THE MASTER
CROSSWORD PUZZLE
DICTIONARY

The Unabridged Word Bank

Also by Herbert M. Baus

THE EXPERT'S CROSSWORD PUZZLE DICTIONARY
HOW TO WINE YOUR WAY TO GOOD HEALTH
POLITICS BATTLE PLAN
PUBLICITY IN ACTION
PUBLIC RELATIONS AT WORK

HERBERT M. BAUS

THE MASTER CROSSWORD PUZZLE DICTIONARY
The Unabridged Word Bank

DOUBLEDAY
NEW YORK LONDON TORONTO SYDNEY AUCKLAND

To My Wife

PUBLISHED BY DOUBLEDAY
a division of Bantam Doubleday Dell Publishing Group, Inc.
666 Fifth Avenue, New York, New York 10103

DOUBLEDAY and the portrayal of an anchor with a dolphin
are trademarks of Doubleday, a division of Bantam Doubleday
Dell Publishing Group, Inc.

Library of Congress Cataloging in Publication Data
Baus, Herbert M.   1914–
The master crossword puzzle dictionary.
    1. Crossword puzzles—Glossaries, vocabularies, etc.
I. Title.
GV1507.C7B354   793.7'32'014   79–7681
ISBN 0-385-15118-7 (thumb-indexed)

10   12   14   16   17   15   13   11

BG

INTRODUCTION

The crossword puzzle hobby as an intellectually stimulating art form is a 20th-century American invention that has swept the nation and much of the modern world since the first one appeared December 21, 1913, in the old New York *World*.

The first book of crossword puzzles was put out eleven years later, April 10, 1924, by Margaret Farrar, America's first lady of crossword puzzles and crossword puzzle editor of the Los Angeles *Times* syndicate. During that same year the *World* began printing a puzzle a day. Now hardly a daily newspaper anywhere dares *not* to print a puzzle a day.

For example, my friend Walter Hicks, then publisher of a chain of several dozen southern California newspapers, told me, "For one edition we inadvertently omitted the crossword puzzle. The telephone switchboard almost exploded. We'll never do *that* again. I'd rather leave out the advertising. . . ." And when San Francisco's *Chronicle* and *Examiner* merged into a combined Sunday edition, it seemed logical to drop one of the Sunday puzzles. Logical, maybe, but it almost started a riot. Ever since, the combined Sunday *Chronicle* and *Examiner* has published *both* crossword puzzles to keep the readers happy—and quiet.

Crossword puzzle solving demonstrates resourcefulness in using words and also stimulates expanded general word knowledge. Use of dictionaries and standard references grew with the crossword puzzle explosion. And a new literary reference form called "crossword puzzle dictionary" came into being.

Regular dictionaries often have shortcomings as puzzle-solving aids. They flow from single *clue words* into detailed and multiple definitions and synonyms, or *answer words*. For optimum crossword puzzle use, however, dictionaries need also to flow from multiple *clue words* to single *answer words*.

> *Clue words* are those numbered "questions" printed with a crossword puzzle for which specific answers must be written in. *Answer words* are those answers.

Sometimes one elusive *answer word,* once discovered, will unblock an impasse and start a chain reaction permitting solution of the entire puzzle—or will clean up a major pocket that obstructs unraveling of the puzzle.

In checking thousands of printed puzzles, I have found that from 50 to 75 percent of the *clue words* comprise multiple-word terms such as "ship's deck," "Russian hut," "Iowa Indian," and "Peruvian fertility goddess." Multiple *clue words* seldom appear as such in regular dictionaries and standard reference works. Hence the necessity for and resulting invention of the crossword puzzle dictionary.

Most crossword puzzle dictionaries existing as recently as the early 1960s were primitive, skimpy, and erratic. Hence was born my ambition to create the world's biggest, richest, and most complete crossword puzzle dictionary (in English or any other language). My Doubleday editors encouraged me to begin the compilation, which proceeded with the help of a small army of assistants. This unabridged word bank is the final result.

Here it is—a volume with more than 50,000 *clue words,* 150,000 *sub-clue words,* and 1,000,000 (one million) answer words. A wealth of geographic, historic, biblical, literary, foreign-language, archaic, obsolete, scientific, and musical words, and hundreds of other special references are marshaled here to make this volume a weapon that should "break" any crossword puzzle.

IS USING A DICTIONARY "CHEATING"?

Some diehards think so. But when one runs into an absolute block working a puzzle, there are only these alternatives:

1. Quit (the coward's cop-out).
2. Peek at the printed solution (*that's* cheating!).
3. Research (This dictionary is the maximum research tool ever assembled between two covers for crossword puzzle solution.)

Research is the ultimate recourse of the intelligent. Research enlightens the mind and satisfies the curiosity while it helps solve the puzzle. It is the only "puzzle solution insurance" that is *not* cheating.

WHERE DID THIS DICTIONARY COME FROM?

For more than ten years my associates and I assembled more than 150,000 index cards containing more than 1,500,000 words.

HOW TO USE THIS DICTIONARY

Read through this work before using it to become accustomed to the devices employed. The more often you employ it as a research bonanza, the more facile you will become in exploiting its resources.

1. *Clue words* are given in all caps, such as ACADEMY. *Answer words,* even in cases of proper names or initialed names (USA, USSR), are presented in lower case (annapolis, college, eton, institution, lycee, st cyr, usma, usna, west point).

Proper names (and initials) are treated this way because the primary use of this dictionary is for crossword puzzle solution. In crossword puzzles it makes no difference whether an answer word is capitalized or lower case.

2. In double or multiple *clue words* the primary *clue word* is capital-

ized and the secondary word or words—the sub-clue(s)—is/are italicized, such as ARMOR *leg*, HEARING *aid*, SALT *container*. When looking for a multiple *clue word*, if you do not find it the first way (we do not have LEG *armor*), look for it the other way (we do have ARMOR *leg*). (We also have under ARMOR the *sub-clue words body, horse, neck*, and many others.)

Another example: We do not have TERM *of endearment*, but you will find ENDEARMENT *term*.

3. Word alternatives. For *clue word* subtitles we often use *child* for son or daughter; *kin* for any relationship; *parent* for father or mother; *consort* for wife or mistress or girl friend.

Also, for example, if you don't find *cap*, look up *hat* or *headdress;* if you don't find *dross* or *waste*, look up *refuse;* if you don't find *garment*, look up *robe* or *dress* or *vestment*.

In other words, if you don't find the exact word given in your puzzle clue, look up other related words and you will usually find your answer.

4. Frequently, when the *clue word* has many examples or variations, you may not find the variations listed among the synonyms, but you will often find them under *breed* or *kind* in the secondary clues. Under HORSE and HOG you will find many names under *breed*. For various kinds of SAIL or TAX or TEA or ROSE, for instance, you will find long lists under *kind*.

5. Geographic multiple words (continents, countries, states, cities) usually start with the name of the place:

AFRICA *animal*, not ANIMAL *africa;* ALASKA *indian;* ENGLAND *actress;* HAWAII *fish;* OHIO *state flower*.

For vocabulary words from the language of the country, we have used the adjective form: FRENCH, ENGLISH, SCOTCH.

6. A capitalized word among the synonyms indicates that under that word are still other synonyms, some of which may not be given under the *clue word* you are reading. For example, under the clue SAGE you will find among the answer words SAGACIOUS. Under ENFEEBLE you will find ENERVATE.

Sometimes, instead of just a capitalized word, it is indicated in parentheses that you should look under another clue word for answers.

7. Any group of synonyms exceeding 75 in number is arranged by order of length of word, with 3-letter words alphabetized, then 4-letter words alphabetized, 5-letter words, and so on. (For example, see ABUSE.)

8. Cross-references and directions to other entries are supplied in many cases; these will direct you to alternative spellings, new names for countries, alternative names for people, and the like. For instance, under TESTAMENT you will find: "See also NEW *testament* and OLD *testament*"; these entries will give you additional answer words.

Other examples: "HINDU *writings*," where you will find "See HINDU *scripture*"; VAN DIEMAN'S LAND, "See TASMANIA"; and TAGETES, "See MARIGOLD." These devices will help to guide you to the answers you seek without needless repetition of hundreds of words.

9. Among secondary clues the abbreviation *comb.* indicates a combining form, where one or more syllables, usually from Greek or Latin and combined with other syllables, create a word related to the *clue word*. They are usually suffixes or prefixes as in HAIR *comb.* chaet(o), crini, pil(o), or TAWNY *comb.* fusco, or NAME *comb.* onym.

These combining forms are often called for by crossword puzzle *clue words* and they are difficult or impossible to find in standard reference works and dictionaries. Far more of them are contained in this than in any other crossword puzzle dictionary.

10. Also among the secondary clues you will find *pert.,* which means "pertaining to." For example, under RABBIT *pert.* you will find leporine; SAIL *pert.* gives velic; and HADES *pert.* gives avernal, hellish, and stygian.

11. We have used *peak* as a secondary clue for individual mountains, e.g., Mt. McKinley or Mt. Whitney. We use *range* for a mountain range, e.g., Sierras, Rockies, Alps, Andes.

12. Vocabulary words of a foreign language are often in quotation marks under the country. But many are sprinkled throughout our regular lists of synonym-answer words.

13. The English language abounds with acceptable variations in spelling of the same word. The ideal (or lazy man's) dictionary would give each variation. To do so here would make a reference both physically and financially unwieldy. So in most instances we give one version only, thus giving the puzzle solver his clue but challenging him to use resiliency and imagination in working out the actual spelling called for by a given puzzle.

For example, for DEFECTIVE we give "meagre" but not "meager"; for PAYMENT we give "judgement" but not "judgment." In these particular instances we employ the British rather than the American usual version. But either is correct.

Often where the variation consists in dropping a letter, we enclose that letter in parentheses to indicate the variation: for example, "parol(e)," "wo(e)begone," and "earning(s)." Multiple-letter variations include "lament(ation)" and "appoint(ment)."

In this monumental pursuit and organization of information I was backed by a team of Pomona College students, teachers, and faculty wives headed by Mrs. Margaret Mulhauser, who with her late husband, Frederick, has been associated with that California institution of higher learning since 1941. Mrs. Mulhauser's personal contributions in research, compilation, editing, and proofreading of this work are of such dimensions as to make her in essence a coauthor.

The following sources, among many others, were combed for entries —most of them page by page and cover to cover—making this volume the most exhaustively researched crossword puzzle dictionary ever undertaken.

Dictionaries

Webster's New International Dictionary, second edition
Random House Dictionary
Dictionaries of French, German, Spanish, and Latin languages

Crossword Puzzle Dictionaries

Crossword Puzzle Dictionary by Andrew Swanfeldt (both editions)
Unabridged Crossword Puzzle Dictionary by A. F. Sisson
New Practical Dictionary for Crossword Puzzles by Frank Eaton
Newman
New American Crossword Puzzle Dictionary by Albert and Loy
Morehead
Dell Crossword Dictionary by Kathleen Rafferty
New York Times Crossword Puzzle Dictionary by Thomas Pulliam
and Clare Grundman

Thesauri

Roget's International Thesaurus
The American Thesaurus of Slang

Encyclopedias

Encyclopaedia Britannica
Goren's Hoyle: Encyclopedia of Games by Charles H. Goren
Larousse Encyclopedia of Mythology
The Victrola Book of the Opera

Almanacs

The Reader's Digest Almanac & Yearbook
The New York Times Encyclopedia Almanac
The World Almanac and Book of Facts

Literary References

The Holy Bible
The Iliad of Homer
The Odyssey of Homer
Plutarch's Lives
Shakespeare's plays
Hundreds of other fiction and nonfiction works

Newspapers, Magazines, Periodicals

Los Angeles *Times,* daily and Sunday
Wall Street Journal
Many other newspapers, sporadically
U.S. News & World Report
Time
National Geographic
Reader's Digest
The New Yorker
New York
Town and Country
New West
Gourmet

Los Angeles
Smithsonian
Sunset
Westways

Crossword Puzzles

Thousands of crossword puzzles from newspapers and books were combed and plowed into the source mass.

OTHER USES OF THIS DICTIONARY

A General Reference Word Bank

In addition to being the most comprehensive crossword puzzle dictionary ever created, this volume is a versatile mine of information for general reference use.

It is one of the largest books of synonyms ever published.

Under specific countries, there appears classified information on geography, cities, rivers, mountains, famous people, money, weights, measures, rulers, and many other subjects.

Under famous people—historical, mythological, and fictional—will be found friends, enemies, consorts, relations, and a wide and fascinating range of facts.

The dictionary is a voluminous source of information and precise nomenclature for many objects, vocations, people, countries, and other categories, with many breakdowns called for by crossword puzzles.

Brought together under ARMOR, for instance, are numerous different kinds of armor—for the *arm, elbow, face, head, hand, shoulder*—and for the *horse.*

ARROW entries, for example, include not only *kinds* but also the various *parts*, as well as names of *poisonous, spinning,* and *wobbling* ARROWS.

Hundreds of Indian tribes are given, under their precise geographic locations.

Trades have their special words: Under MASON you will find *gear* and *tools;* under CARPENTER are *joints, patterns,* and *tools.*

While this book is the crossword puzzle solver's best friend, it definitely offers invaluable help as a thesaurus of synonyms, both general and by categories. The dictionary is a teeming word bank for writers, editors, speakers, teachers, students, researchers, reporters, executives, and others who make their living with words, who use words as part of their daily work, or make a hobby of words.

Hobbyists—readers, travelers, history buffs, and others—will find this work an inexhaustible mother lode of supplemental information.

For the word-lover, here is a gourmet feast.

Bon appétit.

HERBERT M. BAUS
Los Angeles, California
1978

A

AA aphrolite, lava
AACHEN aix-la-chapelle
AAH *mother* nut
AAL eel, morindin, mulberry
AALII akeake, shrub
AANI ape, cynocephalus
AAR *city on* solothurn
AARDVARK ant-bear, ant-eater, earthhog, earthpig, edentate, fodientia, orycteropus
AARDWOLF hyena, proteles
AARON, AARON'S cuckoo-pint, har(o)un, levite, priest
associate hur
beard geranium ivy, jerusalem star, rose of sharon, saint-john's-wort, strawberry-geranium
beloved tamara, tamora
burial place hor
kin amram, miriam, moses
miracle worker rod
offspring abihu, eleazar, ithamar, nadab
rod mullein, plant, talisman
wife elisheba
AARU See PARADISE.
ABA abayah, altazimuth, fabric, garment
ABACA canamo, fiber, hemp, linaga, lupis
ABACAY calangay, parrot
ABACISCUS abaculus, tessera, tile
ABACK ago, aloof, short
ABACTION cattle stealing, rip-off, rustling, theft
ABACTOR abigeus, cattle-thief
ABACUS booth, box, buffet, compartment, cupboard, soroban, stone, suan(pan), trough
small abaciscus, abaculus
ABADDON abyss, apollyon, hell, lucifer, pit, satan

ABAFF, ABAFT aft(er), astern, back, rearward
ABAISANCE obeisance
ABAKAN *river tribe* sagai
ABALIENATE estrange, transfer, withdraw
ABALONE ass's-ear, awabe, awabi, haliotis, mollusk, nacre, ormer, palia, sea-ear
shell money u(h)llo
ABAMA narthecium
ABANDON abdicate, abjure, abstain, allay, back out, bail out, banish, beleave, betray, break, bury, cast, cede, defect, depart, desert, desist, devest, discard, discontinue, dismiss, disuse, ditch, divest, drop, evacuate, expel, exuberance, flee, for(e)go, forhoo, forhow, forswear, freedom, give up, jettison, jilt, junk, laxness, leave, let go, maroon, nonchalance, quit, rashness, reject, relinquish, renege, renig, renounce, resign, riotousness, scrap, scuttle, shake, stop, subdue, surcease, surrender, swear off, throw off, unrestraint, vacate, waive, withdraw, yield
duties bug out
hope despair
ABANDONED ahull, bad, corrupt, depraved, derelict, desolate, discarded, dissolute, empty, flagrant, forlorn, forsaken, free, hardened, immoral, incontinent, incorrigible, irreclaimable, irredeemable, left, lorn, lost, obdurate, outcast, profligate, rampant, reprobate, riotous, shameless, unbridled, uncontrolled, unprincipled, unrestrained, unruly, wanton, wicked, wild

ABANGAH mancala
ABANTES euboeans
ABANTIDAS *kin* aratus, paseas, prophantus, soso
slayer aristoteles, dinias
victim clinias
ABARBAREA *son* aesepus, pedasus
ABAS *kingdom* argolis
parent celeus, eurydamas, metanira
slayer diomedes
son acrisius, proetus
ABASE avile, bemean, cast down, debase, decrease, decry, degrade, deject, demean, demit, demote, denigrate, depose, depreciate, depress, diminish, dimit, disgrace, dishonor, grovel, humble, lessen, lower, meeken, mortify, reduce, shame, vail
ABASEMENT demission, exinanition, humiliation
ABASH amaze, astonish, avale, awe, baze, bewilder, bother, browbeat, bully, chagrin, confound, confuse, cow, dash, daunt, discomfit, discompose, disconcert, discourage, dismay, embarrass, esbay, humble, humiliate, intimidate, mate, mortify, nag, shame
ABASHED ashamed, blank, cheap, foolish, shamed, sheepish
ABATE abolish, allay, alleviate, annul, assuage, blunt, calm, cassare, chancer, check, decrease, defalk, demolish, diminish, discount, dull, ease, ebb, end, extinguish, faik, fall, hush, lessen, let up, lighten, loosen, lower, lull, mend, mitigate, moderate, nullify, omit,

pacify, palliate, quiet, rebate, reduce, relax, remit, slacken, slake, slow, soft, subside, suspend, swage, temper, void, wane

ABATEMENT allay, deadening, decrease, delf(t), demulsion, discount, fall, gusset, letup, meiosis, miosis, modulation

ABATTOIR butchery, shambles, slaughterhouse

ABATWA abatoa, abatua, bushman

ABAXIAL dorsal

ABB wool, yarn

ABBA bishop, ecclesiastic, father, god, patriarch

ABBACOMES See MONK.

ABBACY abthain

ABBAI blue nile

ABBAS *nephew* mohammed

ABBAS EFFENDI abdul baba

ABBE cleric, curate, monk, priest

ABBESS amma, nun, superior, vicaress

ABBEY abbadia, abbaye, badia, cloister, convent, monastery, nunnery, priory
business manager cellarer
laird debtor
lands abadengo
pert. abbatial

ABBOT abbas, archimandrite, coarb
assistant prior
of unreason See LORD *of misrule.*

ABBREVIATE abridge, abstract, bobtail, boil down, capsulize, clip, compress, condense, contract, curtail, cut short, dock, elide, epitomize, foreshorten, pollard, prune, reduce, retrench, shorten, snub, stunt, telescope, truncate

ABBREVIATED bobtail, cryptic, short

ABBREVIATION abridgment, contraction, lapse, reduction, siglum, symbol

ABBREVIATURE abbreviation, abridgment, abstract, compendium, outline

ABC, ABC'S alphabet, fundamentals, primer, roots, rudiments
power argentina, brazil, chile

ABDAL mohammedan, saint, sufi

ABDALLAH *son* mohammed

ABDERITE democritus, simpleton, stupid, yokel

ABDERUS *father* hermes

ABDI *parent* elam

ABDICATE abandon, cast off, cede, demit, depose, disclaim, disinherit, disown, divest, expel, for(e)go, give up, leave, quit, remit, renounce, repudiate, resign, retire, surrender, vacate, withdraw

ABDITIVE hidden, hiding, remote

ABDOMEN alvus, appetite, belly, bouk, bulge, gut(s), mirac(h), paunch, pleon, rumen, stomach, tharm, venter, viscera, vitals, womb
comb. ventro
fluid ascites
having narrow stenogastric
obesity ventrosity
part epigastrium

ABDOMINAL celiac, coelic, gastric, hemal, stomachic, ventral, ventricular, visceral

ABDON *parent* micah

ABDUCT capture, carry off, crimp, impress, kidnap, lure, ravish, shanghai, snatch, spirit, steal, take

ABDUCTION apagoge, capture, enlevement, theft

ABDUCTOR muscle, thief

ABECEDARIAN amateur, anabaptist, apprentice, beginner, beginning, fundamentalist, learner, literal, novice, primary, primer, rudimentary, teacher, tyro

ABEDNEGO *companion* daniel, meshach, shadrach

ABEIGH aloof, cautious

ABEL *brother* cain, seth
nephew enos
occupation shepherd
parent adam, eve
slayer cain
son hamite

ABELARD *beloved* heloise

ABELE poplar

ABELIA honeysuckle

ABELMOSK algalia, hibiscus, mallow, musk, okra
fiber castuli
seed ambrette

ABERDEEN *angus* beef, black doddy, cattle, doddie

ABERDEVINE bird, siskin

ABERRANT abnormal, clammy, deviant, straying, variable, wild

ABERRATION abnormality, delirium, delusion, deviation, disorder, divergence, eccentricity, error, fault, hallucination, illusion, irregularity, lapse, slip, straying, unsoundness, wandering, warp
mental daze, doldrum, fog, haze, insanity, lapse, madness, mania, stupor

ABESSIVE caritive

ABET advocate, aid, answer, assist, avail, back, beset, bestead, coach, connive, contribute, countenance, egg, encourage, endorse, espouse, favor, foment, forward, further, help, incite, instigate, promote, second, serve, set on, spur, support, sustain, uphold, urge

ABETO acxoyatl

ABETTOR accessor(y), accomplice, advocate, aide, ally, auxiliary, backer, bottleholder, confederate, conspirator, fautor, helper, partner, promoter, supporter

ABEYANCE cessation, dormancy, expectancy, inactivity, pause, stagnation, suppression, suspension

ABEYANT inert, latent

ABGAR *kingdom* edessa

ABHISEKA coronation, lustration

ABHOR abominate, agrise, despise, detest, dislike, execrate, hate, irk, loathe, shun

ABHORRENCE anathema, antipathy, aversion, disgust, dislike, hate, hatred, horror, odium, repugnance, wlat(i)e

ABHORRENT abominable, detestable, disgusting, hateful, infamous, loathsome, nasty, offensive, repugnant, shocking, ugsome, unlikable

ABI *husband* ahaz
parent hezekiah, zechariah

ABIA *nurse to* hercules

ABIAH *husband* hezron
kin ashur, samuel

ABIATHAR *companion* david

ABIB nisan

ABIDA *parent* midian

ABIDE accept, acquiesce, await, bear, conform, continue, delay, dwell, endure,

face, inhabit, keep, lend, lie, live, pause, remain, reside, rest, sojourn, stand, stay, submit, suffer, sustain, swell, tarry, tolerate, wait, win, withstand
by acknowledge, acquiesce, hold, observe
ABIDING durable, fast, lasting, perdurable, permanent, resident, stable
ABIEGH aloof, cautious
ABIEL *grandson* abner, saul
son kish, ner
ABIES abeto, acxoyatl, balsam-poplar, black gum, conifer, evergreen, fir, mastictree, pine
ABIGAIL maid, servant, server
father jesse
husband david, ithra, nabal
son amasa
ABIGEUS See CATTLE *thief*.
ABIHAIL *husband* rehoboam
nephew mordecai
ABIHU, ABIU *father* aaron
ABIJAH *parent* david, maacah, zechariah
son asa
ABILITY adequacy, aptitude, brainpower, brilliance, caliber, can, capability, capableness, capacity, class, competence, cunning, efficacy, efficiency, energy, faculty, flair, force, naught, potency, power, skill, strength, stuff, sufficiency, talent, verve, virtu(e)
creative imagination
ABIMELECH *commander* pichol
father gideon, jerubbaal
friend ahuzzath, ochozath
kingdom gerar
ABINADAB *father* jesse, saul
ABINOAM *son* barak
ABIOGENESIS See GENERATION.
ABIOTROPHY degeneration
ABIPON coronado
ABIRRITANT balm
ABISHAI *kin* david, zeruiah
ABISTON asbestos
ABITAL *kin* david, shephatiah
ABITUB *father* shaharaim
ABJECT base, beggarly, cast down, contemptible, contrite, cringing, degraded, despicable, forlorn, grovel-

ing, helot, hopeless, humble, ignoble, low, mean, menial, miserable, obsequious, paltry, poor, rejected, scurvy, servile, slavish, sordid, sunk, supine, vile, wretched
ABJECTION turpitude
ABJURE abandon, avoid, deny, disavow, ejurate, eschew, forswear, give up, nit(e), nitte, recant, reject, relinquish, renounce, repudiate, resign, retract, revoke, shun, spurn
ABKHAZIA *capital* duripsh, sukhum
ABLACH dwarf, rascal
ABLASTOUS budless, germless
ABLATE cut, remove
ABLATION aciurgy, deduction, removal, surgery
ABLAZE, ABLEEZE afire, alow(e), ardent, burning, emotional, gleaming, glowing, inflamed, on fire, radiant
ABLE adept, adequate, adroit, apt, artful, can, capable, capacious, clever, competent, dextrous, doughty, effective, effectual, efficient, expert, facile, fere, fine, fit(ted), good, habil(e), ingenious, powerful, proficient, qualified, ready, skilled, smart, talented, there, versatile, vigorous
-bodied athletic, yal(d), yauld
ABLEPSIA amaurosis, blindness
ABLING(S) perhaps
ABLUENT cleansing, detergent
ABLUTION baptism, bath, cleansing, washing, widu, wudu, wuzu
ABNAKI *indian* algonquian, arosaguntacook, etchimin, malecite, norridgewock, passamaquody, penobscot
ABNEGATE abjure, deny, disavow, disclaim, for(e)go, forswear, immolate, refuse, reject, relinquish, renounce
ABNEGATION self-denial, temperance
ABNER *kin* abiel, ner, saul
leader saul
ABNET scarf
ABNORMAL aberrant, adelomorphic, amorphous, anom-

alous, ataxinomic, atypic (al), deviating, deviative, divergent, eccentric, enorm, erratic, exceptional, extraordinary, freakish, heteroclite, heteromorphic, irregular, odd, queer, unnatural, unusual, utter, wandering
comb. allotri(o), anom(alo), anomo, dys
ABNORMALITY ataxia, ataxy, dementia, heterology, teratism
ABO turku
ABOARD across, afloat, aloft, here, on deck, onto, topside
ABOBRA gourd
ABODE abidal, address, biding, cantonment, cell, cot, cottage, dar, domicile, dwelling, estate, flat, habitance, habitat(ion), home, house, howff, hut, inhabitancy, inn, lodgement, lodging, nest, pad, place, reset, resiance, residence, seat, shelter, sojourn, stay, tenement, won
animal menagerie, zoo
earliest cunabula
miserable doghole, sty(e)
of blessed arcadia, eden, goshen, heaven, paradise
of dead aaru, abaddon, abyss, aralu, chaos, chasm, dar, hades, heaven, hell, orcus, purgatory, shades, sheol, xibalba
of delight elysium
of gods asgard, asgarth, meru, olympus
of love shalimar
of souls limbo
of snow himalaya
ABOLISH abate, abrogate, annihilate, annul, blot, cancel, countermand, destroy, discard, do away with, efface, eliminate, end, erase, evacuate, exterminate, extinguish, extirpate, finish, fordo, invalidate, kill, neutralize, nullify, quash, recall, remove, renounce, repeal, rescind, reverse, revoke, rub out, scratch, stamp out, suppress, vacate, void, wipe out
ABOLITION abrogation, destruction, end, extinction
ABOLITIONIST garrison, lundy, stevens

ABOLLA chlamya, cloak

ABOMASUM bag, belly, read, reed, stomach

ABOMINABLE abhorrent, bad, base, beastly, detestable, disagreeable, evil, execrable, foul, goshawful, hateful, heinous, horrible, inferior, loathsome, maledict, odious, offensive, poor, repugnant, revolting, rotten, rusty, terrible, unpleasant, vile

ABOMINATE abhor, execrate, hate, loath

ABOMINATION abhorrence, anathema, aversion, corruption, crime, curse, depravity, detestation, disgust, evil, hatred, horror, loathing, loathsomeness, odium, plague, repugnance, wrong

A BON MARCHE bargain, cheap

ABOON above

ABORIGINAL adamite, ancestral, ancient, antepatriarchal, autochthonal, autochthonous, first, indigenous, natal, native, natural, patriarchal, preadamite, prehistoric, prehuman, primary, prime(val), primigenial, primitive, pristine, protohistoric, savage, yao

ABORIGINE abo, adibasi, aino, ainu, alfuro, andamanese, aranda, aranta, arunta, autochthon, baiga, balawa, binghi, boong, caveman, chinhwan, dasyu, dravidian, indian, kipper, kodaga, maori, myall, native, sakai, savage, toda, vedda(h), warragal
boy atua-kurka
extinct taino
female gin, jin, lubra
hatchet gweeon, mogo
hut goondie
rite alkira-kiwuma, bora, lartna
weapon boomerang, gidgee

ABORTION brutum fulmen, castling, dud, failure, misbirth, miscarriage, misconception, misfire, slip
inducer abortient, abortifacient, oxytocin, prostaglandin

ABORTIVE addle, blind, bootless, fruitless, futile, idle, ineffective, ineffectual, inefficacious, lame, sterile, stickit, stillborn, unfortunate, unsuccessful, vain

ABOU, ABU father

ABOUND bristle, bustle, crawl, creep, exuberate, fleet, flow, luxuriate, overflow, overrun, pour, rain, redound, shower, snee, sny, stream, swarm, teem

ABOUNDING abundant, copious, plentiful, replete, rife, routh, teeming
comb. acious, acity, ful, ous, poly, ulant, ulent

ABOUT abroad, adjacent, after, almost, anen(s)t, approximately, apropos, around, astir, away, bordering on, circa, circum, close to, concerning, contiguous, current, environ, going, hereunto, near(ly), over, pertaining to, prevalent, proximate, regarding, relative to, respecting, say, some, throughout, touching, toward, umbe, upon, whereon
comb. amb(i), amph(i), ish, peri, umbe
-face change, flop, pivot, reverse, tergiversation
ship tack
to ready
to be imminent

ABOVE abeen, aboon, abune, airborne, aloft, atop, before, beyond, ditto, dorsal, earlier, en haut, exceeding, foregoing, heaven, high(er), oer, over(head), paradise, past, superior, supra, surpassing, transcendent, uber, upon
all primarily, surtout
comb. hyper, super(o), supra
ground aerial, alive
par superior
suspicion pure

ABOVEBOARD frank, honest, open(ly), overt

ABRA defile, pass

ABRACADABRA gibberish, incantation, jargon, nonsense, spell

ABRADE abrase, bark, chafe, erase, excoriate, exhaust, file, fray, frazzle, fret, gall, grate, graze, grind, irritate, pulverize, rasp, raw, raze, rub, sand, score, scrape, scratch, scuff, skin, wear

ABRADED erased, flat, level, raw, smooth

ABRADER emery, file, grinder, rasp, sander, scraper

ABRAHAM, ABRAHAM'S
ally aner, eshcol
bosom heaven, paradise, rest
burial site machpelah
concubine hagar
descendent hebrew
eye charm
kin esau, haran, huz, lot, nahor
master montague
mountain arfaday, moriah
parent adna, azar, terah
religion hanifiya
son isaac, ishbak, ishmael, jokshan, medan, midian, shuah, zimran
wife hagar, keturah, sara(i), sarah, shua

ABRAMIS bream, carp, fish

ABRASION attrition, blasting, bruise, burn, gall, graze, hurt, pulverization, scar, sore

ABRASIVE abradant, arrosive, attritive, chafing, erodent, fretting, galling, gnawing, grinding, harsh, polish, rasping, refractory, rough
kind aloxite, alumina, alundum, carborundum, corundum, emery(board), file, garnet, nail file, pumice, quartz, rasp, rottenstone, sand(paper), scouring-pad, scrubber, silica, silver polish, tripoli

ABRAXAS abrasax, abrastas, amulet, charm, gem

ABREACTION catharsis, sublimation, suppression

ABREAST afront, against, alongside, beside, equal, even, opposite, parallel, side by side
of the times current, modern, popular

ABRET bread, kisra, wafer

ABRI cover, dugout, entrenchment, refuge, shed, shelter

ABRIDGE abbreviate, abstract, alter, boil down, breviate, brief, capsulize, compress, condense, contract, curtail, cut, decrease, deprive, digest, diminish, divest, dock, edit, elide, epitomize, lessen, limit, outline, rasee, razee, reduce, retrench, rewrite, shorten, shrink, simplify, summarize, synopsize

ABRIDGEMENT, ABRIDGMENT abstract, brief, compend(ium), condensation, digest, epitome, pandect, precis, summary, summula, synopsis

ABROACH afoot, astir, diffused, propagated, running

ABROAD about, abreed, abrode, afield, afoot, apart, asea, astir, astray, at large, away, circulating, distant, extensively, far away, off, offshore, outward, overseas, remote, widely

ABROGATE abolish, annul, cancel, dissolve, end, invalidate, nullify, overrule, put aside, quash, remit, repeal, rescind, revoke, set aside, vacate, void

ABROGATION cassation, rescission

ABROTANUM artemesia, southernwood

ABRUPT bluff, blunt, bold, brief, broken, brusk, brusque, choppy, craggy, crusty, curt, disconnected, fast, hasty, headlong, hurried, ictic, immediate, impetuous, perpendicular, precipitate, precipitous, prompt, quick, rough, rude, rugged, sharp, sheer, short, steep, stunt, sudden, surly, terse, unceremonious, uneven, unexpected, vertical, violent

ABRUPTLY bang, sharp, short, slapbang, steeply, suddenly

ABSALOM *captain and cousin* amasa
parent david, maacah
sister tamar
slayer joab

ABSCESS apostasis, aposteme, gumboil, impostume, lesion, moro, parulis, quinsy, squinacy, ulcer, vomica

ABSCIND cut, dock, rend, sever

ABSCISSION apocope, deduction, frustration, pruning, termination

ABSCOND absquatulate, bolt, conceal, decamp, depart, desert, eloi(g)n, elope, escape, flee, fly, hide, levant, quit, run, scram, sh(l)-emozzl, smoke, welsh, withdraw

ABSENCE abstraction, blank, cut, defect, deficiency, furlough, hooky, lack, leave, nonattendance, truancy, vacancy, vacuum, want, withdrawal

leave of absit
license for exeat

ABSENT about, abroad, absorbed, abstracted, away, awol, desert, ditch, dreaming, engrossed, gone, inattentive, lacking, lost, minus, missing, musing, nonexistent, nowhere, off, omitted, out, preoccupied, wane, wanting

-minded distrait, dreaming, oblivious, preoccupied

-mindedness abstraction, bemusement, brown study, daydreaming, forgetfulness, moonraking, musing, oblivion, pipedreaming, preoccupation, reverie, stargazing, woolgathering

without leave awol, truant

ABSENTEE no-show, truant

ABSINTH(E) ajenjo, green, sagebrush, wormwood

ABSOLUTE absolved, arbitrary, authoritative, autocratic, blank, brahma, categorical, certain, clear, complete, dead, definite, despotic, dictatorial, disengaged, dogmatic, downright, elative, entire, evendown, exact, explicit, fair, fine, fixed, free(d), full, fundamental, god, great, imperious, implicit, independent, intrinsic, mear, meer, mere, one, open, outright, peremptory, perfect, plenary, plum(b), positive, potent, pure, rank, real, severe, sheer, simple, square, supreme, sure, tao, tat, thorough, top, total, true, ultimate, unadulterated, unconditional, unqualified, unrestricted, utter, very, whole

not conditional, finite

ABSOLUTELY cold, dead, entirely, evendown, exactly, flatly, greatly, plat, positively, quite, really, sheerly, simply, slap, stark, wholly, yea, yes

ABSOLUTION absolving, acquittal, amnesty, exculpation, excuse, forgiveness, pardon, release, remission, shrift, shriving

ABSOLUTISM caesarism, despotism, imperialism, totalitarianism

ABSOLVE accomplish, acquit, assoil, cancel, clear, confess, discharge, disentangle, exculpate, excuse, exonerate, explain, finish, forgive, free, justify, liberate, loose, pardon, quit, release, remit, set free, shrive

ABSONANT contrary, discordant, dissonant, unreasonable

ABSORB amuse, assimilate, assume, consume, cushion, destroy, devour, digest, drink, engage, engross, engulf, enthrall, enwrap, exercise, fascinate, fill, filter, fix, grip, hold, imbibe, immerge, incorporate, infiltrate, ingest, insorb, intercept, interest, involve, inwrap, merge, monopolize, occlude, occupy, osmose, pay for, preoccupy, receive, rivet, seep, soak, spellbind, sponge, stifle, strip, suck, swallow, take, understand, unite

ABSORBED absent, bemused, buried, deep, engaged, engrossed, fixed, gone, hipped, immersed, incorporated, intent, lost, monopolized, occupied, plunged, preoccupied, rapt, riveted, spellbound, sunk, swallowed, thoughtful, wrapped

ABSORBENT antacid, antiacid, assimilative, base, bibacious, bibulous, blotting, endosmotic, exosmotic, fomes, imbibitory, osmotic, spongeous, spongy, thirsty

ABSORPTION application, assimilation, attention, autism, brown study, concentration, consumption, devotion, endosmosis, engagement, engrossment, exosmosis, immersion, incorporation, infiltration, ingestion, intentness, involvement, occupation, osmosis, percolation, preoccupation, seepage, sorption, sponging, submersion, thought *agent* absorbefacient, blotter *unit* sabin

ABSQUATULATE abscond, beat it, decamp, elope, flee, sit, squat

ABSTAIN abandon, avoid, cease, constrain, control, curb, decline, deny, desist, discontinue, dispense with, disuse, do without, eschew, fast, forbear, for(e)go, hold back, limit, pass, quit, refrain, refuse, reject, renounce, reserve, restrain, restrict, spare, spurn, stay, teetotal, waive, withhold

ABSTAINER apostolic, ascetic, banian, banya, hindu, hydropot, rechabite, tote, water-drinker

ABSTEMIOUS abnegatory, abstinent, ascetic, austere, dry, moderate, restrained, sober, sparing, temperate, virtuous

ABSTENTION See ABSTINENCE.

ABSTERGE bathe, clean, purge, rinse, wipe

ABSTERGENT abstersive, cleansing, detergent, soap

ABSTINENCE abstemiousness, abstention, ascesis, asceticism, avoidance, continence, control, denial, encratism, encraty, eschewal, forbearance, frugality, gymnosophy, moderation, nephalism, pythagorism, restraint, sacrifice, self-control, self-restraint, sobriety, stoicism, teetotalism, temperance, virtue, willpower *day* friday

ABSTINENT See ABSTEMIOUS.

ABSTRACT abbreviate, abridge, absorb, abstruse, argument, breviate, brief, compend(ium), concentrate, cull, deduct, deed, detach, difficult, discrete, divert, docket, draw, epitome, essential, excerpt, general, grab, ideal, outline, part, picture, precis, pure, purloin, remove, separate, steal, summarize, summary, syllabus, synopsis, take, theoretical, vidimus, withdraw

expressionism action-painting

ABSTRACTED carried, oblivious, remote

ABSTRACTION absentmindedness, deduction, entity, inattention, prescission, quoddity, study, theft, theory, universal

ABSTRUSE abstract, acroamatic, anagogic(al), arcane, cabalistic, concealed, dark, deep, difficult, esoteric, hidden, metaphysical, metempiric(al), mysterious, mystical, obscure, occult, profound, recondite, remote, sage, secret, subtle, transcendent(al), wise

ABSURD asinine, bizarre, crazy, dissonant, dotty, droll, egregious, extravagant, false, fantastic, farcical, fatuous, flagrant, foolish, funny, gross, highflown, hot, illogical, impossible, inane, inconceivable, incongruous, inconsistent, inept, irrational, laputan, ludicrous, meshugge, monstrous, nonsensical, outlandish, outrageous, outre, poppycockish, preposterous, quoz, ridiculous, screwy, senseless, silly, stupid, unbelievable, unheard of, unimaginable, unreasonable, unthinkable, untrue, wild

ABSURDITY betise, fatuity, folly, foolery, foppery, maggotry, nonsense, unreason

ABSYRTUS *kin* medea

ABU-BAKR *daughter* aisha, ayesha
son-in-law mahomet, mohammed, muhammad

ABUBUS *son* ptolemaeus

ABUJAH *son* elisha

ABULIC irresolute

ABUNA father, metran, priest, reverend

ABUNDANCE affluence, amplitude, bellyful, bounty, copiousness, depth, endowment, exuberance, fluency, foison, fouth, fullness, galore, generosity, lashin(g)s, mort, oodles, opulence, overflow, plenitude, plenteousness, plenty, plethora, pl(e)urisy, power, profusion, quantity, riches, rimption, river, routh, rowth,

scads, scouth, sonse, store, sufficiency, superfluity, uberty, wamefou, wealth, wone
comb. ose
emblem cornucopia

ABUNDANT affluent, ample, aplenty, bounteous, bumper, copious, demoid, fertile, flush, fruitful, fulsome, galore, generous, great, hefty, large, liberal, luxuriant, many, much, numerous, opime, productive, rank, replete, rich, rife, routh, rowth, store, teeming, uberant, uberous

ABUSE 4 cuss, damn, drub, gali, harm, hurt, maul, rail, rate, teen 5 bully, cheat, crime, curse, fault, galee, rough, scold, smear, snash, wrong 6 assail, attack, batter, berate, bruise, buffet, defile, harass, ill use, injure, injury, insult, malign, missay, misuse, molest, punish, ravish, revile, tansel, tirade, vilify 7 affront, asperse, assault, backjaw, belabor, calumny, censure, chew out, deceive, lampoon, obloquy, offense, outrage, pervert, slender, traduce, upbraid, violate 8 atrocity, ballyrag, bullyrag, diatribe, dishonor, illtreat, maltreat, misapply, mistreat, penalize, reproach, slapdash 9 blaspheme, contumely, deception, desecrate, disparage, invective, manhandle, mishandle, objurgate, profanity 10 blackguard, calumniate, corruption, detraction, intimidate, misimprove, opprobrium, perversion, revilement, scurrility 12 billingsgate, vilification, vituperation

ABU-TALIB *nephew* mohammed

ABUT adjoin, border, bound, butt, join, juxtapose, meet, project, rest, straddle, touch on

ABUTA moonseed

ABUTILON flowering maple, mallow

ABUTMENT alette, buttress, crib, fortification, pier

ABUTTAL adjacency, boundary, butting, limit

ABUTTING adjacent, adjoining, conterminous, contiguous, coterminous, near, nigh, touching

ABUZZ alive, bursting

ABWAB cess, fine, impost

ABY continue, endure, last

ABYSMAL, ABYSSAL bassalian, bottomless, deep, dreary, great, immeasurable, plumbless, profound, unending, unfathomable, unfathomed, wretched, yawning
zone bassalia

ABYSS, ABYSM abaddon, abime, apsu, bisme, cavity, chaos, chasm, cleft, deep, depth, downfall, gap, gehenna, gulf, hades, hell, hole, pit, sheol, space, void, vorago, wasteland

ABYSSINIA See ETHIOPIA.

ACACALLIS *son* amphithemis, garamas

ACACIA bablah, babul, bluebush, boobyalla, boree, brigalow, broom, buffalothorn, cashcuttee, cat(s)-claw, catechu, chapparo, cooba(h), garad, gidgea, gidgee, gidjee, gidy(e)a, gum, hashab, ironwood, jurema, kameeldoorn, kar(r)oobush, locust, mimosa, mulga, myall, myoporum, rosewood, saltbush, siris, thornbush, timbe, verek, wattle, yarran, yellow
compound acacatechol
extract catechu
gum amrad
thorny broom-wattle, kar(r)oo

ACADEME See ACADEMY.

ACADEMIC abstract, classic, conjectural, donnish, erudite, formal, hypothetic(al), ideal, impractical, ivy, learned, quodlibetic, rigid, scholastic, speculative, theoretical
costume cap and gown
world campus

ACADEMICIAN dean, docent, doctor, don, prof(essor), scholar, tutor

ACADEMY annapolis, association, college, eton, institute, institution, lycee, lyceum, manage, plato's grove, sandhurst, school, seminary, society, st cyr, university, usafa, usma,

usna, west point, woolwich, yeshiva

ACADIA, ACADIE nova scotia

ACADIALITE chabazite

ACADIAN cajun
dialect cajun
flycatcher empidonax
owl saw-whet

ACAJOU cashew, cedar, mahogany, marinheiro, tree

ACALEPH coelenterate, jellyfish, medusa, sea nettle

ACAMAS *companion* aeneas
kin archelochus, munitus
parent phaedra, theseus
victim promachus

ACANA almigue, sapota

ACANACEOUS prickly

ACANTHA fin, prickle, spine, thorn

ACANTHACA caricatureplant, graptophyllum

ACANTHITE argentite, silver sulphide

ACANTHODIAN See SHARK.

ACANTHOID, ACANTHOUS spiny, spinous

ACANTHURUS surgeon-fish

ACANTHUS andrographis, aphelandra, bear's-breech, bearskeiters, bearwort, brankursine, cow-parsnip, justicia, plant, spicknel

ACAPU chaperno, walnut

ACAPULCO *diver* clavadista
launch la punta, la quebrada
suburb pichilingue

ACARID acarine, acarus, arachnid, dibranch, insect, mite, nymph, octopod, tick
first stage protonymph

ACARNAN *father* alcmaeon

ACARPOUS barren, sterile, unproductive

ACASTUS *brother* alcestis
daughter laodamia, sthenele
father pelias
rival peleus
slayer peleus
wife cretheis, hippolyte

ACATALEPSY skepticism

ACAUDAL, ACAUDATE anurous, bobbed, ecaudate, tailless

ACCAD achad, akkad

ACCADIAN sumerian
lord bel

ACCEDE accept, accord, acknowledge, acquiesce, adhere, agree, allow, approve, assent, attain, comply, concede, concur, conform, con-

sent, grant, install, let, submit, yield

ACCELERATE advance, antedate, atomize, bustle, dispatch, drive, expedite, favor, force, forward, further, gear up, get cracking, gun, hasten, hie, hurry, hustle, increase, jazz, precipitate, push, quicken, race, railroad, rev, run, rush, SPEED, step up, urge, zip

ACCELERATION pickup, quickening, speedup, stepup
unit milligal, stapp

ACCELERATOR betatron, bevatron, booster, gas, speeder, throttle

ACCENT accentuate, acute, arsis, beat, blas, brogue, burr, cadence, character, dialect, emphasis, emphasize, grave, ictus, language, manner, mark, meter, modulation, pitch, pronounce, pronunciation, pulse, rhythm, speech, stress, symbol, thesis, time, tone, twang, verge, word
without atonic, proclitic

ACCENTED marcando, marcato, pronounced, sforzato, sfz, strong, tonic

ACCEPT abide, accede, accommodate, acknowledge, acquiesce, adjust, admit, adopt, affirm, agree, allow, answer, approve, assent, assume, avouch, believe, buy, concede, condone, consent, contain, countenance, eat, embrace, endure, espouse, expect, fang, grin and bear it, honor, jump, marry, nostrificate, pocket, ratify, receive, reconcile, resign, settle, submit, tae, take, tolerate, understand, undertake, will, yield
readily swallow
responsibility answer for

ACCEPTABLE adequate, admissable, agreeable, allowable, al(l)right, authentic, bearable, bueno, comfortable, desirable, eligible, expedient, fine, lief, okay, okeh, passable, pleasant, pleasing, safe, satisfactory, sightly, tolerable, unobjectionable, welcome, worthy

ACCEPTANCE aditio, credence, currency, pass, passage, snaff

ACCEPTED approved, canonical, conventional, credited, going, orthodox, standard, usual

ACCESS accost, adit, admission, admittance, advance, ague, approach, attack, avenue, door, entrance, entree, entry, opening, outburst, paroxysm, passageway, path, portal, road, route, seizure, street, way

ACCESSIBLE affable, approachable, attainable, available, comeatable, convenient, easy, gettable, handy, navigable, near, obtainable, open, passable, patent, penetrable, pervious, present, procurable, public, reachable, securable, sociable, within reach

ACCESSION acquisition, addition, adherence, adjunct, advance, agreement, alluvion, approach, assent, assumption, attack, augmentation, consent, enlargement, entrance, illapse, inaugural, increase, joining, onset, reinforcement, seizure, usurpation

ACCESSORY abettor, accidental, accompaniment, accompanying, accomplice, additional, additive, adjunct, aid, ally, ancilla, appendage, appurtenance, appurtenant, attachment, auxiliary, collateral, contributory, enclave, extra, fixture, nonessential, ornament, participant, subordinate, subservient, subsidiary, supplementary
ornamental parergon

ACCIDENCE chance, inflection

ACCIDENT act of god, befalling, calamity, case, casualty, CATASTROPHE, chance, contingency, contretemps, disaster, error, event, fortuity, fortune, grief, hap(pening), happenstance, hazard, incident, injury, irregularity, luck, misadventure, misfortune, mishap, pile-up, slip
-prone reckless

ACCIDENTAL accessory, additional, adscitious, adventitious, by chance, casual, chance, collateral, conditional, contingent, dependent, extraneous, extrinsic, fortuitous, freakish, incidental, involuntary, nonessential, occasional, odd, parenthetical, random, secondary, spontaneous, subordinate, subsidiary, sudden, undesigned, unforeseen, unintended, unmeant, unplanned, unpremeditated, unprompted, unpurposed, unwitting

ACCIDIE acedia, apathy, indifference, laziness, sin, sloth, torpor

ACCIPITER bandage, goshawk, hawk

ACCITE arouse, cite, excite, summon

ACCLAIM acclamation, announce, applaud, applause, approbation, approval, approve, cheer, clap, compliment, cry, declare, eclat, encore, endorse, extole, greet, hail, hand, hosanna, huzza, laud, ole, ovation, plaudit, praise, proclaim, root, salute, salvo, shout, welcome

ACCLAMATION See ACCLAIM.
carried by unanimous

ACCLIMATE accustom, adapt, adjust, habituate, harden, inure, season

ACCLIVITY abruptness, ascent, bank, brow, climb, grade, hardship, height, hill, incline, pitch, rise, rising, slant, slope, steepness, talus, upclimb, upgo, upgrade, uphill, uplift

ACCOLADE award, blessing, ceremony, dubbing, embrace, emmy, garland, gree, honor, kiss, knighthood, kudos, laudation, medal, notice, oscar, praise, recognition, salutation, sign, symbol, token, tony

ACCOLENT neighbor

ACCOMMODATE accept, adapt, adjust, advance, aid, assist, bed, billet, board, bow, camp, conform, contain, credit, facilitate, fashion, favor, fit, furnish, harmonize, help, hold, lend, lodge, mend, oblige, orient, provide, put up, reconcile, repair, serve, settle, sort, suit, supply, yield

ACCOMMODATING considerate, helpful, indulgent, kind, polite

ACCOMMODATION adaptation, adjustment, agreement, aid, bearings, bed and board, bedroom, berth, board, cabin, capacity, convenience, fitting, food, furnishing, giffgaff, keep, loan, lodging, passage, room, seat, settlement, subsistence

ACCOMPANIMENT adjunct, alba, concurrence, descant, incidental, instrumentation, obligato, oompah, ornament, supplement, support
without acapella

ACCOMPANIST escort, jongleur, pianist

ACCOMPANY associate, assort, attend, bring, chaperon, companion, conduct, consort, convey, convoy, couple, escort, fair, fere, follow, go with, join, lead, pilot, play for, see, sort with, squire, synchronize, tend, wait on

ACCOMPLICE abettor, accessory, aide, ally, assistant, associate, bonnet, buddy, canary, chum, cohort, confederate, conspirator, crony, feodary, feudary, helper, louke, pal, participator, partner, shill(aber), stall, steerer, tiler

ACCOMPLISH achieve, afford, attain, bring about, carry out, chevise, compass, complete, consummate, contrive, discharge, dispatch, dispose of, earn, effect(uate), enact, encompass, end, engineer, equip, execute, explete, fetch, fill, finish, fulfill, furnish, knock off, manage, negotiate, operate, perfect, perform, produce, realize, render, succeed, swing, turn the trick, win, work

ACCOMPLISHED able, adept, apt, artful, attained, beseen, capable, completed, consummate, done, effected, ended, expert, gifted, perfected, skilled, talented, wrought

ACCOMPLISHMENT achievement, acquirement, art, attainment, completion, consummation, craft, deed, discharge, earning, effect, end, execution, fait accompli, feat, finish, fruition, fulfillment, grace, implementation, knowledge, learning, performance, production, proficiency, quality, realization, skill, talent

ACCORD accede, adjust, affinity, agree(ment), alliance, allow, amity, assent, assonate, atone, attune, award, befit, bestow, beteem, blend, chime, chord, communion, community, compact, compatibility, comply, concede, concert, concord(ance), concur (rence), congeniality, consent, consonance, consonate, corde, correspond, empathy, fit, gee, give, grant, harmonize, harmony, jibe, jump, likemindedness, pact, peace, permission, permit, rapport, rapprochement, reciprocate, reconcile, settle, suit, sympathy, symphonize, symphony, synchronize, tally, treaty, truce, unanimity, understanding, union, unison, unite, unity
complete unanimity
mutual compact, contract, pact, understanding

ACCORDANCE agreement, concert, concord, concurrence, conformity, consent

ACCORDANT agreeable, at one, attuned, coherent, compatible, conformable, congenial, consistent, consonant, correspondent, en rapport, even, harmonious, of one mind, reconcilable, suitable, sympathetic, understanding

ACCORDING *to* after, a la, alla, aux, emforth, enforth, evidentially, pursuant, secundum
to custom ex more
to hoyle conformably, correct(ly), fair(ly), right
to value ad valorem

ACCORDINGLY consequently, correspondingly, ergo, hence, igitur, in that event, that being so, then, therefore, thus, wherefore

ACCORDION flutina, lantum, melodeon, solitaire

small flautino

ACCOST abord, access, address, approach, board, broach, call, confront, greet, hail, halloo, hello, mash, meet, solicit, speak, waylay

ACCOUCHEUR midwife, obstetrician

ACCOUNT anecdote, answer, assign, audit, balance, basis, battel, BILL, calculation, cause, check, chronicle, client, computation, compute, consider, credit, customer, deem, description, enumeration, esteem, estimate, explain, explanation, importance, impute, information, item, judge, motive, narrate, narrative, nick, note, opine, profit, rate, recital, recitation, reckon(ing), record, rede, rehearsal, relate, render, rendition, report, sake, score, state(ment), STORY, tab, tail(zie), tale, tally, terrier, text, think, tick, tot(al), treatise, valuation, value, worth
accurate griff(in)
analytical explication
book codicil, ledger, log, terrier
call to impeach
detailed play-by-play
for attribute, explain, save, vindicate
lengthy megillah

ACCOUNTABLE amenable, answerable, comprehensible, explicable, liable, responsible

ACCOUNTANT actuary, auditor, bookkeeper, clerk, cpa, defender, examiner, kulkarni, mutsuddy, peshkar, putwari, reckoner, recorder, registrar, relater, sircar, sirkar, teller
general daftar, dar, defterdar

ACCOUNTING audit(ing), bookkeeping, costing, reason, task
form billhead

ACCOUNTS assets, expenditures, liabilities, receipts

ACCOUTER arm, array, attire, bedight, clothe, dress, equip, furnish, gird, harness, outfit, provide, rig

ACCOUTERMENTS attire, dress, gear, graith, tire

ACCREDIT affirm, allot, appoint, approve, ascribe, attribute, authorize, believe, certify, clear, commission, confirm, credit, depute, endorse, license, provide, ratify, sanction, send, trust, vouch

ACCRESCENT growing, increasing

ACCRETION accession, accrual, addition, adhesion, coherence, deposit, enlargement, extension, gain, growth, increase, sum
injurious rust

ACCROACH acquire, appropriate, assume, usurp

ACCRUE accresce, accumulate, acquire, add, arise, collect, cumulate, earn, ensue, enure, gain, grow, increase, incur, inure, issue, mature, pile, redound, result, spring, stitch, vest, win

ACCUMBENT leaning, lying, reclining

ACCUMULATE accrue, acquire, aggregate, amass, assemble, buy, cluster, collect, draw, fund, garner, gather, grow, harvest, heap, hive, hoard, increase, mass, muster, pile, preserve, save, scrape, stack, store, total

ACCUMULATION acervation, acquisition, agglomerate, agglomeration, aggregation, amassment, anlage, backlog, batch, budget, buildup, bulk, collection, congeries, conglomeration, cumulus, debris, dump, garner, gathering, gob, increase, interest, lump, mass, pile, stack, stock(pile), store

ACCUPRESSURE jin-shinjyutsu

ACCURATE alright, careful, close, correct, exact, faithful, faultless, flawless, flush, impeccable, just, leal, meticulous, nice, on the beam, particular, perfect, perqueer, precise, proper, punctual, right, rigid, scrupulous, severe, strict, true, truthful, unerring

ACCURATELY closely, correctly, exactly, fairly, faultlessly, insooth, just so, rightly, straight

ACCURSED blasted,

damned, doomed, execrable, fey, maledict, waried
ACCUSATION attack, beef, blame, charge, delation, point, scandal, threap, threep, wite
false calumny
unjust slander
ACCUSATORY wrayful
ACCUSE appeach, appeal, argue, arraign, attack, berate, betray, bewray, blame, call, calumniate, censure, charge, chide, criminate, defame, delate, denounce, file, frame, impeach, implead, impugn, incriminate, indict, murmur, peach, recriminate, redargue, report, reprehend, reproach, show, slur, smear, taint, tax, wray, wry
ACCUSED appellee, defendant
ACCUSER charger, delator, libelant, plaintiff
ACCUSTOM acclimate, acclimatize, ADAPT, addict, adjust, condition, conform, consort, drill, educate, enure, establish, familiarize, habit(uate), haft, harden, haunt, inure, naturalize, season, set, tame, toughen, train, ure, use, win
ACCUSTOMED adapted, addicted, adjusted, attached, characteristic, chronic, conditioned, consuete, current, customary, devoted, enured, familiarized, habited, habituated, inclined, indulged, prone, tame, used, usual, wont(ed)
ACE acme, adept, a-one, apex, atom, authority, aviator, basto, best, bit, brick, brisque, bull(et), burner, card, champ(ion), corker, crack, darb, dilly, dollar, excellent, expert, finest, first(rate), flyer, head, hero, high, hole in one, honey, humdinger, jot, knockout, leader, lulu, magnate, mark, master, nearness, one(r), one-spot, outstanding, particle, peach, pilot, pip, placement, plum, point, prodigy, score, service, single, spot, superior, supreme, sweetheart, tib, top(s), trump, whiz, wonder

and queen tenace
and 10 blackjack, natural, twenty-one
-high a-one, esteemed, great, tops
in the hole advantage, reserve, resource
of clubs basto, puppyfoot
of diamonds bone-ace, bragger
of spades spadille, spadillo
of trumps honor, punto, tib
pair ambsace, amesace, snake-eyes
3 corona, gleek
10 brisque, brisquembille
ACEDIA accidie, apathy, flatfish, indifference, laziness, sin, sloth, symphurus, torpor
ACEPHALOUS headless
ACER box-elder, MAPLE, negundo, sapindale, sugartree
ACERATA aracnid, arthropod, merostomata
ACERB acid, acrid, acrimonious, astringent, austere, biting, bitter, caustic, hard, harsh, rough, severe, sharp, sour, stern, strict, surly, tart, unripe
ACERBAS synchaeus
consort dido, elissa
ACERBATE embitter, harsh, irritate, sour
ACERBITY asperity, BITTERNESS, harshness, severity
ACEROUS hornless
ACERVATE clustered, heaped
ACESCENT acidulous, sour
ACESIUS See APOLLO.
ACES UP firing squad, solitaire
ACETABULUM cupule, holdfast, pan, pyxis
ACETAL butyral, formal, ketal, ketate
ACETAMINOPHEN tylenol
ACETATE celanese, ester
amyl banana oil
crude pyrolignite
ACETES *leader* dionysus
sister circe
ACETIC acetous, acid, sharp, sour, vinegary, zoonic
acid salt acetate
ACETOMORPHINE See HEROIN.
ACETONE acetol, butanone, ketone
ACETUM vinegar

ACETYLENE alkine, alkyne, ethin(e), ethyn(e), gas, tolan(e)
linkage triple-bond
source calcium carbide
welder blowtorch
ACEY-DEUCY backgammon
ACHAD accad, akkad
ACHAIA ahhiyawa, greece
city mycenae
ACHAR condiment, pickle, relish
ACHATE agate, stone
ACHATES *friend* aeneas
ACHAZ See AHAZ.
ACHE afflict, agonize, ail, ake, anguish, crave, desire, eche, gall, hache, hurt, long, misery, nag, nip, pain, pang, pine, smart, soreness, stang, stitch, stoun(d), suffer, sympathize, throb, throe, twinge, twitch, warch, wark, werk, wish, yearn
ACHELOUS *daughter* See SIREN names.
wife melpomene
ACHENE akene, beggar's-lice, cypsela, fruit, samara, utricle
ACHENODIUM cremocarp, schizocarp
ACHERON See HELL.
ACHETE calonyction, moonflower
ACHEUS *kin* ajax, telamon, teucer
ACHEWEED goutweed
ACHIEVABLE practicable, practical
ACHIEVE accomplish, arrive, attain, bring about, bring off, carry out, cheve, chevise, commit, compass, complete, conclude, consummate, contrive, earn, effect(uate), end, fetch, finish, fulfill, gain, get, make, obtain, perform, perpetuate, produce, pull off, reach, realize, render, score, succeed, triumph, win
ACHIEVEMENT act, adventure, career, deed, feat, job, performance, result
ACHILLEA ball-of-snow, bloodwort, milcoil, ptarmica, sneezewort, yarrow
ACHILLES pelides, pelion
advisor nestor, odysseus, ulysses
armor-maker hephaestus

betrothed polyxena
captive briseis
charioteer automedon
consort briseis, deidamia, hippodamia
descendant alexander the great
foster father phoenix
friend patroclus
heel danger, downfall, vulnerability, weakness
horse balius, xanthus
of England wellington
of the west roland
parent peleus, thetis
protectress athena, hera
reflex ankle-jerk
rescuer ajax
slayer paris
soldier myrmidon
son neoptolemus, pyrrhus
spear pelias
teacher ch(e)iron, phoenix
tendon hamstring
tomb sigoeum
tutor ch(e)iron, phoenix
victim hector, memnon, mynes, penthesilea, rhigmus, thersilochus, thersites
vulnerable part heel

ACHIMELECH See AHIMELECH.

ACHIOTE achuete, annatto, arnatto, bixa, bixin, oleana, oncoba, orellin, tree

ACHIRA canna

ACHISH *kingdom* gath
protected david

ACHITOPHEL See AHITHOPHEL.

ACHMETHA ecbatana, hamadon

ACHONDRITE aubrite

ACHRAS safota

ACHROITE tourmaline

ACHROMATIC colorless, gray, neutral, pale

ACHROMYCIN tetracycline

ACHSAH *father* caleb
husband othniel

ACHTUNG attention, beware

ACICULAR needle-shaped, pointed, splintery

ACICULUM bristle, pin, seta, spine

ACID acerb(ic), acescent, acetic, acetose, acetous, acrid, acrimonious, algin, allin, astringent, biting, bitter, caustic, cauterant, citr(o)us, dial, dope, dry, eager, harsh, ill-natured,

keen, lad, lysin, mordant, narcotic, oleate, serine, sharp, sour, tart, tweaky, vinegary, vitriolic, yar
acridic auinoline
amino asparagine, proline, valine
anti magnesia
boric sassolite
colorless abietic
comb. acer(o), aceto, olic, oxy
crystalline abietic, alanine, aspartic, aspartyl, atrolactic, benzilic, berberonic, bilianic, citraconic, comanic, erucic, eupitonic, felic, galleine, isoleucine, kynurenic, paraconic, usnic
drop candy, sourball, sweet
fatty arachic
-head See ADDICT.
kind alkapton, amino, aquafortis, arabin, arsonic, butyric, carbolic, chloric, chlorous, chromic, citric, cyanic, filicin, formic, gallic, hydrochloric, iridate, lactic, malic, muriatic, niacin, nicotinic, nitric, oleic, oxalic, perchloric, phenol, phosphoric, picric, pittacal, prolin, prussic, salicylic, selanic, sulphuric, ulmic, uric, valine, vinegar, vitriol
neutralizer alkali
organic carboxylic
pert. oleatic
protein amino
radical acetyl, acyl, benzoyl, malonyl
removing edulcorant
salicylic aspirin
test assay, showdown, trial
unsaturated, pert. acrylic
wood soot asbolin

ACIDEMIA acidosis

ACIDICE *daughter* tyro

ACIDITY acerbity, acor, alkalinity, sourness, tartness, verdure, verjuice

ACIDOSIS acidemia

ACIDULATE embitter, sour

ACIDULOUS, ACIDY acescent, caustic, sour, tart

ACINIFORM acinose, acinous, clustered

ACINUS alveolus, berry, currant, drupelet, grape, kernel, lobule, sac, seed

ACIPENSER beluga, cetacean, delphinapterus, fish, hausen, sturgeon

ACIS *beloved* galatea

parent faunus, symaethis
rival and slayer polyphemus

ACIURGY ablation, surgery

ACKNOWLEDGE accede, accept, admit, adopt, agnize, agree, allow, answer, appreciate, assent, aver, avow, beknow, bow, concede, confess, confirm, consider, couthe, declare, disclose, face, grant, kithe, kythe, nod, notice, own, publish, recognize, reply, respect, reward, rsvp, settle, sign, testify, thank, warrant, yield

ACKNOWLEDGED conventional, recognized, traditional

ACKNOWLEDGEMENT, ACKNOWLEDGMENT admission, agnition, apology, avowal, confession, credit, gratitude, receipt, recognition, recu, rsvp, shrift, thanks, voucher

ACLE hardwood, ironwood, irul, jamba, pyengadu, xylia

ACLYS hurlbat

ACME ace, apex, apogee, cap(sheaf), capstone, climax, comble, consummation, crest, culmination, cumulus, height, heyday, high, ideal, ne-plus-ultra, paragon, peak, pinnacle, pitch, point, prize, quintessence, submit, SUPREME, tip, tittle, top, ultimate, zenith

ACMITE aegirine, aegirite, aegyrite

ACMON *companion* diomedes
defied aphrodite

ACNE pimples, pustules, whelk

ACOCANTHERA dogbane, shrub

ACOCOTL clarin

ACOLYTE accensor, altar boy, assistant, attendant, candlelighter, follower, helper, learner, novice, patener, satellite, tyro
vestment cotta

ACOMIA atrichis, baldness

ACONITE adam and eve, annona, atis, atta, badgersbane, bikh, bish, monkshood, nabee, napellus, wolfsbane, woodbane

ACOR acidity, sourness, tartness

ACORN ballote, barnacle, bellote, camata, finial, knob, mast, nut, ovest, pannage
barnacle balanoid, balanus, scuta, scute
-bearing balaniferous
comb. balan(o)
cup cupule, involucre, valonia
moth valentinia
-shaped balanoid
shell balanoid
sugar quercitol
weevil balaninus
worm balanoglossid, enteropneusta
ACORUS arum, calamus, herb, sweet-flag
ACOUPA cynoscion, weakfish
ACOUSTICON hearing aid
ACOUSTICS cataphonics, diaphonics, sonics
instrument appuun's reed, lamella, sirene
ACQUAINT advise, apprise, communicate, familiarize, inform, introduce, know, notify, possess, present, relate, school, teach, tell, verse
ACQUAINTANCE associate, companion, cousin, familiar(ity), fellowship, friend, gossip, information, intimacy, intimate, kith, knowledge, practice
ACQUAINTED acquent, conversant, friendly, knowledgeable, versant
ACQUARIUS carrier
ACQUIESCE abide, accede, ACCEPT, agree, assent, back down, bend, chime, come around, comply, concede, concur, conform, consent, deign, give in, obey, submit, vouchsafe, yield
ACQUIESCENCE consent, resignation, submission
ACQUIESCENT complaisant, compliant, complying, deferential, docile, gentle, manageable, obedient, passive, resigned, subject, unresistant, unresisting
ACQUIRE accumulate, add, adopt, affect, amass, annex, appropriate, attain, bag, buy, capture, catch, chev(e)y, chiv(v)y, collect, come by, conquer, contract, cultivate, derive, develop,

draw, earn, establish, gain, garner, get, glean, grab, harvest, have, incur, learn, make, net, obtain, procure, profit, reach, reap, receive, sack, secure, seize, snatch, steal, take, win
ACQUIREMENT(S) accomplishment, learning
ACQUISITION accession, accumulation, acquest, acquirement, acquist, asset, attainment, bargain, company, conquest, dishonest graft, find, gain, lucre, obtention, possession, procuration, procurement, securement, theft, wealth, win, windfall
ACQUISITIVE avaricious, grabby, grasping, greedy, mercenary, predaceous, rapacious
ACQUIT absolve, assoil, behave, bestow, cancel, clear, comport, conduct, discharge, dismiss, exculpate, excuse, exempt, exonerate, finish, forgive, free, fulfill, justify, let off, liberate, overlook, pardon, parole, pay, perform, purge, quiet, quit, ransom, release, remit, render, repay, requite, satisfy, settle, shrive, uncharge, vindicate
ACQUITTAL absolvitor, amnesty, compurgation, excuse, quietus, release, settlement, verdict
ACRACY anarchy
ACRAEA aphrodite
ACRASIA excess, intemperance
ACRE arpent, bitter, collop, colp, estate, farmhold, field, pasture, piece, plottage, ptolemais, quantity, sharp, stang
¼ rood
½ erf, erven
⅔ cover
10 decare, furlong
100 hectare
120 hide
bob country gentleman
-fight duel
god's cemetery, churchyard
-man carucarius
-shot land-tax
ACRID acerb, acid, acrimonious, arum, bask, biting, bitter, caustic, corrosive, harsh, irritating, keen, pun-

gent, reeking, rough, sharp, sour, stinging, unsavory, vinegary, virulent
ACRIDITY asperity, pungency, sarcasm, virulence
ACRIDONE acridinium, acridonium, adrenalone, ketone
ACRIMONIOUS acid, acrid, angry, astringent, biting, bitter, blistering, caustic, cutting, edged, escharotic, gruff, harsh, irate, keen, mad, mordacious, mordant, piercing, rough, scathing, severe, sharp, snell, stabbing, stinging, surly, tart, trenchant, virulent, vitriolic
ACRIMONY acerbity, acidity, acridity, anger, animosity, asperity, astringency, bite, bitterness, choler, crabbedness, edge, harshness, keenness, mordacity, mordancy, pungency, roughness, rudeness, severity, sharpness, sourness, sting, tartness, trenchancy, virulence
ACRISIUS *kin* danae, lynceus, perseus, proetus
kingdom argos
parent abas, aglaia
slayer perseus
ACROAMATIC abstruse, esoteric, oral, profound
ACROBAT athlete, balancer, clown, contortionist, gymnast, kinker, leaper, performer, schoenobatist, stuntsman, switcher, toppler, tumbler, zany
garment leotard
net trampoline
ACROGEN archegoniate, cryptogram, fern, liverwort, moss
ACROLITH caryatid, statue
ACRONYM *famous* aid, anzac, care, cod, core, fad, fight, flak, gag, gestapo, inri, jeep, job, laser, nabu, nasa, nazi, posh, quark, quasar, roar, snafu, sonar, sos, sro, swak, tip, wac, wasp, wave, who, wrens, zip
ACROPHONY hieroglyphics
ACROPODIUM pedestal
ACROPOLIS cadmea, citadel, fort, height, hill, larissa, polis, stronghold
temple erectheum, parthenon
ACROSE fructose, sugar

ACROSPIRE bud, plumule, sprout
ACROSS amiss, athwart, awry, beyond, crossways, crosswise, oer, opposite, over, span, thwart, transverse, traverse, yonder
comb. dia, tra(ns)
the board comprehensive, general
ACROSTIC abc, agla, dora, game, puzzle, tanach, tanak
ACROTATUS *father* areus
slayer aristodemus
son areus, aristodemus
ACRYLIC *fiber* orlon
resin lucite, plexiglass, propenoic
ACT 3 ape, bit, gag, job, law 4 bill, blow, bout, coup, deal, deed, fact, feat, fiat, hock, jest, move, part, play, show, skit, turn 5 award, bluff, doing, edict, emote, feign, geste, model, scene, serve, shift, stunt 6 action, affect, answer, appear, behave, bestir, decide, decree, demean, effort, factum, finale, manage, number, patter, record, result, sketch, stanza, stroke, troupe 7 actuate, animate, comport, conduct, execute, exhibit, exploit, fulfill, operate, perform, portray, pretend, proceed, process, produce, resolve, statute 8 ceremony, decision, document, exercise, function, maneuver, pretense, progress, prologue, register, simulate 9 adventure, barnstorm, judgement, pantomime, procedure, represent, slapstick 10 accomplish, enterprise, instrument, masquerade 11 achievement, counterfeit, dissimulate, impersonate, legislation, performance, transaction 12 capitulation, emotionalize, fait accompli 13 determination 14 accomplishment
affectedly mim(p), simper
blindly blunder
ceremonial rite
comb. ade, ado, age, ance, ancy, ency, tion, tious, ure
deceitfully deceptive, double (cross), feint
end of curtain
foolishly foleye, fon(ne) footer, footle

for represent, substitute
frivolously fribble
holy hierurgy
indecisively dither
in theater gaff
like ape imitate
mischievous cantrap, dido, prank
of faith auto da fe
of god accident, birth, damnum fatale
of grace clemency, favor
of replevin avowry
out dramatize
playful ra(i)llery
playfully banter, dally, gambol, sport
rashly rackle
shyly mim
stupid betise
sullen mope
symbolic charade
the part of masquerade, mimic
timidly nesh
together agree, concord, concur, cooperate
toward treat
up carry on, cut up, emote, grandstand, misbehave, show off
violent bensel, bensil
with restraint underplay
wrong derelict(um)
ACTA deeds, proceedings, records, transactions
sanctorum editor bollandist
ACTAEA baneberry, bryony, bugbane, cohosh, herb
ACTAEON *dog* alce, canache, ladon, lycisa
parent aristaeus, autonoe
slayer hounds
spied on artemis, diana
ACTIFY activate, activize, start
ACTING active, agent, astir, characterization, deputy, doing, energic, execution, fulfilling, functioning, impersonation, make-believe, mummery, operation, performance, performing, personation, playing, portrayal, practicing, pretense, pro tem, serving, sham, simulation, temporary, working
against adverse
by turn altern
oddly haywire
out catharsis
tragic cothurnus
ACTINIAN opelet, vestlet
ACTINOID radiate, raylike

ACTINOLITE amphibole, amphibolite
ACTINOZOAN seaflower
ACTION activity, affair, agency, animation, attack, battle, behavior, bout, brush, business, case, cause, ceremony, combat, conduct, confrontation, contest, dap, deed, demeanor, deportment, doing, effect, energy, engagement, enterprise, event, exercise, exertion, expression, fact, fight, fray, geste, gesture, influence, issue, job, litigation, maneuver, manner, mechanism, movement, operation, performance, play, ploy, position, practice, practise, praxis, proceeding, process, program, push, rite, show, skirmish, suit, tanquam, vitality, way, work
absurd nonsense
aggressive power play
capricious freak
comb. ade, ado, ance, ancy, asia, asis, ence, ency, iasis, praxia, ure
cooperative synergism
cruel ruth
exaggerated theatrics
extempore schediasm
fatal kiss of death
faulty parapraxia
field arena, bowl, coliseum, scene, stadium, stage, theater, theatre
final catastrophe
inevitable forceput
legal actus, assize, gravamina, querela, replevin, res, suit, trover
maniacal psychokinesia
military sweep
painting abstract expressionism
pert. practical
place of venue
playful frolic, fun
put into actuate
put out of disable
sudden flisk
symbolic charade
tactless gaucherie
unavoidable forceput
unintended automatism
violent affray
word verb
ACTIS *parent* helius, rhoda
statue colossus of rhodes
ACTIVATE, ACTIVIZE actify, arm, arouse, atomize,

begin, elicit, energize, excite, generate, hasten, launch, open, organize, spark, start

ACTIVATOR catalyst

ACTIVE 3 yal, yap, yep 4 busy, fast, lish, live, pert, spry, trig, yald, yare 5 agile, alert, alive, brisk, chirk, deedy, doing, lingy, lusty, nippy, peart, peppy, quick, ready, smart, snell, vital, wight, yauld 6 acting, breezy, clever, feeril, lively, living, moving, nimble, prompt, semmit, snappy, speedy, sprack, sproil, sprunt, wimble 7 causing, chipper, deedful, dynamic, engaged, hopping, humming, in force, kinetic, sthenic, throddy, turning, working 8 animated, athletic, changing, diligent, erupting, exerting, involved, smacking, spanking, spirited, vigorous 9 assiduous, effective, effectual, energetic, mercurial, on the move, operative, practical, sprightly, strenuous, vivacious 10 proceeding, productive 11 going places, industrious, progressive

ACTIVIST advocate, enthusiast, kochleffl

ACTIVITY action, ado, agency, animation, briskness, business, bustle, busyness, buzz, caper, coil, creation, deed, doing(s), energy, enterprise, event, feat, fizz, force, function, gog, goings-on, hustle, industry, life, motion, movement, operation, parergon, pep, proceedings, process, program, rajas, sproil, stir, trade, vigor, vir, vitality, work
continuous perseveration
freedom from recess, respite, rest
mental brainwork
showy razzle-dazzle

ACTON haqueton, hogton

ACTOR advocate, agent, aisteoir, artist(e), barnstormer, cabotin, character, diseur, doer, dramatizer, entertainer, extra, feeder, foil, grimac(i)er, guiser, ham, heavy, hero, histrion, impersonator, ingenue, lead,

matinee idol, mime, mimic, movie star, mummer, pantomimer, pantomimist, participant, performer, personator, player, pleader, pretender, primomo, protagonist, protean, puppet, roscius, simulator, stager, star, stooge, straight man, stroller, super, thespian, tommer, trouper, vaudevillian, vaudevillist
brother sugeas
cast dramatis personae
club lamb's
consort molione
cue hint, prompt, word
group afra, aftra, cast, company, panel, retinue, troop, troupe
inept ham
kingdom phthia
parent myrmidon, pasidice
part lead, role, support, walk-on
son cteatus, eurytion, eurytus
status stardom
substitute understudy
supporting bit, ripieno, super
valet dresser

ACTRESS chorine, diva, farceuse, ingenue, star(let), thespian

ACTUAL bodily, carnal, certain, concrete, corporeal, current, definite, existing, factual, fleshly, genuine, good, hard, material, physical, positive, practical, present, real, somatic, substantial, sure-enough, tangible, true, undoubted, veritable

ACTUALITY being, ease, entelechy, existence, fact, reality, realness, substance, substantiality, verity

ACTUALLY but, de facto, done, ex facto, fairly, really, truly

ACTUARY accountant, clerk, computer, registrar

ACTUATE agitate, animate, arouse, draw, drive, effect, egg, energize, engender, enliven, excite, exert, generate, impel, incite, induce, inspire, instigate, motivate, MOVE, open, operate, persuade, propel, rouse, run, start, stir, trigger, trip, turn on

ACUATE acuminate, needle-shaped, pointed, quicken, sharpen(ed), stinging

ACUITY See ACUMEN.

ACULEATE acuate, incisive, severe, spiny, stinging

ACULEUS prickle, sting

ACUMEN acuity, acuteness, capacity, discernment, discrimination, edge, fineness, insight, keenness, penetration, perception, perspicacity, sagacity, sense, sharpness, shrewdness, wit

ACUS needle, pin

ACUSHLA darling

ACUTE accented, acid, argute, astute, bright, brilliant, clever, critical, crucial, cunning, discerning, discriminating, distressing, incisive, ingenious, intelligent, intense, keen, knowing, penetrating, perceptive, perspicacious, poignant, pointed, profound, sagacious, sage, sapient, sensitive, severe, sharp(witted), shrewd, shrill, smart, snack, snell, subtle, sudden, urgent, violent, wise
comb. oxy

ACUTENESS acuity, acumen, depth, nostril, sagacity, sense, subtlety

ADA(H) *husband* cain, esau, lamech
parent elon
son eliphaz, jabal, jubal

ADAD ramman

ADAGE aphorism, apothegm, axiom, bromide, byword, dict(um), epigram, gnome, homily, law, maxim, moral, mot(to), precept, proverb, saw, saying, sentence, slogan, sutra, theorem, truism, wheeze

ADAIAH *father* shimei
offspring jedidah

ADAM, ADAM'S *ale* water
and eve aconitum, arethusa, corallorhiza, crawfoot, orchis, plant, pulmonaria, putty root
apple crape-jasmine, fig, guzzle, larynx, throatboll, thyroid
bede, author george eliot
bede, beloved hetty sorrel
bede, character mrs poyser
bede, occupation carpenter
bede, wife dinah morris
burial place aboucala
cup huntsman's horn, pitcher-plant, saracenia
descendent adamite, human

fig plantain
flannel mullein, verbascum
grandchild enoch, enos
home eden, paradise
needle beargrass, scandix, shrub, thorn, yucca
profession agriculture, gardening
rib eve, wife, woman
son abel, cain, seth
teacher raisel
wife eve, lilith
wine water
ADAMANT cast-iron, diamond, firm, grim, hard, immovable, immutable, inexorable, inflexible, iron, loadstone, magnet, obdurate, obstacle, obstinate, perverse, recalcitrant, refractory, relentless, rigid, rigorous, rocky, solid, stern, stiff, stone, stony, stubborn, unalterable, unbending, unmoved, unrelenting, unyielding
ADAMANTINE (See also ADAMANT.) boron, vajra
ADAMAS corundum, diamond, sapphire
foe antilochus
slayer poseidon
ADAMS, JOHN *birthplace* braintree, merry mount
burial site quincy
party federalist
profession lawyer
vice-president jefferson
ADAMS, JOHN QUINCY publicola
birthplace braintree
burial site quincy
party republican
profession lawyer
vice-president calhoun
ADANSONIA baobab, cream-of-tartar tree
ADAPT accommodate, accustom, adjust, agree, alter, amend, apply, arrange, assimilate, attemper, attune, capacitate, change, comply, compose, condition, conform, convert, doctor, dovetail, edit, enable, equalize, equip, fit, furnish, gear, harmonize, humor, match, modify, mold, orient, ply, prepare, qualify, reconcile, regulate, settle, shape, sort, suit, temper, trim, tune, turn, vary
ADAPTABLE adaptive, elas-

tic, flexuous, labile, pliable, tractable, versatile
ADAPTATION accommodation, bearings, harmonization
to environment, pert. autoplastic
ADAR SHENI veadar
ADBEEL *kin* ishmael
ADD accrete, accrue, adject, adjoust, advene, affix, aggravate, aggregate, annex, append, appose, attach, augment, bolster, burden, calculate, cast, clap on, combine, compute, confer, contribute, eik, eke, encumber, enlarge, enumerate, figure, foot, fortify, gain, hitch, include, increase, join, plus, postfix, reckon, recruit, reinforce, saddle, subjoin, sum, summate, super(im)pose, supervene, supplement, supply, tack on, tag on, tot(al), tote, unite
alcohol spike
fuel to the flame agitate, beet, ignite, increase
sound dub
to adorn, augment, enrich
ADDA lizard, scincus, scink, skink
ADDAX antelope, pygarg(us)
ADDED adjunct, and, eked, plus
ADDENDUM addition, adjuncy, appendix, extension, sequel, summand, supplement
ADDER, ADDER'S ather, elapid, elapoid, hagworm, hypnale, krait, nadder, nedder, serpent, snake, viper
kind banded, checkered, puff, sea
-meat cuckoopint, stitchwort
-mouth malaxis
-tongue achillea, arum, cock'scomb, coxcomb, dogtooth violet, erythronium, fern, geranium, lily, ophioglossum, orchis, peramium, roosters
ADDERSPIT brake
ADDERWORT bistort, blueweed
ADDICT accustom, acidhead, alcoholic, apply, attach, bluff, bummer, case, cokey, cokie, devotee, dipsomaniac, dopefiend, dope-

head, dopie, dopy, drunk (ard), enslave, ENTHUSIAST, fan, fiend, glue-sniffer, habituate, habitue, hook, hophead, hoppy, hype, junker, junkie, junky, lush, mainliner, pothead, potlush, slave, snifter, snowbird, speed-freak, triad, tripper, user
treatment center synanon
ADDICTED accustomed, bibacious, bibulous, disposed, given, habituated, hooked, prone, wont
ADDICTION alcoholism, barbiturism, bibacity, cacoethes, cocainism, dipsomania, habit, monkey, morphinism
conquer kick the habit
ADDISON atticus, clio
and steele periodical spectator
and steele squire coverley
ADDITION accession, accessory, accidental, accrue, addend(a), additive, adjection, adjunct, affix, also, and, annexation, another, appendage, auctary, augend, augmentation, auxiliary, codicil, computation, contribution, eik, eke, ell, else, encore, enlargement, expansion, farce, farse, gain, gansel, improvement, income, increase, joining, juxtaposition, mantissa, paragoge, plus, prefix, reinforcement, result, rider, sum, tab, tail, too, total, uniting
comb. super
reversionary annuity
trivial fil(1)ip
ADDITIONAL accessory, ancillary, another, auxiliary, besides, collateral, contributory, else, extra, farther, fresh, further, more, new, other, plus, spare, supernumerary, supplemental, supplementary, surplus, tither, tother
ADDLE agitate, amaze, befuddle, bewilder, confuse, curdle, earn, empty, filth, fruit, mire, muddle, ripen, rot, spoil, thrive, unsound, upset
ADDLED asea, bemazed, bemused, blank, confused, empty, flighty, foolish,

fruitless, harebrained, illogical, intoxicated, mired, muddled, putrid, rotten, scatterbrained, silly, spoiled, unsound
ADDLEPATE draykop(f), scatterbrain
ADDLEPLOT marplot, spoilsport
ADDRA dama, nanger
ADDRESS 3 sue, wit, woo 4 call, ease, form, hail, home, mint, pray, send, tact, talk, tulk 5 abode, apply, array, board, court, erect, greet, lodge, point, poise, raise, skill, speak, title 6 accost, aplomb, appeal, assign, betake, direct, eulogy, halloo, invoke, khutba, manner, number, salute, sermon, speech 7 arrange, bearing, begrace, behight, bespeak, consign, entrust, lecture, oration, prepare, request, tutoyer 8 approach, argument, behavior, dedicate, delivery, demeanor, dispatch, domicile, dwelling, facility, harangue, inscribe, location, perorate, petition 9 attention, dexterity, direction, discourse, ingenuity, residence, statement 10 administer, adroitness, cleverness, deportment, expedition, letterhead, management, salutation 11 benediction, destination, inscription 12 apostrophize
familiarly tutoyer
oneself to undertake
saucily chayack, chyak
to remind
ADDRESSEE correspondent, inhabitant, occupant, resident
ADDUCE advance, allay, allege, argue, assign, bear, bring forward, cite, counter, give, infer, mention, name, offer, plead, present, produce, quote, show
ADDUCT attract, draw
ADE squash
ADELA *father* william the conqueror
ADEN *gulf port* berbera, djibouti
ADENANTHERA barbadospride, beartree, flowerfence, peacock-flower, sandlewood, tree

ADENOSTOMA cedar, chamiso, china-tree, ribbonwood
ADEPHAGIA bulimia
ADEPS fat, lard
ADEPT able, ACE, apt, artist, capable, conversant, crafty, dabster, dextrous, efficient, expert, fit, handy, mahatma, master(ful), mystic, proficient, sage, sharp, skilled, versed
ADEQUACY ability, capacity, competence, plenty, utility
ADEQUATE able, acceptable, ample, capable, commensurate, common, competent, condign, decent, digne, due, effectual, enough, equal, fit, full, meet, proper, proportionate, roomy, satisfactory, satisfying, sufficient, sufficing, suitable, tolerable, utile, wally
ADER benjaminite
ADERMIN pyridoxine
AD ESSE here, present
AD EXTREMUM, AD FINEM at last, end, finally, finish
ADHARMA uprighteousness
ADHEM *son* abou
ADHERE accrete, affix, agglutinate, annerre, apply, associate, attach, bind, braze, cement, clag, clam, clasp, cleave, cling, cohere, freeze, fuse, glue, grasp, gum, hang on, hew, hold, hug, join, link, lute, paste, persevere, persist, solder, stay, stick, unite, weld
ADHERENCE accession, adhesion, allegiance, attachment, cling, fidelity
ADHERENT adept, aide, ally, believer, devotee, disciple, faithful, fan, follower, ist, ite, partisan, retainer, rooter, satellite, sectary, servitor, supporter, upholder, votary
comb. ist, ite
ADHESION adherence, adsorption, agreement, assent, attachment, attraction, bond, clinging, coherence, concurrence, fidelity, grip, stickage, sticking, synechia, tenacity, union
comb. ankyl(o)
ADHESIVE allyl, amino-

plast, bandaid, birdlime, bond, cement, clam, clingy, dabby, dauby, emplastic, epoxy, glue, gluey, gluten, gum, lime, lute, mastic, mucilage, paste, plucky, putty, sealing wax, silicone, size, smeary, stickum, sticky, tacky, tape, tar, tenacious, viscid, viscous, wax
ADHIBIT administer, admit, affix, apply, attach, let in, use
AD HOC temporary
ADIANTOPSIS bird's-foot fern, rock-brake
ADIANTUM fern, MAIDENHAIR
ADIAPHORISM indifference, tolerance
ADIATHERMAL athermanous, diathermic, transcalent
ADIEU See GOOD-BYE.
ADIGE *city on* trento
AD INFINITUM ad nauseam, ake, endlessly, eternally, forever, without end
AD INTERIM in the meantime, meanwhile, temporary
ADIPOSE adepescent, fat (ty), lard, obese, pursy, squat, suet, tallow, unctuous
ADIPOSIS fatness, obesity, oiliness, steatosis
ADIT access, admission, approach, channel, door, entrance, entry, passage, sough, stulm, tunnel
ADITI *consort* varuna
offspring aditya
ADITYA mitra, varuna
mother aditi
ADJACENCY abutment, abuttal, conjunction, contiguity, contiguousness, junction
ADJACENT abutting, adjoining, beside, bordering, close, conterminous, contiguous, handy, hard by, immediate, juxtaposed, meeting, near, neighboring, next, nigh, proximal, touching, vicinal
but opposite back to back
ADJECT add, annex, join
ADJECTIVE accessory, adjunct, adnoun, dependent, diptote, epithet, modifier, nominal
comb. ant, ate, ative, ent, est,

fic, ial, ian, ical, ile, ine, ious, ish, ive, ous, ular
demonstrative these, this, those
-*jerker* author, writer
limiting the
verbal gerundive

ADJOIN abut, accost, add, append, approximate, attach, border, butt, connect, contact, join, juxtapose, meet, neighbor, tack, touch, trench, unite, verge

ADJOURN break up, close, defer, delay, dissolve, end, postpone, prorogue, put off, recess, rise, shut, stay, suspend, transfer

ADJUDGE, ADJUDICATE arbitrate, assign, award, behight, condemn, consider, decern, decide, decree, determine, esteem, find, give, grant, hear, hold, judge, ordain, order, pass, pronounce, rate, reckon, regard, rule, sentence, settle, sit, think, try, value

ADJUNCT accession, accessory, added, addendum, additament, addition, additive, additory, additum, aide, allonge, ancilla, annex(ed), appanage, appendage, appendix, appurtenance, associate, attach(ed), attachment, attending, augment, auxiliary, colleague, complement, conjoined, consequent, continuation, corollary, extension, fitting, fixture, help, increment, offshoot, ornament, part, patch, pendant, pertain, piece, plus, postscript, prefix, reinforcement, rider, satellite, subscript, suffix, supplement, tab, tag, teacher, tuck, wing

ADJURE appeal, ask, beg, beseech, bid, bind, charge, command, conjure, contest, crave, entreat, plead, pray, request, swear, unswear

ADJUST accept, accommodate, accord, accustom, adapt, admit, align, alter, angle, arrange, assess, assimilate, attune, balance, cast, center, conform, coordinate, correct, determine, dispose, ease, equal(ize), fit, fix, form, frame, free, gear, harmonize, justify,

line, modify, order, orient, pare, patch, prepare, range, rate, reconcile, reduce, regulate, remedy, repair, set (tle), shape, size, sort, square, suit, temper, tram, trim, true, tune, wangle
sail flatten, trim

ADJUSTMENT accommodation, adaptation, arrangement, change, compromise, concession, correction, disposition, fit, harmony, indemnification, modification, rectification, regulation, settlement, trim

ADJUTAGE nozzle, opening, pipe, spout, tube

ADJUTANT aide (de camp), ally, argala, assistant, auxiliary, crane, helper, hurgila, marabou, officer, stork

ADJUVANT adjunct, aide, assisting, auxiliary, helper, helpful

ADLAI coix, job's-tears
seed camadulla
son shaphat

AD LIB extemporaneous, fake, impromptu, improvisation, improvise, makeshift, offhand, spontaneous, unrestricted

ADMAH adama

ADMAN huckster, publicist

ADMETE *father* eurystheus

ADMETUS *helper* apollo
kingdom pherae, thessaly
wife alcestis

ADMINICLE aid, auxiliary, help, proof, support

ADMINISTER adhibit, aid, apply, assist, bestow, chair, conduce, conduct, contribute, control, deal, deem, direct, dispense, distribute, dose, execute, furnish, give, govern, husband, impose, manage, minister, move, officiate, oversee, pass, perform, preside, rule, run, serve, settle, superintend, supervise, supply, tender, treat

ADMINISTRATION adhibition, application, bestowal, bureaucracy, cabinet, conduct, council, delivery, direction, directorate, dispensation, disposal, disposition, distribution, execution, government, helm, imposition, infliction, management, managers, ministry, officia-

tion, performance, policy, regime(n), regulation, rule, sway, tahsil, term
branch agency, arm, bureau
pert. dispensative

ADMINISTRATOR caid, curaca, director, dispenser, executive, executor, helm, manager, overseer, provicar, qaid, supervisor, trustee

ADMIRABLE amiable, brave, capital, commendable, divine, elegant, estimable, excellent, good, grand, great, high, laudable, lummy, marvelous, praiseworthy, proud, ripping, wonderful
doctor roger bacon
name meaning miranda

ADMIRAL amrel(le), butterfly, commander(-in-chief), emir, flagman, flagship, general, logwood, officer
famous dewey, farragut, halsey, king, leahy, nelson, nimitz, porter, spee, togo
togo darwin-tulip, flower

ADMIRATION adoration, adulation, affection, appreciation, approbation, approval, awe, craze, esteem, furor, glory, liking, love, marveling, rage, regard, respect, reverence, wonder, worship

ADMIRE adore, adulate, approve, cherish, delight, dig, esteem, extol, idolize, laud, like, love, marvel, prize, regard, respect, revere, salute, value, venerate, worship

ADMIRED popular, precious

ADMIRER amateur, beau, devotee, fan, follower, idolator, lover, swain

ADMISSIBLE acceptable, allowable, eligible, entitled, logical, permissible, tolerable, worthy

ADMISSION acceptance, access, acknowledgment, acquiescence, adit, admittance, apology, charge, concession, confession, consent, entrance, entree, entry, fee, immission, inauguration, ingress, initiation, installation, intromission, permission, price, rate, statement, testimony, ticket
receipts gate

to the bar call
ADMIT accede, accept, acknowledge, adhibit, agree, allow, assent, aver, avouch, avow, believe, concede, confess, consider, enroll, enter, face, grant, immit, inaugurate, include, initiate, inlet, install, instate, intromit, ken, let, open to, own, pass, permit, profess, receive, recognize, suffer, take in, ticket, trust
as member induct
error eat crow
ADMITTANCE See ADMISSION.
ADMIXTURE alloy, blend, composition, compound, dallop, dash, dollop, infusion, leaven, mixing, MIXTURE, olio, potpourri, shade, soupcon, streak
ADMONISH advise, apprise, caution, censure, chide, counsel, dissuade, enjoin, exhort, jog, monitor, notify, preprove, rebuke, remind, reprehend, school, scold, tutor, warn
ADMONITION advice, caution, caveat, counsel, hint, homily, instruction, lecture, notice, rebuke, reminder, reproof, summons, warning
ADNAH ednas
chief for jehoshaphat
ADO activity, agitation, bearm, blather, blether, bother, business, bustle, coil, confusion, deed, doing, effort, energy, excitement, flurry, fuss, howdedo, hubbub, hullaballoo, hurry, noise, pother, rout, ruckus, sputter, stir, storm, to-do, trouble, tumult, turmoil, uproar, upset
ADOBE brick, clay, dobe, doby, earth, gumbo, house, loamy, marly, mud, silt, soddy, tapia
lily fritillaria
tick argas
ADOLESCENCE awkward age, juvenile, minority, nonage, puberty, teens, youth
ADOLESCENT callow, hebetic, immature, lad, minor, nubile, prebetic, pubescent, subdeb, subteen, teenager, youth
girl bobby-soxer

ADONIJAH adonias
father david
slayer solomon
ADONIS buttercup, dandy, herb, plant, thammuz, wig
beloved aphrodite, persephone, venus
festival adonia
flower anemone, pheasant's-eye, poppy, rose
mother myrrh(a)
slayer ares, boar, mars
ADOPT accept, acquire, advocate, affect, affiliate, appropriate, approve, arrogate, assume, borrow, choose, copy, embrace, employ, espouse, father, follow, foster, imitate, maintain, mother, naturalize, receive, select, simulate, steal, take, undertake, use, welcome
ADORABLE admirable, angelic, beautiful, caressable, charming, cuddlesome, cuddly, delightful, exquisite, kissable, likable, lovable, lovely, precious, seraphic, winning, winsome
ADORATION devotion, dulia, homage, hyperdulia, latria, love, obeisance, regard, reverence, veneration, worship
ADORE admire, cherish, dote, enjoy, esteem, exalt, extol, glorify, honor, idolize, land, love, praise, regard, respect, revere, reverence, venerate, worship, wurth
ADORER See SWEETHEART.
ADORN anorn, array, attire, attrap, beautify, bedeck, bedight, bedizen, bedub, begem, belace, bespangle, blazon, border, braid, caparison, deck, decorate, depaint, dight, dignify, dill, dink, dress, embellish, emblazon, enamel, enhance, enrich, fig, finify, foil, garnish, gaud, gild, glamorize, grace, hight, honor, jewel, mensk, ornament, ornify, paint, pink, prank, prettify, primp, prink, rouge, spangle, splay, suborn, tassel, tire, trap
ADORNED bepranked, clad, clothed, colored, daedal, figured, ornate, pinked

ADORNMENT beautification, decor, decoration, dress, ornament, ounding, pranking, prettification, pride, tahali, tinsel, tirement
ADRAMMELECH *father* sennacherib
ADRASTEA nemesis
father melisseus
reared zeus
ADRASTUS *brother* mecisteus
companion amphiaraus, capaneus, hippomedon, parthenopaeus, polynices, tydeus
enemy thebes
father talaus
horse arion, cerus
kingdom sicyon
offspring aegia, aegialeus, argia, deipyle
sister eriphyle
AD REM apt, pertinent
ADRENAL *hormone* aldosterone
stimulant acth
ADRENALINE adrenine, epinephrine
ADRESTUS *captor* menelaus
father merops
slayer agamemnon
ADRIAN, ST. *symbol* anvil, axe, sword
ADRIANA *husband* antipholus
servant luce
sister luciana
ADRIANOPLE *old name* edirne
ADRIATIC *boat* bracozzo
city bari, rimini, venice
coast illyria
gulf quarnero, trieste
island bua, eso, lagosta, lastovo
peninsula istria
plateau karst
port brindisi, fiume, pesaro, pescara, pola, rimini, trieste, zara
queen venice
region, ancient illyria
resort lido
river into adige, bosna, drin, kerka, livenza, piave, reno, rubicon
wind bora, levantera, tramontana
ADRIEL *wife* merab
ADRIFT afloat, aimless, asea, awaft, aweigh, confused, derelict, floating, in-

constant, lost, unanchored, unfastened, unmoored, unstable, wafted

ADROIT able, adept, apt, artful, bright, clever; cunning, deft, dexterous, easy, expert, good, habile, handy, ingenious, neat, nimble, ready, resourceful, right, skillful, smart, tight, trick

ADROITNESS address, art, dexterity, ease, facility, knack, skill

ADSCITITIOUS added, additional, adventitious, nonessential, supplemental

ADUEL *parent* gabael

ADULARIA moonstone, orthoclase

ADULATE blandish, butter, cajole, fawn, flatter, glaze, gloze, honey, kneel, laud, praise, softsoap, wheedle

ADULATORY blandishing, buttery, cajoling, complimentary, courtly, finespoken, flattering, honeyed, insincere, mealy-mouthed, obsequious, oily, smoothspoken, soapy, sycophantic, unctuous, wheedling

ADULT big, developed, full-blown, full-fledged, grown up, imago, man(ly), marriageable, mature, maturescent, mellow, nubile, of age, ripe, seasoned, thriven, woman

ADULTERATE alloy, alter, artificial, contaminate, corrupt, counterfeit, cut, deacon, debase, defile, denature, dilute, doctor, extend, falsify, mix, seduce, sophisticate, taint, vitiate, weaken

ADULTERATED corrupt, cut, illicit, impure, sham, spurious

ADULTERESS *husband* cuckold

ADULTERY avoutry, cuckoldom, faithlessness, lewdness, unchastity, unfaithfulness

symbolic color yellow

ADUMBRATE cloud, etch, foreshadow, image, obscure, outline, overshadow, portend, prefigure, shade, sketch, suggest, symbolize

ADUMBRATION omen, outline, phantasm, shade, shadow

ADUNCOUS bent, curved, hooked

ADUST burnt, dried, fiery, gloomy, sallow, scorched, sunburnt, tan

ADVANCE 3 aid, fee, pay 4 abet, cite, come, dash, gain, grow, help, inch, laud, lead, lend, loan, move, near, nose, push, show, step 5 avant, boost, creep, exalt, extol, favor, forge, march, money, offer, place, press, raise, serve, speed, stake 6 adduce, admove, allege, ascend, assign, assist, attach, avaunt, better, breast, elapse, exceed, growth, hasten, incede, prefer, prepay, supply, tender, thrive, vaunce 7 develop, elevate, enhance, forward, furnish, further, glorify, headway, improve, magnify, payment, proceed, promote, propose, prosper, provect, quicken 8 addition, approach, flourish, heighten, increase, motivate, overture, progress, propound 9 encourage, influence, postulate, spearhead 10 accelerate, aggrandize, appreciate, contribute, underwrite 11 accommodate, improvement, progression 12 breakthrough, press release

by leaps saltation
creeping proreption
difficult slog
gradual illapse
guard van
military anabasis
obliquely sidle
payment arles
slowly crawl, creep, drag, hobble, inch, worm
sudden sweep
upon trespass

ADVANCED aged, ahead, along, far, forward, imprest, intensified, liberal, modern, outer, premature, progressive, vanward
equally abreast
in years aged, antiquated, elderly, old, senior
most extreme, farthest, foremost, headmost

ADVANTAGE account, ascendancy, avail, bargain, behalf, behoof, benefit, better, boot, bot(e), bulge, bunce, capital, derive, edge,

exploit, favor, foothold, fordeal, frame, further, gain, good, handicap, hank, head start, increase, inside track, interest, jump, kinch, leverage, odds, plus, primacy, privilege, profit, promote, sake, service, start, stead, superiority, upper hand, use, vail, van(tage), whip hand
accidental fluke
slight toe hold

ADVANTAGEOUS bargain, beneficial, expedient, favorable, golden, good, handy, joli(e), lucrative, plummy, propitious, speedy, useful
situation catbird seat

ADVENE add, come, reach

ADVENT approach, arrival, coming, future, incarnation, income, parousia

ADVENTIST *leader* miller

ADVENTITIOUS accidental, acquired, added, adscititious, casual, chance, epenthetic, episodic, extrinsic, foreign, fortuitous, incidental, nonessential, parasitic, spontaneous, strange, supervenient

ADVENTIVE alien, exotic, foreign, immigrant

ADVENTURE achievement, act, aunter, auntre, chance, danger, deed, emprise, enterprise, escapade, event, excitement, experience, exploit, feat, fortune, gest(e), happening, hazard, incident, lark, luck, peril, quest, risk, seek, speculation, undertaking, venture
land poictesme
story geste, yarn

ADVENTURER almogavar, argonaut, aventurier, beau sabreur, carpetbagger, condottiere, daredevil, entrepreneur, gambler, landloper, palliard, routier, speculator, traveler, upstart

ADVENTURESS courtesan, demimondaine, demirep, gold digger

ADVENTUROUS aggressive, audacious, auntrous, casual, dangerous, daring, enterprising, errant, foolhardy, fortuitous, hazardous, perilous, presumptuous, rash, reckless, risky, venturesome

ADVERB *comb.* ally

ADVERSARY antagonist, devil, enemy, foe, opponent, rival, satan

ADVERSE afflictive, against, antagonistic, awkward, calamitous, con, conflicting, confronting, contrary, counter, cross, disinclined, diverse, evil, froward, hostile, ill, inimical, loath, opposed, opposing, opposite, overwart, reluctant, thraw (art), thwart, unfavorable, unfriendly, unpropitious

ADVERSITY affliction, bad luck, calamity, catastrophe, disaster, distress, hardship, hard times, misery, misfortune, reverse, sorrow, suffering, trouble, wither, woe

ADVERT allude, attend, comment, designate, heed, notice, observe, recur, refer, remark, return, revert, turn

ADVERTENT attentive, careful, heedful

ADVERTISE announce, back, ballyhoo, bark, bill, blazon, bluff, blurb, boast, boost, bruit, call, circularize, cry, declare, display, emphasize, exploit, inform, make known, notify, observe, offer, parade, placard, plug, post, praise, press agent, proclaim, promote, promulgate, propagandize, publicize, publish, puff, spiel, spotlight, star

ADVERTISEMENT affiche, bill(board), blurb, cachet, circular, commercial, dodger, handbill, notice, poster, spread, stuffer, teaser

ADVERTISER publicist, sandwichman, sponsor

ADVERTISING ballyhoo, barnumism, billing, build-up, bush, promotion, puffery
space measure agate line, column inch
subtle soft-sell

ADVICE admonition, adviso, advocacy, announcement, aviso, avys(e), caution, charge, consideration, consultation, counsel, deliberation, determination, direction, exhortation, expostu-

lation, guidance, hortation, information, injunction, instruction, intelligence, judgment, knowledge, lore, monition, news, notice, opinion, par(a)enesis, persuasion, plan, pointer, prudence, recommendation, rede, reminder, remonstrance, steer, suggestion, tip, urging, warning, wisdom
seek consult, huddle

ADVISABLE befitting, desirable, expedient, favorable, fit, meet, politic, proper, prudent, sensible, suitable, wise

ADVISE acquaint, adjure, admonish, advocate, alert, apprise, aread, areed, berede, bethink, caution, coach, confer, consider, consult, counsel, deliberate, dictate, direct, dissuade, enjoin, enlighten, exhort, familiarize, guide, inform, instruct, kibitz, mention, notify, prescribe, read, recommend, rede, remind, report, reveal, review, tell, tip, urge, warn, weise, weize, wise up

ADVISED calculated, considered, contemplated, deliberate, intentional, meditated, studied, weighed

ADVISER aide, attorney, coach, counsel, director, egeria, lawyer, mentor, monitor, nestor, preacher, starets, teacher, tout, tutor
group board, braintrust, cabal, cabinet, camarilla, clique, committee, council, directorate, panel

ADVISORY hortative, mentorial, prudent, urging

ADVOCATE abet(tor), abogado, actor, adopt, agent, angel, apologist, approve, argue for, attorney, back(er), barrister, boost, campaign, champion, commend, contend, counsel, counselor, defend(er), defensor, deputy, endorse, ENTHUSIAST, espouse, exponent, favor, intercessor, lawyer, lobbyist, maintain, paraclete, partisan, patron, plead, pleader, plug, preacher, proctor, proponent, scholar, solicitor,

speak for, sponsor, support(er), sustain, uphold, urge, vindicate, vogt
comb. arian, ist, ite

ADVOWSON benefice

ADYNAMIA asthenia, debility, weakness

ADYTUM alter, chamber, oracle, retreat, sanctuary, sanctum, shrine

ADZ(E) axe, cut, dress, eatche, hatchet, thixle, tool

ADZHARISTAN *capital* batum

AE ane, one

AEACIDES *consort* phthia
enemy cassander
father-in-law menon
offspring deidamia, pyrrhus, troas
parent arybas, troas

AEACUS *descendants* aeacides
grandson achilles
parent aegina, zeus
son peleus, talamon
subjects myrmidons
wife endeis

AECAMEDE *father* arsinous

AECHMAGORAS *father* hercules

AECIUM caeoma, rust

AEDICULE enclosure, niche, room, shrine

AEDILE edile, magistrate, official

AEDON *brother* amphion
father pandareus
husband zethus
kin itylus, niobe
victim itylus

AEETES *offspring* absyrtus, medea

AEGAEON briareus
brother cottus, gy(g)es, uranids
enemy titans
parent gaea, uranus

AEGEAN *civilization* cycladic, helladic, hellenic, minoan, mycenaean
gulf argolis, saros
island (See also GREEK *island.*) andros, armogos, astropalia, calchi, calino, caso, castellorizo, castelrosso, chios, cos, cyclades, delos, dodecanese, evvoia, icaria, imros, ios, ipsara, kariot, karpathos, kasos, khio, lemnos, leros, lipsos, melos, milos, misyros, mykonos, mytilene, mytilini, nikaria, nios, nisyros,

paros, patmos, psara, rodi, samos, samothrace, santorini, scarpanto, scio, simi, siros, sporades, stampalia, sykros, syme, tenos, thera, tilos, timos
people, ancient lelege, psara, psyra, samian, samiote
people, warlike carians
port enos
river to maritsa, struma, vardar
rock aex
town chios, mytilene, vathy
AEGEON *son* antiphilus
wife aemilia
AEGER excuse, ill, sick
AEGEUS *consort* aethra
kin pandion, theseus
kingdom athens
victim androgeus
AEGILIA *lover* cometes
AEGIMIUS *parent* dorus
AEGINA *lover* zeus
son aeacus
temple panhellenium
AEGIOCHUS zeus
AEGIR gymir, hler
wife ran
AEGIRINE acmite, aegirinolite, aegirite
AEGIS accoutrement, aid, auspice, breastplate, defence, defense, protection, safeguard, shield, sponsorship, symbol
AEGISTHUS *beloved* clytemnestra
kingdom mycenae
parent pelopia, thyestes
slayer orestes
victim agamemnon, atreus
AEGLE *consort* zeus
offspring graces
AEGYPTUS *brother* danaus
kingdom libya
parent anchinoe, belus
son lynceus
AELANA aqaba
AEMILIA *husband* aegeon
AENEAS *adviser* nautes
ally evander
birthplace mt ida
companion acamas, anchises, archelochus, cloanthus, cupavo, eumedes, eumelus, eurytion, evander, gyas, sergestus
consort creusa, dido, glauce, lavinia
defended troy
epic aeneid
friend acamas, achates, archelochus

kin assaracus, brut(e), brutus, capys
parent anchises, aphrodite, venus
rival camilla, turnus
son ascanius, iulus, romus, silvius
steersman palinurus
victim turnus
AENEID *author* vergil, virgil
character acestes, erulus, euryalus, iarbas, nisus
first word arma
hero aeneas
AENGUS eros
parent boann, dagda
AEOLIAN *lyricist* sappho
poet alcaeus
AEOLUS *brother* dorus, xuthus
daughter alcyone, calyce, canace, halcyone
descendants aeolides
parent arne, hellen, hippotes, poseidon
son cretheus, salmoneus, sisyphus
wife enarete, eriboea
AEON aevum, age, aion, cycle, eon, era, eternity, kalpa, period
pair syzygy
AEONIAN eonian, eternal, everlasting, infinite, lasting
AEPYTUS *charge* evadne
parent cresphontes, merope
AERATE actify, activate, activize, aerify, air, bubble, charge, foam, inflate, vaporize, ventilate
AERIAL aerie, aery, airy, antenna, chimerical, ethereal, graceful, high, imaginary, lofty, unreal, unsubstantial
AERIE aery, ayre, brood, company, dwelling, eyrie, eyry, family, nest, perch
AERODONE glider
AERODROME See AIRPORT.
AERODROMICS See AERONAUTICS.
AERONAUT See AVIATOR.
AERONAUTICS aerodromics, airplaning, astronautics, AVIATION, balloonery, ballooning, barnstorming, cruising, flight, flying, gliding, planing, skyriding, soaring, volation, volitation, volplaning
science aerodynamics, aerology, aeroscopy, avionics,

climatology, hydraulics, hydrostatics, kinematics, kinetics, meteorology, photometry, pneumatics, supersonics
term amplitude, bearing, camber, contrail, decalage, flight path, prop wash, slip(stream), stagger, sweepback, tail force, vapor trail, vortex, wake, wash
AEROPE *brother-in-law* thyestes
consort plisthenes, streus, thyestes
seducer thyestes
son agamemnon, menelaus
AEROSTAT aircraft, airship, BALLOON
AERUGO patina, rust, verdigris
AERY aerial, aerie, ethereal, incorporeal, nest, visionary
AES bronze, copper
AESACUS *beloved* hesperia
parent alexirrhoe, priam
AESCHINES *rival* demoathenes
school rhodes
AESCHYLUS *drama* agamemnon, choephori, eumenides, persians, prometheus, psychostasia, seven against thebes, suppliants
trilogy crest(e)ia
AESCULAPIAN doctor, medical, medicinal, physician
AESCULUS buckeye, glabra, horsechestnut, tree
AESEPUS *kin* abarbarea, pedasus
slayer euryalus
AESIR, VANIR aegir, alaisiages, asynjur, balder, baldur, beda, bori, bragi, donar, eir, erda, fenir, fimmilina, forseti, frea, freja, frey(a), frigg, frija, gefjon, gerth, gullveig, heimdall, hel, hermod, hler, hod(ur), hoenir, hoth, idun, ithun(n), jord, kvasir, lodur, loke, loki, lothur, mimir, nanna, nerthus, njord, njorth, norn, odin, odur, ragnarok, ran, reimthursen, saeter, saga, sif, siguna, skadi, skathi, thinscus, thor, tiu, tiwaz, tyr, tyrl, ull, urd, urth, vali, van, vayu, vidar, vitharr,

vor, wider, wili, woden, wotan, ymir, ziu
chief alfader, niord, odin, othin, wodan, woden, wotan
goddesses' abode vingolf
hall valhalla
home asgard, gladsheim
AESON *brother* amythaon, pelias, pheres
father cretheus
son jason
wife alcimeda, alcimede
AESOP *fables compiler* babrios, babrius
item fables, sour grapes
master iadmon
of england john gay
of india bidpai, pilpay
AESTHETE amateur, art lover, connoisseur, dilettante
AESTHETIC artistic, attic, beautiful, chaste, classic (al), cognoscente, connoisseur, dilettante, elegant, pure, tasteful
AESTHETICS connoisseurship, dilettantism, epicureanism, taste, virtu
AESYETES *son* antenor
wife cleomestra
AETHALIDES *father* hermes, mercury
AETHER *parent* chaos, erebus
AETHERIA heliadite
parent clymene, helius
AETHRA *captor* castor, pollux
consort aegeus, atlas, poseidon
father oceanus, pittheus
offspring hyades, hyas, theseus
AETHUSA *father* poseidon
AETHYLLA *brother* priam
AETNA *beloved* hephaestus
AETOLIAN *king* thestius
prince tydeus
AETOLUS *father* endymion
kingdom elis
son calydon, pleuron
victim apis
wife promoe
AFAR away, danakil, dankali, distance, ferne, ferren, hamite, off, remote, saho, yferre
AFFABLE accessible, amiable, benign, bland, civil, clever, complaisant, compliant, cordial, courteous, easy, facile, fluent, forthy, friendly, genial, gentle,

goodhumored, goodnatured, gracious, likable, mild, pleasant, polite, responsive, sociable, social, suave, sweet, urbane
AFFAIR action, amour, behalf, blowout, brawl, business, cause, circumstance, comether, concern, contest, dealing(s), doing(s), doment, duel, effeir, endeavor, engagement, entanglement, event, fight, flirtation, function, gathering, goings-on, hoedown, hypothec, incident, interest, intrigue, job, levee, liaison, matter, object, occasion, occurrence, operation, palaver, party, performance, ploy, proceeding, rank, reception, relationship, rendezvous, reunion, rite, romance, salon, scandal, setout, shauri, shebang, sociable, social, soiree, thing, topic, triangle, tryst
confused schemozzle
critical kankedort
love amour, intrigue, liaison, tryst
social at-home, ball, formal, junket, party, social, supper
AFFECT acquire, adopt, ail, allot, alter, aspire, assign, assume, attack, attaint, attinge, choose, color, concern, counterfeit, cultivate, desire, disposition, distemper, emotion, entail, excite, fake, fancy, feeling, feign, frequent, haunt, hypothecate, imitate, impel, impress, inclination, incline, influence, interest, like, melt, mince, modify, move, passion, penetrate, play-act, pose, prefer, pretend, profess, put on, seize, sham, shock, simulate, soften, stir, sway, tell, thrill, touch
each other interact
strongly hit, hold, surprise
AFFECTATION airs, artificiality, assumption, cant, conceit, dandyism, elegance, euphemism, euphuism, fondness, foppery, frounce, gongorism, grandiosity, insincerity, loftiness, mannerism, ostentation, overniceness, pietism, pose, posture, preciosity, preciousness, pretense, pre-

tension, primness, put-on, sanctimony, sham, unnaturalness
AFFECTED afflicted, ailed, airy, apish, artificial, assigned, assumed, attacked, beloved, canting, cherished, chichi, diseased, disposed, exquisite, false, feigned, feisty, grandiloquent, impaired, impressed, inclined, influenced, ladeda, lahdidah, minikin, missish, moved, moy, posey, precieux, pretended, pretending, pretentious, quaint, seized, stilted, taffeta, taffety, tainted, touched, unnatural
AFFECTER hypocrite, pretender
AFFECTIBILITY sensibility, sensitivity
AFFECTION (See also AFFECTATION.) ailment, aloha, amity, attachment, attribute, bent, bosom, charity, cherte, devotion, disease, disposition, elegance, emotion, feeling, fondness, friendliness, good will, heart, inclination, kindness, leaning, liking, love, loving, malady, melicera, partiality, passion, prejudice, pretense, primness, propensity, property, regard, show, state, tendency, tenderness, waff
parental storge
AFFECTIONATE adoring, amorous, ardent, attached, biased, dear, devoted, disposed, doting, favorable, fond, friendly, liking, loving, partisan, passionate, tender, warm, zealous
AFFEER assess, assure, confirm
AFFERENT advehent, bear, centripetal, esodic, sensory
AFFIANCE affy, assure, betroth, confidence, contract, engage, faith, hope, pledge, plight, promise, reliance, spouse, troth, trust
AFFIDAVIT,   AFFIDAVY affirmation, certificate, davy, declaration, deposition, oath, statement, testimony
maker affiant
taker notary (public)
AFFILIATE adopt, ally, ascribe, associate, attach,

auxiliary, branch, connect, fix, fraternize, join, receive, subsidiary, unite

AFFILIATION association, combination, family, relation(ship), sect

AFFINITY accord, agreement, alliance, attraction, avidity, chemism, conformity, connection, consanguinity, empathy, friendliness, intimacy, kin(dred), kinship, liking, magnetism, rapport, relation(ship), resemblance, sympathy, tolerance

AFFIRM accept, affy, allege, announce, annunciate, approve, assert, assever, asseverate, attest, aver, avow, confirm, contend, declare, depose, endorse, enunciate, maintain, predicate, profess, pronounce, protest, ratify, say, state, swear, tell, testify, threap, threep, vouch

AFFIRMATION assertion, averral, dixit, oath, ponent, testimony, vow, word, YES *by understatement* litotes *expression of* amen, aye, m-hum, rather, umhum, unhuh, yes

AFFIRMATIVE absolute, amen, assent, aten, averment, aye, cataphatic, declarative, dogmatic, emphatic, litotes, nod, okay, positive, pronunciative, pronunciatory, roger, thumbs up, yea(h), YES

AFFIX add, adhibit, adjunct, anchor, annex, append, attach, case, clip, connect, fasten, fix, impose, impress, join, pin, plaster, prefix, put, seal, settle, stamp, stick, subjoin, unite

AFFLATUS breathing, frenzy, furor, impulse, inspiration, revelation, vapor, vision, wind

AFFLICT ail, anguish, beset, blight, bore, chasten, curse, debilitate, derange, devitalize, disable, disorder, distress, disturb, enfeeble, extenuate, grieve, gripe, harass, harm, harry, humble, hurt, incapacitate, indispose, infect, inflict, injure, lacerate, molest, offend, oppress, pain, pester, pine, plague, ply,

rack, remord, rue, scold, scorch, scourge, sicken, smite, strain, stress, torment, trouble, try, tryst, tuke, vex, weaken, woe, wound

AFFLICTION adversity, anger, anguish, bane, bitter pill, bore, buffet, burden, calamity, care, catastrophe, chagrin, cross, curse, disaster, discomfort, disease, distress, duress, encumbrance, ennui, evil, gall, grief, grievance, hardship, hurt, illness, load, loss, malady, millstone, misery, misfortune, mishap, onus, oppression, pain, pathos, pest, plague, scourge, sickness, sore, sorrow, stress, suffering, teen, thorn, torment, trial, tribulation, trouble, vexation, weight, woe, wretchedness

AFFLUENCE abundance, assets, concourse, ease, flowing, fortune, influx, opulence, plenty, profusion, property, riches, richness, supply, wealth

AFFLUENT abundant, copious, fat, flowing, flush, rich, wealthy

AFFORD achieve, bear, confer, cost, endure, furnish, give, grant, incur, manage, offer, produce, provide, spare, stand, supply, support, thole, yield

AFFRAY alarm, altercation, assault, battle, brawl, broil, combat, contention, contest, discord, dissension, disturbance, encounter, enfrai, feud, fighting, fray, frighten, melee, quarrel, riot, scare, scuffle, startle, strife, struggle, terror, tumult

AFFRICATE abrade, grate, rasp, rub

AFFRIGHT aghast, agrise, alarm, appall, confuse, cow, daunt, dismay, far, frighten, scare, startle, terrify, terror

AFFRONT abuse, aspersion, beard, brave, brickbat, challenge, confront, contempt, contumely, cut, defy, despite, dishonor, disoblige, disrespect, embarrass, flout, harass, humiliate, illtreat, impertinence, indignity, in-

jure, injury, insolence, insult, irritate, nettle, offend, offense, outrage, peeve, provocation, provoke, rudeness, scorn, scurrility, slight, strunt

AFFUSION baptism, infusion, pouring

AFFY affiance, affirm, betroth, confide, espouse, join, trust

AFGHAN blanket, carpet, chippendale, cover, coverlet, rug, wrap

AFGHANISTAN *ameer* shere
bath hammam
capital kabul
carpet herat, isfahan, kabul
chief sirdar
city asmar, baghlan, balkh, bamiyan, cabul, chaman, dilaram, doshi, ghuzni, herat, jurm, kabul, kunar, kunduz, maruf, matun, mazar-i-sherif, mukur, nani, nauzad, pahra, panjaro, rui, rustak, sangan, sarobi, tukzar, tulak, urgan, wama, washir
coin abaze, abbasi, afghani, amania, pul, riyal, rupee
council jirga(h)
craftsman patragar
division achakzai
fox corsac, corsak
frontier garrison khyber rifles
garment chapan, posteen
goat markhor
gun je(u)zail
herb isfand
language balochi, baluchi, dari, pashto, pushto, pushtu
measure jerib, karoh
nomad See *people*, below.
parliament shura
pass khaibar, khyber
people aimak, aymak, baloch, baluch, beluchi, belucki, durani, ghilzai, hasara, hazara, kaf(f)ir, kirgiz, pakhton, pathan, pukhtun, rohilla, safi, shinwari, sistani, tajik, turkoman, ulus, uzbek
pony yaboo, yabu, yurga
prince See *ruler*, below.
province badakhsan, farah, ghazni, ghor, herat, kabul, kafiristan, kapisa, kunar, kunuz, logar, nuristan, parwan, wardak, zabul
range chagai, himalayas,

hindu kush, pamirs, safed-koh
river amu darya, cabul, farah, hari, harut, helmund, indus, kabul, khash, kokcha, kunar, lora, murghab, oxus
ruler ameer, amir, emeer, emir, sharif, sherif
sea darya
stitch tricot
stock semitic
title khan
weight karwar, khurd, pau, paw, ser, sir
wind afghanets

AFICIONADO amateur, devotee, ENTHUSIAST, fan, follower

AFIELD abroad, apart, astray

AFIKOMEN matzoth, passover bread

AFIRE ablaze, aflame, alow(e) ardent, burning, flaming

AFLOAT aboard, about, adrift, asea, awaft, awash, buoyed, floating, flooded, happening, moving, natant, reported, unfixed, unstable, volatile, wafted, waterborne

AFOOT about, abroach, abroad, ambulating, a pied, astir, brewing, brooding, forthcoming, in progress, pedestrian, toward, walking

AFORESAID antecedent, ditto, named, previous, prior, same, supra

AFORETHOUGHT deliberate, designed, premeditated, prepense

AFOUL colliding, conflicting, entangling, fouled, tangled

AFRAID adrad, afeared, afrit, aghast, alarmed, anxious, appalled, apprehensive, ascared, askeered, atremble, breathless, cowardly, craven, disquieted, faint-hearted, feared, fearful, fraid, frightened, g(h)astful, haunted, pusillanimous, rad, redde, rede, reluctant, scared, shrinking, shy, skeered, terrified, timid, timorous, tremulous, unwilling, wrothe

AFREET, AFRIT demon, devil, efreet, giant, ifrit, jinnee, jinni, monster, ogre

AFRESH again, anew, anon,

denovo, encore, newly, repeated

AFRICA, AFRICAN (See also SOUTH AFRICA.)
aardvark fodientia
almond brabejum
ancient country cyrenaica, numidia
ancient name libya
animal (See also *antelope* and *monkey*, below.) aardvark, aardwolf, admi, antelope, arui, auodad, ayeaye, ayu, camel, civet, genet, giraffe, ichneumon, linsang, lion, mongoose, okapi, pangolin, potto, quagga, ratel, serval, suricate, zebra, zebu, zenu, zoril(la)
animal, game (See also *antelope*, below.) buffalo, elephant, giraffe, hippo (potamus), leopard, lion, monkey, rhino(ceros), tiger, wildebeest, zebra
anteater aardvark, fodientia
antelope addax, alcelaphus, asse, beira, b(e)isa, blesbok, bohor, bongo, bontebok, bontebuck, bubalis, buib, bushbuck, cephalophus, cervocapra, chiru, defassa, dikdik, duiker, eland, etaac, gemsbok, gnu, grimme, grysbok, guevi, guib, hartebeest, impala, kob(a), kongoni, konze, koodoo, kudu, leche, madoqua, nagor, nyala, oribi, oryx, oterop, pallah, peele, poku, puku, redunca, reedbuck, reitbok, rheeboc, rheebok, roan, saiga, sassaby, sitatunga, sitwanga, springbok, steenbok, steinbok, suni, tiang, tolo, topi, tora(s), tragelaphus, tsessebe, wanto
ant thrush pulish
ape baboon, barbary, chacma, drill, koolokamba, mandrill
arab tribe battakhin
arrow poison haya
ash artar
ass quagga
baboon See *ape*, above.
barbet barbion
bass iyo
battleground alamein
bean calabar
beer pombe
beetle toktokje, toktokkie
berry abolifruit

big five buffalo, elephant, hippo(potamus), lion, rhino(ceros)
bird adjutant, buphaga, coly, courser, crane, diedric, hammerkop, hoopoe, kwe, lo(u)ri, lory, marabou stork, moro, napecrest, pochard, quelea, taha, touraco, turaco(u), turakoo, umbrette, xurakoo
bishop donatus
blackwood akee, dalbergia
blaubok antelope, etaac
boat almadia, almadie, bong, bungo, dhow
bogie mumbo jumbo
boss baas, bwana
bowstring hemp ifa, murva, pangane, sansevieria, sparmannia
bread maize, kankie, kisra
breadfruit treculia
bread wafer abret
bride price lobola
british colony basutoland, bechuanaland, cameroons, gold coast, kenya, mahdi, nyasaland, rhodesia, sierra leone, swaziland, tanganyika, uganda, union of south africa, walvis bay
brown chippendale
buck impala, pallah
buffalo bushcow, niare
bulb plant ixia
bustard houbara, k(n)orhaan, kori, paauw
camp boma, la(a)ger
canary fink, moro
cane imfe, imphee, pearlmillet
cannibal bachichi
cape guardafui, juby, ras, verde, vert, yubi
cat civet
catfish docmac, s(c)hal
cattle niata
cattle pen kraal, zareba
charm greegree, grigri, juju, obe(ah), obi, saffi, safie, saphie
cherry orange citropsis
chief caboceer, kaid
chief's residence tata, zimbawe
child's disease kwashiorkor
city (See also under individual countries.) accra, addis ababa, alexandria, algiers, bangui, bobolasso, brazzaville, cairo, capetown, casablanca, dakar, dar es salaam, elat, elisabethville,

freetown, ibadan, isa, khartoum, lagos, leopoldville, lubumbashi, monrovia, oran, rabat, stad, timbuctoo, tripoli, tunis, windhoek
civet nandin(e)
civilization ghana, kush, mali, songhai
cloak See *garment,* below.
cloth huccatoon
coast barbary
cobra ringhals
coffee arabian
coin (See also under individual countries.) ackey, macuta, maidin, medin, medino, pesa, rupie, toque
colonist boer
cony boomdas, daman, das(sie), dassy, dendrohyrax
cormorant shag
corn ear mealie
corn lily ixia
council raad
country See *nation,* below.
crane balearica
crater kibo
cubeb ashanti pepper, cayenne
cuckoo diedric
cycad kaffir bread
cypress callitris
daisy arctotis, dimorphotheca, gazania, gerbera
desert areg, elerg, igidi, kalahari, libyan, nyika, reg, sahara
dialect akan, bantu, fantee, fanti, geechee, gullah, hausa, saho, swahili, taal, twi
disease nenta, yaws
dish couscous
dog basenji
dogbane acocanthera
dominoes dice
dove namaqua
drink afrikoko, omeires, skokiaan
drum bamboula, dar(a)-bukka, derbukka
duck geelbec(k)
dunes erg
dust storm habo(o)b, hab(b)ub
dwarf tribe (b)abongo, obongo
dynasty aghlabite, albusaid, benin
eagle bataleur, bateleur, berghaan
ebony euclea
elephant loxodonta

enclosure boma, kraal
engineer, mining barth
explorer burton, grant, livingstone, speke, stanley
eyeworm loa
fabric, burrah, kitenge
fairy yumboe
falls victoria
farmyard werf
fence boma
fern mother-spleenwort, todea
fetish See *charm,* above.
fever dengue
fig samh
finch senegal, serin
fish anabas, jewelfish, karmouth, kelb-el-bahr, mormyr(e)
flower bloodlily, cornpoppy, gillyflower
fly glossina, kivu, seroot, tsetse, zebub, zimb
food cassava, pawpaw
fox asse, caama, fennec
french colony algeria, cameroons, issa, madagascar, morocco, senegal, wadai
fruit cubeb, pecego, terfa, terfez
fruit bat epaulet
game mancala
game area (See also KENYA *game area.*) crater, lake manyara, ngorongoro, serengeti
gangster tsotsis
garden shamba
garment dashiki, djelab, djellab(ah), haik, jelab, jellab(ah), jellib(ah), kanzu, kaross, tobe
gazelle admi, ariel, cora, dama, dibatag, korin, kudu, mohr, oryx, springbok
general botha
genet berbe
ghost juba
giant antaeus
gift dash
gillyflower marigold
god abiala, cagn, cogaz, coti, gewi, hyrax, ikaggen, makambi, mumbo jumbo, nyambe, nzambi
gold coast city accra, akkra
gold field rand, witwatersrand
gown See *garment,* above.
grass alfa, apluda, camelhay, cane, drinn, esparto, fundi, millet
grassland veldt
greenhorn ikona

groundnut gobbe
guard askar
gulf babes, guinea, sidra
gully donga, nullah
gumbo lalo
gum resin bis(s)abol
gun roer
hammock machila
harp nanga
hartebeest See *antelope,* above.
harvest celebration kwanzaa
hawk bullet
headland kop, ras
headman caboceer
helmet topee, topi
hemp bowstring, ife, l(h)iamba, murva, pangane, sansevieria, sisal, sparmannia
herb acidanthera, agapanthus, anthospermum, arctotis, atropa, blumea, cape, cowslip, ethiopian sage, flame-flower, kalanchoe, nemesia, okra, renealmia, sesamum, tansy, thistle, torch-lily, valerian
hill kop
honeysuckle halleria
hornbill bucorvus, tock
horse barb, kumrah
horse disease n(a)gana, surra
hottentot nama
hunt safari
hunter shikari
hut kraal, tembe
ibex jaal-goat
incense elemi, tacamahac
islamic sect almohades
island ascension, azores, bourbon, canaries, cape verde, comoro, djerba, fernando po, madagascar, madeira, mauritius, prince edward, principe, reunion, sao tome, seychelles, socotra, st helena, zanzibar
jackal dieb, thos
javelin assagai, assegai
king negus, numidia, selassie
king, imaginary cophetua
kingdom See *nation,* below.
kingdom, ancient mauretania
knife panga
kral zimbawe
lake abayo, albert, asal, bangweulu, chad, chott, debo, dembel, didolo, edward, inongo, leopold, lifu, malumba, moero, mweru, ngami, nyanza, nyasa, rirwa, rudolf, rudolph, shat,

shirwa, shott, stephanie, tana, tanganyika, tchad, tsana, tumba, victoria
land plot erf
language (See also *people,* below.) afrikaans, akim, akka, ashanti, bambara, bantu, bemba, berber, egba, egbe, ewe, somali, sudanic, taal, yao, yoruba
leader banda, luthuli, tshombe, youlou
lemur angwantibo, arctocebus, bushbaby, galago, kinkajou, maholi, potto
lethargy sleeping sickness
lily agapanthus, alde, tulip
locust nitta
lynx caracal, syagush
magic juju
magician grigiman
mahogany cailcedra, khaya
marigold gillyflower, khakibos, tansy
martyrs agonistici, agonists, circumcellions
master baas, bwana
measure cape-foot, curba, darah, doti, mkono, morgen, muid, rood, rope, rotl, schepel, ton
meat, dried biltong(ue)
milkbush synadenium
millet eleusine, kaffir, raggee
millet beer pombe
money bracelet manilla
monkey colobin, colobus, douc, galago, grivet, guenon, guereza, malbrouck, mona, nisnas, patas, potto, talapoin, tamarin, teetee, vervet, waag
monsoon kaskazi
moor maugrabee
mortar swish
moslem habab, moor
moslem vip sidi
moth anaphe
mountain pass nek
mud house tembe
musical instrument akalimba, balafo, gora(h), kayamba, nanga, rebab, zanze
narcotic dagga
nation abyssinia, algeria, angola, bamangwato, barotseland, basutoland, bechuanaland, benin, biafra, botswana, bouar, burundi, cameroon(s), cape colony, chad, congo, dahomey, egypt, eritrea, ethiopia, fernando po, gabon, gambia,

gazaland, ghana, guinea, ivory coast, kaffraria, katanga, kenya, lesotho, liberia, libya, madagascar, malagasy, malawi, mali, mashonaland, matabeleland, mauritania, mauritius, morocco, mozambique, niger(ia), rhodesia, rwanda (burundi), sahara, senegal, sierra leone, somalia, south africa, sudan, swaziland, tanganyika, tanzania, togo, transkei, tunisia, twanda, uar, uganda, volta, zaire, zambia, zanzibar
national park kasanka
nurse aja, ayah
nut tree cola, kola
oak sophora, teak, turtosa
official jemadar
oil palm elaeis
orchid baldberry
ostrich rhea, struthio
oxhide riem
palm borassus, doom, d(o)um, elaeis, gingerbread tree, raffia, raphia
palmyra ronier
parrot agapornis, jako
peak cameroon, kenya, kibo, kilimanjaro, stanley, tizi
peasant kopi
people 3 abo, edo, ewe, fan, ibo, ijo, jur, kru, vai, vei, yao 4 absi, afar, akan, akim, akka, akra, arab, asha, bari, boer, boni, doko, eboe, egba, exoi, fang, fiot, fula, golo, ibok, issa, leda, lori, lozi, luri, madi, majo, moor, nama, nuba, riff, sari, suku, susu, suto, taal, tibu, tshi, viti, xosa, zulu 5 afifi, bafot, bantu, batwa, dinka, felup, fulah, fulup, habab, hausa, igara, inkra, kafir, masai, mende, nandi, nilot, pondo, pygmy, sanye, serer, sotik, tembu, tibbu, tursi, volta 6 achuas, bakuba, bakutu, basuto, berber, bertat, damara, djerma, dorobo, fellup, fulani, hamite, igbara, igbira, kaffir, kanuri, kikuyu, nilote, obongo, somali, sonhai, sousou, tuareg, ubangi, wahehe, wochua 7 aboongo, achango, akwapim, ashango, ashanti, bacongo, bakongo, bakunda, bakwiri, balante, bambute, bapindi, barotse,

batonga, borassu, bushmen, dahoman, giriama, kabonga, kindiga, koldaji, malinke, sandaww, sudanic, sukkiim, swahili, voltaic, wangoni, witbooi, zongora 8 abarambo, andorobo, bechuana, gabunese, hadendoa, quaequae, wambutti, wangatta, wapogoro 9 apollonia, battakhin, hottentot, wasandawi 10 boschneger 11 almoravides
pepper cayenne, cubeb
pheasant tragopan
pig aardvark
pigeon namaqua
plant aizoon, aloe, anthericum, arg(h)el, asclepias, cacoon, calla, carrion flower, cassava, corn lily, euphorbia, giner, ixia, kaffir bread, okra, rue, stapelia, sugar cane, swallowwort, uzara, zilla
plateau karoo, niare
poet senghor
poison calabar
polecat musang, zoril
port casablanca, dakar, freetown, ibo, lagos, oran, sidiifni, tunis
prickly ash artar
pygmy See *people,* above.
quicksand syrtis
range atlas, drakensberg, ruwenzori
ravine donga, kloof, wadi, wady
reedbuck bohor, nagor, reitbok
region barbary, damaraland, nubia, rand, ruanda, senegambia, tibu
region, ancient punt
rhinoceros keitloa, umhofo
river atbara, athi, beira, benue, blue nile, calabar, chinde, chobe, congo, crocodile, gambia, gebe, job, joliba, juba, kagera, kongo, kubango libo, limpopo, niger, nile, nun, nyanza, okovanggo, orange, rovuma, sabaki, semliki, senegal, shari, shire, tana, ubangi, uele, volta, zambezi, zamesi
river bed donga, wadi
rodent anomalure, jumpinghare
root, medicinal calombo, calumba, colombo, columbo

rose corn poppy
rosewood lingoum, molompi
rue aegle, citropsis, peganum
rug kaross
ruins zimbawe
saffron podalyria, satinbush
salt lake chott, shat, shott
satinbush podalyria, saffron
secret society egbo, maumau, poro
sect abelite, coptic, donatist
sedge umbrella plant
sheep aoudad, arui, barbary, udan, zenu
shrike puffback
shrub aalii, acocanthera, alhagi, almond, anthospermum, bocca, boxthorn, camel's-horn, caper, cherry-orange, dogbane, hemp, honeysuckle, iboga, madder, milkbush, saffron, satinbush, selago, tea tree, turkeybush, unoma, vanqueria
sisters hesperides
skin decoration keloid
sleeping sickness lethargus, trypanosomiasis
snake ball python, bitis, black mamba, boa, cobra, elaps, gaboon viper, mamba, puff adder, schaapsteker
snowdrop tree royena
soldier askari, spahi
somali hashiya
sorcery obe(ah), obi
sorghum imfe, imphee
soup powder lalo
southernmost point agulhas
spanish province ifni
spear assagai, assegai
spectres lamies
spider ananci, annancy, nancy
spirit, evil abambou
spiritual power ngai
squirrel xerus
starling ox pecker, spreeuw
state See *nation,* above.
statesman abubakar, adhidjo, adoula, alhaji, balewa, dacko, danquah, eboue, houphouet-boigny, ironsi, kabaka, kasavubu, keita, kenyatta, lumumba, margai, mobutu, nkrumah, nyerere, obote, ojukwu, padmore, senghor, soglo, tafawa, tombalbaye, toure, tshombe, yekka
stockade boma, keddah, kraal, post, zare(e)ba
stork marabou, simbil

storm habo(o)b, hab(b)ub
strait bab el man-deb
sugar cane imphee
swallowwort stapelia
tableland karoo
tansy marigold
teak oak, oldfieldia, sophora
tea tree lycium
tick tampan
timber tree baku, ebony, diospyros, lovoa, mahogany
title baas, bwana, sidi
toad xenopus
touraco alarm bird
tragacanth kutira gum
tree aalii, abura, aegle, afara, akee, almique, artar, assagai, assegai, athel, atlas cedar, balm of gilead, balsam, baobab, berberine, billetwood, bito, blackwood, baphia, brabejum, breadfruit, bumbo, chandelier tree, cola, copaifera, copaiva, cork oak, dakuma, dalbergia, ekki, etua, funtumia, lilac, mafur(r)a, malekola, moli, mopane, njave, odum, olax, pigeon plum, pooli, samandura, sangasanga, sapele, sassywood, shea, siris, snowdrop, tarfa, teak, walnut, yellowwood, yohimbe
tsetse fly glossina, kivu
tulip agapanthus, blood lily
valley congo, elgon, kenya, kilimanjaro, laagte, nile, ruwensori, wadi, wady
village dorp, draal, stad(t)
vine bagflower, basella, buaze, colocynth, ecanda, elephant's foot, palay
violet saint paulia
viper atractaspis, puff adder
volcano elgon, cameroon, kenya
warbler pincpinc
war dance calinda
weaverbird bengali
weight rotl
wheat imphere, sorghum
whip koorbash, kurbash
wild ass quagga
wildcat chaus, servel
wild dove tambourine
wind cape doctor, hamseen, harmattan, kamsin, samiel, simoom, simoon
witchcraft bean calabar
wolf aard
wood avodire, ebony, oak, sapele, teak
woodland mvombo belt

woody vine buaze, bwazi
worker volk
worm loa
yellowwood podocarpus
AFRIKAAN boer, (cape) dutch, taal
AFRO-ASIATIC hamito-semitic
AFROGAEA abyssinia, ethiopia
AFT abaff, abaft, after, ala, astern, back, baff, baft, behind, rear, stern, tail
opposite fore
AFTER abaff, abaft, about, according to, aft, anon, apres, arter, astern, attendant, baff, baft, behind, below, beyond, chasing, concerning, conformable, consecutive, dopo, eft(er), ensuing, following, for, hinder, imitation, infra, in search of, junior, later, on the scent, out for, past, post, posterior, posthumous, pursuing, resembling, searching, second, sequent, since, subsequent, successive, tailing
all considering, nevertheless, therefore
awhile anon, by and by, later, soon
comb. meta, post
dinner postcenal, postprandial
dinner drink brandy, cafe brulot, cognac, liqueur
the event ex post facto
the flood postdiluvian
the manner of ala, alla
the war postbellum
AFTERBIRTH heam, secundine, sequel, sooterkin
AFTERBODY tonneau
AFTERBREAST metathorax
AFTERDAMP carbon dioxide, gas, vapor
AFTEREFFECT backwash, hangover, sequel(a)
AFTERGLOW primrose, shine, twilight
AFTERGRASS fog(gage)
AFTERIMAGE purkinje, spectrum
AFTERMATH arrish, backwash, consequence, eddish, edgrew, edgrow, effect, fog, issue, profit, result, rowen, rowet(t), sequel, stubble, upshot, yield
AFTERNOON arvo, evening,

pomeriggio, post-meridiem, tarde, teatime, undern
nap siesta
AFTERPIECE epode, exode, exodium, postlude
AFTERSWARM cast(ling), spew, spue
AFTERTHOUGHT footnote, reflection, regret, remorse, rue, sequel
AFTERWARD afterhend, apres, eft(soon), later, post, sith, subsequently, then, thereafter, tomorrow
AFTERWHILE anon, by and by, later
AFTERWRIST metacarpus
AGAG *slayer* saul
AGAIN adversus, afresh, agin, anew, anon, another time, ayin, back, besides, bis, consequently, de novo, eft(soon), encore, freshly, further, in addition, iterum, more(over), newly, often, on the other hand, once more, over, recently, re-peated(ly), then, twice, uber
comb. ana, contra, counter, pali
AGAINST abreast, adverse, anen(s)t, anti, at cross pur-poses, athwart, ayens, be-side, con(tra), contrariwise, counter, cross, facing, fer-nent, forenenst, forninst, gainst, gin, near, opposed, opposite, toward, upon, versus
comb. ana, ant(i), anth, cat(a), cath, kat(a), kath, non, para
hope aglee, agley
one's will reluctantly, un-willingly
the grain backward(s), con-trary
AGA KAHN karim
son aly
AGAL *cord,* (head)rope
AGALINIS aureolaria, false foxglove, figwort, gerandia, scrophularia
AGALLOCH agalwood, agar(agar), aggur, aguila-wood, aloeswood, calam-bac, eaglewood, garroo, garrow, gelatin, incense, isinglass, lignaloes, linaloa, perfume, tambac
AGAMA aga(mid) agha, guana, iguana, lizard, tantra
AGAMEDE *father* augeus

AGAMEDES *kin* erginus, trophonius
profession architect
slayer trophonius
AGAMEMNON *avenger* orestes
burial site mycenae
consort cassandra, clytem-nestra
daughter chrysothemis, elec-tra, iphianassa, iphigenia, laodioe
friend polyphides
herald talthybius
kin atreus, menelaus, pelops
kingdom argos, mycense
parent aerope, atreus, eri-phyle, plisthenes
prize cassandra
rival aegisthus
slayer aegisthus, clytemnes-tra
son crestes
victim adrestus
AGAMID agha, balete, baliti
AGANUS *parent* helen, paris
AGAPANTHUS herb, lily, loveflower, tulbaghia, tulip
AGAPE agaze, aghast, agog, astir, athirst, avid, curious, desirous, eager, gaping, love, open, staring, vigilant, yawning
AGAPEMONE *member* prin-ceite
AGAPENOR *father* ancaeus
AGAPORNIS lovebird, par-rot
AGAR (See also AGAL-LOCH.) gelose, gelosin(e)
-agar source algae, gracilaria
AGARIC amanite, amani-topsis, armillaria, blewits, blusher, death cup, flybane, fomes, fungus, lepiota, touchwood, tricholoma
genus panillus, pholiota, pleurotus
AGARICIN(E) choline
AGARITA algerita, mahonia, shrub
AGASTROPHUS *father* paeon
slayer diomedes
AGASTYA *father* varuna
AGATA amberina
AGATE achate, aggie, anthraconite, catalinite, chalcedony, marble, mig, onyx, pebble, ruby, stone, taw
symbol of health, longevity
zodiac sign scorpio

AGATHA, St. *symbol* knife, salver, shears
AGATHOCLES *grandson* ar-chagathus
patron damas
ruler of syracuse
slayer maeno
AGATHYRSUS *father* her-cules
AGATI sesbania
AGAVE agaua, aloe, amaryllis, amole, cantala, century plant, datil, hemp, henequin, istle, jiniquen, karatto, keratto, maguey, mescal, pulque, soapweed, tequila, zapupe
fiber henequen, istle, pita, sisal
husband echion
juice aguamiel, mescal, pul-que
parent cadmus, harmonia
sister autonoe, ino, semele
son pentheus
victim pentheus
AGAWAM blackberry, grape, pennacook
AGE aeon, aetat, ald, an-cienty, antiquate, autumn, century, cycle, date, de-cline, develop, duration, eld, eon, epoch, era, eter-nity, fade, fossilize, genera-tion, get on, lifetime, ma-jority, maturity, mellow, obsolesce, olam, older, out-date, period, ripen, secle, seculum, senesce, senility, seniority, shrivel, siecle, sink, superannuate, time, void, vorhand, wane, waste, wither, wizen, wrinkle, years, yuga
advanced dotage
come of majorize
great antiquity, grandevity
group senior citizens, teens
modern atomic
of discretion maturity
of the same coeval
old dotage, eld, senectitude, senescence, senility, senium, vetusty
old, science of geriatrics, gerocomy, gerontology, nos-tology
pert. anile, eral, geriatric, senile
AGED advanced, along, an-cient, anile, decrepit, dod-dering, doddery, effete, eld-erly, feeble, fossilized, gothic, grayhaired, hoary,

infirm, mature, moss-backed, nestorian, ogyian, old(en), passe, patriarchal, ripe, rusty, seasoned, senectuous, senile, stale, timeworn, tottering, tottery, venerable, wintry, wrinkled, yeared

AGEE See AWRY.

AGELAUS *master* priam
parent hercules, omphale, phradmon
slayer diomedes
wooed penelope

AGELESS enduring, eternal, everlasting, timeless, undying

AGENCY action, activity, arbitor, arm, bureau, business, commission, company, comptoir, department, desk, diet, division, efficiency, enterprise, facility, firm, force, franchise, function, hand, influence, installation, instrument, intercession, intermediation, lever, management, means, mechanism, medium, moyen, office, operation, organ(ization), plant, section, staff, wing
comb. ancy, ator, eer, ency, fic, ier, ific
public authority

AGENDA, AGENDUM calendar, card, docket, list, memorandum, outline, plan, program, record, ritual, schedule, slate
item topic

AGENOR *brother* belus
city carthage
descendant dido
kingdom phoenicia
offspring cadmus, cilix, europa, phoenix
parent antenor, libya, neptune, poseidon, theone
rescued hector
twin belus
wife argiope, telephassa

AGENT 3 spy 4 amin, doer, gene, tool 5 actor, ameen, cause, check, clerk, envoy, fence, force, means, organ, power, proxy, reeve, slave, walla 6 adurol, atopen, author, broker, bursar, commis, dealer, deputy, factor, kehaya, lawyer, medium, minion, muktar, peskar, seller, syndic, vender, wallah 7 bailiff,

channel, contact, coucher, facient, liaison, manager, mooktar, muktear, mutagen, proctor, reactor, scalper, servant, steward, trustee 8 advocate, attorney, aumildar, catalyst, delegate, emissary, gomashta, henchman, institor, licensee, official, quaester, retailer, salesman, virucide 9 canvasser, comprador, detective, expediter, go-between, middleman, operative, performer, principle, publicist, secretary, solicitor, substance 10 instrument, missionary, mouthpiece, procurator, substitute 11 functionary 12 intermediary 14 representative
appoint depute, deputize
comb. ant, ator, nik, ster
confidential ameen, amin
fiscal steward
narcotic nark
native aumilder
press flack
provocateur instigator
purchasing circar, sircar, sirkar
secret courier, provocateur, spy
servile minion

AGERATUM balsamroot, billy-goatweed, boltonia, eupatorium, herb, mistflower

AGES *hesiod's* brazen, golden, heroic, iron, silver
lucretius's bronze, iron, stone
middle moyen-age

AGESILAUS *ally* xenophon
co-ruler agesipolis, cleombrotus
diviner diopithes
friend cleonymus, etymocles, megabates
kin agib, cynisca, melesippidas, teleutias
lieutenant herippidas, lysander, megabates, pisander, scythes, sphodrias, spithridates, xenocles
offspring archidamus, eudamidas, eupolia, prolyta
parent eupolia, zeuxidamus
rival antalcidas, conon, iphicrates, tisaphernes, tolmides
wife cleora

AGGER earthwork, fort, mound, prominence, rampart, ridge, tide

AGGEUS haggai

AGGLOMERATE accumulation, chaos, cluster, coherence, collect(ion), gather, heap, lump, mass, pile, rock, slag

AGGLOMERATION congeries, congery, favella, horde

AGGLUTINATE adhere, cement(ed), glue(d), obtected, unite

AGGLUTINATION adhesion, coherence, union

AGGRANDIZE advance, augment, boost, dignify, enlarge, exaggerate, exalt, expand, extend, glorify, increase, magnify, overexpand, promote, widen

AGGRAVATE aggrege, ampligy, anger, annoy, bedevil, bother, bristle, brown off, burden, burn, deepen, discompose, distemper, disturb, enhance, enlarge, exacerbate, exasperate, exercise, feed, grate, gripe, heighten, increase, intensify, irk, irritate, load, magnify, miff, nag, nettle, pain, peeve, pester, pique, plague, provoke, rile, roil, ruffle, taunt, tease, torment, try, twit, vex, worsen

AGGRAVATED acute, bad, worse

AGGRAVATION irritation, provocation

AGGREGATE accretion, accumulate, add, all, alliance, amass, amount, assemblage, band, bulk, bunch, clone, club, cluster, collect(ion), combination, complete, composite, composition, compound, congregate, deme, ensemble, gross, group, mass, mixture, multeity, sum, total(ity), unite(d), volume, whole
comb. ade, ado, age

AGGREGATION accumulation, AGGREGATE, association, bundle, clump, colony, congeries, eumerism, family, flock, gang, herd, nation, sorites, swarm, system

AGGRESSION assault, assertion, attack, compulsion, encroachment, enterprise, force, incursion, initiative, injury, inroad, intrusion, invasion, offense, provocation, pushing, raid, rapine, violation, war

AGGRESSIVE adventurous, ambitious, assertive, attacking, encroaching, energetic, enterprising, forward, go-ahead, gumptious, hustling, militant, offensive, provoking, pugnacious, pushing, rapacious, up and coming, venturesome, venturous

AGGRIEVE afflict, aggravate, distress, domineer, harm, harry, hurt, inflict, injure, offend, oppress, pain, persecute, trouble, try, wrong

AGGRIEVED distressed, offended, sore, troubled, woeful

AGHAST afraid, agape, agog, appalled, astonished, awe(d), breathless, horrified, open-mouthed, spellbound, struck, terrified, thunderstruck, wide-eyed

AGILAWOOD See AGALLOCH.

AGILE active, adept, alert, athletic, brisk, deft, dexterous, easy, elfin, expert, fast, feerie, feirie, fleet, fragile, light(footed), limber, lish, lissome, lither, lively, nimble, quick, sprightly, springy, spry, wanle, withy

AGING *premature* geroderm(i)a

AGIO allowance, batta, commission, discount, exchange, fee, percentage, premium, speculation

AGIS *ancestor* agesilaus, archidamus, eudamidas, eurypon
consort timaea
friend amphares, arcesilaus, damochares
kin agesilaus, archidamus, hippomedon
parent agesistrata, lampido, zeuxidamus
rival leonidas
son leontychides

AGITATE 3 fan, irk, jar, wey 4 beat, fire, fret, fuss, jolt, move, rile, riot, roil, seek, stir, teem, whip 5 alarm, broil, churn, drive, harry, impel, pique, rouse, shake, upset, whisk 6 arouse, betoss, buskle, bustle, debate, excite, flurry, foment, frenzy, harass, incite, jabble, jostle, jumble, justle, lather, madden, nettle, paddle, rattle, ripple, ruffle, seethe 7 actuate, canvass, concern, discuss, disturb, ferment, inflame, perturb, provoke, revolve, roughen, stagger, subvert 8 activate, convulse, disquiet, distract, distress, irritate 9 electrify, galvanize, infuriate, instigate, stimulate 10 discompose, exacerbate, exasperate, perturbate

AGITATED anxious, churning, shaky

AGITATION 3 ado, gog, jar, jog 4 boil, fear, fret, fume, fuss, gust, heat, itch, jerk, moil, riot, roil, rout, stir, to-do 5 alarm, churn, dance, hurry, quake, storm, stour, whirl 6 bustle, debate, dither, energy, flurry, foment, hubbub, jabble, mutiny, nerves, pother, pucker, quiver, revolt, ruffle, seethe, tremor, tumult, unrest, uproar, urging 7 anxiety, bluster, emotion, ferment, fluster, flutter, quibble, rampage, stickle, swither, tempest, trouble, turmoil 8 conflict, disquiet, paroxysm, struggle, upheaval, violence 9 carfuffle, commotion, estuation, maelstrom, rebellion, trepidity 10 brainstorm, combustion, ebullition, excitement, hurlyburly, inquietude, turbulence 11 controversy, disturbance, embroilment, hurryscurry, trepidation 12 perturbation, restlessness
and propaganda agitprop
prone to emotional

AGITATOR hog, instigator, mixer, rebel, troublemaker

AGLAIA *beloved* hephaestus
parent eurynome, jupiter, zeus
sister euphrosyne, thalia
son acrisius, proteus

AGLAOPHON *son* polygnotus

AGLAUS *parent* naiad, thyestes
slayer atreus

AGLEAF mullein

AGLET aiglet, aiguillette, hawthorn, hazel, lace, ornament, pendant, plate, sheath, spangle, staylace, stud, tab, tag

AGLEY aglee, amiss, aside, askew, awry, wrong

AGLOSSA amphibian, mollusk, pipa, toad

AGLOW burning, luminous

AGMATINE guanidine

AGMINATE aggregated, clustered

AGNAIL corn, hangnail, whitlow

AGNATE akin, allied, cognate, kindred, kinsman, related, relative

AGNATHOUS jawless

AGNEL mouton

AGNES, St. *symbol* lamb

AGNI *parent* aditi, angiras, brahma, kasyapa
son pavaka, pavamana, suci
tongue kali
wife avaha

AGNOMEN alias, cognomen, epithet, name, nickname, surname

AGNOSTIC atheist(ic), atheous, denier, disbeliever, doubter, faithless, heathen, iconoclast, infidel, minimifidian, mullifidian, nescient, pagan, secularist, skeptic(al), unbeliever, unchristian

AGNOSY See IGNORANCE.

AGO aback, agone, back, erst, gone, past, sens, since, sinsyne, syne, ygoe, ygone, yore

AGOG agape, aghast, anticipating, astir, attentive, avid, curious, desirous, eager, excited, expectant, keen, lively, vigilant, wondering

A GOGO galore, plenty

AGON argument, conflict, contest, debate, games, struggle

AGONID apogon, cardinal fish, seapoacher, seapoker

AGONISTIC combative, strained, striving

AGONIZE ache, bear, bleed, brood, depress, despond, distress, excruciate, fret, grieve, moan, mope, mourn, pain, pine, rack, sorrow, strain, strive, struggle, suffer, torment, wrack, writhe

AGONIZING consuming, desolating, excruciating, grinding, harrowing, heartbreaking, racking, rending, tormenting, torturous, unpleasant

AGONY ache, anguish, anxiety, cruciation, crucifixion, distress, grief, gripe, pain, pang, panic, paroxysm, rack, stour, struggle, suffering, thraw, throe, torment, torture, travail

AGORA assembly, marketplace, square

AGORAEA athena

AGORAEUS hermes, zeus

AGOUTA solenodon

AGOUTI acuchi, capa, cavy, dasyprocta, paca, rodent

AGPAITE kakortokite, lujauvrite, naujaite

AGRA *tomb* taj mahal

AGRAEUS apollo

AGRAFFE clasp, cramp, eyelet, hook

AGRARIAN agricultural, campestral, farm, pastoral, rural, rustic, wild

AGRAULOS *husband* cecrops
parent actaeus, agraulos, cecrops
sister horse

AGREE accede, accept, accord, acknowledge, acquiesce, adapt, admit, allow, arrange, assent, assort, atone, bargain, bend, blend, capitulate, click, close, coincide, comply, comport, concede, concur, condone, conform, congrue, consent, consort, contract, convene, correspond, engage, fadge, favor, fay, fit, gee, gibe, grant, gree, gybe, harmonize, hitch, jibe, jump, jutty, match, neet, please, promise, quadrate, reconcile, resemble, settle, sort, square, stipulate, submit, suit, tailye, tailzee, tailzie, tally, toady, understand, yield
with like, side, sit, tail

AGREEABLE acceptable, accommodating, accordant, adaptable, amabile, amenable, amene, amiable, bland, bonny, canny, charming, comformable, compatible, compliant, concordant, considerate, consonant, couthie, cowdie, desirable, disposed, divertissant, dulcet, easy, fair, favorable, fine,

friendly, gracious, grateful, indulgent, lief, likable, likesome, melodious, plausive, pleasant, pleasing, queme, ready, sapid, savory, simpatico, sociable, suant, suave, suitable, thankful, welcome, weme, willing
render dulcify
unpleasantly saccharine

AGREEABLENESS compliance, douceur, eutony

AGREED d'accord, settled

AGREEMENT accession, accommodation, accord, appointment, assonance, assumpsit, atonement, ausgleich, axis, bargain, bond, capitulation, cartel, cause, cautio, compact, concord, concurrence, conformity, connection, contract, correspondence, covenant, covin, deal, dicker, entente, fit, harmony, ikrar, instrument, league, lease, match, meeting, mise, pact(ion), pactum, peace, pledge, rapport, resemblance, sanction, sortance, stipulation, sympathy, tack, tail, treaty, truce, tryst, unanimity, understanding, unison, unity
international convention, treaty
secret cahoots, collusion, conspiracy, covin
written cartel, contract

AGREMEN(T)S amenities, embellishments, graces, ornaments

AGRESTIC rural, rustic

AGRICOLIST See AGRICULTURIST.

AGRICULTURAL campestral, farm, geoponic, pastoral, rural, rustic

AGRICULTURE (See also FARM references.) agrology, agronomy, cultivation, farming, gainage, geoponics, horticulture, husbandry, tillage
area breadbasket
caste meo
college student aggie
comb. agro
establishment estancia, farm, grove, hacienda, orchard, ranch, spread
god, goddess See VEGETATION *god, goddess.*
machine awner, baler,

binder, breaker, combine, compactor, cottonpicker, cultivator, disk, drag, drill, gin, harrow, harvester, header, mower, planter, plough, plow, rake, reaper, rototiller, scooter, seeder, spreader, tedder, thrasher, thresher, trencher, turnplow, windrower
management husbandry
overseer agronome
pert. agrarian, geoponic, georgic, rural, rustic
system kolkhoz
technology agrotechny
worker See FARM *worker* and PEASANT.

AGRICULTURIST agricole, agrologist, agronomist, crofter, cultivator, farmer, granger, grower, husbandman, kulak, peasant, planter, plowboy, plowman, rancher, ranchman, rustic, santal, sharecropper, tiller, yeoman

AGRIMONY ageratum, beggar-tick, bidens, borwort, bur marigold, clive, eupatorium, hempweed

AGRIOPE *wife* eurydice

AGRIOTES beetle, wireworm

AGRIPPA *battle* actium
enemy anthony, cleopatra
friend coriolanus, octavius
wife julia

AGRIPPINA *husband* claudius
parent germanicus, julia
son nero

AGRITO agarita, ashberry, mahonia

AGRIUS *foe* hercules
parent circe, odysseus, ulysses
son thersites

AGROTERA artemis

AGROTIS bogong, cutworm, moth

AGROUND ashore, beached, beneaped, neaped, stranded, stuck

AGRYPHA logion

AGRYPNIA ahypnia, insomnia, sleeplessness

AGUA bufo(nid), toad, water

AGUACATE ahuaca, avocado

AGUAMAS pinguin

AGUAR *son* val

AGUE chill, cold, fever, ma-

laria, paroxysm, shaking, shivers
drop fowler's solution
grass colicroot
tree sassafras
AGUEWEED boneset, comfrey, eupatorium, gentian, hempweed, thoroughwort
AGUJA gar, makaira, marlin, needlefish, sailfish, spearfish, tetrapturus, tylosurus
AGYIEUS apollo
AHAB achab
father omri
kingdom israel
offspring ahaziah, athalia(h), ochozias
quest moby dick
ship pequod
successor ahaziah, ochozias
wife jezebel
AHAD HAAM ginzberg
AHALYA *husband* guatama
AHARTALAV ivy, milfoil, yarrow
AHASUERUS arsicas, artaxerxes, assuerus, combyses, cyaxares, longimanus, mnemon, oarges
advisor terizazus, tisapherenes
agent artasyras, sparamizes, timocrates
brother cyrus, ostanes, oxathres
commander conon, iphicrates
consort esther, hadassah, statira, vashti
courtier ismenias, timagoras
daughter amestris, apama, atossa, rhodogune
enemy evagorus
eunuch abagtha, bagoas, bigtha, bogatha, harbona, masabates, mehuman
kingdom media, persia
minister (h)aman
parent darius, parygatis, xerxes
slayer bagoas
son ariaspes, arsames, darius, ochus
successor arses, ochus
victim darius
AHAZ *kin* abi, helekia, micah
AHAZIAH *kingdom* israel, judah
kin ahab, jehoram, jehosheba
AHAZZATH ochozath
friend abimelech

AHEAD adelante, advanced, advantageous, afore, alee, anterior, before, beyond, dormie, earlier, early, first, fore, forward, in front, leading, onward, prior, superior, supreme, top, van, winning
comb. for, pre
of time beforehand, early, fast
straight foreright
AHER *ancestor* benjamin
AHI dragon, serpent, vritra
leader gad
mother hathor
AHIAH *parent* ehud
AHIAM *father* sacar, shemidah
AHIJAH *father* phineas
leader solomon
AHIKAR *kin* tobit
AHIMAAZ achimaas
father zadok
AHIMELECH *friend* david
slayer saul
AHIMSA nonviolence
AHINOAM *husband* david, saul
offspring amnon, jonatuan, merab, michal
AHIRA *son* enan
AHKANATON *wife* nefertiti
AHOLIBAMAH *husband* esau
AHRIMAN *angel* deev, deva, div
opponent ahura mazda, o(h)rmazd
AHSAN talak
AHU boundary, gazelle, marker, memorial, waymark
AHUEHUETE cedar, cypress, sabino
AHULL abandoned
AHURA MAZDA o(h)rmazd, ormuzd
attendant (arch)angel
creation gayomart
offspring spenta mainyu
opponent ahriman, angra, mainyu
AHUZZATH *friend* abimelech, ochozath
AHYPNIA agrypnia, insomnia
AI sloth
consort shamash
AIAH *kin* rizpah
AID abet, accommodate, accommodation, adjuvate, adminicle, advance, ancilla, assist(ance), auxiliary, aux-

ilium, avail, back, beet, befriend, benefactor, benefit, boost, coach, comfort, encourage, endorse, expedite, facilitate, favor, finance, forward, foster, further, grant, hand, help, indorse, lief, maintain, ministration, ministry, oblige, patronize, payment, pension, pony, profit, promote, queme, relief, relieve, remedy, second, secours, serve, service, spell, subsidize, subsidy, subvention, succor, support, treat, welfare
AIDA celeste, ieda
composer verdi
father amonasro
lover radames
rival amneris
setting egypt
AIDE adjunct, adjutant, assistant, beagle, deputy, follower, help(er), orderly, second, subaltern
group staff
-memoire memorandum, summary
AIDENN See PARADISE.
AIDONEUS *kingdom* thesprotia
AIGRETTE egret, feather, heron, jewelry, ornament, plume, spray, tuft
AIGUIERE buire, ewer, jug, pitcher
AIL ache, afflict, bother, complain, distress, eyle, fail, falter, ile, indisposition, pain, suffer, trouble
AILANTHUS picramnia, sumac(h), tree-of-heaven
silkworm samia
AILILL *consort* medb
AILING craichy, creachy, doncy, donsie, donsy, sick, sickly, unweel, unwell
AILMENT affection, affliction, disease, disorder, distemper, ill, illness, indisposition, infirmity, malady, sickness, weakness
AILURUS See PANDA.
AILWEED clover dodder
AIM acies, address, aspiration, aspire, attempt, bead, beam, bear(ing), bent, butt, cast, conjecture, consider, course, design, desire, direction, drive, end, endeavor, essay, esteem, estimation, ettle, glee, goal, guess, guidance, head, hold, intend, in-

tent(ion), lead, mark, mint, mission, object(ive), plan, point, position, prick, purpose, scheme, scope, seek, strive, target, tentamen, train, try, view, visie, vizy, vizzy, wink

AIMEE beloved

AIMLESS blind, casual, chance, drifting, haphazard, idle, indiscriminate, lost, promiscuous, purposeless, rambling, random, undirected

AIMLESSNESS flanerie

AINOKO halfbreed, lovechild

AINTAB antep, ayntab, gaziantep

AIPI cassava

AIR aerate, aerify, aether, affectation, appearance, artificiality, aspect, atmosphere, attitude, aura, ayre, bearing, behavior, blast, breath, breeze, bring out, broach, cachet, carriage, character, demeanor, deportment, discharge, disclose, display, divulge, effluvium, element, ether, expose, fan, freedom, freshen, gas, give out, haughtiness, heavens, left, lilt, look, manner, melody, mien, open, oxygen(ate), ozone, pew, piaffer, presence, pretense, publicize, radio, refresh, regard, reveal, scent, semblance, sky, stir, style, tell, utter, vanity, vapor, vent, ventilate, voice, waves, welkin, wind, winnow

a grievance complain
bladder bag, lung, sac, tracheole
blow water-gas
boastful parado
-built chimerical, phantom
carried by aloft, flying
chill night snelly
comb. aer(o), atm(o), pneum(a)
component argon, helium, krypton, neon, nitrogen, oxygen, xenon
-condition cool, ventilate
-conditioner climatiseur
confident bravura
containing pneumatic
-cool refrigerate
current breeze, downwash,

draft, draught, pew, thermal, wind
deity ariel, enlil, ninlil, ruchiel, shu
description aerography
downward motion, pert. katabatic
-drawn phantom
drop parachuting
exhaled flatus
expose to weather
fear of aerophobia
force unit anac, arf, atc, ats, casu, feaf, fourth arm, mats, nad, nats, norad, raaf, raf, rcaf sac, squadron, usaaf usaf, usnas
foul reek
fresh ozone
hole spiracle
hunger, cause acidosis
lane skyway
-like aeriform, gaseous, unreal, unsubstantial
measuring device aerometer, airometer, barometer
mephitic carbon dioxide
movement, horizontal advection
musical aria, arietta, brawl, canto, cantus, cavatina, descant, melody, musette, solo, song, tune
passage blowhole, flue, louver, spilehole, spiracle, trachea, transom, ventage
personification aether, amen, ammon, amon
pert. aerial, aural, pneumatic
plant epiphyte, lifeleaf, liveleaf
pocket bump, hole
pore stoma
raid cover, mission, sortie, umbrella
raid alarm alert
raid defense blackout
raid shelter abri, cellar, refuge
raid signal all clear
screw propeller
-sick nauseated
-sickness bag whoopee cup
sleeve windsock
spirit ariel, genie, sylph
stifling smore
stone aerolite
stream See *current*, above.
strip lily, runway, tarmac
swallowing aerophagia
-to-air missile aam
trip flight, hop
upper ether
vent breather

vesicle aerocyst, alveolus
warm oam
without apneumatic

AIRCRAFT 3 cub, jet, mig, sst 4 giro, kite, spad 5 avion, blimp, drone, flier, flyer, jenny, liner, plane, scout, snoop 6 bomber, canard, copter, ferret, fessel, fokker, glider, hunter, jalopy, pusher, ramjet 7 aeronef, aviette, balloon, biplane, chopper, clipper, cruiser, fighter, flivver, helibus, penguin, propjet, snooper, spotter, trainer 8 aerodyne, airliner, autogiro, concorde, gyrodyne, mosquito, parseval, repulsor, seaplane, triplane, turbojet, warplane, zeppelin 9 aeroplane, amphibian, dirigible, freighter, landplane, monoplane, sailplane, transport 10 helicopter, helivector, hydroplane, pathfinder, triphibian, waterplane, whirlybird 11 grasshopper, interceptor 14 reconnaissance
bomber superfortress
cabin cockpit
carrier flattop
commandeer skyjack
commuter airbus
crew member airedale, avigator, bombardier, kicker, machine gunner, meteorologist, navigator, photographer, pilot, stewardess, tail gunner
defense barrage balloon
door clamshell
electronic gear avionics
fighter messerschmitt, mig, spitfire
fleet formation echelon
glider sailplane
group armada, echelon, escadrille, fleet, flight, squad, wing
incline bank
instrument accelerometer, aerograph, altigraph, altimeter, ammeter, anemograph, anemometer, anemoscope, aneroid, autosyn, bombsight, calorimeter, camera, chronometer, climatometer, compass, controls, direction-finder, dynamometer, flight-recorder, galvanometer, gauge, gosport, gyrocompass, hypsometer, inclinometer, joy-

stick, machmeter, micrometer, nephoscope, octant, ozonometer, pelorus, photometer, pluviometer, pyrometer, quadrant, radar, sextant, spirit level, stick, tachometer, throttle, turnmeter, yawmeter
inventor wright (brothers)
keel fin
landing three-point
lever control stick
lubricant castor oil, ricinus oil
maneuver acrobatics, aerobatics, bank, barrelroll, buzz, carhop, chandelle, crab, dip, dive, feather, fishtail, flathat, glide, hedgehop, immelman, lazy-eight, loop, nosedive, pique, plow, porpoise, pullout, pushdown, roadhop, roll, sideslip, skid, spin, spiral, splits, tailspin, volplane, wingover, yaw
manufacturer american, astra, bendix, boeing, cessna, convair, curtis, douglas, grumman, hughes, lear, lockheed, mcdonnell, northrop, republic, united, vega, vultee, wright
marker flare, pylon
motor, kind compound, compression, gas-jet, jet, pancake, propeller-drive, pulsejet, radial, ramjet, reciprocating, resojet, rocket, rotary, supercharged, turbine, twin-engine, v-type, w-type, x-type
navigation term avigation, loran, navar, omnirange, shoran, var
non-rigid parseval
operator ace, aeronaut, aviator, flier, flyer, pilot
part aerofoil, afterburner, aileron, airfoil, astrodome, bay, blister, body, bombbay, bonnet, bow, bubble, cabane, cabin, canopy, catstrip, chassis, cockpit, controls, cowl, deceleron, deck, de-icer, dihedral, drag-strut, ejector, elevator, elevon, empennage, fin, flap, float, fuel-injector, hatch, hood, jackstay, jury-skid, keel, landing gear, longeron, monocoque, nacelle, nose, pontoon, rotor, rudder, runner, spinner, spoiler, sta-

bilizer, stay, stringer, strut, tail, truss, turret, turtleback, undercarriage, wheel, wing
pilotless drone
plunge nosedive
pontoon hydroplane
rescue airlift
restraining force wave-drag
rigid zeppelin
science of aeronautics, avigation
shelter drome, hangar
speaking tube gosport
speed mach
speed measurer machmeter
spin autorotation, vrille
takeoff decollege
throttle gun, rev, warmup
training jenny
turn bank
unidentified bogey, bogie, bogy, ufo
vapor contrail
wing part aileron
wing support cabane
AIRFOIL aileron, blade, elevator, flap, rudder, stabilizer, wing
AIRINESS animation, delicacy, ostentation, sprightliness
AIRING display, exposure, publication, revelation, ride, walk
AIRLESS breathless, breezeless, close, oppressive, stifling, stuffy, suffocating, unvented, windless
AIRLINE carrier, feeder, skyway
porter skycap
AIRMAIL par avion
AIRMAN birdman, flyboy, pilot
AIRPLANE See AIRCRAFT.
AIRPORT aerodrome, air(drome), croydon, drome, dulles, fiumicino, gatwick, heathrow, helidrome, heliport, idlewild, international, kennedy, la guardia, landing field, le bourget, leonardo da vinci, lod, midway, niest, o'hare, orly, scuttle, shannon, templehof
observation post control tower
runway apron, strip, tarmac
weathervane sock, wind-tee
AIRS affectation, dog, haughtiness, ostentation, pretensions, swank

given to prim, prissy, snobbish
AIRTIGHT close, hermetic, impenetrable, impermeable, impervious, sealed, secure, solid
AIRWAY corridor, lane, line, skyway, windroad, windway
AIRY aerial, affected, alfresco, animated, atmospheric, breezy, brisk, chimerical, cool, debonair, delicate, empty, ethereal, exposed, flippant, fluffy, fresh, gay, graceful, haughty, insubstantial, jaunty, jocund, light, lofty, merry, meteoric, open, pneumatic, rare, roomy, speculative, sprightly, thin, trifling, visionary, vivacious, volatile, windy
AISHA *father* abubekr
husband mahomet, mohammed
AISLE access, allee, alley, corridor, feedway, ile, lane, nave, pass(age), path(way)
without apteral, apterygial
AISLING dream, vision
AIT eight, eyot, holm, ile, island, isle, islet, oat
AITU See DEMON and SPIRIT.
AIX-LA-CHAPELLE aachen
AIZLE ember, soot, spark
AJAJA bird, jabiru, spoonbill
AJAR contradicting, discordant, inharmonious, open
AJAX aias, explosive, jakes, powder
author sophocles
beloved helen
butterfly swallowtail, zebra
conqueror ulysses
enemy troilus
festival aianteia
kin aecus, teucer
parent eriboea, oileus, periboea, telamon
rival odysseus, ulysses
son eurysaces
AJONJOLI See SESAME.
AJOWAN aiwain, ajava
AJUGA brown-bugle, bugleweed, bugloss, herb, lycopus
AKAKALLIS *beloved* hermes
AKALI shahidi
AKAN *deity* ngame, odomankoma
state akwamu, bono, isanda yoruba

AKASA ether, sky, space
AKEAKE aalii, ake, hopbush, ironwood, olearia
AKELA *friend* mowgli
AKELEY aquilegia
AKHA burmese, kaw
AKHNATON See AMEN-HOTEP.
AKIHITO *father* hirohito
AKIMBO akenbold, angled, angular, obliquely
AKIN agnate, alike, allied, analogous, becousined, close, cognate, consanguine, cousin, enate, germane, kindred, kinsman, like, near, nigh, related, same, sib(bed), similar, united
AKKADIAN *god* anu, apsu, irra, ishum, kulla, nergal
goddess aruru, thiamat
sage adapa, atrahasis, ziusudra
AKKUB *parent* elioenai
AKMOLINSK *capital* omak
AKONGE burbark, shrub, triumfetta
AKRA inkra, vetch
AKU katsuwonus, victorfish
AKULE fish, goggler, trachurops
ALA axil(la), drum, nosewing, recess, wing
ALABAMA *capital* montgomery
city anniston, athens, bessemer, birmingham, corona, decatur, dothan, enterprise, gadsden, homewood, huntsville, jasper, linden, marion, mobile, piper, prichard, samson, scottsboro, selma, sylacauga, talladega, tuscaloosa
county bibb, blount, butler, chilton, clay, coffee, coosa, dale, dallas, elmore, etowah, geneva, greene, hale, henry, lamar, lee, marion, morgan, perry, pike, shelby, sumpter, wilcox
indian creek, koasati, tohome, tuskegee
native lizard
nickname cotton state, yellowhammer state
peak cheaha
port mobile
river cahaba, conecuh, coosa, mobile, pea, sepulga, sipsey, tennessee, tombigbee
slider terrapin, tortoise
state bird yellowhammer
state fish tarpon

state flower goldenrod
state tree longleaf, pine
ALABAMINE astatine, ekaiodine
ALABASTER alabastrine, aragonite, calcite, gypsum, onychite, onyx, tecali
A LA CARTE individually
ALACRITY briskness, celerity, cheerfulness, eagerness, enthusiasm, haste, liveliness, promptitude, quickness, rapidity, readiness, speed, sprightliness, willingness, zeal
ALLADIN *magic object* lamp, ring
spirit genie, jinni
ALAISIAGES beda, fimmilina
ALALITE diopside
ALALONGA albacore, alilonghi
ALAMANDITE garnet
ALAMEDA mall, path, promenade, walk
ALAMO battle, cottonwood, fort, mission, poplar, shrine
hero colonel travis, davy crockett, jim bowie
river san antonio
vine ipomoea, morningglory
A LA MODE chic, fashionable, modish, smart, stylish
ALAND *islands* ahvenanmaa
port mariehamm
ALANG-ALANG cogon, kogon
ALANGE dismal, dreary, dull
ALANI pelea, tree
ALANS ghuz, oghuz, scythians
ALANTIN inulin, starch
ALAR axillary, pteric, winged, winglike
ALARCON *partner* coronado
ALARIA badderlocks, honeyware, murlin, seaweed
ALARM affright, agitate, agitation, alert, appall, apprehension, arouse, attack, bell, broil, bugbear, buzzer, clock, consternation, cow, daunt, din, dismay, disquiet, distress, disturbance, dread, excite, fear, freeze, foghorn, fray, fright(en), gast, gloppen, horn, hue and cry, klaxon, larum, mountee, noise, outcry, panic, perturb(ation), rouse, scare, signal, siren, sos, start(le),

surprise, suspense, terrify, tocsin, trepidation, upset, warcry, warning, whoop
bird lobibyx, touraco
ALARMED afraid, disquieted, fearful, frightened, gastful, scareful, scar(e)y, startled, streaked
ALARMIST pessimist, scaremonger
ALAS ach, eheu, hech, helas, heu, las, neb(b)ech, neb(b)ish, och(one), ohone, oime, ototoi, ullagone, vae, waesuck(s), welladay, wellaway, woe
ALASKA *animal* bear, kodiak
auk arrie, murre
bear kadiak, kodiak, polar
bird arrie, auk, ptarmigan
blizzard purga
boat angeyck, bidarka, bidarkee, kayak, omiac, umiak
cape nome, prince of wales
capital juneau, sitka
city anchorage, barrow, cordova, eek, fairbanks, juneau, kenai, ketchikan, klawock, kodiak, kotzehue, latouche, metlakatla, nenana, nome, petersburg, seward, sitka, skagway, spenard, umiat, valdez, wrangell
cloudberry molka
cod gadus, wachna
dog husky, malamute, siwash
fish aburabozu, inconnu, salmon, wacha
flower forget-me-not
garment parka
glacier muir
goose emperor
highway alcan
house barabara, igloo
indian ahtena, akkhas, aleut, amerind, haida, han, ingalik, karluk, khotana, koyukon, kutchin, sitka, tanaina, tetlin, tlingit, unakalett, venetie
insect no-see-em, noxeam
island adak, aleut, amchitka, atka, attu, diomede, kiska, kodiak, nunivak, pribilof, riska, tanaka, umnak, unimak
island group aleutian, andreanof, fox, near, pribilof, rat
lake iliamna, naknek
liquor hoochino
national monument katmai

native ahtena, aleut(ian), auk, eskimo, ingalik, koyukon, tlingit
nickname great land, sourdough
northern tip barrow point
oil field beaufort sea, gwydre bay, prudhoe bay
pass chilkoot, white
peak ada, blackburn, bona, denali, fairweather, foraker, katmai, mckinley, muir, pavlof, spurr, veta
peninsula kenai, seward
pine tsuga
port ketchikan, nome, valdez
prospector sourdough
range baird, brooks, chugach, crazy, kaiyuh, kilbuck, st elias, wrangell
red-tail hawk
river atna, chena, chulitna, colville, copper, innoko, kobuk, koyukuk, kuskokwim, matanuska, noatak, porcupine, susitana, tanana, whitehorse, yukon
sable raccoon, skunk
sea bering
state bird ptarmigan
state fish tarpon
state flower camelia, myosote
state tree spruce
storm burga
terrace benchland
volcano katmai, wrangell
ALASTOR zeus
ALASTRIM amaas, glasspox, smallpox
ALATERN barren-privot, buckthorn, evergreen, houseleek, rhamnus
ALB aube, camisia, chrisom, vestment
embroidery apparel
ALBA dawn, poem, song, white
ALBACORE alalonga, alalunga, alilonghi, bonito, fish, german, longfin, mackerel, maguro, scombrid, tuna, tunny
family thunnidae
ALBAINN albyn, SCOTLAND
ALBA LONGA *king* numitor, tarchetius
ALBAN, St. *symbol* crown, sword
ALBANIA *capital* tirana
city avlona, berat, bitsan, chimara, coritza, dardhe, dukat, durazzo, durres, el-

basan, fier, klos, korce, koritza, kruje, opp, pecin, peqin, preshe, preyesa, puka, puke, qukes, rubic, scutari, shkoder, spash, tepeleni, tirana, tirane, valona, vlore
coin franc, lek, qintar
dialect cham, g(h)eg, hish, tosk
foothills maje jezerce
hero scanderbeg
island saseno
king scanderbeg, zog
lake matia, ochrida, scutari
people arna(o)ut, cham, geg, gheg, gueg, skipetar, tosk
people, ancient illyrian
port durazzo, valona
premier hoxha
promontory acroceraunium, cape glossa
river arta, drin
ruler ali pasha
soldier arna(o)ut, palikar
ALBANY *father-in-law* king lear
wife goneril
ALBARCO cariniana, mahogany
ALBARDINE esparto, grass, lygeum
ALBARELLO jar, vessel
ALBATROSS bluebird, cape sheep, diomedea, fabric, gony, goon(e)y, mallemuck, nelly, quaker, seabird, stinkpot, worsted
black nelly
kind layson, quakerbird, sooty, wandering
ALBAY legaspi
ALBEDO lunule, white(ness)
ALBEIT albee, altho(ugh), but, even, howbeit, notwithstanding, tho(ugh)
ALBEMARLE *sound, river into* roanoke
ALBERENE soapstone
ALBERGO hotel, inn
ALBERICH *chief of* nibelungs
possession tarnkappe
slayer siegfried
ALBERT *lake, people* luri
ALBERTA *capital* edmonton
city banff, calgary, edmonton
indian sarsi
ALBERTITE asphalt, byerite
ALBETAD galbanum, gum resin
ALBINISM alphosis

ALBINO colorless, leucrethiop, octoroon, white
pert. leucous
ALBINURIA chyluria
ALBION anglia, britannia, england, giant, phlox, scotland
brother dercynus
father hercules, poseidon
giant king gogmagog
slayer hercules
ALBITE feldspar, pericline, peristerite
ALBIZZIA mimosa, silk tree, siris
ALBOIN *kingdom* lombardy
ALBORAK *master* mohammed
ALBORNOZ burnoose, cloak
ALBULA bananafish, chiro, elops, ladyfish, menhaden
ALBUM albe, book, list, record set, register, tablet, volume
ALBUMEN, ALBUMIN aleurone, phaselin, protein, syntonin, white
iodized gorgonin
ALBUMINOID collagen, elastin, fribroin, gorgonin, keratin, protein, sericin
ALBURNUM sapwood, splintwood
ALBURNUS blay, bleak, fish
ALBYN albainn, albion, SCOTLAND
ALCAEUS *descendant* alcaid, hercules
enemy pitticus
kin androgeus, antimenidas, minos
offspring amphitryon, anaxo
ALCAIDE cade, caid, commander, gaid, jailer, judge, keeper, warden
ALCALDE executive, judge, mayor
ALCANDRE *husband* polybus
ALCATHOUS *helper* apollo
kingdom megara
parent hippodamia, pelops
son callipidis
ALCATRAS frigate bird, pelican
ALCATRAZ the rock
ALCAZAR alhambra, fortress, palace
ALCESTIS *father* pelias
husband admetus
rescuer hercules
ALCETAS *kin* arybas, tharrhypas

ALCHEMIST adept, artist, chemick, chemist, hermetic
iron mars
silver luna
solvent alkahest
ALCHEMY chymia, magic, sorcery, spagyric, trumpet
book almagest
furnace athanor
god hermes, mercury
pert. hermetic, spagyric
process diplosis
vessel gripe's egg
ALCHITRAN, ALKITRAN bitumen, pitch, resin, tar
ALCHORNEA dovewood
ALCIBIADES *ancestor* ajax, alemaeon, eurysaces
consort hipparete, nemea, phrynia, timaea, timandra
defeat notium
enemy agis, androcles, dioclides, phrynichus, teucer, thessalus, thrasybulus
eulogist critias
friend diomedes, socrates, tissaphernes
guardian ariphron, pericles
informer astyochus
kin callias, euryptolemus, hipponicus
lieutenant antiochus
nurse amycla
parent clinias, dinomache
rival hyperbolus, midias, nicias, phaeax, timon
son leotychides
teacher socrates, zopyrus
victory abydos, cynossema, cyzicus
ALCIDES hercules
ALCIDICE *husband* salmoneus
son tyro
ALCIMEDE *husband* aeson
kin clymene, jason
ALCIMEDES *parent* jason, medea
ALCIMEDON *kin* laerces, philao
ALCIMUS *friend* demeter
ALCINOUS *gardens* scheria
grandfather poseidon
offspring laodamas, nausicaa
parent nausithous, periboea
people phaeacians
wife arete
ALCIPPE *father* ares
ALCIS dioscuri
kin androclea, antipoenus
ALCITHOE *father* minyas
ALCMAEON *brother* amphilochus

consort alphesiboea, arsinoe, callirhoe
parent amphiaraus, eriphyle
purifier phegeus
pursuers erin(n)yes
son acarnan, amphoterus
victim eriphyle
ALCMAON *father* thestor
slayer sarpedon
victim glaucus
ALCMENE *brother* licymnius
consort amphitruo, amphitryon, zeus
handmaid galinthias
parent anaxo, electryon
son hercules, iphicles
ALCOFRIBAS rabelais
ALCOHOL alky, aqua vitae, booze, bug juice, kohl, liquor, spirits
and amine alcamine, alkin(e)
basis ethyl
colorless phytol
crystalline alniviridol, anisoin, calciferol, guaiol, idite, iditol, isoborneol, perseitol, talite, talitol
denaturer brucia, brucin(e)
desire for dipsomania
ethyl ethanol
fat soluble calciferol
flavorer congener
god siris
increase content needle, spike
kind acritol, adonite, amyl, amyrol, androl, anisoin, borneol, carbinol, carotol, cedrol, decanol, dehydrated, denatured, erythrol, ethal, ethanol, ethyl, fenchol, glycol, grain, guaiol, heptite, hexitol, hydrol, idite, industrial, inosite, ledol, linalool, methanol, methyl, nerol, phytol, rubbing, scopine, sorbite, sterin, sterno, talite, terpine, tropine, vinic, vinyl, xylitol
lamp etna
liquid androl, farnesol
oily rhodinol
perfume linalool
pert. vinic
radical amyl, bornyl
secondary benzohydrol
solid cholesterol, rhamnite, sterno, sterol
standard proof
terpene borneol, bornyl, camphol, camphor
unsaturated calciferol, cit-

ronellol, nerol, sterol, tremetol
vinyl ethenol
wood methanol, methyl
ALCOHOLIC addict, beery, carouser, dipsomaniac, drunk(ard), sot, vinic, wino, winy
beverage See **DRINK** alcoholic.
comb. itol
control group alanon, alcoholics anonymous
sugar trosse
ALCOHOLISM dipsomania
treatment keeley cure
treatment drug doxepin
ALCON *friend* hercules
slayer odysseus
ALCOTT *heroine* amy, beth, meg
work little men, little women
ALCOVE alhacena, apse, bay, bower, carrel, corner, cubicle, dinette, dormer, gable, gazebo, niche, nook, oriel, recess, retreat, servery, snuggery, stall, summer house, tablinum
shallow tokonoma
ALCYONE pleiad
consort ceyx, poseidon
parent atlas, pleione
ALCYONEUS *parent* gaea, uranus
slayer hercules
ALDEA hamlet, villa, village
ALDEHYDE acrolein, aldol, alkanal, chloral, citral, cogener, congener, decanal, furfural, glyoxal, hexanal
colorless acrolein
comb. ald(o)
crystalline piperonal
derivitive acetal
imino aldim(in)e
sugar aldose
ALDER alnus, arn, birdcherry, dogwood, elder, owler, padius, rhamnus, sagerose, tree
bark frangula
black holly, winterberry
extract frangulin
flycatcher empidonax
grove carr
ALDERMAN archon, bailie, chief, councilman, halfcrown, magistrate, officer, patriarch, prince, ruler, senior, superior, turkey, viceroy
ALDRICH, HENRY ezra stone

ALE alegar, beer, beverage, bitter, bock, brew, clink, darby, flip, hugmatee, jough, lager, liquor, morocco, mum, nappy, nog, october, pharaoh, porter, purl, scud, stingo, stout, swanky, swat, tipper, yell, yill
adam's water
and honey bragget
and oatmeal stoory
and porter half and half
and stout black and tan
brackish tipper
brewing bummack, bummock
-conner inspector, tester
cup yill-caup
half pint nip
hoof ground ivy
house barley island, barroom, mughouse, pothouse, pub, saloon, tavern
inferior swank(e)y
knight sot, tippler
mug black pot, stein, toby
new swats
sour alegar
source barley
spiced swig
strong burton, huff(cap), merry-go-down, mum, nog(g), stingo
sweetened bragget
tester conner
vinegar alegar
weak twopenny
ALEA athena
ALEC herring, pickle, sauce
ALECTO See FURIES.
ALECTRION nassa, snail
ALEE *opposite of* aweather, stoss
ALEICHEM SHALOM peace to you
ALEIDAMEA *consort* hermes
son bunus
ALEKSANDROPOL leninakan
ALELAPHUS antelope, bubal(is), hartebeest, topi
ALEMAR bema, bimah
ALEMBIC cucurbit, cup, distiller, furnace, limbec(k), purifier, refiner, retort, still, transformer, vessel
ALEMENE *son* hercules
ALENCON *product* lace
ALEPPO beroea, haleb
fabric agabanee
stone eye-agate
ALERA athena

ALERT active, acute, advise, agile, alarm, alive, apt, attentive, awake, aware, breme, bright, brisk, careful, caution, gleg, hep, keen, leery, lively, nimble, observant, peart, peert, pert, prepare(d), prompt, quick, ready, remind, sharp, siren, sleepless, slippy, smart, spirited, sprack, sprightly, swift, tocsin, unsleeping, vigilant, wacker, wakeful, wakerife, warn (ing), wary, watchful, wide-awake, with it, yald, yauld, yepe
first yellow
second blue
urgent red
ALERTNESS aptitude, attention, caution, nous, snap, wakefulness, wit
to change weather eye
ALETES *ancestor* hercules
city mycenae
parent aegisthus, clytemnestra
ALETTE abutment, jamb, wing
ALEURITES ama, bankulnut, candlenut
ALEUS *kingdom* tegea
offspring amphidamas, auge, cepheus, lycurgus
ALEUTIAN atka, eskimauan, eskimo, orarian, unalaska, unungun
boat bidar
indian attu
island adak, amchitka, atka, attu, kiska, kodiak, umnak, unalaska
island group andreanof, fox, near, rat
sod hut barabara
volcano shishaldin
ALEWIFE allice, aloofe, alosa, bang, buckie, fish, grayback, herring, pomolobus, pompano, sawbelly, shad, skipjack, walleye
ALEXANDER *ancestor* achilles, aeacus, hercules
artist stasicrates
battle arbela, chaeronea, gaugamela, granicus, issus
biographer antigenes, aristobulus, aristoxenus, chares, clitarchus, hermippus, ister, onesicritus, polyclitus, potamon, sotion, stroebus
birthplace pella
bodyguard argyraspides

captain neoptolemus
chamberlain proxenus
conquest asia, sogdiana, syrmus
consort barsine, campaspe, cratesipolis, roxana, thais, timandra
conspirator hermolaus, limnus, statira
cupbearer iolaus
diviner aristander, cleomantis, pythagoras
dog peritas
enemy bessus, darius, paul, porus
father-in-law artabazus
favorite hephaestion
friend alcetas, antipater, ariston, attalus, bagoas, coenus, craterus, demaratus, erigyius, exathres, hagnon, harpalus, hephaestion, leonnatus, limnaeus, nearchus, parmeno, perdiccas, peucestes, philotas, phocion, proteas, ptolemy, serapion
general antigonus, antipater, clitus, nearchus, polysperchon
horse bucephalus
informer balinus, nicomachus
kin amyntas, apame, arymbas, barsine, dionysius
kingdom macedonia
lifeguard aristophanes
master diomedes, paris, troilus
mediator hagnon, philoxenus
messenger ladas, leonnatus
parent olympias, philip
physician alexippus, glaucus, pausanias
rival darius
savior clitus
servant athenophanes, parmenion
son aegus, hercules
teacher anaxarchus, aristotle, calanus, callisthenes, harpalus, leonidas, lysimachus, xenocrates
the great game, la belle lucie, midnight oil, solitaire
victim bessus, callisthenes, clitus, clytus, darius, medes, menander, orsodates, oxyartes, persians, polymachus
ALEXANDER II *beloved* catherine dolgoruky
ALEXANDRIA *beauty* hypatia

bishop arius, athanasius
clover berseem
column pompey's pillar
island pharos
laurel poon tree
library destroyer amrou, caliph omar
library founder ptolemy
lighthouse pharos
magistrate alabarch
patriarch papa
philosopher philo-judaeus, plotinus
pleiad apollonius, aratus, callimachus, homer, lycophron, micander, theocritus
ruler araspes, ptolemy
teacher origen
theologian arius, philo-judaeus
wonder catacombs
ALEXANDRITE chrysoberyl
ALEXIA amnesia, aphasia
ALEXIARES *parent* hebe, hercules
ALEXIPHARMIC alexiteric, antidotal, antidote, counterpoison, disinfectant, prophylactic
ALEXIS, St. *symbol* habit, staff
ALFA esparto, grass, stipa
ALFADIR odin
ALFALFA burgundy trefoil, fodder, grass, hay, lucerne, medicago, spanish trefoil
butterfly colias
disease crownwart, yellowtop
hopper stictocephala
weevil phytomomous, snout beetle
ALFILARIA erodium, filaree, filaria, herb, pin clover, pinweed
ALFIO *wife* lola
ALFONSO *queen* ena
ALFORJA alfarga, bag, pouch, saddlebag, wallet
ALFRESCO airy, exterior, openair, outdoor(s), outside
ALGA, ALGAE *acid* fucic
blue-green anabaena, calothrix, cyanophyce, gloeocapsa, nostoc
brown chorda, cutleria, ectocarpus, elachista, fucales, fucus, gulfweed, padina, rockweed
carbohydrate fucosan
coralline nullipore
description phycography
disease red rust

edible fatchoy, sloke
envelope ceramidium
extinct cryptozoon
feeding on algivorous
fertilizer seaware
fossil fucoid
freshwater anabaena, desmid, nostoc, spirogyra, tribonema
green acetabularia, bulbochaete, caulerpa, chlorella, chlorophyce, cladophora, codium, enteromorpha, frogspit, gomontia, iceland seagrass, palmella, pediastrum, redrust, rock violet, stonewort, tetradesmus, trentepohlia, ulothrix, valonia, vaucheria
group akontae, isokontae
kind alaria, anabaena, aquatic, badderlocks, botrydium, brown, carrageen, confervoid, desmid, diatom, fallen star, fernleaf, funori, gelidium, green felt, kelp, nori, nostoc, oarweed, pondscum, red, rockweed, seabeard, seabloom, seaweed, silkweed, slake, sloak, sloke, sporogen, stonewort, thallophyta, whipcord, zoogloea
marine caulerpa, dasya, funori
node bulbil, chara
pigment algocyan, fucoxanthin
primitive cyanophyce
red ahnfeltia, ceramium, chondria, corallina, dasya, floridean, frogspawn, frogspit, furcellaria, gigartina, gloiopeltis, gloiosiphonia, grinnellia, iridescent seaweed, lemanea, nemalion, pincerweed, rhodosperm, rhodymenia, rosetangle, threadweed, wormmoss
rock biolite, biolith, biotherm
spore akinete
study algology
tropical peacock's tail
tufted ahnfeltia
yellow-green tribonema
ALGAL confervoid, fucoid, fungiform, fungoid, fungous
ALGALIA abelmosk, hibiscus
ALGARROBA calden, carob, ceratonia, cybistax, honey mesquite, jacaranda, locust,

mesquite, prosopis, raintree, st john's bread
ALGEBRA *system* abelian
term equation, nome, nomial, square, vector
theorem abel's
ALGERIA numidia, pomaria
berber kabyle, shawia, tuareg
camel mehari
capital algiers
cavalryman spahee, spahi
city abadla, aflou, algiers, annaba, arzew, aumale, barika, batna, bechar, bejaia, benoud, biskra, blida, boghari, bona, bone, bougie, constantine, dellys, djanet, djelfa, dzioua, eloued, frenda, ghardaia, guelma, laghouat, mascara, medea, miliana, negrine, nemours, oran, ouargla, saida, setif, sidi-bel-abbes, skikda, tebessa, temes, tlemcen, touggourt
commune setif
conqueror bugeaud
department algiers, constantine, oran
desert sahara
dolman senam
governor dey, disawa
grass diss, esparto
hero abd-al-kadir, abd-el-kader
hill tell
holy man marabout
island ios
leader abd-al-kadir, abd-el-kader, boumedienne
measure pik, rebis, tarri, termin
monastery ribat
name, ancient numidia, pomaria
national anthem kassaman
native quarter casbah, kasbah
oil minister abdes.alam
peak ahaggar, aissa, atlas, aures, chelia, dahra, djurdjura, kabylia, mouydir, tahat
people arab, berber, haratin, kabyle, tuareg
pirate corsair
plane mitidja
plant barilla
plantation owner colon
poet abd-el-kader
port bona, bone, oran, orel
president ben bella
river cheliffmedjerda

roman name pomaria
ruler bevlerbay, bey, dey
sect sunnite
senam dolman
settler colon, piednoir
ship xebec, zebec
slum bidonville
soldier arbi, sepoy, spahee, spahi
statesman ben bella
tirailleur turco
warrior abd-el-kader
weight rotl
ALGERINE coolooly, koolooly, pirate
ALGERITA agarita, mahonia
ALGESIA ache, pain
ALGID chilly, clammy, cold, cool, gelid
ALGODONCILLO majagua, tree
ALGOLAGNIA algophilia, masochism, sadism
ALGONQUIAN *dance* cantico
divinity earth-mother, glooscap, manito(u)
fish-curing site agawam
friend netop
indian abitibi, abnaki, adirondack, algic, appomattoc, bersiamite, blackfoot, blood, brotherton, cahokia, canarsee, cheyenne, conoy, cree, delaware, fox, illinois, kaskaskia, kickapoo, mahican, manhattan, mashpee, massachuset, mattapony, miami, michigamea, micmac, missisaca, mohican, moingwena, monsoni, montagnais, montauk, nascapee, nascapi, nauset, niantic, nipissing, nipmuck, nipmuk, nishoskan, ojibway, ottawa, pamlico, pamunkey, patuxent, peoria, piquot, piankashaw, piegan, podunk, quinnipiac, rockaway, sac, sauk, scaticook, shawnee, shinnecock, sihasapa, siksika, sokoki, stockbridge, sutaio, wampanoag, wappinger, wea, weanoc, weitspekan, wewenoc
smoke kinnikin(n)ic(k)
spirit hobomoco, hobomoko, huaca, manito(u), michabo, nokomis, thunderbird
spirit, great gitchi-manito(u)
wampee pickerelweed
ALGOR bloom, chill, coldness

ALGORISM arithmetic, mathematics
ALGUM almug, sandalwood, tree
ALHAGI camel's thorn
ALHET ashamnu, confession
ALI lion of god
boxer clay
cousin mohammed
descendants alid(e)s, fatimid
father-in-law mohammed
horse dhuldul
son has(s)an, husain
sword zulfagar
wife fatima
ALIAS anonym, ayless, else, epithet, name, nom de plume, otherwise, penname, pseudonym, sobriquet
ALI BABA *brother* cassim
magic word sesame
slave morgiana
ALIBAMU wetumpka
ALIBANGBANG bauhinia, tree
ALIBI apology, cop out, defense, excuse, explanation, eyewash, plea, pretext
ALIBIER kvetcher, kvetcherkeh
ALIBLE nourishing, nutritive
ALICE IN WONDERLAND
author carroll, dodgson
cake words eat me
cat dinah
character bandersnatch, carpenter, caterpillar, cheshire cat, dodo, dormouse, duchess, gnat, gryphon, humpty dumpty, king, knight, lion, mad hatter, mock turtle, mouse, queen, rabbit, rockinghorse fly, tweedledee, tweedledum, unicorn, walrus
poem jabberwocky
ALIDADE diopter, index
ALIDES *ancestor* ali
ALIEN adverse, alaunt, alltud, antagonistic, auslander, barbarian, different, estrange(d), exotic, extraneous, foreign(er), frammit, fremd, furriner, ger, gringo, hostile, immigrant, incongruous, inconsistent, invader, irrelevant, metic, opposed, other, outlander, outlandish, outsider, perigrene, remote, strange(r), tramontane, transfer, uitlander, ultramontane, unsympathetic
comb. xen(o)

ALIENATE annaly, antagonize, convey, deed, demise, devest, disaffect, dispossess, disunite, divert, divide, embitter, estrange, forfeit, freeze, mortmain, part, separate, set against, subvert, transfer, wean, withdraw
ALIENATION breach, break, conveyance, disaccord, disunion, division, donation, enmity, estrangement, insanity, transfer
ALIENIST psychiatrist, psychopathist
ALIGHT aflame, arrive, burning, descend, dismount, drop, get down, kindle, land, latch, lodge, rest, roost, settle, stay, stoop, stop, swoop
ALIGN, ALINE adjust, ally, arrange, array, dress, join, level, line, marshal, parallelize, range, tram, true
ALIGNMENT adjustment, affiliation, association, grouping, kelter, kilter
ALIKE agnate, akin, congruent, duplicate, equally, identical, like, resembling, same, similar, twins, uniform, yliche
comb. iso
ALIMENT alimony, allowance, broma, food, maintenance, manna, nourishment, nutriment, pabulum, pap, rations, sustain, sustenance, support, viands
ALIMENTARY *canal* foodtube
canal, lacking asplanchnic
canal part esophagus, intestine, mouth, pharynx, stomach
ALIMONY aliment, allowance, maintenance, subsidy
ALIPIN See SLAVE.
ALISON herb, sweet alyssum
ALISONITE cuproplumbite
ALIVE abuzz, active, agile, alert, animate(d), astir, aware, breathing, brimming, brisk, bursting, busy, charged, current, extant, fresh, green, keen, lively, living, operating, quick, sensible, sensitive, slippy, sprightly, spry, swarming, swiftly, unexpired, vibrant, vital, vivacious, vive, vivid, warm, well

with swarming, teeming
ALIZARIN anthragallol
source anthracene, anthracon, anthraquinone, madder
ALKALI base, brack, caustic, lime, lye, magnesia, reh, salt, soda, usar
disease botulism, milk sickness
element francium
flat plain(s)
grass puccinellia, zygadenus
metal cesium, francium, lithium, potassium, rubidium, sodium
mustard jackass clover
pegmatite bowralite, mineral
trachyte beringite
volatile ammonia
ALKALINE lime, oxide
remedy antacid
salt borax
ALKALOID arabine, aricine, atarine, atropine, base, bebeerine, boldine, brucin, caffein, cevine, cicutin, cocaine, codeia, codeine, conin(e), curare, ditamin, emetine, ergot, eserine, jervine, kairine, morphine, nicotine, physostigmine, quinia, quinine, sinapin, solanine, sophora, strychnine, violine
artificial apocodeine, apomorphin(e)
bitter achilleline, boldine
cadaveric ptomaine
colorless pelletierine
crystalline apoatropine, apomorphine, aporphine, berbamine, berberine, cephaeline, ether, globulin, hydrocarbon, imperialine, indaconitine, ketone, phenol, rubijervine, rutaecarpine, salt, theophylline, trigonelline, tropacocaine, xanthaline, yajeine, yohimbine
emetic alangine
liquid anatabine, isopelletierine
mixture adonidin, jaborine
narcotic pellotine
poisonous aconitin(e), amarine, anagyrine, anthorin(e), aristolachin(e), atropine, boldine, conin(e), coninine, curare, daturine, jervine, nicotine, taxine, thebaine, thorin(e), tropine
red achilleline
sirup mescaline
solution lye

ALKANET alkannin, bugloss, puccoon, redroot
ALKEKENGI ground cherry, lantern plant, physalis, winter cherry
ALKENE olefin
ALKINE alcamine
ALL aggregate, alone, altogether, any, apiece, aught, complete(ly), consumed, cosmos, each, entire, every, exclusively, final, finished, full, gone, gross, just, omnes, only, ought, plenary, plenty, quantity, solely, sum, total(ity), toto, totum, tout, tutto, universe, very, whole, wholly
about around
absorbing paramount
along always, forever
anyhow chaotic
around blanket, broad, complete, comprehensive, everywhere, exhaustive, handy, inclusive, serviceable, thorough, versatile
at once simultaneously, suddenly, together
but almost, barely, nearly, scarcely
comb. omni, pan(to)
ears attentive, vigilant
-embracing all-inclusive, blanket, complete, comprehensive, exhaustive, global, infinite, sweeping, thorough
-expense package
eyes attentive, vigilant
fired excessive, extreme, infernal, inordinate, tremendous
fives dominoes, muggins, seven-up
forty maximum
fours auction-pitch, california-loo, cinch, creeping, double pedro, high-low-jack, old sledge, pedro, pitch, razzle-dazzle, seven-up, shasta-sam, sixty-three, smudge, snoozer
fours term gambler's point, gift, refuse, rob, run
get out imaginable, maximum, possible, the limit
hot and bothered anxious, confused, dismayed, upset
in committed, exhausted, fatigued, finished, inclusive, spent, tired
in all altogether, everything, generally, substantially, wholly

-inclusive See *-embracing*, above.
in one's head illusory, imaginary
in the wind confused, flurried, uncertain
-knowing almighty, omniscient
off cancelled, ended, erroneous, wrong
one equal, identical, same
one can take bellyful
out altogether, complete, exhausted, exhaustive, swiftly, thorough, total, unqualified
over dispersed, ended, entirely, everywhere, irregular, straggly, thoroughly, wholly, widespread
-overish anxious, apprehensive, shaky, sick, uneasy, upset
-overs creeps, fidgets, thrills
over with dead, ended, finished
right acceptable, accurate, agreed, bien, bueno, buono, cava, certainly, correct, fine, good, great, okay, okeh, okeydoke, reliable, safe, satisfactory, sobeit, sound, tolerable, well, yes
round See *around*, above.
shook up discombobulated, shaky
the rage See POPULAR.
there alert, informed, normal, on the ball, quick-witted, sane, smart, well-informed
the same identical, nevertheless, notwithstanding
the while forever, invariably
threes dominoes, muggins
thumbs awkward
-time record
-told altogether, in all
washed up discarded, done, ended, exhausted, failed, fatigued, finished, spent, tired
wet mistaken, wrong
-wise almighty, supreme
ALLAH *in the name of* bismillah
offspring al-lat, al-uzza
word of kalam
ALLAN-A-DALE *friend* robin hood
ALLANITE bagrationite, bucklandite, cerine, epidote, orthite, silicate
ALLANTIASIS botulism, sausage poisoning
ALLASCH kummel

AL-LAT *father* allah

ALLATU *consort* nergal

secretary belit-seri

ALLAY abandon, abate, aid, alleviate, appease, assuage, calm, check, compose, cool, defer, dilute, ease, help, hush, lessen, lighten, mitigate, moderate, mollify, pacify, palliate, quench, quiet, relieve, repress, salve, satisfy, slake, soften, solice, soothe, staunch, subdue, temper, weaken

ALLBONE alsine, chickweed, stitchwort

ALLEGATION assertion, assumption, averment, charge, citation, count, declaration, essoin, fiction, profert, quotation, statement, surmise, testimony, vouch

ALLEGE adduce, advance, affirm, ascribe, assert, asseverate, assign, assume, attest, attribute, aver, avow, charge, cite, claim, declare, depose, feign, infer, ledge, maintain, offer, plead, present, pretext, profess, propose, purport, quote, recite, say, state, swear, testify, urge, vouch

ALLEGHENY appalachia

evergreen fraser fir

indian cayuga, delaware, huron, mahican, mohawk, mohican, nipmus, oneida, onondaga, seneca, susquehanna

vine fumitory

ALLEGIANCE adherence, adhesion, attachment, bond, devotion, duty, faithfulness, fealty, fidelity, homage, honor, legiance, loyalty, obedience, obligation, respect, servage, tie, tribute, truth

violation of treachery, treason

ALLEGORY anagoge, apologue, emblem, fable, fiction, image, metaphor, myth, narrative, parable, story, tale

collection physiologus

ALLELUIAH cheer, hallelujah, hymn

ALLEMANDE folk dance, landler

ALLEN, HERVEY *novel* anthony adverse

ALLENARLY only, sole(ly)

ALLENE hydrocarbon, propadiene

ALLERGY anaphylaxis, antipathy, atopy, atrophy, aversion, hypersensitivity, idioblapsis, reaction, sensitivity, susceptibility, tendency, vulnerability

cause allergen

determinant scratch test

remedy antihistamine, coricidin, cortisone

ALLEVIATE abate, aid, allay, allege, assuage, calm, compose, cure, decrease, diminish, disburden, disencumber, ease, help, lenify, lessen, lighten, mitigate, moderate, modify, pacify, palliate, quiet, relax, relieve, soften, soothe, succor, temper, tranquilize, unburden, unlade, unload

ALLEVIATION abatement, decrease, palliation, relief, solace

ALLEY airway, aisle, allee, blind, byway, lane, mall, marble, mews, mib, mig, passage, peewee, road, street, tewer, vennel, vent, walk, way, weent, went

back slum

blind cul de sac, impasse, loke, pocket, stop

cat slattern

oops excelsior, onward, up-a-daisy, upsydaisy, upward

ALLHEAL mistletoe, panacea, valerian, woundwort, yarrow

ALLIANCE accord, affiliation, affinity, agnation, agreement, association, axis, band, bloc, bund, cactales, coalition, combination, compact, concurrence, confederacy, confederation, connection, consortium, correspondence, covenant, federation, fusion, group, league, marriage, merger, pact, partnership, relationship, society, symmachy, treaty, union

anti-communist nato, seato

triple dreibund

war symmachy

ALLICE alewife, alosa, pompano, shad

ALLICIENT alluring, attracting

ALLIED agnate, akin, analogous, associated, cognate,

connate, cousin, federal, germane, joined, kin(dred), linked, related, relative, sib, similar, united

ALLIGATE attach, tie, unite

ALLIGATOR alagarto, cacao, caiman, cayman, crocodile, crotch, fishmouth, hellbender, hellgramite, jacare, lagarto, lizard, loricate, niger, sled, theobroma, travois, travoy, yacare

bonnet waterlily

fish agonida, podothecus, seapoacher

head buttonweed, diodia

lizard gerrhonotus, sceloporus

male bull

pear aguacate, avocado, zaboca

snapper terrapin, tortoise, turtle

tree sweet gum

turtle loggerhead

wampee pickerelweed

ALLITERATION paromoeon

ALLIUM chives, garlic, leek, lily, onion, shallot

ALLNESS entirety, omnitude, totality, universality

ALLOCATE allot, apportion, assign, award, deal, distribute, dole, fix, locate, mete, rate, share

ALLOCATION allotment, apportionment, arrangement, draw, placement, share

ALLOCHROITE andradite, aplome, garnet

ALLOCUTION address, speech

ALLONYM pen name, pseudonym

ALLOT allocate, allow, apply, appoint, apportion, appropriate, assign, attribute, award, bestow, billet, cast, cavel, consign, deal, dedicate, design, destine, detail, distribute, divide, dole, fix, give, grant, intend, locate, mark, mete, ordain, parcel out, portion, prescribe, prorate, quarter, rate, ration, reserve, set, share, specify, split, spread, tribute

ALLOTMENT allocation, appointment, apportionment, appropriation, assignment, budget, cavel, consignment, cut, distribution, dividend, dole, lot, ordainment, ordinance, pittance, plot, portion, ration, share, subsidy

ALLOW abate, accept, accord, acknowledge, admit, approve, assign, authorize, bear, bestow, beteem, concede, confess, deduct, defer, enable, endure, give, grant, land, leave, let, loan, low, permit, ratify, recognize, sanction, say, stand, suffer, suppose, think, thole, tolerate, yield
for condone, consider, extenuate

ALLOWANCE abatement, acknowledgment, agio (tage), aliment, allotment, amount, appenage, apportionment, arras, batta, bot(e), bouche, bounty, budget, burse, clearance, cloff, confession, corrody, deduction, discount, divergence, dole, edge, exchange, expenses, extra, fee, fodder, gift, grant, leave, odds, pension, permission, pin money, pittance, portion, prebend, premium, ration, retainer, salary, sanction, share, size, stent, stint, stipend, subsidy, tantum, tare, tolerance, tret, viaticum
traveling mileage
weight beamage, bug, draft, draught, scalage, tare, tret

ALLOY (See also *kind*, below.) abate, admixture, adulterate, aich, allay, amalgam, combination, composition, corrupt, debase, dilute, garble, impair, lay, loy, mixture, moderate
black metal niello
cover with terne
fusible solder
gold-like doralium, occamy, oreide, oroide
heat-resistant illium
kind acieral, albata, alnico, alumel, amalgam, arsedine, babbitt, biddery, bidri, bidry, brass, britannia, bronze, caracol, carboloy, castiron, chrome, chromium, constantan, cupronickel, dental-gold, doralium, duriron, electrum, elinvar, flint, gridmetal, gunmetal, hypernik, iconel, invar, kamacite, mettallide,

mokum, monel, muntz, nichrome, occamy, paktong, permalloy, perminvar, pewter, pigiron, rhodite, romanium, solder, spiegeleisen, steel, stellite, tambac, tombac, tutenag, wrought iron
magnetic alnico, bismanol
native iridosmine
non-ferrous tula
pewter-like bidree, bidri, bidry
principal base metal
silver-like billon, occamy

ALLOYED base, spurious

ALLSEED burstwort, goosefoot, flaxseed, knotweed, radiola

ALLSPICE pimento

ALL'S WELL THAT ENDS WELL *author* shakespeare
character bertram, diana, helena, lafeu, mariana, parolles, violenta
clown lavache
hero bertram
heroine helena

ALLTHORN junco

ALLTUD alien, foreigner, slave

ALLUDE advert, attribute, connote, designate, glance, hit, imply, indicate, insinuate, intimate, mention, point, refer, relate, suggest

ALLURE agacerie, air, allect, appeal, attract, bait, beguile, bewitch, bribe, captivate, charm, coax, coy, decoy, draw, ensnare, entice, entrap, fascinate, gait, induce, inveigle, invite, lure, move, persuade, seduce, sex appeal, sway, tempt, tice, tole, toll, trap, wile, win, woo

ALLUREMENT agacerie, appeal, attraction, bait, bewitchery, bribe, captivation, enchantment, enthrallment, fascination, glamo(u)r, gudgeon, inducement, interest, inveiglement, invitation, seduction, sex appeal, tantalization, temptation

ALLURING allicient, attracting, captious, catching, charming, come-hither, fetching, mouth-watering, seductive, sirenic, takeful, taking, winsome
gland androconium

ALLUSION glance, hint, im-

plication, indication, inkling, innuendo, instance, intimation, mention, reference, touch, twit

ALLUSIVE canting, figurative, metaphorical, punning, suggestive

ALLUVIAL estuarine, fluviomarine
clay adobe
deposit cone, fan, mud, placer, silt
fan delta
plain bajada

ALLUVIUM accretion, deposit, detritus, earth, gravel, sand, sediment, wash

ALLY accomplice, akin, alliant, analogue, associate, backer, combine, confederate, connect, federate, friend, fuse, helper, join, kinsman, league, marry, pal, partner, relative, union, unite, wed

ALMACK'S brooks's, willis's

ALMAGEST *author* ptolemy

ALMAIN allemande, alman, armor, dance, german(y)

ALMA MATER ceres, college, cybele, school, university

ALMANAC annual, calendar, calends, chronogram, compendium, ephemeris, kalends, ordo, paddy, poor richard's

ALMIGHTY all-knowing, all-wise, awesome, divine, extreme, god, great, infinite, irresistible, jehovah, omnipotent, omniscient, overpowering, potent, powerful, puissant, sovereign, strong, supreme, ubiquitous, unlimited.

ALMIQUE acana, alamiqui, almon, hardwood, makilkara, philippine mahogany, sapote, shorea, solenodon, tree

ALMIRAH bahut, buffet, cabinet, cupboard, wardrobe

ALMOND almendron, amygdala, badam, chufa, doe, kamani, kanari, pawnee, pili, rosacean, talisay, tonsil, valencia
bitter amarine
color biscuit, brown, tan
confection marzipan
emulsion amarin(e), orgeat
enzyme emulsin

-eyed oriental
furnace alman
kernels tonsils
liqueur creme de noyau, orgeat, orzata, ratafia
milk amygdalate
oil amarin(e)
paste marzipan
pert. amygdalate, amygdaline, amygdaloid
protein amandin
shape mandorla
tumbler pigeon
willow black-maul, salix
ALMONER ecclesiastic, philanthropist, purse, social worker
ALMOST all but, amaist, anear, approximately, barely, close, feckly, mostly, muchwhat, nearly, nigh, wellmost, wellnear
comb. pen(e)
ALMS almoign, almoin, almous, awmous, benefaction, beneficence, bounty, charity, corban, dole, donation, gift, gratuity, handout, maundy, money, offering, passade, pittance, relief
box arca
fee peter's pence
giver almoner, almsman, eleemosynar
giving See CHARITY.
seeker beggar, beneficiary, bluecoat, pauper
ALMSHOUSE asylum, beadhouse, bedehouse, poorhouse, workhouse
ALMUCE amice, cape, cowl, headdress, hood, tippet, vagas, vakass, varkas, vestment
ALMUG algum, sandalwood, tree
ALNUS alder, aliso, birch, buckthorn, tree
ALOADAE ephialtes, giants, otus
enemy olympians
parent iphimedia, poseidon
slayer apollo
ALOCASIA apii, aroid, arum
ALOE agalloch, agave, century plant, furcraea, lily, maguey, pita, purgative, succulent, tambac, tombak
creole furcraea
substance aloemodin, aloin, orcin(ol), picra
wood agalloch(um), agalwood, agar, aquilaria, eagle-

wood, incense, lignaloes, sebestan
ALOEUS *parent* canace, neptune, poseidon
sons aloadae, ephialtes, otus
wife iphimedia
ALOFT aboard, above, aheight, airborne, aloof, high, o'er, overhead, skyward, upstairs, upwards
ALOHA farewell, goodbye, greetings, hello, kindness, love
ALONE apart, azygous, bare, companionless, desolate, detached, ensile, exclusive, forlorn, friendless, homeless, insular, isolated, kithless, lonely, lonesome, lorn, matchess, one, only, separate, simply, single, singular, sole, solein, solitary, solo, solus, sullen, unaccompanied, unaided, unequalled, unexcelled, unique
all leelane, leelone
comb. mono, soli
fear of being monophobia
ALONG advanced, ahead, beside, during, forbye, forward, lang, onward, parallel, through, together, via, with, yond
comb. par(a)
in years aged, old
the way enroute
towards near
with and, through, together
ALONGSIDE abreast, aside, beside, close, forenenst, parallel, sidelings, sidlins, together
ALONSO *kin* ferdinand, sebastian
ALONSOA figwort, maskflower, plant
ALOOF aback, abeigh, abiegh, aloft, apart, arrogant, cold, cool, disinterested, distant, dry, exclusive, frigid, frosty, impartial, inaccessible, indifferent, olympian, otiose, proud, remote, removed, reserved, reticent, secluded, seclusive, standoffish, unapproachable, unfriendly, uninvolved, withdrawn
ALOPE *consort* poseidon
kin cercyon, hippothous
ALOPECIA atrichia, baldness, hairlessness, pelade
ALOPECURUS foxtail
ALOPEX fox

ALOSE commend, praise, shad
ALOW ablaze, afire, ardent, below
ALOXITE abrasive, alumina
ALOYSIA lemon verbena, lippia
ALP bullfinch, demon, mountain, nightmare, peak, witch
ALPACA coat, guanaco, l(l)ama, paco
-like guanaco, viouna
-like fabric brilliantine
ALPENSTOCK bergstock, staff
ALPHA beginning, chief, debut, deneb, first, start
and omega all, entire, whole
ALPHABET abc, bisaya, brahmi, crossrow, futhorc, glagol, gujarati, kaithi, kufic, language, letters, order, peshito, primer, rudiments, sarada, visaya
board ouija
book abecedarium, abecedary
character ofham, ogun, rune, sarada
cyrillic kirillitsa
early runes
learner abecedarian
pert. abecedarian
plant para cress
principle acrology
runic futhorc, futhork
sign rune
teacher abecedarian
ALPHAEA artemis
ALPHEUS *parent* oceanus, tethys
quest arethusa
ALPHOSIS albinism
ALPINE See also ALPS.
beardtongue pentstemon
bogplant felwort
campion viscaria
cattle celtic ox
cranberry bog bilberry
cress cardamine
fir pumpkin tree
flora and fauna cryoplankton
forget-me-not eritrichium
goldenrod solidago
harebell bluebell, campanula
lake tarn
larch larix
lousewort pedicularis
molewort rock cress
plant bistort, edelweiss, sea pink, thrift
poppy papever
primrose auricula

rock cress arabis, bishop's wig, molewort
rose edelweiss, rhododendron
sandstone flysch
shrub heather
sled luge
spring beauty claytonia
spruce hemlock
umbrella plant eriogonum
undershrub crowberry
wallflower erysium
ALPS See also ALPINE.
activity skiing
beyond tramontane
chain rhaetian
dance gavot
dress dirndle
dwelling chalet
flower edelweiss
goat bouquetin, ibex
granite protogine
herb rock-beauty
herdsman senn
native grison
pass brenner, cenis, col, eiger simplon, st bernard
peak bernina, jungfrau, matterhorn, mont blanc, monte rosa, monte viso, pilatus, weisshorn
peak, highest mont blanc
pert. alpestrine, alpine, cisalpine
range bernese, cottian, dinaric, dolomites, maritime, ortler, pennine, tyrol
sound echo, yodel
structure fanfold
tunnel See TUNNEL *famous.*
valley moon-gorge
wind bise, bora fo(e)hn
AL QAHIRAH cairo
ALREADY before, done, een, even, now, previously, since
ALSACE bas-rhin, haut-rhin
lorraine reichsland
patron saint odile
ALSATIAN clover alsike, herb, trifolium
coin baetzner
wine charmant, chasselas, crystal, fleur d'alsace, gewerztraminer, klevner, muscat, pinot blanc, riesling, sylvaner, tokay, zwicker
ALSINE allbone, bird's-tongue, bog stitchwort, chickweed, herb
ALSO als, and, besides, ditto, eke, erst, even, further, in addition, incidentally, item,

likewise, moreover, same, similarly, thereto, too, yet
-ran candidate, hare, loser, mediocrity, second
ALSOS felsos, kalaber, kalabrias, klaberjass
term bella, bettli, cassa, forty-four, tous les trois, uhu, ultimo, volat
ALSTONIA bitter bark, cascara buckthorn, dogbane
ALSTONITE bromlite
ALTAR acerra, ara, autere, bema, bomos, chancel, chantry, communion table, credence, eschara, gradin, haikal, hestia, lord's table, mensal, omphalos, predella, prothesis, reposoir, scrobis, shrine, table, thymele, tripod, vedika, weved
area apse
boy acolyte, thurifer
boy's coat cotta
bread wafer
candle percher
carpet pedale, pedecloth
cloth antimension, bisso, catacarka, cerecloth, cerement, chrismal, coster, dossal, ependytes, frontal, haploma, pall(a), riddel, superfrontal
corner ministerium
curtain coster, parafront, riddel
decoration antependium
enclosure bema
funeral pyre acerra
hanging dorsal, dossal, dossel
offering altarage
part desk, gradin, mensa, predella, rail, retable, slab, stair, stead, stone
piece ancona, diptych, reredos, screen, triptych
platform predella
portable acerra
rail septum
sacrificial eschara
screen reredos
top frontal, mensa
vessel pyx
ALTE *der* konrad adenauer
ALTE FRITZ frederick the great
ALTER abridge, adapt, adjust, adulterate, affect, blue-pencil, braid, censor, chaffer, change, cook, correct, corrupt, deacon, deform, differentiate, doctor,

duff, edit, emend, geld, hocus, hoke, immute, jigger, juggle, load, manipulate, modify, move, mutate, mutilate, neuter, neutralize, other, qualify, rase, shape, shift, sophisticate, turn, vary, wend
appearance wry
-ego alternate, carbon copy, deputy, friend, second self, stand-in, substitute
garment bushel
ALTERATION change, commutation, deduction, difference, mutation, upheaval
ALTERCATE bicker, contend, dispute, spat, tiff, wrangle
ALTERCATION affray, argument, bicker, boil, brabble, brawl, broil, contention, contest, controversy, debate, dialogue, discord, dispute, dissension, disturbance, fight, fracas, fray, fuss, jangle, quarrel, spat, strife, struggle, tiffitilt, tumult, wrangle
ALTERNATE alternative, back and fill, change, ebb and flow, else, exchange, interchange, intermit, mutual, oscillate, other, periodic(al), reciprocal, reciprocate, recur, relieve, replacement, reverse, ringer, rotate, second, seesaw, shift, shuttle, spell, substitute, sway, swing, teeter-totter, to-and-fro, understudy, vacillate, vary, waver, wigwag, zigzag
ALTERNATELY by turns, every other, in rotation, off and on, reciprocally
ALTERNATION ebb and flow, interchange, reciprocation, seesaw, teeter-totter, ups and downs
ALTERNATIVE choice, disjunct, either, election, escape, fork, lorn, opportunity, option, preference, recourse, selection
ALTERNATOR booster, dynamo, generator
ALTHAEA healer, hibiscus, hollyhock, lucasta, mallow, marshmallow, plant, rose of sharon
consort oeneus
father thestius

offspring deianira, meleager, toxeus, tydeus

ALTHORN alto, altus, sax(horn)

ALTHOUGH albeit, alif, despite, een, even(if), granting that, howbeit, notwithstanding, that, though, whenas, whereas, while

ALTILOQUENCE bombast, grandiloquence, loftiness, pomposity, rhetoric

ALTITUDE apex, ceiling, celsitude, clearance, elevation, excellence, height, highness, loftiness, peak, prominence, rank, stature, tallness, top

measuring device altimeter, arbalest, astrolabe, orometer

parallel almucantar

sickness soroche

ALTO althorn, contralto, elevation, halt, height, hill, singer

ALTOGETHER agreat, all, au naturel, collectively, completely, entirely, exactly, freely, generally, holus-bolus, nude, quite, sheer, thoroughly, totally, tout ensemble, utterly, whole, wholly

ALTOMETER theodolite

ALTRUISM beneficence, benevolence, bigheartedness, brotherly love, charity, dogoodism, generosity, grace, humanitarianism, philanthropy

ALTRUISTIC almsgiving, beneficent, benevolent, bighearted, charitable, eleemosynary, generous, gracious, heroic(al), humanitarian, philanthropic(al)

ALUDEL condenser, pot, udell, vessel

furnace bustamente

ALUKAH horseleech, jinni, vampire

ALULA calypter, lobe, lobulus, squama, tegula, winglet

ALUM alme, astringent, aum, emetic, kalinite, migite, styptic, tscher

burnt terra alba

compound boral

feather alunogen

rock alunite, mineral

schist shale, slate

ALUMINA abrasive, aloxite, argil, corundum

ALUMINITE websterite

ALUMINUM *alloy* acieral, alnico, alumel, dural (umin), partinium, romanium, wolframinium

borate boral, jereme, jevite

bronze abyssinian gold, talmi gold

coated alclad

compound alumide, boehmite, carpholite, corundum, epidote, gibbsite, thermite, wavellite

discoverer davy, wohler

family gallium, indium, thallium

phosphate augelite, berlinite, callainite, ceruleolactite, evansite, palmerite, sphaerite, wardite, wavellite

silicate allophane, allushtite, andalusite, cimolite, cyanite, kornerupine, mullite, sillimanite, staurolite, weinbergerite, xenolite

source bauxite

yellow-green epidote

ALUMNA, ALUMNUS graduate, pupil, student, ward

ALUMROOT chocolate flower, coralbells, crane's-bill, heuchera

ALURE ambulatory, gallery, passage, walk

ALUTACEOUS brown, coriaceous, cracked

AL-UZZA *father* allah

ALVEARY apiary, beehive, beescap, beeskop, gum tree, hive, meatus, praesepe, skep

ALVEOLA acinus, cavity, cell, depression, faveolus, peritheceum, pit, pore, socket

ALVEOLATE favose, favous, honeycombed, pitted

ALVEUS bed, channel, duct, trough, utriculus

ALVUS abdomen

ALWAYS algates, alwise, aye, but, constantly, continually, een, eer, eternally, ever(more), forever, habitually, invariably, permanently, perpetually, sempre, simle, unceasingly, uniformly

AMA (See also AMAH.) amula, candlenut, chalice, cruet, cup, vessel

AMABILE armigerous, balmy, bland, gentle, tender

AMADAVAT tigerbird, waxbill

AMADELPHOUS gregarious

AMADIS *beloved* oriana

country gaul

AMADOU punk, tinder

AMAH maid, nurse, servant

AMAIMON See DEVIL.

AMAIN anon, at once, bang, exceedingly, forcibly, greatly, suddenly, swiftly, violently

AMALEK *grandfather* esau

king agag

parent eliphaz

AMALGAM alloy, combination, compound, mixture, union

AMALGAMATE blend, blunge, coalesce, combine, commingle, communify, compound, consolidate, fuse, join, marry, merge, mingle, mix, unify, unite

AMALTHEA *consort* melisseus

foster-child zeus

horn cornucopia

AMANITA agaric, death cup, fungus

AMANITOPSIS agaric, mushroom

AMANUENSIS copier, penman, recorder, scribe, scrivener, secretary, steno, transcriber, typist, writer

AMAPA gum tree, parahancornia, tabebuia

AMARANTH achyranthes, acnida, beetroot, bloodleaf, careless(weed), celosia, chenopodium, cockscomb, coxcomb, floramor, flower, herb, jataco, joseph's coat, love-lies-bleeding, pigweed, prince's feather, purpleheart

AMARANTHINE everlasting, undying, unfading

AMARELLE cherry, fruit, prunus

AMARGOSO balsam apple, goatbush bark

AMARIAH *parent* ezias

AMARYLLIS agave, bomarea, clivia, crinum, datil, hippeastrum, lily, mistress, narcissus, polianthes, shepherdess, snowdrop, sprekelia, sweetheart, vallota

AMARYSIA artemis

AMASA *cousin* joab

leader absalom, david

parent abigail, hadlai, ithra

AMASIAH *commander* jehoshaphat

AMASS accumulate, aggregate, assemble, collect, compile, congest, gather, heap, hill, hoard, mass, overheap, pile, save, stack, stockpile, store

AMASSMENT accumulation, build-up, storage

AMATA *daughter* lavinia
husband latinus

AMATE daunt, dishearten, ficus, match, subdue

AMATERASU *kin* susanowo

AMATEUR admirer, aficionado, apprentice, athlete, beginner, dabbler, devotee, dilettante, enthusiast, fancier, follower, greenhorn, ham, inferior, innocent, jackleg, laic, mediocre, non-professional, novice, prentice, tiro, tyro, varment, volunteer, votary

AMATI *pupil* stradivari(us)

AMATIVE See ARDENT.

AMATORY amorous, ardent, erotic, gallant, loving, philter, potion, tender
gesture pass

AMAUROSIS ablepsia, blindness

AMAZE alarm, astonish, astony, astound, awe, awhape, bewilder, confound, confuse, dumfound, ferly, impress, overwhelm, perplex, stagger, stam, stun, stupefy, surprise, wonder

AMAZED aghast, astonished, bushed

AMAZEMENT alarm, astonishment, awe, bewilderment, consternation, ferly, frenzy, perplexity, stam, stupefaction, surprise, wonder
expression of gore-blimey, wow

AMAZIAH amasias
kin joash, uzziah
kingdom judah

AMAZON aella, aleria, ant, antiope, hummingbird, orellana, parrot, river, solimoes, thalestris, virago, warrior
adversary bellerophon, hercules, theseus
ant polyergus
discoverer orellawa
estuary para

fish candiru, catfish, electric eel
gum cumay
indian tapajo, tupi, tupy, xingu
island marajo
jungle green hell
lily eucharis
mat yapa
plant cumay
queen antiope, calafia, hippolyta, penthesilea, radegund, thalestris
rain forest selva, silvas
sea snake yacumama
slayer hercules
source andes
stone feldspar
tidal bore pororoca
tributary apa, ica, madeira, maranon, napo, purus, tapajos, xingu
turtle arrau
vine timbo
vs. greeks amazonamachia
woodland rain forest

AMAZONITE feldspar, microline

AMAZONS solitaire

AMBAGE ambiguity, circumlocution, convolution, quibble

AMBAGIOUS anfractuous, circuitous, circumlocutory, devious, roundabout, tortuous, turning, winding

AMBARY cordage, fiber, hemp, hibiscus, kanaff, kenaf, nalita, sunn

AMBASSADOR agent, capucius, deputy, diplomat, elchee, elchi, envoy, intermediary, legate, messenger, minister, nuncio, representative, vakil
aide attache
papal internuncio
pert. legatine
representative vakil
temporary charge d'affaires

AMBATCH aeschenomene, herminiera, sudd, tree

AMBER aumer, awmer, brass, burmite, electrum, fustic, hypericum, lammer, liquidambar, medregal, resin, st-john's-wort, succin, sunstone, sweetgum, yellow
black jet, labdanum
comb. succino
islands electrides, glessariae
jack See AMBERFISH.
mica phlogopite

pear ambrette

AMBERFISH amicore, carangid, caraux, coronado, jurel, kahala, kingfish, mackerel, medregal, mokuleia, runner, seriola

AMBIDEXTROUS clever, deceitful, double-dealing, facile, falsehearted, skillful, switch-hitting, treacherous, versatile

AMBIENCE atmosphere, character, environment, milieu, mood, quality, surroundings, tone

AMBIENT atmosphere, circulating, encompassing, environing, surrounding

AMBIGUITY ambage, ambilogy, amphibology, amphilogism, deceptiveness, double-entendre, duplicity, equivocality, equivocation, equivoque, obscurity, paradox, pun, sophistry, uncertainty, vagueness

AMBIGUOUS amphibolic, bifarious, changing, cryptic, dark, debatable, delphic, double, doubtful, dubious, equivocal, forked, indefinite, indeterminate, indistinct, indistinguishable, irregular, obscure, problematic, puzzling, questionable, slippery, spurious, uncertain, unclear, unsettled, vague

AMBISINISTER clumsy, lefthanded, unskillful

AMBIT boundary, bounds, circuit, circumference, compass, extent, limit, precinct, scope, sphere

AMBITENDENCY ambivalence

AMBITION ardor, aspiration, ate, desire, eagerness, energy, enterprise, fire, goal, hope, intention, longing, purpose, spirit, striving, willingness, wish, yearning
without drifting, feckless, lazy, slothful

AMBITIOUS aggressive, aspiring, avid, bold, creative, desirous, eager, emulous, enterprising, ettle, high, keen, showy, venturesome

AMBITUS bribery, edge, extension, periphery, tenor, test

AMBIVALENCE ambitendency, bipolarity, fluctuation, uncertainty

AMBIVALENT equivocal, two-faced

AMBLE gait, meander, mooch, move, pace, padnag, saunter, stroll, tripple, walk, wander

AMBLYOPSIS blindfish, cavefish

AMBO desk, pulpit

AMBOINA kiabooca, lingoa
button yaws
pine agathis, galagala
pitch kauri resin
wood andaman

AMBOS incus, malleus

AMBOSEXOUS hermaphrodite

AMBROSE chenopodium, oak, teucrium, wood sage
saint, symbol beehive, scourge

AMBROSIA beebread, blackweed, bloodpink, bluecurls, chenopodium, eau secree, haemanthus, honeydew, kingweed, manna, nectar, perfume, ragweed, sugar water, wormseed
beetle corthylus, scolytid, xyleborus

AMBROSIAL delicious, delightful, divine, fragrant, paradisic, pleasing, savory, sweet

AMBRY almery, almonry, armariolum, armarium, armoire, armory, aumbry, chest, closet, cupboard, niche, pantry, press, recess, repository, safe, storeroom

AMBSACE amesace, bad luck, black ox, misfortune, TRIFLE

AMBULANCE auxilium, carrier, vehicle
chaser lawyer, shyster

AMBULATE foot, gad, hike, move, shift, walk

AMBULATORY alure, cloistor, gallery, passage, peramble, portico, walk (ing)

AMBURAJA See VARUNA.

AMBUSH ambuscade, artifice, attack, await, blind, booby-trap, bushwhack, busse, catch, concealment, cover, disguise, enbusshe, forelay, inbush, lay for, lure, lurk, nab, scupper, shoma, snare, stale, sur-

prise, threat, trap, trojan horse, watch, waylay
bug phymatid
shooter sniper

AMCHOOR amhar, mango

AMEIRUS bullhead, catfish

AMELCORN emmer, plant, speltz, triticum, wheat

AMELIA *friend* becky sharp
husband booth

AMELIORATE amend, better, emend, help, improve, mend, perfect, promote, reform

AMELIORATION bonification

AMEN amon, approval, assent, assuredly, aye, euouae, okay, sanction, so be it, truly, verily, yea, yes
corner pew
kingdom thebes
oracle site ammon
son bast, khensu, khons(h)u
temple karnak
wife mut

AMENABLE agreeable, answerable, capable, docile, easy, liable, manageable, open, pleasant, pliable, pliant, responsive, subject, submissive, tractable, willing

AMEND adapt, alter, ameliorate, atone, beete, better, change, chastise, convert, correct, doctor, emend, enlarge, heal, improve, modify, ratify, rectify, redub, reform, remedy, repair, repeal, rephrase, restore, revise, right, skift

AMENDE apology, fine, penalty, reparation

AMENDMENT alteration, atonement, codicil, correction, recovery, restoration, revision, rider, sleeper

AMENDS apology, asseth, assyth, atonement, boot, bote, compensation, expiation, indemnification, recompense, redress, reparation, requital, retribution, revenge, reward

AMENE agreeable, pleasing

AMENHOTEP akhnaton, amenophis, ikhnaton
parent hapu
queen nefertiti
statues colossi of memnon

AMENITY civility, comity, courtesy, ease, geniality, gentleness, joy, manners,

mildness, pleasantness, suavity

AMENT cachrys, catkin, cattail, chat, gosling, idiot, imbecile, iulus, jul, moron, nucament, simpleton

AMENTI See HELL.
genii amseti, duamutef, hapi, imsety, kebhsenuf

AMENTIA idiocy, imbecility, rapture, trance

AMERCE affeer, condemn, fine, forfeit, mulct, penalize, punish, sconce, treat

AMERCEMENT bloodwit, mulct, unlaw

AMERICA(N) (See also NORTH AMERICA, SOUTH AMERICA, UNITED STATES.) ami, gringo, jonathan, sammy, yank(ee), yanqui
aborigine amerind
abscessroot bluebell, flower
alkanet hoary puccoon, lithospermum
alligator caiman, cayman
allspice strawberry shrub
aloe century plant
animal argali, armadillo, assapanic, badger, bassariscus, bison, buffalo, chickaree, coyote, deer, marten, martin, musquaw, opossum, prairie dog, puma, sable, taira, tapir, tayr, vison, wapiti
anteater tamandua
antelope pronghorn
apple baldwin, ben davis, esopus, fameuse, northern spy, rome beauty, roxbury, winesap
arborvitae cedar, thuja
arrowwood viburnum
art glass agata, amberina, tiffany, vasa murrhina
ash rowan, rowen
aspen auld wives' tongue, poplar, tulip tree
aster beeweed, frostflower
aven bennet
badger mistonusk
balsam tolu
bat nycteris, vespertilio
bean, tropical sieva
bear black, grizzly, musquaw
beauty red rose
big horn cimarron
bird ani, avocet, avoset, bafflehead, baltimore oriole, blackbird, cardinal, colin, condor, crow, eagle, fulmar, grackle, nuthatch,

pigeon, rhea, roadrunner, robin, shrups, sora, squealer, tanager, tern, thick-knee, thrush, toucan, trogon, troupial, turkey, urubu, vireo, woodcock, woodpecker
bird, extinct baptornis
bird painter audubon
bittern dunkadoo, thunder-pumper
bitterwood paradise tree
black currant quinsyberry
bladdernut staphylea
bluebird sialia
bob white colin
boneset eupatorium, herb, thoroughwort
brooklime veronica
broomrape squawroot
buffalo bison
bullfrog bloodnoun
bunting dickcissel
buttercup crowfoot, ranunculus
butterfly admiral, banded purple, citron, lemonias, mourning cloak, papilio, pipe vine, swallowtail, viceroy
buzzard buteo, condor, vulture
cactus bisnaga, bleo, cardoncillo, epiphyllum, rhipsala, tasajillo
canary burion, chewink, junco, linnet, towhee
carp quillback
carriage buckboard, buggy, carryall, dearborn, surrey
cat angora, bob, jaguar, margay, ocelot
catamount cougar, lynx
catfish amiaurus, bullhead
cattle texas longhorn
cavy paca
cedar arborvitae
centaury bitterbloom, sabbatia
century plant agave, alde, maguey, toddy-ladle
chair carver, cogswell
cheese cheddar, jack, tallamock, velveeta, vermont, wisconsin
chicken dominique, rhode island red
chinaroot greenbrier, smilax
coin, early rosa
colonial administrator hutchison
colonial clergyman mather, wheelwright, williams
colonial governor amherst,

andros, argall, winslow, winthrop
colonial hall faneuil
colonial official elihu yale
colonial patriot allen, hale, otis, revere
colonial rebel bacon
colonial settler miles standish
colonists dutch, pilgrims, puritans
columbo gentian, frasera, monument plant
coot crowduck, eider, pulldoo, tule-hen
cornelian tree dogwood
cougar catamount
cowboy buckaroo, vaquero
cowslip caltha, cyclamen, dodecatheon, marsh marigold, shooting star
cuckoo ani, blackbird, coccyzus, kobird
cudweed pearly everlasting
cut money sharpshin
dabchick diddikai
daggermoth apatela
dance big apple, blackbottom, breakdown, bunnybug, cakewalk, charleston, chicken, dan tucker, foxtrot, frug, hoedown, lindy, mashed potato, monkey, twist, twostep, virginia reel
date plum persimmon
deal pine
deer caribou, elk, moose, wapiti
discoverer brendan the navigator, cabot, columbus, d'orkeney, glooscap, leif ericson, madoc, sinclair, votan, zichmni
dish cornpone, fritters, mush, steak
dog, wild agouara
dragonfly snakefeeder
duck bluebill, cayuaga, cinnamon teal, redhead
eagle bald
ebony granadilla
eider coot
elder sambucus
elk wapiti
elm springwood
elm, false celtis, nettletree
epic columbiad
everlasting balsamweed
falcon pigeon hawk
falls niagara
farkleberry bluet
featherfoil hottonia
federalists bluelights

federation of labor president gompers, meany
fern adiantopsis, asplenium, basket, bird's foot, cheilanthes, clayton, lace, nephrolepsis, pellaea, rock brake, sword
feverfew parthenium
finch burion, chewink, graybird, junco, linnet, spizella, towhee
first child virginia dare
fish angler, barb, cavalla, con(e), crappie, cunner, darter, jumprock, redhorse, robalo, rockbass, salmon, soup, snook, stoneroller, studfish, tautog
flounder fluke
flycatcher empidonax, tyrant
gallinule blue coot
gem arizona ruby, turquoise
gentian columbo, frasera
germander betony
ginseng panax
globeflower trollius
goatsucker nighthawk
golden-eye cobhead, copperhead
golden plover troutbird
goldfinch yellowbird
gooseberry heterotrichum, houghton, melastoma, miconia
gopher thomomys
gourd sicana
grape catawba, concord, delaware, fox, muscadine, scuppernong
grass axonopus, bluejoint, bouteloua, camalote, creekstuff, distichlis, gama, nimble will, poa, rye, sesame
ground laurel trailing arbutus
ground squirrel flickertail
grunt roncador
guinea pig paca
gum tree gumbo-limbo
hat stetson, ten-gallon
hawk black warrior, caracara
hellebore bearcorn, bugbane, tickleweed, veratrum
hemp jute, mallow
hemp, false datisca
hepatica ivyflower
herb 4 arum, cous 5 camla, nondo 6 acnida, cosmos, cowish, ipecac, napaea, sagina, stevia 7 angelon, antigon, anychia, balmony, caapeba, dogbane, figwort, hedeoma, liatris, lopezia, lopseed, puchero, verbena 8

agalinis, ageratum, amaranth, amorpham, apocynum, argemone, baptisia, bartonia, beachpea, bluelips, boltonia, calathea, canaigre, cupplant, feverfew, gesneria, manyroot, stokesia, toadflax 9 allinonia, bouvardia, brookweed, colicroot, fortyknot, indiancup, ionoxalis, jacobinia, mistletoe, nicotiana, queenroot, rattlebox, searocket, silverrod, snakehead, spikenard, stargrass 10 balsamroot, bluehearts, clammyweed, four-oclock, joepyeweed, rabbitweed, spiderwort, springbell, turtlehead, watercress 11 contrayerva, deathcamass, featherfoil, globeflower, justiceweed, rupturewort 12 mosquito bill, tradescantia 13 thimbleflower
herdsman llanero
hickory mockernut
hog duroc, hampshire, hereford, razorback, victoria
honeycreeper guitguit
hornbeam blue beech, carpinus
horse appaloosa, cob, morgan, mustang, narraganset, palomino, tennessee walker
horse chestnut buckeye
horse race hambletonian, kentucky derby
hound blue tick, redbone
hummingbird jacobin
hyacinth blue dicks
idol almighty dollar
indian See under individual states.
ipecac gillenia
iris flag
ironweed flattop
ironwood bumelia, hop hornbeam, ostrya
island hawaii(an), santa cruz, st croix
ivy joy, virginia creeper
jade californite
jasmine cypress vine, quamoclit
joy ivy, virginia creeper
ladybird coccinella
larch hackmatack, larix, tamarack
larkspur delphinium
laurel kalmia
leopard jaguar
linden black lime, bois blanc
lion cougar, puma

lizard anolis, sceloporus, teioid
locust clammy, grasshopper, schistocera
lotus nelumba, water chinquapin
lungwort virginia cowslip
lynx catamount
magnolia cucumber tree, umbrella tree
mahogany quail b(r)ush
mallow altea
mandrake may apple
manna, false pinitol
martagon turk's-cap-lily
meadow mouse vole
mercury lobelia
merganser morocco-head, tweezer
mezereon leatherwood
milk pea galactia
mink vison
minnow fallfish, peamouth, stoneroller
mint agastache, bitter bugle, herb, peppermint
missile See ROCKET *names.*
money See UNITED STATES *money.*
monkey acari, aotus, beelzebub, grison, marmoset, miriki, orabassu, ouakari, saki, teetee, titi
montaigne emerson
monument plant columbo
moose original
mussel yellowback
nettle ortiga
nettle tree celtis, false elm
nightshade ditch stonecrop, pokeweed, prairie berry, solanum, trompillo, weed
novel, first wieland
nutmeg calabash, monodora
oak bartram, blackjack, emory, lea, live, macrocatalpa, white
olive devilwood
orange calamondin, navel, temple, valencia
orchid adder's mouth, boatlip, cattleya, coralroot, miltonia, sobralia
oriole bananabird, cacique, icterus
ostrich rhea
palm astrocaryum, attalea, bactris, baytop, corozo, coyol, geonoma, palmetto
pansy bird's-foot-violet
parakeet conuropsis, conurus
parrot amazona
partridge helmet quail

pasqueflower anemone, badgerweed
pear bartlett
pepperroot dentaria
periwinkle myrtle
pert. columbian, yankee
phlox moss pink
picnic barbecue, clambake, cookout
pigeon quail dove
pilgrim leader bradford
plains prairie(s)
plan demi-pension
plane tree sycamore
plant adam-and-eve, agave, alonsoa, ananas, anglepod, aniseroot, anthurium, aphelandra, arrowroot, arum, aster, baby-blue-eyes, baldrush, basketflower, bitterbrush, brittlebush, bromelia, cabomba, cacoon, caladium, cammass, cerveza, cohosh, coontie, cosmos, cube, feverweed, figwort, fitweed, fleabane, frostweed, isoloma, larkspur, lotus, puttyroot, ragweed, rhododendron, romerillo, sarracenia, snakeweed, spanish moss, tagetes, tillandsia, tradescantia, tuckahoe, tumbleweed, yarrow, yucca, zinnia
plant, aquatic cabomba, fanwort
plant, tropical aroid, caladium, calceolaria, figwort, kalaki, maholtine
plover frostbird, killdeer
pocket gopher camass rat
pondweed philotoria
poplar aspen, tulip tree
potato early rose, idaho, irish cobbler, russet
quail colin
rabbit cottontail
raccoon agouara, coati
rail clapper, meadow hen
reindeer caribou
revolution assembly continental congress
revolution battle bennington, brandywine, bunker hill, camden, concord, cowpens, eutaw springs, germantown, guilford courthouse, king's mountain, lexington, monmouth, moore's creek bridge, princeton, saratoga, savannah, ticonderoga, trenton, white plains, yanktown

revolution cause boston massacre, townsend acts

revolution commander alexander, dekalb, gates, greene, herkimer, huger, knox, lee, lincoln, marion, montgomery, morgan, pickens, putnam, schuyler, stark, st clair, sumter, thomas, washington, wayne, wooster

revolution commander, british burgoyne, cornwallis, ferguson, gage, howe, rawdon, tarleton

revolution commander, french de grasse, de rochambeau, lafayette, rochambeau

revolution commander, german kalb

revolution commander, polish kosciusko

revolution commander, prussian steuben

revolution hero nathan hale

revolution leader chase, gwinnett

revolution money continental

revolution soldier buckskin, continental, ethan allen, minuteman, redcoat

revolution spy, major john andre, nathan hale

revolution supporter whig

rodent capybara, gopher, mole, paca, sewellel

ruby garnet, pyrope

sable lemming, marten

saffron safflower

saibling sunapee trout

salamander amphiuma, axoltl

saltwort batis

salvia chia

sanicle heuchera

scorpion vinegarroon

scoter butternose

sea rocket cakile, herb

sedge baldrush, knifegrass, nutgrass

service club kiwanis, lions, optimist, rotary, toastmaster

shark grayfish, thrasher, thresher

sheep columbia, delaine

shorebird yellowlegs

shrub adelia, agarita, algerita, apache plume, arrowwood, artemisia, ascyrum, atriplex, baccharis, barberry, batodendron,

bearbrush, berberis, blackbrush, blueblossom, boggale, broomwood, bumelia, burningbush, calfkill, camara, cat's-claw, cenizo, cestrum, coffeeberry, coralberry, dahoon, deerberry, dockmackie, dogwood, farkleberry, fetterbush, forestiera, fringetree, greasewood, hardhack, ilex, indian arrow, jujube, lippia, lotebush, mahalamat, mahonia, matico, myrica, ninebark, quina, quininebush, ramona, ratstripper, rockbush, salal, saskatoon, savinre, silverberry, snowball, staggerbush, stevia, strongbark, tarbush, titi, toothwort, torolillo, wahoo, yaupon, yew

smoke tree chittamwood, cotinus

snake aboma, blue racer, boa, boma, coachwhip, copperhead, cottonmouth, garter, king, moccasin, mussurana, racer, rattler, rattlesnake, water moccasin

snakeroot bugbane, sanicula

sneezewort helenium

snowball styrax

socrates ben franklin

spider black widow, tarantula

spikenard aralia

spindle tree wahoo

spurge adelia

squirrel assapanic, copperhead, glaucomys

staghorn dividivi, sumac

stakedriver bittern

star mullet

sticky grass purpletop

stock yuma

strawberry dunlap

sumac dividivi, staghorn

sunfish roach, warmouth

surf-scoter blossomhead

swamp lily lizard's-tail

swamp plant cowbane

sweetheart See PICKFORD, MARY.

tarantula eurypelma

thrift sea lavender

tiger jaguar

titmouse verdin

toad agua, bufo, fowler's, rana

toadflax linaria

tobacco burley

token, bronze barcent

tragedy, author dreiser

tree 3 apa, bay, elm, fir, oak 4 ceba, guao, majo, titi 5 alamo, aspen, balsa, beech, cacao, cedar, ceiba, maple 6 acacia, achras, amyris, andira, annona, baboen, balsam, baobab, bustic, carica, cashew, cedron, colima, dagame, laurel, locust, mammea, mammee, myrtle, oncoba, papaya, redbud, tupelo 7 achiote, annonce, annotto, buckeye, calabur, catalpa, caulote, cypress, gateado, guazuma, hemlock, lapacho, licania, liveoak, redwood, serenoa, soursop, surette 8 allspice, bindoree, blackgum, calabash, cecropia, mulberry, palmetto, silkwood, tisswood, varronia 9 arrowwood, butternut, cauchillo, copaifera, cottongum, crabapple, marlberry, marmalade, muntingia, quebracho, quinquino, simarouba, theobroma, tibourbou 10 anacardium, limoncillo, manchineel, marinheiro, pepperwood, silverbell, yellowwood 11 trumpetwood, whistlewood

tree, timber acapu, amarillo, andira, axemaster, billy webb, bongo, cedrela, coffeewood, quira, tamarind

tree, tropical acapu, amarillo, baboen, balsa, caimitillo, dalli, floripondio, grigri, grugru, guama, guara, mammee, manchineel, pawpaw, sapote, sweetsop, wacapou

trillium wakerobin

turtle alligator-snapper, cooter, malaclemys, mobilianer, terrapin, tortoise

umbrella tree magnolia

ungulate tapir

valerian cypripedium, lady's-slipper, polemonium

velvet-leaf indian mallow

vervain verbena

vetch buffalo-pea

vine abute, abutilon, allamanda, amaryllis, basketwithe, bignonia, bladapple, bomarea, calabazilla, ceanothus, coongrape, coriman, cupseed, dogbane, earthpea, grape, guaco, jasmine, lemon vine, monstera,

moonseed, pereskia, trumpet-flower, serjania, supplejack, wild pumpkin, wisteria
vole meadow mouse
vulture carrion-crow, condor
wakerobin green dragon
warbler baybreasted, flycatcher, gnatcatcher, polioptila, yellowthroat
wasp cicada-killer
watercress cardamine
water snake copper-belly
wayfaring tree hobblebush
weed blue vervain, bristly carrot, sandbur, spurge
weevil plum curculio
widgeon anas, baldhead, baldpate, zuisin
wildcat eyra
wild plum sloe
wind pampero
wine catawba
wisteria kidney-bean tree
woodcock shrubs
wormseed mexican tea
wren bewick's
yew hemlock
AMERIND See **ESKIMO** and *indian* under states.
AMERISTIC undifferentiated, unsegmented
AMETHYST corundum, gem, onegite, quartz
planet venus
symbol of sincerity
zodiac sign sagittarius
AMETROPIA astigmatism, hypermetropia, myopia
AMFORTAS *beloved* kundry
father titurel
healer parsifal
wounded by klingsor
AMI blackbird, friend, lover
AMIA apogon, bowfin, grindle, mudfish
AMIABILITY affability, benignity, bonhommie, compliance, cordiality, douceur, friendliness, generosity, geniality, gentleness, goodhumor, goodness, graciousness, kindness, mildness, thoughtfulness
AMIABLE affable, agreeable, amicable, bland, charming, cordial, courteous, engaging, friendly, genial, gentle, good, gracious, indulgent, kind(ly), lovable, loving, mellow, pleasant, pleasing, smooth, sweet, tender, warm, winsome
AMIANTHUS amosite, am-

phibole, asbestos, asbestus, chrysotile, crocidolite, curtain
AMICABLE friendly, harmonious, kind, peaceable, peaceful
AMICE almuce, amictus, amit, cape, cowl, domino, ephod, hood, tippet, vakass, vestment
AMID amell, among, between, during, imelle, midst, through, with
AMIDA amit(abha), BUDDHA
AMIDE anilide, arylide, lactam, sultam
pert. amic, amidic
AMIDIA bowfin, fish
AMIDISM rebirth, salvation
AMIGO friend
AMIL cuscuta, dodder, dye
AMINA *mother* teresa
AMINI mango
AMINO *acid* alanine, arginine, creatine, cysteline, glycine, histidine, isoleucine, leucine, lysine, methionine, norleucine, phenylalanine, proline, protein, sarcosine, serine, threonine, tryosine, tryptophane, valune
compound adenine, aniline, aspartyl, diamide, diamine, triamine
AMIR noble, prince
AMISS agate, agley, askew, astray, awry, bias, disorderly, erroneous, faulty, haywire, ill, improper, inaccurate, incorrect, mistake, wrong
AMITAHBA amida, amidism, BUDDHA
AMITTAI *kin* jonah
AMITY accord, attachment, concord, friendliness, friendship, harmony, peace
AMLI bauhinia, tamarindus, tree
AMLONG pothos, raphidophora, vine
AMMA abbess, mother
AMMI bishop('s)weed, goutweed, water mint
AMMIACE apium, carrot, celery
AMMINADAB *kin* david, uzziel
AMMO See **AMMUNITION.**
AMMON zeus
father david

gift cornucopia, horn of plenty
AMMONIA cleanser, fertilizer, hartshorn, medicine
compound amid(e), amin(e), ammoniate, ammoniuret, anammonide, anilid(e), diamine, imide
compound, comb. amine
molecule ammine
plant dorema, oshac
AMMONITE azotine, baculite, baculiticone, caculoid, ceratite, fertilizer, fossil shell, phylloceras, polypod, saligram
god milcom
king hanun, uzziah
triassic meekoceras
AMMONIUM *carbonate* hartshorn, sal volatile, smelling salts
purpurate murexide
AMMONOID ammonite, bactrite, baculite
AMMOPHILA grass, marram
AMMUNITION advice, ammo, ammu, argument, arms, bomb, buckshot, bullet, cannonball, cartridge, data, facts, fodder, grenade, information, material, materiel, missile, munition, ordnance, powder, projectile, shell, shot, shrapnel
belt or box bandoleer, bandolier
case cartridge
chest caisson
depot arsenal
powderless blank
toy pistol cap
wagon caisson
AMNERIS *rival* aida
AMNESIA agnosia, agraphia, alexia, blackout, disorientation, lapse, paranomia
AMNESTY absolution, dowle, exculpation, excuse, exemption, exoneration, forgetfulness, forgiveness, grace, immunity, impunity, indemnity, oblivion, pardon, remission
AMNION caul, fluid, indusium, membrane, sac, serosa
AMNON *parent* ahinoam, shimon
AM NOT ain't, amn't, an't, hain't
AMOEBA am(o)ebula, cell,

organism, proteus, protoplasm, protozoan, rhizopod
cytoplasm plasmasol
AMOK See AMUCK.
AMOLE agave, amouli, chlorogalum, emol, manfreda, nahuatl, soaproot, yucca
AMOMUM awapuhi, cardamon, herb, zingiber
AMON See AMEN.
AMONASRO *daughter* aida
kin jedidah, josiah, manasseh
AMONG amang, amell, amid(st), amongst, associated, between, bimong, during, entre, imelle, intermingled, mang, midst, mixed, mong, mutually, surrounded, through, within
comb. epi, inter, meta
AMOR amoroso, cupid, eros, LOVE
mother aphrodite, venus
AMORC See ROSICRUCIAN.
AMORET paramour
AMORETTO amorino, amourette, cupid, inamorato, lover, poem, putto
AMORIST casanova, don juan, gallant, lover, romeo
AMORITE canaanite, palestinian, syrian
king sihon
AMOROSA beloved, courtesan, sweetheart
AMOROSO lover
AMOROUS affectionate, amative, amatorial, amatory, amiable, anacreontic, ardent, cadgy, enamored, erotic, fervent, fond, gallant, gamy, hot, impassioned, lovesome, loving, passionate, sexy, smicker, tender, warm
AMORPHOUS, AMORPHIC abnormal, chaotic, deformed, formless, hyaline, indeterminate, irregular, resinous, shapeless, uncrystallized, unorganized, vague
AMORT dejected, lifeless, spiritless
AMORTIZE alienate, destroy, extinguish, liquidate, mortise, pay off, settle
AMOS *home* tekoa
AMOSITE anthophyllite, asbestos
AMOTION deprivation, feck, ousting, removal
AMOUNT aggregate, allow-

ance, ante, arise, ascend, body, cast, come, degree, dosage, dose, draw, extent, feck, figure, measure, mess, mise, number, plenty, price, quantity, ratal, reach, rise, signify, slather, soud, sowd, stack, store, stuff, sum, supply, total, unit, vallidom, whole
due bill, debt, liability, obligation, score, tab
exact nick
extra bonus
fixed rate
gross slump
held capacity
inadequate deficiency
indefinite any, bait, snag, some
large bonanza, chunk, gob, hantle, infinity, mickle, might, mint, mountain, muchness, muckle, sea, slater, snag, somd(i)el, spate, swag
largest maximum
lavish slather
made batch, lot
measured unit
overflown spillage
paid cost
relative degree, ratio
small ace, atom, beans, canch, cantlet, chip, continental, crumb, dab, dash, dight, dite, dole, dose, dot, drab, dram, drappie, drib (ble), driblet, drop, fleck, flitter, flow, flyspeck, fragment, fritter, glimmer, grain, groatsworth, hair, handful, hint, hoot, kenning, lick, might, minim, mite, modicum, molecule, morceau, morsel, mote, nip, nutshell, patch, pennyworth, pinch, pittance, scrat, shred, smidge, smidgin, snippet, spoonful, taste, tot, trace, trifle, wisp
smallest grain, iota, jot, least, minimum, steever, st(u)iver, whit
to average, cost, equal, match, mean, signify, total
yearly annuity
AMOUR affair, druery, intrigue, LOVE, paramour
propre conceit, egotism, pride, self-love, vanity
AMOX *son* isiah
AMOY See FUKIEN.
AMPELOPSIS creeper, ivy

AMPER blemish, blotch, pustule, tumor, varicose vein
AMPERSAND also, ampassy, and, ipseand, plus
AMPERY rotten
AMPHEROTOKY anthogenesis, parthenogenesis
AMPHETAMINE benzedrine, biphetamine, dexamobarb, dexamyl, dexedrine, diphetamine, methamphetamine, methedrine, narcotic, preludin, stimulant
pill bennie, benny, cartwheel, christmas tree, copilot, crystal, dex(ie), dexy, football, greeny, heart, meth, orange, peach, pep pill, roses, speed, upper, wake-up, water, white
AMPHIARAUS *charioteer* baton
consort eriphyle
enemy periclymenus, tydeus
offspring alcmaeon, amphilochus, demonassa, eurydice
parent hypermnestra, oicles
AMPHIBIAN aglossa, agua, aistopod, amtrac(k), anamniote, anura, apoda, batrachian, caecilian, caudate, cyclostome, eft, eriopid, fish, frog, gymnophiona, hellbender, hyla, newt, olm, polliwog, proteus, rana, salamander, salientia, seaplane, siren, tadpole, toad, tractor, urodela
age of carboniferous
extinct aistopoda, archegosaurus, eryop, trematosaurus
family ranidae
tailed salamander
tailless rana, ranida, toad, treefrog
wormlike caecilium
young polliwog, tadpole
AMPHIBOLE actinolite, ambiguity, barkevikite, breislakite, byssolite, crossite, edenite, grunerite, hornblende, nephrite, oralite, richterite, silicate, tremolite, uralite
AMPHIBOLIC ambiguous, changing, equivocal, irregular, uncertain
AMPHICTYON *parent* deucalion, pyrrha
AMPHIGORY doggerel, nonsense, parody, poem, rigamarole, verse

AMPHILOCHUS *brother* alcmaeon
parent amphiarus, eriphyle
sister eurydice
victim eriphyle, mopsus

AMPHILOGISM ambiguity, equivocation

AMPHIMACHUS *leader* epean

AMPHIMARUS *beloved* urania
father poseidon

AMPHINOMUS *beloved* penelope

AMPHION *brother* zethus
nephew itylus
offspring amyclas, chloris
parent antiope, iasus, zeus
sister aedon
wife niobe

AMPHISARCA calabash, gourd, melon

AMPHISSA *parent* echetus

AMPHISSUS *father* apollo

AMPHITHEA *daughter* anticlea
husband autolycus

AMPHITHEATER arena, astrodome, auditorium, bowl, caves, circus, cirque, colosseum, oval, stadium

AMPHITHEATRUM FLAVIUM colosseum

AMPHITHEMIS *husband* poseidon
parent acacallis, apollo
son caphaurus

AMPHITHYRON curtain, door, veil

AMPHITRITE *consort* poseidon
parent doris, nereus, oceanus, tethys
son triton

AMPHITRYON *parent* alcaeus, astydamia, hipponome
servant sosia
son hercules
wife alcmene

AMPHORA amphoniskos, cadus, diota, jar, jug, measure, pelike, urn, vase, vessel

AMPHOTERUS *father* alcamaeon

AMPICILLIN amcill, omnipen, penbritin, polycillin, principen

AMPLE abounding, abundant, adequate, big, bounteous, broad, capacious, copious, enough, extensive, fair, free, full, generous, good, great, handsome,

large, lavish, liberal, much, munificent, overflowing, plenteous, plentiful, plenty, profuse, prolix, rich, roomy, spacious, sufficient, triple, vast, wally, wealthy, wide

AMPLECTANT amplexicaul, clasping, clinging, coiling, entwining, surrounding, twining

AMPLIATE amplify, dilate(d), enlarge(d), expand(ed)

AMPLIFICATION development, enlargement, expansion, explanation, extension, gain, increase
device bullhorn, loudspeaker, maser

AMPLIFIER booster, maser, repeater, transistor

AMPLIFY aggravate, ampliate, augment, broaden, descant, develop, dilate, discourse, enlarge, evolve, exaggerate, expand, expatiate, explicate, extend, increase, lengthen, multiply, pad, stress, stretch, swell, widen

AMPLITUDE, AMPLENESS abundance, argument, breadth, capacity, copiousness, expanse, extent, fullness, greatness, largeness, opulence, plenty, size, sufficiency

AMPOLLOSITY bombast, turgidity, turgidness

AMPOULE, AMPUL bottle, bulb, container, flask, tube, vial

AMPULLA bladder, bottle, cruet, flask, sac, vase, vesicle, vessel

AMPULLACEOUS ampullar(y), ampullate, ampulliform, dilated, flask-shaped

AMPUTATE curtail, cut, dock, lop, prune, remove, sever

AMPUTATION apocope, deduction, surgery

AMPYCUS, AMPYX *father* pelias
son mopsus
wife chloris

AMPYX band, fillet, headdress, trilobite

AMRA hog-plum, spondias, tree

AMRAM *offspring* aaron, miriam, moses

parent bani, dishon
wife jochebed

AMRITA elixir, rasa

AMSEL blackbird, ring ouzel, turdus

AMSHAPEND ameretad, arbidihisi, asha-vahishta, bahman, kashatra-vairya, khordadh, mourdad, shahriver, sipendarmidh, spenta-armati, sraosha, vohu-mano

AMSONIA dogbane, herb

AMSTERDAM *airport* schiphol
boulevard damrak
redlight district gecellig, rosse buurt, zeedijk

AMUCK amok, crazed, crazy, frenzied, homicidal, mad, uncontrolled, violent

AMU DARYA oxus

AMULA ama, vessel

AMULET amalett, antinganting, charm, fetish, gem, hagstone, ligature, ornament, periapt, protection, saffie, saphie, scarab, scroll, symbol, talisman, token
druidic adderbead
kind apotropaion, greegree, grigri, ichthus, ichthys, juju, mascot, menat, mojo

AMULIUS *brother* numitor
father procas
nephew lausus

AMUNDSEN *ship* fram, gjoa

AMURATH murad

AMUSE absorb, beguile, charm, cheer, convulse, delight, disport, distract, divert, engage, enjoy, enliven, entertain, exhilarate, game, gratify, play, please, puzzle, recreate, regale, relax, slay, sport, stir, tickle, titillate, wow

AMUSEMENT avocation, cottabus, diversion, enjoyment, entertainment, fad, fun, game, jest, lake, laughter, mirth, pastime, play, pleasure, recreation, relaxation, sport
place arena, astrodome, carnival, casino, cinema, circus, field, funfair, midway, park, stadium, theater
ride ferris wheel, rollercoaster

AMUSING comic(al), delicious, diverting, divertive, droll, farcical, funny, humorous, laughable, lively,

ludicrous, mirthful, risible, sportful
person card, cutup
AMYCLAE *brothers* castor, dioscuri, gemini, pollux
festival hyacinthia
statue apollo
AMYCLAS *kin* cynortes, niobe
AMYCUS *parent* melie, poseidon
slayer pollux
AMYDALOID calcite, chalcedony, mineral, quartz, zeolite
AMYGDALA tonsil
AMYL alcohol, amydon, isoamyl, pentyl, starch
acetate banana oil
oxide ether
AMYLACEOUS starchy, thick, viscid
AMYLAMINE ptomaine
AMYLASE amylopsin, diastase, enzyme, ptyalin
AMYMONE *consort* enceladus, poseidon
father danaus
son nauplius
AMYNTAS *father* philip
kingdom macedonia
son alexander, amyntiades, aristotle, perdiccas, philip
victim pausanias
wife eurydice
AMYRIS balsam, baumier, candlewood, fir, ocimum, rhodeswood, rosewood, rue, tree, trigonella
AMYTHAON *brother* aeson, pheres
parent cretheus, tyro
son bias, melampus
wife idomene
AMZI *father* bani
AN anybody, anyone, article, one, someone
ANA collection, events, memorabilia, omniana, sayings
ANABASIS advance, expedition, journey, march
ANABATHMOS psalm, song
ANABIOSIS reanimation, reincarnation, resuscitation
ANABO abroma, anabong, fiber, nabo, shrub
ANABOLITE anabolin, anastate
ANABRANCH tallywalka
ANACAMPSIS reflection
ANACAMPTICS catoptrics
ANACANTHOUS spineless, thornless

ANACARDIUM caracoli, cashew, mango, occidentale, pistachio, sumac, varnishtree
ANACES castor, dioscuri, gemini, pollux
ANACHRONISM error, metachronism, misdating, mistiming, parachronism, prochronism, prolepsis, solecism
ANACHRONOUS beforehand, behindhand, mistimed, overdue
ANACLASTICS dioptrics
ANACLETE julian the apostate
ANACLISIS decubitus
ANACONDA abolla, aboma, boa(constrictor), camoudie, constrictor, eunectes, poker, python, snake, sucuruju, sucury
gourd hercules' club
ANACREON *birthplace* teos
consort bathyllus
patron hipparchus, polycrates
ANACREONTIC amatory, convivial, gay, poem, teian
ANACUSIA deafness
ANADEM chaplet, coronet, crown, diadem, fillet, garland, wreath
ANADYOMENE aphrodite, astarte, cytherea, venus
ANAGALLIS maddog, pimpernel, primrose, skullcap
ANAGENESIS regeneration, reproduction
ANAGEP kalumpit, terminalia, tree
ANAGLYPH cameo, ornament, relief
ANAGNOST lector, reader
ANAGOGICAL abstruse, idealistic, mystical, occult, spiritual
ANAGRAM game, logogriph, puzzle, rebus, transposition
ANAGUA anama, anaqua, ehretia, knackaway
ANAGYRIS bean-trefoil, buckbean, coral tree, laburnum, shrub
ANAH *husband* esau
ANAKTORON *goddess* demeter, kore
site eleusis
ANALABOS cloak, habit
ANALCIME analcite, zeolite
ANALECTS collectanea, collection, excerpt(s), glean-

ings, miscellanea, passages, selections
ANALGESIC abrastol, acetanilide, amygdophenin, analgen(e), anodyne, antipyrin, apolysin, aspirin, atropia, atropine, bromamide, codein(e), opium, phenalgin, sedative
ANALGESIS insensibility
ANALOGICAL analogous, figurative, normal
ANALOGION desk, lectern, pulpit, stand
ANALOGOUS agnate, akin, alike, allied, cognate, comparable, corresponding, like, related, similar
ANALOGUE associate, cogener, cognate, correlate, correlative, counterpart, equivalent, parallel
ANALOGY agreement, comparison, correspondence, inference, kinship, likeness, qiyas, relation, resemblance, similarity
close parity
ANALPHABETIC illiterate
ANALYSIS anatomy, assay, autopsy, breakdown, clarification, commentary, conspectus, diagnosis, discussion, dissection, docimasy, estimate, investigation, outline, reduction, resolution, scansion, separation, solution, study, synopsis, table, test, therapy, titration
logical syllogism
situational game theory
situs topology
ANALYST head-candler, psychiatrist, shrink
ANALYTIC clinical, holomorphic, regular, subtle
ANALYZE anatomize, assay, assess, break down, case, describe, determine, diagnose, dichotomize, discuss, dissect, distinguish, divide, examine, explicate, expose, investigate, parse, part, reduce, resolve, sense, separate, sift, solve, study, test, titrate, unpiece, weigh, winnow
ANAMA anagua, anaqua
ANAMIRTA moonseed, vine
ANAMNESIS case history, prayer, recollection, remembrance, reminiscence

ANAMNIOTE amphibian, cyclostome, fish
ANANAS bromelia, pineapple, pinquin, plant
ANADA bliss, paradise
ANANI *parent* elicenai
ANANIAS liar, shadrach, sidrach
cured saul
wife sapphira
ANANISM karaism
ANANTA endless, infinity, serpent, shesha, snake
ANAPEST antidactyl
ANAPNEA breathing, respiration
ANARCHISM See ANARCHY.
ANARCHIST bolshevik, bomb-thrower, nihilist, red(shirt), revolutionary, revolutionist, sacco, terrorist, venzetti
doctrine bakuninism
society black hand
ANARCHY acracy, anomy, bakuninism, broil, chaos, confusion, disorder, lawlessness, license, lynch-law, misrule, mobocracy, mob rule, nihilism, ochlocracy, rebellion, revolt, revolution, riot, terrorism, unruliness
ANARHICHAS catfish, wolffish
ANARTHRIA inarticulateness, inaudia
ANARTHROUS jointless, limbless
ANAS baldhead, baldpate, blackie, bluewing, duck, mallard, teal
ANASARCA dropsy
ANASAZI plateau, pueblo
ANASTASIA *husband* ivan
saint, symbol faggots, stake
ANASTASIS convalescence, recovery
ANASTATE anabolin, anabolite
ANASTOMOSE connect, inosculate, interjoin
ANASTOMOSIS association, circulation, combination, communication, glomus, inosculation, merging, union
ANASTOMUS bird, openbill
ANAT *consort* anu
daughter nanai
ANATHEMA abhorrence, abomination, aversion, ban, blasphemy, censure, curse,

denunciation, detestation, execration, imprecation, malediction, oath
ANATHEMATIZE accurse, ban, censure, comminate, curse, denounce, execrate, maledict, sentence
ANATID duck, goose, merganser, swan
ANATIFA cirriped, crustacean, goose-barnacle
ANATMAN anatta
ANATOLIA armenia, asia minor, turkey
carpet konia, ladik, melas, meles, tuzla
goddess cybele
language luwian
ANATOMIST analyst, dissector, prosector
ANATOMIZE analyze, break down, discriminate, dissect, examine, resolve
ANATOMY analysis, body, breakdown, constitution, figure, make-up, physiology, physique, skeleton, somatology, structure, topology, zootomy
comb. entero
human anthropotomy
microscopic histology
part See BODY *part.*
quick vivisection
vegetable phytotomy
ANATREPTIC defeating, overthrowing, refutative
ANATRON saltpeter
ANATUM *consort* ana
ANAUDIA anarthria
ANAX *son* asterius
ANAXIBIA *brother* agamemnon, menelaus
consort helios, nestor, pelias
daughter alcestis, pelopea, pisidice
parent atreus, bias
son acastus
ANAXIMANDER *1st principle* apeiron
ANAXITHEA *consort* zeus
ANAXO *father* alcaeus
ANAY termite, white ant
ANBA amba, bishop, clergyman, father, patriarch, saint
ANCAEUS *parent* astypalaea, lycurgus, poseidon
ship argo
son agapenor
ANCESTOR adam, antecedent, apetus, archetype, ascendant, atavus, author, begetter, beldame, belsire, eber, elder, eponym, fam-

ily, father, forebear, foreelder, forefather, forerunner, grandfather, grandparent, influence, inspiration, manu, model, parent, patriarch, precursor, predecessor, primogenitor, procreator, progenitor, prototype, relative, root, sept, sire, stock
cult manism
female beldame, foremother
having same consanguineous
law stipes, stirps
soul fravashi
worship ancientism
ANCESTRAL antecedent, atavic, atavistic, aval, avital, familial, forerunning, genealogical, hereditary, lineal, parental, patriarchal, patrimonial, phyletic, prototypal
spirit anito, lares, manes
ANCESTRY antecedence, aristocracy, athel, birth, blood(line), branch, breed, derivation, descent, extraction, family, genealogy, history, house, inception, kindred, line(age), origin, parentage, paternity, pedigree, race, stem, stock, strain, tree
pert. atavic, atavistic
ANCHESMIUS zeus
ANCHINOE *consort* belus
father nilus
son aegyptus, danaus
ANCHISES *beloved* aphrodite
burial site eryx
grandfather assaracus
parent capys, themiste
son aeneas
ANCHOR affix, attach, berth, bind, bolt, bower, brake, cockbill, connect, curb, drag, drogue, fasten, fix, grapnel, grouser, hold, hook, kedge, kelleg, killick, moor, mudhook, reliance, rest, rivet, secure, slug, spud, stability, stop, support, tie
at leeward, motionless, windward
barb flue, fluke
baulk cathead
bed billboard
bill peak, pee
chain catfall, painter
hoist capstan
hold cathead

hove in astay
kind baldt, bower, deadman, drag, dunn, floating, kedge, killick, martin, mushroom, sheet, trotman
knot fisherman's bend
lashings bow-stoppers
lift cat
lifter capstan, dandy
light kedge
line roding
man commentator, editor, emcee, key, mainstay
part arm, bill, cat, fluke, nut, palm, peak, pee, shank, stock
plant colletia
position atrip
ring annulus, tore, toroid, torus
-shaped ankyroid
small grapnel
steady at holsom
tackle cat
timber grouser
without adrift, drifting, unsettled
ANCHORAGE abutment, berth, dock, fee, grapple, ground, gunkhole, harbor, haven, location, moorage, mooring, port, refuge, retreat, riding, roadstead, roothold, security, toll
quiet gunkhole
ANCHORITE anchoret, ascetic, diorite, eremite, hermit, MONK, pillarist, recluse, stylite
abode anchorage, monastery
ANCHOVY alice, bocon, engraulis, fish, herring, sardine, sprat
pear grias, mango
sauce alec
ANCHUSA borage, forgetmenot, oxtongue
ANCIENT aboriginal, aborigine, aged, ageold, antediluvian, antiquated, antique, archaic, archeau, auld, autochthon, caveman, dateless, eld(erly), former, grandeval, historic, hoary, immemorial, noachian, noachic, noetic, obsolete, patriarch, preadamite, primal, primeval, primitive, pristine, remote, senior, traditional, venerable, vetust, yore
comb. archaeo, arche(o), paleo
mariner, author coleridge

mariner, bird albatross
of days deity, god
times past, yore
ANCILE palladium, shield
ANCILLA accessory, adjunct, auxiliary, handmaid, helper, maidservant
ANCILLARY accessory, additional, adjuvant, auxiliary, subordinate, subservient, subsidiary
ANCIPITAL two-edged, twofold
ANCON console, corbel, crossette, elbow, olecranon
ANCONA altarpiece, niche, picture, recess
ANCYLOSTOMA hookworm
AND above, added to, additionally, adjunct, along with, also, altogether, ampersand, as if, as well as, besides, ditto, eke, else, erst, etc, further(more), in addition, including, item, likewise, moreover, plus, similarly, them, therewith, though, to boot, too, with, yet
all besides, in addition, truly
not neither, nor
or optionally
others et alia, etcetera
so consequently
so forth etc(etera)
symbol ampersand
ANDALUSIA *dance* cachucha, flamenco
ANDAMAN *division* balawa
island capital port blair
people balawa, bogigiak, bojig-ngiji, mincopie, minkopi
redwood amboina
ANDEAN (See SOUTH AMERICA references.) andesic, andine, grand, lofty, peruvian
ANDELUSIA *song* saeta
ANDERSON, HANS C.
story ugly duckling
ANDERSON, MAXWELL
drama winterset
ANDERSON, SHERWOOD
work poor white, tar, winesburg ohio
ANDERUN See HAREM.
ANDES See SOUTH AMERICA references.
ANDESITE boninite, feldspar, timazite
ANDIRA angelin, cabbage tree
ANDIROBA crabwood, mahogany

ANDIRON chenet, cobiron, firedog, hessian
pair creepers
ANDORRA *language* catalan
native andosian
river valira
ANDREANOF *island* adak
ANDREW *burial place* amalfi
kin anne, jonah, simon-peter
symbol cross, gospel
ANDREWS *cicily* rebecca west
ANDREWS *sisters* la verne, maxene, patti
ANDROCLEA *kin* alcis, antipoenus
ANDROCLES *friend* lion
ANDROGEUS *parent* minos, pasiphae
resurrector aesculapius
slayer aegeus
son alcaeus
ANDROGYNE eunuch, hermaphrodite
ANDROGYNOUS bisexual, epicene, hermaphrodite, hermaphroditic, timtum
man eunuch
woman amazon
ANDROMACHE *consort* hector, helenus, neoptolemus
father eetion
son astyanax, cestrinus, molossus, pergamus, pielus, scamandrius
ANDROMEDA heath, moorwort
husband perseus
monster p(r)istris, p(r)istrix
parent cassiopeia, cepheus
rescuer perseus
son electryon, sthenelus
ANDRON apartment, passage
ANDRONICUS *friend* paul
ANDROPHONOS aphrodite
ANDROPOGON bluegrass, bluestein, broomsedge, palmetto
ANDROSACE See PRIMROSE.
ANDROSEME hypericum, st-john's-wort
ANECDOTE account, event, haggada(h), item, joke, narrative, sketch, story, tale, yarn
collection ana
comb. ana
ANELE anoint, shrive
ANEMIA hyphaema, hyphae-

mia, hyphemia, ischemia, pallor, spanemia, surra(h)
kind aplastic
ANEMIC bloodless, cadaverous, ghastly, lifeless, low, pale, sallow, sickly, wan, watery, weak
ANEMONE adamsia, bowbells, buttercup, emony, opelet, pasqueflower, snowdrop, thimbleweed
sea actinia
ANENT about, against, before, beside, close to, concerning, in re, opposite, regarding, toward, with
ANESIDORA demeter
ANESTHESIA block, dullness, insensibility, insensitivity
ANESTHETIC analgesic, anodyne, deadener, desensitizer, dull, insensible, insensitive, knock-out, narcotic, numb(ing), obtuse, opiate, painkiller, relaxant, sedative, stolid, stupefacient
comb. algin
kind acoine, alypin, apothesine, benzocaine, butacaine, butyn, chloral, chloroform, cocaine, cyclopropane, ether, ethylidene, freezing, laughing gas, menthol, morphine, novocaine, paraform, scopolamine, spinal, thiopental
local chloral, coryl, dibucaine, eucaine, novocaine, nupercaine, procaine, rhigolene, toponarcosis
spinal dibucaine, nupercaine
ANESTHETIZE analgize, chloroform, deaden, desensitize, drug, etherize, freeze, knock out, narcotize
ANEURIA neurasthenia
ANEW afresh, again, anon, encore, newlings, newly, once more, over, recently, repeatedly
comb. ana
ANFRACTUOUS bending, circuitous, flexuous, serpentine, sinuous, spiral, tortuous, turning, winding
ANGAKOK angakut, medicine man, shaman
ANGARE(E)B bedstead, framework, stretcher
ANGEL advocate, ange, apollyon, ariel, arioch, backer, belial, bishop, cha-

muel, cherub, cherubim, daeva, ebus, egregor, financier, genius, guarantor, guardian, israfel, jophiel, mah, messenger, monkir, munkar, nakir, nekkar, pastor, patron, principal, prophet, raphael, saint, seraf, seraph, spirit, sponsor, supporter, underwriter, uzziel, yaksha, zadkiel, zophiel
air and winds ruchiel
apostate See *fallen,* below.
biblical gabriel, michael, raphael
bottomless pit abaddon, apollyon
death azrael, gabriel, sammael
destroying amanita, danite
dust pcp, phencyclydine
evil ahriman, DEMON
-eye bluet, germander-speedwell
fallen adrammelech, ariel, arioch, azazel, beelzebub, belial, eblis, ibleis, lucifer, ramiel, reprobate, satan, uriel
footstool jolly-jumper
guardian yaksa, yakshi
group choir, fravashi, host, seraphim
hair dodder
hebrew abdiel
holy abdiel, gabriel, michael, raguel, raphael, simiel, uriel
jupiter zadkiel
koran el khidr, sijill
music israfe(e)l, israfil
of schools thomas aquinas
orders archangels, cherubim, dominion, powers, principalities, seraphim, thrones, virtues
paradise lost abdiel, arioch, belial, uriel, zophiel
rebel See *fallen,* above.
recording sijil(1)
red colcothar
shark squatinid
trumpet datura
water perfume
worship dulia
ANGELFISH butterfly fish, catalineta, chaetodipterus, flatfish, holocanthus, isabelita, kingston, mongrelskate, monkfish, munk, pomacanthus, portugais, quott, shark, spadefish, squat(ina), teleost
ANGELIC adorable, beatific,

beneficent, celestial, chaste, cherubic, divine, heavenly, holy, incorporeal, innocent, pure, saintly, seraphic
ANGELICA archangel, confection, herb, jellica
tree hercules' club, prickly ash
ANGELINE andira, cabbagetree, pacay, surinamine, yaba
ANGELITO honeybee, melipona
ANGELO *betrothed* mariana
deputy escalus
leader vincentio
ANGELUS bell, call, devotion
painter millet
ANGEOTRIBE forceps, hemostat, vasotribe
ANGER 3 arr, ire, irk, vex **4** bile, bite, boil, burn, crab, fell, fire, fret, fume, fury, gall, grim, heat, huff, miff, rage, rant, rave, rile, roil, sulk, teen, tiff **5** annoy, blaze, chafe, flare, gripe, growl, hatel, irish, pique, smoke, snarl, snort, sponk, spunk, stora, thraw, wrath **6** bridle, choler, dander, enrage, excite, grouch, madden, nettle, offend, rancor, rankle, simmer, sizzle, spleen, temper **7** affront, bluster, bristle, carry on, dudgeon, emotion, explode, flounce, incense, inflame, offense, outrage, provoke, smolder, tantrum, trouble, vitriol **8** acrimony, ill humor, irritate, sourness **9** animosity, distemper, infuriate, irateness **10** antagonism, conniption, irritation, resentment **11** biliousness, displeasure, indignation, provocation **12** belligerence, exasperation, inflammation
ANGERBODA *consort* loki
offspring fenrir, hel, midgard, serpent
ANGICO copal, courbaril, curupay, piptadenia, resin
ANGINA croup, infection, inflammation, mumps, prunella, quinsy
ANGKOR *attackers* thais
discoverer mouhot
empire khmer
gateway tasom
monument bayon
river siem reap

subject laos, thailand, vietnam
temple banteay srei
underworld god yama
wat builder suryavarman
ANGLE 3 bob, ell, tee, vee, wro 4 axil, beam, bend, cant, coin, draw, fish, fork, hade, hook, iron, keen, knee, nook, peak, site, wick 5 ancon, arris, axial, bevel, bight, choil, coign, crank, crook, elbow, epaul, facet, fleam, groin, guise, ingle, phase, point, quoin, slant, wedge 6 adjust, akimbo, allure, aspect, branch, cornel, corner, cuneus, direct, epaule, hading, laggen, laggin, octant, scheme, square, steeve, tornus, zigzag 7 azimuth, deviate, diamond, distort, draught, gimmick, knuckle, lozenge, outlook, perigon, ravelin, salient, tangent 8 argument, attitude, crotchet, decalage, dihedral, fishhook, intrigue, maneuver, position, shoulder, talisman 9 advantage, direction, specialty, viewpoint 10 appearance, divaricate, inflection, standpoint
acute akimbo
at an obliquely
berry meadow pea, tuberculosis
branch and leaf axil
comb. angulo
equal, pert. isogonal, isogonic
external cant
for solicit
45 degrees octant
geological hade
iron bar, brace, cleat, l-bar, l-beam
kind acute, oblique, obtuse, reflex, right, salient, spherical, straight
mathematical incidence, octant, radian
measure mil
measurer clinometer, graphometer, quintant, semicircle
oblique bevel
obtuse bullnose, heel
on lure
pert. angular, angulate, canted, nooked
placed at sharpest
ratio sine
right all

round bullnose, perigon
salient arris
sharp arris
stem axil
without agonic
ANGLER allmouth, fisherman, frogfish, goosefish, izaak walton, lophius, lophlid, monkfish, piscator, round robin, toadfish
gear bait, creel, lure, pole
ANGLESMITH blacksmith, slabman
ANGLETWITCH earthworm
ANGLEWORM earthworm, ess, fishworm
ANGLIA albion, ENGLAND
kingdom deira
week day feria
ANGLO-INDIAN See INDIA references.
ANGLO-IRISH See IRISH references.
ANGLO-SAXON See also ENGLAND references.
aristocracy edhilingi
armor hauberk
army fyrd
assembly gemot(e), moot, mote
coin mancus, ora, sceat, styca, thrymsa
council heptarchy, witan
court gemot(e), leet
deity eostre, frey(r), ing, thor, tiu, woden, wyrd
epic beowulf
freeman thane, thegn
hawk hafoc
hero beowulf, offa
king bretwalda, edgar, egbert, harold, ine
kingdom mercia
letter edh, eth, thorn, wen, wynn, yogh, yok
lord's attendant thane, thegn
lower class lazzi
measure amber, ell
meeting gemot(e)
middle class frilingi
minstrel scop
money ora
monster grendel
nobleman earl, thane, thegn
official gerefa
parliament witenagemot
penalty weregild
poet caedmon, cyn(e)wulf, kynewulf, scop
prince adeling, atheling
property alod
ruler basileus, bretwalda
scholar bede

sheriff gerefa, reeve
slave esne
thane gesith
village ham
warrior earl, thane, thegn
weight demimark
writer bede, gaelfric
ANGO dye, turmeric
ANGOLA *bantu* eshikongo
capital cabinda, luanda
city benguela, kampala, lobito, luanda, malanje, mossemedes
coin angolar, centava, escudo, macuta, macute
enclave cabinda
kingdom bakongo
language bantu, kimbundu
mahogany khaya
party fnla, mpla, unita
peak loviti
people bantu, kikongo
plateau planalto
port lobito, luanda
river coanza, congo, cuito, cuneme, kunene, kwango, kwanza
seed jequirity bean
weed archil
ANGORA cat, cloth, goat, rabbit, shawl, wool
goat chamal
wool camlet, mohair
ANGOSTURA bark, bitters, tonic
ANGRY acrimonious, acute, aroused, badtempered, birsit, bitter, black, boiling, browned off, burned up, chafed, choleric, contentious, crook, cross, crouse, enraged, fuming, fumous, furious, grame, grim, griped, grouchy, grum, het up, hopping, hot, huffy, illhumored, impatient, incensed, indignant, inflamed, infuriated, iracund, irascible, irate, ireful, irked, irous, irritated, keen, mad, morose, petulant, provoked, rabid, ratty, resentful, riled, riley, roid, sharp, shirty, snuffy, sore, spleenful, splenetic, stunt, sulfurous, sultry, turbulent, upset, vexed, warm, waxy, wemod, wild, wrathful, wraw, wroth, wrought up
ANGST angor, anguish, anxiety, distress, dread
ANGUISH ache, affliction, agony, angor, angst, angus, angwich, anxiety, bale, bit-

terness, desolation, difficulty, discomfort, distress, dole, dolor, dread, extremity, grief, grieve, heartache, heartbreak, infelicity, lamentation, misery, pain, pang, prostration, rack, regret, remorse, sadness, sorrow, suffering, throe, torment, torture, travail, tray, trial, woe, worry

goddess angerona

ANGULAR abrupt, angulose, angulous, awkward, bony, cadaverous, clumsy, cornered, crooked, crotched, dovetailed, edgy, forked, gaunt, geniculate(d), hooked, lank(y), lean, pointed, prismal, prismatic, pyramidal, rawboned, scrawny, skinny, slim, spare, stiff, thin, unbending, ungraceful, zigzag

ANGURIA cucumis, gourd, watermelon

ANGUS *parent* dagda

ANHELATION aspiration, desire, dyspnea, panting

ANHIMA bird, screamer

ANHYDRIDE fulgide, glucosan, lactam, lactide, mannitan, sorbitan, sultam, sultone

ANHYDROUS arid, desiccated, dry, waterless

ANI blackbird, crotophaga, cuckoo, jewbird, keelbill, keelbird, tickbird

ANIAM *father* shemidah

ANIBA bois de rose, laurel

ANICETUS *father* hercules

ANIL indigo, shrub, tephrosia

ANILE infirm, old-womanish, senile

ANIMA life, soul, spirit

ANIMADVERSION blame, monition, perception, punishment, warning

ANIMAL beast, bestial, biped, bodily, brute, brutish, carnal, carnivore, corporeal, creature, critter, fauna, fleshly, gross, inhuman, invertebrate, lusty, mammal, marsupial, physical, quadruped, rodent, ruminant, savage, sensual, stray, vertebrate, wanton, zoon

anatomy zootomy

and plant life bios, biota

anemia surra(h)

appendage tentacle

aquatic See *water*, below.

arboreal dasyure, koala, lemur, marten, sloth, tarsier, unau

armored apara, armadillo, peba, poyon, tortoise, turtle

arthritis carpitis

back chine, rig, terga, tergum

badger-like pahmi, ratel

behavior study ethology

biblical behemoth, reem

body soma

bovine boss, brute, cow, oxen

broken-down crock

burrowing armadillo, badger, gopher, mole, rabbit, squirrel, wombat

capture sool

carnivorous See **CARNIVORE.**

carrying young marsupial

castrated gelding, seg(g), spado, spay

cat-like linsang

coat fur, hair, hide, pelage, pelt, skin, wool

cold-blooded ectotherm

comb. faun, zoo

crawling REPTILE, serpent, snake, worm

crossbred hinny, hybrid, metis, mule

dehorned pollard

description zoography

disease anthrax, aptha, aspergillosis, asthenia, babesiosis, bighead, blackleg, blackwater, blind staggers, braxy, charbon, coath, coe, colic, dartars, distemper, farcy, foot and mouth, garget, glanders, heaves, hoose, loco, mange, megrims, milk-sickness, milzbrand, murrain, myxomatosis, nagana, nenta, parrot-fever, pip, pirophasmosis, psittacosis, rinderpest, rot, rout, rye, sacbrood, scabies, sheeprot, spavins, springhalt, stringhalt, surra, takosis, texas fever, tularemia

dissection zootomy

doctor vet(erinarian)

domestic cat, cattle, cow, critter, crittur, dog, hog, horse, mare, mule, pet, pig, ram, sheep, sow, stock

domestication zooculture

draft a(i)ver, elephant, horse, mule, oxen

driver drover, herdsman, skinner

eczema crustosis

enclosure alvearium, alveary, apiary, aquarium, atajo, aviary, bearpit, beehive, booley, brooder, cage, cancha, chickenhouse, coop, corral, cote, crawl, cruive, fence, gotra, hive, hutch, keddah, kench, kennel, kraal, menagerie, par, pasture, pen, pound, runway, sheepcote, stall, sty, tiergarten, vivarium, weir, yair, yard, yare, zoo

equine ass, horse, zebra

extinct auk, dinosaur, dodo, mastodon, quagga, seacow, urus

fabled acephal(us), achech, alborak, bagwyn, bandersnatch, basilisk, bicorn, bunyip, catawampus, catoblepas, centaur, dingmaul, dragon, faun, garuda, griffin, griffon, gyascutus, hippogriff, hippogryph, hircocervus, hodag, jumart, kylin, minotaur, moonack, onocentaur, rosmarine, semitaur, snark, splacknuck, tragelaph(us), unicorn, yale, yeti

fables author aesop, bidpai, pilpay

fat adeps, adipescent, adipose, cetin, grease, lanolin, lard, suet, tallow

fear of zoophobia

feathered bird, fowl

feed bonemeal, corn, ensilage, fodder, forage, grain, grass, mash, oats, provender, silage, slops, soilage, swill

feeder avener

feline cat, cheetah, jaguar, pard, tiger

female biddy, bitch, cow, cusha, dam, doe, ewe, filly, gyp, heifer, hen, hind, jenny, lady, mare, nanny, partlet, roe, sheder, slut, sow, tigress, vixen

feral cimaroon, cimarron

flesh-eating sarcophile

footless apod(a)

forehead frontlet

fossil zoolite

free-swimming nekton

gilled branchiata

gill-less abranchiata
grasshopper-eating whangam
grazing herbager
greedy gorb
group brit, clutch, covey, drove, family, flock, herd, menagerie, nide, nye, pack, school, trip, zoo
guest inquiline
hairless pelon
hard-backed apar, armadillo, tatou, tortoise, turtle
having jointed limbs arthropoda
headless acephal(us)
hibernating bear
hide pelt
hole wallow
hoofed bison, buffalo, camel (opard), cow, dromedary, giraffe, gnu, hartebeest, kaama, oont
horned antelope, bull, deer, elk, gnu, goat, moose, reem
horse-like zebra
hunted game, prey
husbandry apiculture, beekeeping, breeding, horsecraft, manege, pisciculture, ranching, stockbreeding
hybrid catalo, hinny, mongrel, mule, zebec, zebrass, zebrinny, zebrula, zebrule
hypnosis catalepsy, cataplexy
hypothetical gastraead, proavis, unicorn
imaginary See *fabled* and *hypothetical,* above.
inferior dogie
invertebrate zoophyte
lair form
land and water amphibian
lean ribe, rickle
leg gamb
leporine hare
life bios, biota, fauna
life, comb. alia
life, god of faunus
long-bodied annelid(ian)
lover zoophile, zoophilist
lumbago chine gall
magnetism allure, charisma, hypnotism, mesmerism, tellurism
male bachelor, billy, boar, buck, bull, hart, jack, johnny, mas, ram, stag, stallion, steed, steer, stot, stud, tom(cat), wether
many-footed centipede, decapod, hexapod, insect, multiped(e), octopod
marine antedon, anthozoa, aporosa, archimedes, asterias, asterid, asterinid, asteroid, balanoglossus, basket star, batocrinus, beroe, blastid, brit, coral, crinoid, cryozoa, ctenophore, dolphin, dugong, echinoderm, estrangia, fish, inia, jellyfish, lancelet, manatee, orc, otter, polychaeta, polyp, polyzoa, pterobranchia, rhodope, rotifer, salpa, seal, sedentaria, walrus, whale
microscopic acarid, am(o)eba, animalcule, monad, protozoan, rhizopod
midriff apron
molt exuviae
multicellular gastrotrich
mythical See *fabled,* above.
nearing extinction alligator, elephant seal, sea lion, sea otter, whale, wild horse
nocturnal bat, coon, menur, opossum, owl, possum, raccoon, ratel, tapir
noxious vermin
odd splacknuck
odor, pert. capryllic
one-celled am(o)eba, monad, protozoa(n)
order, comb. ini
ovine sheep
oviparous monotreme
pack ass, burro, camel, donkey, horse, hunia, llama, mule, sumpter
parasitic entozoan
park zoo
peculiar splacknuck
pert. bovine, canine, feline, leonine, ovine, porcine, ursine, vulpine, zoic, zooid, zoologic, zoonic
pet cade
plantigrade bear, man
plump bilch, bilsh
porcine boar, hog, pig, swine
prehistoric brontops, dinosaur, ichthyosaur, machairodus, mammoth, mastodon, megather(e), phytosaur, pterodactyl, pterosaur, saber-toothed cat, smilodon, stegodon, triceratops
prickly hedgehog, porcupine
protection group aspca, humane society, spca
protein arginine
radiated actinozoa, coral, polyp, sea anemone
realm, comb. alia

representation protoma
reproduction zoogamy
reverence for zoism
ruminant antelope, camel, cow, deer, vicuna
sacrifice sphagion
salt source deer lick
science zoology
scrawny scrag
secretion mush
skin fell, hide
skin affliction mange
slaughterer sho(c)het
sluggish drumble
small beastie, polyp, toto, toy
solid-footed soliped
sound bark, buzz, chirp, cry, mew, neigh, roar, trumpet
spirit-inhabited guaca, huaca
spirits exuberance, vivacity
spotted calico, dapple, piebald
starch glycogen
stomach craw, rumen
structure anatomy, zootomy
study zoology
stuffing taxidermy
stunted runt, shargar, wallydrag
symbol totem
tailless acaudal, tenrec
10-footed decapod
thigh hair culotte
timid deer, hare, sheep
totem eponym
track abature, feute, foil, slot, spoor
trainer dompteuse
2-footed biped
2-horned bicorn(e)
unbranded slick
undersized durgan, durgen, runt
unweaned sucker
ursine bear
vegetable-feeding phytophaga
vertebrate agnatha
vulpine fox
warm-blooded endotherm, haematherm
water aquatile, beaver, coral, desman, dolphin, fish, otter, polyp, seal, walrus, whale
weak downer, drag
whisker vibrissa
wild savage
winged bat, bird
work ass, donkey, mule
worship idolatry, zoolatry
young babe, bruin, calf, chick, chipling, chit, colt, cub, fatling, fawn, filly,

foal, gilt, hog(g), joey, junior, kid, kitten, konet, lamb, lionet, littlin(g), pup(py), shoat, shote, stot, suckling, toto, whelp

young-carrying marsupial

ANIMALCULE am(o)eba, diatom, fly, infusorian, microbe, mouse, rotifer, speck

ANIMALISTIC bodily, carnal, fleshly, physical, sensual

ANIMALIZE brutalize, sensualize

ANIMA MUNDI archeus, weltgeist

ANIMATE act(ivate), actuate, alive, arouse, breathing, bright, brisk, catalyze, cheer, comfort, develop, drive, dynamize, encourage, energize, enliven, ensoul, excite, exhilarate, fire, flush, fortify, imbue, impel, incite, infuse, inspire, inspirit, invigorate, jazz up, kindle, liven, living, mobilize, move, pep, perk, prompt, quick(en), rouse, spirited, stir, urge, vital(ize), vivify

ANIMATED active, alive, ardent, bouncing, bright, brisk, buoyant, dynamic, effervescent, gay, jocular, lifesome, lively, living, quick, sparky, spirited, sprightly, sthenic, vif, vigorous, vital, vivacious

ANIMATION action, activity, ardor, breeziness, briskness, buoyancy, ebullience, energy, enthusiasm, excitement, exhilaration, ginger, inspiration, life, liveliness, pep, spirit, sprightliness, verve, vigor, vim, vitality, vivacity

suspended torpor

ANIME bright, copal, elemi, oleoresin, resin, rosin

ANIMOSITY abhorrence, abomination, acrimony, animus, antagonism, antipathy, bad blood, bitterness, choler, dislike, enmity, feud, grudge, hate, hatred, hostility, ill will, malevolence, malice, opposition, pique, rancor, resentment, spite, spleen, venom, virulence, vitriol

ANIMUS animosity, attitude, bias, disposition, effort, inclination, inspiration, inten-

tion, mind, onde, prejudice, purpose, spirit, temper, will

ANIPPE *consort* poseidon

ANIRUDDHA *grandfather* vishnu

ANISE anet, anisum, cumin, dill, fennel, finocchio, licorice, pimpinella, s(h)ikimi

-flavored drink See LICORICE *-flavored drink.*

hyssop agastache

liqueur kummel

plant seseli

root collinsonia, sweet cicely

-scented goldenrod blue-mountain-tea

ANISETTE aguardiente, cordial

ANISOMEROUS unequal, unsymmetrical

ANISOPHYLLOUS diversified

ANISOPTERA dragonfly

ANISTASIMON resurrection

ANITO demon, fetish, idol, spirit

ANIUS *consort* dryope

daughter elais, oeno, spermo

kingdom delos

parent apollo, creusa, rhoeo

son andron, andrus

ANJOU *pert.* angevin

ANKH cross, crux ansata, tau

ANKLE coot, cuit, hock, queet, quit, walk

bone astragal, calcis, hucklebone, malleolus, talus, tarsalia, tarsus

comb. tal(o), tars(o)

cover spat

-deep shallow

iron basil, fetter, shackle

jerk achilles reflex, clonus

joint coot

pert. talaric, tarsal

ANKLET achsa, band, bangle, brace, circlet, fetter, ring, shackle, sock

ANKYLOSTOMA lockjaw

ANLACE dagger

ANLAGE base, basis, bent, blastema, embryo, foundation, incept, inclination, primordium, proclivity, proton, rudiment, source

ANNA coin, hoazin, stinkbird

daughter mary

husband tobit

¼ pice

pupil mongkut

sister dido

16 rupee

ANNALS almanac, annual, archives, chronicle, chronology, history, record, register

ANNAM See also NORTH VIETNAM, SOUTH VIETNAM.

boat gaydiang, gayyou

city hanoi, hue, quangtri, tourane, vinh

coin quen, sapek

division cochin-china, tonkin, tonquin

measure chai, con, dam, gon, hao, mao, mau, ngu, phan, quo, sao, shita, tao, tat, that, thuoc, truong

people ch(i)am, moi, tzaam

river songka

weight binh, can, dong, fan, hao, nen, quan, yen

ANNAPOLIS *graduate* ensign

river severn

student midshipman, plebe

ANNAPURNA devi

ANNAS *son* aseas

ANNATTO achiote, achuete, bixa, bixin, orellin, orlean(s), otter, salmon, tree, urucu

ANNE *attendant* berkeley, tressel

husband joachim

ANNEAL bake, endurate, fuse, harden, heat, inflame, smelt, temper, toughen

chamber leer, lehr

oven calcar

ANNECTANT connecting, linking

ANNELID earthworm, leech, lugworm, sandworm, serpulan

freshwater naid

marine aphrodite, autolytus, lurg, terebella

ANNESLIA calliandra

ANNET kittiwake, seagull

ANNEX acquire, add(ition), adject, adjunct, affix, append(age), appose, appropriate, attach(ment), connect, dependence, ell, extension, fasten, increment, join, postfix, steal, subjoin, subsidiary, superstructure, unite, wing

ANNIE OAKLEY freebie, mozee, pass, ticket

ANNIHILATE abate, abolish, annul, blast, cancel, defeat, delete, demolish, desolate, destroy, devastate, devour, discreate, efface, end, erase, expunge, exterminate, extinguish, extirpate, kill, napoo, nought, nullify, obliterate, quench, ravish, raze, reduce, rub out, ruin, slay, smash, uncreate, undo, vanquish, wreck

ANNIHILATION death, decreation, destruction, extermination, extinction, fana, negation

ANNIVERSARY annual, birthday, celebration, commemoration, feast, festival, fete, jubilee, yahrzeit, yearday, yearly
1st paper
3rd triennial
5th wooden
10th decennial, tin
15th crystal
20th china, vigentennial
25th semijubilee, silver
30th pearl
35th coral
40th emerald, ruby
45th ruby, sapphire
50th golden, jubilee, semicentennial
75th diamond
100th centenary, centennial
150th sesquicentennial
200th bicentennial
1000th millenial
2000th bimillenary

ANNO DOMINI solitaire

ANNONA aconitum, atees, atis, atta, custard-apple, grain, produce, provisions, soursop, sweetsop, tree
fiber anoncillo

ANNOTATE apostil, benote, comment, construe, edit, elucidate, explain, expound, footnote, gloss, gloze, illustrate, interpret, mark, memo, note, postil, record, remark

ANNOTATION apostil(le), comment(ary), exegesis, explanation, footnote, gloss, memo, note, reference, rubric, scholion, scholium

ANNOUNCE acclaim, advertise, affirm, annunciate, assert, aver, beep, betoken, bid, blaze, blazon, bode, broach, broadcast, bruit, call, cern, claim, declare, deem, disclose, divulge, enunciate, expound, fore-

tell, harbinger, herald, inform, intimate, introduce, knell, notify, preach, present, proclaim, promulgate, publicize, publish, report, reveal, state, steven, tell, voice, write
beforehand bode, foretell, portend, presage

ANNOUNCEMENT advertisement, alarm, ban(n)s, bill, blurb, bulletin, circular, commercial, decision, declaration, dictum, edict, gazette, manifesto, mention, message, notice, proclamation, pronouncement, pronunciamento, release, tidings

ANNOUNCER bellman, commentator, crier, disk jockey, emcee, gongman, grinder, harbinger, herald, informant, mikeman, nebo, nunciate, nuncio, proclaimer, prophet, radioman, seer, speaker, spieler, spruiker, trumpeter

ANNOY 3 bug, dun, egg, get, hox, ire, irk, nag, noy, nye, tax, try, vex **4** bait, bogy, bore, burn, fash, fike, fret, fuss, gall, grig, hale, harm, haze, huff, miff, nark, pain, rasp, rile, roil **5** beset, chafe, chase, chevy, chivy, devil, grame, gramy, grate, harry, peeve, pique, stite, sturt, tease, upset, weary, worry **6** abrade, badger, bother, caddle, chivvy, enrage, fester, gravel, harass, heckle, hector, injure, madden, molest, needle, nettle, offend, pester, plague, pother, rankle, rattle, rehete, ruffle **7** bedevil, cheppeh, disturb, perturb, provoke, terrify, torment, trouble **8** distress, irritate, tcheppeh **9** aggravate, displease, embarrass, incommode, obfuscate, persecute **10** exasperate

ANNOYANCE bogy, bore, botheration, cross, discomfort, disturbance, fashery, grief, inconvenience, insect, nuisance, pest, resentment, spite, stall, thorn, umbrage, weed

ANNOYER harrier, noier, nudni(c)k, pest, trier

ANNOYING acrid, aggra-

vating, bad, beastly, bothersome, corrosive, disturbing, exasperating, fashious, fretsome, galling, harrassing, importunate, irksome, irritating, nerve-racking, pesky, pestiferous, pestilent, plaguy, provocative, provoking, spiteful, tarsome, teasing, thorny, tiresome, tormenting, troublesome, unpleasant, vexatious, vexing, worrying

ANNUAL book, etesian, flower, perennial, periodic(al), plant, publication, quotennial, report, yearbook, yearly
register founder burke

ANNUITANT beneficiary

ANNUITY censo, concol, income, investment, pension, rente, stipend, subsidy, tontine

ANNUL abolish, abrogate, adnul, annihilate, avoid, blank, blot out, cancel, cashier, cass(are), delete, destroy, disaffirm, dissolve, elide, erase, invalidate, negate, nullify, obliterate, override, quash, recall, repeal, retract, reverse, revoke, toll, undo, vacate, void

ANNULAR, ANNULOSE banded, cingular, circular, cyclic, orbicular, ringed, round

ANNULATION annulus, belt, hoop, ring, sput

ANNULET bandelet(te), bandlet, circle, fillet, molding, ridge, ring

ANNULMENT avoidance, cassation, obrogation, repeal, retroversion, revocation, undoing

ANNULOID cestode, echinoderm, nematode, rotifer, trematode, worm

ANNULUS annulation, armilla, circle, collar, gyroma, indusium, ring

ANNUNCIATE See ANNOUNCE.

ANNUNCIATION announcement, declaration, ladyday, marymass, proclamation
lily madonna
observance angelus

ANNWFN elysium, fairyland, utopia
lord arawn

ANOA buffalo, oxen, sapiutan

ANODYNE acopon, analgesic, anesthetic, antikamnia, aspirin, assuager, balm, belladonna, bromal, calmative, eugenol, narcotic, nepenthe, opiate, pain-reliever, palliative, remedy, salve, sedative, soother

ANOESIA anoia, idiocy

ANOINT alyne, anele, anoil, balm, bless, chastise, chrism, consecrate, cream, crown, dedicate, enshrine, fat, grease, hallow, int, inunct, latch, lubricate, medicate, nard, oil, oint, pomade, pomatum, rub, salve, sanctify, shrive, smear, spread, unguent

ANOINTMENT chrismatory, greasing, lubrication, oiling, unction

  room alipterion, ceroma

  treatment iatraliptics

ANOMALOUS aberrant, abnormal, atypic(al), awkward, azygous, deviating, difform, eccentric, exceptional, heteroclite, irregular, monstrous, odd, peculiar, prodigious, singular, strange, unique, unnatural, unusual

ANOMALY abnormality, antinomy, departure, deviation, eccentricity, epiloia, exception, incongruity, inconsistency, oddity, paradox, peculiarity

ANOMITE biotite, mica

ANON again, anew, at once, bedeen, bedene, directly, encore, forthwith, hence, immediately, instantly, presently, shortly, soon, straightway, then(ce)

ANONYM alias, pseudonym

ANONYMOUS blind, incognito, innominate, nameless, unknown, unnamed, unsigned, unspecified

ANOPLANTHUS broomrape, herb, indianpipe, orobanche, thalesia

ANORTHITE amphodelite, feldspar

ANORTHOCLASE anorthose, feldspar, microline, orthoclase

ANOTHER additional, alias, anither, different, extra, fresh, further, new, noch,

one more, remaining, second, separate, that, tidder, tother

ANOUNOU lepidium, peppergrass

ANOUS noddie, tern

ANOXIA asphyxia, blackout

ANQUET *husband* khnemu, khnum

ANSA handle, loop

ANSER duck, goose, merganser, swan

ANSEROUS dull, foolish, gooselike, silly, stolid, stupid

ANSTOSS check, limitation, obstacle

ANSWER accept, account, acknowledge, act, antiphone, atone, avail, comeback, conform, correspond, counter, cover, defense, discharge, disprove, echo, fulfill, jawab, justify, letter, maintain, meet, plea, pleading, react, rebut(tal), receipt, recognize, refute, rejoin(der), repartee, reply, report, rescript, response, result, retort, return, reverberate, ripost(e), satisfy, say, serve, solution, squelcher, suffice, suit, talk back, vindicate

  back backtalk, chop, retort, sass

  decisive sockdolager

  for engage, represent, sponsor, vang, vouch

  legal duply

  to objection anthypophora

ANSWERABLE accountable, adequate, amenable, commensurate, correlative, corresponding, equal, liable, proportionate, responsible, suitable

ANSWERER apocrisiary, respondent, ushabti

ANT ampt, anai, anay, aner, atta, camponotus, eciton, emmet, formicid, gyne, hymenoptera, microergate, microgyne, minim, mire, myrmicid, pismire, siafu, slave, termes, termite

  acacia myrmecophyte

  bear aardvark, edentate, erdvark, myrmecophaga, tamanoir

  bird anteater, antshrike, bush-shrike, formicarius, grallaria, microrhopias, pitta, thamnophilus

  bristle ammochaeta

  cattle aphid, plant lice

  comb. myrmeco

  cow aphis

  enslavement dulosis

  feeding on formicivorous

  food beltsbody

  genus camponotus, eciton, formica, monomorium, pheidole, polyergus, solenopsis, tapinoma

  group colony, nest

  hill bank, formicary, tump

  kind agricultural, amazon, argentine, army, brown, driver, kelep, soldier, worker

  king grallaria

  leaf-cutting atta

  -like myrmecoid

  lion doodlebug, myrmekoleon

  male aner, ergatandromorph, ergataner, micraner

  nest formicary, hill

  non-worker drone

  pert. formic(ine)

  pipit conopophagida, gnateater

  plant myrmecophyte

  poison formicide

  queen gyne, microgyne

  -resisting wood amuguis

  rice aristida, texas grass

  shrike batara, thamnophile

  slave-making amazon

  stinging kelep, ponerine

  study myrmecology

  symbol of frugality, industry

  thrush formicarius, pitta, pulish

  tree hormigo, myrmecophyte, triplaris

  velvet cow-killer

  venemous solpugida

  white anai, anay, termite

  wood bulelia, myrmecophyte, shrub

  worker ergate, maxim, minim, neuter, plerergate, pterergate

  wren microrhopias, thamnophilus

ANTA ivory-nut, pedestal, pier, pilaster, porch, TAPIR, tupian

ANTAEA cybele, demeter, rhea

ANTAEUS *parent* gaea, poseidon

  slayer hercules

ANTAGONISM anger, animosity, animus, antipathy, aversion, conflict, contrariety, enmity, hostility, opposition, quarrel, rancor, resistance, war

ANTAGONIST adversary, attacker, battler, combatant, competitor, contender, copemate, enemy, foe, opponent, opposite, rival, warrior, wrangler

ANTAGONISTIC adverse, alien, antergic, antipathetic, averse, clashing, conflicting, contradictory, contrary, counter, cross, discordant, dissonant, hostile, incompatible, inimical, opposed, opposing, opposite, oppugnant, repugnant, resistive, unfriendly, warlike

ANTAGONIZE affront, alienate, attack, combat, contest, disaffect, displease, embitter, envenom, estrange, incite, infuriate, instigate, madden, offend, oppose, outrage, provoke, resist

ANTARANGA dharana, dhyana, samadhi

ANTARCTIC *cape* adare
bird penguin, skua
coastal region adelie, enderbyland, wilkesland
explorer byrd, cook, james, ross, scott, shackleton, wilkins
gull skua
island alexander, south orkney, south shetland
peak erebus, marklam, siple
penguin adelie
peninsula grahamland, palmer
range admiralty, edsel ford, queen maud
region adare, ross sea
russian base mirnyvostok
sea ross
seal ross, sea-elephant, sterrinck
shearwater ice-petrel
shrub diddledee
sound mcmurdo
u. s. base mcmurdo

ANTE before, bet, blind, contribution, cough up, former, hand over, kick in, kitty, money, pay, plank down, post, pot, previous, prior, produce, put up, share, stake, wager
bellum prewar

ANTEA See ANTIA.

ANTEATER aardvark, aardwolf, antbird, dasyurid,

echidna, edentate, manis, numbat, pangolin, smutsia, tamandua, tapir, vermilinguia

ANTECEDE go before, precede, surpass

ANTECEDENT ancestor, ancestry, antecedaneous, anterior, anticipate, cause, determinant, forefather, foregoing, foretaste, former, precedent, preceding, precess, premise, previous, prior, procatarctic, whence

ANTEDATE anticipate, precede, predate, preexist, premundane

ANTEDILUVIAN ancient, antiquated, antique, archaic, before the deluge, obsolete, old fogy, oldster, preflood, primitive, venerable

ANTELOPE See also AFRICA *antelope*, SOUTH AFRICA *antelope*.
ancient addax, pygarg
brown ngor
brush purshia, shrub
bubaline bleekbok, blesbok, blesbuk, bontebok
chamois-like rhebok
chipmunk ammospermophilus
extinct blaubok, pygarg
female doe
forest bongo
4-horned chikara, chouka, chousingha, tetracerus
gazelle-like beira, gerenuk
genus aepyceros, egocerus, oryx
goatlike chamois, goral, serow
golden impala
harnessed boschbok, guib
himalayan chiru, goral
kind 3 doe, gnu, goa, kid, ram 4 bisa, buck, doda, gnoo, guib, ibex, koba, kudu, mohr, oryx, poku, puku, roan, suni, topi, tora, yale 5 addax, baira, beira, bekra, bohor, chiru, eland, gemsf, goral, guiba, ipete, kemas, korin, lichi, mhorr, nagor, oribi, peele, peron, royal, sable, saiga, sasin, serow, takin, yakin 6 bagwin, bhokra, bubale, cabree, chouka, dikdik, duiker, duyrer, dzeren, gooral, grimme, herola, inyala, lechwe, nakong, nil-

gai, nylgau, oterop, ozanna, pallah, pasang, pookoo, pygarg, rhebak, sakeen, shammy 7 algazel, blaubok, blesbok, chamois, chicara, gazelle, gerenuk, greenuk, madoqua, nilghai, nilghau, nylghau, sassaby 8 agacella, korrigum, nilghaie 9 pronghorn, sitatunga, springbok 10 alcelaphus, antidorcas, hartebeest, wildebeest
large addak, aste, beisa, bongo, bubalis, defassa, eland, gemsbok, gnu, hartebeest, impala, impofo, kudu, nilgai, nilgau, oryx, sassaby
-like bovid, bovine, bubaline
male buck
mountain chamois
mythic yale
pied bontebok
pronghorn cabree, cabret, cabrie
redbuck pallah
reddish grysbok
royal ipete, kleeneboc, madoqua
sheep-like saiga
short-maned gnu, grysbok
small duiker, grimme, grysbok, klipspringer, steenbok
state nebraska
striped bongo
tawny oribi
tiger-like agacella
young kid

ANTEMERIDIAN forenoon, morning

ANTENNA aerial, appendage, arista, cercus, conductor, dish, doublet, feeler, horn, loop, nodicorn, palp, parabola, tactor, tentacle, touch, whisker, yagi
end clava
having 2 dicerous
insect clava
radar bedspring, mattress, scanner, sontenna
without acerous

ANTENNARIA cat's-ear, cat's-foot, cudweed, thistle

ANTENOR *guest* menelaus, odysseus, ulysses
parent aesyetes, cleomestra
son agenor, antheus, archelochus
wife theano

ANTEP aintab

ANTERIOR antecedaneous, antecedent, anticus, atlantal, atloid, before, earlier, foregoing, former, forne, forward, front, inferior, lower, preceding, previous, prior, prorsal, ventral

ANTEROOM antechamber, entrance, entry, foyer, hall, leewan, liwan, lobby, lounge, narthex, presence-chamber, prostas, salle d'attente, vestibule, waiting room

ANTEROS *brother and opponent* eros

ANTETEMPLE narthex, portico

ANTEVORTA porrima, prorsa

ANTHAS *father* poseidon

ANTHEIA aphrodite

ANTHELION antisun, aureole, countersun, halo, nimbus

ANTHELMINTIC antiscolic, azedarach, brayera, calomel, chinaberry, cunic, embelin, herb, prophylactic, quicksilver, vermifuge

ANTHEM agnus, antiphon(y), asperges, canon, canticle, hymn, introit, kimigayo, laud, motet, offertory, psalm, respond, responsory, song

ANTHEMIDEA sagebrush, tansy, thistle, yarrow

ANTHEMIS c(h)amomile, morgan, thistle

ANTHER chive, microsporangia, pollen, stamen, theca, tip
opening stomium
smut fungus, ustilago

ANTHESIS bloom, blossom, (ef)florescence, inflorescence

ANTHESTERIA choes, chytroi, dionysia, pithoigia

ANTHEUS *father* antenor

ANTHIAS barberfish, surgeonfish

ANTHOCYANIN betanin, cyanin, denin, enin, oenin, pigment, punicin, violanin

ANTHODIUM calthidium, capitulum, involucre

ANTHOGENESIS ampherotoky

ANTHOLOGY album, ana, chapbook, chrestomathy, collection, compilation, corpus, florilegium, garland, miscellany, poetry, posy, reader, sylva, syntagma, thesaurus, treasury

ANTHONOMUS applecurculio, beetle, boll-weevil

ANTHOZOAN anemone, coelenterate, coral, coryl, gulinula, polyp, seapen

ANTHRACITE coal, culm
size barley

ANTHRACONITE agate, limestone, marble, stinkstone, swinestone

ANTHRAX anthracia, aptha, blackleg, blight, boil, carbuncle, charbon, garnet, gem, pustule, ruby, thrush

ANTHRENUS buffalo, buffalo moth, bug

ANTHROPOID ape, chimpanzee, gibbon, gorilla, lar, man, monkey, orangutan, pliopithecus, primate
pert. pithecan

ANTHROPOPHAGITE cannibal, maneater, savage

ANTHROPOS humanity, man

ANTI adverse, against, contra, opposed, opposite

ANTIA sthenboea
consort bellerophon, proteus
father iobates

ANTIAIRCRAFT ackack, aerogun, archie, bofors, pompom, skysweeper

ANTIBIOTIC bacitracin, drug, circulin, citrinin, clavacin, clavatin, fradicin, gramicidin, herquein, humulon(e), neomycin, novobiocin, nystatin, penicillin, rifamyicin, streptomycin, subtilin, sulfa, tetracycline, tetracyn, tyrothricin

ANTIBODY agglutinin, anticatalyst, antilysin, antitoxin, blocker, glutinin, precipitin, reagin

ANTIC bizarre, buffoon, caper, caprice, clown, comedian, comic(al), dido, fool, gambade, gambado, gay, grotesque, merry, mischief, play, prank, stooge, stunt, toy, trick, wild, zany

ANTICHRIST mohammed, nero, pope, pretender, supervillain

ANTICIPATE answer, antedate, apprehend, augur, await, balk, beat, consider, devance, divine, expect, forefeel, foresee, forestall, foretell, hope, intend, jump, nullify, obviate, omen, portend, preclude, predict, prepare, presage, prevene, prevent, realize, sense, stall, suppose, thwart, wish

ANTICIPATING agog, astir, desirous, eager, expecting, pregnant, vigilant

ANTICIPATION augury, expectation, foreboding, foresight, foretaste, hope, preconception, prejudice, prescience, presentiment, prospect

ANTICLEA camass, cammas, herb, quamash
consort laertes, sisyphus
father autolycus
son odysseus, ulysses

ANTICLIMAX bathos

ANTICLINE arch, dome, overfold

ANTICOUS introrse

ANTICYCLONE high

ANTIDACTYL anapaest

ANTIDEPRESSANT amphetamine, aventyl, elavil, marplan, nardil, norpramin, parnate, pertofrane, presamine, sinequan, tofranil, triavil, vivactil

ANTIDOTE alexipharmic, alexiteric, alkalizer, annuller, antacid, antitoxin, bezoar, cacoon, check, chrysolite, coprolite, corrective, counteractant, counteragent, cure, deletery, emetic, galena, guaco, medicine, mithridate, neutralizer, nullifier, offset, prevent (at)ive, prophylactic, remedy, restorative, serum, soda, theriaca, toxin

ANTIFEBRILE antipyretic, febrifuge

ANTIFEBRIN acetanilide

ANTIFORMIN deodorant, disinfectant, solvent

ANTIGEN agglutinogen, antitoxin, biologic, hapten, lysogen

ANTIGONE *brother* eteocles, polynices
consort haemon, peleus
kin creon, ismene
parent oedipus
slayer hero

ANTIGONON buckwheat, mountain-rose

ANTIGONUS *captain* archelaus, theophrastus
consort paulina, stratonice
friend medius

son demetrius, poliorcetes
victim eumenes
ANTIGORITE baltimorite, bowenite, serpentine
ANTIGUA *capital* st john's
dependency barbuda
port st john's
ANTIHISTIMINE coricidin
ANTIKNOCK toluene
ANTILIA brazil, west indies
ANTILLES *bird* trembler
god zeme
island aruba, barbados, cuba, hispaniola, jamaica, puerto rico, saba, trinidad
native carib(ee), ineri
pearl cuba, martinique
queen cuba
ANTILOCAPRA pronghorn
ANTILOCHUS *father* nestor
friend achilles
slayer memnon
victim atymnius
ANTILOGY contradiction
ANTIMACASSAR cover, doily, tidy
ANTIMENIDAS *brother* alcaeus
ANTIMONY kohl, marcasite, stibium, stibnite, sunray, valentinite
and copper babbitt metal
blende bermesite
bloom valentinite
comb. stib
compound algaroth, allemontite, bezoar, boulangerite, cervantite, stibine
glance stibnite
ocher cervantite
salt algaroth
source stibnite
sulphide kermes, kohl, soorma, stibnite, surma, vulcanizer
ANTINEURALGIC bromamide
ANTINOMY anomaly, contradiction, denial, opposite, paradox, variance
ANTINOUS *patron* hadrian
slayer odysseus, ulysses
suiter to penelope
ANTIOCH antikiya
bishop ignatius
lord thaliard
patriarch eudoxius
ANTIOCHUS *commander* alcibiades
enemy ptolemy
father hercules
friend lucullus
kingdom syria
pupil cicero

ANTIOPE *consort* lycus, theseus, zeus
foe dirce
sister hippolyte
son amphion, hippolyte, zethus
ANTIOXIDANT sesamol
ANTIPAS *father* herod
ANTIPASTO appetizer, hors d'oeuvre, smorgasbord
ANTIPATER *friend* alexander
mother thessalonica
son cassander, iolaus
ANTIPATHETIC antagonistic, averse, contrary, distasteful, hostile, loathsome, opposed, repellent, revolting, unsympathetic
ANTIPATHY abhorrence, anathema, animosity, animus, antagonism, aversion, contrariety, detestation, disgust, disinclination, dislike, disrelish, distaste, dyspathy, enmity, hate, hatred, horror, hostility, loathing, nausea, odium, opposition, rancor, reluctance, repugnance, repulsion
ANTIPERIODIC addadd, apiol(e), berberine, celastrus, counteractive
ANTIPHAS *father* laocoon
ANTIPHLOGISTIC antipyrotic, antiseptic
ANTIPHOLUS *attendant* dromio
parent aegeon, aemilia
sister-in-law luciana
wife adriana
ANTIPHONY anthem, canon, canticle, chant, composition, hymn, laud, prayer, psalm, response, song, verse
ANTIPHUS *father* priam
victim leucus
ANTIPODAL antarctic
ANTIPODES antonym, australia, contrary, downunder, opposite
ANTIPOENUS *daughter* alcis, androclea
ANTIPYRETIC analgen(e), apolysin, malarin, salol, thalline
ANTIPYRINE analgesic, antirheumatic, aspidospermin, aspirin, febrifuge, remedy, sedative
ANTIPYROTIC antiphlogistic, antiseptic

ANTIQUARIAN antic, archaist, archeologist, collector, dryasdust, herr teufelsdrockh, jonathan oldbuck, medievalist, palaeophile
ANTIQUATED aged, ancient, antediluvian, archaic, arky, bygone, dated, fossilized, fusty, gothic, medieval, mid-victorian, mossy, noachian, noaic, obsolete, old(fashioned), outdated, outmoded, passe, superannuated, timeworn, venerable, victorian, voided
ANTIQUE aged, anachronism, ancient, ANTIQUATED, bibelot, blank, blind, bric-a-brac, curio, early, emboss, fossil, knickknack, noachic, noetic, obsolescent, obsolete, oldster, past, period piece, refinish, refurbish, relic, venerable, virtu
bronze cacao, cocoa
drab fox
red canna, chaudron
ANTIQUITY ancience, anciency, ancientness, bronzeage, eld, iron-age, old(ness), past, yore
study archeology, paleology
ANTIRRHINUM figwort, snapdragon
ANTISCOLIC anthelmintic
ANTISELENE halo
ANTISEPSIS antiseptic, disinfection, immunization, prophylactic, sterilization, vaccination
pioneer lister
ANTISEPTIC alcohol, antitoxin, bactericide, bacteriophage, colytic, disinfectant, fumigant, germicide, phage, prophylactic, sterile
acid boric
kind acriflavine, alphol, alumnol, amadol, amido, amine, anethole, antitoxin, arbutin, argenol, argentamide, argyrol, aseptol, benzoin, benzosol, borax, boric acid, bromol, camphor, carvacrol, cava, colytic, creosote, cresol, egal, eupad, eusol, iatrol, ichthyol, iodin(e), iodol, kava, krelos, leukin, loretin, lysozyme, merthiolate, metaphen, phenol, picrol, plakin, retinol, salol, tachiol,

terebrene, teucrin, thallin(e), thimerosal, thymol
powder acetaminol, argentol, formin
salt fluoborate
ANTISOCIAL antagonistic, averse, cynical, eremitic, hostile, menacing, misanthropic, unfriendly
ANTISPASMODIC adiphene, antipyretic, asafetida, camomile, carapine, castor(eum), hing, k(h)ellin, sambul, sedative, sumbal
ANTISTES bishop, presbytor
ANTISTROPHE antimetabole, counterturn, repetition, reverse, revert
ANTITHALIAN killjoy
ANTITHESIS antilogy, antipodes, antonym, comparison, contrariety, contrast, opposite, opposition
ANTITHETIC antagonistic, opposite
ANTITOXIN antiabrin, antibody, antigen, biological, remedy, serum
comb. sero
ANTLER bosset, dag(ue), horn, knob, rial, spike, tray, troche, troching
-bearing beamy
branch advancer, bay, beam, bez, brow, croche, knag, point, prong, royal, snag, speller, sur-royal, tine, trestine, troching, tyne
branched rusine
burr coronet
covering velvet
knob croche
moth charaeas
point See *branch*, above.
royal trestine, treztine
trestine tray
unbranched dag(ue), greenhorn, horn, pricket, spike
ANTLERED beamy, branchy, cavicorn, damine, ramifying
ANTONINUS marcus aurelius
ANTONIO *brother* leonato, prospero
friend bassanio, gratiano, salanio, salarino, salerio, sebastian
lender shylock
servant panthino
son proteus
ANTONY AND CLEOPATRA *author* shakespeare
character agrippa, alexas,

antony, caesar, candidus, charmian, cleopatra, demetrius, dercetas, diomedes, dolabella, enobarbus, eros, euphronius, gallus, iras, lepidus, mardian, mark antony, mecaenas, menas, menecrates, octavia, philo, pompey, proculeius, scarus, seleucus, silius, taurus, thyreus, varrius, ventidius
ANTONY, MARK *advisor* clodius, hybreas, lepidus
ally archelaus, bocchus, mithridates, philadelphus, polemon, sadalas, tarcondemus
ambassador euphronius
brother caius, lucius
commander caesar
consort cleopatra, fulvia, octavia
descendant claudius, germanicus, nero
enemy augustus, cicero, eurycles, octavian
entertainer anaxenor, metrodorus, xuthus
favorite god bacchus
freedman hipparchus
friend aristocrates, caesar, cassius, claudius, clodius, cotylon, curio, demetrius, dolabella, domitius, enobarbus, euphronius, gabinus, geminius, hippias, lepidus, lucilius, munatius, philo, plancus, pompey, scarus, sergius, titius, varius, ventidius
in-law domitius, drusus, juba
lieutenant aenobarbus, agrippa, arruntius, canidius, censorinus, coelius, gallus, labienus, marcus insteius, marcus octavius, publicola, sossius, statianus, ventidius
messenger dellius
naval defeat actium
offspring antonia, antony, antyllus, cleopatra
parent antony, julia
rival agrippa, archelaus, aristobulus, cicero, marcellus, menecrates, octavian, pompeius, pompey
servant dercetaeus, eros
son-in-law caesar
stepdaughter claudia, clodia
steward theophilus
sword philippan
victim arsinoe, hortensius, lachares

ANTONYM antithesis, opposite
ANTRIN occasional, rare
ANTROSTOMUS bird, caprimulgus, goatsucker, whippoorwill
ANTRUM cavern, cavity, sinus
ANTWERP anvers
brown congo
native anversois
ANU *consort* anat, anatum, antu
daughter nanai
enemy tiamat
home eanna
parent anshar, kishar
ANUBIS *brother* horus
city cynopolis
commander iosiris
form black jackal
kin isis, kebehut
parent nephthys, osiris
ANUKIT *husband* khnemu, khnum
ANURAN amphybia, batrachia, frog, salientia, toad
ANUROUS acaudal, tailless
ANVIL ambos, anfeeld, beakiron, bickern, bickiron, block, incus, jaw, snarl, stake, stethy, stith(y), teest
beak beck
bone ambos, incus
city nome
horn beakiron, bickern, bickiron
miniature stake, stump
part stock, web
striker smith
tinsmith's teest
ANXIETY agitation, alarm, allovers, angor, angst, anguish, anomie, apprehension, care, caution, chagrin, concern, creeps, diffidence, disquiet(ude), distress, disturbance, doubt, dread, eagerness, fanteeg, fantigue, fear, fidgets, foreboding, impatience, inquietude, kiaugh, misery, misgiving, nerves, panic, perturbation, pucker, qualm, restiveness, restlessness, scruple, shakes, solicitude, suffering, suspense, tension, thought, trouble, uncertainty, uneasiness, vexation, worry
tranquilizer miltown, reserpine, valium
ANXIOUS afraid, agitated, agog, alloverish, appre

hensive, bothered, breathless, careful, carking, concerned, desirous, diffident, disquieted, disturbed, eager, earnful, edgy, expectant, fearful, fretful, fretting, harassed, impatient, impetuous, keen, misgiving, on edge, on tenterhooks, perturbed, restless, solicitous, thoughty, tidious, toey, troubled, uneasy, upset, watchful, worried

ANY air(y), all, ary, aught, each, either, oni, ony, over, part, sone, whatever, whichever
minute imminently, soon
more additional, further, hereafter
part aught
time always, imminently, invariably, whenever
way carelessly, haphazardly, nohow

ANYBODY anyone, someone
ANYCHIA chickweed, whitlowwort
ANYHOW always, haphazard, noway
ANYTHING aught, ought (lings)
ANYWHERE einwer, owhere, ubique, wherever
ANZAC australian, new zealander
ANZANIAN elamite
AOIFE *consort* ler
A-ONE ace(-high), best, bully, excellent, finest, first class, seaworthy, superior, tops
AORNIS *river to* styx
AOUDAD ammotragus, argali, arui, bighorn, chamois, sheep
APA eperua, wallaba
APACE fast, hastily, promptly, quickly, rapidly, speedily, swiftly
APACHE cocoa, criminal, dance, desperado, gangster, hoodlum, indian, killer, ruffian, thug
beverage tiswin
chief cochise, geronimo, victorio
indian arivaipa, athapascan, chiricahua, cibecue, jicarilla, mescalero, mohock, paduca, querecho, tonto, vaquero, yuma
jacket bietle
state arizona

APALIT lingoum, narra, pampango, tree
APAME *lover* darius
APARA armadillo, bolita, mataco, tolyeutes
APARGIA leontodon
APART abroad, afield, alone, aloof, aroom, aside, aspar, astray, asunder, atwain, away, bout, disassociated, distant, divorced, else, enisled, independently, individually, isolated, off, remote, removed, riven, separate, severed, solus, split, sundered, sundry, ytwyn
comb. dia, dis
APARTHEID discrimination, segregation
APARTMENT andron, block, bower, building, cabin, calefactory, cell, chamber(s), compartment, coop, digs, dingle, dorm (itory), duplex, ephebeum, flat, insula, lodgings, penthouse, quarters, rent, room(s), salon, saloon, single, solarium, spence, stanza, stew, suite, tenement, thalamus, walk up, wene, wone, woon
owned condominium
private mahal
rented let
small maisonette
upper sollar
APATETIC camouflaged, imitative
APATHETIC anesthetic, blase, bloodless, calm, casual, cold, comatose, cool, dead, disinterested, dowff, dull, emotionless, hardened, impassive, indifferent, inert, insouciant, languid, lethargic, listless, passive, phlegmatic, sluggish, stoic, stolid, supine, torpid, unconcerned, unemotional, unfeeling, uninterested, unmoved, untouched
APATHY accidie, acedia, cafard, calmness, comatoseness, coolness, disinterest, dispassion, doldrums, dullness, ennui, impassivity, inappetence, indifference, inertia, languidness, languor, lassitude, laziness, lethargy, listlessness, numbness, oscitancy, phlegm, sloth, sluggishness,

stoicism, stupefaction, stupor, supineness, torpor, unconcern, unfeeling
APATITE fertilizer, ijolite, mineral, moroxite
APAYAO isneg
APE (See also *kind*, below.) aani, alalus, anthropoid, boor, copycat, emulate, gunnera, imitate, imitator, mime, mimic, mock, parrot, pongid, portray, primate, rival, sham, simian, simid, simulate
comb. pithecus
cry gibber
dog-headed aani, cynocephalus
extinct dryopithecus
kind baboon, berok, camper, catarrhine, chimpanzee, durukuli, gelada, gibbon, gorilla, kra, langur, lar, magot, maha, mantegar, marten, monkey, o(u)rang (utan), pan, pongid, siamang, soko, tailless, wouwou
largest gorilla
-like animal lemur
long-tailed kra
man akut, alalus, pithecanthropus, primate
pert. pithecan
red o(u)rangutan
sacred aani
study pithecology
symbol of cunning, uncleanness
APEAK vertical
APELLES *friend* paul
APEMIUS zeus
APEMOYSYNE *brother* althaemenes
father catreus
ravisher hermes
APEPSIA indigestion
APER boar, buffoon, clown, copycat, imitator, mime, mocker, snob
APERCU conspectus, digest, glance, glimpse, impression, insight, outline, perception, precia, sketch, summary, understanding
APERIENT aperitive, calendula, dejectory, deobstruent, laxative, purgative
APERITIF absinthe, appetizer, arak, bartissol, boissiere, bonal, byrhh, campari, carpano, cassis, chambraise, cinzano, cocktail, cynar, dubonnet, duperrier,

ferrero, gran torino, kir(sch), martini, noilly prat, opener, ouzo, pastis, perroquet, pikina, positano, punt e mes, raki, retsina, sherry, spirits, stimulator, tomate, vermouth, wine, xeres

APERITIVE See APERIENT.

APERTURE bole, bore, breach, break, cavity, chasm, cleft, crack, cutout, eye, fissure, gap, hiatus, hole, hollow, interstice, keyhole, louver, mouth, opening, orifice, ostiole, passage, perforation, pinhole, pore, puncture, rima, slit, slot, spiracle, stoma, trompil, vent, window

APEX acme, apogee, auge, cacumen, climax, crest, crisis, culmination, cupula, cusp, epi, everest, genion, height, macron, meridian, noon, peak, pinnacle, pitch, point, ruff, spire, summit, tip, tittle, top, vertex, zenith
comb. apic(o)
ornament finial
pert. apical, apicifixed, apicillary
rounded retuse
toward apicad

APHAIA britomartis, dictyuna

APHAREUS *consort* arene
father perieres
grandfather perseus
son idas, lynceus

APHASIA alalia, alexia, allolalia, aphemia, asyllabia, speechlessness

APHESIUS zeus

APHID ant-cattle, aptera, blackfly, blight, chermes, collier, dimeran, greenfly, gynopara, homopter, insect, lice, louse, migrans, prociphilus, puceron
female fundatrix
honey tube siphonet
secretion honeydew
wingless alienicola

APHONIA aphrasia, aphthongia, dumbness

APHONIC mute, noiseless, silent, unvoiced, voiceless

APHORIA sterility

APHORISM adage, apothegm, axiom, byword, dictum, epigram, gnome, maxim, motto, pishogue, precept, proverb, rule, saw, saying, sententia, sutra

APHORISTIC axiomatic, crisp, epigrammatic, gnomic, piquant, pithy, platitudinous, pointed, proverbial, sententious, succinct, terse

APHOTIC black, dark, lightless

APHRIAM *father* joseph

APHRODISIAC amatory, amorous, ardent, erogenous, erotic, philter, philtre, potion, stimulating, venereal
kind almond, ambergris, artichoke, asparagus, beetle, cantharis, capon, castorum, caul, celery, chocolate, cinnamon, clove, cocoa, damiana, dewtry, feverfew, garlic, ginseng, honey, hyena eye, lizard, marjoram, morel, mushroom, nettle seed, nutmeg, onion, orchis, parsley, peppermint, pheasant, pimento, pistachio, quince, rhinoceros horn, roe, snail, spanish fly, sparrow-tongue, sweetbreads, testosterone, thyme, venison, vinegar, watercress, wild cabbage, yohimbe bark, yolks, yuhimbin
madame dubarry's artichoke, asparagus, capon, celery, clove, ginseng, morel, mushroom, nutmeg, peppermint, pheasant, pimento, sweetbread, thyme, venison
ovid's egg, honey, onion, pineapple
petronius's onion, snail, wine
pliny's dill, hyena eye, licorice, lizard ashes

APHRODITE acraea, anadyomene, androphonos, antheia, aphrogeneia, apostrophia, as(h)tarte, cnidia, cytherea, doritis, erycina, genetrix, limenia, love, melaenis, mignonitis, morpho, murcia, mylitta, nymphaea, pandemos, paphian, peitho, praxis, scotia, urania, vacuna, venus, victrix
beloved adonis, anchises, ares, dionysus, hephaestus, hermes, poseidon, vulcan
birthplace sea, suprus
carriage scallop-shell

companion cymodoce, pothos
daughter harmonia
defier acmon
girdle cestus
isle cythera, melos, milo
of melos venus de milo
oracle site aphaca, paphos
parent dione, jupiter, uranus, zeus
priestess hero
sacred bird dove, sparrow, swallow, swan
son aeneas, amor, cupid, eros, rhodos
temple acrocorinth, aphrodision, aphroditeum, cerigo, cyprus, cythera, kythera, paphos

APHROGENEIA aphrodite

APHTHA thrush

APHTHONGIA aphonia, aphrasia, dumbness

APIARY beehive, beeyard, hive, skep

APICIAN epicurean, glutton(ish)

APICULATE pointed, tipped

APICULTURE beekeeping

APIECE distributively, each, individually, per, respectively, seriatim, severally

APINOID clean, sterile

APIO arracach(a)

APIOLE antiperiodic, apiolin, emmenagogue, ether, parsley-camphor

APIS hapi, ptah
kingdom argos
manifestation serapis
parent apollo, laodice, phoroneus
slayer aetolus, cambyses

APISH affected, apelike, foolish, foppish, imitative, silly, slavish

APISHAMORE bed, blanket

APIUM celeriac, celery, herb, umbel

APLITE granite, haplite

APLOMB address, assurance, balance, ballast, composure, confidence, control, cool(ness), discipline, equanimity, equilibrium, imperturbability, nerve, poise, possession, presence, resolution, restraint, self-assurance, self-control, stability, skill, surety, tact, verticleness

APLOME allochroite, andradite, garnet

APNEA apnoea, asphyxia

APOCALYPSE disclosure, discovery, prophecy, revelation, showing, vision
beast dabbat

APOCALYPTIC anagogical, arcane, august, disclosing, exposing, imaginary, inscrutable, mysterious, mystic, prophetic, revealing, scriptural, visionary

APOCARP etaerio, gynoecium, strawberry

APOCATASTASIS restitution, restoration, subsidence

APOCOPATE curtail(ed), dock(ed), elide, shorten(ed)

APOCOPE abscission, amputation

APOCRYPHA *books* abgar, agrapha, baruch, daniel, ecclesiasticus, enoch, esdras, ezra, jubilees, judith, maccabees, manasses, tobit

APOCRYPHAL assumed, counterfeit, doubtful, dubious, fabulous, false, fictitious, heterodox, legendary, mythic(al), questionable, sham, spurious, unauthentic, unorthodox, unreal, unsanctioned

APOCYNACEA dogbane, oleander, periwinkle

APODA amphibia, caecilian, cirriped, leech, worm

APODAL footless

APODICTIC certain, demonstrable, demonstrative, inevitable, necessary, proved, tested, uncontestable

APOGAMY apomixis, homogamy, interbreeding, parthenogenesis

APOGEE acme, apex, climax, culmination, meridian, peak, pinnacle, summit, top, zenith

APOGRAPH copy, ectype, imitation, replica, transcript(ion)

APOLAUSTIC hedonistic, pleasure-loving

APOLLO acesius, agraeus, agyieus, alexicacus, archegetes, argyrotoxus, boedromios, carneus, caster, citharoedus, cynthius, delius, delphinios, dolphin, epibaterius, eulalon, grynaeus, helios, hunter, loxias, lykeios, moeragetes, moonshot, musagetes, paean, parnopius, patrous, phoebus, phyteus, plananistius, sauroctonos, smintheus, spacecraft, spodius, sun
abode helicon
attribute bow, lyre, tripod
beloved amphissa, calliope, chione, clytie, daphne, hyacinth, leucothoe
birthplace delos
challenger marsyas
consort aria, cassandra, coronis, creusa, cyrene, evadne, manto, psamathe, urania
enemy niobe
festival apollonia, carne(i)a, daphnephoria, delia, delphinia, didymaea, pyanepsia, thargelia, theophania
grandson caphaurus
horse pegasus
instrument bow, lute, lyre
master laomedon
nurses thriae
oracle site abae, delos, delphi
parent jupiter, latona, leto, zeus
pert. amphrysian, apollinarion, apolline, delian, delphic, paeonion, phoebean, pythian
priest abaris, calchas, chryseis, laocoon, panthous
priestess phoébad, pythia
rival idas
sacred spring castalia
sister artemis, diana
son aesculapius, amphissus, amphithemis, anius, apis, aristaeus, ascelepius, branchus, galeus, garamas, hymen(aeus), iamus, idmon, ion, laodocus, miletus, mopsus, orpheus, phaeton, philammon
spacecraft director petrone
spacecraft module intrepid
spacecraft parts columbia, eagle
teacher claucus
temple builder agamedes
temple site See *oracle site*, above.
tree bay, laurel
twin artemis
vale tempe
victim aloadae, caenthus, coronis, ephialtes, otus, phorbas, tityus

APOLLYON abaddon, demon, devil, fiend, lucifer, satan

APOLOGETIC defensive, deprecatory, excusatory, explaining, justifying, polemic(al), regretful, sorry

APOLOGETICS argument, debate, polemics

APOLOGIST advocate, champion, defender, excusator

APOLOGIZE acknowledge, beg pardon, defend, take back

APOLOGUE allegory, fable, fiction, myth, narrative, parable, story
pert. fabular, fabulous

APOLOGY acknowledgment, alibi, amends, atonement, confession, defense, excuse, explanation, extenuation, glozing, justification, makeshift, pardon, plea, pretense, pretext, regret(s), remorse, reparation, sorrow, vindication, whitewash

APOMIXIS apogamy, parthenogenesis, reproduction

APOMYIUS zeus

APOPHIS apepi, darkness, evil, serpent

APOPLEXY esca, fit, poplesie, seizure, shock, stroke
plant esca

APOROSA astrangia, coral

APOSEMATIC conspicuous, warning

APOSTASY abandonment, abjuration, backsliding, defection, disavowal, dissent, diversion, fall, heresy, lapse, perversion, reactionism, recantation, relapse, renunciation, reversal, withdrawal

APOSTATE backslider, bolter, convert, crawfish, deserter, dissenter, faithless, false, forsaker, heretic, lapse, mugwump, opportunist, pervert, rat, reactionary, recidivist, recreant, recusant, renegade, reversionist, revulsionary, revulsive, runagate, runaway, schismatic, seceder, secesher, secessioner, separatist, slippery, timeserver, traitor, transfuge, trimmer, turncoat, turntail
the julian

APOSTAXIS discharge, exudation

APOSTEME See ABSCESS, ULCER.

APOSTILE annotation, note

APOSTLE disciple, enthusiast, evangelist, follower, missionary, preacher, revivalist, teacher
bird catbird
canaanite simon
christ's andrew, barnabas, denis, didymus, james, john, judas, jude, levi, luke, mark, matthew, matthias, paul, peter, philip, simon, thomas
creed symbolum
of germany boniface
of indies xavier
of ireland saint patrick
of rome neri, scholar
of the franks remi
of the goths ulfilas
teaching of didache
zealot simon
APOSTOLIC ascetic, catholic, papal, scriptural
king stephen
manual didache
see papacy
APOSTROPHIA aphrodite
APOTELESM fulfillment, issue, result
APOTHECARY chemic(k), chemist, dispenser, dosologist, druggist, gallipot, pharmaceutist, pharmacist, spicer
weight dram, grain, obole, pound, scruple
APOTHEGM adage, aphorism, axiom, byword, dict(um), epigram, gnome, maxim, motto, precept, proverb, remark, saw, saying, sutra, suttah
APOTHEOSIS ascension, consecration, deification, elevation, exaltation, glorification, ideal, idolization, nonpareil, paragon, phoenix
APOTHEOSIZE canonize, deify, exalt, glorify, idolize
APOTROPAION amulet, charm, offering
APPALACHIAN allegheny
part cumberland plateau
peak mitchell
people melungeons
range alleghenies, blue ridge, great smokies, green mountains, shenandoahs
APPALL affright, astonish, astound, awe, confound, daunt, depress, discourage, disgust, dismay, distress, dum(b)found, enfeeble,

frighten, horrify, nauseate, offend, overcome, pain, reduce, repel, revolt, shock, sicken, stun, terrify, unman, weaken
APPALLED afraid, aghast
APPALLING awesome, awful, fearful, terrible, terrific
APPANAGE adjunct, allowance, appurtenance, birthright, dependency, endowment, grant, perquisite, prerogative, privilege, right
APPARATUS apparel, appliance, baggage, contraption, contrivance, device, dingus, engine, equipment, gadget, gear, graith, implement, instrument, machine(ry), material, materiel, mechanism, organ, outfit, paraphernalia, system, tackle, tool, utensil
criticus glossary, text, variants
APPAREL accouter, adorn, appearance, aspect, attire, clobber, clothe, clothing, costume, deck, dress, duds, embellish, equip, fare, furnish, garb, garment, gear, graith, guise, habiliments, habit, harness, invest, livery, outfit, panoply, raiment, robe, tire, togs, trappings, vesture, wardrobe, wear, wede
rich array
APPARENT breem, breme, clear, conspicuous, discernible, distinct, entitled, evident, exposed, glaring, indubitable, inescapable, manifest, notorious, obvious, open, ostensible, outward, overt, palpable, patent, perceivable, plain, plausible, probable, seeming, semblant, shallow, superficial, surface, tangible, unconcealed, unhidden, unmistakable, visible
APPARITION appearance, aspect, assign, blue devil, demonstration, display, doppelganger, dream, eidolon, epiphany, fantasy, fetch, figure, form, ghost, hallucination, ha(u)nt, hobgoblin, hue, idolum, illusion, image, larva, phantasm, phantasy, phantom, phasm, phenomenon,

revenant, semblance, shade, shadow, sowlth, specter, spirit, spook, sprite, stound, swarth, taisch, thurse, vision, wraith
APPARITOR beadle, officer, paritor, parure, summoner
APPEAL accuse, address, adjure, allure, application, apply, approach, ask, attract(ion), avouch, beg, beseech, bid, call, captation, charm, clamor, clepe, conjure, crave, cry, demand, entreat(y), fascinate, imperate, implore, imprecate, invocation, invoke, obsecration, obtestation, petition, piquancy, plea, pray(er), reference, request, rogation, seek, solicit, suit, summon, supplication
for judgment anacoenosis
pert. appellate
to prejudice ad hominem
APPEALING attractive, beseeching, catchy, cunning, cute, delightful, heartwarming, imploring, irresistible, nice, pleasant
APPEAR act, affront, answer, arise, arrive, attend, basset, beseem, blossom, bob up, bow, break, come, compear, crop up, dawn, develop, emanate, emerge, enter, fade in, fare, feel, flair, issue, kithe, kythe, look, loom, manifest, materialize, meet, occur, outcrop, peep, peer, perform, regard, rise, seem, show, sound, spring, surface, turn up, visualize
briefly glint
comb. phane
for represent
large bulk
likely bid fair
suddenly break, burst, irrupt
APPEARANCE advent, air, arrival, aspect, attendance, attire, blush, break, cast, coming, condition, countenance, cut, demeanor, disclosure, display, dress, effect, eidos, emergence, exposure, farrand, fashion, feature, figure, form, forthcoming, front, garb, ghost, glimpse, guise, hue, idea, illusion, image, impact, impression, issuance, leen, likeness, lineament, look(s),

manifestation, manner, materialization, mien, occurrence, ostent, phase, phasm, phenomenon, presence, presentation, pretense, prospect, resemblance, scene, seeming, semblance, sham, shape, showing, sight, spice, state, style, superficies, trait, view, visage, vision, vista
comb. phany
distinctive aura
first dawn, debut, premiere, spring
outward face, seeming, show, surface
personal presence
vague blur

APPEASE abate, allay, alleviate, assuage, atone, calm, concede, conciliate, content, defray, disarm, dulcify, extenuate, gratify, hush, lay, lighten, mease, mediate, meeken, mitigate, moderate, modify, molligy, pacificate, pacify, palliate, pay, pease, placate, propitiate, quiet, reconcile, relieve, sate, satisfy, slake, smooth, soften, soothe, stickle, suffice, sweeten, tranquilize, yield

APPEASEMENT *dishonorable* munich

APPEASER conciliator, pacifier, peacemaker

APPELLANT accuser, challenger, plaintiff

APPELLATION brand, calling, cognomen, denomination, description, designation, epithet, identification, label, metronym, name, nickname, nomenclature, sobriquet, style, surname, tag, term, title

APPEND add, adjoin, affix, annex, appose, attach, augment, clip, fasten, hang, join, pin, postfix, prefix, subjoin, superadd, supplement, suspend, tack, tag, unite

APPENDAGE accessory, addition, adjunct, adnexus, annexment, antenna, appendicle, appendix, appurtenance, aril, arista, arm, attachment, auxiliary, awn, barb, beard, caud, codicil, endite, extremity, feeler, filament, fin, flapper, follower, hanger-on, hook,

horn, leg, limb, lobe, nonessential, palpus, pappus, part, pedipalp, pendant, pendicle, pinna, pinnule, process, rider, satellite, spur, stipel, stipule, subordinate, suffix, swimmer, tab, tail, tentacle, trailer
ear-shaped auricle
having lobar

APPENDANT added, adjunct, annexed, associated, attached, consequent, incidental, subordinate

APPENDICITIS epityphlitis

APPENDIX addendum, addition, adjunct, annex, append, codicil, epilogue, index, outgrowth, pendant, process, projection, rider, sequel, supplement, vermix, vestige, vitals
operation appendectomy

APPERCEPTION assimilation, comprehension, identification, recognition

APPERTAIN apply, bear, belong, concern, fall, lie, pertain, refer, relate

APPETITE abdomen, appetence, alimentiveness, belly, craving, cupidity, desire, edacity, emptiness, famine, fondness, gorge, greed, gulosity, gusto, hollowness, hunger, inclination, liking, longing, lust, maw, orexis, palate, passion, penchant, polydipsia, propensity, relish, stomach, sweet tooth, taste, tendency, thirst, tuck, twist, urge, void, voracity, want, will, wish, yearning, yen, zest
abnormal asitia, b(o)ulimia, edacity, gulosity, hyperphagia, parorexia, pica, polyphagia, rapacity
canine phagedena
controller amphetamine, appestat
deficiency anepithymia, anorexia, anorexy, asitia
excessive gluttony, greed, gulosity, polyphagia
loss anorexia
reducer anorexiant
without stomachless

APPETITIVE famished, hungry, orectic, wanting

APPETIZER antepast, antipasto, aperitif, canape, caviar, ceviche, foretaste, hors d'oeuvre, kickshaw, night-

cap, releve, relish, sashimi, savory, smorgasbord, whet(ter)
wine dubonnet, madeira, port, sangria, sherry, vermouth

APPETIZING desirable, gustful, gusty, moreish, mouth-watering, nice, palatable, piquant, provocative, relishing, sapid, saporous, savory, spicy, tangy, tantalizing, tasty, tempting, toothsome

APPIADES concord, pallas, peace, venus, vesta

APPINITE diorite, monzonite, syenite

APPLAUD acclaim, approve, call, celebrate, cheer, clap, commend, compliment, endorse, extol, hozanna, hurrah, huzza, laud, praise, root, ruff

APPLAUDER cheerer, clapper, claque, patron, rooter

APPLAUSE acclaim, acclamation, approval, bis, bravo, call, cheer, clapping, eclat, encore, euge, hand, ovation, plaudit, praise, rooting, salvo, shout
paid claque
-seeking captation, esurience
sound bravo, hurrah, huzza, ole, rah

APPLE malus, pippin, pome
acid malic
autumn wealthy
baked biffin
bee wasp
berry billardiera, dumpling, vine
big new york
bitter colocynth
blight eriosoma
box eucalyptus
brandy applejack, calvados
canker bitterrot, fireblight
cider-making coccage
crab powitch, wharre
crushed pomace
curculio anthonomous, quadrigibbus, weevil
custard anona
disease anthracnose, bitterpit, blight, blister, brownheart, canker, mildew, rosette, rust, scab, scale
dried beefin, biddin, schnitz, snits, snitz
duck for bob
dumpling cob, grunt

emu colane
family malaceae
fly rhagoletis
genus malus, photinia
golden bael, bel, hog-plum, tomato
grunt cobbler, dumpling, pandowdy, pudding
juice applejack, cider, sidar
kind ambarella, ampalaya, astrachan, baldwin, beaufin, ben davis, coccagee, codling, cortland, costard, crab, custard, delicious, emeu, fameuse, gano, golden, granny smith, gravenstein, greening, grimes, guarender, hevi, jonathan, karela, kavika, macintosh, macupa, manzanilla, newtown, nonesuch, northern spy, ohia, oldenburg, paradise, pearmain, pippin, pome(roy), poropore, quarenden, queening, rambure, rennet, ribston, rome beauty, rose, roxbury, russet, saddle, shea, sorb, spitzenberg, spy, stayman, sweeting, wagener, wealthy, whitsour, winesap, york imperial
leaf-hopper empoasca
-like fruit bel, kei, pome, quince
liquor calvados
love tomato
maggot rhagoletis
mildew podosphaera
moss bartramia
of cain arbutus, strawberry tree
of discord contention, issue
of discord winner aphrodite
of hesperides quince
of peru jimson weed, physalis, shoofly
old rennet
pastry strudel
peeled dumpling
pert. malic, pomaceous
picker atalanta
pie hairy-willow
pie bed short-sheet
-polish bootlick, brownnose, court, fawn, flatter, make over
-polisher backscratcher, bootlicker, flatterer, sycophant, toady, yes-man
pudding See *grunt*, above.
pulp pomace, pug
ribbed costard
rot frogeye

sauce absurdity, bunk, nonsense
seed, johnny john chapman
seedling pippin
-shaped maliform, pomiform
shell ampullaria
shriveled crumpling
small codlin(g), griggles
-squire gallant, pimp
tart bowla
thorn datura, metel
-thrower eris
tree augophora, malus, pawpaw, shea, sorb
tree aphis eriosoma
tree borer amphicus, chrysobothris, saperda
winner aphrodite
winter esopus, pearmain, ribston
wood b(a)el
APPLEJACK brandy, cider
APPLEJOHN deusan, deuzan
APPLIANCE apparatus, application, appurtenance, contrivance, device, engine, equipment, gadget, gear, hardware, implement, instrument, machine, refrigerator, stove, tool, utensil
APPLICABLE apposite, appropriate, apropos, apt, catholic, felicitous, fit (ting), germane, happy, meet, pertinent, practicable, proper, relative, relevant, right, suitable, usable, useful
universally catholic
APPLICANT aspirant, candidate, contestant, petitioner, postulant, prospect, requestor, seeker
APPLICATION absorption, addition, adjunct, appeal, apposition, aptitude, assiduity, attention, bearing, bid, blank, concentration, connection, diligence, dressing, drudgery, effort, engrossment, epitheme, extension, form, industry, intentness, lenitive, perseverance, persistence, pertinence, petition, plaster, poultice, practice, relationship, relevance, remedy, request, salve, sedulity, solicitation, study, suitability, toil, tourniquet, usage, use, utilization
APPLIED accumbent, employed, practical, used, utile, workaday
APPLIQUE adorn, dag(ge),

decoration, ornamentation, overlay, superimpose, superpose
APPLOT apportion, divide
APPLY accommodate, adapt, addict, address, adhibit, adjust, administer, adopt, allot, appeal, appose, appropriate, ask, assign, attend, attribute, avail, bear, begin, bestow, betake, buckle, busy, carry out, clap, compare, comply, concentrate, conform, credit, da(u)b, deal, dedicate, devote, direct, employ, enforce, engage, entreat, exert, give, grind, hold, impress, labor, lay, liken, mind, minister, overlay, persevere, pertain, petition, ply, practice, pronounce, refer, relate, request, seek, serve, slather, smear, solicit, spend, spread, sue, superpose, tender, tip, toil, undertake, use, utilize, visit, work
for review appeal
furring brander
oneself attend, concentrate, intend, muckle
to consult, contact
APPOGGIATURA acciaccatura, backfall, gracenote
APPOINT accouter, accredit, allot, arm, arraign, array, assign, attach, authorize, award, berth, billet, choose, commission, constitute, decree, delegate, deputize, designate, destine, determine, dight, elect, elevate, empower, engage, entail, equip, establish, fix, furnish, gazette, indicate, install, make, name, nominate, ordain, ordinate, outfit, pick, place, prepare, prescribe, provide, resolve, select, settle, slate, specify, stall, steven, tailye, tailzie
as agent delegate, depute, deputize
APPOINTED destined, determined, forecast, foretold, predicted, prescribed
APPOINTMENT(S) accord, accoutrements, agreement, allotment, appurtenances, arrangement, assignation, assignment, berth, billet, charter, command, commission, date, decree, delegacy,

designation, direction, dispensation, employment, engagement, equipment, establishment, fittings, furnishings, interview, meeting, nomination, office, order, ordination, placement, position, post, rendezvous, reservation, set, station, steven, trappings, tryst

APPORTION admeasure, allocate, allot, allow, applot, arrange, assess, assign, award, balance, bestow, budget, carve, cast, deal, detail, dispense, distribute, divide, divvy, dole, give, grant, measure, mete, parcel, part(ition), portion, prorate, quarter, rate, ration, share, sort, split, weigh

APPORTIONMENT allocation, allotment, allowance, assessment, assignment, deal, dispensation, distribution, dividend, division, partition, repartition, share, sharing

APPOSE add, apply, compare, juxtapose

APPOSITE applicable, appropriate, appurtenant, apropos, apt, cogent, connected, fit, germane, incident, material, opportune, pat, pertinent, relative, relevant, suitable, timely

APPOSITION addition, application, appulse, conjugation, connection, junction, juxtaposition, relationship, syzygy, union

APPRAISE adjudge, apprize, assay, assess, audit, commend, consider, deem, determine, discover, estimate, evaluate, examine, gage, inspect, judge, mete, price, prize, rate, scrutinize, size up, survey, value

APPRECIABLE any, apparent, competent, considerable, enough, evident, palpable, perceptible, plenty, ponderable, sensible, tangible

APPRECIATE acknowledge, admire, advance, apprehend, apprize, approve, boom, cherish, comprehend, conceive, detect, dig, enhance, enjoy, esteem, estimate, evaluate, expand,

feel, flourish, grow, increase, judge, ' know, like, love, measure, multiply, prize, rate, realize, recognize, regard, relish, respect, savor, taste, treasure, understand, value

APPRECIATION appraisal, commentary, criticism, critique, discrimination, estimation, eye, gratitude, growth, gusto, recognition, respect, review, sense

APPRECIATIVE aware, cognizant, conscious, grateful, thankful

APPREHEND anticipate, appreciate, arrest, attach, behold, believe, capture, catch, comprehend, conceive, cop, detain, discover, dread, endoute, expect, fear, foresee, get, grab, grasp, gripe, imagine, intue, intuit, know, lag, misdoubt, nab, note, overtake, perceive, pick up, pinch, recognize, scan, see, seize, sensate, sense, suppose, suspect, take, understand

APPREHENSION abduction, alarm, anticipation, anxiety, arrest, awe, capture, care, comprehension, conception, concern, detention, distrust, doubt, dread, fear, foreboding, fray, idea, intellection, intelligence, intuition, meaning, misgiving, mistrust, noesis, observation, opinion, pain, pang, panic, perception, phobia, premonition, presage, presentiment, scan, seizure, solicitude, suspense, suspicion, understanding, uneasiness, worry

APPREHENSIVE afraid, all-overish, anticipative, anxious, apt, bright, cognizant, conscious, diffident, discerning, distrustful, disturbed, doubtful, fearful, jittery, jumpy, knowing, misgiving, morbid, nervous, perceptive, qualmish, qualmy, quick, solicitous, streaky, uneasy, upset, worried

APPRENTICE amateur, aprendiz, assistant, beginner, bind, boot, bound, boy, bursch(e), cub, grommet, helper, indenture, jackaroo, journeyman, learner, neo-

phyte, novice, novitiate, postulant, probationer, squarecap, subordinate, tiro, trainee, turnover, tyro, underling, understrapper

APPRENTICESHIP indenture, servitude

APPRISE acquaint, advise, betray, brief, certiorate, disclose, discover, divulge, inform, instruct, notify, orient, proclaim, publish, reveal, teach, tell, warn

APPRIZE appraise, appreciate, assess, price, value

APPROACH abord, access, accost, address, adit, advance, advent, aggress, anear, appeal, approximate, appulse, argument, arrival, arrive, attempt, begin, board, bid, breast, broach, close, come, coming, commence, consult, converge(ence), court, cultivate, draw, ease, edge up, entrance, entree, essay, forthcome, gain, gather, impend, influence, initiate, introduce, loom, method, near, negotiate, nere, nigh, offer, oncoming, overture, passage, path, present, proach, propose, proposition, road, sidle, solicit, sound, stalk, step up, style, succeed, trench, try, verge, way, woo

shot chip

APPROBATE approve, commend, sanction, smile on

APPROBATION acclaim, admiration, applause, approof, approval, authority, credit, esteem, favor, loange, plaudit, praise, proof, regard, repute, respect, sanction, test, trial

APPROPRIATE accroach, acquire, add, adopt, allocate, allot, annex, applicable, apply, apportion, apposite, apropos, apt, arrogate, asself, assign, assimilate, assume, attribute, becoming, befitting, belonging, borrow, burglarize, claim, comely, commandeer, condign, confiscate, conformable, convert, copy, correct, devote, digest, due, embezzle, expedient, expropriate, felicitous, fit(ting), fitty, germane, grab(ble),

happy, idonesus, impound, individual, inspired, intrinsic, just, kosher, legitimate, meet, monopolize, neat, pat, pertinent, preempt, proper, relative, relevant, right, secrete, seemly, seize, separate, special, suitable, take, timely, usurp, worthy
illegally convert, embezzle, heist, lift, loot, pilfer, pirate, purloin, rob, steal

APPROPRIATION adoption, allotment, annexation, arrogation, assumption, attachment, embezzlement, financing, fund, grant, money, piracy, plagiarism, possession, preemption, subsidy, subvention, taking, theft, usurpation

APPROVAL acceptance, acclaim, amen, applause, approbation, approof, assent, blessing, commendation, compliment, confirmation, congratulation, consent, countenance, credit, eclat, endorsement, esteem, favor, homage, kudos, permission, plaudit, praise, ratification, regard, sanction, suffrage, support
automatic rubber stamp
exclamation of aha, amen, attaboy, aye, bis, bravo, bully, encore, evviva, fine, good, great, hotcha, hurrah, swell, viva
sound See APPLAUSE.

APPROVE accept, acclaim, adopt, advocate, affirm, allow, applaud, appreciate, approbate, attest, authenticate, authorize, bless, boost, buy, canonize, certify, clear, commend, compliment, concur, confirm, consent, convict, corroborate, countenance, endorse, evidence, esteem, exhibit, favor, homologate, like, manifest, okay, okeh, pass, praise, prize, ratify, recommend, sanction, support, test, try, uphold, validate, value, vote

APPROVED accepted, authentic, conventional, groovy, orthodox, popular, standard

APPROXIMATE about, adjoin, almost, approach, circa, close, estimate, general, near, resemble, rough, similar, simulate

APPROXIMATELY about, adjacent, almost, around, circa, crudely, generally, hereabouts, more or less, much, nearly, nigh, practically, roughly, roundly, say, toward

APPROXIMATION approach, counterfeit, proximity

APPULSE apposition, approach, collision, conjunction

APPURTENANCE(S) accessory, accretion, additum, adjunct, annex, apparatus, appendage, appointments, belongings, chattels, duds, effects, equipment, gear, furnishing, instrument, nonessential, paraphernalia, pendicle, perquisite, possession, property, things, trappings, traps

APRICOT ansu, anzu, blenheim, mebo, orange, peach, prunus, titian, ume
-colored armeniaceous
confection meebos
cordial aprivette, persico(t)
dried meebos
palm cocos
plum amygdalus
scale lecanium
vine maypop

APRIL *birthstone* diamond
first all fool's day
fool dupe, gowk, pasqueflower
13th black monday

A PRIORI categorical, deductive, dialectical, non-analytic, presumptive, presupposed, pure
knowledge intuition
principle premise

APRON barmcloth, barmskin, bib, bishop, boot, brat(tle), canvas, cap, cover, daidl(i)e, dick(ey), ephod, flap, gaberdine, gremial, hoover, pinafore, praskeen, protection, protector, ramp, runway, shield, skirt, slop, smock, tablier, tarmac, tayo, tier, touser, vat
leather barmfel, barmskin, barvell, dick, dick(e)y
-man mechanic
silk gremial
top bib

APROPOS about, applicable, apposite, appropriate, apt, fit, germane, happy, incidentally, material, meet, opportune, pat, pertinent, pointed, proper, relevant, suitable, timely

APSE alcove, apsidiole, apsis, arch, chevet, concha, niche, recess, throne, transept
pert. apsidal

APSINTHION wormwood

APSU chaos
consort tiamat
son and messenger mummu

APSYRTUS *father* aeetes
sister and slayer medea

APT adaptable, ad rem, adroit, alert, apposite, apprehensive, appropriate, apropos, aspert, astucious, befitting, brainy, bright, capable, capacious, clever, consonant, deft, dextrous, disposed, expert, fain, feat, felicitous, fit(ting), germane, given, handy, happy, idoneus, inclined, intelligent, kittle, liable, likely, meet, neat, opportune, pat, pertinent, probable, prompt, prone, proper, qualified, quick, ready, relevant, skillful, smart, suitable, to the point, toward, willing

APTERAL finless, limbless, wingless

APTERYX bird, ioa, kivi(kivi), kiwi(kiwi), moa, oweni, ratite

APTITUDE ability, aptness, art, bent, brilliance, capability, capacity, craft, faculty, felicity, fitness, flair, genius, gift, head, inclination, instinct, intelligence, knack, leaning, liability, potential, predilection, proclivity, propensity, quickness, readiness, sense, skill, talent, tendency, turn, verve, wit

APTYALISM asialia

APULEIUS *work* golden ass, metamorphoses

APULIA *capital* bari
horse poille

APUS apodis, bird of paradise, crustacean, cypselus, micropug, swift, triops

AQABA elath, helana

AQUA aqueduct, fountain, liquid, solution, spring, water

caelestis barbados water, cordial, rain water
fortis nitric acid
AQUAMARINE beryl, blue, chrysolite, gem
AQUANAUT frogman, skindiver
AQUARIUM bowl, fishery, fishpond, globe, pond, pool, tank
plant parrot's feather
AQUARIUS skinker, waterbearer
father pegasus
gem onyx
AQUATIC abyssal, aqueous, bathysmal, fluvial, fluviatile, grallatorial, hydatoid, lacustrian, marine, natant, natatory, neritic, oceanic, pelagic, water-living, watery
AQUATICS balneation, bathing, natation, swimming
AQUATINT engraving, etching
AQUAVIT akvavit, alcohol, brandy, spirits, water of life, whiskey
ingredient anise, caraway, coriander
AQUEDUCT aqua, arroto, arterial, canal, channel, conductor, conduit, passage, specus, trench
of sylvius iter
AQUEOUS aquatic, hydatoid, waterish
AQUICULTURE hydroponics
AQUILA eagle
friend paul
AQUILAWOOD See AGALLOCH.
AQUILEGIA capon's-feather, columbine
AQUILINE curved, curving, eagle-beaked, hooked, prominent, roman
AQUINAS, THOMAS angelic doctor, dumb ox
work summa theologica
AQUIVER agitated, shaking, trembling, trepidation
ARA altar, ararauna, blackbird, macaw, parrot, screwpine
ARAB See ARABIA(N).
ARABA alouatta, cab, coach, monkey, vehicle
ARABESQUE decoration, design, motif, ornament, pattern
ARABIA(N) aba, anezah, arabesque, bedouin, bedu,

brown, egyptian, gamin, himyarite, horse, ibad, nejdi, nomad, oman, quraish, saracen, saudi, semite, sleb, steed, tatar, urchin, vagabond, waif, wanderer, yemen(ite)
abode dar
alchemist geber, jabir
alphabet ain, alif, ayn, dad, dal, dhal, gaf, ghain, ghayn, jim, kaf, kha, lam, mim, nun, sad, s(h)in, tha, waw, zay
ancestor kahtan
ancient saha, sheba
animal fair akad
antelope addax
author antar(a), lokman, sandabar
banquet diffa
bazaar sook, suq
beads mizbah
biblical country sheba
bird, fabled hameh, phoenix, roc
bliss, state of kaif, kef
boat baggala, baghla, boutre, d(h)ow, sambuk
caliph ali, has(san), shereef, sherif
camel belool, deloul, dromedary, hejeen
camp douar
cap chechia
caravan cafila
chief ameer, amir, emeer, emir, ras, reis, say(y)id, shereef, sherif, shiek, sultan
city (See also under specific countries.) abha, aden, anaiza, beda, bera, buraida, chafra, damanh, damar, damietta, damma, dubai, hail, hauta, hofuf, irem, jidda, kuwait, manama, mareb, matrah, mecca, medina, mekka, mocha, mukalla, oneizah, qatif, riad, riyadh, sabye, salala, sana, saqqara, shaqra, sharjah, taif, wejh, yenba
coat See *garment*, below.
coffee mocha
coin carat, commassee, dinar, kabik, kohl, lari, peisa, riyal
commando See *guerrillas*, below.
cord agal
cosmetic kohl
country aden, afars, alg, asir, bahran, dhupar, egypt, hira, irak, iraq, jed, jordan, ku-

wait, lebanon, libya, mauritania, minaean, morocco, muscat, nej(e)d, oman, qashran, qatar, saudi arabia, sudan, syria, trucial states, tunisia, yemen
country, ancient hejaz, mareb, saha, sheba
date fardh, knola
deity alilat, allat, aluzza, ankarih, atthar, chai-alkaum, el-lat, el-makum, elozza, haubas, hobal, isaf, itha, khol, kozah, manar, naila, nasr, raham, ruda, sin, sowa, wadd, yaghut, yauk
demon afreet, afrit(e), djinn, eblis, ginn, jann, jin(n), jinnee, jinni
desert ankaf, bedu, dahna, nafud, nefud, nejd, nyd, petraea
dialect See *language*, below.
disease bejel
dish couscous
division asir, faiyum, hadramaut, hasa, hedjaz, mah(a)ra, mecca, medina, nejd, oman, sinai, suez, tehama, yemen
division, ancient deserta, felix, petraea, taima, tema
doctrine avicennism
drink bosa, boza(h), leb(b)an
drum taar, tarabooka
dynasty aghlabid, aglabite, hashimite, idrisid, idrisite
eden aidenn
epic moallakas
exclamation bismillah, mashallah
fabric abas, haik
fairy See *demon*, above.
father abba, ab(o)u, abuna
festival huffly
fighter plane mig, sukhoi
flour samh
flower bela, jasmine
fruit juice dibs
garment ab(b)a, burnoose, burnous, cabaan, ferijee, galabia, haik, ihram, thawb, thobe
gate bab
gazelle ariel, cora
gem aromatite
giant algebar, gabara
giraffe xirapha
greeting effendi
guerrillas al fatah, al saiqa, arab liberation front, black september, fedayeen, pflp,

plo, popular democratic front
gulf aden, kutch, oman, persian
gum acacia, kafal
headgear cord agal
headpiece kaffiyeh
hell's bridge al-sirat
herb anastatica, mustard, trefoil
hero antata-el-absi
hill tel
historian abd-al-hakam, al-bakri, ibn-khaldun, muqadassi
holy city fez, mecca, medina
holy flight hegira, hejira
holy land hejaz
holy war jihad
honor sharaf
horse anazeh, ilderim, kadischi, kochlani, kohl, nubian, palomino
horsemanship display fantasia
hut barasti
idol hubal, isaf, lat, near
infantryman askar
inn serai
island socotra
jasmine bela, sampaquita
javelin jereed
jinni See demon, above.
judge cadi, kadi
king faisal, ibn-abdul-aziz, ibn-saud
knife jambiya
land feddan
language lihyanite, mahri, sokotri
larch ithel
leader koleyb
league egypt, iraq, jordan, kuwait, lebanon, libya, morocco, saudi arabia, sudan, syria, tunisia
leather mocha
letter See alphabet, above.
lightship phare
lock dubbeh
lyric g(h)azel
marriage baal
mascara kohl
measure achir, ardeb, artaba, assbaa, barid, cabda, cafiz, caphite, covid(o), cuddy, den, farsakh, farsang, feddan, ferk, foot, ghalva, hariba, kiladja, kist, makuk, marhale, mille, nusfiah, qasab, saa(s), teman, woibe, zudda
milk, sour leb(b)an
mirage sarab, serab

mosque masjid
musical instrument arghool, kit(t)ar
myrrh commiphora
name ali
name, prefix ibn
nights barber abu sir
nights bird roc
nights character abu hasan, agib, ahmed, aladdin, alasnam, ali baba, alnaschar, amine, badawi, badoura, barmecide, beder, bedredd, bukhayt, danhasch, fatima, ghanem, haroun(al rashid), houssain, iram, judar, julnar, kafur, kalandar, kamar al-zaman, khalifah, king shahryar, labe, larrikin, maimoune, morgiana, nur al-din ali, schacabac, shahriman, shariah, sinbad, zobeide
nights cobbler maaruf
nights dervish agib
nights dreamer al naschar
nights dyer abu kir
nights fairy pari-banou
nights false caliph abu has(s)an
nights fisherman khalifah
nights hero aladdin, ali baba
nights merchant abu hassan, sinbad
nights narrator scheherazade
nights nobleman barmecide
nights prince alasnam
nights sailor sinbad
nights slave morgiana
nights sorceress amine
nights woodchopper ali baba
nights youth aladdin
noble See chief, above.
nomad bedouin, kababish, saracen, sleb
oasis alhasa, douma, jowf, qatif
official cadi, sheik
oil field abu saafah, ghawar, marjan, safaniyah, zuluf
oil minister yameni
pagan sanctuary kaaba
palm doom, d(o)um
panther fahd
paradise aidenn
peak djebel, horeb, nebo, sinai
peasant fellah
peninsula qatar, sinai
people See tribe, below.
people, ancient amalekite, midianite
philosopher al farab(ius), averroes, avicenna, farabi

physician avicenna, rhazes
pilgrim's dress iram
plant kat, retem
poem mathnavi, qasida
poet antar, kaab
porridge samh
port aden, mocha, suez
primrose arnebia, borage
prince emir, say(y)id, shereef, sherif
protectorate aden
puritan wahhabi
rain idol hubal
river bed wadi, wady
robe abayeh
romance antar(a)
ruler See chief, above.
sacred place harem
sacred writing moallakas
scarf cabaan
scholar ulema
scripture alcoran, koran
sea, river into indus, naraba, nerbudda
seashore tehamah
sect antidicomarian, coptic, druze, kihwan, wahibi
servant abd
sheep blackhead
sheikdom koweit, kuwait, qatar
shrine kaaba
shrub alhaj, camel's-thorn, kat, maalesh, retem
shrub leaves kafta
socialist brathist
spirit See demon, above.
strait bab el man-deb
sultanate mahra, oman
sun aldebaran
tamarisk talh
tambourine daire, taar
tea kat
teacher ulema
temple site abu simbel, ipsambul
title abuna, sheik(h), sidi, wazir
town, extinct mareb
tree ben, kafal
tribe absi, anezeh, asir, aus, beni abbas, dedanite, diendel, hagarene, harb, irad, jaalin, kedar, koreish, marabut, nebaioth, omani, shik, shukria, sleb, tema
turkoman shik
united republic See EGYPT.
utopia kaif, kef
viper echis
wagon araba
war cry tamaman
weight artaba, bahar, bokard, cheki, crat, danik, dir-

hem, farsalah, farzil, kella, maund, miskal, nasch, nevat, ocque, oukia, ratel, rotl, toman(d), vakia
wind samiel, simoom
woman's garment galabia
worry beads mizbah
yeoman yemen
ARABIC carshuni, garshuni, karshuni, thamudic
glottal stop hamza
grammar ajrumiya
script nastiliq, nesk(h)i
ARABIS molewort, mustard, rockcress
ARABLE cultivatable, farmable, fertile, plowable, tillable
land earth, farm, laine
ARACA guava, terminalia, tree
ARACARI bird, pteroglossus, toucan
ARACEAE arad, arum, calla lily, jack-in-the-pulpit, skunk-cabbage, sweet-flag, taro
ARACHNID acerata, arthropod, bug, cartare, carter, chigger, crab, eggmite, fag, gigger, harvestman, jayhawk, longlegs, louse, mite, nancy, octopod, pedipalp, phalangid, pique, sandworm, scorpion, solpugid, spider, stinger, taint, tampan, tarantula, tick, weaver
genus acarapis, acarus, acerae, araneida, argiope, attidae, ixodidae, lycosa, pholcus, uloborus
trap web
ARAFURA *sea island* aru
ARAGONITE alabaster
ARAH *father* ulla
ARAKAN *language* maghi
peak victoria
ARAL *river* oxus
ARALIA fatsia, hercules'-club, oxtongue, picris, sarsaparilla, spikenard
ARALIACEAE ginseng, hedera, herb, ivy, panax, shrub, spikenard
ARALU *ruler* allatu, nergal
ARAM syria
children gether, hul, mash
city arphad
deity rimmon
father esrom, shem
grandfather noah
language mandaean, syriac
nomad akhlame
script kharoshthi

tribe geshurites
ARAMAIC, ARAMEAN See ARAM, SYRIA.
translation targum
ARAMIS *companion* athos, d'artagnan, porthos
ARAN *island* irisheer, irishmaan, irishmore, kilronan
kin dishan
ARANEIDA See ARTHROPOD, SPIDER.
ARAPAIMA fish, pirarucu
ARAPUNGA bellbird, campanero
ARARA cockatoo, macaw, prosbosciger
ARARAT aghri-dagh, urartu
ARAROBA andirawood, centrolobium, goa-powder, sickingia, tree, zebrawood
ARATION plowing, tillage
ARATUS *agent* caphisias, euphranor, mnasitheus, polygnotus, xenophilus
ally pantaleon
chronicler polemon
enemy aristippus, aristratus, cleomenes, lydiades, megistonus, nicocles
father clinias
friend antigonous, arcesilaus, aristomachus, aristoteles, neacles, philip, timanthes
messenger xenocles
painter timanthes
rival speratus, timoxenus
servant senthas, technon
ARAUCANIAN *indian* auca(nian), huilliche, mapuche, moluche, pampa, puche, moluche, pampa, pampean, pampero, pehuenche, picunche, purelche, ranquel
ARAUCARIA bunyabunya, monkey-puzzle
ARAWA aoter, matatua
ARAWAKAN *indian* achaqua, apolistan, araua, arawak, aruac, atorai, bainoa, baniva, baniwa, bare, baure, campa, caqueto, chane, changoan, ciboney, goajiro, guana, guinau, ineri, javitero, jucuna, jumana, lorenzan, lucayo, maipure, moxo, paiconeca, passe, piro, puquinan, puru, siusi, tacanan, taino, tariana, ticunan, uaraycu, uarekena, uran, wapisiana, waura, ypurinan
ARBALEST crossbow, sling
ARBITER See ARBITRATOR.

ARBITRAMENT See ARBITRATION.
ARBITRARY absolute, authoritative, autocratic, despotic, discretionary, dogmatic, firm, highhanded, imperious, irresponsible, magisterial, masterful, masterly, oracular, peremptory, rigorous, severe, spontaneous, summary, thetic, tyrannical, uncontrolled, unrestricted, willful
ARBITRATE adjudge, adjudicate, appease, conciliate, decide, determine, intervene, judge, mediate, placate, settle
ARBITRATION adjudication, arbitrage, arbitrament, award, bargaining, conciliation, dayment, decision, diplomacy, diplomatics, intercession, intervention, mediation, negotiation, parley, settlement, umpirage
ARBITRATOR adviser, arbiter, conciliator, critic, daysman, decider, gobetween, judge, mediator, moonsif, munsif, odd(s)-man, overman, ref(eree), settler, umpire
ARBOR axis, axle, bar, berceau, bower, frescade, garden, grove, latticework, lawn, mandrel, orchard, pandal, pergola, ramada, recess, retreat, shaft, spindle, summerhouse, tonnelle, tree, trellis, walk
shaft cardan-joint
vine morning glory, operculina
vitae akeki, cedar, libocedrus, thuja, tree of life
ARBOREAL arboresque, dendral, dendriform, dendroid, sylvan, treelike, woodlike
ARBORETUM garden, nursery
ARBUSCULE cilia, hairs
ARBUSTUM copse, orchard, plantation
ARBUTUS epigaea, groundlaurel, heath, herb, ivy, mayflower
trailing ground-sweet
ARC azimuth, bend, bow, compass, curve, foil, folium, frostbow, halo, hance, octant, orbit, radian, rainbow, spark, swing

boutant buttress
curve sine
horizon azimuth
lamp monophote
measurer cyclometer
prismatic rainbow
ARCA arcida, arcula, box, chest, clam, dish, mollusk, paten, reliquary, shell
ARCADE ambulatory, arcature, arch, avenue, cloister, colonnade, dome, gallery, hall, lesche, loggia, passage, peristyle, portico, vault
ARCADIA arcady, eden, paradise, utopia
ancestor arcas
boar, pert. erymanthian
city alea, tegea
general teuthis
god ladon, pan
huntress atalanta
king aepytus, arcas, cercyon, cypselus, echemus, lycaon
man, poorest aglaos
nymph syrinx
peak cyllene, erymanthus, maenalus
peasant aglaos
princess auge
river neda
warrior ereuthalion
widow cecropia
ARCADIAN agrestic, bucolic, georgic, ideal, innocent, pastoral, rural, rustic, shepherd, simple
nightingale ass
ARCANE abstruse, cabalistic, esoteric, hidden, inscrutable, mysterious, mystic(al), obscure, occult, recondite, secret
ARCANUM elixir, mystery, remedy, secret
ARCAS *consort* erato
kingdom arcadia
parent callisto, zeus
son aphidas, azan, elatus
ARCE *ally* titans
kin harpies, iris, thaumas
ARCESIUS *grandson* odysseus, ulysses
parent euryodia, zeus
son laertes
ARCH alveolar, arcade, arcature, bend, bow, bridge, calcar, camber, chamber, chief, clever, concameration, concha, cope, cove, coy, crook, cunning, cupola, curve, diadem, dome, eminent, fauld, fogbow, fornix, gateway, great,

hance, hoop, hunch, impish, inbow, keystone, leer, loop, mantel, memorial, mischievous, mocking, opening, pauky, pawky, pend, pert, playful, pokey, prime, principal, roach, roguish, round, saucy, skewback, sly, span, squinch, support, sweep, testudo, vault, voussoir, waggish, wicket, zygoma
abutment alette
center coom
curve extrados, intrados
decorative bonnet top
fiend devil, satan
keystone quoin
kind basket-handle, equilateral, fixed, flat, horseshoe, lancet, ogee, ogive, primitive, rampant, round, rowlock, segmental, shouldered, trefoil, tudor
memorial pailoo, pailou
molding accolade, bandelette
part keystone, springer, voussoir
pointed lancet, ogee, ogive
roman alette
solid voussoir
surface soffit
ARCHAIC aged, ancient, antediluvian, antiquated, antique, dated, fossil, historic, obsolete, old(fashioned), passe, past, primitive, prior, venerable
ARCHANGEL angelica, cherub, gabriel, horehound, michael, raphael, satan, seraph, uriel
ARCHBISHOP becket, ecclesiastic, hatto, metropolitan, ordinary, prelate, primate
ARCHBISHOPRIC See BISHOP *chair*, BISHOPRIC.
ARCHDEMON beelpeor, belfazor, belphegor
ARCHDIOCESE eparchy
ARCHDUKE erzherzog
ARCHEBANC bench, settle
ARCHED bowed, cambered, camerated, concave, convex, coped, domed, embowed, hooplike, vaulted
ARCHEGETES apollo
ARCHEGONIATE acrogen, bryophyte, cryptogram, fern, liverwort, moss
ARCHEGONIUM calyptra, ooangium
ARCHELOCHUS *brother* acamas

companion aeneas
parent antenor, theanor
slayer ajax, promachus
ARCHEMORUS opheltes
nurse hypsipyle
parent eurydice, lycurgus
ARCHEOLOGY assyriology, egyptology, epigraphy, paleography, paleology, paleontology
ARCHER bowman, bowyer, butty, clim, clym, cupid, fish, marksman, sagittarius, sagittary, shooter, toxophilite
chief ahiezer
cuff fender
deity apollo, artemis
equipment tackle
famous robin hood, william tell
outlaw adam bell, caco
saint sebastian
screen pannier
skilled acestus
ARCHERY artillery, toxology
locker ascham
shot best-gold
target clout, hoyle, rover, white
term scud
ARCHETYPE ancestor, barre, ectype, essence, example, figure, founder, fravashi, idea, image, model, original, paragon, prototype, sample, standard
ARCHEUS anima mundi
ARCHIDAMUS *consort* eupolia, lampido
father zeuxidamus
father-in-law melesippidas
kingdom sparta
son agesilaus, agis, endamidas
ARCHIDUM fungus, moss
ARCHIL angolaweed, canary moss, capeweed, corcir, corker, cudbear, lecanora, orcein, orchilla, orsseille, persis, roccella, weed
source lichen
ARCHIMAGE enchanter, MAGICIAN, priest, wizard
ARCHIMANDRITE abbot, celibate, priest, superior
ARCHIMEDES *exclamation* eureka
friend hiero
invention screw
ARCHIPIN bursera, gumbolimbo, resin

ARCHIPPUS *butterfly* viceroy
correspondent paul
ARCHITECT artificer, artisan, artist, author, builder, contriver, creator, designer, deviser, founder, inventor, maker, originator, producer, strategist
famous adam, alberti, bernini, bezaleel, bramante, bruer, bulfinch, eiffel, gropius, klenze, luckman, mckim, mead, palladio, paxton, saarinen, speer, sullivan, von mises, wren, wright
ARCHITECTURAL architectonic, oecodomic, tectonic
angle quoin
apex acroterium
base dado, patten, plinth, socle
canopy baldachin, baldoquin, baudekin
convexity entasis, tectonic
design blueprint, diagram, draft, epure, plan, print
edge arris
feature belvedere
figure atlantes, atlas, caryatid, telamon
fillet annulet
molding architrave, bandelet
order attic, composite, corinthian, doric, gothic, ionic, modern, norman, roman
ornament See ORNAMENT architectural.
parapet bahut
pedestal acroter(ion)
pier anta
plan epure
presentation rendering, rendu
rib formeret
screen spier
style academic, baroque, bauhaus, bourbon, byzantine, cape cod, classic, colonial, coptic, egyptian, empire, english, etruscan, florid, french, georgian, gothic, greco-roman, italian, lancet, latin, medieval, modern, monterey, moorish, moslem, norman, palladian, persian, regency, renaissance, rococo, roman(esque), saxon, spanish, tudor
support baluster

topping abacus, architrave, capstone, coping, corona, crown, drip, entablature, epistyle, fastigium, frieze, frontispiece, head(board), header, hoodmold, larmier, lintel, pediment, sconce, tympanum, zoophorus
ARCHITECTURE (See also ARCHITECTURAL.) constitution, construction, structure, tectonics, workmanship
patron saint thomas
pert. architectonic, oecodomic, tectonic
ARCHIVE(S) annals, c(h)artulary, chronicle, collection, depository, document, gallery, library, muniment, museum, record, register, tabulary, tabularium, thesaurus, treasury
keeper scriniary
ARCHLUTE theorbo
ARCHON alderman, director, executive, magistrate, officer, official, ruler
ARCHWAY arcus, entrance, pailoo, pailou, passage
ARCITE *rival* palaemon
ARCTIC bleak, boot, boreal, chilly, cold, cool, freezing, frigid, frosty, galosh, gelid, hyperborean, icy, north, northern, ocean, overshoe, polar
animal throng savssat
archipelago franz joseph land
base etah, thule
bird arrie, auk, brant, fulmar, longspur, tern, xema
bluebell campanula, flower, harebell
bramble blackberry, raspberry
canoe kaiak, kayak, oomiak, umiak
cetacean narwal, narwhale
current labrador
daisy aster, chrysanthemum
dog husky, samoyed
duck eider
explorer amundsen, baffin, bering, button, byrd, davis, eric, franklin, frobisher, greely, hudson, kane, mcclure, nansen, parry, peary, rae, ross, stefanson, wilkins, willoughby, wrangel
fish bib, charr, flounder, liopsetta

gull xema
headland odden
herb arctotis, bartsia
island axel heiburg, ellesmere, jan mayen, spitzbergen, wrangel
jacket anorak
lichen famine-bread
lights aurora borealis
native alaskan, aleut, eskimo, hyperborean, laplander, lapp
ocean, river to coppermine, kolima, kolyma, pechora
penguin auk
plain tundra
plant ledum, marsh-tea
rocket parrya, plant
sea baffin bay, barents, beaufort, chukchi, greenland, kara, laptev, white
seal rabbit-fur
ship sealer
shrub bearberry, crowberry
transportation oomiac, sled, umiak
whale musticete
whirlpool maelstrom
willow salix
ARCTICTIS bearcat, binturong, cat, civet, panda
ARCTIUM bardane, burdock, thistle, weed, xanthium
ARCTOCEBUS angwantibo, lemur
ARCTOID bear, carnivore, raccoon, ursine, weasel
ARCUATE arched, bent, bowed, curved, hooked
ARCUATION arching, bending, bow, curvature, incurvation
ARD *parent* bela
ARDALUS *father* hephaestus
ARDEIDA bittern, heron
ARDENCY ardor, eagerness, fervor, intensity, love, passion, vehemence, warmth, zeal
ARDENT ablaze, adoring, affectionate, afire, aflame, aglow, alow(e), amatory, amorous, anacreontic, aphrodisiac, avid, biased, breathless, burning, convivial, cordial, corrosive, delirious, desirous, devoted, eager, enamored, enthused, enthusiastic, erotic, febrile, feeling, fervent, fervid, feverish, fierce, fiery, flagrant, flaming, flushed, forward, gledy, glowing, hearty,

heated, hot(blooded), impassioned, impetuous, intense, intoxicated, keen, loverly, loving, passionate, perfervid, red-hot, rethe, scalding, sensitive, sharp, shining, strong, torrid, vehement, violent, warm, wild, zealous
spirits alcohol, liquor
ARDILLA See SQUIRREL.
ARDON *father* caleb
ARDOR ambition, animation, calenture, dash, desire, edge, elan, enthusiasm, estro, feeling, fervor, fire, flame, fougue, glow, gusto, heart, heat, love, mettle, passion, pzazz, quickening, spirit, spleen, tapas, vehemence, verve, vivacity, warmth, zeal, zest
ARDU See SLAVE.
ARDUOUS burdensome, difficult, energetic, exhausting, hard, laborious, lofty, onerous, oppressive, steep, strenuous, tiresome, tiring, toilsome, tough, trying, vigorous, wearisome
AREA acreage, banlieu, belt, borough, capacity, circuit, close, compass, confines, country, department, diggings, digs, dimension, district, division, enciente, enclosure, environ(s), expanse, extent, faubourg, field, ground, kingdom, land, locale, locality, measure, neighborhood, part, piece, place, premises, province, purlieu, quarter, range, realm, region, scene, scope, section, sector, size, soil, space, sphere, spread, stretch, superficies, surface, terrain, territory, tract, tref, turf, vicinage, vicinity, volume, zone
combat arena, glacis, pit
diked slushpit
fenced compound, enclosure, fold, sept
fertile hammock
measure acre, are, arpent, braza, centiare, hectare, parish, perch, plethron, plowgang, pole, radius, rood, tan, virgate, yoke
open campus, court, haggard, laund, square
overgrown cogonal
paved causey

pert. areal, spatial
ploughed break
small areola
swampy slash
tidal clamflat
transition ecotone
treeless slick, steppe
uncleared bush
AREAR backward(s), exalt, raise, set up, stir up
ARECA arak, archa, betel, catechu, palm
disease anaberoga
AREFY dry, wither
AREIA athena
ARELI *parent* gad
ARENA amphitheatre, area, armageddon, battlefield, beargarden, bowl, bullring, campus martius, champ de mars, circus, cockpit, coliseum, colosseum, course, court, diamond, drome, field, focus, gridiron, gym (nasium), hippodrome, list, oval, palaestra, pit, platform, region, ring, rink, scene, space, sphere, stadium, stage, terrain, theater, tilting-ground, tiltyard, turf, walk
wall spina
ARENACEOUS arenoid, granular, gritty, sabulous, sandlike, sandy
ARENARIA catacomb, chickweed, sandwort, turnstone
AREOLA area, armlet, cavity, cell, circle, interstice, pit, ring, space, spot
AREPA griddlecake, pancake
ARES enyalius, gradivus, gynaecothoenas, mars, quirinus, theritas
accuser poseidon
companion enyo
conqueror diomedes, hercules
consort aphrodite, bellona, eos, pleiades
daughter alcippe, harmonia, hippolyta
gem ruby
nurse thero
oracle site thrace
parent enyo, hera, juno, jupiter, zeus
priests salii
rescuer hermes
sister eris
son ascalaphus, avenue, cycnus, cyenus, eros, eury-

tion, phobus, remus, romulus, thestius
victim halirrothius, pelorus
ARETAS *son-in-law* herod
ARETE character, crest, excellence, manliness, peak, ridge, top, valor, virtue
husband alcinous, dion, timonides
kin dionysus, hipparinus
ARETHUSA adam-and-eve, flower, nereid, nymph, orchid, rose
fountain site ortygia
pursuer alpheus
ARETUS *father* priam
slayer automedon
AREUS *brother* leodocus, talaus
father bias
ARGALA adjutant, bird, marabou, stork
ARGALI ammon, aoudad, arkar, bighorn, ovis, sheep, wool
ARGAN ironwood
ARGANTE morgain le fay
kingdom avalon
ARGEIPHONTES hermes
ARGEL asclepias, plant, solenostemma
ARGEMONE cardosanto, poppy
ARGENT blanch, cash, luna, money, moon, pearl
ARGENTINA brown, capelin, fish, herb, mirador, silverweed, smelt
alliance abc powers
ant iridomyrmex
arcade galeria
armadillo peludo, quirquincho
barge chalana
bird chunga
bourse bolsa
capital buenos aires
city acha, avellaneda, azul, bahia, bolivar, buenos aires, catamarca, cordoba, dolores, formosa, goya, jujuy, junin, labanda, lanus, la plata, la rioja, lujan, mar de plata, mendoza, metan, monte caseros, neuquen, oran, parana, posadas, puan, quilmes, rafaela, resistencia, rio cuerto, rosario, salta, san juan, santa fe, santa rosa, tigre, tucuman
cloth tarlatan
cocktail clarito
coin argentino, centavo, peso

corral tambo
cowboy gaucho, vaquero
dance cuando, tango
desert patagonia
dish chivitos, criollo, empanada, luna, parrillada, puchero
estuary plata
falls grande, iguazu
fiber plant caraguata
first lady evita peron
fruit cock's-egg
garment chiripa
general belgrano
indian abipon, api, lule, puelche, quarani, querendi, querendy, ranquel, taluhet, vejoz, vilela
lake cardiel, fagnano, musters, viedma
lake district bariloche
leader ellider, juan peron
liberator jose de san martin
measure cuadra, fanega, legua, manzana, sino, vara
mesquite algarroba, calden
native porteno
peak aconcagua, chato, conico, famatina, laudo, murallon, olivares, pissis, rincon, tronator, tupungato, zapaleri
physiologist honsay
plain pampa(s)
plant bromelia, caraguata
port bahia-blanca, corrientes, la plata, rosario
president aramburu, frondizi, illia, mitre, peron, rosas
province catamarca, chaco, chubut, cordoba, corrientes, entre rios, estero, formosa, jujuy, larioja, mendoza, newquen, pampa, patagonia, rioja, salta, san juan, san luis, santiago, tucuman
ranch estancia
range andes
resort bariloche, lalucila, mar del plata, miramar, riviera, villagessel
river atuel, bermejo, chico, chubut, colorado, coyle, cuarto, deseado, dulce, flores, grande, limay, mendoza, negro, paraguay, parana, picomayo, plata, quinto, rio grande, salado, sali, senguerr, tercero, teuco, tunuyan
statesman drago, saavedra-lamas

tableland patagonia
tree ambay, coco, curupay, tala, timbo
village tolderia
volcano domuyo, lanin, maipo, peteroa
weapon bola, machete
weight grano, last, libra, quintal, tonelada
wind pampero, zonda
wood curupay
wool cordova
worker descamisado
writer banchs, borges, echeverria, guiraldes, hernandez, lugones, wast
ARGENTINE calcite, capelin, fish, myctophum, pearlside, silver(y), smelt
ARGENTITE acanthite, argyrite, argyrose, silver sulphide
ARGIA *husband* polybus
parent oceanus, tethys
son argus
ARGILLACEOUS clayey, cledgy, doughy, pasty, slaty, spongy
ARGIOPE *husband* anegor
offspring cadmus, europa
parent teuthras
ARGIPHONTES hermes
ARGIVES danai
ARGO See also ARGONAUT references.
builder argus
helmsman ancaeus, glaucus, tiphys
leader jason
ARGOLIS See ARGOS.
ARGON *source* air, atmosphere
ARGONAUT acastus, admetus, adventurer, aethalides, amphidamas, ancaeus, areus, ascalaphus, asterion, asterius, augeas, butes, caeneus, canthus, castor, cepheus, eurydamas, fortyniner, hercules, idmon, iphitus, jason, miner, nauplius, nautilus, phalerus, phlias, pollux, polyphemous, wanderer
destination aea, colchis
goal golden fleece
hazard symplegades
leader jason
pilot tiphys
ship argo
ARGOS argolis, peloponnesus
capital mycenae
citadel larissa
enemy sparta

hero amphiaraus
island calauria
king abas, acrisius, adrastos, adrastus, crotopus, danaus, gelanor, inachus, lynceus, phid(i)on
monster hydra
princess danae
valley nemea
ARGOSY armada, craft, fleet, flotilla, ragusye, ship, supply, vessel
ARGOT cant, dialect, jargon, lingo, patois, patter, slang, vernacular, vulgate
ARGUE accuse, adduce, advocate, affirm, agitate, argify, argle-bargle, argufy, argy-bargy, arraign, assert, attack, attest, aver, bargle, bargy, bespeak, betoken, bicker, brabble, caffle, cavil, chop, contend, contest, controvert, convict, counter, debate, declare, deduce, demonstrate, disagree, discept, discuss, dispute, ergotize, evince, expostulate, fight, flubdub, fuss, hassle, implead, imply, indicate, infer, insist, jaw, maintain, manifest, mean, moot, move, orate, persuade, pettifog, plead, protest, prove, quarrel, question, quibble, ratiocinate, reason, rebut, refute, remonstrate, show, signify, spar, testify, wrangle
ARGULUS branchiura, carplouse
ARGUMENT abstract, address, affray, agon, altercation, ammunition, angle, apagoge, apologetics, approach, argy-bargy, barney, beef, brief, cajolery, case, clamper, combat, composition, contention, controversy, debate, defence, defense, demurrer, disagreement, discourse, discussion, dispute, dustup, elench, essence, evidence, fuss, ground, hassle, leitmotiv, lemma, litigation, logomachy, matter, opposition, pilpul, plaidoyer, plea, polemic, presentation, proof, quibble, reason, rebuttal, refutation, rhubarb, setto, spar(ring), subject, summary, text, theme, tiff,

topic, trilemma, tussel, words, wrangle
conclusive clincher, corker, crusher, dialectic, finisher, floorer, knockdown, sockdolager, squelcher
fallacious sophism
hater misologist
hatred of misology
heated battle royal
negative con
positive pro
sophistic fallation
specious claptrap, elench, moonshine, paralogism, pseudosyllogism, rot, solecism, sophism, sophistry
starting point premise
subject to moot
with alternative polylemma
ARGUMENTATIVE battlesome, cantankerous, contentious, disputatious, eristic, forensic, fratchy, quarrelsome
ARGUS giant, guardian, panoptes
bird peacock
-eyed jealous, keen, possessive, vigilant, watchful
fish scat
owner odysseus, ulysses
parent agenor, arestor, inachus, niobe, phrixus, zeus
pheasant peacock, rheinardia, tragopan
shell cypraea
slayer hermes, mercury
ARGUTE acute, astute, sagacious, sharp, shrewd, shrill, subtle
ARGY-BARGY See ARGUMENT.
ARGYRA *lover* selemnus
ARGYROL antiseptic, argenol
ARGYROTOXUS apollo
ARHAT lohan, mahatma, monk, rakan, saint
ARIA air, ariette, bravura, cantabile, melody, solo, song, sortie, sortita, tune
consort apollo
son miletus
3-part form dacapo
ARIADNE *consort* dionysus, theseus
gift to theseus thread
parent minos, pasiphae
slayer artemis
son thoas
ARIANRHOD *consort* gwydion
mother don

ARID bald, bare, barren, dehydrated, desert, desiccated, droughty, drouthy, dry, dull, empty, jejune, juiceless, lean, lifeless, parched, prosaic, sterile, thirsty, unfertile, unimaginative, uninteresting, unproductive, vapid, withered
ARIDITY drought, drouth, siccity
ARIEL gazelle, jerusalem, messenger, phalanger, spirit
adversary abdiel
master prospero
opposite caliban
planet uranus
toucan rhamphastos
ARIES ram
ARIGHT correctly, exactly, properly, rightly
ARIKARA *indian* caddo, ree
ARIL arillode, coating, pod, testa
ARIOCH *adversary* chedorlaomer
kingdom ellasar
ARION *father* poseidon
ARIOSE melodious, songlike
ARIOSTO *work* orlando furioso
ARISAEMA arum, greendragon, jack-in-the-pulpit, snakeroot
ARISBE *consort* dardanus, hyrtacus, priam
father teucer
ARISE accrue, amount, appear, ascend, attain, awake (n), bechance, begin, bristle, climb, come, derive, develop, emanate, emerge, exist, exsurge, flow, form, get up, grow, happen, issue, jump, levitate, lift, mount, occur, originate, pile out, proceed, raise, rear, rebel, redound, result, revolt, riot, rocket, roll out, soar, spring, stand, start, stem, stir, sourdre, surge, tower, upheave, uprear, waken, wax
ARISTA antenna, awn, beard, bristle
ARISTAEUS *consort* autonoe, eurydice
parent apollo, cyrene
son actaeon
ARISTARCH critic, grammarian
ARISTATE awned, pointed, spined, tipped
ARISTIDES *beloved* stesilaus

enemy themistocles
friend clisthenes
kin lysimachus, myrto, polycrite
tribe antochis
ARISTIPPUS *chronicler* dinias
enemy aratus
slayer tragiscus
ARISTOBULUS *pupil* ptolemy
ARISTOCRACY ancienne noblesse, aristoi, baronage, best, bluebloods, elite, fourhundred, gentry, haut monde, high life, knighthood, kwazoku, lords, nobles, nobility, oligarchy, patriciate, peerage, plutocracy, royalty, samurai, second estate, society, uppercrust
ARISTOCRAT best, blueblood, boyar, elite, eupatrid, gentleman, grandee, lord, noble(man), parvenu, patrician, peer
imitator buckeen
ARISTOCRATIC cavalier, high, noble, quality, tony
ARISTODEMUS *ancestor* hercules
kingdom messenia
son eurysthenes, procles
ARISTOLOCHIA birthwort, calico-flower, dutchman's-pipe, gooseflower
ARISTOPHANES *comedy* acharnias, birds, clouds, frogs, knights, lysistrata, plutus, wasps
enemy cleon
english foote
french moliere
son araros, nicostratus, philippus
ARISTOPHANIC broad, comic, mocking, satirical, witty
ARISTOTLE *beneficiary* theophrastus
birthplace macedonia, stageira, stagirius, thrace
category action, passivity, place, position, possession, quality, quantity, relation, substance, time
causes efficient, final, formal, material
cousin callisthenes
disciple peripatetic
element air, earth, fire, water
friend hermias
lantern (sea)urchin's-jaws

lectures acromatics
of china tehuhe
of 19th century cuvier
parent amyntas, nicomachus, phaesti(a)s
patron hermeias, philip
pupil alexander
school lyceum
teacher plato
wife pythias
work de anima, ethics, organon, poetics, politics, rhetoric
ARITHMETIC algorism, augrim, computation, numbers, sums
ineptitude acalculia
rules allegations
symbol cipher, minus, plus, zero
ARIUS *disciple* arian
protector eusebius
ARIZONA *buckthorn* bumelia
cactus pitahaya, saguaro
capital phoenix
city ajo, bisbee, blytheville, cortaro, eloy, flagstaff, fredonia, glendale, kingman, leupp, mcnary, mesa, morenci, naco, nogales, phoenix, prescott, safford, salome, scottsdale, tempe, toltec, tucson, winslow, yuma
county apache, cochise, coconino, gila, maricopa, mohave, navajo, pima, pinal, yuma
dam boulder, davis, hoover, roosevelt
desert painted
fish spikedace
gourd calabazilla
indian allentiacan, apache, arivaipa, cahuilla, cocopa, hano, hopi, hualapai, maicopa, mojave, moki, moqui, nambe, navaho, navajo, papago, pima, tewa, tulkepaia, walapai, yavapai, yuma
jay aphelocoma
lake mead
monument petrified forest
motto ditat deus
nickname apache, grand canyon, ocotillo
palm date, fanleaf
peak bangs, groom, hualapai, lemmon, meridian, pastora, san francisco, turret
range aquarius, buckskin, galiura, gila, hualapai, kofa, mohawk

region painted desert
river colorado, gila, puerco, salt, verde, zuni
ruby garnet, pyrope
ruins casa grande
sandstone coconino
shellac sonora-gum
state bird cactus wren
state flower saguaro cactus
state tree paloverde
ARJUAN arjan, kumbick, terminalia, tree
ARJUNA *brother* See PANDU *son.*
charioteer and helper krishna
father pandu
grandfather indra
wife draupadi, subhadra
ARK asylum, barge, basket, bin, boat, box, broadhorn, chest, coffer, flatboat, haven, hutch, receptacle, refuge, retreat, sanctuary, shelter, ship, wan(i)gan, wangun
builder noah, noe
holy aron-kodesh
landing place ararat
porter ben
ARKANSAS quapaw
capital little rock
city alicia, alma, blytheville, bono, camden, casa, dell, diaz, enola, hot springs, jonesboro, keo, little rock, moro, ola, perla, pine bluff, roe, rondo, texarkana, ulm
county baxter, clay, cross, desha, drew, izard, pike, polk, pope, sharp, stone, yell
indian caddo, cherokee, choctaw, osage, quapaw, wichita
lake conway, greeson, nimrod, norfolk, ouachita
motto regnat populus
native toothpick
nickname bear state, bowie state, land of opportunity
peak blue, gaylor, magazine
range ouachita, ozarks
river buffalo, cossatot, current, ouachita, saline, white
river, city on dodge city, hutchinson
state bird mockingbird
state flower apple blossom
state tree short-leaf pine
stone novaculite, whetstone
ARKOSE arenite, sandstone
ARLINGTON oklahoma, rummy

ARM accouter, activate, appoint, authority, auxiliary, blade, bough, branch, bras, cove, crane, equip, fin, fiord, firth, fit, fjord, flapper, flipper, force, fortify, frettum, furnish, gardy, garnish, gun, harness, inlet, instrument, jib, limb, member, might, oar, outfit, part, pinion, power, prepare, projection, protect, provide, radial, ready, rifle, service, sickle, sleeve, snord, soupbone, stock, strength, support, tappet, tentacle, transept, vane, weapon, wing
band brassard, maniple
bone humerus, radius, ulna
comb. brachio
guard bracer
having 8 octopod
lack abrachia
muscle biceps, triceps
of the law police(man)
oneself heel
on the free
ornament bracelet
pad manchette
part ares, chelidon, elbow, wrist
pert. brachial
pitching soupbone
small pistol, rifle
-twisting barley-sugar
upper brachium
vein basilic, cephalic
ARMADA armament, fleet, flotilla, navy, squadron
ARMADILLO apar(a), bolita, cabalassou, dasypodida, edemtate, kabassou, loricate, mataco, mulita, pangolin, peba, peludo, pichiciago, poyou, tatou (ay), tatu, tolypeutes, xenurus
giant peludo, tatou(ay), tatu
-like animal gryptodon
shell cuirass
small peba, quirquincho
ARMADO page moth
ARMAGEDDON battle, conflict, megiddo
contestant gog, magog
ARMAMENT ammunition, armada, armor, arms, artillery, battery, equipment, munitions, ordnance, provisions, weapons
works dupont, krupp, skoda, vickers

ARMAMENTARIUM apparatus, equipment, instruments, paraphernalia

ARMARIUM ambry, armary, closet, pantry, storeroom

ARMCHAIR bergere, cacqueteuse, caquetoire, fauteuil, windsor

ARMDET armilla, band, bracelet, ornament, tablet, torque

ARMED blazoned, equipped, forewarded, fortified, heeled, protected, ready, weaponed
band army, askari, posse
bullhead pogge
conflict combat, war, warfare
force armament, military, service

ARMENIA anatolia, minni, urartu
angel worshipper yezedi
apostle gregory
cap calpac
capital erivan, yerevan
capital, ancient ani, artashat, artaxata
city bitlisarzurum, erivan, sivas, trabizond, trabzon, van, yerevan
cracker bread lahvosh, paraghatz, peda
cucumber guta
dish sou-beoreg
fortress erebuni
game barbout
gypsy bosha
hero ara(me), haik, vartan
king ara, artabazes, artakias, artashes, artavasdes, artaxas, ashot, dikran, gagik, tigranes, trdat, zariades
kingdom ardsruni, cilicia, sophene, urartu, vannic
lake sevan, urmia, urumiyah, van
language haikh
monastic order mechitarist, mekhitarist
native armen, ermyn, gomer, hadji
peak aladagh, aragats, ararat, karabakh, taurus
priest's headdress saghavart
revolutionary group dashnakist
river ara, araks, aras, araxes, cyrus, euphrates, halys, kizil-irmak, kura, razdan, tigris, zanga
saint mesrop, sahak

stone emery
volcano aragats
ARMET helmet
ARMFUL lock, plenty, quantity, yaffle
ARMHOLE oxter, scye
ARMIGER armorbearer, (e)squire
ARMILLA annulus, bracelet, frill, ligament
ARMILLARIA agaric
ARMISTICE cessation, halt, lull, pacification, pax, peace, respite, suspension, treaty, truce
ARMOIRE clothespress, cupboard, wardrobe
ARMOR aegis, armature, arms, caparison, coat of mail, cortex, covering, defense, egis, graith, harness, mail, materiel, panoply, plate, protect(ion), sheathing, shell, shield, weapons, weed
arm bracer, brassart, brazzard, gardebras, mainferre, rerebrace, vambrace
armpit pallette, roundel
attired in panoplied
band tapul, tonlet
-bearer armiger, custrel, squire
body acton, backpiece, braguet(te), brigandine, broigne, byrnie, cataphract, corium, cors(e)let, cuirass, culet, demisuit, dossiere, ecrevisse, gambeson, harbergeon, hauberk, lamboys, lorica, mameliere, pansiere, plastron, surcoat, tace, tapul, tasse(t), tonlet
breast cuirie, mameliere
buckle bouchette
cap cerveliere
chain mail
clasp agraf(f)e
collar pizaine
comb. hoplo
cuirass anime
divest of demail
elbow couter, cubitiere, moton, passe-garde
face aventail, beaver, buffe, mentonniere, ventail
finger gadling
fluted maximilian
foot chausse, sabbaton, solleret
full bard(e), brigandine, cataphract, cuirass, jazerant, mail, maximilian, panoply, placcate, weed

garment under ac(k)ton, aketon, haqueton
hand gauntlet, main-de-fer, manifer
head and neck armet, aventail, aventayle, basinet, beaver, buffe, burgonet, cabasset, camail, capeline, casque, cerveliere, coif (fette), gale(r)a, gorge (let), gorgerin, gorget, hausse-coln heaume, helm(et), mentoniere, morion, pallet, pickelhaube, pizaine, salade, sallet, sconce, secret(e), tippet, ventail
hip brichette, culet, tuilette
hood camail, coiffe
horse bard(e), cataphract, chamfron, crinet, criniere, croupiere, crupper, flanc-(h)ard, peytral, poitrail, poitrel
horse's head chamfron, frontstall, testiere
jacket acton, gipon
kind chain, decorative, plate
knee genouillere, poleyn
lance rest faucre
leather corium
leg boot, braconniere, chausse, cuisse, greave, jamb(eau), jamber, tuille
light allecret, corselet
loop vervelle
neck and shoulders collar, colletin, gorget
ornament ailette
padded gambeson
pert. heraldic, heraldry
plate besage, cuisse, lame, maximilian, moton, tuille
rivet heads grains d'orge
scale cataphract
shield strap guige
shin schybald
shirt byrnie, hauberk
shoulder ailette, epauliere, monnian, spaulder
shoulder to hand ailette, armlet, brassard, cubitiere, epauliere, gardebras, gauntlet, monnian, passegarde, pauldron, rerebrace, roundel, spaulder, vambrace
16th century braconniere
skirt braconniere, lamboys, tace, taslet, tasse(t), tonlet
skullcap pot-de-fer
suit, half allecret
surcoat cyclas, jack
thigh to foot brichette, brigandine, chausse, cuish,

cuissard, cuisse, fauld, genouilliere, gorget, greave, jamb(eau), pallette, sabbaton, solleret, tace, tasse(t), tuille
undergarment ack(e)ton, acton, aketon, haqueton
without baresark, berserker
wrist bracelet, bracer, brassart, vambrance
ARMORACIA horseradish, mustard
ARMORED bulletproof, encuirassed, ironclad, loricate, panzer, protected, safe, secure
ARMORICA See BRITTANY.
ARMORY arsenal, depot, headquarters, heraldry, magazine, storehouse
ARMPIT ala, axilla, chelidon, oxter
pert. axillary
ARMS (See also HERALDRY.) ammunition, apparatus-belli, armament, armor(y), artillery, crest, gunnery, munitions, musketry, ordnance, panoply, tackle, war, weapon
blazoning armory
depository arsenal
exhibition wappens(c)haw
lack abrachia
limitation talks salt
of morpheus sleep
under equipped, trained
with open cordially
ARMSTRONG, LOUIS *nickname* satchmo
ARMY array, battalion, camp-royal, chivalry, cohort, crowd, crush, ferd, force(s), group, her(s)e, horde, host, impi, legion, military, militia, mob, multitude, press, ranks, rout, soldiery, throng, troops
address apo
advance vanguard
ant driver, foraging, legionary
award dsc, dso, fourragere, purple heart, silver star
brown khaki, rosario
camp barracks, etape, fort, stockade
camp head commandant
chaplain padre
clothes blue flannel, fatigues, gi's, khaki, monkey suit, od's, olive drab, uniform
coat blouse, capote, sagum

color khaki, olive drab, tan
commission brevet
core cadre
depot base
elite shock troops
engine See ENGINE *war.*
engineer pioneer, sapper
enlisted man gi-joe, mustang, nco
follower sutler
food chow, mess
front lines, sector
headquarters shaef
high-ranking personnel brass
horse cavalry, hussar, uhlan
horse, outfit castor
hostile enemy, foe
installation base, depot, camp, fort, post, station
kettle dixie, dixy
man See SOLDIER.
messenger courier, estafet(te), orderly
officer adjutant, aga, aide-decamp, ataman, banneret, brass hat, brigadier, captain, centurion, colonel, commandant, commander, cornet, field marshal, general(issimo), hetman, jemadar, lieutenant, luff, major, marechal, marshall, quartermaster, ressaidar, ressaldar, seraskier, sirdar, subahdar, subaltern, tab
officer, noncommissioned cadet, corporal, ensign, havildar, kick, lance-jack, maik, nco, sarge, sergeant, top kick, warrant officer, yeoman
organization cadre
pert. martial, military, stratonic
post exchange canteen
provisioner sutler
punishment strappado
quarters barrack(s), billet, casern, fort
school academy, ocs, ots, vmi, west point
signaler bugler
special forces green berets
staff officer aide
storehouse armory, arsenal, depot, etape
supplies materiel, ordnance
supply service quartermaster corps
survey reconnoiter
transport air-lift
troop arrangement echelon
uniform See ARMY *clothes.*
unit anzac, array, band, bat-

talion, battery, brigade, cadre, caterva, cohort, column, command, company, corps, detachment, detail, division, echelon, file, host, jansco, legion, lochus, maniple, mora, panzers, phalanx, platoon, ranks, regiment, sabaoth, shock troops, squad, task force, troop, wing
vehicle amtrac, caisson, camion, carroccio, jeep, tank
weapon ballista, bazooka, catapult, croc, onager, rifle, robinet
woman wa(a)c, wraf, wren
worm cirphis, grassworm, pseudaletia
ARNA arnee, arni, buffalo, buffelus
ARNA *father* uzzi
ARNE *consort* poseidon
son aeolus, boeotus
ARNEBIA borage, herb, primrose
ARNICA embrocation, leopardsbane, plant, stimulant, thistle, tincture
ARNOLD, BENEDICT *wife* peggy shippey
ARNOLD, MATTHEW *poem* dover beach, scholar gypsy, thyrsis
AROD *parent* gad
AROEIRA astronium, schinus, tree
AROID alocasia, apii, araceous, arad, arum, caladium, cunjevoi, konjak, krubi, mocomoco, pinuela, tania, tanier, taro, yautia
AROINT avaunt, away, begone, scram, stand off
AROMA bloom, bouquet, fetor, flavor, fragrance, huisache, nidor, odor, perfume, redolence, savor, scent, smell, spice, stench
AROMATIC ambrosial, balm(y), drug, flavorful, fragrant, fruity, mastic, mellow, musky, odoriferous, odorous, perfume(d), perfumy, piquant, pungent, redolent, sapid, savory, scented, smelling, spiceful, spicy
substance balm, balsam, bucco, buchu, myrrh, tolu
ARONIA chokeberry, pear
AROO indeed, really
AROSTOLOCHIA bathroot, bathwort, birthflower,

birthwort, bloody-nose, bumblebeeroot, trillium

AROUET voltaire

AROUND about, approximately, binding, circa, circum, close, confining, encircling, encompassing, enfolding, enveloping, environ, enwrapping, girdling, near, somewhere, surrounding, through, umbe, via *comb.* ambi, amph(i), circum, peri *the clock* constantly, continually, continuously, full-time

AROUNDIGHT owner, lancelot

AROUSE abraid, accite, activate, actuate, adawe, agitate, alarm, alert, anger, awake(n), call, challenge, cite, drive, elicit, enliven, escape, evoke, excite, fire, flee, foment, galvanize, heat, impel, incense, incite, induce, inflame, inspire, inspirit, instigate, interest, kindle, move, pique, provoke, raise, rally, rear, revive, rise, rouse, shake, spur, steer, stimulate, stir, summon, thrill, transport, turn on, wake(n), whet

ARPACHSAD, ARPHAXAD *father* shem

ARPEGGIO embellishment, flourish, roulade, sweep *effect* rasgado

ARQUEBUS *support* croc

ARRACACHA apio, arra

ARRACK araki, rack(apee)

ARRAH but, now, really

ARRAIGN accuse, appoint, argue, censure, charge, cite, criminate, criticize, demand, denounce, have up, impeach, impute, incriminate, indict, indite, interrogate, non-pros, peach, prosecute, summon, test, try

ARRAIGNMENT accusation, censure, charge, hearing, impeachment, indictment, presentment, truebill

ARRANGE 3 fix, lay 4 case, cast, comb, edit, file, form, line, plan, plat, rail, rule, size, tier, tift 5 adapt, agree, align, aline, array, besee, ettle, grade, group, order, place, range, ready, score, setup, shape, shift, stack,

stage 6 adjust, appose, assort, assure, codify, daiker, deacon, deploy, design, devise, divide, lineup, manage, ordain, scheme, settle, tailye 7 address, appoint, collate, compose, dispone, dispose, gradate, marshal, permute, prepare, provide, seriate, tailzie 8 classify, conclude, contract, contrive, organize, regulate, tabulate 9 catalogue, determine, harmonize, methodize, stipulate 10 articulate, distribute, straighten 11 systematize *beforehand* for(e)lay, preconcert *for* bespeak *in flocks* hirsel, hirsle *in folds* drape *in order* coordinate *in piles* cock, stack *in row* race *mutually* agree, concert *side by side* appose

ARRANGEMENT adjustment, allocation, appointment, array, attitude, cast, classification, collection, collocation, compact, composition, condition, contract, date, deal, design, direction, disposal, disposition, distribution, file, fix, gradation, grouping, harmonization, hookup, index, layout, method, order, ordinance, ordination, plan, positure, rank, scheme, sequence, setup, steven, structure, system, tontine, treaty *comb.* tax(eo), taxi(s), taxo, taxy *geometrical* lattice *pert.* tactic(al) *traditional* akol(o)uthia

ARRANT bad, base, brazen, confirmed, downright, evil, notorious, obvious, outlaw, outright, rascally, thief, thorough, unmitigated, utter, vagrant, wandering

ARRAS ariste, backdrop, curtain, drapery, hanging, lace, orris, screen, tapestry

ARRAU jurara, podocnemis, turtle

ARRAY accouter, acies, address, adight, adorn, affaite, aguise, align, aline, apparel, army, arrange(ment), assemblage, assemble, assem-

bly, atour, attire, bedeck, bedight, busk, clothe, clothing, company, deck, decorate, display, dispose, doll, don, draw up, dress, dub, equip, exhibit, fettle, fig, finery, furnish, fyrd(ung) garb, graith, grouping, habit, harka, host, line(up), marshal, multitude, muster, number, order, organization, ornament, panoply, parade, parel, place, pomp, quantity, raiment, range, reparel, robe, series, setout, show, vesture

ARRAYAN eugenia, gaultheria, icacorea, myrica, myrtis, pernettia, psidium, rapanea, shrub, wax-myrtle

ARREAR arriere, backward, behind(hand), late, overdue, remainder, unpaid

ARREARS debit, debt, default, deficit, indebtedness, liability, obligation, shortcoming

ARRECT attentive, direct, erect, lifted, raised

ARRENOTOKY partenogenesis

ARREST absorb, apprehend, attach, balk, bridle, caption, capture, catch, check, collar, confine, control, cop, curb, custody, deadlock, delay, detain, detention, dwarf, end, engage, finger, fob, frustrate, grab, halt, hinder, hindrance, hold, imprison(ment), incarcerate, intercept, interfere, interrupt, jail, lag, nab, nick, nip, obstruct, occupy, pick up, pinch, reest, restrain, retard, rivet, run in, secure, seize, seizure, sist, slough, slow, stalemate, standstill, stay, still, stop, stunt, suspend, take, thwart, vag *attention* attract, impress *writ* capias

ARRESTING bold, impressive, magnetic, pleasing, striking

ARRIBA cacao

ARRIDE elate, gratify, please

ARRIE auk(let), murre

ARRIERE behind, rear *-pensee* reservation, sequel

ARRIS angle, arridge, hip, line, peen, pien(d), ridge

ARRISH eddish, sequel, stubble

ARRISWAYS diagonally, ridgewise

ARRIVAL achievement, advent, appearance, approach, attainment, call, comer, coming, emergence, ikbal, incoming, reaching, venue, visitation
time eta

ARRIVE accomplish, achieve, alight, appear, approach, attain, blow in, bob up, check in, come, debark, disembark, enter, find, gain, get in, happen, hent, join, land, lend, light, moor, obtain, occur, parvenu, pop up, pull in, punch in, reach, rive, show up, strike, turn up, upcome, upstart, visit
at bring, educe, estimate, fetch, guess
at settlement agree

ARRIVEDERCI See GOODbye.

ARRIVISTE nouveau riche, parvenu, snob

ARROGANCE affront, airs, assumption, audacity, bobance, boldness, disdain, effrontery, egotism, haughtiness, hauteur, hubris, hybris, insolence, pride, succudry, surquidry, swank, tumor

ARROGANT affected, aloof, assuming, audacious, bold, brazen, cavalier, cocky, contemptuous, contumelious, coxy, disdainful, domineering, fastuous, forward, haughty, hautan, highfaluting, highhat, hoitytoity, huffy, imperious, impertinent, impudent, insolent, insulting, lofty, lordly, magisterial, masterful, officious, overbearing, overweening, peremptory, pompous, presumptuous, pretentious, proud, snobbish, stately, stuck up, supercilious, superior, surly, toplofty, tumorous, uppish, uppity, upstage, vain, wanton, wlonk

ARROGATE adopt, appropriate, ascribe, assign, assume, attribute, claim, confiscate, grab, preempt, presume, seize, take, usurp

ARROW barb, bolt, dart, director, fishtail, flane, flo, flower, fly, forkhead, ganyie, garrot, missile, pin, pointer, projectile, quarrel, reed, rod, rover, sagitta, shaft, shoot, shot, sign, spinner, sumpit(an), vire, zoom
arum peltandra, tuckahoe
barbed pheon
barbless butt shaft
body stele
bundle sheaf
case ascham, quiver
comb. belo
discharge twang
feathered vire
fire malleolus
fit to string nock
grass aristida, triglochin
handle stele
kind bobtail, broad, chested, dogbolt, fishtail, footed, forkhead, pheon, self, sprite
maker boyer, fletcher
notch nock
part barb, butt, feather, head, nock, penma, pile, shaft, stele
pert. sagittal, sagittate, sagittiform
point barb, beard, hook, neb, wing, witter
poison antiar(in), curare, curari, echugin, erythrophleine, haya, inee, ourari, sumpit(an), upas, urari, wagogo, woorali
-shaped beloid, mastate, saggital, sagittate
shooter bow
short sprite
spinning vire
stone belemnite
string nock
thrower anisocycle
wobbling fishtail

ARROWHEAD artifact, broadhead, bunt, crowbill, dart, fluke, forkhead, iztle, neolith, pheon, pile, sagittari, spiculum

ARROWROOT ararao, araru, arum, calathea, canna, coontie, curcuma, maranta, mehl, musa, pia, sagu, starch, tacca, tapioca, thalia, tikor

ARROWWOOD alder, pluchea, sericotheca, viburnum, wahoo

ARROWWORM chaetognath, sagitta

ARROYO barranca, brook, canyon, channel, creek, draw, gap, gorge, gulch, gull(y), hondo, ravine, stream, watercourse, zanja

ARSAPHES hershef, osiris

ARSENAL ammo dump, armo(u)ry, depot, dump, gun park, magazine, repertory, storage, storehouse, supply

ARSENATE *compound* adamite, adelite, erinite, erythrite, sarkinite

ARSENIC orpiment, poison, realgar
bloom arsenolite
compound alloclasite, arsenide, claudetite, cobalite, erinite, jordanite, mispickel, speiss
white ratsbane

ARSHIN altschin, gaz, gez, guz
1/24th parma(c)k

ARSINOE *consort* lagus, lysimachus, philip, ptolemy
nurse to orestes
parent berenice, lysimachus, ptolemy
sister cleopatra
slayer antony
son ptolemy

ARSIPPE *father* minyas

ARSIS accent, beat, cadence, downbeat, ictus, meter, rhythm, syllable, upbeat
opposite thesis

ARSON burning, cantle, crime, felony, fire, incendiarism, pyromania

ARSONIST criminal, felon, firebug, incendiary, pyromaniac

ARSPHENAMINE salvarsan

ART address, adroitness, aptitude, ars, artifice, artistry, beauty, business, contrivance, craft, cunning, decoration, deftness, depiction, descant, design, device, dexterity, discant, duplicity, engraving, faculty, felicity, field, finesse, genre, handicraft, illustration, ingenuity, knack, kunst, learning, magic, mechanics, method, mister, mystery, painting, plan, practice, practise, principles, profession, quality, readiness, representation, science, sculpture, skill, technic(s), technique, technology, trade, trickery, wile, wit

ancient, pert. paleotechnic
black alchemy, conjuration, demonology, diablerie, evil, magic, necromancy, sorcery, witchcraft, wizardry
brown argentina, mirador
comb. craft, ery, techno
cult dada
deity apollo, minerva, muses
diabolic devil(t)ry
domestic home economics, sewing
dramatic stage, theater
element ethos
experimental avant-garde
for art's sake ars gratia artis
form collage, engraving, etching, mezzotint, painting, sculpture
gallery museum
glass See GLASS *art.*
gray blue-red, quaker, sea-mist
gum cleaner, eraser
hermetic alchemy
leg cheesecake
lover aesthete, collector, connoisseur, dilettante, esthete, votary
magic withercraft
manual craft, sloid, slojd, sloyd
material brush, canvas, chalk, charcoal, crayon, easel, ink, oils, paint (brush), palette(knife), paper, sketchbook, spatula, spray gun, stump
mysterious cab(b)ala, kab(b)ala, qabbala(h)
object bibelot, curio, figurine, vase, virtu
occult theurgy
patron angel, berenson, maecenas, sponsor
plastic sculpture
saint eloi
school american, barbizon, bauhaus, blue rider, bolognese, british, dutch, eclectic, flemish, florentine, french, futurism, honfleur, italian, lombard, milanese, neapolitan, paduan, plein-air, preraphaelite, raphaelite, roman, sienese, tuscan, umbrian, venetian
shoddy bondieuserie
show exhibit, opening, vernissage
song kunstlied, lieder
style abstract, baroque, classical, classicism, cloisonnism, constructivism,

cubism, dada, dadism, divisionism, expressionism, fauvism, futurism, genre, gothicism, idealism, impressionism, intimism, mannerism, modernism, naturalism, neoclassical, nonobjectivism, objectivism, ornamentalism, pointillism, pop, primitivism, purism, realism, representationism, romanesque, romanticism, suprematism, surrealism, symbolism, synthesism, traditionalism, vorticism
taste for virtu
truth in verism
ware knickknack
work acrylic, charcoal, collage, drawing, engraving, etching, oil, painting, pastel, sketch, splatterwork, tempera, watercolor
worshiper artolater
ARTAGUS *country* spain
ARTAXERXES See AHASUERUS.
ARTEGAL *bride* britomartis
ARTEL cooperative, guild
ARTEMAS *companion* paul
ARTEMIS agrotera, alphaea, amarysia, apollousa, astrateia, atalanta, auge, bendis, brauronia, britomartis, calliste, caryatis, cedreatis, cynthia, daphnaea, delia, diana, diane, dictynna, eurippa, hemerasia, huntress, hymnia, iocheaira, laphria, leucophryne, limnaea, lochia, lygodesma, moon, orthia, phoebe, polymastus, pyronia, selene, tauropolos, upis
attribute arrow, bow, quiver
beloved endymion
birthplace delos
brother apollo
companion aura, opis, rhodope, thea
enemy niobe
festival brauronia, munychia, thargelia
parent demeter, dionysus, isis, leto, persephone, zeus
priestess iphigenia
student chiron
temple artemision
victim actaeon, admetus, ariadne, callisto, cenchrias, chione, oeneus, orion
ARTEMISIA budbrush, dusty miller, plant, sagebrush, salvia, shrub, wormwood

ARTERIAL See ARTERY.
ARTERY anonyma, aorta, avenue, blood vessel, canal, carotid, channel, coeliac, conduit, course, dorsalis, drive, emulgent, expressway, freeway, highway, ligament, pass, passage(way), path, profunda, pulse, radial, railroad, river, road, route, sciatic, street, thoroughfare, throughway, thruway, trachea, vessel, way
coating extima
deep-seated profunda
from aorta coronary
inflammation exarteritis
main aorta
neck carot(o)id
pulsation ictus
ARTFUL accomplished, adept, adroit, agile, artificial, artistic, crafty, crooked, cunning, deceitful, deep, designing, dextrous, diplomatic, disarming, downy, foxy, ingenious, ingratiating, knowing, politic, practical, scheming, schemy, shrewd, skillful, sly, smooth, spurious, stealthy, suave, subdolous, subtile, tricky, vulpine, wily
dodger dawkins, deceiver, rascal
ARTHA end, purpose, success
ARTHEL arval, arvel, averil, feast
ARTHRITIS arthralgia, arthrosia, carpitis, gout
counter-irritant veratrine
remedy acth, cortisone
symptom ache, pain
ARTHRON articulation, joint
ARTHROPOD acerata, anthracomartus, appendiculata, arachnid, araneid, belinurus, centipede, chilopod, crab, crustacean, diplopod, eurypterid, golach, goloch, insect, merostome, merostomatus, myriapod, onychophor, palaeostracan, pycnogonid, spider, symphala, trilobite
appendage endite
8-legged arachnid, king-crab, mite, scorpion, spider, tick
group gigantostraca
joint basidodite
mouth arthrostome
wingless aptera, centipede, spider

ARTHUR See KING ARTHUR.

ARTHUR, CHESTER
birthplace fairfield, vermont
burial site albany, new york
party republican
profession lawyer

ARTICHOKE bur, canada, chorogi, crosnes, cynara, girasol, knotroot, thistle, vegetable
base fond
drink cynar
leafstalk chard
relative cardoon

ARTICLE bargain, bind, brief, brochure, budget, causerie, clause, commodity, composition, concern, copy, covenant, descant, detail, discourse, disquisition, dissertation, doctrine, essay, etude, excursus, feature, homily, indenture, item, joint, leader, lucubration, manuscript, matter, memoir, monograph, morceau, object, paper, paragraph, part(icular), piece, plank, point, report, scoop, screed, script, sketch, statement, story, study, subject, ten, theme, thesis, thing, tract, treatise, treatment, typescript
cheap camelot
inferior junk, shoddy
miscellaneous sundries
nondescript doodad
showy frippery
worthless dido, trangam, trash

ARTICULAR itacolumite, sandstone

ARTICULATE arrange, clear, concatenate, distinct, eloquent, enunciate, express, facile, fluent, frame, glib, integrate, join, joint(ed), link, methodize, oral, order, organize, precise, pronounce, say, sound, speak, systematize, unified, unify, unite, utter, verbal, vocal, voluble

ARTICULATED alveolar, dental, jointed, labial

ARTICULATION aspiration, enunciation, integration, joint, juncture, node, scheme, suture, syntaxis, utterance, voice
defective lallation, lamdacism

inability anarthria

ARTIFACT amgarn, audi, birdstone, eolith, guaca, keraunion, racloir, relic, rondelle, sagaie, tranchet
from sky ceraunia

ARTIFICE ambush, blind, cautel, cheat, chicanery, cleverness, conspiracy, construct, contrivance, covin, cozenage, craft, crock, crook, cunning, deceit, deception, design, device, dodge(ry), double, draft, duplicity, evasion, expedient, fakement, feint, fetch, finesse, fraud, gimmick, guile, imposition, imposture, ingenuity, intrigue, invention, machination, maneuver, plan, plot, pretense, red herring, ruse, scheme, shift, shuffle, skill, sleight, stall, stratagem, strategy, subterfuge, trick(ery), wile
symbol fox

ARTIFICER architect, artisan, artist, carpenter, contriver, craftsman, daedalus, deviser, framer, inventor, lapidary, mechanic, opificer, producer, tvashtar, tvashtri, workman, wright

ARTIFICIAL adulterate, affected, artful, assumed, bastard, bogus, campy, contrived, counterfeit, crafty, cultivated, cute, dummy, ersatz, fabricated, fabulous, factitious, fake(d), false, fashioned, feigned, fictitious, forced, forged, histrionic, imitative, insincere, manmade, mannered, overdone, postiche, pretended, pretentious, sham, simulated, sly, spurious, stagy, stilted, substitute, superficial, supposititious, synthetic, theatrical, unnatural

ARTILLERY ammunition, armament, arms, barrage, bombardment, cannon(ade), firearms, guns, munitions, ordnance
emplacement battery
fire barrage, rafale, salvo, stonk
man bombardier, cannoneer, gunner, lascar, marksman, redleg, topechee
piece drake, lantaca, lantaka, saker

plant adicea, burning-bush, dittany, evonymus, fraxinella, mock cypress, pilea, wahoo
saint barbara
science of pyroballogy
16th century culverin
support callfire

ARTIODACTYL antelope, camel, cattle, deer, giraffe, goat, hippopotamus, pig, pronghorn, sheep, ungulate

ARTISAN architect, artifex, artificer, cooper, craftsman, hand, kammalan, laborer, mechanic, operative, opificer, roustabout, tarkhan, technician, workman

ARTIST actor, adept, artificer, artisan, author, brush, composer, dab(ster), dancer, daub(ster), drawer, etcher, expert, fictor, illustrator, magician, master, musician, painter, performer, player, rapin, schemer, sculptor, singer, sketcher, songster, virtuoso, wizard, writer
cap beret
equipment brush, canvas, easel, paint, palette
primitive moses
saint eloi
sidewalk screever
signature word fecit
workshop atelier, studio

ARTISTIC aesthetic, appreciative, arty, beautiful, cultured, daedal, decorative, discriminating, esthetic, excellent, ornamental, pictorial, picturesque, skillful, tasteful
production facture
quality vertu, virtu

ARTLESS candid, childlike, clumsy, confiding, crude, frank, gauche, genuine, guileless, ignorant, inapt, ingenuous, innocent, naif, naive, native, natural, open, plain, rough, rude, seely, simple, sincere, tasteless, trustful, trusting, unaffected, uncontrived, uncultured, undesigning, unskilled, unsophisticated, unsuspecting, unsuspicious

ARTOCARPUS angili, anubin(g), breadfruit, camansi, mulberry, pandanus, screwpine, treculia, tree

ARTOPHORION pyx

ARTS *goddess* athena, muse
liberal grammar, logic, rhetoric, trivia, trivium
self-defense aikido, boxing, judo, karate, kung fu
ARTY chichi
ARU indeed, really
island kangaroo filander
ARUI aoudad, sheep
ARUM acorus, adder's-meat, anthurium, arad, arisaema, arrowroot, bobby and joan, calalu, cuckoopint, dracunculus, dragon, friar's-cowl, green dragon, mandrake, monstera, pistia, starch, taro, tawkee, tuckahoe, wampee
family aracaea
lily calla
pert. araceous, aroid(eous)
ARUNDARIA bamboo, cane, reed
ARUNTA aranda
creation alcheringa, dreamtime
ARVIRAGUS cadwal
father cymbeline
ARX citadel
ARYAN caucasian, indoeuropean, mede, nordic, slav
deity agni, ormuzd
indian hindu
language sanskrit
not anarya(n)
people osset
sage agastya
ARYBALLUS bottle, flask, jar, vessel
ARYBAS *consort* troas
kin aeacides, alcetas
ARZUN cereal, grain, millet, panicum
AS also, because, como, equally, for, how, inasmuchas, into, libra, like, pound, qua(tenus), similar(ly), since, some, suppose, than, that, though, thus, when, which, while
above ditto, utsupra
a matter of course certainly, consequently, generally, necessarily
a matter of fact actually, really
a rule generally, normally
far as into, quatenus, until
good as nearly, practically
if als-ab, quasi, similarly, supposedly
it is accordingly

it may be eventually, perhaps
it seems apparently
it were fairly, figuratively, supposedly, though
like as not probably
long as provided that, since, so-be-it, while
matters stand accordingly
much alsmekill, rising
much as you like agogo
one concurrently, simultaneously, together, unanimously
regards about, concerning
she is dyce, thus
soon alswith, astite, directly
soon as once, when
stated thus
the case may be accordingly, perhaps
the crow flies directly
they say proverbially
to quoad
usual as is, in status quo, normally, solito
well as forbye
written sic, sta, stet
yet hitherto, so far
AS YOU LIKE IT *author* shakespeare
character adam, amiens, audrey, celia, charles, corin, dennis, duke, frederick, hymen, jacques, le beau, martext, oliver, orlando, phebe, rosalind, silvius, touchstone, william
clown touchstone
cynic jacques
hero orlando
heroine rosalind
scene forest of arden
ASA *kin* jehosaphat
kingdom judah
parent abia, maacah
wife azubah
ASAFETIDA antispasmodic, assafoetida, carminative, condiment, devil's-dung, ferula, feryka, hing, laser, perula, resin
source narthex
ASAHEL *mother* zeruiah
ASAK asok(a), saraca, tree
ASANA narra, seat, throne
ASAPH dryden
employer david
ASARUM asarabacca, asarite, asaron, bacc(h)ar, birthwort, bitter, foalfoot, ginger(root), hazel, herb, resin
ASBESTOS abbest, abiston,

absistos, albeston, amianth(us), amosite, amphibole, chrysotile, crocidolite, curtain, woodrock, xylite
ASCALABOTA gekkota, iguana, lizard
ASCALAPHUS *brother* ialmenus
leader agamemnon
parent acheron, ares, astyoche, gorgyra, orphne
slayer deiphobus
subjects minyans
ASCALIS *enemy* sertorius
father iphtha
ASCANIUS iulus
kingdom alba longa
parent aeneas, creusa
son romus, silvius
ASCARID nematode, pinworm, roundworm
ASCEND advance, amount, arise, aspire, breast, clamber, climax, climb, escalate, go up, hoick, incline, levitate, mount, progress, rear, rise, rocket, scale, shinny, soar, spiral, stair, sty, surface, surge, swarm, tower, upgo, uprear, uprise, vault, zoom
ASCENDANCY affluence, authority, command, control, dominance, dominion, influence, mastery, owerance, power, predominance, prestige, sovereignty, supremacy, sway
ASCENDANT acclivity, ancestor, assurgent, begetter, dominant, elder, father, foreparent, grandparent, horoscope, influential, mountant, patriarch, peak, predecessor, primogenitor, procreator, relative, rising, superior, surpassing
ASCENDING anabatic, anodal, anodic, aspirant, assurgent, climbing, inflorescent, mounting, racemose, rising, scandent, scansorial, steep, uphill, uppard, upward
ASCENSION apotheosis, ascent, assumption, resurrection, translation
day holy thursday
island bird frigate
lily madonna
ASCENT acclivity, advancement, aliyah, ascension, clamber, climb, escalade, elevation, eminence, grade,

gradient, hill, inclination, incline, leap, mounting, ramp, rise, rist, scend, slope, stairs, steep, steps, stipe, sty, upcome, updraft, upgang, upgo, uprising, uprush, upsurge, upswing, upway

ASCERTAIN analyze, apprise, assure, attain, calculate, compute, decide, determine, discover, divine, figure, find, get at, glean, learn, measure, prove, settle, solve, tell, unearth

ASCESIS asceticism, austerity, self-denial

ASCETIC abstainer, abstemious, abstinent, adamite, anchoret, anchorite, austere, avadhuta, banian, banyan, bhikshu, cathar, celibate, cenobite, cynic, dervish, devotee, eremite, essene, fakir, fanatic, flaggellant, friar, frugal, hermit, hydropot, marabout, monk, moral, muni, mystic, nun, plain, puritan(ical), recluse, religious, rigid, sabbatarian, sadhu, sannyasi, severe, so(o)fee, sofi, solitary, spartan, sramana, stern, stoic, strict, stylite, sufi, tapasvi, whirling dervish, yati, yogi(n)
mendicant bairagi

ASCETICISM abstinence, anchorism, ascesis, austerity, discipline, mortification, puritanism, sabbatarianism, self-denial, stoicism, temperance, yoga

ASCIDIAN cungevoi, polyp, tethydan, tunicate

ASCIDIUM pitcher, vasculum

ASCLEPIAS arg(h)el, bloodflower, bloodpink, bloodweed, butterfly, haemanthus, milkweed

ASCLEPIUS *daughter* iaso
nurse trygon
parent apollo, coronis
savior hermes
slayer zeus
trainer centaur, chiron
wife epione

ASCOCARP apothecium, ascoma, cupule

ASCOMYCETE fungus, mildew, mold, truffle, yeast

ASCON sponge

ASCOPART *slayer* bevis

ASCORBIC *acid* godnose, ignose, vitamin c

ASCOT cravat, necktie, racetrack, scarf, tie
tan brownstone, chestnut, coconut, kermanshah, sandstone

ASCRIBE accredit, accuse, adduce, allege, arette, arrogate, assign, attach, attribute, blame, charge, cite, conjecture, count, credit, dedicate, entitle, fix, guess, imply, impute, infer, intitule, reckon, refer, relate, ret, surmise

ASCRIPTION credit, laud, praise, repute

ASCRY denounce, descry, escry, espy

ASCUS bag, theca

ASE *son* peer gynt

ASENATH *husband* joseph
offspring ephraim, manasseh

ASEPTIC barren, clean, germless, prophylactic, sterile, unfruitful

ASER *father* jacob

ASEXUAL agamic

ASGARD *bridge* bifrost
deity See AESIR.
plain idavoll, ithavoll
sentinel heimdall
12 mansions bilskirnir, breithablik, folkvang, glathsheim, glitner, himinbjorg, hlithskjalf, jotunnheim, noatun, sessyrmnir, sokkvabekk, thruheim, thrymheim, valaskjalf, valhalla, vanaheim, vingolf, vithi, ydalir

ASH, ASHES als, artar, ase, axan, burn, calx, char, cinder(s), clinker, corpse, dogberry, dottle, dregs, ember, essenhout, frain, fraxinus, gray, hardwood, hoopwood, kelp, lava, pallor, powder, pulverin, remainder, remains, remnants, residue, rowan, ruins, sorb, tree, varec, waste, wicken, winetree, wood, ygrdasyl
black boxelder, eucalyptus, kelp, mulberry
bumpy bunjibunji, flindosa
can bomb, depth charge, dust bin
-colored cinereal, cinereous
comb. spodo, tephro
flowering fringetree, orne
fruit samara
juice manna

-of-jerusalem dyer's-weed, woad
pert. cinerary, cinereal
prickly pellitory-bark, suterberry
pumpkin wax gourd
receptacle bin, box, urn
reduce to burn, cremate
seaweed varec
silky cedar
tobacco dottel, dottle
tray spitkid, spitkit, waiter
tree nymph melia
wednesday pulvering day, shrovetide

ASHAMED abashed, abject, bad, compunctious, confused, contrite, discomfited, distressed, embarrassed, hangdog, hontous, humbled, humiliated, mean, mortified, nace, nais, penitent, repentant, restrained, shamefaced, sheepish, unwilling

ASHANTI *capital* kunasi
pepper cayenne, cubeb
religion obeah, obia

ASHEN, ASHY blanched, bleached, burnt, ceraceous, ceral, cinereal, cinereous, colorless, doughy, drained, ghastly, gray, grim, livid, macabre, pale, pallid, pasty, wan, waxen, white

ASHER *offspring* beriah, isui, jimnah, serah, usul
parent jacob, zilpah

ASHERAH ashtoreth, astarte, baal

ASHERITE *chief* imna

ASHKENAZ *kin* gomer, japath
master nebuchadnezzar

ASHKOKO cony, daman, hyrax

ASHORE acost, aground, aland, beached, stranded

ASHRAMA brahmachari, continent, hermitage
stages brahmachari, grihastha, hermit, householder, mendicant, saunyasi, student, vanaprastha

ASHTHROAT verbena, vervain

ASHUR *mother* abiah
symbol feroher
wife helah

ASHWORT senecio

ASIA, ASIAN, ASIATIC See also ORIENTAL references.
alliance seato

animal ahu, bison, camel, chevrotain, ounce, pahmi, panda, pangolin, rasse, tiger, treeshrew, yak, zebu
antelope dzeren, dzerin, goral, serow
ass loulan, onager
bamboo cana espina
bean gram, mungo
bird amadavat, avadavat, bluethroat, brambling, bushrobin, courser, dotterel, fenghuang, hilltit, ibisbill, mina, minivet, moro, myna(h), pitta, spider-hunter, thrush-tit, titbabbler, treron, turnix
bishop abba
bustard houbara
camel bactrian
cap calpac(k)
cattle zobo
central tatary
cereal arzun, ragee
cholera mordisheen
christian uniat
city (See also under specific countries.) amoy, bagdad, bombay, comilla, dacca, sian, singan, singapore, urga
civet binturong
conjuror shaman
consort iapetus
coucal　　　crow-pheasant, cuckoo
country accad, afghanistan, arabia, araby, armenia, assam, bactria, baluchistan, bhutan, burma, cambodia, ceylon, chaldea, china, elam, india, indonesia, irak, iran, iraq, israel, japan, korea, laos, malaya, nepal, persia, siam, siberia, sri lanka, syria, thailand, tibet, turkey, vietnam
country, ancient colchis
cow zobo, zoh
creeper ampelopsis
crowfoot buttercup
cymbal zel
dandelion koksaghyz
deer ahu, axis, barasingha, chitra, hangul, kakar, kakur, maha, muntjac, muntjak, napu, roe, sambar, sambur, shou, sika
desert gobi, karakum, kyzylkum, qaraqum
disease cholera, kalaazar, malaria, trachoma, yaws
dog, wild dhole
drink airan, kumiss

empire, ancient assyria, babylonia, chaldea, mesopotamia
eskimo innuit, tuski, yuit
evergreen bago, yeddospruce
fabric camlet
falcon laggar, lanner(et), luggar, lugger
fern palapalai
fiber hemp, ramie
finch man(n)ikin
fish climbing perch, kissing gourami
fowl brahma, cochin, langshan, sat
fox adive, corsac
fruit durian, loquat
gangster dacoit
gazelle ahu, cora
globeflower trollius
goat goral, jagla, tahr
goat-antelope serow
goatsucker frogmouth
goddess anta
grass apluda, camelhay, cockscomb, coix, millet, munj, ragi, zoysia
greeting salaam
gum bassora, tragacanth
hemp murva
herb abelmost, aletris, alpinia, alyssum, anethum, apios, arneba, aspidistra, astilbe, bamban, bells of ireland, boltonia, borage, cana, cicer, gouaree, gynura, hemp, incarvillea, kalanchoe, lopsee, murva, puschkinia, rheum, ricebean, skirret, torenia, wasabi
highland pamir, tibet
horse tarpan
inn serai
island borneo, celebes, ceylon, formosa, japan, java, luzon, malay, mindanao, philippines, sakhalin, sumatra, taiwan, wrangel
isthmus kra
jay sirgang
juniper sabine, savin(e)
lake baikal, balkash, issykkul, urmia, van
language lao, pali, shan, t(h)ai, turki, urdu
laurel cinnamomum
legume gram, mungo bean
lemur loris, macaco
lizard fish bombay duck
lynx caracal
mangrove bacao, bacauan
medicine man shaman

millet dari, durra
mink kolinsky
minnow rasbora
minor See ASIA MINOR.
mint perilla
mongoose urva
monk lama
monkey langur, macaque, rhesus, toque
monkshood atis
mother, great agdistis
musical instrument anklung
mystic fakir
nomad kipchak, mongol, tatar
northernmost point chelyuskin
nurse amah
oasis merv
official imam
offspring atlas, epimetheus, prometheus
oil plant odal
orchestra gamelan
orchid aerides
owl utum
ox banting, gaur, gayal, yak
palm areca(les), areng(a), assai, betel, calami, calamus, licuala, nipa, nypa, palmyra, penang-lawyer, rhapis
parade ground maidan
parent oceanus, tethys
partridge chukar, seesee
peak everest, kanchininjinga, nanga parbat, tengri khan
peninsula anatolia, arabia, araby, indochina, kamchatka, korea, malay
people alarodian, altaic, hun, innuit, kui, kurd, lolo, mede, meo, miao, moi, mongolian, oriental, sere, seric, shan, tai, ta(r)tar, tocharian, toda, turki, uzbeg, uzbek, yuit
pheasant tragopan
plague cholera
plain chol, maidan, steppe
plant abroma, akebi, alyssum, atis, aucuba, balloonflower, betel, camellia, fenugreek, ferula, frogsbit, odal, soya, tea, zingiber
plateau pamir(s)
polecat sarmatier
poplar bahan
port bombay, calcutta, hongkong, macao, singapore, sinope
priest abuna
pyrocantha firethorn
range alai, alay, altai, anti-

lebanon, himalaya, hindu kush, tien shan, ural
region baluchistan, chaldea, tartary, turkestan, turkistan
religion brahman, buddhist, hinayana, hindu, islam, mahayana, shinto, tao
resin dammar
river amoor, amudarya, amur, aras, araxes, brahmaputra, chaophya, eelee, euphrates, ganges, helmand, hooghly, ili, indus, irawaddy, irtish, jhelum, khabur, mekong, obi, orkhon, orontes, oxus, putra, salween, sutlej, tigris, ussuri, yalu, yang-tse, yangtze, yeinsei
rodent alactaga, gerbil(le), marmot, pika
salmon taimen
salt marsh rann of kutch
sandstorm simoon, tebbad
sardine lour
sea aral, azof, caspian
sheep argali, bharal, nahoor, oorial, rasse, sha, sna, thianshan, urial, wrasse
shopkeeper bakal
shrine tera, wat
shrub aucuba, azalea, bago, cape jasmine, che, deutzia, exochorda, forsythia, fortunella, gardenia, kafta, kat, ramie, raphiolepis, rose of sharon, ruta, savin(e), skimmia, spiraea, styphelia, sweetleaf, tche, tea, thea, tragacanth, vangueria, vervain, wikstroemia
snail hua
snake bongar, cobra, daboia, jessur, katuka, kerril, psammophis, russell's viper
southeast burma, cambodia, ceylon, indonesia, laos, malaysia, philippines, siam, sri lanka, thailand, vietnam
squirrel jelerang, polatouche
storm bura(n), durio, monsoon, tebbad, typhoon
tableland pamir(s), tibet
tea cha, congo(u), hyson, lapsang, oolong
temple wat
thrush pied-blackbird
thorn bel
title khan, shah
trade wind monsoon
treaty seato
tree acle, aegle, alerites, almond, alstonia, amygdalus, anubing, aquilaria, areng,

arjan, arjun, artocarpus, asak, asok(a), athel, atle, bahan, bakula, banaba, banyan, bito, camphor, camuning, caragana, carambola, catalpa, cork, cydonia, dita, elaeodendron, feronia, garsinia, halmalille, kalumpang, loquat, lordwood, matsu, medlar, narra, ochna, olax, rambeh, rasamala, rata, ricepaper, savin, siris, tamarisk, tche, tragacanth, unona, vateria, wampee, wongshy, xylia
vessel sampan
vine actinidia, air potato, akebi, amphicarpa, basella, benincasa, clematis, lavanga, mosquito-plant, quisqualis, turpeth, uncaria
warbler ruby-throat
warehouse godown
weight picul, tael, tras
wind karaburan
yam air potato, colocasia, dioscorea
ASIA MINOR anatolia, levant
animal daman
cheese bryndza
city abydos, aintab, ararat, bergama, cappadocia, cnidus, cyzicus, ephesus, haran, ipsus, issus, miletus, myra, myus, nicaea, pergamum, sardis, tarsus, teos, tiberias, troy, tverya, tyre, urartu, ushak
coast ionia
country arzava, cappadocia, caria, cilicia, eolis, galatia, ionia, isauria, izmir, lycia, lydia, pamphylia, pergamum, pisidia, pontus, smyrna, trebizond, troad, troas
empire, ancient assyria, babylonia, chaldea, mesopotamia, persia
goat aegagrus
goddess cybele
herb bear's-tail, celsia
island ionia, samos
martyr st george
mountain pass cilician gates
peak ida
people, ancient minni
physician galen
port issus, phocaea
range alai
river caicus, cydnus, halys, iris, monderez, pactolus
roman province galatia

sea aegean
shrub alhabi, camels horn
warrior solymi
woodless region axylus
ASIDE abreast, agley, aloof, apart, aslant, astray, away, beside, beyond, bye, byhand, despite, digression, forbye, forthby, gone, hence, indirectly, interjection, lateral, near, neck and neck, off, past, private, reserved, secretly, separate, sidewise, sottovoce, whisper
from besides, excepting, excluding
ASILID hawk fly, robber fly
ASINEGO ass, fool
ASININE absurd, assish, crass, dense, doltish, dull, dumb, fatuous, foolish, idiotic, inane, inept, laughable, mulish, nutty, obtuse, ridiculous, senseless, silly, simple, stupid, unintelligent
ASK address, adjure, appeal, apply, beg, beseech, bespeak, call for, catechize, charge, claim, consult, crave, demand, entreat, examine, expect, extract, fand, fraist, frayn(e), implore, impose, inquire, interrogate, invite, levy, need, obtest, petition, plead, pray, query, question, quiz, request, require, solicit, speak, speer, speir, spur, spy, sue, tap, thig
advice consult
a favor brace
for beg, bespeak, cry, dun, inquire, lait, request, seek
forgiveness apologize
ASKANCE, ASKANT askew, askile, asquint, awry, crooked, enviously, incredulously, jealously, laterally, obliquely, sideways, sidewise
ASKAR guard, soldier
ASKEW agee, agley, ajee, alop, amiss, askance, askant, aslant, asquint, atilt, atwist, awry, azew, bent, biaswise, buckled, cam, catawampus, cockeyed, collywest, crazy, crooked, curved, distorted, eccentric, erroneous, flooey, gleed, oblique(ly), odd, screwy, sideling, skewgee, skewjawed, turned, twisted, wapperjawed, wry, yawways

ASKOS jar, jug, vase, vessel

ASLANT aside, aslope, athwart, oblique

ASLEEP abed, byelow, comatose, dead, dormant, dozing, idle, inactive, inert, insensible, latent, motionless, napping, numbed, oblivious, offguard, resting, slumbering, unconscious, unprepared, unready, unwary

ASMODEUS lucifer

ASOCIAL averse, egocentric, egregious, inconsiderate, indifferent, selfish, withdrawn

ASOMATOUS immaterial, incorporeal

ASOPUS *daughter* cleone, salamis

ASP aspen, aspic, ceraste, cobra, ophidian, snake, uraeus, viper
headdress uraeus
sacred uraeus

ASPARAGUS lily, sparage, sparrow-grass, sperage, sprue
bean bigna
beetle crioceris
broccoli calabrese
garnish princess
lettuce lactuca
part spear, stalk, tip
pea goa-bean
stone apatite

ASPASIA deianira, milto, omphale
consort cyrus, lysicles, pericles
parent axiochus, hermotimus
son eupolis

ASPECT affect, air, angle, appearance, aura, bearing, carriage, character(istic), color, countenance, decile, demeanor, display, essence, exposure, expression, face(t), facies, favor, feature, figure, form, front (age), glance, guise, hue, image, impression, influence, leer, likeness, lineament, look, manner, mien, nature, norma, ostent, outlook, part, phase, phasis, position, presence, prospect, quality, regard, respect, seeming, semblance, shape, show, side, sight, situation, stage, state, status, view, visage, vista, visor, vizor, vult, way

ASPEN alamo, asp, auldwives'-tongue, nither, popular, populus, quaking, quivering, tree, tremble, tremulous
wood popple

ASPER akcha, akcheh, coin, harsh, othmany, rough

ASPERGE asparagus, baptize, moisten, sprinkle

ASPERGILLUM aspersorium, brechites, brush, hyssop, sprinkler, strinkle

ASPERITY acerbity, acrimony, bitterness, causticity, ire, irritability, mordancy, rigor, roughness, severity, sharpness, sourness, tartness, waspishness

ASPERSE abuse, appeach, assail, attack, besmirch, bespatter, besprinkle, blacken, calumniate, decry, defame, defile, derogate, detract, discredit, disparage, forspeak, lampoon, libel, malign, revile, shower, skit, slander, slur, smear, spatter, splash, spot, spray, sprinkle, tarnish, traduce, vilify, vituperate

ASPERSION abuse, affront, animadversion, baptism, calumniation, calumny, criticism, defamation, derogation, imputation, innuendo, invective, pasquinade, reflection, reproach, scandal, slander, slur, smear, sprinkling, squib, vilification
to cast sklent

ASPHALIUS poseidon

ASPHALT bitumen, congo, cutback, floor, pavement, pitch, tar
black gilsonite, uintaite
curbing berme
kind albertite, brea, byerlite, courtzilite, elaterite, maltha, manja(c)k
lake dead sea
natural elaterite
pure glance-pitch

ASPHODEL daffodil, knavery, narcissus, silver-rod

ASPHYXIA acrotism, apn(o)ea, choking, suffocation

ASPHYXIATE choke, kill, murder, smother, stifle, suffocate

ASPIC asp, cannon, galan-

tine, gel(atin), gelatine, jelly, lavender
mold dariole

ASPIDIUM dryopteris, fern, polystichum, tectaria
compound albaspidin

ASPIRANT applicant, candidate, nominee

ASPIRATE articulate, breathe, inhale, murmur, sibilate, suck

ASPIRATION aim, ambition, articulation, breath(ing), desire, goal, hope, ideal, longing, objective, sights, wish, yearning, yen

ASPIRATOR muzzle, pump, respirator

ASPIRE aim, attain, covet, crave, desire, ettle, hope, hunger, intend, long, mount, pant, pine, progress, pursue, seek, soar, strive, sty, thirst, tower, try, want, wish, yearn

ASPIRIN analgesic, anodyne, antipyretic, bufferin, defervescent, empirin, febrifuge
source salicylic acid, willow

ASQUINT askance, askew, awry, blinking, dubiously, fluttering, laterally, obliquely, slyly

ASRAMA ashram, hermitage

ASS, ASS'S addle(brain), addlepate, arcadian nightingale, asinego, blockhead, booby, burro, chump, cuddle, cuddy, dapple, dickey, dolt, donkey, duff, dunce, equid, fool, gudda, hinny, imbecil, jack, jennet, jenny, khur, kiang, kulan, longear, maltese, missouri hummingbird, moke, mountain canary, mule, neddy, ninny(hammer), onager, putz, quagga, rear, rump, simpleton, soliped, twit
comb. ono
ear abalone, comfry, haliotis
female jennet, jenny
foot herb, monkey's-hand, pothomorphe
in lion skin imposter, misfit
male jack(stock)
parsley chervil
pert. asinine
symbol of sobriety, stupidity
thistle onopordon
wild chigetai, ghorkhar,

hemiffe, kiyand, k(o)ulan, onager

worship onolatry

ASSA caama

ASSAGAI javelin, missile, spear, tree

ASSAI enough, euterpe, manicole, palm, very

ASSAIL abuse, accuse, asperse, assault, attack, batter, bawl out, beat, belabor, berate, beset, besiege, bicker, blister, bombard, buffet, castigate, encounter, excoriate, flay, have at, hoot, hurtle, impugn, insult, invade, jump, lash, malign, molest, nag, pelt, pound, pummel, rebuke, revile, ridicule, roast, sailye, scarify, scathe, scorch, set upon, slash, stone, storm, strike, tonguelash, trounce, vituperate, whack, whang

ASSAM (See also INDOCHINA.)

capital shillong

city gauhati, imphal, ledo, sadiya, shillangle, shillong

gibbon hoolock

language ahom, aka, khami, lhota

mongoloid garo

peak japvo

people ahom, aka, angami, angka, aor, garo, kachari, khamti, koch, kuki, mikir, naga

rubber rambong

silkworm eri(a)

state khasi, manipup

ASSAPAN glaucomys, squirrel

ASSARACUS *kin* anchises, tros

kingdom troy

son capys, ganymede

ASSART clear(ing), grub, thwaite

ASSASSIN bravo, cain, cutthroat, fedali, fidawi, fingerman, gunman, hackster, hitman, killer, murderer, ruffian, sicarian, slayer, stabber, thug, torpedo, triggerman

ASSASSINATE bump off, destroy, dispatch, execute, injure, kill, liquidate, MURDER, slay

ASSASSINATION homicide, magnicide, thuggee

ASSAULT abuse, affray, aggression, alarum, assail, assalto, assay, attack, beat, blitz, blow, bombard, brash, breach, brunt, buffet, charge, combat, cosh, descent, fray, harry, holdup, incriminate, incursion, insult, invade, invasion, lambast, mug, onfall, onset, onslaught, outburst, pound, pummel, raid, rape, ruin, seize, seizure, slug, smite, storm, stound, stour, stoush, strike, tempt, thrust, violate, yoking

signal warison

ASSAY affliction, aim, analyze, appraise, apprise, aspire, assault, assess, attack, attempt, demonstrate, docimasy, effort, endeavor, essay, estimate, evaluate, examine, experiment, hardship, proof, prosult, prove, rate, strive, struggle, test, trial, try, value

vessel cupel

ASSAYER explorer, potdar, tester, tryer

ASSE caama, fox, hartebeest

ASSEMBLAGE aggregate, army, array, ASSEMBLY, bevy, body, bunch, camp, choir, circuit, cluster, collection, colony, complex, convoy, crew, drove, flock, galaxy, group, herd, hookup, host, jamboree, junction, levee, levy, mass, mob, pack, quire, ruck, society, spread, swarm, system, throng, troop

confused farrago

ASSEMBLE accumulate, agglomerate, amass, array, associate, bivouac, bulk, bunch, bundle, cluster, coagulate, coalesce, collate, collect, combine, compile, congregate, connect, convene, convoke, couple, crowd, dredge, encamp, forgather, gather, group, herd, hoard, horde, huddle, manufacture, mass, meet, muster, pack, pod, raise, rally, recruit, rendezvous, rest, round up, rout, sam(m), summon, surge, swarm, throng, unite

ASSEMBLY (See also ASSEMBLAGE.) 3 mob 4 army, band, body, club, diet, feis, mass, meet, shul, ting 5 agora, array, coven, crowd, flock, forum, gemot, party, posse, press, rally, sabha, sobor, synod 6 aenach, assize, caucus, covine, gemote, majlis, muster, plenum, powwow, quorum, seance, steven 7 chamber, chapter, cluster, college, comitia, company, consort, council, eotates, landtag, meeting, reunion, session, sitting, society, synaxis, tabagie, turnout, tynwald, zemstvo 8 audience, conclave, congress, ecclesia, folkmoot, placitum, tribunal, volkstag, wardmote 9 committee, concourse, gathering 10 assemblage, collection, conference, confluence, consistory, convention, eisteddfod, parliament 11 association, conventicle, convocation, get-together, ingathering, legislature 12 attroupenent, congregation

afternoon levee, levy

full plena

legislative See LEGISLATURE.

line factory, plant, production

midnight sabbat

people's folcgemot, folcmot, folkmot(e), folkmoot

place agora, auditorium, bouleuterion, estufa, hall, kashim, kiva, pnyx

private ruelle

ASSENT accede, accept, accession, accord, acknowledge, acquiesce(nce), admit, affirmation, agree(ment), allow, amen, approve, aye, bow, buy, compliance, comply, concede, concur, conform, consent, credit, echo, embrace, endorsement, espouse, give in, grant, nod, sanction, seal, submit, subscribe, support, vise, yield

ASSERT advocate, affirm, affy, allege, argue, asseverate, aver, avouch, avow, betoken, brag, champion, cite, claim, constate, contend, declare, defend, depost, insist, justify, maintain, outstand, pose, posit, postulate, predicate, press, proclaim, protest, say, state, support, swear, threap, threep, vindicate, voice, warrant

ASSERTION averment, claim, fact, hoti, vow
boastful jactation
doubtful plinyism

ASSERTIVE aggressive, blatant, brash, certain, clamorous, cocksure, confident, dogmatic, militant, positive, pushing, sure

ASSESS adjudge, adjudicate, adjust, apportion, appraise, appreciate, apprise, ask, assay, assize, bote, cense, cess, compute, determine, doom, estimate, evaluate, extent, figure, fix, impose, inventory, judge, levy, measure, mise, price, prorate, rate, reckon, sample, scot, tax, tiend, tithe, toll, value, weigh, worth

ASSESSMENT apportionment, appraisal, apprisement, brigbote, call, cess, customs, demand, duty, estimate, evaluation, excise, fee, impost, jumma, levy, price, pricing, ratal, rate, scot, scutage, tac, tariff, tax, teind, tiende, tithe, toll, tribute, valorization, valuation
for repair bot(e)

ASSESSOR adjudicator, judge, jurat, lister, mufti, rater, stentor, taxator, taxer
group fintadores

ASSET, ASSETS accounts, acquisition, appurtenance, belongings, bonds, bonus, capital, cash, credit, effects, estate, fixtures, funds, getpenny, goods, goodwill, holdings, intangibles, inventory, means, money, note, nugget, plum, possessions, principal, property, real estate, resources, riches, securities, stock, strength, substance, supply, treasure, value, wealth

ASSEVERATE affirm, allege, assert, assure, aver, avouch, avow, declare, depone, depose, oath, protest, say, state, swear, testify, vow

ASSHUR *father* shem

ASSI holly, yaupon

ASSIDUOUS active, attentive, busy, constant, continuous, devoted, diligent, energetic, frequent, hardworking, indefatigable, industrious, laborious, painstaking, penible, persevering, punctilious, quick, sedulous, sleepless, strenuous, studious, tireless, unflagging, unremitting, unwearied, zealous

ASSIGN address, adduce, advance, affect, allocate, allot, antedate, apply, appoint, apportion, appropriate, ascribe, attach, attribute, award, cast, cavel, cede, charge, commission, consign, convey, credit, deal, delate, delegate, designate, determine, dight, dispose, dole, draw, endow, entail, fix, give, impute, locate, mete, name, nominate, offer, order, pigeonhole, place, prescribe, pronounce, rate, refer, seal, select, set, settle, shift, show, specify, station, transfer

ASSIGNATION allowance, appointment, apportionment, ascription, assignment, attribution, date, engagement, meeting, order, rendezvous, tryst

ASSIGNEE beneficiary, cessionaire

ASSIGNMENT allotment, appointment, apportionment, assignation, attribution, business, care, chare, charge, chore, commission, drill, duty, errand, exercise, grind, homework, job, lesson, mission, obligation, position, post, practice, round, stint, task, transfer, tunca, work

ASSIMILATE absorb, adapt, adjust, appropriate, blend, commingle, compare, comprehend, concoct, convert, digest, domesticate, embody, fuse, homologize, identify, imbibe, imbue, imitate, incorporate, learn, liken, merge, metabolize, mix, resemble, take in, transform, understand

ASSINIBOIN hohe

ASSISH asinine, doltish, obstinate, stupid

ASSIST abet, accommodate, adjuvate, administer, aid, avail, back, befriend, benefit, bestead, boost, champion, coach, cooperate, escort, favor, further, help, leg-up, lift, nurse, patronize, promote, prompt, relieve, second, serve, speed, squire, stead, succor, support, sustain

ASSISTANCE aid, alms, appropriation, auxilium, avail, benefit, cast, dole, easement, furtherance, giffgaff, gift, grant, heeze, help, largesse, patronage, relief, remedy, secours, service, subsidy, subvention, support, use
mutual coadjument

ASSISTANT abettor, accomplice, acolyte, adjunct, adjutant, aide, ally, associate, attendant, auxiliary, cad, clerk, coadjutant, coadjutor, cohort, commis, deputy, dresser, employee, feldsher, flunky, girl-friday, gomashta, groom, hand, helper, maid, mate, minister, nurse, offsider, padrino, partner, postulate, provost, punk, righthandman, rubbler, second, secretary, servant, servitor, sous, squire, subordinate, tultul, underling, valet
female adjutrice, adjutrix
group crew, staff

ASSIZE appoint, assembly, assess, court, decree, dimension, edict, enactment, entent, fashion, fix, hearing, inquest, inquiry, instruction, judgment, measure, ordinance, oyer, rate, session, standard, statute, trial, tribunal, value, writ

ASSOCIATE accomplice, acquaintance, adjunct, aide, allied, ally, analog(ue), assistant, attach, attendant, auxiliary, blend, bracket, branch, brother, buddy, chum, clique, club, coalesce, cohort, collaborator, colleague, combine, commune, companion, compeer, comrade, concomitant, confederate, confrere, conjoint, connect, consort, copemate, co-worker, crony, fasten, federate, fellow, follower, fraternize, friend, gadshill, group, helper, henchman, hobnob, husband, identify, intimate, join, link, marry, match, mate, meddle, merge, mingle, mix, monk, moop, moup, pal, partner, peer, puisne, relate, share, socius, spouse, supporter, troop, unite, wife, workfellow, yoke

with accompany, befriend, collaborate, know, moop, moup

ASSOCIATES company, crew, entourage, fellowship, firm, gang, partnership, staff, team

ASSOCIATION affiliation, alignment, alliance, artel, assemblage, axis, band, bloc, board, body, bond, brotherhood, bund, cahoot, cartel, circle, club, coalition, combination, combine, comity, communication, community, companionship, company, confederacy, confederation, confraternity, congeries, connection, consolidation, consort(ium), corps, correlation, coterie, council, federation, fellowship, firm, fraternity, freemasonry, friendship, fusion, gang, gild, grange, group, guild, hanse, hong, hui, hunt, league, lodge, mixture, order, organization, partnership, party, plunderbund, pool, relation(ship), ring, school, society, sodality, sonderbund, togetherness, tong, unification, union, verein, zollverein

closed intimacy

football soccer

literary athenaeum, lyceum

religious samaj, sodality

secret cabal, lodge, ring

student burschenschaft, corps, fraternity, sorority

ASSOIL absolve, acquit, atone, deliver, expiate, forgive, free, pardon, refute, release, resolve, rid

ASSONANCE alliteration, clink, correspondence, paragram, paronomasia, pun, rhyme, rime

ASSORT alphabetize, arrange, bolt, classify, connect, cull, distribute, file, group, identify, methodize, order, pigeonhole, rank, separate, sort, suit, systematize, type, winnow

with accompany, associate, dovetail

ASSORTED different, diverse, heterogeneous, hybrid, matched, miscellaneous, mixed, motley, promiscuous, suited, varied, variegated, various

ASSORTMENT bag, batch, blend, collection, combination, compound, group, hodgepodge, jumble, kind, line, lot, miscellany, MIXTURE, set, sort, suite, sundries, variety

ASSUAGE abate, allay, alleviate, appease, attemper, calm, comfort, compose, deaden, delay, diminish, ease, lessen, liss(e), mitigate, moderate, mollify, pacify, palliate, placate, qualify, quench, reduce, relieve, salve, sate, satisfy, slake, soften, solace, soothe, still, swage, temper

ASSUASIVE alleviative, balmy, easeful, emollient, lenient, lenitive, mitigating, qualifying, softening, soothing, tranquilizing

ASSUME absorb, accept, accroach, adopt, affect, allege, appropriate, arrogate, assumpt, attempt, believe, cloak, clothe, confiscate, counterfeit, elect, endue, dare, don, fang, feign, grant, guess, hazard, imply, infer, mask, posit, postulate, predicate, premise, presume, presuppose, pretend, put on, receive, sham, simulate, suppose, surmise, think, undertake, usurp, venture

ASSUMED affected, alias, ARTIFICIAL, connoted, fake(d), false, fictional, fictitious, given, hypothetical, inferred, presumptive, spurious, supposititious, tacit

name alias, anonym, pseudonym

ASSUMING arrogant, audacious, bold, forward, lofty, superior, uppish, uppity

different form protean

ASSUMPTION adoption, allegation, appropriation, arrogance, ascension, belief, brass, claim, conjecture, donnee, fiction, homeosis, hypothesis, implication, imposition, marymass, nerve, opinion, postulate, premise, presupposition, pretense, profession, reception, supposition, surmise, theory, thesis, undertaking

ASSURANCE aplomb, audacity, boldness, bond, brass, cautio, certainty, cheek, cheer, cocksureness, confidence, conviction, coolness, courage, credit, earnest, effrontery, face, faith, firmness, gall, guarantee, guaranty, hope, insurance, intrepidity, mettle, nerve, oath, pledge, plevin, poise, promise, safety, sangfroid, security, self-confidence, self-reliance, solace, spirit, surement, surety, temerity, tenacity, trust, warrant(y)

ASSURE assert, avail, aver, back, certify, certiorate, cheer, cinch, clinch, comfort, confirm, convince, depose, embolden, encourage, enhearten, ensure, guarantee, hight, insure, pledge, promise, secure, sekere, si(c)ker, underwrite, vouch, warrant, witter

ASSURED arranged, ascertained, bold, bound, calm, certain, cold, collected, confident, cool, decided, determined, established, fearless, fixed, probal, reliant, sanguine, secure, set, siccar, si(c)ker, sure

ASSUREDLY amen, certes, indubitably, redely, si(c)ker, sure(ly), truly, undoubtedly, verily, witterly

ASSYRIA ass(h)ur

capital antioch, calah, nineveh, ninus

city akkad, alsur, arbela, as(s)hur, calah, dur-sargon, hara, kalakheveh, opis

dynasty sargonid

founder ninus

general abraha

god adad, ashir, as(h)ur, bel, hadad, ira, nabo, nebo, nergal, ninib, ninip, nusku, shamas, sin, siras

goddess allatu, fury, is(h)tar, nana, nine, sarpanit(u), zerbanit

king adram(m)elech, as(e)napper, ashurbanipal, belus, hosher, osnapper, p(h)ul, pilesar, sargon, sen-

nacherib, shalmaneser, tiglath
language akkadian
measure artaba, cane, foot, ghalva, hariba, hasab, makuk, mansion
official limmu
pantheon anshar, asshur
peak niphates, zagrus
philistines polesati
plum sebesten
queen semiramis
river adhian, caprus, lycus, tigris, zabas
ruler asser, assyr
shrub retem
weight cola
writing cuneiform

ASTARTE anadyomene, aphrodite, asherah, ashtoreth, cytherea, dea, inanna, ishtar, moon, mylitta, semiramis, venus
mollusk chestnut-clam

ASTATINE *source* bismuth

ASTEISM cleverness, derision, irony, raillery, sarcasm

ASTER amellus, arnica, astrofel(l), beeweed, bluedevil, boneset, callistephus, cocash, composite, cytaster, daisy, euaster, fleabane, ironweed, layia, monaster, oxeye, spicule, starwort, stokesir, sunflower, tidytips
disease yellows
family carduaceae, compositae
golden chrysopsis
-like herb erigeron

ASTERIA *daughter* hecate
husband perses
parent coeus, phoebe
sister leto

ASTERISK emphasize, mark, star, windmill

ASTERIUS *kingdom* crete
parent anax, hyperasius, pasiphae
stepson minos
wife europa

ASTERN abaft, aft(er), apoop, backward, baft, behind, hind, rear

ASTEROID astraea, calliope, ceres, dione, echinoderm, egeria, electra, eros, eunomia, flora, fortuna, hebe, hygeia, irene, iris, juno, lutetia, massalia, melpomene, metis, pallas, parthenope, planet(oid), psyche, starfish, thalia, themis, thetis, vesta, victoria

first and largest ceres
nearest earth eros

ASTHENIA debility, weakness

ASTHMA bronchitis, catarrh, phthisic
herb chamaesyce
remedy ephedrine, stramonium
weed indian-tobacco

ASTHMATIC panting, pouc(e)y, puffing, pursy, wheezing, wheezy

ASTIGMATISM ametropia, anop(s)ia, nystagmus

ASTILBE flower, goat's-beard, saxifrage

ASTIR about, abroach, acting, active, afoot, agog, agoing, alert, anticipating, around, asimmer, asteer, eager, excited, going, insomniac, moving, roused, stirring, vigilant, wakeful

ASTOLAT guilford
lily maid elaine

ASTONISH affect, amaze, amerveil, astound, awe, bedaze, bedazzle, bewilder, bowl over, confound, daze, dazzle, dumfound, flabbergast, gloppen, impress, knock, nonplus, overwhelm, paralyze, petrify, shock, spiflicate, stagger, stam, startle, stound, stun, stupefy, surprise, touch

ASTONISHED aghast, bug-eyed, taken aback

ASTONISHING amazing, eyepopping, fabulous, fantastic

ASTONISHMENT dismay, farley, ferly, marvel, muse, stound, surprise, wonder
exclamation marry, whew, wow

ASTOUND alarm, amaze, appall, astonish, bewilder, boggle, confound, dismay, dumfound, excite, ferly, flabbergast, overwhelm, shock, stagger, startle, stound, stun, stupefy, stupend, surprise, terrify

ASTRADDLE See ASTRIDE.

ASTRAEA dike, virgo
constellation virgo
divine aphra behn
parent eos, themis, zeus
sister chastity

ASTRAEUS *parent* crius, eurybia

son hesperus
wife aurora, eos

ASTRAGAL anklebone, chaplet, cornice, molding, talus

ASTRAKHAN apple, boxhara, broadtail, caracul, fur, karakul, mohair, wool
sheep dumba

ASTRAL celestial, ghost, lamp, remote, sidereal, starlike, starry, stellar
body comet, planet, star
fluid odyl(e)
influences fate
soul state bardo

ASTRATEIA artemis

ASTRAY afield, agley, amiss, aside, awry, confused, depayse, deviate, devious, errant, erring, erroneous, faulty, gleed, gone, lost, mistaken, sinning, vanished, wandering, wilsome, wrong, wry

ASTRIDE acheval, astraddle, atop, pickaback, piggyback, spanning, straddleback, straddling

ASTRINGE bind, compress, constrict

ASTRINGENCY acerbity, acrimony, asperity, austerity, contraction, severity

ASTRINGENT acerb, acid, acrimonious, alum(nol), apocrustic, austere, binding, bitter, constricting, contractor, emetic, harsh, piercing, puckery, rigorous, severe, sharp, shrinking, sour, stegnotic, stern, strict, styptic, tart
black kath(a)
extract catechu
gum kino
kind albutannin, alnuin, alum(nol), biacuru, boral, cachou, cashoo, catechu, cornus, coto, gambier, gaub, geranium, geum, kath(a), kino, mastic, pipi, rhatany, salumen, sapan, spleenwort, styptic, tannin, trillium

ASTROFELL aster, starwort

ASTROLABE alidad, pantacosm, planisphere

ASTROLOGER astromancer, chaldean, erra pater, horoscoper, joshi, joti(si), lilly, magi, mathematic, merlin, prophet, shaman, soothsayer, zadkiel

charm lamin
ASTROLOGY astrodiagnosis, astromancy, astrometry, genethliacs, horoscopy, starcraft, stargazing
belief in siderism
concurrence synastry
lord abdevenham
position quincunx
term alkahest, almuten, alnath, anareta, apheta, aspect, house, mansion, mundane, nativity, planetary, sign, synastry, trine, zodiac
work almagest
ASTRONAUT (See also ROCKET and SPACE references.) astronavigator, martian, rocketeer, rocketman, saucerman, spaceman
american aldrin, anders, armstrong, bassett, bean, borman, carpenter, cernan, collins, conrad, cooper, cunningham, eisele, enos, glenn, gordon, grissom, lovell, mcdivitt, schirra, schweickert, scott, shepard, stafford, white, young
apollo 7 cunningham, eisele, schirra
apollo 8 anders, borman, lovell
apollo 9 mcdivitt, schweickert, scott
apollo 10 cernan, stafford, young
apollo 11 aldrin, armstrong, collins
apollo 13 haise, lovell, swigert
apollo 14 mitchell, roosa, shepard
ballast junk
boss slayton, phillips
gemini armstrong, borman, grissom, lovell, mcdivitt, schirra, scott, stafford, young
killed in action chaffee, grissom, white
lunar module columbia, eagle, intrepid
mercury glenn, shepard
problem bends, blackout, meteor(ite), weightlessness
rocket See ROCKET *names.*
russian belyayev, bikovsky, blackie, breezie, feoktistov, gagarin, komarov, kubasov, laika, leonov, nikolayev, popovich, rukavishnikov, shatalov, shonin, terech-

kova, titov, yegorov, yeliseyev
workshop skylab
ASTRONOMER brahe, galileo, halley, hipparchus, jeans, joshi, joti(si), kepler, newton, uranologist
royal airy, bliss, bradley, christie, flamsteed, halley, maskelyne, pond
ASTRONOMIC(AL) celestial, colossal, distant, enormous, far, great, huge, immense, infinite, large, universal, uranic, vast
calendar almanac
cycle saros
find quasar
instrument aba, altazimuth, armil(l), astrolabe, backstaff, coelostat, orrery, sector, sextant, telescope, volvelle
measure apsis, azimuth, parsec
phenomena nebula, supernova
science astrophysics, astroscopy, celestial mechanics, meteoritics, meteoroscopy, uranography, uranology, uranometry
system blackhole, galactic cluster, neutron star, pulsar, quasar, supernova
term albedo, apastron, apogee, colures, ecliptic, epact, equinox, galactic, geocentric, geodetic, heliocentric, meridian, orbit, perigee, quadrature, trajectory, zodiac, zone
ASTRONOMY *branch* selenodesy, selenology
muse clio, urania
ASTUTE acute, apperceptive, appercipient, argute, artful, astucious, canny, clever, crafty, cunning, discerning, farseeing, foresighted, foxy, ingenious, intelligent, keen, knowing, nasute, penetrating, perceptive, percipient, perspicacious, piercing, prudent, quick, sagacious, sharp, shrewd, skilled, sly, smart, understanding, wily, wise
ASTYANAX scamandrius
parent andromache, hector
slayer greeks
ASTYDAMIA *abductor* hercules
parent amyntor

son amphitryon
ASTYOCHE *consort* ares
son ascalaphus, ialmenus
ASUNDER apart, atwain, atwo, distant, divided, divorced, loose, separate, split, sundry, ysowndir
comb. dich(o), dis
ASURA demon, god, spirit, varuna
ASVING *son* nakula, sahadeva
ASWAN assouan, syene
ASYLUM almshouse, alsatia, altar, ark, bedlam, boobyhatch, bughouse, cover, grith, harbor, haven, home, hospice, hospital, hospitium, jail, madhouse, orphanage, poorhouse, protection, recourse, refuge, retreat, safety, sanctuary, security, xenodochium
ASYMMETRY asyntrophy, distortion
ASYNCRITUS *friend* paul
AT about, als, atten, hereat, near, presence, there, toward, unto
a blow suddenly
all any(way), aught, ava, eer, ever, half, however, ought, soever
all events certainly, notwithstanding
all points cap-a-pie, utterly
any cost notwithstanding
any rate accordingly, always, certainly
any time ever
a standstill cornered, immovable, motionless, stationary
a stretch continually, continuously, during
bay cornered
bottom basically
close quarters cramped, crowded, near
cross-purposes against, belligerent, perplexed
daggers drawn belligerent, hostile
ease carefree, content, easy, prosperous, relax(ed), secure
fault erroneous, guilty, imperfect, mistaken, to blame
full speed amain, swiftly
gun point forcibly
hand available, close, handy, hard by, imminent, near, nigh, present
home affair, at ease, casual, comfortable, conversant,

easy, here, levee, party, reception, relaxed
home in expert, skilled
intervals haphazardly, irregularly, occasionally
it busy, occupied
large abroad, escaped, free, fugitive, loose, unloosed
last eureka, finally, ultimately
least merely
leisure free, idle
length endlessly, finally, fully, tediously
loggerheads See *odds*, below.
low ebb depressed, exhausted, insufficient, prostrate, sick, weak
odds belligerent, differing, disagreeing, hostile, out
once alla prima, amain, anon, bang-off, directly, forthwith, immediately, instantaneously, instanter, now, pdq, presto, promptly, rightaway, straightway, suddenly
one accordant, agreeable, agreeing, harmonious, in concord, unanimous
one time previously, simultaneously
pleasure ad lib
rest asleep, dead, idle, inactive, motionless, perched, quiescent, quiet, relax(ed), tranquil
sea afloat, bewildered, confused, launched, lost, underway
short notice impromptu
that and, then, thereat, thereupon, whereat, whereupon
the drop of a hat readily, willingly
the hand of through
the same time and, meanwhile, notwithstanding, simultaneously, when
times occasionally
variance ajar, belligerent, disagreeing
war disagreeing, belligerent, fighting
will ad lib
wit's end confounded, cornered
work busy, operating
ATABAL drum, kettledrum, tabor
ATABYRIAN zeus
ATAHUALPA atabalipa, inca

brother huascar
capital quito
conqueror pizarro
general challcuchima, quizquiz
ATALANTA artemis, huntress
accomplice meleager
butterfly red admiral
consort hippomenes, melanion, meleager, milanion
hunt calydonian boar
parent clymene, iasus, zeus
son parthenopaeus
ATALAYA bantayan, cattlebush, sapinda, watchtower
ATAMAN chief, cossack, headman, hetman, judge
ATARAXIA calmness, imperturbability, tranquility
ATAUNT rigged, shipshape
ATAVISM recurrence, reversion
ATAVISTIC ancestral, primitive, retrorse, reversionary, reverting
ATE impulse, infatuation
companion duessa
father eris, zeus
ATEBRIN quinacrine
ATELES belzebuth, coaita, spider-monkey
ATELIER bottega, gallery, studio, workshop
ATEO waker
ATEUCHUS beetle, scarab
ATHABASCAN See ATHAPASCAN.
ATHALIAH *husband* jehoram, jehoshaphat
kingdom judah
offspring ahaziah
parent ahab, jezebel, omri
ATHAMAS *consort* ino, nephele
father aeolus
kingdom minyae, orchomenus
offspring glaucus, helle, learchus, leucon, melicertes, palaemon, phrixos, portumnus
victim learchus
ATHANSIA deathlessness, immortality, perpetuity
ATHAPASCAN *indian* ahtena, apache, babine, beaver, dene, dogrib, hupa, kuneste, kutchin, lipan, navaho, navajo, sarsi, taku, thotana, tinne, tolowa, wahane, wailaki, whilkut
ATHEISM agnosticism, godlessness, unbelief

ATHEIST agnostic, apikoros, apostate, deist, epicoris, heathen, infidel, nastika, netheist, skeptic, unbeliever, zendik
ATHELING adeling, nobleman, prince
ATHENA agoraea, aiantis, alea, alera, anemotis, apaturia, areia, arela, auge, axiopoenus, celeuthea, chalcioecus, chalinitis, cissaea, ergane, ergave, hippia, hygeia, itonea, meter, minerva, neith, nike, ophthalmitis, oxyderces, paeonia, pallas, parthence, parthenia, polias, poliatas, poliuchos, promachorma, promachos, pronaos, pronoea, saitis, salpinx, sthenias, tritogeneia, xenia, zosteria
aegis head medusa
armor aegis
bird owl
companion chariclo
creation olive tree
feast plynteria, thargelion
festival arrhephoria, dilpolia, panathenaea
foster parent alalcomeneus
invention plow, rake
oracle site mycenae
parent metis, zeus
pert. palladian
priest butes
priestess auge, iodama, pandrosos
shield aegis
statue palladium
symbol aegis, gorgon, staff
temple parthenon
tree olive
victim ajax, pallas
ATHENAEUM association, library, sanctuary, school
founder hadrian
ATHENS, ATHENIAN attic, choragus, metic (See also ATTIC, ATTICA.)
alien resident metic
arbitrators diaetetae
architect attic, ictinus
archon thesmothete
assembly boule, pnyx
astronomer meton
athletic contest pankration
athletic school palaestra
bee plato
captain alcibiades
cemetery ceramicus
citadel acropolis, cecropia
citizenship rights isotely
clan obe

club, men's hetaeria, hetairy
coin chalcus, obolus
colonies cleruchies
commander adimantus, antiochus, cimon, lamachus, menander, nicias, strategos, themistocles, tolmides, tydeus
court areopagus, dicastery, heliaea
courtesan aspasia, hetaera, hetaira, phryne, thais
culture hero triptolemus
demagogue cleon
ditch barathron
emblem violet
enemy sparta, sulla, xerxes
ensign owl
festival amphidromia, anthesteria, apaturia, cronia, dionysia, hydrophoria, kallynteria, plynteria, pyanepsia, oschophoria, scirophoria, thargelia
founder cecrops
fountain callirrhoe
funeral oration epitaphion
game kottados
general alcibiades, cleon, lamachus, miltiades, nicias, philocles, phocion, zenophon
governor callibius
hall odeum, prytaneum
hero theseus
hill acropolis, areopagus, lycabettus, pnyx
historian ister, thucydides, xenophon
intellectual anaxagoras, damon, protagoras, sophocles, zeno
judge dicast
king cecrops, codrus, erichtheus, erichthonius, pandion
lawgiver draco, solon
leader alcibiades, cleomenes, clisthenes, lamachus, nicias, pericles
magistrate archon, basileus, draco, polemarch, strategos, triarch
market place agora
misanthrope timon
mountain hymettus
of america boston
of ireland belfast, cork
of north copenhagen, edinburgh
of south nashville
of switzerland zurich
of west cordoba
on limmat zurich

orator aeschines, isocrates, lysias
pert. attic
philosopher anaxagoras, aristotle, philochorus, plato, protagoras, socrates, stilbides
platform bema(ta)
poet aristophanes, musaeus
port piraeus
potters' quarter agora, ceramicus, kerameikos
precinct, sacred lenaeum
rival argos, corinth, sparta, thebes
room adytum, atrium, cella
ruler archon, cecrops, codrus, draco, pericles, pisistratus
runner pheidippides
sculptor phidias
seer musaeus
shakespeare's timon
slaves, public toxotae
song scolian
spring callirrhoe
statesman aristides, cimon, cleisthenes, draco, nicias, pericles, phocion, solon, themistocles
temple erechtheum, theseum
the just aristides
title alea
tribunal areopagus
tyrant ariston, cleon, hippias, pericles, pisistratus
woman of rank geraera
ATHERINE fish, sandsmelt, silverside
ATHERMANOUS adiathermal, diathermal, transcalent
ATHIRST agog, anticipating, anxious, arid, avid, craving, coveting, dry, eager, desirous, keen, longing, parched, pining, yearning
ATHLETE acrobat, amateur, boxer, competitor, contender, funambulist, gamester, gymnasiarch, gymnast, palaestrian, pancratiast, player, pro, sport (sman), star, tumbler, turner, wrestler
group squad, string, team, varsity
of christendom scanderbeg
ATHLETIC ablebodied, acrobatic, active, agile, beefy, boardly, boordly, brawny, buirdly, burly, energetic, husky, lusty, muscular, powerful, robust, sinewy, stalwart, strapping, strenu-

ous, strong, thewy, vigorous, vital, wiry
contest agon, bout, event, game, gymkhana, heat, meet, olympics, pentathlon, race
field arena, astrodome, coliseum, colosseum, course, court, diamond, green, grid (iron), oval, pitch, stadium, ring, rink
pert. pancratic
prize cup, medal, ribbon
ATHOLD detain, observe, preserve, retain, withhold
ATHOS *companion* d'artagnan
ATHWART aboard, across, against, aslant, awry, contrary, crossways, crosswise, oblique, perversely, sidewise, traverse, wrongly
ATHYMIA despondency, melancholia
ATIA *brother* caesar
ATIS aconitum, annona, atta, monkshood, sweetsop, tree
ATKINS See SOLDIER.
ATLANTA *airport* hartsfield
coliseum omni
street peach tree
ATLANTAL anterior, atloid, cephalic
ATLANTES caryatids, pillars, telamones
ATLANTIC *bay* biscay, buzzard's, fundy
bird skur
fish alewife, bluefish, bughead, bunker, croaker, fatback, fluke, greentail, lookdown, margate, menhaden, mossbunker, oldwife, opah, pearlsides, pogy, pompoon, salema, scup, sheepshead, silver-jenny, squeteague, tautog, timucu, tripletail
flier corrigan, lindbergh
goby mapo
grunt cottonwick
inlet bristol channel, firth of clyde
islands azores, bermuda, canary, cape verde, cuba, greenland, iceland, leewards, tristan da cunha
-pacific passage cape horn, panama, straits of anian
port baltimore, boston, colon, new york, norfolk, philadelphia, savannah
river to amazon, clyde, hudson, parnaiba, peedee, tagus
sea irish, weddell

sisters pleiades
whale finback
wrasse bluehead
ATLANTIDES See HES-PERIDES, PLEIADES.
ATLANTIS santorini, UTO-PIA
ATLAS book, folio, giant, icbm, mainstay, maps, pillar, powerhouse, stalwart, support, telamon, titan, tome, vertebra
beetle chalcosoma
brother epimetheus, prometheus
comb. atlanto, atlo
consort aethra, eos, pleione
daughters alcyone, asterope, atlantides, calypso, electra, hesperides, hyades, kelaine, maiia, merope, pleiades, tayget
-like atlantean, toros
-maker mercator
moth attacus
navigation chart, portolano, rutter
parent clymene, iapetus
powder dynamite, explosive
son hesperus
ATLI *slayer and wife* gudrun
ATMAN atta, brahma, breath, buddhi, essence, jiva(tma), purusha, self, soul, spirit
ATMOSPHERE air, ambience, aura, background, ceiling, character(istic), climate, condition, decor, ether, feel(ing), frowst, hyaline, miasma, mood, nimbus, ozone, quality, savor, smell, space, sphere, surroundings, tone, troposphere, welkin
comb. aer, atmo(s)
disturbance static, STORM
gas argon, eon, nitrogen, oxygen, xenon
god hadad
noxious miasma
phenomenon aurora, meteor
pressure, pert. baric, barometric
pressure measurer barometer
pressure unit millibar
science meteorology
section solenoid
sensitivity aeroscepsis
stale froust, frowst, fug
upper stratosphere
ATMU tem, tum
ATOLL baker, bikini, IS-LAND, reef

pool lagoon
ATOM bit, bodikin, corpuscle, dash, diad, dyad, element, haet, hate, henad, ion(ogen), iota, isobar, jot, mite, molecule, monad, mote, particle, radical, shade, smidgeon, smitch, soupcon, speck, tinge, tittle, touch, trace, trifle, whim, whit
charged anion, gramion, (h)ion
component electron, neutron, nucleus, proton, triton
element dyad, heptad, hexad, monad, octad, pentad, tetrad, triad
kind acceptor, bohr, cubic, discrete, hot, isobar, isotere, isotopic, radical, rutherford, schroedinger, tagged, thomson, tracer
negative and positive zwitterion
nucleus proton
particle alpha, beta, electron, ion, meson, mesotron, neutrino, neutron, photon, pion, positron, proton
pert. nuclear
smasher cyclotron
stimulator maser
ATOMIC bantom, cyclic, infinitesimal, isobaric, isotopic, minute, molecular, nuclear, tiny, triasic, ultimate
accelerator betatron, bevatron, cosmotron, cyclotron, rheotron, synchrotron, swindletron
bomb, kind fission, fusion, hydrogen, neutron, plutonium, thermonuclear
bomb site alamogordo, eniwetok, hiroshima, kwajalein, nagasaki
center hanford, los alamos, oakridge
order ring
pile reactor
science nucleonics, quantum mechanics, radiology
scientist bohr, dalton, einstein, lewis-langmuir, rutherford, schroedinger, thomson
submarine nautilus, sargo, skate, triton
term deuteride, fission, heavy water, isotone, isotope, nucleon, pleiad, protium, tritium, triton

unit kiloton, magneton, quantum, valence
ATOMIZE accelerate, activate, aerate, bombard, cleave, destroy, disintegrate, nucleize, pulverize, spray, vaporize
ATOMIZER aerograph, autospray, odorator, perfumer, sparge, spray(er), sprinkler, vaporizer
ATOMY atom, DWARF, mite, mote, pigmy, pygmy, skeleton, speck
ATONE abegge, absolve, abye, accord, adjust, agree, amend, appease, assoil, beet(e), bye, compensate, conciliate, expiate, harmonize, immolate, make good, mend, pay, propitiate, purge, ransom, recompense, reconcile, redeem, redress, repair, restore, sacrifice, satisfy, shrive
ATONEMENT agreement, amends, compensation, compromise, concord, expiation, indemnification, indemnity, mend, michtam, penance, propitiation, quittance, reclamation, recompense, reconciliation, redemption, reparation, restitution, satisfaction
place canossa
for injury angild
ATOSSA *consort* cambyses, darius, smerdis
kin cambyses, cyrus, xerxes
patron sappho
ATOUT tarot, trump
ATRABILIOUS adust, bad-tempered, blackblooded, crabbed, forlorn, gloomy, glum, hopeless, hypochondriac, irritable, melancholic, moody, morbid, morose, sad, saturnine, splenetic, sullen
ATRAMENTAL black, ink-like, inky
ATRAX *offspring* canaeus, hippodamia
parent bura, peneus
ATREUS *brother* chrysippus, thyestes
kin nicippe, tantalus
kingdom mycenae
offspring agamemnon, anaxibia, atridae, menelaus, pl(e)isthenes
parent hippodamia, pelops
slayer aegisthus

victim agalus, pl(e)isthenes

wife aerope, cleola, pelopia

ATRIDAE *father* atreus

ATRIP aweigh, clear, hoisted, taut

ATRIPLEX goosefoot, greasewood, orach, saltbush

ATRIUM auricle, catacumba, cavaedium, chamber, courtyard, hall, passage, room

ATROCIOUS abominable, awful, bad, barbaric, base, brutal, criminal, cruel, cursed, dank, dark, detestable, devilish, diabolical, dreadful, evil, execrable, felonious, flagitious, flagrant, grievous, gross, heinous, horrible, infamous, monstrous, nefarious, odious, outrageous, rank, savage, tasteless, terrible, vicious, vile, villainous, violent, wicked

ATROCITY abuse, affront, brutality, corruption, crime, enormity, infamy, monstrosity, outrage, sadism, savagery

ATROPHY decline, degeneration, diminution, emaciate, kraurosis, macies, rust, shrink, shrivel, starve, stultify, stunt, sweeny, swinney, tabes, waste, wither

ATTA anona, ant, atman, flour, meal, soul, spirit, sweetsop

ATTACH accuse, add(ict), adhere, adjoin, adopt, affix, alligate, annex, append, appoint, arrest, ascribe, assign, associate, attack, attribute, belong, bewed, bind, bolt, capture, cement, cling, combine, commandeer, confiscate, connect, detain, devote, distrain, entail, espouse, fasten, fix, garnish(ee), glue, grasp, hang, hinge, hitch, hook, impound, impress, indict, inset, interweave, join, latch, lay, levy, link, paste, pend, pertain, preempt, press, put, replevy, screw, seize, sequester, span, splice, stick, subjoin, tache, take, tatch, tie, unite, usurp, vest, weave, weld

ATTACHE aide, diplomat

case bag, etui, etwee, tashie

ATTACHED accustomed,

addicted, adjunct, adnate, adscript, doting, fast, fond, habituated, joined, linked, partial, sessile

ATTACHMENT addiction, addition, affection, affinity, allegiance, amour, appropriation, arm, arrest, confiscation, connection, crush, detention, distraint, doodad, expropriation, fealty, fetish, fidelity, fixation, fondness, garnishment, holding, impound(age), impressment, levy, liking, love, passion, possession, regard, seizure, sequestration, taking

ATTACK 3 bat, fit, hit, hop, hue, sic 4 belt, blow, bomb, bout, claw, cope, cosh, coup, dint, fray, gang, jump, poke, push, raid, rail, ramp, rape, rush, stab, wade 5 abuse, alarm, argue, assay, begin, beset, blame, blast, blitz, brash, brunt, catch, drive, feint, fight, flout, foray, harry, ictus, onset, press, sally, score, scuff, shoot, siege, snipe, spasm, spell, stone, storm 6 accuse, action, affret, ambush, assail, banzai, battle, bicker, charge, crisis, envaye, expugn, have at, impugn, infest, insult, invade, maraud, molest, onfall, onrush, oppugn, pounce, rebuke, savage, sortie, stound, strike, stroke, tackle, thrust, volley 7 advance, aggress, assault, attempt, barrage, battery, belabor, besiege, bombard, censure, crusade, illness, offense, potshot, seizure, swing at 8 betongue, camisado, escalade, paroxysm, skirmish, surprise 9 ambuscade, cannonade, criticize, encounter, irruption, light into, offensive, onslaught, undertake 10 aggression, blitzkrieg, dragonnade 11 bombardment, incriminate

false feint

night camisado

of illness bout, dwalm, dwam, seizure

slight touch, waff

sudden blitz, raptus, surprise

suicidal kamikaze

verbal bludgeon, stoush, tirade

ATTAI *father* rehoboam

ATTAIN accede, accomplish, achieve, acquire, arise, arrive, ascertain, aspire, bump, catch, compass, earn, effect, fetch, gain, get, obtain, overtake, procure, prove, reach, secure, strike, succeed, touch, win

ATTAINABLE accessible, available, obtainable, practicable, practical

ATTAINMENT accomplishment, acquisition, adoption, arrival, avowal, feat, learning, purchase, skill, wisdom

ATTAINT accuse, affect, attainder, banish, brand, charge, condemn, convict, corrupt, damn, defile, disgrace, doom, exile, hit, infect, mark, pollute, proscribe, sentence, spot, stain, stigma, sully, touch, transport

ATTALEA cohune, coquilla, palm, piassava

ATTAR athar, essence, itr, oil, ottar, otto, perfume

ATTEMPER accommodate, adapt, assuage, attune, control, curb, extenuate, mitigate, moderate, modify, mollify, palliate, reduce, regulate, relieve, restrain, soften, soothe, TEMPER

ATTEMPT aim, assail, assay, assume, attack, begin, bid, crack, dab, effort, endeavor, essay, ettle, exertion, experiment, fand, fist, fling, fraist, have a go, job, lick, mind, mint, mird, move, offer, onset, osse, press, prove, pursuit, say, seek, shot, shy, solicit, stab, start, strive, struggle, tentamen, test, toil, trial, try, undertake, venture, wage, whack, whirl, work

ATTEND accompany, administer, aid, appear, apply, assist, audit, await, chaperon, conduct, consort, convoy, delay, escort, expect, follow, foster, guard, hark(en), hear(ken), heed, hoa, hoo, intend, join, keep, lackey, list(en), look after, mind, minister, notice, nurse, observe, participate,

perpend, recognize, regard, remark, result, second, see, serve, shadow, show, squire, stay, tend, treat, turn up, visit, wait, watch, witness
to punish

ATTENDANCE attention, audience, crowd, delay, escort, gate, presence, regard, retinue, service, suit, turn-out

ATTENDANT accompanying, adjunct, agent, assistant, associate, attache, bearer, bellboy, bellhop, bootblack, bostanji, butler, buttons, caddie, caretaker, chokra, clerk, companion, comrade, concomitant, consequent, corollary, corybant, cupbearer, disciple, donzel, employee, escort, famulus, fenella, fewterer, follower, footboy, friend, gillie, hamal, handmaid, heedful, henchman, keeper, khidmatgar, knight, link-man, menial, minister, nurse, orderly, page, patron, peon, present, prosdyte, pursuivant, related, retainer, sequent, servant, spectator, squire, stocah, subsequent, suitor, tender, thane, thegn, tipstaff, trabant, trainbearer, usher, valet, verger, waiter, yeoman
group claque, cortege, coterie, entourage, followers, following, guards, retinue, staff, suite, train
wedding best man, bridesmaid, bridesman, groomsman, maid of honor, matron of honor, usher

ATTENTION absorption, account, achtung, address, advertence, alertness, application, audience, awareness, beware, care, caution, civility, comity, command, concentration, consideration, courtesy, courtship, deference, detail, diligence, ear(nest), gallantry, gaum, hearing, heed, hist, homage, intentness, listen, mark, mind, note, notice, observance, observation, politeness, reflection, regard, respect, scrutiny, sed-

ulousness, study, thought, vigilance
exclamation of behold, hark, harken, hear ye, listen, look, oyez, see
fixed dharana
flattering homage
from superior tashreef, taskrif
-getter ahem, catch-line, oath
military position brace
wandering aprosexia

ATTENTIVE advertent, agog, alert, arrect, assiduous, busy, careful, circumspect, civil, considerate, diligent, gallant, heedful, immersed, intent, johnny on the spot, listful, meticulous, mindful, obedient, observant, observing, on the ball, particular, polite, present, rapt, reactive, regardful, studious, tentie, tenty, thoughtful, thoughty, vigilant, wakeful, wary, watchful

ATTENUATE abate, avianize, constrict, decrease, deflate, dilute, diminish, draw, emaciate(d), enfeeble, finespun, gaunt, lessen, mitigate, rarefy, reduce, retund, sap, shrink, slender, subtilize, tapering, thin, water, weaken

ATTER matter, poison, pus, sting, venom

ATTERY malignant, poisonous, purulent

ATTEST adjure, affirm, allege, approve, authenticate, aver, certificate, certify, chop, confess, confirm, countersign, declare, depone, depose, evidence, indicate, invoke, manifest, prove, record, say, seal, sign, state, substantiate, swear, testify, testimony, verify, vouch, warrant, witness, witten

ATTIC (See also ATHENS.) aesthetic, athenian, celer, celure, classic(al), cockloft, dormer, esthetic, garret, greek, grenier, head, loft, plain, refined, sky-parlor, solar, soler, storeroom, tallet
bee plato, sophocles
bird nightingale
boy caphalos
festival brauronia

hercules theseus
muse xenophon
part skeeling
salt wit
wall bahut

ATTICA (See also ATHENS.)
city athens
division deme
festival diipol(e)ia
founder cecrops
island salamis
king amphictyon, cecrops, ogyges, ogygos
marble quarry pentelicus
resident metic, pelasgian
river cephissus
town deme
tribe argades, geleontes, hopletes

ATTICUS addison
christian heber
pope's dr arbuthnot

ATTILA atli, etzel, hun, scourge of god
defeat chalons
modern adolf hitler
slayer ildico
wife kriemhild

ATTIRE accouter, adight, adorn, aguise, apparel, arm, array, bego, bigan, cleading, clothes, clothing, costume, DRESS, duds, equipage, garb, garment, guise, habit, headdress, livery, ornament, outfit, panoply, raiment, regalia, revest, robe, suit, tire, togs, toilet, vest(ure)

ATTIS See ATYS.

ATTITUDE action, air, angle, aspect, bearing, behavior, bias, carriage, crotchet, demeanor, disposition, feeling, frame, habitude, inclination, manner, mien, mood, opinion, orientation, outlook, phase, pose, position, posture, predilection, presence, regard, respect, sentiment, set, shape, slant, spirit, stance, stand (point), station, tendency, venue, viewpoint

ATTITUDINARIAN assumer, poser, posturer, pretender

ATTITUDINIZE affect, assume, feign, mince, pose, posture, pretend, sham, simper

ATTORNEY advocate, agent, barrister, counsel(lor), dep-

uty, factor, fiscal, lawyer, legist, muktar, proxy, solicitor, substitute, supply, syndic, vakeel, vakil
power of proxy
ATTRACT adduct, allure, appeal, bait, beckon, beguile, bewitch, bring, call, captivate, catch, charm, court, decoy, drag, draw, enamour, enchant, engage, enlist, entice, fascinate, fetch, gather, influence, interest, intrigue, invite, lure, magnet(ize), pique, pull, seduce, solicit, strike, take, tantalize, tempt, titillate, tole, troll, wind
ATTRACTED drawn, smitten
and repelled ambivalent, amphierotic, amphigenous
ATTRACTION adhesion, affinity, allurement, appeal, bail, bond, call, capillarity, charm, clou, cohesion, cynosure, draught, draw, entertainment, enticement, fascination, gravitation, gravity, indraft, influence, lure, magnet(ism), penchant, pull, show, spectacle, spell, sympathy, witchery
capillary adhesion, gravity
center of polestar
strong penchant
ATTRACTIVE allicient, alluring, amiable, attrahent, beauteous, beautiful, bonny, braw, bright, canny, charming, chic, circean, comely, cunning, cute, desirable, drawing, eesome, engaging, eyesome, fair, fetching, flashy, graceful, gracious, heppen, inviting, irresistible, lovely, magnetic, pleasing, pretty, queme, savory, snazzy, sonsy, taking, venerean, winsome
ATTRAHENT attracting, drawing, luring, magnet, sinapism
ATTRIBUTE account, adjunct, affection, allot, allege, allude, apply, arrogate, ascribe, assert, assign, attach, badge, bestow, blame, character(istic), charge, connect, credit, essence, fasten, feature, fix, foist, give, impute, intitule, mark, note, owe, peculiarity, pertain, place, point,

power, predicate, property, put, qualification, quality, refer, regard, reputation, sign, SYMBOL, token, trait, type
godly eternity, glory, goodness, holiness, immutability, infinity, justice, light, love, majesty, mercy, omnipotence, omniscience, power, sovereignty, truth, ubiquity, unity, wisdom
wrongfully foist
ATTRIBUTION application, arrogation, ascription, assignation, attachment, classification, derivation, etiology, identification, imputation, placement, theory
ATTRITION abrasion, anguish, chafing, compunction, decline, decrease, detrition, erosion, friction, galling, grazing, grief, grinding, penitence, rasping, regret, remorse, repentance, rubbing, scraping, scratching, scuffing, sorrow, wear
ATTUNE accord, adapt, adjust, agree, balance, compensate, conform, harmonize, harmony, key, pitch, prepare, reconcile, temper, tune
ATUA demon, god, spirit
ATUM *consort* iusaas, nebhet-horep
sacred animal bull, merwer, mneris
twins shu, tefnut
ATWAIN apart, asunder, atwin, atwo
ATWITTER aflutter, excited, nervous
ATYMNIUS *companion* sarpedon
father zeus
slayer antilochus
ATYPICAL aberrant, abnormal, bizarre, deviating, different, divergent, grotesque, irregular, non-conforming, unnatural
ATYS attis, shepherd
consort cybele
AUBE *capital* troyes
AUBERGINE eggplant
AUBURN abram, bay, cacha, cachou, catechu, chestnut, cutch, flaxen, gambia, gorevan, hazel, titian, tulipwood, zuni-brown
AUCTION barter, bid(ding), block, bridge, cant, coker,

disposal, hammer, offer, outcry, outroop, portsale, roup, sale, sell, trade, vend(ue)
game bridge, cinch, euchre, forty-five, gin rummy, hearts, manhattan, pinochle, pitch, sixty-six, whist
AUCTIONEER crier, cryer, outrooper
helper spotter
AUDACIOUS adventurous, arrogant, bantam, bardy, barefaced, bodacious, bold, brash, brave, brazen, cheeky, confident, courageous, dantonesque, daredevil, daring, dauntless, death-defying, defiant, doughty, fearless, foolhardy, forward, frack, hardy, harebrained, impertinent, impudent, insolent, intrepid, inventive, lively, madcap, original, presumptuous, rash, rebellious, reckless, saucy, shameless, spirited, temerarious, unabashed, unconventional, uninhibited, unrestrained, valiant, valorous, venturesome
AUDACITY boldness, brass, bravado, bravura, cheek, courage, crust, derring-do, effrontery, enterprise, gall, hardihood, mettle, nerve, officiousness, presumption, sauciness, spirit, temerity
AUDIBERTIA ramona, sage
AUDIBLE aloud, articulate, clear, definite, distinct, hearable, heard, loud, plain, rife
AUDIENCE assembly, attendance, clientele, congregation, crowd, ear, fans, firstnighters, floor, following, gallery, group, hearing, house, interview, listeners, patrons, pit, playgoers, public, spectators, tribunal, viewers, votaries
hall aiwan, auditorium
AUDIENT catechumen, hearer, hearing, listening, penitent
AUDIT account(ing), attend, check, estimate, examination, examine, hear, inquire, inspect(ion), inventory, investigation, monitor, probe, reckon, records, report, review, scan, scruti-

nize, statement, verification, verify

AUDITION audience, conference, examination, hearing, reading, trial, tryout

AUDITOR accountant, apposer, assessor, audient, bookkeeper, catechumen, censor, cpa, disciple, eavesdropper, hearer, hospitant, inspector, listener, monitor, student

AUDITORIUM aiwan, amphitheatre, auditory, aula, cavea, hall, house, nave, odeum, playhouse, room, theater, theatre

AUDITORY acoustic, assembly, audile, aural, auricular, oral, otic
canal ear

AUDREY *suitor* touchstone, william

AU FAIT capable, experienced, expert, proficient, proper, skillful, versed

AUF WIEDERSEHEN See GOOD-BYE.

AUGE, AUGIA *assaulter* hercules
consort augeas, hercules, teuthras
parent aleus, neaera
priestess of athena
son telephus

AUGEAN corrupt, filthy
gulf argolis
stable cleaner hercules
stable site elis
task chore

AUGEAS cyeatus, eurytus, helper
kin actor, agamede, eurytus

AUGER bit, boral, bore, borel, borer, gimlet, nauger, ominate, perforate, terebra, terrier, tool, wimble
cutting edge lip
groove pod
kind annular, pod, screw, slotting

AUGEREAU *commander* napoleon

AUGHT acht, anything, cipher, eawt, eight, naught, nothing, nought, ought, owed, possession, property, valiant, worthy, zero

AUGITE algovite, assyntite, pyroxene, silicate
compound augitophyre, carmeloite, cascadite, fassaite

AUGMENT add, adjunct, ag-

grandize, aggravate, amplify, balloon, boost, dilate, eke, enhance, enlarge, exalt, expand, extend, feed, grow, heighten, help, improve, increase, intensify, magnify, majorate, multiply, raise, swell, urge

AUGUR anticipate, auspex, auspicate, badge, betoken, bode, conjecture, denounce, divine, forebode, forecast, foresee, foretell, forewarn, hariolate, inaugurate, indicate, mark, omen, ominate, portend, predict, presage, prognosticate, promise, prophesy, prophet, seer, sign(ify), soothsayer, token, vaticinate

AUGURY auspex, boding, divination, foreboding, foretoken, hansel, harbinger, omen, ore, portent, precursor, prognostic, ritual, sign, sooth, symptom, token

AUGUST awful, bridget, brilliant, dignified, eminent, estimable, exalted, formal, glorious, grand(iose), great, important, imposing, kingly, magisterial, magnificent, majestic, noble, regal, resplendent, ripen, serene, solemn, stately, venerable, wise
birthstone carnelian, peridot, sardonyx
1st lammas, lug(h)nas, lugnasad
meteor perseid
24th bartholomewtide

AUGUSTINE, ST *mother* monica
memoir confessions

AUGUSTUS caesar, octavian(us)
admiral agrippa
agent cornificus
battle actium
enemy antony, lepidus
freedman epaphrotitus, thyrsus
friend agrippa, cornelius, dolabella, gallus, maecenas, masgaba, proculeius
kin caesar, julia, octavia, tiberius
lieutenant eurycles
mother atia
philosopher areius, philostratus
spa capri
wife livia, scribonia

AUK aethia, alca, alcine, alle, arrie, bird, dovekie, elorios, falk, garefowl, guillemot, halycon, kau, lemot, loom, marrot, murre, noddy, penguin, plautis, puffin, pygopod, razorbill, rockbird, rotche, scoot, skout, starik, tinker, uria, willock
family alcidae
pert. alcidine, alcine
razorbill falk, murre

AULA auditorium, court, emblic, hall, room

AULD old
clootie or hornie devil
lang syne past, solitaire
lang syne author burns
reekie edinburgh
sod homeland
-wives'- -tongue aspen

AULOSTOMUS flutemouth, shrimpfish, snipefish

AUNCEL balance, weight

AUNT bawd, caca, gossip, naunt, prostitute, tanta, tante, tia, zia
mary's tree holly
sally scapegoat

AUNTSARY catamaran

AURA air, aroma, atmosphere, bird, breeze, buzzard, emanation, essence, exhalation, feeling, floriole, halo, odor, savor, scent, sensation, smell, surroundings, tone
consort dionysys
friend artemis
personification wind

AURANTIUM citrus, hesperidium, orange

AUREATE baroque, bombastic, brilliant, euphuistic, florid, flowery, golden, gorgeous, grand, magniloquent, ornate, ostentatious, resplendent, rial, rococo, superb, yellow

AURELIA chrysalis, jellyfish
son caesar

AUREOL corona, crown, effulgence, gloria, gloriole, glory, halo, light, mandorla, nimbus, radiance, ring

AU REVOIR See GOOD-BYE.

AURICLE atrium, chamber, ear, pavilion, pinna, trumpet

AURICULA bear's-ear, pinna, primrose, primula, saxifrage, snail

AURICULAR audible, aural, confidential, hearing, hearsay, otic

AURIGA charioteer, waggoner

AURIGNAC *cave* lascaux

AUROCHS aurus, bison, bonasus, bos, buffalo, tur, urox, urus, wisent

AURORA beginning, dawn, EOS, morning, sunrise, trout

borealis corona, northern lights, petty dancers

tears dawn

trout charr, salvelinus

AURORIAN dawn, dawny, eastern, eoan, roseate

AURUM See GOLD.

AUSCULTATOR stethoscope

AUSLANDER alien, foreigner, outlander, stranger

AUSPICE(S) aegis, aid, care, divination, egis, guidance, influence, omen, patronage, portent, prognostication, protection, sign, sponsorship, supervision, support

AUSPICIOUS advantageous, benign, bright, chanc(e)y, cheerful, cheery, dexter, encouraging, fair, favorable, favoring, fortunate, golden, good, halcyon, happy, hopeful, lucky, opportune, optimistic, pat, promising, propitious, prosperous, providential, reassuring, ripe, rosy, sunny, timely, twine

AUSSIE australian

AUSTEN, JANE *heroine* elizabeth, emma

work emma, mansfield park, persuasion, pride and prejudice, sense and sensibility

AUSTERE abstemious, abstinent, acerb, ASCETIC, astringent, bald, bare, bitter, bleak, budge, chaste, cold, earnest, forbidding, formal, frigid, grave, gruff, hard, harsh, inflexible, inornate, moral, obdurate, primitive, puritanical, relentless, rigid, rigorous, rough, rugged, rustic, self-disciplined, serious, severe, sharp, simple, sober, solemn, somber, sour, spartan, stern, stiff, stour, strict, sullen, tetric(al), unadorned,

uncompromising, unembellished

AUSTERITY asceticism, catoism, inclemency, plainness, prudence, rigor, severity, stoicism, stringency, temperance, yoga

AUSTRALIA, AUSTRALIAN antipodes, anzac, aussie, billjim, binge, digger, down under, jindyworobak, kangaroo, mara, sand-groper, warragal, warrigal

aborigine abo, aiawong, aranda, arunta, austroloid, barkinji, binghi, dieri, euahlayi, ilpirra, kipper, koko, maori, mara, melanesian, myall, papuan, warragal, warrigal (For other aborigine terms, e.g., *boy, shelter,* etc., see below.)

aborigine area arnhemland

acacia brigalow, mulga, myall, rosewood, wattle

afternoon arvo

airline qantas

animal bandicoot, carbora, cuscus, dasyure, duckbill, echidna, kangaroo, koala, marten, numbat, panda, phalanger, platypus, tait, tapoatafa, wallaby, wombat

animal, mythical bunyip

anteater echidna, numbat

apple colane

ash tree acronychia, alphitonia, cupania, elaeocarpus, eucalyptus, flindersia, litsea, malaisia, panax, schizomeria

award logie

baby mulgari

back country billabong, outback

"bad" baal-baal

badger wombat

bag dilli, dilly, shammy, swag

bait berley

barker spruiker

bay bight, botany, moreton, port phillip, shark

beach manly

beach grass marram

bean tree bauhinia, castanospermum

bear koala, panda, wombat

bee karbi, kootcha

beef-wood belah

beverage kava

bird ara(ra), berigora, bittern, boobook, bottle-

swallow, bowerbird, bustard, cassowary, catbird, coachwhip, cockatoo, cooey, crake, crane, dabchick, em(e)u, fairy-martin, figbird, friarbird, gannet, grebe, jacky winter, koel, leipoa, lorikeet, lory, lowan, lyrebird, mallee, manucode, morepork, muttonbird, pardalote, pipingcrow, platypus, pratincole, puffinus, redthroat, roa, rockwarbler, sanderling, stint, stipiture, strepera, waybung, wedgebill, weka, whimbrel

bitterbark quinine-tree

bluebell creeper, sollya

boomerang kiley, kyley, wommera

bowl pitchi

box tree eucalyptus

boy ulpmerka

bread damper

brush ake

brush apple ratonia

brushwood millee

budgereegah See *parakeet,* below.

buffalo grass saint augustine

bull nickey

bush back-blocks, cutback

bustard bebilya

cake brownie, damper

calf poddy

call cooee, cooey

canoe lakotoi

cape howe, york

capital canberra

carrotwood currant, leucopogon

cart jinker

carving, sacred churinga

cat dasyure

catfish tandan

cattle stampede rush

cattle thief duffer, gully-raker

cattle, unbranded clear-skins

cave dwelling gibbergunyah

cedar flindosa, toon(a)

ceremony sheepshearing

chaff-flower khakiweed

channel anabranch, billabong, cowal

chevron dog-leg

chicken australorp

child cooboo

children ambaquerka

city adelaide, albury, ayr, ballarat, bathurst, bendigo, brighton, brisbane, broken hill, cairns, canberra, casino, coburg, collingwood, darwin, dubbo, essendon, geelong, hobart, kalgoorlie, kogarah, melbourne, mildura, mitcham, newcastle, perth, port pirie, randwick, ringwood, rockhampton, sydney, toowoomba, waggawagga, whyalla, wollongong, yass

civil servant cadette

clover nardoo

club waddy

cockatoo arara, corella, galah, ganggang

coin dump, pound, shilling, tray, zack

colonist sterling

container pitchi

conversation yabber

cotton tree majagua

countryman billjim

cowboy jackaroo, waddie

cranberry astroloma, lissanthe

crawl trudgen

crayfish yabbie, yabby

cry cooee, cooey

cuckoo boobook, channelbill

currant carrotwood, leucopogon

dairy man cowcocky

dam hume

dawn kyeema

delinquent bodgie

desert gibson, great victoria, simpson, stuart, tanami

dewfall ilarra

dirge tangi

dish coolamon

dog blue-healer, dingo, kelpie, merle

drink arkaloola

duck pinkeye

eccentric hatter

edelweiss flannelflower

emu apple colane

emu eggs kully-koomurra

englishman pommy

eucalyptus bimbil, bloodwood, bluegum, carbeen, jarrah, mallee, peppermintgum

evergreen araucaria, banksia, bunya-bunya, cairn's hickory, cypress-pine, flindersia

everlasting helipterum

explorer mawson, wilkins

falcon berigora

fan palm cabbage-tree

farmer cocky

female bint

fern asplenium, bird's-nest,

nardoo, nardu, todea, umbrella

festivity corrob(b)oree

finch man(n)ikin

fish barraconta, barracuda, barramunda, beardie, bream, cockatoo, dan, dart, drummer, fortescue, girella, grouper, longfin, mado, mako, morwong, porgy, rockling, rock-whiting, schnapper, silver-belly, sparus, trevally, trumpeter, wirrah

fleabane christ's-eye

flour dust

flower waratah

fly korumburra

folk dance dreher

"follow me" kurura

food kai, tucker

forage goitcho

friend cobber, mate

fruit nonda

gale buster

game sye, tambaroora

geranium crane's-bill

girl lubra

glasswort salicornia

goatsucker frogmouth

"go away" koit bau

goby big-head

gold mining site bendigo

gold rush captain bully forbes

gold rush clipper marco polo

gold rush town coolgardie, kalgoorlie

"good" betcheri, budgeree, budgiroo

gourd star-cucumber

grass andropogon, apluda, cockatoo, marram, spinifex, st augustine

grass finch poephila

grayling cucumber-fish

grunt silver perch

gulf carpentaria, joseph bonaparte, spencer's, van dieman

gully gilgai

gum tree coolibah, eucalyptus, kari, tewart, tooart, t(o)uart

harbor botany bay

harebell wahlenbergia

hawk almakeelia, kestrel, kupalupalu

herb alpinia, ammobium, bluelace, brachycome, brunonia, bunchflower, clover, cobbler's-pegs, ginger, goitcho, horokaka, logania, murrnong, nancy,

parakilya, parrotplant, piripiri, prince's-feather, restio, rhodanthe, sheep-pest, starflower, strawflower, swainsona, wedding-flower

hinterland bush, outback

holiday foundation day

honey-eater bloodbird, blueeye, briarbird, myzomela

honeysuckle banksia

hoodlum larrikin

horse brumbee, prad, waler, warragal, warrigal, yarraman

house humpy

hut gunyah, miamia, mimi

immigrant reffo

impudence chya(c)k

initiation rite bora

ironbark eucalyptus, fat-cake

island admiralty, cato, cocos, coringa, flinders, kangaroo, keeling, king, koolan, lacepede, neptune, norfolk, rottnest, tasmania, thursday, timor

jackass clockbird, goburra, kookaburra

jail tench

jeer barrack

job possie

jumper roo

kangaroo bettong, jerboa, joey, potorco, tungo

kangaroo apple gunyang

kingfisher poditti

kiwi roa

kneestrap bowyang

koala carbora

koel cooee-bird

kumquat desert-lemon

kurrajong calool

lake amadeus, austin, barlee, blanche, bulloo, carey, carnegie, cowan, disappointment, dundas, everard, eyre, frome, gairdner, harris, macdonald, mackay, moore, torrens, wells, yammayamma

language yabber

lark mirafra

lean-to skilling

leg of mutton colonial goose

lifeguard beltman

lilac sarsaparilla

lily blandfordia, doryanthes

liquor, bootleg sly-grog

"listen" arvalla

lizard goan(n)a, stumptail

lorikeet parrot, warrin

luggage tucker bag

lyre bird bullenbullen

magpie piping crow

mahogany bangalay, gunnung, jarrah
manna laa(r)p, lerp
marshmallow lavatera
measure arna, saum
mile naut
millet emu-grass, panicum
mineral barkylite
mining center bendigo, broken hill
mintbush prostanthera
mole platypus
money nicker
morepork nighthawk
morwong jackass-fish
moth bogong
mother gunnea
moundbird talegallus
movie flick
mullet flattail
native See *aborigine*, above.
nettle tree gympie, laportea
newcomer jackaroo, ringneck
nightjar morepork
"no" baal, bail, bale
north mugdinberri, top-end
novelist richardson, russell, white
nurse sister kenny
oak beefwood, casurina
"orate" spruik
orchid rock-lily, tongue flower
ostrich em(e)u
outback back-blocks, bush
oven umu
owl boobook, morepoke, morepork, ninox
palm bangalow, kentia, ptychosperma, seaforthia
pansy parrot-kea, viola
parakeet budgereegay, budgerigar, budgerygah, budgie, corella, greenleek, melopsittacus, rosella
parrot cockateel, cockatiel, corella, lorikeet, lorilet, lory
pasture back-run
pathologist florey
pea clianthus, dolichos
peace thoomee
peach quandong
peak augustus, blue, bongong, brockman, bruce, cradle, cuthbert, doreen, garnet, gawler, gregory, herbert, ise, jusgrave, kosciusko, magnet, morgan, mulligan, murchison, olga, surprise
peninsula cape york, eyre

pepper arva, avaava, kava, vine, yava
pest rabbit
petrel muttonbird, titi
phalanger ariel
physician bruse, burnet
physiologist eccles
pianist grainger
pigeon bronzewing, wonga
pine beefwood, callitris, camphorwood, casaurina, celery-topped, kauri, kaury, nipi, phyllocladus, sandarac
pitcher plant cephalotus
plant abroma, aizoon, alstonia, banga, bathurst-bur, blandfordia, blatti, boxthorn, brisbane-lily, burrawang, calomba, cephalotus, correa, flannelflower, gordon-lily, hempbush, macrozamia, musktree, poisonpea, waratah, warratau
plum cargillia
pond billabong, gilgai
poppy blue-thistle
port albany, brisbane, cairns, freemantle, geelong, geraldton, mackay, maryborough, melbourne, newcastle, sydney, townsville, wollongong
prime minister barton, cook, curtin, deakin, holt, hughes, lyons, menzies, reid, scullin, watson
promenade the block
pudding station-jack
quarreling backslanging
ranch hand boundary-rider
range barlee, carnarvon, darling, durack, flinders, grey, hamersley, james, king leopold, macdonnell, musgrave, opthalmia, robinson
rat hapalote, hapolotis
reptile honey-lizard
rifleman yager
river ashburton, avon, barcoo, barwon, brisbane, bullo(o), burdekin, clarence, comet, culgoa, daly, darling, dawson, degrey, derwent, diamantina, drava, drysdale, fitzroy, flinders, fortescue, gascoyne, georges, georgina, gilbert, hay, hunter, isaacs, lachlan, macquarie, mitchell, murchison, murray, murrumidgee, naomi, norman, paroo, roper, saltwater, staaten, swan, thompson, victoria,

warrego, weeribee, wooramel, yarra, yule
river branch tallywalka
rock hole gnamma
rockrose hibbertia
rodent beaver-rat, rabbit-rat
roller dollarbird
rose boronia
rumor furphy
rustler duffer
sarsaparilla hardenbergia
sassafras atherosperma, doryfora, tree
scar, decorative keloid
scrubland pindan
sea arafura, coral, tasman, timor
seaberry rhagodia
sea bream tarwhine
sea holly eryngium
seaweed jelly-plant
settler bass, cook
shamrock menindie-clover
shanty humpy
shark blue pointer, gray nurse, isurus, mako, tope, wobbegong
sheep comeback, jumbuck
sheep dog huntaway, kelpie
shelter breakweather, wurley
shield elemong, heelaman, hielaman, mulga, yeelaman
shoe plimsol
shore plant atriplex
shrike bellbird, squeaker
shrub aalii, acacia, alstonia, amulla, baloghia, banksia, bloompoison, boronia, boxpoison, broom, brushbush, cockatoobush, commersonia, coralbush, correa, daviesia, dogbane, dogwood, eucryphia, gastrolobium, goodenia, gooma, gray plum, grevillea, guitarplant, hoya, jacksonia, musk, myoporum, myrtle, needlebush, olearia, pimelea, piptomeris, pituri, poisonbush, rhagodia, rosemary, rue, scentwood, styphelia, trochocarpa, turmeric, twinebush, wallabybush, wallflower, wattle
sickness barcoovomit
skull cobbra
slum backblock
snake bandybandy, deathadder, elapid
snapper red bass
soldier anzac, anzak, billjim, digger, swaddy
song waltzing matilda
soprano melba, sutherland

sorcerer bo(o)yla
southwest coast the bight
spear wommala,
  wom(m)era, woomerah
spirit bunylda, tyeera
spring namma
spurge balolo
squall cockeyed bob
stampede breakaway
state bananaland, new south
  wales, northern territory,
  queensland, tasmania, victoria
statesman bruce, cook, curtin, evatt, fisher, wentworth
stone gibber
strait bass, torres
supplejack clematis, myoporum, vine
swag bluey, matilda
swamp mahogany gunnung
swampoak beefwood, cas-
  uarina
sweetheart clinah
tablet, secret churinga
tattoo goanna
tea smilax
teak endiandra, flindersia,
  tree
tennis player court, emerson,
  goolagong, hoad, laver,
  newcombe, rosewall, stolle
thicket mallee
thickhead thunderbird
thieves' look-out cocky
thistle akania
threepence tray
throwing stick boomerang,
  hornerah, kiley, kilie, wommala, wom(m)era, woo-
  mera(h), woomerang
timber tree apple gum,
  brushdeal, cupaniopsis, eugenia, myrtle
tongueflower glossodia, orchid
toy weetweet
trash collector garbologist
tree 3 box, oak 4 goai, kari,
  toon 5 aalii, belah, boldo,
  boree, gidia, gidya, karri,
  mulga, myall, nonda,
  penda, tuart, wilga 6 acacia,
  akeake, bimbil, gidgee, kowhai, lebbek, marara, medlar, myrtle, tewart, tooart,
  wandoo 7 alipata, atalaya,
  cajuput, dogbane, eugenia,
  geebung, gmelina, gunning,
  sapinda 8 alstonia, apple
  gum, balanops, ballygum
  baloghia, bangalay, bangalow, beefwood, brigalow,
  bumpy ash, carabean, cider-

gum, cudgerie, curajong,
emu-apple, flindosa, ironbark, longjack, quandong,
tileseed, turmeric 9 blackbutt, brush-deal, cassowary,
casuarina, flametree,
goutystem, greasenut, ivorywood, koorajong, queen-
wood, sourgourd, stave-
wood, stinkbush, stone-
wood, sweetroot, waddy-
wood 10 axebreaker, bitterbark, black sally, brush-
cedar, bunjibunji, bunya-
bunya, butterbush, callistris,
cattlebush, celery-pine, dun-
garunga, eucalyptus, flindersia, lillypilly, silvertree,
stringbark, woodenpear 11
bottlebrush, brush cherry,
callistemon, cupaniopsis,
elaeocarpus, plume-nutmeg,
prickly pine, tulip-flower 12
illawarraash 13 blind-your-
eyes
tribe See *aborigine,* above.
tulip telopea, waratah
tumbleweed roly-poly
turpentine tree brisbane box
twilight noolinga
umbrella tree ginseng
valley burragorang, grose,
  jamieson, kangaroo, me-
  galong
vessel yallah
vine apple-berry, billardiera,
  bloodybark, bluecreeper,
  burdekin, glory-pea, kennedya, lonchocarpus, sarcostemma, sollya, turpeth
wallabie pademelon
waratah lily telopea
warbler grass-wren, malurus
war club waddy
war dance corroboree
water hole billabong
water jar banga
water lily nymphaea
water mole duckbill, platypus
wattle acacia, boobyalla,
  cooba(h), myoporum, willow
weapon boomerang,
  hulla(h), hullanulla, leeangle, liangle, waddy, womal
weaverbird grass-finch
weed calotis
westerner groper
white-eye grape-eater
wilderness kimberleys, outback
wild grape wongawonga
willow geijara

wind brickfielder, buster,
  cockeyed bob, maria
wine barnawartha, clare,
  coonawarra, dalwood, eden,
  griffith, hunter valley, mildura, moyston, mudgee,
  murrumbidgee, musell-
  brook, swan valley, tahbilk,
  wahgunyah, watervale, valley
wine, cheap nelly, plonk
woman bint, lubra, sheila
wombat koala
wool measure bag
wool organization bawra
work dargue, yakka
workman billjim
workman's insurance compo
zone, arid sonoran

AUSTRIA, AUSTRIAN os-
  tereich
alps tirol, tyrol, noric
amphibian olm
architect loos, von erlach,
  wagner
artist klimt, kokoschka
baron freiherr
botanist mendel
brier eglantine
cake sacher torte
capital vienna, wien
chemist pregl, welsbach
cinnabar vermilion
city bregenz, dornbirn, enns,
  graz, innsbruck, klagenfurt,
  krems, lech, leoben, linz,
  modling, ried, salzburg,
  spittal, steyr, traun, vienna,
  villach, wels, wien
coin albertin, crown, ducat,
  florin, groschen, gulden,
  heller, kreutzer, krone, lira,
  schilling, zehner
composer berg, bruckner,
  czerny, diabelli, dittersdorf,
  friml, haydn, krenek,
  mahler, paumgartner,
  schonberg, schubert,
  strauss, suppe, toch, we-
  bern, weingartner, wolf
conductor bodanzky, bohm,
  karajan, kleiber, korngold,
  krauss, krips, mahler,
  strauss, walter
critic bahr
dance dreher, landler, waltz
duchy carinthia, carniola,
  styria
economist menger
emperor charles, ferdinand,
  francis, franz josef, habs-
  burgs, hapsburgs
explorer forrest
fleabane christ's-eye

foreign office ballhaus, ballplatz
general eugene
horse lippizaner
jew galitzianer
knight ritter
lake almsee, bodensee, constance, fertoto, mondsee, traunsee
leader raab
legislature bundesrat, herrenhaus, reichsrat(h)
magistrate burgomaster
mathematician bolzano
measure achtel, becher, dreiling, fass, fuss, futtermassel, halbe, joch, klafter, leipoa, linie, mass, meile, metze, muth, phiff, punkt, seidel, viertel, yoke
native styrian, tyrolese
neurologist braver, freud, frohlich
noble archduke, furst, ritter
pass arlberg, brenner, loibl, plocken
pathologist landsteiner
peak eisenerz, kitzbuhel, rhatikon, stubai
pheasant leipoa
philosopher carnap, mach, popper, wittgenstein
physician barany, mesmer, skodaic, treitz
physicist boltzmann, frisch, mach, pauli
pianist schnabel
playwright bahr, schnitzler, werfel
poet grillparzer, hofmannsthal, rilke
port krems, linz, vienna
premier dollfuss
president schaerf
prince archduke
province bohemia, bukowina, burgenland, carinthia, carniola, dalmatia, galicia, gradisca, istria, moravia, salzburg, silesia, styria, tirol, triest, tyrol, voralberg
psychiatrist adler, freud, rank, reich, wagner-jauregg, weininger
range alps, dolomites, tirols, tyrols
rifleman jager
river danube, donau, drau, drave, elbe, enns, inn, iser, kamp, lech, march, moldau, mur, raab, salza(ch), thaya, traun
roman province noricum, pannonia, raetia

singer jeritza, rysanek, sembrich, tauber
statesman forrest, franz jonas, metternich
surgeon billroth, lorenz
theologian bolzano
title archduke
tunnel arlberg
vermilion cinnabar
violinist kreisler, morini, paur
weight centner, denat, karch, marc, pfennig, pfund, quentchen, saum, stein, unze, vierling
winehouse heuriger
woman marie antoinette
writer anzengruber, bahr, broch, hofmannsthal, kafka, kraus, musil, rilke, sachermasoch, salten, suttner, werfel
zoologist frisch

AUSTROASIATIC *language* See KHASI, MALACCA, MON-KHMER, and MUNDA *language.*

AUSTRONESIA *language* See JAVA, MALAYSIA, MELANESIAN, POLYNESIAN, and TAGALA *language.*

AUTARCH autocrat, despot, ruler, tyrant

AUTARCHY autonomy, freedom, independence, self-sufficiency, sovereignty

AUTEP aintab, ayntab, gaziantep

AUTHENTIC acceptable, actual, approved, authoritative, authorized, bonafide, certain, conclusive, correct, credible, current, dinkum, established, exact, factual, genuine, kosher, official, original, orthodox, pucca, pukka, pure, real, reliable, right, simon-pure, sincere, standard, true, trustworthy, valid, verified, veritable

AUTHENTICATE accredit, approve, avouch, certify, circumstantiate, confirm, corroborate, endorse, legalize, prove, ratify, seal, substantiate, test, try, validate, verify, warrant

AUTHOR agent, annalist, auctor, begetter, best seller, bookman, bookwright, cause, compiler, composer, creator, declare, designer, doer, dramatist, edit,

elohist, encyclopedist, essayist, factor, formulate, founder, freelance, generator, ghostwriter, immortal, inditer, informant, inventor, journalist, litterateur, lokman, magazinist, maker, monographer, novelist, organizer, originator, pamphleteer, parent, penman, planner, poet, producer, progenitor, projector, reviewer, say, scribe, sire, source, spark, start, storyteller, tell, wordpainter, writer
imaginary lollius, slawkenbergius
name by-line
prolific polygraph
unknown anon

AUTHORITARIAN absolute, accepted, authentic, cathedral, classic, commanding, consequential, dictatorial, dogmatic, ex cathedra, expert, grave, imperative, imperious, impressive, influential, magisterial, magistral, masterful, mighty, official, oracular, orthodox, peremptory, positive, potent, powerful, puissant, reliable, ruling, sovereign, substantial, valid

AUTHORITY adept, approbation, ascendancy, bible, certificate, citation, cognoscente, command, commission, competency, connoisseur, control, conviction, credit, critic, dominance, dominion, empery, epicure(an), expert, faith, force, government, headship, hegemony, hoyle, influence, informant, judge, jurisdiction, jus-divinum, justification, law, licence, license, mastery, model, oracle, pattern, police, power, prerogative, prestige, professional, quotation, regent, regime, riche, right, rod, rule, ruling, sage, sanction, sovereignty, stamp, standard, statute, suzerainty, sway, swinge, testimony, title, virtuoso, warrant, weight, witness
complete carte blanche, power of attorney
judicial banc
preponderant hegemony

symbol bannerstone, baton, crown, fasces, fist, hoyle, mace, orb, scepter
unlimited autocracy
AUTHORIZE accredit, allow, appoint, approve, certificate, charter, commission, constitute, decree, delegate, empower, enable, enact, endorse, enfranchise, entitle, establish, formulate, franchise, justify, legal, legalize, legislate, legitimatize, let, license, ordain, permit, prescribe, privilege, ratify, regulate, sanction, seal, suffer, warrant
AUTHORSHIP composition, inditement, instigation, paternity, pencraft, writing
AUTISM dereism
AUTO (See also CAR references.) 3 bug, bus, cab, car, dog, tub 4 boat, coop, drag, hack, heap, jeep, ride, taxi, trap, wynn 5 buggy, coach, coupe, crate, eight, lizzy, lorry, motor, racer, sedan, wreck 6 beetle, berlin, bucket, camion, chummy, hearse, hoopie, hotrod, jalopy, jitney, junker, landau, saloon, tourer, towcar, wheels 7 berline, clunker, compact, flivver, hackney, machine, omnibus, phaeton, steamer, taxicab, torpedo, tractor, trailer, vehicle, voiture 8 brougham, dragster, dumpcart, electric, motorcar, roadster, runabout, squadrol, stockcar, suburban, victoria 9 ambulance, cabriolet, charabanc, landaulet, limousine 10 beachwagon, blackmaria, blitzbuggy, bookmobile, locomobile, touringcar 11 bloodmobile, convertible 12 stationwagon 13 electromobile
army jeep
cheap tin-lizzie
classic lancia, reo, rolls royce
closed coupe, sedan
convertible drophead, landaulet
court motel
early alco, apperson, auburn, autocar, baker electric, bearcat, benz, brush, bugatti, chalmers, chandler, columbia, cord, crane-

simplex, cunningham, duesenberg, dupont, duryea, edsel, emf, flivver, franklin, graham(paige), hayes, hudson, hupmobile, jackrabbit, kissel, knox, lasalle, lizzie, locomobile, lozier, marmon, maxwell, mercedes, mercer, moon, national, oakland, oldfeld-steamer, olds, overland, owen magnetic, packard, peerless, pierce arrow, pope-hartford, premier, rambler, regal, reo, saxon, sear, simplex, stanley steamer, star, stevens(duryea), stutz, thomas, wills st clair, willys(knight), winton
fast hotrod
harp zither
hood bonnet
large gas-guzzler, hog, roadhog
luxurious limousine
midget doodlebug, topolino
part accelerator, ammeter, axle, bearing, bonnet, boot, brake, bumper, camshaft, carburetor, choke, clutch, cowl, crankcase, cutout, cylinder, dash(board), differential, distributor, engine, exhaust, fan, fender, flywheel, gearshift, generator, headlight, hood, horn, ignition, intake, klaxon, manifold, motor, muffler, piston, radiator, rumble seat, running board, shock(absorber), spark plug, speedometer, starter, stator, steering wheel, tailfins, taillight, tonneau, top, transmission, trunk, valve, wheel, windshield
price list blue book
race drag, derby, five hundred, grand prix, indie, indy, mille miglie
race track motordrome
rear tonneau
repair body-work
shelter carport, garage
sport dragster, dunebuggy, roadster
trim chrome
trunk boot
turn signal trafficator
2-door cloverleaf, coupe, roadster
vibration shimmy
AUTOBAHN freeway, motorway, strada

AUTOBIOGRAPHY chronicle, memoir, reminiscences, vita
AUTOCHTHONOUS aboriginal, ancient, edaphic, endemic, indigenous, native
AUTOCRACY absolutism, autarchy, autonomy, despotism, monocracy, monarchy, oppression, tyranny
AUTOCRAT autarch, caesar, czar, despot, dictator, kaiser, mogul, monarch, monocrat, sovereign, torse, tsar, tyrant, tzar
the oliver wendell holmes
AUTOCRATIC absolute, arbitrary, capricious, despotic, imperious, tyrannical, tyrannous
AUTOGIRO helicopter
AUTOGRAPH engross, handwriting, inscribe, inscription, john hancock, john henry, manuscript, name, sign(ature)
book album
AUTOHARP zither
AUTOLYCUS *city* sinope
commander hercules
daughter anticlea
friend demoleon, phlogius
grandson odysseus, ulysses
parent chione, deimachus, hermes
profession thief
sculptor sthenis
AUTOMAT cafe, one-arm bandit, restaurant, slot machine, vender, vendor
AUTOMATIC autogenous, clockwork, disciplined, endogenous, fire-arm, gun, impulsive, independent, instinctive, involuntary, mechanical, pistol, prompt, quick, ready, rifle, self-generated, spontaneous
device gyropilot, laundromat, missile, robot, self-starter, speedometer, televox
AUTOMATIST medium, psychic, spiritualist
AUTOMATON android, golem, machine, puppet, robot
AUTOMOBILE See AUTO.
AUTONOE *consort* aristaeus, pan
kin actaeon, agave
parent cadmus, harmonia
victim pentheus
AUTONOMOUS autarchic, autarkic, autonomic, free,

independent, self-governing, separate, sovereign, spontaneous

AUTONOMY separateness, sovereignty

AUTOPSY analysis, dissection, examination, inspection, necropsy, postmortem, prosection

AUTUMN decline, fall, harvest, indian summer, maturity, old age, st martin's summer
adonis pheasant's-eye
bellflower gentian
blond fawn, seal
catchfly silene
crocus colchicum, meadowsaffron
dandelion hawkweed
flower aster
gentian bitterwort
leaf feuille-morte
sign libra, sagittarius, scorpio
squill scilla
violet bellflower
willow salix

AUXESIA demeter

AUXESIS growth, hyperbole, increase, proliferation

AUXILIARY abetting, accessory, additional, adjunct, adjutant, adjuvant, adminicular, aide, aiding, ally, ancillary, assistant, associate, branch, coadjutor, confederate, contributory, crutch, helper, helping, mate, partner, reserve, secondary, sub, subordinate, subsidiary, supplementary, support, tributary

AVADAVAT amadavat, bird, estrilda, waxbill

AVADHUTA ascetic, mendicant

AVAIL abet, advantage, aid, apply, assist(ance), assure, benefit, beset, bestead, boot, capitalize, dow, efficacy, expedient, exploit, fadge, fulfill, help, inform, inure, prevail, profit, resort, satisfy, serve, service, skill, stead, succeed, suffice, trade on, use, utility, utilize, value
oneself of apply, catch, embrace, employ, move, subserve, use, utilize

AVAILABLE accessible, advantageous, at hand, attainable, convenient, disposable,

efficacious, fit, flush, free, gettable, handy, obtainable, on tap, open, present, profitable, ready, suitable, usable, useful, valid

AVALANCHE descent, glissade, landslide, lawine, mass, overwhelm, slide, snowslide, swamp, vollenge

AVALE abase, descend, dismount, doff, flow, lower, sink, submit, yield

AVALOKITESHVARA bodhissatva, kuan-yin

AVALON *resident* argante, arthur, morgan le fay, oberon

AVANT *courier* forerunner, herald, scurrier
garde advanced, experimental, lead, literati, pioneer, van(guard)
propos exordium, foreword, introduction, overture, preamble, preface, prelude, proem, prolegomenon, prologue, prolusion, protasis

AVAR kyurin, lezghian

AVARICE acquisitiveness, avidity, avidness, closeness, costiveness, covetousness, cupidity, desire, gluttony, greed(iness), insatiability, lust, miserliness, misery, niggardliness, parsimony, penury, piggishness, rapacity, ravenousness, stinginess, voracity
personification erphila
spirit of mammon

AVARICIOUS close, covetous, grabby, grasping, greedy, griping, gripple, having, hungry, itching, miserly, piggish, rapacious, ravenous, sordid, stingy, voracious

AVAST cease, halt, hold, stay, stop

AVATAR balarama, embodiment, epiphany, exaltation, fetish, incarnation, transformation, VISHNU

AVAUNT advance, aroint, away, begone, boast, depart, dismissal, forward, stand off

AVE farewell, goodbye, hail, welcome
maria hail mary, rosary
atque vale hail and farewell

AVELLAN filbert, hazelnut

AVENA grass, oats

AVENGE awreak, bewreak,

chastise, compensate, defend, get even, justify, pay back, punish, repay, requite, retaliate, revenge, right, satisfy, settle, vindicate, visit, wrack

AVENGER alastor, alecto, ate, erinys, eumenides, furies, fury, goel, kanaima, ker, magaera, nemesis, relatiator, vindicator

AVENS barefoot, bennet, burnet, daisy, geum, hemlock, herb, saxifrage, valerian

AVENTURINE glass, goldstone, mineral, quartz, sunstone

AVENUE access, adit, aisle, allee, alley, approach, arcade, arterial, artery, avenida, boulevard, bypath, drive, entry, exit, expressway, freeway, gate, highway, mall, means, method, opening, outlet, parkway, passage, pike, process, riding, road(way), rue, speedway, strada, street, thoroughfare, via, way

AVER acknowledge, affirm, aiver, allege, argue, assert, asserverate, assure, avouch, avow, claim, declare, defend, horse, justify, maintain, possession, property, protest, prove, state, swear, testify, verify, vow

AVERAGE arriage, common, estimate, everyday, fair, general, indifferent, intermediate, mean, medial, median, mediocre, medium, middle, middling, moderate, norm(al), ordinary, par, ratio, ruck, rule, run, soso, standard, typical, usual
man babbitt, bourgeois(e), proletarian

AVERNUS See HADES, HELL.

AVERRHOA caramba, carambola, gooseberry

AVERSE abhorrent, adverse, afraid, against, antipathetic, backward, balky, contrary, disinclined, hesitant, indisposed, inimical, lo(a)th, opposed, perverse, reluctant, unsympathetic, unwilling

AVERSION abhorrence, abomination, allergy, anathema, antipathy, derry, despite, disgust, dislike, distaste, dread, enmity, fear, hate, hatred, horror, indisposition, mislike, regret, repugnance, repulsion

AVERT alienate, averruncate, avoid, bend, check, deflect, deter, divert, dodge, estrange, evade, fend, forefend, forestall, obviate, parry, preclude, prevent, retard, sheer, shield, shift, thwart, turn, twist, ward off, withturn, wry

AVESTA *demigod* yima *text* gatha, vendidad, vispered, yasht, yasna *translation* zend

AVIARY birdcage, columbarium, columbary, dovecote, ornithon, perch, pigeonhouse, roost, volary

AVIATOR ace, aeronaut, birdman, flier, flyer, icarus, lufbery, manbird, pilot, skyman *badge* wings *famous* corrigan, earhart, lindbergh, red baron *female* aviatrix, birdwoman *signal* out, over, roger

AVICHI See HELL.

AVID acquisitive, agog, anxious, ardent, athirst, atiptoe, avaricious, craving, dedicated, desirous, eager, grasping, greedy, hankering, hungry, keen, longing, thirsty, warm, yearning

AVIGATION See AERONAUTICS.

AVILE abase, debase, depreciate, vilify

AVION See AIRCRAFT.

AVOCADO abacate, abbogada, aguacate, ahuacatl, alligator pear, avocat, chinin, coyo, custard-apple, midshipman's marrow, palta, persea, zaboca *kind* fuerte, hass, zutano

AVOCATION amusement, diversion, hobby, recreation, sideline

AVOCET barker, bird, bluestocking, cobbler's-awl, godwit, scooper, tilter, yelper

AVOID abhor, abjure, abrogate, abstain, annul, avert, balk, blench, blink, burke, bypass, circumvent, ditch, dodge, eject, elude, emit, escape, eschew, evade, evitate, evite, expel, feign, flee,

fly, forsake, hedge, ignore, invalidate, miss, parry, quash, quit, refute, reject, shift, shirk, shun, shy, sidestep, skirt, skulk, slack, snub, spair, vacate, void, wande, ware, withdraw, wonde *the issue* beat around the bush, waffle *work* goldbrick

AVOIDANCE abstinence, annulment, dodge, elusion, eschewal, evasion, go-by, lam, outlet, removal, runaround, shuffle, subterfuge, withdrawal

AVOLATE escape, evaporate, fly

AVON *bard* shakespeare *city on* bristol, stratford *lord* anthony eden

AVOUCH acknowledge, admit, affirm, assert, aver, avow, confess, confirm, corroborate, declare, depone, depose, guarantee, justify, maintain, own, predicate, profess, promise, protest, sanction, swear, testify, underwrite, warrant

AVOW See AVOUCH.

AVOWED declared, frank, stated, sworn

AWA away, elops, fish, kava, milkfish, ten-pounder

AWAFT adrift, afloat

AWAIT abide, attend, bide, expect, heed, hope, impend, keep, look, pend, remain, serve, stay, suffice, sweat it out, tarry, wait, watch, waylay

AWAKE active, adawe, alert, alive, arise, arouse, attentive, aware, call, careful, conscious, daw, excite, fire, get up, heedful, knock up, lively, quicken, rise, rouse, startle, stimulate, stir, vigilant, watchful

AWARD accolade, accord, act, adjudge, allocate, allot, appoint, arbitrament, assign, bestow, bonus, bounty, confer, consign, crown, decision, edgar, emmie, emmy, gift, give, golden globe, grammy, grant, guerdon, honor, iron cross, jackpot, judge (ment), kiss, medal, meed, mete, oscar, premiate, premium, present, prize,

pronounce, reward, sentence, sweepstakes, verdict *academic* cum laude, degree, diploma, magna cum laude, scholarship *cinema* oscar *honorable mention* accessit *recording* grammy *theater* tony *tv* emmy *tv animal* patsy

AWARE active, alert, alive, apprised, awake, cognizant, comprehending, conscious, hep, informed, intelligent, jerry, knowing, knowledgeable, mindful, observant, perceptive, percipient, reck, sensible, smart, sophisticated, sure, understanding, vigilant, wary, watchful, wise, with it

AWARENESS attention, feel(ing), insight, recognition, sensation, sense

AWASH floating, flooding, overflowing

AWAY about, abroad, absent, adrift, afar, along, apart, aside, astray, avaunt, awa, begone, continuously, distant, elsewhere, elsewhither, far, forth, fro, from, gone, hence, hyne, kill, leave, off, out, overseas, past, remote, scat, scram, thence, via *comb.* abh, abs, apo, cat(a), dis, kat(a), kath *from* alone, aloof, apart, beside *from its time* anachronistic, atavistic

AWE admiration, amaze, appall, astonish, bewilder, buffalo, consternation, cow, daunt, dismay, dread, esteem, fear, freeze, frighten, horrify, horror, inspire, overcome, paralyze, petrify, phobia, regard, religio, respect, reverence, scare, shock, stupefy, subdue, terrify, terror, veneration, wonder, worship *-inspiring* extraordinary, fearsome, godful, olympian, splendid, terrible

AWELESS confident, dauntless, fearless, insolent, irreverent

AWESOME appalling, eerie, eery, fell, holy, ghostly, reverent, solemn, weird

AWESTRUCK blank, confounded, dazed, silent
AWETO caterpillar, cordyceps, weri
AWFUL abominable, aghast, BAD, dire, distasteful, dreadful, extraordinary, extremely, fearful, frightful, ghastly, grave, great, hideous, horrible, impressive, ludicrous, majestic, ominous, revered, sacred, satanic, serious, shocking, sublime, terrible, ugly, unpleasant, venerable, very
AWHILE temporarily, transiently
AWKWARD all thumbs, backhanded, blundering, boorish, bulky, bunglesome, bungling, butterfingered, car, clouterly, clownish, clumsy, cumbersome, cumbrous, dangerous, detrimental, difficult, disconcerting, embarrassing, froward, fudgy, gauche, gaum, gawky, graceless, green, halting, hulking, hulky, ill at ease, inapt, incompetent, inconvenient, ineffective, inept, inexpedient, inexpert, inopportune, left-handed, loutish, lubberly, lumbering, lumpish, maladroit, oafish, perverse, ponderous, rigid, rustic, stiff, thumby, troublesome, ugly, unco, uncouth, uncow, uneasy, ungainly, ungraceful, unhandy, unked, unkid, unmanageable, unpleasant, unskilled, untoward, unwieldy, wooden
age adolescence, teenage, teens
fellow bungler, calf, clod, clot, galoot, lout, tawfy, tumfie
AWL broach, brode, brog, els(h)in, elson, fibula, gimlet, goad, nail, nalle, needle, prog, punch, scriber, stabber, tap, tool
-bird woodpecker
-shaped subulate
AWN ail, arista, avel, barb, beak, beard, bristle, bullen, ear, jag(g), pile
grass chrysopogon
AWNLESS humble, hummel, nott, pollard
AWNED, AWNY aristate,

barbate, barigerous, bearded, hairy
AWNING baldachin, blind, canopy, canvas, marquee, semian(na), shade, shamianah, shelter, sunblind, sunshade, tent, tienda, tilt, velarium
fabric algerienne, canvas, duck
fastening earing
AWREAK avenge, condemn
AWRY agee, agley, ajee, alop, amiss, askance, askew, asquint, astray, athwart, bent, bias, blooey, com(med), crooked, disorderly, distorted, eccentric, erroneous, evil, faulty, flooey, gleed, gleyd, ill, improper, inaccurate, oblique, perverse, skewed, snafu, turned, unreasonable, wonky, wrong
AX, AXE adze, ask, besague, biface, bill, bipennis, boucher, burgoyne, celt, chopper, cleaver, cut, eawe, fasces, francisc, gurlet, hache, halberd, hatchet, inquire, jedding, lochaber, macana, oncin, partisan, poleax, pulaski, thixle, tomahawk, twibill
and mattock matax
battle francisc
blade bit
bronze palstave
butt poll
comb. securi
cut gash, hack, kerf
double-edged besague, labrys
give the See DISMISS.
hammer cavel, kevel, knapper
handle boondoggle, haft, helve
headsman's mannaia
mason's cavel
mountaineering piolet
notch kerf
-shaped dolabriform, securiform
stone jade, nephrite
wooden macana
AXILLA ala, armpit, oxter, shoulder
AXIOM adage, aphorism, apothegm, byword, dictate, dictum, formula(ry), fundamental, golden rule, law, maxim, motto, postulate, precept, prescript, principle, principium, proposition,

proverb, rule, saw, saying, scholium, theorem, truism, truth
AXIOPOENUS athena
AXIS alliance, association, axle, axon, caudex, caulome, center, deer, distaff, fulcrum, league, line, nave, oarlock, partnership, pedicel, pin, rachis, radiant, rowlock, stalk, stem, succula, swivel, sympode, trunnion
cerebrospinal brain, cord, neura, spine
comb. atlo, axi, axo
deer chital, chitra
device rotator
power germany, italy, japan
AXLE axile, axis, bar, bogey, bogie, cod, gimbal, gudgeon, hinge, hingle, hub(ble), mandrel, pin(tle), pivot, pole, shaft, skene, sleeve, spindle, spool
box bushing, journal
part linch pin
steering ackerman
AXON axis, axite, dendrite, neurite
AXUNGE fat, grease, lard
AYA *consort* shamash
AYAH chay, eyah, governess, iya, maid, nurse, portent, servant, sign
AYE affirmative, always, assent, continually, eternal, ever, forever, pro, roger, yea, yes
-aye daubentonia, lemur
AYEGREEN houseleek
AYESHA *novel* she
AYESHAH See AISHA.
AYMARAN *indian* cana, canchi, caranga, cauqui, quilaqua
AYNTAB aintab, autep, gaziantep
AYTHYA blackhead, bullneck, canvas-back, duck, nyroca, scaup-duck
AYU plecoglossus, salmon, sweetfish
AZAFRAN ditaxis, saffron, turmeric
AZALEA bouquet de flore, cardinal, erica, ghent, kurume, minerva, pinkpearl, pinkster, rhododendron, snow, winterbloom
AZAN *kin* obed, saul
AZARIAH *employer* nebuchadnezzar, solomon

parent ethan, jehoshaphat, jehu
AZAZEL devil, eblis, lucifer, scapegoat
AZERBAIJAN *city* baku, kirovabad
AZIMUTH arc, bearing, horizon
AZO *dye source* benzidine, bianisidine
AZOR *parent* eliakim
AZORES *city* horta
island corvo, fayal, flores, formigas, graciosa, pico, santa maria, sao jorge, sao miguel, terceira
port horta, ponta delgado
volcano pico
AZOTE nitrogen, switch, whip
AZOTH mercury
owner paracelsus
AZOV *sea arm* taganrog
AZRIKAM *parent* neariah
AZTEC *bacchus* tepozteco

base cahultepec, tenochtitlan, tlatelolco
capital mexico city, tenochtitlan
commander cuauhtemoc
conqueror hernan(do) cortes, cortez
conquest huastecs, olmecs, otomi, tlaxcalans, toltecs
country aztecan, aztlan
dance macehualiztli
deity camaxtli, centeotle, chalchiuhtlicue, coatlicue, eecatl, mexitli, meztli, mixcoatl, nagual, quetzalcoatl, tepozteco, tezcatlipoca, tlaloc, toci, tonatiuh, tonatiuti, tzinteotl, xipe(totic), xiuhtecutli
dog chihuahua
epic nana, natl
family group calpulli
festival toxcatl
hero nata
heroine nana

king See *leader*, below.
language nahuatl, piman
leader cuauhtemoc, moctezuma, montezuma, netzahualcoytl
marigold tagetes
migration anahuac
mythical home aztlan
rain god tlaloc
ritual ballgame tlachtli
school calmecac
spear atlatl
stone chalcihihuitl
stone, sacrificial temalacatl
temple teocalli, teopan
underworld mictlan
AZURAH *husband* asa, caleb
son jehoshaphat
AZUN *offspring* hananiah
AZURE bice, blue, celeste, cerulean, cobalt, gem, iris, jovial, lapis, sapphire, sky, smalt, ultramarine, yonder
stone lapis lazuli, lazulite
AZYGOUS alone, odd, single

B

BA khu, soul, spirit, tripos
BAA bleat, cry, maa, mae
BAAL(ZEBUB) asherah, idol, massebah, melkarth, moloch
consort baltis
BAALBERITH *god of* schechem
BAANAH *king* solomon
father rimmon
BABA baby, child, dessert, midwife, nurse, spongecake
BABAJAGA demon, sorceress, witch
BABASSU oil, orbignya, palm
BABBITT bourgeoise, businessman, conformist, metal
author lewis
group middleclass
BABBLATIVE loquacious, talkative
BABBLE babil, betray, blab(ber), blat(e), blather, bleat, cackle, chaffer, chat(ter), clack, clatter, clyde, confusion, converse, dither, gab(ble), gash, gibber, glaister, glaver, glock, gossip, guggle, gurgle, haver, jabber, jangle, knap, murmur, nonsense, palaver, palter, patter,

peach, prate, prattle, purl, rave, ripple, smatter, speak, squeal, taiver, talk, tattle, taver, tove, trickle, twaddle, wlaff
BABBLER blateroon, busybody, cackler, dotard, haverel, magpie, stipiture
BABBLING *thrush* timalia
warbler whitethroat
BABBO See FATHER.
BABE baby, beauty, child, chotchke(leh), girl, infant, innocent, pitsel(eh), tchotcke(leh), tsatske(leh)
BABEL bedlam, cacophony, charivari, clamor, clang, confusion, din, discord, disorder, hubbub, hullabaloo, hurly-burly, jargon, medley, mixture, noise, pandemonium, racket, scheme, tower, tumult, uproar
king haroot, maroot
site shinar
BABELIZE bewilder, confound
BABESIA apiosoma, nuttalia
BABICHE lacing, thong, thread
BABIES -*feet* gaywings
slippers bird's-foot trefoil, bloomfel

BABILLARD whitethroat
BABISM *founder* bab el-din
BABOON ape, babian, babuino, brute, chacma, dogape, drill, fright, girrit, hamadryad, mandrill, monkey, pap(a), papio(n), sphinx
female babuina
BABOUVISM communism
founder babeuf
BABU clerk, esquire, gent(leman), man, mister, sir, writer
BABUL acacia, attaleh, baboot, garrat, gonak(i)e, gum, harad, mimosa, nebneb, sant, sunt, thorn, vera
BABUSHKA grandmother, kerchief, scarf
BABY, BABY'S baba, babe, bairn, bambino, bebe, chap, child, chris(o)m, coddle, coward, darling, dear, diminutive, doll, dwarf, enfant, fondle, humor, indulge, infant(ile), jack, jerk, kid(dy), miniature, minikin, moppet, newborn, pamper, papoose, poupee, project, puppet, small, smother, spoil, sweetheart,

tot(o), waddler, wayne, weakling, wean(ii), young(est)
bed bassinette, cot, cradle, creche, crib
beef calf
-blue-eyes nemophila
-breath chalk-plant, grape-hyacinth, gypsophila, houstonia
-bringer stork
bunting sack, sleeping-bag
carriage buggy, cart, coach, gocart, perambulator, pram, stroller, walker
clothes barrow, bib, bunting, crawlers, creepers, diaper, jumper, layette, rompers, sleeper, smalls, swaddle, swaddlings
cry See *sound*, below.
feet gaywings
food milk, pablum, pap
god cuba, domiduca, fabulinus, vagitanus, vatican
kisser candidate
pert. infantile, neonate, newborn
room nursery
shoe bootee, cack
-sit chaperon, hand-hold, nurse, pamper, protect
sound coo, crow, mew, squall
source stork
talk babble
-tears parlor-moss
toy rattle
tub bathinette
BABYISH childish, immature, infantile, puerile, puling, simple, tiddy
BABYLON, BABYLONIAN accad, assyria, astrologer, chaldea, elam(ite), hedonistic, luxurious, magnificent, noisy, scarlet, shinar, sinful, sumer, susiana, tumultuous, vast, wicked
adam adapa
army officer samagarnebo
astral triad ishtar (planet venus), shamash (sun), sin (moon)
bacchus siris
baptism kispu
bible the epic of creation
bird roc
bull, human-headed lamassu
captivity exile, transmigration
captors kassites
chaos apsu
city agade, akkad, babel,

borsippa, calneh, calno, cunaxa, cuthah, erech, eridu, kish, kutha, lagash, larsa, nippur, shuruppak, sippar, umma
coin stater
courtesan mylitta
cycle saros
daniel belshazzar
dead, souls of edimmu
deluge amaru
demon de(a)va
dignity anutu
disk, winged feroher
divine bird imdugud
dragon azhi-dahaka
eagle rider etana
earth goddess aruru, bau, gatum-dug, gula, innini, ishtar, ninkhursag
era nabonasser, sumer
exorcist ashipu
fates anunnaki
feast zagmuk
fire god gibil, girru, nusku
foe assyrian, elamite, hittite
founder semiramis
funeral repast kispu
genie ahura, lamassu, shedu, utukku
god abu, adad, adapa, adda, addu, adrammelech, alalu, anat, anshar, anu(nnaki), apsu, asushu-namir, baal, babbar, bel, belil(i), belmarduk, bunenedagan, damgalnunna, dumuzi, ear, enki, enlil, enmeshara, enzu, gaga, girru, guhkinbanda, hadad, hes, igigi, imdugud, irra, kingu, kittu, lares, marduk, merodach, nabu, namtaru, nannar, nebo, nergal, ninazu, ningirsu, ningishzida, ninib, ninigiku, ninurta, nusku, remphan, shamash, shara, sin, siris, tammuz, teshup, urash, uta(g), utu, zaqar
goddess allatu, anunit, aruru, ashtoreth, astarte, athtar, aya, bau, belit, belit-ili, belit-sert, beltis, ennugi, ereshkigal, erua, erya, gatum-dug, geshtin, gibil, gula, innini, ishtar, kadi, kishar, lakh(a)mu, mami, mammitu, misharu, mylitta, nana(i), nanshe, nina, ningal, nin-karrak, ninkhursag, ninki, ninlil, nintud, siduri-sabitu, tashmetum, tiamat, zarpanit
gods, abode of duku, ezuab

gods, burial site gigunu
gods, servants to enulli
governor appolodorus, harpalus
great gods anu (sky), bel *or* enlil (earth), enki *or* ninigiku (sea)
guardian fravashi
harvest deity dumuzi, nisaba, tammuz
hero adapa, elana, engudi, enkidu, gilgamesh, utanapishtim
king aloros, belus, gilgamesh, hammurabi, nabonassar, nabunasir, nebuchadnessar, nebuchadrezzar, yima
language accad, akkad(dian)
liquor, sacred haoma
lunar cycle saros
man, first adapa
man, mythical engidu
moon god enzu, sin
mother goddess erua
neighbor elamite
northern accad, akkad
palace kasr
peak ararat
people chaldean, elamite, sumerian
priest berossus
priestess entum
priest-king patesi
prince belshazzar
princess leucothoe
region aralu, elam, nituk, sumer, sumir
rival elam
river euphrates, tigris
ruler exilarch, patesi
sacred tree kishkanu
sea nina
slave ardu
soothsayer baru
spirits igigi
storm god adad, adda, addu, hadad, teshu
sun god babbar
temple akitu, bel, esagil, ziggurat, zikurat
tower babel, ziggurat, zikurat
underworld aralu
underworld god allatu
underworld messenger namtaru
wall-builder memmon
war god ninurta
water deity enki, nanshe
waters apsu
weight maneh, mina
wild man engudi
willow bahan

wizard ashipu

wonders hanging gardens, tower of babel

writing cuneiform

BABYLONIANISM popery

BAC cistern, ferryboat, vat

BACACH beggar, cripple

BACALAO abadejo, bird, codfish, grouper, guillemot, murre, scamp

BACAO bacauan, bruguiera, mangrove, rhizophora, tree

BACCALAUREATE ceremony, commencement, degree, sermon, service

BACCARAT chemin de fer, chemmy, red and black, rouge et noir, shemmy, shimmy, trente et quarante

player punter

term banco, natural, point, shoe

BACCATE berried, pulpy

BACCHAE See BACCHANTE.

BACCHANAL carouser, devotee, drunk(ard), reveler

cry evo(h)e

BACCHANALIA carouse, dionysia, orgy, revelry, spree, tear

BACCHANTE frow, m(a)enad, thyiad

BACCHARIS broom-tree, genistra, groundsel

BACCHIDES *friend* demeter

BACCHUS See DIONYSUS.

instrument organ

BACHE rivulet, stream, vale

BACHELOR agamist, baculere, bahur, batch, benedict, cavalier, celibataire, celibate, crappie, degree, free, garcon, graduate, knight, male, misogamist, misogynist, novice, seal, single, unmated, wanter

-button bluebottle, blue-eyed grass, centaurea, cornflower, daisy, knapweed, milkwort, ranunculus

fish calico-bass, crappie, perch

girl old maid, spinster, spinstress

of arts baccalaureate

BACILLUS bacteria, bug, germ, microbe, virus

BACK abaft, abet, advertise, advocate, aft(er), ago, aid, assist, backbone, beck, behind, brace, broad, champion, chine, cistern, countenance, dorse, dorsum, dos,

edge, encourage, endorse, exploit, favor, finance, fro, full, guarantee, guaranty, heel, help, hind(er), hindmost, hinterland, keel, maintain, nape, notum, past, patronize, posterior, promote, rear, recoil, regress, reinforce, resource, retire, retreat, return, reverse, ridge, second, soothe, spine, splat, sponsor, stand by, stern, support, sustain, tail, tergal, tergum, transport, trough, tub, underwrite, uphold, vat, verify, vouch, withdraw

ache See *pain*, below.

alley bye, by-way, clandestine, dirty, sordid

and fill alternate, change, oscillate, tack, vacillate

and forth alternate, changeably, side-to-side, shuttlewise, to and fro

at the abaff, abaft, aft, arear, astern, postern

-comb tease

comb. ana, cat(a), cath, dorsi, dorso, kat(a), kath, noto, notus, retro, terg

country boondocks, boonies, brush, bush, hinterland, interior, outback, sticks, veld(t), wilderness

disorder rheumatism

door byway, clandestine, covert, furtive, illicit, indirect, postern, rear, secret, surreptitious

down acquiesce, give up, recant, reconsider, retract, retreat, surrender, withdraw, yield

go — on abandon, repudiate

head tailstock

lower part loin

lying on passive, supine

muscle multifidus, trapezius

number antique, dodo, has been, oldster, out-of-date, trite

off ebb, recant, recede, relent, retire, retreat, retrograde, reverse

on one's helpless, prostrate, recumbent, sick

out abandon, crawfish, defect, flunk, jib, quit, recant, renege, retreat, welsh, withdraw

pain lumbago, notalgia, rheumatism

pain remedy papain, papaya

-pedal check, retreat, reverse, shift, slow

pert. dorsal, lumbar, notal, tergal

-racket countercharge

room clandestine, inner, inside, secret

-scratcher apple-polisher, bootlicker, flatterer, strigil, sycophant

-seat driver badgerer, browbeater, carper, interferer, kibitzer, meddler

showing aversant, tergant

-slanging recrimination, scolding

-slapper See *-scratcher*, above.

-swimmer boat-bug, insect, notonectid, water-boatman

-talk argument, impudence, lip, sass

to back addorsed, adjacent, behind, close, dos-a-dos, next, sequential, succeeding, together

toward abaft, aft, arear, astern, dorsal, postern, retrad, retral

BACKBITE abuse, asperse, attack, censure, defame, denigrate, detract, malign, sass, slander, vilify

BACKBOARD bank, monitor

BACKBONE axis, base, basis, character, chine, decision, firmness, fortitude, grate, gristle, grit, guts, mainstay, mettle, nerve, pluck, resolution, ridge, rigbane, sand, spinal column, spine, spinule, spirit, stamina, support, vertebra

without invertebrate, pliant, spineless

BACKBREAKING exhausting, taxing, tiring

BACKCHAT repartee, sass

BACKDROP arras, backcloth, curtain, environment, milieu, mise-en-scene, oleo, scenery, setting

BACKER advocate, ally, angel, banker, benefactor, champion, endorser, enthusiast, financer, follower, guarantor, ist, ite, patron, sponsor, supporter, surety, underwriter, upholder

BACKFIELD linebackers, offense, secondary

BACKFIRE archback, boomerang, explode, explosion,

kickback, ignite, rebound, recoil

BACKFLASH gutter

BACKFLOW ebb, refluence, reflux, retroflux, return

BACKGAMMON chouette, coanki, doubled sixes, dubblets, duplicate, fayles, irish, jacquet, ketch-dolt, lurch, puff, revertier, saka, sheung-luk, snake, tabal, tick-tack, tokkadille, trictrac

piece man, stone

player blot, tableman, tabler

point fleche

term ahead, bar, bear off, blot, builders, comfort-station, counter, disk, double(r), enter, gammon, hit, home-table, lover's leap, miss, pip, prime, run(ners), shut-out, table

BACKGROUND antecedent, backdrop, distance, education, environment, experience, exterior, ford, hinterland, lineage, mise-enscene, offing, offscape, origin, rear, scene, seasoning, setting, training

musical support

BACKHANDED ambiguous, awkward, circuitous, devious, dishonest, disingenuous, indirect, insincere, insolent, mordent, oblique, roundabout, sarcastic, sardonic, wry

BACKHEEL trip

BACKHOUSE backhoe, chic sale, privy, pullshovel

BACKING advocacy, aegis, aid, behind, egis, endorsement, financing, hearting, lining, muslin, promotion, refuse, reversing, support

BACKJAW abuse, altercate, flak, sass

BACKJOINT chase, rabbet

BACKLASH boomerang, kickback, react(ion), rebound, recoil, repercussion, shake, slack, snarl

BACKLOG accumulation, jam, reserve, stock, store, supply, surplus

BACKPIECE corselet, dossiere

BACKPLATE reredos

BACKROPE jobline

BACKSET check, cultivate, discouragement, eddy, relapse, reverse, set-back

BACKSETTLER frontiersman

BACK-SEY sirloin

BACKSIDE derriere, duff, hind (part), posterior, rear, rump

BACKSLIDE abandon, decline, degenerate, desert, deteriorate, fall, lapse, quit, recidivate, regress, relapse, retrogress, return, revert, sin

BACKSLIDER apostate, recidivist, recreant, renegade, repeater, turncoat

BACKSPEER crossexamine

BACKSPIN drag, undercut, underspin

BACKSTAB attack, discredit

BACKSTABBING assassination, office politics, treachery, treason

BACKSTAGE coulisse

BACKSTAIRS byway, clandestine, covert, furtive, indirect, intriguing, private, privy, secret, sly, sneaky, stealthy, surreptitious, underhand(ed)

BACKSTITCH pearl, purl

BACKSTOP barrier, butt, cage, catcher, fence, reinforcement, safeguard, screen, support, wall

BACKSTRETCH finish

BACKSWORD cudgel, singlestick

BACKTRACK retrace, return, reverse, withdraw

BACKUP accumulation, overflow, stoppage

BACKWARD ago, ar(r)ear, arsy-varsy, astern, atypic(al), averse, bashful, behind, blate, bygone, chary, contrary, dark, dense, dilatory, disinclined, dull, fro(m), gone, hesitant, hind(wards), ignorant, inapt, inept, laggard, lagging, late, lax, lethargic, lo(a)th, past, perverse, postic, rear(wards), recessive, regressive, reluctant, remiss, retarded, reticent, retiring, retrad, retral, retrograde, retrogressive, retrorse, retrospective, reversed, shy, slow, sluggish, stupid, tailfirst, tardy, thraw, timid, unapt, undeveloped, unwilling, upstage, yon

comb. ana, retro

BACKWASH after-effect, reaction, slipstream

BACKWATER bayou, billabong, cove, ebb, flow, inlet, recall, recant, remote, retract, retreat, reverse, sheave, slew, slough, slow, stagnant, sticks, throttle, withdraw

BACKWOODS brush, bush, country, forest, hinterlands, interior, rural, sticks, uncouth, unsophisticated

BACKWOODSMAN buckskin, frontiersman, hick, hillbilly, pioneer, rustic, woodsy

BACKWORT comfrey

BACON bard(e), flitch, gambone, gammon, hogside, lard, pig, porc, pork, prize, rasher, rustic, sawney, sowbelly, speck, winnings

-covered barded, larded

side flitch, gammon, slab

slice collop, rasher

stuff with lard

BACON, FRANCIS baron verulam, viscount st. albans

pert. verulamian

work new atlantis, novum organum

BACON, ROGER admirable doctor

BACONWEED lamb's quarters

BACOPA bramia, figwort

BACTERIA acetobacter, achromatium, aerobe, aerobian, albococcus, anthrax, bacillus, beggiato, botulinus, brucella, coccus, cytode, fungus, germ, infectant, listeria, microbe, microphyte, pathogen, proteus, rod, sarcina, serratia, spirilla, vibrion, virus

absence asepsis

aerobic bacillus, nocardia

anaerobic pediococcus

chain torula

coating of slime

colorless archromobacter

comb. bacill(o), bacilli

culture agar, alinite

destroyer alexin, ANTISEPTIC, bactericide, germicide, lysin

discoverer leeuwenhoek

dissolver lysin

edema-causing vibrion

exclusion antisepsis, asepsis

extract abortin

free from aseptic, sterile

infection, pert. vibrionic
intestinal alcaligenes, coli
mass slime, symplasm
parasitic actinomyces, borrelia, fusiformis, gaffkyia, neisseria
pathogenic shiga, shigella, staphylococcus, vibrio
pert. microbic
red rhabdomonas
spherical coccus
spiral borrelia, spirochete, thiospira
s-shaped vibrio
stain giemsa
tail flagellum
thread-like spirilla
vaccine bacterin
BACTERICIDE antiseptic, antitoxin, disinfectant, germicide, phage, prophylactic
BACTERIOLOGIST koch, lister, pasteur
BACTERIUM See BACTERIA.
BACTRIA *capital* bactra, balkh, wazirabad, zariaspa
mountain paropomisus
sage zoroaster
BACULUS rod, staff
BAD 3 big, bum, dud, ill, low, sad, spa, 4 base, bath, bunk, evil, hard, lewd, mean, poor, punk, sick, sour, ugly, vile, void, wick 5 awful, black, dirty, false, fetid, gammy, nasty, sorry, unfit, weary, worse, wrong 6 amoral, arrant, coarse, faulty, lither, luther, nought, rotten, severe, sinful, stormy, ungood, unkind, vulgar, wanton, wasted, wicked 7 baleful, baneful, corrupt, decayed, fearful, harmful, heinous, hurtful, immoral, inutile, invalid, naughty, obscene, peccant, spoiled, tainted, unlucky, unsound, vicious 8 annoying, criminal, depraved, diseased, dreadful, fiendish, flagrant, grievous, inedible, inferior, sinister, terrible, unsuited, untoward, weakened 9 abandoned, atrocious, blemished, dangerous, defective, execrable, felonious, inclement, incorrect, injurious, irascible, offensive, perverted, stinkeroo, suffering, unhealthy, worthless 10 abominable, aggra-

vated, inadequate, iniquitous, pernicious, unpleasant, villainous 11 blasphemous, counterfeit, disobedient, distressful, inexpedient, misbehaving, unfortunate 12 disagreeable, dishonorable, disreputable, inauspicious, insalubrious
blood anger, animosity, bitterness, enmity, hate, hostility, resentment, unfriendliness
cess sorra
comb. cac(o), dis, kako, mal, mis
debt default
faith infidelity, treachery
guy criminal, hoodlum, reprobate, rogue, villain
influence jinx
luck adversity, ambsace, badcess, deuce, illfortune, misfortune, rum go, tough break
luck carrier jinx, jonah
luck exclamation chin up, good show, too bad
-mannered boorish, crude, goopish, impolite, unrefined
name caconym, dishonor, illrepute
off destitute, downtrodden, poor, sad, wretched
odor dishonor, disrepute
rather indifferent
-tempered angry, atrabilious, carnaptious, churlish, cranky, cross, foul, grouchy, gruff, grumpy, irate, petulant, short, sour, stingy, surly
turn disservice
very almighty, arrant, execrable, grievous
BADAUD fool, gossip, idler
BADDERLOCKS alaria, henware, honeyware, kelp, murlin, purses, seaweed
BADDOCK coalfish, pollack
BADEBEC *husband* gargantua
son pantagruel
BADGE boutonniere, brassard, button, characteristic, chevron, color, crest, cross, emblem, ensign, epaulet(te), fasces, favor, flag, garter, giglio, hallmark, honor, identification, insigne, insignia, kirimon, label, mark, medal, mon, order, patch, pin, plaque, scapular, scepter, shield,

sign, star, symbol, symptom, tag, tiponi, token, weeper, znak
of honor blue ribbon
sleeve chevron
BADGER afflict, annoy, bait, bandicoot, bauson, bedevil, bother, brace, braireau, brairo, braraw, brock, brush, bullyrag, burrower, carcajou, carnivore, chevy, chivy, das, disturb, extort, fret, grisard, haggle, harass, harry, hawker, heckle, hector, hound, huckster, hyrax, irk, irritate, jag, jar, kid, meles, mistonusk, mustelidum, nag, pahmi, pate, persecute, pester, plague, ratel, ride, sandpig, scold, stinkard, taunt, taxel, taxidea, taxus, tease, teledu, torment, vex, wisconsinite, wombat, worry
bird marbled godwit
burrow set
cape cony, daman, hyrax
game extortion
group cete
-like animal arctonyx, balisaur, bear-pig, meline, phami, ratel
pert. meline
skunk coneptatus
state wisconsin
BADGERWEED pasqueflower
BADIA See MONASTERY.
BADINAGE badinerie, banter, chaffing, fool, joker, joshing, kidding, raillery, persiflage, tease, teasing, trifling
BADLANDS malpais
peak butte
BADLY evil(ly), hard(ly), ill(y), poorly, sadly, sick, unwell, viciously, wickedly
BADMAN bandit, desperado, outlaw
oatmeal hemlock, wild-chervil
BADMINTON poona
BADNESS evil, malice, pravity, unvalue, wickedness
BADOUIN *constable to* king arthur
BAEDEKER directory, guidebook, vade mecum
BAERIA goldfields
BAFF aft(er), baft, beat, blow, strike, stroke, thud, worthless
BAFFLE addle, balk, beat,

befuddle, bewilder, blench, block, boggle, buffalo, cheat, check, circumvent, cod, confound, confuse, deceive, defeat, deflect, delude, disappoint, discomfit, disconcert, disgrace, dumfound, elude, evade, faze, fetter, fickle, foil, fox, frustrate, get, hinder, infamy, lick, mate, mock, mystify, outwit, perplex, pose, puzzle, quibble, rattle, resist, stick, stonker, stop, stump, thwart, trick, undo, upset
painting camouflage
BAFFLEGAB argot, gobbledegook, jargon
BAFFLING elusive, enigmatic, evasive, mysterious, puzzling, shrewd
BAFT aft(er), baff, cotton, fabric, stuff
BAFYOT See BAKONGO.
BAG 3 cod, cop, cut, kit, lop, nab, net, pod, sac 4 bait, case, cell, cyst, etui, fyke, grip, hang, hook, kill, mail, pack, poke, sack, swag, tote, trap 5 ascus, belly, borsa, bouge, bulge, bulse, catch, crone, dilli, dilly, ditty, emery, forte, hussy, peter, pocky, pouch, purse, scrip, seize, snare, sneak, steal, swell, udder, woman 6 blouse, budget, cavity, chagul, clutch, entrap, fasten, follis, fright, matapi, metier, obtain, paggle, pocket, pounce, rennet, sachet, shammy, spoils, valise, wallet 7 acquire, alforja, baggage, balloon, beanbag, bladder, blister, buckram, capcase, capture, cushion, distend, ensnare, gomukhi, holdall, kareeta, luggage, musette, package, pullman, sarpler, satchel, travois, trollop 8 abomasum, carryall, entrails, envelope, follicle, knapsack, nail down, reticule, rucksack, suitcase, wineskin 9 container, gladstone, haversack, weekender 10 pocketbook, receptacle 11 portmanteau
and baggage all, complete, total
and spoon dredge
botanic asci, ascus, sac, spore

bulging swag
burlap crocus-sack, gunny
canvas duffle, musette
comb. sacci, sacco
fabric baline, burlap, canvas, gunny
fishing net blunt, fyke
for letters kareeta, mailpouch, postbag
for tools wallet
grab fish-pond
kind boodle, boston, caddie, carpet, ditty, duffel, gladstone, golf, grab-all, grip, gunny(sack), holdall, kit, kyack, mailpouch, moneybag, nosebag, packsack, rucksack, saddlebag, school, sleeping, tucker, wineskin, yannigan
leather askos, bouget, budge, churrus, jag(g), mussuk
muslin tillot
net garland, snood
sewing hussy
sleeping fleabag, fumba
traveling capcase, gladstone, grip-sack, suitcase, telescope
two-handled boston
water chagal, chagen, chagul
with pockets tide, tidy
BAGASSE beet pulp, begasse, linaga, megasse
BAGATELLE cannon, cockamaroo, fico, fribble, game, mississippi, nothing, pinball, trifle, verse
and pool carombolette
BAGDAD See BAGHDAD.
BAGGAGE arms, bundles, carriage, clothes, cuttage, cutty, dunnage, effects, fardage, freight, gear, harlot, hussy, huzzy, impedimenta, jade, luggage, minx, nasty, pack, plunder, property, prostitute, refuse, rubbish, salmary, saman, shrew, stuff, suitcase, sumpter, swag, traps, trash, trunks, utensils, valises, wench, worthless
car fourgon, wagon
handler bellboy, bellhop, docker, porter, redcap, stevedore
BAGGIE belly, minnow, stickleback
BAGGING baline, drooping, hemp, jute, sacking, soutage
BAGGY drooping, flabby, flimsy, hanging, loose, loppy, pendent, pendulous,

pocky, puffed, pursive, pursy, saggy
BAGHDAD *caliph* abbas(s)ide, al mamun
capital irak, iraq
dynasty abbas(s)ide
explorer al masudi
founder mansur
merchant abudah, sin(d)bad
pact cento
thief ahmed
BAGLEAVES liveforever, orpine
BAGMAN bum, drummer, henchman, payoffman, racketeer, salesman, swagman, tramp
BAGNIO bag, bagne, bathhouse, brothel, hothouse, jail, lavatory, prison
BAGNUT bladderwort, staphylea
BAGO banago, gnetum, shrub
BAGOAS artaxerxes, employer, holophernes
slayer darius
victim artaxerxes
BAGOT *master* richard ii
BAGPIPE bignou, biniou, cornemuse, doodlesack, dudelsack, dulcimer, gewgaw, musette, piva, sambuke, symphonia, titty, zampagna
hole lill
mouthpiece muse
music pibroch
part bourdon, chanter, drone
play sackdoudle, skirl
small musette, sordellina, sourdeline
sound skirl
BAGRE catfish, porcus
BAGS barrels, much, PANTS, plenty, trousers
BAGUIO cyclone, storm, typhoon
BAGULETTE chaplet, gem, jewel
BAH baw, faugh, fiddledeedee, foh, nonsense, pah, poh, pshaw, rats, rot
BAHAI *founder* bahaullah, hussein-ali
head abbas-effendi, adbulbaha
origin babism
BAHAMA *bay rush* coontie, zamia
candy benni-cake
capital nassau
drink carib cup, mobana
fiber sisal

grass bermuda, devil, scutch
hemp sisal
island abaco, andros, bimini, eleuthera, exuma, new providence, san salvador, watling
native conch
redwood colubrina
resort nassau
shrub ant's-bush, granny-bush, quicksilver, saffron
tea lantana
tree jumbee-bean, necklace-tree
whitewood canella
BAHAMONDE franco
BAHAN garab, poplar, tree, willow
BAHAY See HOUSE.
BAHERA myrobalan, tanner, terminalia, tree
nut bedda
BAHIA *arrowroot* cassava, manioc
grass paspalum
BAHIAITE dike-rock, hornblende
BAHIMA hima, huma, wahima, watusi
BAHR river, sea
BAHRAIN *capital* manama
city jidraffs, rifaa
coin dinar, fils
BAHT bat, tical
BAHUT cabinet, chest, parapet, wall
BAIKIE gull, stake, stick
BAIL andi, bale, bar, bestow, bond, bow, bucket, bulwark, confine, court, custody, deal, defense, deliver, dip(per), dish, empty, framework, guarantee, guaranty, handle, hoop, ladle, lave, partition, pledge, pole, release, replevin, replevy, ring, rynd, scoop, secure, security, spoon, spring, support, surety, throw, vadium, wall, yoke
go vouch, wager, warrant
out abandon, assist, escape, jump, parachute, release, rescue, save, set free
up halt, rob, stop, yield
BAILE *father* buan
BAILE ATHA CLIATH dublin
BAILEE conductor, lessee, positor
BAILEY *old* ballium, court, jail, prison
BAILIE See BAILIFF.

BAILIFF agent, bailie, beadle, bobby, bull, bumtrap, catchpole, constable, cop (per), factor, gerefa, grieve, hind, huissier, hundreder, lictor, mace-bearer, magistrate, major-domo, oeconomus, officer, overseer, peeler, policeman, porter, portreeve, prevot, reeve, saffo, schout, scult, seneschal, sergeant-at-arms, sheriff, steward, tipstaff, varlet, wapentake
arresting bumbailiff
farm hind
jurisdiction bailiage, bailiwick
BAILIWICK area, bailiage, domain, field, forte, jurisdiction, metier, office, preserve, province, skill, specialization, sphere, stamping-ground, territory
BAILOR lessor
BAIN bath, direct, forward, limber, lithe, near, ready, short, supple, willing
marie double-boiler, gluepot, saucepan
BAIRAGI ascetic, mendicant, monk
BAIRN butcha, child
BAIT afflict, allure, annoy, attack, badger, berley, bite, bother, bribe, capelin, captivate, cast, cheppeh, chevy, chiv(v)y, chum, cog, cungeboi, dap, decoy, dib, drop, enclosure, entice(ment), exasperate, feed, food, fulcrum, gudgeon, halt, hank, harass, harry, heckle, hector, hook, hound, kibblings, leger, lug, lure, needle, net, persecute, pester, plague, provoke, rag, refreshment, repast, rib, ride, ruffle, shrap(e), slate, sliver, squid, snare, tagtail, tail, tease, tcheppeh, tempt(ation), torment, trap, trickery, try, worm, worry
artificial fly, hackle
basket courge
bird-enticing shrap(e)
cod capelin
drag troll
drop dap, dib
fish chum, gentle
greasy rogue
ground berley
maggot gentle

salmon baker
scented drag
BAIZE bay(es), bayeta, domett, fabric, tablecloth
BAJA CALIFORNIA See MEXICO.
BAJARDO *owner* rinaldo
BAJAU bornean, malayan, sea-gypsy, samal-laut
BAKA boko, demon, devil, familiar, spirit
BAKAL shopkeeper, tradesman
BAKE anneal, barbecue, batch, biscuit, broil, burn, coct, cook, cracker, dehydrate, desiccate, dry, escallop, festival, fire, grill, harden, heat, parch, pistate, pot, roast, scallop, shir(r), stiffen
BAKED -*apple* biffin, cloudberry
in earth oven kalua, kichel
BAKEN beacon, buoy, landmark
BAKER baxter, bird, burner, cook, fly, furnace, furnarius, furner, imu, kiln, o(a)st, oven(bird), ovenman, pistor, roaster, victualer
-*bird* hornero
dozen thirteen
fee furnage
itch psoriasis, rash
kneading trough brake
mop malkin, mawkin
patron saint wilfrid
proofer steam-box
shovel pale, peel
workshop imu, umu, yale
BAKIE trough
BAKING assation, batch, coction, cuit, furnage
chamber kiln, o(a)st, oven
contest bake-off
dish casserole, cocotte, ramekin
goddess fornax
implement pale, peel
ingredient flour, soda, yeast
pit imu, umu
powder leavening soda, saleratus
BAKONGO bacongo, bafyot, fiot
capital mbanzakongo
god deisos
goddess nyambi, nzambi
king manikongo
BAKSHEESH gift, gratuity, windfall
BALAAM *steed* ass

BALACHAN balachong, blatjang, condiment, ngapi
BALAENA bowhead, whale
BALAGAN booth, hut, shelter, stall, tent
BALAN *son* ferumbras, fierabras
BALANCE 4 atry, beam, deis, even, firm, rest, risk, sway, trim, tune 5 agree, check, doubt, equal, level, libra, peise, poise, scale, swing, trone, waver, weigh, wheel 6 accord, adjust, aplomb, attune, auncel, cancel, credit, equate, excess, hazard, juggle, kelter, kelvin, kilter, launce, offset, ponder, sanity, settle, square, strike, weight 7 account, ballast, compare, compute, control, desemer, harmony, librate, measure, parison, remnant, residue, surplus, tension, trabush, trutine 8 complete, equality, equalize, estimate, evenness, hesitate, serenity, symmetry, westphal 9 composure, equipoise, reconcile, remainder, stability, stabilize, trebuchet, trutinate 10 compensate, confidence, difference, equanimity, neutralize, proportion, steadiness 11 countervail, equilibrium 12 counterpoise
beam balk
due arrear
fish hammerhead
grammatical parison
in account credit
lose fall, stagger, trip
medieval auncel
of sails atry
part scale-pan, weight
sheet bilan, statement
BALANCED apoise, calm, complete, composed, even, kittle, level(headed), measured, poised, proportional, quadrate, right, self-assured, self-confident, symmetrical, uniform, weighed
BALANCER acrobat, athlete, gymnast, halter(e), tumbler
BALANDRANA cloak, garment, mantle
BALANGAY barangay, boat, canoe
BALANITE balm, bito
BALAO ballyhoo, dipterocarpus, halfbeak, hemiramphus, tree

BALARAMA *brother* vishnu
BALAT bark, leather, shell, skin
BALATA beefwood, borracha, bullace, bully-tree, chicle, gum, gutta-percha, icica, lumber, mimusops
BALAUSTINE pomegranate
BALAYEUSE dust-ruffle, frill
BALCONETTE balustrade, railing
BALCONY balagan, brattice, cantoria, gallery, garret, gazabo, gazebo, loggia, mezzanine, mirador, oriel, pergola, piazza, podium, porch, portico, poy, sollar, stoop, veranda(h)
railing balustrade
rear peanut heaven
singers' cantoria
BALD acomous, austere, bare, barren, base, beardless, beld, blunt, bold, callow, calvous, chaste, cleanshaven, colorless, crude, depilous, direct, doddy, dull, epilated, epilose, forthright, glabrous, hairless, literal, meager, mere, naked, nude, open, paltry, peeled, pilled, plain, polled, severe, shaved, simple, smooth, stark, stripped, tonsured, ugly, unadorned, undisguised, unvarnished, whiskerless
as a coot
brant goose
buzzard osprey
coot bell-kite, fulica, gallinule
crown widgeon
eagle haliaeetus
locust attacus
money gentian, spicknel
rush psilocarya, sedge
spot tonsure
BALDACHIN, BALDAQUIN baudekin, brocade, canopy, ciborium, fabric
BALDER baeldaeg, bald(u)r
brother hoder, hodur
god of peace
herb amaranthus
home breidablik, breithablik, broadblink
murder weapon mistletoe
parent frigg, odin
rival and slayer hoder, hodur, hoth(r), loke, loki
son forsete, forseti
wife nanna

BALDERDASH balductum, bombast, drivel, flubdub, guff, jargon, nonsense, rigmarole, rot, trash
BALDHEAD fruit-crow, goose, pigeon, pilgarlic, skinhead, widgeon
BALDICOOT bird, monk
BALDNESS acomia, alopecia, atrichia, bareness, calvit(ies), calvity, hairlessness, ophiasis, phalacrosis, whitecomb
BALDPATE poacher, widgeon, zuisin
BALDRIC balteus, band, belt, girdle, lace, necklace, support, zodiac
BALDWIN *parent* ganelon
BALE anguish, bail, block, bunch, bundle, burden, cargo, crate, death, dip, disaster, dole, dolor, evil, fardel, fardo, fire, gib, grief, harm, heap, hurt, ill, injury, lade, mischief, misery, misfortune, package, pain, parcel, pile, ruin, sarpler, sero(o)n, sorrow, suffering, torment, woe
BALEARIC *capital* palma
city ibiza, mahon, palma
island cabrera, conejera, formentera, ibiza, iviza, mallorca, menorca, minorca
language catalan
measure barcella, misura, palmo, quarta, quarte(ra), quartin
tower talayot
weight artal, artel, cargo, corta, libra, mayor, quartano, ratel, rotl
BALEEN sea bream, whalebone
BALEFIRE beacon, bonfire, flame, pyre, signal
BALEFUL bad, calamitous, deadly, destructive, detrimental, evil, fateful, harmful, hellish, inauspicious, infernal, injurious, malefic, malign, menacing, noisome, noxious, pernicious, ruinous, sad, sideral, sinister, wicked, woeful, wretched
BALEK *kingdom* moab
BALFE *opera* bohemian girl
BALI demon, dwarf, monkey, oblation, offering
airline zamrud
capital denpasar
city negana, singaradja
dance ardja, baris, barong,

djanger, kebyar, ketjak, kriss, legong, monkey, sanghyang
dish riasi goring, sate
masked players darma-andjaja
musical instrument gamelan(g)
peak agoeng
religion hinduism
rice field sawaii
strait lombok
temple batur, samantiga
village desa
volcano agung
winged creature garuda
BALIBAGO hau, majagua, tree
BALIGANT *enemy* charlemagne
son malpramis
war cry precieuse
weapon maltet, precieuse
BALINE bagging, fabric, hemp, jute
BALINGHASAY anam, anan
BALIUS *brother* xanthus
master achilles
parent podarge, zephyr
BALK avoid, baffle, beam, beat, begrudge, bilk, block, blunder, boggle, buck, bull, check, circumvent, clamp, codling, cond, crossbeam, defeat, demur, disappoint, falter, flinch, foil, frustrate, gag, gorm, grudge, hade, hinder, hindrance, hue, hunch, impede, isthmus, lick, loft, miss, mistake, mound, object, obstruct, omit, outwit, prevent, prop, rafter, rear, rebel, reest, refuse, retard, ridge, rout, shun, shy, signal, skip, slip, stake, stay, stick(le), stop, strain, thwart, timber, waver
half flitch
BALKAN *bandit* haiduk, heyduke
coin novcic
country albania, bulgaria, greece, rumania, serbia, servia, turkey, yugoslavia
dance kolo
guerilla komitaji
jew spagnuoli
musical instrument gusla, gusle
region bilo
river danube, ibar, jiu(l), morava, olt(ul), sava, tisa

sea adriatic, aegean, black, ionian
BALKIS sheba
BALKY averse, contrary, froward, mulish, nappy, negative, obstinate, perverse, recalcitrant, reesty, refractory, restive, stubborn, wayward
BALL affair, balloon, bead, biscayen, bob, bolus, bubble, bullet, button, cartridge, clew, clue, confuse, conglobation, conglobe, cotillion, dance, earth, fandango, fly, globe, globule, glome, goli, grounder, hooker, hurley, ivory, knappan, knob, knur, leather, mandrel, marble, melon, mig, moonie, nob, orb(it), oval, party, pea, peelee, pellet, pelota, pill, pinda, pommel, pompon, projectile, prom, quenelle, ridotto, rondel, rundle, shot, sinker, slitter, slug, sphere, spheroid, sport
aromatic pomander
boy caddy, retriever
bowled bailer, bumper, creeper, crossover, curve, fizzer, googly, inswinger, kicker, poodle, skyer, snorter, tice, yorker
ceremony grand march
club eleven, nine, team
fern davallia, squirrel's-foot
form into conglobe
game See GAME *ball.*
grinder pebble mill
hard snug
holder tee
-hooter brutter, lumberman
lofted fly, lob
low grounder, liner
masquerade ridotto
meat croquette, pinda, rissole
musket goli, slug
of fire genius, whiz
-of-snow achillea, sneezewort
park diamond, stadium
player athlete
point biro
python calabria, snake
rose cranberry tree
silver pome
smut bunt, fungus
snake rubber boa
spiked calt(h)rop
thistle artichoke
up complicate, confuse, mess, upset

wooden knur
BALLAD air, ballant, bylina, canzon(e), carol, carval, chanty, corrido, derry, gwerziou, jigi, lai, lay, lilt, mele, poem, serenade, singsong, song, sonnet, strephonade
collection percy's reliques
division fit
maker bard, composer, poet, scald, skald
seller busker
singer cantabank, musar
16th century green sleeves
BALLAM boat, canoe
BALLAST aplomb, balance, bed, bottom, brace, bracket, burden, crib, fill, gravel, kentledge, lastage, load, saburrate, sandbag, stability, stabilize, steady, stone, support, trim, weight
BALLERINA dahlia, dancer, danseuse, figurante
prima fonteyn, pavlova, plisetskaya
star prima
BALLET bezant, bourree, choreography, dance, dancing, masque, pantomime
artist ballerina, danseuse, coryphee
enthusiast balletomane
exercise port de bras
figure pas de deux
fixture bar
jump ciseaux, entrechat, jete, pas de chat, salto, sissonne, soubresant, sous-sous
kick battement, fouette
kneebend fly
leap cabriole, jete
movement allonge, aplomb, arabesque, arrondi, assemble, attitude, ballonne, battemont, batterie, brise, broadleap, brush, cabriole, developpe, echappe, flicflac, fouette, frappe, ouvert, passe, plie, releve, renverse, retire, temps-levee
printer degas
pose arabesque, attitude
princess aurora
skirt tutu
slipper toeshoe
step allegro, chaisse, coupe, deboite, flicflac, pas de basque, pas debouree, pas de cheval
term allonge, a terre, barre, bourree, chaine, glissade,

pirouette, plastique, pointe, position, soutenue

BALLISTA crossbow, mangonel, sling, sweep

BALLISTIC *device* See MISSILE.

fruit jewelweed, witchhazel

BALLOON aerostat, airship, bag, ball, belly, bilge, billow, blimp, dirigible, distend, drachen, enlarge, expand, gasbag, increase, inflate, montgolfier, multiply, puff, rockoon, sausage, skyhook, swell, zeppelin

basket chariot, fish box, gondola, nacelle

builder charles, montgolfier

control guide rope

feather vane

fish diodon, porcupine fish

gas helium

gas bag ballonet

hot air montgolfier

part ballonet, basket, car, catwalk, envelope, gondola, nacelle, net, sidecar, valve, wingcar

pilot, famous piccard

sail spinnaker

science aeronautics

sickness anoxemia

trial straw vote

vine cardiospermum, farolito, heartpea, heartseed

BALLOT bale, billet, choice, elect, franchise, poll, proxy, select, slate, solicit, suffrage, ticket, voice, vote

negative secret blackball

BALLOTA horehound

BALLOW cudgel, stick

BALLROOM casino, dancehall, saloon

BALLY bloody, contemptible, damned

BALLYHACK destruction, perdition, ruin

BALLYHOO advertise, balao, clamor, demonstration, fish, halfbeak, hoopla, noise, outcry, pitch, plug, promotion, propaganda, publicity, solicit, uproar

BALLYRAG abuse, bully, harass, intimidate, tease

BALM abirritant, anodyne, anoint, balsam, beeb, besmear, bito, comfort, consolation, cream, daub, demulcent, ease, embalm, embrocation, emollient, fomentation, fragrance, healer, leni-

tive, liniment, lotion, medicine, mitigate, oil, ointment, perfume, pomade, pomatum, relief, remedy, salve, solace, soothe(r), unction, unguent, vulnerary

cricket cicada

kind antiphlogistine, arnica, balm of gilead, bite, brilliantine, camphor, cerate, citronella, collyrium, glycerine, glycerole, harquebusade, gum arabic, lanolin, melissa, menthol(atum), nard, olive oil, petrolatum, petroleum jelly, spikenard, vaseline, vicks, zachun, zinc-ointment

of gilead angico, balsam, canada, commiphora, opobalsam, perfume, tree

of heaven laurel, oleander, spice-tree, umbellularia

BALMORAL boot, cap, castle, petticoat, shoe

BALMUNG *owner* siegfried

BALMY analgesic, aromatic, assuaging, balsamic, bland, bughouse, clement, cracked, crazy, daffy, dreamy, eccentric, fair, flaky, foolish, fragrant, gentle, healing, insane, lenient, mild, moony, odoriferous, pleasant, redolent, refreshing, serene, silly, soft, soothing, spicy, sunny, sweet, temperate, warm

BALNEUM bathhouse, bathroom, hotsprings, lavatory

BALONEY bologna, bunk, bushwa(h), hooey, humbug(gery), megillah, nonsense, rot, sausage, shmegegge

BALOO bear, byelow, lullaby

friend mowgli

BALOR *kingdom* formor

people formorians

BALSA bobwood, corkwood, float, guano, ochroma, pola(c)k, raft, tree

BALSAM ampalaya, ampalea, amyris, balm (of gilead), bdellium, benjamin, bikkia, calaba, calophyllum, commiphora, copaiba, copalm, creeper, embalm, fir, gurjun, impatiens, medicine, ochroma, ointment, oleoresin, restorer, riga, soother, storax, tolu, torchwood, tree, turpentine, umiri, wilga

apple amargoso, ampalaya, balsamine, creeper, karela, momordica

bog azorella, plant

-copaiba wilga

extract toluene

fig clusia, scotch-attorney

fir abies, amyris, balm of gilead, baumier, pine, sapin

fragrant umiri

garden jewelweed, touch-me-not

groundsel seecia

herb costmary

hickory carya

of mecca balm of gilead

pear momordica

poplar amyris, balm of gilead, baumier, tacamahac

resin benzoin, tacamahac

BALSAMIC balmy, mitigative, restorative, soft, soothing

BALSAMROOT ageratum, boltonia, sunflower

shrub torchwood

BALSAMWEED celandine, everlasting, featherweed, fuzzyguzzy, gnaphalium, impatiens, jewelweed, moonshine

BALT esth, estonian, latvian, lett, lithuanian, vod

BALTER clot, stick, tangle, tread

BALTEUS baldric, band, belt, girdle, passage, walk

BALTHAZAR *alias of* portia

master romeo

BALTIC *barge* braam

canal kiel

city danzig, faron, gdansk, liepaja, mariehamp, memel

duchy courland, kurland

finn vod

gulf bothnia, danzig, riga

herring stromming

island ahvenanmaa, aland, alsen, bornholm, dago, faro, gotland, hiiumaa, oesel, oland, os(s)el

language lettic

people See BALT.

port danzig, gdansk, kiel, liepaja, mariehamm, memel, reval, riga, rostock, talinn

river dvina, memel, nemunas, n(i)eman, nyeman, oder, odra, peene, viadua, wilsa

ship galeas

BALTIMORE *nickname* monumental city

belle rose

bird oriole

oriole golden-robin, hangbird, hangnest, icterus

sage h. l. mencken

stove latrobe

BALU wildcat

BALUCHISTAN *capital* kelat, quetta

culture quetta

grain jowar

mountain pass bolan

peak hala, kohistan

people brahui, mar(r)i, murree, reki

province lus

river bolan, dashi, gaj, moola, nal

ruler khan, sirdar

state kalat, khelat, lus

town bagh, beyla, dadur

BALUSTER, BALUSTRADE balconet, banister, bolster, colonnette, columel(la), fence, parapet, post, pulvination, rail(ing), spindle, spoke

BALY *horse* aulay

BALZAC *character* foviot

criminal vautrin

miser pere grandet

work comedie humaine, contes drolatiques, cousin bette, eugenie grandet, gosbeck, pere goriot

BAM bang, blow, cheat, fake, hoax, trick, wheedle

BAMBI *author* salten

BAMBINO See BABY.

BAMBOO achar, arundinaria, bambusa, batak(an), cane, dendrocalamus, dha(one), glumal, grass, guadua, madake, nandina, quila, raphia, reed, spinosa, tonkin, whangee

brier smilax

curtain barrier, border, censorship

fern coniogramme

grass glyceria

hut basha

matting sawali

partridge bambusicola

pickled shoots achar

rat rhizomys, spalax

reed arundo

sacred nandin

screen cheek, chick

sugar tapasheer

woven sawali

BAMBOOZLE befool, beguile, bilk, buffalo, bumbaze, cajole, cheat, confound, cozen, deceive, defraud, dupe, fool, gull, have, hoax, hoodwink, humbug, mislead, mystify, outwit, perplex, spoof, swindle, trick

BAN anathema, banat, banish, bar, block, censor, coin, condemn(ation), curse, damn, debar, denounce, denunciation, edict, embargo, enjoin, exclude, excommunication, execrate, forbid, hinder, imprecation, injunction, interdict, invoke, kokumin, malediction, muslin, notice, objurgate, order, ostracize, outlaw, preclude, proclamation, prohibit (ion), proscribe, summons, taboo, tabu, veto, woe

son lancelot

BANA *conqueror* krishna

daughter usha

BANAK ucuba, virola

BANAL assinine, bromidic, campy, cliche, commonplace, conventional, corny, dull, fatuous, flat, hack(neyed), inane, insipid, jejune, moth-eaten, silly, stale, stock, tiresome, trite, trivial, vapid

BANALITY cliche, corn, platitude, s(c)hmaltz

BANANA ensete, fei, lacatan, musa, plantain, platano, saba, sag(u)ing, sunbeam

bird icterus, oriole, quit

bunch hand, stem

disease big-foot, blackhead, bunch-top, freckle, sigatoka

family musaceae, pesang

fiber abaca

fish albula, ladyfish

fly drosophila

land queensland

leaf frond

-like plantain

moth pisang

oil amyl-acetate, nonsense, rot, softsoap

plant musa, penang

-quit bird, coereba, honeycreeper

root borer cosmopolites, snout(beetle)

shrub michelia

water lily nymphaea

wild fei

wilt panama disease

BANAUSIC mechanical, practical, utilitarian

BANBA See IRELAND.

BANCA boat, canoe, dugout, outrigger

BANCAL saber, sword, tree

BAND 3 bar, bed, gad, hub, mob, set, tie, tub 4 belt, bend, bond, bund, came, club, cord, crew, cuff, ferd, fess, gang, girt, hood, hoop, knot, lace, line, link, list, mark, orle, ring, sash, seam, tape, wisp, zone 5 ampyx, brace, braid, cabal, choir, clamp, combo, covey, covin, crape, crowd, crown, facia, femur, flock, frame, girth, gorge, group, guard, hinge, horde, jatha, label, meiny, order, panel, party, patte, pride, quire, sabot, snood, strap, stria, strip, strop, tapis, tenia, torse, track, tribe, troop, unite, withe 6 anklet, armlet, bendel, binder, border, boyang, bracer, bundle, cestus, cimbia, circle, clavus, cohort, collar, copula, cordon, course, crance, fascia, fetter, fillet, frieze, garter, gasket, girdle, hoople, league, ligula, nipper, pledge, regula, ribbon, screed, strake, streak, string, stripe, surety, swathe, taenia, tether, troupe, volume, weeper 7 baldric, balteus, bendlet, binding, chambul, chaplet, circlet, company, coterie, enomoty, ferrule, frontal, garland, heading, manacle, necktie, orphrey, promise, shackle, society, swaddle 8 alliance, assembly, bracelet, cincture, cingulum, conspire, division, dressing, encircle, ensemble, ligament, necklace, nosering, surround, vinculum, wristlet 9 community, connector, frequency, orchestra 10 cummerbund, escutcheon, restrainer 11 aggregation, association, confederacy, confederate

armed army, askari, host, jatha, navy, posse, troop

armor tonlet

broad fess

circular annule, hoop, ring, wreath

clay cottle

colored lacing, slash, stria

dance combo, orchestra

decorative cornice, frieze, leglet, patte
framing architrave, archivolt
garment-fastening patte
heraldic orle
horizontal fess(e)
iron fret, funnel, gate, strake, truss
lace scallop
leader basie, batoneer, choragus, conductor, maestro, master, pryor, sousa, strauss
narrow stria, tape
ornamental bracelet, ring
plant periwinkle, vinca
small bandelette
straw gad, simmon
together affiliate, combine, gather, join, unite
trouser boyang
wheel rigger
BANDAGE accipter, belt, bind(er), blind(fold), brace, capeline, cincture, clout, collar, cover, cravat, dress, fascia, fettle, fillet, galea, gauntlet, ligament, ligate, ligature, nipper, roller, scapular, sling, spica, stocking, strip, stupe, swaddle, swarf, swarth, swathe, sweathe, taenia, tape, tie, treat, truss, wind, wrap
8-tailed cancer
eye muffler
fastener ligator
finger hovel
jaw funda
limb spica
surgical fascia, spica
BANDANNA calico, cloth, handkerchief, pulicat(e), pullicat, scarf, turban, web
BANDBOX flimsy, insubstantial, substandard
BANDEAU band, bra(ssiere), fillet, strip
BANDELET annulet, molding, welt
BANDEROLE flag, ribbon, scroll, streamer
BANDERILLIST bullfighter
BANDICOOT badger, bielby, bilbi, marl, marsupial, nesokia, perameles, pinkie, quenda, rat
BANDIT bandido, bravo, brigand, burglar, bushwhack, caco, cateran, corsair, crook, dacoit, desperado, footpad, freebooter, gangster, haiduk, heyduk, highwayman, hood(lum),

hooligan, kleptomaniac, ladrone, looter, marauder, maumau, miquelet, mobster, outlaw, pad, picaroon, pirate, racketeer, reaver, robber, rover, sandbagger, thief, thug, tulisan
one-armed slot machine
BANDITRY brigandage, kleptomania, ladronism, larceny, latrocinium, theft, thievery
BANDORE guitar, pandura
BANDSTAND kiosk, shell
BANDY bowed, carriage, cart, chaffer, chat, chop, contend, curved, discuss, exchange, fight, gossip, interchange, join, league, pass, publish, racket, report, strike, strive, swap, tennis, throw, trade, vie
-bandy furina, snake
words chaffer, converse, giffgaff, retort, revie
BANE affliction, ban, bone, curse, death, destruction, evil, grievance, harm, infliction, injury, kill, mischief, murder(er), nemesis, nuisance, pain, pest(ilence), plague, poison, ruin, scourge, slayer spoil(ed)(er), thorn-in-the-flesh, torment, toxin, upas, venom, vexation, virus, visitation, woe
BANEBERRY actaea, byrony, cohosh, bugbane, grapeworth, tamus, toadroot
BANEFUL bad, black, deadly, deleterious, destructive, detrimental, evil, harmful, hurtful, injurious, malefic, mischievous, mortal, noxious, pernicious, ruinous, sinister, swart, toxic, venomous, vile
BANEWORT belladonna, ranunculus, spearwort
BANG 3 bam, hit, pop, rap, tap, vim 4 baff, beat, blow, boot, bump, bust, clap, dash, dock, drub, flap, flop, kick, pouf, scat, slam, slap, sock, swap, whap, whop 5 bhang, blaff, burst, clash, crack, crash, crump, drive, excel, force, impel, knock, noise, pound, powie, salvo, slake, slump, smack, smash, sound, spang, stram, thump, whack, whang,

whump 6 bounce, cudgel, energy, excell, fringe, kerbam, report, spirit, strike, stroke, thrash, thrill, thunge, thwack 7 alewife, collide, sardine, surpass, thunder 8 abruptly, directly, forelock, suddenly, vitality 9 explosion, marijuana, precisely, violently 10 detonation, excitement
-beggar beadle, constable
into collide, crash, hit, smash
-off at once, immediately
on apropos, pertinent
-up blighty, bloody, bosker, crack, excellent, extraordinary, first-rate, tiptop
BANGA cycad, jar, macrozamia, vessel
BANGER firecracker, gun, lie, sausage, whopper
BANGI *kin* suttung
BANGING big, great, huge, whopping
BANGKOK krungthep, venice of asia
BANGLADESH *capital* dacca
coin taka
native bengali
river brahmaputra, ganges
BANGLE anklet, bracelet, flap, fritter, ornament, roam, trinket
BANGSTER braggart, bully
BANGTAIL geegee, racehorse
BANI *son* amram, amzi, imri, uel
BANIAN abstainer, banyan, jacket, shirt, sircar, trader, wrapper
BANISH abandon, bandit, cast out, condemn, confine, deport, dismiss, dispel, displace, dister, divorce, eject, exclude, excommunicate, exile, expatriate, expel, export, extradite, fleme, forsay, lag, ostracize, oust, outlaw, proscribe, punish, relegate, rusticate, transport, waive, wreck
BANISHMENT bannimus, exile, ostracism, outlawry, xenelasia, xenelasy
BANISTER See BALUSTER.
BANK 3 bar, cay, jug, rim, row, tip 4 berm, bink, brae, butt, caja, cant, deck, dike, dune, dyke, edge, fund, ghat, heap, hill, lode, mass,

pile, rack, rake, ramp, reef, rely, ripa, rive, sand, save, seat, tier, weir 5 banco, beach, bench, berme, bluff, brink, coast, count, creel, digue, ditch, earth, group, hover, jurst, knoll, ledge, levee, marge, mound, ridge, saver, shelf, shoal, shore, slope, stack, stock, store, trust, wager, wough 6 banque, barrow, caisse, causey, cradge, depend, margin, pocket, reckon, rivage, shelve, stakes, strand 7 anthill, barrier, cushion, deposit, incline, pottery, sandbag, shallow, terrace, tumulus, windrow 8 barranca, buttress, platform, treasury 9 acclivity 10 depository, storehouse
acceptance certificate
account capital, fund(s)
beaver otter
bird phalarope
canal berm(e), heelpath, towpath
clerk teller
credit cash account
dress barbarea, hedge-mustard
earthen cop, dam, ditch
employee bookkeeper, cashier, guard, teller, watchman
examiner accountant
family rothschild
fish cod
fraud kite
jug bird, willow-warbler
mud bar, scalp
note bill, crisp, flimsy, red-dog, screen
of type font
on count, depend, expect, rely, trust
overhanging brew, hover
pert. riparian
piggy knipp(e)l, pishke, pushke(h)
raised mound
rider bogier
river ripa
roll bills, capital, cash, currency, finance, funds, money, resources, support, wad
sand bar, scalp
slope scarp
snow drift
steep barranca, heuch, heugh, wough
swallow riparia, sand-martin
turf sunk

BANKER backer, banya, cambist, capitalist, cashier, dealer, factor, financier, finder, guarantor, lombard, marwari, moneychanger, moneylender, sahkar, saraf, seth, sett, shroff, soucar, sowcar, sponsor, tailleur, teller, treasurer, underwriter
BANKERA burhinus, curlew
BANKRUPT bare, beggarly, break, broke(n), bung, bust(ed), cracked, debtor, deplete(d), destitute, devour, drain, dyvour, fail (ure), gazetted, impoverish(ed), insolvent, moneyless, on the rocks, pauper, penniless, quisby, ruin(ed), rump, sap, smash, strip, sunk, undone, wanting, without
BANKRUPTCY failure, smash(up)
looting through scam
BANKWEED hedge-mustard
BANLIEU environs, lowy
BANNER badge, banderol(e), beauseant, colors, dominant, ensign, exemplary, fane, flag, foremost, gonfalon, headline, jack, labarum, leading, oriflamb, oriflamme, outstanding, peerless, pennant, pennon, poinsettia, poster, salient, screamer, sign, sovereign, standard, streamer, superlative, supreme, vexillum
cloth bunting
cloud pileus
cry slogan
fish istiophorus, sailfish
funeral bannerd, gumpheon, gumphion
plant anthurium
pompano trachinotus
BANNERET cavalier, flag, knight
BANNERMAN manchu, publicist, standardbearer
BANNIMUS banishment, expulsion
BANNOCK bread, cake, digger, jannock, panak
fluke turbot
BANNS announcement, cry, engagement, notice, proclamation, sibrede, sibret, sibrit, spurrings
BANQUET ahaaina, burrakhana, carousal, convito,

convive, delight, diffa, dine, dinner, entertain, feast, feed, festival, fete, junket, manger(y), meal, regale, regalo, seudah, spread, symposium, syssition
entertainment entremets
room cenacula, cenaculum
BANQUETER convive, symposiast
BANQUETTE bank, bench, booth, embankment, footway, ledge, path, platform, seat, shelf, sidewalk
BANQUO *slayer* macbeth
son fleance
BANSHEE bow, faery, fairy, fay, ghost, goblin, shee, sidhe, spirit
BANTAM banty, chicken, cock, combative, dandy, diminutive, dwarf, feisty, grig, pebble, saucy, sebright, small, swaggerer, testy, tiny
weight boxer
BANTENG bantin, bibos, temadau, tsine
BANTER asteism, badinage, badiner, borak, chaff, cod, delude, deride, devil, drape, exchange, fool, giffgaff, give-and-take, guy, haggle, haze, jape, jest, jive, joke, joking, jolly, josh, kid, mock, nonsense, persiflage, pleasantry, queer, quiz, rag, rail(lery), rally, razz, rib, ride, ridicule, roast, rot, sport, stashie, taunt, tease, trick, twit, wheedle, wit
BANTLING bastard, brat, child, infant
BANTU *bride price* lobolo
dialect chwana, sechuana
language (See also *people*, below.) bantoid, bemba, kikuyu, kongoese, luganda, nyamwezi, nyanaja, ovaherero, ronga, sesuto, shambala, subiya, suto, swahili, wanymawezi
lion simba
magician inianga
mud house tembe
okra kingombo
people 3 ila, kua, rua 4 baya, bube, bubi, bulu, ejam, ekoe, gogo, goma, hehe, huha, jaga, luba, ravi, rori, rory, saga, suku, vili, viri, yaka, zulu 5 bunda, duala, kafir, kamba, kioko, konde, kongo, lamba,

lunda, makua, makwa, pondo, shona, sotho, swazi, warua, xhosa 6 abatoa, abatua, abatwa, bakuba, bakutu, balolo, baluba, banyai, basoga, basoka, basuto, bullom, damara, herero, kaffir, mbunda, ovampo, pokomo, thonga, tswana, wabena, wabuma, waguha, warori, yakala, zaramo 7 baganda, bakunda, bakwiri, bangala, bantoid, banyoro, baronga, barundi, basongo, batekes, batonga, bunyoro, cabinda, makonde, mashona, ndebele, swahili, wachaga, wagweno, wakamba, wanyasa, waregga, wasango 8 abarambo, andarobo, andorobo, angolese, barolong, bechuana, ganguela, matabele, transkei, wasagara 9 batetella, eshikongo 10 bashilange, wanyakyusa 11 shukulumbwe 12 bangwaketsia

BANTY See BANTAM.

BANXRING tana, tapaia, tupais

BANYAN ascetic, banian, bunnia, bur(r), gown, jacket, jaguey, moneylender, shirt, trader, tree, wrapper

BANZAI attack, reckless, shout, suicidal, war-cry

BAOBAB adansonia, calabash, imbondo, monkeybread, mowana, sourgourd, tamarind, tebeldi, tree
leaves lalo

BAP bread, loaf, roll

BAPTISIA bugleweed, herb, indigo, rattlebush

BAPTISM affusion, aspergation, aspersion, bath, christening, cleansing, consecration, dedication, immersion, infusion, initiation, palingeny, perfusion, purgation, purge, sanctification, sprinkling
font basin, laver, piscina, spring
liquid liver, perfusion
opponent catabaptist
robe chrisom

BAPTIST didapper, dipper, traskite

BAPTISTA *daughter* bianca, kate, katherina, katherine
son-in-law petruchio

BAPTIZE asperge, asperse,

christen, cleanse, dedicate, depe, dilute, dip, duck, dunk, heave, immerse, initiate, moisten, name, perfuse, plunge, purify, sprinkle, submerge, volow

BAQUET rod, scuttle, trough, tub, wand

BAR 3 ban, dam, fid, gad, law, leg, pub, rib, rod, tap 4 axle, bail, balk, band, bank, baur, beam, bolt, boom, cafe, char, crow, drag, fess, fish, gate, halt, hide, joke, line, lock, loop, mark, moat, oust, pole, rack, rail, reef, rein, risp, save, sess, shut, slab, slat, slip, slot, snib, stop, tree 5 arbor, bench, betty, bilbo, bilco, block, brace, bride, catch, clasp, close, court, cramp, deter, estop, fence, gemel, hedge, humet, ingot, jimmy, lever, perch, ratch, ridge, shaft, shoal, slote, sprag, staff, stang, stave, steek, strip, strut, swipe, table, trace, yaird 6 barret, billet, bistro, bodega, buffet, column, defeat, doffer, dolley, dollie, evener, except, fasten, forbid, forset, grille, heaver, hinder, impede, lancet, muntin, object, peeler, saloon, stower, stripe, tablet, tavern, toggle 7 barrace, barrier, bolster, bobstay, buvette, canteen, confine, counter, exclude, gallows, grating, mandril, measure, munting, prevent, railing, scratch, shut out, snibble, spindle, tombolo, trundle 8 grogshop, handrail, obstacle, pessulus, preclude, prohibit, sandbank 9 barricade, deterrent, hindrance, interpose 10 impediment 11 barrelhouse, obstruction, rathskeller
acrobat's trapeze
artificial barrage
bullion ingot
door lock, risp, slot, stang
gown lawyer
graph histogram
heraldic fess(e), humet, label
jointed chill
lead came
legally estop
loom backstay, batten, leaser, sword

man See BARTENDER.
millstone rynd
mining moil
money bonk, tang
needlework bride
notched ratch, risp, skey
pair of gem(m)el
pressure-resisting strut
racial color line
river char
rotating axle
screen grizzly
sinister stigma
soap frame sess
spiked herisson
steel bullpoint, bullprick, stirrup
stirring crutch
supporting fid, rod, stanchion, strut
tamping stemmer

BARA, THEDA theodosia goodman

BARADARI mausoleum, palace, tomb

BARAK *father* abinoam, abinoem
enemy canaanites
leader deborah

BARATARIA *governor* sancho panza

BARATHRON, BARATHRUM devourer, extortionist, glutton, hell, pit

BARB arrow(head), awn, barbule, beard, bristle, brocard, bur(r), carping, clip, dart, filament, file, flu(k)e, gibe, hair, harl, herl, hook, horse, jagg, kelpie, kingfish, maxim, mot, mow, nag, pigeon, pinnula, point, projection, proverb, quill, ramus, ridge, sarcasm, scarf, shaft, sharpen, shave, spear, spike, spine, strain, thorn, tippet, witter
anchor flue, fluke
feather flu(k)e, harl, herl, pinnula, ramus

BARBACOAN *indian* cara, cayapa

BARBACOU barbet, puffbird

BARBADOS *cabbage tree* roystonea
capital bridgetown
cherry acerola, bunchosia, malphigia, surinam
earth marl
flower fence poinciana
gooseberry blade-apple, cactus, heterotrichum, lemon vine, pereskia
leg elephantiasis

lily amaryllis, hippeastrum
liquor rum
native bim
peak hillaby
pitch manjack
port bridgetown
pride adenanthera, bear-tree, flower-fence, peacock-flower, poinciana, sandlewood
water citronelle
BARBARA, St. *emblem* lance
BARBAREA campe, cardamine, wintercress, yellow rocket
BARBARIAN alien, BARBAROUS, berber, boor, bounder, brute, cutthroat, foreigner, goth, heathen, hun, lowbrow, philistine, rude, ruffian, savage, untutored, vandal, vulgarian, wild
troops caterva
BARBARIC atrocious, barbarous, bestial, brutal, coarse, crude, cutthroat, fell, ferocious, fierce, flashy, florid, foreign, garish, gaudy, gothic, gross, harsh, heathen, hunnish, ignorant, inhuman, lowbrow, ostentatious, philistine, pitiless, primitive, rough, rude, savage, tasteless, uncivil(ized), uncultivated, untaught, untutored, wild
BARBARISM caconym, cant, catachresis, corruption, datism, ignorance, impropriety, localism, malapropism, misuse, rudeness, savagery, solecism, vulgarism
BARBARITY atrocity, brutality, butchery, cannibalism, carnage, cruelty, fellness, ferity, ferocity, inhumanity, manslaughter, massacre, murder, rudeness, sadism, savagery
BARBAROSSA frederick, red-beard
BARBAROUS See BARBARIC.
BARBARY maghrib, magot, moghrib
ape macaca, magot, simian
buttons snail-clover
fig opuntia, prickly-pear
sheep aoudad
state algiers, morocco, tripoli, tunis
thorn cat's-claw

BARBASCO canella, cube, dogwood, joewood, wild cinnamon
BARBATE barbigerous, bearded, hairy, tufted
BARBEAU bluebottle, cornflower
BARBECUE asado, bake, bocan, brasier, brazier, broil, buccan, carbonado, clambake, cook(out), grid, grill, roast, spit
fuel briquette, charcoal
rod skewer, spit
BARBED acid, bent, echinated, hooked, pointed, prickly, spiked, spiny, uncinate, vitriolic, wattled
BARBEL beard, cirrus, cyprinid, fish, pap, vibrissa, wattle
BARBER catfish, chirotonsor, composer, cut(ter), figaro, haircutter, poller, scraper, shave(r), tonsor, tonsure, trimmer
bug barbeiro, conenose, conorhinus
fifth brother alnaschar
-fish anthias, dorab, fop, surgeon-fish, tang
itch ringworm, sycosis, tinea
of seville figaro
of seville author beaumarchais
of seville character almaviva, bartholo, figaro, rosine
of seville composer rossini
pert. tonsorial
shop quartet
BARBERRY berberis, guildtree, pepperidge, podophyllum
derivative berberine
rust aecium
BARBET barbacou, barbican, barbion, barmkin, bird, bucconid, capitonid, dreamer, ironsmith, pearlbird, poodle, puffbird, thickhead, tigerbird
BARBETTE gunmount, mound, parapet, platform
BARBICAN barbet, fort(ification), outwork, tower
BARBITURATE amytal, barbital, hypnotic, nembutal, phenobarbital, seconal, sedative, veronal
BARBUDO catfish, polynemus, rhamdia, threadfin

BARBULE barb(icel), beard, quill
BARBULYIE confuse, confusion, perplex(ity)
BARCA barge, bark, boat, gunboat
son hannibal
BARCAROLE melody, song
BARCELONA handkerchief, neckcloth
street rambla
BARD bhat, demodocus, druid, ecna, fergus, gleeman, improvisator, improvisatore, jongleur, meistersinger, minnesinger, minstrel, muse, musician, ossian, ovate, poet, rhymer, rhymster, rune(r), runesmith, sagaman, scald, scop, singer, skald, swan, taliesen, troubadour, trouvere, trouveur, versifier
of avon shakespeare
of ayrshire burns
of olney cowper
of rydal mount wordsworth
of twickenham pope
BARDOLPH *companion* falstaff, nym, pistol
BARDY audacious, bold, defiant, insolent
BARE alone, bald, barish, barren, blank, bleak, blunt, callow, crude, denudate, denude(d), deprived, desolate, destitute, disclose, divest, divulge, dry, empty, expose, histie, manifest, meager, mere, naked, napless, natural, nude, open, ordinary, paltry, plain, poor, ragged, reveal, scant, scarry, simple, sole, stark, strip(ped), unadorned, unarmed, unclad, unconcealed, uncover, undisguised, undressed, unmask, unveil, waste, without
comb. nudi
possibility improbability
teeth tuck
BAREFACED audacious, bold, brash, brazen, candid, glaring, immodest, impudent, indecent, shameless, undisguised, unseemly
BAREFISTED brawly, brutal, fierce, punishing, rough
BAREFOOT discalceate, discalced, unshod
BAREHANDED open-fisted, toolless, unarmed, weaponless

BARELY all but, almost, edgeways, faintly, hardly, insufficiently, jimp, just, merely, nakedly, nearly, only, poorly, scantily, scarcely, simply, slightly, solely, uneath, unnethe
BARER callower, delver, feigher, muckman, navvy
BARFISH dorab
BARFLY carouser, drunk, stiff
BARGAIN a bon marche, advantageous, agree(ment), arrangement, barter, beat down, bid, buy, chaffer, cheap(en), compact, contest, contract, cope, covenant, deal, dicker, discuss, engage(ment), fight, good buy, haggle, higgle, horse-trade, huck(ster), indenture, koop, mart, mediate, metsieh, mise, money's worth, negotiate, niffer, out-bid, pact(ion), palter, pen-north, pennyworth, pickup, prig, purchase, rug(g), sell, snap, steal, stickle, stipulate, struggle, swap, trade, traffic, transaction, treaty, trog, troke, truck, understanding, wanworth, whiz(z), wholesale, wod
-*basement* cheap, tawdry
blind pig in a poke
for expect, plan, reckon
hard prig
hunter cheap jack
on count on
penny arles, earnest
BARGAINER chafferer, co(w)per, kite, nip, schnor(r)er, shnorrer
dishonest bushranger
sharp screw
BARGE ark, barca, bark, barque, berate, billyboy, birlinn, boat, budgero(w), bump, burllin, burling, butt, casco, chalana, coach, collide, dory, dredge, drogher, dummy, float, foist, gabbard, galley, gundalow, gyassa, hoy, interfere, lighter, lumber, lump, lunge, lurch, moorpunky, pra(a)m, praham, rebuke, rowboat, scold, scow, shrew, stumpy, tender, termagant, thrust, towboat, trow, tub, tumbler, tumbrel, virago, vixen, walk, wherry
charge lighterage

coal keel
harbor hoy
in blunder, enter, intrude
pilot riverman
BARGEMAN bargee, boatman, hoyman, huffler, pug
cabbage turnip
BARGHEST demon, hobgoblin, padfoot
BARGOOSE sheldrake
BARILLA halogeton, kelp, salsoda, saltwort, soda
ashes pulverin
BARITE barytes, barytine, cauk, cawk, hepatite, spar, tiff
BARIUM *compound* barite, baryta, benitoite, celsian, witherite
BARK aabec, abrade, advertise, aga(mid), alarm, alert, baff, bag, balat, barge, bast(e), bawl, bay, bellow, boat, boof, bowwow, chafe, c(h)inchona, clamor, coat, cortex, coto, cough, cover (ing), cry, detonation, dita, doundake, enclose, encrust, explosion, fell, frangule, gall, girdle, gogo, granatum, growl, grumble, hide, howl, hurt, husk, loja, loxa, massoy, mesenna, mocha, mutter, niepa, open, order, ouf, peel, pelt, periera, phloeum, pinnace, remove, rend, report, rind, rose, rub, shell, shot, shout, sintoc, skin, snap, solicit, speak, strip, tan, tapa, threaten, tranky, utter, waffle, warn, woodskin, woof, wuff, yabba, yaff(le), yamph, yap, yelp, yip, youff
aromatic canella, culilawan, sassafras, sintoc
astringent coto
at berate, rebuke, scold
beetle borer, dendroctonus, engraver, hypothenemus, ipida, scolytid
bitter alstonia, angostura, cascarilla, cinchona, niepa, niota, quinine
canoe cascara
c(h)inchona quina
cloth brachystegia, tap(p)a
comb. cortico
cord aea
dish coolamon
dog's See DOG *bark.*
exterior ross
fiber olona, terap
fish poison akia

goatbush amargoso
having corticated
inner bast, cortex, liber
lesion canker
living on corticolous, epiphloedal
louse aphis
medicinal alconorque, calisaya, canella, casca, c(h)inchona, conessi, copalche, copalchi, coto, madar, mudar, niepe, quinine, sassafras, tellicherry
outer periderm, ross
pert. cortical
remove decorticate, rind, ross, scale, spud
remover rosser, spudder
scaly psorosis, ross
tanning alconorque, alder, termeric
tissue cork, phellem
tonic canella
tree bast, c(h)inchona, niepa
up the wrong tree err, stray
BARKER buffer, charlatan, dog, doorman, grinder, gun, pistol, publicist, solicitor, spieler, spruiker, spudder, tanner, tout
-*bug fever* chagas-disease
BARKERY tanhouse
BARKING bay, latrant, latration, loud, noisy, quest, spud
bird hylactes
deer muntjac
iron spud
pert. hylactic
squirrel prairie dog
BARKLE cake, incrust
BARLEY bent, big(g), cereal, cry, grain, hordeum, licorn, malt, sprat, tisane, truce, tsamba, whitecorn
awn horn
beer chang
beat pail, warm
-*bree, -broo* ale, liquor, whiskey
cake fadge
corn whiskey
disease scald, scale, smut, stripe, take-all
drink ptisan
4-rowed bear, bere, big(g)
globulin byndestin
ground tsamba
hulled ptisan
island alehouse, pub, saloon
parched tsamba
pert. hordeaceous
protein hordein
refuse flints, shag

6-rowed bear, bere
spike chat
steeped malt
straw trifle
water ptisan, tisane
BARLEYBIRD nightingale, siskin, wagtail, wryneck
BARLEYCORN *3* inch
BARLEYSICK drunk, intoxicated, stiff
BARLOW jackknife
BARM alban, boil, bosom, ferment, froth, lap, leaven, yeast
BARMAID tapstress, waitress
BARMAN See **BARTENDER**.
BARMKIN barbican
BARMY flighty, foolish, lightheaded, scatterbrained, shallow, silly
BARN byre, cowhouse, grange, lathe, mew(s), saur, shed, shelter, shippon, skipper, stable, stall, store
bay goaf, skeeling, skilling, skillion
dance hoedown, party, social
dance official caller
door raja, shate
grass ankee, cockspur, millet
gun shingles
owl lulu, madge, padge, strix, tyto
part bay, hayloft, leanto, mow, stall
swallow hirundo
BARNABAS *companion* paul
symbol rake
BARNACLE acorn, anatifa, balanid, bray, brey, cirriped, cling(er), crustacean, cypris, decoy, fasten, gnathopod, goose, incumbent, lepadid, lepas, limpet, nosepincher, parasite, sacculina, swindler
appendage cirrus
back mariner, veteran
body capitulum
eater filefish
larva kentrogon
plate tergum
scale bark-louse
BARNACLES glasses, spectacles
BARNEY argument, blunder, botchery, brawl, contest, dispute, fight, fizzle, foolery, free-for-all, hoax, mistake, mob, nonsense, quarrel, row, rumpus
-clapper lily-of-the-valley

BARNSTORM campaign, stump, tour, travel, troupe
BARNSTORMER actor, campaigner, candidate, office-seeker, politician
BARNYARD backside, bucolic, corny, pightle, strawyard, unsophisticated
golf horseshoes
BAROI grewia, pandanus, pterospermum
BAROMETER altimeter, aneroid, glass, orometer
gauge manometer
line isobar
BARON beef, businessman, capitalist, daimio, financier, freeman, freiherr, husband, industrialist, loin, lord, mogul, noble(man), peer, personage, potentate, sachem, sirloin, vassal
court hallmoot
BARONESS lady, solitaire
BARONET bart, cavalier, esquire, knight, sir
BARONG cleaver, knife, sword
BARONY domain, fief, han
BAROQUE elegant, extravagant, fancy, fantastic, flamboyant, florid, gothic, grotesque, irregular, ornate, outre, rococo
BAROSMA *camphor* diosphenol
leaves buchu
BAROTO boat, canoe, dugout, vinta
BAROUCHE carriage, four-wheeler
BARRACK(S) barracoon, billet, bivouac, bothy, bullpen, camp, can(n)aba, casern(e), cellar, cheer, cuertel, decry, garrison, hut, jeer, lodge, quarters, root, shelter, shout, support, taunt
BARRACOON barrack, jail, prison
BARRACUDA barry, becuna, escolar, fish, guaguanche, kaku, katonkel, pelon, picudilla, scooter, picuda, scoots, sennet, snake, snoek, snook, spet, sphyraena, thyrsites, vicuda
BARRAGAN camlet, fabric, mantle, wrap
BARRAGE attack, barrier, broadside, cannonade, discharge, drumfire, fire, fusil-

lade, obstruction, salvo, shower, umbrella, volley
BARRAMUNDA ceratodus, cycloid, dipnoan, flathead, lungfish, salmon, scleropages
BARRANCA arroyo, gorge, gulley, ravine
BARRAS galipot, linen
BARRATRY fraud, infidelity, simony
BARRE streak, stripe
BARRED ribbed, striped
BARREL bowie, brand, butt, cade, calamus, case, cask, cistern, container, cylinder, drum, fat, fessel, firkin, girnal, girnel, hogget, hogshead, hubkang, keg, kilderkin, knag, package, plenty, quill, receptacle, roller, rumble, rundlet, runlet, shell, speed, tierce, trunk, tumble(r), tun, vangee, vat, vessel
cactus fero
capstan spool
disk daunt
edge chime
herring cade, cran
hoop band, gird, girth
maker cooper, tubber, tubman
organ autophon
part ga(u)ntry, hoop, side, slat, stap, stave
rack jib
raising device parbuckle
row longer
-shaped dolioform
slat lag(gin), stap, stave
small barrico, cade, keg, kilderkin, kit, knag, run(d)let
stave See *slat*, above.
stopper bung
support ga(u)ntry, hoop
tobacco hogshead, tun
with cranks vangee
BARRELFUL oodles, quantity
BARRELHOUSE dive, gutbucket, jazz, pub, saloon
BARREN acarpous, arid, austere, bald, bare, bereft, bleak, blunt, bowy, childless, dead, deaf, desert, desolate, destitute, devoid, dour, drape, dry, dull, dusty, effete, eild, empty, exhausted, fallow, fruitless, futile, gast, gaunt, geld, ghast, histie, hungry, impotent, ineffectual, infertile, invalid, lacking, lean, mea-

ger, naked, nude, poor, prosaic, salt, seck, severe, stark, sterile, stern, teemless, treeless, unfruitful, unproductive, unprofitable, unprolific, useless, vain, void, waste, ye(i)ld
chickweed cerastium
myrtle bearberry
not facile, fecund, fruitful
oak bitter-bush, blackjack
privet alatern, houseleek
shoot apoblast
strawberry potentilla, waldsteinia
BARRENNESS agenesis, emptiness, sterility, vacancy
BARRENWORT bishop's hat, epimedium
BARRET biretta, cap
BARRICADE abatis, barrace, barrage, barrier, block (ade), bound, close, defense, enclosure, fence, fortification, fortify, hurdle, limit, obstacle, obstruct (ion), pale, prison, ramforce, roadblock, shut, stop
BARRICO cask, keg
BARRIE, J. M. *play* admirable crichton, dear brutus, little minister, mary rose, my lady nicotine, peter pan
BARRIER alp, backstop, bank, bar(rage), barricade, boma, boom, bound(ary), buffer, bulkhead, bulwark, chain, confines, cordon, crib, croy, curtain, dam, difficulty, dike, door, dyke, embankment, enclosure, fence, fortress, fosse, frontier, gate, glacis, grille, hedge, hindrance, hurdle, impediment, limit, lock, milldam, mole, mound, obstacle, obstruction, pale, palisade, parapet, partition, portcullis, railing, rampart, restraint, roadblock, screen, stockade, stop, style, traverse, treble, wall, weir
across river kiddle, still
artificial foss(e)
fire barrage
movable bars, blind, curtain, door, shade, shutters, window
traffic separator
BARRIGUDA chorisia, iriartea, palm
BARRIGUDO lagothrix, monkey
BARRING aside from, but,

closed, excepting, excluding, omitting, precluding, save, without
BARRIO district, ghetto, settlement, slum, village
part sitio
BARRISTER advocate, attorney, barman, colt, counsel (or), lawyer, proctor, procurator, serjeant, solicitor, templar, tubman
robe silks
BARROOM cafe, cantina, doggery, dramshop, groggery, grogshop, saloon, tavern
BARROW bank, bier, carrier, carry, dune, embankment, frame, galgal, galt, garment, grave, gurry, hill(ock), hog, hurly, kurgan, mote, mound, mountain, naveta, pushcart, swine, tomb, trolley, tump, tumulus
boy costermonger
2-wheeled hurly
BARROWMAN costermonger
BARSINE statira
father artabazus, darius
consort alexander, memnon
slayer parysatis, roxana
son hercules
BARTENDER barkeep, beast of bourbon, mixer, mixologist, skinker, tapster
BARTER auction, bargain, buy and sell, cambium, chaffer, chap, chop, commerce, commutation, cope, corse, coup, deal, dicker, excambion, exchange, give-and-take, hawk, interchange, jobbing, mang, mong, niffer, permute, reciprocate, scorse, sell, swap, trade, traffic, trog, troke, truck (le), vend
pert. metabletic
BARTERER co(w)per, trucker
BARTHOLOMEW *burial* rome
parent talmai
symbol knife
BARTIMAEUS *father* timaeus
BARTIZAN lookout, tower, turret
BARTON farm(yard) homestead
BARTSIA figwort
BARUCK *friend* jeremiah

BARYE microbar
BARYON hyperon, nucleon
BARYTHYMIA melancholia
BASAL See BASIC.
BASALT anamesite, arapahite, auganite, bandaite, diabase, dolerite, ghizite, kulaite, marble, melaphyre, navite, pottery, sudburite
basic araphite
black tachylyte
coarse dolerite
glassy tachylyte
BASE 3 bad, bed, den, hub, low 4 anil, camp, clam, evil, fake, fond, font, foot, fort, foul, lewd, mean, poor, prop, rank, rely, rest, root, seat, sill, site, sole, stay, stem, step, vile 5 apron, basis, block, build, cause, cheap, dirty, floor, found, grave, gross, lache, lowly, nadir, petty, place, pokey, quoin, small, snide, socle, stand, stool, theme, worse 6 abject, anlage, arrant, bottom, cheesy, coarse, ground, grubby, humble, impure, measly, menial, odious, origin, paltry, perron, rascal, riprap, scabby, scummy, scurvy, shabby, shoddy, sordid, tawdry, vulgar, wicked 7 alloyed, bastard, bedding, bedrock, caitiff, carrier, currish, essence, footing, fulsome, grounds, hangdog, heinous, hilding, housing, ignoble, immoral, radical, roinish, scrubby, servile, slavish, staddle, station, stratum, support 8 backbone, beggarly, churlish, coistrel, compound, cowardly, drawhead, flagrant, infamous, inferior, keystone, maintain, meschant, mopboard, pavement, pedestal, pediment, rudiment, rascally, scullion, shameful, spurious, standard, terminal, terrible, unworthy, wainscot, wretched 9 atrocious, establish, execrable, miserable, monstrous, nefarious, niddering, obnoxious, principle, stylobate, truculent, unrefined, worthless 10 abominable, despicable, foundation, hypostasis, rockbottom, stereobate, terra firma, vil-

lainous 11 cornerstone, counterfeit, fundamental 12 contemptible, dishonorable, disreputable, headquarters, substructure, underpinning
architectural dado, patten, plinth, socle
attached by sessile
chemical acridane, actinine, adenine, agmatine, aldimine, alkaloid, anserine, choline, conyrine, galegine, guanine, ketimine, lepidine, semidine
crystalline acridan, alanine, anserine, carnosine, kynurine, rosaniline, thaline, tropine, tyramine
-dealing broking
fellow carl, churl
isomeric anisidine, parvoline
marker bag
metal alloy
military camp, depot, etape, station
on balls pass, walk
pert. basilar
rocket mignonette
root radix
second keystone
stalk-like cnidopod
third hot corner
tree laburnum
vervain germander-speedwell
wallah See SOLDIER.
BASEBALL apple, cowhide, duster, floater, horsehide, inshoot, leather, pill
area center field, diamond, infield, outfield
catcher backstop
fence backstop
field astrodome, diamond
founder abner doubleday
game shutout, slugfest
game, perfect no-hitter
hit bagger, bingle, blooper, bob, bunt, double, grounder, homer, linedrive, liner, lob, looper, pop-up, single, three-bagger, triple, two-bagger
manager alston, barrow, boudreau, cochrane, comisky, cronin, dark, dressen, durocher, eckert, frick, griffith, grimm, haney, harris, houk, huggins, hutchinson, landis, lasorda, lopez, mack, mccarthy, mcgraw, mckechnie, mcphail, mele, murtaugh, omalley, rickey, robinson,

southworth, stengel, terry, veeck, yawkey
marker bag
memorial cooperstown, hall of fame
official coach, manager, umpire
pitch crossfire, curve, fast ball, knuckle ball, knuckler, screwball, sinker, slider, spitball
player yannigan
position catcher, fielder, pitcher, shortstop
source cricket, rounders
team angels, astros, athletics, braves, cardinals, cubs, dodgers, giants, indians, mets, orioles, padres, phillies, pirates, reds, redsox, senators, tigers, twins, whitesox, yankees
term alley, assist, bag, bat (ter), battery, bench, blooper, box, bullpen, bunt, burn, charge, circuit, cleanup, clout, clutch, coach, curve, delivery, drive, dugout, error, fan, first, floater, fly, foul, glove, groove, high, hook, inside, low, lumber, miss, mound, out, peg, pill, pinch-hit, plate, powdered, punch, rbi, rhubarb, rubber, run(ner), sack, sacrifice, safe, score, series, sidearm, sinker, slab, slide, squeeze, stance, stretch, strike, swing, tap, target, thumbed, top, triple, walk, wild, windup
BASEBOARD dado, easement, plinth, mopboard, skirt(ing), wainscot
BASEBORN humble, ignoble, illegitimate, low(ly), mean, menial, plebeian, proletarian, vile
BASELARD dagger, sword
BASELESS bottomless, empty, false, flimsy, gratuitous, groundless, idle, unfounded, unsupported, untenable, unwarranted, vain
BASEMAN sacker
BASEMENT barracks, cellar, hypogea, subterrane, tahkhana, underground, vault
masonry stereobate
BASENESS beggary, felony, squalor, turpitude, vility
BASEWORT belladonna
BASH abash, bat, beat, blow, bruise, crush, dent, lam,

mash, party, slosh, smash, strike, swat, wham, whap, whop
BASHAW See PASHA.
BASHEMATH *husband* esau
parent elon
BASHFUL abashed, ashamed, backward, blate, blushing, chary, coy, daphnean, daunted, diffident, dismayed, embarrassed, helo(e), modest, pudent, pudibund, reserved, reticent, retiring, sackless, shan, sheepish, sheepy, shrinking, shy, skittish, timid, timorous, verecund
billy slow loris
BASHFULNESS pudor, shyness, timidity
BASHIKIV *capital* ufa
BASIC alkaline, basilar, bedrock, bottom, canonic, capital, cardinal, central, chief, classic, core, crux, elemental, elementary, essential, fundamental, indispensable, key, main, original, primal, primitive, primordial, radical, rudimental, rudimentary, substratal, ultimate, underlying, vital
commodity staple
english, inventor ogden
facts abc's, alphabet
BASIDIOMYCETE bracketcap, fungus, mushroom, puffball, rust, smut
BASIDIUM conidiophore
BASIL ankle-iron, bazel, clinopolium, fetter, herb, mountain-mint, ocimum, ocyme, sheepskin, toolsi, tulasi
mint pennyroyal, pycanthemum
saint, bishopric caesarea
saint, brother gregory
thyme bed's-foot, field-balm, herb, mint
wild horse-thyme
BASILICA basilisk, canopy, church, lateran, shrine, temple
annex chalcidicum
part aisle, altar, apse, atrium, nave, tower
BASILICATA lucania
BASILISK cockatrice, dragon, lizard, serpent
BASILOSAURUS zeuglodon
BASIN basson, bay, bed, bowl, bullan, cavity, cesspool, chafer, cirque,

comb(e), container, cove, cuvette, depression, dish, dock, font, gemellion, gulf, harbor, hollow, hoya, lagoon, lavatory, laver, lekane, louter, marina, moorage, pan, piscina, plain, pool, pot, reservoir, scalepan, sink, slake, stoup, tala, tank, tub, valley, vanitory, vessel
kind bathtub, bowl, bullen, catch-bowl, cistern, dishpan, ewer, fingerbowl, lavabo, lekane, louter, punch bowl, terrine, tureen, urceole, vat, washbowl, washtub
rock keeve, kieve
-shaped pelviform
BASINET See HELMET.
BASIS account, anlage, authority, axiom, BASE, bedrock, bottom, criterion, fond, foot(ing), form, fund(ament), gravamen, ground(sel), law, postulate, premise, presumption, root, sill, strength, substone, support, theorem, warrant
BASK acrid, apricate, bathe, beek, bitter, enjoy, laze, luxuriate, rejoice, revel, sun, tan, thrive, warm
BASKET ark, bin, bokark, box, caba(s), cage, calabash, calathiscus, calathus, canister, carrier, cassie, cassy, caul, cawl, cest(a), charity, chequeen, cleave, cob(b), container, corf, crane, crate, cresset, dilli, dorsel, gabion, goal, gondola, grate, hamper, hobbit, hoppet, hott, jicara, junket, kibsey, kipe, kipsey, kish, kit, maun(d), molly, murl(a)in, natte, pan(n)ier, pattara, ped, pegall, petana, pottle, punnet, quantity, receptacle, rusty, score, scull, scuttle, seron, skeough, skep, skippet, swill, teanal, tour, trug, tumbril, vessel, watape, weel, w(h)isket, windle, zecchino, zequin
balloon car, nacelle
-bearer canephora, canephorus
birch-bark bokark
boat coracle
bottom slath

carried on head calathiscus, calathus
center slather
coal corb, corf
crumb voider
eel buck
farm skep
fern nephrolepsis
fig caba(s), frail, tap(net)
fish astrophyton, caul, cawl, corf, crail, crate, creel, gabion, hamper, hask, kipe, kreel, maund, pannier, rip, sea spider, swill, weel, wicker
fruit caba(s), calathos, frail, molly, pottle, punnet
grass otate, turkey-beard
hoop croton, shrub
hop-picker's bin
kind bassinet, buck, bushel, caul, cawl, coop, corbeil, corf, crate, creel, dosser, hamper, pan(n)ier, reed, rush, scull, skep, splint, stave, teanal, tumbrel, tumbril, washbasket, wicker, willy, windel, wire, zecchino
lobster corf
maker anasazi
manure hot(t)
material grass, osier, otate, reed, rush, straw, wicker
palm talipot
rod osier, scallom
round murl(a)in
rummy canasta
rush frail
sculptured corbeil
seed hobbet, hobbit, seedlip
shallow punnet
strip rand
twig wattle
water-tight wattape
wicker bassinet, cob, coop, crib, hamper, hanaper, willy
willow osier, prickle
winnowing liknon
withe heliotropium, vine
BASKETBALL casaba, pelota, sphere
founder james naismith
player cageman, cager, cagester, center, forward, guard, hoopman
start tip-off
team five, cagemen
term block, bucket, cage, casaba, dribble, dunker, foul, freeze, hoop, jumper, keyhole, layup, net, palming, shoot, stall, walking weave

BASKETWORK *term* cabas, slarth, slath(e), slew, stake, stroke, tee, wale
BASQUE baskish, biscayan, euskarian, euscaco, iberian, scoter, vascon, waist
cap beret
city bilbao, guernica, irun, pamplona, san sebastian, vitoria
cyclops tartaro
dance auresca, aurescu, zortzico
dialect labourdin, souletin
drink picon-punch
game mus, pelota
guerrillas eta, euzkadi, frap
"hello" alo-nola-zera
language euskara, euskera, eusk(u)ara, uskara
leader extabe
party eta
petticoat basquine
primogeniture indarra
province alava, biscay, quipuzcoa, navarra, vizcaya
separatist movement eta
shirt pullover
song zortizico
walking stick makila
BASS achigan, anabas, bachelor, barfish, barse, belted sandfish, bigmouth, bitterhead, blackwill, bluefish, bordun, brasse, burden, cabrilla, calico, cherna, chub, clay, deep, drone, drum, growler, huron, iyo, jumper, labrax, linden, linesides, low, mat, oswego, perca, perch, redeye, rockfish, serranid, shale, singer, streaker, striper, tallywag, tattler, welshman
black achigan, bronzebacker, huron smallmouth, speckled hen
blue sunfish
drone bourdon
group shoal
killy mayfish
musical continuo, ostenuto
red drum, snapper
sea serranid
walking boogie-woogie
BASSANIO *beloved* lavinia, portia
brother saturnius
friend antonio, gratiano, lorenzo, salanio, salarino, salerio
servant leonardo
BASSARISK cacomistle
BASSET dog, game, outcrop

BASSIA goosefoot
BASSINET basket, bath
(inette)(tub), moses-basket, perambulator
BASSOON curtal, fagot(o), fagotte, oboe
double fagottone
mouthpiece tudel
part reed
small bassonquinte
BASSWOOD bast, daddynut, lin(den), linn, tilia, wahoo, whitewood, wicopy
BAST *father* amon
fiber acacia, agust, anilao, anilau, castuli, catena, daincha, feru, flax, hemp, jute, noseburn, phloem, piassava, ramie
BASTA enough, stop
BASTARD abnormal, adulterate, bantling, baseborn, brat, byblow, bychild, byspell, cannon, cowson, culverin, fake, false, galley, getling, griqua, hybrid, illegitimate, illicit, impure, inferior, irregular, lowbred, mamzer, memzer, misbeget, nameless, natural, spurious, unusual, whoreson, wosbird
acrimony ageratum
bullet tree humiria
chestnut liquidambar
dory boarfish
feverfew broombush, mugwort, parthenium
gidgee myall
granite gneiss
hartebeest sassaby
mahogany bangalay, eucalyptus, jarrah, ratonia, wooly-bull
nettle richweed
pimpernel chaffweed
plantain mudweed
teak dhak, kino, lingoum
wormwood ragweed
BASTE beat, blister, buffet, cane, chastise, cudgel, denounce, drub, flamb, jipper, lard, lash, moisten, pound, pummel, punish, revile, sauce, scold, sew, stitch, tack, thrash, thresh
BASTILE castle, citadel, fortress, jail, prison
BASTINADO beat(ing), blow, cudgel, punishment, stick
BASTION barbette, breastwork, bulwark, fort(ress), jetty, moineau, parapet,

rampart, ravelin, stronghold, torus
part banquette, curtain, face, flank, gorge
BASTON bat, cudgel, molding, staff, stanza, stave, torus
BASUTOLAND lesotho
BAT aliped, back(i)e, baht, bake, bandy, barbastel(le), baston, bate, bauckie, beetle, binge, blink, blow, bludgeon, chiropter, club, cudgel, desmodus, fewl, flittermouse, flutter, flying-fox, fungo, gait, glassophaga, gray, hindustani, hit, jack, kalong, lob, loft, lump, lunatic, mass, noctule, pipistrelle, pommel, prostitute, racket, reremouse, revel, serotine, shale, speed, spree, stick, strike, stroke, swat, toot, vampire, vespertilian, wad, whack, whip, wink
around debate, drift, ponder, rap, roam
big-eared corynorhinus
blood-sucking diphylla
changed to alcithoe
expert chiropterologist
famous louisville slugger
fish-eating noctilio
fruit epaulet, peca
gently bunt
genus diphylla, molossus, mormoops, petalia, plecotus, vespertilio
hearing organ earlet
go to — for intercede
-like vespertilian
-minded blind, obtuse
of an eye instant
specialist chiropterologist
symbol of blindness
the breeze chat, rap, talk
tree evergreen-magnolia
wood ash
BATA child, servant
BATAAN *bay* subic
city balanga, balayan
BATAD sorghum
BATALEUR eagle, ecaudatus, helotarsus, terathopius
BATATA sweet-potato, tuber, yam
BATAVIA djakarta
BATCH accumulation, amount, assortment, bache, bake, baking, brewing, bunch, cast, cluster, collection, formula, group, lot, lump, making, mass, mate-

rial, mess, mixture, number, quantity, setting, sort, stream, volume
BATE abate, bath, beat, beet, contention, decrease, diminish, discount, except, fail, flutter, grain, lessen, mitigate, moderate, omit, rage, relax, remove, restrain, retrench, soak, solution, steep, strife, temper, waste
BATEAU batel, boat, dhow, pontoon, scow, skipjack
BATES *hymn* america the beautiful
BATFISH angler, devilfish, diabolo, malthe, stingray
BATH ablution, bagnio, bain, balnation, balnearium, balneary, balneation, balneum, baptism, bate, bidet, cleansing, dip, douche, immersion, lavacre, laver, mikva(h), mikveh, natation, plunge, resort, sauna, shower, soak, solution, spa, sponge, springs, steep, stew, swim, tosh, treat, tub, wash (ing), water
asparagus star-of-bethlehem
attendant al(e)iptes
comb. balneo
flower trillium
foot pediluvium
hot scald, stew, stufe, stuphe, therm(e)
king of beau nash
luxurious bubble
metal brass, pinchbeck
mud illutation
pert. balneal, balneatory
photographic fixer
public piscine, therm(e)
sitz bidet, insession, semicupe
sponge euspongia, loofah, luffa
steam sauna, turkish
tanning bate, soak
treatment balneotherapy
turkish hothouse, hummum
type acid, bubble, electric, finnish, hip, hot-air, mud, needle, radium, russian, sponge, steam, sulphur, sweat, turkish, wetpack
BATHE apply, bask, cleanse, cover, dowse, drench, envelop, enwrap, foment, imbue, immerse, lave, moisten, permeate, pervade, rinse, soak, souse, splash, steep, stew suffuse, sur-

round, swim, tosh, tub, wash, wet

BATHHOUSE bagnio, balneary, cabana, hammam, lavatory, sauna, stew, stufe, stuphe

BATHING ablution, aquatics, balneation, balneum, lavacre, lavement, swimming
science balneology
suit bikini, maillot, monokini, trunks
therapeutic balneology

BATHOS anticlimax, comedown, inanity, insipidity, mawkishness, melodrama, pathos, poignancy, sentiment(ality), soppiness, triteness, triviality

BATHROBE dressing gown, negligee, peignoir

BATHROOM biffy, hammam, lavatory, loo, potty, priv(v)y, sudatorium, sudatory, toilet, watercloset

BATHSHEBA bethsabee
father eliam
husband david, uriah
son solomon

BATHTUB lavacre, tosh
gin homebrew

BATHWORT birthroot

BATHYSPHERE *realm* undersea

BATIA *consort* dardanus
son erichthonius

BATISTE cotton, fabric, lawn, linen-cambric

BATMAN maund, orderly, servant, soldier, striker
friend robin

BATOID guitarfish, ray, sawfish, skate, torpedo

BATON baguet(te), baston, bend, billy, bourdon, club, cudgel, cylinder, rod, scepter, sceptre, staff, stick, stigma, truncheon, tube, verge, wand

BATRACHIAN amphibian, anura, frog, salientia, toad

BATSMAN batter, hitter, slogger, slugger, striker

BATTA agio(tage), allowance, bonus, discount, exchange, expenses, money, premium

BATTALION army, company, division, group, regiment, squadron, troops, ward

BATTEL account, bill, charges, expenses

BATTEN beat, board, cleat,

close, devour, end, enrich, fatten, feed, fertilize, grow, ledge, luxuriate, prepare, prosper, reeper, rib, secure, sley, strip, thrive

BATTER abuse, baste, batsman, beat, belabor, bombard, bruise, buffet, cannonade, clour, clout, cripple, damage, demolish, dent, destroy, dinge, fritter, frush, hammer, hitter, impair, lash, maim, mangle, mixture, mutilate, paste, pelt, pommel, pound, pummel, ram, ruin, shatter, slope, slug, smash, smite, thrash, thring, tumble, wear, wound
cake flapjack, waffle

BATTERDOCK butter-bur, pondweed, potamogeton

BATTERY accumulator, armament, artillery, assault, attack, beating, blind, bombardment, bulkhead, dry cell, dynamo, exciter, group, guns, parapet, park, pra(a)m, radeau, sinkbox, transistor, wet cell
commander captain
gun swinger
masked ambush
metal lead
part anode, cable, cathode, cell, charger, grid, plate, pole, post, rod, terminal, tube, valve
storage accumulator
terminal anode

BATTLE action, affray, assault, attack, bombard, brush, camlan, collision, combat, competition, conflict, contend, contest, cope, duel, encounter, engagement, feud, fight, fray, hosting, joust, kick, mart, meet, naumachia, object, onslaught, oppose, protest, push, skirmish, stour, strive, struggle, thoomachy, tilt, toil, warfare, wrestle
area arena, champ, front, sector, terrain
arranger cadwallader
array acies, herse, order
arrayed for battailous
-ax fauchard, halberd, shrew, sparth, twibil(l), wife, wif(f)le
-ax culture neolithic
cry aboo, abu, alala, aux armes, banzai, beauseant, catchword, charge, ensign,

geronimo, monjay(e), slogan, to arms
famous 4 ivry, jena, zama 5 adowa, alamo, bulge, crecy, ipsus, issus, jerez, marne, sedan, somme, tours, valmy, xeres, ypres 6 actium, arbela, armada, battan, cannae, cressy, jhelum, lutzen, mukden, naseby, plassy, plevna, sadowa, senlac, shiloh, skager, verdun 7 argonne, bullrun, chalons, concord, flodden, lepanto, lucknow, marengo, massada, megiddo, orleans, panipat, pultowa, salamis 8 antietam, blenheim, borodino, hastings, manassas, marathon, metaurus, poitiers, saratoga, syracuse, taushima, waterloo, yorktown 9 agincourt, balaklava, caparetto, gaugamela, lexington, manilabay, marignano, skagerrak, solferino, trafalgar, vicksburg 10 armageddon, austerlitz, bunkerhill, carchemish, gettysburg, sevastopol, stalingrad, tannenberg 11 chattanooga, chickamauga, thermopylae 14 chateauthierry
formation acies, column, deploy, herse, line, phalanx
god, goddess See WAR *god, goddess.*
last armageddon, meggido
line front
marker catstane, catstone
of alcazar peele
of brothers fontenoy
of frogs vs. mice batrachomyomachy
of giants marignan
of spurs courtrai
of 3 emperors austerlitz
of verdun fort vaux
order array, battalia, regalia
quoit chakra
raid spreagh, spreath
royal argument, fight, free for all, melee, scrimmage
site See BATTLEGROUND.
strong in armipotent
trophy medal, ribbon, scalp

BATTLEDORE bat, beetle, hornbook, paddle, racket

BATTLEGROUND aceldama, akeldama, arena, armageddon, blair, champ (aign), encampment, front (line), issue, no man's land, tahua, theater

BATTLEMENT balcony, castellation, crenel(ation), cresting, embrasure, kernel, machicolation, merlon, parapet, pinion, rampart, wall

embrasure crenel(le)

BATTLESHIP carrier, cruiser, destroyer, dreadnought, salvo, superdreadnought

BATTOLOGIZE iterate, repeat

BATTUE hunting, massacre, search, slaughter

BATTY bats, buggy, crazy, foolish, insane, silly

BATU KHAN *grandfather* ghengis khan

BAUBLE bead, gaud, gewgaw, gimcrack, marotte, plaything, scepter, staff, tinsel, toy, trifle, trinket, trivium, trumpery

BAUCH blate, defective, insipid, timid, weak

BAUCIS *guest* hermes, zeus *husband* philemon

BAUER jack, pawn

BAUHAUS *founder* walter gropius

BAUHINIA amli, beantree, butterfly-flower, liana, schizanthus, tamarind

BAUM *character* cowardly lion, dorothy, ozma, toto, wizard

BAUMIER amyris, balsam, fir, ocimum, tree, trigonella

BAUTA memorial, menhir, stone

BAUXITE diaspore, gibbsite, wocheinite

BAVARDAGE chatter, nonsense, prattle, twaddle

BAVARIA(N) See also GERMAN references.

beer wurzburger

capital munchen, munich

city augsburg, bayreuth, berchtesgaden, frankfort, hof, munchen, munich, nuremberg, nurnberg, ratisbon, regensburg, wurzburg

community passau

division aschaffenburg, franconia, neuburg, palatinate, regensburg, schwaben

dress dirndl

lake ammer, chiem, starbber, wurm

measure dreissinger, fass,

fuss, juchert, linie, massel, metze, morgan, rut(h)e, tagwerk

pants lederhosen

range vosges, watzmann, zugspitze

river altmuhl, eger, iller, inn, isar, iser, lech, regen, saale, wornitz

saint rupert

university site erlangen

weight gran, quentchen

BAVIAN baboon, poetaster

BAVIN brushwood, kindling

BAWD aunt, commode, defile, dirty, gigolo, gobetween hare, mackerel, madam, maquereau, pander, pimp, procurer, procuress, prostitute, purveyor, runner, white-slaver

BAWDRY filth, lewdness, obscenity

BAWDY dirty, filthy, foul, lewd, obscene, unchaste

BAWL bark, bellow, blore, blubber, boohoo, clamor, cry, glaister, golly, hawk, hoot, howl, outcry, proclaim, rout, shout, squall, utter, wail, weep, yaup, yawp, yell

out berate, criticize, jump, rail, rate, rebuke, reprimand, reprove, revile, scold, tonguelash, upbraid, wig

BAY arm, badius, bahia, baize, bank, bark, basin, bathe, bayou, berry, bight, brewster, brown, carol, carrell, chestnut, cod, coil, compartment, corner, cove, creek, crown, cubicle, dam, enclose, estuary, fiord, fjord, garland, gulf, hanuama, harbor, haven, hole, horse, howl, inlet, laurel, loch, login, lough, malabar, niche, nook, oriel, pursue, recess, roan, silanga, sinus, skilling, sound, tract, trap, trave, tree, ululate, utter, wail, wick, window, yaup, yawp

-bay brysonima, locust

bean canavalia, vine

bird curlew, godwit, plover, snipe

bush sweet-gale

camphor laurin

cedar guazuma, suriana, tassel-plant

color bayard, chestnut, roan

coot surf-scoter

fruit laurin

hops seabeach-morningglory

inner ensenada

lamb pine-flower

laurel oleander

lavender mallatonia

lynx bobcat, wildcat

michel de baius

of billows sinus aestuum, sinus iridum

of dews sinus roris

of rainbows sinus iridum

plum guava

poplar nyssa, tupelo gum

rose oleander

rum aftershave, lotion

rum tree bayberry

seething sinus aestuum

state massachusetts

sweet beaverwood, brewster

tree laurel

window alcove, belly, mirador, oriel, paunch

-winged bunting vesper-sparrow

BAYADERE dancer, singer, striped

BAYARD clown, dunce, fool, horse

master amadis de gaul, rinaldo

of india outram

BAYARDLY blind, clownish, foolish, reckless, stupid

BAYBERRY ausu, bay rum tree, comptonia, myrica, pimienta, waxberry, waxmyrtle, wild clove

bark candleberry, myrica, tonic

family myricaceae

oil laurel butter

BAYGALL marsh, swampland

BAYONET couteau, dagger, gore, kill, pierce, poniard, spear, stab, wound

plant agave, datil, yucca

BAYOU arm, backwater, bay, branch, brook, cove, creek, harbor, inlet, lagoon, lake, outlet, passage, river, rivulet, slew, sloo, slough, slue, stream, watercourse

state mississippi

BAZAAR agora, bezesteen, burse, chawk, chowk, conteen, emporium, exchange, exposition, fair, fete, ginza, market(place), mart, sale, sook, souk, store

BAZATHA biztha

BAZE abash, stupefy

BAZOO boasting, braggadocio, kazoo, mouth

BDELLIUM commiphora, googul, gugal, gugul, gum, pearl, resin

BE abide, are, beeth, belong, bes, beth, bist, breathe, consist, continue, exist, lie, live, occur, remain, subsist, worth

BEACH air, ayr, bank, chip, coast, gravel, ground, lakeshore, littoral, moor, nard, plage, playa, praya, ripa, rivage, rive, sand, seashore, seaside, shilla, shingle, shore, slip, strand
afternoon ornos
apple canajong, fig-marigold
aster erigeron, seaside daisy
bird knot, plover, snipe
cabin cabana
comb. thin(o)
flea amphipod, crustacean, sandboy, screw, scud
garment halter, shorts, swimsuit
goldenrod solidago
grass ammophila, arenaria, bentstar, marram, spire, star
gravelly air, ayr, shingle
-la-mar beche-le-mar, jargon, lingua franca
morning caleta
pest crown of thorns, jellyfish, lionfish, sculpin, seasnake, seaurchin, shark, starfish, stingray, stonefish, weeverfish
plover knot, sanderling
projecting cusp
robin knot, sanderling, sandpiper
sap sea-rocket
slipper go-ahead, thong, zori
tan sedge
wormwood artemisia, dusty miller

BEACHCOMBER billow, black-sander, breaker, ripple, roller, scoter, seasoner, strandlooper, tramp, vagabond, vagrant, wanderer, wave

BEACHHEAD foothold, landing, offensive, stronghold, van(guard)

BEACHMASTER bull-seal

BEACON alarm, alert, buoy, cresset, ensign, fanal, flag, guide, hill, illuminate, lantern, light(house), lodestar, needfire, phare, pharos, pike, pilot, precede, ramark, seamark, shine, sign(post), signal, standard, steer, tower, vane, warmer, warning, watchtower
boat lightship
kind balefire, candlebomb, flare, fusee, fuzee, lighthouse, pharos, rocket, skyrocket, watchfire

BEACONSFIELD disraeli

BEAD aggri, aggry, astragal, ave(maria), baguet, ball, bauble, bicune, blob, bubble, bugle, cabochon, cornet, dewdrop, drop, figure, filet, foam, gaud, globule, grain, head, job's-tear, knurl, molding, nib, pearl, pellet, pipper, prayer, quirk, sight, sparkle, sphere, strip, trinket, wampum
black cat's-claw, shrub
cornelian arango
-eye fish, stonecat
flat rondelle
glass bugle
-shaped monilated, moniliform, moniloid
shell sewan
string chaplet, choker, necklace, rosary
trading arango
tree necklace-tree, sandalwood

BEADHOUSE almshouse, beading(s), tasbih, veining

BEADLE apparitor, attendant, bailiff, bedel(l), bed-(e)ral, bumble, crier, harman, herald, mace-bearer, macer, messenger, nuthook, officer, poker, servitor, summoner, usher
harriet tattycoram

BEADLEDOM bumbledum, bureaucracy, officialdom, pomposity, red-tapism

BEADROLL book of life, catalog(ue), list, rosary, roster, series

BEADS aves, chaplet, eyes, necklace, rosary

BEADSMAN beggar, bluegown, clergy, gownsman, hermit, monk, pensioner, petitioner, precular

BEADY bulbous, bulging, glistening, glittery, globular, round, small

BEAGLE constable, cop, detective, dog, hound, policeman, sausage, ship, spy

BEAK awn, beam, beck, bill, capitellum, capitulum, clap, embolon, forebow, horn, jaw, judge, lorum, magistrate, mandible, master, mouth(piece), neb, nib, nose, nozzle, peck, pike, proboscis, projection, promontory, prow, ram, rostrum, schoolmaster, seize, shod, snout, speron, spout, stipendiary, strike, sword, tip, tube, tutel, umbo, weapon
comb. champh(o), rhynch(o), rhynchus, rostri(i)
having rostrate, rostriform
having broad latirostral
having short brevirostrate
iron bickern
-like rostroid
part gena, nib
-shaped rhamphoid, rostroid
shell's umbo
ship's bow, prow, ram, speron
trim with preen
without erostrate

BEAKED aquiline, billed, rhamphoid, roman, rostrate, rostriform, rostroid
corn salad valerianella
nightshade sandbur
parsley chervil
salmon sandfish
whale hyperoodon, ziphiida

BEAKER bareca, biker, bocal, bouse, cup, glass, goblet, horn, jug, tass, vessel

BEAL bellow, bull, mouth, pass, pimple, pustule, roar, suppurate, swell, tumor

BEAM angle, balance, bar, binder, blaze, breadth, buckstay, bumpkin, caber, camber, cantilever, carriage, cylinder, emit, eradiate, flash, flitch, glade, glance, gleam, gleed, glint, glow, grin, herrison, knife, kvell, leam, leg, lever, light, madrier, mantel, needle, patch, pile, plank, plat, pole, post, radiate, ray, rayon, rooftree, shank, shape, shed, shine, shoot, side, signal, sile, skid, smile, smirk, spark, stang, stentrel, streak, stream(er), support, template, templet, tie, timber, transmit, trevis, tyndall, walker, width, yield
and balance scales
high brights

kind axletree, balk, batten, boom, browpost, corbel, crossbar, crosstie, footing, girder, hammer, header, joist, lintel, padstone, pinrail, plowhead, rafter, ridgepole, rooftree, scantling, sill, sleeper, spar, sprit, stringpiece, strut, stud(ding), summertree, tavil, t-bar, tie, template, templet, tram, transom, transverse, trave, traverse, truss, two-by-four
large ba(u)lk, lace, summer
low dim(s)

BEAMBIRD flycatcher, warbler

BEAMING, BEAMISH bright, brilliant, cheerful, effulgent, gay, glowing, gorgeous, joyous, lambent, lucent, luminous, lustrous, radiant, refulgent, rosy, shining, sparkling

BEAMY antlered, beaming, broad, lucent, massive, mirthful

BEAN adsuki, adzuki, bon(avist), brain, calabar, chap, dollar, escort, fellow, gram, guar, haba, head, konk, lablab, lentil, lover, lyon, nib, nipple, noggin, pate, plant, protuberance, pulse, seed, sieva, skull, soja, strike, tepary, thrash, tonka, tornilla, trifle, urd, vegetable
aphis black-fly, buffalo-gnat, similium
blower peashooter
broad faba, fava
buck menyanthes
climbing lima, pole, scarletrunner
cluster guar
coral frijolillo
curd tofu
disease anthracnose, mildew, mosaic, rust
eye hila, hilum
family liquorice, lupine, senna
field pinto
fly midas
genus dolichos, phaselus, vicia, vigna
green haricot-vert
gregoire cockeye-pilot, damselfish
kidney haricot
kind adsuki, broad, cacoon, calabar, caster, faba, fava,

frejol, frijole, frijolillo, goa, green, haba, haricot, kidney, lima, mung, navy, phasemy, pinto, pole, runner, snap, soy(a), string, tornillo, vicia, wax, windsor
-like fabaceous
lima civet, haba, sieva
locust carob
mescal sophora
people papagos
poisonous calabar, eserine, loco
sacred lotus
scar hilum
-shaped fabiform
shrub broom, ilex, ulex
snuffbox cacoon
tonka guaiac
town boston
tree agati, bogum, carob, catalpa, laburnum, sapan, zebrawood
trefoil anagyris, coraltree, laburnum
weevil bruchus, haria, mylabris, obtectus
wild bush phasemy
yam kamas

BEANIE cap, dink, skullcap, tam

BEANLESS broke, busted

BEANO bingo, revel, spree, treat

BEANS *full of* active, energetic, erroneous, misinformed, stupid, vital

BEANSHOOTER catapult, peashooter, slingshot, trunk

BEANWEED butterwort

BEAR, BEAR'S 3 aim, cub, lug, set, use 4 bern, bide, cast, dree, gest, give, have, head, hold, lead, lift, move, push, show, take, teem, tend, tote, turn, ursa, wear 5 abide, allow, apply, beget, breed, bring, brook, bruin, carry, crank, dreie, drive, fetch, force, fruit, geste, guide, issue, point, press, rowdy, shift, stand, stick, thole, throw, touch, trend, ursus, verge, weigh, wield, yield 6 accept, acquit, addict, affect, afford, barley, behave, belong, convey, direct, endure, import, manage, mother, pierce, render, seller, spread, submit, suffer, thrust, uphold, ursula 7 arctoid, brownie, comport, conduct, contain, deliver, dispose, exhibit,

falling, fanatic, incline, pertain, possess, proceed, produce, provide, ruffian, russian, stomach, support, sustain, undergo 8 brandish, exercise, fissiped, fructify, generate, tolerate, transmit 9 carnivore, influence, pessimist, propagate, reproduce, roughneck, transport 10 aficionado, enthusiast, experience, salamander 11 shortseller
astronomical ursa
away tack
-bed moss
black bhalu, musquaw, selenarctos, sloth
-breech acanthus, brankursine, cow-parsnip, skeiters, spicknel
bush inkberry
cat ailurus, binturong, civet, panda
changed to callisto
clover bloat, mountainmisery
comb. arct(o), ursi
corn helebore, veratrum
down approach, attack, clamp, crush, depress, exert, hurry, press(ure), sink, stress, strive
driver bootes
-ear auricula saxifrage
expenses defray, underwrite
false witness frame
famous teddy
fictional balu
flag republic california
-foot christmas rose, helebore, lady's-mantle, oxheal, pegroots, setterwort, shortia
fruit deliver, fructify, prosper, thrive
-garlic ramson
grape bilberry, whortleberry
-grease kokum butter
great ursa major
grizzly ephraim, roachback, silvertip
group sloth
head hure, tooth-fungus
honey melursus
huckleberry blueberry, vaccinum
hug embrace, squeeze
in hole, kirve
investigation wash
kind bhalu, brown, bruang, bruin, dubb, grizzly, kadiak, koala, kodiak, panda, polar, roachback, silvertip,

sloth, ursus, wah, wombat, woobut
lesser ursa minor
-like arctoid, ursine
male boar
mat mountain misery
moss adam's needle, haircap, yucca
northern russia
oak bitterbush, blackjack
off attain, carry, deviate, flee, gain, remove, run, win
out authenticate, confirm, corroborate, defend, proport, substantiate, support, verify
pert. ursine
polar thalarctos
-shaped ursiform
skeiters cow-parsnip
sloth aswail, melursus
state arkansas
symbol of ill-temper, uncouthness
tail celsia
teddy koala
the brunt endure, suffer, sustain, undergo
the cost underwrite
-tongue clintonia
to port tack
trap ambush, pit, trap (door), trapfall
tree adenanthera, barbados pride, flower-fence, peacock-flower, sandalwood
up buoy, comfort, cope, endure, persevere, resist, smile, support, sustain
upon affect, aggrieve, appertain, apply, concern, influence, pertain, refer to, relate, urge
-weed yerba-santa
with condone, endure, suffer, survive, tolerate, undergo
witness attest, blab, depose, sing, speak, teem, testify
wooly wombat
-wort spicknel
young calve, child, cub
BEARBERRY bilberry, buckthorn, cascara, clintonia, cranberry, creashaks, dogberry, foxberry, holly, ilex, uva-ursi, whortle
BEARBINE bilderdykia, bindweed, convolvulus
BEARD affront, ane, arista, avel, awn, bait, barbet, barbule, beaver, bevel, brave, bristle, brush, burnsides, byssus, catch, challenge, charley, charlie, defy,

down, face, fuzz, galway, gill, goatee, hair, imperial, muff, mustache, mutton chops, oppose, pappus, peak, pile, pluck, plume, seize, shadow, sideburns, stiletto, stir, stubble, tassel, tease, torment, tuft, vandyke, whiskers, ziffs
comb. pogon
excessive pogoniasis
fish barbudo
grass andropogon, polypogon
-growing pogonotrophy
-like crinite
-like growth barb(a)
pert. barbal
plant mullein
small barbet
the lion brave, challenge, dare
treatise pogonology
tree hazel
vandyke pickedevant
without bald, imberbe, not(t), pollard
BEARDED aristate, awned, awny, barbate, barbed, barbigerous, crinite, goateed, hairy, hirsute, pappose, pogoniate, stubbled, stubbly, unshaven, whiskered
argali aoudad
crowfoot darnel, fescue, grass, wheat
eagle lammergeier
fescue crowfoot, darnel, grass, wheat
pinnock reedling, titmouse
tortoise matameta
BEARER attendant, beadle, brancardier, burthenman, carrier, chaprasi, escudero, ham(m)el, jampani, macer, messenger, musahar, portator, PORTER, saki, servant, sirdar, squire, supporter, sustainer, toter
of great burden atlas
BEARING address, aim, air, application, apport, aspect, attitude, azimuth, ball, behavior, birth, bushing, carriage, cast, charge, concerning, conduct, connection, course, crop, delivery, demeanor, dependency, deportment, direction, duct, effect, endurance, enduring, fashion, front, fructed, fruiting, fruition, fulcrum, gerent, geste, habit, heading, influence, jewel, man-

ner, meaning, mien, orient, pedestal, poise, port, pose, position, posture, presence, pressure, producing, productive, purport, reference, relation(ship), relevance, setup, stand, strike, support, tack, tendency, tenue, thrust, tournure, trend, vector, yield(ing)
armorial blazonry, coat-of-arms
arrogant huff
comb. fer, gerous, parous, phora
fine belair
heraldic billet, chaplet, clarion, crown, delf(t), delph, demivol, ensign, ente, fusil, gad, gore, goutte, laver, mark, ordinary, orle, pheon, plasque, quentise
lining babbitt
on pertinent
outward efferent
plate gib
rein curb, harness
BEARINGS accommodation, adaptation, adjustment, charge, direction, emblem, location, orientation, whereabouts
BEARISH blunt, clumsy, falling, gruff, grumpy, harsh, irascible, pessimistic, rough, selling
BEARM See ADO.
BEARSKIN busby, cap
BEARWOOD buckthorn, chittamwood, rhamnus
BEAST animal, anti-christ, bete, blighter, brute, burro, creature, hoof, lout, mammal, monster, musimon, opinicus, pard, quadruped, savage
apocalypse pert. bestian
castrated spado
comb. theri(o)
dead morkin
fabled See BEAST *mythical.*
horned rether, rother
king lion
leg gamb
-like carnal, theroid
mythical apepi, bagwyn, bucantaur, buraq, centaur, chichevache, chim(a)era, dingmaul, dragon, echidna, ellops, empusa, epimacus, figfaun, garuda, geryon, giant, gorgon, griffon, gyascutas, harpy, hydra, jabberwock, kraken, minotaur,

ogre, rahab, rahu, scylla, sphinx, thris, tricorn, triton, vale

of burden ass, burro, camel, donkey, dromedary, drudge, elephant, hathi, horse, husky, jument, llama, mule, pack horse, percheron, onager, oont, percheron, sledge-dog, sumpter

royal leo, lion

sturdy nugget

3-horned tricorn

treatise bestiary

wild ferin(1), outlaw

wild, comb. ther(o)

BEASTLY abominable, animal, annoying, bestial, brutal, carnal, coarse, disagreeable, execrable, gross, inhuman, offensive, outrageous, swinish, terrible, unpleasant

BEAT 3 box, bum, cob, cut, hit, lam, lap, mix, ply, tan, wap, win 4 baff, bait, bang, beet, belt, best, blow, bray, buff, bung, cane, cast, club, cuff, dash, drub, dunt, flog, lace, lash, lick, loop, maul, mell, mill, pelt, plug, poss, rout, skin, slap, slat, slug, sock, stir, swat, tart, toss, trim, tuck, tund, twig, walk, welt, whap, whip, whop, wipe 5 abuse, baste, berry, birch, break, broke, cheat, churn, clout, cream, crush, cycle, drash, excel, field, fight, flail, floor, forge, ictus, knock, knout, meter, orbit, pound, pulse, round, route, scoop, scour, sheaf, skelp, smite, sound, spank, spent, stamp, strap, targe, tempo, throb, thump, tired, towel, track, trump, waddy, whale, whang, worst 6 accent, anoint, batter, batula, bensel, bruise, buffet, bundle, circle, cotton, course, cudgel, defeat, domain, dowsel, duties, feague, hammer, larrup, offset, outrun, pommel, pummel, punish, raddle, rhythm, rotate, rounds, scutch, squash, stound, stoush, strike, stripe, subdue, suggil, swinge, switch, tewtaw, tewter, thrash, threap, thwack, wallop 7 agitate, assault, astound, baffled, belabor, blatter, blister, ca-

dence, canvass, circuit, conquer, cowhide, eclipse, exhaust, fatigue, flutter, lamback, leather, lounder, mystify, perplex, precede, pulsate, rawhide, reeshie, resound, routine, schmeer, scourge, shellac, surpass, swabble, swaddle, swindle, ticking, trample, trollop, trouble, trounce, vibrate, wornout, worsted 8 chastise, emulsify, lambaste, lambskin, lammeate, outclass, overcome, slaister, vanquish 9 alternate, bastinado, battyfang, blackjack, exhausted, frustrate, fustigate, horsewhip, overpower, pulsation, pulverize, schneider, territory 10 assignment, flagellate 11 palpitation

about bangle, busk, flounder, search, tack

about the bush digress, dodge, evade, quibble

against blad, contest, counteract

against the wind laveer, tack

back repulse

down abate, bargain, deject, depreciate, depress, domineer, fell, flash, lay, raze, subdue

generation member beatnik

generation spokesman kerouac

into plate malleate

it absquatulate, begone, blow, decamp, depart, flee, get going, lam, leave, run along, scram, skedaddle, skiddoo, vamoose, vamos

off repulse, resist

musical battuta

severely baste, drub, lather, lump, soak, souse, trounce

the bushes scour, scout, search

the drum celebrate, praise

-up dilapidated, mauled, rundown, spent

wings bate, flap

with flukes lobtail

woods tusk

BEATA blessed, canonized, happy

BEATEN batter, bete, mauled, schneidered, spent, trite, whitewashed

BEATER caner, dasher, driver, jack, lacer, lathe, mallet, maul, rab, scutcher,

seal, thrasher, thresher, whisk

BEATIFIC blissful, deific, delightful, elysian, happy, heavenly, saintly

BEATIFY bless, canonize, consecrate, delight, enchant, endow, gladden, glorify, hallow, sanctify, transport

BEATING bastinado, bastine, battery, belting, blow, caning, dressing, drubbing, dusting, hazing, jesse, licking, ribroast, skelpin, strappado, tattoo, welting, whaling, whipping

game battue

BEATITUDE benison, bliss, consecration, ecstasy, felicity, fruition, happiness, joy, macarism, transport

BEATNIK hippy, nonconformist, unconventional

BEATRICE *beloved* benedick, dante

cousin hero

uncle leonato

BEAU admirer, blade, boyfriend, buck, cavalier, courter, coxcomb, cupidon, dandy, dude, escort, fellow, flame, fop, gallant, inamorato, lover, macaroni, nob, paramour, spark(er), squire, suitor, swain, sweetheart, swell, toff, wooer

brummel coxcomb, dandy, fop, george bryan

catcher tress

fils son-in-law, stepson

frere brother-in-law, stepbrother

gregory cockeye, damselfish

ideal beauty, example, exemplar, mirror, model, paradigm, paragon, perfect, richard nash, standard

monde See SOCIETY.

nash king of bath

pere companion, comrade, father, priest

sabreur adventurer, joachim, murat

BEAUMONT AND FLETCHER *play* coxcomb, cupid's revenge, knight of malta, philaster, scornful lady, tamer tamed

BEAUT ideal, lulu, mouche, perfection

BEAUTIFIER cosmetics, lipstick, make-up, mascara, paint, powder, rouge

BEAUTIFUL, BEAUTEOUS

aesthetic, artistic, attractive, belle, blithe, bonnie, bonny, charming, choice, comely, dainty, elegant, esthetic, excellent, exquisite, eye-filling, fair(some), fine, formose, glorious, good-looking, goodly, gorgeous, graceful, handsome, kalon, lovely, mear, meer, mere, ornamental, pleasing, pretty, pulchritudinous, ravishing, seemly, sightly, stunning, sublime, superb, tempean, tokalon, venust, waly, wlity, wlonk

comb. bel, calli, calo

name meaning calista

BEAUTIFY adonize, adorn, bedeck, decorate, decore, dight, doll up, embellish, endow, enhance, fair, garnish, gild, glorify, grace, ornament, paint. preen, prettify, primp, prune, pulchrify, trim

BEAUTY artistry, bantam, beau ideal, belle, bloom, charm(er), charmeuse, comeliness, dazzler, decore, dish, doll, elegance, elite, excellence, exquisiteness, fair(ness), fetcher, finery, fox, glee, gloss, glow, good looks, grace, handsomeness, kalon, knockout, looker, loveliness, lovely, paragon, peach, perfection, phoenix, polish, prettiness, pride, pulchritude, splendor, stunner, style, superiority, tokalon, truth, vision, wlite

comb. calli

berry callicarpa, mulberry

bush kolkwitzia

contest judge paris

famous adonis, antinous, aphrodite, apollo, astarte, balder, cleopatra, dietrich, freya, garbo, graces, hebe, helen of troy, houri, hyperion, narcissus, nefertiti, ninon, peri, venus

goddess aphrodite, freja, freya, lakshmi, shree, s(h)ri, venus

-lover (a)esthete

name meaning ada(h), bell(a), belle

nymph hetera, houri

of form symmetry

of style elegance

parlor hairdresser's, salon

pert. (a)esthetic

prizes callisteia

spot mole, nevus, patch

treatment mud pack

BEAVER armor, beard, bever, bevor, boomer, castor, cloth, coypu, kersey, mushroom, nat, oregonian, praline, rodent, sewellel, top hat

brown camel, mushroom, nutmeg, starling

cloth kersey

dark nutmeg

-eater wolverine

mountain sewellel

poison water-hemlock

skin nutria, plew, woom

state oregon

tree hackberry, sweet bay

young kit

BEBEERU bibiri, bibiru, greenheart, nectandra, sweetwood, tree

BECARD bird, tityra

BECASSINE avocet, godwit, snipe, stilt

BECAUSE being, due to, for(why), inasmuch, in that, on account of, owing to, parceque, perche, porque, since, thanks to, that, therefore, through

of that hence, therefore

BECCAFICO figeater, figpecker, sylvia, warbler

BECHE-LE-MAR jargon, lingua franca, pidgin, trepang

BECHUANA bantu, kaffir, tswana

land See BOTSWANA.

BECK beak, becon, bidding, bow, brook, curts(e)y, gesticulate, gesture, nod, run, stream, summon(s), vat, vessel

and call devotion, summons

BECKET cleat, eye, grommet, hook, oarlock, squil(l)gee

BECKETT, SAMUEL *play* waiting for godot

BECKFORD *work* vathek

BECKON ask, attract, bow, call, command, curts(e)y, direct, entice, gesticulate, gesture, invite, motion, nod, sign(al), summon, waft, wag, wave

BECLOUD bedim, darken, hide, mask, muddle, mystify, obscure

BECOME accord, adorn, befall, befit, begin, behoove, beseem, betide, change,

convert, fit, flatter, get, grace, grow, pass, proceed, prove, rax, set, sit, suit, take, turn, wax, wear, worth

BECOMING appropriate, apt, attractive, befitting, bhava, change, comely, congruous, decent, decorous, due(ful), expedient, fair, farrant, feat, fit(ting), fitty, gainly, handsome, meet, pleasing, presentable, proper, right, seemly, suitable, wise-like.

BECUNA See BARRACUDA.

BED accommodate, apishamore, ballast, base, basin, bassinet, berth, billet, body, boist, bottom, bunk, channel, charping, cot, couch, coulee, cradle, crib, donga, doss, downy, fix, fleabag, floor, flop, form, foundation, grate, ground, hammock, hay, kip, lair, layer, lenticle, libkin, lit(ter), lodge, lodging, matrix, osiery, pad, pallet, pan, plot, reposal, rest, retire, roost, sack, setting, shakedown, sleep, stratum, stretcher, subsoil, support, vein, wadi, wady

ale birth-feast

and board accommodations, lodging

and wall space ruelle

antique four-poster

canopy tester

chamber cubicle

clothes See BEDDING.

coal brat, delf, seam

confinement to decumbiture, lectual

cover See BEDDING.

down doss, groom, retire

drapery coster, pand, sparver, tester

feather tie, tye

folding slawbank

frame stead, stock

hanging hammock

infant's bassinet, cot, cradle, crib

jacket nightingale

kind double, feather, foldaway, folding, four-poster, hammock, hollywood, hospital, in-a-door, king, plancher, queen, roll-away, single, sofa, studio-couch,

tester, tie, trestle, truckle, trundle, twin, tye
linen See BEDDING.
maker biddy, maid
of roses comfort, easy street, luxury, prosperity, rosary, wealth
on the floor futon
pert. thoral
rail rathe, rave
rubble callow
sandwort spurry
seed seminary
small bassinet, cot, cradle, crib, hammock, pad, pallet, truckle, trundle, twin
stay slat
stream billabong, coulee, coulie, donga, draw, wash .
tester sparver
time taps
BEDASH besmear, demolish, obliterate, ruin, splash
BEDAUB bedizen, clag, clat, daub, paint, slaister, slake, smear, soil
BEDBUG bloodsucker, chinch, chink, chintz, cimex, cimice, cimicid, conenose, coreid, hemipter, housebug, punaise, punese, redcoat, vermin, wall-louse
destroyer cimicide
hunter reduvius
BEDDING afghan, base, blanket, bolster, bundle, comforter, counterpane, coverlet, coverlid, covers, domestics, eiderdown, foundation, layer, linen, litter, mat(tress), pad, paillasse, palampore, pallet, pillow(slip), pourpoint, puff, quilt, sheet(ing), spread
course cushion
-picking floccilation
sweetheart hetty sorrel
BEDECK adorn, array, bedo, dight, embellish, gem, grace, lard, ornament, prink, trap
BEDEGAUR dog-rose, gall, sweetbriar, thistle
BEDENE anon, forthwith, straightway, throughout, together
BEDEVIL abuse, afflict, annoy, badger, beset, bewitch, bother, confound, confuse, corrupt, hamper, harass, muddle, pester, spoil, tease, torment, worry
BEDFAST See BEDRIDDEN.

BEDFELLOW ally, associate, collaborator, comrade, mate
BEDIGHT See BEDIZEN.
BEDIVERE *brother* lucan
knight to arthur
BEDIZEN adorn, array, bedight, daub, deck, decorate, dress, equip
BEDKEY wrench
BEDLAM asylum, babel, bethlehem, booby hatch, broil, confusion, din, disquiet(ude), hubbub, hurlyburly, insanity, madhouse, madness, maelstrom, noise, pandemonium, riot, shambles, tumult, uproar
cowslip lungwort, primula, pulmonaria
BEDLOE *island* liberty
BEDOUIN absi, ARAB, bedawee, bedowi, bedu, harb, howeitat, moor, nomad, riff, shammar
law thar
BEDRABBLE bedraggle, befoul, draggle, soil, trachle
BEDRAGGLED dowdy(ish), poky, sloppy, slovenly, tacky
BEDRIDDEN ailing, bedfast, bedrel, confined, decrepit, exhausted, ill, shut in, sick
BEDROCK base, basis, bottom, foundation, hardpan, lowest, nadir, principle, solid, stonehead
BEDROLL bindle, bing
BEDROOM accommodation, berth, boudoir, cabin, chamber, compartment, cubicle, cubiculum, dormer, dormitory, doss, garderobe, kip, pad, pullman, wardrobe
community levittown, suburb
BEDSORE decubitis
BEDSPREAD aleze, candlewick, counterpane, coverlet, coverlid, quilt, strail
BEDSTEAD angare(e)b, angarep, BED, charpoy, hatch
BEDSTRAW cleaverwort, crosswort, crudwort, curdwort, doss, fleaweed, gallium, gull-grass, scrambler, shakedown, tick-trefoil
BEDWARMER curate, priest
BEE apis, dingar, dor, drone(r), fly, frolic, gathering, idea, insect, nomia, notion, ornament, party, ring,

scopiped, shucking, social, torque, waxmaker, yeast
balm monarda, oswego-tea
bird flycatcher, kingbird
bread ambrosia, cerago
butt See BEEHIVE.
carder anthidium
cell(s) honeycomb, pipe
colony bike, byke, flight, hive, swarm, yeast
comb. api, avi
corbicula pollen basket
disease sacbrood, stonebrood
-eater bird, meropid, merops
-eating apivorous
eggs brood
family apidae
fear of apiphobia
female queen
fly bombyliid, bombylius, bumblebee
food royal jelly
genus andrena, apis, colletes, megachili, psithyrus
glue propolis
gum See BEEHIVE.
hairy colletes
hawk honey-buzzard
honey angelito, deseret, dingar, trigona
-killer robber-fly
kind andrenid, angelito, bumble, carder, carpenter, dingar, honey, husking, mason, quilting, worker
-like apian, apiarian
male drone
martin kingbird
milk royal jelly
name meaning deborah, melissa
nettle henbit
odor pheromone
pert. apian, apiarian
plant balm, cleome, figwort, guaco, ramona, scrofularia, stinkweed
pollen basket corbicula
pollen brush sarothrum, scopa
queen's food royal jelly
scap See BEEHIVE.
solitary anthidium, carpenter
sting forebrood
stingless karbi, kootcha, melipona
study apiology
swarm bike
symbol of industry
tree basswood, gum, linden
weed aster, tongue
wild angelito, dingar, kootcha
wine nectar

BEECH birch, buck, carpus, castanopsis, chinquapin, fagus, flindosa, myrsine, myrtle, nothofagus, roble, tree
agario armillaria
black ironwood, leather-jacket
blue hornbeam
cherry trochocarpa
drops epifagus, squawroot
leaf snake copperhead
BEECHNUT(S) buck, fagine, mast, pannage, splitnut
BEEF beeve, betray, bitch, boeuf, brawn, buccan, bull(y), casson, charqui, complain(t), cow, fight, flesh, gripe, grouse, grumble, jerk(y), lire, mustle, pastrami, pipikaula, power, rage, strength, vifda, vivda, weight
and cabbage bubble and squeak
and greens cowslip, primula
apple peanut
boiled bouilli
braised a la mode
broiled churrasco
canned bullamacow, bully
cattle angus, hereford, shorthorn
corn bully
cut aitchbone, aloyau, baron, brisket, buc(c)an, chine, chuck, cutlet, edgebone, fillet, flank, knuckle, loin, miroton, ninsholes, porterhouse, quarter, rattleran, rib, roast, round, rump, saddle, sey, side, shank, short-rib, shoulder, side, sirloin, steak, t-bone, tenderloin
dried buc(c)an, charqui, jerky, vifda, vivda
filet slices tournedos
for slaughter mart
grade choice, prime, utility
ground hamburger
inferior compound
jerked biltong, charqui, tasajo
lean lire
made with bouillon
pickled bully
rump silverside
salted junk, salt-horse, vifda, vivda
shoulder clod
spiced pastrami
-suet tree buffaloberry, bullberry, shephardia

tenderloin undercut
up strengthen
BEEFEATER bird, buphaga, englishman, gin, guard, oxbird, oxbiter, oxpecker, rhinoceros-bird, tickbird, warden, yeoman
BEEFSTEAK chateaubriand, chuck, filet mignon, flank, round, sirloin, skirt
fungus oak tongue
plant begonia, geranium, pedicularis, saxifrage
saxifrage bear's-ear, mother-of-thousands
BEEFWOOD banksia, belah, belar, blolly, bull oak, callitris, casagha pine, casuarina, filao, grevillea, horsetail-tree, mimopsus, stenocarpus, toa, tree
BEEFY athletic, blubbery, brawny, fat, fleshy, heavy, hefty, obese, solid, stolid, strong, thickset
BEEHIVE alvearium, alveary, apiary, bike, byke, butt, gum(e), gumtree, hoppet, praesepe, pyche, scap, scep, skep, swarmer
covering hackle, super
entrance tee-hole
remove comb from geld
ring eke
-shaped alveated
state utah
BEEKEEPER apiarist, apiator, beeherd, hiver, skeppist
BEEKEEPING apiculture
BEELIADA *father* david
BEELINE crosscut, cutoff, shortcut
BEELPEOR belphegor, devil
BEELZEBUB belial, demon, DEVIL, lucifer, satan
BEEP signal, tone, toot, warning
BEER ale, belch, belly-wash, beverage, biiru, bitter, bock, brew, cervesa, cervisia, chang, chicha, cyle, dragol, gail, gatter, grog, grout, gyle, hops, kvas(s), lager, liquor, malt, mild, mum, pangasi, pharaoh, pilsner, pombe, porter, quash, quass(e), stingo, stout, suds, swanky, swipes, wallap, weiss, zythum
add to krausen
ancient zythum
and gin purl
and oatmeal storry

and skittles amusement, enjoyment, fun, play, pleasure
and whiskey boilermaker
barley chang
black danzic
cask firkin, kilderkin, pin
container can, glass, mug, stein
dregs crap
hall alehouse, bar, bierstube, cabaret, cafe, faro, pub, rathskeller, saloon, tavern, tiddlywink
head forth
inferior belch, swanky, tack, taplash
ingredient barley, hops, malt
inventor gambrinus
king gambrinus
maker brewster, maltster
money allowance
mug See DRINKING *vessel.*
parlor See BEER *hall.*
pert. malty
pitcher growler
small grout, tiff
sour beeregar, kuas, quash, quass
strong double, huff, stingo
sweet swats
thin pritch, swipes
unfermented gyle
warm storry
BEERHOUSE tiddlywink
BEERI *daughter* judith
BEERY intoxicated, maudlin, muddled, teary
BEESWAX bronze, buff, bursattee, capping, coat, lubricate
pert. ceresin, cerotic
BEET aid, amend, asa, atone, butter-leaves, chard, correct, dock, improve, kindle, mangel(wurzel), mangold, mend, orach, relieve, renew, repair, repeat, repent, stechling, sugar, vegetable
disease blight, curly-top, heartrot, scab
pulp bagasse
roasted bonka
sugar bolter, sucrose
BEETHOVEN *birthplace* bonn
mass missa solemnis
nickname der spagnol
opera fidelio
overture egmont, leonore
sonata kreutzer, moonlight
symphony choral, eroica, pastoral
BEETLE bat, beater, bug,

bulge, drive, extend, extrude, hammer, jut, insect, lowering, maul, overhang, pestle, project(ing), ram, stick out
aquatic gyrinid
bark borer
black cadelle, cockroach
blind anophthalmus
blister epicauta
bombardier brachinus
boring death-watch, tanbark
bright ladybug
-browed morose, reproachful, scowling, sullen
burying gravedigger, ratel
carpet dermestid
changed into cerambus
click dor, elater, tora
-crusher boot, foot, policeman
destructive carpet-bug, death-watch
diving acilius, cybister
downy buzz
dried cantharides
dung aphodius, cantharid, scaraboeid, sharnbug, tumblebug
family adephaga, cantharidae, carabidae, clavicornes, elateridae, erotylidae, rutelinae, silphidae
fire cucuyo, elater
flea altica
fruit-loving borer
gaudy ladybug
genus adelops, adoretus, agriotes, amara, anomala, calosoma, clerus, coccinella, dendroctonus, eumolpus, fidia, gyrinus, harpalus, ipidae, lucanus, passalus, popillia, pselaphus, ptinus, pyrophorus, sagra, silpha
grain cadelle
grapevine thrip
ground amara, calosoma, carab, caterpillar-hunter, fidia
hard-bodied anobid
-head blockhead, goldeneye duck, plover
-headed god khepri
horny substance chitin
kind 3 dor, 4 boud, doar, dore, dorr, flea, goga, gogo, hang, ipid, pope, stag, trox, turk 5 amara, atlas, borer, carob, fidia, gogga, hispa, laria, lycid, meloe, sagra, tiger 6 chafer, clerid, cucuyo, elater, golach, goloch,

hammer, hister, khapra, lyctid, lyctus, meloid, picudo, pierid, pruner, ptinid, sawyer, scarab, weaver, weevil 7 adelops, agrilus, billbug, bruchid, buzzard, cadelle, carabid, carrion, cucujid, dardaol, elatrid, fiddler, firefly, girdler, goldbug, gyrinid, humbuzz, junebug, ladybug, lampfly, lucanid, paussid, prionid, ptinoid, rosebug, silphid, skipper, soldier, tanbark, tickler, tumbler, vedalia 8 anthicid, ateuchus, cetonian, curculio, dytiscid, engraver, figeater, glowworm, grayback, hardback, ladybird, lampyrid, rutelian, scolytid, searcher, sharnbug, skipjack, sphindid, squasher, squeaker, symphile, toktokje, whirlwig, wireworm 9 cantharid, cockroach, dedemerid, leafminer, longicorn, ostomatid, tribolium, tumblebug, twirligig, whirligig 10 cockchafer
large atlas
larva borer, grub
-like coleopteroid
long-legged straddlebug
mustard blackjack
oil meloe
pepper itmo
poisonous buprestis
pubescent mordellid
rhinoceros uang
sacred atenchus, scarab
scarabeid anthobian, pleurostict, rose-chafer
secretion trehala
serricorn ptinida
slender agrilus
small anthrenus, buffalo-bug, carpet-beetle, ladybug, paussid, twigpruner
snout curculio
sound churr, drone
sun amara
symbol of blindness
talisman scarab
weed galax
wing elytrum
wing cover shard
wingless pinacate-bug
wood sawyer
BEEWEED aster, tongue
BEEWORT sweetflag, woodbine
BEFALL astart, bechance, become, befortune, betide,

chance, cheff, clive, come, hap(pen), occur, shape, sort, tide, transpire
BEFIT become, behoove, beseem, betide, dow, serve, sort, suit
BEFITTING apt, becoming, decent, decorous, proper, seeming, sortable, suitable, timely, worthy
BEFLUM deceive, flatter
BEFOG cloud, conceal, confuse, dim, gaum, mystify
BEFOOL assot, burn, colt, crap, deceive, delude, diddle, dupe, elude, fode, fonne, infatuate, jade, sot, squander, trifle
BEFORE advance, afore, against, ahead, air, already, anent, ante(cedent), anterior, avant, awaiting, but, coram, earlier, early, enow, ere, facing, first, forby(e), foremost, former, forne, forthby, forward, from, front, gin, headmost, heretofore, hitherto, ibid, initial, past, preceding, preferably, previously, prior, rather, said, sooner, sopra, till, tofore, until, vanward, within, yet, yore
comb. ante, avant, prae, pre, pro
long anon, by and by, erelong, presently, soon
now enow, ere(now), formerly, gone, over
one's eyes openly
the flood antediluvian
the mast aboard
BEFOREHAND advance(d), aforetime, anachronous, betimes, early, precocious, previously, soon
BEFOUL bemire, besquirt, daggle, darken, defile, dirty, drabble, entangle, fewmand, gruft, pollute, slut(ter), soil
BEFRIEND abet, aid, assist, benefit, countenance, favor, foster, help, succor, support, sustain
BEFUDDLE addle, becloud, besot, bewilder, confound, confuse, fluster, gas, intoxicate, muddle, mystify, perplex, puzzle, stupefy
BEFUDDLED ree
BEG adjure, appeal, ask, assume, avoid, beseech, bid, bum, cadge, cant, coax,

conjure, crave, cry, desire, entreat, evade, exact, implore, importune, long, maund(er), mendicate, mooch, mump, obsecrate, panhandle, petition, picard, plead, pray, prig, request, scaff, schnorren, seek, skelder, solicit, sorn, sponge, sue, supplicate, tease, thig, touch, tram, woo, yearn
indulgence apologize
off balk, decline
pardon apologize, bitte, excuse, sorry
the question dodge, quibble
BEGET acquire, afford, author, bear, bigate, breed, cause, conceive, create, ean, engender, engraff, father, generate, get, have, ken, kind, plant, procreate, produce, propagate, reproduce, sire, yield
BEGETTER ancestor, author, father, mother, parent, pater, procreator, producer, sire
BEGGAR, BEGGAR'S abramman, almsman, armine, arnaeus, asker, bacach(e), badgeman, bairagi, beadsman, bum(mer), cadger, canter, dummerer, dyvour, fakeer, fakir, gaberlunzy, hallanshaker, hobo, idler, impoverish, indigent, irus, jarkman, lazar(us), loafer, maunderer, mendicant, mooch(er), mumper, palliard, pardhan, pariah, pauper(ize), poor, randy, rogue, ruffler, ruin, sannyasi, scaffer, s(c)hlepper, schnorrer, sornari, sorner, sponge, starveling, stemmer, suppliant, thigger, thrum, tinkard, tramp, vagabond, whipjack, wretch
barm foam, scum
blanket mullein
blind bartim(a)eus
brown snuff
brush traveler's-joy
buttons burdock
king carew
-lice achene, bidens, bootjack, cuckold, desmodium, gallium, lappula, stickweed, trefoil
licensed beadsman, bluegown

needle lady's-comb
opera author gay, weil
opera character macheath, peachum
pack bindle
saint alexius, giles
tick See BEGGAR *lice.*
BEGGARLY abject, bankrupt, base, cheap, contemptible, despicable, inadequate, indigent, low, mean, needy, obsequious, paltry, pegrall, petty, pilled, pitiable, poor, scurvy, sordid, sorry
BEGGARWEED desmodium, dodder, knotweed, spurry, tickseed, tick-trefoil
BEGGARY bareness, destitution, indigence, mendicancy, pauperism, penury, poverty, rubbish, thig, trash, want
BEGIN actify, activate, activize, approach, arise, attack, attame, auspicate, become, bourgeon, break ground, broach, burgeon, christen, commence, dawn, derive, dive in, embark, enter, establish, fall to, fang, float, found, front, get going, gin, gyn, handsel, head, inaugurate, incept, inchoate, incipit, induct, initiate, install, institute, introduce, jump, kick off, launch, lead, open, organize, pioneer, proceed, rise, set out, spring, start, streak, take off, undertake, usher, yoke
again renew, restart, revive
comb. esce
to use break in
BEGINNER abecedarian, alphabetarian, amateur, apprentice, boot, candidate, catechumen, clerk, deb(utante), entrant, fledgling, freshman, greenhorn, hatcher, inceptor, neophyte, novice, novitiate, originator, postulate, principiant, probationer, punk, pupil, recruit, rookie, rooky, softa, sophta, starter, student, tenderfoot, tiro, trainee, tyro
nerves buck fever, jitters
BEGINNING abecedarian, aleph, alpha, approach, arising, basic, birth, cause, commencement, cradle, dawn(ing), debut, egg, em-

bryonic, emergence, entrance, entry, exordial, exordium, first, foundation, front, genesis, germ, go off, head, inauguration, inception, inchoate, incipience, incunabular, infancy, infantile, initial, inition, introductory, jump off, kick-off, nascency, nascent, natal, nativity, nucleus, oncoming, onset, opening, origin, outbreak, outset, outstart, prime, primitive, primogenial, primordial, rise, root, rudiment(ary), seed, sendoff, setout, source, spring, start(ing), sunrise, take-off, threshold
and ending alpha and omega
at the ad initium
comb. escent
from the ab ovo
pert. initial
BEGO attire, beset, dress, encompass, environ
BEGONE allez, aroint, avaunt, away, beat it, cheese it, clear out, depart, get lost, git, off, on your way, out, pack off, pike, run along, scat, scoot, scram, shoo, skedaddle, skiddoo, vamoose, va-t'en, via
BEGONIA *kind* beefsteak, gaiety, gayety, rex, tuberous
BEGRIME becoom, bruckle, colly, coom, dirty, ditch, smirch, smudge, soil
BEGRUDGE balk, bethink, covet, deny, envy, grumble, jalouse, malign, pinch, resent, stint
BEGTI nair
BEGUILE allure, amuse, bamboozle, befool, betray, blander, blarney, brigue, cajole, charm, cheat, coax, cozen, deceive, deception, delude, disappoint(ment), divert, doublecross, dupe, elude, ensnare, entertain, entice, entrap, evade, fascinate, flatter, flummer, fool, fox, gull, hoax, hoodwink, lure, mislead, seduce, spend, trick, troll, tryst, vamp, weize, wheedle, while, wile, wise
BEGUILED farchadat
BEGUIN beghard, desire, fancy, infatuation

BEGUM empress, lady, princess, queen, smear, widow
husband aga
BEH *son* iri
BEHALF advantage, affair, benefit, benison, cause, defence, favor, good, interest, matter, part, profit, proxy, sake, score, side, stead, support
BEHAVE abear, acquit, act, bear, carry, comport, conduct, contain, control, demean, deport, direct, disport, fare, function, handle, have, let, manage, make, operate, perform, play, quit, react, restrain, treat, work
awkwardly gaum, hocker
boldly gauster
evasively dodge
foolishly dolt
timidly creep
vulgarly ramp
BEHAVIOR abearance, act, action, address, air, amenance, attitude, bearing, breeding, byronics, carriage, comportment, conduct, countenance, course, decorum, deed, demeanor, deportment, development, education, ergasia, fashion, gestalt, goings, guise, habit, havance, havings, improvement, maintain, manner, mien, morals, observance, pattern, port, practice, praxis, presence, procedure, proceeding, reaction, rule, thew, usage, way(s)
arrogant side, swagger
carefree rhathymia
conventional babbittry
courteous comity, politeness
crude buffoonery
lively tittup
queer princum-prancum
stupid sottise
violent rampage
BEHEAD decapitate, decollate, divert, execute, guillotine, kill, neck
BEHEMOTH beast, giant, hippo(potamus), monster
BEHEN bladder-campion, centaury, horseradish-tree, limonium, sea-lavender
BEHEST bid(ding), command, demand, dictate, directive, injunction, law, mandate, order, request, rule

BEHIGHT address, adjudge, call, certify, command, commit, entrust, intend, name, ordain, promise, pronounce, vow, warrant
BEHIND aback, abaff, abaft, aft(er), ahind, arear, arrear, arrier, astern, back (ward), beyond, derriere, dilatory, duff, following, hidden, hint, late(r), left, owing, passe, past, posterior, promoting, rear, remaining, remote, rump, slow, subsequent, supporting, tail, tandem, tardy, underlying, unrevealed
one's back secretly, treacherously
the eightball endangered, sunk
the scenes hidden, invisible, shrouded
the times antiquated, old-fashioned
BEHINDHAND anachronous, backward, detained, dilatory, hinderly, in arrears, laggard, late, overdue, retarded, sad, slow, tardy
BEHN, APHRA *pseud.* astraea, divine
BEHOLD consider, contain, descry, discern, ecce, espy, eye, gaze, hold, keep, look, maintain, mean, mirror, note, notice, observe, ocule, perceive, regard, remark, retain, scan, see, signify, spy, stop, survey, survise, vide, view, voila, voyez, wait, watch, witness
the man ecce homo
BEHOLDEN bound(en), grateful, indebted, obliged, owing
BEHOOF advantage, benefit, good, interest, profit, use
BEHOOVE become, befit, belong, beseem, need, ought, require, stand on, suit, tharf
BEIGE biscuit, dorado, ecru, grege, greige, hopi, nutria, string, tan
BEING abode, actuality, alive, animal, anteal, because, brahma, character, creature, ens, entia, entity, esse, essence, existence, existing, extant, home, human, jagat, life, living, man, mortal, ontology, organism, person(ality),

place, presence, present, reality, self, shape, since, standing, station, subsistence, substance, system, troll, vivancy
abstract ens, entia
actual esse
animate jagat, life
celestial angel, cherub, divinity, god, seraph
comb. ure
divine demigod, deva, god (dess)
done conventual, popular
evil demon, devil, ghoul, satan
fabulous See BEAST *mythical.*
human adamite, body, creature, jack, soul
ideal immortal
imaginary sylph, termagant
intrinsic essence
perfect god
physiological bion
science of ontology
simple amoeba, monad
small elf, gnome, inchling, sprite
spirit of ens, entia
supernatural adaro, akua, atua, balam, daeva, demon, dev(a), fairy, folletto, garuda, godkin, godling, hamingja, jann, lamassu, sheddu, spirit, troll, wight, zemi
supreme abracax, creator, deity, god, monad, nyambe, nzambi, ousia
three signs of anatta, anicca, dukkha, impermanence, soul
true ousia
BEIRUT berytus, beyrouth
BEJA beniamer, bisharin, hamite, hanendoa
dialect bishari
son iri
BEKEN commend, deliver, entrust, tell
BEL aegle, baal, enlil, golden-apple, heshvan, marduk, quince, tree, woodapple
child ninurta
weapon amaru
wife belit, beltis
BELA *father* benjamin
son ard, ezbon, iri, uzzi
BELABOR abuse, assail, baste, beat, bounce, buffet, cudgel, cuff, drub, hammer, hamper, lash, ply, pound,

pummel, slap, thrash, thwack, work

BELAIT europe

BELATED delayed, detained, obsolete, old-fashioned, overdue, tardy

BELAY adorn, belage, beset, besiege, cease, cover, encircle, fasten, invest, quit, secure, tie up, waylay

BELCH beam, beer, bolch, bolk, burp, cast, disgorge, eject, emit, eruct(ation), erupt, galp, gush, rasp, rift, ructation, spew

sir toby, niece olivia

BELDAM alecto, crone, erinys, fury, grandmother, hag, jezebel, old woman, rudas, tisiphone, virago, vixen, witch

BELEAGUER assault, attack, belay, beset, besiege, blockade, encompass, invest, siege, surround

BELFAST *county* antrin

BELFRY beffroy, bellhouse, campanile, clocher, cloghead, head, steeple, tower

floor belldeck

BELGIUM, BELGIAN belgie, belgique, fleming, walloon

anthem la brabanconne

architect horta

battle site rocourt, waterloo

brassware dinanderie

canal albert, campine, union, yser

capital brussels, bruxelles

cardinal mercier

cave furfooz, grenelle

cheese limburger

chemist solvay

city aalst, aarlen, aat, alost, amay, anderlecht, ans, antwerp, anvers, ardooie, arlon, asse, ath, bastogne, berchem, bergen, bilzem, boom, borgerhout, bree, bruges, brussels, bruxelles, charleroi, ciney, courtrai, deurme, doel, doorwik, eeklo, essen, evere, geel, genk, g(h)ent, heist, herstal, hoboken, hoei, ieper, ixelles, izegem, jette, jumet, kortrijk, leliven, liege, lierre, louvain, malmedy, mechlin, merxem, mol, molenbeek, mons, mouscron, namur, opwijk, ostend, quatrebras, ronse, roulers, schaerbeek, seraing, spa, tielt, tournai, turnhout, uccle, verviers, vise, vorst, waterloo, wezet, ynoir, ypres, zele

coin belga, brabant, centime, crocard, franc

colony See *congo*, below, and CONGO.

commune aalst, alost, ans, ath, boom, evere, geel, gen(c)k, hal, jette, lier, mol(l), mons, namur, ronse, spa, tamines, uccle, ukkle, vorst, zele

composer benoit, ysaye

congo ruanda-urundi, zaire

dialect walloon

dog schipperke

dramatist ghelderode, maeterlinck

drink mandarine-napoleon

endive witloof

fascist party rex

fish soup waterzooi

hare chinchilla, leporide

horse brabancon, princeroyal

king albert, baudouin, leopold

lace fichu

linen brabant

lowland polder

marble rance, ranse

measure aune, boisseau, carat, last, perche, pied, vat

missionary damien

musicologist gevaert

net malines

painter ensor, jordaens, magritte

peak botrange

people walloon

philosopher geulinex

physiologist bordet, heymans

plateau ardennes, hohevenn

poet cammaerts

port antwerp, anvers, ghent, ostend

premier, pierlot, spaak, van zeeland

professor agrege

province antwerp, brabant, flanders, hainau(1)t, liege, limburg, luxemburg

river ambleve, boucq, demer, dender, dyle, escaut, leie, lesse, lys, maas, manjel, mark, meuse, nethe, ourthe, rupel, sambre, schelde, scheldt, semois, vesdre, warche, yser

scientist bordet

sheepdog groenendael

soldier brabanter

spring huy, spa, tongres

statesman beernaert, la fontaine, spaak

tapestry oudenarde

tribe belgae, bellovaci, nervii, remi

village waterloo

violinist vieuxtemps, ysaye

weight carat, charge, chariot, esterlin, last, livre, pound

BELGRADE beograd

BELIAL See BEELZEBUB.

BELIE belong, besiege, calumniate, confute, contradict, controvert, counterfeit, defame, deny, disguise, disprove, encompass, explode, falsify, miscolor, misrepresent, negate, pertain, slander, surround, traduce

BELIEF affiance, assent, assumption, assurance, canon, cause, certainty, certitude, confidence, conviction, credence, credenda, credit, credo, credulity, creed, criance cry, cult, deism, dependence, doctrine, dogma, doxy, ethos, faith, fay, feeling, gospel, ground, holding, hope, ideology, ism, leve, maxim, mind, notion, opinion, orthodoxy, persuasion, precept, principle, reliance, religion, rule, school, sect, stock, store, supposition, sureness, teaching, tenet, troth, trow(ing), trust, truth, view, ween

false delusion, fiction

groundless canard

in spiritual beings animism

instinctive animal faith

liable to credent, credulous

superstitious freet

traditional eikon, icon, ikon

BELIEVABLE authentic, conceivable, credible, downable, likely, plausible, probable, reliable, tenable, tried, unquestionable

BELIEVE accept, accredit, admit, assume, buy, consider, credit, credo, daresay, deem, esteem, fancy, feel, guess, hold, judge, leve, opine, posit, postulate, presume, reckon, suppose, swallow, think, trew, trow, trust, ween, wis

BELIEVER adherent, cultist, deist, devotee, ist, ite, kitabi, orthodox, religionist, theist, votary *comb.* ard, arian, ary, ist, ite *in all religions* omnist

BELIEVING assured, certain, confident, convinced, credent, credulous, gullible, naive, persuaded, positive, satisfied, sure, trusting, undoubting, unhesitating, unquestioning, unsuspicious

BELILI *sister* tammuz

BELINDA *haircutter* lord petre

BELIT, BELTIS *husband* bel, enlil

BELITTLE decrease, decry, denigrate, depreciate, derogate, detract, diminish, discredit, disparage, dwarf, knock, lessen, minimize, minish, pooh-pooh, reduce, scorn, slight, sneer, underestimate, vilipend

BELITTLER zoilus

BELITTLING meiosis

BELL alarm, angelus, beautiful, bellow, boom, bronte, bubble, call, campana, campane, carillon, cascabel, chime, clapper, cloche, clock, codon, corolla, crotal, cup, curfew, dingdong, fair, flare, gong, grelot, jangler, jingle, knell, pavillon, peal, ring(er), roar, signal, skellat, sound, squilla, strike, strobile, stroke, swell, tambour, tantony, tapper, ting, tinkle(r), tintinnabulum, tocsin, toller, tongue, torn, vesper

acton anne bronte

alarm tocsin

axle-bearing cod

-bearer leaf-hopper

book and candle excommunication, incantation

clapper jinglet, striker, tongue

closed crotal

cow leader

crank pump bob

currer charlotte bronte

death tailor

ear cannon

ellis emily bronte

evening curfew

famous big ben, great tom, liberty, tom of lincoln

fastener bewet, bewit

funeral knell, tailor, teller

group peal

hand clag

heather cassiope, erica, plant

in tower signum

kind codon, cow, church, door, electric, gong, hand, school, ship's, tenor

kite bald coot, gallinule

large signum

lip skirt

low-toned bo(u)rdon, tenor

magpie piping-crow

maker yaktayvian

metal bronze, stannite

-mouthed evase

part baldric(k), clapper, jinglet, tongue

passing knell

peal change

pert. campaniform, campanular, campanulate

-ringer activist, carillonneur, clinkum, doer, toll(er)

ring the score, succeed, win

room belfry

science campanology

-shaped caliciform, campaniform, campanular, campanulous, evase

sleigh grelot

small campanella, codon

song singer lakme

sound bong, tingtang, tinkle, toll

the cat attempt, brave, dare, risk, try

tongue clapper

tower belfry, campanile, clocher

town adano, atri

tree snowdrop

vine bindweed

BELLADONNA analgesic, anodyne, atropin(e), banewort, basewort, black choke, doftberry, dwale, dwayberry, herb, manicon, morel, mydriatic, nightshade, poison, spearwort, stimulant

lily amaryllis

poisoning atropism

BELLARMINE bottle, graybeard, jug, longbeard

BELLBIRD arapunga, campanero, cotinga, korimako, mako(mako), procnias, shrike, woodthrush

BELLBOTTOMS trousers

BELLBOY attendant, buttons, chasseur, hallboy, page, porter, redcap

BELLE beautiful, beauty, deb, handsome, lady, maja, peri, spark, toast, venus, woman

amie mistress

aude, lover roland

mere mother-in-law, stepmother

BELLEROPHON gastropod, hipponous

beloved antea, antia

enemy iobates, proteus

grandfather sisyphus

horse pegasus

parent eurymede, glaucus

plain aleian

spring pelrene

victim belerus, chimera

BELLES LETTRES humanities, letters, literature

BELLFLOWER adenophora, allpe, bellwort, bluebell, campanula, daffodil, haskwort, ivybells, milkwort, rampion, uvularia

BELLICENT *half brother* king arthur

BELLICOSE See BELLIGERENT.

BELLIED bulging, corpulent, inflated, puffed

large ventricose, ventripotent

BELLIGERENT aggressive, antagonistic, at odds, at war, bellicose, belliferous, bristly, choleric, contentious, disputatious, factious, fighter, fighting, hostile, irascible, irate, jingoist, litigious, mad, martial, militant, militaristic, pugnacious, quarrelsome, rebellious, truculent, warful, warlike, warmaker, wrangling

BELLINI *opera* norma, puritani, sonnambula

pupil giorgione, titian

sleepwalker amina

BELLMAN town-crier

BELLMOUTHED evase

BELLOW bark, bawl, bell, belve, blare, blart, blore, bluster, buller, cheer, clamor, croon, cry, gape, hue, low, moo, noise, outcry, roar, rou(s)t, rummes, rummish, shout, ululate, vociferate, wail, whoop, yap, yawp, yell

character augie march, citrine, humboldt

BELLOWS blower, bullies, insufflator, lungs, sandbag, sylphon, windbag, winker

fish bugler, snipefish, swellfish, trumpetfish

BELLWARE kelp

BELLWETHER leader, master, ram, sheep

BELLY abdomen, abomasum, alvus, appetite, bag, baggie, balloon, baywindow, bilge, billow, bing(e)y, bloat, bouk, breadbasket, bulge, cod, corporation, craw, crop, fill, gie, gizzard, gluttony, gorge, gut, hunger, ingluvies, inside, interior, kitchen, kyte, manyplies, mary, maw, midriff, omasum, paunch, pelvis, pleon, pod, pot, psalterium, rennet, reticulum, riff, rumen, sack, solar-plexus, stomach, swell, tharm, tripe, tumbrel, tummy, venter, viscera, voracity, wame, weam
big baywindow, breadbasket, paunch
buster dive
-god cormorant, glutton, sybarite
having large abdominous
laugh baff(o), boffola
little ventricle
pert. alvin(e), ventral, ventric, ventrine, visceral
-pinched hungry
-wash beer, beverage, coffee, drink, slop, soda, soup, tea
-whopper dive

BELLYACHE beef, bitch, colic, collywobbles, complain, cramps, grouse, grumble, grump, whine

BELLYBAND belt, girth, wanty

BELLYFLAUGHT headlong

BELLYFUL abundance, plenty, quantity, satiety, wamef(o)u

BELMARDUK See MARDUK.

BELONG affeir, appertain, apply, attach, bear, behoove, belie, concern, fall, fit, group, inhere, join, lie, pertain, relate, rely, subscribe

BELONGING(S) alls, appurtenance, asset(s), baggage, chattel(s), duds, duffle, effects, endemic, estate, fare, furniture, gear, goods, household, means, pertinent, possession, property, purprise, resources, trap (pings), traps, usings
to, comb. aceous, ary, orium

BELOVED adored, aimee, amorosa, amoroso, beliked, bien aime, bosom, cheri(e), cherished, darling, dear, dulcinea, girl(friend), idol, inamorata, jill, lady, lass (ie), love, minion, mistress, precious, sweetheart, sweetie
most alderliefest
name meaning aimee, amy, david, vida

BELOW a(b)low, after, aneath, bajo, behind, beneath, down(stairs), hell, inferior, infra, lower, neath, sotto, under(neath)
comb. infra, sub(ter)
par sick
standard bad, inferior, mediocre, worse, worst
the belt dirty, foul
the salt plebeian
zero cold, freezing, gelid

BELPHEGOR archdemon, beelpeor, devil

BELSHAZZAR *father* nabonidus, nebuchadnezzar

BELSIRE ancestor, grandfather

BELT annulation, apron, area, baldric, balteus, band, beat, bellyband, blow, boondoggle, boundary, ceinture, cest(us), cincture, cingle, cingulum, circuit, cordon, corset, crooper, district, drink, encircle, encompass, fettle, flog, gird(le), girth, lace, lash, layer, lunger, miter, obi, patte, region, ring, sash, strait, strap, strike, strip, surcingle, surround, swath(e), switch, tract, waistband, wall, whack, whip, zonar, zone, zonule, zoster
cartridge bandoleer
comb. zon(o)
conveyor apron, cruper, haul
ecclesiastical balteus
holder keeper, loop
imaginary zodiac
line waist
machine swifter
of calms doldrums
sky zodiac
slip creep
sword baldric, bawdric
tree berm(e)

BELTIS See BELIT.

BELUGA acipenser, caviar(e), cetacean, hansen, huse, huso, marsoon, sturgeon, whitefish

BELUS *consort* anchinoe
kingdom chemmis
offspring aegyptus, cepheus, danaus, dido, phineus, pygmalion
parent libya, poseidon
twin agenor

BELVEDERE gazebo, lookout

BEMA almemar, bima(h), chancel, dais, pace, platform, sanctuary, step

BEMAZED bewildered, confused, dazed, muddled, stupefied

BEMOAN bewail, deplore, grieve, keen, lament, moan, mourn, plain, regret, sigh, sob, sorrow, wail

BEMUDDLE addle, annoy, bemuse, bewilder, bother, confuse, distract, fuddle, mystify, perplex, puzzle, vex, wallow

BEMUSE addle, confuse, daze, distract, sot, stupefy

BEN backroom, hill, inner, inside, interior, moringa, mountain, peak, phaseolus, silene, son, within
teak nanawood, nandi

BENA vetiver

BENAME declare, promise, style, swear

BENASTY soil

BENCH archebanc, banc, bank, banquette, bar, basin, bason, benk, berm(e), bink, board, cassanpanca, chair, court, dais, deas, discard, edge, elevation, exedra, exhibit, forme, judge, lodge, mesa, pew, plank, plateau, platform, reposal, sconce, seat, settee, settle, shamble, shelf, shoulder, siege, sill, stool, table(land), terrace, thoft, thwart, trestle, tribunal, woolsack, worktable, zygon
church pew, pue, sedile
covering bancal
dairy tram
hook cramp
judge's banc(us)
king's bancus-regius
land terrace
long langsettle
-made custom
outdoor exedra, exhedra
player's wood
rower's bank, thoft, thwart, zygon
shoemaker's forme

3-legged trestle

-warmer idler, scrub, sub(stitute)

wooden banker, settle

workman's siege

BENCHER boatman, crewman, oarsman

BEND 3 bow, nid, nod, ply, sag, set, sny, win, wry, yaw 4 abow, arch, bias, bool, buck, clay, cope, curb, dome, faud, fawn, flex, fold, fork, genu, hook, kink, knot, lean, lout, ploy, tend, tilt, turn, vert, warp 5 agree, angle, baton, bight, brace, bulge, clamp, coude, courb, crank, crimp, crink, crook, culge, curve, droop, flect, hinge, hunch, inbow, kneel, quirl, relax, round, scrag, skelp, slant, squat, stoop, sweep, trend, twine, twist, yield 6 accept, bought, bridle, buckle, camber, convex, crouch, deform, direct, divert, fasten, fetter, inflex, pleach, strain, subdue, submit 7 contort, deflect, deviate, dispose, flexion, flexure, incline, recurve 8 flection 9 acquiesce, constrain, influence 10 deflection

an ear listen, prate, talk

around circumflex

backward declination, retort, retroflex

earth's geosyncline

one's steps pursue, travel

over backwards go all out, try

rope bight

sinister stigma

the elbow drink

the knee salaam

timber sny

to one's will dominate

BENDER bower, brannigan, bridge, bum, bust, drunk, flexor, guzzler, inflector, jag, leg, pliers, revel, sixpence, spree, whopper

BENDING anfract, bow, buckling, crook, curve, flection, flexion, fract, hogging, knee, knot, lithe, pliable, pliant, sag, sinuous, supple, twist(y)

forward anteflexion

like a bow arcuation

BENDIS artemis

BENDWISE diagonally

BENDY TREE mahoe, miro, okra, portia-tree, thespesia

BENE boon, fine, good, hog, prayer, well

vale farewell

BENEATH alow, ane(a)th, below, bottom, down, inferior, lower, nether, under (neath)

contempt offensive, paltry

BENEDICITE benediction, benison, bless you, canticle, invocation

BENEDICK *beloved* beatrice

BENEDICT bridegroom, husband

arnold traitor

BENEDICTINE camaldolite, celestine, cluniac

abbey site abingdon, cluny

cellarer dom perignon

head abbot primate

hermit vallombrosan

order maurist

title dom

BENEDICTION aboth, address, amen, amidah, benedicite, benison, blessing, boon, brocho, grace, gratitude, happiness, invocation, nandi, praise, prayer, shema, thanksgiving

hebrew berakah, habdalah, kiddush

BENEFACTION alms, beneficence, benefit, boon, charity, contribution, donation, endowment, favor, gift, good, grant, gratuity, largess(e), philanthropy, present, subvention

BENEFACTOR agent, aid(er), altruist, angel, assister, backer, donor, friend, good samaritan, helper, humanitarian, maecenas, ministrant, patron, promoter, samaritan, savior, sponsor, succorer, underwriter

BENEFICE advowson, beneficum, charge, curacy, cure, donative, favor, fee, few, fief, glebe, incumbency, living, perquisite, preferment, prelacy, rectory, revenue, sinecure, totquot, vicarage

first fruit annale, annat(e)

BENEFICENCE altruism, benefaction, boon, bounty, charity, gift, goodness, grace, kindness

BENEFICENT amiable,

beneficial, good, gracious, kindly

BENEFICIAL advantageous, aidful, benign(ant), bonitarian, commodious, constructive, desirable, edifying, enjoyable, favorable, functional, good, healthful, healthy, helpful, hygienic, implemental, instrumental, lucrative, practicable, practical, profitable, remunerative, rewarding, salubrious, salutary, sanitive, serviceable, singular, useful, utilitarian, wholesome

BENEFICIARY almsman, annuitant, assignee, cestui, cestuy, devisee, donee, ecclesiastic, feoffee, feudatory, grantee, heir(ess), incumbent, inheritor, legatee, pensionary, pensioner, recipient, remainderman, remittanceman, resident(iary), stipendiary, usuary, vassal

BENEFIT advance, advantage, aid, ameliorate, assist (ance), avail, befriend, behalf, behoof, bespeak, bestead, better, bid ale, blessing, boon, boost, boot, charity, commorth, concert, contribute, convenience, deserve, equity, favor, fringe, fruit, gain, gift, good, help, improve, interest, performance, prize, profit, prow, reap, sake, selth, serve, service, stead, usance, use, utility, value, worth

BENET ensnare, exorcist, trap

BENEVOLENCE altruism, benignity, charity, favor, generosity, goodness, goodwill, humanity, kindness, liberality, love, munificence, philanthropy, regard

BENEVOLENT altruistic, amiable, benign(ant), bounteous, bountiful, charitable, complaisant, generous, good, humane, kind(ly), liberal, loving, obliging, philanthropic

BENG See DEVIL.

BENGAL See also INDIA references.

ant thrush nurang

bay, river to ganges, godavari, irrawaddy, kistna

beggar baul

bison gaur

boat batel, bat(t)eau, baulea(h), panchway
capital dacca
caste baidya
city barisal, calcutta, dacca, madras, patna, rangoon, tittacarh
cotton adati, adaty
cultivation joom, jum
district dacca, nadia
fish cuchia
gentleman baboo, babu
gram chick pea
grass millet
groom saice, syce
hemp sunn
isinglass See AGAR.
measure chattack, chittack, cotta(h)
people banian, eboe, kol, tipura
physician baidya
poet tagore
quince bael, bel, bhel
revenue officer deshmuk(h)
root cassumunar
sage meriandra, mint
sect or singer baul
soldier sepoy
state cooch behar
thrush nurang
tree bola
BEN HUR *author* wallace
leader solomon
BENI See SESAME.
BENIGHT blind, cloud, darken, dazzle, obscure, overpower, shroud
BENIGHTED blind, ignorant, unenlightened
BENIGN affable, auspicious, benedict, beneficial, benevolent, bland, boon, compassionate, cordial, favorable, friendly, genial, gentle, good, gracious, healthful, humane, innocent, kind(ly), mild, pleasant, propitious, salubrious, salutary, suave, sweet, tender, wholesome
BENIGNANT bland, genial, gracious, kind, liberal, merciful
BENISON beatitude, benediction, blessing, invocation
BENJ See BHANG.
BENJAMIN balsam, benzoin, trillium
brother joseph
clan head iri
descendant aher
parent harim, jacob, rachel
son ard, ashbel, becber, bela,

ehi, gera, huppim, muppim, naaman, rosh
tree spicebush, styrax
tribe belaites
tribe leader ahiezar, jeuz
BENJY benny, petticoat, straw-hat, vest, waistcoat, weskit
BENNE See SESAME.
BENNET avens, clovewort, daisy, geum, hemlock, herb, saxifrage, valerian
weed foxtail
BENNU See BENU.
BENNY amphetamine, benjy, benzedrine, hat, headdress, overcoat, pill, tablet
BENONI *father* jacob
BENT 3 aim, bow, set 4 bias, cast, firm, gift, moor, turn 5 bound, bowed, bowly, coude, crank, crump, field, fixed, flair, frame, gouge, grass, habit, heath, humor, knack, lurch, prone, squat, swing, taste, tract, trend 6 akimbo, anlage, bennet, biased, braced, common, courbe, course, dogleg, energy, flexed, genius, hooked, intent, liking, necked, squint, swayed, talent 7 ability, angular, buckled, crooked, curvant, embowed, faculty, flexion, flexure, impetus, intense, leaning, leveled, pasture, pronate, purpose, stooped, tension 8 aptitude, arcuated, capacity, crumpled, declined, flection, hillside, penchant, reflexed, resolute, resolved, slouched, tendency 9 direction, endurance, prejudice 10 determined, partiality, proclivity, propensity 11 camptodrome, disposition, inclination 14 predisposition
aside declinate
at end grypanian, hamate, hogged
backward inverted, resupinate
comb. curvi, ɾyph(o), cyrt(o)
downward bowed, incumbent, inflexed, pronated, reclinate
easily lithy
grass agrostis
in incavate
mental affection, geme, talent

natural predisposition, swing
upward antrose
BENTEM sarasvati
messenger serpent
BENTHAMISM utilitarianism
BENU osiris, phoenix
BENUMB binomen, blunt, chill, cumber, daver, daze, deaden, dunt, fretish, fretize, hebetate, nip, scram, shram, stiffen, stound, stun, stupefy, torpedo
BENUMBED chill, clumse, clumsy, frozen, leaden, scram, shrammed, stupefied, torpid
BENVENUTO greetings, welcome
BENVOLIO *friend* romeo
uncle montague
BENZEDRINE See AMPHETAMINE.
BENZENE benzol, phene(ne), solvent
derivative cymene
BENZOIN antiseptic, asaduleis, balsam, benjamin(bush), fixative, lindera, resin, spicebush
BEOWULF *character* finn, grendel, higelac, hrothgar, unferth, wiglaf
hall heorot
kingdom geata
uncle higelac
victim grendel
BEQUEATH bequest, bestow, commend, commit, demise, devise, dispose of, endow, entrust, give, hand down, leave, legate, offer, pass on, quethe, transmit, will
BEQUEST birthright, devisal, devise, endowment, estate, gift, heritage, inheritance, legacy, will
BER elb, jujube, zizyphus
BERAIAH *father* shimei
BERAT patent, privilege, warrant
BERATE abuse, assail, baste, betongue, blackguard, censure, chastise, chew out, chide, clapper-claw, criticize, drub, fulminate, jaw, lash, nag, objurgate, rag, rail, rebuke, reprimand, reproach, reprove, revile, scold, score, slate, tell off, tongue-lash, upbraid, vilify, vituperate, wag, yell
BERAY befoul, defile

BERBER hamite, har(r)atin, kabyl(e), moor, mozabite, riff, shilha, shilluh, shlu(h)
assembly jemaa
chief caid, qaid
dynasty hafsid, hafsite
historian ibn-khaldun
home algeria, kabylia
king tankamamin
language senhaja, shilha, tamashek, tuareg, zenata
tribe arsh, beni-abba, chawia, daze, riff, senhaja, teb, teda, tib(b)u, tuareg, tuarek, zaghawa
BERCEAU arbor, bower, cradle
BERCEUSE cradlesong, lullaby, wiegenlied
BERCHMIA buckthorn, supplejack
BEREA aleppo
grit sandstone
BEREAVE deprive, despoil, dispossess, divest, rob, sadden, strip, widow
BEREAVEMENT orbitude, orbity, viduation
BERECHIAH *father* zerubbabel
BEREFT barren, bereaved, bestraught, cut off, denuded, deprived, destitute, divested, forfairn, forlorn, indigent, lacking, less, lorn, lost, minus, orb(ate), pauperized, poor, quit, shorn, wanting, widowed, without
BERENGENA eggplant, solanum
BERENICE *brother* herod
consort antiochus, archelaus, aristobulus, herod, ptolemy
father agrippa, magas
kin cleopatra, ptolemy
BERET(TA) basco, cap, tam
BERETANIA See ENGLAND.
BERG adder, barrow, floe, iceberg, mountain
alban, opera wozzeck
BERGALL bergylt, cunner, rosefish
BERGAMA pergamum
BERGAMASCA tarantella
BERGAMOT bose, essence, mint, monarda, orange, pear, perfume, rug, snuff
camphor bergaptene
BERGERE armchair, shepherdess, sofa
BERGYLT bergall, cunner, rosefish

BERIAH *parent* asher, elpaal, ephraim
BERIBERI dropsy, kakki
BERING *sea fish* popeye
sea island group andreanof, diomede, pribilof
BERITH briss, brit(h)
BERKELIUM *source* americum
BERLIN *airport* gatow, tegel, tempelhof
boulevard kurfurstendam
district tempelhof
gate brandenberg, checkpoint charlie
park tiergarten
police vepos
prison spandau
pubs kneipen
street wilhelmstrasse
BERLIOZ *opera* beatrice and benedict, benvenuto cellini, damnation of faust
BERM bank, bench, brim, edge, heelpath, ledge, lisiere, path, shelf, shoulder, terrace
BERMUDA *arrowroot* ararao, araru
barracuda spet
berry soapberry
bird cahow
buttercup oxalis, wood-sorrel
capital hamilton
catfish coelho
ceremony gombay
chub chopa blanca
coin hog-money, shilling
fern adiantum, maidenhair
flag iris, blue-eyed grass
grass cynodon, devil grass, doob, doub, scutch
grouper rockfish
juniper potloo-cedar
mulberry callicarpa
shilling hog-money
shrub snowberry
snowberry chiococca
triangle hoodoo-sea
BERNADOTTE *commander* napoleon
BERNECIA *founder* ida
BERNSTEIN *work* mass
BEROE *nurse for* semele
parent adonis, aphrodite
BERRY abhal, acinus, acrosarc, aley, allspice, bacca, bay, beat, black, bramble, burrow, caper, cowberry, cran, cubeb, currant, dew, dollar, egg, elder, etaerio, fruit, grape, haw(bake), hill(ock), hip, holly, kernel, landolphia, lansa(t),

lanseh, mound, pass, poha, produce, rasp, sabine, salal, savin, seed, straw, thresh
acid currant
bearing baccate(d), bacciferous
coffee cherry
comb. bacci
disease blue stem
dried cubeb, pasa
-eating baccivorous
jumper abhal
laurel bay
medicinal cubeb
part drupe
pert. baccaceous, baccate, coccoid
poisonous baneberry
-shaped bacciform
wild aley
BERSAGLIERE marksman, rifleman, sharpshooter, soldier
BERSERK amok, amuck, bravo, enraged, frantic, frenetic, frenzied, mad, maniacal, pirate, violent, warrior
BERTH accommodation, anchor(age), appointment, bed, billet, bunk, cabin, cot, dock, harbor, job, lodging, lower, mooring, office, place, position, post, quarters, rank, reservation, secure, shelf, situation, slip(way), space, upper
BERTHA bright, cannon, cape, collar, gun, perchta
BERTRAM *beloved* helena
follower parolles
BERYL aeroides, aquamarine, chrysolite, davidsonite, emerald, gem, goshenite, heliodor, morganite
colorless goshenite
zodiac sign capricorn
BERYLLIA glucina, glucine
BERYTUS beirut
BESEECH adjure, appeal, ask, beg, bid, conjure, crave, cry, entreat, halse, impetrate, implore, importune, obsecrate, obtest, petition, plead, pray, solicit, sue, supplicate, woo
BESEEM become, befit, behoove
BESET abet, allot, annoy, arrange, assail, assist, attack, avail, become, bedangled, befit, bego, belay, beleaguer, besiege, bestead, bestow, bestud, bigan, block-

ade, bother, decorate, employ, encircle, enclose, encumber, enthrong, harass, harry, help, importune, infest, obsess, obstruct, ornament, overrun, overset, peril, perplex, persecute, pester, plague, ply, press, sail, siege, sit, spend, stud, surround, waylay, worry

BESHOW baddock, coalfish, cudden, cuddie, cuddy, skil(fish)

BESHREW corrupt, curse, deprave, execrate

BESIDE abreast, adjacent, against, along(side), anent, aside, fernin(s)t, forby, fornen(s)t, inby, juxtaposed, near, neck and neck, sidelong, toward
one's self crazy, distraught, emotional, excited, fey, frantic, rabid, rapturous
the mark amiss
the point irrelevant

BESIDES above, again, also, and, beyond, but, else, except, forby(e), further (more), in addition, inby, likewise, more(over), other(than), over(and above), supra, then, thereto, too, unto, what's more, withal, without, yet
comb. para

BESIEGE assail, attack, belay, beleaguer, belie, beset, compass, congregate, coventrize, encircle, encompass, envelope, gird, girt, harry, importune, leaguer, obsess, obside, pester, plague, solicit, storm, surround

BESLAVER beslubber, flatter, slobber

BESMEAR apply, balm, beblot, bedash, bedaub, bedizen, beslime, beslubber, besmatter, besmirch, bespatter, coat, cover, daub, defile, discolor, grime, gruft, muddy, paint, platch, slake, slander, smother, smotter, soil, stain, sully, taint

BESMIRCH asperse, besmear, blacken, blaspheme, dash, dirty, draggle, slander, slur(ry), smear, soil, sully, turpify

BESOM bisme, broom, drab,

heath(er), hussy, mop, sloven, strigil, sweep

BESOT befuddle, deaden, dull, infatuate, intoxicate, muddle, stupefy

BESOTTED asinine, crass, drunk, dull, fatuous, fond, foolish, silly, simple, stupid

BESPANGLE adorn, decorate, enstar, figure, jewel, ornament, star, stud

BESPATTER asperse, begarie, begary, besmear, besmirch, blot, brand, dash, discolor, jaup, moisten, muddy, plash, reproach, slander, smotter, soil, sparge, splash, spot, sprinkle, stain, sully

BESPEAK address, argue, arrange, ask, attest, benefit, betoken, cite, discuss, employ, engage, evince, exclaim, foretell, hint, imply, indicate, mean, order, request, reserve, show, steven, tryst

BESPOKE custom-made, engaged, ordered, reserved

BESPRINKLE asperse, bequirtle, bestrew, drop, powder, sprinkle

BESSARABIA moldavian republic

BEST ace, acme, a-one, apex, apogee, aristocracy, aristos, beat, capital, champion, choice, circumvent, conquer, cream, creme de la creme, defeat, elect, elite, excel, finest, flower, gem, good, greatest, kohinoor, lace, largest, leader, matchless, most, nonesuch, nonpareil, optimal, optime, optimum, outmootch, outstrip, outwit, peerless, pick, prime, prize, queen, quintessential, select, subdue, sunday, superior, superlative, tiptop, top(s), unequaled, utmost, vanquish, wale, whip, win, worst
bower joker
comb. arist(o)
friend mainman
man paranymph
part core, essence, heart, milk
-seller book, hit, rave

BESTEAD abet, arranged, assist, avail, benefit, beset, boot, established, help, lo-

cated, placed, profit, serve, substitute

BESTIAL animal, beastly, belluine, brutal, brute, brutish, carnal, cruel, debased, depraved, feral, filthy, inhuman, low, savage, sensual, vile, wild

BESTIR arouse, awake, hustle, shift, steer, stir

BESTLA *son* odin

BESTOW accord, add, administer, allot, allow, apply, attribute, award, bequeath, beteem, bless, cast, collate, confer, deal, demise, deposit, devote, dispense, dispose, divide, donate, dotate, dote, entail, erogate, give, grant, impart, impose, indulge, lodge, partake, place, present, put, quarter, render, send, shower, spend, stow, thole, tip, tribute, use, vouchsafe, ware
lavishly heap

BESTRAUGHT bereft, distracted

BESTRIDE bestraddle, defend, horse, mount, protect, straddle, support

BESUGO porgy, whale

BET ante, back, blind, box, brag, call, chip, come in, copper, cover, fade, gage, gamble, hazard, hedge, hold, kick in, lay, make book, manque, milieu, noir, pari-mutuel, parlay, paroli, pike, play, pledge, plot, plunge, post, pot, punt, pyramid, raise, risk, rouge, set, sleeper, sport, stake, straddle, sweepstakes, venture, vie, wad, wager
boldly bluff
broker bookmaker
chip check
fail to pay renege, renig, welch, welsh
faro sleeper
hedging sleeper
long odds skinner
poker ante, blind, feed the kitty
roulette bas, carre, dernier, encarre, enplein, milieu, noir, rouge
unclaimed sleeper

BETA beet, chard, goosefoot, mangel, star, two, zingiber
geminorum pollux
particle electron

BETAKE address, apply, as-

sume boun, catch, commend, commit, deliver, entrust, get, give, grant, hie, journey, move, remove, repair, resort, seize, withdraw *oneself* haunt, leave, pike, refer, resort, seek, teem, yield
BETE beast, foolish, silly, stupid
-noire abhorrence, abomination, anathema, bugbear, hate, terror
rouge chigger
BETEEM accord, allow, bestow, consent, grant, permit, vouchsafe
BETEL areca, bonga, buyo, cashoo, catechu, ikmo, itmo, penang, pepper, pinang, piper, pupulo, seri, siri(h)
leaf buyo, pan, paun, pawne
nut areca, bonga, bonya, bunga, supari
nut compound acacatechol
pepper ikmo, itmo
seed catechu
BETHABARA greenheart, noibwood
BETHEL bethesda, chapel, church, hostel, luz, refuge, sanctuary
BETHFLOWER bethroot, birthroot, birthwort, trillium
BETHINK advise, begrudge, consider, devise, mind, recall, recollect, reflect, regret, remember, remind, take
BETHLEHEM bedlam
manger cratch, creche
stable representation creche
BETHROOT trillium
BETHUEL *offspring* laban, rebecca
BETIDE befit, betoken, chance, hap(pen), occur, presage
BETIMES anon, at once, early, forthwith, quickly, rath(e), soon, speedily
BETISE folly, stupidity, trifle
BETOKEN attest, augur, evidence, evince, forebode, import, indicate, mark, note, portend, presage, show, sign, symbolize
BETONY broomwort, germander, stachys, teucrium
BETOYAN *indian* curetu, pioxe, tama, tucano, yahuna

BETRAY accuse, babble, beef, beguile, bewray, blab(ber), blackleg, blat, blow, blunder, blurt, boil, collaborate, corrupt, cross up, debauch, deceive, delude, descry, desert, disclose, display, divulge, doublecross, evince, expose, falsify, gull, hoodwink, inform, knife, leak, let down, malign, manifest, mislead, peach, quatch, quisle, report, reveal, round, seduce, sell out, sile, sing, show, snare, snitch, spill, split, squeal, stab, swick, swike, talk, tattle, tell, trap, trick, two-time, uncover, undo, unmask, wray
BETRAYER brutus, informer, judas, rat, recreant, seducer, skunk, snitch, squealer, tattletale, telltale, traitor
BETRAYING telltale
BETROTH affiance, affy, commit, contract, despouse, earl, engage, ensure, handfast, pledge, plight, promise, propose, token, truth
BETROTHAL affiance, banns, contract, engagement, espousal, promise, proposal, sponsalia, subarr(h)ation, troth, tryst
goddess vor
BETROTHED affianced, assured, committed, engaged, fiance(e), handfast, intended, promised, sure, vowed
BETTER advance, advantage, aid, ameliorate, amend, beet, bigger, choicer, correct, defeat, exceed, excel, gamester, greater, healthier, help, improve(d), increase, larger, meliorate, mend, more, preferable, promote, rectify, redress, reform, relieve, remedy, safer, superior, support, surpass, top, transcend, victory, wagerer, wiser
-half mate, spouse, wife
BETTING gambling
adviser tout
equalization handicap
figures odds, price
house tote-shop
machine pari-mutuel

system alembert, parlay, paroli, martingal(e)
BETTOR See GAMESTER.
BETTY dessert, dotard, elizabeth, florence-flask, jimmy, jocrisse, mollycot, solitaire, wifecarl
BETULA See BIRCH.
camphor beulin(ol)
BETWEEN amell, amid(st), among(st), atween, atwixt, average, betwixen, betwixt, connecting, emel, entre, fra, intermediate, mesne, midst, separating, tween, tweesh, twixt, ytwyn
-brain diencephalon
comb. dia, inter, meta
-maid tweeny
scylla and charybdis, choice, dilemma, hobson's choice, perplexed, perplexity
the lines latent, secret
times occasionally
two seas bismarine
us confidentially, entre nous, inter nos
BEULAH israel, jerusalem
BEVEL angle, aslant, bank, beard, bezel, blow, cant, chamfer, cut, edge, fleam, fleem, incline, miter, mitre, oblique, push, rake, ream, rhymer, shelve, slant, slope, snape, splay
corners splay
edge beard, wane
jacking flat
out ream
BEVER drink, liquor, lunch, quiver, shake, snack, tremble
BEVERAGE (See also DRINK references.) brew, cup, draft, drink, liquid, liquor, potable, water
BEVIS *victim* ascopart
sword morglay
BEVUE blunder, boner, error
BEVY assembly, batch, brood, charm, company, covert, covey, drove, flight, flock, gaggle, group, herd, multitude, muster, mye, pack, plump, school, shoal, siege, skein, spring, suite, swarm
BEWAIL bemoan, complain, cry, deplore, grieve, keen, lament, moan, mourn, plain(t), rame, regret, repent, rue, sigh, sorrow, thrope, wail, weep, wey
BEWARE actung, avoid,

cave, eschew, garde, gare, heed, look out, shun, spend, stop, take care, tent, war, warning, watch(out)
let the buyer caveat emptor
the dog cave canem
BEWILDER abash, addle, astonish, baffle, beat, bemist, bemuse, bother, buffalo, bumbaze, confound, confuse, daze, dazzle, deave, dim, disconcert, dismay, distract, disturb, dizzy, dudder, dumfound, embarrass, entangle, flasker, flummox, fluster, fog, foil, fox, gaum, involve, mar, maze, moider, momble, muddle, mystify, nonplus, obscure, overmuse, perplex, perturb, pother, puzzle, rattle, squatter, stagger, stump, stun, surprise, wander, wilder
BEWILDERED agape, asea, bushed, dazed, helpless, lost, mang, mazed, perplexed, puzzled, stupent, willyard, wilsome
BEWILDERMENT amazement, awe, confusion, daze, dilemma, fog, hobble, mismaze, perplexity, pucker, quandary, stew, stickle, wonder
BEWITCH allure, attract, bedevil, beguile, blink, captivate, charm, delight, demonize, diabolize, enamor, enchant, enmesh, enrapture, ensorcel, enthrall, entice, entrance, excite, exorcise, fascinate, forspeak, greegree, grigri, hagride, hex, hoodoo, infatuate, magic, maleficiate, obeah, obsess, overlook, please, possess, spell, strike, take, thrill, transport, voodoo
BEY governor, officer, ruler
BEYLE, HENRI *pseud.* stendhal
BEYOND above, across, after, aside, ayond, ayont, behind, beneath, beside(s), beyant, farther, forby, forthby, free, further, greater, hereafter, more, outgate, outre, over(more), passing, past, superior, surpassing, ultra, without, yond(er), yonside
all expectation successfully
all praise perfect

belief amazing, incredible
comb. hyper, meta, preter, sur, tra(ns), ultra
compare peerless
comprehension closed book
control impossible, refractory
doubt absolutely, assured, certain(ly)
help done for, finished
limits excessive, out of bounds
price dear, valuable, worthy
question absolute, certain
reach inaccessible
reason absurd, impossible
recall hopeless, long ago
seas abroad, travelling
the alps ultramontane
the great future, hereafter, tomorrow
the pale too far, too much
the sea ultramarine
the threshold ultraliminal
this moreover, still
understanding unintelligible
BEYROUTH beirut
BEZALEEL beseleel
father uri
BEZEL basil, bevel, chaton, crown, edge, face(t), flange, inarquise, ocimum, ouch, rim, seal, template, templet, top
BEZIQUE *-like game* alsos, belot(t)e, cinq cents, clabber, clob, eight-pack, felsos, five hundred, gaigel, hundertspiel, jass, jo-jotte, klab(erjass), marriage, penchant, peneech, rubicon, six-pack, sixty-six
term back-door, brisque, close
BEZOAR antelope, antidote, calculus, coprolite, goatstone, hippolith
goat pasan(g)
BEZONIAN rascal, recruit, scoundrel, soldier, wretch
BEZZLE consume, drink, gluttonize, plunder, revel, steal, waste
BHAGAVAD-GITA *character* arjuna, krishna
BHAGAVAT See VISHNU.
BHAIRAVA See SILVA.
BHANG bang, beng, benj, hashish, hemp, marijuana
BHARAL burrhel, nahoor, sheep, tur
BHARATA india(n)
descendants pandavas
half-brother rama(chandra)

BHAT bard, go-between, minstrel, scholar
BHIKSHU gelong
BHUMI DEVI *husband* vishnu
BHUNGI bhangi, bungy, mehtar, scavenger, sweeper, untouchable
BHUTAN dragonland, drukyul
assembly tsongdu
city para, thimbu, thimphu
coin paisa, rupee
disease dha
dish thugpa, tsamba
drink butter-tea
fortress dzong
king wangchuk
language dzongkha, lhoke
leader dharma-raja
monastery taksang
monk zhabdrung
pass dochula
recruit jawan
religion bon, shamanism, witchcraft
river amochu, machu, manas, pachu, thinchu
robe bakkhu, kho
scroll thanka
temple gompa
BIA *brother* cratus, zelos
captive prometheus
parent pallas, styx
sister nike
BIADICE *husband* cretheus
BIAFRA *airport* uli
general effong
leader ojukwu
people annang, efik, ibibio, ibo, ijaw, ogoja
town abakaliki, awomama, bonny, ekwereazu, emekuku, ikwerre, kalabari, nimo, nkwerri, ohaozara, okwu, onitsha, opobo, owerri, uli, umuahia
BIANCA *beloved* cassio
father baptista
sister katherina
suitor gremio, hortensio, lucentio
BIAS amiss, animus, awry, bend, bent, bigotry, cant, clinamen, color(ing), complex, crook, deflect, desire, deviate, diagonal, disposition, favor(itism), inclination, incline, influence, injustice, leaning, oblique, partial(ity), partisanism, penchant, ply, poise, preconception, predilection, predisposition, preference,

prejudice, prepossess, proclivity, propensity, sheer,
skew, slant(ing), slew,
slope, suggest, sway,
swerve, swing, tendency,
transverse, turn, twist, unfairness, veer, warp, wrong,
wry
brother melampus
freedom from cando(u)r
parent amythaon, idomeul
son areus
BIASED bigoted, colored, diagonal, disposed, minded,
partial, prejudiced, slanted
BIB apron, bavette, bibb-
cock, bishop, brat, cloth,
cover, drink, pout, sip, tipple, tucker
and tucker dress
leather barmskin, dick
BIBBER carouser, drinker,
tippler, toper
BIBELOT curio, ornament,
trinket, virtu
BIBI lady, mistress, mrs,
woman
BIBLE, BIBLICAL (See also
HEBREW references.)
book(of books), gospel,
holystone, revelation, scripture, text, vulgate, word,
writ
acre acco
angel gabriel, micah, raphael
animal ass, behemoth,
daman, hydrax, shapan,
reem
apocrypha baruch, bel, daniel, ecclesiasticus, esdras,
esther, jeremiah, jeremy, judith, maccabees, manasseh,
septuagint, sirach, snake,
solomon, song of the three,
susanna, syriac, tobit
battle armageddon, jericho
behemoth hippopotamus
book, last apocalypse
book, new testament acts,
colossians, corinthians,
ephesians, galatians, he-
brews, james, john, jude,
luke, mark, matthew, peter,
philemon, philippians, revelation, romans, thessalonians, timothy, titus
book, old testament amos,
apocrypha, chronicles, daniel, deuteronomy, ecclesiastes, esther, exodus, ezekiel, ezra, genesis, habakkuk, haggai, hosea, isaiah,
jeremiah, job, joel, jonah,
joshua, judges, kings, lam-

entations, leviticus, malachi,
micah, nahum, nehemia,
numbers, obadiah, prov-
erbs, psalms, ruth, samuel,
song of solomon, zechariah,
zephaniah
books, first torah
books, first seven heptateuch
books, omitted apocrypha
cave adullum
chamberlain carcas
charioteer jehu
christian bryanite, methodist
city accad, accho, acre,
agaga, ain, akkad, arad,
arvad, ashkelon, ashur,
assur, aven, babylon,
bethel, bethlehem, biblos,
cana, dan, elim, elon, ga-
dara, gath, gaza, geba, gomorrah, jericho, jerusalem,
joppa, maon, nazareth, nineveh, rome, shelah, shiloh,
sidon, sodom, tadmor,
tarsus, tyre, zeboim
clan senaah, shelah
classes baraca
cloth shaatnez
coin beka(h), daric, mite,
shekel, talent
contempt word raca
country ammon, aram, bela,
canaan, chaldea, elam, ellasar, galilee, gath, hali, israel, judah, judea, moab,
nod, ophir, pul, samaria,
seba, seir, shinar, sumer
desert paran
disease leprosy, plague
eagle gier
eunuch carcas
exile kir
field ager, aner
fire god moloch
fortress dathema
garden eden, gethsemane,
uzza
garment beged, cesuth, peth-
igi
giant anakim, behemoth,
emim, goliath, leviathan,
nephilim, samson, zamzum-
min, zuzim
giant killer david
gold source ophir
greek codex sinaiticus
greek version septuagint
harlot aholah, aholibah
hippopotamus behemoth
hunter nimrod
hypocrite pharisee
invocation maranatha
judge abdon, elon, jephthah
king agag, ahab, ahaz, amon,

asa, bera, birsha, david,
herod, iva, jehoram, jeroboam, omri, reba, saul, solomon, tidal
land of riches ophir
law, pert. levitic
leaf costmary
liar ananias, sapphira
measure ephah
mountain ararat, carmel,
ebal, ezem, ezra, gadi, gilead, heres, horeb, moriah,
nebo, olivet, peor, phud,
phut, pisgah, seir, shigion-
oth, sinai, sion, thanach,
zion
musician asaph, david
navigator noah
nomad jabal
oasis elim
original language aramaic
ornament thummin, urim
passage capitulum, pericope,
text
patriarch enos, israel, peleg
people ammon, amorite, anamin, arpakhshad, ascenez,
ashkenaz, asshurim, do-
danim, gadarene, moabite,
phut, seba
plague locust schistocerca
plains jericho, mamre, pilar
plenty, land of goshen, ophir
plotter haman
pool siloam
priest See ECCLESIASTIC
hebrew.
prince orab
proconsul gallio
pronoun thee, thine, thou,
thy
prophet See PROPHET *famous.*
queen abi, esther, jezebel,
sheba, vashti
reading kri
region bashan, enon, ophir,
perea, sepharad
reproach word raca
river abana, amana, arnon,
geon, kishon, jordan, nile,
pharpar, zab
scapegoat azazel
scholar elohist
sea dead, galilee, gennesaret,
tiberias, red
shepherd abel, david
slavonic ostrog
society gideon
song book jashar(er)
spice frankincense, myrrh,
stacte
spurious writings pseudepigrapha

spy caleb
stone ezel, ligure
study group baraca, philathea
syriac peshitta
tent-dwellers kedar
text mikra, miqra
thief barabbas
transgression averah
translation, english douay
translator coverdale, tyndale, wycliffe
tree almug, sandlewood, shittah
valley aijalon, baca, elah, hela, shaveh, siddim
version apocrypha, bohairic, douay, geez, geneva, italia, king james, new english, peshitta, syriac, targum, vulgate
villain cain, haman, herod, pontius pilate, snake
warriors gammadim
well ain
wilderness zin
witch endor
word amen, mene, selah
worship bibliolatry
writer elohist
BIBLIOPHILE bluestocking, bookworm, collector, reader
BIBULOUS addicted, bibacious, drinking, drunk(en), intemperate, liquorish, sot(tish), spongy, tippling, toping, wine-bibbing
person carouser, drunk, sot, toper
BICE azurite-blue, malachite-green
BICHO chigger, insect, redbug
BICKER argue, assail, attack, battle, bowl, brawl, cavil, contend, contention, contest, dispute, fight, flicker, flutter, fuss, glitter, hurry, jar, pettifog, pickeer, quarrel, quibble, quiver, skirmish, spar, sprint, squabble, tiff, war, wrangle
BICKERN anvil, beakiron
BICYCLE bike, boneshaker, jigger, mount, ornary, quad, tandem, two-wheeler, wheel
early penny-farthing
for two tandem
inventor michaux
rider cyclist, scorcher, wheelman
BID adjure, announce, ask, attempt, auction, bede, beg,

bode, buy, call, charge, cheapen, cite, clepe, command, court, declare, direct, dropvie, effort, enjoin, enjoy, entreat, estimate, express, hest, hist, instruct, invitation, invite, nap, offer(ed), order, overture, pray, present, proclaim, proffer, proposal, quotation, request, require, reveal, solicit, suggestion, summon(s), tender, try, utter, wish, woo
ale benefit, commorth
defiance resist, withstand
fair bargain, court, intend, promise, solicit, volunteer
farewell depart, take leave
in cards See CARD *game bid.*
no trick nullo
BIDDABLE amenable, compliant, docile, obedient, obliging, tractable
BIDDANCE auction, beck, behest, call, command, direction, invitation, summons
BIDDY bedmaker, char (woman), chicken, dame, dowager, fowl, fussbudget, hen, maid, matron, servant
-biddy piripiri
BIDE attend, await, bear, continue, delay, dwell, encounter, endure, face, remain, sojourn, stay, suffer, tarry, tolerate, wait, watch
BIDENS beggar-tick, cuckold, manzanilla, marigold, tickseed, spanish-needle, sunflower, water-daisy
BIDET horse, pony, sitz-bath
BIDRI biddery, bidree, bidry, pewter, tutenag
BIELD bilbie, bold(ness), confidence, courage, cozy, den, dwell, enhearten, refuge, shelter(ed)
BIEN comfortable, fine, genial, good, pleasant, prosperous, thriving
aime beloved
etre comfort, well-being
tot soon
venue welcome
BIER catafalque, cist, coffin, corpse, feretory, feretrum, frame, handbarrow, hearse, grave, litter, pyre, tabut
BIERSTUBE See TAVERN.
BIFF blow, hit, punch, strike
BIFID bipartite, divided, split

BIFURCATE bisect, branch, divide, fork, split
BIFURCATION branch, crotch, dichotomy, fork (ing) split, wye
BIG adult, august, bad, barley, baro, beefy, boasting, bold, bouncing, brimming, bulky, bumping, burly, capacious, chief, colossal, consequential, eminent, enormous, extensive, falstaffian, fat, filled, free, gaucie, gaucy, gawsie, generous, gigantic, grand(iose), great, gross, haughty, heavy, huge, humming, husky, immense, important, imposing, indulgent, kindly, king-size, large, leading, liberal, loud, magnanimous, massive, mighty, monstrous, notorious, outstanding, overflowing, plumping, pompous, powerful, pre-eminent, pregnant, pretentious, rotund, sizable, swanking, swapping, swelling, teeming, thick, thumping, vast, violent, voluminous
apple new york
ben clock, clover, solitaire
bend state tennessee
bertha cannon
bug hickory mockernut
cheese mogul, vip
comb. magni
d dallas
drink ocean, sea
-eyed astonished, impressed, wondering
-foot elephantiasis, yeti
game prize, quarry
h See HEROIN.
-hand acclaim, applause
head conceit
-hearted altruistic, charitable, free, generous, good-natured, gracious, kind, indulgent, liberal, magnanimous, open-handed
house jail, penitentiary, prison
idea aim, intention, plan, proposal, purpose
it braggart, personage
-league important, major
lick roanoke
lie propaganda
muddy mississippi
one lie, story, whopper
push attack, drive, offensive
shot biggie, biggy, brass, ce-

lebrity, fat cat, head, grandee, king pin, leader, lion, lord, macher, magnate, mogul, muckamuck, personage, power, somebody, star, tycoon, vip, wheel
show barnum and bailey, circus
sky country montana
stick despotism, force, power, terror, tyranny
stink tarrarom, terrarom
talk bluster, bragging, noise, rhetoric
ten illinois, indiana, iowa, michigan(state), minnesota, northwestern, ohio(state), purdue, wisconsin
time broadway, important, major
top barnum and bailey, circus, tent, theater
very bonzer
BIGEMINAL double, paired
BIG EYE catalufa, priacanthus, redfish
BIGGIE big shot
BIGGIN(G) building, home, house, outhouse
BIGGITY conceited
BIGHEAD electris, fish, goby, sculpin
BIGHORN aoudad, argal(i), cimarron, sheep
BIGHT angle, bay, bite, coil, corner, cove, curve, gulf, hollow, inlet, loop, noose, pocket
BIGNONIA carajura, catalpa, cat's-claw, chica, tecoma, trumpet-creeper
BIGOT cafard, fanatic, hater, mumpsimus, racist, sectarian, zealot
BIGOTED biased, hidebound, illiberal, intolerant, narrow(minded), partial, prejudiced, sectarian, unfair
BIGOTRY blind spot, discrimination, dogmatism, insularity, intolerance, littleness, meanness, narrowmindedness, pettiness, purblindness, smallness, unfairness
without broad-minded, liberal, tolerant
BIGROOT bitterroot, dogbane, manroot
BIJOU jewel, trinket
BIK aconite
BIKE beehive, bicycle, crowd, hornet's nest, storehouse, swarm

BIKH aconite
BIKINI atoll, bathing suit, trunks
BIKUKULLA bicuculla, bleeding-heart, dicentra, dutchman's-breeches
BILBERRY bearberry, blackwort, blaeberry, heathberry, vaccinium, viburnum, whortleberry, withe rod
BILBO fetter, rapier, shackle, sword
BILDAD *friend* job
BILDAR digger, excavator, servant
BILE anger, atrabile, boil, choler, gall, hump, illtemper, peevishness, spleen, venom
black gloom(iness)
comb. chol(e), cholo
cyst gall bladder
deficiency acholia
pigment bilirubin, biliverdin
BILGE billage, bouge, bulge, fail, nonsense, pump, rubbish, scum, seepage, thurrock
BILHAH *child* naphtali
husband jacob
BILIMBI camias, cucumber, kamias
BILIMENT band, headdress, lace, ornament
BILINGUAL diglot, polyglot
BILIOUS bitter, choleric, cranky, gallious, gallish, illtempered, irritable, liverish, peevish, unpleasant
BILIRUBIN *complication* kernicterus
disease jaundice
BILITIS *consort* sappho
BILK balk, cheat, cozen, deceive, defraud, delude, elude, evade, fleece, fraud, frustrate, gyp, hoax, swedge, swindle, thwart, trick
BILL account, act, advertise(ment), announcement, bank note, beak, boom, broadside, broadsword, budget, bulletin, card, caress, carte, catalogue, charge, check, chit, circular, clap, damage, debt, deed, dertrum, docket, DOLLAR, draft, dun, facture, flyer, indict, inventory, invoice, kite, LAW, list, manifest, mattock, measure, memorandum, menu, money, neb, nib, nose, note,

notice, papal-bull, pea, peck(er), pee, performance, petition, pickax, placard, point, post, poster, prescription, program, reckoning, remanet, schedule, score, shot, statement, statute, strike, tab, throw-away, voucher, waybill, weapon
anchor peak, pee
and coo court, kiss, woo
collector creditor
counterfeit stiff
5-dollar fin, vee
hooked dertrum
-like beaked
of complaint querela
of divorce get(t)
of exchange devise, hundi, sola
of fare carte, list, menu
part cere
revolutionary assignat
BILLABONG anabranch, backwater, channel, creek, slough, waterway
BILLBOARD advertisement, anchor bed, announcement, hoarding, notice, poster
BILLBUG calendra, grasseater, sitophilus, weevil
BILLET allot, appointment, ballot, bar, berth, bloom, bunk, capacity, cess, club, coalfish, document, enroll, epistle, firewood, gad, harbor, house, hut, job, letter, libbet, lodge, lodging, log, loop, missive, note, notice, office, order, pass, place, pocket, pollack, position, post, put up quarter(s), requisition, shide, sprag, stay, stick, strap, ticket
-doux capon, love-letter
soldiers' cess
BILLFISH gar, longjaws, needlefish, sailfish, saury, spearfish
BILLFOLD pocketbook, purse, wallet
BILLHOOK dhaw, knife, pawpaw, scimitar, slasher
BILLIARDS pills, trucks
ball ivory, snooker, spot
cue mace, mast
cue tip leather
cue wood arboloco
game bouchon
lawn troco
rod cue, mace
shot bricole, carambole, carom, masse, reverse-english

spin english
table rim cushion
term cue ball, eight ball, spot-barred
BILLINGSGATE abuse, fishmarket, invective, obloquy, profanity, ribaldry, scurrility, slapdash, vilification, vituperation, vulgarity
BILLINGS, JOSH henry shaw
BILLION baw-bee, milliard
-dollar grass sanwa millet
BILLIONAIRE capitalist, getty, hughes, hunt, ludwig, macarthur, milliardaire, nabob, perot
BILLIONTH *comb.* bicro
BILLOW blow, bore, breaker, bulge, cloud, comb(er), float, heave, resaca, ripple, rise, rock, roll(er), sea, surge, swell, toss, undulate, undulation, wallow, wave
BILLY baton, blackjack, bludgeon, brother, can, chap, club, comrade, cudgel, fanny, fellow, goat, jackshay, male, mate, neddy, nightstick, truncheon, weapon
blind demon, game, spirit
brighteyes germander-speedwell
-button burdock, campion, daisy, geranium, scabious
clipper bindweed, convolvulus
the kid william bonney
white's brother stitchwort
BILLYBOY barge, coaster, ketch, sloop
BILLYCOCK bowler, derby, hat, wide-awake
BILLYWIX tawny owl
BILSH brat, monster, nonentity
BIMA(H) See BEMA.
BIMBO fellow, man, slut, tramp
BIN ark, basket, bing, bleacher, box, bunker, canch, carton, case, casket, chest, coffer, crate, crib, cub, flute, frame, hamper, hutch, kench, manger, pocket, pungi, stall, trough, vina, within
-burn discolor, heat
coal bunker
fish canch, kench
BINARY binate, compounded, coupled, double,

dual, dyadic, geminate, paired, two(fold)
BIND 3 fix, gag, jam, lap, oop, sew, tie, wap, wed 4 frap, gird, gyve, hold, hoop, iron, join, knit, knot, lash, link, moor, nail, rope, stop, tape, tile, trap, yerk 5 brace, cadge, chafe, chain, cinch, dress, edder, girth, leash, marry, snake, stick, strap, thirl, truss, unite 6 adhere, attach, border, bridle, bundle, cement, cohere, commit, engage, fasten, fetter, freeze, garter, girdle, hamper, hinder, hobble, hogtie, hopple, ligate, muzzle, oblige, picket, pinion, secure, strain, string, swathe, tether, thrave, writhe 7 article, astrain, bandage, betroth, confine, connect, control, embound, enchain, grapple, manacle, shackle, swaddle, trammel 8 astringe, catenate, conclude, encircle, handcuff, innodate, ligature, obligate, restrain, restrict 9 condition, constrain, constrict, entrammel, indenture, obstringe, restringe, vinculate 10 apprentice, catenulate, hamshackle 11 predicament
by pledge gage, swear
comb. desmo
in a trapped
oneself adhere
over indenture
together astringe, cement, fag(g)ot, glue, lime, religate, seize
up astrict, bandage, bavin, bundle, kilt, truss, upband, wrap
BINDER agreement, baler, band, beam, bond(stone), bookmaker, bracer, caddis, cement, coagulant, contract, cord, cover, fillet, folder, frame, girder, girdle, harvester, header, lignin, receipt, ring, rope, tarmac, wrapper
BINDING astringent, band, bounden, braid, caddice, caddis, colligation, compulsory, cord, cover(ing), edging, faithful, fastening, fent, galloon, gard, imperative, lear, ligative, mandatory, mousing, obligatory, restraining, ribbon, rope,

stringent, stygian, tag, tape, thickening, valid, webbing, wrapper, yapp
dress fent
fabric selvage
gold bisset
limp yapp
machine baler
BINDLE bedroll, bing, bundle, package
-stiff hobo, nomad, tramp, vagabond
BINDWEB neuroglia, stroma
BINDWEED bearbine, bellbine, bilderdykia, billyclipper, bittersweet, bryonia, bryony, convolvulus, cornbine, creeper, hellweed, lonicera, milkmaid, polygonum, senecio, sheepbine, smilax, solanum, soldanella, tamus, tievine, withywind, woodbine
BINDWITH clematis, traveler's-joy
BING bedroll, bin(dle), cherry, heap, leave, pile
BINGE bat, blow, bow, bust, carousal, cringe, party, soak, souse, spray, spree
BINGO bam, bang, beano, brandy, game, keno, lotto, ring, screeno, tango
BINK bank, bench, rack, shelf, wasps nest
BINNACLE binocle, bittacle, channel, compass, millpond, millrace, needle, pyx, stream
BINOMIAL dionym
BINT daughter, girl, woman
BINTANGOR poon
BINTURONG arctictis, bearcat, civet
BIOGRAPHY chorology, chronicle, history, life, memoir, recount, vita
saints' acta sanctorum, hagiography
BIOLOGICAL antigen, antitoxin, biotic(al), drug, medicinal, pharmaceutical, serum, vaccine
class genera, genus, species
comb. anatomic(o)
factor gene, idant
structure isogen
BIOLOGIST See LIFE *scientist.*
BIOLOGY See LIFE *science.*
BIONDELLO *master* lucentio
BIOPLAST micella, micelle
BIOSIS life, vitality
BIOTA flora and fauna

BIOTECHNOLOGY ergonomics

BIOTITE anomite, caswellite, meroxene, mica

BIPARTITE divided, joint, shared

BIRCH ainus, alder, ansu, beat, betula, birk(en), bundle, cane, canoe, carpinus, flog, gumbo-limbo, hornbeam, punish, rod, stick, swish, switch, tawhai, tree, whip

ament chat

bark canoe

camphor betulin(ol)

-leaf mahogany hardtack

man schoolmaster

partridge grouse

BIRD, BIRD'S airplane, amniote, aves, avifauna, bomber, boo, bronx cheer, chap, chick, chotchke(leh), dandy, dotard, faygeleh, feathered friend, fellow, fowl, gink, girl(friend), guy, kate, mag, man, nester, ornis, plane, raspberry, ridicule, shoot, shuttlecock, singer, tchotchke(leh), tsatske(leh), wing, youngster

accipitrine See *of prey*, below.

adjutant argala, hurgila, marabou, stork

alcidine auk, guillemot, murre, puffin

aquatic alcatras, auk, avocet, baptornis, bidcock, coot, crane, dabchick, dipper, diver, duck, flamingo, gallinule, gaviformes, godwit, goose, grebe, gull, her(o)n, ibis, jacana, loon, osprey, ousel, pelican, penguin, puffin, rail, snakebird, snipe, sora, stilt, stork, swan, tern(e)

aquiline eagle

arboreal curassow

bait shrap(e)

baker hornero

beak bec, bill, cordylanus, neb, nib, lorum, rostrum

beak base cere

beak covering rhamphotheca

beak edge tomium

biblical gier, raven

bill See *beak*, above.

black See BLACKBIRD.

blue See BLUEBIRD.

bolt burbolt, quarrel

bone deformity synsacrum

bread sedum, stonecrop

breast pectus

brier dogrose

brilliant plumage jacamar, jalep, kirombo, minivet, oriole, parrot, peacock, pheasant, tanager, tody, toucan, trogon

butcher shrike

cactus slipper-plant

cage aviary, devil's-box, dice-box, chuck(-a-)luck, paddock, pinjra, volary, volery

call cackle, carol, caw(k), chatter, cheep, chirk, chirp, chirr(up), chitter, chuck(le), clack, clang, clink, cluck, cock-a-doodle(-doo), coo, croak, cronk, crow, crunk, cuckoo, gabble, gaggle, gobble, guggle, honk, hoo(t), jug, peep, pip(e), pluck, quack, roll, sing, squawk, trill, twee(t), twit(ter), warble, weet, whistle, yap

carnivorous raptor

carrion buzzard, urubu, vulture

catcher clapnet, fowler, limer

changed to aesacus, picus

cherry dogwood, eggberry, hackwood, hagberry, padius

clamatovial baker, becard, tityra

class aves

comb. avi, orni, ornith(o)

coraciform See *non-passerine*, below.

corvine crow, daw, magpie, nutcracker, raven, rook, waybung

covering down, feathers, indumentum

covert(s) tectrices, tectrix

covey See *group*, below.

crane-like chunga, grus, wader

crest copple(crown), tuft

crested coppy, hoatzin, hoopoe, kagu, kinglet, topknot

crop ingluvies, maw

crying limpkin, ramage

cuculoid ani

decorative peacock, peafowl

diving alcid, auk, dopper, ducker, goldeneye, grayling, grebe, loon, murre, pelican, plungeon, whistler

dog hunter, investigate, retriever, setter

domesticated poultry

down comb. ptilo

ear part columella

-eating aviculous

edible capon, chicken, drake, duck(ling), fryer, gander, goose, gosling, guinea, hen, peacock, pigeon, poult(ry), roaster, rooster, squab, turkey

egg collector oologist

egg study oology

extinct aepyornis, apatornis, archaeornis, auk(let), didus, dodo, gastornis, hespornis, jib(i), kiwi, mamo, moa, offbird, roc, rukh

-eye briza, comprehensive, cuckooflower, cursory, fabric, general, gilia, hasty, maple, nemophila, panoramic, plant, primrose, primula, superficial, toweling, veronica

fabulous aboulomri, akbaba, fum, ganza, hansa, huma, kerkes, offbird, phoenix, roc, rook, rukh, simurg(h)

false wing alula

feather quill

feather area pteryla

female hen, jenny

fictitious jayhawk, phoenix

finch-like canary, chewink, grosbeak, palila, serin, tanager

fish-catching cormorant, crabier, osprey, sea eagle

flightless apteryx, callow, cassowary, dodo, emu, gor(b), horlin(g), ihi, kagu, kiwi, moa, moorup, nandu, nestler, notornis, ostrich, penguin, ratite, rhea, roc, solitaire, weka

flock See *group*, below.

flower oswego-tea

fly-catching redstart, solitaire

flying backward hummingbird, swallow

food ant egg, seeds

-foot clover baby's-slipper, bloomfell, butter-jag, cat's-claw, fenugreek, ornithopus, serradella, trigonella

foot covering podotheca

-foot trefoil See *-foot clover*, above.

foot webbing palama

frigate ioa, iwa, tropic

fringilline crossbill, grassquit, longspur, redpoll, siskin

frog-mouth podargue
fruit-eating coly, toucan
full-fledged fligger
gallinaceous curassow, francolin, peacock, perdicine, phasianid, rasor, turkey
gallows hempie, hempy
game bustard, colima, dove, duck, flapper, grouse, pheasant, ptarmigan, quail, snipe
genus alca, anser, apatornis, certhia, icterus, moris, otis, phaeton, pitta, rhea, sterna, sula
giant aepyornis
go-away kwe
gooney albatross
group aerie, bank, bevy, brood, cast, covert, covey, drove, flight, flock, gaggle, litter, nye, plump, sord, spring, volary
gruciform coot, crake, gallinule, rail, weka
head pileum
honey-eating florisugent, iao, manuao, noho, tui
horn-headed kamichi
horny-beak epithema
house aviary, box, brooder, cote, nest, nid, ornithon
humming See HUMMING-BIRD.
hunting falcon
insectivorous flycatcher, owl, peewee, tody, vireo
-in-the-bush prickly-poppy
jaw part mala
-killing avicide
kind 3 ani, daw, ern, jay, nun, pie, qua, tit 4 coot, crow, dove, erne, gled, guan, huia, ibis, jacu, kago, kahu, kaki, kala, kite, koko, kulm, lark, mall, monk, moro, osel, pape, quit, rook, ruff, shag, stag, stib, taha, tern, tody, wren 5 ajaja, boonk, brant, chuck, crane, egret, finch, glede, goose, hobby, junco, mavis, oriel, pewee, pewit, raven, robin, sacer, saker, snipe, stilt, terek, twite, vireo 6 bulbul, dunlin, falcon, godwit, guinea, hoopoe, jacana, jaypie, linnet, loriot, martin, oriole, pappia, phoebe, plover, shrike, thrush, trogon, waybug, whewer, wranny, yawper 7 babbler, bittern, bluejay, bustard, buzzard, catbird, courlan,

flicker, grackle, halcyon, irrisor, jacamar, jackdaw, minivet, ortolan, peacock, quiller, sakeret, skylark, sparrow, starnel, swallow, tanager, tinamou, warbler, waxwing, whiskey 8 amadavat, bargoose, bluebird, boatbill, bobolink, bobwhite, chepster, cocorico, firetail, garganay, grosbeak, killdeer, oxpecker, pheasant, poorwill, preacher, starling, swamphen, tapacola, titmouse, trembler, umbrette, whinchat, woodcock 9 capercail, chickadee, goldfinch, mallemuck, partridge, sandpiper 10 chiffchaff, meadowlark, turtledove 11 hummingbird, mockingbird
king of eagle
knee suffraso
lamellirostral duck, goose, flamingo, merganser, swan
lanioid shrike
large bustard, condor, curassow, curlew, eagle, em(e)u, guan, jabiru, kite, kiwi, megapod, moa, ostrich, peacock, pelican, rhea, roc, seriema, shoebill, turkey, willet
largest lammergeir
lark-like pipit
legbone tibiotarsus
leg ring verval
-life avifauna, ornis
-like agile, anserine, anserous, avian, avicular, fragile, gallinaceous, goosy, light, quick, ornithoid, rasorial
limicoline avocet, avoset, capella, glaredo, plover, pratincole, redshank, snipe, stilt
long-billed courlan, limpkin, pelican, snipe, toucan
long-legged avocet, avoset, crane, curlew, flamingo, heron, seriema, snipe, sora, stilt, stork, trumpeter, wader
long-necked agami, crane, goose, ostrich, swan, trumpeter
long-tailed thrasher
loon-like grebe
louse mallophaga, menopon, philopterus, trinoton
lyre bullen-bullen

male chanticleer, cob, cock, drake, gander, rooster, tom
mantle stragulum
marsh alca, alle, arrie, auk(let), bittern, guillemot, halcyon, murre, silt, snipe, sora
membrane allantois
mimic mocking bird, thrasher
mound leipoa, megapod(e)
mouse coly, shrike
name meaning ava, avis
neck part auchenium
nest nidus
nest fungus nidularia
nest plant indian pipe
nest study caliology
nocturnal goatsucker, nightingale, nightjar, owl, potoo, thick-knee
noisy crow, pist
non-passerine bee-eater, hoopoe, hornbill, kingfisher, motmot, roller, tody, trogon
northern auk, gannet, puffin
of freedom eagle
of ill-omen raven
of love eagle
of paradise apodis, apus, bowerbird, canary-flower, cardinal-flower, cincinnurpus, heteroma, lophorhina, lyrebird, manucode, oswego tea, poinciana, regent, riflebird, spiraltail, strelitzia
of passage migrator, rollingstone, transient, wanderer
of peace dove
of prey accipiter, accipitrine, buteo, buzzard, condor, eagle(t), elan(e)t, falcon, glead, glede, goshawk, gyrfalcon, harrier, hawk, kestrel, kite, musket, owl, peregrine, saker, stooper, vulture
of the year hornotine
of wonder phoenix
oldest known archaeopteryx
one-year-old annotine
oscine accentor, artamus, bowerbird, bunyah, buphaga, chat, crow, drongo, flowerpecker, lark, oriole, peppershrike, pipit, tanager, thickhead, timalia, titmouse, trembler, vireo, wagtail, warbler, whistler, wren-thrush
ostrich-like cassowarie, em(e)u, moa, rhea

parrot-like budgereegah, budgerygah
parson poe, tue, tui
part of body alula, ambiens, auchenium, bill, breast, cere, crissum, crown, gastraeum, gigerium, knee, larum, lora, lore, mala, neb, nib, pecten, pectines, pileum, pinion, rosta, scapular, syrinx, tail, wing
passerine ant-thrush, campanero, chat, chatterer, coachwhip, cock-of-the-rock, cuckoo-shrike, drepanid, drongo, falconet, finch, gnateater, grallina, hoopoe, irena, manakin, palmchat, parid, penthestes, pitta, quit, rock-wren, sharpbill, sparrow, starling, starnel, sturnid, swallow, tanager, tapacula, thrush, titmouse, waxwing, woodhewer, xenicus
passerine family cotingidae
pelican-like solan
pepper capsicum, lepidium
pert. avian, avicular, avin(e), ornithic, ornithologic, oscine, volucrine
pink flamingo
plant canary-flower, heterotoma, oswego-tea
plover-like drome, lapwing
plumage ptilosis
plumed egret
pox sorehead
predatory cormorant, falcon, kite, owl, shrike, yager
psittaceous parrot
puff barbet
quail-like seed-snipe, tinamou, turnix
raptores eagle, hawk, owl, vulture
rare lulu, whooping crane
rasorial scratcher
ratite apteryx, cassowary, em(e)u, moa, ostrich, rhea
-rearing aviculture
reed bobolink
reptile-like archaeoptery
running courser, roadrunner
sacred ben(n)u, cuntur, ibis, stork
science neossology, oology, ornithology
sea albatross, auk, booby, cahow, cormorant, eider, ern(e), fulmar, gannet, gony, goony, gull, hagdon, osprey, pelican, petrel, puffin, scaup, scoter, shear-

bill, shearwater, skua, smew, solan, sula, tern
shore auk, avocet, avoset, calicojacket, curlew, gull, petrel, plover, rail, ree, ruff, sandpiper, snipe, sora, stilt, tattler, turnstone, wader, willet, wrybill, yellowlegs
singing See SONGBIRD.
singing organ syrinx
skin apterium
small chat, cocorico, creeper, dick(e)y, didapper, gnatsnap, humming, linnet, peggy, pipit, shorelark, siskin, sparrow, starling, tit(lark), tody, tomtit, tydie, vireo, wheatear, wren
snake annhinga, thelotornis
snarer limer
song trill
spider mygale
stitch ihi
stomach crop, gigerium, maw, ventriculus
stork-like heron, ibis, pelargic
student ornithologist
swallow-like hirundine, martin, martlet, swift, tern
swift-footed courser
swimming See *aquatic,* above.
talking crow, mag(g), magpie, mina, myna(h), parrot
tattler telltake
thigh muscle ambiens
3-toed rhea, stilt, turnix
timaline rock-warbler, tit-babbler, whistling-thrush
toe, part loma
-tongue joint-grass, maple, scarlet pimpernel, stitchwort, strelitzia, tree
toothed ichthyornis
tropical ani, barbet, bos(a)n, guan, jacamar, jacana, jalap, koae, longtail, manakin, motmot, saltator, toco, tody, toucan, trogon, wigtail
turkey-like curassow, leipoa
unfledged babbling, eyas, gorlin, nestling, squab
unsightly spinturnix
upupoid hoopoe
voracious cormorant
wading avocet, avoset, bittern, boatbill, crab-plover, crane, curler, egret, flamingo, godwit, gralatores, ibis, jacana, limpkin, rail, sandpiper, shoebill,

snipe, sora, stilt, stork, tern, umber, umbrette
water See *aquatic,* above.
wattle caruncle
web-footed albatross, avocet, avoset, drake, duck, gander, goose, swan
whidah veuve
white-tailed egret, ern(e)
wing joint flexure
wingless apteryx, kiwi, weka
wing part alula
-witted flighty, shallow, silly
-woman aviatress, aviatrice, aviatrix
woodpecker-like jacamar
world featherdom
young birdikin, chick, flapper, fledgling, gull, nestler, nestling, piper, poult, pullus, squab
BIRDBRAIN dolt, dunce, fool, scatterbrain
BIRDCLAPPER scarecrow
BIRDLIME adhesive, cleavers, glue, snare, trap, viscum
source aulu
BIRDMAN ace, aviator, flyer, fowler, ornithologist
BIRDS aves, avifauna, polymyodi, praecoces
BIRDSEED groundsel, hemp, millet, phalaris, senecio
seedeater chickadee, grosbeak, junco
BIRI beedi, bidi, cigarette
BIRL move, rattle, revolve, rotate, spend, spin, toss, whirr
BIRLE carouse, drink, pour
BIRLING *game* roleo
BIRMA calaba
BIRMINGHAM brummagem
BIRR blow, burr, emphasis, energy, force, impetus, push, sound, thrust, vigor, whirr, wind
BIRSE bristle, irritation, rage, temper
BIRSHAKING *kingdom* gomorrah
BIRSLE broil, scorch, toast
BIRTH accouchement, ancestry, bear(ing), beginning, blessed event, blood, borning, childbed, confinement, creation, delivery, descent, fall, family, genesis, geniture, hatching, heredity, heritage, line(age), lying-in, nascency, natality, nativity, origin, parentage, parturition, start, travail

after postnatal, postpartum
before prenatal
false sooterkin
feast bedale
feast food blithemeat
flower arostolochia, bathroot, bathwort
flower, january carnation
flower, february primrose
flower, march violet
flower, april daisy
flower, may lily-of-the-valley
flower, june rose
flower, july sweet pea
flower, august gladiolus
flower, september aster
flower, october dahlia
flower,' november chrysanthemum
flower, december holly, poinsettia
goddess genetyllis, lucina, parca, taweret
illegitimate, mark bar sinister
new regeneration, renaissance, renascence
pert. natal, primogenitive
test agpar
BIRTHDAY anniversary, borning
ode genethliacon
pert. genethliac(al)
suit altogether, skin
BIRTHMARK blain, blemish, mole, naeve, n(a)evus, port-wine stain, spiloma, strawberry
BIRTHPLACE brooder, cradle, hatchery, hotbed, incubator, nest, nidus, nursery, rookery
BIRTHRATE fertility, natality
BIRTHRIGHT appenage, bequest, coparcenary, coparceny, descent, entail, gavelking, heir(dom), hereditament, heritage, inheritance, patrimony, perquisite, prerogative, primogeniture, privilege, reversion
BIRTHROOT arostolochia, asarum, bathroot, bethflower, bloodynose, clematite, deathroot, dishcloth, squawroot, trillium
BIRTHSTONE *january* garnet
february amethyst
march aquamarine, bloodstone, jasper
april diamond, sapphire
may agate, emerald
june agate, alexandrite, car-

nelian, cornelian, emerald, moonstone, pearl
july onyx, ruby, turquoise
august carnelian, cornelian, peridot, sardonyx
september chrysolite, sapphire
october aquamarine, beryl, opal, rozircon, tourmaline
november topaz
december ruby, turquoise, zircon
BIRTHWORT asarum, birthroot, guaco
BIS again, duplicate, encore, linen, refrain, repeat, repetition, replica, twice
BISACODYL dulcolax
BISAYAN See VISAYAN.
BISCAY *bay city* biarritz
island oleran, yeu
native basque
port bilbao
BISCUIT abernathy, bake, bath oliver, bisk, bisque, bread, bun, cake, cookie, cracker, cracknel, dodger, galette, graham cracker, hardtack, hardtommy, panal, pantile, parfait, pitcher plant, pretzel, ratafee, ratafia, roll, rusk, scone, simnel, snap, soda cracker, wafer, zwieback
beef dodger
brittle cracknel
broken dunderfunk
color almond, doe, pawnee, tan
cutter punch-barrel
leaves greenbrier, smilax
ship's bonne-bouche, crackerhash, hard-dog, pantile
sweet cookie, nabisco, ratafia, rusk
BISCUITROOT camass, cogswellia
BISECT cleave, cross, cut, divide, fork, halve, intersect, separate, split
BISEXUAL androgyne, androgynous, epicene, hermaphrodite
BISHOP, BISHOP'S abba, angel, antistes, beverage, burn, bustle, churchman, clergyman, confirm, denis, ecclesiastic, eparch, epus, exarch, hatto, inspector, lawn, magpie, metropolitan, ordinary, overseer, papa, pontifex, pope, prelate, presul, priest, primate, sanction, tulchan, weaverbird

anglican magpie
apron gremial
assistant coadjutor, verger
burned at stake latimer
buskin caliga
cap berretta, hura, miter, mitre(lla)
chair apse, bema, cathedra, faldistory, faldstool, see, tribune
chair, pert. cathedral
chess alfin, alphin, alphyn, archer
coptic anba
cotton lawn
court consistorial
1st year revenue annat
garment See robe, below.
glove guantus
group bench
hat barrenwort
leaves water-betony
murder episcopicide
mythical golias
office dataria
of hippo augustine
of rome pope
pert. lawny
precursor alfil
pursued by mice hatto
ray obispo
robe alb, chimar, chimer(e), cope, dalmatic, gremial, omophorion, rochet, tunicle
room accubitus
seat See chair, above, and BISHOPRIC.
servant familiar
shoe campagus
staff baculus, cambuca, crook, crosier
stocking buskin, caliga
title abba, amba, anba, excellency, prelate, primate
wig rockcress
worship episcopolatry
BISHOPRIC apse, bema, diocese, episcopacy, episcopate, see
BISHOPWEED am(m)eos, ammi, bolewort, bullwort, goutweed, khella, mint, toothpick, william
BISHOPWORT love-in-a-mist, migella, water-mint, wood-betony
BISKOP brusher, steenbras
BISLEY solitaire
BISMARCK *archipelago islands* admiralty, new britain, new ireland
brown bunny, havana
BISMER disgrace, mock, scorn, shame

BISMUTH marcasite, tinglass, wismuth
compound atelestite, badenite, bismanol, eulytite
salt benzobis
source bismite
BISON aurochs, bonasus, bovine, bubalus, buffalo, bugle, gaur, gayal, mithan, syncerus, tsine, wild ox, wisent
BISQUE biscuit, bisk, ceramics, ice cream, point, soup
BISTORT adderwort, astrologe, blueweed, buckwheat, patience, snakeweed, snakewort
BISTRO bar, boite, cafe, estaminet, nightclub, pub, restaurant, saloon, tavern, wineshop
BISULCATE cleft, cloven (-hoofed), split
BIT, BITS 3 ace, act, cut, dab, dot, fid, fig, gru, jot, nip, ort, pip, pod, rag, rap, tag, wee 4 atom, baud, bite, blob, cast, chip, coin, curb, dash, dite, doit, dole, dose, drab, dram, drib, drop, fico, flaw, grue, haet, hair, hang, hate, hoot, iota, item, lick, mite, mote, orra, part, role, slip, snap, snip, spot, tate, tiny, tool, whit 5 auger, beans, blade, canch, check, crumb, dight, drill, fleck, grain, groat, minim, minor, patch, pezzo, piece, point, scrap, shard, share, sherd, shive, shred, snack, snede, snick, spark, speck, sprig, steek, taste, touch, trace, wight 6 amount, bittie, cantle, dablet, detail, gobbet, morsel, nibble, nicety, number, pelham, pellet, period, pickle, pitsel, screed, shadow, shiver, sippet, sliver, smidge, smitch, snatch, stitch, stiver, tatter, tittle, trifle 7 bridoon, cantlet, dribble, fritter, glimmer, granule, handful, harness, modicum, morceau, pallion, portion, remnant, routine, scatche, smatter, smidgen, smither, snaffle, snippet, soupcon, toddick, traneen 8 flyspeck, fraction, fragment, minutiae, molecule, nearness, nutshell, particle, pittance, quantity,

scuddick, smitchen, somewhat, splinter, spoonful, twopenny, victuals 9 suspicion 10 restrainer, scrimption, smithereen, sprinkling, supporting, thimbleful
¼ gill
2 quarter
4 forbes, half-dollar
and pieces gubbing(s), oddments, orts
by bit by degrees, gradually, piecemeal
cutting chaser
drill crown
fippeny sixpence
horse's bastonet, cannon, kevel, pelham, scatch, snaffle, snode
least fico, fig, ghost, groat, hang, lick, rap, rizzom
part walk-on
small bittock, bleb, dribble, glimmer, jot, lick, rap, remnant, scrinch, smatter, soupcon, speck, spunk, stitch, toddick, touch
thick unbelievable
tuppenny twopence
BITCH beef, bellyache, bick, botch, brood, cheat, complain(t), confuse, dog, female, grouse, gyp, slattern, slut, snafu, spoil, trollop, virago
BITE 3 cud, cut, eat, jaw, nip 4 bait, cham, chaw, chew, edge, etch, food, gash, gnap, gnaw, grab, grip, hold, hurt, knap, meal, pain, pang, quid, rive, snap, take, tear 5 anger, catch, chack, chamm, champ, cheat, chomp, clamp, drive, erode, gnash, hanch, munch, piece, pinch, punch, seize, sever, share, slice, smart, snack, sting, tooth, trick, wheal, wound 6 adhere, crunch, impact, morsel, nibble, noshen, pierce, savage 7 corrode, craunch, deceive, impress, munchet, portion, scrunch, slander 8 acerbity, acrimony, lacerate, macerate, mouthful, puncture, strength 9 denticate, occlusion, penetrate, perforate, sharpness 12 incisiveness
one's nails fret, stew, worry
small munchet
the hand that feeds betray, injure, malign
BITING acerb, ac(r)id, acri-

monious, bitter, bleak, caustic, censorious, clearcut, cold, crisp, cruel, cutting, discourteous, hoar, hot, incisive, keen, mordant, morsure, nipping, nippy, painful, penetrating, piercing, poignant, pungent, quick, racy, sarcastic, scalding, scathing, severe, shrewd, smarting, snell, stinging, stingy, subacid, teethy, trenchant, tweaky, wound
clematis traveler's-joy
dragon tarragon
gnat midge, punkie
knotweed water-pepper
one's flesh autophagia
one's nails phaneromania
BITO agialid, balanites, balm, hajilij, zachun
BITT block, bollard, knight, post, rangehead, wrap
BITTER acerb(ate), acerbic, acid(ulous), acre, acrid, acrimonious, aigre, alum, amara, amer, angry, asarum, aspen(sive), aspre, astringent, austere, bask, bilious, biting, bleak, blistering, caustic, choleric, cold, crabbed, cruel, cutting, disagreeable, distasteful, distressing, dyspeptic, exceedingly, extremely, fervent, fierce, furious, galling, grievous, griping, hard, harsh, hating, hostile, incisive, irate, jaundiced, keen, malicious, mara, negative, nipping, painful, picric, piercing, piquant, poignant, pungent, relentless, rough, rude, ruthless, salt, sarcastic, sardonic, scornful, severe, sharp, sore, sour(tempered), stinging, tart, unpleasant, vinegarish, virulent
almond badam, benzaldehyde
apple colocynth
as gall, soot
ash evonymus, quassia, wahoo
bark alstonia, cascara
bit smallpox
buttons tanacetum, tansy
clover yellowtop
comb. picrin, picro
cress cardamine
cucumber colocynth

cup affliction, disappointment, woe
dock petasites, rumex
earth magnesia
-*ender* diehard, extremist
fitch ers, vicia
gentian baldmoney, spicknel
gourd colocynth
grass colicroot
head calico bass, golden shiner
name meaning mara, mari(e), mary, moll(y), moya, omar, poll(y)
oak blackjack, cerris
orange bigarade
pecan water-hickory
pill affliction, defeat, disappointment, disaster, humiliation, rejection
pit baldwin-spot, stippen
rot anthracnose, apple-canker
spar dolomite
trefoil bogbean, bogmyrtle, buckbean
vetch black pea, ers, lathyris, vicia
wintergreen chimaphila, pipsissewa
BITTERBLAIN vandellia
BITTERBLOOM centaury
BITTERBUR colt'sfoot
BITTERBUSH bearoak, blackjack, picramnia, snakeroot
BITTERHEAD calico-bass, shiner
BITTERN bitore, blitter, bogblitter, bogbull, bogjumper, boonk, botaurus, bottlebird, bumble, bummle(r), bump, butor, buttal, dunkadoo, ericius, gruiform, heron, kakkak, longneck, mosshammer, stakedriver, weaverbird
cry bill
flock sedge, siege
BITTERNESS acerbity, ache, acor, acridity, acrimony, amaritude, amarity, anguish, animosity, asperity, atter, bad blood, bile, choler, cold, enmity, fell, fervency, gall, hate, hostility, malevolence, malice, marah, pain, rancor, resentment, rue, severity, smart, sorrow, virulence, wormwood
BITTERNUT hickory, pignut
BITTERROOT dogbane, lewisia, tobaccoroot

BITTERS aigre, amer, angostura, c(h)amomile, flavoring, tonic
pert. amaroidal
BITTERSWEET bindweed, celastrus, chocolate, dogwood, dulcamara, fellen, felonwood, fevertwig, lobster, nightshade, solanum, tether-devil, waxwork, withywind, wolfberry
BITTERWEED helenium, horseweed, leptilon, ragweed, sneezeweed
BITTERWOOD paradise-tree, quassia, wahoo
BITTERWORT dandelion, felwort, gentian
BITUMEN alchitran, alkitran, asphalt, carbene, congo, elaterite, naptha, pitch, slime, tar
shale bat
BITWISE responsive, tractable
BIVALVE anomia, brachiopod, clam, cockle, diatom, mollusk, mussel, nuculid, oyster, pandora, pinna, scallop, spat, toheroa, unio
fossil palaeoconcha
hinge articulus, cardo
marine ark-shell, nucula, nuculid, toheroa, tridacna, xylophaga, xylotrya
mollusk anisomyarian
tropical iphigenie
BIVOUAC assemble, camp, encamp(ment), etape, gather, rest, shelter, watch
BIXA anatto, arnatto, orellin
BIZARRE absurd, antic(al), curious, d(a)edal, deranged, distorted, eccentric, exotic, extravagant, extreme, fanciful, fantastic, garish, gauche, grotesque, kitsch, odd, outlandish, outre, quaint, queer, ridiculous, rococo, strange, uncomfortable, unusual, weird, wild
BIZET *opera* carmen, pecheurs de perles
BJARMALAND nifl(e)heim
BLAB babble, betray, blart, blate, blow, chat(ter), cheep, chin, clack, clatter, disclose, divulge, GOSSIP, inform(er), klap, nark, nonsense, peach, prate, prattle, rat, reveal, sell out, sing, snitch, spill the beans,

squeal, stool, taletelling, talk, tattle, tell, testify
-*mouth* busybody, informer, meddler, tattler
BLACK 3 bad, dhu, ink, jet, mel, sad, wan **4** calo, crow, dark, dour, ebon, evil, foul, inky, noir, piky, sloe, soil, soot **5** colly, cruel, dingy, dirty, dusky, ebony, funky, gypsy, murky, noire, raven, sable, shine, sooty, sully, swart, tarry **6** atrous, cloudy, dismal, gloomy, inkish, morose, murrey, pitchy, sinful, smooch, soiled, sombre, sullen, tragic, wicked **7** abaiser, baneful, colored, doleful, extreme, harmful, hateful, hostile, inhuman, melanic, nigrine, piceous, shvartz, stained, swarthy, unclean **8** devilish, fiendish, funereal, horrible, infernal, mournful, mourning, sinister, tragical **9** atrocious, monstrous, nefarious, shvartzer **10** calamitous, deliverate, depressing, disastrous, forbidding, traitorous, villainous **11** inexcusable, pessimistic, treacherous **12** dishonorable
alloy niello
amber jet, labdanum
and blue bruised, discolored, ecchymotic, livid
and blue spot bruise, ecchymosis, mouse, shiner
and tan constable, terrier
and white grizzle(d), patrol car, print, writing
archangel angelica, horehound
art alchemy, burglary, conjuration, evil, magic, necromancy, sorcery, witchcraft, wizardry
as coal, crow, ink
ash box-elder. eucalyptus, hoopwood, mulberry
bass achigan, growler, huron, ochigan, trout
bead cat's claw
beech ironwood, leatherjacket
-*bellied sandpiper* dunlin
bent foxtail, switch grass
-*berried* heath crowberry
-*blooded* atrabilious, melancholy, moody
bone spodium
bream tarwhine

-browed forbidding, gloomy, morose, scowling
brownish lava
buck antelope, sasin
bully sapodilla
bunch grass galleta
cabbage tree melanodendron
calla arum, solomon's lily
canker ink disease, melanosis
cat fisher, omen
centaury knapweed
cinnamon bayberry, pimenta
cod beshow, bishow, sablefish
cohosh actaea, baneberry, bugbane, sanicle, wild ginger
comb. afro, ater, atro, mel(a), melan(e)(o)
couch grass foxtail, rhode island bent
country midlands
crappie calico-bass
croaker roncador
cushion zafu
dammer canarium, resin
damp chokedamp, miasma, styth(e), vapor
dance cakewalk, calinda, juba, rhumba, ringshout
death epidemic, plague, typhus
diamond coal, oil
dog despondency, melancholy, blues
dot dartrose
draft assi, cathartic, ilex, senna
drink ya(u)pon
drongo king crow
-eared pondfish blue-gill, bream
earth ampelite, cannel coal, chernozem, mold
elder hackberry
eye bruise, cowpea, disgrace, rebuff, scandal, setback, shame, stigma
-eyed bean cowpea
-eyed susan bladder-ketmie, coneflower, gaillardia, jequirity, ketmie, rudbeckia, thunbergia
eyes sunfish
fellow yammadji
fever kala-azar, typhus
forest schwarzwald
friar dominican
greenish corbeau
grouper aguaji, bonaci, jewfish, garrupa, mero, warsaw
guillemot cutty, dovekey, puffinet, scrabe(r), tyste

gum hornpipe, stinkwood, tupelo
hag sooty-shearwater
hand camorra, la mano nera
harry sea-bass
hazel hop-hornbeam
-hearted corrupt, malevolent, malicious
hole dungeon, lockup, penitentiary, prison, solitary
horehound archangel, henbit
horse cycleptus, sucker(el)
ironwood ax(e)master
ivory abaiser
jack billy club, john logan, john pershing, twenty-one
land egypt, texas
larch larix, tamarack
lead graphite, plumbago
leader abernathy, brooke, brown, carmichael, chisholm, cleaver, jackson, king, malcolm-x, marshall, muhammed ali, newton, powell, randolph, seale, stokes, wilkins, young
-letter gothic, inauspicious, old english, out-of-date, unfortunate, unlucky
ling calluna, heather
linn cucumber-tree
-list ban, boycott, censor, ostracize, veto
magic diablerie, necromancy, sorcery, witchcraft
magic substance hellbroth
mamba dendraspis, snake
mangrove courida
margate grunt, pompon
maria coal box, paddy wagon, patrol car, queen of spades, shell
mark demerit, stigma
market illegal, racket, underground
maul almond-willow, salix
maupa pittosporum
medic hop, nonesuch, shamrock, smut-grass, trefoil
mercury poison ivy
mica biotite
mitcham peppermint
-mouthed foul-speaking, slanderous
muslim leader elijah muhammed
muzzle dartars
neb carrion-crow, scab
nightshade blueberry, duscle, huckleberry, moonshade, morel, solanum, trompillo, wonderberry

nonesuch hop clover, shamrock
note a sharp
oldwife triggerfish
olive oxhorn
organization action, black muslim, core, naacp, operation breadbasket, sclc, urban league
-out amnesia, anoxia, censor (ship), conceal, darken, darkness, faint, falter, game, hearts, obscure, skit, suppression, swoon, unconsciousness
ox misfortune
pagoda site kanarak, konarak
pan hoddle, manavelins
panther battle cry right on
perch blackbass, seabass, tripletail
pert. ebon(y), negrine
pilot cockeye, rudderfish
prince edward
pudding blood sausage
-purple aubergine
rod usher
rush piassava
sally eucalyptus, gum, muzzlewood
sampson coneflower, echinacea
-sander beachcomber, goldminer
sap melaxuma
sassafras oliver's bark
sea pontus euxinus
sea arm azof, azov
sea city batum, odessa
sea country cimmeria, circassia, crimea, thrace
sea devil ceratiid
sea peninsula crimea
sea, pert. euxine, pontic
sea port anapa, balaklava, odessa, sochi, trebizond, varna, yalta
sea, river to bug, danube, dnepr, dnieper, dniester, don, ingur, kuban, phasis, prut, rion
sea strait bosporus
sea tribe abkhas, jagyzes, sarmatian
separatist movement black muslims, nation of islam
shank lanas
sheep deviate, disgrace, reprobate, scapegrace
shirt fascist
skimmer cutwater, shearbill
soap knapweed, scabious
speck dartrose

spice blackberry
spot anthracnose, scab
-spotted trout cut-throat
spurge fluxweed
storm karaburan
swallower chiasmadon
tern darr, starn
-tie semiformal, tuxedo
toner aspergillin, lampblack
turnip lion's-leaf
twinberry honeysuckle
vulture corbie, urubu, zopilote
walnut juglans, nogal
widow latrodectus, pokomoo, spider
wrack rockweed
BLACKAMOOR bleck, cattail, ethiopian, morian
BLACKBALL ballot, debar, deny, disbar, eliminate, exclude, negate, ostracize, pill, pip, rule out, suspend, thumbs down, veto
BLACKBEARD buccaneer, edward teach, pirate
BLACKBELLY herring, pomolobus
BLACKBERRY agawam, bilberry, bramble, bumblekite, crowberry, dewberry, dogrose, lawton, mulberry, pennacook, raspberry, rosacean, rufus
bush more
disease cane-gall
BLACKBIRD agelaius, amsel, ani, ara, blackie, blacky, coll(e)y, cowbird, crotophaga, crow, cuckoo, darr, daw, grackle, jackdaw, kanaka, kidnap, maizer, merl(e), myna, ossel, ousel, ouzel, raven, redwing, rook, thrush, troopial, turdus, woofell
dish pie
BLACKBIRDER kidnapper, slavetrader
BLACKBOARD chalkboard, slate
trough chalkrail
BLACKBUTT box, eucalyptus
BLACKCAP cattail, chickadee gull, haybird, jackstraw, mockbird, raspberry, stonechat, sylvia, titmouse, typha, warbler
BLACKCOAT clergyman, ecclesiastic, preacher
BLACKDAMP chokedamp, miasma, styth(e), vapor
BLACKEN asperse, befoul,

besmirch, besmut, blatch, bleck, brand, calumniate, cloud, colly, darken, defame, denigrate, injure, ink, japan, malign, obscure, polish, shine, slander, smear, smeeth, smirch, smoke, smolder, stain, sully, tar, traduce, vilify
BLACKENED reechy, smeared
BLACKFIN cisco, coregonus, sesi
BLACKFISH borlase, bottlehead, bream, dallia, dogfish, galjoen, girella, grampus, grind, hardhead, pothead, salmon, seabass, swart, tautog, whale
school grind
BLACKFLY gnat, simulid
BLACKFOOT gobetween, matchmaker
indian algonquian, kainah, piegan, sihasapa, siksika, sioux
BLACKGUARD abuse, berate, blaggard, bleck, catso, criminal, demon, devil, gamin, knave, ladrone, larrikin, menial, rapscallion, rascal, revile, rogue, rotter, scamp, scoundrel, scullion, shag, slander, smear, snuff, sweep, vagabond, vagrant, villain, vilify
BLACKHEAD blemish, cattail, comedo, scaup-duck, sheep
BLACKHEART cherry, whortleberry
BLACKING atrament, blatch, bleck, shoepolish
BLACKJACK beat, beetle, billy, bitterbush, blende, bludgeon, bombard, burnt sugar, caramel, cerris, club, coerce, compel, cosh, cudgel, duck, flag, game, hearts, hit, jerkin, mug, oak, pound, quercitron, quercus, ruddy duck, sandbag, sap, sphalerite, strike, threaten, twenty-one, vessel, vingt et un, weapon
term bust(ed), creve, hit(me), insurance, natural, soft, split a pair, stand
variant farm(er), fifteen, macao, onze et demie, pachter, pontoon, post and pair, quince, quinze, seven-and-one-half, thirty-five,

trenta-cinque, twenty-one, van-john, vingt-et-un
BLACKLEG anthrax, apostate, betray, blacknob, deceive, gambler, knobstick, neb, rat, scab, sharper, strikebreaker, swindler
BLACKMAIL bleed, booty, bribe, chantage, chout, coerce, exact, extort, hushmoney, intimidate, payment, threat(en), tribute
BLACKMAILER briber, ghoul, leecher
BLACKMORE *novel* lorna doone
BLACKPOT mug, sausage, toper
BLACKROOT colicroot, comfrey, cotton-wilt
BLACKSMITH blackfish, brookie, burnewin, burn-the-wind, damselfish, farrier, gow, horseshoer, ironsmith, lohar, plover, shoer, smithy, smug, stithy, striker, vulcan
helper backhander, striker
implement anvil, pritchel
personified brontes
shop smith(er)y, stith(y)
tongs tueiron
BLACKSNAKE blueracer, coluber, colubrid, elapid, quirt, racer, runner, whip
BLACKSTRAP knotgrass, molasses, mother, oil
BLACKTAIL dassie, dassy, godwit, mule-deer, ruff
BLACKTHORN crataegus, gribble, haw, scrog, sloe(bush), snag(bush), walking-stick
BLACKTOP asphalt, centaurea, pavement, paving, willow
BLACKWATER pyrosis, texas-fever
state nebraska
BLACKWEED ambrosia, burweed, lamb's-quarters, RAGWEED, sparganium
BLACKWOOD acasia, biti, dalbergia, mangrove, lightwood, logwood, rosewood
BLACKWORT bilberry, comfrey
BLAD blotter, blow, fragment, portfolio, slap, spoil
apple barbados gooseberry, cactus, pereksia
BLADDER ampulla, bag, blather, blister, bubble, cyst, float, inflate, sac,

urocyst, utricle, vesica, vesicle

absence acystia, amastia

air poke, singally, swim

-and-string bumbass

campion beh(e)n, bird's-eggs, bull-rattle, cowbell, cow-rattle, latifolia, rattlebox, silene, snapper, wahlbergia

comb. asco, cyst(o)

fern filix

green reseda

inflammation cystitis

kelp See *wrack*, below.

ketmie black-eyed susan, modesty

-like ampulary, ampulate, ampullaceous, cystoid, dilated, flask-shaped

surgery epicystotomy

worm coenurus, cysticercus, hydatid

wrack bottle-ore, cutweed, kelp(ware), seaweed

BLADDERNUT bagnut

BLADDERPOD indiantobacco, isomeris, physaria, vesicaria

BLADDERSEED ligusticum

BLADDERWORT popweed, stomoisia, utricularia, vesiculina

BLADE arm, bayonet, beau, bit, bone, blood, blunge, brand, bucket, buster, conductor, cutter, damascus, dandy, doctor, dude, edge, float, fluke, foible, fop, gallant, grain, head, heddle, knife, lamina, lance, leaf, limb, mace, oar, propeller, rafter, rapier, saber, saw, scalpel, scapula, scythe, shiv, sickle, sled, sorage, spark, spear, spire, sport, SWORD, tang, toledo, vane, weak, web

bone scapula

indentation choil

maker cutler

part bit

surgical leucotome, scalpel

BLAE bleak, blue, livid, sunless, unbleached

BLAGUE claptrap, humbug, raillery

BLAH bland, bunk, dull, empty, insipid, NONSENSE, rubbish, uninteresting

BLAIN blister, bulla, inflame, pustule, ruby, sore, swelling

BLAINE, JAMES *nickname* plumed knight

BLAIR battlefield, plain

BLAKE colorless, mckay, pale, shoe, wan, yellow

BLAME accuse, animadversion, ascribe, aspersion, attack, attask, attribute, blast, blemish, bumble, burden, call, censure, challenge, charge, chide, chop, condemn(ation), confound, credit, criticize, culpability, culpate, curse, denounce, derogate, dirdum, dispraise, fault, guilt, impeach, implicate, indict, involve, lack, liability, obloquy, odium, onus, pinch, plight, rebuke, reprehend, reproach, reprobate, reproof, responsibility, revile, sake, scance, shend, sin, slander, snape, stricture, swick, swike, task, twit, upbraid, w(h)ite, withnim

deserving culpable, guilty

free from absolve, acquit, clear, exonerate, relieve

BLAMELESS entire, faultless, flawless, guiltless, impeccable, innocent, perfect, righteous, sackless, spotless, witeless

BLAMEWORTHY criminal, culpable, guilty, reprobate

BLANC white

de chine porcelain

BLANCH appall, argent, avoid, bianca, blandish, bleach, blench, blenk, cheat, deceive, decolor(ize), etiolate, evade, fade, fallow, flinch, gloss, lead, pale, parboil, scald, shrink, white(n), whitewash

uncle king john

BLANCMANGE flummery, pudding

BLAND adulatory, affable, agreeable, amenable, amiable, balmy, benign, breezy, buttery, casual, cold, colorless, diplomatic, dull, favonian, flat, genial, gentle, glib, gracious, honeytongued, hypocritical, indifferent, ingratiating, insipid, kind(ly), lenient, mealy-mouthed, mild, obliging, oily, oleaginous, open, polite, politic, sleek, smooth, smug, soapy, soft, soothing, suave, unctuous,

unemotional, urbane, vapid, wishy-washy

BLANDISH allure, blanch, bewitch, cajole, captivate, charm, coax, delude, entice, flatter, fondle, honeyfug, importune, influence, lure, seduce, smooth, soothe, urge, wheedle

BLANK absolute, aim, annul, astounded, bare, barren, blind, blot, brindle, bull's-eye, bur(r), chasm, clean, close(d), colorless, complete, confused, coupon, dazed, delete, disconcert(ed), divert, document, downright, dud, dull, dumfounded, emptiness, empty, false, foil, form, free, harmless, impotent, lacking, nonplus(sed), nothing, object, obscure, open, pale, paper, plain, pure, range, shook, shot, simple, space, speechless, tabula rosa, target, thoughtless, turn, unadulterated, unbroken, unfilled, unmitigated, unmixed, unqualified, unreal, unrelieved, utter, vacancy, vacant, vacuous, vacuum, vapid, void, waste, white

check carte blanche, discretion, go-ahead, opportunity, permission

wall barricade, cul de sac, impasse, obstacle, obstruction

BLANKET afghan, all-embracing, barraclade, bedding, bluey, brot, chiripa, comprehensive, conceal, cooler, corona, cotta, cover (let), cum(b)ly, doubler, dressing, inclusive, kambal, layer, mackinaw, manta, mantle, maud, obscure, obstruct, overwhelm, pattoo, pattu, poncho, puff, puttoo, quilt, rug, saturate, serape, sheet, smother, soogan, stifle, stroud, sugan, suppress, tilpah, throw, whittle, wrap

coarse cotta, cumbly, sugan

cowboy's soogan, sougan, sugan

deposit mango

drill nap

fabric duffel, duffle

fish devilfish, manta

flower firewheel, gaillardia

horse apishamore, manta

indian stroud
leaf mullein
moss alga, scum
piece dagon
plucking carphology
quilted brot
roll bindle, shiralee, sleeping-bag
saddle corona
stiff itinerant, migrant, vagrant
trading stroud
wet drip, killjoy
wool barraclade
BLANKLY completely, directly, flatly, fully, pointblank, totally, utterly, vacuously
BLANQUETTE fricasee, mince, ragout, soda
BLARE beep, blart, blast, blazon, blear, blow, bray, brightness, brilliance, clarion, cry, fanfare, flamboyance, flourish, glare, honk, jangle, klaxon, noise, ostentation, peal, pipe, proclaim, roar, scream, sound, tantara, tattoo, toot(le), trumpet, whistle
BLARNEY apple-polishing, beguile, butter, cajolery, con, flatter(y), wheedle
BLART bellow, blab, bleat, roar
BLASE bored, casual, easy(going), devil-may-care, indifferent, insensible, insouciant, lackadaisical, nonchalant, offhand, sated, satiated, surfeited, unimpressed, veteran, weary
BLASH flash, nonsense, plash, shower, splash
BLASPHEMY anathema, calumny, curse, cursing, desecration, execration, impiety, imprecation, irreverence, malediction, profanation, profanity, reviling, sacrilege, swearing
BLAST annihilate, attack, bang, blame, blare, blight, blist, blore, blow, bluster, break, bub, bugger, burst, censure, charge, criticize, curse, cyclone, damn, denounce, despoil, destroy, detonation, discharge, discredit, dislodge, draft, dynamite, explode, explosion, fire, flaw, forbid, frap, freeze, gale, gust, hurricane, injure, jet, nidder,

nip, nither, noise, outburst, pressure, pryse, rebuff, rebuke, rip, ruin, rust, screech, shatter, shock, shoot, shot, shrivel, sneap, snifter, sound, split, spoil, squall, stop, storm, stream, stunt, thwart, toot, typhoon, volley, wap, whirlpuff, wind, wither
cold sneap
furious snifter
furnace smelter
furnace foreman blower
furnace lamp blow torch
furnace nozzle tuyere
furnace part bod, bosh, bott, tymp
windy gust, perry, pirrie, rise, ventosity
BLASTED accursed, blamed, blighted, blinking, confounded, damned, detestable, drugged, drunk, ruined, sere, shriveled, withered
BLASTING stellation
cap detonator
fuse bickford-match
material carbonite, dynamite, gunpowder, tnt
method mudcap
oil nitroglycerin
BLASTOMA neoplasm, tumor
BLASTULA blastocyst, blastosphere, embryo, metazoan, placula, planula(n)
BLASTUS *master* herod
BLAT betray, bleat, blurt, utter
BLATANT aggressive, assertive, bellowing, bleating, boisterous, brash, brawling, brazen, clamorous, coarse, conspicuous, crude, garish, gaudy, glaring, glib, gross, loud, meretricious, noisy, obstreperous, obtrusive, obvious, ostentatious, pushing, screaming, silly, strident, tasteless, tawdry, tomant, vocal, vociferous, vulgar
BLATE blab, blunt, dull, ghastly, insensible, pale, prate, sheepish, slow, spiritless, timid
BLATHER babble(ment), bleat, blither, hoohah, hullaballoo, nonsense, prattle, stir, waffle
BLATHERSKITE bobber, nonsense, ruddy duck, talker

BLATTA, BLATTID beetle, cockroach, purple
BLAUBOK antelope, bluebuck, etaac, hippotragus
BLAVER blindeyes, bluebottle, corn-poppy, violet
BLAWORT bluebottle, harebell, wood-hyacinth
BLAZE bleeze, blow, bonfire, brilliance, burn, burst, conflagration, describe, effulgence, exhibit, explode, fire(brand), flame, flare, flash, glance, glare, gleam, glory, glow, hack, ignite, illuminate, ingle, lead, light, low, mark, notch, outburst, pioneer, pointer, portray, proclaim, publicize, publish, ratch, shine, shoot, shot, signal, spark(le), splendor, spot, stare, steam, stripe, torch
away shoot
great halliblash
BLAZING afire, burning, conspicuous, fiery, flaming, flamy, light, resplendent, shining
star aletris, attraction, button snakeroot, chamaelirium, comet, cynosure, gayfeather, grubroot, liatris, mentzelia, nova, nuttallia, snakeroot, tritonia
up blash
BLAZON adorn, blare, boast, celebrate, coat of arms, cry, deck, declare, decorate, delineate, depict, describe, display, embellish, emblazon, escutcheon, exhibit, herald(ize), inscribe, promulgate, publicize, publish, proclaim, shield, shout, show, thunder, trumpet
BLAZONING *art* armary, heraldry
BLEACH blanch, bleak, blench, blondine, chalk, chlore, chlorinate, croft, decolor(ize), etiolate, fade, lighten, pale, patch, peroxide, poach, purify, sun, wash, whiten(er)
kind blankit(e), blueing, chlorine, chlorox, graysour, hydrosulphate, indigo, javelle water, lime, peroxide, purex
vat keir, kier
BLEACHER scaffold, seat, stand, whitster
BLEAK ablen, ablet, alburn,

arctic, bare, biting, bitter, blae, bleach, blue, cheerless, cold, cutting, depressing, desolate, dim, discouraging, dismal, dour, dreary, empty, exposed, fish, frigid, gloomy, gray, hopeless, pale, pallid, piercing, raw, sprat, stark, swale, windswept

fish blay, bley, sprat

house author dickens

house character boythorn, deadlock, flite, guppy, jarndyce, skimpole, tulkinghorn

BLEAR blur, cloudiness, deceive, dim, dull, film, hoodwink, indistinct, sore, vague

-eyed herring alewife

BLEARED dusky, inky, rheumy, vague

BLEAT baa, babble, blart, blat(e), blather, bluster, complain, cry, prate, whicker, whine, yarm

BLEAUNT blouse, shirt, tunic

BLEB blister, blob, bubble, bulge, bulla, pimple, pustule, swelling, vesicle

BLEE color, complexion, form, hue, likeness

BLEEBOK antelope, oribi

BLEED agonize, blackmail, blood, cry, cup, deprive, die, diffuse, drain, emit, empty, escape, exploit, extort, exude, flow, flux, hurt, leak, leech, milk, mulct, ooze, overcharge, pity, run, shed, smear, sorrow, spend, strip, suffer, sweat, swindle, teicher, transfuse, weep

BLEEDER hemophiliac, leech, parasite, phlebotomist, resistor, sponge, sticker, usurer, valve

BLEEDING bloody, sanglant

arrest hemostasis

heart bikukulla, butterfly-banner, caladium, coralpea, dicentra, do-gooder, dutchman's-breeches, eardrop, evonymus, fiddle-flower, kennedya, taro, wahoo, wallflower

-heart pigeon gallicolumba

BLEMISH amper, birthmark, blackhead, blame, blister, blot, blotch, blur, botch, breach, breck, bubukle, bruise, cicatrice, cicatrix, cloud, crack, damage, deface(ment), defame, defect,

deformity, dent, disfigurement, failing, fault, fissure, flaw, fleck, frailty, freckle, gall, impair, imperfection, injure, injury, knot, lack, lentigo, macula, macule, maim, mar(k), mayhem, moil, mole, n(a)evus, pock(mark), rift, rot, scab, scar, scratch, slur, smirch, speck, spot, stain, stigma, sully, sunspot, tache, taint, tarnish, tash, verruca, vesicle, vice, want, wart

comb. macul

in fabric amper, sully

in paper fisheye

wood knot, mote

BLENCH avoid, baffle, blanch, bleach, deceive, elude, eschew, evade, flinch, foil, pale, quail, quake, quiver, recoil, retreat, scruple, shake, shirk, shrink, shudder, shun, tremble, trick, whiten, wile, wince

BLEND agree, amalgamate, associate, blot, blunge, coalesce, combine, commingle, commix(tion), compound, confuse, consolidate, contemper, convert, corrupt, cream, cuvee, fade, fit, fondu, fuse, gradate, grade, harmonize, hybrid, immingle, integrate, intermingle, join, meld, melt, meng, merge, mingle, mix(ture) mould, pollute, relate, run, scumble, seel, smear, stain, syncrasy, temper, tincture, tinge, tone, unify, unite

color scumble, soften

BLENDE sphalarite

BLENDING fusion, hotchpot, meld, mix

BLENDWATER distemper

BLENHEIM *adversary* england, france

general marlborough

BLENNY brotula, bully, butterflyfish, eelpout, gunnel, kelpfish, jugular, quillfish, senorita, shanny, wolfish, wrymouth

BLESBOK antelope, blesbuck, bontebok, nunni, oribi

BLESS adore, anele, approve, beatify, bensh, bestow, canonize, cleanse, condemn, confer, congratulate, consecrate, cross, curse, damn, dedicate, devote, embliss,

endow, enshrine, esteem, exalt, extol, favo(u)r, felicitate, gladden, glorify, guard, hallow, invoke, keep, macarize, praise, pray, preserve, protect, purify, sain(t), sanctify, thank, thrash, visit, wave, worship, wound

you benedicite

BLESSED beata, beatified, benedetto, benedict(us), benedight, benedikt, benito, benoit, bhagavat, blest, blissful, blooming, consecrated, cursed, damned, divine, favored, fortuitous, fortunate, hallowed, happy, heavenly, holy, joyful, lucky, religious, sacred, sacrosanct, seelful, seely, spiritual

bread eulogia

event birth

herb avens, bennet, hemlock, valerian

name meaning ben(edict), bennie, benny, dixon

BLESSING approval, baraka, beatitude, benediction, benefice, benefit, benison, berachah, bliss, boon, charm, consecration, damning, darshan, duchan, dukan, favor, felicity, fortune, gain, gift, good, grace, mercy, praise, rebuke, sain, scolding, sorra, spell, wealth, windfall, worship

BLETHER See BLATHER.

BLEU *d'azur* smalt

de hue See MARIJUANA.

de roi sevres

BLIGHIA akee

BLIGHT afflict, bane, blast, brant, canker, death, decay, destroy, destruction, disease, dry-rot, erosion, fire, freeze, frost, frustrate, fungus, impairment, injury, insect, mildew, mold, moth, must, nip, nither, ophthalmia, pest, plague, rash, rot, ruin, rust, seer, smut, sneap, soka, spoil, taking, wilting, wither, worm

BLIGHTBIRD white-eye, zosterops

BLIGHTED blasted, blown, froe(z)y, frowsty, fusty, maggoty, mildewed, moldering, moldy, musty, spoiled, wormeaten

BLIGHTER beast, bloke,

chap, fellow, guy, rascal, wretch

BLIGHTY england, excellent, first-rate, furlough, homeland

BLIMP airship, balloon, dirigible, fatty, official, swaggerer, zeppelin

BLIND 3 bet, dim, pot 4 ante, blur, boma, dark, dead, dull, hide, hood, rash, ruse, seel, trap, veil 5 bisme, blank, bluff, cieco, cover, decoy, dense, drunk, dunch, shade, stake, stall, trick, vague, wager 6 ambush, bisson, blende, closed, covert, darken, dazzle, obtuse, screen, secret, stupid 7 aimless, bandage, benight, blinker, conceal, curtain, eclipse, eyeless, hideout, obscure, pretext, rayless, shutter, unaware 8 abortive, artifice, bayardly, bedazzle, disguise, execate, heedless, hoodwink, ignorant, involved, jalousie, outshine, purblind, reckless, umbrella, unseeing, venetian 9 amaurotic, anonymous, benighted, concealed, defective, oblivious, persienne, senseless, sightless, stratagem 10 ableptical, camouflage, insensible, irrational, nyctalopic, subterfuge, uncritical 11 hemeralopic, nearsighted, smokescreen, thoughtless, unobserving 12 shortsighted, undiscerning, unidentified, unperceptive, unreasonable

alley close, cul de sac, deadend, hopeless, impasse, loke, pocket, stop

as a bat, beetle, mole

bargain chance

dolphin susu

goby pinkfish

hawk's eyes seel

in one eye gleed, gleyd, peed

language braille

man mole

part slat

patron saint cecilia

pig saloon, speakeasy

set ambush, trap

shaft winze

simon johnny darter

spot bigotry, hang-up, ignorance, prejudice, scotoma

staggers barleyhood, drunkenness, gid, vertigo

tiger saloon, speakeasy

writing aid cecograph

-your eyes alipata, excoecaria, gang-wa, mangrove, tree

BLINDER blinker, bluff, eyeflap, flap, hood(wink), lunet(te), winker

BLINDEYES blaver, cornpoppy, papaver

BLINDFISH brotulid, catfish, cyprinid, goby

BLINDFOLD bandage, blinder, blink, bluff, concealed, dark, heedless, hoodwink, muffle, obscure, rash, reckless, scarf, unthinking

BLINDING bisme, bisson

BLINDNESS ablepsia, ablepsy, amaurosis, anopsia, bisson, cecity, darkness, ignorance, meropia, sightlessness, typhlosis

color achrobia, daltonism, monochromatism

day hemeralopia

night nyctalopia

partial hemiopsia, meropia

red-green daltonism

science of typhology

snow chionaolepsia

symbol bat, beetle, mole

temporary moonblink

tendency cecutiency

to truth avidya, avijja

BLINDSTITCH fell

BLINDWEED shepherd's-purse

BLINDWORM adder, anguid, caecilian, hagworm, orvet, slowworm

BLINK avoid, bat, blindfold, blinter, blush, cheat, condone, disregard, elude, evade, flash, flicker, flinch, flutter, glance, gleam, glimmer, glimpse, glitter, ignore, neglect, nictate, obtuse, overlook, pink, scruple, shine, shirk, shun, signal, slight, sour, sparkle, suffer, tolerate, trick, twink(le), twitter, wapper, wink

BLINKER blind(er), bluff, eye, flasher, goggles, hoodwink, light, macherel, signal, tinker, winker

BLINKING blooming, complete, utter

BLIP echo, five cents, nickel, warning

BLISS beatitude, bless, bless-

edness, cloud nine, contentment, delectation, delight, ecstasy, felicity, gladness, glory, happiness, heaven, joy, kaif, ke(i)f, kif(f), paradise, pleasure, rapture, seil, transport, utopia

perfect ananda

place of eden, elysium, heaven, paradise, utopia

BLISSFUL beatified, blessed, blithe, glorified, holy, seely, utopian

BLISTER aphtha, assail, beat, bladder, blain, bleb, blemish, blibe, blob, bluster, boil, bubble, bulge, bulla, burn, criticize, cupola, lash, phlyctena, punish, pustule, quat, rebuke, reprove, scalder, scorch, skeller, sotter, spank, swelling, tetter, vesication, vesicle, whip

beetle cantharis, lytta, meloid, spanish-fly

plant ranunculus

-producing epispastic, vesicant

small phlyctena

BLISTERING acrimonious, burning, hot, scathing, scorching, torrid, withering

BLISTERWORT cursed crowfoot

BLITE good-king-henry, goosefoot

BLITHE airy, bonnie, bonny, buoyant, buxom, carefree, cheerful, cheery, gay-(some), glad, happy, heedless, jocular, jocund, jolly, jovial, joyous, lighthearted, lively, merry, mirthful, sprightly, volatile, winsome

BLITTER bittern

BLITZ assault, attack, bomb (ardment), hit, raid, surprise

BLIZZARD blow, buran, gale, purga, retort, snifter, snow(storm), squelcher, storm, wind

state south dakota

BLOAT balloon, belly, billow, blast, blow(n), bowden, bulge, distend, drunkard, expand, ferment, hoove, hoven, inflate, puff(y), smoke-cure, swell, tumefy

clover mountain-misery

BLOATED brosy, convex,

cured, distended, elated, foggy, fozy, gotchy, hoven, obese, pompous, puffed, replete, sodden, swollen, tumefied, tumescent, tumid, turgid

BLOATER cisco, herring, mackerel, mooneye, whitefish

BLOB bead, BLEB, blister, blot, boil, bubble, clot, dallop, daub, dollop, drop, glob(ule), gout, lump, mass, pimple, pustule, splotch

BLOCK 3 bar, box, cob, cog, dam, die, dog, hob, hub, jam, nog, pad, row, toy, vol 4 bale, balk, base, bilk, bitt, bloc, buck, bunt, cake, clog, cube, dolt, dook, foil, form, foul, glut, halt, head, jamb, lump, mask, mass, mold, plan, plot, quad, quar, sett, snag, stay, stop, trig 5 baulk, beset, brick, bunch, check, cleat, close, deter, dolly, dunce, embar, estop, horst, perch, piece, shape, solid, space, spike, stamp, stand, stock, stump 6 arrest, dentel, dentil, domino, emboss, fipple, hamper, hangup, hinder, impede, invest, kibosh, muffle, mutule, oppose, outwit, pulley, scotch, sheave, square, street, stymie, taplet, thwart, waylay 7 auction, barrier, bollock, casting, condemn, inhibit, outline, portion, prevent, ramhead, section, stonker, trammel, trolley 8 keystone, obstacle, obstruct, platform, quantity, stoppage, suppress, withspar 9 apartment, barricade, frustrate, hindrance, interfere, interrupt, promenade, rectangle, simpleton 10 impediment, projection 11 obstruction, suppression 12 neighborhood

architectural dentel, dentil, dosserft, drum, impost, mutule, plinth, stone

bring to the execute

-buster bomb, knockout, speculator

chopping hacklog

clay drawbar

falconry perch

fault massie

felted damper

flat mutule, tile

fulcrum glut

furnace bloomery

fuse cutout

granite set

grooved bull's-eye

hawser bitt

hole-containing euphroe, wapp

ice cube, serac

iron anvil, bitt, vol

logging jumbo, lead

mechanical pulley

metal quad, quod

molded briquette

nautical chock, deadeye, fairlead, heart, saddle, stock

ornamental boss

out arrange, excavate, outline, prepare, roughcast, screen

paving cube, sett, stone, wheeler

pedestal dado, die, plinth, socle

perforated nut

plaster batter

polishing buff, float

printing cut, quad(rat), riser

pulley crawl

rope bull's-eye

small tessera

squared mitchel

tackle calo, tongue

ten solitaire

timber bolt, juggle

topmast bollock

up bar, dam, foreclose, quirt

vaulting buck, horse

vocal stammer

wheel scote

wood beset, bust, cube, fid, loon

BLOCKADE arrest, bar(ricade), beleaguer, beset, bottle up, clog, close, dam, embar, embolus, ferm, infarct, invest, obstacle, obstruct(ion), seclude, seige, shut in, stop, surround

BLOCKHEAD ass, bakehead, block(pate), bonehead, bullhead, bungler, bust, chump, clodpate, clodpoll, clot, coof, cuddy, cuif, daff, dimwit, disard, doddypoll, dolt, dullpate, dummkopf, dunce, dunderpate, fool, gamphrel, golem, halfwit, hardhead, hoddy(doddy), hoddypeak, idiot, jackass, klutz, knucklehead, lackwit, loggerhead, lug, lunkhead, moke, mome, nincompoop, ninny, noodle, nowt, numbskull,

oaf, screwball, simpleton, squarehead, stub, stupid, thickskull, tomfool, turnip

BLOCKHOUSE fort, garrison, puntal, stronghold

BLOCKING dunnage, jam(b)

BLOKE blighter, bloak, chap, cove, fellow, joker, man, toff

BLOLLY balata, beefwood, corkwood, horsetail-tree, porkwood, torrubia

BLOND auricomous, bawn, fair, fawn, flaxen, golden, leucous, light(colored), platinum, stramineous, towhead, yellow

BLONDI *master* hitler

BLOOD ancestry, aristocracy, birth, blade, blude, bluid, blut, claret, clot, cruor, dandy, dextran, dextrone, energy, erythrocytes, extraction, family, fluid, gallant, gore, grume, hemoglobin, heritage, humor, ichor, juice, kainah, kin(sman), kinship, koko, leucocytes, life, lineage, manslaughter, mood, murder, passion, plasma, profligate, race, rake, relation, sang, sank, sap, serum, slaughter, sludge, spark, stock, temper(ament), trophema, vigor, youth

abnormality See *disorder*, below.

and guts patton

and iron bismarck

and thunder bluster, melodrama, uproar, violence

antibody gamma globulin

bad anger, enmity, hate

bank plasmapheresis center

bath abattoir, massacre, slaughter

-boltered clotted, cruor

brother friend, intimate

cancer leukemia

cell corpuscle, hemocyte, macrocyte, microcyle, platelet

cell component hemoglobin

cell, immature hematoblast

cell part opsonin

circulation discoverer harvey

-clam arca

clot ball-thrombus, crassamentum, embolus, phlebitis

clot, comb. thromb(o)

clot medicine varidase

clotted boltered, cruor
clotting factor prothrombin
color sanguine
coloring matter arterin, cruor, hemachrome
comb. haem(o), haemato, hema(to), hem(o), lympho, sangui, sero
corrupt youstir
-cup peziza, sac-fungus
-curdling frightening, gory, horrible, terrifying
decreased flow venostasis
defective anhematosis
deficiency an(a)emia
deprive of dehematize
diagnostic instrument chromatograph
discharge h(a)emorrhage
disorder acidemia, acidosis, anemia, anhematosis, dyscrasia, hydr(a)emia, hyperglycemia, leucemia, leukemia, sapr(a)emia
drawing of cupping, h(a)emospasia
dust hemoconia
emulsion chyle
enzyme sgot
excessive plethora, poly(a)emia
fear of hematophobia, hemophobia
feud vendetta, vengeance
field of aceldama, akeldama
fine bloodwite, wergild
fluid opsonin, plasma, serum
fluke bilharzia, worm
god's ichor
half demisang
horse thoroughbred
infection septicemia
lily ambrosia, asclepias, cape-tulip, haemanthus
lipids cholesterol
man of charles, david
mixed mestizo
money breaghe, cro, galanas, wergild
of good thoroughbred
oxygen deficiency anoxemia
parasite hematozoon, tryp
part arteriole, granucocyte, lymphocyte, monocyte, plasma, platelet, red cell, thrombin, white cell
particle embolus
pert. h(a)emal, h(a)ematoid, h(a)emic
pheasant ithagine
plasma serum
plasma component fibrinogen, gamma globulin
platelet thrombocyte

plum sumac
poisoning cach(a)emia, py(a)emia, septicemia, toxemia
pressure disorder addison's disease
pressure, high hypertension
pressure, low hypotension
pressure medication aldoclor, aldomet, aldoril, anhydron, aquatag, diupres, esidrix, esimil, eutonyl, eutron, exna, hydrodiuril, hydropres, ismelin, oretic, propranolol, raused, renin, reserpine, serapes, serpasil
pudding sausage
purge massacre
red golf, incarnadine, sanguine, venous
red cell hemoglobin
relationship consanguinity
scavenger platelet
scientist buchanan, erasistratus, hewson, landsteiner, lieutaud, malpighi, newmann, virchow
serum part butyrinase, thrombin
specialist hematologist
stagnation clot, cruor, grume, h(a)emostasia, stasis
stoppage hemostasis
strain family, race, stock
study hematology
sugar glucose
transfer transfusion
vessel aorta, artery, capillary, capillation, comes, hemad, vas, vein
vessel coil glomus
vessel, comb. angi(o), arteri, vas(i), vaso
vessel description angiography
vessel inflammation angiitis
vessel, lacking anangioid
vessel layer externa, extima
vessel, pert. vasal, vascular, vasotonic
vessel rupture rhexis
vessel science angiology
vessel surgery angiostomy
vessel tumor angioma
vessel ulcer angionoma
wedding author lorca
white cell leukocyte
BLOODALP bullfinch, olp
BLOODBIRD honeyeater
BLOODDROPS wind-poppy
BLOODED pedigreed, thoroughbred

BLOODFLOWER ambrosia, asclepias, bloodweed, haemanthus, hippo, redhead
BLOODHOUND bandog, leamer, limer, ly(a)m, lyme, pursue, sleuth, sloth, tiedog
BLOODLEAF aerva, amaranth, iresine
BLOODLESS anemic, cold(hearted), colorless, dead, exsanguine, ghostly, inane, inhuman, insipid, irenic, lifeless, pacific, pale, peaceable, sallow, spiritless, turnipy, unemotional, unfeeling, vapid, wishywashy
BLOODLETTING carnage, cupping, leeching, phlebotomy, venesection
BLOODLINE ancestry, descent, family, lineage, pedigree, progeny, sib, strain
BLOODNOUN bullfrog
BLOODROOT bolo(root), coonroot, indian paint, potentilla, puccoon, redroot, sanguinaria, tetterwort, tormentil, turmeric
BLOODSHED carnage, death, gore, hostilities, killing, murder, slaughter, violence, war(fare)
BLOODSHOT inflamed, red
BLOODSTAIN ensanguine, imbrue
BLOODSTAINED gory
BLOODSTANCH horseweed
BLOODSTOCK thoroughbreds
BLOODSTONE chalcedony, heliotrope, hemachate, hematite, sanguine
symbol of courage
BLOODSUCKER bedbug, blackmailer, calotes, extortioner, harpy, leech, lizard, parasite, sponger, tick, usurer, vampire
BLOODTHIRSTY carnal, feral, ferocious, fierce, gory, murderous, sanguinary, savage, tigerish, violent, wild
BLOODWOOD ajhar, baloghia, croton, eucalyptus, jarool, lingoum, vismia
BLOODWORT burnet, centaury, dock, elder, indianpaint, potentilla, puccoon, redroot, tormentil, turmeric, waterdock, yarrow
BLOODY bally, bleeding, blode, brutal, butcherly,

contemptible, crimson, cruel, cruent, damned, deathful, ensanguined, exceedingly, feral, ferocious, gory, h(a)emotose, hematic, hemic, homicidal, hurt, imbrued, infamous, inhuman, mangled, merciless, murderous, mussed, rare, redwat, ruddy, rude, ruthless, sanglant, sanguinary, savage, stained, very violent
-*back* red-coat, soldier
bark lancepod
bones hobgoblin, specter
fingers foxglove
noses birthroot
BLOOM anthesis, beam, blooth, blossom, blow(th), blurt, blush, brauty, bud, cast, chill, coating, dew, down, floreate, flourish, flower, flush, glow, grace, haze, health, heyday, knot, pink, prime, produce, ripen, shine, thalia, thrive, vigor, vitality, yield, youth
BLOOMER(S) blooper, blower, blunder, boner, brodie, bull, drawers, error, failure, faux pas, howler, knickers, lapse, mistake, pantalets, pants, scourer, slip
BLOOMERY chafery, forge, foundry, furnace, hearth
BLOOMFELL baby's-slipper, butter-jags, trefoil
BLOOMING anthesis, blessed, blinking, blossoming, blowing, florid, flush, fresh, full-blown, gorgeous, green, pert, prime, prospering, roseate, rosy
BLOOPER See BLOOMER.
BLORE bellow, blast, blow, bluster, cry, low, wind
BLOSSOM bell, blob, bloom, blow(ing), b(o)urgeon, bud, chip, develop, floret, flourish, flower, fruit, lehua, open, posy, produce, proliferate, prosper, silk, succeed, thrive, yield
-*bill* surf-scooter
blighted blast
blue ceanothus, lilac, myrtle, periwinkle, vinca
heraldic fraise, frase
withy phlox
BLOT absorb, bespatter, black, blank, blemish, blend, blob, blotch, blote, blur, brand, damage,

darken, daub, defect, delete, destroy, disgrace, dishonor, dry, eclipse, efface, erase, error, expunge, failing, flaw, ignominy, impair, inkstain, macula, mar, obliteration, obloquy, obscure, paint, pollution, remove, reproach, shadow, shame, smirch, smouch, smudge, smut, soil, speck, splotch, spot, stain, stigma(tize), sully, taint, tarnish
out annihilate, annul, cancel, deduct, dele(te), destroy, efface, erase, expunge, extinguish, kill, obliterate, obscure
BLOTCH amper, blain, bleb, blemish, blot, blur, bulla, dab, dash, eruption, gout, macula(te), mark, monk, mottle, obscure, patch, plotch, pustule, smear, smirch, soil, splash, splat, splotch, spot, stain, stigma, variegate
red adustiosis
BLOTCHY scabby, scabrous, scovy
BLOTTER blad, book, pad, police-log, soaker
BLOTTO blind, drunk, stoned
BLOUSE bleaunt, bodice, camisa, camisole, casaque, casaquin, cassock, dickey, draping, garment, guimpe, jacket, jerkinet, middy, overgarment, shirt(waist), smock, sweatshirt, tee, t-shirt, tunic, vareuse, waist
bushman's bluey
front jabot
medieval bleaunt
BLOW 3 bat, bob, box, cop, cut, dab, dad, dub, egg, fan, gas, hit, jab, jar, lam, nap, pat, peg, pop, rap, tap, tip, wap 4 baff, bang, bash, beat, belt, biff, blab, blad, blaw, boil, brag, brew, buff, bump, butt, chop, clip, conk, coup, crig, cuff, dash, daud, ding, dint, drub, dunt, dush, faff, flap, fleg, fume, funk, gale, gowf, gust, hack, honk, huff, hurt, klap, klop, knee, lash, left, lick, louk, lush, paik, pain, palt, pant, pelt, pirr, plug, poke, puff, push, rage, rant, scat, scud, slam, slap, slat, slug, sock, swat, swop, swot, thud, toot, waft, welt,

whop, wind, wipe, yerk 5 binge, blare, blast, bloom, blore, boast, brunt, burst, clour, clout, clump, clunk, crack, crunt, curse, douse, dowse, dunch, erupt, flack, gowef, impel, knock, larva, pandy, paste, plump, plunk, pound, punch, right, scoot, scram, shock, skite, slash, smack, smash, spank, spout, spree, storm, swack, sweep, swipe, throw, thump, vaunt, weary, whack, whang, whiff 6 attack, belter, bensel, bounce, breeze, buffet, conker, dirdum, dunder, expand, fister, frolic, gather, huffle, larrup, siffle, squall, squash, stoush, stream, strike, stroke, switch, thrust, thwack, thwart, tootle, wallop, wheeze, wuther 7 afflate, assault, beating, bellows, bensail, bensall, bensell, blossom, bluster, boaster, bombast, clinker, crusher, debacle, destroy, display, enlarge, explode, freshen, inflate, lamback, lounder, publish, shatter, spanker, whample, whiffle, whistle 8 blizzard, bludgeon, calamity, confound, demolish, disaster, disclose, knockout, reversal, surprise 9 bastinado, chmallyeh, hurricane, windstorm 10 misfortune 14 disappointment
by blow detailed, first-hand
case egg
cover appear, emerge, erupt, expose, identify
down demean, deprecate, disparage, fell, raze, shatter
glancing scuff
heavy bash, belter, buckhorse, clout, clump, dad, devel, dong, drub, dunt, flewit, knock, oner, plumper, reemish, slam, slog, slug, souse, squabash, squat, stave, stot, stound, swack, swash, twitcher, womp, yank
hot and cold change, fluctuate, quibble, vacillate, waver
in arrive, enter, squander
mock feint
noisy clinker, dunder, dunner

nose snite
off blowhard, boast, brag, erupt, explode, explosion, hiss, snift
oneself to buy, purchase, splurge
on head clour, conk(er), nobb(l)er, topper
on nose canker, nozzler, smeller
out burst(ing), disgorge, erupt, extinguish, feed, festival, fete, flameout, flattire, gala, party, rupture, snuff, spree, tantrum, valley
over cease, disappear, dissipate, end, pass, subside, vanish
pipe aeolipile, aeolipyle
sharp bat, click, clinker, flewit, flick, knap, nap, slap, slog, spat, stinger
sky-high disprove, upset
smart flip, skelp, skite, yanker
sound kerwham
the duke err, fumble, lose
the gaff betray, blab
the whistle disclose, expose, reveal, sing, spill the beans, stop, tell
to treat
up berate, blast, bomb, burst, damage, demolish, destroy, detonate, dynamite, enlarge(ment), exaggerate, excite, expand, explode, explosion, fail, generate, inflate, laud, mine, organize, outburst, praise, promote, shatter, stir, sufflate, swell, vesuvius
with fist belt, bop, box, buffet, clout, hook, peg
with foot boot, kick, spurn
BLOWBALL dandelion, pappus
BLOWER bellows, bloomer, booster, braggart, drier, dryer, fanner, fumarole, gaffer, machine, mumbler, puffer, sacheverell, supercharger, swellfish, whale
BLOWFISH puffer, wall-eyed pike
BLOWFLY bluebottle, calliphorid
BLOWGUN pea-shooter, sarbacane, sumpit(an)
projectile dart
BLOWHARD braggart, plosher, shvitzer, tromben(y)ik

BLOWHOLE gloup, nostril, spiracle, spout
BLOWN betrayed, blighted, burned out, breathless, destroyed, distended, exhausted, expanded, fatigued, flyblown, grown, inflated, misshapen, opened, proclaimed, puffed, ruined, spoiled, stale, swollen, tainted, tired, winded
BLOWZE slattern, trull, wanton
BLOWZED flushed, red, ruddy
BLOWZY blousy, coarse, disheveled, dowdy, fat, frowzy, slatternly, slipshod, sloppy, tawdry, unkempt, vulgar
BLUBBER bawl, blobber, bluster, boil, boohoo, bubble, contort, cry, fat, howl, keen, lipper, medusa, nettle, seethe, slobber, sob, speck, spick, swell, swollen, thick, wail, weep, whimper, whine, yowl
grass soft chess
piece flense, flitch, lipper
refuse fenks, footing, fritters
whale cant, fenks, muktuk, speck
BLUBBERHEAD See BLOCKHEAD.
BLUBBERY fat, gelantinous, protuberant, quivering, swollen, unctuous
BLUCHER creedmore, shoe
BLUDGEON bat, billy, bully, club, coerce, cudgel, extort, harass, hit, mace, nightstick, sap, shillala(h), shillelagh, shillelah, stick, strike, threaten, towel, truncheon, weapon
BLUE 3 jay, low, sad, sea, sky 4 aqua, bice, bleu, ciel, cyan, delf, glum, iris, paon, teal, woad, zinc 5 azure, beryl, bleak, cadet, capri, copen, delft, drake, etain, livid, nikko, ocean, orion, pearl, perse, royal, seedy, slate, smalt, vanda, waget 6 canton, cobalt, cyanic, dismal, ensign, gloomy, indigo, lupine, marine, morose, pewter, risque, sailor, severe, sevres, strict, trypan, venice 7 azurine, azurite, celeste, cyanine, doleful, fearful, gentian, gobelin, hyppish, learned,

liberty, matelot, mistolu, peacock, prudish, quimper, sistine, unhappy 8 cerulean, dejected, distance, downcast, electric, hopeless, hyacinth, indecent, larkspur, lazulite, literary, mazarine, pavonian, pedantic, sapphire, thorough, wedgwood 9 celestial, depressed, malachite, pompadour, righteous, turquoise, unionarmy, wedgewood 10 despondent, dispirited, melancholy 11 lapis lazuli, puritanical, ultramarine 13 straightlaced
ash fraxinus, lilac
ball nilgau, scabious, succisa
beech carpinus, hornbeam
billy petrel
bindweed bittersweet, solanum
-black atroceruleous, blo(o)
blood aristocrat, lord, noble, thoroughbred
bloods See SOCIETY.
blossom ceanothus, lilac, myrtle, periwinkle, vinca
book atlas, four-hundred, society
brant See GOOSE *blue.*
bream See BLUEGILL.
brush See *blossom,* above.
button centaurea, periwinkle, scabious, titmouse, vinca
cerulean coelin
chip exemplary, leading, prestigious, solid, valued
-collar worker laborer, unionist
comb. cyan(o)
creeper love
-curls ambrosia, camphorweed, fleaseed, fleaweed, ragweed, selfheal, trichostema
dark marine, navy, perse, royal, sapphire, ultramarine, woad
deep cobalt
devil amytal, apparition, bugloss, chasseur alpin, delirium tremens, demon, depression, doldrums, viper's bugloss
dicks brodiaea, hyacinth
dull haw, livid
dye plant woad
eddoes tania
-eye honey-eater
-eyebright forget-me-not, myosotis
-eyed babies bluets

-eyed grass pigroot, sat-inflower

-eyed mary collinsia, inno-cence, navelwort, ompha-lodes, spiderwort

-fin bass, herring, saury, tuna, tunny, weakfish

funk depression, dumps, fear

-gas ozone

glede harrier

goose See GOOSE blue.

-gown beadsman, beggar

-gray azurine, bice, blae, ce-sious, cesium, merle, pearl, perse, slate

-green aeruginous, aqua-marine, beryl(line), calo-mine, cobalt, cyan, email, mesange, saxe, teal, tur-quoise, venice

grotto site capri, italy

ground kimberlite

gum eucalyptus, fevergum, tree

-head thalassoma, wrasse

hen state delaware

heron crane, nailrod

hill phlox

indian indigo

indigo rattlebush, ynde

-in-the-face exhausted, frantic

jaundice cyanosis

jay cyanocitta, road-monkey

jeans chinos, denims, levis

joe bream, lepomis, sunfish

johnny fish, rainbow-darter

kite hawk, hen harrier

law state connecticut

light alice

lips collinsia

lucy selfheal

man in fireman, policeman, sailor, umpire

marine navy

medium dresden, russian, sevres, sistine

melilot trigonella

men's-cup columbine

moon eternity, never, rarely

mountain tea goldenrod

myrtle See blossom, above.

nile, city on khartoum

nile section abbai

nile source t(s)ana

pale caesious

-pencil abridge, alter, edit, redact, revise

perch cunner

peter coot, glag, gallinule

-point oyster, siamese cat

-pointer isurus, mako, shark

-purple grape

racer columber, constrictor

-red ageratum, amethyst,

anemone, ardoise, argyle-purple, ashes of roses, bi-shop's violet, burgundy, cadet, cattleya, cyclamen, damson, gris-de-lin, hyacin-thine, indigo, maroon, matelot, mulberry, nymph pink, quaker, rose, sea-mist, smalt, wisteria

ribbon award, best, distinc-tion, first, prime, supreme, top, winner

rocket delphinium, monks-hood

royal hathor

ruin gin

runner caranx, fish, jurel

-sailors chicory

skies kaiserwetter

-skinned cyanotic

-sky dubious, fanciful, im-practical, theoretical, un-sound

slate skaillie, teal

spar lazulite

starry aquilegia, columbine

streak lightning

stuff kimberlite

succory catananche, cat-nache, cupidone, cupid's dart, plant

-tailed skink See LIZARD blue-tailed.

tarweed pennyroyal, selfheal, trichostema

tit nun, stonechat

titmouse tidye, yaup

tongue fever, heartwater, thickhead

vervain ironweed, verbena

vinny dorset

vitriole chalcanthite

BLUEBACK herring, salmon, trout

BLUEBEAD quintonia

BLUEBEARD caryopteris, chevalier raoul, landru, monster, murderer, ogre, spiraea, wife-killer

author perrault

character sister anne

french landru

tongue pentstemon

wife fatima

BLUEBELL abscessroot, bellflower, blawort, cam-panula, columbine, crow-bell, harebell, hyacinth, lungwort, scilla, veronica

BLUEBERRY bilberry, clin-tonia, cockatoo, cohosh, currant, dianella, huckle-berry, juniper, myoporum, myrtle, ohelo, palberry, pa-

pooseroot, rabbiteye, sour-top, squawroot, stoner, vac-cinium

BLUEBILL scaup duck, wid-geon

BLUEBIRD irena, sialia, sooty albatross

BLUEBONNET buffalo clover, cornflower, lupine, northiella, parrot, scot (sman), titmouse, trifo-lium

BLUEBOTTLE bachelor's-button, barbeau, blaver, blawort, blowfly, blueblaw, bluecap, bluecup, bluet, brushes, calliphora, cam-panula, centaurea, corn-binks, cornflower, fly, har-dock, hyacinth, lucilia, mus-cari, periwinkle, police-man, scilla, titmouse, vinca

BLUEBUSH acacia, cean-othus, saltbush, wattle

BLUECAP periwinkle, sal-mon, scot(sman), titmouse, tomtit, vinca

BLUECOAT almsman, jay, policeman

BLUEFISH bass, cunner, darzee, elf(t), fatback, girella, iridio, pomatomus, puddingwife, saury, seabass, shad, skipjack, squeteague, sunfish, tailor, tuna, weakfish

young snapper, whitefish

BLUEGILL bream, dollar-dee, lepomis, pondfish, sunfish

BLUEGRASS agropyron, aira, andropogon, poa

state kentucky

BLUEJACKET dragman, gob, mariner, matlow, rat-ing, sailor, seaman, tar

BLUEJOINT bluetops, red-top

BLUELEGS curlew

BLUENOSE moralist, nova scotian, prude, puritan, snob

BLUEPRINT cyanotype, dia-gram, draft, map, outline, plan, plot, project, schedule, sketch, trace

BLUES boogie woogie, ca-fard, dismals, doldrums, dolefuls, dumps, gloom, horrors, jazz, mare, me-grims, melancholy, misery, mopes, mulligrubs, sadness, song, sulks, uniform, vapors

composer handy

BLUESIDES harp seal
BLUESTEM andropogon, bent grass, gumbo grass, palmetto
BLUESTOCKING avocet, bas-bleu, cerulean, intellectual, pedant, scholar
BLUET engeleye, bluebottle, bright-eyes, chrysanthemum, cloth, cornflower, eyebright, farkleberry, houstonia, innocence, pissabed, quaker-ladies
BLUETHROAT pikeblenny, warbler
BLUETOP knapweed, nettle, solanum
BLUEWEED adderwort, bistart, cat's-clover, cattail, chicory, echium, ironweed, larria, viper's bugloss
BLUEWING shoveler, teal
BLUEWOOD chaparral, condalia, logwood
BLUEY blanket, bundle, swag
BLUFF abrupt, act, bank, barranca, blindfold, blinker, blunt, bluster, bounce, brag, brave, brusque, burly, candid, churlish, cliff, crude, crusty, curt, deceive, deter, direct, facade, fake, feint, fool, forthright, frank, gruff, headland, hearty, hill, hoax, honest, hoodwink, impolite, impostor, impudent, mislead, open, outspoken, plain, precipice, pretend, pretext, quackery, rough, rude, sham, short, stall, steep, surly, trick, unceremonious, uncivil, windy
king hal henry viii
BLUISH cyanic, cyanotic
-gray merle
BLUNDER abort, balk, barney, betray, bevue, bloomer, blooper, bobble, boggle, bone(r), boob(oo), botch, breach, break, brodie, bubu, bull, bumble, bungle, cobble, confuse, dolt, err(or), etourderie, failure, fault, faux pas, floater, flounder, flub, fluff, folly, foozle, fudge, fumble, gaff(e), gaucherie, goof, hash, hobble, howler, indiscretion, lapse, lumber, maffle, mess, mingle, miscarry, miscue, misdo, mismanage, mistake, muddle, muff, mull, roil, screamer,

skew, slip, slubber, solecism, sottise, stagger, stumble, stupidity, trip, violation
BLUNDERBORE demon, ogre
BLUNDERBUSS blockhead, bungler, espingole, gun, musket, stupid, trabuc(h)o, trombone
BLUNDERER bumbler, bummler, dummy, fool, knothead, lumberer
BLUNDERING awkward, bumbling
BLUNT abate, abrupt, assuage, bald, bare, bate, benumbed, blate, bluff, brash, brittle, brusk, brusque, callous, candid, cash, categorical, cavalier, cham, churlish, clumsy, crude, crusty, curt, damp, deaden, deter, difficult, dim, direct, discourteous, disedge, dubby, dull(ify), edgeless, flat, forthright, frank, gruff, hackney, harsh, hebetate, impair, impolite, inert, insensitive, mere, money, morne, mull, needle, numb, obtund, obtuse, plain, pointless, quahog, repress, retund, rough, rounded, rude, severe, sheathe, short, slow, snippy, snub(bed), stunt, stupefy, stupid, surly, thick, unceremonious, uncivil, unfeeling, unsharp(ened), weaken
comb. ambly
-headed morned
mentally hebetate
BLUR befog, blear, blemish, blind, blob, blot, blotch, cloud, coma, confuse, darken, defect, dim, fade, feather, fog, fuzz, hum, indistinctness, mackle, macule, mist, obscure, slur, smear, smudge, soil, spot, stain, stigma, sully
BLURB advertisement, announcement, brief, build-up, commendation, critique, notice, praise, publicity, puff, rave, review
BLURRED clouded, dim, faint, fuzzy, muzzy, obscure, smeared, smudgy, vague, wooly
BLURT betray, blat, blunder, bolt, divulge, ejaculate, exclaim, snore, weep

BLUSH blink, bloom, color, crimson, erubescent, flush, gleam, glow, mantle, paint, redden, rouge, rubescence, shamefaced, sheepish, suffusion, tinge
fear of erythrophobia
first beginning, dawn
BLUSHING ablush, flushing, red, rosaceous, roseate, rosy
BLUSTER agitation, anger, babble, beef, bleat, blore, blow, bluff, boast(ing), boisterousness, bombast, bounce, braggadocio, bravado, bravura, bully, bunk, bustle, challenge, commotion, conceit, confusion, dare, ding, fanfaronade, flurry, fluster, fraple, fuss, gas(conade), gauster, harass, hector, heroics, hot air, huffle, jactation, noise, rage, rant, rave, roar, rodomontade, roister, rollick, slangwhang, sp(l)utter, storm, swagger, swank, swash (buckle), tall-talk, threaten, tumult, turbulence, uproar, vanity, vapor, vaunt(age), violence, whither, wuther
BLUSTERER flash, frapler, hector, huffcap, huffer, swag, tearcat
BO buddy, captain, chief, fellow, hobo, man, tramp, vagabond
tree bodhi, pipal
BOA abolla, aboma, adjiger, anaconda, boid, boma, camoodi, corallus, giboia, joboya, python, scarf, snake, stola, throw
arboreal epicrates
constrictor anaconda, giboia, python
BOADICEA boudicca
people iceni
BOANN *cousin* dagda
BOAR, BOAR'S aper, barrow, brawn(er), bristler, grise, guinea-pig, hog(get), peccary, pig, sanglier, sounder, suid(ian), swine, tusker, varaha, wilrone
avatar varahavatara
cry fream
ensign of rome
fish john dory
flesh brawn
group singular
head hure
head drawer francis
head hostess mistress quickly

hound great dane
nest hut
pert. aprine
2nd-year hogget
slayer hercules
sty frank
3rd-year hoggaster, hogsteer
tree poison sumac
wound ganch, gore
young grise, hogget, sounder
BOARD accommodate, accost, address, approach, assembly, attack, border, bred, brett, buird, cabinet, chamber, committee, common, couch, council, court, cover, crimper, dail, deal, diet, directorate, eat(s), edge, embark, enplane, enter, entrain, exchange, face, fare, feed, flip, group, hack, harbor, house, join, keep, kneeler, lath, lodge, lumber, meals, mount, nourish, palette, panel, planch(e), plank, raid, ratch, room, sheet, shelter, side, siding, slab, slat, stage, stall, stave, swale, table, tack, theal, tray, tribunal, tucker, whatman
and room accommodations
blockhead doll
cover with berth
drawing coquille
exhibition frame
game See GAME *board.*
grooved coulisse
handled clapper
heart-shaped planchet
mystic ouija
notched horse
of trade chamber of commerce
poling runner
pressed felt
pulp-pressing couch
rabbeted shiplap
rubber eraser
sheathing sarking
thin sarking, shide
warping bartree
worker wig-maker
BOARDER eater, grainer, guest, mealer, pensioner, tabler, transient
BOARWOOD chewstick
BOAST advertise, aggrandize, avaunt, beef, blaw, blazon, bleeze, blow, bluster, bog, bombast, brag, brave, clamor, crake, crow, devaunt, display, exaggerate,

extol, exult, flaunt, flourish, gab, gas, gasconade, gloat, glorify, glory, jactation, kaena, menace, outcry, parade, plume, pomp, possess, prate, preen, pride, puff, rave, rodomontade, roose, show off, skite, splore, spread-eagle, swagger, swank, vant(erie), vapor, vaunt(ery), voust, wost, yelp, yolpe
BOASTER blatherskite, blow(hard), bouncer, braggadocio, braggart, bragger, bravado, cacafuego, cacofugo, cracker, egoist, fanfaron, fonfer, fourflusher, gasbag, gascon, huff, jingo, pedant, pretender, rodomont, roisterer, ruffler, skite, strutter, swaggerer, swasher, tartarin, wouster, woustour
BOASTFUL big, bombastic, braggy, fanfaron, inflated, jactant, large, magniloquent, parado, pompous, proud, thrasonic, toplofty, vainglorious, vauntie, vaunty
speech gasconade, kompology, rodomontade
BOAT (See also BOAT *fishing;* NAVY *vessel;* SHIP; VESSEL *sailing.*) 3 ark, cat, gig, hoy, tub, tug 4 acon, bark, dory, gufa, hulk, kufa, mule, pahi, plat, prah, prao, prau, punt, raft, scow, ship, waka 5 accon, aviso, balsa, banca, banka, barge, bidar, birch, bungo, canoe, casco, dingy, donga, dunga, ferry, fifal, float, funny, goofa, jolly, kaiak, kayak, kelek, liner, moses, pilot, praho, pungy, racer, rasee, razee, scull, shell, skiff, umiak, vinta, waapa, yacht 6 argosy, baidak, ballam, baroto, bateau, bilalo, bireme, bugeye, caique, cayuca, cayuco, cockle, corial, cutter, dingey, droger, dugout, galley, goupha, jangar, kuphar, launch, lerret, mailer, nuggar, nugget, oomiak, oumiac, pitpan, pungey, randan, robroy, sampan, torpid, umiack, vessel, wherry 7 almadia, almadie,

angeyot, bidarka, buckeye, caracoa, carrier, cascara, cruiser, currach, curragh, currane, dinghie, drogher, fouroar, gondola, jangada, lakatoi, lighter, lymphad, masoola, pinnace, pontoon, scooter, sculler, seasled, skippet, steamer, trireme, vidette, wanigan 8 balangay, ballahoo, barangay, bidarkee, bullboat, caracora, cockboat, duckboat, gundalow, pinnacle, runabout, schooner 9 birchbark, broadhorn, bucentaur, catamaran, outrigger, toothpick, transport 11 cockleshell
abandoned derelict
assault lst
basket coracle, corita
brace thwart
building setwork
cabin baulea(h)
canopy tilt
captain rais
chain sling
chief's birling, birlinn
clumsy drogher, hooker
comb. scaph(o)
deck orlop, poop
dispatch aviso, oolak, packet
duck-hunting dink, skag, sneakbox
8-oar torpid
ferry bac, cutt
15th century balinger
fishing baldie, banker, barcolongo, baris, bawley, bovo, bracozzo, buss, caravel, chebacco, coble, cog(gle), coracle, crabber, dhole, dhoni, dogger, doni, drover, fleeter, follyer, harookuh, kuphar, matinicus, mumblebee, nickey, nobby, pookaun, pykar, sandal, scaffie, scaffy, sealer, seiner, sexern, sharpie, shrimper, skaffie, sloop, smack, tosher, trawler, trow, vinta, volyer
flag officer's barge
flat-bottom ark, bac, barge, baris, bateau, bugeye, bun, coble, dor(e)y, float, gayyou, gondola, hundelow, johnboat, lighter, moses, plat, pra(a)m, punt, puteli, schuit, scow, shout, shrimper
fly buss, flute
freight barge, lighter
front bow, prow, stem
garbage hopper, scow

group armada, fleet, navy, squadron, tow
gun barca
half-decked wherry
harbor barge, bumboat, tug
heavy ballatoon, canaler
hire matelotage
holdfast rypeck
hook gaff, hitcher, stower
ice skeeter
incense navicula, nef
joint jerl
jolly yawl
landing lci, lst
lateen-rigged d(h)ow, mistic, setee, speronara
line guest rope
load burden, cargo
mail aviso, packet
man-of-war brig, pinnace
merchant argosy, holcad
military pontoon
moorage basin, dock, harbor, roadstead
mortar palander
1 bank of oars unireme
1-masted See *single-masted,* below.
open galley, lerret, punt, shallop, whiff
ornamental navicella
paddle sternwheeler
part beam, bilge, bow, bridge, cabin, capstan, companionway, deck, hold, gunnel, gunwale, keel, ke(e)lson, painter, prow, rail, saloon, scupper, skeg, stern, thwart
passenger bilalo
patrol spitkid, spitkit
pin thole
pirate brigantine
pole poy, rypeck, sprit
post biff, bollard, capstan
power tug
propellant oar, motor, peddle, pole, scull
punting skerry
racing scull, sculler, shell, single, skull, torpid
refueling bowser
ride cruise, row, sail
river baidak, barge, bateau, bauleah, billyboy, ferry, oolak, packet, wheeler
round goofa, gufa, kufa
row birlinn, canoe, dory, quincy, randon, scull, shell, skiff, skull
sailing See VESSEL *sailing.*
sealskin baidarka, bidarka, bidarkee
seams, to fill ca(u)lk

seat taft
shallow cockle
-shaped cymbiform, navicul(ar),(oid), naviform, scaphoid
shell cymbium, sweetmeat
ship's dingey, dinghy, gig, jolly, launch, mosos, pinnace, tender, yawl
single-masted balandra, catboat, hoy, sloop
6-oar sexern
16th century balinger
skin angeyok, baidar(ka), bidar(ka), bidarkee, bullboat, umiak
slave dhow
small acon, barca, bilander, canoe, cockboat, cog(gle), dinghy, dink, dory, punt, rowboat, scull, shallop, skiff, skippet, skull, yawl
song barcarole
square-rigged brig, snow
steer conn, pilot
3 banks of oars trireme
3-hulled trimaran
3-masted bark(entine), barque(ntine), tern
3-oar randan
timber keel
tow tug
trading baggala
treadle-propelled podoscaph
2 banks of oars bireme
2-masted baggala, bilalo, bilander, brig(entine), bully, bum
undersea sub(marine), submersible, u-boat
wicker coracle, goofa(h), kufa
woven coracle, corita
BOATMAN barcajuolo, bargeman, bargemaster, barger, bencher, charon, cobleman, dandi, dandy, ferrier, ferryer, ferryman, gondolier, hobbler, hoveller, huffler, lighterman, oarsman, phaon, rower, yachter, voyageur, waterman, yawler
BOATSETTER coxswain, helmsman, pilot, steersman
BOATSWAIN bird, bos(u)n, jaeger, serang, tindal
mate buffer
BOAZ *grandson* david
parent rahab, salma, salmon
son obed
wife ruth
BOB bab, ball, bingle, blow, bobble, bow, buffet, bunch,

calf, caper, cheat, clip, clod, cluster, coiffure, coin, crop, curtsy, cut, dab, dance, delude, dib, dobber, dock, duck, filch, fish, float, flout, grub, haircut, hobble, hod, jeer, jerk, jest, jog, jounce, knob, knot, leap, lop, mock, modification, motion, move, nod, oscillate, pageboy, pat, pendant, plum(met), pommel, popple, pump, rap, refrain, shake, shilling, shingle, shorten, sled(ge), sleigh, strike, suddenly, tail, tap, taunt, thump, trick, trim, truncate, weight, worm, wrap
short bingle, shingle
to and fro popple
up arrive, emerge, lollop, surprise
BOBBER blatherskite, cork, deadhead, dropper, duck, float, ruddy-duck
BOBBERY brawl, disturbance, hubbub, noise, squabble, tumult, uproar
BOBBIN braid, broche, coil, cone, cord, cuckoopint, cylinder, hanger, pin, pirn, ratchet, reel, skreel, spindle, spool, tavell, torchon
and joan arum, cuckoopint
frame creel
lace See LACE *bobbin.*
machine spinner
pin spindle
BOBBLE blunder, ern(or), fumble, jerk, juggling, mistake, oscillate, shake
BOBBY bailiff, bull, calf, catchpole, constable, cop (per), gendarme, officer, peeler, policeman
-soxer girl, teenager
BOBCAT lynx
BOBOLINK bird, bunting, butterbird, conquedle, deer, maybird, ortolan, reed (bird), ricebird, sucker
BOBSLED boblet, dray, ripper
BOBTAIL abbreviated, curtail, cut, deficient, dock(ed), rabble, sheepdog, strunt
BOBWHITE bird, colin, partridge, quail
BOCAGE copse, thicket, woodland
BOCARDO See JAIL.
BOCCACCIO jack, rockfish, tomcod, trecentist

beloved fiammetta
tales decameron
BOCHE deer, german, hardhead, hun, soldier
BOCK ale, beer, lager,
leather, porter, sheepskin,
stout
BOCKEREL falcon
BODACH bugaboo, bugbear,
churl, clown
BODACIOUS bold, insolent,
reckless
BODAI enlightment, salvation
BODE announce, auger, bid,
delay, forecast, foreshow,
foretell, halt, herald, indicate, message, messenger,
offer, portend, presage,
sign, stop
BODEGA grocery, storeroom, wineshop
BODGE botch, patch
BODGER huckster
BODHISATTVA avalokita,
avalokitesvara, bodhisat,
BUDDHA, kwannon, kwan-
yin, maitreya, manjusri,
padmapant, virupaksa
BODICE basque, choli, corset, gilet, jabot, jelick,
jumps, lyfkie, overbody,
slipbody, stays, vest, waist
BODIERON boregat, greenling, rock-trout
BODIES *seven* See SEVEN
bodies.
BODILY actual, animal, carnal, corporeal, external,
fleshly, incarnate, material,
personified, physical, sarkical, sensual, solid, somal,
somatic, systemic, visceral
BODING black, ominous,
prediction, prognostic, sinister
BODKIN awl, broach,
dagger, eyeleteer, hairpin,
needle, pin, poi(g)nado,
poinard, point, poniard,
popper, puncher, stiletto
BODY amount, anatomy, assemblage, association, band,
bati, bed, bole, bones,
bouk, buck, bulk, cadaver,
carcass, class, collection,
committee, company, con-
ference, consistency, core,
corps, corpus, corsaint,
council, crew, crux, cuerpo,
deha, demarchy, density,
enceinte, essence, extent,
flesh, force, form, frame,
fullness, group, hull,

human, khet, lich(am), majority, mass, material, mob,
mold, mortal, mould, multitude, nave, organism, person, quantity, reality, resonance, rind, rupa, sarira,
sect, shank, shell, size, skeleton, skinful, solid, stem,
stiff, soma, substance, sup-
tion, texture, thickness,
throng, torso, trunk, waist
abnormal enlargement acromegaly, elephantiasis,
gi(g)antism
administrative bureaucracy
cavity atresia, coelom(e),
sinus
comb. dema, soma(tic), so-
mato
corporate society
dead cadaver, carcass, carrion, corpse, lich(am),
mort
fat epiploon
fluid bile, blood, chyle,
colostrum, humor, ichor,
lachryma, lymph, matter,
milk, mucus, phlegm, pi-
tuite, plasma, pus, rheum,
saliva, sanies, serum, sweat,
tear
fruiting ascocarp, clava,
conk
governing decarchy, directory, durbar, kahal, senate,
synod
heavenly asteroid, comet, luminary, luna, meteor,
moon, planet, satellite,
sphere, star, sun
hyalin druse
immaterial ghost, specter,
spectre
injury to mayhem, trauma
joint ankle, elbow, hip, knee,
shoulder, wrist
judicial court, forum
legislative assembly, chamber, congress, council, diet,
lagthing, parliament, senate
linen underclothes
long-limbed hypermorph
-mind psychosomatic, yoga
mortal khet
motion gesture
network rete
odor asmidrosis, bromi-
(hi)drosis
of followers retinue
of law code, halacha, halaka,
shar(iat)
of men army, corps, force,
navy, posse, retinue
of principles calculus

of rules canon
part 3 arm, ear, eye, gum,
hip, jaw, leg, lid, lip, orb,
rib, toe 4 back, bone, bree,
bust, calf, cell, chap, chin,
cusp, derm, duct, face, fist,
foot, hair, hand, head, heel,
iris, jowl, knee, limb, lobe,
loin, nail, nape, neck, nose,
palm, root, rump, shin,
skin, sole, vein 5 ankle,
belly, blood, bosom, brain,
canal, caput, cheek, chest,
cutis, derma, digit, elbow,
gland, inion, joint, lymph,
mouth, nares, nerve, nuque,
oxter, pelma, pinna, pupil,
serum, shank, sinus, thigh,
thumb, torso, trunk, uvula,
velum, waist, wrist 6 an-
trum, armpit, artery, basion,
breast, cornea, cortex, dactyl, dorsum, eyelid, finger,
gullet, haunch, lunule, marrow, meatus, oculus, palate,
paunch, pollex, retina,
scruff, temple, thorax,
throat, tongue 7 abdomen,
auricle, eardrum, eyeball,
eyebrow, eyelash, forearm,
gingiva, metopon, nostril,
occiput, papilla 8 brachium,
calvaria, cerebrum, fore-
head, omphalos, shoulder,
sinciput 9 epidermis
pert. physical, somal, somatic, systemic
petrified anthropolith
politic commonwealth, community, electorate, population, society, state, voters,
weal
religious church, congregation, convent, monastery,
sect
rhythm, pert. circadian, cir-
camensual, circannual, ul-
tradian
science anatomy, anthropology, anthropometry,
physiology, somatology
scraping device strigil
segment acron, arthromere,
merosome, metamere, so-
matome, somite
sensibility somesthesia
servant valet
shop garage
small nanoid
stalk-like podetium
stimulant hormone, tonic
structure build
swelling boss

type ectomorph, endomorph, mesomorph
wall, part apodeme, paries, septum
weakness somatasthenia
zoological soma
BODYGUARD antrustion, burkundaz, convoy, escort, housecarl, huscarl, protector, retainer, retinue, thane, thingman, trabant, wardcors, yeoman
BOEBERA dyssodia
BOEDROMIOS apollo
BOEOTIAN crude, dull, fool, obtuse, philistine, stupid
chief leitus
city tanagra, thebes
king clymenus
mountain ptous
prophet bacis
region ionia
BOEOTUS *parent* arne, poseidon
BOER afrikaner, takhaar
council raad
dialect taal
general botha, cronje, dewet
leader pretorius
republic graaff reinet, swellendam
war event jameson raid
BOETHIUS boece
patron theodoric
BOG bemire, boast, bold, cantina, car(r), cess, cripple, dub, fen, flow, forward, gog, hag, letch, marsh, meadow, mire, mizzy, moor, morass, muskeg, ooze, peatery, quag(mire), saucy, sink, slade, slew, slough, slue, spew, stodge, stog, submerge, swamp, syrt, turbary, wash
asphodel knavery, narthecium
bean bitter-worm, buckbean, sweet gale, trefoil
berry cranberry, raspberry, whortleberry
birch buckthorn, rhamnus
blitter or *bumper* bittern
cotton eriophorum, sedge
down cotton-grass, mire, stall
featherfoil hottonia
glede marsh harrier
grass carex, sedge
hop buck bean, sweet gale
iron ore limonite
jumper bittern
land ireland, slade
manganese lampadite, wad

moss aulocomnium, sphagnum
myrtle See *bean,* above.
onion jack-in-the-pulpit, owenia
orchid arethusa, malaxis
peat cess, moss, yarpha
pink cuckooflower
plant abama, butterbur, featherfoil, narthecium, trefoil
rush juncus, schoenus, sedge
shrub autumn willow, sweet-gale
star grass-of-parnassus
sucker bird, rubicola, woodcock
torch golden club, orontium
BOGEY (See also BOGY.) demon, devil, hag, one over par, spook
BOGGLE alarm, astound, baffle, balk, bauchle, blench, blunder, bogy, botch, bungle, demur, dissemble, equivocate, falter, flinch, flounder, foil, goblin, hesitate, jib, kick, object, perplex, protest, quail, quibble, scare, scruple, shock, shrink, shy, spectre, stagger, start, stick(le), stop, strain, stumble, waver
BOGGY deep, fenny, foggy, gouty, haggy, marshy, mossy, quaggy, queachy, slobby, snapy, spewy, squashy, swampy, wet
BOGHEAD cannel coal
BOGHOLE dump
BOGO abil(a)o, garuga, hamite
language bilin, hamitic
BOGOMILE patarin(e)
BOGTROTTER irishman, mosstrooper, refuge
BOGUS counterfeit, fake, false, fictitious, phony, sham, spurious
BOGWORT cranberry
BOGY annoyance, bodach, bogey, boggard, boggart, boggle, bogie, bogle, booger, bugaboo, bugbear, cow, gnome, goblin, harassment, haunter, hobgoblin, phantom, scarecrow, specter, spectre, spirit, spook, ufo
BOHEMIA(N) (See also CZECHOSLOVAKIA references.) artistic, arty, cechy, chichi, gypsy, hus(s), informal, intel-

lectual, nonconformist, picard(y), unconventional
chatterer waxwing
deity byss
district eger
earth terre verte
garnet pyrope
girl character arline, mimi, thadeus
glass moldavite, schmelze
king frederick, polixenes, wenceslaus
olive oleaster
prince florizel
ruby rock crystal, rose quartz
saint wenceslaus
sulfate slavikite
tartar gypsy
BOHNENSPIEL mancala
BOHOR antelope, cervi, nagor, redunca, reedbuck, reitbok
BOHORT *uncle* lancelot
BOHUNK boor, laborer, lubber, worker
BOID anaconda, boa, python, snake
BOIL agitate, agitation, anger, anthrax, barm, bealing, betray, bile, blister, blob, blow, boll, botch, bran, brede, breeder, brew, bubble, bulama, buller, burble, carbuncle, cathair, churn, coct, coddle, cook, cowl, cyst, decoct, ebullate, effervesce, elixate, erupt, estuate, ferment, foam, froth, fry, furuncle, inflame, kyle, leep, oxidize, pearl, pet, phlegmon, quat, rage, sanitize, seed, seethe, simmer, soak, sore, steam, stew, storm, sty(e), sutter, swiel, teem, tottle, vesicle, wabble, walm, well, wobble
almost scald
down abbreviate, abridge, brief, condense, contract, reduce, shorten
in lye buck
syrup pearl
unsteadily bump
BOILED drunk, estuated, sod(den)
BOILER alembic, autoclave, ca(u)ldron, cook, copper, evaporator, furnace, kettle, pan, pipe, reef, retort, still, tank, teache, urn, vessel, yet
circular kier
disk sput

head engineer
-maker beer and bourbon, chaser, dog's-nose, drink
plate sput, stereotype
room bucket shop
salt weller
BOILING agitated, ardent, batch, cluster, coction, ebullience, ebullition, elixation, fervent, fervid, fuming, heaving, hot, irate, party, scalding, seething, simmering, stewing, swelling, torrid, walm
BOIS wine, wood
blanc linden, tree
cotelet fiddlewood
d'arc osage orange
de fer hop-hornbeam, ostrya
de vache buffalo chip
inconnu hackberry
puant catalpa, sycamore
BOISTEROUS blatant, blustering, brawling, burly, clamorous, clangorous, clattery, coarse, cumbrous, excessive, excitable, furious, gurl, high, impetuous, larrikin, loud, massive, noisy, obstreperous, rackety, rambunctious, rampagious, roaring, roistering, rollicking, roritorious, rory-tory, rough, rowdy, rude, shandy, stormy, strident, strong, tempestuous, tonant, tumultuous, turbulent, unrestrained, unruly, uproarious, vehement, violent, vociferous, wild, windy
BOITE bistro
BOITO *opera* mefistofele
BOKADAM See **CERBERUS.**
BOKARDO dokamo, dokhma, prison, tower
BOLA majagua
BOLD 3 big, bog, yep 4 derf, hard, keen, loud, pert, rash, rude, tall, yepe 5 apert, bardy, bield, bossy, brant, brash, brave, brent, broad, frack, freck, freek, gally, hardy, large, manly, nervy, pawky, peart, pokey, saucy, showy, steep, stout, wlonk 6 abrupt, audace, bossed, brassy, brazen, chased, crouse, daring, fierce, flashy, heroic, manful, plucky, strong 7 assured, buckeye, dashing, defiant, doughty, epilose, forward, grivois, haughty, massive,

roaring, valiant 8 apparent, arrogant, familiar, fearless, immodest, impudent, intrepid, malapert, manifest, powerful, resolute, temerous 9 audacious, bodacious, clamorous, dauntless, heartsome, shameless 10 courageous, forritsome 11 challenging, conspicuous, imaginative, uninhibited, venturesome 12 rumgumptious, unhesitating
as a bear bernard, bernie
friend baldwin
name meaning archibald, leopold
BOLDLY crank, crouse, hard(i)ly, roundly, strongly
BOLDNESS assurance, audacity, bield, bravery, brow, cheek, confidence, courage, dare, effrontery, face, freedom, hardihood, nerve, pluck, temerity, vigor
in speech parrhesia
BOLE bolus, brown, clay, crypt, cupboard, dose, ruddle, soil, stem, timber, trunk
BOLERO dance, jacket, music, waist
composer ravel
BOLETUS cepe, fistulina, fungus, mushroom
BOLEWEED centaura, knapweed
BOLEWORT goutweed
BOLEYN *daughter* elizabeth
BOLIDE bolia, fireball, meteor(ite)
BOLIVIAN (See also SOUTH AMERICAN references.)
animal vicuna
author arguedas
boat balsa
capital la paz, sucre
city chuquisaca, cliza, cochabamba, guaqui, icla, itau, ivo, la paz, llica, mojo, oruro, potosi, quime, santa cruz, saya, sucre, tarija, uyuni, vallegrande, yaco, yata, yura, zongo
coin bolivar, boliviano, centavo, tomin
district chuquisaca, cochabamba, colinas, elbeni, el chaco, la paz, oruro, pando, potosi, santa cruz, tarija
dried mutton chalone
indian apolista, arawak, ashluslay, aymara, baure, cani-

chana, cavina, cayubaba, charca, chicha, chiriguano, chunko, colla, inca, ite, iten, itonama, ixiama leca, maropa, maskoi, mojo, moxo, otuke, pacaguara, paiconeca, puquina, quechua, quillaqua, quitemoca, sirione, tacana, tiahuanacan, toromona, tumupasa, ugarono, uran, uro, uru
lake aullugas, coipasa, desaguader, poopo, rogagua, titicaca
measure celemin, league
panpipe sicu, siku
peak ancohuma, cusco, cuzco, illampu, illimani, jara, pupuya, sajama, sorata, zapaleri
plateau altiplano
president sucre
range andes, sansimon, santiago, sunsas
river abuna, apere, baures, benecito, beni, boopi, cordillera, grande, guapore, ichilo, inambari, itenez, itonama, lauca, machupo, madidi, madre di dios, mamore, mizque, orton, paraguay, parapeti, pilcomayo, san miguel, tarija, yacuma, yata
salt deposit empexa, uyuni
statesman arguedas
swamp izozog
tower chulpa
volcano ollague
weight libro, marco
BOLL bubble, bulb, capsule, knob, onion, pericarp, pod, snap
weevil anthonomus, pest, picudo
BOLLARD apostle, bitt, deadhead, dolphin, kevel
BOLLIX See **BUNGLE.**
BOLO defeatist, knife, machete, pacifist, rafflesia, sundang, sword
BOLOGNA baloney, boloney, sausage
ancient name bononia, felsina
stone barite
BOLSA bourse, exchange
BOLSHEVIST anarchist, bolo, bolshie, bolshy, collectivist, communist, nihilist, radical, revolutionary, socialist
leader lenin
BOLSTER add, aid, baluster,

bedding, bulwark, chisel, compress, cushion, jack, maintain, pad, pillow, repair, shore, stiffen, support, uphold

BOLT 3 bar, jag, jet, key, lue, nab, pen, pin, rod, run 4 beat, cram, dart, dash, drop, dump, fall, flee, gulp, lock, pawl, roll, rush, shut, sift, skip, slot, snib, spar, stud 5 arrow, bilbo, blurt, break, catch, close, elope, flash, flour, gorge, latch, plate, rivet, screw, shaft, shoot, sieve, stock 6 assort, bundle, decamp, desert, devour, dredge, escape, fasten, flight, ganyie, garble, gobble, mooter, pintle, purify, quarry, refine, riddle, safety, screen, searce, secure, snibel, spring, streak, strike, stroke, toggle, winnow 7 examine, missile, quarrel, refusal, shackle, slabber, snibble, thunder 8 crowfoot, dislodge, fastener, flathead, separate, stampede 9 cartridge, desertion, discharge, lightning, scantling 10 ranunculus 11 gloveflower
companion nut
fiery resheph
from the blue lightning, surprise
in imprison
sliding pawl
thunder fulmen
top t-nut

BOLTEL bottle, fractable, ovolo, torus

BOLTER apostate, boultel, deserter, dresser, eloper, fugitive, mugwump, sieve

BOLTHEAD matrass

BOLTONIA ageratum, balsam-root, herb

BOLUS ball, bite, clay, clod, cud, lump, mass, pill, rock, wad
alba clay, kaolin

BOMA enclosure, kraal, stockade

BOMB ammunition, attack, barrage, bat, blare, blitz, bombard, booby trap, boom, camouflet, cannonade, container, crump, dud, egg, enfilade, explosive, fail(ure), flop, football, frag, fusillade, grenade, missile, oil can,

pepper, petard, pineapple, prang, projectile, rake, salvo, shell, squib, strafe, surprise, torpedo, vone, whizzbang
air to surface bull pup
anti-personnel butterfly
blast measure megaton
guide fin
hole crater
kind aerial, antipersonnel, antisubmarine, ashcan, atomic, azon, bat, blockbuster, citybuster, concussion, demolition, depth, dynamite, electron, fire (ball), fragmentation, gas, hedgehog, hydrogen, incendiary, marmite, plutonium, razon, roc(ket), smoke, stink, tear-gas, time
lance harpoon
old marmite
-proof impervious, secure
pump stirrup
release toggle
repository bay
shelter abri, casement, dugout, refuge
-thrower anarchist
trench minnie

BOMBA ferdinand, puffcheek, windbag

BOMBARD assail, assault, atomize, attack, batter, blackjack, bomb, bombardoon, cannon, catapult, crump, launch, shell, strafe, tankard, toper

BOMBARDMENT attack, blitz(krieg), cannonade, rafale, shelling, siege, strafing

BOMBARDON bassoon, brummer, horn, nicolo, oboe, pommer, sax(horn), tuba

BOMBAST ampollosity, balderdash, blow, bluster, boast(ing), bounce, bravado, buncombe, buncum, flatulence, fustian, gas, grandiosity, hot air, inflated, magniloquence, padding, pomposity, pontificate, puff, rage, rant, rave, rhetoric, rodomontade, stuffing, tell-talk, tumidity, tumor, turgidity, tympany, wind

BOMBASTIC aureate, declamatory, euphuistic, extravagant, flatulent, flowery, fluent, fustian, gassy, grandiloquent, grandiose-

mouthy, heroic, inflated, mouthy, orotund, pompous, pretentious, puffy, ranting, stilted, stuffy, swelling, swollen, tumid, turgid, vocal, windy, wordy

BOMBAY *arrowroot* tikor
city miraj, poona, surat
division sind
duck bummalo, harpadon, lizard-fish
hemp ambari, ambary, sunn
sect parsi
seed kanagi, nux vomica
state edar, gujarat, maharashtra
vessel patamar

BOMBE bulged, curved, mold, puffed, rounded

BOMBINATE boom, buzz, drone, hum

BOMBSHELL sensation, surprise

BOMBUS bumbee, bumblebee, bumbler

BOMBYX eri(a), moth, silkworm

BON bean, bond, complaisant, fine, good, grass, note, shamanism
aire complaisant, courteous, gentle
ami friend, lover, sweetheart
chretien bartlett pear
homme amiability, peasant
marche bargain
mot crack, jest, pun, quip, witticism
silene tea rose
ton breeding, elite, fashion, society, style
vivant boulevardier, companion, epicure(an), friend, gastronome, glutton, gourmet, sensualist, sport
viveur flaneur
voyage See GOODBYE.

BONA damia, fauna, gynaecea
brother faunus
consort faunus
namo tip
roba courtesan, wanton
son bacchus, midas

BONACE *tree* noseburn

BONACI aguaji, grouper

BONAFIDE authentic, dependable, fraudless, genuine, level, pure, real, reliable, true, trustworthy, veritable

BONAGH See SOLDIER.

BONANZA eureka, golconda,

jackpot, mine, mint, treasure, wealth, windfall
state montana
BONASSUS auroch, bison
BONAVENTURE boat, mast, sail, vessel
BONBON candy, caramel, chocolate, confection, confetto, snapper, sugarplum, sweetmeat
BOND accord, adhesion, adhesive, agreement, allegiance, association, assurance, attachment, attraction, bail, band, binder, bound, captivity, cement, certificate, chain, cohere, collateral, compact, conductor, confiner, connect(ion), connex, contract, couple, covenant, debenture, duty, engage, escrow, fastener, fetter, friendship, glue, guarantee, gyve, join, knot, league, liaison, ligament, ligature, link(age), manacle, mortgage, nexus, note, obligation, overlap, paper, pledge, relation(ship), rente, seam, security, shackle, snare, solder, statute, stock, surety, swathe, tache, tie, union, vadimony, valence, vinculum, vow, yoke
comb. desm(o), syndesm(o)
BONDAGE captivity, chains, confinement, dependence, enslavement, helotism, helotry, imprisonment, obligation, peonage, prison, restraint, serfdom, servitude, slavery, subjection, subjugation, subservience, surfdom, thirling, thrall(dom), vassalage, vassalism, villeinhood, yoke
free from affranchise, emancipate, enfranchise, manumit
pert. captive
BONDER assembler, bondstone, brick, freeholder, freeman
BONDLAND copyhold
BONDS assets, chains, holdings, irons, khakis, securities, trammels
BONDSMAN bailor, carl, chattel, churl, esne, helot, peasant, peon, serf, slave, sponsor, stooge, thrall, vassal, villein

BONDSTONE binder, keystone, perpend
BONE baleen, beg, blunder, cannon, capitatum, cartilege, cram, demand, dib, dollar, domino, framework, issue, ivory, obstruction, ossa, ossicle, osteel, plug, shalo, slate, steal, study, take
adhesion ankylosis
ankle astragalus, talus
anvil ambos, incus
arm epipodiale, humerus, radius, ulna
back spine, vertebra
black abaiser, charcoal
bolt-like pessulus
box bier, casket, coffin
breast gladiolus, sternum, xiphoid
brown bracken
cancer multiple myeloma
cartilage ossein
carved scrimshaw
cavity antrum, cavern, lacuna, sinus
cavity tissue marrow
cell osteoplast
center marrow
change into ossify
cheek malar, zygoma
china porcelain
collagen ossein
comb. osseo, ossi, ost(eo)
corpuscle astroblast, astrocyte
curvature kyphosis, lordosis, scoliosis
decay caries
defect achondroplasia, ankylosis, anostosis, varus
depression fossa
disease acromegaly, arthritis, caries, eburnation, osteitis, osteomyelitis, rachitis, rickets
diseased fragment sequestrum
dorsal ilia, ilium
-dry anti-alcohol
ear ambos, anvil, incus, stapes, stirrup
-eater bonito, sarda
face malar, mandible, maxilla, zygoma
finger digit, phalange
flank ilium
formation ostosis, parostosis
fossil odontolite
fragment spicule
girdle sphenethmoid
group skeleton
heap breccia

hip acetabulum, huggin, ilium
-idle indolent, lazy
-jack bonito, sarda
jaw articular(e), maxilia
junction dacryon, syssarcosis
kind 3 hip, jaw, rib 4 back, heel, shin, soup, ulna, wish 5 aitca, ambon, ancon, ankle, anvil, cheek, chine, costa, femur, funny, hyoid, ilium, incus, jugal, malar, meros, nasal, pubis, ramus, skull, spine, talus, tibby, tibia, ulnar, vomer, wrist 6 breast, canine, cannon, carpal, carpus, coccyx, collar, costal, cuboid, epural, fibula, hallux, haunch, lumbar, magnum, nuchal, pecten, pelvis, rachis, radius, rotula, sacrum, stapes, tarsal, tarsus, tripod, zygoma 7 cochlea, cranium, ethmoid, femoral, frontal, hamatum, humerus, ischium, kneecap, knuckle, lunatum, malleus, mastoid, maxilla, osselet, otolith, patella, phalanx, scapula, sciatic, sternum, stirrup 8 clavicle, lacertus, mandible, otosteon, parietal, phalange, scaphoid, sesamoid, shoulder, sphenoid, temporal, unciform, vertebra 9 cancaneus, cuneiform, lachrymal, maxillary, occipital, rachidial 10 astragalus, metacarpal, metatarsal
layer cementum, lamella
leg femur, fibula, patella, shin, tibia
-like ossal, osteoid
manipulator chiropractor, osteopath
mend knit
nose ethmoid
of contention argument, dispute, issue
oil lanose, olanin
pelvis ilium, pichium
pert. ossal, osteal
plowshare pygostyle, vomer
pot urn
process inion, mastoid, tubercle
prophet's spealbone
rump aitchbone
scraper xyster
separation diastasis
setting apothesis, reduction
shank epipodiale
shin cnemis

sinus antrum
skull frontal, mandible, maxilla, sphenoid, temporal, vomer
small osselet, ossicle, sesamoid
spine coccyx, sacra, vertebra
spur exostosis
thigh femur
thoracic rib
tumor endosteoma, enostosis, periosteoma
turned abnormally valgus
turquoise ivory, odontolite
ulceration caries
up plug, study
wormian epactal, epipteric
wrist carpal(e)
BONEBREAKER bird, fulmar, lammergeier, osprey
BONEFISH albula, grubber, ladyfish, macabi, oio
BONEHEAD See BLOCKHEAD.
BONEHOUSE casket, coffin, ossuary, tomb, urn
BONER bloomer, blooper, blunder, booboo, brodie, bubu, bull, error, faux pas, howler, lapse, mistake, slip, steeler, stum(o)ur
BONES body, dice, dominoes, frame, money, refuse, remains, skeleton
BONESET ageratum, agrimony, agueweed, comfrey, crosswort, eupatory, feverwort, gentian, hempweed, mistflower, sage, teasel, thoroughwort
BONESETTER doctor, healer, surgeon
BONESHAKER bicycle
BONESHAW sciatica
BONEWORT daisy, goldenrod
BONEYARD bank, cemetery, repository, scrapheap, stock, storage, store, supply
BONFIRE balefire, blaze, flame, needfire, tandle, tawnie
BONGO antelope, beetle, dor, drum, tree
BONIFACE host, innkeeper, landlord
BONITO aku, albacore, bone-eater, bonejack, cobia, katonkel, mackerel, nice, pretty, robalo, sarda, scombrid, skipjack, victorfish
BONKERS crazy, mad, unbalanced

BONNE maid, nurse, servant
amie lover, sweetheart
foi fidelity
fortune success
nuit farewell, goodnight
BONNET accomplice, bongrace, calash, cap(ote), casing, chamber, chapeau, commode, coronet, cover, cowl, decoy, doff, hat, headgear, hood, leghorn, mobcap, poky, reticulum, roof, scone, slouch, sowback, spatter-dock, top, toque, voluper
black emberiza, reed-bunting
brim poke
18th century calash
glass monteith
grass redtop
-like mitrate
limpet calyptraea
monkey macaco, macaque, munga, rilawa, sati, toque, zati
rouge extremist, radical, redcap, revolutionist
shark See BONNETHEAD.
string bride
BONNETHEAD hammerhead, shark, shovelhead, sphryna
BONNETMAN highlander, scot
BONNEY, WILLIAM billy the kid, outlaw
BONNY agreeable, attractive, beauteous, beautiful, blithe, braw, budgeree, charming, comely, fair, fine, gay, handsome, healthy, lovely, merry, placid, pleasing, plump, pretty, sweet, taking, tranquil
BONNYCLABBER clot, curd, skyr, sour milk
BONO, JOHNNY englishman
BONTE civility, good nature, goodness, kindliness
BONTEBOK antelope, bantebuck, blesbok, blesbuk, damaliscus
BONTOK igorot
BONUS award, batta, coot, bountith, bounty, bribe, bunce, bunts, cash, cumshaw, dividend, douceur, extra, gift, gratuity, guerdon, honorarium, lagniappe, meed, money, overpayment, overtime, pilon, pique, premium, present, prize, regalo, re-

ward, solatium, spiff, subsidy, tantieme, tip, windfall
BONXIE skua
BONY angular, hard, lank(y), lean, napoleon, osseous, ossicular, ossiferous, ossified, osteal, rawboned, scraggy, skeletal, skinny, solid, stiff, thin, tough, underweight
BONYFISH chiro, menhaden
BONZE See MONK.
BONZER a-one, first-rate, remarkable, wonderful
BONZERY monastery
BOO bird, bronx cheer, catcall, cry, disapproval, goose, hiss, hoot, jeer, low, moo, pooh(pooh), raspberry, razz, ridicule
BOOB See BOOBY.
tube television
BOOBOO See ERROR.
BOOBOOK cuckoo, mopoke, morepark, ninox, owl, peho, ruru
BOOBY ass, camanay, chump, clod, dunce, dupe, FOOL, gannet, gawk, golem, goon, goop, goosecap, idiot, loser, neddy, nincompoop, nitwit, noodle, piquero, prize, s(c)hmo, s(c)hmuck, simpleton, sleigh, stupid, sula, yold
bird redfoot
BOOBYALLA dogwood, longifolia, myoporum, tree, waterbush, wattle, willow
BOOBYHATCH asylum, jail, prison
BOOBYTRAP ambush, bomb, mine
BOODLE bribe, booty, buddle, caboodle, counterfeit, crowd, graft, group, loot, MONEY, newmarket, noodle, plunder, spoil, swag
BOOGEYMAN bugbear, demon, hobgoblin, menace, padfoot, tankerabogus, threat
BOOGIE WOOGIE blues, jazz, walking bass
BOOJUM cirio, snark
BOOK album, annual, arrest, best-seller, bible, brochure, canon, canto, catalog(ue), chapter, charge, codex, composition, detur, diary, dissertation, document, enchiridion, engage, enter, folio, garland, gospeler, guide, hard-cover, herbal,

hire, hora(e), indite, in-scribe, journal, juvenile, lexicon, liber, libretto, lil, list, log, magnum-opus, manual, manuscript, missal, monograph, narrative, novel, opus(cle), order, pamphlet, paperback, pasto-ral, primer, psalter, publica-tion, quair, quire, reader, record, register, reserve, schedule, script(ure), speller, synaxary, text, ticket, tome, tract(ate), treatise, triodion, volume, work, writing
agent drummer
alphabet abecedary
announcement blurb, flyer
back dorso, spine, verso
beginning incipit
best selling bible
binder bibliopegist
binding bibliopegy, string, stub
binding material assiette, bock, buckram, buffing, canvas, cloth, leather, paper, velum
binding style aldine, ara-besque, byzantine, etruscan, fanfare, grolier, harleian, jansenist, maioli, majoli, roxburgh, yapp
binding tool edge-roll
biographical who's who
blank album, diary, tablet
closed incomprehensible
collection bible, canon, library, set
comb. biblio
commonplace adversaria
cover binding, dust jacket, for(r)el, recto, reverse, sleeve, versel, verso
cover ornament plaquette, tooling
dealer bibliopole, bon-guiniste
decorating art fraktur
design format, layout
destroyer biblioclast
devotional bible, diurnal, gospel, missal, psalter
division chapter
early printing gutenberg bible, incunable, in-cunabulum, mainz psalter
edge-covering ferrule
elementary abc, primer
end part afterword, back matter, colophon, epi-log(ue), explicit, finis
extract pericope

extra-illustrate grangerize
factory bindery
folded orihon
heraldic armorial, armory
hidden apocrypha
hoarder bibliotaph(e)
introduction isagoge, preface
jacket notice blurb
large folio, tome
leaf folio, insert, page, plate
lining doublure
liturgical antiphonalm mis-sal, synaxarion
louse corrodentia, troctes
-lover See BOOKWORM.
madness bibliomania
manuscript codex, draft
map atlas, gazeteer
miniature bibelot
mutilate grangerize
navigator's log, portolano
obscene pornography
of account bilan, day, jour-nal, ledger, liber
of books bible
of feasts ordo
of hours hora, nones
of instruction manual
of kings shah namah
of life beadroll
of moses' law pentateuch
of nobility almanach de gotha, burke's, peerage
of questions quare
omitted from bible apocry-pha
page folio
palm corypha, taliera, tali-pot, tara
part binding, chapter, cover, fascicle, folio, gathering, index, introduction, jacket, leaf, page, preface, section, signature, spine
peddler colporteur
pert. bibliographic, bibliog-raphy
poetic canto
prayer horae, portas(s), porthors, siddur
pre-1500 incunabula
production bibliogenesis, bib-liogony
psalms psalter, tehillim
rare incunabulum
record tickler
reference almanac, concord-ance, dictionary, encyclo-pedia, gazeteer, glossary, thesaurus, vade mecum
religious bible, breviary, gos-pel, gradual, horary, kitab, koran, kyrial(e), megillah,

missal, ordinary, prosar, quran, synaxary
review analysis, commen-tary, criticism, critique, de-scription, evaluation
rule hoyle
sacred scripture
school arithmetic, geography, grammar, primer, reader, speller
scorpion chelifer
selection excerpt, extract, pericope
shape and size format
shelf pluteus, press
ship's log
size duodecimo, folio, oc-tavo, quarto, sexto, twelvemo
slipcase forel
small brochure, manual, pamphlet, quire
song hymnal
title page rubric
translation pony, trot
unbound cahier
BOOKCASE for(r)el, plu-teus, press, scrine, stack
18th century chiffon(n)ier
group stack
BOOKING contract, engage-ment, registration, reserva-tion
BOOKISH academic, belle-tristic, erudite, formal, learned, literary, pedagogic, pedantic, scholarly, stilted, studious
BOOKKEEPER accountant, auditor, cpa
BOOKKEEPING *term* bal-ance, capitalize, carry-over, charge, credit, debit, docket, enter, entry, log, post, statement
BOOKLET brochure, folder, pamphlet, tract
BOOKMAKER bet-broker, bookie
establishment wire room
BOOKMAN author, bookie, dealer, litterateur, pub-lisher, scholar
BOOKMARK register, tassel
BOOKPLATE ex libris, label
collection ex librism
BOOKSELLER bibliopole, colporteur, drummer
group conger
BOOKWORK reading, re-search, study
BOOKWORM academician, beetle, bibliolater, biblio-mane, bibliophage, biblio-

phile, browser, catorama, grind, reader, scholar, student

BOOKWRIGHT author, writer

BOOM barrier, beam, bell, bombilate, bombinate, boost, bowsprit, brail, bump(kin), buzz(ing), cable, campaign for, cannonade, cathead, chain, cord, crane, croon, din, drone, drum, explosion, float, flourish, good times, grow, grumble, hum (ming), increase, inflation, jib, lever, manipulate, move, outrigger, peal, pipe, pole, popularity, probe, progress, promote, propel, prosperity, prow, push, reel, resound, reverberation, roar, roll, rumble, rumbling, spar, speed, sprit, support, thrive, thunder
crane arm, gib, jib
iron crance, withe

BOOMER hobo, kangaroo, sewellel, worker
state oklahoma

BOOMERANG atlatl, backfire, kiley, kylie, leeangle, leewill, react, rebound, recoil, resile, ricochet, solitaire, trombash, womerah, woomera

BOON bene(diction), benefit, benign, blessing, bound, bounteous, bounty, congenial, convivial, donation, fairing, favor, gay, gift, goodly, gracious, grant, gratuity, intimate, jolly, jovial, kind, largess, merry, petition, prayer, present, windfall
companion bloodbrother, bullyrock, chum, friend, mate, pal
service See SERVICE *feudal.*

BOONDOCKS boonies, bundoc, bundocks, country, sticks, tulies, wilds

BOONDOGGLE belt, cord, goldbrick, trifle

BOONE, DANIEL *biographer* james fenimore cooper
biography leatherstocking tales
court judgment-tree
discovery cumberland gap, ouasioto

friend john findley, john floyd, mingo
indian foe blackfish, captain will, cornstalk, shawnee
settlement cantucke, kentucky
title syndic

BOONK bittern, botaurus, bottle, bottlebird, weavebird

BOOR barbarian, boeotian, bore, bosthoon, bounder, buffo(on), bumpkin, cad, caliban, carl(ot), cauboge, chuff, churl, clod(hopper), clown, clunch, clusterfist, comic, countryman, fool, grobian, hick, hoblob, jack, jester, jobson, joskin, kern(e), lout, lubber, lummox, oaf, peasant, peon, pill, rube, runt, rustic, slob, tike, tramontane, villain, yokel
mustard pennycress, peppercress

BOORISH awkward, bohunkish, boobyish, brutal, carterly, churlish, cloddish, clodpolish, clumsy, coarse, countrified, crabbed, discourteous, farmerish, gawky, hoblike, hobnailed, hoosierfied, ill-mannered, impolite, inelegant, inept, kernish, loutish, lubberly, maladroit, obtuse, peakish, prost, raffish, roister, rough, rowdy, rude, ruffianly, runty, rustic, savage, stupid, sullen, surly, uncouth, uncultivated, uncultured, ungainly, unmannerly, unpolished, unrefined, vulgar, wool(l)en

BOOST abet, advance, advertise, advocate, aggrandize, aid, assist, back, boom, cheer, coach, commend (ation), elevate, encourage, endorse, enhance, exalt, heave, heighten, help, hoist, hoosh, increase, inspire, jigger, kite, lift, plug, promote, push, raise, rear, rise, surge, thrust, uplift

BOOSTER accelerator, aficionado, cheerleader, detonator, dose, dynamo, enthusiast, fan(atic), follower, flack, panegyrist, promoter, publicist, pump, shoplifter, shot, supporter, synergist

BOOT advantage, alternative,

amends, avail, balmoral, benefit, bestead, blow, blucher, bonus, booty, bot(e), bottekin, bottine, buskin, calcitra, casing, catapult, chukka, cothurn, covering, crakow, cure, dismiss(al), eject(ion), enrich, error, evict(ion), extra, fire, footwear, forehearth, fumble, gain, gaiter, galosh, gratuity, help, hessian, kamik, kick, larrigan, mukluk, napoleon, overshoe, pad, pedule, plunder, profit, punt, receptacle, recruit, relief, relieve, remedy, repair, satisfaction, sheath, shoe(pac), sloat, sock, spoil, stogy, thrill, thrust, tip, torture, trunk, tube, vantage, wader, wellington
dealer bottier
14th-century crakow
half blucher, bottine, buskin, cocker, cothurnus, pac(k), skilty
heavy balmoral, brogan, pac(k), stoga, stogy
high-water wader, wellington
hill cemetery
hobnailed bat, cherry-red
hose spatterdashes, stockings
laced high-low
lady's bottine
logger's pac(k)
loop strap
loose-topped wellington
lumberman's cruiser, larrigan
marine skinhead
19th-century napoleon
out discharge, dismiss, eject, expel, fire
reindeer-skin finnesko
riding gambado, jemmy, jimmy, jodhpur
rubber arctic, galosh, wellington
sealskin kamik
small bottekin, bottine
torture squeezer
trapper's larrigan
winged talaria

BOOTBLACK shiner, shoeboy, shoeshiner

BOOTH balagan, banquette, bothy, box, butin, cabin, casing, cockshy, compartment, coop, crame, hut, kiosh, liwan, lodge, loge, newstand, pagoda, pandal, paybox, seat, shed, shop,

sook, souk, stall, stand, succah, sukkah, suq, tienda
edwin, epithet prince of
players

BOOTJACK bidens, molding,
notch

BOOTLEG clandestine,
hooch, illegal, illegitimate,
illicit, liquor, moonlight,
moonshine, mountain dew,
shyisly, smuggle, unlawful

BOOTLEGGER blindpigger,
moonshiner, rumrunner
wares poteen, rotgut

BOOTLESS abortive, fruitless, futile, incurable, invalid, unavailing, useless,
vain

BOOTLICK apple-polish,
back-scratch, brown-nose,
fawn, flatter, leech, parasite, sponge, sycophant,
toady, truckler, wardheeler

BOOTS attendant, black-haw,
bull's-eye, caltha, marsh-
marigold, overs, servant, viburnum

BOOTY blackmail, boodle,
butin, cheat, creagh, fang,
filch, fleece, foray, gain,
grab, graft, haul, lift, loot,
money, patronage, pelf,
perquisite, pickings, pillage,
plunder, pork barrel, prey,
prize, reif, seizure, spoils,
spreaghery, spreath, spulzie, stealage, stealth, swag,
take

BOOZ See BOAZ.

BOOZE alcohol, bout, budge,
drink, fuddle, liquor, spree,
whiskey
fighter drug addict, drunk
(ard)

BOOZER bouser, carouser,
drunk(ard), pub, saloon,
toper

BOP blow, hit, jazz, strike

BOR *son* odin

BORACHIO *friend* conrade,
don john

BORAGE alkana, anchusa,
arnebia, asperugo, cerinthe,
cochranes, lappula,
primrose, symphytum

BORAK banter, chaff, make-
believe, mockery, ridicule,
sarcasm

BORAX boracous, flux, junk,
pyroborate, sodium, tincal
source kernite

BORDEAUX *ancient name*
burdigala
wine barsac, bourg, carbon-

nieux, chianti, claret, cosne,
cotes, graves, margaux,
medoc, palus, sauterne, st
emilion
wine broker courtier
wine district gironde

BORDELLO bawdy-house,
brothel, house of ill fame,
whorehouse

BORDER 3 end, hem, lip,
mat, rim, tip 4 abut, bind,
brim, brow, curb, dado,
eave, edge, line, list, mark,
mill, oree, orle, purl, rand,
roon, rund, side, trim,
wage, welt 5 adorn, board,
bound, braid, brink, cheek,
coast, costa, flank, forel,
frame, frill, ledge, limit,
march, marge, marli, shore,
skirt, strip, swage, touch,
verge 6 accost, adjoin, edging, emboss, fillet, flange,
forrel, fringe, impale, labium, labrum, limbus, li-
sere, margin, purfle, region
7 affront, bordure, confine,
curbing, edgeing, enframe,
floroon, marches, margent,
orphrey, selvage, valance,
wayside 8 befringe, boundary, district, frontier, labellum, marchese, neighbor,
ornament, outskirt, skirting,
surround, terminus, tressure
9 extremity, kerbstone, periphery 11 enframement,
ironcurtain 13 bamboocur-
tain
decorative entrelac, frame,
fringe, matting, tressure
distinctive limbus
flowered floroon
fluted frill
fringed fimbria
heraldic orle
lace picot
land near marches
-line debatable, frontier, indeterminate, uncertain
making tool edger
minstrel walter scott
ribbon frilac
rider freebooter
rock salband
state arkansas, delaware, estonia, finland, kentucky,
lithuania, maryland, mis-
souri, north carolina, poland, tennessee, virginia
wall cornice, dado, ogee

BORDERED limbate, orle

BORDERING about, adjacent, approximate, coastal,

contiguous, fringing, frontier, littoral, margent, marginal, near, neighboring,
proximate, rimming, skirting

BORE affliction, aiguille, an-
noy(ance), auger, bit,
bother(ation), bromide,
button-holer, caliber, chink,
commonplace, crevice, cut,
diameter, discomfort, drag,
drill, drip, droop, dryasdust,
eagre, eat, ennui, enter, fatigue, flat-tire, gauge, gim-
lit, gouge, headache, hole,
hollow, humdrum, irk,
jump, nudni(c)k, nuisance,
ought, pain, pall, penetrate,
perforate, pest, pierce, pill,
plague, poke, pororoca,
prick, proser, punch, push,
ream, shlump, sink, stale,
stood, talent, tap, terebrate,
tewel, thrust, tide, tire, tool,
trial, tube, tunnel, twaddler,
vexation, vexatiousness,
wave, weary, wet blanket,
wimble
from within maneuver, undermine
of cannon chase, soul
tidal eagre

BOREADES calais, zetes

BOREAL, BOREAD cold,
northern

BOREAS aquilo(n), north
wind
brother eurus, notus, zephyrus
consort orithyia
offspring butes, calais, cleopatra, zetes
parent astraeus, aurora, eos
victim orithyia

BORED ennuyee, satiated,
weary

BOREDOM annoyance, apathy, doldrums, ennui, en-
nuye, indifference, languor,
lassitude, lethargy, poco-
curantism, tedium, yawn

BOREE acacia, myall, wattle-
tree

BOREGAT bodieron, greenling, hexagrammose, rock
trout

BORELE black rhinoceros,
keitloa, upeygan

BORER anarsia, aspergillum,
augur, bardee, beetle, flathead, hagfish, lithodomus,
mole, ovipositor, saxicava,
scolytus, shipworm, tam-

bark, termite, terrier, tool, wimble, woodworm, worm
BORGHILD *husband* sigmund
BORGIA *brother* cesare, pedro, rodrigo
pope alexander, alonso, calixtus, rodrigo
sister lucrezia
BORGO neighborhood, street, suburb
BORING broach, chip, dim, dry, dull, earthsample, filing, flat, fragment, hackneyed, hole, lumpish, poky, slow, stodgy, stupid, tedious, tiresome, tiring, trite
communication bumf
tool aiguille
BORN borg, burg, delivered, hatched, innate, nascent, nate, native, natural, nee, original, renewed
again regenerate(d)
before its time abortive, premature, slink
days lifetime, long-time
dead stillborn
fool simpleton
out of wedlock bastard
tired indolent, lazy
to the purple aristocratic, noble, regal, royal, thoroughbred
under lucky star fortunate
well eugenic, free, noble
with silver spoon wealthy
yesterday inexperienced, naive
BORNE berne, bourn, burnish, carried, endured, limited, narrow(minded), rode
BORNEO kalimantan
ape orang(utan)
bay adang, kumai, sampit
camphor ngai
cape aru, datu, lojar, puting, sambar, selatan
city ketapang, kumai, malinau, pagatan, sambas, sampit, sanggau, sintang, tarakan
insectivore moon rat
island near alor, bali, java, natoena
measure gantang
monkey kalasie
moslem kadayan
north sabah
peak kinabalu, nijaan, raja, saran, tebang
pepper plant ara
pirates bajau

port balik, ban(d)hermasin, brunei, miri, papan, pontianak
range iran, muller, schwaner
region brunei, sabah, sarawak
river arut, bahau, baram, barito, berau, bruni, iwan, kahajan, kajan, kapuas, mahakam, mendawi, padas, pawan, pembuang, sebuku
rubber gutta susu
sea sulu
serpent boiga
squirrel shrew pentail
sultanate baunei
timber tree billian
tree kapor, kapur
tree shrew tana
tribe bakatan, bukat, dajak, d(a)yak, dusun, iban, illano, illanum, punan
weight chapah, para
BORNHOLM *disease* pleurodynia
port ronne
BORO *indian* See MIRANHA *indian.*
BORODIN *opera* prince igor
BORON borax, boric, ulexite
nitride aethogen
BOROROAN *indian* corabecan, coroado, covarecan, curavecan, curucanecan, curuminacan, otuquian, tupian
BOROUGH area, borg, burg(h), citadel, city, county, district, fortress, municipality, town(ship), village
comb. burgh
head borsholder, tithingman
BORR *kin* bure, odin
BORRACHA balata, rubber, sorva
BORROW adopt, appropriate, bank, bite, borgh, borh, bot, cadge, chevise, copy, desume, hire, introduce, kick, loan, luff, mutuate, pawn, pit, pledge, protect, redeem, rescue, schnorren, security, shin, steal, subtract, surety, take, thig, tithing, touch, use
trouble fret, stew, worry
BORROW, GEORGE *work* lavengro, romany rye
BORROWER mutuary
BORS *nephew* lancelot
BORSCH, BORST ragout, soup
base beets

BORSTAL *boy* delinquent
BORT *uncle* lancelot
BORZOI wolfhound
BOS beef, bison, calf, cow, neat, taurus
BOSCHBOK antelope, bushbuck
BOSH botch, bushwa, butterine, end, figure, flaunt, galbanum, humbug, joke, nonsense, pooh, poppycock, rot, show, spoil, talk, taunt, thicket, tosh(ery), trash, trivia, trough, twaddle
BOSK(ET) grove, thicket, wood
BOSKY bushy, drunk, fuddled, intoxicated, shadowy, shady, sylvan, tipsy, woody
BOSNIA See YUGOSLAVIA.
BOSOM affection, barm, breast, bust, cavity, cherish, close, conceal, confidential, desire, dick(e)y, embrace, friend, heart, inclination, inclose, inside, intimate, lap, pectoral, recess, secret, waist
false plumper
friend alter ego
pert. gremial
BOSPORUS *city on* byzantium, constantinople, chalcedon, istanbul
inlet golden horn
BOSS anchor, baas, bold, botch, bovine, buhr, bulge, bulla, bully, bur(r), button, bwana, cacique, capatez, captain, cask, chase, chief, controller, cow, cushion, czar, decoration, dictator, direct(or), domineer, emboss, employer, empty, excrescence, first-rate, foreman, hassock, head(man), hollow, hub, jewel, kingmaker, knob, knop(s), knot, leader, manage(r), master, nail, nob, orb, order, ornament, overseer, owner, pad, padrone, patera, pellet, phalera, politician, pop, projection, protuberance, relief, ridge, sachem, shield, sponsor, stone, stud, super, superintend(ent), supervisor, taskmaster, tsar
fire gasman
leather button
mining shifter, shiftman
political cacique, caudillo, croker, crump, daley,

hague, hanna, pendergast, sachem, tweed
shield umbo
BOSSY authoritative, bold, brock, calf, cow, dictatorial, dominant, domineering, imperious, nagging
BOSTANGI attendant, gardener, guard, oarsman
BOSTHOON boar, clout, dolt
BOSTON athens of america, beantown, game, hub of the universe, waltz
airport logan international
aristocracy bluebloods, brahmins
bag satchel, valise
culture symbol beacon street
dish baked beans
district back bay, beacon hill, fens, hub
district, financial state street
founder john winthrop
fraternal society royal arcanum
game term independence, keep, preference
landmark bunker hill, faneuil hall, fenway park, old ironsides, old north church
leader brahman, brahmin
market faneuil hall
name, first trimontain
pink soapwort
plant fern
resident brahman, hubbite
rocker windsor chair
saint botolph
slum waterfront
BOSWELL, SAMUEL *nickname* bozzy
friend samuel johnson
BOT See BOTE.
BOTANIST dendrologist, herbalist, herbarian, herbist, horticulturist, pomologist
famous brown, linnaeus, mendel, phillips, ray
BOTANY dendrology, floristics, herbarism, horticulture, phytology, pomology
bay worcester college
bay gum acaroid
bay oak casuarina
bay tea smilax
classification taxonomy
collection herbarium
comb. ome
descriptive phytography
orders, comb. ales
specimen case vasculum
BOTCH barnaby, barney, bitch, blob, blunder, bob-

ble, bodge, boggle, boil, bollix, booboo, bosh, brodie, bugger, bumble, bungle, butch(er), cobble, fail, fiasco, flub, fluff, foozle, foul up, fudge, goof, gum up, hash, hodgepodge, jumble, louse, mar, mend, mess, misdo, mismanage, mucker, muddle, mull, mux, patch, repair, scamble, sclatch, slubber, sore, spoil, stagger, stumble, swelling, tinker
BOTCHER bungler, clouter, cobbler, grilse, patcher, salmon, tailor, tinker
BOTE advantage, amends, assessment, boot, brigbote, burghbote, compensation, frithbote, help, kinbote, plowbote, remedy, repair, satisfaction, wainbote, wer, wite
BOTFLY canopid, dipteran, gadbee, gadfly, hypoderma, nitter, oestrian, oestrid, torsalo, warblefly
larva bot(s), bott, torcel, wabble
BOTH alike, all, baith, couple(t), each, equally, pair, twain, two
comb. ambi, amphi(o)
-handed ambidextrous
BOTHER ado, aggravate, ail, annoy, badger, bait, bedevil, beset, bewilder, bore, bug, bullyrag, chagrin, chev(v)y, confuse, cumber, deave, devil, distract, distress, disturb, dither, effort, fash(ery), faze, flurry, fuss, gravel, grizzle, harass, harry, hassle, heckle, hector, impose, inconvenience, infest, irritate, jade, meddle, mither, moider, molest, muckle, nag, needle, nuisance, pain, perplex, persecute, perturb, pester, phase, pick on, plague, plaque, pother, putter, puzzle, ride, tamper, tantalize, tease, to-do, torment, trachle, trade, trial, trouble, uproar, upset, vex, work, worry
BOTHY, BOTHIE barrack, booth, bourock, cot(tage), hut, lodge
BOTOCUDO aimore, aymoro, borun, tapuya
BOTSWANA bechuanaland
city gaberone(s), kanye, lo-

botsi, mochudi, orapa, palapye, serowe, thamaga, tsane
coin rand
desert kalahari
lake dow, ngami
language bantu, click, khoisan, setswana
leader seretse-khama
peak tsodilo
people bamangwato, bantu, bushman, tswana
president khama
river chobe, cuando, cubango, limpopo, molopo, nata, nosob, okavango, okwa, shashi
BOTTEGA atelier, shop, studio, workshop
BOTTICELLI *painting* birth of venus, primavera, spring
BOTTLE aludel, ampul(la), aryballus, askos, bacbuc, betty, biberon, bocal, bombola, borachio, buire, buret, calabash, canteen, carafe, carafon, carboy, caster, chagul, clavelin, cooja, costrel, crewet, cruet, cruse, decanter, demijohn, doruck, enclose, entrap, ewer, fessel, fiasco, fifth, flagon, flask(et), goglet, gourd, guttus, haystack, jar, jordan, jug, kit, lagena, lota, magnum, mariotte, matara, mussuk, olla, phial, pig, preserve, rehoboam, seal, skin, split, thermos, vessel, vial, viol, woulff
bottom indentation kick
brush callistemon, chimney-sweep, equisetum, horsetail, mare's-tail, ribwort, sirmuellera, tree
carrier fascet
case canteen, cellar
cod caper
double gemel
-dwelling demersal
earthenware bombonne
empty deadman, marine
gourd calabash, lagenaria
grass fox tail, rabbit-foot clover
holder abettor, backer, supporter
holy bacbuc
hot water pig
imp cartesian devil, genie, jinni
imperfection heel tap
large balthazar, jeroboam
leather boot, budget, dubba,

dubber, dupper, matara, whinnock, wineskin
nursing biberon
opener corkscrew
ore bladderkelp, bladderwrack, seaweed
pair gem(m)el
priestess bacbuc
-shaped ampullaceous
size baby, balthazar, barrique, demijohn, feuillette, fifth, jeroboam, liter, magnum, methuselah, nebuchadnezzar, nip, pint, pipe, quart, queue, rehoboam, salmanazar, tappit, tonneau, tregnum
small amp(o)ule, costrel, cruet, decanter, doruck, flacon, phial, split, tickler, vinaigrette, vial
spirit genie
swallow fairy-martin
tree kurrajong, skreulia, sourgourd, sterculia
2-quart magnum
up blockade, censor, confine, cramp, repress, restrain, suppress, trap
vacuum thermos
wicker-covered carboy, demijohn, fiasco
BOTTLEBIRD bittern, boonk, botaurus, weaverbird
BOTTLEHEAD blackfish, doegling, plover, whale
BOTTLEMAN butler, sommelier
BOTTLENECK barrier, blockade, confine, congest(ion), hamper, hinder, obstruct, slow-down, stop, throttle
BOTTLENOSE cetacean, dipsomaniac, dolphin, grogblossom
whale hyperoodon
BOTTLER cooper
BOTTOM abyss, ballast, base(ment), basis, bed (rock), belly, breech, butt(ocks), cause, cellar, coil, dale, deep, derriere, discover, doup, downside, dregs, duff, empty, establish, exhaust, fathom, finish, floor, fond, foot, found(ation), fundament(al), fundus, ground, gutter, hardpan, holm, hull, laigh, last, leegte, lees, lowest, lowland, marsh, nadir, neth(most), origin, playa,

rest, root, rump, sike, sink, support, tetrapod, underside, understand, vessel, wind
-dwelling demersal
gear low
get to fathom
land carse, marsh, sike, strath
marshy sike
rake clearance
rock hardpan
sea benthos
sinking to demersal
BOTTOMER footman, stationman
BOTTOMLESS abysmal, abyssal, baseless, boundless, deep, mysterious, soundless, unfathomable, unlimited
BOTTOMS dale, dregs, grounds, lees, marsh, residue, sediment, slag, valley
BOTULISM allantiasis, lamziekte, poisoning
BOUCHAL See BOY.
BOUCHER axe, bursar, coup-de-poing, sack, treasurer
BOUCHON billiards, bush, cork, plug, stopper
BOUDOIR bedroom, bower, cabin(et), room, solitaire
BOUFFANT bulging, full, puffed
BOUGE bag, bilge, bulge, food, hump, provisions, swelling, wallet
BOUGH arm, blink, branch, breakwind, chuck, gallous, leg, limb, offshoot, part, phyllis, ramage, shoot, shroud, spray, sprig, strip, twig
BOUGHT bend, coil, curve, enclose, flexure, keft, pen, pew, sheepfold, store, turn, twist, zebina
BOUGIE antropora, candle, collyrie, filiform, filter, suppository
BOUILLABAISSE chowder, fish stew, soup
BOUILLON broth, consomme, soup
BOUK abdomen, belly, body, buck, bulk, carcass, lye, pail, paunch, psalterium, size, trunk, volume
BOULDER boother, dornick, erratic, hardhead, gibber, kelk, knob, megalith, nob, potstone, rock, stone
bast bulrush
dam site lake mead

head sea wall
iron dornick
monument megalith
transported by ice erratic
BOULE birne, buhl, game, inlay, parliament, senate
BOULEVARD arterial, avenue, drive, mouse-gray, parkway, prado, road, street, terrace, thoroughfare, viale
BOULEVARDIER bon vivant, dandy, flaneur, idler, lounger, rake, roue
BOULTER line, spiller, spillet, trawl
BOUNCE bang, blow, bluff, bluster, boast, bob, bombast, bound, brag, bully, carom, cashier, chounce, chuck, crack, dap, ding, dird, discharge, discuss, dismiss(al), dribble, drop, eject, elasticity, energy, expel, fire, gate, haul, hop, impudence, jump, knock, leap, lie, liveliness, outburst, persuade, rebound, recoil, resilience, ricochet, sack, scold, shake, spirit, spring, stot, strike, suddenly, swagger, thump, toss, verve, vitality
around brainstorm, confer, consider, discuss, dribble
back rebound, recoil, recover
BOUNCER boaster, bounder, braggart, bully, chucker, lie, liar, scrouger, whopper
BOUNCING big, buxom, exaggerated, excessive, exuberant, hale, healthy, hearty, lusty, stout, strong, vigorous
bess herb, soapwort
BOUND 3 end, hop, lop, run 4 abut, bind, bond, brow, butt, dart, edge, girt, jump, leap, list, lope, mere, move, race, ramp, rise, scud, skim, skip, stot, sure, tear, term, tied, wall 5 ambit, bourn, caper, fixed, going, limit, march, ready, sally, skirt, speed, start, stend, sworn, tiled, vault, verge 6 border, bounce, bourne, buttal, cavort, define, domain, finish, gambol, girder, hurdle, intent, liable, oblige, prance, recoil, spring, united 7 affined, assured, barrier, certain, chained, closure,

confine, contain, costive, delimit, gambado, include, obliged, saltate, secured, termine, trussed 8 articled, beholden, confined, destined, enclosed, fasciate, ferrered, frontier, handfast, indebted, limitate, precinct, prepared, resolved, restrict, ricochet, shackled, surround 9 compelled, demarcate, obligated 10 determined, imprisoned, indentured 11 apprenticed, constrained 12 circumscribe
back carom, resile
by oath sworn
not solute
up in devoted, habituated, inseparable
BOUNDARY abuttal, ahu, ambit, barrier, border, bound, bourn(e), butting, close, compass, confines, curb, dole, dool, edge, end, fence, frontier, hedge, land-imore, landline, landmark, limits, list, march, margin, mark, mear, meith, mere, mete, octrol, octroy, pale, perimeter, periphery, rim, run, side(line), stake, term(inal), termination, trig, tropic, umstroke, verge, wall, wike
comb. horo, ori
contiguous abuttal
fortified lines
indefinite twilight zone
lines butts and bounds
natural, having arcifinious
BOUNDEN beholden, binding, compulsory, obligatory, obliged
BOUNDER barbarian, boor, cad, churl, cub, dogcart, looby, lout, mucker, rake, reprobate, ribald, roue, rough(neck), rowdy, ruffian, smuthound, upstart, vulgarian
BOUNDLESS bottomless, enormous, eternal, illimitable, immense, infinite, prodigious, unlimited, untold, vast
BOUNDS ambit, circumference, circumscription, compass, confines, edge, ends, fringes, limitations, limit(s), marches, metes, outlines, outskirts, pale, perimeter, periphery, restraint, rim, skirts

BOUNTEOUS abundant, ample, beneficent, benevolent, boon, bountiful, charitable, extravagant, fertile, generous, lavish, liberal, lush, munificent, plentiful, prodigal, productive, profuse, rich, teeming, valiant
BOUNTIFUL See BOUNTEOUS.
BOUNTY award, benefaction, beneficence, bontee, bonus, boon, charity, donative, generosity, gift, goodness, grant, gratuity, guerdon, kindness, largess(e), largition, liberality, meed, premium, present, prize, reward, subsidy, subvention, valor, virtue, worth
commander william bligh
BOUQUET aroma, aura, bloom, bob, boughpot, boutonniere, busket, buttonhole, chaplet, compliment, corsage, festoon, flowers, fragrance, garland, lei, nosegay, odor, pos(e)y, redolence, scent, sheaf, sheath, spray, wreath
de flore azalea, cardinal, kurume, minerva, rhododendron, snow
garni fag(g)ot, herbs
small boutonniere, buttonhole
BOURBON conservative, royalist, whisky
red turkey
tea faham
BOURDER jester, joker, mocker
BOURDON baton, cudgel, spear, staff
BOURGEOIS babbitt, boorish, burgher, businessman, capitalist(ic), citizen, common, conservative, conventional, hidebound, inelegant, mammonish, materialist, merchant, middle-class, orgon, philistine, shopkeeper, stupid
BOURGOGNE See BURGUNDY.
BOURNE aim, boundary, brim, brook, burn, destination, domain, goal, realm, rill, rivulet, stream
BOURNONITE endelionite
BOUROCK cluster, crowd, heap, hut, mound
BOURSE bolsa, borse, cam-

bio, exchange, market, purse
BOUSE, BOWSE booze(r), brannigan, brawl, carouse, drink, drunk(ard), haul, lift, liquor, roister, sot, squabble, tope(r)
BOUSTRAPA napoleon
BOUT act(ion), aside, assault, attack, booze, brash, carouse, circuit, conflict, contest, course, crash, essay, except, fall, fight, fracas, illness, job, match, outside, period, pluck, revel, round, session, set-to, spell, spree, trial, turn, venny, venue, without, yoking
drinking bat, bender, binge, bust, carouse, gaedown, potation, splore, spree, tire, wassail
BOUTADE caprice, composition, dance, outbreak, prank, whim
BOUTIQUE market, shop, store
BOVARY, MADAME *character* emma, delphine, delamare
author flaubert
BOVENLANT capetown
BOVID 3 ewe, keb, kid, kyl, mug, mul, not, pur, que, ram, tap, teg, tip, tup, tur, yak, yow, zac, zoh 4 anoa, apis, arna, arui, aver, boss, buck, bull, buss, cade, calf, cush, dogy, gaur, gour, hapi, hogg, ibex, kail, lamb, lonk, moil, mugs, mull, nata, nott, ouse, oxen, quey, reem, ship, tagg, tahr, tair, teap, tegg, tehr, thar, toro, toup, udad, uroy, zebu, zobo, zobu 5 agnus, ammon, argal, arnee, audad, beden, billy, bison, bobby, bossy, brawn, capra, caure, crony, cusha, dogie, dumba, gayal, gemse, goral, gyall, heder, jaela, jagla, kaama, nanny, niata, pasan, pesah, poddy, sanga, slink, sooky, steer, stirk, sucky, takin, thave, urial, vache, yakin 6 ankoli, aoudad, argali, aurocs, bantin, barhal, barwal, bharal, bident, braman, bramin, buffle, bulkin, cabree, calver, catalo, chamal, cosset, cotsol, crummy, dinman, doddie,

eweteg, gimmer, hawkey, heifer, hieder, hogget, hogrel, humlie, jersey, jharal, maille, mazama, merino, moiley, moolly, mouton, muflon, muskox, musmon, mutton, nahoor, nayaur, pasang, paular, paulie, putter, romney, sarlak, sheder, taurus, theave, wedder, wether, wisent, wooley 7 aurochs, berendo, bighorn, bleater, brahman, buffalo, bullock, caracul, cheviot, chilver, delaine, dishley, eanling, karakul, mouflon, mufflon, singler, slinker, taurine

BOVINE bangtail, beast, bison, bos, BOVID, bull, calf, complacent, cous, cow(ish), dull, humlie, hummel, oxlike, patient, rother, slow, sluggish, steady, steer, stolid, stupid, taurine

hybrid catalo, mule

BOW 3 act, arc, bob, leg, nod, rod, tie, yew 4 arch, bail, beak, beck, bend, cave, duck, fawn, fold, jouk, knee, knit, knot, lath, loff, loop, luff, play, prow, rodd, stem, true, turn, wend, yoke 5 binge, bulge, cline, conge, crook, crush, curve, debut, defer, entry, frame, goura, greet, guard, honor, kneel, noeud, salam, shiko, stoop, yield 6 archer, assent, buckle, cringe, crouch, curtsy, kowtow, relent, ribbon, salaam, salute, scrape, subdue, submit, swerve, tourte, weapon 7 courtsy, curtsey, depress, incline, inflect, succomb, worship 8 arbalest, bentwood, courtesy, crescent, entrance, fogeater, truelove 9 arcograph, genuflect, obeisance, prostrate, surrender 10 appearance, capitulate, decoration 11 acknowledge, fiddlestick, genuflexion, inclination, performance 12 genuflection, triggerguard

and arrow container ascham, locker

and arrow maker bowyer, fletcher

and arrow use archery

and scrape fawn, kowtow, sala(a)m

bells anemone, cockneydom, wood

ceremonious conge

comb. arc(i), arco

down alout, humble, salaam, surrender

extension sprit

file riffler

kind arbalest, ballista, catapult, crossbow, fiddle, gora(h), goura, longbow, mangonel, onager, quarrel, rodd, trebuchet

line fargood

low binge

of promise rainbow

out dismiss, exit, quit, withdraw

outward convex

part loof, luff

pin cotter

seller bowyer

-shaped arc(u)ate

ship's beak, head, prow, stem

toward afore

violin stick

with the arco

BOWDLERIZE blue-pencil, censor, expurgate, paraphrase

BOWED arcate, arched, arciform, arco, arcual, arcuate(d), bandy, bent, bulging, convex, curvant, curved, embowed, gibbous, humbled, hump-backed, humped, hunched, hunchy, kneed, shamble, stooped, vaulted

down melancholy, sad

BOWELS belly, colon, commiseration, compassion, empathy, entrails, guts, interior, intestine, kindness, pity, ruth, sympathy, tenderness, viscera, vitals

BOWER anchor, arbor, bender, berceau, boudoir, cabinet, chamber, cottage, dairyman, enclose, grotto, jack, joker, knave, lodge, musician, nook, pandal, pergola, retreat, shelter, stooper, summer-house, trellis, violinist

best joker

bird bird-of-paradise, catbird, collarbird

leafy levesel

plant pandorea, vine

snake kisi

BOWERY farm, plantation, shady

BOWFIN amia(calva), amidia, choupic, dogfish, ganoid, grindle, lawyer, morgay, mudfish, sawyer, sesi

BOWIE bowl, cask, knife, pail, sword, tub

death site alamo

state arkansas

BOWK bucket, cleanse, soak, steep, wash

BOWL acerra, amphitheater, aquarium, arena, ball, basin, beaker, bicker, bowie, bridecup, brimmer, cap, carry, cast, cavity, censer, chawan, convey, cootie, coupe, crater, cup, delivery, depas, depression, dish, ditcher, drum, duggler, fessel, hollow, jack, jicara, kitty, knock, laver, lekane, mazard, mazer, monteith, mortar, pan, patina, pelt, pitch, propel, race, rogan, roll(er), scale(pan), scyhus, skyphos, speed, stadium, strike, stummel, tanoa, tass, tazza, theater, theatre, throw, thurible, treem, troll, trough, trundle, tun, tureen, whiskin, vessel, yark

along pace, roll, speed

drinking tass, tun

illegally jerk

mythological depas

oblong pitchi

out york

over astonish, astound, fell, start(le), surprise, upset

pedestaled salver, tazza

shallow cap, coupe, whiskin

small jack

2-handled cap, depas

wooden bassie, bowie, cootie, kitty, mazer, rogan

BOWLEG outknee

BOWLEGGED bandy, bowhough'd, deformed, valgus, varus

BOWLER billycock, boxer, derby, hat, kegler, pinman, spinner, trundle

BOWLINE fargood

BOWLING bocc(i)e, boule, bowls, candlepins, kegling, skittles

ball dodo, jack

division frame

goal pins

machine spotter

mark tenpin

pin deadwood, duck, head, king, skittle, sleeper
place alley, green, rink
player See BOWLER.
score spare, strike
term cincinnati, split
BOWMAN archer, cupid
BOWSPRIT boom, spar
angle steeve, steeving
bar whisker
part bee, chock, heel
rest apron, stem
BOWSTRING beam, execute, girder, kill, serving, strangle, truss
hemp ife, mudar, murva, pangane, sansevieria
BOX 3 ark, bin, car, gig, hit, kit, lob, lug, mix, pen, pix, pyx, tye 4 arca, binn, blow, body, cage, caja, case, cist, crib, cuff, drab, etui, file, flat, inro, loge, mill, mull, pack, pung, scob, seat, slap, slug, spar, stow, swat, till, trap 5 block, boist, booth, buist, buxus, caddy, capsa, chest, clout, crate, fight, frame, hutch, miter, piano, punch, smite, stall, trunk 6 ascham, buffet, bunker, caisse, carton, casket, coffer, coffin, corner, dorine, hamper, hopper, incase, locker, lycium, mocuck, pillar, recess, sagger, shrine, socket, strike, vanity 7 cabinet, caisson, canteen, casquet, cassone, confine, confuse, cottage, enclose, fostell, freezer, hanaper, housing, package, pitarah, present, scatula, shelter, topiary, trummel, wherret 8 bursaria, canister, fostelle, junction, lavarium, position, slipcase, solander, wardrobe 9 container, enclosure, rectangle, situation, tristania 10 eucalyptus, receptacle 11 compartment, predicament 13 pitcher's mound
alms arca
ammunition caisson, bandolier
berry hallock
birchbank mocuck
book-shaped solander
bread barge
brier berry, indigo, inkberry, randia
candle bark
canyon cajon
cigar boite nature, humidor

circular thimble
-cloth melton
compass binnacle, kettle
coot surf-scoter
crab calappa
cutlery canteen
document hanaper
elder maple, negundo, tree
elder bug sapsucker
fancy etui, etwee
fire clay, saggar, sagger
fish car, nid
floating caisson
food mocuck
foundry frame
girdle inro
holly butcher's broom
in confine, contain, coop, cramp, trap
iron hanger
kite hargrave, solitaire
money arca, ladle, perlie, safe
nest inro
off compartmentalize, tack
opener pandora
papers cartonnier, hanaper, serre-papier, solander
poison oxylobium
prickly gorse
printing turtle
sacred cist
salt drab
seed skippet
shallow backet, flat
sleigh pung
small inro
snuff mill, mull
tea caddy, canister
tin canister, trummel, wasculum
tobacco butt, cady, doss, humidor, saratoga
tools chest, kit
turtle cistudo, cooter, terrapene
-wallah peddler
BOXCAR gondola, lowry, stockcar
BOXER bantam, bowler, bruiser, buffeter, champ, chinese, derby, dog, fighter, fisticuffer, gladiator, hat, heavyweight, miller, nobber, prizefighter, pug(ilist), slugger, sparrer, tanker, welter
attendant bottleholder
partner stablemate
BOXFISH chapin, cowfish, shellfish, trunkfish
BOXHEAD squawfish
BOXING bout, case, casing, fight, fistfight, match,

prizefight, pugilism, ring, sparring
blow backhand, bolo punch, counter, feint, haymaker, hook, jab, knockout, left, long melford, one-two, poke, punch, right, round-arm, roundhouse, short-arm, sidewinder, swing, uppercut
champion ali, baer, carnera, clay, corbett, dempsey, ellis, foreman, frazier, liston, louis, marciano, muhammad ali, patterson, schmeling, sharkey, sullivan, tunney, willard
class bantam, feather, fly, heavy
glove cestus, mitt, muffle
match bout, set-to
partner stablemate
period round
pert. fistic, pugilistic
term kayo, mitt, spar, tko
world fistiana
BOXOFFICE gate receipts, take
hit boffo(la)
BOXWOOD buxus, dogwood, dudgeon, knysna, pachysandra, seron, zapalero
BOY apprentice, bellhop, birkie, bouchal, bub(by), bube, bud(dy), buttons, calf, callan(t), chokra, colt, cub, fag, fellow, gamin, garcon, gossoon, groom, guy, him, hobbledehoy, houseboy, kid, knave, lad(die), mafu, mannie, muchacho, nacket, nino, nipper, page, puer, pup(py), putto, rascal, rogue, sapling, servant, shaveling, shaver, slip, sonny, spadger, spalpeen, sprig, sprout, stirra, stripling, swain, tad, tot, trick, urchin, varlet, waiter, whelp, young man, youth
altar acolyte, thurifer
awkward calf, cub, grummet
beautiful adonis
bishop st nicholas
blind cupid
bold spalpeen
book author henty
cleaning busboy
collier's hodder
dressed as woman malineke
effeminate sissy
freeborn camillus
gentile shegetz

ill-mannered cub
native mowgli
office duft(e)ry
on burning deck casabianca
orator bryan
patron saint nicholas
pope benedict ix, john xii
roguish gamin, urchin
saucy nacket
scout award merit badge
scout founder baden-powell
scout gathering camporee, jamboree
scout leader akala
scout motto be prepared
scout rank cub, eagle, rover, tenderfoot, webelos
serving chokra, gossoon, knave, mousse, pedee
small buddy, nipper, sonny, spadger
stable mafoo, mafu, mehtar
BOYCOTT avoid, blackball, blacklist, coerce, cut, debar, mite, ostracize, shun, snub, strike
BOYFRIEND beau, date, escort, fellow, lover, mainman, steady, sweetheart
BOYISH immature, juvenile, puerile, youthful
BOYLA koradji, sorcerer, witch-doctor
BOYS *and-girls* dutchman's-breeches
in blue eli's, navy, northerners, union army, yankee
town founder flanagan
BOZ charles dickens
BRABANT crocard, linen
duchess elsa
BRABANTIO *daughter* beademona
kin gratiano, lodovico
son-in-law othello
BRABBLE argue, brangle, brawl, cavil, contest, dispute, fight, lawsuit, quarrel, quibble, wrangle
BRACE angle-iron, anklet, back, band(age), bend, bind, bitstalk, bitstock, bottine, brache, bracket, bridging, buckle, buttress, case, clamp, clasp, clench, cord, couple, crossbar, crutch, discipline, duo, dwang, encircle, fasten, fathom, firm, fix, fortify, frap, furnish, gig, gird, girth, grip, hold, jack, knee, leg, ligament, nerve, pair, prop, refresh, reinforce, rod, rope, secure, shore, spanner, spur, stabi-

lize, stay, steady, stem, stiffen, stimulate, strain, strengthen, string, strut, stud, support, tauten, tense, tie, tighten, tom, truss, two, vice, wimble, wire, yoke
airplane longeron
-and-a-half leash, three, tierce
connecting tie-rod
game fraud, swindle
up accinge, brave, buck up, cheer up, encourage, rebound, recuperate, sharpen, spunk up
BRACELET armil(la), armlet, band, bangle, calombigas, chain, circle(t), collar, grivna, handcuff, manacle, muffetee, poignet, racette, sankha, wristlet
ancient armil
item charm
pert. armillary
shell sankha
-wearing armillate(d)
wood jacquinia
BRACER armguard, band, binder, blocker, drink, guard, hair-of-the-dog, pick(-me)-up, refresher, reviver, shot, stiffener, stimulant, strengthener, support, tonic
BRACERO farm worker, immigrant, laborer, wetback
BRACES galluses, straps, suspenders
BRACHIOPOD atremate, atrypoid, mollusk, spirifer
BRACHYLOGY brevity, conciseness
BRACHYURE cacajao, crab, crustacean, monkey, ouakari, pitta
BRACING airy, chilly, cold, crisp, invigorating, quickening, salubrious, stimulating, strengthening, tonic
BRACK breach, brine, briny, crack, crag, flaw, opening, quarrel, rock
BRACKEN brake, fern, plaid, pteris, tartan
BRACKET ancon(e), associate, beckett, bibb, brace, bragwort, bridge, candle-holder, category, class (ification), cock, conch, conk, console, corbel, couch, couple, crane, crotchet, derrick, fixture, fork, gate, group(ing), gusset, hook, join, ladder,

ledge, level, link, lookout, match, parenthesis, projection, punk, rank, saddle, sconce, shelf, speckled, sponson, sporophore, spotted, straddle, strut, support, tier, timber, truss, vinculum, wall-iron, yoke
kind ancon, angle(-cleat), angle-iron, brace, cantilever, cheek, consol, corbel, cul-de-lampe, dog-ear, gusset, modillion, shoulder
BRACKISH breachy, briny, distasteful, foist, nasty, nauseous, saline, salty, unpleasant, yar
BRACT glume, husk, leaf, lemma, palea, palet, phyllary, scale, spadix, spathe
without ebracteate
BRACTEOLE prophyll(um)
BRAD nail, pin, prig, rivet, sprig
BRADLEY, EDWARD
pseud. cuthbert bede
BRAE bank, bray, brow, cleeve, cleve, declivity, hillside, slope, valley, wough
BRAG blaw, bleeze, blow, bluff, bluster, boast, bounce, BRAGGART, bravado, brisk, buck, bukh, bull, conceited, crow, defy, face, flaunt, flourish, gas(conade), gauster, jet, parade, pique, plume, prate, prattle, preen, pretense, pretentious, pride, puff, rave, roister, skite, splore, sprose, squirt, strut, swagger, threaten, valiant, vapor, vaunt, wind, wost, yelp
on praise
BRAGGART bangster, bazoo, blower, blowhard, blowoff, bluffer, blusterer, boaster, boastful, bobadil, braggadocio, bravado, burgullian, cacafugo, egocentric, ego(t)ist, fanfaron, fifer, fonfer, gasbag, gascon(ader), hector, know-it-all, parolles, potgun, pretender, puckfist, puff, rodomont, shlemiel, shlepper, shvitzer, skipjack, skiter, stuck-upper, swaggerer, swellhead, thraso, vaporer, windbag, windjammer
BRAGGING jactance, rodomont, roose, thrasonic
BRAGI *skald of* odin

wife idun(a), ithunn
BRAHMA ananda, atman, being, bliss, bull, chicken, c(h)it, cow, creator, demiurge, devotion, essence, fowl, god, intelligence, power, prayer, sat, self, soul
bliss sat
bull zebu
child daksha, manu, menu, vedas, viraj
consort brahmi, bramani, gayatri, sarasvati, satarupa, savitri, shakti
egg hiranyagarbha, sphere, universe, world
first woman ahalya
four faces caturanana
reunion with nirvana
three traits ananda, chit, sat
vehicle hansa
BRAHMAN aristocrat, aryan, bostonian, hindu, intellectual, noble, pundit, snob, zebu
deity See INDIA *god, goddess.*
duck ruddy shelldrake
kite haliastur
precept netineti, sutra, sutta
scripture aranyaka, bhagavad-ghita, purana, rigveda, samaveda, shastra, smriti, sruti, tantra, upanishad, veda, yajurveda
temple vestibule antarala, jagamohan
title aya
trinity brahma, siva, vishnu
BRAHMANI *husband* brahma
BRAHMIN See BRAHMAN.
BRAID adorn, alter, band(ing), bind(ing), bobbin, brandish, bread, brede, broad, bullion, bun, caprice, chignon, coil, combine, complect, confine, cord, crochet, cue, deceitful, decorate, entwine, fancy, freak, frog, galon, gimp, inkle, interlace, intertwine, jerk, jiffy, knit, knot, lace(t), onset, ornament, orris, pigtail, pla(i)t, pleat, plight, queue, rattail, reproach, ribbon, soutache, start, string, tagal, tail, tat, topknot, trace, tress, trick, trim(ming), twine, twist, vomit, waterfall, wattle, weave, wreath(work)
for hats sennet, sinnet

gold and silver orris
hair queue
hemp tagal
knotted lacet
linen inkle
ornamental aiguillette
pert. lacet
straw lisere
BRAIDING frog
BRAIL boom, chain, confine, cord, fasten, haul, line, rope, thong
BRAIN bean, blackjack, capacity, cerebellum, cerebrum, conceive, cranium, encephalon, furious, genius, grey-matter, ha(i)rn, haurn, headpiece, intellect, intelligence, kill, mad, mind, noddle, noggin, noodle, pate, prodigy, psyche, sconce, sense, sensorium, sensory, skull, thinker, understand(ing), upper-story, utac, vitals, wit(s)
absence anencephalia
activity cerebration
and spinal cord axion
band frenulum, funiculus, ligula
box cranium, pan, skull
canal iter
cavity coelia, encephalocoele
cell neuroblast, neuron
chemical serotonin, tryptophan
child idea, manuscript, opus, product, work
comb. cereb(ro), encephal(o)
condition, comb. encephalia
convolution cuncus, gyrus, insula
coral meandrina
coral ridge colline
covering dura mater
disorder alexia, diaschisis, encephalitis, encephalopathy, paranoia, paresis, phrenitis, schizophrenia
electronic computer, eniac
energy cerebricity
fever phrenitis
fissure zygon
groove sulcus
layer cortex, obex
membrane dura, obex, pia mater, tela
opening lura, pyla
operate on trepan
pan cranium, harnpan, pannicle, skull
part alacinerea, arbor vitae,

aula, cerebellum, cerebrum, colline, cortex, diencephalon, epencephalon, gray matter, harnpan, hypothalamus, lobe, lura, mantle, medulla(oblongata), metacoele, obex, pia, pons, stem, thalamus, tree of life
pert. cerebellar, cerebral, cerebric, encephalic, neuroendocrine
removal excerebration
ridge gyrus
sand sabulum
-sick crazy, disordered, insane, mad
softening dementia
storm agitation, confusion, derangement, discuss, idea, inspiration, rap, thought
-storming discussion, spitballing
substance paramyelin
surgery lobotomy
term alba, dura, obex, pan, pyle, utac
tissue tela
tumor encephaloma, psammoma
ventricle diacoele, paracoele, thalamocoele
ventricle opening pyla
x-ray encephalograph
BRAINISH delerious, hotheaded
BRAINLESS anencephalio, boneheaded, dumb, flighty, foolish, mindless, nutty, shallow, silly, stupid, thoughtless, unintelligent, witless
BRAINWASH convert, indoctrinate, persuade, propagandize, proselytize, snowjob
BRAINWORK cerebration, imagination, mentation, reasoning, study, thought
BRAINY astute, bright, brilliant, clever, habile, ingenious, intellectual, intelligent, smart
BRAISE cook, fish, pagrus, roach, rutilus, sea-bream
BRAKE adder-spit, anchor, aruke, block, bracken, break, bridle, bull, bur(r), cage, check, clog, copse, cow, crossbow, curb, deadman, decelerate, deter, dilemma, drag(rope), fern, halt, handle, harrow, hinder, lock, pteris, rack, retard, skid, slacken, slow,

snare, sprag, stay(er), stop-
(per), tara, thicket, trap,
vomit, warabi
part drum, shoe
van caboose
BRAKEMAN brakie, dillier,
dillyman, nipper, shack,
shake, snapper, swamper,
trainman
BRAKY brambly, ferny,
overgrown, shrubby
BRAMBLE berry, black-
berry, brier, bumble, dewberry, dog-rose, jagger, lawyer, mayberry, nessberry,
rhamn, sticker, thief, thorn,
whin
bush granjeno, tutu
BRAMBLY prickly, spiny,
thorny
BRAMIA bacopa, figwort,
herb
BRAMIMONDE *husband*
marsile
BRAN beeswing, carrion-
crow, chaff, chisel, coat,
darak, grit, husk, pollard,
pollen, powder, seed, soak,
topping, treat, treet
and meal shorts
brother evnissyen, manawyddan
father llyr
fine pollen
kingdom britain
-like furfuraceous
sister branwen
unsorted rubbles
BRANCH 3 arm, bud, leg,
ray, run 4 barb, bine, brog,
bush, fork, limb, part, post,
rame, rice, rise, snag, spur,
stem, stud, tang, twig, unit,
wing, yard 5 adorn, axite,
bough, brook, class, creek,
frond, group, local, lodge,
organ, prong, ramus, shoot,
shrag, spear, spray, sprig,
sprit, vimen, withe 6 cladus,
crotch, detour, divide, family, greave, member, office,
offset, outlet, phylum, raddle, ramage, ramify,
runner, sprang, spread,
sprout, stolon, stream,
sucker, switch, tapoun 7
article, burgeon, channel,
chapter, deviate, diverge,
furcate, rivulet, section, tendril 8 affluent, anaphyte,
category, decorate, division,
effluent, offshoot, railroad,
sprangle 9 affiliate, associate, bifurcate, confluent, fla-

gellum, sarmentum, tribu-
tary 10 department, sub-
sidiary 11 compartment,
subdivision 14 classification
angle formed axil
antler advancer, speller
comb. clad(o), ram(i)
dead flag
family sept
grass creek sedge
having 2 biramous
having 3 triskele
having spreading brachiate,
brachiferous
herring alewife, pomolobus
leaf-like cladophyll
-like ram(e)al, ramose,
ramous
out expand, extend, spread
palm lulab
pert. cladose, comal, forked,
ramate, rameal, ramose,
ramous, troched
small ramulus, rice, spiller
trailing stolon
BRANCHED cladose, forked,
forky, ramate, ramose,
troched
BRANCHING dendritic, dichotomy, forking, furcate,
ramose
BRANCUSI *sculpture* bird
in space
BRAND attaint, barrel, bespatter, birm, blacken,
blemish, blot, buist, burn,
character(istic), chop, cinder, class, defame, defect,
defile, dishonor, ember, emblem, expose, fagot, fix,
flambeau, flaw, gibbet,
grade, impress, inure, iron,
kind, label, lighter, make,
mark, marque, note, pil-
lory, quality, scar, scear,
scorch, sear, slur, smear,
smit, smot, soil, sort, stain,
stamp, stick, stigma(tize),
sully, sword, taint, tarnish,
torch, trademark, variety,
vent, vilify, wipe
goose brant
iron cauter(ant), cauterizer,
cautery, gridiron, mordant,
searer, sword, trivet
-new fresh, novel
sheep smit
stolen cattle duff
BRANDISH bear, bless,
braid, brangle, coruscate,
dart, display, exhibit, flaunt,
flourish, glitter, hurtle, irradiate, manipulate, parade,
ply, ruffle, shake, show, stir,

swagger, swing, thrash,
wag, wave, wield, winnow
BRANDLING earthworm,
parr, salmon
BRANDRETH fence, gridiron, tripod, trivet
BRANDY aguardiente, anisado, applejack, aquavite,
armagnac, bingo, boof, calvados, cinder, cognac, dop,
eau de vie, fine, grappa,
jack, marc, metaxa, mobby,
nants, pingo, pisco, pupelo,
quetsch, raki(j)a, slivovic,
slivovitz, visney
and soda peg
and sugar cherry bounce
and water mahogany, pawnee
cherry kirsch(wasser)
cider pupelo
cocktail alexander, rosolio,
sidecar, stinger
glass snifter
liqueur angelica, noyau, rosolio
mastic rakee, raki
mazzard cherry
peach boof
plum slivovitz
poor dop
spiced alkermes
unaged grappa
BRANGLE brandish, brawl,
fight, impulse, shake,
squabble, tangle, totter,
waver, wrangle
BRANGWAINE *mistress*
isolde
BRANK bridle, caper, mumps,
pillory, prance, strut
BRANNIGAN brawl, ca-
rouse, squabble
BRANT bold, chen, clear,
erect, goose, high, proud,
quink, rought, rout, scoter,
shear, showgoose, smooth,
steep, straight
bird turnstone
goose brent
snipe dunlin
-tail redstart
BRANWEN *brother* bran
husband matholwich
parent iluud, ilyr
BRASH attack, blunt, bold,
bout, brazen, brittle, eructation, eruption, facy, forward, gay, hasty, headlong,
heartburn, impertinent, impetuous, impudent, in-
trusive, nervy, pile, pyrosis,
rainstorm, rash, reckless,
rubbish, rubble, saucy,

shameless, shower, storm, tactless, temerarious

BRASHY broken, crumbly, showery

BRASQUE steep

BRASS administration, alloy, amber, assurance, audacity, bathmetal, brazen, bronze, cash, cheek, effrontery, elite, establishment, gall, generals, impudence, insolence, magnate, maslin, money, nerve, officer(s), ormolu, placque, presumption, tablet

alloy bristol metal, mannheim gold, orichalch, orichalcum

alpha-beta muntz-metal

artisan brasier, brazier

buttons buck's-horn, swine's-cress

decorative ormolu

farthing trifle

gold-like ormolu

hat general, officer

inlay tarkashi

-like aeneous, brazen

-like alloy latten, platen

made of brazen

man talos, talus

ornamentation braze

player windjammer

pert. aerose

rubber chalcotript

tacks essentials, facts, fundamentals, realities

ware dinanderie

BRASSBOUND brazen, impudent, inflexible, rigid, set, unyielding

BRASSERIE See RESTAURANT; SALOON.

BRASSICA broccoli, brussel sprouts, cabbage, cauliflower, cole, collard, kale, mustard, rape, rutabaga, turnip, watercress

BRASSY aerose, bold, brazen, bronzy, cheap, clamorous, fresh, harsh, impudent, loud, noisy, reedy, sassy

BRAT apron, bairn, bantling, bastard, bib, bilsh, brachet, broll, child, cloak, devil, elf, enfant-terrible, gaitt, garment, get, imp, infant, mantle, minor, minx, nacket, puck, pup, terror, urchin, whelp, whippersnapper

group passel

BRATTICE boarding, breastwork, bretesse, burlap, cre-

ating, gallery, partition, planking, wall, woodwork

BRAVADO bluster, bombast, bravery, bravura, courage, gasconism, hector, pomp, pretension, pride, storm, swagger(er), talltalk, vauntery

BRAVE 4 bear, bold, braw, dare, defy, face, fine, game, good, hero, meet, posh, tall, wild 5 adorn, beard, boast, bravo, bully, felon, front, gutsy, hardy, jolly, manly, natty, nobby, orped, roman, smart, stiff, stout, vaunt, wight 6 bedare, brawly, brazen, breast, dapper, daring, endure, gritty, heroic, indian, manful, plucky, sporty, spruce, sturdy 7 affront, bravado, bravura, brawlie, defiant, doughty, gallant, hautain, martial, outdare, outface, soldier, swagger, toffish, valiant, venture, warrior 8 atlantan, cavalier, confront, embolden, fearless, intrepid, stalwart, superior, valorous, virtuous 9 admirable, audacious, challenge, chivalric, confident, dauntless, excellent, undaunted, venturous 10 chivalrous, courageous, untimorous 11 lionhearted 12 stouthearted

BRAVERY array, audacity, backbone, beau, boldness, bravado, bravura, courage, display, finery, fortitude, grit, guts, heroism, magnificence, manhood, mettle, nerve, parade, pluck, pomp, prowess, sand, show, spirit, splendor, spunk, valor

drunken pot-valor

BRAVO applause, assassin, bandit, bis, brave, bullyrock, cheer, cutthroat, desperado, euge, gangster, good, gunman, hoodlum, killer, mohock, murderer, ole, rah, ruffian, shabash, thug, triggerman, villain, well done

BRAVURA aria, BRAVADO, bravery, dash, display

jazz bop

BRAW chic, dapper, dashing, excellent, fair, fashionable,

fine, good, handsome, natty, nobby, smart, sporty, toffish

BRAWL affray, altercation, barney, beef, bicker, bobbery, brabble, branle, brannigan, broil, carouse, chide, clamor, clash, clem, complain, contention, contest, din, discord, disorder, dispute, dissension, disturbance, donnybrook, embranglement, embroilment, fight, flite, fracas, fray, habble, hubbub, imbroglio, melee, noise, quarrel, rangle, revel, revile, riot, row, ruffle, rumpus, scold, scrap, scuffle, shindig, shindy, squabble, stoush, stramash, strife, struggle, tumult, turbulence, uproar, wrangle, yatter

BRAWLER frampler, fratch, nicker, nightcap, outcrier, squarer

BRAWLING blatant, boisterous, fliting, noisy, quarrelsome, scambling

fine flitwite

BRAWN beef, boar, callous, flesh, lire, meat, muscle, sinews, strength, thews

BRAWNY athletic, beefy, burly, callous, flesh(l)y, hard, husky, lusty, muscular, powerful, robust, sarcous, sinewy, stalwart, strong, sturdy, swollen

BRAY beat, bruise, comminute, crush, cry, grate, grind, heehaw, jangle, levigate, mix, noise, outburst, outcry, pestle, pound, pulverize, rasp, rout, rub, spread, stamp, thrash, utter, whinny

BRAZEN aenean, arrogant, audacious, aweless, blatant, bold(faced), brash, brass(y), brittle, callous, calm, cheeky, clamorous, defiant, forward, hard(y), harsh, immodest, impudent, indecent, indurated, insolent, loud, metallic, nervy, noisy, pert, rash, sassy, shameless, unabashed, unblushing, vulgar

BRAZIER barbecue, brasero, chest, heater, hibachi, pan, reredos, scaldino

BRAZIL antilia, bersil, brasil, brazir, hardwood, roset, verzin

aborigine carib
airline varig
animal anta, apa, epurua, tapir, wallaba
ant tucandera
anthropologist freyre
architect niemeyer
armadillo tatu
arrow poison ourari
arrowroot cassava
barbecue churrasco
bay guanabara, igrande, marajo, sepetiba
beer cassiri, shopee
bird agami, arara, cariama, chaja, darter, iva, jacamar, macaw, maracan, mitu(a), seriema, soco, tiriba, toucan, urubu
cape blanco, buzios, frio, gurupy, orange, saoroque, saotome
capital brasilia, rio de janeiro, salvador
capital creator oscar niemeyer
cassava aipi
city (See also BRAZIL *port*.) acu, alegrete, anapolis, araquari, bage, baiao, bauru, belem, brasilia, campinas, campos, citoria, croumba, curitiba, exu, faro, floriano, goiania, ibia, ico, ijui, itabuna, itapetininga, jequie, jundiai, lapa, lins, londrina, macapa, mossoro, neves, passofundo, petrolina, piui, salvador, santarem, sao paulo, sorocaba, tupa, uberaba, uberlandia
clover alfalfa, lucerne
club moss piligan
coffee rio
coffee plantation fazenda
coffee port santos
coin conto, cruzeiro, dobra, dump, halfjoe, milreis, moidore, pataca, reis
composer villalobos
cotton matta
cow tree massaranduba
crane cariama, seriama
cult macumba
dam furnas, peixoto
dance batuque, bossa nova, carioca, maxixe, samba
diamond bahia
diamond locale cascalho
dictatorship ditabranda, ditadura
discoverer cabral
dish churrasco, farinha de

mandioca, farofa, feijoada, galinha aomolho pardo, muqueca de peixe a baiana, xinxin de galinha
drink assai, batida, cachaca
emerald chrysoberyl, chrysolite, peridot, tourmaline
estuary para
exploration agency cprm
falls iguassu, iguazu
fiber curratow, imbe
fiber plant caroa
fish arapaima, piaba
flour shaker farinheira
flycatcher yetapas
foot fight capoeira
forest caatinga, matta
god agnen, anatina, apoiaueue, ariconte, bretata, igpupiara, kurupira, mairemonan, nanderevusu, sommay, tamendonare, tupan yurupari
goddess maireata, nandecy
grass jaraqua
he-man machao
herb araonis, bertolonia, manihot, nolana, sinningia, zebra-plant
hummingbird ruby, starthroat
hydroelectric plant furnas
indian acroa, amiranha, anta, apiaca, apinaoe, araquaju, arara, araua, arawak, aueto, bare, bororo, botocudo, bravo, braz, bugre, caboclo, caboculo, caingang(s), canamary, caraja, carayan, carib, carira, catoquina, cavina, cayapo, chambioa, coroado, diau, guana, guarani, guato, guaycuru, hauri, inca, jacunda, javahai, jucuna, kaingang(s), katukina, kustenav, macusi, maku(a), manao, mayorma, mura, omagua, oyana, parukutu, pianokoto, pocaguara, porokoto, puinauis, puri, puru, siusi, tapajo, tapuya, tariana, tupi, TUPIAN, waraycu, waura, yao, yuruna, zaparo
inn pousada
iron ore deposit serra dos carajas
island bananal, cardoso, caviana, comprida, maraca, marajo, mexiana
kitchen midden sambaqui
lake aima, feia, mirim
land crab horseman

leader geisel, goulart, medici, vargas
leaf hopper bell-bearer
macaw maracan
mahogany carapa, plathymenia, yellowwood
measure almud(e), alqueire, alquier, braca, canada, covado, cuarta, fanga, garrafa, league, legoa, milha, molo, oitava, palmo, passo, pipa, pollegada, quartilho, quarto, sack, tarefa, tonel, vara
medicine alveloz
mestizo mameluco, paulista
monkey belzebuth, maraco, miriki, sai, teeter
moss piligan
music bossa nova, choro
musician sayao
national dish feijoada
native caboclo, carioca, curiboca, huari, mameluco, paulista
novelist amado
nuclear power project nuclebras
nut castana, juvia
nut tree almendron
oil monopoly petrobras
ore jacutinga
painter portinari
palm assai, babassu, bacaba, barriguda, carnauba, copernica, inaja, jacitara, jara, jupati, miriti, muriti, paxiuba, tucum(a), uracuri
parrot ara(ra), tiriba
paste guavana
peak bandeira, corcovado, itatiaia, sugar loaf, urucum
pepper tree christmas-berry
peridot See BRAZIL *emerald*.
phosphate arrojadite
plant aveloz, ayapana, bignonia, carajura, caroa, chico, eupatorium, euphorbia, imbe, para, vellozia, yage, yaje
plantation fazenda
plateau mato grosso
poet bilac
politician aranha
port aracaju, bahia, belai, belem, ceara, cuiaba, cuyaba, florianopolis, fortaleza, ilheus, itajai, joao pessoa, joinville, maceio, manaos, natal, nictheroy, niteroi, para, paranagua, parnaiba, pelatas, pernambuco, porto alegre, recife,

rio, santos, sao salvador, teresina

president castello branco

promontory frio

prospector garimpeiro

puffbird dreamer

rain caju

range acarai, amambai, carajas, geral, gradaus, gurupi, orgaos, parima, piaui, roncador, tombador

resort amcora, buzios, cabo-frio, copacabana, gravata, guaruja, ipanema, man-guinhos, ossos, petropolis

restaurant churrascaria

river abuna, ajuana, amazon, anaua, apore, araguaya, arinos, balsas, branco, can-uma, capim, claro, contas, corua, corumba, cuiaba, cuyaba, doce, geio, grajau, grande, gurupi, ibicui, ica(na), iguacu, iguassu, ijui, iriri, itapi, ivai, japura, jari, javari, juruna, jutai, madeira, manso, mearim, mortes, mucuri, negro, orinoco, para(catu), para-guai, paraiba, parana, pardo, parnaiba, paru, piaui, preto, purus, river of doubt, sangue, solimoes, sono, tacutu, tapajos, ta-quari, tarauaca, tefe, teo-doro, tibagi, tiete, tocantins, turvo, uatuma, uaupes, urubu, uruguay, velhas, verde, xingu

rock carnoeira

rodent rock-cavy

rosewood cavina, dalbergia, palisander

rubber caucho, ceara, hule, para, seringa, ule

rubber plant seringa

rubber region ica

rubber tree hevea, hule, ule

ruby rose-spinel, rose-topaz

sassafras nectandra

sauce morcela

serpent jararaca, jararacussu

shrub mate, partridge-pea, snakeroot, uvalha, yellow-ball, yerbe-sagrada

sociologist freyre

sore buba

spa araxa

spider monkey ateles, belzebuth

state acre, alagoas, amapa, amazonas, bahia, ceara, espirito santo, goias, goya, guapore, maranhao, mato

grosso, minas gerais, para(hiba), paraiba, parana, pernambuco, piauhy, piaui, randonia, rio grande, rorai-ma, santa catharina, sao paulo, sergipe

statesman vargas

stew feijoada

tapir anta

tea lantana, mate, yerba

territory acre, amapa, gua-pore, rio branco

terrorist marighella

title cavalheiro

toucan ariel, rhamphastos

tourist agency embratur

tradition cashinaua

tree aba, alcomoque, anda(asou), andira, an-natto, apa, araca, araroba, assai, assu, avaremotemo, babassu, bakupari, balata, barbatimao, barriguda, be-cuiba, biriba, boxwood, brauna, buriti, cabreuva, castilla, caucho, dal-guarabu, embira, embuis, gomavel, hevea, icica, mate, monkeypot, munguba, oi-ticica, paraiba, peroba, pinkweed, pottery tree, sa-tine, seringa, tinge, tulip-wood, ucuuba, u(h)le, urucu, wallaba

turtle matamata

underdog zebra

venice recife

vine calico-flower, flannel-flower

voodoo candomble

wallaba apa

walnut cordia, embuia

warrior cayapo

wax carnauba

weapon cayapo-club

weight arratel, arroba, bag, citava, libra, onca, quilate, quintal, tonelada

wildcat eyra

wind minvano

wood brasilette, caesalpinia, divi-divi, embuia, hypernio, kingwood, mahogany, peachwood, verzino, yel-lowwood

yellowwood mahogany

BREA asphalt, caesalpinia, canarium, elemi, maltha, resin, tar, tree

BREACH alienation, aper-ture, assault, brack, break, broach, bruise, burst, chap, chasm, cleft, crack, crevasse, dispute, disrup-

tion, dissension, error, fissure, flaw, fraction, frac-ture, gaffe, gap, gool, hiatus, infraction, inroad, interruption, interval, open-ing, pause, quarrel, rent, rift, rupture, schism, screed, separation, severance, slap, sluice, solecism, split, stave, transgression, trespass, vac-uum, violation, wound

of contract assumpsit

of duty barratry

of faith treason

of peace burg-bryce

pin tige

BREAD aliment, anadama, azyme, bannock, bap, batch, baton, biscuit, bun, chapati, chapatty, chapon, cocket, cush, damper, diet, dika, dodger, fare, food, hallah, hardtack, host, kan-kie, kisra, limpa, liveli-hood, loaf, maintenance, maslin, matzos, matzoth, money, pain, pan(ada), pane(tonne), piki, pita, pone, popover, roll, rooty, rusk, simnel, sippet, staple, stollen, substance, suste-nance, tammie, toast, toke, yannam, zweiback

and cheese sorrel

and milk panada, pobbies, pobs, saps

and wine eucharist

batch cast

beetle bookworm, catorama, ptinus

board panel

boiled cush, panada

box panetiere, trummel

broth-soaked brewis

browned crouton, sippet, toast

buttered caper

comb. arto

communion azyme, body, host

cornmeal anadama, pone

crisp rusk

crumb mealock, panure

cube crouton

dark boston brown, pumper-nickel, rye

dough sponge

dry toke

-eating panivorous

fried crouton, french toast

fruit, false ceriman

grain cereals

holy antidoron, azyme, body, host

kind ashcake, cocket, corn, damper, french toast, gluten, graham, hardtack, hearth, hoecake, kisra, matzoth, melba toast, pannam, potato, pumpernickel, raisin, rye, sourdough, tommy, white, whole-wheat

line charity, dole, handout, queue, relief

loaf bap, baton, cob, fadge, hallah, miche, tammie, tommy

maize piki

mold rhizopus

oatmeal anak, bannock, jannock

passover azyme, matzos, matzoth

pert. panary

piece canch, mealock, sippet, slice, tartine, tommy, trencher

plant samh

potato boxty, fadge

pudding randa

quality paneity

quick biscuit, scone

ration tommy

roll bap, bun, gemmel, manchet, muffin, tammie

rye pumpernickel

sesame ring coloura

slice See *piece,* above.

soft spoonbread

sopper brewis, browis, miser

spread butter, conserve, jam, jelly, margarine, marmalade, oleo

stick baguette

sweet brownie, bun, stollen

toasted sippet

unleavened azym(e), bannock, chapatti, clod, matzah, matzoth

wafer abret, kisra, melba toast

wheat cheat, cocket, hovis, manchet

white manchet

with butter and cheese caper

with butter and jam tartine

BREADBASKET artophorion, belly, paunch, stomach

BREADFRUIT antipolo, artocarpus, camansi, capomo, castana, chestnut, dug-dug, irvingia, nangca, nanka, pandanus, rima(s), screwpine, treculia

BREADNUT ram

tree capomo

BREADROOT cinnamon-

fern, pomme blanche, prairie-apple

BREADTH amplitude, brede, expanse, extent, girth, grossness, largeness, liberality, scope, size, space, spaciousness, span, width

and depth thickness

BREADWINNER earner, employee, father, husband, money-maker, wage-earner, worker

BREAK 3 cut, gap, lop, rip, run 4 beat, bolt, boon, bust, chip, dash, dawn, drop, fail, fall, flaw, halt, hint, hurl, open, part, rend, rent, rest, rift, rise, ruin, rush, slip, snap, stop, tack, tame, tear, tide, turn, undo 5 annul, begin, blank, burst, calve, cease, check, cleft, crack, craze, crush, daunt, fault, frush, issue, lapse, occur, pause, sever, smash, solve, split, spoil, start, stave, train, wound, yield 6 appear, breach, bruise, cabble, chance, change, cleave, cranny, cut out, decode, defeat, demote, depose, differ, divide, escape, gentle, hiatus, ignore, impair, lacuna, mutate, pierce, recess, reduce, schism, shiver, shrend, subdue, submit, sunder, tewtaw, tewter, unfurl, weaken 7 blunder, brisure, caesura, cashier, conk out, contest, crackle, crevice, crumble, decline, destroy, disable, dismiss, disrupt, divulge, exhaust, express, faux pas, fissure, fortune, grittle, infract, interim, opening, parting, release, respite, rupture, scatter, shatter, torture, violate 8 bankrupt, breather, collapse, crevasse, decipher, demolish, disclose, disfavor, disperse, dissolve, division, fracture, fragment, infringe, initiate, interval, lacerate, overcome, separate, solution, splinter, straiten, stramash, vacation 9 advantage, interrupt, penetrate, severance, subjugate 10 contravene, depreciate, disruption, separation, suspension 11 domesticate, opportunity 12 disaffection, disin-

tegrate, estrangement, interruption 13 discontinuity

a lance joust, tilt

a leg exert, strive, try

away bolt, depart, escape, secession, separation, stampede

bread eat with

cover emerge

down analysis, analyze, articulate, catabolism, cataclasm, classify, collapse, confess, conk, convulse, crack up, crickle, crock, crush, cry, debacle, decompose, demolish, destroy, diagnosis, dissect, erosion, fail(ure), founder, integrate, outline, overwhelm, psychastnenia, qualify, raze, reduce, refract, resolve, separate, smash, sob, subdue, torture, traik, tumble, weep, wrack

even split, tie

for start

force baffle

ground begin, pioneer, weigh anchor

in accustom, begin, blunder, burglarize, bust, discipline, domesticate, enter, force, gentle, initiate, interrupt, intrude, invade, irrupt, master, open, raid, start, stave, subdue, tame, train, vanquish

into pieces chip, craze, crumble, demolish, dice, diffract, disjoint, fritter, shiver, smash, smatter, splinter, stramash

it up cease, separate, stop

of day dawn, morn(ing), sunup

off cease, dirempt, drop, nub, snap

one's heart agonize, grieve

one's neck exert, hurry, hustle, strive, try

one's word deceive, lie

open bust, chop, force

ore cob, spall, spawl

out analyse, arouse, begin, burst, erupt, escape, explode, flash, flee, free, loosen, open, outbreak, overrun, project, rash, spread, start, strike, unstow, upsurgence

out anew recrudesce

promise renege

shell pip

shine borrow

silence quatch, quetch, speak
skin gall
the back of complete, disable, defeat, overcome, paralyse
the ice begin, cultivate, prepare, start
the law abduct, blackmarket, bootleg, extort, fence, moonlight, murder, pirate, plunder, rob, smuggle, steal, transgress, trespass
the news broadcast, divulge, release, report, reveal
the tape win
through advance, attack, beat, force, intrude, open, triumph, victory
up debacle, decay, degrade, destruction, diffuse, disband, disintegrate, disjoint, disperse, dissect, dissolution, dissolve, disturb, divide, fall, fragment, laugh, melt, powder, pulverize, refract, scarify, scatter, separate, sever, spall, split, stash, thaw, upset
with bolt, differ, fall out, repudiate, separate

BREAKABLE brittle, brockle, bruckle, crumbly, delicate, frail, fragile, frangible, friable, shelly, shivery

BREAKAX hardwood, ironwood, quebracho, sloanea, tree

BREAKBONE FEVER dengue

BREAKBONES ossifrage

BREAKER bareca, bareka, beachcomber, beaker, billow, cask, comber, jump, ledgeman, ripple, roller, scrapper, sledger, stockman, surf, tank, tub, wave
circuit cutout

BREAKFAST brunch, disj(e)une, petit-dejeuner
nook dinette
pert. jentacular
roll brioche, croissant

BREAKNECK dangerous, destruction, hazardous, precipitate, reckless, ruin, steep

BREAKSTONE burnet, calculus, parsley-piert, pearlwort, saxifrage

BREAKWATER bulwark, buttress, cob(b), croy, dam, dike, groyne, harbor, jetty, mole, pier, pile, quay,

refuge, revetment, seawall, sluice

BREAM abramis, archosargus, baleen, barwin, braise, broom, carp, chad, cyprinid, flatfish, golden shiner, lepomis, oldwife, porgy, roman, rosefish, sailor's-choice, sargus, scup, shad, snapper, steenbras(s), stumpnose, tai, tarwhine, warehou, zope
family sparidae
red-breasted blue gill, sunfish
young chad

BREAST affections, bosom, brave, brisket, bump, bust, chest, climb, confront, courage, crop, dug, face, forebows, heart, meet, pectus, petto, spirit, stem, thorax
absence of amastia
-beating doubt, emotionalism, remorse
comb. mast(o), stern(o)
-feed nourish, nurse, suckle
hook crutch
like mastoid
ornament aegis, pectoral, phalera
pang angina pectoris
pert. mastoid, pectoral
pin brooch, clasp, pectoral
surgery mastectomy
timber wale

BREASTBONE sternum, xiphoid

BREASTPIECE bib, chemisette, rabat, rabbi

BREASTPLATE aegis, cuirass, egis, ephod, gorget, lintel, lorica, palette, pectoral, plastron, poitrail, poitrel, shield, tapul, thummim, urim

BREATH air, ande, aspiration, atman, breeze, flatus, gasp, gulp, halitus, hint, huff, inhalation, instant, life, murmur, onde, pant, pause, pech, puff, rale, respiration, respite, scent, sigh, smell, sough, spirit, stain, suspiration, tarnish, touch, trace, trifle, triviality, utterance, vapor, vitality, waft, whiff, whisper, wind
bad halitosis, ozostomia
comb. pneuma
divine nephesh
name meaning abel
-of-heaven adenanda, diosma

of life pneuma, prana, spirit
shortness dyspnea, tift
stoppage apn(o)ea, asphyxia
sweetener cachou, catechu
-taking exciting, hair-raising, spine-tingling, startling, stimulating, thrilling

BREATHE afflate, ande, aspirate, blow, divulge, emanate, exercise, exhale, exhaust, exist, expire, express, exude, gasp, gulp, halitus, huff, infuse, inhale, inject, inspire, live, manifest, mean, onde, pant, pause, puff, respire, rest, say, sigh, smell, sniff(le), snort, snuff(le), sough, speak, spite, subsist, suspire, tell, utter, vent, wheeze, whisper
comb. pneo, pneuma
hard fnese, gasp, pant, pech, sough, throttle
noisily snore, snotter, sough
one's last die, expire, pass
upon calumniate, soil, tarnish

BREATHER armistice, break, delay, lung, nose, pause, recess, repose, respite, rest, snorkel, truce

BREATHING alive, anapnea, aspiration, exhalation, expiration, gasping, inhalation, inspiration, insufflation, moment, pant, pause, phlebotomy, pneuma, puff, rale, respiration, spiration, spiritus, sternutation, stridor, utterance, vent(ilation), voice
comb. pnea, pneo, pnoea
difficult asthma, dyspn(o)ea, hyperpnea, orthopnea
disease asthma, emphysema
harsh rale, stridor
heavily suspirious
impair asphyxiate
mark comma
organ gill, lung, mouth, nares, nose, nostril, pore, spiracle, stoma
place caesura, pause, vent
pore stoma
rapid polypnea
recorder atmograph
slow sponopnoea
smooth lene, lenis
sound rale, snore, snort, stridor
spell armistice, delay, rest, truce
upon insufflation

BREATHLESS afraid,

aghast, airless, anxious, ardent, blown, broken-winded, dead, dyspneal, eager, exhausted, lifeless, mute, pumped, spent, suffocating, winded

BRECCIA ataxite, stone
limestone calico-marble

BREDE boil, braid, breadth, broaden, embroider, extend, plait, roast, spread, toast

BREE broth, brow, commotion, disturbance, eyelash, eyelid, juice, liquor, scare, terrify, water

BREECH blemish, block, bore, bottom, brick, butt(ocks), culotte, derriere, doup, dowp, posterior, rear, rump, tige, troddum

BREECHBLOCK ventpiece

BREECHCLOTH clout, dhoti, diaper, dydee, g-string, hippen, hipping, loincloth, malo, moocha, pagne, string

BREECHES bombards, brac(c)ae, bragas, breeks, breekums, britches, buckskin, chaps, cords, denims, gaskin, hose, jeans, jodhpurs, kicksies, levis, pantaloon, PANTS, slops, smallclothes, smalls, stock, tights, trews, trousers, trunkhose
buoy life-preserver

BREED bear, beget, brood, caste, cause, character, class, create, develop, educate, engender, family, gender, generate, genus, get, group, grow, hatch, ilk, impregnate, instruct, issue, kind, line(age), mate, multiply, nourish, nurture, originate, pedigree, posterity, procreate, procure, produce, progeny, propagate, race, raise, rear, reproduce, sire, sort, species, stock, store, strain, train, variety, young
small toy

BREEDBATE troublemaker

BREEDER aurelian, boil, gin, herdsman, horseman, parent, rancher, stockman, tulip, whitlow
fish milter
small-scale backlotter, backyarder

BREEDING amenity, behavior, bonton, civility, cour-

tesy, culture, demeanor, deportment, descent, development, education, elegance, extraction, genteelness, gentility, gentlemanliness, improvement, manners, mien, nurture, origin, poise, polish, procreation, propagation, refinement, savoir-faire, tact, training, tupping, unbringing
place nest, nidus, rookery
science eugenics

BREEZE air, aura, blast, blow, breath, catspaw, cinch, disturbance, doctor, duck soup, easy, facility, flaw, flurry, fracas, gadfly, gale, gust, muzzler, pirr, quarrel, rebat, report, rumor, slant, slatch, snap, speed, stir, terral, uproar, virason, whisper, wind, zephyr
carry on waft
cool doctor
fly whame
gentle air, aura, pirr, zephyr
lake ora, rebat
land terral
stiff stour, tifter
tropical sea doctor
warm cefiro

BREEZY active, airy, blow, brisk, debonair, drafty, fresh, light, lively, peppy, sprightly, vivacious, windy

BREME apparent, brilliant, clear, cruel, distinct, fierce, severe, sharp

BRENT bold, brant, clear, goose, high, smooth, steep, unwrinkled

BRES *consort* brigit
parent elatha

BRESLAU wroclaw

BRESSUMMER beam, girder, lintel, support

BRET brill, flatfish, turbot

BRETHREN brotherhood, congregation

BRETON See BRITTANY.

BREVE bird, brief, compose, mark, minim, note, order, pittid, precept, short, tell, writ(e)
rest silence

BREVET appoint, certificate, commission, decree, honor, message, patent, permit, promote, warrant

BREVIARY abstract, compend, coucher, cursus, digest, epitome, ledger, ordo,

portas(s), portesse, porthors, porthouse, psalter, summary
medieval portass, portesse
part temporale
prayer itinerarium

BREVIATE brief, compendium, note, summary

BREVIGER friar, monk

BREVIT fidget, hunt, prowl, search

BREVITY brachylogy, briefness, compactness, conciseness, laconism, pithiness, shortness, succinctness, syntomy, terseness, unlength
of speech breviloquence

BREW ale, bank, beer, blend, blow, bock(beer), boil, browst, coffee, compound, concoct, contrive, cook, cure, cyle, develop, devise, dilute, foment, form, gather, hatch, impend, incline, liquor, make, mix, plot, prepare, seethe, soak, steep, stew, stout, tea
home samogon
medical tisane
sour alegar

BREWER, BREWER'S *grain* barley, corn, hops, malt, rye
grackle blackbird
grits rice
patron king gambrinus
sparrow spitzella
yeast barm, leaven

BREWERY distillery, tavern, winery
worker brewster, hopper, tunner

BREWING afoot, browst, concoction, gaal, gail, gyle, imminent, malting
ferment lob(b)
haze trub
impurities slummage
refuse draff, dregs
tool vellinch
vat gyle, kive, tun

BRIAR, BRIER barb, burl, erica, health, inkberry, oak, pipe, plant, rose, rubus, saw, smilax, spine, thorn, zarzuela
extract scrap
-hopper frontiersman
pipe bulldog
sensitive beshamed mary, ganderteeth
tree piper

BRIAREUS *father* uranus

BRIBE allurement, anount,

approach, bait, baksheesh, bonus, boodle, buy, coima, corrupt, cuddy, douceur, extort, favor, fee, fix, gift, graft, gratuity, gravy, grease. handy-dandy. hire, hush-money, inducement, lolly, lure, meed, moll, mordida, noddle, offer, oil, palm, payola, price, propina, purchase, reach, reward, tob, schmeer, seduction, soap, soborno, sop, square, steal, suborn, sugar, swag, sweeten, tempt, tickler, tip, touch, vail, venalize, wage

BRIBER bagman

BRIBERY (See also BRIBE.) ambitus, bite, bustarella, corruption, embracery, extortion, graft, mordida, payoff, purchase, robbery, subornation, theft

BRIC-A-BRAC bibelot, bijouterie, curio, knickknack, trinket, trockery, trumpery, vertu, virtu
holder etagere, whatnot

BRICK ace, adobe, bar, bat, block, bonder, build, burnover, clinker, die, dobe, doby, dook, face, fellow, fletton, fill, glut, good-egg, header, ideal, line, marl, nog, pament, paragon, pave, pavior, quarl, split, tile, top-notcher, trump, wall
best stock
burnt bur(r), clinker, shuff
carrier hod
clay malm
color lateritious, saravan
course rowlock
cracked chuff, shuff
dried adobe, bat
group stack
half jack
handfer hacker
imperfect burnover
-making term scintle, scove
mix clay for pug
mold kick
molder bumper
oven kiln
pattern american, blind, block and cross, bond, clip, common, cross, diagonal, english, flemish, herringbone, plumb, raking, running, scintle, skintle, split
pile clamp, hack, lift, scintle, stack

pulverized soorkee, soarky
red saravan
refuse samel, sandal
rounded bullheader, bullnose
second-rate grizzle
small briquette
soft cutter, picking, rubber
square quadrel
unburnt adobe, bat
vitrified burr, clinker
wood dook, nog, scutch

BRICKBAT affront, aspersion, bird, critician, insult, raspberry, slur

BRICKFIELDER bu(r)ster, wind

BRICKLAYER See MASON.

BRIDAL marriage, nuptial, wedding
wreath spir(a)ea

BRIDE, BRIDE'S anemone, bonnetstring, helpmate, kallah, kolleh, loop, newlywed, rain, rose, shulamite, spouse, tie, wed, wife
attendant bridesmaid, flower girl, maid of honor
belt cestus
gift dowry
god hymen
laces dodder, ribbon-grass
of lammermoor lucy ashton
of the sea aphrodite, venice, venus
price lobola

BRIDEGROOM benedict, cha(u)ssen, chossen, hassen, husband, newlywed, spouse
gift to bride handsel

BRIDESMAID paranymph

BRIDEWEED meadowsweet, toadflax

BRIDEWELL gaol, jail, milldoll, prison, workhouse

BRIDGE arch, bascule, bifrost, brig, channel, connection, cross, culvert, duplicate, footlog, gallery, game, gangplank, gangway, gantry, jetty, link, magas, overlie, overpass, passover, pinnock, platform, ponceau, pons, pont(oon), prop, ridge, runway, scaffold, sirat, span, stepping stone, support, tie, towie, traject, transition, traverse, trestle, viaduct, walkway, way, wien
arcaded rialto
asses dilemma, pons asinorum
bid blackwood, defensive,

demand, denial, double, forcing, jump, no trump, pass, psychic, shut-out, slam
bid, final contract
bird peewee, phoebe
builder pontifex, pontist
combination tenace
contract ghoulie, plafond
coup slam
defeat set
error renege
famous ambassador, arrabida, arthurkill, bayonne, bear, birchenough, brooklyn, cornwall, dee isle, elsa, forth, fort pitt, gladesville, golden gate, hell gate, hobart, hood canal, howrah, lion's, london, mackinac, menai, meric, miapimi, mirabeau, narrows, nibelungen, oakland, plougastel, ponte vecchio, quebec, queensboro, rainbow, rialto, sando, severin, sighs, st johns, story, tancarvillo, tappanzee, tower, transbay, triborough, verrazano, volta river, voulte
5-handed quintract
flue altar
forerunner biritch, whist
game auction, bridgit, contract, cut-throat, double, dummy, draw, drive, duel, duplicate, easy aces, echo, ghouli, goulash, hollandaise, honeymoon, individual, lindy, mayonnaise, misery, party, percentage, pirate, pivot, plafond, progressive, quintract, reverse, royal, rubber, short, strip, towie, triumph
gateway gout
hand evaluation point count
hand, honorless milkbottle, yarborough
hose jumper
kind bailey, bascule, bateau, cantilever, covered, draw, floating, foot, pontoon, suspension, swing, toll, trestle, truss
lever bascule
-like game five hundred, vint, whist
longest golden gate, verrazano (narrows)
maker pontiflex
master culbertson, goodman, goren, morehead, schenken, sheinwold, sims, vanderbilt

musical instrument magas, ponticello
of death giallar
of pain kuchuchiao
paradise al sirat
part arch, cable, caisson, crown, deck, hangar, jowel, pier, pylon, shoe, spandrel, tressel, trestle, trunnion, truss
pier end nosing
plank chess
play cross ruff, finesse, high-low
position east, north, south, west
rope joola
round rubber
score leg
support pier, trestle, truss
suspension joola
table four
temporary bailey, pontoon
tender ebbman
term 3 bid, bye, leg, set 4 bete, book, cash, down, duck, game, hook, jump, open, pass, ruff, slam, suit, void 5 count, dummy, entry, major, minor, pivot, raise, rebid, renig, round, sneak, split, swing, trick, trump 6 assist, comeon, demand, double, honors, pickup, renege, revoke, rubber, swings 7 bracket, declare, defense, finesse, no-trump, overbid, penalty, preempt, premium, reentry, shutout, squeeze, take out, throw in 8 contract, declarer, defender, jettison, longsuit, overcall, redouble, response, sequence 9 blackwood, challenge, cross ruff, doubleton, falsecard, grand slam, overtrick, part score, sacrifice, short suit, singleton 10 fourchette, invitation, little slam, quick trick, under trick, vulnerable 12 below the line, distribution
toll pontage
wilder's san luis rey
BRIDGEHEAD base, breach, foothold, landing, offensive, opening, stronghold, toehold, vanguard
BRIDGET, St. *symbol* book, crozier
BRIDLE anger, bend, bind, bit, brake, brank(s), bristle, caper, cavesson, chain, check, clevis, control, cord,

curb, direct, flange, frenum, govern(or), guard, guide, hackamere, halter, harness, inhibit, leash, link, lorain, master, mince, pillory, pose, rein, repress, restrain, ruffle, rule, scratch, shackle, simper, slip-spring, snaffle, strut, subdue, summarize, suppress, swagger, tame, trimmer
bit scatch, snaffle
flap blinder
maker lorimer
noseband cavesson, musrol
part bit, bridoon, cheekpiece, curb-strap, headstall, noseband, rein, snaffle, stirrup, throatlatch
path spurway
strap rein
-wise obedient, responsive
BRIEF abridge, abrupt, abstract, advise, argument, blurb, breve, breviate, capsule, case, catalogue, charm, common, compact, compendious, compendium, concise, condensed, conspectus, cryptic, curt(al), ephemeral, epitome, few, fleeting, flitting, inform, initiate, laconic, list, little, mandate, material, memorandum, momentary, orient, outline, passing, pithy, plan, precept, prevalent, quick, report, rife, short(-lived), small, snatched, snippety, span, spell, statement, succinct, sudden, summary, syllabus, synopsis, taciturn, terse, transient, transitory, writ
case dispatch case, portfolio, tashie
encounter brush
hold — for advocate, defend
BRIEFLY enfin, fleetingly, flittingly, in fine, in short, quickly, shortly
BRIER See BRIAR.
BRIG geordie, JAIL, prison, rig
BRIGADE band, campoo, division, group, terzo
BRIGAND bandit, bedouin, cateran, footpad, highwayman, kettrin, ladrone, marauder, picaroon, pirate, robber, routier, ruffian, soldier, thief, uskok
band tchetnitsi

BRIGANDAGE banditry, depredation, plunder
BRIGHT 3 apt, gay 4 airy, cute, fine, gild, glad, gleg, keen, live, naif, rosy 5 acute, aglow, alert, anime, beamy, blaze, brave, clear, crisp, fresh, glary, happy, jolly, light, lucid, nitid, palmy, quick, riant, sharp, sheen, shiny, sleek, smart, smolt, sunny, vivid, white, witty 6 adroit, aglare, agleam, bertha, cheery, clever, flashy, florid, fulgid, garish, glossy, lively, lucent, nimble, silver 7 beaming, beamish, diamond, dilucid, flaming, fulgent, glaring, halcyon, hopeful, lambent, radiant, ringing, shining 8 animated, cheerful, colorful, dazzling, flashing, gleaming, glittery, glorious, gorgeous, lightful, luminous, lustrous, pleasant, polished, sanguine, splendid, sunshiny 9 effulgent, favorable, ingenious, on-the-ball, promising, refulgent, sparkling, sprightly 10 attractive, auspicious, bedazzling, discerning, epiphanous, flamboyant, glistening, optimistic, precocious 11 conspicuous, illustrious, intelligent, quickwitted, resplendent, translucent, transparent
as silver
-colored serrano
comb. lampr(o)
name *meaning* albert, bertha, bertram, clara, clare, hubert
BRIGHTEN animate, break, burn(ish), cantle, cheer, clear, dawn, embrave, encourage, engild, enliven, flame, furbish, gild, glaze, illume, illuminate, illumine, light(en), liven, polish, shine, snuff, smarten
BRIGHTEYES bluet, chrysanthemum, houstonia
BRIGHTNESS acumen, blare, blaze, brilliance, candor, cheerfulness, clarity, eclat, effulgence, flamboyance, fulgo(u)r, glare, glitter, gleam, glory, gloss, light, luster, nitency, nitor, radiance, refulgence, sheen,

shine, sparkle, splendor, sun, vividness
unit nit, stilb
BRIGIT brigantia
father dagda
husband bres
BRIGUE beguile, cabal, faction, intrigue, quarrel
BRILL bret, flatfish, turbot
BRILLIANCE ability, aglaia, aptitude, blare, blaze, braininess, brightness, capacity, distinction, eclat, effulgence, excellence, fame, genius, glare, glitter, glory, grace, keenness, luster, magnificence, oriency, pre-eminence, quality, radiance, renown, shine, smartness, sparkle, splendor, talent, vivacity
BRILLIANT alert, aureate, breme, bright, brittle, clever, coruscating, dazzling, diamond, discerning, eminent, erudite, flaming, funny, gay, gem, glaring, glorious, good, gorgeous, illustrious, inspired, keen, lambent, lamping, lively, luculent, luminous, meteoric, prismal, radiant, refulgent, sage, scintillating, shining, signal, smart, splendid, stone, vivid, wise
BRILLIANTINE pomade
BRIM bluff, border, bream, brink, edge, fill, lip, marge, margin, ocean, rim, rut, sea, skirt, strumpet, turnup, verge, water
of hat brink, flap, leaf, poke, tarfe
BRIMMING big, bumpered, crowned, full, overflowing, topful
BRIMO demeter, hecate, persephone
BRIMSTONE shrew, spitfire, sulfur, sulphur, virago
comb. thio
BRINDLED branded, dappled, flecked, spotted, streaked, tawny
BRINE alkali, brack, deep, leach, main, marinade, ocean, pickle, preserve, salt (water), sea, tears
fly ephydra
fly egg ahuatle
gauge salinometer
pit salt well, wych
preserve with corn, cure, salt
shrimp or worm artemia

BRING adduce, advance, apport, arrive, attract, bear, call, carry, cause, command, compel, conduce, conduct, convey, convince, deduce, deliver, draw, drive, entail, escort, evoke, fetch, firk, get, guide, impel, incur, induce, institute, lay, lead, obtain, persuade, prefer, procure, produce, rise, sell for, take, tee(m), transport, win, yield
about accomplish, achieve, beget, brew, carry out, catalyze, cause, complete, consummate, create, dight, effect(uate), engender, finish, frame, generate, infer, inspire, make, occasion, produce, prompt, realize, reverse, shape, succeed, swing, tack, transact
action litigate
around convince, cure, persuade, restore, revive
back fetch, occasion, recall, reduct, refer, relate, remember, restore, retrieve, return, revive
before haul
charge appeach
down abase, abate, capture, decline, depress, dismount, drop, fell, kill, lay, lessen, raze, reduce, simplify, stop
down upon incur, inflict, invoke, sic
forth bear, beget, beteem, calve, cast, cause, deliver, ean, educe, elicit, engender, evoke, foal, generate, hatch, incur, issue, kid, produce, profer, publish, rise, spawn, teem, throw, yean
forward adduce, adjoust, advance, allege, assign, call up, carry, cite, confront, improve, infer, introduce, lead, present, produce, propose, show
home convince, prove, show
home the bacon accomplish, earn, prevail, succeed, triumph, win
home to charge, condemn, impress, prove
in adhibit, cost, earn, enable, gather, harvest, import, induce, introduce, present, produce, reap, report, return, submit, usher, yield
into being create, generate

into court accuse, amend, arrest, indict, indite, litigate, sist, sue
low abase, avale, degrade, depress, dishonor, supplant
near appose, approach, approximate, juxtapose
off accomplish, achieve, carry out, complete, consummate, finish, fordo, fulfil, succeed
on adduce, attract, create, entice, improve, incur, induce, infer, lure
out accent, announce, attract, debut, demonstrate, detect, disinter, display, divulge, draw, elicit, establish, evoke, expose, heighten, introduce, issue, manifest, manufacture, present, print, produce, publish, reveal, set forth, submit
over convert, convince, persuade, win
pressure compel, induce, influence, thrust, urge
round cast, convert, convince, cure, persuade, restore, revive, tack, win over
to convert, halt, resuscitate, revive
to account punish
to an end cease, complete, dissolve, dock, expire, finish, foredo, halt, surcease
to bay corner, engage, trap, tree
to bear apply, concentrate, exert, focus
together adduct, aggregate, amass, assemble, bulk, collate, collect, compile, comport, conflate, convoke, engage, enlink, ensemble, gather, join, muster, raise, reconcile, summon, unite
to light dredge up, disclose, discover, divulge, elicit, expose, grub, print, publish, reap, reveal, unearth
to mind recall, remind, resemble
to naught confute, dash, destroy, foil, negate, undo
to pass achieve, cause, create
to stop arrest, cease, curb, end, halt
to terms coerce, compel, conquer, force, overcome, reconcile, settle, subdue
up breed, broach, confront, educate, evoke, foster, halt,

introduce, mention, mobilize, nurse, nurture, propose, raise, rear, regurgitate, retch, stop, summon, train, uprear, vomit
up to date brief, inform, modernize, post
BRINJAL eggplant
BRINK border, bound, bourn, brim, brow, coast, ditch, edge, end, eve, foss(e), lip, marge(nt), margin, rim, sea, shore, strand, verge
on the about to, near, ready
BRIO vigor, vivacity
BRIOCHE bun, cushion, dough, roll, savarin
BRISEIS *captor* achilles
father briseus
lover achilles, agamemnon, mynes
BRISINGAMEN *owner* freya
BRISK active, agile, airy, alert, alive, allegro, animated, brag, breezy, budge, busy, canty, cheery, cocket, cold, cool, crisp, crouse, dapper, dynamic, effervescent, energetic, ephemeral, fast, fleet, flicky, fresh, frisk, gay, humming, kedge, keen, lively, nimble, nippy, peart, perk(y), pert, prompt, quick, racy, rapid, rash, ready, sharp, smacking, smart, snappy, spanking, spirited, sprightly, sprunt, spry, stimulating, swift, trig, trotty, vivacious, vive, windy, yern(e), zippy
BRISKLY busily, crouse, yern(e)
BRISTLE acicula, aciculum, aggravate, anger, arise, arista, awn, barb, bedeg(u)ar, birse, bridle, brush, chaeta, feller, flaunt, frenulum, glochis, hair, jag(g), palpus, pique, plume, preen, pride, provoke, quill, resent, rib, ruffle, seta, seton, setula, setule, spiculum, spine, stiver, stover, striga, strut, stubble, stylet, swagger, tela, vibrissa, whisker
arrangement chaetotaxy
comb. seti
covered with setose
fern trichomanes
grass setaria
having See BRISTLY.

-like aristate, hairlike, hairy, setal, setarious, setiform, setose, styloid
moss orthotrichum
pert. See BRISTLY.
pointed apiculate
-shaped setiform, styloid
small barbellula
with abound, teem
without eremochaetous
worm chaetopod
BRISTLY, BRISTLING barbellate, birsy, briery, echinate, glochidiate, hairy, hirsute, hispid, horrent, horrid, packed, rough, scopate, scrubby, setaceous, setal, setose, spinous, sticky, strigal, stubbled, stubbly, studded, teeming, thorny
BRISTOL solitaire
channel, river to severn
fashion orderly, shipshape
metal brass
milk sherry
stone quartz, rock crystal
weed dog's mercury
BRIT herring, sprat
BRITAIN See also ANGLO-SAXON and ENGLAND references.
founder brut
germanic founders angles, saxons
king, mythical artegal
ruler bretwalda
BRITANNIA See ENGLAND.
BRITCHES See PANTS.
BRITISH See also ANGLO-SAXON and ENGLAND references.
african protectorate gambia, kenya
columbia See CANADA references.
empire personified britannia
guiana See GUYANA.
gum dextrin
honduras bay chetumal
honduras capital belize, belmopan
honduras city cayo, corozal, stann
honduras range maya
new guinea papua
north america canada
north borneo sabah
square solitaire
tobacco coltsfoot
warm overcoat
BRITOMARTIS aphaia, artemis, chastity, dyctynna
consort artegal, minos

parent carme, jupiter, zeus
BRITON brython, celt, pict, scot
early people angles, silures
god ardena, belinus, belisarna, esus, taramis, teutates
king cymbeline
ogre rounfi
prince vortigern
ruler bretwalda
BRITTANY armorica, bretagne
bagpipe bignou, bin(i)ou
ballad gwerziou
king ban
language armorican, breton, brezonek, celtic, cornish, welsh
magic forest broceliande
native armoric(an), breton
nine fays corrigans, korrigans
pert. armoric, breton
poetry sonious
standing stones carnac
BRITTLE brash, breakable, brickle, britchel, bruckle, candy, carbonous, confection, crackable, crackly, crisp(y), crumbling, crump(y), crushable, delicate, difficult, dry, feeble, fickle, fissile, fracturable, fragile, frail, frangible, fratile, friable, frough, frow(y), frush, ginger, hard, inconstant, infirm, irritable, lacerable, perishable, redsear, rigid, scissile, shatterable, shattery, shivery, short, slight, smopple, snappish, spalt, splintery, thin, ticklish, weak
as glass
bush encelia, plant
star echinoderm, ophiuran, ophiurid
stem aralia, sarsaparilla
BRITTLEWOOD buckthorn, rhamnus
BRITTLEWORT diatom
BRIZA birds'-eyes, cuckooflower, quaking-grass
BRIZE, BRIZZ crush, gadfly, press
BROACH accost, advance, air, attame, awl, begin, bodkin, boring, brooch, careen, cress, cut, decant, drain, draw, dress, drill, driver, enlarge, fibula, finish, gimlet, incision, introduce, issue, launch, men-

tion, move, offer, open, ouch, perforate, perforation, pierce, pin, prick, propose, publish, reamer, rhymer, rimer, rod, shape, shed, spear, spindle, spit, spool, spur, stab, strike, submit, suggest, tame, tap, utter, veer, vent(ilate), violate, voice, widener

BROAD all-inclusive, ample, beamy, belcher, big, bold, braid, breezy, candid, catholic, chotchka, clear, coarse, comprehensive, deep, dialectical, essential, expansive, extended, extensive, evident, fat, free, full, general, generous, girl, global, grivois, gross, immense, improper, indecent, indelicate, large, liberal, main, obvious, open, outspoken, plain, prostitute, ranging, roomy, spacious, splay, squab, stout, tchotchke, thick, tolerant, trollop, tsatske, unconfirmed, unfettered, unrestrained, vague, vast, vulgar, wide(spread), woman
and flat platoid, tabulate
arrow pheon, stigma
band fess
comb. eury, lati
-footed platypod
-gauged See *minded*, below.
-leaved ginger zerumbet
-loom carpet
-minded generous, lenient, liberal, tolerant
-mouth raya
-ribbed laticostate
-toothed latidentate
-winged latipennate
BROADBILL bird, boatbill, duck, gaper, heron, raya, scaup-duck, shoveler, swordfish
dipper ruddy duck
BROADBRIM friend, quaker
BROADCAST advertise, air, announce, blazon, cast, circulate, declare, diffuse, disseminate, divulge, plant, present, proclaim, program, promulgate, publish, radio, scatter, seed, send, sow, spatter, speak, sponsor, spread, strew, televise, transmit, troll, widespread
BROADCLOTH castor, fabric, material, suclat, suiting, taunton, wool, worsted

BROADEN amplify, brede, deepen, dilate, enlarge, ennoble, expand, extend, increase, out(spread) (stretch), spread(out), widen
BROADHORN ark, flatboat
BROADIE cow, steak
BROADLEAF griselina, puka, tobacco
BROADSIDE barrage, bill, circular, crossfire, enfilade, fusillade, garland, lateral(ly), salvo, spray, spread, volley
to the wind athwart
BROADSWORD bill, brackmard, cimeter, claymore, cutlass, ferrara, glaive, hanger, kris, montanto, scimitar, scimiter, spatha
BROADTAIL astrachan, astrakhan, caracul, fur, mohair, parrot, persian-lamb, platycercus, sheep, wool
BROADWAY big time, great white way, tawdry
awards obies
BROBDINGNAG *capital* lorbrylgrud
BROBDINGNAGIAN See HUGE.
BROCADE acca, baldachin, baldoquin, baudekin, broche, brocotel(le), cloth, damassin, kincob, kinkob, nishiki
BROCARD barb, ellipse, gallicism, gibe, maxim, principle, proverb, rule, sarcasm
BROCCOLI brassica, calabrese, marijuana
brown goat, loam, plover, rabbit
BROCHAN oatmeal, porridge
BROCHETTE brooch, skewer, spit
BROCHURE booklet, leaflet, pamphlet, tract, treatise
BROCKET coassus, deer, mazama, pita, pito, spitter, stag
BROCKLE breakable, fragments, refuse, rubbish, variable
BROD goad, incentive, pierce, prick, poke, pole, sprout, thorn, urge
BRODIE bloomer, blooper, blunder, boner, botch, error, flop
BRODYAGA vagabond, vagrant

BROG awl, broggle, goad, prick, prod
BROGAN boot, brogue, shoe, stogie, stogy
BROGUE accent, brogan, dialect, fraud, prank, shoe, trick
BROIL affray, alarm, altercation, bake, barbecue, birsle, bloodwit, braise, brander, brawl, brouhaha, brulyie, brulzie, carbonado, char, clamor, conflict, confusion, contention, contest, cook, discord, dispute, disturbance, feud, fracas, fray, frizzle, grid, grill(ade), heat, melee, quarrel, roast, row, scorch, scrap, simulty, splore, stramash, struggle, swelt(er), toil, tumult, turbulence, turmoil, uproar
BROILER chicken, grate, gridiron, grill, mushroom, poussin
BROKE bankrupt, beanless, beat, break, bust(ed), deal, dry, flat(busted), fragment, hog, insolvent, moneyless, negotiate, oofless, penniless, penurious, poor, ragged, skirting, ston(e)y, strapped, traffic, wound
BROKEN bankrupt, blown, brashy, bung, burst, cashiered, contrite, cracked, crushed, disconnected, disjasked, disjaskit, dispersed, disrupted, down, fract(ur)ed, fragmentary, fragmented, gappy, gentle, hackly, haywire, impaired, incomplete, infringed, intermittent, interrupted, irregular, on the blink, out of order, reduced, rent, rompu, rough, rude, ruined, ruptured, shaken, shattered, subdued, tamed, tattered, torn, trained, uneven, vicious, violated, weakened, whipped, zigzagging
-backed chinked, hogged, sagged
-bellied ruptured
comb. fracto
-down collapsed, dilapidated, disjaskit, haywire, infirm, out-of-order, shattered
-hearted depressed, grieving, sad(dened), sorrowful
in stoven
-mouthed toothless
wind heaves

BROKER agent, brogger, cambist, changer, corser, crimp, dealer, factor, forestaller, go-between, huckster, jobber, licensee, merchant, middleman, money-changer, peddler, realtor, retailer, salesman, scalper, schatchen
BROKERAGE agio, commission, fee
fraudulent bucket shop
BROLLY See UMBRELLA.
BROMELIA ananas, caraguata, pinguin
BROMIAN dionysian
drink wine
BROMIDE adage, bore, cliche, commonplace, platitude, truism
BROMIUS dionysus
BRONCHIAL *ailment* bronchitis, bronchiolitis, hoose, hooze, husk
BRONCO broomtail, buckjumper, cayuse, estrapade, mustang, pony, sunfisher
-buster cowboy, buckaroo, horseman, ginette, stockman
grass brome, bromus
BRONTASAUR See DINOSAUR.
BRONTE *anne, pseud.* acton bell
charlotte, pseud. currer bell
charlotte, novel jane eyre, shirley, villette
emily, pseud. ellis bell
emily, novel wuthering heights
home haworth
BRONX *cheer* bird, boo, raspberry
BRONZE aes, alloy, beeswax, brass, brazen, brown, bust, coin, color, latten, pigment, sculpture, statue, sunburn, tan
age cemetery urnfield
age culture harappa, ubaid
age, late larnaudian
age, pert. helladic
antique cacao
-backer black bass
coinage aesgrave
-colored aeneous
film patina
gilded ormolu, vermeil
heavy desgrave
-like brazen
medal calabash
new brussels brown
nude olive-brown
pert. aeneous

BRONZEWING squatter
BROO broth, inclination, juice, water
BROOCH adorn, armilla, boss, broach, brochette, cameo, clasp, crotchet, fibula, morse, nouche, ornament, ouch, pectoral, pendant, petalon, pin, plaque, preen, prop, shield, spray, sprig, sunburst
large stomacher
BROOD aerie, agonize, bevy, breed, cherish, children, cletch, clutch, cogitate, cover, covey, dwell on, eye, family, flock, fry, group, hatch, hover, incubate, issue, kind(le), kindling, languish, litter, meditate, mope, multitude, nest, nid(e), nye, offspring, ponder, posterity, progeny, race, sedge, set, siege, sigh, sit, species, team, trip, weep, worry, young
bud bulbil, gemma, soredium
cell gonidium
smallest of reckling, runt
BROODER birdhouse, birthplace, chickenhouse, hover, kill-joy, mother, nursery
BROOK abide, arroyo, bear, beck, bourn(e), branch, burn, canada, comport, creek, doke, endure, ghyll, gill, purl, quebrada, rill(et), rillock, rindle, rivose, rivulet, runlet, runnel, sicket, sike, stand, stell, stomach, stream, suffer, tchai, tolerate
celandine impatiens, jewelweed
farm founder ripley
flower waterleaf
runner water-rail
salt lick
sunflower bur marigold
BROOKED dirty, spotted, streaked
BROOKIE char(r), fish, trout, sooty
BROOKLIME gratiola, horsecress, speedwell, veronica, wall-ink, watercress
BROOKLYN *bridge designer* roebling
bridge jumper steve brodie
canal gowanus
BROOM baccharis, besom, bisme, bream, brush, cow,

crush, cytisis, deerweed, dogwood, fray, genista, hackweed, hagweed, heather, hirse, mop, plant, shrub, spart, splinter, swab, sweep(er), tree, ualis, whisk, woodwaxen
brush st john's-wort
bush fever-few
cypress goosefoot, toadflax
dyer's dyewood, genet
hickory pignut
palm cohune
sage rabbit-brush
sedge andropogon, arrowgrass, beard-grass
small whisk
squire gypsy(squatter)
tea tree manuka
twig besom
BROOMCORN hurl, kaoliang, shallu, sorghum
millet hirse, kadikane, panic (le)
BROOMRAPE anoplanthus, chokeweed, conopholis, hellroot, herbbane, indianpipe, orobanche, squawroot, strangletare, thalesia
BROOMROOT sacaton, zacaton
BROOMWEED corchorus, scoparia, sida, triumfetta
BROOMWORT orobanch, water betony
BROSIMUM breadnut, capomo, cowtree, leopardwood, ramon
BROSY fat, slow, thick
BROTEAS *father* tantalus
BROTH bouillon, bree, brewis, broo, caldera, consomme, cullis, elixir, imrich, imrigh, jussel, kail, kale, pishpash, possodie, pottage, powsowdy, skillagalee, skilly, souchie, soup, stock, supping
of oblivion mi-hun-tang
BROTHEL bagne, bagnio, bath, bawdyhouse, bordel(lo), bullpen, cathouse, cowyard, crib, dive, hookshop, hothouse, joint, joyhouse, jukehouse, kip, lupanar(e), panelden, rookery, seraglio, shinjuku, stew(house), whorehouse
pert. stewish
BROTHER associate, bhai, billy, boy, brer, brethren, bruder, bub, bud(dy), cadet, chaver, comrade, fellow, fra, fraile, frate(r),

frere, friar, friend, khaver, kin, layman, male, member, monk, oblate, pal, peer, sib (ling)
comb. adelpho, frat(r)
husband's levir
-in-law beau-frere, maugh, shvoger
lay scolog
little hurricane
religious fra, friar, monk
wife's affine
younger cadet
BROTHERHOOD association, bratstvo, brodhull, chishti, companionship, confraternity, fellowship, fraternity, friary, group, g(u)ild, order, profession, society, sodality, thiasos, union
literary felibrige
BROTHERWORT pennyroyal, thyme
BROUGHAM cab, carriage, landaulet, pillbox
BROUHAHA brawl, broil, clamor, confusion, turmoil, uproar
BROW boldness, border, bound, brae, brink, countenance, crest, edge, effrontery, eyebrow, forehead, front, gangplank, inion, mien, ridge, slope, snab, summit, top
point antler
BROWBEAT abash, bulldoze, bully, cow, depress, disconcert, domineer, dumbcow, face, harass, hector, intimidate, nag, oppress, outface, scare, swagger, terrify
BROWN acorn, arab, argus, asphalt, bark, bay, bister, bole, braise, bronze, brunet(te), bruno, bure, burn, chestnut, cocoa, coin, cook, copper, dark, drab, dun, dusky, ecru, fairy, fawn, fox(y), fry, gloomy, harvest, hazel, kaffa, lama, malage, mirador, mushroom, oxblood, pablo, paloma, penny, pongee, quail, redwood, russet, saute, scorch, seal, sear, sedge, sennet, sienna, sepia, sorrel, suntan, tan(ned), tawny, tenne, tiffin, toast(ed), tobacco, turtle, umber, unbleached, wigwam
and white roan

as a berry
bess gun, musket, wakerobin
betty coneflower, daisy, pudding
bill halbert
bright spadiceous
brush st john's-wort
caledonian gypsy
castillian tanegra
condor tiffin
dark bister, bistre, brunneous, burnet, chocolate, puce
-eyed susan gaillardia, rudbeckia
george biscuit, bread, vessel, wig
john, raid site harpers ferry
jolly brinja(u)l, eggplant
light aloma, alesan, beige, biscuit, ecru, fawn, string, tan, tenne, toast
madder castilian, tanagra
name meaning bruno
-nose apple-polish, fawn, flatter, toady
off aggravate, anger
olive autumn, bark
reddish ambrosia, auburn, bay, bole, bronze, bure, coppa(g)h, chestnut, cinnamon, copper, crotal, cuba, ginger, hazel, henna, khaki, mahogany, mordore, roan, ruddle, russet, rust, sepia, sorrel, terracotta, umber
rustic eskimo
shirt fascist, nazi, stormtrooper, sturmabteilung
stone chestnut, coconut, kermanshah
study absorption, musing
yellowish alderney, almond, aztec, bamboo, beeswax, blonde, pablo, tan, tawny
BROWNBACK dowitch(er), snipe
BROWNE, CHARLES *pseud.* artemus ward
BROWNE, THOMAS, *work* religio medici, urn burial
BROWNIE banshee, cake, camera, cookie, demon, dobby, dwarf, elf, fairy, fay, girl scout, goblin, kobold, kodak, leprechaun, nis(se), nix(ie), pixie, puck, sandpiper, shee, spirit, sprite, urisk, uruisg
ceremony fly-up
BROWNING, ROBERT *character* gigadibs, pippa, pompilia

deity setebos
dog flush
home asolo
poem asolando, fra lippo lippi, my last duchess, paracelsus, pippa passes, prospice, ring and the book, sordello
BROWNWORT figwort, selfheal
BROWSE bite, brut, crop, dip into, eat, feed, glance, graze, leaf, look, nibble, pasture, read, scan, thumb, twigs
BROZ, JOSIP tito
BRUCKLE begrime, breakable, brittle, changeable, dirty, frail, inconstant
BRUISE abrasion, abuse, bash, batter, beat, black eye, bray, break, brize, brizz, bubu, buffet, bung, chotchke, contund, contusion, crush, curry, dammish, dent, dinge, disable, discolor, dunt, ecchymosis, hatter, hurt, ictus, injure, injury, intuse, jam(b), maim, mangle, maul, mawl, mouse, pain, pounce, pound, pulverize, shanty, shiner, sore, spoil, squeeze, stound, suggil, tchotchke, triturate, tsatske, tund, wale, wound
remedy arnica
BRUISED battered, black-and-blue, discolored, ecchymotic, froisse, humble, hurt, livid
BRUISER boxer, bully, crusher, gangster, grinder, hoodlum, pugilist
BRUIT blazon, clamor, declare, din, fame, hearsay, noise, publish, rale, report, roar, rumor, sound, tell, voice
BRUMAL cold, hiemal, sleety, wintry
BRUME fog, haze, mist, smog, vapor, winter
BRUMMAGEM counterfeit, gaudy, inferior, showy, spurious, tinsel, worthless
BRUNEHILDA See BRUNHILD.
BRUNET black, brown, dark, gipsy, gypsy, melanous, morena, morenita, olive, swarthy
BRUNHILD *consort* gunnar, gunther

home isenstein
mother erda
BRUNT attack, blow, burden, clash, collision, effort, face, force, impact, jar, load, molt, onset, outburst, shock, strain, stress, tension, violence
BRUNWEN *brother* bran, evnissyen
BRUSCUS box-holly, butcher's-broom
BRUSH 3 dip, dub, rub, tip **4** card, comb, flap, fray, kiss, kiyi, move, rush, skim, swab, tail, tuft **5** beard, besom, broom, chape, clean, copse, fight, fitch, graze, groom, paint, scopa, scrub, scuff, shave, speed, sweep, swoop, touch, whisk, woods **6** action, bottle, brosse, combat, dabber, dauber, duster, gallop, glance, hasten, mogote, polish, putois, remove, rustle, shrubs, sponge, sticks, stroke, tassel, teasel, tickle, tulies **7** contest, country, foxtail, grainer, groomer, stipple, sylvage, thicket **8** branches, bushwood, skirmish, smoothen, stippler, strobile, struggle **9** backwoods, brechites, encounter, sarothrum, wasteland **10** coneflower, engagement **11** aspersorium, undergrowth **12** aspergillium
aside dismiss, disregard, ignore, repudiate, scuff, skip
box tristania
breaker moldboard-plow
cleaning groomer
comb. scopi
dense boondocks, bundocks
drag harrow
electric doctor
flesh scraper, strigil
growth sylvage
-like aspergilliform, scopulate
maker flicker, flirty
off boycott, cut, dismiss, ignore, ostracize, snub
pollen sarothrum, scopa
popper cowboy
shunt pigtail
small fitch(ew)
turkey leipoa, maleo, megapode
up cram, furbish, groom, review, study
BRUSHWOOD boscage,

brake, bush, coppet, coppice, copse, frith, garsil, hag, mallee, rammel, reise, rone, roughie, rush, scrog(s), scrub(s), scrunt, shrog(s), slack, teenet, thicket, tin(n)et, tinsel, undergrowth, woodland, woodris
bundle bavin
BRUSQUE abrupt, bluff, blunt, burly, candid, cavalier, curt, discourteous, gruff, harsh, hasty, impolite, rough, rude, short, terse, uncivil, violent
BRUSSELLS *bisquit* zwieback
brown bronze
patron saint gudula, gudule
point bobbin-lace
BRUSTLE crackle, dry, parch, rustle
BRUT browse, dry
grandfather aeneas
BRUTAL barbarian, barbaric, barbarous, beastly, belluine, bestial, boorish, caddish, callous, carnal, coarse, crude, cruel, feral, ferocious, fierce, gross, harsh, inhuman(e), insensate, irrational, mad, primitive, rough, ruthless, sadistic, savage, unreasoning, untamed, violent, vulgar, wild
BRUTE animal, baboon, barbarian, beast, bestial, caliban, carnal, cruel, gorilla, gross, harsh, hoodlum, inanimate, ogre, ruffian, savage, scoundrel, sensual, soulless, uncivilized, unconscious, unpolished, yahoo
BRUTUS chrysanthemum, traitor, wig
armor-bearer dardanus
enemy antony, vatinius
friend acilius, cassius, cato, favonius, ligarius, lucilius, messala, statilius, titinius, volumnius
kin cassius, cato, junia
lieutenant antistius, camulatus, cicero, herostratus, hortensius, labeo, volumnius
servant claudius, clitus, dardanius, lucius, strato, varro
stepson bibulus
victim caesar, theodotus
wife porcia, portia

BRYAN, WILLIAM J. *cause* free silver
sobriquet the commoner
BRYANT, WILLIAM C. *poem* thanatopsis
BRYONY alraun, cowbind, hop, mandrake, nep, vine
black baneberry, bindweed, oxberry, tamus
BRYOPHYTE anophyte, liverwort, moss
pert. mossy
BRYTHON briton, cambrian, celt, cymry, WELSH
BUB blast, boy, brother, bubble, buddy, gust, liquor, meal
BUBALIS alcelaphus, antelope, hartebeest, topi
BUBALUS bison, buffalo, wild ox
BUBASTIS artemis
kin horus, isis
BUBBLE air, ball, bead, bell, bladder, blain, bleb, blister, blob, blubber, boil, boll, bulge, bulla, burble, caper, cheat, chimera, deceive, delusion, delusive, dome, dream, dupe, effervesce, empty, fantasy, ferment, fizz(le), foam, glob(ule), guggle, gurgle, hiss, hotter, illusion, imagination, mirage, plop, pop(ple), pustule, ripple, scheme, scum, seed, seethe, simmer, snap, sotter, sparkle, speculation, stir, swindle, trifle, vesicle, wallop, work
and squeak beef and cabbage
snail bulimoid, bulimus, bulla, physa
up boil, intumesce
BUBBLER drumfish, promoter, swindler
BUBBLING *up* agush
BUBBLY aerated, champagne, effusive, foaming, gay
jock turkeycock
BUBINGA dedelotia, kevazingo
BUBO bird, emerod, owl, swelling
BUCCA cheek, fool, hobgoblin, sprite
BUCCANEER corsair, freebooter, mariner, marooner, picaroon, pirate, rifler, robber, spoiler, viking
famous edward teach
standard jolly roger

BUCCINOID fulgur, gastropod, snail, whelk, winkle

BUCEPHALA buffleduck, butterball

BUCEPHALUS *owner* alexander

BUCHANAN, JAMES
birthplace stony batter, penn.
burial site lancaster, penn.
party democratic
profession lawyer
vice president breckenridge

BUCHAREST *airport* otopeni
newspaper scinteia

BUCHNERA bluehearts, figwort

BUCK antelope, balk, basket, beech, bleach, blood, bouk, brag, bring, bukh, bull, butt, canter, carry, charge, contest, dandy, deer, dollar, dude, etaac, fop, gamble, hart, jerk, jig, kick, leap, lye, macaroni, male, man, mast, nob, object, oppose, pass, pitch, pricket, prig, pulverize, resist, risk, sasin, sawhorse, skip, soak, sorrel, spark, spring, stag, steep, strive, sunfish, support, swell, throw, thrust, toff, transport, wash, youth
and ball cartridge
and wing tap dance
bean boghop, bognut, moorflower, sweet-gale, trefoil
black sasin
blue blaubok, etaac
fat goat-lard
fever jitters, nerves
1st year fawn
4th year sore
grass brass-buttons, plantain, swine's cress
group herd
off unhorse, unseat
-passer dodger, evader, shifter
private rookie
red impala, pallah
2nd year pricket
slip memo
3rd year sorrel
up brace, cheer, encourage, rally, refresh, revive, stir

BUCKAROO broncobuster, cowboy, horseman, stockman

BUCKBOARD carriage, four-wheeler, wagon

BUCKBUSH ceanothus,

coralberry, purshia, wolfberry

BUCKER carrier, dollyman, hammer, lifter, loader, mule, sawyer

BUCKET awe, bail(er), basket, bowie, bowk, bushel, cage, can(nikin), carry, cheat, clamshell, coal scuttle, dipper, draw, drench, drive, grapple, hedgehog, hod, hoppet, hurry, kibble, ladle, lift, paddle, pail, paintpot, pour, push, say, scoop, scuttle, situla, skeel, skip, snapper, socket, soe, stoop, stoup, swindle, tub, vane, vessel
brigade firemen
famous old oaken
glass-making cuvette
gravel grab
handle bail
hoisting hudge
molten glass cuvette
shop boiler room, brokerage
wheeled skip
wooden bowk

BUCKEYE aesculus, bold, butterfly, canoe, chestnut, loud, shrill
state ohio

BUCKHORN brass-buttons, cinnamon fern, club moss, lycopodium, mussel, plantain, swine's cress

BUCKLE bend, bow, brace, bulge, catch, clasp, close, collapse, confine, contend, crumple, curl, distort(ion), equip, fasten, fermail, fibula, hasp, kink, marry, ornament, ouch, shrivel, strap, struggle, surrender, tach(e), tack, tie, twist, warp, yield
down concentrate, determine, exert, focus
part chape, tongue
-shaped scutate

BUCKLER aegis, block, buckram, crab, defense, rondelle, rotella, roundel, scute, shield, shutter, targe(t)
play fencing

BUCKO bully, chap, companion, fellow, spark, swaggerer

BUCKRAM bocasine, cuckoopint, fabric, formal(ity), linen, precise, ramson, starchiness, stiff(ener)

BUCKS See MONEY.

BUCKSKIN backwoodsman, breeches, cloth, horse, leather, purse, soldier

BUCKSTALL deertrap, net, toil

BUCKTHORN alatern, bearwood, bumelia, cascara, ceanothus, chaparral, chittamwood, colubrina, coma, frangula, lotebush, rhamn, scrog, stinkberry, stinkwood, wahoo, waythorn
bark cascara

BUCKWHEAT antigonon, bistorta, brank, brunnichia, coccolobis, crap, fagopyrum, persicaria, sarrazin, teetee, titi, wright
climbing bindweed
wild beefeed

BUCOLIC agrestic, arcadian, barnyard, cowherd, eclogue, farmer, geoponic, georgic, herdsman, idyl, local, naive, natural, pastoral, poem, rural, rustic, simple, unsophisticated

BUCOLION *parent* laomedon

BUD acrospire, begin(ning), blast, bloom, blossom, bourgeon, boy, brother, bulb, bulbilla, burgeon, button, caper, child, cion, clone, clove, dehisce, develop, eye, floret, flower, fem(ma), gemmule, germ (inate), graft, grow, imp, knop, knot, oculus, pip, plumule, propagulum, protuberance, scion, shoot, source, sprit, sprout, spurt, stem, tendron, youth
arrangement aestivation
blighted blast
brood soredium
comb. blasto
first plumule
internal statoblast
pickled caper
-shaped gemmiform
social deb(utante)
-time spring
underground bulb
undeveloped eye
without ablastous

BUDDHA See *classifications* and *names*, below, and BUDDHIST.
birth story jataka
classifications, dhyani akshobhya, amitabha, amitayus, amoghasiddhi, avalokitesvara, kshitigarbha,

maitreya, manjusri, ratnapani, ratnasambhava, samantab(h)adra, vairocana, vajrapani, visvapani
classifications, manushi dipankara, kanakamuni, krakuchanda, ksyapa, maitreya, vipasyin, visvabhu
company yaksha
cousin ananda, devadatta
death place kusinagara
disciple ananda, kassapa, kasyapa, mogallana
emanation brahma, mahesvara, narayana, sarasvato, varuna
equerry chandaka
falcon sibi-jataka
father suddhodhana
feminine aspect kuanyin, kwannon
footprints sripada
half-brother nanda
horse kantaka
human becoming boddhisattva
image amida, amita, butsu, daibutsu
kin devadatta, mahanama, rahula
king prasenajit
miracle sravasti
monastery changsa, outaichan
mother maya
mother, adopted mahaprajapati
mountain dwelling kukkutapada
mountain with 5 peaks pancasika, pancasirsha
musicians gandharvas
names (See also *classifications*, above.) adibuddha, amida, amitabha, arhat, ashuku, bodhisattva, butsu, cunda, daibutsu, dipankara, foh, gautama, jataka, kanakamuni, krakuchanda, kshitigarbha, ksyapa, kumara(bhova), kurukulla, maitreya, manjughsha, manjugri, miroku, myoo, nyorai, sage, sakya(muni), shakyamuni, siddhartha, sikhin, sramana, tathagata, vaisravana, vipasyin, virudhaka, virypaksa, yakushi
paradise sukhavari
patron bimbisara
philosophy the great vehicle
preaching site deer park
relic tooth
seat vajrasana

sermon sutra
squire chandaka
statue bodhisattva
story barlaam and josaphat, jataka
tempter mara
title blessed one, mahatma, sramana, teacher
tree of wisdom bodhiyaya
wife ahalya, gopa, yasodhara-devi
writings abidharma, karandavyuha, s(o)utra, svayambhuprana, tripitaka, vinaya
BUDDHI discernment, intellect, soul
BUDDHISM (See also BUDDHIST references.) chanism, daijo, foism, hinayana, kegon, lamaism, mahayana
BUDDHIST *altars* butsudan
angel deva, diva
birth cycle samsara
birth-death cycle nidana
building tope
church tera
city, sacred lassa, lhasa, nara
code vinaya
column lat
community sangha
deity bodhisattva, deva, diva, tara
delusion moha
demon mara, yaksha
desire tanha
dialogues sutra
divinity dhrtarastra, vaisravana, virudahka, virupaksa
doctrine amidism, amitabha, anatman, anatta, dharma, sunyate, sutta, trikaya
dryad yaksha, yakshi
duty dharma
eightfold path action, concentration, effort, intention, livelihood, mindfulness, speech, views
enemy mara
enlightenment bodhi, eightfold path
evil spirit mara
existence cause nidana
fate karma
fertility spirit yaksha, yakshi
festival bon, wesak
festival of dead obon
final beatitude raga, nirvana
form rupa
founder gautama, sakya(muni)
goal nirvana, turya
god deva, diva

hatred dosa
heaven chingtu, gokaruku, jodo
hell naraka
initiate mahatma
justice dhurna
king of india asoka
knowledge, supreme bodhi
language pali, sutta
law dharma
leader bodhidharma
legend source sutra
life cycle anicca
mantra dharani
meditation dhyana, yoga, zen
mendicant bhikku, bhikshu, gelong
mind manas
mind-state vihara
minister rinban
missionary bodhidharma
monastery bonzery, gompas, kyaung, lamasery, tera, vihara
mongol eleut
monk arhat, bhikku, bhikshu, bonze, dalai lama, gelong, goyin, grand lama, mahatma, panchen, poong(h)ee, poonghie, talapoin, yahan
monument amaravati, stupa
mountain, holy o(1)mei
nirvana-attaining arhat
novice goyin
oblivion nirvana
paradise chingtu, gokaruku, jodo
passion raga
philosophy madhyamika
pilgrim center sarnath
pillar lat
power, occult siddhi
prayer mani
priest See *monk*, above.
recitation panchasila
reincarnation hutukhtu
relic mound amaravati, stupa
retribution karma
rock temple rath(a)
saint ar(a)hat, lohan
sayings nikaya
school chan, dhyana, kyaung, ritsu, sanfron
scripture See BUDDHA *writings.*
sect jodo-shu, shin, shingon-shu, tendai, zen
self atman
semi-divine boddhigattva
shrine See *temple*, below.
sitting position asana, padmasana, yogasana

status bodhisattva
stories avadana
study buddhology
stupa amaravati
symbol wheel of life
teaching device upaya
temple ajanta, boro-budur, chorten, dagaba, dag-(h)oba, pagoda, ratha, stupa, tera, tope, vihara, wat
temple gateway toran(a), torii
tendency samkara, samskara
text dhammapada, sutra
three baskets tripitaka
throne asana
title mahatma
tree, sacred botree, pipal
triad triratna
triad parts buddha, dharma, sangha
virtue dharma
will to live tanha
wood, sacred champak

BUDDLE boddle, frame, marigold, slimer, strike, trough, tye, wash

BUDDY boy, brother, bub, chum, compadre, companion, comrade, co-worker, crony, dad, digger, jack, mate(y), pal, teammate, tentmate

-buddy chummy, familiar, intimate

BUDGE austere, bogy, booze, brisk, fur, jee, jocund, liquor, move, mudge, nervousness, pompons, solemn, stiff, stir, thief

BUDGERIGAR See BUDGIE.

BUDGET accumulation, allotment, allowance, apportion, bag, batch, bill, bogie, bogy, boot, bunch, bundle, cost, estimate, fund(s), pack(age), parcel, plan, pouch, program, ration, roll, sack, schedule, socket, stock, store, sum, wallet

entertainment booze allowance

BUDGIE budgereegah, budgerigar, budgerygah, parakeet

BUDZAT good-for-nothing, jerk, rascal

BUENOS AIRES *resident* porteno

BUFF addict, beat, blond, blow, bob, buffet, bug, bullhide, burnish, chamois,

clean, coat, cowhide, deaden, devotee, enthusiast, fan, fellow, firm, follower, furbish, hide, leather, nonsense, polish, pounce, pumice, rooter, rub, scour, shine, skin, slap, spark, stain, stammer, steady, steerhide, strike, sturdy, stutter, tan, tawny

tilleul alabaster

BUFFALO anoa, arna, arnee, arni, aurochs, baffle, bamboozle, bewilder, bison, bluff, bubalus, bugle, bulldoze, bumbaze, bushcow, cajole, carabao, caribou, confound, confuse, hamper, intimidate, kerbau, mango, mumah, mystify, overawe, perplex, sapiutan, seladang, stag, timarau, wild ox, wisent, wuntee, zamouse

apple ground plum
berry beef-suet tree, bullberry, rabbitberry, shepherdia, silverleaf
bill william f. cody
bird buphaga, starling, sturnopastor
black rooter
bug carpetbeetle
bush See *berry,* above.
chips bodewash, bois de vache
clover bluebonnet, trifolium
disease barbone, cholera
female arnee
fish bigmouth, carp(sucker), gourdhead, ictiobus, rooter, sucker
gnat bean aphis, black fly, horn fly, simulium
gourd calabazilla
hunter cibolero
hybrid cattalo
jack caranx, jurel
large arna, arnee
mange texas-itch
meat biltong, fleece
milk butter ghee, ghi
pea bluebonnet, ground plum, vetch
short-horned tapir
small timarau
sword sabre
tree elk nut, oil nut, rabbitwood
water carabao
wild anoa, arna, arnee, gaur, saladang, s(e)ladang

BUFFALOBACK whitefish

BUFFER barker, barrier, brush, bumper, cushion,

dog, ease, fellow, fender, frog, incompetent, neutralizer, pad, pistol, polisher, protector, rack, reserve, safeguard, shield, shock absorber

BUFFET abuse, bar, baste, batter, battle, beat, belabor, blad, blow, box, bruise, buff, cabinet, cafe, colpheg, concussion, contest, counter, credence, credenza, cuff, cupboard, drive, filip, flewit, gowf, hassock, hit, knock, meal, plat, pound, pummel, refreshments, restaurant, scuff, server, set out, shock, sideboard, slap, smack, smite, smorgasbord, spanghew, squelch, stool, strike, strive, struggle, table, thrash, toss, wardrobe

BUFFLEHEAD butterback, butterball, cannonball, clown, dipper, dopper, duck, fool, merrywing, shoveler, woolhead

BUFFLE-HEADED dull, stupid

BUFFOON actor, antic, aper, archimime, balatron, boor, buffo, clown, columbine, comedian, comic, dor, drole, droll, fool, funnyman, hanswurst, harlequin, humorist, jackpudding, jape, jester, joker, macaroon, merryandrew, mime(r), motley, mountebank, mummer, naar, narr, owlglass, pantaloon, pickleherring, pleasant, polichinelle, pulcinella, punch (inello), ridicule, scaramouch, stooge, tomfool, wag, wit, zany

BUFFOONERY clownery, drollery, harlequinade, horseplay, humor, japery, monkeyshines, pantagruelism, shenanigans, slapstick, tomfoolery, zanyism

BUFO See TOAD.

BUG afflict, amplifier, annoy, bacterium, BEETLE, bog(e)y, bother, buff, bulge, capsid, conceited, defect, demon, distract, eavesdrop, elater, emblem, enthusiast, fan(atic), fault, fiend, flashlight, germ, hemipter, idea, INSECT, lis-

tener, microbe, mite, obsession, pester, pompous, rooter, spy, tease, torment, wire
aquatic belostoma
bloodsucking conenose, triatoma
blue argas, chicken-tick
juice bellywash, coffee, liquor, whiskey
kind adelges, altica, anasa, aphid, aphis, bedbug, beetle, bicho, blight, boatman, borer, chermos, chinch, chink, chintz, cicad(a), cigala, cimex, cimicid, coccid, conenose, coreid, corixa, corsair, crawler, dimera(n), dor(re), emesa, hemipter, hoglouse, icerya, jarfly, jassid, jugate, laap, lacebug, lerp, louse, lygus, lyreman, mealybug, naucorid, nepa, nepid, nit, pela, psylla, psyllid, puceron, punaise, punee, punese, punie, punice, ranatra, roach, saldid, scale, skater, strider, taenia, tetrix, tettix, thrip(s), tingid, vinchuca, waterbug
lightning firefly
long-legged water strider
-out bulge, defect, desert, flee, quit, play hooky, retreat, withdraw
red bete rouge, bicho, chigger, cotton-stainer, jigger
river, city on brest
study entomology
BUGABOO See BUGBEAR.
BUGANDA *ruler* kabaka, mutesa
BUGBANE actaea, baneberry, cimicifuga, cohosh, hellebore, rattleroot, richweed, sanicle, snakeroot, tamus, wild ginger
BUGBEAR abomination, alarm, anathema, betenoire, bodach, bogey(man), boggard, boggart, boggle, bogie, bogy, booger(man), boogy(man), bugaboo, bugger, bullbeggar, caddy, fearbabe, fee-faw-fum, goblin, goga, gogo, hobgoblin, mormo, mumbo jumbo, ogre, poker, scarebug, scarecrow, specter, sprite, terror, turk, worricow
BUGGER booger, botch, bugbear, buzzard, caitiff, chap, child, cur, disable,

fellow, heretic, man, person, rascal, reprobate, rogue, scum, sod, spoil, wretch
BUGGY auto, caboose, calesa, calesin, car(riage), cart, clarence, crazy, demented, eccentric, foolish, infested, insane, lousy, nutty, odd, shay, stanhope, trap, truck, van, vehicle, verminous, wagon
BUGHOUSE asylum, insane
BUGLE ajuga, bead, bersaghorn, black, blare, buffalo, bugloss, bullock, call, clarion, cornet, hatchet, horn, jet, reveille, summon, trumpet
blare tantara(ra)
call alerte, boots and saddles, dian, retreat, reveille, tantara, taps, tat(t)oo, warison
note blare, mot, tiralee
ring virole
yellow iva
BUGLEWEED ajuga, baptisia, bugloss, indigo, iva, lycopus, mint
BUGLOSS alkanet, anchusa, blueweed, hawkweed, lycopus, madwort, oxtongue, puccoon
BUGS See INSANE.
BUILD assemble, base, compile, constitution, construct, create, develop, drive, edify, erect, establish, extruct, fabricate, fashion, figure, form, found, frame, graith, habitus, increase, joint, make, phyisque, proportions, raise, rear, set, shape, stature, strengthen, structure, synthesize, taille, teld, throw, timber
body habitus
nest nidify
quickly clap
up accumulation, advertise, aggrade, aggravate, amassment, ballyhoo, commendation, concentration, development, encourage, enhance, exaggerate, flatter (y), growth, increase, increment, pitch, praise, promote, promotion, publicity, puff, strengthen
BUILDER bigger, carpenter, constructor, contractor, creator, epe(i)us, erector, maker, producer, tectonic

comb. tecto
knot clove-hitch
BUILDING assembly, biggin(g), construction, dwelling, edifice, fabric, insula, pile, rookery, structure, tonement
addition annex, apse, ell, lean-to, wing
aircraft dock, hangar
art of architecture
circular rotunda, thole, tholos
columned peripteros, peristyle
decaying ruin
dilapidated firetrap, rattrap, rookery, tenement
end gable
exhibition gallery, museum
facing placage
farm barn, castle, crib, hacienda, shed, silo, stable
fortified castle
gateway pylon
grain elevator, garner, silo
kind aedes, apartment, arena, armory, auditorium, barn, basilica, biggin, block, brewery, carbarn, casa, chancery, chapel, church, college, court, crib, dome, dwelling, elevator, ephebeum, factory, firetrap, flat, folly, foundry, gallery, garage, gashouse, hall, hammam, hotel, hothouse, house, igloo, iglu, jail, jawab, mansion, museum, nympheum, palace, prison, residence, school, shed, shop, skyscraper, station, store, synagog, tenement, toolhouse, villa
material adobe, ashlar, ashler, brick, brownstone, celotex, cement, clinker, concrete, firebrick, flooring, glass, iron, lath, lumber, paving, pise, plaster, roofing, sandstone, siding, steel, tapia, tile, walling, wood
medieval castle
movable mobile home, trailer, turret
on posts pataka
part apse, ell, joist, roof, stor(e)y
poor firetrap, hut, rookery, shanty
prehistoric broch
projection alette, annex,

apse, cornice, dormer, ell, lean-to, oriel, wing

protective fort(ress), redan, stockade

public aedile, auditorium, capitol, casino, church, coliseum, edile, hall, museum, temple, theater, theatre

quadrangular tetragon

quarantine lazaret

rib tierceron

round rotunda

ruined masure

sacred aedes, basilica, cathedral, church, edicule, fane, mosque, pantheon, sacrary, sarapeum, synagogue, temple

sacred, study of naology

site lot, pad

small aedicule, coop, edicule, hock, hut, shed

sports arena, stadium

stately castle, chateau, dome, edifice, mansion, palace, villa

stone cashel, kaaba, nuraghe, trullo

story attic, cellar, chess, deck, entresol, etage, flat, flight, floor, mansard, piano, solar, stage

tall high-rise, skyscraper

tradesman artisan, bricklayer, carpenter, craftsman, decorator, electrician, glazier, hodcarrier, lather, mason, mechanic, painter, plasterer, plumber, roofer, steamfitter, stonecutter, tilesetter, timer, wallpaperer

type adobe, a-frame, apartment, auditorium, barn, blockhouse, carbarn, castle, chapel, chateau, fort, garage, hall, hotel, house, igloo, mausoleum, palace, rotunda, school, shed, skyscraper, villa

wing allette

BUILT boukit, made, set, stacked, timbered

in belonging, cupboard, incorporated, inherent, natural

loosely gangling, rangy, quarry

strongly buirdly, burly, gross, quarry

BUIST box, brand, chest, mark

BUKH brag, buck, prate, prattle, talk

BULB amp(o)ule, ampul,

bud, bulbil, clove, corm, globe, helion, ixia, knob, lamp, luminary, root, scilla, sphere, tube(r)

develop a bottom

edible garlic, onion, potato, sego, yam

fly merodon

light helion

small bulbule, chive, cormel, crocus, propago

BULBIL broodbud, bulblet, chara, chive, gemma, soredium

BULBOUS bulging, extrusive, jutting, round, swollen

BULBUL buhlbuhl, kala, leafbird, luscinia, nightingale

BULGARIAN *assembly* sobranji, sobranye

cape emine, kuratan, sabla

capital sofia, vldin

church head exarch

city aytos, bleven, burgas, butan, byclu, dulovo, elena, gabrove, iskra, karlovo, khaskovo, levsky, pleven, plevna, plovdiv, rila, ruse, rustchuk, shumen, shumla, silistria, sistova, sliven, slivno, sofia, stara, tirnova, varna, widden, yambol, zagora

coin lev(a), lew, stotinka

commission sistova

commune sistova, sliven, slivno

finn cheremiss, chuvash, mordvinian

gulf burgas

king boris, ferdinand

liquor clivova

measure krine, likhe, oka, oke

milk yoghurt

moslem pomak

mountain pass shipka

party exarchist

peak botev, musallah, sapka, vikhren

people cheremiss, chuvash, pomak, slav, ta(r)tar

port burgas, varna

prime minister dimitrov, zhivkov

range balkans, pirin, rhodope, rila

river arda, danube, isker, lom, marica, marista, mesta, ogosta, osma, struma, stryama, tundzha, vit

ruler asen, boris, czar, ivan, tsar

sect bogomil(e)

weight oka, oke, tovar

BULGE abdomen, advantage, bag, balloon, beetle, belly, bend, bilge, billow, bleb, blister, bloat, blob, boss, bouge, bow, bowden, bubble, buckle, bug, bulla, bump, burl, button, cask, cockle, convex, dilate, distend, extend, extrude, flask, gibbosity, gnarl, hump, hunch, increase, jut, knob, knot, knur(l), lump, mole, nevus, nubbin, overhang, pooch, pouch, project (ion), protrude, protuberance, ridge, rise, sag, stave, stomach, stru(n)t, stud, swell(ing), vesicle, wale, wallet, wart, welt, whelp

upward mushroom

BULGING bagged, baggy, bellied, billowing, bombe, bouffant, bulbose, bulbous, bumpy, bunched, bunchy, convex, distent, full, gibbous, googly, gouty, pouching, pudgy, puffy, round, swelling, swollen, torose, tumid, ventricose

BULK accumulation, aggregate, all, amplify, assemble, bigness, body, bouk, cargo, dimension, enlarge, expand, extent, figure, food, form, freight, gather, goods, gross, heap, heft, hold, hulk, hull, increase, lump, magnitude, majority, mass, might, mix, pad, pile, plenty, plurality, power, quantity, shape, size, stall, structure, swell, thickness, total, volume, whole

comb. onc(h)o

having boukit

store warehouse

BULKHEAD barrier, battery, check, fence, partition, penthouse, portal, projection

BULKY awkward, big, burly, clumpish, clumsy, cumbersome, elephantine, fleshy, great, gross, hippopotamic, hulking, hulky, husky, large, lumping, lumpish, massive, massy, policeman, ponderous, portly, pudgy, solid, stodgy, stout, substantial, thick(set), unwieldy, weighty

BULL ace, apis, beef, big, bloomer, blunder, bobby, boner, bovine, brag, brute, buck, bulla, bullock, bushwah, cajolery, charge, cheat, constable, cop, critter, decree, edict, error, exaggerate, exaggeration, flattery, fluff, force, howler, humbug, jest, large, letter, leverager, male, minotaur, mistake, nonsense, officer, optimist, papal letter, peeler, policeman, push, roan, rot, rotche, seal, segg, shove, slip, solecism, speculator, stag, stot, stud, tom, toro, taurine, taurus, zebu

angry gorer
area querencia
baiter picador, prod
bat nighthawk
bay magnolia
blue nilgai
buttercup caltha, marsh marigold
calf bulchin
castrated bullock, steer, stot
cell toril
chain jack ladder
comb. taur(o)
cry bellow
grape muscadine
-grip smilax
-headed god apis, menthu, mont, osorapis
hornless doddie, doddy
human-headed camassu, shedu
in a china shop bungler
-killing volapie
-like taurine
lily spatterdock
mackerel chub
-man minotaur
moose leader theodore roosevelt
nettle blue top, solanum
noon midnight
oak beefwood, casuarina
of bashan oppressor
of the bog bittern
papal edict, letter
peep sanderling, sandpiper
pen barracks, cage, enclosure, jail, prison, quarters
pert. taurian, taurine
plum sloe
rattle campion
ring See ARENA.
ring cell toril
ring fence barrera

-roarer bummer, buzz(er), thunderstick toy, tu(r)ndun, whizzer
run battle manassas
run hero lee
sacred apis, zebu
sacrifice taurcobolium
2nd-year stirk
session brainstorming, chinfest, rap
-shaped tauriform
son minotaur
sucker cactus, opuntia
symbol of england, prosperity, strength
tongue cultivator, plow, scooter
trout dolly varden, salmo, truff
victim dirce
young bugle, bullock, mickey, stirk, stot(t)

BULLA blain, bleb, blister, boss, bubble, bulge, case, knob, ornament, pendant, seal, stud, vesicle
small bullule

BULLACE damson, grape, muscadine, plum, prunus

BULLATE blistered, bulliform, inflated, puckered, vaulted

BULLBERRY beef-suet tree, rabbitberry, shepherdia

BULLBIRD rotche

BULLDOG attack, bulldoze, cannon, determined, gun, horsefly, obstinate, pistol, revolver, snapdragon, stubborn, throw
pipe brierwood
wrench alligator

BULLDOZE browbeat, bully(rag), clear, coerce, cow, demolish, dig, force, harass, harry, intimidate, level, menace, press, push, ram, restrain, scoop, threaten

BULLDOZER bully, grader, tractor

BULLER bellow, boil, flatterer, roar, seethe, turmoil

BULLET ace, ball(e), cartridge, dingbat, lead, missile, mushroom, pellet, pellock, pill, projectile, shot, sinker, slug, spitzer, towel, tracer, wadcutter
conical minie ball
diameter caliber, calibre
expanding dumdum
fake dud, pellet
group canister

kind buckshot, cannon ball, chase-me-charlie, expanding, explosive, fish, grape(shot), langrage, langrel, man-stopping, mitraille, pellet, rifle ball, round, shell, shot, shrapnel, slug, swan shot, torpedo, wadcutter
-proof impenetrable, impervious
soft lead dumdum
sound bang, bing, phit, phud, phut, piff, ping, pouf, prut, thud, zap, zip
tree balata, humiria
tree extract umiri

BULLETIN advertise, announcement, bill, calendar, dispatch, flash, item, journal, memo, monograph, news(cast), notice, pamphlet, periodical, poster, program, release, report, scoop, statement

BULLETS ammo, ammunition, lead, money

BULLFIGHT corrida, cuadrilla, faena, novillada
amateur spontano
area ring, toril
attendant See BULLFIGHTER.
cape work media, rebolero, veronica
cry ole
kill faena
movement pase, suerte, veronica
parade paseo
seat barrera, sol, sombara
technique tauromachy
term lidia, spontano, venga
weapon banderilla, estoque, muleta

BULLFIGHTER banderillist, capeador, matador, picador, puntillero, tauromachian, toreador, torero
adversary toro
cloak cape, capote
follower cuadrillero
staff muleta
sword estoque
thrust estocada
troup cuadrillo

BULLFIGHTING rejoneo

BULLFINCH blood-alp, hedge, hoop, mawp, monach, monk, nope, olf, olp(h), pogge, pope, pout, pyrrhula, redbird, redhoop, shirley, tanny, tawny, tonyhoop

female tonyhoop
male redhoop
BULLFIST puffball
BULLFOOT claw bar, colts-foot
BULLFROG callula, rana, solitaire
BULLHEAD beetlehead, blindfish, bungler, catfish, cottus, cur, duck, electris, goby, larimus, miller's-thumb, plover, pout, sculpin, tadpole, tee, wide-mouth
kelp sea otter's cabbage
lily spatterdock
BULLHEADED balky, dogged, headstrong, mulish, obstinate, pertinacious, stiffnecked, stubborn, stupid
BULLHOOF jamaica, passionflower
BULLHORN loudspeaker, megaphone
BULLIMONG farrage, fodder
BULLION bar, billion, billon, billot, cast(ing), dore, gold, ingot, lace, mint, silver
state missouri
BULLISH favorable, headstrong, hopeful, obstinate, optimistic, rising, stiff, stupid
BULLNECK ruddy-duck
BULLNOSE clam, plane, quohog
BULLOCK bovine, bugle, bully, hog(g), labor, neat, nowt, steer, stirk, stot, work
-eye houseleek
-heart custard-apple
BULLPOUT catfish
BULL'S-EYE aldebaran, block, candy, center, circle, cloud, crown, crux, daisy, decisive, gold, hit, lantern, lens, marigold, mirror, objective, oxeye, plover, right-on, roundel, score, shot, spot, target, white, window
BULLWHACK whip
BULLWORT bishop's-weed, waterbetony
BULLY abash, abuse, ballyrag, bangster, barrater, beef, blenny, bludgeon, bluster, boat, boss, bounce(r), brave, bravo, browbeat, bruiser, buck, bulldoze(r), bullyrag, burgullian, cavel, cow, cuttle, darling, dashing, disconcert,

domineer, excellent, face, fanfaron, fine, frampler, frighten, gallant, gauster, good, great, harass, hector, hoodlum, huff(cap), huffer, intimidate, intimidator, jolly, jovial, major, mate, merry, nag, nightcap, ole, oppress, pest, plague, pomfret, rabiator, ròister, rubiator, ruffian, ruffle(r), scare, shanny, snool, soldier, swagger, sweetheart, threaten, tiger, torment, two-master, tyrant, vapor, well-done
-black sapodilla
mastic acoma
tree balata, bansalague, beefwood, bullace, manilkara, mimusops, sapodilla, star-apple
BULLYRAG abuse, badger, bother, harass, intimidate, scold, tease, vex
BULLYROCK bravo, companion
BULRUSH akaakai, bumble, cattail, cyperus, glumal, juncus, papyrus, reed, risp, rush, scirpus, sedge, tule, tussock, typha
BULWARK bail, barrier, bastion, breakwater, breastwork, buttress, citadel, defence, defense, fence, fort, jetty, manta, mound, parapet, protect(ion), rampart, safeguard, sconce, sea wall, stronghold, support, tower, vallation, wall, warder, werewall
BUM alcoholic, bad, beat, beg(gar), bend, boat, boom, buttocks, cadge, deadbeat, debauch, derriere, din, ditch, drink, drive, drone, drunk(ard), duff, dun, false, frolic, good-for-nothing, guzzler, hobo, hum, hurl, idler, inferior, lazzarone, loaf(er), lousy, mooch(er), ne'er-do-well, nogoodnik, orgy, poor, punk, revel, rump, s(c)hnorrer, slouch, soak, sot, sponge, spree, squeef, stiff, sundowner, swagman, toper, tramp, truant, two-master, vagabond, vagrant, wastrel, worthless, wretch
a ride hitchhike
around idle, loaf
BUMBAILIFF policeman

BUMBASTE beat, spank, whip
BUMBAZE See BAMBOOZLE.
BUMBLE beadle, bee, bittern, blame, blunder, botch, bramble, bulrush, bungle(r), bustle, drone, error, idler, muddle, muffle, stagger, stumble, veil
BUMBLEBEE beefly, bombus, bombylius, bumbee, bumbler, carder, dor
coot ruddy duck
fish goby
BUMBLEDOM beadledom, beadlery, bureaucracy, pomposity
BUMBLEKITE blackberry, bramble fruit
BUMBLEPUPPY nineholes, whist
BUMBLING incompetent, ineffective
BUMCLOCK dorbeetle
BUMELIA buckthorn, hornbeam, ironwood, ostrya, sapodilla
BUMF bureaucratese, gobbledegook, memoranda
BUMMER beggar, bullroarer, bum, loser, skidder, truck
BUMP bang, bittern, blow, boil, boom, bounce, buck, bulge, bunt, clash, clour, clout, coincide, collide, collision, contusion, cry, dance, demote, dird, discard, dislodge, dismiss, dunch, fire, hip, hit, impact, increase, inion, jab, jolt, jounce, knob, knock, knurl, lump, matting, misplace, nob, nodule, promotion, protuberance, raise, reject, shock, strike, swelling, thrust, thud, thump, touch, whap, whop
heads collide, differ
into barge, jar, meet
off die, kill
on head clour
BUMPER abundant, big, bowl, brimmer, buffer, carangid, casabe, cup, cushion, dingman, disk, drink, facer, fender, fine, fish, glass, goblet, good, guard, hurter, keltie, large, pad, rail, rim, rouse, safeguard, successful, toast, whopper
BUMPKIN beam, boom, boor, bucolic, carl, cauboge,

churl, clod(hopper), clown, dz(h)lob, dzlub, farmer, gawk, hawbuck, hick, joskin, lout, lummox, outrigger, peasant, robin, rube, rustic, shlub, slob, spar, swab, swain, tike, tyke, yahoo, yap, yokel, zhlob, zhlub

BUMPO, NATTY deerslayer, hawkeye, leatherstocking, pathfinder, trapper

BUMPTIOUS insolent, obtrusive, pert, self-assertive

BUMPY corduroy, irregular, jolty, nodous, rough, rutted, uneven, unlevel

BUMTRAP bailiff

BUN biscuit, boat, bread, brioche, chervil, cookie, cooky, drunkenness, hairknot, head, jag, muffin, popover, punt, roll, scone, stack, stalk, stem, stubble, tail, tipsiness

BUNAEA hera

BUNCH aggregate, assemble, bail, bale, batch, bevy, block, bob, boss, budget, clew, club, clue, clump, cluster, cluther, collection, coma, coterie, crowd, fagot, fardel, flock, gaggle, gather, GROUP, hobble, huddle, hump, kick, knob, knoll, knot, lot, lump, multitude, number, pack(age), pahil, parcel, quantity, set, stem, swad, swell(ing), tuft, wisp
grass andropogon, elymus, fescue, festuca, stipa
hits boast, concentrate, score, try
pert. comal
pink sweet william
small wisp
up assemble, combine, shrug

BUNCHBERRY cornel

BUNCHFLOWER amianthium, angillaria, chrosperma, melanthium

BUNCHY truss, tufted

BUNCO See BUNKO.

BUNCOMBE See NONSENSE.

BUND alliance, band, confederacy, dam, dike, embankment, group, harbor, league, praya, quay, society

BUNDLE aggregation, assemble, bag(gage), bale, band, battin, bavin, bedding, bindle, birch, bluey, bolt, bulto, bunch, bung,

collection, cuddle, dorlach, drum, fadge, fag(g)ot, fardel, fasces, fascicle, garb, gather, glean, group, hank, hurry, hustle, kid, litch, loggin, lot, nestle, nicky, nuzzle, pace, pack(age), packet, pad, parcel, quantity, roll, sack, sheaf, shook, skein, snuggle, speed, start, swag, thrave, tie, tod, trace, tract, truss, turse, wad(ge)
bind into bavin, kid
-maker baler
off dismiss, leave, start
of arrows sheaf
of boards bolt
of firewood bavin
of flax beet, head
of grain sheaf, wap, wase, windling, wisp
of hides kip
of sacks badger
of tobacco carrot
of wood bavin, fag(g)ot, pimp
of yarn hank, haul, slip

BUNDWEED cow parsnip, knapweed, ragwort, scabious

BUNG bag, bankrupt, beat, broken, bruise, casing, close, cork, dead, falsehood, hemp, hit, hole, hurt, lie, maul, pickpocket, plug, plumb, purse, shive, smashed, spile, squarely, stopper, throw
-starter flogger, mallet, stave

BUNGALOW bush house, cabana, cottage, house, kockalayn

BUNGARUM bongar, krait, snake

BUNGLE bauchle, blunder, blunk, boggle, bollix, bollox, botch, bumble, butcher, err(or), fault, flub, fluff, foozle, fudge, fumble, goof, mess, momble, mucker, muddle, muff, shammock, spoil, stagger, stick, stumble, tailor, toggle
shooting tailor

BUNGLER blunderhead, boggler, bosher, botcher, bumbler, bummler, butterfingers, clumse, daubster, fool, foozler, fumble-fist, fumbler, incompetent, klotz, klutz, lubber, lummox, muffer, puddle, slubberer, tinker

BUNGLING awkward, botchery, bunglesome, clumsy, fudgy, inept, slipshod, tinkery, unskilled

BUNION onion, wyrock

BUNK abide, applesauce, baloney, barracks, bed, berth, billet, blaa, blah, bluster, bunco, buncombe, bunko, bunkum, butterboat, case, chicory, claptrap, cot, doss, dwell, hemlock, hokum, hooey, hot air, humbug(gery), jabberwocky, junk, leave, lodge, malarky, nonsense, rot, sack, skeddaddle, sleep(er), stay, swindle, timber, twaddle

BUNKER abri, bin, box, chest, crib, entangle, entrenchment, fort, hazard, obstacle, mound, pillbox, sandpit
hill battle site breed's hill

BUNKHOUSE bullpen, dormitory

BUNKO cheat, deceive, deception, fraud, humbug, misrepresent(ation), swindle
man sharper
steerer decoy, swindler
trick pigeon-drop, scam

BUNN *opera* bohemian girl

BUNNY drain, rabbit, squirrel
rabbit snapdragon

BUNT bat, butt, fungus, hit, propel, push, sift(er), smut, swell, tail, tap, thrust

BUNTAL bangkok, buri

BUNTING bird, bobolink, chink, cirl, cotton, cowbird, dumpy, emberiza, estamene, estamin, etamine, fabric, finch, flag, lark, oatfowl, ortolan, pape, passerina, plump, prusiano, ricebird, ringbird, rounded, slovenly, stocky, towhee, untidy, yellow-hammer
black-throated dickcissel
iron blowtube
painted nonpareil
reed ringbird
snow oatfowl
varied prusiano

BUNUS *parent* aleidamea, hermes

BUNYAH bird, cacique

BUNYAN, JOHN *character* apollyon, christian, faithful, giant despair, greatheart,

hopeful, mercy, pliable, timorous, worldly-wiseman
work pilgrim's progress
BUNYAN, PAUL *companion* babe, blue ox
creation grand canyon, puget sound
poet carl sandburg, robert frost
sponsor laughead, red river lumber company
BUNYARO *ruler* kabarega
BUNYIP counterfeit, humbug, imposter, phony, sham
BUONARROTI See MICHELANGELO.
BUOY baken, bear up, bell, dan, deadhead, dolphin, elate, encourage, float, hearten, hope, lagan, levitate, makefast, mark(er), raise, rise, signal, support, sustain, upbear, uphold, uplift, upraise, waft
fishing dan
kind bell, nun, nut, spar, whistling
mooring dolphin
BUOYANT afloat, animated, blithe, bouncy, cheerful, corky, debonair, effervescent, elastic, expansive, floating, floaty, gay, happy, hopeful, jocular, levitate, light, lilting, lithe, lively, resilient, spirited, sprightly, springy, superfluent, supernatant, supple, vigorous, vivacious, volatile
BUPHAGUS hercules
BUR See BURR.
marigold baclin, cuckold
BURA *son* atrax
BURBANK cherry, cross, graft, improve, modify, plum, potato, tomato
BURBARK akonge, boxbush, burbush
BURBERRY raincoat, waterproof
BURBLE boil, bubble, confuse, flow, jabber, muddle, pimple, ripple, trickle
BURBOT alekey-trout, birdbolt, cod, coney, cusk, dogfish, eelpout, gudgeon, lawyer, ling, loche, lota, lote, maria, morgay
BURDASH neckcloth, sash
BURDEN 3 jag, lug, tax, vex 4 bale, bass, birn, care, cark, clag, clog, core, crop, drag, duty, fare, gang, gist, lade, load, muck, onus,

pack, task, tone 5 birth, blame, cargo, chore, crowd, crush, drone, labor, theme, verse 6 charge, chorus, cumber, entail, fardel, hamper, impose, impost, lading, saddle, thrack, weight 7 ballast, bourdon, burthen, conveth, essence, expense, fraught, freight, hagride, incubus, onerate, oppress, refrain, sumpter, trouble 8 capacity, carriage, encumber, engregge, handicap, hardship, overcome, pressure, quantity, rumbelow 9 aggravate, cumbrance, millstone, substance, undersong 10 affliction, impediment, obligation, oppression, ritornelle 11 encumbrance, incumbrance, restriction 13 accompaniment, inconvenience 14 responsibility
-bearer amasa, amos, atlas
of complaint gravamen
of proof demonstration, obligation, onus
of song holding, overturn, overword, refrain, ritornelle, wheel
with impose
with care cark
BURDENED fraught, gravid, harassed, heavy, laden, loaded, saddled
BURDENSOME carking, cumbersome, cumbrous, difficult, distressing, exacting, exhausting, grievous, grinding, hard, heavy, irksome, loadsome, onerous, oppressive, ponderous, tiring, troublesome, weighty
BURDIGALA bordeaux
BURDOCK agrimony, anthium, arctium, bardane, billybutton, buzzies, cadillo, campion, cleavers, clite(s), clive, clotbur, clots, cuckoobutton, daisy, geranium, gobo, hardock, harebur, haulback, hurrbur, lappa, scabious, xanthium
-like lappaceous
root lappa
BURE *brother* borr
BUREAU agency, association, chest, committee, commode, department, desk, dresser, office, sideboard, unit
BUREAUCRACY adminis-

tration, authorities, beadledom, bumbledom, directorate, ministry, officialdom, red-tapery, system
BUREAUCRAT incumbent, mandarin, office-holder, official
BUREAUCRATESE bumpf, gobbledygook, nice-nellyism
BURFISH atinga
BURG, BURGH borough, city, community, district, enclosure, town
grass cockspur, sandbur, sandspur
BURGEE coal, flag, pennant
BURGEON begin, branch, breed, bud, develop, erupt, gemmate, grow, leaf (out), proliferate, shoot, sprout
BURGESS citizen, commoner, freeman, gorgibus, magistrate, portman
BURGESS, GELETT *creature* goop, purple cow
BURGHER citizen, freeman, townman
BURGLAR cracksman, filcher, gopher, housebreaker, loidman, looter, pete(r)man, picklock, raffles, rifler, robber, safeblower, safecracker, sneakthief, stealer, thief, yegg(man)
amateur raffles
-proof impervious, secure
BURGLARIZE burgle, cop, despoil, lift, loot, pilfer, pinch, plunder, ravage, rifle, rob, sack, snitch, steal, swipe, thieve
BURGLARY break, crack, larceny, robbery, stealage, stealing, theft
BURGONET helmet, morion
BURGOO gruel, oatmeal, porridge, pudding, soup, stew
BURGOYNE mantlet, spade
defeat schuylerville
nickname brag
BURGUNDY bourgogne, wine
monk valliscaulian
warrior hagen
white chablis, (pinot) chardonnay
wine barbera, beaune, chambertin, charbono, clos de bougeot, corton, gamay, macon, meursault, montrachet, musigny, pinot,

noir, pommard, riche-bourg, volnay, vougeot
BURHEAD cleavers
BURIAL commitment, deposition, earth bath, entombment, funeral, funerary, grave, inhumation, interment, inurning, sepulture, tomb
alive, fear of taphephobia
bier catafalque, hearse, litter
case bier, casket, coffin, pall, sarcophagus, urn
ceremony dirge, elegy, epicedium, exequies, funeral, obsequies, requiem
comb. taphe
mound barrow, grave, huaca, tola, tor, tumulus
pert. funerary
pile pyre
place ahu, barrow, bier, boneyard, campo santo, catacombs, cemetery, charnel, churchyard, crypt, dolmen, gigunu, golgotha, grave(yard), huaca, laystall, laystow, mausoleum, mound, necropolis, ossuary, pantheon, potter's-field, pyramid, sepulcher, sepulchre, temenos, tomb
preparation cere, pollincture
wrapper cerecloth, cerements, shroud, winding-sheet
BURIED absorbed, hidden, humate, imbedded, sepult
BURKE dispose of, kill, murder, rid, shelve, slay, smother, suffocate, suppress
BURKUNDAZ bodyguard, escort, policeman, retainer
BURL blob, bulge, burr, dress, excrescence, finish, kha(u)r, knot, lump, pimple, pustule, roe, wart
BURLAP bagging, crocus, gunny, hemp, hesslan, jute, sacking, wrapping
BURLESQUE ape, buffoon, burlecue, burletta, burly, callithump, caricature, comedy, comic(al), copy, doggerel, droll, farce, farcical, hudibrastic, imitation, incongruous, ironic, jest, jocular, lampoon, ludicrous, macaronic, mime, mimic(ry), mock, mockery, odd, overact, overdo, parodic(al), parody, pastiche, revue, ridicule, satire, satir-

ic(al), satirize, slapstick, take-off, travesty, vulgarization
composition macaronic
serenade charivari
BURLET coif, hood
BURLETTA burlesque, drama, farce, opera, play
BURLY bluff, boisterous, bowerty, brawny, brusque, bulky, coarse, corpulent, excellent, fat, gross, heavy, hefty, husky, imposing, large, lusty, massive, mastiff, muscular, noble, obese, policeman, rough, sinewy, stately, stout, strapping, sturdy, thick
BURMA, BURMESE *bay* bengal, heanzay, hunter
buddhist mon
canopy tazaung
capital rangoon
capital, ancient ava
city akyuh, ava, bassein, bhamo, hemzada, hsemw, hsipaw, katha, lashio, mandalay, maymyo, minbu, monywa, moulmein, myingyan, pakokku, papun, pegu, prome, rangoon, tavoy
coin kyat, pya
dagger dan, dhao, dout, dow
deer thameng, thamin
deity gautama
demon nat
dice anzamia
division arakan, pegu, shan, toungoo, yeu
garment engi, tamein
gate toran
gibbon lar
girl mima
governor See *ruler*, below.
gulf martaban
hill chin, kachin, kaga
hill dweller lai
hoodlum dacoit
jadeite feitsui
kneeling gesture shiko
knife See *dagger*, above.
language chin, kachin, karen, kuki, lai, pegu
measure byee, chaivai, dain, dha, lamany, lan, ngu, okthabah, palgat, phan, seit, taim, tao, tat, taun, teng, that, truong
musical instrument tarau, turr
peak nattaung, popa, saramati
peasant tao

people akha, akhlame, arakanese, birman, chin, kachin, kadu, kakhyen, karen, kaw, khmer, kuki, lai, lolo, miao, mon, naga, palauna, peguan, rengma, shan, t(h)ai, tsin, was
plant paukpan
plateau shan
port akyab, bassein, henzada, mergui, moulmein
prime minister newin, uni
range arakan, chin, dawna, kachin, karenni, peguyona
river chindwin, hka, indawgyi, irawadi, irrawaddy, kaladan, myitnge, salween, salwin, schweli, sutang
road, city on kunming, yunnan
robber dacoit
ruby peony
ruler boa, sawbua, woon, wun
sash tubbeck
sea andaman
shelter zayat
shrimp balachan, napee
spirit nat
statesman u thant
stock breeder choliar
tree acle, maidou, rosewood, yamanai
weight abucco, bahar, binh, candy, kait, kyat, mat, moo, pai, peiktha, ruay, tical, ticul, vis(s)
BURN 3 dry, tan **4** bren, brew, char, fire, glow, heat, hurt, pain, raze, rill, sear, sere, tend, tind **5** adust, anger, blaze, bourn, brand, broil, brook, brown, cense, chark, cupel, flame, flare, parch, plout, roast, scald, scaum, singe, smart, speed, sweal, swelt, toast, waste, yearn **6** bourne, brenne, crozle, damage, desire, ignify, ignite, injure, injury, kindle, redden, scorch, seethe, sizzle, stream, swinge, tingle **7** blister, burnish, calcine, comhure, combust, consume, cremate, crozzle, destroy, execute, explode, flicker, frizzle, incense, inflame, oxidate, oxidize, rivulet, scorify, scowder, smolder, swelter, torrefy **8** approach, endanger, flagrate, overcook, squander, vesicate **9** carbonize,

cauterize, vulcanize 10 deflagrate, incinerate
balm carron oil
candle at both ends dissipate, overdo, overtax
down destroy, raze
feebly flicker, gutter
let bishop
midnight oil cram, labor, lucubrate, study
off clear, dissipate
out blow, consume, debilitate, destroy, exhaust, fail, gut(ter), overdo, overtax, weary
remedy amigen, antiphlogistic, antipyrotic
surface scorch, sear, singe
-the-wind blacksmith
up adust, aggravate, anger, enrage, exust, infuriate, speed
BURNED adust, ashen, ashy, baked, dried, parched, seared, sunburnt, ustulate
out bushed, consumed, exhausted, extinct, spent
sugar blackjack, caramel
up See ANGRY.
BURNER ace, baker, beak, blowtorch, bude, calciner, censer, heater, incinerator, koro, pilot, thurible, tops, wick
kind argand, bunsen, filament, fishtail, gasjet, gaslight, jet, mantle, moderator, welsbach
BURNET bloodwort, brown, clover, fabric, pimpernel, poterium, sanguisorba, selfheal, weed, woodwort, wool
saxifrage avens, bennet, breakstone, hemlock, parsley-piert, pearlwort, pimpinella, valerian
BURNING ablaze, adurent, afire, aglow, alight, angry, ardent, ardurous, arson, auto-da-fe, blaze, calcination, calid, carbonization, caustic, cautery, comburent, combustion, conflagrant, conflagration, cupellation, eager, ebullient, exciting, fervent, fervid, feverish, fiery, fire, flagrant, flame, flushed, glaring, gledy, glowing, hot, incandescent, incendiary, inflaming, inustion, irate, live, living, luminous, mad, mordant, near, overheated, oxidation, parching, passionate, pip-

ing, quick, red-hot, reeking, scouther, scowder, shining, sizzling, smarting, suttee, sweltering, sweltry, thermogenesis, torrid, unquenched, urent, ustion, white-hot, zealous
bush artillery-plant, burstingheart, dittany, evonymus, fraxinella, gas-plant
for heresy bonnering
malicious arson
mock-cypress wahoo
no longer extinct
site ghat
BURNISH brighten, buff, develop, furbish, glaze, gloss, luster, polish, rub, shine
BURNISHER agate, buffer, frotton, glazer, polisher
BURNOOSE albornoz, cloak, mantle
BURNS, ROBERT *birthplace* alloway
burial site dumfries
horse jenny geddes
poem jolly beggars, tam o'shanter, to a louse
BURNSIDES beard, mustache, whiskers
BURNT (See BURNED.) adust, ashen, ashy, baked, dried, parched, seared, sunburned
almond coconut-brown
ocher light red, tangier
offering sacrifice
out exhausted, extinct
rose pompeii
russet wallflower-brown
terre verte vandyke-brown
work pyrography
BURNTWEED hart's-tongue
BUR, BURR accent, banyan, barb, birr, blank, boss, brake, briar, brier, buhr(stone), burstone, buzz, chisel, circle, clinker, corona, cut(ter), drill, excavate, excrescence, fin, grip, halo, hull, hum, jangle, knob, knockeroff, knot, meatus, millstone, nap, nut, parasite, pile, pod, reamer, rib, ridge, ring, rove, saw, sinker, slug, sticker, strobile, sweetbread, teasel, teazel, thistle, thorn, threads, thrust, washer, weed, wharl, whetstone, whirr
clover medic(ago)
cucumber cucumis, gherkin, sicyos

island naitauba
-like prickly, rough
marigold agrimony, baclin, beggar-tick, bidens
plant teasel
thistle cocklebur
BURR, AARON *penname* old patroon
victim alexander hamilton
BURRO ass, burrito, donkey, fish, grunt, mule, pomadasys
BURROUGHS, EDGAR R. *character* jane, tarzan
BURROW bed, berry, borough, bury, cave, clapper, conceal, couch, devi, dig, excavate, furrow, gallery, heap, hide, hole, lodge, mine, moil, mole, mound, nuzzle, passage, penetrate, pipe, refuge, retreat, root(le), sap, search, set (tle), shelter, tube, tunnel, undermine, wormhole
BURROWEED goosefoot
BURSA capsella, cavity, dormitory, pouch, sac, shepherd's-purse, vesicle
BURSAR boucher, bowser, cashier, oeconomus, purser, student, terrar, treasurer
BURSARIA box(thorn), lycium, matrimony-vine
BURSARY scholarship, treasury
BURSE allowance, bag, bazaar, boucher, case, fund, pack, pocket, pouch, purse, scholarship, shop
BURSERA archipin, gumbolimbo, pistachio
BURST bang, blast, blaze, blout, blow, brash, breach, break, broken, bust, crack, dash, detonation, erupt, exertion, expanse, explode, explosion, fissure, fit, flare, flash, fly, gap, gush, implode, injury, loss, outbreak, pop, pululate, reave, release, rend, rive, rupture, salvo, scat(t), shatter, shout, spasm, splinter, split, spree, sprint, sprout, spurt, start, stave, stretch, sunder, tear, teem, upbrast, volley
forth balloon, begin, blossom, bob up, bud, burgeon, develop, emerge, erupt, flare, flash, gleam, pop, proliferate, sally, spring, sundered
apart outrive, sunder

artillery graze, rafale
in implode, irrupt
into flame burn, catch fire, ignite, light
into pieces flitter
into tears blurt, cry, sob
inward implode, implosion
open crack, upbrast
out buff, laugh, prorump, roar, yell
the bubble disillusion
upon meet, startle, surprise
BURSTING abuzz, alive, blowout, congested, dehiscence, drenched, erupting, full, lavish, overfed, overstuffed, plethoric, ruption, saturated, stuffed, tumid
comb. rrhage, rrhagia
forth erumpent
inward implosion
BURT butt, dent, gore
BURTON, ROBERT *penname* democritus junior
work anatomy of melancholy
BURUNDI ruanda-urandi
capital usumbura
city bujumbura, bururi, kitega, muyinga, ngozi
coin franc
lake rugwero, tshohoha
people bantu, hutu, pygmy, tutsi, watusi
river akanya, rukagera, ruvuvu, ruzizi
BURWEED burdock, cocklebur, galium, sparganium, triumfetta
BURY abandon, bedelve, burrow, cache, camp, cloak, coffin, conceal, cover, deposit, earth, engross, ensepulcher, enshrine, entomb, funeralize, funerate, hearse, hide, immerse, inearth, inhume, inter, inurn, lay to rest, lose, manor, mool, overwhelm, pithole, plant, rake, repress, secrete, sepult(ure), shroud, submerge, tomb, turf, vault, veil, whelm
the hatchet make up, pacify
BUS bush, camion, coach, convey, jeepney, jitney, omnibus, transport, vehicle
boy piccolo
conductor cad
BUSH boscage, bos(c)h, bouchon, branch, brush, burse, butt, chaparral, clump, cluster, country, cover, exhaust, fatigue,

foliage, fox tail, grove, jungle, outback, plain, plant, plash, scray, shrub, spread, tail, thicket, thorn, tod, undergrowth, waste (land), wineshop
baby galago, lemur
burning wahoo
cat civet, serval
clover hagi, lespedeza
clump tod
country, pert. stringybark
cow buffalo, tapir, zamouse
disease creeps
dog icticyon, potto
dweller hatter
forest chaparral
grass woodreed
hook bill
lawyer bramble
-league amateur, inferior, mediocre, rustic, semi-pro, small-time, two-bit
sickness tauranga
stunted scrog
telegraph grapevine, rumor
trefoil beggar's-tick, desmodium
BUSHBEATER ivory hunter, scout
BUSHBUCK antelope, boschbok
BUSHCRAFT fishing, hunting, woodcraft
BUSHED beat, bewildered, exhausted, overcome, spent, worn
BUSHEL alter, basket, bucket, emer, firlot, fou, gob, hide, lot, measure, met, quantity, ream, repair, strick
1/32 quart
¼ peck
½ tovet
¾ cabot, skipple
1.6 fanega
3 to 5 sack
8 seam
40 wey
BUSHELS gobs, lots, reams
BUSHING abrid, bearing, boucle, coaka, collet, drill, ferrule, grommet, liner, lining, padding, pintle, sleeve
BUSHMAN abatoa, abatwa, frontiersman, gung, heikum, khuai, kung, negrillo, nomad, pioneer, qung, rustic, sa(a)n, strandlooper, swagman, whaler
blanket or garment bluey
poison ordeal-tree

BUSHMASTER curucucu, snake, surucucu, viper
BUSHRANGER footpad, highwayman, hoodlum
BUSHROPE liana
BUSHVELDT See BUSH.
BUSHWAH bodewash, bosh, bull, nonsense, rubbish, trash
BUSHWHACKER ambusher, forerunner, guerrilla, pa(w)paw, scout, scythe, waylayer
BUSHY bosky, dumal, dumose, dumous, hairy, hirsute, overgrown, queachy, shady, shaggy, spreading, thick, woody
hair mop, shag
heap tod
master richard ii
BUSINESS account, activity, ado, affair, agiotage, art, assignment, besoigne, biz, calling, care(er), cause, chore, commerce, company, concern, corporation, craft, custom, dealings, diligence, disturbance, duty, employ (ment), enterprise, errand, establishment, facility, factory, feat, firm, function, fuss, game, gear, industry, installation, interest, job, labor, lay, line, lookout, matter, metier, mission, negoce, occupation, office, palaver, partnership, patronage, practice, profession, project, racket, rickmatic, service, specialty, stint, store, task, thrangity, topic, trade, trading, traffic, transaction, truck, undertaking, venture, vocation, work
arithmetic accounting
character ampersand
combination cartel, consortium, syndicate, trust
comic lazzo
custom patronage
cycle terms boom, crash, crisis, deflation, depression, fluctuation, hard times, infession, inflation, inflump, liquidation, prosperity, recession, recovery, shakeout, slump(flation), stagflation
degree mba
dishonest racket
exchange bolsa, bursa, bourse
machine computer, duplica-

tor, tabulator, typewriter, xerox

pert. commercial, industrial, mercantile, vocational

place emporium, market, mart, office, plant, shop(pe), store

BUSINESSLIKE concise, efficient, methodical, orderly, practical, pragmatic, precise, realistic, regular, systematic, thorough

BUSINESSMAN baron, bourgeois, captain of industry, executive, industrialist, investor, nabob, owner, tycoon

group chamber of commerce

BUSIRIS *father* poseidon

kingdom egypt

slayer hercules

BUSK array, corset, dress, entertain, festival, fix, hasten, hie, prepare, seek, shift, stay, stir, tack, urge

BUSKIN boot, bottine, brodekin, brodequin, caliga, costume, cothurn(us), shoe, tragedy

BUSS boat, calf, deck, dress, kiss, smack, transport, vessel

BUST bang, bankrupt(cy), binge, blockhead, bosom, break, breast, broke, bronze, bump, BURST, chest, collapse, decline, degrade, demote, depose, depression, dismiss, domesticate, downgrade, explode, fail(ure), figure, flop, flunk, frolic, hit, klinker, protome, punch, reduce, revel, ruin, sculpture, spree, statue, tame, train, yarborough

cover bodice, bra

in enter, intrude, open

up dissolution, divorce, failure, outbreak, rupture, separate, separation

BUSTARD bebilya, gompaauw, houbara, korhaan, kori, otidid, otis, paauw, tarda, tetrax, thick-knee, turkey, wato

quail hemipode, turnicid, turnix

BUSTER blade, crab, frolic, hammer, mister, reveler, spree

BUSTIC ausubo, cassada

BUSTLE abound, accelerate, activity, ado, agitate, agitation, bishop, bluster, bother,

bumble, buskle, buzz, clatter, clutter, commotion, cushion, dither, energy, ferment, fidget, fike, fisk, fissle, fistle, flurry, fluster, flutter, fray, frisk, fuss(tle), haste, hubbub, hum, hurry, hustle, hyper, jump, knock, louster, motion, movement, pad, pavie, pother, racket, restlessness, rush, rustle, scowder, scuffle, speed, splutter, spuffle, sputter, steer, stew, stir, struggle, tatter, tear, teem, throng, to-do, tournure, tumult, uproar, whew, whir

woman's bishop, tournure

BUSY absorbed, active, applied, apply, assiduous, brisk, cluttered, confusion, crowded, diligent, disturb, doing, eident, employ(ed), engage(d), engrossed, fast, fell, fussy, gauche, hard(working), hopping, humming, indefatigable, industrious, intent, kinetic, laborious, lively, loud, meddlesome, occupied, occupy, officious, on the go, operose, ornate, painstaking, persevering, prying, quick, rococo, sedulous, steery, throng, tireless, toiling, trouble, unremitting, untiring, working

aces solitaire

oneself set about, undertake, work

BUSYBODY ardelio, babbler, blabber, bluenose, buttinsky, chatterer, detective, earwig, factotum, gossip, granny, hen, inquirer, interferer, intruder, kochleffl, marplot, meddler, newsmonger, nosebody, nosy parker, polypragmatist, pragmatic, pry, querier, questionbox, quidnunc, quiz, rubberneck, rumormonger, scandalmonger, snoop(er), spoffy, tabby, tattler, tattletale, telltale, tittle-tattler, yachna, yachne, yenta, yente

BUT aber, also, always, arrah, barring, besides, bit, except, excluding, hence, howbeit, however, if not, just, kitchen, lacking, mais, mere(ly), nevertheless, nonetheless, notwith-

standing, objection, only, on the contrary, other than, outer, outside, rather, restriction, save, sed, still, than, that, unless, without, yea, yet

and ben back and forth, everywhere

a step near

for without

just barely

BUTCHER, BUTCHER'S botch(er), britten, bungle, charcutier, cutthroat, dress, flesher, hack, kill, killcalf, killer, legger, mangle, meatman, merchant, murder, pigstick, ruin, slaughter, slay, spoil, trainsman, vendor

broom box holly, bruscus, ruscus

dermatitis swine-itch

hook cammock, gambrel

needle tier

rabbi shochtim, shohet

stall abattoir, shambles, slaughterhouse

tool cleaver, knife, saw, skewer, skiver, steel

BUTCHERBIRD bulestes, cracticus, derwent-jackass, lanius, matagasse, reedling, shrike

BUTCHERY abattoir, bloodshed, carnage, killing, massacre, pogrom, shamble, slaughter(house)

BUTEO buzzard, falcon, hawk, vulture

BUTES *parent* boreas, pandion

rescuer aphrodite

sibling erechtheus, philomela, procne

victim coronis

BUTLER boteler, bottle-man, boy, cellarman, consumah, khansama, lackey, majordomo, manservant, servant, somler, sommelier, spencer, stephano, steward, wineserver

BUTLER, RHETT *wife* scarlett o'hara

BUTLER, SAMUEL *novel* erewhon, hudibras

BUTSU See BUDDHA.

BUTT 3 aim, end, fag, hut, jur, jut, lug, pit, put, ram, tup 4 abut, blow, buck, bump, bunt, burt, cart, cask, dish, dobe, doss, duff, dupe, edge, fool, game, goad, goal, goat, grip, heel, horn, jest, join, joke, jolt, jurr, mark, meet, poll, puck, push, quiz, rump, scag, shmo, stub, tope, trim, turr, weed 5 bound, hinge, joint, limit, mound, ridge, roach, schmo, scope, scorn, shove, smoke, snipe, stock, stump, touch 6 adjoin, barrel, bottom, breech, handle, monkey, object, propel, selion, strike, target, thrust, victim 7 beehive, extreme, halibut, mockery, parapet, project, remnant, stummel, tipcart 8 derriere, flatfish, flounder, ridicule, sackbutt 9 cigarette, extremity, objective, remainder 13 laughingstock

black eucalyptus
cigarette bumper, snipe
-headed hornless, obstinate
in interfere, interlope, intervene, intrude, meddle, mediate, obtrude
of joke cockshy, game, jest, scoggin, sport, stale

BUTTE dune, hill, knoll, mound, mountain, picacho, ridge

BUTTER bambuk, beurre, blarney, cajole(ry), clart, coat, cocum, flatter, fulwa, ghee, illipe, mahua, oil, phulwa, pulp, shea, s(c)hmaltz, shortening, spread, suavity, unctuousness

-and-eggs linaria, narcissus, owl's-clover, ransted, toadflax
artificial bos(c)h, butterine, margarin(e), oleo, suin(e)
basket globeflower
blend with sugar cream
browned in noisette
clarified ghee
coloring annatto, annotto, arnatto
comb. butyro
component butyrin
fat caprin, glycerides, oleo
-flour mix roux
-like butyraceous
lump pat
measure span
melted beurre fondu
muslin cheesecloth
oily ghee
pear avocado, beurre
pert. butyric
print mallow

receptacle firkin, ruskin
scraper quirl
substitute See *artificial,* above.
test babcock
tooth incisor
tree fulwa, illipe, phulwara, shea
tub cool, firkin, ruskin
up beguile, brownnose, flatter, softsoap, sweettalk

BUTTERBALL bucephala, buffleduck, bufflehead, duck, shoveler

BUTTERBILL coot, scoter

BUTTERBIRD bobolink

BUTTERBOX bufflehead, duck, dutchman, shoveler

BUTTERBUR batterdock, cleat, clote, eldin, fleadock, gal(l)on, giltcup, oxwort, pondweed

BUTTERBUSH pittosporum, poisonberry

BUTTERCRES See BUTTERCUP.

BUTTERCUP adonis, anemone, atragene, bolt, craisey, craizey, crawfoot, crazy, crowfoot, crowtoe, cyme, frogwort, giltcup, goldcup, goldilocks, horsegold, kingcob, kingcup, pheasant's-eye, windflower

BUTTERFINGERED awkward, bungling, careless, clumsy

BUTTERFISH blenny, ephipus, gunnel, kelpfish, lafayette, palometa, pompano, silverrag, skipjack, whiting

BUTTERFLY frenata, lepidopterid, trifler
banners bleedingheart, bokukulla, dutchman's-breeches
breeder aurelian, lepidopterist
brush-footed anglewing, comma, fritillary, mourning-cloak, nymphalid
bush buddleia
dock butterbur, petasites
fish angelfish, blenny, flatfish, mojarra, pantodon, paru
flower bauhinia, schizanthus
genus argynnis, basilarchia, brenthis, cecropia, colias, heliconius, melitaea, morpho, phycoides, pieris, polygonia, vanessa
kind admiral, alpine, anglewing, antiopa, aphrodite,

apollo, argus, arthemis, baltimore, buckeye, cabbage, caligo, checkerspot, citron, comma, copperwing, crescent, danaid, dolphin, duskywing, elfin, emperor, ghost, grayling, harvester, junonia, kiho, monarch, pierine, pipevine, red admiral, satyr, skipper, swift, thecla, tortoiseshell, troilus, tussock, ursula, vanessa, viceroy, zebra
large caligo, morpho
larva beanleaf roller, caterpillar, eudamus, goniurus, proteus
lily hedychium, mariposa, segro
nymphalid argynnis, fritillary, idalia, zebra
orchid epidendrum, gymnadenia, platanthera
phaeton baltimore
satyr wood-nymph
secretion acraein, acrelin
spotted fritillary
table dropleaf
weed asclepias, canada-root, fluxroot, milkweed, pleurisy-root, windroot
winghooks hami
wing scale androconium

BUTTERINE bos(c)h, oleo(margarine)

BUTTERLEAVES beet, dock, orach

BUTTERMILK jocoque, sourdook, whig
and water bland

BUTTERNOSE coot, scoter

BUTTERNUT juglans, souari, white walnut

BUTTERSCOTCH candy, toffy

BUTTERWEED fireweed, groundsel, horseweed, lactuca, mallow, ragwort

BUTTERWORT beanweed, bog-violet, ecclegrass, pinguicula, rotgrass, sheepweed, steepgrass

BUTTERY adulatory, bland, botry, flattering, larder, pantry, spence, spicery, storeroom, sycophantic, unctuous, wheedling
account battel

BUTTINSKI intruder, meddler, pest

BUTTOCKS backside, behind, bottom, breech, bum, bunny, butt, can, cheek(s), counter, croup(on),

crupper, curpin, derriere, dock, doup, duff, fanny, fud, fundament, heinie, keister, nates, prat, rear, rump, seat, stern, tail, tochis, tot, tuchis
fat steatopygia
shapely, pert. callipygian, callipygous
BUTTON badge, bauble, boss, buckle, bud, bulge, cast(ing), catch, chin, confine, crown, decoy, dewdrop, diminutive, disk, dome, doorbell, fasten(er), glide, globule, hook, horn, key, knap, knicker, knob, knop, landmine, marker, mine, mushroom, olive (tte), pearl, pressel, prill, regulus, secure, shiner, specie, spur, stud, toggle, trifle, troche, tuft, washer
chrysanthemum bluet, bright-eyes
detachable stud
down nail, secure, tie
flower gomphia
grass bog-sedge, crabgrass, digitaria, meadow-oat
material mother-of-pearl, nacre
ornamental stud
part shank
snakeroot liatris, sawwort
tree conocarpus, mangrove, plane tree, sycamore
up bag, capture, close, complete, confine, fasten, naildown, obtain, secure, settle, sew up
BUTTONBALL plane tree, sycamore
BUTTONBUSH buckbrush, ceanothus, cephalanthus, coralberry, crane-willow, purshia, swampwood, sycamore, wolfberry
BUTTONHOLE accost, address, apostrophize, boutonniere, detain, eye(let), harangue, hart's-tongue
stitcher barreroff, loop, slit
BUTTONS attendant, bellboy, page, sour
BUTTONWEED alligatorhead, bluet, diodia, knapweed
BUTTONWOOD cotonier
BUTTRESS abutment, arcboutant, brace, bulwark, counterfort, embankment, encourage, jetty, mole,

outcast, outshot, pier, pile, prop, rampart, reinforce, seawall, shore, shoulder, spur, stay, strengthen, support, tambour
BUTTWOMAN fishwife
BUTTY chum, companion, friend, miner, partner, worker
BUXOM bouncing, cheerful, chubby, crumby, crummy, fattish, flexible, fullbosomed, humble, jolly, junoesque, lively, merry, mild, obedient, obliging, plump, prone, rosy, sonsie, sonsy, submissive, tractable, yielding, zaftig
BUY abegge, accept, acquire, agree, assent, bargain, believe, bid, bribe, chaffer, chap, coff, corrupt, coup, fix, gain, get, hire, invest, obtain, pay, procure, purchase, ransom, reach, redeem, remunerate, secure, shop, snip, steal, treat
and sell barter, trade
back ransom, redeem, reprise
cheaply snup
into invest, speculate
off appease, bribe, fix, reach
refuse to boycott
to sell at profit regrate, speculate
up coempt, corner
BUYER achatour, agent, bull, cater, chap(man), client, coemptionator, coemptor, consumer, customer, emptor, marketer, patron, prospect, purchaser, shopper, vendee
beware caveat emptor
of stolen property fence
option call
BUYING ac(h)ate, emption
mania oniomania
BUZI *son* ezekiel
BUZZ activity, beetle, bombilate, bombinate, boom, bumble, burr, buzzle, call, chirr, churr, creak, crick, cut, dive, drone, empty, fancy, ferment, fling, gossip, greet, hearsay, hiss, hum(ming), huss, incite, jangle, murmur, notion, phone, question, report, ring, rumor, signal, speak, stridulate, summon, talk, tattle, telephone, tittletattle, whirr, whisper, whiz

along dash, depart, leave, speed
bomb rocket
session discussion, rap
BUZZARD archibuteo, aura, beetle, bromvogel, buteo, cockchafer, condor, crank, curlew, dorbeetle, dotard, falcon, fool, glade, gled(e), gleed, harpy, hawk, oldster, pern, puddock, puttock, senseless, stoop, stupid, tesa, vulture
bald osprey
clock dorbeetle
grass pearl-millet
honey beehawk, beekite, chalcedony, pern
moor harpy
turkey john
BUZZER alarm, bee, bell, burrer, generator, howler, hydroextractor, pickpocket, signal, summoner, talebearer, telegraph, trembler, whisperer, whistle, whizzer
electric howler
BUZZGLOAK pickpocket
BUZZING acouasm, boom, carhopping, flathatting, hedgehopping, roadhopping
BUZZWIG See BIGWIG.
BWANA boss, master
BY abut(ting), according to, after, ago, along(side), anon, apart, aside, at hand, away, beside, beyond, born of, close, concerning, during, finished, forby, into, over, near, next, par, pass, past, per, secondary, through, till, toward, via, with
a long shot certainly, greatly
all means algate(s), certainly
and by afterwhile, anon, before long, belive, bimeby, eventually, future, immediately, later on, presently, soon, tomorrow
and large broadly, generally, on the whole, substantially
-bidder capper, decoy, funk, puffer
-blow by-child, bastard, lovechild, mischance
-channel bayou, branch
-child See *-blow,* above.
degrees bit by bit, gradually, little by little, piecemeal
far easily
fits and starts capriciously,

haphazardly, intermittently, irregularly
halves inadequately
heart memoriter, memorized, perqueir
hook or crook habnab, somehow
itself alone, per se
jerks intermittently, irregularly
leaps and bounds swiftly
legal right ex jure
me pass
means of from, moyenant, per, through, with
no means negative, never, no way, on no account
-product crop, effluvium, incidental, offshoot, outgrowth, repercussion, result, scrap, shorts, side-issue
reason of because, ex capite, hence, hereat
stages by degrees, gradually
the book according to hoyle, conformably, conventional, correctly
the by also, in addition, incidentally, in passing
the same token accordingly, and, similarly
the skin of one's teeth barely, hardly, narrowly
the way accidental, also, apropos, by the by, casual, incidentally, in passing, occasional, parenthetical, rambling, through
this time already
virtue of amain, because
way of through, via
-wipe raillery, sarcasm
BYBLIS *brother* caunus

parent cyanee, idothea, miletus
BYBLOS *king* malcandre
BYGONE ago, ancient, backward, bypast, departed, elapsed, forepast, forgotten, former, olden, out of date, past, preterit, yore
BYHAND aside, casual, done with, incidentally, underhand
BYLAW ordinance, regulation, rule
BYLORUSSIA *city* brest, litovsk, minsk
BYNAME cognomen, nickname, sobriquet, surname
BYPASS avoid, burke, circuit, circumvent, cutoff, detour, evade, ignore, jump, omit, outflank, overlook, shun(pike), shunt, side road, sidestep
BYPATH byway, detour, diverticle, lane, way
BYRE barn, cowhouse, shed
BYROAD boithrin, boreen, shortcut
BYRON, GEORGE *beloved* teresa
castle chillon
character don juan, haidee, harold, inez, lara
death site missolonghi
poem childe harold, don juan, lara, manfred, mazeppa, prisoner of chillon, sardanapalus
prisoner bonivard
BYRONIC contemptuous, energetic, melancholy, melodramatic
BYSPELL bastard, parable, proverb

BYSTANDER doppess, innocent, neighbor, onlooker, spectator, tsitser, witness
BYWAY alley, bypass, byroad, bywalk, detour, lane, outway, path, road, shortcut, sidestreet, street, thoroughfare
BYWORD adage, aphorism, apothegm, axiom, byname, catchword, diverb, epithet, maxim, motto, nayword, nickname, phrase, proverb, reproach, saw, saying, shibboleth, slogan
BYWORK moonlighting, overtime
BYZANTINE complex, involved, labyrinthine
capital nicaea, ravenna
chapel antiparabema
coin bezant, follis, nomisma, solidus
emperor alexius, anastasius, heraclius, justinian, michael
empire anatolia
empress irene, theodora
festival brumallia
image eikon, icon, ikon
law manual hexabiblos, prochiron
mosaic icon
officer logothete
ornament bez(z)ant, solidus
ruler catapan, exarch, palaeologus
scepter ferula
speedwell veronica
BYZANTIUM constantinople, istanbul
founder byzas
restorer constantine
BYZAS *father* poseidon

C

C cee, doh, hundred
mark cedilla
CAAM heddles, loom
CAAMA asse, fox, hartebeest, silver
CAANTHUS *father* oceanus
sister melia
CAAPEBA herb, pareira, piperaca, pothomorphe
CAB araba, arana, brougham, cabin, carriage, compartment, coupelet, crawler, crib, enclosure, fiacre, fly,

gharri, hack(ney), hansom, herdic, jitney, judka, purloin, shelter, showfull, taxi, translation, vehicle
driver cabby, cabman, cocher(o), hack(man), mush(er)
4-wheeled bounde(r), bouquet, growler, herdic
2-wheeled herdic
CABA See CABAS.
CABACK See TAVERN.
CABAL association, band,

bloc, brigue, camarilla, chatter, clique, combination, complot, conspiracy, conspire, consult, coterie, council, cult, dispute, faction, frame-up, group, intrigue, junta, junto, party, plot, ring, scheme, secret, talking, tradition, unite
pert. factional
CABALA mystery, mysticism, occultism
author moses de leon

book sefer-yecirah, zohar
CABALASSOU armadillo, priodontes
CABALETTA cavatine, melody, song
CABALISM mysticism, obfuscation, obscurantism, occultism, traditionalism
god ensof, ensoph
CABALISTIC anagogical, arcane, cryptic, enigmatic, esoteric, mysterious, mystic, recondite
CABALLERO admirer, cavalier, escort, gentleman, horseman, knight, lord, lover
CABANA bathhouse, beachhouse, cabin, cottage, poolhouse
CABARET beerhall, boit(de nuit), cafe(chantant), casino, entertainment, floorshow, go-go bar, inn, jukejoint, night club, restaurant, roadhouse, saloon, stand, table, tavern, tray
CABAS basket, handbag, reticule, workbasket
CABASSET helmet, morion
CABASSOU tatouay, xenurus
CABBAGE appropriate, borecole, bowkail, brassica, caul, chou, cole(wort), colza, compress, cos, crib, crout, crucifer, cultigen, drumhead, filch, head, kail, kale, keal, kerguelen, kohlrabi, knol-knol, money, oxheart, pakchoi, palmito, pechay, perquisite, pilfer, press, purloin, savoy, slaw, steal, stock, stolen goods, tailor, vegetable, wort
bark angelin
bug calico back, harlequin
butterfly pierida
butterfly larva kale worm
curculio quadrideus, weevil
daisy globeflower
disease black-leg, wilt, wirestem, yellows
dish coleslaw, sauerkraut, slaw
family brassicaceae
fermented sauerkraut
genus cos
gum eucalyptus
-like vegetable brussels sprouts, rape
looper measuring worm
moth diamond-back, mamestra, noctuid

palm areca, assai, palmiste, roystonea, sabal
plant nape, wahoo
salad coleslaw, kraut, slaw
seed colza
soup borecole, borsch, borscht, borsht, bortsch, kale, shchi, shtchee, stchi
stalk castock, custock
stuffed holishkes
tree andira, angelin, cordyline, fan palm, hat, livistona, nuytsia, ti, yaba
variety cale, colewort, colza, drumhead, kale, kohlrabi, savoy
warmed over cloyer, platitude
white butterfly, colewort
worm caterpillar, herb, looper, othonna, pieris
CABBAGEHEAD dolt, dunce, fool, numbskull, screwball
CABBAGEWOOD privet, ligustrum, silk-cotton tree
CABBY dirty, driver, hack(man), sticky
CABELL, JAMES B. *setting* poictesme
work domnei, jurgen, silver stallion, smirt
CABER beam, pole, rafter, spar
CABERNET claret, wine
district geronde
CABESTRO halter, lariat, lasso, rope
CABEZA chief, head(man)
CABEZONE fish, larimus, porichthys, sculpin, toadfish
CABILLIAU codfish
CABIN accommodation, apartment, bedroom, berth, bohawn, booth, boudoir, box, cabana, capsule, casita, cave, cell, choza, coach, cockpit, compartment, confine, cot(tage), cramp, crew, crue, cuddy, den, enclose, felze, house, hovel, huddock, hut, izba, litter, lodge, mudsill, pad, partition, quarters, refuge, room, saloon, shack, shanty, shed, space, tilt, wigwam
berth baulk
boat baulea(h)
boy crewman, grummet
car caboose
court motel
cozy huddock

cruiser criscraft, pleasure boat, power boat
double saddlebag
CABINET advisors, almirah, ambry, baffle, bahut, birdsnest, board (of directors), bower, box, buffet, buhl, bureau, case, cellaret, chamber, chest, closet, committee, commode, confidential, console, council, cupboard, depository, dressoir, etagere, file, furniture, group, high-quality, hut, icebox, jukebox, ministry, private, repository, room, sanctum, secret, showcase, sink, soviet, stall, summerhouse, tent, vargueno, whatnot
d'aisance toilet
18th century dressoir
filing bus, buss, morgue
large breakfront
-maker carpenter, ebenezer, framer, joiner, woodworker
open-shelved etagere, whatnot
renaissance papelera
wood calamander
CABIRI *helpers of* hephaestus
cult center anthedon, imbros, lemnos, samathrace, thebes
CABLE assembly, boom, catenary, chain, coaxial, cord, fast, fasten, ganger, gunline, guy, hawser, junk, line, link, message, painter, rope, stay, strand, telegram, telegraph, tether, tow, transmit, wire, wireless
car teleferique, telfer, telpher(age)
derrick backstay
fake tier
length scope, shackle
lifter wildcat
loop elliot eye
measure naut
pert. coax(i)al
post bitt
railway ascenseur, funicular, railroad, telpherage, tramway
spliced shot
vault chamber
wheel wildcat
wound keckling
CABLED rudented
CABLING molding, rudenture

CABOCHON carbuncle, gem, ornament, shell, stone
cut buff-top

CABOODLE bag, boodle, calabash, collection, group, kit, lot

CABOOSE braker, brakevan, buggy, cab, car, cookroom, crummy, deckhouse, doghouse, galley, hack, oven, palace, tail, van

CABRILLA bass, cony, fish, gaper, grouper, red-hind, serranus

CABRIOLET cab, carriage, convertible, coupe

CABSTAND hasard, hazard

CABUJA cajun, hemp, lily, piteira, sisal

CACAO arriba, broma, chocolate, cocker, çocoa, criollo, forastero, theobroma
disease black pod
extract butter, fat, martol
seed powder broma

CACHALOT physter, spermwhale

CACHE bury, cash, coin, conceal, deposit, depot, ensconce, hide, hole, refuge, safekeeping, screen, secrete, stash, store(house), stow, treasure, trove
-cache snipe

CACHET capsule, design, essence, handstamp, konseal, mark, pill cover, prestige, seal, slogan, stamp, standing, wafer

CACHEXIA emaciation, wasting, weakness

CACHEXIC deathly, ill, morbid, sick

CACHOT dungeon

CACHOU auburn, catechu, dye, pastil, pill

CACHRYS ament, carrot, catkin

CACHUCHO etelis, red snapper

CACHUNDE antidote, lozenge, pastil, stomachic, troche

CACIQUE bird, boss, bunyah, cassican, cazique, chief, hangnest, landowner, oriole, ruler

CACK discharge, dung, muck, saddle, shoe, void

CACKEREL mendole, smaris

CACKLE babble(ment), cank, chat(ter), chortle, chuckle, clack, cluck, conk, gabble, gaggle, giggle, gob-

ble, gossip, idle talk, keak, keckle, laugh(ter), loquacity, noise, prattle, snicker, talk, titter, twaddle

CACODEMON demon, devil, nightmare

CACOEPY mispronunciation

CACOETHES desire, itch, mania, ulcer

CACOGRAPHY error, inelegance

CACOMISTLE arctoid, bassarisk, cacomixle, cat-squirrel, civet, ringtail(ed cat)

CACOON segra, sequa

CACOPHONOUS discordant, dissonant, harsh, jangling, raucous, strident, unmelodious

CACOPHONY babel, discord, dissonance, jangle, mixture, noise, racket

CACTUS agave, airampo, alfilerillo, alicoche, anhalonium, aporo, barrel, bavoso, beavertail, belly flower, bisagre, bisnaga, biznaga, bleo, cacanapa, cardon(a), cardoncillo, carnegiea, cephalocereus, cereus, chende, chichipe, cholla, cochal, dildo, echinocereus, harrisia, hedgehog, indian-fig, maguey, mammillaria, moscal, nopal, opuntia, organpipe, peyote, peyotl, pitahaya, prickly pear, rattail, rhipsalis, saguaro, santamarta, senita, squaro, tasajillo, tasajo, teddybear, thorn, turk's-head, xerophil
aborescent barbados gooseberry
apple prickly pear
branched chende
bushy pitahaya
cane opuntia
climbing queen of the night
columnar cereus, torch-thistle
dahlia attraction
drug peyote
edible saguaro
fruit cochal, muyusa, prickly pear, sabra
giant cardon
joint phylloclade
-like cochal
pert. xeric
plantation nopalry
prostrate airampo
saguaro carnegiea, pitahaya
small mescal

spineless ariocarpus, chaute
treelike tasajillo
unarmed rhipsalis
yucca adam's needle

CACUMINAL cerebral, inverted, pointed, retroflex, top

CACUS *father* hephaestus, vulcan
slayer hercules

CAD assistant, boor, bounder, chum, churl, conductor, cur, dastard, employee, friend, gyp, heel, hick, mucker, peasant, rascal, reprobate, rotter, rube, schmuck, scoundrel, scout, shmuck, skip, townsman, yokel

CADAVER body, carcass, corpse, deceased, remains, scrag, skeleton, stiff

CADAVEROUS careworn, consumptive, corpselike, deathly, emaciated, gaunt, ghastly, haggard, livid, pale, pallid, pinched, poor, thin, wan, wasted, worn

CADDICE See CADDIS.

CADDIE, CADDY attendant, ball boy, box, cadet, can, chest, hat, lad, nacket, odd-jobber, tea-warmer

CADDIS braid, caseworm, crewel, floss, fly, lint, rags, ribbon, shreds, stonefly, twill, yarn
fly cadew, dun, sedge
worm cadbait, caddice, cadew, piper, strawworm

CADDISH ill-bred, low-bred, presuming, ungentlemanly, vulgar

CADDLE annoy, confuse, confusion, disarray, embarrassment, fuss, gossip, tease, trouble, worry

CADDO *indian* adai, andarko, arikara, arikaree, eyeish, hainai, hasinai, ioni, kichai, nachitoch, pawnee, rees, texas, waco, wichita

CADDOW jackdaw

CADDY See CADDIE.

CADE barrel, cask, coddle, domesticated, foal, indulge(d), juniper, keg, lamb, pet(ted), rebel, spoiled child, tame(d)
lamb sock

CADEAU gift, present

CADENCE accent(uation), anapaest, arsis, beat, clausula, close, dactyl, differentia, emphasis, fall, flow, iamb, ictus, jingle, lilt, measure, meter, metre, modulation, movement, pace, pulse, rhythm, sound, stress, swing, tempo, thesis, throb, tone, trill

CADENT descending, falling, glowing, heated, measured

CADENZA bariolage, flourish, melisma

CADET caddy, dodo, gentleman, goat, junior, lad, midshipman, navy man, pimp, pleb(e), procurer, pupil, recruit, soldier, son, student, trainee, west pointer, youth
first year doolie

CADGE beg, bind, borrow, bum, cage, carry, frame, hawk, impose on, mooch, parasite, peddle, scrounge, sponge, tie

CADGER beggar, carrier, cozier, dealer, hawker, huckster, packman, scrounger, sponger, vendor

CADGY amorous, cheerful, kedgy, lustful, merry, mirthful, wanton

CADIZ gulf, river to guadalquivir, guadiana
pert. gaditan

CADMIUM *blende* greenockite, ocher
lemon yellow
source greenockite

CADMUS agenorides
cousin harmonia
daughter agave, autonoe, ino, semele
founder of thebes
kingdom phoenicia, thelephassa
parent agenor, argiope, telephasa
sister europa
son illyrius, polydorus
sowed dragon's teeth
wife harmonia

CADOR *son* constantyne

CADRE care, directorate, frame(work), group, list, outline, scheme, skeleton, source, unit

CADUCEUS insigne, kerykeion, scepter, sceptre, staff, symbol, wand
group ama, amc
staff of hermes, mercury

CADUCITY feebleness, frailty, infirmity, lapse, perishableness, senility, transitoriness

CADUCOUS deciduous, dropping, falling(off), fleeting, lapsed, perishable, shedding, transitory

CADUS jar, kados, situla, vessel

CAECILIA amphibian, apoda, blind-worm

CAECUM cavity, cecum, cell, cul-de-sac, gut, perithecum, pit, pocket, pore, pouch, sac, socket, typhlon

CAELUM graving-tool

CAENIS, CAENEUS *adversaries* centaurs
lover poseidon
parent coronus, elatus

CAESALPINIA bauhinia, brasiletto, brazilwood, brea, cassia, copaifera, divi-divi, senna, tree

CAESAR autocrat, dictator, emperor, general, historian, kaiser, politician, ruler, salad, solitaire, statesman, tomtate, tyrant
accused dolabella, publius
assassin albinus, artemidorus, brutus, casca, cassius, cinna, labeo, marcus, tillius
aunt julia
beloved cleopatra
brother-in-law antony, marcellus
capital roma, rome
captive arsinoe
colleague bibulus, paulus, piso, pompey
conquest britain, gaul
consort servilia
conspirator brutus, casca, cassius, cinna, flavius, ligarius, metellus, murellus, trebonius
cousin marius
critic cato, catulus, favonius
daughter cornelia, julia
death site forum, nola
enemy crassus, ligarius, pompey
fatal day ides of march
father-in-law cinna, piso
first augustus
follower curio, mark antony, paulus
friend agrippa, amanteus, antony, asinius, balbus, calvisius, cinna, curio, dolabella, gallus, maecenas, mark antony, nicomedes, proculeius, thidias, thyreus, trebatius
general taurus

last words et tu brute
legion alauda
lieutenant antony, calvinus, corfinius, crassinius, dolabella, domitius, hortensius, labienus, pollio, sallutio, taurus
message site zela
mother attia, aurelia
patron vetus
rival abriorix, ariovistus, clodius, domitius, isauricus, lentulus, marcellus, piso, vergentorix
river rubicon
robe toga
rubicon words anerriphtho kubos, the die is cast
sister ancharia, attia, octavia
soldier acilius, cassius
son caesarion
son-in-law pompey
sword crocea, mars
teacher apollonius
title imperator
victim anchillas, pothinus
victory actium, pharsalus
weed aramina, cocklebur, urena
wife calpurnia, cornelia, pompeia, uxor

CAESAREA *bishop* basil(ius), eusebius

CAESARISM absolutism, imperialism

CAESURA break, diaeresis, division, interruption, interval, pause, rest, stop

CAFAR kaffir

CAFARD bigot, blues, depression, humbug(gery), hypocrite

CAFE automat, barroom, beanery, bierstube, bistro, buffet, cabaret, canteen, cantina, chophouse, chuckwagon, coffeehouse, coffeeshop, cookhouse, diner, drive-in, eatery, estaminet, grill(room), hashery, hashhouse, lunch counter, luncheonette, lunchroom, mess hall, nightclub, one-arm joint, osteria, restaurant, tavern, tearoom, trattoria, wineshop
au lait alesan
creme suede
noir espresso, musk

CAFFEINE diuretic, kola, thein, theina, theine
nut cola
source coffee, cola, kola, tea, yocco

CAFFLE argue, wrangle
CAFUSO half-breed, sambo, zambo
CAG insult, keg, offend
CAGAYAN ibanag
CAGE aviary, backstop, bars, basket, box, brake, bucket, bullpen, cadge, car(riage), cavea, chantry, chapel, confine(ment), coop, corf, crib, cylinder, elevator, enclose, enclosure, flight, fold, frame(work), gig, goal, grate, hutch, imprison, jail, lantern, mew, pen, pinfold, prison, receptacle, restrain, retainer, scaffold, score, shelter, shut(in), tumbrel, tumbril
bird aviary, pinjra, volary
hawk's meute, mew
hen's cavey, cavie
lobster corf, creel
CAGER basketball player, onsetter
CAGEY clever, coony, shrewd, wary
CAGGY spoiled, tainted
CAGMAG crank, goose, inferior, kegmeg, meddler, poor, rubbish, unwholesome
CAGNAZZO devil
CAGOT agote, leper, outcast, pariah
CAHIER exercise book, journal, notebook, paperback, report
CAHITA *indian* maya, pima, tehueco, yaqui
CAHOOTS association, collusion, conspiracy, league, participation, partnership
CAHOT bulge, pitchhole, pothole
CAHOW petrel, seabird, shearwater
CAHUILA *indian* shoshone
CAILLEACH crone, hag, witch
CAIMAN alligator, cayman, crocodile, jacare, yacars
CAIN crops, eggs, fine, killer, murderer, poultry, produce, rent
and abel table
brother abel, pur, seth
descendant enoch, enos, lamech
granddaughter aholibamah, anah
land nod
nephew enos
occupation tiller

parent adam, eve
son enoch
wife adah
CAINA See HELL.
CAINAN *parent* enos
CAINGANG aweikoma, bugre, coroado, goyana, tapuyan
CAIRD gypsy, tinker, tramp, vagrant
CAIRN catstone, galgal, landmark, mark(er), memorial, mound, pike, stoneman, tombstone
CAIRO al qahirah, fustat
old al fustat, el fostat
CAISSON box, camail, camel, carriage, case, chest, coffer, crib, lacunar, mine, pont(on), pontoon, reservoir, saucer, wagon
disease bends
CAITIFF bad, base, captive, coward(ly), dastard, despicable, mean, prisoner, vile, wicked, wretched
CAIUS coriolanus
kinsman titus-andronicus
servant mistress quickly, rugby
CAJA bank, box, cash(ier), chest, funds
CAJANUS catjang, pigeonpea
CAJEPUT, CAJUPUT kajeput, melaleuca, paperback, paperbush, punk-tree
CAJOLE bamboozle, beguile, blander, blandish, bumbaze, butter(up), carn(e)y, cheat, coax, cog, con, curry, deceive, decoy, delude, entice, flam, flatter, flum, fraik, fraise, importune, induce, ingle, inveigle, jig, jolly, kid, lure, palaver, palp, persuade, tease, trick, tweedle, wheedle, whilly
CAJOLERY blarney, butter, daub(e)ry, flattery, fraise, palaver, sooth, sycophancy, taffy
CAJON canyon, gorge, pise
CAJUN acadian
CAKE arval, bake, bannock, barkle, batty, biscuit, block, boxty, brownie, bun(n), caraway, cimbal, coagulate, coca, concrete, congeal, consolidate, cookie, cooky, crust, damper, eclair, fadge, fix, floe, fool, french pastry, fuse, galette, gateau, hallah, hamantash, harden, jelly-

roll, jumble, kichel, koji, kyaak, lump, mass, mole, nacket, parkin, pastry, patisserie, pone, popadam, scone, set, shortbread, simnel, simpleton, solidify, sponge, stiffen, sunket, tart, tort(e), torten, wafer, wedge, wig(g)
almond macaroon
barley fadge
boiled in honey teiglech
clay platten
coffee bear-claw, blueberry, buckle, danish, kuchen, snail, strudel
corn fritter, hush puppy, pone
custard creampuff, eclair
day hogmanay
decoration frosting, icing, non pareil
dough batter
-eater dilettante, sissy, trifler
filled flan, tart
flat See CAKE *thin.*
fried bismarck, cruller, cymbal, doughnut, fasnacht, flitter, fritter, olycook, olykoek, simball, sinker, twister
fruit simnel
funeral arthel, arval, arvel, averil
ginger bolivar
griddle bannock, crumpet, flapjack, flipper, fritter, hotcake, latke, pancake, scone, slapjack
hard, brittle cracknell
honey lekach, teiglech
kind angelfood, batty, bruit, cheese, chiffon, coffee, crumpet, devil's food, fruit, griddle, hoe, kuchen, layer, loaf, marble, napoleon, nut, pancake, popper, pound, short, sponge, stolen, upsidedown, wedding
lamb and wheat kibbe(h)
mango juice amsath
mixture batter
new year's hagmena, hogmanay
oatmeal clapbread
part farl(e), icing, layer
plum baba
potato fadge
raisin babka
rich cala
rock tabnabs
round barapicklet, charlotte, torte
rubber biscuit

rum baba
sacrificial hallah
seed wiff, wig(g)
small batty, biscuit, bun, cupcake, jumble, ladyfinger, nacket, tart
sweet simnel
tea sally lunn, scone
thin bannock, bunuelo, chrimsel, damper, farl(e), galette, jumble, matzo, peeta, placent, plate, tortilla, wafer
topping frosting, icing, streusel
unleavened damper, matzo, tortilla, wafer
wheatmeal fadge
with sauce cottage pudding
yeast koji
CAKED clit, clotted, hard, solid
CAKES *and ale* comforts, enjoyment, pleasure
CAKEWALK dance, march, promenade, strut
CAKILE beach-sap, herb, mustard, sea-rocket
CALABA brima, calophyllum, fir, galba, gamboge, santa maria tree
product balsam
CALABAR *bean* esere, isere, ordeal-bean, physostigma
ebony diospyros
extract eserine
CALABASH basket, bottle(gourd), caboodle, calabaza, crescentia, curuba, dipper, drum, gourd, jicara, kettle, rattle
mrs., friend durante
tree baobab, crescentia, higuero, jicara
CALABAZILLA gourd, pumpkin, squash
CALABOOSE bastille, brig, caboose, can, gaol, jail, jug, lock-up, prison, stir
CALABUR *tree* capuli(n), silkwood
CALADIUM aroid, bleedingheart, kaladi, taro
CALAIS *brother* zetes
enemy harpies
parent boreas, orithyia
slayer hercules
CALAITE turquoise
CALAMARY loligo, squid
CALAMBAC See AGALLOCH
CALAMINE cadmia, coat, hemimorphite, smithsonite
CALAMITOUS adverse, bad,

baleful, bitter, black, deplorable, dire, dismal, evil, fatal, grievous, hapless, ruinous, sad, tragic(al), unfortunate, unhappy, unlucky, woeful, wretched
CALAMITY accident, adversity, affliction, bale, blow, casualty, cataclysm, catastrophe, cross, disaster, distress, doom, evil, fatality, hardship, hydra, ill, misadventure, mischance, mischief, misery, misfortune, mishap, oncome, reverse, ruin, sorrow, storm, trial, tribulation, trouble, unhappiness, woe, wrack, wreck, wretchedness
howler pessimist
CALAMONDIN calamansi, orange
CALAMUS acorus, cane, feather, palm, pen, quill, rattan, reed, rotang, sweetflag
CALANDRINA purslane, herb
CALANGAY abacay, cockatoo
CALASH bonnet, caleche, calesa, carriage, four-wheeler, galeche, sailor
driver calesero
CALAVERITE telluride
CALCANEUS heelbone
CALCAR furnace, oven, prehallux, spur, tube
CALCARATE spurred
CALCAREOUS *sinter* coral, spar, travertine
spar calcite
CALCED shod
CALCEOLARIA fagelia, figwort, ionidium
CALCHAQUI *indian* diaguite
CALCHAS *daughter* cressida, criseyde
father thestor
rival mopsus
CALCIFY cretify
CALCIMINE paint, whitewash
CALCINE burn, decrepitate, disintegrate, frit, heat, ignite, oxidize, powder, purify, roast
CALCITE agaric, alabaster, amygdaloid, aphrite, argentine, calcareous, calc-spar, hispolite, spar, stalactite, stalagmite
animal skeleton

deposit spar, stalactite, stalagmite, ta(r)tar, tufa
double-refracting iceland spar
skeleton coral
soil with marl
CALCITRANT defiant, stubborn
CALCIUM lime
borate borocalcite, colemanite, inyoite, pandermite
carbide acetylenogen
carbonate ankerite, aragonite, bog lime, calcite, calcspar, chalk, dolomite, dripstone, limestone, tufa, whiting
chloride apatite, preservative
compound acerdol, afvillite, arduinite, atopite, bakerite, bavenite, belite, cebolite, chanite, pascoite, perovskite, scheelite, sphene, titantite, whewellite
cyanamid fertilizer, nitroline
-iron andradite, aplome, calcioferrite
light limelight
nitrate fertilizer, nitroline, saltpeter
oxide quicklime
phosphate apatite, baking powder, brushite, churchite, fertilizer, isoclasite
source gypsum
sulphate anhydrite, annaline, bassanite, gypsum, hepar
CALCULATE account, adapt, add, aim, algebraize, ascertain, average, calk, callate, cast, cipher, compute, consider, count, design, detail, determine, divide, dope out, enumerate, estimate, evaluate, expect, figure, forecast, frame, gauge, guess, imagine, inventory, itemize, keep tabs, lump off, multiply, number, plan, ponder, prepare, presume, rate, recapitulate, reckon, recount, rehearse, ruminate, score, study, subtract, summarize, summate, suppose, tally, tell, think, tot, total, tottle, weigh
inability to acalculia
on count on, expect, rely
CALCULATED adapted, advised, cold, conscious, contrived, discounted, fitted, intentional, meant, measured, petty, premeditated, small, studied, suited

CALCULATING brittle, careful, cautious, chary, circumspect, cold, crafty, cunning, deliberate, designing, judicious, scheming, shrewd, sly, wary, wily, wise
art algorism, algorithm
CALCULATION account, addition, care, caution, circumspection, computation, computerization, concern, counting, discretion, enumeration, forecast, foresight, forethought, hindcast, numeration, prudence, sagacity, scheming, selfishness, share, solitaire, wariness, wary
CALCULATOR abacus, accountant, adding machine, arithmograph, arithmometer, cash register, comptometer, computer, counter, isograph, log, napier's bones, pari-mutuel, slide rule, soroban, suanpan, table, tabulator, totalizator
inventor babbage
CALCULIST mathematician
CALCULOUS gritty, hardening, sandy, stone, stony
CALCULUS analysis, computation, concretion, stone, tartar, urolith
kind absolute, differential, directional, infinitesimal, integral
CALCUTTA city of palaces
docks kidderpore
hemp jute
measure dhan, jaob, kunk, raik
police station thana
prison black hole
river hooghly
road kalighat
station wayrah
weight hubba, pally, pank, raik
CALDERA broth, caldron, crater, stew
CALDRON alfet, boiler, caldera, copper, kelder, kettle, kohua, morocco red, pot(stone), red, tripod, vat, vessel
CALDWELL, ERSKINE *play* tobacco road
CALEB *association* joshua
daughter achsah, axa
descendants eshtaulites,

ithrites, mishraites, shobal, shumathites, zareathites
leader moses
son ardon, elah, gazez, haran, hur, iru, jesher, mareshah, mesha, moza, naam, shaaph, shebar, sheva, shobab, tirhana
spy for moses
wife azubah, ephah, eprath, jerioth, maacah
CALEDONIA See SCOTLAND.
CALEDONIAN *brown* gypsy, red-yellow
CALEDVWLCH *owner* king arthur
CALEFACTION cauma, heat(er), stove, warming
CALENDAR agenda, agendum, almanac, bulletin, calends, catalog(ue), chronicle, chronogram, chronology, diary, direction, docket, ephemeris, fasti, guide, journal, kalends, list, log, menology, ordo, pattern, press, program, record, register, repertory, schedule, table
church ordo
deficiency epact
former julian, mayan
present-day gregorian
primitive clog-almanac, runic-staff
proposed change cotsworth
CALENDER canroy, dervish, machine, press, roll, schreiner, tabby
worker canroyer, smoother
CALENDRA bill-bug, grasseater, weevil
CALENDS calendar beginning, kalends, record, register
CALENDULA aperient, diaphoretic, herb, marigold, thistle
CALENTURE ardor, fever, fire, glow, infect, passion, sunstroke
CALEPIN dictionary, lexicon, reference
CALESCENT heating, warming
CALETOR *master* hector
CALF, CALF'S bob(by), boss(y), boy, buss, cow, dogie, dolt, fatling, fledging, fool, foreleg, heifer, ice, island, leather, leg, lubber, maverick, moggy, poddy, ranny, shin, sleeper, sooky,

veal, weaner, yearling, youth
atrophy acnemia
cry baa, belat, blat
days salad days, youth
female sterile freemartin
flesh veal, veau
-foot cuckoopint, plant, wake-robin
-foot jelly fisnoga, gelatin, sulze
head pitcher plant
leather slinkskin
-like vituline
love affection, infatuation
meat veal
motherless dogie, dogy, maverick
-mouth snapdragon
muscle plantaris
pert. sural, vitular, vituline
premature slink
-snout snapdragon
stomach vell
stomach lining rennet
symbol of cowardice, lumpishness
unbranded longear, sleeper
yearling caure, deacon
young buss
CALFKILL calico-bush, kalmia, leucothoe, sheeplaurel, shrub, velvet-grass
CALFSKIN corova, grasser, kid, kip(p), korova, suede, tulchan, vealskin, vellum
CALIBAN beast, brute, monster, slave
adversary prospero
deity of setebos
mother sycorax
opposite ariel
CALIBER ability, appetency, bore, breadth, capacity, character, compass, degree, diameter, dignity, gauge, habilitation, importance, intelligence, measure, merit, mettle, pincers, quality, rank, size, talent, thickness
rule calipers
CALIBRATE check, divide, mark, measure, standardize
CALIBURN *owner* king arthur
CALICHE calcrete, nitratine, tepetate
CALICO blay, chintz, cloth, croydon, girl, goldfish, mosaic, mottled, pinto, print, sallo(o), spotted, woman (kind)
aster wiseweed
bass bachelor, bitterhead,

crappie, golden shiner, pomoxis
bird turnstone
bush calfkill, kalmia, mountain-laurel
clam macrocallista
flower aristolochia, calfkill, five-spot, kalmia
horse piebald, pinto
jacket turnstone
mix colors for teer
pigment canarin(e)
print bandanna
printing fondu, lapis, teer
CALICOBACK harlequinbug, stinkbug, turnstone
CALID burning, hot, warm
CALIFORNIA el dorado, golden, the promised land
animal bobcat, cacomistle, dire wolf, mountain lion, sabertooth
bandit black bart, vasquez
barberry mahonia, oregon grape
bay monterey, san diego, san francisco
bay tree laurel
bluebell phacelia
buckthorn coffeeberry, rhamnus
bulrush marsh-sedge, scirpus, tule
calycanth spicebush
cape mendocino
capital benicia, monterey, sacramento
capital, first molina del ray, molley del ray, monterey
cedar redwood
christmasberry holly, toyon
city 4 lodi, napa 5 azusa, chico, chino, indio 6 blythe, carmel, colton, covina, downey, eureka, fresno, laguna, lompoc, merced, novato, oxnard, pomona, sonoma, tulare, upland 7 alameda, anaheim, arcadia, banning, barstow, brawley, burbank, concord, elcajon, fremont, gardena, hayward, la habra, la jolla, lynwood, modesto, needles, norwalk, ontario, salinas, san jose, vallejo, visalia 8 alhambra, altadena, beaumont, berkeley, coronado, daly city, el centro, glendale, glendora, lakewood, monrovia, monterey, palo alto, pasadena, petaluma, redlands, san diego, san mateo, santa ana, stockton, torrance,

whittier 9 buena park, costa mesa, cucamonga, escondido, fullerton, inglewood, lancaster, livermore, long beach, menlo park, oceanside, riverside, santa cruz, sausalito 10 bellflower, burlingame, chula vista, culver city, los angeles, sacramento, san raphael, santa clara 11 bakersfield, carpenteria, castroville, garden grove, palm springs, san clemente, san fernando, santa monica 12 beverly hills, hermosa beach, newport beach, san francisco, santa barbara 13 san bernardino, san luis obispo
coffee bearberry, cascara-buckthorn
college chapman, mills, occidental, pepperdine, pitzer, pomona, scripps, whittier
condor gymnogyps, vulture
county alameda, calaveras, colusa, inyo, kern, lassen, los angeles, marin, merced, modoc, mono, napa, orange, placer, plumas, san diego, shasta, siskiyou, solano, sonoma, sutter, tehama, tulare, ventura, yolo, yuba
cress hedge-mustard
dam boulder, hoover, shasta
dandelion cat's-ear, weed
date fardh
desert colorado, death valley, mohave, mojave
evergreen torreya, umbra
everlasting cudweed
explorer cabrillo, de anza, drake, heceta, junipero serra
fan palm erythea, washingtonia
farm region imperial valley
fish bocaccio, cabrilla, chi, corvina, fringehead, garibaldi, grunion, queenfish, rasher, re(i)na, silversides, sprat, sur, tuna, tunny, viuva
flower creamcups, poppy
fraternity clampers, e clampus vitus
geranium groundsel, senecio
gold town angels camp, aqua fria, bodie, camp seco, china camp, columbia, dry creek, eureka, grass valley, hangtown, igo, jackson, marysville, mokelumne hill,

murderer's gulch, nevada city, ono, placerville, sonora, volcano, whiskey flat
greasewood iodine bush
gulf sea of cortez
gulf, river to colorado
gulf wind collada
hare bell campamula
herb amole, baby-blue-eyes, baeria, bird's-beak, bird's-bill, bloomeria, bluebell, cordylanthus, creamsacs, evening snow, fairy fan, fawn lily, golden eardrop, gold fields, ground pink, ithuriel's spear, layia, morning star, nieveta, poppy, purple sage, romero, skyrocket, stinkbell, tidytips, yerba buena
holly christmasberry, toyon
hyacinth brodiaea
indian achomawi, aguacaliente, atsugewi, cahuilla, chemchvevi, chemehuevi, chumash(an), constanoan, digueno, esselen, gitanemuck, hokan, hoopa, hupa, karok, klamath, koso, kulanapan, kuneste, luiseno, maidu, mattole, mission, miwok, modoc, mohave, mono, nozi, paiute, palaihnihan, panamint, patwin, pericui, pit river, pomo, puvunga, salina, salinan, sastean, seri, waicuri, wailaki, wappo, washo, weitspekan, whilkut, wintun, wishoskan, wiyot, yana(n), yokuts, yuki(an), yuma, yunan, yurok
indian deity acaragui, amayicoyondi, cucumunic, naparaya, purutabui, quaryayp
indigo bush mock-locust
island alcatraz, anacapa, catalina, coronado, farollone, goat, mare, nicholas, san clemente, san miguel, santa barbara, santa catalina, santa cruz, santa rosa, treasure
jack seven-up
jay aphelocoma
lake buena, eagle, goose, honey, mono, owens, salton sea, soda, tahoe, tulare
laurel balm of heaven, bayberry, cajeput, cajuput, myrtle, oleander, pepperwood, sassafras, spice-tree, umbellularia

lilac blueblossom, bluebrush, ceanothus, periwinkle, vinca
lily bloomeria
live oak encina
lizard anniellid
lower baja
lupine sheep-poison
maidenhair adiantum
mint pitcher-sage
motto eureka
myrtle See CALIFORNIA laurel.
named by cortez
national park king's canyon, lassen, redwood, sequoia, yosemite
nickname golden state
oak encina, roble
observatory lick, mt. wilson, palomar
onyx aragonite
pass donner, sonora
peak baldy, el capitan, hamilton, lassen, muir, shasta, telescope, whitney, wilson
pitcher plant calf's-head, chrysamphora
plant bracken fern, brodia, elderberry, escobita, fringepod, golden stars, hookera, sword fern, tarweed, thimbleberry, tidytips, yellow bells
poppy creamcups
port long beach, los angeles, oakland, richmond, sacramento, san diego, san francisco, san pedro
president nixon
pride of campo pea
prison alcatraz, folsom, san quentin
privet ligustrum
quail lophortyx
queen, legendary calafia
range panamint, san bernardino, sierra nevada
ray thornback
river eel, feather, kern, king's, klamath, little, mad, merced, owens, pit, putah, rubicon, russian, sacramento, salinas, salmon, san jacinto, san joaquin, smith, stanislaus, stony, trinity, truckee
rockfish bocaccio, corsair, rasher, re(i)na, viuva
rose bay rhododendron
sagebrush artemisia
sassafras See CALIFORNIA laurel.
scaly bark psorosis

sculpin cabezon(e)
sheep poison lupine
shrub alkali-heath, bush poppy, ceanothus, chamiso, chaparral, deer brush, flannel bush, frankenia, jojoba, kumquat, manzanita, mulefat, myrtle, quailbrush, rosilla, sneezeweed, spicebush, tarbush, toyon
soaproot amole
state bird quail
state flower poppy
state symbol grizzly bear
state tree redwood
stingray batfish
strait golden gate
strawberry shrub spicebush, sweetshrub
sweetshrub spicebush
tortoise ellachick
tree alder, blue oak, brisbane box, fanleaf palm, green wettle, gum myrtle, live oak, lucia fir, madrone, manzanita, myrtle, oak, orange gum, paloblanco, redwood, sequoia, sycamore, torrey(pine), toyon, wellingtonia
trout boregat
university cal tech, stanford, ucla, usc
volcano lassen
vulture condor
westermost part mendocino
wheat shallu
wild plum islay
wind, hot santa ana
wine area cucamonga, livermore, lodi, modesto, monterey, napa, santa clara, sonoma, st helena
woodpecker carpenter-bird, carpintero
CALIFORNIUM source curium
CALIGA boot, buskin, shoe, stocking
CALIGINOUS dark, dim, foggy, misty, obscure
CALIGULA caius caesar
general petronius
horse incitatus
parent agrippina, germanicus
patron tiberius
slayer cassius, cornelius
wife caesonia
CALINAGO carib
CALIPASH carapace
CALIPER(S) clip, jenny, measure, oddlegs, rod, rule
kind hermaphrodite, keyway, slide, transfer, vernier

CALIPH abbasid(es), abu, ali, bekr, calif, imam, omar, ommiads, othman, sultan, umayyad
first ab(o)u-bekr
office caliphate
CALISTHENICS exercise, gymnastics, judo
system delsarte
CALIX chalice, cup
CALIXTINE hussite, utraquist
CALK calculate, caltrap, caltrop, chinse, close, copy, cork, fill, flag, injure, jag, nap, occlude, projection, silence, sleep, snug, stop, tighten, tool
material oakum
CALKER corker, dram, drink, staver, tool
CALKING oakum, wicking
CALL 3 ban, bet, bid, cry, dub, hey, see 4 cite, deal, dial, duty, look, lure, meet, name, need, note, page, pass, pist, psst, ring, roup, sell, solo, sook, stay, stop, taps, term, tone, toot, vote, yell, yelp 5 abuse, alarm, awake, bedub, blast, bring, bugle, claim, clepe, decoy, draft, drive, elect, equal, evoke, hallo, judge, knock, match, noise, order, phone, rouse, scold, shout, speak, stand, style, title, utter, visit, voice, waken, yodel 6 accuse, agenda, alarum, appeal, arouse, awaken, cancel, career, change, choice, decide, demand, divert, drop in, elicit, expose, gather, halloa, halloo, induct, invite, invoke, muster, notice, option, outcry, quethe, rebuke, recall, reckon, regard, remain, revoke, signal, strain, strake, summon, yoohoo 7 acclaim, address, angelus, appoint, attract, behight, betitle, bidding, censure, collect, command, conduct, conjure, convene, convoke, declare, entitle, impeach, inquire, itemize, mention, predict, recruit, reprove, request, require, summons, warrant, whistle 8 announce, appelate, applause, assemble, consider, contract, decision, denounce, estimate, forecast, foretell, judgment, vo-

cation 9 advertise, challenge, criticize, designate, determine, mating cry, reprimand, telephone, terminate, utterance 10 assessment, denominate, disapprove, employment, invitation, occupation 11 declaration, fascination, requirement, requisition 12 characterize, conversation
a bet see, stay
a spade a spade be candid, be frank, level, speak out
attention to remind
away extricate, remove, summon
back recall, recant, remember, repeal, retract, retrieve, reverse, revive, revoke, summon, withdraw
bird decoy
bird's tweet, weet
box telephone booth
bugle post
by name page
close touch
distress mayday, sos
down bawl out, berate, brawl, censure, chide, denounce, devocate, execrate, imprecate, invoke, rebuke, reprimand, reprove, scold
for ask, claim, collect, cry, date, demand, desire, entail, escort, exact, fetch, need, oblige, page, pick up, request, require, solicit, summon, take out, visit
forth appeal, arouse, attract, avail, awake, conjure up, elicit, evocate, evoke, excite, induce, invoke, prompt, signal, stir, suggest, summon
girl courtesan, fancy woman, lady of the evening, prostitute, taxi girl, wanton
hoarsely roop, roup
hogs sooey, sook
hunting hallo, hoicks, rechate, recheat, yoicks
in admit, consult, gather, invite, summon, withdraw
in question challenge, doubt, impugn, protest
into play create, effectuate
it a day cease, close, complete, go home, quit, stop
it square agree, settle
loudly acclaim, cry, hail, shout
money loan
morning matin

names abuse, affront, belittle, excoriate, smear
nautical ahoy
off cancel, count, discontinue, distract, end, number, stop, summon, terminate, wind up, withdraw
of the wild wanderlust
on ask, command, demand, meet, order, petition, request, require, suggest, visit
on telephone buzz, ring up
on the carpet See CALL down,
one's bluff challenge, see
out ascry, challenge, cry, elicit, evoke, gollar, goller, hail, holler, hulloo, invoke, lure, muster, recruit, summon
public attention advertise, announce, promote, publicize
signals command, direct, order, run
summoning come hither
the turn augur, command, run
to accost, address, ascry, greet, hail, halloo, salute
to account arraign, blame, book, control, indict, reprimand
to arms alar(u)m, mobilize, rappel, recruit
to attention hop, remind
to battle challenge
to cow coboss, sook(ie)
together assemble, convene, convoke, gather, muster, rally, summon
to horse hie, hup, proo, way
to mind bethink, cite, envisage, envision, ming, recall, recollect, record, remember
to order command, open, preside
to prayer azan
to the colors enlist, enroll
to witness appeal
trumpet berloque, sennet, sinnet
up advocate, assignation, conjure, draft, elicit, mobilize, phone, prompt, recruit, remember, summon
upon address, appeal, beseech, command, depose, engage, enjoin, grede, halse, implore, petition, see, urge, visit
CALLA aracae, arum, dragon, lily, mayflower, solo-

mon's lily, waterlily, zantedeschia
CALLANT boy, customer, fellow, lad
CALLE See STREET.
CALLER cool, drive, floorman, fresh, guest, refreshing, visitant, visitor
CALLET gossip, prostitute, rail, scold, shrew, strumpet, trull, virago
CALLICARPA beauty-berry, beauty-fruit, mulberry, vervain
CALLICEBUS callithrix, hapale, jacchus, marmoset, monkey, titi
CALLID crafty, cunning
CALLIGRAPHER copyist, engrosser, penman, writer
CALLIGRAPHY chirography, handwriting, lettering, penmanship, script, writing
CALLING appellation, art, avocation, business, career, circumstances, condition, convocation, evocation, forte, function, impulse, inclination, invitation, job, line, metier, mission, name, naming, occupation, outcry, position, profession, pursuit, rank, reading, scolding, shouting, specialty, station, summoning, summons, trade, undertaking, utterance, vilification, vituperation, vocation, warning, way, work
pert. vocative
CALLIOPE asteroid, hummingbird, muse, stellula
consort apollo, oeagrus
emblem book, stylus, tablet
parent jupiter, mnemosyne
son orpheus
CALLIPOLIS *father* alcathous
CALLIRRHOE poppy mallow
husband alcmaeon, chrysaor, tros
parent achelous, scamander
son assaracus, ganymede, ilus
CALLISAURUS zebra-tailed lizard
CALLISTE artemis
CALLISTO arctos, bear, nymph
changed to bear
companion artemis
consort zeus

enemy hera
father lycaon
moon of jupiter
slayer artemis
son arcas
CALLITHRIX See CALLI-
CEBUS.
CALLITHUMP burlesque,
charivari, parade, serenade,
shivaree, uproar
CALLITRICHE star-grass,
starwort, weed
CALLITRIS black pine, camphorwood, cape cedar, sandarac
CALLOSITY callus, chestnut,
seg, sitfast, tylosis
CALLOUS adamant, anesthetic, blunt, brawny, brazen, brutalize, brutify, case-
harden(ed), cold-blood,
cold-hearted, cruel, dedo-
lent, firm, flinthearted,
hard, harden(ed), heartless,
horn(y), impassable, im-
pervious, indifferent, in-
durate(d), inflexible, insensible, insensitive, inure(d),
obdurate, obtuse, ossified,
ossify, pachydermatous,
sear(ed), solid, steel(ed),
steely, stonyhearted, strong,
stun, tenacious, thick-
skinned, torpid, tough, unfeeling, unmerciful, waukit
CALLOUSED brawny
CALLOW artless, bald,
boyish, crude, featherless,
green, immature, inexpe-
rienced, ingenuous, juvenal,
low-lying, marshy, meadow,
naive, natural, puerile, raw,
rough, rude, simple, squab,
unfledged, unformed, un-
sophisticated, untrained,
young, youthful
CALLUS callosity, callous,
corn, hardening, hardness,
induration, insensitivity,
poroma, seg, tyloma
formation porosis
CALM 3 lay 4 cool, dill,
ease, easy, even, fair, hush,
lown, lull, meek, mild,
mold, rest, soft, stay, tame
5 abate, allay, balmy, blase,
charm, level, lithe, lound,
mease, peace, poise, qualm,
quell, quiet, salve, smolt,
sober, staid, still, stoic,
strew 6 aplomb, docile, gentle, glassy, irenic, meeken,
pacify, placid, sedate, serene, settle, smooth, sof-

ten, soothe, steady, subdue
7 appease, assuage, com-
pose, dulcify, halcyon, mollify, pacific, patient, placate, quiesce, relaxed, restful, subside, unmoved 8
balanced, composed, de-
corous, doldrums, patience,
peaceful, placable, restrain,
security, serenity, suppress,
tranquil, unshaken 9 col-
lected, composure, nerve-
less, quiescent, sangfroid,
temperate, unruffled 10
motionless, nonchalant,
phlegmatic 11 anticyclone,
levelheaded, nonchalance,
selfassured, tranquility, tranquilize, undisturbed, un-
flinching 13 dispassionate,
philosophical, selfpossessed
down abate, console, cool
off, relax, repose, rest, subside
CALMATIVE anodyne,
balm, cradlesong, lullaby,
miltown, nervine, opiate,
pacifier, palliative, paregoric, placebo, sedative,
soother, sop, tranquilizer,
valium
CALMNESS apathy, ata-
raxia, ataraxy, compo-
sure, coolness, dispassion,
equanimity, impassiveness,
imperturbability, indifference, insensibility, listlessness, lull, peace(fulness),
phlegm, placidity, poise,
quiet(ness), repose, rest,
self-control, serenity, sluggishness, stillness, stoicism,
supineness, tranquility, unconcern, unfeelingness
CALNO calneh, kullani
CALOCHORTUS flower,
globe-tulip, mariposa-lily,
tulip
CALOMEL quicksilver, turpeth
CALOOL kurrajong
CALOPHYLLUM balsam,
calaba, santa maria tree
CALORIE *counter* dieter
1,000 great therm
CALORIMETER See THER-
MOMETER.
CALOTTE cap, coif, cupola,
glacier, hood, icecap, semidome, skullcap, summit,
zucchetto
CALOYER See MONK.
CALPE gibralter

CALPURNIA *husband* caesar
CALTROP bullhead, ca(u)lk,
crowfoot, crowtoe, galtrap,
guaiacum, kallstroemia,
puncture-vine, saligot, spicule, thistle, trapa, tribulus,
water-chestnut
CALUMET overture, peace-
pipe
CALUMNIATE abuse, ac-
cuse, asperse, attack, befoul, belie, belittle,
blacken, blaspheme, blot,
decry, defame, derogate,
disparage, libel, malign, revile, scold, slander, slur,
teen, traduce, vilify, vituperate
CALUMNIATOR thersites
CALUMNY animadversion,
aspersion, backbiting, black-
wash, blasphemy, defama-
tion, denigration, detraction,
lampoon, libel, misrepre-
sentation, obloquy, scandal,
slander, slur
CALVARIA sinciput, skull
CALVARY cemetery, golgotha, skull, suffering
clover medic
CALVE bear, break up, cave
in, collapse, detach, fall,
freshen, separate, splinter
CALVIN, JOHN pope of
geneva
CALVINISM predestination
CALVINIST berean, gene-
van, gomarian
CALX ashes, broken glass,
cullet, heel, lime, oxide,
residue
CALYCE *consort* poseidon
parent aeolus, enarete
son endymion
CALYDON *king* oeneus
parent aetolpus, promoe
CALYDONIAN *boar slayer*
meleager
hunter axastus, meleager
CALYPSO cytherea, nymph
captive odysseus, ulysses
home trinidad
island gozo, malta, ogygia
music goombay
CALYPTER alula, squama
CALYPTRA archegonium,
calyx, cap, epigonium,
hood, rootcap, veil
CALYX covering, culot, cup,
hull, husk, leaf, sepal(s),
shuck
division sepal
flower's perianth

part petal
-shaped caliciform
without acalycinous, acalycine
CALZADA highway, road
CAM askew, awry, catch, cog, crooked, cylinder, disc, gear, granta, knockoff, lifter, lobe, move, perverse, rollback, shape, snail, trig, trippet, twisted, wiper
lever moved by tappet
CAMAGON diospyros, mabolo
CAMAIL aventail, guard, hood, mail, mantle, mozzetta, tippet
CAMALDOLITE benedictine
CAMALIG cabin, hut, storehouse
CAMALOTE echinocloa, gynerium, hymenachne
CAMANCHACA fog, garua
CAMARA chamber, fruit, hardwood, house, lantana, nutmeg, shrub, tonka-bean
CAMARADERIE cheer, comradery, conviviality, fellowship, friendship
CAMARILLA advisers, cabal, cell, chamber, clique, coterie, council, junto, ring
CAMARIN office, room, storehouse
CAMARON crayfish, shrimp
CAMAROON *capital* yaounde
port douala
CAMASS anticlea, bear grass, biscuit root, cogswellia, lobelia, plain, prairie, quamash, zygadenus
rat pocket-gopher, thomomys
CAMBER arch, beam, bend, convexity, crossfall, curve, dock, roundup, set, sweep
CAMBERWELL *beauty* butterfly, mourning cloak
CAMBISM commerce, exchange, trade
CAMBIST banker, broker
CAMBIUM barter, exchange, juice, tissue, trade
CAMBODIA cambodge, camboja, khmer empire
cape samit
capital angkor, p(h)nompenh
city kampot, kohnieh, kracher, kratie, phompenh, pursat, rovieng, samrong, siemreap, sisophon, takeo
coin piaster, puttan, quan, riel

gulf siam
invasion point fishhook, parrot's beak
kingship devaraja
lake tonlesap
lender khien-samphan, lonnol, sihanouk
native cham, khmer
ox kouprey, kouproh
paper money riel
peak aural, pan
port kampot
range cardamom, dangrek, elephant
river bassac, mekon, porong, san, sekhong, sen, srepok, tonlesap
temple ruins angkor wat
weight mace, tael
CAMBRAI *swan* fenelon
CAMBRIA See WALES.
zone olenus
CAMBRIAN *preceding* arch(a)ean, archeozoic, azoic
CAMBRIC batiste, percale, ramie
grass ramie-plant
leaf pond-lily
CAMBRIDGE *boat races* lent
college official bedell
commencement orator prevaricator
council caput
examination little-go, tripos
flag grand union
grounds backs
pert. cantabrigian
scholarship holder by-fellow, sizar
servant gyp
student by-fellow, cantab(rigian), optime, sizar, subsizer, tab
CAMBUCA club, crook, staff
CAMBYSES *brother* smerdis
father cyrus
kingdom persia
sister atossa
son cyrus
victim apis, smerdis
CAME band, bar, caingain, comb, ribbon, rod
CAMEL, CAMEL'S animal, bactrian, beaver-brown, caisson, colt, deloul, dromedary, float, giraffe, mammal, oont, ruminant, tylopod
-back deformed, deformity
bird ostrich, struthio
corps infantry
cousin llama
disease mbori, surra

driver cameleer, drover, sarwan
female naga
fermented milk koumyss, kumiss, kumys
-foot moccasin-flower
-giraffe alticamlus
grass choenanth, sweet hay
group herd
hair cloth aba, camlet, fabric
hair garment aba
hay cymbopogon
horse mantis
insect mantis
keeper obil
kind bactrian, deloul, dromedary, hageen, hagein, mehari, protylopus
lip chiloma
litter mahmal
1-humped dromedary
pert. bactrian
prehistoric alticamelus
rider shutur, sowar
symbol of submission
thorn alhagi
2-humped bactrian
CAMELINA gold-of-pleasure, mustard
CAMELLIA flower, japonica, red, shrub, thea
CAMELOID llama, okapi
CAMELOPARD giraffe
CAMELOT newsboy, peddler, vendor, winchester
lady enid
lord arthur
magician merlin
CAMENAE antevorta, carmenta, egeria, porrima, postvorta, pronsa
CAMEO anaglyph, anaglypton, camaieu, carving, gamahe, gem, onyx, ornament, painting, phalera, relief, relievo, rilievo, sculpture
conch cassis, mollusk
cutting tool spade
encrustation sulphide
glass portland vase
material onyx, sardonyx
natural gamahe
ware jasper
CAMERA brownie, chamber, department, gobo, kodak, panoram, polaroid, shutterbox
dark obscura
enthusiast shutterbug
eye lens, retention
in privately, secretly
inventor edwin herbert land
kind astrograph, box, candid,

cinematograph, data, flash, folding, hand, iconoscope, instamatic, lucida, miniature, minicam, motion-picture, obscura, photochronograph, photomicroscope, photopitomer, photostat, pinhole, polaroid, precision, spectrograph, stereo, still, telescopic, television, tripod, verascope, x-ray
light lucida
movie akeley
panoramic cyclograph
part bellows, fader, finder, lens, shutter, viewfinder
platform dolly
revolving panoram
shot flash, snap, still
small brownie
stereoscopic verascope
tracking baker-nunn, ballistic
tube vidicon
CAMERAMAN camerist, lensman, operator, photographer, projectionist
CAMERATED arched, vascular, vaulted
CAMERIERE See WAITER.
CAMEROON *capital* yaounde
cathedral site malabo
city bafia, douala, poli, yoko
island fernando poo, nanny poo
native sara
president ahidho, ahmadou
river dja, nyong, sanaga, shari
tribe abo
CAMILLA *father* metabus
rival aeneas
servant to diana
slayer aruns
CAMILLE *hero* duval
CAMION bus, cart, dray, truck, wagon
CAMISA chemise, garment, shirt, waist
CAMISIA alba, case, covering, rochet, shirt, tunic
CAMISOLE chemise, corsetcover, jacket, jersey, negligee, waistcoat
CAMLET angora, barracan, cloak, decorate, fabric, mark, mohair, poncho, wrap
CAMMED awry, camused, crooked, cross, flat, ill-tempered, short
CAMMOCK crook, fleawort, gambrel, hockey, ragwort,

restharrow, stick, st-john's-wort, yarrow
CAMO *father* pythagoras
CAMOENS *work* lusiad
CAMOMILE anthemis, antispasmodic, arnica, bitters, calendula, disphoretic, marigold, matricaria, morgan, oxeye, starwort
CAMORRA blouse, extortion, mafia
CAMOUFLAGE anticryptic, cloak, conceal, cover, dazzle, deceive, deception, disguise, fake, falsify, hide, mask, masquerade, misrepresent, muffle, pretense, protective coloration, redherring, screen, smokescreen
CAMOUFLAGED apatetic, imitative, incognito
CAMOUFLET bomb, explosion, mine, pocket, stifler
CAMP accommodate, artificial, barrack(s), battle, bivouac, boma, casern, castle, company, contend, contest, coterie, division, douar, encampment, etape, exaggerated, expedition, extravagant, faction, fight, gossip, group, horde, hut(ment), inappropriate, jungle, la(a)ger, leaguer, lodge, mahalla, maple grove, palanka, pitch, post, quarters, rough it, scold, settle, shelter, siege, sleep out, stop, tabor, tent, war, wrangle, zare(e)ba
cooking pan billycan
david shangri-la
earth ridge rideau
enclosed carre
equipment tentage
fever typhus
flux dysentery
follower bildar, girl, gudget, prostitute, sutler, sympathizer, tramp
guard askar(i)
hobo jungle
it up display, flaunt, show off
lumber chantier
master colonel
on the trail of follow
pert. castral, castrensian
pot billy, dixy
protected boma, laager
provisioner sutler
recruit's bootcamp, training
robber jay

root yellow avens
royal army, host
CAMPA *indian* anda, andi, anti
CAMPAGNA campaign, champaign, plain
CAMPAGUS sandal, shoe, slipper
CAMPAIGN advocate, barnstorm, blitze, canvass, cause, competition, contest, crusade, drive, electioneer, espouse, expedition, fight, jehad, jihad, journey, operation, organization, plain, plan, politick, prop-stop, service, solicit(ation), solitaire, stillhung, stump, warfare, whistlestop, whoop
trail hustings, mashed potato circuit
CAMPAIGNER candidate, electioneer, muckraker, orator, politician, politico, runner, soapboxer, stumpster, whistle-stopper
CAMPANA bell, gutta
CAMPANERO arapunga, bellbird, cotinga, cotingid, shrike, wood-thrush
CAMPANILE belfry, belltower, carillon, clocher, steeple
CAMPANILLA allamanda, floripondio, ipomoea, morning-glory
CAMPANULA bellflower, bellwort, bluebell, bluebottle, canterbury bell, daffodil, harebell, rampion
CAMPASPE *lover* alexander, apelles
CAMPE *prisoner* tartarus
CAMPEADOR cid, guy de bivar
CAMPEPHILUS ivorybill, woodpecker
CAMPER ape, gossip, talker, wouwou, wrangler
CAMPESINO countryman, farmer, peasant, rustic
CAMPESTRAL agrarian
CAMPHOR alant, apiol, asarone, borneol, disphoretic, ketone, methol, pyrotechnic, racemic, remedy, sedative, stimulant
anise anethole
ball moth ball, naphalene
levo pyrethrin
source camphane, feverfew, tansy
tree cinnamomum, kadur, kapor, kapur, laurel

weed ambrosia, blue-curls, herb, ragweed, vinegarweed
CAMPHORWOOD black-pine, callitris
CAMPION bullrattle, caryophyllus, cowbell, greek rose, herb, lychnis, plant, robin, silene, thunderflower
red billy-button, burdock, catchfly, geranium, scabious
CAMPLE fight, scold, wrangle
CAMPO field, grassland, piazza, plain(s), square
pea pride-of-california
santo cemetery, graveyard, holy field
CAMPUS academia, arena, college, confine, field, gate, grounds, punish, quad, terrace, university, yard
fad pantyraid, streaking
martius arena, field of mars
CAMPY affected, artificial, banal, bizarre, conspicuous, eccentric, excessive, extravagant, mannered, off-color, outlandish, theatrical, weird
CAMSHACH crooked, cross, distorted, ill-tempered, perverse
CAMSTEARY perverse, refractory, stubborn, willful
CAMUS concave, flat, pugnosed, short
albert, novel the plague, the rebel, the stranger
CAN ability, able, bathroom, biffy, billy, bucket, buttocks, caddy, canister, cannikin, capable, cleverness, conserve, container, could, cup, cylinder, depth charge, destroyer, discharge, dismiss, eshin, fire, give up, jail, jar, jug, know(how), knowledge, may, mow, mun, oiler, package, pail, pot, preserve, prison, receptacle, sack, skill, stop, tankard, tin, understand, vessel, weight
bulged flipper, swell
defective springer
garbage dustbin
it don't, silence, stop
perforated leaker
tin destroyer
CANA bamboo, bambusa, cassia, drumstick-tree, puddingpipe, uva-grass
CANAAN heaven, israel, land of promise, palestine, paradise, utopia

army commander sisera
city adullam, gezer, hazor, lachish
conqueror deborah
enemy barac, barak, deborah
father ham
giant race anak
people amorite, arkite, arvadite, girgasite, gizrite, hamathite, hivite, jebusite, sinite
son heth, sidon
CANABA barrack, hut
CANACE *brother* macareus
lover poseidon
offspring aloeus, triopas
parent aeolus, enarete
CANADA balm of gilead, brook, canyon, elecampane, glen, herb, jerusalem artichoke, populus, tree, valley, waterway
airport gander
asphalt albertite
author mcluhan, service
ballerina hayden
balsam turpentine
battlefield plains of abraham
bay fundy, georgian, griper, hecla, hudson, james, minas basin, ungava
blueberry sourtop
boat bat(t)eau, bun
buffalo berry shepherdia
cabin berth abulk
cake athabaska, athapaska
canal soo, welland, wellington
cap tuque
cape canso
capital ottawa
catamaran auntsary
cattle pen corral
cheese cheddar
city banff, calgary, charlottetown, dawson, edmonton, fredericton, guelph, halifax, hamilton, hull, kingston, laval, london, moncton, montreal, moose jaw, nanaimo, niagara falls, oshawa, ottawa, peterborough, port arthur, prince albert, prince george, quebec, regina, sarnia, saskatoon, sherbrooke, st catherine's stratford, sudbury, toronto, val d'or, vancouver, victoria, welland, windsor, winnipeg
club civitan
coin dollar
college simon fraser
conductor pelletier

court decree arret
crookneck cucurbita, cushaw
district franklin, keewatin, mackenzie
emblem maple leaf
expellee cajun
explorer cartier
falls horseshoe, niagara
fern california gold
fir balsam
first settlement annapolis royal, port royal
fish charr, trout
fleabane horseweed
football rouge
free grant district muskoka
french colony acadia, acadie
fur company man voyageur
gannet margot
geologist dawson
goose blackie, brant, bustard, honker, hutchin's, outarde, white-cheeked
governor alexander, buchan, byng, frontenac, massey, vanier
grape isabella
grouse spruce-partridge
halfbreed boisbrule
herb elkclover, elkgrass
hillside coteau
humorist leacock
indian 3 aht, han 4 cree, dene, hare, moka, nass, riel, taku 5 haida, hares, huron, kaska, niska, sarsi, sioux, slave, stalo, tinne 6 abnaki, atsina, babine, beaver, dogrib, haisla, lassik, micmac, nahane, nahany, nootka, ojibwa, oneida, ottawa, piegan, salish, sarcee, sekane, sekani, sokoki, tinneh 7 abitibi, beothuk, carrier, gitksan, goasila, kaigani, khotana, koyukon, lilooet, nanaimo, naskapi, sanetch, shuswap, siksika, songish, tahitan, tahltan, tlingit, tuchone 8 abittibi, algonkin, bearlake, chippewa, chisedic, coeichan, cowichon, heiltsuk, kimsquit, kwakiuti, kwakiutl, malecite, okanagan, salteaux, thompson, tsattine 9 algonquin, athabasca, chilcotin, chipewyan, hochelaga, semiahmoo, squawmish, tsimshian 10 athabascan, bellacoola, montagnais, tionontati 11 assiniboine, caughnawaga, yellowknife 12 passamaquoddy

indian game bagataway
inland sea hudson bay
island anticosti, baffin, banks, bathurst, belcher, breton, bylot, campobello, coats, devon, grand, magdalen, manan, manitoulin, mansel, parry, read, sable, southampton, vancouver, victoria
island group bathurst, belcher, magdalen, parry
jay campbird, camprobber, meatbird, moosebird, whisky-jack
judas tree cercis, red bud
lake abitibi, athabaska, bear, cree, dubawnt, garry, gras, great slave, kootenay, louise, manitoba, mistassini, nipigon, nipissing, okanagan, rainy, reindeer, seul, simcoe, slave, st john, testlin, winnepegosis, winnipeg
land measure arpent, roture
lark alouette
lyme grass wild rye
lynx carcajou, loup-cervier, lucivee, pishu
maritime province new brunswick, nova scotia, prince edward island
mayfair bead-ruby, lily
measure arpent, chainon, minot, perch, point, ton
monseed menispermum, parilla
national park acadia, banff, elk island, glacier, jasper, kootenay, laurentian, prince albert, revelstoke, waterton lakes, wood buffalo, yoho
native canuck
novelist callaghan, connor, costain, morley, parker, roberts
official reeve
painter pellan
pass chilkoot
pea vetch
peak logan, robson, royal, st elias, tremblant
penalty, legal dedid, dedit
peninsula botthia, gaspe, labrador, melville
physician banting, osler
pianist gould
pioneer sourdough
plain barren-lands
plum cheney
poet carman, drummond, roberts
policeman mountie
pondweed waterweed

poplar liard
porcupine cawquaw, urson
port churchill, hamilton, quebec, st johns, victoria
potato jerusalem artichoke
prime minister bennett, borden, bowell, diefenbaker, king, laurier, macdonald, mackenzie, meighen, pearson, st laurent, thompson, trudeau, tupper
prospector sourdough
province alberta, british columbia, manitoba, new brunswick, newfoundland, nova scotia, ontario, prince edward island, quebec, saskatchewan, sorel, yukon
range cariboo, cascade, columbia, laurentian, mackenzie, notre dame, rockies, selkirk, shickshock, skeena, stelias, stikine
reed bluejoint
region barren grounds, barren lands, ungava, yukon
resort banff, lake louise
revolutionary riel
river albany, assiniboine, athabaska, athapaska, churchill, columbia, coppermine, fraser, hay, kootenay, liard, mackenzie, nelson, nicola, ottawa, peace, peel, petawawa, red, richelieu, saguenay, skeena, slave, st john, st lawrence, st marys, thames, thelon, yukon
robin cedar-waxwing
rockies, highest peak robson
rockrose frostweed
root butterfly weed
sailor fishhead
scrubland brule
sled jumper
sleigh car(r)iole
snakeroot herb, wild ginger
soup rubaboo
squaw mahala
statesman borden, bowell, tupper
strait belle isle, cabot, dease, georgia, hecate, hudson, juan de fuca
symbol maple leaf
tea herb, wintergreen
territory yukon
thistle cirsium, cocklebur, xanthium
tundra barren grounds, barren lands
turpentine balsam
university dalhousie, mcgill, toronto, ubc

violet juneflower
warbler flycatcher, wilsonia
whiskey rye
whitefish cisco
writer mcluhan, service
yew ground-hemlock
CANADIAN canuck, jean baptiste
french pea-souper
CANAILLE canaglia, doggery, flour, hoypolloi, mob, proletariat, rabble, riffraff, shorts
CANAL acequia, aphodus, aqueduct, arterial, bayou, cano, channel, conduit, cove, cut, ditch, drain, duct, estero, estuary, firth, forebay, foss(a), furrow, graff, groove, irrigant, kennel, klong, lode, lynn, meatus, millrace, narrows, opening, pipe, prosodus, raceway, scala, shat, skipway, strait, trench, trunkway, tube, volkmann, watercourse, waterway, zanja
alimentary enteron, gut, intestine
anatomical meatus, scala
bank berme, heelpath, towpath
boat ark, barge, broadhorn, gondola
broad shat
carinal lacuna
dredger couloir
famous corinth, erie, kiel, morris, panama, soo, suez, welland
footpath towpath
irrigation acequia
of wirsung pancreatic duct
slackwater lode
worker bateauman, boatpuffer, canaller, flatboatman, hoggie, keelboatman, lockhand, navigator, navvy, poleman, steersman, sweepsman, tolltaker, towpath driver
zone See PANAMA.
CANAPE appetizer, salpicon
CANARD airplane, cheat, circulate, duck, exaggeration, fabrication, grapevine, hoak, humbug, lie, rumor, smear, story, wood-duck
CANARIUM almond, brea, dammar, elemi, resin, torchwood, tree
CANARY cayenne, dance, diamond, dicky, finch, frill, informer, jonquil, lizard,

quandary, roller, serinus, singer, songster, squeak, stool-pigeon, vidonia, weakling, wine
balm cedronella, dragon's herb
bellflower campanula, canarina
bird campanini, convict, dendroica, finch, jailbird, nasturtium, roller, serin(us)
broom cytisus, genista
bush mohua, yellowhead
food cuttlebone, seeds
forerunner serin
grass birdseed, lepidium, peppergrass, phalaris
hybrid mule
island allegranza, clara, ferro, fuerteventura, gomera, graciosa, hierro, inferno, lanzarotte, la palma, lobos, rocca, tenerif(f)e
island capital santa cruz
island city arrecife, laguna, valverde
island commune icod
island language silbo
island measure fanegada
island peak el cumbre, gran canaria, la cruz, tenerif(f)e, teyde
island port las palmas, san sebastian
island province las palmas
island shrub afernan, hare's-ear, tagasaste
island tea queensland hemp
island tribe guanche
island volcano teide, teyde
moss archil, corkir, parmelia, roccella
seed alpist
stone carnelian
tree dragon tree
vine climbing fumitory, irish ivy
wine aristippus, tenerif(f)e, vidonia
wood eucalyptus, mulberry, persea, pine, whitewood
yellow capucine, meline
CANASTA bolivia, cutthroat, mexicana, pennies from heaven, quinella, rummy, samba, tampa
play meld
term ask, base, concealed hand, force, freeze, frozen pack, prize pile, stop card
CANAVALIA awikiwiki, baybean, jackbean
CANCEL abolish, abrogate, absolve, acquit, adeem,

annul, balance, belay, blot, call off, clear, compensate for, confine, counteract, countermand, cross out, dash, deduct, deface, dele, delete, destroy, efface, eliminate, erase, expunge, extinguish, invalidate, kill, lattice, limits, mark, natural, negative, neutralize, nullify, obliterate, offset, omit, perforate, postmark, quash, recall, remit, remove, repeal, repudiate, rescind, retract, revoke, score, scratch, scrub, sponge, strike, stroke, sublate, suppres-s(ion), undo, vent, void, whitewash, wipe out, write off
CANCELER bumper, stamper
CANCELLATE divided, latticelike, netlike, reticulated
CANCELLATION cassation, deduction, extinction, moratorium, repeal, termination
CANCELLI crossbars, latticework, rails
CANCER abscess, bandage, blight, canker(sore), carcinoma, constellation, crab, crustacean, curse, eat into, equinox, evil, growth, hodgkin's disease, jonah crab, kashyapa, lymphoma, lymphosarcoma, malignancy, moon mansion, pestilence, plague, sarcoma, tumor, ulcer, wolf, zodiac sign
blood leukemia
bone multiple myeloma
cause carcinogen, nucleic acid, virus
chicken sarcoma
comb. carcin(o)
drug amygdalin, camptothecin, laetrile
gem emerald
jalap pokeberry
-like cancroid, crabby
meteor cancrid
-producing carcinogenic
skin epithelioma
star cluster beehive, manger, praesepe
stick cigarette
study oncology
treatment alveloz, chemotherapy, cobalt, gamma ray, radium
CANCERROOT beechdrop, broomrape, orobancha, squawroot

CANCERWEED premanthes, sage, salvia, white lettuce
CANCERWORT beechdrop, fluellin, kickxia, squawroot
CANCH bit, caunch(e), cut, descent, part, piece, pile, rick, rise, slice, stack
CANCHA cattleyard, enclosure
CANCION lyric, song
CANDELABRA candlestick, column, girandole, lampstand, menorah, pharos, stonewort
ornate girandole
plant stonewort
stand gueridon
tree chandelier-tree, pandanus
CANDENT glowing, heated, hot
CANDESCENT dazzling, glowing, luminescent, luminous, shining
CANDIA See CRETE.
CANDID aboveboard, artless, bluff, blunt, broad, brusque, clear, direct, downright, evendown, explicit, fair, flat-footed, forthright, frank, free-speaking, genuine, guileless, heart-to-heart, honest, honorable, illustrious, immaculate, impartial, informal, ingenuous, innocent, jannock, just, naive, open, outspoken, plain, pure, sincere, splendid, straight(forward), transparent, truthful, unbiased, unequivocal, unposed, unpretended, unreserved, upright, veracious, white
CANDIDATE also-ran, applicant, aspirant, babykisser, contestant, dark horse, favorite son, graduand, handshaker, hasbeen, hopeful, jobseeker, lame duck, nominee, office seeker, petitioner, politician, proposant, prospect, requestor, ringleader, running mate, seeker, stalking-horse, standard-bearer
for knighthood esquire
list ticket
unlisted write-in
CANDIDE *author* voltaire
tutor pangloss
CANDIED coated, congealed, crystallized, flattering, glace, glazed, granu-

lated, honeyed, incrusted, preserved, sugared, sweet
CANDLE bougie, cierge, dip, examine, filter, glim, light, luminary, mortar, pastil, percher, piper, planet, pricket, rushlight, serge, shamus, size, slut, sperm, suppository, tallow, taper, test, tolly, tortis, wax
box bark
cactus ocotillo
drip catcher bobeche
end doub
holder See CANDLESTICK.
imitation judas
ingredient abilla, cetin, stearin, tallow, wax
kind bayberry, cathedral, roman
larkspur delphinium, flower
light dusk, nightfall, twilight
-lighter acolyte, spill
maker chandler, tallower
melt sweal
pins game, rubberneck
plant kleinia, mullein
seller chandler
-shaped bougie
snuffer douter
square quarrier
stand torchers
store chandlery
tree ama, catalpa, myrtle, parmentiera
wax catcher bobeche
CANDLEBERRY wax myrtle
CANDLEFISH beshow, eulachon, hoolakin, odlachan, sablefish, skil(fish)
CANDLEMAS marymass
CANDLENUT aburagiri, ama, bankul, biabo, fruit, iquape, kekuna, kemipi, kukui, lama, lumbang, shrub, tree
fiber aea
CANDLESTICK bracket, bugia, candelabra, candelabrum, chandelier, chandler, crusie, dicerion, dyker, epergne, flambeau(x), girandole, jesse, lampad, lustre, menorah, mortar, paschal, pricket, sconce, spider, standard, tricerion, tricerium, trikerion
shaft baluster
CANDLEWICK cattail, flannelleaf, match, mulle(i)n, snast(e), velvet-plant, weed
charred par: shroud, snot, snuff(ing)

CANDLEWOOD amyris, cactus, cirio, coachwhip, diporidium, fouquieria, ocote pine, ocotillo, rhodeswood, tabauco
CANDOCK equisetum, nymphaea, spatterdock, water lily
CANDOR artlessness, bluffness, bluntness, brightness, brusqueness, directness, fairness, forthrightness, frankness, freedom, guilelessness, honesty, impartiality, ingenuity, integrity, kindliness, kindness, openness, plain-dealing, plain-speaking, probity, purity, sinceriy, truth(fulness), veracity, whiteness
CANDY (See also *kind,* below.) barbiturates, beefood, bonbon, brittle, cocaine, comfit, confection, congeal, conserve, crystallize, dulce, gundy, honey, incrust, preserve, solidify, stickjaw, sugar-coat, sweet(en), sweetmeat, sweets, taffy
almond marzipan
base fondant
cheap squib
chewy nougat, taffy
chocolate bonbon, non pareil
container bonbonniere
decorative dragee
hard rock, sourball
ingredient chocolate, cornsirup, cornstarch, gelatin, nuts, sugar
kind alphenig, barley, bonbon, brandy ball, brittle, butterscotch, caramel, chocolate(bar), chocolate drop, cream, crisp, divinity, dragee, dump, fondant, fudge, glace, gumdrop, halvah, honey-crisp, horehound, humbug, jujube, kiss, licorice, lollipop, lolly, lozenge, marchpane, marshmallow, marzipan, mint, nogada, nougat, panocha, pattie, peanut-brittle, penidepenochi, peppermint, praline, rock, sugar-plum, taffy, toffee, toffy, torrone, turkish delight, tutti-frutti
mixture fourre
nut brittle, praline
pecan nogada
peppermint bull's-eye
pulled sugar penide, taffy

small kiss, life-saver
sugar alphenic, caramel, sucrose
sugar coated dragee
tart acid drop, lemon drop
wafer mint
CANDYSTICK coral snake
CANDYTUFT crucifer, golddust, iberis, plant
CANDYWEED milkwort
CANE arundinaria, bamboo, beat, bejuco, birch, calamus, crab, crook, cylinder, dart, flog, gibbey, gibstaff, grass, gundy, herb, hickory, hit, jambee, kebbie, kippeen, lance, lash, liana, malacca, palm, pikestaff, pipe, plant, punish, rattan, reed, rod, scourge, sorghum, sorgo, spank staddle, staff, stem, stick, sucrose, swish, tolly, tree, tube, vine, waddy, walking staff, walking stick, wand, warp, whangee, whip, wicker
apple arbutus, strawberry tree
-bearing arundiferous, arundinaceaous, baculiferous
black japan
borer beetle, oberea
brimstone roll sulphur
cactus opuntia
cutter machete
dense growth canebrake
disease black knot, sereh
end fraze
fruit blackberry, raspberry
grass bamboo, glyceria, herb, potamogeton
killer melasma
knife machete
-like arundinaceous, arundineous
osier salix, willow
part ferrule
rat ground pig, hutia
sugar sucrose
trash bagasse
withy golden willow
CANEBREAK thicket
CANELLA barbarasco, cinnamon, dogwood, joewood, whitewood
CANELO cinnamon, cixo
CANENS *father* janus
husband picus
CANEPIN chamois, leather
CANESCENT hoary, white, whitish
CANFIELD china, demon,

fascination, klondike, pounce, solitaire
term mine, nugget, stock, tableau
CANGLE dispute, fight, quarrel, wrangle
CANHOOP ilex, winterberry
CANICULA sirius
CANID 3 cur, DOG, fox, gip, gyp, mut, pom, pug, pup, tod, toy, wap 4 alan, alco, bick, chow, dane, dieb, fist, hund, leam, lobo, lyam, lyme, mutt, peke, puli, rach, skye, tyke, wapp, wolf 5 bawty, bitch, boxer, brach, caama, caleb, canus, colly, dabuh, dhole, dingo, doggy, dumby, feist, fyste, hound, husky, hyena, kiote, lyome, masty, merle, pooch, puppy, rache, ratch, swift, vixen, zerda, zorro 6 aguara, alaunt, bandog, barbet, basset, beagle, bowwow, bratch, briard, buffer, cocker, colfox, collie, corsac, coyote, cusser, doggie, fennec, fenrip, hyaena, isgrim, jackal, kaberu, kelpie, koulan, kratim, lapdog, lucern, lycaon, mastis, messan, messet, mooner, poodle, ratter, renard, saluki, samoed, samoid, scotty, seizer, setter, shakal, sigrim, siwash, sommer, talbot, tangue, tanrec, tenrec, toller, towser, vulpes, yapper 7 bulldog, charlie, courser, griffon, harrier, mastiff, mongrel, pointer, samoyed, scottie, terrier, whippet, yapster
CANIDIA courtesan, poisoner, sorceress, witch
CANINE (See also CANID and DOG.) bitch, canis, coyote, cur, cuspid, DOG, doggish, doglike, fang, fise, fist, fox(like), foxy, hyena, jackal, laniary, pug, pup, tike, tooth, wolf(ish), wolflike
female bitch
madness rabies
tooth laniary
CANING beating, birching, rattan, wickerwork
CANIO *wife* nedda
CANISTEL eggfruit, ties
CANISTER basket, box, bullets, case, enclose, shot, solitaire

CANK cackle, gabble
CANKER abscess, blight, cancer, cancrum, catarrh, caterpillar, consume, corrode(r), corrupt(er), destroy(er), dog-rose, eat, infect, lesion, noma, rust, scab, smutch, sore, tarnish, toadstool, ulcer, verdigris, virus
black ink-disease, melanosis
lettuce consumption weed, false wintergreen
rash scarlet fever
rose corn-poppy
CANKERBERRY cornpoppy, dog rose, solanum
CANKERBIRD cedar waxwing
CANKERED corroded, crabbed, debased, depraved, envenomed, evil, fretful, gangrened, ill-tempered, infected, irascible, malignant, poisoned, rotten, rusted, tainted, ulcerated
CANKERFRET corrode, diseased
CANKERROOT cancerwort, goldthread, marsh rosemary, rumex, sorrel
CANKERWEED ragwort, rattlesnake root, senecio
CANKERWORM paleacrita, rucel
CANKERWORT dandelion
CANNA achira, antique red, arrowroot, cannach, cannot, carmine beauty, flower, goldbird, hungaria, plant, red, turmeric
-down eriophorum, sedge
edible tous-les-mois
CANNABIS bhang, charas, drug, ganja, guaza, gunja, hashish, hemp(wort), herb, marijuana, thc
cousin fig, hop, nettle
drug bhang, charas, marijuana
tops takrouri
CANNED dismissed, drunk, fired, intoxicated, preserved, recorded, reproduced
CANNEL cask tap, channel, cinnamon, coal, gutter, kennel, pipe, tap, tube, watercourse
bone clavicle, furcule
coal ampelite
CANNIBAL anthropophagite, brute, carnivorous, flesh-eater, killer, lestrigon,

maneater, omnivorous, ruffian, savage, thyestean, windigo
secret society bacchichi
victim long pig
CANNIBALISM barbarity, cruelty, endophagy, exophagy
CANNIKIN bucket, can, cup
CANNINO *prince* lucien bonaparte
CANNON (See also *kind*, below.) artillery, aspic, bagatelle, basilisk, bastard, bicorn, big bertha, bit, bomb, bone, bore, canon, carambole, carom, carronade, caster, collide, collision, crack, curl, curtal, drake, ear, firearm, gun, hoist, horsebit, howitzer, minion, mortar, moyen, ordnance, persuader, pickpocket, quill, rerebrace, roaring meg, sacre, sacri, saker, serpent, seventy-five, shaft, shank, spindle, spitfire, stinger, swing, thief, tube, vambrace
ammunition chest caisson
anti-aircraft pompom
ball ammunition, bufflehead, bullet, duck, express, gunstone, missile, pellet, pill, shot, speed(er), train
ball, human hugo zacchini
basket gabion
boss trunnion
breech end knob cascabel
breech sight hausse
butt knob grape
carriage nadrier
charge grapeshot
cleaner merkin
dummy quaker
early aspic, bombard, moyenne, robinet, saker
fire barrage
firing pin linstock
fodder infantry, soldier
handle anse
group artillery, battery, ordnance
kind aspic, culver(in), howitzer, lantaca, licorn, minnie, moyenne, oerlikon, pompom, saker, unicorn, zumbooruk
long culverin
merchant ship bow-chaser
mop merkin, swab
muzzle plug tampion
part bore, breech, cascabel, chamber, chase, frette, lin-

stock, muzzle, rimbase, trunnion
pivot trunnion
platform terreplein
plug tampion
renaissance aspic
short-barrelled curtal
shot grape
16th century bastard, culverin, lombard, veuglaire
small carronade, fowler, minion, robinet, sling, veuglaire, zumbooruk
support mike, trunnion

CANNONADE artillery, attack, barrage, batter, bombardment, boom(ing), enfilade, salvo, volley

CANNULAR, CANNULATED hollow, tubular

CANNY agreeable, astute, attractive, careful, cautious, clever, comfortable, considerable, coony, cozy, cunning, dexterous, expert, fortunate, frugal, gentle, gently, humorous, knowing, lucky, nice, occult, pawky, pleasant, pretty, prudent, quiet(ly), sagacious, sharpwitted, shrewd, skillful, sly, snug, steady, thrifty, wary, watchful, wily, wise
moment childbirth
wife midwife

CANOE almidia, almidie, baidar(ka), balangay, ballam, banca, barangay, baroto, bidar(ka), boat, bong, buckeye, bungo, canader, canka, caracoa, caracora, caracore, cascara, cockle, coracle, cunner, curiara, currane, dugout, faltboat, foldboat, horouta, kaiak, kayak, kiak, kolek, kyak, oomiak, outrigger, paddle, pahi, paopao, piragua, pirogue, pitpan, prah, prahu, prao, prau, proa, pungey, rob roy, skiff, tanee, terawa, thamakau, tonee, toup, umiak, vinta, waapa, waka, woodskin
air chamber sponson
bark birch, cascara
cedar arborvitae, thuja
dugout banca, baroto, caroto, corial, pambanmarche, piragua, pirogue
flat-decked rob roy
large bungo, pahi
outrigger banca
oystering buckeye

sailing prah, prao, prau, proa
seagoing pahi
sewing root watap(e), watapeh
skin-covered baidar(ka), bidar(ka), bidarkee, kayak, kiak, kyak
war prah(u), prao, prau, proa
wood tulip tree

CANOEIRO *indian* tupian

CANON action, adage, anthem, antiphon, axiom, belief, bible, book, cannon, canticle, canyon, catalogue, clergyman, code, commandment, composition, confession, constitution, criterion, decision, decree, dignitary, discipline, doctrine, edict, formula, fuga, fundamental, gap, gauge, gnomon, gorge, gulch, hymn, laud, law, library, list, maxim, measure, model, nodus, ordinance, prebendary, precept, principle, psalm, quitrent, regulation, rule, sacred books, sacrifice, science, screed, scriptures, song, stagiary, standard, statue, table, tenet, test, tithe, touchstone, tribute, type-size, yardstick
body chapter
consequent comes
enigmatical nodi, nodus
hood domino
resident stagiary

CANONICAL accepted, authorized, orthodox, recognized, religious
garment See VESTMENT *religious.*
hours compline, lauds, matins, nones, prime, sext, tierce, vespers
not apocryphal
official antistes
punishment degradation, excommunication, penance
sin adultery, heresy, idolatry, murder

CANONICALS See VESTMENT *religious.*

CANONIZE apotheosize, approve, beatify, consecrate, deify, ensaint, glorify, install, ordain, ratify, sanctify, sanction

CANOODLE caress, fondle, pet

CANOPUS *steersman for* menelaus

CANOPY awning, baldaccino, baldachin(o), baldaquin, baldoquin, basilica, baudekin, cecle, ceil(ing), celure, chupa, ciborium, cope, cover(ing), crown, dais, finial, firmament, gablet, heaven(s), hood, hovel, huppah, marquee, overhang, overwood, pavilion, shade, shadow, shelter, shield, sky, sparver, tester, tilt, vault
altar ciborium
bed sparrer, tester
church basilica
ecclesiastical baldachin(o), baldaquin
hearse majesty
livestock hovel
wagon tilt

CANOROUS clear, melodious, musical, sonorous

CANT 3 beg, pet, tip 4 bank, bias, cast, coax, heel, lean, list, nook, push, sale, sing, slab, song, talk, tilt, toss, turn 5 angle, argot, bevel, chant, drift, fling, frame, grade, hield, humor, idiom, lingo, lusty, merry, niche, pitch, scold, share, slang, slant, slope, speak, strip, throw, utter, whine 6 cannot, careen, corner, cutoff, divert, flitch, gossip, hearty, intone, jargon, lively, patois, patter, snivel, thrust 7 auction, deflect, dialect, incline, leaning, portion, revolve, segment, singing, slander, snuffle, wheedle 8 cheerful, gradient, pretense, singsong, vigorous 9 barbarism, hypocrisy, hypocrite, sidepiece, trade talk, vulgarism 10 intonation, pharisaism, sanctimony, vernacular, vocabulary 11 affectation, inclination, stockphrase 13 colloquialism
across tack
hook peav(e)y, peev(e)y

CANTABILE aria, flowing, melodious, songlike

CANTALA agave, century plant, maguey

CANTALOUPE cucumis, melon, muskmelon

CANTANKEROUS brabagious, cankered, contentious, contrary, crabbed, crossgrained, cursed, cussed,

grouchy, ill(natured), irascible, irritable, kickish, malicious, ornery, peevish, perverse, quarrelsome
man buzzard
CANTATA serenata, villancio
highlight aria
pastoral serenata
CANTATRICE diva, singer
CANTED aslope
CANTEEN bar, bazaar, box, cafe, cantina, chest, commissary, container, flask, post exchange, vessel
CANTER amble, aubin, beggar, buck, canterbury-gallop, caracole, frisk, gait, gallop, hypocrite, job, lark, lope, move, pace, prance, puritan, rack, ride, rogue, run, single-foot, skip, snuffler, trip, trot, vagabond, walk, whiner
CANTERBURY *archbishop* anselm, becket, cranmer, dunstan, lanfranc, lang (ton), laud, ramsey
archbishop, first augustine
bell campanula, cuckoo-flower, cup-and-saucer, milkwort
gallop aubin, canter
palm umbrella palm
saint anselm
story fable, legend, yarn
tales, author chaucer
tales inn tabard
tales knight palamon
tales pilgrim carpenter, chaucer, clerk, cook, doctor, dyer, franklin, friar, haberdasher, knight, manciple, man of law, merchant, miller, monk, nun, pardoner, ploughman, priest, prioress, reeve, sergeant of law, shipman, squire, summoner, tapicer, webbe, wife of bath, yeoman
tales prioress eglentyne
CANTHARIS blister-beetle, lyssa, lytta, spanish fly
CANTICLE anthem, antiphon, bravura, canon, cantilena, cantion, canto, cantus, canzon(e), canzonet, chant, hymn, laud, ode, poem, psalm, song of solomon, song of songs
church benedictus, magnificat, nunc dimittis, te deum, venite

CANTICO dance, party, social
CANTILENA graceful, legato, melody, song
CANTILEVER beam, bracket, cartouch(e), lookout, semibeam, truss
CANTINA bog, cafe, canteen, pocket, saloon, store, tavern
CANTING affected, false, hypocritical, pharisaical, pious, sanctimonious, snuffling, whining
CANTION canticle, charm, incantation, song
CANTIQUE NOEL *composer* adam
CANTLE bit, brighten, cheer, corner(piece), crown, divide, join, nook, piece, portion, raise, segment, slice
CANTLET fragment, part, piece, shred
CANTO air, book, canticle, division, duan, fit, melody, pace, passus, song, soprano, stanza, stave, tenor, verse
CANTON allot, angle, corner, district, divide, division, kwangchow, part, pilaster, portion, quarter, section, separate, state, subdivision, union, volost
flannel cotton, fabric, swan-skin-calico
half esquire
CANTOR baal kore, chanter, chaver, chaz(z)an, hazzan, khaver, leader, precentor, psalmist, singer, soloist, vocalist
CANTRIP charm, magic, mischief, spell, trick
CANTUS air, canticle, song
firmus plain-song
CANTY brisk, cheerful, lively, sprightly
CANUTE *consort* emma
kingdom denmark, england, norway
CANVAS ada, apron, bagging, burlap, catch, cloth, coast, drabbler, duck, entangle, fly, glut, lining, muslin, painting, pata, picture, poldavy, sailcloth, sails, scrim, soutage, tarp(aulin), tent, tewke, toile, towcloth, tuke, vandelas, vitry, wigan
artist's pata
-climber sailor, salt, tar
coarse medrinacks
conveyor apron

cover awning, tilt
-like fabric wigan
old rombowline, rumbowline
rubberized tosh
stuffed cushion
tarred coat
waterproof tarp(aulin)
CANVASBACK aythya, bullneck, cheval, diver, duck, pochard, ruddy-duck
CANVASS agitate, ballot, beat, campaign, case, castigate, comb, consider, count, criticize, debate, discuss, drum, examine, hawk, inquire, investigate, lash, peddle, poll, questionnaire, randy, rejection, repulse, review, scrutinize, scrutiny, search, seek, shock, sift, solicit(ation), still-hunt, study, survey, toss in, trounce
CANVASSER agent, poller, pollster, roadman
CANYON arroyo, cajon, canada, canon, chasm, gap, glen, gorge, gulch, ravine, valley, waterway
box cajon
live oak encina
mouth abra
small canada
wall dalle
wren catherpes mexicanus
CANZONET air, ballad, canticle, cento, lyric, madrigal, melody, poem, song
CAOBA guarea, mahogany, muskwood, swietenia
CAOUTCHOUC caucho, ceara, elaterite, gutta-percha, rubber, ule
oil source caucho, ule
CAP 3 bid, fez, HAT, how, lid, mob, taj, tam, tip, top 4 acme, bowl, caul, coif, cork, cowl, dish, dome, eton, head, hood, hure, joan, kepi, mate, nose, seal, topi 5 apron, beret, boina, busby, chief, cover, crown, curch, excel, houve, kulah, match, mutch, outdo, phano, repay, seize, shako, topee, trump 6 arrest, barrad, barret, beanie, biggin, bonnet, calpac, chullo, climax, cloche, cockup, collar, cornet, galera, helmet, jinnah, pileus, puzzle, summit, tabard, turban 7 alopeke, beretta, biretta, bycoket, calotte, calpack, camauro,

capital, captain, cerevis, closure, ferrule, forager, galerum, galerus, keffieh, overlie, perplex, pillbox, section, surpass, yamilke 8 balmoral, bearskin, biggonet, bycocket, calyptra, capeline, complete, coonskin, headgear, phrygium, skewback, skullcap, surprise, tarboosh, yarmulka, yarmulke 9 balaclava, detonator, explosive, glengarry, headpiece, souwester, yarmulkah 10 bluebonnet, cerveliere 11 braidbonnet, mortarboard, tamoshanter
and bells bauble, costume, marotte
-a-pie head to foot, throughout, utterly
band screed
bishop's hura, hure
brim visor, vizor
case bag, chest, receptacle
child's biggin, bonnet, mutch, toque
close calotte, cloche, coif, toque
cloud pileus
colonial curch
covering havelock
cylindrical chechia
ecclesiastical bar(r)et, berretta, bir(r)etta, hura, hure, galerum, lagerus, mitre, pillion
flagstaff truck
flat balmoral, barret
forked mitre
foxskin alopeke
fur bendigo, busby, shtreimel
helmet-like alopeke, phrygium
heraldic chapeau
hood-shaped coif
hunter's montera, montero
ice brae, calotte
ignition fuse, fuze
in hand humble, solicitous, sycophantic
jesters coxcomb, foolscap
knitted tam(o'shanter), thrum
material coonskin
military busby, havelock, kepi, shako
mountain scalp
muslin mutch
night biggin, mutch
part bill, brim, crown, peak, visor
percussion capsule

pert. pileate
piledriver punch
pope's camauro
root calyptra
round balmoral
seaman's blackball-cheeser
-shaped pileate
sheepskin calpac(k)
16th century byco(c)ket
skull beanie, callot, chechia, coif, houve, pileus, yarmilke, yarmulka(h), yarmulke
small beanie, dink
square mortarboard, trencher
steel cerveliere
tall busby
tassel toorie
visorless beret, biretta, cloche
warmer earlap
watch crown, dome
winged pegasus
woman's biggonet, caul, commode, joan, kell, mutch, sowback, voluper
wool balaclava, bluebonnet, boina, toque, tuque
CAPABILITY ability, capacity, conduct, potency, stroil
CAPABLE able, accomplished, adapted, adequate, amenable, apt, au fait, can, capacious, competent, comprehensive, effectual, efficacious, efficient, endowed, equal to, expert, fendy, fit(ted), good, ingenious, proficient, qualified, roomy, skillful, suited, susceptible, there, up to snuff, wide
legally capax
of inclined, liable, predisposed
of being cut sciccile, sectile
of being defended tenable
of being heard audible
of being molded plastic
of being thrown missile
of being touched tangible
of endurance tough, wiry
of extension tensile
of flying volant
of self-nourishment autotrophic
of singing cantoral
of speech articulate
of submission amenable, tractable
of suffering passible, sensitive

of two meanings amphibolous
person ball of fire, hotshot
render enable
CAPACIOUS ample, big, broad, capable, captious, commodious, comprehensive, continent, exiguous, expansive, extensive, full, generous, goodly, large, much, roomful, roomy, spacious, voluminous, wide
CAPACITATE enable, prepare, qualify, train
CAPACITOR condenser
CAPACITY ability, absorptiveness, accommodation, adequacy, agency, amplitude, aptitude, area, bent, berth, billet, brain(s), brilliance, burden, caliber, calibre, capability, capacitance, character, compass, competence, content, dimension, duty, endowment, energy, expanse, extent, faculty, fitness, flair, force, function, genius, gift, give, hollow, influence, instinct, intellect, intelligence, job, knack, knowledge, limit, maximum, measure, module, office, output, place, position, possibility, post, potential, poundage, power, qualification, readiness, relation, room, situation, size, skill, space, spread, standing, stowage, strength, susceptibility, talent, tankage, tonnage, turn, volume, wisdom
civil caput
comb. ile
special knack
unit abfarad, barrel, bushel, cask, cran, farad, gallon, kighen, kilderkin, lagen, liter, medimnus, mud, muid, orna, peck, pint, quart, ton
CAPANEUS *enemy* thebes
father bellerophon, hipponous
slayer jupiter, lightning, zeus
wife evadne
CAPARISON adorn(ment), armor, armour, bard, clothing, cover, covering, deck, dress, endowment, equip (ment), harness, minstrel, outfit, poet, singer, trap (pings), wardrobe
CAPE amice, bertha, byrrus,

cabaan, capote, cappa, chapel, cloak, collar(et), cope, dido, dolman, fanon, fichu, gape, garment, head (land), hook, huke, inverness, lambskin, leather, look, mantle, mozetta, nase, naze, neck, ness, orale, pelerine, peninsula, point, promontory, ras, sagum, salient, scaw, sealskin, sheepskin, skaw, sontag, stare, stole, tabard, talma, tang, tanjong, tippet, vandyke, wrap, writ
acute or angled point
anteater aardvark
armadillo anteater, pangolin, smutsia
ash essenhout
asparagus lattice plant
beech myrsine
buffalo bison, bubalus, syncerus, wild ox
bulb ixia, sparaxis
bullfighter's capa
cart carriage
chestnut calodendrum
clerical cope, fanon, orale
cod lily of the valley barneyclapper
cod indian nauset
cod turkey codfish
colony magistrate landdrost
colony plateau karoo
cowslip lachenalia
crocheted sontag
doctor wind
dressing toilet
dutch afrikaans
ebony euclea
elk eland
feather ahuula
forget-me-not anchusa
fox corsac
fur palatine, stole
gaullish sagum
gooseberry ground cherry, physalis, poha
gum acacia, karroo bush
hen catharacta, petrel, skua, stinker, stinkpot
holly elaeodendron
honeysuckle tecomaria
hooded almuce, amice, domino, huke, tippet
horn cape stiff
horn fever malingering
horn island diego ramirez, digger ramrees
horn native ona
hunting dog cynhyena, lycaon
jasmine gardenia

kennedy canaveral
knitted sontag
lace bertha, collaret, fichu, mantilla, visite
lancewood assagai
land head, ness, promontory, ras
large pelerine, talma
low tang
marigold dimorphotheca
may warbler dendroica
merchant supercargo
of good hope cape colony
of good hope discoverer diaz
of good hope spirit adamaster
otter aonyx
pigeon petrel, pintado
polecat muishond, zoril
pondweed aponogeton, water hawthorn
pope's fano(n), fanum, orale, phano
primrose streptocarpus
province people amafingo, amakosa, kaffir, pondo, xosa
rain capote
ruby garnet, pyrope
seal arctocephalus
sheep albatross
silk vigite
stiff cape horn
straw mino
three-cornered fichu
town bovenland
tulip blood-lily
verde capital praia
verde island fago, sal
verde native brava, serer
verde volcano fogo
weed archil, cat's-ear, roccella
woman's mantilla, pereline
CAPEADOR bullfighter, matador, toreador
CAPEK *creature* robot
play rur
CAPELINE bandage, skullcap, hat
CAPER antic, berry, bob, bound, brank, bud, caltha, capparis, capriccio, capriole, captain, caracol(e), cavort, condiment, corsair, courant, curlycue, curvet, dance, dido, escapade, falcade, fling, flisk, flounce, friscal, frisco, frisk, frivolity, frolic, gambade, gambado, gambol, gamond, hoit, hop, jet, jump, leap, marigold, monkeyshine, nip up, play, prance, prank(le),

prink, privateer, ramp, rollick, romp, sauce, shrub, skip, skit, spring, stunt, theft, tittup, trip, vagary
bud capot
genus cleome, polanisia
silly shine
spurge catepuce, tithymalus
CAPERCAILLIE cock, grouse, tetrao
courtship lak
CAPERNOITED crabbed, intoxicated, irritable, muddleheaded, peevish
CAPERNOITIE head, noddle
CAPESKIN goatskin, kid, leather
CAPHAURUS *grandfather* apollo
parent amphithemis
CAPHITE kist
CAPHTORIM cretens, philistines
CAPIBARA See CAPYBARA.
CAPILLARY blood vessel, filiform, fine, minute, slender, stringy, tube, vascular, vessel
disease telangiosis
pyrites millerite
CAPISTRATE cowled, hooded
CAPITAL 3 ace, cap, top 4 best, cash, city, fund, gold, good, head, main, rare, seat 5 asset, basie, chief, crack, crown, fatal, first, funds, great, major, means, money, muang, stake, stock, vital 6 choice, corpus, deadly, impost, letter, mortal, primal, supply, uncial, wealth 7 central, chattel, fortune, leading, literal, primary, radical, serious, weighty 8 bankroll, cabecera, cardinal, catallum, champion, chapiter, dosseret, foremost, net worth, property, superior, treasure 9 admirable, essential, excellent, financial, first rate, majuscule, ownership, paramount, principal, prominent, resources, substance, uppercase 10 courthouse, investment, metropolis, preeminent, primordial 11 fundamental, scrumptious 12 municipality, wherewithall
ancient roma
bonus dividend
city, man-made brasilia, can-

berra, islamabad, washington
heavenly amaravati
hell pandemonium
impairment deficit, depletion
inadequate shoestring
letter majuscule
levy property tax
part abacus, agoricus, antefix, astragla, bell, console, corbel, corona, cymatium, dentil, echinus, gorgerin, gutta, metope, modillion, mutule, taenia, triglyph
provide angel, back, finance, support, underwrite
punishment execution
style byzantine, corinthian, doric, gothic, greek, ionic, moorish, roman(esque), tuscan
CAPITALISM business, commercialism, free enterprise, lanocracy, mercantilism, moneyocracy, plutocracy
CAPITALIST banker, baron, billionaire, bourgeois, financialist, financier, have, investor, man of means, millionaire, moneybags, nabob, parvenu, plutocrat, richling, rich man, tycoon
CAPITAN chief, headman, hogfish
el gran gonsalvo de cordoba
CAPITATE cephaloid, enlarged, globose, headlike
CAPITATUM magnum
CAPITELLUM knop
CAPITO barbet, bird, fish
CAPITOL city hall, headquarters, statehouse, temple
hill congress
CAPITOLINE saturnian
hill church ara coeli
CAPITONIDA barbacou, barbet, barbican, barbion, honey-guide, piciformes, puffbird
CAPITULARY heading, index, member, ordinance, title
CAPITULATE abandon, agree, bow, cave, defer, relent, settle, submit, surrender, waive, yield
CAPITULATION agreement, armistice, articles, convention, document, enumeration, instrument, munich, review, settlement, statement, stipulation, submis-

sion, summary, surrender, terms, treaty
CAPITULUM anthodium, beak, blossom, body, capitellum, chapter, end, flower, head, inflorescence, knob, passage, reading, rostrum, section, tip
CAPLE horse, mare, nag, stone
CAPOCCHIA chipochia, fool, simpleton
CAPON billet-doux, castrate, cock, eunuch, rabbit, red herring, rooster
feather aquilegia, columbine, flower
grass festuca, rattail-fescue
tail valeriana
CAPORAL overseer, superintendent, tobacco
CAPOT score, slam, win
CAPOTE bonnet, bud, caper, cappo, cloak, hood, mantle, overcoat, top(per)
CAPPADOCIA *city* pteria
governor ariarathes, eumenes
king gordius
CAPPARIS burro, caper, cod, jamaica, plant
CAPPER by-bidder, corker, decoy, end, informer, sealer, steerer
CAPPY tallowy
CAPRA goat, ibex, pasang
CAPRI *cave* blue grotto
CAPRICCIO caper, caprice, fancy, freak, prank, trick
CAPRICE antic, boutade, braid, capriccio, change, conceit, crank, crotchet, escapade, fad, fancy, fit, flimflam, freak(ishness), humor(esque), idea, impulse, irrationality, kink, maggot, megrim, mood, notion, outbreak, passing fancy, perverseness, phase, prank, quip, quirk, spleen, tantrum, temper, toy, vagary, vein, whim(sey), whimsicality, whimwham
CAPRICIOUS arbitrary, captious, contrary, crotchety, dizzy, doddy, eccentric, effervescent, episodal, erratic, fanciful, fantasied, fantastic, fickle, fitful, flighty, fluky, freakish, frivolous, humorous, humorsome, inconsistent, inconstant, irregular, irresolute, kinky, kittle, maggoty, mer-

curial, moody, moonish, notional, peevish, platty, protean, skittish, uncontrolled, undisciplined, unreasonable, unrestrained, unstable, unsteady, vagarious, vagrant, variable, viewy, volatile, wanton, wayward, whimsical
CAPRICORN goat, nanny, zodiac sign
gem beryl
star within deneb
CAPRIFOLIACEA elder, honeysuckle, lonicera, rubiales, sambucus, snowberry, symphoricarpos, viburnum
CAPRIMULGID antrostomus, frogmouth, goatsucker, guacharo, nightjar, whippoorwill
CAPRIOLE caper, headdress, leap, spring
CAPRIPEDE goat, satyr
CAPRYL decanoyl, rutyl
CAPSA box, pyx, repository
CAPSELLA bursa, mustard, shepherd's-purse
CAPSICUM aji, chili, paprika, pepper
condiment tabasco
CAPSID mirid
CAPSIZE cant, careen, coup, founder, go down, heel, keel, list, overturn, purl, roll, scuttle, sink, subvert, tip, upset, upturn, wrong
CAPSTAN crab, cylinder, dandy, drum, hoist, lever, windlass
catch pawl
CAPSTONE coping, finale, lech, topstone
CAPSULE abridged, ampoule, ampule, barrow, boll, brief, cabin, cachet, cartridge, case, compact, concise, condensed, container, cover(ing), cup, cyst, detonator, encapsulate, enclose, envelope, fruit, integument, lozenge, membrane, oocyst, otocyst, outline, package, pearl, pellet, pericarp, perle, pill, pod, pyxidium, repository, scorifier, seal, seed, sheath, shell, short, silique, small, sporangium, summarized, tablet, tabloid, theca, thoche, urn, vessel, wafer
medicinal perle
CAPTAIN baas, barak, boh,

cap, caper, capitan, capo, chief(tain), commander, fluellen, foreman, governor, gurnard, headman, head-waiter, leader, lord, manager, master, naaman, officer, patroon, pilot, principal, rais, reis, ritmaster, skipper, sotnik, vip, wafter

allowance paid to primage

boat gig

cabin coach

cavalry ritmaster

edward teach black-beard, pirate

fictional kidd, nemo

-general commander-in-chief, governor, viceroy

hook's aide smee

kidd pirate

of industry capitalist, entrepreneur, head, manager, nabob, president

strict sundowner

to the host joab

CAPTION arrest, cavilling, cutline, describe, entitle, head(ing), headline, inscription, leader, left-to-right, legend, quibble, rubric, seizure, sophism, subhead, subtitle, taking, taxation, title

CAPTIOUS alluring, capacious, capricious, carping, catching, caviling, censorious, choleric, contrary, crafty, critical, cynical, entangling, entrapping, exceptive, faultfinding, fretful, hypercritical, insidious, irascible, peevish, perverse, petulant, severe, taking, techy, testy, tettish

CAPTIOUSLY tutly

CAPTIVATE allure, attract, bait, becharm, bewitch, capture, catch, charm, coax, delight, enamo(u)r, enchant, enrapture, enslave, enthrall, entrance, fascinate, infatuate, intrigue, magnetize, overtake, please, ravish, spellbind, subdue, subjugate, surprise, take, transport, win

CAPTIVATED epris(e)

CAPTIVATING catching, charming, killing, taking, winning, winsome

CAPTIVE brisies, caitiff, charmed, confined, convict, daniel, dominated, enslaved, held, imprisoned, in-

communicado, prisoner, restrained, slave, subject, sweetheart, thrall

queens solitaire

CAPTIVITY bond(age), chains, confinement, duress, imprisonment, irons, serfdom, servitude, slavery, subjection, thrall(dom)

CAPTOR catcher, taker, victor

CAPTURE acquire, apprehend, apprehension, arrest, bag, bring down, button up, captivate, captive, carry, catch, clutch, collar, cop, corral, detention, ensnare, entrap, exchange, fall, fang, fix, get, grab, grasp, hold, hook, land, lowbell, lure, nab, nail, net, obtain, occupy, piracy, prey, prize, purse, raven, realize, reduce, secure, seize, seizure, settle, sew up, snare, snip, subdue, swoop, take(possession), trap, tree, undernim, win(ning)

backgammon hit

birds toodle

trout tickle

CAPUCHIN cay, cebus, cepid, cloak, franciscan, garment, monk, monkey, pigeon, sai, sajou, sapajou, weeper

CAPUCINE color, flower, nasturtium, trapaeolum, yellow

CAPULET *daughter* juliet

nephew tybalt

servant gregory, sampson

CAPULIN cereza, chaparral, condalia, plant

CAPUT chapter, citizen, council, crown, division, doomed, fallen, felled, finished, head, legal status, paragraph, protuberance, section, top(pled)

mortuum death's-head, skull

mundi roma, rome

CAPYBARA capibara, capivara, carpincho, cavy, guinea pig, hog, hydrochoerus, rodent

CAPYS *companion* aeneas

father assaracus

grandson aeneas

son anchises

CAR (See also AUTO.) awkward, buffet, buggy, bus, cab(oose), cage, carriage, carrier, carry, cart,

chariot, coach, diner, dingey, dinghy, dipper, drag, dump, flivver, gondola, goodswagon, heap, hopper, horsecar, jeep, jigger, jingle, jitney, left-hand, machine, motor, perverse, quadriga, rath, saloon, sedan, sidecar, sinister, sleeper, smoker, trailer, tram, trolley, truck, unnatural, van, vehicle, wag(gon), wrong

altered for speed hotrod

armored tank

baggage blind

barn depot, station

cable telfer, telpher

carnival dodgem

electric telfer, telpher, trolley

empty idler

group caravan, train

hopping buzzing

jaunting sidecar

log bunk

low-wheeled hutch, truckle

monorail gyrocar

observation buggy

old adams-farwell, american, atlas, auburn, bentley, bugatti, columbia, cord, cunningham, duesenberg, edsel, essex, flanders, franklin, frontmobile, graham, harding, hollier, hupmobile, jones, jordan, kleiber, krit, marmon, maxwell, michigan, moon, nash, overland, packard, philion, pierce arrow, reo, rolls royce, stanley steamer, stutz(bearcat), thomas flyer, worldmobile

on rails tram, trolley

parent cerdo, phoroneus

police black-and-white, cruiser

price list blue book

railroad baggage, box, buffel, caboose, camboose, chair, club, coach, daycoach, diner, express, flat, freight, furniture, gondola, hopper, mail, oil, parlor, passenger, pullman, refrigerator, sleeper, tank, tourist, trolley, zulu

service demurrage

-sick nauseated

used crate, dog, klunker, sled, wreck

CARAACOA canoe, caracore, proa

CARABAO buff(alo), mango
CARABINEER carabinero, policeman, soldier
CARACAL cat, fur, gorkun, lynx, pelt, syagush
CARACARA buzzard, carancha, carancho, chimango, hawk, ibycter, milvago, polyborous
CARACOLE antic, canter, caper, career, frisk, half-turn, prance, shell, snail-flower, staircase, turn-wheel
CARACT character, charm, mark, sign, symbol
CARADOC bala, cradock
CARAFE bottle, croft, decanter, jug, vessel
CARAGUATA chaguar, guzmannia
CARAHO *indian* cayapo, tapuyan
CARAJA *indian* carayan, chambioa, javahai
CARAJURA chica
CARAMBOLA averrhoa, balimbing, blimbing, caramba, gooseberry
CARAMEL blackjack, candy
CARANCHA See CARA-CARA.
CARANGID amberfish, cavalla, pompano
CARANX blue runner, buffalo jack, cavalla, fish, jurel, ulua
CARAPA crab(wood), crappo
CARAPACE calipash, carapax, case, crust, lorica, shell, shield
CARAPATO amblyomma, gar(r)apata, tick
CARAPO eel, fasciatus, giton, gymnotus
CARAT carob bean, estimate, value, weight, worth
weight silique
CARAVAN cafila, coffle, company, conestoga wagon, convey, convoy, expedition, fleet, journey, kafila, procession, safari, trailer, train, travel, trek, trip, van, vehicle, voyage, wagon
CARAVANSARY chan, choultry, hostel(ry), hotel, imaret, inn, khan, rest-house, seraglio, serai, zayat
CARAVEL beetle, boat, nina(h), pinta, vessel
CARAWAY cake, carum, carvi, carvy, cheese, cookie,

herb, seed(cake), sweetmeat, umbel
liquor akvavit, aquavit
CARBINE drago(o)n, escopet, gun, musket, rifle, sten
CARBOHYDRATE cellulose, saccharide, starch, sugar
comb. ose
kind albose, altrose, amylan, arbinose, beet sugar, cellobiose, cellulin, cellulose, dextrin(e), dextrose, erythrose, fructose, fruit-sugar, fucosan, galactose, gelose, glucide, glucose, glycogen, graminin, grape sugar, gulose, idose, inulin, lactose, levulose, lyxose, maltose, malt sugar, mannose, maple sugar, melibiose, milk sugar, pentosan, raffinose, ribose, saccharose, sorbose, starch, sucrose, tagarose, talose, trehalose, triticin, xylose
solid starch
starch-like isolichenin
CARBON black, charcoal, cliftonite, coal, coke, copy, crayon, diamond, ditto, dupe, duplicate, fuel, graphite, lead, norit, plate, remainder, replica, schungite, soot, tree, trichilia
allotrope charcoal, diamond, graphite
comb. but, carbo
compound phosgene, steroid, thiosphosgene
copy ditto, dupe, duplicate, replica, second
deposit soot
dioxide after-damp, chokedamp, dry ice
dioxide deficiency acapnia
dioxide measurer anthracometer, biometer, carbacidometer
facing blacking
fine gas-black
glowing coal
-like anthracoid
plus oxygen barboxide, carbonyl
process autotype
source graphite
tet detergent, extinguisher, solvent
CARBONADO barbecue, black diamond, boart, bort, broil, coal, gut, hack, slash
CARBONATE aerate, alkali, burn, char, charge, enliven,

fizz, gasify, oxygenate, ventilate
of calcium chalk
of iron black band
of lime cave pearl
of potash pearlash
CARBONATOR gasman
CARBORUNDUM abrasive, emery
CARBOY bottle, flagon, jug
CARBUNCLE abscess, anthrax, boil, cabochon, charbocle, garnet, jewel, london-brown, pimple, pyrope, ruby, sore
comb. anthrac(o)
zodiac sign gemini
CARBURETOR diffuser, vaporizer
part choke, float, nozzle, valve
CARCAJOU badger, cougar, glutton, lynx, wild cat, wolverine
CARCAN(ET) chain, collar, headband, necklace, ornament
CARCASS beef, body, bouk, cadaver, carrion, case, corpse, cull, dead body, frame(work), mummy, remains, skeleton, stiff, trunk
hanger for stang
pert. carrion
CARCEL jail, lamp, prison, streetlight
CARCER jail, prison, stall
CARCHAROID dogfish, euselachius, galeida, odontaspis, shark
shark blue, cub, dusky, ground, macherel, man-eater, requiem, tiger
CARCINOMA See CANCER.
CARD, CARDS (See also particular cards: ACE, JACK, JOKER, etc.) 3 ace, kem, map, mix, pam, ten, tum, wag 4 club, comb, dame, hand, jack, king, list, menu, miss, move, plan, play, scat, skat, stir, trey 5 asset, balop, basto, blank, blind, bower, brush, carte, chart, clown, cutup, deuce, dress, enter, fiche, heart, joker, knave, loser, menel, mines, paper, pedro, plate, queen, spade, stamp, stiff, stock, talon, taroc, tarot, tease, trick, widow 6 agenda, amuser, bender, cartel, datary, domino,

filler, karten, knight, ladons, mingle, naipes, oddity, postal, ticket, towser 7 bragger, brisque, diamond, laysuit, nuggets, pidgeon, program, tarocco, torture 8 bookmark, greeting, handicap, schedule, squeezer, stripper 9 advantage, character, eccentric, indicator 10 adulterate, attraction, fehlkarten, invitation, pasteboard 11 disentangle, entertainer 13 communication 14 correspondence, identification
aviator's carnet
best ace, command, soda
calling carte de visite
cheat harry
club coffee-house, oak
combination build, flush, set, spread, straight
compass fly, rose
dead sleeper
discarded crib
dominoes fantan
drawing blowoff
face jack, king, knave, queen
faro soda
fortune-telling tarot
4 cater, quatre
4th case
game 3 loo, pam 4 also, faro, hock, jass, keno, nada, rook, ruff, scat, skat, slam, snap, solo, spin, vint, vole 5 agnes, bange, beast, bingo, chico, cinch, comet, craps, crimp, decoy, gilet, monte, omber, ombre, passe, pedro, pique, pitch, poker, rummy, stops, stuss, tarok, tarot, twoup, waist, whist 6 acesup, belote, boston, brains, bridge, casino, chemmy, commit, ecarte, elfern, elgato, euchre, flinch, hearts, loadum, masset, pokeno, quinze, reddog, rounce, smudge, trumps 7 angehen, auction, authors, belotte, bezique, binocle, boneace, canasta, cayenne, chicago, cooncan, fanfare, havanna, oldmaid, sevenup, sizette, sprypal 8 allfives, allfours, baccarat, baseball, bassetta, binochle, briscala, canfield, commerce, contract, cribbage, ginrummy, handicap, klondike, michigan, napoleon, penchant, pinochle, seisillo, tresillo,

videruff 9 accordion, arlington, bierspiel, blackjack, cinqcents, dutchbank, lanterloo, newmarket, schafkopf, solitaire, spoilfive, two-two-two, vingt-et-un 10 angelbeast, klaberjass, lansquenet, sheepshead, venderruff 11 blindhookey, chemin de fer, everlasting, funfzehnern, russian-bank, speculation 12 ablewhackets, accomodezmoi, ace-deuce-jack, calabrasella, carombolette 13 beat-the-dealer, concentration 14 earl-of-coventry 15 banker-and-broker 17 alexander-the-great
game bid blucher, boston, command, contract, cue, degend, demand, denial, frage, frog, jump, misere, nullo, schmeiss, shift, shutout, slam, smudge, solo, support
game, child's birkie, old maid, pounce, slapjack
game, gambling baccarat
game, old brag, comet, commit, ecarte, gilet, hoc, hombre, loo, omber, ombre, pam, penneech, penneeck, primero, reversi, riversi, ruff, trump, whist, wipperginny
game score pic
game term 3 bid, cat, cut, dry, pet, pie, run, say, set 4 book, buck, bust, byme, card, cash, clip, coup, deal, deck, down, draw, drib, duke, edge, fill, fish, fold, gaff, game, hand, laps, lead, meld, null, pass, push, rank, shed, show, solo, suit, void, vole 5 blaze, blind, blitz, bonus, bunch, catch, check, clear, color, count, cover, crack, elder, entry, fille, flash, flush, force, harry, honor, kitty, nullo, opera, point, raise, regle, remis, score, serve, smear, table, tally, trump, widow 6 bonair, boodle, borrow, boston, breaks, brelan, bruler, bunche, casing, chelem, couper, dealer, duffer, equals, kibitz, misere, misery, redeal, renege, tenace, tricon 7 captain, command, condone, counter, demblee, discard,

fuzzing, gimmick, laydown, milking, misdeal, oneeyes, palooka, partner, reentry, renvier, shuffle, shutout, squeeze, stopper, support 8 colddeck, crimping, facecard, forehand, kibitzer, maldonne, notation, opponent, primiera, proposal, rentrant, retourne, rotation, sequence, skinning, straight 9 breakeven, cutthroat, doubleton, establish, falsecard, fourflush, promotion, singleton, underplay 10 boobyprize, followsuit, quicktrick 13 coffeehousing
game, 2-handed jass
group baraja, blaetter, deck, hand, kartenspiel, pack, stack
hand flush
hand, poor bust, milkbottle
high ace, honor
holder member
holding tenace, triplet
last in box hack(elty)
layout tableau
low guard
marked stamp
number pip, spot
player right of dealer pone
playing ace, basto, deuce, jack, joker, king, knave, pam, queen
playing, old pam, taroc(c)o, tarot
postal cover
ranking ace, facecard, trump
rules author culbertson, goren, hoyle, sheinwold
run sequence
shark crossroader
slam vole
spare hand cat, pot, widow
spot pip
stacked cold deck
stock talon
suit actor, bastos, braun, carreau, churchmen, circle, clubs, coeur, color, couleur, cracks, craks, crowns, diamonds, dots, eagles, eckern, eckstein, eicheln, espadas, farbe, farmers, hearts, merchants, palo, royals, soldiers, spades
table basset
thistle teasel
3 trey
3 face gleek
3 in sequence fourchette, tierce

3 of a kind pairal, tricon, trio, triplet
trump pam
2 deuce
up one's sleeve advantage, reserve, surprise
uppermost soda
wild bug, comet, crazy, freak, joker
wool comb, rove, tease, toom, tum
CARDAMINE barbarea, (bitter) (water) (winter) cress, herb
CARDAMOM knobwood
CARDBOARD blank, bogus, bristol, pall, papiermache, tagboard
box carton
CARDED adulterated, doctored, mixed
CARDER gamester, teaser, tozer, tummer
bee anthidium
CARDIAC tonic, visceral
cycle heartbeat
neurosis soldier's-heart
CARDIACEAN bivale cardium, cockle
CARDIALGIA flatulence, heartburn
CARDIGAN corgi, fabric, jacket, sweater, wampus
CARDINAL alefnull, alefzero, alepha, alephnull, azalea, basal, basic, bird, bouquet de flore, campeius, capital, central, chief, churchman, cleric, cloak, datary, ecclesiastic, essential, fish, fundamental, grosbeak, important, indispensable, key, kurume, leading, main, master, minerva, necessary, number, paramount, pre-eminent, prince, principal, radical, red, requisite, rhododendron, snow, superior, underlying, vital
assembly college
bird grosbeak, redbird, redlegs, redshauk
blue herb lobilia
cap berrettino, galero, zuchetto
cape mozzetta
chairman camerlengo
ending eth
fish agonida, alfoncino, apogon, fucinita, mullet
flower bird of paradise, lobelia, oswego tea
genus richmondena

notification biglietto
number centillion, potency, power
office dataria, hat
points cardo, east, four directions, maximum, minimum, nadir, north, optimum, south, west, zenith
rank hat
sauce veloute
scullcap zucchetto
sign aries, cancer, capricorn, libra
smallest transfinite alephnull
symbol red hat, scarlet hat
title eminence
vestment capa, magna, red babat, scarlet hat
virtues charity, faith, fortitude, hope, justice, prudence, temperance
woolsey little boy blue, little tom tucker
CARDINALATE purple
CARDIOID cordate, cordiform, heart-like, heart-shaped
CARDIUM See CARDIACEAN.
CARDO hinge, joint, turning point
santo argemone, poppy
CARDON cactus, cereus, pachycereus, trichocereus
CARDOON cynara, vegetable
CARDSHARP cheat, gambler, gamester, greek, sharper, spieler, swindler, tramposo
CARDUACEAE aster, boltonia, centaurea, chrysanthemum, compositae, coreopsis, eupatorium, fleabane, goldenrod, helianthus, senecio, solidago, thistle, vernonia
CARDUELIS canary, crossbill, finch, goldfinch, siskin
CARE *3 how 4* cark, coin, cure, fash, fear, feel, fret, heed, howe, keep, kepe, love, mind, reck, tend, tent, wear, wish, yeme *5* aegis, chore, grief, guard, nurse, pains, rowan, sorge, think, trust, vigil, worry, yearn *6* attend, burden, charge, cumber, desire, effort, esteem, foster, grieve, lament, notice, prefer, regard, sorbus, sorrow *7* anxiety, auspice, caution, cherish,

concern, culture, custody, keeping, respect, scruple, thought, trouble, tuition *8* auspices, business, consider, disquiet, distress, interest, periergy, prudence, takeheed, tendance, tendment, tutelage, vexation *9* attention, oversight, rowantree, suffering *10* affliction, assignment, management, protection, provide for, solicitude *11* inclination, mindfulness, safekeeping, supervision *12* apprehension, watchfulness *13* consideration *14* circumspection, responsibility, thoughtfulness
for attend, baby-sit, chaperon, cherish, esteem, father, foster, guard, keep an eye on, know, like, look after, love, matronize, mind, minister to, mother, nurse, nurture, provide for, reck, regard, relish, savor, see after, serve, shepherd, support, tend, ward, watch
nothing for scorn, spurn
requiring fragile, ticklish
under another's apprentice, charge, protege, ward
CARECLOTH bridal-veil
CAREEN bicker, broach, calk, cant, capsize, clean(se), gip, heave, heel, incline, keel, lean, list, lurch, overset, overturn, pitch, refit, repair, slant, slope, speed, sway, tilt, tip, turn, upset, veer, yaw
CAREER business, call(ing), charge, course, encounter, field, flow, frisk, full speed, gallop, gambol, life, lists, living, occupation, orbit, profession, progress, pursuit, race(course), road, run(ning), rush, specialty, speed, success, trade, vocation, way, work
CAREFREE at ease, blase, blithe, debonair, degage, easy, frank, happy, holiday, lighthearted, secure, unanxious
CAREFUL accurate, advertent, alert, anxious, assiduous, attentive, busy, calculating, canny, cautious, chary, choice, circumspect, close, concerned, conscientious, considerate, criti-

cal, dainty, diligent, discerning, discreet, eident, exact, eyeful, fabian, farsighted, fearful, foresighted, frugal, gingerly, grieving, guarded, heedful, hooly, judicious, leery, meticulous, mindful, mournful, narrow, noncommittal, on guard, painful, politic, provident, prudent, punctilious, punctual, regardful, regardless, safe, scrupulous, solicitous, sorrowful, studious, tenty, thorough, thoughtful, thrifty, troubled, vigilant, wary, watchful, worried

CAREFULLY cannily, charily, choicely, gingerly, hooly, narrowly

CARELESS butterfingered, casual, cool, cursory, desultory, dropper, forgetful, haphazard, hasty, heedless, hit or miss, imprudent, impulsive, inaccurate, inadvertent, inattentive, inconsiderate, indifferent, indiscreet, languid, lash, lax, listless, loose, madcap, mindless, neglectful, negligent, offhand, overly, perfunctory, pococurante, rakish, random, rash, reckless, regardless, remiss, rumblegarie, slack, slatterly, slipshod, slipslop, sloppy, slovenly, spontaneous, supine, thoughtless, unconcerned, unconsidered, unheedful, unmindful, unstudied, unthinking, unthoughtful, untidy, unwary, yemeless
weed amaranthus, pigweed
worker botcher

CARELESSNESS incaution

CARESS bill, canoodle, cherish, chuck, cocker, coddle, cosher, cosset, cuddle, cully, dandle, daut, dawt, embrace, endearment, enfold, flatter, fondle, fondling, hug, ingle, kiss, love, neck, nuzzle, pamper, pat, pet, rub, spoon, squeeze, stroke, touch(ing)

CARETAKER attendant, curator, custodian, guardian, janitor, keeper, shammes, sham(m)us, superintendent, supervisor, warder

CARETTA loggerhead, turtle

CAREWORN cadaverous, exhausted, fagged, haggard,

harassed, jaded, pinched, scrawny, skinny, troubled, tuckered, waster

CAREX bog-carnation, boggrass, sedge

CARF notch, slit

CARFUFFLE agitation, disarrange, disorder, flurry, ruffle

CARGADOR carrier, porter, stevedore

CARGO bale, boatload, bulk, burden, cargason, carload, cartload, charge, content, freight, goods, impedimenta, jag, lading, last, load, lug, mail, merchandise, payload, portage, property, shipload, shipment, traffics, truckload, wagonload
compression estivage
discarded flotsam, jetsam, lagan, ligan
discharge strike
loader longshoreman, stevedore
ship carrier, freighter
space bottom, hold
stabilizer ballast
take on lade, load
weight burden

CARGOOSE grebe

CARIAMA chunga, seriema

CARIB(AN) *indian* akawai, aparai, apiaca, arara, arecuna, arekuna, bakairi, calinago, caribisi, chayma, cumanagoto, galibi, macusi, maquiritare, mayana, oyana, parukutu, pianokoto, porokoto, tamanaco, tao, trio, woyaway, yao, yauapery

CARIBBEAN See also WEST INDIES.
bird tody
garment jupee
gulf darien, gonaives, honduras, san blas
indian See CARIB(AN).
inlet ria
island See WEST INDIES
island.
language creole, papiamento
lizard anole, anoli
snook roba
trade wind brisa

CARIBE characine, charicinid, fish, piranha, piraya, pital, serrasalmo

CARIBOU rangifer, reindeer, stag
-eater chipewyan, tinne

CARICA *tree* jacaratia, papaya, pawpaw

CARICATURE ape, burlesque, cartoon, copy, deride, distortion, exaggeration, farce, humor, imitate, irony, lampoon(ery), libel, mimic, mock, overdo, parody, pastiche, ridicule, satire, simulate, skit, squib, takeoff, travesty
musical extravaganza
plant acanthaca, graptophyllum

CARIDEA crustaceans, decapoda, prawns, shrimp

CARIES cavity, decay, rot, saprodontia

CARILLON bells, chimes, glockenspiel, organ stop, peal, tune
keys clavecin

CARILLONNEUR bellmaster, campanist

CARINA keel

CARIOCA rumba, samba

CARIOLE carriage, cart, sleigh

CARIRIAN *indian* sabuja

CARK anxiety, burden, care, charge, harass, heed, labor, load, pains, trouble, vex, worry

CARKING anxious, burdening, burdensome, corroding, distressing, fretting, miserly, moiling, niggardly, perplexing, stingy, toiling, troubled, worrying

CARL bondman, boor, churl, fellow, hemp, laborer, lad, miser, peasant, pinchpenny, rustic, snarl, villein

CARLINE crone, hag, old woman, witch, woman

CARLOTA *husband* maximillian

CARLOVINGIAN *hero* malagigi

CARMAGNOLE jacket, revolutionist, soldier

CARME *consort* zeus

CARMELITE extern, friar, monk, teresian

CARMEN cigarette-maker, gypsy, incantation, opera, poem, song
author merimee
composer bizet
lover jose

CARMI *father* judah, reuben

CARMINATIVE anethole, asaf(o)etida, calamus, camphor, ginger, laxative, valerian

CARMINE color, crimson, dye, lake, red, scarlet, stain
beauty canna

CARNAGE barbarity, battue, bloodshed, butchery, carcasses, destruction, flesh, manslaughter, massacre, murder, pogrom, slaughter, strage
place of shambles

CARNAL actual, animal(istic), beastlike, beastly, bestial, bloodthirsty, bodily, brutal, brute, brutish, coarse, concupiscent, consaguineous, corporeal, crow, earthly, erotic, flesh-eating, fleshly, gross, human, lascivious, lecherous, lewd, libidinous, lustful, material, mundane, natural, pandemic, physical, profane, secular, sensual, sensuous, sexual, somatic, swinish, temporal, theroid, unregenerate, voluptuous, vulgar, wanton, wordly

CARNALITY the beast, the old adam

CARNARIA carnivore, chiroptera, insectivore

CARNATE See INCARNATE.

CARNATION bizarre, caryophyllus, daybreak, dianthus, flake, flesh, flower, gillyflower, grenadine, indy, jack, malmaison, pickeral, picotee, pink, self
grass carex

CARNAUB caranda(y), copernica, wax-palm

CARNELIAN canary-stone, chalcedony, copper-red, sard
bead arango

CARNEUS apollo

CARN(E)Y cajole, wheedle

CARNIFEX executioner, hangman

CARNIVAL apokrea, apokreos, canvas, carny, fair, fasching, fastnacht, feasting, festival, fete, mardi gras, masquerade, merry-making, midway, revelry, show, shrovetide
lace reticella
last days jour gras
performer geek
ride chute the chute, dodg-em, roller coaster

speech spiel
water aquacade

CARNIVORE arctoid, badger, bear, cacomistle, cat, civet, coon, cougar, dasyure, dog, ermine, felid, feline, ferret, fisher, foussa, fox, genet(te), glutton, hyena, ichneumon, jackal, jaguar, leopard, lion, lynx, marten, meateater, meerkat, mink, mongoose, ocelot, opossum, otter, panda, pekan, polecat, possum, predacean, puma, raccoon, ratel, sable, sarcophile, seal, serval, stoat, tasmanian devil, tiger, tigress, tuatora, ursus, weasel, wolf, zoophagan
arboreal marten
musteline grison

CARNUS *slayers* heraclidae

CARNWENHA *dagger of* king arthur

CAROB algar(r)oba, bignonia, carat, ceratonia, cybistax, husk, jacaranda, locust-pod, st-john's-bread, tree

CAROL aguinaldo, alcove, ballad, bay, carrell, celebrate, chant, circle, compartment, croon, cubicle, dance, ditty, embrasure, enclosure, harmonize, hymn, lay, madrigal, niche, noel, nook, oriel seat, praise, recess, rejoice, ring dance, seat, sing, song, study, trill, warble, wassail, yodel
joyce, pseudonym oates
singer wait

CAROLINA allspice, calycanthus, strawberry shrub
ash fraxinus
bean lima
beechdrops sweet pinesap
catchfly silene, wild pink
chinaroot greenbrier, smilax
grasshopper dissosteira
junco finch
parakeet conuropsis
pink dianthus, silene
poplar balsam, cottonwood
rail sora
rosebay rhododendron, shrub
water shield fanwort
woodbine jasmine, jessamine

CAROLINE *island* hall, oroluk, palau, palu, peleliu, peleu, ponape, pulap, truk, uap, woleai, yap

island town garusuun, koror, lot, malakal, mutok, nip, ponape, runu, tomil

CAROLINGIAN karling

CAROM billiard, bounce, cannon, carambole, collide, collision, glance, rebound, ricochet, shot, strike

CAROUSAL banquet, bender, binge, birle, bouse, debauch, drinking-bout, feast, festival, frolic, gell, jamboree, lark, orgy, randy, revel(ry), riot, romp, shindy, splore, spree, tear, toot, wassail

CAROUSE bat, bender, birle, booze, bouse, bowse, branigan, brawl, carousal, courant, cupful, debauch, dissipate, draft, drain, draught, drink, drinking(bout)(match), go on a spree, hell, jollify, liquor, paint the town red, party, play, quaff, randy, rant, revel, roister, rouse, spree, squabble, tear, toast, toot, wassail

CAROUSEL merry-go-round, roundabout, torator, tournament, whirlabout, whirligig
inspiration lilliom

CAROUSER alcoholic, bacchanal(ian), barfly, bibber, boozer, bouser, dipsomaniac, drunkard, fuddler, guzzler, inebriate, lovepot, oenophilist, player, reveler, soaker, sot, swigger, swiller, tippler, toper, tosspot, tun, wassailer, winebibber, wino

CARP bite, cavil, censor, censure, chatter, chub, complain, criticize, cyprinid, cyprinus, dace, discourse, drum, find fault, fish, gibel, goldfish, grumble, koi, loach, nag, nibble, objurgate, orf, pan, pinch, prate, quibble, quillback, recite, reproach, roud, rud(d), say, scold, sea bream, sing, snag, speak, talk, tell, yerk
comb. endo
cousin gace
crucian bibel
lake drum
-like fish ide
louse argulus, branchiuria
pert. cyprinoid
sucker buffalo fish, car-

poides, catostomid, quill-back
CARPAL actinost
CARPATHIAN *gorge* iron gate
pass moravian gate
peak gerlachovka
range tatra
river san
wizard proteus
CARPEL achenium, carpid, carpophyll, coccu, leaf, megasporophyll, mericarp, pistil
mass core, sorema
CARPENTER ant, artificer, bee, builder, cabinetmaker, constructor, fitter, framer, houser, howsour, idler, indenter, joiner, lohar, pitwright, squareman, tectonic, timberer, woodman, woodworker, workman, wright
ant camponotus
bee xylocopa
bird woodpecker
brace knee
comb. tecto
fictional adam bede
fish hammerhead
grass yarrow
herb prunella, selfheal
joint miter
machine lathe, planer, shaper
moth goat moth, prinoxysus
patron saint joseph
pattern strickle, template
piece tenon
pin dowel
ship's chips
square figwort, scrophylaria
tool adz(e), auger, awl, axe, axhammer, backsaw, bit, bob, carlet, carriage wrench, case stake, celt, cestrum, chisel, gimlet, hammer, handsaw, hatchet, level, nail, plane, pliers, plumbbob, plumbline, plummet, punch, rule, saw, scriber, square
CARPENTERIA flower, hydrangea, shrub
CARPENTRY woodwork, wrightry
joint mitre, tenon
CARPET (See also ORIENTAL *rug*, PERSIAN *rug*.) cloth, cover(ing), dilettantish, drugget, effeminate, fabric, floor, footpace, mat, rebuke, reprimand, rug,

runner, scold, spread, tapestry, tapet(e), tapis
beetle anthrenus, attagenus, buffalo bug, dermestida
border susanee
caucasian See CAUCASIAN *carpet.*
cut pile axminster
design medallion
golden erawan, erewan
handwoven axminster
holy kiswa
industrial amritsar
kind afghan, agra, amritsar, axminster, broadloom, brussels, cashmere, caucasian, dari, derbend, dhurrie, drugget, giordes, guendje, hamadan, herat, ingrain, isfahan, ispahan, kali, karabagh, kashan, kilim, kirman, kuba, lavehr, moghan, moquette, namdah, nammad, oriental, persian, runner, sarouk, saruk, saxony, seljuk, shag, shemaka, smyrna, sumak, tapestry, tapriz, teheran, tekke, turkoman, ushak, velvet, venetian, wall-to-wall, wilton
knight dandy, sensualist
moth larentiid, trichophaga
oriental See ORIENTAL *rug.*
persian See PERSIAN *carpet.*
pileless geleem, kilim
pink catchfly, silene
prayer melas, meles
seamless broadloom
shark wobbegong
shell clam, eerock, pullet, tapes, venerid
shiraz afshar
snake brachyaspis, notechis, python
tapestry weave aubusson
wool chenille
yarn source argali
CARPETBAGGER intruder, politician, profiteer, sharp(er)
ally scalawag
CARPETWEED aizoaceae, ficoid(al), mollugo
CARPING captions, caviling, censorious, crabby, critical, faultfinding
CARPINUS beech, betula, birch, hornbeam
CARPOGONIUM ascogonium, cystocarp, procarp, sporocarp

CARPOID buffalo fish, carp sucker, catostomid
CARPOPHORUS demeter
CARPSUCKER quillback
CARPUS *father* zephyr
bone capitate, centrale, wrist
CARR bog, fen, pool
CARRACK galleon, ship
CARRAGEEN alga, killeen, moss, seaweed
CARREFOUR carfax, crossroads, crossway, junction, plaza, square
CARRIAGE (See also VEHICLE references and *kind*, below.) address, administration, air, attitude, baggage, bearing, behavior, burden, comportment, conduct, conveyance, convoy, demeanor, deportment, disport, drain, equipage, execution, fare, frame, freight, front, furrow, gait, import, load, management, manner, mien, poise, position, presence, rig, sense, significance, signification, support, transit, transportation, vehicle, vettura, voiture(ette), waftage, wagon
ammunition caisson
baby buggy, coach, gocart, perambulator, pram, stroller
closed brougham, cab, calash, caleche, clarence, hack, taxi
covered berlin, bobbyhutch, calash, calesin, carryall, dearborn, jinrikisha, landau, ricksha, stanhope
dog dalmatian
elevated lift
entrance portal, porte-cochere
4-wheeled barouche, brougham, buckboard, buggy, cariotee, carry-all, clarence, coupe, dearborn, diligence, gladstone, landau, limousine, phaeton, rockaway, stanhope, surrey, tarantas(s), victoria, whisk(e)y
handpress coffin
gearing hornbar
hood calash
house remise
kind 3 fly, gig 4 biga, cart, chay, dray, duke, ekka, hack, sado, shay, trap 5 bandy, brake, break, brett,

buggy, chair, coach, coupe, jutka, midge, sadoo, stage, sulky, tenue, tonga, wagon 6 berlin, calash, chaise, charet, charri, cisium, dennet, fiacre, gharry, gocart, hansom, kosong, landau, limber, spider, surrey, tandem, telega, troika, whisky 7 berline, britzka, caleche, calesin, cariole, caroche, carreta, carroch, carroza, chariot, coachee, concord, croydon, dogcart, dosados, droshky, growler, hackney, phaeton, poschay, ricksha, sidecar, tilbury, trolley, tumbrel, tumbril, visavis, whiskey 8 barouche, britchka, britzska, brougham, carretel, carreton, carretta, carriole, carryall, clarence, curricle, dearborn, dormeuse, rockaway, runabout, sociable, stanhope, tarantas, tournure, victoria 9 cabriolet, carroccio, carromata, charabanc, chariottee, charrette, kittereen, limousine, wagonette 10 four-in-hand, jinrikisha, postchaise, shandrydan 11 barouchette, fourwheeler, one-hoss-shay
livery remise
log drag
luxurious caroche
maker wheelwright
military limber
1-horse buggy, car(r)iole, dennet, fly, gig, jingle, shay, stanhope, sulky, trap
open britska, britz(s)ka, dogcart, dosados, jauntingcar, sociable
piece roughstring
public fly, omnibus
shaft limber, sill, thill
sleeping dormeuse
step footplate
support futchel
3-horse troika
trade See SOCIETY.
2-wheeled caleche, forecar, caretella, carret(t)a, carromata, chaise, chariot, cisium, dennet, essed, gig, hansom, jinrickishaw, kingle, shay, stanhope, sulky, tilbury, tonga, trap, volante
CARRIED abstracted, borne, giddy, puffed up, ravished, toted
away rapturous

CARRIER aircraft, aquarius, barge, barrow, basket, bearer, bheesty, bhisti, boat, boxcar, boy, bucker, busboy, cadger, car, cargador, carryall, cart(er), catalyst, chair, coach, conduit, conveyer, coolie, current, drain, dray(man), drougher, express, ferry, flattop, float, follower, freighter, ham(m)al, hod(man), jagger, kahar, machine, mailman, messenger, newsboy, omnibus, packer, pick-up, pigeon, plane, porter, raft, RAILROAD, receptacle, redcap, roller, runner, sabot, ship, sled(ge), spool, stevedore, tamen, teamster, train, transmitter, trotter, truck, van, vehicle, vessel, wagon, waterbearer, waterboy, wave, weasel, wheelbarrow
endless tailer
snail xenophora
CARRION carcass, corpse, corrupt(ion), crowbait, dead body, dogmeat, hoodie, ket, loathsome, offal, refuse, rotten(ness), vile
bettle burying sylph, necrophorus, silpha
bird scavenger
buzzard caracara, cathartida, hawk
crow blackleg, blackneb, corby, corvus, dowp, gallinazo, gercrow, hoodie, hoddy, scab, urubu, vulture
disease oroya fever
flower catbrier, greenbrier, morel, smilax, stapelia
fungus stinkhorn
CARROLL, LEWIS charles lutwidge dodgson
character alice, carpenter, cheshire cat, dormouse, duchess, humpty dumpty, jabberwock, mad hatter, march hare, mock turtle, queen of hearts, rabbit, red queen, snark, tweedledee, tweedledum, walrus, white queen
creation noncewords
illustrator john tenniel
inspiration alice liddell
snark boojum
work alice's adventures in wonderland, hunting of the snark, jabberwocky, phantasmagoria, the new

belfry, through the looking glass
CARROT aegopodium, aethusa, ammiace, anethum, angelica, angelique, anise, apium, arracach, astrantia, bupleurum, buplever, cachrys, carum, conium, daucus, drias, enticement, hilltrot, plant, root, secrete, umbel
beetle ligyrus
deadly drias
family ammiaceae
genus bupleurum, carum, cicuta, cogswellia, erigenia, cuta, cogswellia, erigenia, legu[sic]sticum, pastinaca
prepared with crecy
ridges juga
tree madeira, melanoselinum
weed ambrosia, ragweed
wild crow's-nest, hilltrot, laceflower, queen anne's lace
wood cupania
CARROTING secretage
CARROTTOP redhead
CARROUSEL merrygoround, quadrille, ride, tournament, whirligig
CARROW gambler, gamester
CARRY 3 car, fly, lug, sky, win 4 bear, bowl, cart, dray, fare, gest, haul, hump, lead, move, pack, pass, port, ride, show, sway, take, tick, tote, tump, urge, waft, wear 5 barge, bring, brook, cadge, cover, drift, ferry, fetch, geste, guide, impel, imply, offer, range, reach, scent, shift, stock, sweep, trust, weigh, yield 6 barrow, behave, bucket, convey, delate, demean, deport, derive, endure, escort, extend, follow, obtain, propel, remove, thrust, uphold 7 capture, conduct, contain, entrust, exhibit, incline, involve, portage, produce, publish, schlepp, sponsor, succeed, support, sustain, undergo, vehicle 8 continue, distance, movement, postpone, progress, transfer, transmit 9 direction, firmament, influence, penetrate, prosecute, transport 11 communicate
along drift
arms fight, serve
away abduct, ablate, asport, charm, delight, drain,

eloi(g)n, fascinate, firk, kidnap, kill, move, reave, remove, seize, steal, swarm, sway, sweep, take, tote, transport, win
by storm triumph
coals to newcastle duplicate, overdo
forward extend
off abduct, asport, fetch, hent, kidnap, kill, ravish, rifle, sack, scour, seize, shanghai, spirit, swoop, take, win
on act up, advance, agye, anger, apply, behave, caper, conduct, continue, create, cut up, direct, drive, emote, endure, ensue, farewell, follow, good bye, keep up, maintain, manage, misbehave, occupy, operate, perform, persevere, play, practice, proceed, prosecute, pursue, rampage, rant, rave, resume, run, storm, train, transact, wage, wait, war, work
oneself bear, hold
one's point convince, score, win
out accomplish, achieve, act, apply, bring about, bring off, complete, deliver, discharge, effect, enrapture, execute, fulfill, honor, meet, obey, perform, produce, put in motion, put into motion, ravish, satisfy, sustain, work out
over contango, defer, extend, persist, postpone, shelve, table, tide, transfer
sail navigate
silk race
the ball direct, operate, run
the banner campaign, lead
the day overcome, prevail, triumph, win
through complete, conclude, execute, finish, persevere, persist, produce, sustain
too far exaggerate, overdo
weight bear, influence, matter, persuade
young gestate
CARRYALL bag, buss, carriage, case, etui, pack, patrol car, purse, tote, wagon
CARRYTALE gossip, scandalmonger
CART arba, bandy, barrow, birota, bogey, bogie, butt, caddie, caddy, camion, car,

caretta, carrier, carrus, carry, chaise, convey, coop, coup, dandy, dilly, dollie, dolly, dray, dumper, gharri, gharry, gujerat, hackery, haul, jang, jigger, jinker, jinrikisha, kuruma, lead, load, lorrie, morfrey, palanquin, plough, plow, putt, rickshaw, ruth, spider, sulky, tonga, tote, trolley, truck, tumbrel, tumbril, two-wheeler, vehicle, wagon, wain
body sirpea
bullock bandy, hackery
costers troll
covered carlole, jingle
end gate, tib
farmer's gambo, morfrey, morphrey, putt
freight careton
hauling charge haulage, porterage
horse cartaver
ladder rack, zave
license caroome, caroon
load burden, cargo, fother
log bunk
lumber bummer, gill
milkman's pram
ox reckla
pert. plaustrel
racing sulky
rope wanty
rough tumbrel, tumbril
rugged bogie
strong dray
3-wheeled porter
tip coup(e)
-track plant plantago, plantain
2-pony kosong
2-wheeled bin, birota, butt, carretela, carret(t)a, dandy, gig, reckla, shay, sulky, tonga, tumbrel, tumbril
underslung float
CARTAGENA la ciudad heroica
CARTE bill (of fare), card, chart(er), diagram, map, menu
and tierce thrust
blanche blank(check), discretion, free hand, permission
du pays lay of the land, map
CARTEL agreement, bargain, card, challenge, combination, combine, compact, concordat, consortium, contract, convention, corner, covenant, deal, defy, en-

tente, enterprise, letter, merger, mise, monopoly, pact, paper, pool, ship, syndicate, treaty, trust
CARTER carman, drayman, driver, fish, harvestman, jagger, lademan, leader, marysole, teamster, trucker
CARTESIAN *curve* cardioid, limacon
devil bottle-imp
parabola trident
CARTHAGE cartago, junonia
apple pomegranate
capital caralis
citadel bozra, bursa, byrsa
city near tunis
commander asdrubal, hamilcar, hanno, mago
deity adonis, baal-hammon, bes, eshmun, tanit
destroyer scipio
dictator suffete
district mara
division taenia
emblem palm
family barca
foe cato, rome, scipio
fort goletta
founder aeneas, dido
general hannibal, hanno
god moloch, vaal
goddess tanit(h)
governor suffete
inhabitants poeni, punici
language punic
lion hannibal
magistrate suffete
of north lubeck
pert. punic
queen dido
ruler barca, dido, hannibal, hasdrubal
statesman hanno
subjects libyans, nomads
suburb megara
theologian tartulian
warrior mago
CARTHAMUS safflower
CARTHUSIAN eremite, monk
chronicler ferrari
founder st bruno
monastery certosa, pavia
noted hugh
superior prior
CARTILAGE copula, cricoid, epipubis, epiural, gristle, hypohyal, radiale, sesamoid, sternum, tarsale, tissue, turbinal
comb. chrondr(io)
cutter ecchondrotome

growth endochondroma
inflammation chondritis
malformation achondroplasia, dwarfism
ossification endostosis
ossified bone
pert. chondral, chondric
CARTILAGINOUS chondric, firm, gristly, hard, solid, tough
CARTOGRAPH chart, map, plat
CARTOGRAPHER chartist, mercator
CARTON bin, box, bull's-eye, case, casket, chest, coffer, container, crate, enclose, package, papiermache, pasteboard, shell, shot
CARTOON caricature, comic(s), comicstrip, design, drawing, epure, funnies, funny paper, picture, satire, sketch, study
CARTOONIST arno, buell, capp, caricaturist, conrad, gagman, gagster, kelly, kirby, low, nast, rea, schulz, soglow, steig
CARTOUCHE cantilever, cartridge (box), case, console, corbel, durango, escutcheon, hieroglyphic, modillion, oakwood, ornament, roll, scroll, shield, tablet
CARTRIDGE ammunition (case), bag, ball, bolt, brickbat, buck and ball, bullet, capsule, cartouch(e), case, cassette, countermissile, cylinder, handload, hull, magnum, missile, package, pick-up, projectile, rocket, shell, shot, sinker, trajectile, tube
belt bandoleer, bandolier
box cartouch(e)
buff putty
die sizer
holder clip
without bullet blank, dud
CARTULARY coucher
CARTWHEEL clogwheel, coin, dollar, handspring, overturn
CARTWHIP lash, punish
CARUCATE arable, carve, field, hide, land, plowland
⅛th bovate, oxgang, oxland
CARUNCLE comb, excrescence, gill, growth, protuberance, strophiole, wattle
CARVE alay, apportion,

behew, bit, castrate, chisel, chop, circumcise, cleave, create, cut, disjoint, divide, enchase, engrail, engrave, fashion, form, furrow, hew, incise, kirve, make, malahacky, mince, part, quinse, sculp, sculpt(ure), separate, serve, shape, shear, shred, slash, slice, slit, splay, spoil, stroke, subdivide, thwite, trench, unlace, whittle
chicken frush
goose rear
hen spoil
one's way forge ahead
peacock disfigure
plover mince
swan lift
CARVEL hymn, jellyfish
CARVER bodger, ciceleur, cropper, froster, ivorist, kirver, trencher
mixture compo
CARVING cameo, entail, glyph, intaglio, ivory, maskoid, nicking, scrive, triptych
art anaglyphy, anaglyptics
in intaglio engrail
ornamental anaglyphy, billethead, cameo, engrailing, jalee work, scrive, sculpture
pert. glyphic, glyptic
relief cameo
stone incision, intaglio
technique bori
CARYA bitternut, hickory, hicoria, juglans, pecan, pignut, shagbark, shellbark
CARYATID atlantes, canephora, pillar, telamon
male cap, telamon
part gaine
CARYATIS arthemis
CARRYCAR souari
CARYOPHYLLUS babies'-breath, campion, carnation, catchfly, chenopodiale, dianthus, gillyflower, gypsophila, jambosa, lynchnis, pink, silene
CARYOPSIS seed
CARYOPTERIS blue beard, spiraea, vervain
CAS umbrella, vanity bag
CASA See HOUSE.
CASABA melon, muskmelon, winter melon
CASABLANCA *section* anfa
CASANOVA amorist, don juan, gigolo, lothario, lover, rake, roue

CASAQUE blouse, casaquin, cassock
CASATE hide, land, plot
CASCA *victim* caesar
CASCABEL pommel(ion)
CASCADE cataract, descend, downrush, fall, firework, force, lin(n), precipitation, series, spout, vomit, waterfall
CASCADES *peak* adams, rainier
CASCARA bearberry, bearwood, bitter-bark, buckthorn, california cobbel, canoe, chittamwood, coconut husk, cranberry, holly, laxative, rhamnus, shittim, wahoo
CASCARILLA croton, goatweed, sweetwood
CASCO barge, lighter
CASE 3 bag, box, hap, pod, pot, pyx, set 4 bind, body, boot, bunk, burr, cask, cope, deed, dock, fact, form, fuse, hide, inro, pack, pair, roll, skin, suit, test, tray 5 affix, brace, brief, bulla, burse, caddy, cause, check, claim, cover, crate, event, folio, forel, frame, hussy, hutch, order, plate, press, pyxis, shell, state, strip, study, theca, trial 6 action, addict, affair, amount, barrel, binder, carton, chance, coffin, couple, forell, locket, lorica, matter, penner, petard, plight, sample, sheath, shrine, survey, tashie, valise 7 analyse, arrange, cabinet, camisia, capsule, carcass, enclose, envelop, examine, example, history, holdall, humidor, inspect, lawsuit, meaning, package, patient, problem, protect, satchel, sheathe 8 accident, allative, argument, carapace, cartouch, carryall, category, covering, exemplar, gardevin, incident, instance, knapsack, portfire, quantity, question, sickness, solander, specimen, tantalus 9 cartouche, cartridge, character, condition, container, framework, occurrence, situation, statement 10 apostrophe 11 infatuation 12 circumstance, illustration
bony carapace, shell

book-holding for(r)el
card shoe
cigar humidor
compartmented riddle
cosmetic compact
court lawsuit
divinity casuistry
document hanaper
egg ootheca, ovisac
explosive firecracker, lance, petard, shell
grammatical ablative, accusative, caritive, dative, essive, equative, ergative, factive, genitive, illative, instrumental, locative, nominative, possessive, vocative
-hardened accustomed, callous, insensitive, inveterate, obdurate, strong, tough
history anamnesis, record, story
hopeless goner, loser
in point example
jewel tye
kind bandbox, bandoleer, bin, boot, box, bunker, caisson, canister, capsula, capsule, cardcase, carton, casket, cedar chest, chest, coffer, crate, crib, etui, etwee, file, folio, hatbox, holster, hope chest, housewife, hussy, huswife, hutch, kit, letter file, pillbox, pod, portfolio, powder box, quiver, rack, satchel, scabbard, sheath, skippet, socket, tinderbox, valise, vanity, vasculum
liquor cellaret, dozen, tantalus
mummy sledge
ornamental etui, etwee
paper coffin
pistol holster
pully block
sewing hussy
shot canister, cartouche, shrapnel
small bulla, etui, etwee, inro, trous(s)e, tye
wicker barrow, hanaper, hask
CASEIN clot, legumin, protein, protoid, rennet
holey swiss cheese
CASEMATE bombshelter, enclosure
CASEMENT cavetto, covering, dormer, frame, luket, oriel, sash, scotia, window
CASEOUS cheesy, clotted
CASERNE See BARRACKS.

CASEWEED shepherd's-purse
CASEY JONES See JONES, CASEY.
CASH argent, asset(s), bonus, cache, caisse, caja, capital, cashier, change, chien, clear, clink, coin(age), currency, darby, dismiss, dough, dust, exchange, exchequer, funds, hemlock, honor, legal tender, MONEY, pay, receive, road, settlement, specie, wherewithal
account bank credit
book log
box caisse, coffer, till, treasury
in convert, take profit
keeper bursar, cashier, teller, treasurer
note melt
on delivery cod
register damper, greffier, recorder, regest, till
short of broke, hard up
CASHAW cushaw, mesquite, prosopis
CASHEW anacardium, maranon
bird curassow, pauxi, spindalis, tanager
fruit acajou, anacard(ium)
lake See AUBURN.
nut sedge
nut oil cardol
CASHIBO *indian* buninahua, carapache, puchanahua
CASHIER banker, bounce, break, bursar, cash, cashkeeper, cass, cast, checker, collector, dealer, depose, deprive, discard, discharge, dismiss, dispossess, drop, eject, eliminate, expel, fire, officer, oust, paymaster, potdar, purser, reject, reprimand, sack, teller, treasurer
CASHIERED broken, canned, degomme, fired
CASHMERE prunell, rug, ulvan, wool
shawl amlikar
CASING anacard, body, bonnet, boot, booth, boxing, bung, cachepot, case, coffin, collet, cover(ing), derma, doorframe, ephod, frame (work), gaine, hull, jacket, kishke, liner, lining, partition, pipe, plowshoe, rim, sausage cover, sheath(ing), shirting, shoe, skin, staving,

stock, thimble, trunk, volute, walls, windowframe
brain harnpan
spool calf-wheel
CASINO ballroom, cabaret, card game, country house, dance hall, game room, garden house, hall, pink, rotunda, saloon, summerhouse, ten
game callabra, papillon, scoop, scopa, scopone, trail
game term build, card, cash point, combine, last, overs, sauterelle, scoop, scopa, spades, sweep, take
CASK anker, bareca, bareka, barrel(et), barrico, boss, bowie, breaker, bulge, butt, cade, cardel, case, casque, cassette tape, container, cowl, dolium, drum, firkin, foist, fooder, fostell, hogshead, keg, kilderkin, knag, octave, package, pipe, puncheon, quardeel, rier, roundlet, rundlet, sackbut, shell, slip, stand, store, tierce, tub, tun, vat, winger, wood
brewing union
bulge bilge
contents ullage
42-gallon tierce
headpiece cant
large hogshead, puncheon, tierce
locked tantalus
maker cooper
oil rier
orifice bunghole
part bilge, bouge, chime, lag
perforated pot
rim chimb, chime, chine
small keg, knag, rundlet, stoop, stoup
stave lag
support stillage
tap can(n)el
water longer
wine barrel, boss, butt, fust, hogshead, pipe, tierce, tun, vat
CASKET acerra, bonebox, bonehouse, box, buist, case, casquet, cassette, chasse, chest, cist, coffer, coffin, confine, crate, enclose, fostell, gasket, pall, pix, pyx, reliquary, sarcophagus, shell, shrine, till, tomb, tye, wooden kimono, wooden overcoat
CASPER MILQUETOAST

s(c)hlemie(h)l, shlemihl, shmendrick

CASPIAN *language* gilaki, mazanderani, samnani, talishi, tat
port baku
region parthia
river to aras, emba, kima, kura, terek, terra, ural, volga

CASQUE cask, casket, casquetel, casquette, galea, hat, headpiece, helmet, horn

CASS annul, cashier, discharge, dismiss, quash, void

CASSABANANA curuba

CASSANDER *enemy* aeacides
son antipater
wife thessalonica

CASSANDRA alexandra, chamaedaphne, prophetess, seeress, shrub
admirer apollo
booty of agamemnon
lover apollo
parent hecuba, priam
sister helenus
slayer aegisthus, ajax, clytemnestra

CASSARE abate, annul, quash

CASSAREEP caxiri

CASSATION abrogation, annulment, cancellation, reversal, serenade

CASSAVA aipi, casiri, cazibi, juca, manihot, manioc, starch, tapioca, typyoca, yucca
juice casiri
starch arrowroot
syrup cassareep

CASSEROLE bake, cocotte, dish, marmite, mold, ragout, saucepan, terrine, tureen, tzimmes, vessel
fish king crab
shell-shaped coquille

CASSIA acapulco, caesalpinia, cinnamon, drug, drum-stick-tree, herb, kezia, laxative, lignea, mogdad coffee, ringworm-bush, senna, shrub, sicklepod, tree
leaves senna
nut cashew

CASSIDONY goldilocks, lavandula, lavender, linosyris

CASSIM *brother* ali baba

CASSIMERE zephyr

CASSINO See CASINO.

CASSIO *enemy* iago

friend othello
mistress bianca

CASSIOPEIA *consort* cepheus, zeus
daughter andromeda

CASSIS black currant, cassidida, conch, fruit, liquor, mollusk, plant, ribes, shell, syrup

CASSITERITE tinstone

CASSITES kushshu

CASSIUS *colleague* brutus
enemy antony
freedman pindarus
friend brutus, cato, lucilius, messala, titinius
messenger titinius
servant demetrius, pindaris
victim caesar

CASSOCK casaque, clergyman, coat, gown, jacket, pelisse, priest, soutane, vest, zimarra

CASSOON caisson, coffer

CASSOWARY bird, casuariid, casuarius, emu, moorup, murup, ratite
tree casuarina

CASSYTHA rhipsalis, woevine

CAST 3 add, aim, bit, hue, lot, set, sum, tap, tax, tie, tot 4 bear, beat, bent, bowl, clap, copy, dash, drop, emit, fish, form, give, help, hurl, jilt, junk, kind, lift, look, lose, mold, molt, plan, plot, pure, rate, ride, role, seek, shed, sort, spew, suit, tack, tilt, tint, tone, toss, tube, turn, type, veer, vote, warp, whip 5 allot, batch, bloom, clear, color, eject, expel, fling, found, fusil, guise, heave, image, impel, moult, pitch, place, scrap, shape, sling, slink, slope, stamp, strew, style, swarm, taste, throw, tinge, total, trace, twist, vomit, yield 6 actors, adjust, amount, aspect, assign, bestow, chance, charge, chaste, chorus, confer, course, decide, defeat, degree, design, device, devise, direct, divide, exhale, figure, funnel, fusile, glance, impost, intend, pellet, ponder, reckon, sample, scheme, search, slough, troupe 7 agarwal, arrange, bearing, cashier, company, compute, condemn, convict,

deposit, discard, dispose, fashion, fortune, incline, pattern, perform, plaster, project, scatter 8 addition, consider, contrive, distance, dressing, entangle, estimate, exuviate, forecast, partwith, polytype, quantity, specimen, sprinkle, tendency, tincture 9 broadcast, calculate, give birth, overthrow, sculpture, send forth 10 afterswarm, appearance, assistance, commitment, complexion, conjecture, distribute, embodiment, expression, impression, performers, stereotype, strabismus, trajectory 11 arrangement, contrivance, disposition, electrotype, inclination 12 conformation, construction, reproduction 14 characteristic 16 dramatis personae
about consider, plan, search, tack, try, turn
a glance look, peer, see
anchor moor, stop
aside See CAST *away.*
aspersions appeach, belittle, downgrade, malign, sklent, slur, smear
away abandon, discard, dismiss, dump, exile(d), jilt, junk, maroon, nomic, reject, scrap, shed, shipwreck(ed), squander, stranded, thrown away, waste, weigh anchor, wreck
back impede, reflect, retroject, revert
ballot vote
dice whirl
down abase, abate, abattue, abject, amort, dash, decast, deject(ed), demolish, depress, destroy, disappoint, discourage, dispirit, dump, eclipse, fell, humble, hurl, lower, melancholy, raze, ruin(ate), sad(den), sink, sunk, thring
eye strabismus
forth belch, disembogue, disgorge, emit, launch, speu, spew, vomit, warp
gloom cloud, darken, depress, sadden
-iron adamant(ine), hard(y), inflexible, rigid, solid, strong, unyielding, yetling
loose let go, release, set adrift, set free

lots cavel, gamble, speculate, venture

metal yet

of dice coup, throw

off abandon, abdicate, castaway, daff, depart, derelict, devest, discharge, dismiss, disown, ditch, doff, eliminate, estimate, free, jilt, laid aside, launch, let go, loose, mo(u)lt, put off, refuse, reject, remove, renounce, shake, shed, slough, sluff, spew, throw, toss, unmoor, untie, waive, wastements, weigh anchor

off skin desquamate, exuviate, slough

out abandon, abject, banish, discard, dismiss, egest, eject, exorcise, expel, extrude, fall out, force out, ostracize, reject, shed

out nines check, test, verify

over consider, ponder

overboard jettison

plaster cuirass

shadow adumbrate

shadow over obscure

spell bewitch, entrance, trap

the die decide, determine, settle

the parts deal out, parcel, ration

theatrical actors, company, players, troupe

up abandon, add, appear, bring up, compute, eject, erect, levy, lift, measure, reckon, reproach, spew, sum, taunt, throw up, tot(al), turn up, upbraid, vomit

CASTALIA *site* delphi, parnassus

CASTALIDES muses

CASTANA brazil nut, breadfruit, chestnut, tree

CASTANEA beech, chestnut, fagaca, shrub, tree

CASTANET crotalum, knacker, knocker, snapper, tchapan

CASTANOSPERMUM bean tree, carob, catalpa, chestnut, laburnum, tree, zebrawood

CASTAWAY abject, bum, crusoe, derelict, outcast, pariah, reject, reprobate, tramp, waif

CASTE agarwal, ahir, aroras, bais, balija, banian, bice, brahman, breed, chetty, chuhra, class(ification),

color, degree, dhanuk, division, dom, dosadh, durzee, estate, gola, grade, harijan, jati, knubi, kori, kuli, kumhar, ladha, lohana, magi, mal(i), meo, mina, order, pallar, pariah, pasi, prabhu, pulaya, race, rajbansi, rajput, rank, singh, sphere, station, status, stock, stratum, sudra, tanti, teli, vaisya, varna, vellala

agricultural meo, vaisya

artisan sonar, sudra

aryan vaishya

cowherd ahir

gardener mali

group varna

healing ambastha

high amelu, babhan, bibar, kshatriya

hindu gati, kula, shudra, sudra, varna

kingly kshatriya

labor dosadh, holeya, shudra, sudra

low bhat, bhil, dom, koli, kori, kuli, lodha, madiga, mahar, mali, panchama, pariah, teli

medical ambastha, baidya

mercantile agarwal, banian, banyan, chetty, marwari, vaisya

minor gati, kula

priestly brahman, magus

slave shudra, sudra

swineherd passi

thieves sansi

top cream, elite, four hundred

trader balija

warrior kshatriya

weaver kori

CASTELLAN battlement, fortress, governor, guardian, senator, warden

CASTER account, bottle, cannon, cloak, container, cruet, cruse, dredger, founder, horral, hurler, machine, master, muffineer, phial, pitcher, pulley, roller, stand, swivel, trolley, truckle, trundle, vessel, vial, wheel

surf squidder

CASTIGATE admonish, amerce, assail, beat, berate, canvass, censure, chasten, chastise, correct, criticize, discipline, dress down, emend, fine, flog, fustigate,

lambaste, lash, leather, punish, rail, rebuke, reprove, revise, scare, scold, score, strafe, subdue, thrash, wig

CASTIGLIONE *work* il cortegiano, the courtier

CASTILE soap

hero cid

king alfonso

northern vieja

province avila, soria

river douro, duero, ebro, esla, xucar

southern nueva

CASTILLEJA birthroot, bloody-noses, bloody-warrior, figwort, painted cup, scrophularia, trillium

CASTILLO castle, cave, fort

CASTING billet, block, bullion, bumper, button, chock, chuck, cocilage, die, font, ingot, matrix, mold, mould, pig, projection, regulus, separator, sowing, spider, tymp, vomit, warping

cavity pipe

horoscope apotelesm

iron yetling

line leader

lots sortition

mold die, matrice, matrix

place foundry

rough pig

CASTLE abode, alcazar, bastille, camp, casbah, castellar, chateau, citadel, court, donjon, earthwork, elsinore, enclose, fastness, fort(ification), fortress, hall, hideaway, home, house, keep, manor, manse, mansion, morro, palace, residence, retreat, rock, rook, schloss, starosty, stronghold, tintage, tower, udolpho, village, windsor

build dream

builder dreamer, visionary

-building absentmindedness, dreaming

chess judge, juez, rook, tour, tower

gilliflower matthiola, stock

in the air daydream, dream, fantasy, imagining, vision

of indolence solitaire

outwork bawn

part bail, bailey, ballium, bawn, donjon, drawbridge, fosse, keep, moat, portcullis, tower, turret

small castlet, chatelet, peel, tower
tower keep
wall bail(ey)
warden castellan, disdar, dizdar
CASTOR anax, antispasmodic, barkstone, bean, beaver, broadcloth, callosity, castoreum, castoriet, chestnut, cruet, fabric, hat, leather, rodent, st elmo's fire, star, truckle, trundle
and pollux dioscuri, gemini, twins
bean oil seed
bean meal fertilizer
bean poison ricin
brother pollux
gray yellow-green
horse cyllaros, harpagos
-oil plant kiki, mamona, palma christi, palmcrist, ricinus
oil plant eater eri(a)
opponent idas, lynceus
parent leda, zeus
slayer idas
CASTRATE alter, capon(ize), carve, change, cut, desex, effeminize, emasculate, eunuch, evirate, expurgate, geld, gib, glib, mutilate, neuter, pinch back, prune, saturnize, spay, sterilize, swig, trim, unman, unsex
CASTRATED cut, gibbed, unpaved
CASTRATO tenorino
CASUAL accidental, adventitious, aimless, apathetic, at home, bland, blaze, blithe, byhand, careless, cas(s)alty, cas(s)elty, casuistic, cazelty, chance(ful), chancy, contingent, cursory, desultory, drifter, easy, extemporaneous, fickle, folksy, glib, haphazard, heedless, hit-or-miss, incidental, indifferent, indiscriminate, infirm, informal, insecure, irregular, lax, leisure, natural, negligent, nonchalant, nonessential, occasional, offhand, parenthetical, pauper, precarious, random, running, shaky, slack, stray, suave, uncertain, unconcerned, undependable, unexpected, unforeseen, unpremeditated, unreliable, vagrant
CASUALS loafers, slacks

CASUALTY accident, blow, caduac, calamity, cataclysm, catastrophe, chance, contingency, death, debacle, disaster, injury, happening, hazard, loss, misadventure, misfortune, mishap, precariousness, uncertainty, victim
CASUARINA beefwood, cassowary tree, oak, toa
CASUIST jesuit
CASUISTRY fallacy, paralogism, sophistry
CAT (See also CATS, CAT'S.) ailuroidea, artictus, baudrons, carnivore, catamountain, caterpillar, catling, chessy, civet, dasyurid, felid, felis, felix, fissiped, flog, fur, game, gato, gossip, grimalkin, jazz fan, kit, kitling, kitten, kitty, lion, lynx, malkin, mawkin, mewer, miauer, miss, moggy, mouser, prostitute, purrer, puss(y), quadruped, ratter, shrew, snit, tabby, tackle, tibert, tiger, tom, tractor, tripod, vessel, vomit, whip
-and-dog contentious, destructive, inharmonious, quarrelsome, vicious
-bed centranthys, red valerian
breed abyssinian, angola, angora, archangel, burmese, cheshire, chinchilla, coon, egyptian, geoffroy's, maltese, manul, manx, margay, pallas, persian, russian, siamese, tabby, tiger, tortoiseshell, turkish
brier carrion-flower, smilax
burglar second-story man
characteristic nine lives
-chop fig marigold, flower
civet-like genet, rasse
claw acasia, una
-clover bird's foot trefoil, lotus
comb. aelur(o)
cry hiss, meow, mew(l), miaou, miau(l), purr, waul, waw, yelp, yow, yowl
ear gosmore
fancier aelurophile
family felidae
fat See MAGNATE.
fear of aelurophobia
female grimalkin, lady, queancat, wheencat
fever distemper
fit caniption, tantrum

-footed stealthy
genus felidae, felis
group clowder
ham thigh
hater aelurophobe, ailurophobe
-headed goddess bast, mut, pacht
house bagnio, brothel, mouser
killing felicide
kind alley, bay lynx, binturong, bobcat, bondar, bushcat, cacomistle, caffre, caracal, catamountain, cheetah, civet, cougar, dasyure, eyra, genet(te), hyena, jaguar, kuichua, leopard, linsang, lion, lynx, margay, ocelot, ounce, pajero, panther, pard, polecat, puma, ringtail, serval, tiger, wildcat, zibet(h)
large tawny cougar, mountain lion, panther, puma, tiger
-like feline, noiseless, sly, tigrine
-locks cotton-grass, eriophorum
-lover aelurophile, a(i)lurophile
male gib, tom
nap doze, snooze
-o-nine-tails flogger, lash, whip
paw loof
pea plant, vetch, vicia
ringtailed cacomistle
shark dogfish, scylliorhinus
silver See MICA.
skinner engineer
snake tarbophis
sound See CAT cry.
spotted genet, lynx, margay, tiger
squirrel cacomistle
symbol of deceit
thyme germander, hulwort, teucrium
tree evonymus, spindle tree
typhoid distemper
walker attid
whisker smeller, vibrissa
-whistle equisetum, horsetail, plant
wild balu, bobcat, caffre, catamountain, chaus, civet, eyra, jaguar, lion, lynx, manul, ocelot, panther, puma, serval, tiger
-witted conceited
CATACHRESIS abusion
CATACLYSM calamity, ca-

tastrophe, debacle, deluge, disaster, flood, misfortune, revolution, tragedy, upheaval

CATACOMB arenaria, cellar, cemetery, crypt, grotto, hypogeum, locule, loculus, tomb, vault
chamber cubiculum
niche arcosolium, locule, loculus
roman arenaria

CATADROMOUS seagoing

CATAFALQUE bier, platform, scaffold, tomb

CATALECTIC hemiamo, truncated

CATALEPSY cataplexia, catatony, hypnosis, hypnotism, immobility, seizure, shock, trance

CATALINETA angelfish, anisotremus, holocanthus, porkfish

CATALOG(UE) arrange, beadroll, beadrow, bibliotheca, bibliotheke, bill, book, brief, bulletin, calendar, canon, census, class(ify), didascaly, diptych, enter, enumeration, file, flier, flyer, index, inventory, invoice, leaflet, list, pamphlet, pie(book), pinax, pye(book), ragman, record, register, roll, rosary, roster, rota, schedule, table, tariff
saints' menology

CATALONIA *dance* sardana
marble brocatel(le)

CATALPA bignonia, candle tree, catawba, indian bean, paulownia, trumpet creeper

CATALUFA big eye, scad, toro

CATALYST accelerator, agent, blender, carrier, dissolution, hopcalite, organizer, ziegler
negative inhibiter

CATAMARAN auntsary, balsa, boat, float, jangada, monitor, nagger, raft, scold, trimaran, trow, vessel

CATAMITE bardash, ganymede, gunsel, ingle, ningle, pathic

CATAMITUS See GANYMEDE.

CATAMOUNT(AIN) cat, cougar, leopard, lynx, panther, puma, wildcat

CATAN See SWORD.

CATANA *invader* hiero
tyrant mamereus

CATAPHRENIA dementia

CATAPLASM dressing, pap, poultice

CATAPLEXIA See CATALEPSY.

CATAPULT alacran, ballist(a), bible, boot, bounce, bricole, crossbow, discharge, dondaine, hurl, hurtle, launch(er), mangonel, martinet, onager, pedrero, project, robinet, scorpion, shoot, sling(shot), springal, stonebow, sweep, take off, throw, thrust, torment, trabuch, trepan, warwolf
boy's beanshooter, peashooter

CATARACT cachoeira, caligo, cascade, cast, catadupe, controller, deluge, descend, downpour, downrush, fall(s), flood(gate), force, lin(n), opacity, overfall, pearl, portcullis, rush, sluice, superabundance, thrust, waterfall, waterspout

CATARRAH canker, cold, coryza, hypersecretion, inflammation, influence, mur(r), rheum, roup, secretion
fever blue-tongue, heartwater, influenza, pinkeye, thickhead

CATASTA scaffold, stage, stocks

CATASTROPHE accident, affliction, calamity, cataclysm, climax, close, conclusion, debacle, defeat, denouement, disaster, disturbance, end(ing), failure, fiasco, finish, misadventure, misfortune, mishap, rout, storm, trial, tribulation

CATAWAMPOUS askew, catercornered, cattycornered, fierce, kitty-corner(ed), ravenous

CATAWBA grape, red, sioux, wine
tree catalpa

CATBERRY gooseberry, holly, nemopanthus

CATBIRD bowerbird, dumetella, mimida

CATCALL assail, boo, deride, disapproval, hoot

CATCH 3 bag, cob, cop, get, hit, kep, nab, net, nip, see, win 4 bolt, burn, draw, fang, find, fowl, gain, game, glom, grab, grip, hasp, haul, hawk, hear, hent, hold, hook, land, lock, mesh, nail, pawl, rope, sack, save, snag, snap, snib, snug, song, stop, take, trap, tree, vang, view 5 beard, charm, chase, check, clasp, cleek, click, decoy, error, fault, fetch, grasp, hitch, incur, ketch, knack, lasso, latch, limit, lodge, marry, noose, prize, reach, round, scrap, seize, sight, snare, sneck, snick, spear, stick, trick, troll 6 ambush, arrest, attack, attain, attend, buckle, button, canvas, clutch, collar, corner, corral, detect, detent, engage, enmesh, entrap, guddle, hasten, immesh, nobble, please, retard, sicken, snatch, sprent, sprout, strike, tangle, turnel 7 acquire, attract, capture, deceive, enchant, ensnare, gimmick, grapnel, harpoon, ratchet, receive, release, seizure, sniggle, springe, trigger 8 conceive, contract, crannage, eligible, entangle, fastener, flourish, fragment, hold fast, obstacle, overtake, restrain, surprise, treasure 9 apprehend, captivate, fascinate, intercept 10 sweetheart 11 germination
-all bag, basket, closet, receptacle
as catch can hit or miss
at straws hope, overestimate
attention flag, signal, wave
a wink nap, sleep
basin cistern, drain, reservoir, vault
-cry slogan
fire burn, blaze, flame, ignite, kindle
hinged ratch
-line slogan
off guard surprise
of fish fare, haul, shack, shot, string, tack, trip
on fathom, figure out, follow, get, please, register, seize hold, succeed, take, understand, win favor
one's breath chink, gasp, pause, rest
ratchet click

ride hitchhike
safety clevis
short surprise
sight of descry, espy, see
the 10 hearts, whist
up (to) gain on, interrupt, overhaul, overtake, reach, seize

CATCHER backstop, batterymate, birder, fanger, larker, receiver, taker

CATCHFLY campion, carpet pink, caryophyllus, flower, flybane, gentleman's-hat, luchnis, plant, silene, viscaria

CATCHING alluring, changeable, confiscatory, contagious, deprivative, infectious, precarious, seizure, taking, uncertain

CATCHMENT reservoir

CATCHPENNY cheap, paltry

CATCHPOLE bailiff, bobby, bull, constable, cop(per), gendarme, officer, peeler, police(man), publican, puttock, sheriff, staff, taxgatherer

CATCHUP ketchup, ketsup, tomato sauce

CATCHWEED cleavers, galium, thorn

CATCHWORD byword, clew, clue, cry, cue, formula, motto, phrase, shibboleth, slogan, starter, tag

CATCHY appealing, deceptive, fetching, fitful, insidious, irregular, pleasant, treacherous, tricky

CATECHISM belief, carritch(es), confession, creed, doctrine, dogma, guide, manual, questions(-and-answers), tenet, view

CATECHIZE ask, examine, inquire, instruct, interrogate, query, question, quiz, speer, teach

CATECHU auburn, cash cuttee, cotch, cutch, dye, gambier, gum, khair, kino, yellow
tree gambier, mangrove, pegu

CATECHUMEN audient, auditor, beginner, competent, convert, devotee, instructee, layman, neophyte, novice, pupil, tiro, tyro

CATEGORICAL absolute, definite, demonstrative, dia-

lectic(al), direct, dogmatic(al), downright, explicit, express, knockdown, positive, specific, ultimate, unconditional, unmitigated, unqualified
imperative conscience

CATEGORY aspect, branch, case, caste, class(ification), department, division, family, field, genre, genus, group(ing), league, mode, order, principle, rank, rubric, series, species, state, style
highest idea
include in subsume
primary substance
taxonomic cohort, family, form(a), genus, legion, order, subclass, subfamily

CATENATE bind, chainlike, connect, link

CATER accouter, appoint, content, cut, diagonally, equip, feed, forage, four, furnish, humor, indulge, move, obliquely, pamper, pander, place, procure, provender, provide, provision, purvey, satisfy, serve, supply, treat, victual
-cornered catawamp(o)us, catawamptious, diagonal(ly)
-cousin friend, intimate, pal

CATERAN freebooter, marauder, soldier

CATERCAP mortarboard, student

CATERPILLAR astragalus, aweto, canker, cutworm, eruca, forget-me-not, hangworm, larva, lepitopter(on), looper, muga, oubit, palmer, porina, risper, scorpiurus, silkworm, tailor, tractor, webworm, weri, wooly-bear, worm, wortworm, woubit
comb. campa, eruci
disease flacherie, pseudograsserie
eater beetle, calosoma
fern hart's-tongue
fungus cordyceps
hair seta, weri
hunter beetle, calosoma, carabida, crow shrike
kind armyworm, bagworm, cabbageworm, cankerworm, cutworm, palmerworm, tent
organ mastigium

plate pinaculum
vegetable aweto

CATERWAUL court, cry, howl, miaul, screech, wail, woo

CATES dainties, delicacies, food, vianda, victuals

CATFACE arr, skar

CATFISH ameiurus, anarchichas, aspredo, bagre, barber, barbu(do), berycoid, blindcat, bullhead, bullpout, candiru, catulus, channelcat, chimaera, clarias, cobbler, corydora, cusk, cuttlefish, docmac, dorad, elod, fiddler, flathead, glanis, goonch, goujon, hassar, haustor, horned pout, ictalurus, madtom, mathemeg, mudcat, mudfish, octopus, pladuck, plotosid, polymixia, polynemus, porcus, pout, prenadillas, pygidid, raad, raash, rhamdia, saccobrachnus, shal, silveroid, silurid, sheatfish, squeaker, stargazer, stonecat, tandan, teleost, threadfin, wallago, weever, wolffish
electric malapterurus, torpedo
family aemeiuridae, ariidae loricariida, siluridae
freshwater madtom
pert. siluroid
row lovers bess, porgy

CATGUT catling, cord, goat's-rue, herb, rope, string, tephrosia, thairm, tharm, violin whipcord, wild sweet pea

CATHAR See ASCETIC.

CATHARI albanenses, albigenses, bulgari, concorrezanes, credentes, neomanichaeans, patarines, perfecti, tesserants, the pure

CATHARIZE clean, cleanse, purify

CATHARSIS ablution, abreaction, discharge, discipline, elimination, lustration, moderation, outlet, psychodrama, purgation, purification, release, relief, sublimation

CATHARTIC aloin, aperient, blackdraft, blackdrink, bryony, calomel, caroba, castor oil, dejectory, euonymus, evacuant, gum resin, guttagum, hydragog, lapactic, laxative, physic, purgative, purge, purifying, scammony, senna, solutory, yaupon

CATHARTIDA carrion buzzard, catharta, condor, falconiformis, king vulture, turkey buzzard, vulture

CATHAY See CHINA.

CATHAYAN kitan

CATHEDRAL authorative, basilica, center, church, dom, duomo, lateran, martyry, memoria, minister, official, see, sobor, temple
chapter house cabildo
close enciente
endowment prebend
famous amiens, canterbury, chartres, cologne, durham, notre dame, reims, salisbury, st marks, st peters, st sophia, wells
-like ecclesiastical
part aisle, altar, chevet, cloister, crossing, font, nave, porch, sacristy, tower, transept
passage slype
staffer bishop, canon

CATHER, WILLA *novel* lost lady, my antonia, shadows on the rock

CATHERINE DE MEDICI
daughter margot, marguerite, queen of navarre
husband henry ii
rival diane de poitiers

CATHERINE THE GREAT
husband paul
lover potemkin
son paul

CATHEXIS charge

CATHLEEN *ni houlahan* IRELAND, roisin dubh

CATHODE electrode, filament, hydrogode
ray electron, particle
ray tube braun tube

CATHOLIC apostolic, applicable, broad(minded), calotin, christian, cosmic, cosmopolitan, diffuse, ecumenical, general, liberal, orthodox, papal, papish, papist, papistic(al), popish, prevalent, roman(ish), romist, tolerant, ultramontane, universal
altar top mensa
cassock soutane, zimarra
church, pert. romish
church seat rome
dissenter waldenses

eastern uniat(e)
forbidden books index
fraternal order knights of columbus
frog notaden
greek uniat(e)
mass missa
palace lateran
prayer ave maria
prayer book missal
priest abbe, father, monsignor, sacerdos
shrine fatima, lourdes
skullcap zucchetto
society, secret hibernians
theologian aquinas

CATHOLICON panacea, remedy, treatise

CATILINE *biographer* sallust
conspirator cethegus, manlius, marcius, lentulus
enemy antonius
prosecutor cato, cicero, silanus

CATJANG cajanus, herb, pigeonpea

CATKIN aglet, ament, cachrys, cattail, chat, gull, iulus, pussy, rag, spike, tag
bearer alder
-bearing amentiferous

CATNIP cataria, catmint, catnep, cat's-heal-all, cat's-wort, herb, nep, nepeta, nip

CATO *admirer* favonius
ally pompey
brother caepio
brother-in-law lucius, lucullus, silanus
commander gellius, rubrius, tiberius
consort atilia, lepida, marcia, porcia
enemy clodius, memmius, metellus, scipio, sylla, trebonius, varus, vatinius
emulator statyllius
father-in-law philippus, soranus
freedman butas, cleanthes, quintio
friend bibulus, candidius, cicero, curio, favonius, hortensius, lollius, lucius, lucullus, marcellus, marcus, minucius, munatius, murena, thermus
kinsman brutus, domitius, livius
lieutenant rubrius
nephew brutus
offspring marcus, porcia, salonius
patron fabius, valerius

rival scipio
servant chilo
sister porcia, servilia
teacher antipater, athenodorus, sarpedon

CATOISM austerity, harshness

CATOSTOMID buffalo fish, catostomus, cyprinid, carpsucker, fish, sucker

CATREUS *daughter* apemosyne, clymene
kingdom crete
parent minos, pasiphae

CATS, CAT'S *and dogs* securities
-claw acacia, batocydia, bignonia, black bean, escambron, long-pod, mimosa, trefoil, vetch
clover blueweed, blue-thistle, bugloss
-concert noise, uproar
-cradle hei, herb, ribwort
-ear antennaria, calochorius, capeweed, cudweed, dandelion, flatweed, gosmore, pussy's-toe
-eye chatoyant, chrysoberyl, gem, herb, marble, speedwell, veronica
-faces flower, pansy
-foot antennaria, herb, ivy, pussy toe, thistle, wild ginger
-grass sun spurge
-paw agent, amarantha, breeze, cully, dupe, gull, hitch, instrument, pigeon, plant, ruffle, stooge, tool, trichinium
-tail blueweed, bugloss, cirrus, grass, timothy
tongue herb, priva, velvetbur, verbena
-wort catnip

CATSKILL *peak* slide mountain
resorts borscht-belt, borscht circuit

CATTAIL ament, bayon, blackcap, blackhead, bleck, blueweed, bulrush, candlewick, carbungi, catkin, cirrus, cloud, clubgrass, clubrush, cooper's-flag, cooper's-fly, cotton-grass, ditchdown, dod(d), equisetum, flag, flaxtail, gladen, gladdon, horsetail grass, marsh-beetle, matreed, murray-down, musk, plant, raupo, reed(mace), reree, rush, timothy, totora, tule,

typha, viper's-bugloss, wonga
fungus ascomycete, epichloe, hypocrea, rust
CATTLE aphids, beef, beeves, bestial, bossy, bovi, bovine(s), bullamacow, bullock, bulls, butthead, calf, canaille, chattel, cow, crowd, cush, dhan, dogie, fee, followers, gaur, gelding, gour, guernsey, heifer, humans, kine, leppy, maverick, milch(er), mob, mulley(head), nata, neat, niata, nowt, oxen, pecora, property, riffraff, rother, steer(s), stock, stot, taurus, top-cow, tubicorn, yearling, zebu, zobo
black angus, kerry
breed aberdeen, africander, afrikander, alderney, angoni, angus, ankoli, ayrshire, barotse, beefmaster, belted(galloway), boran, bradford, brahma(n), brahmany bull, brangus, campagna di roma, cattabu, cattalo, cattleyak, charbray, charolais, coaster, criolla, devon, dexter, durham, dutch(belted) fjall, french canadian, friesian, fulani, galloway, guernsey, guzerat, hariana, hereford, highland, holstein, jersey, kangayam, kerry, longhorn, nata, niata, normande, red poll, sahiwal, sanga, sangu, santa gertrudis, schwyz, shorthorn, sindhi, south devon, sussex, swiss, teeswater, welsh, zebu, zobo
breeder ahir, alur
bush atalaya, sapinda
call sook
carried off spreath
colic guttie
comb. bovi
damara herero
dealer couper, cowper, drover, herder, rancher
dehorned muley, mulley
disease actinobacilosis, actinomycosis, anaplasmosis, anthrax, bangs, blackleg, blackquarter, blendwater, brucellosis, catarrh, circling, closh, coath, coth(e), farcy, foot-and-mouth, footmange, gid, hoose, hooze, mawbound, miltsick, murrain, rinderpest, texas fever,

trembles, turnabout, undulant fever, vibriosis
dog blue heeler
driver trail boss
dung casson
dwarf devon, nata, niata
earmark bit, overbit, overcrop, oversharp, underbit, undercrop, undersharp
egret ardeola ibis
enclosure See CATTLE *pen.*
extinct ureoxen
feed for hire agist
felon fetlow, whetlow
food bhoosa, chaff, ensilage, fodder, mash, silage
genus bos, neat, taurus
goddess bubona
grass eatage
group creaght, drove, head, herd
grub warble fly
herd creaght, wrangle
hide buff, croupon
hornless aberdeen angus, red poll
humped zebu
humpless ankoli
hybrid battalo, cattabu, cattleyak, zobo
intestine casing
leader nose ring
-like beevish, bovine
long-haired dishley
long-horned ankoli, chillingham
man byreman, cowboy, fazendeiro, rancher, stockman, vaquero
mange texas itch
market saleyard, triste, tryst
marking jinglebob
neat bos, nowt
pen barn, barth, bawn, bool(e)y, byre, corral, hammel, hovel, kraal, reeve, stell
plague murie, rinderpest
poison slangkop, staggerbush
raid spreagh, spreath
rake pasture, range
rump natch
run station
shelter See CATTLE *pen.*
stealing abaction, abigeat
tender byreman, byrewoman, cowboy, cowgirl, gaucho, herder, neatherd
thief abactor, abigeus, rustler
thick annulatus, boophilus, carapato, garapata, margaropus
trail chisholm

unbranded clearskins
whitlow fetlow
wild gaur
wild young kangaroo
yard cancha
CATTY effeminate, gossipy, katy, kin, malicious, mean, spiteful, stealthy, treacherous, weight
CATTYMAN logger
CATWALK footway, monkey-bridge
CAUBOGE beer, bumpkin
CAUCASIAN, CAUCAS colchis, european, griffin, haole, iranian, japhetic, melanoi, paleface, white, xanthochroid
carpet baku, chila, dagestan, derbend, kabistan, karabagh, kazak, khila, khilim, kuba, lezghian, shirvan, sumak
chechen galga, ingush
chinese lolo
family aryan
goat bharal, tehr, tur, zac
hero shamil
herb moss-campion
ibex zac
knife kindjal
language adighe, andi, avar, kartli, laz(e)(i), ossete, semitic, udi(c), udin, udish
liquor kefir, kephir, kumiss
moslem laz(zi)
mountaineer lak, pshav
peak adaikhokh, elbruz, kazbek
people avar, budukha, darghian, gurian, imer (itian), kabard, kizikumuk, kubachim, kumyk, kurd, kyurin, lak, laz(e), lazi, lezgin, mingrelian, moschi, nogai, osset, pshav, sarmatian, svan(e), sythian, tabasarin, tat, tatar
pert. armenoid
race anglo-norman, anglo-saxon, arab(ian), aryan, basque, bedouin, berber, bohemian, celt(ic), creole, georgian, gypsy, hamite, hamitic, hebrew, hindu, indian, indoaryan, indoeuropean, iranian, israelite, jew, kelt(ic), latin, nordic, norman, norse, northman, osset, romany, scandinavian, semite, semitic, slav, teuton(ic), viking, white

silk moff
volcano kazbek
CAUCHO castilla, mulberry, rubber, tree, ule
CAUCON *father* poseidon
CAUCUS council, election, meeting, politick, primary
CAUDATA amphibia, congo snake, newt, salamander, urodela
CAUDEX axis, base, stem, stipe, tree trunk
CAUDILLO captain, chief (tain), leader
CAUDLE diet, drink, gruel, mix, refresh
CAUGHT entangled, grippit, trapped
CAUK barite, cawk, chalk, cog, limestone, spar, tenon
CAUL basket, cap, creel, crepine, dorlot, form, galea, hat, houve, kel(i), kercher, membrane, net(work), omentum, pericardium, plate, sillyhow, tressour, tressure, trug, veil, web
CAULD cold, dam, weir
CAULDRIFE chilling, chilly
CAULICLE axis, rostellum, scapel, stem
CAULIFLOWER brassica, broccoli, cabbage, choufleur, plant, snowball
disease shiptail
CAULK See CALK.
CAULKING *mixture* blare
needing leaky
CAULOPHYLLUM barberry, cohosh, herb
CAUNUS *parent* cyanee, miletus
sister byblis
CAUSAL at the bottom of, constitutive, creative, effectual, etiological, genetic, germinal, institutive, occasional, originative, productive
CAUSE account, action, activity, actuation, aetiology, affair, agent, agreement, aim, animation, antecedent, arche, author, base, basis, beget, beginning, behind, birth, bottom, breed, bring about, bring to pass, business, call, campaign, case, causality, chat, cheson, chesoun, conceive, concern, consideration, contrive, create, crusade, destination, determinant, determinative, disease, drive, effect, ele-

ment, elicit, end, engender, evoke, fact(or), fate, father, foment, force, frame, gar, generate, gestate, goad, goal, gossip, ground(s), hoti, ideal, induce, influence, instance, intention, interest, invoke, ism, issue, key, lawsuit, lead, let, make, malady, manner, matter, means, motive, move(ment), moving, object, occasion, originate, parent, party, precipitate, presupposition, principle, procure, produce, prompt (ing), provoke, quarrel, question, reason, resort, root, sake, score, sire, skill, slake, source, spring, spur, subject, suit, trigger, warrant, way, wherefore, work, wreak, yield
comb. aetio, aitio, etio
final end
impelling mainspring
lost disaster, goner
pain hurt, urn
primal urgrund
science of etiology
without chance
CAUSING *comb.* able
CAUSTIC abrasive, acerb (ic), acid(ulous), acrid, acrimonious, acute, alkaline, alum, biting, bitter, branding iron, burning, cautery, corrosive, cruel, curve, cutting, di(a)eretic, erodent, erosive, escharotic, gruff, incisive, keen, lime, lye, malevolent, mordacious, mordant, nipping, painful, penetrating, phenol, piercing, pugent, pyrotic, quick, salty, sarcastic, satiric(al), scathing, scorching, severe, sharp, snappish, snell, sour, stabbing, stinging, tart, trenchant, withering
agent cauterant, cautery, erodent
creeper euphorbia, milk plant
poison phenol
solution lye
vine sacrostemma
CAUSEWAY chausse, dike, highway, road
CAUSEY areaway, bank, dam, highway, mound, pave, sidewalk, street
CAUTELOUS cautious,

crafty, deceitful, prudent, sly, smart, wary, wily
CAUTERANT acid, brand (ing) iron, caustic, corrosive, escharotic, heating, mordant, radium
CAUTERIZATION inustion, ustion
CAUTERIZE brand, burn, char, fire heat, inust, sear, singe, sterilize
CAUTION admonish, advice, advise, alert(ness), anxiety, attention, calculation, care, cautel, caveat, character, chariness, circumspection, counsel, diligence, discretion, exhort, fear, forebode, forecast, foresight, forewarn, guarantee, guard, heed, monition, notice, notify, oddity, pledge, precept, providence, proviso, prudence, reservation, security, surety, threaten, tip off, top-notcher, vigilance, wariness, warn(ing), watchfulness
CAUTIOUS abeigh, abiegh, active, alert, cagey, canny, cantelous, careful, chary, circumspect, curious, discreet, fabian, fearful, ferdful, gingerly, guarded, hesitant, hoolie, prudent, safe, shy, sicker, siker, suspense, tender, vigilant, ware, wary
exclamation beware, careful, danger, easy, look alive, look out, look sharp, mind, take care, watch out, watch your step
money deposit, down payment
CAVALCADE company, journey, march, pageant, parade, procession, raid, ride, safari
CAVALIER bachelor, banneret, baronet, blunt, brave, brusque, caballero, cavalero, cavy, chamberer, chevalier, cisisbeo, coin, commander, companion, courtier, curt, debonair, disdainful, easy, escort, esquire, fellow, fine, frank, gallant, gay, haughty, horseman, knight(errant), lover, mount, offhand, proud, rider, ritter, royalist, soldier, spark, supercilious
famous don quixote, gala-

had, gawain, lancelot, sidney

poet carew, herrick, lovelace, suckling

servante follower

CAVALLA caranx, cero, crevalle, fish, jack, jurel, mackerel, scombrid, toro, ulua

CAVALRY chivalry, equites, heavies, horse(guard), horsemen, horses, knighthood, lancers, turm(a), yeomanry

body foragers, troop

horse lancer

-man argolet, carabineer, carabinero, carabinier, courier, dragoon, forager, gendarme, horseman, hussar, jinete, lancer, plunger, sabreur, soldier, sowar, spahee, spahi, stradiot, suwar, trooper, u(h)lan

-man's case sabretache

raid chevachie

retinue sowarry

twill tricotine

weapon lance, saber

CAVATINA air, cabaletta, melody, song

CAVE antre, beware, burrow, cabin, cache, calve, castillo, cavern, cavity, cell(ar), chamber, collapse, cove, croft, crypt, debacle, delve, den, dugout, dungeon, excavate, fall, fogou, grotto, hidden, hole, hollow, lair, larder, lookout, mine, mithragual, opening, overturn, pantry, plunge, rear, recess, reserve, retreat, secession, shelter, sink, slade, spelunk, speos, stakes, store(room), subterrane, subway, surrender, tip, toss, tube, tunnel, underground, upset, watch, weem, wine cellar

archaic antre

comb. antr(o)

cricket ceuthophilus, hadenoecus

dweller aborigine, ancient, horite, neanderthal, taurus, troglodyte

-dwelling natufian

explore spelunk

explorer spelunker

fish amblyopsis, blindfish

icicle stalactite, stalagmite

in bow, calve, capitulate, collapse, colt, concave, debacle, defer, delation, fall,

give in, hollow, prostration, relent, stove, submit, succumb, surrender, weaken, yield

-inhabiting spelaean, spelean

man See CAVE *dweller.*

of 1,000 buddhas chien-fo-tung

of triphonius despair

painting site altamira, lascaux

pert. spel(a)ean, speluncar

researcher speleologist, spelunker

science of spel(a)eology

village ellora

CAVEAT admonition, beware, caution, disengage, notice, precaution, proviso, warning

emptor let the buyer beware

CAVEL allot(ment), bully, cast lots, fate

CAVENDISH henry jones

CAVERN (See also CAVE.) antrum, cavity, croft, den, grot(to), hollow

limestone carlsbad

CAVERNOUS alveolate, chambered, concave, deepset, erectile, hollow, porous, roomy, spacious, vast

CAVESSON chain

CAVETTO gorge, gula

CAVIAR appetizer, belugo, delicacy, eggs, ikary, ikra, ova, relish, roe, sturgeon

source shad, sterlet, sturgeon

CAVICORNIA antelopes, bovida, goats, oxen, pronghorns, ruminants, sheep

CAVIL bicker, caption, cark, carp, censure, chicane, complain, criticize, expostulate, find fault, formalize, haft, haggle, marl, nag, object, objurgate, pettifog, protest, quarrel, quibble, quiddity

CAVILER critic, girder, hafter, zoilus

CAVILING brabblement, caption, captious, censorious, critical, criticism, demanding, discord, exacting, kicking, picayune, quarreling, quibbling

CAVITY 3 bag, cup, dip, pit, sac, vug 4 abri, antu, aula, axil, bowl, case, cave, cell, dalk, dent, duct, hole, mine, pore, sink, vein, void, voog, vugg 5 abyss, antre, basin, bosom, bursa, celom,

crump, crypt, druse, fossa, geode, gouge, lumen, mouth, orbit, scoop, sinus 6 antrum, areole, atrium, axilla, boring, caecum, camera, caries, cavern, coelia, coelom, cotyle, crater, deblai, grotto, hollow, lacuna, pocket, socket, vacuum, vomica 7 abdomen, alveola, chamber, cistern, coelome, cyathus, kyathos, loculus, mortise, opening, vacuity, vacuole 8 alveolus, broodsac, epicoele, follicle, wellhole 10 depression, excavation 11 alveolation, compartment, peritheceum 12 displacement

air somatocyst

body abdomen, antrum, armpit, aula, belly, coelom, epicoele, fossa, sinus, stomach, thorax

bone antrum, cavern, lacuna

brain coelia

casting pipe

chest thorax

comb. antr(o), coele, sinu

filler bone-plombe, cement, foil, gold, porcelain, silver

gun bore

having 2 dicoelious

heart atrium, ventricle

lode vug

mine bag

nasal cavun

pert. atrial, geodic, sinal

rock geode, lode, voog, vug(g), vugh

saclike bursa, vesicle

shell flue

skull aula, fossa, sinus

tooth caries

CAVORT bound, caper, curvet, dance, dido, frisk, gambol, play, prance, prank, romp

CAVY agouti, aperea, capibara, capybara, cayuse, guinea pig, hencoop, mara, paca, pig, pony, rodent

female sow

CAW croak, cronk, cry, jangle, kaak, plunk, quawk

CAWK barite, mineral, spar

CAWQUAW porcupine

CAXI fish, snapper

CAY island, islet, key

CAYAPO *indian* apinage, caraho, caraja, chambioa, javahai, juya

CAYENNE canary, cap-

sicum, copepod, pepper, whist
cherry surinam
incense elemi
oil bois de rose
pepper chili, condiment, cubeb
pepper extract capsicin
rose pottery-bark-tree, sassafras
CAYMAN See CAIMAN.
CAYUSE bronc(h)o, cavy, mustang, pony, waillatpuan
CAZELTY See CASALTY.
CEANOTHUS bluebush, blugeblossom, buckbush, buckthorn, buttonbush, california lilac, coralberry
CEASE abstain, avast, balk, belay, blin, bow, break, cessation, close, conclude, culminate, cut, desist, devall, die, disappear, discontinue, dowse, drop, end, expire, fade away, fall, fine, finish, forget, give over, go phut, halt, hold, intermit, lay off, leave, lift, lin, liss(e), outgive, pass, pause, perish, peter out, pretermit, quit, refrain, relinquish, rest, shut, stay, stint, stop, stow, surcease, suspend, swick, terminate, waive, wonde
efforts call it quits
fire armistice, truce
hostilities mediate, pacify
temporarily lift, postpone
without endless, incessant
CEASELESS constant, continuous, endless, eternal, ever(lasting), immortal, incessant, unending
CEBRIONES *master* hector
CEBUS capuchin, monkey, sai
CECILIA sis(su)
CECROPIA ambay, blast, fiber, mulberry, tree, trumpetwood
moth samia, silkworm
CECROPS *daughter* agraulos, herse, pandrosos
founded athens
kingdom attica
wife aglauros, agraulos
CECUM See CAECUM.
CEDALION *aided* hephaestus
parent hephaestus
CEDAR acajou, ahuehuete, arborvitae, atlas, calantas, callitras, cedrela, cedrus, chamaecyparis, crypto-

meria, cypress, deodar, ehretia, guazuma, juniper, kaikawaka, librocedrus, mahogany, pahautea, red, ribbonwood, savin(e), sequoia, sugi, tabebuia, thuja, toon(a), tumion, waxwing
camphor cedral
green cedre, color
-like cedrine, cedry
moss hornwort
nut cembra
of lebanon cedrus, deodar
red arborvitae, canoe, flindosa, sabine, savin(e), thuja, toon(a)
swamp greening
waxwing bombycilla, canada robin, cankerbird, cherrybird, recollect
yellow alaska cypress
CEDE abandon, accord, assign, award, capitulate, cess, communicate, concede, convey, deed, forgo, give up, give way, grant, impart, leave, part with, pass, relinquish, render, renounce, resign, submit, surrender, transfer, vouchsafe, waive, yield
CEDILLA tittle
CEDREATIS artemis
CEDRELA cedar, mahogany
CEDRIC *son* ivanhoe
CEDULA certificate, permit, schedule, security, tax
CEIBA, CEIBO bentang, bombaca, bombax, bulak, eriodendron, erythrina, god tree, gossampine, kapok, pochote, shrub, silk-cotton tree
CEIL line, overlay, plaster, syle, top, wainscot
CEILE client, farmer, tenant, wassal
CEILIDH gathering, musical, party, visit
CEILING altitude, astel, astesonado, atmosphere, chutt, cover, cupola, curtain, deckhead, dome, height, lacunar, limit, lining, loft, maximum, paneling, plafond, plancher, record, roff(ing), soffit, syling, testudo, top, vaulting, visibility, wainscoting
arched testudo
beam trave
covering calcimine, kalsomine
division trave

fan punkah
gothic severy
mine astel
ornament rosace
paneled artesonado, lanunaria
unlimited cavu
wooden plancher
CELADON green, lover, porcelain
CELAENO harpy
consort poseidon
star in pleiades
CELANDINE felonwort, ficaru, impatiens, jewelweed, killwort, pilewort, wartweed, wartwort
CELASTRA catha, kat, sapindale, shrub, staff-tree
CELASTRUS bittersweet, vine
leaves add-add
CELEBES minahassa, sulawesi
animal anoa, buffalo
capital macassare
city buol, luwuk, makasar, manado
gulf bone, tolo
island boetoeng, butung, kabaena, moena, muna, peleng, sulawesi, wangiwangi, wowoni
language alfurese
macaque moor-monkey
ox anoa
people alfuro, bugi, macassar, makassar, minahussa, tora(d)ja
port macassar, makassar, menado
sea banda
wind barat, broeboe, brubru
CELEBRATE applaud, besing, blazon, carol, chant, chaunt, commemorate, commend, communicate, ditty, elegize, emblazon, eulogize, execute, extol, fete, glorify, hallow, honor, jubilate, jubilize, keep, kill the fatted calf, laud, maffick, magnify, make merry, mark, memorialize, observe, perform, play, praise, proclaim, publish, revel, sacre, signalize, solemnize, speak
CELEBRATED conspicuous, distinguished, eminent, fabulous, famed, famous, farfamed, feasted, great, honored, illustrious, immortal, kept, laureate, marked, notable, noted, notorious, observed, of note, out-

standing, popular, prominent, renomme, renowned, signal, storied, well-known

CELEBRATION beanfeast, beano, bination, birthday, blowout, ceremony, commemoration, coronation, doment, festa, festivity, fete, fiesta, gala, hogmanay, hogmena, holiday, hoolaulea, jubilation, jubilee, makahiki, observance, paschal, potlatch, powwow, revel, shindig, shivaree, simchas, simche, simhah, solemnization, spree, yomtov, yontif(dig), yontiff

CELEBRITY big name, cynosure, eclat, fame, figure, glory, hero(ine), honor, immortal, lion, luminary, magnate, man of note, name, notability, notable, notoriety, personage, rara avis, renown, repute, social lion, somebody, star, vip, worthy

group brass, elite, four hundred, upper crust

treat as lionize

CELEOMORPH bird, woodpecker, wryneck

CELERITY acceleration, activity, alacrity, briskness, dispatch, haste, hurry, liveliness, rapidity, speed, sprightliness, swiftness, velocity, zip

CELERY ammiace apium, celeriac, karpas, salary, smallage, umbel

-like plant udo

pine phyllocladus

wild ache, aneth, smallage, tape-grass

CELESTIAL aerial, airy, angel(ic), asteroidal, astral, astrologic(al), astrologistic, astrologous, astronomical, blue, chinaman, chinese, cynthian, divine, empyreal, empyrean, equinoctial, ethereal, ethered, godlike, godly, heavenly, heliac, holy, intercosmic, interplanetary, intersidereal, interstellar, lunar(y), lunate, lunular, lunulate, meteoric, nebular, nebulose, nebulous, olympian, planetal, planetarian, planetary, planetesimal, sider(e)al, sphery, spiritual, starry,

starspangled, stellar, solar, uranic, zodiacal

being angel, archangel, cherub, seraph

body ball, comet, meteor, nebula, planet, quasar, star

body, pert. spherical

city jerusalem, zion

conjunction appulse

elevation of mind anagoge

empire china, tienchao

juno caelestis

matter nebula

mechanics astronomy

pert. empyreal

space blue, heavens, infinity

teacher heavenly preceptor, master of heaven

CELESTINE benedictine, heavenly, pelagian

CELESTITE apotome, coelstine

CELEUS *guest* demeter

kingdom eleusis

offspring abas, andromeda, demophon, triptolemus

patron demeter

CELEUTHEA athena

CELIA *father* frederick

CELIBACY abstention, abstinence, anaphrodisia, bachelorhood, chastity, continence, maidenhood, misogamy, misogyny, monachism, monasticism, purity, single-blessedness, singleness, spinsterhood, virtue, virginity

CELIBATE androgyne, archimandrite, ascetic, bachelor, capon, chaste, continent, epicene, eunuch, maiden(ly), misogamist, misogynist, monachal, monastic, monk, old maid, single, sole, spinster(ish), steer, unmarried, unwed(ded), vestal, virgin(al)

CELL agamete, alveola, alveolus, amebula, amoeba, anaxon, apartment, apocyte, body, box, cabin, caecum, cage, cavity, ceptor, clink, coccus, compartment, confinement, corpuscle, coterie, cubicle, cup, cytode, cyton, depression, disc, disk, dungeon, egg, erythroblast, fiber, frame, gamete, germ, gland, gonium, group, haploid, hematid, hole, inaxon, interstice, jail, jar, kil(l), leucocyte, loculus, lymphocyte, macrogamete,

macrophage, myocyte, neuron(e), normocyte, ootid, organule, ovum, peritheceum, pit, pollen sac, pore, prison, room, socket, sperm(ule), spore, stirps, theca, tmema, toril, vault, vessel, zooblast, zooid, zygote

alga autospore

animal zooblast

bridge plasmodesm

bull toril

cavity vacuole

clump sludge

coloring endochrome

colorless achroacyte, lymphocyte

comb. cyte, cyto, ont

connecting hereocyst

content cytoplast

contractile myocite

dentention bullpen

destroyer cytolysin

destruction abiotrophy, cataplasia, cytoclasis, cytolysis, lysis

disease sicklemia

division amitosis, cleavage, cytodieresis, linin, mitosis, spirem(e)

embryo zygote

excretory nephrocyte

family coenobium

first division blastomere

fragmentation clasmatosis

free-moving zooid

generative gamete

granule blepharoplast

group blastema, cascade, ceptor, epithem

hermit's clochan

immunizing leucocyte, leukocyte

interior endosmosis

iridescent iridocyte

isolated idioblast

kernel nucleus

layer blastoderm, blastula, cambium, cortex, ex(t)ine

lens-shaped lenticel

-like cytoid

mass cancer, cumulus, stalace

membrane epicyte

migratory leucocyte

multiplication epimorphosis

naked protoblast

nucleus cytoblast, karyon

nucleus, comb. cary(o), kary(o)

nucleus part. achromatin

olfactory amacrine

part axon, cytoplasm, cy-

tosome, energid, karyosome, linin, membrane, mitone, nucleolus, nucleus, plastid, protoplast, vacuole
part, lifeless metaplasm
pert. cytoid
pigmented chromocyte
plant meristem
prison bing, clink, cooler, hole, jigger, sweatbox
protoplasm centrosome
red erythrocyte
reproductive agamete, gamete, gonoblast, sperm
series cascade
spindle-shaped closter
star-shaped astroblast, astrocyte
study cytology
substance chromatin, endolysin, linin
thin-walled stomium
transfer metastasize
unit biogen
voltaic battery
wall cytoderm, periplast
wall constituent callose
white leucocyte, leukocyte, macrophage
CELLA naos
CELLAR basement, bodega, case, cave, favissa, fraid hole, funk hole, hold, hypogee, hypogeum, last, matamoro, receptacle, serdab, spudhole, storeroom, subterrane, underground, vault(age), wine room
entrance areaway
room catacomb, coalbin
CELLARER butler, manager, steward
CELLARMAN butler, sommelier, wine-server
CELLINI *statue* perseus
halo heiligenschein
CELLULAR alveolate, areolar, faviform, favose, vascular
tissue parenchyma
CELLULOID film, motion picture, movie, xylonite
hardener bakelite
ingredient camphor, guncotton, pyroxylin
CELLULOSE amyloid, carbohydrate, crumb, lignose, tamidine, viscose
acetate acetose
comb. cello
elastic rayon
CELOSIA amaranth, coxcomb, heatherbell, herb

CELSIA bear's-tail, figwort, herb
CELSIUS centigrade, thermometer
CELT breton, briton, brython, chisel, cornish, cymry, eolith, erse, gael, gaul, goidel, irish, kelt, kymry, manx, palstaff, palstave, pict, scot, welsh (man)
abbot coarb
alphabet oghams
bard taliesin
black dhu
book ballymote, conquests, dun cow, hergest, lecan, leinster, rhydderch
cerberus gurme
chariot essed
chieftain tanist
church iona
clan sept
dart colp
dirge keen
feast beltain, imbolc, lugnas, samhain
fairy leprechaun
giant domnu, fionn, fomors, hymer
giant land ysbaddaden
giantess domnu
goblin pooka
god aengus, amaethon, angus og, arawn, artor, beal, belinus, bran, camulus, cenn cruaich, ceridwen, craiwy, crom cruaich, crom dubh, dagda, dea, dylan, esus, gobniu, govannan, gwydion, gwyn, hafgan, lamfhada, leir, ler, lleu, lludd, llyr, lug(h), mannan, midir, nuada, nudd, oengus, pryderi, pwyll, ruad rofhessa, taranis, teutates
goddess ana, anu, arianrhod, badb, bodb, bridget, brigantia, brigid, brigit, dana, danu, don, macha, morrigan, rhiannon, tailtiu
gods tuatha de dannan
gods' abode brugh na boinne
harp clairschach, telyn
hero cuchulainn, finn mac cumal, goll, ossian, setanta
hero's sword calad-bolg
homer ossian
horse abakur
island aval(l)on
king aillill, brennius, lud
landholder tanist
land-holding system rundale
language brythonic, cornish,

cymric, gaelic, irish, manx, welsh
literature (See also CELT *book.*) duan, lebor gabala, mabinogion
may day rite beltane
mountain ben
nard spikenard, valerian
nation aedui
otherworld mag mel, tir fothuinn, tir nanoc
paradise avalon
pasture collop, colp
peasant kern
people belgae, boii, britons, brythons, cymrians, iceni, senones, volcae
pert. goidelic
priest druid
prophetess ganna
queen branwen
ruler pendragon
sea robber fomor
shrine avebury, stonehenge
soldier kerne
spirit banshee, kelpie, kelpy
string instrument crowd
sword sax, seax
warrior dagda, fenian, kern
whiskey uisgebaugh
CELTIS elder, false elm, hackberry, nettletree
CEMBALO dulcimer, zimbalon
CEMENT adhere, adhesive, agglutinate, albolite, albolith, asphalt, attach, badigeon, ballast, binder, bond, coat, cohere, combine, concrete, cover, fasten, filler, floor, fuse, glue, grout, gulgul, gum, gunite, gypsum, hadigeon, hard, heal, imbed, join, kibosh, knit, lime, lute, maltha, mastic, merge, mortar, mucilage, ooglea, paar, paste, pave (ment), plaster, putty, slab, slip, solder, solid(ify), stick, tabby, unite, weld
and stone bumicky
bookbinding paste
egg ooglea
hydraulic paar, roman
infusible lute
mixer temperer
pasty mastic
plaster stucco
plastic albolite, albolith
quick-drying mastic
substance celite
well-lining steen
window-glass putty
work covering

CEMETERY ahu, barrow, boneyard, boot hill, burial ground, calvary, campo santo, catacomb, charnel, churchyard, god's acre, golgotha, grave(yard), holy field, howf, kill, kurgan, lair, lich gate, litten, low, marble city, memorial park, necropolis, polyandrium, potter's field, tumulus, urnfield
ancient urnfield, urnyard
for strangers aceldama
CENCHRIAS *father* poseidon
CENCHRUS bur-grass, hedgehog-grass, sandbur
CENOBITE anchorite, ascetic, eremite, essene, friar, hermit, monastic, monk, nun, recluse, religious, synodite
CENOBY abbey, cloister, convent, monastery, priory
CENOTAPH memorial, monument, tomb
CENOZOIC *epoch* eocene, miocene, oligocene, paleocene, pleistocene, pliocene, recent
period quaternary, tertiary
pert. paleogene
CENSE assess, estimate, perfume, position, rank, rating, thurify
CENSER incensory, thurible
CENSOR blacklist, blue-pencil, bowdlerize, cato, conceal, conscience, critic, deduct, delete, detractor, examine, expurgate, faultfind(er), launder, overseer, psyche, restrict(or), scold, screen, stifler, supervisor, suppress(or), syndic
CENSORIOUS blameful, blaming, captious, carping, caviling, chiding, critical, culpable, denunciatory, derogatory, faultfinding, reproachful, severe, slashing
CENSORSHIP assize, blackout, censure, comstockery, deduction, iron curtain, pall, smothering, suppression, wraps
CENSURE abuse, accuse, admonish, animadversion, animadvert, arraign, attack, ban, berate, blame, blaming, blast, blister, call, carp, castigate, castigation, charge, chasten, chastise, chide, condemn(ation), correction, criminate, criti-

cism, critique, cry down, curse, damn(ation), declaim, decrial, decry, deduct, deem, denounce(ment), denunciation, disallow, disapproval, disapprove, dislogy, dispraise, drub, excoriate, excoriation, exprobate, fault(find), flay, hit, impeach, impugn, inveigh, judge, judgement, lecture, object(ion), opinion, perstringe, rap, rate, rebuke, recension, remord, reprehend, reprimand, reproach, reprobate, reproof, reprove, scold, sentence, shame, slang, slap, slash, slate, slating, stricture, targe, task, taunt, tax, tirade, tonguelash, traduce, upbraid, wig, wite
spirit of momos, momus
CENSUS cense, count(ing), enumeration, list, luster, lustrum, number(ing), poll, registration, rent, tax
CENT brownie, coin, copper, counter, duit, hundred, penny, sant, sou, stuiver, trifle
1/10th mill
12½ levy
CENTAUR agrius, bucentor, chiron, eurytion, nessus
adversary lapithae
bull's head bucentaur
hercules' attacker agrius
home pelion
parent ixion, nephele
wine-guarder pholus
CENTAUREA blawort, boleweed, knapweed
CENTAURIUM awiwi, bloodwort, blushwort, erythraea, gentian, herb, trichosporum, turtle-head
CENTAURY behen, behn, betten, blawort, bloodwort, boleweed, canchalagua, chlora, earthgall, herb, knapweed, milkwort, polygala, sabbatia
CENTAVO *100* cordoba, cordova, peso
CENTENARIAN See MAN *old.*
CENTENNIAL anniversary, centenary, century, hundred(th)
state colorado
CENTER adjust, axis, bull's-eye, cathedral, collect, concentrate, converge, core,

dot, equidistance, essence, eye, focus, gib, glome, heart, hub, interior, intermediate, kernel, linchpin, marrow, medulla, mid, middle, midst, midway, moderate, modify, nave(l), nucleus, omphalos, pass, pinhole, pith, pivot, point, polestar, seat, shape, snap, snap(per)back, source, spine, stage, staple, target, temple, umbilic(us), yolk
away from distal
collection entrepot
commercial machi, mart, wall street
-directed centripetal
hard knot
of activity crossroads
of attraction cynosure, focus, stage
of interest focus, mecca
nerve brain
proceeding from centrifugal
proceeding toward centripetal
toward entad, orad, mesial
vital heart, hearth
CENTERPIECE dormant, epergne, ornament, rosace
CENTESIMAL hundredfold, hundredth
unit grad(e)
CENTESIMO *5* soldo
CENTETID tenrec
CENTIGRADE celsius thermometer
CENTIMANES See HECATONCHEIRES.
CENTIME gourde, rappen
5 sou
100 franc
CENTIMETER *cubic* mil
CENTIPEDE arthropod, chilopod, earwig, geophilus, golach, goloch, insect, multiped, myriapod, polypod, santapee, scutiger, veri
fang toxicognath
plant muehlenbeckia, ribbon bush, shrub
CENTRAL accessible, axial, basic, capital, cardinal, caucho, centroidal, chief, dominant, equidistant, focal, geocentric, leading, main, median, mid, middle(most), midmost, nuclear, omphalic, pivotal, primary, prime, principal, telephone operator, umbilical
CENTRAL AFRICA sahel

CENTRAL AFRICAN RE-PUBLIC ubangi-shari
capital bangui
city bambari, bangui, birao, bouar, ngoto, obo, paoua, rafai, zemio, zemongo
coin franc
deity bieri, bumba, libanza, mebeli, mokadi, nkokon, nzame, otukut, phebele, zamba, zambi
leader bokassa
native banda, banziri, baya, bwaka, mandjia, sango, sara, yakoma
river bomu, chari, chinko, kotto, lobaye, mbari, mpoko, nana, ouaka, ubangi
CENTRAL AMERICA *agave* sisal
animal coati, sloth, tapir
ant kelep
bird condor, corvine, crow, curassow, daw, guan, jacamar, puffbird, quetzal, raven, rook, tragon, urubu
boa emperor
boat cayuco, pitpan
cactus cochineal-fig
cat eyra
catfish barbudo
country costa rica, el salvador, guatemala, honduras, nicaragua, panama
flycatcher pitangua
goby aboma de rio
gopher guachil
grass teosinte
guavina aboma de mar
gum tree tuno, tunu
herb barajillo, desmodium, lopezia, tronador
hummingbird amizilis
hurricane cordonazo
indian (See also under particular countries.) carib, maya, popoloco, ulva
lizard anole, anoli, galliwasp, iguana
measure cantaro, manzana
monkey mono
mullet bobo
palm acrocomia, cohune, pacaya
people ladino, maya
porcupine coendou
rattlesnake cascavel
rodent agouti, paca
rubber caucho
sash tobe
shark tiburon
snake bushmaster
statesman morazan

stockade boma
tortoise hicatee
tragon bird, quetzal
tree amate, balsa, banak, cortez, coyo, cypress, ebo(e), primavera, sapodilla, tuno, tunu, ule
village boma
weight libra
wind papagayo
CENTRALIZE concenter, concentrate, converge, focus
CENTRARCHID See FISH centrarchid.
CENTRANTH spurflower, valerian
CENTRIC central, cylindrical, ocellar, oolitic, terete
CENTRIFUGAL efferent, eyme, radiating
CENTRIFUGE cyclone, separator, whirl
CENTRISCUS bellowsfish, hemibranchus, macrorhamphosus, shrimpfish
CENTROSEMA bradburya, butterfly-pea
CENTRY center, middle
CENTUNCULUS herb, knotweed, primrose, primulace, weed
CENTURY age, eon, era, eternity, hundred, secle, siecle
10 millennium
13th duecento
14th renaissance, trecento
15th quattrocento
16th cinquecento
plant ade, agave, aloe, cantala, maguey, monocarp, pita
plant distillate tequila, pulque
plant fiber pita, pito
CEORL boor, churl, freeman, peasant, slave, thane, villein
CEPANEUS *consort* evadne
CEPE boletus, fungus, mushroom
CEPHALALGIA headache
CEPHALIC anterior, atlantal, atloid, cerebral, cranial
CEPHALOID capitate
CEPHALON See HEAD.
CEPHALOPUS antelope, duiker(bok)
CEPHALOPHOLIS ephipus, (butter) (dollar) (kelp) fish, guativere, gunnel, poronotus
CEPHALOPOD ammonite, architeuthis, argonautica, baculite, baculiticone, cut-

tle(fish), gyroceras, ink (fish), mollusk, nautilus, octopus, scaphite, spirula, squid
secretion ink
CEPHALUS pteleon
consort eos, procris, procne
parent deion, diomede
victim procris
CEPHAS peter, rock, simon, stone
kin jonah
CEPHEUS *daughter* andromeda
father aleus, belus
kingdom ethiopia, tegea
wife cassiopeia
CERAMIC china, clay, enamel, faience, glass, porcelain
black basalt, bucchero
box sagger
flaw black core
ingredient boric acid, ceria, frit
kiln, kind acid, brick, cement, enamel, lime, muffle
low firing petit feu
material adobe, clay, flux, glaze, kaolin, potter's earth, terra cotta
metal selenium
ornament on adorno, sigillate
oven kiln
paste barbotine
sieve laun
study ceramography
unglazed bisk, bisque(tte)
ware bowl, bucchero, crock(ery), jug, pot(tery), tile, urn, vase
wheel, kind kick, pedal, potter's, power
CERAMACIST glass blower, potter
equipment archetto, furnace, kiln, oven, stove, wheel
CERASTES asp, viper
CERATE lard, oil, ointment, salve, unguent, wax
base beeswax
CERATODUS barramunda, epiceratodus, lungfish, neoceratodus, salmon
CERATOMIA catalp, moth, sphinx
CERATONIA carob, senna
CERATOPSIA dinosaur, ornithischia, triceratops
CERATOSE horny
CERANUIA arrowheads, axes, stones
CERBERUS bokadam, custo-

dian, dog, guard(ian), helldog, warden, watchdog
brother chimaera, gorgon, hydra, nemean lion, orthus, scylla, sphinx
guard of hades, hell
parent echidna, typhon
CERCOCEBUS mangabey, monkey
CERCOPES dwarfs, gnomes, goblins
captor hercules
CERCOPID froghopper, homopterid, spittle-insect
CERCYON *daughter* alope
father hephaestus, poseidon
slayer theseus
victim alope
CERDO *husband* phoroneus
CERE anoint, wax, wrap
CEREAL arzun, atole, barley, bean, bran, breakfast food, corn(flakes), crowdy, farina, flummery, frumenty, grain, granola, grass, grits, gruel, hasty pudding, hominy, loblolly, maize, millet, mush, oatmeal, oats, pablum, porridge, post toasties, rice, rie, rolled oats, rye, samp, secale, soybean, spelt, supawn, teff, wheat
bowl porringer
coarse bran
coating bran
disease ergot, flagsmut, footrot
fertilizer alinit
fungus ergot
grass See GRASS *cereal.*
leaf flag
named after ceres
spike cobb, ear
CEREBELLUM parencephalon
part vermis
CEREBRAL cephalic, intellectual, intelligent, mental, psychic
anemia milk fever
apophysis pineal body
cortex pallium
cortex, pert. pallial
defect agyria
peduncle crus-cerebri
stimulant anhaline, hodenine, lophophorine, mescaline, pellotine
CEREBRATE cogitate, ponder, think
CEREBROSIDE kerasin
CEREBROTONIA intellectuality, introversion
CEREBRUM brain, en-

cephalon, forebrain, midbrain
layer capsule
CERECLOTH, CEREMENT chrismal, shroud, sparadrap, winding-sheet
CEREMONIAL conventional, form(al), liturgical, liturgy, order, precise, prim, procedure, punctilious, rite, ritual(istic), solemn, splendor, stiff, studied, system, triumph, upanaya
cleansing emundation
CEREMONIOUS academic, comme il faut, courteous, decorous, formal, grand, impressive, lofty, moving, polite, precise, proper, punctilious, ritual, seemly, solemn, stately, stiff, studied
leave-taking cong(e)
CEREMONY accolade, act (ion), augury, baccalaureate, baptism, berit(h), bridal, burial, celebration, civility, commencement, confirmation, crown, dance, display, duty, encaenia, etiquette, exequy, exercise, fete, form(ality), formula, formulary, function, gaud(y), gesture, gombay, graduation, hako, homage, inaugural, induction, initiation, institution, keriah, kiddush, liturgy, malkah, marriage, maundy, mummery, mystery, nipter, observance, occasion, office, ordinance, ovation, panagia, parade, performance, pomp, portent, powwow, practice, prodigy, re-enactment, review, rite, ritual, sacrament (al), sceptor, seal, service, show, sign, solemnity, sraddha, usage
marriage espousal, wedding
post-baptismal apol(o)usis
sprinkling asperges
CERES See DEMETER.
CEREUS cactus, cardon(a), plant, saguaro, waxen
CEREZA capulin, cordia, fruit, malpighia, plant, prunus
CERIANTHID actinarius, cerianthus, sea animal, vestlet
CERILLO cogwood, zapatero
CERIMON *servant* philemon
CERINTHE honeywort
CERION land-snail

CERISE cherry, red
CERIUM *metal* allanite, cerite, lanthanum, neodymium, praseodymium, promethium, rare earth, samarium
source monazite
CERNUOUS drooping, inclining, nodding, pendent, pendulous
CERO cavalla, kingfish, mackerel, pintado, scomberomorus, searer, sierra
CEROPLASTICS waxworks
CERRUS turkey-oak
CERRO highland, hill
CERTAIN 3 yea 4 amen, cold, cool, dead, fast, firm, free, real, some, sure, true 5 bound, clear, exact, fated, fixed, plain, siker 6 actual, beyond, poised, secure, sicker, stated, witter 7 assured, decided, implied, obvious, perfect, precise, settled 8 absolute, cocksure, constant, decisive, definite, destined, grounded, in the bag, official, positive, question, reliable, resolved, sanguine, unerring 9 avoidless, believing, confident, convinced, doubtless, necessary, satisfied, steadfast, undoubted, unfailing 10 dependable, determined, guaranteed, inevitable, particular, undeniable 11 apodictical, determinate, established, indubitable, ineluctable, inescapable, irrefutable, irrevocable, trustworthy, unavoidable 12 indefeasible, indisputable 13 incontestable, unpreventable 14 unquestionable 16 incontrovertible
absolutely apod(e)ictic
CERTAINLY actually, all right, amen, at all events, beyond doubt, by all means, certes, come what may, definitely, doubtless, evermore, for fair, forsooth, for sure, hardily, in any event, indeed(y), in truth, iwis, just so, necessarily, no doubt, notwithstanding, of course, perdie, positively, really, siccar, si(c)ker, soon, sure, surely, true, truly, undoubtedly, verily, veritably, wat, wis, without fail, yea, yes, ywis

CERTAINTY absoluteness, aplomb, assurance, belief, certitude, cinch, confidence, constancy, credence, definiteness, fact, faith, inevitability, infallibility, lead-pipe cinch, pipe, pledge, policy, positiveness, proof, security, sureness, sure thing, surety, truth, warranty, yea
lack of doubt, scruple

CERTIFICATE acceptance, aegrotat, affidavit, affidavy, amparo, attest(ation), authority, authorization, authorize, bill of exchange, bound, brevet, cedula, celebret, certify, check, cheque, chit, coupon, credential, credit-slip, debenture, deed, demit, deposition, deposit slip, diploma, docket, document, draft, draught, due bill, hundi, judgment, jurat, libel, license, money, navicert, note, order, paper, patent, permit, postal order, potah, register, scrip, security, sheepskin, stock, talon, tescaria, testamur, testimonial, tezkirah, ticket, timebill, title, token, treasury bill, verify, visa, vise, voucher, warrant, waybill, witness
cargo navicert
debt bond, debenture, iou
illness aegrotat
invention patent
land amparo, deed, title

CERTIFY accredit, affirm, approve, assert, assure, attest, authenticate, avouch, avow, behight, confirm, corroborate, depone, depose, determine, endorse, evince, guarantee, license, make certain, okay, prove, ratify, sanction, swear, testify, verify, vouch for, witness, witter

CERTITUDE assurance

CERULEAN azure, blue (stocking), ceruleous, coelin(e), cyanean, cyaneous, heavens, sky-blue
warbler dendroica

CERUMEN earwax

CERVALET rackett, sausage

CERVANTES *hero* don quixote

CERVELAT rackett, sausage

CERVID alce, antelope, axis, brocket, caribou, cervine, cervus, chital, dauw, deer, doe, elk, fawn, guemac, guemul, hangul, hart, havier, hearst, hind, hine, kakar, kakur, kidang, losh(e), maha, maral, moose, mort, muist, munjak, musk, napu, olen, pita, pito, pudu, rascal, ratwa, reindeer, roe, royal, rusa, sambar, samboo, sambur, shou, show, sika, sorrel, spado, spay, stag, surre, tarand, thamin, venade, venison, wapiti

CERVINE See DEER.

CESARIO viola

CESIUM *source* pollucite

CESPITOSE clustered, matted, sodded, tangled, tufted, turflike

CESS abwab, assess(ment), bog, cede, customs, duty, estimation, excise, impost, levy, luck, measure, peat bog, rate, slope, surrender, tax, teind, tithe, toll, tribute, turf, yield
bad sorra

CESSATION abandonment, abeyance, armistice, arrest, blackout, break, breather, cease, ceasing, close, closure, cloture, death, demise, desisting, desition, deval, discontinuance, disuse, end, halt, hiatus, hitch, hoo, idleness, inactivity, intermission, interruption, interval, letup, liss(e), lull, offset, pause, qualification, recess, remission, respite, rest, shutdown, slack, stacy, stint, stop(page), surcease, suspension, truce
arms armistice, truce
of being death, desition

CESSION ceding, qualification, surrender, transfer, yielding

CESSPOOL cistern, jawhole, pump, septic tank, sewer, sink(er), sump, suspiral

CESTODA monozoa, tapeworm

CESTRUM jasmine, matrimony vine, poisonberry, shrub, solanace

CESTUS band, belt, ctenophore, gauntlet, girdle, plant, venus's-girdle, whirlbat

CETACEAN acipenser, apod, beluga, cete, dowfish, delphinapterus, dolphin, grampus, hausen, inia, narwal, narwhal(e), orc(a), porpoise, sturgeon, susu, whale
blind susu
comb. ceto

CETO *brother* phorcys
lover phorcys
offspring euryale, gorgons, graeae, hesperides, medusa, stheno
parent gaea, pontus

CETONIA beetle, sap-chafer

CETORHINUS basking-shark

CETUS whale

CEUTA cibta, sebta
citadel jebel musa, monte acho
neighbor melilla

CEYLON lanka, serendip, sin(g)hala, sri lanka, taprobane
aborigine toda, vegga(h)
animal bandicoot, barking-deer, buffalo, elephant, langur, leopard, loris, maha, sambar, sloth, spotted-deer, stag, white deer, wild boar
ape langur, maha
athens kandy
bay palk
bird bee-eater, peacock, wanderoo
boat balsa, d(h)oni, done(y), warkamoowee
buddhism hinayana, mahayana
capital colombo, kandy
capital, ancient anuradhapura, polonnaruwa, sigiriya
chronicle mahavamsa
city anuradhapura, badulla, colombo, galle, jaffna, kandy, mannar, matara, moratuwa, polonnaruwa, puttalam, uva
coin cent
district dambulla, sri lanka, taprobane
dravidian tamil
fish danio
food curry, egg-hopper
foot soldier peon
fortress sigiriya
game area wilpattu
garment comboy, sarong
gooseberry ketembilla, kitambilla
government dissava

governor disawa
grass chena, patana
gulf mannar
hemp aloe, ifa, murva, pahgane, sansevieria, sina-wa
hill-dweller toda
holiday poyaday
king ravana
language english, pali, sin(g)halese, tamil
langur maha
lemur lori(s)
lion race sin(g)halese
litter tomjon, tonjon
lizard cheecha
lotus nelumbo
mail delivery tappall
market place pettan
marriage beena
measure amunam, para(h), parrah, seer
monkey langur, maha, rilawa, rillow, toque, wanderoo
moonstone adularia
moss agar, gracilaria, gulaman, jaffna, seaweed
national park ruhuna, wilpattu
nelumbo lotus
oak kusam, schleichera
pageant esala, perahera
palm talipat, talipot
paper money rupee
people burgher, cingalese, dravidian, eurasian, gin(g)halese, tamil, vedda(h), weddah
pert. sin(g)halese
point pedro
poontree domba
port batticaloa, colombo, galle, trincomalee
prime minister bandaranaike
prince, patricide kasyapa
rat bandicoot
resort bentota, hikkaduwa, mount lavinia, ruhuna, trincomalee, wilpattu
rest day poya
rest house ambalam, tissamaharama
rice paddy, padi
rose oleander
ruins See *capital, ancient.*
sarong comboy
sea sands paar
sedan tomjon, tonjon
shrub kitambilla
skirt reddha, sarong
snake adjiger
snakeroot arisaema, herb, jack-in-the-pulpit
soldier peon

strait palk
tea pekoe
temple asokharamaya, dagoba, kelaniya, lankatilaka
tree allaeanthus, domba, doon, hora, palu, shimahabodhi, tala, talipot
zircon jargon
CEYLONITE spinel
CEYX *parent* hesperus
  wife (h)alcyone
CHA chais, tea, tsia
CHABLIS chenin blanc, folle blanche, pinot blanc, pinot chardonnay, wine, white pinot
CHACK bite, clack, snack, snap, wheatear
CHACMA baboon, bavian, bobbejaan
CHAD *capital* fort lamy, ndjamena
  city areche, ati, bol, bongor, fada, faya, lai, largeau, mao, mongo, moundou, moussoro
  coin franc(cfa)
  leader malloum
  native arab, kamadja, kreda, massa, moundan, sara, toubou
  part wadai
  plateau ennedi
  president tombalbaye
  river bahraouk, chari, logone
CHADDO *indian* hainai, ioni
CHADOR phulkari
CHAETA bristle, seta, spine, stalk
CHAETOCHLOA setaria
CHAETOPOD annilid, bristle worm, scaleback
  larva atrocha
CHAFE abrade, anger, annoy, banter, bark, bind, burn, chaff, champ, exasperate, excite, excoriate, fret, friction, fridge, frig, frot, fume, fuss, gall, grate, grind, harass, heat, hurt, incense, inflame, irk, irritate, itch, nettle, provocation, provoke, rage, raillery, rankle, rub, scold, snuff(le), stew, sweat, vex, warm, wear, worry, wring
CHAFF badinage, banter, bhoosa, borak, bran(ner), chip, chyak, dross, glume(s), grain, grit, guff, guy, hulls, husk, jest, jolly, josh, kid, mock, persiflage, pug, pulu, quiz, raillery, rally, razz, refuse, remain-

der, rib, ridicule, riffraff, rot, rubbish, slack, stour, straw, stuff, tailling, tantalize, tease, teasing, trash, trivia, twit
  blow off winnow
  -like See CHAFFY.
  particle palea
CHAFFER bargain, buying, chatter, dicker, exchange, haggle, higgle, kid(der), market, merchandise, negotiation, palter, sieve, trade, traffic, wares
CHAFFINCH chick, roberd, robinet, scobby, skelly, snabbie, spink, twink wetbird
CHAFFY acerate, acerose, acerous, bantering, needleshaped, palaceous, paleate, scaly, spade-shaped, trivial, worthless
CHAFING abrasion, abrasive, attrition, galling, heating, impatience
  dish choffer
CHAGRIN abash(ment), affliction, anxiety, balk, blow, bother, confound, confuse, confusion, disappointment, discomfit(ure), discomfort, disconcert, distress, disturbance, embarrass(ment), envy, frustration, humiliation, let-down, melancholy, mortification, mortify, put out, shame, spite, trouble, vex(ation), worry
CHAGRINED ashamed, mortified, sick
CHAIN albert, attach, bind, bobstay, bond, boom, bracelet, brail, bridle, cable, carcanet, catena, catfall, chignon, combine, concatenation, connect, cordillera, cordon, curb, embrace, enslave, fast(en), fastener, fetter, file, fog, ganger, gleipner, group, guy, gyve, hanger, hobble, jacker, jigger, join, lashing, leash, line, link(er), linkwork, manacle, moor, necklace, net(work), painter, pendant, progression, rackan, range, restrain, ridge, rigwiddy, sautoir, seal, secure, sequence, series, set, shackle, slang, sling, soam, string, strobila, succession, suite, tackler,

tether, tew, tie, toe, toggle, torac, torque, trace, train, tug, tye, wrase
anchor hole hawse
binding jacker, tackler
cable boom
collar torc, torque
convicts slang
decorative festoon
endless creeper
fern anchistea
forminto catenate
grab wildcat
key chatelaine
length shot
-like catenate, catenulate
link copula, shut, swivel
log bull, jack-ladder
magic gleipner
-mail byrnie, habergeon, hauberk, linkmail
maker linksmith
mountain range, ridge, rockies, sierras
nautical type
ornamental bracelet, carcanet, lavaliere, locket, necklace, pendant, sautoir
pert. catenarian, catenary
reaction disasters, dominoes, vicissitudes
rock reef
-shaped catenoid, filiform
short shank
steps cascade
store supermarket, supermart
suspended catenary
10 square acre
together enlink
CHAINMAN clashee, clashy, lineman, tapeman
CHAINS bondage, bonds, enslavement, fetters, helotry, irons, servitude, shackles, slavery, trammels
lady in andromeda
CHAIR administer, bench, cacolet, carriage, cathedra, chaise, commode, conveyance, enthrone, gondola, install, institution, kago, keep, klismos, office, preside, pulpit, rocker, saddle, seat, sedan, see, shinza, sitter, speaker, stool, support, throne, tonjon, voyeuse
back splat
bath vinaigrette
bishop's cathedra, faldstool
chippendale ribbon-back
cover antimacassar, tidy
designer eames
easy cogswell, coxwell

18th century bergere, fumeuse, ribbon-back
folding faldstool
jacobean acorn chair
kind acorn, arm, arrowback, barrel, bergere, boston rocker, bowback, brewster, campaign, captain's, club, cogswell, comb-back, coxwell, deck, dining, easy, faldstool, fanback, fauteuil, folding, gaddi, high, howdah, ladder-back, lawn, lounge, morris, overstuff, recliner, rocker, sedan, sgabello, steamer, straight, swivel, throne, tub, voltaire, windsor, wing
kneeling prie-dieu
knob pommel
litterlike kago, sedan
material plastic, rattan, steel, wicker, wood
occupy preside
of state shinza, throne
on wheels bath, vinaigrette, part arm(rest), leg, rung, seat, splat
pole-borne kago, sedan, talabon
portable sedan
reclining chaise longue
renaissance panchetto, sgabello
seat bottom
spring perch
throne shinza
-warmer idler, loafer, lounger
wicker guerite
windsor fanback
CHAIRMAN administer, convener, director, emcee, head, introducer, leader, moderator, preses, president, presider, speaker, supervisor, symposiarch, toastmaster
CHAISE calesin, carriage, chair, gig, shay
longue daybed, duchesse
1-horse calesin
CHAJA screamer
CHAL fellow, man, person
CHALAZA gallature, tread(le)
CHALCEDONY agate, amydaloid, beekite, bloodstone, carnelian, carneol, cat's-eye, copper-red, enhyros, heliotrope, hematite, honey buzzard, jasper, onyx, opal(ine), prase, quartz, sard(ine), sardius

nodule enhydros
pseudomorph beekite, honey buzzard
CHALCIOPE *sister* medea
CHALCIS *parent* asopus, metope
CHALDEA, CHALDEAN astrologer, babylonian, enchanter, kaldani, seer, soothsayer
astronomical cycle saros
capital babylon
hero amelen, amenon, amphis
measure artaba, cane, foot, gariba, ghalva, makuk, mansion, qasab
river euphrates, tigris
CHALET cabin, cottage, house, hut
CHALICE ama, amula, blossom, bowl, calix, cup, goblet, grail, krasis, regal
cover aer, air, animetta, pall
flower daffodil
mixed krasis
pall animetta
veil aer, air
CHALINITIS athena
CHALK account, blanch, bleach, cauk, cork, crayon, credit, creta, flour, gesso, hurlock, limestone, mark, pale, picture, rubble, scar, score, talc, tally, tick, whiten, whiting
and clay malm
board blackboard, greenboard, slate
convert to cretify
green prasine
hard hurlock
-like cretaceous
plant babies'-breath, baby'sbreath
red bole, rubric, ruddle
rubbing frottage
sponge ascon
stone tophus
surveyor's keel
talker lecturer
up charge; earn, record, score
CHALKY calcareous, cretacic, grayish, powdery, pulverable, whitish
CHALLENGE accuse, affront, appeal, arouse, arraign, banco, blame, bluster, brag, brave, call, cartel, censure, champion, charge, cite, claim, confront, contest, controvert, dacker, daiker, dare, defial,

defiance, defiant, defy, demand, descry, double-dare, doubt, exception, face, flout, forbid, gage, gauntlet, glove, impeach, impugn, invite, object, protest, provoke, query, question, recuse, reproach, solicit, stimulate, stump, summons, vie
judge recuse

CHALLENGER duelist, pugilist

CHALPHI *son* judas

CHAM albanian, bite, champ, chew

CHAMBER ager, alcove, apartment, arch, assembly, atrium, auricle, bedroom, bonnet, boudoir, bower, cabinet, camarilla, camera, cave, cavity, cavum, cell, channel, cist, coffer, committee, compartment, council, court, cubicle, cylinder, digs, flat, fold, gomer, group, hall, hollow, house, iwan, kiva, legislature, loculus, mihrab, oda(h), pad, pocket, room, salle, senat(e), shaft, socket, sol(l)ar, soler, stanza, tenement, tomb, wardrobe
air sponson
annealing leer
bombproof casemate
burial catacomb, cubiculum, tomb
comb. thalam(o)
council consistory
drying kiln, oven
-fellow comrade, roommate
fire arch, cockle, stove
furnace doghouse, shaft
having 2 bicameral
judge's camera, inn
king's camarilla
member booster, jaycee
of commerce board of trade
open lantern
organ swell
ornamented gloriette
pert. cameral
pot jeroboam, jordan
private adyta, adytum, conclave, sanctum
small loculus
underground cave(rn), crypt, hypogee
water tight caisson

CHAMBERLAIN attendant, camerlengo, chamberer, factor, officer, palatine, polonius, servant, steward, superintendent, treasurer

papal camerlengo, camerlingo

CHAMBERMAID bedmaker, servant

CHAMELEON anole, anoli, eft, lacert, lizard, newt, opportunist, saurian, solitaire, timeserver
-like colorful, inconstant, vacillating, variegated

CHAMFER bevel, channel, chimb, chime, chine, flute, furrow, groove

CHAMOIS antelope, aoudad, canepin, gems, gemse, izard, rupicapra, sarau, shammy, shamoy, sheet
-like leather buff
male gemsbok

CHAMOMILE cammomile, mayweed

CHAMP bite, chaw, chew, chomp, field, grind, munch, trample
at the bit await, chafe, flare up, fume, wait
de mars arena

CHAMPAGNE belleek, bubbly, shampen, sillery, simkin, wine
bottle size jeroboam, magnum, methuselah, nebuchadnezzar, rehoboam, salmanazar
center troyes
deposit griffe
inventor dom perignon
kind blanc de blanc, brut, doux, dry, extra dry, natural, sec
semi-dry sec
sweet doux, gooseberry-juice
very dry brut
worker remuer

CHAMPAIGN See PLAIN.

CHAMPION abet, ace, advocate, aid, ally, apologist, assert, attend, back(er), best, boss, capital, challenge, choice, combatant, defend(er), defy, espouse, expert, exponent, fan, fighter, first-rate, ghazi, guard, help, hero, kemp, knight(errant), maintain, master, medalist, nonpareil, oak, paladin, palmerin, paragon, partisan, patron, perseus, prize(man)(winner), protect(or), sponsor, squire, support(er), sympathizer, the best, titleholder, unbeaten, unexcelled, un-

holder, victor, vindicator, winner

CHAMPIONSHIP advocacy, laurels, leadership, supremacy, title
winner grand slammer, titleholder

CHAMPLEVE inlaid

CHAN khan, lord, resthouse

CHANCE 3 hap, lot 4 case, cast, dint, draw, fate, joss, line, luck, odds, pass, risk, shot, show, tide 5 blind, break, ettle, fluke, happy, lucky, occur, stake, wager, whack 6 befall, betide, casual, fairgo, gamble, happen, hazard, kismet, mishap, raffle, random, squeek, toss up, turn up 7 aimless, bargain, fortune, opening, outlook, potluck, scratch, stumble, vantage, venture 8 accident, casualty, distance, eventual, fortuity, lady luck, prospect, question 9 adventure, causeless, haphazard, happening, hit or miss, irregular, liability, mischance, tempt fate, transpire 10 accidental, casualness, contingent, fortuitous, incidental, likelihood, occasional, touch and go, unexpected, unforeseen 11 contingency, opportunity, possibility, probability, speculation, uncertainty 12 adventitious, happenstance, inexplicable 13 indeterminate, unintentional 14 throw of the dice
adverse hazard
by accidentally, casually, habnab, haphazardly, incidentally, spontaneously, suddenly, unexpectedly
comb. tycho
equal even break, toss up
game of betting, gambling, gaming, pool, sweepstakes, wagering, wheel
god tyche
good likelihood, odds-on
-medley haphazard, potluck, random
upon alight, encounter, meet, run across

CHANCEL *area* apse
part altar, bema, communion table
screen jube
seat sedile, sedilia
table altar

CHANCELLOR chief, executive, head, judge, logothete, premier, prime minister, principal, ruler, secretary
pert. cancellarian
seat woolsack
CHANCO wolf
CHANCY auspicious, canny, casual, contingent, haphazard, hazardous, lucky, precarious, random, risky, rocky, uncertain, unpredictable
CHANDELIER candlebranch, circlet, corona, crown, electrolier, gasolier(y), luster, pendant, pharos
tree pandanus
CHANE ara wakan, khan, orejon
CHANG beer, din, noise, row
and eng siamese twins
CHANGE 4 cash, flop, flux, mart, molt, move, muta, peal, sour, sway, tack, turn, vary, veer, warp 5 adapt, alter, amend, break, coins, emend, money, moult, shift, swing, taint, throw, trade, waver 6 adjust, barter, become, dacker, differ, evolve, immute, modify, mutate, obvert, remove, revamp, revise, seesaw, switch, tamper, teeter, wabble, wamble, wissel, wobble, wrixle 7 alembic, caprice, commute, convert, develop, deviate, fluxion, novelty, shuffle, stagger, transit, variety 8 becoming, demarche, denature, exchange, flounder, innovate, modulate, reversal, revision, transfer, transume, variance 9 deviation, diversify, diversion, diversity, fluctuate, oscillate, pendulate, transform, turnabout, vacillate, variation, volte-face 10 adjustment, alteration, assimilate, difference, innovation, revolution, substitute, transition 12 metamorphose, modification, teetertotter 13 differentiate 15 diversification
abnormal lesion
appearance disguise, obvert, transfigure
back return, revert
character denature
color blush, dye, fade, flush, pale, redden, take fright, turn
comb. meta, tropo
course angle, bear away, break, cant, deviate, gybe, jibe, kant, knee, sheer, shift, tack, turn, veer
for See SUBSTITUTE.
form develope, metamorphose, metastasize, transmute
for worse bedevil, decline
gait break
god vertumnus, vortumnus
gradual drift
hands devolve, transfer
hatred of misoneism
house alehouse, inn
into become, metamorphose
-maker boxman
mind budge, convert, repent
musical muta
of belief conversion, turncoat
of heart regeneration, repentance
of life climacteric, menopause
of policy turnaround
opposition to conservatism, philistinism, reaction, standpattism
order transpose
over See CONVERT.
position fleet, hotch, move, stir
pressure allobar
radical revolution
resist stand pat
resistance to inertia
shape creep, deform, develop
small chicken feed, pin money
strangely transmogrify
sudden burst, saltation, switch(eroo)
time of crisis, transition, turning point, zero hour
CHANGEABLE alterable, alterative, amenable, amphibolic, bruckle, capricious, catching, chameleonic, checkered, choppy, eemis, erratic, fickle, fitful, fluid, frivolous, gerful, giddy, glibbery, immis, inconstant, kaleidoscopic, ketchy, light, many-sided, mercurial, metamorphic, mobile, modifiable, moody, motile, motley, moveable, mutable, opportunistic, permutable, plastic, protean, shifty, skittish, ticklish, time-serving, transilient, uncertain, unstable, variable, variant, various, veerable, versatile, wavering
as april showers, chameleon, kaleidoscope, mercury, moon, proteus, quicksilver, rolling stone, shifting sands, weathercock, weathervane
in color allochroic
in form metabolic
CHANGEABLY back and forth, in and out, off and on, on and off, round and round, to and fro
CHANGELESS consistent, constant, permanent
CHANGELING auf, awf, child, dolt, double, dunce, elf, fool, idiot, imbecile, inconstant, killcrop, oaf, renegade, ringer, simpleton, substitute, turncoat, waverer
CHANGER alembic, alterant, alterative, alterer, modificator, modifier, transformer
CHANGING active, alternate, ambiguous, amphibolic, amphibolous, catching, equivocal, floating, fluxible, irregular, uncertain, variable
color allochroous, alloc(h)romatic
pattern and color kaleidoscope
CHANNEL 3 bed, cut, gap, gat, ree, rut, tun, way 4 adit, band, cano, dike, duct, geat, gool, lane, leaf, pipe, race, road, tube, vein, wadi, weir 5 agent, bayou, canal, chase, chute, ditch, donga, drain, drove, flume, flute, glyph, gulch, gully, means, organ, rigol, route, sewer, sinus, sound, spout, stria, swash, water 6 airway, alveus, arroyo, artery, avenue, branch, bridge, canyon, convey, course, estero, funnel, furrow, groove, gullet, gutter, kennel, medium, outlet, rabbet, siphon, slough, sluice, stream, streat, strial, throat, trench, trough 7 acequia, conduct, conduit, culbert, culvert, fissure, narrows, opening, passage, raceway, scupper, silanga, straits, strigal, tideway 8 aqueduct, gunkhole,

headrace, penstock, pipe-line, riverway, spillway, tailrace, watergap, water-way 9 pentrough, stream-way 10 instrument, passage-way 11 watercourse
aqueduct specus
artificial gat, gout
bone caniculus, clavicle, col-lar
brain iter
cat catfish
communication artery
drainage gaw
formed by cutting scarf
goose gannet
inclined shoot
in cloth flute
inland canal, gat
iron bar, hook
irrigation acequia, auwai, ditch, drove
island alderney, guernsey, herm, jersey, sark
island cattle alderney
island measure cabot, cade
island seaweed vraic
longitudinal rabbet
lymph cisterna
marker buoy
mill leat, race
narrow furrow, gat, strait
near port deeps
open fairway
river alveni, alvenus, bed
secondary binnacle, binocle
shallow lagoon
ship gat
sloping chute, shute
underground emissarium, ka-tabothron
vertical glyph
vital artery
water aqueduct, canal, con-duit, drain, flume, gat, gote, leat, millrace, pipe, race, sluice, tailrace, weir
CHANNELBILL cuckoo, rainfowl
CHANNELED champered, confined, fluted, furrowed, voluted
CHANSON ballad, lyric, re-frain, SONG
CHANT alleluia, anthem, an-tiphon(y), cant(icle), can-tillate, cantus, carol, croon, drone, hymn, intone, introit, lilt, litany, mele, melody, prosode, psalm, re-quiem, response, sing(ing), singsong, song, sough, war-ble, worship

plain cantus firmus, cantus planus
religious agnus dei
triple agnus dei
CHANTER bagpipe, cantor, chalumeau, chorister, oboe, precenter, singer, stick
CHANTEY ballad, ditty, lay, SONG
CHANTICLEER cock, roos-ter
CHANTING autiphoney, chazzanut, hazanut
CHAOS abyss, anarchy, apsu, babel, chasm, clutter, con-fusion, disarray, disorder, formlessness, gulf, havoc, hyle, improglio, jumble, kore, lawlessness, matter, mess, mixture, muddle, nun, pandemonium, pie, shambles, snafu, snarl, tail-spin, tohubohu, tophet, tu-mult, turmoil, void
daughter night, nox, nyx
personification anarch, hun-tun, ymir
son aether, erebus
utter tophet(h)
wife night, nox, nyx
CHAOTIC amorphous, balled up, confused, formless, fouled up, hay-wire, helter-skelter, hig-gledy-piggledy, hugger-mug-ger, inchoate, jumbled, messy, mixed up, mom-mixed, muddled, ramble-scrambled, scattered, shape-less, snafu(ed), topsy-turvy, turbulent, unformed, up-sidedown
CHAP baby, barter, bean, beat, bird, blighter, bloke, blow, bohunk, boy, breach, break, bucko, bugger, bully, buy(er), callan(t), chaft, chink, chip, choose, chop, cleft, codger, cove, crack, cuffin, customer, dick, duck, fellow, fissure, gaffer, gal-lant, geezer, gent, guy, hus-band, jaw, jerk, john, kerel, kibe, kipper, knock, lad, lover, man, mash, mate, merchant, pound, rap, red-den, roughen, rummy, scout, shaver, snap, split, sport, spray, strike, stroke, swipe, trade, turnip, wag, youth
fine bully
-hands rack, spray
odd galoot

old gaffer, geezer
young punk
CHAPARRAL bluewood, buckthorn, bush, chamisal, condalia, macchie, maqui, monte, shrub, thicket
cock ground-cuckoo, road-runner
CHAPARRO yaya
CHAPBOOK anthology, chrestomathy, corpus, flori-legium, garland, pamphlet, thesaurus, treasury
CHAPE case, crampet, loop, mordant, mounting, scab-bard, sheathe
CHAPEAU See HAT.
CHAPEL altar, bethel, bethesda, cage, capella, chantry, chatri, chhatri, choir, church, conventicle, deaconry, diaconia, fere-tory, galilee, haikal, morada, oratorium, ora-tory, printing office, sacel-lum, sacrarium, sacrary, sanctuary, service, shrine, sistine, sodality
byzantine antiparabema
dissenters', pert. pantile
part oratory
CHAPERON accompany, at-tend, care for, convoy, dragon, duenna, escort, gooseberry, governante, governess, griffin, guard (ian), hood, matron(ize), protect(or)
CHAPFALLEN chagrined, dejected, dispirited, down-cast, embarrassed, ex-hausted, sullen
CHAPLAIN altarist, clergy-man, ecclesiastic, levite, or-dinary, padre
CHAPLET anadem, astragal, band, bead, circle(t), coronal, coronet, crown, fillet, garland, jamber, jammer, molding, necklace, orle, prayer, rosary, stud, trophy, wreath
CHAPMAN buyer, customer, dealer, hawker, merchant, peddler, trader, vendor
john johnny appleseed
CHAPPED coarse, cracked, harsh, humble, kibed, kiby, rough, split
CHAPPY cleft, gaping
CHAPS breeches, chops, flews, jaws, leggings, mouth, overalls
CHAPTER assembly, body,

branch, cabildo, camp, canon, capital, capitulary, caput, cell, circle, correct, court, division, lodge, mark, meeting, part, portion, post, quotation, reprimand, section, topic, unit, wing
and verse fully
house cabildo
member capitular
of book capital
pert. capitular, chapteral
CHAR assignment, blacken, broil, burn, carbonize, cart, chariot, chark, chore, clean(ing woman), coal, daily, duty, fix, job, redbelly, repair, saibling, salmonid, sandbank, scorch, sear, singe, stint, task, tea, trout, work
CHARA bulbil, muskgrasy, stonewort
CHARABANC bus, coach, vehicle
CHARACIN bloodfin, dorado, dourade, fish
CHARACTER 3 air, ilk 4 bent, card, case, clef, dash, elan, form, kind, mark, mold, note, part, role, rune, sign, sort, tone, trim, type 5 actor, arete, brand, breed, class, ethos, fiber, habit, heart, humor, neume, savor, stamp, tenor, token, trait, write 6 accent, aspect, caract, cipher, emblem, figure, genius, kidney, letter, madcap, makeup, manner, mettle, nature, number, oddity, repute, spirit, stripe, symbol, temper, traits 7 courage, engrave, essence, portray, probity, quality 8 capacity, describe, ethology, function, identity, inscribe, ligature, property 9 attribute, eccentric, integrity, represent 10 atmosphere 11 description, disposition, distinction, peculiarity, personality 13 impersonation 14 recommendation
assumed figure, incognito, role
bad budmash, drole
chief hero, heroine, lead, star
comb. iose, ity
comic gracioso
common community
defect hamartia
distinguishing ethos

firm backbone
fundamental nature
group ethos
hereditary strain
physical armenoid
racial ethos
science of ethology
shiftless deadbeat
stock maccus
vein streak
vulgar onmun
without blah, dull, mediocre, weak
word-representing logogram, logograph, logos
CHARACTERISTIC accent, accustomed, angle, aroma, aspect, attribute, badge, brand, cast, depiction, distinctive, earmark, egohood, endemic, feature, flavor, foible, grace, habit, hallmark, identity, idiocrasy, idiosyncrasy, impress(ion), individual(ism), kink, lineament, mannerism, mark, mein, nature, oddity, oneness, originality, particularity, pathognomonic, peculiar(ity), personality, point, property, quality, quirk, savor, selfness, singularity, slant, smack, special(ty), species, specific, stamp, stand, stroke, symbolic, tache, taint, tang, temper, token, tone, trait, trick, type, typical, vein
distinguishing birthmark, hallmark, species
individual idiopathy
CHARACTERIZE call, define, delineate, depict, describe, differentiate, distinguish, earmark, enact, engrave, entitle, eulogize, feature, impersonate, imprint, indicate, inscribe, mark, name, portray, represent, style, title, typify
CHARCO pool, puddle, spring
CHARCOAL blacken, carbon(ligni), chark, drawing, fuel, fusain, lignite, pencil, picture, remainder, scribbet, spodium, xylanthrax
animal bone-black
burner charbonnier
gas from oxan(e)
-like carbonous
reduced to char
refuse breeze
rubbing frottage

CHARE alley, business, CHAR, chary, finish, job, lane, occasion, perform, return, street, task, time, turn, work
CHARGE 3 ask, bid, fee, ram, tap, tax 4 beef, bill, book, buck, bull, call, care, cark, cast, cost, cram, dash, doom, dues, duty, fill, gibe, keep, lade, levy, lien, load, nick, note, onus, rack, rate, rush, soak, task, tilt, toll, twit, urge, ward, wike 5 blame, blast, cargo, cause, chalk, count, crime, debit, exact, extra, flank, onset, oomph, order, pinon, power, press, price, prime, punch, refer, run at, score, sneak, spark, steam, stick, sting, taunt, tithe, trust 6 accuse, adjure, advice, aerate, allege, appeal, assess, attack, burden, career, client, course, credit, damage, defame, demand, direct, enjoin, enurny, hurtle, impose, impute, indict, office, report, saddle, surtax, tariff, wallop, weight 7 accusal, arraign, article, ascribe, assault, censure, command, conjure, custody, expense, impeach, intrust, mandate, mission, precept, prorate, protege, request, require, slander, warhead 8 benefice, casualty, cathexis, chastise, complain, denounce, instruct, overload, question, reproach, shotsize, stampede, tutorage 9 challenge, complaint, dependent 10 accusation, assignment, commission, denunciate, dependence, imputation, indictment, injunction 11 attribution, encumbrance, impeachment, incriminate, supervision 12 denunciation 13 counterattack
against tilt
anchorage boomage, dockage, moorage
cover couvert
criminal accuse, attaint, impeach, indict
customary dues
depth can
explosive blast, booster, burster, cap, igniter, snake, squib

false calumny, slander
grazing agist
legal costs, dues, fee, retainer
money-coining brassage
-off See DISCOUNT.
spiritual cure
wine corkage
with gas aerate
with lance tilt
CHARGED electric, hot, hyperthyroid, tense, uptight
CHARGEHAND blaster, clicker, foreman
CHARGER accuser, courser, dish, horse, mount, plate, platform, platter, steed, warhorse
CHARICLO *consort* everes
son tiresias
CHARIOT auto, biga, buggy, car, carriage, cart, char, curre, essed(a), rath(a), seven, triga, vehicle, wagon, wain
ancient curre, essed(a), rath(a)
driving aurigation
driving, pert. diphrelatic
4-wheeled quadriga
god-carrying rath(a)
of the gods sierra leone
poetic wain
religious rath(a)
3-wheeled troga
top calash
2-horse biga
2-wheeled essed(a), gig
CHARIOTEER auriga, automedon, ben hur, cartare, carter, driver, iolaus, jehu, myrtilus, pilot, wagoner
pert. aurigal
CHARIS *beloved* hephaestus
CHARISMA appeal, impact, leadership, oomph, personality, power
CHARITABLE altruistic, beneficent, benevolent, benign, bounteous, bountiful, caritative, clement, compassionate, considerate, eleemosynary, forgiving, generous, humane, humanitarian, indulgent, kind, lenient, liberal, magnanimous, mild, munificent, open-handed, philanthropic, sympathetic, tender, tolerant
CHARITONETTA bucephala, buffleduck, bufflehead, butterback, butterball, glaucionetta, namer-duck.
CHARITY alms, altruism,

basket, benefaction, beneficence, benevolence, benignity, bounty, caritas, consideration, dole, donation, forgiveness, generosity, gift, good works, grace, handout, humanity, kindness, largess, lenience, lenity, liberality, love, mercy, oblation, open-heartedness, patience, philanthropy, pity, quarter, relief, ruth, sympathy, tenderness, tzedakah, welfare, widow's mite, works
case pauper
dispenser almoner
pert. eleemosynary
place almshouse, arca, home
symbol pelican
symbolic color red
CHARIVARI babel, callithump, chivari, noise, serenade, shallal, shivaree, uproar
CHARLATAN cabotin, cheat, counterfeiter, empiric, fake(r), feigner, fraud, humbug, imposter, magician, montebank, pretender, quack(salver), sycophant
-astrologer astrologaster
CHARLEMAGNE *adviser* alcuin
brother carloman
capital aachen, aix-la-chappelle, ingelheim, nymwegen, regensburg
conquest avars, bavarians, lombards, saracens, saxons, spaniards
daughter melisendra
enemy baligant, corsuble, desiderius, marsile, nicephorus, widukind
father pepin III
father-in-law desiderius, galaire
godchild mitaine
grandparent charibert, charles martel
hero roland
horse tencendur
knight See *paladin,* below.
mother berta, bertrada
nephew gwyferos, orlando, roland
paladin acelin, anseis, aspremont, astolfo, astor, balan, berengier, enfrances, engeber, fierambras, florismart, gaifer, ganelon, gaston, geoffrey, gerard, gerier,

guarinos, g(u)erin, guillaume, hoel, ivoiere, ivon, lambert, malagigi, maugis, milon, montrogon, naimes, nami, ogier, oliv(i)er, orlando, otes, otuel, richard, rinaldo, riol du mans, roland(o), samson, thi(e)ry, turpin, wolf
pert. caroline, carolinian
romance anseis de carthage, chanson de roland, fierebras, gaidon, guiteclin, les saisnes, macaire, otinel, weihenstephan
shield biterne
son charles the young, lewis the pious, pepin
sword falmberge, joyeuse
sword-maker galas
teacher albinus, alc(h)uin(e)
traitor ganelon
12 peers See *paladin,* above.
war cry montjoie
wife adalinda, blanchefleur, desiderata, frastrade, galerana, galienne, gersuinde, hamiltrude, hildegarde, himiltrude, irene, luitgarde, maltegarde, regina
CHARLES *pert.* carlovingian, carolean, caroline, carolingian, carolinian
CHARLES I jack sprat
advisor strafford
dwarf richard gibson
enemy roundhead
supporter cavalier
CHARLES II curly locks, david
courtesan nell gwyn(ne)
son, illegitimate monmouth
CHARLES V *admiral* andrea doria
brother ferdinand
daughter katharine
empress isabel
nephew maximilian
servant bodard, philip ii
son don juan, philip ii
CHARLES VIII *horse* savoy
CHARLES X *battle* poltava
CHARLES MARTEL the hammer
ally eudes, odo
enemy abd ar rahman, plectrude, ragenfrid
grandson charlemagne
parent chalpaida, pippin
realm alemannia, austrasia, bavaria, burgundy, neustria, provence
son carloman, pippin

victory agde, beziers, maguelonne, narbonensis, poitiers, tours
CHARLES, NICK *dog* asta
wife nora
CHARLES'S *wain* bear, dipper, ursa
CHARLESTON *fort* sumter
name holy city
title colonel
CHARLEY beard, fox, watchman
horse cramp, crick, kink, pain, pang, seizure, stiffness, stitch
CHARLOCK chedlock, crowd-grass, crowdweed, crunchweed, kedlock, kerlock, kraut(weed), mustard, runch, sinapis, skedlock, skelloch, yellows
CHARM 3 hex, key, obi 4 calm, chic, hand, jinx, juju, jynx, luck, lure, mojo, rune, snow, song, take, zogo 5 allay, brief, catch, favor, freet, freit, grace, lamin, magic, obeah, saffi, safie, spell, wanga, weird 6 allure, amulet, appeal, attach, beauty, caract, deasil, dessil, enamor, engage, entice, fetish, glamor, grigri, mantra, mascot, please, ravish, saphie, scarab, soothe, subdue, symbol, voodoo, votive 7 abrasax, abraxas, assuage, attract, beguile, bewitch, cantion, cantrip, charact, delight, enchant, enthral, flatter, glamour, gratify, handsel, heitiki, periapt, philter, philtre, sorcery 8 blessing, breloque, coquetry, glaumrie, greegree, inveigle, madstone, pishogue, scarabee, sudarium, swastika, talisman, veronica 9 captivate, carry away, delectate, fascinate, gammadion, magnetism, sweetness 10 brimborium, likability, lovability, loveliness, lucky piece, mumbo jumbo, phylactery, rabbit foot 11 adorability, apotropaion, enchantment, incantation, winsomeness 12 antinganting, lovesomeness
jewel breloque, brimborion, brimborium
magic abraham's eye, conjuration
metal lamin

protective amulet
-*struck* spellbound
CHARMED captive, enamored, garchadat, glad, ravi, spellbound, taken
CHARMER allayer, calmer, enchanter, lorelei, magician, siren, sorcerer, wizard
CHARMING adorable, amiable, darling, delicate, eyesome, golden, graceful, lepid, lovely, magical, sweet, winning, winsome
CHARMION *companion* iras
CHARNEL cemetery, ghostly, golgotha, mortuary
CHARON ferryman
parent erebus, nox, nyx
pay obolus
river styx
CHARPENTIER *opera* louise
CHARQUI jerky, xarque
CHART arrangement, card, carte, cartogram, chorography, design, diagram, dopebook, emagram, explore, graph, list, map, mercator, outline, plan, plat, plot, presentation, project, record, rutter, scheme, sheet, sketch
a course pilot
book wagoner
mariner's rose
mark vigia
thermodynamic emagram
weather analogue
CHARTER authorize, book, certificate, code, constitution, contract, conveyance, deed, diploma, engage, fix, franchise, fuero, grant, grundlov, hire, immunity, lease, let, license, monopoly, pact, panchart, patent, permit, rent, sanad, sunnud, treaty
CHARWOMAN daily, domestic, janitress, portress
CHARY calculating, careful, cautious, chere, choosy, circumspect, curious, dainty, dear, deliberate, economical, fastidious, frugal, hesitant, loath, prized, provident, prudent, reluctant, saving, scant, shy, skimpy, spare, sparing, thrifty, treasured, vigilant, wary
CHARYBDIS eddy, galofalo, garofalo, rock, whirlpool
father poseidon

mother gaea
partner scylla
slayer hercules
CHASE annoy, backjoint, boss, caccia, catch, channel, chevy, chiv(v)y, chouse, course, court, dissipate, drive, emboss, engrave, escort, expel, fetch, follow, frieze, furrow, gallop, groove, harass, harry, hasten, hound, hunt, hurry, indent, intaglio, jerl, pursue, pursuit, quarry, quest, repulse, run, rush, scorse, seduce, shag, shoo, sic, sue, tag, tail, trach, trail, trench, woo
along depart, scat, scram
away repulse, rout, shoo
deity apollo, artemis, diana, ull
women cat
CHASER chasse, drink, hound, hunter, jager, johnnie, philanderer, pursuer, ram
CHASM abysm, abyss, aperture, blank, breach, brief, canon, canyon, chaos, cleft, crater, crevas(se), crevice, fissure, flume, gap, glut, gorge, gulf, hiatus, hole, interval, megaron, opening, pit, ravine, reft, rift, swallow, vacancy, void, yawn
CHASSE dismiss, glide, reliquary, shrine
CHASSEUR attendant, bellboy, doorman, footman, hunter, huntsman, soldier
alpin blue devils
CHASSIS figure, frame, landing-gear, railway
CHASTE aesthetic, angelic, austere, bald, bare, cast, celibate, classic, clean, continent, decent, honest, immaculate, innocent, intermerate, leal, loyal, maidenly, modest, moral, neat, plain, proper, pudical, pure, refined, reprove, restrain, righteous, severe, simple, stark, subdue, undefiled, unmarried, unpretentious, vestal, virgin(al), virginly, virtuous
name meaning agnes, catherine, karen, katharine, kay, kit, trina
CHASTEN abase, abash, afflict, blame, castigate, censure, chastise, correct, disci-

pline, humble, moderate, prove, punish, purify, rate, refine, restrain, simplify, slap, smite, smote, sneap, sober, spank, subdue, swinge, taunt, temper, trim, try, whip

CHASTISE accuse, amend, anoint, beat, berate, blame, castigate, censure, charge, chasten, correct, discipline, ferule, firk, flog, lash, punish, purify, rebuke, refine, restrain, scold, scourge, slap, slate, spank, strap, suspect, swinge, taunt, temper, thrash, trim, whip

CHASTITY artemis, britomartis, celibacy, goodness, honesty, honor, innocence, modesty, naivete, pudicity, purity, simplicity, virginity, virtue

mother cher

symbol olive, tortoise

symbolic color silver, white

CHASUBLE amphibalus, casula, deacon, infula, paenula, pianeta, planet, vestment

CHAT ament, babble(ment), bat the breeze, bird, catkin, cause(rie), chaffer, CHATTER, chin, chitchat, collogue confab(ulate), converse, coose, cose, coze, dally, essence, essential, gab(ble), gas, gibber, gossip, goster, hobnob, jabber, jaw, mag, patter, pitch, point, potter, prate, prattle, prittle-prattle, prose, pross, samara, shoot the breeze, speak, spike, talk, tell, tete-a-tete, thrush, tittle-tattle, tove, twig, visit, wheatear, yarn

CHATEAU castle, chatelet, estate, fortress, house, mansion

CHATELAINE brooch, clasp, decoration, etui, key chain, mistress, ornament, purse, solitaire, torque

CHATHAM pitt

CHATHAM ISLANDS *native* moriori

CHATON basil, bezel, bezil, coating, setting, stone

CHATTEL(S) appurtenances, capital, cattalum, cattle, bondman, effects, farleu, farley, fixture, gear, goods, livestock, money, pledge,

principal, property, slave(s), stuff

distraint of naam

lent commodatum

tenant's farleu, farley

to recover detinue

CHATTER 3 gab, gas, jaw, mag, yak, yap 4 blab, blah, blat, carp, CHAT, chin, clap, clat, dish, gaff, goon, guff, gush, hack, magg, talk, yack, yirr 5 cabal, clack, click, garre, haver, prate, run on, speak, spout 6 babble, cackle, caquet, claver, gabble, gibber, gossip, hot air, jabber, jangle, jargon, palter, patter, rattle, shiver, speech, tatter, yammer, yatter 7 blabber, blether, chackle, chaffer, chitter, clatter, clicker, clitter, nashgob, palaver, prattle, reel off, smatter, thattle, twattle, twittle 8 blahblah, schmoose, spout off, verbiage 9 amphigory, bavardage, rigmarole, yaketyyak 10 amphigouri, babblement, caqueterie, talkytalky 11 rigmarolery, yacketyyack 12 bibblebabble, gibblegabble, ribblerabble, talkeetalkee, tittletattle 14 prittleprattle

conjurer's hanky-panky

inane pribble-prabble

noisy brabble

symbol of jay

tree lebbek

CHATTERBOX bluejay, bucco, chattermag, chewet, clack, gabber, gasbag, gossip, jay, mag(pie), piet, talker

CHATTY chirrupy, colloquial, conversational, gabby, garrulous, intimate, loquacious, piebald, pyot, talkative

CHAUCER *character* See CANTERBURY *tales pilgrim.*

hen partlet

inn tabard

of painting albert durer

patron john of gaunt

work canterbury tales, troilus and criseyde

CHAUFFEUR driver, shover, tester

CHAUTAUQUA assembly, lyceum, oratory

CHAUVINISM jingoism

CHAW bite, champ, chew, envy, jaw, masticate, mull, ponder, trick, vex(ation)

-bacon rustic

CHAYOTE chocho, huisquil, mirliton, pepinella, tallote

CHEAP abashed, abject, a bon marche, at cost, bad, barato, bargain, base, beggarly, bid, brummagem, cheesy, chinchy, chintzy, close, common, contemptible, crumby, crummy, dime-a-dozen, disconcerted, five-and-ten, fleece, frugal, gain, gaudy, ignoble, inexpensive, inferior, kitch, light, low (-priced), mean, mediocre, miserly, moderate, nasty, nominal, paltry, pennorth, pennyworth, pitiable, plentiful, plenty, poor, price, purchase, reasonable, schlock, shmatte, shmotte, shoddy, sixpenny, small, snide, sordid, sorry, stingy, tatty, tawdry, tight, tinhorn, tinny, trade, twopenny, undear, value, vile

item twofer

-jack hawker, huckster, peddler, vendor

-skate miser, piker, s(c)hnorrer, skinflint, stiff, tinhorn

CHEAPEN abase, bargain, belittle, bid, chaffer, debase, decline, degrade, depreciate, depress, devalue, drop, fall

CHEAT 3 bam, bob, cog, con, fob, fub, gip, gyp, jig, lie, nip, rip, rob, tap 4 beat, bilk, bite, burn, clip, colt, crib, dish, do in, duff, dupe, fake, firk, flam, flum, fool, geck, gull, hoax, jilt, jink, milk, mock, nail, nick, pick, ramp, ream, rook, sell, sham, sile, skim, skin, snow, swiz, take, trap 5 booty, bunko, cozen, crimp, crook, cully, dodge, evade, fraud, fudge, gleek, gouge, guile, mulct, pinch, pluck, renig, rogue, shark, sharp, shave, shill, stick, sting, swick, touch, trick, yentz 6 befool, bilker, bubble, bucket, chisel, chouse, conman, deceit, delude, diddle, fleece, humbug, jockey, outwit, renege, ripoff, shicer, snudge, topper, tre-

pan 7 beguile, deceive, defraud, diddler, do out of, finagle, grifter, mislead, plunder, sharper, skinner, swindle, tellbox, verneuk 8 artifice, blackleg, chiseler, delusion, hoodwink, imposter, mechanic, stripper, swindler 9 bamboozle, deception, fainaigue, goldbrick, nogoodnik, victimize 10 thimblerig 11 doublecross, hornswoggle, shortchange 12 stack the deck
at cards blackleg, crimp, crossroader, mechanic, milk, philosopher, shark, shill, snow, stack
at craps blanket-roll
blustering bullyrook
CHEATER (See also CHEAT.) bilker, finagler, knave, topper, treacher
CHEATERS falsies, glasses, spectacles
CHEATING barrat, fubbery, juggling, michery, odling, roguery, shtickl(ech), shtik(eleh)
CHECK 3 bit, end, hap, nab, nip, pay, tab, try 4 balk, bill, case, chit, curb, damp, halt, rein, rout, slow, snub, stay, stem, test 5 abort, agent, annul, audit, block, brake, catch, cease, choke, crack, delay, deter, draft, embar, limit, pause, plaid, prove, quell, repel, score, snape, split, spoke, stall, stunt, tally, token, train, trial 6 arrest, baffle, bottle, bridle, damage, dampen, damper, hamper, hinder, impede, rebuff, retard, review, scotch, stanch, stifle, stymie, tartan, ticket, tryout, verify 7 analyze, anstoss, aweband, balance, barrier, control, counter, curcuma, examine, harness, inhibit, inspect, measure, reagent, receipt, repress, saccade, snaffle, suspend 8 obstacle, obstruct, overhaul, research, restrain, withhold 9 frustrate, interrupt, inventory, reckoning, restraint, take stock, variegate 11 certificate, demonstrate, investigate, retardation
bad bouncer, kite
bad, passer kiter
forged stiff, stumer

in arrive, punch the clock, record, register
out depart, die, leave, vanish
over comb, examine, inspect, investigate, verify
rein curb, harness, saccade
stone chuck
CHECKBIRD wheatear
CHECKED (See also CHECKERED.) beaten, captive, closed, stopped
CHECKER counter, damper, draugh, freak, freck, piece, tessellate, variegate
bloom mallow
board dambrod, table
spot butterfly, melita
CHECKERBERRY drunkard, jinks, teaberry
CHECKERED changeable, diversified, inconsistent, mosaic, pied, plaid, vacillating, vair, variegated
CHECKERS *board* dambrod, table
game chequers, contract, dama, dame(s), damenspiel, dam(m)spiel, dices, drafts, draughts, elevenman ballot, giveaway
opening alma, ayreshire, black doctor, boston, bristol, center, cross, defiance, denny, douglas, dundee, dyke, edinburgh, farmer, fife, glasgow, goosewalk, huff, kelso, laird and lady, nailor, orthodox, paisley, pioneer, single corner, souter, switcher, tillicoultry, wagram, waterloo, whilter, white doctor, will-o-thewisp
piece black, counter, dame, king, man, morel(le), queen, red
term barred, big stroke, block, bridge, capture, cook, counter, cramp, crown, cut, double corner, draughtsman, draw, exchange, jump, king row, lock, man off, opening, position, problem, row, shot, single man, sprag, squeeze, star move, steal, stroke, system
CHECKERWORK tessel, tessera
CHECKMATE baffle, corner, deadlock, defeat, foil, frustrate, gain, lick, outwit, overthrow, rout, scotch,

standstill, stop, stymie, suimate, thwart, tree, undo
CHECKSTONE chuck, jacks, pebble, stonechart
CHEEK audacity, boldness, border, brass, bucca, chap(s), choke, chop, chyak, crust, effrontery, face, flank, gall, gena, gleg, haffet, haffit, impudence, insolence, jamb, jaw(bone), jole, jowl, leer, nerve, sass, sauce, side, temerity, wang
and tongue buccolingual
bone haffet, malar, zygoma
by jowl intimate, side by side, tete-a-tete, together
comb. bucco, mel
having distended buccate
muscle buccinator
pert. buccal, genal, jugal, malar
pouch alforja
spur shank
CHEEP chip, chirp, hint, peep, pip, pule, squeak, tattle, tweet, twitter, yap, yip
CHEER 3 aha, aid, ave, cry, hip, joy, ole, rah, ray, wow 4 clap, face, hail, hoch, laud, root, viva, yell 5 amuse, boost, bravo, bully, chirk, drink, elate, huzza, liven, mirth, shout, sport, tiger, whoop 6 assure, banzai, buoy up, cantle, credit, encore, gaiety, gayety, hooray, hurrah, hurray, huzzah, praise, rehete, repast, salute, solace, spirit, viands 7 acclaim, all hail, animate, applaud, cherish, comfort, console, enliven, feeling, gladden, hearten, hosanna, inspire, jollity, lighten, plaudit, refresh, rejoice, support, welcome, whoopee 8 alleluia, alleluja, applause, brighten, hilarity, inspirit, reassure, vivacity 9 alleluiah, animation, encourage, geniality, hiphurrah, rejoicing 10 exhilarate, halleluiah, hallelujah 11 camaraderie, countenance
burst salvo
on urge
pine chil, chir
up brace up, buck up, liven, perk up, revive, snap out of it, take heart
CHEERER comforter, solace
CHEERFUL auspicious, beaming, blithe(some),

bright, buoyant, cadgy, canty, cheerly, chipper, chirk, chirpy, crouse, debonair, douce, ebullient, eupeptic, gawsie, gay, genial, glad(some), gleg, good-humored, good-natured, happy, heartsome, high, homelike, jaunty, jocund, jolly, jovial, joyful, joyous, laughing, light(some), lively, merry, ost, pe(a)rt, pleasant, radiant, reddy, riant, rident, rosy, sanguine, smiling, sparkling, sprightly, sunny, sunshine, vaudy, vivacious, willing, winsome

name meaning hilary

CHEERFULNESS euphrasy, levity, optimism, sunniness

symbol lark

CHEERLESS blae, bleak, cold, dejected, desolate, dire, disconsolate, dismal, doleful, dour, drab, drear(y), dull, forlorn, gloomy, glum, joyless, melancholy, sad, unhappy, wintry

CHEESE 3 oka, pot 4 bleu, blue, brie, dick, edam, feta, hand, jack, kose, sage, tybo 5 brick, cream, darby, dutch, gouda, grana, swiss 6 barrie, bonbel, bondon, brynza, cantal, dunlop, grated, gratin, leyden, mysost, romano, tilsit, zieger 7 angelot, babybel, baronet, boursin, bryndza, caraway, cheddar, chevret, cottage, fontina, fromage, gjedost, gruyere, kebbuck, limburg, munster, new york, primost, process, ricotta, sapsago, stilton, truckle, windsor 8 american, beancurd, bel paese, cheshire, emmental, longhorn, parmesan, pecorino, tilsiter 9 camembert, leicester, limburger, mousetrap, port salut, provolone, roquefort, schweizer, smearcase, tillamook, wiltshire 10 appetitost, caerphilly, emmentaler, fontinella, gloucester, gorgonzola, mozzarella, neufchatel 11 liederkranz, wenzleydale 12 capiocavallo 13 schweizerkase

and milk product gervais

barrel-shaped truckle

big See MAGNATE.

blue danish, gorgonzola, mycella, pipocreme, roquefort

box quadrangle

brown mysost

cake dessert, gam, leg, photo(graph)

cement glue

cloth butter muslin

comb. caseo, tyr(o)

cream philadelphia, smearcase

curdy trip

dessert triple creme

dish cake, fondue, omelet, rabbit, rarebit, souffle, welsh rabbit

flower mallow

green moon, sapsago

hard asiago, cheddar, cheshire, fontinella, jack, kasseri, mysost, parmesan, romano

head souse

inferior dick

ingredient casein

it beat it, begone, don't, leave, look out, stop, warning

knife spatula

large kebbock, kebbuck

lip pillbug, rennet, wood louse

lover caseophile, turophile

maggot skipper

mild trappist

pale yellow gruyere, swiss

pert. caseic, caseous

poached gnocchetti

rennet cotherstone

say smile

semi-hard tilsit

soft babybel, baronet, bel paese, bonbel, boursin, brie, camembert, cream, fontina, neufchatel, sanglier, tybo

strong gorgonzola, limburger, pont l'eveque, roquefort

swiss emmenthaler, gruyere, jarlsberg, samsoe, sapsago

tenpin-shaped caciocavallo

toaster sword

unpressed camembert

vat chessart, chessel

vegetable bean curd

whey primost, ziega, zieger

white cottage, cream, neufchatel

whole milk dunlop, port salut

yellow cheddar, cheshire, process, trappist

CHEESEPARING close (fisted), economical, frugal, mean, miserly, niggardly, parsimonious, penny-pinching, penurious, skimping, stingy, thrifty, tight (fisted)

CHEESEWOOD bonewood, pittosporum, whitewood

CHEESY base, caseous, cheap, inferior, paltry, punk, worthless

CHEETAH cat, guepard(e), youse, youze

CHEF See COOK.

d'oeuvre masterpiece

hat toque-blanche

CHEFOO yentai

CHEKHOV *play* cherry orchard, sea gull, three sisters, uncle vanya

CHELA claw, disciple, hand, manus, novice, pincer, servant, spicule, talon

CHELICERA appendage, claw, falcer, falx, fang, mandible

CHELKIAS *parent* eliab

son elias, ezerias

CHELUB *son* ezri

CHEMICAL See also specific chemicals and *kind*, below.

agent catalyst

alkaloid abrotin(e)

bonded adherend

cleansant krypton

comb. aci, amid(e), amido, amino, ane, ene, enol, ical, ide, idin, ile, imino, ine, ion, ite, oic, ole, olic, ose, oxa, oxo, oxy, uret, ylene

compound adamsite, amid(e), amin(e), azine, azo(le), borid(e), ceria, diol, elaterin, ester, imid(e), imine, inosite, iodide, isomer, leucine, linin, metamer, purin, quassin, stearate, toluene, ytterbia

container aludel, ampul(e), beaker, bell jar, cucurbit, cupel, etna, matrass, phial, retort, test tube, vial

element See ELEMENT chemical.

indicator aurin(e)

instrument acetometer, alembic, aspirator, blowpipe, bunsen burner, buret(te), crucible, desiccator, distiller, etna, reagent bottle, retort, still, test tube

kind acetate, acetone, alcohol, aldehyde, amine, ammonia, anhydride, arsenate, arsenite, benzoate, bicarbonate, bisulfate, bisulfide, borate, borax, bromide, carbide, carbohydrate, carbonate, chlorate, chloride, chlorite, chromate, citrate, copperas, cyanide, dioxide, disulfate, disulfide, est(h)er, ethyl, fluorid, formaldehyde, fulminate, halide, halogen, hydrate, hydride, hydrocarbon, hydroxide, iodide, ketone, lactate, methyl, monoxide, niter, nitrate, nitride, nitrite, oxalide, permanganate, peroxide, phosphate, phosphide, phosphite, potash, sal ammoniac, salt(peter), silicate, sodium, sulfate, sulfide, sulfite, sulphate, sulphide, sulphite, tartrate, tetroxide, thiosulfate, trioxide

lubricant silicone

measure dram, gram, liter, titer

medieval alchemy

messenger autacoid, autocoid, hormone

process catalysis, titration

radical benz(o)yl, butyl, carbonyl, ethyl, methyl, oxalyl, tolyl

salt abietate, acetate, acrylate, adipate, borate, ester, formate, niter, nitre, sal, sinigrin

test assay

unit titer

variability allomerism

warfare weapon arsine

CHEMIN DE FER baccarat, railroad, railway

CHEMISE ark, camisa, camisole, lingerie, shift, shimm(e)y, shirt, simar, slip, smock

CHEMISETTE bodice, dress, guimpe, partlet, sham, tucker

CHEMIST analyst, apothecary, assayer, chemick, druggist, pharmaceutist, pharmacist

workroom lab(oratory)

CHEMMIS *king* belus

CHEN bird, brant, snowgoose, wavey

CHENAANAH *son* zedekiah

CHENANIAH *chief of* levites

CHENDE cactus, chinoa

CHENFISH kingfish

CHENILLE cord, fabric, henbane, snail

CHENOPODIUM alapasotes, ambrosia, goosefoot, jerusalem oak, lamb's-quarters, pigweed, saltbush, wormseed

oil ascaridole

CHEOPS khufu

CHEPPEH annoy, bait, nag, provoke

CHEQUEEN basket, cecchine, sequin, zecchino, zequin

CHERAN *parent* dishon

CHERAW sara

CHEREMIS mari

CHERIE See SWEETHEART.

CHERIMOYA See SUGAR *apple.*

CHERISH admire, adore, aid, appreciate, bosom, brood, care, caress, cling, comfort, defend, dote, embosom, embrace, encourage, enjoy, enshrine, entertain, esteem, faddle, fondle, foster, harbor, have, hold dear, hope, hug, idolize, indulge, inspirit, keep, like, love, nestle, nourish, nurse, nurture, nuzzle, pamper, pet, preserve, prize, protect, regard, respect, revere, save, shelter, shield, support, sustain, treasure, value, venerate, woo, worship

enviously grudge

CHERNA red-grouper, serranid, stone-bass

CHEROOT cigar, stogie, stogy, trichi, trichy

CHERRY amarelle, bigarreau, bing, brandy-mazzard, burbank, capulin, chapman, cordia, cornel, drupe, duke, duracine, eggberry, egriot, fuji, gean, lambert, lukeward, mahaleb, marasca, may duke, maz(z)ard, merry, morel(lo), napoleon, oxheart, padus, phantom-red, pitanga, prunus, rosacean, ruddy, tartarian, windsor

acid cerasin

bird cedar waxwing, hawfinch

black belladonna, marasca, tartarian

clammy gouttree

color cerise, red, scarlet

drink kirsch(wasser)

extract cherasein

genus padus, prunus

gum cerasin

heart-shaped bigarreau

holly islay

laurel cerasus, oleander

orange kumquat

perfumed mahaleb

plum myrobalan

sour amarelle, egriot, giotte, may duke, montmorency, morello

st lucie mahaleb

stone clam, oyster, paip, pip, pit, quahog

sweet bigarreau, bing, gean, lambert, marmotte, maz(z)ard, napoleon, oxheart, queen anne, tartarian, whiteheart

tree disease black-knot

wild marasca, maz(z)ard

CHERT boone, whinstone

CHERUB(IM) amor(etto), amorino, angel, child, cupid, eudemon, fatty, punchinello, roly-poly, rubi, saint, seraph(im), spirit, star

CHERVIL arfoil, bun, cicely, cowmumble, cowparsley, cowweed, honewort, keck, milkweed, ratsbane

CHESAPEAKE *bay boat* bugeye, flattie

bay, river to potomac, rappahannock, susquehanna

canoe pung(e)y

CHESS ajedrez, brome-grass, brumus, chaturanga, checkers, darnel, echecs, game, layer, row, scaachi, schachspiel, shatranj, shogi, skittles, story, tier

ancestor chaturanga

blindfold sans voir

board table

capture, exemption fidate

capture, exposed to enprise

capture, mutual exchange

castle judge, juez, ledge, rook, tour, tower, udge

checkmate suimate

defense alekhine's, budapest, cambridge springs, carokann, dutch, french, indian, nimzowitsch, petroff, philidor's slav, stonewall

draw game stalemate

finish checkmate, draw, endgame, mate, stalemate

gambit danish, evans, fork, king's, muzio, queen's
goddess caissa
knight horse, chevalier
master alexander, bisguier, botvinnik, capablanca, fischer, hoban, morphy, nimzovitsch, reshevsky, spasskey, tal
mate check, conditional, direct, fool's, help, reflex, scholar's, self, smothered
move castle, check, cook, coup de repos, fianchetto, fork, gambit, mate, rochade, zugzwang
opening albin counter, catalan, center game, colle, debut, defense, english, falkbeer, gambit, irregular, king's gambit, king's pawn, maclange, orthodox, pillsbury, reti, ruy lopez, scotch, vienna
pert. scacchic
piece alfin, alphin, archer, bauer, bishop, castle, cavalier, chevalier, dame, fers, four, horse, king, knight, konig, konigin, laufer, lumber, man, officer, pawn, pon, poune, queen, rook, springer, tour(rook), tower
player, mediocre woodpusher
promotion queening
queen fers, fiers, phearse
set meinie, meiny
soft blubbergrass
term capture, castle, center, check(mate), combination, cook, defense, development, diagonal, double-check, double-pawn, echiquier, endgame, en passant, en prise, exchange, fianchetto, fidate, file, guard, heavy piece, in hock, interpose, jadoube, line, mat(t), mate, maximate, opening, opposition, passed pawn, pat(t), pin, problem, promotion, protection, queening, rank, remis, retractor, schachmatt, stalemate, straddle, tempo, threat
variant chaturanga, fourhanded, four knights, giveaway, kriegspiel, pa(r)chisi, parche(e)si, schach(spiel), shatranj
CHESSMAN See CHESS piece.
CHEST almoin, ambry, arca, ark, armoire, bahut, basket, bin, bosom, box, breast, brisket, buist, bunker, bureau, bust, cabinet, caddy, caisse, caisson, caja, cajeta, canteen, capcase, carton, case, cash, casket, cassone, caxon, chiffonier, cist, coffer, coffin, commode, container, contention, controversy, crate, cupboard, cyst, deposit, drawers, dresser, enclose, forcelet, forcer, fund, girnal, girnel, hamper, highboy, hoard, hutch, jordan, kist, kit, locker, lowboy, manifold, pix, pyx, razee, safe, scob, semainier, shrine, stow, strife, thorax, toolbox, treasure, treasury, trunk, wangan, wanigan
animal's brisket
bird's pectus
bone costa, sternum
carved bridewain
comb. seth(o), thorac(o)
covering pectoral
cutlery canteen
holy ark
human thorax
maker arkwright
meal girnal, girnel
miniature bible-box
of drawers commode, dresser, highboy, lowboy
-on-chest highboy, tallboy
ornament pectoral, stomacher
pain pectoralgia
part bosom
pert. midriff, pectoral, thoracic
renaissance cassone
sacred arca, ark, cist, kist
sepulchral larnax
sound rale
stone cist, kist
supplies wangan, wan(n)igan
CHESTNUT ascot tan, auburn, bay, brown(stone), calodendrum, castanea, castaneous, castor, chinquapin, coconut, corn, crenata, dentata, fagaca, horse, humor, joe millerism, joke, kermanshah, ling, marron, oldie, platitude, rata, rechauffe, red-haired, sandstone, sandy, sativa, tan, titian
and gray roan
blight bark-disease

clam astarte
-colored auburn, bay, roan, titian
disease black canker
dwarf chinquapin
horse conker
in syrup marron-glace
pert. castanean, esculic
water ling, stripe, tapa
CHESTY conceited, proud, self-confident, self-important
CHEVALIER cadet, cavalier, gallant, greenshank, horseman, knight, lord, noble, tattler
d' industrie sharper
raoul blue beard, murderer
CHEVRON angle, beam, flexuosity, mark, molding, rank, stripe, vee, wound, zag, zig, zigzag(gery)
narrow couple-close
CHEVROTAIN boomorah, deerlet, kanchil, meminna, musk-deer, napu, peesoreh, plandok, ruminant, tragule
CHEVY, CHIVY annoy, badger, bait, bother, chase, chivvy, cry, flight, game, harass, hector, hound, hunt(ing), maneuver, nag, pursue, pursuit, race, ride, run, rush, scamper, tease, torment, trail, try, vex, worry
CHEW bite, blister, cham(m), champ, chavel, chaw, chomp, chonk, chumble, coca, cr(a)unch, cud, denticate, eat, fletcherize, gnash, gnaw, grind, grouze, gum, manducate, masticate, meditate, mouth, mumble, munch, nibble, quid, rally, rumen, ruminate, scold, scranch, scrunch, taw
inability to amasesis
noisily chank, grouze
out bawl out, berate, brace, call down, dress down, eat out, excoriate, rebuke, reprimand, rip, scold, tell off
the rag chat(ter), discuss, gossip, jaw
up the scenery emote, overact
CHEWINK finch, grasset, joree, towhee
CHIA beverage, oil, sage, salvia
CHIANG CHING *husband* mao tse-tung

CHIAPANECAN chapanec, dirian, mangue, orotinan

CHIAPAS *indian* tapachula

CHIAROSCURO black and white, grisaille, shaded

CHIAUS cheat, messenger, sergeant, swindler

CHIBCHAN *chief* zipa
indian aruac, betoya, colima, doraskean, duit, guatuso, guaymi(e), muysca, muzo, pioxe, rama, talamaca, tama, tucano, tuenbo, yahuna, zaque, zipa

CHIC brave, braw, chichi, current, dapper, dashing, elegant, fashion(able), kippy, modish, natty, nifty, nobby, pert, posh, smart, spruce, stylish, trig, trim

CHICAGO porkopolis, windy city
airport midway, o'hare
district gold coast, loop
irishman studs lonigan
landmark water tower
park grant, lincoln
planetarium adler
street, financial la salle

CHICANERY artifice, beguilement, cavil, collusion, connivance, corruption, cozenage, deception, dirt, dodgery, double-dealing, duplicity, espieglerie, feint, foul play, fraud, intrigue, jobbery, jockeyism, knavery, pettifoggery, ruse, sharp practice, shuffling, skullduggery, sophistry, stratagem, subterfuge, superchery, trick(ery), trimming, villainy, wile

CHICHI arty, bohemian, effeminate, fancy, smart, sporty

CHICK babe, bird, CHICKEN, child, chotchke(leh), chuckie, fledgling, fowl, girl, peep, poulet, pullet, pullus, screen, sequin, sweetheart, tchotchke(leh), tsatske(leh)
pea chich, chit, cicer, cowgram, garavance, garbanzo, garvanzo, gram, herb, sowgram

CHICKADEE black cap, parus, penthestes, titmouse

CHICKAREE squirrel

CHICKEN, CHICKEN'S araucana, biddy, broiler, capon, child, chook, chuck, cock, coq, coward(ly), craven, deedy, dom, effeminate, fainthearted, fowl, fryer, girl, hen, huhnchen, kip, kuchlein, layer, manoc, phasanid, pollo, poule, poult(ry), poussin, pullet, roaster, rooster, silky, springer, timid, weakling, young, youth
bird turnstone
breed ancona, andalusian, austrolorp, bantam, black spanish, brahma, cochin bantam, cornish, dominique, leghorn, minorca, new hampshire, plymouth rock, rhode island (red), sultan, sussex, wyandot(te)
coop cavie, cavy
disease asthenia, leukosis, perosis, pip, roup
fat schmaltz
group brood, clutch, poultry
head lousewort
heart cold feet
-hearted base, cowardly, timid
house brooder, hencote, henhouse, hennery
hybrid rock cornish
in wine sauce coq au vin
out falter, quit, renege
pepper buttercup
pox sorehead, varicella
prairie grouse
small bantam
snake boba
soup caldo-tlalpeno
tail piece pope's nose
tick argas, blue bug
-toes coralroot, glasswort
white-skinned minorca
young broiler, chick, deedy, fledgling, fryer, poult, pullet

CHICKWEED allbone, alsinace, alsine, arenaria, blink(s), cerastium, herb, margeline, pennypies, sandwort, silverhead, spurry, starwort, stitchwort
red pimpernel
wintergreen starflower, trientalis

CHICLE gum, latex

CHICO sapodilla

CHICORY arnoseris, bluedaisy, blue thistle, blueweed, bunk, coffeeweed, crepis, echium, endive, hemlock, lapsana, picris, root, succory, witloff

CHIDE abuse, admonish, berate, blame, censure, chafe, heck, chew out, contend, criticize, exprobate, flite, flyte, fret, fume, fuss, harass, lambaste, lecture, objurgate, rail, rate, rebuff, rebuke, reprimand, reproach, reprove, school, scold, sneap, threap, threat, upbraid, vilify, vituperate, wrangle

CHIEF 3 ace, aga, big, boh, cap, cid, dux, jam, mir, top, vip 4 agha, alii, amir, arch, boss, caid, cham, chef, dain, dato, datu, dean, duce, duke, emir, head, hier, high, inca, jarl, jefe, kaid, khan, king, main, moro, most, naik, qaid, rais, raja, rana, reis, seid, skip, tyee, zaim 5 alder, alpha, ameer, ariki, astur, dateo, datto, doyen, elder, emeer, first, front, great, major, pombo, prima, rajah, ruler, sayid, sunck, thane, titan, vital, zippa 6 ataman, cabeza, deputy, flaith, fuhrer, hetman, kubera, kuvera, leader, luluai, master, old man, pakhan, prabhu, primal, sachem, sayyid, senior, sheikh, sherif, sirdar, staple, sudder, suncke, sundic 7 big shot, cacique, capital, capitan, captain, central, crucial, fuehrer, general, headman, kingpin, officer, primary, skipper, stellar, supreme, supremo, tribune 8 alderman, caboceer, capitano, cardinal, caudillo, dominant, foremost, governor, hierarch, kingfish, palatine, panglima, sagamore, superior 9 numero uno, paramount, personage, potentate, principal, principle, top sawyer 10 head honcho, preeminent 11 first fiddle 12 kalanianaole 13 cock of the walk
clan toisech
comb. arch(i)(y)
executive boss, chairman, governor, leader, mayor, president, ruler
magistrate avoyer, syndic
native jam
of state king, president, ruler
provincial khan

CHIEFTAIN See CHIEF, LEADER.

CHIEN FO TUNG caves of one thousand buddhas

CHIGGER bete-rouge, bicho, chigga, chigoe, enigua, flea, gigger, harvest mite, insect, jigger, leptus, pique, redbug, sandboy, sandworm, screw, sika, wheelworm

CHIGOE See CHIGGER.

CHIHUAHUA *dictator* pancho villa

CHILBLAIN blain, frostbite, kibe, mools, mouls, mule, pernio, sore

CHILD (See also CHILDREN.) 3 ace, aga, big, boy, cap, cid, dux, jam, mir, top, vip 4 arab, baba, babe, baby, bata, brat, chit, cion, girl, gyte, lamb, mite, nino, punk, puss, tike, tiny, trot, tyke, wean 5 bairn, broll, chick, chiel, gamin, issue, keiki, minor, poult, scion, scrap, sprat, sprig, trick, whelp, youth 6 bugger, butcha, cherub, enfant, infant, kitten, moppet, nipper, peewee, proles, pullet, shaver, squirt, urchin 7 alannah, bambino, darling, gangrel, gytling, kitling, lambkin, papoose, product, progeny, stichel, toddler, younker 8 baldling, bantling, daughter, duckling, innocent, juvenile, littling, nestling, nursling, prattler, suckling, weanling, whimling 9 dandiprat, little one, offspring, posterity, youngling, youngster 10 changeling, descendant, pickaninny 11 butterprint, chickabiddy 12 little fellow 13 breadsnatcher

advancement precocity
apron bib, biswop, slipper, tier
bad-mannered goop
blouse middy
care pediatrics
chubby butterball, rolypoly
comb. paedo, ped(o), tecno
dainty elf, fairy
della robbia bambino
dirty arab, ragamuffin, urchin
disease chicken pox, glandular fever, glycogenosis, herpangina, measles, mumps, rachitis, rickets
expert gesell, spock

foster dalt, dault, norry, nurry, rearling, ward
good bon enfant
hater misopedist
homeless waif
illegitimate bantling, bastard, by-blow, love-child, mishap, natural
incorrigible enfant terrible
innocent chrisom
killing filicide, infanticide
last dilling
-like artless, bab(y)ish, biddable, docile, dutiful, ingenuous, innocent, meek, naive, obedient, puerile, submissive, trusting
lively scopperil
medical practice pediatrics
merry sunbeam
mischievous devil(kin), dickens, elf, hellion, imp, limb, rascal, rogue, royet, scamp, smatch, tike, urchin
mixed blood mestee, mustee, octoroon
naked scuddy
-naming festival amphidromia
nurse amah, ayah, nana, nanny, sitter
of light and day eros
only ewe-lamb
parentless orphan
pauper minder
pert. filial
playful elf, wanton
plump chunk, fob, fub
precocious prodigy, wunderkind
protector adeona
-rearing breeding, nurture, pedology, pedotrophy, upbringing
roguish hellion, imp, scamp, smatchet, terror, urchin
rowdy hoodlum
small babe, baby, gaitt, kid(dy), peewee, spud, tacker, tot
spirit of taran
spoiled bantling, brat, cade, cockney, darling, mammothrept, mardy, smatchet
street arab, gamin
stunted urf
sun inca
tend baby-sit
toy bauble, gewgaw, plaything, trinket
troublesome smatchet, stichel
unborn embryo, f(o)etus, humunculus

vehicle babybuggy, baby carriage, perambulator, pram, sled, stroller, tricycle, trike, wagon
young baby, bantling, gangrel, infant, innocent, joey, nestler, squirt, suckling, toddler, wrig

CHILDBED jizzen

CHILDBIRTH accouchement, confinement, delivery, eutocia, inlying, labor, lying-in, oxytocia, parturition, travail
assist at accouche
assistant accoucheur, accoucheuse, auxesia, bonadea, damia
comb. toco
deity apet, artemis, auge, auxesia, carmenta, damia, eileithyia, levana, lucina, matuta, upis, virbius
feast food blithebread, blithemeat
pert. obstetric, puerperal
quick oxytocia
technique lamaze
woman in puer pera

CHILDHOOD babyhood, boyhood, cradle, girlhood, infancy, nursery, teens, youth
second dotage, twichild

CHILDISH asinine, babyish, brattish, chitty, credulous, dansy, foolish, immature, juvenile, kiddish, naive, panty-waist, pedomorphic, peevish, petty, puerile, puling, senile, silly, simple, weak, weanly, young

CHILDLESS barren, orbate, sterile, unproductive

CHILDREN (See also CHILD.) family, generation, issue, kinder(lach), offspring, posterity, progeny, proles, seed, spawn, strain, youth
dislike of misop(a)edia
game authors, barnyard, bob cherry, cat and mouse, cat's-cradle, concentration, duckoo, donkey, fish, hide and seek, i spy, kukuk, memory, pig, pushpin, slapjack, snap, tag, tic-tac-toe, war
goddess abeona, adeona
medical science pediatrics
of heaven and earth titans
of light christians

patron saint nicholas, santa claus

room nursery

study of pedology

CHILE *aborigine* See INCA.

admiral cochranea

arborvitae alerce, cedar

armadillo quirquincho

bay cook, darwin, desolate, dyneley, eyre, inglesa, inutil, lomas, moreno, nena, otway, sarco, skyring, stokes, tarn, tongoy

bells copihue, lapageria

cape bascunan, carranza, choros, deseado, dyer, horn(os), quilan

capital santiago

channel ancho, beagle, cheap, cockburn, moraleda

city angol, arauco, boco, calama, caldera, cauquenes, chillan, cobija, concepcion, copiapo, coquimbana, curico, cuya, gatico, lebu, lota, ocoa, osorno, ovalle, puerto montt, rancagua, san bernardo, santiago, serena, talca, temuco, tome, valdivia, vallenar, valparaiso, vicuna, vina del mar, yumbel, yungay

clover alfalfa

clown drougette, zapata

coconut coquito

coin condor, escudo, libra, peso

dance cueca

deer pudu

desert atacama

evergreen alerce, boldo, boldu, monkey puzzle, plum fir

fort maipu

god cherruve, chonchonyi, colocolo, heucuvu(s), meuler, pillan

gulf ancud, arauco, guafo, penas

indian alikuluf, arauca(nian) atacameno, auca, chango, inca, mapuche, moluche, ona, onan, pampean, patagon, picunche, puegian, ranquel, tsonecan, uahgan

island angamos, byron, campana, chiloe, clarence, dawson, easter, guafo, hanover, hoste, huamblin, lennox, luz, mocha, nalcayec, navarino, nuevo, nunez, piazzi, picton, prat, quilan, refugio, riesco, stosch, tal-

can, traiguen, tranqui, vidal, wellington

island group chaques, chonos, hermite, pajaros

lake puyehue, ranco, rupanco, toro, yelono

marxist allende, alleudl

measure cuadra, fanega, legua, linea, vara

mineral bath colina, toro

national police carabineros

palm coquina, coquito

palm seed coker-nut

peak apiwan, burney, chalo, chaltel, cochrane, conico, copiapo, fitzroy, jervis, juncal, maca, maipo, paine, palpana, poquis, potro, pular, rincon, toro, torre, tronador, tupungato, velluda, yanteles

peninsula hardy, lacuy, taitao, tumbes

pianist arrau

pine monkey-puzzle

poet huidobro, neruda

point angamos, cachos, galera, gallo, lavapie, liles, lobos, loros, molles, morro, talca, tetas, toro, vieja

port arica, coquimbo, iquique, laserena, lota, talcahuano, tocopilla, tome, valdivia

president alessandri, allende, frei

proletariat roto

province aisen, arauco, arica, atacama, aysen, biobio, chiloe, coquimbo, curico, linares, maleco, maule, nuble, o'higgins, osorno, santiago, talca, tarapaca, valdivia

range almeida, andes, darwon, domeyko

resort portillo, vina del mar

river alhue, azapa, biobio, bravo, bueno, camina, choapa, choros, cisnes, colina, copaibo, elqui, huasco, illapel, itata, laja, lauca, limari, lluta, loa, lontue, maipo, maule, morado, palena, poscua, puelo, rahue, rapel, tolten, valdivia, vitor, yali

rodent chinchilla, cururo

secret police dina

shrub boldo, bridal wreath, lithi, litre, maqui, pepino

statesman o'higgins

strait magellan, nelson

tree alerce, alerse, boldo, brea, cedar, coigue, coleu,

fitzroya, muermo, patagua, pelu, rauli, roble, ulmo

volcano antuco, calbuco, lanin, lascar, lincancabur, llaima, maipo, oyahue, peteroa, socomap, tacora

weight grano, libra, quintal

wind sures

writer pablo neruda

CHILI bush-pepper, capsicum, goat-pepper

dish size

CHILIAST millenarian

CHILION *mother* naomi

wife orpah

CHILL ague, air-condition, algid, algor, benumb, bite, bloom, check, cloud, cold(ness), cool, cut, dampen, dash, daver, dazy, depress, deter, discourage(ment), dishearten, enmity, frappe, freeze, fretish, frigid(ity), frisson, frost, frosty, gelid(ity), ice, malaria, melancholy, nip, numb, penetrate, pierce, raw, refrigerate, rigor, schel, shake, shiver, shudder, snelly

CHILLED acold, cooled, frozen, hardened, refrigerated, starven

CHILLON *prisoner* bonivard

CHILLY aguish, algid, arctic, bleak, bracing, cauldrife, cold, cool(ish), freezing, fresh, frigid, frosty, frozen, gelid, glacial, hush, icy, invigorating, lash, leepit, nippy, raw, shivery, stimulating, unfriendly, wintry

CHILOPOD arthropod, centipede

CHIMAERA, CHIMERA belue, bubble, catfish, doodskop, dragon, dream, fancy, fool's paradise, illusion, imagination, mirage, monster, pipe dream, placoid, pomato, ratfish, rattail

father typhon

killer bellerophon

mother echidna

CHIMAKUAN *indian* hoh, quileute

CHIME accord, agree, bell, carillon, chimb, chine, cloche, concord, cymbal, din, edge, glockenspiel, gong, harmonize, harmony, jingle, melody, music, peal, rim, ring, speak, suit, ting

in interrupt

CHIMERA See **CHIMAERA**.

CHIMERICAL absurd, aerial, air(built), airy, cloudborn, deceptive, delusive, ethereal, fabulous, fanciful, fantastic, illusory, imaginary, insane, mythical, phantasmal, pretentious, quixotic, romantic, utopian, vain, wild

CHIMNEY cleft, fireplace, fissure, flue, fumiduct, funnel, gap, gully, hearth, louver, lum(m), opening, pipe, smoker, smokestack, stack, stovepipe, tewel, tube, tun(nel), vent
bird stork
board fender
cap abatvent, turncap
corner fireside, hearth, inglenook
cover cowl, jack, turncap
deposit soot
flue uptake
hood jack
jack cowl
lining parget
lug fireside
partition with(e)
piece ingle, mantel, parel
pink soapwort
pipe flue, tallboy
plant bellflower
post speer
pot cowl
seat sconce
sweep bottlebrush, chummy, flueman, ramoneur, ribwort
sweep's helper chummy
swift chaetura

CHIMOR *capital* chan-chan

CHIMPANZEE animal, ape, baboon, drill, jacko, jocko, monkey, nchega, pigmean, pigmen, pygmy

CHIN burmese, button, chat, chatter, choller, converse, jabber, jaw, mentum, talk, tsin
comb. genio, mento
double buccula, choller, dewlap
fest bull session, talk
music speech
pert. mental
point button, menton, pogonian
under submental
-wag gossip
whelk sycosis
-whisker rural

whiskers beard, goatee, imperial

CHINA, CHINESE cathay, cheeney, cinchona, crockery, dishes, earthenware, figurine, maid(servant), orange, orient, porcelain, pottery, serica, woman
abacus suan(pan)
abode of gods kun-lun mountain
aborigine heh(miao), mans, mantzu, miao(tse), miaotze, yao(min)
accidents, town of those who died in wang ssu cheng
alloy packtong, paktong
ancient cataia, cathay, seres, sinoe, tsao
animal, magic dragon, lung, phoenix, tortoise, unicorn
animal, symbolic fum, funghwang
anise badian, illicium
annals bamboo-books
antelope dzeren
arch pailoo, pailou, pailow
area measure, mow, m(o)u
aromatic root ginseng
arrow poison aconite
art treasure flying horse of kanshu
artichoke chorogi, crosne(s), knotroot, stachys
assembly hui
aster callistephus, fall-rose
backgammon double sixes, sheung-luk
bamboo whangee
bandit manza
banker schroff
barbarians esin
barrier bamboo curtain
bay hangchow, laichow
bean adzuki, cowpea, soy
bed platform kang
bird, mythical feng-huang, phoenix, shang-yang
blue nikko
boat bark, junk, sampan, toko
bovine zebu
brick bed kang
bridge of pain kuchu chiao
brigand hunghutze
broth of oblivion mi hun tang
buddha foh
buddhism foism
buddhist amban
buddhist divinity amitbha (buddha), avalokitesvara, dhrtarastra, mahasthama-

prapta, vaisravana, virudhaka, virupaksa
buddhist paradise chingtu
bunting ricebird
buttress wuta
cabbage michihli, pakchoi, petsai, wongbok
cakes col(l)yba
calculator suan(pan)
canton hsein
cape olwanpi
capital chang, hsien-yang, loyang, peiping, peking, taipei
caucasian lolo, nosu
celestial dog tien kou
channel bashi
chaos personified huntun
chestnut ling
chopsticks fiejie
cinnamon cassia(bark)
city 3 bai, noh 4 ahpa, amoy, fuyu, guma, hami, huma, ipin, kian, kisi, lini, loho, luta, moho, moyu, niya, noho, omin, rima, saka, sian, taku, tali, tayu, wuhu, yann 5 chiai, fusin, kirin, koklu, lhasa, linyu, macao, penki, shasi, soche, taian, talai, tihwa, tuyun, wuhan, wusih, yenan, yenki, yulin, yumen 6 anshan, antung, canton, dairen, fuchau, fuchow, fushih, fushun, hankow, harbin, kalgan, loyang, luchun, mukden, nanhai, ningpo, peking, singan, sining, taipei, talien, tsinan, yangku, yunnan 7 fatshan, hanyang, kunming, lanchow, mengtze, nanking, nanning, paoshan, peiping, soochow, taiyuan, urumchi, urumsti, waichow, wuchang, yenping 8 chinchow, fengkieh, fengtien, hangchow, kingchow, liaoyang, nanchang, shanghai, shenyang, siangtan, tientsin, tungchow, wanchuan, wanhsien 9 chungking, kiangling, tsingyuan 10 chiangling, port arthur
city, walled peiping, peking
civet rasse
clay kaolin
cloth moxa, nankeen, nankin, pulo, sha, silk
cloth stiffening haitsai
clover milk-vetch
club tong
coin candareen, cash, cent, dollar, fan, fen, haikwan-

tael, kupingtael, liang, mace, sen, sycee, tael, tiao, ticket, tsien, yuan
comb. sinic, sinico, sino
commercial place hong
commissioner lin
communist leader chen-pota, chou-en-lai, chu-teh, kang-shen, lin-piao, mao tse-tung
compassion jen
concubine tsip
condiment balachan, balachong, napee
cooking cantonese, fukien, honan, mandarin, peking, shantung, szechuen, szechwan, yangchow
cooking vessel wok
cosmic order tao
court uemen
cult amidism
cult image joss
customs haikwan
customs collector hoppo
date jujube
deer elaphure
dependency tibet
depression turfan
desert alashan, gobi, ordos, shamo, taklamakan
dialect amoy, canton, foochow, hakka, hsiang, kanhakka, mandarin, min, ningpo, swatow, wenchow
dice shik-tsz
dignitary celestiality
diplomat koo
dish ame, bao, bean curd, bird's-nest soup, buddha's feast, bumbum, chanchiang-mein, chingpoa, chop suey, chow mein, dimsum, egg fooy(o)ung, egg roll, eight-jewel, fooy(o)ung, funga, funsee, gai bao, gingko nut, hungshao-yee, king poa, lichee, ling, lion's-head, mooshi, mooshu-pork, paperwrapped chicken, peking duck, pickled cabbage, pig's-stomach, rice, sakwaya, seaweed, shark's-fin, shrimp toast, snow peas, sour-hot soup, suanlatang, subgum, suimai, sweet and sour, thousand-year eggs, trepang, wochoy, wonton, yangchao
divination book i ching
divine path tao
division canton, chow, foo, hsein

dog chow, peke, pekin(g)ese, shar-pei
doll pu-tao-wang
dominoes kwatpai, ngapai
dragon chilin, lung
dragon king ao chin, ao jun, ao kuant, ao shun
drink bean wine, shamshu
duck mandarin, pekin
duck eggs pidan
duke sung
dulcimer yang-kin
dumpling dimsum
duty likin
dwarf chemah
dynasty chin(g), chou, chow, ghos, han, hao, heh, hsia, hsin, kin, lan, liao, ming, mongol, shang, shu, sui, sung, tang, tsin, wei, yin, yuan
dynasty, first hsia
dynasty, last ching
eating utensil chopsticks
8 immortals See IMMORTALS 8.
elements, 5 earth, fire, metal, water, wood
emperor chien-lung, fu hsi, hsuan tsung, huang ti, kang hsi, liu pang, li yuan, pu-yi, tai tsung, yao
emperor, first cheng
emperor's adviser kaochao, kao tsu, lissu, mandarin, sang yung hang
empire, pert. celestial
enemy tatars
ensign dragon
evergreen waterplant
exchange medium sycee
exercise kwai-tai-chuan, tai-chi-chuan
explorer cheng ho
fabric crepe de chine
factory hong
fan palm bourbon, latania
father god yuti
festival ching ming
feudal state wei
fiber kohemp
fiddle urheen
figure puzzle tangram
figurine magot
financier kung, soong
fine dresden, lenox, limoges, meissen, sevres, spode, wedgwood
fir nikko
fish snakehead, trepang
flower camellia, chrysanthemum, chulan
flute (t)che

food See CHINA *cooking* and *dish.*
forbidden city peking
foreign devil fankwai, yiangkweitse
foreign establishment hong
founder fu-hsi
4 gentlemen bamboo, chrysanthemum, orchid, plum tree
frontier heavenly mountains, tien-shan
fruit apricot, kiwi, lichee, litchi, longan, mandarin, peento, wampee
fryer wok
gambling cube po-tsz, shik-tsz
game fantan, hoi-tap, kaptai-shap, kong-poh, mah jongg, nautin kau, pat cha, pie-gow, shing kuto, sing luk, tiuu, tsung shap
gate of demons kuei men kuan
gateway pailoo, pailou
gelatin agalloch, agar(agar), haitsai, isinglass
general chu teh, sun tsu
giant chang
ginger galingale
glue agar
goat yamens
god (See also DRAGON *king,* HAPPINESS *gods,* IMMORTALS 8.) august personage of jade, chao, cheng-huang, chin-shu-pao, confucius, ehr-lang, fankuei, father heaven, fengpo, ghos, great general pa cha, heng-ha-ehr-chiang, hou chi, hsuan-tien, hushen, jos(s), juant, juanti, kou-hun-shih-che, ksitigarbha, kuan-ping, kuanti, kuan-yu, kuei-hsing, leikung, lu-hsing, lung-wang, lupan, lu-tung-pin, mamien, men-shen, millet hou-chi, niu-tou, pa-cha, shen, shentu, shih-tien-yenwang, shouhsing, shou-tsang, shuikuan, sun-pin, tai-yueh-tatiu, tatior, tiao-chia-kuan, tien hou, tien kuan, tienkuan-ssu-fu, tien-wang, ti kuan, ti-tsang wangpusa, transcendent pig, tsai-shen, tsao-wang, tseng-fu-tsaishen, tung-tueh-tati, tungyueh-ta-ti, tu-ti, wen-chang, wu-chang, yama kings, yenwang-yeh, yu-chih-ching-te,

yu-huang-shang-ti, yu-lu, yun-tung, yu-ti, yutzu
god, buddhist See *buddhist divinity*, above.
god, christian shen
god, supreme august personage of jade, shang-ti
goddess ama, chango, chang-wu, chih-nii, feng-popo, hengo, kuan-yin, lady horse-head, mao-ku, mei-chou, nu-kua, pi-hsia-yuan-chun, sheng-mi, tien-hou, tien-mu, wang-mu-niang-niang
gods' guardian wang
gong tamtam
good and evil fengshui
gooseberry averrhoa, barambola, caramba, coromandel
grape wampee
grass bon, manie, rhia
grass linen barandos
green lokao
groom mafoo, mafu
group guild, hui, tong
gruel congee, conjee
gulf chihli, liaotung, pechili, pohai, siam, tonkin
harbor chefoo
hat haeltzuk, heiltsuk
headquarters yamen
heaven kunlun mountain
heavenly empress tien hou
"hello" ni-had
herb ginseng, nandina, primrose, spider lily, tea
hero chuko-liang, hai-jui, tsao-tsao
hoodlum quaijai
houseboat tanka
household god joss
idol joss, pagoda
illustrious sovereign kublai
immigrant hakka
indigo isatis
invention gunpowder, lacquer, paper, porcelain
inventor tsae
isinglass See CHINA *gelatin.*
island amoy, chouchan, chusan, coloane, formosa, hainan, hungtow, kulangsu, maco, matsu, namki, pratas, quemoy, staunton, taipa, taiwan, tinian, tungsha, yuhwan
island group chushan, flyspecks, miaotao, paracels, penghu, pratas, spratleys, tachen
jade lady touwan
jute chingma
karate kung fu

king hoang
kingdom shu wei
knock-head cotow
laborer coolie, cooly
lake bamtso, bornor, chaling, chao, ebinor, erhhai, hulunnor, hungtse, kaoyu, karanor, khanka, kokonor, lopnor, montcalm, namtso, oling, poyang, tai, taroktso, telli(nor), tienchih, tsinghai, tungting
lake, dry lopnor
language cantonese, mandarin, shan, sinitic
language, pert. sinological
lantern cloth haitsai
lantern plant alkekengi, winter cherry
lawn grass eremochloa
leader chiang ching-kuo, chiang kai-shek, ching chun-chiao, chou en-lai, hua kuo-feng, iao kuan-hua, lin piao, liu shao-chi, mao tse-tung, teng hsiao-ping, wang hai-jung
lemon citron
letter mana
limestone sinian
linen kompow
liquor rice wine, samshu
literature god wen chang, wen-ti
mafia heaven and earth society, pih-lien-kiao, tien ti hui, triads, water lily society
magistrate mandarin
magnolia yulan
mandarin's residence yamen
mark moth, nymphula
marten pahmi
measure catty, chang, chek, chih, ching, cho, chupak, fan(g), fen, kish, kungchih, kungching, kungfen, kungho, kungli, kungmu, kungshih, kungyin, para, pau, quei, sheng, shih, shing, tching, teke, tou, tsan, tsun, tun, yan, yin
medical practice acupuncture
medicine senso
medieval cathay, kitai
mender patragar
merchant soong, taipan
merchant's corporation hong
military academy whampoa
military organization manchu
military writer sun tzu
mineral petuntse

mirror of the wicked nieh ching tai
mist bai
monetary unit ien-min piao
mongol dynasty yuan
monkey douc
moon goddess chango, hengo
mosque official ahong
musical instrument cheng, kin, samisen, sang, sheng
nationalist party kuomintang
native lolo, pat, punti
native agent comprador
negative principle yin
news agency hsin-hua
newspaper people's daily
noodles mein
numbers (1) yih, (2) urh, (3) san, shan, (4) sze, (5) woo, (6) liu, luh, (7) tsi(eh), (8) pa, (9) chiu, kew, (10) shi, tsu, (100) pih, (1,000) tseen
nurse amah
nut lichi, litchi
oasis khotan
official ahoub, amban, kuan, kwan, mandarin, taoyan, tutu(h)
official residence yamen
oil tung
old man of the moon yuelaou
omelet egg fooyung
orange kumquat, mandarin
ounce tael
ox zebu
pagoda taa, taag
pan wok
paradise amitabha, chingtu
paradise god amitabha (buddha), avalokitesvara, mahasthamaprapta
parasol tree aogiri
part turkistan
partridge bambusicola
party kmt, kuomintang
pavilion crescent
peach peen-to
peak everest, kailas, muztabh, om(e)i, pobeda, sung(shan)
pea tree caragana
peninsula kowloon, leichu, liaotung, luichow
people cataia(n), hakka, hoklo, johnny, lolo, miao, mongol, seres, serian, sinaean, sinic
people, ancient mantzu, us(s)un, uzun
pert. cataian, senesian, serian, seric, sinaean, sine-

sian, sinian, sinic, sinisian, sinitic, sino

philosopher chuang-tzu, chu hsi, chwang-tse, confucius, laotse, laotzu, mencius, moti, motzu, shang-yang

physicist yang

pine tree matsu

plant dragon's gall, ginseng, ramie, tche, tea, udo

poet li-po, li-tai-po, su-tung po

political leader sun yat-sen

pony griffin

porcelain blanc de chine, celadon, eelskin, grain of rice, nankeen, sang de boeuf

porgy tai

port aigun, amoy, antung, canton, changsha, chefoo, dairen, foochow, hangchow, hunchun, ichang, kiukiang, kongmoon, kwangchow, luichow, nanking, ningpo, pakhoi, samshui, santuao, shanghai, shasi, soochow, swatow, tengyueh, tientsin, tsingkiang, tsingtao, wanhsein, weihaiwei, wenchow, wuchow, wuhu, yinkkow, yungkia

positive principle yang, yochow

potter chun

pottery boccaro, chien, chun, kuan, ming, tang, ting, tzuchou

pound catty

premier chou en-lai

prince wang

principle tao, yang, yin

province anhwei, antung, chekiang, chinghai, fukien, hokiang, honan, hopei, hsingan, hunan, hupen, jehol, kansu, kiangsi, kiangsu, kirin, kokonor, kwangtung, kweichow, liaoning, liaopeh, manchuria, mongolia, shansi, shantung, sheng, shensi, sikang, sinkiang, suiyuan, sungkiang, szechwan, taiwan, tibet, tsinghai, yunnan

provincial chief taoyin

provincial unit hien

public kung

punishment cangue, chab(o)uk

puzzle enigma, tangram

race dard, khitan, lolo, mongol, sinic, soyot

range alashan, altay, bog-
doula, great khingan, himalaya, ku(e)nlun, meiling, minshan, nanling, nanshan, tanglha, tapashan, tayuling, tienshan, tsin(g)ling, wuylishan

red bittersweet, chrome, scarlet, vermillion

region dzungaria, hien, jenol, manchuria, sericana, turkestan

religion buddhism, caodaism, confucianism, maoism, shinto, taoism

religious book i ching, i king, yi ching

reservoir sungari

rice congee

river amur, argun, cherchen, chukiang, chumar, drechu, fenho, han(kiang), hoangho, huai, huang, hungshui, hwangho, ilo, kerulen, khotan, kialing, kumara, liao(ho), lono, machu, manass, mekong, min(kiang), nen, ochina, pei(ho), salween, sikiang, sungari, tarim, tsangpo, tumen, tung, urungu, wei(ho), wukiang, yalu, yangtze(kiang), yarkand, yellow, yuan, yuen, yukiang

river, pert. kiang

roller sirgang

rooster's strut lak

root, dried galangale, ginseng

rose banks, bansia, bengal, burbank, hibiscus, manetti

ruler wang, yao(u), wau

sacred book chong-yong, lun-yu, meng-tse, ta-heo

sage fu-hsi, lao-tzu, sun-wa

salaries, god lu-hsing

salutation bow, kowtow

sand pear pyrus

sauce soy

scholar hu shih

script kai shu

scripture five kings, tao-te-ching

sea echina, schina, yellow

sea gulf siam

seasons chunchi

secret society hui, hung, tong

secretariat neiko

sect taoism, taou

sedge kali, mati

servant amah

shop toko

shrub che, crape myrtle, fatsia, forsythia, goumi, kerria, nandina, pearl bush,
ramie, rea, sas(s)anqua, star anise, tas, tche, tea

sidestreet hutang

silk pekin, pongee, shantung, tasar, taysaam, tsatlee, tussah

silk plant ramie

silk worm ailanthus, sina, tasar, tussah, tusser

silk worm moth bombycid, pernyi

silver sycee

skiff sampan

sky tien

sleeping platform kang

society boxer, hoey, huey, hui, hung, tong, triad

sovereign kee, kubla(i), yaou

speech, colloquial kuoyu

spirit hsien, kuei, kwei

squash cushaw

state, ancient cathay, tsao

statesman li hung-chan

steelyard dotchin

stocks cangue

stone agalmatolite, lithophone, petunse

store toko

street hutung

student of sinologist, sinologue

sugar cane sorgo

sumac tree of heaven

supply line burma road

taa pagoda

tartar tribe toda

tax likin

tea bohea, cha, congo(u), emesa, hyson, oolong, oopak, padra, tsia

tea substitute faham

temple joss house, pagoda, taa(g)

thousand san, shan, tsan

3 friends bamboo, plum, pine

title hsien sheng

toast yam seng

tourist attraction forbidden city, great wall, ming tombs, peking, summer palace, temple of heaven, trade fair

toy tangram

trade guild hong

travel service luxingshe

treaty port amoy, ichang

tree ailanthus, apricot plum, amygdalus, azedarach, bandoline, bead, chestnut, epaullette, hagbush, ginkgo, kaya, kinkan, kumquat, larch, lilac, litchi, matsu,

nahuong, nikko, pagoda, pear, soapberry, yulan
tribe heh, hei, lolo, miao, shan, toba
truth tao
vegetable udo
vermilion pimento
vernacular paihua
vessel junk
vine cinnamon, jasmine, kudzu, yangtao
walking stick whangee
wall builder cheng
war lord tuchun
-*ware* ceramic(s), cinchona, crockery, delft, dishes, dresden, earthenware, eggshell, enamel, faience, limoges, porcelain, pottery
-*ware, fine* limoges, sevres, spode, wedgwood
warehouse godown, hong
watermelon wax-gourd
wax cere, pela
way tao
weather, god of chao of the dark terrace, tsai-shen, tseng-fu-tsai-shen
weight candareen, catty, chee, chi(e)n, dong, fan, fen, haikwan, hao, kin, kungchin, kungfen, kungli, kungssu, kungtun, kupingtael, picul, shih, ssu, tael, tan, tchin, tsien, tsin, yin
wife tsai
wind instrument cheng, sheng
wine shao hsing
woman symbol phoenix
wonder great wall
wood tung tree
world creator pan-ku
wormwood moxa
writer chu tzu-ching, han-yu, kuan nan-ching, lin yutang, ly hsun, shen chi-chih, su shih, tao chien, tao yuan-ming
yellow sil
yellow mist bai
zither chin
CHINABERRY azedarach, emetic, lilac, soapberry
CHINAMAN celestial, chow, johnny, klondike, pounce, sinian, solitaire, tanka
tricky ah sin
CHINAWARE ceramics, cinchona, crockery, delft, dishes, earthenware, pottery
CHINCOUGH kinkhorst, pertussis
CHINE back(bone), bulge,

chink, cleave, crack, crest, crevice, fissure, ikat, ravine, ridge, silk, spine, sprout, vertebrae
CHINESE (See also CHINA.) asian, asiatic, baba, cataian, celestial, cerai, chinois, chow, manzas, mongol, sangley, seres, seric, sinic(o)
CHING tsing
CHINGACHBOOK *son* uncas
CHINK aperture, bore, cash, chaffinch, chap, check, chine, cleft, clink, coin, crack, cranny, fissure, fit, furrow, gap, grike, groove, interstice, jingle, jink, kink, knack, money, open(ing), rent, rift, rime, scar, sprain, stop, tinkle
CHINOOK *chief* tyee
god tamanoas
indian clackama, clatsop, wasco, watata
people tilikum, tillicum
powwow wawa
salmon quinnat
state washington
wind snoweater
woman klootchman
CHINQUAPIN beech, bonnet(s), candock, castanopsis, chestnut, rattlenut, wankapin, yokernut
CHINTZ calico, pintado, salampore
CHIOCCA blolly, snakeroot, snowberry
CHIONE *consort* apollo, hermes, neptune, poseidon
parent boreas, daedalion, orithyia
slayer artemis, diana
son autolycus, chionides, eumolpus, philammon
CHIOS *inhabitant* sciot
man of homer
CHIP bit, bone, bonnet, boring, break, chap, check, cheep, chisel, clip, counter, crack, cut, deride, dib, fiche, fish, flake, fragment, gag, gallet, hack, harrow, hew, hoe, jeton, key, knap, marker, mille, nick, nig, part, piece, quarrel, rally, sand, scrap, shaving, skin, slice, snip, snub, spall, spalt, specie, spell, splinter, taunt, tease, token, waste, whitling

in ante, contribute, interrupt, participate, settle
off the old block descendant, duplication, offspring, sib (ling)
CHIPEWYAN *indian* athapascan, caribou-eater, montagnai, thilanottine, yellowknives
CHIPMUNK chippy, gopher, grinnie, grinny, hackee, squirrel, tamias
CHIPPENDALE afghan, brown
CHIPPER active, agile, babble, brisk, chatter, cheerful, chirp, chirrup, cockie, cocky, debonair, fierce, gay, hacker, healthy, jaunty, kipper, lively, perky, pert, quick, sprightly, spry, twitter, vivacious
CHIPPY dry, harridan, pickup, prostitute, squirrel, tasteless, trollop, wanton
CHIPS crewmen, money, wealth
CHIRK active, cheerful, chirp, chirrup, creak, croak, lively, pert, squeak
up cheer, enliven
CHIRO albula, bonyfish, elops, fish, francesca, ladyfish, menhaden, seering
CHIROGRAPHY See HANDWRITING.
CHIRON centaur, philyrides, sagittarius
friend hercules
home mt pelion
parent cronus, philyra, saturn, tamora
pupil achilles, asclepius, castor, dioscuri, jason, peleus, pollux
teacher apollo, artemis
CHIROPODIST corncutter, pedicure, pedicurist
CHIROPTER See BAT.
CHIRP boom, cackle, call, caw, chatter, cheep, chip, chirr, chirrup, chitter, chuck, chuckle, churr, clang, cluck, cock-a-doodle, coo, croak, cronk, crow, cuckoo, cur, gabble, gaggle, gobble, hiss, honk, hoot, peep, pew, pipe, plunk, pue, quack, scream, screech, sing, squall, squawk, trill, tu-whit, tu-whoo, tweet, twink, twitter, warble, whistle, whoop
CHIRPY See CHIPPER.

CHIRRUP See CHIRP.

CHIRU antelope, saiga, sus

CHISEL bargain, bolster, bran, broad, bruzz, bur, burin, calking-iron, carve, celt, cheat, chipper, create, cut, drove, engrave, etch, fabricate, firmer, flour, form, furrow, gad, gouge, gradine, gravel, grubber, haggle, hardy, hew, moil, pare, point, pommel, quarry, roughhew, scoop, scorper, scrimp, sculpt(ure), seat, sett, shingle, slick, spitstick, splitter, stiff, swindle, tang, tool(er), twibil
blacksmith's hardie
blade bezel
broad drove
corner bruzz
dress with drove
edge basil, bezel, face
engraving scooper, scorper
flint tranohet
ice spud
in intrude
jeweler's scauper, scorper
-like tool adz(e)
mason's pommel
metal-working cold-set
mine gad, peeker
paring skew, slick
prehistoric celt, tranchet
sculpture ebauchoir, gradine
-shaped scalpriform
stone broach, celt
stonemason's drove, pommel, splitter
toothed gradine, jagger
triangular bur(r)
wheelwright's bruzz(iron)

CHISELER cheat, coyote, crook, gouger, shnorer, s(c)hnorrer

CHISION *son* elidad

CHIT bill, check, child, correspondence, dab, draft, hoyden, infant, intelligence, iou, letter, memo(randum), mind, note, offspring, recommendation, rice, romp, shoot, sprout, tab, tomboy, voucher

CHITCHAT babble, banter, gash, gossip, guff, small talk

CHITON diplois, exomion, exomis, gown, limpet, mollusk, robe

CHITTAMWOOD bearwood, buckthorn, cascara, cotinus, ironwood, smoke tree

CHIV knife, sword

CHIVALROUS brave, civil, courteous, courtly, dauntless, faithful, fearless, gallant, genteel, gentle, knightly, loyal, mettlesome, noble, polite, spirited, true, valiant

CHIVALRY caballeria, cavalry, courage, courtesy, courliness, gallantry, knighthood, nobless(e), oblige, valor
saint george

CHIVE allium, anther, bulbet, chip, civet, clove, cut, filament, garlic, knife, leek, onion, shallot, sithe, sive, stab

CHIV(V)Y See CHEVY.

CHLAMYS abolla, cloak, garment, mantle

CHLOE demeter, shepherdess
lover daphnis

CHLORDIAZEPOXIDE librium

CHLORIDE alembroth, butter, calomel, muriate

CHLORINATE bleach, disinfect, purify, sanitize, sterilize

CHLORINE element, gas
family bromin(e), fluorin(e), iodin(e)
remover antichlor
source salt

CHLORIS *brother* amyclas
consort ampucus, ampyx, neleus, zephyr
parent amphion, niobe
personifies spring
son nestor

CHLORITE amesite

CHLORO *toothpaste* phyll

CHLOROFORM an(a)esthetic, antiseptic, deaden, gas, kill, murder
discoverer guthrie, liebig, soubeiran
ingredient acetone
-like chemical bromoform

CHLOROPAL gramenite

CHLOROPHYL etiolin, leafgreen

CHLOROSIS anemia, iron deficiency, yellowing

CHOAT complete

CHOCHO chayote, zapotecan

CHOCK block, chuck, cleat, cog, scotch, spoke, sprag, tight, wedge
-a-block crowded, full, jammed, packed
-full brimming, crammed, replete

CHOCOLATE assonia, bittersweet, bonbon, cacao, candy, cocoa, confection, jacolatt, norfolk, sugarplum
color amber, brown, cafe-aulait, coffee, norfolk
corn dura
discoloration bloom
family sterculiaceae
flower alpine bloom, alum bloom, alumroot, crane'sbill, geranium
machine conche
mixer molinet
powder cocoa, pinole
seed cacao
tree cacao, cola, theobroma

CHOCTAW *indian* ahepatokla, apalachee, oklafalaya, six towns

CHOICE alternative, a-one, best, chary, chosen, cream, dainty, decision, delicate, desire, determination, dilemma, discretion, discrimination, drather, druther, eclecticism, election, elegant, elite, excel(lent), fastidious, fine, frugal, good, mind, odd, option, peerless, permiss, pick(ed), pleasure, plummy, pole, popular, precious, predilection, preference, preoption, prime, rare, rather, resistless, select(ion), supreme, surpassing, uncommon, unique, valuable, voice, volition, vote, wale, weal, will
deliberate proairesis
lottery gig
without alternative hobson's

CHOIR band, chapel, chorale, chorus, company, concert, kapelle, psalmody, quire, singers
boy chorister, clergeon
invisible angels, dead
leader cantor, choragus, chorister, precentor
loft gallery
member alto, bass(o), chorister, songman, soprano, tenor
screen reredos
stall stasidion
vestments cotta

CHOKE bottleneck, burke, check, cheek, chock, clog, close, congest, dam, damp, enose, extinguish, gag, gob, impede, jaw, kill, muffle, neck(cloth), obstruct, plug, quackle, quar, queasom, queazen, querken, repress, retard, scrag, scumfish, silence, smolder, smother, squeeze, stifle, stop(page), strangle, stuff, suffocate, suppress, surfeit, swarve, throttle, warp, worry, wring, yoke

coil reactor

damp blackdamp, carbon dioxide, miasma, stythe, vapor

off beset, gag, stifle, suppress

weed broomrape

CHOKEBERRY aronia, dogberry, soapberry

CHOKED clotted, foul, wool(l)y

up inert, mute, overcome, paralyzed, pressured, scared, silenced, still, stopped

CHOKER collar, cravat, neckcloth, necklace, stock

CHOKEWEED broomrape, orobanche

CHOKIDAR porter, watchman

CHOKY See JAIL.

CHOL mayan, plain

CHOLER acrimony, anger, animosity, asperity, bile, bitterness, distemper, foam, fury, gall, humor, ire, rage, rancor, rankling, soreness, spleen, temper, virulence, wrath

CHOLERA bile, mordisheen

bacillus comma, vibrio

goddess mariamman

morbus corporal forbes, gastroenteritis

CHOLERIC anger, belligerent, bilious, bitter, cranky, cross, enraged, fiery, fumish, huffy, impatient, indignant, iracund, irascible, irate, ireful, irritable, mad, peevish, peppery, petulant, querulous, splenetic, techy, testy, touch, waspish, wrathful

render enrage

CHOLESTEROL hyperlipoproteinemia, sterol

pill cholestyramine, clofibrate

CHOLINE agaricin(e), amanitine

CHOMP bite, champ, chew

CHOOSE adopt, affect, anoint, appoint, chap, coöpt,

crave, cull, decide, desire, destine, determine, elect, embrace, espouse, extract, fancy, fit, glean, like, list, op(ate), pick, please, prefer, select, separate, settle, take, try, vote, wale, want, weal, will, winnow, wish

CHOOSY choicy, conscientious, dainty, discriminating, eclectic, fastidious, finical, finicky, fussy, hair-splitting, particular, per(s)nickety, picky, prissy, queasy, select(ive)

CHOP argue, axe, barter, blow, carve, change, chap, chip, cleave, cleft, clip, cotelette, crack, cut, cutlet, dice, eat, exchange, gash, hack, hash, hew, incise, jaw, jowl, knock, lop, mangle, meat, mince, permit, quality, rive, shift, side, slash, slit, split, stamp, trademark, truck, vacillate, whang

-chop quickly, promptly

down fell, level, raze

eye of noisette

fine devil, dice, mince

off lop, snig

pork griskin

up hackle

CHOPFALLEN See CHAPFALLEN.

CHOPHOUSE cafe, restaurant

CHOPLOGIC argue, contend, sophisticate, vie

CHOPPER axe, buster, canary bird, child, helicopter, lumberman, mincer, slasher, trancet

CHOPPING lusty, shifting, strapping, vigorous

block hacklog

instrument axe, cleaver, hatchet, sax

CHOPPY bumpy, changeable, inclement, incoherent, irregular, loppy, lumpy, pecky, rough, uneven, unstable, variable, violent, wild

CHOPS cheeks, jaw, jowls, mouth, muzzle, snout

CHOPSTICK fiejie, hashi

CHOR rob, steal, thief, thieve

CHORAL cantabile, hymn, lyric, melic, operatic, singing, vocal

music cantata, motet

CHORD accord, cadence,

clef, diameter, dyad, filament, gamut, hamonize, harmony, key, lace, line, nerve, play, roll, rope, scale, string, sympathy, tendon, tetrad, tone, triad, trine

arc sine

common triad

harplike arpeggio

kind dominant, major, minor, ninth, seventh, tonic

musical major, minor

ninth none

seventh tetrad

succession cadence

three-toned triad, trine

CHORE assignment, business, char(e), difficulty, drag, duty, errand, handful, job, knack, large order, stint, task, work

CHOREA convulsion, jerks, jumps, st vitus dance

CHOREOGRAPHY dancing, terpsichore

CHORINE chorus girl

CHORISTER chanter, choirboy, singer

CHORTLE cackle, chuckle, giggle, guffaw, laugh, snort

CHORUS accord, agreement, bagpipe, burden, cast, choir, chorale, drone, echo, ensemble, glee club, holding, kapelle, liederkranz, liedertafel, quire, refrain, response, ritornelle, sing (ing club), unison, voices

girl actress, beauty, chorine, chorister, dancer, rockette, singer

leader cantor, choir director, choragus, conductor, coryph(a)eus

re-entry epiparodos

CHOSEN elect(ed), elite, KOREA, picked, selected, sorted

CHOTCHKE(LEH) babe, bird, broad, bruise, chick, contusion, fifth-wheel, gewgaw, misfit, nobody, playgirl, plaything, trinket, tsatske(leh), wound

CHOUGH bird, chank, chevet, chocard, chow, corbie, crow

group chattering

CHOUSE cheat, chiaus, defraud, dupe, gull, imposition, sham, swindle, trick

CHOW dog, eats, fodder, food, forage, grub, meal,

mess, provender, provisions, viands, victuals

CHOWCHOW cuckoo, hodgepodge, miscellaneous, mixed, mixture, olio, pickles, preserve, relish, slaw

CHOWDER *party* squantum

CHOWRY cowtail, whisk

CHRESTOMATHY anthology, collection, corpus, florilegium, garland, thesaurus, treasury

CHRISM anele, anoint(ment), cream, creme, muron, myron, officiate, ointment, unction, unguent

CHRIST, CHRIST'S adonai, adoney, anointed, drighten, drightin, emmanuel, good shepherd, ihs, inri, jesus, king, lamb, logos, lord, mediator, messiah, only-begotten, pantocrator, prince of peace, rabbi, ransome, redeemer, savio(u)r, shepherd, son of god, son of man, the life, the way, verity
acronym ihs, inri
agony gethsemane
betrayer judas
birthplace bethlehem
brother simon
burier joseph
childhood home nazareth
church the house
cross-carrier simon
crucifixion golgotha
crucifixion observer joanna, joseph of arimathaea, mary (magdalene)
disciple See **APOSTLE** *christ's.*
execution, induced by caiaphas
eye fleabane
follower nicodemus
gift frankincense, gold, myrrh
hair hart's-tongue
herb christmas rose
home capernaum, egypt, nazareth
humbling kenosis
image angel, baba, baby, bambino, bata, crucifix, sudarium
infant bambino
jericho host zacchaeus
king of peace
ladder centaury
language aramaic
letters inri
life of gospels, heliand
ministry capernaum
miracle cana
miracle beneficiary bartimaeus, jairus, joanna, lazarus, mary magdalene, simon, susanna
miracle words ephphatha, talitha cum
name boanerges
parent joseph, mary
passover meal last supper
pert. dominical
resurrection observer cleopas
salvation through redemption, soteriology
sayings agrapha, logia
2nd coming advent, millennium, parousia, resurrection
society of See **JESUIT.**
stopped at eboli
symbol asp, fish, ihc, ihs, jls, lamb, pelican, unicorn
thief crucified near desmas, dismas, dysmas
thorn carissa, jujube, nabk, nubk, zisyphus
words on cross eli, eli, lama sabachthani
wounds stigmata

CHRISTEN baptize, clep, godfather, kirsen, launch, name

CHRISTENING *feast* gossiping

CHRISTIAN catholic, colossian, copt, devotee, devout, faithful, galilean, gentile, gracious, holy, melchite, nazarene, nazarite, orthodox, pious, paragon, protestant, stoneite, traditor, uniate, upright
convert priscilla
creed apostles, athanasian, nicene
denomination adventist, amish, baptist, brethren, disciples of christ, episcopal, evangelical, friends, greek orthodox, jehovah's witnesses, lutheran, mennonite, methodist, moravian, nazarene, pentecostal, presbyterian, reformed, roman catholic, russian orthodox, unitarian, universalist
destination celestial city
early alogi, galilean
eastern uniate
emblem agnus dei
fathers, pert. patristic
fellowship koinonia
feast agape, eucharist
festival epiphany
group acephali, congregation, faithful, flock
holy city jerusalem
holy season advent
invocation agnus dei
leaderless acephali
love feast agape
manual didache
mendicant euchite
monasticism founder st anthony
persecuted martyr
preceptor athanasius, augustine, chrysostom, origen
prophet agabus
purity symbol holy grail
science eddyism
science founder mary baker eddy
science principle divine mind, life, love, mind, soul, spirit, truth
scientist mind-healer
sect, early abelite, alogi, aquarian, audean, audian, cathar
sect, heretical docetae
society civitas dei
symbol cross, ichthus, lamb, orant
theologian aquinas, augustine, bonhoeffer, bultmann, de chardin, kierkegaard, kuhn, niebuhr, origen, tillich
tribute to turks caratch
unity ecumenicalism, irenics

CHRISTIANA oslo

CHRISTMAS holiday, nativity, noel, xmas, yule(tide)
berry toyon
bonus aguinaldo
carol adeste fidelis, joy to the world, noel, nowel, silent night, we three kings
carol author dickens
carol character scrooge, tiny tim
carol family cratchit, fezziwig
carol saying bah humbug
carol singing caroling, hodening
day after boxing day
drink egg nog, tom and jerry
entertainment bummack, bummock
flower aconite, hellebore, poinsettia
4 sundays before advent
mass supper reveillon

mummer guiser
plant mistletoe
rose bearfoot, boar's-foot, hellebore, lungwort, melampodium, pedelion
symbol bay, box, holly, ivy, lights, mistletoe, poinsettia, SANTA CLAUS, tinsel, tree
CHROMA color, hue, quality, shade, tinge, tint
CHROMATIC cold, colorable, colorative, colored, colorific, cool, diatonic, enharmonical, hueful, pigmentary, prismatic, tinctorial, tingible
CHROMATIN protoplasm, spireme
CHROMIUM element, mineral, trim
discoverer vauquelin
group element molybdenum, tungsten, uranium
CHROMOSOME allowsome, gene, homolog, idant, idiosome, karyomere, leptonema
component chromatin, dna, protein
sexless autosome, euchromosome
CHRONIC confirmed, constant, continual, continuous, deep-rooted, deep-seated, disagreeable, established, fixed, incessant, indurated, intense, inveterate, lasting, lingering, prolonged, rooted, settled, severe, stubborn
CHRONICLE account, adventures, almanac, annals, archives, autobiography, biography, brut, calendar, confessions, diary, enact, experiences, fortune, history, journal, letters, life(story), memoir, memorabilia, memorials, narrative, necrology, obituary, profile, recital, record, register, registry, report, story, timecard, timetable, version
CHRONICLER analist, autobiographer, biographer, boswell, chronist, compiler, historian, historiographer, layamon, memorialist, narrator, recorder, writer
CHRONOLOGY almanac, annals, calendar, chronometry, chronoscopy, horology, horometry, menology

according to datal
error anachronism, prolepsis
CHRONOMETER clock, dial, metronome, timekeeper, timer, watch
CHRYSAL fret
CHRYSALIS aurelia, cocoon, kell, larva, nymph, pupa
CHRYSANTHEMUM arctic daisy, azalea(mum), brutus, kiku(mon), kirimon, mum, pompon, pyrethrum, spoon
pompon brutus, golden west
CHRYSAOR *mother* medusa
wife callirrhoe
CHRYSIN flavone
CHRYSIPPUS *kin* atreus, pelops
teacher cleanthes
CHRYSOBERYL alexandrite, cat's-eye, cymophane, tourmaline
CHRYSOLITE aquamarine, asbestos, asbestus, beryl, chrysopal, mineral, olivine, peridot
CHRYSOSTOM, JOHN golden mouth
CHTHONIAN hadean, hellish, infernal, stygian, tartarian
worship sorcery
CHUB bass, chevin, chopa, cyprinid, dace, dolt, fallfish, fool, hornyhead, kiyi, lout, mackerel, poll, shiner, spawneater
mackerel hardhead, scombrid, tink(er)
-sucker creekfish
CHUBBY buxom, chuff, corpulent, dumpy, fat, fleshy, fubsy, obese, plump, portly, rolypoly, rotund, squat, stout, stubby
person butterball
CHUCK bounce, brush, cant, caress, charles, chock, chug, chunk, clap, cluck, collet, discard, dismiss(al), ejection, eliminate, eviction, expel, flip, food, grub, hen, hurl, log, lump, out, pat, pet, pig, pitch, quit, stroke, tap, throw, tickle, toss, twirl
-full replete
hole cahot
-luck bird cage, crown and anchor, hazard, sweat
wagon cafe, restaurant
CHUCKLEHEAD blockhead, fool, lubber, plover

CHUD mongol, tavastian, veps(e), vote
CHUDDARD mantle, phulkari, shawl
CHUFA cypress, earthnut, galangal, glumal, groundnut, sedge, tigernut
CHUFF boor, brick, chubby, churl, conceited, cross, elated, fat, illtempered, miser, proud, rustic, sulky, surly
CHUG bang, fish, pull, throw, tug, vibration
CHUKARD See PARTRIDGE.
CHUM aikane, associate, bait, berley, buddy, butty, cad, catercousin, cobber, companion, comrade, copain, crony, feller, fellow, fish, friend, mate(y), pal, pard, pardner, roommate, tole, toll bait
around hobnob
CHUMMY buddy-buddy, chimneysweep, close, confidential, familiar, friendly, great, intimate, pally, palsywalsy, sociable, thick
CHUMP ass, blockhead, boob(y), dolt, dupe, endpiece, flat, fool, goof, goon, head, jerk, lump, munch, mutt, piece, prize, pumpkin, sap(head), schlemiel, sucker, victim
CHUMPY chunky, stocky, thickset
CHUNCO chama, tiatinagua
CHUNK chuck, claut, dab, dad, dornick, fid, fragment, gob(bet), hurl, junt, knuckle, lump, lunch(eon), pat, piece, portion, slug, throw, wad, whang, whank
CHUNKY blocky, chubby, chumpy, dumpy, lumpy, obese, plump, short, squat, stocky, stout, stubby, thick(set)
CHURCH abbey, aedes, autem, basilica, bethel, body, cathedral, chapel, charge, clergy, communion, congregation, conventicle, creed, crypt, cult, denomination, dominical, ebenezer, ecclesia, edifice, faith, fanacle, fane, flock, fold, hieron, house of god, iglesia, kil(l), kirk, kovil, kurk, lateran, masjid, meetinghouse, minister, mission,

monastery, mosque, oratory, pagoda, pantheon, parish, parsonage, persuasion, rectory, religion, samaj, sanctuary, sect, shrine, synagogue, tabernacle, temple, tera, zion
aisle ambulatory
-ale feast
altar end apse
attendant altarboy, choirboy, sexton
balcony contoria
baptistry font
bench pew, pue, seat, sedile, sedilia
bishopric see
body of nave
book missal, psalter, triodion
calendar ordo
candlestick tricerion
caretaker verger
celebration candlemas, christmas, easter, encaenia, synaxis
ceremony book ordinal
chapel oratory
choir scola cantorum
comb. ecclesio
congregation fold, synaxis
contribution offering, tithe
corner amen
council synod
court colloquy, presbytery, rota
courtyard parvis
crime simony
crossing plage, transept
cupboard ambry
curtain endothys, ependytes, riddel
deputy curate, vicar
dignitary abbot, archbishop, bishop, canon, cardinal, dean, ecclesiarch, pope, prelate, prelatist, primate
dish paten
-disrupting ecclesioclastic
dissenter sectary
district diocese, parish
division schism
dominion of sacerdotium
doorkeeper ostiary
doxology gloria
early christian basilica
eastern See EASTERN church.
endowed benefice
entrance chapel galilee
episcopacy prelacy
father ambrose, augustin(e), barnabus, basil, bernard, clement, cyprian, cyril, gregory, hermas, ignatius, jerome, justin, origen, polycarp, tertullian
feast See CHURCH *celebration.*
fountain columbeion
furnishing altar, baldacchino, baldachin, bell, cannel, cerecloth, chrismal, corporal(e), fanon, font, jube, lectern, organ, paten, pew, piscina, priedieu, pulpit, pyx-cloth, reredos, rood screen, stoup
government archiepiscopacy, episcopacy, hierarchy, prelacy
group uniat
head catholicos, catholicus, katholikos
historian justin martyr
house convent, deaconate, deanery, manse, parsonage, pastorate, presbytery, priory, rectory, vatican, vicarage
jurisdiction deanery, diocese, parish, see
land glebe
laws nomocanon
leader See CHURCH *dignitary.*
-like ecclesiastical
living benefice, prebend
man See CHURCHMAN.
obligation tithing
of england anglican
of scotland presbyterian
of the brethren dipper, dunkard, dunker
offering altarage, collection
official See CHURCHMAN.
official's seat sedile
part aisle, altar, ambry, amen corner, apse, apsidiole, apsis, baptist(e)ry, bells, bema, blindstory, cantoria, chancel, choir, clearstory, clerestory, cloister, confessional, crossing, crypt, diaconicon, font, narthex, nave, nef, parvis, plage, presbytery, porch, retrochoir, roodloft, sacrarium, sacristy, solea, spire, steeple, tower, transept, triforium, vestry
platform pulpit, solea
poe's lateran
porch parvis
prayer kyrie eleison
property glebe
reader lector
reading desk lectern
recess apse, apsidiole, apsis

retreat See MONASTERY.
revenue annat, benefice, tithe
seaman's bethel
seat See CHURCH *bench.*
screen jube, parclose, reredos
servant beadle
service compline, evensong, mass, matins, nocturn, rite, tenebrae, vespers
service, annual encaenia
side, pert. cantoral, decanal
small oratory
stall stasidion
stand ambo
steward erenach, herenach
stipend prebend
treasures cimelia
transept plage
vault crypt
vessel ama, amula, columba, colymbion, font, monstrance, piscina, pix, pyx
vestment See VESTMENT *ecclesiastical.*
vestry room sacristy
wall cashel
wash basin lavabo
window jesse
woman nun, priestess, rectress, religieuse
CHURCHGOER(S) congregation, devotee, flock, parishioner, worshiper
CHURCHILL *daughter* sarah
order garter
salute v-sign
skill oratory, prose, style
son randolph
son-in-law soames
trademark brandy, cigar
CHURCHLESS unaffiliated
CHURCHMAN 4 abba, abbe, amba, anba, cure, dean, papa, pope 5 abbot, angel, canon, clerk, elder, frock, padre, prior, rabbi, saint, vicar 6 beadle, bedral, bishop, cleric, curate, deacon, divine, exarch, father, gallah, layman, lector, levite, musset, mullah, paroch, pastor, priest, reader, rector, sexton, verger, warden 7 acolyte, almoner, bederal, cassock, dominie, erenach, pontiff, prelate, primate, prophet, sacrist, stallar 8 anagnost, antistes, cardinal, chaplain, clerical, diocesan, herenach, hierarch, minister, preacher, reverend, sermoner, shepherd, sidesman,

superior, thurifer 9 black-coat, capitular, clergyman, coadjutor, moderator, patriarch, precentor, predicant, prelatist, presbyter, pulpiteer, religious, sacristan, sermonist, squareson, succentor, suffragan 10 archbishop, archdeacon, capitulary, evangelist, high priest, holy father, prebendary, sermonizer 11 abbreviator, beneficiary, ecclesiarch 12 ecclesiastic, metropolitan
group clergy, ulema
house manse, parsonage, priory, rectory, vicarage
CHURCHWARDEN ecclesiastic, pipe, sexton, warner
aide hoggler, sideman
CHURCHYARD cemetery, graveyard, haw, litten
entrance lich-gate
CHURL bodach, bondman, boor, bounder, bumpkin, cad, carl(e), carlot, ceorl, chuff, clodhopper, clown, freeman, gnof(f), haskard, hind, husband, knave, lout, lubber, man, miser, niggard, oaf, peasant, rascal, rough, rustic, serf, servant, slave, tightwad, vassal, villain, villein, yeoman
CHURLISH bluff, blunt, boorish, brusque, carlage, carlish, chuffy, crabbed, crabby, crusty, curt, discourteous, dour, gruff, ill-mannered, impolite, irascible, mean, peevish, rough, rude, runty, rustic, sordid, sour, sulky, sullen, surly, uncivil, ursal, violent, vulgar
CHURN agitate, agitation, baratte, beat, boil, bubble, convulse, cream, drill, emulsify, joggle, jolt, kirn, moil, seethe, shake, stir, trundle, whip
drill jumper
part dasher, staff
supper harvest home
CHURNSTAFF dasher, sunspurge, toadflax
CHURRUS See MARIJUANA.
CHUTE channel, decline, descent, downfall, fall, flume, hopper, hurry, incline, parachute, passageway, rapid, rush, shoot, slide,

slip, stampede, telegraph, trough, tube
mining pass, telegraph
-the-chute roller coaster
CHUTZPA effrontery, impudence
CHUZA *steward to* herod
wife joanna
CHUZZLEWIT fips
victim tigg
CHYLE *deficiency* achylia
CHYME *deficiency* achymia
CHYPRE perfume
CIA the pickle factory
CIBOL onion, shallot, sybo(w)
CIBORIUM canopy, cimboris, civory, coffer, goblet, pix, pyx
CICADA cad, cicala, cigale, cricket, harvestfly, homopter, jarfly, locust, lyreman, tettix
killer digger wasp
noise chirr
symbol of poetry
CICATRICLE gallature
CICATRIX blemish, eye, mark, scab, scar, seam
CICATRIZE fester, heal, restore, scar, scarify
CICELY myrrh, parsley
CICERO *brother* quintus
city tusculum
client cluentius, herennius, milo, munatius, popillius, roscius, sextius
colleague antonius
enemy antony, clodius, crasus
essay de amicitia, de legibus, de oratore, de republica, de senectute
friend hirtius, ligarius, lucullus, pansa, pompey, pomponius, publius, vergilius, vibius
mother helvia
offspring marcus, tullia
prosecuted manilius, verres
protege charas, diopithes, leosthenes
rival chrysogonus
sister-in-law fabia
target catiline
teacher apollonius, clytomachus, diodorus, dionysius, menippus, mucii, phaedrus, philo, posidonius, xenocles
villa astura
warner fulvia
wife pubilia, terentia
CICERONE conductor,

courier, dragoman, guide, mentor, orator, pilot, sightsman
CICISBEO bow, cavalier, gallant, knot, ribbon, streamer
CID bivar, campeador, chief, commander, hero, leader, rodrigo, ruy diaz de vivar
horse babieca, bavieca
sword colada, tizona
CIDER apple wine, coccagee, kvas, perkin, perry, pommage, quas, swanky, syddir
girl ida
hard applejack
inferior swanky
pulp pomace
CIDEVANT former, late, past, prior
CIE See COMPANY.
CIEL heaven, paradise, sky
CIENAGA marsh, swamp
CIGALA See CICADA.
CIGAR belvedere, breva, bunco, cheroot, cigarro, claro, colorado, concha, corona, cremo, culebra, habana, havana, heater, locofoco, londres, madura, manila, panatella, perfecto, pickwick, puritano, puro, regalia, rope, se(e)gar, shuck, smoke, stinker, stogie, stogy, toby, trabuco, trichi(nopoly), twofer, weed, woodbine
black maduro, toscano
cheap broom, cabbage, el ropo, heater, pickwick, stinker, stogie, toby, twofer, woodbine
crude cheroot, culebra, trichi
dark black beauty, colorado, maduro
factory buckeye
factory rejects odd lots, throw-out
fish quiaquia, round robin, scad
grader escojedore
group box, bundle, humidor
light claro
long thin panatela, panatella
maker noodle twister, tabaquero
medium colorado claro, puritano
merchant dunhill
mild claro
pioneer demetrio pela, ignacio haya
process curing, fermentation
salesman drummer
self-lighting locofoco

shape belvedere, bonanza, bonita, breva, corona, imperial, lonsdale, monte carlo, palma, panetel(1)a, perfecto, shamrock, stogie, swagger, vitola
size barcelona, cheroot, churchill, cigarillo, jaguar, kohinorr
small cheroot, cigarillo, cigarito, tipperello
smoking term aroma, exhaling, globes, gulp, inhaling, retention, rings, whiff
spot frogeye
store, 1st demuth's
store statue wooden indian
strong maduro, toscano
tapered delicioso, perfecto
tobacco broad leaf, havana
tree catalpa
twisted end super
wrapper candela
CIGARETTE birdwood, biri, brain tablet, coffin nail, cubeb, dope stick, dream stick, fag, gasper, greenie, hump, jigger, jump stick, lung duster, pill, poison sausage, reefer, skag, smoke, weed
additive menthol
break respite, rest
butt bumper, roach, snipe
defective farole
half-smoked castaway
inhale drag
king-sized longie, longy
marijuana joint, pot, reefer, stick
medicinal cubeb
pack bale of hay, herd
paper blanket, prayer book
re-smoked blincher, butt, snipe
roll twist a dizzy
stale fast burner
stub butt, snipe
unlit dry smoke
CILIUM barbiee ciliolum, eyelash, filament, hair, lash, quill, uncinus
CILIX *sister* europa
CILLA *brother* priam
slayer priam
CIMA dome, height, peak, top
CIMARRON bighorn, dog, maroon
author edna ferber
CIMBRI acanthia, bedbug
CIMBRI *destroyer* marius
king boerix
CIMICIFUGA bugbane,

crowfoot, hellebore, snakeroot, snakeweed
CIMMERIAN black, dark, gloomy
CIMON *accuser* pericles
chronicler phanodemus
companion polygnotus
consort asteria, clitorium, isodice, mnestra
diviner astyphilus
enemy persians
parent hegesipyle, miltiades
parent-in-law euryptoleumus, megaoles
patron aristides
poet archelaus, melanthius
rival ephialtes, pausanias, themistocles
sister elpinice
son eleus, lacedaemonius, miltiades, thessalus
summoner pericles
surname coalemus
CINCH assure, belt, breeze, certainty, child's play, dupe, easy mark, facility, fasten, fix(ed), gird, girth, gravy, grip, harness, nail down, pianola, picnic, pipe, plum, prove, push-over, saddle, set, sew (up), sinecure, snap, sure thing
game term pedro, protection, rob the pack
CINCHONA bark tree, china, quina, quinidine, quinine
bark calisaya, guina
bark, pert. quinic
CINCINNATI *nickname* porkopolis
CINCTURE baldric, band, belt, center, cestus, collal, compass, encircle, enclosure, environment, fillet, girdle, girth, halo, ring, surcingle, surround, zone
CINDER(S) ash(es), chark, clinker, coal, dander, dross, ember, foxtail, gleeds, gray, lapillus, remainder, remnant, residue, scar, scoria, slag, smithydander, tap
refuse breeze
CINDERELLA *suitor* prince charming
vehicle pumpkin
CINEMATOGRAPH camera, kino, projector, veriscope, vitagraph
CINERARIA senecio
CINERATOR ashery, crematory, furnace

CINGLE belt, girdle, girth
CINGULAR annular, circular
CINNABAR mineral, ore, vermil(1)ion
derivative quicksilver
CINNAMON barbasco, canel, canella, canelle, cassia, flavoring, ishpingo, sanela, spice, stagte
apple sweetsop
bark canella
black bayberry
fern bread root, buckhorn
flower cassia bud
honeysuckle swamp azalea
oak bluejack
root fleawort, flybane
sedge sweet flag
stone essonite, garnet
tree canela, canella
tree extract camphor
wild barbasco, bayberry, dogwood, joewood
wood sassafras
CINQUEFOIL clover, comarum, cowberry, fivefinger, frasier, hardhack, herb, plant, potentilla, quintfoil, rosacean
CINYRAS *daughter* myrrha
father apollo
kingdom cyprus
son adonis
CION bud, cutting, descendant, graft, imp, sarment, scion, shoot, slip, uvula
CIPANGO See JAPAN.
CIPHER albam, athbash, aught, calculate, code, decode, device, figure, key, letter, monogram, naught, nil, nobody, nonentity, nothing, nought, null(ity), number, ought, sign(ature), vigenere, zero, zilch
disk decoder
system code
CIRCA about, approximately, around
CIRCASSIAN *dialect* abkhasian, adighe, cherkess, kabard(ian)
king sacripant
tribe adighe, kabard
CIRCE aeaea, magician, siren, sorceress, tempter, temptress, titania
brother aeetes
captive odysseus, ulysses
changed men to swine
island aeaea
lover odysseus, ulysses
niece medea

parent helios, perse
son comus, telegonus
CIRCLE 3 dot, lap, orb, red,
set 4 band, beat, clue, cult,
disk, eddy, gird, gyre, halo,
hoop, iris, loop, maru,
nimb, orbe, pals, ring, rink,
roll, rond, tour, turn, zone
5 carol, class, crowd,
crown, cycle, fetch, field,
frame, globe, group, kreis,
lasso, monde, noose, orbit,
party, realm, rhomb, rigol,
round, rowel, scope, swirl,
twirl, wheel, whirl, whorl 6
areola, areole, bezant,
brough, circus, cirque,
clique, collet, colure,
cordon, corona, diadem,
equant, girdle, gyrate, radius, region, rondel, rotate,
rundle, sphere, spiral, system, tropic, washer, wreath
7 annulus, azimuth, chuk-
kar, chukker, circlet, circuit,
company, compass, coronet,
coterie, enclose, friends,
garland, horizon, looplet,
monthon, revolve, ringlet,
rondure, roundel, society 8
deferent, ecliptic, frostbow,
rondelle, surround 9 curvature, influence, intimates 10
millaround, roundabout 13
circumference
altitude almucantar
astronomical epicycle, equant
banded with annular(y), annulose
celestial almucantar, colure
circumference, part arc
comb. cycl(o)
dance galley
fairy ringlet
flower parts verticil
geographic tropic
great ecliptic, equator, meridian
heavenly zodiac
imaginary deferent
-like cycloid
longest chord diameter
luminous aura, corona, halo,
nimbus
monolith cromlech
move in mill
parhelic frostbow
parquet orchestra
part arc, center, chord, degree, diameter, octant, radian, radius, secant, sector,
segment, tangent
red guze
reasoning in dialellus

squaring cyclometry, cyclot-
omy
stone carol, gorsedd, hurler
symbol yin and yang
two cachet
vicious rat race
CIRCLET anklet, annulet,
band, bangle, bracelet,
chandelier, corona, coronet,
eye(let), grommet, halo,
headband, hoop, ring(let),
roundlet, vallary, verge
of light aureola, aureole
ornamental anklet, bangle,
bracelet
CIRCUIT accepter, address,
ambage, ambit, area, beat,
bout, chain, circle, circulate, circumambulate, circumference, curcummigrate,
circumnavigate, comarca,
compass, cycle, detour, diocese, district, double, encircle, encompass, eyre, flank,
go about, gyre, hookup,
iter, journey, lap, loop,
orbit, perimeter, periphery,
periplus, progress, revolution, round, route, skirt,
sphere, tour, turn, umgang,
viron, walk, wend, zodiac,
zone
assembly breadboard
branch leg
connecting tieline
court eyre
drive home run
electric doubler, leg, loop,
secondary, squelch
electronic gate
heterodyne autodyne
inductance henry
interrupter breaker
one-input buffer
rider preacher
CIRCUITOUS ambagious,
ambigatory, anfractuous,
backhanded, crooked,
curved, deceitful, deviating,
devious, digressive, discursive, errant, excursive,
flexuous, indirect, labyrinthine, mazy, oblique,
out-of-the-way, rambling,
roundabout, serpentine, sinuous, spiral, tortuous, turning, twisted, twisting, vagrant, wandering, winding
course circumduction
method windlass
CIRCULAR annular, bill,
broadside, cingular, com-
pass, complete, corre-
spondence, cycloid, discoid,

dodger, dopebook, dope-
sheet, encyclic, flier, flyer,
folder, globular, handout,
indirect, infinite, leaflet, letter, mail, orbal, orbed, orbicular, orblike, pamphlet,
piece, publication, ringed,
rond, round(ed), spheri-
cal, spheroid, terete,
wheely
enclosure lis(s)
indicator dial
letter encyclical
nearly penannular
pert. arc, gyre
tread volt
CIRCULATE air, bring out,
bruit, canvass, circuit, convect, convolve, defuse,
diffuse, disseminate, distribute, encompass, gyrate,
issue, mill around, mix,
monetize, move, pass, propagate, publish, rise, rotate,
scurry, sphere, spread, troll,
turn, walk, wander, wind
publicly announce, broadcast, report
CIRCULATING afloat, cur-
rent, stirring
CIRCULATION course, cov-
erage, currency, issue,
readers, subscription
test apgar
CIRCUMCISED apellous
CIRCUMCISION berit(h),
brit(h), deduction, perit-
omy, purification
stages mezizah, milah,
periah
CIRCUMCISOR mohel
CIRCUMFERENCE ambit,
apsis, arc, auge, border,
boundary, bounds, circle,
circuit, compass, contour,
girth, limits, outline, perimeter, periphery, surround,
verge
CIRCUMFUSE bathe, dif-
fuse, distribute, envelop,
scatter, surround
CIRCUMLOCUTION am-
bage, circuit, paraphrase,
periphrasis, pleonasm, prolixity, redundancy, tautology, verbiage, verbosity,
winding, wordiness
CIRCUMSCRIBE bound,
capture, check, confine,
conscribe, cram, curb,
define, delimit, demarcate,
determine, encircle, en-
close, encompass, environ,
fence, fetter, fix, hamper,

inclose, inhibit, lay off, limit, mark off, restrain, restrict, surround, trammel

CIRCUMSCRIBED insular, limited, narrow, provincial

CIRCUMSPECT alert, attent(ive), calculating, careful, cautious, chary, discreet, gingerly, guarded, judicious, prudent, scrupulous, thoughtful, vigilant, wary, watchful

CIRCUMSPECTION attention, caution, deliberation, prudence, respect, wariness

CIRCUMSTANCE affair, calling, case, component, condition, contingency, detail, element, environment, episode, event(uality), fact (or), fix, footing, happening, incident, instance, item, note, occasion, occurrence, particular, phase, pickle, point, pomp, position, situation, start, state, status, strait, surroundings, thing
critical extremes
favorable auspice

CIRCUMSTANTIAL accurate, coincidental, complete, concomitant, concurrent, cumulative, detailed, exact, ex parte, formal, full, hearsay, incidental, itemized, minute, nonessential, nuncupative, particular(ized), precise, presumptive

CIRCUMSTANTIATE authenticate, confirm, establish, evidence, particularize, support

CIRCUMVENT avoid, baffle, balk, beat, by-pass, capture, cheat, check, cozen, deceive, defraud, delude, dupe, elude, ensnare, entrap, evade, foil, forestall, frustrate, hinder, hoodwink, ignore, nobble, outgo, outsmart, outwit, overreach, prevent, stave off, surround, thwart, trick, underfong, ward off

CIRCUMVOLVE revolve, rotate

CIRCUS arena, big top, carnival, circle, cirque, cockpit, coliseum, colosseum, court, diamond, field, gridiron, hippodrome, lists, ring, rink, show, theater
barrier spina

employee clown, flea, roustabout, tamer
flying aeronautics
gear ring, tent, trapeze
hanger-on shillaber
lot tober
post meta
rider desultor, hippodromist
ring arena, tanbark
wagon gilly
wall spina

CIRIO boojum

CIRQUE basin, circle(t), CIRCUS, coomb, corrie, cwm, erosion, recess

CIRRIPED anatifa, apoda, barnacle, crustacean, peltogaster

CIRROSE curly, hairy, stringy

CIRRUS cloud, coil, filament, tendril

CIRSIUM cocklebut, thistle, xanthium

CISCO blackfin, bloat(er), bluefin, coregonus, finisco, fish, grayback, herring, kiyi, longjaw, mackerel, mooneye, tullibee, whitefin

CISSA sirgang

CISSAEA athena

CIST box, casket, chest, kist(vaen), pit, quoit, tomb

CISTERCIAN *abbey* port royal
order bernardine
rule law of love

CISTERN bac(or), back, cavity, chultun, cuvette, feedhead, impluvium, laver, pump, rainbarrel, raintub, reservoir, sac, steeper, sump, tank, tub, urn(a), vat, well

CISTUDO box turtle, terrapene

CIT civilian, civit, shopkeeper, townsman, tradesman

CITADEL acropolis, alamo, arx, blockhouse, borough, bursa, byrsa, castle, fastness, fort(ress), hall, height, kremlin, solitaire, stronghold, toothill, tower

CITATION authority, cital, encomium, eulogy, evocation, honor, mention, monition, notice, panegyric, reference, summons, ticket, tribute

CITE accite, acclaim, accord, accuse, adduce, advance, allay, allege, apprehend,

arouse, arraign, arrest, assert, avouch, bespeak, call, convoke, demonstrate, detain, enumerate, evoke, excite, exemplify, extract, honor, illustrate, impeach, indicate, instance, invoke, laud, mention, muster, name, narrage, notify, quote, recite, refer, repeat, sample, sist, specify, subpoena, summon, tell

CITHAERON brother, helicon

CITHARA lyre, phorminx

CITHAROEDUS apollo

CITHER cithara, cittern, phorminx, zittern

CITIZEN american, burgess, burgher, cit, citoyen, citybred, civilian, cleruch, commoner, conscive, denizen, domestic, dweller, elector, flatcap, freeman, inhabitant, national, native, occupant, oppidan, resident, subject, townman, voter
average joe blow, joe doakes
comb. ese, ian, ist, ite
foreign-born alien
king louis philippe
native domestic
naturalized denizen
world cosmopolitan, cosmopolite

CITIZENSHIP *admission to* enfranchisement, naturalization
pert. civic
principle civism, ius soli

CITRAL geranial, neral

CITRIL carduelis, finch

CITRINE rhubarb

CITRON butterfly, cedra(te), esrog, et(h)rog, fruit, lemon, lime, melon, yellow
fruit buddha's-hand

CITRONELLA collinsonia, grass, horsebalm

CITRUS *belt* california, florida
black fly bean aphis, buffalo gnat, similium
disease anthracnose, blackfly, blast, buckskin, canker, exanthema, inspissosis, mal di gomma, melanose, mottle-leaf, nematode, psorosis, rust mite, scab, tristezza, white fly
drink ade
fruit bigarade, calamansi, calamondin, cedrat(e), citrange, citron, grapefruit,

hesperidium, kumquat, lemon, lime, mandarin, orange, shaddock, tangelo, tangerine
hybrid limequat, tangelo
pest rust mite
rind part albeda
CITTERN cithern, laud, penorcon
CITY borough, burg(h), burh, calno, capital, ciudad, cuthah, dorp, ekron, eldorado, hamlet, megalopolis, metropolis, municipality, place, polis, sette, stad(t), stead, suburb, town, urban, urbs, village, ville, won, woon, zion
ancient pergamum
besieged solitaire
block square
cathedral canterbury, coventry, durham, ely, lincoln, norfolk, paris, rheims, salisbury, wells
celestial zion
center downtown
chief cabecera, capital, megalopolis
crescent new orleans
district barrio, block, business, chinatown, downtown, east side, ghetto, precinct, redlight, residential, shopping center, skid row, slums, square, suburb(s), suburbia, tinpan alley, uptown, ward
dwelling in urbicolous
eternal roma, rome
forbidden peking
golden prague
hall ayuntamiento, capitol
heavenly jerusalem, sion, zion
holy benares, fes, mecca, medina, jerusalem
large megalopolis
man metropolitan, slicker, sophisticate, townsman, urbanite
mythical hotzeplotz, schippishok
nymph poliad
of angels bangkok, los angeles
of bells strasbourg
of bridges bruges
of brotherly love philadelphia
of chance las vegas
of churches brooklyn
of david jerusalem
of dead cemetery, graveyard, necropolis, pompeii

of elms new haven
of god civitas dei, heaven, paradise, zion
of gods asgard
of golden gate san francisco
of guitars paracho
of hundred towers pavia
of joseph nauvoo
of kings lima
of lights paris, perth
of lilies florence
of luxury sybaris
of magnificent distances washington
of masts london
of palaces calcutta, rome
of palm trees jericho
of plain admah, gomorrah, sodom, zaboim, zoar
of prophet medina
of rams canton
of refuge medina
of roses pasadena, portland
of saint michael dumfries
of saints montreal
of seven hills rome
of straits detroit
of sun baalbek, balbec, heliopolis, rhodes
of victory cairo
of violet crown athens
of violets toulouse
official aedile, alder(man), amphodarch, councilman, mayor, reeve, ward boss
oldest damascus
pert. civic, civil, metropolitan, municipal, urban
petrified ishmonie
pink jaipur
problem crime, ghettos, noise, riots, slums, smog, traffic, transportation, violence, zoning
rat-infested abdera, hamlin
red petra
sacred See CITY *holy.*
slicker busker, townsman
-state athens, civitas, polis, rome
treasure raamses
ward watchman
white helsinki
wicked babylon
windy chicago
CIUDAD DE LOS REYES lima
CIVET arctictus, bearcat, binturong, bondar, cat, dedes, fanaloka, fossane, fosse, foussa, genet(te), linsang, mongoose, musang, nandine, paguma, panda,

perfume, polecat, rasse, tangalung, zibet(h), zibetum, zinsang
cat dandy, fop
palm bondar, musang, nandine, paguma, paradoxure
relative genet(te)
CIVIC lay, metropolitan, municipal, public, secular, suave, urban
CIVIL affable, amiable, bland, complacent, courtly, decent, fair, gallant, gracious, hend(e), humane, kind, obliging, orderly, polished, polite, politic(al), refined, respectful, secular, sober, suave, urbane, wellbred
disobedience noncooperation, passive resistance
engineer bridgebuilder
rights workers freedom riders
wrong tort
CIVILIAN cit, citizen, civie, civvy, gownsman, lay, nonmilitary, pekin, private citizen, subject, teacher
dress civvies, mufti
CIVILITY amenity, attention, bonte, ceremony, comity, courtesy, gentility, good nature, goodness, kindliness, manners, notice, urbanity
CIVILIZATION breeding, cultivation, culture, kultur, refinement, urbanization
CIVILIZE domesticate, educate, elevate, enlighten, humanize, polish, refine, tame, teach, train, urbanize
CIVIL WAR *adventurer* carpetbagger
battle antietam, bull run, chancellorsville, chattanooga, chickamauga, cold harbor, fredericksburg, gettysburg, kennesaw mountain, murfreesboro, nashville, rapidan, shiloh, spotsylvania, vicksburg, winchester
bullet minie
coin copperhead
confederate admiral semmes
confederate commander beauregard, bragg, breckinridge, buckner, early, ewell, hampton, hill, hood, jackson, lee, mosby, pickett, smith, stuart, toombs
confederate guerrilla bushwhacker

confederate guerrilla leader quantrill

confederate note bluejack

confederate prison andersonville

confederate soldier butternut, grayback, (johnny) reb

confederate statesman benjamin

flag-waver barbara fri(e)tchie

fort moultrie, pickens, pulaski

guerrilla redleg

guerrilla leader quantrill

gun rodman

heroine barbara fri(e)tchie

historian catton

money greenback

northern volunteer zouave

photographer brady

postwar period reconstruction

prison andersonville

profiteer carpetbagger

ship merrimac, monitor

siege, vicksburg

soldier, plundering bummer

southern sympathizer copperhead

spy belle boyd, elizabeth van lew, pauline cushman, pinkerton, rose greenhow

surrender site appomattox

treasury note seven-thirty

union admiral dupont

union commander banks, buell, burnside, butler, custer, foote, grant, halleck, hancock, hooker, logan, maury, mcclellan, mcdowell, meade, pope, porter, sheridan, sherman

CLABBER clauber, clot, congeal, curdle, lop, lopper, mire, mud

CLACK babble, cackle, chatter, gossip, nonsense, ratthe, talk, tongue

CLACKDISH clicket

CLAD adorned, arrayed, attired, beseen, cledde, clothed, coated, covered, decked, dight, dressed, drest, has on, plated, robed, sheathed

in purple porporate

in white candidate

scantily singly

CLADOPHORA alga, blanketmoss, blanketweed, scum

CLADOSE branched, ramose

CLAIM adduce, allege, arrogate, ask, assert, assume,
assumption, aver, avow, call, case, challenge, collect, declaration, declare, demand, derecho, desire, dibs, document, draft, draught, droit, due, elicit, equity, exact, extort(ion), hak(h), homestead, intend, interest, justify, license, lien, maintain, mine, name, need, patent, plea, plead, pretence, pretend, pretension, pretext, privilege, proclaim, profess, reckon, reclaim, require, right, shout, solicit, title, usurp

false jactation

formal condictio

-jump appropriate

just right

-man adjuster

to land amparo

CLAIMANT pretender, usurper

CLAIRVOYANCE divination, insight, lucidity, penetration, sagacity, telopsis

CLAIRVOYANT clearsighted, fey, medium, omener, prophet, psychic(al), sagacious, seer (ess)

CLAM adhere, adhesive, band, base, bivalve, clamp, clangor, clog, clutch, crash, daub, dummy, glam, grasp, grope, hush, mean, mollusk, shell, silence, smear, solen, sphynx, spout, sticky, sulk(er)

freshwater three-ridge, washboard

giant chama, tridacna

-killing snail winkle

kind bear's-paw, blunt, bullnose, calico, carpet shell, chama, cherrystone, coquina, gaper, geoduck, gweduc, littleneck, macrocalista, mega, mya, nanninose, pahua, quahaug, quahog, razor, round, shipworm, solen, steamer, tapes, venerida

long mya, razor

razor solen

round quahog

shell bucket, grab, grapple, shuck

shell opening gape

up hush

CLAMBAKE clamaroo, festival, gathering, jam session, picnic, rally, squantum

CLAMBER ascend, claver, climb, rammack, scale, scrabble, scramble, scrauchle, scrawm, sprauchle, sprawl, struggle

CLAMCRACKER stingray

CLAMJAMFRY crowd, rabble, rubbish

CLAMMY damp, dank, moist, sammy, soft, squidgy, sticky, viscous, wack, waughy, wet

cuphea waxweed

sage clary

CLAMOR babel, ballyhoo, bawl, bellow, bere, blare, bluster, boast, bowwow, braggadocio, brawl, broil, brouhaha, bruit, bunk, chide, chirm, complain, confusion, cry, din, exclaim, gaff, hubbub, hue, hullabaloo, noise, noration, outas, outcry, philliloo, protest, pullalue, quethe, racket, rane, rerd(e), roar, roup, rout, rumor, shout, snarl, stashie, tumult, turmoil, uproar, utas, wail, yatter

against decry

for appeal, demand, desire, need

CLAMOROUS ambitious, blatant, boisterous, bold, brassy, brawling, brawly, brazen, clamant, decrying, demanding, dictatorial, dinsome, imperious, importunant, impudent, loud, noisy, obstreperous, strident, turbulent, urgent, vocal, vociferous, voluble, yelling

CLAMP agraf(f)e, bail, bend, block, bolt, brage, bury, clam, clasp, clinch, clothespin, clump, clutch, cramp, dog, fasten(ing), glam, gland, glaum, grab, grave, grip, heap, hog, holdfast, jack, lug, mollusk, mute, nail, nip(per), pile, pin, pinchcock, spur, stack, stirrup, tie, tramp, vice, vise, yoke

CLAN abusua, aimak, ayllu, calpulli, caste, class, clique, collection, coterie, cult, division, family, fraternity, gen(s), genos, genus, group, han, hapu, horde, kin, name, obe, party, phratry, phyle, race, sat-

suma, sect, sept, set, sib, siol, society, stock, tribe, unit, zadruga
division obe
emblem tartan, totem, xat
head alder, chief, elder, tanist, thane, toisech
member calebite
pert. septal, tribal
CLANDESTINE backalley, backdoor, backstairs, bootleg, bye, clancular, concealed, covert, foxy, furtive, hedge, hidden, hidlings, illicit, privy, quiet, secret, sly, sneak, stealthy, surreptitious, underhand(ed)
CLANG clank, clash, dang, din(g), jangle, noise, peal, resound, ring, shrill, stroke, timbre, tonk
CLANGOR clam, din, hubbub, jangle, noise, roar, uproar
CLANGOROUS brazen, blangent, ringing
CLANGULA duck, glaucionetta, harelda, squaw
CLANK clatter, rackle, ring
CLANNISH cliquish, close, exclusive, inbred, indirected, introvert(ive), restricting, restrictive, secret, select, tribal, united
CLAP acclaim, applaud, applause, bang, cast, chatter, cheer, chuck, clapper, clink, close, crack, crash, dint, explosion, flap, flatten, fling, hurl, noise, pat, peal, plank, plaudit, plop, plump, plunk, poster, pounce, slap, smite, spat, strike, stroke, tack, throw, thrust, thunder, tongue, toss
eyes on see
hands acclaim, applaud, rejoice
CLAPBOARD framing, knapple, lathing, sheathing, siding
CLAPNET daynet
CLAPPER backer, bell, cheerer, clack, end, jinglet, knacker, knocker, patron, rattle, stick, supporter, tongue
support baldric(k)
CLAPPER *claw* abuse, revile, scold, scorn
CLAPTRAP blague, bunco, buncombe, bunkum, cheap, eyewash, fustian, humbug(gery), insincerity, non-

sense, paltry, pretentious, showy, trash, trickery, trivia
CLAQUE crush hat, group, opera hat, patrons, praisers, rooters, sycophants
CLARE *county seat* ennis
CLARE, ST *symbol* palm branch
CLARENCE carriage, growler, william iv
cousin landau
daughter margaret plantagenet
CLARET blood, bordeaux, cabernet(sauvignon), grignolino, lafite, milk of the aged, red, wine, zinfandel
with soda badminton
CLARIFY clean, cleanse, clear, depurate, despume, distill, eliquate, elucidate, explain, fine, free, get across, glorify, illuminate, purge, purify, put(across)(over), rarefy, refine, render, resolve, settle, snuff, solve, transfigure, untangle
CLARIN acocotl, trumpet
CLARINET aulos, been, ben, bon, bone, clareone, pungi, reed
low register chalumeau
mouthpiece birn, reed
snake charmer's been
socket birn
CLARION blare, clarino, clary, clear, loud, proclaim, shout, sufflue, trumpet
CLARITY clearness, elegance, intelligibility, limpidity, lucency, lucidity, pellucidity, precision, simplicity, splendor, strength, trenchancy
CLART daub, mud, sloven, trash
CLARTY bedaubed, dirty, foul, muddy, sticky
CLARY clarion, clarre(e), herb, salvia
CLASH affray, argument, bang, battle, bolt, brawl, brunt, bump, check, collide, collision, combat, conflict, contend, contest, counteract, crash, cut, dash, differ, disagree(ment), discord(ance), encounter, fight, fray, frush, gossip, grate, hostility, hurtle, impact, jangle, jar, jolt, jostle, knock, mass, misunderstanding, noise, prate,

quantity, rift, rupture, scandal, shock, slam, sound, strife, strike, swear at, tattler, telltale, thrust, thwart
of arms contest
with differ
CLASHING antagonistic, collision, conflict, discord(ant), friction, harsh, hostility, inharmonious, jarring, off-color, opposition
rocks planctae
CLASHY chainman, miry, muddy, noisy, sailor, servant, showery, talkative, wet
CLASP accole, adhere, agraffe, amplex, barrette, belt, brace, broach, buckle, catch, cinch, clench, cling, clip, clutch, dalk, embrace, enfold, fasten, fermail, fibula, fold, gimmer, glue, grab, grasp, grip, hasp, hold, holding, hook, hoop, hug, infold, jimmer, keep, morse, mousing, ouch, pin, preen, seize, snatch, spang, stay, stick, surround, tach(e), tendril
CLASPING amplectant, perfoliate
CLASS (See also CLASSIFICATION.) assort, bracket, brand, breed, caste, catalog(ue), categorize, category, chop, circle, clan, congregation, course, describe, description, division, echelon, estado, estate, estimate, excellence, faction, family, form, gen, gender, genera, genre, genus, geomoroi, grade, group, heimin, ilk, kidney, kind, league, lecture, mister, mold, nation, order, phylon, phylum, quality, race, range, rank, rate, rating, reckon, remove, school, sect, seminar(y), sort, species, sphere, state, station, strain, stratum, stripe, style, subject, suit, tribe, type, variety, varna, year
animal genera, genus
biological genera, genus
choicest robur
consciousness discrimination
hereditary caste
laboring paraiyan, toil
learned clerisy, intelligentsia, meritocracy, vates

lower gente
lower middle petite bourgeoisie
lowest canaglia, canaille, rabble, scum
member coed, freshman, junior, senior, sophomore
member, comb. ander
middle bourgeois(ie)
name, comb. aet(o), ales, ander, ane
peasant jacquerie
pert. generic
social shizoku
CLASSIC ancient, book, chaste, masterly, masterpiece, model, standard, venerable, vintage
CLASSICAL academic, aesthetic, ancient, archaic, attic, augustan, chaste, elegant, esthetic, greek, hellenic, latin, liberal, literary, masterly, pure, roman, scholastic, simple
revival renaissance
CLASSICS belles-lettres, humanities, letters, literature
commentator scholiast
edition bipont(ine)
CLASSIFICATION (See also CLASS.) analysis, arrangement, attribution, biotaxy, bracket, branch, breakdown, caste, cataloguing, categorization, category, codification, denomination, department, distribution, division, echelon, estate, family, file, genre, genus, grade, grading, group(ing), kingdom, nomenclature, order, organization, phylum, pigeonholing, placement, rank(ing), rate, rating, section, sept, series, sort(ing), species, state, status, system(atics), taxis, taxonomy, variety
CLASSIFIED assorted, confidential, restricted, secret, sorted
CLASSIFY account, alphabetize, arrange, assort, bracket, break down, catalog(ue), categorize, code, codify, digest, dispose, distribute, divide, draft, draught, file, grade, group, label, list, marshal, pigeonhole, order, range, rank, rate, register, size, sort, suit, ticket, tribe, type
together slump

CLASSY admirable, elegant, excellent, ostentatious, posh, stylish, superior
CLATTER babble, ballyhoo, blatter, brattle, chatter, clack, clangor, crash, din, gabble, gossip, jar, noise, pandemonium, prate, prattle, racket, rackle, rattle, reeshle, roar, rumor, shatter, slambang, tattle
CLATTERTRAPS knickknacks
CLAUDIA *husband* pilate
CLAUDIO *beloved* juliet
sister isabella
CLAUDIUS *adopted son* nero
chamberlain polonius
courtier cornelius, guildenstern, osric, rosencrantz, voltimand
enemy cicero
nephew hamlet
poisoner locusta
wife gertrude, messalina
CLAUSE article, close, commata, conclusion, condition, item, part, passage, petition, phrase, plank, provision, proviso, rider, sentence, sleeper, stipulation, tenendas, tenendum, trope
conditional protasis
consequential apodosis
in will devise
CLAUSTRAL cloistered, conventical, conventual, monachal, monasterial, monastic
CLAUSULA cadence, conclusion
CLAVATE clubshaped
CLAVER chatter, clabber, claiver, clamber, GOSSIP, prate
CLAVICHORD clarichord, clarigold, clavier, manicord, monochord, unichord
effect bebung
CLAVICLE collarbone, fircule
comb. cleid(o)
CLAVUS band, bunion, callus, corn, ergot, heloma, stripe
CLAW chela, clee, cloof, clufe, clutch, court, crab, cratch, crubeen, dig, falcula, fang, fawn, fingernail, flatter, grasp, griff, hand, hook, nail, nipper, ongle, peg, pincer, pull, scrabble, scrape, scratch, seize, talon,

tear, unce, uncus, ungual, ungues, unguis, ungula, wheedle
away revile, scold
-back sycophant
bar bull-foot
comb. chel(i), unci
crustacean chela
curved falcula
great megalonyx
having acronychous, ungual
-like hooked
off get rid of
pad pulvillus
sharp falcula
sickness footrot
CLAY adobe, argil, bass, bentonite, binder, blue mud, body, bole, bot(t), brick, camstone, cledge, cloam, clunch, cob, earth, enamel, ga(u)lt, gley, gumbotil, kaolin(e), laterite, leck, loam, loess, lute, malm, marl, mire, moulder, mud, ocher, ochre, palolo, papa, paste, pug, rabat, sagger, sinopite, slip, smit, stilt, tasco, till, wad, wax
absorbent fuller's earth
alluvial adobe
and magma buchite
and straw cob
articles ceramics
baked adobe, brick, tasco, tile
band cottle
bed ga(u)lt
block sillar
box sagger
-brained dull, stupid
building adobe, tapia
burned piece testa
-casting slip
-cold inanimate, lifeless
comb. argillaceo, argillo, pel
constituent alumina
covered with lutose
deposit loess, marl
drab brown
earthy ochre
fever scratches
fired tile
firing box sagger
fragment bat
hard bend
hardened metal
hard-fired stilt
house adobe
indurated bass, clunch
iron bull
layer flucan, gley, gouge, pinnel, selvage, sloam, sloom, varve

lump clam, clod
made of fictile
melting pot tasco
mineral attapulgite, nactire
mixture cob, slip
mold dod
molded brick, pug
molding plate dod
name ali
nodule bob
pack with tamp
paste barbotine
pert. argillaceous, argilliferous, bolar
piece brick, tile
pigeon cinch, dupe, easymark, target
pipe camstane, camstone
plastic pug
plug bott
polishing rabat
potter's argil, slip
pottery kaolin(e)
red laterite, sinopite
remove unlute
rich malm, marl
semivitrified porcelanite
slab bat, tile
sticky bumbotil
stiff till
stone argillite, leck
stratum pinnel
target skeet
tough leck
tropical laterita
ware glost
white kaolin

CLAYMORE broadsword, ferrara
CLAYWEED coltsfoot
CLEAM daub, plaster, stick, smear
CLEAN absterge, apinoid, bathe, bream, bright, brush, buff, censor, chamois, char, chaste, clarify, cleanse, clear, clear out, comb, correct, curry, decent, delouse, depurate, deterge, dirtless, dust(off), elutriate, empty, entire, entirely, expert, expurgate, fair, fay, feigh, fey, furbish, groom, immaculate, innocent, kosher, launder, lave, legible, lustrate, mop, neat, perfect, plain, police, pure, purge, purify, redd, renovate, rout out, sanitary, sanitize, scavenge, scour, scrub, shapely, smart, smug, snowy, spandy, spic-and-span, spotless, stainless, sterile, sterilize, swab, sweep, swingle, taintless,

terse, thorough, tidy, toshy, total, trim, undefiled, unsoiled, unstained, wash, weedless, wipe
boat careen
cannon scale
-out clear, crisp, distinct, evident, exact, shapely, trim, well-defined
-fingered deft, honest, scrupulous
fur drum
gun worm
in acid blanch
-lined spruce, trim
out empty, exhaust
ritually kosher
ship's bottom bream, grave, hog
slate blank, innocence, nothing, tabula rasa, vacuum, void
up cash in, complete, dispatch, gain, get rich, killing, muck-up, police, profit, redd, tidy, wipe out

CLEANER borax, cleanser, flueman, janitor, purer, ramrod, scaler, soap, spotter, sweeper, washer
CLEANING *agent* See CLEANSER.
device besom, broom, brush, carpet sweeper, comb, dish (cloth), dishmop, dishwasher, doormat, dustcloth, duster, dustpan, feather duster, hackle, hose, mop, napkin, rake, ramrod, scraper, scrubber, serviette, sponge, sudarium, swab, sweeper, swob, toothbrush, toothpick, towel, vacuum cleaner, washboard, washcloth, washer, washing machine, whisk(broom)
woman biddy, char, daily
CLEANSE absterge, baptize, bathe, bless, bran, card, careen, catharize, clarify, clean, clear, comb, debride, depurate, deterge, dight, disinfect, expiate, fay, feigh, heal, launder, mundify, pick, purge, purify, refine, renovate, rinse, soap, sponge, wash
CLEANSER (See also CLEANING *device.*) ammonia, art gum, benzene, benzine, benzol(in), bluing, borax, carbon tet, detergent, detersive, lye, sal soda, scouring powder,

soap, soda, sodium (bi)carbonate, washing powder
CLEANSING abluent, ablution, abstergent, abstersive, acquittal, bath, clysmic, detergent, flush, lavation, purification, purifying, soap(ing), wash(ing), washup
ceremonial lavabo, purgalion
CLEAR 3 fay, net, rid, top, way 4 cast, easy, fair, fine, free, gain, grub, jump, keen, loud, neat, okay, open, over, pass, pure, pute, quit, redd, rife, shut, void 5 acute, atrip, brant, breme, brent, broad, chuck, clean, crisp, drive, empty, fresh, light, lucid, naked, plain, prune, scour, sharp, sheer, smolt, sunny, sutel, untie, vivid 6 acquit, assart, assoil, aweigh, bright, cancel, candid, excuse, exempt, lauter, let off, limpid, lucent, patent, profit, purify, refine, serene, settle, shet of, shrill, simple, spared, unstop 7 absolve, acclaim, approve, audible, certain, clarify, clarion, crystal, defined, deliver, evident, excused, explain, express, graphic, lighten, obvious, paid off, precise, release, reshape, visible 8 accredit, apparent, brighten, bulldoze, canorous, clean-cut, definite, distinct, explicit, liberate, licensed, luminous, manifest, pellucid, relevant, tangible, thorough, univocal 9 cloudless, eliminate, establish, exonerate, extricate, unsullied, vindicate 10 articulate, disphonous, hotglaring, privileged 11 crystalline, disentangle, perceptible, perspicuous, translucent, transparent, unambiguous, unequivocal, unqualified, well-defined 12 disembarrass, intelligible, recognizable, transpicuous, unmistakable 14 understandable 15 distinguishable
as crystal, glass
as crystal evident, manifest
away banish, clean, dispel, eliminate, evacuate, fay, feigh, fey, remove, vanish, wash out
coast clean slate, facility
-cut apparent, chisel(l)ed,

concise, decided, definite, direct, distinct, evident, exact, incisive, lucid, manifest, nice, open, precise, sharp, trenchant, unconfused, well-defined

decks prepare, set up, tidy

-eye clary, herb

-eyed bright, penetrating, sagacious

for action prepare

from aloof

hurdle break through, go ahead, manage

-obscure chiaroscure

off distant, evacuate, flee, fly, leave, quit, remove, rid, scram, withdraw

of mud slutch

of scum skim

of trees delignate

of water bail

out begone, blow, clean(up), discharge, eliminate, empty, escape, evacuate, flee, hightail, leave, skiddoo, throughout, utterly

path bushwhack, fray, hack

-sighted discerning, perspicacious

skirts See ACQUIT.

stage opportunity

the way advance, facilitate, prepare

throat hawk, hoick, hough

up assoil, clarify, dissolve, explain, make clear, police, resolve, settle, solve, unshadow, tidy(up)

CLEARANCE allowance, backlash, clearing, margin, permit, profit, room, runby, sale, tolerance, windage

CLEARING assart, field, frith, milpa, pruning

in woods glade, ridding, riding, slashing, tract

of land (as)sart

pan clarifier

stone knife sharpener

CLEARLY cleanly, decidedly, definitely, distinctly, evidently, frankly, plainly, redly, witterly

CLEARNESS clarity, finesse, lucidity, precision, simplicity

CLEARSKINS cattle

CLEARSTORY See CLERESTORY.

CLEARWAY apron, runway

CLEARWEED richweed

CLEARWING aegerid, moth, sesiid

CLEAT angle iron, batten, belay, bitt, block, bollard, butterbur, chock, coltsfoot, coxcomb, grouser, heel plate, joint, kevel, ledge, piton, riffle, sirmark, spike, strip, stud, support, surmark, wedge

angle bracket

CLEAVAGE cleft, division, fission, fissure, fragment, mitosis, parting, partition, rift, scission, separation, split(ting), wedging

CLEAVE adhere, atomize, basket, bisect, break, carve, chine, chop, clave, cleft, cliff, cling, cohere, crack, cut, dispart, divide, divorce, fasten, fix, furrow, halve, hew, join, link, open, part, penetrate, pierce, plow, rely, rend, rift, rip, rive, separate, sever, shale, shear, sleave, slice, slit, slive, split, stab, stick, sunder, tear, thrust, unite

CLEAVER axe, barong, billhook, burdock, cite, clive, froe, frow, frower, parangi, tool

CLEAVERS birdlime, burhead, clithe, clote, clots, galium, goosebill, gravelgrass, grip, hairif, hairup, loveman, pigtail, thorn

CLEAVERWORT bedstraw, CLEAVERS, galium

CLECK hatch

CLEDGY clayey, sticky, stiff, tenacious

CLEE claw, hoof, redshank

CLEEK club, clutch, crook, firehook, fishhook, hook, iron, link, pluck, pothook, seize, shadow, snatch

CLEF character, chiavetta, key

base eff

treble gee

CLEFT abysm, abyss, aperture, blasted, breach, break, chap(py), chasm, chawm, chink(y), chop, cleave, clough, cloven, crack(ed), cranny, crease, creek, crena, crenelated, crevice, crotch, cut, dehiscent, divide(d), fault, fent, fissure(d), fissury, flaw, forked, fracture, gap(e), gap(ing), gash, gulch, gulf, hole, incision, leak, lissom, nock, notch, opening, parted, per-

forate, reft, rent, rictus, rift, rill(e), rima, rime, rimulose, riva, rive(n), rupture, scissure, sinus, slit, split, sulcate, yawn

-beaked fissirostral

branchial gill slit

comb. fissi, schist(o)

-lip harelip

CLEITUS *consort* eos

CLEMATIS bagflower, bindwith, birthwort, crowfoot, curlyhead, jasmine, jessamine, pipestem, plant, traveler's-joy, viorna, virgin's-bower

CLEMENCEAU *nickname* tigre de france

CLEMENCY charity, compassion, fairness, forgiveness, grace, indulgence, kindness, leniency, lenity, love, mercy, mildness, ore, pity, quarter, ruth, sympathy

CLEMENS, SAMUEL *home* hannibal

newspaper territorial enterprise

pseud. mark twain

river boat creole belle, delta queen

work connecticut yankee, huckleberry finn, innocents abroad, mysterious stranger, pudd'n-head wilson, tom sawyer

CLEMENT balmy, benevolent, benign, compassionate, forebearing, gentle, humane, indulgent, kind, lenient, merciful, mild, soft, sympathetic, tender, tolerant, warm

saint, symbol anchor, papal crown

CLENCH clasp, clenk, clinch, clint, clutch, contract, constrict, constringe, fist, grasp, grip, grit, nail, seize

CLEOBIS *brother* biton

mother cydippe

CLEODAEUS *grandfather* hercules

CLEOLA *husband* atreus

son plisthenes

CLEOME beeplant, figwort, plant

CLEOMENES *brother* euclidas

colleague demaratus

enemy clisthenes, nicagoras

father-in-law gylippus

friend fanteus, hippitas, therycion, xenares
general damoteles, panteus
kingdom sparta
parent ageipolis, anaxandrides, cleombrotus, cratesiclea, leonidas
rival antigonus, aratus
son acrotaxus, cleonymus
stepfather megistonus
teacher sphaerus
victim megalopolis
wife agiatis
CLEOMESTRA *husband* aesyetes
son antenor
CLEON *enemy* brasidas, spartans
father asopus
governor of tarsus
opponent pericles
successor clinias, timoclides
wife dionyza
CLEONYMUS *father* cleomenes
son leonidas
CLEOPATRA *attendant* alexas, charmian, diomedes, iras, mardian, seleucus
brother alexander, ptolemy
consort caenus, caesar, mark antony, meleager, philip
cosmetic kohl
downfall asp
father ptolemy
friend archibius
kingdom egypt
lieutenant achillas, apollodorus, pothinus
maid charmion, iras
needle obelisk
physician olympus
river nile
secretary diomede
sister arsinoe, berenice
son caesarion
steward seleucus
CLEOPHAS *wife* mary
CLEOTHERA *father* pandareus
CLEPE bid, call, christen, clupien, cry, name, shout
CLEPSYDRA clock, dial, ghurry, gurry, horologe, water clock
CLERGY apostleship, church, clericals, clerisy, cloth, crape, desk, fingerpost, ministry, prelacy, presbytery, priest(hood), pulpit, spirituality
body of college, pulpit
office canonry, curacy, cure,

ministry, pastorate, priorship, rectorate
vestment See VESTMENT ecclesiastic.
CLERGYMAN See CHURCHMAN.
CLERIC See CHURCHMAN.
non laic
pert. diaconal, ministerial, secretarial
office See CLERGY *office.*
CLERICAL clerkish, parsonic, parsonly, secretarial
CLERK accountant, acolyte, actuary, agent, amanuensis, assistant, attendant, baboo, babu, biller, bookkeeper, carcoon, clergion, clergyman, cleric, commis, dopster, ecclesiastic, filer, gomasta, greffier, hermit, kitman, layman, mapper, mediocrity, monitor, monk, munshi, notary(public), nun, pandit, penman, piarist, priest, pundit, recorder, registrar, salesman, saleswoman, scholar, scorekeeper, scribe, scrivener, secretary, shipper, shopman, stenographer, teller, timekeeper, write(r), yeoman
-ale feast
pert. scribal
CLERKLESS unlearned
CLERKLY clergial, clerical, learned, scholarly, scribal
CLETCH brood, clique, clutch, family, hatching, nest, young
CLEUGH clough, descent, ravine
CLEVE brae, cliff, hillside, slope
CLEVELAND, GROVER
burial site princeton
party democratic
profession lawyer
vice president hendricks, stevenson
CLEVER able, adroit, affable, agile, alert, apt, artful, astute, brainy, bright, canny, clean, clear, crafty, cunning, cunny, cute, deft, dext(e)rous, expert, featy, fell, fendy, fine, foxy, funny, good, habile, handsome, handy, heady, hend(e), hep(pen), intellectual, intelligent, keen, kittle, lithe, neat, nimble, oily, parlish, parlous, quick,

resourceful, sharp, shrewd, skillful, slick, slim, sly, smart, snack, spry, stalky, subtile, talented, welldevised, with it, witty
dangerously parlous
CLEVERNESS address, brilliance, calculation, can, chic, craft, cunning, dexterity, industry, ingenuity, nous, sagacity, shrewdness, skill, wisdom
CLEVIS bridge, bridle, catch, dee, hake, hook, muzzle, plowhead, shackle
CLEW See CLUE.
CLICHE banal(ity), bromide, commonplace, hackneyed, platitude, stereotype, trite, truism
CLICK agree, blow, catch, chatter, dash, detent, dot, fit, forge, forging, function, pallet, paul, pawl, purr, rap, ratchet, snap, snick, sound, succeed, suit, take, work
beetle doar, dor(r), elater, elator, tora
catch pawl
CLIENT account, brief, buyer, ceile, charge, customer, henchman, jajman, patient, patron, protege, responsibility, retainer, ward
CLIENTELE audience, following, patrons, public
CLIFF arete, bluff, cle(e)ve, clogwyn, col, crag, height, heuch, heugh, hill, hoe, klip, krans, krantz, nip, pali, palisade, piskun, precipice, rock, scarp, shore, slope, steep, traverse
brake fern, pellaea
broken crag
-hanger melodrama
ice iceblink
line of scarp
rose statice, thrift
tombs site beni-hasan
CLIMATE atmosphere, attitude, clime, condition, environment, heaven, latitude, mood, public opinion, realm, region, sky, status, temper, weather, zone
study climatology, phenology
CLIMAX acme, apex, apogee, ascend, blow off, cap(sheaf), capstone, catastasis, conclusion, crest, crown, end, epiploce, epitasis, everest, finish, grada-

tion, head, height, high point, meridian, mount, peak, pinnacle, scale, shinny, shut, summit, top, zenith
rhetorical epiploce
CLIMB acclivity, arise, ascend, ascent, breast, clamber, coon, creep, escalade, gad, grade, grimp, incline, mount, ramp, rise, scale, sclimb, scrabble, scramble, scrawm, shin(ny), skin, sklim, soar, speed, speel, spele, sty(e), surmount, swarm, swarve, swerve, traverse, twine
aboard hop
down condescend, dismount, fall, light, retreat, unscale, withdraw
on board, mount, scale
on bandwagon accept, follow
one's frame punish, rebuke
over scramble, surmount
CLIMBER akala, akela, alpinist, crampon, creeper, rigger, scaler, steeplejack
CLIMBING *adapted for* scansorial
fern agsam, nito
fumitory cypress vine
iron crampbit, crampet, crampit, crampon, creeper, prick(er), spur
palm rattan
pepper betel
CLINCH assure, bind, clamp, cling, clink, clutch, complete, conclude, confirm, embrace, establish, fasten, fix, grapple, grasp, grip, hold(fast), hug, lock, nail, pun, rest, rivet, scuffle, seal, secure, seize, settle, snatch, take, toe
CLING adhere, bank, cherish, clasp, cleave, clinch, cohere, continue, contract, dangle, depend, embrace, endure, fasten, grasp, hand, hitch, hold, hug, last, nourish, rely on, shrink, shrivel, stick, trust, wither
CLINGFISH remora, sucker, suckfish, testar, tetard
CLINGING adamant, adherent, amplectant, coherence, hugging, osculant, retentive, tenent
name meaning ivie, ivy
CLINGSTONE amygdalis, peach

CLINIS *lover* apollo, artemis
CLINK ale, beat, blow, brig, cash, clap, clinch, coin, instant, JAIL, jingle, jinglin, jug, klink, latch, lockup, money, move, prison, rap, rhyme, ring, seize, slap, strike, time, ting, tinkle
-down sit
CLINKER blow, brick, buhr, bur, bust, error, failure, flop, mistake, rouge, scar, slag, specie, waste
-built lapstrake, shingled
CLINKERS ashes, cinders, embers, money
CLINKSTONE phonolite
CLINTONIA bearberry, beartongue, bluehead, calfcorn, cowtongue, dogberry, hounds-tongue, lily-of-the-valley
CLIO addison
consort pierus
CLIP abbreviate, barb, barrette, bat, beak, binder, blow, bob, brush, caliper, chip, clasp, cluppe, clutch, crop, crutch, curtail, cut, deduct, diminish, dock, dod(d), dress, embrace, encircle, encompass, fasten(er), force, gaff, hit, hodd(er), hook, hug, lop, lunet, mow, nig, nip, pare, part, poll, prune, punch, rate, scissor, shave, shear, shorten, shrip, snip, sock, speed, steek, strike, trim, whack
at a swiftly
coin shorten
spring jack
wings disable, slow, stymie, thwart
wool crutch
CLIPPER boat, clammer, docker, grabman, gripper, shearer, ship, slicer, snapper, speeder, vessel, workman
feature sail
CLIPPERMAN shinglemaker
CLIPPING abbreviation, clasping, excellent, firstrate, scrow, shortening, snipping, trimming
CLIQUE bloc, cabal, camarilla, circle, clan, cletch, club, combination, combine, conclave, coterie, crowd, faction, gang, GROUP, junto, know, mob,

party, plot, ring, schism, set, society, sodality
CLIT close, heavy, sticky
CLITE burdock, cleaver
CLITELLUM cingulum, girdle, saddle
CLITUS *abductor* eos
beloved eos
father mantius
friend and slayer alexander
CLOAK 3 aba, hap 4 brat, capa, cape, cope, haik, hide, hood, huke, izar, jupe, mask, pall, robe, slop, veil, wrap 5 bauta, blind, burka, capot, choga, cover, frock, grego, guise, jelab, manta, manto, plaid, sagum, shawl, shuba, tilma 6 abolla, ahuula, assume, bautta, bavary, birrus, byrrus, caftan, camail, capote, caster, chamma, chimer, dolman, joseph, jubbah, kimono, kirtle, mantle, mantua, masque, pharos, poncho, rhason, screen, serape, shield, shroud, tabard, visite 7 alicula, bavaroy, burnous, cassock, chlamys, chuddar, conceal, courtby, garment, kaitaka, manteau, manteel, paenula, pelisse, pellard, pretext, protect, shelter, surcoat, wrapper, zimarra 8 albornoz, analabos, burnoose, capuchin, caputium, cardinal, courtepy, disguise, intrigue, mantelet, mantilla, mozzetta, palliate, pelerine, pretense 9 bursattee, dissemble 10 balandrana, mantellone, roquelaure 11 dissimulate, houppelande, overgarment
and dagger conspiratorial, intrigue, secret(ive), sensational
and dagger man spy
armor-covering tabard
baptismal chrisom
bishop's mantelletta
clerical analabos, cappa magna, cope, habit
coarse brat
18th century rokelay, roquelaure
feather ahuula, mamo
fur pelisse
hooded almuce, anabata, bautta, bavaroy, birrus, burnoose, byrrus, camail,

capot(e), capuche, capu-
chin, caputium, cardinal,
cowl, domino, huke, moz-
zetta, parka
large-sleeved witzchoura
long pelisse
loose See OVERCOAT.
man's rokelay, roquelaure
military paludament, sagum
monk's analabos
room vestiary
short mandillion, mantelet,
mantilla, talma
sleeveless dolman, paenula,
poncho, serape
soldier's sagum
traveler's balandrana
12th century balandrana
waterproof gossamer, loden
woman's dolman, manteau
CLOAM clomb, crockery,
daub, earthenware
CLOANTHUS *companion*
aeneas
CLOBBER apparel, beat,
clothing, cobble, devastate,
gear, lambaste, patch, rout,
strike
CLOCHARD hobo, tramp
CLOCHE bell, cover, hat,
jar
CLOCK alarm, beetle, bell,
bundy, call, chronometer,
cluck, crouch, dial, ghurry,
gong, gurry, hatch, horo-
loge, hurry, incubate,
knock, measure, meter, nef,
pendule, orlage, quirk,
skelper, solitaire, taximeter,
telltale, ticker, time, timepiece, timer, uhr, verge,
watch
arrangement cal(l)iper
astronomical sidereal
-case window lenticle
clapper striker
electromagnetic buhl, bulle
face table
kind balloon, banjo, bracket,
cuckoo, grandfather, man-
tel, riefler
maker horologer
part balance spring, balance
wheel, bundy, detent, dial,
escapement, face, foliot,
jewel, pendulum, recorder,
weight
self-winding atmos
ship-shaped nef
stocking gushet, gusset, quirk
striking repeater
tower horologium
watcher goldbrick, idler

water clepsydra, ghurry,
gurry, solarium
weight peise, poise
CLOCKBIRD jackass
CLOCKWISE deaseal, deasil,
dessil, positive, right,
round, sunwise
comb. dextro
CLOCKWORK automatic,
regular
CLOD bait, blockhead, bob,
boor, bread, clat, clatch,
clot, clout, clown,
clump, divot, dolt, dullard,
earth, fool, glebe, golem,
ground, imbecile, inept,
loam, lubber, lump, oaf,
peasant, piece, rustic, slob,
sod, soil, turf, yokel
CLODDISH boorish, gross,
stupid
CLODHOPPER blockhead,
boor, bumpkin, churl,
CLOD, clown, dolt, hob-
nail, infantry, lout, lump,
plowman, rube, rustic,
shoe, yokel
CLODIA lesbia
CLODIUS *enemy* caesar, cicero
sister olodia, quadrantia, tertia
slayer milo
CLODPATE blockhead,
CLOD, clodpoll, dolt, fool,
imbecile, ramhead
CLOELIA *captor* porsena
swam tiber
CLOG adhere, baffle, balk,
ball, bar, bedaggle, begum,
blind, block(ade), check,
choke, chopin(e), clag,
clam, cobcab, congest,
curb, daggle, dance, daub,
difficulty, drag, fetter,
freeze, fur, gum, hamper,
hinder, hobble, hog-tie, impede, impediment, jam,
lead, load, lumber, lump,
manacle, obstruct(ion),
overshoe, patine, patten,
remora, restrain, sabot, sandal, seeque, shoe, skid,
snaffle, snag, spancel,
spoke, stop, trammel, trash,
trigger, weight
almanac runic staff
dance black bottom
rim calker
up choke, congest, glut, stop,
stuff
with mud daggle, daub
wooden geta(s)
CLOGGED begummed, clot-

ted, foul, frozen, furry,
pinny, stuffed
CLOGGY dull, heavy,
lumpy, sticky
CLOGHAD belfry, tower
CLOISSONE inlay, shippo
CLOISTER abbey, aisle, ambulatory, arcade, cell, close,
confine, convent, corridor,
ermitage, friary, gallery,
hall(way), hermitage, im-
mure, monastery, nunnery,
passageway, priory, retreat,
seclude, stoa
and hearth author reade
courtyard garth
gallery ambulatory
pert. claustral, cloistral
walk al(l)ure
CLOISTERED claustral,
confined, enclosed, pro-
tected, recluse, sheltered
heart closed gentian
CLONE desma
CLOOF claw, hoof
CLOP clump, drub, hobble,
limp, pace, stamp, stomp,
thud
CLOPAS *wife* mary
CLOSE 3 air, ban, bar, cap,
dam, end, gum, hot, key 4
akin, area, bang, beat,
bung, calk, chop, clap, clit,
coda, daub, dear, fast, fill,
firm, fold, grip, hide, limp,
lock, louk, meet, near, nigh,
pent, plot, plug, quit, seal,
seam, seel, shut, slam, snap,
snug, stop, taut, tine, warm,
yard 5 anear, blank, block,
break, caulk, cease, cheap,
coapt, debar, dense, estop,
fence, final, finis, forby,
garth, heavy, latch, muggy,
plumb, put up, sneck, solid,
stale, steek, stivy, thick,
tight 6 at hand, batten,
buckle, button, chinse,
chummy, clench, fasten,
finale, finish, fold up, forbye, frugal, hard by, hobble, inward, narrow, near
by, retire, scarce, sealed, secret, secure, settle, shut up,
silent, stanch, stingy, stuffy,
sultry 7 adjourn, airless, arrange, compact, concise,
cramped, exclude, grapple,
literal, miserly, niggard, occlude, padlock, pockety,
puthery, shutter, similar,
stopper 8 accurate, adja-
cent, airtight, approach,
blockade, clausula, com-

plete, compress, conclude, confined, faithful, familiar, finalize, hairline, hermetic, imminent, intimate, obdurate, obstruct, preclude, reserved, reticent, surround, taciturn 9 barricade, niggardly, terminate 10 completion, contiguous, meticulous, oppressive, unfriendly, watertight 11 approximate, suffocating, tightfisted 12 cheeseparing

as possible chock

by around, beside, for(e)by, forthby, hereby, near, proximal, proximate

call narrow escape, shave

comb. crebri, sten(o)

down shut, terminate

eyes seel

firmly bar, batten, bolt, cement, lock, seal

-fitting hard, meet, narrow, snug, succinct, theat, theet, thight, tight

-hauled near the wind

hawk's eye seel

knit trussed

in on besiege, surround, take, trap

musical coda

off barricade, obstruct

out dispose of, sale, sell

over ceil

partially hood

ranks cooperate, prepare, serry, unite

shave narrow escape

stitch buttonhole, feston

to about, against, almost, anear, approximately, inbye, near(ly), nigh

up cork, dit(t), fill, fold, near, serry, shut, stop

with adhere, arrange, bind, collide, converge, encounter, engage, fight, seal, sign

CLOSED blank, blind(alley), blocked, caecal, covered, dark, dead(end), inaccessible, lucken, plie, shut, unopened, unvented

at one end blind

comb. cleisto

passage atresia

CLOSEFISTED handfast, mean, miserly, near, niggardly, penny-pinching, penurious, snippy, stingy, tenacious, tight

CLOSELY attentively, barely, compactly, economically, fast, hardly, junctly, just,

narrow(ly), near(ly), privately, secretly, strictly

CLOSEMOUTHED cautious, reserved, reticent, secret(ive), silent, taciturn, tight-lipped

person clam

CLOSENESS fidelity, intimacy, literalness, narrowness, nearness, parsimony, proximity, secrecy, stinginess, strictness, tightness

CLOSET amariolum, ambry, ambush, ark, armarium, armary, cabinet, conceal, conclave, confident, confine, cubby, cuddy, cupboard, den, ew(e)ry, gardevin, linen, locker, office, pantry, press, private, refuge, repository, room, safe, sanctum, secret(e), shut up, store (house), wardrobe

cynic recluse

CLOSING claudent, closure, cloture, coda, end, slam

device bolt, bung, button, cork, fly, hook, lace, latch, lid, lock, plug, snap, stopper, tampon, tap, zipper

CLOSURE atresia, bar, blockade, bolt, bound, clausure, cloture, conclusion, embolism, embolus, end, entrenchment, finale, finality, gag, limit, occlusion, seal, tension

comb. cl(e)sis

CLOT balter, bonnyclabber, cake, casein(ogen), clabber, clag, clart, clat, clodder, clodpate, coagulate, coagulum, concrete, congeal, cotter, crassamentum, cruor, curd, embolus, gel, gob, gout, grume, jell, lapper, lopper, lump, mass, mole, paracasein, solidify, stick, thicken

bur burdock

formation embolism, phlebitis, thrombosis

CLOTEN stepfather cymbeline

CLOTH (See also FABRIC.) bib, bolt, canvas, clergy, coat, ditto, drab, drap, dress, felt, garment, goods, handkerchief, livery, material, napkin, rag, raiment, sacking, seam, sheeting,

stuff, textile, towel, uniform, ware

altar bis(so), catasarka, pallium, pendle, towel, vesperal

ancient byssus

baptismal chrisom

bark tapa, tappa

black kiswa(h)

blemish amper, rip, snag, sully, tear, yaw

chalice burse

cheap mungo

checkered plaid, tartan

clerical oral

coarse See FABRIC *coarse.*

coat bath, bombazette, cheviot

communion corporal, fanon, sindon

consecrated antimension

cord insertion shirr(ing)

cotton See FABRIC *cotton.*

crimson cramasie, cramoisy

crinkled crepe, seersucker

dealer cogman, draper, mercer, ragman

decoration technique batik, plangi

design print

dressing stupe

dull stary

dye method batik, tie

finisher beetler

flawed brack, rase

flaxen See LINEN.

fold plait, pleat

glass doron

glazed chintz, tammy

goat wool sling

green kendal

gunny tat

hair aba, abba, cilice

hemp pinayusa

homespun kelt, khaddar, khadi, pattu, puttoo

hood bashlik, bashlyk

knot burl

lap gremial, napkin

layer ply

linen See FABRIC *linen.*

lining sarcenet, sarsenet, serge

made of clootie, clouty

measure ell, meter, nail, yard

measuring officer alnager

medieval ratteen

mourning crape, crepe

narrow braid, edging, ribbon, tape

old acca, cheyney, samite, tewke, tuke

organic wool(en)

ornamental dossal, dossel, gimp, lace, lampas, riband, tapestry
pack manta
packing soutage
piece apron, banner, capot, clout, godet, gore, langooty
printer candroy
puckered plisse
raised design brocade
remnant bolt end, fent
rich scarlet
roll bolt, carding, slub
rug mat, matting
saddle panel
selvage fag-end, listing, roon
sheets batting
shop mercery
sifting boultel
silk See FABRIC *silk.*
soaked buck
stage backdrop
starched guimpe
straining cheese, tamis, tammy
stretcher tenter
strong canvas, durance
synthetic See FABRIC *synthetic.*
tapered piece gore
toweling terry
triangular gore
twilled gambroon, jean
undyed hodden
unsold remnant
washing chamois, shammy
waste ganzie
wax mumjuma
winding ceres
wool See FABRIC *wool.*
worker fuller, stenterer
worn rag
worsted bombazet, rash, shag
wrapping burlap, tillot
wreath bourrelet
CLOTHE accouter, address, adorn, apparel, array, attire, bedizen, bewrap, clead, cleed, clover, dandify, deck, don, drape, dress, dub, endue, flesh, frock, garb, gird, gown, habilitate, habit, indue, invest, lap, outfit, primp, prink, provide, rig, robe, shride, shroud, spruce, swaddle, swathe, tog, vest(ure)
with power authorize, delegate
CLOTHED beclad, clad, dressed, habited
CLOTHES (See also CLOTHING.) apparel,

array, attire, baggage, bedizenment, bib and tucker, braws, burel, caparison, cleading, clobber, costume, drapery, dress, duds, fardel, fatigues, feathers, fig, finery, frippery, frock, garb, garments, gear, guise, habiliment, habit, impediment, indument, outfit, rags, raiment, regalia, rig, robes, shroud, suit, toggery, toilette, trim, trog(g)s, vestment, vesture, wardrobe, wear(ables)
business needle trade, shmata
cast-off duds, frippery, hand-me-downs
closet armoire, press, wardrobe
coarse burel
conservative grey flannel
dealer See CLOTHIER.
dressy go-to-meeting
dryer airer, tenter, tumbler
fine bravery, braws
informal bermuda shorts, blue jeans, denims, levis, shirtsleeves
label etiquet
maker See CLOTHIER.
moth larentiid, tinea, trichophaga
mourning dole
pert. vestiary, vestural
protective armor
rack armoire, valet
showy finery, lugs, sheen
spy keek
washed in lye buck
work fatigues
CLOTHESHORSE fashion-plate, frame, rack, trestle
CLOTHESPIN clamp, peg
CLOTHESPRESS armoire, chest, closet, kas, tallboy, wardrobe
CLOTHESPRESSER sadiron, valet
CLOTHIER cloak-and-suiter, costum(i)er, couturier, draper, dressmaker, fripper(er), furrier, glover, haberdasher, hosier, linen draper, mercer, outfitter, ragman, tailor
CLOTHING (See also CLOTHES.) brat, cleading, coat, covering, dress, garb, habit, knitwear, livery, ornament, outwall, robing, sails, stuff, vestiary, vestry, weedery

cheap slopwork
nautical clops
odd rig
sheer flimsies
women's frillies
CLOTHO See FATE.
CLOTTED caked, caky, caseous, clabbered, clouted, coagulated, congealed, curded, curdled, gargety, gelatinized, gory, grumous, incrassated, inspissated, jellied, knotted, livered, lumped, lumpish, lumpy, thickened
CLOTURE closure, gag
CLOUD adumbrate, arcus, bedim, befog, bemist, benight, bewilder, blacken, blemish, bloom, blur, cocktail, coma, conceal, confuse, crowd, damage, darken, defame, defect, dim, drift, drisk, dust, eclipse, enmist, envelope, film, fog, fool, gauze, gloom, haze, helm, hide, lot, messenger, mist, muddle, nebula, nightcap, nuage, nubecula, nubia, nubilate, obfuscate, obnubilate, obscure, odumbrate, overcast, overshadow, poother, pother, rack(s), reek, scarf, screen, scud, shade, shadow, smaze, smog, smoke, smother, smur(r), stain, stigma, sully, sunspot, swarm, taint, tarnish, vapor, veil
-born airy, chimerical, ethereal, gossamer, imaginary, unsubstantial
broken rack
-built airy, imaginary, unsubstantial
cap pileus
-capped high, lofty
cirriform capillatus
comb. cirro, nepho
comets coma
cumulus woolpack
dense arcus
dust smother, stew
filmy cirrus, nubia
funnel-shaped tuba
gaseous nebula
god, goddess See SKY *god, goddess.*
gray zinc
group gashes, rack, scud, soup
height-measurer ceilometer
horizontal stratus

kind altocumulus, alto-stratus, arcus, banner, calvus, capillatus, cat's-tail, cirro-cumulus, cirro-stratus, cirro-velum, cirrus, coal-sack, colt's-tail, cumulo-nimbus, cumulus, funnel, goat's-hair, granule, mack-erel, mare's-tail, nebula, nimbus, nubia, nue, oxeye, pileus, scud, strato-cirrus, strato-cumulus, stratus, thunderhead, tornado, wa-tercarrier, woolpack
land See UTOPIA.
-like nebular
-like mass nebula
luminous nebula, nimbus
masses cumuli, racks, strati
mist sop
morning velo
movement carry
nebulous coma
nine bliss, happiness, well-being
nuclear fireball, mushroom
over mountain helm
pert. nebular, nephological
photograph nephogram
plume-shaped banner
-producing nubiferous
rain cumulus, nimbus
roll-shaped arcus
stars nebula
stone meteorite
study meteorology, nephol-ogy
thunder cumulonimbus
under subnubilar, sub-nuvolar
vapory scud
white cirrus
wind-driven rack, scud
without azure, bright, clear, crystal, light

CLOUDBERRY akpek, averin, bake(d)apple, hjor-tron, molka, multe, noop, suomuurian

CLOUDBURST rainfall, shower, storm, torrent

CLOUDED dirty, dusty, filmy, gloomy, hazy, in-fumate, mottled, mucky, nebulous, shady, spotted, striped, veined

CLOUDY bleak, blear, con-fused, dark, dim, dismal, dull, filmy, foggy, gloomy, hazy, lackluster, lowery, misty, muddy, murky, neb-ular, obscure(d), opaque, overcast, roily, shady, smurry, sunless, turbid, un-

certain, vague, vaporous, veiled

CLOUGH cleft, cleuch, cleugh, cluf, gap, hill, ra-vine, valley

CLOUR batter, blow, bump, dint, thump

CLOUT bandage, bat, beat, blow, bosthoon, box, breechcloth, bump, clobber, cloth, clothes, club, cold, cuff, dab, force, fragment, hit, influence, klowet, mend, muscle, nail, patch, piece, power, pull, pummel, punch, rag, shred, slap, slug, smack, smite, strike, swat, target, thrash, wallop, washer
-shoe peasant, rube, rustic

CLOVE bulb, button, cleave, cleft, gap, ravine, weight
brown eagle
⅛th pound
pepper allspice
pink carnation, dianthus, gelofer, grenadin(e)
spikenard cinnamon root
treacle garlic

CLOVEN cleft, slit, split
-hoofed bisulcate, devilish, evil, fissiped, reprehensible, satanic, sinful, slit, wicked

CLOVER alfalfa, alsike, ber-seem, bersim, big ben, bur-net, carldoddy, claiver, comfort, comfrey, cow-grass, curldoddy, ease, hagi, harefoot, herb, hubam, la-dino, lotus, lucern(e), lux-ury, medic, melilot, napo-leon, nardoo, pussy(cat), red, shamrock, solitaire, suckling, trefoil, trifolium, trifoly, wealth, yellowtop
bur medicago
crimson napoleon
disease black patch, crown-wart
dodder ailweed, epithyme, hailweed, hairweed, hale-weed
leaf automobile, crossway, fan, freeway, good luck, intersection, la belle lucie, solitaire
prairie thimbleweed
rabbit-foot pussycat
sweet melilot

CLOVEROOT bennet

CLOVES *isle of* zanzibar

CLOWN, CLOWN'S 3 hob, oaf, sop, wag, wit 4 aper, bobo, boor, bozo, card,

fool, gaum, gawk, goff, joey, lout, mime, mome, naar, narr, rube, swad, zany 5 antic, beppo, buffo, churl, comic, cutup, droll, drone, feste, hodge, idiot, joker, mimer, patch, punch, wamba, yahoo, yokel 6 au-gust, bodach, footer, galoot, hobbil, jester, lubber, mummer, roarer, rustic, stocah, stooge, zannie 7 ac-robat, boddagh, bounder, buffoon, bumpkin, charley, costard, koshare, lavache, lobster, mudhead, pierrot, playboy, tomfool 8 come-dian, coviello, dotterel, gra-cioso, jokester, koyemshi, larrikin, merryman, quipster, 9 bergomask, blockhead, drawlatch, harlequin, pa-gliacci, pantaloon, simple-ton, whiteface 10 clodhop-per, mountebank, ragamuf-fin, scaramouch 11 merry-andrew, punchinello, wise-cracker 14 tatterdemalion

CLOWNHEAL hedge-nettle, stachys

CLOWNING shtik(eleh), shtickl(ech)

CLOWNISH awkward, bay-ardly, boorish, churlish, clumsy, coarse, gauche, gawky, green, hoblike, kern-ish, lobbish, loutish, raw, rough, rude, rustic, swad-dish, uncivil, ungainly, zan-nie, zany

CLOY burden, choke up, claw, clog, fill, glut, gorge, nail, pall, pierce, prick, sate, satiate, satisfy, satu-rate, surcharge, surfeit

CLOYER nauseant, overdose, sickener, snap, surfeiter, thief

CLOYING gooey, luscious, oversweet, rich, sweet, va-nilla

CLUB (See also *kind,* below.) alliance, arum, as-sociate, association, athe-neum, baffy, bandy, bat, baton, beat, billet, billy, blackjack, bludgeon, brith, bunch, cabaret, cafe, cam-buca, cane, clique, clout, coterie, council, cudgel, dog, eleven, fraternity, fus-tigate, group, hetaery, he-tairy, hit, join, kebbie, ma-caba, mace, mashy, mass,

maul, menage, mere, muckle, nine, nullah, set, social, society, sodality, sorority, sorosis, stick, strike, taiaha, tawkee, team, thump, towel, union, unite, verein, weapon, zonta
ace basta, basto, matador, oak, puppyfoot
baseball farm, nine, team
boys' hi-y, scouts
-carrier claviger
comb. cordyl(o), rhopal(o)
crooked cambuca
famous friars, garrick, lambs, white's
fungus sparasis
golden bog-torch
golf See GOLF *club.*
grass cattail, reed mace
kind alpeen, arum, bastinado, bat, billy, blackjack, bludgeon, boomerang, cambuca, cane, catstick, cudgel, espantoon, kiri, knobkerrie, libbet, macana, mace, maquahuitl, marree, mashie, mashy, mere, morgenstern, nullah(nullah), pantoon, patu, pogamoggan, polt, quarterstaff, shillala(h), shillela(g)h, spantoon, spar, spontoon, staff, stick, taiaha, tawkee, tawkin, tertulia, truncheon, waddy
law anarchy, despotism
literary atheneum
member eranist
moss buck-grass, buckhorn, crowfoot, fernwort, lycopod(ium), piligan, selaginella
police billy, pantoon, sap, spontoon, truncheon
political hetaery, hetairy, rota
rush cattail, deerhair, glumal, reed mace, sedge
service friars, junior league, kiwanis, lions, optimists, rotary, uso
-shaped clavate, claviform
social bridge, card, cercle, clique, fraternity, sodality, sorority
suit bastos, braun, eckern, eicheln, farmers, kreu(t)z, puppyfoot, trebolés, treff, trefle
suit, 4 devil's bedposts
suit, jack knave, knocher, mistigri, pam
suit, 9 comet

suit, queen spadilla
together associate, combine
war mace, waddy
woman's sorority, sorosis
CLUBFOOT bumblefoot, cyllosis, deformity, poltfoot, taliped, talipes, talus, varus
CLUBROOT ambury, hanbury
CLUBSTART stoat
CLUBWOOD casuarina, wamara
CLUCK call chicken, chuck, clack, clew, click, fuss, hen, thread
CLUCKER tsitser
CLUE, CLEW ball, catchword, cocoon, cue, evidence, glode, guide, hint, idea, indication, inkling, innuendo, intimation, key, lead, prompt, scent, sign, skein, solution, suggestion, tell tale, thread, tint, tip, token, twine
misleading red herring
CLUMP blow, bluff, bulge, bunch, bush, clot, clunch, cluster, dollop, drub, group, grove, heap, hit, hobble, knot, limp, lump(er), mass, moss, mott(e), patch, piece, plump, scuff, sole, sop, stomp, stump, tangle, thicket, thud, tod, tope, tread, tuft, turb, walk, wudge
CLUMSY ambilevous, ambisinister, artless, awkward, big, blunt, boorish, bulky, bunglesome, bungling, callow, chockle, clouterly, clownish, cumbersome, cumbrous, flob, footless, gauche, gaumy, gawky, graceless, great, green, handless, heavy(handed), hoggy, hulky, inapt, inept, jumbo, left-handed, lubber, lumberly, maladroit, massive, misshapen, noggen, oafish, ponderous, rigid, rude, rustic, scram, slipshod, splay, stiff, stogy, stupid, tactless, tense, thumby, ugly, uncouth, unfit, ungainly, unhandy, unready, unskilled, unwieldy, weedy, wooden
person booby, boor, clown, clunch, gawk, lout, lubber, oaf, s(c)hlemiel, shlemi(e)hl

CLUNCH boor, clump, hand, lout, lump(y), stiff
CLUNIAC benedictine
product guipure, lace
CLUNK lump, piece, thud
CLUPEID See FISH *clupeoid.*
CLUSTER aggregation, anadem, assemble, bob, boiling, bourock, bunch, bush, clot, cluther, collection, colony, cone, cyme, fascicle, foliage, gather, glomerule, group, hassock, hattock, knock, knot, lump, morula, nep, nucleate, pleiad, plump, raceme, sheaf, shock, sorus, sprig, stook, surround, troche, tuft, tussock, wisp
bean guar
compact fascicle
confused splatter
cup aecium, lichen
fern spore sorus
fibers nep
flower ament, anthemia, anthemy, corymb, cyme, glomerule, panicle, raceme, umbel
grape-like aciniform, acinous
growing in acervate, racemose
of bananas hand
pine bordeaux, pinaster
seven stars pleiad
small sprig
suspended swag
CLUSTERED acervate, aciniform, acinose, acinous, aggregate, agminate, cespitose, coacervate, glomerate, grumose, racemose, tufted
bluet buttonweed
grains grumose
CLUSTERFIST boor, miser
CLUTCH brood, capture, catch, clam, clasp, claut, claw, cleach, cleek, clem, clench, cletch, click, clinch, clip, clum, control, cop, coupling, crampen, crisis, emergency, fasten, fist, glam, glaum, grab, grasp, grip, grisp, group, hatch, have, hold, hug, lever, nab, nest, own, possess, power, retain, seize, set, snatch, take, talon, young
of eggs brood, laughter, lawter, laying set(ting), sitting
CLUTTER bustle, chaos, clatter, confusion, cumber,

disarray, disorder, jumble, litter, mess, muddle, pie, rattle, rubbish, snarl, stuff
CLY pocket, purse, seize, servant, steal
CLYDE *firth* bute
firth island ailsa craig, arran
CLYDESDALE dog, horse, stir, terrier
CLYMENE *abductor* paris
companion helen
consort helios, iapetus, nauplius, phylacus
daughter aetheria
parent catreus, minyas, oceanus, tethys
relative menelaus
son alcimede, atlas, helios, iphiclus, menoetius, oeax, phaethon, prometheus
CLYMENUS *daughter* harpalyce
CLYSTER injection, lavement
CLYTEMNESTRA *ancestor* lacedaemon
brother castor, dioscuri, pollux
husband agamemnon
lover aegisthus
offspring aletes, electra, iphigenia, orestes
parent leda, tyndareus
sister helen
slayer electra, orestes
victim agamemnon
CLYTIE *beloved* apollo
changed to heliotrope
father oceanus
CLYTIUS *brother* priam
companion jason
slayer hercules
CNIDIA aphrodite
CNUT canute
parent magnus
COACH advise(r), araba, baby buggy, brief, bus, cabin, car, CARRIAGE, carrier, chariot, counsel, diligence, direct, dormeuse, drag, fiacre, flier, fly(er), go-cart, gondola, guide, hack, help, jarvey, jitney, lead, perambulator, pilot, pram, prepare, prime, rattler, saloon, stage, tallyho, taxi, teach(er), train(er), tutor, vehicle, vetura
-and-four rig
dog dalmatian
driver's seat box
fast flier, flyer
hackney fiacre, jarvey
heavy drag

railway car, pullman, sleeper
17th century caroche
slow slowpoke
stop inn
3-wheeled tricycle
COACHMAN charioteer, coachee, coacher, coachy, driver, fly, fish, jehu, pilot, temschik, whip, yamshik, yemschik
assistant postillion
COACHWHIP bird, candlewood, flag, lash, snake
COADJUTOR adjutant, aide(-de-camp), assistant, associate, co-worker, ecclesiastic, helper, prior
COAGULANT binder, coagulum, curd, gelatine, rennet, styptic
COAGULATE cake, clod, clot, clotter, congeal, cotter, curd(le), gel, jel, lapper, lobber, lopper, pectize, posset, quail, set, solidify, thicken, yearn
COAGULATED crudy, curdy, livered, set, solidified, viscous
COAHUILTECAN *indian* comecrudo
COAK bushing, dowel, pin, tenon
COAL anthracite, bass, black diamond, brat, burn, carbon(ado), char(k), cinder, cob, coke, coom, culm, duff, ember, fuel, ghost, gleed, jet, landsale, lignite, smut, stoke, swad
agent fitter
bad smut, swad
bed blossom, seam
bin bunker
black anthraconite, atrous
block jud(d)
boghead torbanite
bony slate
box black maria, dan, hod, jack johnson, scuttle, shell
brass iron pyrite
broker crimp
brown bovey, lignite
cannel ampelite, boghead
car hutch, jimmy, tender, wag(g)on
car part hopper
carrier flatiron
chute cock
comb. anthrac(o)
constituent benzene, carbon, clarain, creosote, ethene, naphthalene, phenol, pyrene, vitrain

dealer collier
derivative cresol, lysol, paraffin, pitch
dirty rash
drawer putter, trammor
dust coom(b), culm, slack, smut, soot, sut, swad
fine duff, screenings
from the altar genius
gas acetylene, methane, miasma, pintsch
goose cormorant
hard anthracite, splint
heat-treated coke
heaver danner
immature lignite
impure swad
joint cleat
kind (See also COAL *size*.) anthracite, bituminous, blind, boghead, bovey, brown, burgee, byerite, cannel, dant, durain, glance, glead, grate, hard, jud, lignite, lithanthrax, lump, soft, splint, steamboat, stove, tasmanite, torbanite
layer in vitrain
-like anthracoid, jet
-like substance anthraxolite
live coffin spark, ember, gleed, gleyd
lump cob, nubbling
mass jud(d)
measure chalder, chaldron, corf, keel, ten, ton
measuring instrument billy-fairplay, billy-playfair
mine pit
mine direction endon
mine explosive bobbinite
mine gas damp, methane
mine shaft heugh
miner collier
mineral lithanthrax
miner's tb anthracosis
mining implement breaker
mining system bo(a)rd and pillar, pillar and breast, stoop and room
oil kerosene, paraffin, petroleum, photogen
opening in pillar jenkin, junking
pillar stook
plant fossil
-producing carboniferous, carbonigenous
rake freggin, fruggan, hoe, scrapple
refuse ash, backing, breeze, cinder, clinker, coke, coom(b), culm, dust, goaf, gob, slag, smut, soot, thurst

scuttle bucket, hod
seam ridge horseback
size barley, broken, buckwheat, chestnut, cob, egg, flaxseed, lump, mustard seed, nubbling, nut, pea, rice, slack, steamboat, stove, wallsend
slab skip
slaty bass, bone, bony
slice jenkin, junking
soft bituminous
soot coom
stratum bench
substance geocerite
tar base aniline
tar comb. pheno
tar derivative alizorin, creosote oil, cresol, dye, eosine, indigo, lysol, phenol, pitch
tar distillate toluene
tar paraffin decane
trade vessel cat
unsalable rash
volcanic scoria
wagon corb, corf, tram
white metaldehyde, tasmanite, water power
worker chaffman, geordie, hurrier
yard ree
COALESCE amalgamate, blend, cleave, cling, clog, cohere, combine, consolidate, embody, fuse, gather, join, league, merge, mingle, mix(ture), stick, unite
COALESCENCE combination, fusion, joining, league, mixture, synanthy, union
COALFISH baddock, beshow, billet, bluefish, cod, cudden, cuddy, glashan, glassin, parr, piltock, podler, pollack, rock salmon, sablefish, saithe, sey
young comamie, grayfish, piltock, podler, podley, poodler, sillock
COALITION alliance, association, combination, confederacy, confederation, entente, federation, front, fusion, league, merger, trust, union
COARSE 3 bad, fat, low, raw **4** base, dank, foul, hard, hask, lewd, lowd, rank, rude, ruff, sour, vile **5** bawdy, brash, broad, burly, crass, crude, dirty, dowdy, green, groff, gross, harsh, hasky, heavy, loose, randy, rough, routh, rowty, ruddy,

stogy, stour, thick, unorn **6** blousy, blowsy, blowzy, brazen, brutal, callow, carnal, common, dudgen, earthy, frowzy, grainy, gritty, impure, obtuse, randie, ribald, rudous, rugged, rustic, severe, sultry, uneven, unfele, vulgar **7** blatant, boorish, carlage, carlish, chapped, goatish, grained, loutish, lowbred, obscene, raploch, raucous, roinish, sensual, unkempt **8** granular, homespun, immodest, indecent, inferior, plebeian, slovenly, stubborn, unchaste **9** barbarian, inelegant, ingrained, offensive, tasteless, unrefined **10** blotesque, disheveled, granulated, indelicate, slatternly, unpolished **12** crossgrained
-grained gruff, unrefined
person baboon, boor, lout
COARSELY inelegantly, meanly, roughly, rudely, uncivilly
COASSUS brocket, mazama, samer deer
COAST approach, bank, beach, bobsled, border, cleve, drift, float, flow, glide, glissade, land, littoral, ripa, rivage, roll, run, sail, seaboard, seashore, seaside, shore, skid, sled, slide, slip, slither, stand, sweep, toboggan, warth
area beach, seaside, shore (line)
bird gull, tern
blite goosefoot
dweller orarian
grass job's tears
guard boat cutter
guarder navyman, spar
land maremma
live-oak encina
pert. littoral, orarian, riparial, riparian, riverain, riverine
projection cape, headland, ness, peninsula
trade cabotage
COASTER container, cradle, creeper, dolly, mat, salver, ship, sled, toboggan, tray, waiter
COAT (See also *kind*, below.) achkan, alpaca, bedaub, besmear, blue, bran, buff(y), bursatte, bursautee, butter, cape, cement,

cloak, coney, cony, cover, crust, da(u)b, enamel, feathers, flash, foil, fur, garment, gild, glace, glaze, gloss, hackle, hair, hide, husk, jack, jerkin, lacquer, lamina(te), lay, layer, mail, mantevil, membrane, overly, paint, patina, pee, pelage, pelt, petticoat, plaster, plate, protect, rind, scab, seal, shell(ac), simar, skift, skin, slough, smear, spread, stain, stucco, tar, tegument, terne, toga, tunic, varnish, veneer, vesture, wool
alloy terne
animal hair, hide, pelage, pelt, shell, skin
armor blazonry, escutcheon
artery extima
bird-skin temiak
blanket mackinaw
buff soldier
camel's hair aba
caribou-skin kooletah
claw-hammer swallow-tail
coarse capot(e)
double-breasted edwardian, prince albert, redingote, reefer
downy lanugo
-dress redingote
eye(ball) choroid, sclera
fabric melton
fastener button, frog, toggle
flap labie
flower saxifrage-pink, tunica
food dredge
fur shuba
fur-lined pelisse
goat's hair aba
gravel blotter
hair melote
hanger shoulder
hooded capote, grego
hunter's pink
kind **3** fur, mac, pee **4** jama, jupe, mail, mino, robe, sack **5** armor, cloak, frock, habit, jamah, jemmy, ruana, tails, wooly **6** alpaca, blazer, blouse, bolero, coatee, dolman, duffle, duster, enamel, jacket, jerkin, joseph, jumper, kirtle, mantle, melote, parget, poncho, reefer, rocket, sacque, sealer, tabard, topper, trench, ulster **7** cassock, courtby, crispin, cutaway, doublet, haubeck, norfolk, paletot, pelisse, rokelay,

spencer, surcoat, surtout, swagger 8 benjamin, capuchin, chaqueta, courtepy, mackinaw, overcoat, panolone, sealskin 9 brunswick, fingertip, gaberdine, newmarket, norwester, pea jacket, redingote, shadbelly, ski jacket, spiketail 10 clawhammer, messjacket, roquelaure, sportscoat 11 shadbellied, swallowtail, windbreaker 12 chesterfield, dinner jacket, prince albert, strambouline
lining fabric merveilleux
long dyibbah, jibba, kapote, redingote
long-sleeved caftan
loop tab
loose cassock, inverness, mantevil, overcoat, paletot
maker furrier, tailor
man's cutaway, mackinaw, prince albert, surtout, swallowtail, tails
metal anodize, calorize, enamel
military blouse, buff coat, tunic
monk's cassock, melote, paletot
neck george
of arms bearings, blazonry, crest, escutcheon
of arms, bearing armigerous
of arms, pert. heraldic
of mail armor, brinie, byrnie, cataphract, frock, hauberk
ornament frog
outer See OVERCOAT.
part collar, cuff, george, lapel, lining, pocket, skirt, sleeve
plaster arriccio, intonaco, set
rack valet
riding joseph, newmarket
sealskin netcha, sealchie, sealkie
seaman's grego, monkey jacket
seed bran, husk
17th century buffy
sheepskin zamarra, zamarro
short blazer, bolero, cardigan, doublet, eton, jacket, jerkin, jumper, lumberjack, parka, pea, reefer, sack, sacque, shrug, smoking jacket, spencer, tabard, tunic, windbreaker
sleeveless sobrevest
soldier's blouse, tunic

tail labie, lappet
¾ length achkan
waterproof burberry, bursattee, bursautee, mac(k)intosh, nor'wester, oilskin, poncho, slicker, tarpaulin
with cape macfarlane
with pitch pay
woman's brunswick, caraco, dolman
COATED backed, candied, furred, glace, glazed, loaded, painted, waterproof
COATI arctoid, mammal, narica, nasua, pisote, tejon
-like animal raccoon
COATING aril, bloom, cladding, covering, covert, crust, dope, emulsion, enamel, encrustation, facing, film, finish, flash, flor, fur, gilding, glace, glaze, hair, hoar, icing, jacket, lacquer, lamina, paint(ing), patina, pellicle, rust, scale, scum, skin, veneer
boiler fur
tongue atter
wounds collodion
COAX argue, banter, beg, beguile, blandish, cajole, cant, captivate, cog, coy, croodle, crowdle, cruddle, cuitle, cutter, dupe, egg, entice, exhort, fage, fawn, flatter, fleech, fondle, implore, importune, induce, inveigle, jolly, line up, lure, persuade, pester, pet, prevail on, seduce, tease, tempt, urge, wangle, wheedle, worm
COB axis, basket, beat, breakwater, chief, chignon, dollar, ear, excel, gull, heap, herring, hit, horse, leader, lump, magnate, mass, mole, muffin, nut, peapod, piece, pier, seagull, spider, surpass, swan, thresh, toss
black-backed gull
COBALT blue, smalt
arsenide flystone
bloom erythrite
blue azure, smalt
compound alloclase, alloclasite, bieberite, danaite, linnaeite
glass smalt
gray smaltite
red erythrite
source smaltite
yellow aureolin, azure

COBBLE blunder, botch, bungle, cobstone, coggle, darn, loon, mend, patch, pave, repair
stones pavement, paving
COBBLER, COBBLER'S beverage, bootmaker, botcher, catfish, cobnut, cozier, crispin, dessert, drink, fortescue, fruit pie, killifish, mender, nut, pie, pompano, scorpion, shoemaker, soler, souter, sutor
awl avocet
pegs bidens, thistle
pert. souterly
pitch code
tool fudge wheel
wax code, pitch, rozet
COBBLERFISH pompano, shoemaker, sunfish
COBCAB clog
COBHEAD goldeneye
COBIA bonito, fish, sergeant
COBNUT cobbler, conker, hazel(nut), hognut, ouabe, pignut
COBRA asp, elapid, haje, krait, mamba, naga, naia, naja, ringhals, snake, uraeus, viper
king siva snake
COBWEB, COBWEBBY arachnoid, fiction, filament, gossamer, intricacy, net, snare, trap, wevet
pert. arachnoid, araneose, araneous
COCA chew, cuca, flavor, khoka, leaf, shrub, truxillo
COCAINE anesthetic, candy, coke, dust, narcotic, snow, speedball, white stuff
addict cokey, dope fiend
source coca, cuca
substitute butyn
taking snuffing up
COCALUS *guest* daedalus
kingdom sicily
victim minos
COCCULUS cebatha, fish berry
COCCYGIUS zeus
COCHIN CHINA (See also VIETNAM.) mekong delta
COCHINEAL blanco, castilian-red, coccus, lake, sylvester
fig nopal
insect verm(e)il, vermilion
refuse granilla
wax ciccerin
COCK, COCK'S alectryon, bank, calk, capon, chan-

ticleer, cog, coil, collect, coque, cox, craven, erect, faucet, fight, fowl, fugie, gallo, gather, hammer, haystack, heap, jermonal, leader, lump, mass, master, nozzle, petcock, pile, prime, rick, rooster, shell-fish, shock, spout, stack, stand up, stick up, strut, swagger, tap, tee, valve, vane, yawl, yowle

-a-hoop askew, awry, boast-ful, defiant, elated, exultant, lively, out of kilter

-and-bull story canard, fable, lie, tall tale, yarn

chaparral roadrunner

claw raisin-tree

comb adder's-tongue, carun-cle, celosia, crest, erythrina, foolscap, lousewort, prick-leback, yellow-rattle

-crow dawn

divination by alectromancy

ensign of gaul

fighting alectryomachy, fu-gie, heeler, turnpoke

foot millet

gun nab

of hay hipple

of the walk chief, cotinga, kingfish, master

of the wood capercaillie, cap-ercailzie, tetrao, wood-pecker

robin merganser, redbreast

sorrell sour dock

spurless muckna

symbol of insolence, vigi-lance

the ear listen

the eye squint

up arise, cap, protrude

weather fane, vane

COCKADE badge, cocarde, insignia, knot, rosette

state maryland

COCKAIGNE See PARA-DISE and UTOPIA.

COCKATOO abacay, ara(ra), arra, cacatua, calangay, cockie, cocky, corella, farmer, fish, galah, ganggang, jacatoo, kakatoe, macaw, parrot

bush blueberry

COCKATRICE basilisk, de-ceiver, dragon, serpent

COCKBOAT cog, tender

COCKCHAFER buzzard, dorbeetle, humbuzz, oak web

COCKER caress, coddle,

cogger, dog, fighter, indulge, legging, pamper, pet, quiver, reaper, shoe, spaniel, wrin-kle

COCKEYE *pilot* beau gre-goire, beau gregory, dam-selfish, pintano, rudderfish

COCKEYED alop, askew, awry, drunk, esophoric, foolish, squinting, strabis-mic

bob squall

COCKFIGHT contest, game, match, spar, welsh main

COCKHORSE astride, exult-ant, lofty, proud, upstart

COCKLE boat, canoe, car-diacean, cardium, compress, cuckhold, darnel, gall, gith, kakel, kiln, mollusk, nuc-ula, oast, palour, pucker, ripple, shell, stove, wabble, whimsical, wrinkle, zizany

bur burdock, burweed, ca-dillo, clotbur, clotweed, cots, ditchbur, thistle, xanthium

oast kiln

of the heart depths, essence

COCKLIGHT dawn, twilight

COCKLOFT attic, garret

COCKLOREL rascal, rene-gade

COCKNEY array, dialect, londoner, londonese, milk-sop, ortheris, pamper, pet, plebeian, proletarian

locale bow bells, london

workman arry

COCKPADDLE lumpfish

COCKPIT arena, cab(in), circus, court, field, gallera, gridiron, lists, nacelle, nose, ring, rink, seat, well

of europe belgium

COCKROACH beetle, blatta, blattid, bug, drum(mer), mill-beetle, knocker, peri-planeta, roach

COCKSPUR acacia, frin-grigo, garabata, hawthorn, thorn, tree

grass millet

COCKSURE assured, certain, confident, decided, decisive, positive, pretentious, san-guine, showoff, stuckup

COCKTAIL See DRINK

mixed.

lounge See SALOON.

originator peychaud

COCKWEED corncockle, peppergrass

COCKY arrogant, chipper,

conceited, crank, dapper, debonair, ego(t)istic, for-mer, impudent, insolent, jaunty, natty, nervy, over-weening, perky, pert, proud, saucy, self-assured, self-confident, smart

COCO(A) apache, broma, brown, chocolate, coconut, coker, head, mahal, nut, palm, patashte, sapucaia, taro, theobromine, yautia

palm leaves cadjan

plum hicaco, icaco

preparation broma

sedge nutgrass

yam eddo

COCONUT ascot tan, brown-stone, chestnut, copra, co-quito, kermanshah, mafadu, nargil, noggin, pate, sand-stone

brown burnt almond

fiber cayar, coir(e), kair, kyar

husk cascara, coir(e)

meat calapit(t)e, copra

tree koko, niog

COCOON clew, clue, d(o)upion, follicle, in-cunabulum, kell, larva, pod, pupa, scab, shed, shell

double d(o)upion

thread bave, silk

waste cappadine

COCOROOT taro

COCOTTE casserole, trollop, wanton

COCOWOOD kokra

COCT bake, boil, cook, di-gest

COD bacalao, bag, bankfish, belly, bib, bitterling, boce, burbot, cabeliau, cabilliau, cape cod turkey, coalfish, codger, cor, cultus, cush-ion, cusk, dolefish, droud, fool, gadus, glashan, hake, hoak, husk, kabbelow, klipfish, milwell, mulvel, pillow, pod, pollack, poor, pouch, pout, rock, scrod, torsk, wachna

bait capelin, mammotus

black beshow, bishow, sa-blefish

buffalo ling

cured dunfish

dried buckhorn, stock(fish), yaffle

-head fool

-like bib, gadus, hake, ling, pout

-liver oil substance gaduin

pert. gadid, gadoid
salted cor, haberdine, klipfish
young codling, scrod, sprag
CODA bob, cauda, codetta, epilog(ue), finale, mark, rondo
CODDLE baby, boil, cade, caress, cocker, cook, cosset, cotton, fondle, humor, indulge, love, much, nurse, pamper, parboil, pet, poach, ptisan, smalm, spoil, steam
CODE canon, charter, cipher, codex, constitution, corpus juris, cryptography, decalogue, digest, discipline, dogma, doombook, equity, ethics, fuero, key, law, multeka, pandect, pitch, principles, rule, secret, signal, standards
chivalric bushido
filler null
inventor morse
legal ada(t), doombook, pandect
message cipher, cryptogram
of rules vinaya
telephone area
CODGER churl, cod, crank, cuff, fellow, miser, oddity, old man, oldster
CODICIL annex, appendix, bequest, diploma, label, postscript, provision, rider, script, sequel, tablet
CODIFY analyze, classify, digest, index, organize
CODLING apple, cod, hake, moth, youth
moth carpocapsa, tortricida
COELENTERATE acaleph(e), medusa, polyp, radiate
COENOCYTE symplasm, symplast, syncytium
COERCE blackjack, blackmail, bludgeon, boycott, browbeat, bulldoze, bully, check, coax, cohert, compel, constrain, cow, curb, distrain, dragoon, drive, enforce, force, hijack, impel, intimidate, inveigle, make, menace, oblige, order, persuade, press, push, repress, restrain, restrict, sandbag, strong-arm, threaten
COERCION command, constraint, duress, force, heat, pressure, restraint, violence

COEUR D'ALENE skitswish
COEUS *offspring* asteria, leto
parent gaea, uranus
COEVAL coincident, concomitant, concurrent, contemporary, simultaneous, synchronous
COFFEE bellywash, beverage, brew, bugjuice, cafe, coho, cohu, java, mocha, mud
after dinner demitasse
alkaloid caffeine
and snack
and brandy gloria
and cream cafe creme
and milk cafe au lait
bean nib, quaker
berry buckthorn, cascara, coprosma, jojoba, peaberry, rhamnus, soybean, yerbadeloso
black cafe noir
break intermission, respite, rest
cake blueberry buckle, kuchen
-chocolate flavor mocha
corn durra
cup finjan
cup holder zarf
disease viruela
extender chicory
extract caffeine
filtered cafe filtre
flamed cafe brulot
flavoring abelmosk
grind drip, electroperk, regular
kind arabica, black, bogota, bourbon, brazil, chaoua, diable, drip, espresso, filtre, instant, irish, jamoke, java, kona, maracaibo, mazagran, medellin, mild, mocha, rio, santos, sumatra, trillado
liqueur creme de cafe, creme de moka, kahlua
maker chemex, dripolator, filter, meleta, percolator, pot, silex, urn
plantation cafetal
pot biggin, cafetiere
refuse gailings, triage
senna cassia, stinking weed
small demitasse
substitute decaff, sanka, seenie bean
tree bonduc, buckthorn, chicot
COFFEEHOUSE cafe, estaminet, inn
COFFEEHOUSING chatter, gossip, talk

COFFEEWEED chicory, curled dock
COFFEEWOOD brown ebony, wamara
COFFER ark, box, caisson, cash box, casket, cassoon, chest, ciborium, coffin, dam, forcet, funds, hutch, pyx, store, treasure, treasury, trench, trunk
COFFERDAM patardeau
COFFIN basket, bier, bone house, box, bury, case, casing, casket, cist, confine, crust, hoof, kist, mold, ossuary, pall, sagger, sarcophagus, shell, trough
-bearing pole spoke
boat sink box
carrier gull, pallbearer
cover cloak, coom, pall
lead cope
nail cigarette
prehistoric chest, cist
stand bier, catafalque
varnish liquor
COG cajole, cam, catch, cauk, cheat, chuck, coak, cock, cockboat, cogue, cozen, deceive, deception, dovetail, fabricate, falsehood, fang, gear, hoax, jest, lie, money, palm off, prong, quibble, scotch, ship, tenon, tine, tooth, trick, tusk, wedge, wheedle
-wheel ore bournonite, sulphide
COGENT conclusive, convincing, effective, forceful, forcible, good, legitimate, persuasive, pithy, potent, powerful, puissant, sound, strong, suasive, telling, valid
COGITATE connate, consider, deliberate, meditate, mull, muse, plan, ponder, reason, reflect, ruminate, speculate, study, think, weigh
COGNAC brandy, liquor, spirit
region angoumois, bois
COGNATE affiliated, akin, alike, allied, analog(ue), apophonic, bandhava, cogener, generic, identical, kin(dred), related, relative, similar, universal
COGNIZANT alive, awake, aware, cognoscent, conscious, conversant, in-

formed, knowing, sensible, versed, ware, wise

of apprised of, hep to, informed of, in the know, let into, next to, on to, privy to, undeceived, wise to

COGNOMEN agnomen, appellation, by-name, coparcener, epithet, name, nickname, parcener, patronym(ic), sobriquet, surname, title

COGNOSCENTE authority, connoisseur, judge

COGON grass, illuk, imperata, kunai, lalang

COHEIR coparcener, joint, parcener

COHERE adhere, agglutinate, agree, attach, bind, blend, bond, cement, cleave, cling, coalesce, coincide, combine, connect, fasten, fit, fuse, glue, glutinate, hang together, join, merge, seize, stick, suit, unite

COHERENCE accretion, adherence, adhesion, adhesiveness, agglomeration, agglutination, agreement, cementation, clearness, clinging, coagulation, cohesion, cohesiveness, compactness, concretion, congelation, conglomeration, congruity, consent, consistency, consolidation, context, glueyness, glutinosity, gumminess, integrity, lucidity, set, solidarity, solidification, stickiness, sticking, strength, tackiness, tenacity, toughness, union, unity, viscidity, viscosity

COHESION adhesion, bond, COHERENCE, hardness, strength, union

COHESIVE gluey, tenacious

COHIBIT restrain, restrict

COHORT band, company, GROUP

ten legion

COHOSH actaea, baneberry, bugbane, cimifuga, ginseng, papooseroot, sanicle, snakeroot, snakeweed, squawroot

COHUE crowd, mob, rout

COHUNE corajo, corozo

COIF beggin, biggonet, burlet, calotte, cap, cervel(l)iere, hairdo, headdress, hood, houve, how, quaif, skullcap, top

COIFFURE bang, bob, bouffant, COIF, hairdo, headdress, marcel, pompadour, roach, shag, shingle, tressure, tutulus, wave

17th century tete de mouton

COIL ado, ansa, bobbin, braid, circle, cirrus, clew, clue, confusion, convolution, convolve, corkscrew, crimp, crisp, curl(icue), difficulty, eel, encircle, enroll, enwind, fank, flake, frizz, frizzle, furl, glomus, gyration, hank, helix, inductor, involution, kink, length, link, loop, marcel, mesh, plait, querl, quile, quoil, ringlet, roll, round, rundle, screw, serpent, snake, spiral, spire, tangle, tendril, tesla, tickler, toil, trouble, tuft, tumult, twine, twirl, twist, upwind, viper, volute, whorl, wind, wip, worm, wreath(e), wring

comb. spiro

hair bun, pug, ringlet

induction jigger

wire bobbin, solenoid

COILED gyrate, tortile, twirled, writhen

COIMPLICANT equipollent

COIN (See also under individual countries.) angle, bit, bob, brass, bronze, cache, caroon, cash, change, clink, compose, conceive, corner, currency, die, doit, fabricate, gill, harp, invent, issue, joe(y), lit, mint(age), money, originate, quoin, rap, red, silver, specie, stamp, strike, talent, tanner, tender, two bits, wedge, wen

aluminum beshlik, forint, pruta(h), yen

base black money, brockage, commassee, counterfeit, rap, shand, sheen, sinker

blank planchet

box cash register, meter, pyx, till

bronze avo, boudle, cent (avo), centesimo, centime, eyrir, farthing, filler, follis, grain, groschen, grosz, halfpenny, hapenny, heller, lepton, litra, macuta, mil, millieme, mouzouna, obol, ore, para, penny, pfennig, pie, quintar, reichspfennig, santims, sen, sou, tempo, triens, uncia

collector numismatist

commonwealth breeches money

compound potin

copper atchison, ban, batz, besa, bodle, brown, cent(avo), centime, drachma, equipaga, fugiocent, heller, kopeck, novcic, penny, pesa, peso, pul, pya, soldo, tornese, tuppence, twopence

counterfeit brummagem, gray, grey, rap, sheen, shoful, slip, slug, stumer, stumo(u)r

date exergue

debased See COIN *base.*

defect brockage, fault

design beading

edging knurling, milling, nig, reeding

15th century plack

front head, obverse

game pitch-and-toss

gold 3 lat, lev, yen 4 demy, kran, lira, oban, onza, peso, pond, rand, rial, ryal 5 broad, daric, dinar, dobra, ducat, eagle, libra, mohur, noble, obang, oncia, pengo, pound, rebia, rider, ruble, ryder, sucre, tanga, toman, unite 6 amania, aureus, azteca, condor, doblon, dobrao, dollar, doppia, ducato, escudo, laurel, mancus, octave, ongaro, specie, stater, stella, triens, ungaro 7 alfonso, angolar, ashrafi, carolus, duplone, jacobus, lempira, marengo, milreis, moidore, oncetta, pahlavi, pistole, ruddock, solidus, unicorn 8 augustal, cruzeiro, denarius, doubloon, henri d'or, hyperper, louis d'or, maravedi, morocota, napoleon, pistolet, sultanin 9 argentino, chervonet, philippus, tremissis, zermahbub 10 krugerrand, sovereigne

hole slot

honorary fader

imperfect brockage

inscription sigla

medieval banco, ducat

metallic specie

mill nurl

money get rich, profit, succeed

nickel franc, girsh, lek, lev, lew, lira, piaster, real, rupee, sent, shahi, stiver, zloty
official issue piedfort
of the realm specie
old ducat, galley-halfpenny, pistole
overstruck surfrappe
part exergue
pert. numismatic(al), nummary
pewter at(t), tra
refuse breeze
reverse reverse, tail, verso
ringer sharp(er)
roll rouleau
science chrysology, numismatics, numismatology
-shaped nummiform
side heads, obverse, reverse, tails
silver 3 bit, hog, lat, leu, ley, lit, sol, yen 4 baht, batz, dime, doit, dump, kran, lira, mark, peso, pina, real, rial, ryal, tael, tara, yuan 5 bezzo, colon, crown, dalger, fanam, franc, fuang, girsh, groat, krona, krone, kroon, liard, litas, litra, medio, mohar, obole, pengo, rebia, riyal, ruble, rupee, rupia, sceat, soldo, sucre 6 abbasi, balboa, carlin, dinero, dirhem, dollar, ducato, escudo, florin, fuerte, gourde, gulden, heller, obolus, peseta, puttan, rouble, salung, specie, stater, talari, teston, tostao, toston, tugrik, turner 7 afghani, altilik, angolar, bolivar, carline, chakram, cordoba, cordova, daalder, drachma, mahmudi, piaster, quarter, quetzal, stooter, tallero, testone, tornese 8 chuckrum, cuarenta, denarius, didrachm, ducatoon, gigliato, giustina, marcello, medjidie, shilling, sixpence, sterling, tetrobol, tuppence, twopence, yirmilik 9 boliviano, dandiprat, didrachma, dubbelite, fourpence, half-crown, rigsdaler, rixdollar, schilling 10 half-dollar, reichsmark, threepence, thruppence 11 cistophorus, decadrachma 12 reichsthaler, rijksdaalder
silver amalgam pina, tester
small dump, mite, orkey, silverling, solidare
square klippe

stamper mill
substitute slug, stamp, token
tail verso
tester saraf, shroff
tin tra
toss birl, match
trifling doit, mite, rap, soumarque
trim nig
weight shekel
words neologize
worthless skillagalee
COINAGE fabrication, fiction, invention, mintage
COINCIDE accompany, accord, agree, bump, concur, correspond, fit, gee, harmonize, identify, jibe, jump, match, synchronize, tally
COINCIDENCE coetaneousness, coevality, concomitance, concourse, concurrence, conjunction, correspondence, isochronism, simultaneity
COINCIDENT concurrent, congruent, consonant, even, together
COISTREL base, groom, peasant, servile, varlet
COJA khaja, khodja, khojah, schoolmaster, teacher
COKE ash, chark, coal, cocaine, core, dope, fuel
COKY See ADDICT.
COL depression, gap, has, joch, neck, nek, pass, saddle, swire
COLANDER bolter, colatorium, refiner, sieve, sifter, strainer
COLCHIS *king* aeetes
princess medea
COLCOTHAR angel-red, coromandel, saffron, tuscany
COLD 3 flu, icy, mur, nip, raw 4 ache, ague, blue, cool, dead, dull, flat, hard, hask, hoar, keen, murr, roup, sure 5 acale, algid, algor, aloof, bleak, brisk, cauld, chill, crisp, fishy, froid, frore, frost, gelid, glace, nippy, oorie, ourie, parky, polar, poose, rheum, rigor, shaky, sharp, solid, stiff, stony, urled, virus 6 aching, arctic, biting, bitter, boreal, brumal, chilly, clammy, coolth, coryza, creeps, freddo, frigid, frigor, frosty, frozen, hiemal, marble, severe, snappy,

stecky, wairch, winter, wintry 7 brittle, callous, catarrh, chilled, cinched, costive, cutting, didders, disease, distant, glacial, gravedo, iciness, inhuman, morfond, nipping, numbing, rawness, shivers, shivery, strange, subzero 8 algidity, coolness, freezing, gelidity, hibernal, insolent, keenness, morfound, piercing, pinching, reserved, reticent, rhigosis, rigorous, severity, siberian, sniffles, unheated 9 apathetic, bloodless, briskness, chromatic, frigidity, inclement, shivering, subboreal, unfeeling 10 chilliness, inclemency, insensible, lackluster, melancholy, thieveless, unenthused 11 hyperborean, indifferent, passionless, penetrating, unconscious, unemotional 12 discouraging 13 dispassionate 15 undemonstrative
as charity, ice
as a frog
biting algid, gelid
-blooded brutal, callous, dispassionate, frozen, heartless, heterothermic, imperturbable, poikilothermal, steady, stonyhearted, unfeeling
chap chilblain, kibe
cock deaden, flatten
comb. cry(o), frigo, gel, psychro
cream balm, cleanser, salve
creeps trepidation
deck ice
extremely arctic, frigid, peevish
fear of cheimophobia, psychrophobia
feet apprehension, chicken heart, cowardice, doubt, faint heart, fear, weak knees, yellow streak
-hearted bloodless, callous, flinty, frozen, hard, stony, unfeeling
in the head catarrh, coryza, gravedo, poose, pose, rhinitis, roup, sniffles, snifters, snivels
mist drow
pack icebag
pert. frigid, frigoric, gelid, icy
pinched with urled
preventative ascorbic acid,

interferon, propanediamine, vitamin c
producing algific
region arctic, niflheim, niflhel
remedy antihistamine
sensation rhigosis
set chisel
severe morfound
shivers fear, shakes, trepidation
shoulder disregard, indifference, snub
shrivel with shram
sore virus herpes-simplex
spell snap
steel bayonet, dagger, sword
storage coolhouse, frigidaire, frigidarium, ice plant, locker
sweat dread, trepidation
symptom ache, drip, sneeze, sore throat
therapeutic use crymotherapy
war event berlin wall
water, throw deprecate, discourage, disparage
with hoarseness murr
COLDFINCH flycatcher
COLDNESS algor, chill, distance, enmity, froideur, frost, phlegm, stiffness
COLE See COLEWORT.
COLEOPTERA See INSECT.
COLERIDGE, S. T. *sacred river* alph
work ancient mariner, biographia literaria, kubla khan
COLETTE *heroine* gigi
COLEWORT brassica, cabbage, cale, colza, kail, kale, rape, ribe, stock
sprout stoven
COLHOZEH *kingdom* mizpah
son baruch, shallun
COLIC bat(ts), bellyache, enteralgia, fret, guttie, pain, tormina, visceral
remedy philonium
COLICROOT ague grass, aletris, aloeroot, bitter grass, blazingstar, comfrey, huskwort, starwort, unicorn
COLICWEED dutchman's-breeches, squirrel-corn
COLIMA ironwood, tapa
COLIN bobwhite, quail, rustic, shepherd, swain
COLISEUM arena, bowl, colosseum, hall, stadium, theater

COLL clip, embrace, hug, poll, prune
COLLABORATE aid, assist, betray, coact, concert, concur, cooperate
COLLABORATOR associate, bedfellow, bedmate, coactor, coauthor, cooperator, quisling, traitor
COLLAPSE bankruptcy, break(down), buckle, bust, capsize, cave(in), comedown, contract, crack-up, crash, cropper, crumble, crumple, debacle, defeat, deflate, deflation, depression, downfall, explosion, fail(ure), fall, fold(up), flummox, founder, implode, pratfall, prostration, ruin, shatter, slump, smash, spoil, succumb, tailspin, telescope, topple, tumble, wreck, yield
COLLAPSIBLE folding
COLLAR (See also *kind, below.*) arrest, band, bobeche, bracelet, cang(ue), cap, cape, capture, catch, chain, choker, circlet, dickey, fur, gorget, grab, harness, hawse, nab, neckband, poke, ring, ruff, saddle, seize, shackle, tackle, take, torque, trap, yoke
angle stapling
beam spanner, spanpiece
bone clavicle
button stud
cell choanocyte
clerical rabat(o), rebater, rebato
close-fitting turtleneck
convict's cang, carcan, carcanet
deep bertha, rebato
edging fraize
frilled jabot, ruff
furniture bracelet
iron carcan, joug(s), pothook(s)
jeweled carcanet
kind bargham, bertha, buster brown, cangue, carcan(et), chevesaile, collum, dickey, eton, fanon, fanum, fichu, fur, orale, panuelo, partlet, phano, rabat(o), rebater, rebato, ruche, ruff, stock, tucker, turndown, turnup, van dyke
lace scallop
old rabat(o)
pad afterwale
papal fanon, orale

part hame, lapel
pert. accollee, torquate
plaited ruche
queen's ruff
17th century rabato, piccadil
starched buster brown, eton
stiffener starch, stay
turned down rabat(o), rebato
twisted torque
wheel-shaped ruff
wide stiff rabat(o), rebater, rebato
wooden cang(ue)
COLLARDED accolle(e), caught, torquate
COLLATE assemble, bestow, compare, confer, contrast, organize, verify
COLLATERAL accessory, accidental, additional, allied, back-up, branch, bond, credit, dependent, deposit, eventual, faith, hostage, margin, oblique, parallel, reciprocal, related, secondary, security, side, subordinate, succursal, surety
COLLATION address, collection, comparison, conference, consultation, contrast, contribution, dejeuner, hotchpot, lunch(eon), meal, reading, repast, sermon, tea, treatise
COLLEAGUE adjunct, aide, ally, assistant, associate, cohort, compeer, comrade, confederate, confrere, consort, conspire, deputy, friend, partner, socius, unite
COLLECT accrue, accumulate, acquire, aggregate, amass, assemble, bag, call in, center, cluster, compact, compile, conclude, conflate, congest, congregate, convene, crowd, cull, dig up, draw, flock, garner, gather, get(together), glean, group, heap, hoard, impound, levy, lift, mass, muster, nob, pick, pile, pool, prayer, raise, rake up, rammass, round up, sam(m), save, scamble, scare up, scrape, up, scrounge, semble, sheave, store, sweep, synapte, take up, tax, uplift, uptake
communion prayer
food forage
grain gavel
on delivery cod

COLLECTED calm, composed, confident, cool, levelheaded, present, quiet, serene, sober, temperate, tranquil, unruffled

COLLECTION 3 ana, bag, kit, lot, set 4 band, bevy, body, clan, crop, exam, file, heap, levy, mass, olio, pile, raft, sort 5 album, batch, block, bunch, crowd, depot, FLOCK, GROUP, hoard, kitty, sheaf, stack, store, suite, virtu 6 bundle, corpus, mishna, parcel, ragbag, recule, rosary, sorite 7 exhibit, fistful, flutter, gallery, garland, library, mishnah, omnibus, quotity, sorites, sylloge 8 analecta, antiques, archives, assembly, caboodle, delectus, donation, fascicle, glossary, romescot, syntagma 9 aggregate, americana, anthology, bircabrac, collation, congeries. gathering, symposium 10 assemblage, miscellany, repertoire 11 compilation, examination, knickknacks, miscellanea, onomasticon 12 accumulation, chrestomathy, mobilization
animal head, herd, menagerie, zoo
center entrepot
comb. ana
confused clutter
large cloud
literary ana(lects), repertory, rhapsody
miscellaneous fardel, olio, smytrie
poems anthology, cancionery, divan, sylva

COLLECTIVE aggregate(d), coop(erative), gathering, kibbutz(im)

COLLECTOR antiquer, bibliophage, bibliophile, cashier, compiler, douanier, dustman, exciseman, gatherer, gauger, governor, pack rat, philatelist, teller, treasurer, whipper-in, zamindar

COLLEEN belle, blonde, damsel, girl, lass(ie), maid(en)

COLLEGE academy, assemblage, alma mater, brevet, campus, clergy, company, graduate school, guild, gymnasium, institute, lycee, lyceum, madrasa, normal (school), prison, school, seminary, tol, university, varsity
absence permit exeat
accounts battel
barracks dorm(itory), fraternity
building dorm, gym, library, student union
campus quad(rangle)
cap mortar board
cheer yell
course major, minor, seminar
court quad
exam blue book, collection
girl coed
grad alum(na), alumni, alumnus, doctor, master
grounds campus, lawn, quad
group fraternity, sorority
hall aula, dorm
hypothetical siwash
ice sundae
kind electoral, pontifical
official beadle, busar, dean, docent, don, president, proctor, registrar
oldest u.s. harvard
oldest women's, u.s. mt holyoke
pert. academic
professor docent, doctor, don
provincial siwash
servant gyp, scout
student academic, coed, collegian, diplomate, graduate, scholar, underclassman, undergraduate
term semester, trimester
treasurer bursar
tree elm

COLLICULUS postgeminum, pregeminum

COLLIDE bang, barge, beat, bump, cannon, carom, clash, crack up, crash, dosh, differ, encounter, foul, graze, head into, hit, hurt(le), impinge, knock, meet, ram, run foul of, run into, shock, sideswipe, slam, smack, smash, smite, smudge, strike, thrust, wreck

COLLIE beardie

COLLIER boat, coal miner, coal seller, coal ship, coil-year, flatiron, fly, geordie, miner, plover, scutcher, vessel
boy hodder

lung disease anthracosis
purchase foothold

COLLINS, WILKIE *novel* moonstone, woman in white

COLLINSIA blue-eyed grass, blue-eyed mary, bluelips, innocence, navelwort, spiderwort

COLLIQUATE dissolve, fuse, liquefy, melt

COLLISION accident, appulse, brunt, bump, cannon, carom, clash, concussion, conflict, confrontation, contest, crack(up), crash, encounter, engagement, headon, hit, hostility, hurtle, impact, impingement, jar, jolt, meeting, misfortune, opposition, percussion, shock, sideswipe, smash(up)

COLLOCATE arrange, place, set

COLLOP acre, lamina, part, piece, rasher, slice

COLLOQUIAL cant, chatty, common, communicative, conversational, dialectal, everyday, familiar, idiom(atic), informal, substandard, undignified, unliterary, unstudied, vernacular, vulgate

COLLOQUY chat, confab, conference, conversation, court, dialogue, discourse, parley, talk

COLLUDE collogue, connive, conspire, plot, scheme

COLLUSION agreement, cahoots, chicanery, complicity, connivance, conspiracy, cooperation, deceit, duplicity, guilt, intrigue, machination, plot, practice, scheme, secrecy
law covin

COLLYWOBBLES jitters, nerves

COLOGNE (See also PERFUME.) toilet water
earth pigment, vandyke brown
ingredient neroli
king balthasar, caspar, gaspar, jasper, magi, melchior
plant costmary
spirit alcohol, ethanol

COLOMBIA darien, new granada
artist ariza

author arciniegas, isaacs, marquez
cape aguja, augusta, marzo, punta gallinas, vela
capital bogota
cay roncador, vela, vigia
city amza, barranquilla, bello, bogota, bucaramanga, buenaventura, buga, cali, cartagena, cartago, chinu, cucuta, girardot, guapi, ibague, ipiales, leticia, maganque, manizales, medellin, mitu, monteria, muzo, neiva, paez, palmira, pasto, pereira, popayan, quibdo, sangil, sipi, tado, tolu, tulua, tunja, yari
coin centavo, condor, peseta, peso, real
deity bachuo, bochica, chaquen, chibchacum, cuchavira, fomagata, guesa, nencatacoa, thomagata
diplomat arciniegas
dish ajiaco
gulf cupica, darien, tibuga, tortugas, uraba
hummingbird trainbearer
indian achagua, andaqui, arawak, bellacoola, betoya, boro, calima, carib, catio, chibcha, chimila, choco, churoya, cocanucos, coconucan, coconuco, cofan, cogui, colima, cubeo, cuna, duit, guahibo, guajiro, guane, guarauno, haida, hoka, ingano, macu, mirana, mocoa, motilone, muso, muzo, paez(e), panaquita, panches, pijao, puinave, puinavis, puitoto, quechua, quimbaya, saliva, seona, sinsigas, shuswap, tahami, tairona, tama, tapa, telembi, ticunu, tucano, tunebo, witoto, yagua, yahuna
inlet tumaco
island baru, cusachon, fuerte, gorgona, naipo
lake tota
liquor aquardiente
mahogany albarco, caniniana
measure azumbre, celemin, vara
musical instrument bandola, tiple
pastry empanada, pastelito
peak chita, huila, purace, tolima
peasant campesino
plains llanos

plant yocco
point caribana, cruces, gallinas, lacruz, solano
poncho ruana
port barranquilla, buenaventura, cartagena, lorica, santa marta, tumaco
president valencia
province amazonas, antioquia, arauca, atlantico, bolivar, boyaca, caldas, caqueta, cauco, choco, cundinamarca, guarjire, huila, magdalena, meta, narina, putomayo, santander, tolima, valle, vaupes, vichada
range abibe, andes, ayapel, baudo, chamusa, cocuy, oriengal, perija, tunahi
river amazon, apapois, arauca, ariari, atrato, atroto, bita, caguan, caqueta, casanare, cauca, cesar, guainia, guaviara, inirida, isana, magdalena, mesai, meta, muco, nechi, pattia, pauto, putumayo, sinu, sucio, tomo, truando, uva, vichada, yapura, yari
river sucker big lip
tree arboloco
volcano huila, pasto, purace, tolima
weight bag, carga, libra, quilate, quintal, saco
writer arciniegas, isaacs, marquez
COLOMBO *airport* bandaranaike
COLON coin, hemistich, husbandman, mesymnion, planter, viscera, vitals
surgery colectomy
COLONEL campmaster, officer, solitaire, tribunus
blimp swaggerer
COLONIST boor, colon, emigrant, immigrant, nudist, pioneer, planter, settler
friend netop
COLONIZE establish, found, gather, inhabit, migrate, plant, pre-empt, settle, squat
COLONIZER ant, oecist, planter, settler
COLONNADE arcade, choultry, cloister, hall (way), parvis, passage (way), pergola, peristyle, piazza, pillar, portico, row, stoa, terrace
COLONUS litus, serf

birthplace of sophocles
refuge for oedipus
COLONY apoikia, cenobe, cenobium, community, cormus, dependency, dominion, gannetry, group, hive, mandate, possession, protectorate, skep, society, state, stock, swarm, territory
proprietary delaware, maryland, pennsylvania
COLOPHONITE andradite, garnet
COLOR aspect, badge, banner, bepaint, bias, blee, blush, cast(e), cause, chroma, chromogen, complexion, crimson, decorate, depaint, dip, disguise, distemper, distort, dramatize, dye(stuff), emblazon, ensign, exaggerate, extenuate, fake, falsify, flag, flare, flush, game, glaze, gloss, gouache, grain, guise, hue, jack, illuminate, imbrue, imbue, impaste, infect, influence, ingrain, kind, locket, mantle, medium, misrepresent, ornament, paint, pennant, pigment, prejudice, pretend, raddle, redden, ripen, shade, shadow, sham, slant, speckle, stain, streak, taint, tarnish, taste, tempura, tenne, timbre, tinct(ion), tincture, tinge, tint, tone
achromatic black, gray, white
band lacing, slash, sock, stria, stripe
bar discrimination
biscuit doe
blind achromate, monochromate
blindness achropsia, daltonism, parachromatism
blindness, blue-yellow achromatopsia
blindness, green achloropsia, deuteranopia
blindness, red protanomaly, protanopia
blindness, red-green daltonism
blindness, yellow xanthocyanopia
carrier lurrier
cell chromoblast, chromocyte, endochrome
change iridesce, opalesce, tinctumutation

-changing allochromatic, allochrous
chart broca scale
comb. chromato, chrome, chromia, chromo
dark puke
deprive of achromatize
deviation abrash
dull drab, dun, favel, khaki, mat(te), terne
expert artist, dyer, painter
fast grain
full of chromatic
gradation sfumato, shade
grizzled agouti, agouty
guard flag-bearer
having different chatoyant, heterochromous, motley, piebald, pied, varied, variegated
healthy tan
heraldic sable
increased pleiochromia
intensity brilliance, saturation
iridescent schiller
lead plomb
light achromatous, pastel, tint
line apartheid, bigotry, discrimination, prejudice, streak
lose blanch, bleach, etiolate, fade, pale
malachite bice
mark nebulation, rivulation
mat white alabaster
mulberry morello
neutral beige, black, ecru, gray, white
nickel nimbus
organ clavilux
painter titian
pale See COLOR *light.*
pert. chromatic
-photography inventor ives
play kaleidoscope, opalescence
primary blue, red, yellow
-producing chromogenic
protective camouflage
quality achromaticity, achromatism, chromism, keeping, key, note, value
science chromatics, chromatology, colormetry, spectrology
secondary green, orange, purple
set palette
shade of difference nuance
spectrum order vibgyor
stratum fahlband
streak fleck, plaga

subdued undertone
tone hue, shade, timbre, tint
unhealthy sallow
varying allochromatic, iridescent, opalescent
vehicle magilp, megilp(h), meguilp
without (See also COLORLESS.) achromatic, bleached, pale, plain, wan
COLORADO cigar, reddish, solitaire, yampa
army camp carson
bean pinto
bird lark bunting
capital denver
city alamosa, arvada, aspen, aurora, boulder, colorado springs, delta, denver, durango, golden, greeley, gunnison, lamar, loveland, pueblo, purgatory, salida, silverton, telluride, trinidad, vail
college regis
county baca, chaffee, gilpin, mesa, otero, ouray, routt, yuma
fish bonytail
fort collins, logan
gorge grand canyon
grass texas millet
hydroelectric plant boulder, hoover
indian arapaho(e)
national park dinosaur, estes, mesa verde, rocky mountain
native rover
nickname centennial state
pass alpine, argentine, book, cottonwood, elk, independence, park, raton, roan, sawatch
peak arapahoe, audubon, baldy, blanca, castle, elbert, estes, ethel, evans, grays, harris, harvard, holy cross, james, longs, maroon bells, oso, pikes, princeton, ptarmigan, rosalie, snowmass, summit, torreys, wilson
range book, elk, laramie, park, raton, roan, rockies, sangre de cristo, san juan, sawatch
region garden of the gods
resort aspen, estes park, manitou, vail
river apishapa, arikaree, arkansas, bear, colorado, dolores, gila, grand, green, gunnison, laramie, purga-

toire, smoky hill, south platte, white, yampa
river explorer alarcon
river fish flannelmouthed sucker
river tributary gila, green
state flower columbine
state tree spruce
valley estes
COLORATION blee, clouding, flash, pile, schiller
abnormal chromatism, chromism
COLORATURA diva, run, soprano, trill
COLORED biased, faw, glossed over, hued, partial, piebald, pied, plausible, prejudiced, pretended, rubricated, simulated, specious, stained, variegated
brightly chromatic
COLORFUL blatant, brave, bright, chamelonic, exotic, florid, gauche, gaudy, gay, golden, gorgeous, intense, juicy, psychedelic, rich, variegated, vivid
COLORING alkanet, alkannin, blee, camouflage, chameleonic, dye(ing), emblazonry, falsification, painting, pigmentation, qualification, staining, tinction, tincture, tinge(nt), tint(ing)
agent ruddle
matter alnein, arterin, chlorophyll, clorofil, dye, endochrome, morin, pigment, tinction
COLORLESS achromatic, achromatous, achromic, achroous, albino, ashen, ashy, blake, blanched, blank, bleached, characterless, clear, common, drab, drained, dull, etiolate, gray, hueless, lackluster, mousey, neutral, nondescript, pale, pallid, pasty, plain, toneless, wan, washed out, waxen, white
comb. achromato
COLORS banner, ensign, flag, jack, pennant, pennon, standard, streamer
COLOSSAL big, cyclopean, enormous, gargantuan, giant, gigantic, great, huge, immense, large, mammoth, monstrous, monumental, prodigious, superb, supreme, titanic, vast

COLOSSEUM amphitheater, amphitheatrum flavium, arena, coliseum, stadium, theater

COLOSSUS giant, monolith, monster, powerhouse, prodigy, stalwart, statue, strong man, titan, tower

COLPORTEUR bookseller, evangelist, hawker, vendor

COLT, COLT'S beat, boy, equuleus, foal, filly, fledgling, greenhorn, gun, hogget, horse, pistol, poleyn, potro, rope, sapling, stag(gie), staig, stater, wanton, whip, yearling, youngster
distemper strangles
group rag
-pixie hobgoblin, sprite
-tail cirrus, cloud, horseweed
-tooth wantonness, wild oats
yearling, hogget

COLTER cutter, knife, laver

COLTSFOOT asarum, bullsfoot, clayweed, cleats, clote, dock, farfara, foalfoot, galax, hoofs, horsehoof, lagwort, sowfoot, tobacco, tussilago

COLUBER, COLUBRID black racer, black runner, blue racer, carphiophiops, carphophis, serpent, wormsnake

COLUMBA dove, pigeon
dove of noah

COLUMBARY, COLUMBARIUM aviary, dovecote, niche, pigeonhole, vault

COLUMBIA sinkiuse
river, city on richland
river fish chiselmouth
river indian shahaptian
river tributary deschutes, snake, willamette
river valley grand coulee

COLUMBINE aquilegia, bluebell, blue starry, buffon, calumba, capon's-feather, chuckies, colenbell, dovelike, dovesfoot, flower, rockbell
lover arlechino, harlequin, pulcinella
state colorado

COLUMBITE annerodite, dianite, niobite
source niobium

COLUMBUS *banner* green cross

birthplace genoa
brother bartholomew, diego, ferdinand
burial place havana, santo domingo, seville
colony isabella, la navidad
companion ojeda
destination cipangu, indes
embarkation port cadiz, palos, puerto de santa maria
father-in-law bartolomeo perestrelo
1st land sighted san salvador
flagship santa maria
fleet surgeon chanca
funeral place vallodolid
historian peter-martyr
name for new world dominica
navigator pinzon
of skies herschel
patron ferdinand, isabella
port of gold zaiton
prayers to virgin of milagros
school pavia
2nd voyage port la grande anse
ship nina, pinta, santa maria
son diego
spanish name colon
successor nicolas de ovando
supporter juan perez
title admiral of the mosquitoes
wife filipa moniz perestrello

COLUMN asokan, bague, bar, candelabrum, colonnade, cylinder, feature, file, formation, fust, gnomon, goal, lally, lat, line, memorial, obelisk, part, pilaster, pillar, pole, post, procession, scapus, shaft, stela, stele, string, support, synema, torse, torso, tower, troops, trunk, wurtz
annulated ring bague
arrange in marshal, sum, tabulate
arrangement accouplement
base dado, patten, plinth
comb. ciono
convexity entasis
corner anta
curve scape
decoration cil(l)ery, volute
double row dipteral
drum tambour
figure atlantes, atlas, caryatid, telamon
fluting channel, striga
form entasis, galbe

groove flute
having 2 distyle
having 12 dodecastyle
part anta, architrave, baluster, base, capital, epistyle, fust, pilaster, plinth, scape, scotia, shaft, socle
ring bague
rock hoodoo
set in tabular
shaft fust, scale, scape, tige
small stele
spinal backbone, spine, vertebrae
square anta, pilaster
style attic, corinthian, doric, ionic, tuscan
sub-base stylobata
support socle
top abacus, capital
twisted torse, torso
without astylar

COLUMNAR stelene, terete, vertical

COLY mousebird

COMA blackout, blur, bunch, carus, catalepsy, chevelure, faint, insensibility, sleep, stupor, subeth, syncope, torpor, trance, tuft, unconsciousness

COMATOSE apathetic, asleep, drowsy, impassive, languid, lethargic, listless, out, phlegmatic, sleepy, sluggish, stuporous, supine, torpid, unconscious

COMATULID antedon, crinoid, echinoderm, featherstar

COMB beatille, billow, break, brush, cambe, canvass, card, caruncle, clean, coneflower, coomb, crest, curry, disentangle, flisk, gill, hackle, hatchel, heckle, kame, pecten, rack, rake, ransack, rasp, ravel, redd, ridge, scold, scour, scrape, seek, slack, smooth, strigil, tease, thrash, toze, wallop, wave, wraithe
-back windsor chair
-bearer ctenophore
comb. cten(o), pect(i)
cotton card, tease
-fern curly grass
flax hackle, hatchel, heckle
jelly ctenophore
-like pectinal, pectinate
pert. pectinal
rat gundi
-shaped cteniform, pectinate

teeth-filer burrgrailer
wool tease, toze

COMBAT action, affray, antagonize, argument, assail, attack, battle, belligerence, belligerency, blow, bombard, bout, brush, clash, conflict, contend, contest, cope, counter, deraign, dispute, duel, engagement, fight(ing), fray, fury, hostilities, joust, meet, oppose, repel, resist, rush, scuffle, skirmish, storm, stour, strife, struggle, tilt, war (fare), withstand
branch arm
code duello
futile sciamachy
group task force
single duomachy

COMBATANT battler, champion, contender, contestant, dueler, enemy, fighter, gladiator

COMBATIVE agonistic, antagonistic, bantam, bellicose, belligerent, militant, pugnacious, strained, striving, warlike

COMBED crested, scraped, tufted

COMBER billow, breaker, kempster, ripple, roller, wave

COMBINATION addition, affiliation, aggregation, alliance, alloy, amalgam(ation), anastomosis, association, blend(ing), bloc, brew, cabal, camarilla, cartel, clique, coadunation, coalescence, coalition, collection, combine, combo, composite, compound, concurrence, confederation, conglomerate, conjunction, connection, consolidation, consort(ium), corner, coterie, crasis, embodiment, ensemble, faction, federalization, federation, fusion, gang, group, hash, hook-up, incorporation, inosculation, joining, junction, junto, league, medley, merger, mixture, monopoly, package deal, pact, party, pool, ring, solidification, synaeresis, syndicate, syndication, synizesis, synthesis, tie-up, trust, underwear, unification, union

harmonious concord, cooperation, coordination
unlawful monopoly

COMBINE absorb, accrete, add, amalgamate, associate, band, bind, blend, bloc, braid, bunch, cabal, cartel, club, coadunate, coalesce, combination, compound, concur, condense, conglomerate, conjoin, conjure, connect, consolidate, construe, cooperate, cumulate, faction, federate, fraternize, fuse, gang up, group, hook up, incorporate, interfuse, intermix, join, junto, league, link, lump, marry, meddle, merge(r), mingle, mix, nick, pair off, pool, relate, ring, splice, stand together, team up, thresher, tie in with, total, unify, unite, wed
against boycott
efforts concur, coordinate, cooperate

COMBINED bound, conjoint, cooperative, fixed, fused, joined, joint, united

COMBINING amphimixis, synthesis, systasis

COMBO See COMBINATION and MIXTURE.

COMBUSTIBLE ardent, burnable, conder, excited, fiery, flammable, fuel, hotheaded, inflammable, irascible, piceous
material coal, coke, gas, oil, peat, tinder, wood

COMBUSTION agitation, burning, candescence, confusion, consuming, cremation, fire, flame, heat, ignition, inflammable, oxidation, therm, tumult
residue ash(es), brand, calx, carbon, charcoal, cinder, clinker, coal, coke, coom(b), culm, dross, fume, gas, lava, reek, scoria, slag, smog, smoke, smudge, smut, soot
spontaneous thermogenesis

COME accrue, advance, advene, appear, approach, arise, arrive, befall, burst, chance, chive, coop, develope, draw, emanate, emerge, ensue, fall, fare, fetch, flare, get, happen, issue, lay, light, near, obtain, occur, pass, proceed,

reach, rise, spring, stem, turn out
about arise, chance, happen, occur, pivot, rally, result, tack
a cropper collapse, fail, fall
across ante, confess, contribute, encounter, find, meet
across with admit, advance, cough up, deliver, deposit
after ensue, follow, succeed, sue
again ante, bye-bye, farewell, good-bye, recur, rejoin, repeat, return, revisit
along fare, improve, manage, progress, prosper, succeed
alongside board, breast
and go alternate, approximate, commute, fluctuate, oscillate, recur, seesaw, vacillate
apart break, fray, shed, stave
around acquiesce, agree, give in, go along, recover, revive, surrender, visit, yield
at arrive, attack, attain, rush at
back (See also COMEBACK.) answer, better, improve, rally, rebound, reciprocate, recover, recur, re-enter, remigrate, reply, resume, retaliate, retort, return, revive
before antecede, antedate, appear, face, forerun, precede, present, prevene
between alienate, estrange, interpose, separate
by accrue, accumulate, acquire, amass, enter, gain, get, inherit, obtain, receive, visit
-by-chance bastard
clean confess, tell
close approach, approximate
down alight, avalanche, collapse, depreciate, descend, deteriorate, discipline, dismount, land, rain, reverse, sink, swoop
down on discipline, oppose, punish, rebuke, reprimand, scold
down with catch, contact, sicken
face to face with See MEET.
first lead, open, precede, start
forth accede, appear, begin, break, emanate, emerge,

emerse, emit, forthgo, gush, issue, jet, spew, turn up
forward accede, appear, emerge, offer, reveal, splurge, volunteer
from accrue, derive, ensue, hail from, result
-hither alluring, enticing, invitation, summons
-hither look coquetry, flirtation, gaze, ogle
home to affect, impress, realize
in appear, arrive, crash, enter, immigrate, intrude, produce, win, yield
in for acquire, deserve, get, inherit, receive
in second fail, lose
into acquire, enter, get, incur, inherit, join
into being appear, begin, emerge, happen, spring, start
into bloom blossom, burst, flower
into money flourish, prosper, succeed, win
into one's own grow up, make it, mature, succeed
into possession acquire, inherit
into view appear, emerge, loom
into vogue make it, score, take
it accomplish, blab, divulge, lend, manage, reveal, speed, succeed
it over bully, deceive, dominate, trick
it strong exaggerate
near approach, approximate
of age majorize, mature
-of-will bastard, incomer
off conclusion, escape, evasion, event, excuse, finish, happen, harl, issue, materialize, occur, pass off, quit, result, succeed, take place, turn out, work
off it desist, quit, stop
off with flying colors triumph, win
on advance, allurement, appear, approach, attack, bait, begin, challenge, decoy, develop, dupe, enter, fare, find, flourish, hurry, impend, inducement, lure, manage, mature, meet, near, please, progress, prosper, seize, succeed
out act, appear, begin, bow,

bourgeon, burgeon, debut, egress, emanate, emerge, emerse, end, exit, extend, introduce, issue, outcome, protrude, result, reveal, surface, terminate
out of it cheer up, rally, recover, resuscitate
out on top hit, prevail, score, succeed, win
out with admit, bring out, confess, disclose, divulge, reveal, say, speak, spill, tell
over acquiesce, affect, agree, convert, cross, defeat, influence, surpass, visit
round accept, acquiesce, buy, change, convert, deceive, pacify, rally, recover, recur, relent
through perform, rise, score, succeed, survive, triumph, win
to acquiesce, agree, amount to, anchor, attain, betide, consent, equal, extend to, luff, match, recover, revive, total, undertake, yield
to a head climax, culminate, mature, suppurate
to anchor moor, settle
to an end cease, die, perish, stop
to an understanding agree
to a point converge, focus
to conclusion decide, end, finish
together accord, add, amass, assemble, bump, clash, collect, collide, combine, concur, convene, converge, couple, gather, herd, join, meet, muster, pacify
to grief fail, fall, founder, suffer
to hand appear, arrive, emerge, materialize, offer
to life awake(n), wake
to light develop, materialize, surface, turn up
to mind occur, strike
to nothing cease, disappoint, end, fail, fall through, fizzle out, perish, stop
to one's senses cool down, cool off, sober(down)
to pass befall, betide, break, eventuate, happen, light, occur, sort
to rest (a)light
to terms accord, acquiesce, agree, approve, assent, bargain, coincide, compose, consent, join, make up, pac-

ify, settle, submit, tryst, understand, yield
to the fore lead, precede, prevail, score, succeed, win
to the point be brief, particularize, speak
true occur, realize
under belong to, subvene
up appear, arise, ascend, ease off, emerge, occur, recover, rise, slacken, spring
up against encounter, engage, meet
up short halt
up to approach, equal, match, near, overtake, total
up with approach, catch, overtake, present, produce, propose, reach, supply
upon alight, attack, befall, chance upon, cross, discover, encounter, find, invade, invent, strike, surprise
what may certainly, earnestly, necessarily, no matter what, notwithstanding

COMEBACK answer, guineafowl, rally, recovery, renewal, repartee, retort, return, taunt

COMEDIAN actor, antic, areoi, arioi, buffa, buffo, buffoon, card, clown, comic, comoedus, dramatist, droll, farceur, funnyman, gagman, harlequin, humorist, jester, joker, merry andrew, pantaloon, patterer, stooge, thalia, wag, wit, zany

COMEDOWN bathos, descent, disappointment, drop, humiliation, letdown, setback

COMEDY burlesque, burletta, drama, exode, farce, harlequinade, humor, lazzo, revue, slapstick, temacha, travesty
character pantaloon
heroic nataka
improvised commedia dell' arte
masked scapino
muse thalia
pert. thalian
rustic atellan
symbol cap and bells, coxcomb, motley, sock

COMEDY OF ERRORS *author* shakespeare
character adriana, aegeon, aemilia, angelo, antipholus,

balthazar, courtezan, dromio, gaoler, luce, luciana, pinch, solinus
duke solinus
goldsmith angelo
merchant aegeon, balthazar
schoolmaster pinch
setting ephesus
twins antipholus, dromio
COMELY appropriate, attractive, beautiful, becoming, bonny, decorous, fair, farrant, fitting, formful, good, goodly, graceful, handsome, hend(e), likely, lovely, pert, pleasing, pretty, proper, queme, seemly, shapely, sightly, soncy, sonsie, sonsy, suitable, tall, tidy, venust, weme
name meaning al(1)an, allen
COMESTIBLES eatable, eats, esculent, fodder, food, forage, manna, provender, provisions, viands, victuals
COMET meteor(oid), shooting star
christmas kohoutek
discoverer barnard, biela, borelli, brooks, brorsen, coggia, darrest, de vico, donati, encke, faye, finlay, forges, giacobini, grigg, halley, holmes, kohoutek, kopff, olber, perrine, pons, schaumasse, swift, tempel, tuttle, westphal, winnecke, wolf
envelope coma
head, part coma, envelope, nucleus
name ikeye-seki, kohoutek, xappho
sword-shaped xiphias
tail streamer, train
COMEUPPANCE chastisement, deserts, due, punishment, rebuke, revenge
COMFIT candy, confection, praline, preserve, suckle, sweet(meat)
COMFORT aid, aise, alleviate, animate, assist, assuage, assure, bear up, bedquilt, bien etre, calm, cheer, cherish, condole, console, content, convenience, corroborate, delight, ease, encourage, enliven, euphoria, fortify, gladden, hearten, inspirit, light, mitigate, nepenthe, please, pleasure, prosperity, quilt, reassure,

refresh, rejoice, relief, relieve, repose, rest, restore, scarf, solace, soothe, sop, stay, succor, support, sustain, untrouble, visit, wellbeing
producing eudemonic
symbol old shoe
without desolate
COMFORTABLE acceptable, at ease, at home, bien, canny, cheerful, comfy, commodious, content(ed), convenient, cosh, cosy, couth(y), cozy, cushioned, easeful, easy, euphoric, feil, friendly, gratifying, heppen, homelike, homely, homey, in clover, lithe, lived-in, luxurious, peaceful, pleasing, prosperous, queme, quilt, relaxed, relaxing, reposeful, restful, rich, roomy, satisfied, scarf, snug, soft, soncy, sonsie, sonsy, sufficient, trig, voluptuous, warm, welcome, well off, wristlet
COMFORTER bedspread, blanket, cheerer, cover-(let), eider(down), nahum, pacifier, puff, quilt, scarf, tippet
COMFORTLESS cheerless, desolate, dreary, eithless, forlorn, sad, uncouth
COMFREY agueweed, assear, blackwort, boneset, colic-root, culver's root, daisy, eupatorium, knitback, slippery root, thoroughwort
wild dogbur
COMIC(AL) absurd, amuser, amusing, base, boor, bouffe, buffo, buffone, buffoon, burlesque, capricious, cartoon, clown, COMEDIAN, cut-up, diverting, droll, facetious, farcical, fool, funny, gagman, humorist, humorous, jester, jocular, laughable, low, ludicrous, merry(andrew), mockheroic, odd, pantaloon, queer, ridiculous, risible, splitting, stooge, strange, thalian, ticklish, wag, whimsical, wit, witty, zany
afterpiece exode
character ally slopper, billiken, harlequin, merry andrew, pantaloon

performance antimasque, burlesque, pantomime
strip cartoon, funnies, funny paper
strip box frame
COMICE pear
COMING advent, appearance, approach(ing), arrival, becoming, deserved, due, forward, future, imminence, imminent, impending, nearing, next, noil, overhanging, parousia, prospective, resulting, sprouting, successful, toward, venue
after later
and going fitful
before antevenient
in beginning, entrance, entry, income, revenue
into being aborning, birth, genesis, origin
-on compliant, yielding
out appearance, debut, egress, inauguration, issuance, issue, sortita
to adit
together congress, coupling, gathering, seance
COMITY affability, amenity, attention, civility, commerce, courtesy, dealings, gallantry, geniality, politeness, suavity, urbanity
COMMA point, virgule
COMMAND 3 bid, gee, haw, hup, law, saw 4 beck, boon, call, come, easy, fiat, halt, head, hest, hete, lead, mush, rule, stop, sway, toho, toll, warn, whoa, will, word, writ 5 beken, canon, check, edict, exact, force, hight, order, power, range, say-so, tower, ukase 6 beckon, behest, charge, coerce, compel, corner, decree, demand, direct, enjoin, giddap, govern, impose, manage, master, oblige, oracle, ordain, presto, ruling, steven 7 appoint, behight, bidding, concern, control, dictate, jussion, jussive, mandate, mastery, officer, possess, precept, require, skipper, statute, summons 8 biddance, coercion, dominate, domineer, instruct, restrain, subpoena 9 about face, authority, direction, mandament, ordinance, pre-

scribe, prescript 10 ascendancy, injunction, invitation, regulation 11 appointment, call to order, instruction 12 jurisdiction
allied aef, eto, nato, shaef
military echelon
module columbia
respect awe
supreme hegemony
COMMANDANT See COMMANDER.
COMMANDEER appropriate, attach, compel, enjoin, enroll, impress, press
COMMANDER adalid, ag(h)a, alcaide, alcayde, caid, captain, chief(tain), cid, commendador, commandant, decarch, dekarch, drungar, duke, dux, emeer, emir, emperor, general, head(man), khalifa, killadar, leader, lord, marshal, master, navarch, officer, phylarch, rammer, risaldar, seraskar, sirdar, skipper, tartan, tetrarch, warden
-in-chief admiral, field marshal, general, president, sirdar, tartan
of 20 men vintener
of 1,000 men chiliarch
supreme generalissimo
COMMANDING arresting, authoritative, dominant, imperant, imperial, imposing, lofty, mandatory, paramount, striking
COMMANDMENT bod(e)-word, decree, dictate, edict, law, mitzvah, order, precept, rule
10 decalog(ue)
COMMANDO fedayee, guerilla, raider, ranger, soldier
COMME IL FAUT conventional, decent, decorous, demure, fit(ting), formal, meet, nice, proper, seemly
COMMEMORATE feast, honor, remember, remene
COMMEMORATION award, celebration, encaenia, jubilee, medal, memorial, mention, plaque, service
COMMENCE arise, arrame, arrange, begin, bring, embark, establish, file, found, inaugurate, incept, initiate, launch, move, open, set out, spring, start, streak, streek
COMMENCEMENT bacca-

laureate, beginning, ceremony, entrance, graduation, kick off, novitiate, onset, opening, origin, outset, source
COMMEND acclaim, adorn, advocate, alose, applaud, approve, beken, bequeath, bespeak, bestow, beteach, boost, celebrate, commit, compliment, confide, deliver, entrust, extol, grace, greeting, intrust, ken, laud, pat, praise
highly eulogize, extole, panegyrize
publicly preconize
to favor ingratiate
COMMENDABLE creditable, exemplary, expedient, good, laudable, lowable, praiseworthy, worthy
COMMENDATION applause, approval, aproof, blurb, boost, build-up, citation, compliment, greeting, laud, plug, praise, puff, vassalage
effusive palaver, slaver
COMMENSAL epizoon, messmate
COMMENSALISM communism, symphily, synoecy
COMMENSURATE adequate, answerable, appropriate, comparable, compensating, corresponding, enough, equal, even, offsetting, proportionate, relevant, sufficient, tolerable
COMMENT addendum, annotate, annotation, aside, barb, buzz, caption, construe, criticism, critique, descant, dictum, dilate, discuss, elucidation, exegesis, explain, explanation, explicate, expound, gibe, gloss, gloze, gossip, interpret (ation), jibe, kib(b)itz, mention, notate, note, obiter, observation, observe, postil, reference, remark, report, review, rubric, scance, scholion, speech, state(ment), talk, word
adverse animadversion
adversely harrumph
marginal scholium
COMMENTARY account, analysis, annotation, criticism, critique, editorial, exegesis, footnote, gloss(ary), memoir, memoranda, note,

notice, observation, postils, remark(s), report, review, satire, treatise, write-up
COMMENTATOR analyst, annotator, columnist, critic, descanter, discourser, editor, essayist, expositor, expounder, glossarist, glossator, glossist, glossographer, glozer, monographer, news analyst, observer, publicist, reviewer, scholiast
COMMERCE barter, business, change, commune, communication, conversation, correspondence, dealing(s), exchange, free enterprise, free trade, industry, interchange, intercourse, market, mercature, merchandising, merchantry, private enterprise, trade, traffic, truck
game accomodez-moi, help-me-neighbor
god hermes, mercury, teutates
term coemption, emption, preemption, purchasing power, refusal
COMMERCIAL advertisement, announcement, break, industrial, mercantile, merchant, mercurial, retail, spot, store, trading, trady, wholesale
COMMINATE anathematize, curse, denounce, threaten
COMMINGLE amalgamate, blend, coalesce, combine, comeddle, cominge, embroil, fuse, immix, join, merge, mingle, mix, unite
COMMINUTE crush, grind, mill, pound, powder, pulverize, smash, triturate
COMMISERATION compassion, condolence, empathy, humanity, mercy, pity, ruth, sympathy, yearning
COMMISSARY canteen, market, ministry, post exchange, store, supplier, sutlery
COMMISSION accredit(ation), agency, agio, allot, allowance, appoint (ment), assign(ment), authority, authorization, authorize, bid, board, bonus, brevet, brokerage, charge, charter, command, commit (ment), consign, convey (ance), delegate, delega-

tion, demand, deputation, depute, deputize, detach, detail, diploma, dividend, elect, employ(ment), empower, encharge, engage, enjoin, enlist, enroll(ment), entrust, errand, establish, exequatur, fee, gosplan, hire, indenture, install, instruction, invest, mandate, mission, office, ordain, payola, percentage, performance, permit, perpetration, post, power of attorney, procuration, proxy, rake-off, recompense, repair, send, share, task, trust, warrant
out of broken, disabled, ill, laid up, sick

COMMISSIONER agent, arrayer, commisar, delegate, envoy, justice of the peace, officer, official, pristav, pristaw, trier

COMMISSURE joint, junction, seam, sitre, suture

COMMIT accomplish, achieve, allot, arrest, arret(te), assign, behight, bequeath, beteach, command, commend, commission, confide, consign, decide, dedicate, delegate, deliver, deposit, engage, entrust, give, imprison, institutionalize, intrust, jug, lag, move, perform, perpetrate, promise, refer, relegate, remand, remove, send(up), shift, stow, take, teach, transfer, transport, trust, wreak
burglary rob, steal, thieve
crime break the law, transgress
oneself cross the rubicon
to memory con, learn, memorize

COMMITMENT agreement, cast, confinement, consignment, constraint, contract, engagement, imprisonment, mittimus, pledge, remand, restraint, undertaking, warrant

COMMITTAL burial, consignment, engagement, interment

COMMITTEE bench, board, body, bureau, cabinet, chamber, council, court, delegacy, executors, group, guardians, junta, jury, mis-

sion, soviet, staff, syndicate, table

COMMODE bawd, chest(of drawers), cupboard, fontange, procuress, sink, stool, washstand

COMMODIOUS ample, beneficial, big, broad, capacious, cavernous, comfortable, deep, fit, great, large, roomy, spacious, suitable, useful, wide

COMMODITY article, drug, export, feature, goods, item, leader, merchandise, object, product, shipment, special, staple, stuff, thing, vendible, ware
equivalence parity
market term cash grain, new crop, old crop, scalper, pit, trader
principal staple

COMMON (See also COMMONS.) abundant, average, banal, base, bourgeois, brief, cheap, coarse, colloquial, current, customary, demoid, ejido, familiar, famous, frequent, general, generic, green, grimy, gross, habitual, homely, homespun, ignoble, inferior, joint, low, mean, mediocre, merged, middling, mutual, natural, noa, nondescript, often, ordinary, ornery, paltry, pandemic, philistine, plain, pleb(eian), plentiful, popular, prevalent, prost, prosy, public, raffish, reciprocal, recurrent, regular, rife, shared, simple, slack, stale, trifling, trite, trivial, universal, usual, vernacular, vile, villain, vulgar
comb. ceno, coeno, hono, hyo, pre
effort cooperation, teamwork
fellow bourgeois, carl, ruck
fund pool, pot, purse
law tradition
man bourgeoisie, plebeian, proletariat
market euromart
market originator monnet
people rabble, ruck, vulgus
ruck rabble
sense acumen, discretion, gumption, judgment, marbles, nous, practical(ity), sachel, salt, wisdom, wit
sort rabble, ruck
stock blue chip, securities

COMMONER burgess, ceorl, citizen, lawyer, participator, pleb(e), proletarian, routuier, simple, student

COMMONLY familiarly, normally, often, plainly
accepted popular, vulgate
thought putative, reputed

COMMONPLACE average, banal(ity), bromide, cliche, colorless, daily, dully, everyday, garden, hackneyed, homely, humdrum, inanity, mediocre, memo(randum), middling, modern, ordinary, plain, platitude, plebeian, prosaic, prose, prosy, rumtytoo, stale, tedious, tripy, trite, trivial, truism, unimportant, usual, wellknown, worn

COMMONS commonality, dining hall, fare, food, green, grounds, hall, keep, pabulum, park, provisions, quarters, rations, square

COMMONWEAL republic, welfare

COMMONWEALTH body politic, citizenry, commonty, community, country, estate, polis, population, public, republic, res publica, society, state
coins breeches money
country australia, canada, new zealand, rhodesia
idea utopia

COMMORANT abiding, dweller, dwelling, inhabitant, resident, residing, sojourner

COMMOTION ado, agitation, alarm, blather, bluster, bree, bustle, cathro(w), catouse, chop, clatter, concussion, confusion, convulsion, din, disorder, dust, eruption, excitement, ferment, fissle, fistle, flare, flurry, fracas, fray, furor(e), fuss, heat, hoopla, hubbub, hurlyburly, hurry, kippage, mutiny, perturbation, pother, riot, ruckus, ruffle, rummage, rumpus, shindig, shindy, shtuss, splore, squall, stir, storm, stour, stramash, to-do, toss, tummel, tumult, turbulence, turmoil, unrest, upheaval, uprising, uproar, upstir, welter, whirl

COMMUNE advise, area,

commerce, communicate, communior, community, confer, consult, conversation, converse, dealings, debate, deme, discuss, district, divulge, impart, kibbutz, kol(k)hoz, mir, negotiate, parley, realm, reveal, share, society, soil, speak, stanitza, talk, township, traffic, treat

COMMUNICABLE catching, contagious, diffusible, frank, infectious, sociable

COMMUNICANT adorer, celebrant, churchgoer, congregation, idolater, worshiper

COMMUNICATE acquaint, address, apprise, break, breathe, carry, catch, cede, celebrate, converse, convey, correspond, declare, dictate, disclose, divulge, give, impart, infect, inform, intimate, narrate, phone, reach, relate, relinquish, render, reveal, say, show, sign(ify), speak, tell, yield

COMMUNICATION address, association, cable, call, card, comether, commerce, communion, congress, conversation, converse, correspondence, exchange, information, intelligence, intercourse, language, letter, message, missive, news, note, report, speech, statement, telegram, tidings, traffic, transfer, wire
boring bumf
comb. tele
divine oracle
friendly comether
means drum, flag, letter, mail, memo, movies, note, phone, post, radio, smoke, speech, telegraph, telephone, television, tomtom
occult psychomancy
satellite relay
stoppage blackout

COMMUNION accord, affinity, aspheterism, church, communication, concord, converse, creed, cult, ecstasy, empathy, eucharist, faith, homily, host, interchange, intimacy, lord's supper, mass, nachtmaal, nagmaal, persuasion, rapport, rapture, religion,

sacrament, sect, sympathy, transport, unity, viaticum
anthem introit
cake wafer
case burse
cloth corporal(e), dominical
consecrated food hagia, obley, wafer, wine
cup ama
plate paten
service eucharist, mass
table altar
table screen altar piece, reredos
vessel pyx
wafer obley

COMMUNIQUE bulletin, message, news, release, story

COMMUNISM aspheterism, babouvism, collectivism, leninism, sovietism
father of lenin
philosopher of marx

COMMUNIST anarchist, bolshevik, bolshevist, card-carrier, collectivist, comrade, nihilist, pink, red, socialist, soviet
community brook farm
council soviet
dissenter djilas, pasternak, solzhenitsyn
group cell
newspaper daily worker, isvestia, pravda
organization cominform
promotion agitprop
sympathizer fellow-traveler
youth organization comsomol, komsomol

COMMUNITY affinity, anthill, association, body, bratsvo, brotherhood, burg, cenoby, city, clan, colony, commonty, commonwealth, convent, dessa, district, family, firca, group, hamlet, kingdom, kinship, likeness, mark, mir, nation, order, partnership, polity, population, province, public, society, sodality, state, thorp, town(ship), village
biotic biome
center town hall
character ethos
comb. socio
environmental biome
gathering bee
isolated colony
native brolga
of interests accord

plant alterne, enclave, forest, heath
religious cenobium, cenoby, convent, lamasery, monastery, sangha
village ikhwan

COMMUTE alter, change, compensate, convert, exchange, interchange, substitute, swap, switch, travel

COMORO *island* anjouan, mayotte, moheli
islands capital moroni

COMOSE brush, hairy, tuft

COMPACT accord, agreement, alliance, arrangement, bargain, beetle, bind, bond, brief, capsule, cartel, case, close, compendious, compress, concentrate, concise, concord, condense(d), contract, convention, covenant, covin, crowded, deal, dense, dicker, etui, fast, federation, firm, gross, hard, heavyset, horny, intente, knit, league, mise, pack(ed), pact, paction, pithy, plot, polymicrian, press, promise, protocol, sententious, serried, short, shrink, snug, solid, spiss(y), stipulation, stocky, succinct, terse, thick, tie, tight, treaty, trig, trim, true, understanding, unify, united, vanity, whizz
private covin

COMPACTNESS body, density, intensity, solidity, unity

COMPANION achates, ally, alter ego, amigo, associate, attend(ant), beaupere, billy, brolga, buddy, butty, cavalier, chaperon, chum, cobber, cohort, comes, compadre, compeer, comrade, confidant, consort, crony, cully, double, escort, fellow, fere, friend, gossip, husband, kimmer, marrow, match, mate(y), maugh, pal, partner, peer, playfere, second self, shadow, sociate, sport, spouse, steady, synodite, twin, wife
at table convictor, convive
drinking aleknight, cupmate
star comes

COMPANIONSHIP affinity, company, fere, society

COMPANIONWAY stair(s)

COMPANY aerie, agency, alliance, assemblage, assembly, association, band, battery, bevy, body, business, camp, caravan, cast, cie, circle, clique, club, college, comrade, concern, concourse, consort, corps, cortege, coterie, coven, crew, crowd, crue, cry, enterprise, fere, firm, flack, flote, gang, gathering, get, GROUP, guest, herd, horde, host, league, line, mob, party, performers, phalanx, posse, push, retinue, rout, set, society, soldiers, sort, squad, suite, team, thiasus, troop, troupe, turm(a)

business cartel, cie, concern, consortium, corporation, firm, house, monopoly, partnership, pool, societe, syndicate, trust

combination cartel, trust

exclusive clique, crowd

suitable besort

COMPARABLE akin, analogical, analogous, commensurate, equipollent, equivalent, like, parallel, proportionate, relative, same, similar, uniform

COMPARATIVE equal, like, parallel, relative, similar, than

comb. est, ier, ior

COMPARE allude, analogize, apply, appose, approach, assimilate, balance, bracket, collate, confer, confront, contrast, equal, equate, estimate, even, examine, juxtapose, liken, match, measure, oppose, parallel(ize), parify, relate, resemble, scale, semble, similize, size, tally, test, tival, vie, weigh

notes confer

COMPARISON analogy, antithesis, assimilation, balance, contrast, discrement, dissimile, likeness, likening, parable, parallel(ism), resemblance, similarity, simile, similitude

beyond superior, supreme, unique

by contraries dissimile

COMPARTMENT abacus, alcove, apartment, area, ballonet, bay, bin, boot, booth, box, branch, bunker, cab(in), cabinet, capsule, carol, cavity, cell(ule),

chamber, corner, crib, crypt, cubicle, division, flue, hatch, hold, hole, hollow, hopper, hutch, manger, muffle, niche, nook, part, pew, pod, section, slot, smoker, stall, steerage, vault, volet, well

coal bunker

granary grintern

sleeping berth, cubicle, roomette

COMPASS accomplish, achieve, ambit, area, attain, bearing, boundary, bounds, caliber, calibre, cincture, circle, circuit, circumference, circumscribe, complete, degree, diacle, dial, distance, effect, embrase, encircle, enclose, environ, extent, field, fulfill, gain, gamut, gyro, horizon, imagine, ken, limit, needle, orbit, perimeter, periphery, practice, purview, radius, range, reach, room, scope, sphere, spread, surround, sweep, tour, trammel, volume

about protect, surround

beam trammel(head)

box binnacle, kettle

brick adobe

card pedrero, perrier, rose

case binnacle

corrector compensator, magnet

direction bearing, course

dummy pelorus

horizontal circumferenter

kind beam, gyro, mariner's, solar, sun, vernier

mariner's dial

needle end lily

part airt(h), gimbal, needle, pen, rhumb, trammel, vane

-plant pilotweed, prairie lotus, rosinweed, wyethia

pocket diacle

point airt(h), azimuth, rhumb

quarter plage

ring gimbal

ship's cabin telltall

sight vane

stand binnacle

suspender gimbal, vane

COMPASSION charity, clemency, commiseration, condolence, empathy, forgiveness, grace, heart, humanity, karuna, kindness,

lenity, love, mercy, misericordia, piety, pity, rachmones, remorse, rue, ruth, sympathy, tenderness

COMPASSIONATE clement, gentle, gracious, human, kind, pietoso, piteous, pitiful, ruth, soft, sympathetic, tender

name meaning ruth

COMPATIBLE accordant, agreeable, akin, appropriate, artistic, congenial, congruous, consistent, consonant, harmonious, harmonizing, suitable, sympathetic

COMPATRIOT fellow, native, synethnic

COMPEER comrade, equal

COMPEL actuate, bring, cause, coact, coerce, command, constrain, dragoon, drive, enforce, enjoin, exact, extort, force, gar, impel, incite, make, motivate, move, necessitate, oblige, obsess, order, press, require, shove, urge

accounting bring to book

by threat blackjack, blackmail, menace

COMPELLING compulsory, congent, forceful, necessary, stringent, strong, telling, urgent

COMPENDIOUS abridged, brief, compact, concise, condensed, direct, laconic, pithy, short, succinct, summarized, summary

COMPENDIUM abbreviation, abridgment, abstract, apercu, breviary, brief, catalog(ue), contraction, digest, economy, epitome, landskip, lexicon, list, medulla, outline, pandect, precis, reparation, short cut, sketch, summary, survey, syllabus, sylloge, synopsis, talmud

COMPENSATE abrogate, atone, balance, cancel, commute, correct, counterbalance, countervail, cover, equalize, indemnify, jibe, make amends, make good, offset, pay, recompense, recoup, redeem, redress, remunerate, repay, reprise, requite, restore, return, reward, satisfy, square, tally

COMPENSATION adjustment, amends, angild, atonement, balm, bonus, bot, breakage, consideration, correction, counterpoise, damages, earnings, gratuity, guerdon, hire, honorarium, income, indemnification, indemnity, interest, meed, offset, pay(ment), penalty, pittance, price, quittance, recompense, redress, remuneration, reparation, requital, requitment, restitution, retribution, return, reward, salary, salvage, satisfaction, setoff, settlement, solatium, stipend, toll, utu, wages
for murder manbot(e)
small pittance
COMPETE clash, contend, contest, cope(with), emulate, fight, kemp, match, outvie, pit, race, rival, strive, struggle, tend, vie
with buck
COMPETENCE ability, adequacy, capability, capacity, faculty, income, plenty, qualification, skill, suitability, supply
COMPETENT able(bodied), adept, adequate, apt, can, capable, capax, competible, effectual, efficient, enough, expert, fit, good, lawful, meet, needful, plenty, proficient, qualified, requisite, sane, skilled, skillful, smart, sufficient, suitable, tight, worthy
COMPETITION campaign, concours, conflict, confusion, contest, emulation, feis, game, heat, jump, kemp, match, prize, rat race, rivalry, strife, trial, wager
retailer's price war
COMPETITOR antagonist, athlete, candidate, contender, contestant, corrival, emulator, enemy, entrant, favorite, fighter, foe, match, opponent, player, rival, wager
COMPILATION ana, anthology, book, casebook, cento, code, collection, compilement, digest, directory, gathering

COMPILE add, amass, anthologize, arrange, assemble, build, classify, collate, collect, compose, construct, edit, file, gather, group, prepare, select, unite, write
COMPILER author, editor, gatherer, glossist
COMPLACENT assured, bovine, calm, complaisant, compliable, compliant, confident, considerate, content, ego(t)istic, fat, fatuous, kind, lenient, obsequious, polite, priggish, proud, self-satisfied, smug, vain (glorious)
COMPLAIN ail, beef, bellyache, bewail, bitch, bleat, brawl, carp, cavil, charge, chunner, clamor, cotter, crab, crake, create, criticize, croak, cry, deplore, fret, fuss, grieve, gripe, grizzle, grouch, grouse, growl, grumble, grunt, grutch, holler, howl, inveigh, keen, kick, kvetch(er), kvetcherken, lament, moan, moot, murmer, mutter, nag, peenge, pinge, protest, pule, rage, rail, remonstrate, repine, scream, snivel, squawk, storm, take on, tetter, threap, thrope, twank, wail, whimper, whine, yammer, yell, yelp, yip, yirn
COMPLAINING doleance, expostulative, grumbly, latrant, petulant, plaintive, puly, querent, querolous, whining, whiny
COMPLAINT affection, ailment, beef, bellyache, bitch(ing), cavil, clamor, cry, declaration, disease, disorder, fuss, gravemen, grievance, gripe, grouch, grouse, growl, grudge, grumble, grumbling, holler, howl, illness, indignation, indignity, jeremiad, kick, lament, malady, moan, molligrant, murmur(ing), plaint, protest(ation), quarrel, rap, remonstrance, repine, round robin, rumble, squawk(ing), virus, wail, whine
COMPLAISANCE affability, amenity, civility, contentment, facility, smugness, suavity, urbanity

COMPLAISANT acquiescent, affable, amiable, bland, bon, bonair, buxom, civil, complacent, compliant, diplomatic, easy, genial, good(natured), gracious, indulgent, kind, lenient, obliging, pleasant, pleasing, polite, smooth, smug, suave, submissive, supple, urbane
COMPLEMENT accessory, adjunct, alexin, allowance, amount, completion, correlate, crew, force, gang, obverse, parallel, personnel, supplement, tally
military strength
of parallelogram gnomon
COMPLETE 3 all, cap. end, tot 4 done, do up, fair, fine, full, just, seal, sole 5 blank, close, crown, gross, large, mop up, plain, plumb, pucca, pukka, quite, ripen, round, sheer, siker, sound, stark, total, utter, whole 6 clinch, deadly, effect, eke out, entire, fill in, finish, global, intact, make up, plenal, proper, refill, single, strict, top off, wind up 7 achieve, clean up, confirm, execute, fill out, fulfill, perfect, perform, plenary, realize, replete 8 absolute, blinking, button up, carry out, circular, conclude, finalize, finished, infinite, integral, make good, outright, overcome, piece out, thorough 9 out and out, replenish, terminate, versatile 10 accomplish, consummate, exhaustive 11 acatalectic, unqualified, well-rounded 12 carry through
comb. hol, tele(o)
COMPLETELY all(out), bag and baggage, bare, blankly, cap-a-pie, clean, close, directly, entire(ly), fair, flat, from a to z, fully, gainly, heart and soul, in tote, jam, outright, plumb, purely, quite, root and branch, sheer, slam, slap, smack, spang, thoroughly, throughout, totally, to the limit, utmost, utter, whole hog, wholly

comb. cat(a), cath, dia, kat(a), kath

or not at all all-or-nothing

COMPLETENESS allness, depth, fullness, integrity, ripeness

COMPLETION accomplishment, achievement, close, conclusion, consummation, development, end (ing), finish, fulfillment, integration, maturation, maturity, perfection, performance, realization, ripeness, termination

comb. teleuto

COMPLEX adduct, balled up, being, bias, biome, blended, building, complicated, composite, compound, daedal, economy, equation, ethos, field, fouled up, hard, intricate, involute, involutional, involved, knotty, manifold, maze, mazy, merged, mingled, mixed, network, organism, samkara, samskara, scheme, sinuous, syndrome, synthesis, system, tangled, thorny, twisted, whole

of communities biome

progressively anamorphic, anamorphous, developing, evolving

psychological electra, inferiority, mania, nuclear, oedipus, persecution, superiority

COMPLEXION aspect, blee, cast, character, color(ing), disposition, guise, hue, humor, individuality, kind, look, mood, nature, personality, rud(d), temper (ament), tenor, tinge, tint, vein

having dark melanochrous

light blonde

poor dyschroa

red-brown aithochroi

COMPLIANCE acquiescence, adherence, agreeableness, amiability, assent, cession, civility, complaisance, conformity, consent, decency, docility, graciousness, harmony, indulgence, keeping, kindness, morigeration, munich, obedience, obsequy, resignation, submission, yielding

COMPLIANT acquiescent, ameable, available, buxom,

coming on, commode, docile, ductile, dutiful, easy, facile, indulgent, obedient, oily, passive, pleasant, pliable, pliant, resigned, soft, subdued, submissive, supple, tame, towardly, tractable, willing, yielding

COMPLICATE ball up, befoul, bewilder, embrangle, embroil, foul(up), intort, intricate, intrigue, involve, perplex, puzzle, snag, snarl, tangle, worsen

COMPLICATED abstruse, complex, crabbed, cramp, difficult, disordered, entangled, gordian, hard, heavy, intricate, involved, knotted, knotty, obscure, perplexing, prolix, puzzling, recondite, snarled, steep, tangled, tough

COMPLICATION intrigue, knot, node, nodui, nodus, plot, predicament, problem, snarl

COMPLICITY collusion, connivance, guilt(iness), intrigue, involvement

COMPLIMENT acclaim, adulate, adulation, applaud, approval, approve, blandish, blarney, bouquet, butter up, commend, congratulate, douceur, encomium, eulogize, eulogy, extol, flatter(y), flummery, gift, laud, panegyric, posy, praise, saloam, salute, tradelast, tribute

COMPLIMENTARY adulatory, fortuitous, free, gratis, gratuity

COMPLINE apodeipnon, service

COMPLOT cabal, confederacy, conspiracy, conspire, crowd, frame-up, intrigue, machination, throng

COMPLY abide, accede, accept, accord, acquiesce, adapt, agree, apply, assent, cede, conform, consent, embrace, obey, observe, submit, yield

with obey, satisfy

COMPONENT bit, conjunct, constitutent, detail, element, factor, form, given, ingredient, integral, item, key, member, part(icular), piece, portion, simple, unit

chief basis, principle

COMPORT accord, acquit, act, agree, bear, behave, behavior, brook, carry, conduct, conform, demean, deport, dish, dovetail, endure, harmonize, hold, involve, jibe, keep, quit, square, suit, tally

COMPORTMENT accordance, bearing, behavior, conduct, dealing, demeanor

COMPOSE abate, accomodate, accord, adapt, adjust, allay, arrange, assemble, author, breve, brief, calm, compile, comprise, concoct, conform, consist of, constitute, construct, couch, create, design, dight, dite, draft, draught, fashion, form, frame, graith, harmonize, indite, instrument(ate), lull, make, melodize, orchestrate, order, originate, pen, piece, prepare, produce, quiet, reconcile, redact, regulate, score, set(type), settle, soothe, steady, stick, still, transcribe, transpose, typeset, write

COMPOSED balanced, calm, collected, cool, decorous, demure, entente, imperturbable, level-headed, nonchalant, placid, quiet, sedate, serene, set, settled, smooth, sober, staid, still, temperate, tranquil, unruffled, written, wrote

COMPOSER arranger, artist, author, ballader, balladmaker, bard, conteur, contrapuntist, creator, elegist, harmonist, harmonizer, hymnist, hymnographer, hymnologist, lyrist, madrigalist, maestro, melodist, melodizer, monodist, musician, odist, orchestrator, penman, phantast, poet, scorer, tone poet, tunesmith, typesetter, writer

famous bach, beethoven, brahms, gershwin, handel, haydn, ives, mahler, mozart, palestrina, prokofieff, ravel, schubert, schumann, shostakovich, strauss, stravinsky, vivaldi, wagner

COMPOSITE complex, composed, concrete, hybrid, integral, mixture, motley

COMPOSITION accord,

acrostic, antiphony, argument, arrangement, article, atmosphere, atonement, badigeon, balance, book, burlesque, canon, cento, collage, compound, consistency, constitution, construction, contents, design, diction, display, dissertation, dite, ditty, drama, embodiment, epistle, essay, etude, eulogy, exercise, filler, formation, fugue, getup, grouping, haikai, lesson, maggot, make-up, manuscript, mass, misture, monody, nome, opus, organization, picture, piece, presswork, product(ion), rondo, scene, sheetwork, sonata, structure, suite, synaeresis, synizesis, synthesis, technique, theme, thesis, tone, treatment, typesetting, vulgus, work, writing

choral anthem, cantata, motet, oratorio

dramatic play

for 2 duet(ino), duetto

humerous burla

imperfect sooterkin

impromptu maggot

instrumental air, berceuse, canzone, concerto, fancy, fantasia, fugue, gato, ground, nome, overture, prelude, rhapsody, rondo, sketch, sonata, symphony, tiento

literary article, book, cento, comedy, debat, drama, essay, novel, ode, piece, play, poem, review, satire, sketch, theme, thesis, tragedy, treatise

magic hellbroth

metrical ode, poem, poesy, rhyme, rime, verse

mournful dirge

musical See MUSICAL COMPOSITION.

9 instruments nonet

pert. synthesis, synthetic

plastic cement

poetic ballad, elegy, epic, lyric, POEM, ode, stanza, verse

rubber gum

rules rhetoric

sacred anthem, cantata, chorale, hymn, motet, oratorio

¾-time valse, waltz

vocal anthem, aria, canon, solo, song

COMPOSITOR adman, bankman, caseman, printer, setter, stoneman, typo

COMPOST compote, compound, dressing, fertilizer, manure, mingle, mixture, pelf, plaster, soil, stucco

COMPOSURE aplomb, balance, bond, calm(ness), constraint, cool(headed)ness, countenance, equanimity, imperturbation, mien, nonchalance, peace(fulness), phlegm, placidity, poise, posture, quiet(ude), repose, reserve, restraint, sangfroid, savoirfaire, serenity, tranquility, union

COMPOUND adjust, admixture, alloy, amalgam, blend, combination, combine, complex, compose, composite, composition, compost, constitute, create, element, enclosure, farrago, fill, fuse, increase, join, jumble, merge, mingle, mix(ture), multiply, prepare, settle, synthesis, temper, union, unite

adhesive salve

alcohol-soluble alkaloid

aliphatic olefin, paraffin

alkaline soda

ammonia amine

amorphous phenose

antihistamin phenylephrine

aromatic anthracene, benzene, napthalene

astringent boral

basic part gravamen

binary alkide

chemical amid(e), amin(e), anilide, azin(e), azola, borid(e), ceria, chloride, diazo, ester, imid(e), imin(e), inosite, leucine, metamer, osone, oxide, pyran

chemical-warfare phosgene

crystalline aciculite, aconite, aikinite, alban, aloin, aloric, amarine, anemonin, anisil, anonal, apothesine, asarite, asaron, asparagine, atophan, atropine, benzoin, biurea, biuret, bixin, camphor, capsaicin, crocetin, cyanamide, epinine, ergotamine, furil, furoin, gontisin, gossypol, haemin,

idrialin, imidazole, indigo white, indirubin, indole, indoxyl, inositol, iodoform, iodol, isatide, isatin, juglone, morin, murexide, oscin(e), quinone, ricinine, rotlerin, serine, tanghinin, tariric, tartramide, taurine, terpinol, theobromine, thialdine, thiamine, thymine, tolan, urazine, urethan

cyclic furomonazole

dual bonded triene

"e" cortisone

"f" hydrocortisone

fatty phosphatide

for See SUBSTITUTE.

hypnotic trional

hypothetical julol(e)

interest anatocism

isomeric biphenol, thioxene

medicinal pamaquine

oily saponule

organic alkaloid, amid(e), amin(e), enol, ester, ketol(e), ketone

poisonous arsenate, cacodyl, glycine, helenin, muscarine, stibine, toxin

synthetic androgen, sorbitan

word bahuvrihi

yellow anisil, galangin

COMPOUNDER jacobite

COMPREHEND apperceive, appreciate, attain, compass, comprise, conceive, conclude, contain, cover, digest, discern, embody, embrace, enclose, envolve, fathom, follow, get, grasp, hold, imagine, implicate, imply, include, know, latch(on), perceive, pierce, savvy, see, seize, sense, subsume, swallow, take, trammel, twig, understand

inability acatalepsia, asemia

COMPREHENSIBLE accountable, apprehensible, cognizable, conceivable, discoverable, exoteric(al), explicable, fathomable, include, intelligible, knowable, penetrable, scrutable, sensible, understandable

COMPREHENSION appreception, erudition, grasp, hold, insight, intellect, intelligence, knowing, knowledge, learning, noesis, savvy, science, sense, synecdoche, understanding, uptake

COMPREHENSIVE across-the-board, all-embracing, all-inclusive, all-round, big, bird's-eye, blanket, broad, capable, capacious, catholic, complete, comprising, concise, embracing, encompassing, encyclopedic, exhaustive, full, general, generic, generous, global, grand, large, omnibus, over-all, panoramic, scopic, spacious, sweeping, thorough, universal, wide

COMPRESS abbreviate, abridge, astringe, bale, bandage, bind, bolster, bundle, cling, cockle, compact, concentrate, condense, consolidate, constrict, constringe, contract, cram, cramp, crowd, crush, curtail, decrease, deflate, densen, densify, digest, draw(in), dressing, embrace, firm, gather, knit, narrow, nip, pad, pinch, pledget, preparation, press, pucker, ram down, reduce, repress, restrain, shorten, shrink, smash, solidify, squeeze, squinch, strain, stupe, suppress, syncopate, tamp, throng, tie, tighten, wrap, wrinkle
medical bandage, bolster, pledget

COMPRESSION condensation, constraint, crush, pressure, squeeze, thlipsis

COMPRISE comprehend, conceive, confer, consist of, constitute, contain, cover, embody, embrace, enclose, hold, imply, include, involve, muster, seize, subsume

COMPROMISE adjust (ment), arrangement, commit, compound, concession, contemperation, discredit, endanger, fine, medium, meet halfway, settle(ment), surrender, temper, trim
opposed to bullheaded, intransigent

COMPT neat, polished, spruce, tidy

COMPULSION coaction, coercion, constraint, distress, drive, duress, enforcement, exaction, exigency, force, impulse, mania, necessity, need, obligation, obsession, perforce, press(ure), requirement, restraint, stress, urge

COMPULSIVE forced, involuntary, irresistible, obsessive, obtrusive

COMPULSORY binding, bounden, coactive, coercive, compelling, compulsive, driving, enforced, forcible, imperative, imperious, importunate, irresistible, mandatory, necessary, obligatory, peremptory, requisite, spontaneous

COMPUNCTION conscience, contrition, demur, guilt, heart, pangs, penitence, qualm(s), regret, reluctance, remorse, repentance, rue, scruple, shame, sorriness, sorrow

COMPUTATION account, calculation, estimate, estimation, numeration, reckoning

COMPUTE account, add, assess, balance, calculate, capitalize, cast, cipher, count, estimate, figure, ga(u)ge, item, number, rate, reckon, sum, tally, total, value

COMPUTER abacus, eniac, ibm, quipu, slide rule, univac
billionth of second nanosecond
circuit channel
data input, printout, readout
data holder memory, storage
date by pair up
digital eniac
information data, input, output, readout
information unit byte
inventor babbage
kind analog, arithmograph, arithmometer, audrey, binac, binary, digital, eniac, eniad, erma, ibm, ida, idp, oarac, raydac, teleplotter, telereader, tristimulus, univac
language algol, basic, fortran
plan program
principle binary
product printout
program software
program symbol block
symbol system code
term access time, binary, bit, data, feedback, hardware, input, message, noise, play, punch-card, quantity, signals, software, sound-level
unit adder, analyzer, bit, byte, coder, collator, decoder, detector, differential, divider, fosdic, integrator, multiplier, receptor, relay, transmitter

COMRADE ally, aim, associate, attendant, beaupere, bedfellow, bedmate, billikin, billy(can), brother, buddy, bunkie, camarade, chamberfellow, chum, classmate, colleague, comate, communist, comorado, companion, company, compeer, confederate, confrere, consociate, consort, convive, copartner, copemate, cousin, crony, engidu, fellow, frater, friend, hearty, kamerade, leftist, mate, messmate, paisano, pal, pard(ner), partner, peer, playfellow, playmate, roommate, shipmate, sidekick, teammate, tovarich, workfellow, yokefellow, yokemate

COMUS *god of* joy, mirth
mother circe

CON against, anti, cheat, convict, cunne, deceive, direct, examine, guide, inspect, knock, know, lead, learn, look, memorize, opposed, peruse, pore, rap, read, regard, scan, shark, steer, strike, study, swindle, think, trick, understand, versus
-man sharper, swindler

CONATION, CONATUS effort, endeavor, exertion, impulse, inclination, striving, tendency, unrest, volition, will

CONCATENATE articulate, chain, combine, connect, fuse, integrate, join, link, merge, organize, relate, unite

CONCAVE arched, calathiform, camus(e), cavernous, crescent, cupped, cupshaped, dented, depressed, dimpled, dished, dishing, hollow(ed), incurvate, incurved, incurvous, minus, notch, retiring, retreating, scyphate, scyphiform, simous, sunk(en), vaulted, vaulty

CONCEAL becloud, befog,

bescreen, black out, blanket, blind, blot out, bosom, burrow, bury, cache, camouflage, censor, cloak, closet, cloud, couch, cover(up), curtain, dern(e), disguise, dissemble, eclipse, eloi(g)n, enscone, enshroud, envelope, feal, feign, harbor, hide, hugger, hush(up), imbosk, join, keep back, keep from, lain, layne, lene, mantle, mask, masquerade, mew, miche, obliterate, obscure, occult(ate), pall, palm, plant, pocket, quash, repress, screen, scug, secrete, shade, shadow, shield, shroud, sile, sit on, smother, squash, stifle, stow, suppress, veil, vest, withhold, wrap, wry
information layne

CONCEALED abstruse, blind, clandestine, covered, covert, cryptous, dern, doggo, hidden, inner, larvate, latent, latescent, masked, occult, perdu(e), privy, recondite, scug, secret, snug, under wraps, unseen, untold, veiled, wrapped
comb. adelo

CONCEALMENT ambuscade, ambush, celation, cover, fraud, mew, privacy, refuge, secrecy, stealth, surprise, trap, velation, waylaying

CONCEDE accept, accord, acknowledge, acquiesce, admit, agree, allow, appease, assent, award, begrudge, beteem, capitulate, cede, confess, consider, discount, give, grant, ottroye, own, relinquish, resign, submit, surrender, vouchsafe, waive, yette, yield

CONCEIT amour-propre, arrogance, bighead, bluster, bovarism, bovaryism, caprice, chestiness, cockiness, complacency, conceive, concept, concetto, crotchet, ego(t)ism, fancy, fantasy, flam, flimflam, folly, idea, imagination, imagine, judgment, knack, notion, opinion, outrage, perkiness, pertness, pride, quip, quirk, seizure, self-esteem, side, stuck-upness, suppose,

swelled head, think, thought, trick, vagary, vainglory, vanity, whim
symbol goose, jackdaw

CONCEITED arrogant, biggity, biggoty, bigheaded, botty, briggety, bug, catwitted, chesty, chuff, clever, cocky, coxcomical, coxy, dandified, dandy, dogmatic, floppish, flory, huffy, know-it-all, opinionated, otherwise, peacockish, penseful, perk(y), pert, priggish, proud, puffed up, saucy, set up, snobbish, stuck up, swellheaded, toffee-nosed, vain(glorious)

CONCEIVABLE believable, cogitable, comprehensible, contingent, earthy, eventual, plausible, possible, potential, thinkable

CONCEIVE apprehend, beget, begin, cause, coin, compose, comprise, construct, contrive, couch, create, deem, design, devise, dream, envisage, envision, fancy, form, formulate, frame, gestate, guess, hold, ideate, image, imagine, intend, know, make, originate, perceive, picture, phrase, plan, ponder, realize, suppose, teem, think, understand, ween

CONCENTRATE absolute, absorb, aim, apply, arrest, assemble, attend, bring to bear, buckle down, center, centralize, coact, compact, compress, condense, congregate, consolidate, contemplate, contract, converge, decoct, distill, elixir, engross, essence, extract, fix, fixate, focus, gather, heap, heed, increase, mass, pay attention, pile, purse, render, syrup, thicken, think, unify
inability to psychataxia

CONCENTRATED dense, fixed, hard, intense, intent, rich, strong

CONCENTRATION absorption, application, attention, build-up, center, centralization, contemplation, contraction, convergence, engrossment, extract, fixation, increase, intentness, preoccupation, raptness, reflec-

tion, samadhi, study, thoughtfulness
camp See NAZI *concentration camp.*

CONCEPT absolute, abstraction, begriff, conceit, consideration, disposition, fancy, idea, image, opinion, percept, plan, supposition, theory, thought
abstract archetype

CONCEPTION abstraction, beginning, belief, comprehension, conceit, design, embryo, ens, entity, fancy, idea, image, impression, inkling, notation, opinion, origin, picture, procreation, project, purpose, rational, understanding, universe, view
comb. ideo
false delusion, idol

CONCERN affair, affect, agitate, answer to, anxiety, appertain, apply, bear, belong to, bother, bug, business, care, cause, charge, company, consideration, corporation, correspond to, deal with, direct, disquiet, disturb, drive, employ, enterprise, event, fear, firm, gear, grief, heart, import, influence, interest, involve, matter, pertain, plant, reck, regard, relate to, respect, rickmatic, sake, shop, solicitude, sorge, stand, sway, thing, thoughtfulness, touch, treat, trouble, weight, worry
industrial colossus, company
oneself with attend, deal, intermit, pass, touch
unselfish altruism, charity, philanthropy

CONCERNED affected, anxious, atwitter, bothered, careful, disturbed, engrossed, impressed, intent, interested, involved, solicitous, troubled, versant, worried

CONCERNING about, after, anen(s)t, apropos, as for, as regards, as to, between, for, in re, pertaining to, regarding, related, respecting, till, touching

CONCERT accord, arrange, bend, benefit, choir, collude, combine, concur(rence), conjoin, consort, consult, cooperate, debate, devise, discuss, harmony, musical(e), negotiate, oneness, plan, pop, popular, recital, unanimity, unite, unity

hall academe, auditorium, lyceum, odeon, theater

CONCERTINA accordion, bandonion, lantum, melophone, organ, squiffer

CONCESSION adjustment, admission, allowance, assent, boon, cession, consent, discount, favor, gambit, gift, grant, leniency, octroy, privilege, qualification, tolerance

CONCH bracket, chank, cockle, conk, ear, mollusk, mussel, punk, shell, stromb(us)

meat scungli

queen heavyback

CONCHA apse, cigar, dome, ear, semidome

CONCHOBOR *captive* deirdre

nephew cuchulainn

wife medb

CONCIERGE doorkeeper, janitor, landlady, landlord, manager, porter, suisse, warden

CONCILIATE abate, acquire, adjust, appease, arbitrate, atone, calm, concile, ease, gain, honey, mollify, pacify, persuade, placate, prevail on, propitiate, reconcile, satisfy, soften, soothe

CONCILIATOR appeaser, arbitrator, go-between, make-peace, pacificator, peacemaker, propitiator, reconciler

CONCILIATORY gentle, giving, irenic(al), lenient, lenitive, mild, mollifying, pacific, persuasive, soft, winning

CONCILIATRIX bawd, trollop

CONCINNITY elegance, fitness, harmony

CONCION assembly, oration

CONCISE brief, businesslike, capsule, close, cogent, compact, compendious, compressed, condensed, crisp, curt, cut, efficient, epigrammatic(al), laconic, mutilate, neat, piquant, pithy,

pointed, practical, precise, pregnant, realistic, sententious, serried, short (and sweet), succinct, summary, taciturn, terse, thorough, to the point, trenchant, trig

CONCISENESS brachylogy, brevity, concision, economy, syntomia, syntomy

CONCLAVE areopagy, assembly, closet, conference, convention, meeting, sit-down, sit-in, sitting, sober

CONCLUDE achieve, analyze, arrange, clinch, close, collect, complete, culminate, decide, deduce, derive, determine, dispatch, embrace, enclose, end, estop, expire, extract, fetch, fine, finish, gather, glean, guess, induce, infer, judge, limit, period, ratiocinate, reason, reckon, resolve, rest, settle, speculate, stop, suppose, surmise, take, terminate, top off

CONCLUDING conclusive, destitive, final, last

CONCLUSION amen, apodosis, arrangement, bitter end, catastrophe, clausula, climax, close, closure, coda, completion, consequence, consummation, corollary, culmination, curtain, decision, deduction, denouement, derivation, diagnosis, end, envoy, epilog(ue), ergo, event, extraduction, extremity, finale, fine, finis(h), illation, induction, inference, issue, last, loose, opinion, outcome, pay-off, period, point, quaesitum, resolution, resolve, result, sentence, sequel(a), settlement, term, termination, thirty, upshot

final issue

random surmise

weak anticlimax

CONCLUSIVE apodictic, assuring, authentic, certain, cogent, convincing, correct, damning, decisive, definite, definitive, determinative, evident(ial), extreme, final, first-hand, impressive, indicative, inevitable, last, mandatory, necessary, overwhelming, persuasive, satisfactory, satisfying, signi-

ficant, telling, testatory, ultimate, valid, weighty

CONCOCT blend, brew, compose, compound, confect, conjure up, contrive, cook, create, devise, digest, dream up, fabricate, fake, fashion, form, frame, hatch, intrigue, invent, make, manufacture, mingle, mix, originate, plan, plot, prepare, produce, project, refine, scheme, vamp

CONCOCTION blend, brew, compound, device, digestion, mixture, mummia, plan, plot

CONCOMITANT accessory, accompanying, associate(d), attendant, attending, coeval, coincidental, companion, concurrent, conjoined, contemporaneous, escort, incident, joined, linked, related, satellite, sequela, simultaneous, synchronous

CONCORD accord(ance), agreement, amity, atonement, calmness, community, compact, concert, consensus, consonance, covenant, diapason, goodwill, grape, harmony, oneness, pact, peace, placidity, rapport, serenity, sympathy, terms, treaty, truce, unanimity, union, unison, unity

CONCORDAT bargain, cartel, compact, contract, convention, covenant, entente, mise, pact, treaty

CONCOURSE assembly, coincidence, company, concurrence, confluence, conjunction, convergence, crowd, flow, frequence, gathering, hall, resort, road, station, terminal, throng

CONCRETE actual, beton, cake, CEMENT, clot, coalesce, combine, congeal, corporeal, definite, firm, floor, grout, hard, individual, mortar, palpable, particular, pavement, physical, plaster, positive, real, solid(ified), special, specific, substantial, tangible, unite

component ballast

deposition laitance

depositor tremie

fact, comb. ance, ancy, ence, ency

mixer paver
rough brut
structure blockhouse, caisson, pillbox
CONCRETION arthrolite, bezoar, calculus, clot, coherence, flint, fusil, hardening, knot, lithite, mass, nodule, pearl, sebolith, stone, tabasheer, tabishir
stony calculus
CONCUBINAGE hetaerism, kaaro, karewa
CONCUBINE das(i), doxy, hagar, mistress, odalisk, odalisque, paramour, rispah, sultana, wanton
famous chang wu
CONCUPISCENCE appetence, appetite, desire, hunger, longing, lust, passion, urge, yearning, yen
CONCUPISCENT antsy, carnal, lascivious, lustful, sensual, wanton
CONCUR accede, accompany, accord, acquiesce, agree, approve, assent, check, chime, coact, coadunate, coincide, collaborate, combine, conjoin, consent, conspire, converge, cooperate, correspond, cowork, ditto, echo, gee, go along with, harmonize, jibe, join, meet, reciprocate, subscribe, synchronize, synergize, unite
CONCURRENCE adhesion, admission, agreement, alliance, assent, association, ayes, combination, concert, concomitance, concordance, concourse, confluence, conjunction, consent, consilience, consort, convergence, junction, meeting, syndrome, synergy, union
CONCURRENT circumstantial, coeval, contemporary, copunctal, incidental, meeting, parallel, simultaneous, unanimous, united
CONCUSSION brunt, buffet, bump, clash, collision, commotion, hurt, impact, jar, jolt, jounce, percussion, pounding, repercussion, shock, succussion, trauma
CONDALIA blue-wood, capulin, chaparral, hardwood, shrub, tree
CONDEMN adjudge, amerce, attaint, awreak, ban(ish),

blame, bless, castigate, censure, chide, convict, criminate, criticize, damn, decry, deem, denounce, denunciate, detest, disparage, doom, file, find guilty, fine, hiss, judge, penalize, proscribe, reprehend, reproach, reprobate, sentence
CONDEMNATION animadversion, blame, censure, decrial, disapprobation, doom, judgment, rap, seizure, sentence, verdict
CONDEMNED damned, doomed, fatal
CONDENSATION abridgement, abstract, brief, capsule, dew, digest, outline, precipitation, precis, rainfall
CONDENSE abbreviate, abridge, adsorb, boil down, brief, combine, compact, compress, concentrate, constrict, contract, cut, decoct, decrease, deflate, densen, digest, distil(l), harden, lessen, liquify, mix, narrow, reduce, shorten, shrink, solidify, telescope, thicken, unite
CONDENSED brief, capsule, compact, concise, curt
CONDENSER aludel, balancer, capacitance, capacitator, pot, reflux
CONDESCEND accomodate, assent, climb down, concede, deign, demean, descend, favor, grant, oblige, patronize, specify, stoop, submit, unbend, vouchsafe
to acquiesce
CONDESCENDING patronizing, snobbish, snobby, superior
CONDESCENSION concession, courtesy, disdain, stoop
CONDIDDLE steal, waste
CONDIGN adequate, appropriate, deserved, due, equitable, fair, fit(ting), just, merited, rightful, suitable, worthy
CONDIMENT dressing, flavoring, herb, relish, seasoner, seasoning, spice
container cruet
kind achar, aiwain, allspice, apple butter, assaf(o)etida, balachan, balachong, bell pepper, blatchang, blatjang,

canella, caper, capsicum, cardamon, catchup, cumin, curry, devil's dung, dill (seed), garlic, ginger, horseradish, kari, ketchup, leek, mace, marjoram, mayonaise, mint, mustard, nutmeg, onion, oregano, paprika, parsley, pepper (mint), piccalilli, pickle, pim(i)ento, pimpernel, potherb, radish, sage, salad dressing, salsa, salt, sambal, sauce, savory, shallot, soy sauce, spice, tabasco, tartar sauce, thyme, turmeric, vanilla, vinegar
mixture tamara
CONDITION 3 and, tie, way 4 bind, case, form, mode, mood, pass, rank, rote, side, term, tone, trim 5 adapt, angle, cause, class, color, covin, estre, facet, joker, limit, phase, place, shape, stage, state, tenor, terms, theat, train, whack 6 agency, aspect, clause, define, degree, estate, fettle, morale, nature, plight, repair, repute, sphere, status, string, temper 7 article, calling, codicil, feather, footing, grounds, posture, premise, prepare, provise, specify, station 8 accustom, covenant, function, occasion, position, protasis, standing 9 affection, character, determine, postulate, provision, requisite, situation, status quo, stipulate, ultimatum 10 appearance, atmosphere, definition, limitation, obligation 11 arrangement, contingency, requirement, stipulation 12 circumstance, prerequisite 13 determination, qualification, specification
chance accident
comb. ance, ancy, ate, blasty, dymus, ence, ency, hood, ile, ness, ose, osis, red, tude
critical emergency
depressed downbeat, illth, low
favorable odds
indispensible sine qua non
in good healthy, kilter, up to scratch, up to snuff
intermediate mesomorphic
miserable penury, squalor

permanent hexis
static entropy
sublime heaven, paradise
weather fog, haze, heat, rain, smog, snow, sunshine
CONDITIONAL accidental, connexive, contingent, dependent, dialectic, eventual, fixed, fortuitous, given, iffy, incidental, limited, provisional, provisory, qualified, questionable, relative, specificative, specified, stated, stipulated, subject, tentative
CONDITIONING education, training
CONDOLENCE comfort, commiseration, compassion, consolation, empathy, pity, ruth, solace, sympathy
CONDOMINIUM apartment
CONDONE absolve, accept, acquit, allow for, bear, blink at, connive, disregard, endure, exculpate, excuse, forget, forgive, ignore, overlook, pardon, pass over, remit, tolerate, wink at
CONDOR buzzard, catharta, cathartid, coin, falconiformis, tiffin, vulture
CONDOTTIERI See MERCENARY.
CONDUCE accomplish, accrue, administer, advance, aid, bring, conduct, confer, contribute, effect, engage, forward, further, guide, help, hire, lead, lend, promote, redound, tend
CONDUCT accompany, act, action, address, administer, affair, attend, baton, bear, bearing, behave, behavior, bring, call, carriage, carry(on), channel, compere, comport(ment), conduit, conn, convey, convoy, course, deed, demean, demeanor, deport(ment), direct, direction, drive, escort, execute, fare, firk, form, gost(e), gover, guard, guide, habit, lead, manage, maneuver, manner, marshall, mayne, mien, operate, operation, play, practice, regulate, rule, run, shepherd, show, sithe, squire, toke, train, transact, transfer, transport, usage, use, usher, wage

appropriate dharma
comb. ery
disorderly randan
evil malversation, moral turpitude
reckless devil(t)ry
right tao
scandalous esclandre
usual praxis
wanton ruff
CONDUCTANCE *unit*
abmho, mho, micromho, millimho, siemens
CONDUCTOR aqueduct, bailee, band major, batonist, blade, bond, brush, bus bar, cad, cantor, captain, carman, carrier, cathode, channel, choir master, chorister, cicerone, commander, concert master, conveyor, convoy, director, escort, guide, hirer, kapelmeister, konzertmeister, lead, leader, maestro, main, operator, shunt, stickman, trainman
electric filament
famous barenboim, beecham, bernstein, bjoerling, boulez, charry, corelli, furtwangler, klemperer, koussevitzky, lane, mahler, mehta, muck, munch, nikisch, ormandy, ozawa, previn, queler, rudolf, solti, stokowski, toscanini, von karajan, walter, weingartner
stick baton, wand
CONDUIT adit, aqueduct, cable, carrier, channel, chimney, culvert, cundy, drain, duct, exhaust, gout, main, opening, passage, pipe, race, sewer, sluice, trough, trunk, tube, waterway, wire
CONE bevel, bobbin, bur(r), conoid, cop, cornet, frustum, funnel, galbulus, nuraghe, pina, pyramid, strobil(e), thimble
cloth vane
half forme, nappe
inverted hopper
paper coffin, spill
pert. strobilaceous
pyromatic montre
retorting pina
-shaped conic(al), pineal, pyramidal
silver pina
tip vertex

tree conifer, fir, larch, pine, spruce
CONEFLOWER black-eyed susan, brown betty, brush, comb, daisy, echinacea, golden glow, lepachys, rudbeckia, sampson
CONENOSE barbeiro, barber bug, bedbug, bloodsucker, conorhinus, kissing bug, triatoma
CONEY chervil, daman, guatibero, hyracid, hyrax, parsley, rabbit
CONFAB chat, converse, powwow, prattle, talk
CONFECTION alhet, angelica, barley candy, bonbon, brittle, butterscotch, candy, caramel, chocolate, cimbal, cockle, comfit, compound, dainty, dolce, dragee, dulce, fondant, fudge, halvah, majoon, marshmallow, marzipan, medicine, me(e)bos, nougat, pomfret, praline, preserve, spun sugar, succade, sugar plum, sweet (meat), taffy
colored ribbon candy
fluffy cotton candy
fruit tutti-frutti
CONFECTIONARY comfit, confiserie, sweetmeat
CONFEDERACY alliance, association, band, bloc, body, bund, coalition, combination, complot, covenant, covin(e), dixie, federation, fusion, group, kedar, league, society, south, union
capital richmond
CONFEDERATE (See also CIVIL WAR.) abbetter, abbettor, accessory, accomplice, aid, ally, associate, auxiliary, band, butternut, colleague, combine, conspire, federal, federary, federate, feodary, league, pal, partner, reb(el), santar, snill, stall, steerer, unite
flag stars and bars
rose chinese mallow
soldier grayback, graycoat, johnny (reb)
CONFEDERATION See CONFEDERACY.
CONFER accord, advise, afford, argue, award, bestow, bless, cast, collate, collogue, commune, com-

pare notes, comprise, conclave, confab(ulate), consult, contact, converse, counsel, debate, discourse, discuss, donate, dub, endow, feoff, give, grant, huddle, impart, meet, negotiate, palaver, parley, powwow, present, sit (with), spend, take up with, talk, treat, vouchsafe
degree cap
knighthood accolade, dub
rank brevet, commission
CONFERENCE assembly, audience, audition, body, caucus, circuit, colloque, colloquium, colloquy, conclave, confab, congress, consultation, convention, convocation, council, counsel, deliberation, diet, discussion, hearing, huddle, indaba, interview, korero, meeting, palaver, parley, parliament, parvis, pour parler, powwow, reception, seminar, session, sit-down, sit-in, sitting, summit, symposium, synod, talk, treat, tribunal, tutorial
technique brainstorming
CONFESS absolve, acknowledge, admit, allow(as), attest, avouch, avow, know, break down, come across, come clean, concede, cop out, cough up, couthe, disbosom, disclose, discover, divulge, grant, kithe, lay bare, manifest, open up, out with it, own (up), plead guilty, profess, regret, remit, render, repent, reveal, rue, shrift, shrive, sing, spill the beans, spit it out, squawk, squeak, talk, tell, unburden
CONFESSION alhet, allowance, apology, ashamnu, atonement, avowal, canon, catechism, cognovit, credo, creed, peccavi, shrift, shrive, symbol, viddui
of faith credo, creed
of sin alhet, ashamnu
CONFESSIONAL creedal, lectern, malchus, pardon chair, pardon stall, shrift, whispering office
CONFESSOR father, penitent, priest, shrift, shriver
CONFETTI bonbons, candy,

confections, ribbon, streamers, sweetmeats
carrier cascaron
CONFIDANT chum, companion, crony, eminence grise, friend, intimate, privado, privy
CONFIDE affy, believe, commend, commit, consign, depend, divulge, entrust, give, grant, hope, intrust, let in on, lippen, relegate, rely, repose, tece, tell, trust
CONFIDENCE aplomb, assurance, belief, betrothal, bield, boldness, certainty, certitude, cheek, cool(ness), courage, credence, credit, dauntlessness, dependence, face, faith, fearlessness, fiduce, hark, hope, mettle, morale, poise, privity, reliance, secret, security, self-assurance, spirit, stock, surety, tip, trust
game bunco, bunko, deception, fraud, swindle
in sub sigillo
lack diffidence, distrust, fear, shyness, timidity
man sharp(er), swindler
whispered hark
CONFIDENT assured, audacious, aweless, believing, bold, brave, certain, cocksure, convinced, crank, dauntless, dreadless, expectant, fearless, fiducial, hardy, hopeful, impudent, intrepid, overweening, poised, positive, presumptuous, reassured, reliant, sanguine, secure, self-assured, self-reliant, smug, soignee, sure, traist, trustful, trusting, unafraid, undoubting, unfaltering, unfearful, unfrightened, unwavering, valiant
CONFIDENTIAL arcane, auricular, backdoor, backstairs, between us, bosom, close, closet, covert, esoteric, familiar, fiduciary, hushhush, inside, intimate, inward, low-down, off the record, private, privy, restricted, secret, thick, trustworthy, unquotable
CONFIDENTIALLY between us, entre nous, in camera, off the record, secretly, sub rosa
CONFIGURATION arrange-

ment, conformation, constellation, contour, design, figure, form, geometry, gestalt, outline, pattern, positure, profile, shape
CONFINE 3 bar, box, dam, end, hem, mew, pen, pin, sty, tie 4 area, bail, bind, cage, coop, crib, curb, edge, hasp, jail, keep, lace, shut, span, stop, stow, term, yard 5 bound, bourn, braid, brail, cabin, chain, check, cramp, crowd, delay, hem in, house, lay up, limit, march, pinch, pound, verge 6 arrest, border, bottle, buckle, button, casket, circle, closet, coarct, coerce, coffin, commit, corral, encage, entomb, fetter, hamper, hole in, immure, impale, intern, kennel, pinion, rail in, tether 7 astrict, compass, enclose, fence in, impound, inhibit, manacle, poister, reclose, seclude, shackle, trammel 8 boundary, cloister, distrain, frontier, imprison, restrain, restrict, straiten 9 carcerate, enclosure, restringe 10 quarantine 11 hospitalize 12 circumscribe
CONFINED abed, bedridden, bound, caged, captive, circumscribed, close, cramp(ed), cribbed, fast, ill, impent, implicit, interned, invalided, jailed, limited, local, narrow, pent, pentit, petty, provincial, restrained, sealed, shut in, sick, small-minded, squeezy, two-by-four
to select group esoteric
CONFINEMENT accouchement, birth, bond, bondage, cage, captivity, cell, childbirth, clausure, commitment, delivery, detention, durance, gating, hold, incarceration, jail, jankers, limit(ation), lying-in, mew, parturition, restriction, solitary, ward
place asylum, brig, cage, calaboose, caup, coop, corral, dungeon, gaol, jail, jug, limbo, mew, pen(itentiary), prison, stir
CONFIRM accredit, accustom, acknowledge, adminiculate, affeer, affirm,

approve, assent, assure, attest, authenticate, avouch, back, bear out, bishop, certify, circumstantiate, clinch, convince, corroborate, document, endorse, entrench, establish, fix, harden, justify, officiate, probate, prove, ratify, reable, sanction, seal, second, settle, stable, strengthen, substantiate, support, sustain, thicken, track down, uphold, validate, verify, vouch, warrant *by evidence* adminiculate

CONFIRMATION ceremony, corroboration, proof, rite, sacrament, sanction, verification
candidate catechumen
money arles
ritual alapa

CONFIRMED arrant, certain, chronic, deep-rooted, deepseated, encouraged, established, fixed, habitual, habituated, hardened, inveterate, ratified, rooted, set, settled, stable, sworn

CONFISCATE appropriate, arrest, arrogate, assume, attach, attaint, condemn, confisk, distrain, expropriate, grab, pre-empt, proscribe, seize, take, usurp

CONFISCATION escheat, incension, seizure, taking

CONFLAGRATION blaze, burning, fever, fire, flame, holocaust, inferno, wildfire

CONFLICT action, agitation, agon, attack, battle, bout, broil, brush, clash, combat, contend, contest, controversy, counteract, differ, disagree, discord, dispute, dissension, duel, encounter, engagement, faction, fight, fray, friction, hostility, incompatibility, meet, militation, mutiny, oppose, quarrel, rift, riot, scape, scuffle, skirmish, stour, strife, struggle, tussle, war(fare)
final armageddon
in literature agon
pert. internecine
psychological war of nerves

CONFLUENCE assembly, concourse, conflux, connection, convergence, crowd, flow, fork, infall, joining, junction, meeting

CONFORM abide, accede, accept, accomodate, acquiesce, adapt, adjust, agree, answer, assent, attune, chime in with, comply, comport, compose, confirm, fall into line, fit, harmonize, hew, jibe, keep in step, lean, meet, obey, reconcile, settle, shape, square, submit, suit, tally, toe the line, tune, walk the chalk, yield
to answer, behave, keep, meet, observe, satisfy
with dovetail

CONFORMABLE congruent, consistent, conventional, done, obedient, orderly, proper, pursuant, regular, similar, suitable, suited, tractable, uniform

CONFORMATION build, form, shaping
mental samskara

CONFORMIST babbitt, bromide, bromidite, compiler, conventionalist, formalist, methodologist, orthodox, pedant, philistine, precisian(ist), purist, routinist, traditionalist

CONFORMITY acceptance, accord, accuracy, acquiescence, affinity, agreement, compliance, congruity, convention, dharma, equity, harmony, justice, justness, likeness, symmetry
to law dharma, legality

CONFOUND abash, addle, amaze, astonish, astound, awhape, babelize, baffle, bewilder, blast, blow, chagrin, confuse, confute, contradict, corrupt, curse, dash, destroy, dismay, distract, drat, dudder, dum(b)found, faze, flummox, frustrate, mate, maze, mingle, mistake, mix, muddle, mystify, nonplus, perplex, puzzle, rattle, refute, rout, shend, shock, spoil, stam, stun, stupefy, surprise, thwart, trap, waste, whip

CONFOUNDED at a loss, bamboozled, blame(d), blank, blasted, buffaloed, consarned, darned, dazed, deuced, dummered, execrated murrain, mystified, peevish, switched, wonderstruck

CONFRATERNITY body,

confrairy, group, society, sodality, union

CONFRERE associate, cobrother, cohort, colleague, comrade, friend, partner

CONFRONT accost, affront, beard, brace, brave, breast, challenge, compare, cross, dare, defy, encounter, envisage, face, lay before, meet, nose, oppose, present, propose, resist, threaten, visage

CONFUCIUS *analects* lun yu
disciple mencius
doctrine shu
name, chinese k'ung futse
name, personal kung chiu
symbol plum
truth tao
works analects, lun yu

CONFUSE 3 box, fog, mis 4 ball, dash, daze, doit, doze, faze, fuss, gaum, harl, maze, muss, rout, stun 5 abash, addle, amaze, befog, bitch, cloud, deave, dizzy, mix up, shame, shend, shent, snarl, steer, stump, twist, upset 6 baffle, ball up, bedaze, bemuse, bother, burble, caddle, dazzle, dudder, duddle, flurry, foul up, fuddle, gravel, jingle, jumble, maddle, maffle, mingle, mizzle, moider, momble, muddle, pother, put out, puzzle, rattle, ruffle, twitch, wimple 7 becloud, bedevil, blunder, break up, buffalo, bumbaze, chagrin, derange, diffuse, disturb, fluster, flutter, garboil, giddify, mystify, nonplus, perplex, perturb, scatter, shatter, shuffle, stagger, unravel 8 bedazzle, befuddle, bemuddle, bewilder, conflate, confound, disorder, distract, dumfound, entangle, squatter, unsettle 9 barbulyie, discomfit, disorient, disparple, embarrass, frustrate 10 demoralize, discompose, disconcert 11 disorganize 12 razzledazzle

CONFUSED abroad, addlebrained, addled, addlepated, adrift, asea, astray, at sea, balled up, bemazed, bemused, blank, blotto, blurred, brangled, busy, chagrined, chaotic, clouded,

cloudy, cockeyed, deranged, disconcerted, disordered, disorderly, dizzy, doiled, drumly, farchadat, fartootst(er), flurried, flustered, foggy, foolish, groggy, harebrained, hazy, hurrisome, illogical, in a hobble, in a stew, lost, macaronic, misty, mixty-maxty, muddy, mussy, muzzy, obscure, rattled, shaggy, silly, tavert, throughother, topsyturvy, tsedoodelt(eh), tsedraydelt, tsetummelt, turbulent, upset, vague, westy, wooly
heap bourock

CONFUSING baffling, blinding, dizzy(ing), mazeful, mystifying, perplexing

CONFUSION ado, anarch, ataxia, ataxy, babble(ment), babel(ism), ballup, barbulyie, bedlam, bluster, bouleversement, broil, brouhaha, busyness, caddle, chagrin, chaos, chevy, chivy, clamor, clutter, coil, commotion, confutation, defeat, deray, din, disarray, discord, disorder, disturbance, embarrassment, fog, foul up, fuss, harl, hassle, havoc, hobble, hoorush, hubbub, huddle, hullabaloo, hurly, jabble, jumble, kippage, louster, mess, mismaze, mixture, mix-up, mizmaze, moil, mucker, muddle, noise, overthrow, pandemonium, perplexity, pie, pother, riot, rookery, ruffle, ruin, rummage, rumpus, scaddle, scowder, s(h)lemozzl, snafu, snarl, strow, tohubohu, topheth, tumult, turmoil, uproar, welter, whemmel, widdrim
of tongues babel

CONFUTE conclude, confound, convince, deny, disprove, evict, evince, expose, falsify, improve, overcome, rebut, refute, silence, subvert

CONGE apophyge, apophysis, bow, curtsy, curve, dismissal, hypophyge, leave, scape

CONGEAL cake, candy, clabber, clot, coagulate, concrete, cotter, cruddle,

curd(le), dense, fix, freeze, gel, gelatinate, gelatinize, harden, incrassate, inspissate, knot, jell(ify), jelly, lopper, lump, pectize, set, solidify, stiffen, stroken, thicken

CONGENER acid, aldehyde, beaver, dott(e)rel, ester, ketone, phenol, tannin

CONGENIAL accordant, affable, agreeable, amiable, boon, companionable, compatible, consistent, convivial, cordial, en rapport, friendly, gemutlich, gracious, happy, kindred, jovial, natal, native, pleasant, sib, simpatico, social, sympathetic, warm

CONGENITAL connate, genetous, hereditary, inborn, inbred, inherited, innate, native

CONGERIES accumulation, aggregation, assemblage, calculary, collection, group, heap, mass, pile

CONGEST choke, clog, glut, obstruct, overburden, stop up, stuff, surfeit

CONGESTED bursting, chock-full, crowded, hyperemic, jammed, massed, obstructed, overcrowded

CONGESTION bottleneck, heap, jam, lampas, lampers, mass, obstruction, plethora, stoppage

CONGLOMERATE ball, banket, big business, cartel, clustered, collection, combine, corporation, crowded, gather, heap, hoard, mass, nagelfluh, pile, psephite, puddingstone, rock, solid, stack, trust, zaibatsu

CONGLOMERATION accumulation, aggregate, aggregation, collection, glommox, huddle, imbroglio, miscellany, mixture, synergism

CONGO amadi, asphaltum, bitumen, brown, eel, mummy, river, snake, susu, tea, zaire
animal okapi
beer garapa
capital boma, brazzaville, kinshasa
cataract stanley falls
city albertville, boma, brazzaville, bukavu, coquilhat-

ville, djambala, dolisie, enyelle, epena, ewo, holle, jacob, kamina, kikwit, kindu, kinsangani, kolwezi, leopoldville, lubumbashi, luluabourg, lusambo, makoua, manoco, mbandaka, mitwaba, okoyo, ouesso, sandoa, sembe, souanke, stanleyville, zanaga
coin franc, franccfa
councillor macota
deity mebele, phebele
discoverer cam
drizzle cacimbo
eel wrymouth
fish lulu
lake albert(nyanza), leopold, mweru, stanley, tumba, upemba
language bangala, fiote, susu
mahoe ambary
mist cacimbo
peacock afropavo
plant manioc
plateau bateke
port brazzaville, cabinda, matadi, pointe-noir
premiere adoula
president kasavubu, lumumba
province kasai, katanga, knu
pump trumpetwood
pygmy achuas, akka
river aruwimi, kasal, kouilou, kwango, kwenge, loange, lualaba, lubilash, lulua, ngoko, niari, sanga, swilu, ubangi, uele, wamba, zahir, zaire
river, city on boma, brazzaville, leopoldville
river tributary aruwimi, itimbiti, lomami, lualaba, luapula, ubangi
season bangala, cacimbo, kundey
shrub bocca
snake amphiuma, blind eel, siren
statesman adoula
tobacco hemp
tribe ababua, akka, amadi, bacongo, bafyot, bakongo, bangala, bantu, bateke, batetla, figot, mantu, manyema, mbochi, nzambi, pygmy, rua, susu, wabuma, warua, zambi

CONGRATULATE bless, compliment, felicitate, flatter, greet, hug, laud, macarize, praise, salute

CONGRATULATION(S)

compliment, good wishes, mazel tov, parabien, seventy-threes

CONGREGATE assemble, besiege, collect, concentrate, convene, forgather, gather, group, herd, mass, meet, muster, pack, summon, swarm, teem, throng, troop

CONGREGATION assembly, audience, body, brethren, cenacle, chapelry, church(goers), class, communicants, company, flock, fold, following, gathering, herd, host, laity, laymen, meeting, parish(ioners), people, samaj, settlement, sheep, shul, society, swarm, synaxis, temple, throng

CONGREGATIONALISM brownism
founder barrowe, browne

CONGRESS assembly, association, boot, capitol hill, caucus, communication, conclave, conference, connection, convention, convergence, convocation, council, dail, diet, duma, gorsedd, group, house(of representatives), legislature, lower house, majlis, meeting, mejlis, mod, oblast, ouyezd, parliament, powwow, rada, senate, shoe, society, solitaire, soviet, synod, uyezd
headquarters capitol

CONGRESSMAN legislator, representative, senator

CONGRUITY accord, agreement, coherence, coincidence, concord, fitness, harmony, keeping, merit, symmetry

CONGRUOUS agreeable, appropriate, compatible, congenial, consistent, consonant, expedient, fit(ting), harmonic, harmonious, meet, proper, seemly, suitable, sympathetic

CONIBEAR trap

CONIFER cedar, evergreen, fir, larch, pinal, pine, spruce, thuja, torrey, tsuga, yew
disease blueing, bluerot, bluestain, heartwood rot

CONJECTURAL hypothetical, putative, reputed, stochastic, supposititious

CONJECTURE aim, assumption, augur, belief, cast, concur, deduce, divine, ettle, fancy, gather, guess, hindcast, hypothesis, imagine, infer(ence), meet, opine, opinion, plot, posit, presume, rove, shot, speculation, stab, supposal, suppose, supposition, surmise, suspect, suspicion, theory, think, view

CONJOINED conjunct, jugate(d), linked, overlapping, together, touching, united

CONJUGAL connubial, marital, matrimonial, nuptial, spousal

CONJUGATE connect(ed), couple(d), dwell upon, harp upon, inflect, join(ed), repeat, unite(d), yoke(d)

CONJUGATION assemblage, combination, conjunction, fusion, joining, syngamy, synopsis, uniting, zygosis

CONJUNCTION adjacency, and, appulse, association, but, combination, concurrence, connection, consort, joint, nor, since, than, though, tie, und, union, unity, yet
omission asyndetion

CONJUNCTIVITIS pink eye, syndesmites
remedy terramycin

CONJURATION art, charm, conspiracy, exorcism, incantation, jugglery, juggling, magic, seance, sorcery, spell, supplication, voodoo
practitioner exorcist

CONJURE adjure, appeal, ask, beg, beseech, bring, call (up), charm, conspire, contrive, deceive, enjoin, entreat, envisage, envision, evoke, exorcise, halse, imagine, implore, importune, invent, invoke, levitate, plead, pray, raise, recall, remember, sue, summon, supplicate, wish
man cunjah, cunjer, goofer, guffer

CONJUROR coswearer, dowser, exorcist, hocuspocus, jongleur, juggler, mage, magician, pellar, powwow, pythonic, seer, shaman, sorcerer, voodoo,

warlock, wielare, witness, wizard

CONK bean, blow, bracket, decay, fail, head, hit, nose, stall, strike
out break, die, fail, faint, perish, spoil, stall, stop, weaken

CONLAECH *parent* aoife, cuchulainn

CONNACHT *king* ailill

CONNECT adjoin, affix, ally, anastomose, apply, assemble, associate, assort, attach, attribute, bind, bond, bridge, cascade, catenate, catenulate, cement, chain, cog, cohere, combine, continue, couple, dovetail, enchain, enlink, fasten, fix, gear, glue, hitch, integrate, involve, join, knit, knot, link, relate, span, splice, succeed, tie, unite

CONNECTICUT *capital* hartford
city ansonia, avon, bethel, bridgeport, bristol, danbury, darien, enfield, greenwich, hamden, hartford, manchester, meriden, milford, mystic, naugatuck, new britain, new haven, new london, niantic, norwalk, norwich, sharon, shelton, stamford, storrs, stratford, tolland, torrington, wallingford, waterbury, westport, windsor
college trinity
county tolland, windham
founder hooker
indian mohegan, niantic, pequot, quinnipiac
nickname blue law, freestone, nutmeg
peak bear
river housatonic, thames
state bird robin
state flower mountain laurel
state tree oak
university wesleyan, yale

CONNECTION accouplement, affiliation, affinity, agreement, alliance, application, apposition, association, attachment, attribution, bearing, bond, bracketing, bridge, buckle, coherence, combination, commerce, concatenation, confluence, congress, conjugation, conjunction, connexus, contact, correlation,

coupling, descent, family, friendship, go-between, hitch, hook up, hub, interdigitation, intimacy, isthmus, joiner, junction, kinsman, kinship, liaison, ligation, link(age), marriage, meeting, nexus, node, passage(way), pusher, relation (ship), relative, relevance, sibness, span, suture, swivel, tie, trussing, union, yoke
anatomical anastomosis, diarthrosis
electrical ground
CONNECTIVE and, but, conjunction, junction, ligative, nor, sutural, syndetic, vincular
CONNELLY, MARC *play* green pastures
CONNIPTION fit, hysteria, rage, tantrum
CONNIVE abet, assent, blink, cabal, collaborate, collude, condone, conspire, cover, disregard, foment, incite, instigate, intrigue, overlook, plan, plot, scheme, wink
CONNOISSEUR adept, aesthete, authority, cameist, cognoscente, critic, dilettante, epicure, expert, gourmet, judge, maven, mavin, virtuoso
CONNOTE denote, designate, evidence, hint, imply, insinuate, intimate, mean, signify, suggest
CONNUBIAL conjugal, domestic, marital, matrimonial
CONOCARPUS buttontree
CONON *enemy* pisander
helper evagoras
refuge cyprus
son timotheus
CONOR *consort* deirdre, medb
CONQUER acquire, balk, beat, best, crush, daunt, debellate, defeat, down, evict, firk, foil, gain, get, humble, lick, master, outwit, overcome, overgang, overpower, reduce, rout, subdue, subject, subjugate, surmount, surpass, tame, triumph, vanquish, whip, worst
CONQUERABLE defeatable, pregnable, superable, vincible, vulnerable
CONQUEROR champion,

conquistador, master, victor, winner
of men andronicus
the william (of normandy)
CONQUEST defeat, enchantment, mastery, rout, seduction, surrender, sweetheart, triumph, victory, win(ning)
CONRAD, JOSEPH *hero* axel, jim, lord jim
heroine lena
novel heart of darkness, lord jim, nostromo, secret agent, typhoon, youth
ship otago
CONRADE *leader* don john
CONSANGUINITY affinity, agnation, blood, cognation, enation, filiation, kinship, nasab, relationship
pert. parentelic
CONSCIENCE censor, compunction, erinys, fastidiousness, grace, heart, inwit, monitor, probity, psyche, punctilio, qualm, scruple(s), scrupulosity, scrupulousness, sense, superego, syndeidesis, thought, virtue
money tax
personification aidos
-stricken apologetic, sorry
CONSCIENTIOUS careful, choicy, choosy, dedicated, devoted, discriminating, discriminative, dutiful, eident, ethical, exact, exacting, fair, faithful, fastidious, honest, honorable, just, meticulous, moral, nice, painstaking, particular, perfectionist(ic), picky, precise, principled, punctilious, punctual, religious, rigid, scrupulous, selective, strict, thorough, upright
objector conchie, conchy, pacifist
CONSCIOUS active, alive, appreciative, attentive, awake, aware, calculated, cognizant, deliberate, feeling, intentional, keen, knowing, known, mindful, percipient, premeditated, quick, rational, sensible, sentient, sentimental, shy, studied, supraliminal, ware, watchful, witting
CONSCIOUSNESS aniruddha, anoesis, attention, awareness, ego, feeling, limen, recognition, sensation, sense, spirit, wits

-altering psychedelic
loss apoplexy, apsychia, coma
pure c(h)it
restore to bring around, revive
return to anabiosis, reanimation, reincarnation, resurrection, resuscitation
CONSCRIPT choco, draft(ee), dragoon, enlist, enroll, force, impress, jeanjean, levy, muster, press, recruit
CONSECRATE anoint, apotheosize, bless, canonize, consacre, dedicate, deify, devote, enshrine, fain, hallow, ordain, sacrate, sacred, sain, sanctify, seal, taboo, venerate, vow
CONSECRATED blessed, blest, hallowed, hieratic, holy, oblate, sacred, votary, votive
object sacrum
CONSECRATION apotheosis, beatification, beatitude, blessing, canonization, dedication, devotion, enshrinement, exaltation, glorification, grace, hallowing, ihram, justification, ordination, psychiasis, purification, sacre, sacring, sacry, sanctification, sanction
CONSECUTIVE after, continual, continuous, discrete, following, sequent(ial), serial, seriate, succeeding, successive
CONSECUTIVELY hand running, in a line, in tune, running, sequentially, seriatum, serially, step by step, together
CONSENSUS agreement, concord, confession, cooperation, harmony, likemindedness, unanimity
CONSENT accede(nce), accept(ance), accession, accord, acquiesce(nce), agree(ment), allow, approval, approve, assent, beteem, coherence, compliance, comply, concede, concession, concur(ence), discretion, endorse(ment), goodwill, grant, hear to, hold with, permission, permit, relent, sanction, subscribe, support, willingness, yes, yield

age of maturity
by common unanimously
expression okay, okeh, righto, umhum, unhunh, yeah, yes

CONSENTIENT accordant, amenable, unanimous

CONSEQUENCE aftermath, apodosis, attendant, concern, conclusion, dignity, distinction, effect, end, entail, event, force, fruit, growth, import(ance), inference, influence, issue, moment, outcome, prestige, produce, repute, result, sequel(a), sequent, significant, upshot, value, weight, worth
bad evil
of conduct browst
of little trifling, trivial, unimportant

CONSEQUENTIAL authoritative, big, deducible, eventual, great, heavy, important, indirect, influential, meaningful, pompous, self-important, significant, vain, weighty

CONSEQUENTLY accordingly, and so, as a result, consecutively, ergo, hence, inevitably, it follows that, later, naturally, naturellement, necessarily, of course, of necessity, presently, pursuant, then, therefore, thus

CONSERVATION abstinence, custody, husbandry, maintenance, preservation, protection, safekeeping, salvation

CONSERVATISM bitterendism, bourbonism, fogyism, golden mean, hunkerism, intransigence, irreconcilability, laissezfaire, moderation, philistinism, reaction(aryism), right-wingism, standstillism, temperance, toryism

CONSERVATIVE bitterender, bourbon, bourgeois, defensive, diehard, fogram, fogrum, fusty, hardshell, hidebound, hunker, lamellar, middle-of-the-road, moderate, old fogy, oldline, preservative, protective, reactionary, right(ist), right-wing(er), safe, square-toed, stable, staid, standpat(ter), tory
super fuddyduddy, mossback, stick-in-the-mud

CONSERVATORY academy, art school, college, dancing school, greenhouse, music school, nursery, salle de danse, storehouse

CONSERVE can, candy, confection, defend, guard, husband, jam, jelly, maintain, medicine, preserve(s), protect, safeguard, save, secure, shield, sustain, sweetmeat, uphold, uvate

CONSIDER account, acknowledge, admit, advert, advise, aim, allow, appraise, attribute, believe, besee, bethink, calculate, call, canvass, cast, cogitate, concede, consult, contemplate, count, debate, deem, deliberate, digest, discuss, ear, esteem, estimate, ettle, excogitate, figure, gaum, give, grant, heed, hold, inspect, judge, meditate, mull, muse, poise, ponder, prepend, provide for, rate, reason, reckon, reflect, regard, respect, revolve, ruminate, see, seem, study, suppose, take into account, think, treat, turtinate, view, vise, volve, weigh
probable daresay
the source discount

CONSIDERABLE abundant, ample, appreciable, authoritative, canny, consequential, estimable, fair, gay, gey, good(ly), great, handsome, healthy, important, large, many, notable, numerous, powerful, pretty, remarkable, several, smart, substantial, substantive, unlittle

CONSIDERATE accommodating, agreeable, attentive, careful, charitable, companionate, complacent, complaisant, deliberate, delicate, discreet, gentle, gracious, heedful, indulging, judicious, kind(ly), mild, mindful, nice, obliging, patient, prudent, reflective, regardful, serious, solicitous, sympathetic, tender, thoughtful, well-disposed, well-meaning

CONSIDERATION advice, aspect, attention, care, cause, charge, charity, commission, compensation, concern, count, courtesy, debate, deference, deliberation, delicacy, eminence, esteem, fee, gratuity, idea, influence, insight, kindness, motive, notice, opinion, payment, premium, qualification, reason, reflection, regard, remittal, remuneration, respect, sake, sanction, scruple, significant, study, subject, tact, thought(fulness), tip, topic, verdict, weight
basic bedrock
brief short, shrift
private avizandum

CONSIDERED advised, deliberate, designed, express, intentional, premeditated, studied, voluntary, willful, witting

CONSIDERING after all, on the whole, seeing, since, therefore, wherefore
everything all told

CONSIGN address, allot, assign, award, bequeath, beteach, commission, commit, confide, confirm, delegate, deliver, deposit, devote, dight, dispatch, doom, entrust, forward, give, intrust, issue, mail, move, relegate, remand, remit, send, shift, ship, subscribe, surrender, transfer, transmit, yield
again remand
to a place locate
to oblivion bury, expunge, forget, shred
to perdition condemn, damn, excommunicate

CONSIGNEE agent, awardee, broker, factor, receiver, shipper

CONSIGNMENT cargo, goods, invoice, shipment

CONSIST compose, comprehend, comprise, constitute, contain, dwell, embrace, exist, hold, include, inhere, insist, involve, lie, rely, reside, rest, stand

CONSISTENCY agreement, body, coherence, compages, concord, congruity, correspondence, degree, evenness, firmness, harmony, keeping, sameness, solidity, symmetry, union

CONSISTENT accordant, coherent, compatible, congruous, consonant, constant, durable, enduring, even, firm, harmonious, homogeneous, logical, of a piece, rigid, settled, steady, suitable, uniform

CONSOLATION comfort, condolence, relief, solace, sop

prize booby

slight cold comfort

CONSOLE allay, alleviate, ancon, assuage, brace, bracket, cabinet, calm (down), cartouch(e), cheer, comfort, commiserate, encourage, grieve(with), mitigate, organ, relieve, solace, soothe, sorrow with, support, sustain, sympathize, table, weep (with)

CONSOLIDATE ankylose, band, blend, cake, close, coalesce, cog, combine, compact, compress, condense, conjoin, fuse, harden, increase, join, knit, league, mass, merge, mingle, mix, pool, settle, solidify, splice, strengthen, unify, unite, weld

CONSOMME argenteuil, broth, lucette, madrilene, royale, soup

cold madrilene

CONSONANCE accord, agreement, coincidence, compatability, concord, congruity, consistency, diapason, diapente, harmony, symphony, unison

CONSONANT accordant, agreeable, alveolar, aspirate, atonal, bilabial, compatible, conformant, congruous, consistent, dental, ejective, fortis, geminate, harmonic, harmonious, labial, lateral, lene, lenis, letter, liquid, palatal, sonant, spirant, stop, suitable, surd, sympathetic, tonic, unified, unison, waw

aspirated sonant, surd

hard fortis, fricative

hissing sibilant

loss ecthlipsis

pert. fricative, palatal

replacement lenition

smooth lene, lenis

sound surd

strong fortis

voiceless atonic, lene, spirate, surd

CONSORT accord, aide, ally, assembly, attend, colleague, combination, companion, company, comrade, concert, damkina, date, empress, escort, group, harmonize, husband, join, mate, mingle, partner, princess, spouse, troop, unite, wife, yoke

CONSORTIUM alliance, amalgamation, association, cartel, corporation, enterprise, group, merger, partnership, union

CONSPECTUS abridgement, abstract, analysis, apercu, brief, digest, epitome, impression, insight, list, outline, precis, resume, sketch, summary, survey, syllabus, synopsis, theoric

CONSPICUOUS aposematic, apparent, arrant, arresting, big, blasing, blatant, bold, bright, campy, clear, eminent, evident, famed, famous, flagrant, glaring, important, lionized, manifest, marked, notable, noticeable, obvious, open, outstanding, overt, patent, plain, pointed, prominent, pronounced, remarkable, salient, sightly, signal, staring, stary, striking, visible

CONSPIRACY artifice, cabal, cahoots, champerty, collusion, compact, complot, concurrence, conjuration, connivance, counterplot, coup, covin(e), frame-up, intrigue, junto, machination, perfidy, plan, plot, ring, scheme, sedition

CONSPIRATOR abettor, accessory, accomplice, catilinarian, confederate, fawkes, plotter, saboteur, schemer

CONSPIRE abet, cabal, collude, complot, concur, confederate, conjure, connive, contrive, cooperate, intrigue, league, plan, plot, scheme, unite

CONSTABLE alguazil, bailiff, beadle, beagle, bobby, bull, catchpole, cop,

coroner, dogberry, dozener, harman, kavass, keeper, officer, peeler, policeman, rancelman, ranselman, sheriff, slop, subashi, tipstaff, warden

petty borrowchief, borrowhead, borsholder, tithingman

CONSTANCY ardor, attachment, determination, devotion, durability, faith, fealty, fidelity, homeostasis, honesty, loyalty, oneness, regularity, resolution, sameness, stability, steadfastness, truth, uniformity, zeal

symbol diamond, garnet

CONSTANT assiduous, ceaseless, certain, chronic, consistent, continual, definite, diligent, durable, enduring, equable, even, everlasting, faithful, fast, firm, fixed, gravity, immutable, incessant, inveterate, just, lasting, leal, loyal, parameter, permanent, perpetual, persevering, positive, regular, resolute, scrupulous, set(tled), solid, stable, sta(u)nch, standing, steadfast, steady, still, tight, tried, true, trusty, uniform, unwavering, weight

CONSTANTINE *birthplace* naissus, nish

enemy licinius, maxentius

mother helena

CONSTANTINOPLE See ISTANBUL.

CONSTANTLY always, at all times, ceaselessly, continually, daily, day after day, day and night, ever, forever, hourly, incessantly, on and on, perennially, perpetually, regularly, steadfastly, steadily, unceasingly, year after year

CONSTELLATION See also STAR IN.

air pump antlia

altar ara

archer sagittarius

argo division vela

arrow sagitta

atlantides pleiades

balance libra

bear ursa major, ursa minor

berenice's hair coma berenice

bull taurus

cancer crab

champion perseus
charioteer auriga
charles' wain dipper
clock horologium
compass circinus, pyxis
crab cancer
crane grus
cross crux, cruz
crow corvus
crown corona
cup crater
dimmest cancer, crab
dipper charles' wain
dog canis
dog, greater sirius
dogs, hunting canes venatici
dolphin delphinus
dove columba
dragon draco
eagle aquila
easel, painter's pictor
fish, flying piscis volans
fly musca
foal equuleus
fox, little vulpecula
furnace fornax
giant aesculapius, ophiuchus
giraffe camelopardalis
goat capricorn
goblet crater
goldfish dorado
hare lepus
harp lyra, lyre
herdsman bootes
horse equuleus
horse, winged pegasus
hunter orion
keel carina
lady, chained andromeda
lady, in the chair cassiopeia
lion leo
lion, little leo minor
lizard lacerta
long-winding eridanus
lyre lyra
maiden virgo
mariner's compass pyxis
mast malus
milky way argo
monarch cepheus
mountain, table mensa
nautical box pyxis
net reticulum
noah's dove columba
northern andromeda, aquila,
aries, auriga, bootes, cancer, canes, cassiopeia, cepheus, cetus, coma, cygnus,
delphinus, draco, equuleus,
gemini, hercules, hydra, lacerta, leo, lynx, lyra, orion,
pegasus, perseus, pisces, sagitta, serpens, sextant,

square of pegasus, taurus,
ursa, virgo, vulpecula
orion's hound canis major
paradise bird apus
peacock pavo
pert. asterismal
pictor painter
pleiades atlantides
pump antlia
rabbit leporis
ram aries
rescuer perseus
river eridanus
rule norma
sails vela
sculptor's tool caelum
sea monster cetus, hydra
sea serpent hydra
serpent bearer ophiuchus
sextant sextans
shield of sobieski scutum
ship argo
southern altar, antilia,
apodus, apus, aquarius, ara,
argo, bird of paradise, caelum, canis, capricorn,
carina, centaurus, cetus,
chameleon, circinus, co-
lumba, corvus, crater, cross,
crux, dorado, fornax, grus,
horologium, hydra, indus,
lepus, libra, lupus, mensa,
microscopium, monocerus,
mons mensae, musca,
norma, orion, pavo,
phoenix, pictor, pisces,
puppis, pyxis, reticulum,
sagittarius, scorpius,
sculptor, sextans, sextant,
tucana, vela, virgo, volans
southern cross crux
square norma
stern puppis
swan sygnus
swordfish dorado
table mensa
toucan tucana
twins gemini
unicorn monoceros
ursa bear, dipper
wagoner auriga
wain, charles' dipper
water bearer aquarius
water snake hydrus
whale cetus
winged horse pegasus
wolf lupus
wreath corona australis
zodiacal aries, cancer, gemini, leo, libra, taurus, virgo
CONSTERNATION agita-
tion, alarm, amazement,
awe, confusion, dismay,

dread, fear, fright, horror,
panic, shock, stupefaction,
terror, trepidation, trepidity
CONSTITUENCY borough,
electorate, following, patronage, retinue, train
CONSTITUENT atom, component, detail, elector, element, essence, factor, feature, ingredient, integral,
integrant, item, matter,
member, part(and parcel),
piece, portion, principal,
simple, suffragan, voter
CONSTITUTE appoint, authorize, compose, com-
pound, comprise, create,
depute, enact, establish,
fashion, fix, forge, form,
found, frame, graith, legislate, make, ordain, set,
shape, spell, station
CONSTITUTION appoint-
ment, being, canon, character, charter, code, composition, content, crasis, design,
disposition, establishment,
estate, formation, frame,
grondwet, grundlov, health,
humor, ingredients, iron-
sides, law, legislation,
magna c(h)arta, make-up,
nature, personality, phy-
sique, sett, setup, solitaire,
state, structure, system,
temperament
author madison
internal temperament
of basil prochiron
opponents anti-federalists
ship old ironsides
state connecticut
supporter cartist
CONSTITUTIONAL amble,
congenital, daily dozen, essential, exercise, healthful,
inherent, innate, intrinsic,
legal, perambulation, stroll,
walk
CONSTRAIN abstain, actuate, astrict, bend, bind,
chain, check, clasp, coart,
coerce, compel, compress,
confine, cramp, curb, deter,
drive, enforce, exact, fain,
force, hale, hold, impel,
lead, moderate, oblige, obstringe, oppress, press, religate, repress, require, restrain, secure, thrast, tie,
urge
CONSTRAINED bound,
coacted, cramped, fain,

forced, formal, tied, uneasy, vain

CONSTRAINT bond, coercion, commitment, compulsion, confinement, cramp, distress, duress, embarrassment, force, moderation, pressure, reserve, restriction, stress, violence

CONSTRICT astringe, bind, choke, clench, compress, condense, confine, constringe, contract, cramp, curb, deflate, distrain, grip, hamper, limit, narrow, press, restrict, shrink, snaffle, squeeze, stiffen, strain, straits, strap, tauten, tense, tie, tighten, tuck

CONSTRICTED bound, compressed, contracted, cramped, held, strait, strict

CONSTRICTOR aboma, anaconda, astringent, boa, guavina, king snake, python, snake, sphincter

CONSTRUCT arrange, artifice, build, combine, compose, concept, confect, construe, craft, create, design, devise, dight, engineer, erect, fabricate, fashion, form, frame, idea, levy, make, manufacture, model, originate, produce, put together, put up, rear
by art artifice

CONSTRUCTION architecture, arrangement, aspect, building, cast, composition, constitution, definition, dwelling, erection, explanation, fabric, frame, interpretation, meaning, production, rendition, structure, synesis. translation, version
abstract stabile
begin break ground
pert. tectonic

CONSTRUCTIVE creative, factive, helpful, illative, implicit, implied, inferential, inferred, interpretive, involved, suggestive, virtual

CONSTRUE analyze, deduce, define, dissect, elucidate, explain, explicate, expound, infer, intend, interpret, paraphrase, parse, render, resolve, translate, translation, understand

CONSUBSTANTIATION

change, eucharist, transformation

CONSUETUDE custom, habit(ude), practice, usage, wont

CONSUL comes, counselor, count, earl, judice, magistrate, officer, official, praetor, senator
first napoleon

CONSULT advise, ask, confer, consider, counsel, debate, deliberate, discuss, emparl, imparl, look, negotiate, parley, plan, resolve, seek, talk, treat
one's pillow delay

CONSULTANT adviser, conferee, counsel, discusser, doctor, expert

CONSULTATION advice, conference, council, counsel, deliberation

CONSUME absorb, bezzle, bolt, burn, canker, corrode, decrease, deplete, destroy, devour, dispose of, dissipate, drain, drink, dwindle, eat, engross, ete, exhaust, expend, fare, feed, finish, flame, fret, gulp, hog, idle, imbibe, impoverish, ingurgitate, inhale, kill, monopolize, raven, run out of, rust, spend, squander, sup, swallow, swig, swill, take, toss down, toss off, tuck, use, vanish, waste, wear

CONSUMED all, burnt(out), combust, exhausted, outworn, spent, used

CONSUMER buyer, customer, eater, purchaser, spender, user
society coop(erative)

CONSUMING agonizing, burning, corrosive, engrossing, flaming, using, wasting
by combustion comburivorous

CONSUMMATE absolute, accomplish(ed), achieve, acme, arrant, best, complete, consume, crowned, destroy, effect, end, entire, fine, finish(ed), flawless, fulfill, full, great, ideal, impeccable, intact, meridian, peerless, perfect, perform, ratify, ripe, sheer, superlative, supreme, thorough, top, whole

CONSUMMATION accomplishment, acme, climax, conclusion, end, goal, perfection, upshot

CONSUMPTION absorption, atrophy, decay, decrease, decrement, deglutition, depletion, dissipation, drain, exhaustion, expenditure, expense, impoverishment, phthisic, phthisis, spending, tuberculosis, use, wastage, waste, wasting, white plague
pert. phthisical
remedy alcornoque
weed canker lettuce, false wintergreen, indian lettuce

CONSUMPTIVE cadaverous, emaciated, lungy, patient, phthisical, predatory, sick, skeleton-like, thin, wasted

CONSUS neptune
associate ops

CONTACT abut, adjoin, agent, arrive, bridge, brush, collision, commerce, connection, contingence, cross, customer, drop, fence, graze, hit, holding, impact, impinge, impingement, kiss, meet, osculate, osculation, relationship, rub, scrape, skim, spy, strike, syzygy, taction, tangency, touch (ing), truck, union
electrical hub(b)
fleeting brush
mine magnetic, sonic

CONTAGION epidemic, miasma, plague, poison, pox, taint, virus
preventive alexiteric, antidote, prophylaxis shot, vaccination, vaccine

CONTAGIOUS catching, communicable, endemic (al), epidemic, epizootic, impartible, infectious, infective, inoculable, mephitic, noxious, pandemic, pestiferous, pestilential, smittle, sporadic, spreading, taking, toxic, virulent, zymotic

CONTAIN abstain, accept, accommodate, admit, carry, check, close, comprise, embody, embrace, enclose, enfold, enseam, harbor, harness, have, hold, house, include, involve, keep, measure, receive, restrain, retain, shelter, stow, subsume, take

CONTAINER 3 bag, box, can, cup, hod, jar, jug, keg, kit, lug, pan, pod, pot, pyx, tin, tub, urn, vat 4 bail, bata, bomb, bowl, cage, case, cask, crib, drum, pack, pail, pint, poke, sack, tank, tube, vase, well 5 ampul, basin, billy, caddy, chest, crate, cruet, dewar, flask, glass, hutch, pouch, scoop, stoop, stoup, trunk 6 ampule, barrel, basket, bottle, bucket, bushel, carafe, carboy, carton, casket, caster, coffer, cooler, cradle, hamper, holder, hopper, manger, mortar, shaker, sheath, tea cup, tierce, vessel 7 ampoule, bandbox, bladder, blunger, canteen, capsule, cistern, compact, feedbox, hanaper, holdall, holster, humidor, inkwell, luggage 8 billican, canister, canniken, demijohn, envelope, hogshead, knapsack, puncheon, reticule, slipcase 10 jardiniere, receptacle, tabernacle 11 artophorion
comb. angio
drying saltpan
5-gallon jer(r)ican
pottery stean
shipping bale, kit, trunk

CONTAMINATE adulterate, alloy, attaint, befoul, corrupt, debase, debauch, defile, deprave, desecrate, dirty, disease, dishonor, foul, harm, impair, infect, injure, poison, pollute, profane, slur, soil, spoil, stain, sully, taint, tarnish, violate, vitiate

CONTAMINATED degraded, dirty, infected, polluted, unclean

CONTANGO interest, premium

CONTE crayon, narrative, novelette, story, tale

CONTEMN despise, disdain, disregard, flout, hate, heer, misprize, neglect, reject, repudiate, scoff, scorn, scout, slight, snub, spurn, vilipend

CONTEMPLATE advise, aim, cherish, cogitate, concentrate, consider, deliberate, descry, dream, envisage,

envision, examine, excogitate, expect, face, feature, focus on, foresee, intend, look, meditate, muse, note, notice, observe, plan, ponder, pore over, propose, reflect, regard, revolve, ruminate, scan, see, study, survey, talk of, think, view, weigh

CONTEMPLATION attention, consideration, dhyana, expectation, insight, intention, meditation, mooning, musing, petition, prayer, regard, request, study

CONTEMPLATIVE broody, engrossed, gloomy, intent, meditative, moody, pensive, rapt, reasoning, reflective, speculative, studious, theoretical, thoughtful

CONTEMPORARY coetaneous, coeval, coexistent, coincident, concurrent, current, equal, fellow, living, mod(ern), monochronic, present, simultaneous, stylish, synchronous, topical
comb. neo

CONTEMPT affront, aversion, contumely, defiance, derision, despect, despisal, despite, disdain, disgrace, dishonor, disregard, figo, geck, hate, hething, insolence, loathing, misprize, mockery, repugnance, ridicule, scorn, shame, slight, sneer, snobbery, snobbism
exclamation bah, faugh, fico, fough, fouter, pah, pho(h), phoo(ey), pish, yah, yuk

CONTEMPTIBLE abject, bally, base, baubling, beggarly, bloody, caitiff, cheap, damned, despicable, detestable, dirty, grubby, ignoble, infamous, lousy, low, mean, measly, miserable, muck, odious, paltry, paskudne(h), peevish, petty, pitiable, pitiful, ruddy, scorned, scummy, scurvy, shabby, snotty, sordid, sorry, squalid, swinish, terrible, unworthy, vile, worthless, wretched, yellow
person bauchle, bounder, brock, bum, butt, caitiff, crumb, cur, heel, roue, scrub, scum, skate, sneak, swine, wretch

CONTEMPTUOUS arrogant, cavalier, contumelious, defiant, disdainful, disrespectful, flouting, haughty, insolent, lightly, melancholy, sardonic, scaffing, scornful, slighty, sneering, sniffy, snippy, snobbish, snooty, toplofty, upstage, withering

CONTEND advocate, affirm, argue, assert, bandy, bargain, bate, battle, bicker, brawl, buckle, buffet, camp, chide, claim, combat, compete, conflict, contest, cope, counter, deal, debate, differ, digladiate, dispute, fight, flite, frab, grapple, hold, insist, jostle, justle, kemp, maintain, mean, meddle, oppose, plea, race, reason, resist, rival, scuffle, squabble, state, struggle, tug, vie, wage, war, withstand, wrestle

CONTENT amount, appease(d), at ease, blessed, blissful, capacity, cargo, cloy, comfortable, complacent, composition, cubage, delight, ease, easygoing, essence, gist, glad, gratified, gratify, happy, matter, paid, pay, please(d), rath(e), replete, sans souci, sated, satiate, satisfaction, satisfied, satisfy, smug, soothed, subject, substance, suffice, surfeit, text, theme, thesis, undisturbed, wilcweme, willing
oneself with See ACCEPT.
symbol cornelian

CONTENTED See CONTENT.

CONTENTION affray, altercation, argument, bait, bate, bicker, broil, chiding, claim, colluctation, combat, conflict, contest, controversy, crawl, debate, disagreement, discord, dispute, dissension, disturbance, estrif, feud, flight, fray, jangle, opinion, quarrel, question, riot, rivalry, squabble, strife, struggle, strut, tiff, toil, tumult, variance, war, wrangle

CONTENTIOUS angry, argumental, argumentative, bateful, bellicose, belligerent, cantankerous, cat-and-

doggish, competitive, controversial, cross, disputatious, dissentious, eristic, fighty, litigious, peevish, perverse, polemic(al), pugnacious, quarrelsome, scrappy, warlike, wrangling **CONTENTMENT** bien aise, bien etre, bliss, ease, fulfillment, gratification, happiness, heaven, pleasure, satisfaction
CONTENTS bale, bottle, capacity, filler, filling, guts, inlay, innards, insides, lading, lining, load, pack(ing), padding, size, space, stuffing, volume, wadding
CONTEST 3 bee, sue, try, tug, vie, war 4 agon, bout, buck, cope, deny, duel, feud, fray, game, kemp, meet, play, pull, push, race, show, spar, suit, tiff, tilt 5 agony, argue, brawl, break, broil, brush, clash, derby, event, fight, joust, match, melee, mix up, rodeo, scrap, set to, sport, trial, wager 6 action, adjure, affair, affray, battle, bicker, bixley, boxing, buffet, combat, debate, defend, oppose, racing, resist, rubber, runoff, seesaw, strife, strive, tussle 7 bargain, brabble, compete, contend, content, deraign, dispute, grapple, playoff, protest, quarrel, regatta, rivalry, scuffle, shutout, tourney, warfare, wrangle 8 argument, biathlon, campaign, concours, conflict, dogfight, fighting, handicap, litigate, olympiad, scramble, skirmish, slugfest, squabble, struggle, tug of war 9 bickering, challenge, champerty, cockfight, collision, encounter, rencontre, scrimmage, trackmeet, wrangling 10 contention, dimication, engagement, free-for-all, rencounter, tauromachy, tournament 11 altercation, competition, controversy, disputation, embroilment, spelling bee
athletic decathlon, meet, olympiad, olympic games, pentathlon, trackmeet
division heat, inning
endurance marathon
final play-off

futile sciamachy
kind beauty, lawsuit, litigation, tryout
log-birling roleo
personal rencounter
racing drag
reaping kemp
rifle bisley
tied draw, stalemate
wordy altercation
CONTESTANT competitor, disputing, entrant, fighter, finalist, player, rival, vier
CONTIGUOUS about, abutting, adjacent, adjoining, close, conterminous, juxtaposed, nearby, nearest, next, nigh, tangent, touching
CONTINENCE abstinence, celibacy, chastity, moderation, platonism, purity, sobriety, temperance, virginity, virtue
practitioner brahmachari
CONTINENT abstinent, africa, antarctica, asia, australia, capacious, capacity, cascadia, chaste, content, continuous, decent, earth, europe, good, greenland, land, lemuria, main(land), moderate, north america, pure, receptacle, restrained, restrictive, sober, south america, temperate
covering all epeiric
dark africa
hypothetical cascadia
legendary atlantis, cascadia, gondwanaland, lemuria
lost atlantis pacifica
super pangaea
CONTINENTAL bit, currency, european, picayune, soldier, trifle
congress president read
CONTINGENCY accident, adjunct, case, casualty, chance, circumstance, contact, event, fortuity, happening, incident(al), juncture, liability, possibility, prospect, venture
dependent on aleatory
CONTINGENT accidental, adventitious, casual, chance, conceivable, conditional, dependent, depending, doubtful, eventual, exposed, fortuitous, inchoate, incidental, in the cards, liable, likely, nonessential, occasional, open, part, pos-

sible, probable, provisional, provisory, relative, share, subject to, touching, uncertain, unforseen
CONTINUAL around-the-clock, assiduous, ceaseless, chronic, consecutive, constant, continuous, endless, enduring, eternal, everlasting, frequent, incessant, interminable, lasting, minutely, never-ending, nonstop, obstinate, perennial, permanent, perpetual, persevering, persistent, recurrent, regular, repeated, repetitive, round-the-clock, stable, steady, straight, stubborn, successive, tenacious, twenty-four-hour, unbroken, unceasing, undying, unending, uniform, uninterrupted, universal, unremitting
CONTINUALLY always, at a stretch, aye, constantly, endless, eternal, ever(ly), forever, hourly, on and on, on end, still, without a break
CONTINUANCE abidance, deferment, delay, durability, durance, duration, lasting, permanence, postponement, sequel, stay, survival
CONTINUATION adjunct, breakover, contango, delay, extension, jump, protraction, sequel
CONTINUE abegge, abide, aby, beleave, bide, break, carry(on), drag on, dure, endure, extend, go along, go on, hold, keep going, last, linger, live, maintain, outlast, outlive, perdure, persevere, persist, proceed, prolong, protract, pursue, push on, remain, retain, run on, stay, stick, subsist, sue, survive, sustain, tarry, unite
CONTINUED chronic, constant, protracted, repeated, resumed, serial, still
CONTINUITY cohesion, CONTINUATION, continuum, duration, identity, persistence, progression, scenario, script, sequence, tract
break in saltus
CONTINUOUS anend, chronic, CONTINUAL, ei-

dent, endless, entire, even, eydent, progressive, running, steady, unbroken, uninterrupted

CONTORT bend, coil, cringe, curl, deform, distort, gnarl, obvolute, pervert, screw, squinch, turn, twist, warp, wind, wrap, wrest, writhe, wry

CONTORTED awry, bent, coiled, convuluted, knotty, obvolute, perverted, screwed, twisted, wound, wried, wry

CONTORTIONIST acrobat, tumbler

CONTOUR boundary, cartouche, configuration, curve, figuration, figure, form, galbe, graph, isobase, limb(ament), outline, periphery, profile, shape, silhouette, sweep, tournure
outline configuration

CONTRA against, contrariwise, counter, offset, opposed, opposite

CONTRABAND forbidden goods, hot, illegal, illicit, prohibited, schvartzeh, smuggled, taboo, unlawful, verboten

CONTRACEPTIVE birth control, pill, prevent(at)ive

CONTRACT 3 bag 4 bond, book, call, deal, deed, draw, hale, knit, mise, pact, sale, tack, take 5 agree, catch, close, coact, cramp, incur, lease, limit, pinch, yield 6 bridge, cartel, cringe, engage, gather, hiring, indent, lessen, narrow, pledge, policy, pucker, reduce, shrink, sicken, treaty 7 abridge, acquire, agganage, bargain, capture, compact, crumple, curtail, deflate, dwindle, entente, execute, mandate, promise, scrunch, shorten, shrivel, wrinkle 8 compress, condense, covenant, decrease, diminish, handfast, restrict, straiten 9 agreement, assumpsit, betrothal, concordat, constrict, indemnity, indenture, stipulate 10 abbreviate, constringe, convention, obligation, suretyship 11 aggangement 13 understanding
addition clause, codicil, rider
for bag, book, button up,

capture, employ, nail down, obtain, provide, schedule, settle, sew up
furnishing slaves assiento
marriage affiance, betrothal, handfast, ketuba, sponsalia
matrimony marry, unite, wed
part clause, proviso
unlawful chevisance

CONTRACTION abridg(e)-ment, astriction, astringency, blend, compendium, compression, concentration, condensation, constriction, constringency, coup, cramp, crasis, elision, epitome, fist, gather, knitting, narrowing, puckering, pursing, reduction, restriction, shortening, spasm, stricture, systole, twitch, wrinkling
common aint, arent, cant, een, eer, hadnt, hasnt, its, oer, oft, mustnt, shant, tis, wont, wouldnt
heart systole
pert. systolic
rhythmic systaltic

CONTRACTOR astringent, builder, butty, constructor, declarer, knot, mediator, supplier

CONTRADANCE solitaire

CONTRADICT belie, confute, contravene, controvert, counter(act), cross, deny, disaffirm, disprove, dispute, downface, forbid, gainsay, impugn, negate, negative, oppose, oppugn, rebut, recant, refute, resist, reverse, traverse, withsay

CONTRADICTION antilogy, antiloquy, antinomy, denial, inconsistency, opposition, paradox

CONTRADICTORY antagonistic, antinome, antinomy, antipodal, antithesis, antithetic(al), antonym(ous), counter, irreconcilable, negating, negative, opposing, opposite, paradoxical, reverse, thwarting

CONTRAPTION apparatus, appliance, contrivance, curwhibble, device, gadget, instrument, jigger, machine, rig, tool, utensil

CONTRARIETY antagonistic (al), antithesis, contrast, disagreement, hostility, in-

consistency, opposition, repugnance

CONTRARILY backward, crisscross, elsehow, elseways, elsewise, on the other hand, otherways, otherwise

CONTRARY adverse, against, antagonistic(al), antilogous, antilogy, antipathetic, antipede, athwart, averse, balky, captious, conflicting, contra, contradictory, contrair, contumacious, counter, crabbed, crossgrained, denial, discordant, discrepant, enemy, froward, hostile, hostility, inimical, insubordinate, intractable, inverse, kicky, negative, obstinate, opposed, opposite, ornery, peevish, perverse, pig-headed, rebellious, repugnant, restive, reverse, shaman, singular, snivy, stubborn, thrawn, wayward
to fact false, untrue
to law criminal, illegal, unconstitutional
to reason absurd, irrational, silly

CONTRAST antithesis, clash, collage, compare, comparison, contend, contradistinction, contrariety, difference, differentiate, discord, discriminate, distinction, distinguish, division, oppose, opposite, opposition, parallel, strife
pert. against

CONTRAVALLATION See FORT.

CONTRAVENE break, combat, contradict, counteract, defy, deny, disprove, dispute, disregard, hinder, impugn, infringe, negative, obstruct, oppose, refute, resist, thwart, transgress, traverse, violate

CONTRAVENTION breach, crime, infraction, offense, opposition, sin, trespass, vice, violation

CONTRETEMPS accident, boner, embarrassment, goof, hitch, mischance, misfortune, mishap, scrape, shtuss, slip, syncopation

CONTRIBUTE abet, accrue, administer, advance, aid, ante, benefit, bestow, cause, chip in, conduce, confer, cooperate, cough up, dole

out, donate, fork up, furnish, further, give, grant, hand out, help, kick in, participate, present, provide, redound, subscribe, supply, sweeten the kitty, tender
money pungle

CONTRIBUTION additament, alms, ante, article, benefaction, bit, boon, charity, collation, donation, exaction, gift, grant, impost, input, largess(e), levy, offering, participation, pay (ment), present, romescot, romeshot, share, subsidy, subvention, sum, tax, tip, tithe
forced assessment, demand, duty, exaction, excise, impost, levy, tax, tithe, toll, tribute
small widow's mite
voluntary peter's pence, romescot, romeshot

CONTRIBUTORY accessory, additional, adjuvant, ancillary, auxiliary, concurring, incidental, secondary, subservient

CONTRITE abject, humble, melted, penitent(ial), remorseful, repentant, rued, rueful, softened, sorrowful, sorry, touched, worn

CONTRITION attrition, compunction, confession, grief, humiliation, penance, regret, remission, remorse, repentance, self-reproach, shrift, shriving, sore, sorrow

CONTRIVANCE adaption, apparatus, appliance, art, artifice, cast, contraption, cunning, deceit, deception, design, DEVICE, devisal, dingbat, engine, expedient, fangle, gadget, hickey, implement, industry, instrument, intrigue, invention, jigger, machine, make-shift, origination, plan, policy, produce, project, resource, rig, scheme, shift, stratagem, subtlety, tool, witcraft
intricate tirlie-wirlie, tirlywhirly

CONTRIVE accomplish, achieve, brew, cast, compass, concoct, conjure, conspire, consult, design, devise, draw, fashion, figure,

find, firk, forge, form, frame, hatch, imagine, induce, intrigue, invent, machine, make, manage, originate, plan, plot, project, scheme, shape, stage, start, wangle, weave, work

CONTRIVED artificial, calculated, constrained, factitious, forced, hokey, pat, slick, stages, strained, unnatural, unreal

CONTRIVER architect. daedalus, engineer, originator

CONTROL abstain, abstinence, administer, aegis, amenage, arrest, ascendancy, authority, beck, bind, bridle, check, clutches, coaction, command, conn, curb, custody, determine, direct(ion), discipline, dominate, domineer, dominion, drive, empery, govern(ment), grasp, grip, hand(ling), hank, head, hegemony, helm, hold, influence, jurisdiction, law, lead, manage(ment), manipulate, manurance, master(y), moderate, monopolize, monopoly, pilot, power, predominate, preside, rede, regiment, regulate, regulation, rein, repress(ion), restrain, restrict, rule, run, steer, subject, subjugate, supervise, supervision, supremacy, sway, theat, upper hand, wield, wirepull
device bit, governor, leash, pedal, regulate, rein(s), robot, switch, treadle
mechanical servo
panel plugboard
position of chair, conn(ing tower), helm, saddle
post helm
remote telemechanics
subject to rulable
symbol apron strings, baton

CONTROLLER boss, bursar, commander, cpa, governor, master, rheostat, ruler, starter, steersman, steward, treasurer, wirepuller

CONTROVERSIAL apologetical, arguable, contentious, controvertible, debatable, disputatious, disputed, dubious, eristic, moot, polemic(al), questionable

CONTROVERSY agitation, altercation, argument, battle, chest, combat, conflict, contention, contest, debate(ment), disagreement, disceptation, dispute, fight, forensic, furor, hassel, hassle, polemic, quarrel, spat, strife, suit, tussle, wrangle
addicted to philopolemic
pert. eristic

CONTROVERT argue, combat, contest, contravene, debate, defend, deny, discuss, disprove, dispute, face, gainsay, impugn, moot, oppose, oppugn, rebut, refute, traverse

CONTUMACIOUS contrary, disobedient, factious, headstrong, insolent, insubordinate, intractable, mutinous, perverse, pig-headed, rebellious, riotous, seditious, sharp, stubborn, unruly

CONTUMELIOUS abusive, arrogant, contemptuous, demeaning, derogatory, disdainful, disgraceful, insolent, opprobrious, overbearing, profane, scoffing, scurril(e), scurrilous, shameful, vituperative

CONTUMELY abuse, affront, contempt, disdain, humiliation, insolence, insult, reproof, rudeness, scorn, upbraid

CONTUSE beat, brain, bruise, injure, pound, squeeze, thump

CONTUSION blow, bruise, bump, chotchke(leh), mouse, tchotchke(leh), tsatske(leh), wale

CONUNDRUM conceit, crochet, enigma, mystery, poser, problem, puzzle, riddle, whim

CONVALESCENCE anastasis, rally, recovery, recuperation

CONVENE agree, assemble, call, cite, collect, come, congregate, convent, converge, convoke, gather, harmonize, hold, meet, muster, rally, sit, summon, unite

CONVENIENCE(S) accommodations, appliances, availability, benefits, cakes and ale, comforts, commodity, ease, equipment, facili-

ties, gain, handiness, leisure, luxury, utilities
public restroom
CONVENIENT accessible, adapted, advantageous, appropriate, available, avenant, clever, comfortable, commode, congruous, expedient, fit, handy, helpful, hend(e), nearby, proper, ready, serviceable, suitable, suited, timely, useful
CONVENT abbey, assemblage, assembly, cenoby, cloister, convene, friary, lamasery, meeting, monastery, nunnery, priory, recluse, summon, tekke, tekya
dweller brother, cenobite, friar, monk, nun
head abbess, abbot, hegumene, hegumeness
pert. claustrial, friary
reception room parlatory
CONVENTION accord, agreement, assembly, asiento, babbittry, bargain, biensence, capitulation, cartel, caucus, compact, conclave, conference, conformity, congress, contract, convocation, correctness, covenant, custom, decorum, diet, etiquette, fashion, feis, form(ality), gathering, grundyism, main street, meeting, mise, mores, mrs grundy, pact, powwow, practice, propriety, rally, rule, synod, tabu, treaty, usage
established tradition
headquarters hotel
CONVENTIONAL accepted, acknowledged, approved, artificial, being done, bourgeois(e), ceremonial, comme il faut, common, conformable, correct, customary, decent, decorous, de rigueur, established, fixed, formal, groovy, habitual, hackneyed, humdrum, nomic, ordinary, orthodox, popular, precise, proper, recognized, regular, right, seemly, solemn, stipulated, traditional, trite, usual
expressions cant
CONVENTIONALITY form(ality), grundyism, stuffiness
CONVENTUAL monk, nun

CONVERGE approach, assemble, center, centralize, close (in on), concenter, concentrate, concur, corner, descend, fall in with, focus, funnel, join, meet, rally, unite
CONVERGENCE asymptote, concentration, concourse, concurrence, confluence, conflux, congress, encounter, focalization, focus, meeting
CONVERGING asymtotic, centripetal, connivent, focal
at both ends amphicentric
jaws aristotle's lantern
to a center centrolinear
CONVERSANT accustomed, acquainted, adept, at home, busied, erudite, expert, familiar, informed, occupied, practiced, proficient, skilled, used (to), versed
CONVERSATION affair, assembly, association, backchat, cackle, call, causerie, chat(ter), chin(wag), chitchat, colloquy, commerce, communion, confab, debate, dialogue, discourse, disputation, gam, giffgaff, gossip, harangue, jabber, palaver, parlance, powwow, rune, speech, talk, tete-a-tete, yabber
light causerie, chat, chinchin, chitchat
of 2 dialogue
of 3 trialog(ue)
pert. interlocutory
private ceilidh, collogue, tete-a-tete
water liguor
CONVERSATIONALIST causeur, deipnosophist, talker
CONVERSE air, associate (with), bandy words, broach, cackle, chat(ter), chew the rag, chin(chin), chitchat, collocution, collogue, colloquice, colloquy, commerce, commune, communicate, communication, communion, confab (ulate), confer, contrary, convert, descant, dilate, discourse, discuss, dwell, express, gabble, gossip, interlocution, opposed, opposite, palaver, parley, propose, reason, shoot the

breeze, speak, talk, ventilate, voice
CONVERSION change, exchange, metamorphosis, redemption, substitution, transfiguration, transformation, transition, transmogrification, transmutation
factor value
instrument alembic, anvil, blowpipe, cladron, crucible, lathe, melting pot
into coal carbonification
into flesh carnification
into gold transmutation
into steel acieration
into stocks capitalization
into sugar amylolysis
mortar potter's wheel, retort
religious regeneration
CONVERT activate, aline, alter, amend, ansar, apply, appropriate, assimilate, become, blend, bring over, capitalize, cash in, catchumen, catholicize, change, christianize, commute, concoct, convict, convince, decode, detect, devotee, direct, disciple, exchange, forge, ger, geshmat, geshmott, invert, make over, melt into, merge, metamorphose, neophyte, novice, novitiate, persuage, proselyte, proselytize, protestantize, redeem, reduce to, reform, regenerate, render, renew, resolve, restore, reverse, romanize, sell, settle into, theist, transform, translate, transmute, transpose, turn, use, wax, wean, wend, win over
into leather tan, taw
into money realize
into steel acierate
recent neophyte, novice
to catholicism romanize
to islam ansar
to judaism ger
CONVERTIBLE auto, bond, cabriolet, car, complementary, correlative, coupe, debenture, interchangeable, reciprocal, security
CONVEX arched, bellfaced, bombed, bombus, bowed, bulge(d), bulging, bulgy, curved, embowed, excurvate(d), gibbous, gibosse, humped, rounded
shaft entasis

CONVEXITY camber, entasis

CONVEY alien(ate), assign, barter, bear, bowl, bring, caravan, carry, cart, cede, channel, commission, communicate, conduct, consign, convey, deed, demise, dispone, eloi(g)n, fetch, giggit, grant, guide, impart, imply, lad, lease, mean, move, pass, relegate, restore, sell, shift, steal, take, tote, trade, transfer, transmit, transport, vend, wain

forcibly hustle
secretly crim

CONVEYANCE auto, bus, car, carriage, cart, cession, deed, demise, kago, load, machine, omnibus, piracy, sale, surrey, taxi, theft, trailer, train, transportation, van, vehicle, waftage

public airplane, bus, cab, car, elevated, ferry, jinricksha, jinrikisha, liner, metro, omnibus, railroad, ricksha(w), steamer, subway, taxi, trailer, train, tram, transfer, trolley, underground

CONVEYER belt, carrier, chain, elevator, ladder, lift, scraper, thief, worm

CONVICT accuse, approve, argue, attaint, captive, cast, condemn, convert, convince, criminal, culprit, defeat, doom, expiree, felon, forcat, jailbird, lag (ger), lifter, malefactor, prisoner, redargue, termer, transport, trusty

chain slang
collar carcan(et)
fish hinalea, manini, pointed greenling

CONVICTION assurance, authority, belief, certainty, certitude, credence, credit, credo, creed, confession, faith, hope, judgment, opinion, persuasion, regeneration, sense, sentiment, tenet, view

demonstration of act of faith

CONVINCE assure, bring over, bring round, confute, convert, convict, disprove, drive home to, expose, fetch, overcome, overpower, persuade, prevail

on, refute, resolve, satisfy, sell, subdue, sway, vanquish, wean, win over

CONVINCING cogent, forceful, forcible, potent, powerful, sound, telling, valid

CONVIVIAL agreeable, amatory, anacreontic, boon, companionable, congenial, cordial, festal, festive, free and easy, friendly, fun-loving, gay, genial, gregarious, hail-fellow-well-met, hearty, hospitable, jocular, jolly, jovial, merry, sociable, social

CONVOCATION assembly, calling, congregation, congress, convening, convention, council, diet, gathering, meeting, summons, synod

CONVOKE assemble, bid, call, cite, collect, congregate, convene, hold, invite, marshal, muster, summon

CONVOLUTE coil, curl, roll, tangle, twist, wind, writhe

CONVOLUTION ambages, ambagiousness, circumvolution, coil, crinkle, curl, curvature, flexuosity, fold, gyroma, gyrus, intorsion, involution, meander(ing), rivulation, sinuation, sinuosity, swirl, torsion, tortility, tortuousness, turn(ing), twirl, twist(ing), undulation, wave, whirl, winding

CONVOLVULUS bearbine, bilderdykia, billy clipper, bindweed, herb, morning glory, scammony vine

CONVOY accompany, attend, bodyguard, caravan, chaperon, conduct, escort, guard, guide, lead, pilot, protect, safeguard, shield, waft, watch

CONVULSE agitate, amuse, discompose, disturb, double up, entertain, excite, laugh, pain, perturb, rock, shake, spasm, stir, torment

CONVULSION agitation, algospasm, attack, bouleversement, commotion, disturbance, eclampsia, fit, laugh(ter), outburst, paroxysm, quake, revolution, seism, seizure, shock, shrug, spasm, spastic, tantrum,

throe, tumult, upheaval, uproar

CONVULSIONS chorea, jerks, tics, tremors, twitching

CONVULSIVE epileptic, fitful, paroxysmal, spasmodic, upheaving

CONY asakoko, ashkoko, badger, boomdas, burbot, cunny, daman, das, dassie, dupe, fur, ganam, gazabo, gazebo, hare, hutia, hyrax, klipdach, klipdas, lapin, lapus, pika, rabbit, red hind, simpleton, wabber

catcher cheat, sharp(er), swindler

COO chirr, chizz, chough, crood(le), cruddle, curr, murmur, woot

COOF blockhead, dolt, lout, ninny

COOK alter, bake, barbecue, baste, bawarchi, boil, braise, brew, broil, brown, chef, cochinero, coct, coddle, concoct, crouch, cuisinier(e), curry, cusinero, delay, devil, disappear, escallop, falsify, fire, fix, fricassee, frizz(le), fry, griddle, grill, heat, hide, jipper, magirist, oven-bake, pan(broil), parboil, percoct, perspire, poach, prepare, roast, ruin, saute, scald, scallop, scorch, sear, seethe, shirr, simmer, sizzle, spoil, steam, toast, warm

bull flunkey, greaser
camp doctor
chief chef
excellent cordon bleu
famous beard, careme, childe, escoffier, francatelli, point, soyer, ude, vatel, weltje
helper slushy
island rarotonga
lightly braise, saute
male native bawarchi
one's goose defeat, fix, ruin, spoil, undo
out barbecue, roast
partially parboil
stove calefactor, range
up build, concoct, contrive, fabricate, falsify, improvise, originate, plot

COOKHOUSE bakery, cafe, cuddy, galley, grill(e), kitchen, restaurant, rotisserie

COOKIE, COOKY animal cracker, biscuit, brownie, bun, cake, caraway, confection, crescent, date bar, dear, fruit bar, gingersnap, hermit, kichel, kipfel, lebkuchen, lorna doone, macaroon, nabisco, oatcake, rock, seedcake, shortbread, snap, sweetheart, teacake, tollhouse, wafer
child's animal cracker
COOKING *art* cuisine, magirics
contest bake-off
device baker, barbecue, boiler, brazier, broiler, chafer, chafing dish, coffee maker, corn popper, dutch oven, etna, grill, oven, range, rotisserie, samovar, steamer, stove, toaster, waffle iron
fat s(c)hmaltz
method baking, barbecuing, boiling, clear-simmering, cold-mixing, deep-frying, drying, frying, grilling, heating, pan-frying, pickling, pot-stewing, red-cooking, rinsing, roasting, salting, sauteing, shallow-frying, sizzling, smoking, splashing, steaming, steeping, stewing, stir-frying, torching
mixture batter
odor nidor
oil source babassu
pert. culinary
room cuddy, galley, kitchen(ette)
spoon kochleffel
style a la bearnaise, a la bonne femme, a la bourgeoise, a la cocotte, a la creole, a la croissy, a la diable, a la florentine, a la francaise, a la jardiniere, a la julienne, a la king, a la marengo, a la matelote, a la mode, a la perigord, a la polonaise, a la ravigote, a la reine, a la russe, a la suisse, a la vinaigrette, au fines herbes, au fromage, au gratin, au jus, au maigre, au naturel, au vin blanc, en casserole, fricandeau, maitre d'hotel
vessel autoclave, bain marie, baker, broiler, casserole, cassolette, caster, chafer, colander, double boiler,

dutch oven, etna, fleshpot, griddle, olla, pan, percolator, pot, pressure cooker, roaster, skillet, spider, steamer, tureen
COOL air condition, algid, aloof, arctic, calm, cautious, chill(ing), chilly, chromatic, cold, collected, composed, deliberate, deter, distant, dull, emotionless, faint, fan, fresh, frigid, frosty, gelid, halfhearted, icy, impassive, indifferent, insolent, lukewarm, mitigate, moderate, nervy, nonchalant, passive, philosophical, phlegmatic, placid, quiet, refrigerate, reticent, sedate, self-composed, self-possessed, sensible, slow, smooth, stoic, temperate, tranquil, unconcerned, unemotional, unfeeling, uninterested, unresponsive, unruffled, weak
as a cucumber
headed commonsensical, composed, level, self-composed, sensible, stoic, temperate, well-balanced
one's heels mark time, wait
COOLER ade, airconditioner, can, coop, drink, fan, icebox, icer, jail, jug, keelfat, lockup, olla, prison, refrigerant, refrigerator, sinker
distilling alcogene
COOLEY'S *anemia drug* desferoxamine
COOLIDGE, CALVIN
birthplace plymouth, vermont
party republican
profession lawyer
vice president dawes
COOLIE carrier, changar, madrasi, mazdoor, peasant, porter, servant
COOLING *agent* alcogene, algefacient, ammonia, carbon dioxide, dry ice, ether, ice cube, refrigeration
off period armistice, truce
COOLNESS apathy, aplomb, calmness, composure, disinterest, dispassion, enmity, frost, indifference, insensibility, listlessness, nerve, phlegm, serenity, sluggishness, swale, unconcern, unfeelingness
COOM(BE) begrime, cirque, coal dust, corrie, culm,

cwm, gaum, grime, hollow, peat, ravine, refuses, sawdust, shavings, slack, smut, soot, valley, vat
COON, COON'S animal, cat, climb, fur, mapach(e), raccoon, rascal
age eternity, forever, long time
bear giant panda
skin congressman, colonel davy crockett
COONTAIL hornwort
COONTIE arrowroot, bay rush, comptie, plant, sago, zamia
COOP artel, auto, cage, case, cavie, confine, coob, corral, cote, cramp, cub, encase, enclosure, fold, hutch, jail, market, mew, pen, pinfold, prison, store, sty
fly the escape, flee
up confine, cramp, enclose, immew, pen
COOPER, COOPER'S cook, cowper, grogshop, hooper, spoil, tubber, tubman
flag or fly cattail, reedmace
heroine cora
novel the deerslayer, the last of the mohicans, the pathfinder, the pilot, the pioneers, the prairie, the spy
product barrel, cask, tub, vat
river indian ahtena
tool howel
COOPERATE accept, accord, agree, chip in, coact, coadjute, coadjuvate, coincide, collaborate, combine, concert, concur, conduce, conjoin, conspire, contribute, coordinate, co-work, get with the program, go along, hang together, join, play ball, pool, share, synchronize, tend, unite, work together
secretly collude, connive
COOPERATION coaction, coadjuvancy, collaboration, give and take, logrolling, participation, synergism, synergy, teamwork, union
COOPERATIVE artel, association, gracious, gregarious, helpful, kibbutz(im), market, sociable, social, store, synergic
workers' artel, guild, union
CO-OPT appoint, choose, elect, pre-empt
COORDINATE adapt, ad-

just, arrange, co-equal, conduce, equal(ize), ensemble, harmonize, pool, symmetrical, synchronize, syntony, time, tune
inability to abasia
COORDINATION bond, harmony, liaison, organization skill
lack abasia, asynergy, dysergia
loss (locomotor)ataxia
COORG kadaga
COOS *indian* anasitch
COOT beltie, blue peter, dolt, duck, eider, fetlock, fool, fulica, full, gallinula, gorhun, ionornis, lobiped, lunatic, oddity, pelick, pulldoo, queet, rail (bird), scoter, simpleton, smyth, splatterer, surf duck, swamphen, tule hen
bald bell-kite, beltie
group covert
pied winged velvet scoter
COOTER idle, loiter, tortoise, turble
grass cabomba, water-shield
COOTFOOT phalarope
COP bag, blow, bobby, bull, capture, catch(pole), cone, constable, copse, crest, entrap, filch, flic, gendarme, grab, hasp, head, heap, lift, mound, nab, outdo, peeler, pile, pinch, policeman, rob, shock, snare, snatch, spider, steal, stock, strike, swipe, thicket, top, trap, yarn
-out alibi, avoidance, confess, defect(ion), quit, retreat, withdraw(al)
COPA copita, lancewood, landmark, yaya
COPACETIC capital, dandy, fine
COPAIBA copaifera, jesuits' resin
COPAIN See FRIEND.
COPAL anime, boea, chakazi, congo, cowrie, kauri, loba, resin
COPE bargain, barter, battle, bend, canopy, cappa, cloak, combat, compete, contend, contest, cover, emulate, encounter, exchange, fight, get by, grapple, heavens, height, manage, mandyas, match, meet, muzzle, notch, oppose, resist, sky, struggle, vault, vertex, vestment, vie, war, withstand

clasp morse
hooded anabata
with buffet, compete, equal, match, rival, struggle, vie
COPEHAN *indian* patwin, wintun
COPEMATE antagonist, associate, comrade, opponent, partner
COPENHAGEN *island* skeland, zealand
park tivoli
shopping district stroget
COPEPOD calamid, cayenne, diaptomid
COPESTONE completion, crown
COPHETUA *beloved* penelophon
COPIER amanuensis, scribe, secretary, stat, stenographer, xerox
COPING cap(stone), course, flue, skew
COPIOUS abundant, affluent, ample, diffuse, exuberant, fertile, flowing, free, full, fulsome, lavish, lush, luxuriant, many, numerous, plenteous, plentiful, plenty, prodigal, profuse, rank, replete, rich, teaming, uberous
COPLAND *ballet* appalachian spring, billy the kid, rodeo
opera the tender land
COPPER aes, bet, bobby, boiler, ca(u)ldron, carnelian, cent, change, coin, cuprum, hedge, maroon, metal, penny, POLICEMAN, red cent, terra cotta, vellon, venus
acetate verdigris
alloy babbitt metal, barberite, beryllium, brass, bronze, duralumin, everdur, oroide, pac(k)tong, pewter, rheotan
arsenate bayldonite, ceruleite, clinoclasite, erinite, euchroite, tyrolite
-belly natrix, watersnake
black melaconite
blue azurite, malachite
brass chalco
brown armenian red
carbonate azurite, bice, gem
chloride atacamite
coin See COIN *copper.*
-colored cupreous
comb. chalco, cupra
compound algodonite, ataca-

mite, bisbeeite, bornite, caledonite, carrollite, domykite, ehlite, enargite, litbethenite
cup dop
engraving mezzotint
gilded vermeil
glance chalcocite
-gold alloy shakudo
gray tetrahedrite
green ehlite
lead sulphate caledonite
-like bronzy, cupreous
-nickel alloy constantan, niccolite
-nose blackscoter, bluegill, wellington
ore bornite, chalcocite, chalcopyrite, cuprite, malachite, melaconite
phosphate arakawaite, ehlite, libethenite
planet venus
plush chalcotrichite
purple bornite, erubescite
pyrite foolsgold
red carnelian, cuprite
rust canker, verdigris
rust, pert. aeruginous
selenide berzelianite
silicate bisbeeite
source cuprite
sulphate antlerite, arzrunite, bluejack, bluestone, boothite, brochantite, burnt brass, chalcanthite, copperas, sandstone, vitriol
sulphide covellite, ferretto
telluride rickardite
-tin alloy bell metal
-zinc alloy alpha-beta brass, arsedine, brass, dutch gold, muntz, oroide, tombac
zinc carbonate auriehaleite
COPPERHEAD beech-leaf snake, coin, goldeneye, moccasin, pilot snake, pit viper, redeye, squirrel
COPPERSMITH barbet, tinkerbird
COPPICE bluff, bosca, boscage, bosk, brow, coppet, coppice, copse, covert, firth, forest, frith, grove, hag, holt, hurst, shackle, thicket, wood
COPSE arbustum, clasp, clevis, coppice, coupling, cut, droke, fasten, hasp, holt, hurst, plant, shackle, shut in, spinny, trim
COPT christian, egyptian
dialect ahkmimic, bash-

muric, bohairic, fayumic, memphite

patriarch anba

title amba, anba, father, saint

COPY adopt, advertising, ape, apobraph, article, calk, calque, carbon, cast, context, ditto, draft, dummy, dupe, duplicate, ectype, edition, effigy, emulate, ensample, estreat, extract, facsimile, flimsy, image, imitate, likeness, manifold, manuscript, matter, mime(r), mimeograph, mimic, mirror, model, oyer, pasticcio, pattern, photostat, picture, plan, portrait, record, reflect, replica, reproduce, reproduction, reprograph, rubbing, sample, similitude, simulacrum, stat, text, trace(ry), transcribe, transcript(ion), type, write, writing, xerox

kind carbon, ditto, duplicate, ectype, estreat, extract, facsimile, mimeograph, pattern, protocol, replica, xerox

machine duplicator, hectograph, mimeograph, multigraph, multilith, pantograph, xerox

process xerography

small microfilm

true estreat, oyer

writer publicist

COPYCAT imitator, mimic

COPYIST calligrapher, copycat, imitator, plagiarist, scribe, scrivener, transcriber

pert. clerical

COPYREAD edit

COPYREADER editor, rimman

COPYRIGHT patent

infringe pirate, plagiarize

COQUETRY agacerie, charm, coyness, dalliance, flirtation, sheep's eyes, side glance

COQUETTE blinker, celimene, dally, flirt, hummingbird, nereni, philander, toy, trifle

COQUILLA attalea, cohune, palm, piassava

COQUINA clam, donax, limestone

CORA kore, nayarit, persephone, proserpine

mother demeter, persephone

CORACLE boat, canoe, curagh, currane, scow

CORAL (See also *kind*, below.) acropore, akori, alcyon, anthozoan, astraean, caratophyta, favosite, fuchsia, fungian, oculina, palule, pearl, pink, polyp, porite, red, rose, staghorn, stalacite, tubipore, zoophyte

bean frijolillo, sophora

bells alumroot, heuchera

berry buckbush, buttonbush, ceanothus, purshia, wolfberry

black gorgonian

blue aggri, aggry, heliopora

branch ramicle

cavity calyculus

cup-shaped zaphrentis

division aporosa

drop bessora

enemy acanthaster, crown-of-thorns, starfish

evergreen ground pine

fish dollfish

formation calicle, paar, palus, protheca

fossil alveolites

fungus clavaria, mushroom

genus acropora, favosites, fungia, oculina, porites, stylaster, tubipora

group caratophyta

island atoll, cay, key, reef

kind aporosa, astraean, astrangia, favosite, gorgonia, madrepore, millepore, perforata, porite, puna(luu), seafan, staghorn, starleaf

part. palus, protheca, septum

pea bleeding-heart

reef atoll, cay, island, key, shoal

ridge colline

rock bicherm, biolite, giolith

sea gulf papua

septum palus

skeleton coenosteum

snake bead snake, candystick, elapid, elaps, roller

sumac poisonwood

tissue exotheca

tree dapdap, erythrina, gabgab, pia

tropical madrepore

zooid polypite

CORALROOT crawley, dragon's-claw, orchid

CORBEIL basket, corf, creel, dosser, pannier

CORBEL ancon, bracket, bragger, cartouch(e), knot,

projection, respond, strut, timber

pert. pannier

CORBIE bird, chough, crow, raven

CORBIESTEP catstep, crowstep

CORBIN, MARGARET captain molly

CORCIR archil(la), corke(r), orchil

CORCYRA corfu

consort poseidon

CORD (See also *kind*, below.) aea, agal, amentum, bobbin, boom, boondoggle, bowyang, braid, brail, bungee, cable, chenille, fiador, funicle, heddle, inkle, lace, leash, ligament, ligation, ligature, line, lisere, olona, oxreim, rachis, raip, rope, skirreh, strand, strap, string, strop, tendon, thong, tie, tire, torsade, trine, twine, twist, urachus, welt, whang, wire

ball clew

drapery torsade

electric flex

embroidery arrasene

fringed llautu

goat's hair agal

grass spartina

hammock clew

kind catgut, clew, clothesline, gartel, gut, guyrope, hamstring, laniard, lanyard, lariat, lasso, lead(er), macrame, rain, rope, sennit, shoe lace, shoestring, sinew, stay, thew, trace, tug, umbilical, whipcord

-like funicule, funiform

mason's skirreh

nautical marlin

ornamented aglet, aiglet

parachute ripcord, shroud

piping bobbin

sacred kusti

spinal myelon, nucha, nuke

spinal, comb. myel(o)

spinal, pert. myelic

spinal, x-ray myelogram

strong catgut

twisted torsade

CORDAGE capacity, coir, gear, rigging, ropes, ropework, sennit, tackle

fiber abaca, ambaree, ambari, ambary, anodendron, anonang, ca, coir, cordia, mya, eruc, feru, hamber, hemp, imbe, ixle, jute,

kenaf, kyar, pita, sennit, sisal
fiber source anilao, anilau, grewia
length catenary
tree sida
CORDATE cardioid, hearted, heart-like, heart-shaped
CORDAY *victim* marat
CORDELIA *father* king lear
sister goneril, regan
CORDIA anonang, cereza, cherry, embuia, fruit, sebesten, varronia, walnut
CORDIAL affable, amiable, anisette, aqua caelestis, aqua mirabilis, ardent, barbados water, companionable, convivial, drink, elixir, friendly, generous, genial, glowing, gracious, heartfelt, hearty, hospitable, jovial, liberal, LIQUEUR, medicine, neighborly, open (hearted), persicot, pleasant, receptive, responsive, rosolio, sincere, sociable, warm(hearted), welcoming, wholehearted, zealous
medicinal hippocras
spiced usquebaugh
CORDIALITY ardor, amiability, empressment, friendship, generosity, heartiness, passion, regard, warmth
excessive backslapping
CORDILLERA See RANGE.
CORDON badge, band, braid, circle, coping, enclosure, ensign, group, guard, inclosure, lace, line, star, string, warden
bleu bengalee, chef, cook
decoration, haute cuisine
sanitaire quarantine
CORDS See PANTS.
CORDWOOD bodywood, lumber
measure stere, sterr
CORE ame, body, burden, cadre, center, cob, colk, company, crux, essence, focus, form, gist, heart, hub, kernel, linchpin, matrix, middle, midst, nave, nowel, nucleus, omphalus, pith, rumpf, staple, substance
arbor stalk
earth's nife
inner yolk
mold matrix, nowel
COREGONUS blackfin,

bloater, bowback, buffaloback, cisco, whitefish
COREOPSIS calliopsis, leptosyne, tickseed, tickweed
CORESUS *beloved* callirrhoe
CORF basket, cage, corb, creel, dosser, skip, truck, tub
CORFU curcyra, kerkyra
CORGI cardigan, dog, pembroke
CORIACEOUS alutaceous, cracked, tough
CORINTH, CORINTHIAN
capital ornament acanthus
citadel acrocorinth
colony leucadia, syracuse
commander demaretus, dinarchus, euclides, isias, neon, telemachus
crater kelebe
ensign pegasus
fountain pirene
king polybus, sisyphus
leader timoleon
princess creusa, glauke
rival argos
seer polyidus
tyrant cypselus, periander
CORINTHUS *father* marathon, zeus
CORIOLANUS *author* shakespeare
character caius marcius, cominius, junius brutus, marcius, menenius agrippa, sicinius velutus, titus lartius, tullus aufidius, valeria, virgilia, volumnia
friend agrippa
general aufidius, cominius, lartius
mother veturia
son marcius
wife virgilia, volumnia
CORK balsa, bark, bobber, bouchon, bung, close, confine, float, obstruction, peel, phellem, plug, restrain, seal, shive, soberin, spile, stop(per), stopple, suber, suppress, tampon
cambium phellogen
county resort kinsale
derivative or *extract* cerin
flat shive
fossil amianthus
helmet topee, topi
jacket life preserver
-like suberose, suberous
noise cloop
pert. suberic, suberous
source oak, suberin
tissue suber

tree millingtonia
tree bark suber
wax cerin
CORKER ace, ca(u)lker, stopper, top-notcher
CORKING excellent, fine, great, pleasing
CORKSCREW coil, convolute, convolve, defect, helical, opener, spiral, wind, wormer
CORKWING goldfinny, wrasse
CORKWOOD balsa, blolly, guano, harefoot, leitneria, majagua
CORKY buoyant, debonair, dry, light, lively, shriveled, skittish
CORM bulb, freesia, root, stem, uintjie
CORMORANT animal, bird, coal goose, duiker, duyker, glutton(ous), gormaw, greedy, guanay, norie, phalacrocorax, sea raven, scarfe, scart(h), shag(let), urile, voracious
-like snakebird
CORN banality, callus, cereal, chestnut, clavus, durra, ear, formity, frument(y), grain, granulate, heloma, hominy, induration, intoxicate, kafir, kanga, keep, kernel, maize, mealie, money, nocake, nubbin, para, platitude, preserve, rag(g)e, salt, seed, s(c)hmaltz, wyrock, zea
and beans succotash
-ball bumpkin, campy, hick
beads job's tears
belt country, middle west, midwest
black cornwheat
bread anadama, ash cake, bannock, cracklin bread, dodger, hoecake, hushpuppy, johnnycake, kankie, pone, tortilla
bundle shock, stack, stook
bunting ebb, lark
cake See CORN *bread.*
centaury bluebottle
cob ear, pipe
cockle agrostemma, cockweed, gith, hardhead, popple, melanthy
crake cornbird, crex, rail
crib bin
crow colicroot
crowfoot goldweed, hellweed, jackweed, joy

crushed stamp
crusher quern
cutting helotomy
dealer cornmonger
deity ceres, demeter
disease black bundle, boil smut, earrot, stewart's
dodger bread, dumpling, pone
dried pinole
ear abib, cob, icker, mealie, mealy, spike, tiponi, tucket
ear, comb. stachyo
ear, small nubbin
flag gladiolus, iris, levers
gromwell alkanet, painting plant, salfern
ground grist, meal
guinea d(h)urra
handful songle
having helosis
house corncrib, granary
hulled hominy, samp
husk cap, shuck
indian maize, samp, zea
juice whiskey
kale charlock
knife machete
leaf blade
lily bindweed, ixia
marigold boddle, boodle, buddle, gold(ing), golland, gools, gowlan, herb
meal atole, hoecake, masa, mealie, pinole, pone, samp, sofk(i)
meal, boiled atole, mush
meal, fried hoecake
mush atole, porridge
mustard charlock
parched graddan, hok(e)age, nocake, rokeage, rokee
parsley umbel
part cob, ear, husk, silk
pest bollworm, earworm
planter's tribe senecas
poppy blaver, blind eyes, canker(berry), cockle, coprose, earache, ponceau, redweed, rheadine, soldier, thunderflower
salad fetticus, milkgrass
shock stack, stook
silk floss
spike cob, ear
spurrey yara
stack hovel, hut
string trace
sugar dextrose
violet specularia
weevil calandra, kapra
whisky bourbon
woundwort stachys
CORNAGE horngeld

CORNCRACKER state kentucky
CORNEA comb. cerato, kerato
deposit arcus
disorder pinguecula
excision keratectomy
flattening aplanation
inflamation keratitis
opacity leukoma
pain in kratalgia
protrusion keratectasia
spot on nebula
thickening pannus
ulcer fossette
CORNEILLE character camille
drama cinna, horace, le cid, le menteur
CORNEL angle, cherry, corner, dogwood, redbrush
dwarf bunchberry, crackerberry
CORNELIA husband caesar
sons caius, gracchi, tiberius
CORNELIAN sardonyx
planet jupiter
symbol of content(ment)
CORNELIUS leader peter
CORNER alcove, angle, bend, cant, canthus, canton, coign(e), coin, control, cove, cranny, cubby(hole), edge, elbow, gloryhole, halk, herne, hole, impasse, ingle, inn, jam, jambe, manipulate, margin, monopolize, monopoly, niche, nook, part, pigeonhole, pose, quoin, recess, refuge, region, trap, tree, turning, verge, wick, wro
furniture encoignure
lower clew, clue
obscure nook
CORNERED angular, at bay, difficult, floored, graveled, nonplussed, treed
CORNERPIECE bumper, cantle, design
CORNERSTONE base, basis, coign(e), coin, coyn, curbstone, diatonus, foundation, headstone, quoin, solitaire, support
receptacle time-capsule
CORNET horn, twist, zink(e)
fish flutemouth, hemibranch
CORNFIELD mow
CORNFLOWER bachelor's button, barbeau, blaewort, blaver, bluebonnet, bluebottle, bluet, ixia, zea
pigment cyanin

CORNHUSKER state nebraska
CORNHUSKING shucking
CORNICE ancon, astragal, band, crown, drip, eave, geison, jowpy, molding, swanneck
basket caul
ornament antefix
part. cymation, cymatium, stagline
projection ortho
soffit plancer
support ancon
underside plancier, soffit
CORNISH See CORNWALL.
CORNSTALK karbi
CORNSTARCH binder
CORNUCOPIA coffin, horn of amalthaea, horn of plenty
CORNUS bloodyrod, buckbrush, buckbush, bunchberry, buttonbush, ceanothus, coralberry, crackerberry, dogwood, dwarf cornel, pigeonberry, purshia, redbrush, wolfberry
CORNWALL capital truro
cape tintagel
castle tintagel
crow aylet
diamond quartz
father-in-law king lear
giant cormoran
king mark
mine bal(1), wheal
native celt, cousin jack, kelt
ore whits
port bude
prince constantine
town penzance
western tip land's end
wife regan
CORNWALLIS dance, general
surrender site yorktown
CORNY banal, barnyard, buckeye, dull, mawkish, mickey, stale, trite
joke chestnut
COROEBUS father mygdon
slayer diomedes
victim poena
COROLLA bell, cup(ule), ligule, perianth, petals
part galea, petal, unie
rim annulus
COROLLARY adjunct, attendant, conclusion, concomitant, consequence, effect, porism, result, theorem, truism

geometric porism
COROMANDEL colcothar
gooseberry caramba, carambola
wood calamander
CORONA aureola, aureole, aurora borealis, blanket, bur(r), chandelier, cigar, circle(t), crown, fillet, garland, halo, merry dancers, northern lights, rosary, scyphus, solitaire, tonsure, wreath
australis southern crown
borealis northern crown
lightning andes glow, andes light
lucis chandelier
sun aureola, aureole, bishop's ring
CORONATION abhiseka, crowning, inaugural, installation, investiture
gulf tribe eskimo
robe armil(1), armilla, colobium, tunic
stone lia fail, scone
CORONER elisor, examiner, searcher
CORONET anadem, band, chaplet, circle(t), crown, diadem, fillet, garland, tiara, wreath
CORONIS *consort* apollo
slayer apollo
son aesculapius, asclepius
CORPORAL animal, bodily, carnal, fano(n), fanum, fleshly, material, missile, naigue, nayak, nco, personal, physical, sensual, sindon, somatic, tindal
famous hitler, napoleon
forbes cholera morbus
little napoleon
punishment death, flogging, spanking, whipping
violet napoleon
CORPORATION belly, body, business, city, company, concern, enterprise, firm, guildry, paunch, potbelly, pouch, society, stomach
officer controller
CORPOREAL actual, bodily, carnal, fleshly, hylic, material, objective, palable, phenomenal, physical, real, sensible, somal, somatic, tangible
CORPSE anatomy, ashes, body, bones, bulk, butt, cadaver, carcass, carrion, coil, crowbait, deadman, dece-

dent, lich, majority, mummy, relic, remains, stiff, wormfood, zombie
attraction to necrophilia
comb. necro
fat of adipocere
goddess libitina
light indian pipe
-like cadaverous, deathly
plant indian pipe
washing taharah
CORPULENT adipose, bellied, brawny, bulky, burly, chubby, chunky, dumpy, fat, fleshy, gross, husky, obese, plump, portly, rotund, stout, thick(set), weighty
CORPUS anthology, body, capital, collection field, florilegium, garland, group, literature, thesaurus, treasury, writings
christi fete-dieu
juris code
CORPUSCLE atom, blood, cell, electron, ghost, globule, hematid, hemocyte, leucocyte, molecule, particle
colorless leucocyte
destroyer globulicide
lack anemia
numbering blood count
red blood h(a)ematid, megaloblast, megalocyte, schistocyte
red, deficiency anemia
white leucocyte, plasmocyte
CORRAL atajo, capture, confine, coop, enclose, herd, kraal, pen, pound, seize, stockade, sty, surround, tambo
CORRECT accurate, actual, adjust, all right, amend, appropriate, aright, beam, beet, bete, better, careful, castigate, chasten, clean, conventional, cure, discipline, disillusion, due, edit, emend(ate), erect, exact, factual, fix, flawless, inform, legitimate, mend, meticulous, okay, order, orthodox, penalize, perfect, precise, proper, punish, rebuke, rectify, redress, reform, remedy, repair, reprimand, revamp, right, scold, set right, set straight, smug, strict, tame, tic, train, true, truthful, warn
comb. orth(o)

CORRECTNESS accuracy, convention, decorum, elegance, fitness, justice, veracity
CORRELATE analogue, collate, counterpart, parallel
CORRELATIVE analogue, answerable, correspondent, equal, mutual, neither, nor, reciprocal, redditive
CORRESPOND accord, agree, answer, assimilate, circularize, coincide, communicate, comport, concur, conform, dispatch, drop a line, equal, fit, gee, harmonize, jibe, mail, match, parallel, quadrate, reciprocate, square, suit, tally, write
in sound assonate
CORRESPONDENCE accord, analogy, answer, assonance, billet, bulletin, card, chit(ty), circular, communication, concord, consonance, dealings, dispatch, encyclical, epistle, harmony, homology, letter(writing), mail, message, missive, note, postcard, reply, rescript, resemblance, similarity, symmetry, tally, traffic
exact register
incomplete assonance
CORRESPONDENT accordant, addressee, communicator, complementary, conformable, contributor, epistolarian, letterwriter, like, pen pal, reciprocal, reporter, similar, stringer, sufficient, writer
CORRESPONDING akin, analogous, answerable, comparable, conformable, kin(dred)
in sound rhymic, rimic
part. isomere
CORRIDA bullfight
CORRIDOR aisle, arcade, cloister, coulisse, couloir, gallery, hall(way), passage(way)
CORRIE cirque, coomb, cwm, hollow
CORRIGENDUM erratum, error, mistake
CORROBORATE approve, back, confirm, prove, second, substantiate, sustain, validate, verify
CORRODE abrade, begnaw, bite, burn, canker, con-

sume, decary, eat(into), erode, etch, fret, gnaw, impair, mordicate, oxidize, rust, spoil, waste

CORRODING carking, esurine, harmful

CORROSION abrasion, attrition, decay, embayment, erosion

CORROSIVE acid(ulous), acrid, biting, caustic, cauterant, diabrotic, eating, erodent, erodine, fretful, harmful, mordant

CORRUGATE crimp, crinkle, crisp, crumple, furrow, rumple, wrinkle

CORRUGATION crease, crinkle, fold, furrow, groove, pucker, wrinkle

CORRUPT abandoned, abased, alloy, attaint, augean, bad, base, bedevil, beshrew, betray, blackhearted, bribe, buy, canker, carrion, contaminated, crafty, criminal, crooked, dark, debase(d), debauch(ed), decadent, decay(ed), deceive, defile, degenerate, degrade, demoralize(d), deprave(d), diseased, dishonest, dishonorable, dissolute, false, falsify, fishy, fix, foul, fraudulent, immoral, impure, infamous, infect, insidious, knavish, loose, monstrous, pervert(ed), poison, pollute, profligate, prostitute, putrid, questionable, ravish, rot(ten), ruin, seduce, shady, sick, sinister, soil, sophisticate, spoil, sully, taint(ed), traitorous, treacherous, ulcerate, unconscienced, underhanded, unethical, unfaithful, unprincipled, unreliable, unscrupulous, venal, venum, vile, vitiate(d), wemmy, wicked, wreck

CORRUPTION abuse, atrocity, barbarism, betrayal, bribery, dirt, dishonesty, carrion, chicanery, criminality, crookedness, decay, depravity, dirt, filth, fraud(ulence), improbity, indirection, infamy, infection, infidelity, inquination, lubricity, perfidy, perver-

sion, pus, putrescence, soil, solecism, squalor, taint, treason, turpitude, venality, vice, villainy

CORSAC adive, karagan

CORSAGE bouquet, canezou

CORSAIR buccaneer, bug, caper, cursaro, freebooter, picaroon, pirate, privateer, robber, rockfish

ship xebec

CORSELET ahl(l)ecret, allecret, armor, bodice, breastplate, cover, thorax

CORSET belt, bodice, busk, foundation, girdle, jupes, panty girdle, stays, support, two-way stretch, underbody

bone busk

cover camisole, chemise, underwaist

stay source whalebone

strip bone, busk, stay

CORSICA *capital* ajaccio

city ajaccio, aleria, bastia, calvi, corte, sartene

patriot paoli

peak cinto, rotondo

pine larch

plant baby tears, maqui

port bastia

river golo, gravone, taravo

vegetation maquis

CORTEGE company, funeral, group, parade, pomp, procession, retinue, suite, train

CORTEX armor, bark, cover, pallium, peel, periblem, peridium, rind, shell

cerebral area-striata

gray matter ectocinerea

primary periblem

CORTEZ marques del valle, tibourbou

beloved isabel, malinche

captain alvarado de leon, olea, olid, sandoval

friend duero, medina

historian claviero, diaz, gomara, ixtlilxochitl, oviedo, sahagun, tezozomoc

interpreter aquilar, dona marina

patron ovando, velazquez

school salamanca university

sea of gulf of california

secretary francisco lopez de gomara

victim cuantemoc, cuauatemac, montezuma

wife catalina juarez

CORUNDUM abrasive,

adamas, alumina, amethyst, barklyite, emery, mineral, ruby, sand, sapphire

synthetic emerald

CORUSCATE blaze, brandish, flash, glance, gleam, glint, glister, glitter, radiate, scintillate, shimmer, spark(le), twinkle

CORVUS See CROW.

CORYBANTIC agitated, dissipated, frenzied, unrestrained

CORYCIA *consort* apollo

CORYDALIS capnoides, dobson, fumewort, hellgramite

CORYNETES periphetes

CORYPHAEUS zeus

CORYPHASIA athena

CORYPHEE dancer, premiere danseuse, star

CORYTHUS *beloved* helen

foster son telephus

parent oenone, priam

slayer priam

CORYZA catarrh, cold

sign sneeze

COS lettuce, romaine

pert. coan

COSAM *parent* elmadam

son addi

COSA NOSTRA mafia, syndicate

COSCET cotarius, cotsetle, cottar, cottier, peasant

COSETTE *patron* valjean

COSH blackjack, bludgeon, cottage, friendly, happy, hit, hovel, husk, lively, neat, quiet, snug, still

COSMETIC angel water, ceruse, clown white, cold cream, compact, crayon, cream, cream base, enamel, eyebrow pencil, eye shadow, foundation, fucus, grease paint, henna, kohl, kuhl, liner, lipstick, makeup, mascara, mudpack, nail polish, paint, pomade, powder, rouge, stibium, stibnite, talcum(powder), war paint

bismuth blanc de ford, blanc d'espagne

eyelash mascara

medicated lotion

paste pack

source aubepine, babassu oil, benzoin, benzyl

white lead ceruse

COSMIC catholic, cos-

mogonal, cosmopolitan, ecumenical, great, harmonious, infinite, mundane, orderly, universal, vast
cycle eon
dust meteor
fog nebula
opposed to acronycal
order rita, tao
principle urgrund
COSMOGRAPHIC See COSMIC.
COSMONAUT See ASTRONAUT.
COSMOPOLITAN allaround, amphigean, ecumenic, liberal, many-sided, pandemic, progressive, sophisticated, versatile, worldly
COSMOS earth, globe, harmony, heaven, macrocosm, order, plant, realm, universe, world
symbol mandala
COSSACK ataman, hetman, russian, soldier, tartar, tatar, zaporogue
captain sotnik
cavalry sotnia
chief ataman, hetman, mazeppa
conqueror ermak
district steppes, voisko
elder ataman
leader hetman, mazeppa
mount charger
people chernomorish
post guard, warden
squadron sotna, sotnia
unit stanitsa
village stanitza
whip knout
COSSET caress, coddle, cuddle, darling, fondle, lamb, pamper, pet, tiddle
COSSETTE chip, schnitzel, slice, strip
COST afford, amount to, bring in, budget, characteristic, charge, come to, costmary, damage, detriment, disposition, entail, estimate, expense, fetch, load, loss, manner, means, outlay, penalty, price, quality, reprise, run to, sacrifice, scathe, sell for, spend, suffering, tansy, tax, value, way, yield
at cheap
COSTA midrib, rib, ridge, vein

COSTA RICA *cape* blanco, elena, velas
capital san jose
city alajuela, bagaces, boruca, canas, cartago, colorado, golfito, guapiles, heredia, liberia, limon, negrita, nicoya, san jose, vesta
coin centimo, colon
dance punta, torito
gulf dulce, nicoya, papagayo
indian boruca, bribri, guatuso, guaymi, voto
island coco
lake arenal
measure caballeria, cafiz, cahiz, cajuela, cantaro, fanega, manzana, tercia, vara
nightshade paradise flower
peak blanco, chirripo
peninsula nicoya, osa
people guaymie
point cahuita, galonos, llerena, quepos
port limon, puntarenas
president figueres, orlich
river irazu, matina, poas, sixaola, tarcoles, tenoria
volcano barba, irazu, poas
weight bag, caja, libra
COSTERMAN barrowboy, hawker, pearly, peddler, vendor
COSTIVE bound, close, cold, dry, emplastic, hard, niggardly, reserved, unyielding
COSTLY dainty, dear, dearthful, dispenditious, expensive, extravagant, gorgeous, high, lavish, luxurious, opulent, precious, priceless, prodigal, rich, splendid, sumptuous, valuable
COSTMARY alecost, maudlin, mint geranium, rosemary, tansy
COSTREL bottle, flask, head, keg
COSTUME apparel, attire, bloomers, buskin, cap and bells, clothes, clothing, disguise, domino, dress, duds, ensemble, garb, get up, habit, masquerade, motley, outfit, raiment, rig, robe, sari, scenery, sock, suit, theatricals, tights, tog, toilet, truss, tutu, uniform, wardrobe
COSTUSROOT pachak
COSY See COZY.
COT bed, berth, boat, bothy, bunk, charpai, charpoy,

coop, cotquean, cottage, cover, hut, mat, pen, shelter, stall, tangle
COTA See FORT.
COTE coop, cottage, hillside, homestead, house, hut, outrun, outstrip, shed, shelter, surpass
d'azur riviera
d'or wine burgundy, chambertin, conti, montrachet, musigny, romance, vougeot
COTERIE association, bunch, cabal, camarilla, circle, circuit, clique, group, junto, monde, platoon, set, society
COTHURNUS boot, buskin, footwear, tragedy
COTILLION dance, german, quadrille, solitaire
COTINGA bird, campanero, chatterer, cock of the rock, umbrella bird
COTINUS chittamwood, smoke tree
COTTAGE bach, bari, blockhouse, bohawn, bothy, bower, bungalow, cabana, cabin, cape cod, chalet, chaumiere, cosh, cot(e), house, hut, lodge, log cabin, lonquhard, shack, shed, shelter, shieling, thalthan
cheese skyr, smearcase
partition hallan, speer
tulip bouton d'or
COTTAR See PEASANT.
COTTER bowpin, clot, coagulate, complain, congeal, cottager, forelock, linchpin, mat, peasant, potter, pucker, shrink, shrivel, tangle, toggle, vex, villein, willwin, wither, worry
COTTID fish, miller's-thumb, sculpin
COTTON (See also FABRIC *cotton.*) accord, adati, agree, algodon, bayal, beat, bolly, coddle, cossypium, derry, drab, dressing, flog, fraternize, gossypium, harmonize, maco, mata, pima, prosper, sak, silesia, succeed, susi
and linen fustian
ball bolly, lint
blight black arm, weevil
boll snap
cleaner willow, willy
clearer gin
cloth See FABRIC *cotton.*
cloth blemish nit

coarse bagging, baline, bunting, canvas, hemp, jute
disease anthracnose, blackarm, bollrot, hybosis, stenosis
dye copperas, sulphide
fiber lint, linter, stapel, viscose
fiber knot nep, slub
filament thread
filling batt(ing)
flannel canton, swans's-down, swanskin
flowered calico
gauze cypress, cyprus, leno
gin charkha
gin attachment moter
gin inventor eli whitney
grass bogdown, canna(ch), catlocks, drawling, eriophorum
handkerchief bandana, malabar
injured by frost bolly
jersey t-shirt
kind maco, pima
knot in neb, slub
last picking top crop
lawn batiste
layer batting
light etamine, pima
long-staple maco
machine bale-breaker, candroy, gin, mule, twiner
mass fussock
measure hank, lea
mercerized burberry, silkaline
moth alabama
napped lambskin
painted indienne
pest boll weevil, snout beetle
-picking confounded, damned, worthless
plant lamb
printed calico, indienne, sarong
printing dye alizarin
raw bayal, lint
rebaled city crop
refuse grabbots
sheet batting, drilling, manta, muslin, percale
shoot ratoon
silk floss
square tzut(e)
staple matta
state alabama
striped bengal, bezan, express
strong denim, duck, scrim
sugar raffinose
teal pygmy-goose
thread lisle

to like, love, take to
treat with alkali mercerize
tree black poplar, bombax, ceiba, maco, majagua, simal
twilled beaverteen, chino, fustian, jean, sallo(o), silesia
twisted roll slub
wad tampon
warp cloth satinet
waste blowings, card strip, grabbots, linter, noil
wick grunt
wilt black root
wool caddice, caddis
worker baler
worsted zanella
COTTONMOUTH snake, water moccasin
COTTONSEED *kernel* meat
oil test becchi test
principle gossypol
remover gin, mule
tree groundsel
vessel bole, boll
COTTONTAIL cony, hare, leveret, rabbit
group nest
COTTONWOOD alamo, necklace-poplar, paulownia, poplar, populus, tree
COTTUS bullhead, sculpin
COUCH bed, bend, biclinium, burrow, canape, conceal, cot, crouch, davenport, daybed, depress, divan, dormeuse, express, feuter, hide, incude, kip, lair, lay, lie(down), lodge, lurk, pallet, phrase, press, put, recline, repose, rest, screen, secrete, settee, skulk, slink, sneak, sofa, squat, state, stoop, word
dining room biclinium
grass cutch, foxtail, kutch, quack, quick, quitch, scotch, scutch, stroil, twitch, withvine
in terms phrase, word
nuptial thore
pert. sofane
reclining on accubation
COUCHANT dormant, prone, prostrate, reclining, recumbent, supine
COUCI-COUCI mediocre
COUGAR badger, carcajou, cat, catamount(ain), lynx, mountain lion, panther, puma, wolverine
COUGH baff, bark, begma, chank, croup, exhalation, hack, hawk, heck, hoast,

hoose, hooze, tussis, whoop, yex, yox
caused by tussive
drop lozenge, pastil(le), troche
dry hoose, hooze
hoarse croup
medicine eclegma, herb tobacco, horehound, sapa
pert. bechic, tussal, tussive
syrup eclegma, linctus
syrup ingredient glycerin
up ante(up), blurt out, cede, confess, contribute, deliver, divulge, expectorate, give, hand over, reveal, surrender, vomit, yield
COUGHROOT wakerobin
COUGHWEED ragwort
COULEE bed, couloir, draw, gap, gorge, gulch, ravine, valley
COUMA hyahya, sorva
COUMADIN warfarin
COUNCIL assembly, board, body, brain trust, bule, cabal, cabildo, cabinet, camarilla, conference, congress, convention, curule, dael, diet, divan, duma, durbar, folkmoot, fono, gathering, gerusia, husting, indaba, jirga(h), junta, lukiko, majlis, meeting, musnud, parliament, powwow, rigsraad, sabha, sanhedrin, senate, sobor, soviet, state, synod, taryba, tribunal, witan, yuan
chamber balai, balei, bouleterion, camarilla, divan
ecclesiastic chapter, church, classis, congregation, consistory, conventicle, presbytery, session, synod, vestry
hall balai
national congress, dail, diet, parliament
pert. cameral, synodal
political cabal, caucus, junto,
table cover tapis
COUNCILLOR enduna, faipule, induna, senator, vizer, vizier
COUNCILMAN alderman, concionator, deputy, legislator, selectman
COUNSEL abogado, admonish, advise(r), advisor, advocate, attorney, barrister, caution, chide, coach, confer(ence), consultant, deliberation, design, direct, echevin, egeria, enduna, guide,

intent(ion), instructor, kibitzer, lawyer, leader, lecture, monitor, nestor, nobleman, plan, proctor, prudence, recommendation, rede, reed, scheme, silk, solicitor, starets, suggestion, tip, ucalegon, verbum sapienti, warn, witan, word to the wise

good, name meaning alfred

ill aboula

king's silk

sacred torah

COUNSELOR adviser, advisor, advocate, COUNSEL, gonzalo, lawyer, mentor, proctor, redesman, sage, starets, wite

woman egeria

COUNT add, ascribe, calculate, canvass, cast, census, comes, compt, compute, comte, consider(ation), depend, earl, enumerate, estimate, figure, foot, graf, impute, influence, inventory, judge, lord, matter, nobleman, number, numerate, points, reason, reckon, regard, rely, score, sum, tale, tally, tell, tot, total(ize), tottle, trust, value, weigh

down calculate, launch time, start

of monte cristo edmond dantes

of monte cristo author dumas

on aim for, depend on, expect, lite, plan on, rely

out disqualify, exclude

pert. comital

COUNTENANCE abet, accept, aid, appearance, approval, approve, aspect, back(ing), bearing, befriend, behavior, brow, cheer, composure, conduct, demeanor, encourage(ment), endorse, face, favor, goodwill, invite, looks, mien, mug, patronize, physiognomy, puss, sanction, suffer(ance), support, visage

out of disgraced, embarrassed

COUNTER adverse, against, answer, antagonistic(al), antipodal, bar, bench, bone, carom, check, chip, coin, combat, computer, contend, contrary, controvert, field

goal, fish, geiger, hostile, inimical, jeton, man, marker, money, oppose(d), opposite, parry, pawn, point, react, reply, retaliate, run, score, shamble, shelf, shopboard, showcase, stand, stern, stop, table, tally, thwart, token, touchdown

-agent antidote

blast reciprocation

blow retaliation

-charge backracket, cathexis, rebut, recriminate, retort

comb. ant(i)

-current backset, eddy

-glow gegenschein

instrument See MATHEMATICS *instrument.*

kind bone, card, checker, chip, domino, man, piece, poker chip, tally, tile, token

plot intrigue

-stamp punch mark

-stroke reciprocation, riposte

-sun anthelion, halo

tendency reaction

theme undersong

to against, opposed

COUNTERACT antagonize, balance, cancel, check, clash, compensate, conflict, contradict, contravene, correct, counterpoise, countervail, cross, defeat, defend, destroy, frustrate, go against, hinder, interfere, negative, neutralize, nullify, offset, oppose, oppugn, react, resist, thwart, traverse

COUNTERACTANT alkalizer, antacid, antidote, antihistamine, antiperiodic, irritant, neutralizer, remedy

COUNTERATTACK answer, charge

COUNTERBALANCE cancel, compensate, counterpoise, neutralize, offset, set off, stabilize, weigh

COUNTERCHECK bumper, censure, curb, hinder, rebuke, stop

COUNTERCLOCKWISE against the sun, backward(s), direct, left, round

COUNTEREARTH antichthon

COUNTERFEIT act, affect, artificial, assume, bad money, base, bogus, boodle, brummagem, bunyip, cheat,

chemic(k), coin, copy, dissemble, duffing, dummy, ersatz, fabricate, fake, false, falsify, feign(ed), forge(ry), fraud(ulent), gaudy, green goods, imitate, impostor, inferior, kite, mint, mock, phony, postiche, pretend, queer, rubber check, sham, showy, simular, simulate, snide, spurious, supposed, tin, tinsel, worthless

apparatus for bogus

COUNTERFEITER coiner, imitator, jackman, jarkman, scratcher

COUNTERFOIL check, stub

COUNTERIRRITANT antidote, arnica, ginger, iodine, liniment, moxa, mustard, pepper, seton, silver nitrate, stupe

COUNTERJUMPER salesman, shopman

COUNTERMAND abolish, annul, cancel, forbid, recall, repeal, rescind, revoke

COUNTERMARK signature

COUNTERMINE entrenchment, fortify, frustrate, plot

COUNTEROFFENSIVE attack

COUNTERPANE bed cover, bedspread, coverlet, quilt, spread

COUNTERPART analog(ue), complement, copy, correlate, cousin, doppelganger, double, duplicate, equivalent, facsimile, image, match, mate, obverse, opposite, parallel, pendant, replica, rescript, shadow, tally, twin

COUNTERPOINT accompaniment, arrangement, contrapunto, contrast, descant, foil, fugue, juxtaposition, song

COUNTERPOISE balance, ballast, compensate, counteract, counterbalance, counterweight, equalize, equilibrium, offset, stabilize, steady, trim

COUNTERPOISON alexipharmie, antidote, antitoxin, mithridate, orvietan

COUNTERPOLE antithesis, opposite

COUNTERSIGN back, confirm, consigne, corroborate, endorse, grip, guarantee, mark, password, ratify,

sanction, seal, sign(al), signature, watchword
COUNTERSINK bevel, chamfer, dish, imbed, ream
COUNTERTENOR alto, falsetto, male alto
COUNTERVAIL balance, compensate, counteract, neutralize, offset, poise, stabilize
COUNTERWEIGHT tare
COUNTERWORK counteract, frustrate, hinder, oppose, thwart
COUNTESS comtesse, contesa, lady, olivia
husband earl
COUNTLESS incalculable, infinite, limitless, numberless, teeming
COUNTRY area, backwoods, boondocks, boonies, borderland, brush, bundu, bush, champaign, corn belt, cotton belt, cush, district, dominion, dust bowl, earth, forest, frith, frontier, grass roots, hick(dom), highlands, hinterland, home, hoosier belt, hoosierdom, hotzeplotz, kith, land, locale, lowlands, march, nation, outback, outpost, pais, people, province, realm, region, rural, rustic, scrub (land), soil, state, sticks, territory, timbers, tract, tulies, upland, vale, veld(t), weald, wheat belt, wide open spaces, wilderness, wild(west), woodlands, woods, yokeldom
ancient aeolis, aram, elam, elis, eolis, etruria, sheba, tarshish
bred in, name meaning silvester
bumpkin carl, churl, clod, rube, yahoo, yokel
dance barn dance, blue grass
division canton, county, department, province, shire, state, territory
father of See **FATHER** of his country.
festival ale
gallant swain
gentleman allworthy, bob acres, sweetcorn
gentlewoman lady bountiful
girl amaryllis, minnie pearl
gooseberry bilimbi
house bastide, casino, cassine, chalet, chateau, dacha,

estancia, grange, quinta, villa
imaginary brobdingnag, cockaigne, lagado, laputa, leonnoys, lilliput, svithiod, swithiod, teutonia, utopia, weissnichtwo, wonderland
law pais
lost atlantis
man billjim, boor, bumpkin, campesino, churl, clown, compatriot, farmer, gibaro, granger, hayseed, hick, hob, inhabitant, jake, kern(o), landsman, paisano, patriot, peasant, plowman, rube, rural(ist), rustic, swain, yahoo, yokel
man without nolan
maritime maremma
open bled, field, heath, moor, range, veld(t), weald, wold
party barn dance, cornhusking, husking bee
pepper stonecrop
pert. agrestic, predial, rural, rustic
place estate, farm, fief, hacienda, ranch, seat, spread, villa
pygmies lilliput
reside in rusticate
road byway, lane, path
town hamlet, village
tract basin
undersea atlantis, lyonesse
walnut candlenut
world's highest tibet
COUNTY amt, aristocracy, borough, bute, canton, district, domain, elite, fylke, gentlefolk, gentry, lan, parish, province, seat, shire, society
administrators board of supervisors
division barony, hundred, rape
house poorfarm
seat capital
COUP act, attack, barter, blow, buy, capsize, cut, drain, feat, overturn, ploy, putsch, scoop, slash, spill, stroke, upset
de grace death blow, end
de main attack, stratagem
de maitre masterpiece, masterwork
de pied check, disgrace, kick, repulse
de plume satire
de poing boucher, handstone
de soleil sunstroke

d'etat arrogation, revolution, stratagem, take-over, usurpation
d'oeil glance, glimpse, look, peek, peep, sight, survey, view
COUPE auto, cabriolet, carriage, convertible, cut, ice cream, landau(let)
COUPLE assemble, board, bond, both, brace, bracket, case, combine, come together, connect, cover, doublet, duo, dyad, fasten, gemel, gemini, join, leash, link, man and wife, marry, match, mate, newlyweds, pair, serve, shackle, span, splice, team, tie, twain, twins, two(some), unite, wed, yoke
loving darby and joan
of shakes jiffy, short time
COUPLED double, gemel(ed), geminate, joined, paired, united, wedded, yoked
COUPLER bobber, drawbolt, janney, link(er), ring, shackle(r), snapper, uniter
COUPLES *growing in* binate
COUPLET beyt, brace, copla, distich, elegiac, pair, poem, two(-liner), verse
COUPON certificate, sample, securities, token, twofer
clipper bondholder, retiree, shareholder
COURAGE arete, audacity, backbone, bield, boldness, bravado, braveness, bravery, breast, chivalry, confidence, daring, doughtiness, firmness, fortitude, gallantness, gallantry, greatheartedness, grit, guts, hardihood, hardiment, heart, heroism, intrepidity, intrepidness, knightliness, lionheartedness, liquor, manfulness, manhood, manliness, manship, mettle, mind, nerve, peker, pluck, prowess, rashness, resoluteness, resolution, sand, soul, spirit, spunk, stoutheartedness, stoutness, strength, temerity, tenacity, valiancy, valiantness, valor, virtue, will
deprive of unman, unnerve
of one's convictions confidence, resolution, stamina
personification arete, virtus

symbol bloodstone, horse, lion

COURAGEOUS adventurous, audacious, bold, brave, daring, dauntless, devilish, doughty, enterprising, fearless, fiery, gallant, game, gutsy, hardy, heroic, impavid, intrepid, manful, manly, martial, mettlesome, plucky, resolute, spartan, spunky, stalwart, staunch, stout(hearted), trojan, two-fisted, unafraid, undaunted, valiant, valorous
name meaning neal, neil

COURBARIL cuapinole, guapinol, jatoba, locust

COURIER cicerone, dragoman, estafet(te), express, guide, intelligencer, kavass, messenger, patamor, post(er), runner
horse bidet
mounted estafet(te)
relay system angaria

COURLAN bird, jacamar, limpkin, tinamon

COURSE aim for, ambit, approach, artery, assiette, bearing, beeline, career, cast, channel, chase, circuit, class, conduct, current, curry, cycle, dart, dash, direction, dish, distance, drift, drive, entree, flight, flow, flux, gallop, girder, gutter, hask, heading, heat, highway, hunt, itinerary, journey, lap, lapse, layer, leg, method, mode, movement, ongoing, onrush, orbit, pass(age), path, plan, point, policy, procedure, process, progress, pursue, race, road, rote, rout(e), run, rush, sail for, scope, sequence, series, set, speed, stratum, stream, street, study, subject, system, tack, tendency, tenor, tier, track, traject, travel, trek, trend, trip, vector, voyage, way
alter detour, veer
blocking parapet
change deviate
charting pilotage
circular chukker, compass, sweep
comb. agog(ue)
downward decline, slide, toboggan
easy cinch, gut, pipe, sinecure, snap

first antipasto, hors d'oeuvre
habitual bias, groove, regimen, rote, routine, rut
masonry coping, heading, skewback, stilt
meal antipasto, dessert, entree, salad, soup
oblique skew
of action career, custom, demarche, procedure, routine
of sprouts training
of study college, curriculum, seminar, syllabus
on underway
regular routine, rut
roundabout detour, diversion, indirection
turn off yaw

COURSER charger, crocodilebird, cusser, horse, mount, racer, steed

COURT (See also *kind*, below.) 3 bar, bid, soc, sue, woo 4 area, bail, date, dock, eyre, fawn, leet, ring, rink, road, rota, suit, wale, ward, wind, wynd, yard 5 alley, arena, bench, chase, close, curia, curry, dairo, divan, diwan, favor, field, forum, gemot, judge, levee, patio, spark, spoon, suite, train, yamen 6 allure, atrium, bailey, circus, dargar, durbar, follow, gemote, homage, hustle, invite, palace, pander, parvis, pursue, sudder 7 adawlut, address, assizes, attract, barmote, bethdin, classis, compass, flatter, husting, mansion, probate, retinue, society, solicit, truckle 8 approach, audience, bootlick, make up to, markmoot, markmote, pay court, play up to, run after, serenade, townhall, tribunal, woodmote 9 caterwaul, committee, cultivate, enclosure, shine up to 10 quadrangle 11 apple polish 13 pay attentions
action case, suit, trial
arbiter judex
assistant amala, amlah, beadle, clerk, crier, elisor, eyre, juror, marshall, staff, staves, talesman
before the at the bar
body jury
bouillon stock
bring to arraign, arrest, subpoena, sue
calendar docket

call arraignment, oyes, oyez, subpoena, summons
church audiencia, classis, consistory, curia, rota, synod
circuit eyre, iter
city municipal
complaint querele
crier bailiff, beadle
criminal assizes, bureo
cry oyes, oyez
dance pavan
danger dare
decision adjudication, arret, decree, guilty, judgment, ruling, verdict
district soke
ecclesiastical See COURT church.
exemption essoin
exercise ephebium
fee fine
fine amerce
hearing oyer
inner atrium, patio
kind admiralty, appeals, appellate, assizes, bar, bench, bethdin, chancery, claims, common pleas, criminal, domestic relations, judgment seat, judiciary, martial, municipal, police, small claims, star chamber, tribunal
ladies bedoyo
local gamot(e)
-martial drumhead, trial, try
mikado's dairi
minutes acta
-noue roncet
of equity chancery
officer bailiff, byrlawman, clerk, crier, cursitor, dempster, examiner, extractor, feodary, filacer, jurat, macer, mehamander, surrogate
of 100 centumvir, mall(um)
old arret, gemot(e), leet, mote, woodmote
order brief, capias, decree, injunction, nisi, process, rule, ruling, subpoena, summons vacator, writ
panel jury
participant advocate, crier, defendant, defender, elisor, judge, jury, lawyer, plaintiff, pleader, prosecutor, talesman
pert. aulic, forensic, fornaecus, judicial, judiciary, rotal

plaster bandage, dressing, tape
proceeding placitum
reformed classis
room banc
section witness box
security bail
session assizes, oyer, sedurunt, trial
shoe pump
tyrannical star chamber
writ See COURT *order*.
COURTEOUS affable, attent(ive), bonaire, ceremonious, civil, complaisant, considerate, cordial, courtly, deferential, diplomatic, dutiful, gallant, genteel, gentle(manly), gracious, honorific, ladylike, mannerly, obliging, polite, refined, regardful, respectful, smooth, suave, thoughtful, urbane, well-behaved, well-bred
COURTESAN adventuress, amorosa, aspasia, bona roba, delilah, demi-mondaine, demimonde, demirep, devadasi, hetaera, jezebel, lais, lorettas, madame, messalina, mylitta, paramour, phryne, plover, prostitute, pucelle, stallion, sweetheart, thais
COURTESY affability, amenity, attention, bienseance, bonton, breeding, ceremony, chivalry, civility, comity, complacency, complaisance, curtsy, deference, favor, gallantry, generosity, gentility, good manners, graciousness, gratuity, help, indulgence, mannerliness, manners, mensk, politeness, politesse, refinement, respect (fulness), savoir faire, savoir vivre, suavity, tashrif, urbanity
title bey
COURTHOUSE capital, county seat, cutch(ery)
COURTIER attendant, butterfly, cavalier, flatterer, follower, hanger on, henchman, iachimo, kuge, osric(ic), polonius, sycophant
COURTLY aulic, chivalrous, civil, conventional, courteous, dignified, elegant, finished, formal, gallant, graceful, hend(e), obsequi-

ous, polished, polite(ly), refined
COURTMANTLE henry ii
COURTSHIP amour, attention, dru(e)ry, plight, romance, sparking, suit, wooing
COURTYARD atrium, bailey, ballium, cortile, curtilage, enclosure, patio, quadrangle, solitaire, tetragon, trance, wynd
open garth
COUS bovine, cowlike
COUSIN akin, allied, coz, kuzin(eh), onkel, shvesterkind
COUTURIERE dressmaker, modiste
COVE arm, bay, bight, bloke, cave, chap, corner, estuary, fellow, firth, frith, gunkhole, gypsy, haven, hollow, inlet, molding, niche, nook, pass, recess, retreat, sump, valley, waterway
COVENANT accord, agreement, bargain, bind, bond, bris, brith, cartel, compact, concord(at), contract, convention, entente, handfast, indenture, mise, pact, patise, pledge, stipulate, treaty, true, understanding
COVENTRY *horsewoman* lady godiva
patroness godiva
send to exclude, ostracize
COVER (See also *kind*, below.) 3 aim, bet, cap, dim, hap, lap, lay, lid, top 4 aech, bury, bush, ceil, coat, cope, cowl, face, film, furl, heal, hele, hide, hood, line, mask, pall, pave, peel, pelt, rime, rind, roof, scum, seal, sell, sile, skin, span, stop, tent, tidy, tilt, veil, wrap 5 apron, armor, blind, board, cloak, drape, front, guise, house, kiver, paint, put on, reach, shade, sheet, strew, umbra 6 ambush, armour, binded, bonnet, casing, cement, clothe, couple, encase, entail, incase, invest, jacket, mantle, muffle, pelage, refuge, screen, shield, shroud, spread, swathe, thatch, veneer 7 asphalt, bandage, binding, blanket, capsule, coating, conceal, contect, curtain, embrace, housing, include,

involve, obscure, overlay, retreat, scutate, sheathe, shelter, shutter, smother, tegumen, thicket 8 bewilder, disguise, envelope, preserve, pretence, sericate, slipover, vestment 9 caparison, indemnify, overwhelm, vestiture 10 camouflage, substitute, subterfuge 11 superimpose
a bet fade
a fire bank, damp(er)
a hatch batten
charge couvert, fee
comb. stego
dark umbra
eyes blindfold
ground advance, progress, speed, travel
kind altar cloth, antimacassar, awning, baize, baldachin, bed spread, blanket, blind, canopy, carpet, centerpiece, cerecloth, cerement, chrismal, cloth, coom, corporal(e), cosy, cowl(ing), cozy, curtain, doily, dossil, doyley, elytron, fannel, fanon, fingerstall, hood, housing, manta, mantle, marquee, marquise, mask, pall, pavilion, pilch, pledget, purdah, pyx cloth, quilt, rug, scarf, screen, shamianah, shard, sheet, shield, shroud, shutters, smokescreen, tablecloth, tarp(aulin), tester, tidy, veiling
over becloud, hid, quelme, rake, sheathe, sheugh, smother, welme, whelm, withhele
partly debruise
protective apron, armature, armor, bib, camouflage, cocoon, helmet, scale, shell, smokescreen
-shame sawin(e)
thin film, veneer
up belie, bely, conceal(ment), put on, salve, sleek
up for front, protect, take the rap
with bacon strips lard
with crumbs bread
with mud belute
with oakum fother
with straw thatch
with water douse, dowse, drown, flood, soak, whelm
COVERED armor(ed), blind, clad, cleithral, covert, encrusted, hidden,

ironclad, ivied, loricated, obtected, panoplied, protected, screened, scutate, sericated, shielded, shod
comb. crypto, stegano
wagon boxcar, conestoga, white top
COVERING (See also COVER *kind.*) apron, aril, armor, asphalt, awning, bark, binding, boarding, booth, canopy, capsule, casement, cloaking, curtain, envelopment, fur, hide, incubation, overlaying, painting, pall, pargeting, peel, pelage, pelt, pericarp, plasterwork, protection, rind, roof, screening, sheathing, shelter, skin, smokescreen, stuccowork, superimposition, tagumen(t), tent, testa, tile, umbrella, upholster, vesture
coarse caddow, canvas, tillet
defensive See COVER *protective.*
membrane caul
oramental antemacassar, caparison, doily, doyley, tidy
outer bark, carapace, coat, crust, fur, hide, hull, husk, skin, testa
winter hibernaculum
COVERLET afghan, blanket, buffalo robe, caddow, colcha, coverlid, dagswain, heler, lap robe, ligger, rezai, robe, rug, spread, throw
COVERT asylum, backdoor, backstairs, blind, clandestine, cloaked, concealed, den, disguised, feline, furtive, hangdog, hidden, hole-and-corner, huggermugger, insidious, involved, lair, latent, lay, lie, masked, mystic, private, privy, refuge, screened, secret, shelter, shifty, shrubbery, skulking, slinking, slinky, sly, sneaking, sneaky, stealthy, subrosa, surreptitious, thicket, undercover, underground, underhanded, under the counter, unobtrusive
coat duster
COVET aim at, aspire, begrudge, crave, desire, envy, grudge, hanker, long, lust, pant, pine, want, wish, yearn, yisse

COVETOUS acquisitive, avaricious, avid, desirous, eager, envious, frugal, gluttonous, grasping, greedy, gripple, jealous, mean (-spirited), mercenary, miserly, ravenous, stingy, voracious
COVEY bevy, brood, company, covert, drove, flight, flock, gaggle, group, herd, multitude, pack, school, set, shoal, swarm
COVIN band, company, convene, crow, fraud, group, tuckery
COW abash, awe, beef, bogy, bos, boss(y), bovine, broadie, broak, browbeat, bulldoze, cattle, crummie, crummy, daunt, discourage, dismay, dispirit, dolt, dompt, faze, frighten, harass, hawkie, heifer, intimidate, mulley, overawe, poll, prune, quey, raft, rattle, simpleton, terrify, terrorize, threaten, vaca, vach(e)
ant aphis
barn barth, byre, saur, shippon, shed, vaccary, vachery
barren drape
bell bladder campion
call coboss, sookie
comb. vacci
cud rumen
disease vaccinia
divine audumla
double chin dewlap
dry key, sew
dung upla
fat valerian
foot ulcer foul
grass red clover
group cattle, herd, kine
-headed goddess hathor, isis, nut
hide beat, buff, whip
hornless doddie, doddy, humlie, mailee, moîl, moulleen, muillie, mul(l)ey, pollard
house See COW *barn.*
hybrid cattabu, cattalo
-killer velvet ant, wasp
kind sacred
-like bovine, cous
lily marsh marigold, spatterdock
lowing moo
mother calver, incalver
mumble wild chervil
mythical chichivache
noise low, moo

nourishing ymir audhumia
oak basket tree
parsley chervil
parsnip bear's breech, bearvort, bundweed, cadweed, heracleum, hogweed, knapweed, madnep, pigweed, ragwort, scabious, towcock
pasture vaccary
pert. vaccine
pilot chirivita, damselfish, fish, pintano
protectress bubona
raiser byre-man
rattle campion
sacred favorite, pet, taura
sea See COWFISH.
shed See COW *barn.*
-tongue clintonia
tree balata, couma, galactodendron, karaka, massaranduba, mimusops
udder disease core
unbranded maverick
vetch canada pea, cat pea, herb, vicia
white-faced hawkey, hawkie
young calf, heifer, stirk
COWARD baby, caitiff, chicken, coof, cowheart, craven, daff, dastard, flunker, fraid(y)-cat, fugie, funk(er), jellyfish, lache, meacock, milksop, niddering, nithing, panurge, piker, poltroon, quiter, rabbit, recreant, scaredy-cat, sissy, sneak, softy, turntail, weakling, white-feather, white-liver
COWARDICE chicken-heart(edness), dastardy, faintheart(edness), fear, funk, pusillanimity, recreancy, yellowness
symbol calf, chicken, pigeon
COWARDLY afraid, apprehensive, argh, base, caitiff, chicken(hearted), cowed, craven, dastardly, fearful, gutless, hilding, niddering, nidget, pigeonhearted, poltroon, pusillanimous, recreant, shy, spiritless, timid, timorous, yellow
COWBIND bryony
COWBIRD becco, blackbird, bunting, cokewold, cuckhold, lazybird, molothrus, oxbiter
COWBOY baille, broncobuster, brushpopper, buckaroo, buckayro, charro, cowpoke, dallyman,

gardian, gaucho, hazer, herder, herdsman, horseman, jackaroo, llanero, neatherd, paniolo, puncher, ranchero, rider, roper, vaquero, waddi, wrangler
blanket sugan
contest rodeo, round-up
friend pard(ner)
garment chaparajos, chaps, jodhpurs, levis
gear cola, riata
roping nooser
strap latigo
whip chicotte
COWCATCHER bumper, front, guard, pilot, protector, safeguard
COWER blench, coorie, cringe, crouch, cruddle, fawn, flinch, grovel, hug, hurkle, quail, recoil, shool, shrink, shrug, stoop, toady, truckle, wince
COWFISH becco, cuckold, dolphin, grampus, manatee, porpoise, ray, sirenia, toro
COWHEART coward
COWHERB cockle, cowfat, soapwort
COWHERD bucolic, herdsman, neatherd
COWL boil, bonnet, cap, capuche, cover, cucule, hat, headdress, hood, miter, nightcap, scuttle, soa, soe
pert. cucullate
staff stave
CO-WORKER associate, cohelper, colleague, mate, partner, shop-mate, teammate, yokefellow
COWPEA black-eye (bean), frijol(e), sitao, towcock, vigna
COWPOX kinepox, pappox, vaccinia
COWPUNCHER See COWBOY.
COWRIE cypraea, money, shell, venus, zimbi
COWSLIP auricula, beef-and-greens, culver-key, cyclamen, herb peter, marsh marigold, paigle, primrose, primula, shooting-star
COWTAIL chowry, horseweed
COWWEED chervil
COX See COXSWAIN.
COXCOMB amaranth, beau, buck, cleat, dandy, dude, elegant, exquisite, fool, fop, herb, jackanapes, macaroni,

nob, pate, popinjay, princock, princox, swell, toff
COXSWAIN crewman, helmsman, pilot, steersman
COY allure, aloof, arch, bashful, blushing, caress, cautious, chary, coax, coquettish, decent, decorous, demure, diffident, entice, hoax, modest, nice, pat, proper, quiet, reserved, retiring, shy, skittish, stroke, timid, wary
COYO avocado, chinin
COYOTE brush wolf, canine, prairie wolf
state south dakota
COYPU degu, nutria, rodent
COZBI *father* zur
slayer phineas
COZE chat, converse, gossip, talk
COZEN bamboozle, beguile, cheat, chisel, deceive, defraud, delude, dupe, fool, grease, gull, hoax, hoodwink, mislead, swindle, trick
COZIER cadger, codger, cosier
COZY bield, canny, comfortable, contented, covering, cushy, easy, familiar, homelike, homey, intimate, intime, quilt, restful, rug, safe, satisfying, secure, snug, sociable, toasty
place den, nest, snuggery
CRAB (See also *kind,* below.) anger, apple, ayuyu, beef, bellyache, boco, brachyura, buster, cancer, claw, complain, crank, crosspatch, crustacean, foul up, gin, gripe, grouch, maja, malcontent, mollusk, ocypode, oxystome, polypod, queer, ruin, seafood, sour, spoil, sulk, surique, tanfish, winch, zodiac sign, zoea
abdomen apron
apple coling, malus, scrab, scrog, solitaire
apple liquor wherry
beach sanite
beckoning fiddler
claw chela, nipper
comb. carcin(o)
-eating cancrivorous
extinct trilobite
family niachidae
fiddler uca
fresh-water thalphusa

front metope
genus belinurus, birgus, grapsus, lithodes, maia, ocypode, pinnotheres, portunus, squilla, uca
giant marcochira
grass button grass, darnel, digitaria, drawk, eleusine, fonio, panic(le)
hermit pagurid, parapagurid
horseshoe king, lumulus, trilobite, xiphosura(n)
horseshoe, pert. limuloid
kind blue, box, brachyura, buckler, bucklum, crayfish, fiddler, hermit, horseshoe, king, limulus, maia, maja, partan, pungar, sargassum
king aglaspis, horsefish, horseshoe, limulus, panfish
land gecarcinus
-like cancroid, carcinomorphic
louse morepeon, morpion, phthirius
mantis squilla
middle metope
parasite rhizocephala
pert. carcinomorphic
plover drome
-shaped cancriform, cancroid
shore ochidore
spider maia, maja
split-shelled buster
stick cane, crank, cudgel
the deal queer, spoil, wreck
tree bitterbark, gribble
wood andiroba, carapa, mahogany, poisonwood
yaws frambesia
CRABBED bitter, boorish, brusque, cankered, cantankerous, capernoited, complicated, contrary, cronish, crooked, cross, crusty, difficult, dour, fractious, glum, gnarled, grouchy, huffy, irascible, irritable, knotted, morose, peevish, petulant, rugged, sour, splenetic, sulky, sullen, surly, teethy, testy, ugly
CRACK 3 ace, cut, gag, mot, pop, rap, tap, try 4 bang, blow, chap, chip, chop, clap, fine, flap, good, jape, jest, joke, kibe, quip, rend, rift, rime, seam, slam, slap, slit, snap, whap, whop, yerk 5 brack, break, burst, check, chine, chink, clash, cleft, crash, craze, crump, great, jibek, knock, slash, smack, solve, split, taunt,

whack 6 bangup, bon mot, bounce, breach, choice, cleave, cranny, damage, deluxe, expert, furrow, groove, remark, report, second, shiver, strake, strike, thwack 7 attempt, blemish, capital, crevice, fissure, instant, opening, thunder 8 fracture, hairline, nearness, slambang, slapbang, splinter, stramash, superior 9 alligator, excellent, fishmouth, witticism 10 detonation, interstice
a book study
-brain crackpot, lunatic, screwball
-brained crazy, erratic, foolish, nutty, senseless, unreasonable
down on attack, brace, discipline, suppress
fill calk
of doom day of judgment, doomsday, fate, future, gotterdammerung, tomorrow
on accelerate, speed
pert. alutaceous, coriaceous
sail accelerate
shot ace, expert, marksman
the whip discipline, guide
up break(down), collapse, collide, collision, crash, debacle, extoll, fall apart, go mad, laugh, misfortune, praise, shake, tout, wreck
CRACKED balmy, bankrupt, bughouse, chapped, crazy, croaky, flawed, gruff, harsh, injured, insane, mad, rimose, roupy, touched
on enthusiastic
CRACKER biscuit, boaster, braggart, breakdown, bun, cookie, duck, frontiersman, georgian, liar, pretzel, rusk, saltine, smash, snapper, wafer
berry bunchberry, dwarf cornel
bread lahvosh
broken dunderfunk
state georgia
CRACKERJACK ace, expert, fine, great, syperios, topnotcher, trump
CRACKLE break, brustle, craze, crepitate, crink(le), crisp, dry, rustle, snap, sparkle, sputter
CRACKLING cremant, crespitant, critling, greaves, grieben

CRACKNEL simnel
CRACKPOT eccentric, erratic, impractical, insane, lunatic, nut, oddball, screwball, tsedoodelt(eh), tsedrayt(en)
CRACKSMAN burglar, housebreaker, thief, yegg
CRACOW krakau
CRADLE babybed, bed, beginning, berceau, birthplace, cadar, cader, cadre, cot, creche, crib, cunabula, foster, hamper, infancy, matrix, nativity, pannier, protect, refiner, rock(er), slee, solen, source, support, trough, truss
book incunabulum
of liberty faneuil hall
song berceuse, lullaby, schlummerlied
wicker bassinet
CRADLING brack
CRAFT ability, aptitude, argosy, art(ifice), boat, business, cleverness, cunning, deceit, deception, dexterity, forte, guild, ingenuity, magic, manual art, metier, mister, profession, proficiency, ship, skill, strategy, struse, subtlety, talent, trade, trick, vessel, vocation
comb. techno
gentle fishing
society artel, cooperative, guild
CRAFTSMAN architect, artificer, artisan, artist, bricklayer, builder, cabinetmaker, carle, carpenter, chandler, contractor, cooper, forger, founder, fuller, glassblower, glaz(i)er, hand, journeyman, laborer, mason, master, mechanic, miller, navvy, operative, plubber, potter, puddler, puttier, spinner, steeplejack, stonecutter, tanner, technician, tinker, tinner, weaver, welder, worker, workman, wright, writer
valley of ono
CRAFTY acute, artful, artificial, astute, callid, captious, cautelous, clever, corrupt, cunning, deceitful, dern, designing, dexterous, enginous, falsehearted, foxy, fraudulent, ingenious,

insidious, keen, plotting, quaint, scheming, sharp, shrewd, skillful, slape, sleekit, sly, smart, solert, subdolous, subtle, tod, tricky, vafrous, vulpine, wily, wise
CRAG arete, brack, cliff, craig, craw, heck, heuch, heugh, huuahu, knee, neck, precipice, rock, scar(p), stone, throat, tor
above glacier nunatak
CRAGGY abrupt, cliffy, knotty, rocky, rough, rugged
CRAKE cornbird, crow, rail(bird), raven, rook, sora
CRAKOW boot, poulaine, shoe
CRAM agrote, bone(up), bulldoze, charge, compress, crowd, crush, devour, fool, force, glut, gorge, jam, learn, lie, mug, multitude, pack, prepare, press, ram, squeeze, stech, stow, study, stuff, surfeit, swot, tutor
down the throat convince
CRAMFUL chockful, replete, satiated
CRAMMER liar, lie, tutor
CRAMP bottle up, box up, cabin, charley horse, complicated, compress, confine, contract, corner, crick, crimp, crowd, difficult, dogtie, hamper, hinder, kink, limit, narrow, pain, pang, pressure, restraint, restrict, seizure, shackle, spasm, stitch, vise
iron agraf(f)e
one's style frustrate, queer, restrain, thwart
CRAMPED close(quarters), confined, illegible, little, pent, stiff, two-by-four
CRAMPFISH electric ray, torpedo
CRANBERRY acrosarc, bearberry, bogaberry, bogbilberry, cascara, ericad, raspberry
bush pimbina
disease end rot
fungus exobasidium
habitat bog
mountain lingonberry
scald blast
small bogwort
tree ball rose, guelder-rose

pembina, snowball, viburnum

CRANE, CRANE'S alectoride, balaerica, bird, cormorant, crab, davit, demoiselle, derrick, elongate, erector, extend, gib, gruid, grus, heron, jack(screw), jenny, jib, jigger, kulang, kulm, lifter, pulley, sarus, siphon, spread, stretch, tackle, titan, windlass
arm cotterel, gib(bet), jib, ramhead
bill alumroot, dovefoot, geranium, gluxweed
charges cranage
clip cal(l)iper
cry cronk, crunk
family gruidae
fly tipula
follower spotter
gray coolung
ichabod, pursuer headless horseman
ichabod, rival brom bones
-like bird chunga, grus, seriema, wader
old-world demoiselle
pert. gruine
ship's davit
small demoiselle
stephen, novel maggie, red badge of courage
the neck gaze, stare
travelling jenny, titan
willow buttonbush

CRANIUM braincap, braincase, brain pan, brains, cerebrum, head, skull
nerve vagi, vagus
nerve root radix
part. calotte, calvaria
suture bregma, dacryon, glabella, inion, malar, metopion, nasion, orphryon, pogonion, prosthion, pterion, sphenion, stenion
vault cornix

CRANK angle, bear, bend, brace, buzzard, caprice, crab, crosspatch, crotchet, dragon, eccentric, enthusiast, fanatic, fireeater, fury, fussbudget, grouch, handle, hothead, hotspur, lively, lusty, malcontent, meanie, monomaniac, nut, quip, shaky, sick, sorehead, spitfire, start(er), stickler, tartar, tseddodelt(eh), tsedrayt(eh), turn, unstable, vagary, weak, whim(sy), winch, wind up, wit, zigzag

case sumps
CRANKING *device* winch
CRANKLE ossillate, turn, wrinkle, zag, zig, zigzag
CRANKY atrabilious, badtempered, bilious, cantankerous, choleric, crabby, cronk, cross, crotchety, eccentric, fifish, grouchy, illtempered, infirm, irascible, irritable, jittery, peevish, perverse, petulant, short, sickly, splenetic, sullen, surly, techy, testy, tortuous, touchy, ugly, unsteady
CRANNY channel, chink, cleft, corner, crack, crevice, fissure, groove, hang, hole, nook
CRANTS corance, garland, wreath
CRAP buckwheat, cast, darnel, dice, dregs, drivel, gallows, greaves, hazard, lie, money, nap, nonsense, relax, rest, rubbish
out die, fail, quit, yield
-shooter gambler, gamester
CRAPE clergy(man), crimp, curl, fabric, friz, shroud
band scarf, weed
-hanger kill-joy, pessimist, spoilsport
jasmine adam's apple, nero's crown
myrtle astromeda, bloodwood, japonica
needle lady's comb
CRAPPIE bachelor, calico bass, campbellite, sacalait, sunfish
CRAPS dice, hazard
5 phoebe
term back line, bande, box cars, buck it, cane, crab, drag, fade, field, gag, hard way, larry, line, lumber, main, manna from heaven, miss, natural, nick, nina, pass, phoebe, point, rail, sister, sleeper, stickman, string
CRAPULENT gluttonous, intemperate, intoxicated
CRASH bang, burst, clap, clatter, cloth, collapse, collide, collision, crack(up), crock up, crush, debacle, defeat, fabric, fail(ure), fall, fiasco, hurtle, impact, intrude, linen, misfortune, peal, ram, roar, ruin, shatter, shock, smash(up),

splinter, stentor, stramash, thunder
-land ditch
CRASIS combination, composition, constitution, makeup, nature, temperament
CRASS boorish, coarse, crude, dense, dull, dumb, gross, illiberal, indelicate, loud, lowbrow, oafish, obtuse, philistine, raw, rough, rude, stupid, thick, vulgar
CRASSUS *accuser* plotinus
associate caesar, pompey
city reduced zenodotia
consort licinia
deceiver andromachus, ariamnes
diviner onatius
enemy ateius, cinna, marius, spartacus
friend metellus, sylla, vibius
impersonator caius-paccianus
lieutenant censorinus, heironymus, megabacchus, mummius, nicomachus, octavius, petronius, quintius, roscius
rival caesar, pompey, spartacus, surena
slayer pomaxathres
victim appollonius
CRATAEGUS azarole, blackthorn, haw(thorn), sloe, walking stick
CRATAEIS *husband* phorcys
offspring scylla
CRATE auto, bar, basket, box, cacaxte, car, casket, cradle, crib, encase, hamper, pack(age), quantity, seron
bar slat
CRATER abyss, caldera, cavity, celebe, chasm, cone, cup, fovea, hell, hole, hollow, kelebe, linne, maar, pit, yawn
edge lip, rim, somma
lunar linne
CRATUS *parent* gaea, pallas, styx, uranus
CRAUNCH bite, chew, gnash, grate, pulverize, scranch
CRAVAT ascot, bandage, crumpler, dressing, necktie, scarf, stock, teck, tie
lace steenkirk, steinkirk
pin tietack
CRAVE appeal, ask, beg, covet, demand, desire, dun, greed, hanker, hunger for,

itch, letch, long(ing), need, pine, plead, require, seek, solicit, thirst, want, wish, yammer, yearn

CRAVEN afraid, coward(ly), dastard(ly), fainthearted, fearful, overcome, poltroon, pusillanimous, recreant, scared, terrified, timid, timorous

CRAVING appetance, avid, desire, letch, likerous, longing, thirst, tickling
abnormal boulimia, bulimia, bulimy, pica

CRAW belly, crop, gorge, gullet, ingluvies, maw, stomach, throat, viscera

CRAWDAD See CRAYFISH.

CRAWFISH (See also CRAYFISH.) apostate, back, kreef, recant, recede, retract, retreat, sidle, ula, withdraw, yabbie, yabby

CRAWFONT buttercup

CRAWFORD, JOAN lucille lesueur

CRAWL clamber, creep, cringe, drag, fawn, grovel, inch, kraal, lag, recant, reprove, retreat, scrabble, scramble, shug, slither, snail's pace, snake, sniggle, trail
in retire
out of quit, retreat
with abound, infest, permeate, teem

CRAYFISH astacis, camaron, cambarus, crab, crawdad, crawfish, crustacean, ecrevisse, kraftkalas, langosta, lobster, ula, yabbie, yabby
burrowing yabbie, yabby

CRAYON chalk, conte, drawing, keel, pastel, pencil, sanguine, sketch
geoffrey washington irving

CRAZE break, bug, crack(le), cry, custom, derange, dernier cri, destroy, fad, fashion, flaw, furor, impair, infatuation, madden, maddle, mania, maze, mode, monomania, rage, shatter, style, vogue, weaken, whimsey
comb. -itis

CRAZINESS mishegoss

CRAZY, CRAZED absurd, amok, balmy, bats, batty, beany, bereft, berserk, be-

side one's self, bonkers, brainsick, buggy, bughouse, bugs, coocoo, crackbrained, crackers, cuckoo, daffy, daft, deleerit, delieret, demented, deranged, disordered, distraught, dottle, dotty, eccentric, foolish, goofy, halucket, insane, loco, looney, lunatic, luny, mad, manic, mental, meshuga, non compos mentis, nutty, off one's rocker, off one's trolley, potty, ree, round the bend, scatty, scranny, screwy, shatterwit, tetched, touched, unbalanced, wacky, weird, wild, wood, wowf, zany
about enamored, enthusiastic, in love
idea bee (in one's bonnet)
like a fox cunning, shrewd, sly
person beehead, CRACKPOT
quilt patchwork, solitaire
water liquor

CREAK cheep, chirr, complain, craik, crank, crepitate, croak, fratch, g(e)ig, girg, grate, grind, groan, jarg, screak, screech, scrike, scroop, shraik, squeak

CREAKING jarg, screak, scrike

CREAM anoint, balm, beat(up), bonbon, churn, creme, damage, elite, emulsify, foam, froth, gist, grease, lambaste, lubricate, oil, pomade, ream, select, skim, top, whip
and milk half and half
and wine sillabub
clotted clout, devonshire
clouted fool
cooked with a la king, shir(r)ed
curded junket
-faced pale
measurer lactoscope
of tartar adansonia, argol, cathartic
of tartar tree baobab
puff duchesse, effeminate, profiterole, sissy, weakling

CREASE cockle, crimp, crumple, crunkle, engrave, fold, plait, pleat, pucker, rigosity, rimple, ruck, ruga, runkle, scarpa, seam, stria, suture, wrimple, wrinkle

CREATE author, breed, build, carve, cause, chisel, coin, compact, compose, compound, concoct, construct, design, devise, discover, elaborate, erect, evolve, fabricate, fashion, forge, form(ulate), frame, generate, get up, invent, make, manufacture, originate, plan, prepare, produce, raise, rear, scheme, shape
a disturbance rampage, riot
confusion garboil
for oneself carve out

CREATION activity, alcheringa, appointment, bereshit(h), business, composition, cosmos, edition, facture, fashion, invention, lila, making, manufacture, manuscript, masterpiece, nature, poiesis, product(ion), universe, world
mental fantasy, phantasy
six days of hexa(e)meron

CREATIVE causative, constructive, demiurgic, fertile, formative, germinal, ideaed, inventive, original, originative, poietic, pomative, productive, prolific

CREATOR architect, artificer, artist, author, brahma, builder, composer, demiurge, father, god, inventor, lord, maker, mani, operator, originator, poet, producer, supreme being, tagaloa, tiki, varuna, writer
the brahma, god, lord

CREATURE agent, animal, being, cat's-paw, craythur, dabba, dependent, gangrel, hellicat, instrument, man, manikin, minikin, minion, offspring, organism, pawn, product, puppet, tool, wretch
comforts conveniences
evil devil, satan
fabled centaur, dragon, elf, faerie, fairy, gnome, mermaid, merman, pixie, wyvern
imaginary whangdoodle
mechanical golem, robot
nonsense snark
small atomy, beastie, elf, grig, mite
stunted wirl(ing), wrling
worthless sculpin, snipjack

CRECHE crib, manger, nursery

CREDENCE altar, belief, buffet, confidence, conviction, creance, credit, credenza, cupboard, faith, reliance, sideboard, trust

CREDENTIAL certificate, credance, document, recommendation, testimonial, voucher
carrier breviger

CREDIBLE authentic, believable, faithful, likely, logical, plausible, possible, probable, reliable, reputable, trustworthy

CREDIT accommodate, account, apply, ascribe, asset, assign, attribute, belief, believe, blame, certainty, charge, cheers, credence, credibility, endow, entry, esteem, faith, honor, impute, influence, izzat, laud, loan, mensk, merit, praise, prestige, rating, refer, renown, reputation, repute, standing, sway, tenet, tick, trust, weight
card american express, bankamericard, carte blanche, charge-plate, diners, master charge, visa
instrument bond, certificate, check, coupon, draft, note
line of account
on hire purchase, installment plan, mace, never-never
risk fly-by-night
term never-never, time
transfer cash-letter, giro

CREDITABLE credible, estimable, honest, honorable, praiseworthy, reputable, respectable, upright

CREDITOR apprizer, banker, collection agent, cransier, creancer, debtee, dun(ner), moneylender, mortgagee, shylock

CREDO See CREED and FAITH.

CREDULOUS believing, gullible, simple, spoony, trustful, trusting, undoubting, unsuspecting, unsuspicious

CREED belief, catechism, confession, conviction, credo, doctrine, dogma, faith, ism, kalimah, kelima, platform, symbol, tenet, trowing
apostle's symbolum

christian apostle's, athanasian, nicene
comb. dosy, ism

CREEK arroyo, bache, bayou, billabong, bogue, branch, brook, burn, canada, cleft, cove, estero, estuary, geo, gio, gut, indian, inlet, kill, passage, rill, rio, rito, rivulet, run, slake, slough, slue, spruit, stream, vlei, vley, voe, wick, zanja, zanjona
bed vado
duck gadwell
fish chub-sucker
grass pondweed
indian chief selocta
indian festival busk
indian halfbreeds forgotten moors, red bones
sedge branch grass, thatch

CREEL bank, basket, caul, cawl, hask, jack, junket, kell, trap

CREEP cramble, crammel, crawl, drag, fawn, grapnel, grovel, gumshoe, inch (along), insinuate, itch, jerk, lurk, prickle, pussyfoot, rizzle, scrabble, scramble, scride, shift, skulk, slide, slink, slip, sniggle, steal, tarry, tauranga, tingle, worm
geological solifluction
into good graces flatter
up on See SURPRISE.
with abound, infest, permeate

CREEPER bindweed, bird, crope, ivy, jiti, lice, odul, pito, reptile, shoe, snake, sneaker, vine, worm
kind foxglove, honey, picucule, quitquit, woodbine

CREEPING allfours, atiptoe, crawling, inching, on hands and knees, reptant, reptatorial, reptile, scramble, servile, slow, sneaking, stealing, sycophantic, trailing, wile
bur ground pine
charlie moneywort, stonecrop
crowfoot sitfast
jennie ground ivy
sickness orgotism
snowberry ivory plum, moxa, teaberry

CREEPS all-overs, fornication, gringles, jimjams, shivers, trepidation, willies

CREEPY dreadful, eerie, itchy, jittery, jumpy, nervous

CREESE crena, cress, crise, dagger, kris, sword, weapon

CREMATE burn, calcine, incinerate

CREMATION *wife's* suttee

CREMONA amati, violin

CRENATE cleft, notched, scalloped, serrated

CREOLE criollo, dialect, fish, haitian, janissary, mestizo, patois
condiment file powder, rougail
dish gumbo, jambalaya
jargon petit-noir
state louisiana

CREON *brother-in-law* oedipus
father menoeceus
kingdom corinth, thebes
nephew eteocles, polynices
niece antigone
offspring creusa, glauce, harmon
sister hipponome, jocasta
son-in-law jason
victim antigone

CREOSOTE bush larrea

CREPE chirimen, CRAPE, crinkled, nacarat, pancake, wrinkled
fabric aeroplane
myrtle astromeda, tree

CREPITATE crackle, grate, rattle, roll, snap

CREPUSCULE evening, twilight

CRESCENT demilune, halfmoon, horseshoe, lunar, lunate(d), lunoid, lunula, lunule, meniscus, moon(ed), semicircle, sickle, solitaire, waxwand
city new orleans
-like bicorn
point cusp, horn
-shaped bicorn, corniform, cusp, horn-shaped, horny, lunar, lunate, lunula(r), lunulate, menisciform, meniscoid(al), moony, semicircular, semilunar, sigmoid, two-horned

CRESIUS dionysus

CRESOL frother

CRESPIE whale

CRESS crucifer, eker, kers(e), madwort, molewort, peppergrass, roripa, whitetop
mouse-ear turkey-pod
weed sandrocket

CRESSET beacon, crisset, flambeau, signal, torch
CRESSIDE criseyde
consort diomedes, troilus
father calchas
servant alexander
uncle pandarus
CREST acme, apex, apogee, arete, chine, climax, comb, cop, copple, crown, eckle, ectolph, finial, head, height, helmet, knap, mane, mountain, notching, panache, peak, pinnacle, plume, ridge, seege, symbol, top(knot), tor, tuft, whitecap
imperial kikumon
rugged arete, sawback
wave feather, whitecap
CRESTED coppled, coronate(d), cristate(d), muffed, pileate(d), topknotted, tufted
grebe cargoose
quail coppy
screamer chaja
CRESTFALLEN cowed, dejected, depressed, dispirited, down(cast) (hearted); embarrassed
CRETA *consort* helius
offspring pasiphae
CRETE candia, khandah, kiridadasi
airport maleme
animal, sacred pig
bay kanca, kisamo, mesara, suda
cape buza, krio(s), liano, lithinon, salome, sidero, sidheros, spatha, stavros
capital canea
city anoyia, candia, canea, hag, heraclion, heraklion, kasteli, khania, khora, lato, lisamo, malemi, mallia, meleme, nikolaos, palaiophora, retimo, sitia, sphakion, tympakion, zakro
city, ancient cydonia, gortyna, knossus, phaistos
conqueror metellus
culture, ancient minoan
earth spirit curete
flier icarus
giant talos
goddess apjaia, britomartis, dictynna
gulf khania, merabello
herb dittany
inhabitant candiot(e)
inventor daedalus

king carmanor, catreus, idomeneus, minos
language minoan
minoan site gournia
monster minotaur
nymph britomartis, cynosura
peak dikte, ida, juktas, lasithi, psiloriti, theodore
people candiot, caphtorim, philistines, sphakiots
people, ancient kefti(an), minoan
people, mythical curetes
pert. candiot, keftian, khania
philosopher epimenides
poet epimenides
port candia, canea, herakleion
range madaras, phino
spikenard cut-finger, phu, valerian
CRETHEIS *husband* acastus
slayer peleus
CRETHEUS *companion* aeneas
offspring aeson, amythaon, hippolyte, pheres
parent aeolus, enarete
realm iolcus
wife biadice, tyro
CRETIN fool, idiot, myxedema, simpleton
CRETISM falsehood, lie, lying
CREUS *offspring* pallas
wife eurybia
CREUSA glauce, glauke
consort aeneas, apollo, jason
offspring ascanius, ion
parent creon, hecuba, priam
slayer medea
CREVASSE bergschrund, cleft, fissure, gap, hole, opening
CREVECOEUR *pseud.* j hector st john
CREVICE bore, break, chine, chink, cleft, crack, cranny, creek, cunne, fissure, grike, gunnies, interstice, kravers, leak, nook, opening, peephole, rime, seam, split, vein
CREW band, cabin, covin, crue, eight, faction, gang, ging, group, hands, herd, hovel, hut, meinie, members, men, mob, oars, party, pen, retinue, shearwater, staff, team, throng, workers
cut butch, flattop
CREWEL caddice, caddis, worsted

CREWMAN bakehead, bungs, cabinboy, conner, cox(swain), deckhand, deckie, drudge, gunner, hand, helmsman, mess steward, navigator, purser, ship(s), steersman, steward(ess), stoker, torpedoman, wheelsman, yeoman
CREX bird, corncrake
CRIB bassinet, bed, bin(n), boose, boosy, brothel, bunk(er), cab, cheat, compartment, confine, cot, cratch, crate, creche, critch, deceive, dive, granary, horse, hovel, hut, key, manger, pilfer, plagerize, pony, purloin, rack, raft, silo, skin, stall, steal, theft, translation, trot, weir
CRIBBAGE *jack* nob
score nob(s), peg
term combination, count, heel, home, knave, last, lay away, lurch, muggins, nob(s), noddy, noddy boards, off, peg(out), prial, proil, run, show, starter
CRIBBER shorer, stumpsucker
CRICK cramp, creek, garganey, hitch, jackscrew, kink, spasm, stitch, stream, twist, wrench
sand marsh
CRICKET equity, fair, footstool, good form, grig, gryllid, insect, mole, right, snob, twiddler
ball edger, shooter, snick
ball, bowled tice, yorker
ball core quilt
captain skipper
family gryllidae
genus acheta, achetidae, gryllotalpa, gryllus
hit slog
mole churrworm
player batsman, fag, fieldsman
position leg, mid-off, slip, square-leg
rod stump
run bye
score blob, duck egg, zero
side offs, ons
sneak grub
sound stridulate
teal garganey
team elevens
term backplay, bail, bye, edger, legbreak, offs, ons,

over, rot, snick, stonewall, tice, tye, york(er)

yorker tice, tye

CRIER announcer, beadle, herald, huer, muezzin, wailer, wrawler

CRILE dwarf

CRIME abuse, accuse, arson, atrocity, caper, enormity, evil, fault, felony, folly, forfeit, iniquity, libel, malefaction, misdemeanor, murder, offense, outrage, simony, sin, stickup, tort, trespass, vice, villainy, wickedness, wrong(doing)

basic element corpus delicti

ecclesiastical simony

fighter batman, bond, green hornet, gunn, hammer, hoover, ironside, mannix, marvel, ness, smart, superman, tracy, wilson

goddess ate

organized See UNDER-WORLD.

scene of venue

student of criminologist, penologist,

CRIMEA krym

city kerch, sevastopol, yalta

people cimmerians, tauri

port balaklava, kerch, yalta

river alma

sea azof, azov

strait kerch

tribe inkerman

war battle balaklava

war commander lord cardigan, lord raglan

CRIMINAL apache, arsonist, bad, bandit, blackguard, bravo, burglar, convict, corrupt, cracksman, crook, culprit, dacoit, delinquent, desperado, dipper, disgraceful, evil, evildoer, felon(ious), fugitive, gallows bird, gangster, gaolbird, guilty, hood(lum), hooligan, illegal, jailbird, lawbreaker, mafioso, malefactor, malfeasant, nocent, outlaw, proscrit, public enemy, racketeer, rampsman, scofflaw, screwsman, sinful, sinner, slayer, snakesman, spadassin, stickman, swindler, thief, thug, unlawful, wargus, wicked, wrong(doer), yegg

accomplice canary, crow, stall

act caper

burning arson

court bureo

famous bonney, billy the kid, capone, chessman, clyde, dillinger, james, manson, slasher, speck, strangler, sutton, zodiac

female bonny, emma barnes, gun moll

forte alias

group amalaita, black hand, la cosa nostra, mafia, mob, syndicate

habitual recidivist, repeater

identification bertillonnage, fingerprint

intent dole, dolose

refuge alsatia, whitefriars

CRIMINATE accuse, arraign, charge, impeach, indict

CRIMP abduct(or), arrest, cheat, check, clamp, coil, crinkle, crisp, curl, flute, fold, friable, friz(z), gash, gauffer, goffer, hinder, north, notch, plait, pulverable, queer, ruffle, swirl, weak, wind, wrinkle

CRIMSON bloody, blush(ing), carmine, flush, jockey, lac, mantle, pink, red(den), ruby, sanguinary, scarlet

clover napoleon

manuka tea tree

CRINE hair, mane, shrink, shrivel

CRINGE bend, binge, blench, bow, buckle, cower, crouch, fawn, flinch, grovel, kneel, quail, retreat, scringe, shrink, sneak, snool, stoop, submit, toady, truckle, wince, yield

CRINGING abject, hangdog, servile

CRINGLE circle, disk, eyelet, grommet, orb, rope, terret, withe

pass rope through reeve

CRINKLE cockle, convolution, crankle, crepe, crimp(le), crisp, curl, fold, kink, ruffle, rumple, rustle, seam, turn, twist, wind, wreathe, wrinkle

CRINKLED buckled, contortuplicate, crimp, curly, encomic

CRINOID camerate, comatula, feather star, polyp, sea lily

genus actinocrinus, batocrinus

CRINOLINE hoop

CRIPPLE bacach, batter, damage, disable, enfeeble, halt, hamstring, handicap, harm, hobble, hook, hough, hurt, impair, incapacitate, injure, kalikeh, kolyyika, lame(ster), lamiger, lamiter, maim, mutilate, paralyze, sap, scotch, spavine, spoil, weaken

saint giles

CRIPPLED disabled, gimpy, lame

CRISEYDE cressida

CRISIS apex, climacteric, climax, clutch, conjuncture, contingency, crise, crux, eleventh hour, emergency, epitasis, exigency, extremity, hinge, hump, jump, juncture, panic, pass, pinch, point, push, rub, squeeze, state, strait, trial, turn, zero hour

commercial depression, recession

CRISP aphoristic, biting, bracing, brisk, brittle, clean, clear, coil, cold, concise, crump, crunchy, crusty, curl(y), firm, fold, fragile, frangible, fresh, friable, friz, hard, incisive, lively, neat, nippy, pithy, pulverable, rumpled, sharp, short, smopple, snappy, spalt, stiff, terse, trenchant, wavy

CRISPIN coat, shoemaker

CRISSCROSS awry, confused, network, patchwork, reticulation, tick-tack-toe

CRITERION axiom, canon, check, comparison, evidence, gauge, law, measure, metric, model, norm, plummet, principle, proof, rule, standard, test, touchstone, trial, type, yardstick

CRITIC aristarch, authority, boaster, booer, carper, censor, commentator, connoisseur, debunker, exegete, expert, faultfinder, judge, literator, mome, momus, pundit, reviewer, scold, slater, syndic, zoilus

CRITICAL abusive, acerb, acute, bordering, captious, carping, caviling, cen-

sorious, climacteric, conclusive, crucial, cunical, dangerous, deadly, decisive, deprecative, deprecatory, difficult, discriminate, disparaging, edgy, exacting, exigent, faultfinding, fussy, grave, hairsplitting, hazardous, important, integral, judicial, meticulous, momentous, nagging, nervous, objurgatory, parlous, perilous, precarious, repoachful, risky, severe, strategic, ticklish, touchy, urgent, vituperative, weighty
mark obelsik, obelus
CRITICISM animadversion, aspersion, blurb, brickbat, carping, cavil(ing), censure, comment(ary), critique, disapproval, faultfinding, gaff, hairsplitting, hit, imputation, judgment, knock, nagging, notice, objection, obloquy, opprobrium, puff, rap, reflection, report, review, slam, slating, stricture, thrust, vitriol, zoilism
random pot shot
CRITICIZE accuse, animadvert, arraign, assail, attack, berate, blame, blast, blister, call, canvass, carp, castigate, cavil, censure, chide, complain, condemn, critique, denounce, disapprove, evaluate, examine, faultfind, flay, hit, judge, kibbitz, knock, nag, pan, rap, rebuke, reprehend, review, roast, scan, scarify, scold, slam, slash, slate, taunt, tear apart
CRITIQUE criticism, review
CRIUS *offspring* astraeus, pallas, perses
parent gaea, uranus
wife eurybia
CROAK caw, complain, creak, cronk, cry, die, forebode, gasp, grumble, hawk, jangle, kill, krechtz, portend, squawk
CROAKER bubbler, cabezon(e), corvina, crocus, doctor, drumfish, frog, grunt, hardhead, kingfish, parson, preacher, queenfish, roncador, tomcod
CROAKY harsh, hoarse, raucous, roupy, stertorous

CROATIA, CROATIAN bosnian, chorwat, chrobat, h(e)rvati, sclav, serb, slav, slovene, sorb, wend
capital zagreb
city agram, fiume
governor ban
peak kapela
river bednya
rock shelter krapina
soldier pandour
territory banat
CROCHET braid, crotchet, hook, knit, plait, spin, tat, twill, weave
stitch afghan
CROCIDOLITE asbestos, asbestus, fabric
CROCK beanpot, chatty, critch, dud, ewe, failure, flop, goolah, injure, intoxicate, jar, pig, pot(sherd), smut, soil, soot, stean, steen, terrine
CROCKERY ceramics, china, cloam, dishes, earthenware, piggery, potware
CROCKET, DAVEY *last stand* alamo
CROCODILE aetosaurus, alligator, cayman, diapsid, gator, gavial, gharial, goa, goniopholis, jacare, loricate, mugger, reptile, saurian, yacare
bird courser, messmate, plover, sicsac, trochil(us)
common mugger, nilotic
ensign of egypt
-headed god amemait, sebek, sobk
-like gavial, nako(o)
marsh goa, mugger
nile vulgaris
river limpopo
symbol of hypocrisy
tears hypocrisy, insincerity
CROCUS irid, iris, lily, saffron
bulb corm
of mars colcothar
of venus cuprous oxide
sack burlap bag
CROESUS (See also MAN rich.) dives, midas, millionaire, nabob
CROFT bleach, bottle, cavern, cottage, craft, crypt, farm, field, garth, parrock, plot, torp, vault
CROMLECH circle, crommel, cyclolith, dolmen, gorsedd, memorial, quoit, stone

CROMWELL *agent* agitator
nickname ironsides
parliament barebones
porter daniel
soldier ironside
son-in-law ireton
title lord protector
victory naseby
CRONE aunt, beldam(e), cailleach, cailliach, crony, ewe, gorgon, hag, harridan, old woman, ribibe, witch
CRONUS saturnus
daughter demeter, hera, hestia
parent gaea, uranus
son chiron, hades, poseidon, zeus
victim uranus
wife rhea
CRONY associate, billy, buddy, chum, companion, comrade, eme, friend, gimmer, gossip, gossy, intimate, pal
CROOK abgle, akimbo, badman, bend, bias, cambuca, cammock, cane, cheat, chiseler, criminal, cromb, crosier, crummie, crummy, curvature, curve, deflect, deviate, deviation, distort, felon, filcher, gonef, gonif, gonov, hinge, hood, hook, hunch, indent, knave, knee, meander, pedum, pervert, pilferer, pothook, scoundrel, shake, sharper, slither, staff, steal, swindle(r), tendril, thief, twist, wind, yentzer, zigzag
an elbow drink
-backed crouchie, deformed
shepherd's crotch
CROOKED agee, akimbo, angular, artful, askance, askew, aslant, awry, bad, bandified, bent, cam(med), camshach, circuitous, contorted, corrupt, crafty, cranky, criminal, crump, curved, curvous, deceitful, devious, dishonest, distorted, dogleg, false, fraudulent, galleywest, game, gleed, gnarled, hooked, kam, kicky, knurly, nefarious, oblique, rotten, skywest, thraw(art), thrawn, tortile, tortuous, tricky, turning, twisted, vicious, warped, weewaw, weewow, winding, wry, zag
comb. ankyl(o), cam

stick crank
symbol dogleg
wood buttonbush
CROOKNECK cashaw, cushaw, squash
CROON bellow, boom, carol, chirm, chirp, complain, hum, lament, low, lull, mourn, murmur, sing, song, teedle, wail, whine
CROP bearing, belly, bob, breast, browse, burden, clip, crap, craw, curtail, cut, deduct, emblement, farm, feed on, finial, fruit, gebbie, gorge, graze, group, gullet, hair, handle, harvest, hide, lash, lop, maw, output, proceeds, produce, product, prune, rabi, reap, rop, rowen, shank, shave, shorten, silage, stomach, top, trashify, trim, whip, yield
destroyer army-worm
forage alsike, clover, rape
fowl's craw, gebbie, ingluvies, maw
grass lea, ley, swarth, swath(e)
hunting quirt, rop, whip
management agrology, agronomics, agronomy, arviculture
out appear, basset
paid as rent cain
profits emblement
renew rotate
2nd growth rowen
up appear, begin, occur, rise, surface, turn up
yearly annona
CROPPED docked, gotched, shaved
CROPPER collapse, disaster, failure, fall, grinder, misfortune, mucker, plumper, pouter pigeon, purler
CROPSHIN herring
CROQUET jeu de mall, roque, sport of stings
chronicler pepys
entrepreneur mister jaques
london patron mr spratt
pioneer miss mcnaughten
term arch, bisque, breakdown, cannon, crush shot, mallet, roquet, rover, tice, triple peel, wicket
CROQUETTE cecil, cutlet, kromeski, oyster, roque
CROSS 3 cut, mix, tau 4 ankh, crux, funk, rood, sail, span, ugly 5 angry, cangy,

chuff, corse, frank, graft, humpy, irate, staff, sulky, surly, teaty, techy, testy, thraw, trace, trial 6 bisect, bridge, cammed, chuffy, crabby, cranky, flyfot, grumpy, modify, oppose, patchy, potent, snaggy, sullen, symbol, teethy, thwart, touchy 7 against, burbank, calvary, crabbed, grouchy, peevish, saltier, saltire, waspish 8 anchored, camshach, churlish, crantara, crucifix, insignia, memorial, navigate, petulant, swastika 9 crostarie, cruciform, hybridize, intersect, irascible, irritable, signature 10 affliction, counteract, disappoint, impediment, interbreed, misfortune 11 bad-tempered, ill-tempered, tribulation 12 antagonistic
ansate ankh, crux ansata
arm ends split patonce
as two sticks
-barred trabeculate
-bearing cruciferous
-bombard atomize
christ's tree
cleavers wild licorice
comb. stauro
-examine grill, question, third degree
-eye esotropia, squint, strabismus
-fertilization allogamy, phytogamy, pollination
fiery crantara, crostarie
-fire interchange, overreach
flower milkwort
form urde, urdy
-grained cantankerous, churlish, coarse, contrary, crossways, gnarled, hickory, ill-tempered, intractable, irascible, nurly, patchy, perverse, self-willed, stubborn, ugly
guard chaps
heraldic botonne, cleche, couped, crosslet, fitche, fleury, humette, maltese, moline, pate, potence, potent, trefle, urde
hooked swastika
latin crux immissa
oneself sain
one's heart depose, swear
one's mind occur to, think of
out blank, cancel, deduct, dele(te), eliminate, erase, obliterate, remove, rub out

over span, traject, transcend
purposes difference, misunderstanding
-question backspear, backspeer, backspier, examine, ta(i)rge
-rib arch, lierne
rubicon burn bridges, decide, determine, make up one's mind
-section part, representation, sample, selection, slice
-shaped cleche, crucial, cruciate, cruciform
southern crosier, crux
spar bougar
-staff crozier, radius
st anthony's tau
stone chiastolite, harmotome, staurolite
stroke beard, bind, ceriph, serif
swords combat, duel, fight
symbol of st andrew
talk backchat, chatter, interference
tau ankh, crux (commissa), tace
the line score, transgress, trespass
the path of encounter, meet
thread trame, weft, woof
timber spale
transom patible
type ankh, avellan, botonee, celtic, egyptian, formee, fourchee, greek, jerusalem, latin, lorraine, maltese, moline, papal, patee, pommee, potent, quadrate, swastika
up betray, deceive
way of via crucis
wires confuse, reticle
worship of staurolatry
x-shaped crux decussata
CROSSARM wishbone
CROSSBAR axle, baton, beam, horizontal, jugum, locket, round, rung, stempel, stemple, transom, transverse
CROSSBEAM balk, bar, bolster, girder, grill, spur, trave, traverse, treve
CROSSBILL finch, loxia
CROSSBOW arbalest, ballista, brake, latch, manubaliste, piece, prod(d), rodd, weapon
arrow bolt, quarrel
man balistarius
CROSSBREED cape boy, generate, husky, hy-

brid(ize), metis, mixture, mongrel, sanga, sangu
CROSSCURRENT conflict, opposition, surging
CROSSCUT beeline, coupure, drift, offset, tunnel
saw briar
CROSSHATCH engrave, shade
CROSSING bisecting, chiasma, cruciation, decussation, diagonal, fork, horizontal, intersecting, intersection, passage, sailing, traject, transverse, transversion, traversal, voyage
of the bar death
CROSSPATCH bear, crab, crank, grouch
CROSSPIECE bar, beard, buck, chopstick, cleat, crowfoot, doubletree, evener, footrail, grill, headrail, lintel, rung, spar, toggle, transom, transverse, yoke
on wicket bail
CROSSROAD carfax, carrefour, comitum, hub, intersection, leet, vent, vilage, weent, went
goddess hecate, trivia
of the world lisbon
CROSSROW alphabet
CROSSRUFF oscillate, saw, seesaw, trump
CROSSWAY (See also CROSSROAD.) rotary, traffic circle, transverse
CROSSWAYS across, athwart(wise), contrar(i)-wise, contrawise, diagonal, obliquely, overthwart, side-(ways), sidewise, thwart(ly)(ways), transverse(ly)
CROSSWISE acrostic, athwart, diagonal, perversely, traverse, weftwise
CROSSWORD *puzzle* acrostic, anagram
CROSSWORT boneset, loosestrife, maywort, mugweed, mugwort
CROTALUS cascavel, rattler, rattlesnake, venum
CROTCH bifurcation, branch, cleft, crutch, detour, deviation, fork, notch, post, prong, ramification, turning
CROTCHET angle, caprice, corchat, crankum, eccentricity, fad, freak, hook, irritation, oddity, quirk, vagary, whim(sey)

CROTCHETY cranky, kinky, odd
CROTON basket hoop, bloodtree, bloodwood, cascalote, cascarilla, cockroach
CROTOPUS *daughter* psamathe
kingdom argos
victim psamathe
CROTUS *companions* muses
father pan
CROUCH bend, bow, cook, coorie, couch, cower, cringe, croodle, curb, dare, fawn, grovel, huddle, hunch(down), hunker, hurkle, quail, rook, ruck, scrooch, scrouch, scrunch, squat, stoop, truckle, wallow, welter
CROUP angina, catarrh, cough, croak, crup(per), cynanche, hives, rump
CROUSE bold, brisk, cheerful, cocky, lively
CROUTON bit, garnish, sippet, toast
CROW, CROW'S absaroka, aga, aylet, babble, blackneb, blow, boast, brag, bran, carnal, carrian, chough, corbie, corvine, corvus, crake, crone, cry, daw, dowp, exult, gas, gavelock, gloat, grapnel, graypack, guggle, gurgle, hag, hoodie, hoody, kelly, kokako, laugh, lever, raven, rook, triumph, vapor, vaunt, whoop
bait carrion, corpse
black rook
blackbird grackle
carrion black neb
changed to coronis
constellation corvus
corn colicroot
cry caw, craw, daw
duck coot, pulldoo, tule hen
family chough, jackdaw, jaypie, pie, raven
garlic wild onion
-like corvine, pie, rook
ling heath(er)
mythical hugin, munin
nest aerie, eyrie, lookout, outlook, wild carrot
pert. corvine
pheasant coucal
piping flutebird
shrike magpie, organbird, squeaker
symbol of longevity

to pluck issue
white vulture
CROWBAR gablock, gavelock, handspec, jemmy, jimmy, lever, pry, setup, suape, tool
CROWBERRY heathberry, heather
family empetraceae
CROWD accelerate, army, assemble, atef, audience, bike, boodle, bourock, charge, chorus, compress, congest, coterie, cram(p), crush, drove, fill, fry, gate, group, heap, herd, hoi polloi, horde, host, house, hug, hurry, jam, legion, mass, meiny, mob, moider, multitude, pack, populace, posse, press, push, rabble, ram, rout, ruck, saturate, scrouge, scruze, serry, shoal, shove, slue, squeeze, surfeit, swad, swamp, swarm, thicken, thrave, threat, throng, thrust, thrutch, troop, turb, urge
around besiege, flock
-boulder barker
comb. ochlo
fear of ochlophobia
grass charlock
in enter, intrude, shove
noisy rout
number three
out displace, supplant
penetrate elbow, needle
sail accelerate, speed
together clutter, contrude, hotter, howder, huddle, hug, serry
CROWDED bunched, busy, close, congested, cooped up, crammed, dense, elbowed, jam-packed, numerous, opplete, packed, serried, spiss, stuffed, teeming, thick
place beehive, subway
CROWDWEED charlock, field cress
CROWFOOT banewort, batrachium, buttercress, buttercup, caltrop, catha, cimicifuga, clematis, club moss, cuckoo bud, exogen, furrow, goldcup, golland, gowan, headline, hellweed, joy, king cup, paigle, ram's-claws, ranunculus, wrinkle
CROWN adorn, atef, basil, bay, bezel, button, cantle,

cap, capital, capsheaf, caput, chandelier, chaplet, circle, climax, complete, consummate, copestone, corona(l), coronate, coronet, crest, diadem, enthrone, fillet, finishing touch, garland, glorify, grace, head (dress), honor, inaugurate, install, invest, laurel, metier, miter, palm, pate, perfect, pinhead, pinnacle, potong, reward, ruler, scepter, summit, taj, tiara, tonsure, topknot, top off, trophy, vertex, wreath

and anchor chuck-a-luck

comb. stephano

crane balearic

forfeited to deodand

half alderman, george

name meaning stephen

northern corona borealis

of east antioch

of head cantle, foretop, pate, pommel, skull

of st stephen hungary

of-the-field corn-cockle

of thorns affliction, caraunda, curse, spurge, starfish

pert. coronal, coronate, laureled, rosated

piece bull, coin

plant stool

post upright

prince atheling, heir(apparent)

-shaped coroniform

southern corona australis

symbol of st alban

vetch axseed, coronilla

wheel contrate, gear, ratchet

CROWNED browbound, consummate, coronate, crested, cristated, incoronate, perfect, sovereign

head caesar, emperor, kaiser, king, potentate, tsar

CROWTOE buttercup, caltrop, toothwort, wood hyacinth

CROZER chucker

CROZIER *bearer* crociery

CRU growth, land, vineyard

CRUBEEN claw, paw, trotter

CRUCIAL acute, bull's eye, climacteric, critical, decisive, demonstrative, determining, final, important, menacing, momentous, severe, supreme, telling, threatening, trying, vital

CRUCIBLE cruset, dish,

etna, foyer, hearth, melting pot, pot, retort, shoe, test

lining brasque

CRUCIFIX cross, crux, pax, rood

ebony black rood

CRUCIFIXION *hymn* stabat mater

road via dolorosa

site calvary

CRUCIFY excruciate, execute, hang, harry, ill-treat, kill, martyr(ize), mortify, persecute, subdue, torment, torture, vex

CRUD curd, NONSENSE, refuse

CRUDE artless, bald, barbarian, bare, blatant, bluff, blunt, brutal, callow, coarse, crass, doggerel, earthy, fallow, graubyer, graubyon, green, gross, harsh, illbred, immature, impolite, incult, indelicate, lowbred, misleared, primeval, primitive, raw, rough(hewn), rude, rustic, savage, tactless, tasteless, uncooked, uncouth, undeveloped, unfledged, unpolished, unrefined, unripe, untrained, vulgar, wild

CRUEL atrocious, barbarian, barbarous, bestial, bitter, black, bloodthirsty, bloody, boarish, breem, breme, brutal, brute, brutish, callous, caustic, cutthroat, demoniac, despiteous, devilish, diabolic(al), divers(e), draconian, dreadful, fell, feral, ferocious, fiendish, fierce, gril, grim, harsh, hellish, inclement, inconsiderate, infernal, inhuman, malevolent, malicious, merciless, murderous, painful, rethe, ruthless, sadic, sadistic, satanic, savage, sensual, stern, strict, swinish, tartarean, tyrannic, unkind, unmeek, violent, wroth

CRUELTY atrocity, barbarity, barbarousness, bestiality, bloodthirstiness, brutality, brutishness, cannibalism, devilry, duress, ferociousness, ferocity, fiendishness, fierceness, maltreatment, mistreatment, oppression, rigor, ruthlessness, sadism, savagery, severity,

truculence, viciousness, violence

lover of sadist

symbol wolf

CRUET ama, ampul, ampulla, bottle, buret(te), caster, crewet, cruse, guttus, urceole, vessel, vial

CRUISE coast, fly, jaunt, junket, navigate, prowl, ride, sail, soar, trip, voyage, wander

CRUISER battleship, patrol car, police car, power boat, prowl car, ship, squadcar, streetwalker, traveler, vessel, warship, yacht

CRULLER doughnut, olycook, olykoek, twister, wonder

CRUMB bit, boor, cad, dab, dash, fragment, grain, mealock, morsel, murl(ack), oaf, part(icle), piece, remnant, seed, speck, sweep

CRUMBLE collapse, crush, decay, decompose, decrease, disappear, disintegrate, dissolve, fall(apart), fragment, grush, mash, mo(u)lder, murl, mush, particle, perish, powder, pulverize, rot, shatter, slough, spall, spoil

CRUMBLY brashy, bruckle, friable, murly, pulverable

CRUMP bang, blow, brittle, cavity, crack, crisp, crook(ed), crunch, curve, deviate, friable, grate, thud, thump, thwack

CRUMPET cake, cripple, head, muffin, pikelet

CRUMPLE buckle, collapse, contract, crinkle, fold, frumple, furrow, mool, muss, raffle, rool, ruck, ruffle, rumple, scrunch, shrink, shrivel, wrinkle, yield

CRUNCH beat, bite, bruise, champ, chew, cranch, crump, crush, gnash, granch, grate, grind, growse, masticate, munch, pulverize, scrunch, trample, tread

CRUNCHWEED charlock

CRUOR blood, gore

CRUPPER curpel, curpin, harness, rump, tailband

bone sacrum

CRUSADE campaign, cause,

croisee, expedition, jahad, jehad, jihad, mission, war
chivalric order knights templar
cry deus vult
leader tancred
CRUSADER pilgrim, reformer, templar
famous ademar, baldwin, tancred
foe infidel, saladin, saracen, turk
headquarters acre, rhodes
CRUSH bash, beat, beloved, bow, bray, break(down), brize, brizz, bruise, burden, comminute, compress, craze, creem, crowd, crumble, crunch, defeat, defoil, defoul, demoralize, destroy, doll(e)y, dollie, drink, grind, hoard, hug, humble, infatuation, jam, love affair, mash, mob, mortify, mow(down), multitude, overwhelm, powder, press(ure), pulp, pulverize, put down, quash, quell, refute, rout, rumple, scrunge, sink, smush, squabash, squash, squeeze, squelch, squiss, stamp, steam-roller, subdue, suppress, thring, throng, trample, tread, unman
have a — on See LOVE.
in stave
room foyer
CRUSHED broken, contrite, despairing, dispirited, hopeless, overcome, shattered, subdued, tame, upset
CRUSHER bruiser, nibber, policeman
CRUSHING breakback, conclusive, decisive, embarrassing, fierce, humiliating, pulverization, smashing
CRUST abaisse, armo(u)r, bloom, brass, cake, caliche, carapace, cheek, coat(ing), costra, cover, earth, eschar, gall, lorica, nerve, pellicle, rondle, scab, scruff, scutulum, shell, skin, surface, wineball
CRUSTACEAN (See also *kind*, below.) amphipod, arthropod, copepod, decapod, isopod, phyllopod
antenna, comb. cerite
antenna joint carpocerite
appendage exite, palpus
aquatic anostraca
blind well-shrimp

claw chela
egg sac swimmeret
extinct archaeocyathid
feeler antenna
5th segment carpus
footless apus
fossil trilobite
fresh-water cladocera, conchostraca, crawfish, crayfish, notostraca, spiny lobster
genus astacus, calappa, cancer, caprella, copepoda, eryon, gammarus, hippa, protocaris, triops
gill arthrobranch, podobranch
group caridea
isopod gribble, limnoria, slater, wood louse
kind acorn, alima, anatafia, anomura, artemia, asellus, ayuyu, balanid, barnacle, box crab, buckler, burster, buster, calappa, camaron, cancer, carida, caridoid, copepod, crab(fish), crawdad, crawfish, crayfish, craylet, crevette, dad, daphnid, decapod, eryon, fiddler, flea, gammarid, grapsoid, grapsus, gribble, hippa, homard, inach(o)id, kingcrab, lernaean, limulid, limulus, lobster, macrura, maia(n), maya, mudcrab, mys(o)id, mysis, ochidore, ocipode, oniscus, pandle, panfish, peacrab, peeler, pillbug, pillworm, prawn, pungar, racer, ranian, scud, shedder, shrimp, slater, sowbug, sprite, squagga, squilla, uca, wood louse, yabber, yabbie, yabby, zo(a)ea
larva alima, glasscrab, metanauplius, nauplius
limb pleopod, podite, walking-foot
limb segment carpos
marine barnacle, callianassa, emerita
one-eyed monocule
phyllopod artemia, branchipus
science of carcinology
shrimp-like anaspida, krill
small amphipod, anostraca, barnacle, copepod, cyclops, fiddler crab, nebalia, sand flea, whale louse
stalk-eyed podophthalmia
10-footed crab
thorax pereion

CRUSTY bluff, blunt, brusque, choleric, crabbed, cranky, curt, fretful, gruff, hard, harsh, impudent, irascible, irritable, obstinate, peevish, prickly, rude, short, starchy, surly, testy, touchy, waspish
CRUTCH clutch, cratch, fork, prop, scatch, staddle, staff, stick, stilt, support
CRUX ankh, body, brunt, bull's eye, core, crisis, cross, difficulty, essence, essential, gist, hitch, nub, pinch, pith, pivot, point, puzzle, riddle, rub, squeeze, stress
ansata ankh
CRY 3 baa, boo, caw, fad, hep, hoa, hue, low, moo, sob, yap 4 bark, bawl, blat, bray, bump, call, cawk, evoe, honk, hoop, hoot, howl, keen, mewl, moan, mode, oyes, oyez, pish, pule, rage, reem, rerd, roar, scry, sign, test, toot, wail, weep, yawl, yawp, yell, yelp, yipe, yoho, yowl 5 avast, blare, bleat, bleed, blore, cheer, clepe, cooee, cooey, craze, croak, greet, groan, hollo, mourn, rumor, shout, style, trial, vogue, wahoo, whine, whoop, yodel 6 banzai, barley, bellow, bewail, blazon, boohoo, chivvy, clamor, halloo, lament, murmur, mutter, plaint, scream, shriek, shrill, snivel, sorrow, squall, squeal 7 acclaim, blubber, catcall, deplore, fashion, implore, protest, screech, spraich, whimper, yoowhoo 8 complain, jeremiad, scronach 9 break down, catchword, caterwaul, complaint, ululation
about issue, publish, report, spread
aloud blart, grede, sob, wail
ancient evoe
animal baa, bark, blat, bleat, pheal(e), pheel, trumpet, whoof, yelp
back revert
bird bill, boom, caw(k), clang, coo, pew, qualm
cattle hoy
child's mewl, pule
child's, newborn vagitus

derisive bah, boo, catcall, hiss, hoot, phooey, rats
disgusted ugh
down belittle, censure, condemn, depreciate, disparage, dispraise, forbid
drinking rivo
for demand, desire, need
for truce barla, barl(e)y
hailing hola
harsh croak
havoc mobilize, warn
hawking au vol
hoarsely croup
hunting chev(v)y, chivy, hey go bet, pillloo, tallyho, tantivy, tivy, yoick(s)
introductory hear ye, oyes, oyez
of approval bravo, hoch, ole, rah
of attention hey, holla
of grief keen, tangi, ullagone
of pain ouch
of relief phew, whew
of sorrow alack, alas, woe
of surprise hein
of triumph aha, hurrah
off abandon
on appeal, beseech
out blame, blat, blazon, bray, breathe, call, censure, clamor, complain, decry, disclaim, escry, exclaim, gale, lament, proclaim, protest, scream, shout, steven, suffer, threap, thrope, vociferate, yell
out against accuse, blame, censure, dissuade, incriminate, protest
party shibboleth, slogan
quits surrender, yield
shrill screech, skirl, squeak, squeal, yallock
to implore, pray
up crack, extol, laud, praise
war alala, slogan
western wahoo
wild evoe
wordless keen, ululu
CRYBABY complainer, whiner
CRYING blatant, blubbering, clamant, clamorous, conspicuous, demanding, flagrant, glaring, heinous, in tears, lachrymal, lachrymatory, lachrymose, notorious, plaintive, pressing, puling, recreant, snivelling, sobbing, tearful, teary, urgent, vagient, wailing, weeping, weepy

bird limpkin
hare pika
out childbirth, confinement
CRYMMYONIAN *sow* phaea
CRYOMETER frigorimeter
CRYPT cavity, compartment, croft, follicle, gland, grave, grotto, mausoleum, pit, recess, refuge, shroud, tomb, treasury, urn, vault
CRYPTIC abrupt, ambiguous, arcane, cabalistic, dark, elliptic(al), enigmatic, equivocal, esoteric, hidden, mysterious, mystical, obscure, occult, oracular, perplexing, puzzling, recondite, secret, short, sibyllie, terse, vague
CRYPTOGAM acrogen, alga, fern, liverwort, moss, thallophyte
CRYPTOGRAM cipher, code
CRYPTOGRAPHER vigenere
CRYSTAL clear, dial, diamond, glass, goblet, ice, lucid, mirror, needle, pellucid, quartz, transparent, water
cavity vug(g)
clear apparent, evident, manifest, obvious, open, patent, pellucid, plain
cluster druse
comb. hedron
covered with drusy
fine beryl
form bisphenoid, disphenoid
-gaze foresee, predict, scry
-gazer prophet, scryer, seer(ess), skryer
-gazing catoptromancy, divination, scry
ice frazil
needle-shaped raphides
pendant prism
planet moon
rock bristol
rodlike bacillite
studded druse
tea cinquefoil, wild rosemary
twin baveno, druse, macle, twindle, twoling
variation of seriate
vision esp
CRYSTALLINE clear, pellucid, pure
acid See ACID *crystalline.*
alkaloid akuammine, amarine, apoatropine, apomorphine, aporphine, atropine, berbamine, codamine,

codeine, cinchonicine, conhydrine, cotarnine, cryptopine, cusconine, cytisine, daturine, ecgonine, emetine, ephedrine, galegine, gelsemine, geneserine, glaucine, jervine, muscarine, papaverine, pilosine, piperine, protopine, pseudomorphine, pseudotropine, psychotrine, pukateine
base alanine, anserine, gerontine, guanidine, guanosine
colorless acacetin, ergosterol, erythrin, orcine
compound See COMPOUND *crystalline.*
diacid azelaic
fat cetin
globulin avenalin, edestin, excelsin, vitellin
glucoside acacin, androsin, antiarin, apiin, asperuloside, baptisin, esculin, gentiopicrin, gitalin, gitonin, gitoxin
hydrocarbon retene
material impactite
mineral spar
monoacid atropic
poison amarin
solid tetracaine, thiourea, thymol
sterol anthesterin, anthesterol
structure siderite, sparry
substance alban, amarine, bergaptene, dulcin, orcine, scopoline, urea
white berberine, gallic acid
CRYSTALLITE acrulite, bacillite, belonite, scopulite, tricite, whinstone
CRYSTALLIZE candy, come together, congeal, definitize, fix, form, gather, solidify, sugar, take form, take shape
CRYSTALLY drusy
CRYSTALWORT hepatica
CTEATUS *father* actor
CTENOPHORE beroe, beroid, cestida, cestus, cydippid, jellyfish, nuda, rib
CUADRA manzana
CUATEMOC guatemoc, guatemozin, guatemuz(a), quautemoc
CUB baby, bear, boy, brat, child, codling, coop, eam, fledgling, fry, lionet, novice, pen, pup, reporter, shed, stall, toto, whelp
scout leader akela

shark carcharias, carcharrinus, galeid, lamia
CUBA, CUBAN *asphalt* chapapote
ballerina alicia alonso
bay guantanamo, nipe, pigs
beverage pina
bird tocororo, trogon
cape cruz, lucrecia, maisi
capital havana
castle morro
chess master capablanca
cigar havana
city artemisa, baracoa, bayamo, camaguey, cienfuego, colon, guantanamo, guayabal, guines, havana, holguin, manes, marianao, matanzas, palmira, pinar del rio, puerto principe, santa clara, santiago
coin centavo, cuarento, peso
composer lecuona
conqueror velazquez
dance comparsa, conga, danzon, guajira, guaracha, habanera, pachanga, r(h)umba, samba, tango
dictator batista, castro
disaster bay of pigs
document ostend manifesto
dollar gourde
ebony granadilla
falls agabama, caburni, toa
fish bacalao, diablo, escolar, palu, viajaca
fortification morro, trocha
gulf anamaria, batabano, mexico
hutia pilori
indian arawak, carib, ciboney(e), taino
island camaguey, de pinos, pines, sabana
leader batista, castro, urrutia
lily scilla, squill
measure caballeria, cocoy, cordel, fanega, tarea, vara
motto patria y libertad
municipality palmira
patriot marti
peak copper, guaniguanico, pico turquinos, pinar del rio, turquino
port baracoa, cardenas, cienfuegos, duabi, manzanillo, matanzas
president batista, dorticos, machado y lorales
prince cazique
province camaguey, havana, matanzas, oriente, pinar del rio, santa clara

range cristal, maestra, organos, trinidad
region vuelta abajo
revolutionary castro, che guevara
river cauto, zaza
rodent hutia, pilori
root malanga
rum bacardi, ron
secret police porra
shirt guayabera
shrub aroma, aromo, huisache, peregrina
snake juba
solenodon alamiqui, almique
song comparsa, guajira
spinach indian lettuce
storm bayamo
swamp zapata
terrorist che guevara
tobacco broadleaf, capa, havana, vuelta
tree almendro, culla, cuya, guacacoa, jique
trogon tocororo
ward barrio
weapon machete
weight libra, tercio
wood fustic
writer marti
CUBBYHOLE corner, nook, refuge, retreat
CUBE angle, ba(r)basco, block, DICE, die, hexahedron, knob, masik, nob, quadrate, tessella, tessera
magic nasik
small dice, die
spar anhydrite
CUBIC isometric, solid, three-dimensional
centimeter fluigram
contents capacity
decimeter liter, litre
measure cord, kilo(meter), stere
meter stere
shape cuboid
CUBICLE alcove, bay, bedroom, booth, cabin, carol, carrell, cell, embrasure, niche, nook, recess, room, study
CUBISM *founder* picasso
CUBITIERE elbowpiece
CUCHULAINN *country* ireland
court conchobor
enemy queen medb
father sualtaim
poet amairgin
son conlaech
teacher cathbad, fergus, scathach, sencha

victim conlaech
wife e(i)mer
CUCKOLD actaeon, becco, beggartick, cokewold, cornute, cornuto, cowbird, cowfish, hornify, husband, ramhead, tup, weed, wittol
dock burdock
symbol stag
CUCKOO ani, ano, bird, boobook, chataka, chowchow, clock, coccygus, coel, coucal, cowk, crazy, crotophaga, di(e)dric, fool (ish), gowk, imitator, insane, kobird, koel, koil, larus, mad, picarian, rainfowl, roadrunner, silly, simpleton, sirkeer
bee nomada
black-billed rainbird
bread sorrel
buds crowfoot
button burdock
channel-bill rainfowl
family cuculidae
flower bird-eye, bog pink, briza, canterbury bell, head(ache), lady's-smock, milkmaid, pa(i)gle, quaking grass, ragged robin, sorel, spink
fly cuculus, ruby wasp
fool wryneck
gillyflower ragged robin
kind coccyzus, coucal, ko(w)bird, rainbird, wryneck
-like piririgua
maid shrike, wryneck
shrike blue pigeon, campephagia
spit woodsere
terrestrial roadrunner
vulgate larus
word platitude
yellow-billed rainbird
CUCKOOPINT aaron, adder's-meat, arum, bobbin and joan, bobbins, bobby, buckram, dragon, mandrake, oxberry, priest's-hood, ramp, wake-robin, waterlily
CUCULLATE covered, cowled, hooded
CUCUMBER conger, cucumis, cucurb(it), earth apple, ecballium, gherkin, gourd, pedata, pepino, peop, peponida, pickle, vegetable
bitter colocynth
fish grayling

rot cottony-leak
shriveled crumpling
small gherkin
squirting touch-me-not
tree bilimbi, black linn, magnolia, tulip tree
wild creeper

CUCUMIS anguria, cacur, cantaloupe, cucumber, gourd, muskmelon, watermelon

CUCURBIT alembic, flask, matrass, vessel

CUCURBITA calabazilla, cassabanana, crookneck, cucumber, curuba, cushaw, gourd, pumpkin, sicana, squash, watermelon

CUD bite, bolus, chew, merycism, queed, quid, rumen
chewing merycism
chew the rumination

CUDBEAR cork, persio, persis

CUDDLE bundle, caress, cosset, curl up, dandle, embrace, fondle, hug, kiddle, kiutle, nestle, nuzzle, pet, snoozle, snuggle
-me-to-you pansy

CUDDLY draper, peddler

CUDDY ass, bribe, cabin, coalfish, cudeigh, cupboard, donkey, gift, hedge-sparrow, lout, pantry

CUDGEL alpeen, ballow, baste, bastinado, baston, bat(on), beat, blackjack, bludgeon, bourdon, club, drub, fustigate, kebbie, kevel, pound, rung, sandbag, shillala(h), shillela(g)h, staff, stave, stick, swaddle, swingle, thump, towel, truncheon

CUDWEED antennaria, catfoot, cat's-ear, enaena

CUE braid, clew, clue, function, hint, jog, mast, mnemonic, mood, nod, pigtail, plait, presa, presto, prod, prompt, queue, remind, rod, role, signal, tag, tail, tip, twist, twit, watchword, wattle
billiard mast, stick
script prompt book
shot masse
shuffleboard shovel
tip leather
word presto

CUERNAVACA cuauhnahuac

CUERPO body, hulk, naked, torso, uncovered

CUFF blow, box, buffet, clout, colpheg, fender, fight, gauntlet, glove, gowf(f), hit, manacle, miser, mitten, old man, punch, scuff(le), slap, slug, souse, strike, swat, turnup
embroidered epimanikia
fastener link, tab
off the ad lib, impromptu

CUIF coof, dolt, lout, ninny

CUIRASS anime, armor, curace, curate, curiet, lorica, mail, plate, thorax
articulated anime
part backplate, blackpiece

CUIRASSIER See SOLDIER.

CUISINE cookery, cooking, food, kitchen, menu, table
variety grande, haute, minceur

CUL-DE-SAC blank wall, blind alley, bracket, c(a)ecum, dead end, impasse, pocket, strait

CULL assort, choose, cully, dupe, elect, handpick, garble, gather, glean, gull, inferior, opt, pick, pike, pluck, prefer, reject, select, separate, sift, single out, sort, try, winnow

CULLIS channel, groove, gutter

CULLY cheat, deceive, trick

CULM, CULMS coal dust, coolm, deposit, refuse, shoal-water, sirky, slack, stalk, stem, top

CULMEN acme, ridge, top

CULMINATE cease, climax, complete, conclude, end, top

CULMINATION acme, apex, apogee, auge, blow off, climax, completion, conclusion, crest, crown, end, meridian, noon, peak, pinnacle, roof, summit, top, vertex, zenith

CULPA carelessness, fault, guilt, neglect, negligence

CULPABLE blameable, blame-worthy, censurable, criminal, faulty, guilty, immoral, laches, reprehensible

CULPER, SAMUEL robert townsend

CULPRIT convict, criminal, felon, malefactor, offender, sinner

CULT belief, church, communion, creed, denomination, devotion, doctrine, fad, faith, ism, mania, persuasion, religion, ritual, school, sect, veneration, worship

CULTIVATE acquire, affect, approach, backset, better, cherish, civilize, court, curry, cut, develop, dress, ear, educate, fallow, farm, fertilize; foster, get next to, grow, harrow, hoe, improve, instruct, labor, make up to, manage, manure, mature, mulch, nourish, nurse, nurture, play court to, play up to, plow, prepare, prune, raise, rake, ratoon, rear, refine, ripen, run after, school, scratch, study, teach, teel, teil, tend, till(the soil), train, weed, woo, work

CULTIVATED artificial, civil(ized), cultured, domesticated, educated, elegant, hoed, polite, politic, refined, tame, taught, tilled, toiled, trained, urbane, well-bred

CULTIVATION agriculture, background, breeding, crop, culture, delicacy, finish, manurage, polish, refinement, taste, tillage, tilth, tilture
method goom, jhum, joom, jum
science agrology, agronomics, geoponics

CULTIVATOR agriculturist, farmer, florist, grubber, harrow, husbandman, mamoty, plough, plow, tiller
blade duckfoot, sweep
gang rig

CULTURE abashev, agar, art, breeding, civilization, cultivation, delicacy, education, eugenics, euthenics, humanism, knowledge, kultur, polish, refinement, scholarship, schooling, society, starter, taste, tillage, tilth
center athens
hero prometheus, theseus, triptolemus
medium agallock, agar, arabinose, gelatin, isinglass, pectin, pectinose
pattern folkway
pert. tribal

stone age acheulean, aurignacian, azilian, chellean, combe-capelle, cro-magnon, eolithic, magdalenian, mousterian, neolithic, paleolithic, solutrean
study anthropology, archeology, ethnology
vessel for petri dish
CULTURED aesthetic, artistic, bookish, civil(ized), erudite, learned, lettered, literary, profound, scholarly, tasteful, well-bred, well-read
person brahmin
CULVER dove, pigeon
house dovecot
CULVERFOOT columbine, cranesfoot
CULVERIN bastard, cannon, lantaca, musket, pelican, spirole
CULVERKEY columbine, cowslip, samara, wood hyacinth
CULVERROOT comfrey, false ipecac, gillenia, indian(hippo)(physic), leptandra, spurge, whorlywort
CULVERT bridge, channel, conduit, drain, gout, overpass, sewer, sluit
CUMBER burden, cummer, defeat, hamper, hinder, inconvenience, overload, perplex, shackle, trouble, vex
CUMBERLAND *disease* anthrax
gap ouasioto
poet wordsworth
tributary stone
waterfall lodore
CUMBERSOME awkward, bulky, burdensome, clumsy, cumbrous, distressing, great, heavy, hefty, leaden, lugsome, massive, onerous, ponderous, troublesome, unwieldy, weighty
CUMHAL slave
CUMMER companion, female, friend, girl, godmother, intimate, kimmer, lass, midwife, witch, woman
CUMMERBUND band, belt, obi, sash
CUMSHAW bonus, gratuity, tip
CUMULATE (See also ACCUMULATE.) combine, gather, heap
CUMULATIVE additive,

amassed, augmenting, chain, circumstantial, increasing, multiplying, summative
CUNABULA cradle
CUNCTATION delay, procrastination, tardiness
CUNEATE cuneiform, triangular
CUNEIFORM bone, hieroglyphics, sphenoid, triquetrum, ulnare, wedged, wedge-shaped
character sphenogram
inscription site behistun, bisitun
study of sphenography
writing sphenography
CUNNER bergall, berggylt, bluefish, burgall, canoe, chogset, corkwing, gilthead, goldney, nibbler, nipper, perch, rosefish, surffish, wrasse
CUNNING 3 art, sly 4 arch, cute, foxy, keen, ruse, slim, wily, wise 5 acute, cagey, canny, craft, dedal, feint, guile, leery, pauky, pawky, pokey, sharp, skill, slick, smart 6 adroit, artful, astute, callid, clever, crafty, daedal, dainty, deceit, feline, foxery, shifty, shrewd, smooth, subtle, supple, tricky 7 darling, devious, finesse, knowing, politic, skilled, slyness, tricksy, varmint, vulpine 8 artifice, deeplaid, dextrous, foxiness, skillful, sleighty, slippery, subtlety, trickish, wiliness, yepeleic 9 acuteness, cageyness, canniness, chicanery, deception, dexterity, duplicity, ingenious, insidious, sagacious, sharpness, slickness, stratagem 10 artfulness, attractive, cleverness, craftiness, diplomatic, serpentine, shiftiness, shrewdness, subtleness, trickiness 11 serpentlike, well-devised 12 disingenuity, slipperiness 13 circumvention, insidiousness, machiavellian
one slyboots
symbol ape, fox
CUNNINGLY yepley, yeply
CUP ama, bleed, bucket, bumper, calix, calyx, cappie, capsule, cavity, cell, chark, cotyla, crater, cruse,

cupel, cupula, cyathus, demitasse, depas, dobbin, dop, fate, fessel, finjan, goblet, godet, grail, half-pint, holmos, horn, kotyle, kyathos, ladle, lota(h), mazard, mazer, mug, naggin, noggin, oxhorn, portion, quoniam, rumkin, scyphus, skyphos, stein, tass(ie), tig, tjanting, trophy, tumbler, tyg, vessel
-and-saucer campanula, canterbury bell
assaying breaker, cupel
-bearer ganymede, hebe, pincern, saki
comb. scypho
covered hanap
diamond-cutting dop(p)
drinking bowl, bratina, cylix, dobbin, facer, godet, kylix, mug, quaich, quoniam, stein, tankard, tass(ie), tig, toby, toss, trinket, tun
eared quaich, quaigh
earthenware mug
edge lip
fairy coolwort
-feast anthesteria
filled bumper
flower bell, calyx
fungus aecium
gem-cutting dop(p)
handle ear, lug
holder zarf
horn-shaped holmos
iron culot, mushroom
large facer, grail, jorum
leather gis, pin, well
-like depressing, calicle, calycle
long-handled cyath(us), dipper, kyathos
looped handle cantharus, kantharos, kylix
loving award, prize, tyg
nautical thief
of tea dish, forte, metier, oyster, speed, thing
olympus depas
ornamental tazza
paper dixie
pastry dariole, patty shell
prize pewter
sacred grail
17th century tig, tyg
shallow capsule, cylix, taster, tazza
-shaped calathiform, concave, cotyloid, cyathiform, pezizoid, pociliform, pociliform, scyphate

-shaped structure calycle, calycule, calyculus
small acetabulum, calicular, cannikin, chark, cruse, demitasse, dobbin, dop(p), nipperkin, nog(gin), pannikin, shot, tass(ie)
square madder, mether
stand zarf
standing goblet
2 pint
2-handled cylix, depas, kylix, tig, tyg
wooden capper, cappie, cog(ue), mether, quaich
CUPBOARD abacus, almirah, ambry, aparador, armoire, bole, buffet, bunker, bureau, cabinet, canterbury, case, catmalison, cellaret, chest(of drawers), chiffonier, chifforobe, closet, clothespress, commode, credence, credenza, cuddy, davenport, desk, drawer, dresser, escritoire, etagere, highboy, kas, kitchen cabinet, larder, locker, lowboy, press, repository, safe, secretaire, secretary, shelf, shelves, sideboard, skibbet, storehouse, trostera, vargueno, vitrine, wardrobe, whatnot
hood tremor
CUPEL burn, refine, test
CUPID, CUPID'S amor (etto), amorino, amour (ette), cherub, dan, eros, love, putto
beloved psyche
dart catananche, succory
delight wild pansy
flower cypress vine
infant amoretto, amorino, putto
parent aphrodite, mars, mercury, venus
torch brandon
CUPIDITY appetite, avarice, avidity, covetousness, desire, greed(iness), longing, lust, rapacity
demon mammon
CUPOLA belfry, calotte, cimborio, cockloft, dome, kiln, lantern, lookout, turret, vault
CUR black sheep, bobtail, bum, canine, dog, fice, mixture, mongrel, mut(t), ne'er-do-well, reprobate, sneak, tike, tyke, whappet, worm, wretch

CURACAO capital willemstad
jargon papiamento
CURARE oorali, poison, urari, woorali
CURASSOW cashew-bird, crax, mitu(a), pauxi(pauxi)
CURATE abbe, bedwarmer, clergyman, dominie, ecclesiastic, overseer, poker, priest, vicair, vicar(e)
CURATIVE healing, iatrical, physical, remedial, salutary, sanative
CURATOR caretaker, custodian, guardian, keeper, manager, overseer, steward, superintendent, supervisor, treasurer
CURB abstain, anchor, arrest, balk, bit, border, brake, bridle, check, clog, coerce, collar, compesce, constrain, countercheck, discipline, drag-sail, foil, govern, hamper, hamshackle, harness, hogtie, hold back, inhibit, kerb, leash, martindale, moderate, obstacle, pavement, puteal, rein, remora, repress, restrain, restrict, scotch, shackle, slack, slow, snaffle, snub, stay, stifle, stock exchange, stop, strain, subdue, suppress, tame, thwart, withhold
CURCH cap, (hand)kerchief
CURCULIO peach, snout bettle, turk, weevil
CURD(S) casein(e), cheese, clabber, clot, coagulum, congeal, crud, dahi, fleetings, oast
and whey pinjane, slip
bean tofu
dish from skyr
in milk ziega
CURDLE acerbate, acidify, acidulate, clabber, clot, coagulate, condense, congeal, earn, lapper, lobber, lop(per), posset, quail, quar(l), rennet, sam(m), sour, spoil, thicken, turn, unite, yearn
causing agent rennet
the blood frighten, horrify, terrify
CURDLED quarred, shotten
CURE antidote, apeutics, barbecue, boot, bring around, charge, churchman, corn, correct, disinfection, dose, drug, dun, ecclesiastic,

guerison, heal, help, instauration, jerk, kipper, medicament, medicate, medicine, nostrum, panacea, physic, pickle, preserve, priest, proprietary, recovery, recuperate, reest, relieve, remedy, restorative, restore, salt, serum, smeek, smoke, souse, specific, stay, temper, therapeutic, therapy, treacle, treat(ment), vaccine, vulcanize
-all avens, balm, catholicon, elixir, panacea, remedy, theriac
by salting corn
cough sapa, sape
fish dun, rouse
having power to sanative
herrings bloat
in smoke bloat, gammon, smudge
in sun dry, rizzar
science of iamatology
skins dress, tan
CUREMA mullet
CURETES aetolians, gegeneis, imbrogeneis, phoenicians, priests of crete, priests of rhea
CURIA court, rota, tribunal
CURIO bibelot, objet d'art, ornament, souvenir, virtu
friend orsino
CURIOSITY freak, interest, marvel, nicety, nosiness, oddity, peculiarity, phenomenon, rara avis, rarity, wonder
burn with begape, gape
CURIOUS agape, agog, eccentric, erratic, freakish, inquisitive, intrusive, meddlesome, meddling, meticulous, nos(e)y, odd, open-eyed, pandora, peculiar, prying, quizzical, rare, remarkable, rubberneck, searching, selle, selly, singular, snooping, snoopy, strange, unique, unusual
person gossip, pandora, quidnunc
CURIUM source plutonium
CURL berger, buckle, cannon, coil, convolution, criddle, crimp(le), crinkle, crip, crocket, cr(o)uche, cruddle, curve, earlock, feak, flexure, flourish, friz(zle), frounce, kink, lock, lovelock, mullet, purl, ringlet,

ripple, snake, spiral, squirm, swirl, tendril, toupet, tress, twist, wind, wrinkle, writhe
blue fleaweed
comb. cirri, cirro
fringe frisette
hair crook, frizz, marcel, wave
metal chip
one's teeth taunt
remove decatize, straighten
tight friz(z)
up crump, crunch, cuddle, huddle, hunch, shrink, snuggle
CURLED cockled, coiled, crimped, frizz(l)y, helicine, kinky, savoyed, scrolled, spiry, twisted
CURLEW bankera, bird, blue-legs, burhinus, bustard, doebird, fute, godwit, jack, kioea, marlin, numenius, smoker, snipe, spow(e), thick-knee, whaup, whimbrel
black ibis, plegadis
bug corn-billbug
jack whimbrel
pink spoonbill
CURLICUE caper, coil, curl, curve, ess, flourish, gyration, helix, paraph, quirk, spiral, squiggle, squirl, twist
CURLING *captain* skip(per)
term besom, button, hack, hog, house, iron, loofie, port, potlid, soop, spiel, stone, tee, wick
CURLY crimpy, crisp(ed), crispy, crull, frizzed, frizzly, frizzy, kinked, kinky, oundy, ripply, swirly, undy, wavy
-haired wooly(headed)
-head clematis, viorna
locks charles ii
top beet blight, virus
CURMUDGEON churl, crab, crosspatch, gleyde, grouch, miser, tightwad
CURMUDGEONLY cheeseparing, close(fisted), crabby, mean, miserly, penurious, stingy, sullen, surly, tight-fisted
CURRANT berry, blueberry, corinth, raisin, ribes, rissel, rizzar, rizzle
black cassis
bun wig(g)
jam barleduc
liqueur creme de cassis
red rissel

substance alite
tree shadbush
CURRAWONG squeaker, strepera
CURRENCY cash, cater, circulation, coin(age), fashion, greenbacks, legal tender, mod, money, publicity, scrip, specie, style, timeliness
substitute token
CURRENT about, accepted, actual, afoot, alive, au courant, carrier, coetaneous, coeval, common, contemporary, course, direction, doing, draught, drift, eddy, electricity, existing, familiar, flow, flux, going, habit, happening, instant, in the air, juice, lively, living, millrace, motion, ordinary, passing, popular, present, prevailing, prevalent, rapid, reported, rife, roust, run, stream, tendency, tenor, tide, topical, trend(y), undertow, universal, up-to-date, usual, waft, well-known, widespread, wind
air breeze, downflow, draft, draught, sheet, thermal
carrier fuselink
collector trolley
comb. rheo
direction axis
electric stray
event activity, affair, news
generator electromotor
living in lotic
measuring device ammeter, rheometer
ocean agulhas, aleutian, antilles, benguel(l)a, brazil, gulf stream, japanese
pert. voltaic
rapid tongue
regulator rheostat
reverser spacer
strong gale, roost, roust
warm el nino, gulf stream
CURRY beat, bruise, brush, cajole, carree, clean, comb, condiment, cook, dress, drub, food, groom, kari, powder, prepare, rub down, tarkeean, tend
favor apple polish, brownnose, cajole, cotton, court, fawn, flatter, smoodge, smooge
vegetable tarkeean
CURSE abuse, accidente,

afflict(ion), anathema (tize), ban, bane, beshrew, blame, blaspheme, blasphemy, blast, bless, blow, calamity, commination, condemn, confound, cuss, damnation, dang, darn, denounce, denunciation, excommunicate, execrate, execration, forspeak, hex, imprecate, imprecation, makutu, maledict(ion), malison, marantha, oath, objurgation, pestilence, pize, plague, profanity, proscribe, proscription, revile, scourge, shrew, sinze, spell, swear (ing), torment, trouble, wanion, whammy
CURSED all-fired, bally, blamed, blasted, blessed, confounded, cussed, damnable, damned, darned, dashed, deuced, devilish, execrable, flagitious, heinous, hellfired, hellish, infernal, odious, wicked
CURSORY brief, careless, casual, desultory, discursive, fast, fitful, haphazard, hasty, irregular, passant, passing, perfunctory, quick, rambling, random, rapid, roving, shallow, short, slapdash, small, speedy, superficial, swift, uncritical
CURT abrupt, bluff, blunt, brief, brusk, brusque, cavalier, churlish, concise, crusty, gruff, irritable, laconic, offhand, peremptory, rough, rude, sharp, short (ened), snappish, squab, succinct, summary, taciturn, terse, unceremonious, waspish
CURTAIL abbreviate, abridge, bobtail, clip, crop, cut, decrease, decurt(ate), deprive, diminish, dock, lessen, lop, pare, reduce, retrench, shorten, slash, stunt, trim, trunk
CURTAIN act, arras, barrier, blind, censorship, conceal, cover, drape(ry), drop, end, hanging, hide, lambrequin, mask, opening, portiere, rideau, screen, shade, sheet, shroud, trideau, valance, veil, velum, wall
casement vitrage
fabric algerienne, algerine,

gauze, leno, ninon, scrim, voile
half brise-bise, cafe
line tag
raiser forepiece, inauguration, opener, prologue
rod tringle
stretcher scray, strainer
style cafe, tier
CURTILAGE area, court (yard), enclosure, yard
CURTIS *master* petruchio
CURTMANTLE henry ii
CURTSY beck, bob, bow, conge, dip, dop, drop, greet(ing), honor, jouk, obeisance, respect, salaam, scrape
CURULE chair, council, seat
CURVATED hooked
CURVATURE aduncity, aquilinity, arc, arch, arcuation, bend, bool, camber, circularity, concameration, convolution, curl, CURVE, cyrtosis, entasis, extropism, gryposis, kyphosis, lordosis, rhebosis, rotundity, scoliosis, sinus, vaulting
abnormal gryposis
axis polar line
center locus evolute
convex camber
inwards aduncity
surface plane
CURVE arc(h), ball, bend, bight, bought, bow, bulge, camber, catacaustic, catenary, caustic, circle, circuit, coil, concave, contour, convex(ity), crescent, crook, crump, curl(icue), deflect, deviate, diacustic, divert, dome, ellipse, embow, entasis, ess, festoon, flex, gram, gyrate, helix, hook, horseshoe, hump, hunch, hyperbola, inflect, loop, ogee, ogive, parabola, pitch, quirk, reflex, round, sag, scallop, sinuate, sinus, snake, sny, spiral, spring, sweep, swerve, swirl, throw, tracery, tractrix, trend, turn, twist, vault, veer, wind
arch extrados, intrados
ball's drop, snake
comb. scolio
cricket swerve
cusp spinode
diocles' cissoid
double cima, cyma, ogee
double point acnode

kind memniscate, parabolic
looped folium
mathematical plane polar
parallel to ellipse toroid
part arc, arch
pert. toric
plane ellipse
point tachnode
quartic limacon
quick descent brachistochrone
reverse ogee
rise camber
ship's plank, sny
space knot
verticle ramp
CURVED adunc(ous), anchored, aquiline, arciform, arcuate, arrondi, bendified, bent, biarcuate, circuitous, circular, concave, convex, corbe, crooked, cygneous, elliptical, falcate, geanticlinal, geosynclinal, hamate, hooked, looped, loopy, nowy, obvolent, round(ed), scrolled, sigmate, sigmoid, sinuous, s-shaped, tortuous, turned
bay hanuama
comb. campyl(o)
in adunc(ous), concave, hooked
out bandy, bombe, bulged, bulgy, convex
slightly miconcave
twice biarcuate, biflected
CURVET bound, caper, cavort, corvetta, courbette, croupade, frisk, frolic, gambol, hop, leap, lollop, lope, pannade, play, prance, prank, ricochet, skip, turn, vault
half-turn caracole
CURVING aquiline, concave, simous, spiry, turned, twisty
inward adunc
CUSCUTA dodder, parasite, plant
CUSH cassite, cow, ethiopia, money, sorghum
father ham
language galla
son havilah, nimrod, ramah, sabtah, sabtechah, seba
CUSHAT bird, dove, pigeon
CUSH-CUSH cara, yampee
CUSHI *parent* gedaliah
son shelemiah
CUSHION bedding, bolster, boss, bott, brioche, buffer, bumper, bustle, check, cod,

cosshen, cutidur, dashpot, deaden, fender, forestall, gaddi, hassock, ignore, insulate, jockey, mat, muffle, neutralize, offset, pad, pig, pillow, protect, puff, pulvillar, seat, seclude, sham, shock-absorber, soften, softening, squab, support, suppress
black zafu
coronary cutidure
lace-makers bott
-like pulvinar
pin princod
pink moss campion
plant polster
stuffing baru, down, feathers, foam rubber, kapok
tailor's ham
CUSHITIC (See also CUSH.) ethiopian, nubian
CUSHY easy, pleasant, soft
CUSK burbot, catfish, eel, fish, torsk, tusk, wrymouth
CUSP apex, cantle, cone, corner, ectocone, edge, end, horn, paracone, peak, point, spinode, style, tooth
comb. cone
molar protocone
CUSPIDOR crachoir, garboon, spittoon
CUSS abuse, curse, fellow, rebuke, reprobate, swear
word oath
CUSTARD blancmange, charlet, dessert, doucet, dowcet, dowset, flan, flawn, flummery
apple annona, asimina, bullock-heart, corazon, pawpaw, sweetsop
cake creampuff, eclair
dish quiche lorraine
frozen ice cream
pudding caramel, creme, creme brulee
tart flan
tree annona, ates, atta, sweetsop
CUSTODIAN caretaker, clariger, concierge, curator, guard(ian), jailer, janitor, keeper, protector, sexton, supervisor, warden, warder
CUSTODY bail, care, charge, confinement, conservation, detention, durance, guardianship, handfast, hold, imprisonment, incarceration, keep(ing), possession, responsibility, safe

keeping, safety, trust, tuition, ward, watch

take into apprehend, arrest

CUSTOM asal, assessment, business, canon, consuetude, convention, dastur, dharma, dues, dustour, duty, endogamy, establishment, fad, fashion, folkway, form, formula, habit(ude), halakah, impost, institution, law, levy, manner, market, minhag, mode, more, mos, observance, patronage, practice, praxis, prescription, rite, ritus, routine, rule, tariff, tax, thew, toll, tradition, tribute, ure, usage, use, vogue, way, wont(ing)

bad cacoethes

binding law

comb. nomo

-made bespoke, tailored, tailor-made

of peoples mores

temporary fad, trend, vogue

with force of law mos

CUSTOMARY accustomed, classic, common, conventional, current, everyday, general, habitual, habituated, inclined, natural, normal, orthodox, prone, regular, rife, routine, traditional, typical, used, usual, wont(ed)

CUSTOMER account, buyer, callant, chap(man), client, contact, eccentric, fellow, man, patient, patron(izer), prospect, purchaser, shopper, sucker

group clientele

CUSTOMHOUSE aduana, chophouse, dogana, douane, tollbooth

CUSTOMS aduana, assessment, cess, dogana, douane, duty, excise, impost, levy, rate, tariff, tax, teind, tithe, toll, tribute

document carnet

goods list bill of entry

officer douanier, ga(u)ger, shark, surveyor, tidesman, waiter

union benelux, common market

CUT 3 adz, bag, bob, bur, dag, dap, dig, dod, gap, hag, hew, hob, lap, lob, lop, mow, nig, rip, saw, sny, way 4 adze, beat, bore,

burr, chip, chop, coup, dice, dock, fell, form, hack, hurt, kerf, mark, melt, miss, mode, nick, open, pain, pare, part, pink, reap, rent, shag, slap, slit, snee, sneg, snip, snub, stab, stop, trim 5 bevel, canch, carve, cater, cease, chive, cleft, elide, frith, gouge, grave, halve, knife, lance, lower, notch, prune, scalp, scarp, scind, sever, share, shear, shirl, slash, slice, slish, slive, sneed, split, style, taunt, vogue 6 ablate, ajoure, bisect, chisel, cleave, deduct, depart, dilute, escarp, excise, flitch, furrow, groove, lamina, lesion, lessen, mangle, pierce, rabbet, reduce, remove, sculpt, secant, secude, slight, snathe, strike, swinge, thrust, thwite, trench, trepan, weaken 7 abridge, absence, affront, curtail, dismiss, dissect, engrave, escarpe, harvest, pattern, sarcasm, scissel, scissor, serrate, shorten, tailzie, whittle 8 decrease, discount, dissolve, excavate, incision, scission, thwittle 9 carbonado, cultivate, dimidiate, economize, engraving 10 abbreviate, depreciate, exasperate

above superior

across economize, intersect, slice, transcend, transect

a figure flaunt, parade, peacock, pirouette, show off, splurge

along See SPEED.

a melon allot, apportion, dispense, measure, partition, share

and dried canned, ordinary, trite

and run depart, flee, vanish

and thrust attack

angled bevel, miter

apart anatomize, separate

a rug dance, jive

a shine rampage

a swath succeed

away abate, concise, cope, resect, slit, undo

back decrease, economize, reduce, retrench, save, spur

capable of being sectile

capers See PLAY.

comb. sect, temno

corners (See also CUT

back.) chamfer, champher, skirt

dead slight, snub

deep dig, shank

down abash, abridge, clear, decrease, destroy, economize, fell, humble, kill, lessen, level, machine-gun, mow, pare, rasee, raze, reduce, remodel, retrench, scarp, shorten, slash, slice, stag, stub

-finger figwort, periwinkle, spikenard

grain bag, fag, mow, swinge

hair bob, shear, style

in dance, interpose, interrupt, introduce, intrude, mix

in small pieces chop, cube, dice, hash, mince, sliver

in squares cube, dice

in strips fletch, flitch, jerk, julienne

in two bisect, dimidiate, halve, secant, sever

it out don't, stop

loose escape, extricate, go berserk, rampage, run(amuck)(riot)(wild)

loss salvage

meat (See also MEAT *cut.*) bone, mince, slice

off abdicate, abrade, abridge, abscind, absciss, amputate, apocopate, beeline, belee, bereft, bob, cant, cast off, clip, couped, crop, curtail, decrease, deduct, depost, deprive, diminish, disclaim, disinherit, disown, dispossess, divorce, dod(d), drib, elide, eliminate, end, excise, exempt, ex(s)cind, exterminate, intercept, interrupt, isolate, kill, lop, mow, mutilate, nip, pare, peel, poll, pollard, precide, prune, renounce, resecate, retrench, roach, scind, separate, sever, shave, shear, shield, shive, shorn, skive, snick, snip, snub, stop, tail, top, truncate

of one's jib appearance, look

on a bias miter

open fendu, incise, mine, operate, splay

out arrange, broach, cease, clip(ping), contrive, debar, deduct, delete, desist, dess, dink, discontinue, disuse, eliminate, excerpt, excide, excind, excise, exsect, exterminate, extract, leave, omit, operate, oust, plan, remove, stop, supplant, win

-outs, decorating with decoupage

-rate cheap, discount, inexpensive, low-priced, nominal, reduce

roughly butcher, hack, jag, snag

short abbreviate(d), abort, arrest, atajo, bang, bob, bobtail, check, clip(t), concise, crop, curtail, destroy, dock(ed), end, hashed, hogged, jimp, mow, poll(ed), prune, scantle, snib, strunt, trim, truncate

slanting bias, bevel, miter, mitre

the mustard make it, manage, succeed

thinly curl, shave

timber log

to pieces britten, chop, decimate, defeat, destroy, dice, dissect, fritter, mince

to the quick exasperate, hurt, insult, pain

up anticker, apportion, caper, card, carve, clown, dice, dissected, grieve, harry, injure, joint, joker, jokester, lacerate, misbehave, overcome, play, prank(ster), rampage, rogue, showoff, slice, slit, spoil, wag, wit, wound

with die blank, dink

wool dod(d), shear

CUTANEOUS cortical, cuticular, dermal, dermic, ecderonic, ectodermal, ectodermatic, endermic, epicarpal, epidermal, epidermic, hypodermal, hypodermic, skinlike, testaceous

CUTAWAY frockcoat, swallowtail

CUTCH catechu, gambi(e)r

CUTE bright, coony, coy, dainty, darling, dinky, ducky, expert, nervy, obnoxious, pretty, shrewd, venturesome

CUTICLE bloom, derm, epidermis, hide, integument, membrance, pelicle, scarfskin, shuck, skin, theca

blister bleb, bulla

CUTIE girl

pie beloved, darling, sweetheart

CUTIS corium, derma, skin

anserina goose-pimple

CUTLASS campilan, curtal, curtaxe, dusack, machete, shabble, SWORD, tesack

fish hairtail, hiku, kalkvis, machete, savola

CUTLERY *chest* canteen

CUTPURSE cloyer, hornthumb, pickpocket, thief

CUTTAIL eucalyptus

CUTTER barber, blade, boat, bravo, butcher, coax, corker, cotter, facer, fondle, fraze(r), hob, incisor, mill, mincer, ruffian, sailboat, schokker, ship, sled, sleigh, slicer, sloop, smack, tooth

-head wabbler, wobbler

CUTTHROAT assassin, barbarous, bitter, bravo, butcher, cruel, destructive, determined, exorbitant, fierce, game, gunman, hoodlum, intense, killer, liquor, murderer, mustang grape, ruffian, ruthless, sworder, violent

trout mykiss

CUTTING acerb, acrimonious, acute, adulteration, biting, bitter, bleak, carf, caustic, clipping, cold, crisp, deduction, excerpt, extract, incisal, incisive, keen, mordant, painful, part, penetrating, phyton, piece, piercing, piquant, polling, probing, pruning, raw, sarment, satiric, scion, scission, secant, sectile, section, severe, sharp, slip, sneeing, stechling, steckling, tart, trenchant, twig, violent, wounding

comb. tom(e), tomic, tomo(us)

edge blade, nusiness end

implement adz(e), axe, billhook, bit, blade, bold, broach, burin, carver, chisel, cleaver, clippers, coping saw, cutlery, file, hacksaw, jigsaw, knife, lathe, machete, mower, plane, razor, reaper, saw, sax, scimitar, scissors, scythe, shears, shinkersee, shredder, sickle, skiver, slicer, switchblade, sword

oblique barbing

off abscission, avulsion, pruning, termination

of last letter apocope

pert. sectile

second rowan

short abortive

teeth carnassial, sectorial

CUTTLEBONE gladius, osselet, sepia(ry), sepion, sepium

CUTTLEFISH catfish, decapod, inkfish, mollusk, octopus, scribe, scuttle, sepia, sepiola, sepiostaire, squid

fluid ink, sepia

genus geoteuthis

CUTWORM agrotis, caterpillar, greasy

CUVETTE basin, bucket, cistern, cunette, pot, tank, trench, tub

CUVY kelp, sea girdle

CWM cirque, coomb, corrie

CYANEE *consort* miletus

offspring byblis, caunus

CYANIDE *source* apricot pits, peach pits

CYANITE blue, disthene, mineral, sappare

CYANOCITTA bluejay, steller's jay

CYANOSIS blue disease, blue jaundice

born with blue baby

CYBELE agdistis, antaea, berecyntia, demeter, dindymene, kybele, rhea

attendant corybant, dactyl

ceremony criobolium

consort attis, at(t)ys, saturn

daughter juno

parent gaea, uranus

priest corybante(s), galli, gallus

son dionysus, midas, neptune, zeus

CYCHREUS *parent* poseidon, salamis

CYCLADES *island* amargos, andros, delos, ios, keos, melos, milos, naxia, naxos, nio, paros, sira, syra, syros, thera, tinos, zea

CYCLAMEN baccar, bacchar, cowslip, primwort, sowbread

CYCLE aeon, age, alternation, baktun, beat, bike, circle, circuit, eon, epoch, era, orbit, pedal, period(icity), phase, recur, rhythm, round, saros, secle, sere, vehicle, wheel

attachment sidecar

business juglar

kind bicycle, dandy horse,

draisine, hobby, hurdocycle, motor, penny-farthing, quadri-cycle, scooter, tandem, tricycle, velocipede, wheel
lunar saros
track velodroma
CYCLIST wheeler, wheelman
CYCLOLITH cromlech, memorial
CYCLONE bag(u)io, blast, gale, gust, hurricane, STORM, tornado, twister, typhoon, waterspout, whirlwind, wind
anti high
cellar basement, refuge, shelter
tropical bag(u)io
CYCLOPEAN colossal, enormous, giant, gigantic, herculean, huge, mammoth, massive, strong, vast
CYCLOPS acamas, arges, asterope, brontes, copepod, gasterocheires, giant, ogre, polyphemus, powerhouse, pyracmon, stalwart, steropes, strong man, tartaro, water-flea
abode mt etna
aides to hephaestus
feature one eye
parent gaea, uranus
slayer apollo
CYCLOSTOME amphibian, anamniote, eel, fish, hagfish, lamprey
CYCLOTRON accelerator, atom smasher
CYCNUS *changed to* swan
father apollo, ares, poseidon
offspring hemithea, tenes
slayer achilles, hercules
CYDIPPE *father* ochimus
lover acontius
son biton, cleobis
CYDON *father* hermes
CYGNUS, CYGNET olor, swan
star sadr
CYLINDER barrel, beam, blanket, bobbin, brode glass, cage, cam, can, cartridge, column, cottle, drum, gabion, inker, pillar, pipe, piston, platen, prism, roll(er), rouleau, screw, shell, spool, stela, stele, tipiti, tube
armored barbette
central stele
diameter bore
glass muss

hollow pipe, tube
perforated flusher
pert. terete
revolving beater, roller
toothed sprocket
CYLLENE *birthplace of* hermes
CYMA arch, doucine, gola, gula, molding, ogee
reversa heel
CYMBA boat, spicule, yet
CYMBAL(S) becken, castanets, chime, doughnut, gong, piatti, tal, zel
CYMBALO dulcimer
CYMBELINE *author.* shakespeare
character arviragus, belarius, cadwell, caius lucius, cloten, cornelius, guiderius, helen, iachimo, imogene, philario, pisanio, polydore, posthumus-leonatus
daughter imogen
son arviragus, cadwal, guiderius, polidor
stepson cloten
CYMBOPOGON camel grass, camel hay, citronella grass, lemon grass
extract carene, terpene
CYMLING pattypan, scallop, simnel, squash
CYMOSE *inflorescence* anthelia
CYMRIC See WELSH.
CYNARA artichoke, ball thistle, cardoon, plant
CYNIC apemantus, ascetic, disbeliever, doglike, doubter, egotist, hangdog, ironic, jaques, misanthrope, pessimist, sardonic, satyr, scoffer, skeptic, snarler, sothic, timon
philosopher antisthenes
CYNICAL acerb, captious, carping, critical, currish, distrustful, doggish, gloomy, jaquesian, misanthropic, misogynic, negative, pessimistic, sarcastic, satirical, scoffing, skeptical, snarling, sullen, suspicious, unbelieving
CYNICISM acerbity, asceticism, incredulity, irony, sarcasm, suspicion
CYNOCEPHALUS aani, dog-headed ape, lemur, papio
CYNORTES *parent* amyclas, diomede
CYNOSURA *nurse of* zeus

CYNOSURE altar, attraction, blazing star, celebrity, focus, hero, lodestar, polaris, polestar
CYNTHIA artemis, luna, moon, queen elizabeth
CYNTHIAN celestial, lunar, lunate, luniform, lunular, moon-shaped
CYPRESS ahuehuete, belvedere, bhutan, cupressus, cedar, fireball, galingale, guadalupensis, jackpine, sipers
bald sabino, taxodium
flowering tamarisk
grass sedge
-like shrub retinispora
mock belvedere
outgrowth knee
pine relative cape cedar
sawara tetinspora
spurge balsam, bonaparte's crown, napoleon, plant, weed
vine jasmine, quamoclit
CYPRIAN lewd, licentious, prostitute
frigid lover anaxarete
green terre verte
maidens propoetides
CYPRINID, CYPRINOID See FISH *cyprinoid*.
CYPRIPEDIUM cordula, lady's-slipper, moccasin flower, nervine, orchid, valerian
CYPRIS aphrodite
CYPRUS kittim
cape andreas, arnauti, gata, greco, zevgari
capital nicosia
castle famagusta
city famagusta, kyrenia, larnaca, limmasol, morphou, nicosia, paphos, polis, salamis
coin para, piaster
governor montano, sergius paulus
levite barnabas
measure cass, donum, gomari, kantar, kartos, kouza, medimno, moosa, oka, oke, pik
merger enosis
native cypriot
peak troodos
port famagusta, limmasol
president makarios
weight kantar, moosa, oka, oke
wind imbat
wine retsina

CYRANO *beloved* roxane
problem nose
CYRENAICA pentapolis, tripoli
biographer xenophon
capital cyrene
city arsinoe, barca, berenice, hesperis, ptolemais, teuchira
measure dra
philosophy hedonism
port apollonia
CYRENE *beloved* apollo
founder battus
parent hypseus
son aristaeus
CYRILLA titi
CYRUS koresh, sun
biographer xenophon
biography cyropaedia
brother artaxerxes, ostanes, oxathres
consort aspasia
daughter atossa
empire persia
friend araeus, ariaeus
march anabasis, babylon, pergamum, sardis
parent cambyses, darius, mandane, parysatis
pert. koreshan
prisoner croesus
slayer ataxerxes
son cambyses
tomb pasargadae
treasurer mithradates
victim artagerses, satiphernes
CYST bag, bladder, capsule, dermoid, hydatid, hygroma, mucocele, pouch, ranula, sac, sheath, steatoma, vesicle, wen
sebaceous steatoma
without head acephalocyst
CYTHEREA anadyomene,

aphrodite, astarte, calypso, orchid, venus
CYTOPLASM diastema, massula, ooplasm
CYZICUS *bishop* eunomius
enemy mithradates
slayer argonauts
wife clite
CZAR autocrat, caesar, dictator, emperor, judge, kaiser, king, nicholas, oppressor, peter, ruler, samodersheta, tsar, tyrant, tzar, umpire
daughter czarevna, tsarevna
edict ukase
murder site ekaterinburg
son czarevitch, grand duke, tsarevitch
wife czarina, tsarina, tzarina
CZECHOSLOVAKIA(N) bohemia, bohunk, slav, slovak, tscekh, zips
archaeologist hrozny
armament works skoda
beer pilsen
capital prague, praha
castle hradcany
chemist heyrovsky
city asch, aussig, austerlitz, bilina, bratislava, brno, brunn, budweis, carlsbad, cheb, eger, jihlava, karlsbad, kladus, koniggratz, kosice, liberee, most, olomouc, opava, ostrava, pilsen, plzen, prague, praha, presov, pressburg, reichenberg, sadowa, tabor, teplitz, tuzla, vsetin
coin crown, ducat, haler, heller, koruna
composer dvorak, haba, janacek, kubelik, martinu, smetana, weinberger

county ung
dance furiant, polka, redowa, talian
engineer skoda
father tatinek
forest bohmerwald
gypsy bohemian
hero benes, masaryk
king charles, wenceslas
martyr huss
measure korec, lan, liket, merice, mira, sah, stopa, strych
munition plant skoda
novelist hashek
peak gerlachovka, ore, sudeten, tatra
people bohemian, slav, slovak
playwright capek
president benes, masaryk, novothy
prime minister gottwald
province bohemia, moravia, ruthenia, slovakia
range carpathian, erz, tatra
reformer jan hus
region slovakia, sudetenland
resort marienbad
river becva, berounka, danube, dunaj, dyje, eger, elbe, gran, hron, isar, iser, labe, luznice, moldau, morava, mze, nisa, nitra, oder, ohre, ondava, sazava, slana, tisza, waag, vag, vah, vltava
saint john nepomuk, wenceslas
scientist cori
spa bilin
statesman benes, masaryk
theologian jan hus
train vindobona
violinist kubelik
writer hashek, kafka

D

DAB adept, artist, attempt, bit, blotch, blow, chit, coat, dhabb, dight, expert, flatfish, flounder, iota, lizard, marygole, paint, pat, peck, pinch, portion, sandling, smear, smooth, spot, stain, tap, touch, wizard
DABBER ball, prod, tampon
DABBLE boggle, boondoggle, daily, delibate, dibble, dirty, draggle, hang, meddle, moisten, muddle, paddle,

potter, putter, smatter, sossle, spatter, splash, splatter, sprinkle, tamper, tap, tinker, toy, trifle, twiddle
DABBLER amateur, dilettante, duffer, quack, sciolist, trifler, tyro
DABBY damp, moist
DABCHICK bird, didapper, diddikai, dipper, dobber, dopchick, dopper, gallinule, grebe, henbill, pennybird, puffer

DACE chub, cyprinid, dare, dart, fish, grayling
DACHA See VILLA.
DACIA See RUMANIA.
DACKER challenge, dare, dispute, potter, saunter, search, stagger, stroll, vacilate, waver, wrangle
DACOIT bandit, dakoo, daku, maraud(er), murder(er), plunder, robber(y)
DACTYL adonic, craftsman,

finger, foot, magician, meter, piddock, toe
attendant to cybele, rhea
home mt ida
reversed anapest
DACTYLOLOGY sign language
DACTYLOPODITE pollex
DACTYLOZOOID palpon
DAD See DADDY.
DADAIST arp, ball, duchamp, ernst, grosz, piabia, tzara
DADDLE cheat, dawdle, deceive, fist, hand, toddle, waddle, walk
DADDY babbo, buddy, father, pal, pap, paw, pop(pa), sire
longlegs arachnid, curlew, phalangid, spinner, stilt, tipulid
DADO base, die, groove, solidum, wainscot
DADUCHUS torchbearer
DAEDAL complex, cunning, expert, ingenious, intricate, skil(l)ful, variegated
DAEDALION *changed into* hawk
daughter chione
parent hesperus, phosphorus
DAEDALUS contriver, craftsman, creator
ancestor erechtheus
construction labyrinth
friend minos
host cocalus
nephew calos, perdix, talos, talus
pursuer minos
slayer talos
son iapyx, icarus
victim talos, talus
DAEMON daimon, demon, eudaemon, ghost, mistress, python
group curetes
DAFF coward, daily, dastard, doff, fool, play, toy
DAFFODIL asphodel, bellwort, campanula, crowbell, dilly, glen, jonquil, lily
DAFFY, DAFT balmy, crazed, crazy, demented, doting, dotty, foolish, giddy, idiotic, imbecilic, insane, loony, mental, potty, silly, wild
DAG antler, edging, pierce, pistol, pricket, scallops, slash, sprinkle, stab
horse hrimfaxi, skinfaksi
parent delling, nott

DAGAME lemonwood, madrona, salamo
DAGDA *consort* boann
offspring a(e)ngus, brigit
DAGESTAN carpet
people lezghian
DAGGER anlace, balarao, balas, bas(e)lard, bayonet, bodkin, couteau, coutel, creese, cris(e), dague, dhu, diesis, dirk, dudgeon, handjar, itak, katar, khanjar, kirpan, knife, krees(e), kris, kuttar, misericorde, obelisk, panade, parang, pinker, popper, puncheon, puntilla, saex, skean(dhu), skene, skhian, snee, snickersnee, spud, stab, stiletto, stylet, tang, tanto
ancient skean, skene, snee
double diesis
handle dudgeon, hilt
hilt dudgeon
magic creese, kri(s)
medieval alace, baselard, basilard
part hilt
plant yucca
reference mark spit
sacred kirpan
short katar, puntilla
single-bladed choora
stroke stab, stoccado
tapering anlace
thin-bladed misericord(e)
wavy-bladed creese, kreese, kris
DAGGLE befoul, draggle, muddy, wet
-tailed dirty
DAGONET *fool to king* arthur
DAGUERREOTYPE calotype, colotype, ferrotype, photo(graph), talbotype, tintype
DAHLIA pompom
tuber jicama
DAHOMEY *capital* porto nova
charm gbo
city abomey, cotonou, kandi, nikki, ouidah
god voodoo
port cotonou
river niger, oueme
tribe ewe, fon(g)
DAIBUTSU buddha
DAIL *land of* Ireland
DAILY constantly, diurnal, gazette, newspaper, per diem, quotidian
bread support, sustenance

double bet
dozen calisthenics, exercise, routine
grind habit, routine, work
meals board
DAIMON See DEMON.
DAINCHA nardoo, nardu, sesbania
DAINTIES cates, diablotin, est(e), sock
fond of friand
DAINTY beauteous, beautiful, bonbon, bonny, cate, chary, choice, cunning, cute, delicacy, delicate, delicious, dentical, elegant, este, ethereal, exquisite, fair, fastidious, fine, finical, finicky, frail, friand, fussy, gentle, light, little, loath, lovely, migniard, mignon, minikin, minion, morsel, naish, neat, nesh, nice, petite, pretty, rare, recherche, regalo, savory, small, squeamish, subtle, taffeta, taffety, tidbit, tryphosa
DAIRA tambourine
father oceanus
DAIRY creamery, deyhouse, farm, lactarium, lactary, milk plant, tambo, vaccary
food butter, cream, milk, yog(h)ourt, yoghurt
house larder, wick
maid dey(woman), milkmaid
man ahir, bower, farmer, milkman, stockman
products milchigs
tool separator
tub bench tram
DAIS alemar, bema, bench, bima(h), canopy, chabutra, estate, estrade, footpace, halfpace, hathpace, hustings, lewan, lissom, pace, platform, podium, pulpit, rostrum, seat, settle, stage, stand, support, table, throne, tribune
DAISY aster, backwort, bellis, bennet, billybutton, blue alpine, blue chicory, boneset, bonewort, bowwort, brisbane, brown betty, brown cornflower, bull's-eye, burdock, campion, cape marigold, chiffon, comfrey, composit, dimorphotheca, dogblow, felicia, geranium, gerbera, globeflower, gold(enrod), gowan, hexafoil, knitback,

marguerite, michaelmas, moonflower, moonpenny, morgan, oxeye, pissabed, shasta, topnotcher
cutter grub
fleabane erigeron, scabious
oxeye kellupweed, shasta
DAKOTA *indian* arikara, arikaree, arikari, caddo, mandan, ree, santee, sioux, teton
DAKSHA *adversary* vishnu
father brahma
son-in-law rudra, siva
DALAI LAMA incarnation, ruler
seat lhasa
DALE bottom, dell, dene, dingle, glade, glen, haw, share, sprout, trough, vale, valley
DALEA parossela
DALLAS big-d
airport grapevine, love
DALLES rapids
DALLIANCE colling, coquetry, delay, fabianism, flirtation, gossip, play, sport, talk, tousel, tousle, trifling
DALLIER pingler
DALLY bide, boondoggle, chat, coquet, daff, dawdle, delay, diddle, dillydally, disport, doodle, dringle, flirt, fondle, frolic, idle, jake, jauk, lag, linger, loiter, peddle, pet, piddle, pingle, play, poke, potter, procrastinate, putter, slidder, sport, swan, toy, trifle, wanton
away waste
DALLYING coquetry, sisseton
DALMATIA (See YUGOSLAVIA.) jugoslavia, servia
DALMATIC tunicle
DAM aboideau, an(n)icut, bar(rier), bay, block, blockade, broodmare, burrock, cauld, causey, clog, close, coin, dike, hamper, hinder, impede, lady, mare, millpond, mother, obstacle, obstruct, parent, pen(head), pound, rampire, repress, restrain, sadd, shackle, spur, stem, stop, sudd, suppress, tappoon, wall, weir
control caterpillar gate

highest in world boulder, hoover
temporary sudd
DAMAGE accident, afflict, bill, blemish, blitz, blot, blow up, burn, check, cost, cream, deface, deterioration, detriment, disadvantage, disserve, evil, expense, fracture, harm, hurt, impair, injure, injury, jeel, lesion, loss, mar, mischief, mistreat, payment, price, ruin, sabotage, scar, scathe, spoil, strafe, tab, vandalism, wreck
causing noxal
pert. noxal, noxious
DAMAGED broken, cracked, hurt, injured, used
DAMAGES amende, award, compensation, fine, forfeit, hamesucken, interest, payment, penalty, punishment, usury, verdict
DAMALISCUS antelope, belsbok, blesbuck, bontebok, bontebuck
DAMAN ashkoko, cherogril, con(e)y, dassy, ganam, hyrax, lamb, rabbit, wabber
DAMA PADEMELON tamar, wallaby
DAMASCENE *work* koftgari
DAMASCENED watered
DAMASCUS See SWORD.
dynasty amayyad, ommiad, umayyad
king aretas, benhadad
mosque umryyad
people syrian
river abana, barada, pharpar
DAMASK cloth, damassin, darnex, dornic(k), drawloom, fabric, linen, pink, rose, steel
violet damewort
DAME biddy, dint, dowager, girl, lady, matron, mistress, woman
correlative sire
DAME'S *violet* eyeweed
DAMIA bona dea, fauna, kore
DAMKINA *child* marduk
DAMMARA agathis
DAMMER canarium, copal, resin
DAMN abuse, anathematize, attaint, ban, blame, blast, bless, burn, censure, condemn, confounded, consarn, curse, darn, dash, dee, denounce, denunciate, destroy,

discipline, doom, durn, excoriate, execrate, goldarn, judge, objurgate, outlaw, proscribe, punish, revile, sentence
yankees temptress lola
DAMNED bally, blankety, blasted, blessed, blinking, bloody, contemptible, darn(ed), dee, detestable, doggoned, doomed, execrable, goldurn, loathsome, lost, outrageous, tarnal, unregenerate
DAMOURITE hydromica
DAMP bloom, blunt, check, choke, dabby, dank, deaden, depress, deter, drippy, drizly, extinguish, gas, humid, irriguous, killjoy, malmy, mochy, moderate, moist(en), muffle, mungy, musty, oozy, quench, rawky, soggy, stifle, thone, vapor, wack, wet
choke stythe
of evening serene
DAMPER discouragement, killjoy, lid, mute, register, spoilsport, suffocator, valve
winding amortisseur
DAMSEL donzella, girl, maid(en), miss, moppet, princess, rucelle, virgin, wench
fish beau gregoire, blacksmith, cockeye-pilot, demoiselle, pintano
fly demoiselle, naiad
DAMSON bullace, bully-tree, grape, muscadine, plum, prunus
DAN buoy, river, title
parent bilhah, jacob
sister una
town elon
tribal head ahiezer
DANAE *consort* zeus
father acrisius, acrosois
rescuer dictys
son perseus
DANAI argives, greeks
DANAKIL afar
DANAUS anosia, asclepias, butterfly
brother aegyptus
daughter amymone, danaid
father belus
kingdom argos
slayer lynceus
DANCE 3 bal, bob, hay, hop, jig, rag, rap, toe, top 4 ball, bump, clog, folk, foot, frug, haka, hoof, hora, hula, jazz, jive, jota, kolo, mask, prom,

reel, rock, shag, siva, trot 5 baile, basse, belly, brawl, caper, carol, conga, fling, galop, gavot, gigue, hopak, lindy, mamba, mambo, pavan, polka, rondo, rumba, sally, samba, skirt, snake, stomp, sword, tango, truck, twist, valse, volta, waltz 6 althea, apache, areito, ballet, balter, berlin, bolero, bouree, branle, bubble, cancan, cebell, cuando, dreher, formal, gestie, hormos, joropo, masque, maxixe, minuet, monkey, morris, nautch, pavane, redowa, rhumba, sextur, shimmy, shindy, square, trepak, tresca 7 auresca, batuque, beguine, bourree, boutade, bransle, buffalo, calinda, cantico, chaccon, chacona, courant, cut-a-rug, czardas, darabee, farruca, flicker, flutter, foxtrot, furiant, furlana, gavotte, halling, hoedown, lancers, lavolta, mazurka, morisco, onestep, pas-seul, romaika, saltate, shuffle, tresche, twostep, ziganka 8 anglaise, big-apple, bobby-joe, bunnyhug, cachucha, cakewalk, chaconne, cotillon, courante, fandango, galliard, guaracha, habanera, hornpipe, hulahula, kanticoy, marengue, pachanga, rigadoon, sailboat, saraband, saradana, serenade 9 allemande, bagatelle, bergamask, bossanova, breakdown, chachacha, chonchina, cotillion, farandola, farandole, gallopade, jitterbug, malaguena, polonaise, promenade, quadrille, tarantell 10 bergamasca, bergerette, caledonian, castle walk, charleston, cornwallis, masquerade, passamezzo, petronello, saltarello, strathspey, tarantella, tripudiate, turkey trot, varsoviana 11 blackbottom, bobbing joan, calathiscus 12 divertimento, virginia reel 13 highland fling 14 hootchykootchy 18 sir roger de coverley
acrobatic adagio
art of choreography, natya, orchesis

attendance apple polish, court, lackey, lacquey, praise, serve
back step reverse
ballroom bunnyhug, castle walk, charleston, conga, cotill(i)on, czardas, foxtrot, lambeth walk, mambo, mazurka, polka, twostep, varsovienne, waltz
band combo
basket-carrying calathiscus
bolero-like cachucha
carnival coo(t)ch, folia
ceremonial areito, basse, bat, cantico, dutuburi
chorus cancan, cordax, strut
circle roundabout, roundel(ay)
clog blackbottom
clumsily balter
college hop, prom, trot
country ace of diamonds, althea, anglaise, argeers, aurrescu, baile, barn, bergamask, bobbing joan, confess, ecossaise, haymaker, landler, reel, saraband, siciliana, tarantella, villanella
court pavan(e)
courtship batuque, cueca, lezgibka
designer choreographer
drama ballet, noh
18th century cassation, cotillion, divertimento, serenade
enthusiast balletomane
exhibition ballet, tap
fiesta akrieros
flamenco alegrias
folk dreher, fado, hora, kolo, newcastle, tarantella
form piva
formal ball, farandola, pavan, prom
gesture siva
girl alma, artiste, ballerina, bayadere, chorine, coryphere, danseuse, devadasi, geisha, nautch, terpsichorienne
god tezcatlipoca
gondolier's furlana
gypsy farruca, flamenco, polo, zingaresca
hall ballroom, casino
high-kicking cancan
highland fling
hobbyhorse calusar
in circle jigger
involuntary tricotee
jazz bebop, shimm(e)y, stomp

jitterbug lindy (hop)
leap salto
leaping lavolta
lively allemande, bolero, bourree, branle, canary, carioca, chasse, coranto, corybantic, farandole, fling, furlana, galliard, gallopade, galop, gigue, hoedown, hornpipe, jig, lavolta, polka, rant, reel, rhumba, rigadoon, rumba, schottis(c)he, shag, shakedown, spring, tamourin, trenchmore, trot
mania chorea, corybantiasm, tarantism
masked ridotto
method laban
mirthful caper, conga, galop
modern chacha, charleston, dump, gogo, frug, hullygully, jitterbug, mashed-potato, monkey, pony, rock, shag, susy-q, tango, toe, twist, twostep, watusi
morris bobby joe, tideswell
mournful dump
movement arabesque, branle, brisse, buck and wing, buzz, chasse, coule, coupe(e), dip, dos-a-dos, drag, entrechat, fishtail, flat, fouette, gambade, gambado, gigue, glide, glissade, grapevine, heel-and-toe, irish, jete, pas, pigeon-wing, pirouette, plie, poussette, quickstep, shag, shuffle, skip, slide, stomp, tap
muse terpsichore
music bebop, boogiewoogie, bop, gymnopedie, jazz, jive, rag, rock (and roll), swing
nimbly canary
1910 turkey trot
1920 big apple, blackbottom, castle walk, charleston
nude bubble dance, fan dance
of death macaber, macabre
old allemande, basse, bource, boutade, branle, canary, carole, cebell, chacona, chaconne, chasson, clog, coranto, courant, faradole, farandola, furlana, galliard, galop, gavotte, hornpipe, jig, jog, lavolta, loure, minuet, morris, pavan, reel, rondo, sarabande, tarantella, turkey trot, volta
orgiastic sikinnis
painter degas

partner gigolo

peasant balitao, danzon, jota, tyrolienne

pert. gestic, nautch, orchestic, saltant, saltatory, terpsichorean, tripudial

polka-like berlin

ragtime texas tommy, turkey trot

round branle, carol(e), charleston, cracovienne, maxixe, newcastle, polka, ray, schottische, turkey trot, waltz

rustic See *country*, above.

sailor's hornpipe, matelote

st vitus chorea

school hop, prom, trot

17th century allemande, passepieds

shoes pumps, slippers, taps

shuffling truck

sinuous coo(t)ch, hootchy-kootchy, hula(hula)

16th century bergerette, cinquepace, pavane

slow adagio, habanero, minuet, passacaglia, polonaise, valeta, waltz

solo pas seul

spear baris

square argeers, caledonian, hoedown, lanc(i)ers, quadrille, reel

stately emmeleia, pavan(e), saraband

step See *movement*, above.

strutting cakewalk

style abhinaya

sword bacubert, flamborough, matachin

tap soft-shoe

violent apache

voluptuous belly, habanera, seven veils

wedding canacuas

weird macabre

DANCER alma, alme(h), artist(e), astaire, baladine, ballerina, ballet girl, bayadere, bedoyo, bolger, chorine, chorusgirl, chorusman, coryphee, danseuse, devadasi, figurante, funambulist, geisha, gestic, gigolo, gofo, hepcat, hoofer, hopper, hula girl, jitterbug, maenad, morricer, nautch (girl), pascola, prancer, sailour, tap, taxi, terpsichore(an), toe, zorina

ballet coryphee, etoile, soliste

biblical salome

exotic stripper

female artiste, ballerina, bayadere, chorine, coryphee, danseuse, devadasi, hoppestere, terpsichorienne

gandy trackman

garment leotard

group corps, gahe, troupe

instrument castanet

kind ahe, gandy, hula, softshoe, tap, taxi, toe

painter degas

pole poy

public baladine

rod crotalum

rope nat

sword matachin

DANCERS *petty* aurora borealis

DANCING *mania* tarantism

DANDELION bitterwort, blowball, blower, canker (wort), cat's-ear, chicory, dindle, gosmore, hawkbit, hawkweed, pissabed, puffball, swine's-snout, taraxacum, yellow gentian

blue chicory

dwarf krigia

head buffball, bullfice, bullfist, puffball, puffclock

root extract taraxacin

stalk scape

DANDER anger, dawdle, hackles, irish, passion, saunter, scurf, stroll, temper, wander

DANDIFIED adonized, buckish, conceited, dashing, foppish, impetuous, lively, spruce

DANDIFY adonize, decorate, ornament, preen, spruce

DANDIPRAT child, coin, midget

DANDLE caress, cuddle, dally, diddle, disport, faddle, fondle, nurse, pamper, pat, pet, play, sport, toy, trifle

DANDRUFF flake, furfur, scurf

galloping fleas, ticks

DANDY adonis, bantam, bean, beau(brummel), bird, blade, blood, boatman, boulevardier, buck, capstan, carpet knight, coxcomb, dildo, dude, elegant, exquisite, fine, fop, fribble, gallant, gentleman, great, jackanapes, jake, jemmy, jessamy, ladies' man, ladykiller, macaroni, majo, man

about town, masher, mendicant, mizzen, nob, palanquin, popinjay, puppy, spark, sport, swell, toff, trif, yawl

female dandisette, dandizette

fever dengue

funk hard tack

horse draisine, velocipede

king murat

DANE dansker, dubhgall, jutlander, lochlin

DANEWORT deadwort, ebulus, lochlin, wallwort

DANGER adventure, chance, crisis, distress, exposure, fear, hazard, jeopardy, liability, menace, peril, pitfall, plight, risk, threat, venture, wathe

pert. sematic

signal alarm, bell, red flag, tocsin

DANGEROUS bad, breakneck, chancy, critical, dicey, dire, doubtful, feral, fickle, foul, grave, haphazard, hazardous, insecure, jeopardous, kittle, mad, murderous, nasty, ominous, parlous, perilous, precarious, random, risky, scathy, touch-and-go, treacherous, ugly, unguarded, unprotected, unsafe, vulnerable

DANGLE display, droop, flap, fluctuate, follow, hang, loll, lop, oscillate, pend(ulate), shoggle, shoofle, sling, suspend, sway, swing, trollop, wave

DANIEL belteshazzar

companion abednego, azariah, hananiah, mishael

dancer miser

dream animals bear, dragon, leopard, lion, ram

parent david, ithamar

prince michael

prophet to belshazzar, nebuchadnezzar

DANISH See DENMARK.

DANITE *band* avenging angels

DANK clammy, coarse, damp, donk, drenched, drizzle, humid, moist(ure), muggy, soggy, soppy, sticky, wet(ness)

DANSEUSE See DANCER *female.*

DANTE *beloved* beatrice

devil alichino, cagnazzo

heaven paradiso

hell caino, inferno
illustrator botticelli, dore
patron scala
tomb ravenna
verse form sestina
work convito, divine comedy, vita nuova
DANU tuatha de danann
DANUBE duna, ister
city on belgrade, blenheim, bratislava, budapest, linz, ulm, vienna
fish huch, huchen, hucho
gibraltar petrovaradin
gorge irongate
irongates djerdad
people dacian
tributary arges, drau, drava, drave, iller, inn, ipel, ipoly, isar, jui, lech, morava, naab, olt, prut(h), raab, sava, save, schyl, siret, taba, temes, tisza, traun, vag vah, waag
DANZIG gdansk
brandy goldwasser, goldwater
coin gulden, phennig
liqueur ratafia
DAP bounce, dab, dib(ble), dip, fish, notch, rebound, skip
DAPHNAEA artemis
DAPHNE laurel, mezereon, nymph
changed to laurel tree
father ladon, peneus
pursuer apollo
victim leucippus
DAPHNIS shepherd
beloved chloe
father hermes
DAPPER brave, braw, chic, dashing, elegant, foppish, jaunty, little, lively, modish, natty, neat, nifty, nobby, posh, prim, smart, smug, sparkish, spruce, stylish, toffish, trim
DAPPLE(D) bedip, brindle(d), dot(ted), fleck(ed), freckled, mark, mottle, piebald, pied, roan, sorrel, spot, stipple, variegated
DARB ace, dandy, expert, lulu, topnotcher
DARBHA kusa, kusha
DARBIES handcuffs, shackle
DARDANELLES hellespont
wind dusenwind
DARDANUS *birthplace* corythus
descendents trojans

kingdom arcadia
parent electra, zeus
DARE adventure, assume, attempt, brave, challenge, dast, daunt, defy, face, fish, hazard, make bold, oser, osse, presume, risk, stump, taunt, venture
say remark, suppose, think
DARED durst
DAREDEVIL adventurer, adventurous, audacious, daring, fire-eater, foolhardy, hardydardy, harumscarum, hellcat, hero, hotspur, madbrain, madcap, rantipole, rash, reckless, stuntman, swashbuckler, temerarius, venturesome
DARES *companion* aeneas
priest of hephaestus
skill boxing
DARIEN terra firma
DARING adventurous, audacious, audacity, bold (hearted), bravado, brave, bravura, courage, dairous, defiant, derf, enterprising, fearless, foolhardy, hardihood, heroic, heroism, intrepid, manly, nervy, pert, prest, rash, reckless, sporty, venturesome, venturous
DARIOLE cup, madeline, pastry, shell
DARIUS *brother* exathres, sogdianus
conqueror alexander
consort apame, parysatis
defeat arbela, gaugamela, marathon, ussus
enemy greeks
father ahasuerus, artaxerxes, hystaspes, xerxes
kingdom persia
lieutenant spithradates
offspring artaxerxes, cyrus, osthanes, oxathres, statira
palace site susa
prince daniel
prizewinner zerubbabel
victim bagoas
DARK 3 bad, dim, dun, mum, sad, wan 4 base, blae, dern, dusk, ebon, evil, inky, mirk, murk 5 black, blind, brown, dingy, dusky, faint, foggy, mirky, misty, murky, shady, sooty, swart, umber, unlit, vague 6 bleary, brunet, cloudy, cyprus, dimpsy, dismal, drumly, gloomy, latent, mo-

rose, mystic, occult, opaque, pitchy, secret, somber, sombre 7 aphotic, blurred, clouded, corrupt, cryptic, eclipse, joyless, melanie, obscure, opacate, shadowy, stygian, subfusk, sunless, swarthy, thester, unclear 8 abstruse, brunette, hush-hush, ignorant, melanoid, sinister, starless 9 ambiguous, enigmatic, equivocal, lightless, tenebrose, tenebrous, unlighted 10 adumbrated, cabalistic, caliginous, indistinct, obfuscated, pitch black, subfuscous, tenebrious 12 confidential, extinguished, overshadowed
brown bruneous, brunness
colored carbonous, sad, somber, sombre, swart(h), swarthy
comb. melan(e), meland, nyct(i), nycto
complexioned swarthy
continent africa
depths dungeon, hole, lockup
fear of achluophobia, nyctophobia
haired brunet, melanocomous
horse candidate, longshot, morel, zain
in the blind, concealed, obscure
keep conceal, hide
lady mary fitton
DARKEN becloud, bedim, benight, blacken, blind, blot, blur, cloud, dim, dull, dun, eclipse, embrown, flush, gloam, gloom, obfuscate, obscure, obtenebrate, obumbrate, opacate, overcast, perplex, poche, sadden, seel, shade, shadow, slubber, stain, sully, tarnish
DARKENING scurf
DARKNESS (See also DARK.) black(out), caliginosity, dern, despondency, dusk, erebus, gloaming, gloom, ignorance, iniquity, midnight, mirk, murk, night(fall), nigritude, obscurity, opacity, pitmark, privacy, secrecy, shade, shadow, tamas, tenebra, tenebres, tophet, twilight, umbra, yin
comb. scoto
fear of syctophobia

intense pitmirk
prince of ahriman, devil, satan
realm erebus
spiritual hell, tamas

DARLING acushla, aroon, aruin, asthore, beloved, cheri(e), child, chou, cony, cosset, cushlam, cutie pie, dautie, dawtie, dear, desire, dumpling, dunk, favorite, fondling, idol, jewel, joe, liebchen, lieve, life, love, machree, macushla, mavourneen, mavournin, minikin, minion, moppet, nobs, ochree, peat, peet, pet, pigsney, pinkeny, precious, preference, querida, roon, storeen, sweet(heart), sweeting, teacher's pet
dog nana
pea indico, indigo

DARN anathematize, ban, blow, bugger, curse, damn, dern, dog(gone), drat, durn, goldurn, mend, patch, repair, sew

DARNED blame(d), blessed, deuced, doggone

DARNEL aegilops, cheat, chess, cockle, crap, drank, drawk, dwant, eaver, egilops, grass, ivray, neele, ray, tare, weed

DARNLEY *wife* mary

DART arrow, banderilla, barb, bolt, bound, brandish, bulten, buzz, cane, career, cast, colp, course, dash, elance, fish, flame, fling, flit, fly, gallop, gavelock, gleam, glint, hurl, hurry, jaculate, javelin, jet, jouk, lance(t), leap, lick, missile, pellet, pompany, pop, projectile, rout, run, rush, sail, scamp, scheme, scoot, scud, shaft, shoot, shot, skite, skyte, speed, spiculum, spring, spurt, squirt, start, sting(er), sumpit, throw, verutum
barbed banderilla
board target
-like dartling, spicular
-shaped belemnoid
snake arrow snake
thrower anisocycle, bow

D'ARTAGNAN *companion* aramis, athos, porthos
creator dumas

DARVON propoxyphene

DARWAN doorkeeper, porter

DARWIN *boat* beagle
doctrine evolution
islands galapagos
missing link apemau, krao
tulip admiral togo

DAS badger, cony, dassie

DAS CAPITAL *author* marx

DASH ardor, bang, beat, birr, bit, blank, blow, bolt, bravura, break, breenge, bribe, career, cast, charge, chill, cloud, collide, confound, courage, crash, cut out, dab, dampen, dart, demoralize, depress, ding, disappear, disappoint, dive, drop, eclat, elan, energy, flash, flee, gallop, gratuity, hurry, hurtle, hyphen, lace, line, lunge, mark, moisten, obelus, overthrow, pelt, pinch, plash, poss, punctuation, race, run, rush, scattering, shade, shatter, shiver, smack, smash, sosh, soupcon, spatter, spirit, splast, splinter, splotch, spoil, sprinkle, sprint, spurn, spurt, strain, streak, strike, stroke, style, suggestion, suspicion, swank, swash, swell, tantivy, taste, throw, thwart, tick, tinge, touch, trace, upset, vein, verve, vim, zip
about gad, reel
down quell, stram(ash)
into collide, meet
off author, compose, depart, flee, improvise, leave, write
up flurr
with water blash, jaw, splash

DASHBOARD fa(s)cia, instrument panel

DASHED downcast, switched, upset

DASHEEN See TARO.

DASHING bold, brave, braw, buckish, bully, chic, dandified, dapper, doggy, fashionable, fast, foppish, gay, headlong, impetuous, larking, lively, natty, nifty, nobby, ostentatious, plangent, posh, precipitate, showy, smart, spanky, spirited, sporty, spruce, stylish, swanky, swish, toffish, veloce
fellow blade

DASHPOT damper, shock absorber

DASI concubine, servant, slave

DASSIE blacktail, cony, daman, mule deer, ruffe

DASTARD cad, caitiff, coward, craven, daff, dullard, milksop, poltroon, recreant, slink, sneak, sot, villain, withing

DASTARDLY foul, furtive, malign, pusillanimous, recreant, sinister, sneaking, underhand

DASYLIRION dracaena, sotol, yucca

DASYPUS armadillo, pellido, tatu

DASYURE dapple, tiger, yabbi

DATA dope, dossier, evidence, facts, input, material, memoranda
biographical personalia
processing analyzing, classifying, collating, computing, scanning, sorting, telecomputing

DATE age, antiquate, appointment, archaize, beau, calends, court, day, deadline, drag, engagement, epoch, era, escort, exergue, furit, fuss, gallant, go with, ides, interview, keep company, moment, none(s), obsolete, outdate, outmode, palm, party, period, point, reckon, record, register, rendezvous, sweetheart, time, tryst
between strangers blind
clause teste
erroneous anachronism
juice dibs
kind asharasi, degletnoor, degletnur, fard(h), halawi, jujubi, saidi
pert. datal
plum lotus, sapote, zapote
-ripening khalal, kimri, rutab

DATED antiquated, antique, archaic, given, old-fashioned, outmoded, passe

DATELESS everlasting, immemorial, timeless

DATHAN adversary

DATOLITE bakerite, humboldtite

DATURA jimson weed, stramony, toguacho

DAUB apply, balm, besmear, besmirch, blob, blot, clag, cleam, coat, dab, ditch, dob, gaum, labber, moil, mud,

paint, picture, plaster, sclatch, slaister, slake, slaum, slubber, smear, smirch, smudge, soil, splotch, stain, sully, teer
DAUBED blotted, gaumy
DAUGHTER alumna, bairn, bint, cadette, dame, descendant, dochter, fille, filly, girl, jama, offspring, progeny
-in-law shnir, shnur
name meaning inga
of eve woman
of joy prostitute, wanton
of moon nokomis
pert. filial
DAUNT adaw, alarm, amate, appall, awe, baffle, browbeat, conquer, cow, dare, daw, daze, deter, discomfit, discourage, dishearten, dismay, dompt, faze, feaze, feeze, foil, frighten, horrify, intimidate, overawe, overcome, scare, shake, stop, stun, stupefy, subdue, terrify
DAUNTLESS audacious, aw(e)less, bold, brave, confident, courageous, doughty, fearless, gallant, good, intrepid, persevering, tireless, valiant, valorous
DAUPHIN delphinium, guigo, heir
pert. delphine
DAUT caress, dote, fondle
DAVAO mindanao
DAVENPORT chesterfield, couch, daybed, desk, divan, lounge, loveseat, pouf, sofa
DAVID dawkin, taffy
anointer samuel
archer ahiezer
armor bearer naharai
brother ozem
cave adullam
chief abiel, abiezer, abishai, adina, ahiam, ahijah, amasa, asahel, attai, azmoth, benaiah, dodaian, eleazar, elhanan, eliab, eliahba, eliel, eliphal, elzabad, ezer, gareg, hanan, hashem, heldai, heled, helez, hepher, hezro, hurai, ilai, ira, ithai, ithma, jashoboam, jasiel, jediael, jeiel, jeremiah, jeribai, joel, joha(nan), joshaviah, machbanai, maharai, mishmannah, obadiah, obed, perez, shamhuth,

shammoth, sibbecai, uriah, uzzia, zabad, zelek
chief ruler amasa, ira
city zion
comforter abis(h)ag
companion abiathar, hushai, jonathan
consort abigail, abishag, abital, ahinoam, bathsheba, bathshua, eglah, haggith, lisa, maacah, michal
counsellor achitophel, ahithophel, jonathan
daughter maacah, tamar
employer nabal
epithet the psalmist
father jesse
field supervisor ezri
friend barzillai, ittai, jonathan
general abner, amasa, igal, ira, joab, rei, shammah
grandfather amminadab, boaz, hezron, nashon, obed, pharez, ram, salmon
guard ira
herdsman jaziz, jehdeiah, obil, shaphat, shitrai
instrument harp
kin abigail, absalom, jesse, michal, tamar, solomon
minister ira
musician asaph
nephew amasa, joab
olive master baalhanan, joash
priest zadoc
prince azareel, eliezer, elihu, hoshea, iddo, ishmaiah, jerimoth, omri, shepatiah, zadok
prophet nathan
recorder jehoshaphat
ruler amasa, ira
scribe shavsha
son absalom, adonijah, amnon, beeliada, daniel, eliada, eliphalet, elishama, elishua, elpalet, hattush, hepheg, ibhar, ishar, ithream, japhia, nathan, nogah, shammua, shepatiah, shimea, shobab, solomon
son, favorite absalom
stoned by shimei
supporter achimaas, ahiezer, ahimaaz
sword saadia
traitor to achitophel, ahithophel
victim goliath
vintner sabdi, shemei
water-bringer shammah
weapon slingshot

DAVID COPPERFIELD *author* dickens
aunt betsy trotwood
character agnes, dartle, dora, gummidge, james, micawber, murdstone, peggoty, rosa, steerforth, traddles, uriah heep, wickfield
clerk uriah heep
friend traddles
nurse peggotty
stepfather murdstone
wife dora
DA VINCI *painting* mona lisa
DAVIT crane, hoist
DAVOUT *commander* napoleon
DAW awaken, bird, corvus, daunt, drab, grackle, jackdaw, magpie, revive, simpleton, slattern, sluggard
DAWDLE daidle, dally, dander, delay, diddle, dillydally, drag, drant, driddle, dritch, faddle, falter, finnick, flag, halt, idle, jawk, lag(gard), linger, loiter, muck, mull, piddle, pingle, poke, potter, procrastinate, putter, shammock, slummock, stay, tantle, tarry, toy, trail, trifle, wait
DAWDLER fabius, idler, louther, musard
DAWKINS artful dodger
DAWN alba, aurora, beginning, break of day, brightening, cockcrow, cocklight, creek, crepusc(u)le, daybreak, daylight, dew, eoan, eos, greking, morn(ing), morrow, opening, orient, origin, precursor, prime, spring, start, sunrise, sunup, uprise
before antelucan
deity asvins, aurora, dyaus, eos, heimdall, matuta, usas
on occur to, penetrate
pert. auroral, aurorean, eoan, matin
symbol dew
toward the eastward
DAY, DAY'S age, dia, diem, dies, distance, eon, epoch, era, generation, giorno, jour, lifetime, light, period, tag, time, yom
after day always, constantly, endlessly, long(time), repeatedly
and night always, constantly, kalpa

bed baigneuse, chaise-longue, duchesse, sofa
before eve, yesterday
bird dayal
blindness hemeralopia, nyctalopia
book diary, diurnal, journal, log
comb. hemer(o)
dog canicule, summer
every 3rd tertian
every 9th nonan
every other terian
evil dies mali
fat jour gras
father of erebus
favorable dies faustus
flower cohitre
god horus, janus
half, pert. semidiurnal
holy feast, holiday
hot boiler, roaster, scorcher
in and day out See ALWAYS.
joyful festival
judgment dies irae, doomsday, inquest
last of festival apodosis
lean jour maigre
lily hemerocallis
longest baranaby, bright, d-day
march etape
market fiangue, nundine
meatless maigre
mother nyx
muse phantasm, phantasy, reverie, revery, stargaze, vision, woolgather
nursery creche
of atonement alhet, ashamnu, yom kippur
of origin birthday
of rest sabbath
of yore ago, has-been, past
pert. diurnal, ferial, hodiernal
pulvering ash wednesday
quarter term
reaping bedrip
scholar extern
seize the carpe diem
-sight hemeralopia, nyctalopia
60th ghurry
star sphere, sun
supplemental uayeb
time of horo, hour
12th epiphany
week feria
work darg(ue), diet(a), warday
DAYAK bahau, dusun, dyak,

iban, kayan, kelabit, kenya(h), malay
DAYAL daybird
DAYBREAK dawn, daylight, morn(ing), sunrise, sunup
DAYDREAM absent-mindedness, castle in spain, dwa(l)m, fancy, fantasy, imagination, muse, phantasm, phantasy, reverie, revery, stargaze, vision, woolgather
DAYLIGHT dawn, enlightenment, hope, information, noonday, noontide, publicity, sunbeam, sunburst, sunlight, sunshine
saving inventor ben franklin
DAYS 5 pentad
5 nameless uayeb
7 hebdomad, week
14 fortnight
50 quinquagesima
260 tonalmatl
evil dismal
fast ashura, lent
fateful ides
gone by past
DAYSPRING beginning, dawn, morning
DAYWORKER dilker
DAZE addle, aston(e), astonish, astony, astound, awe, befog, bemuse, benumb, bewilder, blind, blur, confuse, damp, dare, daver, deaden, dizzy, drug, dumfound, fog, maze, muddle, paralyze, perplex, petrify, rattle, shine, shock, stun, stupor, swoon, torpify
DAZED asea, assot, awestruck, besot(ted), dazy, dazzled, dithered, dizzy, donnered, dopey, doyled, doylt, drugged, groggy, mad, narcotized, punch-drunk, rotten, silly, slaphappy, totty, withered, witless, woozy
become dwa(l)m
DAZZLE astonish, astound, benight, bewilder, blind, confuse, daze, eclipse, fulgor, glaik, glare, impress, outshine, shine, splendor, surprise
DAZZLING bright, candescent, dizzying, flashy, fulgent, garish, glaring, gorgeous, radiant, showy
DDT dicophane, pesticide, tde
DEA aphrodite, astarte
priests arvales

DEACON adept, adulterate, alter, churchman, cleric, doctor, ecclesiastic, falsify, layman, levite, load, master, meddle, minister, sophisticate, tamper, vary, weight
prayers ectene, ektene
stole orarion
DEACONESS widow
DEAD ad patres, amort, annihilated, apathic, asleep, at rest, blind, bloodless, breathless, bung, bygone, closed, deceased, defunct, demised, departed, disparu, done(for), dowd, dull, expired, extinct, fallen, fey, finished, flat, gone west, inanimate, inert, inorganic, insensible, kaput, lackluster, languid, late, lifeless, low, mort(e), napoo(h), no more, numb, obsolete, obtund, passe, passed away, perished, phut, pok(e)y, sainted, slain, spent, start, sterile, still, strung, tedious, unconscious, vacant
ahead directly
-alive spent
arm necrosis
as a door-nail
at top rampick
beat bum, parasite, renigger, spent, sponge(r), tired, welcher
body carcass, carrion, corpse
city of necropolis
comb. abio
deity See UNDERWORLD *god, goddess.*
drunk blind
duck goner, loser
end blind alley, closed, cul de sac, impasse, trap
end channel billabong
festival of obon
hand mortmain
heat draw, impasse, tie
home of (See also BURIAL *place.*) ament, aral(1)u, hades, hell, inferno, necropolis, paradise, sheol, utgarthar
lift chore, exertion
light corpse-candle
nettle henbit
pledge mortgage
rap likeness, similarity
right accurate
ringer double, identical, likeness
sea city sodom

sea mountain pisgah
sea pass akrabbin
sea people horite
sea plateau seir
sea scrolls site khirbet qumran
sea territory moab
service black mass
-set determined, stop
shot marksman, sniper
spirit akh, manes, vampire
stand dilemma, standstill
sure absolute, actual, certain
tired exhausted, spent
tree(s) driki, rampick, rampike
turning of famadihana
weight impediment, lading
worship of necrolatry
wrapping fabric, cerecloth
DEADEN amortize, anesthetize, bedaze, benumb, besot, blunt, buff, chloroform, close, cold-cock, cushion, dampen, desensitize, dope, drown, drug, dull, enfeeble, etherize, freeze, kayo, knock out, lay out, moderate, muffle, mull, mute, narcotize, numb, obtund, opiate, palsy, paralyse, petrify, repress, retard, sear, slake, slumber, smother, stifle, stun, stupefy, weaken
scent foil
DEADFALL trap
DEADHEAD bobber, bollard, buoy, empty, hawser, parasite, pass, post, sink(er), sprue, tailstock
DEADHOUSE bonehouse, boneyard, burning ghat, cinerarium, crematorium, crematory, funeral home, lichhouse, morgue, mortuary
DEADLINE boundary, limit
DEADLOCK checkmate, draw, impasse, logjam, stalemate, standoff, standstill, stop(page), tie
DEADLY baneful, capital, dire, fatal, fateful, feral, gory, internecine, killing, lethiferous, malign(ant), mort(al), mortific, noxious, poisonous, ruinous, sanguinary, sanguine, toxic, tuant, venomous, virulent
carrot drias, thapsia
nightshade belladonna
DEADPAN calm, impassive, vacant

DEADWOOD *character* calamity jane
dick robert dickey
DEAF barren, dead, dunch, dunny, empty, muffled, oblivious, sorda, sordo, sterile, surd, unhearing, unheeding
adder copperhead, slowworm, snake
as a post
ear auricle, cotyledon, scab
-mute aphasiac, fenella, laloplegic, surdomute
DEAFEN adeave, deaden, deave, din, dive, dorr, muffle, surd
DEAFNESS amusia, anacusia, anacusis, asonia, barycola, cophosis, surdity
cause deave, stun
DEAL allocate, allot, apply, apportion(ment), arrange(ment), assign, bargain, batten, bestow, broker, compact, contract, dail, dispense, distribute, divide, dole, donne, draw, fetch, give, hand, handle, inflict, lend, market, mete, mix, negotiate, negotiation, operate, operation, partake, pianola, pine, plank, quantity, sale, separate, serve, sever, shake, share, shift, tale, trade, transaction, treat, troke, truck(le), turn, understanding, whiz, wield, wrestle, yield
a blow strike
a deathblow defeat, destroy
cards draw, tally
clandestinely trinket
directly make no bones about
great jugful, loads, lots, might, mort, sight, skinful
harshly discipline, punish
illegally bootleg, smuggle
in include, purvey, trade, truck
of cards coup, goulash, spoil
out administer, scatter
political dicker
shrewdly jockey
square fair play
with accomplish, comment, concern, cope, cover, demean, dight, discuss, entreat, handle, manage, operate, patronize, perform, punish, review, treat
with others negotiate
DEALER agent, badger, bank(er), broker, butcher,

cadger, chapman, collier, co(o)per, couper, cutler, draper, eggler, house, jobber, keelman, licensee, marketer, mercer, merchant, middleman, monger, retailer, salesman, scorser, seller, stickman, tailleur, trader, vender, vintner
crooked mechanic
in provisions chandler, sutler
secondhand goods broker, pawnbroker
slave mango
DEALFISH vaagm(a)er
DEALING(S) act, affair(s), business, commerce, commune, communion, converse, dole, exchange, intercourse, trading, traffic, troke, truck
shrewd chicanery, deceit
DEAN chief, decan, doyen, ecclesiastic, elder, headmaster, preceptor, prefect, principal, provost, senior, teacher, vale, valley, verger
gloomy inge
pert. decanal
residence decanate, parsonage, rectory
the jonathan swift
DEAR achree, agrah, beloved, bosom, cara, chary, chere, cheri(e), cherished, close, costly, darling, dautie, dawtie, esteemed, exorbitant, expensive, familiar, golden, high(priced), hon(ey), inestimable, intimate, invaluable, joe, lamb, lovable, love, pet, pigsney, poppet, precious, priceless, querida, rich, scarce, severe, special, squall, tender, tootsie, valuable, worthy
DEARLY alife, deeply, keenly, richly
DEARTH cherte, deficiency, drought, famine, lack, paucity, poverty, scarcity, solitude, want
DEATH ankou, annihilation, bale, bane, biolysis, blight, casualty, charos, charus, crossing the bar, curtain, decay, decease, dee, demise, depart(ure), dissolution, doom, dormition, end(ing), eternal rest, euthanasia, evanishment, exit(us), expiration, expiry, extinction, extinguishment, fall, fatality, fate, finis, grave, grim

reaper, gruel, journey's end, lethe, mors, mort, murder, necrosis, night, obit, parting, passing, quietus, reaper, release, rest, silence, sleep, thanatos, wagang
adder elapid, elapoid
after posthumous
angel abou jahia, azrael, danite, morded, samael
before ante-mortem
black plague, typhus
blow coup de grace, defeat, end, quietus
-bringing funest
by drowning noyade
camass lobelia
comb. necro, thanat(o)
cup agaric, amanita, mushroom
-defying audacious, bold
eternal perdition
examination after autopsy, necropsy
fear of necrophobia, thanatophobia
feigned catalepsy, cataplexy
god See UNDERWORLD *god, goddess.*
march bataan, cortege, dirge, funeral
means of halter, lapidation, lynch, noose, noyode, rack
meditation thanatopsis
mercy euthanasia
near in extremis
note mort
notice necrologue, necrology, obit(uary)
personification ankou, azrael, charos, grim reaper, mors
portending fey, funest
portent barghest
put to See KILL.
rate mortality, statistic
rattle rale
register necrology
reminder memento mori
representation pale horse
science of thanatology
song dirge, elegy, threnody
stiffening rigor mortis
stroke coup de grace
struggle agony, contest
subject to mortal
sword morglay
symbol orant, yew
throes, pert. agonal
to the utterly
valley of, site crimea
DEATHLESS eternal, immortal, undying
DEATHLIKE ghastful,

ghastly, macabre, moribund, mortuous, thanatoid
DEATHLY cadaverous, corpselike, eerie, fatal, ghastful, ghastly, ghostly, grisly, gruesome, haggard, lurid, macabre, mortal(ly), pale, stygian, wan, weird
DEATHWATCH beetle, insect, vigil, wake
DEB adolescent, girl, newcomer, novice
DEBACLE breakdown, breakup, cataclysm, catastrophe, cave(in), collapse, crackup, crash, destruction, dud, fiasco, revolution, smash(up), washout, wreck
DEBAR ban, bar, blackball, boycott, eliminate, estop, exclude, forbid, hinder, interdict, keep out, obstruct, preclude, prevent, prohibit, refuse, restrain, rule out, seclude, shut out, suspend, tabu
DEBARK arrive, disembark, land
DEBASE alloy, avile, bastardize, bemean, canker, cheapen, corrupt, debauch, defile, degenerate, degrade, delay, demean, demote, denigrate, deprave, depress, deteriorate, devalue, dilute, dirty, disgrace, dishonor, doctor, harm, humble, impair, lower, nidder, nither, pervert, pollute, sap, sink, spoil, taint, vilify, vitiate, weaken
DEBASED bastard, bestial, cankered, decadent, degraded, derogate, low, squalid, vile, vitiate(d)
DEBATABLE arguable, moot
DEBATE agitate, agitation, agon, altercation, apologetics, argue, argument, battle, canvass, confute, contend, contention, contest, controversy, conversation, dialectic, discept, discuss, disputation, dispute, fight, fray, hassle, hesitate, militate, moot(ing), palaver, pilpul, plead, polemicize, polemics, prove, quarrel, reason, rebut, wrangle
art of dialectics, polemics
association lyceum
pert. cloture, forensic, polemical, quodlibet

place forum, senate
stoppage of cloture
DEBATER arguer, dialectician, disceptator, disputant, picador, polemicist, polemist
DEBAUCH betray, bout, bum, carousal, corrupt, deboise, deprave, dishonor, dissipate, dissipation, file, guzzle, harm, injure, lure, mar, mislead, orgy, play, pollute, revel, riot, seduce, splore, spoil, spree, squander, strumpet, stuprate, taint, wassail, whore
DEBAUCHED deboist, dissipated, fast, lewd, profligate, rakehell, wanton
DEBAUCHERY priapism, rakery
DEBENTURE bond, certificate, security
DEBILITATE afflict, devitalize, emasculate, enervate, enfeeble, exhaust, harm, hurt, impair, mar, sap, sink, weaken
DEBILITATED asthenic, feeble, infirm, limp, sapped, seedy, spent, weak
DEBILITY asthenia, astheny, atony, frailty, languor, sickliness, weakness
DEBIT charge, debt, entry, loss
DE BIVAR campeador, cid
DEBLATERATE blabber, gab, prate, tattle
DEBONAIR affable, airy, breezy, buoyant, carefree, cavalier, cheery, chipper, cocky, corky, dapper, elegant, gay, genteel, graceful, gracious, jaunty, light (hearted), lightsome, lithe, lively, perky, polite, resilient, sprightly, suave, urbane
DEBORAH *husband* lapidoth
DEBOUCH disgorge, emerge, fall, mouth, outlet
DEBRIEF examine, interrogate, question
DEBRIS crumble, decay, deposit, detritus, dotter, driblets, eluvium, frush, guck, junk, litter, oddments, powder, refuse, remainder, remains, rubbish, rubble, rudera, ruins, scree(n), screenings, slag, slash, slidder, tailings, thurst, trash, waste
fluffy flue

in wool bur(r)
prehistoric breccia
rocky drift, eluvium, talus
DEBT arrears, charge, debit, due, duty, iou, judgment, liability, obligation, sin, trespass, wanigan
discharge clear, meet
old oblata
secured bond
statement bill, chit, invoice, iou, memo, note, reckoning, score, tab, tally
DEBTOR abbey laird, bankrupt, borrower, dyvour, mortgagee, ower, skip, yielder
detention place sponging house
of record judgment
proceed against excuss
shelter holyrood abbey
DEBUNK debag, disillusion
DEBUT admission, bow, coming out, entree, inauguration, ingress, introduction, opening, performance, presentation, start
DEBUTANTE bud, deb(by), ingenue, rosebud, sophomore
DECADE decennary, decennium, solitaire, ten years
DECADENCE deterioration, paracme
DECADENT corrupt, decayed, degenerate, degraded, depraved, effete, hothouse, overripe
DECALOGUE code, ethics, principles, standards, ten commandments
DECAMP abscond, absquatulate, bolt, depart, elope, escape, evade, flee, fly, go, guy, hike, kite, lam, leave, levant, mizzle, mog, morris, mosey, move, powder, put, quit, scoot, scour, scraff, sh(l)emozzle, vamoose, vamos(e)
DECANT drain, emit, pour, transfer, unload
DECANTER carafe, carafon, croft, ewer, gardevin, ingester, pitcher, urceole
DECAPITATE behead, decollate, execute, guillotine
DECAPOD buster, crab, crustacean, homarus, lobster, mollusk, prawn, shrimp, squid
DECAY addle, atrophy, blet, blight, break up, caries,

conk, corrode, corrosion, corrupt, crock, crumble, decadence, decline, decompose, decrease, defile, dilapidation, disintegrate, doat, dote, doze, druxiness, ebb, erode, erosion, fade, fail, fester, fordwine, gangrene, go bad, impair, marcescence, marcor, milder, mildew, mold(er), mortify, mosker, oxidation, oxidization, phythogenesis, putrefy, putresce, rankle, rot, rox(y), ruin, rust, shank, sicken, sloom, sloum, sphacelate, spile, spoil, wante, waste, wear, wither
comb. sapr(o)
incipient blet
in tree conk, konk
DECAYED bad, carious, corrupt, dead, decadent, dilapidated, disjacked, disjaskit, doty, dozy, frush, marcid, putrid, rotten, roxy, snaggled, spaked, withered
DECEASE death, demise, departure, die, dying, fail, gone, late, lost, obit, pass (age), passing
DECEASED dead, decedent, defunct, departed, extinct, gone, late, umquhile, umwhile
DECEIT abuse, artifice, cautel, cheat(ing), chicane(ry), covin, cozenage, craft, cunning, deception, defrauding, dissait, dole, dolus, double dealing, duplicity, faitery, fake, falsedad, falseness, feint, felony, fiction, flum, fraud, furtiveness, gab, gaff, guile, gull, hoax, humbug, imposture, insidiousness, ruse, sarab, shadiness, sham, shiftiness, spoofery, subtlety, swick, swike, trap, tray, treacherousness, treachery, trumpery, wile, wiliness, woidre
symbol cat, duck
DECEITFUL artful, blind, braid, cautelous, collusive, conniving, covert, crafty, cunning, delusive, dishonest, evasive, false, fictive, fraudulent, furtive, gaudy, gnathonic, guileful, insidious, janus, loopy, scheming, shady, shammish, shifty, sirenic, slape, sleekit,

slidder, sneaky, surreptitious, tortuous, two-faced, underhand(ed), unwrest, wily, winding
DECEIVE 3 bob, cog, con, dor, fob, fub, gab, gas, gum, kid, lie 4 bilk, bite, bunk, crap, do in, dupe, fail, fake, fool, gaff, gull, have, hoax, jape, jilt, jouk, mask, mock, mump, sell, sham, sile, snow, take, trap, wile 5 abuse, blear, blind, blink, bluff, catch, cheat, cozen, cross, cully, dodge, dorre, gleek, gloze, hocus, lurch, patch, spoof, swick, swike, trick, troil, truff, trump, tryst 6 bedote, beflum, befool, betray, bubble, cajole, cloine, cloyne, daddle, delude, desert, diddle, euchre, gammon, humbug, illude, jockey, juggle, niggle, pigeon, seduce, sucker, wimple 7 beguile, conjure, corrupt, falsify, flummox, forsake, gudgeon, mislead, slicker, twotime 8 blackleg, come over, flimflam, hoodwink, outreach 9 bamboozle, overreach, victimize 10 camouflage, circumvent, hocus-pocus, honeyfogle 11 doublecross, hornswoggle
DECEIVER artful dodger, bamboozler, beguiler, betrayer, bilker, bluffer, boggler, charlatan, cheat, chicaner, cockatrice, cogger, faiter, faker, falsary, fonfer, fox, fraud, guiler, imposter, indian giver, janus, japer, jeremy diddler, jilt(er), judas, knave, liar, losenger, lothario, machiavelli, magician, mountebank, picaro (on), rascal, rogue, serpent, sham, sharper, slicker, snake, sneak, snide, trapan, trepan, trickster, trumper, warlock, weasel, wernard
DECEMBER *birthstone* ruby, turquoise, zircon
17th-19th saturnalia
21st mumping day
DECENCY chastity, compliance, decorousness, decorum, delicacy, dignity, gentility, grace, honesty, modesty, properness, propriety, pudicity, respect-

ability, restraint, seemliness, shame, taste, virtue

DECENT acceptable, chaste, comme il faut, decorous, demure, estimable, ethical, expedient, fair, fit(ting), gradely, graithly, honest, indulgent, jannock, maidenly, mediocre, meet, modest, nice, noble, proper, pure, right, seemly, shapely, sightly, sufficient, suitable, tolerable, wiselike

DECEPTION abuse, artifice, bam, bamboozlement, barrat, beguile, blaflum, blind, camouflage, cautel, chicane(ry), cog, covin, cunning, delusion, dole, dolus, dor(re), double-dealing, doubletake, dupery, duplicity, eyewash, fake, falseness, falsity, favel, fiction, flam, flimflam(mery), flum, fraud, gaff, gag, guile, gullage, gullery, hoax, illusion, jape, knavery, legerdemain, lie, maze, obliquity, pettifoggery, phenakism, pretext, ripoff, runaround, ruse, sell, sham, shenanigans, skulduggery, slyness, spoof (ery), stratagem, trick (ery), trumpery, wile

DECEPTIVE artful, astucious, astute, catch(y), crafty, cunning, delusive, delusory, dishonest, fallacious, false, feline, flam, flimflam, foxy, hollow, illusory, misleading, oblique, questionable, shammish, shifty, sirenic, slick, snaky, sneaky, specious, treacherous, trickish, trick(s)y, unsicker, wrong

DECIDE act, adjudge, adopt, arbitrate, ascertain, award, call, cast, cern, commit, conclude, decern, decise, decree, deem, deraign, determine, elect, end, find, fix, govern, hold, induce, judge, rate, resolve, rule, settle, tell, vote, will
upon choose, elect, set, termine

DECIDED assured, certain, concluded, decisive, emphatic, ended, fated, firm, flat, formed, main, peremptory, resolute, resolved, settled, unalterable, unqualified, unshaken

by judge arbitrary

DECIDUA caduca

DECIMA tenth, tithe

DECIMAL denary, numeric(al), repeater, repetend, ten, tenth
base ten
part mantissa
pert. decadic
system man dewey

DECIMATE annihilate, burke, destroy, kill, slaughter, slay, subtract, tenth

DECIPHER break, decode, decrypt, detect, discover, interpret, read, reveal, solve, translate, unpuzzle, unravel

DECISION act, acuerdo, announcement, aplomb, arbitrament, arbitration, arret, award, call, canon, choice, conclusion, decree, determination, diktat, doom, end, fiat, finding, firmness, grit, judgment, mettle, nerve, oracle, placitum, pluck, rede, report, resolution, result, ruling, sentence, umpirage, verdict, volition, vote, will(power)
existential leap
final issue
inability abulia
intermediate interlocutory
maker executive, judge, referee, umpire
of court holding, verdict
sudden impulse, whim

DECISIVE acute, bull's eye, categorical, certain, climacteric, conclusive, critical, crucial, crushing, decretal, definite, definitive, explicit, express, final, mandatory, payoff, positive, sure, telling, terminal, virile
but unreasoned arbitrary

DECK adorn, array, attire, bank, beautify, bedight, bedizen, blazon, buss, caparison, cards, clothe, daub, decorate, dink, dizen, dress, embellish, emblazon, enhance, enrich, equip, fettle, fig, floor, flounce, focsle, garnish, gild, group, hatch, heap, ornament, pack, pink, platform, poop, preen, primp, prink, prow, prune, roof, stud, tiff, tog, trig, trim
hand boatman, crewman, deckie, roustabout, sailor, trimmer

high poop
house caboose, camboose
kind berth, boat, bridge, flight, focsle, forecastle, gun, hurricane, main, orlop, platform, poop, promenade, protective, rasee, razee, shelter, spar, splinter, upper
lower orlop
man leverman, tripper
on ready
out adorn, array, attire, barb, bedight, dizen, fangle, finify, spick, tiff
part scupper
planking spirketing
post bitt
remove razee
ring crance
ship's See DECK *kind.*
space bay
space between lazaret

DECKED beseen, clad, dressed, laureled
out ornate, spiffed

DECKLE featheredge, frame

DECLAIM air, blazon, bleeze, censure, criticize, elocute, gale, harangue, herald, inform, inveigh, mouth, orate, perorate, rant, rave, recite, roll, speak, spout, utter, vent, voice

DECLAMATION harangue, speech, spouting

DECLARATION affidavit, allegation, announcement, annunciation, avowal, bid, bill, call, claim, complaint, decree, deposition, dick, fuero, manifest, misere, narr, oracle, parol(e), placet, platform, pleading, proces-verbal, promise, publication, resolve, saying, statement, tale, testimony
of faith confession, profession
of policy platform

DECLARE acclaim, acknowledge, affirm, affy, allege, announce, aread, areed, argue, assert, asseverate, assure, aver, avouce, avow, behight, bid, blazon, bruit, couthe, denounce, depone, depose, descry, expone, herald, indicate, intimate, keeth, ken, kithe, kythe, lay, maintain, manifest, meld, nunciate, posit, predicate, proclaim, pronounce, publish, renounce, say, schneider, schwarz, show,

signify, snum, speak, spread, state, swan, swear, termine, trow, upgive, utter, vote, vouch, vow
arbitrarily gavel
invalid annul
off recede, withdraw
one's opinion allow
publicly cry, proclaim
untrue deny
war challenge, dare, defy
DECLENSION bending, decadence, decline, decrease, degeneration, descent, deterioration, devolution, inflexion, refusal, sloping
DECLINATION bend, bias, decay, descent, deviation, obliquity, refusal, regret, slope, southing, swerving
DECLINE 3 age, beg, dip, ebb, end, jib, sag, set, shy 4 balk, bend, bust, deny, down, drop, fade, fail, fall, flag, flop, pine, sink, slip, vail, wane, welk 5 abate, break, chute, decay, demur, droll, droop, dwarf, faint, heald, hield, lapse, lower, pitch, quail, repel, slack, slide, slope, slump, spoil, spurn, stick, stoop, swine, tabes, waive 6 boggle, debase, falter, go down, recede, refuse, reject, renege, sicken, weaken, worsen 7 atrophy, cheapen, descent, dwindle, failure, falloff, letdown, run down, scruple, sinkage, subside 8 decrease, downturn, marasmus, toboggan, withdraw 9 catabasis, declivity 10 cataplasis, depreciate 11 deteriorate, shortcoming
DECLINING awane, bearish, decadent, down(hill), falling, western
DECLIVITY bent, brae, brew, calade, cliff, decline, descent, devex, dip, downhill, drop, fall, grade, hanger, hanging, hill, incline, pitch, scarp, skug, slant, slope
DECOCT boil, cook, excite, extract, kindle, make, plan, prepare, refine, render, smelt
DECOCTION apozem(a), b(h)ang, boiling, cremor, decoctum, dish, drink, extract, infusion, ooze, ptisan, sapa, save, solution, tisane

DECOHERER rotator, shaker, tapper
DECOLOR achromatize, blanch, bleach, etoliate, fade, fume, peroxide, tarnish, tone down, wash out, whiten
DECOMPOSE analyse, analyze, attach, break down, decay, degrade, digest, disintegrate, dissolve, foul, frit, liquefy, macerate, melt, putrefy, putresce, rot, spoil
DECOMPOSITION acidolysis, biolysis, breakdown, decay, exchange, solvolysis
DECOR decoration, motif, scenery, setting, theme
DECORATE adorn, array, band, beautify, bedeck, bedizen, beset, blazon, border, brocade, camlet, chip, cite, color, daiker, dandify, deck, dink, dizen, doll up, dress, edge, embellish, emblazon, emboss, embroider, enhance, enrich, festoon, fig out, flock, flourish, flower, fret, frill, furbish, gadroon, garnish, gaud, grace, heighten, honor, inlay, laureate, miniate, ornament, paint, parget, pink, prank, preen, primp, prink, purfle, rail, rule, scrimshaw, set off, smarten(up), spruce up, suborn, tiff, tire, titivate, trick, trim
garishly bedizen
with letters miniate
with raised pattern brocade
DECORATED adorned, ajoure, cited, demasse, distinct, flambe, floreted, giddy, inlaid, laced, niell(o)ed, ornate, sigilate, wreathed, wrought
DECORATION adornment, applique, arabesque, barbola, bayadere, bibelot, blue ribbon, boss, boule, bow, bucrane, bucranium, buhl, cordon (bleu), decker, decor, doodab, doodad, dsc, dsm, dso, edging, elaboration, embellishment, emblazonment, emblazonry, embroidery, fall, finery, floret, flourish, fluting, fretting, frieze, fuss, garnish(ment), garniture, gesso, gold star, honor, ikat, illumination, insigne, intarsia, lace, medal, niello, ornamen-

t(ation), plaque, pride, purfle, riband, ribbon, tiara, tinsel, tole, trim(ming), trophy
coat brandenburg
cut-out applique
excessive foofaraw
inessential spinach
leafy vignette
military medal, ribbon
mural fresco, topia
musical grace, trill, turn
pert. medallic, ornate
plaster and glass ardish
surface intarsia
technique plangi
waist jabot
wall dado, fresco, tenture, wainscot
DECOROUS becoming, calm, chaste, comely, composed, conventional, decent, demure, douce, expedient, fitting, formal, genteel, good, grave, mannerly, modest, moral, nice, polite, prim, proper, quiet, regular, right, sedate, seemly, sober, solemn, staid, steady
DECORTICATE bark, debark, denude, flay, hull, husk, pare, peel, pill, skin, strip
DECORUM convention, correctness, decency, dignity, etiquette, fitness, form, formality, goodness, gravity, modesty, niceness, order, properness, propriety, seemliness, solemnity, suitability, usage
DECOY allure, bait, barnard, bernard, betrayer, blind, bonnet, bunk, button, bybidder, call(er), capper, catch, crimp, deceive, deception, delude, drill, entice, entrap, goad, inveigle, lure, peter funk, pigeon, plant, ringer, roper, seduce, shill, snare, squawker, stale, stall, steerer, stool(pigeon), straw-bidder, tempt, tole, toll(er), train, trap, trepan, trick
auctioneer's button
bird call-duck
gambler's capper, shill, stooge
swindlers barnard, bernard, sharper
DECREASE 3 cut, ebb, sag 4 bate, drop, ease, loss, melt, pare, sink, wane, wear,

welk **5** abase, abate, decay, erode, lapse, let up, lower, remit, slash, slump, swage, swarf, taper, wanze, waste **6** decess, decrew, deduct, impair, lessen, minify, narrow, recede, reduce, shrink, weaken **7** abridge, atrophy, bedwarf, consume, crumble, curtail, cutback, cut down, deceive, decline, deflate, deplete, depress, erosion, falloff, shorten, sinkage, slacken, subside, swindle, tail off, whittle **8** belittle, compress, condense, contract, decimate, diminish, discount, downturn, languish, lowering, minimize, mitigate, retrench, rollback **9** abatement, alleviate, attenuate, catabasis, decrement, deduction, deflation, downgrade, extenuate, reduction, shrinkage **10** abbreviate, declension, depreciate, diminuendo, diminution, mitigation **11** abridgement, contraction, curtailment, decrescence, decrescendo, dissipation, extenuation **12** depreciation, minification, minimization
in volume ablation
of energy fatigue
DECREE act, adjudge, appoint(ment), aread, areed, arret, assize, authorize, bando, besluit, brevet, bull, canon, command(ment), decern, decision, declaration, decreet, decretal, decretum, destine, dictate, dictum, dit, doom, edict(um), emit, enact, escript, fiat, firman, gezerah, grace, hattihymayun, hattisherif, indict, irade, judge, judgment, law, mandate, manifesto, nisi, ordain, order, ordinance, ordonnance, placit(um), point, proclamation, pronounce(ment), pronunciamento, rede, rescript, rogation, rule, ruling, sanction, saw, sentence, statute, tenet, ukase, verdict, will, wite, writ
authoritative arret, canon
beforehand destine
church canon, synodical
imperial fiat, irade
official rescript
papal bull

DECREPIT aged, anile, bedrid(den), creaky, decayed, forfairn, fragile, frail, infirm, invalid, lame, old, ramshackle, senile, unorn, unsound, wasted, weak, worn
DECRY abase, asperse, barrack, belittle, book, censure, complain, condemn, criticize, croak, debauch, derogate, detract, discredit, disparage, lessen, minimize, protest, reprobate, rogue, slur, traduce
DECUPLE tenfold
DECUSSATION chiasma, crossing, intersection
DEDAN *father* jokshan, raamah
son asshurim, letushim, leummim
DEDICATE allot, anoint, apply, ascribe, baptize, bless, christen, consecrate, consign, devote, devow, direct, entitle, hallow, inscribe, intitule, oblate, sacre, sacri, separate, vote, vow
DEDICATED oblate
DEDUCE analyze, argue, bring, cogitate, conclude, deem, derive, draw, drive, elicit, extract, fetch, gather, infer, interpret, judge, lead, opine, put, ratiocinate, reason, subsume, suppose, take, think, trace
DEDUCIBLE consequential, deductible, deductive, derivable, following, illative, inducible, inferential, sequential
DEDUCT abate, abstract, allow, bate, blot, cancel, censor, censure, cross out, curtail, cut, decrease, defalk, dele(te), detract, diminish, discount, dock, erase, excise, expunge, expurgate, faik, minus, pare, rebate, recoup, reduce, remove, retrench, rub out, rule out, separate, shave, strike off, subduct, subtract, take off, thin, traduce, weed, wipe out, withdraw, write off
DEDUCTION ablation, abscission, abstraction, agio, allowance, alteration, amputation, beamage, bowdlerization, cancellation,

castration, censorship, conclusion, credit, cutting, decrease, decrement, deletion, detruncation, discount, dockage, editing, eduction, erasure, ergotism, excision, expurgation, extirpation, gelding, illation, inference, judgment, minuend, minus(sign), mutilation, negative, offtake, rebate, removal, reprise, retrenchment, salt, spaying, stoppage, subduction, subtraction, tare, truncation
logical ergotism, reasoning
DEED accomplishment, achievement, act, act(a), action, activity, actum, adventure, bill, book, byplay, case, cede, chart(er), convey, coup, document, escrow, exploit, fact(um), fait, feat, fiat, gest(e), heirloom, indenture, instrument, jest, muniments, paper, parergon, pottah, practise, reality, record, remise, sasine, security, starr, stroke, stunt, sunnud, tailye, tailzie, tat, title, transfer
evil harm, hurt, ill, injury, malefaction, sin
good benefice, boon, favor, mitzyah
part habendum
DEEDS acta, doings, muniments, res gestae, service
DEEM account, adjudge, announce, appraise, believe, conclude, consider, estimate, gather, give, hold, hope, imagine, infer, judge, let, opine, ordain, proclaim, reckon, regard, respect, say, suppose, surmise, think
DEEP abstruse, abysmal, abyss(al), astute, baritone, barytone, base, bass, bassalia, benthon, benthos, bold, bottomless, brine, broad, complete, contralto, cunning, depths, dewat, duat, esoteric, grave, great, heavy, hollow, howe, intense, intent, inveterate, low (pitched), mysterious, neal, obscure, ocean(bottom), powerful, profound, rapt, recondite, sage, sea, sepulchral, serious, shrewd, strong, sullen, thorough, unfathomed, wide, wise
bosomed bathycolpian

comb. abysso, bathy
-dye color, engrain, fix
-dyed engrained, established, fast, indelible, thorough, unfading
in implicated, involved
-rooted established
-sea abyssal, bassalian, bathic, bathy(a)l, bathybic, bathysnal, benthal, benthonic, dipsey
-sea tangle driftweed, kelp
-seated chronic, established, implanted, ingrained, intimate, intrinsic, inwrought, profound
-set cavernous
-six abandon, destroy, dispose of, do in, reject(ion), tomb
-toned bass, stour

DEEPEN aggravate, broaden, cloud, darken, dredge, enhance, excavate, heighten, increase, intensify, strengthen, thicken

DEER alce, atlas, axis, barasingha, bobolink, boche, brock(et), browzer, buck, camel's hair, capreolus, caribou, cashmere, cervid, cervus, chital, chitra, coassus, dae, daim, dauw, doe, elaphure, elk, fantail, fawn, guazuti, guemac, guemul, hangul, hart, havier, hearst, hind, hine, huemul, kakar, kakur, kastura, kidang, losh(e), maha, maral, milu, moose, mort, moschus, muist, munjak, musk, napu, olen, para, parrah, pita, pito, plandok, pudu(a), rangifer, rascal, ratwa, red, reindeer, roe(buck), royal, ruminant, rusa, sabir, sambar, sambur, shou, shue, sika, sorrel, sowre, spade, spay, spikehorn, stag, surre, tarand, thameng, thamin, venade, ven(i)son, wapiti, yearling
antler See DEER *horn.*
axis chital
barking muntjac, muntjak
berry buckberry, checkerberry, huckleberry
big caribou, elk, moose, wapiti
black-tailed acerina, dassie, godwit, ruffe
bush soapbush
coat, winter blue
comb. cervi

cry bell
dung fumet
entrails nombles, numbles
fallow, daim, dama
fallow, pert. damine
family cervidae
female doe, hearst, hind, roe, teg
fictional bambi
fly tabanid
forest firth
4-year sore, staggard, staggart
gelded havier
genus alces, cervus, dama, moschus, pudu, rangifer, rucervus, rusa
grass handsome-harry, rhexia
group herd
hindquarters fouch, fourche
hog altas, para
horn antler, balcon, bez, buckhorn, croche, dag, mussel, testine, tine
horn knob croche, offer
-like giraffe, okapi
maha samba
male buck, hart, olen, roebuck, spay, stag(gard)
marsh suacupucu
meat charqui, jerky, venison
muntjac kakar, kakur
pampas mazame
panolia thameng
path run, slot, trail
pert. cervine, damine, furciferine, rusine
pygmy plandok
red axis, brocket, coassus, elaphine, hart, hind, maral, mazama, len, roe, samerr, spay, stag
ring tinchel, tinchill
rusine axis, ring
samba maha
slayer natty bumpo
slayer author cooper
small chevrotain, fawn, muntjak, napoo, napu, plandok, ratwa, roe
spotted chital, kakar
tail scut, shingle
3-year old sorel, sorrel, spade, spay(ad), spayard
tiger cougar
tine cluster troche
trap buckstall
2-year old brocket, hearst, knobber, pricket
unbranched antler dag
weed tanglefoot
young brocket, fawn, kid, pricket, spay, spitter

DEERHAIR bulrush, sedge
DEERLET See DEER *small.*
DEERSKIN buck
DEFACE batter, blemish, blotch, damage, defame, deform, destroy, disfigure, distort, disvisage, foul, hurt, injure, malahack, mangle, mar, mutilate, outshine, ruin, scar, shame, slander, spoil
DEFALCATE abscond, defalk, default, drib, embezzle, filch, loot, peculate, pilfer, plunder, purloin, rifle, rob, steal
DEFAME abuse, asperse, belie, besmirch, blacken, brand, calumniate, decry, defoul, denigrate, detract, dishonor, disparage, forgab, infamize, injure, libel, malign, revile, slander, smear, splatter, suggil, traduce, vilify
DEFAULT arrears, defalcate, defect, deficit, delinquence, delinquency, dishonor, fail(ure), flaw, lack, loss, mora, neglect, offend, repudiate, shirk, shortcoming, want, welch, welsh
on debt levant
DEFEAT 3 bar, fix, top, wax, win 4 balk, bath, beat, best, cast, ding, do in, down, drub, fall, fell, foil, jink, kill, lace, lick, loss, rout, ruin, rush, sink, trap, trim, whip 5 crash, facer, floor, outdo, shend, skunk, smash, swamp, throw, upset, whack, worst, wrack 6 cumber, eucher, larrup, master, reduce, refute, stoush, subdue, thrash, thwack, thwart, waggle, weaken 7 confuse, confute, conquer, convict, destroy, failure, licking, nose out, perempt, quietus, repulse, reverse, scomfit, shellac, snooker, subdual, triumph, undoing 8 collapse, conquest, downfall, drubbing, overcome, repuesto, vanquish, waterloo 9 checkmate, deathblow, frustrate, overthrow, overwhelm, subjugate 10 annihilate, disappoint
contractor's codill(e), codillio, repuesto
decisively blast, cleanup,

drub, flatten, rout, shellac, skunk, whomp
satisfactory moral victory
thoroughly wipe the floor with

DEFEATED beaten, checked, craven, derricked, down, kaput, lost, mated, set, whipped

DEFEATIST bolo, fatalist, gloomy, pacifist, pessimist, quitter, submitter, yielder

DEFECT abandon, blemish, botch, bug(out), coloboma, crack, cry uncle, damage, demerit, desert, disease, drawback, error, fail(ing), fault, flaw, foible, frailty, hick(e)y, imperfection, knot, lack, lacuna, lag, mayhem, minus, mispick, need, quit, renig, scob, shan, snag, twit, vice(ty), vitium, wane, want, weakness, yaw
without perfect, sound

DEFECTIVE bad, bauch, baugh, blind, cacoplastic, cripple(d), deficient, disgenic, dysgenic, faulty, flawed, imperfect, lame, meager, meagre, mutilous, pasul, simpleton, without
article schlack, schlag, s(c)hlock
comb. atel
mental idiot, imbecile, moron

DEFEND advocate, assert, avert, back, battle, champion, conserve, contend, cope, cover, deraign, espouse, expound, fight, flank, fortify, garrison, guard, hold, justify, keep, maintain, oppose, preserve, propugn, protect, resist, safeguard, save, screen, secure, shelter, shend, shield, support, uphold, vindicate, ward, warn, warrant

DEFENDANT accused, appelle, avowant, champion, libelee, litigant, prisoner, rea, respondent, reus, suspect
answer nolo contendere, plea
in replevin avowant

DEFENDER accountant, advocate, apologete, apologist, asserter, champion, guardian, paladin, partisan, patron, protector, sympathizer, tribune, upholder
of men alexander

of the constitution webster
of the faith henry viii

DEFENSE abatis, aegis, alibi, answer, apologia, apology, argument, armor, barrace, barricade, barrier, breasting, breastwork, buckler, bulwark, demurrer, denial, egis, entrenchment, exception, excuse, fort(ification), fraise, galapago, garrison, glacis, grith, guard, haganah, maintenance, moat, munition, objection, outwork, palisade, parados, plea(ding), protection, ravelin, rebuttal, refutation, reply, rock, sconce, security, selfpreservation, selfprotection, sepiment, shelter, shield, stronghold, tower, wall, ward(ing), warrant
armor caparison
castle matchecold
civil system conelrad
colored for aposematic, camouflaged
dike estacade
garment armor, broigne
mechanism autism, dereism, dynamism, escapism, fantasy, negativism, projection, sublimation, withdrawal
movement spar
outpost barbacan, barbican
pert. phylactic
position bridgehead, rampart
self, art aikido, arnis, boxing, judo, jujitsu, karate, kung-fu
slope glacis
wall bailey
warning system dewline, norad
work base, fort, redan

DEFENCELESS bare, cold, desolate, helpless, naked, open, silly, unarmed, unguarded

DEFENSIBLE justifiable, tenable

DEFER accede, acknowledge, adapt, adjourn, agree, assent, bow, capitulate, cave in, conform, delay, fawn, honor, humble, intermit, postpone, prorogue, protract, put off, relent, remand, remit, respect, retard, shelve, slow, stay, submit, succumb, suspend, table, tarry, truckle, waive, yield

DEFERENCE attention, civility, consideration, courtesy, delay, esteem, fealty, homage, honor, obeisance, regard, respect, reverence, submission, vail, veneration, worship

DEFERENTIAL acquiescent, courteous, dutiful, obeisant, polite, subservient

DEFIANCE affront, bravado, brave, challenge, confrontation, dare, defial, disobedience, gage, insurgency, opposition, rebellion, revolt

DEFIANT audacious, bardy, bold, brave, brazen, calcitrant, challenging, contemptuous, daring, disregardful, insolent, mutinous, rebellious, recalcitrant, reckless, refractory, stocky, stout, stubborn

DEFICIENCY absence, anoesia, anoia, blemish, dearth, defalcation, default, deficit, deletion, error, failing, fault, inadequacy, inlaik, lack, scarcity, shortage, shortcoming, sketchiness, ullage, want(age)
comb. penia
mental amentia, idiocy, stupidity

DEFICIENT barren, bobtail, defective, disgenic, exiguous, faulty, feeble, imperfect, inadequate, indigent, inferior, infrequent, lean, meager, meagre, rare, scant(y), short, sparse, unequal, wanting, without
comb. privic
mentally dumb, slow, soft, stupid
to be scantle

DEFICIT arrears, inadequacy, lack, shortage, shortfall, underage
madame marie antoinette

DEFILADE mask, protection, shield

DEFILE abra, abuse, bawd, bedo, befoul, benasty, beray, brand, cleft, contaminate, corrupt, debauch, deprave, dirty, dishonor, distain, filth(ify), filthy, foul, gap, glack, gowl, gullet, gut, hals(e), imbrue, infect, lime, maculate, mess, moil, muck, narrows, nasty, notch, pass, passageway, pervert, poison, profane, ravish, ray, seduce, slander, smear, smouch, smut, smutch, soil, stain, sully, taint, tarnish, violate, vitiate

DEFINE allot, assign, bound, circumscribe, clarify, condition, construe, decide, delimit, demarcate, describe, establish, explain, fix, interpret, limit, mere, name, outline, prescribe, set, settle, term

DEFINITE absolute, actual, approved, audible, certain, clear, decided, distinct, emphatic, evident, exact, explicit, final, firm, fixed, formed, hard, limited, manifest, official, open, plain, positive, precise, punctual, restricted, set, settled, sharp, special, specific, sure, tangible, unqualified

DEFINITION clarity, delineation, description, determination, explanation, gloss, interpretation, limit, meaning

DEFINITIVE conclusive, decisive, determining, final, grand, last, oristic, settling, terminal, ultimate

DEFLATE collapse, condense, contract, decrease, deplete, depreciate, drain, empale, empty, exhaust, humble, impale, lessen, let down, mortify, prick, puncture, put down, reduce, shrink

DEFLECT avert, baffle, bend, bias, cock, crook, curve, cut, depart, deviate, diffract, diffuse, digress, disperse, diverge, divert, parry, prevent, refract, sheer, skew, swerve, turn, twist, veer, warp, wrest, wring, wry

DEFLECTION aberration, bend, deviation, diffraction, diffusion, dispersion, divergence, diversion, droop, obliquity, refraction, sweep, windage

DEFLOWER breach, broach, defoul, despoil, forlie, possess, ravage, ravish, seduce, unmaiden, violate

DEFOE *character* friday, moll flanders, robinson crusoe, roxana

novel moll flanders, robinson crusoe, roxana

DEFORM blemish, buckle, contort, cripple, deface, disfigure, distort, gnarl, impair, injure, knot, maim, mangle, mar, misshape, mutilate, spoil, twist, warp, wince

DEFORMED bandy-legged, blemished, bow-legged, bunbacked, club-footed, defaced, disfigured, erose, formless, gammy, gibbous, grotesque, hideous, humped, illmade, illshaped, irregular, kyphotic, malformed, marred, misbegotten, misshapen, monstrous, mutilated, paulie, simous, skew, taliped, truncated, unmackly, wrong

comb. cac(o)

DEFORMITY asymmetry, blemish, bowlegs, buckle, camelback, clubfoot, clubhand, crookback, defacement, disfigurement, distortion, flatfoot, gall, gibbosity, harelip, humpback, hunchback, knockknee, knot, kyphosis, lordosis, malformation, misfigure, misshape, monstrosity, mutilation, pravity, splayfoot, swayback, talipes, teratology, truncation, vice, wanshape, warp

grotesque gargoylism

DEFRAUD bamboozle, beat, befool, bilk, boodle, cheat, chouse, chowse, cozen, deceive, dupe, fake, fleece, foil, fool, gouge, gull, gyp, hoax, hoodwink, mulct, outwit, rob, rook, slick, stick, swindle, trick, trim, victimize, wrong, yentz

DEFRAY appease, cover, disburse, expend, pay, reimburse, requite, satisfy

DEFT able, adroit, agile, apt, brisk, capable, clever, dext(e)rous, expert, feat, fit, handy, heppen, meet, neat, nimble, pat, pretty, quick, ready, skillful, sprack, spruce, tall, trim

DEFY affront, beard, brag, bravade, brave, cartel, challenge, champion, confront, contravene, dare, disobey, face, flout, forbid, front, mauger, maugre, mock, oppose, outdare, outface, outscout, renounce, resist, re-

volt, scorn, slight, spurn, stump, tempt, threaten, withstand

danger dare, gamble

DEG dampen, drizzle, sprinkle

DEGEN See SWORD.

DEGENERATE bastardize, corrode, corrupt, debase, debauched, decadent, decay, degender, degrade, deprave(d), deteriorate, deviate, effete, infamous, pervert(ed), profligate, reprobate, rot, rust, sin, sink, unkind, vicious, wilder, worsen, yahoo

DEGENERATION abiotrophy, adiposis, atrophy, devolution, turpitude, waller

of tissue cataplasia

DEGRADATION debasement, decline, degeneration, deposition, disgrace, erosion, humiliation, ignominy, reduction, shame

DEGRADE abase, break, bust, canker, corrupt, debase, declass, demean, demote, deplume, depose, disgrace, dishonor, disparage, displume, embase, foil, humble, humiliate, imbrute, lower, reduce, shame, shend, sink, stoop, strip, supplant, unman, villain, vitiate

DEGRADED abject, base, degreed, demiss, fallen, grieced, outcast, seamy, squalid

DEGRADING base, demeaning, humiliating, shameful

DEGREE amount, bank, caliber, calibre, cast, class, extent, gradation, grade, grado, grece, gree, griece, honor, intensity, interval, level, mark, measure, order, pip, pitch, poane, point, poll, quantity, radian, range, rank, rate, ratio, rung, saenger, scale, scope, shade, stage, stair, standing, station, step, strength, term, tier

academic baccalaureate, bachelor, bsc, dlit, doctor (ate), littd, lld, master(ate), mfa, msc, phd

arrange by gradate, grade

confer cap

conferral graduation, laureation

greatest utmost

highest cum laude, extreme, magna cum laude, nth, pink, sublimity, sum, summit, supreme, utmost

musical space subtonic

of closeness fit

of combining power valence

of contrast gamma

of deviation leeway

of elevation ascent

of engagement depth

of excellence caliber, calibre

of force kick

of height grade

of importance caliber, calibre

of inclination ascent

of lightness value

of mixture alloy

of opacity density

of slope splay

of the soul ruach

rabinnical cemichah, semicha, semikah

-seeker candidate, inceptor, student

small ace, drop, glimmer, gradation, hair, inch, iota, nth, shade, shadow

some bit

to a sickening ad nauseam

utmost acme, extreme, extremity, height, sum

without honors pol

DEGU octodont, rodent

DEHGAN swat(i)

DEHISCE burst, gape, yawn

DEHORN disbud, snub

DEHYDRATE bake, desiccate, dry, evaporate, jerk, parch, preserve

DEIANIRA *brother* meleager, tydeus

consort hercules

parent althea, ceneus

victim hercules

DEICOON *parent* hercules, megrara

slayer hercules

DEIDAMIA hippodamia

consort achilles, evander

father lycomedes

son neoptolemus, pyrrhus, sarpedon

DEIFIC beatific, beatifying, godlike

DEIFICATION apotheosis, idolization

of man anthromorphism, anthropathy, anthropolatry, anthrotheism

DEIFORM divine, godlike

DEIFY adore, apotheosize, begod, divine, divinify, exalt, fetish(ize), glorify, goddize, honor, idolatrize, idolify, idolize, venerate, worship

DEIGN accord, acquiesce, award, concede, condescend, consent, grant, patronize, stoop, vouchsafe

DEIL, DEIL'S See DEVIL.

bit scabious

bread earthnut

oatmeal earthnut

spoons plantain, pondweed

DEIMOS *brother* phobus

father ares

DEION *kingdom* phocis

parent aeoulus, enarete

DEIPHOBE *father* glaucus

DEIPHOBUS *brother* hector, paris

parent hecuba, priam

slayer menelaus

wife helen

DEIRDRE *consort* conor, noise

DEITY See also GOD, GODDESS.

avenging alastor, anteros

descent of avatar(a)

half-fish oannes

half-goat faun

hawk-eyed horus, sokari(s)

heathen idol

incarnate avatar

inferior demiurge, godkin, godling, pettigod

jackal-headed anubis

local numen

primal demogorgon

supreme hansa, monad, ormazd

symbol serpent

3-headed hecate

tutelary cabiri, daemon, genius, hershef, lar(es), numen, penates

winged amor, cupid, eros, mercury, nike

worship theolatry

DEJECT abase, blacken, chill, cloud, depress, discomfort, dispirit, downcast, flatten, humble, lessen, lower, overthrow

DEJECTA egesta

DEJECTED amort, atrabiliar, bad, blue, broody, crestfallen, damp, demiss, discouraged, doleful, down (cast), droopy, dumpish, gloomy, glum, hangdog,

humbled, low, melancholy, miserable, moody, mopy, muddy, pining, poor, repining, sad, somber, sombre, soul-sick, sunk, unhappy, wapped, wo(e)begone, wretched

DEJECTION bleakness, blues, damp, depression, despondency, dismals, dismay, dumps, gloom, lowness, megrims, melancholia, melancholy, oppression, sadness, sloth, vapors

DEJEUNER breakfast, colazione, collation, lunch

DEL nabla

DELAIAH *father* shemiah

DELATE accuse, denounce, report

DELATOR informer, plaintiff

DELAWARE *capital* dover

city acoma, claymont, elsmere, georgetown, lewes, milford, smyrna, wilmington

county kent, newcastle, sussex

indian lenape, len(n)i, munsee, tammany

nickname blue hen state, diamond state

peak centerville

port wilmington

river, city on bristol, easton

river tributary lehigh

state bird blue hen

state flower peach blossom

state tree holly

DELAY 3 lag, 4 bide, blin, bode, halt, hold, hone, leng, ling, lite, mora, sist, slow, slug, stay, stop, wait 5 abide, bline, block, check, dally, defer, demur, deter, laten, pause, sloth, stall, stent, stint, table, tarry, waive, waver 6 arrest, backen, belate, dawdle, detail, detain, dilute, dretch, essoin, extend, falter, hang up, hinder, holdup, impede, linger, loiter, remore, retard, shelve, taigle, tarrow, tempor, weaken 7 adjourn, confine, druttle, forslow, holdoff, red tape, reserve, respite, slacken, suspend 8 continue, hesitate, mark time, obstruct, postpone, reprieve, slowdown, slowness, standoff, stave off, stoppage 9 breathing, dalliance, de-

murrage, detention, tarriance, temporize, vacillate 10 cunctation, dillydally, filibuster, moratorium, pigeonhole, suspension 11 micawberism, prorogation, protraction 12 dilatoriness, postponement 13 procrastinate
indefinitely perendinate
legal dilator, induciae
seeking victory by fabian
undue laches
without sine mora
DELAYED belated, lagged, late, overdue, tardy
DELECTABLE agreeable, beautiful, dainty, delightful, desirous, enjoyable, exquisite, luscious, palatable, pleasing, rare, sapid, savory, tasty
DELEGATE agent, appoint, assign, attorney, authorize, commissar(y), commission(er), commit, delate, depute, deputize, deputy, dubash, emissary, empower, entrust, envoy, legate, messenger, name, nuncio, relegate, representative, send, transfer, vicar
group caucus, convention
DELEGATION delegacy, delia, mission
DELETE blank, blot, cancel, censor, deduct, delate, dele, destroy, edit, efface, eliminate, eradicate, erase, exclude, expunge, obliterate, omit, purge, slash, stonker, strike
DELETERIOUS bad, baneful, deletery, destructive, detrimental, harmful, hurtful, injurious, noxious, pernicious, prave, pravous, prejudiced, ruinous
DELETION apocope, deduction, excision, extinction
DELIA artemis
DELIAN *god* apollo
DELIBATE cull, dabble, pluck, sip, taste
DELIBERATE advise(d), aware, bethink, careful, cautious, chary, cogitate, confer, conscious, consider(ate), cool, discuss, express, intended, intentional, measured, meditate, muse, peel, plain, planned, ponder(ous), pore, prepense, propense, reason, reflect,

regard, rune, slow, studious, study, think, wary, willful, willing, voluntary
DELIBERATION advice, advisement, conference, consideration, contemplation, council, counsel, leisure, lucubration, meditation, musing, pondering, reflection, revolving, rumination, speculation, study, thought, visement, weighing
DELIBES *ballet* coppelia, naila
opera lakme
DELICACY acate, airiness, ambrosia, bon, cate, caviar(e), couche, culture, daintith, daintrel, dainty, decency, delicate, delice, diplomacy, discrimination, finesse, goody, kickshaw, knack, legerete, luxury, manna, nectar, nicety, roe, savory, sickliness, subtlety, sweetmeat, tact, taste, tenderness, tenuity, tidbit, titbit, weakness
lacking boorish, gross
DELICATE airy, araneous, brittle, cashie, charming, choice, consideration, dainty, delectable, delicious, delie, discriminate, dorty, elegant, elfin, epicine, ethereal, exact, exquisite, faint, feathery, filmy, fine(drawn), fine-grained, finical, fragile, frail, gauzy, gentle, gossamer, hothouse, kittle, lacy, lenient, light, meticulous, mild, minikin, minion, nesh, nice, petite, pindling, precarious, puling, queasy, rare, savory, sensitive, slender, slight, slimmer, smooth, soft, subtile, taffeta, taffety, tender, tewly, thin, tiffiny, touchy, twiggy, unlustie, weak, zart
DELICIOUS amusing, appetizing, apple, choice, dainty, delicate, delightful, friand, good, luscious, mellow, nectareous, palatable, rare, sapid, savory, tasty, toothsome
DELICT crime, offense, tort, violation, wrong
DELIGHT amuse, arride, banquet, becharm, bewitch, bliss, captivate, charm, content, delectate, delice, disport, divert, ecstasy, edana,

enchant, enjoy(ment), enrapture, enravish, enthrall, entrance, exult, fascinate, feast, fruition, gladden, glee, grace, gratify, gust(o), joy(ance), lite, mirth, oblectate, please, pleasure, rapture, ravish, regale (ment), rejoice, relish, revel, satisfy, savor, send, slay, smack, thrill, tickle, titillate, transport, treat, wow
expression hoho, whee, whoo, wow
in acclaim, admire, approve, love, relish, savor
of mankind titus
DELIGHTFUL adorable, appealing, beatific, bewitching, cheery, delectable, delicious, divine, dreamy, dulcet, elysian, empyrean, enjoyable, exquisite, fetching, heavenly, intriguing, jammy, jolly, leesome, lovely, savory, sooth, sublime, sweet, taking, winning, winsome
DELILAH courtesan, dalila, prostitute, wanton
betrayed sampson, samson
consort sampson, samson
home sorek
DELINEATE blazon, blueprint, chart, cipher, depict, describe, design, devise, diagram, draft, draw, etch, fence, figure, limn, line(ate), map, outline, paint, picture, plan, plot, portray, relate, represent, show, sketch, stell, survey, touch, trace, traverse, trick
DELINEATION design, draft, draught, picture, sketch, survey
DELINQUENCY default, failure, guilt, misconduct, misdeed, neglect, shortcoming, sin, vice
DELINQUENT criminal, derelict, kalang, remiss, sinner, welsher
DELIQUESCE decay, decompose, decrease, dissolve, fuse, liquefy, melt, ramify, thaw
DELIRIOUS aberrant, ardent, brainish, deleerit, delieret, deranged, deviant, deviate, drunk, feverish, fey, frantic, frenetic, frenzied, gyte, insane, intoxicated, light, lunatic, mad,

maniac(al), manic, off, raving, ree, wandering

DELIRIUM brain-fever, dementia, fever, frenzy, fury, hysteria, incoherence, insanity, lunacy, madness, mania, maze, paraphrenitis, phrenitis, ranting, raving, wandering

kind floccination, tilmus

producing delirifacient

tremens beezie-weezies, blue devils, blue johnies, depression, dipsomania, dt's, fantod, hallucinations, heebie-jeebies, horrors, jimjams, jimmies, jump, penomania, pink elephants, potomania, screaming meemies, snakes

DELIUS apollo

DELIVER assize, assoil, bail, bear, beken, betake, beteach, biteche, born, bring, code, commit, consign, deal, declaim, dictate, discharge, emit, exorcise, express, fetch, fork over, forward, free, give, grant, hand in, hand over, hit, lay, liberate, pass, ransom, reach, redd, redeem, release, relieve, rescue, resign, rid, save, say, succor, surrender, transfer, turn over, utter, vent, voice, yield

ball bowl, pitch

rhetorically declaim, orate

speech address

DELIVERANCE delivery, escape, rescue, riddance, salvation, saving, solution, voidance

DELIVERY accouchement, address, airdrop, bail (ment), birth, bowl, childbirth, enunciation, flier, fly(er), inflection, intonation, issue, labor, liberation, parturition, rescue, salvage, shipment, surrender, transfer, travail

mail tappall, tappaul

man drayman, saoshyant, soter

speaking diction

wagon fly

DELL dale, dean, den(e), dill, dingle, drab, gap, glade, glen, how, ravine, slack, slade, trull, vale, valley, wench

DELLING *daughter* dag

DELOS *birthplace of* apollo, artemis

king anius

mountain cynthia

DELPHI kastri, pytho

cliffs phaedriades

festival stepteria, theophania

league amphictytony

maxim know thyself

oracle's stool tripod

pert. pythian

priestess perialla, pythia, xenoclea

DELPHIC ambiguous, obscure, oracular

DELPHINIOS apollo, dolphins

DELPHINIUM blue-rocket, dauphin, dolphin, larkspur

DELPHUS *parent* melantho, poseidon

DELPHYNE monster, python

guarded zeus

DELTA mouth, plain, point, rocket, star, triangle

material silt

ray electron

DELUBRUM church, font, sanctuary, shrine

DELUDE baffle, bamboozle, banter, beguile, bejuggle, betray, bilk, bob, bubble, cajole, cheat, circumvent, cozen, deceive, diddle, doublecross, dupe, elude, enchant, evade, flam, fool, glaik, gull, hoax, hoodwink, illude, inveigle, jig, mislead, mock, oversile, snare, spoof, trick

DELUGE cataclysm, cataract, catastrophe, chloppeh, diluvy, downpour, flood, flow, immerse, inundate, overflow, plethora, rainstorm, saturate, sea, spate, stream, submerge, swamp, torrent

before antediluvium

pert. clysmian

DELUNDUNG linsang, viverrine, zinsang

DELUSION artifice, bubble, cheat, chicane(ry), chimera, deceit, deception, dream, dwale, einredenish, error, fake, fallacy, fancy, fantasm, fantasy, fraud, hallucination, humbug, illusion, imposture, maze, mirage, misbelief, moha, phantasm, phantom, ruse,

trick, vision, wanhope, wile, will-o-the-wisp

of grandeur megalomania

shared folie a deux

DELUXE elegant, fine, sumptuous

DELVE burrow, cave, den, dig, dint, dip, disinter, ditch, dredge, excavate, exhume, fathom, grub, indent, investigate, mine, pit, plumb, probe, search, spade, study, till

DEMAGOGUE agitator, cleon, instigator, jawsmith, ochlocrat, orator, rabblerouser, speaker, statist, tribune

DEMAND adjure, appeal, application, arraign, arrogate, ask, assessment, bid, bone, call(for), challenge, charge, cite, claim, clamor, cry, demand, desire, direct, draft, drain, dun, elicit, entreaty, exact(ion), exigence, extort(ion), fee, gavel, importune, imposition, inquire, insist, instance, levy, lien, mandate, nag, need, oblige, order, pester, petition, plea, prayer, press, question, rame, request, requirement, requisition, right, rush, sale, solicit, suit, summon, supplication, tax, ultimatum, urge

bill certificate

destructive pound of flesh

payment call, dun

recognition assert, claim

DEMANDING acute, ambitious, clamorous, crying, dictorial, exacting, exigent, hefty, imperative, imperious, importunate, insistent, instant, pressing, urgent

DEMANTOID emerald, olivine

DEMARCATE bound, circumscribe, delimit, demark, discriminate, separate

DEMARIUS *1/12th* assarion, assary

DEMAS *companion* paul

DE MAUPASSANT, GUY *novel* bel ami, boule de suif, pierre et jean, une vie

DEMEAN abase, acquit, bear(ing), behave, behavior, carry, comport, conduct, debase, degrade, deport, descend, exhibit, express, humble, humiliate,

lower, maltreat, mien, portance, quit
oneself condescend, fall
DEMEANOR action, ad-
dress, air, appearance, aspect, attitude, bearing, behavior, carriage, conduct,
deportment, front, garb,
habit, havior, manner,
mien, poise, portance, position
DEMENTED buggy, bug-
house, bugs, crazed, crazy,
daft, deranged, fatuous,
foolish, hysterical, idiotic,
insane, loony, luny, mad,
maniacal, manic, nutty,
screwy, skewed, tsedoo-
delt(eh), tsedrayt(eh)
DEMENTIA cataphrenia, fatuity, insanity
praecox catatonia, he-
bephrenia, paranoia,
paraphrenia, schizophasis,
schizothymia
DEMESNE district, domain,
estate, manor, place, realm,
region, sphere
lands barton
DEMETER anesidora, antaea, auxesia, brimo, carpophorus, ceres, chamyne,
chloe, erinys, hecate, lernaea, lusia, pelasgis, persephone, sitria, stiritis, ther-
masia, thesmophoros
amuser iambe
birthplace enna
brother zeus
consort zeus
daughter artemis, cora, despoina, kore, persephassa,
persephone, pherrephatta,
prosperpine
festival cerealia, eleusinia,
thesmophoria, triptolemus
flower narcissus, poppy
follower of socrates
headdress polos
mocker abas
parent cronus, ops, rhea, saturn, vesta
priest celeus, eumolpus
sacred pit megaron
shrine ahaktoron, argos
son plotos
stone agelasta
symbol corn-ears, poppy,
torch
DEMETRIUS nicator,
phalereus, poliorcetes, sotor
brother philip
captain alcimus, bithys
consort anticyra, chrysis,

cratesipolis, deidamia,
demo, eurydice, helena,
helepolis, hermia, lamia,
phila, ptolemais
daughter stratonice
enemy antiochus, balas, cassander, lysimacus, plis-
tarchus, ptolemy, seleueus
father-in-law aeacides, antipater
friend alcimus, bacchides,
cleaenetus, damocles, sosi-
genes
general apollonius, nicanor
parent antigonus, seleucus,
stratonice, tamora
physician erasistratus
rival pyrrhus
son-in-law antiochus,
seleucus
victim cassander, ptolemy
DEMIGOD adapa, deity, godling, hero, idol, mobocrat,
satyr, triton, yima
pert. satyric
sylvan satyr
DEMILUNE ravelin
DEMIMONDE See WAN-
TON.
DEMIREP adventuress, courtesan, prostitute, wanton
DEMISE bequeath, convey,
death, decease, end, hire,
lease, passing, transfer, will
DEMIT abdicate, humble,
lower, renounce, resign
DEMOCOON *father* priam
slayer odysseus, ulysses
DEMOCRACY commonalty,
populacy, public
chronicler de tocqueville
DEMOCRAT barnburner,
danite, democraw, hunker,
locofoco, popocrat, snap-
per, wagon
faction locofoco
movement popularism
DEMOCRITUS JUNIOR
robert burton
DEMOISELLE coolen, crane,
damselfish, dragonfly, fish,
fly, girl, heron, kaikara,
kulm, pintano, tiger-shark
DEMOLISH abate, annihilate, batter, blow(up),
break(down), destroy, devastate, dilapidate, disassemble, dismantle, elide, level,
maim, mangle, mutilate,
overthrow, rase, ravage,
raze, ruin(ate), sack, scrap,
shatter, slight, smash,
stramash, subvert, take

apart, tear apart, unbuild,
undo, wrack, wreck
DEMON 3 alp, bug, dev,
hag, imp, jin, nat, oku 4
aitu, akua, asag, atua, badb,
baka, bali, bhut, bodb,
boko, caco, deil, deva,
dook, dust, gyre, hyle, jann,
jinn, ketu, mara, ogre,
okee, puck, rahu, sobk,
surt, wade, wate 5 afrit,
algol, angra, anito, apepi,
asura, bhoot, daeva, deuce,
devil, dhoul, eblis, fiend,
genie, ghost, ghoul, harpy,
ifrit, jinni, jumby, lamia,
leshy, lesiy, naomi, otkon,
satan, satyr, shedu, surtr,
taipo, troll 6 abigor, afreet,
afrite, alukah, arioch,
belial, bilwis, curete, daedal, daemon, daimon, dai-
tya, dybbuk, efreet, genius,
gerard, goblin, jinnee, jumbie, mainyu, mammon, pil-
wiz, pisaca, spirit, thwise,
vritra 7 anhanga, apoplus,
asmoday, demonio, harpier,
hellion, incubus, lucifer,
monster, pisacha, shaitan,
sheitan, vampire, villain,
warlock 8 alichino, apol-
lyon, ashmadai, baalpeor,
babajaga, barghest, beel-
peor, canfield, curupira,
dybbukim, eudaemon, jin-
niyeh, obidicut, succubus 9
ashmodeus, belphegor, blue
devil, solitaire 10 cacodae-
mon, evil spirit 11 angra-
mainyu, blunderbore 15
flibbertigibbet
assembly of sabbat
cunning daedal, imp, ogre
drive off exorcize
evil shedu
fan solitaire
female ataen(t)sic, hag,
lamia, pisachi, succubus,
witch
friendly billy-blind
gate kuei-men-kuan
group dasyus
king ashmodai, asmodeus
kur asag
medieval abigor
orgy sabbat
patience klondike, solitaire
pert. demoniacal
petty imp
possessed by energumen
prince asmodeus, beelzebub,
pasupati, rudra, siva
puny imp

rum liquor
storm ham, heyd
vanity asmodeus
vengeance arioch
weather ham, heyd
woodland lesh(e)y, lesiy
worship idolatry, sorcery

DEMONASSA *husband*
theresander
parent amphiaraus, eriphyle
son tisamenus

DEMONIAC crazy, cruel,
devilish, diabolic, fiendish,
frantic, hellish, infernal, lunatic, maniac, satanic

DEMONSTRATE argue,
bewray, bring out, check,
cite, clear, convince, debate,
disclose, display, establish,
evidence, evince, exhibit,
flaunt, instance, manifest,
parade, portray, prove, reveal, show, speak, symbolize, test, try, verify

DEMONSTRATION agita-
tion, apodixis, ballyhoo,
conclusiveness, darshana,
decisiveness, determination,
display, establishment, exhibition, experiment, explanation, maneuver, manifest,
proof, representation, riot,
scene, settlement, show,
sign, test, trial
absolute apodixis
showy splurge

DEMONSTRATIVE affec-
tionate, apodict(al), categorical, convincing, crucial,
deictic, effusive, evincive,
explanatory, explicit, fiery,
fong, gushing, illustrative,
irresistible, melodramatic,
probative, tender, that,
these, this, those, vehement

DEMOPHOON *beloved*
phyllis
nurse demeter
parent celeus, metanira,
phaedra, theseus

DEMORALIZE abash, confuse, corrupt, crush, dash,
deprave, disconcert, dis-
countenance, embarrass,
frighten, nonplus, over-
come, pervert, prostrate,
shake, undo, unnerve,
unstring, weaken

DEMOS citizens, deme, district, people, populace

DEMOSTHENES sword-
maker
affliction stammer
biographer demetrius,

eratosthenes, hermippus,
pappus, phylarchus, theo-
pompus
briber harpalas
cousin demon
cure pebbles
disciple cineas
enemy aeschines, androtion,
aristocrates, timocrates, timotheus, philip
father alcisthenes
follower bryan, orator
friend demades
guardian aphobus
nickname argas, batalus,
rhopoperperethras
oration philippic
rival aeschines
teacher alcidamas, ctesibius,
isaeus, isocrates, plato, satyrus

DEMOSTHENIC eloquent,
silver-tongued, tullian, well-
spoken

DEMOTE abase, break,
bump, bust, debase, de-
grade, disrate, downgrade,
lower, reduce, unrank

DEMOTIC enchorial, popular

DEMPSEY, JACK manassa-
mauler

DEMULCENT balm, borage,
emollient, emulsion,
ginseng, manna, palliative,
salve, sedative, softening,
soothing

DEMUR balk, boggle, coy,
demeore, disapprove, dis-
sent, doubt, falter, gib, hesitate, interpose, jib, object,
oppose, pause, protest,
qualm, remonstrate, resist,
scruple, shy, stay, stick(le),
stop, strain, suspense,
waver

DEMURE coy, decorous,
grave, mim, modest, nice,
prenzie, prim(sie), proper,
prudish, sedate, serious,
shy, skittish, sober, solemn,
spake, staid, suant, suent

DEN atelier, bield, burrow,
cabin, cave(a), cavern,
cove(rt), dean, dell, dive,
glen, grotto, haunt, hideaway, hollow, hotbed, kennel, lair, library, lodge,
mew, nest, ravine, resort,
retreat, room, sanctum,
shroud, slade, snuggery,
spelunk, studio, study,
workroom
animal lair, wash

foul spital
gambling deadfall
of iniquity domdaniel
of thieves alsatia, whitefriars
of vice brothel

DENARIUS denar, dinder,
penny

DENARY decimal, tenfold

DENDRITES dionysus

DENDROICA canary,
warbler

DENDROID arboreal, arborescent, treelike

DENDROLAGUS boongary,
kangaroo

DENIAL abnegation, defense, dementi, denay, disproof, nay(say), negation,
rebuff, refusal, refutation,
renege, repulse, temper-
ance, traverse
of authority anarchy

DENIER agnostic, coin, denarius, dinero, dinheiro,
filament, negant, negator
half mail(le)

DENIGRATE befoul, belittle, blacken, crucify, defame, slander, slur, smear,
sully, vilify

DENIMS blue jeans, dungarees, levis, pants

DENIZEN cit(izen), domesticate, inhabitant, native,
resident
of hell hellion

DENJONG sikkim

DENMARK *anatomist* steno
ancient name thule
animal aurochs
archæologist thomsen
artist bloch
astronomer brahe, hansen,
huygens
biochemist dam
borough borg
capital copenhagen
cheese blue, mycella, ost,
samso, tybo
chief jarl, yarl
city a(a)lborg, a(a)rhus,
ballerup, copenhagen, dor-
sor, dragor, elsinore, gen-
tofte, glostrup, hals, helsingor, horsens, hov, koge,
kolding, morsens, nibe,
nyberg, odense, randers,
roskilde, skagen, soro,
struer, viborg
coin frederik, fyrk, krone,
one, rigsdaler, skilling
comb. dano
composer buxtehude, nielson, weyse

council rigsraad
county a(a)benraa, aalborg, a(a)rhus, amt, bornholm, maribo, odense, randers, ribe, soto, tonder, velje, viborg
dance sextur
dancer bruhn
dependency faroes
division alt, amt, ribe
downs klitten
drink aquavit, glogg
duchy schleswig(-holstein)
elf erlking
embroidery hedebo
ensign raven
entomologist fabricius
explorer bering, rasmussen, vitus
fine lashlight, lashlite
fiord ise, isse
flag dan(n)ebrog
freeholder junster
goblin nis(se)
goddess merthus
grouse rype
guard housecarl
hero ogier, scyld
historian brandes
inlet fiord, fjord, horsens, ise, lim, logstor, mariager, nissum, odense, velje
island aaro, aero, als, amager, baago, bornholm, falster, fano, faroe, fohr, funen, fyn, laaland, laeso, mo(e)n, mors, romo, rum, samso, sando, seeland, sejero, sudero, zealand
king canute, christian, cnut, ethelred, frederick, frothi, knut, olaf, waldemar
king, first gorm
knighthood order dannebrog
language odan
legislature folketing, landsting, rigsraad, risdag
linguist verner
measure achtel, album, alen, anker, ell, favn, fjerding, fod, kande, korntonmde, landmil, last, linje, mil, ortonde, ottingkar, paegl, pot, rode, sk(i)eppe, tomme, viertel
musical instrument lure
oil seed rape
organist buxtehude
pathologist fibiger
peninsula jutland
philosopher kierkegaard
physician finsen
physicist bohr, oersted
physiologist krogh

politician bajer
port a(a)lborg, a(a)rhus, helsingor, korsor, odense, randers
possession baroe, greenland, iceland, santa cruz, st john, st thomas
prince hamlet, havelok, ogier
queen gertrude
river asa, gelsaa, guden(aa), holm, lilleaa, lonborg, omme, skive, stor, susaa, varde, vorgod
ruler aven, canute, klak, knut, olaf, sven, sweyn
sand ridge scaw, skagen, skagi
scientist bohr
sculptor thorvaldsen
settlers ostmen
ship koff
speech sound stod
strait kattegat, skagerrak
theologian kierkegaard
tip of skagen, skaw
trading post thule
tribe angles, cimbri, danes, jutes, teutons
tribunal rigsrad, rigsret
trumpet lure
weight bismerpund, carat, centner, eser, kvint, last, lisp(o)und, lod, ort, pound, pund, quint(in), skibslast, skipp(o)und, to(e)nde, unze, vog
writer anderson, bajer, dinesen, gjellerup, jacobsen, jensen, nexo, pontoppidan
DENNET carriage, gig
DENOMINATE call, christen, denote, designate, due, entitle, indicate, name, style, term, title
DENOMINATION appellation, category, church, class, communion, creed, cult, designation, faith, kind, name, party, persuasion, religion, school, sect, society, style, title
religious baptist, congregational, episcopalian, lutheran, methodist, presbyterian, unitarian
DENOMINATIONAL sectarian
DENOTE attest, betoken, describe, designate, evidence, express, hint, imply, import, indicate, intend, mean, name, notify, prove, show, signify, specify, suggest, symbolize

DENOUEMENT anagnorisis, catastrophe, climax, conclusion, development, discovery, end, eventuality, issue, moment of truth, outcome, solution, upshot
DENOUNCE accuse, arraign, ascry, assail, ban, baste, blame, blast, censure, charge, condemn, criticize, de(s)cry, detest, disparage, execrate, incriminate, indict, manace, rebuke, reprehend, reprobate, revile, scathe, taunt, threaten, upbraid, vituperate, wray
DE NOVO afresh, again, anew, newly, over (and over), repeatedly
DENSE blind, blockheaded, close, compact(ed), compressed, concentrated, condensed, consolidated, crass, crowded, dewy, dull, dumb, dunch, firm, foggy, gross, heavy, impenetrable, impermeable, imporous, incompressible, intense, luxuriant, massed, massive, murky, obtuse, opaque, packed, piled, populous, rank, serried, silly, solid, spissatus, spissy, stiff, stolid, stupid, substantial, teeming, theet, thick, thight, tight, woofy
comb. dasy, pycno
DENT bash, batter, blow, burt, clour, delve, depress(ion), dimple, dinge, dingle, dint, doke, dunkle, dunt(le), effect, faze, hit, hollow, impression, influence, nick, notch, pit, print, projection, score, stove, tooth
DENTAL odontic, oral, point, tooth
cement guttapercha
construction bridge(work), plate
DENTATE jagged, serrate, toothed
DENTENE ivoire
DENTICULATE serrate(d), toothed
DENTIST jawsmith, orthodontist, radiodontist, stomatologist, toothdoctor, toothdrawer
appliance dam, mirror
child's pedodontist
drill bur(r), cavitron
hand protector thimble
specialty aerodontia, exodon-

tia, orthodontia, orthodontics, periodontia
tool bur(r), cleoid, drill, forceps, scaler

DENUDE bare, despoil, dismantle, disrobe, divest, expose, nudate, shave, strip, unrobe

DENUNCIATION anathema, censure, charge, comminative, condemnation, curse, diatribe, malediction, threat, thunder

DENVER mile-high city

DENY abjure, abnegate, abstain, begrudge, belie, blink, confute, contest, contradict, contravene, controvert, debar, denegate, disallow, disavow, disclaim, disown, disprove, forsake, forswear, gainsay, grudge, impugn, nait, naysay, negate, negative, nego, nick, nite, nitte, oppose, prohibit, protest, rebut, recant, refuse, refute, reject, renay, renege, renounce, repel, repudiate, repulse, sublate, traverse, warn, werene, withhold, withsay
access bar, close

DEODAR cedar, cedrus, tree

DEODORANT acerdol, antibromic, antiforman, bleach, borax, chlorine, chlorophyll, empasm, fumigant, fumigator, lime, ventilator

DEPART 3 cut, die, fly, guy, mog, nip, put, run, wag 4 blow, buzz, dash, dust, exit, flee, flit, hike, hook, move, pack, part, pike, quit, sail, scat, shed, skip, tear, trot, vade, veer, void, walk, wend, wite 5 break, elope, leave, leg it, march, mosey, sally, scoot, scram, sever, slope, split, start, truss, whizz 6 avaunt, begone, decamp, decede, demise, differ, egress, escape, get off, hasten, perish, remove, retire, sashay, sunder, swerve, vamose, vanish, wander 7 abandon, abscond, buzz off, decease, deviate, digress, discede, flounce, forsake, get away, make off, migrate, pull out, retreat, ring out, scaddle, scamper, set sail, shove on, skiddoo, skin out, take off,

up and go, vamoose, whip off 8 check out, emigrate, evacuate, farewell, fling off, hightail, light out, punch out, runalong, separate, weigh out, withdraw 9 cut and run, disappear, take leave 10 make tracks, relinquish, skelter off 11 toddle along
from abandon, break camp, deviate, differ, scram
from harbor embark, set sail, sortie
rapidly breeze, bugger off, bug out, lammas, scram, skive, vamoose
secretly abscond
suddenly decamp, flee, haste

DEPARTED bygone, dead, deceased, defunct, gone, inanimate, late, left, lifeless, napoo, off, past, went

DEPARTMENT agency, area, branch, bureau, category, chancery, commune, district, division, hanaper, intendance, jurisdiction, nomarchy, okroog, okrug, parish, part, portion, province, realm, region, section, sphere, station
part arrondissement
store au bon marche, market

DEPARTURE abandonment, apostasy, bunk, congee, death, decampment, decrease, easting, egress, evacuation, exit, exode, exodus, farewell, flight, going, hegira, leave, leaving, offgoing, outgang, outgo, parting, passing, remotion, removal, retirement, retreat, set off, sortie, trundle, wagang, waygate, waying, withdrawal
comb. abs
emergency bailout
secret guy, slip
speech valedictory

DEPEND bank, confide, count, hang, hinge, incline, lean, lop, reckon, rely, rest on, rest with, revolve on, ride, stand on, suspend, trust, turn

DEPENDABLE calculable, certain, good, reliable, safe, secure, siccar, sicker, siker, silvendy, solid, sound, stable, sta(u)nch, steady, sure(fire), there, tried,

trustworthy, trusty, unfailing

DEPENDENCE adjunct, anaclisis, annex, appendage, bearing, belief, bondage, cliency, confidence, connection, decubitus, ell, faith, leaning, reliance, trust, wing

DEPENDENCY a(p)anage, colony, dominion, mandate, possession, protectorate, province, taluk

DEPENDENT accidental, adjective, aleatory, beggar, child, client, clinging, collateral, conditioned, contingent, enclitic, feodary, feudary, follower, hangby, hanger-on, liable, minion, mutual, open, pendent, pending, pensile, pensioner, proneur, protegee, reciprocal, relative, retainer, satellite, secondary, servant, servile, sponge(r), subject, succursal, tributary, vassal, ward
grammatically enclitic
on illative
on contingency aleatory

DEPICT characterize, delineate, depaint, describe, draw, emblazon, enact, etch, hue, image, impaint, limn, outline, paint, portray, represent, resemble, shadow, sketch, tell, undo

DEPILATE husk, peel, pluck, shave, strip

DEPILATION hairlessness, psilosis

DEPILATORY epilator, pelador, psilatro, psilothrum, rusma

DEPLETE bankrupt, consume, decrease, diminish, drain, empty, evacuate, exhaust, impoverish, lessen, punish, reduce, sap, unload, use up, waste, weaken

DEPLETED bankrupt, debilitated, spent, wasted

DEPLORABLE bad, calamitous, disgraceful, distressing, dolorous, execrable, grievous, lamentable, pitiable, regrettable, sad, shameful, terrible, tragic, unfortunate, wailsome, wo(e)ful, wretched

DEPLORE bemoan, bewail, complain, cry, disapprove, grieve, lament, moan, mourn, regret, rue, sigh, sorrow, wail, weep

DEPLOY display, spread, unfold

DEPONE affirm, asservate, attest, depose, swear, testify

DEPONENT affiant, examinate, witness

DEPORT acquit, ban(ish), bearing, behave, carry, cast out, comport, conduct, demean, dismiss, eject, evict, exile, expatriate, expel, export, forbear, punish, relegate, transport, withhold

DEPORTMENT action, address, air, bearing, behavior, breeding, carriage, comport, conduct, demeanor, development, education, geste, gesture, havance, improvement, manner(s), mien, training

DEPOSE abase, affirm, assert, asseverate, assure, attest, aver, avouch, avow, banish, break, bust, cashier, cut off, declare, degrade, discrown, displace, divest, guarantee, liquidate, oust, overthrow, prive, purge, reduce, remove, retire, secularize, suspend, swear, testify, unfrock, unsaddle, unseat, vouch, vow, warrant

DEPOSIT adhi, alluvia, alluvion, alluvium, ashfall, bank, bed, bestow, bloom, bury, cache, caliche, cast, caution(money), chest, collateral, consign, crud, crust, culm, debris, delta, depose, depot, detritus, diluvium, dregs, drift, drop, dump, flysch, forfeit, fur, garner, geest, guhr, hoard, hock, inhume, lay down, lees, lode, lodge, loess, margin, marl, mine, moraine, ooze, pawn, place, placer, plant, pledge, plop, plunk down, put down, remainder, repose, rest, sandbank, save, scoria, scurf, secrete, security, set, silt, sinter, slap down, stake, store, sud, tartar, tophus, tosca, vein

alluvial apron, delta, geest
archaeological lens(e)
bank cash
black soot, stupp
black tissue melanosis
box meter, pyx

calcareous stalactite, stalagmite
clay marl
debris breccia
earthy alluvium, asar, delta, eskar, esker, geest, gobi, guhr, lode, loess, manto, marl, moraine, ore, placer, sand, silt, sludge, trona
geological blanket, bone breccia, horizon
geyser sinter
gravel apron, lead
in earth inhume, inter
loamy loess
muddy sludge, slumgullion
ore bank, flat, lode, vein, voog, vug(g), vugh
roric dew
sedimentary silt
shoal-water culm
skeletal coral
tarry gum
unstratified loess
welding tack

DEPOSITION affidavit, allegation, burial, certificate, declaration, deposure, evidence, opinion, placement, remainder, sediment, silting, statement, testimony

DEPOSITORY attic, bank, cache, depot, drop, ossarium, ossuary, safe, sentine, storehouse, treasurer, trustee, vault

DEPOT arsenal, aurang, aurung, base, cache, depository, fort, gare, magazine, repository, station, stop, storehouse, terminal, terminus

DEPRAVE beshrew, corrupt, damage, debase, debauch, defile, infect, malign, pervert, pollute, revile, seduce, spoil, taint, vitiate

DEPRAVED abandoned, bad, base, bestial, cankered, corrupt, debased, degenerate, dissolute, evil, fast, immoral, perverted, prave, pravous, reprobate, rotten, shameless, shrewd, ugly, vicious, vile, wicked

DEPRAVITY abyss, decadence, degeneration, disgrace, immorality, infamy, iniquity, license, perversion, pravity, vice, villainy, vitosity

DEPRECATE beseech, bewail, condemn, deplore, disapprove, disparage, invoke,

lament, pray, protest, regret, vilipend

DEPRECIATE asperse, base, beat down, belittle, break, cheapen, cry down, cut, decline, decrease, decry, deflate, degrade, depress, derogate, devaluate, discount, disparage, disprize, disvalue, down-talk, drop, fall, impair, lessen, lower, mark down, minimize, minish, pare, pejorate, reduce, sag, shave, shrink, slander, slash, slump, smallen, trim, underrate, undervalue, vilipend

DEPRECIATION agio, decrease, decrial, discount, fall, pejoration, shrinkage

DEPREDATE loot, pillage, plunder, prey, raze, spoil, thieve

DEPREDATOR pillager, robber, spoiler, thief

DEPRESS abase, abate, agonize, ail, appall, bate, beat down, bow, browbeat, cast down, cheapen, chill, couch, cow, crush, damp(en), dash, debase, deboss, decline, decrease, deject, dent, detrude, devalue, diminish, dip, discourage, dishearten, dispirit, drop, enfeeble, fag, fall, fatigue, flatten, humble, hyp, indent, jade, let down, lower, notch, prostrate, reduce, sadden, sicken, sink, slump, sump, trouble, tucker, weaken, weary, weigh

DEPRESSANT anhaline, hellebore, hordenine, mescaline, pellotine, sedative

DEPRESSED areola(te), blue, broody, damp, dejected, dire, dished, dismal, downcast, downsome, dull, exanimous, flat, gloomy, hipped, lonely, low, oblate, prostrate, sad, sunk, triste, wroth

DEPRESSING black, bleak, chill, drear(y), dusky, melancholy, muzzy, ourie, sad, somber, sombre, triste

DEPRESSION alveola, basin, blue devils, blues, bothrium, bowl, bust, caecum, cafard, cavity, cell, chagrin, channel, col, concave, cowal, cupule, debase-

ment, dent, despair, detrusion, diminution, dimple, dip, discouragement, doldrums, dumps, ennui, ephippium, fossa, fossette, fovea, foveola, funk, furrow, gloom, groove, gully, gutter, hard times, hollow, hypochondria, jawfall, jimmies, low spirits, melancholia, melancholy, nadir, notch, oppression, peritheceum, pit, pore, ravine, recession, reduction, salar, saucer, sink hole, sinking, slough, slump, socket, tedium, trough, vapors, variole
articular glene
between hills swire
in ground charco, dalk, delk, gully, swag, swale, well
oblong circus
small dent, dimple, follicle, lacuna
subject to moody
DEPRIVATION amotion, bereavement, cost, curtailment, deprival, divestment, loss, mayhem, misture, ousting, privation, removal, taking
DEPRIVE abridge, amerce, bankrupt, bate, bereave, bleed, cashier, curtail, cut off, debar, dement, denude, deny, depose, desolate, despoil, devest, disentitle, dispossess, divest, dock, empty, exhaust, exute, for(e)bar, geld, gudgeon, mulct, relieve of, rob, seize, strip, take, wrong
by trickery mulct, nose
fraudently cheat, gudgeon
of individuality fordize
of strength enervate, exhaust
DEPRIVED amerced, bankrupt, bereft, desolate, reft, sans, shorn, without
DEPTH abysm, abyss, acumen, deep, drop, expanse, extent, fathom, ga(u)ge, gulf, hole, holl, intensity, measure, middle, moho, ocean, pit, profoundness, profundity, sagacity, sea, sidth, sounding, strength
charge ash can, mine, projectile
comb. batho, bathy
finder bathometer, fathomer, fathometer, lead, plumb (bob) (line)

interview psychoanalysis
measure sound(ing)
moral abyss
of water draft, draught
pert. bathic
record fathogram
DEPTHLESS shallow, small
DEPUTATION legation, mission
DEPUTE accredit, allot, appoint, assign, authorize, commission, delegate, devote, send
DEPUTY advocate, agent, aide, alter ego, alternate, amphyctyon, angelo, attorney, bailiff, caimacam, champion, commis, curate, delegate, dummy, emissary, envoy, escalus, exarch, exponent, factor, go-between, kehaya, lawyer, legate, lieutenant, locum-tenens, messenger, middleman, minion, nabob, negotiator, proxy, pylagore, qamaqam, representative, secondary, stand-in, substitute, surrogate, teniente, vicar
DERACINATE eradicate, extract, isolate, uproot
DERANGE afflict, confuse, craze, deraign, disease, dislocate, disorder, disorganize, displace, distrait, disturb, madden, perturb, ruffle, turn, unsettle, unwit, upset
DERANGED buggy, bughouse, crazed, crazy, frantic, furious, gyte, insane
DERANGEMENT aberration, alienation, deliration, delirium, disorder, frenzy, insanity, lunacy, madness, mania, phrensy, rummage
DERBY billycock, bowler, boxer, cad(d)y, contest, dicer, hat, kelly, pot, race, shire
site churchill downs, epsom
DERELICT abandoned, astray, castaway, castoff, deserted, dogie, faithless, flotsam, forsaken, foundling, jetsam, jettison, lapse, lax, neglectful, negligent, orphan, outcast, slack, stray, tramp, unfaithful, waif, wastrel, wreck, wretch
DERELICTION abandonment, failure, infidelity, neglect, nonfeasance, reliction, sin

DERIDE banter, boo, catcall, chaff, drape, expose, fleer, flout, geck, gibe, gird, guy, hoot, illude, irride, jape, jeer, jibe, kid, knack, lampoon, laugh at, lout, lowbell, make fun of, mock, rage, rally, razz, ridicule, scoff, scorn, scout, sneer, taunt, tease, twit
DE RIGUEUR conventional, essential, imperative, necessary, required
DERISION asteism, contempt, geck, hoker, irrision, jeer, mockery, ridicule, scorn, sport
DERISIVE insolent, irrisory, jeering, jeery, mocking, mowing, ridiculous, sardonic, satanic, scoffing, scornful, sneering, snide, taunting, twitting
DERIVATION attribution, descent, etymology, family, origin, pedigree, source
DERIVE acquire, arise, borrow, bring, conclude, deduce, descend, desume, draw, educe, elicit, emanate, evolve, extract, flow, gather, get, infer, issue, obtain, originate, proceed, receive, rise, spring, stem, take, trace, traduce
DERMA corium, dermis, integument, intestine, kishke, layer, skin
DERMATITIS cascado, cutitis, itch
DERN conceal(ed), darkness, determined, dire, dour, durn, earnest, hidden, hide, secrecy, secret, somber, underhand
DERNIER darrein, final, last, ultimate
cri fashion, latest, novelty
ressort expedient, recourse
DEROGATE annul, belittle, decry, denigrate, deteriorate, detract, diminish, disparage, fall, lessen, minimize, reduce, repeal, slander, withdraw
DEROGATORY bad, calumnious, censorious, defamatory, deprecatory, depreciative, detractive, disparaging, libelous, pejorative, scandalous, scurrile, scurrilous, slanderous, vilifying
DERRICK crane, davit,

erecter, gallows, hoist, jenny, jib, lever, lift, rig, spar, steeve, stiffleg, tackle, tower
hand jenny-winch
part boom, gin, leg
small jinnywink

DERRIERE behind, bottom, duff, fanny, rear end, seat, tochis, tot, tuchis

DERRING-DO audacity, geste

DERRY ballad, song

DERVISH agib, ascetic, calender, darwesh, fakeer, fakir, hermit, mendicant, monk, sadite, santon, whirler, yogi
arabian nights agib
cap taj
meeting dhikr
mendicant calender
moslem calender, sadite
robe khirka(h)
wandering agib

DESCANT air, amplify, article, comment, copula, counterpoint, dilate, discourse, enlarge, expatiate, melody, note, observation, prelude, quinible, remark, review, sing, song, soprano, tune, warble
in fifths auinible

DESCARTES *pert.* cartesian
principle cogito ergo sum

DESCEND alight, avale, cascade, cataract, chute, coast, come down, delapse, derive, deteriorate, devall, devaul, devolve, dip, dismount, dive, drop, fall, go down, gravitate, land, parachute, pitch, plummet, plunge, settle, shed, sink, slide, squat, stoop, subside, swampt, swoop, sye, topple, tumble

DESCENDANT branch, breed, child, cion, daughter, epigonus, gens, ghuz(z), grandchild, heir, issue, offspring, posterity, progeny, scion, seed, slip, son(ny), strain
from same ancestor agnate, agnatic, consanguineous, enate, enatic
insignificant tag

DESCENT abseil, ancestry, assault, attack, avatar, birth, bloodline, breeding, canch, chute, cleuch, cleugh, comedown, declension, declination, decline,

declivity, defluxion, degression, devolution, dip, dive, downfall, drop(ping), escarp, fall(ing), family, glissade, gravitation, header, hill, humiliation, incline, issue, jet, jump, kindred, line(age), lurch, origin, parage, pedigree, pitch, plummet, plunge, posterity, progeny, rappel, reverse, scarp, schuss, set, shute, slide, slip, slope, strain, succession, swoop, tailspin, tumble
familiar havage
from one pair monogenism
lines phyla
overwhelming avalanche
parachute bailout, jump
parental filiation, havage
plunging spin

DESCRIBE analyse, blaze, blazon, caption, characterize, define, delineate, denote, depencil, depict, draw, explain, express, form, image, limn, name, narrate, outline, paint, parse, picture, point, portray, rehearse, relate, report, represent, sketch, state, storify, style, titule, trace, write, yarn
briefly kodak
grammatically parse

DESCRIPTION account, appellation, character(ization), class, definition, delineation, depiction, discourse, explanation, explication, ilk, image(ry), kind, landskip, monograph, name, nature, painting, pastel, photograph, picture, portrait, portrayal, recital, report, representation, sketch, sort, species, treatise, type, version, vignette, word picture
brief caption, legend
formal exphrasis
personal prosopography
rustic idyll

DESCRIPTIVE depictive, detailed, expositive, expressive, life-like, realistic, specific, suggestive, true to life

DESCRY ascry, behold, betray, denounce, detect, discern, discover, display, espy, ken, note, notice, observe, perceive, recognize,

remark, reveal, see, sight, spot, survey, view

DESDEMONA *father* brabantio
husband othello
slayer othello
traducer iago

DESECRATE abuse, contaminate, defile, dishallow, misuse, pervert, pollute, profane, temerate, unhallow, violate

DESERT abandon, abscond, apostate, areg, arid, badlands, barren, beach, betray, bold, bolt, chicken, clear out, deceive, defect, demerit, depart, desolate, due, empty, erg, excellence, expose, forsake, go back on, guerdon, hornada, leave, let down, lurch, maroon, meed, merit, plain(s), punishment, quit, rat, reg, renege, renounce, reward, run out on, sand, scram, secede, sell out, sert, solitary, solitude, talion, tih, tundra, unproductive, waste(land), western, wastine, wild, wilderness
beast burro, camel, coyote
candle ocotillo, plant
driver cameleer, camelteer
dweller arab, bedouin, eremite, nomad, sourdough
famous annafud, arabian, aralkarkum, arunta, atacama, black rock, borrego, colorado, dahama, dahna, dashtilut, death valley, elhamad, gibson, kalahari, karakum, libyn, mohave, mojave, nefud, painted, qarqqum, sahara, sechura, shamo, thar
fish killfish, pupfish
flower chuperosa, creosote, encilla, foxtail, larrea, pincushion, sand verbena
fox rommel
hallucination mirage
herb bluebell, phacelia
-inhabiting eremophilous
lemon kumquat
-like arid, dry, eremic, sere
plant afernan, agave, alhagi, black bush, brittle bush, cactus, catclaw, century plant, encelia, eremophyte, euphorbia, incienso, joshua tree, manzanita, mesquite, ocotillo, r(e)etem, saltbush,

smoke tree, sotol, tarbush, yucca
rat miner, prospector
region eremian, erg, reg
salt pan playa
sandy erg, hornada, reg
science eremology
ship of camel
train caravan
valley bolson
watering spot oasis
wind chamsin, khamsin, simoom, simoon, sirocco
DESERTED abandoned, cast off, dead, desolate, empty, forlorn, forsaken, homeless, left, lonely, lorn, marooned, solitary, stranded, vacant, wysty
DESERTER apostate, bolter, bugout, bushwhack, fugitive, rate, recreant, renegade, transfuge, turncoat, turntail
masasitte adnah, ednas
DESERTION apostasy, betrayal, bolt, bugout, defection, disloyalty, perfidy, rattery, recreancy, treachery
DESERVE asserve, benefit, earn, meed, merit, promerit, rate, win
DESERVED condign, due, just, merited, worthy
DESICCATE arid, bake, dehydrate, drain, dry, parch, preserve, sear, sere
DESICCATION xeransis
DESIGN aim, allot, arabesque, art(ifice), aspire, blueprint, calculate, cartoon, cast, compose, composition, contrivance, contrive, create, decor, destine, device, diagram, doodle, draft, draught, drawing, end, engineer, ettle, figure, form, function, goal, idea, insigne, intend, intent(ion), invent, layout, model, monogram, motif, object(ive), obtent, pattern, picture, plan, plat, project, propose, purport, purpose, scheme, shape, sketch, system
burned on wood pyrograph, pyrogravure
by intentionally, purposely
cup-shaped husk
decorative vignette
emblematic impress, symbol
inlaid niello
of scattered objects seme
perforated pounce, stencil

repeated motif
school bauhaus
scribbler doodlebug
scroll-like cartouch(e)
shaded ombre
skin tattoo
striped stria, strie
structural architechtonic
tesselated mosaic
DESIGNATE allot, allude to, anoint, appoint, assign, blaze, call, choose, denominate, denote, depute, deputize, earmark, elect, entitle, finger, hail, identify, indicate, intend, mark, mean, name, nominate, pick, point out, refer to, select, settle, show, signify, single out, specify, stipulate, style, surname, tick off, title
DESIGNATION address, appellation, appellative, appointment, caption, homonym, identification, kind, label, name, nomenclature, style, tag, title
DESIGNER architect, author, engineer, organizer, planner, plotter, schemer
DESIGNING artful, cunning, jesuitic, planning, plotting, scheming
DESIPIENCE conceit, folly, trifling
DESIRE 3 aim, ask, beg, eye, yen 4 ache, burn, care, eros, goal, hope, idol, itch, kama, like, long, love, lust, mind, need, pant, pine, urge, want, will, wish, zeal 5 ardor, brame, covet, crave, fancy, go for, greed, groan, heart, mania, nisus, quest, yearn, yisse 6 affect, appete, aspire, beguin, behest, choose, cry for, demand, hanker, hunger, libido, orexis, pothos, psyche, pursue, take to, target, thirst, utinam, yammer 7 anxiety, avarice, avidity, craving, darling, entreat, erotism, fantasy, himeros, impulse, inkling, longing, oestrus, passion, request, wanting 8 ambition, appetite, cathexis, coveting, cupidity, gluttony, pleasure 9 appetence, appetency, cacoethes, clamor for, eagerness, nostalgia, objective, prurience 10 aphrodisia, aspiration 11 infatuation

12 desideration 13 concupiscence
abnormal onomania
ardent thirst
basis appet
comb. orexia
concentration cathexis
god himeros
inborn conatus
irritating itch
lack of inappetence
personified himeros, pothos
pert. appetent, orectic
removal catharsis, sublimation, suppression
strong cupidity, slavering
uncontrollable cacoethes
DESIROUS agog, ambitious, anticipating, anxious, appetent, aspirant, astir, avid, eager, envious, fain, frack, freck, gluttonous, greedy, itchy, jealous, lickerish, lief, lustful, lusty, optative, panting, vain, vigilant, willing, wishful, wistful, zealous
DESIST abandon, abstain, avoid, cease, discontinue, disuse, don't, ease, forbear, forfeit, halt, lin, pause, quit, refrain, relinquish, remit, resign, sist, spare, stop, subsist, surcease, swick, swike, whoa, wonde, yield
DESK ambo, board, bureau, caisse, clergy, console, desse, escritoire, kneehole, lectern, pluteus, pulpit, rolltop, scob, scribanne, secretaire, secretary, standish, table, vargueno
kneeling prie-dieu
one-keyed monocleid(e)
small davenport
DESMA clon(e), spicule
DESMANTHUS acuan, herb, scrub
DESMID closterium
DESMODIUM barajillo, beggartick, beggarweed, (tick) trefoil
DESOLATE abandoned, alone, annihilate, barren, cheerless, cimmerian, defenseless, dejected, deprived, deserte(d), despairing, destroy, devastate(d), disconsolate, drear(y), empty, forlorn, forsaken, friendless, gaunt, gloomy, godforsaken, goustie, gousty, grieve, gubat, heart-

sick, heartsore, helpless, homeless, inconsolable, kithless, lacking, lone(ly), lonesome, lorn, miserable, remote, sack, sad, solitary, soulsick, start, tragic, unhappy, unked, unkie, unkit, waste, wasty, wild, wilsome, wo(e)begone, wretched, wysty

DESOLATION anguish, desert, despair, disconsolation, forlornness, gloom, grief, havoc, inconsolability, misery, ravage, ruin, sadness, vacancy, waste(land), woe
area desert, wasteland

DESPAIR dejection, depression, desolation, desperation, despond(ency), disappointment, disillusion(ment), falter, forlornness, futility, gloom, grief, hopelessness, melancholy, sadness, sorrow, unhope, wanhope

DESPATCH See DISPATCH.

DESPERADO blade, CRIMINAL, daredevil, harumscarum, hector, hotspur, lawbreaker, scapegrace

DESPERATE baffled, balked, bold, cornered, despondent, dire, exorbitant, extreme, foiled, foolhardy, forlorn, frantic, futile, headlong, hopeless, mad, outwitted, perilous, rabid, rash, reckless, thwarted, trapped, treed, useless, vain, wretched
straits beam-ends

DESPERATION See *DESPAIR.*

DESPICABLE bad, caitiff, contemptible, dirty, fouty, ignoble, mean, miserable, offensive, orra, paltry, reptile, scaly, shabby, sordid, terrible, unworthy, vile, wretched

DESPISE abhor, abominate, condemn, contemn, detest, disdain, disprize, forhoo, forhooy, forhow, hate, loathe, misprize, repudiate, scorn, scout, spurn, vilipend

DESPITE affront, anger, aside, contempt, grudge, hate, malevolence, malgre, malice, mauger, meanness, scorn, spite, spleen, vex

DESPOENA See also PERSEPHONE.
parent demeter, poseidon

DESPOIL bereave, booty, deflower, denude, deprive, disrobe, divest, fleece, harry, hespel, huspel, injure, pelf, pillage, plunder, poll, raid, ravage, ravish, reave, rip, rob, rope, sack, seduce, spoil, spoliate, spuilzie, steal, strip, strub, stuilzie, take, trice, unclothe

DESPOND agonize, despair, droop, languish, lose heart, sink, touch bottom

DESPONDENCY athumia, athymia, athymy, blues, defection, depression, despair, desperation, dumps, dysthymia, gloom, melancholia, misery, oppression, pressure, sadness

DESPONDENT blue, dejected, depressed, desperate, dispirited, downcast, forlorn, gloomy, grieving, hopeless, mourning, negative, pessimistic, sad, sorrowing

DESPOT anarch, autarch, autocrat, caesar, czar, dictator, hitler, kaiser, monarch, nero, oppressor, satrap, tsar, tyrant

DESPOTIC absolute, arbitrary, authoritarian, autocratic, capricious, dictatorial, dominant, domineering, dominical, imperious, lordly, masterful, tyrannical, tyrannous

DESPOTISM absolutism, autocracy, big stick, dictatorship, domination, iron boot, iron hand, oppression, reign of terror, sultanism, terrorism, totalitarianism, tyranny

DESPUMATE foam, froth, scum, skin

DESQUAMATE layer, peel, scale, strip

DESSERT afters, babka, baked alaska, baklava, barquette, bavarian cream, bavaroise, betty, blanc mange, bombe, boston cream pie, cake, cream puff, crepe, dolce, dumpling, eclair, flan, flummery, fool, fruit, frumenty, glace, grunt, ice(cream), jello, jelly, junket, mousse, napoleon, parfait, pastry, peche, pie, pudding, sherbet, sillabub, skyr, slump, snow, sorbet, souffle, sponge, spumone, strudel, sweet, trifle
eggs and milk custard
fermented milk lacto
frozen bombe, icecream, lacto, mousse, sherbet, sorbet, spumone
gelatin spanish cream
milk and wine sillabub, sillibub, syllabub
pancake crepe-suzette

DESTINATION address, aim, billet, bourn(e), cause, design, end, fate, goal, last stop, lot, mark, object(ive), port, purpose, stop, terminal, terminus, will, wish

DESTINE aim, allot, depute, design, devote, doom, eure, fate, intend, mark, mean, ordain, plan, purpose, sentence, shape, slate, weird

DESTINED appointed, bound, certain, designed, doomed, fated, foregone, foreordained, inevitable, intended, marked, ordained, planned, predetermined, prescribed, purposed, reserved, set apart, written

DESTINY afterlife, bahi, dole, doom, end, eure, expectation, fate, foredoom, fortune, future, goal, horoscope, k(h)arma, kismet, lot, moira, portion, prospect, star(s), terminus
deity moira, norn
man of napoleon
name meaning carma
stone liafail

DESTITUTE bankrupt, bare, barren, beggared, bereft, clean, deficient, depleted, devoid, down-and-out, empty, homeless, indigent, lacking, landless, moneyless, nace, naked, needy, pauper, penniless, poor, sans, sur le pave, viduate(d), void, wanting, waste, without

DESTITUTION adversity, beggary, distress, exigency, famine, impoverishment, indigence, lack, misfortune, necessity, need(iness), pauperism, pennilessness, penury, poverty, privation, straits, want, wolf at the door

D'ESTREES, GABRIELLE *headquarters* auvergne, besse, carlat, usson
lover henry iv

DESTROY 3 axe, bag, end, fix, gut, nip 4 blow, burn, damn, do in, frap, full, kill, null, rase, raze, root, ruin, sack, sink, slay, stry, tear, tine, undo, void 5 blast, break, erase, erode, havoc, prang, quade, quell, shend, shoot, smash, split, spoil, stroy, swamp, waste, wrack, wreck 6 cancel, canker, deface, defeat, devour, finish, mangle, murder, ravage, reduce, settle, starve, unmake, uproot, uptear 7 abolish, atomize, blot out, consume, corrode, enecate, marplot, mortify, nullify, ruinate, shamash, shatter, swallow 8 cut short, decimate, demolish, desolate, immolate, knock out, lay waste, mutilate, sabotage, stramash 9 devastate, dismantle, dispose of, overthrow, shipwreck 10 annihilate, extinguish, obliterate 11 exterminate
oneself commit suicide
totally cumber, scuttle, smash, sweep

DESTROYED blown, flat, kaput(t)

DESTROYER apollyon, bane, blast, blight, can, death, flivver, hun, iconoclast, nihilist, pest, plague, saboteur, shiva, siva, spoiler, tin can, undoer, vandal, victor, warship, wrecker

DESTRUCTION ballyhack, ballyw(r)ack, bane, blight, breakup, carnage, collapse, crash, crush, death, debacle, decay, defeat, demolition, desolation, devastation, doom, downfall, end, eversion, expery, extinction, fall, fate, fire, genocide, havoc, hew, holocaust, killing, loss, massacre, obliteration, perdition, rack (and ruin), ravage, ruin, sabotage, shambles, smashery, smash(up), stroy, stry, tala, vandalism, wrack and ruin, wreckage
deity ara, sekhmet, siva

gradual corrosion, erosion
malicious sabotage

DESTRUCTIVE an(a)eretic, baleful, baneful, catawampous, cutthroat, deadly, deathly, exitial, exitous, fatal, fell, hun-like, hunnish, mortal, noisome, noxious, pernicious, poisonous, ruinous, wrackful, wreckful

DESULTORY aimless, capricious, casual, chance, chancy, cursory, disconnected, disorderly, fitful, haphazard, hasty, hit-or-miss, idle, inconstant, irregular, loose, mercurial, rambling, random, roving, slight, spasmodic, unsteady, wavering

DETACH abstract, calve, cut, disconnect, disengage, disjoin, dissolve, divide, divorce, isolate, loose, loosen, part, prescind, separate, sever, sunder, unfasten, unfix, unglue, unhinge, withdraw, woan

DETACHED abstract, alone, aloof, candid, clinical, cold, cool, deadpan, discrete, disinterested, emotionless, fair, impartial, indifferent, insular, isolated, objective, portato, remote, reticent, sciolto, spiccato, unbiased, unconcerned, unemotional
comb. aph

DETACHMENT aloofness, ataraxia, avulsion, boredom, brown study, dispersion, distance, disunion, group, indifference, isolation, item, outguard, outpost, part(y), piece, portion, posse, reverie, sector, squad, unconcern

DETAIL account, allot, appoint, article, bit, calculate, circumstance, commission, count, crew, develop, division, doodad, fact, fraction, fragment, group, instance, item(ize), megillah, member, minutia, narrate, nicety, parcel, part(icular), patrol, piece, plan, plot, portion, recital, relate, respect, sector, segment, specific, specify, technicality, trivia, unit, work force
leaf-like phyllomorph

DETAILED amplified, blow-by-blow, closeup, complete, copious, elaborate, full, itemized, meticulous, minute, particular, prolix, replete, tiresome

DETAIN arrest, athold, attach, capture, catch, check, collar, constrain, contain, cop, curb, delay, hinder, hold, intern, jail, keep, nab, reserve, restrain, retain, retard, slacken, slow, stay, stop, taigle, tarry, withhold
during war intern

DETECT appreciate, catch, decipher, descry, discern, discover, distinguish, divine, espy, expose, find, hear, make out, nose, notice, observe, perceive, recognize, scent, see, sense, smell(out), spot, spy, trap, twig, uncover

DETECTION accusation, exposure, revelation
device dowser, radar, sonar

DETECTIVE agent, beagle, bull, busy(body), dick, eye, fbi(man), ferret, flatfoot, fly bull, g-man, gumshoe, hawkshaw, house dick, investigator, manhunter, mouchard, mouser, nose, operator, pinkerton, plainclothesman, plant, policeman, private-eye, runner, scenter, scout, shadow, shamus, sleuth, snoop(er), spotter, spy, tail(er), tec, t-man, tracer, trap
famous ackroyd, archie goodwin, arsene lupin, bertha cool, black mask, charlie chan, columbo, ellery queen, gascoyne, goldfinger, hercule poirot, inspector vautain, ironside, irwin blye, james bond, kojak, lew archer, maigret, mike hammer, mike shayne, miss marple, moses wine, moto, nero wolfe, nick carter, perry mason, peter wimsey, philip marlow, philo vance, pinkerton, sam spade, sherlock holmes, simon templar, teddy villanova, the saint, trent, vidocq
writer christie, doyle, fleming, gardner, queen, sayers, spillane

DETECTOR coherer, rea-

gent, sferics, spherics, spotter, tracer, tracker
defect troubleshooter

DETENT catch, click, dog, fall(et), fence, paul, pawl, pin, ratch(et), stop, stud, tongue

DETENTE ostpolitik

DETENTION apprehension, arrest, capture, confinement, delay, detainer, detinue, immurement, imprisonment, internment, retardation, stoppage

DETER bar, block, bluff, blunt, check, chill, cool, damp(en), daunt, dehort, delay, discourage, disincline, dissuade, divert, frighten, hinder, preclude, prevent, quench, repel, restrain, scare, stop, turn
from

DETERGENT abluent, abstergent, abstersive, annite, cleaner, cleanser, gardinol, purge, purging, rhyptic, saponin, smectic, soap, solvent, syndet, wash

DETERIORATE alloy, appair, bastardize, come down, corrode, corrupt, debase, decay, decline, degenerate, depreciate, derogate, descend, drop, ebb, erode, fail, fall, firefang, get worse, go to pot, impair, lapse, let down, pervert, regress, retrocede, retrograde, retrogress, rot, rust, sicken, sink, slip, slump, sour, spoil, vitiate, wane, wear, worsen, worst

DETERMINATE certain, definite, established, fixed, oristic, resolute, specific, unqualified

DETERMINATION act, assay, backbone, bioassay, cause, character, conclusion, courage, decision, definition, demonstration, firmness, fortitude, grit, guts, hest, intention, judg-(e)ment, limit, opinion, pluck, resolution, resolve, sentence, settlement, solution, verdict, volition, will (power)

DETERMINATIVE conclusive, decisive, final, formant, limiting, precipitant, restrictive, settling, shaping
most dominant

DETERMINE adjudicate, adjust, analyse, analyze, appoint, arbitrate, arrange, ascertain, assess, assign, bound, calculate, call, certify, circumscribe, cognosce, conclude, condition, contrive, decern, decide, define, dijudicate, direct, discover, dispose, end, establish, find, fit, fix, govern, impel, learn, limit, prove, purpose, resolve, rule, run, seal, settle, solve, test, think, will
fineness set, sett
rate assess

DETERMINED assured, bent, bound, certain, decided, decisive, dern, dogged, firm, foregone, given, grim, gritty, hard-set, mulish, obstinant, perverse, resolute, resolved, set, settled, stout, stubborn, sturdy

DETERRENT bar, bridle, leash, preventive, rein, warning

DETEST abhor, abominate, condemn, curse, damn, despise, dislike, execrate, HATE, loathe, reject, repudiate, scorn, spurn

DETESTABLE abhorrent, abominable, accursed, blasted, despicable, execrable, foul, hateful, heinous, horrid, infamous, infernal, loathsome, monstrous, odious, offensive, scurvy, sorry, terrible, vile

DETESTATION antipathy, hatred, horror, loathing, odium

DETHRONE depose, divest, oust, remove, strip, topple, uncrown, unseat

DETONATE belch, blast, explode, fire, go off, shoot

DETONATION ambitus, bang, bark, bingo, blast, burst, crack, discharge, explosion, fulmination, gunshot, knock, percussion, pinging, pinking, pop, repercussion, shot

DETONATOR booster, cap, exploder, fuse, fuze, initiator, primer, priming, squib, torpedo

DETOUR ambages, bypass, byroad, byway, circuit, circumbendibus, crotch, deviate, deviation,

digress(ion), diversion, divert, excursion, fork, go around, roundabout, shunpike, turn(ing)

DETRACT asperse, belittle, besmirch, decry, deduct, defame, depreciate, derogate, diminish, disparage, dispraise, distract, lessen, libel, malign, reduce, ridicule, rundown, slander, smear, subtract, traduce, vilify, vilipend
from impede

DETRACTION abuse, backbiting, calumny, defamation, harm, hurt, injury, ridicule, scandal, slander, zoilism

DETRIMENT cost, damage, damnum, disadvantage, disfavor, disservice, evil, expense, harm, hurt, impediment, injury, jacture, loss, mischief, prejudice, sore, wound

DETRIMENTAL adverse, awkward, damaging, deleterious, disadvantageous, harmful, hurtful, inexpedient, injurious, invidious, lossful, noxious, prejudicial

DETRITUS chaff, debris, deposit, garbage, outwash, powder, refuse, remainder, rubbish, sheetwash, shingle, tuff, waste

DETROIT motown
founder cadillac
park belle isle

DEUCALION *kingdom* phthia, thessaly
offspring amphictyon, hellen, protogenia
parent clymene, prometheus
wife pyrrha

DEUCE adin, demon, devil, diantre, dickens, plague, two
-ace three
wild freak

DEUS deity, divinity, god
fidius jupiter, zeus

DEVA angel, deity, demon, dewa, div, divinity, god, sura

DEVAKI *offspring* krishna, vishnu

DEVALUATE cheapen, debase, depreciate

DEVANCE anticipate, forestall, outstrip

DEVASTATE annihilate, demolish, desolate, despoil, destroy, harry, havoc, lay waste, loot, pillage, plunder, rape, ravage, raze, rifle, rob, ruin, sack, scourge, spoliate, strip, waste, wreck

DEVASTATING crushing, deadly, effective, ferocious, gorgeous, lethal, ravishing, savage

DEVASTATION destruction, exile, havoc, rapine, ravage, ruin, sacca(d)ge, sackage, waste

DEVELOP advance, age, blossom, boom, bourgeon, breed, brew, bud, burgeon, burst, cook, cultivate, detail, dilate, disclose, educate, elaborate, engender, enlarge, evolute, evolve, expand, expound, finish, flourish, flower, follow, form, fulfill, gather, gemmate, generate, germinate, grow(up), improve, increase, incubate, manifest, maturate, mature, mellow, mushroom, open, originate, outgrow, perfect, polish, print, progress, pullulate, refine, result, ripen, shape(up), shoot(up), spring, sprout, stem, take shape, thrill, till, train, uncoil, unfold, unfurl, unreel, unroll, unwind, upshoot, upspring, vegetate, wax
cracks alligator, craze
into amount
rapidly mushroom
well cotton

DEVELOPED adult, advanced, deep, forward
after birth acquired
fully adult, bold, florid, formed, summed
imperfectly abortive

DEVELOPER amidol, builder, elon, glycin(e), kachin, reagent, rodinol, solution, soup
photographic dope

DEVELOPMENT advance(ment), amplification, behavior, blossoming, breeding, elaboration, enlargement, evolution, evolvement, expansion, explication, flowering, furtherance, generation, genesis, growth, improvement, increase, manners, maturation, matu-

rity, opening, progress(ion), ripening, rise, stature, training, unfolding, unrolling, upshot, wax
abnormally slow retardation
arrested aplasia, fixation, hypoplasia
backward retrogression
comb. plasia
defective agenesis
faulty aplasia
full blown, maturity, ripeness
highest bloom
individual ontogeny
monstrous anamorphosis
normal aphanisia
pert. evolutive, genetic
thematic continuity
total eosere
unexpected accident

DEVEREUX, PENELOPE stella

DEVI annapurna, bhavani, bhowani, chandi, durga, gauri, haimavati, himavat, kali, lady, madam, mahadevi, mrs, parvati, shakti, uma
consort siva
father himavat

DEVIATE aberrant, angle, avert, bear off, bend, bevel, bias, black sheep, branch, break, contrast, crook(en), crump, decline, deflect, depart(from), detour, differ, digress, divagate, divaricate, diverge, divert, err, go astray, hade, heel, heretic, lapse, lean, lie, misbelieve, miss, mutate, oblique, pervert, rove, run, sheer, shift, sin, skew, slew, slue, squint, stray, sway, swerve, tack, trend, turn, twist, variant, variation, vary, veer, waive, wander, warp, wry, yaw
from the vertical hade

DEVIATING aberrant, anomalous, circuitous, erratic, indirect, sinuous, skew

DEVIATION aberration, abnormality, abrash, anomaly, bend(ing), branch, brisure, change, circuity, crotch, declination, departure, detour, devarication, distortion, divagation, divergence, diversion, double, drift, excursion, excursus, exhorbitation, fork, helm, indirection, jump, lapse, license, obliquity, quirk, rambling,

sheer(ing), shift(ing), skew, solicism, straying, sweep(ing), swerve, swerving, tack, turn(ing), variance, variation, veer(ing), wandering, yaw
standard sigma

DEVIATIVE different, eccentric, irregular, out-of-the-way, rambling

DEVICE alarm, apparatus, appliance, art(ifice), axiom, badge, bit, boat, carrier, cast, chat, contraption, contrivance, design, desire, dodge, doohickey, emblem, expedient, figure, fraud, gadget, gimcrack, insigne, instrument, intention, letter, machination, maxim, motif, motto, opinion, pattern, plan, project, purpose, rule, ruse, scheme, signature, slogan, symbol, tool, trio, type, view, wile, will
boring auger, drill, tiger
catching net
centrifugal cyclone
clever coup, knack
curve measuring rotameter
gripping come-along, pincers, tongs
hampering hobbles, shackle
heating etna
holding clamp, vise
mixing crutcher
polishing wagwag
protective bonnet
pyrotechnic fireworks
sighting alidade
skillful art
theatrical sloat, slote

DEVIL (See also DEVIL'S.) 3 imp, ned, wat 4 baka, bang, beng, bhut, bogy, cook, deil, dule, haze, mahu, nick, ogre, puck, qued, wolf, wond 5 afrit, annoy, bogey, bwana, chort, cloot, demon, deuce, eblis, enemy, fiend, harry, horns, hugon, pluto, rogue, satan, scrat, shedu, taipo, tease 6 afreet, amamon, amayon, azazel, banter, belial, bother, daemon, dahack, diablo, goblin, hornie, pester, raboin, roarer, rotter, spirit, sprite, terror, teufel, thurse, wretch 7 abaddon, ahriman, amaimon, anhanga, clootie, dickens, dracula, evil one, gremlin, hellcat, hellion, hoodlum, lucifer, mahound, monster, old nick, ormazed, raboino, serpent, shaitan, tempter, torment, warlock, wendigo, windigo 8 apollyon, beelpeor, belfagor, cagnazzo, curupira, mephisto, obidicut, plotcock, sathanas, worricow 9 arch enemy, beelzebub, reprobate 10 holy terror, oldscratch 11 auld clootie 14 mephistopheles

belief in diabolism

bird drongo, goatsucker, owl, swift

bottomless pit apollyon

change into diabolify

chaser moralizer, reformer

dante's cagnazzo

disguised friar rush

-diver dabchick, grebe

-dodger ecclesiastic, preacher

-dog marine

female demoness

fish manta, octopus, ray, sea bat, whale

god idol

grass bahama, bermuda, gum succory, scutch

-in-the-bush love-in-a-mist

kin imp

lore demonism, demonology, diablerie, diablery, diabolism, satanism, sorcery, witchcraft

-may-care blase, cavalier, defiant, indifferent, reckless

nickname auld clootie, deil, deuce, dickens, old bendy, old clootie, old gooseberry, old harry, old horny, old ned, old nick, old scratch, scrat, teufel, the adversary

personification archimago

pert. diabolical, satanic

possession by diabolepsy

prince of azazel, eblis

printer's apprentice

raise the celebrate, revel

ruler diabolarch

symbol dragon, serpent, swine

the bog(e)y, bogie

tree abroma, alstonia, dita

white nailrod

wood american olive

worship black magic, black mass, satanism, sorcery

DEVILISH black, chthonian, clovenhoofed, cruel, demoni(a)c, diabolic(al), excessively, execrable, extreme, fiendish, fiendly, hellish, impish, infernal, inhuman, nefarious, plutonic, saturnine, serpentine, vicious, wicked

DEVIL'S *apple* jimsonweed, mandrake

apron kelp, laminaria

bird wagtail, yellowhammer

bit scabious, snakeroot

bite hellebore

bones dice, wild yam

books cards

broth starch

candle mandrake

candlestick stinkhorn

club fatsia

coachhorse dardaol, rove beetle, wheelbug

corkscrew daemonelix

cotton tree abroma

darning needle esparto, lady's-comb, virgin's-bower

dozen thirteen

dung asaf(o)etida, assafetida, condiment

dust shoddy

garter bindweed

godmother baba

guts bindweed, dodder

horse praying mantis

milk celandine, spurge, wartweed, wartwort

needle dragonfly

oatmeal chervil

pincushion pineapple-cactus

pitchfork beggar-tick

posy ramson

shoestrings goat's-rue, turkey pea

snuffbox puffball

son imp

toenail belemnite

tree abroma, alstonia, dita

triangle bermuda triangle, hoodoo-sea

turnip bryony

walking stick ailanthus

DEVILTRY art, black magic, diablerie, enchantment, fiendishness, magic, meanness, mischief, sorcery, villainy, wickedness, witchcraft

DEVIOUS aberrant, ambagious, circuitous, circumlocutional, crafty, crooked, cunning, deceitful, deep, deviating, deviatory, digressive, discursive, errant, erratic, erring, flexuous, foxy, fraudulent, havering, indirect, louche, mazy, meandering, oblique, out-of-the-way, periphrastic, plaited, rambling, roundabout, roving, scheming, shifty, sinful, sly, stray, subtle, swerving, tortuous, tricky, twisting, undirected, vagrant, wandering, winding

DEVISE aim, arrange, array, bequeathe, bequest, bethink, cast, concoct, contrive, convey, create, decoct, demise, design, endow, excogitate, fancy, fashion, form, frame, imagine, invent, leave, legate, make, meditate, originate, plan, plot, prepare, project, scheme, think up, warp, will

DEVISER architect, artificer, finder, producer

DEVOID bare, barren, destitute, destroy, dismount, empty, expel, free, lacking, leave, shun, sincere, vacant, wanting, without

of bout, empty

DEVOIR duty, respect, service, task

DEVOLUTION declension, decline, degeneration, descent, deterioration, passing, transference

DEVOLVE blossom, fall, overturn, pass, result, shift, succeed, transfer, transmit

DEVONSHIRE *boat* mumblebee

cream clotted

fairy pixie, pixy, puck

river exe

treat cream-tea

DEVOTE addict, administer, allot, ally, apply, apportion, appropriate, bestow, bless, consecrate, consign, dedicate, destine, devove, devow, direct, give, hallow, intend, set apart, spend, study, venerate

oneself apply, attend, determine, practice, undertake

time bother, busy

DEVOTED addicted, adherent, adoring, affectionate, ardent, assiduous, attached, consecrated, constant, dedicated, destined, devout, doting, engrossed, faithful, fast, fervid, firm, fond, habituated, jealous, leal, liege, loving, loyal, mad, obedient, oblate, pious, sta(u)nch, tried (and true), true, votive, zealous

DEVOTEE adherent, aficionado, amateur, believer, bhagat, bigot, bopster, buff, cat, catechumen, christian, churchgoer, churchman, convert, devotary, disciple, enthusiast, fan(atic), fiend, follower, habitue, hepcat, hipster, hound, ist, monk, neophyte, nun, partisan, pietist, proselyte, receiver, religionist, saint, shavia, supporter, truster, votarist, votary, voteen, yati, zealot
comb. ist, nick, nik

DEVOTION absorption, addiction, adherence, adoration, affection, allegiance, angelus, ardor, attachment, bhakti, blessing, brahme, consecration, constancy, cult(ism), dedication, devoutness, enthusiasm, fealty, fervor, fidelity, idolatry, jealousy, kavvanah, kawwanah, love, loyalty, novena, pietism, piety, religion, worship, zeal
excessive cult
fervent adoration
object of fetish, idol, totem
parental progenity
religious novena
selfless bhakti
to others altruism, philanthropy

DEVOUR afrete, batten, bolt, consume, cram, destroy, dispatch, dispose(of), down, eat, engorge, engulf, enjoy, fraunch, fress, fret, glut(tonnize), gobble, gorge, gulp, guttle, guzzle, imbibe, ingest, ingurgitate, jaw, overeat, put away, raven, stuff, surround, swallow, swap, swop, take in, tuck away, vour, waste, whale down, wolf down
comb. vorous
greedily swill

DEVOURING avid, consuming, edacious, greedy, ligurition, voracious, vorant

DEVOUT adorant, adoring, ardent, believing, christianly, devoted, devotional, dutiful, faithful, fanatic(al), fervent, froom, godly, good, gracy, holy, kosher, pietistic(al), pious, regenerate, religious, reverent(ial),

saintly, sanctimonious, solemn, venerative, worshipful, zealotic, zealous

DEW bloom, dag, moisten, moisture, prime, refresh, rime, rosee, viridity
-beater footh, pioneer, shoe
congealed rime
goddess herse
measurer drosometer, pagoscope
pert. roric

DEWBERRY blackberry, mayes

DEWDROP pearl

DEWEY *victory* manila bay

DEWLAP bell, choller, fold, gullet, jollop, jowl, palea, wattle(s)

DEWY damp, drusy, moist, misty, roral, roric, rory, roscid, roy, sparkling, vaporous
-eyed innocent, sentimental, visionary

DEXADRINE See AMPHETAMINE.

DEXAMETHASONE decadron

DEXTERITY ability, address, adroitness, agility, aptitude, art, chic, craft, deftness, ease, expertness, facility, finesse, knack, magic, nimbleness, quickness, readiness, skill, sleight, stroil, tact

DEXTEROUS adept, adroit, agile, apt, artful, bright, canny, clever, cunning, deft, draft, expert, facile, fly, handy, hend, jimmy, nimble, quick, ready, sleight(y), smart, tight, wise, yare
comb. ambi

DEXTEROUSLY handily, yarely

DEXTROSE ame, cerelose, glucose, sugar

DHAK butea, dak, palas, peatree, pulas
extract butein

DHAL lentil, split pea

DHARMA doctrine, duty, gospel, idea, the law, virtue
son yudhishthira

D'HERBLAY amadis, aramis

DHOLE cuon, cyon, dog, kolsun

DHOW bateay, batel, bugala, lateen(er), pontoon, samb(o)uk, scow, skipjack, vessel

DHRTARASTRA See BUDDHA.

DIA noxos
parent cioneus

DIABETES *bronze* hemochromatosis
cause glucagon, sumatotropin
remedy antimellin, hypoglemic, insulin, orinase, somatostatin, tolbutamide

DIABLOTIN bonbons, dainties, guacharo, imp, petrel

DIABOLICAL cruel, demonic, devilish, fiendish, hellish, infernal, inhuman, satanic, violent, wicked

DIABOLISM See DEVIL *worship.*

DIABOLUS See DEVIL.

DIACOPE cut, incision, thesis, wound

DIACRITICAL See MARK *diacritical.*

DIAD digonal, pair, twofold

DIADEM anadem, circle, coronet, crown, empire, fillet, headband, mind, monarch, rigol, tiara

DIAERESIS breakup, c(a)esura, dialysis, mark, meter

DIAGNOSE analyze, identify, interpret, prognose

DIAGNOSIS analysis, conclusion, examination, interpretation, verdict
uncertainty of acatalepsia

DIAGONAL bendwise, bias(ed), catabiased, catacorner(ed), catercorner(ed), cattycorner(ed), counter, hypotenuse, incline, kittycorner(ed), oblique, slant, slash, solidus, transverse, virgule

DIAGRAM blueprint, carte, chart, design, draft, drawing, epure, gamut, graph, icon(ograph), isotype, layout, map, outline, picture, plan, plat, plot, schema, scheme, section, sketch, symbol, trace, yantra

DIAL azimuth, clock, crystal, diacle, gnomon, horologe, jigger, knob, solitaire, telephone, tune, watch
pin gnomon, style

DIALECT (See also *dialect* and *language* under individual countries.) accent, argot, brogue, cant, idiom,

jargon, language, patois, patter, phraseology, southern, speech, talk, tongue, vernacular
group aeolic
strange gibberish
DIALECTIC(AL) a fortiori, a posteriori, a priori, broad, categorical, conditional, deductive, discursive, epagogic, hypothetical, inductive, pilpul, soritical, syllogistic, synthetic(al)
DIALECTICS argument, debate, discussion, logic, pilpul
DIALOGUE apology, arito, colloquy, epilog(ue), exchange, lazzo, parlance, patter, phaedo, phaedrus, repartee, script, sutra, sutta, symposium, talk, timaeus
between gods bhagavad-gita
dramatic stichomythia
funny lazzo
having nature of conversational, interlocutory
DIAMETER bore, breadth, caliber, calibre, chord, ga(u)ge, gear, middle, module, moot, radius, ray, spoke, width
half radius
inside bore
DIAMETRIC adverse, remote, utmost
DIAMOND adamant(ine), adamas, arena, ballpark, boort, bort(z), brilliant, briolet, carbon, carreau, cockpit, court, crystal, dorje, field, figure, gem, gridiron, ice, ja(e)ger, jewel, lask(e), lasque, lozen(ge), mineral, premier, rhombus, ring, rink, rock, rondel(le), sancy, shiner, sparkler, treasure, vajra
bird pardalote
black carbonado, coal
black moth cabbage moth, mamestra, noctuide, plutella
blue hope, ja(e)ger
card correau, pick
center golconda, kimberley, luderitz, well
coarse bort
corner base
crystal ballas, glassie
cutter brilliandeer
cutting cup dop, dopp
cutting process bruting
cuttings bort

cut too thin fisheye
engraving shanp '
facet bezel, crown, culet, girdle, pavilion, table
famous chapada, cullinan, debeers, dudley, dutoit, eugenie, hope, hornby, jonker, jubilee, kohinoor, kollur, matan, mogul, orloss, pigott, pitt, regency, regent, sancy, starojaprica, stewart, tennant, tiffany
flat lasque
flaw carbon-spot
fragment bort, chips, cleavage
geometrical lozen(ge), rhomb
glazier's emeril, quarrel
hard adamant
high grade wesselton
holding device dop(p)
imitation paste, schlenter
imperfect bort, bywater
industrial bort
inferior grade bo(a)rt, borty, bortz, flat
jack fool, gimbarde
-like naif
molder dop(p)
native carbon
necklace riviere
9 of bragger, comet, curse of scotland, pope joan
oval briolette
perfect paragon
planet sun
pure white river
queen guinguette, nazarene
ring solitaire
rough brait
7 of peneech
-shaped pattern argyle
single solitaire
6 of brilliant
small melee
snake carpetsnake, copperhead, python
splinterlike rose
state delaware
suit carreau, coins, cuadros, diamantes, eckstein, gelb, merchanes, oros, ruthen, schellen
surface See *facet.*
symbol of innocence
table cut baguette
10 of big casino
transparent crystal
wheel skive
yellow canary, silver cape
zodiac sign virgo
DIAMORPHINE See HEROIN.

DIANA (See also ARTEMIS.) cynthia, delia, lucina, moon, titania, trivia, victrix
attendant camilla
brother apollo
cult, pert. arician
goddess of ephesus
grove nemus
monkey roloway
observer actaeon
oracle site colchis
parent jupiter, latona, zeus
temple site ephesus
twin apollo, leto
DIANTHUS carnation, caryophullus, flower, pink
DIAPASON concord, harmony, montre, range
DIAPER breechcloth, breechclout, clout, dhoti, didie, didy, hippen, hipping, loincloth, napkin, nappie, nappy
DIAPHANOUS clear, limpid, lucid, pellucid, sheer, translucent, transparent
DIAPHORETIC asclepidin, asclepin, borage, bucco, buchu, bucko, calendula, camomile, camphor, chamomile, expectorant, hidrotic, remedy, sudatory
DIAPHRAGM apron, decker, iris, membrane, middle, midriff, partition, phragma, phren, platen, riff, skirt, tympanus, wafer
pert. phrenic
DIARIST evely, historian, pepys, scribe
DIARMET *consort* btianne
DIARRHEA delhi-belly, flux, gurry, lask, lax, lientery, montezuma's revenge, scour, sprue, squirts, trots, turista
DIARY blotter, chronicle, daybook, diurnal, ephemeris, hemerologium, journal, log, minutes, record, register
DIAS footpace
DIASKEUAST critic, editor, reactor, reviser, revisor
DIASPORA dispersion, exile, galut(h), golah
DIASPORE migrule
DIASTASE amylase, amylopsin, enzyme, malt, ptyalin
DIATOM alga, animacule, animalculum, asterionella, brittlewort, centrale, centrica, planckton, plant

cell frustule
covering perigloea
fresh-water meridion
genus navicula, pleurosigma, synedra, tabellaria
reproductive cell auxospore
DIATONIC achromatic, chord, scale
opposed to chromatic
run tirade
scale gamut
DIATRIBE harangue, invective, jeremiad, philippic, screed, tirade
DIAZ DE BIVAR *title* cid
DIB(BLE) bit, bob, dap, dibstone, dip, fish, game, kippen, money, rupee, token, trifle
DIBLAIM *offspring* gomer
DIBS claim, cockal, juice, money, syrup
DICE angle, anzamia, astragals, bones, checker, chop, craps, cube, dees, devil's bones, devil's teeth, dominoes, flats, goads, indoor golf, ivories, kabat, mince, mississippi marbles, rice, shiktsz, tats, wurfeln
box birdcage
cheater cogger, topper
cheat with cog
double ace ambsace
false goad, gourd, graviers, squarier, stopdice, tats
game acey out, alea, backgammon, barbooth, barbudi, baseball, battleships, bingo, birdcage, cameroon, canoga, centennial, chicao, chuckaluck, cootie, crag, craps, crown and anchor, destroyers, deuces wild, drop dead, elf hoch, esperance, everest, fifty, garanguet, hamburgen, hazzard, hooligan, klondike, multiplication, mumchance, newmarket, odd and even, patcha, qualify, quinquenove, raphe, see-low, singluk, wurfelspiel, yacht
game naturals sevens
goddess peace
highest throw aphrodite
loaded doctor, fulham, fullam, high runner, langret, tat, tops
lowest throw ambsace
paired numbers doublets, duplet
player tatsman, throwster
set bale

6-throw boxcars, sice, sise
term ambsace, baseball-bum, bones, boxcar, cockeyes, cog, come, craps, crosseyes, dick, dispatcher, doublet, fade, field, flat, float, joe, miss, natural, nick, phoebe, point, raffle, roll, shoot, sice, sise, sister, yacht
throw ambsace, cast, crabs, craps, hazard, natural, nick, roll, shot
trick cog
weighted loads
DICENTRA bicuculla, bikukulla, bleeding-heart, dutchman (s-breeches)
DICER See GAMESTER.
DICERION candlestick, dyker
DICEY See DANGEROUS.
DICHOTOMIZE analyze, halve
DICHOTOMY cleft, division, duality, split
DICK agent, detective, lad, whip
DICKENS, CHARLES *alias* boz
character 3 amy, bet, pip, pot, tox 4 baps, bray, dora, fang, fips, fogg, gamp, heep, jowl, kags, mell, nell, prig, tigg, veck, wegg 5 baloo, bates, betsy, bevan, brick, choke, drood, fagin, flite, guppy, krook, lucie, miggs, nancy, noggs, peops, pinch, pross, quilp, rogue, rudge, sikes, slyme, smike 6 bailey, barkis, boffin, bucket, bumble, buzfuz, carter, carton, cuttle, darnay, dartle, dobson, dombey, dorrit, fat boy, harmon, jarley, jingle, lammle, maylie, merdle, nipper, pirrip, pogrom, redlaw, sleary, tapley, wardle, weller, winkle 7 baillee, blimber, browdie, dawkins, dedlock, defarge, estella, gargery, grimwig, jaggers, jeddler, jellyby, manette, mowcher, nadgett, nubbles, peggoty, pipchin, podsnap, scrooge, slowboy, slumkey, snagsby, snubbin, spenlow, squeers, stryver, tiny tim, trotter, wemmick 8 bagstock, chadband, cratchit, crummles, cruncher, fledgeby, gummidge, havisham, hortense, humphrey, jarndyce, lir-

riper, magwitch, micawber, nickleby, pickwick, skimpole, swiveler 9 bill sikes, gradgrind, headstone, mantalini, pecksniff, riderhood, sairy gamp, sam weller, uriah heep, wickfield 10 little nell, steerforth 11 bob cratchit, oliver twist, pumblechook 12 artful dodger, sidney carton 13 charles darnay 16 david copperfield, martin chuzzlewit, nicholas nickleby 17 cheeryble brothers
club pickwick
mistress ellen ternan
novel barnaby rudge, bleak house, christmas carol, david copperfield, dombey and son, great expectations, hard times, little dorrit, martin chuzzlewit, nicholas nickleby, old curiosity shop, oliver twist, pickwick papers, tale of two cities
pen name boz
residence gads hill
sister-in-law mary
wife catherine
DICKER bargain, barter, chaffer, cheapen, compact, daker, dakir, deal, exchange, haggle, icre, negotiate, swap, ten, trade
DICKEY apron, bib, bird, collar, donkey, front, gilet, haddock, jacket, pantlet, petticoat, plastron, poop, rumble seat, shaky, sham, starcher, tucker, vestee, waist, weak
DICOTYLEDON exogen
DICTATE advise, axiom, behest, bidding, canon, command, compose, convention, decree, direct, dite, enjoin, impose, indite, injunction, law, octroy, ordain, order, precept, prescribe, rule, statute, suggest, tell, warrant
DICTATOR autocrat, boss, caesar, caudillo, czar, despot, duce, franco, fuhrer, governor, hitler, kaiser, lenin, mikado, mussolini, oppressor, pendragon, peron, salazar, shogun, stalin, sulla, tito, trujillo, tsar, tyrant
DICTATORIAL absolute, arbitrary, bossy, despotic, dogmatic, domineering, imperious, lordly, magisterial,

magistral, masterful, oracular, overbearing, pompous, positive, tyrannical

DICTION composition, dialect, enunciation, expression, formulation, idiologism, idiom, language, locution, parlance, phrase (ology), phrasing, rhetoric, speech, style, talk, tongue, verbiage, vocabulary, wording

bad acrylology, cacology

DICTIONARY calepin, compendium, gloss(ary), gradus, idioticon, lexicon, onomasticon, polyglot, thesaurus, vocabulary, wordbook

geographical atlas, gazetteer

poet's gradus

sanskrit amara-kosha

DICTUM adage, apothegm, axiom, dictate, effatum, maxim, opinion, principle, saying, say-so, statement

DICTYNNA aphalia, artemis, britomartis, diana

father zeus

protectress of hunters, seafarers

DID ded(e), dyde

not didna, didnt

DIDACTIC academic, donnish, dry, educational, instructive, preachy, preceptive, sermonic, teacherly

DIDACTICS instruction, pedagogy

DIDAPPER baptist, dabchick, grebe

DIDDER dither, oscillate, quake, quaver, quiver, shake, shimmy, shudder, sway, totter, tremble, trepidation, waver

DIDDLE befool, cheat, dally, dawdle, deceive, gin, hoax, jerk, jiggle, kill, liquor, potter, ruin, swindle, toddle, undo

-daddle dawdle, fiddlefaddle, fussing, trifling

DIDO antic, caper, elissa, frolic, monkeyshine, prank, trick

aunt jezebel

brother pygmalion

consort acerbas, aeneas, sichaeus

father belus

kingdom carthage

rejected suitor iarbas

sister anna

uncle acerbas

DIE angle, base, bite the dust, bleed, block, boss, brick, cease, chance, check out, conk, croak, cube, dado, decay, decease, dee, depart, dice, dod, drop, drown, end, exit, expire, fade, fail, go west, hang, hazard, hob, hub, intaglio, kick the bucket, lapse, matrix, mold, mullar, napoo, pass(on), patay, perish, pike, pile, pip, pop off, puncheon, quit, rot, seal, shuffle off, sica, stall, stamp, starve, succumb, swelt, tat(t), tessera, tine, torfel, torfle, trespass, trussell, vanish, wane

at one's post persevere

away decrease, disappear, end, fail, faint, languish, persevere, recede, swoon

-back exanthema, staghead

by hanging swing

coining sicca

down flit, sink, subside

for See DESIRE.

for drawing wire whirtle, whortle

from hunger affamish, starve

-hard blimp, conservative, persevere, resist, tory

hollow gourd

improper flat

is cast anerriphtho kubos

loaded doctor, fulham, fullam, fullom, highman, langret, tat

mold dod

on the vine fade away, languish, weaken

out disappear, stop

pipe dod

revolving dreidel

DIEGO See SWORD.

father columbus

DIET aliment, allowance, assembly, bant, bantingize, board, caudle, congress, council, fare, fast, food, gruel, hoftag, kreistag, landtag, legislature, pap, ration, regime(n), riksdag, seim(as), seym, slenderize, slim, viands, victuals, victus, volkstag

convalescent broth, gruel

deficiency anutraminosa

laws kashruth

reducing banting(ism)

science of sitology

DIFFER battle, break(with), clash, collide, conflict, con-

tend, cope, depart from, deviate, disaccord, disagree, discrepate, dispute, dissent, divaricate, diverge, divide, fall out, fight, jangle, jar, jostle, oppose, part, resist, separate, square, vary, withstand

DIFFERENCE anomaly, breach, brisure, change, chasm, clash, cross-purposes, dash, debate, difficulty, disagreement, discord, discrepancy, disparity, dispute, dissimilarity, distance, divergence, diversity, division, epact, fight, imparity, misunderstanding, nuance, odds, total, variance

angular explement

comb. ant(i)

graded gradient

of opinion argument, disagreement, dissent

small hairline, nuance, shade

wide chasm, gulf

DIFFERENT another, atypical, contrary, deviative, disaccordant, disagreeing, discordant, discrepant, disparate, dissimilar, dissonant, distant, distinct, distinguished, divergent, divers(e), fresh, heterogeneous, inconsistent, inconsonant, manifold, many, new, novel, original, other(than), otherwise, particular, peculiar, screwy, separate, sere, several, single, strange, sundry, unequal, unlike, unusual, variant, various, wild

comb. aph, apo, hetero

in nature allogeneous

DIFFERENTIAL conductor, difference, fluxion, tangent

DIFFERENTIATE alter, change, characterize, contrast, discern, discriminate, distinguish, haplite, separate, set apart, speciate

DIFFERENTIATION anaboly, deviation, dichotomy, distinction

from the normal, comb. all(o)

DIFFICULT arduous, augean, awkward, blunt, brittle, clumsy, complicated, cornered, crabbed, cramp, crank(y), cryptic, cumbrous, endangered, fiendish,

formidable, hard, herculean, ill, involved, knotted, knotty, laborious, mean, messy, murderous, obscure, obstinate, onerous, painful, perplexed, perverse, puzzling, rocky, rough, rugged, spiny, squeamish, steep, stickle, sticky, straitened, strenuous, stubborn, thorny, ticklish, toilsome, tough, trappy, troublesome, uneasy, uneath, unnethe, uphill, weneth, wick(ed)
comb. dys, mogi
to bear bitter, sad
to comprehend abstruse, strange
to grasp fugitive
to handle spinous
to please captious, curious, picky
to satisfy choos(e)y
to understand abstract, abstruse, complex, crabbed, deep, esoteric, high, strange, subtle
DIFFICULTY ado, anguish, aporia, asperity, barrier, bunker, cavil, chore, clog, coil, crus, crux, difference, dilemma, fix, gordian knot, habble, hardship, hobble, hotwater, ill, imbroglio, impasse, jam, kasheh, knot, lock, misunderstanding, node, obstacle, pass, pickle, pinch, plight, predicament, problem, rigor, rub, scrape, snag, sore, squeeze, stour, strait, struggle, task, tifter, trial, trouble
clear up iron out
lack of ease
pert. crucial, spiny
sudden facer
unexpected snag
with hardly, scarcely
DIFFIDE distrust
DIFFIDENCE anxiety, distrust, doubt, modesty, reserve, scruple, shyness, timidity
DIFFIDENT anxious, apprehensive, backward, bashful, blate, chary, coy, doubtful, modest, reluctant, reserved, retiring, sheepish, shrinking, shy
DIFFUSE bleed, broadcast, circulate, copious, deflect, diffund, dilate, diosmose, disperse, effusive, expand, extravagant, exuberant,

exude, general, gushing, gushy, large, lavish, nervous, patulent, permeate, perplex, pervade, pleonastic, prevalent, profuse, profusive, prolix, publish, radiate, redundant, scatter, shed, slack, spangle, sparkle, sprawly, strew, verbose, wordy
not compact, strict
DIFFUSION bleeding, deflection, distribution, osmosis, pervasion, propagation, radiation, spread
subject to osmose
DIG absorb, bedelve, burrow, claw, costean, delve, dike, disinter, dredge, drudge, dwell, excavate, fathom, gault, get, gouge, graft, grave, grout, grub, harvest, hoe, hollow, howk, jab, mine, moot, nip, pion, pit, poach, poke, probe, prod, punch, relish, root, rout, sap, scoop, scrape, search, sheugh, shovel, spade, speed, spud, stock, study, sump, swot, taunt, thrust, trowel, tunnel, understand, unearth
beneath undermine
carelessly spuddle
in begin, fortify, intrench, start
into explore, investigate, research, study
out depart, disinter, excavate, exhume, extract, learn, mine, research, scoop, shovel, spade, stump
out crevices fossick
peat sheugh
potatoes lift
trenches costean, grip
up cast, collect, disclose, discover, disinter, exhume, find, grub, spade, stub, unearth, upgrave
DIGEST abridge(ment), absorb, abstract, apercu, appropriate, assimilate, breviary, brief, classify, coct, code, compendium, condense, consider, conspectus, decoct, endue, epitome, heat, indue, metabolize, outline, pandect, ponder, precis, shorten, sketch, study, summary, survey, swallow, syllabus, system, understand

DIGESTION absorption, classification, coction, eupepsia, eupepsy, pepsis
agent maltase, pepsin, rennin
aid bromoseltzer, peptic
ailment acidosis, cardialgia, colic, constipation, dyspepsia, gripes, pyrosis, tormina
good eupepsia
having good eupeptic
pert. chyme, cyle
primary protopepsia
product amphopeptone
sac archenteron, enteron, gastrula
unit alimentary canal, bile, gastric glands, liver, pancreas, saliva
DIGESTIVE assimilative, digerent, magnesia, peptic
DIGGER australian, bildar, borer, delver, dog, dredge, driller, excavator, groundhog, miner, mole, navvy, peatman, pioneer, plodder, quarrier, sandhog, sapper, shoveler, soldier, trencher, wasp
post hole loy
DIGGING *fitted for* fodient, laniary
pert. fodient, fossorial
tool bailer, bulldozer, dikage, dredger, drill, dykage, loy, mattock, pick, plough, plow, scoop, shovel, slick, spade, steamshovel, trowel, wimble
DIGGINGS, DIGS area, establishment, flat, lodgings, mine, pit, property, quarters, room
DIGHT adorn, appoint, bit, clad, consign, construct, dab, deck, dicht, dink, dite, dress, equip, manage, order, perform, prepare, raise, repair, rub, treat, winnow, wipe
DIGIT cipher, dewclaw, doight, figure, finger, hallux, integer, medius, number, thumb, toe, unit
binary binit
cleft dissidactyl
dog's dewclaw
extra prepollex
5th minimus
having equal length isodactylous
having flat platydactyl
human finger, thumb, toe
podal toe

shield for cot, fingerstall, stall, thimble
vestigial dewclaw
DIGITALIS *source* foxglove
DIGLADIATION disputing, fencing, fighting, wrangling
DIGMEAT duckweed
DIGNIFIED aristocratic, august, courtly, decorous, elevated, ennobled, formal, grand, grave, imposing, kingly, lofty, lordly, magisterial, majestic, noble, portly, princely, queenly, regal, royal, sedate, sober, solemn, stately, togate(d), venerable
DIGNIFY adorn, crown, dub, embellish, ennoble, exalt, grace, honor, ornament, promote, raise
DIGNITARY canon, don, grandee, hutuk(h)tu, lion, magnifice, officer, personage, prelate, priest, raja(h), shereef, sherif, somebody, vestiary, wig
DIGNITY augustness, bearing, bench, chic, courtliness, decency, decorum, dog, elegance, eminence, face, fitness, glory, grace, grandeur, gravity, highness, honor, izzat, kingliness, loftiness, majesty, merit, nobility, perfection, prestige, pride, propriety, rank, repute, sedateness, sobriety, solemnity, standing, stateliness, station, status, value, virtue, worth
accidental hayz, joy
bishop's lawn
papal tiara
DIGOXIN lanoxin
DIGRESS aberrate, circumlocute, depart, deviate, digress, divagate, excur(se), go astray, maunder, periphrase, ramble, stray, swerve, turn aside, veer, wander
DIGRESSION aside, deviation, ecbasis, ecbole, episode, evagation, excursus, loop, obliquity, passage, sideslip, tangent, vagary
rhetorical ecbole
DIGS See DIGGINGS.
DIKE astraea, bank, barrier, bund, causeway, channel, cradge, dice, dick, digue, ditch, estacade, fortification, furrow, gap, gulf, gully,

jetty, levee, linn, mine, moat, mole, mound, obstacle, pier, pond, pool, powdike, spreader, trench, trough
military estacade
parent themis, zeus
rock banakite, beresite, odinite
up dress
DIKETOUE benzil, biacetyl, dimedone
DILACTONE anemonin, lactide
DILAPIDATE decay, destroy, disintegrate, havoc, impair, neglect, rot, ruin, slight, squander, waste, wrack, wreck
DILAPIDATED battered, beat-up, broken, craichy, creachy, creaky, decayed, desolate, faded, gone to seed, ragged, ramshackle, ruined, rundown, scarred, shabby, tattered, tumbledown, weatherbeaten, woebegone, wrecky
DILAPIDATION decay, decrepity, depreciation, disintegration, disrepair, ruin
DILATE amplify, argue, augment, broaden, bulge, delay, descant, discourse, discuss, distend, enlarge, expand, expatiate, explain, extend, grow, increase, inflate, lengthen, plump, protract, spread, stretch, swell, widen
DILATOR diopter, dioptra, dioptry, speculum
DILATORY behindhand, dawdling, delaying, fabian, inactive, indolent, laggard, late, latrede, lax, lingering, moratory, negligent, remiss, slack, slow, sluggish, tardy, tedious
DILEMMA alternative, asses' bridge, bewilderment, brike, choice, cornute, difficulty, disjoint, dulcarnon, fix, fork, gordian knot, impasse, jam, jeopardy, mire, node, nodus, option, paradox, perplexity, pickle, plight, plunge, polemics, ponsasinorum, predicament, problem, puzzle, quandary, question, scrape, snare, snifter, sorties, strait, trap
person with dulcarnon
DILETTANTE admirer,

aesthete, amateur, authority, connoisseur, dabbler, dabster, enthusiast, esthete, lover, novice, sciolist, smatterer, superficial, trifler, tyro, virtuoso
DILIGENCE application, assiduity, attention, business, care, carriage, caution, dilly, earnestness, heed, hie, horning, industry, painstaking, perseverance, prudence, sedulity, stagecoach, vehicle, vigilance
DILIGENT active, assiduous, busy, careful, constant, eident, hardworking, heedful, ithand, laborious, operose, painful, painstaking, persevering, persisting, sedulous, steady, studious, tidy, tireless, unflagging, workful
DILL anet, anise, calm, herb, pickle, soothe, soya, umbel
seed anet, anise, fennel
DILLY ace, daffodil, duck, pip, top-notcher, tree
-dally dawdle, delay, idle, lag, loaf, loiter, procrastinate, sport, stall, tarry, toy, trifle, vacillate
DILOGY redundancy
DILUTE adulterate, allay, attenuate, baptize, blunt, brew, cut, delay, diminish, dissolve, enfeeble, fuse, irrigate, lengthen, moderate, qualify, rarefy, reduce, temper, thin, water, weaken
liquor brew, split
wine gallize, water
DIM befog, bemist, bewilder, bleak, blear(y), blind, blunt, blur, caliginous, cloud(y), cover, crepuscular, dark(en), darkle, darkling, daswen, dimpsy, dreamy, dull, dusky, eclipse, enmist, envelope, fade, faint, filmy, fog(gy), hazy, indistinct, mat, mist (y), mysterious, nebulous, obscure, obtuse, opacate, overcast, pale, pall, shadowed, shadowy, stupid, tarnish, twilit, vague, veil, wan, weak
become daswen
name meaning derrick
not fresh
-sighted cecil, moonblind, purblind
sun yamcha
view objection

-wit simpleton

-witted blunt, dull, slow, stupid, thick, weak-minded

DIME coin, disme, hog(g), ten cents, tenpence, tenpenny, tenth, tithe

-a-dozen cheap, plentiful, plenty

half nickel, picayune

novel penny-dreadful

-store cheap, five-and-ten, woolworth's

DIMENHYDRINATE dramamine

DIMENSION(S) body, bulk, capacity, degree, extent, ga(u)ge, girth, importance, magnitude, measure, proportion, scope, size, space

4th space

DIMINISH abate, abridge, alleviate, amoinder, bate, condense, contract, curtail, cut, dampen, decrease, deplete, diminute, discount, dwarf, dwindle, ebb, erode, fade, fail, fine, fret, fritter, lessen, lighten, melt, minorate, mitigate, moderate, pare, peter(out), pink, ploy, rebate, recede, reduce, relieve, retrench, sap, sink, slack, slough, subside, tail, taper, temper, wane, wear, wither

DIMINUTION abatement, contraction, decrease, decrement, fall, mitigation, moderation, relief, shrinkage, waste

DIMINUTIVE baby, bantam, banty, bit, button, byname, duodecimo, dwarfish, exiguous, fingerling, jitney, lightweight, lilliputian, little, manikin, minikin, minnow, minny, minuscule, minute, mouse, nickname, nubbin, peewee, petite, pocket(sized), pony, puny, runt(y), shrimp(y), slip, small(fry), tiny, tit(mouse), tomtit, toy, wart, wee, wisp, young

comb. ale, cula, cule, culus, ette, ita, kin(s), let, ling, ock, ule

DIMLY darkly, dully, feebly, shadowy

DIMMED bleared, bleary, clouded, cloudy, grayed, lessened

DIMPLE ahmadi, ahmedi, dent, depression, doke, fos-

ette, gelasin, indentation, notch, ripple

DIN alarum, babel, bedlam, belder, blast, boom, bruit, bum, chirm, clamor, clangor, clash, clatter, confusion, deafen, deave, deeve, dingdong, fragor, frush, hubbub, hullabaloo, hurlyburly, noise, pandemonium, racket, rerd(e), resound, ring, riot, steven, stun, surge, swell, thunder, tintamar, turmoil, uproar

into drum, hammer, harp on

DINA(H) *brother* levi

parent jacob, leah

DINAR coin, denari, maravedi, money

1/100th para

20 bisti

100 rial

gold ahmadi, ahmedi

DINDLE hawkweed, thistle

DINE banquet, consume, eat, fall to, fare, feast, feed, regale, sup

DINER eater, epicure, gourmand, gourmet, lunchroom, restaurant

DING beat, clang, dang, dash, drive, dun, fling, kick, knock, noise, pitch, pound, punch, sound, stroke, thrash, thrust, thump, urge, veto, whip

-a-ling eccentric, jingle, tinkle, weirdo

DINGBAT dingus, missile, thingamabob

DINGDONG active, busy, earnestly, monotonous, nag, redundant, tedious

DINGE batter, bruise, dent, dint, tarnish

DINGHY rowboat, shallop, skiff, snowbird

DINGLE dale, dell, den, dimble, dumble, glen, jingle, portal, ravine, ring, storeroom, stormdoor, tinkle, tremble, vale, valley

DINGO warrigal

DINGUS doohickey, GADGET

DINGY black, blae, cold, dark, dirty, drab, dreary, dun, dusky, dusty, grim, grimy, murky, ourie, smirched, smoky, subfusc

DINING *comb.* deipno

room cafe, cenacle, cenaculum, eatery, grill, mess, oecus, refectory, restaurant,

salle a manger, salon, spence, triclinium

science aristology

DINK beanie, boat, cap, cut out

DINKA janghey

DINKUM fair, genuine, honest, reliable

DINKY cute, finicky, little, locomotive, neat, poor, small

DINNER banquet, beanfest, beano, feast, feed, function, kale, meal, pranzo, puchero, repast

ceremonial seder

course antipasto, appetizer, dessert, entree, fruit, hors d'oeuvre, salad, soup

jacket black-tie, formal, tux-(edo)

pail blickey

pert. cenatory, prandial

DINOSAUR allosaurus, anchisaur, apatosaur, branchiosaur, brontosaur, camarasary, camarasaurus, ceratops, ceratosaur, cetiosaur, claosaur, diapsid, diplodocus, duckbill, gigantosaur, gorgosaur, iguanodon, megalosaur, megatherium, monoclonius, morosaur, nodosaur, orinthopod, orithischia, palaeosaur, predentata, pterodactyl, sauropod, scelidosaur, stegosaur, theropod, thespesius, titanosaur, torosaur, trachodon, triceratops, troodont

carnivorous allosaurus, gorgosaur, tyrannosaur

herbivorous atlantosaurus, iguanodon

hornless protoceratops

period jurassic, mesozoic, triassic

small anchisaur

3-horned triceratops

DINT attack, blow, clour, delve, dent, dinge, dunt, efficacy, effort, force, imprint, indentation, nick, notch, power, press, print, shock, strike, striking

DIOCESE bishopric, center, district, eparchy, episcopate, jurisdiction, parish, prebend, province, see, stall

change exeat

church cathedral

division parish(en)

DIOCLES *ruler of* syracuse

DIODE kenotron

DIOGENES cynic, recluse
home tub
search honest man
symbol lantern
DIOMEDES tydides
companion acmon
enemy aeneas, hector
horse dinos, lampon
kingdom aetolia, thrace
parent cyrene, deipyle, mars, tydeus
theft horses
victim abas, agastrophus, coroebus, eniopeus, xanthus
wife aegialea, euippe
DION *brother* leptines, megacles
brother-in-law dionysius
captain marsyas, saesylus
enemy dionysius, heraclides, philistus, sosis
friend callipus, cimonides, eudemus, hicetes, miltas, ptoeodorus, speusippus, synalus
messenger archonides, hellanicus, telesides
niece arete, sophrosyne
pilot protus
sister aristomache
son hipparinus
teacher plato
DIONE *brother* titan
consort zeus
daughter aphrodite, venus
father oceanus, zeus
moon of saturn
DIONYSIA(N) anthesteria, bacchanal(ia), frenzied, orgiastic, uninhibited
DIONYSIUS *admiral* nypsius
brother diocles, erginus
brother-in-law dion, polyxenus
consort aristomache
construction lautumiae, prison
father-in-law hermocrates, hipparinus
friend archytas
offspring apollocrates, arete, dionysius, syphrosyne
parent doris, hermocrates
sister arete, theste
tyrant of syracuse
DIONYSUS bacchus, bromios. bromius, cresius, dendrites, dithyramb, eleutherios, evius, lacchus, lenaeus, liber, liknites, lyaeus, mitrephorus, pyrigenes, thrianbus, zagreus
altar thymele
aunt ino

birthplace thebes
companions bacchae, bacchant(e), bassarae, bassariedes, centaur, clodones, lenae, m(a)enads, mimallones, pan, satyr, thiasos, thiasus, thyiad
consort ariadne, aura
cry for joy iacchus
daughter artemis, diana
feast participant comoedus
festival agrania, agrionia, anthesteria, bacchanalia, bromalia, brumalia, thiasos, thiasus
follower acetes, satyr, thiasos, thiasus, thyiad
foster father silenus
friend silenus
garment nebris
grandfather cadmus
mocker arsippe
nurse brisa, coronis
parent demeter, jupiter, persephone, semele, thyone, zeus
pert. bacchic(al), bromian
priest coresus, eumolpus
protector acetes
sacred animal ass, dolphin, lynx, panther, serpent, tiger
sacred plant asphodel, ivy, laurel
sacrifice ram
shrine baccheion
skin worn by nebris
son comus, phlias, thoas
symbol ivy, panther, thyrsus
victim eurytos, pentheus, rhaetos
worshippers bacchante, clodones, mimallones, threskeuein, thyiad
DIONYZA *husband* cleon
servant leonine
DIOPSIDE alalite, malacolite, pyroxene, violan
DIORAMA panorama, scene, view
DIORITE appinite, corsite, diabase, ornoite
DIOSCURI alcis, anaces, anakes, anax, castor, gemini, pollux, polydeuces, twins, tyndaridae
horse cyllaros
parent leda, tyndareus, zeus
sister clytemnestra, helen
teacher chiron
victim amycus, lynceus
DIOSPYROS alintatao, amaga, camagon, persimmon, plum, sapote
wood calamander, ebony

DIP bail, baptize, candle, cavity, dap, decline, declivity, delve, descent, dib, dish, dop(p), douse, downturn, drop, duck, dunk, hat, hollow, immerse, incline, lade, ladle, lave, load, lower, merse, moisten, penetrate, pickpocket, pitch, plunge, scoop, set, signal, sink, slope, soak, sop, souse, spoon, submerge, subside, swim, taint, thief
and throw bail, bale
into browse, sample, scan
in water douse, rinse, souse
out bail, keach
slip fault
DIPENTINE cajaputene, cinene
DIPHENHYDRAMINE benadryl
DIPHETAMINE See AMPHETAMINE.
DIPHTHONY bivocal, breaking, ligature
DIPLOMA certificate, charter, codicil, commission, degree, document, paper, sanad, sheepskin, sunnud
highest summa cum laude
DIPLOMACY arbitration, delicacy, discretion, discrimination, eclat, expedience, finesse, politics, protocol, style, tact, wisdom
DIPLOMAT ambassador, attache, charge d'affaires, consul, doyen, emissary, envoy, legate, minister, nuncio, plenipotentiary, proconsul, proxenus, solitaire, statesman, vice-consul
corps head dean, doyen
DIPLOMATIC artful, bland, crafty, cunning, discriminate, fecial, fetial, polite, politic, shy, smooth, suave, tactful, urbane
DIPLOPIA ambiopia, polyoba
DIPODY diiamb, meter, metre, syzygy
DIPOLIA b(o)uphonia, festival
DIPPER bail, baptist, bucket, calabash, car, dunkard, dunker, gawn, gourd, grebe, ladle, ouzel, pickler, pickpocket, piet, piggin, plough, plow, scoop, septentrion, simpulum, spoon, tunker, ursa

astronomical wag(g)on
big charles's wain, ursa major
little ursa minor

DIPPY crazy, fónd, FOOL-ISH, insane, mad, obsessed, preposterous, silly, unreasonable

DIPSOMANIA alcoholism, bibacity, bottlenose, delirium tremens, enomania, intemperance, intoxication, oenomani, oinomania, potomania

DIPSOMANIAC addict, alcoholic, boozer, bouser, carouser, drunk(ard), inebriate, soak, sot, tippler, toper, tosspot

DIPTERA anopheles, anthomyid, bat-tick, botfly, flea, gnat, housefly, insect, mosquito, tsetse
wing lobe alula

DIPWARE pottery

DIRAE See FURIES.

DIRCE *husband* lycus
mother antiope
slayer amphion, farnese bull, zethus

DIRDUM blame, blow, outcry, punishment, rebuke, scolding, tumult, uproar

DIRECT 3 aim, bid, con, fix, ken, lay, run, set 4 agye, airt, bain, bald, beam, bend, boss, cast, conn, heap, helm, hold, lead, main, nigh, open, rein, rule, send, show, sway, tell, turn 5 airth, apply, aread, bluff, blunt, coach, cover, ettle, exact, frank, guide, hight, level, order, pilot, refer, right, short, speed, steer, teach, train, utter, weise 6 advise, arrect, candid, charge, devote, enjoin, govern, graith, handle, homely, honest, lineal, master, oneway, steady, streck, temper, witter 7 address, appoint, command, conduct, control, convert, counsel, deictic, express, marshal, present, sincere 8 engineer, manuduce, manduct, outright, regulate, shepherd, straight, unbroken 9 determine, dunstable, immediate, prescribe, supervise 10 administer, forthright, horizontal, mastermind, unswerving 11

categorical, undeviating 15 straightforward
against launch, sic
attention to attend, caution, remind
horse hup
into channels canalize
itself tent
one's course aim, hit, travel
sideways sklent

DIRECTION address, administration, advice, aegis, aim, airt(h), angle, appointment, arrangement, aspect, bearing, bent, bidding, calendar, carry, channel, command, conduct, control, counsel, current, deleatur, design, dictate, directive, directorate, disposition, drift, duct, east, eaver, egis, formula, gate, government, guidance, heading, helm(age), inclination, instruction, kibla, lay, lead, leadership, lie, line, management, mandate, north, order, pattern, pilotage, point(er), precept, prescript (ion), program, quarter, range, regulation, reins, route, rudder, run, sense, set, south, steerage, steering, stewardship, stretch, supervision, tack, tendency, tenor, track, trend, way, west
biblical selah
change in jog, knee, step
comb. ling
court order, verdict
dance call
finder compass
horizontal azimuth
in opposite antidromic, antidromous
line of See RANGE.
musical See MUSICAL *direction.*
oblique skew
opposite counter
outward beam
pole to pole axial
without astatic

DIRECTIVE circular, dictate, instruction, orders

DIRECTLY anon, aright, at once, bang, blankly, bolt, due, even, exactly, expressly, fast, flat, forthright, forthwith, immediately, instantly, openly, outright, personally, plumb, point, promptly, quickly,

right, sheer(ly), simply, slapdash, soon, souse, spang, square, stang, straight, wholly
comb. even

DIRECTOR administrator, archon, auditor, boss, chairman, coach, comptroller, curator, floorman, governor, guide, head, impresario, leader, manager, master, monitor, pilot, prefect, producer, rector, starets, sterner, steward, superintendent, tetrarch, trainer, warden
group administration, board, cabinet, management
theatrical regisseur

DIRECTORY atlas, baedeker, bluebook, bradshaw, gazetteer, guidebook, handbook, index, itinerary, list, manual, murray, ordo, phone book, reference, register, roadmap

DIRGE coronach, death march, elegy, epicede, epicedium, funeral march, grief, hearse, hymn, jeremiad, keen, kinah, lament (ation), linos, linus, monody, qinah, requiem, song, tangi, threne, threnody, trental, ullagone
-like elegaic(al), epicedial, funereal, threnetic(al), threnodial

DIRIGIBLE aerostat, airship, balloon, blimp, steerable, zeppelin
famous akron, graf zeppelin, hindenburg, shenandoah
framework nacelle
part fin
pioneer rosendahl

DIRK dagger, obelisk, sica, skean, skeanockle, skhian, skiver, snee, sny, sword

DIRL thrill, tingle, vibrate

DIRT clay, corruption, dregs, dust, earth, feculence, fen, filth, gore, gossip, grime, ground, grout, guck, muck(ment), mud, mullock, refuse, seuch, seugh, soil, sump, trash, vileness
attraction to mysophilia
bird woodpecker, vulture
comb. myso, ryo
dauber wasp
dread of mysophobia, ryophobia
-eating geophagy

free from apinoid, clean
symbol pig
DIRTY 3 low, 4 base, evil, foul, hory, lewd, mire, muck, rile, roil, soil, vile, wory 5 bawdy, black, cabby, dingy, dusty, grimy, gusty, horry, messy, mucky, muddy, mussy, nasty, pousy, smoky, sooty, sully 6 bedust, bemire, besoot, bleary, clarty, clatty, defile, dreggy, filthy, frousy, frowsy, fulyie, fulzie, greasy, grubby, impure, muck up, opaque, scrimy, slashy, sloppy, slummy, slurry, smudge, smutty, snuffy, soiled, sordid, untidy, vulgar 7 begrime, bemuddy, beslime, brooked, brookie, bruckle, drabble, draggle, grufted, imbroin, muddied, obscene, profane, roynous, slotter, slubber, smirchy, smutchy, spatter, squalid, stained, sullied, tarnish, unclean 8 begrimed, besmirch, bruckled, draggled, ordurous, paskudne, polluted, slovenly, soapless 9 paskudneh, 10 bedraggled 12 contaminated, pornographic
dig See TAUNT.
look frown
DIS god, hades, horn, orcus, pluto, underworld, valkyrie
DISABLE afflict, batter, becripple, break, bruise, bugger, chink, cripple, crock, damage, debilitate, demoralize, disarm, dismay, disqualify, enervate, enfeeble, gag, gruel, hamstring, handcuff, harm, hock, hog tie, hurt, impair, inactivate, incapacitate, injure, kibosh, knock out, lame, maim, mangle, muzzle, paralyze, pinion, prostrate, queer, ruin, sap, silence, spike, strangle, throttle, unable, undermine, unfit, weaken, wing, wrack, wreck
DISABLED crippled, halt, hors de combat, injured, invalid, lame
DISACCHARIDE biose, lactose, maltose, sucrose
DISADVANTAGE damage, drawback, handicap, hindrance, hurt, impediment, inconvenience, injury,

lurch, miss, penalty, risk, strike, trouble, unselth, unspeed, worry
put at lee-bow
DISADVANTAGEOUS adverse, contrary, detrimental, harmful, hurtful, inconvenient, inopportune, objectionable
DISAFFECT agitate, alienate, debauch, disturb, divorce, estrange, sever, sunder, wean
DISAFFECTION deceit, disease, disgust, dislike, disorder, hostility, mutiny
DISAFFIRM annul, contradict, deny, disclaim, repudiate, reverse
DISAGREE argue, battle, bicker, clash, conflict, differ, discept, dispute, dissent, fight, hate, jar, quarrel, row, vary, war, wrangle
DISAGREEABLE bad, bitter, chiselly, chronic, cross, fulsome, ghastly, harsh, hateful, ill, ingrate, irascible, irksome, kindless, nasty, naughty, offensive, repugnant, rotten, snuffy, ugly, ungenial, unlovely, unlusty, unpleasant, unsavory
DISAGREEMENT argument, bicker(ing), bree, clash, controversy, difference, discord, discrepancy, dispute, dissent, dissonance, division, faction, fight, fissure, friction, incongruity, mislike, quarrel, rift, spat, squabble, strife, variance, war(fare), wrangle
DISALLOW censure, deny, disclaim, disprove, forbid, prohibit, reject
DISAPPEAR cease, depart, die, disparish, dispel, disperse, dissipate, dissolve, drop, evanesce, evanish, evaporate, fade(away) or (out), faint, flee, fly, get lost, go away, immerge, lapse, melt, pass, perish, recede, resolve, retire, scram, sink, snuff, vanish, wend, whop
gradually dim, drain, ely, evanesce
suddenly burst, cook, duck, mizzle
DISAPPEARANCE eclipse, fadeaway, flight, vanishing
DISAPPOINT baffle, balk,

beguile, belie, bilk, cast down, chagrin, cheat, cross, dash, defeat, destroy, discomfit, disenchant, disgruntle, disillusion, displease, dissatisfy, fail, fall, foil, frustrate, let down, mock, nullify, put out, snape, sour, thwart, undo
DISAPPOINTMENT ba(u)lk, beguile, blow, chagrin, comedown, denial, despair, discontent, disillusion, failure, frustration, heartscald, letdown, lurch, rue, sour grapes
expression of drat, rats
DISAPPROBATION See DISAPPROVAL.
DISAPPROVAL ban, bird, blackball, blacklist, boo(h), boycott, brickbat, catcall, censure, condemnation, criticism, disfavor, disgrace, dislike, displeasure, hiss, objection, odium, razz, the bird, veto
expression of by no means, god forbid, heaven forfend, phooey, thunder, yuk
DISAPPROVE call, censure, condemn, criticize, decry, deprecate, disallow, discountenance, disfavor, disparage, frown at, groan, hiss, mistake, nag, object, oppose, protest, reject, reprehend, take exception, thumbs down
DISAPPROVER wowser
DISARM appease, deactivate, demilitarize, disable, paralyze, subdue, unsteel
DISARRANGE carfuffle, clutter, confuse, derange, discompose, dishevel, disjoint, dislocate, disorder, disturb, garble, mess(up), misplace, muss(up), mux(up), overturn, ruffle, rummage, slatter, tiffle, tousle, unsettle, upset
type scramble, squabble
DISARRAY caddle, derange, despoil, discreate, dishabille, dishevel, disorder, disturb, fuffle, huddle, mess, strip, undight, undress, upset
DISARRAYED unkempt
DISASSEMBLE demolish, demount, dismount, strip, take apart
DISASTER accident, adver-

sity, affliction, bale, blow, calamity, casualty, cataclysm, catastrophe, exigency, misadventure, mischance, misfortune, mishap, reverse, ruin, stroke, tragedy

DISASTROUS bad, calamitous, catastrophic, fatal, ill, sinister, tragic(al), weary

DISAVOW abjure, abnegate, decline, deny, disclaim, disown, disvouch, recant, refuse, renounce, retract

DISBAND adjourn, cashier, chase, discharge, dismiss, dispel, disperse, dissolve, reduce, reform, release, rout, scatter

DISBAR blackball, cashier, depose, dismiss, exclude, shut out, suspend

DISBELIEF agnosticism, atheism, incredulity, infidelity, nihilism, rejection, scruple
in god atheism

DISBELIEVE discount, discredit, doubt, ignore, refuse, reject, suspect

DISBELIEVER agnostic, apostate, atheist, doubter, doubting thomas, heretic, infidel, skeptic, thomas
in fall of man antilapsarian

DISBURDEN alleviate, clear, deliver, discharge, disload, ease, expend, lighten, relieve, rid, spend, unload

DISBURSE acquit, defray, distribute, expend, outlay, pay, spend, waste

DISC cam, co(u)lter, dial, discoid, discus, DISK, harrow, lamina, mad, medal (lion), paten, plate, platter, quoit, record, rondel, spangle, trochus
plastic frisbee

DISCANDY dissolve, melt

DISCARD abandon, abdicate, bait, bilge, cashier, cast(away), chuck, desert, discharge, dismiss, dispose of, disuse, divest, do away with, drop, dump, eject, eliminate, excuss, expunge, exuviate, forsake, get rid of, give away, jetsam, jettison, jilt, junk, molt, omit, oust, part with, reject, relegate, remove, repudiate, riddance, scrap, shed, shuck, slough, sluff, spurn, throw away, trash
in bridge echo
pile boneyard, dump, heap, pack, trash

DISCARDED cast(off), dormant, limbo, refuted, rejected, shed, thrown out

DISCARNATE immaterial, incorporeal, spectral

DISCERN apprehend, behold, deem, descry, detect, diagnose, discover, discriminate, distinguish, divine, espy, judge, ken, know, note, notice, observe, penetrate, perceive, probe, read, remark, scan, scerne, see, spy, survey, view, wit

DISCERNIBLE apparent, evident, manifest, obvious, visible

DISCERNING acute, apprehensive, astute, bright, brilliant, careful, clever, intelligent, judicious, nice, penetrating, perceptive, sage, sapient, sharp, shrewd, understanding, wise

DISCERNMENT acuity, acumen, astuteness, buddhi, comparison, divination, evaluation, eye, flair, gout, insight, intellect, intuition, judgment, penetration, perception, percipience, reason, refinement, sagacity, sharpness, shrewdness, skill, tact, taste, understanding, vision

DISCHARGE 3 air, axe, can, pay 4 boat, bolt, cass, drop, dump, emit, fire, flow, flux, free, give, oust, quit, riff, sack, shot, spew, teem, vent, void 5 annul, blast, bleed, break, conge, eject, empty, erupt, evict, expel, exude, frush, gleet, ichor, issue, loose, ozena, purge, repay, rheum, salvo, shoot, speed, vomit, whiff, yield 6 acquit, answer, assoil, bounce, cancel, emerge, excern, exempt, feeder, launch, lay off, lochia, ouster, parole, settle, shower, square, ticket, unlade, unload, volley 7 cashier, deraign, disband, discard, dismiss, excrete, exhaust, explode, fulfill, license, mission, perform, quietus, release, skitter 8 acquital, catapult, despatch, detonate, disgorge, dispatch, displode, emission, enfilade, evacuate, liberate, persolve, separate, solution, unburden 9 apostaxis, catharsis, excretion, expulsion, exudation, fusillade, purgation 10 accomplish, disembogue, observance, profluvium 11 performance
abnormal apostaxis
comb. cenosis
concentrated barrage
dishonorable bobtail, cashier
electric effluce, leader, lightning, spark, static, streamer
heavy storm
matter weep
simultaneous broadside, fusillade, salvo
suddenly hike

DISCHARGER excitator

DISCIPLE adherent, ananda, apostle, attendant, chela, convert, devotee, discipline, enthusiast, fan, follower, hearer, ist, ite, learner, murid, partisan, proselyte, punish, pupil, satellite, scholar, sectary, sectator, sravaka, student, supporter, teach, train
beloved john
christ's See APOSTLE christ's.
comb. ist, ite

DISCIPLINARIAN authoritarian, martinet, militarist, ramrod, teacher, trainer, tyrant

DISCIPLINARY corrective, educational, penal, punitive, punitory, strict

DISCIPLINE aplomb, break, bridle, canon, catharsis, chasten, chastise, check, come down on, control, correct(ion), course, curb, doctrine, drill, education, ethics, government, guide, heavy hand, innure, instruct, lead, learning, order, pedagogy, possession, punish, regulate, restrain(t), rule, scourge, selfcommand, selfcontrol, selfdenial, system, tairge, tame, teach (ing), thew, tight rein, train(ing), tutor(ing), virtue, whip
mental yoga
religious church, penance, sadhana

strict regimentation

DISCLAIM abdicate, abjure, abnegate, cut off, deny, devow, disallow, disavow, disown, recant, refuse, reject, renounce, repudiate

DISCLOSE air, announce, avow, babble, bare, betray, bewray, blab, blazon, blow, break, broadcast, call, come out with, declare, descry, develop, dig up, discover, discuss, disinter, dismask, display, divulge, evolve, exhibit, explain, expose, impart, indicate, know, lay bare, make clear, manifest, ope, open, publish, reveal, rip, root up, show, shrive, spill the beans, squeal, tattle, tell, turn up, unbundle, unclose, uncover, unearth, unfold, unhasp, unkennel, unlock, unmask, unroll, unsecret, unthatch, unveil, unwry, ventilate, voice

DISCLOSURE apocalypse, appearance, descrial, discovery, exposure, overture, revealing, revelation, shrift

DISCOLOR bedaub, besmear, besmirch, bespatter, bruise, burn, dull, fade, fox, mark, slander, smirch, smoke, soil, spot, stain, streak, tarnish, tinge

DISCOLORATION argyria, black eye, blemish, blight, bloom, blot, blotch, blur, browning, chloasma, cyanosis, dyschroa, foxing, livedo, mark, melasma, mildew, parachroma, rust, scald, speck, stain

by sun bronzing, burning, tanning

of turkeys blueback

on cured fish rust

small freckle, speck

DISCOLORED bin-burn, black and blue, bruised, dingy, dirty, doty, ecchymotic, foul, haw, livid, old, rusty, scorched, stained, tarnished, ustulate

by decay doty, foxed

DISCOMFIT abash, abave, abawe, agitate, annoy, battle, bother, chagrin, confuse, disappoint, disconcert, dismay, disturb, embarrass, faze, feague, foil, frustrate, irk, rattle, rout, shend,

shent, squash, thwart, upset, worst

DISCOMFORT ache, affliction, agony, anguish, annoyance, bore, chagrin, confusion, disaffection, disease, disgust, disquiet, dissatisfaction, distress, embarrassment, malaise, malease, misease, pain, provocation, sorrow, torment, trial, trouble, uneasiness

DISCOMMODE annoy, bother, disturb, flurry, fluster, inconvenience, irk, molest, perturb, trouble, upset, vex

DISCOMPOSE aggravate, agitate, confuse, disarrange, disquiet, excite, perturb, rattle, unsettle

DISCONCERT abash, alarm, baffle, bash, bewilder, blench, bowl, browbeat, bully, chagrin, confuse, daunt, dismay, disturb, embarrass, faze, feeze, flummox, flurry, fluster, fuss, hack, intimidate, misput, nag, nonplus, perplex, perturb, phase, puzzle, rattle, ruffle, squelch, thwart, upset, worry

DISCONNECT detach, disengage, disjoin, dissolve, divide, separate, sever, uncouple, undo, unyoke

DISCONNECTED abrupt, broken, choppy, cursory, desultory, disjointed, incoherent, interrupted, irrational, rambling, scattered, separate, staccato

DISCONSOLATE cheerless, dejected, desolate, distressed, doleful, downcast, forlorn, gloomy, hopeless, inconsolable, melancholy, miserable, sad, uncouth, woeful

DISCONTENT anger, disappointment, disgruntlement, displeasure, disquiet, dissatisfaction, envy, ill-humor, sourness, unhappiness, vexation

DISCONTENTED disaffected, disgruntled, displeased, dumpy, malcontent, unhappy

DISCONTINUE abandon, abstain, arrest, break up, cease, check, desist, disuse, drop, end, halt, intermit, in-

terrupt, letup, pause, quit, renounce, stay, stop, sunder, surcease, suspend

DISCONTINUOUS alternate, broken, chopped-off, decousu, discrete, disjunct, fitful, gaping, intermittent, irregular, periodic, recurrent, saltatory, spasmodic

DISCORD affray, argument, atonality, brawl, broil, cacophony, caviling, clash, conflict, contention, difference, din, disaccord, disagree, disharmony, dislike, dissension, dissonance, disturbance, enmity, fight, fray, friction, grate, harshness, hostility, inharmony, jangle, jar, jostle, mischief, mistone, misunderstanding, noise, quarrel, quibbling, rancor, schism, strife, struggle, tension, tumult, unsaught, variance, war

deity ate, eris, loki

DISCORDANT absonant, ajar, cacophonic, cacophonous, charivari, clashing, colliding, conflicting, contrary, cronk, diaphonic, different, disagreeing, discrepant, dissident, flat, frowzy, grating, harsh, hoarse, incongruous, inconsistent, inharmonious, jangling, jarring, off-color, off-key, off-pitch, rude, scordato, squawky, uncongenial

DISCOTHEQUE agogo, cabaret, nightclub

DISCOUNT abate(ment), agio, allow(ance), bate, batta, belittle, breakage, charge-off, concede, concession, contango, cut, deduct (ion), depreciate, disbelieve, discompt, discredit, disregard, drawback, ignore, lessen, percentage, poundage, rebate, reduce, reduction, reject, salvage, scout, setoff, shave, strike off, take off, tare, undersell, write off

DISCOUNTENANCE abash, disapprove, disconcert, discourage, embarrass, oppose, shame, thwart, veto

DISCOURAGE abash, alarm, appal(l), carp, cast down, chill, cow, damp, dampen, dash, daunt, deject, depress, deter, dishearten, dismay, dispirit, dissuade, flatten, freeze, frost, inhibit, oppose, prevent, shake, stifle

DISCOURAGEMENT cold, damper, daunt, depression, letdown, obstacle, oppression, putdown

DISCOURAGING bleak, chill, depressing, dreary, melancholy

DISCOURSE account, address, amplify, argue, argument, article, carp, catechesis, colloquy, comment, confer, converse, declaim, deliver, descant, dilate, discuss, dissert(ate), drool, entreat, eulogy, expound, homily, lecture, locution, loquence, monologue, narrate, orate, parlance, parley pr(a)elect, preach, rant, read, review, rhetoric, saw, screed, sermon, speak, speech, tale, talk, tell, theme, thesis, tract(ate), treatise, word
enthusiastic rhapsody
laudatory panegyric
long descant, philippic, screed, tirade
prolonged diatribe
serious homily
simple pap
unprofitable mataeology

DISCOURTEOUS blunt, boorish, brash, brusque, cheeky, churlish, crusty, curt, gruff, ill-behaved, ill-mannered, impolite, insolent, rude, scurvy, uncivil, ungracious, unhende, unrefined, vulgar
person boor, bounder, cad, churl, clown

DISCOURTESY cut, disrespect, incivility, rudeness, slight

DISCOVER apprehend, ascertain, bare, betray, communicate, confess, create, declare, descry, detect, determine, discern, disclose, discure, distinguish, divulge, espy, explore, expose, find, get, hit, impart, invent, learn, manifest, notice, observe, overgo, perceive, recognize, reveal, see, spy, strike, twig, uncover, unearth, unhide, unkennel

DISCOVERER columbus, explorer, inventor, scout, spy

DISCOVERY analysis, apocalypse, deduction, descry, detection, disclosure, espial, find, retrieval, revelation, treasure, trove
by chance accident
exclamation eureka
logic of heuretic

DISCREDIT asperse, backstab, belittle, blast, blemish, deface, defect, disbelieve, disgrace, dishonor, disparage, disrepute, distrust, doubt, ignominy, impeach, obloquy, odium, question, repel, reproach, revile, scandal, shame, smear, suspect

DISCREET careful, cautious, chary, circumspect, civil, considerate, discriminate, expedient, foresighted, guarded, heedful, judicious, polite, politic, provident, prudent, reserved, reticent, silent, wary, wise

DISCREPANCY difference, disagreement, discordance, divergence, incongruity, variance

DISCRETION calculation, caution, choice, consent, courtesy, diplomacy, discrimination, finesse, foresight, forethought, freedom, free will, judgment, liberty, mense, option, politics, providence, prudence, reserve, sense, tact, taste, will, wisdom

DISCRIMINATE anatomize, demarcate, demark, differentiate, discern, distinct, distinguish, divide, favor, incline, judge, part, penetrate, recognize, screen, secern, segregate, select, separate, set apart, set off, sever, sift, winnow

DISCRIMINATING acute, artistic, choice, choosey, conscientious, critical, explicit, exquisite, fastidious, finical, good, judicious, nice, particular, select(ive), sharp, tactful

DISCRIMINATION acumen, address, apartheid, appreciation, bias, bigotry, choice, color bar, color line, delicacy, diplomacy, discernment, discretion, distinction, elegance, eye, finesse, grace(fulness), injustice, insight, intolerance, judgment, nicety, penetration, perception, preference, prejudice, racialism, racism, redbaiting, refinement, sapience, savoir-faire, segregation, sense, sensibility, sensitivity, subtlety, tact(fulness), taste, wisdom
symbol of hansa

DISCURSIVE cursory, desultory, devious, dialectic(al), rambling, roving, wandering

DISCURTAIN uncover, unveil

DISCUS discoid, disk(os), plate, quoit, trencher
thrower discobolus

DISCUSS advise, agitate, air, analyse, argue, bandy, bargain, bespeak, brainstorm, canvass, chat, chew the rag, comment, confer, conjobble, consider, consult, controvert, cover, dandy, deal with, debate, deliberate, descant, dicker, dilate, discant, discept, discourse, dispute, dissert, emparl, examine, explain, explicate, expound, handle, imparl, interpret, investigate, kick around, moot, narrate, parley, reason, review, roun, rune, sift, study, talk, thresh out, tract, treat, ventilate
at length bat
bombastically harangue
casually mention
earnestly agitate
hastily skip
lightly bandy
secretly roun, rune
terms bargain, chaffer, dicker
thoroughly exhaust

DISCUSSION analysis, argument, article, brainstorming, buzz session, canvass, chinfest, colloquy, conference, consultation, debate, dialectic, diatribe, disceptation, dispute, excursus, forum, homily, huddle, moot, parley, pribble, symposium, talk, treatise
bombastic harangue
controversial argument, debate, dispute, wrangle
group brainstorming, class, forum, panel, seminar, symposium

open to moot

DISDAIN antipathy, arrogance, aversion, contemn, contempt, contumely, defy, despise, disregard, haughtiness, hauteur, ignore, insolence, pride, reject, repudiate, scorn, scout, slight, snoot, spurn, tut
expression of tsk, tush

DISDAINFUL arrogant, cavalier, contemptuous, contumelious, coy, deignous, digne, insolent, lordly, overbearing, proud, saucy, scornful, scorny, sniffish, sniffy, snuffy, supercilious, toplofty, tossy

DISEASE affection, affliction, ailment, alloverishness, blemish, blight, collapse, complaint, complication, crud, defect, derange, disability, disorder, dolor, epidemic, evil, fever, flaw, illness, indisposition, infection, infirmity, languor, mal(ady), malaise, malease, morbidity, morbus, necrosis, pathema, pathology, pest, plague, pox, rot, seediness, seizure, sepsis, sickliness, sickness, the pip, unhealth, virus
beginning, pert. pathoformic
black braxy
blue cyanosis, tick-fever
cause bacterium, contagium, germ, microbe, virus
cereal take-all
chagas' barberbug-fever
change in character alloeosis
chronic addison's
classification noseography, nosology
comb. agra, algia, itis, nos(o), nosus, oma, path(ia), pathic, patho
contagious alastrim, chickenpox, diphtheria, flu, glasspox, impetigo, measles, mumps, scarlet fever, smallpox, typhoid fever, typhus
contagious, pert. prosodemic
convulsive ergotism, raphania
crippling arthritis, polio, rheumatism, sclerosis
crisis apostasis
cutaneous eczema, herpes, impetigo, tetter
declining stage catabasis
defense antibody, sozin

deficiency beriberi, pellagra, scurvy
description pathography
detection radiography, xray, xrg
end of lysis
eruptive exanthema
fatal cooley's anemia
fatal lyssa, malignancy, pest, plague
favorable termination lysis
fear of nosophobia
febrile typhoid fever, typhus
1st period anabasis
fly-caused african lethargy, sleeping sickness, trachoma
foreign ecdemic
fungus ergot, jellyend rot, tinea
glandular addison's
hansen's leprosy
heat treatment thermotherapy
hereditary anemia
investigator etiologist
jumping lata(h), tic
kissing mono(nucleosis)
malignant cancer, plague
mental psychosis
mild, pert. subclinical
nervous botulism, chorea, pellagra, tic
origin of etiology
pert. clinic, endemic, loimic
prediction about prognosis
prevalent endemic
prevention antitoxin, immunization, prophylaxis, shot
primary idiopathy
-producing zymotic
recognition diagnosis
reigg's pyorrhea
return of relapse
science etiology, nosology, pathology
science, children's pediatrics
spreader bacteria, carrier, fly, germs, mosquito, vector, virus
subject of case, patient
transmission contagion
treatment antibiotic, antilepsis, homeopathy, therapy
treatment, by water hydropathy
treatment, drugless naturopathy
tropical jungle rot, malaria, sprue, yaws
virus cancer, cold, creutzfeldt jakob syndrome, ebola fever, flu, influenza, kuru, lassa fever, legionnaire's disease, measles, multiple

sclerosis, rocky mountain spotted fever, sspe, swine flu
wasting cancer, phthisic, tuberculosis
wide-spread epidemic
without asymptomatic
yeast-caused saccharomycosis

DISEASED ailing, bad, cachexic, contaminated, corrupt(ed), critical, evil, indisposed, infected, infectious, morbid, morbific, morbose, pathological, peccant, pestiferous, poisoned, poorly, septic, sick(ly), stricken, tainted, traumatic, unhealthy, unsound, unwell, upset, vicious, vitiated, weak(ly)
comb. cace, cac(o)

DISEMBARK alight, arrive, debark, deboat, deplane, detrain, disboard, go ashore, land, unbark, unboat

DISEMBARRASS clear, disencumber, extricate, free, liberate, release, relieve, rid, untangle

DISEMBODIED discarnate, fleshless, immaterial, separate, spectral
one ghost, phantom, poltergeist, spectre

DISEMBODIMENT soul, spirit

DISEMBOGUE discharge, disgorge, eject, emerge, flow, pour out

DISEMBOWEL eviscerate, garbage, gralloch, gut, hulk, paunch, untripe

DISENCHANT disabuse, disillusion, dismay, set straight

DISENCHANTED disillusioned, sour

DISENCUMBER alleviate, detach, disengage, ease, educe, extricate, free, liberate, lighten, redd, release, rid, unclutch, untangle, untie

DISENGAGE clear, cutover, detach, disembroil, disjoin, evolve, extricate, free, liberate, loose(n), part, release, separate, unclutch, unravel, untile, wean, withdraw

DISENTANGLE card, clear, comb, detach, disembroil, disencumber, divorce, extricate, free, liberate, loose, part, ravel, release, scutch, separate, sever, simplify, sleave, solve, straighten, sunder, tease, tose, toze, undo, unravel, unreave, untangle, untie, untwine, untwist

DISESTEEM disfavor, dishonor, disrespect, disvalue, slight, umbrage

DISFAVOR break, disapprove, disesteem, disfigure, dishonor, dislike, disregard, disrepute, dutch, malgrace, objection, offense

DISFIGURE batter, blemish, blot, blubber, blur, deface, deform, disgrace, distort, foul, gnarl, hurt, impair, injure, maim, mangle, mar, mutilate, scar, warp

DISFIGURED defect, deformed, foul, mutilated, scarred

DISGORGE belch, cast forth, debouch, discharge, disembogue, ejaculate, eject, empty, eruct, erupt, exhaust, expel, extravasate, jet, outpour, pour out, relinquish, send out, spew, spout, spurt, squirt, vent, vomit

DISGRACE abase, attain(ure), baffle, befoul, besmear, blot, brand, defile, degrade, discredit, disfavor, dishonor, disrepute, foil, foul, gibbet, humble, humiliation, ignominy, infamy, mortify, notoriety, obloquy, odium, offense, opprobrium, reproach, scandal, scorn, shame, shend(ing), shent, slander, slur, spite, stain, stigma, sully, taint, tash, villainy
mark with blot, brand, scar, stigmatize

DISGRACEFUL criminal, defamous, evil, filthy, ignoble, indign, infamous, inhonest, mean, opprobrius, scandalous, shameful, shocking, sour

DISGRUNTLED disaffected, discontented, displeased, grumpy, malcontent, peevish, petulant, sore

DISGUISE affect, ambush, belie, blend, camouflage, cloak, color, conceal, costume, cover(t), deacon, dissemble, dissimulate, doctor,

domino, facade, false front, falsify, feign, glass, gloze, hide, illusion, incognito, inmask, lain, layne, mantle, mask, masque(rade), misrepresent, mumm(ery), obscure, palliate, pretence, pretend, pretense, shade, sham, shroud, simulate, smoke screen, transvest, travesty, umbrella, veil, visor, vizor
information layne

DISGUISED camouflaged, cloaked, covert, fucate, gilded, incognito, latent, mystic, palliate, travesty

DISGUST abhorrence, antipathy, appal(l), augh, aversion, degout, detestation, disaffection, discomfort, distaste, irk, kreistle, loath(ing), nausea(te), offend, repel, revolt, scandalize, shock, sicken, surfeit
exclamation of aug(g)h, avoy, faugh, feich, feigh, fie, foh, pah, phew, pish, poot, psha(w), pugh, rats, ugh, weloo, yah, yuk

DISGUSTING abhorrent, anathematic, beastly, foul, fulsome, gruesome, hateful, hideous, horrid, loathsome, loathly, lousy, macabre, mawkish, monstrous, mucky, nasty, nauseous, noisome, obscene, odious, offensive, outrageous, pert, repulsive, scrimy, shitten, shocking, vile

DISH basin, basque, batea, beauty, blazer, boat, bowl, casserole, caup, charger, cheat, choffer, comal, compote, compotier, concoction, course, critch, crock, cruse, depress, dip, entree, epergne, food, frustrate, girl, lade, ladle, lanx, luggie, mo(u)ld, nappy, patella, paten, patera, patina, piece de resistance, pinax, plat(e), platter, porringer, preparation, quoit, ramekin, receptacle, recipe, saucer, scoop, serve, shape, shelve, spoil, spoon, terrine, thwart, timbale, tureen, vessel
baking casserole, cocotte, ramekin, scallop, scollop
braised haslet
by dish a la carte

chafing chafer, choffer
cooking blazer, casserole, pot
footed comport, compote, compotier
gravy boat
main entree
-mustard pennycress
out administer, give, hollow, mete, serve
pan basin, keeler
pyramid style buisson
rack fiddle
sailor's scouse
serving platter, trencher, tureen
shallow scuttle
side entremets
silver hollow ware
spiced salami, salmi, sausage
stemmed compo(r)t
sweet dessert, flummery, junket
tasty morsel
the dirt gossip
wooden bassie, bicker, bourie, bowie, ca(u)p, goggan, kickshaw, luggie

DISHABILLE bathrobe, brunchcoat, disarray, disorder, dressing gown, housecoat, kimono, negligee, peignoir, robe(de chambre), tea gown, undress, wrapper

DISHAN son aran

DISHARMONY adharma, clash, discord(ance), disorder, dissonance, fraction, incongruity, schism

DISHCLOTH gourd loofah, luffa, patola

DISHEARTEN amate, cast down, daunt, deject, depress, deter, discourage, dispirit, displease, flatten, indispose, shake, unheart, unman, unnerve

DISHEARTENED depressed, downcast, dull, gloomy

DISHEVEL disarray, disorder, let down, let hang, loosen, make untidy, mess up, muss, ruffle, rumple, tumble

DISHEVELED blousy, blowsy, blowzy, coarse, deranged, disarrayed, disordered, disorderly, dowdy, fat, frowzled, frowzy, mussed, rooky, ruddy, ruffled, rumpled, sheveled, slatternly, slipshod, slovenly, tattered, tousled, tumbled, uncombed, unkempt, untidy

DISHON *son* amram, cheran, eshban, ithran

DISHONEST bad, cheating, corrupt, cozening, cronk, crooked, deceitful, faithless, false, fishy, fraudulent, knavish, lying, mendacious, oblique, perfidious, shady, shameful, sinister, snide, swindling, thievish, treacherous, unfair, unhonest, unjust, unscrupulous, untrue, untruthful

DISHONESTY crookedness, deceit, deviousness, fraud(ulence), improbity, knavery, racket, roguery, skulduggery, thievery, villainy

DISHONOR abase, abuse, affront, attainder, attaint, blot, brand, corruption, debase, debauch, defame, default, defile, degrade, deplume, discredit, disesteem, disfavor, disglory, disgrace, displume, disrespect, flout, foul, fraud, humiliate, ignominy, illrepute, infamy, obloquy, odium, opprobrium, reproach, scandal, shame, spite, stain, stigma, villainy, violate, wrong

DISHONORABLE bad, base, black, corrupt, crooked, deceitful, devious, disreputable, evil, false, foul, ignoble, ignominious, inglorious, low, mean, miscreant, nasty, scandalous, shabby, shameful, shameless, unhonest, unworthy, yellow

discharge bobtail, cashiering, dismissal

DISHWASHER domestic, flycatcher, swiller, wagtail

DISHWATER dregs, offal, refuse

DISILLUSION awaken, correct, debunk, disabuse, disappoint, disenchant, disillude, dismay, disquixote, enlighten, expose, free of, prick the bubble, put straight, set right, sour

DISINCLINATION aversion, dislike, distaste, nill, unlust, unwill

DISINCLINED afraid, averse, backward, balking, hesitant, indisposed,

lo(a)th, opposed, reluctant, unwilling

DISINFECT clean, cleanse, fumigate, sanitize, scrub, sterilize, sweeten

DISINFECTANT acerdol, alexiteric, antidotal, antiformin, antiseptic, argenol, bactericide, bleach, borophenol, bromol, chlorine, creolin, cres(s)ol, cressyl, eugenol, formaldehyde, fumigant, germicide, halazone, iodin(e), lysol, manganite, paraform, peroxide, phenol, prophylactic, tachiol

DISINHERIT abdicate, cut off, deprive, disclaim, disheir, disown, dispossess, exheredate

DISINTEGRATE atomize, beat, break, calcine, collapse, corrode, crumble, decay, decompose, deliquesce, disband, disorganize, disperse, dissipate, dissolve, erode, grush, melt, molder, powder, pulverize, putrefy, resolve, rot, scatter, separate, shatter, slake, split, spoil, waste away

DISINTEGRATION biolysis, breakup, catalysis, collapse, decay, dialysis, dispersion, erosion, heartrot, hydrolysis, proteolysis, pulverization, thermolysis

DISINTER delve, dig, disclose, discover, disentomb, excavate, exhume, grub, resurrect, spade, unbury, unearth, ungrave, untomb

DISINTERESTED aloof, apathetic, candid, detached, fair, impartial, indifferent, lackadaisical, negative, neutral, perfunctory, unconcerned

DISJOIN detach, disengage, dissociate, dissolve, disunite, part, separate, sever, sunder, undo, untack, unyoke

DISJOINED diazeutic

DISJOINTED incoherent, irrational

DISJUNCTION breach, break, caesura, division, divorce, isolation, parting, rent, rift, separation, split

DISK aten, bobeche, burr, c(h)akra, checker, circle, clipeus, dial, eye, harrow,

knob, medal, nob, orb, pan, paten, pellet, plate, platter, pook, puck, record, riffle, rondel(le), rosette, rotator, sequin, sheave, sput, token, tondino, tondo, tuft, wafer, washer, wax, zecchino, zequin

admitting light bull's-eye

boiler-patching sput

bull's-eye carton

choked papilledema

coin-making flan, planchet

cut trepan

eccentric sheave

fleshy sarcoma

handled riffle

hocky puck

-like discal, discoid

medicated lamella, troche

metal flan, ghurry, gong, medal(lion), sequin, slug, tag, token, zecchino

paper confetti

revolving wafter

rotating scanner

solar aten, aton, c(h)akra

trochal corona

wax agnus

winged feroher

DISLIKE antipathy, aversion, derry, despisal, detest, disapproval, disfavor, displeasure, distaste, hate, hatred, loathe, loathing, objection, odium, regret, repugnance, resent(ment), scunder, scunner, spite, spleen, stomach

comb. mis(o)

exclamation of foh, fough, pah, pew, phew, ugh

irrational scunder, scunner

object of anathema

of children misopedia

DISLOCATE break, derange, disjoint, dislock, displace, lux(ate), slip, splay, unhinge, unjoint, unset, unwrest, upset

DISLOCATED shotten

DISLOCATION break, shift, slide

DISLODGE beat, blast, bolt, buck, bump, discard, dishabit, DISLOCATE, dismiss, displace, disroot, evict, expel, extricate, move, oust, overthrow, remove, shake, shift, stir, swoop, topple, unhorse, unseat

by blasting brush

DISLOYAL disleal, faithless, felon, fickle, inconstant,

perfidious, punic, recreant, snaky, traitorous, treacherous, unfaithful, unstable, untrue

DISLOYALTY betrayal, defection, infidelity, lese majesty, perfidy, recreancy, sedition, swick, swike, treachery, treason, unlewty

DISMAL alange, black, bleak, blue, calamitous, dark, desolate, dingy, dire, dolesome, dolorous, dowff, drab, dreadful, drear(y), dree, dreich, dreigh, dull, eery, funereal, gash(ful), ghastly, gloomy, glum, gousty, grave, gray, groanful, joyless, lonesome, lurid, melancholy, ominous, ourie, pocosin, sad, saturnine, sinister, solemn, somber, sombre, sombrous, sorry, swamp, swart, terrible, triste, uncouth, unhappy, unlucky, wan, waste, weariful, wearisome, weary, wisht, woeful
-looking gash, woebegone

DISMANTLE bare, demolish, denude, deprive, destroy, dismount, divest, rase, raze, strike, strip, undress, unravel, unrig

DISMAY abash, affright, alarm, appal(l), astony, astound, awe, bewilder, chill, confound, consternation, daunt, defection, discomfit, disconcert, discourage(ment), dishearten, dispirit, dread, faze, fear, fright(en), horrify, panic, perplex, puzzle, rattle, scare, stop, terrify, terror, trepidation
expression of oops

DISMEMBER discerp, disjoint, dissect, limb, maim, mangle, mutilate, part, quarter, rend, sever, torture, unlimb

DISMISS abandon, acquit, amand, axe, banish, boot, bounce, break, brush off, bump, bust, can, cash(ier), cast out, chuck, conjee, dejob, demit, deport, depose, disband, disbar, discard, discharge, disemploy, disgrace, dispatch, displace, dispoint, ditch, drop, drum out, eject, expel, fire, flunk, forget, gate, give the axe,

idle, ignore, kick out, lay off, let go, loose, ostracize, oust, pack off, pension, punish, quash, red-line, refute, reject, release, relegate, remove, remue, replace, retire, sack, scorn, scout, shed, shelve, slough, swap, swop, turn away, vaik, withdraw
evil spirits exorcize
lightly poohpooh

DISMISSAL air, axe, bobtail, boot, brush, bum's rush, cashiering, conge(e), coventry, deposal, discharge, dispatch, dispersion, exile, exorcism, firing, kickaxe, layoff, manumission, mittimus, ouster, pink slip, removal, retirement, sack, scat, suspension, walking papers
word of begone, out, scat, scram, shoo, vamoose

DISMISSED canned, degomme, fired

DISMOUNT alight, avale, descend, dislodge, get down, land, light, unhorse, unseat, unstride

DISNEY *dog* pluto
duck donald
mouse mickey, minnie

DISOBEDIENT bad, contrary, defiant, disorderly, fractious, froward, insubordinate, insurgent, lawless, mutinous, naughty, perverse, rebellious, recalcitrant, refractory, restive, seditious, transgressive, unbain, unbuxom, undutiful, ungodly, unready, unruly, violative, wayward

DISOBEY break, defy, disregard, ignore, infringe, reject, resist, revolt, transgress, violate

DISOBLIGE affront, neglect, offend, refuse

DISORDER afflict, anarchy, bouleversement, brawl, carfuffle, chaos, clutter, commotion, confusion, deraign, derange, deray, disease, disharmony, dishevel, distemper, disturb, garboil, hash, ill, illness, jumble, litter, malady, mess, misbehaviour, misrule, muddle, mux, outrage, perturb, pie, puddle, revel, riot, ruff, shatter, sickness, snafu,

snarl, split, taissle, topsy-turvy, tousel, tout, trouble, tummel, tumult, turbulence, unsettle, upset
complete chaos
god susanowo
mental insanity, paranoia, psychosis
mental, comb. phrenia
place of mare's nest, pigpen

DISORDERED blotto, brainsick, chaotic, confused, crazed, crazy, deranged, diseased, feverish, flurried, frowsy, frowzy, gaumy, ill, inchoate, incult, insane, messy, morbid, sick, tumbled, unrid

DISORDERLY amiss, askew, awry, chaotic, confused, disheveled, disorganized, immethodical, indecent, irregular, larrikin, lawless, matted, messed up, messy, mussed, noisy, out of kilter, out of order, rand(y), riotous, rowdy, ruffled, rumblegarie, rumpled, shaggy, slipshod, slovenly, sluttish, stormy, tousled, tously, tumbly, turbulent, uncombed, unrid, unruly, untidy

DISORGANIZE confuse, contuse, derange, disarrange, disarray, disintegrate, disorder, disrupt, dissolve, shock, spoil, unsettle, upset

DISORIENTATION anomie

DISOWN abdicate, abnegate, cut off, deny, disavow, disclaim, dispossess, recant, reject, renay, renounce, repudiate, retract

DISPARAGE abuse, asperse, backcap, belittle, blow down, cry down, debase, debauch, decry, defame, degrade, demerit, denigrate, depreciate, derogate, detract, disapprove, discredit, dishonor, dispraise, downcry, knock, libel, lower, malign, minimize, misliken, object, run down, slander, slight, slur, smear, vilipend

DISPARAGING critical, defamatory, derogatory, pejorative, slighting, snide, unfavorable

DISPARATE different, discordant, dissimilar, distinct, diverse, incongruous, inconsistent, inconsonant, separate, unequal, uneven, various

DISPARITY difference, dissemblance, dissent, distance, inequality

DISPASSION apathy, calmness, coolness, disinterest, indifference, insensibility, phlegm, sluggishness, stoicism, supineness, unconcern, unfeelingness

DISPASSIONATE calm, clinical, coldblooded, cool, equitable, fair, impartial, indifferent, just, moderate, neutral, objective, sedate, serene, steady, stoic, temperate, unbiased, unfeeling

DISPATCH accelerate, accomplish(ment), address, alacrity, aviso, breviate, brief, bulletin, cable, communication, consign, correspond(ence), deliver, devour, diligence, direct, envoy, execute, expedite, expedition, express, haste(n), hurry, issue, item, kill(ing), letter, mail, message, missive, murder, news, note, perform(ance), post, promptitude, report, rid, send, shoot, slay, speed, swiftness, telegram, transmit, velocity, wing, wire
bearer messenger
boat aviso, packet
case attache case, bag, etui

DISPEL banish, blow off, cast forth, chase, disappear, disband, dismiss, disperse, dissipate, dissolve, eject, expel, fray, oust, rout, satisfy, scatter, shoo, vanish

DISPENSATION absolution, allotment, appointment, disposal, distribution, economy, exemption, faculty, fate, giving, government, grace, law, license, lila, plan, provision, quienel, release, scheme, totquot

DISPENSE absolve, acquit, administer, allocate, allot, apply, apportion, arrange, assign, deal, disperse, distribute, divide, dole, dribble, excuse, exempt, forego, free, give, issue, manage, mete, minister, parcel, por-

tion (out), prorate, ration, relieve, scatter, sell, vend
with abstain, miss, spare

DISPENSER apothecary, bomb, manager, merchant, pharmacist, steward
information stoolpigeon, tipster, tout

DISPERSE baffle, bestrew, break, broadcast, centrifugate, decentralize, defeat, deflect, diffuse, disappear, disband, discharge, dismiss, dispel, dispense, disseminate, dissipate, dissolve, distribute, divide, dribble, evanesce, face, fray, fritter, loose, part, propagate, rout, scatter, separate, sever, shatter, shed, skail, sow, sparple, sparse, sperple, sperse, spread, sprinkle, squander, strew, unknit, vanish, winnow

DISPERSION breakup, broadcast, debacle, deflection, demobilization, detachment, diaspora, diffusion, disbandment, dismissal, dissolution, distribution, emulsoid, parting, propagation, radiation, release, scatter, separation, solution, splitup, spread, stain, stampede

DISPIRIT chill, cow, damp, daunt, deject, depress, discourage, dishearten, flatten, mate, mull

DISPIRITED abattu(e), blue, dowie, downcast, downsome, dowy, gloomy, letdown, sackless, shotten, unhearty, wo(e)begone

DISPIRITING chill(y), cold, dismal

DISPLACE banish, bump, change, depose, dislocate, dislodge, dismiss, displant, dispose, edge, eject, expel, expulse, fire, mislay, misplace, move, oust, relegate, remove, reverse, shift, stir, succeed, supersede, supplace, supplant, transfer, transpose, unsettle, uproot, winkle
laterally heave

DISPLACED atopic, depayse
person fugitive, outcast

DISPLACEMENT bump, cubage, eviction, falling, heave, scend, shift, slip, start, upslip

DISPLAY air, array, aspect, bare, betray, blaze, blazon(ry), blow, boast, brandish, bravery, ceremony, dangle, deploy, deray, descry, disclose, discover, eclat, emplazon, estate, etalage, evidence, evince, exercise, exhibit(ion), expand, expose, extend, fanfare, fanfaronade, feature, flash, flaunt, flourish, gaud(ery), grandstand, indicate, manifest, muster, open, ostent (ation), outlay, pageant(ry), panorama, parade, paraffle, pomp, pose, present(ation), reveal, scene, setout, show, sight, spectacle, splash, splay, splendor, splurge, sprank, spread, swank, tinselry, uncase, unfold, unfurl, unveil, vaunt, wave
boastful jactation
daring bravura
emotional gush
empty eyewash, gaud
impressive swell
ostentatious dog, gaudery, swagger
radar scan

DISPLEASE anger, annoy, antagonize, disappoint, discontent, disgruntle, dishearten, dislike, dissatisfy, dissuit, fret, frustrate, gall, irritate, miff, mislike, misset, offend, pique, provoke, put out, repel, vex

DISPLEASED glum, put off, uneasy, unfain, unhappy

DISPLEASURE anger, discontent, disfavor, disgrace, dislike, distaste, indignation, injury, ire, misery, mumps, offense, petulance, pique, repulsion, resentment, strunt, trouble, umbrage, unlust, unthank
exclamation of bother(ation), darn, drat, rats, rot, tchu, tck
show cry, frown, mope, pout

DISPORT amuse, caper, divert, entertain, frisk, frolic, gambol, merriment, play, recreate, rollick, romp

DISPOSAL administration, arrangement, assignment, auction, bestowal, cleanup, dispatch, disposition, distribution, propine, sale, transference, use, vending
quick washway

DISPOSE accomplish, apply, appoint, arrange, array, bear, bend, bequeath, bestow, bias, cast, consume, destroy, devour, dight, discard, dispense, dispone, eat, eliminate, end, give, govern, incline, induce, influence, kill, locate, market, order, perform, place, posit, prevent, refute, regulate, relinquish, set, settle, stand, sway, temper, tend, upload, yark
of deep-six, dump, eliminate, finish, handle, scrap, sell, unload

DISPOSED addicted, apt, arranged, bent, biased, fain, fit, fixed, given, inclined, lief, minded, mindful, partial, proclive, prone, propend, protense, ready, set(tled), sold, subject, talented, tending, willing, wrast

DISPOSITION adjustment, affect(ion), animus, aptitude, attitude, bent, bequest, bias, cast, character, complexion, custom, disposal, ergasia, ethos, faculty, grain, habit(s), heart, idiosyncrasy, inclination, individuality, leaning, make-up, mind, mood, morale, nature, organization, personality, placement, plan, predilection, proclivity, propensity, ptyxis, sale, set, slant, sort, spirit, stomach, strind, tache, talent, temper(ament), tendency, trim, turn, twist, use, warp, will
angry choler
evil the old adam
generous heart
kind charity, humanity, philanthropy
natural grain, indoles, tarage
ultimate fate

DISPOSSESS bereave, cashier, cut off, depose, deprive, disendow, disinherit, dismiss, disown, disseise, disseize, divest, eject, evict, expel, expropriate, foreclose, oust, separate, strip, wrong

DISPOSSESSED alienated, evicted, lumpen

DISPRAISE blame, censure, deprecation, detraction, disparage

DISPROOF answer, censure, clincher, elench, negation, rebuttal, refutation, reproof, retort

DISPROVE belie, blow up, break, confute, contradict, contravene, controvert, convince, demolish, deny, destroy, disallow, discredit, explode, expose, falsify, impugn, invalidate, negate, negative, oppose, overthrow, puncture, rebut, redargue, refute, repel, show up

DISPUTABLE debatable, doubtful, dubious, fallible, indefinite, moot, precarious, questionable, uncertain, unsure, vague

DISPUTANT arguer, brawler, contender, debater, enemy, fencer, fighter, mooter, obstructionist, opposer, polemic, wrangler

DISPUTATION argument, controversy, debate, dialectic, exercise, forensic(s), parvis, pilpul, polemic(s), problem

DISPUTATIOUS argumentative, belligerent, captious, contentious, eristic, quarrelsome, sassy

DISPUTE agitate, altercation, argle-bargle, argue, argument, argy-bargy, bicker, brabble, brawl, breach, broil, cabal, call, cangle, carp, catfight, chop, conflict, contend, contention, contest, contradict, controversy, controvert, dacker, debat, debate, deny, digladiate, disagreement, discuss, dissent, doubt, feud, fight, flite, flyte, fray, fuss, gainsay, haggle, hassle, higgle, impugn, jar, negate, odds, oppose, pribble, protest, quarrel, refute, sharry, skirmish, spar, squabble, squall, squeal, strife, threap, tiff, tilt, wrangle
minor velitation
poetical flyting, partimen
subject of bone of contention

DISQUALIFY debar, deprive, disable, disbar, disfranchise, impair, incapacitate, invalidate, outlaw, unfit

DISQUIET agitate, agitation, alarm, annoy, anxiety, bother, concern, discomfort, discompose, disrest, distress, disturb, excite, fear, flurry, fluster, fret, frighten, harass, harry, irk, pain, perturb, trouble, turmoil, unease, unpeace, unquiet, unro, upset, vex, worry

DISQUIETUDE agitation, anxiety, uneasiness, wanrest, wanrufe

DISQUISITION article, inquiry, piece, search, speech, treatise

DISRAELI *earl of* beaconsfield
nickname dizzy
novel coningsby, endymion, sybil, tancred

DISREGARD blink at, cashier, cold-shoulder, condone, connive, contravene, defy, despise, discount, disdain, disfavor, disobey, dispense, dissemble, flout, forget, forheed, hubris, ignore, indifference, insult, let pass, licence, license, mock, neglect, omission, omit, overhale, overlook, oversee, oversight, pass, pay no attention, play possum, scorn, slight, swallow, unheed, unregard, vilipend, waive, wane, wink at

DISREPUTABLE bad, base, discreditable, disgraceful, dishonorable, gam(e)y, ignoble, ignominious, infamous, low, notorious, raffish, scandalous, seamy, shady, shameful, shoddy, waff
person bad hat, bimbo, bum, scoundrel

DISREPUTE discredit, disfame, disfavor, disgrace, dishonor, ill-fame, infamy, notoriety, obloquy, odium, reproach, scandal, shame

DISRESPECT affront, blasphemy, contempt, discourtesy, disesteem, dishonor, disregard, flippancy, impertinence, impiety, impudence, incivility, insolence, irreverence, outrage, rudeness, sacrilege, slight

DISRESPECTFUL flip(pant), fresh, impertinent, impious,

impolite, impudent, insolent, insulting, irreverent, rude, sassy, saucy, snippy, uncivil

DISROBE change, despoil, divest, strip, undress

DISRUPT break(up), disorganize, distract, gash, hamper, rend, rip, spoil, tear

DISRUPTION breach, break(up), cataclasm, debacle, rupture

DISSATISFACTION agitation, complaint, disapproval, discomfort, discontent(ment), distaste, dysphoria, ennui, fretfulness, malcontent, pain, uneasiness, unrest, vexation

DISSECT analyse, analyze, break down, cut, disjoin, examine, exscind, exsect, inspect, penetrate, pierce, probe, scalpel, scrutinize, slice, unpiece

DISSECTION analysis, anatomy, breakdown, resolution

DISSEMBLE act, affect, assume, boggle, cloak, conceal, counterfeit, disguise, disregard, feign, hide, mask, pretend, sham, simulate, simulize

DISSEMINATE bear, broadcast, circulate, diffuse, disperse, distribute, effuse, propagate, publish, scatter, sow, sparple, spread, strew, teach

DISSENSION affray, altercation, brawl, breach, broil(ery), conflict, contention, debate, discord, dispute, dissent, distraction, disturbance, disunity, division, faction, fight, fraction, fray, friction, quarrel, sedition, strife, struggle, tumult, variance, wrangle

DISSENT apostasy, balk, brouillerie, demur, differ, disagree(ment), disparity, dissension, dissidence, exception, faction, fight, heresy, nonconformity, object, opposition, protest, recusance, recusancy, take exception, vary

signal of nay

DISSENTER apostate, heretic, maverick, nonconformist, protestant, protester, raskolnik, recusant,

schismatic, sectarian, sectary, separatist

house, pert. pantile

DISSEPIMENT partition, phragma, replum, septum

DISSERTATION article, composition, debate, descant, discourse, disquisition, essay, excursus, lecture, screed, sermon, study, theme, thesis, tract(ate), treatise

on roast pig, author lamb

DISSERVICE bad turn, damage, detriment, harm, hurt, injury, mischief, prejudice, wrong

DISSIDENCE disagreement, dissent

DISSIDENT different, discordant, dissenting

DISSIMILAR different, difform, diverse, mismatched, mismated, odd, out, unlike(n), unrelated

comb. allo

DISSIMULATE act, cloak, conceal, counterfeit, disguise, dissemble, fake, feign, hide, mask, pretend, unliken

DISSIMULATION cunning, deceit, duplicity, fakery, guile, hypocracy, irony, make-believe, play-acting, pretense, sham

DISSIPATE burn, carouse, chase, crumble, debauch, destroy, disappear, dispel, disperse, dissolve, divide, embezzle, evanesce, expend, fray, fritter, go to pot, indulge, lavish, melt, part, rake, scatter, separate, spend, squander, swattle, tarnish, vanish, wallow, wander, wanton, waste, whore

DISSIPATED corybantic, debauched, dissolute, fast, high, intemperate, licentious, loose, lost, orgiastic, profligate, rackety, riotous, saturnalism, spent, sporty, squandered, wasted

DISSIPATION consumption, decrease, distribution, extravagance, free-living, improvidence, orgy, saturnalia, sensuality, sybaritism, wastage, waste

DISSOCIATE disjoin, disunite, separate, sever

DISSOLUTE abandoned, corrupt, depraved, desolate,

dissipated, drunk(en), evil, fast, immoral, inebriate, lax, lewd, libertine, licentious, loose, profligate, rackety, rakehell, rakely, rakish, reckless, reprobate, shameless, uncurbed, vicious, wanton, weak, wild

DISSOLUTION biolysis, break-up, bust-up, death, decay, decease, dialysis, dispersion, divorce, end, liquifaction, ruin, turpitude

DISSOLVE abolish, abrogate, annul, break(down)(up), cancel, close, colliquate, crumble, cut, decompose, delapidate, deliquesce, destroy, disappear, disband, discandy, disintegrate, disjoin, disperse, disunite, divorce, end, evanesce, fade, fluidize, fuse, liquefy, liquesce, liquidize, loosen, melt, release, relent, render, revoke, separate, sever, solute, terminate, thaw, unbind, unglue, unknit, vanish

out leach

DISSONANCE cacophony, diaphony, discord(ance), incongruity

DISSONANT absonant, absurd, atonal, different, discordant, discrepant, grating, harsh, incongruous, inconsonant, jangling, jarring, ragged

DISSUADE admonish, advise, bluff, caution, deprecate, dehort, deter, discourage, divert, exhort, expostulate, remonstrate, warn

DISSUASION dehortation, expostulation

DISTAFF axis, axle, female, rock, woman

DISTAL distant, remote

DISTANCE afar, aloofness, background, blue, breadth, circuit, coldness, compass, cosescant, diameter, draught, extent, far cry, farness, footstep, gap, gate, handspan, height, hence, hinterland, horizon, interval, length, light-year, long way, mileage, offing, offscape, outskirts, outstrip, perspective, piece, purlieu, radius, range, reach, remoteness, reserve, shave, space, span, spell, step, stretch, stride, way(s), yardage

angular anomaly, latitude, longitude

at a abroad, afield, far away

between battens gag

between rails gage, gauge

between ship and shore berth

comb. tel(e)

earth's surface latitude, longitude

end to end length

from equator height, latitude

great infinity

hauling leadage

long country-mile

measure coss, kilo(meter), kos, mile, parasang, yojan

measuring device cyclometer, micrometer, odograph, odometer, pedometer, ruler, stadia, stenometer, tachymeter, telemeter, viameter, yardstick, yojan(a)

perpendicular altitude, camber, drop, height

pert. metric

safe berth

short cockstride, footstep, hair, inch, outbye, spell, spit, step

side to side breadth, width

DISTANT afar, aloof, antipodal, apart, asunder, away, chill, cold, cool, coy, distal, far away, far off, farther, ferne, ferren, foreign, further, haughty, hence, inaccessible, outlying, out of reach, remote, removed, reserved, reticent, strange, terminal, thither, ulterior, utmost, withdrawn, yon(d), yonder

comb. tel(e), teleo, telo

more yond(er), ulterior

opposite of close, near, nigh, proximal

DISTASTE aversion, degout, disgust, dislike, displease, displeasure, hate(red), mislike, mistaste, offend, repugnance, repulsion, unlust

expression of rot, tchu, ugh, yuk

DISTASTEFUL abhorent, beastly, bilious, bitter, brackish, hateful, invidious, loathsome, nauseous, objectionable, obnoxious, offensive, repellent, repugnant, revolting, shocking, sour,

unappetizing, unpleasant, unsavory

DISTEMPER aggravate, ailment, anger, cat fever, cat typhoid, choler, color, dilute, disease, dyscrase, garget, gargil, gargle, illness, malady, paint, panleukopenia, sickness, strangles, unsettle

DISTEND amplify, bag, balloon, bloat, blow, bulge, dilate, enlarge, expand, extend, fill, grow, heft, increase, inflate, lengthen, plump, spread, stretch, strut, swell, widen

DISTENDED bloated, blown, dilated, distent, dropsical, edematous, enchymatous, expanded, full, gravid, incrassate, patulent, patulous, pent, plethoric, pooch, puffy, pursy, swollen, taut, trig, tumid, ventose

DISTENSION bloat, diastole, dilatation, dilation, dropsy, edema, flatulence, flatus, inflation, intumescence, meteorism, puff(ing), stretching, sufflation, swelling, swollenness, tumescence, tumidity, turgidity, tympany, windiness

DISTICH couplet, proode, sloka, two

DISTILL alembicate, brew, clarify, dissolve, drop, elix, emit, expel, express, extract, ferment, infuse, instill, leak, limbeck, melt, purify, rate, refine, render, still, trickle, vaporize

DISTILLATE benzin(e), essence, extract, gundy, rosin, run, singlings, spirits

DISTILLER abkar

DISTILLERY jigger, still

device alembic, matrass, retort, still

DISTINCT apparent, articulate, audible, breme, clear, concrete, crystal-clear, definite, different, discrete, disparate, diverse, dividual, evident, individual, legible, lucid, manifest, obvious, open, palpable, particular, patent, peculiar, plain, prominent, separate, several, sharp, single, sole, special, sundry, transparent, unattached, unique, visible

comb. idio

DISTINCTION aristocracy, brilliance, class, consequence, credit, demarcation, difference, divergence, division, earmark, elegance, eminence, feature, figure, glory, grandeza, honor, importance, laurel, luster, mark(ing), note, quality, quillet, rank, renown, separation, uniqueness, unlikeness, variation

academic hono(u)rs

without common

DISTINCTIVE characteristic, diacritical, discrete, discriminate, individual, particular, peculiar, phonemic, proper, signal, single, special, specific, talented, typical, unique

DISTINGUISH analyse, analyze, characterize, contrast, decern, deen, deliniate, describe, descry, detect, devise, differentiate, discern, discover, discrepate, discriminate, ensign, honor, judge, know, label, mark, note, perceive, recognize, secern, see, separate, sift, skill, sort, stamp

DISTINGUISHED banner, celebrated, clear, conspicuous, different, eminent, eximious, famed, famous, gentle, great, honored, illustrious, important, insigne, marked, notable, noted, outstanding, prominent, renowned, signate, splendid, storied, swell

DISTORT angle, bend, blubber, buckle, camshachle, cloud, color, contort, cringe, crook(en), deform, falsify, garbel, gnarl, grimace, injure, knot, mangle, mar, misconstrue, misinterpret, misshape, outimage, pervert, screw, shachleys, shackle, shevel, skew, slant, torture, turn, twist, warp, wiredraw, wrench, wrest, wring, writhe

DISTORTED askew, awry, camshach, crank, crooked, deformed, degraded, rubato, skewed, strained, tortious, warped, writhen, wry

DISTORTION anamorphism, anamorphosis, asymmetry, buckle, caricature, contortion, crookedness, deformity, detorsion, deviation, error, exaggeration, falsehood, falsification, flutter, garbling, gnarl, grimace, hog, irregularity, knot, loxia, misrepresentation, perversion, quirk, sag, screw, sophistry, strain, torsion, torture, turn, twist, warp, wrench, wrest, wryness

DISTRACT addle, agitate, amuse, baffle, balk, bewilder, confound, craze, detract, divert, dumfound, embroil, fluster, fuddle, harass, imbroil, madden, mither, moider, mystify, nonplus, perplex, perturb, puzzle, scatter, tosticate, twitch

DISTRACTED amused, bestraught, confused, crazy, distraught, frantic, gyte, heedless, insane, irrational, mad, rabid, raving, scranny, stract, wild

DISTRACTION alar(u)m, blind, dissension, ecstasy, frenzy, tumult

DISTRAIN attach, bind, coerce, confine, confiscate, constrain, constrict, distress, drive, na(a)m, poind, poundage, punish, rend, seize, tear, torment

DISTRAUGHT absent-(minded), addled, agitated, bewildered, confused, crazed, deranged, distracted, distrait, flustered, frantic, insane, perplexed, preoccupied, rabid, rambling, straught, wandering, wild

DISTRESS ache, agitate, agonize, agony, ail, alarm, anger, angst, anguish, annoy, anxiety, appal(l), attachment, barrat, bother, calamity, care, cark, chagrin, danger, daymare, destitution, difficulty, disaster, discomfort, disquiet, distrain, disturb, dolor, dread, duress, embarrassment, fine, forehail, grief, grievance, grill, grudge, harass, hardship, harrow, heed, misease, MISERY, pang, pass, penance, pester, pinch, plague, poverty, press, rack, rigor, sorrow, straiten, stress, stur-

ble, throng, torment, travail, trial, tribulation, trouble, try, tryst, tweak, unquiet, upset, wandreth, woe, worry, wound

exclamation of aie, haro, harrow, oime

mental psychalgia

signal mayday, sos

DISTRESSED bitter, concerned, downgone, exercised, inconsolable, miserable, poor, sad(dened), wrung

DISTRESSING affecting, afflicting, bitter, burdensome, carking, cumbersome, deplorable, dolorous, grievous, grim, griping, heavy, lamentable, mournful, moving, onerous, painful, pathetic, piteous, pitiable, rueful, sad, severe, sharp, sore, thorny, touching, troublesome, unpleasant, weighty, woeful

DISTRIBUTE administer, allocate, allot, apportion, arrange, assign, assort, cast, deal, devise, disburse, dispend, dispense, dispose, divide, divvy, dole, dot, erogate, expend, hand out, impart, job, mete, parcel, portion, prorate, ration, scatter, seed, separate, share, sow, spread, sprinkle

DISTRIBUTION administration, allotment, apportionment, arrangement, array, broadcast, circumfusion, classification, compartition, diffusion, dispensation, dispersal, dispersion, disposal, disposition, dissemination, dissipation, dividend, division, divvy, dole, doling, issuance, parting, peppering, placement, propagation, sale, share, sowing, spattering, spread(ing), sprinkling

DISTRIBUTOR carrier, sharer, sower, zanjero

DISTRICT aimik, area, barrio, belt, border, borough, burg(h), bowery, canton, cercle, circle, circuit, coila, commune, community, country, county, curragh, demesne, department, diocese, division, enclave, exurb, field, gau, ghetto, jagheer, jag(h)ir, locale, locality, mahal(la), malacca,

markaz, merina, neighborhood, okroog, okrug, pale, paramo, parcel, parish, party, pollam, precinct, province, purlieu, quarter, realm, region, section, sector, shire, sircar, site, slum, soc, soke(n), sphere, syssel, taluk, teman, territory, thanage, tract, upriver, vicinage, vicinity, ward, wene, wick, woon, zillah, zone

burned quemado

court leet

ecclesiastical classis, diocese, parish, see, synod

judicial circuit

of columbia flower rose

of columbia motto justice to all

of columbia peak tenleytown

of columbia river anacostia, potomac

of columbia section anacostia, capital hill, georgetown

poor slums

rural boondocks, boonies, outback, sticks, wayback

theater broadway, rialto

tribal gau

DISTRUST apprehension, defide, diffide, discredit, disfaith, doubt, dubiety, envy, fear, foreboding, jealousy, misfaith, misgiving, suspect, suspicion, uncertainty, unfaith

DISTRUSTFUL cautious, cynical, jealous, leary, leery, shy, wary

DISTURB aggravate, agitate, badger, bewilder, bother, check, churn, commote, commove, concern, confuse, convulse, derange, discomfit, discommode, discompose, disorder, disquiet, distract, distress, drove, drumble, excite, faze, feeze, fluster, fret, fuss, garboil, hinder, interfere, interrupt, jostle, meddle, mismake, molest, move, perplex, perturb, pother, rattle, rile, roil, roust, ruffle, scare, scuffle, shake, shift, start(le), stir, sturble, tamper, tempest, toss, trouble, uncalm, unease, unsettle, upset, vex, worry

suddenly start(le)

the peace broil, riot

DISTURBANCE affray, agitation, alarm, altercation,

annoyance, anxiety, bobbery, bother, brawl, bree(ze), broil(ery), brulyie, brulzie, business, catastrophe, cathro(w), chagrin, clatter, clutter, confusion, contention, convulsion, desray, discord, dissension, ferment, fight, foofaraw, fracas, fraise, fray, hubbub, incident, kickup, pother, quarrel, quibbling, reelrall, riot, ripple, rooker, row, rumble, rumpus, shindy, shine, shock, squabble, squall, static, stir, storm, stramash, strow, struggle, sturt, touse, travally, trouble, tumult, turbulence, turmoil, turnup, upheaval, uproar

atmospheric grinder, storm, turbulence
emotional neurosis
mental delirium, frenzy, phobia, phrensy, psychosis
ocean tsunami
seismic earthquake, seaquake, temblor, tidal wave, tremor
DISTURBED agitated, anxious, apprehensive, cracked, makadoo, perturbed, streaked, troubled, uneasy, upset
DISUNITE alienate, break, disband, discerp, dissever, dissolve, divide, divorce, estrange, part, rend, rift, rip, separate, split, sunder, unsolder, unteam, unyoke
DISUNITY discord, division
DISUSE abandon, cease, cut out, desist, desuetude, discard, discontinue, dismantle, drop, give up, idle, lay up, leave off, misapply, neglect, obsolescence, obsoleteness, obsoletism, outrage, quit, relinquish, reserve, shelve, spare, stop, vacancy, waive
DITCH abandon, absent, acequia, begrime, canal, channel, chase, conduit, daub, delf, delue, derail, dike, drain, dyke, entrenchment, evade, fleam, flume, foss(e), foul, furrow, gaw, graff, graft, grave, grindle, gripple, gully, gurt, gutter, guzzle, haha, hide, hole, holl, land, loet, lose, mine, moat, pit, pudge, quit, relais, rheen, rhine, rine,

rut, sap, sheuch, sheugh, sink, slonk, sluice, sluit, smear, sough, stank, stell, tajo, trench, vanfoss, zange, zanja, zanjona
big panama
-down cattail, reed-mace
flanking bastione
grass enalid
herb isnardia
millet hureek, paspalum
muddy letch
narrow grave, relais, trench
open stell
part graffage, scarp
reed bennel, cane, grass, spire
side scarp
stonecrop nightshade, pokeweed
DITHER bother, didder, dodaw, excitement, flap, fluster, flustration, flutter, fuss, jitters, lather, nerves, pother, pucker, quake, quiver(ing), shake, shimmy, shiver, shudder, stew, teeter, tizzy, totter, tremble, trouble, twitter, vacillate, vibration, whirl, wobble
DITHYRAMB dionysus, hymn, ode, poem, poetry
inventor arion
DITHYRAMBIC boisterous, enthusiastic, poem, poet, wild
DITTANY artillery-plant, ballota, burning-bush, cunilla, evonymus, fraxinella, frostweed, gas-plant, mint, mock cypress, wahoo
DITTO above, aforesaid, again, concur, copy, dupe, duplicate, image, imitate, likewise, match, refrain, repeat, same
DITTY dite, dyte, lay, poem, saying, sing, song, verse, vinetta, vocal
DIURETIC adonidin, antihydropin, aparteine, arbutin, bastard balm, bucco, buchu, caffeine, cava, copaiba, drosera, emictory, kaya, lappa, nasrol, pichi, sabal, zea
DIURIL chlorothiazide
DIURNAL butterfly, daily, daybook, diary, ephemeral, journal, newspaper, periodic(al), quotidian
DIUTURNAL aeonian, agelong, centuried, endless,

eternal, infinite, lasting, secular
DIVA cantatrice, prima donna, singer, star
famous bori, pons
DIVAGATE digress, stray, wander
DIVAGATION deviation, digression, episode, excursus, wandering
DIVAN book, canape, couch, council, court, davenport, daybed, leewan, saloon, seat, settee, sofa
DIVARICATE bifid, branch, deviate, differ, digress, divagate, diverge, diverging, fork, ramble, range, spread(ing), staddling, stray, wander
DIVE bar, barrelhouse, brothel, buzz, clipjoint, crib, deave, den, dop, drop, drum, duck, dump, explore, fall, gainer, header, hole, honkytonk, joint, penetrate, pique, pitch, plop, plummet, plump, plunge, plunk, pounce, saloon, scatter, shebang, spin, submerge, submersion, subway, swoop, underpass
bomber stuka
fancy full gainer, full twist
into begin, hurry, investigate, start, take on, test, try, undertake
kind backflip, belly whopper, gainer, isander, jackknife, swan, twist
DIVER ama, bird, ducker, frogman, loon, pearler, plungeon, plunger, submarine, swimmer, thief
comb. dytes
disease bends, caisson
gear aqualung, flippers, scuba, snorkel
DIVERGE alter, bend, branch, contrast, devaricate, deviate, differ, digress, disagree, divagate, diverse, divide, err, fork, part, ramify, separate, spread, swerve, turn, vary, veer
DIVERGENCE aberration, abnormality, allowance, branch, change, contrast, crotch, deflection, detour, deviation, dip, diverication, diversion, error, fork, obliquity, parting, radiation,

separation spread(ing), vagary
point axil
DIVERGENT abnormal, apart, contrary, different, disparate, eccentric, off, opposite, remote, tangent, variant, various
more farther
DIVERS cruel, different, differing, evil, manifold, many, miscellaneous, multifarious, numerous, perverse, several, sundry, various
colored variegated
DIVERSE contrary, contrasting, different, disparate, distinct, evil, incomparable, manifold, motley, opposite, perverse, separate, sere, several, sundry, unlike, variegated, varietal, various
comb. vari
DIVERSIFY alter, assort, change, check, dapple, dot, freck, fret, modify, spot, sprinkle, variate, variegate, vary
with colors begarie, begary, bespatter
DIVERSION amusement, apostasy, deduit, deflection, deviation, disport, divertisement, entertainment, escapism, feint, frisk, game, hobby, jeu, laughs, maneuver, move, pastime, play, pleasure, recreation, red herring, solace, sport, variorum
DIVERSITY change, contrast, difference, discord, dissent, variety
DIVERT abstract, alienate, alter, amuse, arride, avert, avoid, beguile, bend, call away, change, curve, deceive, deflect, delight, derail, deter, deviate, digress, dissuade, distract, entertain, estrange, head off, modify, occupy, parry, pastime, please, recreate, regale, relax, sheer, shunt, sport, sublimate, swerve, switch, syphon, tickle, turn, twist, veer, wring
water flume
DIVERTING amusing, distracting, droll, entertaining, foolish, pleasant
DIVEST abridge, bare, bereave, delawn, denude,

depost, deprive, despoil, dismantle, dispossess, doff, empty, exute, reave, reft, remove, strip, tirl, unclothe, uncover, undress
of abdicate
of sham debunk
DIVIDE alienate, aliquot, allot, apportion, arrange, assign, atomize, balkanise, balkanize, bepart, bifurcate, bisect, branch, break, britten, calculate, cantle, canton, carve, cast, chop, cleave, cleft, cut, deal, detach, devise, differ, dimidiate, dirempt, discriminate, disparple, dispense, dissect, dissent, distribute, divorce, divvy, dole, estrange, fissure, fork, fraction, halve, hemisect, joint, lot, mammock, measure, mere, multisect, open, parcel, part, partition, portion, prorate, raly, ration, rend, rift, rive, scan, scind, select, separate, sever, share, shear, sort, split, summit, sunder, watershed
in 2 parts bifurcate, bisect, halve
in 4 parts quadrisect, quarter
into districts canton
into parts bifurcate, bisect, gobbet, paly, quarter, scantle, septinate, trisect
land stint
DIVIDED aerolate, apart, bifid(ate), bipartite, camerate, cancellate, cancellous, cleft, cloven, dividual, ente, fissate, forky, fourche(e), gyronny, halved, parted, partial, partite, prongy, reft, septate, split, zoned
at extremities bourche(e)
comb. fid, fissi, schist
evenly bendy
having ribs fissicostate
in 2 dimidiate, fourche, halved
in 4 paly, quartered
not global, one, solid, united
vertically paly
DIVIDEND allotment, apportionment, assessment, bonus, commission, earning, income, part, plum, portion, rake-off, return, royalty, share, yield
comb. paly
DIVIDER bunting, bunton,

compass, dividant, merist, severer, sharer
DIVI-DIVI brazilwood, caesalpinia, libidibi, sumac, tree
DIVIDUAL distinct, fragmentary, shared
DIVINATION acumen, angang, astrology, augury, clairvoyance, discernment, divinail, dowsing, foretelling, fortunetelling, hariolation, insight, intuition, magic, mantic, mantology, metagnomy, omen, palmistry, penetration, perception, prediction, prophesy, pythonism, soothsaying, sorcery, sors, sort(es), taghairm
by animal shoulders armomancy
by animals theriomancy
by arrows belomancy
by ashes spodomancy, tephramancy
by barley meal alpitomancy
by birds ornithomancy
by bones astragalomancy, osteomancy
by books bibliomancy
by brass vessels chalcomancy
by burning coals anthracomancy
by casting lots cleromancy
by cheese tyromancy
by dice astragalomancy, cubomancy
by dreams oneiromancy
by fig leaves sycomancy
by figures geomancy
by fire empyromancy, pyromancy
by flour aleuromancy
by footprints ichomancy
by forehead metopomancy
by fountains pegomancy
by hand examination chiromancy, palmistry
by handwriting graptomancy
by human entrails anthropomancy
by leaves botanomancy, phyllomancy
by letters onomancy
by lines stitchomancy
by lots cleromancy, sors, sortes, sortilege
by mirror enoptromancy
by monstrosities teratoscopy
by numbers arithmancy, arithmomancy
by objects psychometry

by pebbles psephomancy, thrioboly
by plants botanomancy
by playing cards cartomancy
by rods rhabdomancy
by rooster alectryomancy
by shield aspidomancy
by shoulders armomancy, spatulamancy
by smoke capnomancy
by south wind anstromancy
by spasmodic movements spasmatomancy
by stars astromancy, sideromancy
by straws sideromancy
by sword machairomancy
by thunder brontoscopy, keraunoscopia
by verses rhapsodomancy
by walking ambulomancy
by wand rhabdomancy
by weather aeromancy
by wild animals theriomancy
by wind austromancy
by wood zylomancy
circular gyromancy
comb. mancy
pert. mantic
practice of mantic(ism), mantology
science mantic
ventriloquistic gastromancy
DIVINATOR See PROPHET.
DIVINE almighty, ambrose, angelic, anticipate, areed, arioate, auger, blessed, canonist, celestial, christ-like, christly, clergyman, cleric, conjecture, deify, delightful, detect, determine, devise, discern, divus, ecclesiastic, foreknow, foresee, foretell, godful, god-like, godly, gorgeous, guess, halsen, heavenly, holy, immortal, interpret, learn, minister, parson, pastor, perceive, pious, portend, predict, presage, priest, prophesy, religious, sacred, scholastic, schoolman, solve, spae, spiritual, superb, suppose, supreme, theologian, theological, theologist, theologue, twig, ubiquest
artificer tvashtar, tvashtri
attribute See ATTRIBUTE *godly.*
being deity, deva, god
comedy angel beatrice
comedy author dante

comedy guide virgil
comedy part inferno, paradiso, purgatorio
favor grace
law fas
render deify
right authority
sarah bernhardt
word grace, logos
work theurgy
DIVINER aruspex, augur(er), haruspex, prophet, seer, sibyl, wizard
DIVING haurient, urinant
bell bathysphere, nautilus
bell inventor eads
bird See BIRD *diving.*
equipment, aqualung, aquascope, bathysphere, bell, benthoscope, gangava, periscope, scuba, snorkel
hazard bends
suit gangava
DIVINING *rod* doodlebug, dowser, twig, wand, witch stick
rod, to use dowse
DIVINITY (See also GOD, GODDESS.) adonai, celestial, deity, elohim, god, godhead, godship, idol, jah, jehovah, joss, nymph, power, sanctity, theologumenon, theology, yahwe
beneficent ahura, asura
DIVISIBLE discerpible, partible, secable
DIVISION abteilung, allotment, apportionment, area, band, barrio, bifurcation, branch, break(down), butt, caesura, camp, canton, caput, caste, category, clan, class(ification), cleavage, cleft, cohort, compartment, concision, degree, department, disconnection, discord, disjunction, dismemberment, distinction, distribution, district, divergence, divvy, dole, eogaea, fascicle, field, fight, fork, fraction, geld, gelt, group, hien, hold, hsien, lith, meer, mere, mitosis, neighborhood, parcel, part, parting, partition, party, piece, portion, realm, rift, roulade, schism, scissure, sect(ion), sector, segment, shard, share, split, subclass, variance
administrative charge, circle,

county, custody, diocese, district, eyalet, lathe, parish, township
anthropological stock
army mora
astrological face
comb. schizo
ecclesiastical parish, precinct, schism, society
geological arnusian, epoch, era, laramie, lias, ludian, malm, richmond, series
hinged leaf
in parts merotomy
into 100 centuriation
into small pieces morcellation
line boundary
many eogaea
nuclear fission
pert. di(a)cretic
political ato, borough, city, country, county, district, hundred, lathe, parish, purchase, state, ward
population stratum
property gavelkind
religious schism
restricted meer, mere
sign obelus
social caste, class, clique, horde, in-group, tribe
taxing gold
time age, eon, epoch, era
tribal clan
DIVORCE ahsan, alienate, annulment, banish, disband, dissolution, dissolve, disunion, disunite, divide, estrange, get(t), hasan, khula, mubarat, part, separate, separation, sever, split up, sunder, talak, unmarry
decree enoch arden, final, interlocutory, nisi
law get(t), talak
mill reno
DIVOT clod, sod, turf
DIVULGE air, announce, bare, betray, bewray, blab, blurt, break, breathe, broadcast, come out with, confide, disclose, discover, disembosom, evulgate, evulge, give out, gossip, impart, make known, out with, proclaim, propale, publish, release, reveal, spill, tattle, tell, unfold, utter, vent, whisper
DIVVY allot, apportion, divide, hack, partition, portion, share, split

DIXIE confederacy, paradise, pot, south, utopia
heart alabama
DIZEN decorate, dress, ornament, overdress
DIZZINESS dinus, giddiness, hilo, megrim, merligo, scotodinia, scotoma, scotomy, swimming, tiego, vertigo, whirling, willness, wooziness
pert. dinic(al), vestibular
with headache scotodinia
DIZZY bewildered, confused, crazy, dunt, faint, farchadat, fickle, foolish, frivolous, giddy, heedless, insane, mad, reeling, sappy, stupid, totty, unsteady, vertiginous, vertigo, westy
dame scatterbrain
round whirl
DJAKARTA batavia, jakarta
DJED osiris
DNA double-helix, mitochondria, plasmid
bases adenine, amino, antigen, cytosine, guanine, thymine
decoder See LIFE *scientist.*
helper ribonucleic acid, rna
DNEIPER *tributary* bug, desna, pripet, psel, psiol, sula
DO accomplish, achieve, act, affair, answer, attend, avail, behave, bilk, bitch, care, cause, cheat, command, commit, complete, cook, cover, dae, deal, deceive, deed, discharge, div, dost, duty, effect, event, execute, exert, fare, festival, guise, make, nobble, overreach, perform, place, produce, prosper, provide, put, render, rite, satisfy, sell, serve, settle, shift, solve, succeed, suffice, suit, swindle, transact, traverse, trick, try, work
a daring deed bell the cat
a fadeout disappear
again duplicate, repeat, reproduce
a good turn benefit, help
a land-office business prosper, thrive
-all factotum
all one can shoot one's bolt
all right get rich, succeed, thrive
as the romans do conform
as told obey

away with abate, abolish, annul, banish, burk, cancel, cashier, consume, countermand, demolish, destroy, discard, discontinue, dissolve, drop, elide, eliminate, erase, finish, kill, liquidate, nullify, quash, repeal, rescind, retrench, slaughter, void, wipe out
business chaffer
carelessly dash off, fake, fudge, huddle, mess around, patch, scamp, scant, skimp, slapdash, slight, slim, slubber, toss off, trifle
duty function, officiate, perform, serve
for defeat, destroy, diddle, fetch, fix, get, jack, kill, napoo, punish, ruin, sink
good aid, assist, benefit, help
-gooder altruist, bleeding heart, give-away, liberal, philanthropist, reformer, welfarist
in beat, cheat, deceive, deepsix, defeat, destroy, fatigue, kill, overcome, punish, thrash, wear out
injury bane, hurt
like ape, imitate, mirror
not dinna, dont
nothing idle, laze, lazy, mark time, rest, sit back
-nothingness faineance
offhand improvise, scamp
oneself proud feast, overcome, prevail, succeed, win
out of See *in* above.
penance regret, satisfy
piecework dacker
poetic didst
poorly dub
proud gratify
-re-mi money, sing
something See ACT.
the honors entertain, introduce, present, preside
the job accomplish, achieve, get results
thoroughly floor
to a turn complete, cook, finish, polish off
up bale, bundle, fatigue, launder, package, prepare, raise, repair, ruin, tidy, tire, wash, wrap
up brown cheat, complete, deceive, hoax, hogtie, polish off, swindle
well go far, prosper, succeed, win

without abstain, dispense, forbear, lack, spare
wrong err, miscarry, sin, transgress
DOBBER bob, dabchick, float, grebe
DOBBIN cup, horse, nag, robert
DOBBY brownie, dolt, dunce, fabric, fool, goblin, spirit, sprite
DOCENT lecturer, teacher, tutor
DOCILE acquiescent, amenable, apt, biddable, calm, compliable, compliant, docious, ductile, dutiful, educable, educatable, facile, flexible, gentle, humble, impressionable, malleable, manageable, meek, moldable, obedient, orderly, plastic, pliable, pliant, putty-like, quick, quist, ready, receptive, responsive, submissive, susceptible, tall, tame, taurie, teachable, toward(ly), tractable, trainable, yielding
DOCK bang, basin, berth, bloodwort, bob(tail), camber, canaigre, clip, coffer, court, curtail, cut(off), deduct, feverfew, fine, hamble, hangar, harbor, jetty, landing, marina, moor, parella, parelle, pen, perforate, pier, quary, rumex, rump, scut, shipside, shorten, slip, sorrel, staith, storehouse, strunt, tail, truncate, weed, wharf
bitter butterbur
cress nipplewort
part bollard, camber, pile
ship's basin, berth, slip
sour cock sorrel
support pile
worker longshoreman, matey, rafler, stevedore
yard arsenal, harbor
DOCKAGE berthage, curtailment, fee, reduction
DOCKED apocopate, bobtail, cut short, shortened
DOCKET agenda, agendum, certificate, digest, label, record, register, schedule
DOCTOR, DOCTOR'S adulterate, alter, bonesetter, breeze, change, chirurgeon, consultant, cook, coroner, croaker, debase, disguise, dope, dose, fake, falsify, fly,

galen, gloss, haikun, hakim, healer, intern(e), leech, load, locum (tenens), medicate, medico, mender, ollam(h), physician, physicker, powwow, repair, resident, sawbones, sophisticate, surgeon, teacher, therapeutist, therapist, treat
admirable roger bacon
angelic thomas aquinas
animal vet(erinarian), veterinary
assistant intern(e), nurse
cherubic thomas aquinas
fictional jekyll, zhivago
group ama, panel, staff
gum tragacanth
inferior barber-surgeon, quack
jekyll's other self hyde
literary johnson
mirabilis roger bacon
oath hippocratic
pangloss pedant
pioneer galen, hippocrates
quack crocus
specialist aurist, chiropodist, chiropractor, cranioscopist, gynecologist, hippiater, intern(e), internist, neurologist, oculist, opthomologist, optometrist, orthopedist, otologist, pediatrician, podiatrist, proctologist, psychiatrist, radiologist, surgeon, urologist
up cook, eyewash, fake
voodoo goofer

DOCTRINAIRE authoritarian, dictatorial, dogmatic, fanatic, impractical, ismy, magistral, oracular, theorist

DOCTRINE (See also *specific,* below.) belief, cabala, canon, catechism, confession, credenda, credo, creed, cult, discipline, dogma, doxy, esotery, faith, fundamental, gospel, ideology, instruction, ism, knowledge, learning, logic, lore, maxim, opinion, position, precept, principle, program, propaganda, religion, rite, rule, sect, system, teaching, tenet, theory
comb. doxy, ism, osophy
contrary heresy
esoteric cabala, cabalism, qabbala
evil moloch
false heresy

good agathism
mystical boehmenism
new neology
occult cabal(a), cabalism, qaballa
of inferiority adlerian
of lawlessness anarchy
of origins archology
of ultimate good agathism
of ultimate reality monism
pert. dogmatic
philosophical panlogism
psychological, behaviorism
skeptic acatalepsy
specific ahimsa, amidism, animism, atheism, babism, cabala, devilism, dharma, dynamism, egotism, fatalism, gobinism, hedonism, heresy, islamism, krypsis, malism, mishna(h), monism, nihilism, noetics, pragmatism, zoism
spreader propagandist
theological arianism, aryanism

DOCUMENT(S) act, annals, archive, article, bill, billet, blank, bond, book, brevet, bumf, cadjan, capitulation, certificate, chirograph, chronicles, contract, covenant, deed, diploma, dossier, draft, estreat, evidence, exhibit, form, helograph, instrument, license, manuscript, memo, monument, palapala, papers, parchment, proof, record, roll, scrip(t), scroll, targe, testimony, thesis, ticket, title, treatise, warrant, waybill, will, writing
addition amendment, codicil, rider
classified top-secret
copy vidimus
file dossier, filace
historical archives
provisional draft, rough, scrip(t)
receptacle hanaper
seal jark
shipping cocket
signed by all syngraph
true copy estreat

DOD cattail, clip, die, fit, huff, lop, poll, sulk, summit
DODAVAH *son* eliezer
DODDER acotyledon, amil, angels'-hair, beggarweed, bride's-laces, cuscata, dother, fideos, flaxdrop,

hairweed, haleweed, hellweed, knotweed, potter, ribbongrass, scad, scald, shake, spurry, tickseed, totter, tremble
laurel devil's-guts, mistletoe, woevine
seed gold-of-pleasure
DODDERING aged, anile, decrepit, doated, dotard, doted, feeble, foolish, inane, infirm, old, senile, unsteady, weak
DODDIE humlie
DODDYPOLL blockhead
DODECANESE *island* kalymnos, kasos, khalke, kos, lipsos, nisyros, patmos, syme, tilos
DODGE artifice, avert, avoid, bilk, duck, elude, equivocate, escape, evade, evasion, expedient, fence, flee, fudge, gilenyie, hedge, jink, jouk, lurch, lurk, malinger, palter, parry, proffer, pussyfoot, put off, quibble, recoil, retreat, sheer, shift, shirk, shrink, shunt, sidestep, sky, stall, swerve, trick, trifle, ward off, wheeze
DODGER buck-passer, flier, flyer, folder, handbill, leaflet, pamphlet, rascal
artful john dawkins
DODGSON, CHARLES *pseud.* lewis carrol
DODO bird, didus, has-been, num(b)skull
-like didine
son eleazar, elhanan
DODONA *oracle of* zeus
priests selloi
DOE almond, biscuit, deer, fawn, female, girl, hind, nanny, rabbit, roe, teg, woman
blue flier, flyer
1st-year fawn
DOEG *herdsman for* saul
DOER actor, agent, author, executor, facient, factor, feasor, maker, manager, medium, mover, operative, operator, performer, perpetrator, practitioner, producer, worker
comb. ant, ast, ator, eer, euse, ist, lier, ster
of odd jobs factotum, jack (of all trades)
DOFF avale, bonnet, divest,

douse, dowse, off, remove, strip, undress, vail

DOG, DOG'S (See also CANID, and *breed*, below.) andiron, bawtie, bawty, bitch, bowwow, cad, cane, canine, canis, catch, chien, crampon, cur, feist, fido, follow, foot, gripper, hound, hunt, male, mastiff, messet, mongrel, mutt, nipper, pariah, pointer, pooch, pug, pup(py), pye, rascal, ratter, shadow, slut, snarleyyow, sport, tailwagger, tike, towser, track, trail, tyke, whelp, wretch, yapper, yelper

age long time

ape baboon

bark alarm, alert, bowwow, braggadocio, clamor, snarl, threat, warning

barkless basenji

bee drone

bird bolter, pointer, retriever, setter, toller

bramble caper, eglantine

breed (See also CANID.) 3 jip, pom 4 alco, chow, dane, peke, puli 5 akito, boxer, coach, cooly, corgi, dabuh, dhole, dingo, husky, pelon, spitz 6 afghan, agoura, barbet, basset, beagle, borzoi, bratch, briard, cocker, collie, colpeo, eskimo, heeler, kelpie, kennet, kuvasz, poodle, ranger, ratter, saluki, setter, siwash, sleugi, sussex, talbot 7 basenji, beardie, bulldog, clumber, griffon, harrier, lurcher, maltese, owtchar, pincher, pointer, samoyed, scottie, shar-pei, spaniel, starter, terrier, tibetan, whippet 8 aberdeen, airedale, alsatian, bluetick, brinjary, chowchow, doberman, elkhound, foxhound, labrador, landseer, malamute, malinois, papillon, pekinese, pinscher, pyrenees, sealyham, sheepdog, shepherd, springer, turnspit 9 boarhound, brabancon, brinjaree, buckhound, chihuahua, dachshund, dalmatian, great dane, greyhound, kerryblue, police dog, retriever, schnauzer, shorthair, st bernard, staghound, wolf-

hound, wolfspitz, yorkshire 10 bedlington, belljeemer, bloodhound, blueheeler, boston bull, chesapeake, clydesdale, fox terrier, manchester, otterhound, pomeranian, rottweiler, schipperke, weimaraner, welsh corgi, wirehaired 11 english bull, groenendael, irish setter, skye terrier 12 cairn terrier, french poodle, gazelle hound, german police, gordon setter, irish terrier, newfoundland, water spaniel, welsh terrier 13 affenpinscher, boston terrier, great pyrenees, prince charles, scotch terrier 14 german shepherd, highland collie 15 blenheim spaniel, golden retriever, mexican hairless, riesenschnauzer 16 doberman pinscher, russian wolfhound

bur comfrey

buster brown's tige

call soss

camomile mayweed

cart bounder, gadabout, gadder, tumtum

chained bandog

chops flews

close-haired boxer, dachshund, pug

coach dalmatian

coat color belton

comb. can(i), cyn(o)

command come, heel, hyke, mush, sit, stand, toho

control collar, lead, leash

crop-tailed cur

daisy mayweed, yarrow

days canicule, summer

decoy toller

disease black tongue, chorea, distemper, mange, rabies

dorothy's toto

duck hunting toller

-ear acroterium, bight, bracket, fold, leather

-face private, soldier

-faced cynocephalous

-faced ape aani, hapi, thoth

famous aleo, argus, asta, balto, belka, checkers, devil, fala, feller, king, lassie, nana, rab, rintintin, strongheart, tige, toby

farm komonder

female bitch, brach(et), gip, gyp, slut

fennel hogweed, mayweed

fierce bandog, kolsun

50-headed cerberus

fight melee, scramble

-fisher otter

-footed cynopodous

fox corsac

fox-like colpeo

group kennel, leash

hauling, dalmatian, husky, malemute, samoyed(e)

headless yeth-hound

hook spanner, wrench

house kennel, lair, limbo, wap(p)

howl arr, grr, ululation, yelp

100-headed cerberus

hunting alan(d), alant, basset, beagle, bloodhound, borzoi, brach, courser, cynhyena, dropper, elkhound, griffon, harrier, hound, kennet, lucern, pointer, rach(e), ratch, retriever, saluki, seizer, setter, slough, talbot, toler, wolfhound

hybrid cur, mongrel

hyena-like simir

in the manger egotist, spoilsport

it idle, laze, run away

john brown's rab

keeper fewterer

lap messan, shough

large alan, bawtie, bawty, boxer, briard, collie, great dane, huskie, komondor, malemute, mastiff, newfoundland, police, rottweiler, shepherd, st bernard, towser

latin gibberish

leash harl, slip, tirret, trash

-like canine, cunic, cynocephalous, cynoid

-like animal coyote, fox, hyena, jackal, wolf

-like goblin barghest

long-eared beagle

long-haired alco, chow, nootka, shock, spaniel

lost stray

mercury bristolweed, sapwort

mixed cur, mongrel, mutt

multi-headed cerberus, garm, orthros

name meaning caleb

non-barking basenji

nondescript cur, malemute, mut(t), pooch

on the job goldbrick, shirk

pack canaglia, canaille

-parsley chervil
parti-colored pie, pye
pert. canicular, canine
pet lapdog, minx, moppet
pointing drahthaar
poodle chien
pouched thylacine
pound greenyard
pug mops
punch and judy's toby
reward hallow
rose bedegar, bird-brier, blackberry, bramble, brier, bucky, canker, eglantine, rubus
rose fruit hep, hip
salmon calico, chum, keta, morgay
shaggy owtchah, rug
sheep beardie, collie, cur, kelpie, malinois, old english, shepherd
shore dagger
short-eared alan(d), alant
short-haired dalmatian, staffordshire
short-legged beagle, dachshund
sled command mush
sled-drawing malamute, malemute
small alco, amertoy, ascob, chihuahua, comforter, f(e)ist, fice, lhasa apso, lion-dog, maltese, melita, messan, messin, papillon, peke, pekinese, piper, pom(eranian), pug, pup, purp, schipperke, shih tzu, shock dog, skye terrier, tike, toy, turnspit, tyke
snapper jocu
star asta, canicula, procyon, sept(i), sirius, sopt, sothis, veps
swift greyhound, whippet
symbol of fidelity
tail bent
thin man's asta
3-headed cerberus
-tired spent, weary
top elite, leader
toy affenpinscher, italian greyhound
trio leash
tropical alco
trot dance, pace, run, walk
upper lip flews
vicious taepo
-wagon diner
whelk nassa, thais, winkle
wild aboli, adjag, agouara, cimarron, coyote, cuon,

cyon, dhole, dingo, guara, jackal, tanate
woolly rug
working husky, malamute, malemute
yelping wappet
young pup(py), whelp
DOGBANE acocanthera, allamanda, alstonia, amsonia, apocynace, aspidosperma, beaumontia, bigroot, bitterroot, dita, echites, flytrap, honeybloom, indian hemp, kendir, kendyr, lewisea, milkweed
fruit aboli
spreading ipecac
DOGBERRY *friend* verges
DOGBOAT pig, sled
DOGE magistrate, ruler
barge bucentaur
headdress toque
medal osela
DOGFISH bluedog, bonedog, bowfin, burbot, carcharias, catfish, cynias, daggar, gabback, galeid, grayfish, hoe, hurse, huss, mange, morgay, mudminnow, mudpuppy, nursehound, roussette, sandshark, seahound, shark, tope(r), triakid
liver extract acanthine
DOGGED dour, inflexible, mulish, obstinate, persevering, pigheaded, resolute, stubborn, sullen
DOGGEREL absurd, amphigory, amphigouri, burlesque, crambo clink, crude, jingle, macaronics, mean, mongrel, nominy, nonsense verse, poem, poor, rhyme, rime, rude, singsong, tasteless, trivia
DOGGERY barroom, canaille, mob, rabble
DOGGONE blessed, darn(ed), drat, hang
DOGIE calf, derelict, fledgling, leppy, maverick, stray
DOGMA belief, cant, conviction, credo, creed, dictum, doctrine, fundamental, ism, levitic, persuasion, principle, tenet
pert. levitical
DOGMATIC absolute, affirmative, arbitrary, assertive, authoritarian, authoritative, categorical, confident, dictatorial, doctrinaire, doctrinary, domineering, magis-

terial, magistral, opinionated, oracular, peremptory, positive, pragmatic, stiffnecked, strait-laced
DOGMATISM bibliolatry, bigotry, fundamentalism, hideboundness, hyperorthodoxy, precisianism, puritanism, sabbatarianism, sabbatism, stiff-neckedness
DOGWOOD aucuba, barbasco, bloddy-twig, boxwood, cornel, cornus, fishwood, gaiter, houndsberry, nyssa, osier, sumac, tua, widbin
black bird-cherry, padius, piscidia
blue pigeonberry
red bloody-rod, bloody-twig
DOILY mat, napkin, pad, tide, tidy
DOING(S) act(ing), action, activity, ado, deed, event, execution, fact, fair, function, gear, happening, hustle, occasion, party, performance, stir, up to
good benefaction, beneficence
wrong malefaction
DOIT bit, coin, confuse, dodkin, lubber, whit
DOLDRUMS bluedevils, blues, boredom, calm, dejection, depression, dismals, dolefuls, dumps, ennui, gloom, inertia, lachrymals, megrims, misery, mopes, mulligrubs, mumps, stagnation, stupor, tedium, torpor
DOLE agony, allot(ment), alms, anguish, bit, charity, deal(ing), destiny, dimensum, dispense, distress, distribution, divide, division, donation, dool, gift, give, goal, gratuity, grief, guile, handout, landmark, lot, mete, misery, mourn, part, pittance, portion, ration, regret, relief, share, sorrow, trial, trifle, vail, welfare, woe
DOLEFUL black, blue, dark, dirgeful, dismal, dolorous, dowie, dowy, drear, dree, flebile, funereal, funest(al), gloomy, heavy, melancholy, miserable, mournful, rueful, sad, tragical, woeful
DOLIUS hermes, mercury
mistress penelope
DOLL array, babe, baby,

dish, girl, kachina, katc(h)ina, kewpie, maiden, maumet, miniature, mistress, moll, moppet, muneca, plaything, poppet, poupee, preen, primp, puppet, sweetheart, toy, woman
black golliwog(g)
cardboard pantine
-like infantile
stuffer rammer
up adorn, dress, prank, preen, prink, prune, smarten, spruce, swank
DOLLAR ace, bean, berry, bill, boffo, bone, buck, cartwheel, coin, daalder, daler, eagle, fish, frogskin, gourde, ironman, loksh, money, note, one, pataca, patacoon, peso, plonk, plunk, rock, scad, simoleon, skin, smacker, taler, wheel, yuan
¼th quarter, two-bits
½ fifty cents, forbes, four-bits
1 buck, frogskin, single, spot
2 deuce
4 stella
5 fin, five(r), vee
10 sawbuck
100 century, c-note
500 monkey
1,000 gee, grand, thou
bill frogskin, greenback, rock
bird roller
gap arrears, deficit
group bundle, fortune, pile
silver cartwheel, sinker
to doughnuts probably
DOLLARDEE bluegill
DOLLARFISH ephipus, gunnel, kelpfish, moonfish, poronotus, shiner, starfish
DOLLOP blob, clump, lump, patch
DOLL'S HOUSE *author* ibsen
heroine nora
DOLLY (See also DOLL.) car, carrier, cart, drab, figure, follower, hobby, maiden, mistress, peggy, punch, shifter, slattern, swage, sweetheart, tray, trolley, truck
DOLLYMAN bucker
DOLLYWAY dock
DOLMEN cromlech, crommel, megalith, memorial, senam, tolmen
DOLOMITE bitter-spar,

brown-spar, magnesite, pearlspar
DOLON *father* eumedes
slayer diomedes, odysseus, ulysses
DOLOR affliction, anguish, distress, grief, misery, mourning, pain, sadness, sorrow, suffering, trial, woe
DOLOROUS dismal, distressing, grievous, melancholy, mournful, pathetic, rueful, sad, woeful
DOLPHIN bollard, bottlenose, bouto, cetacean, cowfish, dorado, gairfish, inia, mahimahi, mereswine, narwhal(e) palach, pellock, porpoise, porpus, pullock, snuffer, soosoo, susu, tursio(ps), whale, wreath
blind susu
bottle-nosed tursio
comb. delphinus, delphis
flower larkspur
fly aphid, collier
river bouto, inia
DOLT ass(head), birdbrain, block(head), blutie, booby, bonehead, bosthoon, cabbage(head), calf, chub, chump, clod(hopper), clodpate, cluck, coot, cow, cudden, dawcock, dimwit, donkey, doodle, duffer, dullard dullhead, dully, dult(ie) dumbbell, dummy, dunce, fool, funge, hobbil, idiot, imbecile, jackass, loon, lout, lunkhead, moke, mooncalf, mut(t), ninny, nump(s), numskull, oaf, patch, peasant, sap(head), schnook, steg, stick, stock, stupidhead, thickwit, yold
cunning sly-boots
DOLTISH besotted, blockish, dull, foolish, peakish, sottish, stupid, tomfool
DOMAIN area, bailiwick, barony, birthdom, bourn(e), deme(s)ne, district, dominion, earldom, empery, empire, estate, field, jurisdiction, medina, orbit, property, province, quarter, region, scope, signory, sphere, starosty, state, territory, zone
nether hell
transcendent heaven
woman's distaff, home, kitchen
DOMBEY AND SONS *char-*

acter bagstock, blimber, carker, cuttle, nipper, toots
DOME arcade, arch, blister, bubble, calotte, cap, cima, cimborio, crown, cupola, curve, edifice, head, house, mansion, pate, rise, roof, span, swell, tholos, top, tope, tower, vault
observation blister
over tomb weli
-shaped domoid
snow-capped calotte
support pendentive, squinch, tholobate, trompe
tomb tholos
top ball, cupola, lantern
DOMESTIC domal, employee, enchorial, esne, familiar, family, hamald, hame(i)ld, hamelt, keyduc(k), homebred, homeloving, homely, homemaking, housal, household, housekeeping, indigenous, inland, inmate, interior, internal, intimate, intramural, khamal, kitchenman, local, maid, menial, mozo, native, naturalized, potwalloper, recluse, scalder, scullion, servant, tabby, tame
animal See ANIMAL *domestic.*
DOMESTICATE adopt, affiliate, amenage, assimilate, break, breed, bust, civilize, corral, denizen(ize), endenizen, entame, gentle, housebreak, nationalize, naturalize, raise, rear, reclaim, settle, tame
DOMICILE abode, address, crib, dwell(ing), habitation, home, HOUSE, mansion, menage, residence, roost, shed
identification doorplate, nameplate
pioneer log cabin, sod house
DOMINA lady
DOMINANCE ascendancy, authority, control, dominion, influence, sway, whiphand
DOMINANT bossy, central, chief, commanding, controlling, dominule, head, influential, paramount, preponderant, prevailing, regnant, salient, sovereign, sovran, superior, supreme, tenor
DOMINATE bestride, bully,

charm, coerce, command, control, domineer, envelope, govern, influence, lead, master, overshadow, oversway, overtop, preponderate, prevail, reign, rule, subject, subjugate, sway, top, tower, vassal

DOMINATION ascendancy, bovarism, bovaryism, control, despotism, dominion, empire, influence, range, strings
by political bosses caciquism

DOMINATOR boss, lord, ruler

DOMINEER aggrieve, beat down, bluster, boss, browbeat, bully, command, compel, control, dominate, grind, hector, henpeck, keep down, lord, nag, oppress, overawe, overbear, overlord, override, revel, ride over, rule, swagger, tower, trample, tread down, tyrannize

DOMINEERING arrogant, bossy, despotic, dictatorial, haughty, imperious, lordly, magisterial, masterful, oppressive, peremptory, surly

DOMINICAN jacobin, jacobite, preacher, predicant

DOMINICAN REPUBLIC
bay calderas, escocesa, isabela, neiba, ocoa, rincon, samana, yuma
cape beata, cabron, caucedo, engano, falso, isabela, macoris
capital cuidad trujillo, santo domingo
city azua, bani, barahona, bonao, cotui, higuey, moca, nagua, neiba, nizao, oviedo, pena, polo, sanchez, santiago, sosua
coin franco, oro, peso
dictator rafael trujillo
island altovelo, beata, catalina, hispaniola, saona
leader balaguer, trujillo
lowland cibao
measure fanega, ona, tarea
peak duarte, gallo, tina
president trujillo
range bahoruco, neiba, oriental
river ozama, yuna
valley neyba, real

DOMINION ascendance, ascendancy, authority, califate, colony, control, coun-

try, crown, dition, domain, dominance, dominancy, domination, duchy, empery, empire, enclave, government, jurisdiction, khanate, mandate, ownership, possession, poustie, power, predominance, preponderance, prepotence, prepotency, primacy, province, realm, regency, regnum, right, rule, seignory, signoria, sovereignty, sovranty, sphere, state, supremacy, sway, territory, upper hand, whip hand
church sacerdotium, see
imperial empery, empire
joint condominium
old virginia

DOMINO amice, bone, cloak, costume, die, disguise, hood, jeton, mask, matador, stone, tile, venetian

DOMINOES bones, cards, dice, ivories, rocks, tiles
bank banks
galloping dice
game all-fives, amazualat, bergen, bingo, doublet, fortress, forty-two, ho-hpai, hoi-tap, matador, muggins, nag-pai, sebastopol, sniff, star, tau-tem, tiddlywinks
term bingo, blank, block, boneyard, deal, lighter, matador, matching, play, rock, set, tableau

DON address, array, assume, change, clothe, dress, endue, get on, indue, invest, nobleman, put on, slip on, teacher, tutor, wear
city on rostov

DONA, DONNA See LADY.
DONALBAIN *brother* malcolm
father duncan
DONAR See THOR.
DONATE accord, award, bestow, confer, contribute, gie, give, grant, present, subscribe
DONATION alms, benefaction, bestowal, charity, collection, contribution, dole, gift, grant, gratuity, handout, offering, offertory, pittance, present, subscription, subvention, tribute, widow's mite
to singers carl
DONAX bamban, mollusk, reed

DONE agreed, cooked, dead, deen, ended, enough said, executed, exhausted, finished, given, mere, over, through
brown cheated
carelessly botched, scambling
for all over, all up, beyond help, dead, dying, exhausted, finished, gone, invalid, kaput(t), napoo, sunk
in exhausted, spent
in plain sight brazen
not being unorthodox
together concerted
unconsciously automatic, instinctive
up exhausted, spent, worn out
with completed, disposed of, ended, finished, through
DONGA channel, gap
DONIZETTI *opera* daughter of the regiment, don pasquale, la favorita, lucia de lammermoor, lucrezia borgia, rita
DON JOHN *brother* don pedro
follower borachio, conrade
DONJON castle, dungeon, fort, jail, keep, prison, rocca, stronghold
DON JUAN casanova, debauchee, jeromin, lecher, libertine, lothario, lover, rake
creator byron, tirso de molina
general quijada, requeseus, sessa
intimate grand conde, princess palatine
mother inez
naval victory lepanto
nurse barbara blomberg, blombes, dona magdalena, plumberger
DONKEY, DONKEY'S ane, asinego, asino, ass, booby, brayer, burro, buss(ock), cardophagus, chump, cuddy, dickey, dolt, engine, equid, ezel, fool, fuss(ock), genet, gudda, hinny, jackass, jennet, jenny, longear, lubber, moke, mule, neddy, onager, ono, simpleton, thistle-eater, yarder
comb. ono
cry bray, hee-haw

engine auxiliary, doctor, dollbeer, roader, yarder
-faced god set(h)
years eternity, long time
DONNYBROOK brawl, confusion, free-for-all, melee, uproar
DON PEDRO *attendant* balthasar
beloved hero
brother don john, don juan
favorite benedick, claudio
servant balthasar
DON QUIXOTE visionary
author cervantes
beloved dulcinea
character basilius, camacho, durandarte, guadiana, malambruno, marcella, maria theresa, maritornes, quiteria, ruydura, toboso, toralva
doctor pedro
giant alifanfaron, caraculiambo
home la mancha
squire sancho panza
steed rocinante, rosinante
wooden horse clavileno
DONSIE ailing, listless, pert, perverse, sad, saucy, sickly, tidy, trim, unfortunate, unlucky
DON'T can it, cut it out, desist, enough, forbear, hands off, ixnay, lay off, nix, prohibition, stop
DONZEL page, squire
DOODAD bauble, dofunny, dohickey, gadget, gimcrack, jimcrack, object, thingumbob, trifle, trinket
DOODLE cheat, dally, dolt, draw, fool, idle, picture, screeve, scribble, trifler
DOODLEBUG divining rod
DOODLESACK bagpipes
DOOHICKEY dingus, gadget, thingumbob
DOOK See DEMON.
DOOM attaint, charge, condemn, curse, damn, death, decision, decree, destine, destiny, destruction, devote, end, fate, foreordain, fortune, future, judge, justice, ker, lot, mercement, portion, predestine, ruin, sentence, statute, steven, tomorrow
palm doum, dum, gingerbread tree
spirit ker

DOOMED accursed, damned, dead, destined, done, fatal, fated, fey, finished, forlorn, goner, illfated, illstarred, kaput(t)
DOOMSDAY future, ragnarok, tomorrow
DOOMSMAN judge, lawman
DOOR anteport, avenue, dar, drop, entrance, entry, fusuma, gate(way), hatch, inlet, janua, jigger, lid, opening, outlet, passage (way), path, portal, postern, posticum, raddle, servidor, stopping, trap, traverse, valve, wicket
airplane clamshell
back postern
bar risp, stang
cross piece lintel, transom
curtain portiere
fastener bar, bolt, catch, hasp, latch, lock
frame buck, casing
half hatch, heck
head derner
hinged slapper
hinge goddess cardea
holy amphithyron
jamb alette, post, reveal
knocker hammer, rapper, risp
latch catch, haggaday, sneck, snick
lay at blame
lock night-latch
lock keeper nab, rasp, stang, tiler
mine stopping
part alette, ansel, butt, durn, jamb, knob, lintel, mullion, panel, pier, postel, rail, reveal, risp, sash, sill, stile, upright
post alette, jamb, pier, postel, upright
rails impages
recess embrasure
show the dismiss
sill soil
sliding arcadia, fusuma, shoji, shut(ter), traverse
storm dingle
-to-door canvass
trap drop, scruto
DOORKEEPER bidello, concierge, durwa(u)n, hasp, huissier, janitor, janitress, janitrix, ostiarius, ostiary, porter, tiler, tilia, tyler, usher, warden, wiskinky
DOORMAN attendant, foot-

man, hallman, porter, servant, shutter
DOORMAT bearskin, cocomat, weakling
DOORSTOP bumper, holdback
DOORWAY aperture, arch, entrance, exit, opening, portal, vestibule
DOPE ass, boob(y), deaden, deceive, donkey, drug, facts, fool, fuel, goff, goon, goop, guess, heroin, hop, information, judge, knock out, load, lowdown, lubricant, lubricate, marijuana, medicate, narcotic, news, opiate, opium, paste, predict, s(c)hmuck, solution, stupefy, truth
fiend See ADDICT.
out calculate, solve
up adulterate, debase, doctor
DOPEY dazed, farchadat, languid, stupid, woozy
friend See DWARF *seven*.
DOPPELGANGER apparition, counterpart, double, hanger-on, spirit, wraith
DOR beetle, bongo, buffoon, bumblebee, clock, deceive, deception, droner, joke(r), mock(ery), scoff(er), trick
DORADO color, cuir, cuit, dolphin, goldfish, xiphias
DORBEETLE bumclock, buzzard, clock, cockchafer, droner
DORCAS gazelle, tabitha
occupation seamstress
reviver peter
DORIAN rustic, simple
festival carnea, carneia
DORIC *accent* plateasm
capital part abacus
frieze part metope, taenia
DORIDEN glutethimide
DORINE *master* tartuffe
DORIPPE *daughter* elais
DORIS *consort* nereus
offspring nereids
parent oceanus, tethys
DORITIS aphrodite
DORMANCY abeyance, latence, latency, stagnation, torpor
by day diurnation
DORMANT abeyant, asleep, comatose, connivent, couchant, fallow, fixed, idle, inactive, inert, latent, lethargic, passive, potential, prone, quiescent, recum-

bent, resting, sleeping, smoldering, supine, torpid

DORMER bedroom, casement, dormitory, window
window eyebrow, gablet, lucarne, lucomb, luthern, oriel

DORMITORY accommodation, apartment, bedroom, bullpen, bunkhouse, bursa, cubatory, dormer, dorter, dortour, hall, hostel, house, quarters
bedroom cubicle
rules, pert. parietal

DORMOUSE dryad, glirid, glis, lerion, lerot, loir, moy, mur, rodent, sleeper
pert. myoxine

DORNICK boulder, cloth, darnix, donack, doney, donnick, linen, stone

DORP city, hamlet, village

DORSAL abaxial, back, dosser, hanging, nerve, neural, notal, posterial, superior, tergal, vertebra(e)
opposed to ventral
region back

DORUS *descendant* hellenes
parent apollo, hellen, orseis, phthia
slayer aetolus
son aegimius

DORY bearfish, boat, fish, pike

DORYMENES *son* ptolemaeus

DOSE bole, bolus, booster, bromide, capsule, datio, doctor, dost, draft, draught, drench, drug, medicate, part, pharmacoposia, portion, potion, quantity, remedy, shot, treat
narcotic bindle, locus(t), shot

DOSITHEUS *son* ptolemaeus

DOS PASSOS *novel* big money, manhattan transfer, three soldiers, usa

DOSS bed(room), bow, bunch, knot, sleep, tuft
house hotel, inn

DOSSER dorsal, pan(n)ier

DOSSERET abacus, pulvino

DOSSIER black book, chart, compendium, document, file, history, list, record, report

DOSSIL dressing, pledget, spigot, tent

DOSTOEVSKY *novel* brothers karamazov, crime

and punishment, the double, the idiot, the possessed
inspector porfiry

DOT bit, clot, dapple, dower(y), endowment, flyspeck, iota, lump, mark, mote, particle, peck, period, point, prick, punctum, scatter, speck(le), spot(tle), sprinkle, stigme, stipple, tick, tittle, tocher, variegate, whit
black dartrose
on forehead bottu
over letter stigme, tittle
with paint stipple

DOTAGE drivel, folly, senility, twichild

DOTARD babbler, betty, dott(e)rel, driveler, fogy, fool, henhussy, imbecile, liripipe, liripoop, old fogy, old man, old woman, radoteur, senile

DOTATE bestow, endow, give

DOTE adore, bestow, decay, drivel, drool, enjoy, fancy, like, love, relish, timberrot

DOTHEBOYS HALL *master* wackford squeers
student nicholas nickleby

DOTING affectionate, anile, decaying, devoted, doddering, fatuous, fond, foolish, loving, senile, silly

DOTTED patchy, piebald, pied, pinto, punctate, seme(ed), speckled, spotted, stellated, stippled, studded, ticked, touchy

DOTTEREL clown, dupe, eudromias, fool, gull, morinel, plover, wind

DOTTY crazy, feeble, insane, spotty, totty, unsteady

DOUBLE alternate, ambiguous, appreciate, bent over, bifold, bigeminal, binary, binate, bivalent, breve, copy, coupled, crack, crease, deceitful, deviation, diploid, doppio, dual, duplex, duplicate, dyad, equal, equivocal, evade, fellow, fold(ed), gemel, geminate, grow, increase, induplo, insincere, level, look-alike, match, paired, sosie, stand-in, substitute, supply, transcript, twice, twin, twofold, understudy
aces ambsace, amesace

and quits monte carlo, solitaire
a point tack
back return, reverse
-barrelled deadly, important
boiler bain-marie
check verify
chin bubbula, choller
cocoon dupion
comb. bini, diphy
-cross betray(al), bitch, cheat, deceive, deception, delude, gyp, mislead, rat, swindle, treachery, twotime
-crosser heel, rat, traitor
dagger diesis
dare challenge
dealing chicane(ry), deceit, deception, duplicity, falsehearted, fraud, mealy-mouthed, perfidy, subterfuge, treachery, trickery, twofaced
dutch enigma, greek, jargon, unintelligible
-edged acerb, acrimonious, keen, sharp
entendre ambiguity, amphibology, joke
-faced ancipital, false, hypocritical
for pass as, substitute
hue bicolor
impression mackle
in brass act, represent
life amphibiety
meaning ambiguity
pedro cinch, game
phantom fetch
point of curve acnode
quick fast, march, speedy, swiftly
reed basanello
ring gemel
-ripper bobsled, bobsleigh, sled
runner skate, sled
salt alum, selenium, soda
-talk babel, equivocation, gobbledegook, jargon, mumbo, nonsense, patter, rigamarole
truck layout, spread
up buck, clench, jackknife

DOUBLED gemel, geminous

DOUBLEGANGER See DOPPELGANGER.

DOUBLENESS duality, plenitude

DOUBLET duplet, gippon, pair, paltock, placcate, pourpoint, sniff, two, undergarment
front peasecod

DOUBLETREE evener, spreader, transverse

DOUBLING artifice, duplation, duplicate, fold, lap, lining, loop, trick
comb. duplo

DOUBLOON ocher, onza
¼th pistole

DOUBLY dually, twice, twofold
comb. duplicate

DOUBT aporia, apprehension, challenge, demur, diffide, disbelief, disbelieve, discredit, dispute, dissent, distrust, dread, dubiate, dubiety, dubiosity, dwere, flounder, hesitate, incredulity, misgiving, mislippen, mistrust, pause, puzzleover, pyrrhonism, qualm, query, question, scruple, shilly-shally, skepsis, skepticalness, skepticism, smell a rat, staggers, suspect, suspense, suspicion, suspiciousness, swither, umbrage, uncertainty, vacilate, waver, weir, wonder
expression of ahem, come now, do tell, go on, hum(ph), in a pig's eye, indeed, like fun, my eye, my foot, nonsense, rats, really, says who
in in dubio
without sine dubio

DOUBTFUL afraid, ambiguous, bogglish, dreadful, duberous, dubious, dubitable, dubitant, equivocal, fearful, fishy, hesitant, improbable, incredulous, jealous, juberous, jubus, perhaps, perilous, problematic, pyrrhonic, questionable, questioning, shady, skeptical, suspicious, unsafe, unsure, vacillating, wilsome

DOUCEUR agreeableness, bonus, bribe, gratuity, pourboire, sop, tip

DOUCHE eyewash, moisten, rinse, shower, soak, sprinkler, wash(ing)

DOUGH batter, cash, change, crust, daigh, duff, leaven, mandlen, money, noodle, pasta, paste, puffpaste, pulp, sponge, spud, teiglach
belly stoneroller
-faced irresolute, pliable, pliant

fermenting leaven
fried spud

DOUGHBOY dumpling, soldier

DOUGHHEAD clodpole, clodpoll, fool

DOUGHNUT bagel, beignet, bismarck, cruller, cymbal, fasnacht, fatcake, olycook, olykoek, simball, sinker, twister
shaped bagel, toroidal, torus

DOUGHTY bold, brave, courageous, fearless, fell, heroic, intrepid, preu, resolute, strong, tall, valiant

DOUGHY ashen, crude, dunch, flabby, pale, pasty, pulpy, sodden, thick, viscid, white

DOUGLAS *fir* spruce
song annie laurie
spruce yellow fir

DOUP buttocks, end, rump, thread, wrap

DOUR crabbed, dern, gloomy, glum, grim, hard, harsh, morose, obstinate, ominous, rigid, rough, severe, sour, stern, strict, strong, sulky, sullen, surly, taciturn

DOUSE beat, blow, doff, downpour, drench, duck, extinguish, immerse, plunge, quit, remove, sluice, souse, stow, strike, stroke

DOVE columba, coo, culver, cushat, doo, inca, innocent, jemima, jonah, kuku, laughter, namaqua, nun, paloma, peace lover, peacenik, pigeon, slumber, talpacoti, tumbler
blue pelican
goddess eurynome, tangaroa
ground rola, talpacoti
-like columbine, gentle, lovable, pure
long-tailed namaqua
name meaning jonah, jonas
pert. columbine
ring cushat, pigeon, toozoo
rock sod
scale inca
sound coo, curr
symbol of innocence
weed spurge
wild tambourine
young doveling

DOVECOTE aviary, columbarium, columbary, doocot, dooket, louver, pigeonry

DOVEFOOT columbine

DOVEKIE alle, auk, bull(bird), guillemot, rotch(e), rotge

DOVETAIL adapt, agree, cog, comport, consort, fit, go with, groove, insert, intersect, jag(g), join, sort with, suit, tenon, tongue

DOWDY blousy, blowsy, blowzy, coarse, disheveled, fat, frowzy, frumpy, poky, pudding, ruddy, shabby, slatternly, sloppy, slovenly, stodgy, tacky, unkempt

DOWEL coag, coak, duledge, joggle, peg, pinion, pin(tle), setpin, skittle, sprig, stenon, stud

DOWER bequest, doarium, donation, dos, dot, endow, endue, equip, gift, grant, heritage, maritage, outfit, portion, talent, toucher

DOWITCHER brownback, driver, fowl, grayback, greyback, longbeak, sleeper, snipe

DOWN absolute, bas, below, bete, descending, descent, dislike, doon, dowl(e), eider, fall, feathers, fell, flix, floor, flue, fluff, fuzz, grudge, hill(ock), hup, lanugo, lint, pappus, pile, plumage, positive, pronate, prone, refrain, set, sick, sour, swallow, under(neath), upland
-and-out destitute, pauper, quisby
-and-outer pauper, wretch
at heels indigent, seamy, shabby, shaggy, slipshod, slovenly
beat gloomy, thesis
comb. bas, cata, cath, cat(o)de, kat(o)
-covered hesthogenous, precocial, tomentose
-cry disparage
east maine
facing pronate, prone, prostrate
far deep(ly)
farthest bottom
feather plume, plumule
feathery dowl
in the mouth depressed, discouraged, glum, low, melancholy, pessimistic, sick, unhappy
market bear
payment advance, binder, earnest money

quilt comforter, duvet, puff
south dixie
stage or stairs below
the ages ab aeterno
the drain dissipated, gone, lost
the line complete, full, unreserved
-to-earth practical, realistic
to the ground throughout, utterly
under antipodes, australia, new zealand, tasmania
wind leeward
with abas
woollike dowl(e)
DOWNCAST abject, blue, chapfallen, chopfallen, crestfallen, dashed, dejected, depressed, despondent, discouraged, disheartened, dispirited, drooping, droopy, gloomy, heartless, hopeless, languishing, low, melancholy, pining, sad, spiritless, sunk, unhappy, woebegone
DOWNCOMER pipe
DOWNFALL abyss, collapse, defeat, degringolade, descent, destruction, disgrace, downpour, drop, eclipse, ecroulement, failure, fate, finish, misfortune, overthrow, pit, precipice, reverse, ruin(ation), trap, undoing
DOWNFLOW deflux, vail
DOWNFOLD saddle
DOWNGRADE abase, bust, declivity, decrease, demote, descending, dipping
DOWNHEARTED dejected, depressed, melancholy
DOWNHILL anticlinal, declined, declining, declivate, declivity, declivous, descending, dropping, falling, pendent, synclinal
rush schuss
DOWNPOUR cataract, deluge, douse, dowse, drencher, flood, flow, rain-(storm), spill, spout, storm, torrent
DOWNRIGHT absolute, arrant, blank, blunt, brusque, candid, clear, completely, curt, direct, explicit, fair, flat, forthright, frank, greatly, honest, open, perpendicular(ly), plain, plumb, positive, pure, rank, sheer, simple, sincere, stark,

straightway, thorough(ly), throughout, unceremonious, unqualified, utter, vertical
DOWNS highland, plains, ridge, upland
DOWNSET rebuke, reprimand, slope
DOWNSIDE bottom, rear
DOWNSWING doldrums, slump
DOWNTOWN center, city, urban
away from upstreet
DOWNTRODDEN abused, browbeaten, henpecked, oppressed, trampled, under
DOWNTURN decline, decrease, dip, fall, sinking
DOWNWARD below, deorsum, lower, netherwards, prone, quaquaversal
DOWNY bed, callow, cottony, cunning, feathery, flocculent, flossy, fluey, fluffy, fuzzy, knowing, lanate, lanuginous, mollipilose, mossy, nappy, pilar(y), placid, plumulaceous, plumy, pubescent, quiet, soft, soothing, velutinous, villous, wary
mildew bremia
poplar cottonwood
DOWRY dos, dot, dower, endowment, gift, maritage, money, nadan, portion, sulka, talent, tocher
pert. dotal
DOWSER waterfinder, watersmeller, waterwitch(er)
DOWSING *rod* See DIVINING *rod.*
DOXOLOGY acoteleutic, gloria, hymn, kaddish
DOXY belief, doctrine, doyen, harlot, opinion, paramour, prostitute, sweetheart, system, wanton, wench, woman
DOYEN chief, dean, senior
DOZE catnap, dorm, dote, dover, drowse, muddle, nap, nod, perplex, rot, sleep, sloom, snooz(l)e, stupefy
DOZEN dizzen, dosain, twelve, xii
2 thrave
5 tally
12 gross
baker's thirteen
short eleven
DRAB arid, besom, bit, box,

cloth, daw, dell, dollymop, drug, dull, dun, everyday, fox, frump(y), heavy, hussy, jade, jezebel, lackluster, malkin, poison, prosaic, prostitute, sad, slattern, stodgy, subfusc(ous), trollop, wanton, wench, whore
DRABBLE draggle, fish, hang, muddy
-tail slattern, sloven
DRACHMA *1/20th* obol
½ triobol
DRACONIAN brutal, cruel, harsh, severe
DRACULA demon, devil, the impaler, vald tepes
actor bela lugosi
author bram stoker
home bran, hunedoara, risnov
principality wallachia
DRAFF dregs, hogwash, lees, offal, refuse, remainder, waste
DRAFF-SACK glutton
DRAFFY waste, worthless
DRAFT abbozzo, bill, check, chit, claim, conscript, copy, current, demand, depth, design, displacement, dose, drain, draught, draw(ing), drink, enroll(ment), epure, glut, gorge, gully, levy, load, manuscript, money, muster, note, outline, pattern, plan, plot, potion, project, protocol, pull, scheme, selection, sinkage, sketch, slock, submergence, submersion, suck, swig, swill, swipe, version, waucht, waught, wind, write
fear of aerophobia
heavy whitter
large carouse, score
of air cooke
of composition score
off shed
of pattern strip
of treaty projet
original protocol
regulator damper
rough brouillon, scantling, sketch
sleeping dorter
DRAG bore, bother, brake, clog, creep, curb, daggle, date, dawdle, dog, draggle, dragshoe, draw, drogue, escort, fish, friction, go slow, grapnel, grapple, hale, hang, harl, harrow, haul,

hone, hook, impediment, inch(along), influence, lag, linger, lug, lurry, nowel, obstacle, pluck, poke, pull, race, rally, remora, retard(ation), road, scent, s(c)hlep, s(c)hloom, s(c)hlump, shuffle, skidpan, sledge, slide, slow, slug, smooth, snake, snig, stagger, stuffed-shirt, taigle, tease, toddle, totter, tow, train, trawl, trayne, trice, tug, weight, worm
along craw, lug, shool, tra(u)chle, trayne
behind chariot defeat, humiliate, subdue
carelessly hike
deer toll, tump
down degrade
feet slodge
into implicate, involve
jerkily snig
logs skid
off harry
on continue
one's freight beat it, flee
out drawl, elicit, extend, prolong, protract
racer hotrodder
reducer boattail
rope guss
-stone mill arrastra, arrastre
through mud bemire, stain
DRAGGLE bedabble, bedrabble, dabble, daggle, dirty, drabble, drail, hang, pull
DRAGNET flue, lasso, seizure, train(el), trap, trawl, web
lead in dum-de-dum-dum
DRAGOMAN agent, guide, interpreter
DRAGON, DRAGON'S ahi, ati, basilisk, cockatrice, crank, dipsas, draco, drake, duenna, earthdrake, fafnir, ketu, ladon, lizard, lung, meteor, monster, musket, nidhog(gr), nithhogg(r), ogre, orc, pigeon, rahu, rehab, reptile, satan, serpent, soldier, tractor, vritra, wivern, worm, wyvern
biblical rehab
biting tarragon
blood resin
brown jack-in-the-pulpit
claw coralroot
cloud shi
darkness rehab
emblem of china, wales

fiery firedrake
flying meteor
head anabilbazon, rahu
king ao chin, ao jun, au kuang, au shun, lung wang
-like draconic, dracontine
many-headed hydra
slayer florent, george, martha, michael, philip, romain
symbol of satan
tail catabilbazon, ketu
-teeth-sower cadmus
tree dracaena
2-legged vivern, wyvern
vedic ahi
DRAGONET fox(fish), gowdnie, gurnard, illect, jugular, loricate, quaviver, sculpin
DRAGONFLY adderbolt, agrionid, anisoptera, darner, libellula, naiad, odonata, skimmer
DRAGOON cavalryman, coerce, harass, oppress, soldier
DRAIN 3 dry, gan, gaw, sap, tap, top 4 coup, dail, dale, delf, draw, gout, grip, leam, milk, pipe, pour, pump, sike, sink, soak, suck, suff, sump, teem, tile, toom, tube 5 bleed, bunny, canal, delft, ditch, draft, dreen, drink, empty, fleet, groop, gully, leach, rhine, seuch, seugh, sewer, siver, sough, stell, strip, waste 6 broach, cloaca, decant, demand, emulge, filter, furrow, gutter, kennel, let out, refine, riggot, sheuch, siphon, sleuce, suck up, swough, syphon, trench, trogue, weaken, zanjon 7 alberca, carouse, carrier, channel, clarify, conduit, consume, culvert, deplete, draught, exhaust, grindle, gripple, piscina, piscine, scupper, suck out, vitiate, zanjona 8 bankrupt, carriage, cesspool, evacuate, sinkhole, thurrock, waterway 9 effluence, headchute, undermine 11 consumption
arched culvert
blood exsanguinate
board sink
covered thurrock
dry jib
forces spend
mine sough

open siver, stell
small trone
DRAINAGE adit, saur, sock, sullage, sumpage
area basin
DRAINED ashen, ashy, colorless, empty, gray, pale, pallid, pasty, spent, wan, waxen
DRAINPIPE leader, quelm, shell, sink, whelm
mold dod
DRAKE cannon, cob, dragon, duck, gadwale, gadwall, gadwell, galley, gander, rooster, sta(i)g
city san francisco
rounded cape horn
ship golden hind
DRAM bit, ca(u)lker, drachm, draft, drink, jigger, mite, nip, nobbler, pony, potation, shot, slug, snifter, sopie, timber, tipple, tot, weight
shop See SALOON.
DRAMA (See also PLAY.) auto, ballet, burlesque, buskin, cliffhanger, comedia, comedy, cothurnus, diorama, extravaganza, farce, footlights, histrionics, kabuki, legit, mask, masque, melodrama, mime, mummery, mystery, nataka, noh, nokaku, opera, operetta, pageant, pantomine, pastoral, piece, representation, review, revue, soaper, spectacle, stage (dom), tableau, theater, theatre, tragedy, vaudeville
action epitasis
allegorical morality play
climax catastasis
court trial
dance ballet, kathakali
division See PLAY *part.*
18th century burletta
expression system delsarte
for single actor monodrama
god dionysus
horror grand guignol
interlude extremes
medieval mystery
muse melpomene, thalia
musical burletta, grand opera, operetta, saynete
part See PLAY *part.*
performer actor, actress, mummer, star, thespian
pert. histrionic
school actor's studio, rein-

hardt, stanislovsky, strasberg
sentimental soaper, soap
opera
short saynete, skit
somber tragedy
spectacular extravaganza
sudden reverse in peripetia
western horse opera
DRAMAMINE dimenhydrinate
DRAMATIC emotional, exciting, histrionic, impressive, makebelieve, ostentatious, protean, scenic(al),
sensational, spectacular,
stagelike, stagy, startling,
stirring, theatrical, thespian,
vivid, wild
representation impersonation, PLAY, wayang
scene cameo
DRAMATIST actor, author,
choreographer, comedian,
dialogist, dramaturge, dra-
maturgist, farce(u)r, farceuse, farcist, gagman, librettist, melodramatist, mi-
mographer, pantomimist,
playwright, scenarist,
screenwriter, scriptwriter,
stagewright, tragedian,
writer
DRAMATIZE color, enact,
extravagate, feature, glamorize, play up, present,
produce, show, stage
DRAMATURGE See
DRAMATIST.
DRANCES *enemy* turnus
DRAPE adorn, barren, cover,
cow, crape, cretonne, curtain, dress, farrow, festoon,
hang(ing), pendant, val-
ance
DRAPER clothier, linenman,
tailor
DRAPERY baize, clothing,
curtain, hanging, mourning,
pand, reredos, scene, swag,
tester, valance
decorative lambrequin
sash tieback
DRASTIC dire, extreme,
harsh, powerful, radical,
rigorous, severe, stern, vigorous, violent
DRAUGHTS checkers
DRAUPADI *husband* See
PANDU *sons.*
DRAUPNIR *owner* odin
DRAVIDIAN andhra, arava,
australoid, badaga, birthor,
brahui, collery, coorg,

gond(i), hindu, kanarese,
kannada, khond, kling, kodagu, kota, kurukh, ma-
layalam, male, malte, nair,
oraon, tamil(ic), telegu,
telugu, toda, tulu
aborigine dasyu
ghost bhut
language tamil
tribe badaga, colleri(es),
collery
DRAW 3 gap, get, lug, tee,
tie, tow, tug, win 4 drag,
duct, etch, gain, gate, hale,
haul, limn, lure, move,
pick, pull, rake, show, span,
till, tire, tole 5 bring, catch,
draft, drain, endue, evoke,
infer, paint, pluck, shirr,
skink, trace 6 abduce, allure, arroyo, broach,
bucket, choose, deduce, depict, design, devise, entice,
gulley, inhale, pucker, remove, select, siphon,
sketch, strike 7 acquire, attract, beguile, detract, extract, lottery, picture, portray, present, prolong, receive, scumble, turnout,
wrinkle 8 charisma,
compress, deadheat, de-
scribe, inveigle, outbraid,
standoff 9 delineate, formulate, frequence, influence,
magnetism, magnetize,
stalemate 10 attendance, attraction
a bead on aim, attack, direct, sight
a blank black out, fail, forget
again remat, replat
air breathe
along track, train
and quarter torture
apart diduce, divel, diverge,
ream, separate
away abduce, abduct,
arac(h)e, distract, divert,
draught, entrain, outdis-
tance, outspeed, pass up,
speed
awkwardly scrawl
back (See also DRAW-
BACK.) arrear, blench,
cringe, crinkle, deduct, defect, detract, discount, fade,
fawn, flinch, hindrance,
protest, rebate, recede, reclaim, recoil, retire, retract,
retreat, revel, revoke,
sheathe, shrink, start, torfel,

torfle, wince, withdraw,
withtee
bead aim
bolt slot
by suction aspirate
card cut
close approach, near
deep breath suspire
down earn, induce, receive
finely engrave, etch
forth deprome, derive,
educe, elicit, exhaust, fetch,
pull, tug
from bottle decant, drain,
extract
game stalemate
in compress, inhale, involve,
retract, retreat, retrieve,
taper, windlass, withdraw
inference conclude, interpret
in horns quit, recant, surrender, withdraw, yield
line challenge
lots gamble, venture
near approach, coast, hie,
impend
off abstract, bleed, decant,
distract, drain, extract, sap,
siphon, syphon, withdraw
on approach, cause, count
on, impend, induce, indue,
lean on, occasion, receive,
rely on, solicit, use
out attenuate, continue, cross
examine, educe, elicit,
exact, exantlate, exhale, extend, extract, interrogate,
lade, lengthen, loosen, milk,
produce, prolong, protract,
pump, shake(up), skink,
slub, tract, tweeze(r)
parallel compare, relate
plan block, outline, prepare
play fake, feint
rein control, halt, slow, stop
the line challenge, dare, discriminate, limit, select
the long bow boast, brag, exaggerate, lie
the teeth of disarm, paralyze
tight bind, brace, cinch, coul,
frap, furl, lace, pull, secure,
strain, stretch, thrap, tie
to a close end, stop
to a head climax, suppurate
together assemble, astringe,
coart, compress, coul, cowl,
frap, gather, lace
up array, assemble, form,
gather, halt, huckle, inknit,
make, outline, prepare,
tuck, uphale
DRAWBACK disadvantage,
discount, fault, flaw, hin-

drance, letdown, liability, obstacle, pullback, out, takeoff
concealed catch
DRAWBAR bullnose, coupler, sliprail
DRAWBRIDGE pontlevis
part bascule
DRAWER artist, bin, caricaturist, cartoonist, delineator, draftsman, draughtman, limner, locker, magnet, receptacle, shuttle, sketcher, till(er), tray
handle knob, pull
DRAWERS calsouns, calzooms, bloomers, panties, pants, shalwar, shintyan, shorts, shulwaurs
chest of SEE CHEST *of drawers.*
DRAWING attractive, attranent, black-and-white, brouillon, cartoon, charcoal, chiaroscuro, crayon, delineation, design, diagram, doodle, draft, draught, ebauche, elevation, etching, freehand, frottage, fusain, graph, illustration, isotype, pen-and-ink, picture, plan, rendering, rendition, sanguine, sketch, speculum, tousche, tracing, traction, tushe, work
absent-minded doodling
away abducent
back retrahent
card attraction, lure
charcoal fusain
comic cartoon, drollery
curve spline
exaggerated caricature, cartoon
instrument clinograph, eidograph, pantograph, perspectograph
line diagram
lots ballot
out battue
pencil crayon
pert. diagraphic
sidewalk screeve
technique silverpoint
with chalk calcography
DRAWING ROOM parlor, salon, saloon, society
DRAWKNIFE jigger, shave
DRAWL drag out, drant, drate, drunt, linger, loiter, prolate, tarry
DRAWLATCH clown, dawdle, eavesdropper, lag, thief
DRAWN draft, draught, etio-

lated, even, eviscerated, exhausted, graphic, haggard, hove, pale, pinched, starved, streit, teind, tense, thin, tied, tired
apart distract(ed)
close strict
off decanted, drained, siphoned, syphoned
out dree, dreich, dreigh, extended, lengthy, long, prolonged, protracted, stretched
DRAWPLATE agate, flatter, follower
DRAWSHEET tympan
DRAWSTRING latch
DRAY camion, carrier, cart, lorry, nest, sledge, sloop, vehicle, wagon
DRAYAGE freight(age), haulage, transportation
DREAD affright, agrise, alarm, angor, angst, anguish, anxiety, apprehension, awe, dismay, distress, doubt, dree, dridder, fear, fray, frunk, gastness, grise, horrible, horror, panic, terrible, terror, trembling, venerable, ward, were
morbid phobia
object of bog(e)y, bogie, bugaboo, bugbear
without confident
DREADFUL awesome, awful, bad, careful, dire, direful, dismal, doubtful, doubtous, dridder, fearful, fiction, formidable, frightful, ghastful, ghastly, great, grimful, grisly, hideous, horrible, horrific, perilous, scareful, scary, seriously, shocking, terrible, tremendous, uncouth, ungainly, very
DREADNOUGHT battleship, dareall, fearless, tank, warship
DREAM aisling, aspire, brown study, chim(a)era, contemplate, delusion, fancy, fantasy, hallucination, illusion, incubus, mete, moon, muse, music, nightmare, nirvana, phantasm, reve, revelation, reverie, romance, scheme, somniate, songe(r), suppose, sweven, topnotcher, trance, vagary, vision, wonder

comb. oneir
girl, author rice
god morpheus, on(e)iros, serapis
interpretation oneirocritics, oneirology
-land sleep, utopia
pert. intersomnial, oneiric, oneirotic, somnial
time alchera, alcheringa
up conceive, create, ideate, originate
DREAMER airmonger, alnaschar, don quixote, fantast, idealist, luftmensh, madman, meter, musard, phantast, poet, romanticist, visionary
immortal john bunyan
DREAMING traumerei
DREAMY dim, entranced, immaterial, inattentive, kef, languid, moony, musing, nodding, oblivious, oneiric, pensive, sleepy, soft, soothing, tranced, vague
DREAR dern, dismal, doleful, gloom(y), melancholy, sadness
DREARY alange, alone, banal, bleak, cheerless, dark, depressing, desolate, dingy, dire, dismal, doleful, dowie, dowy, dree, drury, dull, elenge, forlorn, gloomy, glum, gousty, grievous, insular, lifeless, lonely, melancholic, melancholy, miserable, monotonous, murky, ourie, sad, sinister, somber, sorry, tedious, tiresome, waste, weariful, wilsome, wintry
DRECK dregs, dud, flop, garbage, junk, refuse, trash
DREDGE bulldozer, deepen, dig, drag(ue), dreg, excavate, gangava, mop, raise, scallop, scrape, shovel, sift, sponge, sprinkle, train
DREDGER caster, digger, duster, hedgehog, shovel, steamshovel
DREGS bottoms, crap, dirt, draff, drest, dribble, dross, dunder, faex, grounds, grout, grummel, heeltap, jaups, lag(s), lees, magma, marc, mother, mud, outwale, refuse, remainder, remnants, residue, riffraff, salin, scum, sediment, settling, silt, slag, sludge,

sordes, sordor, squeezing, tailing(s), ullage, vinasse
of liquor taplash
of molten glass bribble
pulpy magma
DREISER *novel* american tragedy, sister carrie, the financier, the genius
DRENCH bathe, bedraggle, blash, bucket, deluge, dose, douse, dowse, draft, drink, droke, drouk, drown, embathe, hose, imbrue, infuse, permeate, potion, ret, saturate, sind, sink, slock, sluice, slush, soak, sog, sop, souse, steep, surfeit, swill, tosh, touse, waterlog, wet
DRENCHED asop, bursting, dewed, dewy, dripping, drunken, intoxicated, inundated, soaked, soused, splashed, wet
DRESDEN *palace* zwinger
DRESS 3 adz, dab, don, dub, dud, fig, fit, kit, nig, rag, ray, rig, tan, taw, tog **4** adze, bego, bind, burl, busk, buss, card, deck, dike, doll, garb, gear, gore, gown, hone, huke, jupe, knap, knot, lump, robe, suit, tack, tiff, tire, trim, wrap **5** array, digan, clean, curry, dight, dizen, drape, endue, equip, fancy, fix up, frock, getup, groom, guise, habit, ihram, jupon, prank, preen, prick, primp, prink, prune, shape, skirt **6** aguise, attire, barber, bedeck, bonnet, broach, buck up, bundle, clothe, doll up, enrobe, enwrap, fangle, fettle, finery, finish, fit out, fraise, invest, jelick, kirtle, muffle, outfit, shroud, smooth, swathe, toilet **7** apparel, bandage, bedizen, bedrape, burdash, clobber, clothes, costume, couture, dallack, garment, garnish, hatchel, prepare, raiment, regalia, sheathe, slick up, smarten, spiff up, swaddle, toggery, turn out, vesture **8** accouter, clothing, decorate, enclothe, enshroud, frippery, ornament, pretty up, spruce up, titivate, toilette, trick out, vestment **9** comparison, embellish, lubricate, wearables **10** habili-

ment **11** put on the dog **12** bib and tucker
animals butcher
best bib and tucker, finery, flash(ery), frippery, gaudery, glad rags, sunday best
bodice corsage, waist
business haberdashery, needle trade, tailoring
civilian mufti
clasp agraffe
clerical See VESTMENT *religious.*
coarse burel
coat simar(re), symar
court robe
down brace, chew out, excoriate, rebuke, reprimand, reprobate, reproove, scold, wallop
elegantly dike, dink
evening formal
fabric agaric, balzarine, barege, bombazet(te), bombazine, broadcloth, cotton, faille, marocain, paramatta, satin, silk, velvet, voile
feather preen
fish calver
flax dizen, ted
fling knap, nap
food garnish, nap, sauce
formal black tie, tails, tux(edo)
fussily priss(up)
gaudily bedizen, dizen, prank, prink
hair barber, coif, tire, truss
hides beam, tan
informal blue jeans, halter, jeans, negligee, shorts, slacks, smock, trunks
kind alb, chemise, decollete, dirndl, dolly varden, ephod, evening gown, farthingale, filibeg, formal, hoopskirt, huke, jumper, kilt, kirtle, lavalava, livery, mantua, mother hubbard, mufti, muumuu, negligee, pannier, peignoir, philabeg, pinafore, polonaise, regalia, sack, sarong, sheath, tailleur, tenue, tunic, weeds
leather curry, tan, tew
looped part pouf
loose mother hubbard, muumuu, sack, sacque, shift
manufacturer cloak and suiter
mean rags, tatters
meat lard, shroud
model mannequin, man(n)ikin

morning peignoir
mourning barb(e), dole
neatly dink
neck-cloth barb(e)
odd getup, rig
old duds
one-piece chemise, princess, sheath, shift
ore van
ornament bouillonne, braid, chequeen, embroidery, frog, gimp, jabot, lace, ruche, ruching, ruffle, sequin, zecchino, zequin
padding bustle
parade promenade, solitaire
part armhole, back, belt, binding, bodice, bust, bustle, button(hole), collar, cuffs, darts, facing, front, hem, innerlining, lining, neck, peplum, placket, ruffle, shoulder, skirt, sleeves, stay, waist, yoke, zipper
pert. habilatory, vestiary
presser sadiron
quickly huddle
rack frippery
riding breeches, habit, jodhpurs
shape a-line, bouffant, empire, sheath, shift, tent
sheepskin taw
showy full feather, full fig
skin wheel
smartly dallack
stand frippery
stone da(u)b, face, ga(u)ge, hack, nidge, nig, point, ray, scabble, scapple, spall
suit formal, tails, tux(edo)
surgically dight
tawdrily bedizen
untidily mab
up adorn, array, beclout, bedizen, busk, deck out, decorate, dill, falsify, fettle, ornament, prank, preen, prig, primp, prink, spick, tog(gle)
vulgarly daub
warmly bundle up
woman's fardel(s)
working denims
worn by man drag
wound bandage, panse, remedy, treat
DRESSED bandaged, bonnetted, breeched, capped, clad, clothed, coifed, combed, decent, decked, goffered, gussied up, habited, hatted, hooded, pantalooned, shod,

titivated, trimmed, trousered
in white candidate, nurse
loosely discinct
richly brocaded
roughly hewn
showily bepranked, sparkish
well braw, dallack, gash, smart, spruced up, stylish
DRESSER appreteur, bureau, cabinet, chest, chiffonier, cupboard, levanter, mallet, sideboard, table, tawer, vanity
leather currier, levanter
scrupulous beau brummel, dude, peacock, preener
DRESSING adhesive tape, application, bandage, band-aid, beating, blanket, bloter, brace, castigation, cataplasm, clothing, compost, compress, condiment, cotton, courtplaster, dossil, emplastrum, epithem, farce, fertilizer, fillet, fingerstall, forcement, gauze, gravy, lint, manure, mayonaise, mustard, ointment, plaster, pledget, poultice, rebuke, remedy, remolade, salve, sass, sauce, scolding, sinapism, sling, splint, sponge, starch, stuffing, stupe, tamp(i)on, thousand-island, tourniquet
gown bathrobe, housecoat, kimono, negligee, peignoir, wrapper
hair lacker, lacquer, pomade, spray
ingredient herbs, oil, vinegar
jacket camisole
room apothesis, camarin, vestry, vestuary
roomer johnnie
stone scotching, skiffling
table beau brummel, vanity
top mulch
DRESSMAKER courturier, modiste, sarta, seamer, seamstress, sewer, stitcher, tirewoman
term fitting, godet, gore, gusset, seam
DRESSY modish, sharp, smart, sporty, stylish
DREYFUS *defender* zola
trial site rennes
DRIBBLE bit, drift, drip, drivel, drizzle, drop, gush, leak(age), saliva, slaver, slobber, spittle, spout, trickle

DRIED adust, burnt, gizzen(ed), sear, sere, shriveled, wizened
out desiccated, stale
DRIFT aim, alluvion, bearing, carry, coast, course, creep, current, dene, deposit, deviation, diphead, direction, dribble, drove, dune, end, float, flock, flow, gly, goal, heap, herd, idle, impetus, impulse, intent(ion), mass, meaning, motion, outwash, pile, podger, progress, punch, purport, purpose, range, relax, roam, silt, slide, sloom, sloum, stray, tendency, tenor, tide, treat, trend, wander, wash, windage, windle
away recede
downward droop
glacial cary, iowan, till
off to sleep bye-low
plug bobbin, dummy
rubble head
sandy dene, esker, wreath
sidewise crab, crescent
snowy wreath
DRIFTER butterfly, casual, drover, floater, maunderer, nogoodnik, rolling stone, s(c)hnorrer, tramp, vagrant, wanderer
DRIFTWAY drove
DRIFTWOOD lumber, spars, wafture
DRILL auger, baboon, bar, bit, bore(r), boxbill, broach, chark, churn, core, decoy, denim, discipline, dreel, drip, enter, entice, excavate, exercise, fabric, furrow, gad, gimlet, grind, instruct, jankers, jar, jig, jumper, paddy, perforate, pierce, plant, practice, prepare, probe, rehearse, rid, school, seeder, sow, spud, stream, tap, teach, thirl, train, trickle, tutor, twirl
bit foerstner
center armo(u)ry
dentist's reamer
man stoper
DRINK (See also BEVERAGE.) 3 ade, ava, bib, bum, nip, nog, peg, pop, pot, sea, sip, sup, tea, tun, wet 4 belt, cola, dram, drop, fizz, flip, grog, gulp, homa, jolt, kava, lush, mate, milk, pony, pull, purl, shot, slug, soak, soda,

sope, sour, spot, suck, swig, tass, tiff, tope, whet 5 assai, bever, birle, booze, bouse, bumbo, cheer, cocoa, crush, draft, drain, facer, flogg, haoma, hocus, julep, lager, lap up, negus, ocean, panal, punch, quaff, setup, skink, sling, slurp, smash, smile, sniff, snort, souse, swill, toast, toddy, tonic, water, whiff 6 absorb, bezzle, bibble, bracer, bumper, calker, chaser, coffee, drench, fuddle, guzzle, imbibe, jigger, liquor, nectar, posset, potion, squash, tank up, tipple 7 beeftea, carouse, caulker, draught, refresh, seltzer, snifter, suppage, swallow, swizzle, tickler 8 aperitif, beverage, cocktail, highball, libation, nightcap, potation, quencher, toss down 9 bellywash, chocolate, eyeopener, fogchaser, phosphate 10 buttermilk 12 bend the elbow
addict See DRUNKARD.
after-dinner armagnac, brandy, cafe brulot, cappuchino, coffee, demitasse
alcoholic (See also *mixed,* below.) 3 ale, ava, bub, dew, gin, lap, nog, pot, rum, rye, tap 4 alky, arak, beer, beno, bino, bock, bosa, boza, bree, brew, chia, corn, flip, grog, lush, mead, nipa, nogg, owse, raki, ruin, sake, saki, soma, swig, tape, tiff, wine 5 airah, bever, bogus, bombo, booze, bouse, bowse, bozah, broth, budge, bumbo, cider, hooch, irish, juice, lager, negus, pombe, posca, punch, rakee, sauce, shrub, sling, snaps, snort, stock, stout, tonic, vodka 6 arrack, arrope, balche, brandy, casiri, caudle, cognac, diddle, eggnog, elixir, fogram, fogrum, fuddle, gimlet, kirsch, likker, liquor, mescal, poison, porter, posset, pulque, rickey, rotgut, scotch, spirit, stingo, strunt, tipple, whisky, zombie 7 akvavit, aquavit, bacardi, bitters, bootleg, bourbon, bragget, cobbler, cordial, courage, crawrot, guarapo, liqueur, potable,

shellac, sloe gin, snifter, spirits, spunkie, tequila, whiskey 8 aperitif, armagnac, blue ruin, bock beer, bugjuice, busthead, calvados, cocktail, demon rum, dubonnet, eye water, highball, hollands, homebrew, joy water, medicine, nearbeer, oil of joy, pilsener, popskull, potation, rice wine, rumbarge, sangaree, schnapps, snake oil, switchel, tequilla, toxicant 9 applejack, aquavitae, cutthroat, firewater, goldwater, inebriant, metheglin, moonshine, nosepoint, ratpoison, schnappes, shipbelly, tigermilk 10 ammunition, barleygree, crazy water, gulletwash, horse's neck, intoxicant, liquid fire, tanglefoot, tanglelegs 11 boilermaker, corn whiskey 12 dutch courage, formaldehyde, kirschwasser, whoopee-water 13 coffin varnish, sorrow drowner 14 embalming fluid, little brown jug 15 jersey lightning

ancient morat
and play beer and skittles
apple bunnell, cider
bedtime nightcap
beer after whiskey boilermaker
beer and buttermilk bonnyclabber
beer and gin dog's nose
beer and gingerale shandy(gaff)
beer and lemonade shandy
beer-like cassiri
bitters americano, angostura, campari, cardinale, fernetbranca, negroni, spritzer
brandy sangaree
brewed ale, beer, bock, lager, porter, stout
buttermilk and water bland
camel's milk k(o)umiss
carbonated cola, fizz, gingerale, pop, rootbeer, seltzer, soda
christmas nog(g), wassail
claret and soda badminton
comb. dipso
container charger, kettle, mixer, separator, shaker, vat
drugged hocus, mickey finn
egg and spirits copenhagen

extract kola
farinaceous ptisan
fermented balche, basi, birchbeer, bosa, boza(h), cassiri, guarapo, k(o)umiss, kumys, mead, mushla, ptisan
final nightcap, one for the road
foe carrie nation, dry, prohibitionist, wctu
fond of bibulous
free shout
fruit ade, assai, bland, julep, lemonade, morat, orangeade, ratafia, rickey, squash
gin fizz, martini, rickey, tom collins
gods' ambrosia, nectar
greedily guttle, guzzle, slop, swack, swill
gruel-like caudle
half-size chotapeg
hastily toss off
heady huffcap
heavily bezzle, bibble, booze, bouse, carouse, quaff, souse, swig, swill, swink, swizzle, toot, tope, waught, waycht
honey hydromel, mead, morat, oenomel
hot bishop, buttered rum, cardinal, caudle, cocoa, coffee, copus, egghot, negus, plotty, posset, rumfustion, salo(o)p, tea, tod(dy)
iced cooler
immortalizing ambrosia, amrita, haoma, rasa, sama, soma
insipid bland, slop, slumgullion, wash
intoxicating (See also *alcoholic*, above.) booze, drappie, grog, kumiss, pairvari, sauce, skokiaan, suck, swizzle
invalid rice-water
long collins, cooler, highball
magic nepenthe, potion
malted wheat zythem, zythum
midday meridian, nooning
milk kefir, kephir, malt, shake
milk, fermented airan
mixed (See also *alcoholic*, above.) alexander, americano, bacardi, bishop, bloody mary, bronx, buttered rum, chaser, cobbler, cocktail, collins, cooler,

cubalibre, daiquiri, daisy, eggnog, fizz, flip, frappe, gibson, gimlet, gin fizz, gin rickey, gin sling, grasshopper, grog, highball, hot toddy, irish coffee, julep, manhattan, margarita, martini, mint julep, moscow mule, negroni, negus, old-fashioned, pims cup, pink lady, piscosour, planter's punch, posset, punch, purl, rickey, robroy, royale, rusty nail, sangaree, sazerac, screwdriver, sidecar, sling, smash, sour, spritzer, stinger, swizzle, toddy, tom and jerry, tom collins, ward eight, wassail, whiskey sour, zombie
mixer barkeeper, barman, bartender, mixologist
molasses swanky, switchel
money bonamano, pourboire
morning antifogmatic, coffee, eyeopener
mulberry and honey morat
noisily slurp
non-alcoholic ade, cocoa, coffee, coke, cooler, gazoz, milk, moxie, squash, tea
off coup
palm nipa
parting bonailie, stirrup cup
pepper kava(kava)
pert. bibulous
pineapple pina
plant juice nipa, soma
poisonous drench
portion dollop, jigger, ounce, shot, two fingers
pulque tepache
quart of shanny
rum bombo, bumbo, cubalibre, daiquiri, grog, tom and jerry
sacred amrit(a), h(a)oma, soma
sacrificial h(a)oma
sassafras saloop
sea island ava
small bull, chaser, dallop, diluent, dram, hum, nip, noggin, peg, pony, shot, sip, sniff, snifter, snort, sopie, suck, tabor, tiff, tift, tot, wetting
soft ade, cider, coke, frappe, gingerale, lemonade, phosphate, pop, rootbeer, soda, squash
sour milk leban, leben, tayir, tyre
sparingly bleb, sip

stand celleret
stimulating bracer
sweet julep, orgeat, posset, stepony
tequila margarita
together birl, hobnob
to person bumper, toast
up carouse, crush, empty, epote, exhaust
vinegar and water posca
warm caudle
weak bool, bull, catlap, diluent, lap, slosh
wine bishop, cardinal, clary, cobbler, kir, negus, punch, sangria, sillabub
wine and fruit cobbler, cup, sangria
wine and soda spritzer

DRINKER barfly, belter, bender, bouser, carouser, cupman, drunkard, imbiber, inebriate, intaker, lapper, lush(er), poter, potter, pot walloper, quaffer, soaker, sot, sponge, tank, toper

DRINKING bever, bibulous, carousal, compotation, draft, guzzle, imbibing, poculation, potation, winebibbery
abstention on the (water) wagon
bout bacchanalia, beano, binge, blow, bouse, brawl, bum, bust, carousal, downsitting, drunk, fuffle, gaedown, godown, hit, orgy, party, potation, prosit, revel, shindig, shindy, skoal, soak, soiree, splore, spree, tear, wassail
cup See *vessel*, below
fear of dipsophobia
fountain bubbler
god bacchus, comus, dionysus, siris
horn rhyton
pert. bibitory, bibulous, potatory
place bar, bistro, cafe, cantina, cellar, cocktail lounge, dive, hangout, saloon, taproom
song brindisi
vessel acetabulum, aleyard, ama, ampulla, barrel, beaker, blackjack, bombard, bottle, bowl, bratina, bugle, can, cannikin, cappie, chalice, cruiske(e)m, cup, cylix, dipper, facer, flagon, flask, glass, goblet, gourd, hanap, holmos, horn, jolly-

boys, jorum, jubbe, jug, keg, kylix, magnum, mazer, mug, noggin, patera, pilsner, pony, pourie, psykter, quaich, quaigh, rhyton, rumkin, schooner, seidel, stamnos, stein, stemware, stoop, stoup, tankard, tanker, tass, teacup, toby, tumbler, tyg

DRIP bore, creep, dribble, drill, drop, eaves, jerk, label, larmier, leak(age), melamed, ooze, pink, rain, s(c)hlep(per), s(c)hloomp, s(c)hlump, seep, sege, shmegegge, sie, sile, sipe, sye, trickle, trinkle, trintle, weep
stone bat, ding, hoodmold, label

DRIVE 3 bum, vim 4 bear, blow, call, cram, ding, drub, drum, firk, goad, hack, herd, hunt, hurl, lane, lash, move, poss, push, ride, road, send, serr, slog, spur, task, tool, tour, urge 5 alley, argue, cause, chase, crowd, feeze, flail, force, guide, hurry, impel, motor, pilot, power, press, repel, roust, shove, skelp, steer, sweep 6 attack, avenue, bensel, buffet, charge, coerce, compel, course, cudgel, direct, ferret, hasten, hustle, incite, motive, oblige, obsess, propel, street, tee off, thrust 7 actuate, crusade, enforce, impulse, operate, overtax, parkway, roadway 8 arterial, beardown, campaign, catapult, excavate, shepherd, tendency 9 boulevard, constrain, incentive, obsession 10 accelerate, compulsion, enterprise 12 thoroughfare
animals haze, herd
at aim, hint, intend
away aroint, bandy, banish, chase, dispel, displace, enchase, exile, exorcise, expel, feeze, firk, fleme, reject, repel, repulse, rid, rout, scatter, shoe, smoke, sweep
away, comb. fuge
back culbut, defend, rebate, rebuff, rebut, refringe, repel, repulse, retund, rout, rush
briskly june

crazy bedevil, bug, enrage, frenzy, madden
down nail, tamp
dull care away cheer, play
fast barrel, bucket, bum, career, race, speed
hard hackney, sweat
home convince, prove
in cafe, cram, dint, enter, hammer, inject, market, nail, open-air, penetrate, pile, restaurant, tamp, theater
mad See *crazy*, above.
morbid obsession
off excoct, lift, peel into
out chase, depel, discharge, dislodge, dismiss, drum, eject, eradicate, evict, exile, exorcise, expel, exturb, fire, harry, ish, knock, propulse, rout, wreak
pin cam
recklessly cowboy
roughly chouse
slantingly toe
stakes build, camp, settle
violently hurtle, smash, thud

DRIVEL blather, doat, dote, dottage, dribble, drool, drudge, eyewash, footle, fritter, humbug, mad(ness), nonsense, saliva(te), slaver, slobber, sonk, twaddle, waste

DRIVELER dotard, gool, idiot, slobberer

DRIVER ant, autoist, bullocky, bullwhacker, cabbie, cabby, cabman, calesero, caller, cameleer, carman, carter, cartman, charioteer, chauffeur, coachman, coachy, cochero, cowboy, cruiser, drabi, dragsman, drayer, drayman, drover, engineer, galloway, gharrywallah, goadsman, hack (man), hacky, hammer, hayward, helmsman, hoodlum, hurrier, impulsor, jarvey, jehu, jittneur, jittneuse, jockey, leader, mahout, mallet, martinet, motorist, motorman, muleskinner, muleteer, mush(er), operator, overseer, phaeton, pilot, propeller, reinsman, sarwan, skinner, spanker, stagecoachman, stager, sumpter, teamster, trucker, tyrant, urger, vetturino, voiturier, wagoner, whip(ster)

fast barney oldfield, hot-rodder, jehu, speeder
of golden chariot helios
seat box, cab(in)
DRIVING appulse, coaching, compulsory, energetic, impellent, pelting, propulsive, scudding, slashing, urging
force capillarity
together drift
toward appulse
DRIZZLE dank, deg, dribble, drip, drish, drop, drow, fog, haze, ling, misle, mist, mizzle, mug, rain, scouther, skew, smur(r), sprinkle, stew
DROGUE anchor, drag, drug
DROICH See DWARF.
DROIT claim, law, right
DROLL amusing, buffoon, clown, comic(al), facetious, farcical, fool, funny, humorous, jester, jocose, ludicrous, merry, odd, punch, quaint, ridiculous, risible, waggish, zany
fellow card, clown, comedian
DROLLERY humor, farce, jest, whimsicality, wit
DROMEDARY camaile, camel(us), clown, deloul, delul, dromond, hageen, hagein, hygeen, mehari, oont
-like bactrian
DROMIA *master* antipholus
DRONE bagpipe, bee, bombilate, bombinate, boom, bum, bumbass, bumble, chorus, dor, dra(u)nt, droll, drum, hum(ming), idler, laggard, leech, loafer, parasite, pipe, shirker, sleeper, sloth, sluggard, snail, soldier
boss bourdon
DRONGO forktail, shrike
DROOL dribble, drivel, enthuse, exult, flat, nonsense, saliva(te), slabber, slaver, slobber
DROOP bangle, bend, bore, dangle, decline, despond, drop, drowk, fade, fail, faint, flack, flag, flitter, hang, heald, hield, lag, languish, lop, mourn, nod, nutate, pine, sag, sink, slouch, slump, swag, weaken, weakling, wilt, wither
DROOPING alop, bagging, baggy, cernuous, floppy, gotch(ed), hanging, lan-

guid, lank, lazy, limp, loose, lopeared, loppy, nodding, nutant, poppied, saggy, slouch, sopite, trailing, weak
on one side alop
DROOPY dreepy, gloomy, sagging, slimpsy
DROP 3 bit, can, dap, die, dip, lay, sie, spy, sye 4 atom, bead, bede, blob, blow, blub, boot, cast, dash, dive, drib, dump, fall, fell, fire, fold, glob, glub, gout, leak, lose, omit, plop, sack, sege, shed, sile, sink, slip, spot, tear 5 agent, break, cloth, drepe, drink, faint, fence, flump, gutta, hance, lapse, leave, lower, minim, pause, pinch, plunk, shoot, slide, slope, slump, sprue, swoon, swoop, weary 6 bounce, cancel, desert, disuse, extill, fumble, gobbet, goutte, morsel, plunge, scoria, splash, tackle, trifle, weaken 7 abandon, cashier, cheapen, contact, decline, depress, descend, descent, discard, dismiss, dribble, dwindle, earring, expunge, globule, guttula, guttule, letdown, modicum, pendant, plummet, spatter, trickle 8 decrease, trapdoor 9 declivity, discharge, eliminate 10 relinquish, 11 deteriorate
a line correspond, write
anchor moor, settle, slip, stop
bait chum, dab, did, lure
by drop guttatim, little by little
curtain greeny
dead get lost, stop
-dry impervious, seaworthy, secure
everything cease, stop
game fraud
gently dap
in arrive, call, enter, happen, instill, stop, surprise, visit
it cease, discard, relinquish, stop
lachrymal tear
-like guttate
off decline, decrease, doze, fall, nap, nod, sleep, slump
out cop out, flounce, leave, quit(ter)
serene amaurosis
-shaped guttiform

small blob, globule
sudden hance, nosedive, plop, thud
syllable elide, elision
theatrical curtain, scrim, tab
DROPLET globule
DROPPER bobber, butterfingers, pipette, sink(er)
DROPPING fall, flyings, scat, shard, skat, soil, spoor
away caducous, caduke, downhill, falling, sinking
sharply abrupt
DROPS dosage, leakage, medicine, rain
DROPSICAL distended, edemic, hydropic, puffy
DROPSY anasarca, ascites, distension, edema, hydrops, tumor
remedy broom-tails, senso
DROPWORT deadtongue, horsebane
DROSS chaff, cinder, dregs, drush, garble, kish, leavings, lees, offscum, refuse, remainder, scobs, scoria, scruff, scum, shruff, sinter, slag, sprue, sullage, trash, waste
DROSSEL drazel, hussy, slut
DROUGHT appetite, aridity, dearth, drouth, dryth, guar, insufficiency, need, soka, thirst
-resistant xerophilous
-fearing xerophobo
plant xerophyte
DROVE assemblage, atajo, bevy, boaster, chisel, crowd, disturb, drift(way), flock, gaggle, group, herd, manada, mob, multitude, pack, school, swarm, trouble
DROVER dealer, driver, herdsman, top(s)man, whacker
DROWN adrench, deaden, deafen, die, drench, extinguish, founder, immerse, inundate, kill, muffle, mute, overwhelm, sink, stifle, suffocate
care play
the shamrock drink
DROWNING demersion, noyade
tragedy chappaquiddick
DROWSE dover, doze, drone, drop off, nap, nod, sleep, slumber, snooze, sog
DROWSINESS dullness, languor, lethargy, oscitance,

sleepiness, sluggishness, torpor

DROWSY comatose, comatous, dormant, dozy, lethargic, logy, nodding, noddy, oscitant, poppied, sleepy, sluggish, somnolent, sopite, stupid, supine, swoony, torpid

become dow

DRUB arrass, bang, beat, belabor, blow, clop, clump, cudgel, curry, defeat, drum, flog, pound, shellac, stamp, stomp, thrash, thump, whale

DRUDGE behama, behayma, behayme, crewman, dig, digger, drivel, droil, droy, drug, endure, fag(ger), grind, grub(ber), hack (ney), hammer, jackal, labo(u)r, moil(er), peg, plod(der), plug(ger), pound, scrub, servant, slave(y), sludge, suffer, sweat(er), toil(er), travail, trachle, tug

literary devil, hack

DRUDGERY effort, exertion, fag(ger), grind, labor, moil, pains, slavery, slog, sweat, swink, toil, trachle, travail, turmoil, work

DRUG analgize, anodyne, aromatic, atropia, biological, cocaine, commidity, cure, daze, deaden, dope, dose, drab, dull, hallucinogen, hypnotic, laxative, medicate, medicine, narcotic, nepenthe, numb, opiate, philter, philtre, physic, relax, remedy, sedate, sedative, simple, sina, spece, specific, stupefy, toxicant, tranquilizer, truck

active principle aloin

addict See ADDICT.

addiction loxicomania

addictive 3 gow, lsd, pot, stp 4 acid, benj, dexy, dope, down, ghow, glue, hash, hops, junk, meth, reds, scag, snow 5 barbs, candy, crank, ether, lotus, nimby, opium, rizla, seccy, smack, speed, stuff, tooie 6 bennie, codeia, downer, goofer, heroin, peyote, reefer, suckie, whites, zigzag 7 bromide, cocaine, codeine, crystal, greenie, hashish, munchie, peanuts, pheenie,

quieter, rainbow, redbird, sominex 8 cannabis, goofball, laudanum, mandrake, morphine, red devil, sedative, sleepeze, snappers 9 dexadrine, marijuana, roach clip 10 benzedrine, blue heaven, hyoscyamus, methedrine, mickey finn, stramonium 11 amobarbitol, amphetamine, barbiturate, green dragon 12 bethesda gold, hallucinogen, TRANQUILIZER, yellow jacket 13 christmas tree, doubletrouble, pentobarbitol, phenobarbitol, sleeping pills

and ship shanghai

anti-heroin methadone

anti-malarial atabrine, quinacrine, quinine

anti-neuralgia tonga

apeptite control amphetamine

bitter aloe, quinine

comb. pharmaco

container capsule, gallipot

controversial dmso, gerovital, laetrile, saccharin

convulsion causing tetanic

crocus saffron

dealer (See also MARIJUANA *exporter*.) mule, pusher

depressant, anhalamine, hordenine, lophophorine, mescaline, pellotine

diuretic asa-dulcis

effect crash, kaif, ke(e)f, kick, kif, rush

forgetfulness nepenthe

habit monkey

hippocratic mecon

homeopathic similimum

hypnotic barbiturate, trional, veronal

injector hypo, needle

jar albarello

list formulary

manufacturer abkar

mood-changing amphetamine, downer, lsd, upper

narcotic heroin, morphine, opiate, opium

nux vomica tetanic

pain-killing aspirin, bufferin, darvon, morphine

psychedelic lsd, marijuana, mescaline, peyote, stp

purgative aloe, laxative

sleeping narcotic, sedative, somnifacient

social pot-party

stimulant amphetamine, an-

haline, cocaine, ephedrine, hordenine, mescaline, pellotine, speed

synthesizer aniline

take cop out, get high, pop pills, smoke pot

taking acid-rap, chemical vacation, hype, injection, lighting up, mainlining, popping, snorting, trip, turning on

tranquilizer equinil, meprobamate, miltown, valium

user joypopper, junkie, speeder, speedfreak

vegetable finger

withdrawal come down, crash

wonder acth, penicillin

DRUGGED acid-rapped, benumbed, blasted, coasting, dazed, freaked out, hyped, kef, keif, kief, kif(f), lit up, narcotized, poppied, pot-high, spaced out, stoned, turned on, wasted, zonked

DRUGGIST apothecary, chemist, gallipot, pharmacist, pharmacopologist

bible usp

implement pestle

pipette stactometer

DRUGSTORE apothecary, chemist's, dispensary, pharmacy

beetle anobid, biscuit-weevil, bookworm

DRUID prophet, saronide, seer(ess)

deity fan, mollac, taulac

leader brenhin, brenn

lodge cove

priestess norma

stone sarsen

symbol mistletoe

war chief brenn

DRUM (See also *kind*, below.) anacara, at(t)abal, bamboula, barrel, beat, boom, bowl, bubbler, bundle, calabash, cannister, carp, conga, croaker, cylinder, dive, drub, dub, hammer, hill, kettle, moulinet, palpitate, patter, pitterpatter, pound, pulsate, rap, rataplan, rat(a)tat, rattattoo, repeat, ridge, roar, rout, ruffle, swag, swash, tattoo, throb, thrum, thump, tympan(um)

bass tamburone

beat alarm, berloque, bre-

loque, dub, flam, rataplan, ruff(le), tattoo, tuck
call to arms rappel
cavalry anacara
codes bush telegraph
fire volley
flourish roulade
hand tabor, timbrel
heated drier, dryer
hollow tree gumbe, gumby
kettle atabal, naker, timpano
kind ala(l), barbukka, bass, bongo, caisse, conga, derbukka, gangsa, gong, gumbe, gumby, huehuetl, kettle, nagara, naker, othrum, snare, stumpan, tabo(u)r(et), tabret, tambour(et), tambourin, tambourine, tamtam, timbal, timbre(l), timpani, tombe, tomtom, toph, tymbal
large tamburone
-like barrel, naker, tabret
-major's hat shako
one-headed tambourine
out discharge, dismiss
player tambour(gi), tympanist
primitive bamboula
revolving gurdy, rattier
roll dian(a), paradiddle, reveille, roulade
small bongo, snare, taar, tabor, tabret, tambour(ine)
sound ratatat, rubadub
string snare
tighten cords frap
up muster
up business hustle
up interest ballyhoo, promote, push
DRUMFISH bubbler, croaker, crocus, drummer, drumsler, gaspergou, pogonia, sciaenid, thunderpump(er)
DRUMHEAD cabbage, eardrum, membrane
DRUMMER bagman, bookseller, cockroach, commisvoyageur, fish, hobo, runner, salesman, taborer, tambo, tambourgi, timpanist, tramp, traveler, traveling salesman, tympanist
DRUMSTICK baguet(te), knapweed, leg, sandpiper, tampon
-like plectridial
tree canafistulo, cassia
DRUNK (See also DRINKING *bout*, DRUNKARD.)

ardent, bacchic, bagged, blah, blasted, blind, blotto, boiled, bombed, boozy, bouse, bout, brawl, bungfu, buzzed, canned, cockeyed, crapulent, crapulous, fluffy, fuddled, full, gone, gooned, groggy, high, hungover, illuminated, inebriated, intoxicated, juiced, lit, loaded, looped, lushy, malty, maudlin, mellow, oiled, pickled, pie-eyed, plastered, polluted, potted, potto, queer, reeling, schnoggered, shicker, shipped, sloppy, smashed, soaked, sodden, sosh(ed), sotted, sottish, soused, sozzled, sprung, squiffed, squiffy, stewed, stiff, stinking, stinko, stoned, swacked, tiddly, tight, tipsy, wet, winy, zapped, zorched
DRUNKARD alcoholic, bacchanal, bacchant, barfly, bibber, bloat, boozer, borachio, carouser, dipsomaniac, fuddler, habitual, inebriate, lush, lusher, potshot, rumbum, rumhound, rummy, rumpot, shicker shikker, sot, souse, sponge, stewbum, stumblebum, swillbelly, swillpot, swilltub, tank, tippler, toper, tosspot, wino
patron saint vincent
street bowery
DRUNKEN (See also DRUNK.) drench(ed), drown, saturate(d), uneven, unsteady, vinolent, wabbly whipcat, woodsere
DRUNKENNESS alcoholism, barleyhood, blind staggers, inebriacy, inebriety, intemperance, intoxication, ivresse, potshot, tipsiness
bout of binge, bust, tear, toot
pert. bacchanalian
preventive dionise
DRUNT drawl, grumble, humor, pet
DRUPE almond, apricot, cherry, drupeole, fruit, peach, plum, pyrenocarp, tryma
stone nutlet, pit, putamen
DRUPELET acinus, grain, nutlet, tryma
DRY 3 sec, sun 4 acid, arid, bake, blot, bray, brut, burn,

dull, fire, hard, hask, kiln, sear, sere, sour, swab, tart, wctu, wipe 5 arify, beath, broke, brush, corky, drain, empty, harsh, hasky, hazle, husky, parch, plain, prosy, sandy, secco, smeet, sober, stale, towel, vapid, wizen 6 aerify, barken, barren, boring, ensear, essene, jejune, rizzar, sapped, scorch, shrewd, soak up, sponge, weazen, wither 7 aneroid, aridian, ascetic, birstle, brustle, crackle, cynical, deplete, drought, dwindle, exhaust, insipid, mummify, parched, prosaic, sapless, shrivel, siccate, skeller, sterile, thirsty, torrefy, xerotic 8 barbecue, insolate, preserve, teetotal, tiresome 9 abstainer, abstinent, acidulous, anhydrate, anhydrous, dehydrate, desiccate, evaporate, exsiccate, juiceless, sarcastic, thirsting, waterless 10 abstemious, antisaloon, dehydrated, desiccated, on the wagon, watertight 11 sarcastical, unmoistened 12 matter of fact, unproductive 14 prohibitionist
as a biscuit, bone, cracker, mummy
as dust boring, dull, pedantic
-bulb See THERMOMETER.
comb. xer(o)
goods drapery, fabrics, linens, napery, notions, textiles
goods dealer draper, mercer
-gulch ambush, betray
herrings deese
ice carbon dioxide
measure bushel, peck
out rizzar, siccate, toast
partly sammy
point engraving
rot blight, powderpost
-shave cheat, defraud
spell drought
-stone diker cowan
up abstain, arefact, dehumidify, dehydrate, desiccate, evaporate, exsiccate, forwelk, languish, mop, sere, shrink, silence, skeller, steam, welk, wither
wit attic salt
DRYAD deity, nymph, woodmaid, yaksha, yakshi

DRYAS *slayer* lycurgus
son lycurgus
DRYDEN asaph
work absalom and achitophel, alexander's feast, all for love, astraea redux, conquest of granada, mac flecknoe
DRYING siccant
agent calcium chloride
frame airer, sess
machine extractor, tedder
rack crib
DRYNESS aridity, desiccation, drought, drouth, haskness, siccity, torrefaction, xerosis, xerotes
abnormal xerosis, xerostom(i)a
DRYOPE *changed to* poplar
consort anius, apollo
father dryops
offspring amphissus, elais, oeno, spermo
DUAD couple, dual, dyad, pair, two
DUAL bifold, binal, binary, binate, double, dualist, duplicate, twin, twofold
DUALITY yin-yang
DUAMUTEF *father* horus
DUAT deep, hell, underworld
DUB adorn, analogue, array, beginner, blow, bungler, call, clothe, designate, dress, drumbeat, duplicate, entitle, knight, lubber, name, ornament, pike, puddle, rub, schlemeil, smooth, strike, style, substitute, tag, term, thrust, thump, title, trim
in substitute
DUBIETY, DUBIOUSNESS confusion, doubt, hesitation, mistrust, skepticism, suspicion, uncertainty, vacillation, wavering
DUBIOUS ambiguous, confutable, contestable, controversial, controvertible, debatable, deniable, diffident, disputable, doubtable, doubtful, doubty, dubitable, dubitative, equivocal, farfetched, fishy, hesitant, iffy, indefinite, juberous, moot, obscure, problematic(al), questionable, refutable, reluctant, seamy, shady, skeptic(al), suspect, suspicious, uncertain, undecided, unsafe, unsure, vague

DUBLIN baile atha cliath
jail kilmainham
organization gaelic league
university silent sister
DUBRIC *crowned* king arthur
DUBROVNIK ragusa
DUCE chief, head, leader
DUCHY ducatus, dukedom
DUCK (See also *kind*, below.) aex, anas, anatid, avoid, baptize, bird, bob, bow, canard, canvas, chap, cloth, cringe, darling, dilly, dip, dive, dodge, douse, dowse, drake, dunk, eider, evade, fabric, fellow, fowl, gadwall, gannet, hen, immerse, lord, lurch, man, mandarin, merganser, merse, mig, oddity, pato, pet, plunge, retreat, scruple, seaplane, shirk, smee, smew, sound, souse, stoop, submerge, truck, vehicle, wamp, webfoot
ant termite
black dusky, ringnecked, scoter, tufted
black-headed naloonga
bluebill scaup
brood team
cooking caneton
dead goner
decoy squawker
disease keel
diving canvasback, nyroca, redhead, scaup, smew
down eider
egg balut, nothing, pidan, zero
eggs, preserved pidan
eider colk, somateria, wamp
extinct labrador
flight skein
flightless nesonetta
flock See *group*, below.
footless cannet, merlette
freshwater aix, anas, mandarin, teal, widgeon
genus aex, aix, anas, anseres, aythya, clangula, glaucionetta, nesonetta, nettion, nyroca, somateria
golden-eye gowdnie, greathead
gray gadwall, mallard, pintail
green bluegrass
group skein, sord, team
harlequin canne-de-roche
hawk falcon
heraldic cannet(te)

hooked bill merganser, weaser
kind aylesbury, barwing, blackjack, blacky, bluebill, bufflehead, bumalo, butterball, cannet, cracker, dabbler, eider, garbill, garganey, geelbec, greaser, indian runner, mallard, marionette, merganser, moonbill, morillon, muscovy, nettion, oldwife, pato, peking, piketail, pintail, redhead, redshank, rouen, scaup, sco(o)ter, sheldrake, shovel(l)er, smee, smethe, smew, sprigtail, squealer, swaddlebill, teal, teuk, waddler, weaser, widgeon, wiretail, yaguaza
large muscovy, pato
-like anatine, coot, decoy
lure decoy
male drake
muscovy pato
old squaw clangula, quandy
old world pochard, cheldrake
-on-the-rock player tenter
out escape, flee, vanish
pert. anatine
-petter hellebore
pintail cracker, piketail, querquedule, smee, smethe, smew, spike, widgeon
ring-necked bunty, woonbill
river anatine, dogy, eider, greenwing, pike, pintail, shoveler, smee, teal
ruddy blackjack, bobber, rook, sticktail
sawbill smee, smew
scaup blackjack, blackneck, bluebill, dosgris, ruddy, widgeon
sea coot, eider, harlequin, scaup, sco(o)ter
sitting decoy
small smee, smew
snipe willet
soup cinch, easy thing, set-up
squaw mommy
stuffed dumpoke
swollen-billed sco(o)ter
symbol of deceit
teal nettion
tree yaguaza
wild canvasback, gadwall, geelbeck, mallard, scaup, teal
wood branchier, canard, decoy
yellow-billed geelbec(k)

young caneton, flapper, flopper, weasel-coot

DUCKBILL mallangong, platypus, tambreet

DUCKER diver, gun, ouzel

DUCKS See PANTS.

DUCKWEED digmeat, frogfoot, glit, grain, lemnad, lentil, spirodela

DUCT alveus, aorta, canal, channel, conduit, downtake, efferent, emunctory, flue, intestine, lactile, lemna, lymphatic, meatus, ostium, passage(way), pipe, pore, race, trachea, tube, vas, vessel

comb. tubi

DUCTILE adaptable, amenaable, elastic, flexible, fluid, liquid, malleable, plastic, pliable, pliant, resilient, responsive, tensile, tractable

DUD abortion, dreck, dress, failure, flop, garment, lemon, nonentity, stumor

DUDE beau, buck, coxcomb, dudine, easterner, exquisite, fop, jackeen, johnnie, marcaroni, nob, spark, swell, toff, traveler

DUDELSACK bagpipe

DUDEVANT *pseud.* george sand

DUDGEON anger, ferment, fume, fury, huff, indignation, ire, malice, miff, offense, pet, pique, pucker, rage, resentment, sniff, stew, temper, tiff, tizzy, umbrage, wrath

DUDS appurtenances, clothes, clothing, wardrobe

DUE appropriate, becoming, charge, claim, comeuppance, coming, condign, custom, debt, desert, duty, equitable, expected, expedient, extent, fair, fee, fit(ting), hak(h), in arrears, interest, just, lawful, mature, meed, meet, merit, obligation, outstanding, owed, owing, payable, payment, prerogative, privilege, proper, redeemable regular, reprisal, reward, right(ful), satisfaction, scheduled, sufficient, suitable, tallage, title, unpaid, unsettled, warranted

to attributable, because, resulting from, worthy of

DUEL affair, affaire d'honneur, affair of honor, bout, combat, conflict, contest, fencing, fight, holmgang, interview, match, meeting, monomachia, monomachy, satisfaction, sparring, swordplay, tilt

DUELIST fencer, fighter, spadassin, swashbuckler, swordsman

aide second

DUENNA chaperon, dragon, escort, instructress

DUES assessment, custom, liability, obligation, tax

DUET dui, duo, pair, two (some)

ballet adagio

lower part secondo

upper part primo

DUFF alter, bottom, bum, cheat, coal, derriere, dough, fake, floor, humus, mishit, paste, pudding, rear, seat, slack, tochis, tot, tuchis

DUFFER blunderbuss, bungler, cobbler, dabaster, dolt, fake, lubber, muff, oddity, oldster, peddler, sham, shicer

DUG breast

-dug breadfruit

DUGONG cowfish, halicore, manatee, seacow, sirenian, yungan

DUGOUT abri, banca, banting, baroto, blindage, boat, bongo, bungo, bunker, bury, canoe, cave, cayuca, cayuco, dongo, entrenchment, foxhole, hut, lipalipa, pirogue, refuge, shed, shelter

canoe wood anacardium, caracoli

DUIKER antelope, cormorant, ipiti

DUKAS *opera* ariane and bluebeard

DUKE cherry, chief, commander, doge, duck, heretoga, herzog, knez, leader, lord, orsino, peer, prince, prospero, ruler, steenie

football team blue devils

frederick, brother duke senior

frederick, courtier le beau

frederick, wrestler charles

iron wellington

realm ducatus, duchy, dukedom

senior, brother duke frederick

senior, lord amiens, jaques

DULCET agreeable, ariose, charming, delightful, harmonious, honeyed, melodious, soft, soothing, sweet, syrupy, tuneful

DULCIFY appease, calm, mollify, soften, sweeten

DULCIMER canun, cembalo, citole, cymbalorn, pantal(e)on, psaltery, santir, santour, sitar, sitol, zimbaloa

5-stringed kantele

oriental canun, santir

DULCINEA beloved, mistress, sweetheart

DULCOLAX biscodyl

DULE See DEVIL.

DULL 3 dim, dow, dry, dun, mat, sad 4 arid, bald, blah, cold, cool, dark, dead, dowf, drab, drug, dumb, flat, logy, mull, poky, slow, tame, thin, weak 5 bland, blank, blate, blind, blunt, campy, crass, dense, dowie, drear, dubby, dusty, gross, heavy, inert, leady, lourd, matte, muddy, murky, muzzy, pokey, prosy, stale, stogy, terne, thick, trite, vapid 6 barren, benumb, bleary, boring, bovine, dampen, deaden, dreary, driech, frigid, gloomy, hebete, jejune, leaden, muffle, obtund, obtuse, oxlike, retund, simple, stodgy, stolid, stuffy, stupid, torpid, vacant, weaken, wooden 7 callous, disedge, doltish, dowfart, humdrum, insipid, languid, palling, passive, patient, prosaic, relieve, subfusc, tedious, vacuous 8 backward, boeotian, boresome, bromidic, comatose, discolor, hebetate, lifeless, listless, moderate, plodding, retarded, slottery, sluggish, tiresome, unlively 9 apathetic, colorless, impassive, lethargic, pointless, ponderous, stuporous, tasteless, unfeeling 10 anesthetic, drearisome, insensible, lackluster, monotonous, pedestrian, philistine, phlegmatic, spiritless, subfuscous, unexciting 11 elephantine, emotionless, indifferent, uncon-

cerned, unemotional 12 uninterested 13 characterless, platitudinous, unintelligent, uninteresting
as dishwater boring
become hebetate, pall, rust
comb. ambly
of mind barren, blear-witted, dopey, dopy, muzzy
scent foil
witted doltish, dumb, feebleminded
DULLARD dastard, dodunk, doldrum, dolt, dulbert, dullhead, dunce, moron, pothead, stupid
DULLED bleared, cloudy, empty, grayed, heavy, jaded, stupid
DULLING abatement, modification, relief, weakening
DULLNESS anesthesia, apathy, coldness, drab, haze, lackluster, languor, mat, obscurity, opacity, oscitancy, phlegm, slowness, stagnation, stupidity, tarnish, weakness
DULSE dillesk, seaweed
DULY appropriately, fitly, fittingly, orderly, properly, regularly, sufficiently, timely
DUM doom palm, gingerbread tree
DUMAH *kin* ishmael
DUMAS *character* aramis, athos, camille, d'artagnan, marguerite gautier, porthos
favorite wine chassagnemontrachet, puligny-montrachet
work camille, the count of monte-cristo, les trois mousquetaires, the three musketeers
DU MAURIER *novel* peter ibbetson, trilby
DUMB apohnic, crass, dense, doltish, dull(witted), foolish, ignorant, inarticulate, mousy, mum, mute, silent, speechless, ston(e)y, stupid, taciturn, tonguetied, voiceless
ox thomas aquinas
-waiter dummy, elevator, hoist, lift
DUMBBELL dimwit, dolt, dullard, dummy, dunce, FOOL, halter, knothead, screwball, stupid, weight
DUMBFOUND amaze, aston-

ish, astound, bewilder, confound, confuse, daze, distract, embarrass, mystify, nonplus, perplex, puzzle, silence, stun, surprise, upset
DUM(B)FOUNDED blank, stupent
DUMBNESS aphonia, aphrasia, aphthongia
DUMDUM bullet
fever kalaazar
DUMMY charlie, clam, copy, counterfeit, decoy, deputy, dumbbell, effigy, fake, figure(head), fool, imitation, maniken, mannequin, mute, numbskull, pell, pendejo, phantom, ringer, sham, silent, sphinx, spurious, stand-in, substitute
whist mort
DUMP arsenal, beat, boghole, candy, clear out, counter, dance, discard, dive, drop, empty, expel, fall, glory-hole, grieve, hut, jail, joint, junkyard, leave, market, muse, plump, plunge, reverie, rubbish heap, sadness, sell, slum, storehouse, thud, tip, tipple, toom, trash pile, tune, unload, wasteyard
edge toe
DUMPCART tumbrel, tumbril
DUMPING *ground* toom
DUMPLING apple grunt, apple slump, cob, doughboy, gnoccho, knaidel, knish, knodel, kreplach, kreplech, pudding, quenelle, sinker
filled piroshki
steamed moomoo
DUMPS blues, dejection, depression, despair, doldrums, gloom, melancholia, melancholy, mopes, sadness, vapors
DUMPY bunting, chunky, gross, plump, pudgy, rounded, squat(ty), stocky, stubby, sullen, thick(set)
DUMUZI *consort* inanna
DUN ask, bill, bother, brown, crave, cure, dark, din, ding(y), dull, ecru, favel, fort, gloomy, gray, grey, horse, importune, jade, khaki, kick, lackluster, mayfly, nag, pester, plague, press, resound, solicit, swarthy, tan, urge

-diver merganser, ruddy duck
DUNBAR council, court, hall
DUNCAN *general* banquo, macbeth
kingdom scotland
slayer macbeth
son donalbain, malcolm
DUNCE ass, blockhead, blockpate, bobby, boob(y), coot, dimwit, dobby, dolt, dope, dullard, dultie, DUMBBELL, dummy, dunderhead, fool, gaby, golem, gony, goon, halfwit, hobbil, idiot, ignoramus, imbecile, lamebrain, lout, meathead, moron, neddy, nincompoop, ninny, nitwit, numskull, oaf, pontic, proxy, simpleton, stunpoll, tomnoddy
famous codrus, flecknoe, margites
DUNDER blow, dregs, lees
DUNDERHEAD See DUNCE.
DUNE bank, bar, barchan, barkan, barrow, dene, down, drab, embankment, hill, knoll, meal, mesa, mound, ridge, saif, seif, terrace, towan, tumulus, twine
DUNEDIN edinburgh
DUNG argal, argol, billet, buttons, cack, casson, droppings, excrement, exhausted, fiants, filth, fumet, gore, lesses, manure, merd, muck, ordure, poppycock, scarn, scummer, sharn, soil, stallage, tath, treddle, trotters, upla
-befouled sharny
-bird hoopoe, jaeger
-eating scatophagous
pert. stercoraceous
DUNGEON bastille, black hole, cachot, cave(rn), crypt, donjon, ergastulum, hell, hole, keep, massymore, oubliette, pistol, pit, prison, revolver, vault
DUNGHILL colluvies, manure pile, midden, mixen, mixhill, muckmidden, stercorary
DUNGON sunclari
DUNK dip, duck, immerse, moisten, saturate, soak, sop, souse, steep, submerge
DUNKER brethren, dipper, dumpler, dunkard, pochard, taufer, tumbler, tunker
DUNLIN bird, leadback, ox-

bird, oxeye, pelidna, plover, purre, redback, sandpiper, stib, stint

DUNSTABLE direct, hat, plain

DUNSTAN, ST *symbol* pincers

DUNT beat, benumb, bruise, dizzy, heartthrob, knock, split, strike, stump, stupefy, stupid, thump

DUO brace, couple, duet, dyad, pair, two

DUODECIMO diminutive, miniature

DUOMO cathedral, dome, temple

DUPE agent, ape, april fool, baffle, bamboozle, befool, beguile, betray, bilk, boob(y), bubble, butt, catspaw, cheat, chicane, chouse, chump, cinch, clay pigeon, come-on, con(e)y, copy, cozen, cull(y), deceive, defraud, delude, dotterel, doublecross, duplicate, dust, fair game, fish, flat, fool, fox, fraud, geck, goat, gobemouche, greenhorn, greeny, gudgeon, gull, heald, hoax, hocus, hoodwink, instrument, jay, mark, mislead, mock, monkey, mug, outwit, pawn, pigeon, plaything, pushover, put, repeat, rook, sap, saphead, sucker, swindle, tool, toy, trick, use, victim

DUPIN, ARMANDINE *pseud.* george sand

DUPLESSIS richelieu

DUPLEX apartment, double, duplicate, dwelling, twofold

DUPLICATE analogue, bifold, biform, bilateral, biparous, bis, bridge, carbon, copy, counterpart, disamatous, ditto, double, doubling, dual, dub, dupe, duplex, estreat, facsimile, flimsy, gemination, imitate, imitation, ingeminate, likeness, manifold, obverse, parallel, redo, repeat, repetition, replica(te), reproduction, second(ary), tally, transcript, twice, twin, twofaced, twofold, twoply

DUPLICITY ambidexterity, ambiguity, art(ifice), chicane(ry), cunning, deceit, deception, dishonesty, dissimulation, doubledealing,

duality, duplexity, faithlessness, falseheartedness, falsehood, fraud, guile, machiavellianism, perfidy, subterfuge, treachery, trickery, twofacedness *having* ambidextrous

DURABILITY abidingness, constancy, continuance, durance, duration, endurance, fiber, fibre, longevity, longstanding, maintenance, permanence, persistence, protraction, stamina, standing, steadfastness, steel, substantiality, survival, wear

DURABLE abiding, consistent, constant, continuing, enduring, firm, lasting, lasty, livelong, permanent, perpetual, persistent, solid, stable, stout, strong, sturdy, tenacious, tough

DURAIN *constituent* attritus

DURAMEN heartwood

DURANCE custody, duress, imprisonment, jail

DURANDEL *sword of* roland

DURANGO cartouch, oakwood

DURANTE *friend* mrs calabash

DURATION age, continuance, date, extent, infinite, length, life(time), period, space, span, stretch, term, time, trice, when *endless* eternity, infinite

DURBERVILLE *lass* tess

DURESS affliction, captivity, coercion, compulsion, constraint, cruelty, durance, force, hardness, harshness, imprisonment, pressure, restraint, stress, violence

DURGA chamunda *husband* siva

DURGAN See DWARF.

DURGON triggerfish

DURING amid(st), among(st), at a stretch, durante, for the period of, in the time of, intra, over, pending, through(out), until, while *the interval* meanwhile *the time* all along, while

DURO peso

DURRA cholum, dari, duri, grain, joar, jondla, jowar, juar, millet, sorghum

DURUM grain, major, triticum, wheat

DURVASAS *cursed* vishnu

DURWAUN See PORTER.

DUSACK See SWORD.

DUSE, DUSIO folletto, incubus, spirit

DUSK candlelight, cocklight, crepuscule, crepusculum, dark(ening), dim, dimmet, dimness, dimpsy, even(ing), gloam(ing), glooming, nightfall, owllight, twilight

DUSKY black(ish), brown, cloudy, crepuscular, dark (ish), darkling, dim, dingy, dull, fusc, gloomy, grimy, melancholy, murky, obscure, opaque, phaeochrous, sad, shadowy, slaty, subfusc, subfusk, swart(hy), tawn(e)y, umbra *shark* carcharias

DUST antelope, ash, beflour, briss, clean, coom(b), coombe, corpse, depart, dirt, disturbance, dupe, earth, eburine, filler, flee, flour, grime, grit, ground, humiliation, levigate, lint, money, particle, pilm, pollen, pouce, powder, remains, row, rubbish, sand, slickens, smeddum, smeech, smut, soil, soot, sprinkle, stive, stour, strew, trash, uproar *bin* ashcan, trashcan *blood* hemoconia *cloud* stew *coal* coom(b), culm *cosmic* stardust *devil* bhoot, bhut, demon *diamond* seasoning *flax* pouce, pouse *gauge* konimeter, koniscope *hole* dump *jacket* cover, wrapper *-like* powdery *-off* helicopter *reduce to* grind, mull, pulverize *roll* fuzzguzzy, kitten *ruffle* balayense, skirt *speck* mote *storm* black blizzard, devil, hab(b)ub, habo(o)b, harmattan, khamsin, peesash, samiel, santa ana, santana, shaitan, simoom, simoon, sirocco *study of* koniology *up* ado, argument, brawl, dirty, melee, setto

DUSTER coat, devil, helicopter, willow, zephyr

DUSTMAN janitor, sweep(er)

DUSTY barren, dirty, dull, filthy, mottle, motty, poucey, powdery, pulverant, sordid, state, stoury
miller artemisia, wormwood

DUTCH See HOLLAND for all geographical references.
brass See *metal*, below.
cheese mallow
east indies See EAST INDIES; INDONESIA.
guiana See SURINAM.
metal arsedine, tombac
pink stil-de-grain, yellow madder, yellowweed
sauce hollandaise
tile azulejo
uncle critic

DUTCHMAN, DUTCHMAN'S batavian, b(e)-landa, butterbox, hans, hogen(mogen), mynheer (closh), sooterkin
breeches bikukulla, bleedingheart, boys-and-girls, butterfly-banners, dicentra, flyflower
flying vanderdecken
pipe big sarsaparilla

DUTIFUL compliant, courteous, debtful, devout, docile, filial, lawful, obedient, respectful, reverent, submissive

DUTY affair, assignment, bailage, blanch, boomage, burden, business, call, ceremony, cess, chare, charge, chore, cocket, concern, customs, dever, devoir, dharma, ermin, excise, exitus, feu, fossage, function, furding, fyrd, heriot, impost, indulto, ingate, job, lastage, levy, liability, lot, malikana, maltolte, must, obligation, office, onus, ought, place, pontage, prest, rate, reddendo, respect, responsibility, rivage, royalty, scavage, service, tariff, task, tax, tie, tithe, toll, tonnage, tribute, trust, wike(h), work
export exitus
feudal heriot
import ermin, indulto
impose assign, bind, enjoin,

exact, look to, oblige, prescribe, require, saddle with
on commodities excise
perform serve
shirking performance of feasance, truancy
spell of hitch, shift, trick, turn, watch
tiring fatigue
tour hitch, term, trick
unfinished arrear

DUVALIER papa doc

DUX chief, heretoga, leader, subject, theme

DWARF 3 elf, fay, nix, pug, urf 4 aeta, baby, bali, crut, grig, pixy, puck, runt, shee, tiny, wart 5 atomy, brokk, crile, crowl, devil, elfin, fairy, galar, gnome, knurl, midge, pygmy, runty, scrub, small, stunt, troll, wally, wight 6 ablach, abongo, alviss, bantam, conjon, droich, durgan, goblin, little, midget, minify, nanoid, peewee, petite, reginn, shrimp, sindri, spirit, sprite 7 andvari, banshee, blastie, brownie, congeon, decline, duergar, ivaldir, manikin, micrify, negrito, overtop, pacolet, scraggy, scrubby, stunted, wratack 8 alberich, belittle, decrease, huckmuck, knurling, mannikin, menehune, nanander, negrillo, nibelung, tom thumb 9 jack sprat, miniature, pigwiggen, undersize 10 dapperline, homunculus, leprechaun, micromorph, smallscale 11 hopomythumb, lilliputian, sesquipedal 15 rumpelstiltskin
animal runt
archaic dandiprat
avatar vaman(avatara)
comb. nano
dandelion krigia
fabled pigmy, pygmy
famous andromeda, aristratos, conopas, primo magri, wormberg, zarate
fan palm erythea, sabal
fish-shaped andvare
king alberich
male nannander
mallow cheese, pellas
pert. See DWARFISH.
race nibelung
raspberry plumbog
seven bashful, doc, dopey,

grumpy, happy, sleepy, sneezy
tribe abongo, babongo, obongo

DWARFING brachysm

DWARFISH diminutive, elfin, knurly, nanoid, pigmy, pygmy, runtish, small, stunted, stunty

DWARFISM ateliosis, nanism

DWELL abide, bide, bield, big(g), bower, brood, build, converse, cot, delay, dig, endure, habitance, haft, harp, house, inhabit, live, lodge, muse, pause, remain, reside, shack, sit, sojourn, staff, stay, stop, teld, tenant, wine, wont
in bedwell, big(g), inhabit, occupy, reside in
irritatingly grate
on bore, brood, emphasize, harp, gloat, muse, protract, repeat

DWELLER denizen, downsman, (in)habitant, occupant, paleman, resident, tenant, wonner
fellow inmate
formicary nat
temporary boarder, lodger, roomer, transient, visitor

DWELLING abode, address, apartment, building, bungalow, cabin, casa, castle, cave, chalet, commorancy, cottage, dar, domicile, domus, dorm(itory), dugout, duplex, farm, flat, fort, habitation, haft, hall, haunt, home, hotel, house, hovel, howf(f), hut, inn, joint, lodging, maloca, manse, mansion, messuage, motel, nest, quarter, residence, roof, see, shanty, slum, teepee, tenement, trailer, triplex, villa, weem, wigwam, won(ing)
attractive bower
crowded tenement
crude humpy, hut, shebang, shed
in groves nemoricole
mean burrow, shanty, slum
neolithic terramara
1-room cell, cubicle
rude bothie, bothy
subterranean weem
temporary lodgings, pied-a-tierre
2-room but-and-ben

DWINDLE abate, consume, contract, decay, decline, decrease, degenerate, diminish, drain, dry, ebb, fade, fail, flag, fordwine, fritter, lessen, melt, mo(u)lder, peter, pine, recede, reduce, shrink, taper, thin, trail, wane, waste

DWINDLING awaste, down, flagging, shrinking

DYAD bivalent, couple, duo, pair, two

DYAK bornean, iban
knife or sword parang

DYBBUK demon, gilgul

DYE (See also *kind*, below.) amaranth, anil, archil, embue, engrain, fucus, fugitive, imbue, indigoid, infect, intinct, lacmoid, lit, logwood, lokao, madder, pigment, stain, tinct(ure), tinger, tint, venom, zambesi
acid alizarin
artificial auramine
azo chrome-yellow
base analine
black guako, nigrosine
blue anil, caruto, cyanine, dicyanine, room, rum, wad, woad
blue-red orchal, orselle, solferino
brown cachou, ifil, sumac
coal-tar azarin, eosin(e), magenta
component alizarin, aniline, azo, diazine, diazo, sal-volatile
cosmetic henna, red
cotton indanthrene
crimson See *red*, below.
delicate tinge, tint
early alizarin(e)
extract catechu
fixative backtan
flavin quercitron
foam flurry
food tartrazine
gum kino
hair henna, rastik
herb woad
indigo a(a)l
kind a(a)l, ango, anil(ine), an(n)atta, an(n)atto, anthracene, archil, aurantia, aurin, azo, chromotrope, crocein, cyanine, dianil, eosin(e), fast, flavin, fuchsin, garance, garanceux, ifil, induline, ipil, isomin, kino, lit, madder, metanil, mordant, naphthol, orchal, orchil, or-

selle, pinachrome, pinaverdol, rum, safranine, stain, stilbene, synthetic, tincture, ting(e), twinsole, weld, woald, wold, ypil
lichen archil, litmus, orchal, orchil
mixer colorman
mordant alizarin
morindin a(a)l
non-fast fugitive
orange crocein(e), kamala
plant alhenna, alkanet, anil, annatto, chay, henna, kamala, madder, orselle, sumac, woad
poisonous aurine, metanil
purple cassius, gallein, murex, turnsole
purple-red punicin
quercitron flavin
red aal, alizarin, alkanet, alkannin, an(n)atto, aurin(e), bordeaux, brazilein, cerise, chay, corallin, crimson, crocein(e), eosin(e), fuchsine, grain, henna, kermes, magenta, morindin, orseilline, ponceau, relbun, rhodamine, rosaniline, rubin(e), safflor, tuly
red-brown henna
red-orange archil, chica, fuchsin, morindin
root pigment madder
silk luteolin
solvent morpholine
soot kohl
source amil, dodder, resorcin(ol), stilbene, tormentil
synthetic curin(e), primula
term pina
tester fadeometer
tree logwood
violet archil(la), cudbear, lacmoid, mauve, orchil
yellow arusa, auramine, chrysin, efisetin, flavin(e), fustic, lawsone, metanil, nankin(g), primuline, quercitron, rhamnetin, romerillo, tartrazine, weld, woald, wongshy
yellow-red anato, annatto
yellow, source amil

DYED ingrain
-in-the-wool black, confirmed, established, thorough
permanently fast

DYEING tinction

DYER, DYER'S dyester,

fielder, lister, skeiner, taintor, tinger, tinter, tintist
apparatus ager, vat
broom woodwax(en)
chamber oast, oven
cleavers beadstraw, madder
furze woodwax(en)
grape pokeweed
moss archil
mulberry fustic
term harass
weed ash of jerusalem, goldenrod, solidago, woad

DYESTUFF alizarin, alkanet, an(n)atto, carajura, chica, cudbear, isatin, litmus, lokao, madder, orcein, orpiment, relbun, saffron, weld, woad, would

DYEWEED greenweed, weld, whin, woadwax(en), woald, woodwax, would

DYEWOOD alder, barwood, brazil, caliatour, camwood, fustet, fustic, hypernic, ipil, sap(p)an, tua, tu(w)i

DYING death, done for, fey, going, last, morendo, moribund, mortal, parting
away calando, diluendo, mancando, perdendo, smorzato
without a will intestate

DYKE dam, dike, haha, lesbian, opening, wall

DYLAN *parent* arianhod, gwydion

DYMAS *companion* aeneas
foe greeks

DYNADAN *lampooned* king arthur

DYNAMIC active, aggressive, driving, effective, energizing, forceful, impelling, intense, isotonic, kinetic, live, potent, powerful, starting, vehement, vigorous, vital

DYNAMICS forces, kinetics, mechanics, science, system, variations

DYNAMITE blast, dangerous, dualin(e), explosive, fulgerite, gelignite, hecla, kieselguhr, nitroglycerin, rendrock, shatter, tnt
inventor nobel

DYNAMO alternator, booster, busy bee, eager beaver, enthusiast, exciter, generator, go-ahead, go-getter, humdinger, hummer, hustler, livewire, man of

action, motor, powerhouse, rustler, tornado
inventor faraday
part arm(ature), brushes, coil, commutator, conductor, limb, rotor, stator, yoke
pulley stator
DYNAST potentate, prince, ruler
DYNASTY dominion, empire, kingdom, lordship, realm, reign, rule, sovereignty
DYNE *per centimeter* barad
DYSENTERY diarrhea, flux, lientery, menison, scour, toxemia
treatment acetarsone, ipecac, lomatil, star-reed, sulfaguanidine, uzaron
DYSLOGY censure
DYSPEPSIA *nervous* gastroxynsis
DYSPEPTIC bitter, gloomy, irritable, patient, sick
DISPHORIA anxiety, disquiet, fidgets, restlessness
DYSPNEA anhelation, breathlessness
DYSPROSIUM *source* rare earth
DYSSODIA boebera, thistle
DYSTHYMIA despondency
DZHUGASHVILI stalin
DZLOB bumpkin, oak, shlub, yokel, zhlub

E

EA deity, each, enki, hea, inlet, ninigiku river
colleague shamash
consort damgalnunna, damkina, ninki
country apsu, eridu
daughter nina
dwelling kishkanu
EACH all, ana, apiece, both, distributively, either, every (one), ilk(a), individually, one by one, per, respectively, severally, uch(e)
and every whole
in its turn interchangeably
to each proportionately
to each his own suum cuique
EAGER acid, agape, agasp, agog, ambitious, anticipating, antsy, anxious, apt, ardent, astir, athirst, atiptoe, avid, breathless, burning, bursting, cormorant, desirous, enthusiastic, excited, expectant, fain, fervent, fervid, frack, freck, forward, gair, hetter, high, hot, hungry, impatient, itching, itchy, keen, lickerish, overzealous, prompt, rad, rath, ready, restive, restless, sharp, snell, solicitous, sour, strenuous, tare, thirsty, thro, vigilant, vigorous, willing, yan, yare, yearning, yern, yiver, zealous, zestful
beaver dynamo, enthusiast
wildly crazy
EAGERLY belive, fast, fell, hotly, hungrily, intently, prestly, yarely, yepely, yern
EAGERNESS alacrity, ambition, anxiety, ardency, ardor, avidity, cupidity, desire, devotion, elan, fainness, fervor, gare, gog, impatience, solicitude, thirst, vehemence, voracity, zeal
EAGLE aar, adler, allerion, aquila, bald, bat-aleur, bateleur, bearcoot, berghaan, bergut, betaleur, bird of freedom, coin, emblem, ern(e), etana, falcon, formal, formel, gier, haliacetus, harpy, helotarsus, hole in one, insignia, nra, ossifrage, raptor, ringtail, terathopius
-beaked aquiline
bearded lammergeier, vulture
biblical gier
brood aerie
changed to periphas
comb. aet(o)
constellation aquila
cry scream
ensign of rome
female formal, formel
fern brake
flower impatiens
golden ringtail
group aerie, convocation, eyrie
hooked aquiline
-like accipital, accipitrine, aquiline, raptorial
lone lindbergh
male tercel
name meaning ajax, arno, arva
nest aerie, eyrie, eyry
of brittany du guesclin
of divines thomas aquinas
owl bubo-bubo, grand duke, horned, katogle
ray aetobatid, obispo
sea ern(e), pygarg(us)
short-tailed bataleur
stone (a)etite, ironstone
strong as, name meaning arnold(o)
symbol of inspiration, majesty
wing solitaire
-winged fast
EAGLET laiglon
EAGLEWOOD agalloch (um), agar, aloes, aquilaria, lignaloes, perfume
EAGRE aegir, bore, flood, flow, hygre, wave
EAM gossip, uncle
EAN See YEAN.
EAR adjunct, attention, audience, auditory canal, auricle, auris, cannon, clip, cob, cochlea, conch(a), corn(cob), croset, crossette, cultivate, epi, handle, hear (ing), heed, hole, knob, lappet, list, listen(er), lobe, lobule, lug, mealie, neb, nubbin, pinna, plow, receptor, sensory, shell, souse, sowse, spica, spike, strium, till, tiu, tiwaz
absence anotia
affecting binotic, dichotic, diotic
and nose, pert. aurinasal
anvil ambos, incus
aperture fenestra
attachment corn, drop, lobe, ring
auricle pinna
bone ambos, incus, malleus, manubrium, stapes, stirrup, tegmen
bone behind mastoid
canal scala
canal part ampull(ul)

cartilage elevation antihelix
cave cochlea, meatus, utricle
chamber saccule
cleaning device aurilave
cockle purples
comb. auri, ot(o)
conch pinna
corn cob, icker, nubbin, spike
covering earlap, earmuff, oreillet
crystal otoconium, otolith
deformity cauliflower-ear
depression scapha
disorder cophosis, mastoid (itis), otalgia, otalgy
doctor aurist, otologist
drop See EARRING.
dust otoconia
external auricle, concha, helix, meatus, pinna
flap earmuff, eartab, lug
fluid perilymph
fungus otomyces
hammer malleus
having aurated, auriculate
having 1 monaural
having 2 binaural
inflammation aerootitis, otitis(media), syringitis, tympanitis
injury barotrauma
interior, pert. entotic
internal cochlea
-leaved auriculate
lobe lap, lug, pendant, pinna
lobe people orejon
lock tress
membrane tectorium
middle drum, tympanum
-minded audile
muff oreillet
muscle auricularis, stapedius
near parotic
opening bur(r)
ornament eardrop, earring
part alveus, antihelix, antitragus, anvil, auricle, bur(r), canal, cauda, cavum, cochlea, concha, cymba, drum, eustacean tube, helix, incus, labyrinth, lobe, lug, malleus, meatus, modiolus, octonium, organ of corti, pinna, stirrup, tragus, utricle, vestibule
passage auditory meatus
pert. auditory, aural, auric(ular), binotic, binural, lobar, lobate, entotic, otic, parotic, periotic
pick auriscalp
-piercing shrill
plug stopple, tembeta

prominence tragus
rim helix
ringing syrigmus, tinnitus
science otology
seize by sool
-shaped auriform
shell abalone, ormer, snail
small microtia
-splitting loud, noisy, uproarious
stone otolite, otolith, sagitta
tick octobius, pinolia
tree conacaste
trumpet auriphone, cornet, topophone
wax cerumen
wheat cape, spica
EARACHE dysaconsia, otalgia, otalgy
EARBOB See EARRING.
EARDRUM membrane, tabo(u)r, tympan(um)
EARL betroth, bind, comes, consul, count, graf, lord, needlefish, noble(man), peer, pledge, siward
duck merganser
of coventry snipsnapsnorum
pert. comital
wife countess
EARLIER anterior, before, elder, ere, erst, first(er), fore, former, further, hither, lower, pioneer, premier, previous, sooner, upper
EARLIEST alert, chief, eldest, erst, first, furthest, initial, maiden, premier, primal, primary, primeval, primitive, primordial, primrose, rathest
EARLINESS anticipation, headstart, prevenience, stitch in time
EARLY aforehand, ahead, ancient, anon, anticipative, anticipatory, beforehand, beforetime, betimes, ere long, erliche, first, forehanded, former, in advance, in anticipation, matutinal, old-time, past, prehistoric, premature, prevenient, previous, primy, prompt, rare, rath(e), rearly, seasonable, seasonal, shortly, soon, sudden, untimely, verty, youthful
comb. paleo
warning system dewline
EARMARK allocate, badge, bit, characteristic, charac-

terize, crop, designate, distinction, identification, identify, label, name, overbit, overcrop, peculiarity, sign, sleeper, split, tag, token, underbit
EARN acquire, addle, chevise, deserve, ettle, fang, gain, get, glear, make, merit, obtain, procure, reach, secure, till, vang, win, work
a living bring home the bacon, make the pot boil
by labor addle, beswink, swink
EARNER breadwinner
EARNEST ardent, arles, arr(h)a, assurance, busy, dern, diligent, eager, emphatic, engaged, fervent, forward, gage, grave, han(d)sel, hearty, heavy, intent, pawn, pledge, promise, sedate, serious, sincere, smart, sober, solemn, staid, warrant, zealous
comb. serio
money arles, arr(h)a, deposit, handgeld, handsel, hansel, security, token
EARNESTLY at all events, at any price, come what may, dearly, determinedly, devoutly, ding-dong, entirely, firmly, hammer and tongs, heart and soul, heartily, intently, resolutely, seriously, staunchly, tooth and nail, wishly
EARNESTNESS animation, devotion, diligence, fervor, glow, gravity, sincerity, sobriety, somberness, studiousness, unction, warmth
EARNINGS addlin(g)s, emolument, gain, get, income, net, pay, picking, proceeds, profits, receipts, revenue, salary, stipend, wages
EARPIECE button
EARRING band, drop, earclip, earscrew, girandole, pendant, pendle
EARSHOT hearing, nearness, range, reach, sound
EARTH adobe, alluvion, alluvium, bury, byon, center, clay, clod, crust, dirt, dobe, dust, e(a)rd, floss, gaea, glebe, globe, groot, ground, horizontal, kokowai, lair, land, lithosphere, loam,

loess, magnesia, marl, midgard, midgarth, mold, mool, muck, orb, planet, regur, rock, sod, soil, sory, sphere, subsoil, terrafirma, terrain, terrene, tierras, topsoil, tripoli, vale, world, yacata, yird
air cover biosphere
almond chupa, peanut
and sky junction horizon
apple cucumber, jerusalemartichoke, potato
axis hinge, pole
ball polysaccum, truffle
black ampelite, chernozen, killow, muck, sory
blue kimberlite
blue iron vivianite
bob grub, maggot
-born autochthonous, human, low, mortal, plebeian, temporal, terrigenous, vulgar, worldly
bring to fell, knock down, land
brown umber
building material adobe, pise
center barysphere, centrosphere, core, pyrosphere
clayey bion, byon, lame, loam
club squawroot
comb. geo, telluro, terra
compound tierras
core nife
cover air, sial
crab molecricket
crust epigene, horst, silica
crust deformation diastrophism
crust part craton
dark chernozen
deposit alluvium, guhr, loam, loess, marl, mold, silt, soil
drake dragon
dry groot, mool
dweller tellurian
end of ultima thule
fall avalanche, landslide
flax amianthus, asbestos
flea chigger, chigoe, jigger
formed on surface epigene
friable mo(u)ld
fuller's creta
gall century, mungo
gem-bearing bion, byon
god cab(e)iri, dagan, geb, kabeiri, keb, shechi, tellus
goddess aruru, auxesia, bhumidevi, ceres, damia, demeter, erda, gaea, gaia, gula, hertha, kore, lua,

mannu, nerthus, semele, sif, tari, terra, vasundhara
hog aardvark
interior See *center*, above.
jinn yaksa
layer loam
like oblate
lodge hogan
loose crumb, geest
lump clod, sot
metal erbium, ore, protore
moist slime
mother hertha, nzambisi
nucleus See *center*, above.
nut See EARTHNUT.
opening in abyss, burrow, cave, cavern, crater, ditch, excavation, grotto, mine, quarry, subterrane, trench, tunnel
opposite side antipodes
partial shadow penumbra
pert. clayey, geal, planetary, seismic, tellural, tellurian, telluric, temporal, terra, terranean, terrene, terrestrial, terrigenous
pig aardvark, erdvark
pigment ochre, umber
poor rammel
prepare for seeding cultivate, harrow, plow, shovel, spade
queen of opal
rammed pise
refuse murgeon
ridge kame, rideau
river bank grewt
sample boring
satellite moon
science geodesy, geology, geography
shadow umbra
shaker poseidon, zeus
-shaking important, loud
small terrella
solid geosphere
spirit(s) annunaki, erdgeist, gnome, igigi
star fungus, geaster
star nearest sun
sun-dried swish
surface crust, geoid, sial, sima
surface gravel eratum, erratice
surface, made on epigene
surface, pert. geomorphic
vitriol infused floss, sory
volcanic lava, tarass, trass, tuff
wall trinchera
wax ozocerite
yellow bismite

EARTHEN cloamen, dirten, fict, yarthen
EARTHENWARE astbury, bennington, buffware, ceramics, china, clayen, cloam, crock(ery), echea, faience, jasper, olla, pottery, raku, stoneware, talavera, terracotta, tickney
glazed delft
ingredient pipe-clay
maker potter
peddler mugger
pert. ceramic
piece of shard
pot crock
EARTHINESS carnality, salt, terreity, terrosity
EARTHKIN terrella
EARTHLING human, iconoclast, man, mortal, tellurist
EARTHLY (See also EARTHY.) carnal, coarse, earthen, fleshy, glebous, global, gross, lairy, low, mortal, mundane, pace, planetary, profane, secular, sensual, subastral, sublunar, tellurian, telluric, temporal, terrene, terreous, terrestrial, worldly
EARTHNUT arnot, arnut, chufa, goober, harenut, hawknut, peanut, pignut, pod, root, truffle, tuber
EARTHQUAKE diastrophism, lindol, seism, shake, shock, temblor, tremor, upheaval
belt pacific rim of fire
comb. seismo
deep bathyseism
famous See *site*, below.
fault palmdale bulge, san andreas-rift
fear of seismophobia
intensity scale mercali
measurement richter scale
measurer laser beams, magnetometer, seismograph, seismometer, strainometer, tiltmeter
not subject to aseismic
pert. seismal, seismic(al)
phenomenon microseismic p waves
point above epicenter
preliminary dilatancy-diffusion
producing seismotic
protectress st agatha
recorder seismoscope
science seismology
severe macroseism

shock tremor
site agadir, alaska, aleppo, assam, china, cutch, dutch east indies, guatemala, iran, ischia, kansu, lisbon, managua, martinique, mukden, peru, quito, san francisco, shensi, tokyo, turkey
slight microseism
theory plate-tectonics
violent megaseism

EARTHWORK agger, bank, breastwork, castle, dike, epaulement, fishworm, fort(ification), mound, parapet, rampart, rath, ridge, terrace, tump

EARTHWORM angledog, angletwitch, annelid, brambleworm, brandling, dewworm, easse, ersenia, ess, ipomoea, lumbricid, maddock, microchaeta, twatchel

EARTHY barnyard, coarse, crude, dull, gross, low, salty, terrene, terreous, terrestrial, unrefined, visceral, vulgar, worldly, wormy
cobalt asboite
sign capricorn, taurus, virgo

EARWIG battle twig, centipede, forficula, golach, goloch, labidura, tip, touchbell

EASE abate, allay, alleviate, approach, assuage, buffer, calm, comfort, compose, content, convenience, decrease, dexterity, diminish, elegance, euphoria, expedite, facilitate, facility, fluency, freedom, knack, leisure, lessen, liberty, lighten, loosen, lull, mitigate, mollify, nonchalance, peace, prosperity, quiet(ude), reduce, relaxation, relief, relieve, repose, rest, sangfroid, satisfaction, security, simplify, slacken, slake, slow, smooth, soften, soothe, unburden
at degage, free, otiose, relaxed
of deprive
off check, relax, retard, slack(en), slough, slow, start
rudder tack
tension render

EASEL frame, scaffold, support

EASEMENT herbage, relief, servitus, turbary, wayleave

EASILY conveniently, dexterously, eath(ly), handily, handsdown, lightly, readily, simply, sleekly, smoothly, swimmingly

EASING abatement, detente, ramp

EAST asia, dawn, direction, est, levant(ine), orient, sunrise
pert. asian, eoan, oriental
queen zenobia
river channel hell-gate
river island welfare
symbol of ormus

EAST AFRICA *antelope* dik-dik, gerenuk, grant's gazelle
bush nyika
business shauri
cedar deodar
coin heller, pesa, shilling, supie
dialect kiswahili
discoverer vasco da gama
former kingdom shoa
garden shamba
hemp pangane
house tembe
lake victoria
masai wakwafi
native ashei, bari, baronga, masai, samburu, somali, sotik, turkana, viti, wakwafi, wambugu
river webi-shebeli
slave vessel dhow
spiritual power ngai
sultanate zanzibar
tool panga
tree moli, podo
tribe See *native*, above.

EASTER eed, eostre, paas, pace, paques, pasch(a), pasqua
anemone pasqueflower
before antepaschal
bell stitchwort
beurre pear
5th sunday after rogation
1st sunday after antipascha, quasimodo
flower daffodil, poinsettia, pulsatilla, stitchwort
40 days after ascension day, holy thursday
giant bistort
island rapaniu
island statues moai
pert. paschal
2nd tuesday after hockday
7th sunday after pentecost
sunday before palm
symbol bunny, egg, fish, lily, rabbit

EASTERN (See also ASIA and ORIENTAL.) asiatic, auroral, ortive

EASTERN CHURCH *altar cloth* catasarka
anthem prokeimenon
bishop sparch
body uniat
cake col(l)yba
calendar melology
candlestick dicerion
ceremony panagia
choir platform solea
cloak mandyas
convent head hegumene
council sobor
dignitary grand steward
diocese eparchy
doxology doxa
eucharist hagia
eucharist wine krama
festival apodosis, koimesis
gong semantron
host vessel maragita
hymn hirmos, sticheron, trisagion
manual typicon
member uniat
monastery laura, mandra
monastic group acoemeti
monk caloyer
novice rhasophore
porch proaulion
prayer cathisma, ectene, ectriche, ektene
priest abba, catholicos, katholikos, protopope
robe sticharion
saint anargyros
screen iconostasis
spoon labis
stole omophorion
teacher didascalos
verse stichos
vespers hesperinon
vestment phelonion, sakkos

EASTERNER dude, levantine, oriental

EAST GERMANY *city* brandenburg, breslau, dresden, leipzig
coin ostmark
leader ulbricht
port rostock

EAST INDIES See also INDONESIA.
agent gomashta, gomastah
animal babiroussa, babirus(s)a, bandicoot, banxring, delundung, napu, tana, tapaia, tarsier, tupaia, zebu
antelope chiru, nilgai, nilgau
army servant lascar

arrowroot tikor
bark lodh, niet .
bead tree margosa, neem(ba), nim
beetle blister-beetle, cantharis, spanish fly
bird baya, falcon, koel, raya, shama, tit-babbler
bison banteng gaur, gayal, tisine
boat dhoni, ding(e)y, dinghy, doni, gallivat, jalor, lota, manche, oolak, patamar
boatswain serang
broadbill raya
buck black, bezoratica
bush sola
cab kosong
calico sallo(o)
carpet amritsar
cashmere ulwan
cattail elephant grass
cattle dhan, gaur
cavalry troop ressala
cedar mahogany, toon(a)
chamois sarau
cheroot lunkah
chickpea gram
chief dato, rana, sirdar
civet dedes, musang, rasse, tangalung
coin bonk, doit, rupee
cotton tree simal
cow, blue nilgai
cypress bhutan
dancing girl dasi
decoration ardish, tracery
deer chital, gerau, muntjac, muntjak, napu, rusa
design method batik
disease lanas
dish biryanis, curry, kedgeree, mulligatawny, papadum, samosas
dodder amil
drink nipa, soma
drinking pot lotah
drug zedoary, zerumbet
dye aal
fabric ban, beteela, jamdanee, mushru, romal, sallo(o), tash
falcon besra, peregrine, redpool, shahin
fan punkah
farmer ryot
fiber plant ambaree, ambary, badaga, corchorus, hibiscus, jute, oadal, nilgiri, ramie, sana, sunn
fig tree banian, banyan
finch hierax
fish archer, darter, dorab,

dourami, pegasus, pomfret, triodon
flower hibiscus, jasmine
flute matacan
fly whisk chowry
food sago
freight boat oolak
fruit bel(leric), bilimbi(ng), cardamon, cubeb, durian, elephant-apple, myrobalan, papaw, pulasan, zanonia
fruit pigeon treron
garment sari
gateway toran(a)
goat markhor, tahr
granary gola
grass glaga(h), hasa, raggee, raggie, raggy
greyhound brinjaree, brinjarry
groom syce
gum tree kino
harbor master shabundar, shabunder
hardwood sal
harvest rabo
hawk bacha, goshawk, shikra
hemp pangane
herb abelmosk, cardamom, cardamon, cardamum, chay, choy, eggplant, ghetchoo, pia, prophetflower, rea, roselle, sesame, sola, til, turmeric
hog babiroussa, bibirussa, pigmy
honeybee dingar
insectivore banxring, tupaia
island adi, arroe, aru, bali, borneo, caram, celebes, java, leti, misal, muna, nias, sumatra, timor
jalap turpeth
juniper berry abhol
lace gota
law adat
liquor arrack
macaque bruh, egret-monkey
madder chay
maid ayah
mail dak
mangrove ceriops, tagal
market pasar
measure bamboo, bouw, coyang, depa, depoh, gantang, kilan, kit, kos, parah, rood, rope, takar, tjenkal, toenbak
millet bajra, dhurra, durra
mint java tea, patchouli
money changer shroff
monkey entellus
moth nacoleia, pisang
mountain ghat

musical instrument bina, ruana, saron, sistrum, vina, upanga
muskmelon wungee
muslin ban, beteela, jamdanee
myrrh commiphora
nilgiri badaga
nose flute upanga
nurse amah
nut ben
official controleur, kotwal
orchestra gamelan(g)
palm atap, book, corypha, gebang, jaggery, nipa(h), palmyra, sago, tala, talipot, tokopat
palm civet musang
panda wah
peasant ryot
pepper betel
pheasant argus
pine chir
plant acanthaca, ambaree, ambary, amil, benne, betel, blatti, chay, choy, columbowood, creat, dal, deutzia, jute, mad(d)ar, mudar, nero's crown, rea, sesame, sila, sola, sunn, turpeth
plant fiber jute
poison bikh, bish
police official daragah, wedana
port damao
post dak, dawk
princess begum
race swat, varna
rat badger, bandicoot
region malabar
religious body saras
relish chutney
remedy amil
resin black-dammar
resthouse passangrahan
road praya
robber dacoit
root atees, atis, gallingale
rose bay crape jasmine, nero's crown
rubber tree saj
ruler akbar, rajah
ruminant zebu
sailor lascar
sardine lile
satin mushru
sea banda
sect jain(a)
servant maty
shaddock pompelmous
shawl slendang
sheep, wild shapu, sna, urial
shell bear's-paw, papboat

shrub ancistrocladus, bastard indigo, carandas, caraunda, carissa, cubeb, dogbane, ipecac, mudar, nunnari, odal, purging-croton, sola, soma, tubeflower, upas

shrub, medicinal celastrus, soma

skipper serang

snake bokadam, cerberus, kupper

snuff rapee

soldier sepoy

songbird shama

songs, holy gitanjali

spectacle tamasha

spider katipo

split pea dal

squirrel taguan

starch sago, tikor

stimulant betel

storm elephanta

sugar glaga(h), gur, raab, talthib

swine babiroussa, babirus(s)a

sword pata

thyme borage

timber tree sal, toon

title raja(h), sahib, shri

town hooghly

tree 3 ach, ber, bet, bih, eng, fig, hur, mee, nim, saj, sal 4 alof, alus, amla, dhak, kino, moli, neem, odal, poon, punk, sain, saul, teak, toon, upas 5 acana, ampac, asoka, butea, chica, dadap, fulwa, ixora, kokan, kongu, lansa, mahua, mesua, mowha, neeba, niepa, piney, press, rohan, ruhun, salai, sapan, simal, siris, tikur, uadal 6 abroma, antiar, bahera, banyan, cassia, chalta, chogak, deodar, engelg, hurjun, illupi, jambol, jambul, kamala, kanagi, nutmeg, sissoo, tikoor 7 benteak, cadamba, cajeput, cajuput, caramba, catechu, champac, dhamnoo, gumihan, hollong, jambool, kajeput, kokoona, koombar, margosa 8 antiaris, averrhoa, carajura, phulwara 9 ailanthus, blackwood, bloodwood, carambola, jointwood, nagkassar, nux vomica, paperbark, paperbush, roseapple 10 cannonball, coromandal,

couroupita, ilangilang, karinghota 11 chaulmaugra, hursinghair 13 anthocephalus

tribe kader, mari, puliar

troop pay batta

umbrella payong

vehicle tonga

vessel See *boat,* above.

vine amil, anamirta, dodder, elephant-creeper, gilo, gulancha, jasmine, moonplant, moonseed, odal, odel, soma, telakucha

viol ruana

viper kupper

walnut lebbek

warrior singh

watercourse nullah

weight candy, catty, ratti, ser, toen, tola

wood benteak, eng(elg), kokra, sal, satin

wood apple bel

wood, incense agalloch, agal(wood), agalloch(um), ag(u)ilawood, aloes, lign-aloes

xylophone saron

EASTLAND eistriche, orient

EASTWARD eassel

EASY accessible, affable, agile, amenable, at home, available, breezy, calm, carefree, casual, cavalier, comfortable, comodo, cozy, eath, effortless, eith, elementary, facile, familiar, free, gentle, glib, gradual, gullible, homelike, indolent, lenient, light, mild, moderate, natural, placid, plain, prone, reposeful, restful, rife, secure, serene, simple, slow, smooth, snap, snug, soft, spacious, suave, tranquil, unforced, wanton, yezzy

come, easy go carefree, prodigal

in mind secure

job bludge, breeze, cinch, pipe, setup, sinecure, snap

mark breather, breezer, chump, cinch, fool, gullible, putz, setup, simpleton, sucker, upe

street bed of roses, comfort, luxury, prosperity, wealth

streeter riley

thing breeze, cakewalk, cinch, duck soup, gravy (train), leadpipe cinch, pic-

nic, pie, pipe, pushover, setup, sinecure, snap, yare

EASYGOING blase, calm, careless, casual, cavalier, complaisant, content, degage, impromptu, indifferent, indulgent, informal, lax, lazy, lenient, loose, nonchalant, offhand, peaceful, placid, relaxed, slow, tolerant, uncritical, unexacting

EAT absorb, begnaw, bite, board, bolt, break bread, browse, burn, canker, chew, chop, chuck(up), consume, corrode, devour, dine, down, erode, essen, fall to, fare, feast, feed, fog, fret, glut, gnaw, gobble, gorge, grub, gulp, gurge, heyt, ingest, kai, manducate, mange, masticate, munch, nibble, nourish, partake, peck, pick, picnic, piece, pitch in, ravage, raven, rust, sate, scoff, slurp, snack, stuff, sup, swallow, tuck, victual

-all glutton

away canker, corrode, erode, fret, gnaw, rankle, rust

between meals bever, nosh, snack

big meal stoke

by regimen diet

comb. phag(e)

crow admit, apologize, bow, condescend, crawl, recant

crunchingly grouze

excessively bezzle, colf, gorge, stuff

grass forage, graze

greedily bolt, chaum, cram, gamp, gawp, glut, gobble, goffle, gorge, gourmand(ize), gudge, gulp, guttle, guzzle, mooch, raunge, raven, ravin(e), sate, scoff, slab, slop, sluice, stuff, tuck, wolf

heartily gorge, thorn

humble pie See EAT *crow.*

in gulps lab

like a bird pick(le)

loving to esurient

mincingly pick(le), piddle

noisily gug, gulch, guttle, slop, slotter, slurp

one's heart out agonize, grieve

one's words recant, retract

out of one's hand go along, submit, yield

pert. dietary, dietetic, edacious

slovenly mummick, slotter, slurp

sparingly diet, mince, pick, piddle

sumptuously regale, stuff

up accept, believe, consume, demolish, devour, engross, enjoy, go for, swallow, take in

with break bread

with pleasure relish, smouse

without chewing bolt, gulp

EATABLE edible, esculent

EATEN cankered, corroded, rusted

away eroded, erose

half semese

EATER board-and-roomer, boarder, cannibal, carnivore, consumer, devourer, diner, gourmand, gourmet, granivore, herbivore, luncher, mouth, omnivore, omophagist, pantophagist, pecker, predacean, trencherman, vegetarian

comb. phag(e), vore

EATERY See RESTAURANT.

EATING bit, canker, carnivorism, caustic, chewing, consuming, consumption, corrosive, deglutition, depascent, devouring, dining, edacity, epulation, erodent, erosive, esurine, feasting, food, fretting, gluttony, gnawing, ingestion, manducation, mastication, omniverousness, pantophagy, phytophagy, rumination, voracity, vorant

comb. phag(o), vore

excessive edacity, polyphagia

fear of sitophobia

flesh carnivorous

out exedent, exesion

place See DINING *room* and RESTAURANT.

EAU aqua, water

benite flattery, holy water

de cologne perfume, toilet water

de vie brandy, spirits

forte etching

sucree ambrosia, nectar

EAVES brow, edge, eyelashes, eyelids, ridge, rim, roof(edge)

tile starter

trough cheneau, gutter

EAVESDROP h(e)arken, listen, overhear, stillicide, trickle

electronically bug

EAVESDROPPER auditor, drawlatch, earwig, lot's wife, peeper

EBAUCHE drawing, plan

EBB abate, backflow, corn bunting, decay, decline, decrease, deteriorate, diminish, dwindle, fail, fall, flow, lessen, neap, recede, refluence, reflux, regress, retreat, retroflex, shallow, sink, subside, wane, waste

and flow (a)estus, alternate, billow, fluidity, tide

sleeper dunlin

tide low water, neap

EBBING awane, refluent, refluous

EBBMAN bridge-tender

EBED *son* gael

EBEDMELECH *eunuch of* zedekiah

EBEL *child* gaal

EBENEZER church, commemoration, memorial

EBER *parent* elpaal, shem *son* joktan, peleg

EBIONITE elkesaite, gnostic

EBLIS devil, iblis, jann, lucifer, satan

EBONITE rubber, vulcanite

EBONY black, diospyros, euclea, gabo(o)n, hebenon, ironwood, tree, wamara

brown coffeewood, wamara

fruit embolo

-like ebeneous

spleenwort fern

EBULLATE boil, bubble, seethe, stew

EBULLIENCE boiling(over) (up), elevation, exhilaration, high spirits, overflow

EBULLIENT boiling, brash, bubbling, burning, fervid, high-spirited, hot, passionate, torrid

EBULLITION agitation, boiling, bubbling, commotion, effervescence, excitement, ferment(ation), outburst, seethe, turbulence

ECAD ecophene

ECCENTRIC aberrant, abnormal, anomalous, atypic(al), awry, balmy, batty, bird, bizarre, bonkers, buggy, card, character, cove, crackpot, crank(y), creep(y), crotchety, cuckoo, curious, cuss, divergent, dotty, droll, erratic, exceptional, extraordinary, freak (ish), funny, gazebo, gink, grotesque, idiosyncratic, inconstant, irregular, kinky, loco, mad, maggoty, misfit, nut(ty), odd(ball), oddity, offbeat, oner, out of the ordinary, outish, outlandish, outre, peculiar, potty, psycho, quaint, queer(fish), quizzical, screwball, screwy, singular, squirrelly, strange, tike, touched, twisted, uncommon, unconventional, unique, unnatural, wacky, weirdie, weirdo, weirdy, whacky, wild

piece cam

ECCENTRICITY aberration, abnormality, caprice, crotchet, deviation, ferly, foible, freak, idiosyncrasy, irregularity, kink, oddity, peculiarity, quiddity, quirk, vagary

ECCHYMOTIC black and blue, bruised, discolored

ECCLESIASTES koheleth, qoheleth

ECCLESIASTIC (See also CHURCHMAN, ECCLESIASTICAL, and PROPHET.) abbe, abbot, archon, clergyman, deacon, father, kirkman, preacher, prelate, priest, vicar

armband maniple

assembly coetua, sederunt, synod

assistant acolyte

banner labarum

belt belt(h)eus

benefice glebe, precarium

cap berettino, biretta, calot(te), pileus, zucchetto

cape cappa

chapter, pert. capitular(y)

cope cape, cappa

corruption simony

council See COUNCIL *ecclesiastic.*

court classis, rota

court order church writ

curse anathema

dignitary dom

garment See VESTMENT *religious.*

head rector

hebrew aaron, bilgah, bilgai, cohen, darshan, eli, high priest, levite, maggid, prophet, rabbi(n), scribe

hindu atharvan, bairagi, ba-

shara, bhikhari, bhikku, bhikkshu, brahman, guru, hotar, mobed, mulla(h), pujari, pundit, purohit, ramanandi, ramwat, sannyasi, shamen, vairagi, yogi(n)
hood amice
income benefice, glebe
instruction book catechism, ordinal
jurisdiction deanery, diocese, parish, see
law canon
lay person oblate
linen amice
living benefice
mass missa
muslim abdal, dervish, fakir, hadji, ima(u)m, kahin, karim, kasis, muezzin, mufti, mullah, murshid, pandita, santon, sheik, wahabi
officer bishop, deacon, dean, priest, rector
order See ORDER *religious.*
pagan daduchus, druid, epopt, flamen, hierodule, hierophant, hieros, mystes
prince cardinal, heirarch
privilege indult
punishment censure
robe epitrachelion, mantelletta, mantellone
seat deanery, sedile, sedilia
shaven crown tonsure
statute capitular
surplice cotta
tax tithe
title See CHURCHMAN.
veil vimpa
vessel censer, thurible
vestment See VESTMENT *religious.*
widow's office viduate
work, benevolent dorcastry
ECCLESIASTICAL apostolic, catedralesque, cathedral, christian, churchish, church-like, churchly, clerical, divine, ministerial, pantheonic, papal, parochial, pastoral, priestly, rabbinical, spiritual, synogogal, synogogical, tabernacular, templelike
ECDYSIAST stripper, stripteaser
ECDYSIS molting, shedding, stripping
ECHECLES *wife* polymelia
ECHEMUS *kingdom* arcadia
victim hercules

ECHETUS *daughter* amphissa
kingdom epirus
ECHEVIN magistrate, scabine, scabinus
ECHIDNA anteater, edentate, monster, nodiak, porcupine
consort typhon
food ants
offspring cerberus, chimera, dragon, eagle, gorgon, hydra, nemean lion, orthus, scylla, sphinx
parent gaea, tartarus
slayer argus
3-toed nodiak
ECHIMYINE cony, hutia
ECHINACEA black-sampson, coneflower, herb, thistle
ECHINATE bristly, prickly, spiny
ECHINOCLOA ankee, barngrass, camalote, cockspur grass, millet
ECHINODERM amphiuroide, annuloid, asteroid, basket star, blastoid, crinoid, cystid, gorgonocephalus, starfish
armed starfish
extinct agelacrinite, blastoid
radial area ambulacrum
ECHION *parent* antianira, hermes, mercury
son pentheus
wife agave
ECHIUM blue, blue devils, blue thistle, bugloss, catsclover, chicory
ECHO answer, ape, chorus, concur, ditto, epanalepsis, gingko, imitate, imitator, iterate, nymph, parrot, react, rebound, repeat, repercussion, reply, resound, respond, response, reverb(eration), ring, second, sing, sympathy, tree, vibrate
beloved narcissus
ECHOING iterant, resonant
ECLAMPSIA convulsion, seizure, spasm
ECLAT acclaim, celebrity, fame, glory, honor, note, notoriety, pomp, praise, prestige, prominence, renown, reputation, repute, score, sensation, splendor
ECLECTIC broad, choosy, discriminating, liberal, sectarian, select(ive)
ECLIPSE beat, blind, blot, cloud, conceal, darken, daz-

zle, dim, hide, obscure, occult, outshine, shade, shroud, stain, sully, surmount, surpass, veil
demon ketu, rahu
kind central, partial, penumbral, total
pert. occulted
point lagna, solstice
shadow penumbra, umbra
ECLOGUE bucolic, idyl(l), poem
ECOLOGIST bionomist
ECOLOGY biology, bionomics, bionomy, environment, mesology
pioneer commoner
ECONOMICAL cheeseparing, frugal, low, moderate, penurious, provident, prudent, reasonable, scrimpy, skimpy, sparesome, sparing, spartan, stinting, thrifty
ECONOMICS finance, housewifery, plutology, plutonomy
element commodity
practioner moneybug
ECONOMIZE crosscut, cut corners, hain, husband, pare, retrench, save, scrape, scrimp, shepherd, shorten, skimp, spare, stint
ECONOMY austerity, complex, foundation, frugality, husbandry, management, managery, network, order, parsimony, plan, productivity, prudence, saving, scheme, structure, system, thrift
bad cacoeconomy
domestic husbandry
ECRU beige, biscuit, doe, tan, unbleached
ECSTASY afflatus, beatitude, bliss, delight, delirium, emotion, enthusiasm, exaltation, felicity, frenzy, fury, happiness, inspiration, joy, madness, pleasure, power, rapture, rhapsody, swoon, trance, transport
spiritual turya
ECSTATIC athrill, beatific, blissful, hot, pythian, rapt (urous), thrilled, wild
ECTODERM epiblast
ECTOMORPHIC ashenic, leptosome, linear, thin
ECTOPLASM aura, ectosarc, emanation, luminescence
ECTOR *son* sir kay

ECTYPE copy, imitation, reproduction

ECU coin, scute, shield
¼th cardecu

ECUADOR *ancient name* quito
animal vicuna
breeze chanduy
cape pasado, puntilla, rosa
capital quito
city ambato, azogues, cayambe, cuenca, guamote, guano, guayaquil, ibarra, jama, loja, machala, manta, napo, pajan, pelileo, pillaro, pinas, piura, puyo, quito, riobamba, salinas, tena, tulcan, yaupi, zaruma
coin centavo, condor, sucre
conqueror huayna-capac
fruit cherimoya, sugar-apple
god umina
indian ardan, barbacoa, canelo, cara, cixo, inca, jibaro, jivaro, maina, mocoa, palta, puruha, quitu
island baltra, chaves, darwin, isabela, mocha, pinta, pinzon, puna, wenman, wolf
island group colon, galapagos
language jibaro, quechua, spanish
measure cuadra, fanega, libra
native montuvio
peak antisana, cayambe, chimborazo, cotacachi, cotopaxi, pichincha, sangay
port esmeraldas, manta
president flores, garcia moreno, plaza lasso
province azuay, bolivar, canar, carchi, colon, cotopaxi, eloro, guayas, imbabura, los rios
range andes
region oriente
river aguarico, bobonaza, coca, curaray, daule, guayas, mira, napo, naranjal, pastaza, pindo, putumayo, tigre, tumbes, zamora
tennis player segura
tree balsa
volcano cayambe, sangay
weight libra

ECUMENE hearth

ECUMENICAL catholic, cosmic, cosmopolitan, liberal, universal
council lyon, trent

ECZEMA dermatitis, earworm, herpes, malanders, rash, tetter

EDACITY appetite, avarice, gluttony, greed, voracity

EDAM cheese
relative gouda

EDDA *dwarf* andvari
god See AESIR.
poem voluspa

EDDISH aftermath, arrish, edgrew, edgrow, eegrass, etch, park, pasture, rowen, sequel, stubble
hen quail

EDDO aroid, cocoyam, taro

EDDY acker, backset, backstream, bore, charybdis, circle, countercurrent, counterflow, counterflux, crosscurrent, curl, galofaro, gulf, gurge, gyrate, maelstrom, pirouette, purl, reel, revolve, rotate, spin, surge, swirl, swoosh, turn, twirl, undercurrent, undertow, vortex, wale, wash, weel, wheel, whirl(pool), wirble, wreathe, writhe

EDEL bentle, humble, modest, noble, refined, sensitive, shy

EDEMA anasarca, bighead, braxy, distension, dropsy, hydrops, intumescence, puffiness, swelling, tumor

EDEMATOUS bloated, distended, hydropic, spongy, swollen

EDEN anthony, arcadia, elysium, garden, glory, heaven, paradise, utopia
east of nod, samarkand
river euphrates, gihon, hiddekel, pis(h)on, tigris

EDENITE amphibole, amphibolite

EDENTATE aardvark, adventurine, antbear, anteater, armadillo, manis, pangolin, sloth, toothless

EDESSA urfa
king abgar(us)

EDESTAN protean

EDGAR *father* gloucester

EDGE acrimony, advantage, allowance, arris, bank, basil, bench, berm(e), bevel, bezel, bezil, blade, board, border, brim, brink, brow, butt, chimb, chime, compass, confine, cusp, deckle, emborder, end, extreme, face, flange, fringe, handicap, hem, hone, jag, kalihi, kant, keenness, labrum, limb(us), limit, lip, list, majority, marge, margin, nerves, odds, outskirt, pearl, periphery, picot, pien, plange, point, rand, rim, ruler, selvage, sharpen, sharpness, shelf, shoulder, side, sidle, sill, skirt, tat, tip, top, touchiness, unstroke, vandyke, verge, whet, zest
beveled cant, chamfer
-bone aitch, rump
cutting shoe
embroidered surfle, surphul
exterior ambitus
forward creep
in enter, interpose, intrude
metal buhr, bur(r)
rough fash
rounded bourrelet, nosing
run along skirt
sharp arris, beard, pien
sloping basil, bevel, bezel, bezil
straight ruler
untrimmed deckle
up to approach, near
without blunt

EDGED acrimonious, crenate, cutting, erose, sharp
by arcs invected

EDGER strander, whetter

EDGING beading, binding, border, coquille, dag, filet, fimbriation, frill(ing), fringe, furbelow, galloon, gimping, hem, lace, motif, picot, puntilla, rickrack, ruche, ruffle, skirting, tatting, trimming, valance
loop picot
make crochet, tat
scalloped pinking

EDGEWISE laterally
set surbed

EDGY angular, anxious, critical, eager, highstrung, nervous, raspy, sharp, snappish

EDIBLE comestible, eatable, edule, esculent, gustable, succulent
arum taro
gallingale chufa

EDICT act, announcement, arret, assize(s), ban, bando, bull(a), canon, command (ment), decree, ecthesis, escript, fiat, irade, law, mandate, manifesto, order, prescript, program, rule, sanad, statute, ukase, writ

EDICULE niche, shrine

EDIFICE building, erection, house, pile, structure, tetragon, turbeh
kind capitol, church, hall, palace, tabernacle, temple

EDIFY brief, build, construct, enlighten, establish, grow, improve, inform, initiate, instruct, organize, prosper, teach, uplift

EDIFYING beneficial, educational, elevating, enlightening, high, illuminating, informative, instructive, savory

EDINA edinburgh

EDINBURGH auld reekie, dunedin, edina, midlothian
castle gun mons meg
port leith
street canongate, princes, royal mile

EDIT abridge, adapt, alter, amend, arrange, author, bluepencil, clip, compile, copyread, correct, emend, issue, package, publish, rectify, redact, revise, reword, rewrite
film cut

EDITION ausgabe, collection, copy, diglot, hexapla, impression, imprint, issue, kind, number, octapla, princeps, print(ing), variorum, version
early aldine, elzevir, incunabulum
first bulldog, princeps
kind bulldog, extra, final, hard-cover, paperback, princeps, reprint, revisal, special
special extra

EDITOR anthologist, commentator, compiler, diaskeuast, journalist, newsman, overseer, redactor, reviser, writer
room sanctum

EDITORIAL article, comment(ary), leader, opinion

EDMONDS *hero* chad

EDMUND *father* gloucester

EDMUND II *nickname* ironside

EDNA *husband* raguel

EDO beni, bini, tokyo

EDOM (See also ESAU.) idumaea, kin, seir, tema(n)
city dedan, pau, teman
district teman
duke aholibamah, aliah,
aran, elah, iram, jetheth, kenaz, magdiel, mibzar, pinon, teman, timnah
king baalhanan, bela, had(d)ad, husham, jobab, samlah, shaul
mountain hor

EDOMITE omar
ancestor esau

EDUCATE breed, coach, develop, discipline, drill, inform, instruct, nurture, prepare, rear, school, teach, train, tutor

EDUCATED bred, cultured, erudite, learned, lettered, literate, profound, schooled, skilled

EDUCATION background, behavior, breeding, cultivation, deportment, edification, improvement, instruction, learning, literacy, manners, nortelry, nurture, pedagogics, rearing, study, training, tuition, upbringing
good eupsychics
institution academy, college, school, seminary, university
liberal humanities
organization lyceum, nea, pta
physical gym

EDUCATIONAL cultural, didactic, disciplinary, edifying, enlightening, homiletic(al), hortatory, informative, instructive, preceptive, tuitional

EDUCATOR coach, instructor, maitre, mentor, preceptor, professor, teacher, trainer, tutor
famous angell, bascom, butler, dewey, eliot, flexner, gilman, hall, harper, hopkins, hutchins, james, kerr, mann, mather, neilson, peabody, pound, pusey, royce, seton, sproul

EDUCE derive, disengage, draw, elicit, evoke, evolve, extort, extract, infer

EDWARD *consort* philippa of ahainaut
son black prince

EDWARD IV *jester* scogan
mistress jane shore
queen elizabeth
son edward, george, richard

EDWARD VI *dwarf* xit
mother jane seymour

EDWARD VII *queen* alexandra
EDWARD *the confessor, sword* curtana
the elder, son edred

EEL aal, agnatha, anguilla, apodan, apodes, carapo, coil, conger(ee), congo, congrio, cuchia, cusk, ele, elver, fasciatus, fausen, giton, grig, gymnotid, gymnotus, kingklip, kwatuma, lamprey, launce, ling, moray, moreia, moringua, muraena, murene, olm, opah, scourge, siren, snig(gle), spitchcock, tuna, vinegar worm, whip, wriggle
amphibian olm
basket buck, courge
boat schuit
bright-colored moray
conger elver
congo wrymouth
cooked spitchcock
fish tandan
fish for sniggle
-like anguilloid, serpentine
marine conger
pot trap
sand crig, launce
-shaped anguilliform, anguilloid
spear elger, pilger
trap (eel)pot
25 stick, swarm
young elver, oliver, yelver

EELGRASS barnacle (grass), drew, enalid, grassweed, (sea)wrack, zostera

EELPOUT bard, blenny, burbot, conger, fish, guffer, ling, lycodes, lycodoid, muttonfish, quab, weasel, yowler, zoarces

EELWARE crowfoot

EELWORM nema(tode)

EERIE arcane, awful, bizarre, creepy, curious, deathly, eccentric, eldritch, fearful, ghoulish, gloomy, goustie, gousty, grotesque, macabre, mysterious, odd, peculiar, pokerish, queer, strange, uncanny, unearthly, weird

EETION *daughter* andromache

EFFACE blot, cancel, dele(te), destroy, dislimn, erase, expunge, rase, remove, sponge, strike, undo, unpaint, wear
oneself shrink

EFFECT accomplish, achieve,

acquire, action, aftermath, aspect, attain, bearing, bring about, causatum, cause, compass, complete, consequence, contrive, corollary, dent, derivative, development, drift, end, enforce, ettle, event(uality), execute, feck, force, fruit, fulfill, gain, grab, growth, harvest, have, impact, implement, import, imprint, induce, influence, issue, make, meaning, obtain, offshoot, operate, outcome, outgrowth, perform, power, pray, procure, produce, purport, reach, reaction, realize, result, secure, sequel, sequence, take, upshot
blurred fuzz
false facade
from cause to a priori
have militate, tell
intense jar, jolt, stress
of past experience mneme
shattering brisance
striking eclat
total ensemble
tremolo bebung

EFFECTIVE able, active, adequate, brilliant, cogent, competent, convincing, deadly, decisive, devastating, efficacious, efficient, feckful, forceful, influential, operative, potent, powerful, real, resultful, salutary, severe, siker, smashing, sovran, striking, substantial, telling, trenchant, valid, vigorous, virtual
very blockbusting

EFFECTIVELY naitly

EFFECTS assets, belongings, dunnage, goods, means, merchandise, paraphernalia, possessions, property, resources, works

EFFECTUAL able, active, adequate, capable, competent, decisive, dynamic, earnest, effective, efficacious, efficient, potent, powerful, toothy, valid

EFFECTUATE accomplish, achieve, bring about, complete, fulfill, perform, produce

EFFEMINATE androgyne, androgynous, betty, bitchy, catty, chichi, chicken, cockney, coddled, creampuff, emasculated, epicene, femi-

nine, gentle, goody(goody), henhussy, ladyfinger, ladylike, lily, lydian, mamma's boy, mild, milksop, molly(coddle), muff, muliebrous, niminy, oversoft, pampered, pantywaist, percy, powderpuff, prissy, silken, sissified, sissy, soft(y), sop, sybaritic, tamecat, tender(ling), timorous, unmanly, weak(sister), woman(ish), womanly

EFFERVESCE aerate, boil, bubble(over), ebullate, ferment, fizz, foam, froth, hiss, sparkle

EFFERVESCENCE agitation, animation, bloom, bubbling, buoyancy, crackle, ebullience, ebullition, elasticity, ferment(ation), flippancy, foam(ing), froth(ing), levity, resiliency, sparkle, volatility, yeast

EFFERVESCENT brisk, bubbling, bubbly, cheerful, ebullient, elastic, exhilarated, expansive, fizzy, hilarious, jolly, merry, quick, volatile

EFFETE aged, barren, decadent, etiolate, exhausted, fruitless, futile, idle, invalid, milky, moribund, old, sere, soft, spent, sterile, tender, tired, unprolific, weak

EFFICATIOUS able, cogent, convincing, effective, efficient, forcible, influential, mighty, potent, powerful, puissant, sound, telling, valid, vigorous, virtuous

EFFICACY ability, availability, cogency, competency, efficiency, energy, dint, feck, force, grace, might, potency, power, strength, utility, vigor, virtue

EFFICIENCY ability, action, agency, aptitude, competence, dispatch, efficacy, facility, power, proficiency, skill

EFFICIENT able, active, adept, business-like, capable, competent, concise, effective, effectual, expert, feckful, good, orderly, potent, powerful, practical, proficient, qualified, realistic, skilled, skillful, systematic, thorough, well-ordered

EFFIGY copy, dummy, fac-

simile, figure, guy, icon, idol, image, likeness, manikin, mask, model, monument, portrait, sign, simulacrum, statue

EFFLORESCE germinate, incrust, powder

EFFLORESCENCE anthesis, bloom, blossom, eruption, powder, rash, roseola, whitewash

EFFLUENCE defluxion, drain(age), efflux(ion), effusion, emanation, flowoff, gush, issue, outflow(ing), outpouring, runoff

EFFLUVIUM afflatus, air, aura, ectoplasm, ectoplasy, efflux, effusion, emanation, exhalation, exudate, flatus, fluxion, miasm(a), nador, odor, ooze, outgoing, reek, remainder, vapor

EFFLUXION effluence, effusion, emanation, lapse, outflow, stream

EFFORT act, animus, assay, attempt, bother, burst, conatus, devoir, dint, endeavor, energy, essay, exertion, force, fuffle, hump, jump, labor, might, molimen, molition, nisus, nitency, pains, pingle, power, puissance, push, reach, splurge, spurt, strain, stretch, strife, stroke, struggle, tensure, throe, toil, travail, trial, trouble, tug, work
abortive fizzle
agonized throe
big hassel, hassle
effective lick
final charette
for oneself fend
initial assay
single heat, solo, trice
violent adit, burst, spasm, strain, struggle
without easy, facile, light, simple, smooth

EFFRONTERY assumption, audacity, boldness, brashness, brass, brow, cheek, chutzpa, discourtesy, forehead, gall, guts, hardihood, impertinence, impudence, nerve, presumption, temerity

EFFULGENCE blaze, brightness, brilliance, flare, glory, glow, luster, radiance, rutilation, splendor

EFFULGENT aglow, beam-

ing, blazing, bright, brilliant, flowing, gleaming, lambent, lucent, luminous, lustrous, radiant, rutilant, shining, splendid
EFFUSE disseminate, dribble, effund, emanate, emerge, erupt, excrete, fling, gush, plenty, rant
EFFUSION effluence, effluvium, exudate, exudation, foison, ooze, spilth, stream
EFFUSIVE bubbling, diffuse, ebullient, exuberant, generous, gooey, gushy, lavish, loquacious, outpouring, sloppy, staturient
display backslapping
EFT after(ward), again, anon, ask, evat, evet, forthwith, lizard, newt, triton, triturus
EFTSOON See EFT.
EGAD adad, by jove, ecod, expletive, igad, sgad
EGBA yoruba
EGBERT, KING bretwalda
EGERIA adviser, asteroid, nymph
EGEST discharge, eliminate, excrete, perspire, void
EGEUS *daughter* hermia
EGG abet, ahuatle, albumen, balut, berry, blow, bomb, clutch, coal, cokeney, darner, easter, embryo, encourage, eyren, fellow, foment, germ, glair, goad, goog, graine, help, incite, instigate, kelk, nit, oeuf, oocyte, ooplast, oosperm, ova, ovule, ovum, peewee, protovum, roe, seed, setting, source, spawn, spur, stimulate, stone, urge, zygote
-and-dart echinus
and spirits copenhagen
bake shirr
beater helicopter, mixer
berry bird-cherry
bird (sooty) tern
bonnet water-shield
case ootheca, ovisac, pod, sac, shell
collector oologist
comb. oario, ovi
cracked check, leaker
deposit blow, lay, spawn
dessert blancmange, custard, zabaglione
dish omelet(te), souffle
dried ahuatle
drink flip, nog(g)

-eater red squirrel
feeding on ovivorous
fertilized oosperm, spermatovum, zoon, zygote
fish berry, caviar, roe
foo yong omelet(te)
formative part animal pole
fruit canistel, lacuma
germinating blastema
goose blob, zero
group clutch
hunt oologize
immature oocyte
infertile clear
insect larva, nit
large blockbuster, bomb
measurer oometer
mushroom chanterelle
nest clutch
on abet, drive, goad, hag, incite, needle, push, spur, stimulate, urge
order easy over, sunny side up
part albumen, archiblast, glair, latebra, shell, white, yelk, yellow, yolk
parthenogenetic pseudovum
pert. ovularium
poached moonshine, shirred
primitive protovum
product zoon
raw avgholemono, prairie oyster
-shaped elliptical, elliptoid, obovoid, ooid(al), oval (oid), ovate, oviform, ovoid
shell cascaron, shard
small ahuatle, caviar, nit, ovule, ovulum, pea, ree
small, comb. oario, ovule
strand chalaza, treadle
tester candler
timer sandglass
tissue blastema
to anger provoke
unfertilized oosphere
white albumen, glair
white and sugar meringue
white protein avidin
yolk lechithin, vitelline, vitellus, yellow
yolkless alecithal
EGGHEAD double-dome, highbrow, intellectual
EGGNOG advocaat, rompope
EGGPLANT aubergine, berengena, bringela, brinja (u)l, brown-jolly, jew's-apple, melanzana, melongena, solanum
EGHBAL *land* iran
EGIL *brother* volund

EGLAH *husband* david
son ithream
EGLANTINE dog-rose, honeysuckle, sweetbriar, woodbine
father pepin
husband valentine
EGLON *kingdom* moab
EGO amour-propre, atman, builder, conceit, fylgja, ideal, jivatma, pride, selfbuilder, selfpride, spirit
alter friend
EGOCENTRIC asocial, braggart, inseeing
EGO(T)ISM complacency, conceit, egomania, individualism, meanness, oneism, ownhood, possessiveness, pride, selfconfidence, selfesteem, selflove, selfness, smugness, vainglory, vanity
EGO(T)IST autothaumaturgist, narcissist, peacock, roadhog, selfadvancer, selfseeker, swellhead, temporizer, timeserver, tufthunter
EGREGIOUS absurd, exorbitant, extraordinary, fine, flagrant, glaring, gross, important, precious, shocking, terrible
EGRESS departure, disembogue, door(way), emanation, escape, exit, exodus, gate(way), gush, issuance, issue, opening, outcome, outgate, outlet, passage, port, proceed, sally, spurt, vent
EGRET aigrette, bird, fowl, gaulding, gaulin, heron, kotuku
-monkey macaque
EGYPT, EGYPTIAN black land, kem, misr, mizraim, nubia, uar, united arabian republic
adam atum, tum
air god shu
alloy asem
amulet menat
ancient copt
ancient city abydos, akhetaton, akhmim, apollinopolis magna, apu, arsinoe, asyut, avaris, busiris, buto, bybastis, canopus, coptos, crocodilopolis, dendera, edfu, heracleopolis magna, hermonthis, hermopolis, karnak, latopolis, letopolis, lycopolis, memphis, nekheb,

ombos, pelusium, perehbet, pharbaethos, sais, sebennytos, shedet, syene, thebes
animal adda, fox, gazelle, genet, hyena, hyrax, ichneumon, jackal, jerboa, lynx
animal, sacred aani, apis, banaded, buchis, lutembi, mendes, menuis, merwer, mnevis, onuphis, osorapis, petesuchos
ape, sacred aani
architect imhotep
army chief sirdar
artist god ptah
arum taro
ascetic pachomius
bay ab(o)ukir, foul
bean lotus
beer zythum
beetle scarab
bird ba-bird, ben(n)u, ibis, sicsac, wryneck
bird, sacred ben(n)u, ibis
boat baris, cangia, dahabeah, felucca, nuggar, sandal
body khet, sahu
bottle doruck
boy-king tutankhamun
bread herisa
bull apis, bacis, mont
bull, sacred apis, hapi, menuis, merwer, mneris, mnevis, onuphis
burial jar canopus
cactus fruit fig
calendar ahet, apap, choiak, hathor, mechir, mesore, pachons, paophi, payni, phamenoth, pharmuthi, shemu, thoth, tybi
canal suez
cap fez
capacity unit ardeb
cape banas, rasbanas, sudr
capital akhetaton, alexandria, alkahira, asyoot, cairo, cutor, elqshira, memphis, tell-el-amarna, thebes
captain rais, reis
catfish bagre, docmac
cat-headed goddess bast, mut, pakht, sekhet
chaos nun
childbirth goddess apet, bes, meskhent, nekhebet, opet, renenet, taueret
christian copt(ic)
city abu simbel, abydos, abydus, akhmin, alexandria, al-fustat, argo, ass(o)uan, aswan, asyut, aven, benha, benisuef, bubastis, bulaq,

bursaid, cairo, canopus, damietta, dumyat, dush, el alemein, el fostat, eltur, esna, girga, giza, gizeh, helwan, idfu, ismailia, isna, karnak, luxor, memphis, meroe, mut, nakhl, noph, pibeseth, port said, qena, raamses, rashid, rejaf, rosetta, sais, salum, sin, siwa, sohag, suez, tahta, tanis, tanta, thebes, zagazig, zoan
city, petrified ishmonie
city, ruined abydos
cloth galabeah, galabia, galabieh
clover berseem
coastal area gaza strip
cobra asp, haje
coin ahmadi, asper, bedidlik, dinar, dirham, fils, fodda(h), gersh, girsh, guinea, junayh, kees, maidin, medin(e), medino, millieme, para, piaster, pound, purse, riyal, tallard
commander sirdar
concubine hagar
conqueror amru, ashurbannipal, hyksos
cosmetic kohl
cotton maco, pima, sak(el), sakelardis
courtesan naucratis
cow-headed goddess hathor, isis, nut
creator khepera
crocodile-headed god amemait, sebek, sobk
crocodile, sacred lutembi, petesuchos
cross ankh
crown atef, pschent
cucumber mango-melon
cult copt, gnostic
culture amratian, badarian, tasian
dam assuan, aswan, sadd, sudd
dancer alma(h), alme(h), ghawazee, ghawazi
date saidi
dead, deity of amemait, amenti, anubis, horus, maat, ophois, osiris, sekhet, serapis, upuaut
dead, devourer of ammut
dead, judge of amemait, anubis, horus, maat, osiris
dead, protector of serket
dead, region of aalu, aaru, amenti
dead, servants of shawabti
dead, spirit of akh

dead, statues of shabtis, ushabtis
decoration colla
demon set(h)
depression quattara of the nile
descendant copt, fellah
desert libyan, nubian, sahara, scete, skete, tih
devil set(h)
diana pakht, sekhet
dish khoshaf, kofte
division markaz, mazor, pathros
dog saluki
dog-faced god hapi, thoth
drink bosa, boza(h)
drug nepenthe
dust storm khamsin
dye plant henna, hinna
dynasty hyksos, old kingdom
dynasty founder menes
earth god geb, keb, seb
elf ouphe
elysium aalu
embalming booth goodhouse
emblem aten, lotus
ennead geb, isis, nephthys, nut, osiris, ra-atum, set(h), shu, tefnut
ensign bull, crocodile, vulture
era, early amratian
estate daira
eternity god neheh(heh)
evil, god of set(h)
eye, symbolic uta
falcon-headed god harakhtera, horus, khonshor, mont, qebhsnuf, raharakhte
farmers fellahin
father atef
fertility symbol serapis
festival bubastis, busiris, bute, butis, hebsed, heliopolis, isis, papremis, sais
fish bagre, bichir, bouri, docmac, lates, mormyrid, siade
flower, sacred lotus
fortress magdala
frog-faced god heket
fruit fig
gambling game faro
garment galabeah, galabia
gate pylon
gecko fanfoot
gem aromatite
general ibrahim pasha, magdoub
genie hapi
giant caligorant
ginger taroroot
god (See also EGYPT *dead,*

deity of; god, animal-headed; sun god.) aah, amen(ra), amon, amun, anaka, anubis, apet, apuat, aten, atum, bast, bes(a), canopus, chnemu, djed, dje-huti, geb, harakhti, hor(us), imhotep, imhtimis, keb, khem, khensu, khepera, khnemu, khnum, knebera, ment, min, mnevis, neph, onnophris, onuphis, opet, osiris, pasht, ptah, re-harakhti, rhe, seb, seker, shu, sutekh, tefnut, tem, toth, tum, zehuti

god, animal-headed aani, aelurus, amemait, amen-ra, am(m)on, anubis, apis, ar-saphes, duamutef, hapi, harakhte-ra, hershef, khepri, khnemu, khons-hor, khunum, knenti, kneph, mont, nefertum, ophois, osorapis, pakht, qebhsnuf, sebek, set(h), sobk, thoth, upuaut

god, evil sebek

god, king amen, amon(ra), amun, geb

god, man-deified amenhotep, imhotep, pharaoh

god, primeval atum

god, queen of sati

god, supreme amen-ra

goddess (See also EGYPT childbirth goddess and god-dess, animal-headed.) amen(ti), anta, anuket, apet, athor, athyr, bast, buto, dor, ensos, hathor, iris, isis, iusaas, ken, kiun, maat, min, mut, nehmauit, neit(h), nephthys, nut, pakht, rat, sati, sekhet, sekhmet, seshat, shait, ta-weret, uert-hekeu

goddess, animal-headed ament, apet, bast, buto, hathor, heket, isis, met-seger, mut, nekhebet, nut, renet, sekhet, sekhmet, sel-kit, selquet, taurt, tefnut, thoueris

governor bey, mudir, pasha

governorate alexandria, ba-harya, bahriyah, sinai

grass halfeh, sadd, sudd

guard ghaf(f)ir

gulf aqaba

hades amenthes

harelike mammal hyrax

hawk-headed god horus

headdress uraeus

healer arabi

heart hati

heaven aalu, aaru, ialu, yaru

heavenly region field of reeds

herb anise

hercules sesortris

hermit saint anthony

hippo-headed deity amemait, apet, tauret

historian manetho

hydroelectric plant assuan, aswan

ibis-headed deity thoth

insignia uraeus

intelligence chu

island elephantine, philae, roda

isthmus suez

jackal-headed god anubis, ophois, upuaut

king (See also PHARAOH name.) akhenatem, akhna-ton, amenhotep, amenophis, arses, bebti, busiris, cheops, chephren, darius, djer, djet, epephus, euergetes, far(o)uk, f(o)uad, hophra, huny, ikhnaton, iti, ity, kebeh, k(h)afre, khufu, knian, meneptah, menes, menkure, meno, merneptah, narmer, nebka, necho, nefer, osorkon, pami, pepi, pharaoh(hophra), philome-tor, poseidon, proteus, psamtik, ptolemy, rameses, saladin, senedi, sesostris, seti, shishak, snefru, teos, thutmose, thuthmosis, tut, tutankhauen, tutenkhamun, udimu, unis, xerxes, zemti, zoser

king, heretic akhenaten

kingdom, ancient sennar

lake birket-el-karun, burul-lus, edku, idku, man-zaleh, mareotis, maryut, moeris

land feddan, goshen, sennar

land measure feddan

language arabic, coptic

leader hegazi, nasser, sadat

lighthouse pharos

lily calla, lotos, lotus

lion-headed goddess mut, ne-fertum, renenet, sekhmet, tefnut

lizard adda, scink, skink

lock dubbeh

lotus nymphaea, water lily

lute nabla

measure abdat, apt, arab, ardab, artaba, aurure, ba-

ladi, choryos, cubit, dari-bah, dira(baladi) (mi-mari), dra(a), farde, fed-dan, hen, kantar, kassabah, keddah, keleh, kerat, kharouba, khet, kilah, malouah, nief, ocha, rob(hah), roub(ouh), sahme, schene, theb, toum-nah, wudu

man deified amenhotep, im-hotep, pharaoh

mercenaries shardana

military class mameluke, mamlukg

millet shallu

monarch pharaoh

monster amemait

month See EGYPT calen-dar.

monument obelisk, sphinx

moon god aah, khons, thoth

moon goddess isis

mouse jerboa

mullet bouri

musical instrument arghool, sistrum

music god bes

musician almeh

name, hebrew mizraim

national party wafd

nature god osiris

nature goddess isis

necropolis valley of kings, valley of tombs

neolithic site al omari, ba-dari, deirtaso, merimde

new kingdom founder ah-mose

oasis bahariya, bahariyeh, dakhel, dakhla, farafra, kharga, khargeh, siwa, wah-el-khargeh

ocean god chaos, nun

official mudir, potiphar

opium thebain(e)

palace kubbeh

paper papyri, papyrus

peak gharib, katherina, sinai, uekia

peasant fellah

pebble jasper

peninsula pharos, sinai

people arab, badarian, berber, copt, gippy, gyppy, gypsy, hyksos, kem, mem-phian, misr, mizraim, mus-lim, nilot, nubian, pharian, tasian, wafd

period amarna, amratian, badarian, tasian

pharaoh See EGYPT king.

physician imhotep

plain asaseff

plant cum(m)in, kiki
plateau tih
pleasure goddess bast(et), hathor
plumb line merkhet
poison record ebers papyrus
policeman ghafir
port alexandria, attur, boolak, damietta, dumyat, el alemein, gaza, hurghada, quseir, raschid, rosetta, safaga, said, sallum, suez, tor
pound rotl
priest arbaces, choachyte, manetho, potipherah, psammetichus, stolist
privet henna, hinna
prostitute naucratis
province aljizah, aswan, asyut, beheira, benisuef, damietta, dumyat, faiyum, gharbiya, giza, ninufiya, minya, nome, qena, qina, sawhaj, sharqiya, sohag, tahrir
pump shadoof
pyramid builder cheops, imhotep
pyramid site giza
queen cleopatra, hatshepsut, khazneh, nefertiti, nofretete
rain goddess tefnut
ram-headed god amen, amon, amun, arsaphes, harsphes, hershef, khnum
ram, sacred banaded, baneb, djedet, mendes
rattle sistrum
reed byblus, papyrus
region nubia
religious center busiris, heliopolis, hermopolis, memphis
religious classic book of the dead
relic mummy
reservoir assuan, aswan
river bahr, nile
romance reciter anteri
rose scabious
royal symbol asp, flail, uraeus
ruins abydos, memphis, miroe, pyramids, sphinx, thebes
ruler ali, khedive, pharàoh, ptolemy, thot(h)mes, thut(h)mes, thutmosis
sage imhotep, ipuwer
sanctuary secos, sekos
sandal tatbeb
scarab god khepera, khepri
scarf yashmak
scorpion goddess selkit, selquet

scribe ani
seal scarab
season ahet, pert, shemu
serpent apepi, apeti, asp, buto, cobra, haje
shrub kat
skink adda
sky goddess hathor, nut
slate tablet palette of narmer
slave, military mamaluke, mameluke
snake goddess mer(t)seger
solar disk aten
somaliland punt
soul sahu
spirit akh, chu, sahu
stone rosetta
storyteller anteri
sultan saladin
sun god amen, amon, anhur(shu), aten, atum(ra), behdety, chepera, haroeris, herakhti, HORUS, khep(e)ra, khepri, osiris, phra, re-harakhte, rhe, shu, tem, tum
symbol ankh, asp, crook, flail, maat, scarab, serapis, uraeus, uta
talisman scarab
tambourine rikk
temple abydos, dendera, edoon, idfu, karnak, luxor, osiris, thoth
temple gate propylon, pylon
thief doxy
thorn babul, gonake, gonakie, kikar, pyracanth
title atef, calif, caliph, pasha, pharaoh, ptolemy
tomb mastaba, pyramid, serdab, syrinx
tomb cell serdab
tomb figurine shawabti, ushabti
tomb jar canopic, canopus
tomb site abydos, gerzean, gizeh, narmer, zer, zozor
tree ambatch, caliph willow, herminiera, kikar, sudd
underworld aaru, amenthes, amenti, duat
underworld god osiris, serapis
union sam-taui
uppers cotton
vegetable lentil, lupin, vetch
vegetation god seker
vessel canopic jar, canopus
viceroy ismail-pasha, khedive, mehemet ali
viper asp, cerates, cobra, haje, ouraios, uraeus
vulture dirtbird, nekhebet,

pharaoh's chicken, pharaoh's hen
war god anhur(shu), mont(menthu), onouris, sutekh
war goddess neith, sutekh
water bottle doruck
water-raising device sakieh, shadoof, tabut
waterwheel sakieh
waterway nile
weight artal, artel, deben, dera, drachma, hamlah, heml, kantar, kat, kerat, ket, khar, minae, minas, oke, ok(i)a, okieh, pound, quintal, ratel, rotl, uckia
well birtaba
wheat shallu
wind chamsim, k(h)amseen, k(h)amsin, samiel, simoon, sirocco
wisdom god thoth
wizard jambres, jannes, manbres
wonder pyramids
EH anan
EHEU alas
EHI *father* benjamin
EHLIS lucifer
EHRETIA anagua, anama, anaqua, cedar, tree
EHUD *parent* gera
son ahiah, gera, naaman
EIDER diver, down, duck, edder, quilt, shoreyer, somateria, wamp
-*down* bedcover, bedspread, fuzz, quilt
duck colk, spectacled, stellar's
EIDETIC remembered
EIDOLON apparition, emanation, ghost, idea, image, phantom
EIDOS form, idea, species
EIDOURANION observatory, orrery, planetarium
EIGHT acht, ait, aught, card, crew, echt, engine, eta, hachi, huit, ocho, octad, octonary, ogdoad, otto, utas
arranged in octamerous
-*ball, behind* in bad, in trouble, periled, trapped, troubled
bit byte
comb. oct(a)(o)
-*day* octan
-*day clock* solitaire
days, occurring every octan
feast days utas
-*fold path* buddhism, hinayana, mahayana

furlongs mile
group of octad, octave, octet(te), octonary, ogdoad
hundred omega
immortals (See IMMORTALS 8.)
multiply by octuple, octuplicate
off solitaire
penny nail
performers octet, octette
pert. octan, octic
pieces of reals
-point brevier
-sided octagonal
-tailed bandage cancer
tones diatonic, uncae
EIGHTEEN benedictions
abot, aboth
-carat genuine
inches cubit
EIGHTH *circle* octant
day after nones ides
feast utas
month august, bul, heshvan
note chroma, croma, quaver, unca
order octic
EIGHTY *-year old* octogenarian
EILD barren, milkless
EINSTEIN *theory* relativity
EINSTEINIUM *source* plutonium
EIONEUS *offspring* dia, rhesus
EIR *goddess of* healing, peace
EIRE See ERIN, IRELAND, IRISH.
EITH easy, eath
EITHER any, edder, ither, optionally, other, whether
of two rulers duumvir
EJACULATE blurt, discharge, disgorge, egest, eject, eliminate, exclaim, excrete, fling, say, spew, state, vomit
EJECT avoid, banish, belch, blow, boot, bounce, cashier, cast, chuck, disembogue, disgorge, dislodge, dismiss, displace, dispossess, drive out, eliminate, emit, eruct, erupt, evict, exclude, exile, expel, expulse, extrude, fire, force out, molt, oust, reject, sack, shed, spew, spit, spue, spurn, spurt, squirt, void, vomit
EJECTION blow, bum's rush, discharge, dispatch, eviction, expedition, expulsion,

extrusion, heave-ho, ouster, rejection, the boot
EKE add, also, appendix, augment, enlarge, etch, husband, imp, increase, lengthen, likewise, piece out, postscript, stretch, supplement, tab
out complete, kvetch(er), protract
ELA *son* shimel
ELABORATE complex, complicated, create, deluxe, detailed, devise, develop, dressy, elegant, embellish(ed), enlarge, expand, expatiate, explain, extend, fancy, fikie, improve, intricate, labor, labored, laborious, luxurious, ornate, painstaking, refine, repeat, specify, splendid
ELABORATENESS curiosity, fineness, grandeur
ELABORATION construction, decoration, development, production, refinement
ELAEOCARPUS blueberryash, brahman bead, quandong, tree
ELAH *father* caleb
steward arza
ELAINE lily maid
beloved lancelot
father pelles
home astolat
son galahad
ELAM susiana
capital shushan, susa
father shem
king arioch, chedorlaomer
son abdi, eliah, jehiel, jeremoth, mattaniah, zechariah
ELAMITE anzanian, susian
ELAN ardor, dash, drive, gusto, morale, pzazz, spirit, style, verve, warmth, zest
vital zoism
ELAND (cape)elk, impofo, taurotragus
ELAPSE advance, die, expire, flit, flow, fly, glide, go by, lapse, pass(by), press on, proceed, roll on, run its course, run out, slide, slip, vanish
ELARA *consort* zeus
son tityus
ELASMOBRANCH ray, shark
ELASTIC adaptable, adaptive, baleen, battledore, buoyant, cheveril, chewing

gum, ductile, expansive, extendible, extensible, extensile, flexible, flexile, garter, gum, limber, lithe, plastic, pliable, pliant, protractile, protractile, renitent, resilient, responsive, rubato, rubber, spring, springy, stretchable, stretchy, supple, tensible, tensile, volatile
filament elater
ELASTICITY adaptability, bounce, buoyance, buoyancy, ductility, flexibility, give, life, rebound, renitence, renitency, resilience, snap, spring, stretch, tensibility, tensility, tone, tonicity, verve
coefficient bulk-modulus
science elaterics
ELASTICIZE stent, stretch, vulcanize
ELATE animate, arride, cheer, delight, elevate(d), enliven, exalt, flush, gratify, left, lefty, please, raise, uplift
ELATED bucked(up), cheerful, chuff, crowing, ecstatic, exalted, exhilarated, exultant, flushed, gleeful, happy, high, inflated, joyful, joyous, perked, piquant, prideful, proud, puffed up, rad, rapturous, spirited, swollen, transported, uppish, vaudy, vogie, wlonk
ELATER beetle, elasticity, filament, skipjack
ELATH aqaba
ELATHA *son* bres
ELATION buoyancy, exultation, glee, happiness, joy, jubilation, triumph
ELATUS *daughter* caenis
ELB ber, jujube
ELBE labe
city on cuxhaven, dresden, hamburg
tribe eger, elde, havel, iser, ohre, mulde, saale
ELBOW ancon, arm, bend, crazybone, crowd, funnybone, hook, joint, jostle, nudge, oelcranon, pierdrop, poke, punch, push, shove, squeeze, thrust
bend drink, tope
bone ulna(e)
capped shoe-boil
cop couter
covers patches, sleeves
grease effort, friction, work
hollow chelidon

joint noop
-like anconoid
muscle anconeus
out at shabby
pain anconagra, anconitis
pert. anconeal, anconoid, ulnar
-piece cubitiere
shaking dicing, gambling
up to engrossed
ELBOWROOM latitude, leeway, scope, space
ELCAJA See MAFURRA.
ELCESAITES *founder* elkai
ELDAAH *parent* midian
ELDER aine, ancestor, ancient, bloodwort, bountree, bour, churchman, danewort, dean, earlier, ebul, ecclesiastic, eller, first (born), forefather, former, iva, mormon, older, oldest, oldster, presbyter, prior, sanbucus, senior, sheik, sire, starost, trammon, tree, udder
black hackberry
fungus jew's-ear
red cranberrytree
statesman genro, mentor, nestor, patriarch, solon
tree sambucus, trammon
ELDERLY aged, alder, ancient, badgerly, gray, hoary, old, senile, superannuated, veteran
ELDEST aine(e), eigne, first-born, oldest, senior
ELDORADO california, chief, treasure-land
capital manoa
ELDRITCH eerie, frightful, ghastly, uncanny, weird, wild
ELEAD *parent* ephraim
ELEASAH *son* sisamai
ELEAZAR *parent* aaron, eliud
son jason, matthan, phine-(h)as
ELECAMPANE canada, elfwort, herb, inula, scabwort, sweetmeat
root liquid alantol
ELECT appoint, best, call, choice, choose, chosen, cull, decide, elite, exclusive, fix, judge, name, nominate, opt, ordain, pick, prefer(red), rare, redeemed, resolve, saved, select, settle, single out, take, vote
to membership co-opt
ELECTION alternative,

choice, decision, option, preference, primary, proxy, runoff, selection, settlement
judge pollwatcher, scrutineer, scrutinizer
majority of votes plurality
-posies castilleja, painted-cup
predictor gallup, pollster
study psephology
ELECTIONEER campaign(er), canvass, speak, stump
ELECTIVE choice, option(al), spontaneous, voluntary
ELECTOR balloter, chooser, constitutent, eligent, elisor, voter
ELECTORATE constituency, people, public, voters
ELECTRA laodice, pleiad
brother orestes
daughter harpies, iris
husband pylades, thaumas
parent agamemnon, clytemnestra, oceanus, pleione, tethys
sister iphegenia
son dardanus
victim clytemnestra
ELECTRIC dynamic, galvanic, galvanizing, stimulating, streetcar, train, voltaic
amplifier maser
appliance blender, dryer, heater, iron, mixer, sparker, stepup, stove, toaster, washer
atmosphere aura
atom anion, electron, ion, kation
battery See BATTERY.
capacity See ELECTRIC *unit.*
carrier conductor, wire
catfish raad, torpedo
charge live wire
circuit conductor bus(s)
circuit, kind closed, complete, galvanic, hot, lateral, leg, loop, multiple, multiplex, mux, open, series, short
circuit regulator booster
coil tesla
column voltaic pile
components circuitry
conductor ohmage, solenoid
connection plug, terminal
current, kind alternating, conduction, convection, direct, exciting, galvanic,

high-frequency, idle, oscillating, reactive, rotary
current measurer ammeter, attenuator, coder, decremeter, ergometer, potamometer, rheometer, voltmeter, wattmeter
current, pert. audio, foradic, voltaic
current strength amperage
detective radar, sonar
device amplifier, anode, armature, capacitator, cathode, coil, condenser, distributor, divertor, dynamo, fuse, generator, ignition, maser, rheostat, rheotome, sensor, socket, sparkplug, starter, switch, timer, transformer
discharge arc, backstroke, flashover, shock, spark
flow current
force elod
generator dynamo
impedance reactance
ion See ELECTRIC *atom.*
light arc, incandescent, neon
light inventor edison
load demand
measure See ELECTRIC *unit.*
motor inventor davenport
motor part commutator
needle acusector
particle See ELECTRIC *atom.*
pole anode, cathode
power amperage, energy, wattage, voltage
power curtailment blackout, brownout
pressure barad, dyne
pressure detector tasimeter
principle ohm's law
property capitance
ray crampfish, numbfish
reluctance See ELECTRIC *resistance.*
resistance ballast, impedance, oerstad, ohmage, reactance, reluctance
resistance unit rel
safety device circuit breaker, fuse
strength amperage
switch mechanism selector
terminal electrode, pole
transmission radio
tube bulb, valve
unit abfarad, abhenry, abohm, abvolt, abwatt, ammeter, amp(ere), barad, begohm, bel, coulomb,

debye, dyne, elod, erg, farad, henry, hertz, joule, kilowatt, mega(dyne), megavolt, megawatt, mho, microcoulomb, milliampere, milliwatt, oersted, ohm, perm, proton, rel, statfarad, stathenry, statohm, statvolt, tesla, volt, watt(age), weber

wave detector cymoscope

wave measurer ondometer

wire cable, cord, lead, line

ELECTRICAL *genius* edison, marconi, tesla, volta

ELECTRICIAN boardman, faultsman, gaffer, groundman, grunt(er), juicer, lineman, rigger, sparks, troubleshooter

ELECTRICITY current, friction, galvanism, juice, pyrogen

ability to collect capacitance

charged with live

constituent anion

fear of electrophobia

static franklinism

ELECTRIFY agitate, amplify, arouse, charge, energize, enthuse, excite, galvanize, provoke, quicken, rally, rouse, shock, short (circuit), startle, stimulate, switch on, thrill, turn on

ELECTRODE anode, base, cathode, crowfoot, dee, dynode, grid, igniter, kathode, plate, rheophore

tube detector

ELECTROMAGNETIC *cylinder* solenoid

unit abampere abs(tat), gauss, gilbert, maxwell, oersted, weber

ELECTRON baryton, duplet, ion, meson, mesoton, negatron, polaron, positron, speck, thermion

and proton atomicule

flow cathode-ray

stream beta ray

ELECTRONIC *apparatus,* *pert.* audio

brain computer

control automation

detector radar, sonar

detonator fuse

device calutron, camera, computer, electric eye, fader, fuze, hearing aid, missile, neon tube, oscilloscope, pacemaker, radar, radio, satellite, tape re-

corder, telephone, television, transistor, vacuum tube, video

scientist ampere, bardeen, brattain, copernicus, edison, franklin, galileo, kelvin, kepler, kirchhoff, newton, ohm, shockley, tesla, thompson, volta

system condor

tube audion, diode, dunatron, excitron, geissler, heptagrid, heptode, ignitron, klystron, magnetron, pentode, phanotron, resnatron, strobotron, tetrode, thyratron, triode, varistor

ELECTROPHONE martenot

ELECTROTYPE cast, cliche, patch

process acrography

ELECTRUM alloy, amber, orichalc

ELECTRYON *grandson* hercules

kingdom mycenae

offspring alcmene, licymnius

parent andromeda, perseus

ELEEMOSYNARY almoner, altruistic, charitable, donee, dependent, free, gratis, philanthropic

ELEGANCE affectation, atticism, attic salt, beauty, chasteness, chastity, chic, clarity, classicism, comeliness, correctness, decency, discrimination, distinction, ease, euphemism, euphuism, fanciness, felicity, fineness, finish, flamboyance, floridness, floweriness, frippery, gentility, good taste, grace(fulness), grandeur, lux(e), luxury, ornateness, overniceness, polish, preciosity, propriety, purism, purity, refinement, restraint, seemliness, simplicity, splendor, style, swank, taste

ELEGANT aesthetic, artificial, artistic, attic, beauteous, beautiful, chic, choice, classical, courtly, cultivated, cultured, dainty, delicate, deluxe, dink, exquisite, fancy, fastidious, fine, finished, gent, good, graceful, grand, grazioso, handsome, lardydardy, luxurious, minikin, nice, noble, opulent, ornate, polished, polite, posh, rare, re-

cherche, refined, sharp, sleek, smart, smicker, splendid, sumptuous, swank(y), tasteful

expression atticism

style bonton

ELEGIAC epicedial, funereal, mournful poem

ELEGIST poet

ELEGY dirge, epicede, kinah, lament, monody, nenia, poem, qinah, requiem, song, threnody

ELEMENT agent, air, bit, carrier, cause, component, constituent, detail, drop, essence, ether, factor, feature, germ, ingredient, item, material, matter, metal, moment, origin, part, portion, principle, rect, rudiment, stuff, substance, trace, unit, woof

air argon, nitrogen, oxygen

alien alloy

alchemist's air, earth, fire, water

binding bond, cement, glue

chemical 3 tin 4 gold, iron, lead, neon, zinc 5 argon, boron, radon, xenon 6 barium, carbon, cerium, cesium, cobalt, copper, curium, erbium, helium, indium, iodine, nickel, osmium, oxygen, radium, silver, sodium, sulfur 7 arsenic, bismuth, bromine, cadmium, calcium, fallium, fermium, hafnium, holmium, iridium, krypton, lithium, mercury, niobium, rhenium, silicon, sulphur, terbium, thorium, thulium, uranium, wolfram, yttrium 8 actinium, aluminum, antimony, astatine, austrium, chlorine, chromium, europium, fluorine, francium, hydrogen, lutetium, nitrogen, nobelium, platinum, polonium, rubidium, samarium, scandium, selenium, tantalum, thallium, tungsten, vanadium 9 americium, berkelium, beryllium, columbium, germanium, lanthanum, magnesium, manganese, neodymium, neptunium, palladium, plutonium, potassium, ruthenium, strontium, tellurium, tintanium, ytterbium, zirconium 10 dyspro-

sium, gadolinium, lawren-
cium, molybdenum, phos-
phorus, promethium, tech-
netium 11 californium, einsteinium
combining power valence
component atom, electron,
neutron, nucleus, proton
decomposed anion
devouring fire, flame
different weight isotope
dominant capsheaf
essential corpus
even valence artiad
5 earth, fire, metal, water,
wood
form of allotrope
4 air, earth, fire, water
gaseous argon, krypton,
neon, nitrogen, radon,
xenon
geometric simplex
halogen chlorine
hypothetical coronium, neb-
ulium, victorium, welsium
inflammable pyrogen
liquid bromin(e)
metallic antimony, cerium,
columbium, copper, gal-
lium, germanium, gold, hafnium, indium, iridium, lead,
radium, rhodium, ruthen-
ium, silver, tantalum, terbium, thallium, thorium,
thulium, titanium, tin, tungsten, yttrium, zinc, zir-
conium
minute monad
mixture didymium
moral daena
nonmetallic argon, boron,
bromin(e), carbon, chlo-
rine, iodin(e), nitrogen, oxygen, phosphorus, silicon,
sulphur
nonvolatile barium
pert. artiad, radical
poisonous arsenic
primal arche, guna, salt
principal staple
radioactive curium, francium, lawrencium, pluto-
nium, polonium, protec-
tinium, radium, radon,
thoron
rare cerium, erbium, hafnium, iridium, lanthanum,
palladium, rhenium, rho-
dium, tantalum, tellurium,
tungsten, yttrium
silver-white rubidium
similar isotope
soft lithium
sulfur-like tellurium

synthetic nobelium
trivalent praseodymium, promethium
white indium, silver
ELEMENTAL basic, fundamental, inchoate, material,
original, physical, primal,
primary, primordial, pure,
rudimental, rudimentary,
simple, ultimate, uncom-
bined
organism mondad
spirit gnome, salamander,
sylph, undine
ELEMENTARY basic, easy,
effortless, fundamental, initial, plain, rudimentary,
simple, simplified, ultimate
reader primer
ELEMI acouchi, anemi,
anime, brea, canarium, conima, elemin(e), matti,
oleoresin, protium, resin
constituent amyrin
source boswellia
ELENCH argument, dis-
proof, index, refutation,
sophism
ELENGE dreary, miserable,
remote, tedious
ELEOTRIS bighead, bullhead
ELEPHANT, ELEPHANT'S
airavata, bruta, bull, calf,
cow, giant, hathi, hatty,
jumbo, koomkie, loxodont,
mammoth, mastodon,
muckna, oliphant, pachy-
derm, proboscidian, punk,
rogue, tusker
apple bel
apple tree feronia
boy sabu
-carrying bird roc
corral kraal
cry barr
decoy koomkie
dentin ivory
driver mahout
ear begonia, dieffenbachia,
dumbcane, fern, taro(root)
extinct archidiskodon, mammoth, mastodon
famous babar
female cow
fictional babar
fish joseph, josup
-foot hottentot-bread, tes-
tudinaria, tortoise-plant
goad ankus
god ganes(h)a
grass cattail, pennisetum,
reed-mace
group herd
keeper mahout

male bull
pen kraal
pert. pachydermic, probos-
cidean
pink hallucination
saddle or seat howdah
shrew jumper
snare kheda
staff ankus
symbol of intelligence, sagacity, wisdom
trappings jhool
trunk proboscis
tusk ivory, scrivello, tooth-
shell
white albino
young calf
ELEPHANTINE big, bulky,
clumsy, colossal, dull, enormous, gargantuan, giant, gigantic, heavy, herculean,
huge, immense, large,
mammoth, titanic, vast
ELETTARIA cardamon, cardamum
ELEUSIS *priests* eumolpides
shrine anaktoron
ELEUT kalmu(c)k, kalmyk,
mongol
ELEUTHERIOS dionysus,
zeus
ELEVATE advance, aggrandize, appoint, ascend, boost,
dignify, dredge, elate,
emboss, enhance, ennoble,
erect, exalt, glorify, grimp,
hain, heave, heft, heighten,
hoist, honor, inspire, jump,
levitate, lift, magnify,
mount, promote, raise,
ramp, rear, refine, rise,
rocket, soar, stilt, tower,
uprear
ELEVATED alpine, amotus,
exalted, fine, grandiloquent,
great, high, lifted, lofty,
majestic, mountainous,
noble, raised, risen, rising,
stilted, uplifted, winged
ELEVATION advancement,
altitude, alto, anagogue, ascent, bugor, dignity, drawing, eminence, erection,
evection, exaltation, furcula, height, hill, importance, incentive, levitation,
lift, lofting, majesty,
mound, mountain, nobility,
plan, preferment, promo-
tion, raise, raising, rearing,
rideau, ridge, rise, shoal,
spur, stature, steep, suble-
vation, sublimation, swell
(ing), tower, upcast, up-

heaval, uplift, upright, upthrow, upthrust, vantage
point, wheal
broad bank
cartilage anthelix
measure bench-mark
measurer abney level, apo-
mecometer
of mind anagoge
skin bleb, blister, wheal
vertical altitude
ELEVATOR ascenseur, bin,
cage, car, crane, dredge,
dumbwaiter, escalator,
granary, hoist(er), lift,
moving, rig, silo, stacker,
stairway, teagle, uplifter,
uptaker, wing
door opener bow-iron
inventor otis
ELEVEN *comb.* hendec(a)
kings angwyshaunce, bran-
degoris, carados, clari-
vaunce, cradilment, idres,
lot, morganoure, nentres,
uryens
ELEVENTH elft
hour crisis, night
zodiac sign aquarius
ELF banshee, blastie,
brat(ling), brownie, changeling, cluricaune, drac, drow,
dwarf, erlking, fairy, fane,
fay, gnome, goblin, hob,
imp, incubus, kobold, leprechaun, nix(ie), oaf, ouph(e),
peri, pixie, pixy, puck,
rogue, shee, sprite, succubus, urchin
bore knothole
child changeling, oaf
dock elecampane
domain alfheim
fire ignis-fatuus
in counsel alfreda
personifying the present verdandi
ruler aubrey, erlking
shelter toadstool
-stricken bewitched
ELFIN butterfly, child, eldritch, fairylike, fey, impish, pixyish, thecla, tricksy,
urchin
ELFLAND fairyland, make-
believe
ELFWORT elecampane
EL GRECO theotokopoulos
ELI *pupil* samuel
son hophni, phine(h)as
ELIAB *parent* jesse
son chelkias
ELIADA *captain of* jehoshaphat

father david
ELIAH *parent* elam
ELIAKIM *son* azor, melea
ELIAM *daughter* bathsheba
ELIAS elijah
son helkias
ELIASAPH *father* lael
ELIASHIB *parent* elioenai
son johanan, joiada
ELICIT arouse, bring forth,
bring out, call out, deduce,
derive, discover, drag out,
draw(out), educe, evoke,
evolve, extort, extract,
fetch, induce, obtain, procure, prompt, pull, pump,
rouse, secure, stretch, summon, wangle, worm out
ELICUS jupiter
ELIDE abbreviate, dele(te),
eliminate, omit
ELIEL *father* shimei
ELIENAI *father* shimei
ELIEZER *parent* dodavah,
harim, moses, zipporah
son joshua
ELIGIBLE acceptable, admissible, apt, authorized, available, catch, competent, desirable, entitled, fit(ted), licensed, marriageable, meet,
nubile, privileged, qualified,
suitable, worthy
ELIHU *father* shemaiah
son jeroham
ELIJACH *parent* harim
ELIJAH, ELIJAH'S elias,
john the baptist, prophet
cup fifth
flight chariot of fire
slayer jezabel
successor elisha
ELIMELECH *wife* naomi
ELIMINATE abolish, blackball, cancel, cast off, chuck,
clear(out), cut(off), dele,
detach, devar, disbar, discard, dismiss, dispose of,
drop, efface, egest, ejaculate, eject, elide, eradicate,
erase, evacuate, evict, exclude, excrete, expel, expunge, exterminate, get rid
of, kill, leave out, liquidate,
omit, oust, pick out, purge,
remove, rid, root, rule out,
scissor, scotch, scrap, scrub,
scuttle, separate, shut out,
sift, suspend, throw over,
uproot, weed out, winnow
ELIMINATION abrogation,
catharsis, deletion, discard,
discharge, disposal, ejection, eradication, expulsion,

extermination, extinction,
homicide, liquidation,
purge, rasure, removal,
strip, withdrawal
ELINOR OF AQUITAINE
husband henri plantagenet,
louis vii
son king john
ELIOENAI *parent* neariah
son akkub, anani, dalaiah,
eliashib, hodaiah, johanan,
pelaiah
ELIOT, GEORGE mary ann
evans
husband george henry lewes,
john cross
novel adam bede, felix holt,
middlemarch, mill on the
floss, romola, silas marner
ELIOT, T. S. *play* cocktail
party, family reunion
poem ash wednesday, burnt
norton, dry salvages, east
coker, four quartets, hollow
men, little gidding, wasteland
ELIPHAZ *friend* job
parent adah, esau
son amalek, gatam, kenaz,
omar, teman, timna, zephi,
zepho
ELIPHELET *parent* david,
hashum
ELISHA *father* abujah, shaphat
home abelmeholah
predecessor elijah
servant genazi
ELISHAH *father* javan
grandfather noah
ELISHEBA *husband* aaron
ELISHUA *father* david
ELISION abridgement, apocopation, haplology, syncope
mark apostrophe
ELISSA See DIDO.
ELITE aristocracy, best, cafe
society, choice, chosen,
county, cream, estab-
lishment, flower, four hundred, galaxy, gentry, high
society, nobility, nobles, patricians, perfecti, privileged,
select, social circle, social
register, society, stars, type
corps green berets, marines
gathering galaxy
guard schutzstaffel
ELIUD *son* eleazar
ELIXER amreeta, amrita, arcanum, catholicon, cordial,
cureall, extract, haoma,
medicine, panacea, quintes-
sense, rasa, sama, spirit

of life ruby
of love letterleaf
ELIZABETH bess, betsy, lizzie, oriana, queen bess
husband zechariah
queen cynthia, little betty blue, little maid, oriana
queen, adviser burghley, burleigh
queen, attempted assassinator babington
queen, courtier devereux
queen, enemy erin
queen, favorite dudley, essex, leicester, walter raleigh
queen, jester patch, wallet
queen, mother anne boleyn
queen, tutor ascham
saint, symbol lamb
ELIZABETHAN *figure* anjou, buckhurst, burleigh, cecil, drake, dudley, effingham, essex, frobisher, harrington, hatton, hawkins, hertford, howard, lady jane grey, leicester, pembroke, raleigh, shakespeare, shrewsbury, walsingham, worcester
jingle cat and fiddle
theater globe
ELIZAPHAN *father* levi
son jeiel, shimri
ELK, ELKS aland, alces, bpoe, cervid, deer, eland, goose, leather, losh, moose, sambar, sambhur, swan, wapiti
bark bay, big-bloom, magnolia
call bugle
group gang
hide losh
nut buffalotree, pyrularia, rabbitwood
tree sorrel
ELKANAH *son* samuel
wife hannah
ELKSLIP marsh-marigold
ELKWOOD umbrellatree
ELL addition, angle, annex, aune, dependence, elbow, extension, measure, ulna, wing
ELLAS See GREECE.
ELLASAR *king* arioch
ELLEN *consort* lochinvar
ELLFISH menhaden
ELLIPSE curve, oblate, oblong, oval, ovoid
ELLIPTICAL oblong, oval, ovate, rectangular
aggregate auge, augengabbro

ELM chewbark, elven, hackberry, mescal, mezcal, orhamwood, orme, shrub, tree, ulm(e), ulmus, wahoo
borer lamiid
fruit samara
genus celtis, planera, trema, ulmus
kind basket, cork, mezcal, slippery, wych
rock or wing wahoo
state tree of massachusetts, nebraska, north dakota
winged wahoo
ELMADAM *son* cosam
ELMIRE *husband* orgon
ELOAH See GOD.
ELOCUTION diction, eloquence, oratory, speech
ELOCUTIONIST improvisator, reader, reciter, speaker
ELOIGN abscond, conceal, convey, remove
ELON *offspring* adah, bashemath
son-in-law esau
ELONGATE extend, lengthen, prolong, protract, remove, stretch
ELONGATED extended, lank, lengthy, linear, oblong, prolate, prolonged, protracted, slender, stretched
ELOPE abscond, decamp, escape, flee
ELOPS albula, awa, chiro, herring, ladyfish, menhaden
ELOQUENCE elocution, expression, facund(ity), fluency, gift of gab, oratory, rhetoric, significance, silver tongue, vividness
deity benten, bragi, hermes, mercury, ogmios, sarasvati
ELOQUENT articulate, ciceronian, demosthenic, expressive, fervid, fluent, glib, grandiloquent, graphic, impassioned, meaningful, mercurial, oratorical, picturesque, potent, powerful, rhetorical, significant, silver-tongued, telling, tullian, vivid, vocal, voluble, well-spoken
ELOTH *builder* uzziah
ELPAAL *son* beriah, eber, heber, hezeki, ismerai, jezliah, jobab, meshullam, misham, shamed, shema, zebadiah

ELPENOR *companion* odysseus, ulleses
ELSA *groom* lohengrin
EL SALVADOR san miguel
city acajutla, corinto, cutuco, izalco, metapan, santa ana, usultan
coin centavo, colon, peso
dance pasillo
gulf fonseca
indian lenca, mangue, matagalpa, pipil
lake guiha, ilopango
measure batella, cafiz, cahiz, cajuela, cantara, fanega, manzana, tercia, vara
point remedios
port acajutla, cutuco
river jiboa, lapaz, lempa
ruins tazumal
volcano izalco
weight bag, caja, libra
ELSE additional, also, and, besides, contrarily, different, ens(e), instead, noch, other (wise), too
ELSENE txelles
ELSEWHERE alibi, away, except, thence
ELUCIDATE clear, construe, explain, explicate, expound, interpret, simplify
ELUDE avoid, baffle, beet, beguile, bilk, dodge, double, escape, eschew, evade, flee, fly, foil, frustrate, outwit, shun, thwart
ELUSIVE baffling, deceptive, eely, elusory, equivocal, evasive, fugacious, fugitive, impalpable, impermanent, lubric, shifty, shy, slick, slippery, subtle, tricky, twisty, volatile
ELUTRIATE clean, purify, refine, strain
ELYSIAN beatific, blissful, delightful, heavenly
ELYSIUM annwin, bliss, eden, paradise, utopia
ELYTRON husk, scale, scute, shard, sheath, sherd
ELYTRUM shard, tegmen
ELZABAD *father* shemaiah
EMACIATED atrophied, cadaverous, consumptive, empty, gaunt, haggard, lean, meager, peaked, poor, skeletal, skinny, tabetic, thin, wasted
EMACIATION atrophy, attenuation, cachexia, cachexy, cancer, lankness, leanness, macies, maras-

mus, niton, reducing, symtosis, tabefaction, tabes, thinning, waste, weakness

EMANATE appear, arise, begin, breathe, come, commence, derive, egress, emerge, emit, exhale, exude, flow, follow, initiate, issue, loom, originate, proceed, radiate, result, rise, spring, start, stem, exit

EMANATION aura(e), beam, blas, breath, ectoplasm, ectoplasy, effluvium, efflux, eidolon, emergence, emission, fug, glory, issuance, issue, light, nidor, niton, odor, outcome, perfume, process, radiation, sephira, vapor, wind
from divine nature azilut
from stars blas
psychic aura

EMANCIPATE affranchise, deliver, discharge, enfranchise, free, liberate, manumit, release, rescue, unfetter, unshackle

EMANCIPATION freedom, release
final nirvana

EMANCIPATOR deliverer, freer, lincoln, redeemer

EMASCULATE castrate, enervate, evirate, geld, neutralize, soften, sterilize

EMATHION *parent* eos, tithonys
slayer hercules

EMBALM balsam(ize), cere, condite, enshrine, mummify, perfume, preserve, season

EMBALMING *booth* goodhouse
jar canopic vase

EMBANK bund, fortify

EMBANKMENT argin, bank, banquette, barrier, barrow, bund, bunker, buttress, dam, digue, dike, dune, dyke, fill, fortificaion, heap, hill, levee, mound, pilapil, pile, quay, rampart, rampire, revet, road, seawall, shore, shoulder, staith, terrace, tumulus
hole gime

EMBARGO ban, blockade, edict, imbarge, prohibition, stoppage

EMBARK board, depart, emplane, engage, enlist, enter, entrain, go aboard, invest, launch, put to sea, sail, send, ship, start, take off, weigh anchor
on begin, set about, set out

EMBARRASS abash, affront, annoy, bewilder, boggle, chagrin, chaw, confuse, cumber, discomfit, disconcert, distress, disturb, encumber, entrike, faze, fease, feeze, flummox, gravel, hamper, handicap, harass, hinder, hobble, impede, impester, involve, mortify, nonplus, obstruct, perplex, rattle, shackle, shame, straiten, trouble, upset
financially stop credit

EMBARRASSED abashed, ashamed, chagrined, chapfallen, chopfallen, crestfallen, encumbered, flurried, hangdog, humiliated, mortified, poor, selfconscious, shamefaced, sheepish, uncomfortable

EMBARRASSING awkward, confused, crushing, disconcerting, disturbing, hideous, messy, mortifying, uncomfortable, unpleasant

EMBARRASSMENT caddle, chagrin, discomfort, discomposure, fix, hobble, humiliation, impediment, implication, lurch, poverty, pudency, puzzle, riches, shame
expression of whoops

EMBASSY errand, inbassat, legation, message, mission, residence

EMBATTLED bretesse, crenele(d), crenelee

EMBAY bathe, detain, encircle, enclose, shelter, suffuse, surround

EMBED bond, charge, embowel, engage, ensconce, establish, fix, immerse, set, stamp

EMBELLISH adorn, amplify, array, beautify, bedeck, blazon, bough, deck, decorate, dress, elaborate, emboss, enhance, enrich, exaggerate, falsify, fudge, garnish, gem, gild, grace, heighten, intensify, mystify, ornament, rouge, trim, varnish

EMBELLISHED brocaded, colored, euphuistic, florid, flowery, focused, gested, highflown, ornate, rhetorical, splendid

EMBELLISHMENT agremen, arabesque, exornation, fil(1)ip, flourish, gilding, grace, ornament, parergon, superfluity, trapping, tricking

EMBER aizle, ash, brand, cinder, clinker, coal, firebrand, gleed, isle, izle, remainder, spark

EMBERIZA black-bonnet, (reed)bunting

EMBEZZLE appropriate, confiscate, filch, lift, loot, misappropriate, peculate, pilfer, plunder, purloin, rifle, rob, steal

EMBEZZLER See THIEF.

EMBITTER acerbate, acidify, acidulate, aggravate, alienate, antagonize, curdle, envenom, exacerbate, poison, provoke, sour, venom, verjuice

EMBITTERED acerbate, farbissen(eh), soured

EMBLAZON adorn, color, decorate, display, exhibit, extol, glorify, laud, praise

EMBLAZONED bristled, cloue(e), crested, crined

EMBLEM attribute, badge, bar, bee, brand, crest, cross, design, device, diadem, eagle, fasces, favor, fetish, figure, flag, image, insigne, insignia, mace, mark, motif, pattern, sabcat, scepter, seal, shield, sign, star, stripes, symbol, token, totem, trademark, trisul, type
carved totem
revolutionary red flag
sacred hierogram

EMBLEMATIC figural, symbolic, typal, typical

EMBLIC amla, aula, myrobalan

EMBODIMENT avatar, cast, combination, composition, conformation, epitome, form, genius, image(ry), incarnation, incorporation, matter, representation, self, son, whole

EMBODY actualize, coalesce, comprise, contain, embrace, express, externalize, identify, incarnate, include, incorporate, involve, materialize, objectify, organize,

personify, realize, reify, symbolize, unite

EMBOLDEN assure, bield, bowden, brave, encourage, enhardy, erect, fortify, hearten, nerve, stiffen, stomach

EMBOLISM, EMBOLUS clot, intercalation, obstruction, occlusion, stoppage, wedge

EMBOSOM cherish, embrace, enclose, foster, secrete, shelter, surround

EMBOSS adorn, block, chase, enclose, exhaust, gauffer, goffer, indent, inflate, knob, knot, ornament, pounce

EMBOSSED antique, bold, champed, raised
cypress water-pine

EMBRACE abrazo, accept, accolade, accoll, adopt, assume, bearhug, bosom, caress, cherish, choose, clasp, clip, clutch, coll, comprehend, comprise, contain, cradle, crush, cuddle, embody, embosom, enarm, encompass, enfold(ment), espouse, grasp, greet(ing), halse, hass, hold, hug, implicate, imply, inarm, include, incorporate, involve, love, press, receive, seize, squeeze, subsume, surround, take, welcome, wrap
rough bearhug
tight clinch

EMBRACING clipping, colling, comprehensive, including, osculant

EMBRASURE battlement, crenel(le), loop, port (hole), recess, vent

EMBROCATION arnica, balm, embroche, fomentation, liniment, poultice, stupe

EMBROIDER adorn, broud, color, couch, darn, embellish, exaggerate, faggot, falsify, fret, frieze, heighten, lace, ornament, purfle, purl, romanticize, sew, smock, stitch, surfle, tambour, tat, work

EMBROIDERED brocaded, brode(e), browden

EMBROIDERY appenzell, bonnaz, brede, crocheting, decoration, hedebo, lace, needlework, ornament,

orphrey, superfluity, tapestry, tatting
fabric arrasene, bolting-cloth
figure etoile, tabouret
frame hoop, ring, tabo(u)ret, tambour
hole eyelet
machine-made bonnaz
mottoed sampler
on tapestry setwork
open spokestitch
stitch bre(a)dstitch, figure of eight, gros point
style appenzell, crewelwork, cutwork, faggoting, orphrey
yarn crewel

EMBROIL confuse, disorder, distract, disunite, embrangle, entangle, involve, jumble, perplex, snarl, trouble

EMBROILMENT agitation, brawl, contest, turbulence, uproar

EMBRYO acanthor, anlage, blastocyst, blastosphere, blastula, bud, cadet, gastrula, germ, larva, neurula, nymph, ovule, principe, rudiment, source
comb. amnio, blasto
fluid amnion, blastochyle
intestine metagaster
metazoan gastrula
opening neuropore
origin theory epigenesis
term blastocoele, blastoderm, blastomere, blastopore, blastula
young blastema, bastosphere, blastula

EMBRYONIC beginning, germinal, microbic, original
vesicle egg

EMCEE host, master of ceremonies

EME aunt, friend, gossip, neighbor, uncle, yeme

EMELYE *husband* palaemon

EMEND adapt, ameliorate, amend, better, correct, criticize, edit, improve, rectify, redress, remedy, repair, revise, right, write

EMERALD beryl, emerant, emeraude, gem, green, jewel, prasine, smaragd
copper dioptase
fish esmeralda, goby
isle eire, erin, ireland
moth hipparchus
nickel zaratite
pert. smaragdine
planet mars

zodiac sign cancer

EMERGE appear, arise, bob, bolt, break(cover), burst forth, dawn, debouch, derive, disembogue, effuse, emanate, erupt, extrude, exude, flow, gush, issue, loom, occur, originate, pend, plunge, proceed, rise, sally(forth), spring, spurt, start, stem, stream

EMERGENCE appearance, beginning, birth, discharge, eclosion, egress, emanation, emission, escape, exigence, growth, issuance, issue, vent

EMERGENCY contingency, crisis, difficulty, exigency, juncture, necessity, need, pass, pend, pinch, push, state, strait, urgency, vicissitude
signal flare
system dew line, hot line

EMERGING budding, emanent, rising

EMERSON *friend* thoreau
philosophy transcendentalism
poem brahma, monadnoc, rhodora
work english traits, nature, representative men, selfreliance, the oversoul

EMERY abradant, abrasive, corundum, file, grind, smiris

EMETIC alangine, alum, anacarthartic, apomorphine, azedarach, caroba, chinaberry, cocillana, evacuant, ipecac, mustard, nauseant, puke(r), remedy, vomit (ive), vomitory
holly yaupon
root spurge
source antidote-lily, crinum

EMEUTE outbreak, revolt, tumult

EMIGRANT alien, colonist, evacuee, exile, exodist, expatriot, migrant, migrator, patarin(e), refugee, settler, stranger

EMIGRATION exodus, hegira, hejira, removal, swarming

EMILIA cacalia, plant, tasselflower
husband iago
mistress desdemona, hermione, perdita
slayer iago
sweetheart peregrine pickle

EMIM giants, moabites

EMINENCE altitude, berg, cardinal, celebrity, crag, dignity, elevation, fame, height, highland, hill, importance, influence, knoll, note, prestige, prominence, protuberance, rank, renown, repute, rideau, rise, scar, superiority, title, tor, upland, upperhand, vip
grise confidant

EMINENT arch, celebrated, chief, conspicuous, distinguished, elevated, exalted, famed, famous, great, high, illustrious, important, lofty, notable, noted, notorious, outstanding, prominent, renowned, shining, signal

EMIR chieftain, commander, dignitary, prince, ruler
province emirate

EMISSARY agent, ambassador, delegate, deputy, envoy, intelligencer, legate, messenger, minister, missionary, nuncio, representative, scout, spy

EMIT beam, belch, cast, discharge, eject, emanate, eruct, excrete, exhale, exhaust, exude, give off, gush, issue, ooze, outpour, pour, puff, radiate, reek, say, shed, smeech, squirt, throw off, utter, void, yield

EMMA *consort* king canute

EMMENTHALER gruyere

EMMER amelcorn, speltz, triticum, wheat

EMMET ant, formicid, pismire

EMOLLIENT balm, demulcent, lenient, lotion, malactic, nard, ointment, salve, softening, soothing, suppling

EMOLUMENT compensation, fee, gain, hire, honorarium, income, lucre, pay, perquisite, profit, remuneration, salary, screw, stipend, wage

EMOTE act, feel, grimace, gush, ham, mug, overact, rant, sentimentalize, slop over, spout

EMOTION affect(ion), agitation, anger, elan, excitement, feeling, heart, ire, love, onde, passion, pathos, sensibility, sentiment, spleen, tremor, tug

center bosom, heart
comb. thymo
controlling leitmotif, leitmotiv
person without apathist
pert. pathematic
vacuum anomie
without aloof, apathetic, cold, cool, dull, impassive, indifferent, passive, phlegmatic, staid, torpid, unconcerned, unfeeling, uninterested

EMOTIONAL ablaze, affectional, affective, attitudinal, demonstrative, drippy, feeling, gooey, inflamed, on fire, sensitive, sensuous, soulful, spoon(e)y, stirring, temperamental, touching
disturbance anxiety, apathy, catatonia, dejection, depression, detachment, euphoria, hypochondria, hysteria, hysterics, indifference, melancholia, preoccupation, stupor, unresponsiveness
release catharsis
stability balance, sanity
tone atmosphere

EMOTIONALISM breastbeating, melodrama, s(c)hmaltz

EMPAISTIC embossed, inlaid, stamped

EMPATHY accord, commiseration, compassion, condolence, fellow-feeling, imagination, passion, pity, ruth, sympathy, transference, understanding, warmth

EMPEROR abkar, atahualpa, baginda, boa, caesar, commander, czar, fish, goose, imperator, imperial, inca, kaiser, king, mikado, mogul, monarch, moth, padishah, penquin, potentate, ruler, sovereign, tenno, tsar, tzar
deceased divus
eastern basileus
of germany solitaire

EMPERY domain, dominion, empire, government, sovereignty

EMPHASIS accent, birr, cadence, charge, energy, force, impetus, meter, push, stress, thrust, vigor, weight

EMPHASIZE accent(uate), advertise, advertize, betone, dwell on, highlight, insist, mark, point up, punctuate,

spearhead, spotlight, star, stress, underline, underscore
by contrast counterpoint

EMPHATIC absolute, accented, accentuated, affirmative, decided, energetic, forceful, forcible, important, marcato, marked, pointed, positive, punctuated, stressed, sure, underlined

EMPIDONAX flycatcher

EMPIRE diadem, domain, dominion, government, kingdom, power, reign, rule, sovereignty, state, sway
ancient assyria, aztec, babylon, mogul
city new york, wellington
cloth cambric, insulation
hidden See ETHIOPIA.
holder of darius
holy roman See HOLY roman empire.
of the rising sun japan
red vermilion
state new york
state of the south georgia

EMPIRIC charlatan, dabbler, dilettante, empirical, experimental, faker, imposter, mountebank, quack, tyro

EMPIRICAL experienced, experimental, observed, practical

EMPIRICISM charlatanry, experiment, observation, quackery

EMPIRICIST virtuoso

EMPLACEMENT localization, location, platform, situation

EMPLASTRUM bandage, dressing

EMPLOY adopt, apply, bespeak, bestow, build, busy, choose, commission, contract for, enclose, engage, engross, enlist, exercise, exert, hire, infold, involve, occupy, pay, pick, place, practice, put on, retain, select, service, sign on, spend, supply, take on, use, utilize, work

EMPLOYEE attendant, cad, clerk, domestic, factotum, hired hand, hired help, hireling, lackey, maid, mercenary, servant, steward, wage earner, waiter, worker, workman

dinner bean-feast, beano
minor assistant, cog, helper, underling
EMPLOYER bloke, boss, director, gaffer, hirer, joss, manager, master, superintendent, supervisor, taskmaster, user
EMPLOYMENT action, adoption, application, appointment, business, calling, career, commission, draft, engagement, field, hire, job, metier, occupation, place-(ment), position, profession, pursuit, retainer, service, trade, usance, usage, vocation, work
agent padrone
EMPORIUM bazaar, etape, market, mart, monopole, shop, store, supermart
EMPOWER accredit, appoint, arm, authorize, capacitate, commission, discipline, enable, endow, endue, instruct, invest, qualify, sanction, teach, train, vest
EMPRESS begum, czarina, imperatrix, kaiserin, maharani, princess, queen (mother), rank, ruler, sultana, tsarina
of india solitaire
tree paulownia
EMPRISE adventure, endeavor, enterprise, prowess, renown, undertake
EMPTINESS appetite, blank, hollowness, inanition, vacancy
EMPTOR buyer
EMPTY abandoned, addle, arid, bare, barren, baseless, blank, bleak, bleed, bootless, bottom, bubble, clean, clear, depleted, deprive, desert(ed), desolate, destitute, devoid, disgorge, dishonest, drain(ed), dry, dull, dump, emaciated, evacuate, exhausted, futile, gaunt, godforsaken, hollow, howe, hungry, idle, ignorant, inane, inexpressive, insincere, invalid, lean, nugatory, null (and void), otiose, pour, rid, scoop, stark, strung, superficial, teem, toom, trivial, unfilled, uninhabited, unload, unoccupied, unpopulated, va-

cant, vacate, vacuous, vain, void, without
comb. ken(o)
head calabash
-headed blank, ignorant, rattlebrained, scatterbrained, stupid, thoughtless, vacant, vacuous
space atmosphere, blank, vacuum, void
talk nonsense
to last drop buzz
EMPUSA fungus, hobgoblin, monster, specter
EMPYREAL, EMPYREAN aerial, aether, airy, blue, celestial, delightful, ether (eal), firmament, heaven (ly), heavens, paradise, sky
EMU apple, bird, dromiceius, millet, ratite, rhea, tree
apple bitterbark, colane
bush berrigan, pholidia
eggs kully-koomurra
grass millet
-like bird cassowary
wren stipiture
EMULATE ape, compete, copy, envy, equal, follow suit, imitate, match, model after, pattern, rival, strive, take after, touch, vie
EMULATION contest, rivalry
EMULOUS agog, aiming, ambitious, aspiring, athirst, avid, eager, keen, panting
EMULSIFY beat up, churn, cream, homogenize, whip
EMULSION demulcent, fluid, liquid, solution, suspension
EMYD, EMYS terrapin, tortoise, turtle
ENABLE adapt, allow, authorize, capacitate, decree, empower, endow, enjoin, implement, invest, let, make possible, ordain, permit, qualify
ENACT accomplish, actuate, authorize, command, decree, depict, effect, enjoin, impersonate, influence, legislate, ordain, pass, perform, play, portray, represent, stage
ENACTMENT assize(s), bill, canon, decree, edict, law, legislation, ordinance, sanction, statute, usage, veto
ENAMEL adorn, aumail, dentine, email, embellish,

glaze, gloss, paint, porcelain, schmaltz(e), shippo, smalto, stain, varnish
call adamantoblast
defect in sagging, scab, scumming
inlaid cloisonne, shippo
source borax
technique bassetaille, champleve
ENAMELWARE cloisonne
ENAMOR captivate, charm, love, smite
ENAMORATO See SWEETHEART.
ENAMORED ardent, bewitched, captivated, charmed, devoted, doting, enraptured, epris(e), fargone, fascinated, fond, hard hit, infatuated, in love, loving, smitten
ENAN *parent* ahira
princess naphtali
ENARETE *daughter* calyce
husband aeolus
son athamus, salmoneus
ENAROPHORUS *father* hippacoon
ENATION affinity, agnation, cognation, consanguinity
ENCAMP assemble, bivouac, lodge, pitch, siege, stop, teld, tent
ENCAMPMENT abode, bivouac, camp, castramentation, etape, laager, location, lodge, tent
ENCASE package
ENCAUSTIC cerograph, painting
ENCEINTE body, close, plot, pregnant
ENCELADUS *moon of* saturn
parent gaea, tartarus, tellus
slayer zeus
wife amymone
ENCEPHALON brain, cerebrum
ENCHAIN bind, encircle, enslave, fasten, fetter, hold, incatenate, lodge, manacle, pin, restrain, rivet, shackle
ENCHANT allure, attract, bedazzle, bespell, bewitch, captivate, catch, charm, delectate, delight, enamor, enrapture, ensorcell, enthrall, fascinate, gladden, gratify, please, rejoice, spellbind, take, transport
ENCHANTER alquife, archi-

mage, charmer, circe, magician, siren, sorcerer
herb vervain

ENCHANTMENT allurement, cantation, caract, charm, conjuration, devilry, hex, incantation, joy, magic, necromancy, sorcery, spell, witchcraft, witchery

ENCHANTRESS charmer, circe, lorelei, medea, siren, sorceress, witch

ENCHASE carve, emboss, enclose, engrave, enshrine, incase

ENCHORIAL demotic, domestic, native

ENCINCTURE encircle, encirclement, enclosure, environment, girdle, surround

ENCIRCLE band, belt, betrend, bind, brace, circle, circuit, circumscribe, clasp, cover, embay, embrace, enclose, encompass, enfold, engirt, enlace, enring, envelope, environ, fathom, frame, gird, girt, hem, inclose, include, inorb, invest, orb, ring, round, span, surround, zone

ENCIRCLEMENT belt, embowment, embrace, environment, maneuver, siege

ENCLAVE enclose, plot, surround, territory, tract

ENCLOSE beset, bottle, bought, bower, box, bught, cabin, cage, capsule, case, circumscribe, contain, coop, corral, curtain, embower, encircle, encompass, enshrine, envelop, fence, frame, harness, hedge, hem, impound, imprison, incase, include, inwall, pen, sheathe, surround, wrap

ENCLOSED barred, bound, cabined, cloistered, confined, cooped, cribbed, fenced, fortified, hedged, hemmed, immured, ingrown, mewed, obtect, paled, penned, pent-up, protected, railed, secure, shut in, walled
places, fear of claustrophobia

ENCLOSING *comb.* peri

ENCLOSURE aedicule, atajo, bait, barnyard, barrier, barton, bawn, boma(r), booly, box, byth,

cab, cage, canaut, cancha, carol, cattlefold, chickencoop, cincture, cloister, cofferdam, compound, confine, coop, corral, court (yard), crawl, crib, croft, cruive, curtilage, delubrum, dooryard, farmyard, fence, hencoop, hutch, jail, kapalama, keddah, kench, kraal, lanai, list, manger, navelle, paddock, pale, paling, pasture, patio, pen, pightle, pigpen, pinfold, pound, quad(rangle), run(way), sekos, sept, seraglio, sheepcote, sheepfold, square, stadium, stall, stockade, stockyard, sty, vivery, warren, wynd, yard
armored casemate, pillbox
circular byth
protective zareba
sacred sekos, shrine

ENCOMIUM acclaim, applause, commendation, compliment, eloge, eulogium, eulogy, extollation, laudation, panegyric, plaudit, praise, tribute

ENCOMPASS accomplish, begird, bego, beleaguer, belt, beset, besiege, circuit, circumscribe, cover, embrace, encircle, gird, girt, include, invest, outwit, pale, ring, round, subsume, surround, wall, wrap

ENCOMPASSED amid(st), bayed, begirt, ringed

ENCOMPASSING ambient, around, circumferent, comprehensive, profound, round

ENCORE acclaim, afresh, again, altra volta, ancora, anew, anon, bis, da capo, de novo, echo, more, next, over, reappearance, recall, repeat, repetition, return, twice
anti boo, catcall, hiss

ENCOUNTER action, affront, assail, attack, battle, bear, bide, breast, brush, bump, clash, close with, collide, collision, combat, come upon, concurrence, conflict, confront, contest, discover, dispute, experience, face, fall foul of, fight, find, fray, greet, impact, joining, jostle, meet(ing), occur, op-

pose, recontre, rencounter, run afoul of, skirmish, stour, struggle, undergo
courageously beard, brave, weather
hostile fight

ENCOURAGE abet, advance, aid, animate, assure, back up, boost, brace up, buck up, buoy, buttress, cheer, comfort, console, countenance, egg, elate, embolden, enforce, exhort, feed, foster, further, hearten, help, incite, inspire, inspirit, invite, nerve, nourish, nurture, promote, rally, reassure, rehete, second, spirit, stimulate, support, uphold, urge

ENCOURAGEMENT blessing, boost, build-up, bulwark, exhortation, impetus, incentive, inspiration, sanction, solace
expression of yoicks

ENCOURAGING auspicious, bright, cohortative, favoring, helpful, inspiriting, propitious

ENCROACH butt in, enter, exceed, extravagate, horn in, impinge, infringe, interfere, interlope, intrude, invade, lap over, obtrude, overlap, overrun, overstep, penetrate, pierce, poach, presume, probe, surpass, transcend, trench, trespass, usurp, violate

ENCROACHMENT breach, impingement, infringement, inroad, intrusion, invasion, overlap, transcendence, transgression, trespass, violation

ENCUMBER add, beset, burden, check, clog, complicate, crowd, embarrass, felter, fetter, hamper, hinder, impede, load, lumber, obstruct, oppress, overburden, overload, retard, saddle, weight(down)

ENCUMBERED congested, embarrassed, heavy, in debt(ed), involved, laden, tied up, weighted

ENCUMBRANCE affliction, burden, charge, child, claim, debt, dependent, impediment, incubus, lien, mortgage, onus, oppression, perplexity, responsibility, trouble

ENCYCLICAL correspondence, letter, literature, pandect, pascendi, piece, study, treatise

ENCYCLOPAEDIA britannica

ENCYCLOPEDIC comprehensive

ENCYCLOPEDIST author, compiler, polyhistor, writer

ENCYST encapsulate, enclose, package

END 3 aim, die, lot, neb, nib, tag, tip, toe, top 4 butt, coda, doom, fate, fine, foot, goal, halt, heel, kayo, kill, over, part, pass, quit, shut, stay, stem, stop, stub, tail, taps, term, wane 5 artha, bound, bourn, cause, cease, check, close, death, envoi, final, finis, issue, lapse, limit, omega, piece, point, share, stall, stump 6 arrest, be done, capper, climax, corker, demise, design, exitus, expire, expiry, finale, finish, intent, izzard, kibosh, lenvoi, object, payoff, period, perish, result, run out, thirty, upshot, wash up, wind up 7 abolish, abuttal, blowoff, call off, cincher, clapper, closing, confine, decline, destiny, destroy, extreme, last lap, lineman, outcome, product, purpose, quietus, remnant, wear off 8 abutment, apodosis, boundary, clincher, complete, conclude, cut short, finality, fragment, knock out, swan song, terminal, terminus, ultimate 9 antipodes, cessation, culminate, determine, dispose of, extremity, flattener, intention, objective, polish off, remainder, terminate 10 armageddon, completion, conclusion, denouement, expiration, put a stop to 11 catastrophe, consequence, coup de grace, culmination, destination, destruction, dissolution, homestretch 12 annihilation, consummation
approaching vergent
at abut
at the ad finem
-brain telencephalon
comb. acro, tel(o)

loose tag
of the line blank wall, terminal, terminus
of the world armageddon, crack of doom, day of judgment, doomsday, gotterdammerung, pralaya
on afoul
paper flyleaf
piece brace, chump
pin button
plea abater
pointed apex, cusp(is), neb, nib, point, prong, spire
remove clip, tip
result product
scraper grattoir
tapering point, spire
tending toward telic
to end adjacent
to the ad fin, jusqu'au bout
upper acme, apex, cabeza, head, top
without leger

ENDANGER burn, compromise, hazard, imperil, jeopardize, peril, risk, threaten

ENDANGERED behind the eight ball, bestead, difficult, fraught, in dutch, in trouble, out on a limb

ENDEARING affectionate, amatory, pet

ENDEARMENT blandishment, caress, soft words, sweet talk
term achree, acushla, agrah, alannah, angel, aroon, aruin, asthor(e), astor, avourneen, babe, baby, bobeleh, bonito, bubby, bubeleh, bunting, cherub, chick, chickabiddy, darling, dear(ie), deary, duck(ling), honey(bunch), lamb, love(r), pet(kins), precious, snookums, storeen, sugar, sweet, sweetheart, sweetie

ENDEAVOR affair, afforce, aim, apply, assay, attempt, determine, effort, emprise, emulate, enterprise, essay, ettle, exert(ion), intend, labor, nisus, pains, resolve, seek, strain, strive, striving, struggle, study, toil, travail, trial, trouble, try, venture, vie, work

ENDED all off, all over, concluded, conclusive, decided, done, final, fini(shed), over, past, settled, terminal, ter-

minated, through, washed up, wound up

ENDEMIC aboriginal, characteristic, contagious, exotic, indigene, indigenous, native, pandemic

ENDING close, coda, conclusion, death, desinent, end, envoi, epilogue, finale, moribund, summation, terminal
comparative ier, ior
having same conterminous, coterminous
slangy eroo
superlative est

ENDIVE chicory, escarole, witloof
-blue iris

ENDLESS ananta, boundless, ceaseless, constant, continuous, dateless, deathless, eternal, eterne, everlasting, immense, immortal, incessant, infinite, innumerable, interminable, limitless, measureless, neverending, perdurable, perpetual, timeless, unceasing, undying, unended, universal, unlimited, unremitting

ENDLESSLY ad infinitum, ad nauseam, always, eternally, forever, perpetually

ENDLONG horizontally, lengthwise, longitudinally, vertical(ly)

ENDMOST farthest, remotest

ENDOCRINE autocoid, gland, hormone, secretion

ENDOGAMY inbreeding, procreation

ENDOPITE petasma

ENDORSE abet, acclaim, advocate, approve, attest, back, boost, certify, champion, confirm, cosign, countersign, endoss, guarantee, join, praise, ratify, recommend, sanction, second, sign, sponsor, subscribe, superscribe, support, underwrite, uphold, vouch for, warrant, witness

ENDORSEMENT allonge, approval, backing, codicil, consent, permission, rider, sanction, support, visa, vise

ENDOW assign, beautify, bequeath, bequest, bestow, bless, charter, clothe, confer, crown, devise, dotate, dote, dower, due, empower, enable, endue, enrich, entail, entalent, equip,

furnish, give, grace, grant, hand down, invest, leave, pass on, provide, settle on, transmit, vest in, will
with bodily form materialize
with power energize

ENDOWED able, capable, gifted, intestate, pensionary, skilled, stipendiary, subsidiary, testamentary, testate

ENDOWMENT ability, appanage, bequest, boon, bounty, capacity, caparison, chantry, charism, dot, dotation, dower, dowry, faculty, foundation, genius, gift, grant, investment, largess(e), portion, present, settlement, talent

ENDSHIP suburb, village

ENDUE accouter, bestow, clothe, confer, digest, dower, dress, ENDOW, enrich, equip, furnish, invest, outfit, supply, teach, vest

ENDURANCE bearance, bent, comfort, durability, gameness, guts, patience, pluck, stamina, strength, substantiality, tolerance
requiring backbreaking

ENDURE abear, abide, aby(e), accept, afford, bear(up), bide, brave, brook, carry(on), cling, condone, continue, dree, dwell, exist, experience, extend, harden, hold on, keep, last, linger, live, maintain, outlast, outlive, perdure, perennate, persevere, persist, prevail, put up with, remain, run on, stand, stay, stick, submit, suffer, support, survive, sustain, swallow, take it, tarry, thole, tolerate, undergo, wait, wear, withstand

ENDURING bearing, continuing, durable, eternal, fast, lasting, immortal, permanent, persevering, remembered, solid, stable, stout, sturdy

ENDWAYS, ENDWISE adjacent, ahead, continuously, erectly, forward, lengthwise, vertically

ENDYMION *beloved* artemis, selene
loved by selene
mother calyce
son aetolus

ENEMA clyster, glyster, lavage, lavement, remedy, sprinkler

ENEMY adversary, antagonist, assailant, combatant, competitor, devil, disputant, feid, fiend, foe(man), frenne, hater, offense, opponent, opposition, philistine, rival, satan, unfriend
public criminal

ENERGETIC active, aggressive, animated, assiduous, brisk, bursting, bustling, busy, byronesque, byronic, dashy, demonic, diligent, driving, emphatic, enterprising, forceful, fresh, industrious, lively, lusty, melancholy, melodramatic, nervous, potent, powerful, pushing, stirring, stout, strenuous, striving, sturdy, vibrant, vigorous, vital, yauld, zippy
person demon, dynamo, eager beaver, fireball, life of the party, trojan

ENERGIZE actify, activate, activize, animate, arouse, brace, electrify, enliven, excite, fortify, galvanize, ignite, innervate, invigorate, launch, mobilize, pep up, quicken, rally, rouse, spark, stimulate, stir, vitalize

ENERGIZER activator, animater, dynamo, force, power, sparkplug, stimulant, stimulator, stimulus

ENERGUMEN demoniac, enthusiast, fanatic, lunatic

ENERGY activity, ado, ambition, animation, arm, atomic power, bang, bent, birr, blood, bounce, bustle, dash, drive, dynamism, edge, emphasis, endurance, enterprise, erg(al), foison, force, fortitude, get-up-and-go, git-up, horsepower, impetus, initiative, input, intensity, jiva, life, mettle, might, momentum, orgone, pep, pizzazz, potency, power, puissance, punch, push, resilience, s(h)akti, sap, snap, spirit, spizzerinctum, stamina, starch, sthenia, strength, thrust, verve, vigo(u)r, vim, vitality, work, zest, zip
emission radiation
emotional cathexis, libido

lack anemia, aneuria, asthenia, atony, debility, inertia, laziness, neurasthenia, sloth
light rad
measure See ENERGY *unit.*
measuring device bolometer, ergometer
mental docity, psychurgy
neural psychokyme
path ergodic
pert. actinic, dynamic, isenergic
potential edar, ergal, latency
-requiring endergonic
source coal, electricity, fuel, gas, geothermal, offshore drilling, oil, peat, shale, solar, steam, sun
unit atomerg, dinamode, dyne, erg(on), energid, footpound, footton, horsepower, joule, kilogrammeter, kilowatt hour, megajoule, megerg, photon, poundal, quantum, rad
vital horme, panzoism
without doless, dud, thewless, thowless, tired

ENERVATE abase, bush, debilitate, demean, devitalize, disable, drain, enfeeble, exhaust, fatigue, jade, mollify, sap, tire, undermine, unman, unnerve, weaken, weary

ENERVATED bedrid, debilitated, decadent, deteriorated, effete, enfeebled, exhausted, lackadaisical, languid, languishing, limp, listless, spent, spiritless, weakened

ENFEEBLE afflict, appal(l), cripple, disable, ENERVATE, harm, impair, injure, mar, sap, soften, undermine, unnerve, unstrong, weaken

ENFILADE barrage, bomb, rake

ENFLE game, rolling-stone, schwellen, stops

ENFOLD clasp, comply, cover, drape, embrace, enlace, enroll, enwind, enwrap, envelop, surround, swathe, umbelap, wattle

ENFORCE administer, administrate, apply, compel, constrain, discharge, execute, force, fulfill, goad, implement, ivoke, lash, levy, oblige, perform, urge

ENFORCED compulsory, obligatory

ENFORCER hitman, muscleman

ENFRANCHISE authorize, deliver, emancipate, free, liberate, manumit, release

ENG *and chang* siamese twins

ENGAGE absorb, accept, affiance, affy, agree, allure, answer for, apply, arrest, assent, attach, attract, bargain, bespeak, betroth, bind, book, busy, charter, commit, consume, contract, covenant, do battle, employ, engross, enlist, enter, fasten, fight, guarantee, hire, hook, induce, involve, join battle, lock, mesh, obligate, occupy, persuade, place, pledge, plight, practice, promise, rent, reserve, retain, subscribe, take on, tie, undertake, use
attention attract
in embark on, join, launch, lead, undertake
in debate stonewall

ENGAGED active, assured, attached, betrothed, booked, busy, earnest, embedded, employed, fast, gone, hired, interested, involved, meshed, occupied, pledged, promised, zealous
in about
in, comb. ary
in thought absorbed

ENGAGEMENT absorption, action, affair, affiance, appointment, bargain, battle, betrothal, brush, combat, commitment, conflict, contest, cowle, date, employment, encounter, espousal, fight, fray, hire, implication, placement, position, push, rendezvous, skirmish, sponsalia, sponsion, surety, troth, tryst, undertaking
short snap
single gig

ENGAGING attractive, charming, delightful, soft, sweet, winning, winsome

ENGENDER arouse, bear, beget, breed, bring about, create, excite, generate, get, occasion, originate, procreate, produce, promote, prompt, propagate, provoke, quicken, reproduce, rouse, sire, start, stimulate, stir, yield

ENGIDU eabani
comrade gilgamesh
creator aruru
insulted ishtar

ENGINE ability, agent, apparatus, appliance, artifice, capacity, contrivance, ingenuity, invention, machine(ry), mallet, means, method, motor, net, rack, skill, tool, trap, turbine, wile
auxiliary booster
cover cowling
hydraulic ram
inventor daimler, lenoir
kind corliss, corvy, diesel, dinkey, dollbeer, donkey, dynamo, dynamotor, generator, gin, helper, hydraulic, hydrojet, jet, locomotive, mallet, mazda, mogul, mule, outboard, piston, pusher, ramjet, rotary, steam, turbine, turbojet, wankel, yarder
lifting noria, ram, sakieh, shadoff
part bearing, boiler, cam(shaft), carburetor, choke, crankcase, cylinder, differential, flywheel, gear, piston, stator, transmission
pilot cowcatcher
pipe slouch
railroad diesel, goat, hog, switcher, yarder
rotary turbine
small puffer, spinning jenny
war arbalest, artillery, ballista, battering-ram, boar, bomb, cannon, catapult, dondaine, dondine, espringal, gun, half-track, helepole, jeep, mangonel, martinet, missile, mortar, onager, ordnance, perrier, ram, robinet, rocket, ribaudequin, scorpion, tank, terebra, trebuchet, trebucket, trepan, turtle, warwolf

ENGINEER accomplish, casey jones, cat-skinner, conduct(or), control, direct, driver, fanner, generate, guide, hogger, hoghead, ingenier, lokeyman, manage, maneuver, motorman, operate, operator, pilot, plot, sapper, seabee, steer
assistant flunk(e)y
place cab

ENGINEERING building, construction, intrigue
device bascule

ENGINOUS crafty, ingenious

ENGLAND albion, angleterre, anglia, beretania, blighty, britain, britannia, egbert, great britain, inghilterra, john bull, limeyland, lo(e)gria, logris, punch, sceptered isle
abbey tintern, westminster
abbot aelfric
aborigine pict
actor arliss, booth, burbage, burton, coward, donat, evans, forbes, garrick, gielgud, grimaldi, guinness, gwenn, hardwicke, irving, maude, olivier, redgrave, richardson, robertson, terry, tree
actress ashcroft, campbell, evans, gwyn, kemble, langtry, lawrence, neagle, redgrave, siddons, terry, thorndike, woffington
admiral beatty, benbow, blake, buckingham, drake, fisher, jellicoe, nelson, penn, rodney, vernon
admirer of anglophile
adventurer brooke, burton, smith, trelawney
airforce raf
airline boac, new caledonian
airport croydon, gatwick, heathrow
air-sea group rnas
ale bitter
allowance tantum
antarctic explorer scott, shackleton
anthologist palgrave
anthropologist haddon, leakey, rivers
apartment flat
apostle augustine, austin
apple beaufin, beefin, biffin, coccagee coling, costard, guarenden, rennet, ribston
apron barmskin
archaeological site sutton hoo
archaeologist evans, lawrence, layard, leakey, petrie, smith, wooley
archbishop becket, lang, laud, pole
architect abercrombie, adam, barry, bodley, denham, eastlake, harrison, hawksmoor, jones, lutyens, nash, scott,

soane, vanbrugh, ventris, wren, wyatt
architect, naval brunel
arctic explorer ross
aristophanes foot
armor corium
army kettle dixie, dixy
army, old fyrd
art critic fry, ruskin
art gallery tate
art historian binyon, clark, gombrich
artist See *painter* below.
artists' society royal academy
assembly folkemoot
astrologer dee
astronomer baily de la rue, dyson, eddington, flamsteed, halley, herschel, lockyer, lovell, mason
astrophysicist jeans
athlete bannister
atticus addison
auto part bonnet, boot, mudguard, windscreen
auto trunk boot
autumn st martin's summer
bacon gammon, streaky
badger hawker
bailiff reeve
bank holiday boxing day, whit monday
banker rothschild
bar association inns of court
bard beowulf, scop
barge trow
barilla black ash, kelp
basket caul, ped, trug
bathhouse hydro
battle agincourt, agned, badon, blenheim, camlann, celidon, crecy, dubglass, evesham, glein, guinnion, hastings, ramillies, saratoga, tribuit, waterloo
battle wagon ornest
bay bideford, bigbury, cardigan, falmouth, lyme, mounts, tremadoc, wash, weymouth
bean mazagan, scarletrunner
bed doss
beer grout, stout
beggar badgeman
bent redtop
berry bramble
bible translation coverdale, douay, king james, tyndale, wycliffe
biochemist haldane, hopkins, martin, sanger, synge

biographer boswell, evelyn, lee, strachey
biologist huxley
biophysicist crick, hodgkin, martin
bird annet, bottlebump, godwit, kestrel, lammergeier
biscuit bathbun, bath oliver
bishop latimer, stubbs, swithin
black country midlands
bluebell wood-hyacinth
bluegrass fescue, poa
boat bawley, billyboy, coracle, keel, trow
bodyguard housecarl
botanical garden kew
botanist bennett, cattley, fraser, lindley
boxer fitzsimmons
boys' school See *public school* below.
brass bathmetal
breadslice canch
bride's gift dos, dot, dower
broadsword fox
brook beck
buffet scuff
bunk doss
bush scray
buttercup crowtoe
butter dish ruskin
cake batty
canal worker navvy
candy sweety
cap mutch
cape tintagel
capers capuchin
capital london
cardinal manning, pole, wolsey
caricaturist ape, beerbohm, cruikshank, rowlandson, spy
carpet kidderminster
carriage fly, growler
cascade ladore
cassandra adversity hume
castle arundel, sandringham, windsor
cat baudrons
cathedral canterbury, coventry, durham, ely, exeter, hereford, lincoln, norwich, salisbury, st paul's, wells, winchester, worcester, york
cattail dod(d)
cattle devon, durham, hereford, longhorn, sussex, teeswater
cattle shelter barth
cattle tender byreman
cavalry yeomanry
central region midlands

chair farthingale
channel bristol, leat, sleeve, solent, spithead
channel boat groper, lerret
channel island alderney, guernsey, jersey, sark
channel port boulogne, calais, dover, dunkirk, folkestone, trouville
channel, river into ouse, somme
channel rocks eddystone
charity scholar blue-coat
cheese cheddar, cheshire, gloucester, stilton, truckle, wiltshire
chemise sark
chemist abel, ashton, cavendish, dalton, davy, frankland, haworth, hinshelwood, hodgkin, perkin, perutz, robinson, smithson, soddy, wilkinson
chest highboy, tallboy
chicken cornish, dorking, orpington, sussex
chieftain caractacus, caradoc, cassibelan, cassivelaunus, pendragon
child tacker
chimney tun
china See *porcelain* below.
choreographer ashton, de valois
chronicle brut, harleian
chronicler bede, eusebius, geoffrey, gildas, holinshed, jerome, nennius, prosper
church caretaker berger
church officer beadle
church seat frith-stool
cigar smoker churchill
circuit court eyre
city 3 ayr, ely rye 4 bath, deal, hull, ryde, ware, york 5 acton, derby, dover, leeds, lewes, ripon, rugby, truro, wigan 6 barnet, barrow, bolton, bootle, camden, durham, ealing, exeter, hendon, ilford, leyton, london, oxford 7 banbury, bedford, bristol, bromley, chelsea, chester, croydon, grimsby, hornsey, ipswich, lambeth, margate, newport, norwich, preston, reading, taunton, walsall, wembley 8 brighton, carlisle, cornwall, coventry, hastings, hereford, hertford, peterlee, plymouth, ramsgate, richmond, st albans 9 aldershot, blackpool, cambridge, doncaster,

leicester, lichfield, liverpool, maidstone, mansfield, newmarket, rochester, rotherham, salisbury, sheffield, stevanage, stockport, tottenham 10 birmingham, canterbury, dorchester, manchester, nottingham, pontefract, shrewsbury, twickenham, warrington, winchester 11 bournemouth, northampton, walthamstow 12 peterborough, stoke on trent 13 burton on trent, bury st edmunds, wolverhampton 15 stratford on avon

civil wars bishops, roses

class form

class, lower oik

classical scholar murray

clergyman becket, donne, inge, keble, kingsley, latimer, law, neale, newman, oates, paley, pusey, smith, stanley, sterne, trench, wesley

cloth See *fabric* below.

coal broker crimp

coal measure corf

code deciphering ultra

coin ackey, angel(et), bawbee, bob, bodle, carolus, crockard, crown, dandiprat, decus, dollar, drake, dubs, farthing, fiver, florin, fourpence, george, groat, guinea, half-crown, ha(lf)-penny, harrington, jacobus, laurel, logger, mag, marigold, mark, mite, monkey, noble, ora, pence, penny, plack, plum, pound, quid, rial, ryal, seskin, shilling, sixpence, sovereign, sprat, tanner, teston, threepence, thrippence, tuppence, tuppenny, twopence, unicorn

college See CAMBRIDGE, OXFORD.

college account battel

colonial capitalist rhodes

colony fiji, grenada, honduras, singapore, st helena

columbine doves-foot

comedian chaplin, gingold, guinness, toole

comic weekly ally sloper

commander-in-chief haig

commonwealth island tobago, trinidad

communistic group agapemone

composer arne, balfe, bax,

britten, burney, byrd, coates, delius, dowland, dunstable, elgar, gay, gibbons, gilbert, goosens, handel, holst, lambert, lawes, leginska, mellers, neale, purcel(le), scott, stainer, sullivan, taverner, tosti, tovey, walton, watts, williams

conductor barbirolli, beecham, boult, lambert, sargent

conqueror caesar, hengist, horsa, romans, william

conservative tory

conspirator guy fawkes

constitution magna charta

converter augustine

conveyance moped, tram, waggon

cookie biscuit

coot bell-kite

coppers pence

coronation desk faldstool

coronation robe dalmatic

coronation sword curtana

corporal lance-jack

cotton city manchester

council witan

country, ancient anglia, dalriada, danelaw, deira, east anglia, essex, hibernia, ireland, kent, mercia, northumbria, pictland, scotia, sussex, wales, wessex

country dance anglaise, popgoes-the-weasel

country festival ale

county bedfordshire, berks(hire), buckingham(shire), bucks, cambridgeshire, cheshire, cornwall, cumberland, derby (shire), devon(shire), dorset(shire), durham, essex, gloucestor, hampshire, hants, hereford(shire), huntingdon(shire), hunts, isle of ely, kent, lancashire, lancaster, lincoln(shire), london, middlesex, norfolk, northampton(shire), northumberland, nottinghamshire, rad, rutland, salop, somerset(shire), southampton, suffolk, surrey, sussex, warwick(shire), westmorland, wight, wiltshire, worcestershire, york(shire)

county division hundred, lath(e), rape, riding, wapentake, ward

county hundreds lathes, rapes

court eyre, forty-days, gemot, hustling, leet, old bailey, soc, soke

court section witness box

cow parsnip bears-breech

cravat crumpler

crib cot

critic arnold, beerbohm, bell, drinkwater, empson, hazlitt, huxley, leavis, lee, lewes, palgrave, pater, quiller-couch, read, ruskin, saintsbury, shairp, sitwell, stephen, strachey, swinnerton

crook critch

crown dick's hatband

crown tax geld

customs officer landwaiter

daisy avens, bennet, bruisewort, burnet, gowan, hemlock, herb bennet, soapwort, valerian

dance althea, anglaise, argeers, bobbing joan, brawle, cebell, hornpipe, lancers, morris, newcastle, trenchmore

dancer ashton, beriosova, dolin, fonteyn, markova

dandy beau brummel, toff

deist tindal

delinquents' school borstal

designer beaton

dessert fool, sillibub, syllabub, trifle

diaper napkin

diarist evelyn, pepys

diplomat bryce, bulwer, digby, eden, elyot, nicolson, stratford

dish bubble and squeak, kidney pie, toad-in-the-hole, yorkshire pudding

dishcloth rubber

ditch haha

dog otterhound, staffordshire

domain manor

donkey fussock

dramatist barrie, beaumont, beddoes, besier, betterton, congreve, coward, dane, decker, dekker, drinkwater, dryden, dunsany, etherege, farquhar, fletcher, ford, fry, gay, gilbert, granvillebarker, greene, heywood, jerome, jones, jonson, kyd, lewis, lillo, lodge, lyly, lytton, marlowe, marston, massinger, middleton, nashe, osborne, otway, peele, pinero, pinter, rat-

tigan, reade, shadwell, shakespeare, shaw, sherriff, shirley, steele, tobin, vanbrugh, webster, wilde, wycherley
dressing table beau brummel
drink ale, squash
duck aylesbury, marionette
dwarf coppernin, decker, gibson, hudson, jarvis, stocker, wanmer
economist angell, bagehot, beveridge, bright, gresham, jackson, jevons, keynes, malthus, marshall, martineau, mill, ricardo, webb
editor addison, mee, steele
editorial leader
educator arnold, birkbeck, colet, shairp, sherriff
elm campestris
emblem lion, rose, unicorn
enclosure barton, croft, hoarding
engineer bailey, baker, bessemer, bramah, brunel, froude, smeaton, stokes, whittle
engraver bewick, hogarth
entertainment busk, ridotto
epic beowulf
epithet perfidious albion
essayist addison, bacon, beerbohm, belloc, de quincey, elia, hallam, hazlitt, huxley, lamb, lang, orwell, raleigh, sala, steele
etcher hadon
evangelist wesley, whitefield
examination eleven-plus, smalls, tripos, viva(voce)
exclamation bloody, by george, cor, gorblimy
executioner ketch
explorer baffin, burton, cabot, cook, drake, franklin, frobisher, hudson, livingston, parry, raleigh, ross, scott, shackleton, stanley
fabric admiralty cloth, batswing, russel, tweed, worsted
falcon hobby, kestrel, peregrine
farm, small bargain, croft
farmer scullog(ue)
fashionable belgravian
fee feod
feminist germaine greer
festival ale, gaudy(night), lammas
feudal tenant radknight
field croft

field marshall alexander, allenby, french, kitchener, montgomery, wolseley
final course afters
financial center lombard street
financier beit, cityman, gresham, rothschild
fire tax fumage
firth solway
fish allice, allis, dragonet, plaice, sewen, sewin, shad, vendace
fishing boat trow
fish trap cruive
5-pound note finnip
5 towns potteries
flood spate
floor covering lino
fluorspar blue-john
flute recorder
food dealer costermonger
fool jack adams
football rugby, rugger
foreign minister bevan
forest arden, exmoor, new, sherwood
forest officer agister, verderer
fortified town berg
fourpence flag
fowl See *chicken* above.
franchise soc
freeman ceorl, chorl, churl, laet, thane, thegn
free tenant dreng
funeral feast arval
furniture designer adam, chippendale, hepplewhite, sheraton
gaiters galligaskins
gallon imperial
game brad, cricket, croquet, darts, fives, hot cockles, loggat, logget, rugby, soccer, troco
garden, small allotment
garganey crick
general baden-powell, braddock, buller, burgoyne, bying, clinton, cromwell, fairfax, gage, gordon, hamilton, napier, oglethorpe, wolfe
geneticist haldane
geographer haklyt
geologist belt, lyell, smith
ghost guytrash
giant bamford, bellerus, blacker, bradley, bushby, daniel, evans, godmer, goemagot, goemot, gordon, hale, holmes, magrath, middleton, miller

gillyflower carnation
golf cart trolly
government downing street, parliament, whitehall
government securities consols
greeting pip-pip
groat flag
guitar zither
gull scull
gun armstrong, bren, brown bess, enfield, snider, sten
gym shoe plimsoll
half-penny bawbee
hamlet dorp
hat benly, billycock, boater, busby, deerstalker, fantail, trilby
hater anglophobe
hazel beard-tree
headland bolerium, naze
heathen ruler penda
hedgehog urchin
hedge sparrow dunnock
heir apparent charles
heirlooms cimelia
hero alfred, bayard, beowulf, offa, robin hood
highwayman dick turpin
hills brendon, cheviot, chiltern, clee, cotswolds, downs, mendip, wolds
historian acton, bede, bryce, buckle, carte, eusebius, freeman, froude, fuller, gardiner, gibbon, gildas, gooch, grote, hallam, jerome, kinglake, laqueur, layamon, macaulay, maitland, mill, nennius, parkinson, rawlinson, saintsbury, selden, stubbs, trevelyan, trevor-roper, wells
hobnail tacket
hog essex, suffolk, tamworth
holiday boxing day, whitsun
homer milton
honor exam tripos
horn cor
horse prad, punch, suffolk
horse dealer coper
horse race ascot, derby, goodwood, oaks, st leger
hospital reformer florence nightingale
houseworker char(woman)
huckster badger
humanist linacre, more
humorist colet, lear, spooner
hunting method battue
hymnist cowper, dykes, easton, heber, neale, watts, wesley
hypnotist braid

idiom anglicism, briticism

illustrator beardsley, caldecott, cruikshank, greenaway, rackham, seton, tenniel

imposter oates

impresario beecham, bing, (d'oyly) carte

installment plan hire-purchase, never-never

invader caesar, dane, hengist, horsa, jute, norman, pict, roman, saxon, william

inventor arkwright, atwood, bessemer, bramh, de la rue, hargreaves, newcomen, siemens, stokes

island alderney, anglesea, anglesey, ascension, bardsey, channel, coquet, farne, foulness, grenadines, hayling, holyhead, ireland, jersey, lundy, man, mersea, scilly, sheppey, st helena, thanet, tresco, walney, wight

ivy bindwood

jacket dickey, eton

jail See *prison* below.

jargon barrikin

journalist gibbs, harmsworth, harris, west, wilkes

jurisprudence danelaw

jurist bentham, blackstone, bryce, campbell, coke, cooke, hale, jeffreys

king alfred, artegal, arthur, belenus, beli(nus), bladud, bran, brennius, bret, bruce, brunt, brut(us), canute, caractacus, charles, cnaut, cnut, coeur de lion, cole, cymbeline, e(a)dgar, edmund, edred, edward, edwin, edwz, egbert(us), elidure, george, gogmagog, gorboduc, hal, harold, henry, james, john, knut, lear, llud, lud(d), nudd, offa, philip, richard, stephen, sweyn, walda, william

king, mythical artegal, arthur, elidure

kingdom, early anglia, dalriada, danelaw, deira, east anglina, essex, hibernia, ireland, kent, mercia, northumbria, pictland, scotia, sussex, wales, wessex

laborer navvy

lake coniston, derwentwater, ennerdale, grasmere, ulls-water, wastwater, windermere

land measure bovate, carucate, sulung, virgate, wist

landed proprietor squire

lane vennel

lapwing tewit, tirwit

law danelaw, esnecy, soke

lawbook fleta

law building chancery, inn of court

lawn billiards troco

law schools inns of court

lawyer barrister, bencher, solicitor

legislator commoner, lord

legislature parliament

letter wen, zed

lexicographer fiorio, fowler, johnson, roget, weekley, wright, wyld

liberal whig

limestone oolite

linguist ogden, sweet, ventris

loaf bap

logician boole

lord chancellor thurlow

lord protector cromwell

lunch tiffin

mace-bearer beadle

magistrate beak, comburgess

maid tweeny

man atkins, britisher, briton, bronc(h)o, cockney, goddam, gringo, john bull, johnny, limejuicer, limey, macaroni, sassenach, saxon, southron, tommy(atkins)

manner a l'anglaise

marshland broads, fen

martyr alban, alben, latimer, ridley, tyndale

masterwort goutweed

mathematician atwood, boole, briggs, cayley, clifford, dee, dodgson, ellis, gunter, hardy, wallis, whitehead

meadow grass rye

measure 3 cut, ell, lea, mil, pin, rod, ton, tun, vat 4 acre, bind, boll, butt, cade, coom, cran, foot, gill, goad, hand, hank, heer, hide, inch, last, line, mile, nail, pace, palm, peck, pint, pipe, pole, pool, rood, rope, sack, seam, span, trug, typp, wist, yard, yoke 5 bodge, cabot, carat, chain, coomb, cubit, digit, float, floor, hutch, jagum, metre, minim, ounce, perch, point, prime, quart, skein, stack, truss 6 alnage, barrel, bovate, bushel, cranne, fathom, firkin, gallon, hobbet, hobbit, league, manent, oxgang, oxland, pottle, runlet, second, square, strike, sulung, thread, tierce 7 auchlet, furlong, kenning, quarter, rundlet, seamile, spindle, tertian, virgate 8 carucate, chaldron, hogshead, landyard, puncheon, quadrant, standard 9 shaftment, shathmont 10 barleycorn, kilderskin, tablespoon, winchester

medical journal lancet

merchant draper

mercury good-king-henry

midlands black country

military authority liddel-hart

military cap busby

military college sandhurst

military commander churchill

militia fyrds

milkwort gangflower

mine wagon rolley

miners' court barmote

miners' judge barmaster

miser scrat, scrooge, silas marner

missel bird sycock

missionary asbury, boniface, winfrid

molasses treacle

mole tape

money lsd

monk b(a)eda, bede, boniface, cuthbert, lydgate

monument cromlech

mosquito gnat

movie director hitchcock

murderer aram, jack the ripper

musician See *composer* above.

musicologist baines, carse, grove, tovey

nail dump

national anthem god save the king, rule britannia

naturalist banks, barrington, darwin, lubbock, sloan, tomlinson, wallace

naval enlisted man rating

naval officer bligh, grenville

naval station portsmouth

naval victory trafalgar

navigator baffin, cabot, cook, dampier, drake, flinders, ross

nazi propagandist joyce

news agency reuters

newspaper area fleet street
nobleman See *title* below.
northeastern danelaw
nothing nawt, nowt
novelist amis, arlen, austen, bennet, blackmore, bronte, butler, collins, conrad, corelli, defoe, de morgan, dickens, douglas, du maurier, durrell, edgeworth, eliot, fielding, ford, forster, galsworthy, gaskell, gissing, golding, freen(e), hardy, hawkins, henty, hewlett, hilton, huxley, isherwood, jameson, lawrence, lessing, lewis, lytton, macaulay, martineau, maugham, meredith, milne, mitford, monsarrat, moore, morgan, oppenheim, orwell, priestly, sabatini, sayers, shreiner, shute, sitwell, smollet, snow, sterne, swinnerton, thackeray, tomlinson, trollope, walpole, ward, waugh, wells, west, white, wodehouse, woolf, wren
numbskull twit
nurse cavell, nightingale, sister
oath crum
occupying army black and tan
orator disraeli, pitt
order garter
orderly batman
organist biggs, burney, byrd, taverner
outlaw bell, robinhood
oyster-catcher trittichan
painter bacon, bonington, burne-jones, constable, cruikshank, fuseli, gainsborough, girtin, greenaway, hogarth, hunt, kent, landseer, leighton, lely, lewis, millais, morris, nash, opie, orpen, poynter, reynolds, romney, rossetti, ryland, sickert, stevens, turner, watts, wright
palace buckingham, hampton court, st james
pamphleteer defoe, swift
pancake round-robin
parish official beadle, meresman
parliament commons, lords
parliament, first woman nancy astor
parliament record hansard
party conservative, grumble-

tonian, labo(u)r, liberal, tory, whig
patron saint anne, george
peak cheviot, scafell, skiddaw, snowdon
pear warden
peasant churl, esne, serf
peddler coster (monger)
peerage See *title* below.
peninsula portland
people john bull
people, ancient angle, brython, celt, iceni, jute, pict, scot, silure
period angevin(e), stuart, tudor
periodical punch, spectator
personification john bull
pert. albion, anglican, britannic, british, brythonic, cymbric
petrarch sidney
philanthropist angell, shaftesbury, tate, whittington
philologist furnivall, junius, murray, onions, skeat
philosopher alexander, ayre, bacon, bentham, berkeley, bosenquet, bradley, broad, burke, godwin, hobbes, hooke, hume, joad, locke, martineau, mill, morgan, occam, russell, spencer, stephen, sweet, whitehead
photographer armstrong-jones, beaton, cameron, carroll, dodgson, talbot
physical education teacher games master
physician addison, barnardo, birkbeck, bright, brown(e), fothergill, fowler, grenfell, hopkins, jenner, linacre, mandeville, sloane
physicist appleton, aston, barkla, barlow, blackett, bragg, cockcroft, crookes, dirac, eddington, heaviside, hooke, joule, moseley, powell, rayleigh, richardson, rutherford, thom(p)son, wheatstone
physiologist adrian, dale, hill, huxley, sherrington
pianist hess, moiseivich, scott
pie flan
pig pen stee
pindar cowley, gray
pirate avery, drake, hawkins, kidd, morgan
plain sedgemoor
plantain ribwort

plateau dartmoor, exmoor
poet 3 gay 4 gray, hood, hugh, hunt, lang, owen, pope 5 auden, blake, byron, carew, donne, eliot, hardy, keats, lewis, lodge, noyes, peele, percy, prior, wyatt 6 arnold, binyon, brooke, butler, cibber, clough, cowley, cowper, crabbe, davies, dobson, dowson, dryden, durrel, empson, gibson, graves, hemans, henley, landor, lytton, marlow, milton, shairp, sidney, surrey, symons, waller, wotton 7 beddoes, bridges, caedmon, campion, collins, coppard, crashaw, drayton, herbert, herrick, hewlett, housman, kipling, langley, layamon, lydgate, marston, marvell, meynell, patmore, peacock, quarles, sassoon, shelley, sitwell, skelton, southey, spender, spenser, thomson, vaughan, withers 8 betjeman, browning, davenant, day-lewis, de la mere, langland, lovelace, rossetti, shadwell, suckling, tennyson, thompson 9 aldington, coleridge, maccaulay, masefield, rochester, shenstone, swinburne 10 drinkwater, wordsworth 11 shakespear(e)
poet laureate austin, bridges, cibber, davenant, day-lewis, dryden, eusden, jonson, masefield, pye, rowe, shadwell, southey, tate, tennyson, warton, whitehead, wordsworth
poets' meeting place the mortal
point dodman, gibralter, hartland, landsend, lizard, lynas, morte, naze, prawle, sales
policeman bobby, constable, copper, peeler
police pioneer sir robert peel
polisher dollier
political philosopher burke, godwin, laski
political satire mother goose
politician adversity hume, harmsworth, selden, steele, tooke
pope (h)adrian
porcelain celadon, chelsea, spode, wedgewood
pork chop griskin

port ayr, barrow, blackpool, bristol, cowes, dover, eastbourne, falmouth, folkstone, gloucester, gravesend, great yarmouth, grimsby, hastings, hull, liverpool, lowestoft, middlesborough, newcastle, penzance, plymouth, poole, portsmouth, preston, scarborough, sheerness, southampton, southport, sunderland, tynemouth, wallasey, whitby

pot herb clary

potato chip crisp

pottery elersware, minton, spode

pound nicker, quid

preacher bunyan, spurgeon, swift

prehistoric mound barrow, tumulus

prehistoric site abury, avebury, piltdown

prestige group order of the garter

prime minister attlee, baldwin, balfour, bentinck, canning, cavendish, chamberlain, churchill, compton, disraeli, douglas-home, eden, fitzroy, gascoyne, gladstone, grenville, grey, heath, jarrow, jenkinson, lamb, law, lloyd george, macdonald, macmillan, montagu, palmerston, peel, pelham, perceval, petty, pitt, robinson, roseberry, russell, spencer, stanhope, stanley, stuart, talbot, walpole, wellington, wilson

prime minister's house chartwell, chequers

primrose cowslip

prince, early aethelbert, alfred, arthur, catigirn, griffith, hengist, henry, oswald, pascent, stuart

principal master

printer baskerville, baxter, caxton, morris

prison bocardo, dartmoor, gaol, ludgate, newgate, old bailey

prophetess mother shipton

protection right mund

psychologist ellis, ogden

public school charterhouse, eton, harrow, rugby, sandhurst, winchester

publisher beaverbrook, blackwood, newberry

pudding stick thivel

puffin coulterneb

pump court-shoe

puritan baxter, cromwell, prynne

quarterly yellow book

queen anne, bess, bloody mary, boadicea, charlotte, eleanor, elizabeth, jane seymour, mab, mary, victoria

queen, informal title ma'am

rabbit tan

rabelais amory, sterne, swift

race track (See also *horse race* above.) ascot, epsom downs

radio wireless

railroad builder brunel

range black, cambrian, cumbrian, downs, pennines

reactionary colonel blimp

ready money prest

rebel cade, cromwell, essex, mortimer, percy, washington, wat tyler

rebellion barons' war

reformation leader cranmer

reformer ridley, spence

refrigerator fridge

regatta henley

regicide pride

regiment black watch

region lake district, north riding, weald, west country

resort bath, blackpool, bournemouth, brighton, cowes, margate, ramsgate, torquay, tunbridge wells

revenue office exchequer

revolution song lillibullero

riffraff ronyon(s)

rifle bandhook, enfield, snider

rifle contest bisley

river aire, aln, anker, avon, boyne, cam, colne, deben, dee, derwent, eden, esk, exe, humber, isis, kennet, lea, lune, mersey, nen(e), nidd, ouse, parrett, penk, ribble, rother, severn, stour, swale, tamar, tees, thames, till, torridge, trent, tweed, tyne, ure, usk, waveney, wear, welland, wensum, wharfe, witham, wye, yare

road, paved tarmac

road, roman watling street

romance king horn

rose, wild briar, brier

royal air force motto ad astra per ardua

royal house blois, hanover, lancaster, plantagenet, stewart, stuart, tudor, windsor

royal forest dean, epping

royal officer equerry, exon

royal residence buckingham palace, windsor

rune wen

sacristan verger

sailor jack tar, limey

saint alban, anne, bede, george, walburge, walpurgis

salmon sewen

sand dune dene, medano

satirist marvell, swift

sausage banger, saveloy

scholar alcuin, ascham, blue coat, elyot

school charterhouse, eton, harrow, merchant taylors, rugby, sandhurst, shrewsbury, st pauls, westminster, winchester

school assistant usher

school award accessit

school boy etonian, fag, scug

school master aram

scientist aston, bacon, boyle, connel, darwin, faraday, fleming, galton, haldane, hogben, kendrew, lindeman, snow

sculptor armitage, epstein, flaxman, gibbons, leighton, moore, stevens

sea atlantic, channel, irish, north, norwegian

sea battle armada, trafalgar

sea kale cole

seaman limey, rating

sedan tudor

serf esne, thrall

serpentary bistort

servant boots, char, cookgeneral, tweeny

settler angle, jute, norman, pict, saxon

sheep cheviot, cotswold, dartmoor, dishley, dorset, exmoor, kerry hill, lincoln, lonk, romney, ryeland, southdown, suffolk, teeswater, wensleydale, wiltshire

sheepwalk foldcourse

shelter scug, skyg

sherry doctor

ship lusitania, maretania, queen elizabeth, queen mary, titanic

ship money prest

shoals goodwin sands

shrub heath, laurustine

sideboard court-cupboard

signal flag blue peter

sinologist backhouse

sixpence sprat

smock overalls

socialist fabian, shavian

social reformer barnardo, ruskin, shaw, webb

soldier atkins, basewallah, bloody-back, carabineer, fusileer, fusilier, gilbert, redcoat, tommy(atkins)

soldier's coat tunic

son of fitz

southermost part landsend, lizard(head)

spa See *resort* above.

spade didle

spaniel clumber

spy andre, benedict arnold, cavell

square dance argeers

squash marrow

squire, ideal sir roger de coverley

stable mews

statesman addington, asquith, attlee, bacon, baldwin, balfour, baring, bentinck, bevan, bevin, birkenhead, bolingbroke, bright, burke, calvert, canning, carteret, castlereagh, cavendish, cecil, chamberlain, churchill, clarendon, clive, cranmer, cripps, curzon, disraeli, dudley, eden, gaitskell, gladstone, godwin, gordon, greville, grey, halifax, hampden, harley, heath, hoare, lloyd george, lubbock, lytton, macaulay, macdonald, macmillan, montfort, morley, morrison, noel-baker, north, peel, pitt, pym, sackville, salisbury, shaftsbury, sidney, simon, spencer, strafford, tablot, thurlow, trevelyan, vane, vansitart, walpole, walsingham, warwick, wilberforce

station wagon brake

stock exchange member orchid

stole armil(l), armilla

stone scree

stone-cutter jadder

stone monument cromlech

stool creppie

strait dover

streetcar tram

street, curved crescent

street-seller coster(monger)

student sizer

suffragist pankhurst

sultanate brunei

surgeon haden, hunter, lister, paget, pott

sweet trifle

sword ferrara, sabre

symbol bulldog, john bull, lion(and unicorn), rose

table cheveret, sheveret

tank landship

tavern local, pub

tax danegeld, excise, extent, fumage, geld, prest

tax collector exciseman

tax on crown lands tallage

tea cake crumpet

tea cart trolley

teacher's fee minerval

temperance society band of hope

tenant laet

terrier bedlington

theater old vic

theatrical director brook, richardson

theatrical producer d'oyly carte

theologian andrews, anselm, bebe, biddle, butler, hugel, newman, paley, pelagius, wycliffe

theosophist besant

thicket spinney

thief moll cutpurse

thistle teasel

thornbeck ray dorn

throne pretender perkin warbeck

timetable bradshaw

tip of land's end

title barron(ess)(et), count (ess), dame, domina, duchess, duke, earl, king, knight, lady, lord, marchioness, marquis, milord, noble, peer, prince(ss), queen, thegn, viscount(ess)

title, ancient pendragon

tormentil bloodroot

tory leader heathe, thatcher

tourist tripper

traffic circle roundabout

tragedy, earliest gorboduc

translator burton, fitzgerald, garnett, wycliffe

travel agent thomas cook

traveler borrow, cook, coryate, ligon, purchas, walking-stewart

treacle germander, hedge-garlic, molasses, syrup

treasury note bradbury, fisher

tribute heriot

trolley tram

trouser cuff turnup

trousers kickseys, kicksies

trout sewen, sewin

truck lorry

tub cowl, soe

turbot windowpane-fish

tutor don

20 shillings broadpiece, pound

typographer baskerville

umbrella brolly, mush

unitarian biddellian

university birmingham, cambridge, liverpool, london, manchester, oxford, sussex

uplands downs

usher black rod

vagabond abraham-man

valley combe, coom(b), coquet, dean, dene, eden, tees, tyne, wye

van kittereen

vessel barge, cat, trendle, trow

veterans organization legion

viceroy, india wavell

village bourg

violin-maker hill

wager of battle ornest

wall builder hadrian

wall tax murage

walnut akhrot, bannut

ware albert(ine), albion

warehouse pantechnicon

weed balder, nettle

weight bag, barge, bushel, cantal, clove, fagot, fangot, firkin, fodder, fother, fotmal, grain, keel, kip, last, mast, maun(d), pocket, pound, quarter, quintal, sarpler, score, stand, stone, tod, ton, truss

weight system avoirdupois

west point rma, sandhurst

wheat squarehead

women's army waac

wonder stonehenge

woolen cloth shoddy

wren tope

writer (See also *essayist, novelist,* and *poet* above.) addison, allen, angell, ascham, bacon, baxter, beaton, beckford, beddoes, beerbohm, belloc, bentley, besant, birkenhead, birrel, borrow, bosanquet, browne, bunyan, butler, caine, carlyle, chesterton, defoe, digby, doddridge, dodgson, doughty, doyle, ellis, etherege, fielding, fox, gladstone, gosse, grenville, grey, hare, hudson, huxley, kipling, lander, lear, le gallienne, lewes, lubbock, lyly, mansfield, opie, paget, powys, reade, rolle, seton, sidney, stanley, sterne, surtees, tennant, walton

wryneck cuckoo-fool
yeoman guard beefeater
zoologist lankester, medawar
ENGLISH (See ANGLO-SAXON and ENGLAND.)
anglican, austral, blighty, british, saxon(ish), southron
homer milton
ENGORGE devour, glut, stuff, swallow
ENGORGEMENT congestion, ingestion, plethora, satiety
ENGRAIL border, edge, indent, ornament, roughen
ENGRAVE carve, character, characterize, chase, chisel, crease, crosshatch, cut, enchase, establish, etch, figure, fix, impress, imprint, incise, infix, inscribe, intaglio, line, lithograph, mark, print, rist, scrape, scratch, sculpture, stipple, tool
ENGRAVER burinist, carver, cerographer, chalcographer, chaser, etcher, glyphographer, inscriber, lapidary, lignographer, lithographer, medalist, xylographer, zincographer
ENGRAVING aquatint, carving, celature, chasing, design, etching, picture, print, stamp
chemical copperas, vitriol
instrument stylet
kind cerograph, color print, copperplate, cut, drypoint, glyptograph, imprint, intaglio, lignograph, lithograph, lithotype, mezzotint, print, xylograph
on gem cameo, glyptograph
on wax cerograph
pert. diaglyphic, glyphic, glyptic
process albertype, aquatint, autotypy, block-print, bori, cerography, crible, demitint, electrotype, etching, intaglio, mezzotint, pyrography, rotograph, stereo-

type, xylography, zincography
stone cameo, intaglio
tool burin, cradle, dabber, mattoir, scauper, stylet
wood xylograph
ENGROSS absorb, apply, bury, conduct, consume, control, copy, employ, engage, enroll, enwrap, immerse, inscribe, involve, manage, manipulate, monopolize, occupy, preoccupy, sink, use, utilize, write
ENGROSSED absorbed, buried in, busy, caught up in, consumed, devoted, diligent, employed, fixed, immersed, industrious, intent, involved, lost, monopolized, rapt, set(tled), submerged, wrapped
ENGROSSING absorbing, enthralling, fascinating
ENGROSSMENT absorption, monopoly, study
ENGULF absorb, devour, engorge, flood, immerse, invade, overwhelm, plunge, quelme, slough, submerge, swallow, swamp, whelm
ENHANCE add to, adorn, aggrandize, aggravate, appreciate, augment, beautify, boom, deepen, elevate, embellish, exaggerate, exalt, extol, greaten, heighten, improve, increase, intensify, lift, magnify, raise, sharpen, strengthen, wax
ENHYDRA latax, sea-otter
ENID *lover* geraint
ENIGMA brain-twister, charade, conundrum, cryptogram, double-dutch, egma, facer, floorer, gibberish, graph, graveler, griph, grueler, jargon, knot, mystery, perplexity, poser, problem, puzzle(r), question, rebus, riddle, secret, sphinx, staggerer, sticker, stumper, why
comb. crypto
ENIGMATIC abstruse, ambiguous, cryptic, dark, delphic, doubtful, equivocal, esoteric, mysterious, mystic, obscure, occult, oracular, perplexing, puzzling, recondite, vague
ENIOPEUS *charioteer for* hector

slayer diomedes
ENISLE insulate, island, isolate, separate
ENISLED alone, apart, isolated
ENJOIN admonish, advise, appoint, ban, bar, bid, call upon, caution, charge, command, counsel, decree, dictate, direct, exhort, expostulate, forbid, forewarn, hinder, impose, inhibit, instruct, interdict, move, order, preach, prescribe, prohibit, prompt, proscribe, remonstrate, require, restrain, urge, warn
ENJOY adore, appreciate, arride, bask in, brook, delight (in), devour, dote on, eat up, fancy, feast on, gladden, gloat, gratify, have, hold, indulge in, like, love, luxuriate, own, please, possess, regale, rejoice, relish, revel in, riot in, savor, taste, tickle, use, wallow in, wield
oneself feast, laugh, rejoice
the moment carpe diem
ENJOYABLE amiable, delectable, delightful, glorious, good, pleasant, pleasurable, preferable, splendid
ENJOYMENT beatitude, beer and skittles, bliss, boot, cakes and ale, delectation, delight, ease, felicity, fruition, fun, gratification, gusto, happiness, joy, joyance, mechaieh, pleasure, rejoicing, relish, satisfaction, skittles, thrill, zest
devoted to apolaustic, hedonistic
ENKIDU *friend* gilgamesh
ENLACE encircle, enfold, entangle, entwine, weave
ENLARGE add, aggrandize, aggravate, ampliate, amplify, augment, balloon, biggen, blow up, bore, broach, broaden, bulk, cumulate, develop, distend, elongate, exaggerate, exalt, expand, expatiate, extend, fill out, huff, increase, inflate, ingreat, largen, lengthen, magnify, multiply, pad, print, prolong, protract, puff (up), ream, spread, stretch, swell, widen
photo blow up
ENLARGED ampliate,

bloated, blown up, capitate, expanded, megascopic, swelled, swollen

ENLARGEMENT accession, addition, aggrandizement, bunion, development, evase, expansion, growth, increase, knop, print, swell(ing)
bony spavin(e), spur
comb. auxe, megalia, megaly
ENLARGING growth, swelling
comb. macro

ENLIGHTEN acquaint, advise, apprise, brief, civilize, clear, disillusion, edify, educate, enkindle, fill in, illuminate, illumine, illustrate, inform, initiate, instruct, school, teach, tell, train, unseel
name meaning jairus

ENLIGHTENING edifying, educational, educative, illuminating, informative, instructive

ENLIGHTENMENT aufklarung, bodai, bodhi, eclaircissement, explanation, information, learning, light, opening, prajna, salvation, samadhi, satori
attainer of bodhisattva, gautama

ENLIL See BEL.

ENLIST employ, engage, enroll, hitch, induce, join, levy, rank, recruit, register, soud, sowd, use, utilize

ENLIVEN amuse, animate, brighten, cheer, dash, divert, elate, encourage, excite, fire, galvanize, inspire, leaven, quicken, refresh, rejuvenate, renew, restore, rouse, stimulate, vitalize, vivify, wake

ENMESH bewitch, catch, ensnare, entangle, implicate, insnare, involve, knot, snare, snarl, trap, web

ENMITY abhorrence, alienation, animosity, animus, antagonism, antipathy, aversion, bad blood, bitterness, chill(iness), cold(ness), coolness, discord, feud, frost, hate, hatred, hostility, illwill, loathing, malevolence, malice, opposition, rancor, uncordiality, unfriendliness, ungeniality

ENNEACANTHUS sunfish

ENNEAD See EGYPT *god, goddess.*

ENNOBLE dignify, elevate, exalt, glorify, honor, lord, noblify, promote, raise, uplift

ENNUI blues, boredom, dejection, depression, doldrums, dumps, fatigue, languor, melancholy, sadness, satiation, satiety, surfeit, tedium, vapors

ENOCH *father* cain, jared, reuben, seth
son irad, methuselah

ENORMITY atrocity, crime, flagrancy, gravity, grossness, heinousness, rankness

ENORMOUS antaean, bad, big, colossal, cyclopean, elephantine, evil, excessive, flagrant, gargantuan, giant, gigantic, great, heroic, huge, immense, inordinate, mammoth, monstrous, monumental, prodigious, stupendous, terrible, titanic, tremendous, vast

ENOS *father* cain, jared, reuben, seth
grandparent adam, eve
son cainan
uncle abel, cain

ENOUGH adequate, ample, aneuch, anogh, aplenty, assai, basta, bus, competent, don't, enow, fully, halt, plenteous, plentiful, plenty, quite, satisfying, stop, suffice, sufficient, tolerably, very
said done, silence

ENOW anew, enough, presently

ENRAGE aggravate, anger, despite, exasperate, frenzy, fry, incense, inflame, infuriate, ire, irk, irritate, madden, provoke, roil, stir

ENRAGED angered, angry, aroused, berserk, choleric, frenzied, furious, hornmad, irate, ired, mad, manic, savage, violent, wode, wood

ENRAPTURE bewitch, captivate, delight, enchant, enravish, entrance, fascinate, trance, translate, transport

ENRAPTURED beatic, delighted, ecstatic, enamored, enrapt, rapt

ENRICH adorn, boot, decorate, endow, fatten, fertilize,

improve, increase, invest, lard, ornament, salt

ENROLL attest, billet, call up, coil, commandeer, conscribe, conscript, draft, engross, enlist, enter, imbreviate, impanel, impress, induct, initiate, join, levy, matriculate, mobilize, muster, poll, press, raise, record, recruit, register, serve, sign on, sign up, subscribe, summon, tally

ENROLLMENT conscription, enlistment, impressment, induction, list, mobilization, recruitment, registration, registry, summons, tally

EN ROUTE along the way, en passant, forwards, in passing, in transit, on the road, on the way

ENS being, entity, essence

ENSANGUINE bloodstain, imbrue

ENSCONCE bury, cache, conceal, cover, defend, enthrone, establish, guard, hide, lodge, protect, safeguard, screen, seat, secrete, settle, shelter, shield

ENSEAM containe, grease, include, sew

ENSEMBLE band, choir, chorus, corps, costume, glee club, orchestra, outfit, together, whole

ENSHRINE bless, bury, cherish, consecrate, ennoble, entemple, glorify, preserve

ENSHROUD conceal, dress, wrap

ENSIFORM bone, ensate, gladiate, swordshaped, xiphisterhum, xiphoid

ENSIGN badge, banner, blue, colors, flag, gonfalon, iago, insigne, insignia, jack, lieutenant, officer, oriflamb, pennant, pennon, regalia, sailor, sign, signal, standard, streamer, symbol
bearer oriflamme

ENSILAGE feed, fodder, silage, silo

ENSLAVE bind, chain, enthrall, indenture, subject, thirl, yoke

ENSLAVED addict, captive, catch, habituate(d), subject, thrall

ENSLAVEMENT bondage, chains, helotry, slavery

ENSNARE bag, benet, betrap, birdlime, capture, catch, cop, decoy, enmesh, entice, entoil, entrap, inveigle, lure, nab, noose, seduce, snarl, sniggle, spring, surprise, tangle, tempt, trap, trick, web

ENSORCEL bewitch, charm, enchant, entrance

ENSPHERE encircle, envelop, inorb, surround

ENSUE arise, chase, derive, develop, emanate, eventualize, eventuate, follow, happen, issue, occur, originate, proceed, pursue, result, rise, spring, stem, succeed, supervene

ENSUING after, consequent(ial), resultant

ENSURE affiance, assure, betroth, espouse, guarantee, protect, secure, warrant

ENTABLATURE trabeation
part architrave, cornice, frieze

ENTAD inward
opposite ectad

ENTAIL affect, attach, birthright, bring, call for, carve, cause, demand, endow, entangle, figure, implicate, imply, impose, inheritance, intaglio, involve, lead to, pattern, require, sculpture, tack, tailzie
lost cost

ENTAL inner
opposite ectal

ENTANGLE befoul, bunker, canvas, cast, catch, confuse, cotter, embrangle, encumber, enmesh, ensnare, entrap, entrike, frankle, hamper, hankle, implicate, involve, mat, mesh, puzzle(r), raffle, snare, snarl, tiffle, trap, twist, web, wraple

ENTANGLED deep, cotty, knotted, snarled

ENTANGLEMENT affair, complication, fortification, hitch, imbroglio, implication, intricacy, involvement, liming, mesh, net, obstacle, quarrel, snare, trap, war, web

ENTASIA seizure, spasm, tetanus, trismus

ENTELECHY actuality

ENTELLUS boxer, hanuman, langur, monkey

opponent darius

ENTENTE accord, agreement, alliance, bargain, cartel, compact, concordat, contract, covenant, convention, cordiale, group, indenture, mise, pact, treaty, understanding

ENTER admit, appear, barge in, begin, billet, blow in, board, book, bore, break in, breeze in, burst in, bust in, card, catalog(ue), come in, compose, creep in, drop in, embark, encroach, engage, enlist, enroll, file, get in, go in, hop in, immigrate, incept, incur, inscribe, insert, insinuate, interpolate, introduce, intrude, invade, irrupt, join, jump in, list, matriculate, nominate, pass, penetrate, pierce, pop in, post, press, probe, push in, put in(to), record, register, share, slip in, start, step in, thrust in, trespass, volunteer
by force break in
hastily bulge
into compose, join, participate
militarily attack, invade
one's mind occur to
slowly ooze, percolate, seep
the lists compete
upon approach, undertake
without ticket crash

ENTERIC intestinal, typhoid, visceral

ENTERING entry, immigrant, inbound, incoming, ingressive

ENTERPRISE achievement, act(ion), activity, adventure, agency, aggression, aggressiveness, ambition, attack, attempt, audacity, business, cartel, company, concern, consortium, corporation, crusade, daring, determination, drive, empire, emprise, endeavor, essay, establishment, exploit, feat, firm, get-up, go-ahead, gumption, holding company, house, hustle, industry, initiative, intercept, iron, management, merger, monopoly, partnership, pool, project, push, quest, scheme, spirit, spunk, stock company, striving, struggle,

tryst, undertaking, utility, venture, venturousness
hard difficulty
pert. capitalistic

ENTERPRISING advancing, adventurous, aggressive, bold, entreprenant, progressive, pushing, pushy, resourceful, venturesome

ENTERTAIN absorb, accommodate, act, admit, amuse, banquet, beguile, board, busk, cherish, cultivate, delight, disport, divert, enthrall, feed, foster, gladden, gratify, harbor, house, imagine, interest, lodge, nourish, occupy, pamper, party, pique, please, preside, receive, record, recreate, regale, shelter, solace, sup, treat, wassail, welcome, w(h)ile

ENTERTAINER actor, artist, badchen, busker, comedian, courtesan, dancer, diseur, diseuse, geisha, harlot, hetaera, hetaira, host, hostess, magician, mime, minstrel, performer, singer, speaker, tummeler, tummuler

ENTERTAINMENT affair, amusement, attraction, ball, banquet, bat, bender, benefit, binge, blowout, board, bummack, bummock, cabaret, dance, dinner, diversion, entracte, feast, festival, fete, fiesta, fun, gaiety, game(s), get-together, glee, lark, party, performance, play, pleasure, randan, rantan, razee, reck, recreation, repast, revel, revue, ridotto, shivoo, show, social, soiree, sport, tea, wattle, xenodochy
musical concert, recital
place amphitheatre, auditorium, cabaret, casino, cinema, circus, gaff, midway, nitery, park, stage, theater, theatre
trite corn

ENTHRALL absorb, captivate, charm, delight, enslave, fascinate, grip, occupy, send, subject, swing, thirl

ENTHRONE crown, establish, exalt, glorify, install

ENTHUSIASM abandon,

afflatus, animation, ardency, ardor, avidity, bigotry, devotion, ebullience, ecstacy, elan, estro, excitement, fanaticism, fervency, fervor, fire, frenzy, furor, fury, heat, heart(iness), inspiration, interest, mania, passion, perfervor, rabidity, rabidness, rapture, spirit, transport, verve, warmth, zeal(otry), zealousness, zest, zing
demonic mynpholepsy
excessive mania
ENTHUSIAST activist, addict, advocate, aficionado, amateur, angel, apostle, arditus, backer, bear, bigot, booster, buff, bug, crank, devotee, dilettante, disciple, doer, dynamo, eager beaver, energumen, exponent, faddist, fan, fanatic, fancier, fiend, follower, fool, highflyer, hobbyist, hound, ist, ite, monomaniac, nik, nut, patron, rhapsodist, rooter, self-starter, shaker, sparkplug, visionary, votary, zealot
ENTHUSIASTIC active, afire, ardent, bugs on, cracked, crackers, crazy about, dithyrambic, eager, ebullient, fanatical, fervent, fervid, glowing, gone, gungho, hearty, hipped, hot about, infatuated, keen, lyrical, mad about, nutty, perfervid, rabid, red-hot, rhapsodic, warm, wholehearted, wholesouled, wild about, worked up, zealous
ENTHYMEME argument, syllogism, thought
ENTICE allure, attract, bait, bewitch, blandish, cajole, catch, coax, coy, decoy, drill, ensnare, incite, instigate, inveigle, lure, magnetize, pique, seduce, snare, tempt, till, tole, train, trap, trepan, troll, wheedle
ENTICEMENT attraction, bait, decoy, inducement, lure, persuasion, seduction, temptation
ENTIRE absolute, all, complete, full, gross, hale, intact, integral, integrated, livelong, perfect, plenary, sound, sum, thorough, total, tutto, unbroken, unified,

universal, unqualified, whole
comb. all, holo, toti
ENTIRELY allover, clear, completely, earnestly, exactly, exclusively, formerly, fully, in full, inside out, in toto, merely, only, simply, solely, tout a fait, wholly
ENTIRETY aggregate, allness, completeness, sum, total(ity), whole, universality
ENTITLE allow, ascribe, assign, authorize, call, caption, dedicate, designate, dub, empower, enable, impute, name, nominate, permit, qualify, term, warrant
ENTITLED eligible, warranted, worthy
ENTITY being, body, energy, ens, entia, essence, existence, individual, one, ousia, single(ton), soul, space, subsistence, thing, unit
ENTOMB bury, confine, hearse, immure, inhume, inter, inurn, shrine
ENTOTROPHI bristle-tail, empusa, lepisma, thysanura
ENTOURAGE attendants, environment, following, retinue, surroundings, train
ENTRAILS bowels, chawdron, gut(s), hallow, harigald, innards, interior, jaudie, paunch, quarry, tripe, umbles, viscera, vitals
pert. splanchnic
ENTRAMMEL bind, confine, embarrass, hamper
ENTRANCE access, adit, approach, archway, atrium, avenue, bewitch, boc(c)a, captivate, cast a spell, commencement, cusp, debut, delight, door, entree, entry, fascinate, foregate, foyer, gate, gorge, hallway, hypnotize, income, incoming, infiltration, ingang, ingate, ingoing, ingress(ion), initiation, inlet, input, insertion, intake, interpenetration, intrado, introgression, introit, mesmerize, mouth, opening, orifice, passage(way), penetration, porch, portal, postern, reception, road, spell(bind), stile, stulm, take-in, thirl, toran(a), trance, vestibule, vomitory, way

forcible inroad
formal debut
ENTRANCED dreamy, enchanted, rapt, transported
ENTRANCEMENT bedevilment, bewitchery, bewitchment, captivation, fascination, obsession, possession, spell, witchery
ENTRANT applicant, beginner, competitor, incomer, newcomer, novice, starter
ENTRAP bag, beguile, bottle, capture, catch, clutch, cop, decoy, ensnare, entice, entoil, lure, nab, seize, snare, taigle, take
ENTREAT adjure, appeal, apply, ask, beg, beseech, coax, conjure, crave, halse(n), implore, importune, obtest, petition, plead, pray, press, request, solicit, sue, supplicant, urge
for release beg off
ENTREATY appeal, application, cry, deesis, petition, plea, pleading, prayer, request, urgency
pert. precatory
ENTRECHAT leap
ENTREE access, admission, admittance, blue plate, boudin, debut, dish, entrance, entrement, entry, incoming, ingress, mazarine, ostium
ENTREMETS dainty, entertainment, side dish
ENTRENCH absorb, consume, encroach, engross, establish, fix, fortify, infringe, interfere, intrude, invade, sconce, set, trespass
ENTRENCHED deep-rooted
position camp
ENTRENCHMENT abri, bunker, closure, countermine, coupure, defense, ditch, dugout, fosse, foxhole, gallery, mine, moat, parallel, sap, trench, vanfoss
ENTRE NOUS between us, confidentially
ENTREPOT depot, storehouse, storeroom, warehouse
ENTREPRENEUR businessman, enterpriser, entrepreneuse, executive, gobetween, industrialist, match-maker, wheelerdealer

ENTRESOL anteroom, mezzanine, story

ENTRUST bank, behight, beken, bequeath, carry, commend, commission, commit, confide, consign, count, delegate, encharge, give, lippen, rely, trust

ENTRY access, adit, antechamber, anteroom, contestant, credit, debit, docket, entrada, entrance, entrant, entree, foyer, hall(way), ingress(ion), item, lobby, memo(randum), minute, narthex, notation, note, passage, post, register, registration, vestibule *wrongful* trespass

ENTWINE braid, clasp, embrace, enlace, fold, interweave, inwind, join, lace, serpent, weave, wind, wreathe

ENTWINED accolle(e), braided, inwoven

ENUMERATE add, calculate, cite, compute, count, detail, estimate, figure, list, mention, name, number, recapitulate, reckon, recount, relate, score, specify, sum, tally, tell, total

ENUMERATION account, aparithmesis, capitulation, catalog(ue), census, list, recital, recounting, score, tale, tally

ENUNCIATE affirm, announce, articulate, declare, deliver, enounce, express, inform, postulate, proclaim, pronounce, say, sound, speak, state, tell, utter, voice

ENUNCIATION articulation, attack, delivery, diction, orthoepy, phonology, pronunciation, tone, utterance

ENVELOP(E) begirt, bemist, besiege, bewilder, bur(r), capsule, cocoon, conceal, cover(ing), dim, dress, encircle, enclose, encompass, ensphere, fold(er), gird(le), hide, invest, involve, inwrap, jacket, lap, mantle, mantling, muffle, obscure, overlay, perianth, pocket, pod, round, sack, sheath(e), shell, shroud, stifle, surround, swaddle, swallow, swathe, vesicle, vesture, wind, wrap(per), wrapping

chemise teddy
fruit bur(r), rind
glass bulb
markings indicia
nebulous chevelure, coma
return sae
type manila, monarch, number ten

ENVELOPED womplit

ENVELOPMENT attack, covering, environment, siege

ENVENOM antagonize, canker, corrupt, embitter, exacerbate, poison, taint, vitiate

ENVIOUS cautious, covetous, emulous, grasping, greedy, grudging, jealous, malevolent, malicious, malign(ant), sparing, spiteful

ENVIRON(S) about, around, banlieu, bego, compass, district, encircle, enclose, envelop, hem, inclose, involve, outskirt, precinct, purlieu, skirt, suburbs, surround(ings)

ENVIRONMENT alentours, ambience, area, atmosphere, aura, backdrop, background, banlieu(e)s, belt, borderland, cincture, circumfluence, circumstances, context, encincture, encompassment, entourage, envelopment, faubourg, habitat, home, influence, locale, locality, milieu, mise-en-scene, neighborhood, outposts, outskirts, precinct, purlieus, range, scene(ry), setting, suburbs, surroundings, terrain, vicinage, vicinity
adaptation to epharmony
adapting to autoplastic
comb. eco, oeco, oiko
science of bionomics, ecology, euthenics

ENVISAGE, ENVISION behold, call up, conceive, confront, conjure up, contemplate, face, fancy, feature, image, imagine, materialize, objectify, picture, realize, see, think, view, visualize

ENVOY ablegate, agent, ambassador, delegate, deputy, diplomat, elchee, emissary, legate, messenger, metatron, minister, nuncio, postscript, substitute, vicar

ENVY begrudge, chaw, covet(ousness), desire, em-

ulate, emulation, evest, greeneyed monster, grudge(ry), grudging, hanker, heartburn, jalousie, jaundice, jealousy, malice, odium, onde, pine, rankle, rivalry, spite, suspect, suspicion, wish, yearn

ENWRAP absorb, convolve, dress, engross, entangle, ENVELOP, implicate, infold, inswathe, involve, surround

ENYALIUS ares

ENYO bellona
son ares, enyalius

ENZYME aldolase, amidase, aminase, aminopherase, amygdalase, amylopsin, arginase, carbohydrase, carboxylase, casease, catalase, cathepsin, crepsin, cytase, cytochrome, diastase, erepsin, esterase, ficin, glutaminase, glycogenase, insulase, invertase, invertin, kinase, laccase, lactase, lipase, lotase, maltase, mutase, nuclease, olease, papain, pepsin, protease, ptyalin, racemase, reductase, rennin, rhamniase, ribonuclease, saccharase, seminase, sulphatase, tannase, trehalase, trypsin, tryptase, tyrosinase, urease, zymase
action zymolysis
comb. ase
inactive zymogen
leather-making tannase
pineapple bromelin
plant laccase
proteolytic pepsin, protease
science of zymology
yeast carboxylase, raffinase, zymase

EOLITH axe, celt, flint, relic, tool

EON age, cycle, epoch, era, eternity, long time, olam, period

EOS aurora, dawn, morning, tithonia
consort ares, astraeus, atlas, cephalus, cl(e)itus, orion, procris, tithonous
horse abraxas, eoos, phaeton
parent eurypha(e)ssa, hyperon, pallas, th(e)ia
son boreas, emathion, eurus, hesperus, memnon, notus, phaeton, phosphorous, zephyrus

EPAENETUS *friend* paul

EPAMINONDAS *rival* agesilaus
slayer anticrates
EPAPHRAS *aide of* paul
EPAPHUS *city* memphis
descendent cadmus, danaus
kingdom egypt
parent zeus
EPARCH bishop, metropolitan, prefect, ruler
EPAULET knot, pauldron, scale, shell, swab, swob, tegula
EPEAN *chief* amphimachus
king endymion
EPEE See SWORD.
EPEUS *construction* | trojan horse
father endymion, panopeus
EPHAH *husband* caleb
1/10th omer
10 homer
parent jahdai, midian
EPHEDRINE *tree* mahuang
EPHELIS freckle
EPHEMERAL awhile, brief, brisk, corruptible, daily, deciduous, diurnal, episodic, evanescent, flashing, fleet(ing), flitting, flying, fugacious, fugitive, impermanent, meteoric, momentary, mortal, passant, passing, perishable, pro tem(pore), quick, shortlived, shortterm, temporal, temporary, transient, transitive, transitory, undurable, unenduring, unstable, volatile
EPHEMERID mayfly, shadfly, smoke
EPHEMERIS almanac, calendar, diary, journal, record, table
EPHER *parent* ezra, midian
EPHESUS *deity* diana
duke solinus
lord cerimon
EPHIALTES demon, giant, nightmare
brother otus
friend pericles
mother iphimedia
slayer apollo
EPHIPUS butter kelp, dollar kelp, fish, gunnel, poronotus
EPHLAL *son* obed
EPHRAIM *descendant* resheph
father joseph
grandson eran

son beriah, elead, ezer, rephah, shuthelah
EPHRATHAT *father* hur
EPIBATERIUS apollo
EPI finial, peak, pinnacle, spire
EPIBLAST ectoderm
EPIC aeneid, beowulf, cid, edda, eneid, epopee, epos, epyllion, grand, heroic, homeric, iliad, kalevala, narrative, noble, odyssey, poem, ramayana, saga, story
poetry epopee, epos
puritan paradise lost
EPICARP husk, peel, rind, skin
EPICARPAL cutaneous
EPICEDIUM dirge, elegy, ode, song
EPICINE androgynous, bisexual, effeminate, hermaphrodite, sexless, womanish
wear slacks
EPICRISIS evaluation, judgement
EPICTETUS stoic
pupil arrian
work enchiridion
EPICURE aesthete, apician, authority, bon vivant, connoisseur, dilettante, feaster, friend, gastronome(r), glutton, gourmand, gourmet, hedonist, pleasure-seeker, sensualist, sybarite
EPICUREAN apiloros, dainty, fastitious, heretic, luxurious, nice, particular, scoffer, sensual, sensuous, sybaritic, voluptuous
EPICURUS *of china* tao-tse
EPICYDES *father* euphemides
rival themistodes
EPIDEMIC attack, black death, bubonic plague, catching, communicable, contagion, contagious, disease, endemic, flu, infectious, murrain, pandemia, pandemic, pandora's box, pest(ilence), plague, plentiful, plenty, prevailing, prevalent, rife, siege, widespread
catarrh influenza
chorea dancing mania
parotitis mumps
EPIDERMIS bark, cuticle, peel, skin, velamen

outgrowth feathers, hair, hoof, horn, wart
EPIDOTE allanite, arendalite, begrationite, bucklandite, delphinite, scorza
EPIGLOTTIS flap, gullet, weezle
EPIGONI aegialeus, alcmaeon, diomedes, euryalus, gromachus, sthenelus, thersander
EPIGRAM adage, aphorism, apothegm, distich, epitaph, joke, maxim, mot(to), poem, posy, proverb, quip, quirk, saw, saying
EPIGRAMMATIC aphoristic, concise, laconic, piquant, pointed, witty
EPIGRAPH imprint, inscription, quotation, slogan, title
EPILEPSY catalepsy, convulsions, falling sickness, fit(s), grand-mal, petit-mal, seizure, spasm
remedy crotalin
EPILOGUE act, appendix, close, conclusion, end, finale, peroration, sequel, summation, swansong
comic exode
EPIMEDIUM barrenwort
EPIMETHEUS *brother* atlas, menoeteus, prometheus
daughter pyrrha
parent clymene, iapetus
wife pandora
EPINEPHRINE adrenaline, andrenin(e)
EPIONE *husband* asclepius
EPIPACTIS serapias
EPIPHANY avatar, feast, manifestation, uphellya
tableau creche, presepio
time twelfth night
EPIPHORA delacrimation, eyewatering
EPIPHYTE alga, billbergia, bromeliad, cactus, fern, karo, lichen, liverwort, moss, orchid
EPIRUS *king* echetus, pyrrhus
native epirote
town dodona
EPISCOPACY bishopric, prelatism, see
EPISCOPAL *parish head* rector
sandal campagus
EPISODE action, affair, attack, chapter, circumstance, deflection, departure, deviation, digression, divagation,

divergence, event, excursus, incident, interjection, occasion, occurrence, scene, section, sequence

EPISTLE billet(doux), bull, canon, circular, communication, correspondence, decretal, dispatch, favor, lesson, letter, line, message, missive, note, postal, postcard, report, rescript
side right

EPISTROPHE abgesang, epode, refrain, repetition, song

EPITAPH commendation, epigraph, hic jacet, inscription, legend

EPITASIS climax, crisis, paroxysm, seizure, spasm

EPITHEM application, dressing, poultice

EPITHET agnomen, akal, appellation, byword, curse, designation, invective, moneta, name, oath, phrase, smear, so(u)briquet, tag, title, vituperation

EPITOME abridgment, abstract, apercu, breakdown, breviary, brief, compendium, concise, condensation, conspectus, digest, outline, precis, scheme, sketch, summula, synopsis

EPITOMIZE abbreviate, abridge, compress, contract, copy, curtail, diminish, embody, exemplify, illustrate, resume, sum, typify

EPIZOOTIC contagious, epidemic

EPOCH aeon, age, arenig, bala, chazy, date, day, ecca, eon, era, erian, formation, generation, kaibab, lias, malm, mauv, oolite, period, point, series, time, uinta
prehistoric See ERA *prehistoric.*

EPODE epistrophe, poem, song

EPONYMOUS *ancestor* eber

EPOPEUS *kingdom* sicyon

EPOPTIC mystic

EPOXY adhesive, glue, resin

EPRATH *husband* caleb

EQUABLE calm, constant, een, equal, equivalent, even, immutable, methodical, orderly, regular, same, serene, smooth, steady,

suant, systematic, tranquil, uniform

EQUAL abreast, accord, adequate, agree, alike, all one, amount to, approach, balance, call, come to, compare, compeer, coordinate, correspond, drawn, emulate, equable, equipollent, equitable, equivalent, even, fair, fellow, fifty-fifty, identic(al), isochronic, isonomic, just, level, like, match, mate, measure, meet, nip and tuck, on a par, on even terms, par, parallel, paregal, pareil, peer, proportionate, quits, rival, same, steady, substitute, sufficient, symmetrical, tally, tantamount, tie(d), touch, uniform
almost approximate
-angled figure isogon
-celled isocytic
comb. iso, equi, pari
distribution balance
-footed equipedal
in rank compeer
odds even money
power equipotential
quantity ana, identical
rule isocracy
-sided equilateral
sides isosceles
to abreast, able, adequate, ample, capable, commensurate, competent, ready, sufficient, up to
weight equiponderance
without non pareil, unique

EQUALITY adequacy, balance, egalitarianism, egality, equation, equipoise, equity, fairness, homology, identity, impartiality, isonomy, isopolity, justice, owelty, par, parage, parallelism, pareil, parity, sameness, tie, uniformity
comb. ent
legal isonomy
of measure isometry
of power isocracy
state wyoming

EQUALIZE balance, equate, even(up), handicap, isochronize, level, match, poise, smooth, trim

EQUALLY alike, both, egally, even(ly), like, pari-passu, same
comb. equi
near equijacent

EQUANIMITY aplomb, balance, calm(ness), composure, control, equipoise, phlegm, placidity, poise, sangfroid, selfassurance, selfpossession, serenity, temper

EQUATE balance, equalize, level, parallelize

EQUATION balance, equality, equilibrium

EQUATOR center, girdle, line, middle
-crossing ceremony polliwog

EQUATORIAL torrid, tropical
constellation cetus

EQUERRY officer, servant, stable, stockman

EQUES knight

EQUESTRIAN chevalier, horseman, jockey, rider
star hippeastrum

EQUIDISTANT central, halfway, middle, parallel

EQUILIBRIUM aplomb, balance, composure, control, counterpoise, equation, equipoise, isostasy, poise, sanity, serenity, stability, tension
being in astatic
lack of astasia
science astatics

EQUINE caballine, colt, filly, foal, horse(like), horsley, horsy, steed, zebra

EQUINIL meprobamate

EQUINOX aries, cancer, capricorn(us), libra, solstice

EQUIP accomplish, accouter, apparel, appoint, arm, array, bar, bedight, belt, buckle, caparison, deck, dight, dress, endow, feat, fettle, fit out, fit up, furnish, garnish, gear, gird, girt, heel, imp, man, mechanize, munition, outfit, plenish, prepare, provide, provision, rig, turn out, staff, stock, supply
a vessel apparel
with wings imp

EQUIPMENT accoutrements, apparatus, appliance(s), appointment(s), appurtenances, armament, arms, baggage, caparison, conveniences, duffel, duffle, equipage, fittings, fixtures, furnishings, furniture, gear, graith, impedimenta, kit, machinery, material, materiel, outfit, panoply, para-phernalia, plant, provision, rig(ging), stores, supplies, tackle, talent, things, trappings, traps

EQUIPOISE See EQUILIBRIUM.

EQUIPPED armed, armored, boden, provided, ready, under arms, weaponed

EQUIPOLLENT coimplicant

EQUISETUM bottle-brush, candock, cat-whistles, horsetail, plant, scouring rush

EQUITABLE bonitarian, decent, dispassionate, even, equal, ethical, fair, honest, identical, impartial, just, objective, proper, proportionate, right(ful), same, unbiased, upright, wise

EQUITY benefit, claim, code, dispassionateness, easement, epikeia, epiky, equality, estate, fairness, fairplay, fairshake, give-and-take, holding, honesty, impartiality, justice, justness, property, rectitude, right(s), settlement, square deal, stake, term, trust, unbias, uprightness, use
goddess astraea

EQUIVALENCE equality, equipollence, par(ity)

EQUIVALENT alike, analog(ue), comparable, convertible, equal, even, identic(al), kind, like, parallel, poecilonym, reciprocal, same, substitute, tantamount, uniform
to as good as

EQUIVOCAL ambiguous, amphibolic, changing, cryptic, dark, doubtful, dubious, enigmatic, evasive, forked, irregular, obscure, puzzling, sibylic, uncertain, vague

EQUIVOCATE boggle, dodge, evade, fence, fib, hedge, lie, mislead, palter, pollyfox, prevaricate, quibble, shift, shuffle, tergiversate, trifle, weasel

EQUIVOCATION ambiguity, amphibology, double-entendre, evasion, falsification, shuffle, tergiversation

EQUIVOCATOR liar

EQUIVOGUE ambiguity, double-meaning, pun

EQUUULUS constellation, fork, gibbet, rack, torture

EQUUS ass, horse

ER, EAR tiu, tiwaz
consort tamar
son almadam

ERA aeon, age, cycle, date, eon, epoch, generation, hegira, period, samvat, stage, time
before life azoic
comb. zoic
emperor's kimigayo
prehistoric archeozoic, azoic, cambrian, cenozoic, cretaceous, devonian, eocene, jurassic, mesazoic, miocene, mississippian, neogene, oligocene, ordovician, paleocene, paleogene, paleozoic, pennsylvanian, permian, pleistocene, pliocene, proterozoic, quaternary, silurian, triassic

ERADICATE abate, abolish, annihilate, annul, blot, dele, delete, demolish, deracinate, destroy, efface, eliminate, epilate, erase, expunge, exterminate, extinguish, extirpate, extract, kill, level, obliterate, outroot, raze, root, slay, supplant, unroot, uproot, weed out, wipe out

ERAN *grandparent* ephraim

ERASE abolish, annihilate, annul, blot(out), cancel, deduct, dele(te), destroy, dispunge, efface, eliminate, excise, kill, obliterate, plane, rub out, scrape, scratch, sponge, unwrite, wipe out

ERASER art-gum, rubber

ERASTUS *aide of* paul

ERASURE deduction, deletion, excision, expunction, obliteration

ERATO *lover* arcas
son thamyris

ERBIUM *source* gadolinite

ERD earth, land, region
shrew ranny, sorex

ERDA hertha, nerthus
goddess of nib(e)lungs

ERE before, earlier, early, erewhile, formerly, preceding, previously, prior, rather, soon(er), yer

EREBUS darkness, hades, hell
abode hades
consort night, nox, nux, nyx
father chaos
offspring aether, charon,

day, eros, hemera, hesperides
sister night, nox, nux, nyx

ERECHTHEID See THESEUS.

ERECHTHEUS *brother* butes
enemy eleusinians
kingdom athens
offspring cecrops, chthonia, creusa, ganymede, merion, orithyia, pandion, procris
parent atthis, dardanus, gaea, hephaestus, vulcan
reared by athena
sister philomela, procne
slayer zeus
wife praxithea

ERECHTITES butterweed, fireweed

ERECT address, alert, arear, arrect, bigg, brant, bristle, build, cast up, cocked, construct, create, elevate, fabricate, hauriant, hoist, lift, make, mure, perpendicular, pitch, put up, raise(d), ramrod, rear, set up, stand(ing), stately, stay, straight, unshaken, upend, upheave, uplift, upright, upstanding, vertical, watchful

ERECTION construction, dome, elevation, house, raising, rearing, structure, uplifting, upraising, uprearing

ERECTOR builder, derrick, muscle

ERELONG anon, soon

EREMITE anchoret, anchorite, ascetic, cenobite, hermit, monk, recluse
hut cell

EREMITISM isolation

EREUTHALION *slayer* nestor

EREWHILE before, formerly, heretofore, once, whilom

EREWHON See UTOPIA.
author butler

ERGANE athena

ERGATOID ant

ERGINUS *son* agamedes, trophonius

ERGO accordingly, argal, because, hence, therefore

ERGOPHOBIA indolence

ERI *parent* gad

ERIBOEA *husband* aloeus

ERIC cro, galanos, honor-price, wergild

ERICA besom, briarroot,

briarwood, broom, calluna, cassiope, heath

ERICHTHONIUS See ERECHTHEUS.

ERIDANUS padus, rhone
parent oceanus, tethys
star in achernar, keid

ERIDU *god* hea

ERIGERON aster, bitterfleabane, daisy, herb

ERIGONE *father* aegistrus, icarus
lover bacchus
mother clytemnestra

ERIN aryan, eire, hibernia, ireland
go bragh ireland forever

ERINY(E)S See FURIES.

ERIOPHORUM bog-cotton, canna-down, cat-locks, cotton grass, drawling, plant, sedge

ERIPHYLE *bribed by* polynices
father talaus
husband amphiaraus
offspring alcmaeon, amphilochus, demonassa, eurydice
slayer alcmaeon, amphilochus

ERIS discordia
brother ares
daughter ate
missile apple
mother night, nox, nux, nyx

ERISTIC apologetic, controversial, disputatious, polemic(al)

ERITE See GAD.

ERITREA See ETHIOPIA.

ERITRICHIUM forget-me-not

ERLKING elf, sprite

ERMINE ermalin, fur, futeret, miniver, mustela, stoat, vair, vare, weasel, white, whitrack, whittret
white lasset, miniver

ERODE abrade, comb, corrode, decay, decrease, decline, eat, scour, waste

ERODIUM alfilaria, geranium, pin-grass

EROS aengus, amor, cupid, love, pothos
brother anteros
consort psyche
friend antony
opponent anteros
parent aphrodite, ares, erebus, hermes, ilithyia, iris, venus, zeus

EROSE notched, uneven

EROSION abrasion, attrition,

blight, break down, corrosion, decrease, nivation, scouring, wear
limit base level

EROTIC amative, amatory, amorous, aphrodisiac(al), carnal, erogenous, fervent, fervid, fleshly, impassioned, lascivious, loving, paphian, passionate, perfervid, romantic, sensual, venereal

EROTICA curiosa, esoterica, pornography

ERR aberrate, blow, blunder, bone, boot, butch, deviate, diverge, do wrong, fall, go amiss, go astray, go wrong, lapse, lose, miscalculate, miscarry, misgo, misinterpret, misjudge, miss, mistake, offend, pull a boner, roam, scrithe, sin, slip, stray, stumble, transgress, trespass, trip, waffle, wander, wrong

ERRAND assignment, charge, commission, message, mission, task
boy bellboy, bellhop, gopher, lobbygow, messenger, page
comb. ance

ERRANT astray, circuitous, devious, erratic, erring, fugitive, offending, planetary, sinning, wandering, wayward

ERRATIC aberrant, abnormal, capricious, changeable, eccentric, errabund, errant, fickle, fitful, fitified, fugitive, inconsistent, inconstant, irregular, mercurial, nomadic, odd, planetary, quaint, queer, rogue, spasmodic, strange, tangent, unusual, vagabond, vagrant, wacky, wandering, whacky, wild

ERRING astray, ERRANT, peccable, sinning, wayward

ERROL, CEDRIC fauntleroy

ERRONEOUS aberrant, all off, amiss, askew, astray, at fault, awry, erratic, falacious, false, faulty, heterodox, illusory, mistaken, off, peccant, straying, untrue, wrong

ERROR aberrance, aberrancy, aberration, albardine, alfa, bevue, bloomer, blooper, blunder, bobble, boner, booboo, boot, bull,

bumble, bungle, catch, clanger, devil, distortion, errata, evil, fallacy, falsity, fault(iness), faux pas, flap, flaw, floater, fumble, gaffe, garble, hash, heresy, howler, illusion, inaccuracy, indiscretion, lapse, lapsus, mehdalim, miscue, misjudgment, miss, misstep, mistake, misunderstanding, peccadillo, perversion, rhubarb, sin, slip, smear, solecism, transgression, trespass, trip, typo, untruth, wrong
grammatical bull, hibernicism, irishism, malapropism, mispronunciation, missaying, misusage, partingtonism, slipslop, solecism, spoonerism
in time anachronism
measuring device aberrometer
to be corrected corrigendum
without accurate, correct, exact, faultless, flawless, impeccable, nice, precise, right

ERS bitter fitch, bitter vetch, vicia

ERSATZ artificial, counterfeit, factitious, makeshift, substitute, synthetic

ERSE celt(ic), gael(ic), irish, scottish

ERSENIA brambleworm, brandling, earthworm

ERST(WHILE) earlier, earliest, first, former(ly), heretofore, once, past, previously, sooner, soonest

ERUA sarpanitu
consort marduk

ERUBESCENT blushing, red(dish), ruddy

ERUCT belch, disgorge, eject, emit, erupt, rasp

ERUCTATION belch, brash, burp, outburst

ERUDITE cultured, didactic, educated, learned, polymathic, profound, sage, scholarly, smart, wise

ERUDITION education, information, knowledge, learning, letters, lore, scholarship, science, wisdom

ERUPT belch, blow out, blow up, boil, break out, burst, discharge, disgorge, eject, eruct, explode, gush, rupture, sicken, spew, spout, vesuviate, vomit

ERUPTION acne, agria, blast, blotch, blowout, blowup, brash, breakout, commotion, ecthyma, emergence, exanthema, explosion, morphew, nirles, outbreak, outburst, pimple, pustule, rash, storm
comb. anthema
ERYCINA aphrodite
ERYNGIUM herb, seaholly, snakeroot, snakeweed
ERYSICHTHON *parent* agraulos, cecrops, tripoas
sister iphimedia
ERYSIPELAS blast, disease, phlogosis, pox, rose, st anthony's fire, wildfire
ERYTHEA fan palm, palmetto, sabal
father besperus
ERYTHRA-THALASSA red sea
ERYTHRINA bucare, dadap, pea, shrub, tree
ERYTHROCYTE corpuscle
ERYX *parent* butes, venus
slayer hercules
ESARHADDON *father* sennacherib
ESAU edom
brother jacob
country edom
descendant edomite
father-in-law elon
grandfather abraham
grandson amalek, omar
home edom, seir
parent isaac, rebecca, rebekah
son eliphaz, jaalam, jeush, korah, reuel
wife adah, aholibamah, anah, bashemath, judith
ESAY See ISIAH.
ESCALADE ascent, climb, escalado, mount, raid, scale
ESCALATE cop out, increase, mount, rise, speed up
ESCALLOP cook, notch, shell, wind
ESCALUS *kinsman* mercutio, paris
ESCAMILLO toreador
ESCAPADE adventure, antic, caper, caprice, dido, freak, frolic, indiscretion, lark, maladventure, prank, revel, runaway, sally, scheme, vagary
ESCAPE abscond, alternative, avoid, avolate, bail out, bilk, blow, blowout,

bolt, break, break loose, breakout, come-off, cut loose, decamp, deliverance, depart, desert, dodge, elope, elude, emergence, eschew, evade, evaporate, evasion, exhaust, flee, flight, fly, free, getaway, get free, issuance, issue, jail-break, jump, lam, leak, liberation, loophole, miss, mistake, ooze, outbreak, outlet, pretext, quit, release, retreat, riddance, run away, sally, scape, scrithe, seep, shun, skip, skirt, slip, sneak out, split, squeak, squeeze, take refuge, throw off, vent, withslip
artist houdini, manzini
earth astronavigate
from fly, illude, shun, steer clear
means loophole
narrow close shave
ESCAPED at large, free, loose, unloosed
ESCAPISM avoidance, flight
ESCARGOT snail
ESCAROLE endive, scarola
ESCARPMENT edge, fortification, precipice, slope, steep
ESCHAR ascher, crust, scab
ESCHAROTIC acrimonious, branding iron, caustic, cauterant, pungent
substance cautery
ESCHEAT booty, confiscation, fall, fine, forfeit(ure), lapse, plunder, reversion, revert, spoils
ESCHEL blue, smalt
ESCHEW abnegate, abstain, avoid, elude, escape, evade, fear, forbear, forgo, refrain, sacrifice, shun
ESCOLAR barracouta, barracuda, becuna, fish, mackerel, palu, plaintail, rovet(to)
ESCORT accompanist, accompany, attend(ant), beau, bodyguard, bring, burkundaz, carry, cavalier, chaperon, chase, comate, companion, company, concomitant, conduct, consort, convoy, date, defend, drag, duenna, flame, gallant, gooseberry, guard, guide, hustle, lead, man, marshal, pilot, protect, safeguard, see, shepherd, shield, show,

spark, squire, staff, steer, take, tend, tote, usher, wait on, warden
ESCRITOIRE See DESK.
ESCROW bond, deed, deposit
ESCUAGE scutage, service
ESCUDERO esquire, page, shield-bearer
ESCUDO *1,000* conto
ESCULENT comestible, eatable, edible
ESCUTCHEON archboard, arms, blazon, cartouch(e), crest, orle, shield
band fess(e)
point chief, color, dexter, fess, heart, honor, navel, nombril, sinister
surface field
voided orle
ESDRAS *angel* uriel
ESHBAAL *father* saul
ESHBAN *parent* dishon
ESHTAULITES *ancestor* caleb
ESKER eiscir, hogback, kame, mound, osar, ose, ridge
ESKIMO aglemiut, agomiut, alask(i)an, aleut, amerind, angakok, esquimau, husky, ikogmiut, innuit, inuit, ita, kidnelik, kinipetu, kunmiut, magemiut, malamute, malemiut, nugumiut, okomiut, orarian, sinimiut, tuski, yuit
aboriginal amerind
aleutian islands aleut, atka, husky, ita
american innuit
and russian creole
asian yuit
assembly house kashga, kashim(a)
boat b(a)idar, b(a)idarka, bidarkee, cayak, kamik, kayak, kiak, oomia(c)k, umia(c)k
boot kamik
chief tonjon
coat kooletah, netcha, parka, parkee, temiak
commune etah
culture dorset, ipiutak, punuk, thule
curlew fute
diomede islands yikirgaulit
dish muktuk, reindeer stew, seal-liver
dog husky, malamute, malemute, samoyed(e), siwash
game amazualat
garment See *coat* above.

god creptus, great spirit, tek-keitserktok, torngarsak
goddess sedna, tootega
greenland ita
hood amowt
house barabara, bar(r)abora, igloe, igloo, igl(o)u, kashiga, kashima, topek, tupek, tupik
hysteria piblokto
ice cream agootuk
indian See ALASKA *indian,* CANADA *indian.*
instrument ulu
knife ulu
medicine man angakok, angakut, angek(k)ok, angekut
memorial post totem pole, xat
mountain nunatak
nomad nunamuit
pantheon innua
race, fabulous tornit
settlement etah
siberian yuit
sledge komatik
sorcerer angakok, anodijum
spirit agoolik, aipalookvik, akselloak, ataksak, aulanerk, aumanil, eeyeekalduk, innua, keelut, kingmingoarkulluk, koodjanuk, noesarnak, nootaikok, ooyarrauyamitok, pukkeenegak, torngak, torngarsak
summer hut topek, tupek, tupik
tent topek, tubik, tupek, tupik
tool manak
tribe aleut, atka, caribou, koniaga, unalaska
ESLI *son* nahum
ESMERALDA *rescuer* quasimodo
ESNE peasant, servant, slave
ESOPHAGUS gula, gullet, meri, weasand
comb. lem(o)
part cardia, epicardia
ESOTERIC abstruse, anagogical, arcane, cabalistic, confidential, inner, mysterious, mystic(al), occult, orphic, private, recondite
doctrine cabala
knowledge gnosis
one epopt
reality mysticism
ESOX fish, miskellunge, pickerel, pike
ESP clairvoyance, foresight, insight, intuition, metapsychosis, premonition, psy-

chometry, second sight, sixth sense
ESPADON sword(fish)
ESPALIER lattice, palisade, railing, trellis
ESPARTO alfa, atocha, grass, halfa, spart, stipa
ESPECIAL chief, peculiar, SPECIAL, uncommon, very
ESPERANTO ido, volapuk
ESPIONAGE espial, espy, intelligence, observation, reconnaissance, spying
agent spy
ESPLANADE drive, glacis, level, maidan, marina, path, road, walk(s)
ESPLANDIAN *parent* amadis, oriana
ESPOUSAL affiance, betrothal, engagement, marriage, matrimony, nuptials, sponsalia, spousage, wedding, wedlock
ESPOUSE adopt, advocate, assume, back, campaign, champion, defend, embrace, husband, marry, mate, plight, suggest, support, take, uphold, wed
ESPRESSO *and milk* cappucino
ESPRIT devotion, elan, humor, morale, spirit, vivacity, wit
fort freethinker
gaulois racy
ESPY behold, describe, descry, detect, discern, discover, locate, note, notice, observe, perceive, see, spot, survey, view
ESQUIRE armiger, armorer, baronet, cavalier, escudero, gentleman, knight, lover, mister, promote, radman, sergeant, shieldbearer, sir, spark
ESROM *son* aram
ESS curve, sigma, sigmoid, worm
ESSAY article, attempt, chria, composition, dissertation, effort, endeavor, experiment, labor, manuscript, paper, piece, prove, screed, strive, struggle, test, theme, thesis, toil, tract, treatise, trial, try, undertake, venture, work, writing
collection festschrift
preliminary prolusion
ESSAYIST author, addison,

commentator, elia, emerson, lamb, litterateur, payne, steele, writer
ESSE being
ESSENCE abstract, amrita, attar, balm, base, being, body, burden, center, chat, cologne, core, crux, distillation, eidos, ens, entity, existence, extract, fiber, fibre, form, foundation, gist, hypostasis, idea, inbeing, jet, juice, kernel, marrow, meaning, meat, nature, nub, odor, ottar, ousia, perfume, pith, point, principal, quiddity, quintessence, rasa, reality, sap, scent, sense, spirit, substance, true being, whole
innermost atman
pert. basic
universal form
ESSENE ascetic, palestinian
ESSENTIAL basal, basic, broad, cardinal, central, chief, critical, crux, distinctive, fundamental, gist, great, important, indispensable, ingrained, inherent, innate, inner, intrinsic, key(stone), landmark, main, material, metal, milestone, mortal, must, necessary, need(ed), needful, nub, organic, pith, primary, required, requisite, salient, sine qua non, substratal
being bhutatathata, suchness
part core, pith
regard as desiderate
ESSENTIALS brass tacks, facts, guts, necessities
ESSEX *earl of* devereux
ESSOIN delay, excuse, exemption, parlying
ESTABLISH accustom, acquire, anchor, appoint, ascertain, authenticate, authorize, base, begin, bring out, build, clear, clinch, commence, confirm, constitute, create, decree, enact, ensonce, erect, firm, fix, foot, form, found, ground, implant, inculcate, initiate, install, instill, institute, instore, invent, locate, lodge, make, moor, ordain, organize, originate, pitch, place, plant, prove, put, radicate, root, seat, secure, set (up), settle, situate, start, station, validate, verify

firmly indurate

ESTABLISHED assured, authentic, based, bestead, bien fonde, certain, confirmed, conventional, deep-dyed, deep-rooted, deep-seated, embosomed, engraved, ensconced, entrenched, etched, fixed, imbedded, implanted, infixed, ingrained, ingrown, inveterate, inwrought, legal, old-line, placed, planted, posited, reliable, rooted, set(tled), situate(d), stable, stabilized, standing, staple, stationed, strong, there, vested, well-grounded

ESTABLISHMENT agency, appointment, authority, business, city hall, company, concern, constitution, custom, decree, demonstration, enterprise, facility, firm, formation, foundation, household, income, ins, installation, institution, joint, law, layout, leadership, market, menage, mill, organization, plant, position, power(structure), rule, shebang, shop, society, state, structure, system

domestic menage
monastic cloister

ESTATE (See also *kind, below.*) acreage, allod(ium), assets, bequest, capital, caste, chak, chateau, class(ification), condition, daira, degree, demesne, devise, domain, dowar, dowry, echelon, effects, endow, equity, esne, feod, fief, finca, fortune, grade, hacienda, ham, heritage, holdings, home, inheritance, land, latifundium, legacy, manor, mode, parcel, pomp, position, posture, property, rank, situation, sphere, station, status, stratum, substance, taluk, villa

1st church, clergy
2nd aristocracy, nobles
3rd commons, people, tiers etat
4th press, newspapers
car station-wagon
child's portion legitim
come to man's grow, mature
feudal benefice
holding tenancy
kind copyhold, equitable, ex-

pectancy, in fee, intail, feod, feud(atory), lease(hold), remainder, reversion
manager administrator, executor, guardian, steward
officer factor, landreeve, steward
owner hacendero, patroon
part legitim
partition boedelscheiding
pert. demesne
purchaser acquereur
rent deduction reprise

ESTEEM account, admiration, admire, adoration, adore, aim, appraise, appreciate, approve, bless, care (for), cherish, consideration, credit, deference, favor, glory, homage, honor, judge, love, opinion, pride, prize, regard, repute, respect, revere(nce), set store by, think highly of, think well of, treasure, value, venerate, wonder, worship, worth

ESTEEMED appreciated, dear, honored, redoubted, reputable, respected, revered, well thought of

ESTER abietate, acetin, congener, ether, formate, fucodin, glycerin(e), glycerol(e), indican, iodide, lactate, lactone, margarin, mellate, nitrate, oil, oleate, olein(e), palmatin, pepside, salt, sarin, selenate, silicate, sorbate, stearate, stearin(e), tropate

ESTHER hadassah, vashti
cousin mardochaeus, mordecai
enemy haman
eunuch hachrathaeus
father aminadab, mordecai
festival purim
foster-father See *cousin, above.*
husband ahasuerus, artaxerxes, assuerus

ESTHETIC See AESTHETIC.

ESTIMABLE august, creditable, decent, good, great, honest, honorable, noble, palmary, praiseworthy, reputable, respectable, solid, upright, valuable, venerable, worthy

ESTIMATE add, adjudge, adjudicate, analyse, analysis,

analyze, appraisal, appraise, appreciate, appreciation, apprize, approximate, ascertain, assay, assess(ment), audit, average, bid, budget, calculate, call, capitalize, carat, cast, cense, censure, class, compute, conjecture, count, critique, decide, determine, discover, esteem, evaluate, evaluation, figure, ga(u)ge, guess, judge, judicate, make, mark, measure, mete, opinion, prize, rank, rate, rating, reckon, repute, scale, settle, size up, stock, sum, surmise, survey, think, valuation, value, weigh
low undervaluation
smallest minimum
too highly overrate
value appraise, capitalize

ESTIMATION assessment, cess, conjecture, count, enumeration, esteem, fame, honor, importance, judgment, numeration, opinion, regard, repute, respect, supposition

ESTIVATE sleep, summer
ESTIVATION praefloration
ESTOC See SWORD.
ESTONIA *bay* narva, parnu
capital reval, revel, tallinn
city dorpat, narva, paide, parnu, petseri, reval, revel, tallinn, tartu, valga
coin estmark, kroon, lat, sent
dialect tartu
island dago, hiiumaa, muhu, oesel, saare, sarema
lake peipus
measure elle, faden, kulimet, liin, lofstelle, pang, sagene, sund, tennland, tool, toop, tun, verchoc, verst(a), verste
native aesti, esth
oxcart kulak
port narva
province saare
river ema, narva, parnu
state assembly riigikogu
strait muhu
weight lood, nael, puud
zoologist baer

ESTOP bar, debar, fill, plug, prevent, stop
ESTOGUE See SWORD.
ESTRADE dais, platform
ESTRANGE abalienate, alienate, antagonize, disacquaint, disaffect, disunite,

divert, divide, divorce, part, separate, sever, sunder, wean, withdraw

ESTRANGEMENT alienation, aversation, break, distaste

ESTRAY dogie, waif, wander

ESTRE condition, estate, place, state

ESTREAT copy, exact, extract, fine, record

ESTRILDA amadavat, avadavat, waxbill

ESTROGEN premarin

ESTRUS heat, season

ESTUARY bay, creek, estero, fiord, firth, fjord, fleet, frith, inlet, liman, loch, mouth, para, plata, ria, wash

ESURIENT greedy, hungry, voracious

ETAGERE cabinet, whatnot

ET AL and(others), elsewhere, others

ETAM *son* ezer, idbash, ishma, jezreel, penuel

ETAMINE worsted

ETAPE bivouac, emporium, stockade, storehouse, supplies

ETCH aftermath, bite, corrode, cut, delineate, draw, eddish, engrave, establish, fix, frost, furrow, impress, incise, inscribe, stamp

ETCHING acquatint, chasing, eauforte, engraving, incising, picture

ETEOCLES *brother* polynices
parent jocasta, oedipus
slayer polynices
son laodamas

ETERNAL ageless, agelong, boundless, ceaseless, continuous, deathless, endless, eonian, ever(lasting), forever, god, illimitable, immortal, imperishable, infinite, perdurable, permanent, perpetual, tarnal, timeless, unceasing, undying, unending
city rome
feminine woman
flower everlasting
home See PARADISE.
sleep death
verities See TRUTH.

ETERNALLY ad infinitum, ad nauseam, always, endlessly, ever, forever, without end, without limit

ETERNITY aeon, aevo, aevum, age, athanasia, blue moon, century, coon's age, donkey's years, eon, ewigkeit, glory, immortality, infinity, lifetime, olam, paradise, perpetuity, time, years
symbol serpent

ETESIAN annual, periodic(al), seasonable, seasonal

ETHAN *son* azariah

ETHBAAL *daughter* jezebel

ETHER acetal, air, akasha, amyl, anesthetic, anisole, apiol(e), asarone, atmosphere, empyrean, epoxide, ester, heaven(s), ozone, paradise, pinole, safrole, sesamin, sky, solvent, space, vapor
complex acetal
compound anisol, ester
crystalline apiol(e)

ETHEREAL aerial, aery, airy, celestial, dainty, delicate, empyrean, exquisite, fairy, fine, fragile, gaseous, heavenly, light, rare, rarified, shadowy, spectral, spiritual, subtle, supernal, tenuous, thin, unearthly, unworldly

ETHICAL correct, decent, equitable, good, honorable, just, kosher, moral, noble, right(eous), upright, virtuous

ETHICS convention, deontology, hedonics, morals, principles
system of hedonics
teacher of moralist
without amoral

ETHIOPIA abyssinia, afrogaea, axum, cush, eritrea, geeze, hidden empire, kaf(f)a, seba
animal baboon, galla, gazelle, gelada giraffe, hippopotamus, impala, jackal, kudu, lion, monkey, oryx, redbuck, sanga, sangu, walie, zebra
ape gelada
banana ensete, musa
battleground adowa
bible version geez
bishop abuna
capital addis ababa, aksum, asmara, axum, meroe
cat shoa
cattle sanga, sangu
cereal teff

church coptic
city addis ababa, adowa, aduwa, ankober, antalo, asmara, assab, axum, bako, dessye, dimtu, diredawa, dori, dunkur, elfud, gambela, gardula, goba, gondar, gore, har(r)ar, jidda, kecha, lalibala, magdala, makale, massawa, mojjo, mustahil, nakamti, napata
coin amole, ashrafi, besa, dollar, girsh, harf, kharaf, levant, maria theresa, pataca, plaster, talari, tallero
depression danakil
dialect See *language*, below.
district See *province*, below.
dollar levant, maria theresa, menelik, talari
emperor ahile, memnon, menelik, negus, selassie
falls blue nile, tisisat
flower brayera
fly zimb
game shum-shir
garment chamma, toga
gazelle aoul
governor ras
grain aamite, agao, beja, teff
grass tocusso
guerrilla group edu, elf, eplf, tplf
hamite afar(a), blemmyes, bogo
ibex saol, walie
in India sidi
island dahlak
jew falasha
junta dirgue
king hailie selassie, lion of judah, memnon, menelik, merops, negus, ras, tirhakah, zerah
lake abaya, abe, dambea, dembea, rudolph, shola, stefanie, tan(n)a, tsana, tzana, zeway
language afar, agow, amharic, galla, gallinya, geez(e), ghese, giz, harari, irob-saho, saho, smali, tigre, tigrinya
leader haile selassie, menelik, mengistu, zauditu
lyre kissar
market harrar
marriage damoz, qurban, semanya
measure cabaho, cubi, derah, entelam, farsakh, farsang, ghebeta, kuba, messe, sinjer, sinzer, tanica, tat
native abigar, abyssinian,

afar, annuak, assamite, beja, blemmyes, cushite, danakil, doko, falasha, galla, hamite, harari, kafa, kala, negro, shoa, somali, tigrai, troglodyte
neighborhood association kebele
nomad galla, shifta
oxen galla, sanga, sangu
party dergue
peak amba, batu, guge, guna, rasdashan, talo
pepper cubeb
port assab, massaua
premier imru
prince asfa-wossen
princess aida, andromeda
province amhara, arusi, bagemder, bana, boron, enarea, eritrea, gamagofa, gojam, gondar, harage, ilubabor, jim(m)a, kaffa, lasta, meroe, ogaden, shawa, shoa, sidamo, tigre, walaga, wallege, wallo
pygmy doko
queen candace, kandrake
range ahmar, choke
revolutionaries eprp
river abbai, akoho, albai, awash, baro, dawa, fafan, gashgash, gibe, gila, juba, mareb, mofer, omo, rahad, tacazze, takkaze, webbe
tableland amba
talari pataca
tea kat
title abuna, negus, ras
torah tetel
training camp field of meat, sigameda
tree cusso, koho, koso
tribe afara, agows, amhara, doko, donakus, galas, galla, gondar, somalis, shoa, tigres
valley rift
violin masinko
weight alada, artal, farasula, kasm, mocha, mutagalla, natr, neter, oket, pek, ratel, rotl, wakea, wogiet
wolf kaberu
ETHNARCH See GOVERNOR.
ETHNIC gentile, heathen, infidel, pagan, paynim, racial
ETHOS character, manner, spirit
ETHYL *compound* emol
cyanide propionitril
derivative alcohol, ether
gas petrol(eum)

hydride ethane
hydroxide alcohol
oxide ether
ETHYLENE elayl, etherin
ETIOLATE blanch, bleach, decolorize, pale, whiten
ETIOLOGY attribution, cause, reason
ETIQUETTE amenities, bearing, ceremony, civilities, code, convention, courtesy, custom, decency, decorum, deportment, dignity, elegancies, form, formalities, good form, manner(s), mien, mores, proprieties, propriety, protocol, punctilio, social graces, suavities
breach of gaff, solecism
required by de rigueur
ETON *boater* wet-bob
cricket player dry bob
debating society pop
food battel
game fives
holiday vac
master beak
student oppidan, tug
ETRURIA See ETRUSCAN.
ETRUSCAN etrurian, rasenna, tuscan, tyrrhenian
black pottery bucchero
chieftain astur
city caere, chiusi, clusium, cortona, faesulae, falerni, sutrium, tarquinii, veii, volaterrae, volsinii, vulci
coiffure tutulus
deity fufluns, menfra, tinia, turan, turms, uni
king lars porsena
noble lucumo
people tyrheni
race founder tarchon
title lars
wine god fufluns
ETTLE aim, aspire, arrange, chance, conjecture, consider, design, direct, earn, endeavor, intend, intent, interest, plan, prepare, suppose, try
ETTRICK SHEPHERD james hogg
ETUDE article, composition, exercise, study
ETUI box, briefcase, case, etwee, reticule, tweeze(r), trousse
ETYM giants, moabites
ETYMOLOGY derivation, eponymy, genesis, glottogony, lexicology, linguistics, philology

ETYMON radical, radix, root
ETZEL atilla, atli
EUAECHME *father* megareus
husband alcathous
EUBOEA evvoia, negropont
city chalcis, eretria
promontory cenaeum
tribe abantes, dryopes, ellopii, ionians
EUBULEUS *father* trochilus
found persephone
helped demeter
EUCALYPTUS applebox, applegum, bastard mahogany, bimbil(box), black ash, blackbutt, bloodtree, bloodwood, bluegum, boxtree, cabbage gum, carbeen, carbun, ironbark, jarrah, mallee, messman, myrtal, redgum, ribbongum, stringybark, yate, yellowjacket, yertchuk
gum kino
insect pest laap, lerp
leaf deposit cerf
secretion laap, larp, lerp
EUCHARIST bread and wine, communion, host, housel, impanation, intinction, last supper, lord's supper, maundy, mystery, oblation, real presence, sacrament, thanksgiving, transubstantiation, viaticum
canopy ombrellion
case artophorion, pix, pyx
celebration mass
cloth fano(m), fanum
cup calix, chalice
element bread, host, loaf, wafer, wine
festival corpus christi
plate paten, patina
spoon labis
table credence, credenza
vessel ama, amula, asterisk, calix, chalice, ciborium, columba, paten, patina, pix, pyx
wafer host
wine cup, krama
EUCHENOR *father* polyidus
slayer paris
EUCHITE adelphian, mendicant, satanist, vagrant
EUCHRE best, defeat, game, outwit
game comet, cutthroat, domino, five hundred, hasenpheffer, jambone, jamboree, malilla, mallillio, manille

term alone, assist, bower, bridge, dutch it, march, next, take up, turn it down
EUCLID *founded* geometry
home alexandria, megara
proposition asses' bridge, pons asinorum
EUDAMIDAS *brother* archidamus
descendant agis
father agesilaus
son archidamus, eurypon
EUDEMONIA happiness, wellbeing
EUDOCIMUS guara
EUDORUS *parent* hermes, polymeda
EUGENIA arrayan, brush cherry, myrtle, rose apple
EUGENICS culture, heredity
EUIPPE *father* daunus
husband diomedes
EULALIA grass, miscanthus, neti, thatch-grass
EULOGIST panegyrist
EULOGISTIC commendatory, eloge, encomiastic, epenetic, laudatory, panegyrical
EULOGIZE acclaim, applaud, boost, compliment, exalt, extol, glorify, laud, magnify, praise
EULOGY address, citation, commendation, eloge, encomium, hesped, oration, paen, panegyric, praise, tribute
EUMAEUS *employer* odysseus, ulysses
herd swine
EUMECES lizard, scorpion, skink
EUMEDES *companion* aeneas
father dolon
EUMENIDES See FURIES.
EUMOLPUS *parent* chione, poseidon
priest of demeter, dionysus
slayer erectheus
son ismarus
EUNEUS *parent* hypsipyle, jason
EUNICE *kin* lois, timothy
EUNOMIA *father* zeus
EUNOMUS *slayer* hercules
EUNUCH androgenus, androgyne, capon, castrate, castrato, gelding, halfman
biblical bukhayt, kafur
one of 7 bazatha, bigtha, biztha, carcas
pert. spadonic

EUPATORIUM agrimony, agueweed, ayapana, boneset, comfrey, hempweed, thoroughwort
EUPHEMISM affectation, bureaucratese, elegance, gobbledegook, nicety, softening
example darn, disadvantaged, gee, golly, lawkes, passing away, powder room, senior citizen, undertaker
use cledonism
EUPHEMIST euphuist, gongorist, pretender
EUPHEMUS *founded* cyrene
parent europa, poseidon
EUPHONIUS melodic, melodious, musical, tuneful
EUPHONY concord, consonance, harmony, melody, meter, musicality, sweetness
EUPHORBIA aveloz, candelilla, caustic creeper, milk plant, spurge
EUPHORBUS *father* panthous
slayer menelaus
EUPHORIA alupag, buoyancy, elation, fog, haze, joy, wellbeing
EUPHORION *lover* zeus
parent achilles, helen
EUPHRATES *tributary* habor, murat, tigris
EUPHROSYNE grace, joy, mirth
EUPHUES *author* lyly
EUPHUIST euphemist, gongorist
EUPHUISTIC aureate, bombastic, figurative, flowery, grandiloquent, magniloquent, overnice, rhetorical
EURALE gorgon, monster
EURASIA burgher, cheechee, feringi
dock parelle
grass arrhenatherum, barrenbrome, quake
grouse capercaillie, capercailzie
herb anthriscus, apium, berteroa, betonica, buphthalmum, carthamus, celery, digitalis, featherfoil, fraxinella, galega, larkspur, lavandula, mother-of-pearl, pheasant's-eye, snakeshead, speedwell, toadflax, veronica, whorlflower
kinglet goldcrest
larkspur stavesacre

mint nepeta
native feringi
pea colutea, ervum
plant blooddock, cyclamen, parelle
rail corn-crake
range urals
region tatary
shrub cinnamon-rose, cistus, honeysuckle, jerusalem-star, lonicera, wayfaring tree, whipcrop, ulex, yew
tree ash, jodas, juniper, redbud
weed wild carrot
EUREKA aha, at last, finally, i have found it, thalassa, thalatta
red puce
EURIPIDES *drama* alcestis, andromache, bacchae, electra, hecuba, helena, heracles, heraclidae, ion, iphigenia in aulis, medea, phoenissae, troiades, trojan women
hero ion
heroine electra, helena, iphigenia, medea
EURIPPA artemis
EURIPUS canal, channel, flow, flux, frith, reflux, strait
EUROPA *brother* cadmus, cilix
consort asterius, poseidon, zeus
moon of jupiter
parent agenor, phoenix, telephassa
son euphemus, minos, rhadamanthus, sarpedon
EUROPE, EUROPEAN anglo, balt, celt, continental, croat, dane, finn, frangi, frank, gaul, german, lapp, latin, lett, magyar, sahib, slav, slovene
agrimony clive
alder irish mahogany
anchovy engraulis
and asia eurasia, scythia
antelope chamois
ape baboon
apple sorb
arum bobby and joan, cuckoopint
ash sorb
-asia straits bosporus, dardanelles, hellespont
aspen black poplar
auto (See also under individual countries.) aston, benz, bmw, denzel, ferrari,

isetta, jaguar, martin, maserati, mercedes, metro, porsche, prefect, prinz, rabbit, skoda, volkswagen, volvo, zodiac
badger brock
barracuda spet
bass brasse
bat barbastel(le), noctule, serotine, vespertilio
bay biscay
bear ursus
beetle cockchafer
bellflower haskwort, rampion
berry tree arbutus
bird 3 ani, daw, emu, ern, mew, qua 4 cirl, darr, emeu, erne, gled, kite, mall, moro, osel, quis, rook, stag, tern, whim, yite 5 amsel, boonk, glede, mavis, merle, ousel, ouzel, sacer, saker, serin, tarin, terek, terin, whaup 6 avocet, avoset, cuckoo, cushat, gaylag, godwit, hoopoe, linnet, loriot, marten, merlin, missel, redcap, turnix, whewer, windle, winnel, wranny 7 bittern, bustard, haybird, jaybird, kestrel, motacil, ortolan, sakeret, starnel, whiskey, winnard, witwall 8 bargoose, chapster, dotterel, fauvette, garganey, redstart, reedling, wheybird, whimbrel, woodlark, wrannock, yoldring 9 babillard, beccafico, brambling, gallinule, goldfinch, goosander, peregrin, stonechat, swinepipe, wheybeard 10 bluethroat, chiffchaff, lammegeyer, turtledove, whitterick 11 capercailie, herring gull, lammergeire 12 capercailzie
birthwort clamatite
bison aurochs
bittern bogblitter, bogbull, bogjumper, boonk, mosshammer
blackbird amsel, merl(e), ousel, ouzel
black currant cassis
boar aper, sus
boxing savate
brandy armagnac, cognac, slivovitz
broadcloth suclat
brooklime horse-cress, wallink
buckthorn alatern(us)

buffalo aurochs, bison
bullfinch redbird
bulrush akaakai, scirpus
bunting cirl, ortolan, yellowhammer
burbot lote
buttercup frogwort
campanula rampion
canal corinth, kiel
canary serin, tarin
cantaloupe rock melon
card game tarok
cattail elephant grass
cavalryman cossack, hussar, u(h)lan
chair varangian
cherry gean, mahaleb
clematis traveler's joy
clover alsike, rabbitfoot, trifolium
coal basin saar
cod bib, bitterling, boce, coalfish
coin ducat, pistole, taler
columbine aquilegia, bluestarry
coot smyth
cormorant shag
country albania, austria, belgium, bulgaria, denmark, finland, france, germany, greece, holland, hungary, italy, latvia, luxemb(o)urg, netherlands, norway, osterrich, poland, portugal, rumania, spain, switzerland, yugoslavia
country, ancient moesia
cress molewort
crow carrian, daw, hoodie, hoody, rook
crowfoot eelware
crustacea branchipus
curlew whaup
cyclamen sowbread
dabchick pennybird
dance koio, polka, tarantella
deer fallow, roe
dogfish nursehound
dogwood gaiter
dormouse loir
dotterel eudromias
dragonet foxfish
duck bar-goose, morillon, sheldrake
eagle owl grand duke
economic community common market
elder bourtree, danewort, sambucus
elk alces
ermine stoat
evergreen firethorn, holmoak

fabric calamanco
falcon kestrel, merlin, saker(et)
fern crest
field vole campagnol
finch serin, tarin, terin, yellowhammer
1st gentleman george iv
fish abramis, alburnus, allice, allis, alosa, alose, angler, atherine, barbel, barse, besugo, bitterling, blay, bleak, boce, bogue, bose, braice, braise, brasse, bream, brisling, chad, dace, dentex, doree, dory, eperlan, gar, graining, gudgeon, homelyn, ide, john doree, john dory, lavaret, lote, lyrie, maiger, maigre, marena, meagre, morgay, osseter, picarel, plaice, roach, rudd, ruffe, sciringa, sennet, shad, silverside, spet, sprat, surmullet, tench, tiru, tope, topknot, trench, umber, wrasse
flatfish bret, brill, turbot
flounder topknot
flycatcher beebird, bee-eater, kingbird, muscicapa, warbler
folk custom egg-rolling
folk hero fortunatus
foodfish atherine, silverside
fowl campine, hamburg
fruit azarole
garlic moly
gentian autumnbells, autumnviolet
geranium cranesbill
germander bastard-hyssop
goat angora
goatsucker dorhawk, evechurr, evejar, nightchurr, nightjar
goldcrest moon, thumbbird
goldfinch foolscoat
goose brant, greylag
grape muscat
grape hyacinth bluebell
grass anthoxanthum, cockscomb, comb-wheat, esparto, golden top, foxtail, lagurus, lamarkia, poa, ripgut, sielingia, whinrack
grayling umber
grosbeak hawfinch
ground squirrel suslik
grouse capercaillie, capercailzie
gulf aegina, riga, saronic
gull mall, mew, pewee, pewit
gum tragacanth
harrier blue-glede

hawk falcon, faller, glede, harrier, kestrel, kite, puttock
hawkweed bugloss
hawthorne albespine
heath broom, erica
hemlock deathin
herb alfilaria, alkanna, anthriscus, apium, arum, astrantia, atropa, axseed, babiesbreath, bassia, bearsfoot, bindweed, birdsbill, birthroot, birthwort, bistort, borage, catbed, catchfly, catsear, chervil, clary, cornsalad, cow-basil, cowfat, dill, dropwort, elecampane, erodium, eryngo, everlasting, eyebright, feverfew, ficaria, fowlfoot, galanthus, galega, garden rocket, glaucium, globularia, goatroot, gosmore, grape hyacinth, gypsum pink, ice pink, iva, jasione, ladys-comb, ladys-mantle, lovage, mandrake, meum, pellitory, pingrass, pussy's-toe, ragged robin, rocket salad, rue, sage, sainfoin, savory, spicknel, squinancy, star-of-bethlehem, sulla, tarragon, thistle, tormentil, weaselsnout, woad, yarrow, yellowwort
herb, poisonous henbane, mandrake, navelwort, nigella
heron ardea, frank
herring sprat
holly acebo, aunt-mary's-tree
honeysuckle goats-leaf, gold-and-silver
hunting dog griffon
hyacinth bluebell
hyssop mint
industrial region ruhr, saar
in indies blijver
invaders alani, arabs, huns, mongols, turks
iris orris
jew ashkenazi(m)
juniper cade, savin
kelp badderlocks
kinglet firecrest
kite gled(e), milvus, puttock
knapweed rhapontic
lake enare, geneva, ladoga
laurel sweet bay
lavender aspic
leek rocambole
lime teil
linden teil
linnet twite

loach beardie, thunderfish
lousewort rattle
madder garance
mainland continent
man, primitive blond beast
maple bird's-tongue
martin martlet
matgrass bastard-spikenard
measure aam, kilometer, liter, metre
merchant ship fluyt
mew gull
military landwehr
military draft landsturm
milkwort crossflower, four sisters
mint ballata, bastard-dittany, bitter-bugle, clare, clar(r)y, dittany, horehound, hyssop, ironwort, iva, lampwick, pennyroyal, sideritis
monkshood jacob's chariot
moslem frangi
moth cochylis, convolulus, emperor, eudemis, notchwing, poplar hawk, sphinx
mountain ash rowan, rowen, sorb
mouse bankvole, loir, vole
navelwort blue-eyed-mary
oak durmast, holm, kermes
orchid badderberry, bee-orchis, bird's-nest, cytherea, foolsstones, neottia
owl cue
ox aurochs, urus
pancake blintze
pear chaumontel
pellitory sneezewort
peninsula balkan, iberian, italian, italy, kola, scandinavia(n), spain
people, early beakerfolk, brunn, teutons, vlach
perch barse, ruff(e), zingel
pigeon ringdove
pink agrostemma
plain steppe
plant alexander(s), alkanet, alyssum, arnica, arnoseris, asphodel, autumn squill, azarole, ball mustard, bastard balm, bevy, bluebottle, borage, burstwort, butchersbroom, capon's-tail, cancerwort, cornflower, damewort, eelware, elderwort, escobilla, frogsbit, herniaria, lavender, motherwort, myrtle, neslia, orpine, rocambole, sawwort, scilla, sharewort, sneezewort, starfruit, succory, toothwort, ulex, valeriana, yarrow

plantain fleawort
plover dotterel
plum orleans, quetsch
polecat ferret, fitchet, fitchew, foulmart, perwitsky, sarmatier
porgy besugo, pagrus, pargo
principality andorra, lichtenstein, luxembourg, monaco, san marino, wallachia
quail wet-my-lip
rabbit con(e)y
ragwort cankerweed, senecio
rail ortolan
railroad car wagon-lit
range alps, apennines, balkans, bohmerwald, carpathian, dolomites, erz, jura, urals
ray homelyn, thornback
rebuilding marshall plan
redstart brantail, firetail
redwing swinepipe
reed donax
resort baden, capri, costa brava, cote d'azur, ems, majorca, mallorca, riviera, spa
ringdove cushat
river arno, elbe, inn, isar, isonzo, maritsa, maros, minho, mures, neisse, oder, ohre, oise, prut(h), san, sirit, struma, rhine, rhone, teiss, tiber, tisza, vardar, volga
river, longest volga
roach braise, sea bream, pagrus, rutilus
robin erithacus, ruddock
rodent erd, hamster
rustic peasant
saltwort barilla
sandpiper ruff
sea adriatic, aegean, aral, azoy, baltic, black, caspian, mediterranean, north
sea bream braise, carp, pagrus, roach, rutilus
sea eagle ern(e)
seaweed badderlocks, henware, honeyware, murlin
sedge bogrush, chufa
service tree checker
shad allice, allis, alosa, alose
shark acrodus, thrasher, thresher, tope
sheldrake bargoose, burrow duck, tadorna
shrew erd, ord
shrub alder, azarole, bastardquince, bladdersenna, broom, cade, caper, cistus, forsythia, furze, heath,

laurel, needle-gorse, poets' cassia, savin(e), sorb, springheath
siskin aberdevine, aberduvine, barleybird, nightingale, wagtail, wryneck
skate thornback
smelt eperlan, sparling
snake aesculapius
snipe ernbleater
soldier landsknecht
songbird goldfinch
soup bors(c)ht, minestrone
sparrow whitecap
sponge badiaga
squill star-hyacinth
squirrel polatouche, sisel, s(o)uslik
starling chepster, starnel
st johnswort androseme, hypericum
stork ciconia
strait bosporus
swallow martin, martlet
swift black martin, squealer
sycamore london plane
teal nettion
tern darr, richelbird
thistle cnicus
thrush mavis, missel, os(s)el, ousel, ouzel, redwing, stonechat, throstle
titmouse coaltit
toad natterjack
train orient express, settebello
tree aspen, blackthorn, corkoak, medlar, sorb, teil, terebrinth, tragacanth
tree, heath briar, brier
trout char(r)
turkey oak cerris
valerian celtic nard, spikenard
vervain frogfoot
vessel, sailing crayer
vetch blackpea, ervil, sicklewort
vetch-like herb axseed
vine traveler's joy
wallflower gilliver
warbler beccafico, blackcap, furzeling, pettichaps
waterlily flatterdock, nenuphar
water rail bilcock, brookrunner
water vole craber
waxtail barleybird
weasel stoat, whitrack
weed alfilaria, blacktop, catsear, cheirinia, cockspur, earlycress, fools parsley, gum succory, knawel, mus-

tard, oxtongue, ragwort, spurry, strapwort
weevil funnel-twister
westernmost part cape roca
wheat einkern, emmer, whizen
whitethroat babilard
whortleberry blackheart
widgeon whewer, whim
willow sallow
willow warbler bank jug
wind bise, mistral, sirocco
wood anemone bowbells
woodcock quis
woodpecker dirtbird, hickwall
wood pigeon cushat
wood sage ambrose, teucrium
worm sao
wrasse ballan, goldfinny, labrus
wren stag
wryneck barleybird, nightingale, siskin, wagtail
yarrow maudelin(e)
EUROPIUM *source* monazite
EUROTAS *father* milos, myles
EURUS *mother* eos
EURYALE *sister* medusa
EURYALUS *friend* nisus
victim aesepus, pedasus
EURYBATES *companion* odysseus, ulysses
EURYBIA *husband* creus, crius
offspring astraeus, pallas, perses
parent gaea, pontus
EURYDAMAS *son* abas
EURYDICE agriope
brother alcmaeon, amphilochus
consort amyntas, aristaeus, orpheus, pan
daughter themiste
parent amphiaraus, eriphyle
EURYMEDON perseus
parent thucles
EURYNOME *consort* zeus
father oceanus
offspring graces, leucothoe
EURYPHAESSA *daughter* eos, selene
lover hyperion
EURYPYLUS *parent* astypalaea, euaemon, poseidon, telephus
slayer hercules
uncle priam
EURYSACES *parent* ajax, tecmessa

EURYSTHENES *father* aristodemus
kingdom sparta
twin procles
EURYSTHEUS *cousin* hercules
daughter admete
kingdom mycenae
parent nicippe, sthenelus
slayer hyllus
EURYTHMY proportion, symmetry
EURYTION centaur
friend aeneas
parent actor, ares
slayer hercules, peleus
son-in-law peleus
EURYTUS *daughter* iole
father actor, augeus, melaneus
kingdom oechalia
slayer hercules
EUSCARO basque
EUTERPE *lover* strymon
parent jupiter, mnemosyne, zeus
son rhesus
EUTOPIA See UTOPIA.
EVA *friend* topsy
EVACUATE abandon, clean out, clear(away)(out), deplete, deprive, desert, discharge, drain, eject, eliminate, emit, empty, exhaust, expel, forsake, leave, nullify, perspire, purge, quit, remove, sweep out, vacate, void, withdraw
EVACUATION clearage, clearance, departure, depletion, drainage, draining, elimination, emptying, excretion, exhaustion, removal, voidance, withdrawal
EVACUEE migrant, outcast
EVADE avoid, baffle, beg, bilk, blench, blink, bypass, cheat, circumvent, ditch, dodge, double, duck, elope, elude, escape, eschew, fence, flank, flee, fly, foil, frustrate, gee, get out of, give the slip, illude, jump, miss, outslip, outwit, palter, parry, quibble, shake, shirk, shuffle off, shun, shunt, sidestep, skip, tergiversate, thwart, waffle
payment bilk
work goldbrick, jouk
EVADED exempted, geed
EVADNE *brother* melantius

consort apollo, capaneus, poseidon
guardian aepytus
parent iphis, neptune, pelias, pitana
son iamus
EVALUATE adjudge, appraise, assay, assess, calculate, criticize, dissect, estimate, ga(u)ge, judge, price, rate, reckon, value
EVALUATION appraisal, assessment, estimate, rating
critical epicrisis
EVANDER *ally* aeneas
parent carmenta, hermes
son sarpedon
EVANESCE disappear, dissipate, fade, vanish
EVANESCENCE anicca, impermanence, vanishing
EVANESCENT brittle, cursory, ephemeral, fleet(ing), fragile, flitting, fugitive, impermanent, infinitesimal, momentary, passing, short-lived, stayless, transient, transitory
EVANGEL good news, gospel, herald
EVANGELICAL gospel, orthodox, protestant, scriptural
EVANGELINE *home* acadia, grand pre
lover gabriel
EVANGELIST apostle, colporteur, disciple, ecclesiastic, edwards, gantry, gospeler, graham, john, luke, mark, matthew, mcpherson, missionary, missioner, patriarch, preacher, propagandist, pulpiteer, revivalist, smith, sunday, writer
EVANS, MARY ANN george eliot
EVAPORATE avolate, dehydrate, desiccate, disappear, dissolve, distil, dry, escape, exhale, fly, preserve, steam, vanish, vaporize, volatilize
EVAPORATING *system* calandria
vat apron
EVASION artifice, circumvention, dodge, equivocation, escape, jink, loophole, quirk, shift, shuffle, shuffling, slip, snatch, twister
EVASIVE cagey, deceitful, dodgy, eely, elusive, elusory, evanescent, malinger-

ing, piking, shifty, shy, slippery, slipskin, sly, stealthy, trick(s)y
EVAT eft, newt
EVE, EVE'S dampen, dusk, evening, eventide, female, herb, iva, rib, sundown, sunset
cup pitcher-plant
grandchild enos
husband adam
new year's hagmena, hogmanay
serpent's tree amanita, flyagaric
son abel, cain, seth
successor lilith
EVEA cephaelis, ipecac, madder, shrub, tree
EVEN abreast, balance(d), but, calm, consistent, constant, continual, deen, direct, drawn, een, equable, equal(ize), exact, fair, flat(ten), flush, grade, horizontal, identical, in accord, just, level(headed), match(ing), moderate, neck-and-neck, neutral, parallel, placid, plain, plane, plumb, proportional, right, same, smooth, square, steady, straight, suant, symmetrical, tho(ugh), tie(d), true, uniform, unruffled, unwrinkled, yet
break tie
chance hope, odds, possibility, toss up, touch and go
comb. homal(o)
if albeit, altho(ugh), spite, tho(ugh)
make steady, true, weigh
money equal odds
now yet
number, comb. artio
numbers pair
off level
on continuously
so notwithstanding
-tempered calm, equable, equanimous, impartial, level-headed, mild, plane, steady, still
tenor order, sameness
the score avenge
though albeit, altho(ugh)
-toed artiodactyl
up solitaire
EVENER doubletree, equalizer, ravel
EVENGLOW twilight
EVENHAND equalibrium, equality, equity

EVENHANDED equal, equitable, fair, impartial, just, unbiased
EVENING abend, afternoon, cockshut, dusk, eventide, gloaming, nightfall, sera, soir, sundown, sunset, tarde, twilight, vespers, vespertime
bell vesper
deity vesper
dress formal
emerald chrysolite
glory moonflower
lovesong serena
party soiree
pert. crepuscular, vesper (tine)
primrose afterglow, anogra, scabious, suncup
religious service hesperionos, vespers
star hesper(us), mercury, moon, venus, vesper
wear black tie, formal, tails
yesterday streen
EVENT accident, achievement, act(ion), adventure, affair, befalling, case, casus, chance, circumstance, come-off, consequence, contest, cool, deed, effect, episode, experience, exploit, fact, factum, fate, feat, fortune, game, hap(pening), happenstance, incidence, incident, issue, milestone, occasion, occurrence, outcome, particular, phenomenon, portent, result, sequel, tiding, tragedy, transpiring, upshot
blessed birth
dreadful tragedy
1st opener, premiere
funny comedy
ghostly seance
grave accident, calamity, disaster
happy godsend, hit, marriage
heroic epic, saga
series of epos
significant crisis
EVENTFUL bustling, important, memorable, notable, outstanding, phenomenal, stirring
EVENTIDE dusk, evening, twilight, vesper
EVENTUAL collateral, coming, conceivable, conditional, concluding, ensuing, extreme, final, future, indirect, last, later, secondary,

stirring, terminal, ulterior, ultimate, vicarious

EVENTUALITY chance, circumstance, consequence, contingency, future, liability, possibility, tossup

EVENTUALLY finally, hereafter, in future, in the long run, lastly, later, sooner or later, tomorrow, utimately, yet

EVENTUATE close, end, ensue, follow, happen, issue, occur, result, succeed, turn

EVENUS *father* ares, mars
offspring marpessa

EVER always, anon, at all, aye, constantly, eer, forever, once, perpetually
and anon constantly
more always, crescendo, forever, increasing
so little slightly
so many numerous
so much greatly
upward excelsior

EVEREST *conquerer* hilary, tenzing
peak ihotse

EVERGLADE marsh, swamp
bird curlew
state florida

EVERGREEN (See also SHRUB *evergreen*, TREE *evergreen*.) gorse, ming, orpine, pipsissewa
bunch clubmoss
state washington

EVERLASTING aeonial, aeonian, ageless, agelong, amaranthine, ceaseless, coeternal, constant, continual, continuous, dateless, deathless, durable, endless, enduring, eternal, eterne, everabiding, evergreen, fadeless, forever, immortal, immortelle, imperishable, incessant, incorruptible, indeciduous, infinite, interminable, lasting, neverending, olamic, perdurable, perennial, permanent, perpetual, sempiternal, tedious, timeless, unceasing, undying, unending, unfading, uninterrupted, unremitting, wearisome, without end
fire hell
flower orpine, waitzia

EVERT invert, overthrow, subvert, upset

EVERY all, any, complete,

each, entire, ilk(a), one and all
bit quite, throughout, utterly
inch throughout, utterly
now and then haphazardly, irregularly, occasionally, repeatedly
other alternate(ly), periodic(al)
which way disordered, irregularly, messy

EVERYBODY all(and sundry), each and every one, everyone, tout le monde, whole kit and caboodle

EVERYDAY colloquial, commonplace, constantly, customary, frequent, homely, ordinary, per diem, prosaic, quotidian, recurrent, routine, usual, workaday

EVERYLIKE continually, frequently

EVERYTHING all(in all), alles, altogether, athing, omni, sum, the works, total, whole(schmeer), wholly
being equal after all, considering, possibly, probably, therefore, wherefore
included overall, tout compris

EVERYWHERE algate, all around, all over, anywhere, but and ben, complete, far and near, from dan to beersheba, from end to end, from pole to pole, generally, handy, high and low, inclusive, overall, the world over, ubique, universally, upstairs and downstairs
comb. omni

EVERYWHERENESS allpresence, infinity, omnipresence, ubiquity

EVIAN *product* eau

EVICT cashier, cast (out), conquer, discharge, dislodge, dismiss, dispossess, eject, eliminate, exclude, expel, fire, oust, put out, remove, sack, shut out, spurn, turn out, unhouse

EVICTION dislodgment, dispossession, ouster, ousting, rogue's march

EVIDENCE affadavit, approve, argument, attest(ation), bespeak, betoken, charter, clew, clue, connote, data, demonstrate, demonstration, denote, depone,

deposition, display, disproof, divulge, document(ation), evince, exhibit, expose, express, facts, grounds, illustrate, imply, indicate, indication, involve, manifest(ation), mark, point to, probate, proof, prove, record, reveal, set forth, shew, show, sign, signify, speak, symptom, testimony, token, trace, voucher, warranty, weigh
kind circumstantial, collateral, constat, corpus delecti, direct, documentary, external, extrinsic, hearsay, incriminating, indirect, internal, intrinsic, oral, presumptive, primary, secondary
of wrongdoing goods
piece of probate
positive constat

EVIDENT apparent, axiomatic, beholdable, broad, cleancut, clear, conclusive, conspicuous, crystal-clear, decisive, defined, definite, discernible, disclosed, distinct, exposed, extant, frank, glaring, in sight, in view, loud, luculent, manifest, noticeable, observable, obvious, open, palpable, patent, perceivable, perceptible, plain, prominent, pronounced, recognizable, revealed, seeable, sensible, staring, tangible, unconcealed, unhidden, unmistakable, visible, welldefined, well-marked, witter

EVIDENTLY clearly, flagrantly, obviously, perceptibly, plainly

EVIL 3 bad, hob, ill, low, mal, sin, woe 4 bale, bane, base, dark, dern, dire, foul, harm, hell, hurt, jinx, mala, poor, qued, rank, sick, ugly, vice, vile 5 black, crime, curse, error, havoc, malum, quede, wrong 6 arrant, cancer, damage, divers, malign, menace, rotten, sinful, unwell, wicked 7 adverse, baleful, baneful, corrupt, diverse, harmful, heinous, hurtful, malefic, naughty, offense, outrage, satanic, vicious 8 atrocity, calamity, cankered, damnable, depraved, disaster, diseased, enormous, improper, infamous, mischief, peccancy, shameful, sinister, vexation 9 atrocious, defective, detriment, diablerie, execrable, flagitous, grievance, malignant, monstrous, nefarious, obliquity, offensive, reprobacy, repulsive, turpitude, villanous, worthless 10 abominable, iniquitous, malevolent, pernicious, scandalous, sinistrous, wickedness 11 abomination, disgraceful, mischievous, unwholesome 12 blackhearted, inauspicious

averter amulet, apotropaion, charm, fetish, symbol
child deev, imp, nis, nixie
comb. male, mis
days hard times
deity girru, loke, loki, set(h), sobk, typhon, varuna
-doer cheat, criminal, crook, culprit, felon, malefactor, miscreant, sinner, villain
eye curse, drochuil, hex, jinx, malevolence, malocchio, spell, whammy
father of See DEVIL.
incarnation of devil, satan
intent dolus, meanness
morally cankered
omen knell, sign
personification apepi, apophis, belial, serpent
pert. belial, devil
root of money
source bane
spell warding of abracadabra
spirit See SPIRIT evil.
star jinx
EVILNESS diablerie
EVINCE argue, attest, bespeak, betoken, betray, breathe, demonstrate, disclose, display, evidence, exhibit, expose, indicate, manifest, prove, reveal, show, signify, suggest
EVISCERATE bowel, degut, disembowel, draw, gut, weaken
EVIUS dionysus
EVOCATION exorcism, sadhana, sorcery, summons
EVOKE arouse, awaken, bring, call forth, conjure (up), educe, elicit, enliven, evolve, excite, extort, extract, induce, move,

prompt, provoke, rally, rouse, stimulate, stir, summon, voice, waken
EVOLUTE develop, evolve, grow, unfold(ed), unroll
EVOLUTION anagenesis, anamorphism, aristogenesis, biogeny, change, cosmism, development, dioecism, drift, expansion, growth, horotely, maturation, speciation, unfolding
regressive catagenesis
theorist darwin, haeckel, lamarck, spencer, weismann
EVOLUTIONARY advancing, developing, evolving, ontogenetic, phylogenetic, physiogenetic, progressing
EVOLVE amplify, blossom, create, deduce, derive, develop, disengage, disentangle, educe, emit, exhibit, extract, give out, grow, unfold, unplight, unroll
EVOLVING anamorphic, anamorphous, developing
EVONYMUS artilleryplant, bitterash, bleedingheart, burningbush, cattree, dittany, fraxinella, gasplant, wahoo
EVULGATE divulge, publish
EVULSE extract, pluck out, root out
EWE chilver, crock, crone, drape, female, gimmer, keb, lamb, rachel, teg, theave, yoe
changed into theophane
daisy tormentil
gowan daisy
lease pasture
old biddie, biddy, crock, crone
young theave
EWER aiguiere, aqua(e)manale, aquamanile, basin, jug, lair, pitcher, udder, urceole, urn, vessel
medieval aquamanale
EXACERBATE aggravate, agitate, embitter, enrage, excite, increase, inflame, infuriate, ire, irk, irritate, provoke, tease, worsen
EXACT absolute, accurate, ask, blackmail, bleed, careful, certain, charge, claim, clearcut, coerce, compel, constrain, correct, definite, delicate, demand, direct, distinct, due, elicit, estreat, even, exorbitant, express,

extort, faithful, fine, force, graith, impose, just, levy, limited, literal, mathematical, meticulous, minute, need, nice, oblige, particular, perfect, pinpoint, positive, precise, press, proper, punctilious, refined, request, require, right, rigid, rigorous, screw, scrupulous, severe, solicit, specific, square, squeeze, stern, strict, subtle, take, true, undeviating, unequivocal, unerring, verbatim, wrest, wring
point tee
EXACTING arduous, burdensome, conscientious, critical, demanding, difficult, exigent, finicky, hard, ironclad, meticulous, nice, onerous, oppressive, pressing, severe, stern, strait, strict, stringent
EXACTION cess, compulsion, coigny, coyne, extortion, fee, gouge, gripe, levy, tax
EXACTLY absolutely, accurately, ad litteram, aright, directly, even, in all respects, minutely, precisely, punctually, quite, right, sharp, spang, squarely, to a tee, truly
EXAGGERATE aggrandize, amplify, blow up, boast, brag, build up, bull, caricature, color, embellish, embroider, enhance, enlarge, extravagate, heap up, heighten, hyperbolize, increase, intensity, lay it on, lie, magnify, make much of, maximize, eutherod herod, outlash, overdo, overstate, overtell, puff, put it on, romance, romanticize, solemnize, strain, stretch
EXAGGERATED bouncing, camp, colored, exceptional, extravagant, fustian, hyperbolical, inflated, magnified, melodramatic, outre, overdone, overwrought, steep
EXAGGERATION amplification, boasting, bull, caricature, distortion, embroidery, fishstory, halftruth, hype(rbole), increase, lie, magnification, overstatement, puffery, reacher
EXALT advance, aggrandize,

arear, augment, bless, dignify, elate, elevate, enhance, ennoble, enthrone, extol, glorify, greaten, halo, heighten, increase, inflate, inheaven, inspire, intensify, laud, lift, magnify, praise, promote, raise, swell, tower, transfigure, uplift

EXALTATION altitude, avatar, celsitude, concentration, ecstasy, elation, elevation, importance, incentive, joy, magnanimity, rapture, refinement

of mars capricorn

to rank of god apotheosis

EXALTED astral, august, elated, elevated, extolled, great, haughty, high (minded), honorable, illustrious, immodest, lofty, lordly, magnificent, noble, pompous, pretentious, proud, rapturous, refined, selfimportant, sheen, sublime

father abraham

EXAMEN inquiry, investigation

EXAMINATION analysis, apercu, assay, audit(ion), autopsy, biopsy, catechism, checkup, critique, divvers, exploration, final, greats, hearing, inquiry, inquisition, inspection, interrogation, investigation, little-go, midterm, midyear, mod(eration), necropsy, observation, opposal, oral, probe, questioning, quiz, reconnaissance, reconnoiter, research, responsion, review, scanning, scrutiny, search, small, study, survey, tat, test, trial, tripos, tryout

oral viva, vivavoce

EXAMINE analyse, analyze, anatomize, appose, ask, assay, audit, auscult(ate), autopsy, bolt, candle, canvass, case, catechize, censor, check, collate, consider, contemplate, discuss, dissect, explore, go over, grope, inquire, inspect, interrogate, inventory, lait, look(over), note, notice, observe, ogle, overhaul, overlook, palpate, peer at, penetrate, peruse, pore(over), postmortem, probe, prospect, prove, pry, query,

question, quiz, reconnoiter, resolve, review, ripe, rummage, run over, scan, screen, scrutinate, scrutinize, search, sift, size up, speer, spy, study, survey, test, try, view, visit

EXAMINER analyst, assayer, auditor, canvasser, censor, checker, conner, coronor, inspector, observer, probator, regarder, scrutator, scrutineer, searcher, surveyer, tester

EXAMPLE archetype, bysen, calendar, case, copy, exemplar, facet, forbysen, foregoer, ideal, illustration, instance, lecture, lesson, mirror, model, norm, notice, paradigm, parallel, pattern, pink, praxas, precedent, problem, purpose, representation, sample(r), specimen, standard, sum, warning

instructive lesson

outstanding beaut, paragon

EXANIMATE languid, lifeless, spiritless

EXARCH bishop, ecclesiastic, governor, patriarch, viceroy

EXASPERATE aggravate, agitate, anger, annoy, bait, bother, chafe, enrage, exacerbate, excite, gall, get one's goat, heat, incense, inflame, infuriate, ire, irk, irritate, madden, nettle, peeve, pique, provoke, rile, roil, sting, vex, wound

EXASPERATED snak(e)y, wroth

EXASPERATION aggravation, anger, disturbance, excitement, irritation, resentment

EXCALIBUR *donor* lady of the lake

owner king arthur

EXCAVATE bur(r), burrow, cave, cut, delve, dig, disinter, dredge, drill, drive, exhume, extract, furrow, gouge, grave, groove, grub, hollow, lower, mine, mole, muck, navvy, pion, pit, quarry, sap, scoop, shovel, sink, spade, tunnel, unearth

EXCAVATOR bildar, digger, (steam)shovel

EXCAVATION cavity, denehole, ditch, dugout, grave,

hole, hollow, mine, muck, opening, pit, redd, shaft, slushpit, stope, sump, trench, trough, tutwork

into bank remblai

EXCEED advance, beat, better, cap, eclipse, excel, go beyond, outdo, outstrip, overdo, overpass, overreach, overrun, overshoot, overtop, pass, predominate, surmount, surpass, top, transcend, win

EXCEEDINGLY all, amain, awfully, beastly, bitter, bloody, excessively, extremely, greatly, heartily, horribly, immoderately, many, parlous, passing, superlatively, tree, unduly, vastly, very

EXCEL beat, best, better, bleck, cap, cob, ding, exceed, master, outclass, outdo, outpeer, outstrip, outvie, overgo, precel, shine, star, surmount, surpass, top, transcend, whale, win

EXCELLENCE altitude, arete, beauty, brilliance, character, class, dignity, eminence, fineness, firstrateness, goodliness, goodness, grace, merit, perfection, price, probity, quality, splendor, superiority, value, virtue, virtuousness, worth

model beau ideal

moral grace, probity

EXCELLENT ace, admirable, a la bonne heure, a-one, artistic, athel, bang-up, beautiful, best, blighty, bosker, brave, bravo, braw, brawlie, brawly(s), bully, burly, capital, choice, classy, corking, crack, deluxe, eminent, expert, exquisite, famous, fine, firstrate, gentle, good, grand, great, jolly, lofty, matchless, nifty, peerless, prime, proper, rare, rial, select, skookum, spiffy, superb, superior, tiptop, tops, unrivaled, virtuous, wizard, worthy

EXCELSIOR alleyoop, ever upward, onward and upward, stuffing, upsydaisy, upward

state new york

EXCEPT bar(ring), bate, besides, bout, but, else, exclude, excluding, forby, forprise, free, object, omit, quality, reserve, save, saving, sever, unless, without

EXCEPTION affront, anomaly, complaint, defense, demur(ral), deviation, doubt, exemption, fallency, forprise, instance, irregularity, license, marvel, objection, oddity, omission, perquisitor, protest, qualification, salvo, saving
take See TAKE *exception.*
without always, ever, generally

EXCEPTIONABLE distasteful, invidious, loathsome, objectionable, obnoxious, offensive, repellent, repugnant, repulsive, revolting

EXCEPTIONAL aberrant, anomalous, conspicuous, excellent, extraordinary, fine, firstclass, good, infrequent, outstanding, prominent, qualifying, rare, remarkable, salient, scarce, signal, singular, strange, sui generis, uncommon, unheard of, unique, unprecedented

EXCERPT analecta, analects, choice, choose, citation, clipping, cull, cutting, extract, fragment, misellanea, miscellany, offprint, passage, pericope, portion, quotation, quote, scrap, select (ion), verse, withdraw

EXCESS acrasia, deluge, dissipation, exorbitant, extra, extreme(s), extremity, exuberance, glut, gluttony, indulgence, intemperance, luxuriance, luxus, nimiety, overabundance, overage, overexpansion, overflow, oversupply, plethora, plus, prodigality, profusion, recrement, redundancy, remainder, riot, sate, spare, superfluity, surfeit, surplus
comb. ard, hyper

EXCESSIVE abnormal, allfired, boisterous, bouncing, campy, exorbitant, extra(vagant), extreme, exuberant, fanatic(al), glut, immoderate, inordinate, intemperate, intense, overabundant,

overflowing, overmuch, plethoric, redundant, steep, stiff, superabundant, superfluous, surplus, terrific, too much, ultra, undue, unreasonable

EXCESSIVELY devilish, enorm, exceedingly, extremely, fanatically, greatly, immoderately, inordinately, overly, passing, too, unduly

EXCHANGE agio(tage), allowance, auction, bandy, bank, barter, batta, board, bolsa, bourse, cambism, cambium, cash, chaffer, commerce, commutation, conversion, convert, cope, corse, curb, deal, dicker, excamb, flyting, give and take, kula, market, pit, premium, rap, reciprocate, repartee, reprisal, requite, retort, rialto, saloon, sell, shuffle, shuttle, store, substitute, substitution, swap, tit for tat, tolzey, trade, traffic, transpose, troke, truck, valuta, wissel, wrixle
financial amex, (big)board, bolsa, borsa, bourse, curb, floor, lombard street, stock market, the street, wall street
foreign agiotage, devise
medium coinage, currency, schuit, shoe, sycee
mutual reciprocity
pert. catallactic
rate agio, batta

EXCHANGEABLE commutable, fungible, returnable, substitutive, synonymous, transmutable

EXCHEQUER bank, chess (board), finance(s), fisc, fisk, fund(s), khalsa, purse, treasury
bill certificate, promissory note

EXCISE alcabala, assessment, cess, customs, cut, deduct, duty, erase, expunge, extirpate, geld, hollow out, impost, levy, rate, remove, retrench, revenue, slash, tariff, tax, teind, tithe, toll, tribute
officer ga(u)ger, revenuer

EXCISION cut, deduction, destruction, erasure, expulsion, exsection, removal, surgery

instrument exsector

EXCITABILITY edginess, erethisia, irritability, nerves, nervousness, skittishness

EXCITABLE combustible, ebullient, fiery, highstrung, hotblooded, hotheaded, inflammable, nervous, passionate, vascular

EXCITANT goad, intoxicant, oestrum, oestrus, prod, stimulant, stimulus, sting, thrill, titillant, whip

EXCITE actify, activate, activize, affect, agitate, alarm, anger, animate, arouse, awake(n), bestir, blow up, call forth, call up, commove, cumflutter, discompose, disquiet, elate, electrify, engender, enkindle, exasperate, explode, ferment, fire, flurry, fluster, foment, frenzy, galvanize, heat(up), ignite, impassion, incense, incite, infect, inflame, inspire, interest, intoxicate, kindle, light up, move, perturb, pique, provoke, quicken, raise (up), rally, roil, rouse, ruffle, seethe, send, spur, start, steam up, stimulate, sting, stir, sublevate, summon, thrill, tickle, titillate, wake(n), warm, wecche, whet, wow

EXCITED ablaze, afire, agog, animated, ardent, aroused, astir, atwitter, avid, breezy, cadgy, combustible, daft, delirious, discomposed, drunk, eager, ecstatic, fired, frenetic, frenzied, gay, haywire, het up, impassioned, inflamed, manic, moved, perturbed, ranty, ruffled, skeered, stormy, thrilled, turned on, wild

EXCITEMENT adventure, aggravation, agitation, animation, bang, bearm, bustle, buzz, charge, commotion, delirium, drama, ebullience, ecstasy, emotion, enthusiasm, exacerbation, exasperation, exhilaration, febricity, ferment, fever, fire, flurry, fluster, flutter, fomentation, frenzy, furor(e), fury, fuss, glow, heat, hoopla, hysteria, inflammation, infuriation, irritation, kick, melodrama,

oestrus, outburst, passion, phrensy, provocation, racket, rage, rampage, sensation, snit, stimulation, stimulus, stir, tension, thrill, tingle, tizzy, to-do, trepidation, twitter, whirl
abnormal mania, parethesis
expression of hoopla, yoicks
EXCITING breath-taking, desirable, dramatic, electric, hair-raising, heady, lurid, provoking, sensational, startling, stimulating, stirring, terrific, thrilling
EXCLAIM call, censure, clamor, cry, ejaculate, say, shout, speak, state, utter, vociferate
EXCLAMATION 3 ach, aha, aho, bah, bam, baw, boo, cry, epa, fee, fie, foh, grr, hah, haw, hay, hem, hep, heu, hey, hic, hip, hoa, hoi, hoy, huh, och, off, oho, ouf, paw, pew, pho, pox, pue, rot, see, suz, tch, tck, tut, ugh, wee, wow, yah, yoi, yow 4 ahem, alas, avoy, blaa, booh, bosh, bunk, chut, drat, ecce, egad, evoe, farn, fore, good, hail, heck, hegh, hist, hoot, huff, hunh, hush, hyke, oime, oons, ouch, ough, pfui, phew, phoh, phoo, phul, piff, pish, poof, pooh, prut, pugh, rats, scat, shoo, siss, soft, soho, sola, swow, tchu, tivy, toga, tosh, tush, umph, wagh, well, wham, what, whee, whew, whit, yipe 5 alack, blimy, bravo, curse, ewhow, fains, fancy, faugh, feigh, goody, heigh, hello, holla, huffa, hullo, humph, huzza, pshaw, right, salve, shish, skoal, sorry, sugar, whoop, woons 6 blimey, clamor, hoopla, indeed, outcry, quotha, rather, righto, shucks, tchtch, whoosh 7 gangway, hosanna, jiggers, nichevo, protest, righton, rubbish, tantivy, whoopee 8 by cracky, gadzooks, holy cats, reproach 9 complaint, expletive, utterance 10 hubba-hubba 12 interjection
derogatory drop it, forget it, never mind, no matter, skip it
interrogatory huh, hunh

point bang, screamer, shout
profane ban, curse
use ecphonesis
EXCLUDE banish, bar, blackball, block(ade), boycott, count out, cut off, debar, deport, disbar, eject, eliminate, embargo, except, exempt, exile, expel, freeze out, keep out, limit, lock out, obviate, occlude, omit, ostracize, outwall, preclude, prevent, prohibit, reject, repudiate, repulse, rule out, shut out, suspend, turn away, ward off
EXCLUDING aside from, but, except, less
EXCLUSION banishment, barring, blockade, boycott, coventry, debarment, embargo, exception, inadmissability, lockout, occlusion, omission, ostracism, preclusion, prevention, prohibition, rejection, repudiation
EXCLUSIVE alone, aloof, aristocratic, beat, clannish, cliquish, elect, elite, hypercritical, individual, limited, limiting, narrow, only, particular, personal, picked, posh, preventive, private, prohibitive, restrictive, select(ive), single, snobbish, snobby, sole, special, unique, whole
brethren darbyites
EXCLUSIVELY alone, entirely, limited, merely, only, simply, singly, solely, wholly
EXCOGITATE consider, contemplate, contrive, deliberate, devise, intent, meditate, muse, ponder, reflect, revolve, ruminate, speculate, study, think, weigh
EXCOMMUNICATE banish, curse, ostracize, oust, unchurch
EXCOMMUNICATION anathema, ban(ishment), bell book and candle, dismissal, ejection, expulsion, herem, interdict, ousting
partial akroasis, aphorismos, hypoptosis, proklausis, syntasis
EXCORIATE abrade, assail, berate, blister, censure, chafe, curse, damage, damn, execrate, flay, fret,

gall, gouge, hurt, injure, lambaste, objurgate, peel, revile, scar, scold, scorch, skin, tonguelash, upbraid
EXCORIATION spoliation, stripping
EXCREMENT appendage, cack, cast, crottels, dejecta, dejection, dejecture, discharge, dreck, dregs, egesta, ejectamenta, ejection, extravasate, extravasation, exudate, exudation, filth, frass, growth, increase, lees, outgrowth, refuse, transudate, transudation, waste(matter)
EXCRESCENCE boss, bur, burl, burr, caruncle, caruncula, excess, exuberance, fungus, fuzee, growth, knob, knurl, lump, nob, nubble, outgrowth, protuberance, pustule, stud, superfluity, tubercule, wart, wattle
EXCRETA egesta, exudate, secreta, waste(matter)
EXCRETE discharge, effuse, egest, ejaculate, eliminate, emanate, emit, evacuate, exhale, expel, extravasate, exudate, exude, give off, pass, perspire, produce, secern, secrete, sweat, transude, weep
EXCRETION discharge, eccrisis, effusion, egestion, ejaculation, elimination, emission, exudation, flux, purgament, secretion, smegma, sordes, transudation
EXCRUCIATE agonize, grind, pain, rack, torment, torture
EXCRUCIATING agonizing, chastening, grinding, grueling, intense, painful, punishing, racking, torturing, torturous, vehement, wracking
EXCULPATE absolve, acquit, clear, condone, excuse, exonerate, explain, forgive, free, justify, pardon, rationalize, remit, vindicate
EXCULPATION amnesty, excuse
EXCURSION canter, circuit, cruise, detour, deviation, drive, escapade, expedition, extension, hike, jaunt, jour-

ney, junket, obliquity, outing, outlope, picnic, pilgrimage, ramble, ride, sail, sally, tour, tramp, transgression, trek, trip, voyage, walk

EXCURSIONIST sightseer, spectator, traveler, tripper

EXCURSIVE devious, digressive

EXCURSUS article, digression, divagation, episode

EXCUSABLE defensible, dispensable, justifiable, pardonable, venial

EXCUSE absolve, acquit, aeger, alibi, amnesty, apologize, apology, beg pardon, condone, defense, discharge, essoin(e), exempt, exonerate, explain, explanation, forgive, free, justification, justify, out, overlook, palliate, pardon, plea, pretext, reason, release, relieve, remit, sunnyie, vindicate, whitewash
for being raison d'etre

EXECRABLE abominable, accursed, atrocious, awful, bad, base, beastly, cursed, curst, damnable, damned, detestable, devilish, diabolical, evil, heinous, hellish, horrifying, infernal, loathsome, low, monstrous, odious, offensive, outrageous, repulsive, revolting, ruddy, terrible, ungodly, vile, wretched

EXECRATE abhor, abominate, ban, berate, censure, condemn, curse, cuss, damn, denounce, detest, hate, objurgate, rate, reprobate, revile, smear, swear at

EXECRATION anathema, blasphemy, curse

EXECUTE achieve, act, administer, assassinate, behead, bowstring, burn, carry out, close, complete, conclude, consummate, contract, crucify, decapitate, decollate, design, direct, discharge, dispatch, effect(uate), electrocute, enforce, fill out, finish, force, fulfill, garrote, gas, gibbet, govern, guillotine, hang, implement, kill, lynch, make, manage, meet, murder, perform, play, produce, prosecute, punish, re-

alize, render, rule, scrag, seal, shoot, sign, slay, speed, strangle, transact, vest

EXECUTION accomplishment, acting, administration, auto da fe, doing, effect, ganch, hanging, killing, observance, performance, practice, production
means axe, block, cross, drop, electric chair, electrocution, firing squad, gallows, gas chamber, gibbet, guillotine, halter, hanging, hemlock, hemp, hot seat, maiden, mecate, noose, rack, rope, scaffold, stake, tree
writ elegit

EXECUTIONER beheader, burrio, carnifex, deathsman, decapitator, garroter, hangman, header, headsman, jack ketch, koko, lockman, lyncher, strangler, topsman

EXECUTIVE administrative, administrator, alcalde, archon, boss, brass, businessman, cashier, chancellor, dewan, directing, director, entrepreneur, governor, industrialist, judge, magistrate, manager, managing, minister(ial), official, podesta, prefect, premier, president, prexy, provost, warden

EXEGESIS anagoge, anagogy, explanation, exposition, haggadah, midrash

EXEGETE adviser, authority, critic, interpreter, leader

EXEMPLAR archetype, copy, eidolon, mirror, model, module, nonpareil, parable, paradigm, pattern, phoenix, prototype, specimen, standard, symbol, type

EXEMPLARY banner, bluechip, commendable, laudable, monitory, praiseworthy, typical, warning

EXEMPLIFY cite, embody, epitomize, illustrate, symbolize

EXEMPT acquit, apart, clear, discharge, dispense, excuse(d), exon(erate), free, immune, privileged, release, relieve, removed, set apart, sever, spare, special

EXEMPTION amnesty,

bloodwit, essoin, freedom, grace, immunity, liberty, license, privilege, qualification, release

EXEQUIES ceremony, dirge, funeral, obsequy, procession, rite, wake

EXERCISE absorb, act(ion), aggravate, athletics, bear, breathe(r), calisthenics, ceremony, constitutional, daily-dozen, deed, discharge, discipline, display, drill, effect, employ, etude, eurythenics, exert, exhibit, gymnastics, handle, lesson, manipulate, nisus, operation, performance, ply, practice, praxis, pursuit, recitation, ritual, show, stretch, study, task, test, trial, ure, use, utilize, wield, work(out)
aerobic cycling, running, swimming
book cahier
equipment barbell
kind isometric, isotomic
musical etude, scales, solfege, vocalise
system aerobics, calisthenics, daily-dozen
vocal solfege, solfeggio

EXERCISED bothered, concerned, distressed, nervous, perturbed

EXERT act(uate), apply(oneself), bear down, buckle down, employ, endeavor, exercise, hump, kvetch(er), lay out, ply, put out, stir, strain, strive, try, use, work
to utmost go for broke

EXERTION action, bout, burst, drudgery, effort, endeavor, exercise, grind, labor, pains, pull, spurt, strain, struggle, toil, travail, trouble, tug, work

EXFOLIATE desquamate, develope, flake, layer, scale, unfold

EXFOLIATION furfur, scaling, stripping

EXHALATION aura, breathing, fume, halitus, malaria, odor, reek, steam, vapor, wind

EXHALE breathe, cast, emanate, emit, expel, expire, perspire, reek, respire, vaporize
moisture transpire

EXHAUST bottom, breathe, consume, deplete, deprive, develop, discharge, disgorge, drain, emit, empty, evacuate, fag, fatigue, hatter, jade, mate, outwear, overdo, overwear, prostrate, sap, smoke, spend, squander, strip, swink, tire, tucker, use, vaporize, waste, weaken, wear out, weary
box muffler
device afterburner
pipe valve cut-out
EXHAUSTED all in, beat, bedridden, blown, breathless, bucked, burned out, bushed, careworn, consumed, depleted, dished, done for, done in, done up, drained, dung, effete, empty, fordone, forworn, foughten, groggy, harassed, laid low, petered, rundown, spent, stank, tired, traiky, weak, weary, worn out
EXHAUSTION consumption, debility, depletion, enervation, expenditure, fatigue, goneness, impoverishment, lassitude, prostration, sooreyn, vacancy, waste, weakness
mental psychasthenia
nervous neurasthenia
EXHAUSTIVE all-embracing, all-inclusive, blanket, complete, comprehensive, full, minute, thorough
EXHIBIT administer, advertise, air, betray, blazon, brandish, demonstrate, diorama, disclose, discover, display, divulge, emblazon, evidence, evince, explain, expose, exposition, feature, flaunt, manifest, ostend, parade, perform, present, produce, project, provide, represent, reveal, shew, show(case), stage, submit, traduce
room cabinet, gallery, panopticon
EXHIBITED ostensible
EXHIBITING ostensive, showing
EXHIBITION allowance, bench, cosmorama, diorama, display, exercise, exposition, fair, maintenance, manifestation, pageant, parade, pension, representation, salary, sale,

salon, scholarship, show, sight, spectacle, sustenance
aquatic aquarium
EXHIBITIONIST flaunter, grandstander, ham(fatter), showoff, swaggerer, vulgarian
EXHILARATE amuse, boost, buoy, cheer, elate, encourage, enliven, fire, gladden, inspire, inspirit, invigorate, quicken, refresh, stimulate, titillate
EXHILARATED gay, joyous, stimulating
EXHILARATION animation, excitement, gaiety, gladness, glee, hilarity, inspiration, jollity, joy(ousness), merriment
exclamation evoe
EXHORT admonish, advise, caution, dissuade, engage, enjoin, incite, induce, persuade, preach, press, spur, urge, warn
EXHORTATION advice, counsel, encouragement, homily, incitement, prophecy, warning
son of barnabas, barnaby, joseph
EXHUME delve, dig, discover, disentomb, disinhume, disinter, excavate, grub, resurrect, spade, unbury, unearth, untomb
EXIES fit, hysterics
EXIGENCY claim, constraint, contingency, crisis, demand, difficulty, dilemma, duress, emergency, essential, hardship, jam, juncture, necessity, need, pass, pickle, pinch, plight, pressure, quandary, requirement, rigor, scrape, strait, urge, urgency, want
EXIGENT critical, demanding, difficile, exacting, necessary, pressing, strict, urgent, vital
EXIGUOUS attenuated, confined, diminutive, fine, little, meager, restricted, scant(y), scrimpy, skimpy, slender, small, spare, sparse, sterile, tenuous, thin, tiny
EXILE attaint, banish(ment), condemn, deport(ation), deportee, diaspora, dismiss, eject, expatriate, expel, expulsion, extradite, fugitive,

ostracize, oust, outcast, outlaw, pilgrim, prescribe, refugee, relegate, ruin, transport, wretch
tree oleander
EXIMIOUS choice, distinguished, excellent, extraordinary, select
EXIST abide, are, breathe, come, continue, dwell, endure, esse, etre, grow, hold, lie, live, obtain, occur, outlast, prevail, remain, stand, stay, subsist, survive
cause to bring on, produce
passively subsist, vegetate
EXISTENCE animation, being, condition, duration, ens, entity, esse, essence, identity, life, occurrence, presence, prevalence, reality, state, status, subsistence, survival
actual in esse
element dharma
eternal sat
ever-changing samsara, sansara
pert. noumenal, ontal, ontic
principle tattva
realized energeia
science of cosmology, metaphysics, ontology
self-originated aseity
EXISTENT See EXISTING.
EXISTENTIALIST camus, sartre
EXISTING actual, alive, being, belonging, built-in, current, existent, extant, going, hard, incorporate, in ease, inherent, latent, living, natural, prevailing, prevalent, real
at the same time contemporaneous
in name only nominal, titular
in the mind apriori
self increate
EXIT avenue, bow out, death, debouche, demise, depart(ure), door, egress, end, escape, exodus, gate, get out, go out, issue, leave, outgate, outlet, passage, vent, withdrawal
EXITUS duty, exodus, issue, outcome, outlet
EX LIBRIS bookplate
EXOCOETUS butterflyfish, flyingfish
EXODUS departure, egress(ion), emigration,

exit(us), flight, forthcoming, going, hegira, hejira, outcome, outgo(ing)

EX OFFICIO authoritative

EXONERATE absolve, acquit, alleviate, clear, exculpate, excuse, exempt, forgive, free, lighten, pardon, release, relieve, remit, unload, vindicate

EXOPHTHALMOS proptosis

EXORBITANCE avarice, greed, irregularity

EXORBITANT absonant, burdensome, covetous, cutthroat, dear, desperate, egregious, exacting, excessive, extortionate, extravagant, extreme, fabulous, fancy, grasping, greedy, high, immoderate, inflationary, inordinate, intemperate, large, monstrous, onerous, oppressive, out of sight, outrageous, outre, preposterous, steep, stiff, superfluous, superlative, tall, too much, unconscionable, undue, unreasonable, unwarranted, usurious

EXORCISE cast out, conjure, expel

EXORCISM charm, conjuration, explusion, exsufflation, incantation, sorcery, spell

EXORCIST benet, wizard

EXORDIUM avant-propos, beginning, foreword, introduction, opening, overture, preamble, preface, prelude, proem, prologue, prolusion, protasis

EXOSKELETON cors(e)let

EXOSTOSIS osselet, poroma, splint

EXOTERIC comprehensive, external, open, outsider, public

EXOTIC alien, colorful, extraneous, foreign, glamorous, outland(ish), outre, peregrine, strange, unfamiliar, unusual

teachings acousmata

EXPAND add, amplify, augment, balloon, bloat, blossom, blow, branch out, broaden, bulk, develop, diduce, diffuse, dilate, dis(s)pread, distend, elaborate, enlarge, expatiate, extend, flan, flue, foam, grow, increase, inflate, lengthen, retch, splay, spread, sprout,

stretch, swell, unfold, unravel

EXPANDING dilatant

EXPANSE amplitude, area, beam, breadth, broadness, burst, depth, domain, extent, field, ocean, orbit, plain(s), range, reach, scope, sea, size, space, span, sphere, spread, stretch, sweep, territory, tract, width

broad acre, breadth, main, spread

vast desert, empire, ocean, sea, sweep

EXPANSION addition, aggrandizement, ampliation, amplification, broadening, deployment, development, dilation, distention, ectasia, ectasis, enlargement, evolution, extension, flare, growth, increase, inflation, magnification, maturation, multiplication, splay, spread(ing), swelling, widening

EXPANSIVE bombastic, broad, buoyant, diastaltic, diffusive, elastic, elated, free, generous, genial, grandiose, lavish, liberal, spacious, sympathetic, uninhibited, unrestrained, volatile, voluminous, wide

EXPATIATE amplify, argue, broaden, converse, descant, dilate, discourse, discuss, enlarge, expand, rant, recite, recount, relate, satisfy, speak, talk, tell, widespread

EXPATRIATE banish, deport(ee), emigrant, evacuee, exile, expel, extradite, migrant, ostracize, outcast, outlaw, proscribe, transport

EXPECT abide, accept, aim, anticipate, apprehend, ask, attend, await, bank on, bargain(for), calculate, contemplate, count on, deem, divine, envision, figure on, foresee, hope, intend, lippen, look(for), plan, prepare, presume, reckon, rely, suppose, suspect, think, wait, watch for, ween, wish

EXPECTANCY abeyance, anxiety, anxiousness, eagerness, hopefulness, impatience, suspense

EXPECTANT agog, antici-

pative, anxious, ardent, atiptoe, awaiting, breathless, eager, gaping, hopeful, impatient, in suspense, openeyed, optimistic, sanguine

EXPECTATION assurance, calculation, confidence, esperance, future, hope, intention, presumption, prospect, reliance, trust, view, wait, ween(ing)

EXPECTED awaited, coming, due, foreseen, future, impending, logical, probable, prospective, reckoned on, supposed

EXPECTING agog, anticipating, astir, atip, awake, awkward, breeding, enceinte, gestating, gravid, laden, parturient, pregnant, teeming, with child

EXPECTORANT cineol(e), creosote, quaiacol, storax, terebene

EXPECTORATE salivate, slobber, spit

EXPEDIENCE advantage, artifice, efficiency, fitness, opportunity, policy, propriety, utility

EXPEDIENT acceptable, advantageous, advisable, advisory, appropriate, artifice, atajo, avail, becoming, beneficial, commendable, congruous, contrivance, convenient, decent, decorous, desirable, device, discreet, dodge, due, feasible, fit(ten), fitting, good, knack, likely, makeshift, means, measure, meet, nice, opportune, pis aller, politic, possible, profitable, proper, prudent, resort, resource, right, ruffle, seasonable, seemly, shift, step, stopgap, stratagem, substitute, subterfuge, suitable, surrogate, timely, useful, utilitarian, way, wise, worthwhile, worthy

EXPEDITE accelerate, dispatch, ease, facilitate, further, grease, hasten, hie, hurry, precipitate, quicken, rush, send, speed

EXPEDITION address, agility, alacrity, camp, campaign, caravan, celerity, chase, cruise, crusade, dispatch, drave, drive, ease, enterprise, excursion, harka, haste, headhunt, hurry, jaunt, jehad, journey, junket, outing, outlope, pilgrimage, progress, promtitude, quest, safari, shikar, speed, suffari, tour, trek, trip, undertaking, velocity, voyage, warpath

EXPEDITIOUS agile, brisk, effective, efficient, fast, fleet, hasty, nimble, quick, rapid, ready, speedy, swift

EXPEL avoid, banish, belch, boot, bounce, cast out, chase, chuck, discharge, disgorge, dismiss, disown, displace, dispossess, egest, eject, eliminate, evacuate, evict, exclude, exile, expulse, extrude, exude, fire, forjudge, heave, kick out, obtrude, ostracize, oust, outcast, outray, profugate, put out, relegate, remove, retch, sack, scratch, seclude, shut out, slirt, spurt, suspend, throw out, toss out, void, vomit

EXPEND blow, consume, defray, disburse, exhaust, pay, shel! out, spend, splurge, use, waste, wreak

EXPENDITOR disburser

EXPENDITURE charge, consumption, disbursement, EXPENSE, outgo, outlay, payment, pense, price, waste

EXPENSE allowance, batta, burden, charge(s), cost(s), damage, disbursement, gaff, load, loss, nut, oncost, onus, outlay, overhead, sum, sumpture
account swindle sheet
indirect overhead

EXPENSIVE costly, dear, exorbitant, extravagant, fancy, high(priced), lavish, luxurious, precious, priceless, rare, rich, steep, stiff, sumptuous, valuable

EXPERIENCE address, adventure, approve, assay, background, bear, bitter pill, brave, empiricism, encounter, endure, enjoy, escapade, event, facility, feel, fraist, have, know, knowledge, lark, meet (up with), nightmare, ordeal, passion, pay, practicality, practice, realize, sample, sa-

voir-faire, sensation, sense, skill, sophistication, spend, suffer(ing), sustain, taste, training, trial, tribulation, try, undergo, wit
based on empiric(al)
painful calvary, via dolorosa
past mneme
trying adversity, ordeal

EXPERIENCED able, accomplished, accustomed, ace, acute, capable, expert, finished, inveterate, met, old, practical, practiced, pro, qualified, salty, seasoned, skilled, skillful, thriven, trained, used, versed, veteran, wise
person cosmopolite, empiric, empiricist, smoothy, sophisticate, veteran, worldling

EXPERIMENT assay, attempt, check, docimasy, docimology, empiricism, endeavor, essay, examination, experience, ordeal, practice, proof, prove, sample, taste, test, trial, try(out), verify

EXPERIMENTAL avantgarde, empirical, peirastic, sample, tentative, trial

EXPERT ace, adept, adroit, agile, apt, artistic, au fait, authority, balmalucha, bamalocha, boffin, canny, capable, champion, clever, cognoscente, connoisseur, conversant, crack(erjack), cunning, cute, dabhand, dabster, daedalian, darb, debt, dexterous, efficient, excellent, experienced, facile, fancy, flash, gainsome, good, graduate, habile, handy, ingenious, likely, marksman, master(ful), masterly, natural, neat, oner, past master, practical, professional, proficient, quick, ready, resourceful, schooled, shark, sharp, shroff, skilled, skillful, slick, smart, sophisticate, specialist, speedful, superior, topnotcher, trained, versatile, veteran, virtuoso, welldone, whizz, workmanlike
comb. ician, ist
group board, brain-trust, cabinet, panel, seminar
technical boffin

EXPIATE amend, appease, assoil, atone, avert, correct, deliver, propitiate, purge,

ransom, rectify, redeem, redress, remedy, save, shrive, skug

EXPIATION atonement, contrition, cross, penitence, piaculum, reparation, satisfaction, trial, tribulation, visitation
requiring piacular

EXPIRATION breath(ing), death, efflux, end, extinction
forced exsufflation

EXPIRE breathe, conclude, die, elapse, emit, end, exhale, expel, fall, inlaik, lapse, perish, run out, terminate

EXPIRED dead

EXPLAIN account for, acquit, amplify, annotate, apologize, aread, areed, clarify, clear(up), comment, construe, defend, define, demonstrate, develop, diagram, discuss, elucidate, enucleate, excuse, explicate, expound, gloss, gloze, illustrate, interpret, justify, make clear, outline, popularize, rationalize, rede, resolve, riddle, show how, simplify, solve, speed, spell out, tell how, unfold, unplight, unwonder, wise

EXPLANATION account, alibi, annotation, answer, apology, caveat, clarification, comment(ary), definition, demonstration, diagram, elucidation, enlightenment, enucleation, excuse, exegesis, exemplification, explication, exposition, footnote, gloss(ary), illumination, illustration, interpretation, justification, key, notation, note, outline, postil, rationale, reason, resolution, scholium, solution, theory, titulus
point shriek
requiring exponible

EXPLANATORY demonstrative, exegetic, exegetical, explicative, expository, scholiastic

EXPLETIVE adjunct, bosh, curse, dang, darn, dear, egad, exclamation, filler, gee, gosh, gracious, interjection, oath, redundancy, there, voila
comic great horn spoon

EXPLICABLE accountable, attributable, comprehensible, construable, explainable

EXPLICATE account, amplify, analyse, analyze, amplify, clarify, clear, construe, elucidate, enucleate, explain, expound, interpret, unfold

EXPLICATION account, analysis, description, development, evolution, explanation, exposition, opening, unfolding

EXPLICIT absolute, accurate, candid, categorical, clear, definite, demonstrative, exact, express, fixed, forthright, implicit, lucid, manifest, open, outspoken, particular, plain, perspicuous, positive, precise, smooth, specific, unqualified, visible

EXPLODE anger, backfire, bang, belch, belie, blast, blaze, blow, bomb, burn, burst, bust, confute, detonate, discard, discharge, discredit, disprove, erupt, excite, fail, fire(up), flame, flare, flash, flush, fulminate, get mad, go off, jet, let off steam, platz, plotst, plotz, pop, rage, rant, rave, refute, reject, seethe, set off, shoot, spread, squib, storm, take fire, tear, temper, touch off

EXPLOIT achievement, act(ion), adventure, advertise, avail, bleed, capitalize on, cash in on, chivalry, clip, consume, deed, enterprise, fare, feat, gest(e), heroism, impose on, make use of, milk, overcharge, perform, presume, profit, promote, publicize, quest, stunt, success, take advantage of, tour, use, utilize, venture, work

EXPLOITABLE gullible

EXPLOITER profiteer

EXPLORE botanize, chart, discover, dive, drag, examine, fathom, inquire, investigate, map, navigate, plumb, probe, range, research, scout, scrutinize, search, seek, sound, spy, test

EXPLORER astronaut, bal-

boa, burton, byrd, cabot, clark, columbus, cook, cortez, dagama, deleon, delong, desota, discoverer, drake, eric, hedin, lewis, logan, navigator, osa, perry, pike, pioneer, rae, raleigh ross, satellite, scott, sputnik, stanley, traveler, vanguard, wilkes

EXPLOSION backfire, bang, bark, blast, blowoff, blowout, blowup, boom, burst, collapse, crump, detonation, discharge, eruption, flare, flash, fulguration, fulmination, outbreak, outburst, pop, report, salvo
auto's backfire
slight pluff
underground camouflet

EXPLOSIVE combustible, dangerous, detonative, eruptive, fiery, irruptive, tense, worked up
blasting cheddite
case trunk
charge blast, booster, burster, cap, igniter, snake, squib, tulip
coal mine bobbinite
comb. ite
crystalline tetryl
device cap, detonator, initiator, petard, torpedo
flameless roburi
high cordite, jovite, pentolite, tnt
igniter fuse
illuminating starshell
kind abelite, ajax, amatol, amberite, amide, ammo(nal), ammonite, amvis, aporia, azotine, ballistite, bobbinite, bomb, brom(o)picrin, cap, carbonite, carcass, ceria, cordite, dynamite, ecrasite, emmensite, fulgurite, gaine, gelignite, guncotton, gunpowder, jovite, lignose, lyddite, maximite, melinite, methane, mine, nitrocotton, nitroglycerin, petard, powder, pyrolite, pyroxylin, roburite, shimose, soup, tetryl, thorite, tnt, tonite, torpex, westfalite
lightning-produced fulgurite
mixture extralite
oil nitroglycerin
planted mine
powder ajax, amide, atlas, ballistite

power brisance
projectile cartridge, grenade, shell, torpedo
solid gunpowder
sound bang, bark, boom, chug, oomph, pluff, vroom

EXPONENT advocate, champion, deputy, devotee, enthusiast, example, explainer, expounder, hierophant, illustration, index, indication, interpreter, ite, mystagogue, note, proponent, representative, second(er), sign, supporter, symbol, symptom, token

EXPONENTIAL base, exhibitive, numeric(al)

EXPORT banish, freight, outcarry, remove, sell, ship, send, vend
duty exitus

EXPOSE advertise, air, bare, betray, bewray, brand, broadcast, declare, demonstrate, denounce, denude, disclose, discover, disillusion, display, disprove, divulge, endanger, evince, exhibit, express, feature, finger, flaunt, inform, introduce, launch, manifest, muckrake, nail, open, oppose, parade, present, proclaim, propine, publish, recital, release, report, reveal, ridicule, satirize, show, snitch, strip, uncover, undress, untruss, utter, vent(ilate), voice
suddenly flash

EXPOSED accessible, airy, apparent, bare, bleak, evident, incident, insecure, liable, manifest, open, prone, raw, sensitive, subject, susceptible, threatened, unguarded, unprotected, unsafe, vulnerable, weak
to against

EXPOSIT See EXPOUND.

EXPOSITION account, analysis, bazaar, display, disquisition, exegesis, exhibit(ion), explanation, explication, exthesis, fair, interpretation, market, mart, pageant, show, spectacle, survey, tract(ate), treatise
hall neorama

EXPOSTULATE argue, combat, debate, declaim, discuss, dispute, dissuade, enjoin, examine, kick, object, oppose, protest, remonstrate, resist

EXPOSTULATION advice, dissuasion, outburst, protest, remonstrance

EXPOSURE appearance, aspect, baring, betrayal, blot, bow, disclosure, frontage, nakedness, nudity, opening, openness, outlook, position, prospect, revelation, susceptibility, susceptivity, vulnerability

EXPOUND analyze, anatomize, construe, develop, discourse, discuss, dissect, elucidate, explain, explicate, exposit, express, harangue, hold forth, illustrate, interpret, lecture, moralize, preach, present, resolve, sermonize, set forth, simplify, state, treat

EXPOUNDER advocate, commentator, exponent, interpretor, mufti, mullah, pitchman, salesman

EXPRESS accelerated, accurate, air, articulate, assert, bid, break, breathe, broach, categorical, clear, considered, couch, declare, definite, deliberate, describe, determine, direct, distill, distinct, enunciate, evidence, exact, explicit, fast, freight, high-speed, indicate, intentional, interpret, limited, mail, manifest, mean, message, messenger, nonstop, outspoken, particular, phrase, plain, positive, posthaste, precise, proclaim, put, quick, render, reveal, say, send, ship, signify, speak, specific, squeeze, talk, tell, testify, train, truck, unqualified, unwavering, velocious, vent(ilate), voice, voluntary, willful, witting, write

excitedly bubble, gush
numerically count, enumerate
train cannonball, flier
volubly blatter, chat, gossip

EXPRESSED said, stated, verbal

EXPRESSION action, aspect, atticism, cast, communication, conveyance, declaration, delineation, description, diction, elocution,

eloquence, idiom, language, locution, manifestation, meaning, parlance, phrase-(ology), representation, saying, show, sign, smile, statement, symbol, term, token, tone, utterance, verbalism, voice, vocalism, vult, word(ing)

algebraic binomial
ambiguous equivoke, equivoque
annoyed tch, tsk
antiquated archaism
approval applause, bravo, clap, ovation, smile
assent placet
concise brachylogy
consent okay, okeh, righto(n), roger
contempt bah, fie, fouter, geck, hiss, phooey, pshaw, sneer, yuk
delight whee, whoo
disapproval fie, thunder
disdain tsk, tush
dismay oops
displeasure tck, tsk
distaste rot, tchu
dull glassy-eyed
elegant atticism
encouragement yoicks
excitement yoicks
facial frown, grimace, grin, laugh, scowl, smile, sneer
gratitude thanksgiving
hackneyed bromide, cliche, saw
impatience tsk, tut
incredulity indeed, really
local argot, idiom, patois
mathematical equation
metaphorical figure(of speech)
negative unh-unh
opinion vote
pedantic inkhornism
pet cant, catchword, slogan
sarcastic gibe, jibe
scorn geck
sorrow alas, lamentation
strange argot, idiom
surprise lawks, tck
symbolic equation, formula
weariness sigh

EXPRESSIONLESS blank, empty, stupid, vacant

EXPRESSIVE ciceronian, eloquent, fluent, graphic, holophrastic, meaningful, oratorical, picturesque, poetic, pregnant, sententious, significant, silver-tongued, soulful, suggestive, vivid

EXPRESSIVENESS delicacy, eloquence, oratory, significance

EXPRESSLY directly, explicitly, formally

EXPRESSMAN carrier, messenger

EXPRESSWAY freeway, road, speedway, thoroughfare, throughway, turnpike

EXPROBATE censure, rebuke, reproach, upbraid

EXPROPRIATE deprive of, dispossess, seize

EXPULSION banishment, bannimus, dismissal, dispossession, ejection, eviction, exile

EXPUNGE blot, cancel, deduct, dele, delete, efface, eradicate, erase, excise, obliterate, scratch, strike out, wipe out

EXPURGATE bathe, bluepencil, bowdlerize, castrate, censor, clean, cleanse, deduct, geld, purge, purify

EXQUISITE affected, acute, beauteous, beautiful, buck, choice, consummate, costly, coxcomb, dainty, dandy, delicate, delightful, discriminating, dude, elegant, entire, ethereal, exact, fine, flawless, fop, impeccable, intense, keen, lovely, macaroni, matchless, nice, overnice, perfect(ed), pert, precious, priceless, rare, recherche, refined, savory, sensitive, spark, subtle, superb, swell, valuable, whole

EXSCIND cut, excise, extirpate, sever

EXSICCATE arid, dry, parch(ed), sere

EXSUFFLATION expiration, exorcism, sorcery

EXTANT alive, being, conspicuous, existent, existing, living, manifest, present, protuberant, subsistent, visible

EXTEMPORANEOUS adlib(item), apt, casual, impromptu, improvisate, improvisatory, improvised, improvisional, improviso, impulsive, mechanical, offhand, prompt, quick, ready, snap, spontaneous, sudden, unrehearsed

EXTEMPORIZE See IMPROVISE.

EXTEND add, advance, amplify, augment, beetle, branch out, brede, broaden, carry(over), cover, crane, delay, deploy, dilate, distend, eke, elaborate, elongate, endure, enlarge, expand, flow, give, increase, jut, lengthen, let out, lie, mantle, offer, proceed, prolong, protract, radiate, reach, renew, span, spread, straighten, strain, stretch, submit, sustain, widen

across traverse

around gird, girth

credit advance, carry, finance, underwrite

horizontally porrect

over bridge, contain, cover, cross, last, span

to reach

EXTENDED assured, broad, drawn out, lasting, lengthy, long, open, spread, stretching, valued, verbose

EXTENSIBLE elastic, pliable, pliant

EXTENSILE productile, protrusile

EXTENSION adjunct, ambitus, annex, area, arm, branch, bridge, cape, dependence, distension, ell, enlargement, expansion, expatiation, increase, limb, range, scope, span, spread, stretching, wing

building annex, ell, lean-to, wing

of time delay, reprieve, respite, stay

trench sap

wing-like ala

EXTENSIVE ample, big, broad, capacious, commodious, comprehensive, diffuse, enormous, farflung, farreaching, generous, huge, immense, large, lengthy, roomy, spacious, sweeping, vast, widereaching, widespread

EXTENT ambit, amplitude, area, body, breadth, bulk, capacity, compass, degree, dimension, distance, duration, expanse, latitude, magnitude, mass, quantity, radius, range, reach, scope, size, space, spread, stretch, sweep, tract, variety, volume

utmost a la riguer, nth degree

EXTENUATE afflict, allow for, color, condone, decrease, dilute, diminish, enfeeble, excuse, forgive, gloss over, gloze, justify, lessen, mince, mitigate, moderate, palliate, qualify, rarefy, reduce, soften, temper, thin, varnish, weaken, whiten, whitewash

EXTENUATION decrease, palliation, qualification, weakening

EXTERIOR alfresco, alien, ambitus, cortical, ectal, exomorphic, exoteric, external, extrados, extraneous, extrinsic, face(t), finish, foreign, margin, open(air), outby, outdoors, outlying, outside, outward, peripheral, polish, rind, scene, shell, skin, superficial, superficies, surface, top

comb. ectal

toward ectad

EXTERMINATE abate, abolish, cut off, demolish, deracinate, destroy, do away with, efface, eliminate, eradicate, erase, execute, extinguish, extirpate, kill, liquidate, obliterate, pull out, purge, raze, remove, root up, sweep away, uproot, wipe out

EXTERMINATION annihilation, expulsion, extinction, killing

EXTERMINATOR aerosol bomb, bug bomb, ddt, destroyer, eradicator, fungicide, killer, microbicide, paris green, pesticide, poison, rodenticide, vermicide

EXTERNAL alien, cortical, ectal, exoteric, exterior, extraneous, extrinsic, foreign, formal, outer, outermost, outside, outward, peripheral, superficial, surface

comb. ect(o), exo

world nonego, reality

EXTERNALIZE actualize, embody, hypostatize, incarnate, materialize, objectify, realize, reify, substantiate

EXTINCT dead, defunct, extinguished, gone, passe, past, quenched, superseded

EXTINCTION abolition, annihilation, blot(ting out),

cancel(lation), death, deletion, destruction, doom, elimination, eradication, erasure, expiration, extermination, extirpation, liquidation, obliteration, purge

EXTINGUISH abate, abolish, annihilate, blanket, blot, blow out, choke, damp, destroy, douse, dout, efface, erase, expunge, nullify, obliterate, out, put out, quash, quell, quench, repress, slack, smother, snub, snuff, squash, squelch, stamp out, staunch, stifle, suppress, uproot, wipe out

EXTINGUISHER acid, carbon tet, fire engine, foam, quencher, soda, water, wet blanket

EXTIRPATE annihilate, dele, deracinate, destroy, eradicate, erase, excise, expel

EXTOL, EXTOLL acclaim, advance, aggrandize, applaud, bless, celebrate, commend, compliment, enhance, eulogize, exalt, glorify, laud, magnify, praise, resound, roose, upraise

EXTORT badger, blackmail, bleed, bludgeon, claim, compel, constrain, demand, drag, draw, educe, elicit, evoke, exact, extract, force, grate, milk, overcharge, pull, rend from, require, screw, shake down, squeeze, steal, tear from, wrench (from), wrest, wring(from)

EXTORTION badger game, blackmail, camorra, chantage, claim, demand, exaction, fraud, gouge, holdup, malversation, overcharge, racket, rending, shakedown, swindle, theft, thievery

group blackhand, camorra

EXTORTIONATE avanious, exorbitant, hard, inordinate, outrageous

EXTORTIONIST barathron, barathrum, blackmailer, bloodsucker, briber, camorrist, harpy, leech, poller, profiteer, shaver, sponger, usurer, vampire, vulture

EXTRA accessory, actor, addendum, addition(al), allowance, bonus, boot, edition, excess, insert(ion), more, nonessential, occasional, odd, over, plus, premium, reserve, spare, special, sub, subsecive, substitute, supe, super(fluous), superior, supernumerary, surplus, unusual

comb. hyper, super

theatrical supe(r)

EXTRACT abstract, ask, attar, avulse, citation, cite, clipping, concentrate, concentration, cull, decoction, deracinate, dig out, distil(late), distillation, drag, draught, draw, educe, elicit, elixir, elute, eradicate, essence, estreat, evoke, evolve, evulse, excavate, excerpt(ion), extort, extricate, flavoring, florescence, get out, grub out, infusion, juice, lift, obtain, ottar, otto, pericope, pick out, pluck, procure, pull(out), quintessence, quote, rake out, remove, require, root(out), select(ion), spirit, summary, take out, tear out, tincture, unearth, uplift, uproot, vanilla, weed out, withdraw

EXTRACTION ancestry, birth, blood, breeding, derivation, descent, elicitation, essence, evaporation, family, genealogy, kin, line (age), origin, parentage, removal, stock, withdrawal

EXTRACTIVE amaroid, arousing, bang, bhang, eductive, elicitory, eradicative, evocative, exactive, extortionate, extortive, uprooting

EXTRACTOR catheter, corkscrew, dryer, forceps, pliers, press, separator, siphon, tweezer(s), wringer

EXTRACTS analecta, analects

EXTRADITE banish, deport, exile, expatriate, ostrasize, relinquish, resign, transport, yield

EXTRAMUNDANE heavenly, immaterial

EXTRANEOUS accidental, adventitious, alien, exotic, exterior, external, extrinsic, foreign, immaterial, incidental, irrelevant, outer, outside, outward

EXTRANEOUSNESS *comb.* all(o)

EXTRAORDINARY abnormal, awesome, awful, awing, bang up, big, bloody, byous, corking, enorm, exceptional, eximious, great, huge, important, incomprehensible, inconceivable, incredible, indescribable, irregular, marked, marvelous, memorable, mighty, miraculous, notable, noteworthy, odd, phenomenal, prodigious, rare, remarkable, rememberable, signal, singular, special, strange, striking, stupendous, tickaninny, unco, unforgettable, unique, unusual, wonderful, wondrous

person oner

EXTRASENSORY clairvoyant, esp, psychic(al), telepathic

EXTRAVAGANCE dissipation, ela, excess, extremism, fanaticism, improvidence, intemperance, lavishness, overage, plenty, prodigality, profligacy, profuseness, profusion, squandering, superfluity, surfeit, wastage, waste, wastefulness

EXTRAVAGANT absonant, absurd, abundant, baroque, bizarre, bombastic, bounteous, bountiful, camp(y), diffuse, dispenditious, excessive, exorbitant, expenseful, expensive, fanciful, fancy, farout, flighty, foolish, immoderate, improvident, inordinate, intemperate, lavish, lush, meshugge, nimius, outre, plush, posh, prodigal, profligate, profuse, rampant, reckless, rococo, romantic, silly, splendid, violent, unreal, wanton, wasteful, weird, wild

EXTRAVAGANZA caricature, drama, fabrication, spectacle

EXTRAVAGATE dramatize, elaborate, exaggerate, exceed, rove

EXTRAVASATE bleed, disgorge, erupt, excrete, exude, pour

EXTREME all-fired, antipodes, bitter end, blue, border, butt, cruel, deadly, dire, drastic, edge, end, eventual, excess(ive), exorbitant, fanatical, far, farthest, final, great, highest, howling, immoderate, inordinate, intense, just, last, latest, limit, maximum, nth degree, outermost, outrageous, outrance, overdone, pitch, rabid, radical, rank, remote, sore, steep, terminal, terrible, terrific, too, top, ultimate, ultra, utmost, uttermost, vile, violent

comb. acro, arch

unction last rites, sacrament

EXTREMELY aplenty, awfully, bitterly, dead, deuced, drastically, greatly, heaps, hopping, majestically, mortally, precious, selly, sopping, sublimely, terribly, too, unduly, utterly, very

EXTREMIST bonnet rouge, fanatic, jacobin, radical, red cap, revolutionary, revolutionist, ultraist

EXTREMITY anguish, appendage, arm, border, bound, bourn, butt, confine, crisis, disaster, edge, end, excess, exigent, finger, foot, hand, impasse, leg, limb, limit, need, pole, push, term(inal), termination, tip, top, verge

comb. acro

disease of acropathy, gout

enlargement of acromegalia

EXTRICATE abstract, clear, cut loose, deliver, detach, disembarrass, disencumber, disengage, disentangle, dislodge, expedite, extract, facilitate, free, help, liberate, loose(en), pull out, release, relieve, remove, rescue, tear loose, untangle

EXTRINSIC accidental, acquired, alien, earned, external, extraneous, foreign, gained, nonessential, outer, outlying, outside, outward

EXTROVERSION objectivity, outgoingness, syntony

EXTROVERT outgoing, syntonic

EXTRUDE eject, expel, force out, press out, project, protrude, push out, spew, thrust out

EXUBERANCE abandon, abundance, animal spirits, copiousness, enthusiasm, excess, luxuriance, luxury, overflow, plenty, profusion, rampancy, rankness

EXUBERANT copious, diffuse, effusive, energetic, fecund, fertile, fruitful, gay, glowing, lavish, lush, lusty, luxuriant, plentiful, prodigal, productive, profuse, prolific, rampant, rank, spirited, thriving, vigorous

EXUDATE, EXUDATION apostaxis, aura, balm, bleeding, copal, dikamali, discharge, effusion, emanation, excretion, extravasion, filtering, filtration, gum, lac, leaching, moisture, ooze, percolating, percolation, pitch, resin, rosin, sap, seep (age), sudor, sweat, tar, transudation

EXUDE bleed, discharge, drip, eject, emit, excrete, expel, flow, give off, ooze, perspire, pour, radiate, reek, secrete, stream, sweat, throw off, weep

EXULT boast, crow, delight, elate, gloat, glory, joy, jubilate, leap, rejoice, spring, triumph, vaunt

EXULTANT agog, cockahoop, ecstatic, elate(d), euphoric, exalted, flushed, glad, gleeful, happy, joyful, joyous, jubilant, ovant, rapturous, sanguine, transported, triumphant

EXULTATION elation, joy, jubilance, jubilation, jubilee, ovation, rapture, triumph

EXUVIATE cast, discard, junk, molt, scrap, shed, slough

EYAH See AYAH.

EYE, EYES appear, auge, behold, blinker, brood, circle(t), daylights, detective, detector, een, exocone, eyne, flirt, glim, glimmers, glimpse, goggle, gudgeon, hilum, hoop, inspect, intention, keekers, lamp, lights, look, loop, mark, mien, observe, ocular, oculus, ogle, opinion, optic, orb, outlook, peeper(s), peephole, pinkany, pinkeny, regard, scan, see, sekhet, shade, sight, spy, stare, stemma, tail, tinge, uta, view, watch,

window, winker, witness, yen, yes
absence anophthalmia
agate aleppo-stone
anesthetic phenacaine
angle canthus
askance fear
bags under blepharochalasis
balm golden-seal
between interocular
black hypopyon, mouse, shiner
blind spot punctum-caecum
cast strabismus
cavity orbit
close seel
coat choroid
color daw
colored part iris
comb. irido, ocul(i), oculo, opthalmo, opto, video
compound ommateum
corner canthus
cosmetic kohl, kuhl, mascara, shadow, surma
covering blindfold, lid, patch
deception trompe l'oeil
defect, comb. itis, opia
defect or disease achromaticity, amaurosis, amblylopia, ametropia, aniridia, anisocoria, ano(o)psia, anopia, anorthopia, ansiometropia, aphakia, aplanation, astigmatism, axanthopsia, blinkard, blinking, buphthalmia, caligo, cast, cataract, cockeyes, coloboma, conjunctivitis, crosseyes, diplopia, esotropia, glaucoma, gutta-serena, heterotropia, hippus, iritis, lippitude, macropsia, micropsia, minuthesis, myopia, nictitation, nystagmus, ophthalmia, pin and web, pinkeye, presbyopia, ptosis, purblindness, retinitis, scleritis, squinch, squint, strabismus, stye, synechia, trachoma, uveitis, walleye, winker, winking, xerosis
drop tear
drop ingredient eserin
dropper pipette
enlargement buphthalmia
evil drochuil, jettatura, malocchio, whammy
examiner ophthalmoscope
fatigue asthenopia
film cataract, nebula, pearl
flap blinder, blinker, goggles, lid, patch, visor
fold epicanthus

for an eye retribution, revenge
hollow orbit, socket
inner coat retina
layer uvea
lens absence aphakia
-like ocellated
little ocellus
loss madarosis
magic radar
mark spectacle
measurer campimeter
medication collyrium, terramycin
membrane conjunctive, retina, sclera
muscle rectus
nerve abducens
of day sun
of greece athens
of heaven sun
of ra sekhet
of storm bull's-eye
-opener drink, surprise
opening apocalyptic(al), pupil, uvea
pain lippitude
parasite loa
part areola, cornea, disc, iride, iris, pupil, retina, sclera, strale, uvea
pert. areolar, corneal, irian, ocellate, ocular, oculate, ophthalmic, optic, retinal
piece lens
piece crosshairs reticle
pigment melanin
pit socket
-popping astonishing
private detective, sleuth
protector See *flap,* above.
pupil absence acorea
pupil defect anisocoria
pupil-narrowing stenocoriasis
retina part cone, rod, yellow spot
science ophthalmology
shade sunglasses
shadow kohl
simple ocellus
socket orbit
spot ocellus
stalk stipe
strings tendons
symbol uta
to eye unanimous, united
tooth canine, cuspid
tumor encanthis
turned upward anoopsia, anop(s)ia
ulcer (a)egilops
water boric(acid), collyrium, gin, liquor, teardrop, tears

-watering delacrimation, epiphora
weakness asthenopia
winker lash
worm loa
EYEBALL glass, glene, globe, look, orb, stare
covering cornea, sclera
movement vergence
protrusion exophthalmos, proptosis
shrinkage phthisis bulbi
EYEBOLT sprig
interlocking snibel
EYEBRIGHT euphrasy, eyewort, herb, indian pipe, indian tobacco, scarlet pimpernel, sundew
EYEBROW bree, dormer, eebree, fillet, molding, supercilium, wriggle
between interciliary
EYEGLASS brills, goggles, lens, lorgnette, lorgnon, monocle, nippers, pincenez, spectacles, specs
EYELASH blinker, bree, brow, cilia, winker
loss madarosis
EYELESS blind, sightless, unsighted
EYELET agraf(f)e, button-

hole, circlet, cringle, grommet, loophole, oillet, peephole, perforation
EYELETEER bodkin, stiletto
EYELID bree, palpebra
absence ablepharia
angle canthus
comb. blephar(o), canth(o)
darkener See EYE *cosmetic,* above.
disease deplumation, scleriasis
droop ptosis
fold epicanthus
hair brills
incision tarsotomy
-like ocellated, ocellus
membrane conjunctiva
part tarsus
pert. blepharal, palpebral
spasm blepharism
trembling cillosis
tumor pladaroma
without ablepharous
EYEROOT goldenseal
EYESHOT range, reach
EYESIGHT observation, view, vision
EYESOME attractive, charming, goodlooking
EYESORE blemish, blot, de-

fect, fright, sight, stigma, ugliness
EYEWASH alibi, applesauce, collyrie, deception, flattery, nonsense, rubbish
EYEWITNESS beholder, bystander, kibitzer, observer, onlooker, spectator, viewer
EYOT(Y) ait, ile, island, isle(t)
EYRA jaguarundi, wildcat
EYRE, JANE *pupil* adele
EYRIE eerie, nest
EZBON *parent* bela, gad
EZEKIAS *son* manasses
EZEKIEL *father* buzi, jeremiah
4 beasts aniel, azriel, haniel, hayoth, kafziel
EZEL ass, juniper, tree
EZER *parent* ephraim, etam
son bilhan, jakan, zavan
EZERIAS *son* saraeas
EZIAS *son* amariah, amarias
EZRA salathiel
dragons carmanians
field ardat
son epher, jalon, jether, mered
woman mourner zion
writer asiel, dibri, ethan, seraiah, shelemiah

F

FAAM faham, tea
FABA bean-vetch, vicia
FABACE cativo, centrosema, pea, prioria, vine, tree
FABES gooseberry
FABIAN careful, cautious, shaw, socialist
mistress olivia
policy delay, inertia, procrastination
FABIUS cunctator, delayer
FABLE allegory, apolog(ue), bestiary, canterbury tale, cock-and-bull story, fableau, fabrication, fiction, figment, figure, invention, legend, lie, myth(ology), parable, story, tale, untruth, yarn
collection bestiary
end moral
writer aesop, andersen, bidpai, grimm, parabolist, parabolizer, pilpay
FABRIC (See also CLOTH.) building, condition, consis-

tency, contexture, edifice, frame, goods, material, mold, skirting, stamp, structure, stuff, suiting, textile, weave
absorbent huck
alpaca-like brilliantine
artificial See *synthetic,* below.
awning algérienne
basket-weave monk's-cloth
brocaded lame, lampas
buckram bocasine
calico sall(o)o
camelhair aba, camlet
canvas poldavy, tewk, tuke
canvas-like wigan
cashmere prunell
cellulose rayon
checked gingham, hound's-tooth, plaid, tartan
clerical armozeen, caddice, caddis
coarse aba, bafta(h), baize, baline, bocking, buffin, bure, burlap, cad(d)is, can-

gan, canvas, cordillat, cotonia, crash, dagswain, denim, drabbet, drugget, duck, duffel, flushing, gunny, haire, hessian, kersey, kharva, linsey (woolsey), mat, putto, raploch, ratine, rugging, russet, sacking, sarcilis, sinamay, stamin, stammel, stroud, tat, yerga
coat bombazette, cheviot
corded bengaline, corduroy, crystalline, ducape, ottoman, pique, poplin, rep(p)
cotton 3 rep 4 crea, duck, jean, lawn, leno, lino, moxa, mull, pima, sela, susi 5 adati, bafta, baize, basin, bluet, caffa, chino, crash, denim, doria, drill, durry, khaki, lisle, manta, pique, rumal, scrim, selah, surat, swiss, toile, vichy, wigan 6 alache, baftah, ba-

line, burrah, byssus, calico, cangan, canvas, catgut, chillo, chintz, cossas, coutil, dimity, dowlas, durrie, humhum, linene, madras, muslin, nankin, oxford, penang, ratine, sateen 7 batiste, buckram, bustian, cambaye, cambric, cantoon, damasse, derries, etamine, flannel, fustian, galatea, gingham, harvard, hickory, holland, jaconet, kitenge, malabar, nanteen, oilskin, organdy, percale, regatta, satinet, silesia, ticking, tiffany, tucking 8 agabaull, anabasse, birdseye, bogotana, bourette, buckskin, coteline, coutille, cretonne, drilling, dungaree, indienne, lambskin, marcella, moleskin, nainsook, osnaburg, seerhand, sheeting, tarlatan, thickset 9 bookcloth, cannequin, huccatoon, percaline, silkalene, soiesette, turkeyred 10 balbriggan, beaverteen, broadcloth, hopsacking, madapollam, marseilles, seersucker, sicilienne, terrycloth 11 covertcloth 12 cavalry twill 13 airplanecloth, brittanycloth

cotton and wool astrakhan, domett, lambsdown, viyella

cotton and worsted paramatta

cotton, glazed argentina, chintz

cotton, knit balbriggan

cotton, light jaconet, leno, organdy, organza, silkalene, silkaline

cotton mixture bombasine, delaine, grusaille, mashru, orleans, satinet, zanella

cotton print agabanee, bat(t)ik, calico, cretonne, percale

cotton, silk-touched agabanee

cotton, twilled denim, fustian, sall(o)o, silesia

cotton velvet fustian

crepe plisse

crinkled crape, crepe, plisse

crisscross network

curtain cretonne, leno, moreen, net, ninon, scrim, silesia, velvet

damask-like caf(f)oy

dealer draper, mercer

decorated batik, diamante

defect barre, brack, gout, scob, smash

delicate hus, jusi, net

design bat(t)ik, stripe

drapery chintz, cretonne, tabaret, velvet

durable chino, scrim, serge

dye an(n)atto, anthraquinone, arnatto, auramine

18th century calamanco

elastic goring, stockinet

embellished lampas

embossed cloque, matelasse

embroidered sampler

embroidery baldaquin, bolting-cloth

felt-like baize

figured brocade, brocatel, damask, moreen, paisley

fine byssus, cashmere, dimity, linen, merino, mohair, mull, percale, pima, silk, susi

finish cire, soleil

finisher beetle

flag bewpers, buntine, bunting

floral dobby

fluted cannele, rep

frieze cothamore

gauze pleasance, tulle

gauze-like barege, gossamer

glazed argentina, chintz, cire, tammy

glossy gloria, sateen, satin

goat's hair camlet, mohair, tibet-cloth

gold acca, lame, soneri, tash, tass

gray blunket

hand-dyed batik

heavy brocade, burlap, canvas, catgut, crash, denim, duck, frieze, gros, linene, tobine, whitney

hemp bagging, burlap, sarpler, tinampipi

herringbone coutil

homespun bandle-linen, kelt, khaddar, khadi, pattu, puttoo, russet

horse-blanket yerga

imitation, comb. een

jute bagging, baline, burlap, crash, velure

knapped ras

knitted balbriggan, barre, boucle, jersey, lisle, tricolette, tricot

lace alencon, mechlin, net, schiffli, val

lawn quintin

light challis, delaine, eta-

mine, fortisan, gloria, leno, lino, tissue, zenara, zephyr

linen barras, bewpers, blancard, bocasine, brabant, brin, brittany, buckram, cambresine, cambric, carde, catgut, corporal, crash, crea, cretonne, damask, dornick, dowlas, drabbet, drill, duck, ecru, forfar, gallipot, holland, huck(aback), lawn, lockram, marcella, nacarat, osnaburg, scrim, silesia, sindon, sinelon, taffeta, toile, tucking, velure

lining cubica, pelon, sateen, shalloon, tammy, zanella

looped pile terrycloth

loose weave eponage, net, ratine

lustrous chintz, lame, poplin, radium, samite, sateen, satin, tinsel

marbled marbrinus

measure aune, centimeter, meter, yard

medieval acca, baldachin, ciclatoun, samite

melton box cloth

mesh See *open*, below.

metallic acca, lame, tash, tinsel

military cadet, khaki

modern acetate, dacron, nylon, rayon, trivera

mottled chine

mourning alma, crape, crepe, radsimir

muslin adati, plumetis, tanjib

napped broadcloth, cantonflannel, ras, rugging

necktie nep

net maline, tulle

non-woven felt

nylon cire

open lace, leno, mesh, net, sinamay, skipdent, tamis, tarlatan, tiffany, tulle

ornamental galloon, gimp, lace, lampas, trap

painted caffa

palm-fiber saguran

patterned allover, armure, pinstripe, vigoureux

pebbled armure, barathea

piled astracan, astrakhan, broadtail, chenille, corduroy, krimmer, mohair, moquette, plush, terry (cloth), velour, velvet

pineapple-leaf pina-cloth

plaid maud, tartan, tattersall

pleated ruche

printed agabanee, allover, bat(t)ik, calico, challis, chintz, cretonne, percale, tournay

raffia rabanna

raised design armure, brocade, broche, matelasse

rayon acetate, alpaca, radium, rep

remnants lint, mungo

rib wale

ribbed cord(uroy), cotele, faille, gros, marocain, mogadore, pique, rep(p), soleil, twill, whipcord

rough homespun, hopsack, terry

sacking burlap

satin camlet, etoile, mushru, pekin

satin-like calamanco, camlet, lustrine, sateen, satinet(te)

serge clay

shaded ombre

sheer batiste, casement cloth, dimity, gauze, gossamer, lawn, net, organdy, organza, souffle, swiss, tiffany, toile, tulle, valence, voile

shroud sindon

silk 3 rep, say 4 acca, alma, crin, fugi, fuji, gimp, gros, husi, ikat, jusi, moff, muga, pang, rash, repp, soie, tash 5 atlas, caffa, carde, china, corah, crape, crepe, honan, moire, ninon, pekin, rajah, rumal, satin, shela, shikh, surah, tabby, tiras, tiraz, tulle 6 alacha, armure, bengal, blatta, broche, cabeca, camaca, camaka, camoca, canton, cendal, chappe, culgee, ducape, faille, khaiki, maline, mantua, patola, piquet, pongee, radium, ratine, samite, sendal, shelah, sindon, souple, tissue, tobine, tricot, tussah, tusser, tussur, velure 7 alachah, alamode, brocade, chiffon, dornick, dornock, epingle, foulard, habutai, hernani, marabou, organza, romaine, schappe, taboret, taffeta, tiffany, tsatlee, tussore, yesting 8 baratbea, baudekin, bourette, cherimen, diaphane, duppioni, eolienne, florence, habutaye, imperial, languent, louisine, marabout, marocain, milanese, mogadore, ormuzine, radsimir, sarcenet, sarsenet, shagreen, siamoise 9 ailantine, alex-

ander, ardassine, baldachin, baldaquin, bombacine, charmeuse, grosgrain, levantine, marceline, matelasse, messaline, stauracin, tartarine 10 baldachino, rumchunder, tricolette 11 merveilleux

silk brocade baldachin, baldaquin, baudekin

silk imitation rayon, satinet

silk mixture acca, albert crepe, baldachin, barathea, bombazine, brocatel(le), challis, crepeline, crepon, crystalline, eolienne, farandine, gloria, grogram, kin, lansdowne, mashru, sagathy, siamoise, tabinet

silk, patterned armure

silk-ribbed epingle, faille, marocain, poult-de-soie, rep(p)

silver tash

16th century caffa, tewk, tuke

sizer algin

soft baratbea, cashmere, duvetyn, fleece, kasha, montagnac, panne, plush, rugine, surah

stiff crinoline, taffeta, wigan

stiffening haitsai, starch

straw mat(ting)

stout brin

striped aba(s), alexander, algeri(en)ne, anabasse, bayadere, coothay, doria, galatea, madras, meraline, susi, tabaret, zenana

suiting acrilan, cassimere, dacron, gabardine, serge, worsted

surface map

synthetic acetate, acrilan, aralac, arnel, celenese, dacron, dynel(o), fiberglass, fortrel, kodel, lycra, milanese, nylon, nytril, organza, orlon, polyester, qiana, rayon, romaine, satinet, sharkskin, silesia, surah, tricolette, trivera, tycora, velon

thick drab, gros, loden

thin crepe de chine, crisp, cypress, delaine, gauze, gossamer, grenadine, hernani, marabou, net, persian, pongee, silkalene, tamise, tarlatan, toile, voile

tie-dyed chunari

towel agaric, huck, terry

twilled alma, bannockburn, beaverteen, bolivia, bom-

basine, bombazeen, bombazet(te), cameline, canotier, canton flannel, cashmere, coburg, corduroy, coutil, covertcloth, denim, diagonal, flannel, gabardine, gambroom, jean, kasha, kerseymere, levantine, louisine, messaline, nankeen, paramatta, pilotcloth, regatta, rep(p), russel, sallo(o), serge, shalloon, surah, ticking, tricotine, venetian, whipcord, zanella, zulucloth

unbleached beige, drabbet, muslin

uncolored blunk, bogotana

uncut loops terry

upholstery brocatel(le), chintz, damask, frieze, frise, lampas, mohair, moquette, tabaret

velvet bagheera, cisele

velvet-like duvetine, duvetyn, panne, plus, tripe, velour, velure, velveteen

vinyl-coated koroseal

waste material lint, mungo

watered silk moire

waterproof burbury, camlet, canvas, cerecloth, cravenette, loden, tarp

white coteline, nainsook

wide-loomed broadcloth, cotele

wool 3 rep, say 4 felt, kash, kelt, repp 5 baize, beige, burel, casha, cotta, doily, duroy, loden, osset, serge, tamin, tamis, tammy, tweed, twill, yerga 6 afghan, alpaca, angora, armure, baline, beaver, buffin, burnet, djersa, duffel, etamin, frieze, frisca, hodden, kersey, mantle, medley, melton, merino, mohair, moreen, motley, oxford, perpet, ratine, russel, satara, saxony, shoddy, stamin, stroud, suclat, tamine, tartan, tricot, vicuna, wadmal, witney 7 batiste, bocking, bolivia, bunting, cheviot, crystal, debeige, delaine, doeskin, dornock, droguet, dunster, etamine, flannel, frisado, frizado, heather, hernani, kashmir, mockado, raplock, ratteen, rugging, shatush, stammel, tabinet 8 algerine, barragan, batswing, bearskin, bombazat, buckskin, burberry, cashmere, cataloon, chiveret, drap d'ete, estamene, harateen, lambskin, mackinaw, maracain, meraline, prunella, rattinet, sanglier, sarcilis, shalloon, shetland, wildbore, zibeline 9 albatross, astrakhan, balzarine, bissonata, calamanco, cassimere, catalowne, cordillat, gabardine, grenadine, harrateen, hauberget, montagnac, pampilion, penistone, petersham, sharkskin, tavestock, zibelline 10 bombazette, broadcloth, fearnought, kerseymere, lady'scloth, perpetuana 11 covertcloth, drapdeberry, dreadnought, harris-tweed 12 cavalry-twill 14 henrietta cloth

wool bunting nun's cloth

wool, coarse bocking, djersa, duffel, kersey, witney

wool, milled beaver, felt

wool mixture circassian, delaine, duvetyn, empress cloth, grisaille, zanella

wool, patterned armure

wool, reclaimed mungo

wool, ribbed marocain, rep(p)

wool, undyed rumswizzle

worsted balzarine, bombazet(te), camleteen, camletine, cas(s)imere, coburg, covertcloth, estamin, etamine, gabardine, plainback, raploch, rash, sagathy, serge, tabby, tartan, tournay, zephyr

woven blanket, broadcloth, broigne, damasse, grogram, lane, leno, pique, sarsanet, textile, tissue, tricot, tweed, twill, valencia

FABRICATE build, coin, concoct, construct, contrive, cook, counterfeit, create, devise, erect, fake, falsify, fashion, feign, fib, fictionize, forge, form, frame, fudge, hatch, hoke up, invent, lie, make (up), manufacture, mint, mix, mythify, organize, originate, pretend, prevaricate, produce, scheme, shape, sham, trump up, turn out, weave

FABRICATION art(ifact), canard, coggery, concoc-

tion, construction, craft, creation, deceit, deception, extravaganza, fable, fiction, figment, forgery, guile, invention, lie, myth, opus, origination, product, romance, tissue, untruth, web, work

FABRICATOR coiner, fabulist, forger, inventor, liar, maker, parabolist

FABULIST (a)esop, andersen, fabler, fabricator, grimm, la fontaine, liar, parabolist

FABULOUS amazing, apocryphal, artificial, astonishing, astounding, exorbitant, extravagant, fictional, fictitious, imaginary, legendary, marvelous, mythical, romantic, spectacular, striking, stupendous, unreal, wonderful, wondrous

FACADE bluff, disguise, face, facia, front(age), frontal, rear, sham, veneer

FACE acknowledge, angle, answer, aspect, basil, bezel, board, boldness, brave, brick, carry off, cheek, cheer, clapboard, confront, countenance, dare, dial, encounter, envisage, exterior, external, facade, facet, facies, favor, features, fiz(z), front(age), glass, glaze, grimace, impudence, index, jib, kisser, lath, level, line(aments), looks, lug, map, mask, mazard, meet, move, mug, mush, muzzle, obverse, oppose, outside, paint, pan, phase, phiz(og), physiogomy, puss, revet, shake, sham, sheathe, shingle, slate, snoot, stone, surface, thatch, tile, value, veneer, visage, visor, vizor, wallpaper

about pivot

-arbor knife, true

artery maxillary

bandage accipiter

boldly brazen out

bone lachrymal, malar, mandible, maxilla(ry), nasal, palatine, vomer, zygoma(tic)

card cavalier, figure, jack, king, knave, konig, paintskin, picture, queen, redskin, roi, royal, tete

-cardless hand beggar, carte blanche, milkbottle, yarborough

covering mask, veil, yashmak

cream balm, moisturizer

curved extrados, intrados

defect harelip

down outstare, prone, prostrate, resist

eastward orientate

false mask

guard beaver, frontal, mask

inner concave

-making gurning

masonry revet

ornament cosmetic, jewel, patch, veil

paint fard, parget, rouge

paralysis bell's palsy

part beard, brow, cheek, chin, eye, jaw, lid, lip, mouth, nose

pert. prosopic

the music brave, endure, suffer

to face, affront, openly, opposite, vis a vis

12-planed dodecahedral

upon overlook

wall revetment

without aprosopia

FACEMAN hagger, hewer, quarrier, winner

FACER bumper, drink, enigma, poser, puzzle, sockdologer, tankard

FACET angle, appearance, aspect, bezel, bezil, collet, culet, example, exterior, face, fillet, front, level, pane, phase, phasis, plane, side, slant, surface, twist

bottom culet

FACETIAE curiosa, jokes, quips

FACETIOUS comical, droll, frivolous, funny, humorous, jesting, jocose, jocular, joking, jolly, jovial, ludicrous, merry, risible, smart, sportive, tongue-in-cheek, waggish, witty

FACETIOUSNESS smartism

FACIA front, nameplate

FACIENT agent, doer

FACILE adroit, apt, articulate, cursory, deft, docile, easy, effortless, flexible, gentle, glib, light, pliable, pliant, quick, ready, shallow, simple, smooth, uncritical, vocal, voluble

FACILITATE accommodate,

aid, assist, ease, expedite, extricate, further, hasten, help, pave the way, quicken, simplify, smooth, speed

FACILITY abandon, ability, address, affability, agency, art, competence, compliance, dexterity, ease, easiness, efficiency, establishment, expertness, fluency, freedom, help, installation, knack, means, pliancy, poise, proficiency, readiness, setup, skill, smoothness, spontaneity, tact, toilet

FACING against, coating, covering, dado, front, harl, layer, leaf, lining, opposite, panel, skirt, surface, toward, veneer

each other affront, affronty, eye to eye

inward introrse

outward extrorse

FACINOROUS atrocious, criminal, wicked

FACSIMILE autotype, carbon, copy, ditto, duplicate, likeness, match, miniature, replica, reproduction, transcript, twin, xerox

FACT actuality, case, cause, certainty, circumstance, datum, deed, donnee, event, evidence, fait, feat, fiat, given, gospel, info, information, keynote, lowdown, particular, poop, reality, scoop, specific, statistic, truth, verity

based on authentic, real, true

collection analecta

comb. ance, ancy, ence

decisive clincher

secondary collateral

support with circumstantiate, verify

FACTION bloc, brigue, cabal, circle, clan, clique, combination, combine, conflict, coterie, discord, dissension, dissent, friction, junto, party, quarrel, ring, schism, sect, set, side, splinter, strife, tumult

FACTIONAL partisan, sectarian

FACTIOUS alienated, contending, demagogic, dissentious, estranged, fighting, insubordinate, litigious, mutinous, quarrelsome, rebellious, recalcitrant, refrac-

tory, seditious, turbulent, warring

FACTITIOUS affected, artificial, assumed, compelled, ersatz, fabricated, forced, made, manufactured, pretended, sham (med), spurious, synthetic

FACTOR agency, agent, aid, attorney, author, bailiff, broker, cause, circumstance, component, constituent, deputy, element, equation, faciend, gene, incitant, influence, ingredient, instrument, major-domo, maker, means, multiple, oeconomous, part, proxy, reeve, seneschal, steward, substitute, thing

heredity gene

FACTORY aurang, aurung, fabrique, forge, hong, mill, officina, plant, shop, workshop

FACTOTUM agent, bonne, comprador, do-all, employee, handyman, servant, slavey

FACTUAL accurate, actual, authentic, correct, empiric, genuine, literal, real, reliable, true

FACULATE authorize

FACULTIES habiliment, smarts, wits

FACULTY ability, aptitude, authority, bent, capability, capacity, cognition, crew, dexterity, felicity, fitness, flair, force, function, genius, gift, ingenuity, knack, leaning, penchant, power, professorate, propensity, property, quality, right, sense, skill, staff, talent, teachers, wit

critical judgment

member lecturer, master, professor, teacher, tutor

FACY fresh, impudent, saucy

FAD caprice, craze, cry, custom, dernier cri, faction, fancy, fashion, foible, hobby, ism, latest thing, mode, passion, rage, rave, style, thing, trend, vagary, vogue, where it's at, whim(sey), wrinkle

FADDISH trendy

FADDIST See ENTHUSIAST.

FADDLE dandle, dawdle,

fussiness, nonsense, pet, trifle

FADE abate, age, bet, blanch, bleach, cease, daver, decay, decline, decolor(ize), die, dim, disappear, discolor, dissolve, dow, droop, dwindle, dwine, dull, evanesce, fail, flat, fly, insipid, languish, lighten, melt, pale, pass, perish, peter, recede, slack off, taper, vade, vanish, wan(e), want, weaken, whiten, wilt, wither

in appear

out disappear, end

FADED dilapidated, dim, dull, faint, insipid, lackluster, passe

FADELESS amaranthine, deep-dyed, everlasting, immortal, lasting, perdurable, permanent, perpetual

FADGE agree, bundle, fagot, farthing, fit, harmonize, suit, trot

FAERIE QUEEN gloriana

author spenser

character abessa, acrasia, alma, amoret, artegal, ate, blat(t)ant, braggadocio, britomartis, calidore, cambalo, cambel, claribel, corflambo, cormorant, duvessa, florimel, gloriana, grill, gryll, guyon, malbecco, malecasta, malegar, lanegin, mammon, medina, mordant, munera, orgoglio, phaedria, phaon, philemon, philotime, pollente, priamond, radegund, ruddymane, sansfoy, sansgoy, sansloy, satyrane, scudamore, talus, triamond, una

enchantress acrasia

giant corflambo, cormorant, orgoglio

hero calidore

monster blat(t)ant

witch duvessa

FAEROES *capital* torshaven

district manager foud

duck eider, puffin

fish char

island bordo, estero, fugio, sando, skuo, stromo, sydero, vaago, videro

judge foud

sheep faar

FAERY See FAIRY.

FAEX dregs, sediment

FAFNIR dragon, giant

brother regin
slayer siegfried, sigurd
FAG cigarette, droop, drudge(ry), exhaust, fatigue, faygeleh, flag, fray, frazzle, hack, harass, jade, labor, liar, menial, serve, sink, slave, smoke, task, tick, tire, toil, tucker, tuft, weary, work, worry
end remainder, ruck, selvedge
FAGACEAE beech, castanea, chestnut, oak, shrub, tree
FAGALES betula, shrub, tree
FAGIN *associate* bill sikes
victim nancy, oliver twist
FAGOT brand, bundle, bunch, cinder, dummy, ember, fadge, firebrand, nicky, nitch, package, pile, pimp, slack, slattern, spiceball, twig
symbol of st anastasia
FAGUS beech
FAIENCE ceramics, earthenware, majolica
FAIL abort, blow, bomb, break(down), burst, bust, collapse, conk, crash, deceive, decline, defect, desert, die, disappoint, droop, dwindle, ebb, err, explode, fade, fall through, fan(out), fizzle, flop, flub, fluff, flummox, flunk, fold, foozle, founder, freak out, go broke, go to the dogs, languish, lapse, lay an egg, lose, miscarry, misfire, neglect, pass, peak, peter (out), pine, poop out, renege, renig, scantle, sicken, sink, slump, stall, strike out, wane, want, waste(away), weaken, wilt, wither, zap out
FAILING bad, blemish, blot, bombing, bust, cadent, defect, dud, error, fault, flaw, flop, foible, frailty, ill, inform(ity), lapse, shortcoming, vice, weakness, without
FAILURE abortion, bankrupt(cy), bloomer, bomb, botch, breakdown, brodie, bust(up), catastrophe, collaspe, crash, cropper, debacle, decline, defeat, disappointment, disaster, downfall, dud, error, false alarm, fault, fiasco, fizzle, flop, flub, flunker, flunky, foil,

frailty, frost, insolvency, klinker, lack, miss, neglect, negligence, no go, omission, ruin, sin, smash, trip, washout, wreck
chance of calculated risk
FAIN apt, contented, desirous, eager, enjoy, fond, glad, lief, reconciled, rejoice, satisfied, well-pleased, willing, wont
FAINAGUE cheat, intrigue, maneuver, plot, revoke, scheme, shirk
FAINEANT idle(r), impassive, inactive, indolent, inert, languid, lazy, lethargic, otiose, slothful, sluggart, sluggish, supine
FAINT aglimmer, black out, cold, conk out, delicate, dim(mish), dimmy, dimpsy, droop, drop, dwain, fade, fail, feeble, fragile, frail, gentle, inaudible, indistinct, irresolute, languish, listless, low, pale, pass out, piano, slight, soft, swelt, swither, swoon, syncope, tender, thin, timid, unconscious, vague, wambly, waugh, weak, weary, wersh, whispered
comb. ambly
FAINTHEART cold feet, fear, qualm
FAINTHEARTED afraid, cowardly, craven, timid, timorous
FAINTING deliquium, syncope, talme
spell drow, dwalm, dwam
FAINTLY dimly, feebly, gently, low, piano, pianissimo, softly, sordamente, sordo
FAIR 4 bawn, beau, bell, braw, calm, even, fine, gala, hend, just, mart, mela, open, show, soso, wapp, well 5 balmy, bazar, belle, blond, bonny, clean, equal, feria, light, right, sunny, woman 6 aenach, aonach, bazaar, blonde, candid, comely, decent, dinkum, evenly, goodly, kermis, kirmes, kosher, likely, lovely, market, medium, pastel, polite, pretty, square 7 average, clearly, equable, exhibit, favored, kermess, logical, quietly, shapely, whitish 8 becoming, charm-

ing, festival, handsome, mediocre, middling, ordinary, pleasant, pleasing, rational, slightly, unbiased 9 agreeable, beauteous, beautiful, equitable, impartial, objective, tolerable 10 exhibition, exposition, legitimate, mensurable, personable, reasonable 11 goodlooking, indifferent, presentable, wellfavored 13 dispassionate
and square dinkum, honestly, justly
as a lily
ball base-hit, hit
complexioned blond(e), light(skinned)
concourse midway
field opportunity
game butt, dupe, patsy, victim
-haired blond(e), favored, sandy, towheaded, xanthochroid
-haired, name meaning boyd, linus
lady belle dame
-lead wapp
maid of perth catherine glover
-minded honest, judicious, just, unprejudiced
-mindedness equity, impartiality
penitent rowe
pert. nundinal
shake good chance, shot
-spoken adulatory, bland, courteous, plausible, soft, soothing
-weather good times, inconstant, sunshine
FAIRFAX *estate* belvoir
FAIRNESS beauty, candor, equality, equity, honesty, impartiality, justice
FAIRY afreet, ariel, banshee, benshee, boggart, bogie, bogle, brownie, bugbear, deev, djinn, dryad, dwarf, efreet, elf(kin), elle-folk, goblin, gremlin, habundia, hamadryad, hob(goblin), imp, jin(n), kelpie, kobold, leprechaun, mab, mandrake, melusina, mermaid, monaciello, naid, nis(se), nix(ie), oberon, ogre, oread, ouphe, peche, peri, pixie, pixy, puck, salamander, shade, shee, spectre, spook, sprite, sylph(id),

sylphidine, titania, troll, una, undine, vila, vily, white merle, will-o-the-wisp, wraith, yaksha, yakshi
air sylph
bad sprite
bell disporum, foxglove
bird little tern, white merle
candle bugbane
cap foxglove
chief puck
creeper fumitory
cup miterwort, primrose, primula
domestic brownie
famous iolanthe, tinker bell
finger foxglove
folk good people, little men, little people, shee, sidhe
fort lis(s), shee
ghost sprite
horse kelpie, kelpy
king mider, oberon
-land annwfn, annwn, eden, elfland, paradise, utopia
-like elfin, sylphid, sylphish
lore mythology
martin bottle-swallow
medieval fata morgana
midwife mab
musical stomkarl
name meaning ella, fae, fala, fay(e), naida, nissa, nixie
potatoes bladder-campion
queen argante, ariel, cleo, gloriana, mab, medb, morgaine le fay, pam, titania, una
realm avalon, shee, sidhe
ring mushroom champignon
shoemaker leprechaun
small elf, imp, pigwidgeon, pigwiggen
smoke indian pipe
spirit of death banshee
stone arrowhead
tale allegory, fabrication, fib, fiction, invention, lie, marchen, narrative
tale prince frog
thimble foxglove
tricky puck
wand blazing-star
woman banshee
FAISAL *consort* iffat
FAIT ACCOMPLI accomplishment, act
FAITERY deceit, pretense
FAITH allegiance, belief, betrothal, certainty, certie, certy, church, communion, confidence, constancy, conviction, credence, credit, creed, cult, denomination,

dependence, doctrine, dogma, doxy, fay, fidelity, gospel, hope, loyalty, persuasion, piety, piousness, reliance, religion, sincerity, stock, tenet, troth, trow, trust
act of auto-da-fe
article credenda, credo, tenet
bad duplicity, infidelity, mala-fides, treachery
deity fides
doctrine pistiology
false miscreance
healing christian science, theotherapy
of the true orthodox
pert. pistic
reliance on fideism
symbol diamond
symbolic color green, yellow
FAITHFUL accurate, close, constant, devoted, devout, exact, fast, firm, good, honest, leal, liege, life-like, like, literal, loving, loyal, obedient, orthodox, reliable, resolute, scrupulous, similar, sincere, sta(u)nch, steadfast, tried, trig, true(blue), trust(worthy), trusty
FAITHLESS agnostic(al), apostate, atheist, deceptive, delusive, disaffected, disloyal, false(hearted), fickle, hollow, inconstant, incredulous, irreligious, mercurial, nullifidian, perfidious, punic, shifting, shifty, skeptical, traitorous, treacherous, unjust, unsatisfying, unstable, untrue
FAITHLESSNESS duplicity, falsity, infidelity, perfidy, treachery
FAITOUR See CHEAT, IMPOSTER.
FAKE (See also FAKER.) affect, bam, base, bastard, bluff(er), bogus, charlatan, cheat(er), cliquant, counterfeit, deceit, deceive, deception, duffer, duffing, dummy, fabricate, false, falsify, feign, fictitious, forgery, fraud, furbish, hoax, hokey, hypocrite, imitation, imposter, lie, loop, make-believe, mock, mountebank, paste, phony, pinchbeck, pretend(ed), pretense, sham, shoddy, simulacrum, simulate(d), spurious, swindle,

tier, tinsel, trick, tromben(y)ik, vendor, wangle
article schlag, s(c)hlock
comb. pseud(o)
FAKER humbug, imposter, peddler, quack, sham
FAKIR ascetic, beggar, dervish, faquir, mendicant, monk, moslem, yogi
FALA refrain, song
FALANGE *leader* el caudillo, franco
FALCATE curved, hooked, sicklelike
FALCHION See SWORD.
FALCON anatum, berigora, besra, bird, bockerel, bockeret, buteo, dhoti, eyas, hawk, hobby, hunt, jagger, jugger, kestrel, laggar, lanner, luggar, lugger, merlin, peregrine, plunderer, raptor, redpool, saker(et), shaheen, shahin, sokol, sorage, tercel
bait lure
bind mail
blind seel
board hack
cosmopolitan peregrine
cry chant
desert lanner
-faced diety harakhte-ra, horus, khons hor, menthu, mont, qebhsnuf
female formel, gentle, lanner
1st year sore(hawk)
group cast
-headed god ment(u)
-like accipital, accipitrine, raptorial
male sakeret, tassel, tercel
old world saker
peregrine game-hawk, great-footed hawk
small besra, hobby, kestrel, merlin
soaring alschain, gamma-aquilae
white icelander
young eyas(s), passager
FALCONER accipitrary, hawker, ostreger
cry au vol
inept marhawk
implement hood, jess
term bewet, bewit, hood, jess, seel
FALDERAL finery, nonsense, refrain, trifle
FALKLAND ISLANDS las malvinas, les malouines
capital stanley
penguin rock hopper

FALL 3 faw, lin, sag, sin, sye 4 bolt, cave, come, dive, drip, drop, dump, dunt, fail, flop, hang, linn, lose, pass, plap, plop, rain, ruin, shed, sile, sink, slip, sway, swop, trip 5 break, calve, cloit, crash, death, lapse, lower, lurch, occur, pitch, skite, slide, slope, spill, stoop, upset 6 arrive, autumn, brodie, defeat, devall, dounce, expire, footer, header, mucker, perish, plunge, settle, sprawl, streek, topple, tumble, wander 7 cascade, cropper, crumble, debauch, decline, depress, descend, descent, dribble, dwindle, founder, harvest, niagara, plummet, relapse, stumble, subside 8 cataract, decrease, derogate, disgrace, overturn, pratfall 9 declivity, dissipate, overthrow 10 depreciate 11 degradation, destruction, prostration, spreadeagle 12 indian summer 13 precipitation 14 bouleversement

abruptly dump

all over oneself hurry, scurry

apart break, collapse, deteriorate, shatter, shiver

at one's feet fawn, salaam

away decline, decrease, defect, fade, relapse, slip, slump

back dim, fade, follow, give way, recede, relapse, resort, retreat

behind backslide, follow, lag, lose

down cave, collapse, descend, die, err, fail, flop, mistake, slip, slump, stumble, swap, swither

duck redhead

due accrue, befall, mature, owe

fish chub, corporal, dace

flat collapse, err, fail

flower aster, cosmos

for bite at, love, tumble

forward pitch, prolapse

from grace err, relapse, sin

gradually drip, ebb, sag

guy goat, scapegoat, s(c)hlemiel, shlemi(e)hl, s(c)hmo, victim, whipping boy

headlong come a cropper

heavily cloit, clyte, ding, dump, plump, soss, swack

herring tailor

in accept, agree, assemble, cave, concur, end, form, gather, lapse, occur, terminate, yield

in price depreciate, drop

into come upon, discover, find, incur, inherit, luck out, undertake

into line queue

into place align, assort, crystallize

in with agree, conform, converge, incur, join, meet

off abate, apostatize, decline, decrease, descent, deteriorate, deviate, die, diminish, drop, lose(ground), perish, relapse, revolt, slacken, slip, slump, step aside, trend, withdraw

of the cards chance

on assail, assault, attack, begin, meet

out argue, chance, contend, differ, disagree, happen, quarrel, radiation, radioactivity, result, turn out

over astreger

rose china aster

short decline, fail, lack, lose, miss, shy, slump, stop, want

snipe dunlin

through collapse, fail, fizzle

to begin, close, eat, fight, follow, launch, meet, set about, start, undertake

to leeward bogue

to pieces break, buckle, collapse, crumble, decay, disintegrate, shatter

under incur

upon ambush, attack, attempt, surprise, warp

victim to catch, sicken

FALLACIOUS ambiguous, crafty, deceptive, delusive, equivocal, false, heterodox, hollow, illogical, illusory, irrational, misleading, sophistic(al), specious, unfounded, unreal, unsound, untrue, wily

FALLACY aberration, casuistry, delusion, error, fault, flaw, heresy, idol, idolum, illusion, misconception, mistake, paralogism, pitfall, sophism, sophistry

formal pseudosyllogism

FALLAL affectation, finery, geegaw, ruff

FALLEN dead, degraded, dropped, kaput, prostrate, rare, ruined, slain, sunken, wanton, wayward

FALLING bearish, cadent, caducous, caduke, decreasing, displacement, downhill, hollow, prolapse, slumping

in drops stillatitious

off abatement, caduce, caducous, leeway

out disagreement, quarrel

-sickness epilepsy, seizure

FALLOW barren, blanch, crude, cultivate, dormant, faugh, favel, felloe, harrow, idle, pale, plow(ed), quiescent, shallow, slack, unplowed, unproductive, unsown, untilled, unused, vacant, virgin, yellow

chat wheatear

deer damine, dapple, teg

FALSE absurd, affected, apostate, artificial, assumed, bad, bogus, bum, counterfeit, crooked, deceitful, deceptive, delusive, dishonest, disloyal, erroneous, faithless, fake, fallacious, feigned, forged, goody (-goody), hypocritical, illusive, illusory, incorrect, insincere, luke, mealymouthed, mendacious, meretricious, misleading, paste, perfidious, pharisaic(al), phony, pietistic(al), pious, pseudo, recreant, renegade, sanctimonious, self-righteous, sham, sophist, spectral, spurious, tartuffian, tartuffish, traitorous, treacherous, truthless, unctuous, unfaithful, unfounded, unreliable, untrue, untruthful, wrong

acacia black locust, honey locust

alarm failure, sham, wolf

as hell

alder winterberry

aloe colicroot

axis sympodium

banana papaw

beechdrops pinesap

box dogwood

breadfruit ceriman

buckthorn shittim

colors camouflage, 'disguise, sham

comb. pseud(o)

crawley pinedrops

dittany fraxinella

elm hackberry

face caricature, disguise, mask
foxglove feverweed
friend iago, judas, traitor
front camouflage, deception, disguise, sham
goat's-beard astilbe
grape virginia creeper
-hearted ambidextrous, crafty, deceitful, double-dealing, fraudulent, janus-faced, machiavellian, perfidious, treacherous, two-faced
hellebore earthgall
hoof dewclaw
horehound archangel, ballota, black angelica, herb
hyacinth camass
ipecac bloodflower, gillenia, indian hippo, spurge
items spuria
lily of the valley bead-ruby
mahogany redbay
mandrake bryony
mercury good-king-henry
mermaid floerkea, limnanth
mustard clammyweed
pennyroyal blue gentian
pimpernel chaffweed
pretense lie, pretext, sham
rampion bellflower
saffran safflower
sanicle miterwort
spring beauty blinks
stargrass colicroot
step faux pas, lapse
sunflower daisy, marsh elder, sneezeweed
sycamore china tree
trail red herring
violet dewdrop
wintergreen canker-lettuce, pyrola
witness liar
wormwood ragweed
FALSEHOOD bouncer, bung, canard, cog, crammer, deception, duplicity, fable, fabrication, fib(bery), fiction, figment, flam, fraud, half-truth, imposture, invention, leasing, lie, mendacity, perfidy, perjury, prevarication, pseudology, romance, roorback, story, strapper, tale, tarradiddle, treachery, untruth, white lie, whopper
FALSENESS deceit, deception, disguise, fabrication, fakery, forgery, fraud(ulence), inaccuracy, infidelity, sanctimony, sham, untruth

FALSIFY belie, betray, camouflage, color, cook(up), deacon, deceive, disguise, disprove, distort, doctor, dress up, embellish, embezzle, embroider, fake, feint, forge, garble, gild, gloss, manipulate, misrepresent, misstate, pervert, twist, varnish, violate, warp
FALSITY disloyalty, error, falsification, infidelity
FALSTAFF *companion* bardolph, gadshill, peto, pistol, poins
lieutenant pistol
meeting place boar's head
page robin
tricker mistress page
FALTER blench, boggle, chicken out, dawdle, despair, dodder, flinch, flounder, fluctuate, flunk, funk, halt, hesitate, mammer, oscillate, pause, quail, quake, quaver, recoil, reel, rock, roll, scruple, shake, shrink, shudder, stammer, stumble, stutter, swing, totter, tremble, vacillate, waver
FALX chelicera, falchion, sword
FAME acclaim, acclamation, applause, celebrity, distinction, eclat, eminence, esteem, glory, greatness, honor, kudos, luster, memory, notability, note, notoriety, prestige, price, prominence, recognition, renown, report, reputation, repute, tongue
symbol bays, certificate, citation, crown, decoration, diploma, garland, laurel, medal, palm, ribbon, wreathe
FAMED See FAMOUS.
FAMILIAR abreast, accustomed, affable, apprised, baka, boko, bold, chummy, close, colloquial, common, confidential, conversant, cosy, couth, customary, dear, domestic, easy, everyday, free, frequent, friendly, habitual, hand-in-hand, homely, informal, informed, insolent, intimate, known, near, ordinary, personal, proverbial, snug, sociable, standard,

thick, usual, versant, versed, vulgar, wellknown
FAMILIARITY acquaintance, affability, concord, freedom, friendship, habit, intimacy, knowledge, liberty, license
FAMILIARIZE accustom, acquaint, adapt, addict, adjust, advise, habituate, haft, inform, inure, let know, orient, season
FAMILY affiliation, aiga, ancestry, birth, bloodline, branch, breed, brood, children, cinel, clan, classification, derivation, descent, domestic, dynasty, extraction, filiation, genos, gens, genus, ging, gotra, group, house(hold), ilk, issue, line(age), lineal, menage, order, origin, parage, parentage, phylum, posterity, progeny, race, seed, sept, side, society, stem(ma), stirps, stock, strain, succession, tribe, zegris
by marriage in-laws
degenerate jukes, kallikaks
division branch
group barangay, clan, tribe
head alder, genarch, goodman, householder, husband, matriarch, mother, pater familias, patriarch
name patronymic, surname
pert. gentilitial, lineal, nepotic
symbol totem
tree genealogy, stemma
FAMINE blight, dearth, drought, hunger, paucity, poverty, scarcity, starvation, want
bread lichen
predictor of agabus
FAMISH deprive, hunger, raven, starve, stint
FAMOUS breme, celebrated, celebrious, distinguished, eminent, famed, foremost, good, great, illustrious, immortal, known, mere, named, notable, noted, notorious, outstanding, preeminent, prominent, renowned, splendent, storied, topflight, well-known
person celebrity, dignitary, hero, immortal, laureate, lion, luminary, notable, personage, somebody, vip

FAN addict, adherent, aerate, aficionado, air, amateur, beat, blower, buff, bug, chamar, circulator, cool(er), dance, devotee, disciple, enthusiast, fiend, flabellum, flabrum, flyflap, follower, foment, habitue, handle, lambaste, nut, ogi, patron, punka(h), rhipidium, rooter, solitaire, spread, stimulate, strike out, supporter, vane, ventilate, votary, wafter, whisker, winnow, zealot

alluvial apron, cone, delta

blade vane

ceiling punka

dancer ecdysiast, stripper, strip-teaser

-flower taccada

form plicate

light transom, window

-like, comb. flabelli

out fail, go hitless, spread

palm erythea, fantree, inodes, talipot, yaray

plate brin

-shaped alary, flabellate, rhipidion

the flame agitate, excite, ignite, stir

FANATIC ascetic, bigot, bug, crank, crazy, devotee, devout, doctrinaire, energumen, enthusiast, excessive, extreme, extremist, fan, fancier, fiend, frenzied, infatuate, inordinate, irrational, ist, lunatic, mad, mani(a)c, monomaniac, nut, over-enthusiastic, overzealous, partisan, phrenetic, rabid, radical, ultra, visionary, wild(eyed), zealot, zealous

comb. ist, nick, nik

religious babaylan

FANATICISM excessiveness, extravagance, extremeness, insanity, overzealousness, rabidness, sanctimony, zealotry

FANCIED affected, conceived, deemed, dreamed, favorite, ideated, imaginary, imagined, ornamental, unreal

FANCIER See ENTHUSIAST.

FANCIFUL absurd, aerial, bizarre, blue-sky, capricious, chimerical, dreamborn, extravagant, fabulous, fantastic, fictitious, grotesque, high-flown, ideal, imaginary, imaginative, laputan, notional, odd, ornate, poetic, preposterous, queer, quixotic, romantic, unreal, visionary, whimsical, wild

FANCY affect, approve, arabesque, baroque, bee, capriccio, caprice, chichi, chimera, conceive, concept, conjecture, crotchet, decorative, desire, dream, elaborate, elegant, endorse, enjoy, excellent, exorbitant, expensive, expert, fable, fad, fantasy, figment, fine, flamboyant, florid, flossy, flowery, foible, fondness, frilly, fussy, guess, idea(l), ideate, image, imagination, imagine, impulse, judge, labored, like, love, luxuriant, luxurious, megrim, notion, ornamental, ornate, ostentatious, over-elaborate, overelegant, overworked, phantasy, quirk, reverie, rich, romance, sanction, suppose, think, vagary, vision, whim(sey), will, wrinkle

dan fop, swell, toff

-free footloose, unattached, uncommitted

groundless chimera

man pimp

passing fike, whim

vain chimera

work crocheting, embroidery, sewing, stitchery

FANDANGLE highfalutin, nonsense, ostentatious

FANDANGO ball, dance, manakin, murciana, tune

FANE banner, basilica, church, flag, sanctuary, shrine, temple, weathercock

FANFARE blare, call, display, fanfarade, fanfaron(ade), festivity, flourish, hurrah, show, tantara(ra), tantaro, tucket

FANFARON boaster, braggart, braggary, bully, fanfare, hector, swaggerer

FANFARONADE bluster, boasting, display, fanfare, festivity, ostentation, swagger(ing)

FANFOOT gecko, lizard

FANG accept, attack, booty, capture, catch, claw, earn, falk, nail, obtain, pangwe, procure, projection, prong, seize, share, sting(er), talon, tine, tooth, tusk, vang

FANGLE contrivance, cut, dress, fashion, geegaw, style, trick out, vogue

FANION banner, flag, symbol

FANON cape, collar, corporal, maniple, orale, phanon, vane

FANTAIL comet, pigeon, shaker, wagtail

FANTAN game, parliament, sevens

FANTASSIN See INFANTRY *man.*

FANTASTIC absurd, alien, antic, baroque, bizarre, capricious, chimerical, extreme, fanciful, freakish, grotesque, illusory, imaginary, inconceivable, incredible, monstrous, odd, outre, queer, rococo, romantic, singular, strange, teratogenic, teratoid, unaccountable, unfamiliar, unimaginable, unreal, visionary

FANTASY caprice, chim(a)era, daydream, delusion, desire, dream, fabrication, fancy, figment, freak, idea, illusion, imagination, invention, nightmare, phantasm, phantom, reverie, vagary, vision, whim(sey)

absorbed in autism

FANTOCCINI figures, puppets

FANTOD fidget, fuss, pet, sulk, vision

FANWORT cabomba, watershield

FAR advanced, away, distant, long, much, progressed, remote, removed, room, way off

across wide

ahead premature

and wide abroad, broadly, extensively, greatly

away abroad, abstracted, aloof, at a distance, at arms length, distant(ly), dreamy, oblivious, remote(ly), widely

between detached

comb. tel, tele(o)

cry distant

down deep

east See ORIENTAL.

-famed celebrated

-*flung* outspread, widespread

-*gone* enamored, exhausted, implicated, intoxicated

off outbye, remote

out bizarre, campy, extreme, odd, outre, unconventional, wild

-*reaching* deep, extensive, great, intense, lengthy, long, profound, vast, wide

-*seeing* telescopic

FARBAUTI *child* loki

FARCE burlesque, caricature, comedy, dressing, exode, fatten, forcemeat, mockery, parody, satire, sham, skit, sottle, stuffing, temacha, travesty, trifle

FARCE(U)R clown, comedian, dramatist, joker, wag

FARCHADAT beguiled, charmed, confused, dizzy, dopey, punchy, shocked, smitten, stunned, surprised

FARCICAL absurd, atellan, buffo, burlesque, comic(al), droll, funny, laughable, ludicrous, ribald, ridiculous, risible

FARD date, gloss over, impetus, motion, onset, paint

FARDEL bale, bundle, burden, clothing, collection, fragment, furl, lot, pack (age), packet, parcel, quarter, wrapper

FARE board, carriage, carte, charge, come, diet, eat, entertainment, fee, fend, fettle, food, get along, journey, make out, manage, menu, passage, pay, prosper, provisions, rate, result, rider, sagaciate, shift, table, thrive, token, travel(er), try, victuals

bill of carte, menu

FAREWELL aloha, bonally, conge(e), departure, leave, leaving, parting, send off, swansong, valedictory

expression See GOODBYE.

FARFETCHED devious, doubtful, dubious, fishy, forced, illogical, incoherent, recherche, remote, roundabout, strained, suspicious

FARINA flour, meal, pollen, semolina, starch

FARINACEOUS mealy, powdery, starchy

food barley, cereal, cornstarch, flour, grain, meal,

oat, pudding, rye, sago, salep, spelt, wheat

FARKLEBERRY bluet

FARM agrarian, asylum, barton, bowery, chacra, cotland, croft, crop, cultivate, dude ranch, estancia, finca, garden, grange, grow, hacienda, haras, hire, homecroft, homestead, jail, kolkhoz, location, mains, messuage, milpa, pen, plantation, plow, podere, raise, ranch, rancheria, rancho, rear, sharecrop, spread, steading, till, toft, torp, truck garden, tydden, vaccary, werf, work

basket skep

building barn, crib, henhouse, shed, silo, soddy

communal ejido, kibbutz, kolkhoz, kvutza(h)

crop alfalfa, corn, rye, wheat

crossing stile

dairy wick

fee manor

grazing ranch

house caserio, grange, hacienda, manor, onstead, quinta, steading, villa

implement disc, disk, harrow, header, plow, rake

land acreage, field, tillage

lease tack

machine See AGRICULTURE *machine.*

out hire, let

outbuildings steding

rented mailing

servant scolog

steward bailiff, granger

tenant aillt, contadino, cott(i)er, cropper, gebur, metayer, sharecropper, shareman, sirdar

wagon wain

work clodhopping

worker beehunter, bracero, bywoner, cornhusker, cornpicker, cowherd, cradler, cropwatcher, dairymaid, drover, fodderer, fogger, gleaner, goosegirl, hand, hayloader, haymaker, haypresser, hind, hired man, hogcaller, limeburner, milkmaid, mower, neatherd, orraman, peasant, plowboy, plowman, reaper, scarecrow, sharecropper, sower, swineherd, thresherman, wheatshocker

yard barton, close, werf

FARMER agricole, agricolist, agriculturist, agronomist, boer, bucolic, bywoner, carl(e), ceile, clodhopper, cocky, colon, contadino, cotter, crafter, granger, grower, harvester, hayseed, husbandman, jibaro, khot, kulak, kyle, meo, muzhik, okie, orraman, peasant, pedologist, pike, planter, plowman, rancher(o), reaper, rube, rustic, ryot, scullog(ue), sodbuster, sower, tiller, yokel

caste meo

deity amaethon, ceres

organization grange

plague goutweed

tenant aillt, colonus, gebur, shareman, sirdar

unskilled buckwheater

FARMING agriculture, agrology, agronomy, cultivation, frugality, gardening, husbandry, hydroponics, pedology, tillage

pert. campestral

FARMSTEAD byre, town, wick

FARO monte, stuss, tiger

bank tiger

bet sleeper

box can

card hock, soda

card combination cathop, split

dealer gut-puller

-*like game* bingo, florentini, garbage, haufeln, landsknecht, monte, pharaoh, pitch and toss, put and take, red and black, schnitt, skinball, skinning, stuss, sussmilch, tempeln, two-up, ziginette

symbol tiger

term box, brace, buck the tiger, case, cathop, chops, colors, copper, drive the hearse, gate, heel, kangaroo, lookout, snowball, soda, split, tell box, turn, whipsaw

FAROES See FAEROES.

FAROUK *father* fuad

FARPOTSHKET bollixed up, messed up, sloppy

FARQUHAR *play* the beaux strategem, the constant couple

character boniface, wildair

FARRAGE bullimong, fodder

FARRAGO medley, mess, mixture, nonsense

FARRELL, JAMES *novel* judgment day, studs lonigan

FARRIER blacksmith, marshal, stockman, veterinarian

FARROW drape, litter, pig, young

FARSIGHTED astute, clairvoyant, cleareyed, coolheaded, divinatory, hypermetropic, levelheaded, precognizant, prescient, provident, prudent, sagacious, shrewd, wise
person prebyope

FARSIGHTEDNESS hypermetropia, hyperopia, presbyopia

FARTHER additional, and, ayond, beyond, distant, remote, yonder
india indochina

FARTHEST downmost, end, extreme, furthermost, furthest, lattermost, longest, outmost, remotest, ultima(te), uttermost
point apogee

FARTHING bit, coin, fadge, ferling, grig, jack, quad (rans), rag, mite, trifle
dip candle
½ cue, mite
3 gill

FARTHINGALE fardegew, petticoat, vertugal

FASCIA aponeurosis, band (age), fillet, membrane, molding, sash, strip, tissue

FASCIATUS carapo, giton, gymnotus

FASCICLE bundle, cluster, division, glomerule, group, part, phalange

FASCINATE absorb, allure, attract, becharm, beguile, bewitch, captivate, carry away, catch, charm, dare, delight, enchant, engross, enrapture, enravish, ensorcel, enthrall, entrance, gladden, hypnotize, impress, influence, interest, intrigue, mesmerize, please, spellbound, take, thrill

FASCINATED besotted, enamored, gripped

FASCINATING bewitching, delightful, enticing, fetching, luring, mesmeric, seductive, sirenic, tempting

FASCINATION appeal, attraction, allurement, call, charm, entrancement, interest, mania, obsession, piquancy, spell, trance, witchery
game canfield, demon, klondike, solitaire

FASCINATOR siren, scarf

FASCINE *bundle* rouleau

FASCIST black-shirt, brownshirt, storm trooper, totalitarian
leader mussolini, ras
song giovinezza
theorist pareto
youth avanguardisti, balilla
youth organization balilla

FASH bother, care, seam, trouble, vex(ation), worry

FASHION adjust, bonton, build, carve, cast, chic, compose, contrive, convention, craze, create, cri, cry, currency, current, custom, cut, dernier cri, design, devise, drift, fad, faddishness, fadism, figure, fit, forge, form, frame, garb, guise, habit, invent, last word, make, manner, method, mode, model, mold, nattiness, pattern, plan, plot, popularity, practice, prevalance, produce, quality, rage, shape, smartness, society, style, suit, swim, system, timber, ton, trend, usage, vogue, way, wont, wrinkle
designer ballenciaga, balmain, beene, blass, bohan, brooks, cardin, chanel, clodagh, courreges, de la renta, dior, gernreich, givenchy, halston, klein, logan, loper, quant, saint laurent, schiaparelli
latest kick, rage
pert. a la mode
symbol brooks brothers, savile row
world See SOCIETY.

FASIONABLE a la mode, brave, braw, chic, chichi, cool, dapper, dashing, faddish, groovy, hot, jaunty, modish, natty, new (fangled), nifty, nobby, opuesto, popular, posh, smart, spruce, stylish, toffish

FASSAITE pyrgom

FAST abstain, accelerated, active, agile, apace, asleep, at once, betimes, cheap, close, dashing, debauched, dharma, dhurna, diet, directly, dissolute, doublequick, ember, engaged, expeditious, express, famish, firm, fix(ed), fleet, hasty, hurried, hypersonic, in a hurry, joined, lent, lickety split, light-footed, lively, loose, mercurial, nimble, post haste, presto, profligate, quick, racy, ramadan, rapid, reckless, reliable, secure, settled, smacking, snappy, solid, spanking, speedy, splitting, sporty, stable, starve, stationary, stuck, summarily, supersonic, swift, tie, tight, ultrasonic, unyielding, velocious, wild, winged, xerophagia, xerophagy
and loose capricious, inconstant
as an antelope, arrow, blue streak, cannon ball, courser, dart, eagle, electricity, gazelle, greased lightning, greyhound, hare, hydrargyrum, light(ning), mercury, rocket, streak, wind
by close, near
day ashura, banyan, dish day, ember, jour maigre, lent, quadragesima, ramadan, sabbath, xerophagia, xerophagy
-dyed ingrain
8-day octaemeron
life rat race
-mass shrovetide
period lent, ramadan
-talking glib, slick

FASTEN affix, anchor, astrict, astringe, attach, bag, band(age), bar, baste, batten, belay, belt, bend, bind, bolt, bond, brace, brail, buckle, button, cable, capture, catch, chain, cinch, clamp, clasp, close, colligate, couple, fix, gird, girt(h), glue, hankle, harness, hitch, join, key, knot, lace, lash, leash, ligate, link, lock, moor, nail, obtain paste, pin(ion), raddle, reeve, rivet, rope, screw, seal, secure, settle, sling, slour, snib, splice, strap, string, suture, swathe, tack, tether, tie, thrap, trap, truss, zipper *below* subnect

comb. desmo

upon attribute, catch, clutch, grab, impose, seize

FASTENER 3 bar, fid, gum, guy, nog, nut, peg, pin, tag, tie, tug **4** band, belt, bitt, bolt, bond, brad, clip, cord, frog, glue, hasp, hook, lace, lash, line, lock, loop, nail, pawl, ring, seal, snap, snib, stud, tack, wire, yoke **5** belay, brace, cable, catch, chain, cinch, clamp, clasp, cleat, click, dowel, hitch, inkle, kevel, latch, leash, noose, paste, putty, rivet, screw, spike, strap, thole, thong, truss, twine, withe **6** anchor, batten, bonder, bridle, buckle, button, cement, clevis, cotter, couple, fillet, garter, girder, hawser, lariat, mortar, sennit, skewer, splice, staple, string, terret, toggle, zipper **7** agraffe, bandage, binding, bollard, bracket, closure, funicle, grapnel, gut rope, hairpin, harness, haywire, kingpin, latchet, padlock, soldier, towline **8** barrette, bobbypin, cincture, forelock, grappler, handcuff **9** cotterpin, paperclip, safetypin, thumbtack **10** clothespin, connection, hook and eye, togglebolt **12** infibulation

split cotterpin

FASTIDIOUS careful, chary, choisy, choosy, clean, conscientious, critical, dainty, delicate, discriminating, exact(ing), finical, fussy, gourmet, nice, overnice, particular, pawky, pernickety, picky, precise, prissy, queasy, scrupulous, squeamish, taffeta, taffety

FASTIGIATE conical, pointed

FASTING abstinence, dharma, dhurna, lenten, quadragesimal, ramadan, starvation

FASTNESS acropolis, castle, celerity, citadel, fixity, fort(ress), retreat, speed, stability, stronghold, velocity

FAT abdominous, adeps, adipose, aliphatic, axunge, best, big, blousy, blowsy, blowzy, blubber, brosy, cerotin, cetin, chubby, chuff, coarse, complacent, corpulent, dika, dowdy, elain(e), ester, falstaffian, flab(by), fleshy, fodgel, frowzy, fruitful, grease, gross, heavy, kedge, kokum, lard(y), lipa, lipid, lucrative, marrow(ed), obese, oil(y), olein(e), pinguid, plenty, plump, porcine, portly, productive, pudgy, pyknic, rich, rotund, saame, saim, s(c)hmaltz, slatternly, slovenly, solid, spick, squabbish, stearin(e), stout, suet, sumen, tallow, thick, unctuous, unkempt, wax, weighty, zaftig

animal adeps, glore, grease, lanolin, lard, saim, suet, tallow

as a hog, pig, porpoise

-bird quachero, sandpiper

city good life

comb. adip(o), lip(o), pingui, pio, sebo, steat(o)

constituent cholesterol, olein, stearin

derivative oleo, sebacic, sebic

-frying corruption, graft

in cells suberin

kind monounsaturated, polyunsaturated, saturated

layer panniculus

-like steariform

liquid elain(e), olein(e)

lump keech

man blimp, dumpling, falstaff, five-by-five, grampus, heavyweight, humptydumpty, lump, man-mountain, porpoise, potbelly, pudge, pudgy, roly-poly, squab, tub, tubby

monounsaturated olive oil, peanut oil

natural ester

of the land See PLENTY.

part elain(e), globule, olein(e)

pert. adipose, lipoid, obese, sebaceous, seba(c)ic

polyunsaturated corn oil, cottonseed oil, safflower oil, sesame oil, soybean oil, vegetable oil

poultry schmal(t)z

render lard, try

saturated butter, cheese, cocoa, coconut oil, cream, egg yolks, meat, palm oil

solid kikuel, lard, stearin(e)

-yielding tree shea

FATAL baneful, capital, deadly, destructive, dire, dispatchful, disural, fey, funest, heavy, killing, lethal, mortal, mortiferous, pernicious, poisonous, ruinous, toxic, unsonsy, virulent

dose hotshot

FATALITY calamity, casualty, disaster

FATA MORGANA luminescence, mirage, morgan le fay

FATE anake, atropos, cavel, chance, consequence, cup, death, destination, destiny, destruction, disaster, dispensation, doom, downfall, effect, end, fatality, foredoom, fortune, hado, heaven, ides of march, imshallah, inevitability, issue, karma, ker, kismet, lachesis, lot, luck, necessity, nona, outcome, paradise, portion, predestination, providence, result, ruin, sort, stars, upshot, whate

god zervan, zurvan

goddess adraste(i)a, adrastia, ananke, atropos, clotho, decuma, ker, moerae, moirai, morta, nona, norn, parca(e), skuld, tyche, urd, urth, verthandi

inevitable adraste(i)a, adrastia

personified ananke, moira, moros, urdar

ultimate ananke

FATED appointed, certain, decreed, destined, doomed, fey, final, foreordained, irreversible, last, predestined, preordained

FATEFUL acute, conclusive, critical, crucial, deadly, decisive, destructive, dire, eventful, fatal, important, inevitable, momentous, ominous, portentous, predestined, prophetic, significant, sinister

FATES atropus, clotho, lachesis, moirai, norns, parcae

father zeus

FATHEAD dolt, imbecile, redfish

FATHEADED dumb, fozy, STUPID

FATHER abba, ab(o)u, adopt, ama, amba, anba, ancestor, apostle, atef, author, baba, babbo, babu, beaupere, beget, breadwinner, care for, cause, churchman, clergyman, create, creator, dad, daddums, daddy, earner, elkanah, founder, generate, governor, hatch, isa, originate(r), padre, pai, pap(a), pappy, parent, parson, pater(familias), patriarch, pere, pop(s), priest, procreate, producer, progenitor, sire, supporter, tata, tateh, tateleh, the old man, vader, vater

brother eme, uncle

christmas saint nicholas, santa claus

church See CHURCH *father.*

god kane

-in-law shver

king abimelech

-lasher bullhead, gundie, loricate, sculpin

neptune ocean

of english prose wycliffe

of geometry euclid

of gods and men jupiter, zeus

of greek prose herodotus

of his country andrea doria, augustus, caesar, cicero, cosimo de medici, gurion, pater patriae, washington

of human race adam, iapetus

of lies herodotus, satan

of music palestrina

of musicians jubal

of plenty abiathar

of the church See CHURCH *father.*

of the gods amen(ra), amon, anshar, ashur, aspu, zeus

of waters mississippi

of wind astraeus

pert. agnate, paternal

relative of agnate

semidivine pitri

-slayer oedipus

time methuselah, oldster, solitaire

time's emblem hourglass, scythe, water jar

wise mentor

FATHERHOOD deity, paternity

FATHERLAND homeland, kith, patria

pert. patrial

FATHERLESS anonymous, bereft, orphaned, sireless

FATHERLY careful, parental, paternal, venerable

FATHOM bottom, brace, delve, discover, divine, figure out, follow, grasp, investigate, know, measure, pinpoint, plumb, plummet, probe, solve, sound, test, try, understand, unravel

FATIGUE beat, bedraggle, bore, bush, deplete, do in, do up, drain, droop, enervate, enfeeblement, exhaust(ion), fag, faintness, fatigate, flag, frazzle, goneness, gruel, hag, harass, jade, knock up, languish, languor, lassitude, overdo, overtax, overtire, poop(out), prostrate, sag, sap, sink, succumb, taigle, tash, tax, tedium, tension, tire(dness), traik, tucker, tuck up, use up, weaken(ing), weakness, wear down, weariness, wear out, weary, wilt, wind, work

FATIGUED beat, blase, bleary, blown, deadbeat, done in, droopy, enervated, exhausted, fagged, footsore, listless, outspent, played out, spent, taskit, tired, weary, wing-weary, worn out

FATIMA *descendant* fatimid, fatimite, sa(y)id, seid

father mohammed

husband ali, bluebeard

sister anne

son has(s)an, husein

step-brother ali

FATIMID *ancestor* ali

FATNESS adiposity, bloom, corpulency, cream, fertility, fruitfulness, obesity, thickness, weight

FATSIA aralia, echinopanax

FATTEN batten, brawn, enrich, expand, farce, feed, fertilize, finish, gain weight, improve, pingueyfy, plump, saginate, stall, thrive

FATTENING battel, battle

FATTY adipescent, adipose, aliphatic, cherub, fertile, greasy, liparoid, liparous, oily, oleaginous, punchinello, rolypoly, sebific, suety

acid adipic, arach(id)ic, lanoceric, valeric

comb. adipo

degeneration adiposis

pert. adipic

secretion oil, sebum

tumor lipoma

FATUOUS asinine, besotted, big-endian, dopey, fond, foolish, futile, idiotic, imbecile, inane, infatuated, insensate, invalid, moronic, silly, simple, stupid, thoughtless, vacant, witless

FAUCES gullet, passage, throat, vestibule

FAUCET bib(b), bibcock, cock, horse, hydrant, nozzle, outlet, peg, petcock, robinet, spigot, spout, tap, valve

upright hydrant

wooden horse

FAULKNER, WILLIAM *novel* absalom absalom, as i lay dying, light in august, pylon, sanctuary, sartoris, soldiers' pay, wild palms

county yoknapatawpha

family snopes

FAULT abuse, blame, blemish, blotch, blunder, bug, carp, catch, cavil, check, clag, cleft, crime, culpa, defect(ion), demerit, dip, displacement, drawback, err, error, fail(ing), failure, flaw, foible, fracture, frailty, guilt, hade, heave, hole, imperfection, infirmity, lapse, mistake, negligence, peccadillo, peccancy, responsibility, shortcoming, slip, snag, tache, taint, vice(ty), vitium, weakness

earthquake balcones, san andreas

my mea culpa

petty peccadillo

FAULTFIND carp, cavil, censure, criticize, nag

FAULTFINDER caption, carper, caviler, censor, censurer, complainer, critic, knocker, malcontent momist, momus, nagger, nagster, repiner, scold, shrew

FAULTFINDING captious, carping, caviling, censorious, censure, critical, criticism, demanding, exacting, exceptive, finical, fussy, hypercritical, particular, pernickety

FAULTLESS accurate, correct, entire, flawless, guiltless, immaculate, impeccable, indefectable, innocent, intact, nice, paragon, perfect, precise, right, spotless, stainless, whole

FAULTY amiss, bad, blamable, culpable, defective, deficient, erroneous, false, flawed, illogical, imperfect, mistaken, narrow, peccant, spurious, unfit, unreliable, untrue, without, wrong

FAUN deity, goat-man, satyr, silvanus, woodwose

FAUNA animals, bona dea, damia, goddess, organism
and flora biota
consort faunus
fossil biochron

FAUNTLEROY cedric errol
mother dearest

FAUNUS lupercus, pan
associate ops
butterfly green comma
consort fauna, marica
deity of agriculture
festival lupercalia
grandfather saturn
parent canente, picus
priest of lupercus
son acis, latinus

FAUST *aria* jewel song
attendant wagner
author goethe
composer gounod
heroine marguerite
tempter devil, mephistopheles, satan

FAUSTULUS *foster-son* remus, romulus
wife acca-larentia

FAUX PAS bloomer, blunder, boner, booboo, break, bulba, bull, error, floater, gaffe, howler, lapse, misstep, mistake, slip

FAVEL cunning, dun, fallow, fraud, horse, yellow

FAVOR 3 aid, woo 4 abet, back, bias, boon, ease, face, fief, gift, gree, help, kind, pity, pull, turn 5 badge, bless, court, fancy, grace, honor, humor, leave, mercy, token 6 aspect, esteem, notice, oblige, pamper, pledge, prefer, profit, regard 7 approve, benefit, bouquet, earnest, fairing, freebie, further, gratify, indulge, largess, memento, present, rapport, respect, revenue, service, support 8 approval, befriend, benefice, blessing, courtesy,

donation, good deed, good turn, gratuity, interest, kind deed, kindness, largesse, look like, nepotism, resemble 9 benignity, encourage, patronage, patronize, privilege 10 admiration, appearance, concession, facilitate, obligation, partiality, permission, perquisite, preferment 11 accommodate, benefaction, benevolence, boutonniere, countenance, labor of love
curry dance attendance on
exchange of backscratching
name meaning gratia
without disgraced

FAVORABLE advantageous, auspicious, beneficial, benign, boon, bright, conducive, dexter, disposed, fair, friendly, genial, good, gracious, healthful, inclined, kind(ly), optimal, optimistic, outgoing, pleasing, predisposed, profitable, promising, propitious, rosy, salutary, timely, trine, wholesome, willing, worthy

FAVORED aided, blessed, faur(e)d, featured, gifted, preferred, supported

FAVORITE beloved, darling, dear, esteemed, front runner, hanger-on, hero, idol, insider, leader, leech, lickspit, minion, parasite, partisan, personna grata, pet, popular, precious, preferred, special, sponge, sycophant, toady
son absalom, candidate

FAVORITISM bias, discrimination, nepotism, partiality, partisanship, prejudice

FAWKES, GUY *incident* gunpowder plot

FAWN applepolish, bend, blandish, blond, bootlick, bow (and scrape), brown, buck, cajole, coax, court, cower, crawl, creep, cringe, croodle, crouch, deer, defer, doe, flatter, flether, grovel, ingratiate, invite, kneel, kowtow, lickspittle, serve, servile, stoop, submit, toadcat, toady, truckle, wheedle, woo, yearling, yield
skin nebris

FAWNER bootlicker,

shmatte, shmotte, sycophant

FAWNING flether, glozing, hangdog, ingratiating, menial, obsequious, servile, sleek, surple

FAY banshee, brownee, clean(se), dwarf, elf, fadge, faery, fairy, faith, fit, gnome, goblin, join, meet, name, nix, pixy, prosper, puck, shee, sprite, succeed, unite

FAYAL *city* horta

FAYGELEH bird, child, fairy, gag

FAZE abash, confound, confuse, daunt, dent, discomfit, disconcert, disturb, dumfound, embarrass, fease, feeze, flurry, fluster, muddle, mystify, nonplus, perflex, perturb, phase, puzzle, rattle, upset, worry

FBI *director* hoover, johnson

FEAK curl, tweak, twitch, wipe

FEAL conceal, faithful, fee, loyal, obedient

FEALTY allegiance, constancy, devotion, duty, faith(fulness), fewte, fidelity, homage, lealty, loyalty, obligation, piety, respect, service, trewage

FEAR affright, alarm, anxiety, apprehend, apprehension, awe, blue funk, boof, care, cold feet, concern, consternation, cowardice, diffidence, dismay, disquiet, distrust, doubt, dread, dree, esteem, feeze, flinch, foreboding, fright, funk, heartquake, hesitation, horror, metus, misdoubt, misgiving, palpitation, panic, peur, phobia, qualm, regard, respect, reverence, scare, shock, stampede, startle, terrify, terror, timidity, tremble, trepidation, venerate, veneration, wonder, worry, worship
personification deimos
struck with alarmed, scared

FEARFUL afraid, alarming, anxious, appalling, apprehensive, awed, awful, blue, careful, concerned, craven, dire, disconcerting, dismaying, disquieting, dreadful, frightening, frightful, ghastly, great, grim, grisly, gruesome, hesitant, horrible, horrific, in awe, lurid, macabre, malign, overawed, pavid, reluctant, scared, scaring, scary, shaky, shocking, shuddery, sinister, skeery, startling, terrible, terrifying, timid, timorous, tremulous, trepid, worried *comb.* dino

FEARLESS audacious, bold, brave, confident, courageous, daring, dauntless, doughty, dreadnought, gallant, harmless, heroic, impavid, intrepid, undaunted, valiant

FEARSOME frightful, timid, timorous

FEASIBLE doable, expedient, fit(ting), likely, politic, possible, probable, realistic, reasonable, suitable, workable

FEAST agape, ahaaina, arthel, arval, azyme, banquet, bon, bridale, carnival, carousal, celebration, chanukah, cheer, christmas, citua, delight, dine, dinner, dirgie, eat, enjoy, entertain, epiphany, eucharist, festival, fete, fiesta, foy, gratify, hanukkah, junket, kirn, luau, mas, maundy, meal, picnic, purim, regale, repast, revel sabbath, satisfy, seder, shabuoth, spread, succoth, treat, tuck

christening bed ale
christian agape, eucharist
day, comb. mas
funeral arthel, arval, arvel, averil, dirgie, dirgy, wake
harvest busk
immovable all saints, all souls, annunication, christmas, epiphany, lady day, mich(a)elmas
movable ascension, ash wednesday, easter, good friday, palm sunday, pentecost, trinity sunday, whitsunday
of booths succos, sukkos, sukkoth
of cups anthesteria
of lanterns bon
of lights chanukah, hanukka(h)
of lots purim
of nativity christmas
of pots anthesteria

of tabernacles succos, sukkos, sukkoth
of tasting anthesteria
of trumpets yom teryah
of weeks pentecost, shabuoth, shevuos
on enjoy
passover seder
place idgah
religious canao, kanyaw
together convive
village tansy

FEASTING comessation, epulation
companion convive

FEAT accomplishment, achievement, act(ivity), adept, adroit, adventure, brisk, conquest, coup, craddy, deed, deft, easy, emprise, enterprise, equip, expert, exploit, facile, fitting, gest(e), miracle, neat, nice, nimble, quest, skilled, skillful, smooth, spry, stunt, trick, triumph, victory
of strength tour de force

FEATHER (See also FEATHERS.) adorn, blur, brail(s), bristle, class, condition, crest, down, eider, err, fledge, fletch, fluff, grow up, hackle, herl, hulu, implume, kind, line, mature, mood, nature, pen(na), pinion, pinna, pluma(ge), plume, plumule, preen, quill, remex, remicle, remiges, sarcel, sickle, spirits, tectrix, tongue, topknot, topping, tread, trifle, trim, vibrissa, wake
alum alunogen, hair-salt, halotrichite
barb flue, harl, herl, pinnula, ramus
barrel calamus
bed tye
-bird whitethroat
-brained foolish, frivolous, giddy, shallow, silly, stupid
cloak ahuula, mamo, temiak
cluster muff
comb. penn(i), penno, pinni, pter(o), ptile
contour penna, pluma
-crowned goddess anukit
description pterography
down dowl(e), plumule
-edged See SHARP.
filament dowl(e)
flight pinion

-footed braccate, plumiped(e)
fringe barbicel
grafting imping
grass stipa
group beard
growth area pteryla
hair-like filoplume
-headed See *brained*, above.
in one's cap accomplishment, achievement, honor, token, triumph, trophy, victory
key spline, stop
large quill
-leaf hottonia
-legged cootie, cooty
mature teleoptile
merchant loafer
neckpiece boa
nest accumulate, amass, prepare, provide, reserve, store, succeed, thrive
new stipule
ornament plume
palm ejoo, howea, irok
part boot, calamus, rachis, shank
-pate scatterbrain
pert. pinion, pinnate, plumeous, plumose
pinion sarcel
powder-down polviplume
quill aigret(te), calamus, covert, panache, rectrix, remex
repair imp
rump brail
scarf boa
shaft barrel, scape
shank boot
shed molt
short cape
shoulder cape
slot spline
small covert, tectrix
soft bedown
space between apteryla
star antedon, comatulid, crinoid
to dress preen
tuft crest, hulu
without deplumate, plucked, squab, unfledged
writing quill
yellow hulu

FEATHERED, FEATHERY braccate, crested, downy, fledge(d), fledgy, fleet, fluffy, granulated, hirsute, light, pennate(d), pinioned, pinnate, plumate, plumed, plumose, plumy, ruffed, swift, tufted, winged

on feet braccate
FEATHERING endysis, foliation, plumage
FEATHERS attire, boot, brail, bush, cape, clothing, crissum, cushion, down, duds, eiderdown, finery, flue, fluff, hackles, mail, panache, plumage, remiges, ruff, sley, spuriae, topknot, tuft, vanity, wings
provide with fletch
remove deplume, dress, pluck, singe
shed mo(u)lt
space between apteryla
web of vane
FEATHERWEED alga, ptilota
FEATHERWEIGHT diminutive, light, small
FEATHERWING plumemoth
FEATLY cleverly, fitly, footingly, graceful, heroic, neatly, nimbly, oddly, strangely
FEATOUS elegant, handsome, well-shaped
FEATURE advertise, appearance, article, aspect, blaze, character(istic), commodity, contemplate, distinction, dramatize, earmark, envisage, envision, favor, film, form, hallmark, headline, highlight, ingredient, item, lineament, mark, mien, motif, peculiarity, plot, point up, present, saliance, shape, specialize, spot(light), star, story, token, trait, underline
chief crux
distinguishing hallmark, stroke, trait
natural geography
FEATURES appearance, contour, countenance, face, geology, lie, looks, outline, visage
FEATY clever, dexterous, neat
FEAZE See FEEZE.
FEBRICITY fever
FEBRIFUGE antifebrile, antipyretic, carapine
FEBRILE ardent, excited, feverish, passionate, pyretic
FEBRUARY *2nd* candlemas day, groundhog day
29th bisextus
30th never
birthstone amethyst

FECKLESS feeble, improvident, ineffective, invalid, shiftless, spiritless, useless, weak, worthless
FECULENT dreggy, filthy, foul, muddy, roily, turbid, turbulent
FECUND bearing, fertile, fruitful, productive, prolific, propagating
FECUNDATE fertilize, impregnate, pollinate
FECUNDITY exuberance, fertility, fruitfulness, invention, lavishness, luxuriance, productivity, prolificacy
god or goddess See FERTILITY *deity.*
symbol guinea pig, rabbit
FED fattened, nourished
up blase, bored, browned off, jaded, satiated, sick of, surfeited, through, tired (of), wearied, weary
FEDAYEEN freedom fighter, guerrilla
FEDERAL allied, confederate(d), leagued
city washington
FEDERALESE gobbledegook
FEDERALISTS *nickname* the well-born
FEDERATE ally, associate, combine, friend, join, league, unite
FEDERATION alliance, association, band, body, bund, coalition, combination, confederacy, council, fusion, group, league, nation, party, union
FEE admission, advance, agio, allowance, anchorage, assessment, blackmail, blood money, bountith, bribe, brokerage, carfare, cartage, cellarage, charge(s), commission, consideration, cost, covercharge, dastur(i), demand, dockage, due(s), emolument, exaction, exactment, expense, fare, few, fief, footing, freightage, gratuity, hansa, hanse, honorarium, hire, hush money, mileage, moorage, pay(ment), percentage, pilotage, portage, price, quitrent, rackrent, reckoning, remuneration, rent(al), requital, retainer, salary, scot, screw, settlement, shot, stipend, storage, tax, tip, toll, towage, trib-

ute, value, wage, wharfage, wite
comb. age
customary dastur
delivery deferred backwardation
-faw-fum bogy, bugbear, ogre, terror
hauling boatage
initiation footing
landowner's terrage
physician's sostrum
shipping freightage
teacher's minerval
welsh manor lord's amobyr
FEEBLE aged, anemic, anile, brittle, crippled, debile, decrepit, disabled, doddering, donsie, doting, dotty, droghlin, dwaibly, faint, flabby, flimsy, fragile, frail, gentle, impotent, impuissant, indistinct, inferior, infirm, irresolute, lame, languid, low, poor, puny, queechy, sapless, semmit, senile, shilpit, sick, soft, tip, unsound, vague, wanky, washy, weak(ly), wonky
-minded anile, defective, dotty, foolish, infirm, irresolute, moronic, retarded, subnormal, vacillating, wanting, weak
-mindedness acatalepsia, amentia, cretinism, hypophrenia, stupidity
FEED agist, bait, barley, board, bran, bread, browse, cater, cherish, chop(s), corn, crops, dine, dinner, eat, encourage, ensilage, fodder, food, forage, foster, fuel, gavage, grain, grass, gratify, graze, groom, hay, lunch, maintain, mash, meat, nourish, nurse, nurture, oats, pasturage, pasture, peck, provender, provision, regale, satisfy, scratch, silage, slops, spread, straw, strengthen, subsist, supper, supply, support, sustain, swill, wheat
board deck
hungrily cram, fraunch
on batten, browse, crop, eat, fatten, graze, pasture, prey, sponge
poultry scratch
the fire agitate, excite
the fish sink, spew, vomit
the kitty ante, bet
to excess agrote, crapulate,

glut, overfill, pamper, satiate, surfeit

FEEDER branch, crammer, dependent, herder, inciter, parasite, railroad, role, shepherd, supplier, trainer, tributary, tutor

FEEDHEAD feeder, riser, sinkhead

FEEDING depascent, foldage, pannage
forced gavage
on small objects microphagous

FEEL affect, ail, appear, appreciate, atmosphere, aura, care, discern, echo, emote, examine, experience, explore, find, finger, grope, handle, impress(ion), palp(ation), perceive, probe, react, respond, savor, search, see, sense, suffer, taction, test, texture, think, tone, touch, understand
ashamed atone, regret, repent, rue, sorrow
better improve, recuperate
chilly creem
confident hope
fine flourish
for empathize, grope, identify with, pity, sympathize, understand
hurt resent
in one's bones believe, foresee, intuit, predict, sense, think
lack of miss
longing yearn
one's way grope, probe, test
out query, sound
pain ail, hurt, suffer, urn
remorse regret
shame blush, suffer
sick wamble
the pulse examine, probe, test

FEELER (See also INSECT *feeler.*) antenna, barbel, barbule, bristle, inquiry, palp(us), prober, quill, tactor, tentacle, test, trial balloon, vibressa, whisker

FEELING affect(ion), ardor, association, atmosphere, attitude, aura, awe, capacity, character, ego, emotion(al), impression, imprint, love, opinion, passion, pathos, perception, pity, premonition, quality, reaction, recognition, re-

sponsiveness, savor, sensation, sense, sensibility, sentiment, sympathy, tone
capable of sentient
comb. pathy
evocative of emotive
ill howlish
imaginary pseudesthesia
intuitive hunch
kindly goodwill
lack an(a)esthesia, analgesia, ap(a)esthesia, apathetic, apathy, insensate, insensibility, insensitive, numbness
shared compathy
show emote

FEET dogs, gunboats, paws
2 metric dipody
3 yard
6 fathom
35 cubic ton
43,560 square acre
cold fear, timidity
having pedate
having large sciapodous
large guffins
number of footage
pert. pedal, pedary, podal
-washing maundy
without apod(al)

FEEZE, FEAZE alarm, beat, daunt, disturb, drive, excitement, faize, fear, fray, impact, impel, roughen, rub, run, rush, turn, unravel, untwist, worry

FEGARY finery, gewgaws, prank, whim

FEIGN act, affect, assume, avoid, bluff, camouflage, cloak, conceal, counterfeit, dissemble, dissimulate, fabricate, fake, falsify, fashion, flinch, forge, garble, hum, imagine, invent, malinger, mask, mint, possum, pretend, sham, shape, shirk, simulate, stall, trick
ignorance connive
sickness malinger

FEIGNED artificial, assumed, colored, counterfeit, devisable, disguised, false, fictitious, imaginary, insincere, make-believe, pretended, pseudo, spurious

FEIL comfortable, neat, soft

FEINT appel, artifice, blind, bluff, diesis, expedient, fakery, fatch, hoax, hoodwinking, make a pass at, make believe, maneuver, pretense, pretext, resort,

ruse, semitone, sham, shift, stall, stratagem, trick, wile

FELDSPAR albite, albitite, amazon(e), amazonite, ambite, andesine, andes(in)ite, anorthite, barbierite, bostonite, bytownite, calciclase, celsian, gneiss, kaolin, leelite, odinite, sanidine, sodaclase
glassy sanidine

FELICITATE bless, congratulate, macarize

FELICITOUS apposite, appropriate, apt, fit(ting), happy, meet, neat, opportune, pat, pertinent, proper, relevant, suitable, timely, well-timed

FELICITY aptitude, beatitude, bliss, delection, delight, ecstasy, elegance, fortune, grace, happiness, joy, pleasure, rapture, success, transport
name meaning naomi

FELINE (See also CAT.) cattish, catty, cheetah, civet, cougar, covert, cunning, jaguar, leopard, lion, lynx, mouser, ounce, puma, rasse, sly, stealthy, tiger, tom, treacherous, wily
breathing purr

FELL axe, bad, baleful, barbarous, bark, blow down, bludgeon, bowl(down), bring down, brutal, bulldog, cast down, chop, crashed, cruel, cut(down), deadly, down, drop(ped), ferocious, fetch down, fierce, fleece, fling down, floor, grass, gravel, great, grim, ground, hew, hide, hill, inhuman, kill, knock down, lay out, level, malefic, malign, merciless, mow down, peel, pelt, pitiless, plain(s), precipitate, prone, prostrate, pull down, rase, raze, relentless, rind, ruthless, savage, sew, shoot, sinister, skin, slay, spread-eagle, supinate, take down, terrible, throw(down), truculent, tumble(d), very, whack

FELLAH peasant, servant

FELLOW (See also PERSON.) 3 boy, bub, bud, cad, cat, don, egg, guy, lad, man, pal, wat 4 baby, bean, beau, bozo, buff, carl, chap, cove, date, dick, dodo, drip,

duck, dude, fool, mate, peer, rake, roue 5 bimbo, blade, bloke, brick, buddy, bully, caddy, catso, clown, dring, equal, fogey, kerel, lover, match, scamp, spark, yahoo, youth 6 beggar, birkie, buffer, bugger, chappy, cookie, coward, double, duffer, friend, gazebo, geezer, glayde, member, person, rascal, sirrah, squirt, worthy 7 bleeder, brother, chappie, comrade, dalteen, gallant, glutton, partner, peasant, scroyle, vaurien, younker 8 bezonian, bon homme, customer, neighbor 9 associate, boyfriend, companion, dandiprat, schlemiel 10 sweetheart 11 academician
active springal
alert sharpie
aloof cold fish, snob, snoot
amusing card, comedian, comedien(ne), comic
annoying terror
antiquated fogg(e)y, fogram, fogrum
arraigned culprit
average john doe
awkward boob(y), bumpkin, clown, club, dromedary, dub, galoot, gawk, gillygaupus, guffin, hobble-dehoy, looby, lout, oaf, slam, slouch, staup, speldring, yokel
bad-mannered goop
bad-tempered crab, crosspatch, grouch, hunks, taistrel
base caitiff, carl(e), cullion, dring, hangdog
beggardly bezonian
big fat gulch
blamed for others butt, scapegoat
blunt tom truth
boring drag, drip
brilliant genius, mastermind, quiz-kid
brutal clubfist, legree, yahoo
bungling foozle
callow gorlin, gosling, smarty, squab
careless poccurante, tassle
changing sides turncoat
charitable samaritan
cheerful optimist
clever gonef, gonif, gonov, litvak, snollygoster
clumsy butter-fingers, cow,

dropper, farmer, hodmandod, jumbo, lubber, meatball
coarse baboon, roughneck, tough, yahoo
cocky rooster, squirt
comb. even
confused foosterer
contemptible bauchle, bounder, brock, cad, dog, heel, hilding, roue, runt, scrub, scut, skate, snake, smatchet, toad, yap
country See FARMER, PEASANT.
-countryman compatriot
crafty sly-cap, tod
craven coward
cringing snool, uriah heep
cruel brute, hellkite, ruffian
cunning fox, slyboots
cynical jaques
deranged lunatic, (mono)maniac, nut, psycho(path)
despicable blackguard, cur, fouter, foutra, hound, rotter, smatchet, stinker
detested anathema
dirty brock, draggletail, howlet, scab, slattern, slut
disagreeable gleyde, pill, schlack, schlag, s(c)hlock
disgruntled crosspatch, sorehead
dishonest rascal
disorderly roit, royt
disreputable ragamuffin, squeef
dissolute debaucher, rake, roue
dull blockhead, clod, codshead, defective, dorbel, drip, dunce, fog(e)y, imbecile, lump, lungis, moron, nebbish, prosaist, slow coach, stock
eccentric character, wack
effeminate smockface
energetic hummer, towser
enterprising gogetter, hustler
evil bad actor, fouter
exhausted trachle
extraordinary rara avis
fat glutton, gulch, pompion, tub
fawning bootlicker, smoothboots, sycophant, toady
fearless dreadnaught, fearnaught, fearnought
feeble crock
-feeling compassion, empathy, sympathy, understanding

fickle chameleon
fictitious jane doe, john(doe) (a-nokes)(o'noakes) (a-stiles), hoit, richard roe
fierce dragon, lion, tiger
fine bawcock, bon homme, brick, bully
flighty fliskmahoy, fly-up-the-creek
foolish clown, dotard, drivel, featherbrain, featherweight, gaby, gander, goff, hoit, howlet, schlemiel, sheepshead, shlemi(e)hl, widgeon, zany
forceful dynamo, stemwinder
frivolous fribble
funny card, clown, wag, wit
futile buffer
gay blade
gentle dove
giddy cockbrain
good brick, bully, prince, trump
gray-headed grisard
greedy slute
grotesque golliwog(g)
guileless babe in the wood
guilty culprit
hateful toad
honest truepenny, trusty
horned cornute
hostile sociopath
idle footer, franion, lollard, skulker, stocah
illbred larrikin
ill-mannered goop, yahoo
impetuous hotspur
important big shot, magnate, pooh bah, vip
impotent spado
impudent jack sauce
inane shaup
inconstant chameleon
inferior underscrub
inscrutable sphinx
insignificant also-ran, dab, nonentity, shurf, sprat, squib, squidgereen, twerp, twirp
irascible curmudgeon
jolly vavaso(u)r
kindly neighbor
lacking faith non-believer
lacking pigment albino
lazy bum, dolittle, donothing, drawlatch, lento, lurdan(e), lusk, slowbelly, slugabed, tool
lean shargar, spindleshanks
little birkie, bub, caddie, caddy, dandiprat, midget, peewee, punk, runt, shaver

lively birkie
loud-voiced stentor
low limmer, mechanic, rag, sweep, varlet, waff, whoreson
mean blighter, boor, bucko, bully, cad, carl, catso, cavel, churl, coistrel, coistril, cullion, fouter, foutre, pleb, reptile, smatchet, snake, sneaksby, spalpeen, spitpoison, stinkard, stinker, yahoo
meddling buttinsky, cagmag
-members brethren, comrades
mentally abnormal mattoid
middle-class babbitt
mischievous imp, pest
narrow-minded mrs grundy
nervous neuropath
niggardly snudge
noisy howlet, mouth
odd codger, rummy, splacknuck
of consequence tallboy, vip
old gaffer, geezer, glyde, moony
old-fashioned fog(e)y, squaretoes
overbearing grimsir
paltry shab, slumgullion
peevish attercop
perfidious serpent, snake, traitor
persevering stick-at-it
petty lilliputian
pious holy joe, zaddik
plucky trojan
prosaic prune
prying nosy parker
puny smaik
puritanical wowser
quarrelsome hector
quick-tempered spunkie
ragged ragamuffin, tatterdemalion
rapacious harpy, shark, wolf
reckless blade, buck, daredevil, hellraker, hotshot
red-headed carrot-top
rough towser
rowdy larrikin, hellion, roarer
rude boor, caveman, jack, rough
scolding catamaran
serious sobersides
sexy casanova, don juan, libertine, roue, sexpot
shabby shab, squeef
sheepish sumph
shiftless bum, drifter, loafer, prog(ger), shack

shifty dodger
shorn monk, priest, shorling
shrewd auld wecht, colt, gazabo, gazebo, sharp cookie, sharpie
shy introvert
silly coof, dotterel, gump, mushhead, nimshi, sheep, smaik, tot, zany
skilled adept, artisan, artist, master, mechanic, talent
slovenly huddroun, slute, streel
slow stick-in-the-mud
sluggish doldrum(s)
sly fox
small lilliputian, midget, posset, sprat, squidgereen
sneaky snudge
sordid hunks
sporty playboy
stingy cheapskate, silas marner, skinflint, tightwad
studious grind, porer
stunted shargar
stupid ass, bayard, blockhead, blunderbuss, blunderhead, boob(y), boodle, bucca, bufflehead, clod, clo(u)t, codshead, coot, daff, dolt, dowfart, duffer, dullard, dumbbell, dummkopf, dummy, dunce, dunderhead, erk, farmer, fool, foozle, gamphrel, gander, gobbin, gump, hash, heavyhead, howfing, ignoramus, moke, moron, muff, mumphead, muttonhead, nitwit, schmo, simp(leton), sockhead, stirk, stock, stunpoll, stupe, sumph
submissive snool
sullen glump
superior brain, genius, topsawyer
talkative chatterbox, chatterpie
tall swabble
thin beanpole, slim-jim
timid milquetoast
traveler communist, commy, fifth columnist, subversive
tricky dodger, greek, knave, rascal, rook, scamp
trustworthy standby
unattractive drip, droopsnoot
uncivil rudesby
uncouth boor, jake, kemp, tike
unknown whoosis
unscrupulous snollygoster
unsophisticated hayseed, innocent, rube

unsound bad lot
unstable psychopath
vain coxcomb, fop
vile rat, skunk
violent spitfire, tartar
vulgar tiger
wanton colt
weak shilp
wealthy nob, toff
wild heller, hellion, skyrgaliard
with no belief nothingarian
without originality rubber stamp
with queer ideas rozum
witless crazy-cat, clabberer
witty bel-esprit
-worker brother, butty, mate(y)
worthless bobtail, brothel, budmash, budza(r)t, bum, cad, crumb, cur, dog, hash, javel, lorel, loser, prog(ger), rip, rogue, scamp, schlemiel, schlemihl, scoundrel, shand, shicer, shoat, snake, spalpeen, spridhogue, tartaret, trash, vaurien
wretched devil, dogbolt
young billy, bucko, caddie, cadie

FELLOWSHIP acquaintance, alliance, association, brotherhood, camaraderie, communion, companionship, company, comradeship, corporation, familiarity, family, friendliness, friendship, guild, intimacy, lodge, membership, partnership, scholarship, sect, society, sodality, union
in suffering compassivity

FELLY bitterly, craftily, cruelly, destructively, felf, felloe, fiercely, keenly, rim, savagely, terribly

FELO-DE-SE See SUICIDE.

FELON bad, brave, bum, convict, criminal, cruel, culprit, disloyal, factor, fetlow, fierce, illegal, knavish, malefactor, mighty, outcast, outlaw, panaris, paronychia, phlegmon, runround, sturdy, sullen, traitorous, villain(ous), whitlow, wicked, wild

FELONY arson, assault, burglary, crime, kidnapping, misdeed, murder, offense, robbery

FELT baize, batswing, beaver

cloth, fabric, fieldfare, filter, hat, hide, groped, pannose, pelt, sensate, sensed, velour
cap calpac(k)
comb. pilo
-like pannose
work network, neuropile
FELTWORT herb, mullein, plant
FEMALE amazon, baggage, broad, dame, distaff, doe, donna, dowager, effeminate, ewe, fem(e), femme, flapper, frail, gal, gin, girl, goodwife, goody, gorgon, grisette, hussy, jade, lady (like), ma'am, madam(e), matron, mulier, pedant, petticoat, she, signora, sister, skirt, sow, squaw, tomato, wahine, wench, wife, woman(ish)
aboriginal gin
ancestor taproot
comb. enne, ette, gyn(e), gyno, ina, thely
figure caryatid
flirtatious coquette
hormone drug estrogen, premarin, progestin
imperfect freemartin
impersonation eonism
naive ewelamb
parthogenetic amazon
quarrelsome barge, panther, shrew, termagent, tiger, virago, vixen, wildcat
silly goose
symbol yin
unkempt dowdy, draggletail, frump, jake, malkin, scarecrow, slattern, sloven
FEME tribunal, wife, woman
FEMININE distaff, effeminate, fair, gentle, gynecic, ladylike, maidenly, matronal, matronly, muliebrile, petticoat, soft, tender, weak, womanish, womanly
nocturnal sign cancer, capricorn
FEMININITY effeminacy, muliebrity, muslin, womanishness, womanliness
FEMINIST freidan, jong, lucy, pankhurst, steinem, stone, suffragette, suffragist
FEMME woman
de chambre chambermaid
fatale lorelei, siren
savante bluestocking
FEN bog, candareen, carr, dirt, filth, forbid, marsh,

moor, morass, mud, quagmire, sud(s), sump, swamp, weight
-duck shoveler
man slodger, webfoot
water suds
FENCE aha, balustrade, battle, bar(rier), boards, boundary, bout, bulkhead, combat, confine, container, digladiate, dispose, dodge, drop, duel, enclose, enclosure, equivocate, espalier, evade, fagin, fight, fortification, fortify, girdle, haha, hawhaw, hedge, hem, hoarding, inclosure, intermediary, joust, match, oxer, pale, paling, palisade, parapet, parr, partition, picket, protect(ion), quibble, raddle, rail(ing), rampart, receiver, scherm, scrime, sell, shuffle, smasher, stockade, swag(s)man, swordplay, tilt, trellis, vallation, wall, weir
cattle scherm, skerm
crossing stile
fishing weir
heavy log bunk, glance
high palisade
interwoven raddle
lifter rainstorm
log glance
-making stick raddle
movable glance, hurdle, stile
part pane
picket pale, paling
rail drawbar
section pane
sitter mugwump
stake palisade
sunken aha, haha, hawhaw
wooden brandreth, brandrith
FENCER duelist, gladiator, parrier, scrimer, sworder, swordsman
FENCING enclosure, escrime, paling, swording
attack assalto, assault, one-two, reprise
breastplate plastron
broadsword montano
code duello
cry en garde, hai, hay, sasa, touche
dummy pel
feint appel
foil blunt, epee, fleuret, floret
hit punto
leap balestra, gait, volt
master lanista

move appel, balestra, butt, coupe, jump, lunge, passado, punto, remise, reprise, riposte
parry counter, quinte, tacau-tac
parry position seconde
pass foin, lunge, punta
position carte, guard, octave, pel, prime, pronation, quarte, quinte, saccoon, seconde, septime, sixte, sixth, supination, tierce
score touche
stroke appel, butt, riposte
sword epee, floret, foil, forte, montanto, rapier, saber, sabre, spathoe, tucke
term bind, caveat, disengage, doigte, imbrocata, lunge, mandritta, octave, paling, parry, pel, plastron, swauf, thrust, tierce
thrust foible, forte, lunge, mandritta, peage, punto, remise, reprise, reverse, ripost(e), stramazon
turn demivolt
FEND avert, fare, forbid, keep off, maintain, parry, prevent, provide, resist, shift, strive, support, work, ward(off)
FENDER buffer, bumper, curb, cushion, fireguard, guard, hearth, kerb, safeguard, shield, skate, sluice(gate), splashboard, splasher
skid glancer
FENESTRA aperture, fenestella, fontanel, foramen, opening, window
FENIAN irishman, revolutionist
heroes fianna
leader finn mac cool
FENKS fritters
FENNEL anis, azorean, azorian, carosella, cowbane, dill, finkel, finochio, hemp, mayweed, nigella, plant, sanfoin, soya
FENNER zerda
FENRIR, FENRIS wolf
bit tyr
brother hel
chain gleipnir, laeding
parent angerboda, loki
slayer vidar
victim odin, tyr
FENS *native* slodger
FENT cleft, slit, remnant
FENUGREEK baumier,

bird's-foot, lotus, mellilot, ornithopus, trigonella
seeds helbeh
FEODARY, FEUDARY accomplice, dependent, servant, subject, tenant, vassal
FERAL bestial, bloody, brutal, cruel, deadly, ferine, ferocious, fierce, funereal, malignant, rapacious, savage, unbroken, untamed, wild
FERASH servant
FER-DE-LANCE bonetail, jararaca
FERDINAND bomba, bull
author munro leaf
beloved miranda
kingdom navarre, spain
lords berowne, biron, boyet, dumain, longaville
patron to columbus
wife isabella
FERETORY bier, chapel, shrine
FERGUSONITE bragite
FERIA fair, ferie, festival, fiesta, holiday
FERMENT ager, agitate, agitation, barm, boil, brew, bubble, bustle, buzz, change, commotion, dander, disorder, dudgeon, ebullition, effervesce, enzyme, excite, fever, fret, leaven(ing), moil, must, mutation, seethe, simmer, sour, stum, sweat, tumult, turbulence, turmoil, turn, uproar, variation, work, yeast, zyme
active principle enzyme
free from dezymotize
FERMENTATION agitation, disturbance, ebullition, excitement, leaven, perturbation, quickening, stimulation, unrest
pert. zymic, zymotic
tank silo
FERMENTING *agent* bacteria, baking powder, barm, buttermilk, carbon dioxide, cream of tartar, diastase, enzyme, mother, pepsin, soda, sour milk, yeast, zyme
cause zymotic
mixture bub
FERN (See also *genus* and *kind*, below.) acrogen, alsophila, amamau, aterach, bracken, brake, dendrite, dugal, ekaha, filicite, gold-

back, kolokolo, mulewort, nardoo, osmund, parareka, pillwort, plant, polypody, pteridophyte, pulu, salvinia, schizaea, sporogen, synange, tara, weki
aquatic ceratopteris
bermuda adiantum
bird's-foot adiantopsis
caudex stipe
cell spore
climbing alice's, nito
cluster sorus
comb. pterido, pteris
description pteridography
edible roi, tara
evergreen california-gold
flowering osmund(a)
fossil caulopteris, glossepteris, lesleya, linopteris, pecopteris
gametophyte prothallium
genus acrostichum, asplenium, blechnum, cheilanthes, cryptogramma, davallia, dryopteris, marsilea, nephrolepis, osmunda, pellaea, polypody, psilotum, pteris, tmesipteris, todea, woodsia
grape botrychium
kind adder's-tongue, adiantum, anemia, basket, birdsfoot, bracken, brake, ceterach, cliff-brake, dogtooth violet, maidenhair, moonwort, nito, onoclea, osmund, palapalai, pitau, royal, staghorn, sword, todea, uluhi, wallrue, wallwort, wheki, woodsia
leaf crosier, frond
-like pteroid pteridophytic
-like plant acrogen, pteroid
maidenhair adiantum
male basket, osmund
owl night jar
paleozoic lepidophyte
part sorus, spore
patches sori
pert. bracky
polypody phlebodium
primitive botryopterid
root pannum, roi
royal bog onion, brake, osmund, pteris
scale ceterach, chaff, ramenta, ramentum
science pteridology
seed spore, talisman
-shape filiform
spore sorus
stem caudex, stipe
tropical marattia

woodland crest
FERNEY *philosopher* voltaire
FEROCIOUS barbarous, bloody, brutal, cruel, fell, feral, fierce, gothic, grim, infuriated, inhuman, lupine, maddened, merciless, ravenous, relentless, rude, ruthless, savage, truculent, untamed, vandalic, vicious, violent, wolfish
FEROCITY brutality, cruelty, ferity, fierceness, savagery, violence
symbol tiger, wolf
FERRAGUS *foe* roland
FERRARA See SWORD.
ducal family este
FERRET animal, gil(l), hob, jill, monk, mustela, polecat, talpe, tape, weasel
female bitch, gil(l), jill
male hob
prey prairie dog
FERREX *brother* porrex
father gorboduc
FERRIC *compound* arizonite, beudantite, geosole, prussiate
oxide crocus
oxide powder rouge
sulphate amarantite
FERRULE armgarn, bushing, collet, cuff, pulley, ring, runner, virl, virole
FERRUM See IRON.
FERRY boat, bridge, carrier, fly, pont, scow, traject, transport, vehicle, wherry
boat bac(k), pont
man boatman, charon
money naulum
FERTILE battel, battle, bearing, breedy, creative, fecund, feracious, fruitful, gleby, hearty, inventive, loamy, luxuriant, mellow, pinguid, plenteous, plentiful, procreant, productive, prolific, rank, rich, stimulating, strong, teeming, uberous, vegetative, yielding
as a cow, hydra, rabbit, warren
land carse
render enrich
FERTILITY bountifulness, copiousness, creativity, fecundity, feracity, fruitfulness, generousness, heart, invention, luxuriance, multiplication, pinguidity, plen-

teousness, potency, pregnancy, productiveness, productivity, proliferation, prolification, prolificacy, pullulation, richness, uberty *deity* (See also EGYPT *childbirth goddess.*) aglauros, annona, apet, aphrodite, ashtoreth, astarte, atargatis, baal, bona dea, briget, brigid, ceres, cybele, dagan, damia, danu, demeter, dionysus, fauna, faunus, frey(a), freyr, isis, istarte, khnemy, khnum, lupercus, mama, min, nerthus, njord, njorth, oro, osiris, picumnus, priapus, tellus, vanir, venus, yaksha
drug clomid, hcg, spanish fly
patron yaksha
rites lupercalia
symbol fish
FERTILIZATION endogamy, fecundation, heterogamy, impregnation, insemination, isogamy, orthogamy, pollination, porogamy
FERTILIZE enrich, fatten, fecundate, fecundify, fructify, impregnate, inseminate, marl, pollen, pollinate, pollinize, prolificate
FERTILIZER alinit, ammonia, ammonite, apatite, argal, argol, argul, baculite, boneash, bonemeal, compost, compote, dressing, dung, enrichener, guano, humus, manure, marl, milt, muck, nitrogen, phosphate, potash, tankage
FERULE collet, fennel, palmer, punishment, rod, ruler
FERVENCY ardency, ardor, cadency, enthusiasm, heat, passion, vehemence
FERVENT, FERVID agog, ardent, avid, boiling, burning, devout, eager, enthused, enthusiastic, excited, fiery, glowing, heartfelt, hearty, hot, impassioned, intense, keen, passionate, perfervid, pious, religious, responsive, sincere, tender, torrid, vehement, warm, whole-souled, zealous
FERVID See FERVENT.
FERVOR animation, ardency, ardor, devotion, enthusiasm, feeling, fire, heat, intensity, love, passion, piety, strength, warmth, zeal, zest

FESCENNINE See OBSCENE.
FESCUE grass, mote, plectrum, pointer, rush, straw, trifle, twig, vester
bearded crowfoot, darnel, wheat
grass blue bunch
FESTAL gala, gaudy, gay, feastful, festive
FESTE *mistress* olivia
FESTER abscess, blister, canker, cicatrice, cicatrize, corrupt, decay, inflame, lesion, pustule, putrefy, rankle, rot, scar, sore, suppurate, swell, ulcer(ate)
FESTERING fretty, inflammation, irritation, rankling, sore(spot)
FESTIVAL (See also FEAST.) agon, agrionia, ale, apollonia, armilustrium, arrephoria, athenaea, bairam, bake, banquet, barbecue, beanfeast, bee, beltane, blowout, bon, b(o)uphonia, busk, carnival, carousal, celebration, clambake, dashahara, delia, dewali, diipolia, eed, encaenia, fair, fasching, feast, feis, feria, fete(champetre), field day, fiesta, fishfry, floralia, fun, gala, haloa, high jinks, holi, holiday, hoolee, huffle, jamboree, jubilee, kermess, kermis, kurmes, lammas, mardi gras, mela, merrymaking, mishnah, moed, muharram, opalia, pesach, picnic, puja, purim, revel(ry), saturnalia, seder, squantum, succos, sukkoth, thiasos, vota, wayzgoose
church candlemas, christmas, easter, epiphany, lent, martinmas, michaelmas
comb. mas
day, last apodosis
epiphany uphelya
of lights dewali, divali, diwali
play festspiel
procession corso
religious all hallows
rural ambarvalia, fete champetre
FESTIVE convivial, festal, gala, gay, glad, holiday, jovial, joyous, merry, mirthful, social, sportive
FESTIVITY celebrating, cele-

bration, commemoration, conviviality, fanfare, fanfaronade, feu de joie, fun, function, gaiety, hilarity, holiday-making, jollity, joviality, joy, joyance, jubilation, jubilee, levity, merriment, merrymaking, mirth, observance, ovation, party, racketing, rejoicing, remembrance, revel, revelment, revelry, revels, salute, salvo, skylarking, solemnization, splore, triumph, whoopee, yomtov, yontif(dig), yontiff
god bacchus, comus, dionysus
lively whoop-de-do
FESTOON bouquet, bucranium, curve, decorate, garland, lei, swag, wreath
FESTUCA capon's-grass, rattail
FETCH accomplish, achieve, apparition, arrive, artifice, attain, attract, bear, bring, call for, carry, cheat, come, conclude, cost, deduce, derive, double, elicit, filch, gasp, get, ghost, haunt, heave, interest, make, move, obtain, phantom, plait, procure, reach, remove, retrieve, revenant, run after, secure, shack, shade, shag, shift, sophism, specter, spirit, spook, steal, strike, stroke, sweep, tack, take, transfer, transport, travel, trick, wraith
a blow strike
about contrive, devise, pivot, tack
and carry serve
down fell, force down, lower
off deliver, drain, drink, rescue
round come to, persuade, revive
up halt, train
up at arrive, discover, elevate, reach, recall, recover, revive, run, sight
FETCHING alluring, attractive, crafty, cunning, delightful, fascinating, pleasing, scheming, sweet
FETE See FESTIVAL.
FETID bad, foul, frowsty, frow(z)y, fulsome, fusty, high, malodorous, mephetic, miasmal, miasmic, musty, nasty, noisome, nosy, odorous, offensive,

olid, putrid, rancid, rank, reas(t)y, reechy, reeking, reeky, repugnant, repulsive, revolting, rotten, smelling, smellsome, smelly, stenchy, stinking, vile, virous, whiffy
bastard ballota, black horehound
buckey horse-chestnut
camomile mayweed
cress peppergrass
hellebore bear's-foot, skunk-cabbage
horehound black angelica
nightshade henbane
shrub papaw, pawpaw
woodwitch stinkhorn
FETISH abraxas, amulet, anito, aphrodisiac, ascon, avatar, charm, grigri, guaca, image, juju, karma, magic, mascot, mojo, mumbo-jumbo, nagual, obe(ah), obi(a), periapt, phylactery, shintai, spell, stimulent, symbol, totem, talisman, voodoo, zeme, zemi, zogo
FETISHER medicine-man, sorcerer
FETISHISM idolatry, sorcery
FETLOCK coot, tuft
FETTER anklet, baffle, balk, band, bar, basil, bend, bind, block, bond, chafe, chain, check, clog, confine, cuff, curb, dam, foil, frustrate, gyve, hamper, handcuff, hinder, hobble, hog-tie, hopple, impede, iron, langle, manacle, obstruct, restrain(t), shackbolt, shackle, snaffle, spancel, strain, swath, thrall, thwart, tie, trammel
FETTERBUSH pipestem, pipewood
FETTLE arrange, attend to, bandage, beat, belt, condition, deck, dress, equip, fuss, groom, harness, line, manage, mull, provide, rope, strike, thrash, trim
up tidy up
FETTLER billyer
FETUS embryo
human homunculus
limbless amelus
FEU benefice, fee, fire, grant, tenure
de joie festivity
FEUD affray, animosity, broil, contention, contest, dissension, enmity, estate,

fief, fight, fray, land, quarrel, spat, strife, vendetta
blood vendetta
FEUDAL lordly, manorial, subject, vassal
benefice feod, feu(d), fief
chief capite
domain feod, feud, fief
jurisdiction feoff, soc, soke
land holding odal
lord See FEUDAL *ruler.*
noble vidame
penalty sursise
ruler daimio, dauphin, liege, lord(ling), overlord, suzerain, vavaso(u)r
service avera(ge), bedrip
service, pert. banal
tax tail(l)age, tallage, tertian, tillage
tenant bordar, cotter, cottier, leud(e), socager, socman, vassal
tenants' fee tailage, tallage
tenure socage
township vill
tribute brennage, heriot
vassal baron, feodary
FEUDATORY beneficiary, dependent, fief, state, tenant, zamindar, zemindar
FEVER ague, ardor, calenture, cauma, delirium, dengue, desire, disease, enecia, excitement, febricity, febrility, ferment, fire, flush, heat, malaria, pyreticosis, pyrexia, sicken, temperature, tertian(a), warmth
abatement defervescence
absence apyrexia, apyrexy
affected with pyretic
-bird roller
black kalaazar, typhus
blister cold sore, herpes
breakbone dengue
bush winterberry
chills and ague
comb. febri, pyr(a), pyro, typh(o)
continued synchus
-cup pitcherplant
intermittent malaria, quartan, sextan
kind ague, amakebe, breakbone, brucellosis, calentural, calenture, dengue, hay, helodes, malaria, malta, marsh, milk, octan, quartan, remittent, rock, rose, scalma, scarlatina, scarlet, sextan, sodoku, spotted, tap, texas, trench,

typhinia, typhoid, typhus, undulant, yellow(jack)
lake malaria
malta brucellosis
marsh helodes
pert. pyretic
plant ocimum, primrose
producer febrifacient, pyrogen
reducer defervescent, febrifuge
remedy antipyretic, aseptolin, aspirin, defervescent, febrifuge, refrigerant
rock brucellosis
slight febricula
slight, pert. subfebrile
sore necrosis, ulcer
spots petechiae
texas tristeza
treatment antipyresis
tree bitterbark, blue gum
tropical dengue, malaria, yellow(jack)
undulant brucellosis, malta, rock
without afebrile, apyretic
FEVERFEW broombush, mayweed, mugwort, parthenium, prairie-dock
FEVERISH agitated, aguish, ardent, burning, delirious, excited, febrile, fidgety, fiery, flushed, flustered, frantic, frenetic, hectic, hot, impassioned, impatient, inflamed, jittery, jumpish, jumpy, nervous, passionate, pyretic, restive, restless, sick, skittish, speedy, torrid, uneasy
FEVERROOT bastard ipecac, genson, horse gentian
FEVERWEED fitweed
FEVERWORT boneset
FEW curn, curran, exigious, handful, hardly any, infrequent, insignificant, less, limited, lite, meager, meagre, middling, minute, not many, paltry, petty, peu, piddling, poco(s), rare, scant(y), scarce, scattering, scrimption, short, some, sparse, sporadic, sprinkling, stingy, thin, trifling, unplentiful, wheen, whone
and far between sparse
comb. olig(o), pauci
FEWNESS dearth, exiguity, handful, infrequency, minority, paucity, rarity, scantiness, scarceness, sparsity

FEWTRIL trifle

FEY accursed, dead, delirious, doomed, dying, elfin, enfeebled, fatal, fated, otherworldly, timid, unlucky, visionary

FEZ busby, caftan, cap, shako, tarboosh, tarbouche, tarbush, turban

FIALIN *friend* napoleon iii

FIANCE betrothed, confidence, intended, promise, spouse, trust

FIANNA fenians, oisin

FIASCO botch, bottle, catastrophe, crash, debacle, failure, fizzle, flask, frost, hash, mess, miscarriage, muddle, mull, washout

FIAT act, command, decision, decree, edict, endorse, law, mandate, order, ordinance, permit, sanction, writ
lux let there be light

FIB beat, equivocate, falsehood, invent, lie, palter, prevaricate, pummel, sklent, story, untruth, white lie

FIBER (See also *kind,* below.) caliber, calibre, catena, character, cilia, cordage, filament, grain, hair, nap, nature, quality, root, shred, sinew, staple, strand, strength, suture, thread
agave zapupe
artificial acrilan, aralac, arnel, dacron, dynel, estron, fortrel, kodel, nylon, nytril, orlon, polyester, qiana, rayon, spandex, vicara
band fillet, lemniscus
bark olona, tapa, terap
basket-making datil, raffia
bast couratari, escobadura, gumihan, marakapas, ramie
black kittul
board beaverboard, celotex
carding of scribble
cellulose rayon
century plant clusters, pita
cluster nep
coarse adad, bassine, kemp
coconut coir, kyar
comb. ino
combing noil
cordage abaca, ambaree, ambary, anodendron, anonang, coir, eruc, feru, hemp, imbe, jute, rhea, sisal
cotton linit, staple
ends, fuzzy nap

flax harl, tow
group rope, spindle
hat datil
hemp harl, sinawa
istle pita, pito
jipijapa toquilla
kind 3 ala, nap, nep, tal, tow 4 adad, aloe, bast, buri, harl, hemp, husi, imbe, ixle, jusi, jute, kair, kyar, lint, marl, noil, pita, pito, rhea, saba, sana, silk, sola, wool, yarn 5 abaca, civil, erizo, floss, istle, ixtle, kapok, linen, mudar, nylon, oakum, orlon, qiana, ramee, ramie, rayon, sisal, velon 6 ambary, amiray, aralac, avisco, cotton, dacron, dynelo, lastex, manila, merino, raffia, staple, thread, tussah, vicara, vinyon, zephyr 7 acetate, acrilan, castuli, chingma, fortrel, haurizo, papoula, sabutan, sarelon 8 celanese, fibrilla, filament, fortisan, keratose, rexenite, toquilla 9 gamelotte, horsehair 10 anodendron, chemstrand, escobadura 11 filamentule
knot nep, noil
length staple
-like byssoid, cottony, towy
loose lint
manufactured See *artificial,* above.
matted shag
matting coir, raffia
measurement grex
mineral asbestos
muscle rhabdium
palm agave, coquito, corozo, coyol, doh, eruc, gebanga, raffia
peacock feather marl
pert. desmoid
piece noil
pineapple pita, pito
plant abaca, aloe, ambary, arusha, caroa, corchorus, creole, ehuawa, flax, istle, ix(t)le, pita, ramee, ramie, rossele, sana, sida, sisal, sunn, totora
pressed felt
pulverized flock
ramie amiray
rope allaeanthus, ambary
sacking chandul
sedge gamelotte
separate scutch
short noil
silky castuli, kapok, kumbi, yachan

source arusha, callicarpa, ribbon tree, urena
spun yarn
synthetic See *artificial,* above.
tampico istle, ix(t)le
textile azlon, ramie, saba
tree ceiba, hau, majagua, yachan
triacetate arnel
tropical istle, ix(t)le
twisted strand
vegetable filasse
waste fly, gout, noil
wood aralac, bast, grain, scutch
wool gare, kemp, nep, pile, staple
yarn filasse, strand

FIBRIL(LA) desmose, filament, hair, myoneme, myophan, roothair, thread
bundle axoneme

FIBRINOLYSIN plasmin

FIBROUS capsular, capsulate, stringy, tough

FIBULA brooch, buckle, clasp, leg bone, ouch, perone, pin
pert. peroneal

FICKLE arbitrary, capricious, cas(s)alty, cas(s)elty, casual, cazelty, changeable, dangerous, deceitful, dizzy, erratic, faithless, false, fitful, flatter, flighty, frivolous, gery, inconstant, irresolute, kittle, light, mercurial, mutable, protean, puzzle, shifty, spasmodic, unfaithful, unstable, unsteady, vacillating, variable, veery, volage, volatile, wankle, wavering

FICO bit, fig, snap, tanti, trifle

FICTILE molded, plastic, pliable, pliant

FICTION allegory, apologue, contrivance, deceit, device, dime novel, drama, dreadful, fable, fabliau, fabrication, fairy tale, fancy, fantasy, feigning, fictitious, figment, grue, imagination, invention, legend, lie, love story, marchen, myth, narrative, nouvelle, novel(a), novelet(te), parable, phantasy, pretending, romance, shocker, short story, soap opera, story, tale, thriller, western, yarn

FICTIONAL allegoric(al),

anecdotal, assumed, bogus, chimerical, fabulous, fake, false, idealistic, legendary, mythical, narrative, parabolic(al), romantic, unreal

FICTITIOUS apochryphal, artificial, assumed, bogus, chimerical, counterfeit, created, dummy, fabricated, fabulous, false, fanciful, fantastic, fashioned, feigned, fictional, figmental, imaginary, invented, legendary, mythical, poetic, spurious, unreal

name alias, pseudonym

story apologue, novel, romance

FICTIVE deceitful, feigned, imaginary

FICUS agamid, balete, banyan, bo-tree, fig, pipal, pyrula, rubber plant

fruit syconium

FID bar, bit, lump, pin, plug, quid

FIDDLE bow, cheat, crowd, dawdle, fithel, fritter, giga, gigue, gudok, humstrum, kit, potter, scrape, swindle, swivel, trifle, urheen, violin

ancient rebab, rebec(k)

-deedee nonsense

-faddle fuss, gossip, nonsense, procrastinate, trifle(r), trivial

flower bleeding heart

-headed foolish, silly

medieval giga, gigue, rubeba

6-stringed crouth, crowd

stick bow

string thairm

FIDDLER crab, duck, fish, flicker, sandpiper, scraper, sixpence, violinist

crab ocypode, racer, soldier, uca

fish ray

unskilled tweedledee

FIDDLESTICKS pshaw

FIDELITY accuracy, allegiance, attachment, bona fides, bonne foi, constancy, devotion, exactness, faith(fulness), fealty, good faith, hold, honesty, lealty, loyalty, naturalism, piety, probity, realism, reality, stanchness, staunchness, steadfastness, troth, veracity, verism

symbol dog, topaz

FIDGET brevit, bustle, chafe, dysphoria, fantod, fike, firk,

fissle, fistle, fret, fuss(er), hotch, jitter, restlessness, shrug, stew, thrill, tiddle, toss, tremble, trifle, twitch, worrit, worry

FIDGETS all-overs, dysphoria, nerves, trepidation, shakes

FIDGETY fantad, feisty, feverish, figert, fussy, hectic, impatient, jittery, jumpy, nervous, restive, restless, shaky, skittish, twitchy, uneasy

FIDUCIARY trustee, trustful

FIDUS ACHATES companion, friend

FIEF benefice, estate, fee, feof, feud, han, satsuma, servant

FIELD acre, ager, area, arena, arrish, bailiwick, beat, bounds, business, calling, campo, career, catch, champ, champaign, champs, circle, circus, clearing, cockpit, court, croft, diamond, district, domain, earth, expanse, extent, farmland, forte, glebe, grid (iron), handle, land, lea, limits, lists, lot, margin, matter, meadow, metier, nilpa, occupation, orbit, outside, paddy, padi, pale, plain, plot, profession, province, range, receive, rowen, savanna(h), scope, space, specialty, sphere, territory, thing, tillage, trade, vocation, wong

ash rowan tree

athletic arena, course, court, diamond, green, gridiron, oval, ring, rink, stadium

balm basil-thyme, ivy, sheepmint

bed four-poster

biblical ager, aner

bird plover

camomile oxeye

comb. agro

common share dale

crane's bill alfilaria

cress crowdweed

crop corn, cotton, grain, hay

day festival, tournament

day, equestrian gymkhana

division rig

duck bustard

-dwelling arvicoline

edge rand

eugene, character calico cat, gingham dog, toy soldier

extensive plain, savannah

garlic wild onion

glass binocle, telescope

god faun, pan, pellervoinen

grassy garston, lea, pen

growing in agrarian agrest(i)al, campestral

gun amusette, artillery

holy campo santo, cemetery

inclosed ager, paddock

kale charlock

laborer (See also PEASANT.) bagdi, bracero, hand

lava pedregal

madder rubiacin, sherardia, spurwort

man hunter

martin kingbird

meeting duel

mint catnip

mouse vole

oak encina

of blood aceldama, ager, akeldama, cannae, sanguinis

of mars arena, campus martius

of stars compostela

of vision See RANGE.

pert. agral, agrarian, agrestic, campestral, champetre

piece amusette, galloper, gun

pine poverty-plant

plowed erd, furrow

rice sawah

scabious billy button, bluebottle, bluecap, burdock, daisy, geranium, periwinkle, vinca

small croft, haw, paddock

stubble arrish, gratten, gratton, hirsh, rowen

tobacco vega

vocational calling, forte, metier, profession

work fortification, lunet(te), redan

worker AGENT, hand, peasant

FIELDFARE felt, hillbird, jack(bird), redleg, redshank, snowbird, thrush, veltfare

FIELDING *novel* amelia, jonathan wild, joseph andrews, tom jones

practice fungo

FIEND addict, amaimon, apollyon, barbason, d(a)emon, devil, devotee, enemy, fan, foe, habitue, imp, mephistopheles, monster, sadist, satan, succuba, titivil, votarist, votary, **wizard**

FIENDISH atrocious, avernal, baleful, black, cruel, demoniac(al), demonic, devilish, diabolic(al), fenden, hell-born, hellish, infernal, malefic, malevolent, malicious, malign(ant), mephistophelean, satanic, sinister, wicked

FIENT devil, oath

FIERASFER carapus, fish, pearlfish

FIERCE active, ardent, barbarous, barefisted, bitter, bold, breme, brim, brutal, catawampous, cruel, eager, farouche, fell, ferocious, fiery, frantic, furious, grim, haughty, hetter, horrible, infuriated, inhuman, lupine, makaha, menacing, orped, proud, raging, rampant, ravening, ravenous, rethe, savage, stark, stern, stour, threatening, thro, truculent, uncurbed, valiant, violent, warlike, wild, wroth

FIERCELY felly, hard

FIERY adust, angry, ardent, burning, candent, candescent, combustible, combustive, conflagrative, demonstrative, empyreal, excitable, fervent, fervid, feverish, fierce, flaming, flickering, furious, gingery, glowing, headlong, heated, hot(headed)(tempered), igneous, ignescent, impassioned, impetuous, inflamed, intense, madcap, mettlesome, passionate, peppery, perfervid, precipitate, red-hot, scorching, simmering, spirited, spunky, torrid, vehement, violent, volcanic, wild

cross crantara

cross user ku klux klan

pert. phlegethontal

FIESTA fair, feast, feria, festival, fete, holiday, party, vacation

costume pollera

FIFE array, bit, flute, piffero, stick, trifle

thane of macduff

FIFTEEN *comb.* pentadec(a)

FIFTEENER incunabulum

FIFTH *amendment* silence

columnist infiltrater, subversive

comb. quint(i)

day thursday

estate scientists

perfect hemidia

wheel chotchke(leh), superfluous, supernumerary, tchotchke(leh), tsatske(leh)

FIFTY *-fifty* divided, equal(ly), half(-and-half), split

men, commander quinquagenarion

per cent half

year celebration jubilee

years old quinquagenarian

FIG agama, agamid, array, balete, bit, breba, clothing, condition, dress, eleme, elemi, fico, form, fouter, fruit, furbish, gondang, peepul, piece, pipal, raisin, retund, rig, smah, trifle, zero

bale sero(o)n

bark doundake

basket caba(s), frail, seroon, tap(net)

bean lupine

blue brisbane, quandong

boy pickpocket

cochineal cactus, nopal

comb. syco

crop mamme

curer hezekiah

degenerate gallflower

disease smut

finch beccafico

1st-crop breba

leaf covering, garment, modesty

-like caricous, ficoid

marigold catchop, ficoid(al), foxchop, mesem, noonflower, plant, samh

out or up decorate, dress, ornament

pecker beccafico

rotting endosepsis

sacred pipal

-shaped caricous, ficiform

smyrna eleme, elemi

tree banyan, gondang, pipal, upas

wasp blastophaga

wild clusia, fatpork

FIGENT fidgety, volatile

FIGHT 3 box, jar, row, vie, war 4 beef, bout, clem, cope, duel, feud, fray, miff, mill, riot, spar, spat, tiff, tilt 5 argue, bandy, brawl, break, broil, fence, joust, match, melee, runin, scold, scrap, setto, snarl, words 6 affair, affray, attack, bar-

ney, battle, bicker, cample, cangle, combat, debate, demele, differ, engage, fracas, fratch, hassle, jangle, jostle, meddle, rassle, rastle, resist, rumpus, strife, strive, tangle, timber, towrow, tussle 7 brabble, brangle, compete, contend, contest, discord, dispute, dissent, grapple, quarrel, rhubarb, ruction, scuffle, stickle, tuilyie, warfare, wrangle, wrestle 8 campaign, conflict, disagree, shemozzl, skirmish, squabble, struggle, vendetta 9 bushwhack, encounter, lock horns, scrimmage, shlemozzl 10 contention, difference, donnybrook, fisticuffs, tournament 11 battleroyal, controversy, cross swords

against buck, challenge, contest

against the gods theomachy

between 2 duel, duomachy

eager to bellicose, belligerent, bloodthirsty

fist rippit, turnup

shy of avoid, scruple

street habble

FIGHTER barrator, battler, belligerent, boxer, brawler, champion, cocker, combatant, competitor, contender, contestant, disputant, duelist, gamecock, gladiator, guerilla, jingoist, jouster, militant, militarist, recruit, rookie, scrapper, scuffler, SOLDIER, struggler, swordsman, tussler, warmonger, warrior, wildcat, wrangler, wrestler

name meaning boris

pilot ace

FIGHTING bellicose, belligerent, combat, conflict, digladiation, game, militant, plucky, pugnacious, sciamachy, strife, warlike

by fire pyromachy

fish betta, plakat

street bovver, brawl, riot

FIGMENT creation, (day) dream, fable, fabrication, fancy, fantasy, fiction, idea, imagination, invention, nightmare

of the imagination apparition

FIGURAL emblematical, metaphorical, numeric(al)

FIGURATION adorning, design, embellishment, form, marking, outline, representation, shape, shaping

FIGURATIVE allegoric(al), allusive, antipathetic(al), catachrestic(al), denotative, euphemistic, euphuistic, flowery, ironic(al), metaphoric(al), metonymic, parabolic(al), pictorial, referential, satiric(al), symbolic(al), tropical, tropal, typical

FIGURE 3 add, sum, wax 4 body, cast, doll, form, mark, plan, rate, sign 5 build, count, digit, dolly, dummy, frame, image, model, motif, price, shape, total, trace, value 6 assess, cipher, design, device, effigy, emblem, entail, expect, isagon, number, puppet, reckon, scheme, statue, symbol, typify 7 anatomy, carving, compute, contour, decagon, diagram, engrave, feather, hexagon, manikin, numeral, outline, pattern, portray, reality, waxwork 8 estimate, likeness, monument, physique, portrait, resemble, similize 9 calculate, celebrity, character, enumerate, fantocine, mannequin, personage, personify, quotation, sculpture, statuette, symbolize 10 allegorize, apparition, appearance, fantoccini, illuminate, marionette, silhouette 12 conformation, constitution
anatomical ecorche, skeleton
architectural atlantes, atlas, caryatid, telamon(es)
carved figurine, glyph, statue
comic billiken
covered with seme
earth geoid
-eight knot
equiangular isagon, isogon
female caryatid, orant
5-angled pentagon
4-angled rectangle, rhombus, square, tetragon
geometrical See GEOMETRY *figure.*
grotesque babcon, gargoyle, magot, maximon
human form atlantes, caryatid, dummy, glyph, mannequin, nude, oran, telamon(es)

many-sided cube, decagon, dodecahedron, hexagon, hexahedron, icosahedron, isogon, nonagon, octagon, octahedron, pentagon, polygon, polyhedron, quadrilateral, tetragon
ideal eidolon
imaginary bogeyman
incised intaglio
odd maumet
of fun butt, eccentric, grotesque
of speech allegory, anaphora, antithesis, antonomasia, aporia, apostrophe, asyndeton, catachresis, ecphonesis, ellipsis, enallage, epitrope, euphemism, euphuism, exclamation, flower, hyperbole, imagery, irony, litotes, metalepsis, metaphor, metathesis, metonymy, oxymoron, parable, personification, pun, rhetoric, satire, simile, synecdoche, trope
on expect
out calculate, catch on, conclude, dope, fathom, follow, get, reason, solve, understand
oval ellipse, swash
pagan icon, idol, image
papier-mache pinata
pear-shaped goutte
praying orant
prehistoric chacmol, chacmool, intaglio
round circle, globe, sphere
shadow skiagram
skating bracket, counter, spiral
stuffed dummy
symbolic emblem
10-sided decagon
3-angled triangle
3-branched triskele, triskelion
3-dimensioned solid
triangular triquet
20-faced icosahedron
winged eidolon, idolon, idolum, spiling

FIGURED adorned, computed, faconne, ornate, patterned

FIGUREHEAD cat's-paw, charlie mccarthy, dummy, front, insignia, puppet, scroll, tool

FIGURINE statuette, tanagra
female orant
movie oscar

FIGWORT agilinis, alonsoa, angelon(ia), antirrhinum, bacopa, bartsia, beeplant, bramia, brownwort, bucknera, calceolaria, collinsia, cutfinger, diascia, euphrasia, foxglove, iceplant, linaria, mullein, pilewort, rhinanthus, selfheal

FIJI *arrowroot* pia
bay mbya, natewa, ngaloa, savusavu
capital suva
chestnut rata
city etumba, lambasa, mau, mba, momi, naloto, namoli, nandi, narata, nasala, navola, rewa, sagara, suva, thuvu, tuvu
dance siva
drink kava, yaqona
drug tonga
feudal service lala
hut bure
island agata, aiwa, eld, kambara, kandavu, kia, koro, lakemba, lau, mali, mamolo, mango, matuku, mbenga, mbulia, moala, naiau, naitauba, naviti, nairai, ngamea, ngau, ono, ovalau, rambi, taveuni, totoya, vanualevu, vitilevu, viwa, waia, yasawa, yendua
island group tonga
leader mara
native vitian
neighbors mamanutha islands
nephew vasu
peak monavatu
point vuya
poon tree dilo
port suva
tree buri, dilo, parinarium, poon

FIKE fidget, flirt(ation), fuss, itch, trifle, trouble, vex, whims(e)y, worry

FILAGO gifola

FILAMENT barb, brin, capillament, capillary, cilia, ciliolum, cilium, cirrus, cobweb, denier, dowl(e), elater, FIBER, fibril(la), flagellum, gossamer, hair, harl(e), nema, phacella, quill, skein, spiderweb, sterigma, strand, tendril, thread(let), vein, web, wire
bivalve byssus
cotton thread
dermal hair
divide sleave

feather dowl(e)

flax harl(e)

having capillaceous, capillary

mineral stringer

silky byssus, byssine

twisted hackle, strand

FILAMENTOUS fibrous, hairlike, hairy, ropy, stringy, threadlike, wiry

FILANDERS backworm

FILBERT cobnut, hazelnut

sieve of prickle

FILCH bob, booty, cop, crib, fetch, grab, grasp, lift, loot, nim, pilfer, pinch, plunder, purloin, rifle, rob, seize, snatch, sneak, snitch, STEAL, swipe, take, thieve

FILCHER See THIEF.

FILE abrade, accuse, archive, arrange, befoul, box, cabinet, carlet, catalog(ue), collection, column, condemn, debauche, dishonor, docket, dossier, enter, exhibit, folder, grail(er), grate, grind, index, label, line, list, march, pace, pickpocket, pigeonhole, polish, quannet, rascal, rasp, rattail, raze, record, risp, roll, row, rub, scrape, sharpen, smooth, soil, stain, store, string, tabulate, thread, topper, train, walk, wire

box solander

carpenter's risp

circular bull's-foot, wastebasket

coarse rape, rasp, rubber

comb-maker's carlet, grail(er), graille, topper

curved riffler

document archive, dossier

finisher ender

flat quannet

half-round grail(le)

rough rasp

single one by one

6 soldiers rot

13 scrap, wastebasket

wood rasp

FILEFISH balistis, foolfish, lija, triggerfish, turbot, unicorn, unie

FILET (See also FILLET.) lace, mesh, net, steak

FILIAL sonly

FILIATION descent, family, offshoot, relationship

FILIBEG kilt, skirt

FILIBUSTER block, buccaneer, delay, freebooter,

hinder, pirate, procrastinate, stall, stonewall

FILIFORM catenoid, stringy

FILIGREE decorative, design, fanciful, figure, filigrant, lace, openwork, unsubstantial

FILING(S) abrasion, attrition, leftovers, limation, limature, powder, rasion, refuse, remainder, smoothing

metal lemel, limaille

FILIPINO See PHILIPPINES.

FILL accomplish, bag, bloat, block, brick, brim(mer), bulge, caulk, choke, complete, cram, dilate, dirt, distend, earth, execute, formation, glut, gorge, hold, implete, include, inflate, kedge, lade, load, occupy, pack (age), pad(ding) pang, perform, permeate, pervade, possess, provide, quar, sate, satiate, satiety, satisfy, stop, stuff(ing), suffuse, supply, swell, trig

by force cram, jam

cracks ca(u)lk, shim

in alternate, complete, insert, post, shoal, silt up, substitute

out complete, distend, enlarge, execute, extend, protract

the bill avail, suffice

the shoes of supplant

to brim bumper, crown

to capacity jampack

up brick, complete, estop, insert, occupy, plenish, restore, shoal, stoak, stodge, stop

with air balloon, blow up, dilate, inflate

with zeal enthuse

FILLE daughter, girl, maiden

de chambre maid

de joie See PROSTITUTE.

FILLED crowded, flush, gravid, loaded, opplete, swollen

FILLER adulterant, content, funnel, pipe, shim, silex, silka, syringe, wrapper

FILLET ampyx, anadem, annulet, band(age), bandeau, batten, chaplet, comble, diadem, dressing, fascia, garland, headband, irlo, listel, molding, orle, orlo, potong, reglet, regula, ribbon, scantling, snood, sola,

stria, strip(e), taenia, tenderloin, tiara, tressure, tringle, turban, vitta, wreath

architectural cimbia, lintel, listel, regula, taenia

frieze regula, taenia

hair band, snood

jeweled diadem, tiara

narrow anadem, listel, orle, reglet, stria

pert. boneless

remnants scissel

wool infula

FILLING bandwork, content, gob, impletion, lading, packing, saturation, stopping, stuffing, warp

dental bridge, crown, inlay

fabric warp, weft, woof, yarn

FILLIP blow, buffet, excitement, flash, flip, incentive, moment, snap, stimulate, stimulus, strike, tap, throw, tonic, toss, triviality, urge

FILLMORE, MILLARD

birthplace summerhill, new york

burial site buffalo

party whig

profession lawyer

FILLY colt, foal, girl, horse, mare

FILM blear, brate, celluloid, cine, cinema, cloud, coating, cover, flick, glaze, haze, hide, kel(l), lamina, layer, leaf, membrane, motion picture, movie, nebula, negative, obscure, patina, pellicle, photo(graph), picture, scale, scruff, scum, sheet, shoot, skin, veil, weft, x-ray

again retake

award oscar

coated with patinate, scummy

container cartridge

developer bath, dope, emulsion, hypo, soup, wash

discarded outtake

green patina

holder cassette

oily slick

thin brat, pellicle

wine beeswing

x-ray bitewing

yeast flor

FILMY cobwebby, delicate, diaphanous, dim, fine, gossamer, hazy, misty, sheer, vague, wispy

fern trichomanes

FILS boy, son
FILTER bougie, candle, clean, colander, colate, colature, drain, felt, ooze, percolate, purify, rape, refine, seep, sieve, sile, strain(er), truckle
in absorb, infiltrate, percolate, seep
press cake cachaza
sugar clay
FILTH bawdry, corruption, dirt, dregs, dung, fen, flop, fulyie, fulzie, garbage, gleet, gore, immorality, impurity, lubricity, lucre, muck, nastiness, obscenity, ordure, pouce, rot, slime, sluttery, soil, sordes, squalor, sullage, swill, vermin
symbol hog, swine
FILTHINESS cenosity, immundity, mucor, squalor, sullage
FILTHY augean, bestial, crummy, defiled, dirty, disgusting, foul, gross, hoggish, immund, impure, lairy, licentious, loathsome, low, nasty, obscene, offensive, polluting, repulsive, sloppy, slovenly, sordid, squalid, unclean, unkempt, vile
lucre gain, money
FIMBRIATE bordered, fringe(d), hairy, hem
FIN acantha, appendage, arm, blade, carve, cut up, end, fish, fiver, flipper, foot, forelimb, hand, kite, limb, pinna, pinnule, rib, spline
comb. pterygo, pteryx
de siecle decadent, modern
-footed pinniped
spinous acantha, dorsal
under ventral
without apteral, apterygial
FINAGLE cheat, deceive, intrigue, maneuver, plot, scheme, trick, wangle
FINAGLER draykop(f)
FINAL caudal, closing, complete(d), concluding, conclusive, darrein, decisive, definite, definitive, dernier, desistive, end, eventual, exam(ination), extreme, farewell, last, latest, mandatory, runoff, supreme, telic, terminal, ultimate, unqualified, utter
not nisi
offer ultimatum
outcome issue, upshot

part capstone
stanza envoi
things doctrine eschatology
FINALE act, bowout, coda, completion, conclusion, end(ing), epilogue, finis(h), peroration, summation, swan song, terminal, windup
FINALLY ad extremum, ad finem, at last, at length, conclusively, decisively, end, enfin, eureka, eventually, in conclusion, in fine, last(ly), once for all, ultimately
FINANCE aid, back, banking, bankroll, capitalize, chrysology, economics, endow, goods, grubstake, invest, money, patronize, pay for, promote, provide for, raise money, revenue, set up, sponsor, stake, subsidize, support, tax(ation), treasure, underwrite
FINANCES accounts, funds, income, purse, resources, revenues
FINANCIAL bursal, capital, fiscal, monetary, nummary, pecuniary, sumptuary
control purse-strings
statement balance sheet, budget
FINANCIER angel, backer, banker, baron, capitalist, enterpriser, entrepreneur, guarantor, moneyman, patron, solitaire, underwriter
FINANCING appropriation, backing, promotion, support, underwriting
FINBACK gibbar, jubartas, rorqual, whale
FINCH aberdavine, aberdevine, aberduvine, acanthis, bird, brambling, bunting, burion, canary, carduelis, carpodacus, chewink, citril, fink, firetail, fringilla, grosbeak, junco, linnet, man(n)ikin, moro, noap, olph, palila, peeweep, redhead, redpoll, senegal, serin, siskin, snowbird, sparrow, spink, tanager, tarin, terin, towhee, waxbill, yellowhammer
canary-like serin
copper chaffinch
falcon hierax
flock charm
gold drawbird

grass poephila
house burion, linnet
-like chewink, grosbeak, tanager
yellow canary, serin, tarin
FIND acquisition, arrive, attain, catch, chance, come on, decide, descry, detect, determine, devise, discover(y), espy, eureka, experience, feel, foundling, gain, get, invent, locate, meet, perceive, pinpoint, procure, provide, reach, regard, scrounge, strike, summon, supply, treasure, trouvaille, trove(r)
by accident blunder on, stumble on
by search ferret, probe
fault arraign, beef, bellyache, blame, carp, cavil, complain, crab, criticise, criticize, fret, gront, grumble, knock, mote, nag, natter, reproach, scold, upbraid
guilty attaint, condemn, convict, sentence
loophole escape
out ascertain, check, decipher, detect, determine, discover, divine, learn, solve, tell, trove, understand
solution solve, unriddle
the key solve
up discover, search for
FINDERS keepers
FINDING award, inquest, judgment, sentence, serendipity, solution, verdict
report of assay
FINE able, abwab, aim, amende, amerce(ment), attenuated, beautiful, betcheri, bien, bonny, brave, brawlie, brawly(s), budgeree, bumper, cain, cavalier, copacetic, copasetic, cool, cro, dainty, dandy, damages, delicate, de luxe, dire, discriminate, distraint, distress, doomage, elegant, end, escheat, ethereal, exact, excellent, exceptional, exquisite, fair, fancy, filmy, finish(ed), firstclass, firstrate, forefeit(ure), furbish, galanas, gauzy, good, gossamer(y), great, handsome, healthy, impost, jake, keen, lager, leger, levy, limit, meticulous, minute, mulct, nice, noble, object,

penalty, pleasant, powdery, pretty, prime, punish (ment), rare, result, rum, satiny, sconce, scot, sharp, slender, small, smarten, smooth, splendid, subtle, sweet, tax, tenuous, thin (spun), tickety-boo, tiny, up to snuff, wergild, wite

arts aesthetics, design, drawing, illustration, painting, sculpture, sketching

arts degree mfa

away diminish, dwindle

-drawn overnice, rentered

for killing cro, wergild

for misdeamor mulct

-headed clever, ingenious, subtle

letter line serif

record of estreat

-spoken adulatory, bland

whack neatness

FINENESS clearness, elegance, excellence, purity

FINERY bauble, bravery, bread, caparison, chiffon, clinquant, clothing, decoration, fegary, folderol, foofaraw, frill(ery), frippery, froufrou, fuss, gaiety, gaud(ery), gewgaws, gilding, gilt, jewelry, panoply, paste, pinchbeck, superfluity, tinsel, togs, trappings, trickery, trimmings, trumpery

bedeck with prink

worthless frippery

FINESPUN hair, thin, twittery, unsubstantial, visionary

FINESSE aplomb, artifice, clearness, competence, cunning, delicacy, discrimination, impasse, maneuver, purity, refinement, savoir faire, schneiden, schnitt, skill, stratagem, subtlety, taste, thinness, trick

FINEST See ACE, BEST.

FINFOOT sunbird

FINGAL *cave site* staffa

kingdom morven

son ossian

FINGER arrest, dactyl, digit(ize), feel, filch, handle, index, informer, meddle, minimum, pilfer, pointer, pollex, purloin, spy, touch, toy

affliction agnail, dactylitis, felon, hangnail, runaround, whitlow

board fret

cap cot, thimble

coldness acrocyanosis

comb. dactyl(o), digit(i)

cymbals castanets

devil's belemnite

disease acropathy

exercising device sthenochire

fern asplenium, hart's-tongue

1st index

flower foxglove

guard cot, stall, thimble

having 6 hexadactyl

inflammation See *affliction*, above.

lake canadice, canandaigua, cayuga, conesus, hemlock, honeoye, keuka, otisco, owasco, seneca, skaneateles

-like dactyl(ose), digitiform, digitate

little auricular(is), minimus, pinkie, pinky, pirlie

-man assassin, bravo, cutthroat, gunman, triggerman

middle medius

pert. annular, digital

-post clergyman, pointer

ring annular(is)

rubber shamer

snap with fil(l)ip

stall cot, dressing

vein salvatella

with digitate, prehensile

without adactyl(ous)

FINGERLEAF cinquefoil

FINGERLING diminutive, parr, thimble, troutlet

FINGERNAIL digger

curvature gryposis

disease flaw

moon lunula, lunule

pert. onychoid

FINGERPRINT dactylogram, dactylograph

mark arch, composite, latent, loop, whorl

science dactylography, dactyloscopy

FINGERROOT foxglove

FINGERSMITH midwife, pickpocket

FINIAL amalaka, apex, crest, epi, knob, knop, pinnacle, tee, top

FINICAL, FINICKY carping, choosey, critical, dainty, dapper, delicate, dinky, exacting, fastidious, fikey, fikie, foppish, fussy, jaunty, meticulous, miminypiminy, mincing, natty, nice, overelaborate, per-

nickety, prissy, prudish, smicker, spruce, squeamish

FINIFY furbish, trick out

FINISH accomplish(ment), achieve, acquit, beauty, be done, bottom, broach, burnish, chare, cheve, clinch, close, come off, complete, completion, conclude, conclusion, consume, consummate, crown, death, defeat, destroy, develop, do in, dress, effect, elaborate, elegance, end, execute, face, fulfill, furbish, glaze, goal, grace, kill, perfect(ion), polish, refinement, refute, settle, shine, slaughter, slay, surface, tape, terminal, terminate, texture, top off, win, windup

carefully neaten

dull mat(te)

glazed lacker, lacquer

glossy enamel

line ribbon, string, tape, wire

off consume, crush, destroy, kill

stucco spatter

FINISHED able, beyond help, climaxed, closed, completed, consummate, cultivated, cultured, dead, done, elegant, ended, entire, exhausted, fine, full(fledged), gone, intact, napoo(h), ornate, over, perfect, plenary, polished, proficient, refined, ripe, skilled, smooth, suave, symmetrical, through, urbane, whole

definitely sunk

ornamentally purfled

FINISHER beetler, edger, enameler, ender, eyer, settler

FINITE bound, circumscribed, conditioned, confined, definable, definite, delimited, fixed, limited, restricted

FINK bird, blab, derb, finch, inform(er), scab, spy, squealer, stool-pigeon, strikebreaker

FINLAND, FINN suomi

air divinity ilma

architect aalto

author sillanpaa

bath sauna

biochemist virtanen

capital helsingfors, helsinki

city aba, abo, enare, espoo, helsingfors, helsinki, imatra, kajaani, kem(i), kotka,

kuopio, lahti, lappeenranta, mikkeli, ouou, pori, rovaniemi, tampere, turku, vaasa, vasa
coin mark(ka), penni
composer sibelius
death goddess kalma
dialect karel, olonets(ian)
disputed territory karelia
division ijore, villipuri, vod
drink mesimarja
dulcimer kantele
earth goddess mother of mannu, mother of metsola
epic kalavala, kalevala
evil spirit hiisi, lempo, paha
field god pellervoinem
folksinger kanteletar
forest god tapio
fortress suomenlinna
fruit cloudberry, suomuurian
gods See KALEVALA.
granite rapakivi
gulf port leningrad
harp kantela, kantele
heroes See KALEVALA.
house-spirit para
illness goddess kipu-tytto
island a(a)land, ahvenanmaa, hailuto, karlo, vallgrund
isthmus karelia
lake enara, enare, hauki, inari, juo, kalla(vesi), kemi, kivi, koitere, ladoga, lappa, lentua, lesti, muo, nasi, nilakka, pielavesi, pielien, puru, puula, pyha, saima(a), simo, sounne, syvari
language avar, estonian, lapp, magyar, ostyak, samoyed, tarast, ugric, vogul
leader kekkonen, paasikivi, ukk
legend sampo
legislature eduskunta
magician vainamoinen
measure fathom, kannor, kannu, ottinger, sjomil, skalpund, tunna, tunnland, verst
moon god kuu
monster surma
musical instrument kantele
nationalist party fenoman
pain goddess kivutar, loviatar, vammatar
peak laltia
people avar, cheremis, estonian, fioun, ijore, inger, karelian, lapp(ish), livonian, magyar, mordvin, ostiak, ostyak, permiak, sa-

moyed, suomi, swekoman, tarast, tavast(ian), ugrian, uralian, veps(e), vod, vot(yak), zyrian
pert. suomic, suomish
pianist palmgren
poetry kalevala, rune(s)
port abo, helsinki, kemi, kokkola, ouli, pori, rauma, turku, vaasa
president See *leader*, above.
province hame, kymi, lappi, vaasa
region, legendary pohjola
resilience sisu
river iijoki, ivalo, kala, kitinen, kokemaki, lapuan, lotta, muonio, oulu, ounas, pasvik, siika, simo, teno, tornoi
sociologist westermark
soul haltija
statesman mannerheim
stone, sacred saite, saivo, sejda
sun god paiva
supreme god jumala, ukko
talisman sampo
tribe chud, hame, karjalaiset, suomalaiset, ugrian, veps(e), vogul, vote, voth
underworld manala, tuonela
underworld deities tuonetar, tuoni
water genii tursas, vetehinen
water god ahto, ahti
water sprite jelpin-tur, nakki, passe-jokka, pyhaj-oki
woods deity mielikki, nyyrikki, tapio, tuulikki
FINNIKIN pigeon
FINNO-UGRIC See FINLAND.
FIONN *son* oisin, ossian
FIORD See FJORD.
FIORIN knotgrass
FIOT bacongo, bafyot, bakongo
FIPPLE FLUTE recorder
FIPS chuzzlewit
FIR abies, conifer, evergreen
beech linden
club moss foxfeet
cone strobil(e), strobilus, yow(ie)
kind algerian, alpine, balm, balsam, baltic, baumier, cedar, cypress, larch, lashorn, sapin
marigold beach(apple) (strawberry)
pole juffer, ufer, upher
red douglas, pine, spruce
tree, changed to attis

FIRBOLG *enemy* fomorians
queen tailte, tailtiu
FIRE 3 can, dry, feu, vim, war 4 agni, bake, bale, burn, char, cook, drop, elan, glow, heat, hell, leye, love, oust, pyre, sack, stir, zeal 5 anger, ardor, blaze, demit, eject, expel, fever, flame, fuoco, heave, ignis, ingle, light, mania, shine, shoot, smart, spark, throw 6 arouse, beacon, blazer, bonner, bounce, excite, ignite, incite, inform, kindle, launch, scorch, signal, spirit, tandle 7 animate, bonfire, burning, cashier, dismiss, explode, flicker, inflame, inspire, passion, provoke, rapture, redline, smolder, sparkle 8 backfire, ignition, luminary, violence 9 calenture, discharge, holocaust, scintilla, vehemence 10 combustion, enthusiasm, excitement, phlogiston 11 inspiration 12 conflagration
abode of muspelheim
apparatus extinguisher
arrow malleolus
artillery barrage
away begin, go ahead
baptism by ordeal
basket cresset, grate
bed grieshoch
beetle cocuyo, cucuyo, elater(id)
boat palander
bolt lightning
-breather dragon
brick grog, quarle
bullet tracer
ceremonial bonfire
charioteer elijah
clay taskos, thill
comb. igni, pyr(o)
containing igneous
cover curfew, curphew
cross gantlet, gauntlet
-cured dark
damp gas, methane, vapor, wildfire
dampen smother
dart phalarica
deity agni, brigit, dyaus, girru, hephaestus, hestia, ishum, loki, moloch, mulciber, nuska, pele, vesta, vulcan
demon surt(r)
destroy by consume
dog andiron
drake dragon

drill chark
-eater crank, daredevil
engine pumper, rig, tub
extinguisher bucket brigade, extinctor, pryoleter, pyrene, squirt
fear of pyrophobia
feeder fueler, stoker
festival shebseze
fighter hotshot, vamp
hazard brush, cigarette, lightning, match, smoker, undergrowth
lily elk grass
line gutter
little sponk, spunk
lock fusee, fuzee, spanner
lover pyrophile
military ack-ack, artillery, barrage, broadside, enfilade, flak, rafale, salvo
off discharge, shoot
offspring jinn
opal girasol(e)
particle arc, spark
peat greesagh
personification loki
pert. igneous, fiery
pike poker
plant painted leaf
raft catamaran
-ravished area brule(e)
room stokehold
sacrificial agni
set on accend, enkindle, ignite, inflame, irritate, kindle
signal bale(fire,) beacon
spirit genie, salamander
st antony's erysipelas
st elmo's corposant, furole
thorn pyracanth
up agitate, arouse, drink, excite, incite, stir
upon attack, snipe at, shoot
warden ranger
water liquor
wheel blanket-flower, gaillardia
worship idolatry, parsiism, pyrolatry, zoroastrianism
worshiper gabor, gheber, idolator, ignicolist, parsee, parsi, pyrolator, zoroastrian
FIREARM See GUN.
FIREBACK pheasant, macartney, reredos
FIREBALL bolide, bolis, bomb, bonditt, grenade, lychnis, maltese cross, meteor(ite), pistol, sun
FIREBRAND agitator, blaze, bleery, boutefew, char, cinder, ember, extremist, fagot, fuel, incendiary, in-

stigator, kindling, lighter, militant, peat, revolutionary, torch
FIREBUG arsonist, incendiary, pyromaniac
FIRECRACKER banger, cherry bomb, devil, petard, salute, skyrocket, snapper, squib, whizbang
box marroon
FIREFLY candlefly, cucuyo, glowworm, lampyrid, lightning bug
FIREGUARD fender, hearth, watch
FIREMAN bakehead, furnacer, stoker, tizeur, vamp
gear axe, hook, hose, ladder
FIREPLACE cheminee, chimney, focus, fogon, forge, foyer, grate, hearth, ingle, tisar
accessory andiron, lighter, poker, tender
back of reredos
ledge hob(b), mantel, shelf
lintel clavel, manteltree
part hearthstone, hob(b), ingleside, ironback, mantel, reredos
FIREPLUG hydrant
FIREPROOF impervious, secure
FIREPROOFING amianthus, asbestos, boric acid, earth flax, mountain flax
FIRESIDE chimlalug, hearth(stone), inglenook, ingleside
FIRESTONE flint
FIRETAIL finch
FIREWEED goat's-chicory, pileweed, pilewort
FIREWOOD bavin, billet, billot, clog, fag(g)ot, kindling, lena, log, lumber, slab, stovewood, talshide, yule log
FIREWORKS bomb, cap, cascade, catherine wheel, cracker, fizgig, flare, flowerpot, gerbe, girandole, petard, pinwheel, riprap, rocket, roman candle, salute, serpent, skyrocket, snake, sparkler, squib, torpedo, tourbillion, whiz-bang
case cartouch(e), lance
display set-piece
FIRING dismissal, ignition, inflammation, kindling, lighting, projection
squad aces up, solitaire
FIRK beat, bring, chastise,

cheat, conduct, conquer, contrive, drive, fidget, flick, freak, frisky, fuss, hasten, help on, lash, lively, strike, stroke, trick, urge
FIRM adamant(ine), anchor, bent, bound, brace, buff, bulldogged, business, close, compact, company, compressed, concern, constant, corporation, crowded, dauntless, dense, determined, devoted, establish(ment), fast, fix, hard, house, hui, immovable, inexorable, inflexible, intent, iron, moor, obdurate, obstinate, orthodox, persevering, persistent, plant, relentless, reliable, rigid, 'rigorous, rivet, robust, rooted, safe, secure, set, settle(d), shop, solid, stable, stabilize, sta(u)nch, steady, stern, stiff(en), strict, strong, substant(ial), swith(e), team, tenacious, tense, thick, tight, tough, true, uncompromising, unrelenting, unyielding
comb. stereo
remain bear, persevere, resist, stand fast, stand pat
FIRMAMENT canopy, foundation, heavens, paradise, sky, sphere, vault, welkin
FIRMAN decree, grant, license, mandate, order
FIRMLY earnestly, fixedly, solidly, steadfastly
fixed established, rooted, solid, stable
FIRMNESS determination, fidelity, resolution, solidity, stability, staunchness, steadiness, substantiality
lack of laxity, looseness, relaxation, vacillation, weakness
FIRN granular, ice, neve, snow
FIRST aboriginal, ace, advanced, ahead, alpha, avant-garde, before, beginning, best, capital, chief(ly), debut, earliest, foremost, front, head, highest, imprimis, initial(ly), leader, leading, maiden, main(ly), new, opening, original, preceding, preferably, premier, primal, primarily, primary, prime, primitive, primor-

dial, primus, principal, ranking, top, virgin
and last alone, altogether
-born aine, ayne, eigne, heir, protogenist, senior
chop See *class,* below.
class (See also *rate,* below.) ace, a-one, bunkum, de luxe, excellent, expensive, first chop, luxury, palmary, prime, superb, tiptop, top-drawer, tophole, tops
comb. archi, proto
fiddle chief, personage, vip
fruits annates, primitae
-hand conclusive, direct, fresh, original
in rank primacy
in time, comb. arch
lady mistress
mate eve
-of-may saxifrage
-rate (See also *class,* above.) ace(high), admirable, a-one, bang up, blightly, blue ribbon, bonzer, bosker, boss, brag, capital, champion, classic, clipping, excellent, good, jake, okay, okey, prime, shipshape, skookum, slap-bang, sound, super (dooper), supernacular, thumping, tiptop, top-drawer, topflight, topnotch, tops, triple-a, wizard
very primoprime
FIRSTLING senior
FIRTH arm, coppice, fiord, fjord, forest, frith, kyle, mouth, thicket, wood
of clyde island bute
FISCAL bursal, financial, monetary, pecuniary
FISH (See also *kind,* below.) angle, bob, brainfood, cast, catch, chug, clam, dap, dare, dib(ble), dollar, drag(gle), drail, draw, dredge, gig, grig, guddle, ligger, net, pescare, pesce, pisces, poisson, probe, search, seine, sniggle, spin, spoon, torch, trawl, troll
acanthopterygian See *percoid,* below.
age of devonian
air-breathing gourami
air sac gas bladder, maw, sound
amber medregal
amulet ichthus, ichthys
anacanthine cod, hake
anadromous salmon
anatomy ichthyotomy

ancient el(l)ops
aquarium orfe, tetra
avatar matsyavatara
backbone grate
bag net fyke
bait caddis, chum, fly, gudgeon, killifish, killy, shiner, worm
baked with sauce coquille
barbed-tail stingaree, stingray
basket caul, cawl, corf, creel, junket, pot, slath
bass-like salele
bat diablo
bathypelagic barrel eye
beaked sauries
bearded barbudo
berycoid barbudo, catfish, threadfin
bigmouth alfiona
billed gar
bin kench
bivalve clam, diatom, mollusk, oyster, pandora, scallop
black swart, tautog
bleak blay, bley, sprat
blennoid prickleback, wrymouth
blind pinkfish
bloody piranha
blue mackerel
boat dory
bone actinost, opercle, solitaire
boneless fil(l)et
bony albula, carp, chiro, elops, ladyfish, lungfish, menhaden, ostelchthyes, teleost
box trunk
breeder milter
briner cobberer
broken-bellied thoke
butter blenny, gunnel
butterfly bennie, paru
carangid amberjack, big-eye scad, bumper, caranx, chad, cavalla, goggle-eye, jack, jurel, pilot, pompano, runner, saurel, scad, seriola, threadfish, tinosa, trevally, yellowjack
carboniferous acanthodes
cardinal apogon
caribe piranha, piraya
carnivorous aimara
cat See CATFISH.
catch fare, gill, gillnet, hang, haul, jab, jig, shack, shot, string, tack, trip
catch with hands grabble, guddle, handfast

caviar-yielding beluga, sterlet, sturgeon
centrarchid blackbass, chaetodon, crappy, sunfish
cephaloptera manta
characin bloodfin, piranha
chimacroid ischyodus
chopped chum
chowder bouillabaisse, cioppino
cleaner giller, scaler
climbing anabas, martinico, (mud)skipper
clinging remora
clinid fringehead
clupeoid herring, lile, menhaden, sardine, shad, teleost
cobia bonito, coal, sergeant
cod See CODFISH.
cod-like beardie, bib, cusk, gadoid, gadus, hake, ling, loach, nemachilus
colorful boce, koi, opah, wrasse
comb. ichthyo, pisci
condiment paste
counting unit mease
cured kipper
cutlass savola
cuttle octopus, sepia, squid
cut up solay
cyprinoid barbel, barbus, bitterling, blay, bleak, bley, blindfish, bream, carp(sucker), chi, chub, dace, gobio, goldfish, graining, ide, loach, lulu, orfe, pap, rhodeus, roach, rud(d), sentoree, spot, sundoree, tench, uit, woundfin
deep sea argyropelecus, blenny, brotula, prickleback
dermatitis ich, ick
devonian arthrodira
dipnoan protopterus
disease ich, ick
dish bouillabaisse, cioppino, mousseline, waterzoi, waterzooie, waterzootje
dresser idler
dried baccala, herring, spalding, spelder
duck merganser
-eater ichthyophagist
-eating piscivorous
edible See *food,* below.
eel-like apod, conger, cuchia, eelpout, lamprey, lant, link, opah
eggs caviar, roe, spawn
elasmobranch chimera, ray, sawfish, shark
electric raad, torpedo

elongated eel, gar, pike, saurel

enclosure crawl, croy, kench, spiller, spillet, warren, yair, yare

escolar palu

extinct arthrodire, placoderm

fabled ihi, mah

female henfish, raun, spawner

fence garth, net, weir

fertilizer milt

fighting plakat

fin, kind adipose, dorsal

fin part ray, spine

finless apoda

flat big-eye, bret, brill, dab, dace, flounder, fluke, halibut, plaice, ray, sanddab, skate, sole, solea, sunfish, torpedo, turbot, yellowbelly

flying butterfly, exocoetus, gurnard, pantodon, saury, volador

food 3 cod, dab, eel, gar, ide, iki, sey 4 bass, baya, boga, carp, cero, cony, haak, haik, hake, ling, mado, scup, sole, tuna, ulua 5 akule, bolti, bream, cisco, coney, grunt, guasa, hilsa, jurel, loach, porgy, siera, skate, smalt, trout, tunny, umbra 6 aimara, baleen, beshow, bichir, bigeye, burbot, cunner, hapuku, hilsah, maigre, meagre, mullet, nonnat, plaice, pompan, salema, salmon, sesele, sparus, tautog, turbot, wahoon, weever, wirrah, wrasse 7 alewife, catfish, cavalla, corvina, croaker, escolar, garlipa, grouper, haddock, halibut, herring, pentado, pompano, pompoon, reddrum, redfish, redhind, rouster, sanddab, sardine, snapper, sunfish 8 cabrilla, catalufa, flounder, hiwihiwi, mackerel, trevally 9 barracuda, ictalurus, papagallo, sablefish, spadefish, swordfish, trumpeter 10 barramunda, redsnapper, squeteague, tripletail 11 yellowgrunt

for seek, solicit

fossil ichthyolite

fresh-water abramis, aimara, anabantid, anabas, arapaima, barb(el), bass, bluegill, bream, bullhead,

carib(b)ee, carp, catfish, charicinida, chub, crappie, dace, darter, esox, gar, ide, inange, loach, mooneye, orfe, pap, perch, pike, piranha, redeye, roach, rudd, ruff(e), sandroller, serrasalmo, sheepshead, stoneroller, stonetoter, sucker, sunfish, tandan, tench, trout, yellowbelly

fry festival, picnic

gadid cod, haddock, pollack, tomood

game bass, blanquillo, cero, goldeye, grayling, grilse, inconnu, lingood, marlin, muskellunge, opaleye, rock bass, salmon, shark, swordfish, tarpon, trout, tuna, tunny, ulua, yellowtail

ganoid bowfin, dipnoi, gar, sturgeon

garth weir

genus amia, apogon, elops, fistularia, lota, mola, perca

gig spear

gill choller

gilless abranchiate

gland milt

globe diodon

glue isinglass

gobioid loter, testar, tetard

gobylike dragonet, puneca

god dagon

gold-colored aurata

group actinopteri, maze, school, shoal, take

hadoid hake

half-beak ihi

handler icer

harpoon grains

haul catch, drave, mess, tack

hawk osprey

head jowl

heraldic chabot

herbivorous girella

herringlike sprat

hook (See also FLY *artificial*.) aberdeen, angle, barb, carlisle, drail, fizgig, fly, foul, gaff, gange, gig, hackle, hang, hitch, kendal(l), kirby, lari(n), limerick, sedge, sleek, snag, sniggle, spoon, sproat, strike

hook leader snell

hook part barb

hook remover gobstick

horned pout

imperfect thoke

in wine sauce matelote

jelly See JELLYFISH.

jugular batrachid

killer benacus, harpoon, nobbler

kind 3 bib, cat, cod, dab, eel, gag, gar, ide, ihi, orf, rud, wet 4 bass, brit, carp, chub, chug, cusk, dace, dorn, esox, fike, flat, fugu, gade, goby, haak, hake, hiku, huss, jocu, kelt, lant, lija, ling, loro, loup, lulu, mado, mapo, masu, mero, mola, monk, odax, opah, orfe, peal, pega, penk, peto, pike, pogy, pout, quab, raia, rena, rock, roud, rudd, ruff, sama, scad, scup, sesi, shad, sier, sisi, skil, sole, spet, spot, susu, tope, tuna, ulua, waha, wels, zant 5 bream, cisco, lance, midge, otter, pargo, perch, porgy, prane, roach, ruffe, scrod, skate, smelt, sprat, trout, tunny, umbra, wahoo, whiff 6 barbel, caribe, darter, kipper, launce, minnow, mullet, plaice, porgie, sanger, saurel, shiner, tomcod, turbot, wrasse 7 alewife, dogfish, grouper, grunion, haddock, herring, machete, pegador, pintado, piranha, poisson, sunfish, teleost, whiting 8 bluegill, cardinal, flatfish, flounder, halfbeak, hardhead, mackerel, menhaden, pickerel, pilchard, porkfish, sturgeon 9 devilfish, gourdhead, sheatfish, whitebait 10 candlefish, dogsnapper, redsnapper, silverside, squeteague 11 muskellunge

labrid tautog

land-traveling anabas

large arapaima, bichir, blanquillo, chiro, cusk, escolar, gourami, maskalonge, maskinongy, muskellunge, opah, sargo, sennett, shark, sturgeon, swordfish, tarpon, whale

large-headed capezon, pout

largest arapaima

lice epizoa

life ichthyofauna

-like ichthyic

linglike cod

long eel, gar, lamprey, pike

lord of the whale

louse gisler

lure bassbug, silver-dollar, spinner, spoonhook

mackerel-like bonito, cerocoelho, escolar, pintado, tinker, tunny

mammal manatee, whale

marine anchovy, angler, apogon, argentina, arius, blenny, bonito, capelin, catalufa, cavalla, chopa, cockatoo, cod, corvina, crevalle, cusk, cutlass, flutemouth, geelbec(k), gilthead, girelia, grunion, grunt, hairtail, hake, jack, john dory, ling, menhaden, mero, opah, palometa, picarel, pigfoot, pollack, ribbontail, robalo, rockling, ronquil, saury, scup, siganus, tarpon, tripletail, torsk, trumpeter, tubesnout, tuna, tusk, whapuku

market billingsgate

measure cran(e), mease, vog

minnow satinfin

moth lepisma, silverfish

needle gar

nest redd

nesting acara, stickleback

net bunt, flew, flue, fyke, sagena, sagene, salemboa, seine, spiller, trammel, trawl

net center bunt

net line meter

net mender beatster

newly hatched fry

offal gurry

oil escolar

olive green blenny, ludefish, lutfisk, shanny

one-horned monoceros

or cut bait choose, decide, determine

ornamental koi, paradise

out of water misfit

-owl ketupa

parasite monazoa

parasitic pega(dor), remora

peddler ripper, rip(p)ier

pelagic blackrag, blackruff, tube-eye

pen See *enclosure*, above.

perchlike anabas, darter

percoid archerfish, bass, bigeye, perch, ronquil

permean acanthode

pert. finny, piscatorial, piscatory, piscine

pickle alec

pickled herring

pie crustade

poison akia, hola, tuba

-poisoning ichthyism

poisonous fugu, trygon

pond aquarium, keep, piscina, vivarium

pound madrague

prepare calver

preserve warren

purple murex

raw ceviche, sashimi

red clee, fathead

refuse chum, gubbins, gurry, shack

relish botargo

-rice dish kedgeree

river arapaima, barramunda, blay, testar, tetard, trout

river-ascending anadrom, salmon, shad

rock See ROCKFISH.

roe caviar(e), kelk

sailor's choice porgy

sale of ichthyopolism

salmonoid char, coregonine, gwyniad, nelma, pollan, powan, trout, whitefish

salted cor

salting bin canch, kench

sauce alec, anchovy, botargo, garum, soy, tartar

scale ganoid

scale covering ganoin

scaleless alepitode, catfish, wolffish

scaly ganoid

sciaenid corvina, croaker, cubbyu

science ichthyology

scombroid bonito, cero, mackerel, pomfret, tuna

scorpaenid thornhead

scorpion See ROCKFISH.

scraps chum

sea See *marine*, above.

serranoid aguavina, bonaci, burbot, coney, creole, graysby, guapena, lates, phoebe, red hind, sea bass, stereolepsis

-shaped ichthyomorphic

shark-eating catfish, pega, som

shore dragonet

sign pisces

silvery mullet, sesele, shiner

small anchovy, atharine, blenny, brit, cunner, dace, darter, fry, goby, guppy, halfbeak, ide, ihi, killfish, limpet, minnow, prim, riggle, sardine, saury, seahorse, sennet, shiner, smelt, spearing, spet, sprat, whitebait

smelt-like cap(e)lin

smoked kipper

snouted saury

soaked in lye lutfisk

soft-finned apodes, eel, gadid

soup See *stew*, below.

sparoid napa, porgy, salema, sar(go), sargon, scup, sheepshead, tai

spawn redd

spawned shotten

spear chug, gaff, gig, granes, leister, trident, waster

spear-snouted gar

speculator bummares

spine epipleura

spiny-finned berycida, blanquillo, carangid, catalufa, fortescue, icosteus, miller's-thumb, perch, sculpin, tilefish

spiny-rayed threadfin

spotted malma, trout

stew bouillabaisse, cacciucco, cioppino, solianka, waterzooi

stock court-bouillon

story bluster, braggadocio, exaggeration, lie

sucking pega(dor), remora

sucking appendage acetabulum

sun See SUNFISH.

surf alfiona

synancioid laff

synodontoid tiru

taboo ichthyophobia

tank aquarium

teleost abdominale, ammodyte, anacarthin, angelfish, apoda, bony fish, catfish, dealfish, eel, iniomi, isospondyli, opah, pediculati, physoclisti, plectognath, ribbonfish

toothed piranha, shark

trap bagnet, coop, cruive, eelpot, fyke, net, pot, pound net, sagene, seine, spiller, trae, weel, weir, willy, ya(i)re

treatise ichthyography

tree-climbing anabas

troll drail

true teleostome

tunicate salpa

25 pounds stick

under water goggle

upholding universe mah

vivaparous poeciliid

voracious barracuda, caribe, louvar, pike, piranha, piraya, shark, tigerfish

warm water grouper, guasa

whisker barbel

wife carp, nag, scold

worship ichthyolatry

young alevin, brit, fry, minnow, parr, smelt, sprod

FISHER animal, bird, eeler, izaak walton, marten, martrix, pekan, sable, seiner, sobol, taira, tayra, troller, wejack
-like marten, weasel
sponge hooker
FISHERMAN angler, disciple, drifter, eeler, gigman, giller, izaac walton, jacker, maimul, netter, peter, piscator(ian), seiner, shanker, smelter, squam, striker, toty, waltonian, weirer
apron barvel(l)
boots waders
deity britomartis
hat squam
hut skeo, skio
FISHING angling, halieutics, harling, piscatology, rod and reel, snelling, snoeking, spillet, trolling
bait angleworm, ant egg, chum, earthworm, fly, worm
bank haaf
basket creel, slarth, slath
boat See *vessel*, below.
bob bab
clip gaff
device tipup
duck merganser
eagle osprey
equipment See *gear*, below.
expedition drave, smear
father of izaak walton
fly See **FLY** *artificial*.
forceps cleammer
gear bait, box-bill, cadar, cader, cork, dogger, flew, float, flue, fly, gaff, gig, gimp, hook, lam, ledger, line, lure, net, reel, rod, sedge, seine, setline, snell, tackle, tew, trot(line), waders
grounds haaf
line See **FISHLINE**.
net See **FISH** *net*.
on shares drave
pert. halieutic, piscatory
prong gaff, pew, pugh
reed donax
reel troll
reel part spool
rod gad
saint elmo
smack dogger
spear gig
stick gad, pole, rod
tackle See *gear*, above.
vessel cayuca, cayuco, dogger, doni, dory, hooker,

luzzu, scow, seiner, smack, trawler
FISHLINE bo(u)lter, bulter, cord, cuttyhunk, dipsy, gangion, ligger, snell, speller, taum, trawl, trimmer, trot, troll
base cadar, cader
float bob, cork, dobber
part snood
weight sinker
FISHMONGER bummaree, pessoner, ripier, ripper, rippier
FISHMOUTH alligator, turtlehead
FISHTAIL arrow, semaphore, skid, urosome
palm caryota
FISHWIFE buttwoman, hag, poissarde, scold, shrew
FISHY corrupt, doubtful, dubious, dull, extravagant, farfetched, finny, funny, glassy, improbable, piscine, shady, smelly, suspicious, vacant
FISSILE brittle, fidget, hiss, rustle, whistle
rock shale
FISSION atomize, breaking, cleavage, cleaving, gamogeny, reproduction, scission, splitting
product cesium, plutonium, strontium
FISSURE abra, apperture, blemish, blowhole, breach, break, chasm, chine, chink, cleft, crack, cranny, crevasse, crevice, flake, fracture, gap, gaug, interstice, leak, lesion, opening, rent, rictus, rift, rima, rime, scissura, seam, slit, split, sulcus, vent, zygon
FIST attempt, clench, clutch, dog, duke, effort, hand (writing), job, mauler, mauley, mitt, neaf, nief, nieve, puffball, strike, tightwad
-fight box, spar, turn up
mailed force
FISTIC pistachio, pugilistic
FISTICUFF blow, bout, boxing, combat, cuff, fight, nevel, strike
FISTULA cavity, egilops, passage, pipe, reed, sinus, tube
FISTULINA boletus, fungus
FIT able, accommodate, adapt, adequate, apposite,

appropriate, apropos, apt, attack, ballad, besort, blend, block, capable, caprice, clothe, competent, conform, convenient, convulsion, decent, dovetail, due, duly, eligible, equip, expedient, exies, fadge, fancy, fay, felicitous, frenzy, gear, gee, hale, happy, hard, healthy, huff, humor, meet, outbreak, outburst, paroxysm, pat, pet, pique, prepare(d), proper, qualified, ready, reconcile, right, ripe, seizure, shock, song, spasm, spell, square, stroke, suit (able), tailor, tantrum, temper, timely, trained, trig, trim, whim
as a fiddle healthy, trim, vigorous
closely snug
company besort
in accord, agree, coincide
like a glove dovetail
maniacal psychokinesia
of temper brainge, grouch, outburst, spleen, tantrum, tiff
out accouter, appoint, arm, busk, clothe, dress, equip(ment), furnish, habille, outfit, prepare, supply
tightly cram, stuff
to be tied angry, furious, livid
together coapt, cohere, dovetail, fay, join, mesh, nest, panel
to live in habitable
FITCHEW polecat, skunk
FITFUL capricious, catchy, changeable, convulsive, cursory, erratic, flighty, impulsive, intermittent, irregular, restive, restless, spasmodic, uneasy, unstable, variable
FITFULLY intermittently, irregularly, jerkily
FITMENT equipment, furnishings, furniture
FITNESS adaptation, adjustment, aptitude, capacity, congruity, decency, decorum, dignity, justness, property
FITTED able, apt, calculated, clever, eligible, engaged, furnished, gifted, suited
FITTEN fib, fiction, lie, suitable, whim
FITTING accommodation,

adapter, adjustment, applicable, appropriate, apt, cap, germane, graceful, just, lug, pat, pertinent, proper, relevant, right, seemly, suitable, tactful

FITTINGS accouterments, appointments, equipment, fixtures, reparel, trappings

FITZGERALD, F. SCOTT *novel* great gatsby, tender is the night, this side of paradise

period jazz age

wife zelda

FIUME rijeka

FIVE cinco, cinq(ue), epsilon, estoile, fin(f), finnif, funf, mullet, pentad, phoebe, quinary, quintet(te)

and 10 cheap

books of moses pentateuch

cents blip, jitney, nickel

comb. pent(a), quinqu(e), quint

-dollar bill fin(if), finiff, finnif, fiver, vee

feet pace

-finger cinquefoil, fish, oxlip, plant

-flowered gentian agueweed

-fold pentamerous, pentangular, quinquefid, quintan, quintuple, quinary

group of cinquain, pentad

-hundred bid nullo

-leaf cinquefoil

-line verse limerick

nations cayuga, cherokee, chickasaw, choctaw, creek, delaware, iroquois, mohawk, oneida, onondaga, seminole, seneca

nations founder hiawatha

of trumps pedro

pert. quinary

senses hearing, sight, smell, taste, touch

sisters loosetrife

-spot calico flower, fin

stones snobs

2 quinas

-year period lustrum, pentad, quinquennial, quinquennium

FIX 3 bed, jam, peg, set, tie 4 bind, busk, deal, dope, firm, form, kill, lock, mend, nail, pack, pose, root, rule, seat, shot, stay 5 amend, brace, bribe, cinch, dress, embed, frame, imbed, lodge, place, plant, posit, prove, rivet,

sew up, stamp, wedge 6 adjust, anchor, assess, assign, attach, decide, defeat, define, direct, entail, fasten, freeze, impact, pickle, plight, punish, scrape, settle, square 7 appoint, arrange, confirm, congeal, destroy, dilemma, engraft, engrave, frameup, implant, impress, prepare, station 8 entrench, intrench, quandary, regulate, renovate, solidify 9 determine, establish, influence, injection, prescribe 11 predicament, circumscribe

amount of affeer

cost of charge, price, settle, tag

firmly anchor, brace, cement, engaff, enroot, freeze, grave, inbed, moor, rampire, rivet, set, stamp

on attribute, choose, decide, resolve, settle

responsibility attribute, blame

up arrange, contrive, cure, decorate, dress, heal, mend, patch, reconcile, renovate, repair, restore, tidy

FIXATION complex, fetish, hangup, installation, mania, obsession, one track mind, regression, relapse

comb. pexy

FIXED assured, certain, changeless, conventional, definite, determinable, dormant, established, explicit, fastened, firm, formal, glued, hard, intent, inveterate, ironclad, jelled, located, motionless, pat, put, quiet, repaired, resolute, rigid, riveted, rooted, set, settled, situated, sot, specific, stable, staid, staple, stated, static, steady, stiff, still, straight, strong, stuck, traditional, unqualified

amount rate, ration, remittance, stipend

comb. aplano, stato

price quotation

star sphere, vega

time appointment, date, era, fast, rendezvous, rut, tryst

FIXER agent, amender, lobbyist, mender, percenter

FIXTURE adjunct, appliance, asset(s), bracket, chandelier, equipment, facility,

faucet, hardware, knocker, sconce

FIZZ activity, bubble, champagne, fuss, hiss, liveliness, seethe, simmer, sparkle

FIZZLE abort, barney, bubble, fail(ure), fall through, flop hiss(ing), miscarry, misfire, sibilate, sputter, weaken

FJORD bay, fiord, firth, frith, inlet, sea arm

-like passage gat

FLABBERGAST amaze, astonish, astound, bewilder, confound, dumfound, faze, floor, nonplus, perplex, rattle, shock, surprise

FLABBY baggy, feeble, **FLACCID,** flappy, flexuous, flimsy, fozy, frush, lax, limp, listless, loose, loppy, pendulous, pulpy, quaggy, relaxed, slack, sleezy, soft, weak, woozy

FLACCID flabby, flaggy, glimsy, inelastic, lax, limber, limp, loose, relaxed, slack, soft, weak, yielding

FLACCUS *assassin* fimbria

FLAG 3 sag, sod 4 alem, fail, fane, iris, jack, leck, limp, pall, pine, poop, sign, sink, stop, turf, waft, wilt 5 droop, faint, flake, floor, groat, roger, shale, stone, woman 6 banner, bougee, burgee, colors, cornet, danger, dawdle, emblem, ensign, fanion, figure, flower, guidon, lessen, muleta, pennon, signal, symbol, weaken 7 bunting, calamus, cattail, decline, dwindle, exhaust, fatigue, gesture, labarum, pennant, poop out 8 banderol, banneret, brattach, gonfalon, languish, masthead, old glory, standard, streamer, tricolor, vexillum 9 banderrole, blackjack, blue peter, coachwhip, oriflamme, sandstone, signalize, union jack 10 jolly roger 11 cobblestone 15 red white and blue, stars and stripes 11 starspangled banner

-bearer guidon

company guidon

confederate stars and bars

corner canton, union

ecclesiastic labarum

knotted waft

merchant vessel burgee
military colors, fanion, guidon, standard
national ensign
navy burgee, ensign
pirate black jack, jolly roger
pole shaft
pole bracket bracciale
ship's duster
signal burgee, cornet
small banneret(te), fanion, pencel
special blue peter
study of vexillology
swallow-tailed burgee
sweet calamus
triangular burgee
truce kartel
-waving chauvinism, patriotism
yacht burgee

FLAGELLANT(S) albi, ascetic, penitentes

FLAGELLATE beat, castigate, ceratium, cudgel, flog, flutter, lash, scourge, thrash, throw, whip
kind eudorina, giardia, leptomonas, monas, noctiluca, volvox

FLAGELLATION asceticism, beating, flogging, penance, scourging, whipping

FLAGELLUM branch, clavola, filament, runner, scourge, shoot, whip
comb. kont, mastig(o)
having mastigate
rim choana
without atrichous

FLAGEOLET basaree, bean, flute, larigot, monaulos, pipe, sibilus, zuf(f)olo

FLAGGING pavement, sidewalk

FLAGITIOUS atrocious, bad, corrupt, criminal, degenerate, disgraceful, flagrant, glaring, gross, heinous, infamous, iniquitous, nefarious, scandalous, shameful, sinful, vicious, villainous, wicked

FLAGMAN judge, warden

FLAGON canteen, carafe, demijohn, ewer, flacket, flask, gun, iris, jug, rehoboam, stoup, vessel

FLAGRANT absurd, ardent, atrocious, bad, base, burning, conspicuous, crying, egregious, enormous, evil, glaring, glowing, great, gross, heinous, infamous, inflamed, monstrous, nefarious, notorious, odious, outrageous, outstanding, profligate, raging, rank, scarlet, terrible, villainous, violent, wanton, wicked

FLAGRANTE DELICTO in the act

FLAGSTONE cobble, favus, leek, pavement, rock, sandstone, shale, slab, walk (way)
layer paver

FLAIL beat, flog, paw, pound, strike, swingle, swip(p)le, thrash
joint capel
part capling, swingle, swip(p)le

FLAIR ability, aptitude, bent, brains, discernment, discrimination, faculty, genius, knack, leaning, liking, ray, scent, talent, taste, wits

FLAKE aphtha, carnation, chip, coil, dandruff, delaminate, exfoliate, flag, fleck, flitter, floc(cule), flocculus, flock, fragment, hurdle, lamella, lamina, layer, paling, paring, peel, plate, rack, scale, scurf, scute, shaving, shive, shove, slate, spall, streak, strip, variegate
out nap, sleep

FLAKY asperous, flocculent, furfuraceous, lentiginous, lepidote, scabby, scabious, scabrous, scaly, scurfy, squamous

FLAM cajole, cheat, deceive, drumbeat, false(hood), humbug, lie, marsh, nonsense, rubbish, trick, untrue

FLAMBEAU candlestick, cresset, kettle, lighter, torch

FLAMBOYANCE blare, brightness, display, elegance, flourish, panache

FLAMBOYANT baroque, brave, bright, dashing, exuberant, fancy, flashy, florid, garish, gaudy, gorgeous, luxuriant, ornate, orotund, ostentatious, pretentious, purple, resplendent, rococo, showy, splendid, wavy

FLAME arc, ardor, beam, blaze, brilliance, burn(ing), crush, desire, effulgence, enthusiasm, escort, excite, fervor, fire, flare, flash, glare, glaze, gleam, glint, glow, holocaust, incandescence, ignite, interest, kindle, leye, light, love(r), passion, radiance, spark, steem, swain, sweetheart, warmth
fire without punk
movement dart, flick(er), lick
small flammule, gleed, spunk
tree dhak, huisache, kurrajong, mistletoe, muytsia, poinciana, rhododendron

FLAMEN *wife* flaminica

FLAMENCO *term* sivillana

FLAMING afire, aflare, ardent, blooming, bright, brilliant, burning, earnest, fiery, flagrant, flamboyant, ignescent, passionate, shining, vivid, zealous

FLAMINGO phenicopter
flower anthurium

FLAMINIUS *master* timon

FLAN blank, custard, dessert, disk, expand, gust, net, pastry, planchet, puff, splay, tart

FLANDERS See FLEMISH.
native fleming, flemish

FLANEUR boulevardier, idler, loafer, loiterer, stroller, trifler

FLANGE bead, bezel, border, boss, bridle, collar, protuberance, rib, rim, shroud

FLANK beat, border, charge, defend, flake, flap, flick, flip, lisk, loin, side, skirt, thigh, wing
comb. laparo

FLANNEL cloth, domett, lana, molleton, saxony, stamin, swanskin, whittle, wool
-leaf candlewick, mullein, velvet-plant
-mouthed oily-tongued, smooth-spoken

FLAP adjunct, aventail, backtalk, bag, bang, bangle, beat, blinder, clap, crack, dangle, dither, drop, fall, fan, flicker, flop, flutter, fly, fold, hang, lamina, lap(pet), leaf, loma, lop, lug, plump, pound, pulsate, rob, slap, slat, sway, swindle, swing, tab, tag, toss, vibrate, wap, wave
-doodle See NONSENSE.
having lobed
loose lappet
membranous loma, lomata
violently flog, slat

FLAPJACK griddle cake, hotcake, pancake, turnover, turtle

FLAPPER arm, backfisch, flipper, flirt, girl, hand, reminder, snicket

-bag burdock

-dock butterbur

FLARE beacon, bell, blaze, blinker, burst, dart, dazzle, expansion, explosion, fire, flame, flash, fleck, flicker, flue, flutter, fusee, fuzee, glance, glare, glint, glitter, glow, kindle, light, outburst, rise, shimmer, shine, shoot, signal, sparkle, splay, spread, spring, torch, trumpet, very(light), waver, widen

up anger, burst forth, color, explode, flush, growl, kindle, mantle, outburst, redden, row, rumpus, snap, snarl, tantrum

FLARING belling, blatant, burning, dazzling, gaudy, glaring, evase, showy, swagger

edge flange, lip

FLASH blash, blaze, box, bulletin, burst, cheap, coruscate, dart, dash, dazzle, explosion, facula, fake, false, fillip, flabby, flame, flare, fly, glaik, glance, gleam, glimmer, glimpse, glint, glisten, glitter, impulse, instant, jiffy, lait, leam, levin, light, look, marsh, minute, news(bulletin), pool, rise, rocket, scintillate, second, shimmer, shine, shoot, signal, smart, spark(le), speed, splash, spurious, spurt, swank, trashy, trice, twinkling, wink

-back answer, cutback

hot flush

in the pan failure, fizzle, nonentity

lamp strobe

lightning levin

lock stanch

note counterfeit

FLASHING blinking, bright, ephemeral, flange, flaunting, forward, gaudy, lamping, meteoric, shining, sporty

FLASHLIGHT bug, glim, penlite, torch

FLASHY arty, bold, catchpenny, dashing, fiery, flamboyant, flat, flaunting,

florid, flossy, frothy, garish, gaudy, gay, glittery, grandiloquent, impetuous, insipid, loud, ornate, ostentatious, showy, snazzy, sporty, tawdry, tinhorn, tinsel, vehement

FLASK ampull(ul)a, aryballus, betty, bottle, box, bulge, canteen, carage, chrismal, cruse, cucurbit, ewer, fiasco, flacon, flagon, girba, gourd, guttus, lagena, matara, matrass, olpe, warburg

glass matrass

leather costrel, girba, matara, olpe

raffia-wrapped fiasco

-shaped ampullaceous, ampullar, ampullate, ampulliform, dilated, lageniform

FLAT apartment, banal, bar, broke, busted, cammed, camus(e), chambers, chump, deflated, digs, directly, discordant, dull, dupe, even, exactly, fade, flush, horizontal, inane, inert, insipid, jejune, lackluster, level, lifeless, low, mol(le), monotonous, oblate, paint, plain, plane, plano, prone, prosaic, prostrate, quarters, sandbank, shallow, silent, simple, smooth, spit, splay, squat, stale, suite, supine, tasteless, tideland, uninteresting, unit, unqualified, vapid, weak, wholly, wishywashy

and short camus(e)

as a board flounder, pancake, prairie

boat ark, barge, pullboat, scow

car idler, lorry, piggyback

comb. plani

foot cop, deformity, detective, policeman

-footed candid, deformed, determined, explicit, firm, forthright, open, shambling

-headed platycephalic

-nosed simous

not brisk

on one's face agroof, agruif, agrufe

out directly, openly

-tailed platurous

-tire bore

FLATFISH acedia, bream, brill, but(t), dab, dace,

flounder, fluke, halibut, hogchoker, marysole, plaice, quiff, ray, sanddab, sole, sunfish, torpedo, turbot, yellowbelly

FLATHEAD salish

FLATIRON goose, steel, sadiron

FLATLY blankly, bluntly, dully, evenly, frigidly, horizontally, plainly, positively

FLATS See DICE.

FLATTEN clap, compress, crush, depress, even, fell, grade, land, level, pat, plane, platten, raze, roll, smooth, splat, squash, squelch, subside

FLATTENED applanate, ecrase, evened, ill, leveled, oblate, planate, planed, sick

FLATTER adulate, applepolish, bedaub, beflum, beguile, beslaver, beslubber, bland(ish), blarney, bootlick, brown-nose, build up, butter(up), bye, cajole, charm, coax, compliment, conceit, court, evener, fawn, flether, flutter, glaver, honey(fogle), ingratiate, insinuate, jolly, oil, palaver, palp, pander to, please, praise, puff, salve, sawder, slaver, slobber, soap, softsoap, string along, sweet talk, toady, truckle to, wheedle, worm in

FLATTERER adulator, applepolisher, backscratcher, backslapper, beguiler, blandisher, bootlicker, buller, cajoler, courtier, damocles, earwig, fawner, flunky, gloze, greasehorn, hanger-on, jenkins, lickladle, lickspit(tle), lickspigot, losenger, parasite, puffer, softsoaper, spaniel, sycophant, toady, truckler, tufthunter

FLATTERING adulatory, buttery, candied, ceremonial, complimentary, courtly, gnathonic, honeyed, ingratiating, obsequious, servile, silken, smarmy, soapy

FLATTERY adulation, blandishment, blarney, bull, bunco(mbe), bunk(um), butter, cajolery, compliment, eyewash, flam, fleech, flether, flummery, grease, gloze, hoomalimali, humbug(gery), kopdrayenish, oil, palaver, panegyrics, puff(ery), praise, salve, sawder, servility, snow, soap, sycophancy, taffy, unction, whillywha

FLATTOP aircraft-carrier, ironweed

FLATULENCE distension, inflation, pneumatosis

FLATULENT bombastic, empty, inflated, pompous, pretentious, rhetorical, shallow, tumid, turgid, ventose, windy

FLATUS air, breath, gas, inflation, puff, vapor, wind

FLATWARE cutlery, silver (ware), tableware

FLATWORM bdelloura, bipalium, cestoda, convoluta, fluke, planarian, platode, polyclad, stylochus, trematode

FLAUBERT *novel* madame bovary

FLAUNT advertise, air, boast, bosh, brag, brandish, challenge, dare, display, exhibit, expose, flourish, flutter, parade, proclaim, publish, reveal, show, taunt, traipse, vaunt, wave

FLAUNTING grandiloquent, sporty

FLAUTO See FLUTE.

FLAVIUS *master* timon

FLAVONE chromone
derivative apigenin

FLAVOR aroma, characteristic, fragrance, gout, gust(o), infuse, lace, mask, odor, pepper, perfume, piquancy, relish, salt, sapidity, sapor, savo(u)r, scent, season, smack, spice, tack, tang, tarage, tincture, zest
trace of soupcon
unpleasant tack
without bland, flat, insipid, stale, tasteless, vapid, waterish

FLAVORFUL, FLAVORSOME appetizing, aromatic, nutty, palatable, rich, sapid, saporous, savorous, savory, tangy, tasty, toothsome

FLAVORING anise, condiment, essence, extract, herb, pepper, salt, seasoning, spice, zest
agent anise, asarum, basil,

bitters, calamus, camomile, cardamom, cinchona, cinnamon, cloves, cocoa, coriander, c(o)umarin, c(o)umarone, curry, diacetyl, elder, gentian, herb, leek, lemon, licorice, mint, nutmeg, orgeat, orris root, rosemary, sage, SPICE, vanilla, wormwood
licorice-like aniseed

FLAVORLESS See FLAVOR *without.*

FLAW bane, blast, blemish, blot, brack, breach, break, breeze, bug, cleft, crack, cyclone, default, defect, error, fault, foible, fracture, gale, gap, gust, hangup, hole, hurricane, hurt, imperfection, intoxicate, lesion, mar, outburst, pitfall, problem, rase, rent, rip, rupture, smear, split, spot, sunspot, taint, tear, tornado, tumult, twister, typhoon, violate, wem, whirlwind, wind, zephyr
tragic hamartia

FLAWLESS accurate, clean, correct, entire, exact, faultless, immaculate, impeccable, intact, nice, perfect, precise, right, sound, whole

FLAX bast, bissyn, breards, cathartolinum, flix, flower, harakeke, harl, hemp, herb, jute, korari, lin(e), linen, linseed, lint, linum, phloem, pita, pito, ramie, scutch, wallop
bundle bait, beat, beet, head, strick
capsule boll
clean card, swingle
cleaning tool card, hackle, hatchel, swingle
cloth canvas, linen
comb See *cleaning tool,* above.
disease browning, pasmo, stem-break, wilt
drying area boom yard
dust pouce
-like byssine, towy
-olive mezereon
prepare ret
refuse hards, hurds, pab, pob, scutch
remove seeds ribble
seed head hoppe
seed product oilcake
snapdragon toadflax
tool hackle, hatchel, swingle

tow codilla
waste product boon, shive, shove
worker tippler

FLAXEN bawn, blond, golden, leucous, stramineous, straw-colored, towy
-haired auricomous, bawn, blond
-haired, name meaning linus

FLAXWEED toadflax

FLAY abrade, afflict, assail, castigate, censure, chafe, chastise, decorticate, excoriate, fleece, grill, pare, peel, punish, rack, reprove, scarify, skin, strip, torture, tyrne

FLAYFLINT miser, skinflint

FLEA chigoe, cootie, cyclops, daphnia, flae, flay, fleck, insect, louse, pest, puce, pulex, pulicid, sandhopper, xenopsylla
beetle altica, systena, thrips
bite bit, irritation, trifle
destroyer pulicide
in the ear counsel, reminder, warning
-like pulicarious
-lugged giddy, heedless, wild
mint pennyroyal
pert. pulicene, pulicose

FLEABANE frostweed, pennyroyal, scabious, skevish, whitetop

FLEADOCK butterbur

FLEAM bevel, lancet, (mill) stream

FLEANCE *father* banquo

FLEAWEED blue-curls

FLEAWOOD sweetgale

FLEAWORT cammock, cinnamonroot, fleaseed, plantain, psyllium

FLECHE arrow, broach, fieldwork, outwork, parapet, spire, tower

FLECK atom, bit, dapple, fat, flake, flare, flea, flit, flock, flutter, freckle, lard, mark, mote, particle, speck(le), spot, stain, stipple, streak, stripe, tuft, variegate

FLECKED spotted

FLECTION, FLEXION bend(ing), fold(ing), turning

FLEDERMAUS *composer* strauss
maid adele

FLEDGE feather(ed), mature

FLEDGLING birdling, calf, catling, chick(ling), chicky, colt, cub, dogie, duckling, fligger, foal, frier, fryer, kid, kit(ten), lamb(kin), nestling, novice, pollyfrog, pollywog, pollywoggle, pup(py), tadpole, weaner, whelp, yeanling, youth

FLEE abandon, abscond, absquatulate, avoid, beat a retreat, beat it, blow, bolt, break out, clear out, cut and run, decamp, depart, desert, disappear, dodge, duck, dust, elope, elude, escape, evade, fley, fly, forsake, guy, lam, leg it, levant, loup, make off, mizzle, mooch off, pull out, run (away), scamper, scram, scur, shirk, shun, skeddadle, skip, slip, slope, sneak off, steal away, take a powder, take flight

FLEECE abb, bleed, cheat, clip, cloth, deceive, despoil, fabric, fell, gaff, gouge, hair, ket, mort, mulct, nap, overcharge, pelage, pile, pillage, plunder, rifle, rob, rook, shag, shave, shear, skin, strip, take, teg(g), toison, wool, yarn
coarse cast

FLEECED indigent, poor, took

FLEECH coax(ing), flatter(y), wheedle

FLEECY floccose, flocculent, fluffy, hairy, lanose, wooly

FLEEING aflight, flemed, fugient, fugitive, hotfoot, running

FLEER deride, flaunt, flout, fugitive, gibe, gird, grimace, grin, jeer, jibe, leer, mock, ridicule, scoff, scold, scorn, smile, smirk, sneer, taunt

FLEET abound, active, agile, argosy, armada, armata, bay, beguile, brief, caravan, creek, dissolve, drain, drift, escadrille, escarda, estuary, fast, flight, flit, float, flotilla, flow, fluctuate, glide, group, hasten, hasty, inlet, light, marine, merchant marine, navy, nimble, pass, quick, rapid, sail, scudding, sewer, shallow, shipping, ships, skim, speed(y), spry,

squadron, stream, swift, swim, tonnage, transitory, vanish, w(h)ile
as racehorse, wind
-tender patache

FLEETING brief, ephemeral, evanescent, flighty, flying, fugitive, passing, short-lived, transient, transitory, volatile

FLEG blow, fling, fright, kick, scare

FLEME banish, fugitive, outlaw

FLEMISH *anatomist* vesalius
beerjug bellarmine
brotherhood beg-hard
capital ghent
cartographer mercator
city lille
composer binchois, de(s) pres, dufay, egidius, lejeune, okeghem, willaert
deity nehallenia
geographer mercator
giant rabbit
horse footrope, roil
imposter warbeck
king, mythical gambrinus
lace binche
magistrate burgomaster
painter bouts, breughel, brouwer, brueg(h)el, goes, gossa(e)rt, jordaens, mabus(e), massys, matsys, memling, moro, oost, patinir, rubens, teniers, van cleve, van der weyden, vandyck, vaneyck, weyden
sloop boyer
statesman arteveld(e)
vessel boyer, frigate

FLESH body, brawn, carnage, carnality, carnation, family, fatten, glut, harden, humanity, kin(dred), man (kind), meat, mortality, muscle, pulp, race, satiate, stock
abnormality sarcosis
and blood kin(dred), materiality, offspring, relative
appendage palpus
-bearing carniferous
brush strigil
-colored carnation, carneous, incarnadine, pink, rosy, sarcoline
comb. cre, kreato, sarco
dead carrion, murrain
deprive of excarnate
dried tapa
-eater creophagist
-eating carnal, carnivorous,

creophagous, omophagia, sarcophagy
flea chigoe
formation sarcosis
human long-pig
kind brawn, carrion, chevon, chiver
-like carneous, carniform
lifeless mummy
pert. carnic, carnose, carnous, sarcous
-shearing carnassial

FLESHLESS lean, scrawny, thin

FLESHLY actual, animal(istic), bodily, carnal, corpor(e)al, gross, lascivious, lecherous, licentious, lustful, material, mundane, physical, sarkical, sensual, sensuous, sexy, sinful, soft, somatic, sybaritic, tender, voluptuous

FLESHPOTS plenty, prosperity

FLESHY adipose, brawny, burly, carnal, carnose, carnous, chubby, corpulent, fat, human, husky, obese, plump, portly, pulpy, rotund, sarcoid, stout, succulent
-stemmed chylocaulous

FLETCHER (See also BEAUMONT and FLETCHER.) *partner* beaumont
play boadicea, bonduca, coxcomb, cupid's revenge, mad lover, maid's tragedy, pilgrim, tamer tamed, women pleased

FLEUR-DE-LIS iris, lily, lis(s), luce, lycy, lys
decorated with liliated

FLEURET epee, flower(et), foil, sword

FLEX bend, bow, curve, deflect, genu(flect), lean, tilt

FLEXIBLE bendsome, docile, ductile, elastic, limber, lissome, lithe, malleable, plastic, pliable, pliant, resilient, springy, supple, tractable, willowy, winding, withy, yielding
comb. campto

FLEXION anaclasis, bend

FLEXUOUS anfractuous, circuitous, flickering, meandrous, relaxed, serpentine, sinuous, softened, tortuous, wavering, winding, zigzag

FLEXURE arch, bend, bent,

crook, curvature, curve, fold, genu, joint, turn(ing), twist, winding

FLEY fright(en)

FLIBBERTIGIBBET chatterer, demon, fiend, gossiper, scatterbrain

FLICK cinema, crack, cut, daub, fat, film, fleck, fleece, flip, flirt, flisk, flutter, hare, jerk, mark, movie, rabbit, snap, stain, streak, tap, throw, whip, wound

FLICKER beam, bicker, bird, blaze, blink, blinter, burn, dance, fail, fire, flame, flare, flit(ter), fluctuate, flunk, flutter, glance, glare, gleam, glimmer, glow, goldenwing, heigh-ho, high-hole, hover, lambency, quaver, quiver, ray, scintillate, shake, shimmer, spark(le), tremble, twinkle, vibrate, waver, whiffle, yucca

FLICKERING burning, fluttering, lambent, unsteady, wavering

FLICKERTAIL spermophile, squirrel
state north dakota

FLIER See FLYER.

FLIES *batting* fungo
lord of See DEVIL.

FLIGHT (See also AERONAUTICS.) airdrop, airlift, bevy, bole, bugout, course, covey, departure, disappearance, drove, escape, evasion, exodus, fleet, flock, flyover, fuge, gaggle, group, hegira, hejira, hop, joyhop, jump, migration, mission, mounting, multitude, nolo, pack, radius, rout, run, school, shoal, shoot, shuttle, skein, soaring, solo, speed, stairs, stampede, swarm, take off, trip, velocity, volation, volee, volitation, wing
holy hegira, hejira
in airborne, aloft
-like phugoid
of birds volary, volery, volley
of fancy imagination, sally
of steps grece, perron, pitch, scale, stairs, stairway, stepway, stoop
operation mission
organ wing
pert. aero, orbital, volar
power of volant
put to rout

range radius
science See AERONAUTICS *science.*
strip runway

FLIGHTY addlebrained, addlepated, barmy, bird-witted, brainless, capricious, confused, delirious, dizzy, fickle, fitful, flippant, foolish, freakish, frivolous, frothy, giddy, harebrained, illogical, light-headed, mad, mercurial, moonish, scatterbrained, silly, stupid, thoughtless, transient, unstable, volatile

FLIMFLAM caprice, conceit, deception, deceptive, freak, hoax, hocus, humbug(gery), nonsense, swindle, trick(y), trifle

FLIMSY baggy, bandbox, baseless, cheap, copy, dupe, feeble, flabby, flaccid, footless, fragile, frail, gimcrack, groundless, jerry (built), lame, limp, loose, manuscript, meager, meagre, papery, rare, shallow, sheet, slack, sleazy, slight, slimsy, superficial, tenuous, thin, trashy, trivial, twittery, unsound, vain, weak
thing butterfly

FLINCH blanch, blench, blink, cower, cringe, crouch, falter, fear, feign, flense, game, hesitate, quail, recoil, retire, retreat, scringe, shrink, slink off, snape, squinch, start, swerve, vacillate, wince, withdraw, wonde

FLINDER fragment, part, piece, smithers, splinter

FLINDERSIA, FLINDOSA beech, bumpy ash, bunjibunji, cudgerie, hickory

FLING attempt, baffle, cast, cheat, chuck, clap, dance, dart, dash, effuse, emit, flounce, heave, hurl, hurtle, kick, pitch, propel, prostrate, rebuff, repulse, revel, rush, send, shove, shy, spree, slat, sling, sneer, spanghew, spirit, swindle, taunt, throw, thrust, toss, try, venture, warp
about agitate, betoss
down fell
down the gauntlet challenge, dare
highland walloch

missiles chunk
off baffle, depart, say, utter
out depart, leave
up abandon, quit, relinquish

FLINGDUST See PROSTITUTE.

FLINT chert, clint, eolith, gratloir, miser, quartz, scraper, silex, stone
artifact audi
comb. silic
-head wood ibis
-hearted callous, hard
impure chert
tool burin

FLINTLOCK fusee, fusil, miquelet, musket, snaphaan, spanner

FLINTWOOD whitetop

FLINTY brassy, brazen, cruel, hard, obdurate, rocky, solid, steely

FLIP cant, chuck, crack, drink, flick, flirt, flop, flutter, fresh, glib, hop, impudent, jerk, limber, nimble, pert, pliant, sassy, saucy, sling, slirt, somersault, tap, throw, toss, trip, twirl
a coin gamble
-flap arm, firecracker, teacake
-flop about face, overturn, sandal, zori
up turn over

FLIPPANT arch, bold, brassy, chatty, fluent, forward, fresh, frivolous, glib, impish, impudent, limber, nimble, pert, playful, roguish, sassy, saucy, snippy, talkative, trifling, volatile, voluble, waggish

FLIPPER arm, fin, flapjack, game, hand, paddle, paw, pinball, springer

FLIRD brag, flirt, flutter, jibe, snear

FLIRT caress, chuck, coquet(te), dally, dart, disport, eye, fike, fillip, flick, fling, gallant, gallivant, gibe, golddigger, hurl, jeer, jerk, jest, jill, jilt, joke, make eyes, mash(er), mock, ogle, pet, philander, play, rover, shy, sport, start, tap, throw, tick, toss, toy, trifle, vamp

FLIRTATION affair, amour, coquetry, fike, passade, romance

FLIRTATIOUS arch, coquettish, coy

FLISK caper, comb, dance, fillip, flick, frisk, jiffy, whim, whisk

FLIT dart, elapse, flicker, flitter, float, flutter, fly, gad, glide, hover, scud, skim, speed, vanish, velocity

FLITCH blubber, cant, cut, flank, flip, gammon, longwood, middling, side

FLITE complain, contend, debate, dispute, gibe, jeer, quarrel, scold, strife

FLITTER See FLIT.

FLITTERMOUSE bat

FLITTING brief, ephemeral, flying

FLIVVER failure, fizzle, ford, model-t

FLIX down, flax, fur

FLIXWEED hedge-mustard, sand-rocket

FLOAT aid, balsa, begin, bladder, bob, boom, bucket, buoy, carrier, catamaran, cork, darby, dart, drift, effleurer, flitter, flood, fly, glide, hover, issue, launch, levitate, lifebuoy, liferaft, loan, lure, peddle, pontoon, quill, radeau, raft, run, sail, scud, skim, slide, slip, soar, start, streel, support, surfboard, swim, trench, vehicle, waft, watch, wave
aloft glide, soar
past glace
wooden camel

FLOATABLE buoyant, light

FLOATBOARD blade, ladle

FLOATER bloomer, blunder, boner, bull, drifter, error, faux pas, howler, lapse, maunderer, mistake, rolling stone, slip, stiff

FLOATING adrift, afloat, awaft, awash, buoyant, drifting, flotant, fluctuant, free, loose, natant, shifting, supernatant, unfunded, waft, wandering, watching, waterborne
bridge ferryboat, pontoon
fern ceratopteris
grass fescue, foxtail
-stone opal
wreckage flotsam, jetsam

FLOCCULENT flaky, hairy

FLOCK assemble, bank, bevy, brood, bunch, church, collection, company, congregate, congregation, covey, crowd, crush, drift, drove, flake, fold, gaggle, gather(ing), gregal, GROUP, hatch, herd, hirsel, horde, huddle, join, lots, many, meinie, meiny, mob, multitude, pack, parishioners, pod, press, progeny, raft, sedge, set, shoal, siege, skein, swarm, team, thicken, throng, troop, troupe, tuft, volary
god of pan
kind covey, gaggle, nid(e), nye, pod, sedge, sord, tribe
pert. gregal

FLODGE pond, pool, puddle

FLOE berg, ice, raft
-rat ringed-seal
scattered panice

FLOG baleise, beat, belt, birch, cane, cat, chastise, cotton, cowhide, drub, excel, ferule, flap, hide, hit, larrup, lash, peddle, punish, scourge, sjambok, slaister, surpass, swish, switch, tan, thrash, tire, urge, urticate, wale, welt, whip, yank

FLOGGING birching, cat-o-nine-tails, tanning, toco, toko, whipping
fond of plagose

FLOOD bore, cataclysm, cataract, current, deluge, downpour, drencher, eagre, engulf, excess, float, flow, flux, freshet, glut, inundate, irruption, niagara, overflow, overrun, overwhelm, plethora, pour on, rainstorm, sea, sluice, spate, storm, stream, submerge, superfluity, surfeit, surge, surplus, swamp, tide, torrent, washout, water, wave, whelm
before antediluvian
highest point crest
light illuminate, kleig, olivet
pert. diluvial, diluvian
plain banco, bench, dambo
tidal eagre

FLOODGATE cataract, clow, drag, gool, hatch, lock, penstock, sluice, staunch, tidegate, weir

FLOOR asphalt, base, beat, bed, blacktop, bottom, causeway, cement, cobblestone, concrete, confound, deck, defeat, drop, etage, fell, finish, flabbergast, flag, flatten, horizontal, kayo, knock down, layer, macadamize, mezzanine, nadir, nonplus, overthrow, pave-(ment), perplex, piano, planch(e), platform, playa, overcome, refute, silence, sollar, stage, story, support
board footling
border coaming, scuttle
cement slab
covering carpet, congoleum, linoleum, mat, plank, rug, tapis, tile
ground basement, terreno
-leader whip
-man floorwalker, manager
ocean seabed
plan blueprint, diagram, outline
plank chess
raised dais, halfpace, leewan, liwan, platform
show act, attraction, cabaret, feature, performance
slab dalle
threshing mowstead
timber batten, solepiece

FLOOZY prostitute, trollop, trull, wanton, whore

FLOP bang, bed, bomb, brodie, bust, change, clap, dog, drop, dud, fail(ure), FALL, fizzle, flap, flivver, flutter, frost, hang, hat, klinker, lemon, lie down, lop, plump, retire, seat, sink, sleep, slump, squab, strike, stroke, swop, tumble, turkey, washout, wave, whop
-top soapwort

FLOPHOUSE dosshouse, inn

FLOPSY cottontail, rabbit
kin mopsy, peter

FLORA asteroid, plant(life)
and fauna biota

FLORAL bloomy, blossomy, flowery
comb. anth(o), anthous
envelope perianth
leaf bract, sepal
leaves perianth
ornament anthemion

FLORENCE *artist* del sarto
bridge ponte vecchio, santa trinita
cathedral duomo
coin florin, ruspone
devotees neri
emblem giglio, lily
family medici, strozzi
father gawain
flask betty
gallery accadamia, bargello, corsini, pitti(palace), uffizi
gardens boboli
iris ireos, orris, treos

river arno
FLORESCENCE anthesis, blossoming, extract, perfume
FLORET bud, sword
bract palea, palet
FLORIA la tosca
FLORID bombastic, colorful, embellished, euphuistic, fancy, flamboyant, flowery, flushed, melismatic, opulent, ornamented, ornate, ostentatious, pompous, pretentious, red, rhetorical, rococo, rubicund, ruddy, showy, splendid, taffeta, vigorous, wordy
FLORIDA *arrowroot* wild sago
balsam torchwood
bay apalachee, biscayne, waccasassa
bird curlew, mockingbird, pelican
cape kennedy, sable
capital tallahassee
city bradenton, brooksville, clearwater, cocoa, coral gables, daytona beach, fort lauderdale, gainesville, hialeah, jacksonville, key biscayne, lakeland, lake worth, melbourne, miami(beach), ocala, orlando, orleans, palatka, palm beach, pompano beach, st augustine, st petersburg, sarasota, sebring, tallahassee, tampa, tice, vero beach, winterhaven, winterpark
college rollins
county alachua, brevard, broward, dade, guff, manatee, osceola, pinellas, sarasota, volusia
cowrie micramock
cranberry roselle
discoverer ponce de leon
eggfruit canistel
fan palm coccothrinax
feature everglades
fish atinga, barracuda, bream, bur(r)fish, chopa, crawfish, crunt, doncella, grouper, salema, snook, tarpon, tetard, tomtate
fishing boat smackee
flower orange blossom
fort pickens
gallinule ricebird
grunt tomtate
heron fly-up-the-creek
indian ais, apalachee, apalachi, calusa, chatot, mika-

suki, ocale, potano, seminole, timucca, utina
indian farmer calusa
island bahama, biscayne, dry tortugas, key largo, key west, sanibel
key biscayne, largo, west
lake apopka, arbuckle, dora, harney, jessup, kissimmee, ledwith, newnan, okeechobee
laurel sweetleaf
lizard rhineura
mahogany red-bay
majarra muttonfish
motto in god we trust
name origin pascua de flores
native conch, cracker, fly-up-the-creek
nickname flower state, peninsular state, sunshine
palm royal
peak iron
plain savannah
plant coontie, pickerelweed
port jacksonville, pensacola, tampa
quinine georgia bark
region everglades
resort hobe sound, palm beach
river apalachicola, aucilla, banana, indian, manatee, ochlawaha, st johns, scambia, suwanee
road tamiami trail
sago arrowroot
shrub ant's-weed, velvet-seed
snake moccasin
song swanee river
squirrelfish matajuelo
state bird mockingbird
state flower orange blossom
state tree palmetto
swamp everglades
threadfin barbudo
tree blolly, gomart, gumbo-limbo, mabi, mangrove, palmetto, royal palm, sabel palm, snakebark
tree louse barnacle-scale
turtle cooter
university stetson, tampa
wetlands glades
FLORIDITY elegance, rhetoric
FLORILEGIUM anthology, chapbook, chrestomathy, corpus, garland, thesaurus, treasury
FLORIST seedsman
FLORIZEL *beloved* perdita
FLORY conceited, vain

FLOSS rushes, silk, sleave, spill, stream, thread
silk caddice, caddis
silk tree samohu
FLOSSY downy, fancy, fluffy, light, ostentatious, showy, stringy, stylish
FLOTATION buoyancy, floating, inauguration, issue, securities
FLOTILLA armada, fleet, group, squadron
FLOTOW *opera* martha
FLOTSAM debris, derelict, driftage, jetsam, wafture, waveson, wilsam, wreckage
FLOTTER float, flood, wet
FLOUNCE caper, falbelo, figure, flap, fling, flounder, fold, frill, furbelow, huff, jerk, pace, play, ruching, ruffle, slam, spring, struggle, turn, twist
FLOUNDER (See also *kind*, below.) addle, blunder, boggle, change, confuse, doubt, fail, falter, fish, flounce, gab, gadoid, grovel, hesitate, labor, lurch, megrim, muddle, obstruct, pitch, plunge, reel, rock, roll, slosh, stagger, strive, struggle, stumble, sway, swing, toil, toss, totter, tumble, vacillate, wallop, wallow, welter
kind bream, but(t), dab, flatfish, fluke, foolfish, halibut, plaice, plunther, sandling, sole, sunfish, topknot, turbot
lantern scaldfish
summer puckermouth
FLOUR amyl, at(t)a, bran, camaille, cribble, farina, hovis, meal, powder, pulverize, semolina, staple, tsamba, whites
and butter roux, thickening
beetle palorus, tribolium
bleach agene
city minneapolis
coarse boxings, chisel, cribble, third
comb. aleuro
diabetic aleuronat
durham wheat semolella, semolina
fine cones, cornstarch, smeddum, sugee
for macaroni semolella, semolina
low grade tail
maker miller

malt smeddum
moth ephestia, phycitid
particle chop
paste beurre manie, roux
potato frow
pudding duff
sifter bolter, farinheira, sieve
sprinkle with dredge, dust
testing device farinometer
wheat at(t)a, semolina
unsorted at(t)a

FLOURISH advance, appreciate, batten, blare, bloom, blossom, boast, boom, brag, brandish, burgeon, catch, cheve, curl(icue), decoration, develop, display, exhibit, fanfare, flaunt, flower, fustian, grow, increase, manipulate, ostentation, parade, paraph, ply, proliferate, prosper, quirk, rhetoric, riot, roulade, shake, show, skirmish, spiral, succeed, sweep, swing, tantara, tantivy, thrash, thrive, touch, twist, vaunt, vigor, wave, wax, wield
musical cadenza, melisma, quaver, roulade

FLOURISHING blooming, bloomy, blossoming, frim, frum, healthy, luxuriant, thriving

FLOUT affront, attack, be-tongue, bob, challenge, contemn, deride, despise, disdain, disregard, fleer, gibe, gird, insult, jeer, jerk, jibe, laugh at, mock, rail at, repudiate, ridicule, scoff, scout, slight, sneer, spurn, taunt, thumb nose, truss

FLOW abound, affluence, afflux(ion), arise, avale, backwash, begin, cadence, career, coast, concourse, confluence, conflux, continuity, course, current, defluxion, derive, downpour, dribble, drift, ebb, emanate, extend, exude, flood, fluency, flush, flux, glide, gush, gutter, issue, juice, melt, millrace, millrun, morass, neap(tide), onrush, ooze, pass, pour, proceed, profluence, progression, quicksand, race, refluence, reflux, rip(tide), rise, roll, run, rush, sequence, slip, spill, spout, spring, spurtle, stem, stream, succession, surge, teem, tide,

travel, trickle, trill, trinkle, undercurrent, wave, well
against bathe, lap, lave
back ebb
comb. rrhagia, rrhe(o)a
in inpour, inrush, pour in
-off effluence
out bleed, emit, exhaust, exude, issue, leak, spill, spread
slowly dribble, drip, exude, ooze, seep, trickle, trinkle

FLOWER (See also *garden,* below.) best, bloom, blossom, blow, bud, burst, choicest, develop, elect, elite, embellish, essence, ferment, fiore, fleur, freshest, froth, mature, pick, posy, proliferate, thrive, unfold
anthology florilegium
apetalus cactus, trema
appendage bract
aromatic camomile
arrangement cascade, corsage, spray
axis prolongation carpophore
band anadem, garland, lei, wreath
basket flasket
-bearing anthophorous floriferous
bed pattern parterre
beetle cetonia
bell-shaped lily, tulip
blooming once a year annual
blue harebell, lupine
border floroon
bract lemma, palea
bud ament, caper, knot, spadix
bud, dried clove
burry teasel
center eye
chaplet anadem
cluster ament, anadem, anthemia, anthemis, anthotaxy, bract, cime, corymb, cyme, glomerule, panicle, paniculate, raceme, umbel
comb. anth(o), anthy, anth(o)lus, flori, florous
compound anthodium
cotton square
-covered fleury
cup calyx, chalice
-cup fern woodsia
cup-shaped scyphus
deformed bullhead
-de-luce iris
description anthography
double burster

dry azalea, brayera, cactus, oleander, yucca
envelope corolla, perianth
everlasting immortelle
expansion anthesis, full-bloom
extract at(t)ar, ottar, otto, perfume
fadeless amaranth, immortelle
fall aster, cosmos
feeding on anthophilious
fence adenanthera, barbados pride, bear tree, peacock flower, sandalwood
festival anthesteria
field gowan, poppy
fly syphid
fond of anthophilian, anthophilious
forgetfulness lotus
fossil antholite
fragrant gardenia, jasmine, rose
full bloom anthesis
garden aster, azalia, bletilla, buttercup, camellia, canna, carnation, chrysanthemum, daffodil, dahlia, daisy, flag, freesia, gladiolus, gloxinia, heliotrope, honeysuckle, hyacinth, iris, ixia, lilac, lily, lupine, marigold, mum, narcissus, olivia, orchid, pansy, peony, petunia, phlox, pink, primrose, ranunculus, rose, solitaire, tulip, verbena, violet, zinnia
girl bouquetiere
girl, blind nydia
goddess antheia, aphrodite, chloris, flora, nanna, thallo
group bed, bouquet, corsage, posy, spray
growing on epanthous, fungus
having affinity for antophilous
head (See also *cluster,* above.) anthodium, bloom, blossom, capitulum, curd, panicle
head, dried anthemis
heath azalea, erica
holder lapel, pot, vase
imaginary amarant(h)
large canna, peony
late-blooming aster
leaf bract, petal, sepal
leaves perianth
-like anthoid, beautiful
meadow bluet, cyme, pratal
medicinal aloe, rue
michaelmas aster

modest violet
motif fleuron
name meaning calla, daisy, fleur(rette), rose, violet
obsolete pense
of an hour bladder-ketmie, shoofly
of bristol lychnis
of death asphodel
of jove campion
of life youth
of paradise camalata, ipomoea
of the levant zante
ornament anthemion, bouquet, boutonniere
part alae, ament, androecium, anther, anthophore, bract, calyx, carpel, corolla, corona, epicalyx, filament, gynoecium, microsporophyll, nectary, ovary, ovule, peduncle, perianth, pericarp, petal, petiole, pistil, pollen, sepal, spadix, spur, stamen, stem, stigma, style, tora, torus
pecker kakawahie
perennial petunia
pert. anthine, floral
pigment anthochlor, anthocyan(in)
pink rhodora, rose, silene
pistel gynoecium
pistel part carpel
poet's chaucer
pot cachepot, jardiniere
producing cauliflorous
purple lilac, orpine, pense, violet
receptacle epergne, pot, torus, vase
scarlet salvia
seed ovule
shape bell, fleuron
sheath spathe
showy anthurium, azalea, bird of paradise, calla, camellia, orchid, rhododendron
6-leaved sexfoil
spike ament, sapdix
spring arbutus, crocus, daffodil, hepatica, hyacinth, iris, lilac, narcissus, peony, tulip, violet
stalk kemp, peduncle, petiole, scape, stem
stamen androecium, anther
state florida
stipe anthophore
striped bizarre
study anthoecology, botany
unfading amaranth
unilateral secund

white barton, calla lily, daisy, gowan
wild anemone, arbutus, baby blue-eyes, black-eyed susan, bluebell, bluet, buttercup, ceanothus, chamise, coreopsis, cuperosa, cyclamen, daisy, dandelion, encilla, gold fields, greasewood, hepatica, innocence, joshua, lupine, marguerite, phacelia, popcorn, poppy, sage, sandverbena
wind anemone
without ananthous
without petals cactus, trema
yellow buttercup, coreopsis, daffodil, daisy, gowan, jonquil, marigold, pense, rue
yellow coloring in xanth(e)in
FLOWERING abloom, anthesis, blooming, blossoming, development
early prevernal
glume lemma
late serotine
FLOWERY aureate, bloomy, blown, bombastic, colorful, eloquent, embellished, euphuistic, fancy, figurative, floral, florid, florient, inflated, ornamental, ornate, prolix, rhetorical, tumid, verbose, wordy
kingdom china
FLOWING abundant, copious, current, cursive, ebb, emanant, fluent, fluid, fluor, flux(ion), fusile, liquified, pendent, running, smooth, tidal
again remontant
freely fluviose
in influent, influx(ion)
out effluent, excurrent
together confluent
FLU influenza
epidemic spanish-lady
FLUCTUATE blow hot and cold, change, oscillate, pendulate, shift, sway, swing, teeter, undulate, vacillate, vary, veer, vibrate, wave(r)
FLUCTUATING erratic, hectic, unstable, unsteady, wayward
FLUCTUATION ambivalence, cycle, fading, flicker, flutter, unsteadiness, ups and downs, variation
FLUE barb, chimney, down (take), expand, feeble, flare, flaring, fluke, funnel, hair,

lint, net, open, passage, pipe, shallow, sickly, smokejack, tewel, thin, tune, tunnel, uptake, vent
bridge altar
cleaner sweep
-cured bright
FLUELLEN cancerwort, mountain parsley, speedwell, toadflax, veronica
FLUENCY ease, facility, floridity, flow, grace(fulness), harmony, loquacity, skill, smoothness
FLUENT apt, articulate, copious, current, easy, eloquent, expressive, facile, flowing, fluid, free, glib, gliding, integral, liquid, prompt, quick, ready, smooth(tongued), solute, stream, talkative, verbose, vocal, voluble
FLUFF blunder, bull, down, err, flash, floc, floss, forget, fuzz, girl, lanugo, lint, miscue, miss, nap, primp, puff, shiv, short change, slip, whiff
FLUFFY creamy, downy, feathery, fleecy, flossy, furry, fuzzy, linten, linty, mollipilose, nappy, velutinous, woolly
FLUID (See also *kind*, below.) aqueous, blood, broth, changeable, dissolved, emulsion, floating, flowing, fluent, flux, gas (eous), glume, gorse, ichor, juice, latex, liquid, liquor, melted, milk, plasma, rasa, sap(py), serous, serum, sol, solution, steam, succulent, vapor, water(y), whey
accumulation ascites, edema, oedema
animal serum
become flow, flux, leach, liquefy, melt
blood plasma, serum
body humor
collection blister, edema, oedema
containing enhydrous
ethereal ichor
inky melena
kind acetone, bile, blood, coaloil, ether, gas(oline), grume, ichor, ink, kerosene, latex, milk, naphtha, nerol, oil, plasma, sap, serum, tar, tear(let), water, wine
liver bile

lubricating oil, synovia
mass fluor
medical serum
medicated elixir, embrocation, liniment, lotion, tincture, tonic
movement through cataphoresis
mythological ichor
ounce floz
pert. humoral
primeval nun
stratification baroclivity
-tapping paracentesis
unit rhe
vital blood, lymph, sap
without aneroid
FLUIDITY changeableness, chylifaction, instability, lactescence. liquefaction, serosity
unit rhe
FLUKE advantage, barb, blade, cercaria, chance, cottrel, fail, flatfish, flatworm, flounder, fortune, grasp, hook, luck, plaice, platode, stroke, windfall, worm
larva miracidium
FLUKEWORT rot grass
FLUKY capricious, uncertain, unsteady
FLUME channel, chute, conduit, gap, gorge, race, ravine, shute, sluice, stream
FLUMMER beguile, humbug
FLUMMERY blancmange, custard, nonsense, pap, sowens, trash, washbrew
FLUMMOX bewilder, collapse, confound, embarrass, fail, thwart
FLUMP fall, plump, sink, thud
FLUNK back out, bust, dismiss, fail(ure), falter, flinch, miss, plow, pluck, retreat, shirk, skew, slip, washout
FLUNKY assistant, bootlicker, cookee, domestic, failure, footman, hangeron, lackey, menial, servant, snob, steward, sycophant, toady, truckler, waiter, wardheeler, worker
FLUOR flowing, fluid, stream
spar blue-john, cand
FLUORESCENCE bloom, epipolism, luminescence
FLUORIDE *hydrous* pachnolite, prosopite
FLUORINE phthor, phtor
source fluorite
FLURRY ado, agitate, agita-

tion, bewilder, blast, bluster, breeze, bustle, carfuffle, commotion, confuse, confusion, disconcert, disquiet, disturb(ance), excite, flusker, fluster, flutter, fooster, fret, fuss, gust, haste, hurry, perturb, pother, quicken, ruffle, speed, squall, stir, swither, tear, whither, wind(flaw)
FLUSH abundant, affluent, bloom(ing), blush, color, crimson, darken, direct, drench, elate, evacuate, even, explode, fever, flare up, flat, fledged, flood, flow, fresh, full, glow, gratify, green, growth, health, hunt, increase, jet, lavish, level, lusty, mantle, moneyed, morass, plain, plane, pool, prodigal, prosperous, raise, redden, replete, rich, rinse, rosiness, ruddle, rush, smooth, soak, spirited, spring, squarely, start, straight, suffuse, thrill, turn color, wash, wealthy, welloff
game serve, start
2nd time retrieve
FLUSHED aglow, ardent, blushing, burning, crimson, eager, elated, exultant, feverish, florid, hot, passionate, prosperous, rapturous, red, rosy, ruby, scarlet, torrid, vigorous
FLUSTER addle, agitate, agitation, befuddle, bewilder, bluster, bother, confound, confuse, disconcert, disquiet, disturb, dither, excite, faze, flurry, fooster, fuddle, fuss, glow, heat, move, muddle, nonplus, perturb, pother, rattle, ruffle, shake, upset
FLUSTERED confused, intoxicated, perturbed, upset
FLUSTRATION dither
FLUTE aulos, bin, breakfastroll, chamfer, channel, crimp, diaulos, doucet, fife, flageolet, flamfew, flauto, fold, furrow, fuye, gauffer, gingras, groove, hemiope, magadis, matalan, monaulos, nay, nei, piccolo, pipe, pungi, quena, recorder, sibilus, sifflot, storeship, styke, tche, tibia, to-

nette, transport, twill, wineglass, zufolo
ancient recorder, tibia
bagpipe chanter
bird piping crow
comb. aulo
double diaulos
eunuch kazoo
fear of auluphobia
fipple flageolet, penny whistle
inventor jubal
-like instrument tche
mouthpiece syrinx
part fipple
player aulete, auletris, flautist, flutist, piper, tibicen, tootler
small flautino
soft-toned recorder
stop ventage
transverse fife
wood for kokra
FLUTEMOUTH aulostomi, cornetfish, shrimpfish, snipefish, trumpetfish
FLUTING coulisse, gadroon, quilling, strigil, strix
space between fil(l)et, gorgerin
FLUTTER agitate, beat(ing), bicker, blink, bustle, confuse, dance, display, dither, drift, flap, flasker, flick(er), flip, flird, flirt, flit(ter), flop, fluctuate, fluster, fly, hover, oscillate, palpitate, palpitation, pitapat, pitterpatter, pulsate, quiver, riffle, ruffle, run, shake, speculation, splutter, sputter, squatter, stir, swing, swivet, thrill, throb, tremble, trepidation, vibrate, waff(le), wave(r), whiffle, wobble
-tonguing growl
FLUTTERING awing, dancing, desultory, flickery, flicky, flying, sp(l)uttering, unsteady, wavery, whutter
FLUTTERY restless, shaky, unsteady
FLUVIAL abyssal, aquatic, bathybic, bathysmal, cacustrine, marine, neritic, oceanic, pelagic, thalassic
FLUX borax, change, current, discharge, dissolve, euripus, flood, flow, fluctuation, fusion, leakage, melt, motion, movement, outflow, purge, shifting, stir, stream,

sway, swing, tide, treat, variable

unit gauss, maxwell, weber

FLY (See also *kind*, below.) abscond, airlift, alert, arise, aviate, avigate, balloon, cab, carriage, carry, cruise, dart, decamp, depart, dipteron, disappear, drift, elapse, escape, evaporate, fade, flap, flee, fleg, flicker, flit(ter), float, flurr, flutter, glide, hasten, hop, hover, hustle, insect, keen, kite, leap, levitate, melt, mount, musca, navigate, nimble, pass, pest, pilot, plane, printer's devil, quick, sail, scud, scurry, sharp, shoot, skim, skir, smart, soar, solitaire, speed, take off, trap, vanish, volitate, volplane, wave, whew, whir, wing

agaric amanita, mushroom

aimlessly bangle

a kite borrow, get lost

anchor drag

artificial abbey, adirondack, alder(man), alexandr(i)a, apple green, ashy hackle, august dun, babcock, baker, barrington, bassbug, beaverkill, bee, black ant, blackdose, black prince, black quill, bluebottle, blue dun, bobfly, brown ant, brown may, brown sedge, bucktail, butcher, buzz, caddice, caddis, cahill, campbell's fancy, canary, catskill, claret, coachman, colonel, doctor, downlooker, dun, evening dun, ferguson, ginger quill, gold spinner, governor, grannom, hackle, hare's-ear, harl, herl, huzzard, jack scott, lure, march brown, miller, nymph, palmer, pink lady, pium, quill, rough olive, sassycat, sedge, silver doctor, tatukira, wasp, wickham's fancy, woodruff, wrentail, zulu

artificial, tail tippet

at attack, charge, spring

-away flighty, free, giddy, light, loose, mirage, restless, streaming, unrestrained

ball blooper, fungo, hit, out, texas-leaguer

-batting, pert. fungo

biting tatukira

black bean aphis, gnat, hippelates, similium

block pulley

bloodsucking seroot, stomoxys, tsetse

blow egg, larva

-blown blighted, contaminated, infested, struck, tainted

bluebottle blowfly, calliphora

boat flight, flute

bull detective

-by-night irresponsible, shifty, slippery, treacherous, unreliable

case elytra

chalcid anastatus, aphelinus, eucharitid, tetrastichus

comb. musci, myi(a), myio

constellation musca

cop detective, plainclothesman, policeman

crane tipula

drone eristalis

egg ahuatle, blow

enemy spider

fishing See *artificial*, above.

flax coolgardie

-flower dutchman's-breeches

genus acrocera, anomalon, calliphora, dacus, drosophila, miastor, microgaster, musca, phora, psila, psychode, trypeta

god achor, beelzebuth, be(e)lzebub, devil, satan

golden-eyed lacewing

green-tail grannom

honeysuckle black twinberry

ichneumon agrictypus, apanteles, aphidiin, parasitica, pimpla, pupivora

in the face of defy, insult, oppose, resist

in the ointment catch, evil, flaw, obstacle, snag

kind alder, bee, bibionid, bluebottle, bot, breeze, butcher, cadew, canopid, caterpillar, ceratitis, collier, dragonfly, eurytoma, fag, fruitfly, gadfly, gnat, gorfly, horse, house, kivu, lacewing, leptid, may, midge, sciarid, sepsid, seroot, shoemaker, silene, tachina, tatukira, trichoptera, tsetse, tyrphid, warblefly, whame, zimb

lacewing chrysopa

larva bloodworm, bott, jointworm

leaf endpaper

life stage adult, imago,

larva(1), maggot, pupa(1), puparium

low buzz, drag, hedgehop

man aviator, loftman, pilot

march bibio

may drake, dun

muscoid phycodromid

mushroom amanita

off break away, revolt, separate

off the handle explode, rage, storm

parasitic compsilura, rhyssa, tachinid

prepare to taxi

press operator bower

rapidly scur, skirr

red chrysops

red, larva filaria

saw horntail

sheep fag, ked

small gnat, midge, plunkie

stone sally

symbol of disease, feebleness, filth, insignificance

the coop escape, flee

thick-headed conopid

tick mite

tsetse glossina

2-winged acalyptrata, asilus, athericera, dipteron, itonidid, pipunculid, resin-gnat, wheat-midge, zimb

whisk chowry, rhipidion

white asterochiton

wings elytra, elytron

yellow huzzard

FLYBANE agaric, catchfly, cinnamonroot, poison, silene, silenus

FLYCATCHER alder, beambird, chebec, elepaio, fantail, fielder, fireball, firebird, forktail, gerygone, grignet, grinder, kingbird, kiskadee, peewee, phainopepla, phoebe, pipiri, pitangua, rafter, redstart, tody, tomfool, tyrannus, tyrant, vireo, wallbird, warbler, web, yellow-bellied, yetapa

pied coldfinch

spotted wall-plat

tyrant tomfool

FLYER ace, advertisement, aeronaut, airman, aviator, bill, bird(man), cannonball, chance, eagle, express, gamble, parachutist, pilot, placard, speculation, speeder, train, venture

eagle-borne etana

garment anti-g-suit

FLYING aerobatics, AER-

ONAUTICS, air-borne, aw-
ing, brief, ephemeral, fast,
flight, flitting, fluttering,
hasty, jet-propelled, soaring,
swift, volant, volation, voli-
tant, volitic
adder dragonfly
around circumvolant
body meteor(ite)
buttress arc-boutant
comb. aero
condition yarak
device airplane, balloon,
glider, kite, parachute,
plane
dutchman mariner, wanderer
dutchman heroine senta
expert ace
fish skipper, volador
fox kalong, pteropid
gurnard angler, batfish,
latchet, lophid, volador
lemur cobego, colugo,
kurong
machine See AIRCRAFT.
maneuver lufbery
pert. aero
phalanger ariel, cuscus,
squirrel
saucer ufo
signal roger
squadron picket(s)
squirrel assapan, taguan
toy kite
FLYSCH macigno
FLYSPECK bit, dot, spot,
trifle
islands paracels
FLYTRAP dogbane, pitcher-
plant
FLYWHEEL wharve, whorl
FO See BUDDHA.
FOAL bear, cade, colt, equuleus, filly, fledgling, young
FOALFOOT asarabacca,
coltsfoot, ground ivy
FOAM aerate, barm, bead,
beat, boil, bubble, churn,
collar, cream, despumate,
effervesce, ferment, fizz,
froth, fume, gush, head,
lather, mantle, offscum,
rage, scud, scum, seethe,
simmer, soapsuds, spindrift,
spoondrift, spray, spume,
suds, surf, trivia, whip,
whisk, yeast
comb. aphr(o)
FOAMY barmy, creamy,
frothy, light, spumescent,
spumous, spumy, sudsy,
yeasty
FOB chain, cheat, deceive,
foam, froth, fub, impose

on, impostor, ornament,
palm off, pocket, sham,
spung, swindler, trick
off delude, impose, put aside,
put off
FOCAL central, decisive,
strategic
point center, hub, nub, omphalos
FOCUS axis, center, centralize, climax, concenter, concentrate, converge, core,
crux, cynosure, fixate, ganglion, heart(h), hub, lodestar, middle, midst, nucleus,
omphalos, polestar
on contemplate, ponder,
think
FODDER alfalfa, barley,
batad, bitter-vetch, chow,
clover, corn, deerweed, ensilage, ers, farrage, feed,
food, forage, fother,
gooma, hay, maize, millet,
oats, podware, provender,
provisions, rape, rye, silage,
stover, straw, vetch, viands,
victuals, wheat
cage tumbrel
plant sainfoin
storage place bakie, barn,
ensilage, (hay)mow, silage,
silo
store of ensilage, ensile
straw stover
trough manger
FODE befool, beguile, lull
FODGEL fat, plump, squat,
stout
FODIENT aardvark, burrower, mole
FOE adversary, antagonist,
assailant, attacker, competitor, contestant, enemy,
fiend, offensive, opponent,
opposer, opposition, rival
FOG aerosol, becloud, bedim,
blue, blur, brume, cloud,
confuse, confusion, daze,
dim, garua, ha(a)r, haze,
mist, moke, murk, obscu-
rity, opaque, pea soup, rag,
roke, salmon, smaze, smirr,
smog, smoke, smother,
smur, soup, stour, stupor,
vapor(s), uncertainty
blue priscilla
-bow mistbow, seadog, stubb
-chaser drink
dense pea-soup(er)
-eater dog, fogbow, mistbow,
seadog
evaporating system fido
frozen barber

light gauze
sea haar, harr
FOG(E)Y antique, conservative, dodo, dotard, fogram,
fogrum, foozle, hunker,
mossback, oldster, stodger
FOGFRUIT lippia, matgrass
FOGGY beclouded, bewildered, bloated, brumous,
cloudy, confused, dark,
dense, dim, dull, fat, flabby,
greasy, hazy, marshy,
misty, moist, moky, mud-
dled, nubilous, obscure,
ro(o)ky, smurry, spewy,
thick, vague, vaporous
place london, san francisco
FOGHORN diaphone, ripper,
signal, siren(e), tyfon
FOGRAM, FOGRUM, con-
servative, fog(e)y, liquor,
oldfashioned, oldster
FOGY See FOGEY.
FOHIST bonze, buddhist,
monk
FOIBLE blemish, defect, deviation, discrepancy, eccentricity, failing, fault, flaw,
frailty, kink, peculiarity,
quirk, vice, weakness
FOIL actor, antithesis, arc,
baffle, balk, blade, blench,
boggle, cheat, check(mate),
circumvent, contrast, curb,
defeat, defile, disappoint,
discomfit, disconcert, disgrace, elude, embarrass,
epee, evade, failure, faze,
frustrate, inhibit, lamina,
leaf, metal, outwit, paillette,
paring, plate, pollute, rattle,
repulse, restrain, rout,
snaffle, soil, stain, stigma,
stonker, stooge, stump,
sword, thwart
fencing blunt, epee, fleuret,
floret
pointed tang
tin tain
tip guard button
FOIST barge, cask, cheat,
fob, fust(iness), fusty, galley, impose, interpolate,
palm, pass off, pickpocket,
put off, rascality, shoehorn,
suborn, swindle, thrust
in interpose, intrude
FOISTED subditititous
FOLD (See also *kind*,
below.) bend, bow, clasp,
cockle, coil, collapse,
collop, congregation, convolution, corrugation, cot(e),
crease, creasing, crimp,

crinkle, crisp, crumple, dogear, double, doubling, drape, drop, duplication, embrace, enclosure, entwine, envelop, fail, flap, flection, flexure, flock, flounce, flute, frill, furdle, furrow, gather, groove, ground, hug, lamina, land, lap, lapel, lappet, pen, pinch, plait, pleat, plica(tion), plicature, plie, ply, pucker, quill, quit, reef, ridge, rimple, ruffle, ruga, rumple, sinus, throw in, tuck, twill, welt, wrap, yard, yield
between interplical
cardiac cusp
comb. farious, plex, stege
geological closure, diapir, exocline, syncline
kind bawn, bight, bought, dewlap, frenum, lapel, loop, octavo, pleat, plica(te), quire, reeve, replicate, tuck
loose lappet
one's arms idle, stand by
restraining fraenum, frenum
up close, collapse, fail
without eplicate
FOLDCOURSE faldage, sheepwalk
FOLDED buttate, closed, cockle, double, fan-like, loopy, plicate, puckery, pursy, shut
and waved gyrose
FOLDER dodger, leaflet, pamphlet
FOLDEROL See FALDERAL and NONSENSE.
FOLIAGE bouquet, bush(es), foliation, frondescence, greenery, leafage, leaves, ramage, spray, umbrage, vernation
carved knot
plant begonia, coleus, geranium, saxifrage
FOLIATE(D) foliaceous, lamellar, lamellate, leafy, lobed, number(ed), spathic
FOLIATION enumeration, leafing, numeration, pagination, stratification
FOLIC *acid* folacin, pga, vitamin-m
FOLIO atlas, book, folder, leaf, number, page
FOLK(S) humanity, inhabitants, kin(dred), nation, parents, people, population, public, race, relatives, tribe

dance movement dos-a-dos
fairy shee, sidhe
singer cantador
song bergerette, blues, bylina, fado, lullaby, tonada, volkslied
tale droll, fable, fabula, legend, marchen, myth
FOLKLORE beliefs, customs, history, legends, mythology, sayings, superstitions, traditions
creature troll
genie sandman
FOLKWAYS customs, mores, mos, patterns
FOLLICLE cavity, cocoon, crypt, depression, fruit, gland, ovisac, tube
FOLLOW accompany, act, adhere, ape, attend, bedog, betise, catch on to, catenate, chase, come after, come next, conform, convoy, copy, court, dangle, dog, draggle, emanate, ensue, fall back, fathom, figure, get, go after, hang about, heed, heel, hound, hunt, imitate, issue, lag, next, nose, obey, observe, parallelize, practice, profess, pursue, result, second, seek, shadow, shag, sleuth, specialize, spoor, stalk, string along, succeed, supervene, supplant, tag (gle), tail, take after, trace, trail, understand
beaten path conform
closely approach, cling, dog, stay near, tag
hounds hunt
in the steps of emulate, imitate
on continue, press on
slowly draggle, straggle
suit ape, copy, emulate, imitate
up attend, debriefing, pursue, reminder, sequel(a), sequelant, sequent, sequitor
FOLLOWER accompanier, acolyte, adherent, aficionado, aide, aper, appendage, associate, attendant, backer, bootlicker, buff, carrier, caudatory, cavalier, chaser, client, copier, courtier, customer, dangler, dependent, devotee, disciple, ensuer, enthusiast, faithful, fan, favorite, grifter, hanger-on, heeler, henchman, homme

de coeur, ist, ite, lackey, lickspit(tle), lover, mimic, minion, myrmidon, partisan, patron, poligar, proselyte, pupil, pursuer, pursuivant, retainer, rooter, satellite, sectary, sequent, servant, servitor, shadow(er), skip-tracer, successor, supporter, sycophant, tagtail, tail, toady, train-bearer, tufthunter, vassal, votary, ward-healer
camp gudget
comb. ist, ite, ni(c)k
group cattle, claque, clique, crowd, gate, retinue, school, staff, train
FOLLOWING after, audience, behind, clientele, consecutive, consequent, custom, deducible, dogging, ensuing, heeling, hounding, last, later, next, patronage, posterior, proximate, public, retinue, rout, sect, sequence, sequent, serial, seriate, seriatim, shadowing since, subsequent, succeeding, successive, tailing, trade, trailing, train, vocation
FOLLY absurdity, betise, blunder, boob stunt, crime, daffing, desipience, dotage, fatuity, foolery, foolishness, foppery, idiocy, imbecility, imprudence, inanity, indiscretion, infatuation, levity, lewd(ness), lunacy, madness, mistake, morology, nonsense, obliquity, rashness, silliness, sin, sotship, sottage, sottise, stupidity, surquidry, unthrift, unwisdom, willness, woodness
personification ate
symbol goose
FOMENT abet, agitate, agitation, arouse, brew, cultivate, excite(ment), fire, foster, galvanize, goad, heat, incite, inspite, instigate, motivate, nurse, nurture, promote, provoke, quicken, relieve, sow, spur, stimulate, stupe
FOMENTATION balm, encouragement, excitation, excitement, instigation, lotion, stupe, turbulence
FOMORIANS, FOMORS
enemy firbolgs
king balot

FOND adoring, affectionate, amorous, ardent, asinine, base, basis, befool, beguile, besotted, bottom, broth, browden, caress, credulous, demonstrative, desirous, devoted, dote, doting, dumb, empty, fain, fatuous, fondle, fool(ish), fount, groundwork, indulgent, infatuated, insipid, juice, languishing, lovelorn, lovesick, lovesome, loving, man-keen, parental, passionate, pleased, romantic, sanguine, sauce, sentimental, silly, simple, soft, spoony, stock, store, stupid, tender, tid, trifling, vain

FONDLE blandish, canoodle, caress, cherish, coddle, cosset, cuddle, dandle, foster, gentle, indulge, ingle, neck, nurse, nuzzle, pamper, pat, pet, pettle, smuggle, stroke, tiddle, twattle

FONDLING caressant, darling, fool, ninny, nurseling, pet, simpleton, waif

FONDNESS affection, appetite, attachment, dearness, desire, feeling, folly, foolishness, gra, liking, love, notion, partiality, predilection, propensity, relish, taste, tenderness, weakness

FONFER boaster, cheater, deceiver, goof-off, lazer

FONT baptism, basin, delubrum, FOUNTAIN, fund, jet, lavacre, laver, origin, piscina, source, spring, stoop, stoup, type

FONTANEL fenestra, mo(u)ld, seton, vacuity

FOOD (See also *kind,* below.) aliment, ambrosia, amrita, bait, bit, board, bread, broma, buffet, bulk, cate(s), cheer, chow, chuck, cibo, comestible, cuisine, diet, dish, dodger, eats, edibles, fare, fauster, feast, feed, fodder, forage, grub, hash, ingesta, kai, kaukau, keep, manna, meal, menu, mess, morsel, nourishment, nurture, nutriment, ort, pab(u)lum, pap, pasta, pasto, peckage, plate, provand, provender, provisions, ration(s), scaff, scoff, scran, snack, stover, sustenance, table, terefa, terefe,

toke, tommy, trencher, tucker, viands, victuals, vivers

additive cyclamate, monosodium glutamate, msg, nitrite, nitrogen, trichloride

and drink bouche, bouge, cheer, diet, fare, found, provisions

and lodging board and room, easement, found

aversion apositia, asitia, cibophobia, sitophobia

bad cagmag

between meals bagging, snack

choice cates

comb. sito, troph(o)

container bowl, box, canister, crock, dish, jar, olla, plate, platter, saucer

craving for appetite, bulimia, pica, sitomania

craving for one kind monophagia

daily bread, tucker

devotee epicure, gourmet

dislike See *aversion,* above.

divine ambrosia, madhu, manna

element carbohydrate, gluten, protein, vitamin

eton battel

extra gash, seconds

filling stodge

flavorless hogwash

fragment ort

garnish gravy, parsley, sauce, socle

gods' ambrosia, amreeta, amrita, manna, nectar

ground dust

health blackstrap molasses, brewer's yeast, fruit, grits, liver, middlings, milk, nuts, peanut flour, rice polish, soybeans, wheat germ, wholewheat, yog(h)urt

invalid broth, custard, gruel, milk-toast, pap

kind acate, ambrosia, ants, aperient, appetizer, balut, beebread, beef, beverage, biscuit, boscage, bouche, bread, broma, bun, cagmag, cake, cereal, cheese, chum, chop, condiment, cooky, cornbread, crumb, dressing, dumpling, egg, farina, fish, forage, fowl, fruit, gruel, hominy, ice cream, jelly, meat, mush, mutton, nuts, pancake, pap, pastry, pemmican, pie, poi, pork, pud-

ding, puree, sago, salep, sandwich, sausage, scaff, shellfish, soup, steak, stew, sweets, tapioca, tripe, veal, vegetable

lack, comb. atrophia

leftover hash

liquid beverage, broth, eggnog, gruel, leban, slop, soup, spoonmeat, supping

list carte, diet, menu

meatless maigre

miraculous manna

mixed panache, salmagundi

pert. cibarian, cibarious, refete

place automat, cafe(teria), diner, diningroom, RESTAURANT

plant soia, taro

protein cheese, egg, fish, meat, milk, soybeans

provide cater, mess, ration, scaff

refuse garbage, swill

scraps scram, swill

seller grocer, viander

semi-digested chyme

semi-liquid swill

sliced leach

soft pap

southern chitterling, greens, grits, hoecake, hominy, okra, pone

special bredi, cabeliau, cabilliau, chowder, colcannon, galantine, haslet, hautgout, hogo, majoon, olla, omelet(te), pandana, pilaf(f), pilau, pilaw, pizza, ragout, rarebit, ravioli, salmagundi, salmis, scouse, shish-kebab, sillabub, souffle, stew, succotash, sukiyaki, sundae, tzimmis

starchy amyloid, macaroni, noodles, pasta, potato, spaetzle, spaghetti, tous-lemoi, vermicelli

strips julienne

unclean terephah, tref

warmed up rechauffe

watery slipslop

worker's tommy

FOOFAROW disturbance, finery, fuss, ornamentation, uproar

FOOL, FOOL'S 3 ass, bum, col, faw, gom, kid, nut, oaf, sap, sop, sot **4** boob, boor, butt, cake, calf, chub, clod, colt, cram, cuif, daft, dolt, dope, drag, dupe, gaby, geck, goon, gowk, gull, gump,

hoak, jape, jerk, joke, marr, mock, mome, narr, nizy, putz, raca, simp, yold, zany 5 ament, antic, bluff, booby, buffo, cheat, chump, clown, comic, cozen, cully, dobby, dummy, dunce, fally, gabby, golem, goose, idiot, looby, moron, ninny, noddy, nonny, patch, schmo, silly, softy, spoof, sumph, totty, trick, yokel 6 badaud, bayard, bedote, buffle, cretin, cuckoo, cudden, delude, dimwit, donkey, doodle, dotard, dummel, fizgig, foozle, hobbil, jester, lubber, nitwit, noodle, putter, simple, spoony, stooge, wampas 7 asinego, becasse, buffoon, bungler, coxcomb, deceive, dizzard, dullard, fathead, flummox, gudgeon, halfwit, juggins, lughead, lunatic, mislead, natural, palooka, saphead, schmuck, stookie, witling 8 boeotian, bonehead, codshead, comedian, dumbbell, hoodwink, imbecile, lunkhead, meathead, mooncalf, numskull, ridicule, sillyass, softhead 9 blockhead, fopdoodle, hoddypeak, hoddypoll, ignoramus, infatuate, lamebrain, pantaloon, philander, simpleton 10 bufflehead, enthusiast, hoddydoddy, jobbernowl, nincompoop, rattlepate 11 blunderhead, chowderhead, merry andrew, ninnyhammer, puddinghead, shallowpate 12 featherbrain, scatterbrain
around dally, experiment, idle, interfere, jive, kibitz, lallygag, meddle, play, skylark, trifle
away spend, squander, waste
bauble cap and bells, geegaw, marotte
born mooncalf
cap cockscomb, coxcomb
coat goldfinch
-fire jack-a-lantern
gold pyrite
hay witchgrass
hen grouse
-large prodigal
learned morosoph
natural innocent
paradise chimera, illusion, limbo, prism

perfect wynn
sage jester
stitch tricot
stones orchid

FOOLHARDY adventurous, audacious, bold, brash, breakneck, daredevil, daring, desperate, harebrained, headlong, heedless, icarian, impetuous, incautious, presumptuous, rash, reckless, temerarious, venturesome, venturous

FOOLISH absurd, addlebrained, addlepated, anserine, anserous, asinine, balmy, barmy, batty, buggy, cockeyed, confused, crazy, daffy, daft, desipient, dilly, dippy, dizzy, dottle, dumb, fatuitous, fatuous, flighty, fond, gaga, goofy, goosy, gowkit, harebrained, harish, idiotic, illogical, imbecile, imbecilic, imprudent, inane, inept, insane, irrational, laughable, lightheaded, loony, ludicrous, mad, maudlin, momish, moronic, noddy, nonsensical, nutty, potty, preposterous, puerile, raca, rash, ridiculous, sappy, sawney, screwy, senseless, shanny, silly, simple, soft, spoony, stupid, trivial, unintelligent, vacant, vain, wacky, witless, zany
render imbecilitate

FOOLISHNESS absurdity, barney, bopkes, buncombe, bunkum, bupkes, fatuity, folly, insipience, levity, lunacy, naarishkeit, narrishkeit, tommyrot

FOOLPROOF easy, impervious, never-failing, plain, risk-free, safe, secure, simple

FOOSTER flurry, fluster, fussiness

FOOT add, base, basis, bottom, cast, dance, discharge, dog, establish, extremity, fetlock, foundation, gambone, goer, heel, hoof, infantry, instep, kick(er), measure, meter, nadir, pace, pad, pastern, pat(te), paw, pay, pedestal, pedestrian, pedicel, pedis, pes, pied, plan, pode, prosaic, pud, rank, rhythm, settle, skip, sole, spurn, sum,

tootsy, tot(al), trilby, trotter, ungula, walk(er)
absence apodia
and mouth disease aftosa, aphthous fever, aptha, murrain
animal hoof, pad, pastern, paw, trotter
bath pediluvium
bench banquette
blower bellows
board treadle
bone astragal(us), calcis, metatarsus, naviculare, scaphoid, tarsus
bone abnormality talipes, varus
comb. ped(i), pedo, pod, pode, podo
corn agnail
covering See FOOTWEAR and SHOE.
cushion brioche
deformity cyllosis, ectodactylism, equinovarus, planus, talipes, varus
disease gout
distorted taliped
doctor chiropodist, podiatrist
dragging slodge
false pseudopodium
fore pud
gear See FOOTWEAR and SHOE.
going on pedality
having pedate
having long dolichopodous
injection quittor
-jaw maxilliped
landraker footpad, tramp
lever pedal, treadle
-licker (See FLATTERER.) sycophant, toady
-licking obsequious
-like pedate
-like part pes
-loose ambulatory, fancyfree, free, nomadic, unattached, uncommitted, untrammeled, wandering
metrical amphimacer, anap(a)est, antibacchius, antidactyl, antispast, arsis, bacchius, choriamb, dactyl, diamb, dochmius, epitrite, iamb(ic), ionic, molossus, paeon, pyrrhic, spondee, syzygy, tribrach, trimacer, tripody, triseme, trochee
metrical, part arsis, semeion, thesis
muscle abductor, opponens, quadratus
oar-shaped remiped

ornamental cabriole
pain talagia
part ankle, arch, astragal, calcis, digit, heel, inch, instep, metatarsus, pastern, scaphoid, sole, tarsus, thenar, toe, unguis, ungula
pert. pedal, pedary, pedate, podal(ic)
pick casc(h)rom
poetic See *metrical*, above.
post mailman
race cross-country, dash, diaulos, marathon, mile, sprint
red boobybird
rot claw-sickness, mal-di-gomma, take-all
-shaped pediform
-slogger infantryman
soldier See SOLDIER *infantry.*
sole planta
pert. plantar, volar
study of podiatry
support hassock, ottoman, stool
tap appel
the bill pay, settle
traveler pedestrian, walker
treatment chiropody, pedicure
tubercle parapodium
-washing nipter
washing rite maundy
worked by lever, pedal, treadle

FOOTAGE board-feet, length, setup
FOOTBALL hurly, leather, pigskin, podosfero, rugby, rugger, soccer
center snapper-back
coach, famous bryant, devine, hayes, jones, layden, leahy, lombardy, mckay, parseghian, rockne, royal, stagg, thornhill, waldorf, wilkinson, yost
field gridiron
group nfl
kick punt, spiral
pass flare, forward, hook, lateral
play block, buck, conversion, crisscross, crossbuck, cut back, fake, pass, spinner
player gridder
position back, center, cornerback, end, fullback, guard, halfback, linebacker, quarterback, slotback, tackle, tailback
rugby fives

score conversion, down, field-goal, goal, safety, touchback, touchdown
team eleven
term blitz, block, bomb, buttonhook, clipping, conversion, cornerback, cover, cut, defense, dive, down, drive, endzone, fake, flanker, flood, fumble, goal, hand-off, hashmark, hitch, hook, inside, interception, interference, kick, line, offside, onside, pass, penalty, pileup, pitchout, pocket, post, punt, red dog, runback, safety, scramble, screen, scrimmage, secondary, slant, snapback, sweep, tackle
trophy heisman
FOOTBOY attendant, page, pedes
FOOTBRIDGE ligger, plank
FOOTED hoofed, pedate, pedigerous
cloven fissiped(al), fissipedate, satanic
large megapod
multiple biped(al), multiped, octopod
FOOTER clown, idle, potter, trifle, walker
FOOTFALL pace, pad, step, tread
FOOTFOLK infantry
FOOTHOLD advantage, bridgehead, footing, overshoe, purchase, sandal, stance, standing, step, toehold
FOOTING base, basis, condition, dance, fee, foothold, foundation, groundwork, progress, purchase, rank, standing, station, status, step, support, terms, total, track, tread, walk
good rapport
regain sprottle
FOOTLE drivel, nonsense, potter, trifle, twaddle
FOOTLESS apod(al), apodous, awkward, clumsy, helpless, inept, inefficient, stupid, unsubstantiated
FOOTLIGHTS broadway, drama, floats, stage, theater
FOOTLOCK bilbo, fetlock
FOOTMAN bottomer, chasseur, doorman, flunky, footpad, hircarra, jeames, lackey, menial, pedestrian,

shackatory, servant, valet, varlet, walker
FOOTNOTE documentation, explanation, memorandum
FOOTPACE carpet, dias, mat, platform, predella, rug
FOOTPAD bandit, brigand, bushranger, gangster, hightoby, highwayman, hijacker, holdup(man), hood, landraker, marauder, robber, stick-up-man, thief, thug, whyo
FOOTPATH drung, jetty, lane, rampire, semita, senda, sidewalk, trail, trottoir
FOOTPRINT ichnite, ichnolite, impression, mark, prick, pug(mark), trace, track, tread
fossil ichnite, ichnolite
fossil, study of ichnology
mold moulage
FOOTREST footstool, hassock, rail, stirrup
FOOTSORE spent, surbate, tired, (way)weary
FOOTSTALK pedicel, peduncle, petiole, stem, strig
FOOTSTALL base, pedestal, plinth, stirrup
FOOTSTEP pace, pad, track, tread, trod, vestige
FOOTSTONE base, memorial, pedestal
FOOTSTOOL buffet, cricket, hassock, mora, ottoman, samble, tut
FOOTWAY banquette, catwalk, path
FOOTWEAR arctic, balmoral, blucher, boot(ee), bootikin, bottekin, bottine, brogan, brogue, buskin, button shoe, caliga, chaussure, chimela, clodhopper, clog, cobcab, cothurn(us), crackow, creeper, finnesko, galosh, gamash, gambado, gumshoe, hessian, hipboot, hobnail, horseshoe, hosiery, huarache, jackboot, juliet, kamil, kick, larrigan, loafer, lounger, moccasin, moggan, mukluk, mule, napoleon, overshoe, oxford, pac(k), pantofle, patten, poulaine, pump, ridingboot, romeo, rubber, rullion, sabot(ine), saddleshoe, sandal, scuff, secque, shoe, slipper, slogger, sneaker, snowshoe, sock, stepin, stocking, stogie, tabi, veldschoen,

wedgie, wellington, wooden shoe

FOOTY mean, paltry, poor, worthless

FOOZLE blunder, booboo, botch, bungle, fog(e)y, fool

FOP adonis, beau(brummel), buck, coxcomb, dandy, dude, dupe, exquisite, fancy dan, fool, gimcrack, jessamy, macaroni, muscadin, nob, popinjay, prig, pup(py), skipjack, spanglebaby, spark, swell, toff, trig

FOPPISH buckish, conceited, dandiacal, dandified, dandy, dashing, finical, foolish, impetuous, lively, sappy, silly, spruce

FOPPISHNESS dandyism, macaronicism

FOR because, concerning, despite, favoring, fornont, inasmuch as, in behalf of, in favor of, in order that, instead, namely, notwithstanding, on account of, on behalf of, per, pro, since, till, toward

a fact certainly

ages forever, long(time)

all that notwithstanding

all time eternal, forever

all voices tutti

a moment briefly

as much as seeing that, since, so far as

a song cheap

a time ephemeral, meanwhile

cash spot

each apiece, per

example incidentally, vide

fear that lest

free gratis

glory ad gloriam

good and all forever, utterly

hire venal

instance say

keeps forever, real

life ad vitam, eternally, forever, lasting

nothing free, gratis, gratuity, lagniappe, lanyap

shame fie, shocking

some time awhile

that reason ergo, hence, therefore

the most part feckly, generally, mainly, normally, substantially, usually

the nonce ephemeral, meanwhile, once, today

the time being temporarily

this case alone ad hoc, temporary

this reason because, ergo, hence, therefore

two a deux

FORAGE cater, chow, eatage, eats, ers, feed, fodder, food, grub, maraud, mast, pillage, plunder, provender, provisions, raid, ravage, russud, scrounge, search, spoil, stover, viands, victuals

plant alfalfa, alfilaria, alsike, barajillo, clover, corn, desmodium, guar, hay, ichu, lucern(e), pin-grass

FORAGER harbinger, messenger, outrider, soldier

FORAMEN aperture, exostome, fenestra, metapore, opening, orifice, perforation, pore

FORAMINIFERA camerina, camerinid, globigerina, gromia, nummulitid, polystomella, rhizopod

FORAY booty, chappow, hership, incursion, inroad, invasion, pillage, rade, ravage, razzia, sally, sortie, spoils, spreagh, spreath

FORBEAR abnegate, abstain, ancestor, avoid, bridle, cease, curb, decline, desist, don't, endure, escape, eschew, forgo, give up, inhibit, lose, miss, parent, part with, pause, refrain, resist, restrain, sacrifice, shun, spare, stop, tolerate, wait, withdraw

FORBEARANCE abstinence, avoidance, charity, clemency, forgiveness, grace, indulgence, leniency, lenity, longanimity, longsuffering, mercy, mildness, patience, pity, placability, resignation, temperance, tolerance

FORBEARING clement, gentle, humane, humanitarian, indulgent, lenient, merciful, mild, patient, tolerant

FORBES fifty cents, four bits, half-dollar

FORBID accurse, ban(ish), bar, blast, challenge, debar, defy, deny, disallow, enjoin, exclude, forestall, forfend, gainsay, hinder, impede, inhibit, interdict, obviate, oppose, preclude, prevent, prohibit, proscribe, refuse,

rule out, taboo, tabu, veto, warn off

FORBIDDEN banned, contraband, denied, out of bounds, prohibited, taboo, tabu, verboten

city lassa, lhasa

fruit allurement, apple, prohibition, shaddock

FORBIDDING austere, black(browed), displeasing, dour, fierce, gloomy, grim, hard, hideous, offensive, repellant, scowling, severe, stern, strict, ugly, unpleasant

FORBYE along, aside, before, beside(s), beyond, close, hardby, in addition, near, over and above, past, superior

FORCE 3 arm, gut, jam, vim, vis 4 biod, birr, body, bull, cram, crew, dint, elod, guts, jamb, main, make, move, odyl, oust, pack, push, tamp, urge 5 agent, brawn, break, brunt, cause, clamp, crush, draft, evict, exact, exert, expel, group, impel, might, order, point, posse, power, press, punch, shock, sinew, speed, staff, stuff, throw, vigor, wrest, wring 6 agency, attack, coerce, compel, duress, effect, effort, energy, enjoin, impact, import, insist, oblige, police, ravish, seduce, spirit, strain, stress, thrust, troops, wrench 7 advance, cogency, command, detrude, dragoon, faculty, headway, impetus, impress, impulse, meaning, obtrude, potency, require, squeeze, tension, torsion, trample, violate 8 activity, affinity, bear down, bludgeon, coercion, emphasis, exaction, exertion, momentum, pressure, strength, validity, velocity, violence, virility 9 blackmail, conscript, employees, extortion, influence, intensity, multitude, personnel, puissance, strongarm, vehemence 10 compulsion, constraint, importance, obligation 11 consequence, necessitate, requirement, steamroller 12 sledgehammer

air blow

alleged biod, elod, odic, odyl(e)
apart sunder
armed army, conrey, marines, navy, posse
back blanch, rambarre, repel
bring by hale
by amain
concentrated pith
creative elan-vital
divine numen
down clew, clue, cram, detrude, jam, stuff, tamp
electromotive becquerel effect
from grab, seize, wrest
god ment, ptah, shu
hypothetical See *alleged*, above.
impelling impetus, impulse, momentum, motive
into smaller space compress, cram, jam
kind army, battalion, bionergy, cadre, dynam, dyne, elod, enemy, fleet, fohat, legion, nature, posse, reinforcement, sanction, steam, task, voltage, wering
life shakti
mental afflatus
onward forge (ahead), propel, urge
open breach, burst, jimmy, ram
opposing yang, yin
out discharge, dismiss, drive out, eject, erupt, evict, expel, express, extrude, extund
overpowering juggernaut
passage bore, squeeze
personification bia
pert. odic
rotation torque
sacred kami
science of dynamics, kinetics, mechanics, physics
special green berets
theoretic See *alleged*, above.
to do without deny, deprive
unit dyne, kinit, newton, volt
vital bionergy
with full amain
FORCED artificial, begrudging, binding, compelled, compulsory, constrained, contrived, falsetto, grudging, involuntary, labored, obligatory, required, spontaneous, stiff, strained, unnatural
FORCEFUL cogent, dynamic, eloquent, emphatic,

energetic, mighty, pithy, potent, powerful, puissant, punchy, stringent, strong, titanic, valid, violent, virile
FORCEFULLY amain, bigly
FORCEMEAT boudin, farce, godiveau, quenelle, stuffing
FORCEPS bulldog, clammer, crowbill, detangra, dog, furca, goosebill, pincette, pinchers, pinsons, pliers, tenail, tongs, vulsella
FORCER chest, coffer
FORCIBLE coercive, compulsory, energetic, forceful, high-pressure, impetuous, impressive, influential, mighty, necessary, obligatory, potent, powerful, strong-arm, valid, vigorous, violent, weighty
FORCIBLY amain, cogently, hardly, mainly, mightily, perforce, potently, strongly, vigorously, violently
FORD bridge, cross(ing), current, flivver, model-t, passage, shoal, span, stean, steen(ing), stream, tin lizzy, wade, wathstead
FORDWINE decay, dwindle
FORE advanced, afore, ahead, antecedent, anterior, because of, before, beginning, earlier, first, former(ly), front, further, past, previous(ly), prior, van
and aft throughout, utterly
and aftbeam carlin(e), carling
comb. anter(o)
FOREARM antebrachium, cubit(al), cubitus, ensure, get ready, insure, prepare
bone radius, ulna
pert. cubital, ulnar
FOREBODE augur, betide, betoken, croak, divine, dread, fear, forecast, foretell, forewarn, import, omen, ominate, portend, predict, premonish, presage, prognosticate, prognostication, prophesy, signify, threaten
FOREBODING anticipation, anxiety, apprehension, augury, black, bodement, croaking, druther, forefeeling, forewarning, gloomy, intimation, menacing, misgiving, omen, ominous, pall, pessimistic, prediction,

premonition, premonitory, presage(ment), presentiment, prognostic, sinister, threaten(ing), warning
FOREBOW beak, breast, pommel, shoulder
FOREBRAIN cerebrum, diencephalon, prosencephalon, telencephalon
FORECAST adumbrate, anticipate, apprehend, augur, auspicate, bode, calculate, calculation, call, caution, conjecture, contrive, design, divine, estimate, figure, forebode, foredeem, foreknow, foreordain, forescent, foresee, foreshadow, fortune, guess, omen, plan, portend, predetermine, predict(ion), prefigure, presage, prognosis, prognostication, prophecy, prophesy, read, scheme, suggest, surmise, umbrate
FORECASTER dopester, meteorologist, nostradamus, oracle, prognosticator, prophet, seer, sibyl, soothsayer, sorcerer, tipster, tout
FORECASTLE focsle
FORECLOSE bar, block, debar, dispossess, hinder, preclude, prevent, shut out
FORECOURT cour d'honneur
FOREDO abolish, destroy, exhaust, kill, ruin, undo
FOREDOOM destiny, fate, forecast, predestinate, predict
FOREFACE cushion
FOREFATHER ancestor, antecedent, elder, for(e)bear, forerunner, grandsire, parent, pitri, progenitor, sire
-cup pitcherplant, sarracenia
FOREFEELING foreboding, premonition, presentiment
FOREFINGER index, pointer
FOREFOOT bind, gripe, paw, pud
FOREFOOTING mangana
FOREFRONT van(guard), vaward
FOREGATHER assemble, consort, convene, encounter, fraternize, meet
FOREGO abdicate, abnegate, abstain, deny, dispense (with), forsake, leave, neglect, overlook, precede, re-

frain, relinquish, renounce, resign, waive

FOREGOER ancestor, example, forerunner, predecessor

FOREGOING above, aforesaid, antecedent, anterior, former, past, precedent, preceding, previous, prior

FOREGONE past, previous
conclusion certainty

FOREHAND(ED) anticipative, early, front, heading, prudent, thrifty, timely

FOREHEAD assurance, brow, frons, front, metopion, modesty, sinciput
bone glabella
comb. fronto
fringe bangs
high leptene
indentation stop
mark kumkum
measurer besiclometer
muscle frontalis
pert. frontal, metopic, sincipital
projection antinion
strap tump

FOREIGN abroad, accidental, adventitious, alange, alien, barbaric, distant, distasteful, ecdemic, epigene, exallotriote, excluded, exiled, exotic, external, extraneous, extraneous, extrinsic, forane, frammit, incompatible, incongruous, inconsistent, inconsonant, obnoxious, outer, outlandish, outside, peregrine, privy, remote, repellent, repugnant, strange, tramontane, unco
aid organization care, oxfam, red cross
comb. xeno
exchange agio(tage), batta
exchange expert cambist
legion center sidi bel abbes
name meaning barbara
office consulate, embassy, legation
quarter barrio, enclave, ghetto
service official ambassador, attache, consul, diplomat, legate
service residence consulate, embassy
to dehors

FOREIGNER advena, alien, barbarian, emigre, gringo, haole, immigrant, outlander, outsider, pardesi,

peregrine, stranger, tramontane

FOREIGNNESS extraneity

FOREKNOW anticipate, apprehend, conclude, divine, foresee, gather, infer, preconceive

FOREKNOWLEDGE foresight, presage, prescience, prevision

FORELAND headland, point, promontory

FORELAY ambush, hinder, obstruct, waylay

FORELIMB arm

FORELOCK bang, cotter, cowlick, daglock, linchpin, quiff, topping, toupet, tuft

FOREMAN boss, bull, capataz, caporal, captain, chargeman, chief, cork, doggy, gaffer, ganger, headman, joss, leader, manager, overman, overseer, ramrod, sirdar, skidder, snapper, steward, strawboss, superintendent, supervisor
office bean-house

FOREMOST ace, acme, banner, before, best, capital, chief, FIRST, forme, front, grand, head, high, important, leading, main, paramount, preceding, preeminent, premier, principal, superior, supreme, top, van
part acron, bow, front, scout, van, vaward

FORENOON antemeridian

FORENSIC argumentative, debate, dialectic(al), disputation, polemical, rhetorical
pert. argument, debate, jurisprudence, law, rhetoric

FOREORDAIN date, destine, doom, forecast, forsay, predestinate, predestine, predetermine, predicate, predoom, slate

FOREPART breast, front, stomacher

FOREPOLE lagging, lath, spile, spiling

FORERUN announce, antecede, anticipate, foreshadow, forestall, harbinger, herald, introduce, outrun, precede, precourse, prefigure, prelude, scout, usher

FORERUNNER ancestor, augury, avant-courier, bushwhacker, forefather, foreganger, foregoer, fourrier,

frontiersman, harbinger, herald, messenger, omen, pioneer, portent, precedent, precursor, predecessor, presage, prodrome, progenitor, prognostic, sign, usher, voorlooper, voortrekker, warning

FORESEE divine, envisage, envision, FORECAST, previse, prospect, purvey, read

FORESHADOW figure, FORECAST, forerun, foretype, herald, hint, prelude, umbrate

FORESHANK shin

FORESHORE beach, coast, littoral, ripa, strand

FORESHORTEN abbreviate

FORESIGHT acumen, anticipation, clairvoyance, discretion, divination, esp, forethought, perception, prediction, prenotion, prescience, prevision, prevoyance, prospect, providence, prudence, sagacity, shrewdness, vision

FORESIGHTED alert, astute, cag(e)y, canny, careful, circumspect, designing, discreet, judicious, knowing, precautious, prescient, provident, prudent, sagacious, sage, sapient, sensible, shrewd, wise

FOREST arden, bois, boscage, bush, caatinga, calydon, cluster, coppice, copse, country, dito, firth, gapo, glade, grove, gubat, jungle, rukh, selva, sherwood, silen(us), silva, sylvan, taiga, timber, tract, trees, waste, weald, wilderness, wold, wood(land), woods
antelope banded duiker, bongo
city cleveland, portland, savannah
clearing camas(s), glade, quamash
decaying floor duff
deity aegipan, ardena, artemis, diana, driad, faun, pan, saturn, satyr, seilenos, silen(us), silvanus, sylvanus, tane, tapio, vidar, viribus, vitharr
demon lesh(e)y, lesiy
destroyed by fire brule
division ward
fire locator alidade
flooded seasonally gapo
fly horsetick

glade camas(s), clearing, quamash
growth underbrush, vert
huge montana
keeper ranger, waldgrave, warden, woodward
land for tillage thwaite
love of nemophily
magic broceliande
pert. nemoral, silvan, sylvan, woodland
rain selva
road ride, riding, trail
small coppice, grove, thicket
stunted caatinga, krummholz
subarctic taiga
warden See *keeper,* above.
waterway igarape
-white penistone
FORESTALL anticipate, avert, beset, circumvent, devance, foil, frustrate, intercept, monopolize, obstruct, obviate, preclude, prevent, thwart, ward off
FORESTER frontiersman, montero, ranger, tineman, treeman, walker, wood(s)-man, woodward
FORESTRY silviculture
FORETASTE antepast, anticipation, antipasto, earnest, gust, hansel, hors d'oeuvre, pledge, prelibation, prospect, teaser
FORETELL augur, bespeak, betoken, bode, caution, disclose, divine, divulge, erst, forebode, forecast, foresay, foreshadow, foreshow, halsen, herald, insee, portend, predicate, predict, prefigure, presage, proclaim, prognosticate, prophesy, read, reveal, soothsay, spae, vaticinate, warn
comb. spae
FORETELLING fatidical, PROPHECY, prophetic
FORETHOUGHT anticipation, calculation, caution, discretion, forecast, foresight, judgment, premeditation, prepense, pronoea, providence, prudence, sense, wisdom
FORETOKEN augur(y), auspicate, badge, forecast, foreshow, foresign, harbinger, herald, indicate, mark, note, omen, presignify, portend, portent, precursor, prognostic(ate),

promise, sign, symptom, token
FORETOOTH biter, cutter, incisor
FOREVER ad infinitum, ake, always, aye, ceaselessly, constantly, continually, endlessly, eternally, eterne, eternity, everlastingly, everly, evermore, for all time, for keeps, in aeternum, incessantly, interminably, invariably, perennially, permanently, perpetually, perpetuity, semper, unceasingly, unchangeably, unendingly, world without end
FOREWARN See FORETELL.
FOREWARNING advice, caution, hint, omen, portent, premonition
FORFEIT abandum, bete, cost, crime, damages, dedit, deodand, deposit, fine, forfault, forgo, ken, lapse, lose, misdeed, mulct, pawn, penalty, relinquish, surrender, tine, wite
paid philopena
FORFEITURE abandum, amercement, confiscation, crime, dedit, fine, loss, mulct, penalty, sin, tinsel, tort, transgression
FORFEND avert, forbid, preserve, prevent, prohibit, protect, secure
FORGATHER See FOREGATHER.
FORGE beat, bloomery, chafery, click, coin, contrive, counterfeit, create, fabricate, factory, falsify, fashion, feign, form, foundry, furnace, frame, imitate, make, manufacture, mint, pound, produce, shape, smithy, steady, stithy, swinge
ahead crowd, drive, hustle, press on, push on
bellows and anvil smithery
tongs teu, tew(el), tuarn, tue
waste dross, sprue
FORGED artificial, bogus, counterfeit, fake(d), fraudulent, mock, sham, spurious
FORGEMAN (black)smith
FORGERY counterfeit, fabrication, fake, feigning, fiction, pseudograph, sham
FORGET absolve, acquit,

charge off, disregard, disremember, draw a blank, excuse, fluff, forgive, ignore, lapse, lose sight of, neglect, oblite, omit, overlook, pardon, remit, slight, unknow, unmind, write off
everything black out
-me-not bluet, caterpillar, eye-bright, myosote, myosotis, oreocarya
oneself anger, muse, neglect
one's lines fluff
FORGETFUL absent-minded, amnemonic, amnesic, amnestic, careless, heedless, inattentive, inconsiderate, insensible, lax, letheian, neglectful, negligent, nirvanic, oblivious, remiss, slack, unmindful
FORGETFULNESS amnesia, carelessness, fluff, fugue, hypomnesia, lethe, manasseh, negligence, oblivion, paramnesia
psychological repression, suppression
river of lethe
tree of lotus
water of lethe
FORGIVE absolve, acquit, assoil, condone, excuse, exempt, exonerate, forget, give up, justify, moichel, overlook, palliate, pardon, purge, remit, reprieve, resign, respite, shrive, spare, vindicate
FORGIVEN excused, overlooked
capable of being venial
FORGIVENESS absolution, amnesty, compassion, condonement, dispensation, disregard, forbearance, grace, immunity, impunity, indulgence, longanimity, magnanimity, mercy, overlooking, pardon, purgation, remission, reprieve, respite
FORGIVING charitable, clement, generous, graceful, humane, magnanimous, merciful, placable
FORGO See FOREGO.
FORGOTTEN bygone, derelict, neglected, out in the cold, past, unminded
man taxpayer
FORHOO abandon, despise
FORK angle, bifurcate, bifurcation, bisect, branch, clitch, croc, crotch, crutch,

dilemma, divaricate, diverge, fourche, fruggin, gaffle, gallows, glack, graip, grom, prong, pump, search, seek, toaster, yoke
-beard hake
kind biprong, croc, evil, glack, graip, pikle, tormentor
out or *up* ante(up), deliver, give, pay, shell out, spend
pert. furcal
prong speam
3-tined runcible spoon
tuning diapason
tuning, relative pitchpipe
FORKED ambiguous, anchored, angular, bifid, bifurcated, branched, cuckolded, equivocal, forficulate, fourchee, furcal, furcate, furciform, horned, liturate, subbifid, zigzag
FORKING aborescence, bifurcation, branching, crotched, dendriform, divarication, furcation, ramification, ramous, v-shaped, y-shaped
FORKTAIL kite, swordfish
FORLET abandon, forsake, hinder, leave, prevent, renounce, yield
FORLORN abandoned, abject, alone, bereft, depressed, deserted, desolate, despairing, desperate, destitute, disconsolate, forefare, forsaken, helpless, hopeless, lone(ly), lonesome, lorn, lost, miserable, oppressed, pitiable, ruined, sad, solitary, stray, vain, vanguard, without, witlosen, wretched
FORLORNNESS blues, dejection, despair, dumps, gloom, loneliness, melancholy, sadness
FORM 3 ame, cut, fix, hew, set, use, way 4 blee, body, brew, cast, caul, chic, kind, make, mark, mint, mode, mold, plan, plot, rite, rule, rupa, seat, thew, turn, type, work 5 arise, bench, blank, block, build, carve, class, dummy, eidos, erect, forge, frame, ghost, grade, guise, image, knead, model, shape, shell, stamp, style, train, usage 6 chisel, create, devise, figure, hammer, invent, manner, method, object, ritual, schema, scheme,

school, settle, symbol, system, taille, tailor 7 address, anatomy, compose, concoct, contour, develop, fashion, gestalt, impress, liturgy, outline, pattern, produce, profile, variety, whittle 8 billhead, ceremony, conceive, contrive, describe, document, likeness, organize, rough out, skeleton 9 character, construct, establish, formation, roughcast, structure 10 apparition, appearance, constitute, convention, embodiment 12 conformation 13 configuration
absence of antropy
ancestral blastaea
assume definite crystallize
carved bust, sculpture, statuary
conventional amenity, etiquette
display manikin, rack
into chain catenate, link
irregular pseudomorph
isometric diploid
literary ballad, drama, epic, epode, essay, novel, ode, play, poetry, romance, saga, satire, sonnet, story, verse
liturgical litany, mass, service
lyrical poem, rondel, sestina
of greeting bow, curtsey, hello, sala(a)m, salute
pert. modal, morphic
pointed angle, triangle
printed acknowledgment, bill(head), blank, discharge, document, questionnaire, receipt, release, voucher, warrant
rough edge burr
spherical ball, circle, globe, orb
spiral gyre
taking different metamorphosis, protean
undeveloped rudiment
FORMAL academic, affected, angular, august, buckram, ceremonial, ceremonious, comme il faut, conventional, court(ly), dignified, exact, external, fixed, full dress, functional, functionary, imposing, lofty, logical, majestic, mannered, modal, outward, pedantic, pompous, precise, prim, proper, punctilious, regular,

rigid, ritual(istic), seemly, set, sober, social, solemn, soup-and-fish, starch(y), stately, stereotyped, stiff, stilted, studied, superficial, surface, systematic
dress black tie, dinner clothes, tails, tuxedo
FORMALDEHYDE formalin, formol, methanal, monose, preservative
FORMALIST conformist, hypocrite, pedant, ritualist, scholar, traditionalist
FORMALITY buckram, ceremony, convention, custom, etiquette, gravity, habit, law, liturgy, mummery, order, precision, primness, punctilio, requirement, rite, ritual, rule, show, solemnity, starch(iness), stereotype, stiffness, tradition, usage, use, wiggery, wont
FORMATION biome, composition, construction, echelon, establishment, file, flight, form, growth, herse, line, organization, plasmation, rock, structure
ecological biome
geological atoll, culm, curtain, ione, ledge, lia, matawan, potomac, schist, tapeats, terrain, terrane
land boothal
military echelon, flight, herse, line, tertia
FORMATIVE creative, derivative, morphotic, plastic, pliable, pliant
FORMED built, constituted, decided, manufactured, matured, organized, settled, shaped, wrought
comb. plast
crudely roughhewn
elsewhere allothogenic
from above catogene
imperfectly abortive
ingeniously d(a)edal
in place authigenic, authigenous
FORMER aforesaid, alder antecedent, anterior, before-mentioned, cidevant, earlier, elder, erst, firster, foregoing, late, nee, old, once, onetime, past, precedent, preceding, previous, prior, quondam, sometime, umwhile, whilom
ages antiquity
FORMERLY aforetime, ago,

autrefois, beforetime, ere, erst(while), heretofore, nee, of old, of yore, once, prior, quondam, then, umquhile, whilst

FORMICATION creeps, paresthesia

FORMICID ant, camponotus, emmet

FORMIDABLE awful, brave, dauntless, difficult, dire, doughty, dreadful, fearful, ferocious, fierce, intrepid, invincible, mean, menacing, overpowering, overwhelming, redoubtable, terrible, threatening

FORMLESS amorphic, amorphous, anidian, arupa, chaotic, crude, deformed, disembodied, doughy, featureless, fluid, inchoate, incorporeal, indefinite, indeterminate, liquid, obscure, raw, rough, rude, shapeless, unbodied, uncut, unhewn, unshaped, unshapen, vague
comb. amorph(o)

FORMLESSNESS amorphia, amorphism, chaos, obscurity, vagueness

FORMORIAN *giant* balor
god elatha

FORMOSA See TAIWAN.

FORMULA axiom, canon, catchword, combination, creed, dhikr, direction, equation, instruction, kekule, kelima, law, lurry, mantra, maxim, method, model, prescription, procedure, receipt, recipe, ritual, rume, theory
magic caract

FORMULATE articulate, assemble, author(ize), compose, create, define, devise, draft, draw, frame, indite, make, manufacture, plan, state, write

FORMULATION aphorism, definition, diction

FORMWORK shuttering

FORNENT against, alongside, beside, facing, for, toward

FORNIX arch, fold, lamella, psalis, scale, vault
-like psaloid

FORSAKE abandon, abdicate, avoid, deceive, deny, desert, discard, forego, forhoo(ie), forswear, leave, quit, refuse, reject, relinquish, renounce, repudiate,

resign, shun, spurn, surrender, withdraw
the world retire

FORSAKEN abandoned, deserted, ditched, forlorn, jilted, lasslorn, lorn, outcast, rejected, unloved

FORSETI *god of* justice, peace
parent balder, nanna

FORSOOTH certainly, even, indeed, in truth, quoth

FORSPEAK asperse, bewitch, forbid, renounce

FORSWEAR abandon, abjure, deny, desert, gainsay, perjure, recant, reject, relinquish, renounce, repudiate, retract, spurn, traverse

FORT abatis, acropolis, agger, akazava, alcazar, balistraria, banquette, barbican, barricade, bartizan, bastille, bastion, battery, battlement, bawn, blockhouse, brattice, breastwork, bretesse, bulwark, bunker, buttress, casemate, castillo, castle, citadel, closure, contravallation, cot(t)a, curtain, doon, earthwork, escarpment, estacade, etape, fastness, garrison, glacis, gota, gurry, hornwork, kame, keep, kota, la(a)ger, lis(s), lunette, machicolation, mant(e)let, merlon, mole, mound, muniment, outwork, pah, palisade, parados, parapet, post, rampart, rath, ravelin, redan, redoubt, rocca, sangar, scarp, scherm, stockade, stronghold, tenaille, tower, vallation, vallum
chamber bunker
circular martello
commander caid, qaid
fairy lis(s), shee, sidhe
garrisoned presidio
gate portcullis, sallyport
gun emplacement banquette
on hill rath
opening balistraria
outwork tenail(le)
part barbette, bastion, caponiere, redan, revelin, talus
ring ceinture
rouille toronto
ruins zimbabwe
slope glacis, talue
small bastide, gurry
trench moat

FORTE ability, aptitude, bag,

bailiwick, call(ing), cup of tea, faculty, gift, loud(ly), metier, speciality, talent, thing, vocation

FORTESCUE cobbler, fortyskewer, scorpion

FORTH abroad, accomplish, away, beyond, forward, manage, onward, outdoors, provoke

FORTHCOMING afoot, appearance, approach(able), approaching, available, exodus, future, imminent

FORTHRIGHT bald, bluff, blunt, brusque, candid, categorical, directly, downright, flatfooted, frank, gutty, immediately, plain, promptly, soon, straightforward, straightway

FORTHWITH anon, away, beden(e), betimes, directly, eft, extempore, immediately, instantly, now, presently, promptly, right away, therewith

FORTHY affable, forward, genial, officious, therefore

FORTIFICATION See FORT.
line of trocha

FORTIFIED armed, bastioned, battlemented, castled, enclosed, escheat, protected, walled

FORTIFY add, arm, bank, barricade, blockade, brace, bulwark, buttress, confirm, consolidate, countermine, defend, dig in, doctor, embank, embattle, engarrison, entrench, fence, garrison, gird, intreat, lace, man, mine, munify, munite, needle, prop up, rampire, refresh, spike, steel, strengthen, wall, ward

FORTITUDE backbone, bravery, courage, fibre, gameness, gaminess, grit, guts, hardihood, hardiness, heroism, intrepidity, mettle, nerviness, pluck(iness), resoluteness, resolution, resolve, sand, spirit, spunk (iness), stamina, strength, tenacity, tolerance

FORTNIGHT halfmonth, two weeks

FORTRESS See FORT.
flying bomber

FORTUITOUS accidental, accidentary, adventitious, casual, chance, chancy, contingent, fortunate, haphazard, happy, hit-or-miss, incidental, lucky, random, undesigned, unrequested, unsought

FORTUNATE advantageous, auspicious, beneficial, benign, blessed, blest, canny, dexter, eurous, faust, favorable, favored, felicitous, fortuitous, in luck, lucky, profitable, prosperous, providential, rosy, shree, successful, timely
islands canary islands, madeira islands
name meaning dexter, evadne

FORTUNE, FORTUNE'S accident, adventure, affair, bahi, blessing, break, bundle, capital, career, cast, chance, chronicle, destiny, doom, estate, fate, felicity, fluke, fortuity, gamble, hail, hap, hazard, hit, king's ransom, luck(iness), lucky strike, millions, mint, money, occasion, opportunity, opulence, pile, portion, pot, prosperity, riches, stake, star(s), ten-strike, the breaks, thousands, tidy sum, treasure, tyche, wad, wealth, whate, windfall
deity fortuna, lakshmi, tyche, venus-felix
favor solitaire
good bonchief, sele, sonse, speed, thrift
hunter adventurer, enterpriser, golddigger, opportunist, pirate
tell dukker
-teller augur, chaldaei, diviner, dukkeripen, gypsy, oracle, palmist, prophet(ess), seer, sibyl, sortiary, sortileger, spaeman, spaewife, spyne, sybil
-telling jadoo, jadu
wheel fate

FORTY two-score
days' fast carene, lent
-5 firearm, gun
-5 degree angle octant
43,560 square feet acre
inches ell
-niner argonaut, goldseeker, miner
piquet points capot
thieves game, napoleon at st helena, solitaire

-2 gallon cask tierce
ways in all directions
winks nap, snooze
-year-old quadragenarian

FORUM assembly, body, discussion, panel, round table, square, tribunal

FORWARD abet, accelerate, active, adelante, advance(d), advancing, afore, ahead, aid, along, arrogant, assist, assuming, audacious, awkward, back, bain, bantam, bardy, before, bold, brash, brazen, bright, champion, coarse, confident, cultivate, deliver, eager, en avant, encourage, flip, fore, forrit, forth, frack, fresh, front, further, hasten, hasty, headwards, help, impel, improve, impudent, insolent, motivate, officious, onward(s), pert, precocious, premature, progressive, promote, prompt, propel, quicken, ready, r(o)udas, saucy, send, ship, spack, speed, support, tellsome, transmit, untimely, uphold, vain, vanward(s), ventral, willing
directed antrorse
end bow
gun bow-chaser
-looking modern, with-it
march en avant, onward
-moving proal

FORWARDNESS assumption, boldness, confidence, eagerness, immodesty, meddling, officiousness, pragmatism, precocity, prematurity, presumption, readiness, zeal

FOSS(E) canal, ditch, entrenchment, graff, grave, moat, opening, trench, waterway

FOSSETTE depression, dimple, hollow, ulcer

FOSSICK potter, rummage, search

FOSSILE adapis, amber, ammonite, antiquated, balanite, calamite, calamosperma, conodont, eolith, fog(e)y, fucoid, graptolite, gyrolith, mimosite, neolith, paleolith, petrification, relic, remainder, rock, scaphite, spongoid, stone, synapsid, tarsioid
ancestral proangiosperm

arthropod trilobite
bone ivory, odontolite
comb. ite
coniferous peucite
coral alveolite, polypite
crinoid encrinite
description paleontography
egg ovulite
eurypteroid king crab, trilobite
fern psaronius
fish berrybone, coccosteus
flower antholite
footprint ichnite
fruit carpolite, carpolith
lemur adapis
locale matrix, shale
mollusk dolite
oil petrol(eum)
plant asterophyllite, calamite
resin amber, copal, retinite
science paleontology
seaweed caudagalli
seed carpolite
shell ammonite, balante, dolite
stem joint entrochite
toothlike conodont
track amphibichnite
tree amber, pinites
tree fern caulopteris
tube sciolite
turquoise ivory, odontolite
vase-shaped ventriculite
worm track nereite

FOSSILIZE age, harden, petrify

FOSTER advance, aid, befriend, breed, care for, cherish, cosset, cradle, cultivate, encourage, favor, feed, fondle, food, gratify, harbor, help, house, indulge, lodge, minister, mother, motivate, nourish, nurse, nurture, nuzzle, oblige, offspring, raise, rear, related, suckle, support, sustain, train, wet-nurse
child dalt, norry, nurry, stepdaughter, stepson

FOSTERITE boltonite

FOU bushel, foul, full, intoxicated

FOUL abusive, bad, base, bedrabble, bedraggle, bemire, beray, besmear, besmut, besoil, black(en), caitiff, clarty, coarse, collide, corrupt, defile, dirten, dirty, dreggy, entangle, evil, fetid, filthy, gross, harsh, hateful, hor(r)y, impure, indecent, loathsome, malodorous, monstrous, mucky, muss, nasty, noisome, obscene, odious, offensive, pollute(d), poor, profane, putrid, rank, repulsive, revolting, roil, rotten, rough, scurrilous, shameful, slottery, sluggish, smear, soil, squalid, stinking, stormy, sullen, sully, taint, terrible, ugly, unclean, unsporting, vile, vulgar, wretched, wrong

fiend See DEMON and DEVIL.

in marbles fulk

play chicanery, homicide, murder, perfidy, unfairness, violence

-smelling fetid, funky, olid, reeky

speaker blackmouth

up botch, bungle, chaos, complicate, confuse, confusion, crab, queer, spoil

weather storm

FOULARD handkerchief, neckerchief, silk, tie

FOULMOUTHED abusive, filthy, obscene, opprobrious, profane, r(o)udas, scurrilous, thersitical

FOULNESS dishonesty, rot

FOUND attach, base, begin, bottom, build, cast, commence, construct, create, depart, endow, equipped, erect, establish, fashion, fix, form, ground, initiate, institute, launch, melt, organize, originate, place, practice, proceed, provided, raise, settle, set(up), start, supplied, try

object trove

wanting imperfect, inferior

FOUNDATION anlage, base, basis, bed(ding), bedrock, beginning, bottom, corse(le)t, endowment, establishment, foot(ing), girdle, ground, hypostasis, installation, legacy, matrix, organization, platform, premise, reason, root(age), settlement, slab, support, underpinning, warrant

forming basal, bedrock

pert. basic, fundamental

projecting socle

wall riprap

FOUNDER archetype, architect, astonish, author, capsize, caster, collapse, crash,

creator, cripple, dismay, dum(b)found, dynast, fail, fall, go down, laminitis, miscarry, originator, planner, producer, sink, strategist, stumble, supporter, swamp, undermine, welter, yet(t)er

metal yet(t)er

pert. fundatorial

FOUNDLING changeling, derelict, find, orphan, waif

FOUNDRY bloomery, forge, furnace, smelter, smith(er)y

mold rod lance

worker's disease spelterchills

FOUNTAIN ain, aqua, fons, FONT, head, jet(d'eau), keld, lode, mine, origin, reservoir, source, spa, spray, spring, sprinkler, syke, upwelling, well

changed into byblis

deity feronia, fons

famous trevi

nymph albunea, egeria, naiad, salmacis

of hippocrene caballine

of hippocrene producer pegasus

of hippocrene site helicon

of the horse hippocrene

of youth seeker ponce de leon

of youth site bimini

pen stylo

pen inventor waterman

sacred aganippe, pierian spring

tree deodar

truthful acadine

FOUNTAINHEAD origin, source

FOUQUIERIA candlewood, ocotillo, plant

FOUR boat, card, cater, cuatro, daleth, delta, little joe, quadrate, quartet, quatre, quatro, shi, tetrad, vier

-angled quadrangular

-bagger homer, homerun, score, tally

bells ten

births quadruplets

books analects, chung-yung, lun-yu, mencius, meng-tzu, ta-hsueh

cards alike mournival

-city federation tetrapolis

comb. quadri, tessara, tetra, tetro, vier(g)

continents solitaire

-cornered quadrangular

corners skittles, solitaire

-eyes anableps

-faced quadrifrous

-5-6 acey-out, see-low, singluk

-flush bluff, deception, sham

-flusher fake, impostor, pretender, quack, tin horn, tromben(y)ik

-footed quadruped, tetrapod, tetrapous

genii of amenti amseti, duamutef, hapi, kebhsenuf

gentlemen bamboo, chrysanthemum, orchid, plum tree

gills pint

group of quadriad, quadric, quartet, quaternary, tetrad

-handed quadrumanous

horsemen conquest, death, famine, war

hundred aristocracy, bluebook, bonton, creme, elect, elite, select, society, upperclass, uppercrust

hundred originator ward mc allister

hundred years baktun

inches hand

-in-hand ascot, coach, necktie, rig, scarf, tie

intruders solitaire

kreutzers batz

-leaf clover solitaire

-man rule quadrumvirate

-metonic cycles callipic

million canaille, hoipolloi, proletariat

noble truths hinaya, mahayana

-o'clock boerhavia, friarbird, herb, marvel-of-peru, mirabilis, tea(time), torrubia

of a kind mournival, pair royal, quatorze, solitaire

of trumps tiddy

parts, divided in quadrifid

pence fippenny, flag, groat, joey

pert. quadrual, quatral

quarts gallon

rods acre

seasons solitaire

-sided quadrilateral, rectangular, square, tetragonal, tetrahedral

-sided sail lugsail

-striper captain

-syllable foot antispast

-toned chord tetrad

weddings solitaire

-wheeler barge, berlin(e), buckboard, calash, carriage, coach

-winged tetrapteran, tetrapterous

-year period pythiad, quadrennium

FOURFOLD quadruple(x), quatern, tetraploid

FOURGON baggage car, tumbril, van, wagon

FOURIERISM socialism

experiment brook farm

FOURSCORE eighty

FOURSOME bridge, quaternion, quartet, tetrad

FOURSQUARE frank, honest, open, quadrangular, rectangular

FOURTH delta, fardel, ferling, forpit, quart(er)

base home-plate

estate press

hour sext

of year raith

FOUTH fullness, fulth, plenty

FOVEA depression, fossa, pit

FOWL bantam, banty, biddy, brant, broiler, campine, c(h)apon, chicken, chucky, cock, coot, dorking, duck (ling), faisan, fryer, gadwall, galeeny, grig, grouse, hen, houdan, hunt, keel, keet, leghorn, malay, minorca, pidgeon, poult(ry), quail, rumkin, snipe, squab, sussex, turkey

castrated capette, capon

coop rip

crested topknot

crop gebbie

disease black-head, bluecomb, bumble-foot, cray, gapes, perosis, pip, pox, roup, sorehead

domestic breed ancona, andalusian, brahma, campine, cochin, cornish, dorking, hamburg, langshan, leghorn, loudan, minorca, orpington, plymouth rock, rhode island red, sussex, wyandotte

domestic pert. gallinaceous

5-toed dorking

grilled spatchcock

group flock, raft, savssat

innard giblets, lights

male chanticleer, cock(erel), drake, gander, peacock, rooster, stag, tom

parts breast, dark meat, drumstick, giblets, gizzard, heart, leg, liver, pope's

nose, thigh, white meat, wing, wishbone

pox sorehead

rump feathers cushion

small bantam, banty

stuffed farci

tailless rumkin

uropygium pope's nose

young chick(ie), poult

FOWLER birdcatcher, cannon, veuglaire

FOX asse, bagman, beguile, brown, caama, canis, corsac, cub, discolor, fennec, fool, intoxicate, karagan, muskwaki, orator, outwit, platinum, rascal, renard, reynard, sham, sour, stag, stain, stupefy, sword, tod, todlowrie, trick(ster), vixen, vulpes, yarn, zorro

and geese merels

breed arctic, blue, cape, silver

brown corsac

brush chape

dung scumber

-ears walloon

female bitch, vixen

fire armillaria, fungus, luminescence

flying kalong

foot pad

grape isabella, labrusca

gray zorro

group skulk

hole entrenchment, kennel

hunter's assistant whipperin

hunter's coat pink

hunter's costume ratcatcher

hunter's cry all on, soho, yoicks

hunter's hazard oxer

-killing vulpicide

-like alopecoid, vulpecular, vulpine

little vulpecula

male stag

pert. vulpine

plum bearberry

symbol of artifice, cunning

terrier wire-hair

trot dance, run

FOXFISH dragonet

FOXGLOVE blob, bloodyfingers, fairycap, fairyfingers, figwort, fingerflower, flapdock, gentian, herb, mullein, orchis, pitcherplant, pokeweed, popdock, thimble

leaves digitalis

FOXHOUND walker

baying belling

FOXTAIL alopeourus, brush,

bush, cauda, chape, couch, flotegrass, gamelot, kneed, pinon grass, setaria, twitch

FOXY artful, brown, crafty, crooked, cunning, deceitful, devious, dishonest, knowing, oblique, rank, retiary, shrewd, slick, sly, sour, tricky, vulpine, wily

FOY assist, faith, feast, gift, pilot

FOYER anteroom, center, crucible, entrance(hall), entry(way), fireplace, greenroom, hall, hearth, home, lobby, narthex, vestibule

FOZY fat-witted, flabby, muggy, spongy

FRA brother, friar, monk, priest

FRAB contend, nag, scold, struggle, worry

FRACAS affray, bicker, brawl, breeze, broil, commotion, disturbance, fight, fray, fuss, melee, noise, quarrel, row, ruckus, ruction, ruffle, rumbullian, rumpus, scrap, set-to, shindy, squabble, squall, stramash, touse, uproar, wrangle

FRACTABLE boltel, bottle, coping

FRACTION bit, breach, break(ing), decimal, detail, division, fracture, fragment, member, moiety, parcel, PART, piece, portion, ruction, rupture, scrap, section, sector, segment, share, uproar

part numerator, quotient

FRACTIONAL aliquot, inconsiderable, insignificant, meromorphic, numeric(al), partial

FRACTIOUS crabbed, disorderly, fretful, huffy, irascible, irritable, mean, peevish, perverse, petulent, querulous, refractory, snappish, unruly, waspish, wayward

FRACTURE breach, break, bulge, bust, cleavage, cleft, crack, discontinuity, fault, fissure, hurt, pilation, rend, rupture, severance, split

setting apothesis, diaplasis, reduction

FRACTURED broken, cracked, splintered, split

FRAGARIA See STRAW-
BERRY.
FRAGILE agile, birdlike,
breakable, brickle, brittle,
crisp, dainty, delicate, eggshell, ephemeral, feeble,
frail, frangible, friable,
frough, frow(y), infirm,
lacy, quick, shivery, short,
slattery, swack, tender,
weak
FRAGMENT ana, bit, blad,
brash, break, cantlet, catch,
chip, chunk, clout, crumb
(le), detail, division, excerpt, fraction, frustum,
gobbet, grot, gubbin, morsel, ort, part, piece, portion,
relic, remainder, remnant,
scrap, section, segment,
shard, shaving, sherd,
shred, sippet, sliver, snip,
splinter, swatch, tag end,
wisp
biographical anecdote
cut off cantle
mass brash
FRAGMENTARY broken,
disconnected, dividual, incomplete
FRAGMENTED broken,
frustulent
FRAGMENTS brockle, fardel, fitters, flinder, frush,
grots, leftovers, orts, pash,
scraps, smithers
literary analect(a), analects
FRAGRANCE aroma, attar,
aura, balm, balsam, bouq-
uet, flavor, incense, nosegay, odor, perfume, redo-
lence, savor, scent, smell,
spice, spiciness
FRAGRANT ambrosial, aromatic, balmy, delicious, delightful, odoriferous, odor-
ific, odorous, olent, redolent,
savory, scented, spicy, sweet
FRAID *hole* bomb shelter,
cellar, refuge, shelter
FRAIDY *cat* coward
FRAIL basket, beat, breakable, brittle, bruckle, crocky,
dainty, decrepit, delicate,
feeble, flimsy, fragile, frangible, gimcrack(y), ginger-
bread(y), girl, gossamery,
impotent, infirm, irresolute,
jerry(built), limp, papery,
pasteboardy, petty, pin-
dling, powerless, puny,
rush, seely, shattery, sickly,
sleazy, slender, slight,
slim(sy), tender, tenuous,

thin, trollop, unchaste, unsubstantial, wanton, way-
ward, weak, woman
FRAILTY adam, blemish,
caducity, defect, delicacy,
failing, failure, fault, flaw,
foible, fragility, humanity,
imperfection, infirmity,
shortcoming, sickliness, sin,
vice, weakness
FRAISE cajole(ry), disturbance, flatter, fray, fuss,
phrase, praise, ream(er),
ruff, strawberry, tool
FRAIST ask, attempt, experience, seek, try
FRAMB(O)ESIA bouba(s),
bubas, pian, sore, yaws
FRAME (See also *kind,
below.*) barrow, bent,
bin(n), body, border, bow,
box, buck, build, cadge,
cage, calculate, calm, cant,
carcass, case(ment), casing,
caum, cell, chasse, chassis,
compose, construct, con-
trive, cratch, crate, create,
design, devise, direct, draft,
draw up, fashion, figure,
float, forge, form(ulate),
frog, gantry, hack, haik,
heck, herse, humor, hurdle,
indite, invent, lattice
(work), make, mold, or-
ganize, originate, pattern,
physique, plan, plot, rack,
railroad, sash, scaffolding,
sess, shape, skeleton, stamp,
stenter, structure, tenter,
timbered, tressel, trestle,
truss, window sash,
wood(en)
circular cadge
cloth-stretching counter,
tenter
coffin bier
counting abacus
diving lunet(te)
drying airer, herse
embroidery hoop, tabaret,
tambour
fishing dredge
fish line cadar, cader
glass-making drosser
harness heald
kind ame, deckel, deckle,
dekle, drosser, easel, gill,
grate, hake, knape, mat,
scray, sess, sime, sley, trave
loom slay, sleigh, sley
metal-casting calm, caum
of mind bent, disposition,
humor, mood
of reference outlook

portable bier, cacaxte
ship's cant
ship's table fiddle
skin-drying herse
square quadra
stretching sledge, tent(er)
supporting horse, tressel,
trestle
timber-carrying gill
torch cresset
-up cabal, conspiracy, intrigue, machination, plot
weaving loom
window chess, sash
FRAMER cabinetmaker, carpenter, joiner
FRAMEWORK anatomy,
bail, bracketing, bustle,
cadre, cage, carcass, carriage, case, casing, chassis,
cradle, crib, design, lattice,
nacelle, outline, rack(e),
replum, scaffold, shell, skeleton, stillage, stroma, structure, support, trestle, truss
bleaching stillage
sculptor's armature
skeletal armature
skirt bustle
FRAMING armature, lathing, production, sheathing,
siding
rod bystake
FRANC *1/20th* centime
5 ecu
20 louis
FRANCE (See also
FRENCH for expressions
in translation.) blefuscu,
gallia, gaul, judy, marianne
abbey cluny, la trappe, mont
saint-michel, st denis
academy members immor-
tals
acadian cajun
actor baron, barrault, chevalier, coquelin, fernandel,
gabin, guitry, michel, mon-
tand, tati
actor, juvenile jeune-
premier(e)
actress bernhardt, rachel, re-
jane
admiral coligny, d'estaing,
grasse, villeneuve
admirer of gallophile
african province territory of
afars and issas
agent commis
airplane avion, spad
airport le bourget, orly
alb aube
albacore germon
algerian pied noire

american revolution ally de grasse, de rochambeau, lafayette

amulet porte-bonheur

animal trainer dompteuse

annuity rente

anteroom entresol

anthropologist bertillon, broca, deniker

anti-nazi maquis

aperitif dubonnet, kir, lillet

apostle st denis

arbor berceau

architect blondel, bruant, delorme, gabriel, le corbusier, le doux, lenotre, levau, mansart, perrault, perret, soufflot, viollet-le-duc

architectural style regency

army officer esterhazy

art critic goncourt

art group barbizon, fauves, fauvists, nab

art style dada(ism), fauvism, impressionism, tachisme

artist arp, barye, bonheur, bonnard, boucher, bouguereau, braque, breton, carriere, cezanne, chagall, chardin, cocteau, cormon, corot, courbet, daguerre, daubigny, daumier, david, degas, delacroix, delaunay, derain, deschamps, deveria, dore, doyen, dubuffet, duchamp, dufy, dupre, fouquet, fragonard, gaugin, gelee, gericault, gerome, greuze, gros, ingres, la fresnaye, latour, laurencin, lebrun, leger, legros, lemoine, lenain, lorrain(e), magritte, manet, matisse, millet, monet, moreau, ozenfant, pascin, pissaro, poussin, prudhon, puvis de chavannes, rapin, renoir, rouault, seurat, signac, sisley, soutine, steinlen, tanguy, tissot, toulouse-lautrec, troyon, utrillo, valadon, vernet, vigee-lebrun, villon, vlaminck, vuillard, watteau

ash laburnum

assembly of nobles champs de mars

astrologer nostradamus

astronomer flammarion, giacobini, leverrier, messier, picard

attack school grand maison

auto citroen, dauphine, pan-

hard, peugeot, renault, simca

aviator bleriot, saint-exupery

award grand prix

bachelor garcon

bacteriologist calmette, guerin, pasteur

bagpipe cornemuse, musette

bailiff huissier

ballad virelai

barn grange

battle agincourt, blenheim, crecy, tours, valmy, verdun, vimy, waterloo

battle cry montjoy(e)

battlefield flower poppy

bay arachon, biscay

beach plage, rivage, rive

bean fauve, haricot, phasel

beauty ninon

bedbug punaise

beef boeuf

beef country charolais

beige hopi

belt patte

best man garcon d'honneur

betrothal fiancailles

bib bavette

bibliophile grolier

bicycle velo

bishop bossuet

bitters amer(tume)

bluestocking bas-bleu

boat bateau, caravel(le), chaloup

bodyguard garde du corps

bond rente, tontine

book cahier

botanist audibert

bottle clavelin

bower berceau

bowl ecuelle, verriere

box caisse

boxing savate

boy garcon

brandy armagnac, calvados, cognac, marc

bread pain

bread and butter tartine

breadstick baguette

breakfast petit dejeuner

brewery brasserie

brigand macaire, routier

brush brosse

bullet mitraille

burlesque comedie bouffe

butcher charcutier

butcher shop charcuterie

cab fiacre

cab driver cocher

cabinet etagere

cafe coffee, estaminet

cake dariole, gateau

calvinist calas, huguenot

camp etape

candy bonbon, dragee

cannon aspic

canvas tente

cape hague, talma

capital paris

card game baccarat, ecarte

cardinal fleury, mazarin, richelieu

caribbean islands indes

carol noel

carpet aubusson, tapis

carriage caleche, dormeuse, fiacre

cathedral amiens, beauvais, chartres, nantes, notre dame, r(h)eims, rouen

catholic organization sillon

cavalryman argolet(ier)

cavalry trousers brogues

cave font de gaume, lascaux, trois freres

chair cacqueteuse, chaise, voyeuse

chalk steatite, talc

chanteuse piaf

chaperon gouvernante

character, bad drole

chasseur blue-devil

cheese babybel, bleu, bonbel, boursin, brie, camembert, fromage, gervais, livaroot, marcillat, marsigny, munster, pipocreme, roquefort, sanglier

cheese pie quiche(lorraine)

chemist barbier, baume, berthollet, curie, flajolet, fourcroy, friedel, gay-lussac, grignard, holbach, lumiere, moisson, monad, pasteur, sabatier

chess player danican

chest bahut, semainier

chestnut marron

chicken coq, houdan, poulet

child enfant

child, incorrigible enfant terrible

chronicler froissart, glaber, joinville

citizen citoyen

city 3 dax, gex, ham, pau 4 albi, auby, caen, laon, metz, nice, orly, sens, st lo, vaux, vimy, vire 5 agens, arles, arras, auchs, blois, brest, dijon, dinan, douai, ernee, laval, lille, lisle, lyons, macon, nancy, nerac, nesle, nimes, ornes, paris, reims, rodez, rouen, sedan, st cyr, tours, tulle, vichy 6 aachen, amiens, angers, annect, calais, cannes, colmar, epinal, grasse, lemans, longwy, menton, nantes, nevers, pantin, rennes, rheims, sarlat, senlis, sevres, toulon, troyes, valoix, vannes, verdun, vienne 7 alencon, antibes, avignon, baretes, bayonne, belfort, bourges, cambrai, chartre, le havre, limoges, lourdes, orleans, roubaix, st cloud, st denis, valence, vouvray 8 asnieres, aurignac, beauvais, besancon, biarritz, bordeaux, boulogne, cantigny, colombes, grenoble, harfleur, mulhouse, narbonne, poitiers, rochelle, soissons, toulouse 9 abbeville, agincourt, compiegne, marseille, montauben, perpignan, st etienne, st nazaire, st quentin 10 argenteuil, carcassone, strasbourg, versailles 11 aix les bains, armentieres, montpellier 12 valenciennes 13 aix en province, aix la chapelle, aubervilliers 15 clermontferrand, st germain en laye

cleric abbe

cloak manteau

cloth See *fabric*, below.

cloud nuage, nue

coach fiacre

cocklebur caesarweed

coffee style au lait

coin agneau(x), agnel, blanca, blank, cavalier, centime, decime, denier, dizain(e), ecu, franc, gros, henri d'or, liard, livre, louis (d'or), mail, napoleon, obole, obolus, parisis, rial, saiga, scute, sol, sou, testo(o)n

colonial governor cadillac

comedian tati

comedy sotie

commune albi, ancre, carnac, cenon, croix, dole, laon, laval, nerac, pau, pessac, reze, rodez, stains, terare, ussel, vichy

composer adam, auber, berlioz, bizet, charpentier, couperin, debussy, de la halle, delannoy, delibes, d'indy, dukas, dupre, faure, franck, gluck, gounod, gretry, halevy, herold, ibert, lalo, lully, martinon, massenet, mehul, messiaen, milhaud,

offenbach, poulenc, rameau, ravel, roussel, saint-saens, satie, spontini, tevrier, thomas, varese, vitry

concrete beton

conductor lamont, martinon, morel

conqueror caesar, clovis

cook See *cuisinier*, below.

cooked meat shop rotisserie

cooking (haute)cuisine

cooking mode a la broche, a la mode, au gratin, au naturel, saute

cordial absinthe, anisette, pernod

cottage chaumiere

cotton jasmine

count comte

counter-intelligence dst

courtesan lenclos, lorette

couturier balenciaga, chanel, courreges, dior, givenchy, gres, molyneux, patou, schiaparelli, st laurent, voinet, worth

cow vache

coward lache

cowboy baille, gardian

cowslip auricula, bearsear

craftsman menuisier

creamcake dariole

critic bayle, brunetiere, diderot, ferdinand, fromentin, gourmont, le maitre, saintbeuve, suares, taine

crusader montfort

cry caira, hein, mon dieu, sacre bleu

cubist braque

cuisinier bocuse, brillatsavarin, careme, escoffier, point

cupboard etagere, secretaire

curate abbe, vicaire

currency assignat

curtain rideau, store, trideau

custom gallicism

custom house douane

daffodil polyanthus

daisy marguerite

dance allemande, apache, bal, bourree, boutade, bran(s)le, brawl, canary, cancan, cotillon, courante, farandole, gavot(te), gigue, lavolta, minuet, pas seul, quadrille, tarantelle, tordion, tripettes, valse

daybed baigneuse, recamier

day of week (1–7) lundi, mardi, mercredi, jeudi, vendredi, samedi, dimanche

dean doyen

decree arret

delicatessen charcuterie

department ain, aisne, allier, alpes-maritimes, alsace, ardeche, ardennes, ariege, aube, aude, aveyron, basrhin, basses alpes, basses pyrenees, bouches de rhon, calvados, cantal, cher, correze, cote d'or, cotes-dunord, deux-sevres, doubs, drome, eure (et loire), finistere, gard, gers, girande, haute(garonne) (loire)(marne)(saone)(savoie), herault, ille-et-vilaine, indre, isere, jura, landes, loiret, loir-et-cher, lot et garonne, manche, marne, mayenne, meuse, morbihan, nievre, nord, oise, orne, pas-de-calais, puy-de-dome, reunion, rhone, saone-etloire, sarthe, savoie, seine(et marne)(et oise) (maritime), somme, tarn, valois, var, vaucluse, vendee, vosges

department head prefet

descendent creole

designer See FRANCE *couturier*.

devil diable

dialect argo, patois

diary journal intime

dining room salle a manger

diplomat cambon, claudel, com(m)ines, de constant, genet, jusserand, lesseps, saint-simon, segur, senet, st john perse

director barrault, dassin, renoir

dish coq au vin, dieppoise, escargots, loup de mer, merguez, snails, soupe de moules, tripe

division, administrative arrondissement, canton, cercle, commune, department

division, ancient aquitaine, aquitania, arelas, arelate, arles, neustria, perche

document acte

dog briard, chien

doorkeeper concierge

double-boiler bain-marie

dramatist anouilh, augier, banville, beaumarchais, coppee, corneille, delavigne, dumas, genet, giraudoux, halevy, hugo, ionesco, labiche, lemaitre, le sage, marivaux, meilhac, moliere,

pagnol, piron, racine, rostand, sardou, scribe, vigny
drawing room salon
dresser commode
dressmaker couturier(e)
drink boire, izarra, kir,
pastis, petanque, vin
duchy aquitaine, burgundy,
luxemburg
duel affaire d'honneur
dugout abri, arai
duke duc
dungeon cachot
dwarf ferry
dynasty bourbon, ca-
pet(ian), frankish, mero-
vingian, orleans, valois
earthenware faence
ecclesiastic abbe, pere, pretre
economist cantillon, monnet,
passy, say, turgot, walras
educator buisson
egyptologist mariette, ma-
spero
elevator ascenseur
emblem fleur de lys, lily
emperor napoleon
empress beauharnais, eugenie, josephine
enamelware email, limoges
encyclopedist dalembert, diderot, voltaire
endearment petit chou
endive chicory, witloof
energy unit ampe
engineer lesseps, peronner,
sorrel, vauban
engraver callot, dore, pastre
entomologist fabre
essayist gide, montaigne
estuary gironde
ethnic group walloons
exclamation hein, mon dieu,
sacre bleu
explorer cartier, chouteau,
joliet, la salle, nicolet
eyeglass lorgnon
fabric blanchard, cambresine, cordillas, cordillat,
drap(d'or), droguet, etoffe,
lame, ras, tissu, toile
fabulist la fontaine
fairy aborde, irac, melusina
faker camelot
fan eventail
farce sotie
farmhouse mas
fashion (haute)couture
fast day jour maigre
fat day jour gras
ferret padou
festival bargemon, fete, les
trois
financier necker

fishwife poissarde
flag drapeau, tricolour
flight volee
floor etage
foie gras country landes
food brioche, canape, crepe,
escargot, mousse, pate, pi-
perade, pot au feu, quiche,
souffle, tournedos
fool's bauble marotte
foreign legion center sidi bel
abbes
foreign office quai d'orsay
forest ardennes, belleau
wood, bois, foret
fortress toul, verdun
fowl crevecour, la fleche, ois-
eau, poulet
fowl country bresse
fox renard
furniture meubles
gala fete
game bouillote, boule,
brelan, jeu, petits chevaux
garden jardin, tapis-vert
general boulanger, carnot,
conde, de gaulle, foch,
gamelin, giraud, grouchy,
guise, hoche, joffre, kleber,
laclos, lafayette, marechal,
montcalm, moreau, napo-
leon, rochambeau, turenne,
vendome, weygand
giant anak, brice, frenz,
louis
gift cadeau
gipsy bohemian
glass lalique, verre
goblin follet
god dieu
godmother marraine
gossip ondit
gourmet lyonnais
government grant octroi
government seat quai d'orsay
grass sainfoin
gravy jus
greenhouse serre
greeting allo, bienvenu, bonjour, bonsoir, comment-
allez-vous
grimace moue
grocer epicier
groundfloor rez-de-chausee
guava ringworm bush
guerillas maquis
guest, professional conte de
bourbonneaux
gun escopet(te)
hairdresser coiffeur, friseur
half-pay demi-solde
handle anse
handwriting batard
hardtack galette

harp harmonica
hat beret, chapeau, nivernois, toque
-hating misogallic
hebrew scholar rashi
hedges haies
helmet heaume
hero amadis of gaul, foch,
roland
high school haute ecole
high society beau monde
historian aulard, blanc,
bloch, braudel, gilson, gui-
zot, hanotaux, michelet,
renan, segur, sorel, taine,
thiers
historical period siecle d'or
hobgoblin king hugon
holiday bastille day
home chez soi, demeure,
logis, maison
homesickness mal du pays
honeysuckle sulla
horse cheval
horsepower force de cheval
horse stable ecurie
hospital hotel dieu, maison
de sante
hotel manager concierge
hour heure
house bastide, maison
house spirit esprit follet,
fada, hada
husband mari
idler flaneur
illustrator dore
impersonation marianne
impressionist cezanne,
manet, monet, pissaro
income rente
income tax office le fisc
infantry nabde noire, zouave
inn auberge, hostel
innkeeper aubergiste
insane person aliene
insurgent camisard
inventor bleriot, coanda,
coulomb, lenoir, niepce,
vernier
island cite, comoro, corse,
corsica, elba, ile, groix,
hyere, langlade, lerins, loos,
marquesas, miquelon, oce-
ania, oleron, ouessant, st
pierre, ushant, yeu
jacket carmagnole
jewelry bijoux orfebrerie
journalist barbusse, hebert
judgment arret
kidney rognon
kidney bean flageolet
king bourbon, capet, clovis,
coeur de lion, eudes,

francis, henri, lothair, louis, odo, pepin, roi
king's eldest son dauphin
king's residence st cloud, versailles
knife couteau
lace alencon, argenton, arras, aurillac, canetille, cluny, colberteen, colbertine, valenciennes
lace-making town cluny
lake annecy, bourget, cazaux
lamb agneau
lamp carcel, veilleuse
lampoon geste
land mass ile
landscapist monet
language catalan, langue d'oc, provencal
lard saindoux
lark alouette
laugh rire, ris
laundry blanchisserie
lavender cassidony, stechados
leader caval, clemenceau, de gaulle, d'estaing, lafayette, pompidou
leather cuir, peau
legislature senat
lent careme
liberty cap bonnet rouge
lightning eclair, foudre
lightning rod paratonnerre
light standard carcel
light verse vers de societe
limestone caenstone
linen linge, toile
liqueur anisette, armagnac, cognac, cointreau, digatif, genepi, pernod, prunelle
literary award prix goncourt
literary society academie goncourt
litter cacolet, panier
lobster homard, langouste
lord seigneur
lottery blanque
love of gallomania
lover, courtly celadon
lyric descort, rondeau, rondel
machine gun chauchat, mitrailleuse
maid bonne, domestique, lisette, servante, suivante
maiden jeune fille
man crapaud, frog(gy), gaul, homme, jean, monsieur, parleyvoo, picard, poilu
manner a la francaise
market halle
market town bourg

marshal bazaine, bernadotte, canrobert, foch, gerard, joffre, jourdan, junot, lyautey, montmorency, murat, ney, petain, save, soult
mask loup
match allumette
mathematician bertrand, borel, cauchy, de moivre, desargues, descartes, fermat, fourier, hadamard, hermite, jordan, lagrange, laguerre, lebesque, l'hopital, liouville, mersenne, monge, pascal, picard, poisson, poncelet, vernier
matterhorn mont cervin
mattress paillasse
measure arpen(t), aune, boisseau, carat, centare, chopine, cotyla, decillion, ell, hectare, hemina, hemine, league, lieue, ligne, line, mine, minot, muid, perch, pied, pinte, point, poisson, pot, pouce, quartaut, quarte, quarteron, requille, sack, setier, stere, toise, tonne, velte
medal croix de guerre
medley tripotage
megalith carnac
memorandum aide memoire
message depeche
metaphysician descartes
microbiologist lwoff
middle class bourgeoisie
midwife accoucheuse
military base etape
military cap kepi
military school saint cyr
milk lait
minerologist boulanger, bournon
mint menthe
misdemeanor delut
misfortune malheur
miss mademoiselle
missile mitraille
mistake malentendu
mistress belle poitrine
mob cohue
mold pariole
monastery cluny, grande-chartreuse, solesmes
monster croque-mitaine
month (1–12) janvier, fevrier, mars, avril, mai, juin, juillet, aout, septembre, octobre, novembre, decembre
moralist joubert, la rochelle
moss stonecrop
mountain troops blue devils

mulberry beauty-fruit, callicarpa, sourbush
murderer landru
museum musee
mushroom champignon, chanterelle, grisatre, morille
musical form allemande, aubade, bourree, chaconne, forlane, morceau, valse
musical theorist cheve
musician boulanger, danican, delsarte
mutton stew navarin
nail clou
national anthem marseillaise
national color bleu de lyon
national holiday bastille day
national socialism etatism
native basque, breton, burgundian, catalan, celt, francien, frank, gallois, gascon, gaul, ligurian, lorrain, norman, picard, provencal
naturalist berthier, buffon, cuvier, lamarck
naval base brest, lorient, toulon
naval officer casabianca, iberville
navigator bouganville, de freycinet
necklace collier, exclavage
neurologist babinski
neuropathologist charcot
newsboy camelot
newspaper article feuilleton
new wave nouvelle vague
night lamp veilleuse
nightmare cauchemar
nobility, old ancienne noblesse
nobleman See *title,* below.
noodle nouille
noon midi
notice annonce, avis
novel roman
novelist apollinaire, ayme, balzac, bazin, benda, bernanos, bourget, camus, celine, colette, coppee, daudet, debamel, dumas, flaubert, fournier, france, gide, giono, halevy, hemon, hugo, huysmans, lacretelle, la fayette, larbau, le sage, loti, louys, malraux, marivaux, martin-dugard maupassant, mauriac, maurois, meissonier, merimee, proust, robbe-grillet, rolland, romains, sade, sagon, sand, sarraute, sartre, scarron, simenon, stendhal, sue, verne, zola

number list itoio

numbers (1–10) un, deux, trois, quatre, cinq, six, sept, huit, neuf, dix

nun bernadette

nursemaid bonne

nursing bottle biberon

oath corbleu, parbleu

official maire, prefet

officer convicted of treason dreyfus

opera carmen, faust, manon, mignon, thais

order mandat

organist couperin, dupre

ornament conge, fleuron

overcoat paletot, pardessus

overnight bag sac de nuit

oyster huitre

paint email

painter See *artist,* above.

pancake crepe

panelling boiserie

pantomime character pierrot

pantomimist marceau

paper streamer serpentin

parkland foret

parliament senat

party bal

passport laisser-passer

pastry abaisse, baba(au rhum), eclair, patisserie, tarte

pastry shop patisserie

patron saint denis, denys

paving brick dalle

peace treaty versailles

peak cervin, chambeyron, cinto, cote d'or, dent, dore, forez, mont blanc, mont cenis, mounier, pelat, puy de dome, puy de sancy, ventoux, vignemale

pear ambrette

peasant jacque bonhomme, truffe

peninsula quiberon

people gens, monde

person, deranged detraque

person, holy sainte

person, sick malade

pert. gallic(an)

pervert sade

petty king roitelet

philologist renan

philosopher abailard, abelard, bayle, benda, bergson, camus, caro, comte, condillac, cousin, d'alembert, descartes, diderot, durkheim, gassendi, helvetius, littre, malebranche, marcel, maritain, montaigne, naude, pascal, rous-

seau, saint-simon, sartre, sorel, taine

phonetician passy

photographer cartier-bresson

physician bichat, celine, laennec, laveran, le forestier, nicolle, pinel, richet, sigaultian

physicist ampere, arago, becquerel, binet, broglie, carnot, coulomb, curie, fizeau, foucault, fourier, lippman, perrin, reaumur

physiologist bernard, cournand, rouget

pianist casadesus, poulenc

pickle cornichon

picture paysage

piece morceau

pig cochon

pilgrim pelerin

pinball machine flipper

pink bluebottle, thrift

pirate john dory

pitcher aiguiere

plane maker dassault

play on words double entendre, mot

playwright See *dramatist,* above.

plebian roturier

plutocrat richard

poem dit, lai, roundeau, vers, virelay

poet apollinaire, aragon, aubanel, banville, baudelaire, bellay, beranger, breton, coppee, corneille, delavigne, duhamel, heredia, jarry, la fontaine, lamartine, lautreamont, leconte de lisle, leger, louys, malherbe, mallarme, mistral, rimbaud, ronsard, rostand, st john perse, scarron, sully-prudhomme, toulon, valery, verlaine, villon, vitry

poker bouillote

police chief's office prefecture

policeman flic, gendarme (rie), surete(nationale)

political club jacobin

political leader orleans, schuman

politician barres, boulanger, darlan, mollet

pope clement

poplar liar

porcelain limoges, sevres

port antibes, bayonne, bordeaux, boulogne, brest, caen, calais, cherbourg, dunkerque, dunkirk, le havre,

lorient, marseille, nantes, nice, quimper, sete, st malo, toulon, trouville

port of call escale

porter suisse

poster affiche

poultry volaille

preface avant-propos

prehistoric people magdalenians, mousterians

prehistoric site aurignac, trois freres

premier blum, clemenceau, daladier, laval, paul-boncour, schuman, viviani

president de gaulle, doumergue, giscard, lebrun, macmanus, mendes-france, millerand, napoleon iii, poincare

president's residence elysee

priest abbe, cure, de paul, la chaise, pere, sieyes, sulpician

prince dauphin

printer estienne, plantin

prison bagne, bastille, devil's island

prisoner detenu(e)

privateer la fitte

prize prix goncourt

promissory note assignat

prostitute peripateticienne, putain

protestant huguenot

province alsace, angoumois, anjou, artois, aunis, auvergne, bearn(aise), berri, berry, bourgogne, bretagne, brittany, burgundy, comtat, dauphine, foix, franche-comte, gascogne, gascony, guienne, guyenne, languedoc, limousin, lorraine, lyon(n)ais, normandy, orleanais, picardie, poitou, provence, touraine

proxy mandat

psychologist binet, janet

psychotherapist coue

pupil ecolier, eleve

purslane portulaca

queen marie antoinette, marie louise, reine

rabbit lapin

rabble canaille

racetrack auteuil, longchamps

railroad chemin de fer, tortillard

railroad station gare

range alps(maritimes), auvergne, cevennes, cottian

alps, dore, ecrins, pyrenees, vosges
rascal coquin
rebellion fronde
receipt recu
reception accueil
recorder greffier
recruit bleu, recrue
reformer fourier
refugee emigre
region (See also *department, province,* above.) agenais, agenois, aquitaine, argonne, bordelais, brie, navarre, perigord
report compte rendu
resistance maquis
resort antibes, bain de mer, cannes, cote d'azur, deauville, juan-les-pines, mentone, midi, nice, pau, riviera, st tropez, trouville, villafranche
restaurant guide gault-millau, kleber, michelin (red guide)
revolt vendee
revolution calendar (1–12) vendemiaire, brumaire, frimaire, nivose, pluviose, ventose, germinal, floreal, prairial, messidor, thermidor, fructidor
revolution cart tumbrel, tumbril
revolution club cordeliers
revolution costume carmagnole
revolution currency assignat
revolution party sans culottes
revolution song caira, carmagnole, marseillaise
revolution statesman mirabeau
revolution sympathizer black neb
revolutionist babeuf, blanqui, bourgeoisie, cloots, communard, danton, desmoulins, girondist, jacobin, marat, robespierre, st-just, sans-culottes, sieyes
rice amelcorn
ridge dos d'ane, viny
rifle chassepot
river adour, ain, aire, aisne, allier, ariege, arve, aube, charente, cher, dordogne, doubs, drac, drome, durance, escaut, eure, gard, garonne, gers, gironde, indre, isere, loir(e), lot, luy, lys, marne, mayenne,

meuse, moselle, oise, orne, rhone, risle, sambre, saone, scarpe, seine, somme, tarn, var, vesle, viaur, vienne, vire, yonne
riviera cote d'azur
riviera coastline corniche, esterel-massif
road chemin
roast roti
roll croissant
romance aucassin and nicolette
roof mansard
room salle
royal family See *dynasty,* above.
royalist bourbon, camelot du roi
royalty reine
saint bernadette, bernard, denis, denys, giles, martin
satirist rabelais
sausage andouille(t)
savant amyot, diderot
savior jeanne d'arc, petain
saying dit, mot
scapegoat ame damnee
scholar abelard, casaubon, ecolier(e), eleve, scaliger
school academie, ecole, lycee
school award accessit
scientist cassegrain, curie, lavoisier, pasteur
sculptor adam, anguier, bartholdi, barye, bouchard, carpeaux, despiau, figuriste, goujon, houdon, lemoyne, maillot, pevsner, richier, rodin, rude
sea mer
seasickness mal de mer
season automne, ete, hiver, printemps
seasoning epice, sel
sect albigenses, cathari
self-mastery author coue
shade jalousie
shelter abri, abro, couvert
shield bouclier, ecu egide, targe
shoe chaussure, sabot, soulier
shopgirl midinette
shooting gallery tir
shoulder epaule
shoulder ornament epaulet(te)
silk gros, soie
silk center arles, lyons
singer calve, cantatrice, piaf, pons, sablon, trenet
sketch croquis
skillet squelette

ski star killy
slang argot
sleeping car wagon lit
smoking room estaminet
snuff tabac
snuffbox tabatiere
socialist cabet, guesde, jaures, proudhon
social leader mme recamier
social reformer rousseau
social scientist st-simon
society (haute)monde
sofa causeuse, veilleuse
soldier assis, bayard, chasseur, fantassin, franctireur, poilu, soldat, zouave
song aubade, bergerette, caira, cantique, chanson, chant, descort, virelai
song, children's alouette, frere jacques
soup garbure, potage
southeastern savoy
southern midi, sud
spa aix, dax, evian
spangle paillete
speculators bande noire
speech, americanized franglais
spice epice
spinach epinard, goosefoot
spirit ame, elan, esprit
spring printemps
stable ecurie
star etoile
state etat
statesman auriol, barthou, bidault, blum, bonnet, bourgeois, briand, broglie, carnot, colbert, constant, coty, debre, delcasse, fleury, gambetta, hanotaux, herriot, lamartine, laval, mazarin, morny, necker, richelieu, sully, talleyrand, tardieu, tocqueville, turgot
steak entrecote
stew cassoulet
stock exchange bourse
stone barrow galgal
stoneware gres
store bon marche, boutique
storm orage
story conte
strait bonifacio
stranger etranger, inconnu
strawberry fraise
street chaussee, rue
string bean haricot vert
summer ete
surgeon broca, carrel, pare
sutler vivandier
sweetbreads ris
sweetheart amant(e),

amoureuse, amoureux, cherie, maitresse
sweetshop confiserie
sword epee
swordsman cyrano de bergerac, spadassin
symbol cock, fleur-de-lis, lily
tale conte, fabliau, histoire
tamarisk salt-cedar
tapestry arras, aubusson, auvergne, felletin
tapestry designer lurcat
tavern buvette
tax patente, taille
taxi fiacre
tea substitute faham
teacher abailard, abelard, maitre(sse)
terrorist regis debray
textile center lille
theatre odeon
theatre box baignoire
theologian abailard, abelard, calvin, fenelon
third estate tiers etat
thread fil
ticket window guichet
tidegate aboideau
tiger of clemenceau
title altesse, comte, duc, marquis, messire, monseigneur, reine, roi, seigneur, sieur
toast a votre sante, salut
tobacco knapweed, tabac
town hall hotel de ville
town, royal fontainebleu
train fleche d'or, mistral
treason crime d'etat
trial essai
tribe aedui, allobroges, arverni, remi, saluvii
tricolor drapeau
troop chasseur
truffle country perigord
tumbler voltigeur
turkey dinde
tuxedo smoking
typographer garamond, plantin
undersea explorer cousteau
underwear dessous
university grenoble, montpelier, sorbonne
upper house senat
vermilion cadmium red
vernacular langue du pays
verse alba, aubade, ballade, descort, lai, rondeau, rondel, vers, virelai, virelay
vessel navette, urne
vile-minded person ame de boue
village bastide

vinegar vinaigre
vineyard clos, cru
violinist francescatti, godard, kreutzer, lamont, martinon
waffle gaufre
wagon fourgon
waiter garcon
wall mur
war cry ils ne passeront pas, montjoie
war memorial belleau woods
warehouse entrepot
watch dog matin
watering trough abreauvoir
water spout jet d'eau
weathercock girouette
weed penny cress, spiderwort
week semaine
weight carat, esterlin(g), gramme, gros, kilo, livre, marc, once, passir, pound, sol, tonne(au), uckia
werewolf loupgarou
wheat ble
whistler siffleur
wicket guichet
wind mistral
wine ambonnay, barsac, blanc fume, bordeaux, burgundy, cabernet, calonsegur, chablis, champagne, chapoutier, chassagne montrachet, chateau neuf-du-pape, claret, condrieu, conthey, crepy de savoie, graves, hermitage, macon, masdeu, medoc, meursault, muscadet, muscat(el), musigny, pavillon, pomerol, pouilly-fuisse, puligny montrachet, rhone, richebourg, roussillon, sancerre, saumur, sauterne, sauvignon blanc, tavel, vermouth, vin, vouvray
wine, beverage vin blanc, vin ordinaire, vin rouge
wine bottle clavelin
wine cup tastevin
wine district alsace, barsac, beaujolais, bois, bordeaux, bordelaise, bourgogne, burgundy, champagne, corton, cote-d'or, cote rotie, cotes du rhone, gironde, graves, loire, medoc, provence, rhone, sauternes
wine estate chateau
wine, local vin du pays
wine st vincent tournante
wine shop bistro
wit bel esprit
witticism jeu d'esprit
wolf loup

woman femme
wood bois
woodland foret
woolens lainage
work table chiffoniere
worker class blouse
workman artisan, ouvrier
writer (See also *dramatist, novelist, poet.*) amar, amyot, anet, aragon, aubanel, ayme, baif, barres, barthou, bazin, beauvoir, bellay, benda, beranger, bernadin, bernanos, boileau, bossuet, boucher, bourget, breton, brieux, brillat-savarin, caboriau, cocteau, crevecoeur, d'alembert, daudet, deschamps, feuillet, gaboriau, gautier, guyon, jouve, labe, la bruyere, laclos, marot, nerval, ohnet, ozenfant, renan, rostand, rousseau, sade, saint-exupery, saint-simon, sevigne, stael, sue, tocqueville, viollet-le-duc, voltaire

FRANCE, ANATOLE *novel* penguin island, thais
character bonnard

FRANCESCA *chronicler* dante
husband lanciotto malatesta
lover paolo

FRANCHISE agency, asylum, authorize, ballot, charter, freedom, immunity, license, patent, permission, privilege, right, suffrage, vote

FRANCIS *of assissi* francesco, il poverello, john bernadone
biographer thomas of celano
body brother jackass
church st damiano
disciple junipero, leo pacifico
father peter bernadone
friends birds
mother pica
nun's order poor clares
order franciscan, tertiaries
painter giotto
poem canticle of the sun
sermon, famous sermon to the birds
symbol stigmata

FRANCISCAN capuchin, minorite
friar bacon
mission alamo
nightshade brunfelsia, lady-of-the-night
nun clarisse, poor clare

FRANCIUM *source* actinium

FRANCO *child* carmencita
friend luis carrero blanco
full name francisco franco y bahamonde
nickname butcher
party falange, movimiento nacionale
shrine valley of the fallen
successor borbon y borbon, juan carlos
title el caudillo
wife carmen polo y martinez valdes
yacht azor

FRANCOA bridal-wreath, spiraea, vine

FRANCOLIN bird, coqui, partridge, redwing, tetur, titar

FRANGIBLE breakable, brittle, frail, weak

FRANGIPANI graveyard-flower, plumeria, red jasmine, shakewood

FRANK aboveboard, artless, bluff, blunt, candid, cavalier, direct, downright, exempt, forthright, free, genuine, guileless, heron, ingenuous, mail, mark, naive, natural, open, outspoken, overt, plain, profuse, sign, simple, sincere, straightforward, undeceiving

FRANKENSTEIN *author* mary shelley

FRANKFURTER dachshund special, hessian, hotdog, sausage, weenie, weiner

FRANKINCENSE galbanum, gum, incense, laserwort, oliban(um), resin, t(h)us

FRANKISH *apostle* remi
dynasty carolingian, merovingian
empire, part austrasia, neustria
ensign bull's head, sword
hero oliver, roland
historian gregory of tours
judge centenar
king charlemagne, clovis, gontran, pepin, pharamond, pippin
kingdom austrasia
law capitularies, salic
peasant litus, liti
people salians, salic
pert. carlovingian, carolingian, salic
ruler charlemagne, charles martel

vassal leud

FRANKLIN, BENJAMIN
nickname bonhomme richard, poor richard
pseud. richard saunders
work dogood papers, poor richard's almanac

FRANKNESS candor, freedom, openness, sincerity

FRANKS See FRANKISH.

FRANTIC avid, berserk, beside oneself, crazed, delirious, demoniac(al), deranged, distracted, distraught, excited, fierce, frenetic, frenzied, fuming, furious, haggard, harrowed, hogwild, hysteric(al), insane, lunatic, mad, mang, maniac(al), passionate, phrenetic, rabid, raging, ranting, raving, turbulent, upset, violent, wild(eyed), wood

FRANZ JOSEF *consort* katherina schratt

FRAP beat, bind, brace, lash, strengthen, strike, tighten

FRATCH dispute, fight, quarrel, wrangle

FRATER brother, comrade, fratry, friar, mendicant, refectory

FRATERNAL brotherly, dizygotic, gracious, society

FRATERNITY association, brotherhood, clan, club, group, lodge, order, society, sodality, tong

FRATERNIZE associate, cotton, hobnob, intrigue, mingle, mix, socialize

FRAU lady, mistress, wife, woman

FRAUD artifice, bamboozling, barratry, bilk, blackmail, bluffer, boodling, brogue, bunco, bunko, cardsharp, cheat, chicane(ry), con(fidence) game, corruption, counterfeit, covin, cozenage, craftiness, deceit(fulness), deceiver, deception, dishonesty, dolus, double-dealing, drop game, duplicity, extortion, fake, fourflusher, gold brick, graft, guile, gyp, hoax, humbug, imposition, impostor, imposture, intrigue, kite, knavery, phony, racket, ramp, ripoff, ruse, scam, shakedown, sham, shark, sharp practice,

shell game, simulacrum, skin game, stellionate, strawbail, strawbond, subreption, subterfuge, swick, swindle, thievery, thimblerig, trick(ery), unreliability, untruthfulness, wile
ecclesiastical barratry, simony
shipping barratry

FRAUDULENT cogged, corrupt, counterfeit, crafty, crooked, cunning, deceitful, devious, dishonest, fake, false, forged, knavish, mock, sham, spurious, stumer, stumo(u)r, treacherous

FRAUGHT beset, big, burden(ed), cargo, charged, equip, fill(ed), freight, full-charged, laden, load, supply, teeming, transport
with woe baneful

FRAULEIN girl, lady, miss, mistress, signorina, woman

FRAXINELLA artillery plant, dittany, evonymus, gas plant, mock cypress, wahoo

FRAXINUS See ASH.

FRAY abrade, affray, altercation, brawl, broil, bruise, bustle, chafe, clash, clear, collide, combat, conflict, contention, contest, discord, dissension, disturbance, engagement, fight, fracas, fraise, frazzle, hassle, melee, quarrel, rag, ravel, rip, rub, ruction, shred, strife, struggle, tear, tiffle, tumult, wear, wrangle

FRAYED ragged, raveled, shabby, worn

FRAZER, J. G. *work* golden bough

FRAZZLE abrade, exhaust, fag, fatigue, FRAY, tire, wear

FRAZZLED shabby, spent, tired

FREA See FREYA.

FREAK aberration, abnormality, antic, caper, capriccio, caprice, crotchet, curiosity, (day)dream, eccentric, fancy, fantasy, flam, fleck, flimflam, frolic, grotesque, heteroclite, humor, idea, megrim, monster, monstrosity, notion, prank, quirk, sport, streak, unnatural, vagary, weird, whim (sey)

of nature monster

out bad trip, crash

FREAKISH accidental, bizarre, capricious, curious, eccentric, fantastic, flighty, inconstant, odd, whimsical

FRECK bold, checker, dapple, desirous, diversity, eager, forward, hale, lusty, ready, stout, strong

FRECKLE blemish, chit, ephelis, ferntickle, heatspot, lentigo, mark, pit, pock(mark), spot, sunspot, tache, variegate

remover adarce

FRECKLED dappled, flecked, lentiginous, nevus, speckled, spotted, spotty

FREDDO cold, passionless, unfeeling

FREDERICK I barbarossa **II** alaric, alte fritz, the great

FREE abandoned, absolute, absolve, abundant, acquit, at large, at liberty, autarchic, autonomous, bail out, beyond, broad, candid, clear, deliver, devoid, discharge, disengage, dispense with, distinct, emancipate, enfranchise, escape, except, excuse, exempt, extricate, footloose, frank, generous, gratis, idle, immune, independent, innocent, lax, let off, liberal, liberate, libre, loose(n), manumit, open, parole, pass, prodigal, profligate, ransom, redeem, release, relieve, remise, remit, rescue, rid, salvage, separate, solute, sovereign, spare, spontaneous, spring, unbound, unchain, uncontrolled, unhampered, unloose, unrestrained, unselfish, untie, untrammeled, vacant, wanton, without

admission annie oakley, comp(limentary), freebie, freeby, pass

and easy blase, bohemian, careless, casual, convivial, debonair, familiar, glib, informal, open, regardless, slack, unconventional

as air

chant recitative

comb. eleuther(o)

enterprise capitalism, commerce, laissez-faire

-for-all barney, battle-royal, brannigan, brawl, competition, contest, fight, foray, fray, melee, race

from devoid, redd, rid

from deceit artless, guileless

hand carte blanche, latitude

-lance author, franc-tireur, mercenary, paparazzo, routier, soldier, writer

land of the america, thailand

living dissipation

-loader guest, parasite, sponger

-love community agapemone

man aire, baron, bonder, burgess, burgher, ceorl, churl, citizen, dedititian, franklin, hauld, independent, laet, latin, liveryman, parolee, probationer, roturier, thane, thegn, tiro, villein

name meaning francis, frank

of charge buckshee, gratis

oneself break, escape, solve

pass annie oakley, comp, deadhead, freebie, freeby

scope carte blanche

sea author grotius

silver advocate bryan

ticket See *pass,* above.

trade commerce, smuggling

wheel coast, glide

will arbitrament, discretion, spontaneous, voluntary

-willer arminian, libertarian

FREEBOARD quickside

FREEBOOTER buccaneer, cateran, corsair, ecorcheur, filibusterer, mosstrooper, pillager, pirate, plunderer, rapparee, rider, snaphance, sote, thief

FREEDMAN laet, leysing, tityrus

FREEDOM abandon, autarky, autonomy, boldness, candor, compass, discretion, ease, eleuthera, exemption, facility, franchise, frankness, frith, generosity, immunity, impunity, independence, largesse, latitude, liberality, liberty, leisure, license, looseness, openness, privilege, profligacy, range, readiness, release, run, sanction, scope, sovereignty, uhuru

deity eleutherius, jupiter, zeus

deprive of confine, fetter, jail, shackle

-desiring person eleutheromaniac

fighter fedayeen, mujahidin

from activity recess, respite, rest

from bias cando(u)r, objectivity, openmindedness, unprejudice

from doubt assurance, certainty, certitude

from error accuracy, perfection

from fraud bonafides, honesty

from pain aponia

from restraint breadth, liberty

from strife peace

games eleutheria

of access entree

of action latitude, scope, swing

symbol open road

zeal for eleutherism

FREEHOLD al(l)od(ial), alodium, barony, copyhold, estate, frankalmoi(g)n, land, mortmain, mulk, odal, property, tenure

FREEHOLDER bonder, franklin, frank-tenant, swain, yeoman

FREELY abundantly, ad lib(itum), at will, cheerfully, copiously, excellently, gladly, gratis, heartily, largely, liberally, nobly, plentifully, readily, spontaneously, very, voluntarily, willingly

FREEMASON frater, morgan, noachite, templar

apron lambskin

FREESTONE bathstone, elberta, hazel, peach

state connecticut

FREETHINKER agnostic, aladinist, atheist, blaster, deist, esprit-fort, heretic, individualist, infidel, latitudinarian, skeptic, unbeliever

FREEZE awe, beice, benumb, bestill, blast, blight, chill, congeal, curdle, deaden, frost, glaciate, glacity, harden, ice, kill, nip, preserve, refrigerate, regelate, rigidify, scare, seize, shock, solidify, stabilize, starve, steeve, take fright *out* drive out, eliminate, exclude

FREEZER icehouse, iceplant, refrigerator

FREEZING algific, arctic, chilling, chilly, congealing, cold, cool, frigerant, frigid, frigorific(al), frosty, gelid, glacial, icy, refrigeration
mixture ammonium nitrate, cryogen, dry ice
science of cryogenics

FREIGHT baggage, burden, cargo, carriage, cartage, consignment, dray(age), express, fee, fraught, goods, haul(age), impedimenta, jag, lading, lighterage, load(ing), lug(gage), onus, pack, payload, poundage, send, shipment, tonnage, tote, traffic, transport(ation)
boat ark, lighter, oiler, tanker
unit carload

FREISCHUTZ, DER *character* agatha, cuno, max
composer weber

FREKI *owner* odin

FREMD alien, foreign, fraim, frammit, hostile, strange, unrelated

FREMESCENT murmurous, noisy

FREMONT, JOHN C. *nickname* pathfinder

FRENCH (See also FRANCE for geographical, etc. references.) creole, franco, gallian, gallic(an)
above en haut
above all surtout
acadian cajun
advertisement annonce
after apres
algerian pied-noire
ancestor belsire
aristophanes moliere
article des, la, les, une
astray depayse
at the onset d'emblee
aunt tante
axe besague, hache
baby bebe, enfant, poupee
bargain bon marche
beast bete
bed couche, lit
beware garde
bill l'addition
bizarre outre
black noir(e)
blessed beni, sacre
blouse casaque

blue bleu, ultramarine
blunder sottise
boldness hardiesse
boy garcon
brother frere
brown bis, brun
bulky gros
by air par avion
by choice de choix
canadian acadian, baptiste, cajun, canuck, jean baptiste
canadian trapper coureur de bois
care coin
carelessly a l'abandon
caribbean islands indes
cashiered degomme
child enfant
cold froid
comfort bien etre
company cie, societe
comrade ami
cooked on skewer a la broche, en brochette
corn mais
corn, mixed meslin
corporation cie
count comte
coward lache
cozy intime
cradle berceau
creek anse
crown ecu
dash elan
daughter fille
dawdling flanerie
day jour
dead mort
dear cher(e), cheri(e)
deathly ill a la mort
decay decheance
deception faux air
defective manque
deed fait
degree agrege
delicacy legerete
desperately a corps perdu
despite malgre
deuce diantre
devil diable
devout religieux
disgust degout
display etalage
dispute debat
down bas
down with a bas
dream reve(r), songe(r)
dressed up en fete
dry brut, sec
easy facile, sans gene
edict arret
egg oeuf
elder aine
elevator ascenseur

enough assai
environment mise en scene
equality egalite
essentially au fond
excellent parfait
expensive cher
extravagant outre, prodigue
eye oeil
eyeglass lorgnon
father pere
fencing escrime
fierce farouche
finally en fin
foolish bete
fop incroyable
friend ami(e)
from bad to worse de mal en pis
furniture meubles
future l'avenir
gift cadeau
given donnee
gladly a bras ouverts
glance, amorous oeil-lade
god dieu
good bon(ne), sage
good-bye a bientot, adieu, au revoir
good looks beaux yeux
good taste bon gout
gossiping commerage
grandfather belsire
gray gris
green vert
head tete
health sante
heaven ciel
hello salute
here ici
here is voici
high haute
his a lui
hope esperance
hour heure
how are you comment ca va
ill-natured acariatre
in a body en masse
in a line en queue
income rente
indeed tiens
infatuated en goue
informally en pantoufles
in jest en badinent
ink encre
in mufti en pekin
insight apercu
in spite of himself malgre lui
in succession en suite
intellect bel-esprit
interest of state raison d'etat
intoxication ivresse
isn't it so n'est-ce pas
it doesn't matter n'importe
just in time a point

keep the faith gardez la fois
laugh rire, ris
leather cuir, peau
leave absence, conge
left a gauche
little peu
lively gai, vif, vivant
long live love vive l'amour
long live the king, vive le roi
look voila
love affair affaire d'amour, affaire de coeur
lover amant(e)
lunch dejeuner
mastery mirtrise
me moi
melancholy a la mort
merry gai
milk lait
mine a moi
misfortune malheur
morning matin
mother mere
mother-in-law bellemere
motion geste
mrs madame, mesdames
my dear mon chere
my house chez moi
nevertheless quand meme
new wave nouvelle vague
not ne pas, non
not at all pas du tout
nothing rien
oceania polynesia
odd impair
oil huile
old-fashioned manner a l'ancienne
on account a compte
on foot a pied
on horseback a cheval
on the carpet sur le tapis
on the contrary au contraire
one says on dit
open ouvert
ordered raisonne
out-moded de mode
out of hors
outside the law hors la loi
overwork surmenage
permit conge
piece morceau
pious devot
please s'il vous plait
pocket poche
poodle chien
pretty joli(e)
pride orgueil
pronoun ces, elle(s), ils, lui, mes, moi, nous, tes, tienne, toi, ton, une, votre, vous
quarrel tracasserie
really ma foi
rear arriere, derriere

reason for being raison d'etre
reckless folle
red rouge
reputed dit
rest repos
reversal volte-face
revolution See FRANCE revolution.
right moment a la bonne heure
right word mot juste
ring cerne
road chemin
room salle
rumor on dit
same egal, meme
sea mere
self-control retenue
self-esteem amour-propre
self-mastery coueism
shabby mesquin
she elle
sister soeur
sister-in-law bellesoeur
son fils
soul ame
spoken here ici on parle francais
spring printemps
step demarche
step-brother beaufrere
step-mother bellemere
step-son beaufils
style ton
suddenly a l'improviste
summer ete
superfluous de trop
taste gout
thank you merci(beaucoup)
that's all voila tout
then alors, donc
thoroughly a fond
time temps
to the utmost a outrance
to the very end jusqu'au bout
to your health a votre sante
trifle peu de chose
true vrai
unforeseen imprevu
up to date au courant
very tres
vigor fraicheur
walking a pied
water eau
welcome bienvenu
who qui
who goes there qui va la, qui vive
willingly de bonne grace
wing aile
with chez

with green peas aux petits pois
with milk au lait
with mushrooms aux champignons
without constraint sans gene
without equal sans pareil
world monde
year annee
yellow cathay, jaune
you toi, vous
FRENCH EQUATORIAL AFRICA chad, gabon
FRENCH GUIANA *cape* orange
capital cayenne
city mana-kourou
native boni, galibi, landuman
port cayenne
river maroni
FRENCH POLYNESIA oceania
island borabora, gambier, huahine, maiao, makateo, mataiva, maupiti, mehitir, moorea, motoite, papeete, ralatea, rangiroa, tahaa, tahiti, tettaroa, tikihau
FRENCH SUDAN mali
FRENCH WEST AFRICA dahomey, niger, senegal, upper volta
FRENETIC crazy, excited, frantic, frenzied, furibund, insane, lunatic, mad, rabid, violent, wild
FRENUM bridle, fold, membrane
FRENZIED amok, amuck, berserk, brainwood, dionysian, enraged, frantic, frenetic, furibund, insane, mad(dened), mang, phrenetic, rabid, turbulent, violent
FRENZY aberration, afflatus, agitate, amok, amuck, attack, corybantiasm, delirium, derangement, distraction, ecstasy, enrage, enthusiasm, fever, furor, fury, hysteria, insanity, lunacy, madden, madness, mania, paroxysm, rage, rapture, seizure, swivet, transport, turbulence
murderous amok, amuck
FREQUENCY abundance, carrier, crebrity, crowd, density, familiarity, iteration, persistence, recurrence, reiteration, repetition, throng
bands airways, channels

range broad band
unit fresnel, hertz
FREQUENT abundant, affect, attend, common, constant, continual, continuous, crebrous, crowd, customary, enhaunt, familiar, fill, general, habitual, habituate, hang around, hang out at, haunt, howf(f), incessant, infest, intimate, iterate, keep, numerous, oft(en), ofttime, persistent, regular, repeated, resort, thick, turn, usual, visit
FREQUENTER guest, habitue, patron
FREQUENTLY commonly, every-like, habitually, hourly, oft(en), oft(en) times, repeatedly, recurrently, unseldom
FRESCO fresh air, mural, paint(ing), shade
artist cimabue, giotto, masaccio
1st coat arricciato, arriccio
last coat intonaco
plaster coat trullisatio
FRESE bend, furl, slack, unbend, untwine
FRESH additional, airy, another, artless, blooming, brand-new, brassy, breezy, brisk, chilly, clear, cool, crude, different, discourteous, energetic, facy, firsthand, flip(pant), flush, further, green, hardy, healthy, impudent, increase, just out, keen, lively, lush, modern(istic), naive, natural, neoteric, new, nouveau, novel, offbeat, original, pert, pure, raw, recent, recruit, remembered, renewed, revived, rude, sassy, saucy, snippy, spanking, sprightly, squall, strange, sweet, thaw, uncommon, unfamiliar, unique, untouched, untrained, untried, unused, unusual, unwilted, vernal, vigorous, virgin(al), vivacious, vivid, windy, young, youthful
and lively racy
-water insignificant, raw, unskilled, untrained
-water cod burbot
-water marshhen rail
-water, pert. limnetic
-water polyp hydra
-water tailor herring

-waterway alawai
FRESHEN air, blow, brace, calve, float, refrigerate, renew, revive, strengthen, sweeten
FRESHET current, flood, inundation, spate stream, tide, torrent
FRESHLY anew
FRESHMAN bejan(t), comp, frosh, greenie, jib, novice, pleb(e), pledge, rookie, student tiro, tyro
FRESHNESS bloom, dew, maidenhood, newness, novelty, verdure, viridity, youth
lose dry, fade, wilt, wither, wrinkle
FRET abrade, agitate, agonize, anger, annoy, care, cark, chafe, colic, complain, consume, corsie, devour, disquiet, disturb, eat, embroider, erosion, fash, ferment, fidget, flurry, fray, frump, fume, furnish, gall, gnaw, grate, grouch, grout, grump, harass, hurt, irk, irritate, kvetch(er), mope, nag, nettle, nudzh(edik), ornament, orp, pique, plague, provocation, provoke, rankle, rasp, ridge, ripple, roughen, rub, ruffle, squall, stew, stop, strait, sulk, supply, tease, ulcer, vex, weep, whelk, whine, worry, yirm, yirn
FRETFUL abrasive, anxious, cankered, captious, corrosive, frecket, girny, gnawing, ill-humored, irascible, irritable, orpit, peevish, pettish, petulant, pindling, plaintive, querulous, spleeny, tatchy, techy, troubled, waspish
FRETTED agitated, chafed, erose, magged, roughened, variegated, vexed, worried
FRETTING abrasion, abrasive, attrition, carking, eating, fretful
FREY freyr, yngvi
boar gullinbursti
consort gerd(a), gerth
friend skirnir
god of crops, fertility, peace, prosperity
home alfheim
parent niord, njord, njorth, skadi
servant skirnir
ship skidbladnir

sister freya, freyja
slayer surt(r)
steed gallinbursti
FREYA freia, freyja, fri(a), frigg
brother frey(r), yngvi
goddess of beauty, fertility, love
hall sissyrmnir
husband oder, odin, odur, othin
necklace brisingamen
parent niord, njord, njorth, skadi
realm folkbang, folkvang
FRIABLE brittle, crisp, crumbling, crumbly, flaky, fragile, frail, frangible, frush, mealy, pulverable, short
FRIAND dainty, epicure
FRIAR, FRIAR'S abbot, ascetic, bhikkshu, bhikku, breviger, brother, capuchin, father, fra(ile), gelong, gosain, jacobin, jacobite, lister, minor(ite), monk, preacher, religious, servite
bird coldong, four-o'clock, honey-eater, monkbird, pimlico, poor-soldier
black dominican
cap monkshood
chair frailero
cowl aconitum, arum, cuckoopint, monkshood
crown wool-thistle
dominican cherubic
franciscan cordelier
goose daneweed
gray franciscan
hood cowl
lantern ignis-fatuus, luminescence, will-o-the-wisp
major dominican
mendicant carmelite, servite
minor franciscan
robin hood's tuck
skate doctor
white carmelite
FRIARY See MONASTERY.
FRIB lock, wool
FRIBBLE dandy, falter, fool(away), frivolity, frivolous, stammer, totter, trifle, trinket, waste
FRICASEE blanquette, cook, mince, potpie, ragout, stew
FRICATIVE buzz, consonant, hiss, open, rustling, spirant, yogh
FRICATRICE harlot, prostitute
FRICTION abrasion, attri-

tion, burnishing, chafe, chirapsia, clash, conflict, disagreement, discord, dissension, drag, elbow grease, faction, grating, opposition, polishing, rubbing, scouring, scrubbing, strife, traction, wrangling

adhesive traction

air windage

as remedy anatripsis

comb. tribo, tripsis

match congreve, lighter

subject to rub

FRICTIONAL anatriptic, chafing, erosive, fricative, rubbing

FRIEND achates, acquaintance, advocate, aikane, ally, alter ego, ami(e), amigo, associate, attendant, benefactor, billy, blood brother, bon vivant, boon companion, boon fellow, brother, broadbrim, buddy, cad, chaver, chum, cobber, cookmate, cohort, colleague, comate, compadre, companion, compeer, comrade, confidant(e), confrere, consort, copain, copemate, cousin, crony, damon, dog, eme, federate, fidus achates, folk, frater, frit, gimmer, hearty, intimate, kith, mate, pal, partner, patron, pickup, playfellow, playmate, pythias, quaker, roommate, sidekick, soce, socius

at church influence, supporter

church founder fox

close alter ego, blood brother, cobber, compadre, crony, cummer, fidus achates, mate(y)

faithful achates, damon, dog, pythias

false brutus, judas

group band, chevra, circle, clique, club, company, coterie, flock, society

man's best dog

name meaning baldwin, elmer

of the court amicus curiae

symbol damon and pythias, david and jonathan, three musketeers

FRIENDLESS alone, desolate, forlorn

FRIENDLINESS affability, affection, affinity, amity, bonhomie, camaraderie,

comradery, generosity, goodwill

display backslapping

FRIENDLY acquainted, affable, affectionate, agreeable, amiable, amicable, benevolent, boon, chatty, chummy, close, comfortable, companionable, congenial, convivial, cordial, cosh, devoted, faithful, familiar, favorable, folksy, fraternal, hearty, hold, home-like, hom(e)y, genial, gregarious, harmonious, intimate, jovial, kind(ly), leal, loyal, matey, neighborly, on good terms, pally, peaceable, pleasant, propitious, sociable, social, steadfast, thick, warm, wellmeaning

island tonga

very buddy-buddy

FRIENDSHIP accord, affection, affability, affinity, alliance, amity, association, attraction, bond, comity, concord, druzhba, empathy, entente, esteem, familiarity, favor, fellowship, fondness, good will, harmony, intimacy, pax, regard, relation, sympathy

famous achilles–patroclus, castor–pollux, damon–pythias, david-jonathan, hercules–iolaus, nisus–euryalus, pylades–orestes, theseus–pirithous, three musketeers

FRIESIAN holstein, sylt

FRIEZE bucrane, bucranium, chase, cloth, down, falding, frisado, friz, kelt, nap

fillet taenia

part metope

FRIGATE ship, vessel, zabra

-bird alcatras, ioa, iwa, pelican

mackerel bonito, sardasarda, skipjack, tassard

FRIGG(A) *abode* fensalir

father fiorgwyn

husband odin, woden

maid fulla

messenger gnas

son balder, baldr, bragi, tyr

FRIGHT affray, affright, alarm, anxiety, appal, awe, baboon, consternation, dismay, dread, eyesore, fear, fley, funk, fray, g(h)ast, gaster, guy, hag, harridan, horror, mess, monster, ob-

ject, ogre, panic, scare, schrik, sight, start, swither, terrify, terror, trepidation, witch

FRIGHTEN afear, alarm, appal(l), awe, baze, bully, consternate, cow, daunt, demoralize, dismay, disquiet, dread, flaite, fley, fray, frecken, funk, ghost, harass, hare, hazen, horrify, intimidate, panic, perturb, petrify, scare, scarify, shake, shock, skeer, spook, stagger, stampede, startle, terrify, terrorize, unman, unnerve, unstring, upset

FRIGHTENED afraid, aghast, alarmed, anxious, eerie, eery, frit, horrified, horrorstruck, panicstricken, scared, shocked, startled, sturtin, terrified

FRIGHTENING alarming, awful, bloodcurdling, creepy, dread, fearful, fleysome, ghastly, horrible, scary, shocking, terrible, terrifying

FRIGHTFUL appalling, direful, disgusting, dreadful, fearsome, ghastly, great, grim, grisly, gruesome, hideous, horrendous, horrible, lurid, macabre, morbid, shocking, sinister, terrible, ugly, ugsome

FRIGID aloof, anoestrous, arctic, bleak, celibate, chill(y), cold, cool, formal, freezing, frosty, frozen, gelid, glacial, ice-cold, icy, lifeless, reticent, stiff, unfeeling

FRIJOLE See BEAN.

FRILL armilla, balayense, border, crimp, curl, dido, edging, finery, fold, furbelow, jabot, ornament, purl, ruche, ruff(le), spinach, superfluity

plaited armilla

FRILLY chichi, fancy, flouncy, sporty

FRIM flourishing, juicy, sappy, soluble

FRINGE beard, border, bound, ciliella, crepine, edge, edging, fas, feather, fimbria, lace, loma, mane, margin, peristome, rim, ruff, skirt, tassel, thrum, trailer, trim(ming), tzitzit, zizith

-cup miterwort
foot uma
part fimbrilla, tassel
pod lacepod
purple cotinus, smoketree
tree shavings
FRINGED fibrillate, jagged, laciniate, rebate
bog bean floating-heart
brome wood-chess
milkwort gaywings
FRINGETAIL goldfish, veiltail
FRINGILLA brambling, chaffinch, finch
FRIPPERY clothes, contemptible, finery, indiscretion, superfluity, trifling, trinkums, trivia
FRISBEE *cousin* beanbag
FRISIAN *apostle* wilbrod, willibrord
sacred grove baduhenna
FRISK brisk, canter, caper, caracole, career, cavort, dance, frolic(some), gambol, hope, jump, lark, leap, play, prance, rejoice, romp, search, skice, skip, sport, steal, tittup
FRISKY coltish, frolicsome, gay, lively, pe(a)rt, playful, spirited, sportive, wanton
FRIT calcine, friend, fuse, waste
FRITH bay, brushwood, coppice, firth, freedom, hedge, help, hurdle, liberate, pasture, protection, security, thicket, wattle, woods
FRITHJOF *sword* angurvadel
FRITILLARY butterfly, lily, plant
FRITTED eaten, eroded, lessened, wasted
FRITTER bangle, cake, cut, dally, dawdle, disperse, dissipate, dribble, drivel, fragment, idle, lavish, part, piece, scatter, shred, squander, slattern, throw away, waste
FRITZ See SOLDIER.
FRIVOLITY caper, flightiness, flippancy, flummery, folly, fribble, fun, futility, gaiety, inanity, jest, levity, liveliness, nonsense, play, sport, trifling, volatility, whimsey
FRIVOLOUS barmy, capricious, changeable, dizzy, fatuous, fickle, flighty, flip(pant), fribble, frothy,

giddy, gimcrack, harebrained, idle, inconstant, lightheaded, mercurial, nidgety, playful, shallow, skittish, sportive, superficial, trifling, trivial, uncertain, undependable, unpredictable, unreliable, volatile, yeasty
FRIZZ coil, cook, crisp, curl, tress, wig
FRIZZED craped, crimped, crispy, curly, fuzzy
FRO See FROM.
FROCK coat, dress, garment, gown, jam, jersey, kirtle, mantle, ordain, robe, smock, soutane, tunic, wrap
FROE cleaver, wedge
FROG amphibian, anuran, braid, creeper, croaker, frenchman, hoarseness, knot, loop, pad(dock), paddy, peeper, polliwog, pollywiggle, pollywog, rana, ranida, ronco, tadpole, tassel, toad, yellowbelly
baby tadpole
cheese puffball
comb. batrach(o), batrachus, rani
crab raninian
-faced god heket
fear of batrachophobia
-fish angler, antennariid, slimer, toadfish
-foot duckweed, vervain
game grand(o), ombre, solo
genus anura, hyla, pelodytes, rana, salientia
grass glasswort, toad-rush
hair cotton grass
hopper cercopid, spittlebug
larva tadpole
-like batrachoid, ranine
marsupial nototrema
pert. anuran, batrachian, ranine
plant orpine
rearing place ranarium
spit red alga
symbol of inspiration
tongue ranula
FROGMAN aquanaut, diver, scavanger, skindiver, swimmer
FROGMOUTH bird, caprimulgus, goatsucker, liveforever, morepork, plant, podangue, snapdragon
FROGSKIN dollar, greenback
FROLIC antic, binge, blow, bum, bust(er), caper, cur-

vette, dido, disport, escapade, fredaine, frisk, frivolity, fun, gaiety, gayety, game, gambol, jest, lark, levity, marlock, mirth, picnic, play, pliskie, ploy, prance, prank, reek, rig, rollick, rollix, romp, scamper, skylark, sport, spree, stashie, wassail
FROLICSOME antic, blithe, daft, espiegle, friskful, frisky, gay, gamesome, gilp(e)y, gleeful, hilarious, impish, jocular, jocund, jolly, jovial, larkish, larky, lively, merry, mirthful, mischievous, playful, roguish, roid, sportful, sportive, sprightly, waggish, wanton
FROM against, away, back(wards), hence, hither, out of, since, whither
a distance aloof
a to z throughout, utterly
authority ex officio
cause to effect a priori
comb. abs, aph, apho, fro
cover to cover thoroughly, throughout, utterly
effect to cause a posteriori, empirical
elsewhere aliunde
front, comb. anter(o)
head to foot cap-a-pie
here away, hence
here on out forever(more), future, thoroughly, throughout, tomorrow, utterly
one side ex parte
one to another between
side to side across, athwart, over
that time thence
the beginning ab ovo, ab initio
the cradle to the grave eternally, forever
the egg ab ovo
the outside ab extra
the sticks boorish
the time that since
this time hence(forward)
time to time now and then, occasionally
top to bottom a capite ad calcem, thoroughly, throughout
which a quo
FROME *beloved* mattie
FROND branch, fern, leaf, shoot, tress

FRONDEUR malcontent, revel, scold

FRONT advance, affectation, ahead, anterior, aspect, advantgarde, bearing, begin(ning), bow, brass, brave, carriage, chief, confront, cover, cravat, demeanor, deportment, dial, dicky, effrontery, facade, face, facet(te), facia, figurehead, firing line, first, forehead, foremost, foreword, forne, go-between, head(ing), impudence, lead(ing), manner, mien, nose, obverse, oppose, outpost, point, port, preceding, preface, presence, primary, prime, priority, promenade, proscenium, prow, sham, van(guard), veneer

comb. anter(o)
for represent
-man go-between
on overlook
-page important, striking
page box ear
-runner leader
sight bead
tapering inswept
toward the anterior

FRONTAGE aspect, exposure, position

FRONTAL facade, headlong, metopic, pediment, sindon

FRONTIER backwoods, barrier, border, bound(ary), bourn, coast, confines, conterminous, country, end, face, limitrophe, march, oppose
boundary limitrophe
cemetery boothill
man backsettler, backwoodsman, boone, howie, briar-hopper, bushman, carson, clark, cody, cracker, desert rat, earp, forerunner, forester, hickok, hillbilly, hinterlander, lewis, logan, mountaineer, ridge-runner, woodlander, woodsman
post fort, stockade

FRONTISPIECE prelude, proscenium, titlepage, unwan

FRONTLET band, chamfron, facade, forehead, frontstall, frown, tiara, valance

FRONTSTALL chamfron

FROOM devout, pious

FROSH freshman, novice

FROST coolness, enmity, failure, freeze, freezing, frigidity, hail, hoar, ice, rime, sleet, snow, top, unfriendliness
comb. cry(o)
-covered iced, rimed
giant gymer, hrym, ryme
hoar rime, rind
jack autumn, cold, freezing, winter
pattern ice-fern
root skevish
smoke barber
snipe dunlin, pelidna, sandpiper

FROST, ROBERT *poem* birches, home burial, mending wall

FROSTBITE chilblains, kibe

FROSTBLITE atriplex, lamb's-quarters, pigweed

FROSTED etched, iced, lactescent, milky, opalescent, opaline, pearly

FROSTFISH kokopu, para, scabbard, smelt, tomcod, whitefish

FROSTFLOWER aster, floating-star

FROSTING icing, topping

FROSTWEED cunila, dittany, fleabane, pluchea, rockrose

FROSTY chilly, cold, cool, freezing, frigid, frore(n), gelid, hoary, hunch, iced, icy, pruinous, rimed, rimy

FROT chafe, rub, soften

FROTH barm, bave, boil, bosh, ebullition, effervescence, ferment, flippancy, foam, frivolity, head, lather, levity, lightness, nonsense, remainder, scum, spit, spume, spurge, suds, trivia(lity), yeast

FROTHY barmy, empty, flighty, frivolous, light, reamy, scatterbrained, shallow, spewy, sporty, spumose, spumous, spumy, sudsy, trivial, unsubstantial, vain, whipped

FROU-FROU finery, hummingbird, lace, rustling, stir

FROW bacchante, brittle, cleaver, fragile, frau, froe, frough, knife, maenad, slattern, wife, woman

FROWARD balky, contrary, disobedient, headstrong, intractable, perverse, petulant, rebellious, refractory, restive, shrewish, stiffnecked, unruly, untoward, wayward, willful

FROWN dirty look, gloom, glout, glower, glunch, lour, lower, moue, rebuke, scowl
at disapprove
of fortune bad luck, jinx

FROWNING dour, glum, glunch, morose, surly

FROWST loll, lounge, sprawl

FROWSTY frowzy, fusty, musty, stale, stuffy

FROWZY blighted, blousy, blowsy, blowzy, coarse, dirty, discordant, disheveled, dowdy, fat, fetid, filthy, lax, musty, raffish, rancid, ruddy, scabrous, slatternly, slipshod, sloppy, slovenly, squalid, stale, unkempt

FROZEN chilly, congealed, fast, fixed, frappe, frostbitten, frore, frory, gelid, glacial, icebound, iced, icy, immovable, snowbound, terrified, unfeeling, unsympathetic

FRUCTIFICATION ascocarp, bearing, badisiocarp, ferilization, fruiting, fruition, sporophore, yielding
asexual acervulus

FRUCTIFY bear, fertilize

FRUCTOSE glycerose, sugar

FRUGAL ascetic, canny, careful, chary, cheap, cheeseparing, discreet, economic(al), husbandly, lenten, meager, meagre, parsimonious, penny-pinching, provident, purdent, saving, scant, spare (some), sparing, spartan, stingy, temperate, thrifty, tight, unwasteful

FRUGALITY abstinence, economy, prudence, temperance, thrift
symbol of ant

FRUIT (See also *kind,* below.) advantage, bear, benefit, blossom, chap, consequence, crop, drupe, echo, effect, fellow, harvest, issue, legume, nut, offspring, outgrowth, posterity, produce, product, profit, result(s), silicle, silique, yield
acid pectic

aggregate etaerio, drupetum, hetaerio, magnolia, raspberry, strawberry, syncarp
apple-like pome, quince
aromatic nutmeg
astringent chebule, gaub, sloe
baccate berry
bat epaulet, kalong, peca, pteropid, pteropus
-bearing carpogenuous, fertile, fructiferous, productive
bearing 2 kinds amphicarpous
beverage ade, crush, punch, squash, wine
blackthorn sloe
blemish blet, spot
bud end eye
bunch hog, strap
buttercup achene, akene
candied conserve
carminative anise, badian
center core, pit, seed
chafer allorhina, beetle, euphoria
citrus citron, hesperidium, kumquat, lemon, lime, orange, tangelo, tangerine
coiled strombus
collective fig, mulberry, pineapple, sorosis, syncarp(ium)
collective, pert. anthocarpous
comb. carp(o), carp(o)us, carpy, fructi
compound pectin
cone-shaped pina
cooked in syrup compote
cordial curacao, framboise, kirsch, ratafia
covering bur(r), epicarp, peel, rind, skin
crow campanera, umbrella bird
dealer frontsman, fruiterer, greengrocer
decay blet, rot, spot
derivative phlorizin
desert region terfa, terfez
desert compote, fool, macedoine
dionysus' wine
discoloration sunburn
disease bitterpit, bitterrot, blight, rot, spot
dots sori
dove kuku
dried cubeb, currant, embilia, mummy, orejon, pasa, prune, raisin, sabal, schnitz, snits, snitz

drupaceous almond, cherry, olive, peach, plum
dry achene, achenocarp, bean, date, fig, legume, milkweed, nut, pea, prune, raisin, regma, samara
early hastings, primeur, rareripe
-eater bananaquie, coereba, honey-creeper
-eating carpophagous, fructivorous, frugivorous
-eating bug bishop's-miter, hemiptera
enlarged tissue anthocarpous
envelope See *covering, above.*
enzyme pectase
explosive seeds ballistic, jewelweed, witch-hazel
fallen shedder
false pseudocarp
first annates, bikkurim, primices
flesh pap, pulp, sarcocarp
fleshy apple, avocado, bacca, berry, cherry, drupe, grape, melon, orange, pear, pepo, plum, pome, sarcocarp, syconium, tomato
fly drosophila
forbidden apple
fungus apothecium, ascocarp
goddess carpo, pomona
grapefruit-like suha
grape-like wampee
grower horticulturist, orchardist, palmologist
hard-shelled gourd, nut
having large macrocarpous
having small microcarpous
having winged pterocarpous
hybrid nectarine, pomato, tangelo
imperfect button, nubbin, spech
indehiscent achene, achenocarp, akene, amphisarca, gourd, melon, pepo, samara
jar mason
jar ring gasket, lute, rubber
jelly quiddany, rhob
juice nectar, omphacy, rob, rohob
juicy apricot, grape(fruit), lemon, lime, orange, peach, pear, pineapple, plum
key samara
kind 3 fig, nut 4 akee, alem, ates, atta, caju, date, duky, gage, gumi, icho, imbu, kaio, kuku, lime, ohia, pear, pepo, plum, pome 5 apple, berry, cacao, grape,

guava, icaco, ilama, lemon, mamey, mango, melon, olive, papaw, peach, prune 6 ananas, banana, casaba, cherry, citron, citrus, durian, feijoa, gingko, jocote, jujube, litchi, loment, loquat, marang, medlar, mombin, muscat, orange, papaya, pawpaw, quince, raisin, sapote 7 apricot, avocado, azarole, capulin, catawba, currant, kumquat, pitanga, plumcot, pulasan, soursop, tangelo 8 barberry, bayberry, bilberry, canistel, catrange, dewberry, etaerion, hagberry, honeydew, mayapple, mulberry, plantain, rambutan, sweetsop, tamarind 9 bearberry, blueberry, cherimoya, cranberry, guanabana, muscadine, muskmelon, nectarine, persimmon, pineapple, raspberry, sapodilla, sugarplum, tangerine 10 blackberry, breadfruit, cantaloupe, elderberry, gooseberry, granadilla, grapefruit, joboticaba, loganberry, manzanilla, strawberry, watermelon 11 boysenberry, candleberry, huckleberry, lingonberry, pomegranate 12 passion fruit, whortleberry 13 alligator pear
layer epicarp
lime and lemon citron
many-seeded amphisarca, gourd, melon, papaya, pomegranate, watermelon
mashed fool
medicinal aiwain, ajowan, alem, embelia
mild acid guava
multiple cone, syconium
of dionysus wine
of jove persimmon
of paradise grapefruit, pomelo
1-seeded achene, achenium, achenocarp, akene, avocado, cherry, date, mango, nectarine, peach, plum, sanara
oily avocado, olive
over-ripe drupe
palmyra punatoo
part peel, pip, pulp, rind, seed, skin
peach-like apricot, nectarine
pear-shaped avocado, fig

pert. pomonal, pomonic
pest olive-fly
pie cobbler, flan
-pigeon kuku(pa), lupe, manuma, manutagi
plum-like carissa, ciruela, sloe
pome apple, azarole, pear
pomegranate-like balausta
preserve compote, confiture, conserve, jam, jelly, marmalade, succade
prickly hedgehog
producing See *-bearing*, above.
prune-like myrobalan
pulp marrow, pap
pulpy berry, drupe, fig, grape, pear, pome, uva
red apple, cherry, haw, plum, raspberry, strawberry
refuse marc
rind epicarp
ripening bletting
rose cynorrhodon
rot blet
science of carpology
seed achene, drupe, pip, pit
self-fertilized autocarp
seller coster, frontsman, greengrocer
skin See *covering*, above.
spike ear
spore aecium
spurge tampoe
squeezer juicer, reamer
stalk peduncle
sterile acarpous
stone apricot, cherry, cob, drupe, nectarine, paip, pip, pit, grune, putamen, pyrene
sugar fructose, levulose
syrup quiddany
tomato-like pomato
tree See TREE *fruit.*
tree framework espalier
tree nymph meliad
tropical ananas, avocado, banana, citrus, date, guard, guava, inca, lemon, lime, mango, papaya, pa(w)paw, sapodilla, sapota
turned into carpo
undeveloped nubbin
vine grape, melon
winged samara
withered nubbin
woody xylocarp
yellow apple, quince, pa(w)paw, papaya
FRUITFUL abundant, bearing, blooming, blossoming, breedy, childing, exuberant, fecund, feracious, fertile,

flourishing, gravid, lush, luxuriant, productive, prolific, propagating, rich, successful, teeming
name meaning ephraim
unusually fructiparous
FRUITFULNESS fatness, fecundity, fertility, prolificacy, uberty
god frey
FRUITLESS abortive, addle, barren, blank, bootless, dry, empty, futile, geld, hollow, idle, illspent, ineffectual, invalid, profitless, sterile, unproductive, unprofitable, unsuccessful, useless, vain
FRUITION accomplishment, achievement, attainment, bearing, delectation, delight, enjoyment, joy, pleasure, realization
FRUMP dowdy, drab, draggletail, flout, fret, gibe, gossip, insult, irritate, mock, oldster, provoke, shrew, slattern, snub, sulk(s), trollop, vex
FRUMPISH, FRUMPY cross, oldfashioned, scornful, sloppy, slovenly
FRUMPLE wrinkle
FRUMPS mopes
FRUSTRATE anientise, baffle, balk, beat, bilk, blight, block, check(mate), circumvent, confuse, counteract, cross, dash, deceive, defeat, disappoint, discomfit, elude, foil, hinder, impede, inhibit, kibosh, neutralize, nullify, outwit, preclude, prevent, scotch, spike, stultify, stymie, thwart, trick
FRUSTRATED hung up, unsated, unslaked, uptight
FRUSTRATER marplot
FRUSTRATION balk(ing), blow, chagrin, circumvention, defeat, disappointment, fiasco, foil, let-down, neutralization, rout
FRY boil, brood, brown, burn, children, cook, electrocute, enrage, ferment, frizz(le), irk, offspring, roe, saute, seethe, sile, simmer, vex, young
FRYER chicken, fledgling, frizzer, springer
FRYING *pan* creeper, griddle, poppy, skillet, spider
size childish

FTATATEETA *nurse to* cleopatra
FUBSY chubby, plump, stocky
FUCHSIA kotukutuku
FUCUS bladderkelp, bladdertangle, bladderwrack, bottle ore, rockweed, sea otter's cabbage, seaweed, wrack
FUD rump, tail
FUDDLE addle, booze, confuse, drink, fluster, fuzzle, intoxicate, liquor, muddle, spree, tipple, tope
FUDDLED bosky, dop(e)y, maudlin, swash, tipsy
FUDDLER carouser
FUDDYDUDDY dodo, fussbudget, fusser, oldster, stodgy
FUDGE blunder, botch, bungle, candy, cheat, contrive, devise, fake, fit in, foist, interpolate, nonsense, penuche, result, turn out
in interpose
together create
up counterfeit, fabricate
FUEGIAN alikuluf, onan, yahgan
FUEHRER chief, head, hitler, leader, ruler
FUEL acetol, anthracite, bait, benzin(e), briquette, carbon, charcoal, coal, coke, combustible, dope, elding, electricity, fagot, feed, fire, firewood, food, gas(oline), inflammable, kindling, lignite, log, oil, peat, peet, petrol, shruff, stoke, turf, upla, wood
antiknock triptane
compartment bunker, coalbin
layer firebed
mixer carburetor
ship oiler, tanker
turf peat, shirrel, vag
FUFF puff, splutter, whiff
FUFFIT See TITMOUSE.
FUFFLE disorder, effort, fuss, mess
FUGACIOUS ephemeral, evanescent, fleeing, flying, impermanent, volatile
FUGGY smelly, stuffy
FUGIENT fleeing, retiring
FUGITIVE bolter, criminal, deserter, elusive, emigre, ephemeral, errant, erratic, escapee, evanescent, exile, fleeing, fleer, fleeting, fleme, flyer, fugacious, hot, imper-

manent, in flight, lamster, levanter, momentary, outlaw, passing, refugee, renegade, runagate, runaway, short(lived), skedaddler, temporal, temporary, transient, transitory, uncertain, unstable, volatile, wandering

FUGLEMAN model, soldier

FUGUE amnesia, ricer car(e), theme

answer comes

elaborate ricercar(e)

exponent bach, handel

kind diatonic, dorian, free, real, strict, tonal

part andamento, development, exposition, stretta

passage stretta

short fughetta

subject dux, proposition, vox antecedens

FUHRER See FUEHRER.

FUJI cherry, volcano, wisteria

FUKIEN amoy

capital foochow

river min

FULAH fellani, fellata, fulbe, peu(h)l, sudanese

division beri

language fulfulde

FULCRUM axis, bait, bearing, carlock, gimbal, gimmal, hinge, lock, point d'appui, pivot, prop, rest, rowlock, shore, stay, support, thole(pin)

pin thole

FULFILL accomplish, achieve, acquit, act, answer, attain, compass, complete, comply, consummate, discharge, effect, execute, finish, gain, honor, implement, match, meet, obey, observe, perform, please, reach, realize, render, satisfy, suffice, suit

FULFILLED delighted, gratified, pleased

FULFILLMENT accomplishment, acting, apotelism, completion, consummation, contentment, effect, flowering, fruition, function, gratification, observance, performance

FULGENT, FULGID bright, dazzling, glittering, radiant, red, shining

FULGOR brightness, splendor

FULGUR buccinid, snail, winkle

FULICA See COOT.

FULIGINOUS darm, dim, dusky, opaque, smoky, sooty

FULL absolute, adequate, ample, bouffant, brimming, broad, bursting, capacious, charged, clogged, cloyed, compact, complete, congested, copious, crowded, diffuse, entire, fulfill, fulsome, glutted, gorged, gravid, great, imbued, inclusive, intoxicated, laden, liberal, loaded, loud, mature, obese, orotund, overflowing, packed, padded, perfect, plain, plenary, plenty, plethoric, replete, resonant, rotund, sated, satiated, satiety, saturated, squarely, stuffed, suffused, surfeited, swollen, teeming, thick, thorough, trig, voluminous, wash

and flowing rotund

bellied paunchy

blast all out, power

-blooded florid, rubicund, strong, thoroughbred

bloom anthesis, maturity

-blown adult, blooming, juicy

-bodied fat, hearty, lofty, rich

comb. itous, ose, ous, pleni, ulent

container brimmer

dress formal

-faced affronte, affronty

-fledged adult, developed, grown(up), mature(d), mellow, ripe, summed

force brunt, power

-grown See *-fledged*, above.

house sro, standing room only

-laden fraught

many numerous

many a time often, repeatedly

-mouth cow, sheep, talker

-mouthed loud, noisy

of beans energetic, gay, healthy, sprightly, vital

of fight pugnacious, warlike

of life active, alive, beany

of pep active, animated, energetic, green, lusty, spirited, vigorous

of promise auspicious, propitious

pelt all out

sized See *-fledged*, above.

speed ahead make headway, pack on sail, swiftly

stop period

tilt high speed

FULLA *mistress* frigga

FULLER, FULLER'S bibcock, blocker, channel, goffer, groove, hammer, roller, thicker, tucker, walker

card teasel

earth bole

earth ingredient attapulgite

grass soapwort

herb soapwort, teasel, teazel

FULLNESS abundance, body, completeness, flair, flare, fleshiness, fulth, much, perfection, plenty, plenum, plethora, plumpness, repletion, satiety, surfeit

FULLY abundantly, all, altogether, amply, at length, blankly, clearly, completely, distinctly, enough, fairly, in detail, in extenso, largely, minutely, outright, particularly, perfectly, totally, wholly

FULMAR bird, bonebraker, lammergeier, malduck, mallemuck, malmock, nelly, noddy, osprey, stinker

giant glutton-bird

FULMEN lightning, thunderbolt

FULMINATE berate, blow, detonate, explode, inveigh, lighten, thunder

against berate

FULMINATION detonation, explosion, lightning, thunder(bolt)

FULSOME base, bland, bombastic, cloying, coarse, excessive, exuberant, fetid, foul, gross, lavish, lustful, lusty, magniloquent, nasty, obscene, offensive, oily, oleaginous, profuse, sleek, suave, terrible, unctuous, wanton

FULTON *folly* clermont, steamship

FULYIE, FULZIE (gold)leaf, manure, sweepings

FUMAGO capnodium, fungus, meleola

FUMAROLE blower, hornito

FUMBLE blunder, bobble, boot, botch, bungle, crowd, err(or), faffle, flub, grope,

huddle, mismanage, muff, mumble, paw, pirl, proddle, stammer, stumble, thrimble, turnover
-*fist* bungler, stumer, stumour
FUME agitate, agitation, anger, boil, bluster, burn, decolor, dudgeon, ewder, flatter, foam, fret, fumigate, gas, odor, praise, preserve, rage, rave, reek, ruff, seethe, smell, smoke, smolder, snuffle, steam, storm, turbulence, vapor(ize)
FUMEROOT corydalis
FUMIGANT cyanide, prophylactic, sulphur
FUMIGATE clean, disinfect, gas, pastil(le), perfume, sanitize, smeek, smoke, sterilize, vaporize
FUMING angry, areek, frantic, irate, mad, raging, reeky
FUMITORY climbing, adlumia, allegheny-vine, canaryvine, fumaria
FUN action, amusement, bourd, chaff, contest, diversion, entertainment, festival, fool, frolic, gaiety, game, gammock, gig, glee, good time, hilarity, hoax, humor, jest, jocundity, joke, jollity, joviality, joy, kicks, merriment, mirth, picnic, play, pleasure, prank, recreation, revel, sport, tournament, trick, whirl, whoopee
-*loving* convivial, gay, merry
FUNAMBULIST athlete, rope-walker
FUNCTION ability, act(ion), activity, affair, agency, behavior, business, calling, capacity, ceremony, character, condition, cosine, cue, design, doing, duty, end, faculty, festivity, gathering, goal, intention, job, mister, object(ive), occupation, office, officiate, operate, operation, part(y), perform (ance), place, position, power, profession, province, purpose, react, relation, rite, role, run, serve, service, sine, task, use, utility, value, work(ing)
comb. ate, ise
essential dharma
hyperbolic cosh, sinh, tanh
loss of abiotrophy

social ball, bash, party, reception, soiree, tea
without otiose, useless
FUNCTIONAL beneficial, dynamic, formal, practical, professional, useful, utile, utilitarian
FUNCTIONARY agent, captain, flunky, official
FUND(S) accumulation, assets, bankaccount, basis, bottom, budget, burse, capital, cash, coffer, deposit, escrow, exchequer, finance, foundation, groundwork, jackpot, kitty, means, money(s), nestegg, pool, provide, reserve, reservoir, resources, securities, security, slush, stock, store, substance, sum, supply, treasure, underwrite
-*raising affair* benefit
FUNDAMENTAL abc, absolute, axiom, basal, base, basic, basilar, bedrock, bottom(line), brasstacks, canon, capital, cardinal, chief, cosine, dominant, elemental, elementary, essential, foremost, hypostatic, important, key, law, necessary, nittygritty, original, orthodox, paramount, primal, primary, prime, principle, radical, rudiment, sine, substratal, substrative, theorem, underlying, vital
FUNDAMENTALISM dogmatism
area bible belt
FUNDY *bay of, island* grand manan
bay of, river into st john
FUNERAL burial, cortege, exequies, interment, last rites, levaya, mortuary, obsequies, requiem, rites, solemnities, tangi
attendant mute, pallbearer
bell knell, mortbell
director blackman, mortician, undertaker
feast arthel, arval, arvel, averil, dirgie, dirgy
goddess libitina
march cortege, crawl, dirge
notice obit(uary)
oration eloge, elogium, encomium, eulogy, panegyric
path lichway
pert. exequial
pyre balefire, pile, suttee
rite obsequy

song dirge, elegie, elegy, elogium, epicede, epicedium, monody, nenia, requiem, threnody
structure catafalque
urn bonepot, ossuarium
FUNEREAL black, cinerary, dark, dirgeful, dirgelike, dismal, doleful, elegiac, exequial, feral, gloomy, grim, lugubrious, mournful, necroscopic(al), obsequial, sad, serious, solemn, somber, tomb-like, woeful
FUNEST dire, doleful, fatal
FUNGICIDE bluestone, blue vitriol, bordeaux, calomel, copperas, dichlone, ferbam, nabam, zineb
FUNGOUS spongy
FUNGUS (See also *genus* and *kind*, below.) blight, brand, mildew, mold, MUSHROOM, puffball, rust, smut, spore, thallophyta, toadstool, tuber, yeast
bird's-nest cornbell
black ergot
blight-causing alternaria
canker-causing valsa
cells asci
cereal ergot
club sparassis
comb. myc(o), mycet(o)
disease athlete's-foot, ergot, eyespot, framboesia, fusariose, mycosis, peck, tinea
dots telia
edible blewits, cepe, champignon, clarvaria, jew's-ear, morel, mushroom, terfez, truffle, turbantop
fruit apothecium, ascocarp, terfez
genus actinonema, agarious, amanita, blastomyces, boletus, calvatia, clathrus, coniophora, coniothyrium, corticium, craterellus, cronartium cytospera, daedalea, erysibe, fusarium, fusicladium, fusicoccum, geaster, gibberella, glomerella, gnomonia, hydnum, isaria, ithyphellus, nidularia, phycomyces, rhizina, rhizoctonia, rhizopogon, rhizopus, rhytisma, russula, sorosporella, stereum, stictis, thielavia, tremella, trochila, tuber
gill agaricus
group archimycetes

growth duvet, mold
imperfect alternaria, botrytis, cercospora, diplodia, glocosprium, oidium, spaceloma, spicaria, stilbella, strumella, tricoderma
kind aecidium, agaric(us), amadou, amanita, aspergillus, blewits, boletus, botrytis, bunt, caeoma, clavatia, earthstar, ergot, erysibe, fomes, fumago, geaster, helvella, hypho, irplex, mildew, monilia, morel, moril, moss, mucor, musci, polypore, saprogen, simblum, stereum, stinker, stinkhorn, truffle, tuckahoe, uredo, valsa, verpa, yeast, zythia
layer hymenium
-like agaric
parasitic achorion, aweto, ergot, phytophthora, rust, smut, tinea
pathogenic venturia
pert. mycetoid
plant uredo
poisonous amanita, amanatine
pore alveola, ceriomyces, daedalea, polyporus
preventing fungistatic
primitive archimycetes, auricularia
puffball calvatia
reproductive organ archicarp
ringworm-causing microsporum
rust aecidium
rye ergot
sac claviceps, verpa
sphere sordaria
spore sac ascus
spots mildew
stinkhorn phallales
study of mycology
tinder amadou, punk
tissue gleba, trama
tooth irpex
yeast-like blastomyces
FUNICLE cord, fiber, filament, ligature, stalk, stem
FUNICULAR See CABLE *railway.*
curve catenary
FUNK coward(ice), dejection, depression, falter, fear, flinch, fright(en), kick, nesh, odor, panic, quail, rage, recoil, shirk, shrink, smell, smoke, spark, stink, terror, touchwood
hole cellar, dugout, refuge, retreat, shelter

FUNKED moldy, rotten
FUNKINESS timidity
FUNKY earthy, foul, panicky, smelly, terrified
FUNNEL cast, channel, cone, converge, flue, hinny, passage, smokestack, tube, tundish, ventilator
-shaped choanoid, conic
-twister weevil
FUNNIES cartoons, comics
FUNNY absurd, amusing, antic, bizarre, brilliant, clever, comic(al), curious, diverting, droll, eccentric, facetious, farcical, humorous, jesting, jocose, jocular, joking, joky, killing, laughable, ludicrous, merry, odd, peculiar, priceless, pungent, queer, rich, ridiculous, risible, rowboat, salty, screaming, sharp, slaying, smart, sparkling, splitting, sprightly, strange, whimsical, witty
bone elbow
man buffoon, clown, comedian, comic, jester, wit
paper cartoon, comics
FUR (See also *kind,* below.) coat(ing), down, fleece, flix, hair, mold, pelage, pell, pelt(ry), pile, skin, stole
-bearer platinum
-bearing animal See *kind,* below.
beaver castor, woom
cape pelerine, stole
coat pelage, pelisse
collection pelts, peltry
comb. dora
durable nutria
14th century miniver, vair
gray crimmer, gris(e), lettice
hat busby
heraldic pean
kind 3 cat, fox, kid 4 calf, cony, flix, lynx, mink, mole, paen, pony, scut, seal, vair, wolf, wool, woom 5 budge, civet, coney, fitch, koala, lapin, llama, otter, pahmi, panda, sable, skunk, tiger 6 alpaca, badger, beaver, cougar, desman, ermine, fisher, galyac, galyak, marmot, marten, martin, merino, monkey, moutin, nutria, ocelot, rabbit, suslik, vicuna 7 cacomix, caracal, cowhide, crimmer, doeskin, fitchew, guanaco, karakul,

krimmer, leopard, marmink, miniver, muskrat, opossum, platina, raccoon 8 antelope, bearskin, buckskin, deerskin, goatskin, karakule, kinkajou, kolinsky, lambskin, ragondin, sealskin, shagreen, squirrel, viscacha 9 astrakhan, bassarisk, broadtail, horsehide, wolverine 10 beaverette, chinchilla
lamb astrakhan, galyak
lamb-like krimmor
measure mantle
medieval vair
number of timber, timmer
pattern agouti, agouty
piece palatine, stole
refuse kemp
regal ermine
seal ursal
tippet victorine
worker sorter
FURBELOW border, dido, edging, falbala, finery, flounce, frill, ornament, ruffle, sea-tangle, trimming
FURBISH amend, brighten, brush up, buff, burnish, clean(se), correct, decorate, finify, improve, polish, recondition, rectify, renew, renovate, restore, scour, scrub, shine, touch up, vamp up
FURCRAEA aloe, cajun, cubaya, fiber, plant
FURCULA fourchette, prong, spring, wishbone
FURFUR dandruff, offal, scurf
FURFURACEOUS branlike, flaky, powdery
FURIES alecto, ate, dirae, eriny(e)s, erinnys, eumenides, ker, megaera, semnae, tisiphone
parent gaea, uranus
FURIOUS angry, boisterous, enraged, fierce, fiery, fit to be tied, flaming, frantic, frenzied, hasty, hopping, infuriated, irate, mad, mankind, rabid, raging, rampageous, ranting, raving, reckless, renish, savage, storming, tearing, turbulent, violent, wood, wrathful
FURL bind, bundle, coil, curl, enclose, fardle, fold, furdle, inroll, lap, roll, stow, swathe, truss, wrap, wrinkle

FURLONG boundary, division, measure, quarentene, shot, stade, stadium, strip

8 mile

FURLOUGH blighty, leave, liberty, passport, permit, vacation

FURNACE bloomery, burner, calcar, caldron, calefactor, cauldron, cinerator, crematorium, crematory, cresset, destructor, etna, firepot, forge, fornax, foundry, heater, incinerator, kiln, oven, refinery, roaster, smelter, tisar, tuel, tymp, volcano

chamber carquaise, doghouse, shaft

door tweel

electric arsem

fiery, 3 thrown into ananias, shadrach, sidrach

flue chimney, pipe, tewel

front breast

glass-heating tisar

industrial calciner

lining basque, fireback

man bustler, drosser, smelter, stoker

nozzle tuyere

opening bocca, glory hole, taphole

ore aludel, bustamente

part bosh, damper, fauld, firepot, flue, grate, howell, pipe, tewel, tuyere

peep-hole eye

pert. fornacic

portable cresset, dandy

reverberatory calcar, flintshire

revolving bruckner

start-up blow-in

stone tymp

tapping bar lancet

FURNISH accommodate, accouter, adapt, administer, advance, afford, apparel, appoint, arm, array, bear, cater, clothe, contribute, dower, endow, endue, equip, favor, feed, fit, fret, give, graith, grant, imp(rovise), invest, lavish, lend, outfit, plenish, present, provide, purvey, render, stock, supply, yield

battlements crenelate

completely charge

crew man

meals board, cater, feed

money back, bankroll, capi-

talize, contribute, donate, endow, fund, support

notes annotate

FURNISHING(S) accommodations, adornment, appliances, appointments, baggage, decor, enrichment, equipment, fitment, fittings, fixtures, gear, mode, movables, ornament, penates, rig, stuff, tackle, tools, wardrobe

FURNITURE accessories, apparatus, decoration, embellishment, equipage, equipment, fittings, goods, graith, merchandise, moble, outfit, supellex, supplies

apron petticoat

carver ciseleur

cheap borax

finisher stainer

foot ball-and-claw

leg baluster, cabriole

ornamentation ball-and-ring, bottle-turning, cabochon

parts shook

pert. supellectile

protector antimacassar

style adam, arkwright, biedermeier, bombay, breakfront, chippendale, colonial, directoire, empire, georgian, hepplewhite, modern, queen anne, regency, renaissance, sheraton, william and mary

wood avodire, calamander, cedar, cherry, mahogany, oak, pine, rimu, teak, walnut

FUROR(E) afflatus, agitation, brouhaha, craze, enthusiasm, excitement, fad, ferment, flurry, frenzy, fury, hoopla, hysteria, insanity, madness, mania, passion, rage, tumult, vogue

FURRED coated, hairy, husky, loaded, thickened

FURROW canal(ize), carriage, carve, chamfer, channel, chisel, corrugate, crack, cut, dike, ditch, drain, drill, field, flute, fluting, fold, gash, gouge, groove, gully, gutter, hollow, incise, intrench, plow, rabbet, ridge, rigol, rill, rout, ruck, rut, score, scratch, seam, seuch, seugh, slit, stitch, sulcus, sulk, thorough, track, trench, trough, vallecula, windrow, wrinkle

bottom sole

comb. aulac(o)

having fluted, grooved, guttery

mark feer(e), scratch

minute stria

notch score

plank rabbet

ridge between restbalk

rod burin

FURROWED canaliculate(d), corduroy(ed), corrugate(d), costate, exarate, ribbed, rivose, rutted, seamed, sulcate(d), trenched, wrinkled

FURTHER abet, accelerate, additional, advance, advantage, aid, and, another, assist, back, besides, beyond, champion, develop, distant, earlier, encourage, engender, expedite, facilitate, farther, favor, former, forward, front, generate, hasten, help, more(over), motivate, promote, propagate, push, quicken, second, speed, strengthen, support, ulterior, uphold, yet, yonder

down beneath

than beyond

FURTHERANCE advancement, aid, development, help, progress, promotion, relief, succor

FURTHERMORE and, also, besides, in addition, likewise, moreover, too

FURTHERSOME advantageous, helpful, rash, venturesome

FURTHEST farthermost, ultimate

FURTIVE arch, backstairs, cautious, clammy, clandestine, cloaked, covert, crafty, cunning, deceitful, disguised, hangdog, masked, meaching, privy, secret(ive), shifty, skulking, sly, sneaky, stealthy, surreptitious, underhand(ed), wary, wily

FURUNCLE boil

FURY (See also FURIES.) afflatus, anger, beldam(e), bluster, breth, crank, delirium, energy, enthusiasm, excitement, ferocity, frenzy, furor(e), hag, harridan, indignation, ire, irish, irritation, madness, might, passion, power, rage, shrew,

spitfire, storm, temper, turbulence, vehemence, violence, virago, widdrim, witch, woodness, wrath
FURZE fuzz, genista, gorse, gorst(e), ling, ulex, whin(chow), whun
lark pipit
FUSAIN charcoal
FUSC dusky, somber
FUSE adhere, amalgamate, anneal, arrange, blend, cake, case, cement, coalesce, combine, commingle, conjoin, deliquesce, detonator, dissolve, frit, join, liquefy, melt, merge, mingle, mix, saucisse, smelt, solder, squib, swage, thaw, unify, unite, weld
FUSEE detonator, flare, flintlock, fusil(ier), gun, lighter, match, musket, pulley, spindle, vesuvian, vesuvius
FUSIBLE soluble
FUSILLADE barrage, discharge, shower, spray, volley
FUSION alliance, association, blend, chiasma, coalition, combination, commixture, cytogamy, flux(ion), fusure, joining, league, mitapsis, mixture, union, uniting
comb. apsis
formed by symphytic
FUSS ado, agitation, bearm, bluster, bother, business, bustle, caddle, chafe, commotion, complain, confuse, dirdum, dispute, disturbance, dither, fantod, fidget, fike, finery, firk, fizzle, flurry, fluster, foofaraw, footster, fracas, fret, friggle,

fuffle, fume, haste, hooray, how-de-do, hurrah, hurry, kvetch(er), nag, nauntle, niggle, perturbation, pother, preen, quarrel, scronach, smuzz, spuffle, solicitude, stew, stir, stroth, to-do, tarrarom, touse, towse, trade, uproar, worry
and feathers display
ceremonial panjandrum
n' feathers winfield scott
FUSSBUDGET biddy, fretter, fuddyduddy, granny, old maid, perfectionist, worrier
FUSSY busy, cranky, dainty, exact(ing), fancy, fastidious, fidfad, fidgety, finical, fretful, garish, gewgaw, gimcrack, irritable, meticulous, nice, ostentatious, overnice, painstaking, pernickety, prissy, querulous, restless, spoffish, spruce, squeamish, sticky
FUST cask, mold, mustiness, pilaster, shaft
FUSTAT cairo
FUSTIAN bombast(ic), claptrap, corduroy, fabric, inflated, marl, moleskin, nonsense, pompous, rant, rhapsody, tumid, twaddle, velveteen, worthless
FUSTIGATE beat, cudgel, strike, whip
FUSTY blighted, dirty, fetid, filthy, foisty, foul, frowsty, malodorous, mo(u)ldy, musty, nasty, noisome, old-fashioned, putrid, rancid, rank, slipshod, sloppy, slovenly, squalid, stale, stinking, stuffy, trite, unkempt
FUTE curlew, whistle
FUTILE abortive, barren,

bootless, effete, empty, fatuitous, fatuous, footless, frivolous, fruitless, helpless, hopeless, idle, inane, ineffectual, invalid, nugacious, nugatory, otiose, sterile, trifling, trivial, unavailing, unprofitable, useless, vain, worthless
FUTILITY despair, inability, nugacity, rat race, vicious circle, worthlessness
exclamation of cui bono, i give up, no use, the hell with it, what's the use
FUTURE advent, afterlife, afterward(s), afterworld, by-and-by, coming, delay, destiny, doomsday, eventual(ity), expectation, final, henceforward(s), hereafter, hope, imminent, impending, judgment day, later, manana, next, offing, posterity, postpone, prospective, skuld, some day, sooner or later, still, the grave, thenceforth, to be, tomorrow, toward, ulterior, ultimate(ly), yet
FUTURES securities
FUTURISTIC advanced, modernistic, ultramodern
FUZZ down, fibers, fluff, fur, hair, lanugo, lint(ers), nap, police(man), puffball
FUZZY blurred, downy, fluffy, foggy, hairy, imperfect, indistinct, hazy, misty, murky, muzzy, spongy, unclear, vague, velutinous, wool(l)y
-guzzy balsamweed
-wuzzy cutie, dog, puppy
FYLFOT amulet, charm, cross, emblem, insigne, swastika

G

GAAL *father* ebel
GAB babble, blab, boast, chat(ter), chinfest, hook, jabber, jaw, lie, mouth, notch, patter, persimmon, prate, prattle, scoff, speak, speech, talk, taste, tongue, vaunt, yap
GABAEL *son* aduel
GABARDINE See GABERDINE.

GABATTA mancala
GABBATHA *eunuch of* susa
GABBINESS loquacity
GABBLE babble(ment), cackle, cank, chat(ter), chuckle, gaggle, gibber, habble, jabber, javer, nonsense, rabble, slipslop, twaddle, twitter, yabber
GABBRO bojite, eucrite, norite

GABBY chatty, fool, loquacious, prating, talkative
GABELLE excise, impost, tax
GABERDINE apron, coat, frock, gown, mantle, pinafore, twill, worsted
GABI See TARO.
GABION basket, cage, corbeil, cylinder, keesh, kish, waling

GABIRIT gauge, model, mold
GABLE dormer, pediment, pinion, roof, wall
half aileron
GABON, GABUN *capital* libreville
cape lopez
chocolate dika bread
city bongo, kango, lambarene, makokou, mitzic, omvane, oyem
lake anengue, azinguo
native adouma, echira, fang, okande
peak mpele
port gentil
president mba
river abanga, ivinda, ngounie, ogoue
tribe vili
GABOON okoume
GABRI *son* gabael
GABRIEL angel, herald
cherub zephon
horse haizum
instrument horn
symbol lily
GABY fool, simpleton
GAD chisel, cruise, gallivant, gaud, goad, gowl, incite, ingot, jaunt, junket, meander, oath, prowl, ramble, range, roam, rod, rove, spear, spike, sting, stray, switch, traipse, urge, wander, whip
chieftain ahi
descendant zia
father jacob
mother zilpah
son areli, arod, eri, exbon, ezni
tribe erites
-zooks egad
GADABOUT dogcart, gallant, gallivanter, haik, kochleffl, rambler, roamer, rover, roving, stram
GADBUSH mistletoe
GADDI cushion, hassock, throne
GADDIEL *father* sodi
GADE fish, pike, rockling
GADFLY annoyer, botfly, breeze(fly), brims, burrel fly, busybody, cleg(g), horsefly, hypoderma, oestrid, pest, stout, tabanid, whame
mythological brize
GADGET contraption, contrivance, device, dingus, dofunny, dohicky, doodad,

gimmick, gismo, hickey, jigger, jimjam, object, thing, thinguma(bob), thingumajig, trangam, widget
GADHELIC See GAELIC.
GADOLINIUM terbium
GADROON fluting, molding, ornament, reeding
GADWALE duck, fowl, rodge
GADWALL redwing, rodge, shuttle, volant
GAEA earth, tellus
consort pontus, poseidon, tartarus, uranus
offspring aegaeon, alcyoneus, anteus, briarius, centimanes, ceto, coeus, cratus, crius, cronus, cybele, cyclopes, echidna, enceladus, erechtheus, eurybia, hecatoncheires, iapetus, kratos, nereus, oceanus, phoebe, phorcys, rhea, thaumas, themis, titans, typhoeus
GAEL celt, goidel, kelt, scot
GAELIC celtic, erse, gadhelic, irish, keltic, manx, scotch
black dhu
clan sept
game pole caber
giant fion
god dagda, ler, mider
hero ossian
land distribution rundale
minerva brigantia
poem duan
spirit banshee, kelpie, kelpy
war cry erin
GAESETAI *king* britomartus
GAFF chatter, clamor, clip, deceit, deceive, fair, fleece, fraud, gaffle, gamble, gavelock, hoax, hook, laugh, ordeal, outcry, slasher, spar, spear, speech, spur, talk, trick(ery), yard
GAFFE blunder, booboo, error, faux pas
GAFFER boy, chap, duffer, foreman, geezer, oldster, overseer, rustic, superintendent
GAG aguaji, anecdote, baff, bind, choke, closure, crack, cut short, disable, fish, grouper, heave, hoax, jab, jape, jerk, jest, joke, kevel, mot, muffle, muzzle, obstruct, pong, project, pun, quip, restrain, retch, scob(e), shackle, shut up, silence, spew, squelch, stifle, stop, strangle, suffocate,

suppress, throttle, vitz, vomit, wheeze, wisecrack, witticism
-man dramatist, jokester, punster, wit, writer
GAGA crazy, cuckoo, insane, mad, nutty, scatterbrained
GAGATE jet
GAGE bet, challenge, defiance, earnest, feeler, fruit, GAUGE, hostage, measure, pawn, pledge, plum, risk, scantle, stake, standard, token, wager
GAGGLE babble, bevy, cackle, covey, drove, flight, flock, gabble, GROUP, herd, pack, shoal, swarm
GAHAM *mother* reumah
GAIETY, GAYETY begonia, delight, festival, festivity, finery, frolic, fun, gala, geniality, hilarity, jest, jollity, joy, levity, liveliness, merriment, mirth, riancy, rollick, show, sport, vivacity
GAILLARDIA (black) (brown)-eyed susan, blanket-flower, fire wheel, rudbeckia
GAILY bravely, finely, lightly, merrily, showily
GAIN accomplish, accretion, achieve, acquire, acquisition, advance, advantage, approach, arrive, attain, avail, bear off, benefit, boot(y), buy, catch, cheap, clean up, compass, conquer, convenient, draw, earn (ings), effect, endeavor, filthy lucre, get, gleanings, good, groove, grow, harvest, improve, income, increase, increment, incut, land, lucre, make, makings, near, net, notch, obtain, overtake, pelf, perquisite, pickings, possess, pot, procure, profit(s), reach, realize, reap, receipts, receive, remedy, return(s), score, secure, spoil(s), take, vantage, win(nings)
advantage best, gleek
command of master
dishonest meed
favor catch on, prevail
ground accelerate, progress
ill-gotten extortion, graft, lucre, payola, pelf, spoil(s)
on approach, beat, catch up, over(haul)(take), reach
strength rally, recuperate

unexpected bonus, bunce
weight fatten
GAINFUL lucrative, productive, valuable
GAINSAY combat, confute, contradict, contravene, controvert, deny, disaffirm, disprove, dispute, forbid, impugn, negative, oppose, refute, resist, traverse, withstand
GAINSBOROUGH *painting* blue boy, pinkie
GAIT amble, aubin, bat, canter(bury), chack, gallop, journey, lope, lounge, pace, rack, rate, run, scuttle, shamble, slouch, stalk, step, stride, tread, trip, trot, volt, walk, wallow, wamble, way
easy lope
leisurely crawl
rapid clip
unsteady shuffle, stagger, toddle, wobble
GAITER(S) antigropelos, boot, bragas, chaparejos, chaps, chivarros, congressboot, cuttikin, galligaskins, gamashes, gambado, gaskin, greave, guelder-rose, guetre, hugger, husion, legging, puttee, shoe, spat, spatterdash, spindletree, strad
GAIUS *aide to* paul
GAIZE malmstone
GALA affair, celebration, festal, festival, festive, fete, fiesta, party, pomp
GALACTIC lacteal, lacteous, lactescent, lactic, lactiferous
circle galaxy
distance parsec
region outer space
GALACTITE milkstone
GALACTOSE cerebrose
GALAGO bushbaby, lemur(oid)
GALAHAD *parent* elaine, la(u)ncelot
quest holy grail
GALAL *son* shammua
GALAM shea
GALANTE *nickname* lillo, the cigar
GALAPAGOS ISLANDS
grosbeak geospiza
tortoise elephant
GALATEA *lover* acis, pygmalion
parent doris, nereus
pursuer polyphemus

sculptor pygmalion
GALATIA *king* deiotarus
people gauls
GALAX beetleweed, coltsfoot
GALAXIAS trout
GALAXY milky way, multitude, nebula, number, quantity, spiral, via lactea
GALBANUM albetad, bosh, ferula, frankincense, gumresin, nonsense
GALBE contour, outline, tournure
GALCHA pamir
GALE blast, blow, bog myrtle, cyclone, declaim, flaw, fleawood, gust, hurricane, nor(th)easter, norwester, outburst, payment, perry, rent, royalty, sail, sing, storm, tempest, twister, typhoon, (whirl)wind
GALEA helmet, mitra
GALECHE calash, caleche, calesa, carriage
GALEID carcharhinus, carcharias, fish, shark
GALEN doctor, physician
GALENA bluelead, theriaca
GALERA tayra
GALERUM cap, GALERA, helmet, periwig, peruke
GALET foussa, spall, stone, viverine
GALGAL cairn, tomb
GALIBI caribi, kalina
GALICIA *native* gallego
river san, styr
symbol cockleshell
GALILEE holy land, mare tyberiadis, porch, portico, stoa, tiberias, vestibule
city cana, capernaum, nain, nazareth, tiberias
prince herod
GALILEO *birthplace* pisa
GALINGALE chinaroot, cyperus, sedge, wanhorn
GALIPOT barras, resin, tacamahac, turpentine
GALIUM bedstraw, birdlime, burhead, catchweed, cleavers, herb, plant, wild licorice
GALL abrade, acerbity, afflict(ion), anger, annoy(ance), bedegar, bile, bitterness, blemish, cecidium, chafe, cheek, choler, chutspa, chutzpa(dik), crust, damage, despite, effrontery, exasperation, excoriate, fell, flaw, fleaseed, fret, gaw, grate, harass,

harm, hurt, hutzpa(h), impudence, injure, irritate, malice, oakberry, provocation, provoke, rancor, rasp, rub, sow, spite, swelling, tacahout, venom, vex, virulence, wound, wring
berry inkberry
bush sweetgale
fly cynipid, cunips, inquiline
of-the-earth lactuca, lionsfoot, pinedrops
on roses bedeg(u)ar
-producing gallicolous
GALLA *ox* sanga, sangu
people boni, hamite
GALLANT amatory, amorist, amorous, beau, blade, bold, brave, bully, carpetmonger, cavalier, chevalier, chivalric, chivalrous, cicisbeo, civil, considerate, courageous, courteous, dandy, daring, dauntless, debonair, doughty, dude, escort, fashionable, fearless, handsome, hero(ic), intrepid, knight(ly), lady killer, lover, polished, polite, quixotic, spark(er), spirited, sporty, squire, suave, suitor, swain, thoughtful, urbane, wooer, younker
GALLANTRY bravery, chivalry, civility, courage, display, dru(e)ry, finery, heroism, mettle, prowess, resolution, spirit, valor, wooing
GALLBLADDER bilecyst, cholecyst
comb. chol(e)
pert. cystic
GALLED infertile, mad, peeved, raw, sensitive, sore, sterile
GALLEON argosy, boat, car(r)ack, galleass, galloon, vessel
GALLERIAN See SLAVE.
GALLERID beemoth, waxmoth
GALLERY aisle, alure, ambulatory, arcade, atelier, audience, balcony, bridge, burrow, cloister, corridor, dedans, entrenchment, hall (way), hypogee, loft, loggia, mezzanine, mine, museum, paradise, passage (way), patio, piazza, platform, porch, portico, poy, public, sollar, salon, stoop, studio, terrace, tunnel, veranda, walk

church jube, laft, loft
mine bord, brow, slovan
GALLET chip, spall, stone
GALLEY aesc, birling, boat, caboose, calan, coin, cookhouse, cromster, foist, galiot, hearth, hexeris, kitchen, pantry, proof, scullery, tray, trireme, vessel, zygite
armed aesc, dromond
bottom slice
chieftain's birling, birlinn
50-oared penteconter
fighting galleass
kind bireme, dromon(d), foist, galiot, galleass, hepteris, hexeris, quadrireme, quinquereme, tessaraconter, triaconter, trireme, unireme, venetian
light foist
medieval dromon(d)
norse aesc
single-masted lymphad
slave drudge, forsado, rower, sforzato
smoke stack charlie noble
-trough char
-west confused, crooked
-worm millepede
GALLIA See FRANCE; FRENCH; GAUL.
GALLIC (See also GAUL.) french(y)
GALLICISM barb, brocard, gibe, maxim, proverb, sarcasm
GALLIGASKINS breeches, gaiters, leggings, pants, trousers
GALLIMAUFRY hash, hodgepodge, medley, mixture, olio, ragout, salmagundi
GALLINAE curassow, grouse, megapode, partridge, peafowl, pheasant, quail, rasores, turkey
GALLINAZO carrioncrow, turkeybuzzard, viru, vulture
GALLING abrasion, abrasive, annoying, attrition, bitter, humiliating, irritating
GALLINULE bald coot, bell kite, bluepeter, coot, dabchick, fowl, gorhen, hen, hyacinth, ionornis, kora, manualii, moho, moorhen, pukerko, rail, ricebird, skitty, stankie, sultana, swamphen
GALLIPOT apothecary, barras, druggist, rosin, sap
GALLIUM *source* bauxite

GALLIVANT cruise, flaunt, flirt, gad, jaunt, kite, meander, prowl, ramble, range, roam, rove, stray, traipse, wander
GALLON(S) congius, gawn, measure
⅛ octarius, pint
¼ quart
128 leaguer
GALLOON binding, border, braid, edging, lace, orris, trimming
GALLOP amble, aubin, canter, career, course, dart, dash, fog, lope, pace, rack, run, rush, scamper, speed, tantivy, tittup, trot, walk
GALLOWS bough, cheat, crap, dashing, derrick, drop, extremely, fine, forches, furca, gibbet, good, great, impudent, rascally, scaffold, stifler, suspenders, tree, very, villainous, warytree, wild, yardarm
bird crackrope, criminal, hempie, hempseed, hempy, widdifow, widdy
cheater sliphalter
fit for widdifow
-grass hemp
pert. patibulary
GALLSTONE calculus, cholelith, chololith
GALLUSES braces, straps, suspenders
GALLWEED gentian, toadflax
GALLWORT toadflax
GALLY bitter, bold, flurry, frighten, gallow, impudent, scare, worry
GALLYBAGGER scarecrow
GALOOT clown, lubber, marine, oaf, oddity, soldier, stiff
GALORE abundance, agogo, aplenty, gobs, lots, plenty
GALOSH arctic, boot, clog, overshoe, patten, rubber, shoe, zipper
GALP belch, gape, gaping, yawn
GALSWORTHY *heroine* irene
novels forsythe saga
GALT See HOG.
GALVANIC affecting, stimulating, voltaic
cell battery
GALVANIZE agitate, arouse, awaken, electrify, enkindle, excite, fire, inflame, kindle,

pique, plate, provoke, quicken, rally, rouse, stimulate, stir, thrill, waken, zincify
GALVANIZED zincic, zincous, zincky
GALWAY BY *isles* aran, inisheer, inishmore
GAM group, herd, leg, mouth, school, socialize, tooth, visit
GAMALIEL pedant, teacher
grandfather gillel
pupil paul
GAMBADE, GAMBADO antic, bound, caper, gaiter, legging
GAMBESON wambais
GAMBET redshank, tattler
GAMBIA *capital* banjul, bathurst
city bintang, kuntaur, mansa
family historian griot
language fulani, jola, malinke, wolof
money dalasi
native diolas, fulani, jola, mandingo, peul, serahuli, wolof
pod babloh
GAMBLE bet, birl, buck, chance, fate, flier, flyer, fortune, gaff, game, hazard, lottery, luck, pike, play, plunge, punt, raffle, rifle, risk, speculate, speculation, sport, squander, stake, take a chance, venture, wager
GAMBLER banker, bookie, carrow, dicer, gamer, gamester, hustler, player, punter, ricker, shark, shill(aber), slicker, speculator, sport
accomplice shill
capital bank, stake
cube dice, die, hazardry
famous female poker alice
itinerant carrow
GAMBLING elbow-shaking, hazardry
device crap table, dice, pachinko, pinball, punchboard, roulette wheel, slot machine, wheel of fortune
game baccarat, backgammon, barbudi, be(a)no, bingo, blackjack, boule, brelan, cards, crack(a)loo, craps, fantan, faro, gluckspiel, guimbarde, hand, hazard, keeno, lotto, macao, monte(bank), panguingui, petits chevaux, pico, pique(t), pitch, poker,

policy, primero, props, put-and-take, rondeau, rondo, rouge-et-noir, roulette, speculation, stuss, tan, twenty-one, two-up, vingt-et-un
house See *place*, below.
house man croupier, dealer, gut-puller, stickman, tab, tourneur
pert. aleatory
place bank, bucket shop, casino, crib, domdaniel, flat, hell, joint, las vegas, nevada, poolroom, reno, sporting house, tripot
pool calcutta
stake ante, bet, kitty, layout, mise, pool, pot
term (See also CARD *playing term*.) banco, bookie, bookmaker, cave, chip, chiseler, clip, consolation, croupier, cut, floorman, freeze-out, frozen, hedge, odds(on), ouverte, pack up, percentage, piker, pique, position, pull down, rake-off, sleeper, slot, stake
GAMBOGE calaba, cambogia, garcina, gum-resin, tree
pigment yellow
GAMBOL bound, caper, career, cavort, curvet, dido, disport, frisk, frolic, hop, leap, play, prance, prank, rollick, romp, skip, sport, spring
GAME (See also DOMINOES; POKER; SOLITAIRE.) amuse(ment), artifice, bet, bold, brave, business, butt, contest, courageous, course, disabled, diversion, frolic, fun, gamble, humbug, intrigue, jest, jeu, joke, lame, match, nervy, pastime, persevering, play, please, ploy, plucky, prank, prey, project, quarry, ramsch, ready, recreation, ridicule, scheme, sport, spunky, strategy, swag, valiant, wager, wathe, willing
amusement park skeeball
ball antiover, antony-over, baseball, basketball, billiards, bocci, boule, bowling, casaba, cat, catch, closh, cricket, croquet, fives, football, fungo, golf, handball, hockey, knappen, pelota, pingpong, polo,

pool, pushball, rolypoly, rounders, rugby, soccer, softball, squash, tennis, trigon, trucks, tut, volleyball
billiard-like trucks
-bird bustard, duck, grouse, guan, partridge, pheasant, quail
-bird group covey
blindfold lang(s)-a-tail
board abangau, acey-deucy, backgammon, bagatelle, bau, bingo, brettspiel, camelot, caroms, chaturanga, checkers, chess, cribbage, crokinole, doppelmuhle, draughts, fox and geese, go bang, halma, i go, keno, lotto, mill, monopoly, muhle, noughts and crosses, nullenspiel, pachisi, parchesi, pegboard, radmuhle, reversi, salta, scrabble, solitaire, squails, table, tic-tac-toe, tit-tat-toe, tivoli
book hoyle
bowling bocci, boule, cocked hat, ninepins, tenpins
boys' cobnut, conker
card See CARD *game.*
carnival darts, hoopla
child's antony-over, bob-cherry, blindman's bluff, cockle-bread, copenhagen, cops and robbers, dib, forfeits, hide-and-seek, hopscotch, hot cookies, red rover, seesaw, simon says, tag
christmas hot cookies
confidence bunco, bunko
counter chip
counting buzz, fourteen, klondike, qualify, twenty-six
court badminton, handball, jai lai, pelota, roque, squash, tennis, volleyball
cube dice, die
deck shuffleboard
dice addition, alea, barbudi, barbotte, cameroon, chuck-a-luck, craps, dominoes, going to boston, hazard, hooligan, ludo, novum, pachisi, raphe, trey-trip
fish See FISH *game.*
-flusher beater
follow beat, dog, hunt, stalk
gambling See GAMBLING *game.*
goal basket, first, homer, home run, score, spare, strike, tally, touchdown

guessing canute, love, mora
hawk falcon
keeper ranger, warden, warmer, warrener
kind beno, carambolette, charades, darts, diabolo, forfeits, hangman, jackstraws, jass, loggats, loggets, ludo, mah-jong(g), marbles, merels, mora, morris, pam, peevers, philopena, pico, quoits, ringtaw, sardine, spillikins, statues, troco, verquere
lawn bowls, croquet, troco
lottery bingo, royal oak, tombola
lumberjack birling
marbles bonce, taw
marching musical chairs
mathematical cheese boxes, cribbage, nim, noughts and crosses, odd and even, thirtyone, triangles, wit and reason
ninepins skittles
nursery pat-a-cake
obsolete alliance, basset(te), beast, belle, bester bube, biribi, bluchern, brandeln, briscan, brisque, cavagnole, culbas, dubblets, emprunt, esperance, fly, guimbarde, haz(z)ard, hoc(a), inn and inn, irish, jacquet, kandsknecht, mouche, pachter, peneech, plain-dealing, pollack, poque, post and pair, puff, put(t), quandrille, quinquenove, reunion, revertier, schnitt, sechsern, sice-ace, sixte, sizette, speculation, spitzeln, susmilch, tatteln, tokkadille, tontine
of chance See CARD *game;* GAMBLING *game.*
official alytarch, judge, linesman, referee, starter, timekeeper, timer, umpire
on ice curling, hockey
outdoor badminton, baseball, cricket, croquet, football, golf, hurly, lacrosse, roque, rugby, soccer, tennis, volleyball
parlor bingo, cards, charades, checkers, dibs, dominoes, jacks, lotto, matador, tiddlywinks
piece checker, chip, dice, domino, man, tile
pin bowling, hob, kegling, ninepins, skittles, tenpins
pole caber

public ludo
racket badminton, bandy, battledore, lacrosse, squash, tennis
remove from bench
rhyming crambo
rural barleybrake, barley-break
sailors able whackets
shelter cover
shipboard deck tennis
shot cannon, carom
sidewalk boxball, hopscotch
site amphitheatre, arena, board, court, diamond, field, rink
skill chess, pool
small bird, fowl
snare tunnel
stewed ragout, salmi
string cat's cradle
swindling thimble-rig
table pingpong, skeeball
trapshooting scoot
war kriegspiel
word acrostic, anagram(s), crambo, double-crostic, ghost, hangman, scrabble, stinky-pinky

GAMECOCK fighter, rooster, stag, staig
handler setter-to

GAMENESS fortitude, guts, pluck

GAMESTER bettor, cardsharp, crapshooter, dicer, elbow-shaker, oraler, player, plunger, punter, sharper, sharpshooter, sport (sman)

GAMETE oocyte, oogamete, oosphere, sperm, zygote

GAMETIC chromatinic, chromosomal, generative, seminal, spermatic, spermatozoal, spermic, sporal, sporogenous, sporoid, sporous

GAMIN arab, blackguard, gavroche, guttersnipe, hoodlum, mudlark, serf, street arab, tad, urchin, vagabond
domain street

GAMMON bacon, bosh, feign, flitch, foot, ham, hoax, humbug(gery), leg, nonsense, pretend, sham, thigh

GAMMONER imposter

GAMP midwife, obstetrician, umbrella

GAMUT compass, horizon, ken, orbit, purview, radius,

range, reach, scale, scope, series, sol-fa, sweep
GAMY amorous, high-flavored, lustful, plucky, strong
GANCH gash, snap, snarl, stammer, stutter, wound
GANDER fowl, gannet, gaze, glance, goose, look, simpleton, stag, staig, steg, stroll, wander
GANDHI *doctrine* non-violence, satyagraha
name ab(b)a, abou, bapu, indira, mahatma
prison poona
publication harijan
GANEF pickpocket, thief
GANELON *foe* roland
friend pinabel
steed tachebrun
stepson roland
sword murgleis
victim roland
GANES(H)A ganapati, gunputty
parent parbutta, parvati, siva
GANG assemblage, association, band, chevra, cluster, coffle, company, course, crew, crowd, gaggle, gait, GROUP, horde, journey, knot, maffia, mafia, mob, number, outfit, pack, passage(way), pasturage, posse, ring, road, set, staff, team, travel, troop, walk
along depart
around assemble
black crewmen, stokers
flower milkwort
head tindal
member bhoy, crook, rowdy, tough, whyo
signal cry whyo
up assemble, combine
up on attack
GANGER foreman, forse, gangrene, stranger, superintendent, walker
GANGES *barge* budgero(w)
boat putelee, puteli
boatman dandi, dandy
city on allahabad, benares
dolphin susu
efflorescence reh
goddess gangadevi, gunga
landing place ghat
GANGGANG cockatoo
GANGLAND underworld
GANGLING awkward, gawky, lanky, lean, slab-sided, spindling, tall, thin

GANGLION cerebrum, gland, nerve cell, tissue, tumor
GANGPLANK bridge, brow, gangboard, platform
GANGRENE canker, decay, garger, mortify, necrosis, phagedena, rot, sphacel(us)
GANGRENOUS cankered, diseased, rotten
GANGSTER apache, bandit, bhoy, bruiser, criminal, desperado, gunman, hood (lum), mobster, mohock, mug, ruffian, thug, tough, whyo, yegg
girl moll
GANGWAY aisle, bridge, catwalk, corridor, couloir, lookout, passage(way), plank, ramp, slip, tunnel, warning, watch out
GANNET bird, booby, fowl, gant, goose, ibis, margot, moris, piquero, solan, sula
deborah robert shurtleff
GANO *foe* roland
GANOF See THIEF.
GANT gannet, gaunt, yawn
GANTRY bridge, frame, platform, span
GANYMEDE aquarius, catamitus
abductor zeus
brother assaracus, ilus
consort hebe
parent assaracus, callirrhoe, erichthonius, laomedon, tros
GAOL See JAIL.
GAP abysm, abyss, aperture, arroyo, blank, breach, break, breck, burst, can-(y)on, chasm, chimney, chink, cleft, cleuch, cleugh, clough, col, coulee, couloir, crack, cranny, crevasse, crevice, cut, defile, dell, donga, draw, fault, flaw, flume, gape, gorge, gulch, gulf, gully, hiatus, interstice, interval, lacuna, meuse, muse(t), notch, nullah, opening, pass(age), ravine, rent, shard, space, split, vacuity, vacuum, wadi, want, waterway
GAPE admire, bilge, cape, chaun, chawn, dehisce, frondesce, GAP, gaum, gawk, gawp, gaze, glare, gloat, grin, hiate, ogle, ope(n), oscitate, peer, re-

gard, rent, see, stare, watch, wonder, yawn, yawp
open dehisce
GAPER broadbill, cabrilla, clam, mya
GAPES gaze, rictus, yawning
GAPING chappy, chasma, cleft, cracked, dehiscence, expectant, galp, gawish, hiant, open, oscitancy, oscitation, pandiculation, ringent, yawning
GAR agujadecasta, agujon, belone, billfish, cause, cherma, compel, force, gorefish, gurdfish, hornbeak, hornfish, longjaws, longnose, make, needlefish, sailfish, saury, snook, spearfish
bony lepisosteus
GARAGE bodyshop, carhouse, carport, hanger, lockup, parking, repair shop
sale item hand-me-down
to house passage breezeway
GARAPATA See CARAPATO.
GARB (See also DRESS.) apparel, array, bundle, carriage, clothing, costume, custom, dress, fashion, garments, gear, grace, guise, method, raiment, sheaf
kind mourning, sackcloth
GARBAGE disembowel, dreck, leftovers, offal, refuse, remnants, rubbish, scraps, slaistery, slop(s), swill, trash, waste(matter)
collector dustman, trashman
GARBLE alloy, bolt, color, distort, falsify, geld, mangle, mess, misquote, misrepresent, mix, mutilate, pervert, refuse, rubbish, select, sift, sophisticate, sort
GARBOIL broil, confuse, confusion, disturb, garble
GARCON boy, man, waiter
GARDA, LAKE *breeze* ora
GARDEN arboretum, arena, chinampa, cultivate, eden, farm, garth, giardino, herbary, hothouse, jardin, leighton, nursery, olitory, outfield, paradise, patch, planting, pomacy, quinta, shamba, verger, vihara, yard
aster callistephus
balm monarda, oswego tea

balsam blue melilot, impatiens
botanical arboretum
bower alcove
buttercup crowfoot
cicely chervil
city chicago, kent
colony natal
cress peppergrass
cypress lavendar-cotton, seawormwood
deity pomona, priapus, vertumnus
flower See FLOWER *garden.*
-gate herb, pansy, robert
ginger cayenne-pepper
glass-enclosed greenhouse, terrarium
green orache
grown in hortensial
heliotrope valerian
herb thyme
house casino, gazebo
huckleberry morel, nightshade, solanum, wonderberry
implement See *tool,* below.
kind botanical, cactus, chinampa, flower, formal, herb(ery), hortyard, kailyard, kaleyard, kitchen, knot, oasis, orchard, terrarium, topiary, truck, vegetable
kitchen croft
of eden See PARADISE; UTOPIA.
of england kent, worcestershire
of europe italy
of france amboise, touraine
of gold apples hesperides
of india oude
of ireland carlow
of italy campania, lombardy, sicily
of spain andalusia
of the west illinois, kansas
orach alpine-dock, beet, butter-leaves
persicary prince's-feather
pert. hortulan
pest aphid, aphis, cutworm, nematode, scale, snail, thrip
phlox beacon
pink dianthus, painted lady
plague goutweed
produced in olitory
purslane portulaca
rocket eveweed
science horticulture
small allotment
spacious pleasance

spider epeira
state new jersey
structure gazebo, scarecrow, trellis
syringa mock orange
tool dibber, dibble, edger, hoe, mattock, mower, rake, scythe, seeder, shovel, sickle, spade, trowel, weeder
variety average, ordinary
wabler beam-bird, bec(c)-afico, fauvette, figeater, flycatcher, haybird, jack, muscicapa, sylvia
GARDENER bostangi, bostanji, horticulturist, mali, ponica
bird bird of paradise, bower bird
delight mullein-pink, rose-campion
garters bride's-laces, dodder, ribbongrass
lady, name meaning hortense
symbol green thumb
underworld ascalaphus
GARE beware, covetous, depot, excitement, keen, piece, pier, station, wharf, wool
-fowl great auk
GARFIELD, JAMES *birthplace* orange, ohio
party republican
profession lawyer
vice president arthur
GARFISH See GAR.
GARGANEY crick, teal
GARGANTUA *abbey* theleme
character bragmardo, picrochole
creator rabelais
parent gargamelle, grangousier
son pantagruel
tutor holophernes, ponocrates
wife badebec
GARGANTUAN big, brobdingnagian, colossal, cyclopean, enormous, giant, gigantic, great, herculean, homeric, huge, immense, mammoth, titantic, vast
GARGLE collutory, mouth wash, prophylactic
GARIBALDI biscuit, goldfish, shirtwaist
cause risorgimento
supporter camicia rossa, red shirt

wife anita

GARISH blatant, bright, broadway, brummagem, cheap, flashy, flighty, fussy, gaudy, gay, gewgaw, gimcrack, glaring, grandiloquent, meretricious, ostentatious, pretentious, showy, tawdry, vulgar

GARLAND anadem, anthology, bays, bouquet, chapbook, chaplet, chrestomathy, circle, collection, corance, corpus, crown, festoon, fillet, florilegium, glory, headband, laurel, lei, palm, prize, rosary, thesaurus, treasury, trophy, wreath

flower daphne, erica, heath, lei

GARLIC allium, chive, clown's-treacle, farce, jig, porret, rocambole

compound allyl

root bulb, moly, ramson

segment clove

smelling of alliaceous

wild moly

GARM (R) *owner* hel

slayer tyr

victim tyr

GARMENT apparel, attire, blanket, clothing, covering, dress, dud, fig-leaf, frock, habit, rag, raiment, robe, robing, tog, vestment, vesture, wearable, wrap, wriel

alterer bushelman

ancient capuchin, chiton, chlamys, ephod, himation, paenula, palla, stola, synthesis, toga, trabea

baby's See *infant's*, below.

bed nightclothes, nightgown, nightie, nightshirt

bishop's See VESTMENT *religious.*

blue mazarine

burial shroud

child's rompers

close-fitting coatee

coarse brat, stroud

dancer's leotard

defensive armor, broigne, gambeson, jack

fitted reefer

foundation corset, girdle, two-way-stretch

gymnastic leotard, romper(s), shorts

hooded anorak, bunting, capuche, cowl, huke, sleeper

infant's barrow, bunting,

crawler, creeper, diaper, sleeper, swaddling clothes, woolly

kind apron, barrow, blanket, cape, capote, cardinal, chamma, coat, cotehardie, cotte, dress, gown, haik, jumper, kimono, mantle, robe, saree, sari, yukata

leather buff

lining underlay

long himation, jibba, jibbeh, mandyas, pelisse, stole

long-sleeved flocket

loop tab, tag

loose burnoose, caftan, camis(e), camus, cloak, cymar, djelab, djellab(ah), flocket, jelib, jellab(a), kimono, mantle, robe, simar, wrapper

loose sleeveless cucula

-making haberdashery, sewing, tailoring

medieval broigne, chausses, dalmatic, gambeson, kirtle, rochet, simar, tabard

men's belt, cap, coat, drawers, hat, jacket, pants, shirt, shorts, slacks, socks, trousers, windbreaker

monk's scapular

mourning black, crepe, cypress, ricinium, sable, sackcloth, weeds, weepers

outer aba, brat, cape, capote, chemise, cloak, coat, coverslut, dalman, dreadnought, dress, frock, galabia, haik, haori, himation, hyke, jacket, jumpsuit, overalls, overslop, paletot, palla, parka, pelisse, pilch, polonaise, robe, rochet, ruana, shawl, skirt, slacks, slop, smock, stole, surcoat, sweater, tobe, trousers, wrap

padded truss

part arm(hole), bodice, bosom, coattail, collar, cuff, fly, lapel, leg, neck(band), pocket, seat, shirttail, skirt, sleeve, stomacher, waist, wristband, yoke

patchwork cento

penitent's sanbenito

pert. vestiary

priest's See VESTMENT *religious.*

protective apron, armor, bib, brat, broigne, chaps, coveralls, cuculla, gabardine, gab-

erdine, overalls, pinafore, raincoat, smock

rain oilskin, poncho, slicker

rehearsal leotard

repairer bushelman

scarf-like tippet

short capelet

skins parka

sleeveless aba, cape, cowl, cucul(l)a, gandurah, jumper, mantle, slipover, sweater, tabard, vest

slit vent

square kaross

tight-fitting cotehardie, cotte, hose, leotard, sheath

tunic-like tabard

under bra, bvd, camisole, shift, shorts, skivvy, slip, teddy, tee-shirt, t-shirt

under armor doublet, haustement

upper blouse, coat, guernsey, jersey, jupon, peplus, shirt, slipover, sweater, tunic, vest, waist

victorian chemisette

women's bloomers, blouse, bodice, bourkha, bra, burga, burk(h)a, burnous, canezou, capote, capuchin, casaque, casaquin, chemise(tte), chiton, cymar, dress, housecoat, izar, kimono, mantua, nabob, negligee, peplos, peplum, peplus, sheath, shift, simar, teddy, visite

GARN go on, worsted, yarn

GARNER accumulate, collect, gather, granary, reap, store

GARNET allochroite, almandine, almandite, andradite, anthrax, aplome, calderite, cape-ruby, carbuncle, demantoid, essonite, grenat, haplome, hessonite, pigeon-blood, olivine, pyrope, red, vermeil, yanolite

berry currant

black melanite

clew rope, tackle

convex carbuncle

green olivine, uvarovite

maganese spesserite

pink rhodolite, rosolite

purple almandine, almandite, rhodolite

red almandine, almandite, rock ruby

symbol of constancy

yellow topazlite

GARNISH adorn, beautify, bedeck, chummage, cress, deck, decorate, doll up, dress, duxelles, embellish, enhance, equip, fetters, furnish, heighten, lard, ornament, parsley, perk up, prank, prink, relish, socle, topping, trim

custard royale

GARNISHMENT attachment, decoration, lien, summons

GAROO agalloch

GARRET attic, cockloft, head, loft, mansard, solar, turret, watchtower

GARRISON defense, fort(ification), fortify, gift, guard, occupy, presidio, store, stronghold, treasure, warden, warnison

pert. presidial

GARROT duck, fowl, goldeneye, tourniquet

GARROTE execute, kill, strangle, strangulation, suffocation, throttle

GARRULOUS articulate, babbly, diffuse, eloquent, fluent, gabby, glib, loquacious, prolix, talkative, talky, verbose, vocal, voluble, wordy

GARRULOUSNESS, GARRULITY babbling, chattering, jabbering, prating, verbiage, volubility

GARRUPA bonaci, garlopa, grouper, jewfish, rockfish

GARRYA bearbrush, feverbush

GARTER elastic, fetters, legirons, leglet, supporter, wooerbab

snake elaps

GARTH close, cortile, croft, dam, girth, hoop, weir, yard

GARUA camanchaca, fog

GARUDA *master* vishnu

GARVEY boat, scow

GARVIE sprat

GAS air, anesthetic, bluster, bombast, brag, chatter, damp, exhaust, flatus, fuel, fume, gossip, humbug, miasma, nonsense, petrol(eum), reek, singe, talk, vapor, wind

apparatus aerator

bag ballonet, balloon, braggart, chatterbox

balloon helium, nitrogen

black carbon

blue ozone

charcoal oxan(e)

charge with aerate

colorless ammonia, arsine, cyclopropane, ethane, fluoroform, germane, keten(e), oxan(e), ozone, stibine

comb. aer(o), ozo

combustion backflash

container bomb, cell, tank

flammable butane, ethane, isobutane, isobutylene, methane, phosphine, propane

hot springs xenon

inert argon, helium, neon, nitrogen, xenon

ionization electromerism

kind acetylene, actinon, ammonia, argon, arsine, benzene, borborygamus, butane, carbon(dioxide) (monoxide), chlorine, damp, ethane, ether, ethine, ethyl, firedamp, fluorin(e), formaldehyde, freon, helium, hydrogen, ketene, krypton, laughing, lox, marsh, methane, mustard, natural, neon, nerve, nitrogen, oil, oxane, oxygen, ozone, phosgene, poison, propane, radon, sewer, sneeze, stibine, tear, vesicatory, xenon

light etherion

-light burner batswing

marsh methane

measurer eudiometer

military adamsite, chlorine

mustard yperite

nerve sarin

non-flammable helium, inert

oxygen ozone

pipe tube

plant artillery plant, burning-bush, dittany, evonymus, fraxinella, mock cypress, wahoo

poison arsine, carbon monoxide, chlorine, cyanogen, ketene, phosgene, stibine

-producing aerogenic

radioactive niton, radon

rating octane

-separating atmolysis

stoker blockman

tear bromoacetone

GASCON braggart, swaggering

GASCONADE bluster, boast, brag(gadocio), crow, vaunt

GASEOUS aeriform, rare, tenuous, thin, volatile

GASH babble, chop, cleft, cut, dawk, furrow, gossip, groove, hurt, incise, incision, knowing, mark, nonsense, notch, score, slash, talkative, tattle, trench, trim, wise, witty, wound

GASKINS bragas, breeches

GASOLINE avgas, benzine, fuel, juice, petrol

ingredient butane, lead

rating octane

GASP blow, breathing, choke, croak, exclaim, gape, hiatus, pant, puff, thratch, yearn

for desire

GASSY bombastic, loquacious, pompous

GASTEROMYCETE puffball, stinkhorn

GASTRIC abdominal, antacid

stimulant capsicum

GASTROINTESTINAL *ailment* diarrhea, giardiasis

GASTROLATOR glutton

GASTRONOME bon vivant epicure, glutton, gourmand, gourmet

GASTRONOMY *capital* dijon

GASTROPOD abalone, ampullaria, aporrhais, appleshell, bleeding-tooth, buccinidum, bucky, cerithium, drill, harpa, limpet, mollusk, nerite, neritoid, oliva, ormer, slug, snail, toxifer, univalve, w(h)elk, wilk

air-breathing achatinella

ear-shaped abalone, haliotis, ormer

extinct bellerophon

land pheumabranchia

marine acera, aplysia, buccinida, conch, conus, cowrie, cowry, limpet, murex, pelican's-foot, tethys, triton

pulmonate geophila

GASTRULA *part* archenteron, blastopore, epiblast, protostome

GAT channel, gun, revolver, roscoe

GATAM *parent* eliphaz

GATE aboideau, arch, attendance, audience, bab, bar(rier), box office,

confine, dar, direction, dismissal, door(way), egress, entrance, entry, fashion, git, gurdwara, herse, income, ingress, intake, journey, judgment, knack, method, money, opening, pass, pasture, path, portal, portcullis, postern, proceeds, receipts, returns, road, route, sallyport, shutter, sluice, sprue, start, street, take, tappoon, toll, toran(a), trimtram, trip, valve, way, wicket
bar ledge, lock, spar
comb. pyle
crasher intruder, uninvited guest
flood sluice
heel harr
irrigation check, tapon, tappoon
-keeper cerberus, concierge, guardian, porter, portitor, stileman, warden, watchman
lich scallage, trimtram
money admission, fee, price
post durn, harr, heel, postel, shaft, upright
rear postern
running funnel
slalom hairpin
sluice hatch, valve
tower barbican
GATEAU cake
GATEHOUSE bar, cerame, lodge
GATEWAY arch, barway, dar, door, entrance, gopura, portal, post(el), propylon, pylon, sluice, toran(a), torii, toril
arch site st louis
double dipylon
GATH *giant* goliath
king achish, maoch
GATHER accumulate, acquire, amass, assemble, blow, brew, bulk, bunch, clot, collate, collect, compile, concentrate, conclude, congest, congregate, convene, corral, cull, decerp, deduce, derive, develop, draw, flock, fold, full, garner, get, glean, harvest, heap, herd, hoard, huddle, impend, increase, infer, kilt, judge, lek, mass, meet, mobilize, muster, pick, pile, plait, pluck, presume, pucker, raise, rally, ram-

mass, reap, she(a)ve, sher, shir(r), stack, store, suppose, take, think, tuck, unite
around crystallize
from interpret
in heap hatter
ye rosebuds carpe diem
GATHERING abscess, accumulation, affair, assembly, bee, boil, ceilidh, collection, company, congregation, convention, crowd, crush, drove, fair, flock, function, galaxy, hall, harvest, horde, hosting, imminent, jamboree, klatsch, meeting, mob, mooting, party, plisse, powwow, press, rout, shivoo, smoker, sum, symposium, tea, throng, turnout
clouds danger, menace, omen, warning
conversational chinwag, gabfest
of cloth shirr(ing)
of the clans solitaire
place amphitheatre, arena, auditorium, hall, lesche, resort, stadium
GAUCHE askew, awkward, bizarre, clumsy, far out, inept, left-handed, maladroit, obtuse, odd, out, skew, tactless, twisted, weird
GAUCHO cowboy, horseman, stockman
knife bolo, machete
lariat bolas
GAUD adorn, artifice, bead, display, fangle, finery, fraud, jest, jewelry, joke, ornament, paint, sport, trick, trinket
GAUDERY display, finery
GAUDY blatant, brankie, branky, brazen, brummagem, catchpenny, cheap, chintzy, coarse, colorful, counterfeit, festal, flashy, flaunting, flimsy, florid, garish, gross, inferior, loud, luxurious, meretricious, obtrusive, paperbox, pretentious, showy, tacky, tasteless, tawdry, tinsel, vulgar, worthless
GAUGE (See also GAGE.) bore, calculate, criterion, dimensions, estimate, extent, fee, feeler, measure, meter, model, moot, norm, quantify, rate, rule, size,

standard, tally, touchstone, type, value, yardstick
kind barometer, calipers, chain, compass, dentin, dial, dividers, gradometer, level, line, log, micrometer, nonius, plumb, protractor, quadrant, rod, rule(r), scale, scantle, sector, sextant, sizestick, square, steel, straightedge, tape(line), tapemeasure, theodolite, transit, vernier, viagraph, yardstick
pointer arm, needle
ring moot
GAUGUIN *book* noanoa
brother theo
GAUL celt, cymry, france, frenchman, gallia, kell, pictone(s)
apostle irenaeus
breeches brac(c)ae, braies
chariot esseda, essede
chieftain vercingetorix
city alesia
coin angelot
deity belenus, belisama, esus, taranes, teutates
deity, 3-headed cernunnos
druid saronide
ensign bear, bull, cock, wolf
fortress alesia
giant perion
hades ifurin
king brennus
magistrate vergobret
nation aedui
peasants bagaudae
priest druid
prince vergobret
prophets vates
river god belisama
ruler brenhin, brenn
soldier's cloak sagum
tribe allobroges, arverni, atrebates, belgae, lemovices, remi, veneti
war god esus
GAULDING, GAULIN bird, egret, heron
GAULTHERIA arrayan, checkerberry, salal, wintergreen
GAUM attention, befog, bewilder, confuse, consider, coom, daub, gape, gom, gorge, handle, heed, hold, lout, paw, pay attention, smear, stuff, understand(ing)
GAUMY daubed, smeary, thick, viscid
GAUNT angular, barren,

bony, cadaverous, desolate, empty, forbidding, gant, grebe, grim, haggard, lank(y), lean, · rawboned, scrawny, sickly, skinny, slender, slight, slim, spare(set), thin, wasted, worn
down slenderize
GAUNTLET challenge, cuff, gainpain, glove, mitt(en), mousquetaire, obstacle, ordeal, test
GAUP, GAWP, GAWK booby, boor, bumpkin, cuckoo, fool, gape, gaze, lout, lubber, lumpkin, oaf, rammack, simpleton, stare, swallow
GAUR bibos, bison, seladang
GAUSTER bluster, brag, bully, gossip, swagger
GAUT pass, range, stairs
GAUTAMA See BUDDHA.
GAUZE bandage, barege, carbasus, cloth, cloud, crepe, dressing, film, haze, leno, lint, lisse, marli, marly, mist, pleasance, tiffany, tulle, umple
black cypress, cyprus
-like tissued
GAUZY diaphanous, fine, pellucid, sheer, thin, transparent
GAVEL hammer, interest, mallet, rent, scepter, sheaf, tribute
GAVELKIND birthright, possession, tenure
GAVELOCK crow(bar), dart, gaff, lever, spear
GAVIA auk, gull, loon, tern
GAVIAL crocodile, gharial, lizard, loricate, nakoo
GAVOTTE bouree, dance, musette, solitaire
GAW drain, gall, gape, trench
GAWAIN *brother* aggravayne, gaheris, gareth, mordred
enemy la(u)ncelot
parent lot, morgause
son florence, gyngalyn, lovel
uncle king arthur
GAWK See GAUP.
GAWKY awkward, clownish, clumsy, gowkit, lean, lubber, oafish
GAWN gallon, pail, tub
GAWP See GAUP.
GAY airy, animated, antic, blithe, boon, bright, bril-

liant, capersome, cheerful, cheery, chipper, colorful, coltish, convivial, debonair, exuberant, fair, festive, fine, first-class, folatre, frisky, frohlich, frolicsome, funloving, gamesome, gaudy, genial, gioioso, glad, happy, high, holiday, jaunty, jocund, jolly, jovial, joyful, lively, loose, merry, pert, playful, pleasant, profligate, riant, rollicking, rollicksome, rollicky, rompish, rorty, rory-tory, showy, skittish, smicker, sparkish, spirited, splendid, sporty, sprightly, tittupy, vivacious, wanton, well, zestful, zippy
as a lark
cat tramp
dog libertine
-feather blazing-star, liatris, prairie pine
john, work beggar's opera, fables, shepherd's week
science poetry
GAYETY See GAIETY.
GAYLUSSACIA black-hurts, buckberry, deerberry, huckleberry, shrub
GAYWINGS babies'-feet, bird-on-the-wing, maywings, milkwort
GAZ arshin
GAZABO boy, eccentric, fellow, guy
GAZE admire, aspect, con, dare, gander, gape, gaup, gawk, gawp, glaik, glare, gloat, glower, goggle, leer, look, moon, observe, ogle, peer, pore, pry, regard, rubberneck, scan, see, stare, survey, toot, twire, watch, wlite
GAZEBO balcony, belvedere, pavillion, summerhouse, tower
GAZELLE addra, admi, ahu, algazel, antelope, aoul, ariel, budorcas, chikara, chinkara, cora, corin(ne), dama, dibatag, dzeren, goa, kevel, korin, kudu, mohr, oryx, springbok, springbuck, tabitha, takin
clark's dibitag
4-horned chikara
hound saluki
name meaning tabitha
GAZETTE courant, journal, newspaper, periodical

GAZETTED bankrupt, posted, sent
GAZETTEER dictionary, glossary, journalist, lexicon
GAZEZ *father* caleb
GAZIANTEP aintab, autep, ayntab
GDANSK See DANZIG.
GE See GAEA.
GEAR accessories, apparatus, apparel, appliances, appurtenance, armor, baggage, belongings, cam, clothing, cog, cordage, dress, duffel, effects, equipment, garb, graith, harmonize, harness, hypoid, kit, machinery, material, paraphernalia, pinion, possessions, rig(ging), tack, tackle, tackling, tools, trilobe, wheel
box transmission
chafing scotchman
kind cogwheel, differential, dynaflow, first, fluid drive, fourth, freewheeling, high, hydromatic, intermediate, low, neutral, overdrive, rack, reverse, speed
military armory
tooth cog
up accelerate
wheel pinion, unilobe, wabbler, wobbler
GEASTER earthstar, fungus
GEATA *prince* beowulf
GEB cronus, keb, s(h)eb
bird form goose
daughter isis, nephthys
father shu
head ornament goose
son osiris, set(h), thoth
successor to thoth
wife not, nut
GEBBIE crop, mouth, stomach
GEBER *governor for* solomon
GECK cheat, deride, dupe, gull, scorn, trick
GECKO fanfoot, lacertid, lizard, tarente, tokay
GEDALIAH *province* judea
son cushi
GEE accord, agree, concur, fit, harmonize, horse, move, right, sulks, sullenness
up spoil
GEEGEE bangtail, horse, nag
GEELBEC salmon, teraglin
GEEZER curmudgeon, oddity, oldster
GEGENEIS See CURETES.

GEGG gag, hoax, joke
GEHENNA See HELL.
GEIGER aloewood, myxa, sebesten, tree
GEISEL, TED dr seuss
GEISHA dancer, hostess, maiko
girdle holder inro
GEIST genius, ghost, spirit
GEL alcogel, congeal, harden, jellify, jelly, pectize, set, solidify
GELATIN agalloch, agar (agar), albuminoid, aspic, bastard-amber, collin, colloid, glutoid, haitsai, isinglass, jelly, norgine, pectin, sericin
plate bat
-silk sericin
transparent film of ice paper
GELATINOUS blubbery, jelly-like, muculent, thick, viscid
hydrate amyloid, starch
GELD alter, barren, caponize, castrate, dry, emasculate, expurgate, fruitless, garble, lib, mutilate, prune, spay, sterile, sterilize, tax
GELDING deduction, eunuch, horse
GELID arctic, chilly, cold, cool, frigid, frosty, frozen, glacial, icy
GELL frolic, fun, spree
GELON *city* syracuse
GELSEMIUM flower, jasmine, jessamine, shrub
GELT gold, lunatic, money, sterile
GEM (See also *kind*, below.) amulet, baguet(te), bijou, bud, ice, jewel, muffin, paragon, precious stone, prize, STONE, treasure
ancient aromatite
artificial birne, boule, chaton, glass, paste, rhinestone, strass
-bearing earth byon
blue aquamarine, benitoite, iolite, sapphire, turquoise
carnelian sard
carved cameo, intaglio
conjugal happiness sardonyx
cut cabochon, emerald, marquise, rose
cutter adamas, cadrans, geniostat
engraved abraxas, crusta
engraving glyptograph
face bezel, bezil, culet, facet
facetted marquise

friendship topaz
fruit false miterwort
goodluck moonstone
green chrysolite, chrysoprase, emerald, hiddenite, jade, peridot
health agate
imitation See *artificial*, above.
immortality emerald
imperfect loupe
iridescent cat's-eye, moonstone, opal, pearl, tiger-eye
kind adamas, agate, alamandine, amber, amethyst, anthrax, aquamarine, bahia, balanite, beryl, bloodstone, briolet, burmite, carbuncle, carnelian, cat's-eye, chalcedony, chrysoprase, citrine, diamond, dorje, emerald, garnet, hematite, jacinth, jade, jasper, jet, kunzite, lapis lazuli, laske, ligure, macle, moonstone, morganite, nephrite, onegite, onyx, opal, pearl, peridot, plasma, prase, prasine, pyrope, quartz, rubelet, ruby, sapphire, sard(onyx), spinel, tigereye, topaz, tourmaline, turquoise, vajra, zircon
light-reflecting asteria
-like lapidacious, lapidarian, lapidary, lapideous
love amethyst
modern jacinth, ligure, zircon
paste strass
peace diamond
pear-shaped briolette
pert. lapidary, lapideous
precious See *kind*, above.
purity pearl
purple amethyst
rectangular baguet(te)
red avena, carnelian, garnet, pyrope, ruby, sard, spinel
relief cameo
rose spinel balas
ruby-colored spinel
setting chase, chaton, collect, ouch, pave, tiffany
single solitaire
state idaho
style cut
stone chevee, crosscut, emerald, fisheye, hyalithe, iolite, jade, spinel, star
support setting
surface See *face*, above.
top facet table
top part crown

translucent moonstone, opal
truth sapphire
2-layered cameo
uncut cabochon, rough
unlucky opal
weight carat, karat
yellow peridot, topaz
youth beryl
GEMARA baraithas, talmud
contents haggada, halakah
GEMARIAH *son* michaiah
GEMATRIA cryptograph
GEMINATE coupled, double, paired
GEMINI castor, pollux, twins
gem carbuncle
GEMMA bud, bulbil, soredium
GEMMATE bud, burgeon, develop, propagate
GEMMULE broodsac, spore
GEMOTE assembly, court, meeting
GEMSBOK chamois, goat, kokama, oryx
GENAZI *master* elisha
GENDARME bailiff, bull, cavalryman, constable, cop, flic, guard, officer, policeman, soldier, trooper, warden
GENDER beget, breed, female, feminine, generate, genus, kind, male, masculine, neuter, offspring, product, sex, sort
GENE allele, allelomorph, cytogene, factor, lethal, modifier, primer
carrier chromosome
mutating allele
GENEALOGY ancestry, descent, family tree, genetics, heredity, history, linage, line(age), order, paternity, pedigree, peerage, stemma
lists begats
tree arbor
GENERA categories, classes, divisions, gens, genus, phyla
GENERAL abstract, accustomed, all(round), approximate, aufidius, average, bird's-eye, brigadier, broad, canidius, catholic, commander, common, comprehensive, customary, diffuse, dominant, encyclic, epidemic, generic, gross, habitual, kaid, major, marshal, natural, normal, officer, ordinary, overall, pandemic, people, popular, prevailing, public, pufidius, rank, regu-

lar, rife, servant, strategos, summary, total, typical, universal, usual, vague, vulgar, whole, widespread, wonted

first women hays, hoisington

GENERALIZATION analysis, average, axiom, bromide, induction, inference, law, ratiocination, universality

GENERALIZE broaden, derive, extend, induce, infer, reason, spread, widen

GENERALLY all in all, approximately, as a rule, by and large, collectively, everywhere, for the most part, in the main, invariably, normally, often, on the whole, thereabouts, roughly, roundly, universally

GENERATE abound, actify, activate, activize, bear, beget, breed, bring about, cause, create, crossbreed, develop, engender, engineer, father, gender, get, give rise to, hatch, inbreed, initiate, kittle, make, mother, multiply, originate, procreate, produce, proliferate, propagate, reproduce, sire, spawn, start, teem, yield

GENERATION age, abiogenesis, biogenesis, breed, creation, descendants, development, eon, epigenesis, epoch, era, family, formation, homogenesis, kind, lifetime, offspring, origination, pangenesis, parthenogenesis, period, procreation, production, progeny, sporogenesis, stock, time

of man humanity

spontaneous abiogenesis

GENERATIVE gametic, genetic, productive, prolific, seedful

GENERATOR alternator, amplidyne, author, buzzer, dynamo, exciter, producer

part stator

GENERIC common, comprehensive, encompassing, general, regular, specific, typical, universal

GENEROSITY altruism, amiability, cordiality, courtesy, friendliness, goodness, grace, graciousness, hospi-

tality, largesse, liberality, magnanimity, neighborliness, open-heartedness, patience, plenty, receptiveness

GENEROUS altruistic, ample, benevolent, big-(hearted), bounteous, bountiful, broad(hearted), capacious, charitable, comprehensive, cordial, expansive, extensive, frank, free, good, gracious, great(hearted), handsome, hefty, indulgent, large, largifical, lavish, liberal, magnanimous, munificent, noble(minded), open (handed), philanthropic, prodigal, productive, profuse, spacious, teeming, unselfish, unstinted, voluminous, wide

GENESIS beginning, bereshit(h), birth, creation, etymology, nascency, nativity, ontogenesis, ontogeny, origin(ation), phylogeny, physiogeny

GENET berbe, dapple, horse, jannet, viverrine

relative civet

GENETICS eugenics, heredity, inheritance

GENETRIX See MOTHER.

GENEVA gin, liquor

gown canting-coat

lake leman

lake breeze rabat

lake, castle on chillon

GENGHIS KHAN *dynasty* yuan

GENIAL affable, amiable, benign(ant), blithe, cheerful, cordial, couthie, douce, expansive, festive, friendly, generative, glad, gracious, happy, hearty, inborn, jolly, jovial, kind(ly), mental, merry, native, nuptial, pleasant, sociable, sunny, warm

become thaw, warm

GENICULATE angular, bend, bent, elbowed, genuflect, kneed, kneel

GENIE, GENII bottle imp, demon, devil, hathor, jann, jinn(i), sandman

GENIP honeyberry, ironwood, jagua, lana, madder, melicocca

GENISTA bridal-veil, broom,

cytisus, furze, retama, woadwaxen

GENIUS ability, afflatus, angel, aptitude, bent, brain(s), brilliance, capability, capacity, d(a)emon, depth, duamutef, einstein, endowment, faculty, flair, fravashi, gaon, geist, gift, grasp, ingine, inspiration, intellect, intelligence, knack, master(y), muse, numen, power, prodigy, prowess, silvanus, skill, soul, spirit, superman, talent, turn, wizard

evil d(a)emon, kali

god lug(h)

GENOA cake, geane

city cuneo

coin genovino, jane

family doria

magistrate abbot, doge

GENOCIDE butchery, extermination, massacre

GENRE category, class(ification), description, genus, kind, school, sort, species, style, type

painting bambacciata, bambocciade, bambochade

GENS clan, family, goyim, house, nomen, people, race

GENTEEL cultivated, decorous, gentle, graceful, nice, noble, polished, polite, refined, stylish, urbane, well-bred

GENTIAN agueweed, autumn-bells, baldmoney, bartonia, bitters, bitterwort, boneset, felwort, feverroot, gallweed, montzelia, orange grass, spicknel

blue false-pennyroyal, soapwort

genus frasera, sabbatia, swertia

green swertia

GENTILE arian, aryan, catholic, christian, ethnic, goi, goy(im), heathen, infidel, pagan, paynim, protestant

apostle st paul

boy shaygets

girl shiksa

pert. ethnic

GENTILITY aristocracy, breeding, courtesy, decency, gentry, heathenism, paganism, polish

GENTLE acquiescent, affable, amiabile, aristocratic, balmy, bland, blue-blooded, break, broken, calm, canny, chastened, chivalrous, clement, courteous, courtly, dainty, deft, delicate, docile, domesticate, easy, edel, ennoble, excellent, faint, falcon, feeble, genial, genteel, granual, honorable, humane, kind(ly), lamb-like, lenient, lent, light, lithe, low(pitched), mansuete, meek, mild, milky, moderate, mollify, noble, pacific, patrician, placid, pleasing, quiet, silken, slow, smooth, soaking, soft(en), soothing, subdued, sweet, tame(d), temperate, tender, tractable, tranquil, well-born

GENTLEFOLK aristocracy, bluebloods, county, elite, gentry, nobility, society

GENTLEMAN('S) amateur, aristocrat, baboo, babu, bayard, caballero, cadet, cavalier, curio, dandy, dom, don, doray, duniewassal, esquire, faithful, galantuomo, gallant, herr, junker, knight, lackey, milord, mister, mynheer, nib(s), noble(man), rye, sahib, seigneur, senhor, senor, ser, signor(e), sir, squire(en), toff, true blue, trusty, tuan, yeoman, yo(u)nker
breeches cowslip
country squire
4 chrysanthemum, orchid, plum, tree
gentleman valet
gypsy rye
hat night-flowering catchfly
jim james corbett
tormentor cleavers, galium
training for knighthood donzel

GENTLENESS amiability, edelkeit, kindness, leniency, lenity, medenagan, moderation, softness, tenderness

GENTLEWOMAN lady

GENTLY adagio, canny, easily, fairly, soave, softly, tenderly

GENTOO hindu, penguin, telugu

GENTRY aristocracy, county, elite, fairies, nobility, people, petite noblesse, society, squirage, squir(e)archy, szlachta

GENU bend, flexure, rend

GENUFLECT bend, bow, curtsey, flex, kneel, salaam

GENUINE actual, artless, authentic, bonafide, candid, certified, dinkum, eighteen-carat, frank, germane, good, graithly, honest, incorrupt, kosher, legit (imate), mccoy, native, natural, official, original, pistic, pucka, pukka, pure, real, right(ful), sheer, simon-pure, sincere, sterling, straight, true, unadulterated, unaffected, unalloyed, uncorrupt, undisguised, valid, veridical, veritable, vrai
not bogus, fake, malafide, sham, tin

GENUS category, class(ification), family, gender, kind, order, sort, type
1-specied monotype
pert. generic
subdivision species

GEODE cavity, druse, nodule, voog, vug(g), vugh

GEOGRAPHER apianus, brunhes, buache, cluvel, humboldt, kant, mela, mercator, munster, ptolemy, ritter, strabo, thales, varen, vidal

GEOGRAPHY chorography, topography, topology

GEOID allipsoid, sphere
angle hade

GEOLOGICAL *age* See ERA *prehistoric.*
comb. cene, ian, oic
deposit varva
division acheulean, aeon, animikean, animiki, aptian, archaean, archeozoic, arenig, argovian, artinskian, arundel, beaufort, benton, bolderian, bretonian, burdigalian, chazy, ecca, eon, epoch, era, erian, gault, glacial, holocene, lias, lyas, muav, quaternary, stade, tertiary, trias, uinta, ventersdorp
eskars osar
fault strainslip
formation aquifer, bedford, boone, ione, terrane, terrene, vicksburg
group bala, caradoc
period See *division*, above; ERA *prehistoric.*
science pal(a)eontology

stage achen, astian, riss, wurm
vein angle hade

GEOLOGIST *famous* huxley, lyell, strabo

GEOLOGY earth science, pal(a)eontology, rocks, tectonics

GEOMANCER See PROPHET.

GEOMETRY *angle* incidence
coordinate abscissas
curve ellipse, evolute, parabola, sinusoid, spiral
father euclid
figure circle, cone, crescent, cube, cuboid, cusp, cylinder, decagon, dodecagon, ellipse, ellipsoid, foursquare, gnomon, heptagon, hexagon, hexahedron, icosahedron, isogon, lozenge, lune, nonagon, oblong, octagon, octahedron, oxygon, parallelepiped, parallelogram, pelcoid, pentacle, pentagon, pentahedron, polygon, polyhedron, prism, quadrangle, quadrant, quadrilateral, rectangle, rhomb(oid), rhombus, sector, solid, sphere, square, tetragon, tetragram, tetrahedron, trapeze, trapezium, trapezoid, triangle, trigon, versor
line(s) loci, locus, secant
premise postulate
proponent euclid, pascal
proportion porism
proposition theorem
solid cone, cube, cylinder, lune, prism, pyramid, sphere
spider aranea, orb weaver
surface nappe, toroid, torus
term cosine, locus, secant, sine, tangent, theorem, versor

GEOMYID See GOPHER.

GEOPHAGY pica

GEOPHILA land-snail, slug

GEOPONIC(S) agricultural, agriculture, georgic, husbandry

GEORGE *henry, concept* single tax
lake horicon
saint, emblem lance
saint, foster-mother kalyb
II, queen caroline of anspach
III, disease porphyria
III, prime minister pitt

GEORGEY-PORGEY king george i
GEORGIA See also GEORGIA (USSR).
bark cascara buckthorn, quinine
capital atlanta
city albany, andersonville, athens, atlanta, augusta, college park, columbus, conyers, cordele, dalton, decatur, gainesville, griffin, jesup, la grange, macon, marietta, moultrie, plains, rome, savannah, sparta, thomasville, valdosta, vidalia, waycross
college emory, georgia tech, mercer, morehouse, spelman
county bibb, cobb, dekalb, fulton, gwinnett, laurens, muscogee, rabon, talbot, tift, troup
flower cherokee rose
founder oglethorpe
indian chiaha, creek, guale, hitchiti, oconee, uchean, yamasee, yuchi
island cumberland, jekyll, ossabaw, sapelo
lake bankhead, harding, hartwell, lanier, martin, nottely, sinclair
national monument fort pulaski
native cracker
nickname cracker state, peach state
peak brasstown, kennesaw, stone
pine longleaf
resort warm springs
river altamaha, chattahoochee, conecuh, etowah, flint, ocmulgee, oconee, ogeechee, pea, pigeon, satilla, savannah, s(u)wanee
state bird thrasher
state flower cherokee rose
state tree liveoak
swamp okefinokee
GEORGIA (USSR) abkhasia, armenia, azerbaijan
capital batumi, tbilisi, tiflis
castle metekhi
cathedral sioni
city adzhar, batumi, iberia, kutaisi, tbilisi, tiflis
conqueror jelel addin
fortress narikala
hat papakhas
king vakhtang-gorgasali
language grusinian

patriarch katholikos
people abkha(sian), adzhar, caucasian, svan(e), tush
prince tsitsianov
queen tamara, thamara
resort sukhumi
sea black
wine ghvino
GEORGIC agrestic, agricultural, arcadian, bucolic, geoponie, pastoral, poem, rural, rustic
GEPHYREAN starworm
GERA *son* ehud, shimei
GERAH 20 shekel
GERAINT *wife* enid
GERANIAL aldehyde, citral
GERANIUM alumbloom, alumroot, beefsteak-plant, begonia, billy-button, blockdock, bloodwort, chocolate flower, cranes-bill, daisy, dovefoot, erodium, fluxweed, pelargonium, red campion, scabious, shameface
creeper japanese ivy
lake nacarat, spark
pink bermuda
strawberry aaron's beard
wild cranesbill, fluxweed, herb-robert
GERAR *king* abimelech
GERARDIA agalinis, aurelaria
GERBIL jird, meriones, rodent
GERD(A) *father* gymer
husband frey
wooer skirnir
GEREFA bailiff, officer, reeve, sheriff
GERENT bearing, carrying, manager, ruler
GERI *wolf of* odin
GERM bacteria, bacterium, beginning, bud, bug, cell, egg, embryo, microbe, organism, origin, ovule, ovum, pathogen, rudiment, seed(ling), seminium, source, spawn, spore, sprout, virus
cell egg, gamete, ovum
comb. blasto
-free ablastous, antiseptic, aseptic, budless
layer mesoderm
plasm genes
seed chit
GERMAN (See also GERMANY for all geographical entries.) aleman(ni), allemand, almain(e),

alman, balt, boche, deutscher, dutch(man), dutchy, fritz(ie), goth, hans, heinie, hun, jerry, kraut, muff, PRUSSIAN, sausage, saxon, tedesco, teuton, tudesque, yekke
and so forth und so weiter
article das, der, die, ein
bavaria bayern
chap kerl
christmas weihnachten
comb. teuto(no)
comrade kamerade
congenial gemutlich
day tag
detente ostpolitik
enlightenment auflkarung
etcetera und so weiter, usw
evening abend
excellent ausgezeichnet
exclamation ach(himmel), donnerwetter, hoch
florence dresden
girl fraulein
gold dutch foil
goodbye auf wiedersehen
good evening gutenabend
good morning guten morgen
gracious lady gnadige frau
heap meiler
hello wie gehts
home heim
homesickness heimwek
horror schrecklichkeit
iliad nibelungenlied
isn't that so nicht wahr
lady frau
law recht
love minne
madwort bugloss
measles masera, rubella
mister herr
new neu(e)
prelude vorspiel
prohibited verboten
pronoun ich, sie, uns
reason vernunft
research arbeit
reverie traumerei
shepherd alsatian
slime schlich
son stammhalter
sorrow weltschmerz
spirit geist
storm and stress sturm und drang
style al allemande
surrender kamerad
sweetheart liebchen
task aufgabe
thank you danke(shon)
to your good health gesundheit, prosit

victory sieg
war krieg
wife frau
work arbeit
yes ja wohl
GERMANDER betony, cat-thyme, foxtail, herb, poly, scordium, sovenez, teucrium, veronica
-*speedwell* angeleyes, base vervain, betony, billy-brighteye, birds-eyes, blue-eye, bluets, eye-bright, scordium, sovenez
GERMANE akin, allied, analogous, applicable, apposite, appropriate, apropos, apt, cognate, comparable, felicitous, happy, kindred, material, pertinent, proper, related, relative, relevant, right, suitable, well-adapted
GERMANIC gothic, gothonic, teutonic
GERMANY See also GERMAN (for phrases in translation) and WEST GERMANY.
ace red baron, von richthof(f)en
admiral canaris, doenitz, raeder, spee, von tirpitz
adventurer munchausen
aircraft albatross, aviatik, gotha, messerschmitt, stuka, taube
aircraft designer junkers, zeppelin
air force luftwaffe
airline lufthansa
airmail luft post
animal tier
anthropologist bastian, sapir, virchow
antiaircraft gun archie
apostle boniface
archaeologist schliemann, seler, winchelmann
archduchess erzherzogin
archduke erzherzog
architect behrens, bohm, gropius, kolewey, van der rohe
aristocracy junker(s)
armament works krupp, skoda
army landwehr, volksturm, wehrmacht
army unit panzer
artist (See also *painter*, below.) ernst, grosz, hausmann, heartfield, schwitters
artist group blaue reiter, blue rider

art nouveau jugenstil
astronomer argelander, bauss, bessel, kepler
auto audi, bmw, borgward, dkw, goliath, golomobile, lloyd wagon, mercedes-benz, opel, porsche, rometsch, taunus, volkswagen, wartburg, weidner
aviator immelmann, richthofen
bacteriologist behring, koch, loffler
bank ufer
banker rothschild
baron freiherr
beaker wiederkomm
beer lager, mum
beer king gambrinus
bill of exchange devise
biologist haeckel, weismann
boar eber
bogy berchta
bomber stuka
botanist boebera, caspary, cohn, floerke, fuchs, schleiden
boxer schmeling
cake kuchen, lebkuchen, pfeffernuss, torte
camp stalag
camp police kapon
canal kiel, ludwig, weser
cannon big bertha
capital berlin, bonn
castle schloss, wartburg
cathedral dom, treve, trier
cathedral city cologne, essen
chancellor adenauer, bethmann, bismarck, brandt, bruning, erhard, hollweg, schmidt, von bulow, von hindenburg
char saibling
cheese limburger, muenster, tilsiter
chemist alder, baeyer, beckmann, beer, bergius, bosch, bottger, buchner, bunsen, butenandt, fischer, freiesleben, freitmann, freundlich, haber, hahn, hoffman, kossel, kuhn, liebig, ostwald, staudinger, von fuchs, wieland, windaus, wohler, ziegler, zsigmondy
chess player lasker
choreographer joos
city 3 aue, ems, hof, ulm 4 bonn, gera, goch, haar, hamm, jena, kiel, koln, lahr 5 aalen, ahlen, emden, essen, furth, gotha, hagen, halle, herne, mainz, neuss,

pirna, trier, worms 6 aachen, altena, altona, berlin, bingen, bochum, bremen, cassel, cleves, coburg, dachau, dessau, erfurt, hameln, kassel, linden, lubeck, munich, plauen, rheydt, speyer, spires, tilsit, treves, weimar 7 bamburg, bautzen, bottrop, breslau, cassell, cologne, crefeld, dresden, gorlitz, hamburg, hanover, kassell, kostanz, krefeld, leipzig, mayence, munchen, munster, potsdam, rostock, spandau, stettin, zwickau 8 augsburg, blenheim, chemnitz, coblentz, dortmund, duisberg, eisenach, freiburg, katowice, liegnitz, mannhaim, nurnberg, schwerin, solingen, wurselen, wurzburg 9 bielefeld, blindheim, brunswick, darmstadt, frankfort, gottingen, heilbronn, karlsruhe, magdeburg, nuremburg, oldenburg, osnabruck, pforzheim, remscheid, stuttgart, wiesbaden, wuppertal 10 badenbaden, dusseldorf, heidelberg, hildesheim, mollendorf, nordhausen, oberhausen, peenemunde, regensburg, wittenberg 11 bremerhaven
civilization kultur
clergyman neimoeller
clock uhr
coach horse giblas
coal region aachen, krefeld, ruhr, saar, sarre
cockroach croton bug
code salic
coffee frustuck, kaffee
coin achtethaler, albus, batz, blaffert, floren, groschen, gulden, heller, kreutzer, krone(n), mark, pfennig, plappert, schilling, silbergroschen, t(h)aler, zehner
colony kamerun, togoland
comb. teuto(no)
commune marl
communist spar'acist
composer abt, bacn, beethoven, blacher, brahms, bruch, egk, gluck, gotz, handel, hasse, henze, hindemith, hoffman, humperdinck, mozart, orff, pepusch, pfitzner, reger,

scharwenka, scheidt, schein, schumann, schutz, spohr, strauss, unger, von flotow, wagner, weber, weill
concentration camp See NAZI *concentration camp.*
conductor bruch, busch, furtwangler, klemperer, mengelberg, muck, orff, rudolf, von karajan, walter
confederation bund
count graf
critic benn, lessing, schlege
customs union zollverein
cutlass dusack, tesack
-czech region sudeten
dam eder
dance allemande, gallopade, landler, waltz
day of the week (1–7) montag, dienstag, mittwoch, donnerstag, freitag, sonnabend, sonntag
deer reh
demon alp, kobold, wode
design school bauhaus
dialect baltisch, bavarian, hessisch, ko(e)lsch
diplomat bernstorff, papen
dirigible hindenberg, zeppelin
division abteilung
dog alsatian, boxer, dauchshund, doberman, drahthaar, rottweiler, schnauzer, shepherd
dramatist barlach, brecht, hauptmann, heyse, kotzebue, lessing, sudermann, toller
drink barenjager, beer, schnapps
duchy franconia
duck gadwall
dumplings klosse, knodel
dwarf alberich, buckinger, colobri, duergar, dwerger, dwergugh, stoberin
dynasty See *royal family,* below.
earnest money handgeld
ecclesiastic bruno, thomas a kempis
economist knies, thunen
editor redakteur
educator froebel
eel aal
egyptologist lepsius
elite guard schutz staffen, waffen ss
emperor frederick, kaiser, otto, wilhelm
engineer diesel, flettner,

lilienthal, roebling, von braun
engraver durer
epic arme heinrich, nibelungenlied
fairy berchta
fairy tale marchen
feast oktoberfest
field marshal blucher, goltz, goring, kesselring, manstein, rommel, von blomberg, von bock, von brauchitsch, von kleist, von mackensen, von manstein, von runstedt, von witzleben
financier fugger, schacht
flutist quantz
flying group jagdstaffel
folk hero till eulenspiegel, tyl(l)eulenspiegel
folklorist grimm
folk song volkslied
folk tale marchen
food knodel, marzipan, rouladen, spa(e)tzle, strudle, wurst
foreigner auslander
forester waldgrave
furniture style biedermeier
game quodliber, radmuhle, schafkopf, tapp-tarok, tippen, wendish, wurfelspiel, zwicken
garment somar
general beck, bernhardi, blumentritt, dietl, groener, guderian, halder, ho(e)pner, hoth, jodl, kalkenhayn, kluck, ludendorff, manteuffel, maurice, ott, speidel, von falkenhorst, von fritsch, von hindenburg, von paulus, von stulpnagel
geographer haushofer
geologist heyne
giant riechart
gingerbread pfefferkuchen
gipsy zigeuner
glass city jena
goblin hinzelmann, hodeken, kobold
gods See AESIR and NORSE *deity.*
governor landvogt
greeting heil, wie gehts
guidebook baedeker
guild hansa, hanseatic league
guild member hansard
gun big bertha, erma, mauser, vierling
hall aula, bursa, diele, saal
heaven himmel
helmet stechelm
herdsman senn

hero arminius, hildebrand, ingomar, offa, siegfried, simplicissimus, tannhauser
high command okh
highway autobahn
historian agricola, dahn, georgius, moser, neander, nieburh, quidde, rank, raumer
house spirit kobold
housewife hausfrau
hunting dog weimaraner
industrialist rathenau, stinness, thyssen
industrial region ruhr
inn gasthof, hasthaus
inventor bunsen, diesel, senefelder
iron region saar, sarre
island alsen, fohr, frisian, hel(i)goland, insel, rugen, usedom, wollin
jews ashkenazim
journalist liebknecht
king ermanaric, frederick, louis, otto, rudolf, rudolph, wilhelm
knight ritter
kobold hodeken
lake ammersee, bodensee, chiem(see), constance, dummer, muritzee, see, wurm(see)
lancer gewebe, u(h)lan
language deutsch, landessprache
leader adenauer, bismarck, brandt, fu(e)hrer, liebknecht
legislature bundesrat(h), bundestag, herrenhaus, landtag, reichstag
letter rune
linguist grassman, sapir
liqueur kirsch(wasser)
liquor See *drink,* above.
literary movement sturm und drang
little theater kammerspiel
lyric poems lieder
machine gun erma
machine-gun nest pillbox
magistrate burgomaster
major dur
manuscript, illuminated fraktur
march goosestep
marshall See *field marshall,* above.
martyr bonhoeffer
massage binde
mathematician bessel, cautor, dedekind, dirichlet, eisenstein, hilbert, jacobi,

klein, kronecker, kummer, lasker, leibnitz, schwarz, weierstrauss, weyl, wolff

measure aam, anker, carat, eimer, fass, fuss, huchart, imi, kanne, kette, klafter, last, linie, ma(a)ss, massel, masskanne, metze, morgen, ohm, oxhoft, rut(h)e, sack, scheffel, schoppen, seidel, simri, stab, strich, stubchen, tagwerk, vierling

menu speisekarte

merchant, rich fugger

metaphysician kant

midwife hebamme

military medal iron cross, purple max

military scientist clausewitz

minerologist beck, ferber, mohs

minstrel hans sachs, meistersinger

missile reprisal, vergeltung

missile site peenemunde, usedom

monk strabo

month (1–12) januar, februar, marz, april, mai, juni, juli, august, september, oktober, november, dezember

mountain region black forest, brocken

movie director lubitsch

music form abendmusik, nachtmusik, zigeunerlied

musical composition stuck

musician reinecke

mystic behmen, bo(e)hme, schwenchfeld

national anthem die wacht am rhein

naturalist forster, hugel, humbolt

naval base emden, kiel

nazi bormann, eichmann, goebbels, hess, heydrich, himmler, hitler, keitel, ley, ro(e)hm, rosenberg, speer, strasser, streicher, von ribbentrop

neurologist krafft-ebing

nobleman adeliger, adlig, billung, edel(man), furst, graf, herzog, junker, ritter, younker

noodles spa(e)tzle

northern language plattdeutsch

novelist auerbach, doblin, grasse, hesse, mann, remarque, seghers, storm,

sudermann, wasserman, zweig

numbers (1–10) eins, zwei, drei, vier, funf, sechs, sieben, acht, neun, zehn

occupation zone bizonia

opera singspiel

organist bach, kuhnau, pachelbel

overture vorspiel

painter altdorfer, baumeister, beckmann, begas, cranach, durer, ernst, grunewald, holbein, huther, jawlensky, kollwitz, liebermann, roos, schongauer, schwitters, stoss, uhde

palatinate phalts

pants lederhosen

pastry shop konditorei

pathologist klebs

peak brocken, feldberg, venusberg, watzmann

people alamanni, alemanni, almain(e), angles, cherusci, cimbri, goth, jute, marcomanni, ostrogoth, quadi, saxon, suevian, teuton, ubii, visigoth, volk(deutscher)

philologist beneke, grimm, lepsius, sievers, vietor

philosopher cassirer, feckner, fichte, haeckel, harrmann, hegel, heidegger, heraclitus, herbart, herder, husserl, jaspers, kant, keyserling, leibniz, lotze, nietzsche, schlegel, schleiermacher, schopenhauer, simmel, spengler, strauss, weiss

photographer leni riefenstahl

physician bartsch, basedow, behring, benn, domagk, erb

physicist born, bothe, braun, clausius, doppler, einstein, erman, fahrenheit, fraunhofer, geiger, guericke, heisenberg, helmholtz, hensen, hertz, kirchhoff, lenard, ohm, roentgen, schrodinger, stark, weber, wien

physiologist loeb, warburg, wassermann, weber, wolff, wundt

pianist backhaus, gieseking, schuman

pietist francke, spener

pigeon taube

pillbox igel

pistol luger

poet angelus, arndt, benn, goethe, hauptmann, heine, herder, hesse, heyse, holderlin, klabund, kleist,

klopstock, rilke, schiller, schlegel, storm, uhland, wedekind, wieland

police gestapo

port bremen, bremerhaven, dusseldorf, emden, hamburg, kiel, lubeck, rostock, schleswig, stettin, stralsund, wilhelmshaven, wismar

postwar boom wirtschaftswunder

prehistoric site heuneburg

president ebert, heinemann, hindenburg

printer gutenberg

prison stalag

psychiatrist fromm, kraepelin

psychologist beneke, kohler

pub kneipe

publisher baedeker, tauchnitz

race stamm

range alps, hardt, harz, hunsruck, ore, rhon

rascal schelm

region (See also *state,* below.) brandenburg, gau, hanover, lauenburg, lusatia, nassau, rhineland, swabia, westphalia

republic brunswick, weimer

resort aachen, baden, ems, wiesbaden

rifleman jager, yager

river aller, altmuhl, alz, danube, donau, eder, eger, eider, elbe, elster, ems, fulda, havel, hunte, iller, inn, isar, jeetzel, kocher, lahn, lech, leine, lippe, main, mosel, mulde, naab, nahe, neckar, neisse, oder, peene, pegnitz, randow, regen, rems, rhein, rhine, ruhr, saale, saar, salzach, sauer, sieg, spree, tauber, ucker, unstrut, vechte, warnow, werra, weser

rocket buzz bomb

rocket engineer werner von braun

royal family hapsburg, hohenlohe, hohenstaufen, hohenzollern, welf

ruler kaiser

sausage wurst

scholar elze, hegel, reuchlin, wolf

school grundschule, gymnasium, realschule, volksschule

scientist baade, caro, ehrlich, fechner, haber

sculptor barlach, kolbe, lehmbruck, lysippus, stoss

season, fall herbst, *spring* fruehling, *summer* sommer, *winter* winter

sect, religious dunker

seeress alruna

shark schurke

sharpshooter ja(e)ger

shooting match schutzenfest

silver albata

silverplate electrum

singers' union saengerbund

singing society liederkranz

sleeping car schlafwaten

socialist bebel, engels, kautsky, lassalle, luxemburg, marx

society bund, gesellschaft, turnverein, verein

soldier boche, jerry, kraut, lansquenet

son stammhalter

song lied(er)

songfest sa(e)ngerfest

soprano lehman, schwartzkoph

spa See *resort,* above.

spy mata hari, von rintelen

squire landjunker

state anhalt, baden, bavaria, bayern, bremen, brunswick, hamburg, hesse(n), lippe, oldenburg, prussia, reich, saarland, saxony, schleswigholstein, thuringia

statesman adenauer, bismark, brandt, ebert, rathenau, stein, tirpitz

stew eintopp

storm troopers schutz staffen, sturm abteilung, waffen ss

stroller spazierganger

student abiturient, fuchs

student cap cerevis

student hall bursa

submarine u-boat, unterseeboot

superman ubermensch

superstition aberglaube

swastika hakenkreuz

sword dusack, schlager

tavern bierstube, weinstube

teacher docent, dozent

theatrical producer reinhardt

theologian arnd, bauer, bultmann, dibelius, eck, eckhart, harnack, luther, spener, strauss

theosophist bohme

thunderstorm donnerwetter

tinder amadou

title graf(f), herr, landgrave, margrave, prinz, von

toast hoch, prosit

tobacco schwarzer krauser

town dorf, stadt

townhall rathaus

tribal leader ariovistus

tribunal vehmgericht

troop panzer

trooper rutter

union with austria anschluss

university freiburg, gottingen, heidelberg, tubingen

university student bursch, fuchs

vernacular volkssprache

veteran group stahlhelm

violinist hindemith, spohr

voltaire goethe

vowel change umlaut

weight drachma, gran, lot(h), lothe, pfund, stein, unze, vierling, zentner

wheat emmer, speltz

wind instrument flugelhorn

wine auslese, bacharach, cabinet, hochheiner, hock, mosel(le), niersteiner, rhine, riesling, rudesheimer, hulander, spaetlese, stein (berger), trocken(beeren) (auslese), wein

wine glass roemer

woman frau(lein), frow, tannakin

woman's duty kaiser, kinder, kuche

world view weltanschauung, weltansicht

writer apel, auerbach, bebel, benn, doblin, ebers, eckermann, engels, fichte, fouque, freytag, fromm, goethe, grimm, hegel, heine, hesse, junger, kant, kastner, lasker, mann, richter, sachs, schiller, seghers, storm, sudermann

writers movement aktivist

zoo tiergarten

zoologist schwann, spemann

GERMICIDE antiseptic, antitoxin, argenol, argyrol, bactericide, benzoic acid, disinfectant, iodine, krelos, prophylactic

GERMINAL beginning, embryonic, incipient, microbic, opening, original, springtime, starting, zaftig

GERMINATE braird, bud, develop, grow, result from, shoot, sprit, sprout, vegetate

GERMINATING *comb.* blastic

GERMINATION beginning, catch, development, ebullition, efflorescence, growth

GERONIMO *boys* parachute troops

GERONTIC aged, old

GEROVITAL novocaine

GERRYMANDER adjust, fix, jigsaw, maneuver, manipulate, politick

GERSHOM *parent* moses, phineas, zipporah

GERSHON *father* jacob, levi

GERSHWIN, GEORGE *opera* porgy and bess

GERTRUDE *husband* claudius

son hamlet

GERUND ing

-grinder pedant

GESSO chalk, gypsum, paste, plaster

GEST(E) act(ion), adventure, bearing, company, deed, deportment, exploit, feat, fiction, jest, kind, lampoon, race, romance, route, saga, tale

GESTALT configuration, conformation, figure, form, pattern, shape

follower holist

GESTAPO police

GESTATE cause, start

GESTATION bearing, breeding, carrying, incubation, pregnancy

GESTION conduct, management

GESTURE accolade, act(ion), beck(on), bere, bow, byplay, caress, carriage, ceremony, chironomy, curtsey, dactylology, dumb show, fig, fillip, gesticulate, high sign, mime, motion, nod, pantomime, pass, posture, pretext, salaam, salute, shrug, sign(al), token, wave, wigwag, wink

of derision snook

of disapproval thumbs-down

GET accept, accomplish, achieve, acquire, annex, annoy, attain, baffle, begone, betake, brat, breed, bring, capture, catch, child, comprehend, contract, cop, corner, delve, dig, discover, earnings, effect, elicit, engender, extort, fathom, fetch, follow, gain, gather, generate, git, grab, grasp, hear, hent, hit, income, incur, induce, inherit, irritate, kill, make, manage, master, obtain, overcome, pen, persuade, possess, prepare, procure, propagate, puzzle, reach, receive, remove, run, secure, seize, sicken, sire, spear, steal, strike, take, trap, understand, vanquish, win, worst

aboard beride, catch, embark, join

about circulate

across clarify, explain, penetrate, sell

ahead advance, anticipate, beat, grow, improve, increase, pass, precede, progress, score, speed, succeed, surpass, win

a head start anticipate

a hold on corner, disable, monopolize, obsess, paralyze, triumph

all available buy up, corner, monopolize

along (See also *ahead, above.*) advance, age, agree, begone, cooperate, cope, fadge, fare, fend, fettle, gee, hurry, manage, speed

a move on hurry, hustle, step on it

around bypass, cajole, circulate, circumvent, cover, deceive, detour, evade, finesse, flummer, issue, mingle, outwit, persuade, recover, socialize, travel

at acquire, affect, ascertain, attain, bribe, effect, influence, mold, reach, tamper with

away depart, elope, escape, evade, flee, fly, lam, leave, scat, shoo, slip, start

away with accomplish, capture, devour, luck out

back recall, recover, redeem, retreat, retrieve, return

back at retaliate

behind back, bankroll, boost, champion, endorse, fall back, lag, promote, support, underwrite

better ameliorate, improve, pick up, recuperate

better of best, daunt, ding, down, overgo, shend, shent, stick, sting, surmount

by cope with, escape, make it, manage, pass, succeed, suffice

by cunning con, whizzle

cracking begin, start, undertake

dishonestly bilk, cheat, firk, STEAL

down alight, crouch, devour, disembark, dismount, eat

down to cases particularize

even avenge, retaliate, revenge, settle, square

fresh challenge, dare, pinch, sass

from elicit, receive

going begin, hurry, move, scram, shake a leg, start, undertake

hep catch on, learn, master

hitched marry, wed

hold of acquire, discipline, learn, master, seize

hot under the collar anger, boil, ire, rage, seethe

in accumulate, amass, arrive, collect, enter, harness, harvest, include, land, mount, plant, reap, secure, store

in a lather emote, excite, perspire, react, respond

in good with brown-nose, cultivate, flatter, play up to

in line conform, obey, queue, salute, wait, yield

in one's hair aggravate, annoy, irritate, rile

in there begin, start

in with cultivate, influence, join, participate

it comprehend, understand

it over complete, end, finish

lost beat it, begone, escape, scram

mad anger, blow up, boil, excite, explode, ire

next to convince, cultivate, flatter, learn, seduce

no better deteriorate

off begin, depart, discharge, dismount, dispose, escape, issue, learn, put forth, remove, speed, start, utter

off the ground fly, launch, start, take off

on age, board, chefe, cheve, depart, don, embark, fare, learn, manage, mount, prosper, shift, succeed

one's back up annoy, bristle, irritate, provoke

on the bandwagon concur, flock, follow, join

on the wagon abstain, dry out, renounce

out begone, elicit, escape, evacuate, exit, extract, extricate, flee, give forth, issue, lam, leak, leave, print, publish, reveal, run, scat, scram, shoo, withdraw

out of avoid, beg off, elicit, evade, shirk

out of kilter break, spoil

out of line dissent, revel, revolt

over end, finish, heal, move, rebound, recover, recuperate, revive, sell, succeed, surmount, triumph

plastered See DRINK.

possession acquire, amass, carry, catch, grab

ready apparel, brace, fettle, frame, prepare, rank

results accomplish, achieve, complete, finish, succeed

rid burke, buy off, cast, destroy, discard, dish, dispel, dispose of, dissolve, ditch, eliminate, eradicate, erase, fling off, kill, liquidate, murder, purge, slough, suppress, throw away, toss, unload

satisfaction duel, make up, requite, settle

set prepare, ready

the best of defeat, skin, surpass, triumph, win

the drift understand

the drop on aim, attack, beat, direct, sight, triumph

the hang of See UNDERSTAND.

the message See UNDERSTAND.

there achieve, arrive, enter, make it, succeed

the show on the road begin, commence, start

through carry off, complete, end, finish

to arrive, begin, bribe, catch, corrupt, effect, extend, reach

to bottom of fathom

together accumulate, affair, agree, amass, assemble, assembly, bee, collect, hobnob, meeting, party, potlatch, social(ize), stag, unite, visit

up approach, arise, arrange, array, arrive, ascend, assembly, awaken, climb, composition, constitution, construct, costume, create, dress, enterprise, fabricate, flush, giddap, harvest, invent, launder, make, mount, prepare, recoup, recover, rise, setout, stack, structure, study, style, wardrobe, turn out

-up-and-go energy, enterprise, vim

well heal, recover, recuperate

wise to learn, see through

with it modernize, undertake

worse decline, deteriorate

GETHER *father* shem

GEUM avens, bennet, blackbur, blessed herb, burnet-saxifrage, daisy, hemlock, herb, plant, valerian

product astringent

GEWGAW bauble, bibelot, brummagem, chotchke(leh), fangle, fegary, flamfew, folderol, gaud, gigger, gimcrack, knickknack, pretentious, showy, tchotchke(leh), tinsel, toy, trangam, trifle, trimtram, trinket, trumpery, tsatske(leh)

GEY considerable, pretty, tolerable, very

GEYSER bore, jet(ter), spring

opening crater

GEYSERITE opal, silica

GEZ arshin

GEZER *king* horam

GEZIRA *capital* wad medani

GHANA gold coast

area agona, akwamy, asokora, bekwai, kokofu, krontior, musta, offinso, tain

capital accra, akkra

chief asantehene, omanhene

city accra, akosombo, antubia, axim, bawku, damongo, dunkwa, enchi, fian, karaga, keta, kintampo, kpandu, kumasi, lawra, legon, mampong, nsawam, obuasi, oda, prestea, sampa, sekondi, sunyani, swedru, takoradi, tala, tamale, tarkwa, tema, wasipe, winneba, yapei

coin ackey

dam akosombo

diety bossum, demonio

drink orangefanta

drum kwatinpomuta, stumpan

elephant-whisk bearer ahoprafo

folktale anansi, nancy

harvest festival odwira

lake bosumtwi, volta

language akan, dagbani, dagomba, ewe, fanti, hausa, tshi, twi

leader otumbuo-opoku-ware ii

money newcedi

nation akan

peak afadjato

people ahafo, akan, akim, akra, akwapim, ashanti, brong, dagomba, inkra, mamprusi

port accra, ada, akkra, keta

president kwame-nkrumah

region ashanti, gold coast, togoland

rite durbar

river afram, ankobra, black volta, daka, kulpawn, oti, pra, tano, white volta

skirt sepiamtama

tong chi, tshi, twi

umbrella akokobaatan, nyankonton, oyokomma

wind harmattan

GHANDI *movement* satyagraha

GHARRY carriage, shigram

GHASTFUL afraid, alarmed, deathlike, dreadful, ghostly, timit

GHASTLY anemic, appalling, ashen, bad, blate, cadaverous, death-like, deatly, dismal, dreadful, fearful, frightful, gashful, ghostly, grim, grisly, grizzly, gruesome, grugous, hideous, horrible, horrid, horrified, lurid, macabre, offensive, pale, pallid, repellant, repugnant, repulsive, sallow, shocking, spectral, terrible, terrified, ugly, uncanny, unearthly, wan

GHAT, GHAUT bank, narrows, pass, stairs

burning crematory

GHAWAZI baramika

GHENT *azalea* cardinal

river lys, schelde

GHERKIN cucumber, pickle

GHETTO barrio, confine, district, quarter, section, slum

GHIBILLINE opposition guelphs

GHOST antaeus, antaios, apparition, appearance, astral, author, banshee, barghest, bhut, boggart, bogle,

breath, bugan, buggane, caddy, churel, corpse, d(a)emon, die, duffy, duppy, eidolon, expire, fetch, form, geist, glimmer, guide, guytrashgytrash, hag, ha(u)nt, hobgoblin, idolum, image, incorporeity, juba, jumby, ker, larva, lemur(es), manes, person, phantasm, phantom, poltergeist, presence, preta, revenant, shade, shadow, shape, soul, sowlth, specter, spectre, spirit, spook, sprite, substitute, taisch, theophany, trace, umbra, vamp(ire), vision, waff, white lady (of avenal)

belief in eidolism, superstition

comb. scio

crab sprite

deity enlil, hecate

dravidian bhoot, bhut, dust-devil

fish chiro, wrymouth

flower indian-pipe

friendly casper

-haunted possessed

moth hepialid, swift

noise-making poltergeist

of a chance improbability

pert. spectral

plant amaranthus, tumbleweed

-ridden possessed

spiritualist's control, guide

story fabrication, lie

study of spectrology

town dead city

weed snow-on-the-mountain

-writer author, spook, substitute

GHOSTLY chthonic, deathly, eerie, eery, eidolic, ghastful, haunted, mystically, pale, shadowy, spectral, spiritual(ly), uncanny, weirdly, wraithy

GHOUL blackmailer, bodysnatcher, demon, devil, fiend, grave robber, harpy, lamia, monster, ogre, resurrectionist, thief, vampire

GHOULISH eerie, hellish, revolting, satanic, vampiric

GHURRY clepsydra, hour, timepiece, water-clock

GI doughboy, infantryman, joe, private, soldier

garb fatigues, khakis, ods, olive drab

GIAI nhang

GIANT (See also NORSE giant.) afreet, afrit, behemoth, brobdingnagian, colossal, cyclopean, demon, devil, dinosaur, elephant (ine), enormous, eten, gigantic, herculean, hippo (potamus), huge, immense, jumbo, leviathan, mammoth, mastodon, monster, ogre, powerhouse, prodigious, stalwart, tall, thurse, TITAN, tremendous, troll, vast
abode utgard
against zeus enceladus
apollo's victim aloadae, ephialtes, otus
arthurian juliance, ritho
atheism kifri
beggar arneos, irus
biblical anak(im), goliath, rephaim, samson, zamzummim
bravest balan
broken-toothed angoulaffre
cactus saguaro
chieftain antiphates
comb. giganto, titano
dance stonehenge
deformed fomors
evil goliath, jotun(n), loki
fairy-tale bellygan, blunderbore, cormoran, galliantus, grumbo, megadore
famous human anak, andronicus, bamford, bates, big sam, blacker, bradley, brice, brusted, busby, charlemagne, cotter, eleazer, evans, frank, frenz, funnum, gabara, gilly, gordon, hale, hardrada, holmes, la pierre, louis, mcdonald, magrath, maximinus, mellon, murphy, o'brien, osen, porus, riechart, salmeron, swann, toller
fictional orgoglio
50-headed aegeon, briareos, gyges
frost hrym
fulmar nelly, stinker, stinkpot
garlic rocambole
granite pegmatite
grass otate
greatest ferumbras, fierabras
hag nickneven
hercules' victim antaeus
heron goliath
100-armed enceladus
100-eyed argus
100-handed aegaeon,

briareus, cottus, cottys, gyges, kottos
100-headed typhoeus
hunter orion
jack's blunderbore, galligantus
king gogmagog
lame periphetes
land of bashan, brobdingnab, utgarther
lily figue, maguey
man-eating cacus, laestrygone
mythological or fabled 3 gog, ott, ran 4 anax, bana, erix, fion, grid, grim, hler, hyrm, irus, loki, maul, myrm, otus, surt, wade, ymer, ymir 5 aegir, argus, ascus, atlas, balan, balor, baugi, cacus, carus, coeus, gerda, gerth, gyges, gymir, hymer, hymir, jotun, kifri, magog, mimir, ogias, orion, ritho, thaon, thrym, titan, yohak 6 acamas, aegeon, agrious, aloeus, bunyan, cottus, coulin, fafnir, fenrir, garion, geomot, godmer, grumbo, jotunn, kottos, maugys, pallas, phidon, thurse, tityus, typhon 7 aegaeon, algebar, aloadae, antaeus, brontes, burlond, clytius, cyclops, despair, eurytus, fiorgyn, galapas, galbara, geirrod, geroneo, giralda, grendel, gunnlod, harbard, hurtali, mugillo, offerus, sittung, skrymir, tartaro 8 ascapart, asterius, bellerus, briareus, colbrand, colossus, cormoran, dondasch, ferregus, gemmagog, goemagot, gogmagog, hercules, hrasvelg, juliance, margutte, morgante, orgaglio, pyracmon, slay good, steropes, typhoeus, utgartha 9 adamastor, alcyoneus, chalbroth, colbronde, cormorant, enceladus, ephialtes, ferracute, ferumbras, fierabras, gargantua, gracassus, grantorto, hapmouche, polybotes, raphsarus, rounceval, treyeagle 10 caligorant, hippolythus, malambruno, montrognon, pantagruel, polyphemus, porphyrion 11 blunderbore, brobdingnag, galligantus, grangousier, hrimthursar, teutobochus

12 caraculiambo, buy of warwick, indracittran, widenostrils
1-eyed arges, brontes, cyclops, polyphemus
pangolin anteater
people anakim
philistine goliath
primeval ymer, ymir
progenitor ymer, ymir
puffball bullfice, bullfist, fuzzball
race aloadae, anak(im), cottus, nephilim, rephaim, zamzummim
sea hymer, hymir, wade
shepherd arges, cyclops
ship naglfar
6-ball mace mugillo
slayer apollo, bevis, jack, ulysses
storm wade
stride distance, league
strongest balan, titan
thieving cacus
30 feet tall teutobachus
1,000 armed bana
300 feet tall polyphemus
ulysses victim irus
GIANTESS angerboda, angerbotha, angribodha, argante, domnu, gerda, grid, groa, norn, nott, skuld, urth, wyrd
athena's victim pallas
GIARDIA lambilia
GIB cat, fasten, gut, prison, salmon, tomcat
GIBBER babble, boulder, chat(ter), gab(ble), hump, jabber, nonsense, prate, prattle, rock, speak, stone, swelling, talk
GIBBERISH abracadabra, barrikin, choctaw, enigma, galimatias, gossip, greek, hocus-pocus, jabberwocky, jargon, nonsense, nonsensical, talk, unintelligible
GIBBET brand, cudge, equuleus, gallows, hang, jebat, jib, scaffold, stob, tree
GIBBLE-GABBLE chatter, nonsense
GIBBON ape, hoolock, hylobates, lar, siamang, ungka, wawa, wou-wou, wuyen
GIBBOUS bowed, bulging, convex, curved, deformed, hulchy, humpbacked, humped, humpy, hunched, protuberant, rounded, swelling

GIBBSITE bauxite, diaspore, mordant

GIBE agree, barb, brocard, deride, fleer, flirt, flout, frump, gallicism, gird, gleek, heckle, jape, jeer, jes, JIBE, kibbitz, maxim, mock, proverb, quip, rally, ridicule, rub, sarcasm, scoff, sneer, taunt, twit

GIBLETS entrails, garbage, innards, vitals

GIBRALTAR calpe, pillars of hercules, the rock, strength, stronghold
founder gebir
of america quebec
port algeciras, ceuta
strait, city on tangier

GIBUS tophat

GIDDINESS dizziness, levity, soorawn

GIDDY changeable, daffy, daft, dizzy, fickle, flighty, foolish, frivolous, furious, glaiket, gowked, gyratory, halucket, heedless, hellicat(e), inconstant, intoxicated, light-headed, reeling, swimming, vertiginous, volage, whirling, wild
-gander orchis
person butterfly, flibbertigibbit, scatterbrain

GIDE, ANDRE *novel* the counterfeiters, the immoralist, the pastoral symphony

GIDEON jerubbaal
enemy midianites
father joash
servant phurah
society cause bible
son abimelech, jotham
victim oreb

GIDGEE, GIDYA acacia, myall, spear

GIER eagle, vulture

GIFFGAFF banter

GIFT ability, alms, aptitude, arras, benefaction, benefit, bent, bequest, blessing, bonus, boon(doggle), box, bribe, buckshee, cadeau, charity, contribution, cuddy, deodate, dole, donary, donation, donative, donum, dora, dow(ry), enam, endowment, etrenne, faculty, fairing, favor, flair, fleer, forte, foy, free, function, genius, gersum, give, grant, gratuity, han(d)sel, honorarium, knack, lag-

niappe, largess(e), largition, legacy, liberality, oblation, offering, potlatch, power, present(ation), prize, skill, sop, sportula, subsidy, talent, tip, token, turn, xenium
-balsam poison-tree
book annual, keepsake
charitable alms, donation, enam, pittance
compulsory sixenia, tithe
exchange kula
name meaning dora, nathan
natural genius, talent
of gab articulateness, eloquence, grandiloquence, loquacity, magniloquence
of god grace
of tongues glossolalia
receiver donee
spiritual charism(a), oblata, missiles
to dignitaries xenia
unreturned boondoggle

GIFTED endowed, ingenious, skilled, talented

GIFTWARE notions

GIG admonish, boat, brace, calesin, carriage, chaise, creak, demerit, dennet, engagement, fool, fun, goad, hilarity, hook, joke, kibble, lure, nap(per), oddity, punish(ment), rig, rowboat, spear, sport, spur, squeak, stanhope, tilbury, top, tub, turn, wanton, whim, whisk(e)y

GIGANTES agrius, anax, centaur, porphyrion, rhoetus, thoas
parent gaea, uranus
subduer hercules

GIGANTIC big, colossal, enormous, GIANT, great, huge, large, monster, monumental, stupendous, tall, titan(ic), vast

GIGGLE cackle, chortle, chuckle, heehaw, keckle, laugh, snicker, snigger, teehee, t(w)itter

GIGOLO bawd, beau, casanova, chic, don juan, escort, fashionable, glamor boy, rake, roue, smart, squire

GI JOE See GI.

GILA *monster* heloderma, lizard
trout hardtail

GILBERT AND SULLIVAN
opera gondoliers, hms pinafore, iolanthe, mikado, pa-

tience, pirates of penzance, princess ida, ruddigore, trial by jury, yeomen of the guard
fan savoyard

GILBERT ISLANDS abaiang, abemama, aranuka, arorae, beru, maiana, makin, marakei, onotoa, tamana, tarawa
capital tarawa

GILBOA *death site of* saul

GILD adorn, aureate, aurify, brighten, coat, decorate, embellish, enrich, falsify, ornament, paint, payment, tax, tempt
the lily exaggerate, lay it on, overdo

GILDA *father* rigoletto

GILDED aurate, inaurate

GILEAD *balm of* See BALM *of gilead.*
descendant ulam
father machir
judge jair
town bezer, casphor, maked

GILGAMESH izdubar
advisor siduri-sabitu, utahapishtim
boatman urshanabi
city erech, uruk
cult lugal-banda
enemy khumbaba
kingdom uruk
mother ninsun
predecessor dumuzi

GILGIG *language* shina

GILL beloved, branchia, brook, choller, coin, collar, cove, fellow, ferret, girl, groat, half-pint, ivy, jaw, lamella, lass, leech, lung, measure, plica, quadrant, stream, sweetheart, tipple, valley, wattle, wench
⅓rd farthing
4 great, pint
comb. branchi(a)(o)
fungus agaric(us)
having branchate, branchiferous
having 2 dibranchiate
without abranchian, abranchiate

GILLENIA culver's root, false ipecac, herb, indian hippo, spurge

GILLIE attendant, follower, henchman, servant, shoe, townman

GILLYFLOWER apple, carnation, caryophullus, clove,

gelofre, gilliver, jezebel, matthiola, stock, wallflower

GILRAVAGE frolic, roister

GILSONITE bitumen

GILT dore, finery, gild(ed) (ing), gold, hog, key, money, pig, sow, thief, yelt
-*edged* best, good, superior
-*head* cunner, fish, melanure, sparus

GIM neat, spruce

GIMBAL axis, axle, fulcrum, gemel, jemble, pastry
-*jawed* loquacious

GIMCRACK bauble, device, fop, frivolous, gewgaw, idea, jimjam, knickknack, scheme, thingmabob, toy, trangam, trifle, trinket, trumpery, whimwham

GIMCRACKY frail, gaudy, paltry, showy, trivial

GIMLET awl, broach, cocktail, piercel, screw, wimbel

GIMMER clasp, ewe, hinge, ring, sheep, woman
-*hog* lamb

GIMMICK aid, artifice, cheating, device, gadget, gaff, means, plan, ruse, setup, shift, shtickl(ech), shtik(eleh), stratagem, stunt, trick

GIMP fabric, fishline, indent, jag, jimp, neckerchief, notch, orris, scant, silk, slender, spirit, spruce, stomacher, thread, trim, vim

GIN against, also, artifice, before, clean, contrivance, device, diddle, female, game, geneva, holland, jacky, jinn, juniper, kangaroo, lace, liquor, machine, max, nearby, rack, rummy, scheme, schiedam, schnapps, sloe, snare, snarl, squareface, tittery, toils, trap, trick, until, whether, whim
and beer dog's nose
block monkeywheel
drink fizz, martini, tom collins
drop of daffy
mill See SALOON.
rummy carousel, chouette, cutthroat, hollywood, kaluki, manhattan, oklahoma, round-the-corner, rummy, tunk
rummy term schneider

GING company, crew, family, rabble, retinue, troop

GINGER alpinia, amomum, asarum, cedar, coltsfoot, eclat, fire, force, jake, lively, mettle, mioga, pep(per), piquancy, plant, pluck, ratoon, sedum, spirit(ed), spunk, vigor, vim, zingiber
cookie snap
drink ale, shandy
genus mioga, renealmia, zingiber
leaf mullein, wintergreen
pine cedar
plant tansy
root coltsfoot, handrace
wild asarum, bugbane, cohosh, coltsfoot, sanicle, snakeroot

GINGERALE *and beer* shandy(gaff)

GINGERBREAD cake, decoration, gimcrackery, money, parkin, pfefferkuchen, spice, superfluity, tinsel, tree, trim(ming), wealth
house child gretel, hansel
tree doom, dum

GINGERLY carefully, cautiously, charily, daintily, dainty, elegant, finically, timidly, warily

GINGERSNAP cookie

GINGHAM chambray, cloth, fabric, solitaire, umbrella

GINGILI See SESAME.

GINK eccentric, oddity

GINKGO echo, fruit, icho, maidenhair, tree

GINSENG acanthopanax, aralia, fatil, herb, ivywort, panax, plant, redberry, sang, shrub
blue cohosh, papooseroot, squawroot
digger sanger

GIOCONDA, LA mona lisa

GIORDANO *opera* andrea chenier, fedora

GIOTTO *fresco site* arena chapel, padua, santa croce
tower campanile

GIPSY See GYPSY.

GIRAFFE camaile, camelopard, dapple, gerfaunt, kameel, okapi, oont, ruminant, spinet, xarapha
-*camel* alticamelus
constellation camelopard (alis)

GIRANDOLE candleholder, clock, earring, mirror

GIRASOLE heliotrope, opal, sunflower

GIRAUDOUX *play* amphityrion, ondine

GIRD accinge, belt, besiege, bind, brace, clothe, cut, deride, encircle, enclose, encompass, environ, equip, fasten, fleer, flout, gibe, girdle, girth, gorden, hoop, invest, jeer, jerk, jibe, mock, moment, pang, prepare, provide, rally, ridicule, ring, rush, scoff, secure, sill, smite, sneer, strap, strengthen, strike, surround, taunt, thrust, trice, twinge, twit, yerk

GIRDER beam, binder, buckstay, caviler, member, mocker, stringer, table, t-bar, timber, truss

GIRDLE baldric, balteus, band, bark, belt, bind, bodice, ceinture, cest(us), cincture, cingle, cingulum, clitellum, corse(le)t, criss, cummberbund, encircle, enclose, environ, foundation, griddle, hoop, kelp, obi, ring, sarp, sash, shingle, solitaire, strap, strengthen, support, waist(band), zoster
bride's cest(us)
ecclesiastic surcingle
little zonelet, zonule
material lycra, spandex
of venus cestus
pert. zonal
royal malo
sacred kusti
saddle cinch

GIRDLER beetle, insect, lumberman

GIRELIA (black)(blue) fish, bream

GIRL babe, baby, belle, beloved, bint, bird, bobbysoxer, broad, burd, calico, chick(en), chit, chowlah, colleen, court, cummer, curve, cutie, dame, damoiselle, damsel, dawtie, deb, deem(ie), demoiselle, doll, duck, fille, filly, flapper, fluss, frail, fraulein, gal, geisha, giglet, hoyden, ingenue, jade, jill, judy, kimmer, kitty, lass(ie), maid(en), mauther, meg, minx, miss(y), mot(t), muchacha, nymph(et), puss(y), queen, roebuck, romp, servant, she, sheila, signorina, sis, skirt, snab,

subdeb, sweetheart, sylph, thrill, tid(dy), tingle, tomato, tomboy, trull, virgin, wench
adolescent bobbysoxer
agile yanker
attractive bonnibel, pigeon
boisterous tomboy
bold hoiden, hoyden
campfire artisan
-chasing kadritsa
clumsy mauther, mawther
cover See MODEL.
dancing dasi, devadasi, ghawazi, kisa(e)ng
flirtatious jade, jillet
flower nydia
foolish tawpie, tawpy
forward chit, strap
-friday assistant, deputy, secretary
-friend See SWEETHEART.
giddy flirtigig, gig(let), gillflirt, jill(et)
goodnight irene
graceful nymph, sylph
handsome bonnibel
lively filly, giglet, wanton
patron saint catherine
pert chit, hussy, minx, snip
play bunny, chorine, showgirl
reckless madcap
scout emblem trefoil
scout founder low
scout rank brownie, tenderfoot
servant biddie, biddy, slut
song adeline, clementine, sal(ly), susan(na)
stunning honey, peach(erino)
unmarried démoiselle, moustmec, towdie
working orisette
young bud, colleen, flapper, groupie, maiden, mauther, mawther, moder, nymphet, rosebud, teenybopper, titty
GIRLHOOD teens, youth
GIRLISH artless, immature, juvenile, maidenly
GIRO aircraft, credit, round, tour, turn
GIRONDE *tributary* garonne
GIRT besiege, bound, cinct, encircled, fasten(ed), fillet, girder, great, secured, surround
up active, eager, prepared
GIRTH band, bellyband, belt, bend, cinch, circumference,, corpulence, encircle, fatness, garth, gird(le),

greth, harness, hoop, perimeter, saddle, size, strap, wanty
GISMO gadget, object, thing
GIST burden, chat, contents, core, crux, effect, essence, essential, heart, jet, kernel, keynote, lodging, marrow, meaning, meat, nub, pasture, pith, point, substance, summary
GIT begone, get, run, scram, vim
GITE gyte, lodging, mad, quarters, shelter
GITON carapo, fasciatus, gymnotus
GIUKI *child* gudrun, gunnar
wife grimhild
GIVE 3 aid, dow, gie, pay, put, set, tip 4 bear, bend, cast, cede, deal, deem, dole, fade, gift, help, hold, lead, look, mete, open, send, slip, weep, will, wish 5 allot, allow, apply, award, dower, endow, fetch, grant, issue, offer, relax, serve, spare, utter, waive, yield 6 accord, afford, assign, bestow, commit, confer, devise, devote, donate, dotate, extend, impart, pledge, remise, render, return, shrink, supply, tender 7 ascribe, concede, deliver, dish out, fork out, furnish, hand out, incline, portray, present, proffer, provide 8 allocate, bequeath, consider, describe, dispense, shell out, transfer 9 attribute, dispose of, pronounce, represent, sacrifice, subsidize, surrender, vouchsafe 10 administer, contribute, distribute, elasticity 11 communicate, flexibility
a bad time bother, harass, pester, ride, tease
a black eye abuse, brand, bruise, smear
a boost bolster, help
a bum steer deceive, mislead
a false color misinterpret, misrepresent, pervert
a free hand authorize
a hand abet, aid, assist, boost, help
a lift boost, cheer, encourage, help up, horse, mount
an account recite, relate, report, tell
and take bandy, banter, compensate, compromise,

equity, giffgaff, interchange, quid pro quo, reciprocate, retaliate, tit for tat, trade
an eye for an eye repay, retaliate, revenge
a turn to change, frighten, scare, startle
away bestow, betray, discard, disclose, divulge, expose, grant, part with, present, relinquish, reveal, sacrifice, telltale
a wide berth avoid, shun
back echo, rebate, refund, remise, remit, replace, restitute, restore, retire, retreat, return
birth bear, beteem, born, bring forth, calve, cast, cause, cub, deliver, drop, ean, farrow, fawn, find, foal, freshen, kindle, labor, lamb, litter, originate, pup, sling, slink, teem, throw, whelp, yean
care nurse, nurture
chase dog, hunt, pursue
ear hark(en), hearken, listen
evidence attest, betoken, testify
for safekeeping commend, commit, confide, consign, entrust
forth afford, belch, blaze, disgorge, edit, emit, eradiate, exhale, proclaim, radiate, shed, sound, spew, vomit, yield
free reign indulge
ground quit, retire, retreat, stop, withdraw, yield
impetus further, impel
in acquiesce, assent, bow, capitulate, cave, collapse, concede, consent, deliver, halt, quit, relent, relinquish, sanction, stop, submit, subscribe, succumb, surrender, yield
in exchange swap, swop, trade
in return reciprocate, render, requite
it a whirl attempt, try
it to admonish, punish, rebuke, reprimand, scold
leave allow, let, permit
notice advertise, advise, apprise, publicize, quit, resign
off beam, belch, cease, effuse, emit, excrete, fling, issue, publish, quit, radiate, shed, vaporize

one's word promise, swear, testify

out administer, air, announce, circulate, collapse, deal, dispense, distribute, divulge, dole, emanate, emit, exude, fail, finish, issue, leak, mete, minister, peter, print, publish, quit, spoil, supply, tell, tender, weaken

over cease, deliver, devote, indulge in, relinquish, stop, transfer

pain aggrieve, hurt, wound

pleasure regale

reluctantly begrudge, grudge

rise engender, generate, make, occasion, originate, produce, start

satisfaction abegge, aby(e), atone, duel, fight, please

sparingly begrudge, inch

support assist, back, champion, promote

the air can, discharge, dismiss, eject, evict, fire, kick out

the business do in, kill

the green light approve, okay, permit, sanction

the lie to deny, disprove

the nod approve, assent, signal

the slip escape, evade

thought to consider, ponder

up abandon, abdicate, abjure, abnegate, betray, bury, can, capitulate, cede, concede, deliver, demit, depose, despair, devote, discard, disuse, dole, drop, emit, fail, flummox, flunk, for(e)go, forsake, hand over, mizzle, present, quit(tance), relinquish, remit, render, renounce, resign, reveal, sacrifice, spare, stop, submit, surrender, transfer, turn over, vacate, waive, yield

utterance announce, proclaim, say, state

way break, buckle, budge, burst, cede, despond, fail, faint, founder, quit, relent, stop, succumb, surrender, swerve, weaken, yield

GIVEN addicted, assigned, bestowed, conferred, determined, disposed, donee, fixed, free, gratis, gratuitous, known, providential, specified, stated

to habituated, inclined, tending

to, comb. able, acious

GIVER almoner, angel, assigner, bestower, consigner, donator, donor, feoffer, philanthropist, settler, testate, testator

of life apheta

GIZA, GIZEH *pyramid builder* khufer

GIZZARD belly, craw, crop, giblet, gigerium, interior, stomach, vitals

shad dorosoma, herring, skipjack

trout gillaroo

GIZZEN parch, shrink, shrivel

GLABRA aesculus, buckey, horse chestnut, shrub

GLABROUS bald, glossy, levigate, satiny, silken, sleek, slick, smooth, velvety

GLACE candied, chilling, cold, dessert, frozen, glide, ice(d), shiny, sleek

GLACIAL arctic, chilly, cold, congealed, cool, frigid, frosty, frozen, gelid, icy

meal rock-flour

GLACIARIUM rink

GLACIATE erode, freeze, score

GLACIATION *stage* See GLACIER *retreat stage.*

GLACIER brae, calotte, ice (cap), piedmont

cleft crevasse

deposit asar, boulder-clay, drift, escar, eskar, esker, kame, moraine, osar, paha, placer, sheet, till

direction stoss

erosion cirque, corrie

facing stoss

fragment serac

hill drumlin, paha

ice firn, neve, serac

lily dogtooth violet

margin snowline

mill moulin

period boulder, wurm

retreat stage achen, cary, elster, gunz, iowan, mankato, mindel, riss, saale, valders, wurm

ridge See *deposit,* above.

shaft moulin

slope stoss

snow See *ice,* above.

structure cipollino

study of cryology

waste diluvium, drift

GLACK defile, fork, ravine, valley

GLAD animated, blithe, bright, charmed, cheerful, cheery, content(ed), elated, fain, gay, gleeful, gratified, happy, intrigued, jocular, jolly, joyful, joyous, lief, loose, merry, overjoyed, pleased, pleasing, proud, satisfied, shining, smooth, thrilled, tickled(pink), rapturous, willing

hand welcome

tidings evangel(ism), gospel, joy

GLADDEN animate, arride, beatify, bless, cheer, comfort, console, delight, elate, encourage, enliven, exhilarate, exult, gratify, happify, lighten, please, quicken, regale, rejoice, solace, tickle, vivify

GLADDON cattail, iris, reedmace

GLADE beam, clearing, dell, flash, gap, laund, marsh, passage, shradd, slade, sunscald, vale, valley, wood

comb. nemo

GLADIATOR andabata, athlete, boxer, combatant, fencer, fighter, lanista, retiary, samnite, secutor, showman, spartacus, swordsman, thrax

blind andabata

competitions ludi

salute morituri te salutamus

trainer lanista

with net retiarius

GLADIOLUS afrikander, flag, iris

bulb corm

GLADLY cheerfully, fain, freely, happily, lief, lieve, readily, willingly

GLADNESS bliss, exhilaration, happiness, joy, mirth, pleasure

GLADSHEIM asgard, valhalla

GLADSTONE bag, carriage, suitcase, wine

GLAIK dazzle, delude, gaze, shine, trifle, wander

GLAIKET foolish, giddy, lightheaded, stupid, thoughtless

GLAIVE spear, sword

GLAMOR, GLAMOUR allurement, appeal, attraction, bewitch, captivation,

charisma, charm, color, enchant(ment), fascination, illusion, interest, magic, mystery, nobility, romance, sorcery, spell, witchery
GLAMORIZE adorn, dramatize, glorify, romanticize
GLAMOROUS alluring, charming, exotic, fascinating, romantic
GLANCE allude, blink, browse, brush, carom, cast, coruscate, coup d'oeil, dart, eye(shot), flash, flicker, flit, gander, gleam, gleek, glent, glim(mer), glimpse, glint, glisten, glitter, gloat, graze, hint, kiss, leer, look, ogle, peek, peep, peer, polish, scan, scance, scime, scry, see, shave, shimmer, shine, sight, signal, skeg, skim, slant, sparkle, stroke, touch, twinkle, view, wink
coal anthracite
copper chalcocite
over sample
pitch asphalt, manja(c)k
GLAND acorn, adrenal, carnel, crumena, endocrine, exocrine, follicle, ganglion, gonad, kernal, liver, lymph, milt, nectary, noix, organ, pancreas, parathyroid, parotid, pineal, pituitary, salivary, scirrhus, sebaceous, spleen, sweat, thymus, thyroid
absence anadenia
adrenal paranephros
alluring androclinium, clinandrium
comb. aden(o), adreno
dissection adenotomy
ductless pineal, thymus, thyroid
edible liver, noix, ris
endocrine adrenal, pituitary, thyroid
enlargement adenia, adenoma
hardening adenosclerosis
inflammation adenia, adenitis, adenophthalmia, bartholinitis
like adenoid
pain adenalgia
part. acinus
racemose bartholin, pancreas
reinforcing accessorius
salivary parotid, racemose
science of adenology
sebaceous tear(pit)(sac)
secretion adrenalin, au-

tocoid, bile, chalone, gall, hormone, insulin, saliva, sebum
sex gonad
study adenology
swelling adenoma, bubo
without eglandular
GLANDERS farcy, malleus, mortersheen
GLARE blare, blaze, blind, blur, bright(ness), cold, dazzle, flame, flare, flash, frown, gape, gaze, glaze, gleam, glisten, glitter, gloat, gloss, glow(er), iciness, light, lower, luster, moon, radiance, scowl, sheen, shine, showiness, splendor, stare
GLARING barefaced, blatant, conspicuous, crying, egregious, excessive, extreme, flagrant, garish, gross, hard, inordinate, obtrusive, protrusive, rank, staring
GLARY blatant, bright, burning, conspicuous, dazzling, evident, frosty, lustrous, shining, slick, slippery, smooth
GLASERITE aphthitalite, arcanite
GLASGOW *waterfront* clyde
GLASHAN coalfish, codfish
GLASS barometer, beaker, bifocal, brimmer, bumper, calx, chark, crystal, cullet, enamel, frit(t), glaze, goblet, lens, microscope, mirror, monocle, mug, pane, parison, perlite, pony, rummer, schmelz, schooner, seidel, smalt, snifter, stein, strass, tallboy, telescope, thermometer, tumbler, uviol, verre, vitro
art agata, amberina, bohemian, cameo, favrile, opaline, tiffany
basaltic palagonite, tachylyte
beads aggri, aggry, bugles
beer seidel, shell, stein
bell-shaped cloche, cup
blower See *maker*, below.
blowpipe matrass
blue smalt
brilliant crystal, paste, strass
broken calx
bubble airbell, bleb, boil, candleball, candlebomb, ream, seed
burning lens, sunglass
cheval psyche

coating foliation, moilos
colored aventurine, opaline, schmelz, smalt(o), tiffany, tinter
-coloring metal selenium
comb. hyalo, vitri, vitro
component alkali, arsenic, baryta, frit, lime, potash, sand, silicon, soda
container bottle, flask, jar, matrass, vase
convert to vitrify
crab spectre
cutter grozing iron
decoration rigaree
decorative millefiori
defect bubble, knot, stone, streak, stria, tear, threads
distilling matrass
drinking See DRINKING *vessel.*
etching fluorography
-eye pomfret, wall-eyed pike
full bumper
furnace calcar, glory hole, leer, lehr, tisar
furnace mouth bocca
fused frit
gall anatron
half split
handling rod punty
heat-resistant corningware, pyrex, vycor
house conservatory
ice-cream slider
jar bocal, mason, tallboy
kind art, blown, crown, cryolite, crystal, cut, etched, flint, fostoria, frosted, hobnail, lalique, milk, opal(ine), plate, plexiglass, pressed, pyrex, safety, sandwich, sheet, stained, steuben, venetian, wireglass
large rummer
layer casing
lead strass
-like hyaline, plass, sanidine, vitric, vitreous
lump bloom
magnifying lens, loupe, microscope, reader
maker footmaker, gangman, glazier, mumbler, shapper, teaser, wetter-off
-making vitrics, vitrifacture
-making device battledore, croppie, drosser, dummy, fascet, ironman, marver, pontee, pontil, punty
-making oven See *furnace*, above.
-making receptacle boot
measuring jigger

milky opaline
molten parison
mosaic smalto, tessera
natural obsidianite
opaque hyalithe
ornament frigger
ornamental See *art*, above.
ornamented lalique
patterned cathedral
pert. filmy, glazy, hyaline, hyaloid, vitreal, vitreous, vitric
piece pane, sheet
piece, hot bit
pox alastrim, smallpox
quizzing monocle
red haematinon
refuse calx, cullet, gall
scum gall, sandiver
sheeted platten
sherbet supreme
showcase vitrine
small pony, shot, vial
snail vitrina
snake lizard
stained vitrail
tear rupert's-drop
threads pele's-hair
tiffany favrile
translucent opaline
transparent uviol
vial ampoule, ampul(e)
volcanic australite, obsidian, perlite, pumice
window pane
GLASSES cheaters, glims, goggles, lorgnette, lorgnon, pince-nez, shades, spectacles, spex
sidepiece temple
-wearer foureyes
GLASSMAN beggar, glazier, peddler, vagabond
GLASSWARE agata, amberina, aurene, burmese, crystal, favrile, opaline, steuben, vitrics
work glaziery
GLASSWORT hyaline, jume, kali, kelpwort, picklegrass, plant, saltwort, samphire
GLASSY blank, brilliant, burnished, crystal, dull, glazy, hyalescent, hyaline, hyaloid, lackluster, shiny, sleek, stupid, transparent, vacant, vitreal, vitreous, vitric, vitriform
GLAUCE *father* creon
husband jason
GLAUCIONETTA bucephala, buffleduck, bufflehead, butterball, goldeneye

GLAUCOMA *treatment* neostigmine
GLAUCUS *brother* learchus
epithet melicertes, palaemon
offspring bellerophon(tes) deiphobe, piren
parent athama, hippolochus, ino, merope, minos, pasiphae, sisyphus
slayer ajax, alcmaon
wife ione, syme
GLAUM clutch, glom, grasp, grope
GLAVER flatter, palaver, wheedle
GLAZE burnish, celadon, coat(ing), coperta, couverte, cover, dip, eelskin, enamel, face, glare, glassen, glidder, gloss, ice, incrust, luster, overlay, paint, polish, sheen, shine, size, sleet, smear, stare, tiger eye, varnish, veneer, vitrify, window
GLAZIER glassworker, puttier
diamond emeril, emery
machine calender
material putty
tack brad
tool grater, ladkin, nipper, sprig
GLEAM beam, blaze, blink, burst, coruscate, flash, flicker, fouldre, glaik, glance, glent, glimmer, glint, glisten, glist(er), glitter, glow, gloze, luster, ray, scance, scintillate, shimmer, shine, spark(le), steem, twinkle, twire, waft
faint scad
GLEAMING ablaze, agleam, bright, clear, faw, luminous, radiant, shining
GLEAN accumulate, bundle, collect(ion), conclude, cull, gather, harvest, lease, pick out, reap, scringe, select, sheaf
GLEANER rake, rubbler, stibber
GLEANINGS analects, collectanea, gain, selections
GLEBE benefice, clod, earth, field, grain, kirktown, land, lump, parsonage, plot, sod, soil, speck, termon, turf
house manse, parsonage
GLEDE bird, buzzard, harri~r, kite, osprey
GLEE delight, descant, elation, enjoyment, gaiety,

gayety, hilarity, jollity, joviality, joy, liveliness, madrigal, merriment, mirth, pleasure, round(elay), song, wassail
club choir, chorus, ensemble
GLEEFUL elated, exalted, exultant, frolicsome, gay, hilarious, jocular, merry
GLEEK cheat, deception, game, gibe, jest, scoff, sneer, trio
GLEEMAN bard, jongleur, minstrel, musician, poet, rhymer, rhymster, scald, scop, troubadour, trouvere, versifier
GLEET discharge, filth, flow, ooze, phlegm, slime
GLEETY ichorous, slimy
GLEN canada, canyon, dale, dell, den, dingle, glen, gorge, griff, heuch, heugh, kloof, pocket, slade, vale, valley
GLENGARRY cap
GLENT flash, glance, gleam, glint, shine, sparkle, spring, squint
GLIADIN glutin, prolamin, protein
GLIB articulate, bland, casual, easy, eloquent, facile, flippant, fluent, garrulous, hypocritical, loquacious, offhand, oily, pat, shallow, slick, smooth(tongued), suave, talkative, unctuous, urbane, vocal, voluble
GLIBNESS bull, hypocrisy, loquacity, suavity
GLIDE bellywhop, coast, dance, elapse, flit, float, flow, fly, glance, glissade, graze, kite, lapse, sail, scrieve, scrithe, scud, shirl, shoot, skate, ski, skid, skim, skip, skirr, slade, sled, sleek, sleigh, slick, slide, slip, slither, slur, snoove, soar, steal, sweep, toboggan, volplane
GLIDER aerodone, aviette, hydroplane, sailplane, scooter
flight study aerodonetics
pygmy flying mouse
GLIDEWORT hemp-nettle
GLIM bit, eye, glance, light, look, luminary
GLIMMER beam, bit, blink, coruscate, fire, flash, flicker, glance, gleam, glimpse, glint, glitter, glow,

hint, leam, mica, ray, scintillate, sheen, shimmer, shine, sparkle, stime, styme, twinkle

GLIMMERING ghost, glooming, inkling, light

GLIMPSE blink, coup d'oeil, dawn, descry, espy, flash, glance, glimmer, idea, inkling, insight, look, peek, peep, see, shim, sight, snatch, spy, stime, styme, tinge, trace, view
brief apercu

GLINKA *opera* life for the czar, russlan and ludmilla

GLINT dart,· flash, glance, GLEAM, glent, glimpse, glitter, peep, see, shimmer, shine, slippery, sparkle, turn

GLISTEN, GLISTER gleam, glitter, shimmer, shine, spangle, sparkle

GLISTENING beady, bright, refulgent, shiny

GLITTER bicker, blink, brandish, brilliance, coruscate, flash, glare, glimmer, glint, glisk, glisten, glister, glow, luster, radiance, scance, scintillate, shimmer, shine, skinkle, skyre, spangle, spark(le), stare, twinkle

GLOAMING dusk, eve(ning), glooming, twilight

GLOAT boast, covet, crow, enjoy, envy, exult, gape, gaze, grudge, look, mediate, preen, rejoice, revel, stare, whoop

GLOBAL round, spheral, spherical, universal, worldwide

GLOBE agger, aquarium, ball, clew, earth, geoid, map, monde, moon, orb, round, sphere
circler, first magellan
half hemisphere
holder atlas
hollow georama
-like globate, globular, orbed
lily spatterdock
pert. capitate, coccoid, coccous, globose, spheric·
thistle artichoke, echinops
-trotter excursionist, expeditionist, migrant, migrator, traveler

GLOBEFISH atinga, blaasop, botete, burfish, diodon, fugu, oopuhue, puffer, tetradon, toado, toby

GLOBEFLOWER bolt, butter-basket, buttonbush, cabbage-daisy, corchorus, golland, gowland, ranunculus, trollius

GLOBOSE coccoid, coccous

GLOBULAR annular, discoid, orbicular, orbiculate, perispheric, round, spherical, stilliform

GLOBULE ball, bead, blob, bubble, button, corpuscle, drop, minim, pill, spherule, tear

GLOBULIN acerin, antibody, arachin, avenalin, biologic, bynedestin, corycin, edestin, excelsin, glycinin, legumin, maysin, musculin, myosin, oryzenin, tuberin, vicilin, vignin

GLOCKENSPIEL carillon, lyra, xylophone

GLOM clutch, GLAUM, look, notice, steal, swipe, take, watch

GLOMERULE fascicle, glome

GLOOM blacken, bleakness, blues, cloud, dark(en), darkle, dejection, depression, desolation, despair, despond(ence), dismalness, dismals, drear(iness), dumps, frown, glower, gravity, lower, luridness, melancholy, menace, midnight, mirk, misery, mope(s), murk, obscure, pall, sadness, scowl, shade, shadow, solemnity, somberness, threaten, vapors, wearisomeness
spirit zozobra

GLOOMY adusk, black, bleak, blue, broody, brown, cheerless, cimmerian, clouded, cloudy, crabbed, crestfallen, cynical, dark, defeatist, depressed, desolate, dim, disconsolate, dismal, dispirited, dolesome, dolorous, dour,· drear(y), dreich, drumly, dun, dusky, dyspeptic, eerie, feral, forbidding, funereal, glum(my), gray, heavy, ill-lighted, leaden, louring, lowering, lurid, melancholy, moody, mopish, morose, muddy, murky, opaque, oppressed, overcast, pessimistic, sad, saturnine, scowling, shvartz(er), sinis-

ter, somber, sombrous, stygian, sulky, sullen, surly, swart, tenebrific, tenebrous, terne, tetric, thester, thrawn, uncheerful

GLOP filth, guck, muck, stare

GLOPPEN alarm, astonish, surprise

GLORIA aureole, doxology, halo, nimbus

GLORIFICATION apotheosis, consecration, praise
ironic pumpkinification

GLORIFY adore, aggrandize, apotheosize, bless, canonize, celebrate, deify, elevate, enlarge, ennoble, enshrine, enthrone, exalt, extole, glamorize, halo, herse, honor, immortalize, kudize, magnify, raise, revere, set up, transfigure, uplife, worship, wurth

GLORIOLE aura

GLORIOUS august, bright, brilliant, ecstatic, effulgent, elated, eminent, famous, gorgeous, grand, illustrious, lofty, lustrous, magnificent, mere, outstanding, peerless, radiant, resplendent, shri, splendid, sri, sublime, superb, superlative

GLORY anticorona, aureola, blaze, bliss, boast, brilliance, celebrity, character, eclat, esteem, exult, fame, figure, grandeur, halo, heaven, honor, importance, kudos, luster, memory, name, nimbus, note, notoriety, paradise, popularity, prestige, pride, radiance, recognition, rejoice, renown, report, reputation, repute, resplendence, skekinah, splendor, worthing, wulder
-hole corner, dump, furnace, locker
old See FLAG.

GLOSS annotaton, blink, bloom, burnish, cloak, comment(ary), construe, cost, deacon, disguise, doctor, elucidate, exegesis, explain, explanation, explicate,· expound, falsify, glare, glaze, gloze, interpret, luster, lustre,· mask, misinterpret, note, observation, paint, polish, pretext, remark, sheen, shimmer, shine, translation, varnish,· veneer *over* blanch, blink, excuse, extenuate, fard, hush, ignore, justify, neglect, palliate, salve, sleek, soothe, whiten, whitewash, wink(at)

GLOSSARY clavis, dictionary, lexicon, onomasticon, synonymicon, wordbook

GLOSSY bright, burnished, glabrous, glace, glib, lambent, lucent, lustrous, nitid, polished, satiny, sheeny, shiny, sleek, slick, smooth, splendent, velvety

ibis black curlew, plegadis

GLOUSTER *son* edgar, edmund

GLOUT frown, scowl

GLOVE berlin, cest(us), challenge, chevron, coffe, cuff, gage, gant, gauntlet, gomukhi, handwear, husker, mit(t), mitten, mousquetaire
body trauk
boxing mitten
gusset piecette
hedger's dannock
leather elk, mid, mocha, suede
maker clasper, domer, fingerer, franker
material cabretta, castor, cotton, kid, lisle, mocha, napa, nylon, pigskin, silk, suede
money bribe, perquisite
shape trank
skin-rubbing strigil

GLOW ardor, beauty, blaze, bloom, blush, brilliance, burn, calenture, corona, enthusiasm, excel, fervor, flame, flare, flush, glare, GLEAM, gleed, glitter, glory, gloss, halo, ignite, illumine, incandesce(nce), kindle, light, radiance, radiate, redness, rutilate, sheen, shine, thrill, twinkle, vehemence, warmth
beetle firefly

GLOWER frown, gaze, glare, gloom, glore, look, lower, SCOWL, stare, watch

GLOWING ablaze, afire, aflame, ardent, ashine, blooming, burning, candent, candescent, enthusiastic, excited, fervent, fiery, flushed, glorious, gorgeous, lambent, luminous, passionate, ruddy, vivid, warm

GLOWWORM firefly,

flyworm, glowbird, lampyrid

GLOXINIA sinningia

GLOZE deceive, disguise, extenuate, fawn, flatter(y), gleam, gloss, glow, light, note, paint, palliate, peer, pore, pretence, shine, smooth, wheedle

GLOZER annotator, commentator

GLUCIDE ose, oside

GLUCK *opera* alceste, armida, orfeo ed euridice

GLUCOSE blood sugar, dextrose, honey, rutin, sirup, syrup

GLUCOSIDE adonin, androsin, anthocyan(in), antimellin, coniferin, durrin, esculin, estevin, fraxin, fustin, gaultherin(e), gein, gratiolin, hederin, helecin, indican, iridin, lotusin, pinipicrin, plumieride, rutin, salicin, tabalin, tencrin
crystalline acacin, androsin, antiarin, apiin, arbutin, asperuloside, baptisin, calycanthine, camellin, coriamyrtin, iridin, isoquercitrin, parillin, phenin, populin, primeverin, prulaurasin, prunasin, prunitrin, robinin, tencrin, uzarin
root gein

GLUE adhere, adhesive, affix, agar, birdlime, cement, epoxy, fasten, fix, funore, mount, mucilage, paste, plaster, stick, taurocol
cell colloblast
comb. coll(o)
ingredient fish, hoof, skins, spetch
-like colloid, viscid
pot bain marie
sheet bat
sniffer addict

GLUEY adhesive, glutonous, gummy, mucilaginous, sticky, tacky, viscid

GLUM atrabilious, badtempered, blue, crabbed, depressed, dour, dumpish, gloomy, grum, low, melancholy, moodish, moody, moping, mopish, mopy, morose, mumpish, overcast, saturnine, sour, sulky, sullen, surly, unhappy

GLUME, GLUMA bract, chaff, husk, leaf, lemma, pile

flowering lemma

GLUT batten, choke up, cloy, cog, congest, cram, deluge, devour, eat, engorge, excess, feed, flood, gorge, gulp, jade, marrow, nimiety, oversupply, pall, pamper, paunch, plenitude, plethora, sate, satiate, satiety, saturation, stuff, surfeit, swallow, too much, wedge

GLUTELIN avenine, oryzenin

GLUTENIN avenin, zymomin

GLUTETHIMIDE doriden

GLUTIN gelatin, gliadin

GLUTINOUS adhesive, gluey, gummy, rop(e)y, sizy, slimy, sticky, tenacious, thick, tough, viscid, viscous

GLUTTER splutter, veer

GLUTTON agee, barathron, barathrum, belly-god, cormorant, crammer, draffsack, epicure, fresser, gastrolater, gorger, gormandizer, greedy-gut, gulch, gulo, guttler, helluo, hog, lurcher, pig, ravener, slowbelly, stuffer, swallower, swiller, trencherman, troben(y)ik, wolverine
bird giant fulmar
famous apicius, gargantua

GLUTTONIZE bezzle, bizle, bolt, cram, devour, gobble, gulp, raven, stuff

GLUTTONOUS covetous, edacious, gorged, grasping, greedy, hoggish, intemperate, omnivorous, piggish, rapacious, ravening, ravenous, voracious

GLUTTONY avarice, belly, crapulence, edacity, gourmanderie, greed, gulosity, hoggishness, intemperance, overeating, overindulgence, ravenousness, sin, surfeit, voracity
symbol cormorant

GLYCERIDE butyrin, oleate

GLYCEROSE fructose

GLYCINE apios, soja

GLYPH channel, groove, pictograph, relief

G-MAN agent, detective, fed, policeman

GNAR growl, snarl

GNARL bend, bulge, contort, curve, deform, distort(ion), gnaw, growl, grumble, knag, knarl, knot, knur(l), nibble, node, nur(r), roughen, sharl, snag, snirl, torture, twist, warp, warre

GNARLED contorted, crabbed, crooked, cross-grained, distorted, knotted, knotty, rugged, twisted

GNASH bite, chew, cr(a)unch, gnaw, granch, grate, grind, scranch, scrunch, tusk

GNAT agaric, blackfly, dipteron, flea, fly, insect, knatte, midge, pest, sciara, smut, speck, stout
comb. culici
-eater antpipit
fungus sciara
group cloud
hawk nightjar

GNATHITE mandible, maxilla, maxilliped, mouth

GNAW befret, bite, champ, chele, chew, chimble, chumble, consume, corrode, crunch, erode, fret, gnash, grind, masticate, mouse, nattle, nibble

GNAWING abrasive, arrosive, eating, pain, pang, rosorial

GNEDE lacking, miserly, scanty, sparing

GNOME adage, aphorism, banshee, bogey, bogie, bogy, brownie, deev, dwarf, elf, erdgeist, faery, fairy, fay, goblin, gremlin, hodeken, imp, kobold, leprechaun, maxim, nisse, owl, pecht, puck, pygmy, reflection, saw, spirit, sprite, tom thumb, tot, troll, vaksha, yakghi
race cercopes

GNOMIC aphoristic, didactic, fairy-(like)
poet phocylides, solon, theognis

GNOMON canon, fescue, index, indicator, nose, pin, rule, stile, style, stylus

GNOSTIC cerdonian, ebionite, knowing, mandaean, perates, sage, sethite, severian, shrewd, simonian, wise
doctrine pan-satanism
founder simon magnus
god abrasax, abraxas, sabaoth

sect bardensanist, marcionite, sethite
wisdom achamoth

GNU antelope, brindle, catoblepas, kokoon, wildebeest
-goat takin

GO 3 act, bet, die, fly, gae, hie, nip, peop, run, tee, try, vai, vim **4** bear, bing, blow, bout, buzz, fade, fail, fare, flee, game, gang, hump, move, pass, quit, read, ride, risk, take, tend, turn, vade, walk, wane, wear, wend, wind, work, yede **5** aller, amble, carry, event, faint, fetch, hurry, leave, match, mosey, offer, reach, sally, scram, slope, sound, stand, track, wager, whizz, yonge **6** affair, belong, betake career, cruise, decamp, depart, elapse, endure, energy, escape, extend, happen, intend, period, quitch, recede, reapir, resort, result, retire, sashay, spirit, spring, strake, travel, weaken **7** abscond, advance, attempt, compare, contest, journey, operate, proceed, purpose, success, venture **8** clear out, diminish, incident, progress, tolerate, withdraw **9** buzz-along, disappear, eventuate **10** enterprise, occurrence **11** deteriorate

aboard embark, entrain, mount

about bigan, circle, jet, perform, pivot, roam, tack, turn, undertake, wander

adrift stray

after chase, come next, ensue, follow, pursue, reach for, strive, succeed

against attack, combat, oppose

against the grain annoy, grate, ruffle

ahead advance, begin, blank check, dynamo, enterprise, hustle, nod, overtake, permission, precede, proceed, progress, speed, surpass

aheads beach slippers, sandals, zoris

all out compete, exert, hustle, persevere, shoot the works, speed, strive, try

aloft fly, soar, take off

along agree, be off, continue, depart, proceed, progress

along with accept, accompany, agree, comprehend, concur, follow, keep pace, parallel, support

around bypass, circle, circuit, circumnavigate, circumvent, detour, skirt, suffice, surround

around in circles flounder

ashore debark, disembark, land

astray aberrate, deviate, digress, diverge, err, lose, mang, miscarry, miss, miswend, sin, stray, wry

at assault, attack, begin, proceed, start, try, undertake, venture

away allez(vous-en), amscray, aroint thee, avaunt, beat it, begone, bugger, clear out, dee-dee, depart, disappear, exit, flee, imshi, jump, leave, recede, retire, run along, scat, scram, shoo, shy, skiddoo, stand off, vacate, withdraw

away bird kwe

back ebb, quit, recede, redress, remember, retire, retreat, retrogress, return, revert

back on abandon, betray, deceive, desert, recede, renege, renig, retrace, turn against, withdraw

bad decay, rot, sour, spoil

bankrupt bust, collapse, fail, sink

before antecede, anticipate, lead, preamble, precede

behind examine, investigate, lose, trail

berserk anger, foam, rage, rave, run amuck, stew, storm

-between agent, arbiter, arbitrator, bhat, broker, conciliator, connection, contact, dealer, deputy, fixer, front man, interagent, intermediary, internuncio, interpose, interpreter, link, mediate, mediator, medium, middleman, mouthpiece, negotiant, negotiator, referee, spokesman

beyond circumvent, deceive, encroach, exceed, outrace, pass, surpass, trespass

broke See *bankrupt*, above.

by call, conform, elapse, lapse, pass, rush on, skirt, vanish *by water* boat, canoe, cruise, row, sail, ship

counter to disagree, disobey, jar, jolt, oppose

courting wench

crazy See *berserk*, above.

dead stall

devil alligator, dart, handcar, scraper, sled, travois

door to door canvass, solicit

down capsize, collapse, decline, decrease, descend, deteriorate, droop, fail, fall, founder, graduate, lose, lower, resist, sag, sink, sound, storehouse, weaken

down the drain disappear, disintegrate, dissipate

dutch no-host, share, split

easy relax

far endure, exceed, progress, rise, soar, succeed, triumph

fast beeline, hurry, speed, split

for abet, accept, agree, assault, attack, attempt, buy, favor, head for, intend, like, love, try for, undertake

forth depart, fare, start

forward advance, fare, improve, proceed, progress

furtively creep, slink, sneak, steal

-getter dynamo, hustler, kochleffl

-go dancer, entada, soapvine

great guns advance, progress, succeed, triumph, win

halfway compromise, mediate, meet, straddle

hand in hand accord, agree, cooperate, synchronize

haywire break down, mar, spoil

head over heels fall, overturn, trip

hence vade

hurriedly dart, dash, hasten, lam(mas), run, scoffle, scram, sprint

in begin, enter, immigrate, ingress, intrude, invade, score

in for adopt, approve of, attempt, begin, engage in, like, practice, specialize, try, undertake

into analyse, analyze, audit, begin, compose, delve, develop, discuss, enter, examine, investigate, join, participate, probe, review, start, undertake

it act, behave, proceed

lightly tiptoe

mad anger, crack up, craze, erupt, maddle, rage, rave, roar, run amuck

near approach

off beginning, decline, detonate, discharge, explode, faint, fall, mog, occur, offset, slip, succeed

off half-cocked err, haste, hurry, prejudge, presume, rush

off on tangent angle, digress

on act, advance, anger, behave, carry on, chatter, continue, depart, further, garn, manage, misbehave, persevere, persist, proceed, progress, rampage, resume, scat, scram, storm

on and on chatter, drool, immortalize, palaver, patter, tarry

on 4 feet quadrupedate

on the globe-trotting, touring, traveling, wandering

on the lam escape, flee, take a powder

on the rocks fail, flounder, sink, wreck

on tick charge

out begone, burn out, date, die, end, exeunt, exit, fail, fall, fan, fizzle, play, quench, snuff, sortie, strike

out for compete, practice, try, vie

out of the way detour, deviate, exert, range, try

over analyze, backtrack, cross, examine, grill, hit, inspect, investigate, probe, read, rehearse, renew, repeat, retouch, retrace, review, revise, scan, sell, study, succeed, surpass, transcend, traverse

over big explode, hit, please, score, sell, succeed

overboard buy, exceed, overdo

phut cease, die, evaporate, fade

pitapat beat, drum, fluctuate, flutter, pulsate, thrill

quickly highball, race, run, scoot, skise, speed, strip

round circuit, circumvent, detour, deviate, digress, suffice, surround

slowly crawl, creep, limp

straight amend, behave, conform, mend, reform

through bear, channel, chill, consume, despoil, eat, endure, enter, examine, execute, exhaust, experience, pass, perform, persevere, persist, rehearse, rob, scrutinize, search, spend, squander, strip, succeed, suffer, undergo, use(up)

through the motions act, pretend, sham

through with complete, persevere

to and fro alternate, fluctuate, shuttle(cock), stagger, totter, waffle, waver, wigwag

to bat for back, endorse, intercede, intervene, sponsor, support

to canossa apologize, submit, yield

together accompany, blend, complement, cooperate, coordinate, correlate, date, dovetail

to glory die, expire, perish, vanish

to it act, begin, hustle, start, strive, try

to pieces blow up, break down, collapse, disintegrate, explode, fall, snurp

to pot decline, deteriorate, die, dissipate, fail, perish, sink

to town accomplish, achieve, hustle, succeed

to work on attack, begin, start, undertake

under fail, give in, lose, perish, set, sink, succumb, yield

up amount, arise, ascend, burn, climb, explode, fail, forget, ignite, increase, mount, perish, raise, rise, vanish

well suit

with accompany, attend, coincide, consort, court, date, dovetail, escort, harmonize, suit

wrong curdle, deviate, err, fault, lapse, miscarry, misfare, miss, sin, stray

GOA crocodile, gazelle, muggar, mugger

butter kokum

capital pangim, panjim

city anjuna beach, panjim

potato kaawi, yam

powder araroba

GOAD ankus(ha), annoy,

badger, bait, brod, brog, decoy, drive, edge, egg, enrage, gad, harry, hotfoot, impel, impetus, impulse, incentive, incite, inducement, inflame, instigate, irritate, lash, motivate, prick, prod, prog, punge, rod, rouse, spring, spur, stimulate, stimulus, sting, thorn, thrust, tool, urge, whip, yerk

GOADS dice

GOAF grain, mow, rick

GOAL ad quem, aim, ambition, aspiration, base, bound, bourn(e), butt, cage, cause, design, desire, destination, destiny, distinction, dole, end, fate, finis, home, hunk, ideal, intention, limit, mark, meta, mete, mission, object(ive), point, port, post, purpose, reach, scope, score, sights, target, term(inus), thule

lack dysgradia

name meaning meta, nyssa

post meta

GOANNA guano, iguana, lizard, monitor

GOAT, GOAT'S aegagrus, angora, beden, bezoar, billy, bouquetin, buck, butt, cabra, cad, capra, capria, capricorn, caprid, cashmere, chamal, chamois, dupe, goral, ibex, jaal, jemlah, kid(dy), kras, lecher, maaer, markhoor, mazame, nanny, scape, s(c)hmo, serow, tahr, tair, tehr, thar, wether

and fish capricorn(us)

angora chamal

antelope chamois, chiru, go(o)ral, serow

-beard aruncus, astilbe, marjoram, noonflower, rosacean, salsify

bezoar pasan(g)

-boy giles

chicory fireweed

comb. aego, capri

cry bleat

disease ecthyma, takosis

domestic hircus

female capra, doeling, nanny

fleece pashm

flesh chevon

god aegipan, pan, satyr

group herd, tribe, trip

hair cloth camlet, kasha, mohair, tibet

hair cord agal

hair sock udo

lard buck fat

leather saffian

-like caprine, hircine, lecherous, lewd

male billy, buck

-man satyr

meat cabrito

milch nubian

-milk cheese chevret

moth (auger) (carpenter)worm, cossid

nut jojoba

pepper chili

pert. capric, caprine, hircine

-ram musimon

rue catgut, herb, wild sweetpea

silky haired angora

skin capeskin, castor, chevrette, crust, kid, leather, suede

star capella

symbol of lasciviousness, lechery, lust

weed ageratum

wild aegagrus, bezoar, ibex, kras, markhor, pasang, tahr, tair, tehr, thar, tur

young kid, yeanling

GOATBUSH *bark* amargoso

GOATFISH moano, mullet, surmullet, upeneus

GOATFOOT oxalis

GOATHERD damon, peter

friend heidi

GOATISH caprine, coarse, hircine, lascivious, lecherous, lewd, libidinous, lustful, salacious

GOATSUCKER antrostomus, caprimulgus, dorhawk, evechurr, evejar, nightchurr, nighthawk, nightjar, pauraque, pewke, poor-will, potoo, puck, spinner

GOB accumulation, bite, blob, bluejacket, choke, clot, goaf, lump, mariner, mass, matlow, mouth(ful), piece, quantity, rating, sailor, salt, seaman, swab, swob, tar, windjammer

GOBAN(G) *term* atari, dame, eye, knot, space, territory

GOBBLE bolt, cackle, devour, eat, gabble, gorble, gorge, gulp, slop, swallow, wolf

GOBBLEGOOK bafflegab, bombast, bumf, buncombe, doubletalk, engineerese, federalese, jargon, nonsense,

officialese, pussyfooting, washingtonese, weasel words

GOBI *desert* shamo

lake hara

part alashan

site asia, mongolia

GOBLET bocal, chalice, crater, cup, glass, hanap, holmos, pokal, rumkin, skull, snifter, stemware, stoop, stoup, tallboy, tass, tumbler, vessel

part bowl, neck, stem

small tass(ie)

GOBLIN banshee, barghest, barguest, bhoot, bhut, bogey, bogie, bogle, bogy, booger, brownie, bugaboo, bugbear, demon, dwarf, elf, fairy, fay, foliot, folletto, gnome, gooseberry, hag, hobgoblin, hurlewayn, knocker, kobold, leprechaun, mare, nis, nisse, nix, ogre, ouphe, padfoot, pixy, pook(a), puca, puck, scarecrow, scrat, shee, specter, spectre, spirit, sprite, troll, trow

doglike barghest, barquest

household kobold

marsh pooka

GOBO burdock, okra

GOBONY compone

GOBY aboma de rio, bighead, bullhead, bully, bumblebee fish, bygo, chalaco, conophorus, fish, gobioid, guavina, mapo, mudfish, pinkfish, sandgoby

blind pinkfish

small mapo

GOCART (baby)buggy, carriage, perambulator, pram, stroller, sulky, wagon

GOD, GOD'S (See also GODS, GODDESSES, and *god, goddess* under countries and function.) abba, adonai, adoncy, agla, allah, all holy, all-knowing, allpowerful, almighty, ancient of days, anima mundi, archeus, baali, creator, daemon, dea, deity, demiurge, deus, deva, devi, dieu, divinity, dominus, duvel, elchim, el shaddai, elyon, eternal, everlasting, father, first cause, great spirit, hero, i am, idol, immortal, infinite, ishi, jehovah, jhvh, king of kings,

logos, lord of lords, mahat, maker, nous, numen, paragon, providence, shen, socius, supreme being, theos, totem, yahweh, yhvh
acre cemetery, churchyard
avenging alastor
belief in theism
be with you adieu, adios, deus vobiscum, goodbye
blind hoder, hoth
blind me blim(e)y, gawblimy
board altar
body bodikin
book bible
bright land of delos
burial place gigunu
by grace of dei gratia
cabalistic ensof
care providence
comb. theo
consecrated to, name meaning elizabeth
craftsman of bach
death-dealing vediovis, veduis, vejovis
-denier agnostic
elevation to rank of apotheosis, deification
false baal(im), idol, mamon, maumet
-fearing devout, pious, religious, reverent
female goddess
forbid chalileh, (c)has vesholem, cholilleh
-forsaken desolate, distant, empty, neglected, remote, wretched
4-faced shiva, siva
gift of, name meaning theodora, theodore, theodosia
giving birth to deiparous
gnostic abrasax, abraxas
government by theonomy
home eden, heaven, langi, paradise
-honoring, name meaning timothy
-horse mantis
incarnation avatar
influence mana
in human form anthropomorphism
is my judge, name meaning daniel
-killing deicide
-king See BRAN.
kingdom heaven, paradise
lamb of agnus dei
loved by theophile
love for man agape
love for amadis, bhaki, piety

lover philotheist
-man demigod, superman, theanthropus
mother of theotocos, theotokos
1-eyed odin
pagan demon, idol
possessed by entheate
power of, name meaning oswald
praise to a(d)scription, laus deo
progenitor buri
ram-headed amon, khnema, khnum
scourge of attila
servants enukki
small microtheos
sunday easter
supreme asur, bel, dagda, ear, fenir, hafgan, joss, jove, jupiter, lleu, llew, lord, marduk, min, odin, ptah, vali, vanir, woden, woten, ymir, zeus
taught by theodidact
thanks to deo gratias
the holy ghost comforter, consoler, dove, paraclete, spirit
the son advocate, annointed, christ, emmanuel, immanuel, jesu(s), lamb, master, messiah, nazarene, only-begotten, prince of peace, redeemer, savior, truth
the word incarnation, logos
3-headed cernunnos
-tree ceiba, deodar
will fate
willing deo volente
winged eros
with us, name meaning emmanuel, immanuel
GODFATHER gossip, padrino, sponsor
GODIVA *husband* leofric
GODLESS agnostic, atheistic, impious, infidel, irreligious, profane, unclean, ungodly, unholy, unregenerative, wicked
GODLESSNESS atheism
GODLIKE deific, deiform, devout, divine, divus, good, holy, immortal, olympian, religious
GODLING demigod, devata, genius, panisc(us)
GODLY celestial, devout, divine, holy, pious, religious, righteous, saint-like, saintly
GODMOTHER cummer, gos-

sip, kimmer, marraine, nammu, sponsor
GODS, GODDESSES (Listed under place, religion, or function.)
answer of oracle
battle among theomachy
blood ichor
comb. dei, theo
cupbearer ganymede, hebe
drink nectar
father amen(ra), amon, anshar, apsu, ashur, odin, taramis, woden, wotan, zeus
favorite of sarpedon
food ambrosia, amreeta, amrita, rasa
geneology theogony
group aesir, ennead, igigi, olympiad, olympians, pantheon, trimurti
home asgard, empyrean, heaven, meru, olympus, valhalla
messenger hebe, hermes, iris, mercury
minor sondergotter
mother allat, amman, ana, anu, brigantia, brigit, chomolongma, cybele, dindymene, erua, frea, frigga, rhea
physician paean
queen hera, juno, sati
secretaries parcae
singer of gandharva
sons angiras, rishis
sword khaled
twilight ragnarok
way of the shinto
GODSON filleul
GODSPEED See GOODBYE.
GODWIT acerina, barker, bird, curlew, goosebird, limosa, marlin, prine, ringtail, scammel, shrieker, spotrump, yardkeep, yarwhelp, yarwhip
GOEL abenger, kinsman, reclaimer, redeemer
GOER doer, patron, pistol, runner, speeder, traveler, walker
GOETHE *associate* schiller
devil mephistopheles
hero faust, hermann, werther
heroine dorothea, gretchen, marguerite, mignon
home weimar
work egmont, faust, wilhelm meister
GOFF See CLOWN, FOOL.

GOFFER crimp, flute, fuller, gaufer, iron, plait

GOFFLE See GOBBLE.

GOG activity, agitation, bog, eagerness, quagmire, stir

GOGGLE bulge, bulging, eye, gaze, guggle, protruding, roll, shake, squint, stagger, stare, staring
-eye calico bass, crappie, rock bass, squinter, warmouth

GOGGLER akule, cicharra, fish, scad

GOGGLES blinkers, eyes, eyeshade, gid, glasses, spectacles, staggers

GOGLET cooja, gurglet, monkey, serai, surahee, surahi

GOGO bantu, bark soap, beetle, bugaboo, entada, gogga, vine

GOGOL *work* dead souls, taras bulba, the inspector general

GOI See GOY.

GOING access, available, behavior, bound, current, demise, departure, dying, exit, extant, fare, functioning, gait, moving, obtainable, passageway, path, road, run (ning), travel, ultra, way, working
around circulating, reported, rumored, said
back on apostasy
light asthenia
nowhere inert
on agate, extant, happening, occuring, operating, toward
out egress, exeunt, exit, exodus
-over rebuke, reprimand
strong abounding, booming, flourishing, thriving, unflagging
the limit brinkmanship

GOITER basedow's disease, bronchocele, struma

GOKURAKU See PARADISE.

GOLA cyma, granary, ogee, sima, storeroom

GOLACH beetle, centipede, earwig

GOLAN HEIGHTS *capital* kuneitra, quneitra

GOLD altun, aurum, bullion, capital, cyme, fortune, gelt, gilding, gilt, marigold, money, ocher, ochre, ormolu, oro, riches, shiny, standard, sunflower, treasure, wealth, yellow
alloy asem, auryl, calaverite, caracoli, electre, electrum, oreide
and-silver-plant honesty
apple tomato
bird canna, plant
black maldonite, oil, petroleum
braid orris
-brick cheat, deceive, evade(r), fraud, loaf(er), malinger(er), shirk(er), slacker, snib, soldier, swindle
burnished pinchbeck brown
cast ingot
chain sedum, stonecrop
cloth of soner
coast ghana
coast fable nancy
-colored metal gilt, ormolu
comb. auri, auro, chrys(o)
compound auride
-containing dore
crab crowfoot
cup butter cress, crowfoot, marsh marigold, renunculus
deposit lode, placer
deposit, richest witwatersrand reef
digger adventuress, flirt, fortune-hunter, hussy, wanton
discoverer sutter
dust alyssum, sedum, stonecrop
dust container shammy
dust tree aucuba
embroidery auriphrygia, orphrey
fabric lame
false oroide
field bendigo, benoni, comstock lode, ophir, rand
flux aventurine
fool's pyrite(s)
greenish aene(o)us
-head pochard
heather poverty plant
imitation asem, ormolu, oroide, tambac
lace filigree, orris
leaf ormolu
-like aureate, GOLDEN
lover chrysophilist
lump nugget
magic hoard rheingold
-making chrysopoetics
measure carat
mine cornucopia, find, lode, plenty, source
miner argonaut, black sander, forty-niner, prospector, sourdough
-of-ophir flower, rose
-of pleasure camelina, flax, madwort, mustard, oilseed
pagoda hoon
pert. aureate, auric, aurous
piece slug, tal
planet sun
plate gild, gilt
powder venturine
-producing aurific
property of aureity
prospect for speck
remnants skewings
rush fraternity clampers, e clampus vitus
seeker argonaut, forty-niner jason, miner, prospector
sheet foil
-silver calaverite, caracoli
source sylvanite
spink yellowhammer
telluride calaverite
thin sheet foil, latten
thread cankerroot, dodder
thread, embroider with purl
-tit verdin
trader goldbug
turn into aurify
uncoined bullion
vein lode
washing lavadero
washing pan batea
washing trough abacus major
-watch spatterdock
weight mark
-yielding auriferous

GOLDCREST kinglet, moon, muddler, thumbbird, tidley, trochil

GOLDEN apple, aureate, aurelia(n), aurelius, aureoline, aureous, auric, auriferous, aurulent, auspicious, blest, blonde, bright, dear, dorado, dore, durry, flourishing, gilten, halcyon, precious, prosperous, sunny, superior, yellow
age siecle d'or
apple bel, hog-plum, tomato
apple claimant aphrodite, athene, hera
apple garden hesperides
apple giver paris
apple guardians aegle, arethusa, atlantides, erytheis, hespera, hestia, ithun
apple winner atalanta
ball globe-flower, guelderrose
bantam sweet corn

bell forsythia
blossom cinquefoil
bough mistletoe
bough author frazer
bug ladybird
calf idol, mammon, riches, wealth
chain laburnum
club bog torch, orontium, plant, tawkee, tawkin, tuckahoe
dream chimera, optimism
eagle ringtail
-eye beetlehead, bullhead, chrysopa, cobhead, copperhead, cur, duck, frogskin, garrot, gowdnie, ironhead, kolea, merrywing, morillon, plover, squealer, whiffler, whistler, widgeon
fleece home colchis
fleece, keeper aeetes
fleece ram aries
fleece seeker argonauts, jason
fleece ship argo
fleece site caucasus
gram mung bean
guineas pilewort
-haired aurelea, auricomous, blond(e)
herb orach
horde tartars
horde leader batu khan
hours halcyon days, overtime
king midas
knop ladybird
maid cunner
mean medium, moderation, temperance
moss stonecrop
mount janiculum
mugweed crosswort
name meaning aurelia, aurelius
oriole loriot, pirol, witwall
plover See GOLDEN *eye.*
polyplody serpent-fern
ragwort liferoot
robin baltimore oriole
shiner bitterhead, bream, calico bass, chub, dace, windfish
shower drumstick, tree, laburnum
spur daffodil
state california
syrup treacle
thread love-in-a-mist
trefoil hepatica
trogon quetzal
wasp cuckoo fly
wattle acacia

willow cane-withy, shrub, tree
wolf chanco
GOLDENROD aaron's rod, blue mountain tea, bonewort, daisy, healing-plant, jimmyweed, solidago, yellowweed
GOLDENSEAL eyebalm, eyebright, eyeroot, keroot, puccoon, yelloweye
derivative berberine
GOLDFINCH canary, flaxbird, foolscoat, greypate, goldy, gowdy, jack, lettucebird, redcap, spinus, yellowbird, yellowhammer
group charm
turned into itys
GOLDFINNY coldney, corkwing, wrasse
GOLDFISH blackback, bluedragon, bubble-eye, calice, celestial, chinyu, comet, cyprinid, dorado, dragoneye, fantail, fringetail, funa, garibaldi, koi, lionhead, miss liberty, moor, narial, old black joe, oranda, pearlscale, pompon, purplecap, redcap, redhead, red tigerhead, ryukin, shubunkin, skywardeye, veiltail
GOLDILOCKS buttercup, cassidony, globeflower, haircap moss, linosyris, mary pickford, plant
host three bears
meal porridge
GOLDSMITH artificer, artisan, aurifex, sonar
crucible crevet, cruset
saint dunstan
tool wagon
GOLDSMITH, OLIVER
friend gynn horneck
pony fiddleback
work she stoops to conquer, the good-natur'd man, vicar of wakefield
GOLDSTONE aventurin(e)
GOLDWATER brandy
GOLDWEED crowfoot
GOLEM automaton, blockhead, booby, dunce, robot
creator lo(e)w
GOLF *attendant* caddie, caddy
ball putty
ball cover balata
blocked shot stymie
club baffy, blaster, brass(e)y, brassie, bulger, cleek, driver, iron, jigger,

lofter, mashie, mashy, midiron, niblick, pitcher, putter, spoon, stick, wedge, wood
club part hosel, neck, toe
course fairway, green, links
course border apron
course part bunker, cup, divot, trap
course, small par-three
cup ryder, walker
cry fore
error baff, chop, hook, sclaff, slice
game round
hazard bunker, stymie, stymy, trap
hole cup
mound cup, tee
pool calcutta
score ace, birdie, bog(e)y, bogie, eagle, hole in one, nassau, par
stroke backswing, baff, chip, cut, drive, loft, put(t), sclaff, slice, undercut
swing waggle
target cup, flag, green
teacher pro
term baff, birdie, bisque, bogey, bogie, bone, bunker, chip, club, cup, divot, dormie, dormy, dubber, eagle, fore, gallery, green, hook, lie, loft, mound, mulligan, par, pitch, putt, sand trap, sclaff, slice, stimie, stimy, stroke, tee, trap
tournament open, pro-am
GOLFER bolt, casper, dubber, hogan, jones, littler, maltbie, nichols, nicklaus, palmer, player, sanders, snead, teer, turnesa, venturi, yancey
GOLGOTHA calvary, cemetery, charnel house, the skull
thief dismas
GOLIATH crane, giant, heron, powerhouse, stalwart
brother lahmi
death site elah
descendant angoulaffre
father galbara
home town gath
slayer david
valley elam
GOMER *father* diblaim, japheth
husband hosea
son ashchenaz, ashkenaz, riphath, togarmah

GOMORRAH *king* birshaking
sister city sodom
GOMUTI areng(a), ejoo, fiber, irok, kitul, palm, sagoweer, sagwire
GONAD germen, gland
GONCALO alves kingwood
GONDAR amhara
GONDOLA barge, boat, cab, car(rier), coach, dghajsa, gunalow, trundle, vessel
cabin felze
race regatta
GONDOLIER barcajuolo, boatman
song barcarolle
GONE absent, ago, away, ackward, behind, broken, departed, drunk, extinct, forfeited, hopeless, irretrievable, left, long ago, lost, missing, napoo, no more, off, out of sight, past, ruined, spent, strayed, vanished, weak, yore
by ago, agone, archaic, behind, bygone, obsolete, o'er, outmoded, over, passe(d), past, yore
for good napoo
on enthusiastic, smitten
out departed, extinct, extinguished, left
GONEF clever one, crook, prankster, shady one, thief
GONER dead duck, hopeless
GONERIL *father* king lear
husband albany
sister cordelia, regan
steward oswald
GONFALON ensign, flag, standard
GONG bell, chime, doorbell, gangsa, tam-tam, tocsin
GONGORISM affectation, cultism, euphemism, euphuism
GONOPHARE medusoid, sporosac
GONY albatross, bird, booby, dunce
GOO glop, liking, mire, sentiment(ality), taste
GOOBER See PEANUT.
GOOD 3 ace, bon, fit, ole, rum 4 beau, bene, best, bien, boon, braw, fair, fine, full, gain, holy, kind, meet, nice, plum, pure, ripe, sage, sake, spur, true, weal 5 ample, avail, bally, bonne, bonny, bonus, bravo, bueno, bully, grand, great,

gweed, merit, moral, noble, pious, prime, right, royal, sound, sweet, valid, value, worth 6 agatha, behalf, behoof, benign, bonzer, bosker, brawly, buckra, clever, devout, edible, expert, facile, famous, honest, mabuti, maikai, nugget, pretty, profit, proper, sacred, superb, tiptop, virtue, worthy 7 benefit, brawlie, brawlys, capital, copious, elegant, ethical, gallows, genuine, gradely, liberal, popular, sincere, slikked, solvent, supreme, tres bon, welfare 8 all right, becoming, blessing, decorous, friendly, gracious, handsome, harmless, interest, pleasant, pleasing, reliable, splendid, straight, suitable, superior, treasure, valuable, virtuous 9 admirable, advantage, agreeable, betcherie, estimable, excellent, expedient, favorable, first rate, gustatory, honorable, marvelous, palatable, righteous, tolerable, wellbeing 10 auspicious, beneficial, benevolent, commonweal, courageous, profitable, sufficient 11 benefaction, wellbehaved 12 advantageous, considerable
afternoon buenas tardes, buona sera
as one's word reliable, trustworthy
comb. agath(a), bene
buy bargain
day gutentag
day See HELLO.
desire to do benevolence
doctrine of agathology
enough acceptable, decent, fair, mediocre, middling, moderate, passable, so-so, sufficient, tolerable
evening gutenabend
faith bona fides, bonne foi, fidelity
fellow ace, brick, trump, worthy
folk brownies, fairies
form comme il faut, convention, cricket, etiquette, polish
for nothing addled, bad, brether, bum, carrion, feckless, fustian, idle, indolent, kapora, kaporeh, keffel,

jackeen, ket, lazy, losel, mean, orra, otiose, rapscallion, ribald, scalawag, scamp, scapegrace, scroyle, shotten, skeezix, skybald, slothful, spalpeen, strackling, tassel, useless, vagabond, worthless, wosbird, wretch
for the public pro bono pulico
friday parasceve
friday cake hot cross bun
gray poet walt whitman
health cheers, prosit, skoal, slainte
-hearted friendly, gracious, kind
highest summum bonum
-humored amiable, cheerful, complaisant, congenial, crouse, pleasant, spirited
-king-henry allgood, blite, chenopod, goosefoot, markery, mercury
-looking beautiful, bonny, comely, eyesome, fair, gawsy, gradely, handsome, lovely, personable, pretty, seemly, stunning, winsome
luck bonne chance, fluke, fortune, hap, mazel, stroke, windfall
luck cap caul
luck charm alraun, amulet, bonus eventus, grigri, mascot, periapt, rabbit foot, talisman
measure solitaire
mighty skookum
morning bonjour, buenos dias, buon giorno, gutenmorgan
name meaning agatha, bonnie
nature affability, bonhomme, bonte
-natured affable, agreeable, altruistic, amiable, benevolent, charitable, kind(ly), obliging, sonsy
news evangel, evangile, gospel
news, name meaning evangeline
night (See also GOODBYE.) bonne nuit, bon soir, buenas noches, buona notte, gute nacht
not bad, worse, worst
old times auld lang syne
one gag, joke, mot, quip, pun
queen bess elizabeth i

samaritan altruist, benefactor, humanitarian, philanthropist
sense sachel
-sized hefty, large
supreme summum bonum
terms accord, rapport
time ball, bash, festival, fete, fiesta, fun, party, soiree
times boom, fairweather, golden age, halcyon days, millennium, past, prosperity, sunshine
to eat flavorful, savory, succulent, tasteful, tasty
very beautiful, bosker, brag, dandy, dicty, grand, hot, immense, nifty, skookum, slambang, slick, splendid, superior, swinging, tiptop, top, tov
will admiration, affection, amity, assets, benevolence, bon accord, brotherhood, charity, comity, esteem, favor, fraternity, friendliness, friendship, gree, heartiness, love, rapport, readiness, regard, respect
working order kilter
works charity
GOOD-BYE abientot, addio, adieu, adios, aloha, a manana, arrivederci, auf wiedersehen, au revoir, ave, bene vele, bonjour, bon voyage, buenas tardes, buona sera, bye(-bye), cheerio, ciao, envoi, farewell, gluckliche reise, godspeed, gutnacht, lebewohl, parting, pippip, proschal, sayonara, see you later, send off, shalom, sholem, sholom, so-long, tata, toodle-oo, vale(diction), valedictory
GOODIE bonbon
GOODLY big, capacious, comely, excellent, fair, gracious(ly), great, handsome, kind, large, pleasant, portly, properly, readily, winne
GOODMAN householder, husband, mister, yeoman
james jacques bonhomme
GOODMAN, THEODOSIA theda bara
GOODNESS beneficence, benevolence, bonte, bounty, class, decorum, excellence, gittel, honesty, honor, integrity, mensk, merit, mo-

rality, nobility, probity, quality, rectitude, sanctity, sattva, value, virtue, worth
goddess of sattva
GOODRICH, SAMUEL
pseud. peter parley
GOODS belongings, bona, bulk, capital, cargo, chaffery, chattels, cloth, commodities, effects, fabric, fee, freight, gear, havings, impedimenta, load, material, merchandise, pelf, possessions, property, stock, stuff, textile, trade, wares, wrack
admission of taking avowal, avowry
aggregation capital
bartered dicker
dry drapery
household insight
imperfect fent
inferior brack
movable chattels
package bale, box, carton
piece cuttanee
secondhand brokery
shipping directions waybill
shipwrecked flotsam, jetsam, jettison, lagan, lagend, ligan
smuggled contraband
stolen booty, cronk, graft, loot, pelf, spoil, waif
sunk in ocean lagan(d), ligan
surplus overage
transportation freightage
valuable swag
GOODY-GOODY effeminate, false, hypocritical, insincere, nicey-nice, overnice, prude, sanctimonious
GOOEY clarty, slimey, thick, viscid
GOOF chump, error, flub, fool, lunatic, mistake, oddity
ball sedative
-off blunder, botch, fonfer, idle, laze, relax, rest, shirk
GOOFY foolish, gullible, silly
GOOGLY bosey, wrongun
GOOK dirt, grime, native, ooze, peasant, sludge, trash
GOOL breach, channel, ditch, fissure, sluice
GOON chump, hood(lum), muscleman, rough(neck), thug, tough
GOONED drunk
GOOP boor, clod, dolt
inventor burgess

GOOSANDER jacksaw, merganser, rantock, titmouse
GOOSE (See also *kind,* below.) brant, dupe, fool, fowl, gander, gannet, gosling, hiss, idiot, iron, nene, ninny, screwball, simpleton
barnacle anatifa, anatifer, crustacean, lepas, pedunculata
-beak dolphin
beakless gannet
blue baldhead, baldpate
cackling greaser
comb. chen(o)
cry cackle, cronk, honk, yang
egg blank, blob, duck, nothing, nought, zero, zilch
fat axunge
fen graylag, grayling
fish angler
flesh cold, duck bumps, pimples
flesh producer arrector, chill, fright, scare
flower aristolochia
genus anser, branta, chen
girl gossard
godwin's ganza
grass cleavers, hariffe, herif
gray lama
group flock, gaggle, plump, raft, skein
kind baldhead, baldpate, bewick's swan, black-headed, brant, bridle, cackling, canada, crested grebe, egyptian, gannet, gray-billed, hansa, knob-billed, nene, neni, outard, pygmy, solan, spur-winged, sula, toulouse, widgeon
liver foie gras
mackerel phalarope
male gander
mythical ganza
neck rooster
pert. anserine, anserous
pygmy goslet
sea gannet, phalarope, solan
snow brant, chen, wavey, whitehead
solan gannet
step march
symbol of conceit, folly
tailor's flatiron
tongue balm, cleavers, sneezewort, spearwort
tough old cagmag
white embden, hansa
white-fronted anser, brant, pied-brant, specklebelly, specklebreast

wild barnacle, brant, elk, ganza, graylag, honker, jacobite

young gosling

GOOSEBERRY acrosarcum, bilimbi, blob, bragas, carberry, catberry, chaperon, currant, dogberry, downing, eatberry, escort, fabes, feaberry, gaskins, goblin, gozill, groser, grozart, grozer, honey-blob, houghton, obstacle, poha, ribes, thape

fool lungwort

old deuce, devil

pert. grossular

stone garnet

GOOSEBILL cleavers, forceps

GOOSEBIRD godwit

GOOSEFOOT allseed, atriplex, bassia, beetroot, beta, blite, blitum, burroweed, chenopodium, french spinach, good-king-henry, greasewood, kochia, orach, pigweed, plant, saltbush, sea blite, shrub, sowbane

seed allabuta, allseed

GOOSEHERD gozzard

GOOSY foolish, nervous, stupid

GOPHER burglar, citellus, geomys, mungofa, quachil, rodent, salamich, sandrat, snake, spermophile, squirrel, thomoys, tucan, tucotuco, tuza

berry gaylussacia, huckleberry

man swamper

plant caper-spurge

pocket quachil, thomomys

snake bull, drymarchon, namer, pituophis

state minnesota

tortoise mungofa

wood fustic

GOPURA gateway, tower

GORB bird, greedy, voracious

GORBODUC *kingdom* britain

son ferrex, porrex

GORDIAN complicated, intricate

GORDYENIAN *king* zarbienus

GORE blood, burt, cruor, dig, dirt, dung, filth, godet, gusset, hollow, hook, horn, killing, mud, nurt, pierce, pike, rheum, slime, spear, stab

king uryens

GORGE appetite, arroyo, barranca, belly, bolt, cajon, can(y)on, cavetto, chasm, choke up, cloy, couloir, cram, crop, defile, devour, fill, flume, gap, gaum, glen, glut, gullet, gully, gurge, khor, kloof, maw, meal, notch, nullah, obstruction, pall, pitcher, pongo, pouch, ravine, sate, satiate, stodge, stomach, strait, strid, stuff, surfeit, swallow, tangi, throat, waterway

with food sate, stech, stuff

GORGED accole, chuck-full, congested, jammed, overfed, replete, satiated, stuffed

GORGEOUS beaming, beautiful, blatant, blooming, bright, brilliant, colorful, dazzling, delightful, devastating, divine, glorious, glowing, heavenly, killing, magnificent, opulent, ostentatious, radiant, raving, ravishing, resplendent, shining, showy, sparkling, splendid, splendrous, stunning, sublime, sumptuous, superb

GORGON euryale, jezebel, medusa, petrifying, phorcydes, repulsive, stheno, terror, ugly

head-covering serpents

-like petrifying, terrible, terrifying

parent ceto, phorcys

watchers deino, enyo, graeae, pehpredo

GORGOPHONE *consort* oebalus, perieres

parent andromeda, peresus

GORGYTHIAN *father* priam

slayer teucer

GORILLA anthropoid, ape, brute, hoodlum, killer, monkey, ngina, thief, thug

GORING cornupete, gusset

GORKI, GORKY alexei peshkov

GORMANDIZE devour, glut, gorge, guttle, overeat, sate, stech, stegh, stuff

GORMANDIZER glutton, helluo

GORMAW cormorant

GORSE furze, juniper, shrub, ulex, whin, whun

bird linnet

duck corncrake

GORSEDD assembly, cromlech, menhir

GORSEHATCH wheatear, whinchat

GORTYS *father* rhadamanthys, stymphalus

GORY bleeding, bloody, imbrued, murderous, red, sanguinary, sanguine(ous)

GOSHAWK accipiter, astur, buteo, gos, tercel

keeper austringer, ostreger

GOSHEN land of plenty, utopia

GOSLING ament, catkin, fool, goose, gull, innocent, novice, pasqueflower, tiro, tyro

grass cleavers

GOSMORE See CAT'S *ear.*

GOSPEL(S) belief, bible, creed, dharmel, doctrine, evangel(ical), evangelium, evangile, fact, good book, kerugma, kerygma, news, principle, scriptural, scriptures, spell, synoptic, truth, verity

4 john, luke, mark, matthew

4, harmony of diatesseron

greek basiliensis, regius

latin book of kells

preaching kerugma, kerygma

symbol of st andrew

truth orthodoxy

GOSSAMER cobweb, fabric, gauze, hat, thread, web

GOSSAMERY cobwebby, diaphanous, filament, fine, flimsy, frail, gauzy, light, mouseweb, stardust, thin, transparent

GOSSIP 3 cat, eam, eme, gab, gup, hen, pie, yak 4 blab, buzz, camp, cant, chat, chin, clat, conk, crow, dirt, gash, piet, tale, talk, tell 5 biddy, cause, clype, frump, noise, ondit, prate, rumor, story, tabby, yente 6 babble, caddle, callet, camper, claver, ferlie, friend, gabble, jabber, magpie, norate, report, shmoos, shmues, spread, tattle, yachna, yakker 7 chaffer, chatter, clatter, clicker, comment, comrade, gauster, nashgab, plosher, prattle, scandal, schmooz, slander, sponsor, tattler, trattle, whisper, windbag 8 busybody, chitchat, jabberer, nonsense, prattler, quidnunc, shvitzer 9 bandarlog, carrytale, companion, godfather, godmother 10 babblement, chatterbox, clishclash, newsmonger, rattletrap, scuttlebut, talebearer 12 acquaintance, tittletattle 13 clishmaclaver, coffeehousing, scandalmonger

GOSSIPER bandarlog

GOSSIPING buzzy, carouse, christening, merrymaking, shanachas, shanachus

GOSSOON boy, lad

GOTH (See also GOTHIC.) suiogoth, visigoth

famous alaric, amal(ing), berig, euric, filimer, leovigild, roderick, theodoric

last roderick

GOTHAM foolish, new york, simpleton, wiseacre

GOTHIC antiquated, barbarian, barbaric, brutal, fierce, germanic, grotesk, grotesque, medieval, ogival, romantic, rough, teutonic

alphabet runes

apostle st ulfilas

arch rib

bard runer

deity frigga, thor, woden

hero wudga

king roderick

letter design fraktur

queen tamora

race amalings

rib lierne

GOTHOLIAS *son* jessias

GOTHONIEL *son* chabris

GOTLAND *capital* visby

dialect gutnish

native geat

GOTTFRIED *sister* elsa

GOUACHE color, painting, pigment

GOUGE bent, cheat, chisel, defraud, excavate, extort, flookan, flukan, fraud, furrow, groove, hollow, imposition, imposter, perforate, pug, scoop, scorper, scuff, selvage, tool, wench

out bulldoze

v-type veiner

GOULASH bridge, game, hash, hollandaise, mayonnaise, pinochle, ragout, stew

GOUNOD *aria* jewel song

opera faust, mireille, philemon et baucis, romeo et juliette

GOUR cattle, koulan, onager

GOURD abobra, amphisarca, anguria, bottle, calabash, chicayota, colocynth, cucumis, cucurbit, dishrag, flask, hechima, jicara, loof(a), luff(a), maraca, melon, patola, peop(nida), peponium, pumpkin, seton, sicana, squash, vine, watermelon, whirlpool

dishcloth loof(a), luffa

-head buffalofish, wood ibis

rattle maraca

tree calabash

wild calabazilla, cucurbita, wild pumpkin, wild squash

GOURMAND apicius, eater, epicure(an), gastronome, gastronomist, glutton, gourmet, sensualist, wold, wolverine

famous bacchus, diamond jim brady, gargantua, henry viii, lucius beebe, lucullus

GOURMANDIZE fress

GOURMET bon vivant, connoisseur, eater, epicure, gastronomer, gourmand, sensualist, taster

GOUT blotch, channel, clot, coagulation, conduit, discernment, disease, ditch, drain, drop, gonagra, podagra, podagry, sluice, splash, taste

comb. agra

deposit chalkstone, tophus

remedy antipodagron, atophan

sufferer podagric

tree clammy cherry, varronia

GOUTWEED acheweed, aiseweed, ammi, axweed, bolewort, goatweed, water mint

GOVERN administer, bridle, command, conduct, control, curb, decide, determine, direct, dispense, dispose, dominate, execute, guide, incline, influence, inhibit, judge, lead, manage, moderate, operate, ordain, order, police, predispose, preside, refrain, regulate, reign, rein, restrain, rule, run, steer, supervise, sway, temper, tend, treat

GOVERNER abbess, amah, aya, chaperon, duenna, fraulein, instructress, mistress, teacher

GOVERNING ascendancy, controlling, dominant, regent, regitive

GOVERNMENT administration, agency, authority, autonomy, bureaucracy, circar, commonwealth, control, dictatorship, direction, discipline, dispensation, domination, dominion, empery, empire, guidance, hegemony, john bull, kingdom, kompeni, maghzen, makhzan, management, policy, politics, polity, power, regency, regie, regime(n), regnancy, regulation, reign, rule, sircar, sovereignty, state, steering, supervision, sway, uncle sam

absence of anarchy

absolute autocracy, caesarism, czarism, despotism, imperialism, oppression, totalitarianism, tyranny

agency authority, bureau, department

agent ambassador, consul, diplomat, envoy, legate, minister

art of politics, statesmanship

by best aristarchy, aristocracy

by church hierocracy, theocracy

by 8 octarchy

by elders gerontocracy

by engineers technocracy

by few oligarchy

by 5 pentarchy

by 4 tetrarchate, tetrarchy

by god thearchy, theocracy, theonomy

by group ocracy

by holy men hagiarchy, hagiocracy

by military stratocracy

by men andrarchy, androcracy, patriarchy

by mob ochlocracy

by 1 monocracy

by people democracy

by planters plantocracy

by pope paparchy

by profligate women pornocracy

by rich plutocracy

by 7 heptarchy

by slaves doulocracy

by 10 decarchy

by 3 triarchy, triumvirate

by 2 biarchy, diarchy, duarchy, duumvirate, dyarchy

by women gynarchy, gynecoc-

racy, matriarchy, metrocracy, petticoat rule
by workers ergatocracy
by worst men kakistocracy
comb. archy, cracy, cratic
control regie, regimen, statism
estates amani
form absolutism, autocracy, centralism, communism, constitutionalism, czarism, democracy, despotism, dictatorship, empire, fascism, federalism, feodality, feudalism, imperialism, monarchism, naziism, parliamentarianism, republicanism, socialism, terrorism, totalitarianism
head czar, dictator, emperor, empress, GOVERNOR, kaiser, king, mukhtar, premier, president, queen, tzar
headquarters capitol, statehouse
house konak
of equal rule isocracy
office agency, bureau
officials bureaucracy
opposition to antarchism
pert. archical, political
popular demarchy, republic
science of archology, politics
system regime
without acracy, anarchism, anarchy
GOVERNOR adelantado, atabeg, beg(lerbeg), bey(larbey), bit, bridle, burgrabe, captain, castellan, catapan, check, chief, collector, commandant, commissioner, comptroller, controller, darogha, decarch, determinant, dey, dictator, director, diwan, eparch, exarch, executive, father, grieve, guardian, harmost, jospodar, khedive, landvogt, leader, lord, magistrate, manager, mandarin, master, monarch, moodir, nabob, oligarch, over(lord), overman, palatine, pasha, pilot, rector, regent, regulator, ruler, satrap, sheikh, shereef, sherif, shogun, stad(t)holder, subahdar, tetrarch, tuchun, tupan, tycoon, vaivod, vali, viceroy, voivod(e)
castle alcaid(e), casellan
-general vali
pert. gubernatorial

provincial ban, ethnarch
GOW narcotic, speed, velocity
GOWAN bellis, daisy, flower
GOWF blow, cuff, stroke
GOWK cuckoo, fool, gawky, gaze, lubber, oaf, simpleton, stare
GOWL defile, gap, ghoul, howl, monster, throat, whine, yell
GOWN (See also DRESS.) cassock, chiton, cyclas, frock, gandoura, garb, garment, jamah, kirtle, manto, matinee, nightie, robe, sack, skirt, soutane, sultane, toga, toosh, wrapper
barrister's silk
dressing housecoat, kimono, peignoir, robe
loose banian, caftan, camise, cassock, chemise, chimer(e), mantua, wrapper
GOY gentes, gentile, infidel
GOYA currant, red, vermilion
painting maja
GRAB apprehend, arrest, beche, booty, capture, catch, clutch, collar, cop, cratch, grapnel, grapple, grasp, jerk, kidnap, nab, seize, seizure, ship, snatch, steal, theft, take
GRABBAG fishpond, lottery
GRABBLE appropriate, feel, grapple, grope, grovel, harvest, scramble, seize, snatch, sprawl
GRACCHI *accuser* drusus
brother caius, tiberius
brother-in-law scipio
enemy annius, fannius, metellus, nasica, octavius, pompeius, popilius
parent cornelia, tiberius
GRACCHUS CAIUS *consort* licinia
father-in-law brutus, crassus
friend drusus, licinius, pomponius, vettius
servant philocrates
GRACCHUS TIBERIUS *consort* claudia
friend crassus, octavius
kin anista, appius
slayer rufus, satureius
GRABBY acquisitive, greedy, rapacious
GRACE accomplishment, adorn, aglaia, amnesty, ballon, beautify, beauty,

become, benediction, benignity, berakah, blessing, bloom, brilliance, charity, charm, clemency, conscience, consecration, crown, decorate, dignity, discrimination, elegance, embellish, enhance, este, excellence, fairness, fate, favor, finish, fluency, forgiveness, garb, goodwill, happiness, hegemone, honor, invocation, joy, kindness, laureate, lenience, lenity, lot, luck, mensk, mercy, ornament, pardon, piety, pity, polish, praise, prayer, quarter, refinement, religion, reprieve, rue, symmetry, tact, taste, tenderness, thanks, venus, virtue
name meaning anne(e) annie, hannah, jane, nan(a), nancy, nina, nita
note acciaccature, appoggiatura, sanglot
symbol of horse, swan
without awkward, crude, cruel, gauche, incorrigible, labored, merciless, tactless, tasteless, ungainly, unregenerate
GRACEFUL aesthetic, airy, beauteous, beautiful, charming, comely, courteous, delicate, discriminate, easy, elegant, feat, fitting, gainly, genteel, gentle, gracious, lovely, mignon, natural, polite, refined, seemly, svelt, sylph(like), tasteful, wispy
comb. habro
GRACELESS See GRACE *without.*
GRACES aglaia, auxo, charities, euphrosyne, thalia
parent aegle, zeus
GRACILE slender, slight, slim, sylphic, thin
GRACIOUS affable, altruistic, amiable, beneficent, benevolent, benign(ant), boon, brotherly, christian, civil, condescending, considerate, cordial, courteous, edmod, favorable, fortunate, fraternal, friendly, generous, genial, gentle, godly, good, happy, human(e), indulgent, kind(hearted), kindly, lucky, merciful, nice, obliging, pleasant, pleasing, polite,

regenerate, sociable, soft-hearted, sympathetic, tender, urbane, warmhearted

GRACIOUSNESS amiability, compliance, generosity, GRACE, gratuity, mensk

GRACKLE beo, bird, blackbird, boattail, daw, jackdaw, mina, myna(h), tinkling, troopial

GRADATIM degree, gradually, step by step

GRADATION ablaut, advance, calibration, climax, degree, hue, nuance, position, progress, rank, stage, step, strength, succession

GRADE acclivity, ascent, blend, brand, cant, class, climb, cuesta, declivity, degree, echelon, estate, even, flatten, form, gradient, graduate, hill, inclination, incline, level, mark, plane, quality, rank, rate, rating, roll, size, slant, slope, smooth, sort, standard, step, value

high super

GRADIENT ascent, GRADE, ramp, slope, walking

GRADUAL antiphon, easy, flat, gentle, grail, leisurely, lentuous, piecemeal, progressive, responsory, slow, stepwise

psalm anabathmos

GRADUALLY bit by bit, deliberately, gently, inchmeal, piecemeal, slowly, step-by-step, stoundmeal

GRADUATE alum(na)(nus), ascend, bachelor, calibrate, climb, collegian, diplomate, divide, expert, fellow, finish, grade, laureate, measure, move up, pass, phd, promote, size, succeed

headpiece mortarboard

GRADUATION ceremony, commencement

GRAEAE deino, enyo, pephredo

GRAFF canal, ditch, fosse, grave, insert, spade, trench

GRAFFER notary, scrivener

GRAFT bite, boodle(ism), booty, bribe(ry), bud, burbank, cion, clave, cross, dig, fix, fraud, hushmoney, imp, improve, inarch, insert, instill, instition, jobbery, join(t), labor, modify, mor-

dida, occupation, payola, plant plunderbund, scion, shoot, slip, spade, splice, spoils, sprout, squeeze, swag, the bite, toil, trade, tribute, unite, work

taker bribee

GRAFTER boodler, politician, spade, worker

GRAHAMITE asphaltite

GRAIL ama, bowl, chalice, cup, gradual, gravel, platter, sangraal, sangrael

seeker bors, galahad, lohengrin, parsifal, percival(e)

GRAIN annona, atom, barley, bead, beat, bit, branch, bran(ner), cereal, chaff, color, corn, crumb, curn, drop, durum, emmer, fiber, fork, glebe, goaf, ganulate, granule(t), gravel, grist, grit, groats, harpoon, husk, inclination, iota, jot, kasha, kern(el), kind, maize, meal, millet, milo, mite, mood, nap, oats, ovule, particle, pearl, powder, prong, pulverize, sand, scrap, seed, shingle, sorghum, spark, speck, spelt, surface, temper(ament), texture, tine, tittle, trace, wale, wheat, whit

beard ail, arista, awn

bearded aristate, awned, rye, wheat

beetle cadelle, cathartus, tenebroides

bind sheave

binder apron canvas

black urd

blade sorage

blight personification

brewing malt

bundle gravel, rip, sheaf, shock

chaff bran, grit

cleaner awner

coarse grits, kibble, meal, samp

coating bran

comb. cocc(o), sito

cradle cadre

dealer cornmaster, cornmonger, swaler

deal in swale

deity annona, ceres, consus, demeter, robigo, robigus

disease ergot, icterus, iliau, russian thistle, smut

dish samp

dried groats, rizzom, straw

ear cape, epi, ressum, risom, rizzom, spike

exchange pit

fields, growing in segetal

food cereal

free annona

fruit caryopsis

funnel hopper

gather glean, harvest, reap

germinated malt, spelt

gold pippin

grass ragis

ground flour, grist, meal

handful reap, single, songle

head icker

hulled grits, groats, shealing, shelling, shilling

husk bran, glume, shealing, shilling, shood

last cut mell

-like frumentaceous

line swath

man-made triticale

man-made, discoverer borlaug

measure bushel, grist, hemine, mite, moy, peck, thrave, toman

merchant lambadi

mixture bullimong, dredge, farrage, fodder, maslin, triticale

mush kasha

outer membrane exine, extine

overripe brit(e)

parched graddan

pit exchange, silo

plant teff

price fiar

processor mill

pulpy drupelet

receptacle bin, elevator, hutch, silo

refuse chaff, pug

rent avenage

sacrificial ador

scoop shaul, wécht

sheaves cop, shock

shock cob, cop, hattock

60 dram

sorghum See SORGHUM.

spike chob, ear

stack hovel, rick, shock

stalk rizzom

stalks haulm

-tin cassiterite

tool flail

24 pennyweight

warehouse elevator

wood bate, beat

GRAINY coarse, granular, oaten

GRAITH apparatus, apparel,

compose, direct, dress, exact, furniture, gear, make, manifest, material, order, plain, possessions, readiness, ready, straight, stuff, wealth

GRAM balmung, chickpea, grain, grandma, iota, jot, khesari, method, mung bean, plant, sword, weight
1/10th decigram
1,000 kilo
black pea, pulse, urd
millionth gamma
owner odin, siegfried, sigmund

GRAMARYE enchantment, grammar, learning, magic, necromancy, sorcery

GRAMERCY thanks

GRAMMAR (See also GRAMMATICAL.) accidence, analysis, conjugation, elements, learning, linguistics, prosody, rhetoric, rudiments, syntax
case abessive, ablative, accusative, dative, genitive, inessive, nominative, objective, vocative

GRAMMARIAN aristarch, literator, priscian, prosodist

GRAMMATICAL *arrangement* syntax, taxis
construction synesis
term accidence, active, analysis, article, case, conjugation, copula, declension, finite, gender, gerund(ive), infinitive, inflection, jissive, mode, mood, paradigm, parse, particle, passive, phrase, praxis, subject, syllepsis, synesis, syntax, telic, tense, transitive

GRAMMATITE tremolite

GRAMPLE crabfish

GRAMPUS blackfish, cowfish, dolphin, killer, orc(a), springer, tongs, whale
blubber melon

GRANADA *fortress* alhambra
king boabdil

GRANADILLA passionflower

GRANARY bin, crib, elevator, firnel, garner, gola, gunge, gunj, hayloft, haymow, hayrick, horreum, lathe, mow, rick, silo, store(house), supply

GRAND andean, august, chief, comprehensive, dignified, eminent, epic, famous, fine, global, good, gorgeous, grave, great, homeric, important, imposing, impressive, kingly, large, lofty, lordly, luxurious, magnificent, main, majestic, monumental, noble, opulent, piano, principal, proud, showy, splendid, stately, sublime, sumptuous, superb, swanky, swell, thousand, wlonk
canyon state arizona
comb. bel
divide rocky mountains
hazard chuck(a)luck
mal epilepsy
sachem boss, chief, head, officer
slam vole
total whole

GRANDCHILD descendant, oye
great ieroe

GRANDEE bashaw, clarissimo, magnate, nobleman, omrah, pasha

GRANDEUR beauty, dignity, elaborateness, elegance, eminence, glory, gravity, hautesse, immensity, importance, impressiveness, luxury, magnificence, majesty, nobility, ostentation, parade, plushness, pomp, proudness, solemnity, splendor, state(liness), sublimity, swankiness, vastness

GRANDEVAL ancient, aged, atavus, avus, old

GRANDFATHER aiel, ancestor, atavus, belsire, bobby, gramfer, gramps, grandfer, graybeard, gudesire, nonno, oldster, patriarch, sayde, zeyde
great besaiel, nono
great-great-great quatrayle
pert. aval, avital
graybeard daddy longlegs, fringe-tree, harvestman

GRANDILOQUENT affected, altiloquent, aureate, bombastic, elevated, euphuistic, flashy, flaunting, flowery, garish, grandiose, heroic, highfalutin(g), highflown, imposing, johnsonian, lexiphantic, lofty, magniloquent, ostentatious, overdone, pedantic, pretentious, rhetorical, sententious, showy, sonorous, turgid

GRANDIOSE affected, august, bombastic, epic, fustian, homeric, imperial, imposing, impressive, magnificent, majestic, noble, ostentatious, pompous, showy, splashy, stately, turgid

GRANDMA MOSES anna mary robertson moses

GRANDMOTHER avia, babushka, beldam(e), bobeleh, bubeleh, gram, grandam(e), grannie, granny, gudame, lucky, nokomis, nonna, oldster, tutu
devil's baba
great elter bugge

GRANDO ombre, skat, solo

GRANDPARENT tupuna, tutu
pert. aval

GRANDSON nepote

GRANDSTAND amphitheater, bleachers, coliseum, colosseum, display, show off, splurge, stadium, strut, swank

GRANGE association, farm (stead), granary, hearth, homestead, lodge, plantation, ranch, society

GRANI *steed of* siegfried

GRANITE alaskite, anoterite, aplite, biotite, frappe, gneiss, greisen, growan, haplite, moorstone, moyite, muscovite, rapakivi, rock, runite, stone
constituent feldspar, mica, orthoclase, quartz
decomposed growan
fine-grained aplite, harlite
graphic pegmatite
lava rhyolite
-like hard, rocky, solid
marking bedway
porphyry elvan
red rapakivi
state new hampshire

GRANNY busybody, fussbudget, grandmother, knot, midwife, nurse, oldster, tutu

GRANT accede, accord, acknowledge, admit, afford, agree, allocate, allot, allow, appanage, appease, assent, assign, award, bestow, betake, beteem, bonus, boon, cede, charta, charter, coincide, concede, concession, concur, confer, confess, consent, consider, contract, contribution, convey, deed, dispense, dispone, donate, donation, enam, extend, feu, firman, gift, give, indulge, largess(e), loan, mise, octroi, patent, permission, permit, present, privilege, purwannah, qualification, remise, stow, subsidy, subvention, suppose, surrender, tithe, vouchsafe, yield

GRANT, ULYSSES *biographer* mark twain
birthplace pt pleasant, ohio
burial site new york city
other name hiram
party republican
profession soldier
scandal credit mobilier
vice president colfax, wilson
wife julia boggs dent

GRANTA cam
GRANTEE beneficiary
GRANTED indeed, just so, licet, yes
GRANTING altho(ugh), remise, supposing that
GRANULAR arenose, firn, grainy, gritty, open, pebbled, pebbly, psammous, sabuline, sabulose, sabulous, sandy
GRANULATE(D) candied, coarse, comminute(d), corn, grain, granular, kern, powder(ed), pulverize(d), rough(en), solid(ify), triturate(d), uneven
rapidly fungate
GRANULE bioblast, grain, grit, lucule, nodule, particle, pill, sporule
GRANULOMA blastoma, growth, tumor
GRAPE acinus, agawam, berry, bullace, cabernet, catawba, cathedral, concord, damson, delaware, fruit, grenache, hamburg, isabella, labrusca, malaga, malvasia, mission, monica, morillon, muscadine, muscat, niagara, pinot, prunus, raisin, riesling, scuppernong, st emilion, sultana, sylvaner, thompson, uva, vine, warden
acid pectic, racemic
black zinfandel
brandy armagnac, cognac, marc
cluster bob, racemation, raisin

comb. botry(o)
conserve jelly, uvate
crusher pisadore
cultivation viniculture, viticulture
curculio black weevil
cure ampelotherapy
derivative enin, oenin
disease anaheim, anthracnose, bird's-eye rot, blackknot, buckskin, coleur, court-noue, erinose, esca, measles, mildew, roncet, rougeau, rougeot, shelling
dried pasa, raisin
drink brandy, dibs, sapa, wine
drying passulation
fermentation cuvage
fern botrychium, moonwort, ophio, todea
fox labrusca
genus muscadinia, vitis
group bob, bunch, cluster, racemation
holly, symbol of resurrection
hyacinth baby's breath, bluebell, musk
hybrid agawam
jelly sapa
juice dibs, must, sapa, stum
juice deposit tartar
-like acinform, uval, uvic
louse phylloxera
muscadine scuppernong
noble rot botrytis-cinerea, edelfaule, pourriture-noble
parasite procris
pear shadbush
pert. botryoidal, uval, uvic
pomace rape
preserve raisine
product enin, oenin, wine
residue bagasse, marc, murk, pomace, rape
root berberis
rot slipskin
seed acinus
-shaped botryoid(al), racemose
sugar dextrose, fructose, maltose
syrup sapa
tokay furmint
white malaga, thompson
GRAPEFRUIT pomelo, shaddock, toronja
GRAPENUTS terrapin
GRAPEVINE bush telegraph, canard, pipeline, report, rumor, underground, vitis
disease apoplexy, erinose
pest phylloxera

study vinology
GRAPEWORT baneberry, bryony
GRAPH chart, contour, design, diagram, drawing, isopleth, locus, map, outline, plan, plot, profile, scheme, sketch, trace
GRAPHIC clear, cogent, descriptive, drawn, eloquent, engraved, freehand, incisive, lucid, monochrome, pastose, photographic, pictorial, picturesque, polychrome, sharp, significant, striking, telling, vivid, written
arts drawing, drypoint, engraving, etching, painting, woodcut
GRAPHITE black lead, gray, kish, lead, lubricant, pencil, plumbago, soot, wad(d)
GRAPHOLOGY bibliotics
GRAPNEL creep(er), crow, drag, grab(ble), grabhook, grapple, snigger
GRAPPA marc
GRAPPLE attack, bind, clasp, close, clutch, dog, fasten, fight, fix, grab, grapnel, grasp, grip, grope, hold, hook, join, knit, latch, lock, oppose, seize, struggle, tongs, tussle, wrestle
bucket clamshell
plant wait a bit
GRAPPLER grab, hand, wrestler
GRAPPLING iron clasp, corvus, cramp(on), creeper, grapnel, harpago
GRASP adhere, apprehend, butt, catch, cinch, clam, claw, cleuk, clutch, comprehend, comprehension, control, cop, embrace, erept, fist, gang, goupen, grab, grapple, grip, handfast, handle, hend, hent, hold, hug, ken, latch, lug, mastery, nab, possession, purchase, reach, seize, smittle, snatch, take, understand, vice
GRASPING acquisitive, avaricious, avid, close, covetous, extorting, grabby, greedy, hard, mercenary, parsimonious, rapacious, ravening, ravenous, retentive, taking
adapted for prehensile, prehensive

GRASS (See also *kind, below.*) abature, bent, boho, bon, cane, cereal, coco, cogon, colieroot, darnel, diss, doob, esparto, gama, grama, greensward, herb(age), ichu, kasa, lawn, mand, marijuana, marram, mung, munj, pasture, pili, poa, pot, quila, raggee, ragi, reed, rhea, rusa, rye, sacaton, sesame, sod, sorghum, spart, spring, sward, turf, ulla, usar, vetiver, zea
among grain drawk
annual italian millet, teosinte
aromatic cuscus, khus(khus)
arrow aristida, esparto, spart
artificial astroturf
bamboo-like reed
barn ankee
beach mat, star
beard awn
beaten down abature
bent agrostis, ammophila, barley, carex, heather, juncus, plantain
bermuda cynodon, devil grass, doob, doub, scutch
bitter colicroot
black foxtail, hop-clover, juncus, shamrock
blade chire, leaf, pile, spear, spike, spire, strap, traneen
blue agropyron, andropogon, poa
blue-bunch festuca
blue-eyed collinsia, herb, innocence, navalwort, pigroot, spiderwort
bog carex
bonnet redtop
border rand
branching nimble-will
brome chess
buffalo buchloe, bouteloua, gramma, st augustine, stenotaphrum
bull gama, slough
bunch stipa, whisk
burden's redtop
button crowfoot, oat
carbohydrate graminin
carpet louisiana, smut
cattail timothy
cereal barley, grain, indian corn, mand, millet, oat, raggee, rag(g)i, rice, rye, secale, surgo, teosinte, vetkousie, wheat
ceremonial kusa
cloth-plant ramie
clump lawn, sward

coarse bent, brome, cogon, fag, gama, quitch, reed, reesk, risp, sedge, sniddle, tath, timothy
corn kaffir, panicum, sedge
couch bermuda, brome, cutch, devil's, foxtail, kweek, quitch, redtop, scutch, squitch, stroil
country veldt
covered with herbaged
creekstuff spartina
creeping beard fescue
crested dog's tail traneen
cure hay
curly comb-fern
-cutting take-off
darnel lolium, rye, tare
dead foggage
deer handsome harry
devil bermuda, couch, joint
disease blackring, copperspot, silvertop
ditch enalid
division sprig
dog's tail bent, cynosurus, traneen
dog's tooth bermuda, couch
dried fodder, hay
-eater billbug
edible See cereal, above.
esparto alfa, ligeum, stipa
family poaceae
feather stipa
fiber bhabar, flax, istle, ramee, ramie
-finch vesper sparrow, weaverbird
flat sage spart
flower spring beauty
flyaway bent
fodder or forage alfalfa, blue stem, bouteloua, clover, corn, dura, gama, ichu, millet, redtop
fragrant schoenanth, teff
fringed brome wood-chess
fruit caryopsis
gama sesame, tripsacum
genus aira, alopecurus, aristida, arundo, avena, axonopus, briza, bromus, coix, danthonia, elymus, festuca, lolium, lygium, panicum, poa, setaria, sieglingia, spartina, sporobolus, stipa, teosinte, vetiveria, zoysia
goose chess, cleavers, clivers, loveman, millet, spear
grain drawk
gumbo bluestem
hay alfalfa, clover, fescue, millet, redtop, timothy

hook sickle
hunger foxtail
hungry-rice fundi
hureek ditch-millet
husk glume
in grain grawk
johnson millet, sorghum
kind 3 awn, eel, emu, fog, nit, oat, ray, rie, rye, uva, zea 4 alfa, baib, blue, boho, bojo, buda, cane, coix, deer, diss, gama, hair, ichu, kans, kasa, koda, kora, kusa, lasa, love, lyme, milo, moha, mung, munj, nard, neti, para, pili, puna, reed, rice, silk, silt, sour, spur, star, tare, tear, teff, tule, ulla, usar, wire 5 adlay, ankee, arzan, arzun, avena, bajra, barit, batad, brome, cogon, drinn, emmer, fairy, float, glaga, goose, grama, heath, hirse, jowar, kafir, kodro, kusha, maize, manna, mouse, otate, panic, pearl, pohna, proso, quake, quick, quila, raggi, roosa, sabai, sassa, sedge, shama, sirki, sirky, sorgo, spart, spelt, spike, stipa, sweet, sword, tenai, toura, wheat 6 aleppo, atocha, bamboo, barley, bhabar, darbha, darnel, doorba, emoloa, enalid, fescue, finger, fiorin, garawi, hureek, jowari, kaffir, kikuyu, lalang, mandua, marram, millet, moonja, pampas, pifine, quitch, raggee, redtop, rhodes, ripgut, sesame, shallu, sleepy, sorgho, sorrel, thatch, tickle, tobosa, toetoe, twitch, uniola, velvet, zacate, zoysia 7 bermuda, bristle, buffalo, esparto, feather, foxtail, galleta, gordura, hariali, hassock, jaragua, lagurus, moonjah, nachani, pilcorn, ragtail, rattail, sacaton, sandbur, shakers, shamalo, sorghum, squitch, talthib, tanglad, timothy, tocusso, tussock, vanilla, vetiver, wallaby, wanghee, weeping, zacaton 8 calfkill, camalote, camelote, fundungi, goldseed, hanequen, kalamalo, lamarkia, manienie, natchnee, poaannua, rolypoly, spinifex, stickers, teosinte, withvine 9 bouteloua,

broomroot, canabrava, cockscomb, comb wheat, danthonia, epicampes, euchlaena, golden top, job's tears, malojilla, paramatta, tambookie, vetkousie, whinwrack 10 andropogon, pilipilula, sieglingia, turkeyfoot, zinyamunga 11 silverbeard
lawn zoysia
leaf blade, spike, traneen
lemon cockspur
-like gramineous
louisiana bena
lyme elymus, hassock, tussock
marsh cane, reed, sedge, spart(ina)
mat nard
meadow alfalfa, bouteloua, clover, fescue, glyceria, grama, poa, timothy, toke
mesquite grama, needle
millet bengal, milium, panic
moor heath
mowed hay
needle aristida
new growth aftermath
nut coco(a)
oat avena, danthonia, trisetum, ulla
of parnassus bog star
oil-bearing vetiver
orchard cocksfoot, dactylis, dogfoot
ornamental eulalia
paper-making alfa
pasture See *meadow*, above.
pea khesari, lang
perennial agropyron, paspalum, rhodes, tripsacum, uniola, usar, vasey
pert. gramineous
plot lawn, meadow
plume erianthus
poverty heath
purple beard aristida, needle
quaking briza, rattlesnake, shaker
quitch couch
reapable swath(e)
reedy bent, carrizo, diss, saccharum
rice zacate
roots country, origin, rank and file, source, sticks
rope soga
rope-making mung, munj, saccharum
rye eaver, marcite, lolium, secale
salt alkali, creek, sedge, spart(ina)

scale glume, palea
science of agrostology
second growth aftermath, fog, rowan
sedge andropogon, broom
seneca vanilla
silt joint, knot
soil-binding vinetie
stem culm, reed
sticky purple-top
stiff bent, reed
stock eatage
study agrostology
swamp See *marsh*, above.
tall arundo, reed, teosinte, zizania
tassel ruppia
thatch alang, bango, cogon
toura tambookie
trampled abature
treatise on agrostography
tree black boy, kingia, lancewood, richea, rush
trembling amourette, briza
tropical imperata, vetiver
tuft hassock, tussock
velvet dog bent, holcus
vetiver bena
water paspalum, reed
weedy ripgut
widow divorcee
wire bent, bermuda, broomroot, nimble-will, poa, reed, um-suff
wrack zostera
GRASSBIRD idlejack, warbler
GRASSHOPPER acridid, acridium, blatta, blattid, bruke, cagn, catydid, ceresa, changa, ckada, cracket, cricket, cub, drum(mer), earwig, empusa, grig, gryllid, gryllus, hadenoecus, katydid, knocker, langosta, locust; mant(oid), mantis, phasma, policeman, prophet, quaker, racer, roach, sawyer, schistocerca, skipper, stick(bug), tettix
changed to tithonus
eater whangam
symbol of old age
warbler cricketbird
GRASSLAND bottom, campo, field, greensward, lea, leyland, mead(ow), pampa, pasture, patana, prairie, rakh, range, savanna(h), schih, sward, vale, veld(t), zuurveldt
plant baccar, bacchar(is)
GRASSQUIT civite, quat
GRASSY cespitose, gramin-

eous, herbid, poaceous, turflike, turfy, verdant, verdurous
GRATE abrade, affricate, aggravate, annoy, bray, broiler, chafe, chark, craunch, crump, crunch, discord, extort, file, firebed, fret, gall, gride, grill, grit, hearth, imprison, irritate, jangle, jar, latticework, offend, pain, pan, pound, prison, pulverize, rasp, rub, scranch, scrape, scratch, screar, screek, scrunch, torment, vex
false dandy
GRATEFUL appreciative, beholden, contented, delighted, desirable, gratifying, indebted, kind, obliged, pleasant, pleased, pleasing, satisfied, thankful, welcome
GRATER nippers, pulverizer, scraper, wrangler
GRATIANO *brother* brabantio
friend antonio, bassanio
GRATIFICATION gratuity, indulgence, pleasure, recompense, relish, reward, satiety, savor
GRATIFY adorn, amuse, arride, baby, content, delight, ease, elate, favor, fee, feed, flush, foster, grace, indulge, make proud, oblige, pamper, pay, please, regale, remunerate, sate, satisfy, tickle, welcome
GRATIFYING agreeable, comely, desirable, good, pleasant, pleasing, satisfying, welcome
GRATING babracot, cratch, crossbars, discordant, displeasing, dissonant, echelle, grid(iron), grill(e), harsh, heck, hoarse, irritating, jarring, lattice(work), partition, rack, rasp(y), rough, strident
GRATIS buckshee, complimentary, eleemosynary, for nothing, free, gifty, given, gratuitous, on the house, scot-free, without charge
GRATITUDE acknowledgment, appreciation, benediction, favor, gift, praise, thankfulness, thanks(giving)
expression of See THANKS.
GRATUITOUS baseless, free, given, gratis, groundless, hazardous, needless,

spontaneous, superfluous, supposed, uncalled-for, unjustified, unprovoked, unrequited, voluntary, wanton, willing

GRATUITY ba(c)ksheesh, backshis(h), bonus, boon, boot, bounty, bribe, buckshee, buona mano, charity, compensation, consideration, cumsha(w), dash(ee), dasturi, dole, donation, douceur, dustoori, fairing, favor, fee, gift, grease, honorarium, lagniappe, mancia, perks, perquisite, pilon, pourboire, premium, present, salve, spiff, spill, sportula, tip, trinkgeld, vail, wages

GRAUB(YER) coarse, crude, ignorant, ill-mannered, insensitive, uncouth, vulgar

GRAVAMEN charge, complaint, grievance

GRAVE ascetic, austere, barrow, base, burial, bury, carve, critical, crypt, cut, death, deep, delf, dig, dignified, dismal, ditch, dour, earnest, excavate, fix, fosse, graf(f), grand, great, heavy, impress, inter(ment), low, mausoleum, momentous, mool, mound, ossuary, pit, ponderous, quiet, sad, sculpture, sedate, sepulcher, serious, severe, shrine, sober, solemn, solemncholy, somber, staid, stern, steward, suant, sullen, terrible, tomb, trench, unaccented, urn, vault, weighty
clothes cerecloth, cerements, linen, pall, shroud, sudary, winding sheet
comb. serio
digger burier, bury-beetle, fossor, pitman, ratel
flower frangipani, plumeria
marker See TOMBSTONE.
mound barrow, tumulus
neolithic cist
pert. sepulchral
-robber bodysnatcher, g(h)oul, resurrectionist, thief
wax adipocere

GRAVEL beach, bother, calculus, check, chesil, chisel, embarrass, fell, geest, grail, grain, overcome, perplex, puzzle, ratchel, refute, rock, sand, shingle, stop

and sand dobbin
chickweed knawel
deposit beachcup, lead
diver burrowing-blenny
grass cleavers
in kidneys arena
loose slither
plant arbutus
ridge eskar, esker
screened hoggins
-stone calculus, pebble

GRAVELED cornered
GRAVELER end, enigma
GRAVELROOT horse balm, joe-pye weed
GRAVER bullsticker, burin, chisel, sculptor, stylet
GRAVESTONE bauta, cippus, headstone, jumper, marker, memorial, monument, plank, sarcophagus, slab, stele, table, tombstone
GRAVEYARD cemetery, churchyard
GRAVID expecting, fruitful, heavy, pregnant
GRAVIMETER doodlebug
GRAVITATE affect, descend, drop, fall, incline, lean, plunge, point, precipitate, settle, sink, subside, tend, tumble
GRAVITY attraction, consequence, decorousness, dignity, formality, geotropism, gloom, grandeur, grimness, heaviness, importance, influence, pull, sedateness, seriousness, severity, significance, soberness, sobriety, solemnity, somberness, staidness, weight
center, pert. centrobaric
instrument hydrometer
knife switchblade
law discoverer newton
science of barology
zero, pert. agravic
GRAVY booty, cream, dressing, facility, jipper, juice, jus, loot, nepotism, patronage, perquisites, sauce
train, pert. handout, perquisites, privileges
vessel argyle, boat, sauceboat
GRAWLS grilse
GRAY achromatic, achromatous, achroous, acier, aged, ash(en), ashy, bat, brindle(d), cinereal, cloudy, colorless, dingy, dismal, dour, drab, drained, dull, dun, elderly, frosty, ful-

vous, gloomy, granite, gris(ly), grizzled, hoar(y), hueless, leaden, lyard, lyart, mature, neutral, nickel, old, pale, pallid, pasty, pilgrim, quaker, sad, sakkara, silver(y), somber, taupe, wan, waxen
antimony stibnite
-blue azurine, cesious, denver, merl, perse
brant goose
brown dun, taupe
cobalt smaltite
crane coolen, cooling
dark charcoal, oxford, taupe
drab acier
duck gadwall, mallard, pintail
fish slaty
friar franciscan
goose lama
-green reseda
-haired aged, badgerly, grizzly, hoary
light ashen, ashy, pearl
matter brains, cortex, intellect, obex
matter, comb. polio
mole taupe
moth sheepskin
mouse sakkara
neutral gunmetal, pearl blue, pelican, plymouth, turtledove
nurse sand shark
-out blackout, faint, swoon
parrot jako, psittacus
pike pickerel, sauger
plaid maud
plover knot
quaker acier
rabbit cottontail
rock andesite
snapper cabellerote, lutianus
squeteague weakfish
walnut butternut
whale hardhead, ripsack
widgeon gadwall, pintail
yellow pongee
GRAYBACK alewife, dowditch(er), duck, herring, hooded crow, knot, louse, sandpiper, whale, whitefish
herring cisco, menominee
GRAYBEARD bellarmine, jug, oldster, virgin's-bower
GRAYLAG anser, goose
GRAYLING bluefish, butterfly, fish, goose, herring, ombre, pink, salmonid, umber, umbrana
GRAYPATE goldfinch

GRAY'S ELEGY *village* stoke poges

GRAZE abrade, agist, browse, brush, collide, contact, crop, eat, feed, fodder, glance, kiss, nick, nourish, pasture, ripple, rub, scrape, scratch, scuff, shave, skim, touch

GRAZING abrasion, attrition *ground* collop, colp, meadow, pascuage, pasture, range

GREASE anoint, axunge, bleck, bribe, cheat, coom, cozen, cream, creesh, daub, fat, fawning, flattery, gratuity, inunct, lanolin, lard, lube, lubricate, money, mort, oil, overreach, pomade, pomatum, saim, smear, spick, suet, tallow, wax
caked seak
coating cambouis
-heels grapes
monkey mechanic
paint makeup
pig's mort
pit lubritorium, lubritory
refuse coom(b)
spot bird's-eye
the palm ante, bribe, pay
the wheels expedite, facilitate, lubricate

GREASEHORN flatterer

GREASEWOOD chamise, chemizo, chico, grayia, lanolin, orache, sage, shrub, striplex, wool degras, yok

GREASY dirty, gross, indecent, oily, oleaginous, porky, slasy, slick, slippery, smeary, smooth, tallowy, thick, unctuous, yolky
grind bookworm, drudge

GREAT 3 ace, big, hot, rum 4 able, acme, baro, best, deep, fine, full, good, high, huge, jake, keen, okay, rich, star, tall, unco, vast 5 ample, awful, bulky, burra, dandy, grand, grave, heavy, large, lofty, mogul, nifty, nobby, noble, noted, socko, solid, stark, stout, super, swell, thick, utter 6 august, cosmic, deadly, goodly, marked, mickle, mighty, peachy, strong, unique 7 banging, capital, eminent, exalted, extreme, fearful, howling, immense, intense, mammoth, perfect, ripping, roaring, rousing, special,

staving, stellar, sublime, supreme, titanic 8 absolute, abundant, almighty, colossal, dreadful, elevated, enormous, generous, majestic, numerous, powerful, precious, profound, slapping, spanking, splendid, superior, swinging, terrible, terrific, thumping, unabated, whacking, whopping 9 downright, estimable, excellent, herculean, hunkydory, important, notorious, ponderous, prominent 10 behemothic, celebrated, consummate, delightful, monumental, out of sight, prodigious, remarkable, stupendous, tremendous 11 crackerjack, illustrious, outstanding, superlative 12 astronomical, considerable 13 consequential, distinguished 14 brobdingnagian
albacore bluefin, tunny
auk garefowl, penguin, pinwing
barrier island otea, shea
bear ursa major
blue heron ardea, arsnicker, crane
britain See ENGLAND.
bulrush boulder-bast, bumble, piassava, sedge
centaury knapweed
comb. arch(i), macro, magni, mega, megal(o)
commoner pitt
dane boarhound
day easter
deal gobs, lots, plenty, quantity
divide crisis, death, watershed
duke wellington
expectations hero pip
goddess demeter, kore, persephone
grandchild iero(e)
grandfather besaiel, besaile, besayle, nonno
gun See *man*, below.
-hearted altruistic, brave, charitable, courageous, generous, indulgent, liberal, noble, philanthropic
lakes erie, huron, michigan, ontario, superior
lakes bay putin
lakes canal welland
lakes fish blackfin, bowback, cisco, coregonus, ictiobus,

kiyi, muskellunge, perch, rooter
lakes indian cayuga, erie, huron
lands alaska
magician sir walter scott
man celebrity, lord, magnate, mogul, personage, ruler, somebody, vip
many See *number*, below.
maple sycamore
mole-rat zemmi, zemni
morel belladonna
mother a(n)gdistis, cybele, dindymene, rhea, semele
number galaxy, heap, host, lac, lakh, legion, myriad(s), plenty, quantity
pacificator henry clay
pompano permit
pondweed water lettuce
ragweed kinghead
salt desert dasht-i-kavir
sea black, mediterranean
serpent apepi
skua bird bonxie
smokies peak clingman's dome
spirit manitou
survey domesday
titmouse sharpsaw
trefoil alfalfa, lucerne
unwashed populace, proletariat
vehicle mahayana
water lily chinquapin
white brother mahatma
white father president
white throne See PARADISE.
white way broadway
willow herb burnt-weed, hart's-tongue

GREATCOAT cothamore, grego, jemmy, joseph, overcoat

GREATER better, beyond, higher, larger, major, mightier, more, superior
antilles cuba, hispaniola, jamaica, puerto rico
comb. meizo
stitchwort head(ache), snapjack, snapper, starwort
than beyond
yellowlegs yelper

GREATEST best, extreme, highest, maximal, maximum, most, supreme, utmost
comb. arch

GREATLY absolutely, abundantly, acutely, amain, by far, considerably, decidedly, downright, essentially, exceedingly, excessively, extremely, famously, glaringly, highly, indeed, infinitely, jolly, largely, much, nobly, notably, only too, passing, perfectly, plenty, positively, preciously, quite, richly, supremely, swythe, unusually, utterly, very much, woundly

GREATNESS abundance, amplitude, bulk, enormity, force, grandeur, grandeza, importance, intensity, magnitude, mass, might, size, strength

GREAVE armor, branch, grove, jamb, puttee, thicket, twig

GREBE arsefoot, cargoose, colymbus, dabchick, didapper, dipper, diver, finfoot, fowl, gaunt, gruiform, henbill, lead, loon, pygopod

GREDE call, cry, proclaim, shout

GREE favor, good will, honor, mastery, pleasure, prize, satisfaction, superiority

GREECE attica, ellas, hellas
abbess amma
actor deuteragonist, protagonist
actor's boot cothurnus
actor's robe syrma
administrator amphodarch, archon, ephor
admiral eurybiades, navarch
alien metic
allies abantes
alphabet alpha, beta, chi, delta, epsilon, eta, gamma, iota, kappa, lambda, omega, omicron, phi, psi, rho, sigma, tau, theta, upsilon, zeta
altar eschara
ancient part achaea, achaia, actium, attica, boeotia, corinth, delphi, doris, elis, epeiros, epirus, hellas, laconia, locris, macedon, megara, megaris, mycenae, paestum, peloponnesus, phocis, pylos, sparta, thebes, tiryns
animal, ficticious tragelaph(us)
apartment andron, thalamos
arcade lesche
archbishop makarios

archeological site argos, asine, athens, corinth, delphi, dodona, epidaurus
archer teucer
archipelago aegean sea
architect callicrates, ictinus, scopas
architectural order corinthian, doric, ionian
archon adimantus
argolis valley nemea
argonaut See ARGONAUT.
aristocracy eupatridai
army corps axis, evzone, hippeis, hoplites, mora, peltasts, phalanx
artist agatharcus, aristophon, dionysius, nichomachus
assembly place agora, boule, pnyx
astronomer anaximander, aristarchus, cal(l)ippus
aurora eos
avenging spirits See FURIES.
ax labrys
badge of aristocracy beard
basin louter
basket calathiscus, calathus, kalathos
basket-bearer canephora, canephoros
battalion taxis
battle chareonea, ipsus, issus, marathon, plataea, salamis
bay eleusis, phaleron, salamis, suda
beauty prize callisteia
belt cestus
bench exedra
biblical codex alexandrinus
bondman penest
bowl depas, kelebe, krater, lebes, lekane
brandy metaxa
bread coloura
bridal escort paranymph
bronze age, pert. helladic
businessman niarchos, onassis
calendar (1–12) hecatombaeon, metageitnion, boedromion, pyanepsion, maemacterion, poseideon, gamelion, anthesterion, elaphebolion, munychion, thargelion, scirophorion
cape akritas, drepanon, grambysa, kolones, krios, malea, matapan, papas, sideros, sounion, spada, tainaron
capital athenai, athens
catholic uniat(a)(e)

cavalryman hipparch
chair klismos, thronos
chamber bouleuterion
chapels hiera
chariot biga, canathrum, griffin, tragelaphus
charioteer baton, helios, phaeton
cheese feta, kasseri
chest larnax
childbirth goddess genetyllis, ilithyia
child's bugbear lamia
choral dance hyporchema
choral ode parabasis, parados, stasimon
chorus leader coryphaeus
church orthodox
church leader arius, origen, papas
church patriarch athenagoras
church reserved section bema(ta)
citadel acrocorinth, acropolis, cadmea, larissa
citizens' meeting ecclesia
city 3 ios, kea, kos 4 arta, dyme, elea, elis, peta, syme, ydra 5 adrea, agyea, argos, asine, canea, chios, corfu, drama, karya, melos, naxos, nemea, pella, poros, psari, pylos, pyrgi, samos, syros, tegea, tenos, vamos, vathy, volos, vyron, zante 6 actium, aegium, athens, candia, daphni, delphi, edessa, ithaca, janina, kozane, kozani, larisa, megara, nikaia, patras, rhodes, serrai, serres, sicyon, sparta, thebes, tiryns, xanthe, yanina 7 athenai, calydon, corinth, eleusis, kavella, kerkyra, larissa, leuctra, mycenae, olympia, piraeus, salamis, stagira, syberis 8 agrinion, ioannina, komotine, marathon, pharsala, salonika, stagiros, trikkala 9 pharsalus, stagirius 12 thessalonika
city, ancient aegina, argos, byzantium, calauria, calydon, cephalleria, chaeronea, chalcis, corcyra, corone, crisa, cyllene, delphi, demetrias, dodona, elea, eretria, helice, hermione, ismarus, ladon, megara, olympia, olynthus, orchomenus, pella, pharsalus, philippi, pydna, pylos, sicyon, thebes, tiryns

city, comb. polis
city, sacred argos, delphi
clan genos, obe(s), phratry, phyle
clerical gown rason
cloak chlamys
club member eranist
coastal region aeolia, aeolis
coin daric, diobol(o)(on), drachma, hecte, lepton, mine, nomas, obol(us), phenix, tetrobol, triobol, stater
colonist oecist
colony aeolis, aeolia, cyrene, elea, ionia
column corinthian, doric, ionic
comb. gr(a)eco, karyo, kilo
commander antiphus, navarch
commonalty demos
communal meal syssitia
commune deme
conductor mitropoulos
conqueror alexander the great
conscience aidos
contest agon, olympic games, panathenaea, pancratium, pythion games
council boule
court dykastery, ephetae
courtesan aspasia, hetaera, thais, thargelia
courtyard hypaethros
counsellor mentor, nestor
coward epeus
critic zoilus
cross sobor
culture hellenic
cup cantharus, cotula, cotyle, cyathus, cylix, depas, holmos, kantharos, kyathos, kylix, phiale, scyphus, skyphos
cupid eros
dagger parazonium
dance calathiscus, cordax, hormos, kordax, pyrrhic, romaika, sikinnis, strophe
dawn eos
death rites thanatousia
debate agon
demon python
dialect achaean, aeolic, arcadian, attic, boeotian, coan, doric, elean, eolic, hellenic, ionic, melian, theran
dictator metaxas
dirge linos
dish arnipsito, avgolemono, baklava, dolmades, doulma,

horyatiki, kalamaria, keftedes, keftethes, mezedes, moussaka, pilaff, psariplaki, skordalia, souvlakia, taramosalata, thyafora
district 4 arta, deme, elis, ilia, nome 5 canea, chios, corfu, crete, drama, evros, fokis, khios, kriti, laris, nomos, pella, salia, samos, zante 6 achaea, achaia, attica, attiki, boetia, epirus, euboea, evvoia, ipiros, kazala, khania, kilkis, kozane, kozani, larisa, lariss, lesbos, lesvos, leukas, levkas, locris, phocis, pieria, serrai, thrace, thraki, xanthe 7 aetolia, arcadia, argolis, corinth, eparchy, florina, imathia, kavalla, kerkyra, laconia, lakonia, larissa, lasithi, mt athos, preveza, rhodope, rodhopi, trikala, voiotia 8 arkadhia, cyclades, ionnania, ionninia, iraklion, karditsa, kastoria, magnisia, messenia, messinia, phlorina, rethymne, rhodophe, salonica, salonika, thessaly 9 acarnania, korinthos, lasithion, macedonia, phthiotis, rethimini, thessalia, zakynthos 10 cephalonia, chalcidice, khalkidike 11 kephallenia
division, ancient achaean, achaian, aeolian, dorian, ionian
doom ker
dragon basilisk, ladon
drama mime
drama catalogue didascaly
drama, final scene exodos
drama founder thespis
drama interlude epeisodion
dramatist aeschylus, agathon, aristophanes, eupolis, euripedes, sophocles, thespis
dream god icelus, phantasus
drinking horn rhyton
drought monster sphinx
dwarf philetas
dynasty seleucid
earth geos
enchantress circe, medea
entertainers hetaer(i)a, hetaira
eparchy doris
epic dionysiaca, iliad, odyssey
epigrammatist meleager
essence ousia

eve pandora
evil spirit momus, python
exclamation babai
fable writer aesop
faithful wife evadne, penelope
fate ananke, atropos, clotho, lachesis, moira(e)
feast master symposiarch
festival agon, aianteia, apaturia, carnea, daphnephoria, delia, delphinia, diasia, didymaea, diipolia, elephebolia, eleusinia, eleutheria, haloa, heraea, hyacinthia, lenaea, thesmorphoria, tonea
figure kouros
fire naphtha
fire hero hephaestus
first man alalcomeneus, deucalion, phanes
flask aryballos, olpe
fleet commander navarch
flute daulos, hemiope
flyer icarus
football podosfero
footrace course diaulos, dromos, stadium
foot soldier hoplite, peltast
fountain nymph abarbarea, arethusa
friend philhellene
furies See FURIES.
galley bireme, trireme, unireme
game agon, kottabos, podosfero
games official gymnasiarch, hellanodic
games site delphi, isthmia, nemea, olympia, pythia
garment chiton, chlamys, diploidion, exomis, fustanella, halma, himation, peplos, tunic
general aratus, eumenes, leosthenes, lysippus, miltiades, pausanias, pelopidas, philopoemen, xenophon
geographer strabo
geometer euclid
ghost ker(r)
giant (See also TITAN.) acamas, aegaeon, agrios, albion, alcyoneus, aloadae, aloeuos, anax, antaeos, antaeus, arges, argus, atlas, briareus, brontes, cacus, clytius, coeus, cottus, crius, cronus, cyclops, enceladus, ephialtes, eurytos, eurytus, gyges, hippolytos, hyperion, iapetus, mimas, orion, otos,

otus, pallas, pelorus, polybotes, porphyrion, rhea, steropes, tethys, thaon, titan, tityus, typhoeus
gifts xenia
girdle estus, zoster
goat amaltheia
god aegeus, aeolus, aether, anteros, apollo(n), ares, asclepius, asklepios, boreas, chaos, comus, cupid, dis, dionysus, endymion, enyalius, eros, euros, faun, hades, helios, hephaestus, hermes, hymen, hyperion, komos, mentu, nereus, notus, olympians, oniros, otus, pan, phaethon, phoebus, phrixos, phrixus, poseidon, pothos, python, satyr, selinus, simois, titans, triton, uranus, zeus
god, abode olympus
goddess 3 ara, ate, bia, eos, ino, nox, nyx, ops 4 aura, cora, dice, dike, enyo, eris, gaea, gaia, hebe, hera, hora, iaso, iole, kore, leda, leta, maia, moer, nike, rhea, upis 5 brimo, brizo, carpo, ceres, cotys, damia, diana, doris, helen, horae, irene, metis, moera, niobe, tyche 6 aethra, athena, aurora, bendis, clotho, cybele, eirene, ergane, hecate, hekate, hestia, moerae, pallas, selena, selene, semele, urania 7 ariadne, artemes, astarte, astraea, atropos, chloris, jacaste, jocasta, majesta, nemesis, nephele, panacea, phaedra 8 adrastea, despoina, lachesis 9 aphrodite, mnemosyne 10 amphitrite, persephone 11 persephassa
god, group cabeiri, kabeiri
gorgon deino, enyo, euryale, graeae, graise, medusa, pemphredo, phorcydes, stheno
governor eparch
graces aglaia, auxo, cleta, euphrosyne, hegemone, pasithea, phaenna, thalia
grammarian aristarch
grape leaves dommathes
gravestone stele
grove altis
guerrilla andart, klepht
guest xenos
gulf arta, athens, corinth, kavalla, khanion, lacon(i)s,

lepanto, mesara, messenia, patrai, patras, rendina, salonika, saronic, strimon, thermaic, toronaic, volos
gymnasium cynosarges, palaestra, xyst
headband ampyx, taenia
headdress miter, stephane, stephanos
healing goddess panacea
helmet alopeke
herald stentor
herald's staff caduceous
hero academus, acamas, achilles, aegialeus, aias, ajax, alcimedon, alcinous, alcmaeon, amphion, androcrates, aristaeus, bellerophon, boeotus, cadmus, castor, cecrops, diomedes, dioscuri, epigonus, erichthonius, euryalus, euryplus, hercules, idas, jason, kolokotronis, leonidas, meleager, nestor, odysseus, oedipus, orpheus, peleus, perseus, promachus, prometheus, protesilaus, sinon, sthenelus, thersander, theseus
hetaira See *courtesan,* above.
historian acestordorus, antiphon, antisthenes, clidemus, ctesias, dinon, diodorus siculus, duris, ephorus, hellanicus, heraclides, herodatus, idomeneus, phanias, phanodemus, phylarchus, polybius, simonides, stesimbrotus, theophrastus, theopompus, thucydides, timaeus, xenophon
history stones arundel, ian
hobgoblin empusa
holy of holies adytumhorse scyphius
horse scyphius
hospitality xenia
hunter acastus, actaeon, adonis, meleager, orion
huntress atalanta
hymn kontakion
immigrant metic
infantryman evzone
initiate epopt(a)
invader dorian
island (See also AEGEAN *island.*) anaphe, anticythera, antiparos, ceos, cephalonia, cerigo, cimolus, corfu, crete, cythera, delos, dia, elis, eubeos, euboea, evvoia, gavdos, hydra, ionia, ithaca, ithaka, ithaki, kalymnos, karpathes,

kea, keos, kerkyra, khios, kimolos, krete, kythera, kythnos, lesbos, leukas, levitha, levkas, myconos, mykonos, myt(h)elene, naxos, paros, patmos, pax(o)i, rhenea, rhodes, rodos, salamis, samos, santorini, saria, serifus, seriphos, siphnos, skiros, symi, syra, syros, telos, thasos, thira, zante, zea
island group cyclades, dodecanese, ionian, sporades, strophades
italian colony cumae, magna graecia
jar amphora, cadus, hydria, lecythus, lekythos, lekythus, pelike
javelin acontium
joint arthros
judge aeacus, dikast, heliast, syndic
justice goddess dike
key pattern meander
king acrisius, agamemnon, cinyras, constantine, george, ixion, nestor, paul, saron, syleus
king of india hermaeus
king's title anax(andron)
lace reticella
ladle cyathus, kyathos
lake copais, karla, kastoria, kopais, prespa, tachinos, topolia, vistonis, volvi
lament kommos
land allotment cleruchy
landowners geomoroi
language, literary katharevusa
lawgiver draco, minos, solon
leader agesilaus, constantine caramanlis, epaminondas, pelopidas, timoleon, timotheus
league of states amphictyony
leather bag ascos, askos
legislation goddess eunomia
legislature boule, senate, vouli
letter See *alphabet,* above.
liquor ouzo
lizard galeus
love philos
love feast agape
lyre barbiton, chelys, cithara, trigon
lyre player arion
magician dactyl, daktyl
magistrate archon, boeotarch, demiurge, eparch, ephor, nomarch

magistrate's hall archeion
maiden canephora
man of brass talos
marble parian, pentelic, rosso antico
marine god aegaeon
marker stela, stele
market place agora, stoa
marriage gamos
marriage song hymen
marsh lerna
mask, part onkos
mathematician archimedes, aristarchus, eratosthenes, euclid, pythagoras
mayor demarch
measure acaena, amphora, bachel, bacile, baril(e), bema, beme, cados, chenica, choenix, chous, condylos, cotula, cubit, cyathos, daktylos, dekapode, diaulos, dichas, digit, diote, dolichos, doron, gramme, hekteus, hemiekton, hemina, koilon, lichas, maris, medimnos, medimnys, metreta, metretes, milion, orgyia, oxybaphon, palaiste, palame, pechys, pekhe, pik(i), plethron, plethrum, podos, pous, pygon, schene, spithame, stadion, stadium, stathmos, stremma, xestes, xylon
meatballs keftethes
meeting place exedra
men's quarters andron
mercenaries armatoles
merger with enosis
missionary methodius
mistress hetaera, lais
monastery laura, stauropegion
monk caloyer
monster argus, briareus, geryon, lamia, scylla, sphinx, tiphoeus
month (1–12) gamelion, anthesterion, elaphebolion, munychion, thargelion, scirophorion, hecatombaeon, metageitnion, boedromion, pyanepsion, maemacterion, poseideon
mortar holmos
mother niobe
murderer cithaeron
musical instrument aulos, barbiton, cithara, epigoneion, heptachord, kithare
musical interval ditone, mesene
musical note mese, nete

musical system neume
musical term ditone
musician arion
mustard sinapi
mysteries site eleusis
mystic hesychast
mythographer euhemerus
nature ousia
noah deucalion
nome See *district*, above.
notary tachygrapher
nurse abia, baubo, beroe
nut jordan almond
nymph (See also *water nymph*, below.) aegina, antiope, arethusa, auloniad, brome, byblis, callisto, cyane, cyllene, cyrene, dryad, galatea, ida, idaea, idothea, mera, napaeae, oread, phthia, rhode, scylla, styx, thoosa
offerings hiera
official alytarch, amphodarch, archon, boeotarch, eparch, ephor, gymnasiarch, hierarch, hipparch, nomarch, strategas
old testament septuagint
oracle sibyl
oracle site delphi, dodona
orator andocides, aeschines, callicles, callisthenes, callistratus, charidemus, cimon, crobylus, demades, demostratus, dromoclides, ephialtes, hyperides, lacritus, moerocles, pericles, phocion, polyeuctus, pytheus, thucydides
outdoor room exedra
overseer ephor
painter aglaophon, apelles, el greco, zeuxis
paradise elysium
pastry baklava(h)
patriarch arius
patriot botsares, bozzaris, klepht, ypsilanti
patron saint nicholas
peak athos, helicon, hymettus, ida, idhi, ithome, lycabettus, oeta, oite, olympus, ossa, parnassus, pelion, pentelicus, smolikas, tagetos, taygetus
peninsula acte, akte, akti, alte, morea, peloponnesus, sithonia
people aeolian, argive, athenian, cretan, danai, demos, hellene, ionian, pelasgian, spartan, suliote
people, father of deucalion

performer acroama
pert. classical, hellenic, ionian, panhellenic
phantom lamia
philosopher See *sage*, below.
philosophic school cynic, stoic
physician aesculapius, archiater, galen, hippocrates
pilaster anta
pipeorgan hydraulus
pit for criminals barathrum
pitcher oenochoe, olla, olpe
plain marathon
platform bema, logeion
playgirl hetaera, hetaira
poem iliad, odyssey
poet agathon, alcaeus, alcman, anacreon, antimachus, archilochus, arion, bacchylides, bion, callimachus, cavafy, colophonian, hesiod, homer, ibycus, ion, kavaphis, musaeus, olen, pindar, seferiades, simonides, sophocles, theocritus, thespis, tyrtaeus, xenophanes
poetess corinna, erinna, sappho
populace demos
port alexandroupolis, aulis, corfu, delium, enos, gallipoli, lepanto, megara, navarino, patrai, patras, pilos, piraeus, pylos, salonica, salonika, saloniki, syra, syros, volos(s)
portico stoa, xyst
precinct temenos
prefecture eparchy
prelate metropolitan
premier karamanlis, papandreou
priest hierophant, myst, papa(s)
priestess auge, caryatid, xenoclea
prime minister venizelos
princess iole, irene
promontory actium
prophet bacis, iamus, tiresias
province See *district*, above.
public disgrace atimy
public record office archeion
queen aedon
race lampadedromy, olympics
race starting line aphesis
range oeta, othrys, pindus, rhodope, rodopi
rattle crotalum
reed pen calamus
region achaia, aetolia, arcadia, arcady, argolis, at-

tica, boeotia, doris, elis, epirus, euboea, laconia, megaris, messinia, thessaly, thrace
religious festival apaturia
resistance group eam, edes, elas
resurrection anastasimon
river achelous, akheloos, alfios, aliakmon, alpheus, arachtus, arda, arta, aspropi, auro, axios, basilipotamo, cocytus, eurotas, evros, evrotas, ilissos, illillus, iri, kephisos, lerna, meda, nestos, peneios, peneus, pinios, raphia, rhouphia, roufias, salambria, saranta, strimon, struma, tano, vardar
river deity achelous, alpheius, asopus, cephissus, eridanus, inachus, ladon, maeander, peneius, scamander, xanthus
robber procrustes
rose campion
ruins acropolis, agora, corinth, delos, eleusis, elevis, lindos, pella, samos
ruler See *official*, above.
runner atalanta, camilla, hermes
sacred city argos
sacred fountain aganippe
sacred grove altis
sacred place abaton, hieron, sekos, temenos
sacred stone baetulus, baetyl(us)
sacrifice hiera
sage abaris, anaxagoras, anaximander, anaximenes, antisthenes, arcesilaus, aristippus, ariston, aristotle, arius, athenaeus, bias, carneades, chilon, chrysippus, cleanthes, cleobulus, democritus, diogenes, elea, empedocles, epictetus, epicurus, galen, gorgias, heraclitus, hypatia, ithagenes, longinus, panaetius, parmenides, plato, pythagoras, socrates, solon, thales, theophrastus, xenocrates, xenophanes, zeno
sages, seven anacharsis, bias, chilon, cleobulus, epimenides, myson, periander, pherecydes, pittacus, sociades, solon, thales
saint hagia
salad horyatiki

sanctuary cella, hiera, sekos
satirist archilochus, lucian
school palaestra
sculptor myron, phidias, praxiteles, rhoecus, scopas
sculpture caryatid, discobolus, kore, kouros, laocoon, xoanon
sea aegean, ionian, mirtoon, thalassa
sea creature ichthyocentaur
sea god glaucus, ino, leucothea, melicertes, nereids, palaemon, phorcys, poseidon, proteus, triton
secret society hetaeria, hetairia
seer amphilocus, calchas, cassandra, melampus, mopsus, nestor, sybil, tiresias
serf helot, penest
serpent seps
settler metic
shawl epiblema
shield clipeus, pelta
ship holcad
shipping tycoon livanos, niarchos, onassis
shrine abaton, amaktoron, hieron, secos, sekos, temenos
silver mines laurium
simpleton margites
siren aglaophone, aglaophonos, molpe, parthenope, thelxepeia
skeptic timon
slab stele
slave baube, baubo, helot, iambe, penest
slave's garment exomis
social gathering lesche
soldier acamas, evzone, hoplite, palikar
soldier's exclamation thalassa
song dithyramb, melos, ode, oicos, paeon, scolion
soothsayer calchas, cassandra
sorceress circe, medea, siren
soul or spirit cer, ker, pneuma
speech rhesis
speech writer tachygrapher
spinner clotho
spring castalia
stage skene
stage wing parascenium
state phocis
statesman aristides, epedocles, pericles, themistocles
stronghold suli

sun god apollo, helios, hyperion, phoebus
sword spatha
symbol orant
tablet parapegm
teacher sophist
temple bassae, heraeum, naos, parthenon, theseum
temple builder agamedes
temple enclosure temenos
temple floor crepidoma, crepis, krepis
temple part cella, epinaos, naos, opisthodome, pronaos
temple slave hierodule
theater epidaurus, odea, odeon, odeum
theater part episcenium, parados, scena, skenai, skene
theologian arius
township deme
tragedy rhesus
tragedy, father of aeschylus
traveler pausanias
trojan war allies abantes, euboeans
trojan war leader agamemnon
troop axis
tunis chiton
tyrant apollodoros, dimitrios, dionysius, gelon, hiero, hipparchus, hippias, periander, pericles, phidion, pisistratus, polycrates
undershirt chiton
underworld river acheron, cocytus, lethe, phlegethon, styx
union enosis
valerian charity
valley nemea, tempe
vase amphora, d(e)inos, diota, loutrophoros
vase painting style black-figure, geometric, idaean, polychrome, red-figure
vernacular demotic, romaic
vessel amphora, aryballos, ascus, askos, cadus, chytra, diota, holcad, olpe, pelike, pithos, stamnos, vaphio cup
victory monument tropaeum
village obe
voting place pnyx
war cry alala(lalai)
warrior See *hero*, above.
warrior's belt zuoave
warship cataphract, trireme, unireme
watchman cerberus
water nymph aganippe, ar-

gyra, calypso, cassotis, castalia, cyane, hago, naiad, pegae, pirene, potamid, salmacis
weight chalcon, chalque, diobol(on), drachma, dramme, kantar, litra, livre, maneh, mina(h), mna, obol(e), obolos, obolus, oka, oke, pound, stater, talanton, talent, tetradrachma
wind l(a)elaps
wind god aello, aeolus, boreas, calais, chimaera, chione, harpies, prodromes, zetes
wine acantria, amorgiano, antika, aresinato, aretsina, athirit, demestica, kokkineli, mavrodaphne, retsina, rumney
wine pitcher oenochoe
wineskin ascos, askos
winged horse pegasus
witch aganice
woman's garment peplos
women's quarters thalamium, thalamus
wooden statue xoanon
workshop ergasterion
world war II group eam
wrestler antaeos
writer aesop, anacreon, hesiod, homer, kazantzakis, lucian, menander, pindar, plato, plutarch, sappho, thales, timon, xenos, zeno
youth adonis, enalus, endymion, ephebe, ephebus
GREED avarice, avidity, covetousness, cupidity, desire, edacity, esurience, exorbitance, gluttony, hoggery, rapacity, selfishness, voracity
symbol cormorant, hog, swine
GREEDINESS avarice, avidity, cupidity
GREEDY acquisitive, avaricious, avid, chintzy, close, covetous, devouring, esurient, gluttonous, gorb, grabby, grasping, gripple, hoggish, hungry, insatiable, insatiate, lickerish, liquorish, miserly, omnivorous, piggish, rapacious, ravenous, stingy, unquenchable, voracious, widemouthed, yiver
GREEK (See also GREECE.) achaean, aeolian, argive, attic, babel, cretan, eolian,

grecian, hadji, hellene, hellenic, ionian, jargon, klepht, koine, metic, mixup, romaic, sharp(er), siceliot
last of philopoemen
life bios
non barbarian
orthodox code nomocanon
orthodox litany ectene, ektene
shame aidos
tense aorist
time chronos
GREEN (See also *shade,* below.) absinthe, amateurish, awkward, bice, blooming, callow, cedre, chartreuse, chlorine, common, crude, cypress, emerald, emeraud, fir, flush, fresh, golf course, grass, gullible, half-baked, hoax, holly, ignorant, immature, incompetent, inexperienced, ingenue, ivy, jade(ite), kelly, laurel, lawn, leafy, leek, lierre, live, mesange, moist, moss, new, nile, olive, peridot, pistache, puerile, raw, recent, remembered, reseda, rough, rude, seafoam, shamrock, sour, tarragon, tilleul, unfired, unripe, untrained, untried, verd(ant), verdet, verdigris, verdure, vigor, viridian, virility, woodland, yearn, yew, young
almond pistachio
amaranth redroot
arrow yarrow
as grass
-back herring cisco
bag lawyer
-bark paloverde
berets elite, special forces
-blue aqua, brittany, ceruleum, clair de lune, cyan, email, mesange, quimper, saxe, sistine, turquoise
bough, name meaning phyllis
broom woodwaxen
chalcedony jasper
chrysolite peridot
cod coalfish
comb. chlor(o), praseo, verdi, vern
copper arsenate erinite
cormorant shag
dark loden
dragon arum, wakerobin
drake mayfly
earth celadonite, terraverde

ebony cocuswood
emerald smaragdine
-eye sea robin
-eyed covetous, envious, jealous
famous gretna
feldspar amazonite
fish bluefish, girella
gables girl anne
goods counterfeit
gray olive, reseda
heraldic vert
heron kialee
inability to see deuteranopia
jack cavalla
light go ahead, permission, signal
mansions heroine rima
master richard ii
monkey guenon
mountain hero allen
mountain state vermont
nile boa
olive loden
olph chloris, greenfinch
oyster sea lettuce
pale aloe(s), celadon, clair de lune
parrot amazon, cagit
peak woodpecker
perch black-bass
permanent terreverte
pike jack, pickerel, sauger
plover lapwing
poppy foxglove
room foyer
sand marl
sap reseda
sauce sorrel
serpentine bowenite
shade apple, bottle, emerald, kelly, kendal, limepeel, loden, mignonette, moss, mousse, nile, paris, parrot, peacock, sap, terreverte, virid
shell turbo
sickness chlorosis
slightly viridescent
spot lawn, oasis, park
stone jade, malachite, nephrite, peridot, pounamu
sunfish redeye
wearer of robinhood
weed woodwax
woodbine peridot
woodpecker eccle, hewhall, hewhole, snapper, speight, sprite, yaffler, yockel, yukkel
yellow absinthe, artichoke, celandine, citrine, gage, glaucous, glauzy, mus-

covite, olive, opalie, rainette, reseda

GREENBACK bill, dollar, frogskin, five, lettuce, money, note, ten

GREENBRIER bread-and-butter, chinaroot, smilax, stretchberry, toadflax

GREENERY herbage, shrubbery, verdure

GREENGAGE plum, reineclaude

GREENHEAD horsefly, mallard, scaup-duck, simpleton

GREENHEADED ignorant, inexperienced, silly

GREENHEART bebeeru, bethabara, bibiri, tree, wood

GREENHORN amateur, buckwheater, cheechaca, cheechaka, colt, dupe, gull, ignoramus, ikona, immigrant, jake, jay, novice, rookie, rooky, softhorn, sucker, tenderfoot, tiro, tyro, yahoo, yap, yekl

GREENHOUSE conservatory, coolhouse, hothouse, nursery, orangery, serre

GREENING apple

GREENLAND *base* etah, thule
bay baffin, disko, melville
cape bismarck, brewster, farewell, grivel, jaal, lowenorn, walker
capital godhaab
city etah, godhavn, godthaab, ivigtut, julianehabb, nord, thule, umanak
discoverer eric the red
district thule
eskimo ita
geological division kome
halibut flatfish
peak forel, khardyu, payer, peterman
reindeer caribou
rock agpaite
settlement thule
spar cryolite
strait davis, denmark
whale bowhead

GREENLEEK parakeet

GREENLING atka, bodieron, boregat, buffalo cod, decagrammus, hexagrammos, loricate, pollack, rock trout

GREENNESS gullibility, immaturity, patina, verdancy, verdure, virescence, viridity

GREENSHANK chevalier, sandpiper, tattler, yellowleg

GREENTAIL fly, grannom, menhaden

GREET accoil, accost, address, appear, buzz, compliment, cry, embrace, encounter, grit, hail, halse, herald, lament, meet, present, receive, salute, smile, sob(bing), wave, weep(ing), welcome

GREETING ahoy, aloha, ave, banzai, benvenuto, bienvenue, bob, bonjour, bow, cheerio, curtsey, ecco, hail, hallo(a), handshake, heigh, hello, hey, hist, hi ya, hoohoo, how(dy), hug, kiss, netop, nod, regards, salaam, salutation, shalom, slainte, toast, welcome

GREGARINE protomerite

GREGARIOUS amadelphous, companionable, convivial, extrovertic, gregah, hospitable, sociable, social

GREGORIAN *chant* cantus firmus, cantus planus, hymn, plainsong, song
doxology euouae

GREGORY *master* capulet

GREMIO *beloved* bianca

GREMLIN dwarf, fairy, hobgoblin, imp, puck, spirit, sprite, troublemaker

GRENADA *capital* st george

GRENADE ammunition, bomb, egg, fireball, missile, pineapple, projectile, shell
bag giberne
plug bouchon

GRENADIER fish, grosbeak, rattail, soldier, whiptail

GRENADINE fabric, fricandeau, fuchsine, red, syrup

GRENDEL *slayer* beowulf
victim hondscio

GREWIA anilao, anilau, baroi, pandanus, pterospermum

GREWSOME See GRUESOME.

GREY See GRAY.

GREYA *husband* oder

GREYHOUND banjara, bringjaree, brinjary, grew, sapling, whippet

GRID barbecue, boocan, broil, buccan, circuit, electrode, grating, grill(age), grille, network

GRIDDLE cook, frying pan,

girdle, grille, pan, spider, torch

-cake arepa, chapatty, corncake, crumpet, flapjack, latke, pancake, slapjack

GRIDIRON arena, brander, brandreth, court, diamond, field, frame, ring, rink, tripod, trivot

-tailed lizard callisaurus

GRIEF abuse, affliction, agony, angry, anguish, care, desolation, disaster, distress, dole, dolo(u)r, dree, failure, grieving, harm, heartache, hurt, lamentation, misery, misfortune, mourning, pain, regret, rue, ruth, sadness, sorrow, suffering, teen, tray, trial, tribulation, trouble, woe
stem kelly
-stricken aggrieved, grieved, sad
symbol ashes, crepe, yew

GRIEG *suite* peer gynt

GRIEVANCE affliction, anger, bane, beef, burden, complaint, cross, displeasure, evil, gripe, hardship, harm, injury, injustice, jeremiad, oppression, roundrobin, tort, trial, tribulation, wrong

GRIEVE afflict, agonize, anger, anguish, bailiff, bear, bemean, bewail, care, chagrin, complain, corsie, cry, cut up, deplore, desolate, discomfort, distress, dole, dump, endure, enrage, erme, ern, harm, hurt, injure, keen, lament, manager, mourn, offend, official, overseer, pain, prostrate, provoke, sign, sorrow, steward, suffer, trouble, try, wail, weep, wound, yearn

GRIEVED afflicted, grame, grief-stricken, pained, sore, sorry, vexed, woeful

GRIEVOUS atrocious, attrite, bad, bitter, burdensome, calamitous, deplorable, distressing, dreadful, dreary, flagitous, flagrant, heavy, heinous, lamentable, onerous, oppressive, painful, sad, severe, shameful, sorrowful, terrible, tragic(al), woeful

GRIFFE mixture, mulatto, spur

GRIFFIN eagle, epimacus,

gripe, gryphon, lion, monster, tyro, vulture
bearded lammergeir
-like epimachus
GRIFTER See THIEF.
helper shill
GRIG annoy, cricket, dwarf, eel, farthing, fish, fowl, grasshopper, heather, irritate, locust, money, tantalize
GRIGRI See FETISH.
GRIKE chink, crevice, ravine
GRILL afflict, bar, barbecue, broil, cafe, catechize, cook, cross examine, distress, grate, grating, grid(iron), harsh, heat, interview, irritate, offend, question, quiz, rack, roast, scorch, sweat, tavern, third-degree, torture, try, vex
opening guichet
GRILSE botcher, finnac, fish, forktail, grawls, salmon, trout
GRIM adamant, angry, bleak, cruel, dire, dour, fell, fierce, forbidding, furious, gash, ghastly, grisly, harsh, horrible, horrid, implacable, lurid, macabre, merciless, morose, obdurate, pitiless, punk, raging, relentless, repellent, ruthless, savage, serious, set, solemn, somber, sour, stern, strict, sullen, terrible, torvous
reality being, existence, facts, life
GRIMACE affectation, distort(ion), emote, fleer, gimble, grin, irpe, make a face, moe, mop, moue, mow(e), mump, murgeon, overact, pretense, scowl, sham, sheyle, simagre, smirk, sneer, snoot, yirn
GRIMALKIN cat, hag, moll, pussy, tom, witch, woman
GRIME colly, dirt, dust, filth, smut(ch), soil, soot, sully
GRIMHILD *husband* giuki
offspring gudrun, gunnar
GRIMMELSHAUSEN *work* simplicissimus
GRIMY augean, collied, colly, dingy, dirty, filthy, foul(ed), grubby, messy, sullied, swarthy, unclean
GRIN beam, fleer, gape, girn, grizzle, laugh, mump, noose, simper, smile, smirk, snare, trap

GRIND abrade, bookworm, bore, bray, bump, champ, chew, comminute, cram, crush, dig, discipline, domineer, drudge(r), drudgery, emery, exertion, file, grate, gristle, grit, grub, harass, joke, labor, levigate, masticate, mill, mull, oppress, pains, persist, plodder, powder, pulverize, pumice, rasp, routine, rub, rut, sand(paper), satirize, scrape, sharpen, steeplechase, study, swink, swot(ter), toil, travail, trouble, whet, work, vex
small bray
teeth gnash, gristbite
whale blackfish
GRINDER bird, bruiser, chopper, crooper, disciplinarian, emery, flycatcher, goatsucker, martinet, mill, molar, pulverizer, sandpaper, tooth, tutor, wheel
GRINDING abrasion, abrasive, attrition, burdensome, excruciating, grating, heavy, imperious, molar
material abrasive, emery
pert. molinary
teeth bruxism
GRINDLE amia, bowfin, ditch, drain, mudfish
GRINDSTONE grit, hone, mano, metate, muller, paver
GRINGLES creeps
GRINGO alien, american, foreigner
GRIP absorb, bag, brace, butt, case, catch, clamp, clasp, clutch, comprehension, control, domination, dominion, etui, flu, gladstone, grab, grapnel, grapple, grasp, gutter, handle, hold, hook, influenza, ken, lug(gage), mastery, obsess, portmanteau, satchel, sceneshifter, seize, seizure, signal, snatch, spasm, strength, tongs, trench, valise, vise
GRIPE affliction, aggravate, annoy, beef, bitch, clasp, complain(t), distress, ditch, frib, graip, grasp, griffin, grizzle, harass, holler, kvetch(er), natter, oppression, pain, pinch, seize, upset, vulture

GRIPER complainer, malcontent
GRIPES tormina
GRIPPE flu, influenza
GRIPPED enthralled, fascinated, held, rapt, spellbound, undistracted
GRIPPER calk, claw, cleat, dog, grabber, handle, holder, keeper, nipper, pliers, tongs, tooth, vise, wrench
GRIPSACK bag, GRIP, suitcase
GRISEL(DE) *husband* gualtiere, wautier
GRISELINA broadleaf, puka, terminalia, tree
GRISETTE trollop, wanton
GRISLY deathly, eerie, ghastly, grim, gruesome, hideous, horrible, horrid, lurid, macabre, terribly, weird
GRISON galictis, huron
dialect romans(c)h
GRIST grain, grind(ing), lot, pabulum, quantity
GRISTLE cartilage
GRIT backbone, bran, bravery, courage, decision, dust, firmness, fortitude, gall, grain, grate, gravel, grind, guts, mettle, nerve, pluck, powder, rubstone, sand(stone), soil, spirit, stamina, texture
GRITH defense, gyrth, mercy, mund, peace, refuge, security
GRITS hominy, kasha
GRITTY coarse, granular, gutsy, persistent, plucky, resolute, rocky, sabulous, sandy
GRIZZLE brick, complain, fret, gray(haired), grin, griseous, laugh, roan, snarl, whimper, wig
GRIZZLY bear, ephraim, gray, hoary, screen, streaked
bear cactus prickly pear
bear state california
GROAN bemoan, bewail, complain, cry, deplore, grank, grunt, jangle, krechtz, lament, moan, rome, sign, sob, sough, stech, suffer, wail, weep, whine
GROAT bit, coin, fourpence, whit
1/4th gill

GROCER bounder, dealer, epicier, spicer

GROCERIES food, merchandise, produce, staples, victuals

GROCERY bakery, bake shop, bodega, butcher shop, delicatessen, drogheria, market, pulperia, store, supermarket

GROG booze, chamotte, drink, liquor, rum(bo)
blossom bottle-nose
server bung
shop See SALOON.

GROGGY dazed, hazy, muzzy, reeling, shaky, staggering, swaying, tipsy, tottering, unsteady, wavering, weak, whirling

GROIN clitch, growl, grumble, grumbling, grunt, grunzie, inguen, jetty, lisk, pier, snout

GROMMET becket, circlet, cringle, eyelet, garland, loop, ring, washer

GROMWELL graymill, redroot, stoneseed

GROOM barber, bed(down), benedict, boy, brush, clean, coistrel, curry(comb), dress, equerry, feed, fettle, hostler, husband, mafoo, mafu, manicure, manservant, marshal, mehtar, newlywed, ostler, page, palfrenier, plume, preen, prepare, prim(e), ready, rub down, sais, sice, sleek, slick up, spruce, stockman, strap(per), swipe, syce, tend, tidy(up), train, wallop, water
horse curry

GROOMING rebuke, toilet(te)

GROOVE bothrium, canal, cannelure, chamfer, channel, chase, chink, corrugation, crack, cranny, croze, cut, dado, excavate, flute, fluting, furrow, gain, gash, gorge, gouge, gutter, habit, incision, joint, kerf, mortise, opening, path, paw, philtrum, pit, pod, quirk, rabbet, raggle, ridge, rigol, routine, rut, scarf, score, scratch, scrobe, slit, stria, sulcus, throat, trench, vallecula, wrinkle
cut in barrel croze, rifle, rifling

make gouge, score
masonry raggle
minute stria
pilaster stria
set in dado
small chamfer
stone jad

GROOVED canalicular, exarate, fluted, furrowed, lirate, striate, sulcate
ring basil, bezel

GROOVY approved, conventional, in tune, modern, okay, on the beam, with it
make elate, enthuse, please

GROPE beat around, claw, examine, explore, feel, finger, fumble, grabble, grapple, grubble, guddle, handle, nail, poke, probe, pry, scrabble, search, sound, tay, test, touch

GROPIUS *school* bauhaus

GROSBEAK bird, bluepop, cardinal, finch, grenadier, guiraca, hawfinch, indigo bunting, moro, pitylus, pyrrhuloxia

GROSS absolute, absurd, aggregate, all, amass, animal, base, breezy, broad, brutal, bulky, carnal, coarse, complete, crass, crude, culpable, earthy, egregious, entire, fate, flagrant, fleshly, glaring, heavy, improper, income, indecent, large, low, lustful, massive, material, measure, obese, obscene, rank, receipts, repulsive, ribald, risque, rough, rude, sensual, shameful, sluttish, sordid, stupid, sum, tasteless, terrible, thick, total, twelve dozen, unqualified, voluptuous, vulgar, whole

GROSSO matapan

GROT See GROTTO.

GROTESQUE abnormal, absurd, antic, baroque, bizarre, clownish, comic(al), deformed, distorted, droll, eerie, extreme, fantastic, flamboyant, freak(ish), ill-made, ludicrous, malformed, misshapen, monstrous, odd, ridiculous, simesque, strange, uncanny, uncouth, unique, weird, wild

GROTTO catacomb, cave(ron), crypt, den, hole, recess, souterrain, speos, subterrane, vault

GROUCH beef, complain, crab, crank, fret, grouse, grudge, grumble, kvetch, malcontent, sourpuss, sulk, whine(r)

GROUCHY angry, bad-tempered, cantankerous, crabby, cranky, cross, growling, grumbling, grumpy, irritable, querulous, snappish, sour, sulky, surly

GROUND area, arena, argument, attitude, base, basis, bed, bottom, cause, clay, clod, cover, dirt, dust, earth, establish, estate, evidence, extent, fell, field, fix, floor, fond, found(ation), greensward, horizontal, initiate, instruct, land, loam, matter, outlook, powdered, premise, prepare, prime, proof, property, pulverized, realm, reason, region, rely, root, soil, station, support, sward, teach, terra firma, terre, territory, testimony, train, turf, tutor
almond chufa
ash angelica, goutweed
bait berley, trap
beam sleeper
beetle amara, calosoma, carabid, carabini
-bird cinclosoma, vespersparrow
boggy marsh, snape, sog
broken hag
burnut caltrop
cedar beach-heather
centaury columbo, polygala
cherry alkekengi, capulin, husk tomato, physalis
chestnut truffle
coat primer, priming
cover dichondra, grass, ivy, pachysandra
cuckoo coucal
depression charco, dalk, delk, ditch, hole, pit, soakaway, swag, swale, trench
dumping tip, toom
elder danewort, dog's-mercury, goutweed
elevated hill(ock), hummock, hurst, hyrst, mesa, mound, plateau, rideau, ridge, terrace
elevation altitude
fallow brise
finch chewink, towhee
firm-holding landfang

fishing haaf
flax gold-of-pleasure
flea springtail
floor pianterreno
flower bitter-milkwort
frozen tjaele
grassy clowre, lawn, links
growing above epigeous
hemlock skinwood, taxus, tree, yew
hog aardvark, digger, marmot, woodchuck
hogday candlemas
holly pipsissewa, wintergreen
honeysuckle baby's-slipper, bird's-foottrefoil, bloomfell, locus
-inhabiting terricole, terricolous
ivy alehoof, bugle, catfoot, crowtread, foalfoot, gagroot, gill-run, hewe, hove, jill, milfoil, periwinkle, tunhoof, twinflower, yarrow
juniper savin
kind acre, arada, bog, calade, cripple, curragh, farm, glebe, lot, maidan, marsh, meadow, moor, park, pasture, patch, plat, range, reseau, swale, tilth
lark pipit
laurel trailing arbutus
lemon may apple
lily trillium
low inch, swale, talao
maple alumroot
mass cement, matrix, paste
middle limbo
nut chufa, gobbe, goober, peanut, phoebe, pignut
original urgrund
parrot kakapo
pasture hirsel
pert. solary
piece acre, lot, plat, plot, solum, tract
pig cane rat
pike sauger
pine ajuga, club moss, foxtail, germander, lycopodium, orange-grass, staghorn
plum buffalo-apple, buffalo-bean, milk vetch
puppy changa, hellbender
raspberry goldenseal
rising See *elevated*, above.
robin chewink, towhee
rubble-covered titi
saligot caltrop
shark carcharhinus, carcharias
sloping cleve, hill, mound

sloth gravigrada, mylodon
spongy bog
squirrel chipmunk, copperhead, gopher, grinny, hackee, sciurid, sciurine, s(o)uslik, xerus
starling meadow lark
swampy cripple, puxy
sweet arbutus
thistle cardoon
thrush pitta
untilled jungle
vine twinflower
water vadose
wet bog, marsh, swamp
wren willow warbler
yew crowberry
GROUNDED ashore, based, beached, certain, fixed, stranded, stuck, suspended
GROUNDLESS baseless, false, flimsy, gratuitous, idle, unfounded, unsupported, untrue, unwarranted
GROUNDMAN grunt, mucker
GROUNDS arena, base, campus, casus belli, cause, conditions, dregs, evidence, field, foundation, greensward, grout, issue(s), lees, motive, premises, proof, property, reason, remainder, residue, sediment, settlings, slag, sward(s), warrant(y)
GROUNDSEL baccharis, bindweed, birdseed, butterweed, dogbush, ragwort, sencion, senecio, simson
climbing ivy
GROUNDWORK base, basis, bottom, fond, foundation, fund(us), fundamentals, homework, preliminaries
GROUP 3 fry, lot, mob, mop, nye, set 4 army, axis, band, bank, bevy, bloe, body, bund, camp, cell, clan, club, crew, crop, deck, file, gang, gate, herd, hive, host, kind, knot, leap, link, mass, meet, pack, pool, push, rank, ring, rope, sect, sort, stew, team, trip 5 array, batch, bench, block, board, breed, brood, bunch, cabal, cadre, chain, charm, class, cloud, clump, corps, covey, crowd, drift, drove, fleet, flock, force, genus, grove, horde, junta, junto, order, panel, party, plump, posse, press, pride, queue,

sabha, shoal, shove, skulk, squad, stack, staff, suite, swarm, train, tribe, troop, trove, union, watch 6 armada, assort, boodle, branch, bundle, bureau, circle, clamor, claque, clergy, clique, clutch, cohort, colony, cordon, detail, family, flight, gaggle, grange, kennel, mindle, league, legion, mulada, muster, number, outfit, passle, people, phlanx, phylum, remuda, school, soviet, string, troupe 7 arrange, battery, bracket, brigade, cabinet, chamber, cluster, combine, company, consort, cortege, entente, flutter, meeting, network, platoon, quotity, society 8 alliance, assemble, audience, caboodle, category, classify, congress, division, flotilla, organize, quantity, sorority, squadron 9 battalion, camarilla, coalition, community, multitude 10 assemblage, chattering, collection, congregate, consortium, detachment, exultation, federation, fraternity 11 aggregation, association, brotherhood 12 organization 13 confederation
assistance aini
atomic ligand
comb. ery, ome
confused snarl
consanguineous clan, family, tribe
core cadre
ecological guild
elite intelligentsia
ethnic achang, balahi, battak, chingpaw
exclusive clique, elect
family gwely
harmonious dovecote
intimate coterie, set
kinship susu
pagan batak, batangan
pert. generic
philosophical academy, cenacle
political bloc, commons, junta, majority, party
related family, phylon
segregated ghetto
social clan, family, kith, sept, tribe
GROUPED agminate
GROUPER aguaji, bacalao, bonaci, cabrilla, cherna,

fish, gag, gar(l)opa, garrupa, gourami, groper, guasa, hamel, hamlet, hind, jewfish, lapulapu, mero, redbelly, redfish, redhind, rockfish, rockhind, scamp, scirenga, serranid, snapper, tripletail, warsaw, yellowfish

GROUPING array, battery, bracket, composition, division, kind(red), organization, sodality, syntagma

GROUSE attagen, beef, bird, bitch, bonasa, canace, capercaillie, capercailzie, clack-cock, cock-of-the-wood, complain(t), ganga, gazelle, gorcock, gorhen, GRIPE, grouch, grumble, heathbird, lyrurus, malcontent, moorbird, moorfowl, muirfowl, mutter, partridge, pintail, ptarmigan, spiketail, sprigtail, tetrao
blue dendragapus
courtship lak
female gorhen, greyhen
group covey
hazel gelinotte
-locust grasshopper, tetrix
male gorcock
pinnated prairie chicken
red lagopus, ptarmigan
ruffed bonasa, partridge
sand attagen
young moorpoot, moorpout, poult, squealer

GROUT beer, cement, dregs, grain, groot, grounds, larry, lees, meal, mortar, plaster, porridge, root, slush, sulk

GROUTY cross, petulant, sulky, sullen

GROVE academy, altis, arbor(et), bluff, boscage, boskage, coppet, coppice, copse, greave, hewt, hurst, hyrst, nemus, olivet, orchard, pinetum, seringal, stand, thicket, tope, underwood, valley, wodeleie, wong, wood
-inhabiting nemoral
pert. nemoral
sacred altis, baduhenna, sarna
small shaw

GROVEL cower, crawl, creep, cringe, crouch, dissipate, fawn, flounder, roll, scrabble, toady, truckle, tumble, wallow, welter

GROVELER lickspit, sycophant, toady

GROVELING abject, obsequious, prone, prostrate

GROW accrue, accumulate, advance, appreciate, augment, batten, boom, bourgeon, branch, breed, bud, burgeon, come, develop, enhance, enlarge, expand, extend, farm, fill out, flourish, germinate, heighten, improve, increase, lead, luxuriate, mature, nourish, plant, produce, pullulate, raise, root, seed, shoot up, sow, spread, sprout, swell, take root, tend, thee, thrive, thro, throdden, tower, upspear, upsprout, vegetate, wax, widen
better improve
dark blacken, cloud, darkle, dim, dusk, fade, gloam, gloom, pale
down decline, decrease, subside
faint dim, fade, wane
fat batten, feed, plim, plump, thrive
light break, brighten, clear, dawn
old age, mature, ripen, senesce
strong convalesce, fortify, storken
together accrete, adhere, ankylose, coalesce, join, knit
up arise, increase, maturate, mature, mellow, ripen
weak faint, sicken

GROWER agriculturist, farmer, horticulturist, planter, producer, rancher

GROWING accrescent, crescent, crescive, increscent, increasing
fast booming, flourishing
hoary canescent, crescive
in clusters racemose
in pairs binate
pains cramp, neuralgia
out enate, enatic
thickly housy
together accrete
vigorously housy, lusty
wild agrestal

GROWL bark, complain(t), flare up, garre, girn, ghar(l), gnar(l), groin, grumble, gurr, howl, jangle, mutter, narr, ogganition, rase, roin, rome, rumble,

snap, snarl, sough, threaten, thunder, yarr, yirr

GROWLER bass, bergy-bit, cab, can, clarence, dog, floe, grouch, iceberg, malcontent, pitcher

GROWN blown, expanded, mature(d), nubile, ripe, seeded, sprouted, thriven
old aged, antiquated, withered
together adnate
-up adult, full-fledged, mature(d), mellow, ripe

GROWTH accretion, beard, bracken, brush, budding, build-up, burgeoning, bush, callus, coat, coppice, development, enlargement, evolution, excrescence, film, gemmation, germination, hair, increase, luxuriation, maturation, pullulation, rise, shoot, sprouting, spur, stature, stubble, surge, swell(ing), vegetation
abnormal callosity, callus, cancer, carcinoma, clavus, corn, cyst, exostosis, felon, fungosity, fungus, intumescence, mole, neoplasm, nevus, paraplasm, proudflesh, sarcoma, tuber(cle), tumefaction, tumescence, tumor, verruca, wart, wen
abundant flush
benign acanthosis
biological allometry
bony exostosis
by added cells accrementition, auxesis
by cell division merisis
comb. aux(o), auxano
dense brush, forest
downy lanugo
early stage, pert. brephic
fatty lipoma
force bathism
fresh sproutage
from within endogeny
fund go-go
in clusters racemose
morbid See *abnormal*, above.
new braird, neoplasm
on another parasite
on surface epigenous
process nascency
promoting nutrient, nutriment
retarding paratonic
rough stubble
second aftermath, ratoon, rowan

sparse scraggle
surface aerugo
transparent druse
vertical, pert. orthotropic
woody burl

GRUB assart, bob, caterpillar, chow, chuck, clear, comestibles, delve, dig, drudge, dwarf, eat(s), essart, excavate, exhume, extract, feed, fodder, food, forage, grind, grugru, hack, larva, maggot, mathe, moil, mudworm, peck, pigroot, plod(der), prog, provender, provisions, root(le), scoff, scran, slave, sneak, spade, spud, stump, toiler, viands, victuals, worm
axe mattock

GRUBBER cultivator, ladyfish

GRUBBLE feel, grope, try

GRUBROOT blazing-star, starwort

GRUBSTAKE finance, provision(s), supply

GRUBBY blowzy, dirty, dwarfish, frowzy, grimy, messy, sculpin, sloppy, slovenly, small, toadfish, untidy

GRUDGE anger, animus, antipathy, attack, bad blood, balk, chatter, complaint, covet, deny, despite, distress, dole, envy, grievance, grouch, grutch, hate, hatred, ill-will, injury, injustice, malice, misgiving, murmur, peeve, pinch, pique, rancor, reluctance, score, spite, spleen, stint, trouble, vex

GRUDGING compelled, envious, forced, involuntary, jealous(y), mean, reluctant, unwilling

GRUE ice, particle, shiver, shudder, snow

GRUEL atole, bleery, burgoo, caudle, congee, crowdy, diet, disable, fatigue, loblolly, mush, porridge, sofkee, wangrace, weaken
-like drink caudel
thick loblolly
thin bleery

GRUELING chastening, demanding, difficult, excruciating, painful, punishing, racking, torturous, troublesome, trying

GRUESOME appalling, baleful, deathly, fearful, frightful, ghastly, gloomy, grim, grisly, hideous, horrible, horrid, lurid, macabre, monstrous, morbid, sinister, sordid, ugly

GRUFF angry, austere, bearish, bluff, blunt, boorish, brusque, churlish, clumpst, clumse, clumsy, coarse, crabbed, cracked, croaky, crusty, curt, discourteous, dour, gloomy, grouchy, grumpy, gutteral, harsh, hoarse, husky, morose, offhand, quarrel, rough, roupy, rude, short, snore, sour, stern, sullen, surly, throaty, truculent

GRUFFS residue, tailings

GRUM glum, guttural, harsh, low, morose, sour, surly

GRUMBLE beef, begrudge, bellyache, bitch, boom, brock, complain(t), croak, fret, gripe, grizzle, groin, growl, gruntle, hone, jangle, maunder, mumble, murgeon, murmur, mutter, peenge, pule, quaddle, repine, roin, rumble, snarl, snivel, squeal, stew, tarrow, whine

GRUMBLER grouch, malcontent, quaddle

GRUMIO *master* petruchio

GRUMOUS clotted, grainy, rooty, thick, viscid

GRUMP fret, ill-humor, mope, sulk

GRUMPY bad-tempered, cross, disgruntled, dissatisfied, glumpish, moody, pettish, surly

GRUNT burrito, burro, complain, croaker, fish, groan, groin, haemulon, humph, koorhaan, kvetch(er), margate, pigfish, pinfish, pomadasys, pompon, porkfish, redmouth, rhoniscus, roncador, ronc(h)o, salema, sargo, tomtate, ugh, umph
black haemulon, lobotes, ronco, tripletail
silver sargo

G STRING breechclout, dhoti, diaper, loincloth

GUACHARO fatbird, oilbird

GUACHONCHO fish, pelon

GUADALQUIVER *city on* cordoba, cordova

GUADELOUPE *archipelago* iles des saintes, los santos,

marie-galante, st barth (elemy), st barts, st martin, terre de haut
capital basse-terre

GUAM *breadfruit tree* nangca, nangka
capital agana
culture chamorro
idol anito
native chamorro
plant acapulco
port agana, apra
tree ipil, nangka

GUAN bird, chacalaca, fowl, jacu, ortalis, penelope, pheasant, pipile

GUANA arawakan, chane, iguana, indian, lizard, majagua, tree
-like reptile tuatara

GUANABANA soursop

GUANACO alpaca, llama

GUANO balsa, dung, fertilizer, goanna, manure, ornithocopros, osite, tree, tuatara
constituent hannayite

GUARANI *indian* caingua

GUARANTEE, GUARANTY assurance, assure, aval, back, bail, bond, cautio(n), certify, depone, depose, earnest, endorse, engage, ensure, gage, hostage, indorse, insurance, insure, pawn, pledge, promise, ratify, scholium, seal, secure, security, sponsor, stand behind, surety, token, undersign, undertake, underwrite, vouchsafe, warrant(y)
written aval, cautio

GUARANTEED assured, certified, foolproof, warranted

GUARANTOR angel, backer, patron, sponsor, surety

GUARANTY See GUARANTEE.

GUARAPUCU bush, peto, shrub, wahoo

GUARD accompany, askari, attend, baffle, bantay, bless, bostangi, bostanji, bracer, brakeman, bridle, bulwark, bumper, care, champion, chaperon, conduct, conserve, convoy(er), cover, custodian, defend, defense, drabant, dragon, escort, fender, gaoler, ghafir, hedge, herd, hood, insure, jailor, kavass, keeper, mind, nurse, pad, patrol, picket, police(man), porter, preserve, protect(ion)(or), rede, restrain, safekeep, screen, screw, sentinel, sentry, shelter, shield, shroud, soulack, tend, tile(r), trainman, turnkey, warden, watch, watchdog, watchman, wite, yeme

axle housing

coach shooter

consular kavass

foil button

group cordon

imperial bostangi, bostanji

keyhole lappet

mounted shomer

native askar(i)

neck camail

of a place genius loci

off one's asleep, blind, dead to, deaf to, napping

on alert, aware, observant, ready, vigilant, wary, watchful

room black hole

spear amgarn

sword bow, tsuba

GUARDED attentive, careful, cautious, circumspect, defended, discrete, excubant, immune, protected, vigilant, wary, watchful

GUARDHOUSE brig, bullpen, clink, gaol, hoosegow, JAIL, lockup, prison

GUARDIAN angel, argus, bartholo, bellarus, caretaker, castellan, cerberus, committee, curator, custodian, defender, eckehart, fravashi, gamekeeper, gardant, governor, GUARD, guide, helper, janitor, keeper, patron, protector, ranger, sentry, shepherd, trustee, tutelary, tutor, warden, warder

heavenly angel

legal trustee

of church relics mystagogue

pert. tutelar(y)

spiritual fravashi

subject of ward

world lokapala, maharaja

GUARDIANSHIP custodia, custody, guardiancy, keeping, tuition, tutela(ge), wardenry

GUARDSMAN *headdress* busby

GUAREA caoba, mahogany, muskwood

GUASA mero

GUATEMALA *ant* kelep

bird quetzal

city achiquimula, antigua, chahal, chisec, coban, cuilapa, esquintla, flores, iztapa, jalapa, jutiapa, progrego, quezaltenango, quiche, salama, san jose, solola, tacana, tecpan, yaloch, zacapa

coin centavo, peso, quetzal

dance elson, guarimba

deity gucumatz, hun-ahpu-vuch, hun-apu-mtye, hurakan, tullan

fruit anay, banana

governor alvarado

grass teosinte

gulf honduras

indian caribe, chol, chorti, chube, itza, ixil, jacalteca, jincan, ketchi, kiche, lenca, mam, maya, pipil, pokomam, quiche, ulva, voto, xinca

lake amatitlan, atitlan, dulce, guija, izabal, peten

language quiche

measure caballeria, cajuela, cuarta, fanega, manzana, tercia, vara

novelist arevalo-martinez

peak agua, atitlan, fuego, pacaya, tacana, tajamulco, toliman

port barrios, champerico, livingston, ocos, san jose

president barrios, estrada cabrera, peralta

river azul, belize, bravo, chiapas, chixoy, dulce, lapaz, motagua, negino, pasion, polochic, samala, san pedro, sarstun

ruins tikal

volcano agua, atitlan, fuego

GUAVA araca, guama, guayaba, guayabo, inga, myrtal

GUAYACAN bethabara

GUAYCURUAN *indian* chaco, payagua, toba

GUAYULE See RUBBER.

GUDDLE gump, handfish, noodle

GUDGEON axis, axle, bait, chalder, cheat, deceive, dupe, eye, fish, gobio, gull, journal, killifish, lure, pin, pivot, quab, trunnion, wheel

GUDGET camp follower, prostitute

GUDRUN *brother* gunnar

consort atli, siegfried, sigurd

guide gilly

GUELDER *rose* cranberry tree, dogberry, dogwood, gaiter, opulus, pincushion, snowball, viburnum, whitten

GUELPHS bianchi

enemy ghibellines

GUENON grivet, monkey, moustache, nisnas, talapoin, tallapoi, vervet

GUERDON bonus, bounty, compensation, crown, honor, meed, pay, premium, prize, recompense, requital, reward

GUERNSEY *capital* st peterport

city st martins, st sampsons

GUERRILLA bushwhack(er) cowboy, fellagha, jayhawk, komitaji, maqui, rebel, skinner, sniper

GUESS aread, areed, assumption, barren, belief, believe, calculate, conjecture, deduce, divine, dope, dry, estimate, fancy, gather, hypothesis, imagine, infer, judge, opinion, reason, reckon, solve, speculate, speculation, stab, suppose, surmise, suspect, suspicion, theory, think, twang, view, ween

GUESSWORK conjecture, hypothesis

GUEST boarder, caller, company, diner, freeloader, frequenter, friend, gatecrasher, habitue, inquiline, lodger, moocher, oyrech, patron, stayer, stranger, transient, traveler, visitant, visitor

comb. xen(o)

gift to xenium

house hostel, inn

master hostler

rope boatline

GUFF chaff, chatter, humbug, nonsense, puff, rot, talk, whiff

GUFFAW heehaw, horselaugh, howl, laugh(ter), scream

GUFFY See SOLDIER.

GUGGLE bubble, gurgle, ripple, trickle, windpipe

GUIANA See GUYANA; SURINAM.

GUIDANCE advice, aim, auspices, counsel, direction,

helmage, leading, navigation, steerage, tutelage

GUIDE advise, advisor, airth, baedeker, barker, beacon, bear, book, bring, calendar, carry, catechism, chart, chauffeur, cicerone, clew, clue, conduct(or), conn, control, convey, convoy, counsel(or), courier, coxswain, direct(or), dragoman, drive, engineer, escort, evangel, fugle(man), genie, ghillie, govern, handbook, helmsman, inspire, key, landmark, lodestar, manage, map, marshal, mentor, mercury, motto, navigate, pilot, pir, pointer, polaris, polestar, precede, regulate, rein, rudder, run, scout, shepherd, skikaree, signpost, steer(sman), superintend, teacher, tip, usher wheel, xenagogue
aeronautic beacon, beam, pylon, racon, radar, radio, trodi, windcone, windsock
spiritual bishop, evangel, guru, pir
traffic mushroom

GUIDEBOOK abc, atlas, baedeker, directory, glossary, itinerary, michelin, ordo, roadbook, thomas

GUIDELINE rope, rule, slug

GUIDEPOST parson, pointer, sign(board), waymark, waypost

GUIDERIUS *parent* cymbeline

GUIDEWAY channel, sley, slide, slot, track

GUIDING directional, dirigent, homing, leading, polar
comb. agogue
rule motto
star lodestar, polestar

GUIDO *note* alamire, alt, are, befa, bemi, cefaut, delasol(re), desolre, doh, ela(mi), esolfa(ut), gammaut, gamut, gesolreut, mese, meson, nete, ray, soh, sol, trite

GUIDON banner, flag, marker, streamer

GUILD basoche, club, cooperative, craft, gremio, group, hansa, hanse, hoey, hong, hui, schola, tong, union
clerks basoche, bazoche
dues hanses

ecological epiphyte, liana, parasite, saprophyte
-hall statue gog, magog
junior member bachelor
medieval hansa, hanse, mattachine
member comacine, hansard
merchants hansa, hanse
tree barberry

GUILE artifice, chicane(ry), craft, cunning, deceit, deceive, deception, doubledealing, duplicity, foul play, knavery, strategem, subtlety, train, treachery, trick (ery), wiles

GUILELESS artless, candid, frank, ignorant, ingenuous, innocent, naif, naive, plain, simple, sincere, unnooked
person babe in the wood, dupe, gull

GUILLEMOT arrie, auk, awk, bacalao(bird), bird, cepphu, coot, cutty, dovekey, dovekie, frowl, grylle, lary, lavy, loom, lungie, maggie, marrot, murre, puffbird, quet, rockbird, scrabe, scuttock, skiddaw, spratter, tarrock, tinker, toist, turr, tyste, uria, willock
black cutty, dovekey, puffinet, scrabe, tyste

GUILLOTINE behead, closure, execute, papercutter
hole lunet(te)
wagon tumbrel

GUILT blame, compunction, crime, criminality, culpability, fault, hamantia, iniquity, liability, nocence, offense, peccancy, penitance, piacle, remorse, repentance, responsibility, sake, shame, sheepishness, sin, wickedness
offering atonement, sacrifice
prove attaint, condemn, convict, indict

GUILTLESS blameless, clean, free, innocent, sakeless, unsaked

GUILTSICK ashamed, contrite, remorseful, repentant

GUILTY answerable, at fault, blameful, blameworthy, cognizant, conscious, criminal, culpable, delinquent, faulty, indicted, liable, nocent, peccant, redhanded, reprehensible, suspect(ed), to blame, wrong
cup ranunculus

GUINEA bean, geordie, george, meg, queed, quid, shiner
bight benin
cape verga
capital conakry
city benty, beyla, cofosso, boke, conakry, coyah, dabola, dalaba, douako, fabala, faranah, fria, kade, kankan, kerouane, kindia, konfara, koule, koumbia, labe, mamou, ouassou, siguiri
coin franc, sily
corn durra, millet
fowl comeback, galeeny, galliney, guttera, keel, keet, meback, numida, pearl (bird), pintado
fowl, sound of potrack
fowl, young keat, keel
grass gamelot, panic(le), panicum, sacaton, zacaton
gulf, river into niger
hen turkey
hen flower fritellaria
hen weed petiveria
island tombo, tristao
measure jacktan
native fulani, guerzi, kissi, kouranke, landuman, malinke, susu, toma
pea jequirity
peak tamgue
pepper capsicum, pimento
pig agouti, capybara, cavia, cavy, midshipman
plant globeflower
port bata, conakry, konakri
president toure
range loma, nimba
river bafing, faleme, konkoure, niger, senegal, tinkisso
rush adrue, cyperus, sedge
sorrel roselle
surf kalema
tamarind baobab
tree akee, dalli
weight aguirage, akey, benda, piso, quinto, seron, uzan
worm dracunculus
yam kaawi

GUINIVERE *burial site* glastonbury, meigle
father leodograunce
husband king arthur
lover lancelot, modred, mordred
refuge almesbury

GUISE apparel, appearance, aspect, behavior, camouflage, cast, cloak, clothes, clothing, color, complexion, costume, cover, disguise, dress, form, garb, likeness, manner, mask, masquerade, mien, pose, posture, pretense, pretext, role, semblance, shape, similitude, turn, way

GUITAR bandore, banjo (rine), bina, calascione, charango, chitama, cithern, gimbri, instrument, jamon, kitar, kittar, mandolin, pandora, pipa, rota, rote, samisen, sitar, uke, ukelele, vina
city paracho
early lute
-fiddle vielle
fish batoid(es), puraque, ray, thornback
home valencia
key dital
manufacturer monrey
originator don vasco quiroga
pick plectrum
play pluck, strum
ridge fret
small uke
soprano tiple
sound plunk, strum, twang
stop fret
10-string tiple
GUITGUIT pitpit
GULA cavetto, cyma, gullet, molding, neck, ogee, throat
GULCH, GULLY arroyo, barranca, cleft, ditch, donga, fall, gap, glutton, gorge, gully, hollow, notch, ravine, sike, sluit, trench, valley, wadi, waterway
GULES mars, ruby, torteall
GULF abysm, abyss, arm, basin, bay, bight, chaos, chasm, cleft, depths, eddy, gap, gulph, hole, inlet, interval, opening, pit, rift, vorage, whirlpool
famous adalia, aden, aegina, alaska, aqaba, bothnia, cadiz, genoa, guinea, kutch, lions, mannar, mexico, panama, paria, persian, riga, sargasso, suez, tonkin, tunis
pert. vortex, vortical
state alabama, florida, louisiana, mississippi, texas
GULFWEED sargasso
GULL allan, annet, bamboozle, befool, beguile, betray, bird, bosun, burgomaster, cheat(er), chouse, chump,

cob(be), cokes, coot, cox, crock, cull(y), deceive, defraud, delude, dotterel, doublecross, dungbird, dupe, ern(e), fool, fraud, geck, gosling, gray, gudgeon, guzzle, gyp, hoax, hoodwink, hoody, imposter, jaeger, kittiwake, lari(d), larus, maa, mall, mew, mislead, mountebank, noio, pale, pe(e)wit, pervee, pigeon, pirr, rissa, scull, seedbird, sell, schooi, skua, teaser, tern, trick, waggel, xema, xeme, yellow
black-backed cob, coffin-carrier, swartback, waggel
black-headed crocker, blackcap, larus, pickmaw, pint, xema
grass bed-straw, cleavers
ivory ice-partridge
jaeger allan, pirate-bird, skua, teaser
-like jaeger, tern
laughing pe(e)wit
pert. larine, laroid
sea See SEA *gull.*
GULLET bronchus, channel, craw, epiglottis, esophagus, gap, gorge, gule, gully, gurgulio, hals(e), lane, larynx, maw, pharynx, swallow, throat, trachea, weasand, wizen
comb. esophag, trache(o)
-wash liquor
GULLIBILITY boobery, easiness, greenness, naivete, naivety, simpleness, simplicity, softness
GULLIBLE believing, credulous, deceivable, deludable, easy, exploitable, foolable, goofy, green, naif, naive, simple, soft, stupid, trustful, trusting, unsophisticated, unsuspicious
person dupe, gudgeon, gull, pigeon, s(c)hlemie(h)l, shlemihl
GULLIVER *author* swift
destination balnibarbi, brobdingnag, glubdubdrib, houyhnhnm, japan, lagado, laputa, lilliput(ia), luggnagg
filthy race yahoos
40-foot girl glumdalclitch
france blefuscu
horses houyhnhnms
imaginary creature splacknuck
island blefuscu, glubdubdrib, laputa, luggnagg

name grildrig, lemuel
nurse glumdalclitch
religious group big endians
GULLY arroyo, barranca, couloir, donga, draught, draw, goyle, GULCH, GULLET, gut(ter), nullah, raik, rake, sheuch, sike
GULP believe, bolt, breathe, breathing, consume, deglutition, devour, drink, eat, gasp, glutch, gobble, imbibe, ingurgitate, ingest(ion), sigh, slorp, sope, swallow, swattle
down believe, bolt, englut
GUM acacia, acacin(e), adhere, adhesive, amapa, amra, asa, balata, bally, bassora, benzoin, carabeen, carob, cattimandoo, cement, cheat, chew, chicle, clog, conima, deceive, dextrine, elastic, eucalyptus, exudate, ghatti, gingiva, glue, gualacum, humbug, impede, karaya, kino, latex, loban, matti, mucilage, myrrh, overshoe, paste, patch, plaster, resin, rubber, smear, stick, talk, t(o)uart, tragacanth, trick, tuno, tunu, ula, wattle, wax, xylan
acacia gedda
animal galago
arabic acacia, acacin(e)
arabic source acacia, egyptian-thorn
arabic tree kikar
aromatic bumbo, frankincense, galbanum, myrrh
artificial dextrine
astringent kino
benjamin benzoin
black hornpipe, nyassa, peppridge, stinkweed, tupelo
bright scouring-rush
bush yerba santa
chewing, ingredient chicle, gutta, wax
cistus rockrose
comb. ule
derivative bassorin, traganth(in), traganthin
disease blueline, scurvy
dragon tragacanth
elastic buckthorn
extract acacia
game fraud
inflammation ulitis
ingredient gutta
juniper sandarac
-like thick, viscid, viscous

-like compound adonin
mahogany jarrah
medicinal arabic, kino
pain ulalgia
pert. gingival, uletic
plant grindelia, ule
rash strophulus
red jamah
resin albetad, antiar, asaf(o)etida, bdellium, bisabol, cava, commiphora, elemi, frankincense, galbanum, gugal, hing, labdanum, loban, myrrh, sagapenum, salban
resin, narcotic hashish
source bahera, caoutchouc
succory hogbite
sugar arabinose
tree brea, eucalypt(us), kar(r)i, nyssa, tooart, touart, tupelo
tumor epulis, uloncus
ungraded sorts
up botch, disable, mess, queer, spoil
white camphor
wood xylan
-yielding guttiferous
GUMBO adobe, clayey, grass, lalo, loamy, marly, melange, mud, ocra, okra, patois, soil, soup
grass bluestem
lily blazing star
-limbo almacigo, archipin, beat, binch, bursera, gomart, jobo, mastic, negrito, resin
GUMBOIL abscess, parulis
GUMDROP jujube
GUMMY adhesive, claggy, gluey, glutinous, lumpy, mastic, mucilaginous, sticky
GUMPTION enterprise, initiative, judgment, megilp, perspicacity, sense, shrewdness, wisdom
GUMSHOE creep, detective, lurk, overshoe, police (man), sneaker, surreptitious
GUMWEED grindella, sunflower
GUN (See also *kind*, below.) accelerate, armor, banger, barker, cannon, carbine, dag, firearm, firelock, fusee, fuzee, gat, heater, hood(lum), hunt, iron, jezail, jingal, marksman, piece, pump, raker, rev, rod, roscoe, shoot(er), shooting iron, soldier, speed

up, spray, syringe, thief, throttle, tube, weapon(ry)
action breeching
anti-aircraft ack-ack, skysweeper
anti-tank bazooka
automatic bofors
barrel chamber
big bertha, cannon, celebrity, gota
bore caliber, calibre
caliber bore
carriage barbette, galloper, lunet, madrier, panel
case holster
catch sear
chamber gomer
cleaner ramrod
cock hammer, nab
cotton pyroxylin
crewman plugman
distance finder replotter
emplacement banquette, pillbox
field long tom, saker
15th-century petronel
fire barrage, broadside, enfilade, fusillade, rafale, rake, salvo, shot, strafe, volley
flint stone
for seek
hand caliver, musket, pistol, revolver
handle stock
hoop frette
-house turret
hunting roer
inventor colt, remington
kind ack-ack, air rifle, amusette, anti-aircraft, archie, armstrong, automatic, baril, bazooka, beretta, bertha, blunderbuss, bofors, bren, brownbess, browning, bulldog, burp, carbine, colt, culverin, derringer, dragon, ducker, dungeon, enfield, escopet(te), espingole, flamethrower, flammenwerfer, flintlock, gatling, gingall, haik, hake, harquebus, jezail, jingal, krupp, lanceflamme, lewis, luger, m-one, machinegun, marlin, matchlock, mauser, maxim, minnie, mortar, mossberg, mug, musket, oerlikon, oscar, pedrero, pistol(et), pompom, quaker, remington, repeater, revolver, rifle, rodman, roer, rohr, sevenshooter, sixshooter, small-bore, snyder,

springfield, sten, tommy, trombone, tupera, vickers, whitworth, winchester, zip
loading device ramrod
lock rowet
lock part catch, doghead, hammer, pawl, sear
lower deck barker
machine See MACHINE gun.
mount barbette, emplacement, platform, turret
mountings furniture
nautical bowchaser
park arsenal
part barrel, bolt, bore, breech, butt, carriage, chamber, chase, choke, cock, comb, cylinder, flintlock, gomer, hammer, lock, magazine, muzzle, nab, rammer, reticule, safety, sear, sight, stock, trigger
platform emplacement, fourquine, sponsion
pointer bead, dotter, sight
repeating mauser
-room quarters
salute salvo
shot detonation, pop
sight bead, hausse, visie
sight setting zero
16th-century currier
small-bore twenty-two
stock blank, tipstock
submachine bren
swiveled amusette
tumbler nut
2-barrelled over and under
GUNBOAT barca, chaloupe, gondola, skip, tinclad
GUNGA DIN *forte* water
GUNGNIR *spear of* odin
GUNK *hole* anchorage
GUNMAN assassin, bravo, criminal, cutthroat, enforcer, gangster, hood (lum), killer, marksman, mobster, murderer, pistoleer, pistolero, pistol pete, sniper, torpedo, triggerman
GUNNAR, GUNTHER *consort* brunhild(a)(e), brynhild
cook rumolt
kingdom burgundy
parent giuki, grimhild, uta
sister chriemhild(a), gudrun, gutrune
slayer kriemhild, hagen
uncle hagen
GUNNEL blenny, butterfish, dollarfish, kelpfish, poronotus, swordick

GUNNER cannoneer, hunter, loon
GUNNERY *science* artillery
GUNNLOD *kin* suttung
GUNNY bag(ging), burlap, sack(ing), tat
GUNPOWDER explosive, green tea, niter, nitro, sulfur, sulphur
cone peeoy
ingredient aigremore, charcoal, niter, saltpeter, sulphur
plot anniversary pope's day, pope's night
plot man guy fawkes
GUNSTONE ogress, pellet
GUNWALE gunnel, portoise
pin thole
GUPPY bellyfish, crool, fish, lebistes, millions, minnow
GUR jaggery, khaur, voltaic
GURGLE babble, bubble, burble, crool, crow, glex, goller, guggle, murmur, purl, ripple, slosh, trickle
GURKHA *sword* kukri
GURNARD batfish, buttterfly-fish, captain, cur, dragonet, ell eck, grunter, hardhead, knorhaan, latchet, lonicate, rochet, sea-robin, soldier, trigla, tubfish
red elleck
GURU guide, maharishi, teacher
pupil shishya
GUSH belch, boil, burst, chatter, come forth, effluence, emerge, emit, emote, erupt, flow, issue, jet, loquacity, pour, rail, rain, run, sentimentalize, slobber, slop, smalm, spew, spirt, spout, spue, spurt, stour, stream, swoosh, vapor, wallow, whoosh
back regorge, regurgitate
GUSHY bathetic, diffuse, effusive, emotional, maudlin, sentimental, sloppy, smarmy
GUSSET bracket, clock, gore, insert, miter, mifre, piecette, quirk
GUST blast, blow, breeze, bub, burst, enjoyment, flaw, flurry, foretaste, fresh, gale, huffle, liking, outburst, pirr, relish, sapor, scud, squall, tang, taste, thode, williwaw, wind(flaw), zephyr
GUSTAVUS I vasa
GUSTO appetite, ardor,

delight, enjoyment, enthusiasm, liking, palate, passion, pleasure, relish, savor, style, taste, zeal, zest
GUSTY blasty, fretful, savory, squally, stormy, tempestuous, windy
GUT abdomen, belly, c(a)ecum, decimate, destroy, dilapidate, disembowel, elision, empty, entrail, eviscerate, gralloch, hollow, intestine, loot, pillage, plunder, ransack, ravage, stomach, strait
fish gib, gill, gip
twisted tharm, therm
GUTE NACHT See GOOD night.
GUTS backbone, contents, courage, entrails, fortitude, grit, innards, insides, mettle, nerve, pluck, resolution, sand, spirit, strength, viscera, vitals, zest
GUTTA campana, drop, golfball, latex, ornament, puan, siak, spot
gum gamboge
kind balata, dujan, gerip, hangkang, jangkar, jelutong, ketapang, percha, pusn, sange(i), semarum, siak, singarip, sundek, sundik, susu, tabanputeh, tre(e)nail, trunnel
mixture soh
percha balata
GUTTER bottom, brook, canal, c(h)annel, cheneau, conduit, cullis, dike, ditch, drain, eaves, flow, grizzle, groove, gully, guzzle, kennel, mire, moat, mud, riggot, river, rone, sink, siver, spout, sulcation, trench, trough, vennel, watercourse
tree cornel
GUTTERMAN swamper
GUTTERSNIPE bounder, cad, gamin, ragpicker, sandpiper, street arab, urchin, vagabond, youth
GUTTLE devour, gourmandize, ravish, stuff
GUTTURAL burr(y), dry, gruff, grum, harsh, hoarse, husky, morose, rasping, thick, throaty, velar
GUY baffle, banter, blighter, bloke, boy, bozo, buffer, cat, chaff, chain, chap, depart, effigy, fellow, flee, fool, gazook, gent, gink,

guide, hombre, joker, jolly, josh, kid, lad, malkin, man, nut, oddity, person, quiz, rag, rally, rib, rope, shore, stay, tease, vang
rope stat, stay, vang
GUYANA *capital* georgetown
coin bit
indian akawai, arawak, taruma
region demerara
GUZZLE bend, bib, carouse, debauch, devour, down, drain, drink, fuddle, gulp, gutter, imbibe, liquor, slosh, sot, spree, swallow, swig, swill, swizzle, throat, tope, tun
GUZZLER bender, boozer, carouser, drunk(ard), sot
GWAWL *beloved* rhiannon
rival pwyll
GWYDION *consort* arianrhod
parent don
son dylan, llew
GWYN, ELEANOR nell
lover charles ii
GWYNN *father* llud
GYLE beer, brewing, vat, wort
GYLIPPUS *father* cleandrides
GYM See GYMNASIUM.
shoe plimsoll, sneaker
GYMER *son* gerd
GYMKHANA contest, race, tournament
GYMNASIUM academy, arena, calistheneum, college, hall, institute, lycee, palaestra, salle d'armes, school, turnverein, xyst
apparatus bars, rope, trapeze, weights
GYMNAST See ATHLETE.
GYMNASTIC(S) acrobatic(s), athletic(s), calisthenics, daily-dozen, exercise, palaestra, physical, work-out
society sokol
stunt handspring, handstand, headspring, headstand, kip(p), tumbling
GYMNODONTES globefish, sunfish
GYMNOGYPS condor, vulture
GYMNOTUS carapid, carapo, carapus, electric eel, fasciatus, giton

GYNERIUM camalote, reed, uva grass

GYP bitch, cad, cheat, deceive, fool, fraud, scout, servant, sharper, steal, swindle(r), trick

-joint schlock-house

-room pantry

GYPSOPHILA baby's-breath, caryophyllus, flower

GYPSUM alabaster, cement, gesso, plaster of paris, satin-spar, selenite, terra-alba, yes(s)o

pink baby's-breath

resembling alabastrine

treat with burtonize

GYPSY aptal, azucena, black, bohemian, bosha(s), broom squire, brown, brunette, caird, cale, calo, chai, cigano, cove, czigany, flamenco, gitano, heidan, hussy, migratory, moonman, nomad, rascal, rani, roamer, rogue, rom(any), rom(n)i, rye, sinte, sisech, tatar, tink(l)er, tzigane, vagrant, walachian, wandering, winch, zigeuner, zincali, zingani, zingaro

big baro

book lil

boy chal, rom, tzigane, zigeuner

camp tan

dance farruca, flamenco, polo, zingaresca

devil bang, beng

fortune bahi

girl chai, chi, gitana

god alako, duvel

great baro

-head winch drum

horse grasni, gri, gry

husband rom

language calo, chib, rom(m)any

man calo, chal, rom, rye

mare grasni

moth perthetria

musical instrument cymbal

non gahjee, gajo, gorgio

onion ramson

paper lil

part diddakoi, diddikai

pert. romanian

pocketbook lil

priest patrico

road drun

rose scabious

sea bajau

song zingaresca

study of gypsology

tent tan

thief chor

tongue chib

trail patrin

tribe aptal, selung

vehicle caravan

village gav

weed speedwell

wife rani, romi

winch crab

woman ch(a)i, rani, romi, romni

word lav

GYPSYWORT lycopus, water horehound

GYRATE circle, circulate, eddy, gyre, mill around, pirouette, revolve, roll, rotate, spin, swirl, turn, twirl, wheel, whirl

GYRE circle, demon, revolution, ring, spirit, vortex, whirl

GYRENE marine

GYRFALCON jerkin

GYROCOMPASS *inventor* sperry

GYRODINE See HELICOPTER.

GYTE child, delirious, mad, pupil

GYVE bind, chain, fetter, shackle

H

H *-shaped* zygal

sound aitch, aspirate

HABAZINIAH *son* jeremiah

HABBLE brawl, confusion, difficulty, uproar

HABEAS CORPUS summons, writ

HABERDASHER clothier, dealer, merchant, ragman

HABERDASHERY gloves, hat, menswear, necktie, sarks, shirt, shop, store, toggery

HABERGEON armor, hauberk, jacket, mail

HABILE able, adroit, apt, clever, dext(e)rous, expert, fit, handy, skillful, suitable

HABILIMENT apparel, attire, biliment, clothing, costume, dress, equipment, faculties, garb, garment, habit, ornament, raiment, uniform, vestment

HABILITATE clothe, dress,

enable, entitle, equip, fit out, qualify

HABIT accustom, array, attire, bent, characteristic, clothe, constitution, consuetude, convention, costume, crotchet, custom, demeanor, dispose, disposition, dress, folkway, form, garb, gate, gown, groove, mannerism, mode, orthodoxy, path, pattern, practice, praxis, routine, rule, rut, second nature, set, state, talent, tenor, thews, tic, tradition, trait, trick, usage, use, way, wont(ing)

bad hank, mistetch, vice

-maker tailor

pert. usitative

riding chaps, jodhpurs, joseph, levis

-shirt chemisette

HABITANT dweller, settler

HABITAT abode, environ-

ment, home, locality, location, range, station

comb. eco, oeco, oiko

natural patria

plant form ecad

HABITATION abode, berth, bield, billet, colony, commorancy, diggings, digs, domicile, dwelling, haunt, home, HOUSE, lodging, occupancy, occupation, pied a terre, purlieu, quarters, region, residence, residing, roost, seat, settlement, tenement

underground burrow, cave, hole, run

HABITED accustomed, arrayed, clothed, dressed

HABITUAL accustomed, addict, chronic, common, confirmed, conventional, customary, deep-seat, established, everyday, familiar, fixed, frequent, general, inveterate, orderly, ordinary, prevailing, prevalent, regular, rooted, routine, set, stock, usual, wonted

HABITUATE acclimatize, accustom, acquaint, addict, discipline, drill, enure, exercise, familiarize, frequent, harden, haunt, inure, practice, school, season, train, use

HABITUATED accustomed, addicted, adjusted, given to, imbued with, inured, permeated, seasoned, used to, wont

HABITUDE attitude, character, condition, disposition, familiarity, HABIT, position, schesis, situation, stand, usage

HABITUE addict, courtier, denizen, devotee, fan, fiend, frequenter, guest, patron, votary

HACATAN *son* joannes
HACHALIAH *son* nehemiah
HACHRATHAEUS *eunuch to* esther
HACIENDA croft, estancia, estate, farm, grange, homestead, house, plantation, ranch
proprietor hacendado
HACK abject, banal, bark, blaze, butch, cab(oose), carbonado, chatter, chip, chop, clip, coach, cough, creeper, cut, devil, drudge, fiacre, frame, grating, grinding, grub, hackle, hackney, haggle, hawk, hew, hireling, hoe, horse, jade, kick, mangle, mark, mattock, mean, mercenary, mutilate, nick, notch, nudge, pick, potboiler, procuress, prostitute, rack, scribbler, slash, sordid, spell, stammer, stroke, stutter, taxi, trial, trim, trite, turn, vehicle, vettura, whoop, writer
gharri shigram
writer devil, grub, penster
HACKBERRY beavertree, beaverwood, bois inconnu, celtis, eggberry, elder, elm, hagberry, oneberry, sweetbay
HACKBUT demihag
HACKEE See CHIPMUNK.
HACKLE bait, bristle(s), chop, comb, cut, feather,

flaxcomb, haggle, hatchel, heckle, plume, rougher, ruff, stickleback
HACKLEBACK sturgeon
HACKMATACK juniper, larch, tamarack
HACKNEY blunt, cab, carriage, coach, coarsen, common, drudge, fiacre, hansom, hasten, hire(d), hireling, horse, jarvey, mean, midge, nag, noddy, race, taxi, vettura, wear out
HACKNEYED archaic, banal, cliche, commonplace, motheaten, obsolete, old, overdone, practiced, saw, shopworn, stale, stereotyped, stock, thin, threadbare, tired, trite, used, vulgar, wasted, worn
HACKTHORN wattle
HAD cheated, conned, fooled, taken in, took
HADAR *kin* ishmael
HADAREZER *captain* shopach
HADASSAH See ESTHER.
founder szold
HADDING *patron* odin
HADDOCK bervie, crail, dickey, finnan haddie, gade, gadid, rizzar, rosefish, scrod, spelding, speldrin
HADES aalu, aaru, a(i)des, aidoneus, aralu, dis, duat, HELL, ialu, orcus, pit, pluto, shades, sheol, tartarus, yaru
assessor aeacus, minos, rhadamanthys
beloved leuce, minthe
brother poseidon, zeus
dweller erebus
entrance aornum, erebus
ferryman charon
gardener ascalaphus
god See UNDERWORLD *god, goddess.*
guard cerebus
herdsman menoetes
inhabitant hellion
judge aeacus
lake avernus
messenger namtaru
parent cronus, ops, rhea, saturn
pert. avernal, chthonian, hellish, infernal, sheolic, stygian
prison tartarus
river acheron, cocythus, lethe, phlegethon, styx
watchdog cerebus

wife kore, persephone, proserpina
HADJI pilgrim, traveler
goal caaba, kaaba, mecca
HADLAI *son* amasa
HADRIAN *favorite* antinous
school athenaeum
HAEMANTHUS ambrosia, asclepias, bloodlily, bloodpink, bloodweed
HAEMON *beloved* antigone
father creon
HAEMOSTATIC adrenaline
HAEMUS *kingdom* thrace
parent boreas, crithyia
turned into mountain
wife rhodope
HAET atom, bit, whiff
HAFGAN *slayer* pwyll
HAFNIUM celtium
source zircon
HAFT accustom, bail, cavil, dudgeon, dwell(ing), familiarize, fix, handle, helve, hilt, hove, put off, settle, stock
HAG beldam(e), bog(y), cailleach, carlin(e), copse, crone, cut, demon, egg on, fatigue, fright, fury, ghost, goad, goblin, gorgon, hack, harpy, harass, harridan, hecate, hellcat, hobgoblin, jezebel, mare, marsh, nickneven, notch, old woman, guagmire, rebes, roudas, rudas, shrew, terrify, urge, vecke, virago, vixen, witch, wood
HAGAR *consort and master* abraham
mistress sarah
son ishmael
HAGBERRY *china* tree
HAGBOAT hogget, hoggie
HAGEN *father* alberich
half-brother gunther
nephew gunnar, gunther
slayer kriemhild
victim siegfried
HAGFISH agnatha, borer, cyclostome, lamphrey, myxine, myxinoid, myzont, placoid, sucker, vecke
HAGGARD anxious, cadaverous, careworn, deathly, drawn, emaciate(d), exhausted, fagged, frantic, gaunt, infirm, jaded, lean, marantic, marasmic, pale, pallid, peaked, pinched, poor, scrawny, shriveled, skinny, spare, starved, starveling, tabetic, tabid,

thin, tired, underfed, undernourished, unruly, untamed, wan, wanton, wasted, weazened, wild, withered, wizen(ed), wizzen, worn

HAGGITH *consort* david

HAGGLE arglebargle, argybargy, badger, bargain, barter, beat down, cavil, chaffer, chop, cut, dicker, dispute, dodge, hack, hail, higgle, huckle, mangle, negotiate, palter, prig, stickle, threep, wrangle

HAGGLER dodger, huckster

HAGGLING arglebargle, argybargy, bargain, chaffer

HAGIOGRAPHA ketubim

HAGRIDE bewitch, harass, scold, torment

HAGTAPER mullein

HAGUE, THE 's-gravenhage

HAGWORM See SNAKE.

HAHA ditch, fence, laugh, trench, wall

HAIDA skittaget

HAIKAL altar, sanctuary

HAIL acclaim, accost, address, ahoy, avast, ave, call, cheer, fortune, frost, goal, graupel, greet(ing), gresil, halloo, health, hello, herald, hoy, ice, salute, shower, signal, sleet, snow, sound, storm, welcome, whole

and farewell ave atque vale

mary ave maria

soft graupel, gresil

storm preventative paragrele

HAILI, CLARA hilo hattie

HAIMISH cozy, informal, unspoiled, warm

HAINAI ioni

HAIR bangs, barba, bit, braid, bristle, bun, bush, capillament, capillus, ciliolum, cilium, coat, crine, crinus, crop, curl, daglock, down, fax, feeler, filament, fleece, forelock, fur, glochis, hackles, kemp, lock, mane, mat, mop, nap, pelo, pelt, pile, pilus, ruff, seta, setula, shag, shock, strand, thatch, tragus, triffle, tuft, vibrissa, villus, whisker, wool

accessory barrette, net, ribbon

animal's fur, pelf, pelt

ball aegagropila, heterolith, phytobezoar

barbed glochis

-bearing comephorous

braid cue, pigtail, plait, queue, tress

brittleness trichoclasis

brown argali

brush shag, toiletry

bundler leech

bushy mop, shag

clasp barrette

cloth aba, cilice

cluster mystax

coarse bristle, cerda, chaeta, kemp, seta, setula, shag

coat fur, hide, melote, pelt

coil bun

coloring auburn, blond(e), brunette, carrot(top), chestnut, red, sandy, titian, towhead

comb. chaet(o), crini, pil(o), tricho

covered with hirsute, pilose

covering net, snood, toment(um)

cue See *braid,* above.

curl buckle, cirrus, guiche, ringlet, tress

cutter barber, beautician

disease alopecia, dandruff, defluvium, furfur, mange, monilethrix, plica, psilosis, scurf, sycosis, trichonosus, trichopathy, trichosis, xerasia

dye henna

excessive growth pilosis

falling psilosis

false See HAIRPIECE.

feeler palpus

fillet snood

frame palisade

fringe bangs, ciliella, frisette, frizette

gray grizzle

growing capilliculture, endysis

having short stiff barbellate, barbulate

having soft mollipilose

head of crine, fleece, mop, suit

in curlers friz(z)

intestinal villus

kinky, pert. encomic

knob toorie

knot bun, chignon

-like capillaceous, capillary, capilliform, ciliate, filamentary, filamentous, filiform, trichoid

lock berger, cowlick, curl, elflock, feak, harigalds, lovelock, ringlet, tag, tait,

tangle, tate, tress, tuft, tuz, wimpler

loose combings

loss See *disease,* above.

mass felting

matted elflock, plica, shag, tomentum

molting ecdysis

mop tousle

neck mane

nose vibrissa

of-the-dog bracer

ornament barrette, bow, comb, coronet, ribbon, tiara

pert. See HAIRY.

plant colletek, pilus, rubes, villus

powder must

-raising breathtaking, eerie, exciting, scary, stunning, terrifying

removal bob, coupage, cut, depilation, depilatory, electrolysis, epilate, shave, tonsure, trim

removing decalvant

rigid seta

roll bun, chignon, crocket, pompadour, puff, roach, rowel, twist

root fibril

rope cabestro, lariat, lasso

salt alum, alunogen, epsomite

sheer off shirl

shirt burden, cilice, penance

short setula, setule

soft down, fluff, fuzz, lanugo, moss, villus

-splitting critical, criticism, distinction, fine, nice, picky, pilpul, schizotrichia, subtle

spray, controversal aerosol

standing pompadour, roach

stiff seta

style See HAIRDO.

tail cutlassfish

tangled elflocks

theatrical crepe wool

thigh culotte

tuft arbuscule, cilia, fetlock, floccus, krobylog, penicel, plume, scopula, verricule

unruly cowlick, mop, tousle

white snow(s)

whiteness canities, poliosis

HAIRBRAINED See HARE-brained.

HAIRBREADTH ace, close, hermele, margin, narrow, near, whisker

HAIRCUT bob, butch, crew, crop, ducktail, flattop, mo-

hawk, pachuco, shag, shingle, tonsure, trim, wedge
pert. tonsorial
HAIRDO afro, bangs, beehive, bob, bouffant, braid, brioche, bubble, bun, chignon, coif(fure), french roll, frisure, glib, goulue, horsetail, marcel, onion, pageboy, payess, peah, peot, perm(anent), pigtail, plait, ponytail, poodle, pouf, psyche knot, set, shingle, tete, upswept, wave, wedge
HAIRDRESSER barber, beautician, coiffeur, coiffeuse, friseur, parruchiere, waver
HAIRDRESSING bandoline, brilliantine, pomade
HAIRLESS atrichie, bald (pated), callow, depilous, glabrate, glabrous, pelon
HAIRLESSNESS acomia, alopecia, baldness, depilation, psilosis
HAIRLINE *point* widow's peak
HAIRNET lint, snood
HAIRPIECE fall, jane, peruke, rat, switch, tete, toupee, transformation, wig
HAIRPIN acis, barrette, bobbypin, bodkin, comose, skewer
HAIRWORM gordi(o)id, gordius, mermis
HAIRY barbate, barbellate, barbigerous, bearded, bristly, capillose, ciliate, cirrose, comate, comoid, comose, comous, crinal, crinite, crinitory, crinose, faxed, fleecy, floccose, flocculent, flocky, furred, furry, hirsute, hirtellous, hispid, jubate, lanate(d), nappy, pilar(y), pileous, piline, pilose, pilous, pubigerous, rough, shagged, shaggy, tressy, trichoid, ulotrichous, unshaven, unshorn, villose, villous, woolly
-back gizzardshad, threadherring
bait lugworm
comb. dasy
laurel wicky
slightly hirsutulous, hirtellous
spicebush jovesfruit
HAITI *aborigine* taino
airport francois duvalier
animal agouta, solenodon

bandit caco
cape foux
capital port-au-prince
channel st marc, sud
city aquin, cayes, furcy, gonaives, gonavel, hinche, jacmel, jeremie, kenscoff, leogane, limbe, port-au-prince, saltrou, tiburon
coin franc, gourde
dance juba, mambo
deity atabei, coatrischie, guabancex, guanatuava, jocahuva, loa, opita, zemis
demon baka, boko
emperor dessalines
group co(u)mbite
idol zemi
indian taino
island gonave, mona, navassa, tortue, tortuga, vache
island group antilles, caymites
isle of dead coaibai
king henri c(h)ristophe
lake saumatre
language creole
liberator toussaint
magic obeah, obi
mart mahogany market
measure aune
oil khuskhus, vetiver
outlaw caco
palace sans souci
peak cahos, lahotte, laselle, noires, nord, troudeau
plain arcahaie, cayes, culdesac, gonaives, jacmel, leogane, nord
police tonton macoutes
port gonaives, jacmel, jeremie, les cayes
priest bocor, houngan
religion voodoo
river artibonite, guayamoul
ruler dessalines, duvalier, henri c(h)ristophe, papa doc
rum tafia
solenodon agouta
soul of dead opita
spirit baka, boko, loa
sweet potato batata
vehicle mammy wagon, taptap
HAKAM cacam, chochem, kahkam, rabbi
HAKE anacanth, codling, fish, forkbeard, frame, gade, gadoid, gun, haddock, harass, hook, idler, kingfish, ling, loiter, merlussius, pester, phycis, pothook,

quodling, silverfish, tramp, trudge, wander, whiting
HAKENKREUZLER swastika
HAKIM doctor, judge, magistrate, physician, ruler
HALBERD axe, bill, glavie, gleave, partisan, pike, polearm, staff, weapon
-shaped gisarme, hastate
HALBERDIER drabant
HALCYON alcyone, auk, auspicious, balmy, bird, bright, calm, carefree, golden, happy, kingfisher, pacific, peaceful, placid, prosperous, quiet, rich, serene, tranquil, wealthy
changed into kingfisher
consort ceyx, poseidon
days good times
parent aeolus, atlas, enarete, pleione
HALE annoy, bouncing, contract, drag, draw, fit, frack, freck, golden, hardy, harass, haul, heal, health(y), hearty, lusty, pull, remedy, robust, rude, rugged, sound, spry, stalwart, stout, strong, sturdy, tow, trail, trig, trim, tug, vex, vigorous, well, yell
nathan spy
HALEVY *opera* la juive
HALF arf, bifidity, bisection, fifty-fifty, hapa, hemisphere, imperfect, incomplete, mediety, moiety, part(ial), partner, piece, portion, recess, rest, section, semester, semisphere, share
and half cream, neutral, solder, solitaire
-ape lemur, tarsier
-baked crazy, doughy, green, premature, sophomoric, superficial
beak balao, ballyhoo, dird, fish, ihi, piper
-blood demisang
-boot blucher, bottekin, bottine, buskin, pac
-breed caboclo, griff(e), harratin, hybrid, ladino, mestee, mestizo, metif, metis(se), mulatto, mule, mustee, octoroon, quadroon, ramona, sambo
-caste topass, topaz
-circumference semicircle
-cocked premature, raw, unprepared
comb. demi, hemi, semi
crazy fifish

crown alderman, cuckolds-knot, george
dark twilight
denier maile, maille
dobra peca
dollar fifty cents, forbes, four bits
eaten semese
farthing cue, minute, mite
fruits slabs
gainer dive, isander
gallon pottle
-*grown* halflin
-*guinea* smelt
-*hearted* cold, cool, indifferent, irresolute, perfunctory
hitch rolling
hose socks
inning bottom
-*man* centaur, eunuch, faun, garuda, minotaur
mask domino, loup
mold valve
-*moon* arc, crescent, cuckold, demilune, lune, lunule, scalare, scimitar, semilunar
more than plurality
note minim
-*pace* dias, landing, platform
pence grocery
penny baubee, brown, coin, dump, gray, grey, hapenny, mag, maille, meg, meke, obol, rap, stuiver, trifle
-*pike* sponto(o)n
-*pint* cup(ful), jack, small
rest sospiro
-*slip* petticoat
sole tap
step chroma
-*tone* dropout, print
tone, pert. chromatic
turn caracol(e), demivolt
way equator, equidistant, equivocal, limited, mid (dle), midship, midst, partial(ly)
-*wit* blockhead, dolt, dunce, dunderhead, fool, gaby, goose, haverel, imbecile, jackass, nimshi, nitwit, simpleton, staumrel, tomfool, underwit
-*witted* cretinous, dotty, dumb, foolish, halucket, imbecilic, moronic, senseless, silly, simple, soft, staumrel, stupid
HALIBUT acedia, but(t), flatfish, flitch, flounder, pleuronectes, turbot
steak flitch
HALICORE dugong

HALIDOM holiness, sanctity, sanctuary
HALIFAX *citizen* haligonian
marquis savile
HALIOTIS abalone, ass's-ear, mollusk, snail
HALIRRHOTHIUS *parent* euryte, neptune, poseidon
slayer ares, mars
HALITUS aura, breath, exhalation, fog, vapor
HALL aisle, aiwan, assembly, atrium, auditorium, aula, balai, building, bursa, camera, cloister, clubhouse, colonnade, corridor, curia, divan, dorm, durbar, entry(way), foyer, gallery, gym(nasium), house, iwan, kursaal, lesche, lobby, loggia, lyceum, manorhouse, meetinghouse, megaron, narthex, odeon, oecus, passage(way), peristyle, raadzaal, room, rotunda, saal, sala, salle, theater, tolsey, valhalla, vestibule, vingolf, xystus
athlete's gym, xystus
justice basilica, court
large aula, rotunda
mission citadel
music gaff, odeon, odeum
reception parlor, salon
student bursa, dorm(itory)
town cabildo, rathaus, socalo, tribunal
HALLELUJAH alleluia, cheer, hosanna, hymn, praise, sorrel, te deum
HALLMARK badge, characteristic, crown, emblem, guarantee, label
HALLOO address, cry, hail, shout
HALLOW anoint, bless, celebrate, dedicate, devote, enshrine, halwe, honor, relic, revere, saint, sanctify, shrine, venerate
HALLOWED blessed, blest, consecrated, holy, inviolable, sacred, sacrosanct
place altar, bethel, cathedral, chapel, church, fane, shrine, synagogue, temple
HALLOWEEN *symbol* jack o'lantern
HALLOWING consecration, dedication
HALLUCINATION aberration, aco(u)asm, acousma, alusia, apparition, chimera, delirium-tremens, delusion,

dream, dwale, error, fancy, fantasy, fantod, illusion, incubus, mirage, nightmare, phantasm, phantasy, phantom, phoneme, vision, wraith, zooscopy
HALLUCINOGEN acetone, benzene, bufotalin, bufotenine, det, dmt, dpt, ether, gasoline, glue, jimsonweed, lsd, mescal(ine), naphtha, nutmeg, peyote, psilocybin, stp, sunflower seed, tolvene, tryptamine
HALLUX digit, talon, toe
HALLWAY entry, foyer, passage
HALO anthelion, antiselene, antisun, aura, aureola, aureole, brough, bur(r), circle, corona, dog, gloria, glory, glow, light, moondog, nimb(us), paraselene, parhelion, ring, sundog
HALOGEN bromine, chlorine, cyanogen, fluorine, iodine
comb. ine
HALOHESH *son* shallum
HALSE col, conjure, defile, embrace, entreat, hug, neck, throat
HALT arrest, arretez, avast, bar, block, brake, break, bring to, cease, check, cripple(d), dawdle, delay, draw up, end, enough, falter, fetch up, hang fire, hesitate, hitch, hold, impasse, lame, leave off, let up, limp, maimed, pause, pull up, respite, rest, shake, stall, stance, stand, station, stay, stick, stop, tenez, toho, whoa, vacillate
HALTER causson, cavesson, hamper, hang, harness, jaquima, noose, restrain, rope, secure, shackle, wanty, widdy, withe
HALTING defective, faltering, hesitant, lame, limping, stiff, wavering
place camp, etape
HALVE bisect, cleave, cut in two, dichotomize, dimidiate, divide, join, share, split, subdivide
HAM actor, amateur, emote, gambone, gammon, hock, manor, overact, pig, pork, thigh, tyro
brother shem
father noah, noe

grandson seba
pert. popliteal
picnic cala, cali
radios cbs
-*shackle* bind, curb, fasten
smoked gammon, serrano
son canaan, cush, mizraim, p(h)ut
sons' country ethiopia
spiced prosciutto
HAMADAN achmetha, ecbatana
HAMADATHUS *son* haman
HAMAL attendant, bearer, porter, servant
HAMAN *enemy* mordecai
father hamadathus, mannedatha
successor mardochaeus
wife zeresh, zosara
HAMATH *deity* ashima
king toi, tou
HAMBURG *part* altona
HAMELIN *ratcatcher* pied piper, rattenfaenger
HAMILCAR *son* hannibal
HAMILTON, ALEXANDER *pseud.* publius
HAMILTON, LADY *lover* horatio lord nelson
HAMITE *ancestor* noah
father abel
people ababdeh, afar, agao, agau, beja, belin, beni amer, berber, bisharin, bogo, boran(a), chamite, copt, cushitic, danakil, dankali, ethiopian, fulah, gaetulian, galla, guanch, hadendoa, hima, kabyle, masai, mauretanian, numidian, saho, shilha, somal(i), tibbu, tuareg, zenaga
religion coptic, moslem
HAMLET aldea, bass, borgo, burg, casal(e), clachan, dorp, dump, grouper, mir, moray, shtetl, thorp, town, tref, village
author shakespeare
beloved ophelia
castle elsinore, helsingor
character bernardo, claudius, cornelius, fortinbras, francisco, gertrude, guildenstern, horatio, laertes, marcellus, ophelia, osric, polonius, reynaldo, rosencrantz, voltimand
country denmark
friend horatio
ghost banquo
king claudius

mother gertrude
slayer laertes
uncle claudius
HAMMEDATHA *son* haman
HAMMELECH *son* jerahmeel, malchiah
HAMMER beat, beetle, belabor, din into, drive, drum, force, forge, gavel, harp on, hit, kevel, malleate, mallet, malleus, marge, martel, maul, mell, peen, plexor, pound, ram, repeat, scold, stammer, strike, trip
and tongs earnestly, hard, violently
away at drudge, persevere
blow martel, pound
bricklayer's scotch, scutch(er)
charles, the martel
face trip
firearm cock, doghead
flatend poll
god mulciber, vulcan(us)
grooving fuller, peen
gumlock cock, dog(head)
hatter's beater
head peen, pene, poll
heavy bully, butt, kevel, mallet, maul, sledge
kind air, ballpeen, beetle, chipping, claw, cross-peen, die, drop, electric, mall(et), peen, pneumatic, raising, riveting, sledge, spalling, steam, stone, tack, trip
lead madge
medical plessor, plexor
miner's bully
of scotland edward i
operator tilter
out anvil, form, make, malleate, shape
paver's reel, tup
percussion plessor
pneumatic buster
presiding officer's gavel
sculptor's marteline
-*shaped* malleiform
shell malleus, mollusk, oyster
slate sax
spreading fuller
steam impacter, impactor
stone kevel, mash, spall
stone-breaking bullset
the charles martel
thief thrym
tilt oliver
toastmaster's gavel
trip oliver
tuning key

wooden beetle, gavel, mallet, maul
HAMMERHEAD balancefish, blockhead, carpenterfish, cornuda, dolt, fish, shark, shovelhead, umbrette
HAMMERKOP umber, umbrette
HAMMERLOCK armlock, bar
HAMMERMAN striker
HAMMETT, DASHIELL *character* nick charles, nora, sam spade
friend lillian hellman
work maltese falcon, thin man
HAMMOCK *bearer-carried* dandy
gear clews
pole-carried machila
wooden kartel, katel
HAMOR *son* shechem
HAMPER arrest, baffle, balk, bar, basket, beat, belabor, bind, block, burden, check, clog, confine, cramp, crate, cumber, curb, curtail, derange, embarrass, encumber, entangle, fetter, foil, frustrate, halt, hanaper, handicap, hinder, hobble, hogtie, hopple, impede, interfere with, load, lumber, manacle, maund, obstruct, package, pannier, ped, restrain, restrict, rusky, seroon, shackle, stop, thwart, tie down, tub, tuck, trammel
straw rusky
HAMPERS fetters, irons, shackles, straits
HAMSTER cricetid, cricetus, rodent
HAMSTRING cripple, disable, enervate, hock, hough, hox, hurt, lame, maim, pinion, tendon
muscle biceps
HAMUTAL *father* jeremiah
husband josiah
kin jehoahaz, jeremiah
son zedehiah
HAN *dynasty founder* han kao-tzu, kao tsu, liu pang
HANAMEEL *father* shallum
HANAN *father* zaccur
HANANI *son* jehu
HANANIAH shadrach
captain for uzziah
father azun, azur, zerubbabel

governor for nebuchadnezzar
son isaiah, pelatiah, shele-
maiah, zedekiah
HANAPER basket, HAM-
PER
HANCH bite, snap
HAND ability, acclaim,
agency, agent, aid, ap-
plause, assist(ance), calligraphy, cards, charm,
chela, clant, claw, cleuk,
clunch, control, crewman,
daddle, deal, deliver, direction, employee, extremity,
famble, famelen, fin, fist,
flapper, flipper, foot, furl,
give, gowpen, help(er),
holding(s), index, laborer,
lead, locality, management,
man(o), manus, palm, part,
pass, paw, penmanship, performance, player, pledge,
pointer, pud, script, side,
signature, skill, source,
span, stiff, stock, supply, talent, till, transfer, transmit,
trend, worker
absence of acheiria
ax boucher, coup de point
baby's spud
back of opisthenar
big maig, paw
clenched fist
-cloth napkin, serviette,
towel
clumsy clunch
comb. ch(e)ria, chiro, mani,
manu
counting zero baccara(t)
covering cestus, gauntlet,
glove, mitt(en), muff
deck hawseman
deformity apehand, ectodac-
tyism, talipomanus
disease acrodynia
down bequeath, deliver,
endow, give, pass on, render, transfer, transmit
dummy board
exposed board, dummy
gestures mudra
grip tuffing
hired braccia
hollow of goupen, gowpen,
gowpin
in deliver, resign, surrender,
yield
in glove concurrently, familiar, friendly, together,
united
it to cede, compliment, concede, inform, surrender,
tell, yield

left gauche, sinister
-length span
lone jambone
loomed hodden
-me-down cheap, readymade,
secondhand
mill grinder, quern
movement, art of chironomy
muscle abductor, opponens
on hip akimbo, obliquely
on the other alternatively,
per contra
open dummy
organ autophone
-out aid, alms, begging, charity, circular, dispense, distribute, distribution, dole,
donate, donation, down,
food, gift, give, leaflet,
meal, mete, pamphlet, press
release, publicity, release,
snack, spend, statement,
welfare
over ante, cede, cough up,
deliver, surrender, yield
over fist fast, hastily, swiftly
pain chiragra
palm loof, thenar, vola
paralysis wrist-drop
part digit, finger, goupen,
knuckle, loof, nail, palm,
pinkie, thenar, thumb
pert. chiral, manual
-pick choose, cull, elect, opt,
prefer, select, single out
-picked best, elite, selected
protector glove, hilt, mitt(en)
pump brake
reading palmistry
right dexter, droite
section snipe
-shaker candidate, sycophant
-shaped maniform, palmate
sleight of legerdemain
stone mano
strap toggel, toggle
stroke tally
study of chirology
-to-mouth improvident
unskilled dabster
using both ambidextrous
without amanous
HANDBAG (See also
BAG.) caba(s), clutch, envelope, etui, etwee, gladstone, grip(sack), pochette,
pocketbook, portmanteau,
PURSE, reticule, satchel,
tote, valise
HANDBALL fives, jai alai,
palm, pelota
point ace
HANDBARROW bier,
handy, truck

HANDBELL skellat, tantony
HANDBILL advertisement,
circular, dodger, flier, flyer,
folder, hook, leaflet, libel,
notice, pamphlet, placard,
poster
HANDBOOK baedeker,
codex, directory, enchiridion, gradus, guide, man-
ual, vade(mecum)
HANDBREADTH shaftmon,
span, spread
6 cubit
HANDCART barrow, dandy,
go-devil, hurly, pushcart,
troll(e)y, wheelbarrow
HANDCUFF bind, bracelet,
darbies, darby, disable, fetter, handbolt, handlock,
iron, manacle, nipper, paralyze, restrain(t), shackle,
stayer, stringer, trammel
HANDCUFFS darbies, irons,
nipper, snaps
HANDED *hundred* briarean
HANDEL *work* larghetto,
largo, messiah, xerxes
HANDFAST betroth(ed),
bind, bound, closefisted,
contract, covenant, custody,
grasp, grip, hold, mana-
cle(d)
HANDFUL bit, bunch, chore,
claucht, claught, claut, few,
gowpen, gowpin, grip(e),
kirn, litch, lock, maniple,
problem, pugil(lus), quantity, wisp, yaffle, yelm
double gowpen
HANDGUN caliver, hake,
pistol, revolver, saturday-
night special
HANDICAP advantage, allowance, bet, burden, disadvantage, drawback, edge,
encumber, encumbrance,
equalize, hamper, hinder,
impede, impediment, knife,
law, lisp, odds, penalize,
punish, race, rate, retard,
stammer, stutter, wager
HANDICAPPED crippled,
disadvantaged, hogtied
HANDICRAFT(S) art, dexterity, skill, trade
goddess minerva
HANDJAR dagger, khanjar,
knife
HANDKERCHIEF bandana,
barcelona, belcher, fogle,
foulard, lachramatory,
madras, malabar, mocketer,
monteith, mouchoir, neck-
cloth, scarf, sneezer, stook,

sudarium, sudary, tignon, vernacle, veronica, wiper
3-cornered fichu
HANDLE (See also *kind*, below.) ansa, appellation, bail, bale, bool, conduct, crank, deal with, designation, direct, discuss, drive, dudgeon, ear, engineer, examine, feel, fettle, finger, fist, gaum, grasp, grip, haft, hank, helve, hilt, hold, label, lifter, lug, manage, maneuver, manipulate, maul, moniker, name, nib, nob, operate, palm, paw, pilot, ply, point, pommel, pretext, rounce, run, sell, shaft, snath(e), snead, stail, stale, supervise, swing, swipe, thumb, tiller, title, tote, touch, trade in, treat, use, wield, woolder, work
awkwardly bungle, fumble, gaum, paw, thumb(le)
axe helve
bucket bail, bale
crank wink
cross hilt, potent
crossbow tiller
cup ear
curved bool, boul
dagger dudgeon
end butt
having ansate
hoop-shaped bail, bale
kind bail, bale, bool, bow, brace, brake, crank, crop, doorknob, grasp, handstaff, helm, hilt, kilp, knob, knocker, loom, lug, pull, rounce, rudder, sally, shaft, shank, snatch, snead, spindle, stock, swipe, tiller, tote, trigger, withe
looped ansa
-making ansation
plane toat, tote
plow hale, staff, start, stilt
pot bail, bale, bools
printing press rounce
rope shackle
roughly grabble, mall, maul, muzzle, towse
scythe snath(e), snead, tack, thole
-shaped manubrial
ship helm, tiller
spade tiller
sword haft, hilt
vase ansa
whip crop
HANDLEBARS mustache, soupstrainer

HANDLED ansate, bantam, dealt, felt, managed, manipulated, palmed, pawed, touched
easily yar(e)
HANDLER driver, engineer, groomer, manager, operator, potter, second, trainer
HANDLESS amanous, clumsy, incapable, inefficient
monster acheirus
HANDLING conduct, control, management, operation, practice, style, treatment, use
HANDLOCK See HANDCUFF, HANDCUFFS.
HANDMAID agent, ancilla, instrument, servant
HANDRAIL banister, bar, manrope, mopstick, safeguard, toadback
HANDS crew, force, men, squad, staff, team
down easily, utterly
off command, don't, forebear, interdict, quit, refrain, taboo
HANDSEL augury, begin, earnest(money), favor, foretaste, fresent, gift, luck, money, omen, pledge, test, token, try, use
HANDSOME adonic, ample, attractive, august, beauteous, beautiful, becoming, belle, betcheri, bonny, bountiful, braw(lie)(lis)(lys), budgeree, comely, convenient, elegant, fair, farand, featous, fewsome, fine, gallant, generous, good(ly), gracious, handy, heppen, large, lavish, liberal, lovely, munificent, noble, pleasing, pretty, princely, prodigal, profuse, ready, smart, smicker, stately, stunning, stylish, suitable, unsparing, weelfard
HANDSPREAD span
HANDSPRING cartwheel
HANDWRITING autograph, backhand, batarde, calligraphy, chirography, ductus, fist, griffonage, hand, john hancock, manuscript, niggle, paw, penmanship, ronde, scrawl, script, scrive, signature
analysis bibliotiks
bad cacography
careless griffonage

imitation isography
on the wall doom, fate, graffiti, warning
on the wall, phrase mene, mene, tekel, upharsin
study graphology
HANDY able, accessible, adept, adjacent, adroit, advantageous, all-around, apt, around, available, capable, central, close, competent, complete, convenient, deft, dextrous, expert, feat, habile, hep(t), lusty, near, nimble, on call, piggin, proficient, queme, ready, skilled, skillful, suited, useful, versatile, wieldy
HANDYMAN greaser, jimaround, jumper, mozo, swamper
HANG adhere, attach, bag, beetle, bit, cleave, cling, crap, crucify, dabble, dangle, depend, drabble, draggle, drape, droop, execute, fall, fasten, flap, flop, flow, gibbet, hover, impend, incline, jut, ketch, knack, lean, linger, loiter, loll, lop, lynch, meaning, neck, noose, patibulate, pend, persist, plan, poise, project, punish, purpose, rely, remain, rest, sag, scrag, sling, stick, stretch, string up, suspend, swag, swing, talter, trail, tree, trine, tuck up
around associate, cling, dring, follow, frequent, hover, knock, loaf, loiter, lounge, slinge
back boggle, delay, falter, hesitate, lag, procrastinate, retreat, scruple
-dog ashamed, bad, base, covert, cringing, embarrassed, fawning, furtive, groveling, mean, obsequious, secretive, shifty, sly, sneak(ing)(y), stealthy, sycophantic, whining
down dangle, dip, droop, festoon, lave, lop, perpend, propend, suspend
fire fizzle, halt, hesitate, pend, stop, suspend
in there cling, defend, hold(on), persevere, pursue, resist, stick
loosely bag, bangle, dangle, flap, flop, flow, loll, lop, paggle, sag
on adhere, attribute, bulldog,

bur, cling, depend, hold, persevere, persist, rely, remain, stay, stick

one's head atone, regret, slink

-out den, frequent, inhabit, joint, lair, lill, place, recess, rendezvous, resort, retreat, spa

over aftereffect, beetle, impend, jut, katzenjammer, morning after, project, remainder, residium, survivor, wauve, whauve

-over remedy prairie oyster

together cohere, connect, cooperate, unite

-up barrier, blind spot, block, dead end, delay, fixation, flaw, hitch, hurdle, obsession, obstacle, obstruction, preoccupation, problem, suspend, thing

HANGAR airdock, dock, garage, housing, mooring, shed, shelter

HANGBIRD baltimore oriole, icterus

HANGER bracket, pendant, seaweed, suspender, sword, tangle, title, whinyard

for carcass stang

-on adjunct, appendage, baggage, bootlicker, bottomer, courtier, dependent, doppelganger, favorite, flunky, follower, heeler, henchman, johnnie, leech, lickspit, onsetter, parasite, satellite, slinger, sponge, sycophant, toady, trencher, truckler, ward-heeler

HANGING arras, celure, curtain, dangling, declivity, dorsal, dossal, dosser, downcast, drapery, drooping, execution, hovering, leaning, loppy, pendent, pending, pensile, pensility, poised, sentence, sessile, slope, suspended, suspensory, tapestry, tenture, verdict

by a thread precarious

cabin hammock

fit for roperipe

gardens site babylon

limply flabby, flaggy, slimpsy

over beetling, imminent, impending, obumbrant

purse aumoniere

rich dorsal, tapestry

HANGMAN carnifex, derrick, executioner, gallows,

game, gregory, hangle, (jack)ketch, scragger, topsman, verdugo

day friday

noose anodyne-necklace

rope caudle of hempseed

HANGNAIL backfriend, whitlow

HANGNEST cacique, oriel

HANGTOWN placerville

HANIEL *father* ulla

HANK bait, bobbin, coil, control, habit, handle, hasp, henry, hold, influence, knot, link, loop, lump, piece, ran, ring, skein, withe

of yarn slip

HANKER aim, aspire, covet, crave, desire, hunger, itch, long, pant, pine, thirst, want, wish, yearn

HANKLE entangle, fasten, twist

HANKY-PANKY chatter, deceit, deception, devilment, flirtation, foolishness, hocus-pocus, jugglery, magic, mischief, trickery

HANNAH *husband* elkanah

son samuel

HANNIBAL *asylum* bithynia

battle cannae, saguntum, trasimeno, trebbia, zama

brother hasdrubal

enemy rome

father barca, hamilcar

lieutenant bareas, bruttain, gisco

war punic

HANOCH *father* reuben

HANOVER *duchess* sophia

dynasty guelph

HANS *consort* ondine

HANSA, HANSE association, goose, guild, soul, swan

HANSEATIC LEAGUE *capital* lu(e)beck, visby

city bremen, cologne, hamburg, koln, lu(e)beck

HANSOM cab, carriage, shoful, showful

HANT See GHOST, HAUNT.

HANUKKAH *candle* shammash

HANUMAN entellus, langur, monkey-god

father vayu

HAP accident, check, cloak, cover, destiny, fate, fortune, HAPPEN, hazard, lot, luck, prosperity, seize, snatch, wrap

HAPHAZARD accidental, aimless, anyhow, casual, chance, chancy, desultory, fortuitous, hit-or-miss, incidental, potluck, random, scrambly, slapdash, slipshod

HAPI *father* horus

HAPLESS sad, unfortunate, unlucky

HAPPEN arrive, bechance, become, befall, betide, chance, come about, come to, cook, eventualize, eventuate, fall, fare, hap, incur, luck, mayhap, occur, perhaps, take place, tide, transpire

again recur

cause to bring on, create

to become of

upon encounter, meet, run into

HAPPENING accident, adventure, casualty, contingency, current, doing, event, fact, fortuity, hazard, incident, milestone, occasion, occurrence, passing, prevailing, prevalent, sporadic, tiding, transaction

sudden clap

HAPPENSTANCE accident, chance, event

HAPPINESS beatitude, benediction, bliss, cheer, content(ment), delight, ecstasy, elation, enchantment, enjoyment, eudaemony, euphoria, felicity, gaiety, glee, joy, jubilance, jubilation, mirth, pleasure, prosperity, rapture, satisfaction, sele, triumph, weal, well-being

god benten, benzaiten, bishamon, comus, daikoku, ebisu, felicitas, fuhsing, fukurokuju, hotei, jurojin, luhsing, pusa, shichi fukujin, shouhsing

goddess lakshmi, shree, shri, sri

incapacity anhedonia

place of eden, elysium, paradise, seventh heaven, shangri-la, utopia

producing eudaemonic

science of eud(a)emonics

HAPPY abeam, appropriate, apt, auspicious, beata, beatific, beatified, benign, blessed, blest, blissful, blithe, bonnie, bonny, bright, carefree, cheerful, content(ed), cosh, delighted, ecstatic, elate(d), enraptured, faust, felix, fitting, fortunate, free, frohlich, gay, glad, halcyon, hauoli, intoxicated, joyful, joyous, lucky, meet, merry, opportune, pertinent, promising, proper, proud, providential, rapt(urous), rhapsodic, seelful, thrilled, timely, willing

as a clam, lark, sandboy

-go-lucky carefree, casual, easy(going), haphazard, improvident, random

hunting grounds See PARADISE.

landings See GOOD *-bye.*

-making, name meaning beatrice

medium moderation

name meaning felicity, felix, ida

valley See UTOPIA.

victory, name meaning eunice

HAPSBURG *dynasty founder* rudolf, rudolph

HAPU *son* amenhotep

HARA-KIRI seppuku, suicide

knife aikuchi

HARAN *brother* abraham

father caleb, shimei, terah

offspring ischa, lot, milcah

HARANGUE accost, address, allocution, bombast, buttonhole, declaim, diatribe, earbash, expound, homily, lecture, nag, orate, oration, perorate, philippic, rant, screed, sermon, speak, speech, spellbind, spout, talk, tirade

pert. demegoric

HARAS farm, horse, stud

HARASS abuse, afflict, agitate, annoy, badger, bait, ballyrag, bedevil, beset, bludgeon, bluster, bother, brace, browbeat, buffalo, bulldoze, bully, chafe, chevy, chiv(v)y, cow, distress, disturb, dragoon, exhaust, fag, fatigue, frighten, gall, gripe, hagride, harry, hase, haze, heckle, hector, hound, huff, huspil intimidate, irk, irritate, jade, molest, mutche, nag, nudge, oppress, perplex, persecute, pester, plague, pother, provoke, rag, raid, ratten, ride, scrape, tantalize, tease, terrorize, threaten, tire, tor-

ment, torture, toss, tosticate, trouble, vex, weary, worry

HARASSED anxious, bestead, careworn, hagrid, harried, heavy-laden, plagued, tormented, vexed, worried

HARBINGER angel, announce, augury, forager, forerunner, foretoken, harborer, herald, host, informant, informer, messenger, omen, precursor, presage, prodrome, sign, usher

of spring crocus, erigenia, robin, swallow

HARBOR abode, anchorage, asylum, basin, bay, berth, billet, board, bund(er), carenage, cherish, conceal, cothon, cove(rt), dock (yard), drydock, embankment, entertain, foster, haven, hide, host, house, jetty, keep, landing, lodge, lodging, manina, mole, mooring, nurse, nurture, pier, port, protect, quarter, quay, refuge, retreat, road(s), roadstead, sanctuary, seaport, secrete, shelter, shield, shiprade, slip, wharf

entrance boca

goddess matuta

master havener, havenor

protection breakwater, bulwark

seal dotant, dotard, ranger, tangfish

small creek, mole

HARD acid, adamant(ine), alcoholic, arduous, austere, bony, brawny, brazen, brittle, callous, cement(al), chondric, clear, close, compact, complex, complicated, concentrated, concrete, corneous, dense, difficult, dour, dry, dure, firm(ly), fit, flinty, granitic, harsh, horny, impenetrable, inflexible, intense, intricate, involved, knotty, laborious, lapideous, lithoid(al), marble, mean, near, obdurate, onerous, oppressive, osseous, perplexing, rigorous, robust, rock(y), rough, scleroid, severe, shotty, solid, sound, sour, steely, stern, stingy, stony, strict, stringent, strong, stubborn,

tight(ly), tiring, tough, unfeeling, unyielding, uphill

and fast aground, binding, rigid

as brick, cement, flint, iron, nails, rock, steel, stone

as nails brawny, solid, sound, strong, tough

-bill seedeater

-bitten callous, dogged, gnarled, grim, insensitive, inveterate, obdurate, severe, stubborn, tough, veteran

-boiled callous, doughty, fixed, impervious, realistic, solid, strict, tough, unyielding, veteran

-bop jazz

by close, forby, forthby, near

cherry bigarreau

comb. dys, sclero

core blatant, fill, obvious, unyielding

corn rye, wheat

-drawn taut, tense

-earned difficult, laborious

-fisted close, miserly, niggardly, ruthless, stingy, tight

-hay st peter's-wort

knocks adversity, trouble

nut to crack dilemma, enigma, problem, puzzle

of hearing deaf, dunch

-pressed burdened, harried, hassled, hurried, oppressed, pressured, pushed, put upon, rushed, straitened, taxed

put to it at a loss, confounded, pressed

salt sylvite

-set determined, firm, fixed, obdurate, obstinate, rigid, stubborn

-shell adamant(ine), baptist, conservative, crab, extremist, intractable, lorica, rigid

sponge zimocca

times adversity, depression, rainy day, recession, stagflation

times, author dickens

to believe incredible

to please finicky, fussy, squeamish

to understand abstruse, arcane, complex, complicated, diffuse, enigmatic(al), esoteric

up broke, hungry, poor, pressed, pressured, starving, straitened

-*witted* stupid
wood See TREE *hardwood.*
-*working* active, assiduous, busy, diligent, eident, industrious, laborious, operose

HARDEN acclimate, accommodate, accustom, adapt, adjust, anneal, bake, beek, brace, braze, cake, calcify, callous, congeal, cornify, crisp, crust, discipline, drill, enure, establisn, fortify, fossilize, freeze, gel, glacity, habituate, hornify, indurate, inure, jell, kern, lapidify, lithify, mineralize, ossify, petrify, planish, seal, sear, season, set, solidify, steel, stiffen, strengthen, taw, temper, thicken, toughen, train, urge, vitrify

HARDENBERG *pseud.* novalis

HARDENED abandoned, caky, callous, compacted, concentrated, crusted, impenitent, impervious, indurated, inveterate, obdurate, reprobate, sclerosed, sclerotic, solidified, tough, veteran

HARDENING poroma, scleroma

HARDHACK cinquefoil, ironbush, poor-soap, shrub, spirea, steeplebush, whitecap

HARDHEAD blockhead, boche, boulder, chub, croaker, duck, fish, gurnard, knapweed, mackerel, menhaden, plant, ribwort, ruddy-duck, sculpin, sneezewort, sponge, steelhead, trigla, trout, whale

HARDHEADED adamant(ine), insensitive, keen, obdurate, refractory, sagacious, set, sharp-witted, shrewd, strict, stubborn, unyielding, willful

HARDHEARTED callous, cold(blooded), cruel, flinty, insensitive, mean, obdurate, pitiless, stern, stony, tough, unfeeling, unsympathetic

HARDIHOOD audacity, boldness, brashness, cheek, courage, effrontery, endurance, fortitude, gall, grit, guts, impudence, nerve, pluck, resilience, sand, strength, temerity, toughness, vigor

HARDING, WARREN G.
birthplace corsica, ohio
burial site marion, ohio
love nan britton
party republican
profession publisher
scandal teapot dome
vice president calvin coolidge

HARDLY barely, harshly, ill, infrequently, only just, rarely, scantly, scarcely, seldom, severely, slightly, uneath
any few, scattered

HARDNESS callosity, callousness, duress, durity, flintiness, hardship, impenitence, induration, obduracy, petrifaction, proof, severity, solidity, steel, stoniness
measuring device durometer
scale mons

HARDPAN bedrock, foundation, moorband, orstein, reality

HARDSHIP acclivity, adversity, affliction, asperity, assay, burden, calamity, catastrophe, curse, difficulty, distress, drudgery, fatigue, grief, grievance, hazard, injury, injustice, jeopardy, mischance, misfortune, need, penalty, peril, privation, rigor, severity, stour, throng, toil, travail, trial, tribulation, trouble, unexpected, unforeseen, unweal, want, vicissitude

HARDTACK biscuit, galette, mahogany, pantile, seabread, tommy
and molasses burgoo

HARDTAIL fish, jurel, mule

HARDWARE appliances, brass, cutlery, equipment, fittings, fixtures, ironmongery, machinery, merchandise, tools, utensils

HARDY audacious, bold, brave, chisel, compact, confident, daring, durable, enduring, energetic, firm, fuller, gaillard, galliard, hale, healthy, intrepid, lusty, manly, rash, resilient, resistant, resolute, rigid, robust, rugged, set, solid, spartan, stalwart, stern, stour, stout, strong, stubborn, sturdy, tough

HARDY, THOMAS *country* wessex
work dynasts, jude the obscure, life's little ironies, mayor of casterbridge, return of the native, tess of the d'urbervilles, woodlanders

HARE, HARE'S bawd, bawtie, bawty, belgion, bunny, con(e)y, frighten, harry, jack rabbit, kliphaas, lagomorph, leporid, lepus, leveret, pika, pug, puss, rabbit, red giant, rodent, run, scut, tapeti, tease, wat, worry
beard mullein
-*brained* addle-pated, audacious, barmy, confused, flighty, foolish, frivolous, giddy, heedless, illogical, inattentive, shallow, silly, volatile
comb. lag(o)
ear modesty, thoroughwax, treacle-mustard
eye campion
female doe, hase
great manabozhs
group flick
-*hearted* timorous
jumping springhaas
-*like* leporine
-*like animal* agouti, hyrax
little chief cony, pika
male buck
meat wood chervil
parsley chervil
ragout hassenpfeffer
symbol of timidity
tail cotton grass
track prick
young leveret

HAREBELL blaewort, bluebell, campanula, herb, thimble, wood hyacinth

HAREBOTTLE knapweed

HAREFOOT avens, clover, corkwood

HAIRLIP lagostoma

HAREM anderun, gynaeceum, purdah, senana(h), seraglio, serai(l), zenana
lady kadein, khanum
male attendant eunuch
room ada, ida, oda(h)
slave odalisk, odalisque

HARHAIAH *son* uzziel

HARICOT bean, hash, ragout, stew

HARIJON panchama

HARI-KARI See HARAKIRI.

HARIM *son* benjamin, eliezer, elijah, ishijah, jehiel, maaseiah, malchijah, malluch, melchiah, shemaiah, shemariah, shimeon, uzziah

HARK attend, attention, confidence, hear, heed, list(en), whisper

back reminisce, return, revert

HARL confuse, drag, entangle, fiber, knot, peel, plaster, scrape(r), snarl, whirl

HARLEQUIN antic, buffoon, clown(ish), comic, droll, fantastic, fool, jester, merry-andrew, opal, pantaloon, pierrot, punch(inello), scaramouche, stooge, variegated, zany

bug cabbage bug, calicoback

duck canne-de-roche, lady, squealer

sweetheart columbine

HARLOT aholah, aholibah, base, buffoon, churl, cocotte, entertainer, hiren, juggler, knave, lewd, low, menial, PROSTITUTE, rascal, rogue, servant, tweak, wanton

lover philopornist

HARLOTRY baggage, filth, lewd(ness), prostitution

HARM abuse, bale, bane, damage, damnum, danger, dere, detriment, disavail, discommode, disease, disserve, disservice, evil, grief, grievance, grieve, hurt, impair, injure, injury, maltreat, mar, misaffect, mischief, misfortune, mistreat, misuse, molest, nuisance, offense, outrage, pain, prejudice, ravage, ruin(ation), sabotage, sap, scatch(e), sorrow, spoil, unquert, violence, wathe, wemmy, werd, wickedness, wound, wrack, wreak, wrong

HARMFUL bad, baleful, baneful, black, corroding, corrosive, damaging, deleterious, destructive, detrimental, dysgenic, evil, hurtful, ill, inimical, injurious, malefic(ient), malign(ant), mephitic, mischievous, nocent, noisome, noxal, noxious, pernicious, predatory, prejudicial, sinis-

ter, teen, traumatic, unsely, vicious, virulent

influence noxa, upas

HARMLESS dovish, good, hurtless, impotent, innocent, innocuous, inoffensive, sackless, safe, seli, unoffending, wholesome

as a dove

HARMONIA *daughter* agave, autonoe, ino, semele

husband cadmus

parent aphrodite, ares, mars, venus

son polydorus

HARMONIC bytone, concordant, consonant, melodious, overtone

close cadence

HARMONICA aeoline, panpipe, syrinx, zampogna

HARMONIOUS accordant, agreeing, at one, balanced, canorous, compatible, concordant, congruous, consonant, cordial, dulcet, euphonious, friendly, homophonic, in accord, in step, in sync, in tune, lydian, mellifluous, melodious, musical, spheral, symmetrical, tuneful, unanimous

HARMONIST arranger, composer, contrapuntist, musician

HARMONIUM organ, vocalion

HARMONIZATION adaptation, arrangement, instrumentation, intonation, modulation, orchestration, phrasing, preparation, resolution, solution, suspension

HARMONIZE accommodate, accord, adapt, adjust, agree, assimilate, assort, at one, attune, blend, carol, chime, combine, comport, compose, conform, consort, convene, cooperate, coordinate, correspond, cotton, fit, gear, hitch, homologate, jibe, key, match, reconcile, set, sing, sort, square, suit, sympathize, sync(hronize), tally, tune, unite

HARMONY accord, adjustment, agreement, amity, attune, balance, chime, chord, concinnity, concord, concurrence, conformity, consistency, consonance, diapason, euphony, flow, friendship, monochord, music,

order, peace, proportion, rapport, rhythm, symmetry, symphony, synchronism, syntony, tone, tranquility, tune, unanimity, understanding, union, unison, unity

bring into attune

goddess concordia

internal concinnity

lack discord

of the gospels diatessaron

HARMOTHOE *husband* pandareus

offspring aedon, cleothera, merope

HARNESS accouter, apparel, arm, armor, array, belt, britchen, caparison, cavesson, draught, drawgear, equipment, fettle, freno, gear(ing), gigtree, graith, gullet, hackamore, halter, heal, hitch, inspan, jaquima, jerkline, lines, lormery, mount, poke, prepare, property, ribbons, rig, simblot, strap, tack(le), tame, toggery, turnback, yoke

adornment horse brass, hounce, phalera

bull policeman

hook sperket

loom heald, leaf, mounting

loop chape

maker knacker, lorimer, loriner, whittaw

ornamental caparison

part backstrap, bellyband, billet, bit, blind, blinker, breastband, breeching, bridle, button, chape, checkrein, chokestrap, cinch, circingle, collar, crouper, crownpiece, crupper, girth, hame, headstall, hitch, knot, martingal(e), quoiler, rein, ridgeband, saddle, snaffle, sperket, surcingle, terret, throatlatch, trace, tug

ring button, terret

shaft heald

trace theat

weaving headle, heddle

HAROLD I harefoot

HARP chrotta, clarsach, guimard, irishman, iterate, kantela, koto, lute, lyre, nag, nanga, nebel, plectrum, repeat, sabeca, sang, scold, seal, sistrum, solitaire, speak, telyn, trump, voice, zither

ancient clarsach, trigon

arthur's vega
-guitar key dital
ivory plectrum
-like instrument arpa, cithara, cither(n), cittern, claviharp, dulcimer, gittern, langspiel, lira, lyre, psalter(y), symphonia, zither
on bore, din, drum, hammer, repeat
plectron fescue
seal beater, bedlamer, bluesides, saddleback, saddler, whitecoat
string chord
triangular trigon(on)
HARPADON bombay duck, bummalo, lizard-fish
HARPALE *consort* poseidon
HARPALYCE *father* clymenus
lover clymenus
HARPIES See HARPY.
HARPINA *child* oenomaus
consort ares, mercury
father asopus
HARPING complaining, monotonous, redundant, tedious, wale
johnny orpine
HARPOON catch, fizgig, gig, grain, iron, javelin, kill, parpago, pierce, spear, strike
barb flue, fluke
explosive headed bomblance
head bomb
HARPSICHORD celestina, cembalo, clavecin, clavicembalo, clavicymbal, clavier, flugel, gravicembalo, haspicol, spinet
composition murky
HARPY aello, bat, bird, cel(a)eno, demon, eagle, extortionist, ghoul, hag, lamia, monster, ocypete, podarge, tormentor, vampire, vulture, xanthippe
attacker argonauts, boreads, calais, zetes
island strophades
parent electra, thaumas
victim phineus
HARQUEBUS caliver, gun, hackbut, hagbut, soldier
fork croc
HARRIDAN brimstone, chippie, crone, fright, fury, hag, hellcat, jezebel, prostitute, scold, shrew, spitfire, streetwalker, strumpet, ter-

magant, trollop, virago, vixen
HARRIER circus, dog, glede, harpy, hawk, hound, pest, puttock, runner
-like accipital, accipitrine, raptorial
marsh harpy, puttock
HARRIS, JOEL *character* brer rabbit, uncle remus
HARRISON, BENJAMIN *birthplace* north bend, ohio
burial site indianapolis, indiana
party republican
profession lawyer
vice president morton
HARRISON, WILLIAM HENRY *battle* tippecanoe
birthplace berkeley, virginia
burial site north bend, ohio
nickname tippecanoe
party whig
vice president tyler
victim tecumseh
HARROW brake, break, chip, cultivate, cultivator, disc, disk, distress, drag, herse, lacerate, oppress, pain, plow, smooth, spader, tear, till, tine, torment, vex, wound
bar bull
crude brush-drag
rest whin
HARROWING agonizing, distressing, heart-rending, painful, tearing, tining
HARRY afflict, annoy, besiege, bother, chafe, distress, fret, gall, grill, hector, henry, hound, maraud, molest, persecute, pester, plaque, plunder, rack, ravage, ravish, rob, sack, steal, tantalize, tease, torment, torture, try, violate
black seabass
old devil, satan
HARSH acerb, acid, acrimonious, asper, astringent, austere, bitter, bluff, blunt, brassy, brazen, brutal, caustic, chapped, clashing, coarse, cracked, croaky, crude, cruel, crusty, discordant, dissonant, dour, dry, dure, grating, grim, grinding, gross, gruff, guttural, hard, hask, hoarse, husky, inclement, jarring, metallic, obdurate, ragged, raspy, raucous, relentless, rigid, rough, roupy, rude, rufty-

tufty, rugged, scabrous, scrannel, severe, sharp, sour, squawking, squawky, stern, stertorous, strict, strident, stringent, strounge, sullen, tasteless, tetric, thick, throaty, uncivil, unkind, unsparing, venomous
HARSHNESS asperity, cacophony, catoism, churlishness, discord, jangle, noise, raucity, raucousness, rigor, screak, severity, stridence, stridor
HARSOMTUS *mother* hathor
HART, HART'S deer, spade, stag
clover medic, melilot
-tongue burnt-weed, buttonhole, finger-fern, longleaf, willow-herb
HARTE, BRET *character* ah sin
HARTEBEEST antelope, asse, bontebok, bubal(e), bubalis, caama, kaama, kongoni, konze, lecama, topi, tora
-like blesbok, sassaby
HARTSWORT sesili
HARUMAPH *son* jedaiah
HARUM-SCARUM daredevil, flighty, irresponsible, rampageous, rash, reckless, rumblegarie, thoughtless, wild
HARUN-AL-RASHID *wife* zobeide
HARUSPEX diviner, extispex, prognosticator, prophet, seer, soothsayer
HARVARD *book award* detur
president bok, lowell, pusey
HARVEST acquire, auslese, autumn, bind, bring in, crop, cut, dig, effect, ernte(n), foison, fruit, gain, garner, gather, get, glean, grabble, growth, hay, ingather, issue, kern, kirn, mow, outcome, output, pick, pluck, proceeds, produce, product, rab(b)i, reap, result, return, reward, solitaire, yield
abundant foison
bell gentian
deity See VEGETATION god, goddess.
festival churn-supper, foy, hockey, horky, kern, kirn, mell, opalia

festival image carline, cliack, doll, kern maiden, kirn baby, knack, mare, mother, nag
fish butterfish, dollarfish, moonfish, peprilus, starfish, whiting
fly cicad
home See *festival,* above.
late spaetlese
lice agrimonia, beggar's-tick, cleavers, galium
lily bindweed
machine binder, reaper, thrasher, thresher
man arachnid, cartare, carter, cocker, daddy long-legs, farmer, spider
mite chigger, red-bug
select auslese, beerenauslese
sharing metayer
tick acarid
time autumn, fall, october
HARVESTER butterfly, cocker, gleaner
HASADIAH *father* jilkiah, zerubbabel
son zedekiah
HASAN *ancestor* mohammed
brother husain
daughter hinda
parent ali, fatima
HAS-BEEN candidate, old-fashioned, old timer, vestige, wuzzer
HASH blunder, botch, bungle, chop, error, fiasco, gallimaufry, goulash, haricot, jumble, mark, medley, mess, mince, mixture, olio, ollapodrida, potpourri, ragout, ramekin, rechauffe, salmagundi, slumgullion, spoil
-house See RESTAURANT.
mark stripe
over discuss
-slinger waiter, waitress
HASHABNIAH *son* hattush
HASHISH assis, bhang, cannabis, drug, gallowsgrass, hemp, marijuana, narcotic, plant
HASHUM *son* eliphelet, jeremai, manasseh, mattathah, mattenai, shimei, zabad
HASK basket, boarse, cold, dry, harsh, hoarse
HASKALAH *follower* maskil
HASKWORT bellflower, campanula
HASLET heart, liver, viscera
HASP clasp, confine, fasten

(ing), gird, hank, skein, spindle, sprent, strap, unite
HASRAH *son* tikvath
HASSAN See HASAN.
HASSAR catfish, dorad
HASSLE argue, argument, brawl, confusion, fight, fray, melee, muddle, quarrel, squabble, struggle
HASSOCK bass, boss, buffet, cluster, cushion, doss, footstool, ottoman, pess, trush, tuffet, tuft, tussock, tut
HASTE alacrity, briskness, bustle, celerity, chase, dash, despatch, dispatch, expedition, flurry, hurry, impetuousity, nimbleness, precipitance, promptness, quickness, rapidity, rush, speed, spurn, swiftness, swivet, urgency, velocity
in great amain
utmost whip and spur
HASTEN accelerate, actify, activate, activize, advance, brush, busk, buss, catch, chase, dispatch, drive, expedite, facilitate, firk, flee, fly, further, hie, hotfoot, hurry, hustle, precipitate, promote, quicken, run, rush, scamp (er), scud, scurry, speed, spur, squirr, streak, urge, withhie
HASTILY against time, amain, apace, cursorily, headlong, helter-skelter, holus-bolus, hotfoot, hotly, hurriedly, hurry-scurry, impatiently, in short order, pell-mell, rashly, slapbang, slapdash, speedily, superficially, swiftly
HASTINGS *battle site* senlac
HASTY abrupt, agile, brash, brisk, cursory, eager, expeditious, fast, feverish, fleet, flying, forward, furious, headlong, hotheaded, hurried, immediate, impatient, impetuous, impulsive, precipitate, premature, quick, rapid, rash, reckless, short, slight, snap, speedy, subitane(ous), sudden, superficial, swift, tearing, urgent
over premature
pudding mush, sepon, stirabout, supawn
retreat bug-out, defeat, rout
HAT baku, ballibuntl, ban-

deau, bangkok, beanie, beaver, bellhopper, benny, beret, bicorne, billycock, biretta, boater, bonnet, bowler, boxer, breton, broadbrim, busby, cap, capeline, capote, cappello, caroline, casque, castor(ida), caubeen, caul, chapeau, claque, cloche, copatain, derby, dicer, dip, fantail, fedora, felt, fez, halacot, headdress, headgear, helmet, homburg, jipijapa, kelly, leghorn, lid, milan, miter, mitre, nabcheat, panama, petasus, pillbox, quaker, sailor, salacot, shtreimel, skimmer, skullcap, snap-brim, stetson, stovepipe, straw, tam(o'-shanter), tarp, top(per), toque, trilby, turban, wideawake, wind-cutter
academic cornercap, mortarboard
band weed, weeper
beaver castor
blocker roper
bowling derby
brim brink, leaf, poke, snap, tarfe
brimangle break
brimless beret, cloche, tam, toque, turban
broad-brimmed benjy, shovel, sombrero, stetson, ten-gallon, terai
brushing pad velure
clergyman's shovel
close-fitting cloche, helmet, toque
cocked bicorne, chapeau bras, ramil(l)ie, scraper, tricorne
cone-shaped cornet(te)
covering havelock
cowboy stetson, ten-gallon
crown poll
crush claque
designer dache
doff vail
ecclesiastic See VESTMENT religious.
fabric felt, toque, turban
felt alpine, billycock, bowler, derby, jerry, stetson, tarai, terai, trilby, wide-awake
fiber felt, soda, straw
fur beaver, busby, shako, shtreimel
fur used in bearskin, beaver, coney, coonskin, ermine, mink

goat's hair cordy
hanger halltree
high silk belltopper, kyl, stovepipe, tile, topper
hunter's deer-stalker, terai
in hand humbly, obsequious, respectfully
iron gossan, gozzan
lady's bonnet, breton, caddie, caddy, cloche, cooie, dolly varden, duck bill, gainsborough, harlequin, leghorn, slouch, toque
low-crowned deer stalker, mushroom
maker milliner
medieval abacot, bycoket
military busby, helmet, kepi, shako
money tampang
oilskin souwester, squam
opera beaver, caroline, claque, crush, gibus, stovepipe, tile, topper
ornament tassel
-palm areca, carnauba, corypha, jipijapa, pandanus, thrinax
palmleaf salacot
pert. castorial
pin pipewort
pith topee, topi
plant sola
quaker broadbrim
renovated moloker
round toque
shabby caubeen
silk beaver, belltopper, catskin, gossamer, kyl, lum, opera, shiner, stovepipe, tile, top(per)
slang for dicer, lid
slouch caddie, caddy
snap-brimmed porkpie
snug toque
soft beret, fedora, trilby
soldier's busby, helmet, kepi, shako, tin
stovepipe See *opera*, above.
straw baku, ballibuntl, bangkok, benjy, benny, boater, brazilian, dunstable, flat, hood, kady, katy, leghorn, milan, panama
sun topee, topi
take off one's honor, praise, recognize, salute
10-gallon sombrero, texas yomulka
30-tasselled galero
3-cornered nivernois, tricorn(e)
top See *opera*, above.
trimming cache-peigne, veil

tropical pith helmet, terai, topee, topi
2-cornered bicorne
unblocked cone
under one's confidential, private, secret
wide-brimmed See *broadbrimmed*, above.
HATCH barrier, breed, brew, brood, conceive, concoct, contrive, covey, devise, door, engrave, fabricate, floodgate, gate, generate, guichet, hack, improvise, incubate, invent, lid, line, make up, mark, opening, originate, outcome, plan, plot, portal, produce, project, scheme, set, shade, skylight, stroke, weir, wicket
covering tarp
HATCHEL flaxcomb, hackle, tease, torment, worry
HATCHET adz(e), axe, gweeon, hache, mogo, thixie, tomahawk
-faced dour, lean
man henchman, highbinder, hoodlum, killer, stooge, tool
stone hache, mogo, tomahawk
HATCHING birth, cletch, clutch, incubation, origination, shading, young
HATCHWAY scuttle
HATE (See also HATRED.) abhor(rence), abominate, animosity, animus, antipathy, aversion, bete noire, contempt, despise, detest, disdain, dislike, dosa, enmity, execrate, horror, loathe, loathing, malevolence, malice, malignity, odium, poison, rancor, recoil, repugnance, revile, scorn, shudders, teen, unlove, venom
castle of chillon
comb. mis(o), phobia
object of abomination, anathema, bete noire, monstrosity
HATEFUL abhorrent, abominable, anathematic, antipathetic, cursed, curst, detestable, disgusting, distasteful, execrable, foul, ghastly, grim, heinous, horrid, infamous, invidious, loathsome, loth, malevolent, malicious, malign(ant), nauseating, nauseous, ob-

noxious, odious, offensive, repellent, repugnant, repulsive, shuddery, spiteful, terrible, unpleasant
HATER adversary, enemy, hitler, misanthrope, ulysses
HATHOR athyr, sekhmet
emblem sistrum
father othniel
husband horus
master mowgli
sanctuary dendara
son ahi, harsomtus, ihi, shu
HATRED (See also HATE.) abhorrence, aversion, detestation, enmity, envy, haine, hell, ill will, jealousy, malignity, odium, rancor, repugnance, scorn, spite
HATTER batter, bruise, eccentric, exhaust, gadger, harass, hurrer, worry
HATTUSAS boazkkale
HATTUSH *father* david
HAUBERK armor, byrnie, coat, mail
HAUGHTINESS airs, arrogance, disdain, hautesse, hauteur, orguil, pride
HAUGHTY aloof, arrogant, assuming, big, bold, cavalier, contemptuous, dain, digne, disdainful, distant, domineering, dorty, exalted, feisty, haught, high, hontish, huffy, insolent, lofty, lordly, lusty, magisterial, noble, orgulous, paughty, proud, scornful, sniffy, stately, supercilious, superior, surly, toplofty, uppity, vain
HAUL bag, booty, bounce, bouse, brail, carry, check, convey, drag, draw, dray, freight, hale, heave, lift, loot, lug, move, pull, rake, remove, reprimand, schlepp, shift, skid, sloop, strain, swag, swamp, tote, tow, tract, transport, travoy, trawl, trek, trice, tug
down lower, strike
in gather
off draw back, run, withdraw
over the coals rebuke, scold
round tack
sail bunt, clew, clue
with tackle bouse, bowse
HAULAGE dock, traction, transport(ation)
fee boatage, freightage, portage, shippage
HAULED *up* arrested, roped, taken in, triced

HAULM culm, litter, stalk(s), stem(s), straw

HAUNCH coxa, fling, hance, hindquarter, hip, huck(le), leg, quarter, rump, side

HAUNT abode, accustom, affect, beset, custom, den, drive, environs, fellowship, fetch, frequent, GHOST, habit, hant, howff, infest, inhabit, lair, lie, nest, obsess, overrun, pad, persecute, possess, practice, purlieu, recur, resort, shade, skill, spector, spirit, spook, stalk, visit

HAUSEN acipenser, beluga, cetacean, sturgeon, whale

HAUTBOY oboe

HAUTE *couture* fashion
ecole dressage, high school
savoie, capital annecy

HAUTEUR arrogance, contempt, contumely, disdain, haughtiness, hight, loftiness, pride

HAUT MONDE See SOCIETY.

HAVANA broad-leaf, brown, cigar, tobacco
castle and fort morro
silk kapok
suburb regia

HAVE accept, accommodate, acquire, admit, affirm, bear, beget, boast, capitalist, cherish, contain, deceive, effect, enjoy, exact, exercise, experience, force, get, hae, hold, include, keep, learn, maintain, obtain, occupy, own, perform, possess, proceed, retain, suffer, swindle, take, teem with, trick, understand, use, wield
a bone to pick argue, differ, disagree, split
a crush on adore, dote, love
a finger in interfere, meddle, participate
a fling at attempt, taunt, try, undertake
all to oneself monopolize
a mind desire, intend, mean, will
and hold cherish, love
at assail, attack
at it attempt, try, undertake
business with concern, deal, treat
cold feet abstain, cringe, dare not, shrink, withdraw
dealings with associate, patronize, trust

done with cease, complete, discontinue, disuse, finish, halt, relinquish, stop
enough cede, fill, give up, quit, satiate, surrender, yield
got must, ought, should
in hand control, dominate, own, possess
in mind aim, contemplate, intend, plan, think of
it out argue, fight, resolve, settle
no choice must
-not disadvantaged, hungry, indigent, lack, needy, pauper, poor, starving
nothing to do with avoid, disregard, refrain, repudiate, spurn
off begone, scram
on wear
one's fling dissipate, play
over entertain, treat
qualms demur, fear, hesitate
rather prefer
some taste, try
the goods on catch, control, dominate, implicate, trip up
to must, ought, should
to do with associate, care, concern, deal, participate, take part, treat
up arraign, investigate, question
words with admonish, bawl out, dress down, fight, rebuke, reprimand

HAVEL *tributary* spree

HAVEN ark, asylum, bay, cove(r), harbor, hithe, home, hope, inlet, lee, pier, port, protection, refuge, rest, retreat, shelter
small hithe

HAVER avena, babble, chatter, holder, maunder, nonsense, oat, possession, twaddle

HAVOC desolation, destroy, destruction, devastation, dilapidation, evil, hobb, lay waste, ravage, ruin, waste, wreckage

HAW (See also HAWTHORN.) berry, bush, close, discolored, enclosure, eyelid, fence, gee, hedge, hem, hesitate, hoi, house, hum, livid, mano, messuage, sloe, turn, wan

HAWAII *apple* maile
baking pit imu
ballad mele

bay halawa, kamohio, kaneohe, kawaihae, kiholo, mamala, maunalua, pohue, waiagua
beach waikiki
beverage kavakava
bird alala, apapani, ava, drepanis, huia, iiwi, ioa, iwa, jibi, kamao, kioea, koae, mamo, moho, nene, omao, ooaa, palila, pikake
bird, extinct mamo
blueberry ohelo
bullrush aka(akai)
canoe waapa
canoe paddle iakus
capital honolulu, lahaina
channel auau, kaiwi, kalohi, pailolo
chant mele
chief alii nui
city aiea, ewa, hana, hilo, honolulu, kahului, kailua, kaneohe, kapaa, kekaha, laie, lanikae, lihue, maili, paia, wahiawa, waianae, wailuku
cliff pali
climber akala, kaiwi, rubus
cloak ahuula, mamo
cloth kapa, olong, tap(p)a
club hui
coffee kona
common noa
cord aea
county hawaii, honolulu, kauai, maui
crater kilauea, punch bowl
cudweed enaena
dance hula
dancer hilo hattie
dead, god of kaneloa
desert kau
discoverer cook, gaetano
district kona, puna
dress muumuu
drink kava, mai tai
duck nene, neni
emblem kahili
farewell aloha
father god wakea
feast ahaaina, luau
fern heii
fern stalks iwaiwa
fiber ehuawa pulu, wauke
fire goddess pele
firm hui
fish ahi, akule, alaihi, awa, humuhumunukunukuapuaa, kaawa, kahala, kava, lania, moano, mokuleia, palani, uku, ula, ulua
fish bait hola
fish poison auhuhu, hola

floral emblem lehua, lei
flower anthruium, dec, emoloa, hibiscus, ilima, lehua,
  plumeria
food apii, kalo, poi, taro
foreigner haole
founder captain cook
frigate bird iwa
fruit pineapple, poha
game hei
garland lei
garment holoku, holomuu,
  muumuu
girdle malo
god kanaloa, kane, lono,
  wakea
goddess pele
goose nene, neni
gooseberry poha
governor, 1st dole
gown holoku, muumuu
grass anounou, emoloa, hilo
green garden island kauai
greeting aloha
harbor pearl
harvest god lono
herb ape, auhuhu, awiwi,
  hola, pia
holiday kamehameha day
house of sun haleakala
indian shot aliipoe
island hawaii, kahoolawe,
  kauai, kaula, kure, lanai,
  maui, molokai, niihau,
  oahu
island, uninhabited kahoolawe
king kalakaua, kamahameha
king's cloak ahuula
lava pahoehoe
liquor awa, kawa
loin cloth malo
love aloha
mahogany koa
majagua hau
man kanaka
massage lomilomi
medicine man kahuna
morning glory koali
mulberry bark kapa, tap(p)a
musical instrument ukalele,
  uke(lele), ukulele
native kamaaini, kanaka
newcomer malihini
nickname aloha state
octopus hee
old name sandwich islands
orange calamondin
origin homeland, owhyhee
pantheon kane
parrot-fish lauia
partnership hoey, hui
paste poi
peacock pikake

peak kaala, kamakou, kea,
  kohala, koolau, lanaihale,
  loa, maunakea, maunaloa
pepper ava
pepper grass anounou
plant ehuawa, hala, ilima,
  kalo, olana, olona, pandanus, pia, pulu, taro
plover kolea
poem mele
porch lanai
port hilo, honolulu
precipice pali
president sanford dole
priest kahuna
primitive menehune
promontory diamond head
pudding haupia
pygmy menehune
queen liliuokalani
rain tree monkey pod
range kohala, koolau,
  waianae
raven alala
religious system taboo
resident kamaaina
root taro
rose akala, flower, shrub
royalty alii
seaweed limu
shaman kahuna
shampoo lomilomi
shrub akala, akia, anapanapa, aupaka, colubrina,
  coprosma, kokio, olona,
  poha
society hui
song mele
squirrel-fish alaihi
staple poi, taro
starch apii, pia, poi, taro
state bird goose, nene
state flower lehua, scarlet hibiscus
state tree candlenut
storm kona
taboo kapu
temple heiau
tern noio
thrush amao, olomao, omao
tree aalii, aiea, akala,
  akeake, alani, amaumau,
  aulu, banyan, bwa, dar, dodonaea, eucalyptus, flindersia, flooded gum, fraxinuts,
  hau(ula), hopbush, ilaihi,
  india, kino, koa, kou,
  kukui, lehua, loblolly pine,
  majagua, mokihana, mon-
  key pod, naio, octopus,
  ohia, pelea, pine, plumeria,
  poinciana, pulu, sal, sloe,
  toona, walahee, wiliwili

tree fern amaumau, pulu,
  sadleria
valley manoa
veranda lanai
victorfish aku
vine awikiwiki, canavalia,
  kaiwi
volcano haleakala, kilauea,
  mauna kea, mauna loa
white man haole
wind kona
woman wahini
worsted tap(p)a
wreath lei
yam hoi
HAWFINCH grosbeak, kate
HAWK, HAWK'S (See also
  kind, below.) accipiter, ag-
  gressor, bark, bird, cadge,
  canvass, chauvinist, cough,
  cry, falcon, fighter, hack,
  hunt, mortarboard, peddle,
  plunderer, predator, publish, reach, sell, sharper,
  slobber, swindler, trade,
  vend(or), vulture, warlover,
  whoop
bell-fastener bewet, bewit
bill pawl, turtle
blind seel
blue hen-harrier, kite
broad-winged buteo, buzzard
cage mew
claw pounce
crop gorge
cuckoo brain-fever bird
disease cray, croak, filanders,
  frounce, rye
-eye natty bumppo, plover,
  quartz
-eyed sharp-sighted
-eye state iowa
feather beam, brail, flag,
  mail, pendent, sarcel
-feet columbine
female formal, formel
fish osprey
fly asilus
genus accipiter, arenda,
  buteo, circaetus, falco
great-footed peregrine falcon
group cast
harrier maximus
-headed god hor(us)
kind allan, arenda, astur,
  aura, badius, beara, beekite,
  berigora, blue glede, blue
  kite, brancher, bull bat,
  buzzard, caracara, carancha, chimango, cooper's,
  eyas, falcon, faller, gerfal-
  con, glede, goshawk, hafoc,
  haggard, harrier, heroner,
  hoby, kahu, kestrel, kite,

lanare, lanrell, merlyn, micrastur, murkyte, osprey, peregrine, pisk, puttock, ramage, redtail, roughleg, sacre, sacrit, shikra, surn, tartaret, tercel, vulture
leash creance, jess, loyn, lune, tirret
-like accipitral, accipitrine, bellicose, belligerent, jingoistic, raptorial
-like bird elanet, osprey, surn
male jack, tassel, tercel
moth sphingid, sphinx
nest aerie
nestling eyas
pair cast
parrot hia
passage tartaret
pert. accipitral, accipitrine
seller cadger
seller's frame cadge
sparrow musket, nisus
-swallow swift
stomach pannel
stomach contents cast
symbol of military aggression, penetration, rapacity, war
tail train
thong brail
toe petty-single
trainer a(u)stringer
wing sail
young brancher, eyas(s), kite, nias
HAWKBIT dandelion
HAWKER auctioneer, badger, cadger, canvasser, chapman, coster(monger), crier, cryer, falconer, glassman, higgler, huckster, mercury, packman, peddler, pether, salesman, seller, solicitor, vendor
HAWKEYE iowan
HAWKING falconry
HAWKINS, JIM *saga* treasure island
HAWKSHAW detective, dick, sleuth, tec
HAWKWEED bugloss, cat's-ear, dindle, fireweed, heracium
HAWSE *bag* jackass
HAWSER cable, headline, rope, warp
block bitt
hole cathole
post bitt, bollard capstan
HAWTHORN a(i)glet, alisier, azarole, black horn, boots, bumelia, cockspur,

crataegus, espino, honeysuckle, maybloom, mayflower, oxycantha, quickset, sheepberry, shrub, sloe, stagbush, tree, viburnum
fruit bird-eagle, cathaw, haw, hazel, peggle
HAWTHORN, NATHANIEL *character* dimmesdale, fanshawe, hester prynne, zenobia
work blithedale romance, marble faun, scarlet letter, tanglewood tales, wonder book
HAY alfalfa clover, dance, feed, fence, fodder, forage, grain, grass, harvest, hit, marijuana, park, pasturage, rip, snare, soilage, stover, timothy
bird blackcap, sandpiper, warbler
bundle bale, botte, gavel, mow, rick, stack, tipple, truss, wisp
fever allergic rhinitis, pollinosis, rose(cold), sneezing
fever cause allergens, allergy, blue grass, box elder, burning bush, ragweed, redroot, red top, roses, sagebrush, spiny amaranth, tumbleweed
fever test rast
field park, rakh
fork evil, pickle, pikel
hit the retire, sleep
line swath, windrow
-maker pickman, punch, swing
mow See HAYCOCK.
pile rack, tumble
rack heck, thripple
rick See HAYCOCK.
roll wake
2nd growth eddish, rowen
source alfalfa
spread(er) ted(der)
stack See HAYCOCK.
stalk risp
storage loft, mow
sweep buck
tit warbler, whitethroat
HAYCOCK cob, coil, doodle, goaf, heap, hipple, hovel, mow, pike, pile, quile, rack, rick, stack, trampcock
HAYDN *oratorio* the creation, the seasons
HAYES, RUTHERFORD B. *birthplace* delaware, ohio
burial site fremont, ohio
party republican

profession lawyer
vice president william wheeler
HAYLOFT granary, mow, scaffold, taller
HAYS, MARY molly pitcher
HAYSEED countryman, farmer, peasant, rube, rural, rustic, yokel
HAYSUCK eysoge
HAYWARD meadsman
HAYWIRE amiss, broken, chaotic, confused, insane, mad, wrong
HAZARD accident, adventure, assume, bet, casualty, chance, chuck(a)luck, contingency, danger, dare, endanger, fortune, gamble, hap(pening), imperil, jeopardy, jump, lot, luck, pawn, peril, risk, speculate, stake, venture, wage(r)
HAZARDOUS adventurous, breakneck, chancy, dangerous, insecure, jumpy, perilous, precarious, queasy, random, risky, risque, speculative, uncertain, unsafe, unsound, unsure, venturous, venturesome
HAZE annoy, banter, beat, brume, calina, cloud, dimness, discipline, drizzle, film, fog, frighten, glin, harass, idle, initiate, loiter, miasma, mist, obscurity, pall, punish, ramble, reek, scold, smaze, smeeth, smog, smoke, vapor
layer fumulus
summer calina
HAZEL a(i)glet, asarabacca, avellaneous, cobnut, corylus, filbert, freestone, muffin, noisette, sandstone, shrub, sweetgum, tree
brown muffin, noisette
hoe pulaski
nut cobnut, filbert, nit, noisette
nut cupule bolster
tree avellano
HAZIEL *father* shimei
HAZING creeling, initiation
HAZOR *king* jabin
HAZY cloudy, dim, dizzy, filmy, foggy, fuzzy, groggy, indistinct, misty, muddled, murky, muzzy, nebulous, obscure, smoky, smuisty, thick, uncertain, vague, whirling

HE buck, bull, cestui, him, ille, lui, male, thon, tom
carved sculpsit
died obit
painted pinxit
wrote scripsit
HEAD 3 ace, bun, cid, man, nob, nut, top, van 4 bead, bean, bear, cape, conk, dato, dome, duce, foam, hair, jefe, knob, lead, pate, poll, scum, tend, tete 5 begin, block, brain, chief, chump, cocoa, crown, datto, first, fount, front, froth, mazer, point, skull, start, tibby, title, topic 6 belfry, cabeza, direct, fuhrer, leader, master, noddle, noggin, noodle, sconce, source, spring, thrust 7 control, costard, costrel, coxcomb, cranium, crumpet, frontal, genarch, magnate, officer 8 cephalon, director, dominant, duffadar, fountain, portrait 9 beginning, chieftain, commander, gravitate, intellect, principal 10 mastermind, upper story
and shoulders completely, utterly
back crown, niddick, noddle, occiput, poll
baked sheep's james, jemmy
bald pilgarlic
bandage gaka, galfa
barbed fluke
bone See SKULL.
borough verges
cavity sinus
cheese souse
cloth potong
comb. cephal(ic), cephalo(us), cephalus, crani
cord agal
covering See HEADDRESS, HAT.
crown cantle, pate, vertex
deformity acrocephaly, hypsicaphaly, loxia, oxycephaly, plagiocephaly
-flattening platycrania
foremost topsail
frame gallows, poppet
having cephalate, cephalophorous, cephalous
having long hypermorph
having 2 dicephalous
into attack, begin, collide, meet
largeness macrocephaly
membrane caul, omentum
muscle occipitalis

narrowness stenocephaly
note syllabus
off block, branch, divert, intercept, prevent, repel, turn back
of house breadwinner, sire
of state See RULER.
ornament See HEADDRESS.
outline cephalogram
over heels engrossed, implicated, involved, obsessed, topsy-turvy, upsidedown
part cranium, earlap, face, lore, lorum, pate, scalp, temple
penny poll-tax
per capitatum
pert. capital, capitate, cephalic, cranial, encephalic
printed boxhead
race channel
science of phrenology
sculpture bust
-shaped capitate(d)
shave tonsure
showing caboshed
spiritual khalifat
shrunken tsantsa
side lore, lorum, temple
smallness acromicria
space outage
-spring fountain, source, start
start advantage, priority
stock poppet
to foot cap-a-pie
top coxcomb, pate, scalp, shode, vertex
toward dephalad
up begin, close, collect, direct, lead, precede
waiter captain, maitre d'
wind muzzler, nos-ender, noser
-work cerebration, mentation, reflection, study, thought
HEADACHE amphicrania, annoyance, bore, bother, busthead, cephalalgia, cephalgy, clavus, encephalagia, hemialgia, hemicrania, megrim, migraine, misery, nuisance, pasqueflower, poppy, stitchwort, trial, trouble
1-sided hemicrania
HEADBAND carcan(et), circlet, coronal, coronet, crown, DIADEM, fillet, frontlet, garland, infula, mitre, sphendone, stephane, taenia, vitta
HEADDRESS 3 cap, fez, fly, HAT, rug, taj, top, toy, wig

4 amit, atef, caul, coif, cowl, hood, katy, pouf, tete, tire, veil 5 ampyx, crown, cupee, egret, gable, lautu, miter, mitre, nubia, polos, poufe, pshem, rumal, shako, shawl, snood, tiara, vitta 6 almice, almuce, bonnet, casque, faille, fillet, hennin, kennel, kullah, mobcap, pinner, tuinga, turban, wimple 7 bandore, bycoket, capuche, coxcomb, fantail, flandan, mortier, pschent, puggree, scraper, tablita, templet, therese, topknot, tresson, tutulus, veiling 8 aigrette, babushka, biliment, binnogue, bycocket, capriole, caputium, coiffure, frontlet, kaffiyeh, kerchief, mantilla, maskette, nightcap, skullcap, stephane, tarboosh, tressure 9 rigolette, sunbonnet 10 boudoir cap, fascinator, pokebonnet
15th century chaperon
18th century pinner, therese
fold on lappet
medieval abacot
old-time mob cap
pin acicula
sacred uraeus
widow's bandore
HEADER binder, dive, fall, knobber, leader, nobber, plunge, stretman, timber
HEADFIRST impulsively, precipitately, rashly, recklessly
HEADGEAR bridle, CAP, HAT, harness, HEADDRESS
fold on lappet
HEADHUNTER ataiyal, italone, killer, lakher, taiyal, uiangan
HEADING banner, bearing, caption, course, direction, lead, preceding, tending, title, trope
HEADLAND bill, bluff, cape, cliff, escarpment, foreland, kop, morro, mull, nase, naze, ness, nook, peak, point, promontory, ras, ridge, scaw, strip, thrum
HEADLESS acephal(ous), beheaded, decapitated, etete, foolish, rash, senseless, stupid, undirected, unintelligent
HEADLESSNESS acephalia

HEADLINE banner, caption, display, feather, label, leader, screamer, sensation, streamer, title

HEADLINER leader, personality, star

HEADLONG abrupt, bellyflaught, brash, desperate, full-tilt, gadakene, hastily, hasty, immediate, impetuous, impulsive, overhasty, pellmell, posthaste, precipitate(ly), precipituous, prone, ramstam, rash, reckless, rough, steep, sudden, tantivy, violently

HEADMAN alderman, ataman, boss, cabeza, caboceer, captain, capitan(o), chief, commander, datto, executioner, foreman, hetman, induna, jarl, komarch, konohiki, leader, lowdah, luluai, malguzar, malik, mokaddam, patel, penghulu, pombo, princeps, starosta, teniente, top man, vidan

HEADMASTER archididascalos, gymnasiarch, principal, protomagister, rector, regent

HEADMOST before

HEADPIECE brains, casket, casque(t)(tel), casquette, chamfron, halter, helmet, lintel, pallet, tester, testiere, tremor, understanding

HEADQUARTERS base, capitol, center, exchange, fondaco, office, precinct, seat, yamen

HEADRAIL kerchief, veil

HEADROPE calk, baulk

HEADSHIP See AUTHORITY.
spiritual khalifat

HEADSTALL bradoon, bridoon, halter, jaquima

HEADSTONE memorial

HEADSTRONG bulldogged, bullheaded, bullish, cobby, contrary, contumacious, dogged, forthright, forward, froward, hotspur(red), intractable, obstinate, perverse, pigheaded, rackle, ramstam, rash, recalcitrant, refractory, selfwilled, stiffnecked, stubborn, stupid, temperamental, ungovernable, unruly, violent, wayward, willful

HEADWATER source, start, upriver

HEADWAY advance, impetus, momentum, motion, pace, progress, room, space, speed, velocity

HEADWEAR See CAP, HAT, HEADDRESS.

HEADY clever, exciting, huffcap, impetuous, intoxicating, precipitate, provocative, rash, reckless, shrewd, stimulating, violent, willful

HEAL amend, cicatrize, convalesce, cure, fix, get well, hale, leech, medicate, mend, pacify, physic, rally, reconcile, recover, remedy, repair, restore, sain, salve, set, skin over, soothe, temper, treat
-all clintonia, figwort, horsebalm, orchis, panacea, remedy
-bite alyssum
over incarn

HEALD camb, dupe, harness, havel, heddle

HEALER althea, asa, balm, balsam, binzuru, DOCTOR, medicine man, naturopath, peai, physician, piay, powwower, practitioner, quack (salver), shaman, witch doctor
name meaning asa, jason

HEALING assuasive, balsamic, comforting, curative, cure, iatric(al), remedial, restorative, sanation, sanative
agent application, balm, lenirobin, medicine, spa
art, pert. aesculapian, medical
-blade houseleek, plantain
divine theotherapy
god apollo, asclepius, belenus, beli, eshmo(u)n, osiris, paeon
goddess bau, damia, eir, gula, hyge(i)a, laso, minerva, salus
herb comfrey, plantain
pert. medical, medicinal
plant bonewort, daisy, goldenrod
science iatrology, medicine

HEALTH bloom, eucrasia, eudaemonia, euphoria, flush, gesundheit, pink, prime, salew, slainte, tone, tonicity, tonus, valetude, verdure, vigor, well-being
comb. sani
concerned about atrabiliar, atribilious, hypochondriac(al)
deity See HEALING *god, goddess.*
good plight, verdure
improver eutrophic
normal eucrasia
out of healless
pert. hygeian, hygienic, salutory
poor dyscrasia, illness, sickness
science of hygienics, prophylaxis
search hatha yoga
station hospital, rest home, sanatorium, sanitarium
symbol agate, pansy, pumpkin
to your bon sante, gesundheit, salute

HEALTHFUL beneficial, benign, hygienic, nutritious, prophylactic, salubrious, salutary, sanatory, sanitary, wholesome

HEALTHY beneficial, blooming, bobbish, bonny, bouncing, chipper, energetic, eudaemonic, euphoric, feirie, fine, fit, full of beans, good, grushie, hale, hearty, hoddy, hygienic, lusty, normal, pe(a)rt, robust, salubrious, salutary, sane, sanitary, sound, strapping, strong, stout, sturdy, tidy, vigorous, well, whole (some)
comb. sani

HEAP accumulate, aggregate, amass, anthill, assemble, auto, bale, bank, bing, bourock, bulk, cairn, car, clamp, clump, cob, cock, collect(ion), congeries, crowd, cumulus, class, dess, embankment, exaggerate, furnish, gather, gob(s), haycock, hipple, hoard, horde, hurrock, jumble, load(s), lump, mass, molehill, mow, multitude, pack, pile, plenty, poke, pyramid, quantity, raff, raft, rick(le), ruck(le), sess, shock, snowdrift, sorite, stack, throng, toorie, tooruck, tummels, tump, wopse
comb. cumulo
combustible pyre
confused bourock

growing in acervate
hay uncock
loose rickle
on bedub, lavish
pert. acerval
together aggest, cumulate, howder, lumber
up accumulate, acervate, amass, exaggerate, gather, hill, hoard, load, mass, pile, sack, save, store
HEAR adjudicate, apprehend, attend, audit, catch, ear, favor, get, hark(en), hearken, heed, hist, learn, list(en), lithe, obey, permit, regard, take in
comb. acou(o)
inability to asonia, deafness
to consent, heed, suffer, yield
ye oyes, oyez
HEARER audient, auditor, disciple, listener
HEARING airing, arbitration, assize(s), attention, audibility, audience, audition, auscultation, case, conference, earful, earshot, examination, heeding, inquest, interview, knowledge, lecture, listening, oyer, probe, range, rebuke, report, scholocation, scolding, trial, tryout
acute hyperacusis
aid acousticon, akoulalion, amplifier, audiphone, auriphone, auriscope, auscultator, dentiphone, ear trumpet, megaphone, otoscope, stethophone, stethoscope
comb. acou(o), acousi(a)(s), oto
court oyer, trial
defect asonia, deafness, diplacusis, hypocusis, otosis, paracusis, presbycusis, surdity
dullness baryecoia
false pseudacusis
judicial trail
measurer acoumeter, audiometer
name meaning simeon
pert. acoustic, audio, auditory, aural, auricular, auriculate, otic
science of audiology, auriscopy, otography, otology, otoplasty, otoscopy
HEARKEN attend, eavesdrop, inquire, HEAR, heed, list, search, tend, wait, whisper

HEARSAY account, bruit, buzz, circumstantial, comment, fame, gossip, on-dit, report, rumor, talk
HEARSE bier, bury, candelabrum, catafalco, coffin, dirge, entomb, grave, hack, monument, shillibeer, threnody, tomb
HEART, HEART'S affection, ardor, bosom, breast, center, cardia, cheer, coeur, compunction, conscience, cor(e), courage, cuore, depths, desire, disposition, emotion, enthusiasm, essence, feeling, focus, fortitude, gist, haslet, hati, hub, intent, interior, kernel, life, love, memory, middle, midst, mood, nerve, nucleus, passion, pith, pump, purpose, quick, raan, soul, spirit, substance, tachlis, temperament, ticker, vitals, wish
abnormality ectocardia, embrycardia, exocardia
aid pacemaker, pacer
and soul earnestly, hard, utterly
attack amour
-bird turnstone
bleeding dicentra, dogooder
-bound devoted
cavity or chamber atrium, auricle, camera, ventricle
cherry gaskins
close to dear, precious, loved
clover melilot
comb. cardi(a)(o), cardium
contraction systole
dear dilis
dilation diastole
disease acleistocardia, aneurysm, angina pectoris, arrhythmia, arteriosclerosis, cardialgia, cardiodynia, carditis, coarctation, coronary (infarct)(occlusion)(thrombosis), endocarditis, murmur, myocarditis, palpitation, pericarditis, stenosis
-ease butterfly-flower, gratiola, kiss-me-quick, lady's-thumb, pansy, peace, selfheal, tranquility, violet, wallflower, wild pansy
enlargement auxocardia
-eye parsnip
in hand readily, willingly
incision cardiotomy
inflammation (par)carditis
interest love

lack acardia
leaf asarum, medic
lower end apex
measurer (electro)cardiograph
medicine acetazolamide, amyl nitrate, cardiant, cardiazol, cardin, carpaine, digitalis, epinephrin, helleborin, quinidine, sparteine, thialdine
muscle myocardium
of palm cabbage-palmetto, carnauba
-of-the-earth selfheal
pain cardialgia, cardiodynia
pea balloon vine
pert. cardiac, cardial, pith
queen elizabeth, guimbarde
record ekg, (electro)cardiogram
recorder cardiograph
sac pericardium
-scald disappointment, heartburn, remorse, trouble
-shaped cardioid, cordate, cordiform, obcordate
sound murmur
specialist cardiologist
stimulant See HEART *medicine.*
study cardiology
suit churchmen
throb beloved, dunt, love(r), sweetheart
-to-heart candid, frank, sincere
trouble See HEART *disease.*
valve, pert. aortic, mitral
-warming gratifying, moving, rewarding, satisfying
-whole courageous, dauntless, fancy-free, sincere, undismayed
HEARTACHE anguish, dole, grief, misery, pang, regret, sadness, sorrow, trouble, woe
HEARTBEAT dunt, emotion, pulsation, pulse, stroke, systole, throb
interval peridiastole
irregular arrhythmia
premature extrasystole
rapid tachycardia
slow bradycardia
HEARTBREAK anguish, grief, misery, pain, sorrow, tragedy, trouble
HEARTBREAKER curl, flirt, lovelock, philanderer, tress
HEARTBREAKING affecting, moving, sorrowful, touching

HEARTBROKEN grief-stricken, inconsolable, overcome, sad

HEARTBURN brash, cardialgia, cardiodynia, discontent, enmity, envy, jealousy, pyrosis, sorrow

HEARTEN animate, buoy, cheer, comfort, embolden, encourage, inspire, inspirit, lift, reassure, refresh, stimulate, strengthen, uplift

HEARTFELT cordial, dear, deep, earnest, genuine, honest, profound, real, sincere, true, unfeigned

HEARTH astre, bloomery, brazier, chafery, chimney, corner, cupel, fender, fire (place), fireside, focus, fogon, foyer, grate, hob, home(stead), house, hub, ingle(nook)(side), residence
accessory andiron, bellows, crane, firedog, grate, gridiron, hob, poker, pothook, shovel, spit, tongs, trivet, turnspit
back reredos
goddess caca, hestia, vesta
gods lares, penates
hook slowrie
money feuage, fumage

HEARTHSTONE fireside, home

HEARTLESS apathetic, brutal, callous, cold, cruel, despairing, despondent, downcast, hard, harsh, hopeless, indifferent, insensitive, listless, merciless, obdurate, oppressive, pitiless, ruthless, sardonic, spiritless, sterile, tough, unfeeling, unkind, unsympathetic

HEARTQUAKE fear, tremor, trepidation

HEARTS blackjack, black lady, cards, churchmen, cirulo, coeur, copas, corazones cups, game, herz, liftsmoke, linger-long, oh pshaw, omnibus, polignac, quatre valets, reverse, rot(h), scotch whist, slobberhannes, smoke out, sorrel, suit
term howell, paint, settlement, sweepstake, take-all

HEARTSICK desolate, despondent, grieved, sore, sorrowful

HEARTSOME animating, cheerful, lively, merry, spirited

HEARTSORE See HEARTSICK.

HEARTWATER blue-tongue, fever
transmitter bont-tick

HEARTWOOD alburnum, brazilette, bubinga, catechu, duramen, guayab, notelaea, sapan, spine, truewood

HEARTY active, ardent, bobbish, bouncing, cant, cobby, comrade, convivial, cordial, deep, devout, earnest, energetic, entire, exuberant, fertile, firm, friendly, glowing, hale, healthy, heavy, lusty, mariner, nourishing, profound, profuse, real, responsive, rich, robust, sailor, sincere, sound, staunch, strong, substantial, unfeigned, vigorous, warm, well, zealous

HEAT achafe, activity, agitation, anger, anneal, ardor, bake, bask, bout, broil, burn(ing), calcine, calor(ic)(ify), condescence, cauma, chafe, cook, degree, effort, enthusiasm, exasperation, excite(ment), ferment, fervency, fervor, fever, fire, flush, foment, grill, hell, ignite, inferno, lap, list, mull, parch, passion, pressure, rage, roast, rut, scald, scorch, spark, steam, stech, strain, temperature, tepefy, tepor, toast, torrefy, trial, warm(th), zeal
comb. calori, therm(o)(y)
detector pyrostat
diffusion radiation
disease calenture, coup de soleil, insolation, siriasis, sunstroke, thermic fever
dispersion thermolysis
-drops rain, sweat, tears
emit glow, radiate
extreme ewder
fear of thermophobia
gentle calor, tepor, warmth
imperviousness adiathermancy
increase incalescence
loss deferescence
measure btu, calorie, calory, centigrade, fahrenheit, therm(e)
measurer calorimeter, pyron-

ometer, pyroscope, thermometer
pert. caloric, calorific, canicular, thermal, thermic, thermotic(al)
prickly rash
-producing calorifacient, calorific, calorigenic, thermogenic
product pyrogen
production pyrogenesis
regulator thermostat
resistant amosite, anthophyllite, transcalent
resistant animal salamander
science calorifics, calorimetry, pyrology, pyrotechnics, thermatology, thermodynamics, thermology, thermostatics, volcanology
-spot freckle
total enthalpy
transfer, pert. metabatic
treatment diathermy
wave dogdays
white candency, incandescence

HEATED burning, candent, fierce, fiery, flushed, het(up), HOT, passionate, rechauffee, recooked, steamy, torrid, warm, warmed-over

HEATER bloomery, boiler, brasier, brazier, (bunsen)burner, calefactor, cigar, cooker, etna, firebox, fireplace, forge, furnace, heat lamp, kiln, oil burner, oven, radiator, range, register, sinterer, stove, sun lamp, tewel, tisar, tuyere

HEATH andromeda, arbutus, azalea, bent, besom, briar, broom, calluna, commons, crowberry, erica, grig, ling, moor(s), pieris, plain(s), polycodium, poverty-plant, savin, shrub, sparrowwort, tamarisk, thicket, wasteland, yeth
bird grouse
box scentwood
bramble dewberry
cypress club moss
inhabiting ericaticolous
-like ericoid
moss cladonia, lichen
native homeland
pea carmele
pert. ericetal
plant erica, ericophyte, mayflower
scrub chaparral

tree briar, brier
HEATHEN agnostic, atheist, ethnic, gentile, godless, idolator, infidel, irreligious, pagan, paynim, profane
deity idol
HEATHER besom, broom, calluna, crowberry, crowling, erica, grig, hadder, ling, plant
area moor(s)
covered with lingy
HEATING burning, calcinatory, calefacient, calefaction, calefactory, caloric, cauterant, cauterizing, chafing, cooking, tepefaction, torrefaction, warming
control thermostat
device burner, radiator, stove
element coils
vessel etna, pan, pot, retort
HEATLESS athermic
HEAVE billow, boost, cast, displace, elevate, exalt, fetch, fling, haul, hoist, hurl, inflate, keck, labor, lift, pant, pitch, puff up, pull, push, raise, rear, recoil, remove, retch, rise, scend, send, spew, struggle, swell, thrill, throw, toss, vomit, wave
down careen
-ho boot, dismissal, ouster
out expel, throw out, unfurl
round tack
the hook anchor, moor
upward scend
HEAVEN(S) aalu, aaru, abraham's bosom, arcadia, asgard, azure, bliss, canaan, canopy, ciel, devaloka, dyaus, ecstasy, eden, elysium, empyrean, ether, fate, firmament, happy hunting ground, himmel, holy city, hyaline, ialu, jenna, jodo, joy, kamaloka, kapiolami, langi, nirvana, paradise, sion, skies, sky, sphere, svarge, svarloka, swarga, uranus, utopia, valhalla, welkin, yaru, zion
-born coeligenous
buddhist See BUDDHIST heaven.
capital amaravati
comb. urano
deity See SKY god, goddess.
description uranography
diagram horoscope
empress tien hou

entrance pearly gates
from supernal
giant invader adamastor
highest empyrean
imaginary zone zodiac
inhabitant afa, angel, celestial, cherub(im), god, goddess, olympian, seraph(im)
instrument harp
mythological asgard, elysium, happy isles, olympus, valhalla
personified anu, nut, uranus
pert. celestial, empyreal, empyrean, orrery, uranian, uranic
queen astarte, belisarna, diana, hecate, hera, isis, mary, moon, sati, trivia
remove to translate
student of uranographist
study uranology
tree ailanthus
way to jacob's ladder
worshipper coelicolist
HEAVENLY angelic, beatific, blessed, celestial, celestine, delightful, divine, edemic, elysian, empyreal, empyrean, ethereal, extramundane, glorious, gorgeous, holy, lovely, olympian, otherworldly, paradisaic(al), sacred, seraphic, sublime, supernal, transcendental, unearthly, unworldly, uranian, uranic
being See HEAVEN inhabitant.
belt galaxy, milky way, nebula, zodiac
body asteroid, comet, luminary, luna, meteor, moon, planet, star, sun
body measurer aba, altazimuth
city new jerusalem, utopia, zion
host angels
name meaning celestine, celia, juno, olympia, sile
object quasar
path orbit
twins castor, gemini, pollux
HEAVER coaly, danner, heftor, lever, stevedore
HEAVES emphysema
HEAVILY cloit, clyte, dully, forcible, grievously, laboriously, sadly, severely, slowly, sorrowfully, soss, souse, swack
HEAVINESS gravity, heft, obesity, oppression,

sadness, sluggishness, thickness, weight
HEAVY actor, afflictive, beefy, big, burden(some), burly, clayey, cloggy, close, complicated, cumbersome, cumbrous, deep, dense, depressing, distressing, doleful, dowf, drowsy, dull, fat, firm, fleshy, gloomy, grave, great, grievous, hard, hearty, hefty, hoggy, idle, inactive, inert, languid, large, leaden, lethargic, lifeless, listless, loud, lumping, massive, massy, obese, obtuse, onerous, oppressive, ponderous, profound, sad, serious, sleepy, slow, sluggish, solid, steep, stout, strong, stuffy, stupid, substantial, sullen, tharf, thick, troublesome, unleavened, villain, violent, viscid, weighty
as lead
-back cassis, queen conch
comb. bary, gravi
-duty durable, strong, tough
earth baryta
-eyed drowsy, sleepy
-footed inficete, leaden, soggy
hand despotism, discipline
-handed awkward, clumsy, oppressive
-headed drowsy, dull, stupid
-hearted despondent, melancholy, sad
-laden burdened, fraught, harassed, oppressed, weighted down
-set fat, fleshy, horsey, obese, thick
-weight boxer, important, personage, ponderous, somebody, superior, vip, wrestler
-wet ale
HEBDOMAD seven, week
HEBDOMADARY weekly
HEBE asteroid, cherry blossom, juventas
consort ganymede, hercules
parent hera, zeus
son alexiares
HEBER *offspring* hotham, japhlet, shomer, shua(h)
wife jael
HEBETATE blunt, dull, obtuse, stupid
HEBETUDE dullness, languor, stupidity
HEBREW (See also BIBLICAL, ISRAEL.) ammonite,

edomite, hebraic(al), hebraist(ic), israelite, jew (ish), judaic(al), judaist, karaite, moabite, pharisee, rabbinic, rabbinist, sadducee, semite, talmudist, zionist
abode of the dead sheol
academy head gaon
acrostic agla
agnostic apiroros, epicoris
air god ruchiel
alien ger, goy
allies habiri
alphabet aleph, ayin, beth, caph, cheth, daleth, gimel, kaph, koph, kuf, lamed(h), mem, nun, pay, peh, resh, sade, sadhe, samekh, s(h)in, taf, tav, teth, vau, vav, yodo, youd, zayin
anagrammatic system atbash
ancestor eber, jacob
anecdotal history elohist
anecdote haggada(h)
angel abdiel, chutriel, dalkiel, gabriel, labatiel, maccathiel, metatron, pasiel, sandalphon, shaftiel
apostate meshumad
archer ahiezer
army, underground haganah
ascetic essene
assembly sanhedrin, synedrion
atonement kapora, kaporeh
automaton golem
avenger goel
bachelor bahur
bath, purifying mikvah
belt zonar
benediction berakah, mizpah, motzi, shema
betrothal kiddushin
bible torah
bible analysis midrash
bible books nebiim
bible prophets haftarah, haftorah
bible reading aid gri, kere, keri, kri, qere, q(u)eri
bible text mikra, miqra
black falasha
blessed gebentsht(eh)(er)
blessing ben(t)sh, broche, dukan, kiddush, motzi, shema
body vaad
book haggada, talmud, tehillim, zohar
bread challa, challeh, hallah, lechem, matzah, matzo(h)
bride kallah
brotherhood essene

bushel emer, epha(h), omer
busybody yente
butcher shochtim, shohet
cabalistic book zohar
cake hallah, hamantas(c)h
calendar (months) 1) ehanim, tishri, 2) bul, heshvan, 3) kislev, 4) tebet(h), 5) shelbat, 6) adar, veadar, 7) abib, nisan, 8) iyar, zif, 9) sivan, 10) tammuz, 11) ab, 12) elul
calf's-foot jelly fisnoga
candelabrum menorah
canonical book talmud
canopy huppah
cantor hazan
cantor's garment kittel
cap mitre, yarmulka, yarmulke
central european ashkenazim
ceremony atonement, (bar) (bas)(bath) mitzva(h), chan(n)ukah, habdala(h), havdala, hanuka(h), kiddush(in), lag-bomer, maarev, mairev, marriv, mincha, minhah, moed, neilah, nusaf, passover, pentecost, pesach, purim, rosh hashona, rosh hoshanah, sedar, seder, sefirah, shabuot(h), sharith, shevuoth, shimath, shivah, simhath torah, succah, succoth, sukkah, sukkoth, tisha-bov, torah, yom kippur, yomtob, yomtov
chariot of fiction golem
circumciser mohel, sandak
citron esrog, et(h)rog
city, holy jerusalem
clean kosher
cloak gabardine, kittel
coat kapote
coin agora, agura, gerah, mil, mite, pruta(h), shekel
collective kibbutz(im)
commandment mitzva(h)
commentary biur
commentator jacob ben asher
communist settlement kevutzah
community aljama, kehillah
community scribe sofer
compassion rachmones
compatriot landsman
confection alhet, halava(h), halvah
confession alhet, ashamnu, yom kippur
confessional poem viddui, vidduy
congratulations mazel tov

congregation aljam, kolel, synagog
congregation official parnas
container mezuzah
conventional pharisee
cooperative kibbutz(im)
cord gartel
council, supreme sanhedrin
court besdin, bet(h)din, sanhedrin
cryptograph gematria
curse choleria
day yom
day of atonement yom kippur
death anniversary yahrzeit
decoration, religious mizrah
dedication, feast of chanukah
deed, good mitzva(h)
demon asmodeus, dybbuk(im), golem
deportation transmigration
descendent chueta
devil belial, teivel, teufel, teuvel
dialect ladino
dinner cholent
dirge kinah
dish babka, cholent, knish, kugel, lox, schav
dispersion diaspora, galus, galut, golah
divine revelation bathkol
divorce bill get(t)
doctrine anamism, karaism, kodashim, mishna(h), shekinah
dowry nadan
drum toph
dumpling knaydl, knish, kreplach, kreplech
education haskalah, maskilin
effrontery chutzpa
eternity olam
ethical principles aboth
evening ereb
exclamation ai-ai-ai, alevai, canary, choleria, chalileh, feh, gevald, gottenyu, mazel tov, mechuleh, nebbech, neb(b)ish, noo-noo, nu-nu, oy-oy-oy, shalom, sholem(aleichem), sholom
excommunication cherem, herem
exile babylonian captivity, diaspora, galus, galut
family mishpochah
fast day asarah, betevet
father abba, abraham, eber
feast or festival See HEBREW ceremony.
flute nehiloth

folklore agada, haggadah
folklore figure golem
food, forbidden hametz, terefa
food inspector mashgiah, shomer
founder abra(ha)m
garment arba-kanfoth, shawl, talis, tallith(katan), tzizi
general abner, barac, barak, joshua
gift-giving shalach-monoth
god adonai, adoshem, adrammelech, baal, bore olam, eloha(i), elohim, en sof, ha-makon, hashem, ihvh, jah(vah)(ve), jehovah, jhvh, jhwh, kedosh, kiddush-hashem, melech-hamlochim, ruchiel, schehinah, sephira(h), shaddai, yah, yahve(h), yahweh, yhvh, yhwh
gods, household teraphim
good deed mitzvah
governor nehemiah
greeting shalom(aleichem), sholem, sholom
group kabbala
halting place marah
harp guimard, nabla, nebel
headdress bashlyk
head of rosh
healer asa
hell abaddon, gehen(n)a, sheol
hercules samson
herdsman amos
heretic doctrine karaism
heroine judith
high priest aaron, ananias, caiaphas, eli, ezra, henaniah
historian josephus
holiday See HEBREW ceremony.
homeland eretz(israel) (visrael), palestine
home service seder
homey heimish
horn shofar, shophar
household gods teraphim
hymn adon-olam, yigdal
immigrant (c)halutz, oleh
infinity adolam
instrument asor, nebel, timbrel
instrument player psalterer, psaltress
insurrectionist bar coch(e)ba, bar kokba
judge abdon, dayan(im), dayen, dayyan, deborah, eli, samson, shophet(in)
juniper exel

king achab, agag, ahab, ahaziah, baasha, david, elah, herod, hosea, hosher, ishbosheth, jehoahaz, jehoash, jehoram, jehoshaphat, jehu, jeroboam, joash, josiah, menahem, nadab, ochozias, omri, pekah(iah), rehoboam, remaliah, saul, shallum, solomon, zachariah, zimri
king, expected messiah
lament elieli
land zion
land of plenty goshen
language yiddish
last stand symbol masada
law chok, chukah, halacha, halakah, kashruth, mitzvot, talmud, torah
lawbook shulhan-aruk
lawbreaker achan
lawbreaking averah
law expert dagan
law giver moses
law, oral cabala, mishna
lax apikoros
leader ahiezer, caleb, gideon, moses, nehemiah
learned man kaham, hakim
lesson haftorah, haphtarah
liturgical poems azaroth, selihoth
liturgical prayer amidah
liturgy maarib, minhag, minhah, shaharith
lots, feast of purim
luck mazel
lyre asor
magistrate alabarch
man bahur, hakam, neshamah, neshoma, neshuma, rab
man of sin devil
marginal note gri, kere, kri, qere, q(u)eri
marriage broker schatchen, shadchan(im)
marriage canopy huppah
marriage contract ketuba, k'tubot
marriage law levirate
marriage terms tenaim
matzo piece afikomen
meadow abel
measure bath, bit, cab, caph, chomer, choros, cor, cubit, digit, epa(h), ephah, ezba, handbreadth, hin, homer, kab, kaneh, kor, letech, log, omer, reed, seah, sher, zareth
meat approval hechsher(im), heksher

meat, forbidden terepha, tref
meat inspector bedikah
melodies chazanut, hazanuth
messiah, false akiba, alroy, bar kockba, benjamin, eldad, hasid, lammlein, menachem, mokhliah, molko, moses of crete, nissim, prossnitz, reuben, reuveni, serene, severus, solomon molko, theudas
mister reb
miter petalon
money talent
monster golem
month See HEBREW calendar.
moses, books of teitch-chumesh
mourning lag b'omer, shibah, shivah
movement haskalah, zionism
musician david, psalterer, psaltress
mysticism cabala, cabbala(h), kabbalah
nation israel(i), jewish autonomous region, judah, judea, khazar(ia)
new year rosh hashanah
next of kin goel
nomads habiri, habiru
non gentile, goi, goy(im)
non-believer apikoros
noodles farfel
not kosher t(e)refah, tref
novelist asch
numerology gematria
offering corban
official gabbai(m)
ok beseder
oppression mizraim
ordeal diaspora, pogrom
order bnai-brith, ito, essene, hadassah
orthodox agudist
palm branch lulab
pancake blintz(e)
parchment mezuza(h)
passover abib, nisan, pasch, pesach, seder
passover story agada, haggadah
patriarch abra(ha)m, david, enoch, isaac, israel, jacob, methuselah, nasi, shem
patriot family maccabee
penitence days yom kippur
pentateuch humash
pentecost shabuot, shevuoth
people israelite, magog, s(h)emite, zion
people in india beni-israel
philosopher avicebron, beth

hillel, buber, criscas, maimonides

phylacteries tefillin, tephillin

pious man chasid(im), hasid(im), hassid(ic)(im), zaddik

pity rachmones

poem azharoth, yigdal

poet avicebron, bialik

pointer yad

potato pie knish

pray daven

prayer abinu, abodah, adon, ahabatholam, alenu, amidah, broche, geullah, hallel, hoshana, kaddish, kedushah, kiddush, kol nidre, mairev, minchah, shachris, shema, shemona esray, yigdal

prayer book mahzor, siddur

prayer shawl tallis, tallit, tallith

prayer straps t(e)fillin

preacher darshan(im), maggid

precept sutra, tora(h)

priest abiathor, a(c)himelech, cohen, eli, ezra, kohen, mattathias, rabbi

priest's assistant levite

priest's caste cohanim, levites

priest's mark thummim, urim

priest's robe ephod

priest's scarf abnet

priest's stone sardius

prophet See PROPHET *famous.*

proselyte ger

proverb mashal

psalms hallel, tehillim

punishment herem

quarter mellah

quorum minyan

rabbi's wife rebbetsen, rebbetzin

ram's horn shofar, shophar

reading baftarah, kri, miqra

reclaimer goel

reincarnation gilgul

relief fund halukkah

religious center shechem

religious law halakha

religious revelation torah

religious service selihoth

religious song zemiroth

revolt masada

revolt chief eleasar ban yair

rite tashlich

ritual tefillin

ritual bath mikvah, mikveh

ritual slaughter shehitah

river, mythological sambation

robe ephod, kittel

robot golem

roll bagel, bialy

roman foe silva, titus

ruler exilarch

sabbath saturday, shabbat

sabbath food cholent, gefilte fish, knaydel, kugel, matzo

sacrament shewbread

sacred book cab(b)ala, haggadah, talmud, torah, zohar

sacred chest ark

sacred objects urim

sacred wrtings hagiographa, ketubim

sacrifice corban

sacrifice laws kashruth

saintly men baal shem

sanctuary bamah

scarf abnet

scholar akiba, amora, gaon, rab, sabora, tanna

scholars, group sabora

school aljamah, (c)heder, schul, yeshibah, yeshiva(h)

scribe ezra, sofer

scribes sopherim

scriptural exegesis midrash(im), midrashoth

scripture bible, gemara, masora(h), mishna(h), torah

scripture box tefillin

scroll megillah, megilloth, sepher-torah

scroll wrapping gelilah

secret marrano

sect assid(a)ean, boethusian, donmeh, dunmeh, essene, haddis, hasid(a)ean, hasidim, mitnagged, mizrachi

seder food haroseth

seder herb maror

seminary See HEBREW *school.*

senate sanhedrin

service selihoth

service for dead yizkor

service part aliyah

settlement kevatzah, yishub

shawl abnet, talithim, tallis, tallit

singer cantor

site, ancient gilgal

skullcap yamilke, yarmulka(h), yarmulke

son ben, kaddishel

song eli-eli, hatikvah, shira, zemiroth

soul meshamah, neshoma, neshuma

soup schav

spirit asmodeus

spirit, evil dibbuk, dybbuk

splendor, book of zohar

spy caleb

strong man samson

student bahur

sun god baal

sweet halvah

symbol star of david

synagogue bes-midrash, beth-hamidrash, beth-midrash, schul

synagogue picture mizrach(i)

tabernacle feast succoth

talmud parts gemara, mishnah

talmud scholar chachem

teacher hillel, melamed, rab, rabban, rabbi, reb(be), rov

temple precentor cantor

temple treasury corban

texts masorah, mechilta, megilloth, mekilta

thanksgiving feast succah, succoth

thief ganof, gonof, gonoph

title abba, adoni, gaon, rab(bi), reb

toast lechayim, lehayim

tribe asher(ite), benjamin, caleb(ite), dan, ephraim, gad, issacher, joseph, judah, levi, manasseh, naphtali, nephtali, reuben, simeon, zebulan

trumpet shofar

unconventional sadducee

universe olam

vestment breastplate, ephod

village shtetl

vowel point tsere

warrior ehud

wedding chasseneh, khasseneh

weekly reading sedra

weight bekah, gerah, manett, shekel, talent

wilderness sojourn provocation

wisdom chachma, hachma, khaukhma

wise man chacham, chachem, kaham

worm, mythological shamir

writer ginzburg, josephus, maimonides, yahwist

young man bahur

zealot sicarious

zionist organization hadassah

HEBRIDES *breeze* caver

island barra, harris, iona, islay, jura, lewis, mull, rum, scarba, skye, staffa, uist, uisy

oyster catcher trillachan
vessel birlinn, craggan
HEBRON *father* levi
king hoham
son amariah, jahaziel, jekameam, jeriah, korah, rekem, shema, tappuah
valley eshcol
HECABE See HECUBA.
HECALEIUS See ZEUS.
HECATE artemis, brimo, demeter, diana, luna, moon, perseis, persephone, phoebe, prosperpine, prytania, selene, tergimina, triceps, triformis, trivia
beloved hermes
consort phorcys
offspring circe, medea
parent asteria, hera, perses, zeus
vampire empusa
HECATONCHEIRES aegaeon, briareus, cenitimani, centimanes, cottus, gyges
brother deiphobus
parent gaea, uranus
HECK cough, dickens, frame, grating, haw, hayrack, manger, oath, rack
HECKHOW hemlock
HECKLE badger, bait, bother, gibe, hack, harass, hatchel, hector
HECKLEPHONE oboe
HECTIC constitutional, consumptive, excited, febrile, feverish, frenetic, frenzied, habitual, heated, hot, passionate, pyretic, restless, warm
HECTOR bait, badger, bluster, bother, braggart, bravado, browbeat, bully, gall, harass, harry, HECKLE, intimidate, irk, molest, nag, pester, plague, roisterer, swagger, tantalize, TEASE, threaten, torment, worry
charioteer archeptolemus, cebriones, eniopeus
companion diomedes
cousin caletor
enemy patroclus
friend polydamas
horse ethon, galathe, podarge
parent hecuba, priam
rescuer agenor
slayer achilles
son astyanax, scamandrius
sword durandana
victim amphimacus, iycophron, patroclus, stichius

wife andromache
HECUBA maera
father cisseus, dymas
husband priam
offspring cassandra, deiphobus, hector, helenus, laodice, paris, polydorus, polyxena, troilus
victim polymnestor
HEDDLE(S) caam, camb, cord, guide, harness, havel, heald, wire
leaf gear
HEDGE adjust, balance, barrier, bleo, boma, border, boundary, bullfinch, clandestine, dodge, edder, encircle, enclose, evade, fence, frith, girdle, guard, haw, hay, hem, hinder, hye, limit, low, obstacle, obstruct(ion), oxer, plant, privet, protect, pull back, raddle, reneg, renig, rew, ring, row, quibble, sepiment, siege, shrub, surround, temporize, thicket, weir
berry bird-cherry
-betty sparrow
binder edder
bindweed convolvulus, creeper, hellweed, woodbine
gap meuse, muse(t), musit
-garlic alliaria, mustard, treacle
hole smeuse
jug titmouse
laurel pittosporum, tarata
-mike sparrow
mustard bank(cress)(weed), barbarea, flix, fluxweed
nettle clownheal, stachys
parsley ben-chervil, herb, hogweed, torilis
pink soapwort
priest patrico
sparrow chanter, cuddy, dick(e)y, doney, dunnock, eysoge, haysuck, philip, pinnock, prunella, titling, warbler
-trimmer gardener, plasher, tacker
vine virgin's-bower
wood layer
HEDGEHOG bucket, dredger, echinus, ericius, gymnura, herisson, hurcheon, lenrec, mammal, orchen, plant, pod, porcupine, pudding, urchin, ylespil
coneflower black sampson
grass sedge

shell murex
HEDGEHOGGY repellent, spiny
HEDGEROW rew
HEDGESMITH tinker
HEDGETAPER mullein
HEDONIST aristippus, cyreniac, epicure(an), sensualist, sybarite
HEDONISTIC apolaustic, pleasure-loving
way of life primrose path
HEEBIE-JEEBIES creeps, jitters, shakes, willies
HEED animadvert, attend, attention, care, cark, caution, consider, drink in, follow, gaum, glom, hang on, lisen, look, mark, mind, note, notice, obey, observation, observe, pay attention, reck, regard, respect, tend, tent, value, vise, ware, yeme
HEEDFUL attentive, careful, cautious, circumspect, considerate, intent, mindful, observant, vigilant, wary, watchful
HEEDLESS blind(fold), blithe, careless, disregardful, distracted, distrait, distraught, dizzy, flippant, forgetful, giddy, impetuous, improvident, impulsive, inadvertent, inattentive, incautious, inconsiderate, indifferent, lax, mad, mindless, neglectful, negligent, precipitate, rash, reckless, regardless, remiss, slack, thoughtless, unmindful, unobserving, unwary, volatile
HEEDLESSLY blindly, headlong
HEEL(S) aft, back, bounder, butt, cad, calcaneum, calkin, calyx, cant, careen, conclusion, crust, deviate, dottle, end, equip, follow, incline, knob, lean, list, obey, pivot, rear, remnant, reprobate, scoundrel, shadow, slant, slope, spur, stern, supply, tag, talon, tilt, tip
bevel rand
bone calcaneum, calcaneus, calcis, fibula(r)
bring to tame
comb. calcaneo
down at frowsy, seedy, shabby, slipshod, sloppy, slovenly
in cover, shough

kick up one's frolic, gambol
kind cuban, french, louis,
  military, spanish, spike
over capsize, careen, seel, tilt
pain talagia
path bank, berm
pert. calcaneal
plate cleat, shod
rim calker
-splitter mussel, proptera
strip rand
take to one's flee
HEELER follower, hanger-
  on, henchman, runner, satellite
HEELTAP dregs, lift, remainder, sediment
HEELTAPPER schooner
HEFT bulk, distend, exertion,
  fasciculus, haft, handle,
  heave, influence, lift, raise,
  strain, weigh(t)
HEFTY beefy, big, burly,
  cumbrous, heavy, husky,
  ponderous, rough, strapping, strong, troublesome,
  vehement, vigorous, violent,
  weighty
HEGEMONIC controlling,
  dominant, leading, predominant, ruling
HEGEMONY authority,
  influence, leadership, mastery
HEGETORIA *son* ochimus
HEGIRA departure, exodus,
  flight
HEIDI *canton* grisons
  creator spyri
  friend peter the goatherd
  original adelheid
  town cuscha, dorfli, maien-
  feld, unter-rofels
HEIFER calf, cow, girl, quee,
  quey, qui, quoy, stirk, terrapin, woman
  young burling, colpindach,
  stocker
HEIGHT acme, acropolis, alt-
  (itude), apex, apogee, ceiling, celsitude, citadel, climax, crest, crown, elevation, eminence, fort, hait,
  hautesse, heat, heyday, hill,
  lift, loftiness, peak, pinnacle, pitch, procerity, rank,
  rise, stature, sublimity,
  summit, supreme, tip, top,
  tower, vertex, vertical, zenith
  comb. acro, aero, alt, batho,
  hypso
  fear of acrophobia, batho-
  phobia

measurement altimetry, hyp-
  sography, hypsometry
measurer altimeter, cath-
  etometer, hypsometer, kathe-
  tometer, yardstick
symbol everest
HEIGHTEN accent, advance,
  aggravate, augment, better,
  bolster, elate, elevate,
  endow, enhance, exaggerate, exalt, hoist, improve,
  increase, intensify, lift,
  magnify, raise, rear, tower,
  upraise, uprear
HEIMDALL *guardian of* bifrost
  home asgard
  slayer and victim loki
HEIMWEH homesickness,
  nostalgia
HEINOUS abominable, accursed, atrocious, base, crying, evil, flagitious, flagrant,
  grievous, gross, hateful, infamous, malicious, mon-
  strous, odious, offensive,
  outrageous, rank, swart,
  terrible, wicked
HEIR beneficiary, cion, coparcener, haeres, hear,
  heres, heritor, inheritor,
  legatee, parcener, posterity,
  remainderman, reversioner,
  scion, son, teind
  accept as adiate
  apparent crown prince,
  prince-regent
  comb. heredo
HEIRLOOM antique, birthright, cimelia, keepsake
HEIST burglary, increase,
  lift, pinch, rob(bery), steal,
  theft
HEJAZ *holy city* mecca, medina
HEJIRA *flight of* mohammed
HEL(A) *bed* kor
  brother fenrir, fenris
  dish hungr
  dog garm
  dwelling elvidna, niflheim,
  niflhel
  kingdom helheim
  knife sullt
  parent angerboda, angerbotha, angrbodha, loki,
  sigyn
  river gjoll
HELD anchored, captive,
  gripped, stuck, tenuto, yield
  up delayed, detained,
  robbed, slow
HELE *father* athamas
HELEKIA *father* ahax

HELEN *abductor* paris,
  pirithous, theseus
  ancestor lacedaemon
  attendant clymene, phylo
  brother dioscuri, castor, pollux
  brother-in-law agamemnon
  caused trojan war
  consort deiphobus, menelaus, paris, theseus
  executioner polyxo
  half-sister clytemnestra
  offspring aganus, dorus, euphorion, hermione, nicostratus
  parent leda, tyndareus, zeus
  relative aileen
  slave aethra
  suitor ajax, leonteus, thoas
HELENA *beloved* demetrius
  son constantine
HELENOR *companion*
  aeneas
  kingdom lydia
HELENUS *brother* hector
  guest aeneas
  parent hecuba, priam
  son cestrinus
  wife andromache
HELGA *husband* hagar the
  horrible
HELI *son* joseph
HELIADAE aetheria, clymene
  brother phaethon
  changed into poplar trees
  parent clymene, helios,
  rhode
HELICAL cochleate, solar,
  spiral, spiry, torse, winding
HELICAON *parent* antenor,
  theano
  wife laodice
HELICE *lover* zeus
  parent lycaon
  son arcas
HELICON poetry, tuba
  fountain aganippe, hippocrene
  resident apollo, muses
HELICOPTER autogiro,
  chopper, duster, dust-off,
  eggbeater, giroscope, gyrodine, gyroplane, puddle-
  jumper, rotocraft, rotor,
  whirlybird, windmill
  landing place helipad, heliport
  part blade, gyro, rotor, vane
HELIOPOLIS matariya
HELIOS, HELIUS apollo,
  hyperion, phaethon, sol,
  sun
  consort anaxibia, clymene,

clytie, creta, gaea, iphiboe, iphinoe, leucothea, naupia-dame, neaera, perse, rhoda, rhode

grandson camirus

kingdom colchis

offspring achelous, actis, aeetes, altheria, augeias, circe, electryone, heliad(e)s, heliadae, lampetia, ochimus, pasiphae, perses, phaethon, phaetusa, tenagis

parent hyperion, thea, theia, thia

sacred isle thrinicia

sister artemis, eos, selene

statue colossus of rhodes

winged horses See HORSE winged.

HELIOSIS sunburn, sunstroke

HELIOTROPE bennet, bloodstone, chalcedony, girasol(e), hematite, marigold, setwall, sunflower, turnsole, valerian

changed into clytie

HELIX coil, curve, snail, spiral, volute

simple unispiral

HELKIAS *parent* elias

son oziel

HELL abandon, abyss, acheron, afterworld, allatu, amenthes, amenti, anguish, aralu, avernus, avic(h)i, barathron, barathrum, below, blazes, caina, cuthah, deuce, dungeon, fire(and brimstone), gehenna, gethsemane, HADES, heat, hereafter, hole, inferno, jahannan, jail, jigoku, limbo, misery, naraka, nastrond, netherworld, nif(e)lheim, niflhel, orcus, pain, pandemonium, perdition, pit, prison, purgatory, sheol, solitaire, tartar(us), tophet(h), torment, trouble, tunket, underworld, war, xibalba

around play, rampage

-bender debauch, salamander, spree, toot, tweeg

-bent dead set, determined, reckless, swift

-bind dodder

bridge al sirat

capital pandemonium

cat daredevil, devil, hag, shrew, vixen, witch

circle of malebolge

descend into harrow

-diver dabchick, grebe

-fire punishment, resentment, spite

gate keeper death, sin

god, goddess See UNDER-WORLD *god, goddess.*

grand-duke abigor

green alabama, jungle

-hound demon, fiend, monster

raise celebrate, object, rage, roar

river styx

HELLAS See GREECE.

HELLE *brother* phrixos, phrixus

parent athamas, nephele

stepmother ino

HELLEBORE arethusa, bear's-foot, bugbane, christmas rose, earthgall, herb, itchweed, lady's-mantle, lingwort, lousewort, lungwort, nosewort, poke(root), sanicle, serap, shortia, veratrum

HELLEN *descendants* hellenes

kingdom phthia, thessaly

parent deucalion, pyrrha

son aeolus, dorus, xuthus

wife orseis

HELLENE, HELLENIC See GREECE, GREEK.

HELLENISTIC alexandrian, archaic, grecian, greek

HELLERI swordtail

HELLESPONT dardenelles

city on abydos

swimmer leander

HELLGRAMMITE clipper, crawler, dobson, sialid, sprawler

HELLION demon, devil

HELLISH acherontic, avernal, chthonian, cruel, demoniac(al), demonic, devilish, diabolic(al), execrable, fiendish, ghoulish, infernal, inhuman, lethean, pandemoni(a)c, plutonian, plutonic, satanic, stygian, styxian, sulfurous, tartarean

HELLO addio, allo, alo nola zera, aloha, bonjour, buon giorno, buona sera, cheerio, dboryden, evviva, gutentag, hola, kaselehlia, ni hao, pronto, shalom, wie gehts

HELLROOT broomrape

HELM conn, control, direct (ion), lead, pilot, reins, rudder, rule, saddle, starn,

steer(age), tiller, timon, wheel

position alee, aport

HELMET armet, aventail, barbel, barbut(e), bas(c) inet, bas(si)net, bourrelet, burgonet, burlet, cabasset, cap, casket, casquet, chapeldefer, crest, elme, galea, galerum, hat, headpiece, heaume, mask, mazer, morion, pallet, salade, sallet, schapska, skullcap, tarnhelm, testiere, topee, topi, turban

bird touraco, turacus

chinpiece barbel

cockatoo ganggang

cover lambrequin

crest comb, hummingbird, oxypogon

fabric kevlar

flower aconite, monkshood, orchid, skullcap

front aventail, aventayle, ventail

hinge charnel

light sallet

open burgonet, chapel de fer

ornament cimier, crest

part aventail, aventayle, barbel, beaver, bell, coif, crest, mesail, mezail, nasal, ventail, visor, vizor, vue

perforation ocularium, oculatus

pert. cassideous, galeate, galeiform

pith topee, topi

plume panache

quail partridge

-shaped cassideous, galeate, galeiform

shell cameo conch, cassis, mollusk, queen conch

visored bas(c)inet, bas(si) net

HELMINTHIC prophylactic, vermifuge

HELMSMAN captain, cond, conn(er), cox(on), coxswain, crewman, guide, leader, operator, pilot, quartermaster, steersman, tiller, timoneer

HELOISE *lover* abelard

HELOMA clavus, corn

HELOT bondsman, esne, peasant, serf, servant, slave, thrall, vassal

master spartan

HELOTARSUS bataleur, berghaan, eagle

HELOTRY bondage, serfdom, slavery

HELP abet, accommodate, adminicle, advance, aid(e), alleviate, assist(ance), assistant, auxiliate, avail, avoid, back, befriend, benefit, beset, bestead, better, boot, bot(e), cast, champion, chevise, comfort, crew, cure, doctor, employee, facilitate, fix, forward, foster, frith, further, hand, heeze, heize, improve, kokua, mitigate, prevent, profit, promote, redress, relief, relieve, remedy, rescue, reset, second, servant(s), serve, sos, staff, stead, subsidy, succo(u)r, support, sustain, tide, uphold
but avoid, fail to, forbear
on advance, further, promote
out firk

HELPER adjutant, aide, ally, ancilla, ansar, apprentice, assister, auxiliary, benefactor, chummy, flunky, galopin, hand, henchman, husband, journeyman, jumper, mate, page, partner, scullion, servant, spouse, subordinate, teammate, underling, wife, worker

HELPFUL adjuvant, aidant, beneficial, convenient, kind, obliging, salutary, speedy, useful

HELPLESS abject, altricial, bewildered, defenseless, dependent, desolate, destitute, disabled, feckless, feeble, forlorn, impotent, incapable, incompetent, inefficient, infirm, irremediable, limp, numb, powerless, prostrate, redeless, shiftless, spineless, unable, unaiding, unguarded, unprotected, unsupplied, weak

HELPING aidant, portion, serving

HELPMATE companion, helper, husband, wife
-me-neighbor accommodez-moi, commerce, game
name meaning ezra
oneself to appropriate, take

HELTER-SKELTER chaotic, disorderly, hastily, pellmell, tagrag, uproar

HELVE haft, handle, helm, shaft
hammer oliver

HELVETIA See SWITZERLAND.

HEM bebay, beset, border, box, confine, cuff, edge, encircle, enclose, environ, fence, fimbriate, fold, hame, haw, hedge, hesitate, hum, impale, inclose, limit, margin, purfle, restrain, rim, seam, sew, stitch, surround, turning, turnup
and haw haver, vacillate

HEMAN *son* bukkiah, eliathah, giddalti, hanani, hananiah, jehiel, jerimoth, mahazioth, malothi, mattahaiah, shebuel, shimei, uzziel

HEMANS *poem* casabianca

HEMATITE bloodstone, chalcedony, heliotrope, limonite, oligist, ore, psilomelane, red ocher, sanguine
pigment amatito

HEMERA *parent* erebus, nyx

HEMERASIA artemis

HEMI half, left, right, unilateral

HEMIBRANCH aulostom, flutemouth, shrimpfish, snipefish, stickleback

HEMICRANIA headache, hemialgia, migraine

HEMINGWAY *nickname* papa
work death in the afternoon, farewell to arms, for whom the bell tolls, sun also rises, torrents of spring

HEMIPODE bustard quail, buttonquail, turnicid, turnix

HEMIPTERA bug, insect, pagiopoda

HEMISPHERE half, realm
division equator, meridian

HEMITHEA *parent* cycnus, proclea
pursuer achilles

HEMLOCK abies, avens, bennet, bunk, cash, cicuta, conium, cowbane, deathin, english daisy, herb, kelk, kex, pine, poison, shinwood, tree, tsuga, yew
fruit conium
poison coniine, conin, conium, heck-how

HEMOPHILIAC bleeder, phlebotomist

HEMORRHAGE apoplexy, bleeding, discharge, flow,

hemophelia, hemoptoe, hemorrhea, nosebleed, petechia, staxis
arrest acupressure, acutorsion
skin petechia

HEMP abaca, ambari, ambary, amy root, baline, bang, bast, bee nettle, benj, bhang, birdseed, bung, burlap, cabuya, cannabis, carl, cordilla, dagga, drug, fiber, fimble, fique, flax, gagfoot, gallows-grass, ganja, gunny, harl, hashish, hurds, ife, i(h)iamba, jute, kaif, ke(e)f, keif, kief, kiff, konopel, locoweed, manilla, marijuana, murva, nalita, neckweed, nepenthe, niyanda, pangane, phloem, pita, piteira, pito, plant, pooa(h), pua, pun, ramie, rine, rogue, rope, sabzi, san, sida, siddhi, sinawa, sisal, sosquil, sunn, tow
agrimony ageratum, eupatory
albany woodnettle
ambary nalita
bowstring ife, murva, neyanda, pangane
bundle bait, beat, beet, bung
cloth burlap, canamo, canvas, pinayusa
coarse chucking
derivative cannabis, ganja
drink subdschi
fiber abaca, agave, jute, sisal
fine lupis
loose oakum
narcotic b(h)ang, cannabis, charas, ganja, ke(e)f, kief, kiff, hashish, marijuana
nettle henbit, ironwort
oil cannabene
pert. cannabic
product birdseed, cloth, cordage, hashish, hay, marijuana, oil, sailcloth, soap, thc
refuse hurds
resin charas
seed gallows-bird, rogue
sheaf glean
smoking See HEMP *narcotic.*
twisting hook whirler

HEMPWEED boneset, comfrey, duckblind, eupatorium, seaweed, thoroughwort

HEN biddy, bird, busybody, chicken, chook, chuck,

cluck, female, fowl, gallinule, gossip, grig, layer, mabyer, nester, partlet, pollo, poulet, pullet, towdie
and chickens columbine, daffodil, houseleek, pliades, trifoil
apple whitebeam
chaucer's partlet
clam mactra, pismo, surf
coop cavie, cavy, chicken-house
cry cackle
extinct heath
-fat lamb's-quarters
goethe's partlet
gorse restharrow
group brood, flock
harrier faller, hawk, katabella, kite, miller, ringtail
hawk buzzard, coot, gallinule, redtail
-hearted cowardly
-hussy dotard, effeminate
mud rail
plan plantago, plantain
roost eve, perch
spayed poulard
speckled bass
water gallinule
HENADAD *son* bavai, binnui
HENBANE chenille, hebenon, hogbean, nightshade, poison-tobacco
content hyoscin
leaves hyoscyamus
HENBILL coot, dabchick, sainfoin
HENBIT beenettle, hemp, lamium, speedwell
HENCE accordingly, avaunt, away, begone, consequently, distance, ergo, forth, frae, from, future, here out, off, out, scram, since, then(ce), therefore, therefrom, thither, whence, wherefore
HENCEFORTH thence, yet
HENCEFORWARDS tomorrow
HENCHBOY attendant, page
HENCHMAN assistant, associate, attendant, disciple, fellow, flunky, follower, gillie, groom, hanger-on, hatchetman, heeler, helper, jackal, lackey, man friday, minion, mobster, myrmidon, page, partisan, politician, retainer, sancho panza, satellite, satrap, sectary, servant, squire, stooge,

supporter, vassal, wardheeler, worker
HENFISH pomfret
HENGEST,   HENGIST
brother horsa
daughter rowena
kingdom kent
son aesc
HENIOCHE See HERA.
HENLEY, W. E. *poem* invictus
HENNA alcan(n)a, camphire, dye, lawsonia, mendy, orchanet, rinse, shrub
HENOCH *parent* midian
HENOTIC harmonizing, ironic
HENPECK annoy, control, criticize, domineer, grind, nag, pick, rule
HENRY II c(o)urtmantle
adversary thomas a becket
daughter margot, marguerite
mistress diane de poitiers, fair rosamund, rose of the world
son john, richard
wife catherine de medici, eleanor
writer montaigne, rabelais
HENRY III balafre
jester chicot
HENRY IV bolingbroke
author shakespeare
birthplace pau
character archibald, bardolph, blunt, bullcalf, colevile, dame quickly, davey, doll tearsheet, douglas, edmund, falstaff, fang, feeble, gadshill, glendower, gower, hal, harcourt, hastings, hotspur, john, lady percy, michael, mortimer, morton, mouldy, mowbray, northumberland, percy, peto, pistol, poins, scroop, shadow, shallow, silence, snare, surrey, travers, vernon, wart, warwick, westmoreland, worcester
country justice shallow, silence
father john of gaunt
foe archbishop of york, colevile, douglas, glendower, hastings, hotspur, morton, mowbray, surrey, warwick, westmoreland
jester chicot
mistress gabrielle d'estrees
queen margaret, marie de medici

son clarence, gloucester, hal, henry, humphrey, john, lancaster, thomas
HENRY V *author* shakespeare
brother bedford, clarence, gloucester, humphrey, john, lancaster, thomas
character alice, bardolph, bates, bedford, charles, court, erpingham, exeter, fluellen, gloucester, gower, grandpre, grey, isabel, jamy, lewis, macmorris, montjoy, pistol, rambures, salisbury, scroop, warwick, westmoreland, williams, york
cousin york
officer fluellen, gower, jamy, macmorris
soldier court, williams
uncle exeter
HENRY VI *author* shakespeare
character alencon, basset, beaufort, bedford, bevis, bolingbroke, bona, buckingham, burgundy, cade, charles, clifford, dauphin, dick, edmund, edward, eleanor, fastolphe, gargrave, george, glansdale, gloucester, goffe, hastings, henry, holland, horner, hume, iden, joan la pucelle, lady gray, lewis, lucy, margaret, montague, mortimer, northumberland, oxford, pembroke, peter, plantagenet, reignier, richard, rivers, rutland, salisbury, say, scales, simpcox, smith, somerset, somerville, southwell, stafford, stanley, suffolk, vaux, vernon, warwick, westmoreland, woodville
queen margaret
son edward
uncle beaufort, bedford, gloucester
HENRY VII *surname* tudor
HENRY VIII defender of the faith, his highness, his majesty, robin the bobbin
author shakespeare
character abergavenny, brandon, buckingham, bullen, butts, campeius, capucius, cranmer, cromwell, denny, gardiner, griffith, guildford, katharine, lovell, merry andrew, norfolk, patience,

sands, suffolk, surrey, vaux, wolsey
jester will somers
physician butts, merry andrew
queen katharine
shilling teston
wives (1st) catherine, katherine, (2nd) ann boleyn, anne bullen, (3rd) jane seymour, (4) anne of cleves, (5) catherine howard, (6) catherine parr
HENRY, O. william sidney porter
HENRY THE NAVIGATOR
exploration teixeira, zarco
parent john, philippa
HENT arrive, carry off, catch, get, grasp, intention, lay hold, obtain, opportunity, reach, seize, until
HENWARE alaria, bladderlocks, murlin, seaweed
HEP heap, hip, informed, knowing, one, wise, with it
cat dancer, swinger
HEPATICA liverwort, marchantia, trefoil, trinity
HEPHAESTION *friend* alexander
HEPHAESTUS lemnian, mulciber, vulcan(us)
abode hiera, imbros, lemnos, lipara, sicily
aides cab(e)iri, cedalion, cyclops, polyphemus, satyrs, sileni, telchines
beloved aetna, aglaia, aphrodite, cab(e)iri, charis, charites, gaea, maia, venus
captive prometheus
emblem cap, chiton, hammer, tongs
god of fire
offspring aethalia, ardalus, cacus, caeculus, cedalion, cercyon, erichthonous, palaemon, palici, pandora, periphetes, pylius
parent hera, zeus
product armor, arrows, chariot, cuirass, goblet, harp, sickle, throne, vase
protectress eurynome, thetis
victim clytius
workshop etna
HEPHZIBAH jerusalem
husband hezekiah
son manasseh
HEPPEN clever, comfortable, deft, fit, handsome, handy, neat
HEPTAD septivalent, seven

HERA anthea, bunaea, henioche, juno, prodromia
allies greeks
bird peacock
brother zeus
consort jove, jupiter, zeus
enemy trojans
helpers hebe, horae
messenger iris
offspring ares, hebe, hecate, hephaestus
parent cronus, ops, rhea
priestess cydippe
reared by oceanus, tethys
rival leto
sculptor polyclitus
symbol peacock, pomegranate, sceptre, veil
temple site argos, plataea, samos
victim antigone, iphianassa, lysippe, trojans
wedding gift golden apples
HERACLES See HERCULES.
HERACLEUM cadweed, cow-parsnip
HERACLIDAE aristodemus, aristomachus, hyllus, oxylus
ancestor heracles, hercules
HERALD announce, beadle, blazon(er), bode, crier, declare, evangel, forerun(ner), foretell, gabriel, harbinger, hermes, introduce, merganser, messenger, page, precurser, preface, prelude, proclaim, rothesay, usher
attendant blue-mantle, pursuivant
garment tabard
of the gods ceryx
HERALDRY, HERALDIC armo(u)ry
animal agacella, aland, alant, allertion, bagwyn, brock, cannet(te), chough, enfield, gray, grice, griffon, harpy, lioncel, loup, martlet, musimon, openicus, popinjay, sanglier, talbot, tyger, wyver, wyvern
animal's head showing caboched, caboshed
animal's position assis, couchant, courant, dormant, flotant, forcene, haurient, issuant, jacent, jessant, naiant, passant, rampant, rousant, salient, sejant, statant, trippant, urinant, volant, vorant
band bar, bend, fess(e), fill, orle

banner banderol(e)
bar inflamed thunderbolt
bar sinister baton
barnacle brey, cirriped
barrulet gemel
bearing annulet, bar(rulet), baton, bend(y), bezant, billet, bordure, canton, chevron(el), chief, closet, cost, cotise, cross, dancette, endorse, fess(e), fil(l)et, flanche, fret, fusil, garter, gemel, golpe, guze, gyron, hurt, label, mascle, ogress, orange, orle, pale, pall(et), pellet, pile, plate, pomey, quarter, riband, roundel, rustre, saltier, saltire, saltorel, scarp(e), shakefork, syke, torteau, tressure, vaire, virole
beast bordure enurny
beast rearing rampant
bend, small cortise, riband, scarpe
bird bordure enaluron
blind seel
boar grice, grise
border bordure
botonee trefle
cadency mark (1–9) label, crescent, mullet, martlet, annulet, fleur-de-lis, rose, moline, quatrefoil
cap bonnet
charge bar gemel, bearing, boterol(l), dragon, drop, enurny, esquire, flanch(e), flaunch(e), gemel, giron, gyron, label, roundel, saltier, saltire, tressour, tressure, vol
circle annulet, bezant
cleche cross, urde
cloth bearing arms banner
collared accolle
color See HERALDRY tincture.
coward coure
cresset beacon
cross(-like) ancre(d), avellan, botone(e), boton(n)y, cercele(e), cleche, crusile(e), crux, erminee, fitche(e), fleury, flory, fourche(e), moline, nowy, pate, patonce, patte, pary, pomme, potent, saltier, saltire, saltorel, sarcelle, urde(e), urdy
crouching couchant
curved arrondi, nebule, nowy
dart head pheon

description blazon
device altier, arms, crest, ente, orle, vair
devouring vorant
disgrace mark abatement
distinctive mark charge
dragon basilisk, wyvern
duck cannet(te)
eagle allerion
embattled breteche, bretesse
escalloped scules
expert armorist
face to face aspectant
facing spectator affronte, gardant, gaze
flying in air flotant
fruit-bearing fructed
full-faced gardant
funeral shield achievement, hatchment
fur ermine, pean, potent, vair(e)
grain sheaf garb, gerb(e)
headless etete
heir See HERALDRY *cadency mark.*
illegitimacy mark bar sinister, baston, baton, bend sinister
knot bourchier, bowen, dacre, harrington, heneage, lacy, stafford, wake
leaping salient
leash lyam
left side sinister
leg gamb(e), jamb(e)
linked braced, conjoined
looking back regardant
lozenge-shaped fusil, mascle, rustre
lying down couchant
manacle tirret
notched raguly
object baton, boterol, brey, escroll, estoile, gerbe, goutte, laver, lymphad, manche, mullet, pheon, seax, syke, tirret, torse, vol, weei
ordinary bend, pale, paly, saltire
overlying brochant
paired gemel
partition line dancetty, dovetailed, embattled, engrailed, indented, invected, nebuly, nowy, onde, potency, raguly, rayonnant, unde, undy, urdy, wavy
pert. armorial, fecial, fetial
pursuivant antelope
rearing rampant
ring annulet(tee)
rising issuing, nascent

rounded arrondi
roundel golp(e), guze
row of squares compone, compony
running courant
sanguine murrey
seated assis, sejant
sewed cousu
s-curved annodated
shield cartouch(e)
shield border bordure, orle
shield boss imbo
shield indentation bouche
shield part canton, chief, ente, flanch(e)
shield-shaped peltate
shield stripe pale
shield surface field
shooting up jessant
silver argent
sleeping dormant
springing salient, saltant
standing statant
star mullet, seme
streamer bande(role)
strewn with flowers seme
stripe bar
striped barruly, burelage, burel(l)e, burelly
succession See HERALDRY *cadency mark.*
surmounting brochant
swimming naiant
term abaisse(d), accole, ad(d)orse(d), affronte, aile, annulet, appaume, assurgent, avellan, aversant, bailone, barrulet, barry, bend(y), bevel, bordure, brisure, checky, cleche, cloue, compone, compony, couped, crescent, debruise, dexter, embowed, enfiled, engouled, ente, fleur-de-lis, forme(e), fracted, gamb, gobony, gore, grined, gusset, gutte, gutty, guze, imbrued, label, martlet, masculy, moline, mullet, nowed, paly, rompu, rose, rustre, sanglant, seme, sinister, tierce, trefle, trussed, unguled, vair, vire, virole, vorant, vuln
3-part division tierce
tincture argent, azure, blanch, gules, guze, jove, murrey, purpure, sable, tenne, vert
traversed See HERALDRY *striped.*
trefoil See HERALDRY *cross(-like).*
upside down renverse
walking passant, trippant

wavy ente, nebule, onde, unde
wings aile, vol
wings joined avol
wings opened rising
without neck caboched, caboshed
wound vuln
wreath orle, torse
zigzag bevilled, dancette

HERB (See also *genus* and *kind,* below.) annual, flora, foliage, grass, plant, seasoning
alpine ice pink
annual borage, corn salad, melilot, nemophila, nettle, nigella, poppy, primrose, purslane, rape, rattle(box), rhocanthe, ricebean, richweed, rocket-salad, roselle, thimbleflower, tidytips, toadflax, tomatillo, winged pea
apiaceous anise, carrot, celery, nondo, parsley
aquatic alisma, alismales, apongeton, batrachium, bladderwort, buckbean, featherfoil, floerkea, hornwort, hottonia, ghetchoo, lemna, limosella, pondgrass, pygmyweed, ranale, saxifrage, water-plantain
aromatic anet, anise, asarabaca, babroot, basil, bayleaf, bezel, caapeba, caraway, carum, catnip, chevril, chives, cicely, cinnamonroot, clary, cress, datura, dill, fennel, french tea, garlic, hemp, horseradish, hyssop, lovage, mace, marjoram, mint, mustard, nard, nondo, okra, oregano, parsley, pycanthemum, rosemary, ruta, saffron, sage, satureia, savory, sheepskin, spearmint, tansy, tarragon, thyme, turmeric, wormseed
-bennet avens, clovewort, daisy, geum, hemlock, saxifrage, valerian
biennial angelica, leek, parsley
bitter aletris, aloe, boneset, centaury, gentian, rue, tansy, turtlehead, woad, yellowwort
bog calla, steepwort
borage alkanna
buckwheat sorrel
bulbous acidanthera, allium,

anticlea, babiana, basketflower, buttercup, canna,
crinum, crocus, dogtooth,
galanthus, garlic, glory-of-
the-sun, lily, nerine, shallot,
slangkop, snowdrop, spider
lily, squill, triteleia, urginea, vallota
bundle bouquet garni
-christopher baneberry, fleabane, meadowsweet, royal
fern
climbing apios, basellace,
faba, lens, vetch, vicia
coarse elecampane, eringo,
eryngo, iva, leafcup, pokeweed, tansy
composite coneflower, ragweed
creeping arbutus, nierember-
gia
cure ayurveda
dish salad
divine vervain
docor naturopath
edible dandelion, dock, parsnip, purslane, rhubarb,
sego, skirret, spinach, yamp
ericaceous arbutus, pinedrops
-eve bugle, iva, plantain,
swine's-crest
fabulous moly, panace,
panax
fetid stinkbell
fleshy peperomía, roseroot
floating frogbit
flowering achimenes, anemone, babies-breath, celandine, daisy, dittane, eardrop, gypsum pink, grape
hyacinth, hepatica, sedum,
stapelia
forage fitches, goitcho
fragrant balm, skyrocket
frankincense laserwort
genus abfa, abroma, acaena,
acanthus, aconitum, actaea,
acuan, aletris, alliaria,
amorpha, anemone, an-
gelica, aphanes, apios, aralia,
arum, asarum, calla, cicer,
cirsium, dondia, ervum, eupatorium, galax, gavra,
geum, gifola, gratiola,
grindelia, hedeoma, ily-
santhes, inula, ionidium,
isoles, iva, jatropha, jeffar-
sonia, kuhnia, lemna, loasa,
manihot, mentha, meum,
nerine, nolana, psoralea,
rheum, rulac, ruta, sagina,
sesseli, shortia, tacca,

thymus, torenia, tovaria,
triosteum, urena
-gerard goutweed
-grace hyssop, rue, vervain
grasslike rush
healing comfrey, plantain
impious downweed, hoar-
wort
-ivy See HERB *-eve.*
kind abscessroot, alumroot,
alyssum, caper, cardamine,
clammyweed, costmary,
croton, cyclamen, deer's-
tongue, dianthus, entada,
ginseng, gloxinia,
goldthread, gossipium,
grindelia, guzmania, hen's-
foot, heuchera, hola, in-
digofera, innocence, ivy,
kale, lens, madder, man-
yroot, mermaidweed, nama,
petunia, pimpernel, poke,
poly, prairie clover, pu-
chero, pyrola, remero, ruta,
sang, sedge, sesuvium, sida,
sinningia, spicknel, teasel,
teucrium, thrift, verbesina,
veronia, vervain, vetch,
waxweed, witchweed, wood-
ruff, wort, yamp, yareta,
yarr(ow)
labiate ground ivy, pot marjoram
liliaceous autumn crocus,
cape cowslip, meadow
saffron, trillium
-louisa lemon verbena
-mastic thyme
medicinal aconite, aloe, arnica, boneset, centaury, coriander, eyebright, galeni-
cal, lovage, rue, sanicle,
selfheal, senna, spigelia,
sumac, tansy, tormentil, tutsan, valerian
milky-juiced dogbane
minty thyme
narcotic hemp, mandrake
of friendship stonecrop
of grace rue
of memory rosemary
of repentance rue
of the cross vervain
onion-like chive, garlic
ornamental basket flower,
sternbergia, stikesia
parasitic anoplanthus, epi-
phegus, mistletoe, pinesap,
rhinanthus
paris oneberry, true(love)
perennial airplant, alkali-
grass, apocynum, asclepias,
balm, brooklime, bugbane,
cachfly, canaigre, clintonia,

coralbell, cow-tongue,
crocus, digitalis, epiphyte,
eyebright, fennel, geum,
gladiolus, globeflower, gold-
enqueen, gold-flower,
gromwell, iris, larkspur,
lopweed, lousewort, mad-
der, mint, mosquito-bill,
nondo, nuttalia, pia, pingue,
poolroot, primrose, prophetflower, raggedrobin, redroot, rockbeauty, sage, sainfoin, sedum, sego, sneezewort, soapwort, talis, toadflax, trillium, umbrella plant,
velvet bur, wallcress, wallflower, watercress, wild vanilla, yellowtuft, yerba
buena
-peter cowslip
poisonous aconitum, conium,
hellebore, hemlock, hen-
bane, loco, mandrake, pokeweed, potagerie
pot cyclamen, wort
prairie redlily, tiny-tim
prostrate camla, catgut, con-
vulvulus
-robert jenny, robin
rock samphire
rosaceous spirea, tormentil
salad chicory, endive, watercress
scaly squawroot
scapose anoplanthus, statice,
thrift
seacoast fingertip
seasoning See HERB *aromatic.*
shoot udo
snake charm mungo
-sophia hedge mustard
spiny xanthium
sprawling cowpea
starch-yielding pia
stinging nettle
stingless false nettle
succulent begonia, navelwort, orpine, sedum, stonecrop, thickleaf
tanning tormentil
tonic boneset, yellowwort
trailing apios, wandering
jew, yerba buena, zebrina
-trinity hepatica, pansy
twining concolculus
-twopence moneywort
weedy centunculus, eringo,
eryngo, gosmore, iva, pearl-
spurry, primrose
woody auhuhu, mother-of-
thyme, red pepper, rue,
tronador

wooly antennaria, cat's-foot, filago, poly, thistle

HERBAGE adonis, foliage, grass, leaves, pasture, pichi, sacate, stems, turf, vegetation, zacate

HERBBANE broomrape

HERBIVOROUS phytophagous

HERCEIUS See ZEUS.

HERCULEAN colossal, difficult, enormous, gigantic, huge, immense, laborious, mammoth, superhuman, titanic, vast

HERCULES alcaeus, alcides, buphagus, charops, cornopion, heracles, herakles, hershef, ipoctonus, oetaeus, ovillus, powerhouse, stalwart, victor, worm-killer

all-heal opopanax

ancestor alcaeus, alcmena, hoppodamia, pelops, perseus

archery prize iole

armor-bearer philoctetes

brother iphicles

captive iole

challenger antagorist

cleaned augean stables

-club angelica-tree, aralia, devil's-walking-stick, ivywort, pigeon tree, ruewort, shotbush

companion abderus, alcon, chiron, hylas, iolaus, lichas, stenelus, telamon

consort astydamia, astyoche, auge, deianira, hebe, hylas, iole, meda, megara, omphale

descendant archias, heraclid

gates of See HERCULES *pillars.*

giant killed antaeus, ephialtes

grandfather electryon

grandson aepytus, cleodaeus

home tiryns

horse arion

insulted by ach(e)mon, basalas

labors, pert. (See also *12 labors,* below.) augean, cerberus, cerynelian, cretan bull, diomedes, erymanthus, geryon, hesperides, hippolyte, lernaean, nemean, stymphalian

lion's home nemea

master eurystheus

mistress omphale

monster slain geryon, hydra

nurse abia

of music gluck

parent alcmene, amphitryon, barsine, jupiter, zeus

pillars abila, abyla, calpe, ceuta, gibraltar

prize iole

servant iolaus

slave to omphale

son aechmagoras, agathyrsus, agelaus, albion, alexiares, anicetus, antiochus, gelonus, glenus, hyllus, lamus, telephus, thessalus

stag cerynea

temple founder abia

tutor amphitryon, autolycus, castor, eurytus, linus, rhadamanthys

12 labors cattle of geryon, ceryneian hind, cretan bull, girdle of hippolyte, golden apples of the hesperides, journey to hades, lernaean hydra, mares of diomedes, nemean lion, stables of augeias, stymphalian birds, wild boar of erymanthus

twin iphicles

uncle licymnius

victim albion, alcyoneus, alebion, amazons, amyntor, antaeus, auge(i)as, busiris, cacus, calais, cercopes, charybdis, chiron, cycnus, diomedes, emathion, ephialtes, erginus, eunomus, eurypylus, eurytion, eurytus, geryon, hippocoon, hippolyte, hydra, iphitus, laomedon, linus, lion, lityerses, megara, melionids, mygdon, nessus, periclymenus, periphete, pholus, sagaris, syleus, thiodamas, thoas, zetes

HERCYNA *friend* persephone

HERD assemblage, assembly, associate, band, bevy, caviya, chouse, corral, covey, creaght, crowd, drive, drove, flight, flock, flote, gaggle, gam, gregal, GROUP, guard(ian), guide, harras, hirsel, huddle, masses, meinie, mob, multitude, pack, pastor, patch, people, pilot, pod, protect, public, rabble, rag, rangale, round up, school, shelter, shepherd, shoal, sounder, spur, swarm,

team, tend, thrave, troop, unite, watch, wrangle

boy bouchal

cattle tail, wrangle

common masses, ruck

god inuus, pan

instinct gregariousness

pert. gregal

together accompany, assemble

HERDSMAN amos, bool(e)y, bootes, bucolic, cowboy, damoetas, drover, garthman, gaucho, herder, llanero, pastor, rancher(o), senn, stockman, thyrsis, vacher, vaquero, wrangler

god pales

HERE aboard, ad esse, at hand, attendant, hic, hither, ici, now, present, ready, somewhere

and now immediately, today

and there about, around, hither and thither, intermittently, irregularly, over, passim, scattered, sparsely, thinly, through

HEREABOUTS approximately, close by, near

HEREAFTER afterlife, beyond, eventually, future, later, paradise, tomorrow, ultimately

HEREBY close, near

HEREDITARY ancestral, congenital, genealogical, inborn, inbred, ingrained, inherited, innate, intrinsic, legitimate, lineal, patrimonial, transmitted

factor dna, gene, idant, rna

group caste, family

HEREDITY atavism, birth, determiner, eugenics, genetics, genesiology, heritage, inheritance, matrocliny, mendelism, patrocliny, transmission

HERESY apostasy, disbelief, error, fallacy, false belief, heterodoxy, infidelity, misbelief, unbelief

chief heresiarch

combatant heresimach

religious arianism, pelagianism

HERETIC agnostic, arian, apostate, atheist, audaean, backslider, bugger, dissenter, freethinker, iconoclast, infidel, ketzer, lollard, misbeliever, nonconformist, patarin, pervert,

renegade, schismatic, sectarian, sectary, skeptic, unbeliever, zindic
burning of auto-da-fe, bonnering
famous arius, pelagius
gnostic basildian
religious agnoites, angelici
HERETOFORE before, ere now, erst(while), former(ly), hitherto, once, past, previous, quondam
HERMAPHRODITE ambosexous, androgyne, androgynus, bisexual, epicene, moph, scrat
HERMAPHRODITUS *lover* salmacis
parent aphrodite, hermes
HERMAS *friend* paul
HERMES acacetus, agoraeus, agoraios, argeiphantes, argephontes, criophorus, cyllenus, diactoros, dolius, herald, logios, mercury, messenger, psychagogos, psychopompus, spelaites
beloved aleidamea
betrayer battus
consort akakallis, aphrodite, chione, hecate, penelope, persephone, phene, polymele
cutlass harpe
footgear talaria
gift to apollo lyre
god of marketplace
nurse cyllene
offspring abderus, aethalides, autoclycus, bunus, ceryx, cupid, cydon, daphnis, eleusis, eros, heryx, myrtilus, pan, polydorus, prylis, saon
parent maia, zeus
personification wind
pert. cyllenian
ravished apemosyne
sacred mountain cyllene
staff caduceus
sword harpe
victim argus, hippolytus, pelops
winged hat petasos, petasus
winged shoes talaria
HERMETIC airtight, alchemical, close, hermaic, magical, sealed
HERMIA *beloved* lysander
father egeus
suitor demetreus
HERMIONE *attendant* emilia
daughter perdita

husband leontes, neoptolemus, orestes, pyrrhus
parent helen, menelaus
son tisamenus
HERMIT anchorite, arme, ascetic, beadsman, cenobite, cookie, eremite, hanif, hummingbird, marabout, minion, recluse, santon, solitaire, solitary, tapasvi
crab pagurian
crow chough
hut cell, clochan
HERMITAGE ashram, asrama, cloister, monastery, retreat, ribat, wine
HERNIA breach, bubonocele, exomphalous, merocele, protrusion, ramex, rupture
surgery celotomy
HERO adventurer, brave, celebrity, champion, cynosure, daredevil, deity, demigod, gallant, god, idol, knight, lead, lion, male, model, paladin, perseus, phoenix, protagonist, soldier, stalwart, star, to(o)a, valiant, victor, vip, warrior
attendant margaret, ursula
beloved leander
cousin beatrice
crusader tancred
deified demigod
eponymous gaedheal
father leonato
hall valhalla
legendary amadis, igor, paladin, roland, tristan, tristram
mythological etana, hercules, leander, otuna, perseus, rustam, rustum
name meaning adolph(us)
of 100 battles nelson
of the nile nelson
suitor don pedro
uncle antonio
worship idolatry
HEROD *brother* archelaus, philip
chamberlain blastus
courtier manaen
father antipater
father-in-law aretas
sister berenice
son alexander, antipas, aristobulus
stepdaughter salome
steward chuza
victim john the baptist
wife herodias, mariamne
HERODIAS *daughter* salome
husband herod

HEROIC bold, brave, courageous, daring, dauntless, enormous, epic(al), exreme, fearless, featly, fell, gallant, great, homerian, huge, illustrious, impavid, intrepid, large, lionhearted, noble, powerful, resolute, valiant, viking
HEROIN acetomorphine, acetonapthone, big-h, brown sugar, diamorphine, dope, horse, junk, narcotic, nepenthe, opiate, scag, skag, smack, snow, stuff
addicted to hooked
antidote methadone
place shooting gallery, skag bar
source opium-poppy, papaver
take inject, mainline, shotgun, skin-pop, snort
HEROINE *name meaning* mathilda
HEROISM bravery, courage, daring, fortitude, gallantry, magnanimity, mettle, prowess, resolution, spirit, tenacity
HERON, HERON'S aigret(te), alba, ardea, ardeida, arsnicker, benu, bird, bittern, boatbill, crabier, craig, crane, demoiselle, egret, frank, gaulding, goliath, handsaw, herle, hern(e), ibis, kialee, kotuku, kulm, paddy, quabird, quaker, shitepoke, soco, squacco, squawk, umbrette, wader, yaboa
bill erodium
crested squacco
flock sedge, seige
great blue arsnicker
green poke
night fishcrane, qua, quawk, soco, yaboa
pert. ardeid
plume aigret(te)
rare boatbill
small bittern
HEROPHILE *prophecy* trojan war
HEROPHILUS *parent* aphrodite, neptune, poseidon, venus
HERPES eczema, lichen, psoriasis, ringworm, shingles, tener
HERR lord, man, mister, signor(e), sir
HERRING alec, alewife, al-

lice, alosa, anchovy, bleak, bloat(er), blueback, brisling, brit, buckling, capon, chub, cisco, clupea, cropshin, dorab, fish, grayling, hilsa, kipper, kiyi, mackerel, maray, matie, nailrod, pilchard, quoddie, raun, rollmop, sardine, scuddawn, shadine, sild, sprat, stromming, tailor, tradine
appetizer rollmop
barrel cade, cran
barrel disk daunt
big-eyed alewife, chiro, elops, megalops, oxeye, pomolobus
blue alewife, nailrod
cast warp
catch tack
common labrador
dry deese
fall hickory shad
family pilchard
female raun
fry sile
green-back cisco
group warp
head cob
-hog porpoise
inferior cropshin
king opah
lake cisco, kiyi
-like anchovy, lile, pollan
measure cade, cran, last, maze
merchant salter
pert. clupeoid
pond ocean
pressing disk daunt
red capon, diversion, ruse, soldier
round stradine
sauce alec
season drave
-shaped harengiform
smoked bloater, bocking, buckling, kipper
young brit, cob, matie, sardine, sile, sill, soil, sperling, sprat, wile
HERRINGBONE cloth, coutil, solitaire
HERSE *father* cecrops
husband hermes
offspring cephalus, ceryx
sister aglauros, agraulos
HERSHEF arsaphes, osiris
HERSHIP foray, raid
HERSILIA *husband* romulus
HERTHA See ERDA.
HERZON *wife* abiah
HESIOD *birthplace* ascra
poem theogony, works and days

HESIONE *brother* priam
consort telemon, zeus
father laomedon
rescuer hercules
son teucer
HESITANT afraid, averse, bashful, cagy, chary, coy, diffident, doubtful, fearful, groping, halting, indecisive, indisposed, irresolute, loath, reluctant, shrinking, shy, timid, undecided, wavering
HESITATE balance, balk, boggle, crane, debate, demur, doubt, ers, falter, flounder, fluctuate, hacker, hang back, haw, hem, hover, linger, mammer, oscillate, pause, procrastinate, scotch, scruple, shrink, shy, stammer, stay, stick(le), stop, swither, teeter, thrimble, vacillate, waver
HESITATION delay, demurral, hank, hink, misgiving, pause, qualm, reluctance, scruples, stand, suspense, sussy
HESPERA *parent* erebus, nyx
HESPERIA italy, spain
HESPERIAN occidental, western
HESPERIDES atlantides, nymphs
dragon ladon
fruit golden apples
names aegle, arethusa, erythesis, hespera, hestia
parent ceto, erebus, hesperus, night, nyx, phorcys, themis, zeus
HESPERUS *offspring* atlantides, ceyx, daedalion, erythea, HESPERIDES, nymphs
parent astraeus, atlas, aurora, cephalus, eos
wrecking reef norman's woe
HESSE *novel* steppenwolf
HESSIAN andiron, boot, burlap, fly, hireling, mercenary, midge, sacking, soldier, ruffian
HEST bid, command, determination, injuction, pledge, precept, promise, will
HESTIA vesta
goddess of hearth
parent cronos, ops, rhea
priestess vestal
HESYCHASTIC calming, soothing
HET *up* angry, excited,

heated, indignant, irate, passionate
HETAERA courtesan, lais, mistress, phryne, thais, wanton
HETEROCLITE abnormal, anomalous, deviation, irregular
HETERODOX agnostic, apocryphal, atheistic, dissenting, erroneous, fallacious, heretical, recusant, schismatic, sectarian, secular, skeptical, unlike, unorthodox, unsound
HETERODOXY apostasy, backsliding, cacodoxy, error, heresy, recusancy
HETEROGENEOUS assorted, different, disparate, dissimilar, divergent, divers(e), foreign, incongruous, indiscriminate, miscellaneous, mixed, motley, promiscuous, varied, variegated, unlike
HETEROTHERMIC coldblooded
HETEROTOPIA change, deviation, dislocation, displacement, transformation
HETEROTROPIA crosseyes, strabismus
HETHIN *foe* hild, hogni
HETMAN ataman, chief, leader
HETTER eager, fierce, severe
HEUCHERA alumroot, coralbells, sanicle
HEUGH bank, cliff, crag, glen, hollow, ravine, shaft
HEW bewitch, carve, chip, chisel, chop, cleve, cut, dress, fashion, fell, form, hack, hag, ninx, rive, sculpt, shred, slash, slice, snag, spell, split, stub, whittle, wound
HEWER faceman, getter, gideon, joey, miner
name meaning gideon
HEWHALL woodpecker
HEX bedevil, bewitch, charm, curse, evil-eye, hag, jinx, magic, spell, voodoo, whammy, witch
HEXAD sestet, sextet, six
HEXAGRAM pentacle
HEXAGRAMMOS bodieron, boregat, fish, greenling, rock trout
HEXAMETER *dactylic* epos, heroic

HEXAPOD housefly, insect, six-footed
HEXASTICH sestet, stanza, strophe
HEXOBARBITAL evipal
HEY hay, high, pst
HEYDAY acme, ardor, bloom, climax, exultation, flush, height, joy, peak, prime, spirits, vigor, virility, vitality, wildness, wonder, zenith
HEZEKIAH ezechias
kingdom judah
offspring abi, aliakim, manasseh
parent abijah, ahaz
recorder joah
scribe shebna
HEZEKIAS *father* thocanus
son ater
HEZRON *father* judah, reuben
grandson david
son aram, arni, ashur, caleb, chelubai, ram, segub
wife abiah
HIATUS breach, break, chasm, col, fissure, gap, interval, lacuna, opening, pause, recess, rift, space, span
HIAWATHA *author* longfellow
friend kwasind
grandmother nokomis
lake gitchegumee
magician paupkkeewis
nurse nokomis
parent mudjekeewis, wenonah, westwind
subdued megissogwon, mishenahma, mondamin
vehicle canoe
wife laughing-water, minnehaha
HIBERNATE latibulize, retire, shack, sleep, slumber, winter
HIBERNIA (See also IRELAND, IRISH.) eire, erin
HIBERNIAN irishman, ivernian, juverna
HIBISCUS abelmosk, algalia, alth(a)ea, ambari, ambary, bladderketmia, kenaf, marshmallow, roselle, rosemallow, rose of sharon
HICCOUGH, HICCUP hick, hocket, singultus, spasm, yex, yox
HICETAON *brother* priam
HICK boor, cornball, farmer, hiccup, jake, peasant, pro-

vincial, rube, rural, rustic, yokel
town village
HICKEY boil, GADGET, pimple, pustule
HICKOK *slaying site* deadwood, number ten saloon
HICKORY bullnut, cane, carya, featherwood, hognut, juglans, nogal, nut, pecan, pignut, shagbark, shellbark, switch, tough, tree, wood
black mockernut, pignut
-head ruddy-duck
nut bullnut, kiskatom, kiskitom, pecan, pignut, tryma
old andrew jackson
-poplar tulip tree
shad fall-herring
upland shagbark
wattle acacia
HICKWALL eccle, heckle, woodpecker
HIDDEN abditive, abstruse, arcane, behind, blind, blotted out, buried, cached, concealed, covered, covert, cryptic, cryptous, deep, dern, innate, inner, latent, masked, mysterious, mystic, obscure, perdu, recluse, recondite, remote, screened, secluded, secret, subtile
aces solitaire
comb. adelo, crypto
thing ambush, stowaway
HIDE bark, beat, burrow, bury, bushel, cache, casate, case, cloak, coat, conceal, cover, deep six, disguise, dissemble, doggo, ensconce, fell, flog, fur, gloss, hele, hit, hod, hole(in)(up), hood(wink), jufti, kip, layne, leather, lie low, losh, mask, obclude, palliate, peel, pelt, plew, refuge, repress, rind, screen, secrete, shadow, shelter, shield, shroud, sit tight, skin, skulk, slough, snug, squirrel, stash, suppress, tapis, veil, wallop, whip, wrap
and hair entirely, utterly, wholly
-and-seek bog(g)le, whoop
bundle kip
-cleaning device slater
comb. dora
dress taw
dressed leather
measuring hidation

-out See HIDEAWAY.
part butt
remove hair from moon, slate
scrapings scutch
tanned crop, leather
undressed kip, pelt, speck
worker tanner
wrapped in seroon
HIDEAWAY blind, cache, cave, covert, den, haven, lair, laterbous, latibulum, mew, refuge, retreat
HIDEBOUND bigoted, bourgeois(e), conservative, conventional, dogmatic, illiberal, miserly, narrow, niggardly, old-line, penurious, prudish, restrained, victorian
HIDEOUS appalling, awful, bad, deformed, discordant, dreadful, fiendish, forbidding, frightful, ghastly, grim(ly), grisly, gruesome, horrible, horrid, loathsome, monstrous, offensive, repelling, repugnant, repulsive, revolting, scabrous, shocking, terrible, ugly, unsightly
HIDING abditive, flogging, miching, perdu, secrecy, skulking
place See HIDEAWAY.
HIE accelerate, busk, diligence, haste(n), high, hurry, incite, prosper, rouse, rush, scud, speed, travel, urge
HIELD cant, decline, droop, inclination, incline, pour, shed, sink, slope, submit, tilt, turn away, yield
HIEMAL chilly, cold, freezing, gelid, wintry
HIERA *father* priam
husband telephus
slayer nireus
HIERAPOLIS pamukkale
HIERARCHY classification, dominion, order, rank
HIEROGLYPHIC acrophony, cartouch(e), cryptic, cuneiform, ideoglyphic, ideographic, ideography, illegible, og(h)am, pictograph, runes, symbolical, symbolography
key rosetta stone
HIEROMONACH See MONK.
HIERONYMUS st jerome
HIFALUTIN See HIGHFALUTIN.

HIGGINS *pupil* eliza doolittle

HIGGLE bargain, chaffer, cheapen, delay, dispute, haggle, hawk, huck, peddle, stickle, vend

-dy-piggledy chaotic, confused, confusion, jumble, mess(y)

HIGH ace, acme, aerial, aerie, airy, aloft, alpine, alto, apex, arrogant, aspiring, best, brant, brent, chief, cloud-capped, colossal, costly, dear, deep, distinguished, drunk, elevated, eminent, exalted, exorbitant, expensive, fetid, first, gamy, grave, great, haught(y), haut(e), heightened, intoxicated, mighty, moldy, mountainous, noble, piercing, polluted, preeminent, principal, profound, prominent, proud, putrid, raised, rancid, reared, rich, serene, serious, sharp, shrill, sky-scraping, soaring, spiring, steep, superior, supernal, supreme, tainted, tall, tipsy, topping, towering, towery, treble, trump, winner

and dry beached, protected, stranded, stuck

and low everywhere

and mighty arrogant, bossy, great, hogen, imperious, important, overbearing, stuck up

ball cocktail, drink, speed, whiskey

caliber classy, first-class, superior

church anglican

-cockalorum leapfrog, snob, snoot

-colored blowsy, blowzy, exaggerated, florid, flushed, rosy, ruddy, strong, vivid

comb. acro, alti, alto, hyps(i)

degree, name meaning erma, herma, irma, irme

-fed beany, pampered

fidelity enthusiast audiophile

-five cinch, double pedro

-flavored gamy

-flier enthusiast, partisan, stagecoach, visionary

-flown absurd, bombastic, elevated, fanciful, grandiose, icarian, inflated, magniloquent, ostentatious, pretentious, proud, tumid, turgid

-flown diction euphemism, euphuism

-go revel, spree

-handed arbitrary, arrogant, cavalier, despotic, dictatorial, dogmatic, domineering, imperious, lordly, opinionated, overbearing, peremptory

-hat aristocratic, arrogant, beaver, snob, snub, tile, topper

-hoe woodpecker

-hole flicker

horse arrogance

-jack See HIJACK.

-jinks celebration, festival, fun, hank(e)y-pank(e)y, high jinx, horseplay, merrymaking, revelry, tantrum

jump eastern roll

-keyed jumpy, nervous

life aristocracy, elite, four hundred, haut monde, society

-low-jack all-fours, old sledge, pitch, seven-up

-minded arrogant, honest, idealistic, proud, upright

-muck-a-muck biggy, big (shot), big wheel, magnate, personage, vip

name meaning alta, ela, elga, helga, holly, olga

-pitched alt(issimo), clarion, inclined, penetrating, piercing, piping, reedy, screechy, sharp, shrill, squeaky, strident, stridulent, thin, treble

places, dread of acrophobia

point altitude, climax, consummation, record

-powered dynamic, important, magnum, potent

-pressure aggressive, coerce, compel, compulsion, forceful, forcible, importunate, insist(ent), intense, pressing, tense, uptight, urge(nt)

-priced blue-ship, costly, dear, expensive, extravagant

priest aaron, annas, bishop, caiaphas, ecclesiastic, eli

-reaching ambitious, aspiring, striving

roller big shot, blade, dice-thrower, dude, magnate, prodigal, roue, show-off

-seasoned exciting, piquant, zestful

society beau monde, elite, four hundred, haut monde

-sounding altiloquent, altisonant, bombast(ic), fustian, grandiloquent, hifalutin, imposing, loud, magnisonant, megalophonous, pompous, sonorant, sonorous

-sounding word amplification, auxesis, hyperbole

speed express, limited, rapido

-spirited audacious, bold, brave, cavalier, courtly, energetic, fiery, gallant, gingery, intrepid, lively, mettlesome, peppery, rampant, spunky

-strung edgy, excitable, mettlesome, nervous, passionate, skittish, spirited, startlish, strained, taut, tense, uptight, wiredrawn

-tail depart, hurry, leave, run

-taper mullein

tide agger, climax, culmination

-toned dic(k)ty, dignified, elevated, fashionable, ostentatious, stylish, tense, tony

-wire tightrope

-wrought intense

-yellow creole, mulatto, octoroon

HIGHBINDER hatchet man, hoodlum, killer, ruffian, spy

HIGHBORN aristocratic, generous, genteel, noble, refined, thoroughbred

HIGHBOY bureau, chest (of drawers)

HIGHBRED classy, refined

HIGHBROW aristocratic, double-dome, egghead, intellectual, intelligentsia, snob(bish), snub

HIGHER above, greater, over, senior, superior, supra, upper(most)

-up boss, superior

HIGHEST acme, apex, best, blue-ribbon, bunemost, first, maximal, summit, supreme, top(most)

comb. acro

point acme, apex, apogee, climax, noontide, top, zenith

HIGHFALUTIN arrogant, blustery, bombastic, bragging, grandiloquent, haughty, ostentatious, paughty, pompous, pretentious, snobbish, snobby, wordy

HIGHLAND andes, bolivia, cerro, nepal, pamir, promontory, rand, ridge, rise, scotch, SCOTLAND, switzerland, tibet
fling walloch
headgear tam(o'-shanter)
moccasin copperhead
HIGHLANDER bairn, bluebonnet, bonnetman, gael, mountaineer, nainsel, plaidman, redshank, scot, soldier, swiss, tartan, trewsman, uplander
HIGHLIGHT adorn, emphasize, feature, heighten, illuminate, salience, stand out
HIGHNESS altitude, dignity, loftiness, stridor
HIGHTOBY See HIGHWAYMAN.
HIGHWAY alcan, appian, arterial, artery, autobahn, avenue, belt, boulevard, calzada, causeway, causey, chaussee, course, drive, expressway, freeway, highroad, iter, lincoln, path, pike, road, route, rte, rumpad, speedway, street, thoroughfare, throughway, thruway, toby, turnpike
improvement tax pavage
intersection cloverleaf, crossroad, roundabout
northwest alcan
HIGHWAYMAN bandit, bandolero, bidstand, brigand, bush ranger, footpad, hightoby, hijacker, ladrone, lanceman, marauder, outrider, pad(der), rider, robber, thief
famous claude duval, dick turpin, jack sheppard, james whitney, jesse james, jonathan wild
mare black bess
HIJACK kidnap, rob, seize, steal
HIJACK(ER) bootlegger, footpad, pirate, robber, rumrunner
HIKE boost, clear out, decamp, depart, hitch, increase, march, mush, raise, ramble, rise, toss, tramp, walk
HIKER marcher, parader, pedestrian, walker
HILAIRA *father* leucippus
priestess to artemis
HILARIOUS amusing, funny, gleeful, jocular, jovial, killing, laughable, merry, mirthful, noisy
HILARITY cheerfulness, devilry, fun, gaiety, glee, jocundity, jollity, joviality, joy, merriment, mirth, play, sport, whoopee
HILD *foe* hethin
HILKIAH *father* shallum
offspring azariah, eliakim, gemariah, hasadiah, jeremiah, shallum, susanna
HILL alto, amass, ascent, bargh, barrow, ben, berg, berry, blugg, brae, bult, bump, butte, cerro, colline, collis, cop(ple), cote, cover, dagh, dene, dod(d), down, drumlin, dune, elevation, fell, grade, heap, height, heuvel, hide, high, hillock, hoe, holt, hone, hummock, hurst, kame, knap, knob, knoll, kop(je), loma, lomita, low, lump, medano, mesa, monticle, monticule, moor, morro, mound, mount(ain), nunatac, otero, paha, peak, picacho, protect, puy, rath, ridge, rise, sand dune, scar, sprunt, swell, tertre, tor, tummock, tump, viminal
bird fieldfare, upland-plover
broad-topped loma, mesa
brow snab
chain of aas, range, ridge
cone-shaped brae, cop(ple), law, low
craggy tor
deity troll
folk bhil, cameronian, covenanter, dogra, elves, toda, trolls
fortified rath
glacial drumlin, kame, paha
gooseberry downy-myrtle
high ben
isolated bargh, butte, hum, toft, tor
last in range strone
lava steptoe
low band, how, sowback, wold
man mountaineer
of beans nothing, trifle
oval drumlin
pasture hoga
residual catoctin
rocky scar, tor
rounded dodd, hone
sharp-pointed kip(p)
small down, dune, knap, knoll, loma, molehill

star hummingbird
steep brew, brow
stony roach
top cop, crest, knoll, paha, peak, pike, summit, tor
-trot wild carrot
wooded holt, hurst
HILLARY *conquest* everest
HILLBILLY backwoodsman, braeman, countryman, frontierman, hayseed, mountaineer, rube
HILLEL *son* saul
HILLOCK boss, copse, croft, heave, hummock, hurst, knoll, kopje, molehill, monticle, morro, mound, rise, tertre, toman, tummock, tump, tumulus
over grave tumulus
HILLSIDE acclivity, bent, brae, brow, cle(e)ve, cliff, cote, falda, grade, scarp, slade, slope, stoss
HILLWORT pennyroyal, thyme
HILLY abrupt, precipitous, steep, tumulose
HILO HATTIE clara haili
HILT haft, handgrip, handle, helve, poignet, shaft
guard bow, pas-d'ane, tsuba
part languet
up to the completely, fully
HILUM eye, hilus, nucleus, porta, scar
HIM hem, hin, man, mun, pikas, yak
HIMALAYAN *animal* bearcat, bhalu, goral, ibex, kail, kyl, marmot, ounce, panda, sackeen, serow, yak
antelope chiru, goral, kemas, serow
bear bhalu
bearcat panda
bird chough
broadmouth raya
cedar deodar
climber hilary, sherpa, tenzing
country bhutan, nepal, sikkim, tibet
cypress bhutan
dweller nepalese
forest bhabar
goat goral, kras, tahr, tair, thar
grassy tract tarai
guide sherpa
ibex kail, kyle, sakeen
legendary creature abominable snowman, gigantopithecus, yeti

liquor chi
marmot pia
monkshood api, atis
native sherpa
oxen yak
panda bearcat
pass leh
peak aku, annapurna, api, cho-oyu, dhaulagiri, everest, kanchenjunga, kongmaala, la chooyu, lhotse, makalu, mansalu, nanda-devi, nanga-parbat
pheasant cheer, monal, monaul
plant nard
river valley arun
sheep bharal, nahoor
shrub barberry, rock spray
sub-ranges siwakiks
swamp terai
tableland tibet
tea plant aucuba
tree deodar, sal, toon
tribe lephcas, pamir
valley dun, mari
walnut corylus

HIMAVAT *offspring* devi, diva, parvati, shakti
HIMYARITE arab(ian), axumite, katabanian, minaean, sabaean
HINAYANA See BUDDHISM.
HIND after, back, cabrilla, chap, con(e)y, deer, doe, domestic, dorsum, fellow, fish, grouper, hearst, lad, peasant, posterior, rear (most), roe, rustic, servant, steward, tergum, venison, worker
deck poop
end backside, breech, buttocks, derriere, rear, rump
-heal germander, tansy
speckled grouper
2-year old hearst

HINDEMITH *work* four temperaments, mathis der maler
HINDER after, arrest, back, balk, bar(ricade), bind, block(ade), bottleneck, check, clog, countercheck, cramp, cumber, curb, dam, delay, deprive, detain, deter, disturb, embar, embarrass, encumber, fetter, filibuster, forbid, hamper, hamstring, harass, hedge, hindrance, hobble, hold back, hopple, impede, inhibit, injure, intercept, in-

terfere, interrupt, manacle, obstruct, pinion, posterior, prevent, prohibit, queer, rear, restrain, retard, set back, shackle, slacken, slow, snag, snub, spike, stay, stop, strait-jacket, taigle, tent, thwart, trachle, trammel, trash, traverse, warn

HINDIC *language* urdu
HINDMOST aftermost, last, rear
HINDRANCE arrest, astriction, balk, bar(rier), block, check, clog, cumbrance, curb, delay, detention, deterrent, difficulty, disadvantage, frustration, hitch, hurdle, impediment, interference, interruption, let, obstacle, obstruction, rampart, restraint, restriction, roadblock, rub, snag, stop, tarriance, trash

HINDU (See also INDIA.)
animist, babhan, babu, brahman, gentoo, jain(a), jajman, kalwar, khatri, kolarian, koli, musahar, nayadi, seik, ser, shudra, sikh, sudra, tamil, thakur, vairagi, vaisya
absolute tat
age cycle kalpa, yaga
altar vedika
ancestor manu
angel deva
ascetic sadhu
association sangh
atheist nastika
black shurdra
bliss ananda, nirvana
body sharira
breath atman, prana
caste See INDIA *caste.*
ceremony samskara, snanayatra, straddha
city, holy ajodhya, benares
consciousness aniruddha, cit, mahat
contemplation samadhi
convert to islam shaikh
cow, celestial kamadhenu
creation lila
cult lingayata
custom sati, suttee
cycle phase krita yuga
demigod devarshi
demon asura, rahu
divine artificer tvashtar, tvashtri
doctrine anatta, dharma, karma

dramatist kalidasa
dualism dvaita
duty dharma
elephant airavata
energy shakti
essence amreeta, amrita, atman, rasa
evil personified vrita
evil spirit kali
female energy devi, shakti
fire god agni
forehead mark tilaka
foreigner mlechchha
gnome yaksha
goal nirvana
god, goddess See INDIA *god, goddess.*
godhead shiva-shakti
group sang, varna
guardian of the north bishamon
heaven devachan, devaloka, dyaus, goloka, kamaloka, kamavachara, nirvana, satyaloka, svarga
hell narac, naraka
hermit vanaprastha
hero rama
holy man sadhu
hymns samhita
idol swami
ignorance tamas
immortality amreeta, amrita
incarnation avatar, rama
infinity ananta
interjection aum
juggernaut krishna
knowledge jnana, vidya
kush peak tirachmir
law dharma
life principle prana, tattva
life stages ashrama, brahmachari, grihastha, sannyashi, vanaprastha
literature darshana, kamasutra, purana, shastra, shruti, smriti, sruti, tantra, veda
male principle purusha
man-bird garuda
man, first yama
mantra dharani
marriage practice hypergamy
meditation dhyana
mendicant sannyasi
mind manas
mister babu, sahib
monastery math
monastery head mahant
monk sadhu, sannyasi
movement, modern brahmasamaj, brahmoism
nature principle guna
nonviolence ahimsa

offering to ancestors lepa, pinda
offering to deity bali
olympus meru
philosopher kapila, shankara
philosophy mimamsa, mimansa, sankhya, vaiseshika, vedanta
philosophy school nyaya
physician to gods dhanvantari
poet valmiki
power devi, s(h)akti
practice purdah
prayer gayatri
prayer rug asana
priest pandarum
progenitor manu
pundit swami
purpose artha
reformer kabir
religious leader vivekananda
religious society samaj
ritual achar, pooja, puja, satyagraha
sacred thunderbolt vajra
sacrificial victim traga
sage devarshi, dharma, katha, maharshi, r(i)shi, rsi
salvation marga, moksha
scripture agama, artharvavedas, brahmaba, samavedas, shastra, s(h)ruti, smriti, tantra, upanishads, yajur-vedas
sect aghori, ahmadiya, ajivika, jain(a), meda, sadh, samaj, seik, shakta, sikh, siva
self atman
slave dasi
sorceress usha
soul atman, brahma, jiva, prana
spiritual exercise dharma
tantra student sadhaka
teacher guru, swami
teachings smriti
temple dancer devadasi
temple official sebait
titan bana
title bahadur, malik(ala), mian
trinity brahma, siva, trimurti, vishnu
twice-born ksatriya
universe koka
unorthodox jain(a)
varna member sudra
virtue dharma
wealth god kubera
woman, first ahalya
world loka
world age yuga

world guardian lokapala
world lord jagannath(a)
world serpent ananta, shesha
worship pooja, yajna
worshipper saiva, sakta
writings See HINDU *scripture.*
HINDUISM animism, brahmanism
HINDUSTAN *dravidian* toda
emperor aurangzeb, aurungzeb
hemp sabzi, siddhi
king akbar, khan, maharajah, rajah
language hindi, lahnda, urdu
magic jadoo, jadu
native dakhini, oordoo, urdu
poet siraj, wali
rice crop aghanee
tribe koeri, toda
HINGE articulus, axis, axle, basis, bend, bivalve, butt, cardo, center, charnel, coxcomb, crisis, crook, depend, flap, fulcrum, garnet, gemel, gimmer, hand, hangle, harr, hasp, hingle, jimmer, joint, juncture, nodus, pivot, rotate, swing, turn, twist
-flower dragonhead
half flap
joint elbow, ginglymus, knee, pivot
ring gudgeon
together scissor
HINK faltering, hesitation, hook
HINNOM gehenna, valley
HINNY burdon, hybrid, jennet, mule, neigh, whinny
HINT advert, allude, allusion, break, clew, clue, eyewink, glance, glimmer(ing), guide, implication, imply, indicate, indication, infer, information, inkle, inkling, innuendo, insinuate, insinuation, intimate, intimation, inuendo, mint, pointer, prompt, pulse-beat, refer, reminder, scent, steer, suggest(ion), supposition, suspicion, tang, taste, telltale, thread, time, tip, touch, whisper, wink, wrinkle
HINTERLAND backwoods, bled, bush, country, frontier, interior, outback, outpost, purlieu, silvan, sticks, sylvan, upcountry, woodland, woods
HIORDIS *husband* sigmund

son sigurd
HIP arris, bump, cheer, coxa, haunch, hop, huck(le), hypochondria, ilia, joint, limp, miss, pseudocarp, shoop, side, skip
and thigh overwhelmingly, unsparingly
bone huggin, ilium
huggers slacks
joint coxa, thurl
muscle iliopsoas, piriformis
pert. coxal, iliac, ischial, sciatic
rose berry, choop, shoop
socket acetabulum
HIPPED depressed, lowspirited, obsessed, peevish
on crazy about, enthusiastic, sold
HIPPEUS knight
HIPPIA athena
HIPPIAS *brother* hipparchus
father pisistratus
HIPPIE acidhead, anti, copout, escapist, horse-tamer, mod, rebel, runaway, unconventional
predecessor beatnik
term grass, groovy, junk
HIPPOCOON *ancestor* lacedaemon
brother tyndareus
parent batea, gorgophone, oebalus
slayer hercules
HIPPOCRATES *birthplace* cos, kos
death site larissa, thessaly
drug mecon, opium
precursor avicenna
profession physician
sleeve refiner, strainer
HIPPODAMIA *consort* pelops, pirithous
father adrastus, atrax, oenomaus
son alcathous, atreus, pittheus, thyestes, troezen
HIPPODROME arena, circus, racetrack, theatre, track
HIPPOLOCHUS *father* bellerophon
HIPPOLYTE *consort* iphitus, theseus
parent ares, mars, otrera
sister antiope, melanippe
slayer hercules
son schedius
subjects amazons
HIPPOLYTUS virbius
parent antiope, hippolyte, theseus

protectress egeria
stepmother phaedra
HIPPOMENES melanion, milanion
ancestor codrus
father megareus
great-grandfather poseidon
wife atalanta
HIPPONICUS *daughter* hipparete
son callias
son-in-law alcibiades
HIPPONONE *son* amphitryon
HIPPONOUS *grandfather* sisyphus
offspring periboea
slayer achilles
HIPPOPOTAMUS behemoth, bundont, seacow, zeekoe
fat speck
-headed deity amemait, apet, taur(e)t, thouris
HIPPOTHOUS *kingdom* arcadia
parent alope, cercyon, poseidon
son aepytus
HIRCINE goatish, lewd, smelly
HIRE allowance, assign, bribe, buy, charter, commission, contract, demise, employ, engage, farm, fee, get, job, lease, let, meed, pay, place, prest, price, remuneration, rent, retain, reward, salary, screw, sign, stipend, take on, wage(s)
HIRED paid, rented, teeka, ticca, waged
HIRELING abject, employee, esne, hack(ney), mean, menial, mercenary, servile, slave, subservient, togt, venal
HIROHITO *reign* showa
son akihito
HIRSEL flock, herd, number, pasture, quantity
HIRSUTE boorish, bristly, coarse, feathery, hairy, rough, shaggy, uncouth
HIS alui, hisn
HISPALIS seville
HISPANIA portugal, spain
HISPANIOLA dominican republic, haiti, hayti
HISPID bristly, hairy, rough, spiny, strigose, strigous
HISS assibilate, blow, boo, bubble, disapprove, fistle, fizz(le), hish, rattle, shish, sibilate, sizz(le), spit, tst

HISSARLIK *excavation* ilium, troy
HISTAMINE ergamine
HISTORIAN annalist, antiquary, archivist, beard, bede, carte, chronicler, cliometrician, diarist, durant, gibbon, griot, herodotus, livy, plutarch, polybius, recordist, sallust, scribe, storier, tacitus, toynbee, wells, xenophon
HISTORIC age-old, ancient, memorable, traditional
period aeon, age, eon, epoch
HISTORY account, annals, background, case, chronicle, drama, legend, lore, memoirs, narrative, ontogeny, past, record(s), story, tale, treatise
based on storial
deity saga
father of herodotus
muse clio
HISTRIO See ACTOR.
HISTRIONIC actor, affected, artificial, dramatic, dramaturgic, melodramatic, theatrical, thespian
HIT 3 ace, bat, bop, box, get, jab, lam, peg, pip, rap, zap 4 beat, biff, blow, bump, bung, bunt, bust, butt, cast, club, conk, coup, cuff, foul, kill, klap, lash, pelt, pink, poke, punt, push, slam, slog, slug, sock, swat, tank, whip 5 agree, baste, begin, clash, clout, homer, knock, occur, paste, punch, reach, score, shoot, slate, smash, smite, snick, spank, stamp, thump, touch, whack 6 affect, buffet, cudgel, glance, impact, larrup, nubber, paddle, pommel, pummel, punish, single, strike, stroke, switch, thrash, thwack, triple, volley, wallop 7 blooper, boffola, collide, contact, fortune, impress, smitten, success, triumph 8 bludgeon, bullseye, discover, favorite, lambaste 9 collision, criticism, criticize, fisticuff, sensation, sideswipe 11 lalapalooza
back get even, retaliate
baseball bingle, blooper, bouncer, bunt, dink, double, drive, fly, foul, foulbagger, four-bagger, fungo,

grand slam, homer, home run, line drive, liner, lob, safety, scratch, single, swat, triple
bunt drag
hard bash, slog, slug, sock, souse, stonker
it off accord, agree, click, like
lightly bob, bounce, carom, drum, glance, kiss, pat, rap, tag, tamp, tap, thrum, tip
oblique glance
off discover, find, imitate, improvise, represent, reproduce, satirize
on bull's-eye gold
on head crown
or miss careless, casual, chance, chancy, desultory, habnab, haphazard, happy-go-lucky, heuristic, random, slipshod, sloppy, solitaire, trial and error
sign of sold out, sro
the ceiling erupt, explode
the hay retire
the high spots abridge, scan, slight, speed
the mark impress, score, succeed
the skids decline, deteriorate, fail, fold, sink, slump, weaken
the spot satisfy
up beg, elicit, loft
HITCH agree, attach, catch, cling, connect, crick, crux, enlist, fasten, flaw, hangup, harmonize, halt, hindrance, hirsle, hobble, hook, hop, impediment, inspan, jerk, join, knot, limp, marry, minnow, obstacle, obstruction, pace, pain, pause, pitfall, problem, pull, snag, stoppage, team, term, tie, trace, tug, unite, wed, yoke
HITCHHIKE bum, thumb
HITCHHIKER pedestrian, stowaway
HITHE haven, port
HITHER earlier, here, nearer
and thither to and fro
HITHERTO ago, as yet, before, past, until, yet
HITLER (der) fuhrer
aerie berchtesgaden
autobiography mein kampf
chosen race aryan
dog blondi
follower brown shirt, nazi
friend eva braun
second man goering

HITMAN enforcer, killer

HITTITE hatti, khatti, tabalian

ancestor heth, hett

capital boazkkale, c(h)archemish, hattusa(s), pterir

deity arinna, irbitiga, ishkur, kalhisapi, samuha, santa, tarhunza, telepinu, teshup, teteshapi

kingdom achaia, ahhiyawa

language arzava, hattic, kaneshite, luian, luish, pala(ic)

storm god teshub, teshup

HIVE alveary, apiary, box, collect, gather, group, gum, multitude, settle, skep, stock, store, swarm

vine partridgeberry

HIVES croup, eczema, eruption, rash, roseola, uredo, urticaria

HIZEN hinado, imari, nabeshima

HIZKIAH *son* amariah

HJORDIS *husband* sigmund

son siegried

HLER *consort* ran

HMONG laoians, meo, miao

HOAR ancient, antiquity, biting, cold, grey, musty, rime, stale, venerable, white

-withy whitebeam

HOARD abundance, accumulate, amass, chest, coffer, collect, deposit, garner, gather, heap, hide, hive, husband, mass, pile, quantity, save, squirrel, stack, stock(pile), store, stouth, stow, supply, treasure

HOARDER husband, miser, niggard, silas marner, storer, uriah heep

HOARDING billboard, gallery, poster

HOARFROST cranreuch, ice, rag, rime, rind

HOARSE cracked, croaky, discordant, grating, gruff, gutteral, harsh, husky, quacky, raspy, raucous, raw, rawky, rokey, rough, roupy, sterterous, thick, throaty

as a hog, raven

HOARSENESS frog, roup

HOARSTONE landmark, memorial

HOARY aged, ancient, canescent, frosty, gray(haired), grey, grizzly, incanous, mossy, mo(u)ldy, musty, old, remote, venerable, white, whitish, wintry

alyssum berteroa

marmot mountain badger

pea goat's-rue

puccoon alkanet

HOAX artifice, bam(boozle), barney, befool, bilk, canard, cheat, chouse, cod, cog, con, cozen, deceit, deceive, deception, defraud, delude, diddle, dupe, fake(ment), flimflam, flivver, fool, fraud, fun, gaff, gag, gull, gunk, hoodwink, hum(bug), joke, legpull, lie, plant, ramp, ruse, sell, sham, shift, string, swindle, trick

HOB clown, countryman, elf, fairy, ferret, havoc, hub, matrix, mischief, peg, punch, robin goodfellow, rustic, shelf, shoe, sprite, target

and nob close, familiar, intimate

-like boorish, clownish

HOBBIL clown, dunce, idiot

HOBBLE bewilderment, bind, blunder, bunch, clog, clump, cramble, crammel, cripple, dance, difficulty, embarrass(ment), fasten, fetter, habble, halt, hilch, hirple, hopple, lame, langle, limp, pace, perplex, postern, predicament, scuff, shackle, shaffle, shuffle, stagger, tolter, trammel, wabble

HOBBLEBUSH dogwood, mooseberry, tanglelegs, triptoe, viburnum, wayfaring tree

HOBBLEDEHOY adolescent, tad

HOBBLER boatman, docker, hoveler, pilot, soldier

HOBBY avocation, bicycle, bug, dandy-horse, dolly, fad, falcon, garran, horse, nag, play, pursuit, recreation, sideline, sport, whim

bird wryneck

HOBBYHORSE buffoon, playmare, prostitute, shoofly

HOBBYIST bug, enthusiast, faddist, nut

HOBE *sound* jupiter island

HOBGOBLIN apparition, bloodybones, bogey, boggart, bogglebo, bogie, bogy, boodie, boogeyman, bucca, bugaboo, bugan, bugbear, coltpixie, cow, demon, dwarf, elf, empusa, ghost, hag, imp, ogre, poker, pook, puck(erel), pug, scarecrow, scrat, specter, spectre, spirit, spook, spoorn, sprite, worricow

HOBNAIL punch, tacket

HOBNAILED boorish, clownish, rustic

HOBNOB associate, chat, fraternize, hit or miss, mingle, mix, play, socialize, toast

HOBO beggar, boe, boomer, bum, clochard, migrant, stiff, sundowner, swagman, tramp, vagabond, vagrant

bundle bindle

HOBSON'S *choice* between scylla and charybdis, dilemma

HOCK ankle, cripple, disable, gambrel, ham(string), hook, hough, hox, huxen, jarret, joint, pawn, peddle, pledge, put up, sell, skink, suffrago, thigh, wine

shop pawnshop

HOCKEY bandy, cammock, game, hurley, shindy, shinn(e)y

ball nun, nur, orr, puck, rubber

cup stanley

goal cage

ice six

player puckster

puck rubber

score goal

stick bulger, caman, cambuca, cammock, cummock, doddart, hooky, hurlbat, hurly, shinny

term bully, cage, faceoff, goalie, icing, offside, penalty, puck

HOCUS adulterate, alter, cheat(ing), drink, drug, fraud, liquor, stupefy, trickery

-pocus abracadabra, cheat, deceive, deception, flimflam, hankypanky, humbug, incantation, juggler, juggling, mumbojumbo, mummery, nonsense, quackery, trick(ster)

HOD bucket, coal scuttle, hide, hold, jog, scuttle, stove, tray, trough, tub

carrier paddy

HODDLE manavelin, stew, waddle

HODDY healthy, pleasant, sound

-doddy blockhead, cuckold, fatty, fool, snail

HODER, HODUR *brother* balder

victim blader

HODGE clown, countryman, rustic

HODGEPODGE botch, cento, gallimaufry, hash, hotchpot, jumble, medley, melange, mess, mishmash, mixture, olio, olla(podrida), potpourri, salmagundi, stew

HOE chip, chonta, clat, cliff, cultivate, dig, dogfish, griffaun, grubber, hill, nidget, padle, pulaski, sarcel, scrape(r), scuffle, shim, tool, trouble, worry

-cake corncake, dodger

-down barn dance, party

handle stail

horse nidget, nigget

HOG, HOG'S babirusa, baconer, barrow, beast, ben(odont), boar, bunodont, cadillac, cormorant, dime, glutton, grunt(er), landrace, monopolize, montana, peccary, pig(gy), pork(er), porket, razorback, self-seeker, shilling, shoat, slattern, sow, suid, swine, tapir, tusker, victoria

ape mandrill

-back arete, esker, flatiron, ridge

bean aster, henbane

brake bracken

breed berkshire, duroc, essex, hampshire, hereford, razorback, tamworth

call hoy, sooey, sook

castrated barrow

-choker flatfish, sole

cholera pneumoenteritis, rouget

deer axis, cervus

ear souce, souse, sowce, sowse

fennel brimstonewort, mayweek

food acorn, mast, slops, swill

garlic ramson

grass swine's-cress

ground See GROUNDHOG.

group drift, herd

horned babirusa

innards haslet

-like animal peccary

lily spatterdock

louse sowbug

meat hogweed, toston

nut earthnut, hickory, ouabe, pignut

peanut earth pea

pen crawl, sty

-physic cardinal flower

plum ambaree, ambarella, amra, jobo

rear quarter ham

side bacon, flitch

skin flask

sucker fish, stone-roller

thigh ham

-tie bind, check, clog, disable, fetter, frustrate, hamper, hinder, impede, manacle, obstruct, paralyse, restrain, secure, shackle, thwart, tie, trammel

wild bene, boar, excited, frantic, frenzied, mad

young sheat, shoat, shote

HOGARTH *engraving* rake's progress

HOGFISH capitan, ladyfish, log-perch, loricate, manatee, porpoise, scorpene, wrasse

HOGG shilling

HOGGET boar, colt, fleece, sheep, weaner, yearling

HOGGISH filthy, gluttonous, porcine, selfish, swinish

HOGGY clumsy, heavy

HOGNI *daughter* hild

foe hethin

victim siegfried, sigurd

HOGNOSE *snake* blowing adder, flathead, puffing adder, sand viper

HOGO stench, taint

HOGSHEAD almud, barrel, cardel, cask, hoggel, measure, pipe, tun, vessel

HOGWASH bilge, draff, nonsense, offal, refuse, swash, swill

HOGWEED ambrosia, cowparsnip, dog-fennel, hedgeparsley, horseweed

HOI haw, yam

-polloi canaille, crowd, herd, masses, mob, multitude, populace, proletariat, rabble

HOIST boost, bouse, cannon, crane, davit, derrick, elevate, elevator, erect, heave, heeze, heist, heize, hoosh, jack, launch, lift, polyspast,

raise, rear, tackle, trispast, whimsey, winch

fish brail

sail hoise, swig

system cableway

the blue peter sail

the white flag quit, surrender, yield

HOISTING *device* capstan, crane, davit, derrick, elevator, gin, jack, lift, parbuckle

pin prop prypole

HOITY-TOITY arrogant, flighty, foolish, giddy, harum-scarum, irresponsible, patronizing, proud, scatter-brained, snooty, thoughtless

HOKER derision, mock, scorn

HOKEY contrived, fake

-pokey See HOCUS-POCUS.

HOKKAIDO *native* ainu

HOKUM acting, blah, bunk, humbug(gery), junk, nonsense

HOLD 3 hug, own 4 bear, bind, bite, bond, bulk, deem, feel, gaum, grip, halt, have, hend, hilt, holt, howe, jail, keep, lair, lock, stay, stop, stow 5 argue, avast, belay, brace, carry, catch, cease, check, clasp, cling, exist, grasp, guard, hatch, house, loyal, pause, seize, stick, think 6 adhere, anchor, arrest, cellar, clench, clinch, clutch, cuddle, decide, defend, detain, direct, endure, fasten, handle, hang on, hinder, intern, manage, occupy, prison, remain, retain, secure, strife, tenure 7 believe, capture, cherish, confine, contain, contend, control, custody, grapple, include, persist, possess, refrain, reserve, seizure, subject, support, suppose, sustain 8 consider, continue, purchase, restrain, treasury 9 influence 11 accommodate, confinement

a brief for abet, advocate, defend, endorse, support

back absorb, abstain, belay, boggle, catch, curb, dam, defer, delay, deny, detain, deter, forbear, hesitate, hinder, inhibit, intern, keep, refrain, repress, reserve, restrain, retain, retard, retire,

shrink, slow, stem, stint, stop, suppress
close cradle, cuddle, hug
comb. ten
dear adore, cherish, love, reverence, treasure
down pinion, rein, repress, suppress
fast belay, catch, clamp, clench, clinch, cling, cohere, hapteron, miser, nail, persevere, restrain, secure, stick, support, tenacious
forth continue, descant, discourse, exhibit, expound, maintain, offer, orate, propose, propound, speak, utter
in curb, hinder, repress, restrain, suppress
in contempt proculate, scorn
in conversation buttonhole
in custody detain, imprison, intern, jail
motionless transfix
off avert, delay, procrastinate, refrain, repulse, resist, scruple
on adhere, cling, continue, endure, forbear, glue, grip, halt, persevere, resist, stick, stop, wait
one's ground See HOLD *on.*
out continue, dangle, defend, deny, dree, endure, exclude, extend, last, offer, persevere, persist, propose, protend, reach, refuse, represent, resist, stay, stretch, strike, sustain
over continue, incumbent, postpone
stationary lay to
together adhere, bond, clip, stick
-up arrest, banditry, bear, boost, buoy, cease, check, cohere, delay, display, endure, exhibit, halt, hijack, hinder, lift, overcharge, pass, persevere, raise, rein, resist, restrain, retard(ation), rob(bery), stand fast, steal, stick-up, stop, support, sustain
water cohere, prove, sound, stand up
with agree, approve, assent, consent
wrestling chancery, crotch, half nelson, hammerlock, headlock, lock, scissors, sidehold, strangle, toe
HOLDER container, dop(p),

haver, owner, payee, possessor, receptacle, tenant, vessel
HOLDING(S) assets, belief, equity, haddin, hand, interest, land, opinion, possession, property, retention, retentive, seat, securities, share, stocks, tenancy, tenement, tenent, tenure
adapted for prehensile
device brace, clamp, clasp, clutch, cradle, forceps, grip(pers), handle, hook, net, nippers, pin, pinc(h)ers, pliers, snap, tongs, tweezers, vice, wrench
HOLE abysm, abyss, aperture, bore, boring, bothross, breach, bunghole, burrow, cache, cave, cavity, channel, chasm, cleft, compartment, concavity, coomb, corner, corrie, cranny, crater, crevasse, cut, den(t), depth, dilemma, ditch, dive, dump, dungeon, fault, gap, geat, gime, gourd, gulf, hell, hollow, howe, hut, impasse, interstice, lacuna, lair, lill, orifice, perforation, pierce, pit, pock(et), pore, predicament, prick, puncture, refuge, score, scye, shaft, sink, sipapu, slash, slit, slot, slum, spiracle, sprue, twel, vacuum, vent, void, well
and corner clandestine, covert, underhand
black See JAIL.
breathing spiracle
comb. trema
-cutter aiguille, awl, bodkin, bore, broach, drill, spade, trepan
deep gourd, pot, well
in one ace
living in latebricole
-proof impervious, secure
sandy bunker
size bore
small ventage
up hide, lair, sleep
volcanic fumerole
HOLIDAY celebration, convivial, feria, ferie, festival, festive, fete, fiesta, gay, jovial, joyous, merry, playtime, rest, shabuoth, vacation, yomtov, yontifdig, yontiff
pert. ferial

spot beach, camp, lake, resort, shore, spa
take laze, relax, vacation
HOLINESS consecration, divinity, halidom, piety, pope, saintliness, sanctity, sanctuary, virtue
HOLL depth, ditch, hold, hollow, middle
HOLLA cease, hello, stop
HOLLAND (See also DUTCH.) frogland, linen, lowlands, netherlands
admiral ruyter, tromp
anabaptist john of leyden
anatomist rau
anthropologist dubois
architect rietveld
art group de stijl
assembly iraad
astronomer blaeu(w), sitter
badger das
bailiff baljew, schout
bargain koop, toast
boat bilander, galliot, hooker, koff, praam, schuyt, treckschuyt, yanky
botanist de vries
breakfast balkenbrij, brey
canal drentsch, juliana, oranje
capital amsterdam, the hague
cask cardel
cattle holstein
cheese cottage, edam, gouda, leyden
chemist vanthoff
chicken kippetje
christmas food eel
church body classis
churchman (h)adrian
city aalsmeer, aalten, alkmaar, amersfoort, amsterdam, apeldoorn, arnhem, asten, breda, delft, deventer, dordrecht, ede, eindhoven, emmen, enschede, groningen, grovenhage, haarlem, heerlen, hilversum, leiden, leyden, maastricht, middelburg, nijmegen, rotterdam, scheveningen, schiedam, the hague, tiel, tilburg, utrecht, velsen, venlo, vollendam, zeist, zwolle
clay zeklei
cloth anabasse
coin albertin, albertustaler, cent, crown, daalder, daler, doit, dubbeltje, ducato(o)n, escalan, escalin, florin, guilder, gulden, oord, raps,

rider, rijksdaalder, ryder, stiver, stooter, stuiver, suskin
colonist boer
colonist .in new york copperhead
colony, former borneo, celebes, java, new guinea, sumatra
commune amsterdam, assen, baarn, breda, delft, dongen, doniawestal. doorn, ede, epe, hague, leyden, oss, rotterdam, sneek, voorst, vught, weert, zeist, zuilen, zwolle
composer obrecht, rontgen, swe(e)linck
concert noise, uproar
conductor obrecht
council heemra(a)d, reemraat
cupboard kas
dialect dietsch, frankish, frisian, saxon, taal
dog keeshond
donkey ezel
drink advockaat, geneva, gin, schnapps, vandermint
dwarf paap
explorer barents, tasman
farm bouwerie
fishing boat dogger, hooker, tode
flea market vlooienmarkt
flower tulip
foil orsede, orsedue
geographer blaeu
gin geneva, hollands, schnapps
gipsy aptal, bazigar, heidenen
gold clinquant
governor in america stuyvesant
gulden florin
hamlet dorp
harlot kippetje
heretic lollard
inlet zuider-zee
inventor fokker
island ameland, arroe, aruba, celebes, madura, saba, schelling, st eustatius, texel, vlieland, walcheren
island group arroe, arrou, ar(r)u
judge schout
jurist asser, grotius
lake haarlem
land reclaimed polder
leader willem i
legislature raad
lessee huurder

liqueur anisette
liquor advocat, geneva, gin, schnapps
liter aam, kan
magistrate amtman, burgomaster, stadtholder
man mynheer (closh)
marsh plant derrie
mathematician brouwer, huygens, stevin
meadow betaw
measure aam, ahm, anker, aum, bunder, carat, duim, ell, kan, kop(pen), leaguer, legger, lood, maatje, mijl, mimgelen, mud(dle), mutsje, okshoofd, roede, rood, rope, schepel, steekkan, stoop, streep, vat, vingerhoed, voet, wigt, wisse, zak
merchant league hanse
merchant vessel galliot
military schuttery
mister heer, van
motto je maintiendrai
musician rontgen
mystic bourignian
naturalist leeuwenhoek
navigator barents
nazi victim anne frank
news agency aneta
nobles kabbeljaws
novelist couperus
official schepen
organist swe(e)linck
painter bosch, cuyp, de hooch, dou, eyck, fabritius, goyen, hals, helst, hobbema, kalf, kroninck, kuyp, lely, leyden, lis, mondrian, mostaert, neer, potter, rembrandt, ruisdael, seghers, steen, ter borch
pancake poffertje
patriots les queus
penny stiver
people flemish, frisian
philosopher brouwer, spinoza
physicist debye, loren(t)z, stevin, waals, zeeman, zernike
physiologist einthoven
piedfort patagon
pile worm navalis, teredo
poet decker
political party cod, geuzen, hoek, hook
port edam, flushing, rotterdam, velsen
possession curacao, saha, surinam
pottery delf(t)

printer elzevir
protestant preacher predikant
province brabant, drenthe, epe, friesland, gelderland, groningen, guilders, limburg, overijssel, utrecht, zeeland
queen eugenie, juliana, wilhelmina
rebels south moluccans
redlight district gezellig, zeedijk
reformer groote
river dintel, dommel, donge, eem, hunse, ijssel, kromme, leck, maas, meuse, rhine, scheldt, waal, ys(s)el
river gravel heibanen
royal house orange
rushes derrie
salad sla
scholar erasmus
scientist swammerdam
sea zuider-zee
sheriff schout
stamp market voorhurgwal
statesman asser, barneveldt, kuyper, maurice, thorbecke
theologian arminius, erasmus, jansen
townhall stadhouse
trooper swartrutter
turf plaggen
uncle eme, oom
vessel See *boat*, above.
village ede, oest, tiel, zalk
weight bahar, esterlin(g), grein, korrel, last, lood, ons, po(u)nd, wichtje, wigt(je)
whaler's cask cardel
woman frau(lein), frokin, frow, vrouw
woman, young tannakin
workman volk
writer bekker, couperus, decker, vondel
HOLLANDAISE bridge, game, goulash, mayonnaise, mousseline, sauce
HOLLANDIA japapura
HOLLER complain(t), cry out, hollow, protest
HOLLOW abyss, basin, boss, bowl, cannulate, capacity, capsular, caval, cave, cavern(ous), cavitary, cavity, channel, chasm, compartment, concave, concavity, corrie, cuppy, dent, depression, dimple, dip, dishonest, doke, dowf(f), empty, excavate, faithless, fallacious,

false, fossette, gore, gouge, grotto, gulf, gully, hole, howe, idle, indent, insincere, niche, notch, nugatory, orifice, otiose, paltry, petty, pit, pocket, pyrrhic, scoop, sinus, slock, socket, sunken, thin, trifling, unsound, vacant, vacuous, vacuum, vain, valley, void, wallow, weak, worthless

as a drum

circular correi, corrie

comb. coelo

-eyed haggard

-hearted deceitful, insincere

long groove

marshy swale

narrow dingle

out bore, chase, corrugate, cut, dent, dig, excavate, excise, furrow, gouge, groove, howk, kerf, notch, pit, rabbet, scoop

small alveolus, pock

-sounding amphoric, amphorous

-stock lion's-ear, mallow

HOLLOWNESS appetite, cavity, vacancy, vacuity, vanity

HOLLOWROOT holewort, moschatel

HOLLY acebo, alnus, assi, aunt mary's tree, bearberry, cascara, cassena, catberry, cranberry, dahoon, holm, hull, hulver, ilex, inkberry, milkmaid, olearia, shrub, tollon, tree, winterberry, ya(u)pon

oak blackjack, holm

pert. ilicic

HOLLYHOCK alth(a)ea, flower, hibiscus, (marsh) mallow, rose of sharon

HOLLYWOOD *award* emmy, oscar

stunt man frank tillman

worker actor, stand-in, stunt man

HOLM ait, bottoms, eyot, holly, island, islet, marsh, oak, sea

cock or thrush missel thrush

oak acorn bellote

HOLMES, SHERLOCK

confidant watson

creator arthur conan doyle

HOLMIUM *source* gadolinite

HOLOCAUST destruction, devastation, sacrifice

HOLOPHERNES *eunuch* bagoas

general for nebuchadnezzar

pupil gargantua

slayer judith

HOLSTER quiver, scabbard, sheath

flap flounce

HOLT copse, grasp, grip, hill, lair, mound, plantation, retreat, woods

HOLUS-BOLUS altogether, hastily

HOLY angelic, awesome, blessed, chaste, christlike, consecrated, devout, divine, godlike, godly, good, hallowed, heavenly, huaca, innocent, inviolable, perfect, pious, pure, religious, revered, righteous, sacre(d), sacrosanct, saint(like), saintly, sanctified, santo, seraphic, shree, shri, sinless, spiritual, sri, unworldly, venerated, vestal, worshipped

all panagia

bark cascara-sagrada

basil toolsy, tulce

bottle bacbuc

bread antidoron, eulogia

breathing prayer

city allahabad, benares, cuzco, fez, heaven, jerusalem, kiev, lhasa, mecca, medina, moscow, rome, zion

clover sainfoin

comb. hagi(o), sacro

communion eucharist

cross star beta crucis

day, christian advent, allhallows, all saints, all souls, annunciation, antipascha, ascension, ash wednesday, assumption, candlemas, christmas, corpus christi, easter, epiphany, good friday, hallowmas, lady day, lammas, lent, maundy thursday, michaelmas, pentecost, pinkster, quadragesima, sabbath, sunday, twelfth-night, whitmonday, whitsun(tide)

day, jewish See HEBREW ceremony.

father pope

fire erysipelas

ghost angelica, comforter, paraclete

ghost enemy pneumatomachian

grail sangraal, sangreal

grail castle monsalvat

grail custodian fisher-king

grail founder bohort, bort

grail knight bors, galahad, percival

grass basil, vervain

green terre-verte

hay lucerne, sainfoin

hill athos

isle guernsey, ireland, lindisfarne, rugen, scattery

joe chaplain, clergyman, minister, pilot, priest

lamb agnus dei

land elis, india, mecca, palestine, st giles

land pilgrim hadji, hajji, palmer

loaf eucharist

man (See also CHURCHMAN.) fakir, sadh(u), tzaddik

mess jumble, predicament

mother of the russians moscow

of holies adyt(um), bema, sanctuary, sanctum

oil chrism

one (See also CHURCHMAN.) alvar, christ, deity, god, jehovah, SAINT, supreme being

orders, convey ordain

place altar, mosque, shrine, temple

roman empire, emperor arnulf, charlemagne, ferdinand, joseph, lothair, louis, otto, wenceslaus

rood cross, crucifix

scriptures bible, canon

see, visit to adlimina

stairs scala santa

statue icon, ikon(o)

terror demon, devil, pest

text zendavesta

things, dread of hagiophobia

thursday ascension day

war crusade, jihad

water vessel asperges, aspergillum, aspersorium, benitier, brechites, brush, canthatur, colymbion, cruet, font, stoup

week matins and lauds tenebrae

wood lignum

words, lord of thoth

writ bible, scripture

HOLYSTONE scrub, wash

HOMADUS *slayer* hercules

HOMAGE allegiance, attention, deference, devotion, encomium, esteem, eulogy, fealty, fee, honor, loyalty, manred, manship, obei-

sance, ovation, respect, reverence, tribute, veneration, worship
render adore, attorn, cheve, venerate, worship
supreme latria
HOMALOIDAL even, flat, horizontal, level
HOMBRE See MAN.
HOME abode, address, astre, asylum, biggin(g), bye, don, domestic, domicile, domus, dwelling, fatherland, fireside, goal, grave, habitat(ion), haft, haunt, hearth(stone), heim, hospital, house, hut, ingleside, kern, locality, natural, nest, original, pied-a-terre, place, plate, quarters, range, residence, rooftree, seat, shelter, village
at chez moi
base den, plate
blessed gimle
dome-shaped igloo
fear of ecophobia, oikophobia
funeral chapel
goddess hestia, vesta
-grown indigenous, local, native
guardian of sif
harvest hockey, kern, kirn, mell
institutional asylum, preventorium
-loving domestic
owner householder
plate rubber
poor hospice
rule independence
run circuit drive, coup, hit, score, swat, swot, triumph
service seder
stall farmyard
stretch end, finish
sweet home author payne
team host
thrust hai, hay
HOMEBORN indigenous, native
HOMEBRED domestic, native, rude, uncultivated, unsophisticated
HOMEBREW bathtub gin, bottled-in-barn, kaffir beer, liquor
HOMECOMING advent, arrival, return
HOMEFELT inward, private, profound
HOMELAND auld sod, blighty, havaiki, mother

country, native soil, vaterland
HOMELESS abandoned, alone, besprizorni, deported, deserted, desolate, destitute, displaced, exiled, outcast, roofless, rootless, vagabond
HOMELIKE cheerful, comfortable, cozy, domiciliary, friendly, hamilt, home(l)y, informal, intimate, peaceful, plain, residential, simple, snug, unpretending, unpretentious, warm
HOMELY comfortable, common, domestic, dudgen, everyday, familiar, homelike, humble, inelegant, informal, intimate, kindly, lowly, mean, modest, oldshoe, ordinary, plain, plebian, provincial, rude, rustic, simple, ugly, unadorned, unattractive, uncomely, unpretentious, unsightly
HOMEMADE coarse, crude, domestic, elemental, kelt, plain, rude, simple
HOMEMAKER baleboosteh, housewife, mistress, wife, woman
HOMEOPATHY *founder* hahnemann, hering
HOMEOSTATIS balance, constancy, stability
HOMER *birthplace* argos, chios, colophon, meles, rhodus, salamis, smyrna
character achilles, ajax, diomede, hector, helen, menelaus, nestor, odysseus, paris, priam, ulysses
epic iliad, odyssey
expert schliemann
father ameon
of philosophers plato
scottish wilkie
translator butcher, lang, purves
verse form hexameter
HOMER, WINSLOW *painting* gulf stream
HOMERIC epic, grand, heroic, imposing, monumental
HOMESICKNESS heimweh, mal du pays, nostalgia, nostomania
HOMESPUN (See also HOMEMADE.) kersey, russet
HOMESTEAD barton, cote, estate, farm(ery), garth,

grange, hacienda, homecroft, mains, mansion, messuage, onset, onstead, pen, place, toft, tref, tydden
HOMESTEADER nester, settler
HOMEWARD inbound, incoming
HOMEWORK assignment, drill, practice, prep
HOMEWORT houseleek
HOMEY comfortable, cosy, friendly, heimish, intimate
HOMICIDAL amuck, bloody, murderous
HOMICIDE assassination, death, elimination, foul play, killing, liquidation, manslaughter, morth, murder
fine cro, eric, galanas, wer(e)gild
HOMILY adage, address, allocution, article, conversation, discourse, exhortation, harangue, lecture, omelie, oration, piece, postil, sermon, speech, talk
HOMINY bran, cereal, corn, grits, nasaump, poi, posole, samp
HOMO ape, lemur, man, monkey
americanus indian
sapiens biped, cro, humanity, man(kind)
HOMOGENEITY equality, identity, sameness
HOMOGENEOUS akin, alike, analagous, comparable, equal, identical, like, parallel, similar, solid, uniform
HOMOLOGATE agree, allow, approve, confirm, ratify
HOMOPHONIC harmonious, monodic, unisonous
HOMOPTERA See INSECT *homopterus.*
HOMUNCULUS dwarf, manikin, midget, pigmy, runt
HONAN *capital* kaifeng
HONDO arroyo, channel, gully, waterway
HONDURAS *capital* belize, tegucigalpa
city catacamas, copan, gracias, juticalpa, laceiba, lapaz, progresso, roatan, san pedro sula, tela, trujillo, yoro, yuscaran
coin centavo, lempira, peso
gulf bonseca

indian carib, chorti, jicaque, lenca, maya, miskito, moreno, mosquito, paya, pipil, sumo, tauira, ulva
island roatan
lake brewer, criba, yojoa
measure caballeria, cajuela, manzana, mecate, milla, tercia, vara
peak ceiba, colon
port la ceiba, puerto cortes, san lorenzo, trujillo
president carias andino, looez, villeda morales
range agalta, celaque, pija
river aguan, chamelicon, choluteca, coco, guavape, lempa, negro, olancho, patuca, santiago, segovia, sico, sulaco, tinto, uluawanks
ruins tenampua
tree cockspur
weight caja, libra
HONE delay, dress, grind(stone), grumble, hill, how, lament, long for, oilstone, pine, sharpen(er), stone, strop, whet(stone), yearn
HONEST aboveboard, bluff, candid, chaste, cleanfingered, conscientious, creditable, dinkum, estimable, fair, faithful, forthright, four-square, frank, genuine, good, guileless, highminded, honorable, just, moral, objective, on the level, open, plain, principled, proper, pure, real, reputable, scrupulous, simple, sincere, square, straight(forward), true, truthful, up-and-up, upright, upstanding, veracious, veridical
injun truly
man abe lincoln, diogenes, worthy
HONESTY bona fides, candor, chastity, equity, frankness, good faith, honor, integrity, justice, justness, morality, probity, rectitude, reliability, scruples, sincerity, truth, veracity, verity, virtue
plant lunaria, mang, moneywort, moonwort, primwort, satinpod, virgin's-bower
HONEY ambrosia, beebread, candy, coax, conciliate, confection, darling, dear, fawn, flatter, hinny,

mel(1), precious, sweetheart, syrup, topnotcher
and mulberry juice morat
and wine mulse
ant pleregate
badger ratel
balm mint
bear kinkajou, melursus
bee See HONEYBEE.
beige dorado
berry genip, hackberry
buzzard beekite, hawk, kite, pern
comb. meli, melli
confection halva
creeper bananaquit, coereba, drepanid, guitguit, iiwi, mamo, palila
drink cenomel, hydromel, mead, morat
eater bellbird, friarbird, iao, manuao, maomao, miner, moho, parsonbird, roster, stitchbird, tenui, tui, wurraluh
feeding on meliphagous
flower melianthus, protea, sweet-sultan
flowing with mellifluent
gland nectary
guide bird, moroc
-like melleous
locust false acacia, mesquite, robinia
lotus melilot
mesquite algar(r)oba, honeypod
-mouthed persuasive, soft, sweet
mushroom agaric, armillaria
name meaning lissa, melissa, millie
palm coquito
pert. hyblaean, hyblan, melissic, mellaginous, sugared, sugary, sweet
plant cleome, figwort, hoya, huajillo
pod mesquite
producing meliferous
source bee, bimbil, nectar
sucking mellisurgent
-tongued adulatory, bland, sweetmouthed, unctuous
HONEYBEE aculeate angelito, cyprian, deborah, deseret, dingar, drane, drone, egates, gyne, kootcha, melipona, melissa, queen, stinger, trigona
disease foulbrood, sacbrood
HONEYBLOB gooseberry
HONEYBLOOM dogbane
HONEYCOMB *cell* alveolus

pert. faveolate, favose
residue slumgum
stomach reticulum
HONEYCOMBED alveolar, favose, perforated, pitted, porpus, riddled
HONEYDEW ambrosia, cantaloupe, meligo, melon, mildew, nectar, orange
HONEYED adulatory, candied, dulcet, saccharine, sirupy, suave, sugared, sugary, sweet
HONEYFOGLE cajole, flatter, sweet-talk, wheedle
HONEYMOONER newlywed
HONEYSUCKLE abelia, azalea, banksia, bindweed, blackhaw, caprifoil, caprifole, caprifolium, clover, diervilla, eglantine, goatsleaf, hawthorne, lonicera, morning glory, pinkster, plant, rewa-rewa, sambuccus, sheepberry, shrub, sulla, trumpet vine, twinberry, viburnum, weigela, widbin, woodbine
ornament anthemion
HONEYWARE alaria, badderlocks
HONEYWORT cerinthe, galium
HONG KONG victoria
airport kaitak
bay mirs, repulse, sheko
coin cent, dollar
district wanchai
gardens tiger balm
island lantao
peak castle, victoria
peninsula kowloon
HONK blare, cronk, cry, ooga, toot, yang
HONKY-TONK See SALOON.
HONOLULU *cliff* diamond head, pali
suburb ewa
HONOR accolade, admiration, admire, adoration, adore, adorn, adulation, athel, authority, award, brevet, celebrate, citation, cite, civility, credit, crown, decorate, decoration, deference, dignify, dignity, distinction, distinguish, eclat, eminence, ennoble, esteem, eulogize, eulogy, exalt, faith, fame, fealty, glorify, glory, grace, grandeur, gree, homage, honesty, integrity, koved,

kovid, kudos, laurel, lionize, majesty, medal, mensk, nobility, notice, obeisance, ornament, point, praise, probity, recognition, rectitude, regard, renown, reputation, repute, respect, revere(nce), reward, title, token, trophy, trust, truth, venerate, veneration, virtue
belonging to another borrowed plumes
guest lion, star
hungering for esurient
pledge parole
society phi beta kappa
symbol red carpet
HONORABLE digne, distinguished, eminent, esteemed, estimable, ethical, exalted, generous, good, honest, illustrious, just, lordly, moral, noble, reliable, respectable, revered, righteous, scrupulous, titled, trustworthy, upright, venerable, virtuous, worthy
HONORARIUM bonus, douceur, fee, gratuity, pay(ment), reward, salary
HONORARY nominal, titular
HONORED celebrated, cum laude, distinguished, famous, good, laureate, laureled, magna cum laude, redoubted, reputable
HONSHU See JAPAN.
HOOCH See LIQUOR.
HOOD bangkok, bashlyk, biggonet, blind(er), bonnet, burlet, calash, calotte, calyptra, camail, canopy, cap, capot(e), capuche, caputium, caul, clee, cloak, cochull, coif, cover, cowl, crook, cucullus, funnel, gangster, hat, hide, HOODLUM, liripoop, mobster, mozetta, protection, seal, shield, top, trotcozy
academic liripipe, liripoop
and cape faldetta
cloth bashlik, bashlyk
18th century nithsdale
-like cuculate
part. camail
riding nithsdale
stirrup tapadera, tapadero
straw java
vehicle bonnet, capote
HOODED capistrate, covered, cowled, crested, cucullate, dressed, galeate

arum friar's-cowl
crow grayback, hoodie, hoody
garment See CLOAK
hooded.
merganser mosshead, smew, snowl, spike, tadpole, towhead
milfoil bladderwort
seal bladderhose, wig
snake cobra
HOODLUM apache, bandit, bravo, brawler, bruiser, bully, criminal, cutthroat, desperado, devil, gangster, goombah, goon, gorilla, gunman, guttersnipe, hatchet man, highbinder, hooligan, larrikin, lurcher, malefactor, monster, mug, muscle man, plug-ugly, quaijai, redman, rip, roisterer, roughneck, rowdy, ruffian, savage, scourer, skolly, strong-arm, thief, thug, torpedo, tough, trigger-man, troublemaker, yap, yegg
teenage cherry-red, hairie, hell's angel, hippie, mod, rocker, skinhead, teddy-boy
weapon gat, rod, switchblade
HOODOO bad luck, bewitch, charm, hex, jinx, jonah, jynx, magic, oppress, sorcery, spell, unlucky, voodoo
sea bermuda triangle, devil's triangle
HOODWINK aveugle, bamboozle, beguile, blear, blind(fold), blinker, bluff, cheat, circumvent, cloyne, con, cosen, cover, cozen, deceive, delude, dupe, fool, gull, hide, hoax, inveigle, mislead, muddle, outwit, trap, wile, wimple
HOOEY See NONSENSE.
HOOF beast, clee, cloof, cloot(ie), clufe, cluve, coffin, dance, foot, pastern, step, tramp, unguis, ungula, walk
beat sound clop
cleft seam
disease brown-scab, coronitis, grease-heels, laminitis
having acronychous, ungulate, unguled
outer layer periople
paring tool butteris
print piste, spoor, track

-shaped ungular, ungulate
under subungual
HOOFER dancer, pedestrian, walker
HOOK agraffe, anchor, angle, bait, barb, bend, blow, catch, clasp, cleek, clevis, clip, cramp, crock, crome, crook, crotchet, curve, decoy, drag, fasten, gab, gaff, gig, gore, grapnel, grapple, grip, hake, hamule, hamulus, hamus, hangle, haunch, hink, hock, huck, meak, nock, persuade, pilfer, point, preen, pugh, reaper, sarpe, secure, sett, sickle, snare, snatch, sperket, steal, strike, trap, uncinus, vulsella
a ride bum, hitchhike, thumb
boat hitcher
chitinous uncinus
comb. an(h)ylo, ankylo, hami, onco
coupling jigger
dagger chape
fireplace cleek, hangle, poker
fish See FISH *hook.*
hemp-twisting whirl(or)
large cleek, gaff, hangle
-like falcate, uncinal, uncinate
line and sinker completely, entirely
money lari(n), larree
musical flag, pennant
-nosed aquiline
pert. See HOOKED.
pot bail, cleek, crook, dracken, hangle, kilp, slowrie, trammel
pruning calabozo, sarpe
reaping hink, twi bill
safety clevis
-shaped ancistroid, ankyroid, hamiform, hamulate, uncinate
stretcher tenter
-up association, chain, circuit, connection, network, system
HOOKAH kalian, narg(h)ile, pipe
part chillum
HOOKED addicted, aduncate, aduncous, ancon(e)al, angular, aquiline, beaked, bent, caught, clawlike, cleeked, crooked, curved, drugged, falcate(d), gaffed, hamate(d), hamiform, hamose, hamular, hamulate,

hamus, uncate, unciform, uncinal, uncinate, uncous, unguiform
HOOKER amish, drink, mennonite, pickpocket, prostitute, thief
HOOKWORM anclystoma, ankylostoma, necator, strongyl
HOOKY absence
player truant
-crooky underhand
HOOLIGAN See CRIMINAL, HOODLUM.
HOOP annulation, arch, bail, band, belt, circlet, clevis, crinoline, cry, embrace, encircle, eye(let), frette, garth, gird, girt, girth, loop, ring, tire, trundle, wicket
ash hackberry
barrel band, gird, girth
form into beck
half bail, bale
ring gem(m)el
skirt crinoline, farthingale, tubtail
snake wampum
wood winterberry
HOOPER bird, cooper, rating, swan
HOOPLA publicity, stir, to-do, uproar
HOOPOE dungbird, irrisor, phoeniculus, picarian, upupa, whoop
turned into tereus
HOOSE, HOOZE cough, hack, husk, wheeze
HOOSEGOW clink, cooler, guardhouse, jail, jug, lockup, prison
HOOSIER See also INDIANA.
poet riley
state indiana
HOOT bit, book, cry, gurr, honk, jeer, laugh, mock, owl, shout, siren, toot, trifle, ululate, utu, whoo(t)
HOOTER owl, siren, whistle
HOOVER, HERBERT
birthplace west branch, iowa
party republican
profession engineer
vice president charles curtis
HOOVERVILLE shantytown, slum
HOP bound, bryony, caper, curvet, dance, drug, flight, fly, frisk, gambol, halt, hip, hobble, journey, jump, leap, limp, lollop, lop, lupulus,

nip, opium, pace, plant, skip(per), spring, stimulate, tittup, trip, vine
back vat
bag sarpler
bush ake(ake), lupulus
clover black medic, shamrock, suckwing, trefoil, trifolium
derivative humulene
flea haltica
flour lapulin
hornbeam bois de fer, bumelia, deerwood, hardhack, ironwood, ostrya, tree
kiln o(a)st
-like lupuline
marjoram dittany
mold fen
o' my thumb dwarf, pygmy
o' my thumb's boots seven-league
picker's basket bin
plant bryony, lupulus, marjoram
plant cone bur(r)
stem bine
tree pickaway anise, ptelea, ruewort, wingweed
up increase
HOPE affiance, aim, anticipate, aspire, assumption, assurance, await, bank, belief, confide(nce), conviction, count (on), desire, esperance, expect(ation), faith, foresee, lean on, long, look (for), optimism, pant, perdue, presume, presumption, promise, prospect, reckon, reliance, rely(on), security, speranza, spes, thirst, trow, trust, wish, yearn
full of sanguine
goddess spes
good spes bona
lack despair
name meaning nada, nadine
sign of silver lining
symbol opal, sapphire
symbolic color blue
vain pipe dream
HOPEFUL assured, auspicious, bright, candidate, confident, expectant, favorable, heartening, optimistic, pollyannish, probable, promising, reassuring, roseate, rosy, sanguine, secure, wenliche
HOPELESS abject, bleak, chilled, crushed, dejected, depressed, despairing, desperate, despondent, dis-

consolate, discouraged, done for, downcast, downhearted, dull, forlorn, futile, gone(r), gloomy, glum, impossible, inconsolable, incorrigible, incurable, irremediable, irreparable, irretrievable, lost, melancholy, morose, no go, pessimistic, psycholeptic, ruined, sad, sardonic, undone, vain
HOPELESSNESS depression, despair, desperation, despondency, gloom, impossibility, melancholy, pessimism, psycholepsy, slough
HOPHEAD See ADDICT.
HOPHNI *brother* phineas
father eli
HOPI banak, bannock, cahuilla, comanche, luiseno, moki, mono, moqui, otoe, paiute, panamint, paviotso, pima, piute, shoshone(an), utah, ute, walpapi, washiki
god huruingwuhti
indian spirit kachina, katc(h)ina
HOPLES *father* ion
HOPPER box, chute, dancer, jack, larva, leaper, macaroni, receptacle, tank
HOPPING angry, furious, mad
dick thrush
HOPPLE bind, entangle, fetter, hamper, hobble, pastern, shackle, sidelang
HOPSCOTCH pallall, peevers, potsy
stone peever
HORACE *birthplace* vinusia
courtesan canidia
patron maecenas
teacher orbilius
wine quadrimum
work ars poetica, epistles, epodes, odes
HORAE dike, eirine, eunomia, irene, thallo
festival thargelia
parent themis, zeus
HORAM *kingdom* gezer
HORATIO *friend* hamlet
HORDE army, assemble, camp, canaille, clan, crowd, crush, gang, group, hoi polloi, legion, mass, mob, multitude, pack, press, proletariat, rout, sept, sib, swarm, throng, tribe, troop(s)
inner bukeyef

HORDEUM barley
HOREB sinai
HOREHOUND angelica, ballota, henbit, holly-fern, marrube, maruel, nigra
black archangel
HORI *kin* lotan
HORITE *chief* seir
HORIZON bound, bourn, compass, confine, distance, edge, end, expanse, finitor, gamut, goal, ken, limit, offing, orbit, panorama, prospect, purview, radius, range, reach, rim, scope, searim, skyline, spread, stretch, sweep, vista
arc of azimuth
glass sextant
on the beyond, expected, imminent
pert. mundance
pole nadir, zenith
HORIZONTAL abed, accumbent, aclinal, even, flat, floor, flush, ground, homaloid, level, lying, parallel, plane, prone, recumbent, straight
bar stunt skin a cat
HORIZONTALLY across, athwart, barwise, endlong, flatly, flatwise, lengthways, lengthwise, level
HORMIC purposive, striving
HORMIGO ant-tree, quira
HORMONE adrenalin, aldosterone, androgen, autocoid, automatin, cortin, cortisone, endocrine, enovid, equilin, estradiol, estriol, estrogen, estrone, florigen, galactin, gastrin, gonadoctrophin, insulin, lactogen, lipocaic, lutein, oestrin, oestriol, parathyrin, progesterone, progestin, prolactin, relaxin, secretin, somatrophin, testosterone, theelin, theelol, thyroxin
adrenal cortin
estrogenic estradiol
female estradiol, estrogen
heart-stimulating automotin
human growth hgh
male androkinin, testosterone
medicine acth
pituitary acth
sex androsterone
HORN alarm, antler, awn, beak(er), beam, belcon, bugle, bull's-feather, casque, clarone, claxon, conch,

cor, cornucopia, croche, cuckold, cup, cusp, dag, drink, gore, hook, hooter, mort, oliphant, outlaw, proclaim, prong, thyton, shophar, signal, siren, spike, spur, stab, tine, tooter, trumpet, tusk
amalthea's cornucopia
ammonian cornucopia
birch bark moosecall
blast beep, blare, fanfare, honk, mort, tantara(ra), toot
budding shoot
comb. cera(s), cerat(o), cornu, kerat(o)
crescent cusp
crooked buccina
cut short cow, dod, poll
deciduous antler
drinking rhyton
fly buffalo gnat, simulium
grey column
growth button, spider
hunter's hutchet
in intrude
insect antenna, feeler, palp
kind crocket, zain
-like corneate
-mad crazy, enraged, furious, raving
mouthpiece bocal
note mort
of plenty cornucopia, metel, valerian
painter's amassette
pert. See HORNY.
pie lapwing
player bugler, cornetist, trumpeter
point broach
poppy squatmore
quicksilver calomel
rudimentary slug
seed ergot
-shaped ceratoid, crescent, cornu(te), cornuted
silver cerargyrite
sound See HORN *blast.*
sounded for kill mort
stag antler
stunted button, scur
tissue keratin, scur
twisted addax
unbranched dag
without acerous, buttheaded, dodded, doddie, hummel, moil, mu(1)ley, nat, not(e), poley, poll(ed)
HORNBEAM beech, caprinus, handhack, hardbeam, hornwood, ironwood, ostrya

HORNBILL bird, bromvogel, buceros, bucorvus, calao, homrai, picarian, tock, toucan, yearbird
cuckoo ani
HORNBLENDE ambonite, amphibole, amphibolite, appinite, bojite, buchonite, edenite, pargasite, siderite, uralite
HORNBOOK battledore, primer
HORNED *dace* chub
pout catfish
screamer anhima, kamachi, unicorn
viper cerastes, wampum
HORNET crabro, insect, vespa, wasp
nest bike, fury, trouble
HORNGELD cornage
HORNPIPE black-gum, dance, matelote, tune
HORNPOUT stickleback
HORNSTONE keralite, quartz
HORNSWOGGLE bamboozle, cheat, deceive, hoax, swindle
HORNTAIL dryssid, sawfly, sirex, tremex, urocerid, woodworm
HORNTHUMB cutpurse, thief
HORNUB *father* thoth
HORNWORT coontail, hornweed, morassweed, ranale
HORNY bony, callous, ceratoid, chitinous, corneous, crescent, hard, kerasine, keratinous, keratoid, solid, waukit
comb. corneo
-head chub, nokomis
scale lorica, nail, scute, scutum
HOROERIS *mother* nut
HOROSCOPE forecasting, prediction
casting apotelesm
HORRENDOUS See HORRIBLE.
HORRIBLE alarming, appalling, awful, bad, black, dire, disgusting, dreadful, eerie, evil, execrable, fearful, formidable, frightening, frightful, ghastly, grim, grisly, hateful, hideous, horrendous, horrid, horrific, loathsome, lousy, obnoxious, offensive, outrageous, repellent, repugnant, repulsive,

revolting, shocking, terrible, terrifying, ugly, unpleasant

HORRID bristling, dreadful, grim, gruesome, **HORRIBLE**, inferior, nasty, rough, rugged, scandalous, shocking, ugsome

HORRIFIED aghast, frightened, ghastly, outraged, scared, terrified

HORRIFY appall, awe, daunt, dismay, frighten, perturb, scare, terrify, upset

HORROR alarm, aversion, awe, consternation, dismay, distaste, dread, fear, fright, monster, panic, recoil, repugnance, shaking, shuddering, terror, torment, trepidation

HORSA *brother* hengist

HORS DE COMBAT dead, done, invalid, killed, spent

HORS D'OEUVRE antipasto, aperitif, appetizer, assiette, barquette, canape, herring, olives, outwork, pupu, relish, zakuska

HORSE (See also *breed* and *inferior*, below.) alsvinn, alsvith, arion, arvak, barb, bay(ard), beast, bidet, block, brock, bronco, broomtail, bucker, buckskin, caballo, cartaver, cavallo, cavalry, charger, cheval, cob, colt, cooser, courser, dobbin, equine, filly, fittielan, foal, furrahin, garran, gee-gee, gelding, gigster, gras, gri, hack, heroin, hoist, hoss, jackstay, jennet, kohl, mare, mount, mustang, nag, pacer, padnag, palfry, pelter, plug, prad, prancer, prod, roan, rouncy, screw, sheltie, stallion, stand, steed, stepper, stud, sumpter, tarpon, thiller, tit, trestle, trotter, waler, warragal, warrigal, wheeler, zain

act manage

and buggy ancient, old-fashioned, old-fogey

ankle hock

ankle joint coot

armor barde, flanchard, frontstall, poitrel, testiere

around caper, fool, misbehave, play, prank

autobiography black beauty

back ridge

back, on a cheval

balm citronella, collinsonia, knobweed, knotgrass, knotroot, monarda, richweed

belt surcingle

bit bastonet, cannon, kevel, pelham, scatch, snaffle, snode

black cycleptus, sucker(el)

blanket apishamore, caparison, manta, namda, rug, saddlecloth, tilpah

blanket fabric yerga

blinder eyeflap

blob marsh marigold

boot scalper

boy tracer

bramble sweetbriar

breast counter

breastplate poitrel, peytrel

breed appaloosa, arab(ian), barb, belgian, cayuse, clydesdale, galloway, hackney, harness, houyhnhnm, hunter, jennet, kohl, lippizaner, morgan, mustang, narragansett, normandy, nubian, palomino, percheron, pinto, poille, punch, quarter, saddle, shetland, shire, spanish, suffolk (punch), tarpan, tennessee-walker, thoroughbred, trotter, turk, waler, welsh pony

breeding farm haras

brown bay, chestnut, roan, sorrel

buckle cowslip

buyer chanter, co(u)per, courger, knacker, scorser, trader

calico piebald, pinto

callous sitfast

cane ragweed

castrated gelding

check, violent saccade

chestnut aesculus, buckeye, conker, glabra, roan, tree

cloth house, housing

collar bargham, brecham

collar ornament hounce

collar part hame

color bay(ard), calico, chestnut, gray, grizzle, palomino, piebald, pied, pinto, roan, schimmel, skewbald, sorrel

comb. eque, equi, hipp(o)

command gee, giddap, haw, huddup, hup(p), proo, whoa

covering caparison

cress brooklime

cry neigh, nicker, whinny

dappled piebald, pinto, roan

dark morel, zain

dealer See HORSE *buyer*.

decrepit plug, skate

-devil indigo

disease azotemia, blind staggers, blue-tongue, botryomycosis, bots, bursattee, caloris, canker, carney, clap, cleft, distemper, dourine, equinia, farcy, foot-mange, frounce, glanders, haw, heaves, influenza, lampas, lampers, leuma, mose, mule, murrina, nagana, parabotulism, pinkeye, pox, quitter, quittor, sarcoid, scalma, scratches, sleepy, spavins, staggers, strangles, strangullion, surra(h), sweeny, thick(head)(wind), thrush, variola, vives, weed

docked-tail cocktail, curtal

doctor hippiater, hippiatrist, quack

draft aver, beetewk, belgian, clydesdale, hairy, percheron, punch, shire, suffolk

driver See HORSEMAN.

duck canvasback

easy padnag

elder elecampane

event race, rodeo, roundup, show

extinct epihippus, miohippus

-eye jack jurel, xurel

eyelid hair brill

eyelid inflammation haw

fallow favel

family dobbin

famous alborak, bayard, black bess, bucephalus, copenhagen, grani, houyhnhnm, incitatus, lipizzaner, lippizzana, lippizzaner, man-of-war, marengo, pegasus, rosinante, sleipnir, vegliantino, xanthus, xeillantif

farm dobbin

fast clipper, ganger

feeder chalcidian, manger, nosebag

female dam, filly, mare, yaud

fennel seseli

fever scalma

flower cowwheat

foot coronet, fetlock, frog, hoof, pastern

foot defect crescent

foot snipe knot, turnstone

forehead chanfrin

forehead mark blaze
4-abreast quadriga
4-toed echippus
gait amble, canter, entrepas, gallop, lope, pace, prance, rack, run, single-foot, step, trot, vott, walk
gear tack
gentian feverroot
genus equus
giant goldfax
gland swelling vives
goddess epona
golden palomino
gowan camomile, daisy, dandelion
gray grizzle, schimmel
group atajo, cartware, caviya, drove, herd, manada, quariga, random, remuda, ruck, span, stable, string, team, troika, unicorn
guard cavalry, sand wasp
guide rope longe, rein
gypsy's gras, gri, gry
hair fetlock, mane, seton, snell
half-man centaur
half-wild mustang
harness pacer, tackle, trotter
-head moonfish, sea-horse
-headed goddess demeter
hired hack(ney)
hobble spancel
hock gambrel, suffrago
hock disease spavin
hoof coltsfoot, ungula
hoof disease canker, frush, mellit, vilitis
hoof parer butteris
hoof print slot
horned gnu, monoceros, unicorn
hydrocephalic dummy
imaginary aullay
immortal balius, xanthus
immunized bleeder
inferior also-ran, balker, cocktail, crock, crowbait, dog, durgan, dweller, garran, gleyde, goat, hack, hatrack, hayburner, jade, keffel, ladino, nag, outlaw, padnag, plater, plug, rackabones, rip, roarer, rogue, rosinante, ruck, scalawag, scrag, screw, shack, skate, stammel, stiff, stumer, stumour, tit, weed, whistler
jump ballotade, capriole, curvet
jumping lepper
keeper groom, hostler
lark corn bunting

last also-ran, thill(er)
-laugh guffaw, heehaw, snort
leap ballotade, capriole, curvet
leech alukah, beggar, farrier, veterinarian
leg disorder curb, sallenders, speedy-cut, thoroughpin, vessignon, windgall
leg growth fusee, fuzee
leg joint flexura
leg part cannon, coronet, fetlock, gaskin, hock, hoof, instep, pastern, shank, stifle
-like equine, equoid
lily spatterdock
lip disease flaps
litter brancard
load seam
-lover hippophile
-lover, name meaning philip
-loving philhippic
mackerel akule, atuke, bluefish, bonito, fish, jurel, saurel, scad, ten-pounder, tunny
male entire, gelding, stallion, steed, stud
mane encolure
market tattersall's
-masher wheatear
mean brock
measure hand
measurer hippometer
medicine hippiatrics
miniature falabella
mint monarda, rignum
mottled appaloosa, piebald, pinto
mounted on equitant
mushroom whitecap
mythological aulay, pegasus
neck withers
neglected tacky
neigh, divination by hippomancy
nettle solanum, trompillo
noseband cavesson
old aiver, aver, crock, crowbait, dobbin, garran, gleyde, hack, harridan, knacker, moke, nag, padnag, plug, prod, rip, rosinante, skate
-opera oater, western
pace See HORSE *gait.*
pack bidet, sumpter
pair span, tandem, team
parsley alexanders
-penny daisy, rattle
pert. caballine, chevaline, equoid, hippian, hippic
piebald pinto
pill bolus
plains mustang

pox grease
prehistoric eohippus, miohippus
race allowance, claiming, derby, handicap, plate, steeplechase, sweepstakes, weight-for-age
race advantage handicap
raceboard tote
race position place, rail, show, win
racing bangtail, entry, favorite, geegee, mudder, mudlark, pacer, plater, pony, speeder, staker, starter, thoroughbred
racing god consus
-radish angel tree, armoracia, beh(e)n, ben, maror, moror, redcoll, wasabi
-radish tree ben
range fantail
rearing pesade
red bay, roan, sorrel
register studbook
relay remuda
rider jockey
riding appaloosa, rouncy, tennessee walker
riding school manege
ring piste
-rooster hippalectryon
rump croup
sacrifice ashvamedha, hippocaust
saddle bidet, cob, mount, palfrey
sea See SEA *horse.*
sense acumen, intelligence, judgment, practicality
shackle fetterlock
shaggy altai
show dressage
skin ailment clay fever, gall, mud fever, scratches
small bidet, bronco, cayuse, cob, colt, galloway, gennet(te), hobby, jennet, nag, pony, shetland, tit
sorrel chestnut, roan
spirited arab, barb, charger, courses, rearer, stallion, steed, stepper
stable ecurie
stealing hoof-snaffling
-stinger dragonfly, gadfly, hornet
stocky cob
stud farm haras
study hippology
sugar sweetleaf
sun alsvinn, alsvith, arvak
swelling capellet

swift arab, courser, pacolet, racer
symbol of grace, speed
tackle harness
talking arion, xanthus
tender groom, hostler, ostler, stabler
thief rustler
3 abreast troika
3, one behind another random
3, team of random, unicorn
tic forest fly
tongue butcher's-broom
tooth tush
trace fastening hame
track slope calcade
trade bargain
trader chanter, sharper
trainer chalan, pinhook, valet
trainer's rope longe
training dressage, manege
transport palander
trapping caparison, harness, tackle
tread volt(e)
trick simon
trotting cob, morgan, paloalto
trunk barrel
tumor ambury, anbury
turn passade
2-year-old twinter
unbroken bronco
vicious ladino
war charger, courser, destrier, steed
western range broomtail, mustang
whale walrus
wheel poler
white streak blaze, reach, shim
wild bangtail, bronco, brumbie, brumby, fuzztail, fuzzy, jughead, kumrah, mustang, tarpan, warragal, warrigal
winged aethon, arion, astrope, bronte, buraq, chronos, eous, hippogriff, lampon, pegasus, phaethon, phlegon, pyroesis
winless maiden
wooden trestle
work aver, dobbin, garran, gelding, percheron
worn-out See HORSE *old.*
worthless See HORSE *inferior.*
wound on leg attaint
young colt, filly, foal, staf(gie), stot, tit

young, group manada, stable, uniform
HORSEBANE dropwort
HORSEFEATHERS See NONSENSE.
HORSEFISH hippocampus, king crab, moonfish, sauger, seahorse, sucker, vomer
HORSEFLESH chevaline, jack
eating equivorous, hippivorous
mahogany sabicu
ore bornite, erubescite
HORSEFLY bot(fly), brachycerus, breeze, bulldog, chrysops, cleg(g), deerfly, gad(fly), indigo, stout, stut, tabanid
HORSEHEEL elecampane
HORSEHIDE baseball, cordovan
HORSEMAN boulanger, broncobuster, buckaroo, bullwagon boss, bullwhacker, caballero, carter, cavalier, cavalryman, centaur, charioteer, charro, chevalier, coachman, courier, cowboy, cowpuncher, dragoon, drayman, equestrian, equestrienne, gaucho, hackmon, hussar, jarvey, jockey, muleskinner, muleteer, nagsman, picador, postboy, postilion, pricker, puncher, rider, ritter, roughrider, spur, sumpter, uhlan, vaquero
headless, quarry ichabod crane
track piste
HORSEMANSHIP cavalry, equitation, manege
term caracole, pesade, piaffe, volt(e)
HORSEMATCH wheatear
HORSENOP knapweed
HORSEPLAY antics, aperies, buffoonery, caper, hank(e)y-pank(e)y, highjinks, hijinks, misbehavior, monkeyshines, prank, tricks
HORSEPOWER energy, force de cheval, soup
HORSESHOE bearpaw, hobber, lunette, plate, ringer
crab trilobite
frame or stall trave, treve
game barnyard golf
gripper calk

heel sponge
part calk, caltrop, sponge, spur, web
shaped hippocrepian, lecotropal
HORSESHOER blacksmith, farrier
helper floorman
HORSETAIL cat-whistles, equisetum, mushroom, plant, prele, snakepipe, toadpipe
dock bob, strunt
lichen freehair
standard toug, utug
tree agoho, agojo, beefwood, balata, blolly
HORSEWEED bloodstanch, butterweed, cocash, colt's-tail, cowtail, fireweed, fleabane, helenium, hogweed, ragweed, scabious, sneezeweed
HORSEWHIP beat, bhabook, cat, chabouk, flog, punish, quirt, scourge
HORTATION advice, exhortation
HORTATIVE, HORTATORY advisory, educational, emotive
HORTENSE *son* napoleon iii
HORTENSIO *beloved* bianca
HORUS behdet, harmakhis, harpakhrad, harpokrates, harsiesis, hartomes, harwer, horbehdet, hormakhu, hormerti, sept(i), sopt
brother anubis, osiris, seth
companion hathor
enemy set(h)
parent isis, nut, osiris
servant thoth
sister bubastis
son amseti, duamutef, hapi, imsety, kebhsenuf, qebhsnuf
victim seth
wife hathor
HOSAH *son* hilkiah, simri, tebaliah, zechariah
HOSANNA blessings, cheer, cry, hymn, praise
HOSE breeches, brogues, drench, gaskin, greaves, HOSIERY, moisten, pipe, socks, sprinkle, stockings, tube, vamp
catch run, snag
HOSEA *offspring* jezreel, loammi, loruhamah
wife gomer
HOSEIN *ancestor* mohammed

HOSHAIAH *son* azariah, jezaniah

HOSIERY anklet, argyles, bobbysocks, boothose, knitwear, nylons, pantyhose, sheers, socks, stockings, sweat socks, tights, work socks
fabric balbriggan, cantrece, nylon, rayon, silk
thread lisle
type stretch
worker looper

HOSPICE asylum, diaconia, hospital, hotel, imaret, inn, monastery

HOSPITABLE accommodating, charitable, convivial, cordial, douce, friendly, genial, gracious, gregarious, jolly, kind, neighborly, social

HOSPITAL asylum, clinic, creche, hospice, hotel des invalides, infirmary, inn, lazaret, maison de sante, maladery, measondue, noscomium, pesthouse, polyclinic, sanatorium, sanitarium, sickbay, sickberth, spital, surgery, valetudinarium
attendant aide, gray lady, nurse, orderly
charity lazaretto, lazar house
fever typhus
insurance blue cross, blue shield
leper leprosery
mobile ambulance
volunteer candy-striper, gray lady
worker almoner

HOSPITALITY cheer, conviviality, cordiality, generosity, mense, warmth, welcome, xenodochy
god dius fidius
patron saint julian
pert. xenial, xenian

HOSPODAR governor, ruler, voivod

HOST army, assemble, balebos, boniface, bread, company, crowd, emcee, entertain(er), fyrd(ung), horde, housel, inn(keeper), jason, landlord, legion, lodging, maitre d'hotel, master, mob, multitude, oast, sacrifice, sacring, server, sum, swarm, throng, viander, wafer, ware, welcomer, wered

consecrated sacrament
eucharistic lamb, sabaoth, sacring
of heaven angels, moon, stars, sun
receptacle ciborium, paten, pyx
unidentified amphitruo, amphitryon

HOSTAGE collateral, earnest, gage, guarantee, hostel, inn, otage, pawn, pledge, security, surety, token
to fortune children

HOSTEL(RY) bethel, hospital, hotel, imaret, inn, lodge, mansion, maret, motel, shelter, tavern

HOSTESS landlady, taupo

HOSTILE adverse, aggressive, alien(ated), antagonistic, antipathetic, asocial, bellicose, belligerent, bitter, chill(y), contrary, cool, deadly, enemy, foe, fremt, frigid, inimical, malevolent, malicious, malign, nasty, opposed, oppugnant, poisonous, repugnant, spiteful, truculent, unfriendly, unquert, vicious, virulent

HOSTILITY aggression, animosity, animus, antagonism, antipathy, bad blood, belligerence, clash, collision, combat, conflict, contrariety, contrariness, disaffection, enmity, feud, grudge, hate, hatred, illwill, inimicality, malice, malignity, opposition, oppugnance, rancor, repugnance, schism, spite, spleen, unfriendliness, venom, virulence, war(fare)
comb. ant(i)
reduction thaw

HOSTLER groom, innkeeper, stockman

HOT angry, ardent, blistering, boiling, broiling, burning, calid, candent, close, contraband, current, eager, ebullient, excellent, excitable, fashionable, fervent, fervid, feverish, fierce, fiery, flaming, flushed, fresh, fugitive, good, great, heated, heavy, impassioned, impetuous, inflamed, intense, lustful, muggy, near, new, novel, overheated, parching, passionate, peppery, pun-

gent, racy, raging, recent, roasting, scalding, scorching, searing, seething, simmering, sizzling, smoking, smouldering, spicy, steamy, stifling, stolen, strong, stuffy, sultry, sweltering, swelt(r)y, thermal, torrid, tropical, vehement, violent, warm, zestful, zesty
air bluster, bombast, braggadocio, bunk, chatter, exaggeration, gossip, nonsense, shmegegge
air artist blowhard, braggart, chatterbox, fonfer
as a coal, fire, oven
-blooded ardent, combustible, excitable, fiery, impetuous, thoroughbred, spirited, vascular
box smoker, stinker
box locator monitor, sensor
cake griddlecake, pancake
comb. therm(o)
day broiler, roaster, scorcher, sizzler, swelterer
dog dachshund special, frankfurter, weeny, whee, wiener(wurst)
flash flush, hunch
off the fire fresh, novel
place equator, furnace, hell, oven, subtropics, torrid zone, tropics
rodder drag-racer, dragster
-shot aggressive, fast, fireman, skillful, speeder, success(ful)
spot hell, night club, oast, oven
spring balneum, geyser, spa
-tempered choleric, fiery, iracund, irascible, peppery, spitfire, touchy
tip low-down, scoop
under the collar angry, furious, livid, torrid
water difficulty, geyser, old faithful, predicament, steam, thermae, trouble, vapor
water bottle pad, pig
ziggety whee

HOTBED birthplace, den, glasshouse, nest

HOTCHPOTCH blend, confusion, hodgepodge, jumble, mass, mess, mixture, stew

HOTEL albergo, auberge, caravansary, fleabag, gasthof, gonda, hospice, hostel(ry), hottle, house, hydro, imaret, inn, lodge,

motel, osteria, parador, posada, ryokan, serai, spatel, tavern
clerk deskman
de ville townhall
dieu hospital
keeper boniface, host, hotelier, master, padrone
manager concierge
waterside boatel, botel
HOTFOOT flee, hasten, hastily, run
HOTH, HOTHR *beloved* nanna
rival bald(e)r
victim bald(e)r
HOTHAM *father* heber
son amal, imna, shelech, zophah
HOTHEAD crank, inciter, raver, reactionary, tinderbox
HOTHEADED angry, brainish, combustible, fiery, hasty, impetuous, madbrained, passionate, peppery, reckless, short-tempered, spunky, volcanic
HOTHOUSE bagnio, brothel, conservatory, fruitery, greenhouse, nursery, pinery
HOTHR See HOTH.
HOTSPUR crank, daredevil, headstrong, henry percy, hothead, impetuous, madcap, rash, reckless, violent
brother-in-law mortimer
father northumberland
wife lady percy
HOTTENTOT balao, balawu, bondelswarts, bondelzwaarts, khoi-khoi, kokana, quaequae, strandlooper, swartzbois, totty, witbooi
apron tablier
bread elephant's-foot
bustle steatopygia
cloak kaross
deity gaunab, tsui-goab
dialect gona, kora, nama
encampment kraal
hero heitsi-eibib
instrument gora(h), goura, ramkee
rug kaross
staff kirvi
tobacco daccha
tribe balao, balawu, damara, gona, goura, griqua, khoikhoin, korana, nama(qua), oerlaam, sandawe, sandawi
warclub knobkerrie
HOTTER bubble, crowd, heap, jolt, mumble, rumble,

seethe, shake, stammer, swarm
HOTTONIA featherfoil, plant
HOUDINI erich weiss
brother theo
wife bess rahner
HOUGH cripple, hamstring, hawk, HOCK
HOUND, HOUND'S afflict, annoy, badger, bait, cerberus, chase, chevy, dog, drive, enthusiast, follow, harass, harry, heckle, hector, hunt, oppress, persecute, pursue, press, reprobate, ride, sleuth, torment, torture, track, treer, try, urge, worry, wrong
berry dogwood, nightshade
bitch brach
breed afghan, barukhzy, basset, beagle, brachet, dachshund, foxhound, greyhound, harrier, lucern, otter, talbot, wolfhound
cry music
fish dogfish, gar(fish), shark
group cry, mute, pack
hunting harrier, redbone, setter
hunting cry glasting
of heaven conscience
of hell cerberus
pert. skirter
sleuth talbot
small basset, beagle
spectral raches, shuck
spotted dogfish
tail stern
tongue clintonia, toryweed
wolf alan
HOUR ghurry, heure, hora, ora, period, stunde, time, wie
book of hora(e)
canonical See CANONICAL hour.
class period
count time
lights out curfew, taps
pert. horal, horary
HOURGLASS clock, shapely
spider black widow
HOURLY constantly, frequent(ly), horal, periodic(al), quickly
HOUSE 3 hut, inn, pad 4 casa, cote, dome, dump, firm, hall, hold, HOME, iglu, isba, line, pent, roof, shop, stow 5 abide, abode, adobe, bahay, basha, berth, board, cabin, cover, domus,

dwell, hotel, humpy, igloo, kiosk, kouba, lodge, place, serai, tembe, tribe, tupek, villa 6 biggin, billet, camara, casino, castle, church, family, gazebo, grange, maison, market, tavern, temple 7 address, barrack, bigging, chamber, chateau, contain, cottage, edifice, enclose, fazenda, kashima, lineage, lodging, mansion, mesudge, protect, quarter, rotunda, shelter, theater 8 ancestry, assembly, audience, barabara, barabora, building, bungalow, domicile, dwelling, hawaghar, pavilion 9 dormitory, residence, synagogue 10 auditorium, habitation, splitlevel
and 5 acres cote
and land demesne, messuage
apartment insula
bawdy bagnio, bordello, brothel, stew
big See JAIL.
block See FORT.
boarding fonda, netherskey, pension(e)
buyer knacker, realtor
chapter cabilda
charnel ossuary, tomb
clay adobe, tembe
cluster dorp, hamlet, village
coach remise
comb. domato, eco
commercial emporium, firm, shop, store
communal morong
country casino, chateau, dacha, quinta, villa
eating cafe, chophouse, cookshop, inn, RESTAURANT, tavern
death See JAIL.
deity lar
dick detective
finch burion, carpodacus, linnet, redhead
-garage passage breezeway
grinding hull
-leek alatern, ayegreen, bullock's-eye, foose, homewort, jubarb, poor-jan's-leaf, privet, sempervivum, sengreen, silgreen, thunderwort
log izba, tilt
manor court, hall, ham, schloss
many-doored baradari
movable camper, caravan, lodge, mobilehome, mo-

torhome, tent, tepee, trailer, wigwam, wikiup, yurt
mud tembe
narrow tome
odds vigorish
of correction bridewell, jail, prison, reformatory
of joy See HOUSE *bawdy.*
cf lords official black rod
of mercy hospital
of 7 gables, author hawthorne
of 7 gables family pyncheon
of worship bethel, bethesda, chapel, church, synagogue, temple
on the free
organ magazine, periodical
part attic, cellar, estre, hall, roof, room
pert. domal
pet cosset
plant aspidistra, begonia, calla, coleus, fern, ivy, violet
public hospice, hostel(ry), hotel, inn, pub, tavern
ranch casa, casita, estancia, grange, hacienda
religious cathedral, chapel, church, convent, kellion, kirk, priory, synagogue, tabernacle, temple
rented let
retreat cenacle
rural chateau, farm, grange, ranch, villa
rustic bower
servant abigail, atriensis, bearer, bootboy, butler, chambermaid, char(woman), chef, cook, domestic, footman, groom, hallgirl, lady's maid, laundress, parlormaid, scullery maid, scullion, valet, washwoman
shabby dump
small bach, cabin, casita, cell, cottage, hovel, hut, shack
smallest in world stockbeck
sparrow passer
spirit banshee, benshee, brownie, duende, dwarf, esprit, follet, fada, feardearg, follet, hada, hinzelmann, kobold, monociello, nis(se)
stately mansion, palace, villa
still chi(c)kee
summer baradari, belvedere, bower, cabin, cottage, gazebo, kiosk, paudal, pergola, shack, trellis, villa

thatched banda
the christ church
timber and plaster calamanco
toy cobhouge
tree nest
-warming infare, party, reception
HOUSEBOAT barge, dehabeah, wangun, wan(i)gan, wannigan
HOUSEBREAK domesticate, train
HOUSEBREAKER burglar, jacob, millken, robber, thief
HOUSEBROKEN civilized, disciplined, domestic, trained
HOUSECARL bodyguard, retainer, thingman
HOUSECOAT dressing gown, duster, kimono, robe
HOUSEFLY bluebottle, brachycera, hexapod, musca
HOUSEHOLD belonging, common, domestic, familiar, family, housal, mainpast, meiny, menage, ordinary, residence, usual
deities hestia, lar(es), penates, seraph, teraphim, vesta
fairy puck
goods chattels, inspreith
regulation economy, husbandry, thrift
HOUSEHOLDER addressee, astrer, bordar, breadwinner, collibert, cottager, cott(i)er, franklin, goodman, homeowner, indweller, master, naukrar, occupant, tenant, villein
HOUSEKEEPER caretaker, daily(woman), domestic, janitor, janitress, maid, matron, mistress, wife
HOUSEMAID duster, servant, tweeny
HOUSEMAN butler, croupier, dealer
HOUSEMAN, A. E. *work* shropshire lad
HOUSEWIFE dame, economize, frau, hausfrau, hussy, mistress, pani, vrouw
HOUSEWORK chore, drudgery
HOUSING address, billeting, box, coat, cover(ing), cowl, drum, hangar, kiosk, lodging, niche, pad, quartering, quarters, shelter, shield, support, tract, trappings

poor barrio, ghetto, slum
HOUSTON *airport* conroe
feature astrodome, greenway plaza, spacecraft center, spindletop
grande dame ima hogg
stadium astrodome, the great indoors
university rice, texas southern
HOUSTONIA baby's-breath, bluet, bright-eyes, chrysanthemum
HOVA imerina
HOVE float, half, heave, ivy, linger, loiter, raise. rise, soar, threw
HOVEL burrow, cabin, canopy, choza, cosh, cottage, crew, crib, cruive, den, dugout, haystack, helm, hood, hulk, hull, hut(ch), lean-to, niche, pig(pen), pondok, shack, shanty, shed, shelter, slum, stack, sty
HOVER cling, drift, flicker, flit(ter), flutter, fly, hang, hesitate, impend, levitate, linger, lurk, poise, sail, skim, soar, suspend, wait, waver
hawk kestrel
HOW by what means, cap, caul, coif, hill(ock), hood, in this way, mound, nightcap, quomodo, thus and so, what, whereby, why
and certainly
come why
-de-do ado, fuss, smuzz, stir, to-do
-so why
HOWADJI merchant, traveller
HOWARD, CATHERINE *husband* henry viii
HOWARD, SIDNEY *play* silver cord
HOWBEIT although, nevertheless, notwithstanding
HOWDAH ambaree, ambari, tower
HOWE deep, depression, empty, hole, hollow, humble, hungry, lowly, valley
admiral black dick
HOWEVER although, but, except, nevertheless, nonetheless, notwithstanding, still, though, yet
HOWITZER cannon, gun, licorn, skoda, unicorn
shell obus
HOWL bawl, bellow, blubber,

caterwaul, complain(t), cry, gowl, gurl, lament, outcry, protest, roar, shriek, sough, steven, ululate, wail, wap, waul, wawl, weep, whewl, whine, wrawl, yawl, yell, yipe, yoll, yout, yowl

HOWLER araguato, blunder, boner, booboo, bull, error, faux pas, floater, lapse, lie, mistake, slip, wailer

monkey alouatte, araba, guariba, quereba, mono, stentor

HOWLING dreary, extreme, great, pronounced, savage, wild

success score, sensation

HOWSOEVER although, nevertheless

HOX annoy, hamstring, hock, pester, trample, worry

HOY barge, crumster, shout, tjalk, vessel

HOYA honey-plant, milkweed, valley

HOYDEN blowze, chit, ill-bred, meg, rigsby, roistering, romp, rude, tomboy, uncouth, youth

HOYLE *according to* correctly, legally

HREIDMAR *son* fafnir, otter, regin(n)

slayer fafnir

H-SHAPED zygal

HUAYNA CAPAC *son* atahualpa, huascar

HUB axis, axle, boss, center, core, focus, heart(h), hummock, hut, kernel, middle, midst, nave, nucleus, omphalos, pith, socket, spider, stock

of the universe boston

HUBBITE bostonian

HUBBLE crowd, hubbub, uproar

-bubble calahan, calean, chatter, confusion, hookah, narghile, waterpipe

HUBBLESHOO commotion, confusion, rabble

HUBBUB ado, agitation, babel, bedlam, bobbery, brawl, brouhaha, bustle, clamor, confusion, din, disturbance, hullabaloo, hurly-burly, noise, pandemonium, racket, rowdydow, rumpus, squabble, stew, stir, tumult, turbulence, uproar

HUBRIS arrogance, insolence, pride, self-confidence

HUCK bend, bargain, haggle, haunch, higgle, hip, hollow, howk, stoop, toweling

HUCKLE bend, haggle, haunch, hip, stoop

HUCKLEBERRY batodendron, bilberry, crackers, ericad, gaylussacia, gopherberry, whortleberry

finn's friend jim

HUCKLEBONE astragal, dibs

HUCKMUCK dwarf, humbug, slattern, strainer

HUCKSTER adman, badger, bargain, broker, cadger, hawker, kidder, middleman, miser, moneygrubber, outcrier, peddler, press agent, publicist, regrater, trucker, vendor

HUDDLE assemble, bunch, bustle, caucus, cling, collect, conceal, confer, confusion, croodle, crowd, disorder, embrace, flock, formation, gather, group, herd, hide, howder, hug, hurry, hush, jumble, miser, muddle, multitude, push, scrinch, scrunch, shuffle, skinflint

on don

HUDIBRAS *author* butler

squire ralph(o)

HUDSON BAY *indian* cree

river cliffs palisades

river, city on cohoes, new york, troy, yonkers

river into churchill, nelson

seal muskrat

HUDSON, W. H. *character* abel, rima

novel green mansions

HUE alarm, apparition, appearance, aspect, balk, bellow, blee, cast, chroma, clamor, color, complexion, cry, figure, form, ghost, guise, outcry, shade, shout(ing), tinct, tinge, tint, tone, whoop

and cry alarm, excitement, publicity, search, stir, uproar

dusky drab, fuscous

HUELESS gray, grey

HUELGA strike

HUFF anger, blow, bluster, boaster, boasting, brag, bully, dudgeon, effervesce, enlarge, expire, harass, hector, inflate, offend, offense, pant, petulance, pique,

pout, provoke, puff, rage, swell, umbrage, wrath

and puff strive, struggle

HUFFCAP ale, blusterer, blustering, bully, drink, heady, strong, swaggering

HUFFY fractious, fretful, irascible, irritable, peevish, pettish, petulant, querulous, shirty, snappish, waspish

HUG adhere, caress, cherish, clasp, cling, coll, coul, cradle, creem, cuddle, embrace, greet(ing), hold, lug, seize, squeeze, welcome

HUGE atlantean, banging, big, brobdingnagian, bulky, bumping, colossal, cyclopean, dinotherian, elephantine, enormous, gargantuan, giant, gigantean, gigantic, great, herculean, heroic, immense, jumbo, LARGE, lolloping, main, mammoth, massive, mastodon, mighty, monster, monstrous, monumental, mountainous, prodigious, slapping, spanking, stupendous, thumping, thundering, titanic, towering, tremendous, vast, whacking, whaling, whopping

HUGGERMUGGER blunder, chaotic, clandestine(ly), confused, confusion, covert, disorderly, hush up, jumble, muddle, privacy, secrecy, secret(ly), sly, stealth

HUGH, ST *emblem* lantern

HUGHES, HOWARD *airplane* spruce goose

HUGIN *crow of* odin

HUGO, VICTOR *character* hernani, javert, jean valjean, quasimodo

group cenacle

nickname olympio

work hernani, les miserables, quatre-vingt-treize, ruy blas

HUGUENOT *leader* adrets, colibhy, conde, mornay, ronan

pope mornay

HUI assembly, firm, guild, partnership, society

HUISACHE acacia, aroma, aromo, cassie, opopanax, popinac, shrub, vachellia, wabi

HUL *father* shem

HULDAH *husband* shallum

HULK chop, corse, disembowel, hull, husk, lubber, ship, vessel, whopper

HULKING awkward, bulky, loutish, lubberly, lumpish, unwieldy

HULL belt, body, bottom, bulk, bur(h), burse, calyx, casco, casing, covering, discorticate, frame, holly, hovel, hulk, husk, hut, loaf, open, peel, pod, rind, saddle, shed, shell, ship, shoot, shuck, strip, throw
grain bran
house founder jane addams

HULLABALOO ado, babel, brouhaha, buzz, clamor, confusion, din, flap, hubbub, noise, pandemonium, racket, tarrarom, terrarom, tumult, uproar

HUM ahem, blur, boom, burn, bustle, buzz, croon, drone, freddon, hoax, HUMMING, huss, imposition, melody, murmur, rustle, sing, sough, sowff, teedle, trill, whir, whiz(z)

HUMAN adamite, being, biped, boy, carnal, child, girl, hominine, homo sapiens, humane, kind, man, merciful, mortal, person, tender, wight, woman
beings humanity, mankind, people
body anatomy
body measurement anthropometry
comb. anthrop(o)(os)
deification anthropolatry
diminutive dwarf, peewee, pygmy, shrimp
figure, ornamental anthropomorph

HUMANE altruistic, benevolent, benign(ant), charitable, clement, compassionate, considerate, forbearing, gentle, gracious, humanitarian, kind(ly), lenient, merciful, mild, philanthropic, polite, sympathetic, tender, tolerant

HUMANITIES arts, belle-lettres, letters, literature

HUMANITY adamhood, anthropos, benevolence, charity, commiseration, compassion, flesh, folks, homo sapiens, mankind, mercy, mortality, mortals, people, persons, pity, populace, public, weakness

HUMBER *tributary* trent

HUMBLE abase, abject, afflict, base, bemean, chagrin, chastise, compliant, contrite, debase, degrade, demean, demiss, demit, depress, discomfit, disgrace, docile, embarrass, gentle, homely, humiliate, inglorious, low(ly), mean, meek, modest, mortify, obscure, penitent, plain, plebeian, poor, resigned, rumble, shame, simple, slight, small, subdue, submissive, unassuming, undistinguished, unpretentious, unpuff
elder danewort
oneself atone, condescend, confess, descend, grovel, repent, repine, stoop, submit
pie humiliation

HUMBLENESS humility

HUMBLY abjectly, lowly, on bended knee, simply

HUMBUG baloney, bamboozle, beguile, blague, blah, bosh, brag, bull, bunco, buncomb, bunk(um), cajole, canard, charlatan(ry), cheat, claptrap, counterfeit, deceit, deceive, fake, flam, flattery, flimflam, flummer, fourflusher, fraud, fudge, gammon, gas, guff, guile, gum, hoax, hocus-pocus, hokum, impostor, imposture, jiggery-pokery, kid, lie, moonshine, mountebank, mummery, nonsense, pah, pretense, pretension, quackery, sham, simulacrum, stratagem, verneuk

HUMDINGER ace, corker, dinger, doozy, dynamo, hummer, oner, snorter, topnotcher

HUMDRUM arid, bore, boring, commonplace, drab, dull, indifferent, insipid, irksome, lifeless, listless, monotonous, prosaic, prosy, redundancy, routine, stupid, tedious, tiresome, treadmill, uninteresting, unrelieved, weary

HUME, JOSEPH *nickname* adversity

HUMECTANT diluting, moistening

HUMERUS arm, brachium

HUMID damp, dank, moist, muggy, soggy, steamy, sticky, sultry, vaporous, wet

HUMIDITY dampness, moisture, wetness
science of hydrometry, hygrology, hygrostatics

HUMILIATE abase, abash, affront, bewilder, chagrin, confuse, dash, degrade, disgrace, dishonor, embarrass, faze, humble, mortify, nidder, nither, nonplus, rattle, shame, squelch, unplume, vilify, wither

HUMILIATION abasement, chagrin, comedown, confusion, contumely, descent, disgrace, downcome, embarrassment, ignominy, letdown, mortification, pudency, shame
site canossa

HUMILITY humbleness, lowlihood, lowliness, meekness, mildness, modesty, plainness, snipe, submission, submissiveness

HUMMER hummingbird, livewire, murmur, mutter, speeder

HUMMING active, agitated, brisk, brool, busy, chiusco, droning, extraordinary, murmur(ing), purring, seething, speedy, spirited, strong, suum, teeming, thrumming

HUMMINGBIRD amazon, ava, bluet, calliope, carib, colibri, coquette, costa, emerald, firetail, froufrou, hummer, jacobin, lilacthroat, lucifer, mango, mimotype, picarian, puff-leg, rackettail, rainbow, roster, ruby, rufous, sapphire, sappho, sheartail, star, swordbill, sylph, tenui, thorntail, topaz, trochilus, vestipedes, warrior, whitetip
bush chuperosa
large amizilis

HUMMOCK hill(ock), hump, knoll, ridge, rise, tussock

HUMOR(S) atticism, attic salt, attitude, baby, blood, buffoonery, cant, caprice, cater, chestnut, comedy, crotchet, delight, disposition, drollery, fancy, favor, fluid(s), fun, gratify, inclination, indulge, irony, jest, joke, moisture, mollycoddle, mood, notion, pamper, pet, pleasantry, please, posi-

tion, prank, pun, quip, quirk, rejoice, repartee, salt, satire, soothe, spoil, stand, temper(ament), tickle, tid, vapor, vein, vitz, whim(sey), wit(tiness)
bad bats, crossness, dudgeon, funk, griping, grumps, ire, pet, pout, spleen, sullenness, tiff, tig, tout
broad farce
4 bile, blood, choler, melancholy, phlegm
good bonhomie
HUMORIST ade, card, clown, comic, farceur, funster, joker, nye, way, wit
HUMOROUS amusing, canny, capricious, comic (al), diverting, droll, entertaining, facetious, farcical, funny, jocose, jocular, playful, ribald, waggish, whimsical, witty
HUMP blues, bulge, bunch, carry, cock, crisis, curve, exert, hulch, hummock, hurry, mound, mountain, protuberance, rush, shoulder, sulks, transport
HUMPBACK crump, kyphosis, salmon, sucker, whale, whitefish
HUMPBACKED bowed, deformed, gibbous, humpty, kyphotic
comb. cyph(o), kyph(o)
salmon haddo, holia
HUMPERDINCK *opera* hansel and gretel
HUMPHREY CLINKER *author* smollett
character bramble, winifred jenkins
HUMPTY DUMPTY richard iii
HUMPY cross, HUT, sulky
HUMUS earth, ground, mold, mor, mulch, mull, soil
HUN avar, barbarian, boche, bulgar, german, magyar, soldier, tartar, vandal
ancestor hiung-nu
chief humber
conqueror avars
king atli, attila, etzel
HUNCH arch, balk, bulge, chilly, crook, crouch, curve, fudge, guess, hump, inkling, jostle, lump, piece, premonition, push, scrunch, shove, thrust
HUNCHBACK See HUMP-BACK.

of notre dame quasimodo
HUNDING *enemy* volsungs
wife sieglinde
HUNDRED cantred, cent(enary), centennial, centum, century, crore, five-score, rho, township, village
by the per cent
comb. cent(i), hecaton, hect(o)
-eyed being argus
-gated thebes
-handed giants HECATONCHIRES
-leaf grass yarrow
-legs centipede
links chain
million, comb. trega
percent entire, genuine, perfect, thoroughing, unalloyed, unquestionable
thousand lac, lakh
years centenary, centennial, century
years war battle agincourt
HUNDREDFOLD bedstraw, centuple, centuplicate
HUNDREDWEIGHT cental, centner, cwt, quintal
HUNG pendent
up frustrated, suspended
HUNGARY pannonia
airline malev
architect breuer
army honved(seg)
canal bega, sarviz, sio
capital bratislava, budapest, esztergom
cattle magyar tarka
cavalryman hussar
cavern okno, vodi
cheese bryndza
chemist hevesy
chieftain arpad
city aba, acs, baja, bekes, budapest, cegled, debrecen, eger, gyor, kecskemet, komlo, mako, miskolc, mohacs, obuda, ozd, papa, pecs, pest, raab, sopron, szeged(in), szentes, tata, ujpest, vac, zirc
cocktail puszta
coin balas, filler, forint, gara, gulden, korona, krone, ongaro, pengo, ungaro
commune mor
communist kun
composer bartok, dohnanyi, goldmark, kodaly, lehar, liszt

conductor dorati, nikisch, reiner, solti
country inn csardak
county arva
critic lukan
dance czardas, kos, varsoviana
dish csipetke, csusza, fatanyeros, fogas, fozelek, galuska, gomboc, goulash, gulyas, halaszle, kocka, kohlrabi, metelt-langos, nockeddli, orja, paprikas, pepper pods, porkolt, rablohus, rantas, rous, rozsa, szegedi edesnemes, tarhonya, toltott kaposzta, turkish pepper
division comitat
dog komondor, kuvasz, puli
drink puszta
dynasty angevin, arpad
family esterhazy
folk song csarda
forest bakony
game alsos, felsos, kalabrias, klaberjass
governor ban
gypsy szigane, tzigane, tzigani
hero arpad, hunyadi, kossuth, nagy
horse lippizaner
hunting guide gilly
inn csarda(k)
king arpad, bela, geza, imre, istvan, kalman, ladisla(u)s, leopold, matthias, saint stephen
lake balaton, blatensee, ferto, plattensee, velence
language finno-ugric
legislature felsohaz, forendihaz
mathematician bolyai
measure ako, antal, hold, huvelyk, itcze, joch, marok, merfold, metze, yoke
musical instrument cimbalom, cymbalom, tarogato
national symbol st stephen's crown
painter moholy-nagy
peak bakony, borzsony, kekes, korishegy
people croat, deak, gypsy, hun, kuman, magyar, serv, slovak, ugrian
pianist liszt, sandor
plain puszta
playwright molnar
premier kadar, nagy
president tildy
queen maria theresa

range alps, bukk, carpathian, gerecse, matra, mecsek, tatra, vertes
regent horthy
regime kadar
region banat
revolutionist bela kun
river berretyo, bodva, danube, drava, drave, duna, henrad, ipoly, kapos, koros, maros, mura, mures, poprad, raab, rab(c)a, sajo, szamos, tarna, theiss, tisza, vistula, zagyva, zala
robbers meat rablo-hus
sausage debreceni, gyuali
servant haiduk
slav croat(ian)
soldier haiduk
statesman andrassy, kossuth
stew gulyas
title ban
transylvanian szekler
travel agency ibusz
violinist auer, joachim, szigeti
weight vamfont, vammazsa
wine eger, szekszard, tokay
wine measure antal, itcze
writer ady, babits, jokai, koestler, molnar, petofi
zither cimbalom, cymbalon
HUNGER acoria, appetite, belly-pinch, clem, covet, crave, craving, desire, edacity, esurience, famine, famish, gluttony, greed, hanker, itch, long, pine, starvation, starve, thirst, voracity, want, wish, yearn (ing), yen
abnormal b(o)ulimia, cynorexia, hyperphagia, pica, polyphagia, sitomania
causing esurine
-controlling brain cells appestat
flower foxtail
insatiable acoria, phagomania
pain belly-pinch
pert. famelic
HUNGRY adephagous, avaricious, avid, barren, bulimi(a)c, craving, eager, edacious, empty, esurient, famished, gluttonous, greedy, hollow, howe, peckish, poor, ravening, ravenous, starved, starving, thirl, unfed, voracious, yappish
as a hunter

vine greenbrier, smilax
HUNK chunk, dad, daud, den, goal, home, hunch, lump, part, piece
HUNKER(S) conservative, crouch, fogy, haunches, squat
HUNKY even, good, laborer, okay, right, square, well
-dory fine, great, nice, okay
HUNNISH barbarous, destructive
HUNT acupate, brevit, chase, chev(v)y, course, dig, dog, drive, falcon, ferret, flush, follow, harry, hawk, hound, persecute, poach, pursue, pursuit, quest, scour, scout, search, seek, shikar, shoot, sport, stalk, start, track, trail, trap
and peck type
-away sheepdog
for fowl acupate
HUNT, LEIGH *poem abou* ben adhem
HUNTER actaeon, bird dog, catcher, chasseur, courser, cuckoo, dog, falconer, ferreter, gunner, horse, hound, huntsman, ja(e)ger, marksman, montero, nimrod, orion, poacher, sealer, shikari, shooter, stalker, trapper, venator, venerer
assistant gillie, gilly
cap montero
coat pink
famous acastus, actaeon, adonis, meleager, orion
golden fleece jason
kill bag, limit, mort
mythological gwyn, orion
name meaning theron
patron saint hubert
ring of tinchel, tinchill
surprised diana actaeon
HUNTING aprowl, battue, beagling, chevy, chivy, coursing, cynegetics, deerstalking, dragnet, falconry, gunning, hawking, hue and cry, shooting, venery, wathe
bird falcon
cry all on, chevy, chiv(v)y, halloo, hoi(c)ks, holloe, see-ho, soho, staboy, tallyho, tantivy, toho, viewholloa, yoi(cks)
district walk
dog alan, basset, beagle, buckhound, deerhound,

dhole, griffon, hound, pointer, setter
dog keeper fewterer
expedition chase, safari, shikar
festival elaphebolia
fond of venatic
game shikar, tir, venery
god apollo, dionysus, mixcoatl, ninip, viribus
goddess artemis, britomartis, diana, diane, vacuna
gun roer
hat terai
horn bugle, hutchet
horn signal gibbet, mort, pryse
pert. venatic, venerial
platform machan
signal seek
weasel ferret
with hounds beagling
HUNTRESS artemis, atalanta, belphoebe, diana
HUNTSMAN (See also HUNTER.) *cup or horn* pitcher-plant, sarracenia
HUPA athapascan
HUR *father* caleb, judah
sister tirzah
son ephrathah, rephaiah, uri
wife miriam
HURDLE barrier, clear, frith, hang-up, hindrance, jump, leap, obstacle, race, stumbling-block, vault
HURDY-GURDY crank, lantum, lira, organ(istrum), rota, sambuke, windlass
HURL break, bum, cast, catapult, clap, drive, fling, haul, heave, howl, hurlyburly, hurtle, overthrow, pash, pelt, pitch, project, riot, roar, rush(ing), send, sling, sock, swither, thrill, throw, toss, tumult, whirl
HURLBAT aclys, cestus
HURLING confusion, hockey, roar, strife, turmoil
stick boomerang, caman
HURLY(-BURLY) agitation, bustle, confuse, confusion, disturbance, storm, tumult(ous), turmoil, uproar
HURRAH acclaim, applaud, bravo, cheer, hail, hooray, huzza(h), ole, rah, root, shout, viva
HURRICANE blast, blow, cordonazo, cyclone, furacana, gale, gust, prester, storm, tornado, twister, ty-

phoon, waterspout, whirlwind, wildwind
center eye
god, goddess See STORM *god, goddess.*
small little brother
HURRIED abrupt, bustling, hard-pressed, hasty, impulsive, precipitate, pressed, reckless, rushed, rushing, snatched
HURRY accelerate, ado, bicker, celerity, chase, convey, crowd, dash, dispatch, dispute, drive, expedite, expedition, festinate, fight, fly, harry, haste(en), hie, hotfoot, hump, hustle, jiffy, plunge, press, quarrel, quicken, race, run, rush, scamper, scramble, scuddle, scufter, scurry, scuttle, sessa, speed, step on it, swithe, tatter, tear, urge, whorry, worry
about scour
away flee, scram, screw
HURST copse, grove, hill(ock), knoll, sandbank, wood
HURT abrasion, abuse, ache, afflict, aggrieve, bark, bloody, bruise, burn, chafe, concussion, crush, cut, damage, deface, dere, detriment, disadvantage, disfigure, disservice, distress, evil, flaw, fracture, fret, gall, gash, grievance, grieve, hamstring, harm, harry, ill, impair, indignant, injure(d), injury, lacerate, lesed, lesion, maim, mangle, mar, miffed, mischief, mischieve, mittle, mutilate, offend(ed), offense, oppress, pain, pang, pierce, piqued, puncture, rend, ruin, rupture, scar, scathe, scotch, scrape, scratch, scuff, skin, smart, sore, sorrow, spoil, sprain, stab, stick, sting, strain, strike, suffer, tear, thorn, throe, torment, tort(ure), trauma, trouble, umbrageous, wathe, whip, wound(ed), wrench, wrick, wrong
easily froisse, thinskinned, touchy
HURTFUL bad, baleful, baneful, deleterious, destructive, harmful, injurious,

malefic, malign, nocent, noisome, noxious, pernicious, scathful, unquert
HURTLE charge, clash, clatter, collide, crash, dash, fling, jostle, lunge, roar, smash, strike, thrust
HUSAIN *brother* has(s)an *parent* ali, fatima
HUSAM *ancestor* mohammed
HUSBAND benedict, consort, cultivate, director, economize, eke, espouse, goodman, groom, guidman, hubby, man, manage, mari, marry, mate, old man, partner, pere, prepare, reserve, sannup, save, spouse, store, till
brother in-law, levir
dowry arras
fond of maritorious
having 1 monandrous
having more than 1 polyandry
murder mariticide
property right curtesy
HUSBANDMAN acre-man, agricole, agricolist, agriculturalist, bond, boor, carl, colon, cultivator, farmer, granger, plowman, rancher, tiller, tillman
HUSBANDRY agriculture, agronomy, economy, farming, frugality, geoponics, homemaking, housekeeping, management, prudence, thrift, tillage
implements wainage
HUSE, HUSO beluga, huchen, whale
HUSH allay, appease, assuage, calm, clam, conceal, console, flush, lull, mum, mute, quiet(ude), repress, rush, shsh, shuch, shut up, silence, soothe, still(ness), suppress, swell
-hush confidential, dark, secret
money bribe
HUSHED noiseless, quiet, secret, silent, soundless, still, whisht
HUSK bark, bhoosa, bran, branner, bur, chaff, coat, colder, cosh, covering, envelope, glume, grain, hoja, hull, leam, peel, pod, rind, scale, shaup, shell, shock,

shood, shuck, shud, shude, skin, slough
bit shiv
comb. lepo
remove decorticate
small silicle
HUSKY athletic, bouncing, brawny, burly, dog, dry, eskimo, furred, gruff, guttural, harsh, hoarse, hulking, muscular, potent, powerful, puissant, raucous, robust, rough, sinewy, stalwart, stocky, stout, strong, sturdy, thickset, throaty, tough
HUSPIL despoil, harass, maltreat
HUSS buzz, dogfish, hum
HUSSAR cavalryman, fish, soldier
headdress busby
jacket dolman
HUSSY bag(gage), besom, case, cutty, drossel, flirt, gipsy, gypsy, housewife, jade, madam, minx, quean, shrew, slut, snip, tit, trollop, wanton, wench
HUSTLE accelerate, bundle, bustle, court, crowd, drive(on), enterprise, escort, fly, forge ahead, go all out, hop to it, hump, HURRY, jostle, peddle, press(on), push, rush, rustle, scramble, sell, shake, skelp, speed, step lively, stir, thrust
HUSTLECAP pinch
HUSTLER chippie, dynamo, fireball, gambler, go-getter, peddler, prostitute, speeder
HUT adobe, balagan, barabara, barabora, barasti, bari, benab, bohawn, bohio, bothy, bourock, bunkhouse, bure, butt, cabin, camalig, can(n)aba, chum, cot(e), cottage, cral, crew, crib, crue, dugout, dump, goondie, gunyay, gunyeh, hammel, hogan, hole, hooden, hovel, huddock, hulk, humpy, hutch, igloo, isba, izba, jacal, jurt, kral, lean-to, linter, miamia, nissen, pagliaio pigpen, pond ok(kie), quonset, rancyo, rondawel, scherm, shack, shanty, shed, shelter, shieling, skeo, skio, soddy, stack, stall, sty, tent, tepee,

tholthan, toldo, tugurium, tupek, wickiup, wigwam, zayat
aboriginal goondie, gunyah, miamia, mimi, wurl(e)y
circular gegurium
fisherman's skeo
hermit's cell
log chantier
mean hovel, humpy, hutch, shanty
mining coe
shepherd's bothy
sod barabara
temporary corf
HUTCH ark, bin, box, chest, coffer, coop, hoard, hovel, humped, hunched, hut, pen, rabbitry, shanty, shelter, store, warren
HUXLEY *novel* antic hay, brave new world, crome yellow, eyeless in gaza, point counterpoint, those barren leaves
HUZ *father* nahor
kin abraham, haran
HUZZAH applaud, cheer, hurrah, root
HYACINTH bird, bluebill, crowfoot, crowtoe, essonite, floater, flower, gallinule, gem, greggle, harebell, jacinth, jacounce, lillium, lily, musk, stone, tenne, zircon
bean bonavist, bonnyvis, dolichos, lablab, tree
feathered purse-tassel
wild camas
HYACINTHUS *beloved* apollo
father amyclas, pierus
loved by zephyrus
slayer apollo, zephyr
HYADES ambrosia, coronis, dione, eudora, pedile, phyto, polyxo, thyene
nurses to dionysus
parent aethra, atlas, pleione
HYALINE glassy, heavens, ocean, sea, translucent, transparent
HYBRID assorted, bigener, blend, cattalo, cross, hash, heterozygote, hinny, liger, mix(ture), mongrel, mule, olio, sobo, varied, zho
growth meterosis
HYDE PARK *bridal path* rotten row
pond serpentine
HYDRA calamity, constel-

lation, evil, monster, polyp, serpent
abode lerna
slayer hercules
-tainted poisonous
HYDRANGEA carpenteria, deutzia, flower, shrub
HYDRANT faucet, pipe, spigot, spout, water-plug
HYDRATE *ethyl* alcohol
HYDROCARBON ambrosine, asphalt(um), benzene, bitumen, bombiccite, butane, butene, cetane, cymene, ethane, indane, melene, methane, octane, pinene, propane, pyrene, resin, retene, trepene, tolane, toluene, tutylene
aromatic arene, carane, chrysene
coal tar pyrene
colorless acetylene, cumene, cumol
comb. ane, ene
crystalline acenaphthene, anthemene, anthracene, bibenzyl, binaphthyl, biphenyl, ditolyl, phenanthrene, retene, terphenyl, tolane
cyclic aceanthrene
ethyl cetane, cetene
fluorescent picene
fluorinated freon
gaseous acetylene, allylene, biacetylene, butadiene, ethane, ethene, fluorine, methane
hypothetical fulvene
inflammable benzene, butane
isotope protium
liquid azulene, cumol, decane, nonane, pristane, toluene, toluol
oily etherin, indane, indene, piperylene, viridine
petroleum octane
radical amyl, aryl, xexyl
solid chrysene
solvent xylene
unsaturated olefine
volatile benzene, benzo, tetrole
white tolan
HYDROGEN *addition of* reduction
compound hydride, imine
having atoms of bibasic
isotope deuterium, protium, tritium
source atmosphere

HYDROID acaleph, obelia, polyp, tracheid, zoophyte
bulb bulbilla
covering perisarc
family sertularia
medusa planoblast
HYDROMETER areometer, cartier, spindle
pert. beek
HYDROPHOBIA lyssa, rabies
HYDROPLANE glider, seaplane
HYENA dabuh, simir, strandwolf
-like animal aardwolf, lycaon, proteles
HYGEIA, HYGIEIA *father* aesculapius, asclepius
goddess of health
HYGIENE prophylaxis, sanitation
branch bacteriology
HYGIENIC aseptic, beneficial, clean, constitutional, healthful, salubrious, salutary, sanitary, uncontaminated, wholesome
HYGLELAC *kingdom* geata
nephew beowulf
HYLA spring-peeper, treefrog, treetoad
HYLAS *companion* hercules
parent menodice, thiodamas
HYLLUS *parent* deianira, hercules
slayer echemus
wife iole
HYMEN cherry, marriage
parent apollo, bachus, urania, venus
HYMENEAL bridal, conjugal, connubial, marital, matrimonial, nuptial, song
rite wedding
HYMENOPTERAN ant, anthophilia, apoidea, bee, bethylid, emmet, formicid, gallfly, ichneumon, insect, pismire, sawfly, wasp, xiphydria
HYMETTIUS zeus
HYMN agnus dei, alabado, alleluiah, allelujah, anthem, antiphony, benedicite, benedictus, canon, cantic(le), carol, carval, carvel, chant, choral(e), dies, irae, doxology, epinicion, gloria, halleluiah, hallelujah, hosanna, introit, laud, lyric, magnificat, miserere, motet, nunc dimittis, ode, offer-

tory, paean, praise, psalm, song, stabat mater, te deum, trisagion, versicle
book psalter
bridal grautlied, hymeneal
collection menaion
funeral dirge
medieval dies irae
missionary greenland's icy mountains
ode-like epinicion
of praise anthem, paean
praising god alleluia, hallelujah, te deum
sacred anthem, ode, trisagion
sung in unison chorale
tune chorale
victory epinicion, epinikion
writer watts
HYPALLAGE metastasis
HYPERASIUS *son* asterius
HYPERBOLE amplification, exaggeration, magnification, overstatement
HYPERBOREAN cold, frigid, northern
people chukchi, eskimo, koryak
sage abaris
HYPERCRITICAL captious, carping, cavilling, censorious, exclusive, fastidious, faultfinding, finical, fussy, nagging, nice, squeamish, supercilious
HYPERENOR *brother* eyphorbus, polydamas
slayer menelaus
HYPERICUM amber, androseme, broom-brush, st john's-wort, tutsan
HYPERION helios, sun, titan
consort euryphaessa, thea, theia
grandson memnon
moon of saturn
offspring aurora, eos, helios, helius, mene, selene
parent gaea, uranus
sister theia
HYPERMNESTRA *father* danaus
husband lunceus
HYPERPHAGIA b(o)ulimia
HYPERTENSION high blood pressure
HYPHEN band, dash, division, mark
HYPNOS *brother* thanatos
parent erebus, nyx
son morpheus
HYPNOSIS catalepsy, cataplexy, magnetod, sleep,

somnipathy, somnolence, somnolism, thanatosis, trance
celebrity bridey murphy
HYPNOTIC amobarbital, amytal, barbital, barbitone, barbituate, bromal, carbromal, chloralose, mesmeric, sedative, somniferous, soporific, thalidomide, tuinal, ural, veronal
state cataplexy, coma, endromed, hypnosis, lethargy, trance
HYPNOTISM auto-suggestion, biod, braidism, elod, magic, magnetism, magnetod, mesmerism, odyl(e), pantod
founder mesmer
receptivity ideoplastia
HYPNOTIST magnetizer, mesmer(ist), operator, svengali
HYPNOTIZE blandish, charm, dazzle, enchant, endorm, entrance, fascinate, influence, mesmerize, spellbind
HYPOCHONDRIA anxiety, dejection, depression, megrim, melancholia, psycholepsy
HYPOCHONDRIAC argan, atrabil(ar)ious, depressed, hippish, melancholic, melancholy, neurotic, nosonaniac, valetudinary
HYPOCRISY blandness, cant, deceit, dissimulation, duplicity, glibness, guile, insincerity, lip service, makebelieve, mummery, oiliness, pecksniffism, pharisaism, pretense, sanctimony, sham, simulation, smoothness, snivel, snuffle, unctuousness, tartuffery, tartuffism
personification archimago
symbol crocodile
HYPOCRITE bigot, blifil, cafard, canter, dissembler, dissimulator, fake, fefnicute, formalist, imposter, lipserver, mawworm, pecksniff, pharisee, phony, pietist, poser, pretender, ranter, religionist, sniveler, snuffler, tartuffe, uriah heep
HYPOCRITICAL affected, assumed, bland, canting, captious, carping, deceptive, false, feigned, fulsome, glib,

goody(goody), insincere, mealy-mouthed, oily, pharisaic, pretended, sanctimonious, shammed, slick, smooth-spoken, specious, tartuffian, unctuous
HYPODERMIS skin
HYPOPHYGE apophysis, conge, curvature, curve, scape
HYPOSTASIS base, essence, material, ousia, sediment, substance, support, suspensor
HYPOSTATIZE actualize, embody, entify, externalize, materialize, objectivity, realize, reify, substantiate
HYPOTHALAMUS acth
HYPOTHECATE affect, assume, guess, imagine, mortgage, pawn, pledge, suppose, theorize
HYPOTHESIS assumption, conjecture, deduction, guess(work), inference, position, postulate, postulatum, premise, presumption, presupposal, presupposition, proposal, proposition, supposal, supposition, surmise, system, theorem, theory, thesis
HYPOTHETICAL academic, assumed, conjectural, dialectic(al), doubtful, dubious, ideal, presumptive, putative, reputed, speculative, supposed, theoretical
force biod, elod, idant, od(yl)
particle magneton
HYPSEUS *kingdom* lapith
parent creusa, peneus
HYPSIPYLE *husband* jason
kingdom lemnos
master lucurgus
parent myrina, thoas
son euneus
HYRACOID, HYRAX animal, cony, daman, das, dassie, klipdas, procavia, rockrabbit, rodent, shaphan, ungulate, wabber, wabur
-like animal badger
HYRMINA *grandfather* endymion
husband phorbas
son actor
HYRNETHO *father* temenus
grandfather aristomachus
HYRTACUS *son* asius, hippocoon, nisus

wife arisba
HYSSOP artemisia, aspergilly, caper, germander, herb, holy water, mint, teucrium
sage devil's-milk

HYSTERIA anxiety, breakdown, convulsion, delirium, emotionalism, excitability, exies, fits, frenzy, mania, nerves, shell shock, tarassis, weeping

cure sagapenum
HYSTERICAL convulsive, emotional, fitful, frantic, overwrought, spasmodic, uncontrolled, wild, wrought up

I

I ego, ich, iota, self, utch(y)
dot over tittle
excessive use egotism, iotacism
have found it eureka
love you te amo
told you so there
understand roger
IACCHUS See DIONYSUS.
IAGO *adversary* othello
dupe of roderigo
friend othello
wife emilia
IALMENUS *parent* ares, astyoche
IALU hades, heaven, paradise
IAMB foot
IAMBIC lampoon, poem, satire, verse
line fourteener
trimeter anapaest, senarius
IAMUS *descendants* iamidae
parent apollo, evadne
IANTHE *husband* iphis
IANTHIA bush-robin, tarsiger
IAO honey-eater, manuao
IAPETUS *consort* asia, clymene, themis
descendant dione, maia
parent gaea, uranus
son atlas, buphagus, epimetheus, menoetius, prometheus
IAPYGIA *inhabitants* daunii, messapii, peucetii
IAPYX *brother* daunius, peucetius
father daedalus, lycaon
IARBAS *beloved* dido
IARDANUS *daughter* omphale
kingdom lydia
IASI See JASSY.
IASION, IASUS *consort* demeter
offspring amphion, atalanta, pluton, plutus
parent electra, zeus
twin dardanus
IBANAG cagayan
IBARRURI, DOLORES la pasionaria

IBERIA georgia, portugal, spain
IBERIAN pict, portuguese, spaniard
IBEX aurochs, beden, bouquetin, capra, eveck, evicke, goat, izard, jaela, kail, kyl, sakeen, saol, steinbok, tek, tur, walie, zac
IBHAR david
IBID ditto, lizard, monitor, same
IBIS bird, ciconiid, gannet, guara, haddad, ironhead, jabiru, stork, turkey
IBN RUSHD averroes
IBRAHIM *ancestor* mohammed
IBSEN *character* ase, brand, gabler, hedda, helmer, nora, pastor manders, peer gynt, rebecca, solveig
play brand, doll's house, ghosts, hedda gabler, master builder, peer gynt, rosmersholm
IBYCTER caracara, hawk
ICARIA See UTOPIA.
ICARIAN daring, foolhardy, rash, reckless
ICARIUS *ancestor* lacedaemon
dog maera
guest dionysus
offspring erigone, penelope, perilaus
parent oebalus
ICARUS *father* daedalus
ICBM atlas, missile, weapon
ICE berg, chill, cool, crystal, dessert, eis, floe, frazil, freeze, frost(ing), gem, glacier, glaze, grue, hail, hoar, jewelry, jokul, lolly, money, neve, payola, refrigerate, serac, sherbet, sish, sleet, slosh, sludge, slush, snow, verglas
age man aborigine
anchor frazil
bag coldpack
bird dovekie, nightjar

-blink reflection
block rubble, serac
boat skeeter
breaker hello, toast, whale
broken brash
cap calotte
cream bar eskimo pie
cream, cheap hokey-pokey
cream cone cornet
cream dish au fait, bisk, bisque, coupe, frappe, frozen yog(h)urt, glace, malt, neapolitan, nesselrode, nougat, parfait, soda, spumoni, sundae, tortoni
cream, served with a la mode
crystal frazil, frost, sleet, snow
duck old-squaw
feathers rime
fish capelin, salangid, whitebait
floating brash, grue
floe avalanche, berg, calf, glacier, hummock, pack, pan, quern, sconce, sturus
fog pogonip
fragment brash
glacial neve, serac, sish
hockey See HOCKEY.
-leaf mullein
mass See *floe*, above.
on thin precarious
partridge ivory gull
patch rone
pellet hailstone
pendant icicle
pert. crystic
petrel shearwater
pile hummock
pinnacle serac
plant figwort
ridge hammock, hummock
river glacier
saint boniface, mamertus, pancratius, servatius
sea glacon, sludge
sheet floe
skater's loop spoon
slide avalanche
slushy or soft lolly, sish, slob

study of cryology
thin brash, floe, grue
ICEBERG bergybit, growler
ICEBOX cooler, deepfreeze, freezer, refrigerator
ICED chilled, frosted, frozen, gelid, glace
ICEHOUSE *worker* airman
ICELAND *author* gudmundsson, laxness, snorristurluson
ballad rimur
bay faxa
bishopric holar, skalholt
capital reykjavik
chronicle landnama-bok
city akranes, akureyri, keflavik, kopavagur
coin aurar, eyrir, krona
dish bloomor, harofisk, skyr, svio
district syssel
epic edda, saga
first settler arnarson
geyser gryla
giant See NORSE *giant.*
glacier hofsjokull, langjokull, vatnajokull
god See AESIR.
golden falls gullfoss
harp langspil
hero audun, bele, eilif, eric, frithjof, grettir, leif, sigurdsson
island heimaey, surtsey
king atli
lake myvatn, thorisvatyn
language norse
legend volsunga saga
legislature althing
measure alen, alin, almenn, almud(e), angjateigur, fathmur, feralin, ferfet, fermila, ferthumlungur, kornskeppa, korntunna, lina, oltunna, pottur, sjomila, thumlungur, tundagslatta, turma
mineral flokite
musician scald, skald
newspaper morgunbladid
parliament althing
patron god grey
peak jokul, orafajokul
poet skald
president asgairsson
republic lyoveldio
river hvita, jokulsa, thjorsa
town pond tjounin
volcano askja, askua, hekla, helgafjell, kirkjufell, laki
waterfall dettifoss, gullfoss
weight pound, pund, tunna, smjors

ICENI *queen* boadicea
ICEROOT goldenseal
ICH DIEN i serve
ICHABOD *father* phineas
ICHO ginkgo, tree
ICHOR blood, discharge, exudate, fluid, magma
ICHOROUS gleety
ICHTHYOSIS fishskin
ICICLE cockbell, icary, ickle, shoggle, shoogle, tangle, yokel
limestone stalactite, stalagmite
ICING frosting, glaze, topping
ICON deesis, effigy, eikon, figure, idol, image, likeness, mask, picture, portrait, simulacrum, statue, symbol
ICONOCLAST agnostic, debunker, earthling, insurgent, irreligionist, materialist, radical, rebel, worldling
ICONOSCOPE view-finder
ICTALURUS bluecat, bullhead, catfish
ICTERID blackbird, bobolink, meadowlark
ICTERUS bananabird, hangbird, hangnest, jaundice, oriole
ICTIC abrupt, sudden
ICTICYON bushdog, potto
ICTIOBUS buffalofish, rooter
ICTONYX polecat, zoril(la)
ICTUS accent, attack, beat, blow, bruise, cadence, contusion, downbeat, fit, meter, pulsation, seizure, spasm, stress, stroke
ICY arctic, cold, freezing, frigid, frosty, gelid, glacial, wintry
ID ego, fish, heredity, idem, instinct, psyche, same, self
IDA *parent* melisseus
IDAEA *husband* phineus, scamander
son teucer
IDAHO *capital* boise
city boise, buhl, caldwell, coeur d'alene, lewiston, malad, moscow, nampa, pocatello, rexburg, twin falls
county ada, benewah, butte, carnas, cassia, gem, kootenai, lateh, power, teton
dam brownlee, oxbow
indian banak, bannock, cayuse, coeur d'alene, kalispel, kutenai, nez perce,

paiute, sahaptin, shoshone(e), shoshoni, snake, spokan(e)
lake bear, greys, priest
nickname gem state
peak big baldy, bluenose, borah, rhodes, ryan, taylor
range cabinet, clearwater, selkirk
river snake
springs hooper, lavahot, soda
state bird bluebird
state flower syringa
state tree western pine
IDAS *brother* lynceus
cousin castor, pollux
opponent castor, pollux
parent aphareus, arene
slayer zeus
victim castor
wife marpessa
IDBASH *parent* etam
IDDO *son* berechiah
IDE *yellow* orf
IDEA abstraction, aim, anonym, apprehension, archetype, association, belief, brainstorm, conceit, concept(ion), consideration, conviction, design, dharma, ectype, eidolon, eidos, essence, fancy, hypothesis, image, impression, inkling, inspiration, intent(ion), meaning, model, notion, observation, obsession, opinion, pattern, perception, phrase, plan, precept, project, recept, reflection, sally, scheme, sentiment, supposition, surmise, theme, theory, think, thought, view, wrinkle
faint glimmer
fixed obsession
good brainstorm
impractical bubble, chim-(a)era, fancy, fantasy, reverie, vagary
main burden, core, essence, gist, kernel, keynote, nub, purport, substance, sum
new breakthrough
prompting action motive
repetition tautology
rudimentary preconcept
stupid stodge
trite bromide, cliche
IDEAL absolute, abstract, acme, arcadian, beauty, cause, complete, conceptual, consummate, domnei, dream(y), edenic, example,

excellence, exemplar, fanciful, faultless, hero, holophrastic, idol, imaginary, impractical, intellectual, limit, mental, millennial, mirror, model, nonpareil, notional, paradigm, paragon, pattern, peerless, perfect(ion), standard, supreme, theoretical, translunary, thule, typical, unreal, utopian, visionary
life asrama
remote thule
republic magna graecia, sicily
state ivory tower, PARADISE, UTOPIA
universal ruler chakravartin

IDEALISM dereism, fancifulness, impracticality, perfectionism, quixotism, quixotry, romanticism, utopianism

IDEALIST romancer, seer, utopian, utopiast, visionary

IDEALISTIC anagogic(al), fictional, mystical, spiritual, visionary

IDEALIZE quixotize, rhapsodize, romantieize, spiritualize, transfigure

IDEATE conceive, fancy, imagine, philosophize, preconceive, prefigure, remember, think, wish

IDEE FIXE mania, obsession

IDENTICAL akin, alike, analogous, comparable, correlative, duplicate, equal, equivalent, even(ly), like, matching, one, parallel, proper, real, same, selfsame, tantamount, twin, uniform

IDENTIFICATION apperception, attribution, badge, calling card, discernment, document, label, name, perception, press card, recognition, tag, title, transference
by epithet antonomasia

IDENTIFY agree, brand, coincide, designate, diagnose, discern, discriminate, embody, entitle, establish, finger, fuse, homologize, incorporate, label, locate, mark, name, prove, rank, recognize, spot, tally, unify, verify
inability to anomia

IDENTITY being, characteristic, coherence, con-

gruence, congruity, equality, exactness, homoousia, individuality, ipseity, name, oneness, personality, sameness, singleness, unity

IDEOGRAM hieroglyph(ic), pictograph

IDEOLOGY belief, creed, dogma, ism, philosophy, rule, speculation, system, tenet, theory, vision

IDES *9th day before* nones

IDIOCY amentia, anoesia, anoia, fatuity, folly, foolishness, imbecility, insanity, irrationality, moronism, morosis, stupidity

IDIOM aeolism, argot, cant, construction, danicism, dialect, diction, expression, jargon, juang, language, lingo, localism, locution, patois, phrase, provincialism, saying, speech, style, tongue, vernacular

IDIOSYNCRASY affectation, characteristic, disposition, distinction, eccentricity, feature, manner(ism), method, peculiarity, pose, way

IDIOT ament, booby, changeling, cretin, dullard, dunce, fonne, fool, hobbil, imbecile, moron, natural, nidget, pinhead, oaf, simpleton, tomfool, witling
delight solitaire

IDIOTIC crazy, daft, fatuous, foolish, imbecile, imbecilic

IDLE asleep, at leisure, baseless, bum, cooter, dally, dawdle, desoeuvre, disengaged, dog it, drift, drone, dull, empty, faineant, fallow, free, fribble, fritter, frivolous, fruitless, futile, gammer, gold-brick, goof off, haze, hollow, inactive, indolent, inert, jobless, kill time, laches, lallygag, languid, laze, lazy, leisurely, lie around, loaf, loiter, loll(ygag), lounge, mooch, moon, nugatory, off, otiant, otiose, passive, petty, resting, rusty, sit, slothful, sluther, sorn, squander, stall, supine, take it easy, thoke, tiffle, trifle, trifling, trivial, truant, unemployed, unoccupied, unused, vacant, vain, vegetate, worthless
talk babble(-bibble), blab, buff, cackle, chatter, gossip,

nonsense, shmoos, shmooze, shmues, yakyak
wheel runner
year accordion, solitaire

IDLENESS faniente, folly, ignavia, otiosity, sloth, triviality, vanity

IDLER abbey-lubber, badaud, bench warmer, blellum, boulevardier, buckeen, bum(ble), clockwatcher, dallier, dawdler, diddler, dillydallier, dolittle, donothing, doodler, drone, faineant, faitour, faniente, indolent, laggard, lazarone, lazybones, lie-abed, lingerer, loafer, loiterer, loller, lounge lizard, lounger, lubber, mope(r), potterer, putterer, rodney, sleepyhead, sloth, slounge, slugabed, sluggard, stalko, stick-in-the-mud, timewaster, trombenik, trombenyik, trifler, weary willie, whiffler

IDMON *parent* apollo, asteria, cyrene

IDOL adonis, anito, baal, bafomet, baphomet, beloved, besan, darling, dear, deity, desire, devil-god, effigy, eidolon, eikon, favorite, fetish, god, golden calf, graven image, guaca, hobal, huaca, idolon, idolum, image, joss, juggernaut, lion, mahomet, maumet, pagod(a), pet, puppet, star, symbol, teraph, tiki, zemi
social lion

IDOLATER admirer, adorer, akkum, baalite, communicant, fetishist, heathen, idolizer, infidel, pagan, worship(p)er

IDOLATROUS baalish, heathen, pagan

IDOLATRY adoration, baalism, bibliolatry, demonism, fetishism, hagiolatry, heliolatry, hero worship, iconoduly, love, maumetry, pyrolatry, sabaism, veneration, whoredom, worship

IDOLIZE admire, adore, canonize, cherish, deify, dote on, esteem, love, regard, respect, revere, reverence, venerate, worship

IDOLOTHYTE offering, sacrifice

IDOLUM apparition, eidolon, fallacy, ghost

IDOMENE *husband* amythaon
son bias, melampus

IDOTHEA *father* proteus

IDUMEA edom

IDUN(A), ITHUNN *husband* brage, bragi
goddess of spring

IDYLL bucolic, composition, eclogue, image, pastoral(e), pastourelle, poem, rural, verse

IDYLLS OF THE KING *author* tennyson
character arthur, bellicent, elaine, enid, gareth, geraint, guinevere, lancelot, lynette, vivien

IERNE See IRELAND.

IF although, and, gif, gin, provided, sobeit, supposing, though, whether
ever once
not but, else, nisi, unless
only alevai, halevai, would that

IFA hemp, murva, pangane, sansevieria

IFFY doubtful, dubious, uncertain

IGAL *father* joseph

IGDALIAH *son* hanan

IGNATIUS *emblem* lion

IGNEOUS combustive, conflagrative, fiery, plutonic

IGNIPUNCTURE pyronyxis

IGNIS FATUUS illusion, luminescence

IGNITE backfire, bank, burn, calcine, conflagrate, enkindle, fire, flash, inflame, kindle, light(en), relume, set fire, spark, start, stoke, touch off, trigger

IGNITED afire, burning, drunk, incandescent, inflamed, kindled, lit, live, living

IGNITION fire, firing, flame, inflammation, kindling, lighting, starting
cap fuse, fuze
premature backfire

IGNOBLE abased, abject, bad, base(born), boorish, churlish, dastardly, debased, dishonorable, disreputable, evil, grubby, humble, infamous, low(ly), mean, measly, menial, paltry, petty, plebeian, puny, shameful, sordid, trivial, unworthy, vile

IGNOMINIOUS base, contemptible, degrading, despicable, dishonorable, disreputable, infamous, low, opprobrius, scandalous, shameful

IGNOMINY chagrin, contempt, disgrace, dishonor, disrepute, infamy, obloquy, odium, opprobrium, scandal, scorn, shame

IGNORAMUS amhaarez, baha(y)ma, behayme, blockhead, bonehead, dolt, dope, duffer, dunce, empiric, fool, greenhorn, idiot, ignatz, illiterate, ingram, knownothing, lowbrow, nitwit, novice, numskull, philistine, sciolist, simple, troglodyte

IGNORANCE agnosy, avidya, barbarism, betise, bevue, blindness, darkness, illiteracy, inerudition, nescience, prejudice, rudity, tamas
philosophy of tamas
study of agnoiology

IGNORANT backward, barbarian, benighted, callow, crude, dumb, empty (headed), graubyer, green, ill-bred, illiterate, inexperienced, ingenuous, ingram, inscient, insensible, knownothing, lowbrow, naive, nescient, philistine, raw, rude, simple, slight, unaware, uneducated, unhep, uninformed, unintelligent, unkenning, unknowing, unlearned, unlettered, unmindful, unread, unripe, unsuspecting, untaught, untutored, unversed, unwitting, verdant, witless

IGNORE avoid, balk, baulk, blink, break, bypass, circumvent, condone, cushion, cut, discount, disdain, disobey, disregard, dodge, duck, elide, escape, evade, forget, misken, misknow, neglect, omit, overlook, poohpooh, reject, scorn, shun, slight, sneeze at, snub, tolerate, wink at

IGOROT bontok, kankanai, nabaloi
chief agp

neighbor ata
town division ati, ato

IGUANA basiliscus, goanna, lizard

IGUANID anole, anoli, basiliscus, basilisk, goanna, horned toad, lizard

IHI fish, halfbeak, skipper, stitchbird
mother hathor

I H S in hoc signo

IKHNATON See AMENHOTEP.

ILAIRA *father* leucippus
sister phoebe

ILE See ISLAND.

ILEX bearberry, canhoop, cassioberry, holly, holmoak, winterberry, yaupon

ILIA See RHEA SILVIA.

ILIAD *author* homer
basis achilleid
boeotian leader prothoenor
carpenter tecton
character agamemnon, ajax, aretus, arsinous, asius, assaracus, atymnius, cassandra, diomede(s), enyeus, odysseus, paris, priam, rhene, rhigmus, stentor, talaemenes, thersilochus, thersites, thoas, thrasdemus, trasymelus, tychius, ucalegon, ulysses
chieftain amphimachus, antimachus
concubine phthia
herald stentor
hero achilles, ajax, diomede(s), hector
king altes, amarynceus, amphidamus, pylaemenes
lake nymph gygaea
priest calchas
river god pelegon
shipbuilder phereclus
trojan ally amphius, antiphus, asteropaeus, pirous, polymelus
trojan warrior antiphates, areithous, podes, polydamas
warrior imbrius

ILIADUM *son* joda

ILIONE *husband* polymnestor
parent hecuba, priam
son deipylus

ILITHYIA *son* eros

ILIUM bone, flank, troy

ILK breed, character, class, family, kidney, kin, kind, nature, sort, stripe, type

ILL abed, adverse, afflicted, ailing, amiss, bad, bale,

cruel, evil, faulty, groggy, harm(ful), harsh, hurt, improper, inauspicious indisposed, injury, mischief, naughty, poorly, sick(ly), unfavorable, unfortunate, unlucky, unwell, wicked, wisht, wrong

-advised foolish, impolitic, imprudent, unwise

at ease ashamed, awkward, discomfited, selfconscious, uncomfortable

-behaved discourteous, gauche, naughty, rude, unthewed

-blood animosity, enmity

-boding dire, dismal, inauspicious

-breeding bad manners, rudeness

-bred boorish, bourgeois, caddish, churlish, clownish, crude, hoiden, hoyden, impertinent, impolite, malapert, plebeian, rude, uncivil, unrefined, vulgar

comb. dys, mal, mis

-considered hasty, impulsive, rash, reckless

-defined unclear, vague

-disposed hostile, malevolent, opposed, unamiable, unfortunate, unfriendly, untoward

-fated doomed, inauspicious, jinxed, prejudiced, starcrossed, unlucky

-favored disagreeable, offensive, ugly, unpleasant, unprepossessing, unsoncy

-fitting baggy, sloppy

-gotten bad, corrupt, evil

-health indisposition, infirmity, invalidism, sickliness, sickness

humor anger, bile, discontent, drunt, dudgeon, grump(s), ire, moodiness, pet, spleen, sullenness, tid

-humored angry, cranky, cross, crouse, fretful, glum, grumpy, mad, morose, peeved, peevish, riled, short, splenetic, stuffy, surly

-lit dark, gloomy

luck ambsace, misfortune

made awkward, deformed, monstrous, sloppy

-mannered boorish, discourteous, graubyer, impolite, prost, rude, uncivil, unrefined

nature malevolence

-natured angry, cantankerous, carping, crabby, dour, fretful, nasty, peevish, snarly, sullen, surly, ugly

-natured one crab

-off poor, sad, unfortunate

-omened dismal, hopeless, inauspicious, ominous

-smelling fusty, stinking, stinky

-starred inauspicious, sad, shvartzeh

-temper anger, animus, spleen

temper symbol bear

-tempered angry, bilious, cammed, camshach, cankered, chuff, cranky, cross, crusty, fess, girnie, grouchy, mad, moody, puxy, short, shrewish, shrill, splenetic, surly, testy

-timed inappropriate, unseasonable

-treat abuse, affront, aggrieve, harm, hurt, injure, maltreat, misdo, misuse, oppress, outrage, persecute, wrong

vaguely howish

will animosity, animus, bad blood, despite, enmity, grudge, hate, hatred, hostility, malevolence, malice, mauger, rancor, revenge, spite, spleen, venom

will, showing bellicose, belligerent, choleric, contentious, disputatious, hostile, irascible, litigious, pugnacious, quarrelsome, spiteful, wrangling

wind bad luck, jinx

ILLATIVE deducible, inferential, then, therefore

ILLEGAL actionable, blackmarket, bootleg, contraband, criminal, crooked, felonious, foul, illegitimate, illicit, invalid, lawless, malfeasant, nonlicit, outlaw(ed), prohibited, proscribed, taboo, tabu, tortious, unauthorized, under-the-counter, unlawful, unlicensed, wrongful

ILLEGIBLE blind, cacographic, cramped, unreadable

ILLEGITIMATE base(born), bastard, bootleg, false, illegal, illicit, improper, misbegot(ten), momzer, natural, nothous, sinistral, spurious,

unfathered, unlawful, wrong(ful)

child bantling, bastard, byblow

ILLIBERAL grudging, mean, mingy, miserly, narrow, small, stingy, tight

ILLICA *opera* la boheme

ILLICIT black, ILLEGAL, sly, unlawful

ILLINOIS *capital* springfield

city albion, alton, aurora, barrington, batavia, berwyn, bloomington, blue island, brookfield, canton, carbondale, chicago, cicero, decatur, dekalb, des plaines, dixon, dolton, downer's grove, elgin, elmhurst, evanston, forest park, galesburg, genesco, glencoe, herrin, joliet, kankakee, kewanee, lagrange, lake forest, lansing, lombard, mattoon, maywood, mendota, moline, niles, nokomis, oaklawn, olney, ottawa, pekin, peoria, quincy, rockford, rock island, skokie, springfield, sterling, streator, urbana, waukegan, westchester, wheaton, wilmette, winnetka

central engineer casey jones

county bond, bureau, cass, coles, cook, dupage, grundy, hardin, iroquois, kane, macon, macoupin, massal, ogle, peoria, sangamon

college aurora, eureka, knox, olivet, quincy, shimer

french settlement cahokia

governor altgeld, stevenson

hills shawnee

indian fox, kaskaskia, sauk

native sucker

nickname prairie state, tall state

nut pecan

peak charles mound

river big muddy, chicago, elkhorn, mackinaw, ohio, rock, sangamon, spoon, wabash

state bird cardinal

state flower violet

state tree burl-oak

university chicago, northwestern

ILLITERATE analphabetic, catachrestic, ignoramus, ignorant, inerudite, nescient, solecistic, uneducated, unlearned, unread, untaught

ILLNESS affliction, ailment, brash, complaint, disease, disorder, distemper, krenk, malady, sickness, traik
attack dwalm, dwam, seizure
comb. agra
cure acupuncture
feigner goldbrick, malingerer
goddess kipu-tytto
mental alienation, psychosis
pretend malinger

ILLOGICAL absurd, addlebrained, addlepated, confused, fallacious, farfetched, flighty, foolish, harebrained, incoherent, inconclusive, incongruous, inconsistent, invalid, irrational, senseless, silly, unfounded, ungrounded, unreal, unreasonable, unscientific

ILLUDE deceive, deride, elude, evade, mock

ILLUMINANT acetylene, benzine, candle, coaloil, electricity, ethine, ethyne, gas(oline), kerosene, petrol(eum)

ILLUMINATE adorn, beacon, belight, beshine, blaze, bright(en), cheer, clarify, color, elucidate, emblaze, enlighten, explain, figure, fire, floodlight, gloss, highlight, illustrate, instruct, intoxicated, irradiate, kindle, light(en), limn, miniate, mystic, overshine, rally, scholar, spotlight, transfigure

ILLUMINATED ablaze, aglow, alight, bespangled, bright, candlelit, decorated, drunk, enlightened, firelit, gaslit, irradiated, lightened, lit up, luminous, spangled, sunlit, torchlit
doctor lully, tauler

ILLUMINATION decoration, elucidation, enlightenment, explanation, glory, knowledge, learning, light, penumbra
device chandelier, flashlight, lamp, lantern, torch
unit foot candle, lux, microlux, microphot, millilux, phot

ILLUMINE See ILLUMINATE.

ILLUSION apparition, bubble, chimera, deception, delusion, deriding, dream, error, fallacy, fancy, fantasy, fool's paradise, hallucination, humbuggery, ignis-fatuus, imagination, mirage, misbelief, misconception, mockery, phantasm, phantom, pipe dream, shadow, trick, vapor, will-o-the-wisp, zollner
optical pseudopsia

ILLUSORY apparent, barmecidal, chimeric(al), deceptive, deluding, delusional, delusive, delusory, erroneous, evanid, fallacious, false, fantastic, hallucinative, imaginary, misleading, ostensible, phantasmal, seeming, specious, spectral, unreal

ILLUSTRATE adorn, beautify, cite, delineate, design, elucidate, embody, epitomize, evidence, exemplify, explain, instance, picture, portray, represent, show, symbolize, typify

ILLUSTRATION case, depiction, design, diagram, drawing, engraving, example, exemplum, explanation, figure, image, instance, painting, photo, picture, print, sample, simile, specimen, vignette

ILLUSTRIOUS bright, brilliant, candid, caste, celebrated, distinguished, eminent, exalted, famed, famous, glorious, great, heroic(al), luculent, lustrous, magnific, noted, radiant, renowned, resplendent, shining, signal, splendent, splendid, splendrous, star
through nobility albert(a)

ILLYRIA *duke* orsino
king bardylis, glaucias

IL TROVATORE *gypsy* azucena

ILUS *grandson* priam
parent callirrhoe, tros
son ganymede, laomedon

IMAGE agalma, agnus, allegory, alraun, apparition, appearance, archetype, aspect, association, cast, concept(ion), construct, copy, counterpart, daibutsu, dap, describe, description, ditto, effigy, efod, eidolon, eikon, ephod, facsimile, fancy, fantasy, fetish, figment, figure, form, god(ling), herma, icon, idea, idol(um), ikon, illustration, imago, joss, katcina, map, mask, medal, miniature, mirror(ing), model, module, notion, percept, phantasm, photo(graph), picture, poppet, portrait, print, reflection, replica, representation, resemblance, sammy, santo, semblance, shadow, shape, shrine, sigil, similitude, simulacrum, sphinx, swami, symbol(ize), teraph, tiki, totem, visage, vision, vorstellung, zoomorph
breaker iconoclast
carved xoanon
comb. icono, idolo, typ(o)
cult joss
distorted anamorphism
good luck alraun, alruna
graven eikon, icon, idol, ikon
heavenly fravashi
-like simulacral
magic sigil
maker iconoplast
mental concept(ion), eidolon, fancy, fantasy, idea, percept, phantasm, recept
mirrored reflection, reflex
of deity godkin, godling, svamin, swami
person with eidetic
pert. iconic
primitive agalma
radar blip
rainbow-like spectrum
religious icon, idol, ikon, orant, pieta, saint, santo(n)
spectral umbra
stone herma
televised video
wooden tiki, totem, xoanon
worship ararati, idolatry
worship(p)er consolater, idolator

IMAGERY description, embodiment, iconism, idolatry, representation, sculpture, statuary

IMAGINABLE cogitable, conceivable, envisaged, envisioned, fanciable, supposable, thinkable

IMAGINARY abstract, apocryphal, artificial, chimeric(al), delusive, delusory, fabulous, fancied, fanciful, fantastic(al), fictitious, ideal, illusory, legendary, mythical, notional, quixotic, romantic, seeming, supposititious, unreal, utopian, visionary

IMAGINATION brain, bubble, chimera, conceit, concept, creation, dream, enterprise, fancy, fantasy, fiction, figment, idea, illusion, image, inspiration, invention, myth, notion, phantasm, phantasy, reverie, romance, thought, verve

creative muse

IMAGINATIVE bold, creative, dreamy, enterprising, extravagant, fanciful, fantastic, fertile, fictive, inventive, original, poetical, productive, unreal, visionary

IMAGINE apprehend, assume, conceive, conjure, create, daydream, deem, dream, envisage, envision, fabricate, fancy, feign, ideate, invent, guess, judge, opine, phantasize, picture, project, propose, suppose, surmise, suspect, think, visualize, ween, wis

IMA(U)M ali(m), caliph, ecclesiastic, mahdi, mufti, priest, prince

IMBECILE, **IMBECILIC** ament, anile, asinine, ass, changeling, childish, congeon, cretin, dope, dopy, dotard, dote, dunce, fatuous, feeble(minded), fool(ish), goon, halfwit(ted), idiot(ic), inane, moron, natural, nitwit, simpleton, stupid, weak, witless, witlet

IMBECILITY absurdity, amentia, anoesia, fatuity, foolishness, idiocy, inability, incapacity, moria, stupidity, weakness

IMBED See EMBED.

IMBIBE absorb, assimilate, bib, consume, devour, drink, gulp, imbue, ingurgitate, inhale, irrigate, partake, permeate, pervade, quaff, receive, sip, soak, souse, steep, swallow, take, tipple

IMBRICATE bent, hollowed, lap, overlap(ping), overlie, overlying, scaled

IMBRIUS *father* mentor *slayer* teucer

IMBROGENEIS See CURETES.

IMBROGLIO brawl, cabal, complication, embroilment, fight, intrigue, plot, predicament, strife, tangle

IMBRUE bloodstain, color, defile, drench, embrew, ensanguine, imbue, infect, insteep, macerate, moisten, saturate, soak, stain, steep, wet

IMBUE animate, charge, color, diffuse, dye, ensoul, fire, imbibe, impregnate, inculcate, inform, infuse, ingrain, inoculate, inspire, instill, leaven, permeate, pervade, saturate, season, soak, stain, stew, suffuse, tinct(ure), tinge, tint

IMHOTEP *father* ptah

IMITATE adopt, affect, ape, borrow, copy counterfeit, ditto, duplicate, echo, emulate, feign, follow, forge, impersonate, mime, mimic, mirror, mock, model, parallel, parody, parrot, pattern, personate, repeat, reproduce, resemble, sham, simulate

father patrizate

IMITATION apism, appropriation, artificial, bogus, burlesque, camblot, copy, counterfeit, dummy, duplicate, echo, emulation, facsimile, fake, forgery, fraud, ghost, hit-off, masquerade, mimesis, mimetic, mimicry, mockage, mockery, model, parody, pastiche, plagiarism, postique, reproduction, satire, schlenter, sham, simulation, travesty

comb. ette

debased travesty

derisive mimesis, mimicry, mockery

pert. apatetic, epigonal, mimetic

IMITATIVE apathic, apish, artful, camouflaged, emulous, mimetic, mimic, mock, reflective, shoddy, simulative, slavish

IMITATOR ape(r), copier, copycat, copyist, counterfeiter, cuckoo, echo(er), emulator, epigone, epigonist, mime(r), mimic,

mockingbird, monkey, parrot, polly(parrot), pretender, shammer, snob

IMLAH *son* micaiah

IMMACULATE candid, chaste, clean, faultless, innocent, perfect, pure, snowy, spick-and-span, spotless, stainless, unsoiled, unstained

IMMANENT indwelling, inherent, subjective

IMMATERIAL asomatous, bodiless, decarnate(d), disembodied, dreamy, extramundane, impalpable, incorporal, incorporate, incorporeal, insignificant, intangible, internal, irrelevant, psychic(al), slight, spectral, spiritual, supernatural, transmundane, trifling, unearthly, unimportant, unsubstantial, unworldly, wraithlike

IMMATERIALIST animatist, animist, herkeleian, idealist, panpsychist, platonist, psychist, spiritualist

IMMATURE boyish, callow, childish, crude, green, half-baked, halfgrown, imperfect, incomplete, infantile, juvenile, lait, larval, neanic, nouveau, premature, primitive, puerile, raw, rude, rudimentary, sappy, small, superficial, tender, trivial, unfinished, unfledged, unformed, unlicked, unmellow, untimely, vealy, verdant, young, youthful

person baby

thing bud

IMMATURITY callowness, chrysalis, crudity, greenness, inexperience, infancy, infantilism, juniority, minority, nonage, puerility, rawness, sappiness, underdevelopment, unripeness, youth

IMMEASURABLE boundless, extensive, illimitable, infinite, limitless, untold

IMMEDIACY directness, instancy, nearness, promptitude

IMMEDIATE abrupt, adjacent, contiguous, direct, hasty, headlong, imminent, impetuous, instant(aneous), instinctive, intuitive, modern, momentary, nearby, nearest, next, nigh, precipitant, precipitate, precipitous, present, presto, prompt, proximal, proximate, quick, speedy, sudden, swift, synectic

IMMEDIATELY anon, at once, away, bang off, close, directly, fast, first, forthwith, hereupon, instantly, just, now, once, pdq, plumb, presto, promptly, right away, soon, straightway, subito, suddenly

IMMEMORIAL ancient, dateless, hoary, old, prehistoric, primeval, traditional

IMMENSE big, boundless, bunyanesque, elephantine, enormous, colossal, fat, fine, giant, gigantic, GREAT, herculean, huge, illimitable, infinite, LARGE, mammoth, measureless, mighty, monstrous, prodigious, stupendous, superb, titanic, tremendous, unbounded, vast(y), wide, whooping, whopping

IMMER *son* hanani, magormissabib, pashur, zadok, zebadiah

IMMERSE absorb, baptize, bathe, bowssen, bury, deluge, dip, dissolve, douse, drench, drown, duck, dunk, engage, engross, engulf, ensteep, imbue, infuse, ingrain, inundate, involve, merge, overwhelm, plunge, saturate, sink, soak, sop, souse, submerge, wet, whelm

IMMERSED absorbed, baptized, deep, engrossed, implicated, innate, submarine

IMMERSION absorption, baptism, bath, dunking *believer in* baptist, dipper

IMMIGRANT alien, arrival, bracero, colonist, comeling, comer, emigrant, emigre, entrant, foreigner, halutz, intruder, metic, newcomer, outlander, outsider, pilgrim, pioneer, settler, stranger, visitant, visitor *illegal* alambre, wetback, wirejumper

IMMINENCE approach, coming, forthcoming, impendence, instancy, threat

IMMINENT approaching, awaited, at hand, brewing,

close, coming, expected, forthcoming, gathering, looming, lowering, immediate, impendent, impending, in prospect, instant, in store, in the wind, likely, looming, menacing, near-at-hand, nearing, on the horizon, on the verge, pending

IMMIT admit, infuse, inject, insert, introduce, receive, send in

IMMOBILE firm, fixed, frozen, immotive, immovable, impassive, inflexible, motionless, quiescent, rigid, set, stable, stationary, steadfast, stolid, tranced

IMMOBILIZE freeze, set, splint, stiffen

IMMODERATE excessive, exorbitant, extravagant, extreme, free, inordinate, intemperate, lavish, overflowing, prodigal, profuse, teeming, unbridled, undue, unmeth

IMMODEST barefaced, bold, brassy, brazen, exalted, free, impudent, indecent, indelicate, lofty, obscene, proud, shameful, shameless, shocking, unblushing, unchaste, unseemly

IMMODESTY brass, impudence, impudicity, indecency, indelicacy, obscenity

IMMOLATE propitiate, sacrifice

IMMORAL abandoned, bad, base, culpable, corrupt, depraved, dissipated, dissolute, evil, fallen, gross, indecent, lascivious, lecherous, lewd, libertine, licentious, loose, lustful, obscene, profligate, rakish, reprobate, ribald, sinful, unchaste, unethical, unprincipled, unscrupulous, vicious, vile, wanton, wicked, wrong *person* baggage, miscreant, rake(hell), reprobate, rotter, roue

IMMORALITY aberrancy, corruption, debauchery, degeneracy, depravity, dissipation, miscreancy, perversion, profligacy, turpitude, vice, villainy

IMMORTAL(S) akal(i), amaranthine, ambrosial, athanasius, celebrated, ce-

lebrity, constant, deathless, deity, divine, endless, enduring, eternal, everlasting, fadeless, famous, glorious, god(like), laureate, neverending, perdurable, perpetual, storied, undying, unfading *bard* shakespeare *8* chang-kuo lao, hanchung li, han hsiang-tzu, hohsienky, lantsaiho, lu tung pin, tieh kuai, tsaokuochiu *name meaning* ambrose *3* dante, homer, milton *tinker* john bunyan

IMMORTALITY ankh, athanasia, athanasy, eternity, fame, memory, perpetuity *beverage* amreeta, amrita, rasa, soma *symbolic color* green

IMMORTALIZE blazon, emblazon, eternalize, eternize, glorify, perpetuate, publicize

IMMOVABLE adamant(ine), changeless, constant, firm, fixed, frozen, immobile, immotile, immotive, inflexible, intransigent, motionless, obstinate, pat, quiescent, set, standpat, standstill, stationary, steadfast, stiff, stubborn, unfeeling, unyielding

IMMUNE allowed, clear, exempt, free, privileged, protected, safe *body* amboceptor, desmon, sensitizer

IMMUNITY amnesty, athrepsia, atrepsy, charter, exemption, exoneration, franchise, freedom, impunity, liberty, license, privilege, prophylaxis, protection, woodgeld *agent* antitoxin, haptene, serum, shot, vaccine

IMMUNIZE haffkinize, inoculate, neutralize, protect, shoot, treat, vaccinate, variolate, vastate

IMMURE cloister, confine, enclose, entomb, imprison, incarcerate, intern, isolate, jail, limit, restrict, seclude, wall

IMMUTABLE adamant(ine), constant, eternal, firm, fixed, inflexible, invariable, permanent, stable, unchangeable

IMNAH *son* kore

IMOGEN *assumed name* fidele
attendant helen
father cymbeline
husband posthumus-leonatus
son cloton

IMP brat(ling), bud, child, cion, demon, devil(et), devilkin, elf, engraft, equip, fairy, fay, fellow, fiend, folletto, graft, hobgoblin, implant, increase, mock, offspring, pixie, plague, progeny, rascal, repair, rogue, scamp, shoot, slip, spirit, sprite, strengthen, terror, tyke, urchin, youth

IMPACT bingo, blow, brunt, clash, collision, concussion, contact, cram, crash, feeze, fix, force, hit, impress(ion), impulse, jar, jolt, meaning, percussion, pulse, ram, reaction, repercussion, shock, slam, slap, smashup, stroke, thrust, wedge
sound plop, slam, slap, thump

IMPAIR blemish, blot, blunt, break, cheapen, cloud, cripple, damage, debase, deface, deform, destroy, devalue, dilapidate, disable, disfigure, distort, enervate, enfeeble, harm, hurt, infringe, injure, labefy, lame, lessen, maim, mank, mar, reduce, ruin, sap, shatter, spoil, taint, undermine, unfit, vitiate, warp, weaken, worsen

IMPAIRMENT akinesia, deficit, dotage, erosion, fault, injury, wearing

IMPALA aepyceros, antelope, redbuck, roodebok, rooibok, rooyebok

IMPALE bait, border, confine, edge, encircle, enclose, ganch, gore, hem in, perforate, pierce, skewer, spear, spit, stab, sting, surround, torture, transfix

IMPALPABLE attenuated, delicate, elusive, fine, immaterial, imprecise, infinitesimal, insensible, intangible, light, nebulous, powdery, rare, rarified, slight, tenuous, thin, unclear, unintelligible, unreal, vague

IMPANATION anartismos, eucharist

IMPAR azygous, odd, unequal, unpaired

IMPART bestow, carry, cede, communicate, confer, convey, discover, dispense, distribute, divide, divulge, give, grant, imbue, implant, inculcate, inform, infuse, instill, intimate, partake, participate, purport, relinquish, render, reveal, say, share, tell, transfer
knowledge instruct, lere, teach, tutor

IMPARTIAL aloof, candid, detached, disinterested, dispassionate, equitable, even, fair(minded), honorable, impersonal, just, neutral, nonpartisan, objective, right, tolerant, unbiased, uncolored, unprejudiced, unslanted

IMPARTIALITY breadth, candor, catholicity, detachment, equity, evenness, fairness, liberality, neutrality, objectivity, tolerance

IMPARTIBLE contagious, inseparable

IMPASSABLE impenetrable, impermeable, impervious, solid

IMPASSE blind alley, block, corner, cul-de-sac, deadend, deadlock, difficulty, dilemma, extremity, halt, hitch, hole, logjam, mire, morass, nonplus, quandary, stalemate, standstill, stop, wit's end
at an cornered, stalled

IMPASSIBLE anesthetic, impassive, insensible, insensitive, unfeeling

IMPASSION arouse, commove, excite, move, rouse

IMPASSIONED animated, ardent, deep, excited, fervent, fervid, fiery, hot, intense, maudlin, perfervid, profound, romantic, sentimental, vehement, zealous

IMPASSIVE apathetic, callous, calm, collected, composed, cool, dull, emotionless, frozen, hard (ened), indifferent, indurated, nonchalant, passive, phlegmatic, placid, reserved, reticent, serene, silent, steady, steely, stoic(al), stolid, taciturn,

unconcerned, unemotional, unfeeling, uninterested

IMPASSIVENESS apathy, calmness, morgue, phlegm, stoicism, stolidity

IMPASTO enamel, pigment

IMPATIENCE anxiety, chafing, disquietude, eagerness, expectancy, fretfulness, fretting, impetuousness, intolerance, lather, restiveness, restlessness, suspense, sweat, uneasiness
expression of chut, nonsense, silence, tsk, tut

IMPATIENS balsam, celandine, herb, jewelweed

IMPATIENT abrupt, angry, anxious, avid, chafing, choleric, eager, feverish, fidgety, fretful, hasty, hectic, impetuous, intolerant, irritable, itching, jittery, jumpy, keen, nervous, nervy, peevish, precipitate, querulous, restive, restless, sudden, testy, tidiose, tired, uneasy, waspish

IMPAVID bold, fearless, intrepid

IMPEACH accuse, arraign, asperse, blame, censure, challenge, charge, condemn, criminate, denounce, discredit, disparage, harm, hinder, impair, impede, impugn, incriminate, indict, prevent, query, question, test, try

IMPEACHMENT accusation, arraignment, challenge, damage, dishonor, harm, hindrance, impediment, injury, obstruction, reproach

IMPECCABLE accurate, clean, correct, entire, faultless, flawless, inerrant, infallible, nice, perfect, precise, pure, right, sinless, spotless, unerring, whole

IMPECUNIOUS penniless, poor, poverty-stricken

IMPEDE baffle, balk, bar, block, check, clog, dam, debar, delay, discomfit, disconcert, encumber, estop, fetter, frustrate, hamper, hinder, hitch, hobble, hogtie, let, obstruct, pester, prevent, rattle, restrict, retard, shackle, slow, snag, stymie, sufflaminate, thwart, trammel, traverse

IMPEDIMENT bar(rier),

block, burden, burthen, cross, difficulty, disability, disadvantage, embargo, embarrassment, encumbrance, hamper, handicap, hardship, hindrance, hitch, imposition, load, lumber, millstone, obstacle, obstruction, onus, pack, penalty, snag, stammer, stop, stutter, weight

speech haar, stammer, stutter

IMPEDIMENTA baggage, equipment, freight, gear, luggage, stuff

IMPEL actuate, animate, blow, bring, carry, cast, compel, constrain, drive, excite, foment, force, forward, goad, incite, induce, influence, instigate, knock, lash, motivate, move, obsess, prick, prod, propel, provoke, push, send, spur, start, stimulate, thrust, urge

IMPEND approach, await, brew, come on, draw near, expend, forthcome, gather, hang(over), hover, loom, lour, menace, near, overhang, pay, portend, threaten

IMPENDING approaching, close, imminent, impendent, likely, menacing, near(ing), nigh, probable, threatening

IMPENETRABLE adamant, airtight, bullet-proof, close, compact(ed), dense, firm, hard, impassable, impermeable, impervious, inflexible, murky, obdurate, solid, thick, waterproof

IMPENITENCE hardness, obduracy

IMPENITENT hardened, incorrigible, lost, obdurate, unashamed, uncontrite, unremorseful, unrepentant, unrueful, unsorry

IMPERATIVE authoritative, autocratic, binding, compulsory, de rigueur, domineering, exigent, imperious, injunction, mandatory, masterful, must, necessary, peremptory, pressing, required, urgent, vital

IMPERCEPTIBLE impalpable, infinitesimal, insensible, insignificant, intangible, invisible, occult, subtle, unintelligible

IMPERFECT at fault, bad,

blemished, crude, defective, deficient, errable, erratic, fallible, faulty, flawed, frail, fuzzy, immature, impaired, inadequate, incomplete, injured, inparfit, lacking, marred, partial, rough, short, stickit, tainted, undeveloped, unfinished, unripe, unsound, unwhole, wanting, warped

comb. atel(o), mal

IMPERFECTION blemish, blotch, bug, defect(ion), deficiency, demerit, drawback, failing, flaw, foible, frailty, inadequacy, kink, peccadillo, shortcoming, spot, stain, vice, weakness, wen

IMPERFORATION atresia, hole

IMPERIAL august, authoritative, beard, coin, dominant, exalted, excellent, fabric, grand, kingly, majestic, noble, princely, purple, queenly, regal, roof, royal, sovereign, stately, superior, supreme, top, tuft

blue smalt

woodpecker ivorybill

IMPERIL endanger, jeopardize, risk

IMPERIOUS ambitious, arbitrary, arrogant, authoritative, autocratic, bossy, clamorous, compulsive, demanding, despotic, dictatorial, dominative, domineering, grinding, haughty, high and mighty, high-handed, imperative, lordly, magisterial, masterful, masterly, oppressive, overbearing, overruling, peremptory, proud, surly, tyrannical, urgent

IMPERISHABLE enduring, eternal, everlasting, immortal, indestructible, lasting, perpetual, undying

IMPERIUM command, empire, power

IMPERMANENCE anicca, brevity, briefness, caducity, evanescence, fleetness, fugacity, fugitivity, mortality, temporality, temporariness, transience, transiency, transitoriness, volatility

IMPERMANENT ad interim, brief, caducous, cursory, deciduous, elusive, ephem-

eral, evanescent, fleet(ing), fugacious, fugitive, impermanent, momentary, mortal, passing, perishable, protem(pore), provisional, provisory, short-lived, sometime, spasmodic, temporal, temporary, tentative, transitory, volatile

IMPERMEABLE dense, firm, hard, impassible, impenetrable, impervious, solid, tight, waterproof, watertight

IMPERSONAL abstract, blind, candid, cold, cool, deadpan, detached, disinterested, fair, general, impartial, inhuman, just, unbiased

IMPERSONATE act, ape, burlesque, caricature, characterize, copy, counterfeit, enact, exemplify, feign, imitate, masquerade, mimic, pass for, personify, play, portray, pose as, pretend, represent, simulate, symbolize, typify

IMPERSONATION act, character, imposture, impression, masquerade, personification, role

IMPERSONATOR actor, mime, mummer, performer, player, thespian, trooper

IMPERTINENCE affront, audacity, effrontery, insolence, pawk, snash

IMPERTINENT arrogant, audacious, brash, brazen, extraneous, fresh, immaterial, impish, IMPUDENT, inappropriate, insolent, intrusive, irrelevant, malapert, meddlesome, obtrusive, offensive, officious, pert, procacious, rude, sassy, saucy, shameless

IMPERTURBABILITY aplomb, ataraxis, ataraxy, poise, sangfroid, self-possession, tranquility

IMPERTURBABLE calm, collected, composed, cool, glacial, immobile, impassive, nonchalant, phlegmatic, placid, serene, smug, steady, tranquil, unmoved, unruffled

IMPERVIOUS adamant(ine), bulletproof, callous, hardened, impassable, impenetrable, impermeable, indurated, inflexible, insensitive, obdurate, opaque, resistant, secure

IMPETRATE appeal, ask for, beseech, entreat, procure, request

IMPETUOSITY ardor, elan, fougue, fury, HASTE, spleen, violence

IMPETUOUS anxious, ardent, boisterous, brash, brothe, buckish, dashing, eager, fervid, feverish, fierce, fiery, flashy, forcible, freck, furious, hasty, headlong, hectic, heedless, hot(blooded), immediate, impatient, impulsive, lively, passionate, powerful, precipitate, quick, rash, reckless, restive, rude, rushing, slapdash, splenitive, spontaneous, sudden, swift, unexpected, vehement, violent, wild

person hotspur

IMPETUS collision, eagerness, emphasis, energy, force, goad, impact, impulse, impulsion, incentive, incitement, life, momentum, motive, pace, power, pressure, push, shock, speed, spur, stimulant, stimulus, swinge, swough, thrust, urge, velocity, vigor

IMPIETY blasphemy, indifference, irreligion, irreverence, profanity, sin, ungodliness

IMPINGE assault, collide, contact, dash, encroach, force, impact, infringe, strike, thrust, touch

IMPINGEMENT brunt, clash, collision, concussion, contact, encroachment, impact, impress(ion), imprint, jar, jolt, percussion, print, shock, stamp, stroke

IMPIOUS atheist, atheous, blasphemous, flagitious, godless, irreligious, irreverent, nefarious, profane, sacrilegious, ungodly

IMPISH arch, bad, cunning, cute, elfish, elvan, malignant, mischievous, naughty, pert, playful, roguish, saucy, sly, sportive, tricky, waggish, wanton, warlock

IMPLACABLE adamant, deadly, grim, inexorable,

inflexible, obdurate, pitiless, relentless, ruthless, stout

IMPLANT engraft, enroot, entrench, establish, fix, graft, imbue, impregnate, impress, inculcate, infix, infuse, inlay, inoculate, insert, inset, inspire, instill, interpose, leaven, penetrate, permeate, pervade, root, set, sow, teach

IMPLAUSIBLE doubtful, improbable, unbelievable, unlikely

IMPLEAD accuse, argue, impeach, litigate, prosecute, sue

IMPLEMENT (See also INSTRUMENT.) accomplish, achieve, agent, apparatus, appliance, arm, article, carry out, complete, contraption, contrivance, device, effect, enable, enforce, engine, equip, execute, fulfill(ment), gadget, gear, graith, INSTRUMENT, kit, machine, material, perform (ance), provide, realize, tackle, thing, tool, utensil

ancient amgarn, celt, eolith, flaker, neolith, paleolith, point, racloir, slice

barbed harpoon

cleaning broom, brush, dustcloth, duster, mop, swab, sweeper, vacuum

climbing creeper, ladder, piton

cutting (jack)knife, mower, pocketknife, razor, reaper, scissors, scythe, shears, switchblade

enlarging dilator, reamer

furcate fork

gardening clippers, hoe, rake, shears, sickle

grasping pliers, tongs, tweezers, wrench

hide-cleaning slater

kind dolly, dredge, fraise, mattock, mortar, paddle, pestle, rabble, sadiron, scraper, shovel, sickle, spreader, tolliker

lifting hoist, lever, pry, tongs

logging peav(e)y, peev(e)y, tode

nap-raising teacle, tease(l), teasle, teazel

plow-like grub-hook

printer's biron, press

reaping mower, reaper, scythe, shears, sickle

shovel-like scoop, spade, spoon, trowel

soldering doctor, gun

surgical See SURGEON *instrument*.

threshing flail

IMPLICATE affect, associate, comprehend, concern, connect, embrace, embroil, entail, entangle, entwine, imply, include, incriminate, infer, interweave, involve, join, link, relate, subsume, unite

IMPLICATION allusion, assumption, claim, connotation, engagement, enmeshment, entanglement, hint, implial, import, inference, innuendo, intimation, involution, involvement, meaning, overtone, presumption, suggestion, supposition

IMPLICIT constructive, covert, gathered, hinted, IMPLIED, inferred, intimated, suggested, tacit, understood, unexpressed, unsaid, unspoken, virtual

IMPLIED certain, deduced, IMPLICIT, inferential, innate, intended, meant, tacit, unqualified, wordless

IMPLORE adjure, appeal, ask, beg, beseech, conjure, crave, entreat, importune, invoke, petition, plead, pray, request, solicit, sue, supplicate

IMPLY allude to, argue, assume, attest, betoken, carry, comprehend, comprise, connote, denote, entail, evidence, hint, implicate, import, include, indicate, induce, infer, insinuate, intimate, involve, mean, predicate, presume, presuppose, promise, signify, subsume, suggest, suppose, understand

IMPOLITE bluff, blunt, boorish, brusque, churlish, crude, curt, discourteous, disrespectful, gruff, ill-mannered, impertinent, inelegant, insolent, loutish, rude, sassy, saucy, uncivil, ungracious, unmannered, vulgar

IMPOLITIC imprudent, inadvisable, indiscreet, unwise

IMPONDERABLE frigoric,

impalpable, infinitesimal, insensible, intangible

IMPOROUS close, dense, solid

IMPORT bear(ing), betoken, bring in, buy, carriage, charge, connote, consequence, denote, design, drift, emphasis, force, hint, implication, imply, importance, indicate, induce, influence, intend, intent, intimate, introduce, involve, matter, mean(ing), moment, moral, pretend, purpose, scope, sense, significance, signify, sound, spell, stress, suggest, tenor, tour, trend, value, weight, wit, worth
tax duty, tariff

IMPORTANCE account, caliber, charge, concern, consequence, dimension, distinction, elevation, emphasis, essence, exaltation, glory, grandeur, gravity, greatness, influence, loftiness, magnitude, mark, matter, moment, nobility, note, pith, prestige, priority, prominence, range, rank, saliency, significance, stress, stroke, sublimity, urgency, value, weight, worth
of prime capital, cardinal
to be of matter

IMPORTANT august, big, cardinal, chief, consequential, considerable, conspicuous, critical, crucial, distinguished, egregious, eminent, emphatic, ESSENTIAL, eventful, extraordinary, front-page, fundamental, grand, grave, great, heavy(weight), high-powered, influential, key, main, major, material, mattery, momentous, necessary, noble, notable, noted, outstanding, paramount, pivotal, principal, prominent, salient, serious, significant, splendid, strategic, strong, substantial, top, urgent, vital, weighty
person big cheese, biggie, biggy, bigshot, big wheel, grandee, high-muck-a-muck, kingpin, lion, magnate, magnifico, mogul, notable, principal, tycoon, vip, wheel, worthy

IMPORTUNATE annoying, burdensome, compulsory, demanding, exigent, overpress, pressing, solicitous, teasing, troublesome, urgent

IMPORTUNE adjure, annoy, appeal, badger, beg, beseech, beset, besiege, blandish, cajole, coax, demand, dun, entreat, flagitate, harry, hector, implore, insist, nag, pester, plague, plead, ply, press, push, request, set upon, solicit, sue, supplicate, tax, tease, terrify, tout, urge, wheedle, work on

IMPOSE abuse, administer, affix, beguile, blaflum, bludge, bother, burden, cadge, charge, deposit, dictate, dupe, encroach, enjoin, entail, exact, exploit, fasten on, fob(off), foist, force, hum, impute, inflict, infringe, lay(on), levy, obtrude, officiate, palm(off), place, play, press, presume, put, saddle with, set, sorn, subject(to), suffer, task, tax, thrust, transgress

IMPOSING august, big, burly, commanding, dignified, formal, grand(iloquent), grandiose, haughty, homeric, imperial, impressive, magnific, majestic, massive, monumental, moving, noble, obese, pompous, portly, pretentious, regal, showy, splendid, stately, stupendous, tall

IMPOSITION accusation, administration, artifice, assignment, assumption, bam, burden, cess, cheating, chouse, command, deception, delusion, hankypanky, hocuspocus, humbuggery, illusion, impediment, IMPOSTURE, intake, sell, taille, tax, teind, wrong

IMPOSSIBILITY fat chance, hopelessness, no way

IMPOSSIBLE absurd, beyond one, beyond the pale, hopeless, IMPRACTICAL, never, out of the question, terrible, unfeasible, unreasonable, unthinkable, visionary

IMPOST abwab, annale, assessment, avania, burden,

cast, cess, chaptrel, customs, duty, excise, gabelle, levy, rate, revenue, tail, tallage, tariff, task, tax, teind, tithe, toll, tonnage, tribute
block dosseret, revetment, spandrel

IMPOSTOR bamboozler, beguiler, bilker, blackleg, blagueur, bluffer, boodler, bunyip, charlatan, cheat, con(fidence)man, counterfeit, cozener, deceiver, empiric, faitour, fake(r), fob, fourflusher, fraud, gammoner, grifter, gyp, hornswoggler, humbug, hypocrite, impersonator, jackleg, misleader, mountebank, mumper, nobbler, pharisee, phony, pretender, quack (salver), ringer, saltimbank, sham, shark, sharp(er), swindler, tinhorn, trickster, wimplor
famous cagliostro, joan(na), macpherson, psalmanazar, romanoff

IMPOSTUME abcess

IMPOSTURE artifice, charlatanry, cheat, counterfeit, deceit, deception, delusion, feint, fraud, humbug(gery), illusion, impersonation, imposition, jugglery, masquerade, quackery, ruse, simulacrum, trick, wile

IMPOTENCE acratia, agenesis, aplasia, barrenness, feebleness, impuissance, inability, sterility, unmight, unwelth, weakness

IMPOTENT barren, crippled, disabled, helpless, impuissant, incapable, incompetent, ineffective, inefficient, powerless, sterile, tillerless, unable, unmighty, unproductive, weak

IMPOUND appropriate, attach, hold, imprison, intern, pen, pinfold, reservoir

IMPOVERISH bankrupt, beggar, consume, depauperate, deplete, depress, drain, exhaust, impoor, pauperize, reduce, strip

IMPOVERISHED destitute, indigent, meager, obolary, poor, poverty-stricken, spent

IMPRACTICAL abstract, blue-sky, crazy, doctrinaire, feckless, IMPOSSIBLE, infeasible, quixotic, theoretical, unrealistic, unusable, useless, viewy, visionary

IMPRECATE appeal, curse, pray, supplicate, wish

IMPRECATION anathema, ban, blame, blasphemy, curse, damning, execration, malediction, malison, oath, objurgation, pize, prayer, profanity, swearing

IMPRECISE inaccurate, vague

IMPREGNABLE defended, fast, formidable, guarded, invincible, invulnerable, protected, safe, secure, shielded, strong, unconquerable

IMPREGNATE boucherize, breed, conceive, drench, fertilize, fructify, imbue, inform, infuse, ingrain, inoculate, instill, leaven, mix, penetrate, permeate, pervade, pierce, season, soak, sog, sop, steep, stock, stuff, tinct(ure), tinge

IMPRESA adage, device, emblem, maxim, motto, proverb, sign, symbol

IMPRESARIO conductor, director, entrepreneur, manager, projector, promoter

IMPRESS abduct, actuate, affect, attach, awe, brand, characteristic, come, conscript, crimp, dent, draft, dragoon, electrify, emboss, engrave, enroll, enthuse, etch, excite, fasten, feel, fix, galvanize, grab, grave, grill, hit, impact, implant, imprint, inculcate, indent (ation), influence, inscribe, levy, mark, move, notch, penetrate, pique, print, provoke, register, seal, seize, smite, stamp, stead, stimulate, strike, sway, thrill, touch

deeply delve

forcefully bedazzle

IMPRESSED affected, bigeyed, indented, moved, stirred, struck

with oneself conceited, stuck-up

IMPRESSIBLE pliable, pliant, sensitive, waxy

IMPRESSION air, apercu, aspect, belief, brand, cast, characteristic, conception, conspectus, dent, ectype,

edition, effect, engram, etching, experience, fancy, feel, form, hollow, idea, image, imprint, incuse, indentation, inkling, insight, mark, moulage, mould, notion, opinion, pattern, premonition, print, proof, pull, recollection, seal, sensation, sense, shape, sign, sketch, stamp, stencil, supposition, thought, token, tooling, trace, track, vestige, view

auditory sound

double mackle, macule

luminous phosphene

mental conception, dream, fantasy, idea, idolum, phantasm

strong hunch, splash

IMPRESSIONABLE docile, easy, emotional, plastic, responsive, sensitive, soft, suggestible, susceptible, waxy

IMPRESSIONIST *painter* bonnard, cezanne, degas, manet, monet, pissarro, raffaelli, renoir, sisley

IMPRESSIVE affecting, affective, arresting, authoritative, awesome, big, conclusive, dramatic, effecting, fat, glorious, grand, imperial, imposing, magnificent, majestic, massive, monumental, moving, noble, portly, remarkable, smashing, splendid, stately, stimulating, stunning, sublime, superb, weighty

IMPRESSMENT abduction, attachment, compulsion, fervor

IMPREST advance(d), bonus, lend, lent, loan

IMPRIMATUR approval, license, permit, sanction

IMPRINT edition, engrave, etch, fasten, fix, impress (ion), indentation, mark, notch, offset, press, pressure, stamp, title, trace

IMPRISON bolt, bond, cage, carcerate, check, clap in, closet, commit, confine, curb, detain, embar, encage, gaol, grate, immure, impound, incarcerate, intern, jail, jug, limit, lock up, occlude, pen, pound, punish, quad, remand, restrain, restrict, shut(in)(up), slough, snaffle

IMPRISONMENT arrest, bondage, captivity, commitment, confinement, constraint, custody, detention, durance(vile), duress, incarceration, internment, occlusion, punishment, reclusion, restraint, solitary, stretch, verdict

IMPROBABILITY fighting chance, long odds, longshot, offbet, offchance, poor bet, unlikelihood

IMPROBABLE doubtful, dubitable, fishy, implausible, inconceivable, marvelous, questionable, rare, unheard of, unlikely

IMPROBITY See DISHONESTY.

IMPROMPTU apt, autoschediastic, by ear, extemporaneous, extempore, glib, improvised, impulsive, offhand, prompt, quick, ready, spontaneous, spur of the moment, sudden

IMPROPER aberrant, amiss, astray, awry, bad, brash, evil, fie-fie, gross, illegitimate, illicit, immodest, immoral, inappropriate, inapt, incorrect, indecent, indecorous, indelicate, pah, paw, perverted, poor, ribald, solecistic, tasteless, unapt, unbecoming, undue, unethical, unfele, unfit, unjust, unseemly, unsuitable, unworthy, vulgar, wrong

IMPROPRIETY aberration, barbarism, illegitimacy, immorality, indecency, indecorum, inequity, injustice, misbehavior, perversity, solecism, wrong

IMPROVE advance, ameliorate, amend, beet, benefit, bete, better, burbank, civilize, correct, cross, cultivate, cure, develop, edify, elaborate, elevate, emend (ate), enhance, ennoble, enrich, fatten, forward, furbish, gain, go ahead, graft, grow, heighten, help, lard, lift, look up, meliorate, mellow, mend, modify, moise, perfect, perk up, pick up, profit, progress, promote, raise, rally, reclaim, rectify, recuperate, refine, reform, relieve, remodel, repair, restore, resuscitate, retouch, revise, teach, touch, train, upgrade, uplift

IMPROVEMENT addition, additive, additory, advance, amends, beterschap, betterment, breeding, correction, development, education, elevation, increase, melioration, profit, promotion, recovery, redress, reform, repair, restoration, training

IMPROVIDENT extravagant, feckless, hand-to-mouth, happy-go-lucky, heedless, lackadaisical, lavish, lax, loose, negligent, prodigal, profligate, rash, remiss, shiftless, slack, thoughtless, thriftless, unthrifty, wasteful

fellow micawber

IMPROVISE ad-lib, compose, contrive, cook up, dash off, devise, extemporize, fake, flash, hatch, invent, jam, knock off, make up, originate, play by ear, pong, strike off, throw off, vamp

IMPROVISED extemporaneous, extempore, impromptu, makeshift, offhand

IMPRUDENT careless, fess, foolish, hasty, ill-advised, impolitic, incautious, indiscreet, officious, prodigal, rash, reckless, thoughtless, unwary, unwise

IMPUDENCE brass, bronze, cheek, gall, mouth, nerve

IMPUDENT airy, arrogant, audacious, bardy, barefaced, biggety, bluff, bold, brash, brassy, brazen, cheeky, chutzpahdik, clamorous, cocky, cool, crusty, discourteous, disrespectful, facy, flip(pant), forward, fresh, gally, IMPERTINENT, impolite, insolent, insulting, intrusive, loud, malapert, nervy, noisy, perking, pert, procacious, rude, sassy, saucy, shameless, smartalecky, smarty, stocky, uncivil, ungracious

IMPUGN asperse, assail, attack, blame, censure, challenge, contradict, controvert, deny, disprove, dispute, gainsay, impeach,

negative, oppose, question, refute, traverse

IMPULSE action, affection, ate, bent, brangle, calling, desire, drive, estro, fancy, flash, force, goad, impetus, incentive, incitement, inclination, inspiration, instigation, instinct, itch, mind, moment(um), motive, notion, propension, propulsion, push, rush, spring, spur, stimulant, stimulus, stirring, thrust, urge, yetzer

blind ate

divine afflatus

traveling wanderlust

IMPULSIVE abrupt, careless, emotional, extemporaneous, hasty, headlong, heedless, hurried, ill-considered, impetuous, impromptu, instinctive, passionate, precipitate, quick, rash, spontaneous, sudden, swift, thoughtless, uncontrolled, unexpected, unpremeditated, unthinking

IMPUNITY amnesty, exemption, freedom, immunity, license, privilege, safety

IMPURE adulterated, alloyed, compromised, contaminated, corrupt, debased, defiled, dirty, filthy, foul, indecent, infected, lewd, maculate, mixed, mongrel, obscene, polluted, profane, tainted, turbid, unclean, unholy, unwholesome

ceremonially defiled, unblessed, unhallowed, unholy

IMPURITY corruption, crud, defect, defilement, dross, fedity, filth, foulness, infection, pollution, taint

free from refine

IMPUTABLE accusable, attributable, culpable, reprehensible

IMPUTATION ascription, attribution, censure, charge, criticism, insinuation, scandal, slur, smear, stigma

damaging aspersion

IMPUTE account, accredit, accuse, adduce, affix, aret, arraign, ascribe, assign, attribute, charge, count, credit, fasten, give, hint, impeach, impose, indict, insinuate, lay, reckon, refer, repute, ret, transcribe, wite

IMRI *son* zaccur

IMSETY *father* horus

IMSHALLAH fate

IN along, at home, available, chic, close, corner, current, dans, dentro, during, elected, enclose(d), faddish, fashionable, favored, furled, harvest, home, influence, mailed, modish, near, nook, on board, plentiful, popular, powerful, pull, seated, stowed, stylish, trendy, within

a bad way exhausted, ill, sick, tired

a body together

a chamber in camera

a dilemma perplexed, puzzled

a fair way inclined, probable, prosperous

a flash immediately, suddenly, swiftly

a flutter pitapat

a groove monotonous

a manner of speaking figuratively, similarly, theoretically

a mess chaotic

a pother anxious, confused, worried

a quiver perturbed, shaky

a rut habituated, monotonous

a series seriatim

a standing position statant

a stew anxious, confused, excited, seething, stirred

a straight line directly, eregione

a tizzy atwitter, fluttery, lost, rattled, upset

a trance spellbound

a vertical line apeak

a whisper sotto-voce

abeyance dormant, latent, pending, postponed, potential, tabled

accordance with, comb. cat(a), cath, kat(a), kath

addition above, again, also, and, aside, besides, beyond, by the way, eke, forby, further, incidentally, in passing, more(over), plus, still, to boot, too, yet

advance ahead, before (hand), early, forth, preceding

agreement together, unanimous, united

all entirely, totally, wholly

all directions around, everywhere, everywhichway, everywhither, forty ways

all likelihood probably

all respects broadly, by and large, exactly, substantially, utterly

-and-out changeably, irregularly, round and round, sinuously

another direction away

anticipation beforehand, early, expectant, forewarned

any event always, anyhow, however, notwithstanding, provided, rain or shine, regardless

arms helpless, infantile, ready, young

arrears behind(hand), due, inadequate

as much because, for, seeing that, since

bad disgraced, distressed, out

being active, actual, alive

between intermediary

blossom abloom, flowering

brief abruptly, bang, in short

cahoots leagued, plotting, scheming, together

camera privately

capacity qua

case lest, provided, supposing

chorus simultaneously, together, unanimously

circulation about, abroad, around, reported, rumored

clover comfortable, prosperous

cold blood deliberately, intentionally

common alike, jointly, public

concert accordant, together

condition fit, healthy, neat, robust, strong

connection with ferninst, fornent

contact against, attingent, near, touching

debt behind(hand), bound, encumbered, mortgaged, owing

disagreement opposed, out

due course opportunely, promptly, sometime, soon, tomorrow

dutch disgraced, endangered, threatened, troubled

earnest agood

effect actually, really

equal shares proportionately

every way completely, entirely, exactly, fully, thoroughly, totally, utterly, wholly

excess beyond, over, superfluous, too much

existence extant

extenso fully, throughout, utterly

fact actually, certainly, de facto, indeed, merely, to be sure, truly, verament, verily

faith efecks, ivads, yfacks

favor for, friendly, liked, pro

few cases seldom

fine fettle brisk, healthy, lively, neat, ready, sprightly, trim

flight airborne, aloft, flying, fugitive

force active, alive, operating

front aface, ahead, anteal, before, forne, leading, opposite, paravant, van

full all, altogether, entire

full swing astir, functioning, going, rolling, thriving

general broadly, by and large, mutual

good faith bona fide

good order bristol-fashion, shipshape

good season betime(s), early

good shape healthy, fit, neat, ready, trim

good spirits bobbish, cheerful, happy, optimistic

good taste See AESTHETIC.

good time betimes, early, eventually, opportunely

great need distressed, straitened

harness busy, ready

haste See FAST.

heat blissom

heaven happy, rapturous

hell below, beneath, troubled

high ready, rolling, swiftly

high feather debonair, dolled up, exultant, healthy

hysterics frantic, MAD

irons bound, chained, fettered, imprisoned, shackled

jest agame, jokingly

juxtaposition beside, ferninst, fornen(s)t, fornint

kind similar, thus

large part almost, chiefly, mainly

lieu instead

line even

loco parentis instead

love devoted, enamored, smitten, taken

manner of a la

name only nominal, supposedly

nothing flat briefly, promptly, quickly, soon, suddenly, swiftly

no way naegates, negative, never, nor, not, nowise

on party to

opposition against, antagonistic, athwart, belligerent, but, counteractive, disagreeing

order ataunt(o)

ovo crude, germinal, original

pairs, comb. dich(o)

passing also, by the way, en route, in addition, incidentally

perpetuity forever

place of for, instead, substitute

plain english candidly, simply

plain sight evident, openly

progress afoot, toward, underway

proportion according, after, compared to, equal

prospect imminent, pending

re about, anent, concerning, pertaining, relative (to)

reason moderately

reserve aside, imminent, on ice, ready

return for against, in exchange

reverse english contrarily

round numbers approximately, average

same place ibid(em)

search of after

shape See IN *good shape.*

short supply inadequate, insufficient, scarce, wanting

snatches haphazardly, irregularly

so far as qua, since

sooth parfey, perfay

spite of against, aside, despite, malgre, mauger, maugre, notwithstanding, over, regardless, yet

step agreeable, conforming, harmonious

stitches amused, laughing

store awaiting, destined, fated, imminent

style chic, current, fashionable, modish, popular, trendy

substance basically

suspense hanging fire, pending

that because

that case accordingly, then

the air aloft

the altogether bare, naked, nude

the background behind, inconspicuous, obscure, unobtrusive

the bag assured, certain, cinch, sure

the balance at issue, undecided

the beginning ab initio, ab ovo, first, once, starting

the cards conceivable, contingent, imminent, likely, possible, probable

the case of in re

the center amid(st)

the clear absolved, free, protected, safe

the clouds aloft, dreaming, oblivious, visionary

the first place imp(rimis)

the gazette bankrupt

the grain inherent

the groove hep, straight, with it

the interim meanwhile

the know aware, hep, informed, onto

the least aughtlins

the limelight important, publicly

the long run eventually, generally, tomorrow

the main altogether, chiefly, essentially, generally, largely, substantially

the matter of about, anent, in re

the meantime ad interim, meanwhile, temporarily

the mood desirous, willing

the name of allah bismillah

the name of another benamee, benami

the near future anon, soon

the neighborhood of about, approximately, around, close, hard by, near

the open al fresco, outdoors

the past ago, of yore, over

the pink See IN *condition*, IN *good shape.*

the presence of before, coram

the raw bare, naked, nude

there alert, alive, on the ball, with it

the rear astern, atergo, behind

the red bankrupt, broke, out

the same period contemporaneous

the same place ibid(em)

the shade also-ran, secondary

the shadow of god, name meaning bezaleel

the style of al(l)a, ese

the swim competing, participating, popular, with it

the thick of amid, among, between

the time of during

the way between, obstructing, underfoot

the works coming, imminent, looming

this herein

this place here

toto all, complete(ly), whole

toward inower

trouble endangered, hurting, in a bind

truth certainly, certes, forsooth, in case(that), indeed, marry, soothly, verily

tune groovy

2 parts, comb. dich(o)

vain to no avail, unsuccessfully, wastely

virtue of because, through

vogue groovy, popular, stylish, with it

want indigent, poor, without

what way how, quo modo

with allied, belonging, friendly, influential, leagued

words of one syllable clearly, plainly

INABILITY disability, disqualification, fatuity, futility, helplessness, impotence, inadequacy, inanity, incapability, incapacity, incompetence, ineffectuality, inefficacy, inefficiency, insufficiency, invalidism, powerlessness, unfitness, weakness

INACCESSIBLE aloof, closed, coy, denied, distant, lost, out of reach, remote, reticent, shadowy

INACCURACY blunder, error, goof, mistake, solecism

INACCURATE careless, defective, erroneous, faulty, imperfect, imprecise, incorrect, inexact, loose, mistaken, slipshod

INACHUS *parent* oceanus, tethys

son argus, phoroneus

INACTION abeyance, apathy, arrest, deadlock, dolce far niente, entropy, faineance, idleness, inertia, inertness, peace, quiet(ude), rest, sloth, stalemate, standstill, suspension, torpor

temporary pause, recess, respite

INACTIVATE arrest, disable, mothball, quiet, still, store, suspend

INACTIVE abeyant, apathetic, asleep, bedfast, bloodless, comatose, deedless, dilatory, do-nothing, dormant, dull, emeritus, faineant, idle, indolent, inert, languid, latent, lazy, lethargic, listless, otiose, passive, peaceful, phlegmatic, potential, quiescent, quiet, recumbent, restful, retired, sedentary, shut-in, slothful, sluggish, stagnant, static, still, supine, torpid, unemployed

INADEQUACY defect, frailty, inability, insufficiency, intolerability, scarcity

INADEQUATE bad, deficient, feeble, halfway, helpless, incapable, incompetent, inferior, in short supply, insufficient, scant(y), short(of), shy, slack, slender, unequal, unfit, unqualified

INADMISSIBLE improper, inexpedient

INADVERTENCE bevue, carelessness, inattention, lapse, neglect, negligence

INADVERTENT accidental, careless, heedless, thoughtless, unmindful, unthinking

INADVISABLE impolitic, IMPRUDENT, unwise

INAMORATA amoretta, beloved, sweetheart

INAMORATO amoretto, lover

INANE absurd, asinine, banal, blank, dizzy, empty, fatuous, flat, foolish, frivolous, futile, idle, imbecile, inept, insipid, invalid, jejune, laughable, meaningless, namby-pamby, pointless, puerile, ridiculous, senseless, sentimental, silly, stupid, thoughtless, trifling, trivial, vacant, vacuous, vain, VAPID, void

INANGA minnow

INANIMATE amort, azoic, brute, dead(ly), deceased, defunct, inert, inorganic, insensate, insensible, insentient, lifeless, nonliving, senseless, slothful, sluggish, soulless, stolid, unconscious, unfeeling

INAPPRECIABLE impalpable, imperceptible, inconsiderable, infinitesimal, insensible, intangible, small

INAPPROPRIATE alien, amiss, camp, discordant, foreign, ill-timed, improper, inapt, incorrect, inept, inexpedient, out of place, unbecoming, unfit(ting), unhappy, unmeet, unseemly, unsuitable, unsuited, untimely, wrong

INAPT awkward, backward, banal, clumsy, flat, footless, gauche, improper, inapropos, incongruous, inept, maladroit, slow, stupid, unapt, unfit, unhappy, unskillful, unsuitable

INARTICULATE aphonic, dumb, indistinct, mousy, mum, mute, reserved, silent, speechless, taciturn, thick, tonguetied, unexpressed, unintelligible, vague

INARTICULATENESS anarthria, anaudia

INARTISTIC See UGLY.

INATTENTION absence, aprosexia, disregard, distraction, neglect, negligence, oblivion, oversight, unconcern

INATTENTIVE absentminded, apathetic, blind, careless, dazed, deaf, dream(s)y, distrait, flighty, giddy, heedless, indifferent, listless, lost, mindless, musing, oblivious, supine, thoughtless, unaware, unheeding, unmindful

INATTENTIVENESS aprosexia

INAUDIBLE faint, indistinct, secret, unclear, unheard

INAUGURAL accession, beginning, ceremony, dawn, opening, start

INAUGURATE augur, auspicate, begin, celebrate, commence, establish, found, handsel, induct, initiate, install, institute, introduce, invest, launch, omen, organize, receive, start

INAUGURATION admission, beginning, debut, embarkment, flotation, initiation, installation, installment, institution, introduction, launching, opener, unveiling

INAUSPICIOUS adverse, bad, baleful, dire, evil, fateful, hostile, ill-fated, ill-starred, malefic, malign (ant), menacing, ominous, poor, portentous, sad, sinister, threatening, unfavorable, unfortunate, unlucky

INBORN automatic, congenital, connatural, essential, hereditary, inbred, indigenous, ingrained, inherent, inherited, innate, instinctive, intrinsic, native, natural, normal, regular, typical

INBRED See INBORN.

INC cie, ltd

INCA ingua, orejon, son of the sun

accounting system quipu
administrator curaca
ambush cahanarca
beaker kero
burial tower chulpa
calculator quipu
capital cuzco
ceremonial center tarahuasi
chronicler hiram bingham
city cuzco, lima, machu-picchu, quito
clan ayllu
conqueror tupa
courtyard cajamarca
deity acomani, apu-punchau, catequil, chasca, choun, cuycha, cuzco, inti, iraya, mama-cocha, mama-cuna, mama-quilla, manco-capac, nina, pachacamac, pachamama, pirrhua-manco, ulracocha, urcaguay, viracocha, virocha
elite curocas, orejones
elite women mamacunas
empire ecuador, peru, tahuantinsuyu
food indian corn, potato
fortress ollantaytambo, sacsahuaman
founder manco capac

gold sweat of the sun
group quechuan
hanging bridge keshwa-chaca
indian ingua, orejon, quechua
king atabalipa, atahualpa, capac yupanqui, huascar, huayna capac, inca roca, lloque, manco capac, mayta capac, pachacuti, sinchi roca, tupa, viracocha, yahuar-huacac, yupanqui
king, last atahualpa
language quechua
leader curaca
ledger quipu
lord son of the sun
love goddess mama
magic flower cantut(a)
massacre cajamarca
medicine man callawaya
noble big ear, orejon
oracle viracocha
predecessor aymara, canari, mochica, nascan, quechua, tiahuanacan, yunca
priest amauta
prince huascar
queen ccoya, mamaocclo
resthouse tauepo
royal orejon
ruins cuzco, machu-picchu
ruler curaca
runners chasquis
sacred hill rumytiana
sacred river urubamba
secret city machu-picchu
shrine cuzco, machu-picchu
solar feast ccapac, cochasitua, raymisitua
successors quechas
sun god inti
tyrant atahualpa
vessel paccha
vestal virgins aclla
vestment borla
worker unit ayllu

INCALCULABLE countless, infinite, uncertain, unknown, untold

INCANDESCE burn, glow, shine

INCANDESCENT bright, brilliant, burning, candescent, glowing, luminous, shining

INCANTATION abracadabra, carmen, chantry, charm, conjuration, dawut, enchantment, exorcism, fetish, greegree, hex, hocus-pocus, magic, mantra, mumbojumbo, open-sesame, sorcery, spell, witchery

INCAPABLE clumsy, crippled, dead, debilitated, disabled, helpless, impotent, incompetent, ineffective, inefficient, numb, powerless, unable, unqualified

INCAPACITATE afflict, cripple, disable, disqualify, hors de combat, lame, maim, napoo, nobble, paralyze, unfit

INCAPACITATED disabled, hors de combat, stricken

INCAPACITY disability, inability

INCARCERATE confine, immure, imprison, intern, jail, limit, restrict

INCARNATE actualize, bodied, embody, enshrined, externalize, materialize, objectify, personified, realize, reify, rosy, substantiate

INCARNATION advent avatar, embodiment, epiphany, hutuktu, impersonation, personification, terton
announcement annunciation
blessed dalai lama, rinpoche
of a god avatar

INCAUTIOUS carefree, hasty, heedless, IMPRUDENT, indiscreet, rash, reckless, thoughtless, unwary

INCENDIARY agitator, arsonist, arsonite, bomb, boutefeu, firebrand, firebug, goon, inflammatory, instigator, petroleur, petroleuse, pyromaniac, seditious

INCENSE (See also *kind*, below.) affront, aggravate, anger, aroma, bouquet, enrage, exasperate, excite, fragrance, incite, inflame, infuriate, instigate, insult, irritate, madden, nettle, odor, offend, outrage, perfume, provoke, redolence, roil, scent, smell, smoke, thymiama
bowl acerra, censer, navette, navicella, navicula, thurible
burn thurify
cedar adenostoma
ingredient gum, onycha, spice, stacte
kind agalloch, aloes, calambach, gum, joss stick, lignaloes, linaloa, matti, myrrh, olibanum, pastille, stacte, storax, tacamahac

tree boswellia, bursera, cicia, protium

INCENSED angry, enraged, fired up, irate, mad, raw, stung, wrathful, wroth

INCENTIVE brod, call, carrot, cause, drive, encouragement, fillip, force, goad, ground, impetus, impulse, incitement, inducement, inspiration, interest, invitation, motivation, motive, offer, prod, provocation, reason, spring, spur, stimulant, stimulus, urge

INCEPTION ancestry, beginning, commencement, origin, provenance, rise, root, source, start

INCESSANT ceaseless, constant, continual, continuous, endless, eternal, everlasting, interminable, perennial, perpetual, steady, timeless, unceasing, unending

INCESSANTLY constantly, continually, continuously, ever, forever, on and on, perpetually

INCH crawl, creep, drag, edge, island, measure, move, prime, steal, unch, uncia, worm
1/3rd barleycorn
1/12 line
1/48th iron
1/100th point
1/1000th mil, point
2¼ nail
4 hand(ful)
7 fistmele
9 hand, span
18 cubit
32 to 43 vara
36 yard
39.37 meter
45 ell
along worm
forward crowhop, edge
meal gradually
pin sweetbread
plant wandering jew

INCHOATE amorphous, beginning, chaotic, elemental, elementary, formless, imperfect, incipient, incomplete, initial, initiate, partly, rudimentary, shapeless, unfinished, unformed

INCIDENT accident, adventure, affair, befalling, case, casualty, chance, circumstance, contingency, episode, event, falling, fortui-

tous, happening, liable, occasion, occurrence, open, pertinent, sensitive, subject

INCIDENTAL accessory, accidental, byproduct, casual, chance, circumstantial, collateral, concurrent, connected, contingent, episodic, extraneous, fortuitous, linked, minor, occasional, parenthetical, related, secondary, stray, subordinate

INCIDENTALLY also, apropos, by the way, en passant, for example, in addition, in passing, obiter

INCINERATE burn, cinder, combust, cremate, incremate

INCINERATOR blowtorch, burner, calcinatory, cremator(ium), crematory, furnace, ghat, wick

INCIPIENT beginning, germinal, inchoate, initial, microbic, opening, starting

INCISE carve, cut, engrave, furrow, notch, open, rase

INCISION aplotomy, broach, cicatrice, cleft, cut, gash, groove, hurt, notch, operation, penetration, scar, slit, snip, wound
comb. otomy

INCISIVE acerb, acid, acrimonious, biting, caustic, clear-cut, concise, crisp, cutting, keen, laconic, penetrating, piquant, pungent, sharp, succinct, terse, trenchant

INCISIVENESS asperity

INCITATUS *master* caligula

INCITE abet, actuate, agitate, animate, arouse, buss, chirk, drive, egg on, entice, excite, foment, galvanize, goad, impel, induce, inspire, instigate, kindle, pique, prick, prod, provoke, quicken, rouse, set on, sic, spur, stimulate, sting, stir, suborn, urge

INCITEMENT goad, impetus, impulse, incentive, inducement, motive, prod, sprint, spur, stimulant, stimulus, stirring

INCITER *hired* agent provocateur

INCIVILITY discourtesy, disrespect

INCLEMENCY asperity,

INCLEMENT cold, cruelty, rigor, severity, tyranny, violence

INCLEMENT bad, cold, extreme, harsh, rough, ruthless, severe, stark, unkindly, violent

INCLINATION acclivity, affect(ion), animus, anlage, appetite, aptitude, assent, attitude, bend, bent, bias, bow, broo, calling, cant, care, cast, conatus, declivity, direction, disposition, grade, gradient, hang, impulse, incline, inkling, intent (ion), lean(ing), liking, mind, mood, nod, notion, partiality, penchant, position, predilection, preference, proclivity, propensity, slant, slaunch, slope, stomach, swag, sway, taste, tendency, threat, tilt, will, yetzer
indulged addiction

INCLINE acclivity, affect, ascend, bank, bear, bend, bias, bow, cant, careen, cast, chute, climb, curve, deflect, deviate, dispose, drive, droop, favor, flect, glacis, grade, gradient, gravitate, hade, hang, heel, helicline, hill(side), induce, influence, intend, keel, lean, like, list, move, nod, pitch, predispose, prejudice, rake, ramp, retreat, rise, scarp, shelve, sidle, skew, slant, slaunch, slope, steeve, swag, swerve, talus, tend, tilt, tip, trend, turn, uprise, veer, verge, volunteer
favorably propend

INCLINED apt, banked, bent, capable, disposed, favorable, given to, leaning, leant, liable, likely, minded, oblique, partial, predisposed, prefer, pronate, propense, ready, sloped, studied, tending, willing

INCLINING alist, bent, beveled, cernuous, disposed, hilly, slantidicular, sloping, tending to, tipping

INCLOSE box, circumscribe, contain, coop, corral, embar, encave, encircle, enclave, fence, gird(le), hedge, hem in, impound, incase, include, insert, pen, pin, ring, shut in, surround, wrap

INCLOSURE case, cincture, close, compound, corral, court(yard), croft, cubbyhole, enclave, field, garth, girdle, pale, patio, prison, quadrangle, sepiment, sept, shed, stockade, wrapper, yard

INCLUDE accommodate, add, admit, attach, compose, comprehend, comprise, confine, consist, contain, count, cover, embody, embrace, encircle, enclose, encompass, fill, hold, implicate, imply, incorporate, involve, occupy, receive, reckon in, subsume, take in

INCLUDED among, belonging, confined, embraced, enclosed, present, with

INCLUSION comprisal

INCLUSIVE all-in, all-round, broad, catholic, complete, comprehensive, extensive, full, grand, sweeping, vast, wide

INCOGNITO alias, allonym, camouflaged, disguised, feigned, nom de guerre, nom de plume, pen name, pseudonym, veiled

INCOHERENT broken, disconnected, disjointed, fuzzy, illogical, inchoate, inconsistent, irrational, rabid, unreasonable

INCOMBUSTIBLE amaiathine, apyrous, asbestic, asbestine, asbestous, nonflammable, unburnable, unflammable
comb. apyro
material amianthus, asbestos

INCOME advent, annuity, avails, beginning, dividends, earnings, emolument, entrance, fee, gain, gate, get (tings), gross, honorarium, intake, interest, living, make, makings, money, net, pay, pension, port, proceeds, produce, profit, receipt(s), rent(e), return(s), revenue, royalty, salary, stipend, take, takings, usance, wages, wealth, yield
annual rentes
pert. rental, tontine
property ap(p)anage, rental
receiver rentier
tax term carryback, deduction

INCOMING accruing, arrival, arriving, beginning, entering, gain, immigrant, inbound, ingressive, profit, receipt

INCOMMODE annoy, block, bother, disquiet, disturb, hinder, impede, inconvenience, irk, molest, obstruct, plague, trouble, vex

INCOMMODIOUS inconvenient, narrow, unsuitable

INCOMMODITY disadvantage, inconvenience

INCOMMUNICADO imprisoned, isolated, quarantined, sequestered

INCOMPARABLE banner, different, disparate, diverse, peerless, preeminent, superlative, SUPREME, surpassing, unequaled, unrivaled

INCOMPATIBILITY antipathy, inconsistency

INCOMPATIBLE adverse, contradictory, contrary, counter, disagreeing, discordant, discrepant, incongruous, inconsistent, intolerant, opposite, uncongenial, unharmonious, unsuited, unsympathetic, warring

INCOMPETENCE disability, inability

INCOMPETENT awkward, buffer, bumbling, clumsy, feckless, green, helpless, impotent, inadequate, incapable, ineffective, inefficient, inept, insane, unable, unmeet, unqualified
person stumblebum

INCOMPLETE abridged, blind, broken, crude, defective, deficient, divided, fragmentary, half, immature, imperfect, inchoate, lacking, part(ial), rough, rude, sketchy, undone, unfinished, unpolished
comb. atel(o)

INCOMPLETENESS deficiency, deficit, inadequacy, lack, omission, shortage, shortcoming, want

INCOMPREHENSIBLE ambiguous, baffling, crazy, dense, enigmatic, equivocal, extraordinary, fathomless, indefinite, indeterminate, indistinct, infinite, irregular, miraculous, mistakable, mysterious, obscure, partial, problematic, puzzling, questionable, uncertain, unclear, unintelligible, unsettled, vague

INCONCEIVABLE improbable, incredible, rare, strange, unheard of, unique, unlikely

INCONCLUSIVE fuzzy, illogical, indecisive, indefinite, ineffective, flimsy, lame

INCONDITE crude, unformed, unpolished, unrefined

INCONGRUITY disagreement, discrepancy, disharmony, dissonance, inconsistency

INCONGRUOUS absurd, alien, bizarre, burlesque, discordant, discrepant, dissociable, dissonant, fantastic, foreign, illogical, inapropos, inapt, incompatible, inconsistent, strange, warring

INCONSEQUENTIAL illogical, immaterial, insignificant, little, small, trifling, unimportant

INCONSIDERABLE careless, insignificant, minimal, negligible, petty, small, trifling, unworthy

INCONSIDERATE asocial, careless, cruel, forgetful, heedless, impolite, outrageous, rash, rude, tactless, thoughtless, unkind, unobliging, unthinking, unthoughtful, wanton

INCONSISTENT absurd, different, discordant, disparate, divergent, diverse, illogical, incompatible, incongruous, inconsonant, warring

INCONSOLABLE desolate, distressed, mournful, rueful, sad

INCONSONANT different, discordant, dissonant, inconsistent, uncongenial

INCONSPICUOUS dim, faint, indistinct, invisible, obscure, subtle, tenuous
position back seat

INCONSTANCY change, infidelity, irregularity

INCONSTANT adrift, afloat, alternating, brittle, bruckle, capricious, changeable, desultory, deviable, disloyal, eccentric, erratic, faithless,

false, fickle, fluctuating, freakish, frivolous, irregular, light, mercurial, mutable, perfidious, protean, rambling, restless, roving, shifting, shuffling, sliding, spasmodic, treacherous, uncertain, uncontrolled, undependable, undisciplined, unfaithful, unfixed, unreliable, unsettled, unstable, unstaid, unsteady, vacillating, vagrant, variable, various, volatile, wanton, wavering, wayward

INCONTESTABLE apodictic, certain, indubitable, sure, undeniable

INCONTINENT abandoned, extravagant, intemperate, loose, profligate

INCONVENIENCE bother, burden, cumber, difficulty, discomfort, discompose, disoblige, disquiet, disturb (ance), harm, incommode, interfere, meddle, mischief, nuisance, pain, stress, trial, trouble

INCONVENIENT absurd, annoying, awkward, improper, irrational, troublesome, unchancy, unfit, unhandy, unked, unkid, untimely, untoward

INCORPORATE absorb, annex, assemble, assimilate, blend, build in, coalesce, combine, conjoin, consolidate, contain, cover, embody, engraft, fold, fuse, identify, include, involve, join, link, materialize, merge, mix, organize, unify, unite

INCORPORATION absorption, assimilation, association, combination, composition, embodiment, incarnation, merger, synthesis, union

INCORPOREAL aery, asomatous, bodiless, discarnate, immaterial, spectral, spiritlike, spiritual, wraithlike
being ghost, ha(u)nt, spirit, wraith

INCORRECT bad, base, erroneous, false, faulty, ill, imprecise, improper, inaccurate, inexact, solecistic, tasteless, ungrammatical, unseemly, unsound, untrue, wrong

INCORRIGIBLE abandoned, graceless, hard, hopeless, irreclaimable, irredeemable, lost, peccant, recidivous, refractory, shriftless, vicious

INCORRUPT honest, pure, sound, untainted, upright

INCORRUPTIBLE amaranthine, everlasting, immortal, just, reliable, upright

INCRASSATE clotted, condense(d), congeal(ed), distended, inspissate, stupefy, swollen, thicken(ed)

INCREASE 3 eke, wax 4 boom, bulk, bump, eche, gain, go up, hike, jazz, jump, rise, rist, soup 5 boost, bulge, exalt, heist, key up, mount, raise, run up, swell 6 access, accrue, ascent, biggen, blow up, deepen, dilate, double, expand, extend, growth, jack up, pick up, profit, return, spread, stepup, triple, upturn 7 accrete, accrual, advance, amplify, augment, balloon, broaden, build up, develop, distend, enhance, enlarge, greaten, inflate, largify, magnify, produce, profits, prolong, pyramid, sharpen, shoot up, thicken, upsurge, upswing, uptrend 8 accresce, addition, additory, elongate, heighten, lengthen, majorate, multiply, protract, redouble 9 accession, accretion, aggravate, expansion, extension, increment, intensify, reinforce 10 accelerate, accumulate, additament; aggrandize, appreciate, exaggerate, strengthen 11 aggravation, propagation 12 accumulation, appreciation 13 amplification
comb. auxo
currency reflate
in pay fogie, fogy, raise
in price appreciate
in sound crescendo
sudden balloon, bulge, leap, spurt

INCREASING accrescent, addititious, crescendo, crescent, crescive, cumulative, enhancing, growing, incremental, increscent, swelling

INCREDIBLE absurd, baroque, bizarre, extraordinary, fabulous, fantastic, fishy, freakish, inconceivable, inexplicable, monstrous, rococo, suspect, tall, teratogenic, teratoid, unaccountable, unbelievable, unimaginable

INCREDULITY disbelief, distrust, doubt, dubiety, dubiosity, humism, pyrrhonism, scoffing, skepticism, unbelief, uncertainty *expression* ahem, hum(ph), indeed, really

INCREDULOUS doubtful, quizzical, skeptic(al), suspicious, unbelieving

INCREMENT accession, accretion, accrual, addition, adjunct, buildup, growth, income, increase

INCRIMINATE accuse, arraign, assault, attack, blame, charge, frame, impeach, implicate, inculpate, indict, involve

INCRIMINATOR plaintiff

INCRUST barken, barkle, candy, coat, effloresce, foul, inlay, loricate

INCRUSTATION crud, crust, eschar, plaque, scab, scale, shale, shell, stalactite, stalagmite, tartar

INCUBATE breed, brood, clock, concoct, cover, develop, generate, gestate, hatch, plan, plot, scheme, set, sit

INCUBATION birthplace, brooding, gestation, hatching, maturation, sitting

INCUBATOR eccaleobion, hatcher, isolette

INCUBUS burden, clog, demon, dream, duse, dusio, encumbrance, hallucination, hindrance, impediment, mare, nightmare, spirit, terror *offspring* cambion

INCULCATE breed, educate, imbue, impart, implant, impress, indoctrinate, infix, infuse, inoculate, inseminate, instill, instruct, leaven, plant

INCULPATE See INCRIMINATE.

INCULT crude, rough, rude, uncivilized, unpolished, untitled, wild

INCUMBENCY benefice, burden, dynasty, liability, position, regime, reign, tenure

INCUMBRANCE See ENCUMBRANCE.

INCUNABULA beginning, cocoon, cradle, fifteener, infancy

INCUR accrue, acquire, afford, bring, catch, contract, entail, enter, fall, gain, get, meet, obtain, risk, run, wage

INCURABLE hopeless, immedicable, inoperable, irremediable, irreparable

INCURIOUS aloof, apathetic, careless, coarse, detached, disinterested, distrait, indifferent, preoccupied, unconcerned, uninterested

INCURSION assault, attack, foray, influx, inroad, intrusion, invasion, irruption, raid

INCURVATION acruation

INCURVE bend, crook, throw

INCUS ambos, anvil(cloud), bone, hammer, thunderhead

INDABA conference, council

INDEBT astrict, bind, obligate

INDEBTED beholden, bound, encumbered, grateful, obliged

INDEBTEDNESS arrearage, arrears, debit, liability, obligation, score

INDECENT bawdy, blue, broad, coarse, gross, immodest, immoral, improper, impure, indecorous, indelicate, intemperate, lascivious, lewd, licentious, naked, nasty, nude, obscene, offensive, profligate, repugnant, revolting, ribald, risque, shameful, unclean, unfit, unseemly, vulgar, wanton

INDECISION acrisy, dilemma, doubt, fluctuation, hesitancy, incertitude, swither, vacillation

INDECISIVE doubtful, dubious, halting, hesitant, inconclusive, indefinite, irresolute, seesaw, teetery, vacillating, vague, wavering, weak-kneed

INDECOROUS coarse, gross, impolite, improper, INDECENT, indelicate, rude, tasteless, unbecoming, un-

civil, unfit, unmeet, unseemly, vulgar, wrong

INDEED actually, aroon, aru, awat, certainly, davvero, forsooth, frankly, greatly, iwis, much, quoth, really, sure(ly), tiens, truly, verily, veritably, wis, year

INDEFATIGABLE active, assiduous, busy, diligent, dogged, energetic, industrious, persevering, persistent, sedulous, strenuous, tireless, unflagging, untiring, unwearied, vigorous, weariless

INDEFEASIBLE avoidless, certain, inalienable, unavoidable

INDEFENSIBLE inexcusable, invalid, unforgivable, unprotected, untenable, vulnerable

INDEFINITE ambiguous, aoristic, blurred, confused, DOUBTFUL, dubious, equivocal, fuzzy, hazy, indecisive, indeterminate, indistinct, intangible, loose, neutral, obscure, smudged, uncertain, undecided, undefined, undetermined, unsure, vague

INDELIBLE deep-dyed, fast, fixed, indestructible, memorable, profound, unforgettable

INDELICATE base, broad, brutish, callow, coarse, crude, earthy, edged, edgy, immodest, impolite, improper, INDECENT, indecorous, lewd, lowbred, offensive, rough, rude, shameful, tactless, unseemly, vulgar

INDEMNIFICATION adjustment, amends, assythment, atonement, compensation

INDEMNIFY compensate, pay, recompense, recoup, redress, reimburse, repay, requite, return, satisfy, warrant

INDEMNITY amends, amnesty, compensation, contract, pay, protection, redress, reparation, restitution, security

INDENT bruise, chase, contract, delve, dent, depress, dint, gauffer, hollow, jag, notch, paragraph, pink, pit, print, rabbet, rut, space, stamp, tooth, wheel

INDENTATION alveolation, alveolus, bow(ed), bulge, choil, chop, cleft, crena, crenelet, dent, depression, dimple, dinge, dint, doke, furrow, groove, hollow, honeycomb, impress(ion), imprint, jab, margin, nick, notch, pit, pockmark, print, recess, score, space

INDENTED alveolar, alveolate, crenate, depressed, dimpled, engrailed, erose, faveolate, grooved, honeycombed, impressed, jagged, notched, pitted, pocked, pockmarked, rasee, serrated, waved

INDENTURE agreement, apprentice(ship), article, bargain, bind(over), cartel, commission, contract, convention, covenant, document, enslave, entente, mise, pact, treaty

INDEPENDENCE autarky, autonomy, freedom, home rule, individualism, liberty, license, reliance, self-government, self-reliance, sovereignty, wealth
absolute alod
political swaraj

INDEPENDENT absolute, alone, apart, autarchic, autarkic, autonomous, divided, freelance, free-spirited, individualist, maverick, neutral, nonpartisan, rich, self-contained, self-reliant, separate, solitary, sovereign, unallied, unrelated, wealthy, well-fixed

INDESCRIBABLE extraordinary, ineffable, inenarrable, inexpressible, nondescript, subtle, termless, unspeakable, unutterable

INDESTRUCTIBLE deathless, imperishable, incorruptible, indelible, ineffaceable, ineradicable, quenchless, undying, unquenchable

INDETERMINATE aoristic, borderline, chance, debatable, equivocal, formless, indefinite, indistinct, infinite, irresolute, racemose, uncertain, undecided, unfixed, vague

INDEX catalogue, characteristic, contents, docket,

exponent, file, finger, fist, gnomon, indicator, list, needle, pip, pointer, preface, prologue, sign, table, token
finger pointer
mark fist
pert. indicial
sundial gnomon

INDIA (See also HINDU.)
. jambudvipa
aborigine dasyas, dravidian, kanwar, toda
absolute tat
"abuse" galee, gali
acrobat nat
actor sabu
agent ameen, amin, aumildar, gomashta(h), muktar
agricultural caste meo, vaisya
alkali plains usar
alphabet devanagari, sarada
ambassador vakeel, vakil
ancestor manu, pitri
ancestor's rite sraddha
ancestral race aryan
anglicized babu
anglo quihi
animal arctonyx, arna, aswail, balisaur, bandicoot, banxring, bear pig, black buck, chitra, dhole, elephant, farsier, gaur, kola, meminna, sambar, saran, sasin, sher, sloth-bear, snow-leopard, tiger, varaha, youse, youze, zebu, zibet(h)
antelope bezoar, cervicapra, chikara, chiru, chouka, chousingha, goral, nilgai, nilgau, nyl, sasin
antimony surma
apartment mahal, zenana
ape kra
aphorisms sutra
aristocracy nayres
army officer jemadar, naigue, naik, tanadar, thanadar
"arrangement" bundobust
art, pert. gandharan
artisan caste sonar, sudra
aryan dehgan, HINDU, swat(i)
ascetic avadhuta, bhikshu, fakeer, fakir, jogi, mahatma, sadh(u) sannyasi, tapasvi, yati, yogi
assessment jumma
association sangh
astrologer joshi
atheist nastika

attendant amah, ayah, syce
attorney muktar
awning shamianah
baby baba
bail andi
bandana publicat
bandit dacoit
banker banian, banya(n), marwari, saraf, schroff, set, soucar, sowcar
barbet coppersmith
bard bhat
bathing place gha(u)t
bazaar chawk, chowk
bean urd
bear baloo, b(h)alu
bearer sirdar
bed charpao, charpoy
bed cover palampore
beer apong
beggar See INDIA *mendicant.*
bible See INDIA *scripture.*
bill of exchange hundi
bird adjutant stork, amadavat, amaduvad(e), argala, avadavat, avis, baya, bulbul, dayal, hawk-owl, homrai, hurgila, kala, koel, kyah, lowa, meninting, mina, munia, myna, ortygan, raya, sarus, seesee, shama, swiftlet, treeswift
bird cage penjra
bison arna, gaur, gayal, tsine
blacksmith lohar
blackwood biti
blanket kambal
blight soka
blouse cholee, choli
boar varaha
boat almadia, budgero(w), dhoni, dingey, ding(h)y, donga, dunga, masoola, masula(h), puteli, shibar
boatswain serang
bodice cholee, choli
bodyguard burkundaz
bond andi
bottle lota, mussuk
bovine zebu
boy chokra, mowgli
bracelet sankha
bread chapatti, chapatty, naan, paratha, piazi, poon, pooree, poori, samosa
breakfast hazri
brick soorkee, soorki, soorky
bridge joola, sangar
british rule raj
bronze octoalloy
"browbeat" dumbcow
buck sasin
buffalo arna, arnee, gaur

bulbul kala
bull zebu
bush kanher
business office dufter
bustard florican
butter ghee, ghi
buzzard tesa
cab judka
cabinet almirah, almura, al-myra(h)
cake amsath
calendar See INDIA *month.*
calico chintz, sallo(o)
camel oont
cannabis See INDIA *hemp.*
canopy shamianah
canvas enclosure canaut
cape comorin, divi
capital (new)delhi, simla
carpet agra, asan, azan, dur-rie, kanara, masulipatam, namda, numda(h), sittingy
carriage bandy, ekka, gharri, gharry, hackery, jutka, rath, rut, tonga
cart bandy, hackery
caste (See also CASTE.) agarwal, ahir(a), am-bashtha, arora, babhan, baidya, bania(n), bhar, bhat, bhil, bibar, brahman, brahmin, caddi, chamar, chuhra, dacoit, dasi, dhan-gar, dhanuk, dhobi(e), dhoby, dom, dosadh, ga-daria, go(a)la, gowlee, harijan, holeya, jain, jat(i), jet, kammalan, koikopal, koli, kori, kshatriya, kuli, kumhar, kurmi, lodha, lo-hana, lohar, madi(ga), mali, meo, palli, pasi, passi, pulaya, purvoe, rajpoot, raj-put, sansi, sonar, soodra soodri, sudra tai, teli, toty, vais(h)ya, vakkaliga, varna, velala
caste mark tilaka
cattle brahman, gaekwar, gaur, gayal, gir, gour, nilgai, tsine, zebu
cattle food bhoosa
cavalry ressala, risala, sowar
cave temple kailasa, rath
celestial light gods aditya
chamber tahkhana
chamois sarau
charm mantra, obeah, obi
cheetah youse, youze
chess chaturanga, shatranj
chevrotain meminna
chief mir(daha), mokad-dam, raja(h), rana, sirdar, sudder

child baba
chinz salampore
church arya, samaj
cigarette beedi, bidi, biri
circle chukker
city 3 ava, diu, mau 4 abad, agra, dama, dhar, gaur, gaya, mahe, mhau, mhow, puna, puri, unao 5 adoni, ajmer, akola, alwar, arcot, arrah, bally, behar, bhera, bihar, dacca, datia, delhi, girot, hansi, impal, kalpi, mysor, nasik, patna, poona, salem, simla, surat, tehri 6 ajanta, ajmerl, ambala, bareli, baroda, bhopal, bombay, chamba, cochin, dumdum, howrah, indore, jaipur, jhansi, kanpur, lahore, madira, madras, madura, meerut, multan, musore, muttra, mysore, nagpur, rajput, rampur, ranchi, ujjain 7 ajodhya, aligarh, banares, belgaum, benares, bikaner, calicut, cawnpur, dinapir, fyzabad, gwalior, jodhpur, karachi, kurnool, lashkar, laswari, lucknow, mathura, patiala, rangoon, rangpur, sialkot, tanjore, udaipur 8 amritsar, bareilly, bhatinda, bhat-para, calcutta, cawnpore, dehradun, dinapore, faiza-bad, golconda, jabalpur, kolhapur, ludhiana, manda-lay, mirzapur, peshawar, shillong, sholapur, srinagar, varanasi 9 ahmedabad, alla-habad, bangalore, bhaun-ager, buddhgaya, hydera-bad, jullunder, moradabad, pathankot 10 ahmednagar, coimbatore, coochbehar, darjeeling, jamshedpur, jub-bulpore, saharunpur, trivan-drum
city, holy banares, benares, lassa, lhasa, varanasi
civet rasse, zibet(h)
claim hak(h)
clan gotra
clarinet been
class See INDIA *caste.*
clerk baboo, babu, carcoon, conicopoly, gomashta(h)
cloak choga
cloth baft(a), baftah, caffa, calico, dewali, dhurrie, humhum, mela, moory, pal-ampore, pata, romal, rumal, rumchunder, salam-

pore, sal(l)oo, salu, surat, tanjib, tat(s), ulwan, zen-ana
club lathee, lathi
coast coromandel, malabar
coat achkan, banian, banyan, choga, chuddar
coconut nargil
coin abidi, adha, ahmed, akhter, an(n)a, cash, cronin, crore, da(w)m, faloo, fanam, fels, gunda, hoon, kano, lac, lakh, mohur, nayapaisa, pagoda, pai(sa), pice, pie, rupee, santhome, shahee, shahi, tanga, tar(a)
college tol
colonist clive
command hookum
common people vaisyas
company jatha
concubine dasi
condiment curry
congregation, religious samaj, somaj
convent math
cook bawarchi
cork tree millingtonia
coronation abhiseka
corporal naik
cosmetic surma
cosmic order rita
costume rajasthan
cot charpoy
cottage bari
cotton (See also INDIA *muslin.*) baft(ah), chintz, cossas, sallo(o)
cotton gin charkha
court adawlut, foujdar(r)y, panchayat, sudder
court official amala, amlah, mehmander, nazir
courtesan asparases
cow gaekwar, nilgai
cowherd caste ahir(a)
cowrie zimbi
crane coolung, kulang, saras, sarus
cremation sati, suttee
crocodile gavial, muggar, mugger, muggur
crop kharif, rabi
cuckoo koel, koil, sirkeer
cucumber tree bilimbi
cushion musnud
custom dastur, purdah, sati, suttee
cymbal tal
dagger choora, katar, kirpan
dais chabutra
dam an(n)icut
dance cantico, nautch

dancer bayadere, davadasi, lasya, nat(araja), nautch girl, tandava
dawn gods asvins
dead, god of yama
deer atlas, axis, barasingha, cervus, cheetal, cheetul, chital, chitra, gerau, kakar, rusa, sambar, sambur
demon See INDIA *spirit.*
dependency taluk
deposit adhi
deputy nabob, nawab
desert thar
devil tree dita
devotee yati
dialect See INDIA *language.*
dias chabutra
dice kabat
dictionary amara-kosha
dill soya
disciple chela, sikh
discount batta
dish achar, aloo, barfi, bhindi-masala, bhurta, biriani, bombay duck, chaat, chappati, chappaty, chattu, curry, dahi, d(h)al, foogath, gajar, gulab-jaman, haleem, kachumbar, kathmandu, kebab, k(h)eema, kheer, khumb, kofta, kulcha, kulfi, kurma, masala, moglai-biryani, muttermasala, nan, pakora, palak(a), paneer-korma, panir, papad, pap(p)adum, podina, pooree, popadam, raita, rasgulla, rasmalai, roghan-josh, saagwalalala, samosa, seekh-kebab, soorkakorma, tanduri, thali, vindaloo
distiller abkar
district agra, berar, daya, diu, gya, malabar, mofussil, nasik, nellore, oudh, patna, sibi, simla, zillah
district head collector
divine artificer tvashtar, tvashtri
divorce law talak
doctrine anatta, dharma, karma
dog buansu, dhole, kolsun, pariah
dog cart tumtum
dowry sulka
dragon ahi, ketu, rahu, vritra
drama nataka
dramatist bhavabhuti
dravidian See DRAVIDIAN.
drink arrack, asha, shrab, soma, sura

drinking pot lotah
driver drabi
drought soka
drug (See also INDIA *hemp.*) charas, sina
drum nagara
dugout dunga
dust storm habo(o)b, hab(b)ub, shaitan, sheitan
duty dharma
dye aal, awl, norindin
dynasty gupta
earth regur
earth jinn yaksa
elephant airavata, hathi
elephant decoy koomkie
elephant driver mahout
elephant goad ankus
elephant-headed god ganes(h)a
elephant, mythological airavata
elephant snare kheda
elephant, white airapadam
elixir amreeta, amrita
elk sambar
emperor akbar, asoka, humayan, ja(e)hangir
enclosure canaut, keddah
english founder clive
epic mahabharata, ramayana, sakuntala
epic hero rama
esplanade maidan
estate talooka, taluk(a)
eternal triangle agra, delhi-jaipur
eternity symbol sesha
european topee-wallah
excavations harappa
exchange rate batta
exercise hathayoga, yoga
fabled mountain meru
fabled people astomoi
fables bidpai, pilpay
factory aurang, aurong
fair mela
falcon bes(a)ra, laggar, lugger, shaheen, shahin
family gotra
fan chamar, punka(h)
farmer hamal, meo, ryot
fasting dharna
fate dharma
father baboo, babu, manu
fennel soya
festival burra khana, dasehra, das(h)ahara, dewali, divali, diwali, durgapuja, dus(h)ehra, dussera(h), holi, hoolee, mela, navaratra, phag, pongol, puja
festival powder abir
feudal chief poligar

fiber agust, ambary, bhabar, jute, kumbi, oadal
fig waringin
fig tree botree, peepul, pipul
fighter gurkha
fine abwab
fire god agni, akal, civa, deva, kama, siva
fire priest atharvan
1st man yama
fish argus, chenas, donio, dorab, hilsa(h), lile, mahseer, scatophagus, seerfish, sulea
fishing boat dhoni, koni
flageolet basaree, larigot
flour at(t)a
flower lotus
flute bin, matalan, poogye, pungi
foot dye alta
"footprint" pug
foot stool mora
forage plant quar
foreigner pardesi
former state kutch
fort gurry
4-armed deity yama
friar See ECCLESIASTIC *hindu.*
frontier bulwark nefa
frost hemanta
fruit amchoor, amhar, b(h)el, lansa, longan, mango(steen)
funeral rite shraddha
gall gambia pod
game bagataway, parcheesi
game preserve shikargah
gardener malee, mali(e)
garment achkan, bania(n), banyan, burqa, choqui, dhoti, jama(h), saree, sari
gate house cerame
gateway dar, toran(a)
gazelle chikara, s(h)ri
gentleman baboo, babu, sahib
geometry text sulvasutra
ghost bhut, preta
giant bana, s(h)esha
giant tribe bouders, boudons
gift dolly, enam, khilat, killut, lepa
gipsy karachee
glove gomukhi
goat markhor, tahr
god aditi, aditya, agni, akal, antaka, apa, asura, asvins, balairama, bhaga, bhrigus, brahma, brihaspati, BUDDHA, chandra, civa, daksha, dandadhara, deva(ta), dewa(ta), dharmaraja,

dyaus, ganes(h)a, hanuman, haoma, INDRA, ishvara, jagannath, juggernaut, kala, kama(mara), karttikeya, khuda, krishna, kritantapasupati, kubera, kumara, kuvera, manu, matarisvan, maya, mitra, narasimha, nasatyas, parjanya, pasupati, pitripati, prajapati, prithivi, puchan, rama(chandra), rudra, samana, samavurti, savitar, savriti, simia, shiva, sishnu, SIVA, skanda, soma, sraddhadeva, surya, tryambaka, tvashtar, VARUNA, vata, vayu, VISHNU, vivasvat, yama
goddess aditi, ambika, amma(n), annapurna, bhairave, bhumi(devi), chandi, cunda, devi, durga, gauri, haimavati, kali, kuanyin, kwannon, lakshmi, matris, parvati, prithivi, sakti, sarasvati, sati, shakti, shitala, shree, shri, sitala, sri, uma, us(h)as
godling deota, devata, dewata
gods' abode meru
gods' artisan ribhus
gods' messenger bhrugi
god's sons angiras, rishis
god, supreme vishvakarma
goglet cooja
goldern triangle cities agra, delhi, jaipur
goldsmith sonar
gorge nullah, tangi
"gossip" gup
government sircar
government lands amani
governor daroga(h)(a), naik, nazim, suba(h)dar
governor general canning, dupleix, hastings
grade chop
grain barngrass
grammarian panini
granary gola, gunge, gunj
grant cowle, enam, inam, jageer, jaghir, jagir, sasan
grass bhabar, darbha, doob, doorba, glaga, kans, kasa, kusha, rag(g)ee, ragi, roosa, usar, vetiver
grassland rakh
greek king hermaeus
greeting namaste, sri
griddle cake chap(p)ati, chappaty
groom oboli, sais, sice, syce

group caste, varna
grove sarpa
guard daloyet
guide shikaree, shikari
guitar bina, sitar, vina
gulf cambay, kutch, mannar
gum amra(d)
guru's pupil shishya
gypsy bazigar, karachee
hall durbar
handkerchief malabar, rumal
hardwood calamander, poon, teak
harem serai, zenana
harvest rab(b)i
hat topee, topi
hawk badius, shikra
hay rakh
headdress puggree, rumal, topee, topi
healing caste ambastha
heiress begum
helmet topee, topi
hemp b(h)ang, beng, carl, chirata, dagga, ganja, hashish, ke(e)f, keif, kief, pie, pooa(h), pua, ramie
hemp oil cannabene
herb (See also INDIA *hemp*.) curcuma, harmel, mat-bean, mongoose plant, mungo, pia, sesame, shevri, sola, zeodary
herbal cure ayurveda
hermit tapasvi
hermitage as(h)rama
hero kuru, nala, prithu, rama, siva
high caste amelu, babhan, bibar
hill dweller bhil, dogra, gond, kol, oraon, pahari, toda
hills garo
hodgepodge kedgeree
"holy" shree, s(h)ri
holy book See INDIA *literature.*
holy center ajodhya
holy city benares, nasik
holy fig tree pipal
holy grove sarna
holy hut bari
holy man alvar, fakeer, fakir, rishi, saddhu, sadh(u)
holy plant banyan, bo tree, creeper, ephedra, kusa, milkweed, millet, periploca, pipal, sarcostemma, soma, valli
holy powder abir
holy river ganga, ganges, yamuna

honey bee dingar
"honor" izzat
hornbill homrai
horse, mythological aulay
house baradari, bari, basha, bungalow, hawaghar, mahal
howdah ambaree, ambari
hunt shikar
hunter shikari
hut bari, basha, toldo
hymn mantra
idiom munda
idol pagoda, swami
idol worship arati
immortality beverage amreeta, amrita
impost abwab
inn choultry
interpreter dubash, moonshee, munshi
invader sacae, saka
irrigation ditch an(n)icut
island agatti, andaman, chilka, laccadive, nicobar
island group amandive
jackal kola
jacket bania
jasmine malati
journalist mohammed ali
jug lota
jungle shola
justice adawlut
kala bulbul
kettledrum nagara
king See INDIA *prince.*
kingfisher meninting
kingly caste kshatriya
king-monkey bodhisattva, mahakapi-jataka
king of serpents sesha
kinsman bandhava, bandhu
knife dah, kukri
knowledge goddess matrika-devis, vidyadevis
laborer begari, duffadar, mazdoor, palli, sudra, toty(man)
laborer caste dosadh, holeya, sudra
lady begum, bibi, devi, memsahib, ranee, rani, sahibah
lake chilka, colair, dhebar, jheel, kolair, sambahr, wular
lancer sowar
land, barren usar
land, common bhaiyachara
land grant enam, inam, sasan
landing place gaut, ghat
landowner zamindar
land reform bhoodan
land rent malikana
land tax malguzari

language agaloch, arura, awadhi, bat, bengali, bhili, bhojpuri, bihari, brajbhasha, dakhini, garhwali, hindi, hindustani, magadhi, maharashtri, maithili, malayalam, malto, marathi, munda, oriya, pali, pamir, pashto, prakrit, punjabi, pushtu, sanskrit, shina, sindhi, siouan, tamil, telugu, urdu, vedic
law book dharmas(h)astra, dharmasutra, mitakshara
law giver manu
law officer moonsif, munsif
lawyer muktar, vakil, yakeel
leader chandra shekhar, indira gandhi, mahatma gandhi, morarji desai, naik, nehru, sirdar
lease patta, pottah
leaseholder ijaradar
legal opinion futwa
legend purana
lentil dhal
leopard cheetah
library bhandar
licorice abrin
limestone kunkur
liquor shrab, soma, sura
literature agama, akhyana, aranyaka, atharva-veda, ayurveda, bhagavadgita, brahamana, gayatri, gita, isha, katha, mahabharata, purana, ramayana, rig-veda, shak(h)a, shastra, shruti, smitri, sruti, sutra, tantra, upanishad, veda(nga), vedanta, yajnavalka, yajur-veda
litter dandy, doly, doolee, doolie, jampan, kajawah, muncheel, polki
living quarters bustees
loam regur
loincloth dhoti, lungi, pata
lord isvara, mian, swami
love god kama
love philosophy tantra
lover indophile
low caste bhat, dom, koli, kori, kuli, lodha, madiga, mahar, mali
lunch tiffin
lute sitar
macaque rhesus
madder aal
madness dewanee
magic jadoo, jadu, maya
magician fakeer, fakir, leopard-man
mahogany toon(a)

maid ayah
mail dak, dauk, dawk
man, educated babu, pundit
manager aumildar
mango bird oriole
mango, dried amchoor, amhar
mangrove goran
man-horses gandharvas
mantra atharva-veda
marauder lootie
mark bottu, tilaka
market gunge, gunj, pasar
marriage arsha, beena, daiva
master mian, saheb, sahib, swami
mat grass seetulputty
matting asan(a), sirki, tat(ta)
mausoleum baredari
meal at(t)a
measure adhaka, adoulie, ady, amunam, angula, bigha, byee, cahar, coss, covid(o), crosa, cudava, dain, danda, denda, depa, depoh, dha(nush), doph, drona, dumbha, erosa, garce, gavyuti, gaz, geerah, gez, gireh, guz, hasta, hath, jaob, jow, khahoon, kos(s), krosa, kunk, lamany, lan, moolum, moot, mushti, niranga, okthabah, ouroub, palgat, pally, para(h), parran, pras(t)ha, raik, rat(t)i, ropani, salay, seit, ser, taun, teng, tipree, tola, unglee, vitasti, yojan(a)
medical book ayurveda
medical caste ambastha, baidya
medical nut malabar
melody raga
mendicant bairagi, dandi, dandy, naga, sannyasi, udasi, vairagi
mendicant, religious fakeer, fakir
mental discipline yoga
mercenary sepoy
merchant banian, banya(n), lambadi, marwari, seth, soudagur, teli
merchant caste agarwal, vaisya
messenger hircarra(h)
midwife dhai
milk, curdled tayer, tayir
millet chena, durr(a), joar, jonda, jowar, juar, koda
mine laborer mita
minstrel bhat
missionary bodhidharma

mistress annapurna
mixture masala
mogul emperor akbar, babar, baber, babur, shah jehan
monastery math
money batta, crore
money-lender mahajan
monkey rhesus
monkey god hanuman
month aghan, asarh, asin, baisakj, bhadon, chait, jeth, ka(r)tik, kuar, magh, pha(l)gun, pus, sa(ra)wan
moon chandra
moral treatise bhagavadgita
mortar soorkee, soorki, soorky
moslem swat
mother goddess amma(n), kali, matris
mountain guard ghatwal
mountain pass ghat(s), ghaut
mountain with 5 peaks pancasika, pancasirsa
mountaineer bhil
mouse metad
mulberry aal, ach, alroot
mungo earthgall
musical composition raga, rasa
musical instrument basaree, been, bina, lute, ruana, sarangi, sarinda, sarod, seringhi, sitar, tamb(o)ur, tambura, vina
musicians gandharva
musket ball goli
muslim leader jinnah
muslin adati, charkhana, dorea, doria, gurrah, madras
mystic bhave, ramakrishna, yogi
myth adi-shesha, purana
narcotic See INDIA *hemp.*
narcotic confection majoon
native See INDIA *people.*
nature principle guna
nco havildar, naik
negro hubshi
newcomer griffin
news agency samachar
nightjar ice-bird
noble ashraf, kshatriya, maharajah, prabhu, rajah
nomad bazigar
number lac(h), lakh
nurse amah, ayah, dhai
nut betel
nymphs apsaras
ocher almagra

officer duffadar, havildar, naik
office servant duftery
officer's son akhundzada
official amala(h), ameen, amin, aumildar, daroga(h), dedan, jemadar, nabob, nawab, nazim, nazir, omlah, patel, ressaldar, shabandar, shabunder, subahdar, tenet
oil vendor teli
oil vessel dubber
okra bandikai
olympus meru
opium chandoo, chandu
opposition leader narayan
opposition party janata
orchard tope
ornament amalaka, bot(t)u, koftgari
outcast chandala
oven tandoor
overseer kangani, kangany
ox gaur, gayal, tsine, zebu
package robbin
pageant tamasha
palace baradari
palanquin dandi, dandy, dooli(e), dool(e)y, palkee
palm nipa, talipot
panda wah
pannier kajawah
papers, official dufter
partridge francolin, kyah, seesee
party See INDIA *political party.*
"passion" rajas
patriarch pitri
paymaster bakshi, bukshee, bukshi
pea, split dal
peak kalahoi, kamet, masharbrum, mastuj, meru, nana-devi, shleiman, tankse, tirach-mir
peasant kisan, ryot
peddler boxwallah
peninsula deccan, kathiawar
people angka, assamese, awan, babhan, baboo, babu(l), badaga, bangash, behac, bhar(ata), bhil, bhumij, bihar, chang, colleri, coorg, dafla, garwali, gentoo, gharwal, gohila, gond, gor, gujar, gujrati, hindu(stani), hubshi, jajman, jat, kadaga, kadu, kalwar, khatri, kotar, kuruba, kurumba, mahratta, male, maratha, maury, meithei, munda, musahar, naga,

nayadi, orakzai, palliyan, saura, savara, sepoy, sherani, shirani, shudra, sikh, sindhi, sudra, tamil, thakur, toda, turi, us(h)tarana, vairagi, vaisya
pepper betel
pewter bidree, bidri, bidry, tutenag
pheasant kallege, mona(u)l, moonal, pukras
philosopher calanus, dandamis, gymnosophist, shankara, sphines, yogi(n)
philosophy advaita, kosha, lokayata, mimansa, tamas, tantra, vedanta, yoga
philosophy books darshana
physicist bhabba, bose, raman
pickle achar
pigeon treron
pilgrimage center gaya
pillar lat, stamba
pink city jaipur
pipe hookah
plains usar
plant mardoo, nardu, spikenard
plant disease sereh
plant stalk amsu
platform chabutra, machan
playwright kalidasa
pleasure garden vihara
plum amra
poem (See also INDIA *epic.*) bhagavadgita, raghuvansa, sloka
poet tagore
poison abrin, bikh, bish, bisk
police chief daroga(h), darogha
policeman peon, sepoy
police station kotwalee
political movement swadeshi
political party congress party, janata people's party, naxalites, swaraj
politician ambedkar, banerjea, krishna menon
poll tax jizya
pony tat(too)
port bhaunagar, bombay, calcutta, cannanore, cochin, daman, damao, kananur, madras, porbandar, puri, surat
porter chokidar, durwaun
pot chatty
pottery uda
powder abir
power sakti
prayer call azan
prayer carpet asan(a), asani

president prasad
priest See ECCLESIASTIC *hindu.*
priest caste brahman
priest's garment dhoti
prime minister dewan, gandhi, nehru, shastri
prince ahluwalia, asoka, bana, bharata, maharaja(h), maharajadhiraja, nala, nawab, nizam, porus, raja(h), rana, s(h)esha, sirdar, taxiles
princess begum, kumari, kunwari, maharani, malikzadi, rah-kumari, ranee, rani, shahzadi
principles See PRINCIPLES *seven.*
progenitor manu
property dhan
property, women's stridhana
proprietor malik
prostitute asparasis
province See INDIA *state.*
provincial districts mofussil
public office cutcherry
punjab founder ranjit singh
punjab people sansi, sikh
queen See INDIA *princess.*
race bharata, dravidian, hindu, jat, nishada, swat, tamil, varna, yadava
raft gharnao
rain god indra
rain snake naga
rainy season monsoon, varsha
rajah's sacrifice abhigit
range aravalli, ghat(s), himalayas, hindu-kush, karakoram, satpura, sitwal(i)k, vindhya
rascal budzat
rat bandicoot
rebellion sepoy
reception durbar
recorder sheristadar
recruit jawans
regiment pulton, pultun
region andhra, canara, carnatic, doab, gandhara, kanara, malabar, oudh
reign nawab, raj
religion brahmanism, buddhism, hinduism, islam, jainism, parseeism, parsiism, s(h)ivaism
religious instructor acharya, guru
religious leader gandhi, gosala, nanak, rammohun, roy

religious shelter ashram(a), dharmsala
relish achar
rent malikana
reply jawab
resort, invalid abu, simla
retreat ashram(a)
revenue jagir
revenue collector au-mil(dar), deshpandee, deshpandi, dessayed, dufterdar, tahsildar, talukdar
rice aus, boro
rice beer apong
river beas, betwa, bhima, cauvery, chambal, chenab, demoh, dor, gandak, ganges, godavari, gogra, hemavati, hooghly, hydaspes, indus, irrawadi, jawai, jhelum, kistna, kosi, krishna, kusi, lumna, mahanadi, narbada, nerbudda, nira, penner, rapti, ravi, rehr, sankh, sarda, sind, son(ar), subansiri, sutlej, tapti, tel, tista, tunga, vindhyas, wardha
river boat oolak
river dolphin bouto
river landing ghat
road praya
road toll rahdaree, rahdari
robber dacoit
robe jama
rodent nesokia
root atees, atis
rope dancer nat
rubber caoutchouc
rug kanara
rule raj
ruler See INDIA *emperor, prince, princess, title.*
saber tulwar
sacred writing See INDIA *literature.*
safari shikar
safflower kusum
saffron turmeric, zedoary
sage agastya, amanda, bharata, bhat, gautama, katha, kishi, mahatma, pandit, pundit, r(i)shi
sailor lascar
saint alvar
salesman brinjaree, brinjary
scarf dopatta, puggree, saree, sari, uparna
scavenger bhungi(ni), bungy, halacor
schoolmaster akhoond, akhund
school, vedanta advaita, tol
science book ayur-veda

score corge
screen jalee, purdah, tattie, tatty
script brahmi, nagari
scripture See INDIA *literature.*
secretary moonshee, munshi, sheristadar
sect aghori, ahmadiya, ajivika, jain(a), meda, sadh, samaj, seik, sikh, siva
seer swami
self-defense varmannie
self-government swaraj
sergeant havildar
serpent adishesha, adjiger, ahi, bongar, bungarus, cobra, daboia, daboya, katuka, krait, naga
serpent king sesha, vasuki
servant amah, ayah, bearer, bildar, dar, dasi, duftery, ferash, hamal, ham(m)aul, hamul, matranee, maty, mussalchee, par, sirdar, syce
servant's wages tunca
share hak(h)
shawl chuddah, chuddar
shed pandal
sheep (See also ASIA *sheep.*) barwal, nahoor, oorial, sha(pu), urial
shepherd gadaria
shirt banian, kurta
shrine dagaba, dagoba, dewal
shrub adhatoda, arus(h)a, callicarpa, crape jasmine, dhanri, jujube, karanda, madar, mudar, odal, snakewood, sunn
silk cabeca, corah, culgee, muga, romal, rumal, tussah
silk worm eri
silversmith sonar
singer bayadere
sitarist shankar
skin disease courap
skipper serang
slave dashara, dasi, shudra
sloth aswail, melursus
small pox goddess shitala
snack muri
snake See INDIA *serpent.*
social division See INDIA *caste* and CASTE.
social structure dharma
soil, rich regur
soldier gurkha, jawan, peon, sebundee, sebundy, sepoy, sikh, sowar
song bhajan
songbird amadavat, amadu-

vad(e), shama, strawberry-finch
sorceress usha
sorghum chena, cush, dari, darra, darso, dhurra, dora, dourah, durr, hegari, milo
soup dal shorba, mulliga-tawny
spirit asura, atman, bali, bhoot, bhudapati, bhut, daitya, danava, dasyus, deva, dust devil, hiranyakasipu, jiva, kali(ka), mara, muktama, naga, pisachee, pisachi, prana, rahu, rakshasa, ravanna, sura, tamas, vibhishana, yaksha
spirit prince pasupati, rudra, s(h)iva
spitoon pigdan
splendor goddess uma
split pea dal, pigeon pea
spring vasanta
spy hiracarra(h)
squirrel taguan
stable khatal
state agra, ajmer-merwara, andhra, assam, baroda, bastar, behar, bengal, berar, bhopal, bihar, bikaner, bundelkhand, bundi, cochin, cooch-behar, coorg, cutch, daman, delhi, dhar, gujarat, gujerat, gwalior, har(yana), himachal, jaora, johor(a), kashmir, kerala, kosala, kurg, kutch, madhya-pradesh, madras, maharashtra, manipur, mysore, nagaland, orissa, oudh, patan, pradesh, punjab, rajasthan, rewa, sikkim, subah, swat, tehri, tonk, tripura, uttar-pradesh
state barge morpunkee
state ceremony durbar
state lands amani
statesman pandit, shastri
steel wootz
steward bhandari, dewan, diwan
stone lingham
stool mora
storehouse bhandar, gola
storekeeper bhandari
storm peesash, tufan
story katha
strait palk
stream-bed nullah
student chela
study of indology
sugar goor, gur, raab
suicide suttee
suit of honor seerpaw

summer residence mahal
sun god aditya(s), agni, mitra, savitar, surya, varuna
sun worshipper parsee, parsi
supreme court sudder
surety andi
swamp terai
swamp deer barasingha
swan hansa
sweeper bhungi(ni), bungy, halacor
sweetmeat balushai
sword khanda, pata, tulwar
tableland balagha(u)t
tablets bogaz-keui, pteria
tailor darzee
tamarisk atle(e)
tapir saladang
tariff zabeta
tavern punch house
tax abkari, abwab, chaukidari
tax district tahsil
taxi tonga
tea assam
teacher akhoond, akhun(d), alfaqui, guru, mulla(h), pir, pundit
temple deul, kovil, mandira
temple ornament amalaka
temple tower gopura, shikara, sikar(a), sikhara, sik(h)ra, vimana
tenant ryot
tent pawl, shooldarry
terrace chabutra
thatched roof shopper
thicket shola
thieves' caste sansi
thrush s(h)ama
tiger sher(e)
title ahluwalia, akhundzada, aya, baboo, babu, bahadur, begum, bibi, burra, cakravartin, dewan, gaekwad, gaekwar, gaikwar, guicowar, haidar ali, huzoor, jam, jemadar, lokindra, maharaja(h), maharana, maharao, memsahib, mian, mir(za), nabob, naig(ue), naik, naique, nawab, nazir, nizam, rai(kat), raikbar, raikwar, rain, raja(h), rana, ranee, rani, rao(bahadur), rawal, sahib(ah), shree, shri, sidi, singh, sirdar, sree, sri, swami, thakur
tomb, saint's dargah, durgah
torch mussal
tortoise kashyapa
tower minar, sikhara, stupa
tracery ardish

tracker puggi
trademark ✦hop
trader banian, banyan
treasury khalsa
tree aal, ach, alus, amboina, amli, ampac, amra, angili, anjan, bael, banyan, bel, bengal quince, benjamin, beyr, buffalo thorn, bur(r), canardium, dadup, dammar, deodar, dhak, dhamnoo, dhava, dita, eng, goran, hollong, hursinghar, kokra, kurung, kurunj, langsat, lin, lodh, longan, mahua, mahwa, majagua, mangrove, margosa, morus, neem, nim, oadal, pipal, poon, quince, sain, saj, sal(ai), sebesten, senna, shoq, simal, sissoo, strychnine, sundari, supa, tala, teak, toon
tribe See INDIA *people.*
troop ressala, risala(h)
trousers shalwar
truck tonga
trumpet narsinga
trustee benamidar
tunic jama(h)
turban lungi, puggree, puggry, seerband
turks afridi
turmeric huldee, huldi
umbrella chatta
underworld patala
untouchable bhangi, bhungi, chandala, harijan, panchama
valley dhoon
vedas, introducer to agastya
vegetable dal, sabzi
vehicle ekka, gharry, rath, tonga
veranda pyal
vernacular apabhramsa
verse form sloka
vessel baggala, doni, lota, patamar, shibar
viceroy curzon, dalhousie, mountbatten, nabob, nawab, nazim, reading
viceroyalty cochin
village abadi, camp(o)dy, mouzah
village chief patel
village lands bhaiyachara, pattidari, zamindari
village meeting place ambalam
vine gila, haoma, lablab, malati, odal, skyflower, snakewood, soma
violin ruana, sarinda, saroh

viper echis
vulture dirtbird
wafer popadam, popper-cake
waistband cummerbund
waist cloth langooty
walnut tree akhrot
ware biddery, bidri
warehouse bankshall
warrior singh
warrior caste kshatriya
warrior god indra
washbasin chillumchee
watchman chokidar, mina, talliar
water carrier bheestie, bheesty, bhestee
water god varuna
water nymph apas
water spirit naga
water vessel chagul, goglet, lota(h), mussuck
wayside stop parao
wealth dhan
weaver tanti
weight abucco, adpad, adpao, bahar, bhar(a), candy, catty, chitta(c)k, dhan, dhurra, drum, hoen, hubba, karsha, kona, mangelin, masha, maund, mod, myat, pai, pala, pally, pank, peiktha, pice, pouah, raik, rat(t)i, ruay, rut(t)ee, se(e)r, tael, tali, tank, tical, ticul, tikal, tola, vis(s), wang, yava
west coast malabar
wheat sujee, suji
wheel chukker
white man goralog
widow sati, suttee
widow's cremation suttee
wildcat chaus
wild life sanctuary fir
wild sheep sestina
wind god marut
window screen tattie, tatty
wine shrab
wine-making abkari
wine-seller abkar
wisdom god ganesha
woman, educated pundita
women's apartment zenana
wood agaloch, benteak, biti, calamander, eng, kokra, sal, sissoo, toon
worship pooja, yajna
writer khidmatgar, moonshee, munshi, sircar
xylophone saron
yogurt dhye
yoke band(h)y
INDIAN (For *tribe,* see under countries and states.)

aborigine, amerind, bharati, brave, injun, maize, native, red(skin), rojo, savage, tamerind, tawny
aboriginal amerind, borinqueno
and white griffe, ladino, mestizo
ascetic tekakwitha
assembly room estufa, kiva
assent ugh
baby papoose
basket bokarak, wattape
basket-makers anasazi
bean bignonia, catalpa, trumpet-creeper, urd
beech kurunj
berry box brier
blanket firewheel, gaillardia, stroud
boat canoe, dugout, kayak
-boys-and-girls dutchman's-britches
brandy pingo
bread cassava, tuckahoe
buzzard tesa
calendar winter-count
ceremonial chamber kiva
ceremonial dance cantico, sundance
ceremonial pipe calumet
ceremony potlatch
chickpea gram
chief cacique, cazique, inca, logan, sachem, sannup, tyee
chief, famous big foot, black fish, black hawk, cochise, cornstalk, crazy horse, ducoigne, geronimo, hoowaunneka, little elk, logan, mahaskah, massasoit, notchimine, ontassete, osceola, ouray, philip, pontiac, powhatan, red cloud, sagamore, selocta, sitting bull, tahgahjute, tecumseh, victorio
child papoose
chronicle walam olum
cigar tree catalpa
clay-eating otomaca, otomaco
club pogamoggan
cloak matchcoat
colonists' friend netop
corn cholum, jagong, kanga, maize, mealies, nocake, rokee, samp, tara, turkeywheat, zea
corn disease boilsmut
corn silk floss
council powwow
cress nasturtium

culture anasazi, oneota
culture hero coyote, raven
currant corralberry
dance areito, buffalo, cantico
dance group matachina
daughter of moon nakomis, nokomis
death spirit chul(l)pa
devil cougar, wolverine
doll kachina, katc(h)ina
drink mushle
drug tobacco
drum calabash
dye goldenseal
eagle, mythical thunderbird
evil spirit windigo
extinct appomattoc, borinqueno, coahuiltecan
farmer calusa, campesino
festival busk, potlatch
fetish manitou, nagual
fiber piassava
fig cactus, sabra
fighter boone, custer, miles
file procession, single file
fish angelfish, flatfish, warmouth
fish poison barbasco
5 nations cayugas, mohawks, oneidas, onondagas, senecas
fog houseleek
food (See also INDIAN corn.) camas(s), cammas, pemmican, samp
forage plant guar
flour source ankee(grass)
friend netop
game bagataway, canute, chunky, double-ball, hubbub, stick-dice
-give deceive, renege
god acaraqui, amyi-coyondi, arch of heaven, ataentsie, atahuata, atira, cucumunk, echo, eithinoha, gahonga, gandayak, gaoh, gendenwitha, gitche-manito(u), great spirit, gunnodoyak, hino, huruingwuhti, ioskeha, kachina, katc(h)ina, kitcki-manitou, manitou, messou, michabo, niparaya, ohdowa(s), orenda, oshadagea, otkon, poia, purubui, quaayayp, sesondowah, shakurur, soatsaki, tamanoas, tawiscara, the great spirit, tirawa, wakan, wakonda
god-animal figure intaglio, mustam-ho
goddess amayicoyondi, atira, nokomis
god tree pipal

gooseberry emblic
gram chick-pea
gravelroot boneset, joe-pye-weed
greeting how, netop, ugh
grindstone mano, metate
guardian spirit totem
halfbreed forgotten moors, red bones
hare manabozho
hatchet tomahawk
hauling device travois
headdress feathers, maekette, tablita, topknot, war bonnet
heart balloon vine
hemp amyroot, dagga, dogbane, jute, kef, kif, mallow, milkweed, sabzi, sunn
hen bittern
herb chaya(root), choya (root)
hero manabozho
hippo false ipecac, flowering spurge, gillenia
hogan earth-lodge
holly assi, ya(u)pon
honey tabasheer
house chikee, cliff dwelling, hogan, te(e)pee, tipi, toldo, wickiup, wigwam, wikiup
jalap turpeth
jewelsmith navajo
labor grant encomienda, repartimiento
laburnum drumstick tree
leader See INDIAN *chief, famous.*
lettuce columbo, consumption-weed, cuban spinach
licorice crab's-eye vine, jequirity, rosary plant
liquor firewater, hoochinoo
lodge See INDIAN *house.*
madder munjeet
magic power manito(u), orenda
magician wabeno
mallow buttonweed, canapina, dagga, hemp, jute, pieprint, sida, velvetweed
man brave, buck, chief, sannup
marauder gaucho
meal bread corn-cake, corndodger
medicine nagual
medicine man peai, shaman
meeting powwow
melon barrel-cactus
memorial post totem, xat, xyst
mestizo griffe, ladino
millet durra, jondla
moccasin pac

money allocochick, beads, hawok, ioqua, peag(e) se(a)wan, shells, wampum
moon daughter nakomis, nokomis
mulberry aal, ach, alroot, awl, canarywood, flowertree, noni, rubra
ocean arm arabian sea, red sea, timor sea
ocean bay bengal
ocean bird crab-plover
ocean gulf aden
ocean island amindivi, ceylon, cocos, diego garcia, keeling, kerguelen, laccadive, madagascar, mahe, maldive, masirah, mauritius, mayotte, minicoy, reunion, socotra
ocean port st denis
ocean, river into juba, murray, tana
ocean stingray sephen
ornament runtee
outlaw belle starr
paint bloodroot, bloodwort, puccoon, redroot, sanguinaria, tellerwort, tormentil, turmeric
peace pipe calumet
pear shadbush
people pomos
people, common tilikum, tillicum
physic See INDIAN *hippo.*
pine loblolly
pink gaywings, painted-cup, silene
pipe anoplanthus, bird's-nest, broomrape, calumet, eyebright, fitplant, orobanche, thalesia, waxflower
plum casearia, flacourtia, osoberry
plume bee-balm, butterflyweed, oswego-tea
poison curare, curari
pole See INDIAN *memorial post.*
pony cayuse, tinder
porridge samp
potato breadroot, groundnut, sunflower, yamp
powwow wawa
prayer stick baho, paho, pajo
praying natick
prehistoric basketweaver, cochise
pre-inca aymara, canari, mochica, nascan, quecha, tiahuanacan, yunca
prophet jessakeed
puberty rite huskanaw

pure-blooded caboclo
purge manroot
queen sunck, sunk(squaw)
red almagra
religious ceremony sundance
religious cult kuksu
remedy birchbark, bloodroot, dockroot, feverwort, pokeberry, sagwa, sarsaparilla, sassafras, white oak, wintergreen
reservation preserve
room kiva
ruler cacique, cazique
rum ocuby
runner duck
saffron turmeric, zedoary
sage boneset
salad waterleaf
sarsaparilla nunnari
scholar sequoya
shaman wabeno
shell money allocochick
shoe moccasin
shot aliipoe, canna
sinister influence bad medicine
sledge travois
slipper moccasin-flower
snake paiute
snake dancer hopi
snakeroot mungo
society, secret midewiwin
sorcery obe(ah), obi
sorrel roselle
spirit (See also INDIAN *god, goddess.*) manito(u), manitu, nagual, totem
squaw See INDIAN *woman.*
stone dish comal
string figure kamut
structure adobe
summer autumn, fall, st augustine's, st luke's, st martin's
supernatural being numeta
tea holly ya(u)pon
tent or tepee See INDIAN *house.*
thong babiche
tobacco asthmaweed, bladderpod, eyebright, gagroot, kinnikinnick, lobella, pukeweed, sourbush, wundtkraut
tomb chul(l)pa
torture hookswinging
tribal queen sun(c)k
trophy scalp
vehicle travois
victorian echuca
village compo(o)dy, pueblo, tolderia
wampum money, peag(e)
war battle wounded knee

war prize scalp
warrior brave, sannup, sitting bull
water lily wocas, wokas
weapon bow and arrow, club, macana, rock, tomahawk
whaler hoh, quileute
wife squaw
wigwam See INDIAN *house.*
woman buckeen, coween, klooch, klootchman, mahala, mahaly, squaw, wench
woman, famous nancy ward, pocahontas, sacajawea
wundtkraut tobacco
yam cushcush
yellow pioury, purree, puri
"yes" how
INDIANA *capital* indianapolis
city bloomington, brazil, columbus, connersville, elkhart, evansville, gary, goshen, hobart, huntington, jasper, kokomo, lafayette, la porte, logansport, marion, mishawaka, muncie, richmond, south bend, terre haute, vincennes, wabash
college ball, bethel, depauw, goshen, marion, notre dame, purdue, wabash
county cass, davies, jasper, jay, tipton, vigo
indian miami, shawnee, wea
lake clear, manitou, michigan, monroe, wawasee
limestone bedford
native hoosier
nickname hoosier state
peak greensfort top
poet riley
port gary
river maumee, ohio, tippecanoe, wabash, white
state bird cardinal
state flower peony, zinnia
state tree tulip
INDIC See INDIA.
INDICATE allude, announce, argue, attest, augur, bespeak, betoken, cite, declare, denominate, denote, designate, disclose, display, evidence, evince, exhibit, express, foretoken, hint, import, intimate, manifest, mark, mean, mention, note, notify, point, prove, register, reveal, show, signify,

specify, suggest, symbolize, tell, testify, token, typify

INDICATION allusion, augury, auspice, brassard, denotation, earnest, emblem, evidence, hint, index, indicium, manifestation, mark, mention, milestone, note, omen, pledge, prognostic, proof, show, sign, suggestion, symbol, symptom, telltale, testimony, token, trace, vestige
vague glimmer, shadow

INDICATIVE auspicious, conclusive, diagnostic, emblematic, evidential, evincive, expressive, ominous, significant, suggestive, symbolic

INDICATOR annunciator, arrow, badge, beacon, blaze, blinker, brazilin, card, cock, detector, dial, earmark, flag, flare, float, gauge, hand, index, label, landmark, mark, pointer, polestar, register, seal, semaphore, sign(post), stamp, stylus, target, telltake, trace, vane
air-speed pneumometer
time gnomon

INDICT accuse, arraign, blame, charge, condemn, criminate, criticize, denounce, impeach, incriminate, panel, peach, summon, warrant

INDICTABLE reprehensible

INDICTMENT arraignment, charge, dittay, presentment, truebill

INDIFFERENCE accidie, acedia, adiaphorism, apathy, calm(ness), coldness, coldshoulder, coolness, disdain, disinterest, dispassion, disregard, froideur, impiety, inattention, inertia, insensibility, insouciance, languor, laziness, lethargy, listlessness, negligence, neutrality, nonchalance, phlegm, sloth, sluggishness, supineness, tepidity, tolerance, torpor, unconcern
expression of so what, what's the diff, who cares

INDIFFERENT aloof, apathetic, asocial, average, bland, blase, callous, careless, casual, cold, cool, detached, devil-may-care, dis-

interested, dispassionate, drab, dull, easy(going), emotionless, fair, frigid, halfhearted, heartless, heedless, idle, impartial, impassive, inattentive, incurious, insipid, insouciant, lackadaisical, languid, laodicean, lethargic, listless, lukewarm, mediocre, medium, middling, mindless, moderate, namby-pamby, negative, negligent, neuter, neutral, nonchalant, passive, perfunctory, phlegmatic, pluckless, pococurante, reckless, regardless, sans souci, soso, spiritless, spunkless, stoic(al), tepid, unbiased, unconcerned, unemotional, unfeeling, uninterested, unmindful, upsitten, vapid, wishywashy

INDIGENCE beggary, destitution, exigency, need, pauperism, penury, poverty, privation, straits, tenuity, want

INDIGENE aborigine, autochthon, endemic, native

INDIGENOUS aboriginal, autochthonal, autochtonous, domestic, edaphic, endemic, exotic, inborn, inherent, innate, native

INDIGENT beggar(ed), beggarly, bereaved, bereft, destitute, fleeced, free, impecunious, impoverished, insolvent, in want, necessitous, needy, pauperized, penniless, poor, poverty-stricken, s(c)hnorrer, stripped, void, wanting
group breadline, queue

INDIGESTION apepsia, apepsy, dyspepsia, dyspepsy, phthisis
cure alka seltzer, bromo seltzer, soda

INDIGNANT acrimonious, angered, angry, aroused, enraged, furious, hot, incensed, infuriated, irate, mad(dened), provoked, resentful, roiled, roused, stirred, wrathful, wroth

INDIGNATION anger, choler, complaint, contempt, disdain, displeasure, dudgeon, exasperation, fury, ire, passion, rage, resentment, scorn, wrath

INDIGNITY abuse, affront,

blasphemy, dudgeon, grievance, incivility, injury, injustice, insult, obloquy, offence, offense, outrage, slap, slight, slur, wrong

INDIGO amorpha, anil(la), bleacher, bluing, color, dye, inde, nill, shoofly, tephrosia, whitener, woad
and zinc indol
bale of serron
berry box-brier, randia, wild box
bird bunting, finch, grosbeak
blue false baptisia, rattlebush
bunting bird, blue pop, finch, grosbeak
bush mock-locust
commercial indigotin
copper covellite
derivative indole, ketole
essence indigotin
pert. anilic
source anil, indican, isatin, woad
wild baptisia, tumbleweed

INDIRECT about, allusive, ambagious, anfractuous, backhand(ed), circuitous, circular, collateral, covert, crooked, deviating, devious, dishonest, eventual, glancing, misleading, oblique, periphrastic, roundabout, secondary, sidelong, sinuous, tortuous, winding

INDIRECTNESS ambages, circuity, circumlocution, obliquity, periphrasis

INDISCERNIBLE imperceptible, infinitesimal, invisible, unintelligible

INDISCREET careless, foolish, hasty, heedless, illadvised, impolitic, imprudent, incautious, misguided, rash, silly, tactless, thoughtless, undiplomatic, unwise, witless

INDISCRETE compact, homogeneous

INDISCRETION blunder, booboo, error, folly, frippery, slip

INDISCRIMINATE aimless, assorted, casual, haphazard, imperceptive, miscellaneous, mixed, motley, promiscuous, shallow, superficial, sweeping, uncritical, unscrupulous, variegated, vast, wholesale, wide

INDISPENSABLE basal,

basic, cardinal, critical, essential, fundamental, imperative, important, key, necessary, needed, needful, requisite, vital

INDISPOSE afflict, disaffect, disincline, disorder

INDISPOSED abed, ailing, antagonistic, averse, disinclined, hesitant, hostile, ill, inimical, loath, reluctant, sick, unfriendly, unwell, unwilling

INDISPOSITION ailment, disease, ill-health, illness, infirmity, invalidism, malady, malaise, sickness

INDISPUTABLE apodictic, certain, evident, incontestable, indubitable, irrefragable, obvious, positive, sure, undeniable, unquestionable

INDISTINCT ambiguous, bleary, blurred, clouded, cloudy, dark, dim, dull, faint, foggy, fuzzy, hazy, inaudible, inconspicuous, indefinite, misty, muddy, murky, nebulous, obscure, pale, shadowy, slurry, smudged, unclear, undefined, unheard, vague, woolly

INDISTINGUISHABLE alike, ambiguous, imperceptible, unintelligible, vague

INDITE compose, describe, dictate, draw, inscribe, pen, phrase, prescribe, prompt, suggest, write

INDIUM source sphalerite

INDIVIDUAL apiece, azygote, azygous, being, bion(tic), characteristic, cog, concrete, different, diploid, distinct(ive), each, eidetic, gee, head, identity, isolate(d), man, monad(ic), morphon, numeric, one, particular, peculiar, person(al), piece, proper, respective, self, separate, several, single, sole, solitary, sort, special, specific, specimen, spirit, thing, unconventional, unique, unit
comb. idio
dull boeotian
immature adultoid
impudent boldface
mosaic gynander

mutant saltant
physiological bion
selfish egoist, egotist
slovenly grobian
smug prig
stupid hobbil
undersized kit(t)
winged alate
young kid, youth

INDIVIDUALISM centricity, disposition, ego(ism) (tism), independence, uniqueness

INDIVIDUALIST braggart, freelance, freethinker, independent, isolationist, loner, mugwump, neutral, nonpartisan

INDIVIDUALITY character, complexion, egohood, ethology, hecceity, identity, nature, particularity, personality, quality, seity, selfdom, selfhood, temper (ament), unit

INDIVIDUALLY a la carte, apart, apiece, each, one by one, respectively, severally, singly

INDIVIDUATION *principle* ahankara

INDIVISIBLE element, indiscerptible, inseparable, undividable

INDO-ARYAN jat, khatri, rajput
deity indra

INDOCHINA (See also VIETNAM.) annam, assam, burma, cambodia, laos, malaya, siam, thailand
agriculture caste meo
bay bengal
bull zebu
city (See also under individual countries.) danang, hanoi, pakse, saigon, vinh
coin piaster, sapek
kingdom an(n)am
language See INDOCHINA
people.
military command arvn, cosvn
people adi, ahom, ak(h)a, amoy, anu, apatani, bama, bodo, bogum, bokar, bomi, bori, burmese, dafla, dagaru, dalbing, gallong, garo, ghao, havi, idu, kami, karkang, karko, kho, lai, lao, longphi, lungchang, lungri, mat(h)un, mayun, memba, midri, mihi, miji, miju, milang, minyong,

mishmi, mitanong, moklong, monpa, moshang, mro, mru, naga, nalobag, nocte, nyubbu, nyullu, palibos, ponggi, ponthai, pwo, rong, rundras, sac, sai, sak, sedang, sgau, shan, sherdukpen, singpho, sulung, tagin, taitangsa, thai, thong, tikhak, vietnamese, wancho
pert. seriform
sea south china
tree eng, mee, teak

INDOCTRINATE brief, coach, edify, imbue, implant, inculcate, initiate, instill, instruct, plant, teach

INDOCTRINATION brainwashing, briefing, inculcation, instruction, summary, teaching

INDO-EUROPEAN arian, aryan, caucasian, czech, lett, serb, slav
language aequian, afghan, anglo-saxon, armenian, balochi, baltic, baluchi, catalan, celtic, cornish, danish, english, gaelic, germanic, gothic, greek, indic, iranian, italian, italic, kafiri, latin, lettic, manx, norwegian, phrygian, polish, sabellian, sanskrit, slav(on)ic, spanish, swedish, welsh

INDOLE ketole

INDOLENCE ergophobia, hoboism, idleness, inertia, languor, laziness, lethargy, musardry, sloth(fulness), sluggishness, spring fever, vagrancy
personified laurence, lawrence

INDOLENT bone-idle, comatose, dilatory, do-nothing, dronish, drony, drowsy, easy, faineant, good-fornothing, idle, inactive, inert, lackadaisical, laggard, languid, lax, lazy, lethargic, listless, ne'er-do-well, otiose, passive, picktooth, remiss, shiftless, slack, slothful, sluggish sorn, supine, sweer, torpid

INDO-MALAYAN See MONGOLIAN.

INDOMITABLE dauntless, dogged, doughty, formidable, impregnable, inexpugnable, intrepid, invincible, invulnerable, refractory,

resolute, stanch, staunch, steadfast, stubborn, undaunted
INDONESIA *aborigine* alfur
administrators priyay, satyra
airline djakarta
animal tarsier
behavior principles musjawarah
bicycle taxi bejak
capital batavia, djakarta, jacarta, jakarta
christian sambal
city bandoeng, bandung, bogor, buitenjorg, djakarta, hollandia, jogjakarta, jokjakarta, makasar, malang, manado, medan, semarang, surabaja, surabaya
coin rupia, sen
communist force vietminh
communist party pki
congress mprs
country bali, java, sumatra
dagger kri(s)
dance horse-trance
discussion musjawarah
drum gangsa
fruit mangosteen, salak
gulf bone, tolo, tomini
gypsy selung
herb aglaonema
hindu empire madjapahit
indian ata
island alor, aras, ar(r)u, bali, ban(a)ka, ban(g)ka, bawean, belito(e)ng, belitung, biak, billiton, borneo, buru, butung, celebes, ceram, flores, halmahe(i)ra, irian, java, kalimantan, komodo, krakatau, lombok, madoera, madura, new guinea, nias, obi, pag(a)i, peleng, rot(t)i, salajar, sawu, sulawesi, sumatra, sumba, sumbawa, ternate, tidore, timor, weh, wetar
island group anambas, aroe, banjak, ewab, molucca, natuna, sabalana, spice, sulawesi, sunda, tabelan
lake ranau, toba, towuti
language bahasa, chamorro, gyarung, igorot, malayan, tetum
law adat
leader suharto, sukarno
lizard komodo-dragon
market pasar
measure depa, depoh
mutual help gotong-royong
news agency aneta

oil monopoly pertamina
oil monopoly head ibnu sutowo
ox anoa
palace kraton
party musjumi
peak bulu, dempo, katopaso, kerintji, leuser, mahameru, menjapa, murjo, napa, niut, ogoamas, raja, rindjani, samosir, slamet, talakmau
people alfur(ata), ata, atta, bagobo, batavian, bat(t)a, battak, bontok, bukidnon, dadayag, dyak, ifugao, igorot(e), kankanai, lampong, manobo, nabaloi, nesiot, sadang, silipan, subanun, tapiro, yami
play wayang
port balikpapan, macassas, semarang, surabaya
president suharto, sukarno
priest caste brahmana
pyramid borobudar, stupa
range barisan, muller, quarles, schwaner
river barito, digul, hari, kajan, kampar, kapuas, mahakam, musi, pawan
sea arafura, banda, celebes, ceram, flores, java, timor
sea gypsy selung
shop toko
soothsayer dukin
strait lombok, makassar, sunda
stupa borobudar
supply base lae
teacher abangan, kijai, santri, ulama
temple borobudur, mendut, prambanan
tree supa
villager abangan
volcano agung, awoe, awu, raung, slamet, tambora
weight catty, ounce, soekoe, thail
wind broeboe, brubu
INDOOR *golf* dice
sports arena astrodome
INDO-PORTUGUESE *half-caste* topas(s), topaz
measure covid(o)
INDORSE See ENDORSE.
INDRA mahendra, meghavahana, sakka, sakra, svargapati, vajri, visvakarma
consort indrani
dragon vritra
elephant airavata
enemy durvasas, tvashtri, vritra

heaven amaravati, svarga, swarga
home mount meru
nymphs apsaras
son arjuna, sitragupta
steed airavata
thunderbolt vajra
INDUBITABLE apparent, certain, evident, factual, manifest, sure, undeniable, unquestionable
INDUCE abet, activate, actuate, allure, bring on, cajole, carry, cause, coax, conclude, contrive, decide, determine, dispose, draw on, drive, effect, elicit, engage, enlist, entice, evoke, exhort, get, impel, incite, incline, influence, inspire, instigate, interest, invite, lead(on), motivate, obtain, persuade, prevail on, procure, prompt, provoke, reason(with), seduce, spur, suborn, sway, urge, wheedle
INDUCEMENT allurement, bribe, come-on, enticement, goad, impetus, impulse, incentive, lure, motive, occasion, reason, seduction, spring, spur, stimulant, stimulus
INDUCIVE suasive
INDUCT begin, bring in, enroll, inaugurate, initiate, install, introduce, invest
INDUCTANCE *unit* henry
INDUCTIBLE inflexible, unyielding
INDUCTION beginning, commencement, conclusion, enrollment, entrance, epagoge, initiation, installation, persuasion
INDULGE arride, baby, cade, cater to, cherish, coddle, cosset, debauch, delight, dissipate, enjoy, favor, foster, gratify, humor, jolly, luxuriate, mollycoddle, oblige, pamper, pet, pettle, please, regale, satisfy, spoil, tolerate, wallow(in), yield(to)
to excess debauch, pamper, surfeit
with furnish
INDULGENCE allowance, binge, charity, clemency, cocker, coddling, compassion, compliance, debauchery, excess, favor(ing), forbearance, forgiveness, glut-

tony, grace, humoring, kindness, lenience, leniency, lenity, liberality, license, mercy, mollycoddling, obliging, pampering, pardon, patent, patience, pleasing, privilege, remission, spree, sufferance, tenderness, thoughtfulness, tolerance
granter church, king, pardoner

INDULGENT accommodating, agreeable, amiable, big(hearted), charitable, clement, complaisant, compliant, condoning, decent, easygoing, fond, forbearant, forbearing, generous, gracious, greathearted, kind(ly), lenient, meek, merciful, mild, obliging, patient, permissive, sympathetic, temperate, tolerant, understanding

INDURATE(D) adamant (ine), callous, harden(ed), inexorable, inflexible, inure, obdurate, rigid, scleroid, stiff, strengthen, stubborn, tough, unfeeling

INDURATION hardening, hardness, insensitivity

INDUS sindon
city harappa, mohenjo-daro
people dard, gor
tributary sutlej

INDUSTRIALIST baron, businessman, entrepreneur, executive, financier, magnate, nabob, producer, shogun, tycoon

INDUSTRIOUS active, assiduous, busy, deedy, diligent, dynamic, eident, laborious, live(ly), painstaking, persevering, persisting, sedulous, skillful, tireless, toiling, untiring, unwearied, virtuous, working, zealous
name meaning amelia, emil(e)

INDUSTRY activity, application, assiduity, business, commerce, diligence, effort, enterprise, gooseberry, ingenuity, labor, pursuit, sedulity, sedulousness, skill, task, toil, trade, traffic, vigor, work, zeal(ousness)
symbol of bee

INDWELL abide, inhabit, inhere

INDWELLER denizen, in-

digene, inhabitant, sojourner

INDWELLING immanent, inherent

INEBRIATE(D) alcoholic, carouser, DRUNK(ARD), drunken, excite, exhilarate, high, intoxicate(d), loaded, sot, souse, squiffy, stupefied, tight, tippler, tipsy, toper, tosspot

INEDIBLE bad, high, poisonous, rank, rotten, spoiled, unfit

INEFFABLE abstract, divine, empyrean, ethereal, heavenly, holy, ideal, indescribable, nameless, sacred, transcendent(al), unutterable

INEFFECTIVE adiaphoral, adiaphorous, awkward, barren, bathetic, bootless, bumbling, clumsy, defeasible, dud, empty, faineant, fruitless, futile, halting, hollow, idle, impotent, inadequate, incompetent, inefficient, inept, innocuous, inoperative, invalid, null(and void), otiose, sterile, unproductive, useless, vain, weak

INEFFECTIVENESS bathos, futility, impotence, inefficacy, useless, vain, vanity, weak

INEFFECTUAL See INEFFECTIVE.

INEFFICACY futility, inability, inefficiency

INEFFICIENCY inability, incapacity

INEFFICIENT clumsy, decrepit, doless, faineant, feckless, feeble, ill, incapable, incompetent, indolent, inept, lame, lax, lazy, neglectful, negligent, poor, remiss, slack, slothful

INELASTIC flabby, flaccid, inductile, inflexible, irresilient, rigid, unyielding

INELEGANT awkward, boorish, bourgeoise, graceless, hoyden, philistine, rude, stiff, tasteless, ugly, ungraceful, unpolished, unrefined, wooden

INELIGIBLE inexpedient, undesirable, unqualified, unworthy

INELUCTABLE apodictic, certain, destined, doomed,

fated, inescapable, inevitable, irresistible, necessary, prescribed

INEPT absurd, artless, asinine, awkward, clumsy, empty, fatuous, foolish, footless, gauche, inadept, incompetent, intrusive, latent, maladroit, pointless, senseless, silly, stupid, supine, torpid, unapt, unbecoming, unfit, unskilled, unskillful, unsuitable

INEQUALITY anomaly, disparity, disproportion, disquiparation, diversity, imparity, inconstancy, unevenness

INEQUITABLE hard, uneven, unfair, unjust, wrong

INEQUITY discrimination, favoritism, injustice, unfairness, wrong

INERADICABLE indelible, indestructible, inerasable, lasting, permanent

INERRANT accurate, certain, correct, dependable, exact, impeccable, infallible, precise, reliable, trustworthy

INERT abeyant, amort, apathetic, asleep, comatose, dead, dormant, dull, flat, foul, heavy, idle, inactive, inanimate, languid, languorous, latent, lazy, leaden, lethargic, lifeless, listless, logy, numb, paralyzed, passive, phlegmatic, slack, sleeping slow, sluggard, sluggish, slumbering, smoldering, stagnant, standing, static, still, stolid, sullen, supine, suspended, tame, torpid

INERTIA apathy, indolence, oscitancy, paralysis, stagnation, stupor, tamas, torpidity, torpor, vegetation

INESCAPABLE apparent, apodictic, certain, ineludable, inevitable, inflexible, necessary, unhidden

INESTIMABLE dear, incalculable, invaluable, priceless, sumless, valuable, worthy

INEVASIBLE certain, inevitable, unavoidable

INEVITABLE apodictic, appointed, certain, decided, decisive, destined, determined, direct, doomed, due, fated, fateful, ineluctable, inexorable, necessary, nemesis, prescribed, settled, sure, unavoidable

INEXACT free, inaccurate, rough, vague

INEXCITABLE calm, coldblooded, collected, cool, philosophical, placid, quiet, serene, sober, steady, stoical, tranquil

INEXHAUSTIBLE infinite, tireless, unfailing

INEXORABLE adamant(ine), firm, grim, immobile, inflexible, merciless, obdurate, relentless, resolute, rigorous, steadfast, stern, stony, stormy, strict, unmovable, unyielding

INEXPEDIENT awkward, bad, detrimental, ill-advised, imprudent, inadmissable, inadvisable, ineligible, infelicitous, infradig, malapropos, objectionable, unfit, unfortunate, unhappy, unqualified, unsuitable, untimely, unwise, wrong

INEXPENSIVE catchpenny, cheap, cut-rate, economical, half-price, marked down, nominal, reasonable, reduced

INEXPERIENCE immaturity, innocence, naivete, verdancy

INEXPERIENCED callow, green, ignorant, inexpert, innocent, naive, puny, raw, sophomoric, strange, unpracticed, unskilled, untrained, unworldly, young
person babe, colt, greenhorn

INEXPERT crude, green, rude, unskilled

INEXPIABLE implacable

:INEXPLICABLE inconceivable, insoluble, insolvable, unaccountable

INEXPRESSIBLE boundless, indescribable, ineffable, infinite, nameless, rare, subtle, tenuous, unspeakable

INFALLIBLE certain, faultless, flawless, inerrable, inerrant, inevitable, necessary, perfect, right, unerring

INFAMOUS base, bleeding, bloody, caitiff, corrupt, degenerate, disgraceful, disreputable, evil, flagrant, foul, ignoble, inglorious, nefarious, notorious, odi-

ous, ruddy, scandalous, shady, shameful, terrible, vicious, wicked

INFAMY abasement, atrocity, discredit, disgrace, dishonor, disrepute, ignobility, ignominiousness, notoriety, obloquy, opprobrium, scandal, shame, stain, villainy

INFANCY babyhood, beginning, childhood, cradle, immaturity, incunabula, minority, nonage, start

INFANT, INFANT'S babe, baby(kins), bairn, bambino, bantling, bastard, bottle-boy, brat, child, chit, chrisom, immature, innocent, milksop, minor, neonate, nestling, novice, nurseling, papoose, pitsel(eh), suckling, tender, tiny, toddlekins, toddler, tot, weanie, weanling, yearling, youth
breath madder, moneywort
cereal pablum
digit piggy
murder infanticide
naked scuddy
newborn neonate, neonatus
premature premie
room nursery
slip gertrude
voracious killcrop
wear bootee, creepers, diapers
wrapper pilch

INFANTILE bab(y)ish, beginning, childish, dollish, kittenish, newborn, puerile
paralysis poliomyelitis
school kindergarten

INFANTILISM ateliosis, puerility, retardation

INFANTRY fanterie, footfolk, foot soldiers, rifles
man askar(i), chasseur, clodhopper, dogface, doggie, doughboy, dragoon, footslogger, fusilier, gi joe, musketeer, pioupiou, slogger, sorefoot, zouave
helmet morion
mounted cavalry
volunteers arditi

INFATUATE befool, besot, captivate, charm, enamor, fanatic, fool, lover, obsess, stupify

INFATUATED assot, beguiled, besotted, captivated, captive, deceived, deluded, dotty, duped, enamored, en-

gouee, enthusiastic, fatuous, fond, foolish, gone, gulled, in love, smitten

INFATUATION beguin, calf love, case, crush, desire, engouement, flame, folly, foolishness, love, madness, mania, mash, pash, passion, puppy love, rave
goddess ate

INFECT affect, canker, color, contaminate, corrupt, defile, deprave, disease, dye, empest, excite, infest, inspire, poison, pollute, smittle, taint

INFECTED cankered, contaminated, corrupt, defiled, diseased, impure, insanitary, poisoned, polluted, septic, tainted, unhygienic

INFECTION bacillosis, cold, contagion, contamination, corruption, disease, dose, epidemic, fungus, implication, inspiration, miasm(a), pollution, septicity, taint, virus
free from aseptic, sterile
treatment antibiotics, antitoxin

INFECTIOUS catching, communicable, contagious, epidemic, infective, mephitic, pestilent(ial), poisonous, smitable, smitting, taking, toxic, virulent

INFELICITOUS gauche, improper, inapt, inexpedient, unfortunate, unhappy, unmeet, unseemly, untimely

INFELICITY anguish, misery, misfortune, pain, unhappiness

INFER argue, assume, conclude, consider, construe, deduce, derive, divine, draw, fetch, gather, guess, imply, interpret, intuit, judge, mean, presume, reason, speculate, suppose, surmise, think

INFERENCE analogy, conclusion, conjecture, corollary, deduction, hypothesis, illation, implication, judgment, presumption, reasoning, sequel(a), sequitur, surmise

INFERENTIAL deducible, hypothetical, illative, implicative, implicit, implied, putative, speculative, suggestive, understood, virtual

INFERIOR amateur, bad (dish), bauch, behind, below, brummagem, bum, bush(league), cagmag, cheesy, coarse, common, counterfeit, crappy, crummy, deficient, dick(e)y, dog(gy), dubious, feeble, gaudy, gross, humble, inadequate, indifferent, junior, less, low(class) (grade)(test), lower, meager, mean, mediocre, menial, minor, nether, off, ordinary, paltry, pedary, petty, picayune, poor(er), puisny, punk, rotten, scrub(by), secondary, second-best, second-class, shabby, shoddy, sleazy, smaller, subaltern, subject, subordinate, third-rate, tin, under, unequal, unsatisfactory, worthless

INFERIORITY diffidence, meanness, mediocrity, subservience
comb. aster

INFERNAL accursed, all-fired, avernal, bad, black, chthonian, cruel, cursed, damnable, demoniacal, demonic, devilish, diabolical, eternal, evil, execrable, fiendish, hadean, hateful, hellish, malicious, malignant, monstrous, nefarious, plutonic, satanic, sheolic, stygian, tartarean, vicious, villainous, wicked
machine bomb
region See HELL, UNDERWORLD.

INFERNO abyss, avernus, fire, hades, hell, limbo, pit, purgatory

INFERRED assumed, implicit, tacit

INFERTILE barren, depleted, drained, exhausted, impotent, lean, poor, sterile, thin, unfruitful

INFEST abound, assail, beset, bother, crawl, creep, frequent, haunt, infect, invade, molest, overrun, pester, plague, ravage, swarm, teem, torment, vex, worry

INFESTATION acariasis, invasion, pediculosis, plague, scale

INFESTED beset, blown, buggy, fluky, grubby, harassed, haunted, lousy, overrun, pedicular, pediculous, plagued, ratty, ravaged, tormented, wormy

INFEUDATION enfeoffment

INFIDEL agnostic, atheist, deist, ethnic(al), free-thinker, giaour, goi, goy (im), heathen, heretic, kaffir, non-believer, pagan(ist), paynim, saracen, skeptic, unbeliever, unorthodox, zendician, zendik(ite)

INFIDELITY adultery, agnosticism, atheism, bad faith, barratry, breach of promise, corruption, dereliction, disaffection, disbelief, disloyalty, faithlessness, falseness, falsity, fickleness, inconstancy, perfidy, recreancy, secularism, trahison, unbelief, unfaithfulness

INFILTRATE absorb, filter, impregnate, penetrate, permeate, saturate, soak, tinge

INFINITE almighty, big, boundless, chaos, cosmic, countless, endless, eternal, everlasting, great, illimitable, illimited, immeasurable, immense, incalculable, indeterminate, innumerable, interminable, limitless, measureless, olamic, sempiternal, shoreless, termless, ubiquitous, unbounded, unending, unfathomable, universal, unlimited, unnumbered
absorption into nirvana

INFINITESIMAL atomic, corpuscular, evanescent, impalpable, imperceptible, imponderable, inappreciable, inconsiderable, insensible, insignificant, intangible, invisible, microscopic, minuscule, molecular, small, tiny, unseeable
bit atom, bicron

INFINITY all-inclusiveness, all-presence, ananta, boundlessness, eternity, immensity, olam, omnipotence, perpetuity, ubiquity

INFIRM aged, ailing, anile, brittle, casalty, casselty, collapsed, craichy, cranky, crippled, cronk, debilitated, decrepit, disabled, doddering, dowless, failing, faltering, feeble, fragile, frail, grey, haggard, ill, insecure, invalid, irresolute, languishing, out-of-order, pale, pathologic(al), peaked, poor(ish), poorly, precarious, run down, senile, shaky, sick(ly), unhealthy, unsound, unstable, unstrong, unsure, valetudinary, wayward, weak (ish)(ly)

INFIRMARY clinic, hospital, surgery

INFIRMITY caducity, disease, failing, fault, frailty, old age, senility, shortcoming, sickliness, weakness

INFIX establish, imbue, implant, impress, inculcate, infuse, ingrain, insert, instill, pierce, set(tle), thrust

INFLAME aggravate, agitate, anger, animate, anneal, arouse, blain, blister, burn, enkindle, enrage, eschaufe, excite, fan, fester, fire, fluster, heat, ignite, incense, incite, infuriate, inspire, intensify, irritate, kindle, light, madden, nettle, provoke, rankle, rile, rouse, spur, stimulate
with love enamor
with rage infuriate, madden

INFLAMED angry, bleezy, burning, emotional, feverish, fiery, flagrant, fretty, hot, passionate, red, torrid, vehement

INFLAMMABLE accendible, ardent, burnable, combustible, excitable, fiery, fuel, irascible, kindling, piceous, tindery, touchy
cinnabar idrialite
gas aliphatic, butane, ethane
liquid acetone, methane
substance amadou, punk, tinder

INFLAMMATION anger, combustion, conflagration, excitement, festering, fire, firing, ignition, irritation, kindling, rankling, scald, sore
comb. itis
kind adenitis, angina, arthritis, arthrosia, bursitis, canker, carbuncle, catarrh, chafing, coxitis, cystitis, encephalitis, felon, fistula, gastritis, gleet, gonitis, gout,

ileitis, iritis, myositis, omitis, otitis, phlebitis, phlegmasia, pimelitis, poliomyelitis, r(h)achitis, rickets, rubor, sacritis, scleritis, sebel, shingles, sunburn

remedy antiphlogistic, antipyrotic, antiseptic

symptom calor, dolor, rubor, tumor

INFLAMMATORY enkindling, incendiary, inflaming, kindling, lighting, phlogistic

INFLATE amplify, augment, balloon, bloat, blow up, dilate, distend, enlarge, exalt, expand, forblow, hove, huff(le), impel, increase, kite, magnify, outswell, overdo, puff, pump, sufflate, swell, tumefy

INFLATED bellied, bloated, blown, blustery, bollen, bombastic, diffuse, dilated, distended, flatulent, flowery, fustian, overblown, pompous, pretentious, prolix, rhetorical, showy, sore, stilted, swollen, tumid, tumorous, turgid, verbose, wordy

INFLATION boom, bullation, distension, expansion, flatulence, overcharge, overprice, pomposity, pompousness, proliferation, spiral, turgidity

INFLECT bend, bow, compare, conjugate, curve, decline, deflect, modulate, sound

INFLECTION accent, accidence, angle, bend, crook, curvature, curve, flexion, flexure, grammar, intonation, modulation, pitch, pronunciation, sign, tenor, tone, turn

of words paradigm

INFLEXIBLE adamant(ine), brassbound, cast-iron, dogged, firm, grim, hard, headstrong, immobile, immovable, immutable, implacable, inductive, inelastic, inexorable, intractable, intractile, iron(clad), irresilient, marble, mulish, obdurate, obstinate, resolute, rigid, rigorous, severe, solid, stark, staunch, stern, stiff, stout, strict, stringent, stubborn, tense, tough, un-

alterable, unbending, unlimber, unmalleable, unpliable, unpliant, unruly, unyielding, wooden

INFLEXIBILITY acampsia

INFLICT add, afflict, bring upon, deal, foist, impose, ramrod, strike, trouble, wreak

INFLICTION bane, disgrace, punishment, scourge, trouble

INFLORESCENCE ament, anthesis, anthotaxy, arrow, capitulum, catkin, cattail, chat, cone, corymb, cyathium, cyme, fascicle, head, panicle, raceme, spadix, spike(let), strobile, tassel, thyrse, thyrsus, umbel, whorl

-bearing umbellate, umbel(l)ed

INFLUENCE action, advance, affect, approach, arouse, ascendancy, attinge, attract(ion), authority, bearing, bend, bias, blandish, bribe, carry, cause, clout, consequence, control, count, credit, dispose, dominance, domination, drive, effect, eminence, force, get at, hold, impel, import (ance), impress, incline, induce, lead, leverage, lobby, magnetize, mastery, moment, motivate, move, outweigh, permeate, persuade, potency, power, predispose, predominance, prejudice, pressure, prestige, prompt, pull, reach, rein, rouse, rule, sanction, soften up, stir, stress, supremacy, sway, swing, touch, upperhand, weigh, weight, whip-hand, win, wirepull, work on

by fixed idea obsess

controlling sway

evil bale, blast, malice

peddling intrigue, mordida

peddling attorney coyote

restraining cord, damper, wetblanket

soothing balm, salve

using wire-pulling

INFLUENCED affected, biased, partial, persuaded, prejudiced, unfair, unjust

easily amenable, plastic, pliable, pliant, pushover, sub-

ject, susceptible, waxen, waxy

INFLUENTIAL ascendant, authoritative, consequential, dominant, effective, effectual, grave, important, inspiring, momentous, potent, powerful, predominant, prepollent, prepotent, prevailing, regnant, ruling, strong, substantial, swaying, telling, weighty

INFLUENZA a-victoria, catarrh, coryza, flu, grip(pe), leuma, pinkeye, swine

epidemic spanish lady

INFLUX illapse, import, indraft, indraught, inflow, inpour(ing), inrun, inrush, mouth, storm, tide

INFORM acquaint, advertise, advise, animate, apprise, avail, blab, brief, caution, edify, educate, endow, enlighten, familiarize, fink, fire, imbue, impart, infuse, initiate, inspire, instill, instruct, invest, kindle, notify, peach, rat, show, signify, sing, squeal, suggest, teach, tell, train, vivify, warn, wise, witter

against betray, blab, blow, fink, peach, sing, snitch, squeal

INFORMAL bohemian, breezy, candid, casual, chatty, colloquial, common, democratic, easy(going), familiar, folksy, free(and easy), homelike, homely, irregular, natural, offhand, plain, simple, sociable, unaffected, unassuming, unceremonious, unconventional, undignified, unofficial

INFORMANT, INFORMER adviser, agent, announcer, authority, betrayer, bird, blab(ber), blabbermouth, canary, finger, fink, herald, insider, messenger, monitor, mouchard, mouthpiece, nark, peacher, propagandist, reporter, rusty, snitch(er), source, spokesman, spotter, spy, squeaker, squealer, stool(pigeon), stoolie, sycophant, talebearer, tanquam, tattler, tattletale, telltale, tipper, tipster, tout(er), traitor, undercover agent, whistle-blower, witness

INFORMATION account, advice, air, ammunition, aviso, briefing, communication, communique, confidence, data, dope, dossier, enlightenment erudition, facts, hint, instruction, intelligence, intimation, knowledge, larnin, learning, light, lore, mention, monition, news, notice, notification, propaganda, report, revelation, scoop, sidelight, statement, tale, tidings, tip, wisdom, word
bit of grif(fin), wrinkle
condensed digest
detailed dossier
giver See INFORMANT.
obtainer bug, wiretap
personal dossier
retrieval data-recovery
secret arcanum
unit bit, byte

INFORMATIVE advisory, descriptive, didactic, edifying, educational, enlightening, instructive, newsy, revelatory

INFORMED abreast, apprized, aware, familiar, hep, hip, knowing, knowledgeable, learned, up on, up to date, wise

INFORMER See INFORMANT.

INFRACTION breach, crime, error, lapse, offense, scandal, sin, slip, transgression, trespass, vice, violation

INFRANGIBLE inseparable, tough, unbreakable

INFREQUENT fugitive, irregular, occasional, rare, scarce, seldom, singular, sparse, spasmodic, sporadic, strange, uncommon, unique, unusual

INFRINGE break, butt in, contravene, disobey, encroach, entrench, infract, interlope, intrude, invade, obtrude, transgress, trench, trespass, violate

INFRINGEMENT breach, foul, infraction, intrusion, invasion, piracy, plagiarism, transgression, trespass, violation

INFURIATE affront, agitate, aggravate, anger, angry, an-

tagonize, bestir, enrage, exasperate, furious, incense, insult, irate, ire, madden, offend, outrage, provoke, roil, vex

INFUSE animate, breathe, distill, drench, fill, fire, imbue, immit, implant, inculcate, infix, inform, ingrain, inoculate, insinuate, inspire, instill, introduce, leaven, macerate, mix, permeate, pervade, pour, saturate, shed, soak, steep, suffuse, tincture

INFUSION admixture, affusion, baptism, decoction, extract, grout, inpouring, inspiration, instillation, tea, tincture, tisane, wort

INFUSORIA acineta(e), animalcule, animalculum, cilia, lepocyte, vorticella

INGA guava, huamuchil, mimosa, tree

INGATHERING assembly, harvest

INGEMINATE duplicate, iterate, redouble, reiterate, repeat

INGENIOUS adept, adroit, artful, ben trovato, bright, capable, clever, creative, cunning, daedal, deft, expert, feat, fine, gifted, handy, intellectual, inventive, mental, proficient, resourceful, sharp, shrewd, skilled, skillful, talented

INGENUE actress, innocent, juvenile, soubrette

INGENUITY address, art (ifice), candor, cleverness, genius, industry, intelligence, invention, originality, resourcefulness, skill, talent, wit

INGENUOUS artless, candid, childlike, clear, frank, guileless, honest, innocent, naif, naive, natural, open, plain simple, sincere, straightforward, transparent, unaffected, unfeigned

INGEST absorb, consume, eat, incept, slurp, swallow

INGLE angle, blaze, cajole, catamite, corner, fire (place), flame, fondle, hearth, wheedle
cheek fireside
nook chimney-corner, hearth

INGLORIOUS disreputable,

humble, infamous, shameful

INGLUVIES belly, craw, crop

INGOT bar, cast(ing), gad, lingot, mold, pig, sycee
brass strip
metal gad, pig
silver schuyt, shoe, sycee, ting
top crophead
worker barman

INGRAIN carpet, color, imbue, infix, infuse, innate, inwrought, native, saturate, suffuse

INGRAINED coarse, confirmed, deepdyed, deepseated, essential, established, fixed, implanted, inherent, inveterate, rooted

INGRATE disagreeable, oppress, snake, thankless, uncongenial, unfriendly, ungrateful, weigh down

INGRATIATE blandish, coax, fawn, flatter, insinuate, toady, truckle

INGRATIATING bland, disarming, fawning, obsequious, servile, silken, silky, sleek, slick, smooth, soapy, soft

INGREDIENT component, constituent, detail, element, factor, integrant, item, part (icular)
fundamental base, basis

INGRESS access, admission, entrance, entree, entry, gate, immigration, influx, portal

INGROWN enclosed, established

INHABIT abide, berth, board, bunk, colonize, cover, dwell, hang out, indwell, keep, live, lodge, nest, nide, occupy, perch, people, plant, populate, possess, remain, reside, room, roost, settle, squat, stay, tenant

INHABITANT addressee, burgher, citizen, commorant, denizen, dweller, householder, incolant, incumbent, inmate, lodger, occupant, resident, roomer, sojourner, tenant, villager
comb. ese, ite
earliest known aborigine
foreign alien(icola), immigrant, straniere

local autochthon, indigene, native

northern septentrion

transient migrant, sojourner, visitor

INHALATION breath, drag, wind

treatment anemopathy

INHALE aspirate, breathe, drag, draw, inhaust, inspire, insufflate, puff, respire, smell, smoke, sniff, snuff(le), suck(le)

INHARMONIOUS absurd, cat-and-dog, conflicting, different, discordant, dissentient, jarring, off-color, unmusical

INHERE abide, belong, cleave, consist, indwell, lie, lodge, reside, stick

INHERENT abiding, basic, belonging, built-in, component, congenital, enorganic, essential, existing, habitual, immanent, inalienable, inborn, inbred, incorporated, indwelling, infixed, ingrained, innate, inner, instinctive, integral, iternal, intrinsic, inward, native, natural, resident, typical

INHERIT acquire, come by, come into, fall heir to, get, receive, succeed

INHERITANCE benefaction, bequest, birthright, coparceny, entail, estate, gift, heirloom, hereditas, heredity, landfall, legacy, parcenary, patrimony, vacantia

acceptance of cerniture

by first-born primogeniture

cattle erf

law annat

portion legitime

restricted entailment

seizer abator

INHERITED bred, congenital, engendered, genetic, genic, hereditary, inborn, inbred, innate, lineal, transmitted

INHERITOR beneficiary, crown prince, heir(ess), legatee, parcener, recipient

INHIBIT arrest, avert, ban, bar, bridle, check, curb, debar, deter, enjoin, forbid, hinder, hold in, keep in, interdict, obstruct, obviate,

preclude, prevent, prohibit, repress, restrain, snaffle, stifle, stop, suppress, trammel, withhold

INHIBITED constrained, reserved

INHIBITION control, constraint, repression, reserve, restraint, sublimation, suppression

comb. ant(i)

INHOSPITABLE aloof, barren, cold, cool, desert, stern

INHUMAN animal, barbarous, bestial, black, bloodless, bloody, brutal, cruel, devilish, diabolical, fell, feral, ferocious, fiendish, fierce, grim, hellish, malicious, malign(ant), manless, merciless, pitiless, relentless, ruthless, savage, truculent, unfeeling, unkind

INHUME bury, entomb, inter

INIA bouto, dolphin

INIMICAL adverse, antagonistic, averse, contrary, hostile, hurtful, unfavorable, unfriendly, warlike

INIQUITOUS bad, corrupt, evil, godless, heinous, ill, infamous, miscreant, nefarious, pernicious, sinful, ungodly, vicious, vile, villainous, wrong

INIQUITY abomination, crime, evil, guilt, harm, injustice, mischief, misdeed, offense, sin, vice, wickedness, wrong(doing)

INITIAL approve, beginning, capital, clear, first, head, incipient, inscribe, letter, maiden, mark, name, okay, opening, original, ratify, sign, start, virgin

design of monogram

interpretation nutrakon

ornamental letter paraph, rubric, rune

INITIATE admit, baptize, begin, brace, break(in), brief, commence, edify, enlighten, epopt, establish, formalize, found, ground, haze, inaugurate, indoctrinate, induct, inform, install, instate, institute, instruct, introduce, invent, invest, launch, novice, open, organize, receive, start, teach

INITIATION baptism, begin-

ning, blooding, bora, bow, ceremony, debut, diksha, entrance, entry, inaugural, inauguration, installation, reception

INITIATIVE act, ambition, beginning, enterprise, getup, gumption, law, mandate, pep, plebiscite, push, referendum

INJECT cast, drive, immit, infuse, insert, interpolate, interpose, interrupt, intromit, offer, propose, suggest, throw

INJECTION booster, clyster, congestion, hint, hypo, intrusion, needle, piercing, shot, vaccination

direct mainline

INJUDICIOUS foolish, illadvised, indiscreet, misguided, rash, unwise

INJUNCTION admonition, ado, advice, ban, bar, behest, bidding, charge, command, denial, dictate, dictation, direction, enjoinder, hest, imperative, instruction, mandament, mandate, order, precept, prohibition, regulation, rescript, rule, taboo, tabu, warning

INJURE abuse, afflict, affront, batter, blast, blemish, break, bruise, burn, calk, cap, caulk, char, cripple, damage, deface, deform, disfigure, distort, gall, grieve, harm, hinder, hurt, illtreat, impair, insult, lame, maim, maltreat, mangle, mar, mistreat, mutilate, offend, outrage, pique, prejudice, scathe, scotch, singe, spite, spoil, sting, strain, sully, teen, terrify, werd, wound, wrong

by exposure ret

INJURIOUS abusive, atrocious, bad, baneful, damaging, deadly, deleterious, detrimental, harmful, hurtful, mischievous, noxious, pernicious, slanderous, unjust, wrackful, wrongful

INJURY abuse, affront, agony, bale, bane, blemish, blight, breach, bruise, burn, damage, dere, detriment, disadvantage, disservice, evil, grievance, harm, hurt, ill(ness), indignity,

injustice, lesion, loss, mayhem, mischief, nuisance, offense, outrage, pain, pang, prejudice, scratch, spurgall, teen, tort, trauma, wathe, wound, wrack, wrong
causing malefic, traumatic
civil tort
pert. noxal, noxious
pressure barotrauma
sense of umbrage
serious mayhem
INJUSTICE bias, damage, discrimination, favoritism, imposition, inequity, iniquity, injury, unfairness, wrong
INK atrament, blacken, bray, daub, encre, fluid, inida, sepia, sign, write
ball dabber, pumpet
black sumi
coloring agent nigrosine
disease black-canker, melanosis
fountain duct
ingredient tannin
knife spatula
-like atramental, atramentous
luminous day-glow
pad dabber, tompion
plant coriaria, pokeweed
slinger author, scribbler, writer
spreader brayer, roller
stone copperas, melanterite
INKBERRY brier, gallberry, holly, indigo, pokeweed, randia
INKER author, brayer, dabber, pad, pen, roller, tompion, writer
INKFISH calamaretti, calamari, cuttlefish, octopus, squid
INKLE braid, cord, spinel, tape, thread, yarn
INKLING clew, clue, cue, glimpse, hint, idea, impression, intimation, notice, scent, suggestion, supposition, suspicion, tip, whisper
INKSTAND fount, standish
small inket
INKY atramental, atramentous, black, colored, dark, dismal, murky, obscure, stained
cap mushroom
fluid malena
INLAND domestic, interior, mauka, midland, upcountry

INLAY boul(l)e, buhl, certosina, certosino, champleve, commesso, contise, couch, enchase, incrust, inse(r)t, intarsia, koftgari, line, lining, mosaic, niello, panel, parquet, pique, tarkashi, tarsia
INLET arm, basin, bay(ou), bight, calanque, canal, centance, cove, creek, estero, estuary, fiard, fiord, firth, fjord, frith, gore, gulf, harbor, lough, narrows, oekloken, opening, passage (way), rae, ria, slew, slough, slue, sound, strait, sump, voe, zee
tidal gap
INMATE beadsman, detenu, felon, inhabitant, intern, lodger, occupant, prisoner, resident, tenant
INMOST deepest, interior, intimate, intrinsic, private, secret
INN abode, albergo, auberge, auto court, boatel, boliche, caback, cabaret, cafeneh, caravansary, choultry, dosshouse, flophouse, fonda (co), fondu(c)k, gasthaus, gasthof, harborage, hospice, hospital, host(age), hostel(ry), hotel, imaret, kaan, khan(jee), locanda, lodge, meson, motel, motor court, ordinary, osteria, parador, pension, posada, resthouse, roadhouse, pub, serai, surahee, tabard, tambo, tavern, venta, wayhouse
of court member bencher
INNARDS contents, gizzards, viscera, vitals
INNATE born, congenital, constitutional, essential, hereditary, inborn, inbred, indigenous, ingrained, inherent, instinctive, intrinsic, native, natural, normal, regular, typical
INNER backroom, central, close, deep-seated, endosarc, ental, esoteric, familiar, focal, indistinct, inside, interior, internal, intimate, inward, mental, middle, obscure, within
circle cabal, claque, clique, coterie, establishment, group, insiders

comb. ent(o), esoter
-directed autotelic, independent
man essence, self, spirit, vitals
meaning core, heart, pith
nature essence
sole rand
INNISFAIL eire, erin, IRELAND
INNKEEPER aubergiste, boniface, caupone, duena, goodman, host(ler), hotelier, khanjee, landlord, master, oste, padrone, publican, tapper, taverner, traiteur, venter
INNOCENCE blue-eyedmary, bluet, cando(u)r, chastity, collinsia, incorruption, navelwort, plainness, purity, simplicity, sinlessness, spiderwort
goddess astraea
patron saint agnes
symbol babe, diamond, dove, lamb
INNOCENT angel(ic), arcadian, artless, babe(in the woods), blameless, chaste, child(like), chrisom, clean, clear, dewy-eyed, dove, dovish, faultless, fool, free, good, gosling, guileless, guiltless, harmless, holy, idiot, ignorant, immaculate, impeccable, incorrupt, infant, ingenue, innocuous, lamb(kin)(like), nafish, naif, naive, nayfish, nefish, pure, sackless, safe, simple, sinless, spotless, square, stainless, unguilty, unsullied, untainted, upright, virtuous, white, without, zaccheus
INNOCUOUS harmless, innocent, inoffensive, simple
INNOVATION change, insurrection, introduction, newfanglement, novelty, revolution
INNOVATOR heretic, revolutionist
INNUENDO allusion, hint, implication, inference, insinuation, intimation, overtone, slur, suggestion
INNUMERABLE countless, infinite, multitudinous, myriad, numberless, teeming
INO leucothea, leukothea
consort athamas

offspring glaucus, learchus, melicertes, palaemon, portu(m)nus

parent cadmus, harmonia

sister semele

stepson phrixos, phrixus

INOCULATE bud, equinate, graft, imbue, immunize, infix, infuse, insert, instill, permeate, seed, suffuse, vaccinate, variolate

INOFFENSIVE harmless, innocent, innocuous, safe

INOPERATIVE broken, dead, ineffective, ineffectual, innocuous, invalid, nugatory, out of order

INOPPORTUNE awkward, contrary, contretemps, clumsy, unfavorable, untimely

INORDINATE all-fired, disordered, enormous, excessive, exorbitant, extra(vagant), extreme, fabulous, fanatic(al), immoderate, intemperate, large, outrageous, superfluous, surplus, uncurbed, undue, unrestrained, wanton

INORGANIC exanimate, inanimate, lifeless, mineral

INPUT contribution, data, entrance, facts, impose

INQUEST assize(s), audit, examination, inquiry, inquisition, investigation, jury, panel, probe, quiz, research, scrutiny, search, trial

official coroner

INQUIRE ask, catechize, demand, examine, explore, interrogate, investigate, pry, pump, query, question, quiz, research, scrutinize, search, seek, speer, study

INQUIRER busybody, catechist, inquisitor, paul pry, querent, snoop(er)

INQUIRY assize(s), canvass, catechism, examen, examination, exploration, inquest, interrogation, interview, investigation, percontation, probe, proceeding, pursuit, query, question, research, scrutiny, search, speering, study, trial

for lost goods tracer

unprofitable mataeology

INQUISITION grilling, inquiry, interrogation, probe, probing, torture, tribunal

burning place brasero

director torquemada

execution auto-da-fe

founder st dominic

officer familiar

INQUISITIVE curious, intrusive, meddlesome, meddling, nosy, personal, prying, searching, snoopy

INROAD breach, incursion, infringement, intrusion, invasion, irruption, raid, trespass

INSALUBRIOUS See HARMFUL.

INSANE balmy, bats, batty, beany, bonkers, brainsick, buggy, bughouse, bugs, cracked, crazed, crazy, cuckoo, daffy, daft, demented, derailed, deranged, detraque, dippy, disoriented, distract, distraught, dotty, eccentric, flaky, foolish, frantic, frenetic, frenzied, gaga, goofy, gyte, hyte, incompetent, irrational, kichigai, loco, loony, loopy, lunatic, luny, mad(dened), maniac(al), moon-struck, morbid, moronic, nuts, nutty, potty, psychotic, queer, rabid, redwood, round the bend, screwball, screwy, senseless, tetched, touched, unbalanced, unhinged, unsettled, unsound, violent, w(h)acky, wild, witless, wood, wud, zany, zonkers

asylum bedlam, boobyhatch, bughouse, loonybin, madhouse, mental institution, nuthouse

delusion appersonation

make dement, demonize, madden

person aliene, crackpot, idiot, loon(y), lunatic, madman, maniac, moron, nut, psychotic

root henbane

INSANITY aberration, alienation, amentia, cacodemonia, daffing, delirium, dementia(praecox), derangement, disorientation, folie, folly, frenzy, furor, hysteria, lunacy, madness, mania, melancholia, pixilation, psychosis, schizophrenia, vesania

circular manic-depressive

homicidal androphonomania

legal alienation

moral pathomania

slight oligomania

temporary amentia

INSATIABLE greedy, unquenchable

INSCRIBE address, blazon, dedicate, emblazon, endorse, enface, engrave, engross, enroll, enter, fix, impress, indite, initial, inscroll, letter, list, mark, record, register, scroll, sign

INSCRIPTION address, caption, dedication, epigraph, epitaph, head(ing), legend, lettering, mention, motto, rubric, slogan, titulus

appropriate motto

crude graffiti, graffito

explanatory titulus

place stele, tombstone

publisher's colophon

rock petroglyph

tomb epitaph

wall graffiti, graffito, menemene-tekel-upharsin

without anepigraphic

INSCROLL See INSCRIBE.

INSCRUTABLE abstruse, abysmal, arcane, baffling, balking, cryptic, dark, deep, enigmatic, equivocal, hidden, incomprehensible, inexplorable, mysterious, obscure, profound, secret, unfathomable, unintelligible, vague

INSECT (See also *kind*, below.) arachnid, arthropod, bug, myriapod, pest, vermin

adult imago

annoying bedbug bicho, chigger, flea, mosquito, nit

antenna feeler, palp(us)

antenna end clava

aquatic backswimmer, corixa, ranatra

armored scale aspidiotus

back notum

beneficial bee, ladybird, ladybug, scarab

bloodsucking corsair, flea, mosquito, tabanid

body thorax

bristles macrochaeta

carnivorous ambushbug, corixa, mantis, rearhorse

chalcidoid blastophaga

chirping cricket

clasper rhabdopod

clypeus prelabrum

comb. entom(o)

control See INSECTICIDE.
cursorial phasmatid, walk-ing-stick
deadly assassin-bug, black-widow, holotricha, reduviid
debris frass
destructive aphid, aphis, lo-cust, predator, redspider, scale, termite
development stage subimago
dipterous beef-fly, bomby-liida, botfly, crane-fly, mos-quito, robber-fly, tabanid, tachina-fly, tick
dissecting entomotomy
ear See INSECT antenna.
-eaters alamiqui, ento-mophaga, hedgehog, mole, moonrat, shrew
edible attacus
eye ocellus, stemma
eyeless campodeid, japygid, proturan
-fearing entomophic
feeler antenna, cercus, palp(us), tentilla
female gyne, queen
-flower chrysanthemum
foot tarsus
foot part plantula
4-winged beetle, tetrapteron
front acron
froth-secreting cuckoo-spit
genus acarus, cicada, cicala, emesa, figitida, mantis, nepa, termes, thripida
grinders malae
group flight, hive, swarm
hard covering chitin
harmful aedes, armyworm, arthropod, blackfly, black-widow, bollweevil, bottlefly, caterpillar, cockroach, cornborer, cutworm, ear-worm, fireant, fruitfly, gyp-symoth, hornworm, japa-nese beetle, junebug, killer-bee, locust, maggot, mos-quito, moth, pinebeetle, rootworm, screwwormfly, shoofly, termite, thrips, tsetsefly, tussockmoth
hemipterous ambushbug, assassinbug, backswimmer, boatbug, calicoback, chig-ger, corsair, kissingbug, murgantia, notonectid, ran-atra, redbug, reduviid, toad-bug, wheelbug
homopterous aleyrod, aphid, aphis, cicada, jarfly, lan-ternfly, leafhopper, locust, plantlouse, spittle-insect, treehopper

hymenopterous ant, bee, gallwasp, ichneuman fly, sawfly, wasp
immature chrysalis, instar, larva, nymph, pupa
inactive stage prepupa
joint cardo
kind acarid, ant, antlion, arthropod, attacus, aurelia, bedbug, bee(tle), bicho, blackwidow, blight, boll-weevil, borer, bug, but-terfly, caddis, cadew, centi-pede, cicada, cicala, cockroach, cootie, cricket, diptera(n), dor, drone, dun, earwig, emesa, ephemerid, eri, figeater, firefly, flea, fly, formicid, gnat, grasshopper, grub, honeybee, hornet, imago, japanese beetle, ka-tydid, laap, ladybird, larp, lerp, loa, locust, louse, mantis, millipede, mite, mosquito, moth, nit, nymph, pela, pismire, roach, sawfly, scorpion, spi-der, stinger, stinkbug, ter-mite, tremex, tsetse, wasp, weevil, yellowjacket, zimb
larva eruca, grub, maggot
leaping daddy-longlegs, grasshopper, podura, springtail
leg setireme
leg segment coxa
lepidopterous butterfly, moth
-like entomoid
linguae glossae
long-legged emesa
luminous glowworm
mature imago
migratory locust
minute scale, thrips
molting ecdysis
mouth trophi
mouth appendage gnathite
nest nidus
neuropterous alderfly, ant-lion
order acarina, aptera, co-leoptera, diptera, hemip-tera, homoptera, lymenop-tera, paleodictyoptera
orthopterous acridid, cricket, katydid
ovipositor aculeus, acus
parasitic anoplura, botfly, chigger, chigoe, flea, lice, louse, mite, pediculus, tick, turicata
part acron, alitrunk, an-tenna, cercus, chirr, clasper, clava, clypeus, corselet,

coxa, feeler, labium, media, notum, nucha, ocellus, palp(us), plantula, prono-tum, scutella, stemma, ten-tacle, thorax
pert. entomic, entomoid, en-tomologic
pest calicoback, termite
plant aphid, aphis, beetle, borer, thrips
pollinated by entomophilous
powder pyrethrum
praying mantis
preservation entomotaxy
primitive ametabola, ap-terygogenea, apterygote, campodeid
proboscis haustellum
pupal pronymph
refuse frass
repellent citronella
saltatorial cricket
sap-sucking aphid, aphis
scale aspidiotus, icerya, polishberry, pulvinaria, ta-chardia
secretion flocoon, honeydew, laap, lac, larp, lerp
sense organ scolophore
shelter domatium
6-legged bee, beetle, bug, fly, chigger, chigoe
slender emesa, mantis
small aphid, aphis, bug, bull-head, chigger, chigoe, flea, garfly, gnat, mico, midge, mite, thrips
slow-moving ambulatoria, phasmid, walking-stick
social ant, bee, emmet, ter-mite
sound buzz, chirk, chirr, churr, creak, crick, hum, katydid, stridor, stridulation
stage chrysalis, cocoon, egg, imago, instar, larva, mag-got, nymph, prepupa, pupa, redio, subimago
sting ictus
stinging aculeate, bee, gadfly, gallinipper, hornet, mos-quito, sciniph, wasp, yellow-jacket
stomach ventriculus
study coccidology, entomol-ogy
thorax alitrunk, corselet
trap web
vein costa, cubitus
wing alula
winged bee, dipteran, drag-onfly, fly, gnat, grass-hopper, hornet, imago, lo-

cust, moth, wasp, yellow-jacket

wingless, anoplura, aphorurid, aptera, apterygot, atropid, boreus, centipede, lepisma, lice, louse, pterygota, silverfish, spider

wing margin termen

wing part alinotum, frenulum, tornus

wing spot isle

wing type frenate

young See INSECT *immature.*

INSECTICIDE aldrin, allethrin, anabasine, arsenic, azobenzene, black leaf forty, blue(copperas)(stone) (vitriol), calomel, chlordane, chloropicrin, culicide, ddt, derris, dieldrin, endrin, flit, isodrin, killer, lindane, mirex, ovicide, parathion, paris green, rotenone, schradan, spray, toxaphene

base antosoly

INSECTIVORE See INSECT *eater.*

INSECURE asea, brittle, cas(s)alty, cas(s)elty, dangerous, diffident, dubious, hazardous, infirm, loose, perilous, precarious, rickety, risky, shaky, treacherous, uncertain, unconfident, unpoised, unreliable, unsafe, wobbly

INSEMINATE dispense, distribute, fertilize, implant, impregnate, inculcate, insinuate, instill, permeate, pervade, saturate, scatter, seed, sow

INSENSATE besotted, blind, brutal, dense, dull, dumb, fatuous, fond, foolish, harsh, inanimate, infatuated, silly, stupid, unintelligent, untouched, unwise

INSENSIBLE anesthetic, apathetic, asleep, benumbed, blase, blate, blind, blunt, callous, comate, comatose, dead(ened), dense, drugged, dull, foolish, forgetful, gradual, ignorant, impassive, inanimate, infinitesimal, insensate, knocked out, numb(ed), obdurate, oblivious, obtuse, senseless, slender, slight, slow, stoic, stolid, stunned, unconscious, unfeeling, unfelt, unrefined

INSENSIBILITY analgesia, anesthesia, apathy, blackout, calmness, carus, catalepsy, coma, coolness, dispassion, faint, indifference, insensitivity, insentience, lethargy, listlessness, narcosis, sluggishness, stoicism, supineness, swoon, syncope, torpor, trance, unconcern, unconciousness, unfeelingness

INSENSITIVE aloof, anesthetic, blunt, boorish, callous, cool, dull, graubyer, graubyon, hardened, impassible, impassive, imperceptive, indifferent, obtuse, stoic, thick-skinned, unfeeling, unresponsive

INSENSITIVITY apathy, callosity, callousness, coldness, cruelty, hardheart, imperviousness, induration, insensibility, inuredness, obduracy, oblivion, thick skin, unconsciousness, unfeeling

INSEPARABLE attached, complete, fixed, impartible, indiscerptible, indissoluble, individable, indivisible, infrangible, infusible, insoluble, joined, secure, united

INSERT collect, dicky, enter, godet, gore, gusset, imbed, imbue, immit, implant, infix, infuse, ingraft, inject, INLAY, inoculate, inset, insinuate, instil, intercalate, interject, interline, interlope, interpose, introduce, intromit, obtrude, panel, put in, record, sandwich, set in, spud, stick in, stop

for growth bud, (en)graft

triangular gore, wedge

wrongly foist

INSERTION addition, dip, embolism, embroidery, empiecement, entrance, godet, gore, immersion, injection, inset, intercalation, interjection, lace, parenthesis, plunge, shim, vee

mark caret

INSET appoint, bed, embed, imbed, infix, inflow, influx, inlay, INSERT, panel

INSIDE backroom, confidential, dope, inbye, inner, interior, internal, inward, keyhole, middle, select, within

and out everywhere, throughout, utterly

dope low-down, scoop

from ab intra

man See SPY.

out entirely, everted, inverted

toward entad, inward

track advantage, favor

INSIDES abdomen, belly, content(s), entrails, guts, viscera, vitals

INSIDIOUS arch, artful, captious, corrupt, covert, crafty, cunning, deceitful, designing, foxy, guileful, sly, snaky, subtle, treacherous, tricky, wily

INSIGHT acumen, apercu, comprehension, conspectus, discernment, divination, esp, goods, impression, inspection, intuition, ken, look, penetration, perception, perspicuity, reason, sensitivity, understanding, view

INSIGNIA ankh, badge(s), brassard, button(s), caduceus, cap and gown, cockade, cross, decoration(s), eagle, emblem(s), ensign(s), figurehead, livery, mantle, mark(s), medal(s), mortarboard, order, paraphernalia, regalia, ribbon(s), stars, swastika, symbol, tau, toga, uniform

ecclesiastical crook, crosier, crown, fillet, keys, miter, mitre, ring, staff, tiara, triple crown

heraldic arms, bar, bearing, bend(sinister), billet, blazon, bordure, canton, chaplet, charge, chevron, crest, cross, escutcheon, fesse, field, flanche, fret, fusil, garland, gyron, hatchment, lozenge, mascle, motto, orle, pale, pall, pheon, pile, quarter, rustre, saltier, scutchen, shield, tressure

military bar, caduceus, chevron, crown, eagle, epaulet(te), oak leaf, star, stripe, wings

royal coronet, crown, diadem, ermine, orb, purple, privy seal, regalia, rod, scepter, seal, signet, tiara, uraeus

INSIGNIFICANCE effacement, inconsequence, non-entity

symbol fly

INSIGNIFICANT contemptible, dinky, foolish, footy, humble, immaterial, imperceptible, inconsequential, inconsiderable, inferior, irrelevant, little, low, mean, meaningless, measly, minim(al), minor, minuscule, minute, naught, negligible, paltry, petit, petty, piddling, pitiful, puny, scrubby, slight, small(time), trifling, tripenny, trivial, unimportant, unimposing, unworthy

pert. bit, iota, molehill, speck, tithe

INSINCERE adulatory, artificial, backhanded, deceitful, deceptive, dishonest, faithless, false, feigned, flattering, hypocritical, kowtowing, obsequious, phony, pretentious, superficial, two-sided, untrue

INSINCERITY affectation, artifice, hypocrisy, pecksniffery, pharisaism, pretense

INSINUATE advert, allude, ascribe, enter, hint, imbue, implant, imply, impute, infuse, insert, instill, interject, interpose, intimate, introduce, intrude, invade, leaven, screw, signify, slur, subinduce, suggest

INSINUATING artful, crafty, disarming, fulsome, ingratiating, oily, politic, smarmy, smooth, snide, soapy, suave, unctuous, winning

INSINUATION allusion, aspersion, hint, implication, imputation, inkling, intimation, innuendo, reflection, suggestion

INSIPID banal, bauch, blah, bland, dead, dry, dull, faded, fatuous, flat, flavorless, heavy, indifferent, jejune, lifeless, mawkish, mild, milk-and-water, monotonous, nambypamby, pointless, prosaic, prosy, sapless, savorless, sentimental, shilpit, slight, soft, stale, tame, tasteless, thin, trite, unflavored, uninteresting, unsavory, vapid, wairsh, weak, wishy-washy

INSIST affirm, argue, assert, aver, contend, craik, demand, emphasize, importune, maintain, persist, press, request, require, stand(on), stress, urge

INSISTENT adamant, demanding, emphatic, exigent, imperious, persevering, pressing, urgent

INSOLENCE arrogance, audacity, cheek, contemptuousness, contumely, disrespect, flair, impudence, lip, presumption, pride, sass, snash, surquidry

symbol cock

INSOLENT abusive, arrogant, audacious, backhanded, bardy, bodacious, brazen, bumptious, calumnious, cheeky, cold, contemptuous, contumelious, cool, defiant, derisive, discourteous, disdainful, disrespectful, familiar, forward, haughty, hubristic, impertinent, impudent insulting, lordly, obtrusive, offensive, overbearing, overweening, pert, presuming, presumptuous, procacious, proud, rude, sassy, saucy, scornful, scurrile, scurrilous

INSOLVENCY bankruptcy, failure, receivership

INSOLVENT bankrupt, broke, failed, lost, ruined, undone

debtor abbey laird

INSOMNIA agrypnia, ahypnia, sleeplessness, vigil(ance), wakefulness

INSOUCIANCE apathy, aplomb, indifference, nonchalance, poise

INSOUCIANT apathetic(al), blase, calm, carefree, cavalier, heedless, indifferent, unbothered, unconcerned

INSPECT ager, audit, browse, case, check, con, consider, examine, eye, inventory, investigate, look, oversee, penetrate, probe, pry, scan, scrutinize, search, shroff, sight, speer, study, superintend, survey, traverse, view, watch

INSPECTION audit, autopsy, checkup, contemplation, examination, inquest, inquiry, insight, overhaul, oversight, overview, perlustration, pe-

rusal, probe, review, runthrough, scrutiny, study, supervision, surveillance, survey, view

INSPECTOR censor, conner, examiner, looker, overseer, policeman, sampler, sealer, searcher, snoop(er), superintendent

INSPIRATION afflatus, animation, animus, assurance, brainstorm, breathing, desire, elevation, emboldening, encouragement, enlivenment, enthusiasm, exaltation, exhilaration, fire, firing, frenzy, furor, fury, genius, heartening, impulse, incentive, infection, inflatus, influence, infusion, inhalation, insight, intuition, lift, motivation, motive, rapture, revelation, sprite, spur, stimulus, transport, uplift, vision

divine theoneusty

poetic pierian

pretender to aeolist

symbol eagle, frog, toad

INSPIRE activate, animate, arouse, awe, blow, boost, breathe, cheer, elevate, embolden, encourage, energize, enliven, exalt, excite, exhilarate, fire, galvanize, hearten, imbue, induce, infect, inflame, inform, infuse, inhale, inspirit, insufflate, kindle, lift, motivate, move, occasion, prompt, provoke, quicken, reassure, sniff, spark, stimulate, sufflate, uplift, vitalize

respect awe

INSPIRED afflated, appropriate, dei plenus, glowing, ingenious, inhaled, visioned

divinely entheal, entheate

INSPIRING affecting, august, awesome, grand, impressive, moving, stirring

INSPIRIT arouse, cheer, comfort, encourage, enliven, hearten, inspire, quicken, rouse

INSPISSATE clot, condense, congeal, evaporate, stiffen, thicken

INSTABILITY failure, fluidity, inconstancy, insecurity, mutability, weakness

INSTALL accede, appoint, begin, chair, commission, crown, enthrone, establish, fix, inaugurate, induct, initiate, instate, invest, locate, lodge, open, ordain, place, plant, receive, seat, set, station

INSTALLATION accedence, admission, agency, appointment, beginning, business, commission, enthronement, establishment, facility, fixation, foundation, inauguration, induction, instatement, investment, lodg(e)ment, part, placement, plant (ation), settlement
military fort, garrison

INSTALLMENT earnest, handsel, kist, token
plan credit, hire-purchase, never-never
seller tallyman

INSTANCE case, circumstance, cite, detail, evidence, example, ground, illustration, importune, instigation, item, motive, occasion, particular, proof, proposal, reason, request, sample, situation, specimen, suggestion, urge

INSTANT breath, crack, current, flash, gliff, glisk, hint, jiff(y), immediate, imminent, minute, moment, point, pop, present, pressing, prompt, quick, sec (ond), shake, split-second, stound, stroke, sudden, tick, time, trice, twinkle, twinkling, urgent, whiff, wink

INSTANTANEOUS immediate, spontaneous

INSTANTLY, INSTANTER anon, at once, directly, forthwith, instantaneously, promptly, right away, slap, suddenly, swith(e)

INSTAR imago, larva, pupa

INSTATE bestow, endow, establish, install, invest, place, receive, set

INSTEAD alternative, either, else, equivalent, faute de mieux, for, in behalf, in lieu, in loco parentis, proxy, rather, substitute, vice
comb. ant(i)

INSTEP acrotarsium, arch, beginning, tarsus, wrist

INSTIGATE abet, activate, actuate, agitate, arouse, egg, foment, goad, hint, impel, incense, incite, invoke, mo-

tivate, plan, plot, prompt, provoke, scheme, set(on) (up), spur, stimulate, stir, suborn, suggest, tempt, urge

INSTIGATOR agent provocateur, agitator, agitprop, author, demagogue, firebrand, incendiary, mischief-maker, provocateur, provocator, provoker, putter-on, rabble-rouser, ringleader, seditionary, seditionist, source, trouble-maker

INSTILL breathe, graft, imbue, implant, inculcate, indoctrinate, infix, inseminate, permeate, pervade, saturate

INSTINCT aptitude, bent, capacity, faculty, gift, intuition, knack, psyche, sixth sense, talent, tendency, turn

INSTINCTIVE automatic, congenital, habitual, impulsive, inborn, inherent, innate, inspirational, intuitive, involuntary, libidinal, natural, normal, reflexive, regular, second nature, spontaneous, typical, wonted

INSTITOR agent, broker, manager

INSTITUTE academy, begin, clinic, college, commence, establish, found, gymnasium, inaugurate, initiate, introduce, law, lycee, ordain, organization, organize, school, seminary, start, university
member piarist

INSTITUTION asylum, ceremony, charity, company, convention, custom, enactment, establishment, foundation, hospital, inauguration, INSTITUTE, library, marriage, organization, shelter, station
charitable almshouse, hospital, pogey
penal reformatory

INSTRUCT acquaint, advise, apprise, assign, bid, breed, brief, catechize, charge, coach, command, direct, discipline, drill, edify, educate, enjoin, enlighten, guide, impart, indoctrinate, inform, initiate, lead, order, pilot, preach, school, show, steer, teach, train, tutor

INSTRUCTION advice, coaching, direction, direc-

tive, doctrine, education, guidance, information, knowledge, learning, lore, monition, nurture, orders, pedagogy, precept, teaching, tuition, tutelage, tutorage
art of didactics, paideutics, pedagogy
divine tora(h)
period quarter, semester, session, term, trimester, year
pert. propaedeutic
place of college, conservatoire, conservatory, lycee, gymnasium, school, seminary, university
preliminary propaedeutics

INSTRUCTIVE advisory, didactic, docent, edifying, educational, enlightening, informative, newsy, preceptive, propaedeutic

INSTRUCTOR acharya, coach, counsel(or), crammer, docent, doctor, don, driller, drillmaster, lector, lecturer, master, mentor, preceptor, prof(essor), teacher, trainer, tutor

INSTRUCTRESS duenna, governess, mistress, preceptress, schoolma'am, schoolmarm, tutoress

INSTRUMENT act, agency, agent, ager, agreement, apparatus, appliance, appurtenance, bond, capitulation, cat's-paw, channel, complex, contract, contrivance, creation, creature, deed, DEVICE, dingus, document, dupe, engine, equipment, fashion, GADGET, gear, handmaid, IMPLEMENT, indenture, jackal, lease, machine(ry), manner, material, means, mechanism, media, medium, method, mode, organ, outfit, paper, pawn, plaything, puppet, rig(ging), slave, stooge, system, tackle, tool, tract, utensil, vehicle, way, wherewithal, will, writ
board panel
boring wimble
calculating abacus, sliderule
collection armentarium, set, trousee
comb. arium, labe, orium, tron

cutting knife, razor, scissors, scythe, shears, sickle
gripping chuck, clamp, clasp, clinch, cramp, dog, forceps, grab, grapnel, grapple(r), grip, holdfast, jaws, nippers, nutcracker, pincette, pinc-(h)ers, pliers, tongs, tweezers, vise, wrench
in proof testimony
kind arm, belt, block, cleat, crane, crow(bar), derrick, helm, jack, jimmy, keystone, knob, lever, oar, paddle, pawl, pedal, pulley, quoin, shim, swingle, tackle, tiller, treadle, trigger, tumbler, wedge
legal contract, deed, testament, will, writ
mathematical sector, sliderule
mechanical pianola
musical See MUSICAL INSTRUMENT.
nautical compass, loran, pelorus, sextant
panel dashboard
percussion glockenspiel
pert. fidicinal
pointed awl, brog, goad, prod
sacred urim
sharp-edged cutlery, knife, razor, scissors, scythe, shears, sickle
string See MUSICAL INSTRUMENT *string.*
surveying transit
tracing perigraph
2-pronged bident
written cautio
INSTRUMENTAL beneficial, conducive, helpful, implemental, serviceable, servient, useful
INSTRUMENTALITY agency, aid, channel, hand, means, media, medium, ministry, organ, vehicle
INSTRUMENTATION harmonization, implementation, tooling
INSUBORDINATE contrary, disobedient, factious, intractable, mutinous, perverse, rebel(lious), refractory, revolutionary, seditious, unruly, unsubmissive
INSUBORDINATION anarchy, disobedience, insurrection, mutiny, rebellion, revolt, riotousness, sedition
INSUBSTANTIAL aerial,

airy, flimsy, footless, frail, frothy, imaginary, intangible, precarious, slender, slight, tenuous, thin, unreal, weak
INSUFFICIENCY dearth, deficiency, deficit, inability, inadequacy, lack, paucity, poverty, shortage, shortcoming
INSUFFICIENT deficient, inadequate, incomplete, lacking, lame, meager, poor, scant(y), scarce, short, skimpy, slack, sparse, stingy, stinted, unequal, wane
INSULAR alone, aloof, contracted, far off, illiberal, isled, isolate(d), limited, local, narrow(minded), nesiote, parochial, petty, prejudiced, remote, removed, restricted, seagirt, secluded
INSULATE cover, cushion, detach, disconnect, enisle, island, isolate, lag, protect, seclude, segregate, separate, shield
INSULATION cork, dielectric, ker(k)ite, lagging, mica, okonite, safeguard, vermiculite
INSULIN iletin
cure for diabetes
discoverer banting, macleod
source pancreas
INSULT abuse, affront, bird, brickbat, bronx cheer, cag, cheek, contempt, contumely, debase, degrade, disgrace, dishonor, disregard, epithet, fig, flout, humble, humiliate, hurt, indignity, injure, innuendo, insolence, jeer, knock, mock, offend, offense, outrage, outray, pan, potch, raspberry, ridicule, scoff, shame, slap, slight, slur, smear, snub, taunt, wrong
INSULTING arrogant, despiteful, infra dig, insolent, offensive, opprobrious, outrageous, rude
INSUPERABLE inaccessible, insurmountable, unattainable
INSURANCE assecuration, assurance, bonus, certainty, coverage, guarantee, indemnity, pledge, promise, security, warranty
adjuster claimsman

applicant risk
computer actuary, adjuster
document bordereau, policy
man agent, twister, underwriter
payee beneficiary
risk moral hazard
system tontine
unemployment dole
INSURE assure, back, compensate, cover, forearm, guarantee, guard, indemnify, prepare, promise, protect, provide, requite, safeguard, secure, shield, underwrite
INSURGENT barrabas, camisard, chourn, iconoclast, insubordinate, mutineer, oakboy, rebel(lious), revolter, revolutionary, seditious, steelboy
INSURRECTION mutiny, putsch, rebellion, revolt, revolution, uprising
INTACT all, complete, entire, flawless, full, imperforate, indiscrete, integral, perfect, permanent, replete, scatheless, sound, unbroken, uncut, undamaged, undefiled, unharmed, unimpaired, uninjured, untouched, whole
INTAGLIO cut, design, diaglyph, die, engraving, entail, gem, matrix, mold, relief
part incavo
process gravure
INTAKE absorption, acceptance, admission, capillarity, contraction, enclosure, entrance, income, input, reception, resorption, suction, swindle(r), understand
INTANGIBLE abstract, abstruse, elusive, evasive, immaterial, impalpable, incorporeal, indefinite, infinitesimal, insensible, insubstantial, rare, slight, slippery, subt(i)le, tenuous, unclear, undecided, vague
INTEGER ace, cipher, digit, entity, gnomon, norm, number, one, sum, whole
INTEGRAL complete, component, composite, constituent, entire, essential, inner, necessary, needful, numeric(al), sum, totality, whole
INTEGRATE articulate, blend, coalesce, combine, conjoin, consolidate, fuse,

merge, mix, organize, unify, unite

INTEGRATED blended, entire, fused, intact, IN-TEGRAL, joined, perfect

INTEGRITY entirety, fidelity, goodness, honesty, HONOR, morality, probity, pureness, purity, rectitude, simplicity, sincerity, solidarity, soundness, strength, totality, truth, union, unity, veracity, verity, virtue, wholeness

INTEGUMENT aril, capsule, coat(ing), covering, cuticle, derm(a), envelope, epiderm, exoderm, husk, perisarc, primine, rind, shell, skin, testa, tunicle

INTELLECT brain(s), brow, cerebration, cognition, discernment, graymatter, head, INTELLIGENCE, inwit, mahat, mentality, mind, noemics, noesis, nous, psyche, reason, sense, soul, thinking, thought, understanding, vernunft, wit(s)
functioning of noesis
impairment dysgnosis
pert. noetic
science of noetics

INTELLECTUAL brahmin, brain(y), cerebral, clever, diagnoetic, egghead, gaon, gnostic, highbrow, ideal, intelligent, literatus, longhair, mental, noetic, psychic, savant, scholarly, sophic, thoughtful
capacity brow
female bluestocking
group academy, avant-garde, bloomsbury, clerisy, cognoscenti, intelligensia, literati, thinktank

INTELLECTUALITY cerebrotonia

INTELLIGENCE acuity, acumen, address, advice, apprehension, aptitude, brahma, brains, brilliance, caliber, capacity, communication, comprehension, esprit, graymatter, information, insight, INTELLECT, judgment, knowledge, mentality, mind, news, noesis, notice, penetration, perception, percipience, precocity, rationality, sagacity, sanity, savvy, sense, shrewdness, skill, spirit, tidings, under-

standing, verstand, wisdom, wit
agent spy
center brain, gray-matter
military data, information
test alpha, beta, binet-simon, stanford-binet
test deviser binet, simon, wechsler
without dull, inane, stupid

INTELLIGENT acute, agile, akamai, alert, apt, astucious, astute, aware, brainy, bright, brilliant, clever, cunning, discerning, gash, informed, intellectual, keen, knowing, mental, penetrating, perceptive, rational, sagacious, sensible, sensitive, sharp, shrewd, skillful, smart, spack, subtle, trenchant, with it

INTELLIGIBLE clear, comprehensible, lucid, pellucid, plain, relevant, understandable, unmistakable

INTEMPERANCE acrasia, acrasy, bibaciousness, bibacity, bibulousness, crapulence, debauchery, dipsomania, dissipation, excess, extravagance, gluttony, indulgence, intoxication, license, overdoing, unrestraint

INTEMPERATE bibulous, crapulent, crapulous, dissipated, dissolute, excessive, exorbitant, extravagant, gluttonous, immoderate, incontinent, indecent, indulgent, inordinate, overindulgent, prodigal, profligate, unbridled, uncurbed, unrestrained

INTEND aim, allot, anticipate, aspire, assay, attempt, behight, bid, cast, contemplate, decree, design, destine, determine, drive, endeavor, essay, ettle, expect, extend, fix to, get at, go for, interest, mean, meditate, mind, mint, ordain, plan, plot, propose, purpose, reckon, reserve, resolve, scheme, stretch, strive, suppose, think, try

INTENDED aforethought, betrothed, fiance(e), implied, meant, supposed

INTENSE ardent, affectionate, charged, chronic, colorful, deep, eager, en-

hanced, enthusiastic. excessive, excruciating, extreme, fervent, fervid, fiery, frantic, great, heightened, hot, immoderate, keen, passionate, perfervid, poignant, powerful, profound, sensitive, sharp, steady, strong, vehement, violent, vivid, warm, zealous

INTENSIFY accent, aggravate, augment, deepen, emphasize, enhance, exaggerate, exalt, heighten, improve, increase, magnify, step up, strengthen, stress, thicken, urge

INTENSITY ardor, blare, colorfulness, degree, density, depth, drive, energy, ferocity, force, heat, loudness, might, power, severity, sonority, strength, stress, vehemence, vigor, violence, volume
pert. isodynamic
reflected albedo

INTENSIVE complete, concentrated, extended, hard, out-and-out, radical, thorough

INTENT absorbed, accuse, aim, ardent, attention, attentive, bent, bound, cause, conation, concentrated, design, desire, determined, drift, eager, earnest, effort, end, engrossed, firm, focus(ed), goal, import, meaning, notion, object, preoccupied, purport, purpose, rapt, riveted, sedulous, set, tenor, theme, vigilant, volition, watchful, will, wish, zealous
to cheat mala fides

INTENTION aim, animus, big idea, cause, concept, counsel, desire, design, determination, end, expectation, function, goal, heart, idea, inclination, meaning, mind, mint, motive, object (ive), plan, pretense, project, proposal, purpose, scope, thought, view, will, wish
and fact animo et facto

INTENTIONAL advised, calculated, conscious, considered, contemplated, deliberate, express, knowing, meant, meditated, planned, premeditated, purposeful, set, studied, voluntary, weighed, willful, witting

INTER bury, ensepulcher, entomb, inearth, inhume, inurn, plant, put under

INTERAGENT medium, middleman, middler

INTERBREEDING amphimixis, apogamy, cross, homogamy, panmixia, panmixy

INTERCALATE insert, insinuate, interject, interpolate, interpose, introduce

INTERCEDE interfere, interpose, intervene, mediate, negotiate, petition, plead, pray, sue

INTERCEPT arrest, block, catch, delay, hinder, interrupt, keep, nab, obstruct, prevent, seize, stop, take, trammel, waylay

INTERCESSION arbitration, entreaty, mediation, moyen, petition, pleading, prayer

INTERCESSOR advocate, agent, bishop, lawyer, mediator

INTERCHANGE alternation, bandy, barter, commerce, commute, convert, crossfire, give and take, metastrophe, quid pro quo, reciprocation, reciprocity, requite, return, reverse, swap, switch, substitute, talk, tit for tat, trade, transpose

INTERCHANGEABLE commutable, fungible, mutual, reciprocal

INTERCLAVICLE episteynom

INTERCOMMUNICATION anastomosis, liaison, merging, union

INTERCOURSE business, commerce, communication, communion, conversation, converse, correspondence, deal(ings), exchange, mang, mong, negotiation, quarter, transaction, truck

INTERDICT anathema, ban, check, curb, debar, enjoin, exclude, forbid, inhibit, prohibit, proscribe, restrain, rule out, snaffle, taboo, utrubi, veto

INTERDICTION ban, decree, excommunication, malison, prohibition, restraint, taboo, tabu, veto

INTEREST absorb, advan-

tage, affair, affect, allure, amuse, arouse, attachment, attention, attract, behalf, behoof, benefit, bent, bug, business, cause, claim, concern, contango, discount, ego(tism), engage, engross, entertain, enthrall, enthusiasm, equity, estate, excite(ment), fascinate, favor, fetch, good, hold, incentive, income, induce, involve, love, money, motivation, motive, part(y), passion, payment, percentage, pique, portion, premium, profit, regard, right, sake, savor, service, share, spark, spirit, stake, study, tantalize, titillate, title, touch, usance, use, usury, vigorish, weal, work

concerned sympathy

exorbitant usury

lose tire

rate yield

special angle

without apathetic, bland, blase, bored, boring, indifferent, jejune

INTERESTED active, all ears, concerned, hipped, hooked, partial, partisan, serious

INTERESTING absorbing, attractive, breezy, challenging, colorful, curious, engrossing, entertaining, exciting, fascinating, inviting, juicy, keen, lively, piquant, provocative, provoking, racy, salty, spicy, succulent, tantalizing, titillating, touching, zestful

INTERFERE baffle, balk, bar, barge in, blanket, block, butt in, clash, collide, conflict, counteract, hinder, impede, intercede, interpose, interrupt, intervene, intromit, intrude, jam, meddle, mediate, molest, obstruct, obtrude, remit, suspend, tamper, thwart

INTERFERER busybody, buttinsky, interloper, marplot, meddler, trespasser

INTERFERENCE balk, bloom, choke, flare, ghost, hum, mush, noise, opposition, rain, snow, static

without laissez-faire

INTERFEROMETER rod etalon

INTERIM diastem, interlude, interval, meantime, meanwhile, pause, period, protem, provisional, temporary, vacancy, while, whilst

INTERIOR achterveld, backland, barysphere, belly, ben, bosom, bowels, cella, center, domestic, endogenous, entrails, familiar, hinterland, inborn, ingrained, inherent, inland, inly, innate, inner, inside, internal, intimate, intrados, intrinsic, inward, mediterranean, middle, midland, midst, penetralia, recesses, upcountry

pert. central, core, ental, inner

remove gut

INTERJECT comment, insert, insinuate, interpolate, interpose, introduce, intrude, mortise, obtrude, remark, splice, thrust

INTERJECTION ahem, ahey, ahoy, alas, aside, bam, bang, criminy, dear, egad, ejaculation, episode, eureka, EXCLAMATION, expletive, goody, heck, hey, hola, injection, insertion, insinuation, interpolation, introduction, lackaday, outcry, parenthesis, pshaw, remark, tenez, tst, whew

INTERJOIN anastomose, inosculate

INTERLACE alternate, braid, complicate, disperse, diversify, knit, link, lock, mix, plait, pleach, twine, twist, unite, vine, warp, weave, wreathe

INTERLOCK clench, connect, dovetail, engage, interlace, interrelate, knit, link, tangle, unite

INTERLOCUTION conference, conversation, converse, interjection, parenthesis, response, speech, utterance

INTERLOCUTOR interpreter, mouthpiece, questioner, talker

INTERLOPE butt in, encroach, intrude, invade, obtrude, trespass

INTERLOPER intruder, trespasser

INTERLUDE break, comedy, drama, entracte, episode,

farce, gap, idyl(l), interim, interruption, interval, overture, pause, period, recess, respite, rest, ritornel, space, spell, stasimon, temacha, triumph, versette
short verset(te), versicle
INTERMEDIARY agent, broker, connection, go-between, henchman, in-between, interagent, link, mediator, medium, mean, middle(man), moyener, negotiator, representative, trampler
INTERMEDIATE average, between, interjacent, interposed, intervening, mean, median, medium, mesne, middle, middling
school junior high
INTERMENT burial, commitment, grave, inhumation, sepulture, tomb
INTERMINABLE constant, continual, continuous, endless, enduring, eternal, everlasting, incessant, infinite, lasting, lengthy, perpetual, timeless, unceasing, unending
INTERMINABLY See FOREVER.
INTERMINGLE blend, braid, mix
INTERMISSION break, cessation, devall, entracte, interim, interlude, interruption, interval, lull, nooning, pause, period, recess, relache, respite, rest, spell, stop, suspension, vacation
INTERMIT abate, arrest, cease, check, defer, devaul, discontinue, interpose, interrupt, lessen, postpone, recur, reduce, stay, stop, suspend
INTERMITTENT alternate, alternating, broken, checked, fitful, infrequent, interrupted, occasional, periodic, recurrent, spasmodic, sporadic
fever remedy aseptolin
INTERMITTENTLY at intervals, brokenly, by snatches, disconnectedly, discontinuously, fitfully, here and there, per saltum, skippingly
INTERMIX See MINGLE.
INTERN confine, detain, doctor, hamper, hold, im-

prison, jail, limit, medic, resident, restrain, restrict, segregate
INTERNAL domestic, essential, inherent, inland, innate, inner, inside, interior, intramural, intrinsic, inward, mental, spiritual, subjective
INTERNALIZE incorporate
INTERNUNCIO ambassador, envoy, legate, minister
INTERPENETRATE impregnate, intersperse, permeate, pervade, saturate
INTERPOLATE add, admit, alter, annex, append, corrupt, enter, farce, farse, foist, fudge, inject, insert, insinuate, intercalate, interpose, introduce, intrude, renew, thrust
INTERPOSE arbitrate, bar, come between, demur, disaffect, drag in, foist, help, implant, inject, insert, insinuate, intercede, interfere, interject, interlie, interpolate, intervene, introduce, intrude, meddle, mediate, object, put in, sandwich, smuggle, throw in, thrust, toss in, work in
INTERPRET annotate, construe, decipher, decode, deduce, define, diagnose, divine, elucidate, explain, explicate, expound, gloss, gloze, illustrate, infer, open, read, rede, scan, simplify, tender, translate, understand, unfold, unravel
INTERPRETATION anagoge, aspect, baraita, construction, definition, diagnosis, dittology, enigraphy, epikeia, exegesis, exegetics, explanation, exposition, gloss(ology), gospel, hermeneutics, light, meaning, metoposcopy, oneirology, pathognomy, physiognomy, prognosis, prophasis, semeiology, semeiotics, significance, solarism, solution, translation, version
aid bohn, cab, clavis, crib, horse, pony, trot
biblical exegesis, hermeneutics
twofold dittology
INTERPRETER cabalist, definer, demonstrator, dragoman, exegete, explainer,

explicator, exponent, expositor, expounder, go-between, haham, hakamin, hermeneut, hierophant, interlocutor, latiner, lingster, linguist, metaphrast, munchee, mystagogue, oneirocritic, paraphrast, selli, selloi, translater, truchman, ulema
professional dragoman
scriptural exegete, hermeneut
INTERROGATE arraign, ask, catechize, debrief, examine, grill, inquire, probe, pry, pump, query, question, quiz, speer, targe
INTERROGATION examination, inquest, inquiry, interpellation, probe, query, quest(ion), quiz, test
mark erotema, eroteme
INTERROGATIVE how, what, when, where, which, who, why
INTERROGATOR inquirer, inquisitor, prober, pumper, questioner
INTERRUPT arrest, break (in)(off), butt in, cease, check, chime in, chin in, defer, derail, discontinue, disrupt, disturb, divide, hinder, horn in, intercept, interfere, intermit, intervene, intrude, meddle, obstruct, postpone, stay, stop, suspend, thwart
INTERRUPTED broken, choppy, discontinuous, snatchy
INTERRUPTION breach, break, caesura, cessation, cutback, diastem, hiatus, hitch, hocket, hoquet, intermission, interval, lapse, letup, pause, recess, stop (over), suspension
polite ahem
INTERSECT bisect, break, cross, cut, decussate, divide, meet, traverse
INTERSECTING compital, crucial, diallel
INTERSECTION cloverleaf, corner, crossing, crossroad, crossway, interval, joint, junction, roundabout
pert. nodal, secant
point foot, staurion
INTERSPERSE diversify, interfuse, interlard, intersow,

intersprinkle, salt, scatter, thread

INTERSTICE aperture, areola, areole, cell, chink, cleft, crack, crevice, gap, interval, orifice, pore, rima, space, spiracle, stoma, vacuity

pert. areolat

INTERSTITIAL interregnal, intervallic

INTERVAL breach, break, caesura, cessation, decima(l), diapason, diastem, distance, entr'acte, gap, hiatus, hole, interim, interlude, intermission, interregnum, interruption, interstice, lacuna, lapse, meantime, parenthesis, pause, period, pitch, recess, respite, rest, season, separation, space, spell, stretch, term, vacancy, void

at irregular sporadically

musical fifth, fourth, ninth, octave, second, seventh, sixth, third

short break, streak

INTERVENE break in, divide, intercede, interfere, interpose, interrupt, intrude, meddle, mediate, obtrude, part, separate, stickle

INTERVENING interfering, interjacent, mediant, mesne, middle, pending

INTERVENTION arbitration, intercession, interposition, mediation, obtrusion.

INTERVERSION metathesis

INTERVIEW appointment, audience, conference, contact, date, duel, examine, hearing, inspection, meeting, parley, question, quiz

formal audience

INTERVIEWER peephole

INTERVOLVE coil, roll, twist, vine, wind, wreath

INTERWEAVE bend, blend, braid, connect, impleach, interlace, intertwine, lace, mat, mingle, mix, plait, plash, plat, raddle, splice, tangle, twine, unite, wattle

INTERWOVEN braided, implicate, netted, retiary

INTESTINAL abdominal, alvine, enteral, enteric, inner, inside, interior, internal, inward, visceral

INTESTINE(S) abdomen, chitlins, colon, domestic,

duct, gut(s), ingangs, inner, internal, native, stomach, tharm, viscera, viscus

comb. entero, ileo

hormone secretin

inflammation colitis

loop knuckle

outside of abenteric

part ile, ileum, ilium, jejunum

pert. alvine, enteric, visceral

INTIMACY affinity, communion, familiarity, friendship, intrigue, liaison, privacy

INTIMATE allude, announce, betoken, boon, bosom, buddy, catercousin, chatty, chief, chum(my), close(up), companion, comrade, confidant, confidential, cosy, cozy, crony, dear, essential, familiar, friend(ly), gremial, hint, homelike, homey, imply, indicate, informal, inmost, insinuate, intime, inward, keyhole, midmost, near, pal, personal, private, privy, refer, secret, sib, signify, suggest, tete-a-tete, thick, tosh, voice, waist

INTIMATION allusion, announcement, clew, clue, cue, foreboding, hint, information, inkling, innuendo, notice, notification, premonition, · scent, supposition, whiff, wind

INTIMIDATE abash, abuse, alarm, awe, badger, bait, ballyrag, bluff, browbeat, buffalo, bulldoze, bully(rag), chevy, coerce, constrain, cow, daunt, discount, force, frighten, harass, hector, hound, menace, nag, overawe, ride, tease, terrify, terrorize, threaten

INTIMIDATION blackmail, browbeating, bullying, commination, demoralization, menace, threat, thunder

INTINCTION dyeing, eucharist, extract, infusion

INTO among, inside, inward(ly), until, unto, within

the bargain and, besides, moreover, to boot

INTOLERABLE enormous, extreme, insufferable, irresistible, unbearable, unpleasant

INTOLERANCE bias, bigotry, discrimination, dogmatism, fanaticism, impatience, narrowness, prejudice

INTOLERANT bigoted, closed, jaundiced, narrowminded, prejudiced, unfair

INTONATION accent, cadence, cant, chant, delivery, fall, harmonization, inflection, modulation, pitch, recitation, sonance, song, tone, tonetics

INTONE cant(illate), chant, croon, drawl, drone, introit, recite, sing, utter

INTORT complicate, curl, twine, twist, weave, wind, wreathe

INTOXICANT alcohol, inebriant, LIQUOR, poison, stimulant

INTOXICATE addle, befuddle, bemuse, besot, boozify, crock, disguise, elate, excite, fire, fuddle, illuminate, inebriate, inflame, inspire, muddle, overtake, plaster, poison, pollute, provoke, soak, souse, stew, swack, thrill, tipsify, tox.

INTOXICATED ardent, barley-sick, beery, bemused, besotted, boiled, boozy, bosky, bousy, buffy, bungfu, canned, capernoited, cockeyed, crapulent, crapulous, delirious, drenched, drunk(en), fargone, flustered, fou, fried, fuddled, full, gay, giddy, glorious, groggy, happy, heady, high, hungover, inebriated, inebrious, in one's cups, jolly, laced, lit, loaded, maudlin, mellow, merry, muddled, nappy, oiled, pipped, potted, reeling, smashed, sodden, sosh(ed), sotted, sozzled, spiffed, spifflicated, squiffy, stewed, stoned, tanked, tight, tipsy, toft, tosy, under the influence, whole-seas, zonked

INTOXICATING exciting, hard, heady, provocative, stimulating

INTOXICATION anesthia, bliss, dipsomania, disguise, dutch courage, ebriosity, frenzy, fuddle, hangover, intemperance, ivresse, joy,

madness, obfuscation, pot-valiance, pot-valor, temulence
of animals dunziekte

INTRACTABLE balky, cantankerous, contrary, dogged, factious, froward, headstrong, inflexible, insubordinate, mulish, obstinate, ornery, perverse, rebellious, recalcitrant, refractory, restive, stubborn, sullen, thwart, unmanageable, unruly, wayward, willful

INTRANSIGENT irreconcilable, radical, uncompromising, unwavering

INTRENCH cut in, dig in, fix, furrow

INTREPID adventurous, audacious, bold, brave, courageous, daredevil, daring, dauntless, doughty, fearless, fiery, game, gritty, hardy, heroic, impavid, lionhearted, plucky, resolute, spirited, valiant, valorous, venturous

INTREPIDITY boldness, brass, bravery, courage, daring, fearlessness, gallantry, guts, heroism, nerve, prowess, valor

INTRICATE arduous, blind, complex, complicated, curious, d(a)edal, difficult, entangled, gordian, hard, involved, knobby, knotty, labyrinthine, mazy, obscure, perplexing, plexiform, tangly, tirlie-whirlie, tirlywhirly, tortuous, tricky

INTRIGUE affair, allure, amo(u)r, angle, artifice, attract, beguile, brigue, cabal, captivate, collusion, complicity, complot, connivance, conspiracy, contrivance, deception, delight, design, enchant, engineering, fascinate, finagle, frame-up, fraud, game, interest, liaison, lobbying, machination, maneuver, manipulation, perplex, plan, plot, puzzle, rendezvous, romance, ruse, scheme, scheming, stratagem, strategy, strings, trick, trinkle, tryst, wile

INTRIGUER jesuit, manipulator, rascal, schemer, strategist, tactician, wirepuller

INTRINSIC absolute, congenital, essential, genuine, immanent, inborn, inbred, ingrained, inherent, inmost, innate, internal, intimate, material, native, natural, normal, pure, real, regular, right, solid, true, typical

INTRINSICALLY per se, really, truly

INTRODUCE acquaint, admit, announce, approach, begin, borrow, bring(in) (up), broach, carry, conduct, enter, expose, herald, immit, implant, import, inaugurate, induct, infix, infuse, initiate, inject, innovate, insert, install, instill, institute, interpose, invoke, lead, meet, preface, present, produce, propose, publish, reveal, sponsor, usher

INTRODUCTION bow, cue, debut, entrance, exordium, explanation, foreword, inauguration, installation, interjection, introit, isagoge, overture, preamble, preface, prelude, proem, prologue, prolusion, protasis
drama protasis
scholarly isagoge

INTRODUCTORY beginning, exordial, prefatory, preliminary, protatic, systatic

INTROIT requiem

INTROMIT admit, insert, interfere, intermeddle, introduce, receive

INTROSPECTIVE autistic, idiotropic, introverted, reticent, self-absorbed, selfish, withdrawn

INTRUDE barge in, bother, break in, bust in, butt in, chisel, crash, crowd, cut in, encroach, entrench, foist, horn in, impose, infringe, insinuate, interfere, interlope, interpose, intervene, invade, meddle, muscle in, obtrude, overstep, press in, push in, squeeze in, tamper, transgress, trench, trespass

INTRUDER buttinsky, carpetbagger, interloper, outsider, scalawag, stranger, trespasser

INTRUSION entry, invasion, seizure

INTRUSIVE curious, fresh, impertinent, meddlesome, nosy, officious, prying, snoopy, spurious

INTRUST See ENTRUST.

INTUIT apprehend, feel, know, sense

INTUITION acumen, anschauung, anticipation, clairvoyance, divination, esp, hunch, insight, inspiration, instinct, penetration, perception, reason, second sight, soul, telepathy, understanding

INTUITIVE direct, immediate, innate, instinctive, knowing, natural, noetic, perceiving, perceptive, seeing

INUNCTION anointing, cream, grease, ointment, pomade, unguent
pert. aliptic

INUNDATE deluge, drench, drown, engulf, fill, flood, glut, immerse, overflow, overwhelm, submerge, surround, swamp

INUNDATION abundance, alluvio(n), cataclysm, deluge, flood, flow, freshet, overflow, spate, water

INURE acclimate, accomodate, accustom, adapt, adjust, avail, benefit, brand, brutalize, brutify, discipline, drill, exercise, familiarize, habituate, harden, school, season, steel, toughen, train

INURED callous, hardened, inveterate, tough

INURN bury, entomb, inhume, inter

INUTILE bad, useless, worthless

INVADE attack, breach, break in, encroach, enter, entrench, foray, infest, infringe, intrude, mauraud, PENETRATE, permeate, pierce, probe, push in, raid, storm, trench, trespass, violate

INVALID bad, barren, baseless, bootless, bum, disabled, done for, effete, empty, false, fatuitious, fatuous, feckless, feeble, frail, fruitless, futile, hog-tied, hors de combat, ill, illogical, inane, infirm, inoperative, nugacious, nugatory, null, patient, shut-in, sick, sterile, vain, valetudinarian, void, weak

food gruel, pap

INVALIDATE abrogate, afflict, annul, avoid, break, cancel, destroy, disprove, disqualify, impair, negate, neutralize, nullify, obliterate, overthrow, quash, repeal, unfit, vacate, veto, vitiate, void, weaken

INVALUABLE costly, dear, helpful, precious, priceless, serviceable, useful, worthwhile

INVARIABLE changeless, constant, immutable, inflexible, unchanging, uniform, unvarying

INVARIABLY all the while, always, ever, forever, generally, often, usually

INVASION assault, attack, breach, break in, encroachment, foray, inbreak, incursion, inroad, intrusion, irruption, raid, trespass, violation

INVECTIVE abuse, aspersion, billingsgate, blasphemy, contumely, curse, diatribe, inveigh, oath, obloquy, profanity, railing, reproach, scurrility, vituperation

INVEIGH abuse, assail, blame, censure, chide, condemn, denounce, rail, reproach, vituperate

INVEIGLE allure, beguile, blandish, blarney, cajole, charm, coax, decoy, delude, entice, lead on, lure, mislead, persuade, seduce, snare, tempt, trap, wheedle, win

INVENT coin, conceive, concoct, conjure, contrive, create, design, devise, fabricate, fashion, feign, forge, form, frame, make, mint, originate, plan, plot, produce, project, scheme, shape, start

INVENTION coinage, commentation, contrivance, creation, creativity, device, fabrication, fancy, fantasy, fecundity, fertility, fiction, figment, forgery, imagination, ingenuity, originality, origination, product, productivity, prolificity

dramatic ibsenism

INVENTIVE adroit, audacious, clever, creative, imaginative, ingenious, original, poetical

INVENTOR author, coiner, conceiver, creator, framer, maker, minter, mintman, producer, starter, talos

protection copyright, patent

INVENTORY account, appraise, asset(s), audit, bill, calculate, canon, catalog(ue), check, count, examine, inspect, line, list, overhaul, record, register, roll, roster, rota, schedule, stock, store, table, tally

method fifo, lifo

INVERSE opposite, reverse, topsy-turvy

relation antistrophe

INVERSION chiasmus, ectropion, entropion, resupination, retroflexion, reversal, reverse, transposal, transposition

INVERT capsize, convert, derange, evert, exchange, overturn, reverse, revert, transpose, turn down, upend, upset

INVERTEBRATE coward, insect, irresolute, mollusk, polyp, spineless, weakling, weakwilled, worm

body wall parisoma

group aptera, arthrozoa, articulata, radiata

marine phoronid

segmented arthropod

INVERTED amphitropal, amphitropous, anatropous, hyperbatic, inside out, outside in, palindromic, topsyturvy, upside-down

commas quotation marks

INVEST ante, apparel, array, attire, belay, beleaguer, besiege, block, buy, clothe, confer, consecrate, corral, dress, don, dub, endow, endue, envelope, feoff, finance, fund, furnish, gird, girt, grant, inaugurate, induct, indue, inform, initiate, install, ordain, place, prove, provide, qualify, raze, risk, robe, settle, sift, sink, spend, surround, tire, trust, venture, wrap

INVESTIGATE ascertain, bird-dog, canvass, delve into, dig into, discuss, examine, excuss, explore,

fathom, indagate, inquire, look into, observe, plumb, poke, probe, pry into, research, scrutate, search, seek, sift, sound, spy, trace, track, wash

INVESTIGATION analysis, audit, delving, examination, exploration, inquest, inquisition, inspection, legwork, observation, perquisition, pilpul, probe, quiz, research, scrutiny, sounding, study, test, trial

pert. heuristic, zetetic

INVESTIGATOR detective, gumshoe, prober, sleuth, snoop, spotter, tracer

group committee, jury, panel

INVESTMENT annuity, bond, capital, clothing, commitment, cover(ing), dress, endowment, flier, garment, habiliments, installation, land, layer, nut, real estate, risk, robe, siege, sinking fund, speculation, stake, stock, venture

income yield

list portfolio

total capitalization

INVESTOR aviador, capitalist, entrepreneur, shareowner, stockholder

INVETERATE accustomed, addicted, casehardened, chronic, confirmed, customary, deep-rooted, deepseated, enduring, established, fixed, habitual, hardened, implanted, infixed, ingrained, innate, inured, obstinate, rooted, set(tled), traditional, usual

INVIDIOUS distasteful, envious, hateful, jealous, malicious, mean, obnoxious, offensive, repellent, repugnant

INVIGORATE animate, brace, cheer, encourage, energize, enliven, exhilarate, fortify, inspirit, liven, quicken, refresh, renew, resuscitate, revive, stimulate, strengthen, vitalize, vivify

INVIGORATING analeptic, awakening, bracing, brisk, chilly, crisp, fresh, hearty, restorative, restoring, tonic, vital, zestful

INVINCIBLE dauntless, impregnable, indomitable, intrepid, irresistible, strong, successful, unassailable, unbeatable, unconquerable, undaunted

INVIOLABLE blessed, consecrated, dedicated, divine, hallowed, holy, irrefrangible, pure, reliable, sacred, sacrosanct, secure

INVIOLATE faithful, sacred, undefiled, unstained

INVISIBLE concealed, hidden, imperceptible, inconspicuous, indiscernible, indistinct, infinitesimal, masked, microscopic, screened, secret, unapparent, unnoticeable, unnoticed, unseen, veiled, viewless

comb. aphan(o)

empire ku klux klan

INVITATION allurement, bid(dance), call(ing), card, come-hither, command, incentive, request, summons

INVITE allure, appeal to, ask, attract, beckon, beg, bid, call, challenge, command, court, encourage, entice, excite, interest, inveigle, lure, order, pray, provoke, request, solicit, sue, summon, tempt, toll, try, urge, welcome, woo

to duel challenge

INVOCATION agnus dei, appeal, benedicite, benediction, bismillah, command, conjuration, deesis, epiclesis, epiklesis, hocuspocus, malediction, malison, prayer, rune, sorcery, summons, wish

INVOICE bill, chalan, manifest, statement

INVOKE address, adjure, appeal, beg, beseech, bless, call, clepe, conjure up, entreat, evoke, implore, plead, pray, solicit, summon, supplicate

devil conjure

evil curse

INVOLUCRE anthodium, covering, cupule, envelope, epicalyx, hull, husk, leaf, rosette, whorl

INVOLUNTARY accidental, compelled, extemporaneous, forced, grudging, helpless, instinctive, mechanical, reflex(ive), spon-

taneous, unconscious, unintentional, unwilled

servitude bondage, slavery

INVOLUTE complex, curled, intricate, involved, rolled, spiraled

INVOLVE absorb, bewilder, care, carry, coil, complicate, compose, comprise, concern, connect, connote, contain, cover, draw in, embarrass, embrace, embroil, encoil, encumber, enfold, engage, engross, enmesh, ensnare, entail, entangle, entrammel, entwine, envelope, evidence, evince, hankle, implicate, imply, import, include, incorporate, incriminate, infold, interest, lap, link, obscure, relate, require, snare, snarl, subsume, surround, tangle, trap, wrap

INVOLVED applied, complex, complicated, confused, deep, detailed, difficult, hard, implicated, intricate, involuted, knotty, labyrinthine, mazy, muddled, obscure, perplexing, puzzling, tangled, winding

INWARD benward, entad, ental, familiar, heartfelt, innate, inner(ly), inside, interior, internal, into, sincere, toward, unfeigned

INWIT conscience, intellect, understanding

INWRAP See ENWRAP.

IO *brother* phoroneus

changed to heifer

consort zeus

father inachus

gadfly brize

guard argus

pursuer gadfly

rival hera

son epaphus

IODINE *antiseptic* eigon, iatrol

bush greasewood

compound iodide

salt iodate

source kelp, saltpeter

substitute aristal

treat with iodate

IOLANTHE char, earl, peri

IOLAUS *friend* heracles, hercules

parent automedusa, iphicles

uncle heracles, hercules

IOLCUS *king* pelias

IOLE *captor* heracles, hercules

consort heracles, hercules, hyllus

father eurytus

moth eurytus

IOLITE cordierite, iberite, peliom(a)

ION amphion, isomer, ligand, molecule, oxonium, particle, speck

current electrojet

duration lifetime

grandmother helen

negative anion

parent apollo, creusa, xuthus

positive cation, kation

son aegicores, argades

stepfather xuthus

IONE *husband* glaucus

rival nydia

IONIA(N) *artist* anacreon, mimnermus

assembly panionia

city chios, clazomenae, colophon, ephesus, erythrae, lebedus, miletus, myus, phocaea, priene, samos, smyrna, teos

coin obol(o)

gulf adriatic, arta, patras, taranto

island cephalonia, cerigo, chios, corfu, ithaca, kai, kei, kythera, laut, let(t)i, leucas, levkas, paxos, samos, taphiae, zante

islands, pert. heptanesian

monk aidan

painter apelles, parrasius

philosopher anaxagoras, thales

promontory mycale

sanctuary panionium

IONORNIS bluecoot, bluepeter, gallinule

IOTA ace, atom, bit, gram, jot, mite, particle, smidgen, smitch, speck, ten, tittle, whit

IOWA *capital* des moines

city amana, ames, burlington, cedar falls, cedar rapids, clinton, council bluffs, davenport, des moines, dubuque, fort dodge, fort madison, keokuk, lemars, marion, marshalltown, mason city, newton, ottumwa, perry, sioux city, waterloo

college coe, cornell, dorot, grinnell, loras, parsons, wartburg *county* adair, ida, keokuk, kossuth, linn, osceola, sac, tama

indian fox, sac, sauk

lake clear, spirit, storm

native hawkeye

nickname hawkeye state

president hoover

religious society amana

river big sioux, cedar, des moines, missouri, skunk

state bird goldfinch

state flower wild rose

state tree oak

IPECAC emetic, feverroot, itoubou, plant

source cephaelis, evea

substance emetine

IPHIANASSA *parent* agamemnon, antia, proteus

sister iphinoe, lysippe

slayer hera

IPHICLES *brother* heracles, hercules

consort automedusa

parent alcmene, amphitryon, cephalus, phylacus

son iolaus

IPHIDAMAS *parent* antenor, theano

slayer agamemnon

IPHIGENIA *benefactor* thoas, thoon

brother orestes

parent agamemnon, clytemnestra, helena, theseus

savior artemis

sister electra

IPHIMEDIA *consort* aloeus, poseidon

son aloidae, ephialtes, otus

IPHIS *beloved* anaxarete, ianthe

offspring evadne

parent alector, ligdus, telethusa

IPHITUS *father* eurytus

sister iole

slayer hercules

son schedius

wife hippolyte

IPOMOEA batatas, batatilla, dawnflower, manroot, morningglory, scammony, vine

IQ *test originator* binet

IRACUND choleric, irascible

IRAD *father* enoch

son mehujael

IRAN See also PERSIA.

capital teh(e)ran

city isfahan, persepolis, shiraz

dynasty pahlavi

oil center abadan

party rastakhiz

people bactrian, bartangi, galcha, persian, sart, shugni, tat

premier mossadegh

ruler king of kings, light of the aryans, shah

shah mohammed-riza-pahlevi

throne peacock

IRAQ See also MESOPOTAMIA.

ancient kish

coin dinar

king faisal, feisal, feisul

leader saddam husayn, zaid hydr

party baath

port basra, fao, ummqass

IRAS *companion* charmian

mistress cleopatra

IRASCIBLE angered, angry, bad-tempered, bearish, belligerent, brash, cankered, cantankerous, captious, choleric, combustible, churlish, crabbed, cranky, cross, crusty, disagreeable, edgy, fractious, hasty, hot, huffy, iracund, irate, irritable, liverish, mean, melancholy, ornery, patchy, peevish, peppery, perverse, petulant, querulous, restive, snappish, spleeny, splenetic, surly, techy, testy, touchy, ugly, waspish

IRATE angered, angry, cross, enraged, furious, hot, incensed, indignant, infuriated, ireful, mad, nettled, piqued, provoked, wrathful, wroth

IRE anger, fury, indignation, passion, provoke, rage, temper, wrath

IREFUL iracund, passionate, wroth

IRELAND (See also IRISH.) banba, bogland, cathleen ni houlahan, eirann, eire, emerald isle, erin, erse, hibernia, ierne, innisfail, irena, roisin-dubh, shan van vocht, ulster

abbess saint bride, saint brigid

abbot brendan

accent blas, brogue

acre collop, colp

actor aisteoir, boucicault

actress mc kenna, woffington

adam partholon

affair comether

agitator o'connell

alphabet ogam

ancestor fir bolg, fir domnann, ish, ith, mil(edh), milesius, tuatha de danaan

anti-british group fenians

apostle st patrick

apricot potato

army black and tan

artist in metals cerd

assembly aenach, aonach, dail, feis

awl elsin

bard aneurin, ecna, fergus, llywarch, ossian

basalt deposit giants' causeway

basket cleave(ful), skeough

battle clontarf

battle cry aboo, abu

battle goddess badb, bodb

battle, mythological magtuireadh, moytura

bay bantry, blacksod, clew, dingle, donegal, drogheda, dundalk, killala, mal, sligo, tralee

bells of malucca balm, molucella, shellflower

bird, protected swan

bit traneed

black dhu

boat boston hooker, coracle, cot, pook(h)aun

boor bosthoon, clout, dolt

bootleg poteen

borrowed stock daer

bribe cuddy

cabstand hazard

cap barrad

cape clear

capital balleathacliath, belfast, dublin, tara, tralee

cardinal wiseman

carriage shandrydan, sidecar

cart jaunting car

castle blarney, tara

cattle dexter, kerry

cattle herd creaght

cattle lord boaire

cattle shelter bool(e)y

chemist boyle

chieftain tanist

chisel celt

church kil

church steward (h)erenach

city adare, athlone, belfast, cobh, cork, donegal, dublin, ennis, kilkenny, killarney, limerick, londonderry, lurgan, mallow, sligo, tipperary, tralee

clan cinel, sept, siol

clansman aire

cloak inar
cloth bandle-linen
club alpeen, shillala(h), shillela(g)h
coin pence, pound, rap, real, shilling, turney
coin, counterfeit rap
comb. hiberno
confetti bricks
constable black and tan
cordial usquebaugh
coronation stone lia-fail
county antrim, armagh, carlow, cavan, clare, cork, donegal, down, fermanagh, galway, kerry, kildare, kilkenny, laoighis, leitrim, leix, limerick, londonderry, longford, louth, mayo, meath, monaghan, offaly, roscommon, sligo, tipperary, tyrone, ulster, waterford, westmeath, wexford, wicklow
critic malone
cudgel alpeen
cup, wooden mether
curse bad cess, bad scran
dagger rinka, skean(dhu), skene(dhu)
dance jig, planxty, rinka (fadda), rinncefada
dane ostman
darling achree, acushla, agran, allanah, aroon, aruin, asthor(e), astor, avourneen, gra, machree, macushla, mavourneen, mavournin, roon
demon amadan, badb, bodb, dhoul
demon race fomorians
dialect agam, ohgam, ogam
dirge coronach, keen, ullagone
disaster potato famine
dish colcannon, stew
district birr
dividend assessment
doctor ollam(h)
dramatist beckett, behan, boucicault, dunsany, gregory, o'casey, shaw, sheridan, synge, wilde, yeats
drink bonnyclabber
dwelling, ancient crannog
early kingdom munster
ecclesiastic erenach, herenach, patric(k)
emblem shamrock
enclosure bawn
endearment term See *darling,* above.
epic tain

eros aengus
exclamation adad, ahey, arah, aroo, arro, aru, begorra, booh, eheu, och(one), orra, whist, wurra
evil eye drochuil
explorer brendan the navigator
explosive paxo
fabric rumswizzle
fair aenach, aonach
fairy amadan, banshee, banshie, cluricaune, leprechaun, lubrican, shee, sidhe
family group cinel
farmer scullog(ue)
feast beltane, beltine, cetshamain, imbolc, lugnasad, samhain
festival beltane, feis
folk daoine
forever erin go bragh, erin go brath
fort lis, rath
freebooter rapparee
freeman aire
free thinker blaster
fuel peat
game hurling
garment inar, lenn
general shea
get-together ceili
giant cotter, fionn, formors, frank, grantorto, mc donald, mellon, murphy, o'brien
giddiness soorawm
girdle criss
girl colleen
god, goddess See CELT *god, goddess.*
good-for-nothing spalpeen
grass traneen
groggery shebeen
hair-do glib
harp clarsach
harvester spalpeen
hat caubeen
headdress binnoque
hero boru, conn of the hundred battles, cuchulainn, emmet, fenian, finn maccool, goll, olwen, ossian
heroine emer
hero's sword calad-bolg
herring scuddawn
hobgoblin pooka
hood cochull
historian lecky
holiday whitmonday
house spirit banshee, benshee
idler buckeen

idol cenn cruaich, crom cruaich, crom dubh
illiterate keelman
imp leprechaun
independence sinn fein
infantryman kern(e)
insurgent oakboy
island achill, aran, bear, clear, holy, man, rathlin, saltee, tory
jug cruisken
junior lord ogaire
king aed, angwyshaunce, ardri, bres(s), brian-boru, enna, eochaid, finn, mac eire, matholwych, nuada, rig
king's home tara
knife skean, skene
laborer mike
lace curragh
lake boderg, capra, conn, cooter, corrib, derg, doo, dromore, ennell, erne, gowna, key, killarney, leane, lough, neagh, oughter, ree, sheelin, tay
lament coronach, keen, ochone, wirra
lament for dead keening
landholding system rundale
language celtic, keltic
lawyer brehon
leader cosgrave, costello, de valera, o'connor, parnell, redmond, sheridan
limestone calp
linen center belfast
liquor pot(h)een
lord aire(ard)(desa)(forgill)(tuise), boaire, ogaire, tanist
lottery sweepstakes
love god aengus, angus og, oengus
luck cess
mahogany alder
mathematician hamilton
measure bandle, crannock, mile
meet feis
melody planxty
mermaid merrow
militia fenian
mineral springs chalybeate
missionary kilian, st columba
moccasin pampootee, pampootie
monk culdee
monk's cell kil(l)
mother of gods ana, anu
mud slob
music festival feis

name, old fodhla, ierne, innis
name, poetic banba, innisfail
national theatre abbey
negative sorra
nobleman See *lord,* above.
oath bedad, begorra, bejabbers
oyster powldoody
painter lover, orpen
party fianna fail, hooley, sinn fein
patriot casement, emmet, healy, oakboy, pearse
peak antrim, caha, donegal, errigal, galtee, keeper, kennedy, keppure, leinster, mourne, mulrea, sperrin, wicklow
peasant frieze-coat, kern(e)
peat ger
people celt(ic), daoine, erse, gael, hibernian
personified irena
pert. celtic, gaelic, hibernian, hibernic, smaragdine
physicist fitzgerald, walton
pig bonav
pig's trotter crubeen
pipe dudeen
pirate fomor(ian)
plant bluet
poem amhran, limerick, rann
poet amairgin, bard, colum, dowden, dunsany, emmet, fili, goldsmith, moore, ossian, pearse, russell, stephens, tighe, wolfe, yeats
point cahore, carnsore
police garda
political group sinn fein
political party fianna fail
politician o'connell, parnell
porcelain belleek
port belfast, cobh, cork, drogheda, dublin, dun laoghaire, limerick, londonderry, shannon, sligo, tralee
potato basket skeough
pouch spleuchan, spleughan
prelate ussher
president hyde, o'kelley
priest druid, soggarth
prime minister costello, de valera, lemass, taoiseach
princess deirdre, iseult, isolde
prison curragh
proprietor tanist
protestant orangeman, sassenach, sassenagh

province connaught, leinster, munster, ulster
queen boadicea, boudicca, cartimandua, medb
race fir bolg
range comeragh, galty, stacks
rascal spalpeen
rebel group ira
reel rinka fadda
refugees fuidhir
religious devotee voteen
republic poblacht
republicanism fenianism
resort kinsale
revolutionary collins, fenian
river bandon, bann, barrow, blackwater, boyne, cavan, clare, deel, erne, feale, flesk, foyle, kenmare, laune, lee, liffey, mull, munster, nore, shannon, suir
robber woodkern
rose tralee
royal family dalcassian, eoghanacht
saint aidan, bridget, brigid, columba, edana, patric(k)
salutation achara
sausage drisheen
sea arm solway firth
sea demon formor(ian)
sea god ler
sea island holy, man
secret society molly maguires, orangemen
servant girl biddy
shield sciath
shilling mint-hog
shop sheBeen
shrew barge
snipe avocet
society aire, sinn fein, siol
soldier ashe, bonagh, galloglass, kern(e), o'higgins, rapparee
soldier's quartering bona-(u)ght
song rann
spade loy, slane
speakeasy shebeen
spirit banshee, banshie
spurge mackenboy
statesman burke, grattan, healy
steward erenach, herenach
stock daer
stone lia-fail
story-teller shanachie
straw load barth
surgeon colles
sweetheart avourneen, colleen, gra
symbol harp, shamrock

tax bona(u)ght, cess
tenant fuidhir, saer
tenpence bit
tenure sorehon, sorren
theater abbey
theologian erigena
thunder god dagda
toast slainte
tramp bogtrotter, caird
tribal division sept
tribe cinel, siol
trout gillaroo
turf for roofing scraw
vehicle noddy
verse limerick, rann
war god bodb the red
war goddess morrigan, morrigu
warrior fenian
warrior band fiana
whiskey poteen, usquebaugh
whitefish pollan
witchcraft pishogue
woman harp
womanhood emer
wretch spridhogue
writer ashe, beckett, bowen, ervine, fili, joyce, lecky, lever, lover, moore, o'connor, o'faolain, o'flaherty, ossian, reid, tighe, shaw, wilde
writing system og(h)am
writings, ancient senchus mor
IRENE *goddess of* peace
parent themis, zeus
IRENIC calm, conciliatory, henotic, pacific, pacifist(ic), peaceful, placating, placatory
IRI *parent* bela
IRID crocus, gladiolus, iris
IRIDESCENT chatoyant, cymorphanous, irid(i)al, iridian, irised, mother-of-pearl, nacre(d), nacr(e)ous, nacry, opalescent, opaline, opaloid, pavonian, pavonine, pearlish, pearly, prismatic, rainbowlike
IRIS acidanthera, alcazar, antholiza, asteroid, azure, babiana, belamcanda, eye, flag(leaf), flower, gladdon, herb, ireos, irid, ixia, levers, lilial, lilium, lis, luce, messenger, moraca, plant, rainbow, orris, sedge, seg(g), shadow, spirit, sunbow, tileroot, variegate
absence aniridia
-adorned fleury

bearded alcazar, crimson king, pogon
beardless apogon
comb. irid(o)
excision iridectomy
family irid
inflammation iritis, uveitis
-like plant avendbloem
paralysis iridoplegia
parent electra, thaumas
part areola, entiris, uvea
patroness hera
pert. irian, iridal
root orris
son eros
surgery coretomy, iridectomy
yellow sedge

IRISH (See also IRELAND for geographical references.) anger, celt(ic), eirann, erse, fury, milesian, temper
-american society clanagael
atticus faulkner
"black" dhu
"climb" scrawm
cobbler potato
daisy dandelion
free state eire, saorstat eireann
"indeed" aru
james shamus
"lift" hoosh
"love" gra
"luck" cess
minerva brigantia, brigit
moss blanc-mange, carrageen, chondrus, cyprus spurge, sloke
"mouth" gob
pennant cow's-tail, reveling, thread
"rascal" spalpeen
"regret" ochone
"scratch" scrawm
"sorrow" sorra
"spank" scud
touchstone basalt
"trifle" traneen
"white" bawn

IRISHMAN aire, bogtrotter, celt, eamon, eireannach, gael, greek, harp, hibernian, kelt, kern(e), mac, manxman, mick(y), milesian, orangeman, paddy(whack), pat, scot(t), shoneen, spalpeen, teague, yreis
learned ollamh
rural bogtrotter
wild matagouri, tumatakuru

IRK aggravate, annoy, bore, bother, chafe, disgust, disturb, fret, fry, itch, nettle, perturb, provoke, rasp, tire, tedium, trouble, upset, vex, weary

IRKSOME annoying, displeasing, dull, fagging, humdrum, onerous, pesky, stupid, tedious, thorny, tiresome, tiring, troublesome, unpleasant

IROK gomuti

IROKO kambala, muvule, odoom, odum, yoruba

IRON adamant(ine), angle, brand, cleek, eisen, element, enduring, ferric, ferrous, ferrum, fetter, firm, gat, goffer, golf club, gun, handcuff, hard, harsh, mangle, mashie, metal, mitis, piece, power, press, robust, rude, severe, shackle, smooth, spike, steel(y), stirrup, strength, strong
affinity for siderophile
age epoch hallstatt, la tene, villanovan
age man aborigine, gollaseccan
aggregate bainite
alloy invar, steel, taenite
angle lath, stiffener
arsenite lollingite, mispickel
ballast kentledge
bar bilbo
beam support torsel
block anvil
boom withe, wythe
boot despotism, tyranny
branding escharotic
bush hardhack
calking chisel
carbide austenite, bainite, cementite
cast mitis, spiegel(eisen), yetling(g)
chancellor bismarck
city cleveland, pittsburgh
climbing creeper, gaff, piton, spur
coated terne
collar caecan(et), joug
comb. ferr(o)(oso), sider(o)
compound beraunite, bilinite, bravoite, cacoxenite, franklinite, gothite, graftonite, ilesite, iserite, mispickel, pyrite, utahite
containing ferric
curtain border
defect seam
deficiency anemia, chlorosis
deposit gossan, iron-hat
disk spinner

driving cleek
dross sinter, slag
duke wellington
-fisted mean, stingy, strong
flower sheep's-bit
forger blacksmith, coachsmith
fragment potleg
free from deferrize
garters fetters, shackles
gates djerdap
glassblowing bait
golf cleek, jigger, mashie, mashy, mid-mashie, niblick, pitcher
grappling clip, crampon, creep, grapnel
hand despotism, discipline
-handed despotic, firm, inflexible, rigorous
hat gossan
hatter's slug
-hearted brave, cruel, unfeeling
hook-shaped croc, kilp
horse bicycle, engine, locomotive, tricycle
hot cauter(ant), cautery
incompatible with antisideric
kind pig, steam
liquid slurry
loop oolly
lump oolly, pig
magnet armature
-man dollar, money, talus
marking brander
mask, man in mattioli
mass bloom
meteoric giderite
millstone rind, rynd
-nickel calite
oak blackjack, cerris
ore dufrenite, gothite, hematite, jacutinga, limnite, magnetite, minette, ocher, ochre, siderite, taconite, turgite
ore sand iserine
oxide franklinite, gothite
pasty sponge
pert. ferric, ferrous
pieces potleg
pig kentledge, spiegel(eisen)
planet mars
plate tramp
pressing tailor's goose
priming drift
pyrite brazil, coalblende, coalbrass, foolsgold, marcasite
rations ammo, ammunition
sand iserin
sediment carr
sheet acicul, plate, terne

soldering copper
source hematite
specular hematite
spinel bercynite
superior osmund
tailor's goose
tamping driver
tree acle, ixora
waste cobble, slag
work ferrament
worker lohar, moschi
wrought bloom, mitis
IRONBARK mugga
IRONBOUND firm, harsh, rigid, rigorous, rugged, shackled, unyielding
IRONCLAD armored, exacting, firm, monitor, rigorous, severe
IRONHEAD duck, goldeneye, knapweed, wood-ibis
IRONIC biting, burlesque, cutting, figurative, hudibrastic, mordant, sarcastic, sardonic, satiric(al), scathing
IRONMONGERY *hardware* store
IRONS chains, gyves, shackles
IRONSIDE(S) edmund ii, oliver cromwell
IRONSMITH barbet, ferrer
IRONSTONE cathead, dogger, eaglestone, siderite
IRONWEED aster, flattop, ragweed, vernonia, vervain, wingstem
IRONWOOD acle, akeake, axmaster, breakax, bumelia, burnwood, cassia, colima, cyrilla, firewood, hele, hornbeam, ixora, joewood, mesquite, millettia, mopane, oceanspray, olive, prosopis, puriri, ridge myrtle, sloanea, snakebark, stopper, titi, tree, wamara
IRONY ambiguity, asteism, caricature, causticity, censure, cynicism, humor, lampoon, mockery, mordancy, pasquinade, ridicule, sarcasm, satire, wit
genteel asteism
IROQUOIS *evil spirit* oki, otkon
god echo, orenda, thunder, wind
indian caughnawaga, cayuga, conestoga, erie, hochelago, huron, mengwe, mingo, mohawk, oneida, onondaga, st regis, seneca, tionontati, tuscarora, wenrohronon, wyandot(te)

leader hiawatha
magic power orenda
morning star gendenwitha
spirit eithinoma, gunnodoyak, hino, onatha, oshadagea, tawiscara
IRRADIATE brighten, diffuse, enlighten, illuminate, radiumize, shed, shine, transfigure, treat, x-ray
IRRADIATION emanation, emission, illumination
IRRATIONAL aberrant, absurd, batty, blind, brutal, brutish, crazy, demented, distracted, distraught, fanatic(al), fatuous, foolish, idealistic, idiotic, illogical, incoherent, insane, loco, mad, nonsensical, odd, preposterous, psychotic, queer, raving, senseless, silly, strange, stupid, unintelligent, unreasonable, unsound, unwise
number surd
IRREDEEMABLE abandoned, incorrigible
IRREGULAR aberrant, abnormal, ambiguous, amphibolic, amphibolous, anaxial, anomalous, arrhythmic, atactic, ataxinomix, atypic(al), baroque, broken, bumpy, capricious, casual, catchy, changing, choppy, confused, crabbed, crooked, deviative, devious, disorderly, diverse, eccentric, equivocal, erose, erratic, fitful, heteroclite, inconstant, informal, lumpy, mutable, odd, peculiar, queer, ragged, rough, scrappy, singular, snatchy, spasmodic, spastic, spotty, strange, uncertain, uneven, unique, unsettled, unsteady, unusual, variable, weewaw
comb. anom, anomal(i)(o), anomo
IRREGULARITY aberration, abnormality, anomaly, arrhythmy, brokenness, choppiness, defect, deviation, distortion, eccentricity, erraticness, exception, fitfulness, fluctuation, imperfection, inconstancy, jog, ruffle, snag, snick, spottiness, uncertainty, unevenness, variability
IRREGULARLY by fits and

starts, now and again, now and then
IRRELEVANT extraneous, immaterial, inapplicable, inapposite, inapropos, incidental, inessential, pointless, remote, unapt, unconnected, unessential, unrelated
IRRELIGION apathy, atheism, doubt, godlessness, heathenism, impiety, infidelity, irreverance, laxity, paganism, secularity, skepticism
IRRELIGIOUS blasphemous, godless, graceless, heathen, immoral, impious, infidel, irreverent, pagan, profane, sceptical, ungodly
IRREPARABLE hopeless
IRREPRESSIBLE abandoned, homeric, refractory, saucy
IRREPROACHABLE blameless, inculpable, perfect, pure, spotless
IRRESOLUTE abulic, capricious, changeable, doubtful, faint, feeble, fickle, frail, halfhearted, hesitant, hesitating, inconstant, indecisive, infirm, laodicean, lukewarm, mutable, pliable, shaky, spineless, uncertain, undecided, undetermined, unstable, vacillating, variable, wankle, wavering, weak(kneed)(willed)
person butterfly, opportunist, shilly-shallier, shuttlecock, time-server, trimmer, turncoat
IRRESOLUTION caprice, fluctuation, instability, shilly-shally, vacillation
IRRESPONSIBLE carefree, careless, feckless, fly-by-night, frivolous, harumscarum, insolvent, reckless, skittish, unreliable
IRREVERENCE blasphemy, disrespect, impiety, profanity
IRREVERENT aweless, disrespectful, impudent, profane, ungodly, unholy
IRREVOCABLE certain, dead, end, final, firm, hopeless, immutable, mandatory, stable, unalterable
IRRIGATE dilute, moisten, refresh, sluice, syringe, water, wet

IRRIGATION *ditch* acequia, an(n)icut, channel, drove, flume, sluice

IRRITABLE bilious, birsy, brittle, cantankerous, capernoited, choleric, crabbed, crabby, cranky, crook, cross, dyspeptic, edgy, erethismic, fiery, fractious, fretful, fussy, huffy, impatient, iracund, irascible, jumpy, liverish, naggy, peevish, pettish, petulant, querulous, sensitive, snappish, spleenful, spleeny, splenetic, splenitive, techy, testy, tetchy, tetty, toitish, touchy, waspish

IRRITANT poison, provocation, sting, venom
susceptible to allergic

IRRITATE abrade, affront, aggravate, agitate, anger, annoy, badger, bother, chafe, embitter, enrage, exacerbate, exasperate, excite, fret, gall, grate, gripe, hector, incense, inflame, infuriate, ire, irk, jangle, jar, madden, needle, nettle, offend, peeve, pique, provoke, rankle, rasp, rile, roil, sensitize, tar(r), tease, teen, try, vex

IRRITATED afret, angry, crabby, cross, grated, huffy, irate, irked, mad, miffed, nettled, rankled, raw, shirty, smartful, smarting, sore, testy

IRRITATING acrid, annoying, irksome, maddening, nettly, provoking, pungent, rankling, stinging, tiresome

IRRITATION anger, annoyance, birse, crotchet, pique, resentment, steam, stimulation, temper, vexation

IRRUPTION break, bursting, foray, incursion, inroad, invasion, raid

IRTISH *city on* tobolsk
tributary tobol

IRU *father* caleb

IRUS arnaeus
errand-runner for penelope
opponent odysseus, ulysses

IRVING, WASHINGTON
character bracebridge, headless horseman, ichabod crane, knickerbocker, rip van winkle
letters jonathan oldstyle

pseud. geoffrey crayon
work legend of sleepy hollow, sketchbook

IS est, exists, hour, nonce, now, personifies, represents
not ain't, isn't, nis, nys

ISAAC *burial site,* machpelah
home beersheba, gerar, lahairoi, rehoboth, sitnah
nickname ike
parent abra(ha)m, sarah
son edom, esau, israel, jacob, kedar
stew pottage
well esek, lahairoi

ISABEL *daughter* katharine
husband charles iv

ISABELLA *brother* claudio
moth larva woolly-bear
patroness to columbus

ISAIAH esaias, esay
parent amos, hananiah
son shearjashub

ISANDER *father* bellerophon
slayer ares

ISCARIOT traitor

ISCHA *parent* haran

ISENLAND *queen* brun(n)hild(e), brunn(e)-hilde, brynhild

ISEULT isolde
consort mark, tristan, tristram
father angush
maid brangwaine

ISHAR *father* david

ISHBAK *father* abraham

ISHBOSHETH *father* saul

ISHI *son* benzoheth, neariah, pelatiah, rephaiah, sheshan, uzziel, zoheth

ISHIJAN *parent* harim

ISHMA *parent* etam

ISHMAEL outcast, pariah, rover
parent abraham, hagar
son adbeel, dumah, hadad, hadar, jetur, kedar, kedemah, massa, mibsam, mishma, nap(h)ish, nebajoth, tema, zebadiah
skipper ahab

ISHTAR ashtoreth, astarte, inana, innina, mylitta, ninni
arabian name athtar
brother shamash
consort anu, dumuzi, tammuz
father sin
goddess of love, war
holy city erech
insulted by eabani, engidu
kin ereshkigal

rescuer asushu-namir, namtaru
sacred women enitu
shrine arbela
victim tammuz

ISHUI *father* saul

ISINGLASS agalloch, agar (agar), carlock, gelatin, huso, ichthyocol, kanten, leaf, mica, pipe
use micate

ISIS aset, eset, star of the sea
brother osiris
consort osiris
disciple apuleius
emblem tat
enemy set
goddess of fertility, navigation
hiding place buto
kin anubis, nephthys
offspring artemis, bubastis, horus, sept
parent geb, nut, rhea, saturn
priest apuleius
shrine ise(i)um, pilae

ISLAM (See also MOHAMMEDAN.) abbasid

ISLAND ait, archipelago, atoll, calf, cat, cay(o), eyot, holm(e), ile, ilot, inch, insula(r), insulate, isla, isle(t), islot, isolate, kay, key, reef, runway
artificial crannog
-born kamaaina
changed to perimele
city montreal
comb. neso
coral atoll
dance hula
enchanted bali, capri
fabled See legendary, below
floating hover
flying laputa
group antilles, archipelago, caroline, faeroe, marshall, samoa, sandwich, thousand
imaginary luggnagg, utopia
inhabiting nesiote
legendary antilia, atlantis, avalon, bimini, brazil, mayda, meru, obrazil, utopia
lost atlantis, caphalonia
lover islomane
low key
of hypocrites chaneph
of saints ireland
of the moon madagascar
of the sun sicily
of thieves ladrones

pert. insular
refuge crannog
river ait, eyot, holm(e)
rocky skerry
sacred ireland
small ait, calf, cay, islet, kay, key, nubble, skerry
snake-free erin, ireland
universe galaxy
ISLANDER insulary, kanaka
ISLANDS *of the blessed* hesperides
ISLE aisle, aizle, ember, ISLAND, soot, spark
ISLE OF MAN *capital* douglas
city castletown, douglas, peel, ramsey
division sheading, treen
judge deemster, dempster
legislature tynwald
measure kishen, kishon
mountain snaefell
part ayre
pert. manx
ISLE OF MIST skye
ISLE OF WIGHT *city* ryde
ISLE OF WINDS ruach
ISM belief, cult, doctrine, dogma, practice, school, style, system, tenet
follower ist, ite
ISMAILIAN sevener
ISMENE *brother* polynices
parent jocasta, oedipus
sister antigone
ISMENUS *parent* asopus, metope
ISMERAI *parent* elpaal
ISOGLOSS *group* bundle
ISOLATE deracinate, enisle, insulate, island, quarantine, seclude, segregate, sequester
ISOLATED alone, detached, enisled, insular, lone, private, quarantined, quiet, secluded, segregated, sequestered, singular, solitary, stranded, unique
place backwater, billabong, sticks
ISOLATION anchoritism, apartness, desolation, detachment, eremitism, hermitism, hermitry, loneness, privacy, quarantine, recess, reclusion, retirement, retreat, rustication, seclusion, secrecy, segregation, separation, sequestration, solitude, withdrawal
desire for agromania
in in vacuo
ISOLDE See ISEULT.

ISOMER cumidine, decosane, dodecane, metamer, pyran, tosyl, xylene
comb. allo
ISOMORPHIC alike, same, similar
ISONOMIC equal, same
ISOPOD armadillidid, bopryid, crustacean, idothea, wharf-monkey
ISOTOPE carrier, ionium
group pleiad
radioactive cobalt, uranium
separating instrument calutron
ISRAEL(I) (See also BIBLE and HEBREW.) beulah, jacob(ite), jew, judaea, palestine, promised land, sabra, sion, tziyon, yishuv, zion
aircraft kfir, messerschmitt, mosquito, phantom, skyhawk
airline el al
airport lod, lydda
anthem hatikva, hattikvah
archeological site gerar, lachish
army haganah, idf
-born sabra
camp etham
canopy chuppah
capital jerusalem, samaria, shechem, tel aviv
city acre, ashdod, batyam, beersheba, bethel, bethsaida, cana, capernaum, hadera, haifa, hazor, hebron, holon, jaffa, jenin, jericho, jerusalem, joppa, lod, megiddo, nablus, natanya, nazareth, rama(tgan), ramla, rehoboth, rehovot(h), safad, samaria, tel aviv, tirzah, tulkarm
civil defense corps haga
coin agora, agura, mil, pound, pruta
commune kibbutz, moshav
commune member kibbutznik
conscience money shilumin
counter-espionage mossad
dance hora
defense line bar-lev
defense minister dayan
desert negeb, negev
dish ajuj, falafel, humus, pitta
district afula, beersheba, hadera, haifa, nahariya, natanya, rehovot, tel aviv, tiberias
doctrine zionism

drink sabra
dust storm khamseen
exclamation tov, yihe beseder
farmer kibbutznik
father of ben gurion
fish ajuj
forbidden food terefa
former name canaan, palestine
founding document balfour declaration
gate of hope petach, tikva
general abner, adan, allon, dayan, elazar, goren, gur, herzog, lahat, rabin, sharon, weizman, yadin
gun uzi
immigration wave aliya(h)
intelligence service mossad, the institution
judge elon
judge's rule kritarchy
labor federation histadrut
labor party mapai
lake galilee, huleh, tiberias
land measure donum, dunam
leader begin, dayan, gurion, meir, peres, rabin, yadin
measure bath, cab, cor, cubit, donum, dunam, epha(h), ezba, handbreadth, hin, homer, kab, kaneh, kor, log, qaneh, reed, seah
missiles tilim
national anthem hatikva(h)
native sabra
parliament knesset, sanhedrin
party democratic movement for change, freedom, haganah, herut, irgun zvai leumi, labor, liberal, likud, unity
peak atzmon, carmel, harif, nafh, ramon, sagi, tabor
people hebrew, jacobite, jew(ish), sabra, yisrael, yisroel
plain esdraelon, jezreel, sharon
port acre, agaba, ashdod, caesarea, eilat, elath, gaza, haifa, jaffa, tel aviv
president benzvi, chaim weizmann
prime minister eshkol, meir, sharett
region negeb
river faria, jordan, lakhish, malik, qishon, sarida, soreq, yarkon
roads goldene wegen
sea dead, galilee

senate sanhedrin
shark karish
sheep daman, tson, tzon
soldier sabra
spice stacte
statesman begin, ben-gurion, dayan, eban, eshkol, maier, meir, rabin, shazar
study center ulpan
tank merkava, the jewish mother
taxi sherut
terrorist organization irgun zvai leumi, national military organization, stern gang
toast l'chaim, lechayim
tree judas
tribesman danite
12 tribes See HEBREW tribe.
undergound irgun zvai leumi, stern gang
underground army haganah
wilderness paran
writer haim gouri, matti golan
youth corps nahal, noar halutzi lohen
ISRAELITE See ISRAEL(I).
ISSACHAR *parent* jacob, leah
son jashub, pua, shimrom, tola
ISSUANCE appearance, distribution, emanation, emergence, escape, publication, sortie
ISSUE 3 end, run 4 blow, come, copy, emit, exit, flow, flux, give, gush, leak, mete, ooze, pour, rise, send, stem, tell, vent, well 5 arise, begin, break, cause, event, float, offer, point, print, spawn, spout, spurt, start, stock, topic, utter 6 appear, broach, derive, egress, emerge, get out, outlet, put out, result, sequel, spring, upshot 7 consign, deliver, edition, emanate, outcome, present, problem, proceed, produce, progeny, publish, scatter 8 blue chip, bring out, decision, dispatch, dispense, monetize, question, security, solution, transmit 9 aftermath, circulate, discharge, flotation, offspring, originate, posterity 10 casus belli, conclusion, distribute 11 controversy 16 bone of contention

final outcome, upshot, utmost
slowly drip, exude, ooze, seep
stock capitalize
without sine prole
IST adherent, believer, devotee, disciple, enthusiast, follower
ISTANBUL byzantium, constantinople, stambul
archbishop athenagoras
bridge eurasia, galata
cathedral hagia sophia
church blue mosque, hagia sophia, mosque of sinan
founder byzas
foreign quarter pera
grand mufti sheikh ul islam
greek quarter fanar
inn imaret, serai
palace topkapi
part golden horn
patriarch eudoxius, ignatius, photius
quarter galata, pera, stamboul, uskudar
schools mahaleh
sea marmara
valley lycus
wonder saint sophia
ISTALCURUS *son* uthi
ISTHMUS balk, narrows, neck, peninsula, point, spit, strait, tarbet, tongue
ISTIOPHORUS aguja, bannerfish, boohoo, sailfish
ISTLE fiber, guapilla, juamave, pita, pito
source agave, bromelia, yucca
ISUI *parent* asher
ISUS *father* priam
slayer agamemnon
ISVARA siva
IT big cheese, big shot, personage, (the)thing
follows that consequently
girl clara bow
is not non est
is so amen
may be haply, perhaps
ITA a(e)ta, negrito
ITALIAN (See also ITALY for geographical references.) etruscan, italici, ligurian, roman, tuscan, umbrian, venetian
alps dolomites
article degli, gli, una, uno
bath bagnio
bit pezzo
cane ditchweed
cheese formaggio

chicken pollo
clams vongole
damsel donzella
"deaf" sordo
"dear" cara, caro
dome cima, duomo
earth burnt-sienna
"enough" basta
feeling sentimento
flower fiore
"fried" fritto
"goodbye" addio, arrivederci, ciao
green terre-verte
harshness durezza
hello addio, buon giorno, buona sera, ciao, pronto
"holy" santo
may spiraea
miss signorina
mister signore
moliere goldoni
ocher raw-sienna
"piece" pezzo
retribution mannaia
rice risotto
rock scaglia
salad insalata, valerian
sauce salsa, sugo
soft dolce, molle, morbido
steak bistecca
"stop" basta
sweet life la dolce vita
"under" sotto
up-date aggiornamento
uproar chiasso
"with love" con amore
woman donna, signora
ITALICIZE emphasize, underline, underscore
ITALY (See also ITALIAN for words in translation.) ausonia, hesperia, saturnia
abbey badia, vallombrosa
actor prim'omo, toto
actress duse, grammatica
admiral andrea doria, columbus
adventurer cagliostro, casanova, cellini
agriculture god picus
aircraft caproni
anarchist sacco, vanzetti
anatomist eustachio, guido, malpighi, morgagni
arcade galleria, loggia, sottoportico
architect alberti, bernini, bibiena, borromini, bramante, brunelleschi, guarini, juvarra, maderno, michelangelo, michelozzo, palladio, peruzzi, sangallo, sanmichel, sansorino, serlio

arctic explorer nobile

army corps alpino, bersagliere

artichokes carciofi

artist See *painter, sculptor,* below.

art patron medici

astronomer amici, galileo, novara, schiaparelli, secchi

auto alfa-romeo, bugatti, ferrari, fiat, lamborghini, lancia, maserati

autobiographer cellini

aviator balbo

ax mannaia

bacon pancetta

bandit brigante, caco

beans fagiolini

bell town adano, atri

bench cassapance

boat barca, gondola, speronara

botanist bertero

bowl tazza

bowling game bocce, bocci(e)

brandy grappa

brazier scaldino

bread pane(ttone)

breeze breva, ora

bridge ponte vecchio, santa trinita

building stone trullo

bull chianina

cafe osteria, trattoria

cape circeo, colonne, falcone, licosa, linaro, miseno, passero, rizzuto, sanvito, testa, teulada, vaticano

capital roma, rome

capital, byzantine ravenna

carriage vettura

castle canossa

cathedral duomo, monreale

cathedral city florence, milan, naples, rome, venice

cattle bue, modica, padolian

cavalier cicisbeo

cemetery campo santo

cheer hurra

cheese asiago, bel paese, caciocavallo, fontina, formaggio, gorgonzola, grana, mozzarella, parmesan, parmigiano, pecorino, provolone, riccota, romano, taleggio

chest arca, cassone

chief duce

child bambino, fanciulla, fanciullo

cigar toscano

city 4 asti, bari, como, este, fano, itri, lodi, nola, pisa, pola, roma, rome *5* anzio, aosta, asolo, avola, capua, cuneo, eboli, fiume, forli, genoa, imola, lecce, lucca, massa, milan, monza, ostia, padua, parma, pavia, prato, siena, terni, turin, udine *6* amalfi, ancona, aquila, arezzo, cannae, cesina, faenza, foggia, genova, mantua, mestre, milano, modena, naples, napoli, novara, rivoli, savona, spezia, tivoli, toreno, trento, urbino, varese, venice, verona *7* assissi, bergamo, bologna, bolzano, brescia, carrara, caserta, cassino, cosenza, cremona, ferrara, fiesole, gorizia, leghorn, livorno, paestum, perugia, pescara, pistoia, pompeii, rapallo, ravenna, san remo, stressa, treviso, trieste, venezia *8* brindisi, cagliari, fiorenze, florence, piacenza, sorrento

city, ancient capua, cumae, heraclea, herculaneum, paestum, pompeii, veii

city council signory

clams vongole

coastal region liguria

coffee caffe, cappuccino, espresso

coin aquilino, augustal, baggatino, centisimo, chequeen, deni, dicato, doppia, grano, julio, lira, lire, marengo, nichelino, paoli, quatrino, ruspone, scudo, soldo, tari, teston(e), tornese, zecchino, zequin

colony dhalak, eritrea, libya, somaliland, tripoli

commune alba, asola, asti, atessa, aversa, bra, dego, eboli, este, firenze, ivrea, massa, meda, nola, paola, rivoli, siena, urbino

communist leader togliatti

composer bellini, boccherini, boito, bononcini, busoni, carissimi, cesti, cimarosa, corelli, dallapiccola, donizetti, gabrielli, galuppi, gesualdo, giordano, guido, landini, leoncavallo, malpiero, marcellus, mascagni, monteverdi, paganini, paisiello, palestrina, pergolesi, peri, piccinni, ponchielli, puccini, respighi, rieti, rinuccini, rossini, sabata, salieri, sammartini, scarlatti, spontini, stradella, tartini, tommasini, torelli, tosti, verdi, vivaldi, wolfferrari

conch scungilli

condiment tamara

condottiere sforza

conductor serafin, spontini, toscanini

country, ancient etruria, italia, latium, oscan, sabine, samnium, tuscany

country house casino, villa

countryside campagna

crepes fritelle

courtesan amorosa

criminologist lombroso

critic croce, valla

culture, 14th century trecento

culture, 15th century quattrocento

cupid amoretto, puto

curse accidente

custom house dogano

cymbals piatti

dance arietta, calata, courante, forlana, furlana, rigoletto, saltarello, tarantella, volta

day breeze ora

day of week (mon.-sun.) lunedi, martedi, mercoledi, giovedi, venerdi, sabato, domenica

defeat caporetto

deity consus, faunus, flora

desk scrivania, stipo

dessert cassata, dolce, fedora, gelato, spumone, torta, zabaglione

dictator mussolini

diplomat castiglione

dish caponata, gnocchi, lasagna, PASTA, peperoni, pizza, polenta, ravioli, risotto, scaloppine, scampi, torta, tortoni, ziti

donkey assino

dramatist alfieri, aretino, betti, goldoni, pirandello

drawing disegno

drink amaretto, campari, cappucino, cynar, espresso, fior d'alpi, gancia, grappa, martini, negroni, sambuca, strega

drug jar albarello

drum tamburone

dumplings gnocchi

dynasty savoy

ecclesiastic abate, arcivescovo, prete, sacerdote

educator montessori
eel anguilla
eggplant melanzana
engraver bartolozzi, piranesi, raimondi
entertainment ridoto
estate latifundium
evening sera
evil eye mal d'occhio
exclamation viva
explorer abruzzi, belzoni, columbus, verrazzano, vespucci
faction bianchi, ghibelline, guelph, neri
fairy befana
family amati, asti, borghese, borgia, cenci, colonna, donati, doria, este, medici, sforza, strozzi, visconti
farce comedietta
festival festa, ridoto
field deity faun(us)
fig fico
15th century quattrocento
flask(s) fiaschi, fiasco
14th century trecento
galley slave sforzato
game mora, pallone, stoppa, tarot, trappola
garlic aglio
general badoglio, balbo, cadorna, farnese
gentleman ser, signore
giant funnum
gipsy zingaro
goblin folletto
god See ROMAN *god.*
goddess See ROMAN *goddess.*
goldsmith verrocchio
gratuity buonamano, mancia
growers' association consorzio
guitar calascione
gulf cagliari, gaeta, genoa, oristano, orosei, salerno, taranto, venice
gun beretta, fabbri, famars fabarm, franchi, fucile, lupara
gypsy zingaro
hall atrio, aulo
ham prosciutto
hamlet borgo, casal(e)
hand mano
headland scilla
helmet elme
hero orlando
highway autostrada
histologist golgi
historian cantu, gerrero, guicciardini, salvemini
holiday festa

honeysuckle woodbine
horse race corso, palio
house casa, casino, villa, villino
humanist ficino, pico della mirandola, politian, poliziano
hut pagliaio
ice cream gelato
imposter cagliostro
infantry arditi, bersagliere
inlay commesso, tarsia
inn albergo, locanda
innkeeper oste, padrone
inventor marconi, volta
island alicudi, asinara, capraia, capri, cos, elba, filicudi, giglio, gorgona, ischia, lampedusa, leros, levanzo, lido, linosa, panarea, pantelleria, pianosa, ponza, salina, sardinia, sicilia, sicily, stromboli, ustica, vulcano
island group egadi, lipari, pelagie, pontine, tremiti, tuscan
jar albarello
journalist alvaro, moneta
judge stradico
king humbert, umberto, victor emmanuel
lace argentella, buratto, reticella
lady don(n)a, signora
lake albano, avernus, avero, bolsena, bracciano, como, garda, iseo, lecco, lesina, lugano, maggiore, nemi, perugia, trasimene, trasimeno, verano, vico
lamb agnello
landlord padrone
language oscan, tuscan, venetic
leader duce, mussolini
leader, socialist matteotti
legislature camera, signory
liberation movement resorgimento
limestone predezzite, scaglia
liqueur arum, galliano, sambuca, strega
liver fegato
lobster aragosta
lordship signoria
lover amoroso
magistrate gonfaloniere, podesta, sindaco, syndic
maid cameriera
marble bardiglio, carrara, cipolin(o), palombino
marshland maremma
mason comacine

mathematician beltrami, cavalieri, peano
mayor sindaco, syndic
measure barile, boccale, braccio, canna, carat, chilometre, etto, giornata, litro, metro, miglie, moggiato, moggio, orna, palma, palmo, pie(de), punto, quadrato, rubbio, salma, secchio, staio, stero, tavola, tomolo
metalsmith cellini
midwife levatrice
military leader borgia
millet buda, moha, tenai
monastery monte cassino
money danaro, denaro
monk abbate, padre, prete, savonarola
month (1–12) gennaio, febbraio, marzo, aprile, maggio, giugno, giuglio, augusto, settembre, ottobre, novembre, dicembre
mosaic inlay certosina, certosino
mother goose pentamerone
mountain troops alpini
movie director antonione, desica, fellini, rossellini, visconti
mushrooms funghi
musical form caccia, furlana, passacaglia, toccatina
musical instrument arpa, colascione
musician alberti, clementi, guido, riccio, rizzio, rosini
naval base taranto
navigator columbus, verrazzano
needlework trapunto
nobleman conte, marchese, principe
noblewoman contessa, marchesa, principessa
novelist alvaro, baccheli, berto, bontempelli, collodi, d'annunzio, deledda, lampedusa, levi, manzoni, moravia, pratolini, silone
oboe piffero
omelet frittata
opera house la fenice, la scala
organist gabrieli, landini, landino
painter ancimboldi, andrea del sarto, bellini, bellotto, bondoni, botticelli, bronzino, cagliari, canaletto, caracciolo, caraggi, caravaggio, carpaccio, carracci,

cimabue, correggio, cortona, crespi, da vinci, del sarto, duccio, fra angelico, fra bartolommeo, fra lippo lippi, gaddi, ghiberti, ghirlandaio, giordano, giorgione, giotto, guardi, leonardo, levi, lippi, lorenzetti, lotto, luini, mainardi, marini, martini, masaccio, michelangelo, modigliani, morandi, perugino, piero di cosimo, piombo, pisanello, pontormo, raphael, reni, ricci, robusti, rosa, rossi, sacchi, sarto, sassetta, severini, signorelli, sodoma, spada, strozzi, tiepolo, tintoretto, titian, uccello, utrillo, vasari, veneziano, zuccari

parricide cenci
pass bernina, brenner, frejus, simplon, splugen, st gotthard
pasta See PASTA.
patriot aleardi, cavour, garibaldi, mazzini
peak bernina, cima, cimone, corno, marmolada, ortler, rosa, vesuvius, viso
peasant contadino
people, ancient ausonian, etruscan, latin, marsi, oscan, picene, roman, rutuli, sabellian, sabine, safini, tuscan, venetian, volsci
philologist castelvetro
philosopher aquinas, bruno, croce, dion, machiavelli, pico della mirandola, rosmini, savonarola, vera, vico
physician lombroso
physicist fermi, galileo, galvani, rossi, torricelli, volta
physiologist galvani
pianist busoni
piccolo ottavino
pie pizza
pineapple anana
plague pellagra
plain campagna
plateau sila
poet alberti, alfieri, ariosto, betti, boccaccio, boiardo, bojardo, carducci, d'annunzio, dante, leopardi, manzoni, marini, metastasio, montale, petrarch, poliziano, quasimodo, redi, tasso
poetic name ausonia
poison aqua-tofana
polemicist gioberti

police headquarters bargello
policeman carabiniere, sbirro
political party bianchi, blue shirts, calderai, ghibelline, guelph, neri
politician farnese
poplar lombardy
porridge polenta
port ancona, anzio, avola, bari, brindisi, fiume, gaeta, genoa, imperia, la spezia, leghorn, livorno, naples, napoli, ostia, pesaro, pola, pozzuoli, rimini, salerno, savona, sorrento, taranto, trani, trieste, venezia, venice
portrait ritratto
pot tazza
pottery faenza, majolica
prayer preghiera
premier de gaspari, moro
president gronchi, saragat, segni
press aldine, bodoni
priest fra, prete
prima donna diva
prime minister crispi
printer aldus, bodoni
procession corso, trionfo
province aosta, bari, cuneo, enna, este, istria, parma, pola, salerno, udine, verona
quartz tarso
queen elena
range alps, apennines, cottian alps, dolomites, maritimes, ortler, ortles
region abruzzi, apulia, basilicata, calabria, campania, carso, emilia, iapygia, latium, lazio, liguria, lombardy, lucania, marca, marche(s), molise, piedmont, piemonte, puglia, puglie, roma(gna) sardegna, sardinia, sicilia, sicily, toscana, tuscany, tyrol, umbria, valle d'aosta, veneto, venetia
republic san marino
resort abitone, agnone, baiae, capri, como, ischia, lido, portofino, positano, san remo, stresa, taormina, vallombrosa
restaurant trattoria
revoluntionary mazzini
rice risotto
rifleman bersagliere
river adda, adige, agri, aniene, arno, belice, biferno, bradano, chienti, crati,

dora, liri, livenza, mannu, metauro, mincio, montone, nera, ofanto, oglio, ombrone, orco, panaro, parma, pescara, piave, rapido, reno, rubicon, salso, sangro, secchia, seimeto, sele, stura, tanaro, taro, tevere, tiber, ticino, tirso, trebbia, volturno
robber cacus
ruler, early theodoric
rye grass marcite
sacred thing bambino, pieta
saint angelica, anthony, benedict, clare, cornelius, francesco, francis, hieronymus, jerome, philip neri
sandwich muffaletta
satirist aretino
sauce salsa
sausage mortadella, salami
scientist avogadro, fermi, molta
sculptor ammanati, bandinelli, belmondo, bernini, boccioni, bologna, borromini, canonica, canova, cellini, della quercia, della robbia, desiderio, donatello, dupre, ghiberti, leoni, manzu, marini, michelangelo, mino da fiesole, pisano, pollaiuolo, rosso, sansovino, verrocchio
sea adriatic, ionian, ligurian
season autunno, estate, inverno, primavera
sharpshooter bersagliere
sheep merino
ship nave, polacca
shock troops arditi
shoe scarpa, scarpetta, zoccolo
shrine town loreto
silk seta
singer albanese, amato, caccini, cantatrice, caruso, farinelli, galli-curci, gigli, patti, pinza, schipa, scotti, siepi, tagliavini, tebaldi, tetrazzini
sketch abbozzo, disegno, schizzo
society, secret camorra, carbonari, cosa nostra, mafia, mano-nera
socialist leader nenni
sociologist pareto
soldier(s) alpini, arditi, bersagliere, carabineer, carabiniere, condottiere, falieri, soldato

somaliland somalia
song canzone, frottola, villanella
soup minestra, minestrone, zuppa
squash zucchini
squid calamari
staple pasta
statesman alberoni, andreotti, balbo, borgia, cavour, ciano, croce, d'azeglio, farnese, gronchi, machiavelli, medici, nenni, nitti, orlando, sforza
steak bistecca
steamboat, small vaporetto
stone marble, pietra dura, travertine
story piano
story, 1st pian-terreno
strait bonifacio, messina, otranto
street corso, strada, via
summerhouse casino
sweet dolce
sweetheart amante, amore, inamorata, inamorato
sword cinquedea, langue de boeuf, schiavone, spada
sword maker ferrara
symbol blue grotto
theologian aquinas, lombard, peronne, socinus
throne seggio
title conte(ssa), marchesa, marchese, ser
toast salute
tour giro, viaggio
train rapido, settebello
troubadour sordello
underpass sottopassagio
university city bari, bologna, florence, milan, padua, pisa, naples, rome, venice
valley sacco
vase lekane
veal vitello
verse form ballata, terza rima
vessel traba(s)colo
violinist corelli, geminiani, paganini, tartini, torelli
violin maker amati, guadagnini, guarneri, stradivari
volcano etna, somma, stromboli, vesuvius, vulcano
waiter cameriere
war boat scampavia
ward contrade
watch towers specchie
water, bottled fuiggi
weight carato, chilogrammo, denaro, etto, libra, oncia, ottava, pound

welfare goddess salus
wheat soglia
wind andar, libecchio, ora, scirocco, sover, tramontana
wine amarone, antoniolo, asti spumante, barbarasco, barbaresco, barbero, bardolino, barolo, bersano, bianco, borgogno, brugo, calisanno, carema, ceretto, chianti, dolcetto, est-est-est, falerno, fontanafredda, francoli, freisa, gattinara, ghemme, giri, grignolino, kiola, lacrima christi, lugani, marsala, moscato, nebbiolo, orvieto, prunetto, ratti, recioto, ricoto, riserva, rosso, soave, spanna, troglia, vallana, valpolicella, verdea, vernaccia, vino
wine bottle(s) fiaschi, fiasco
wine harvest vendemmia
wine measure orna, orne
woman donna, signora
wood inlay intarsia
ITCH chafe, crawl, desire, each, eczema, ewk, formication, hanker, impulse, irritation, long, mange, motive, paresthesia, pine, prick(le), pruritus, psora, psorophthalmia, push, reef, scabies, sting, sycosis, tickle, tingle, urge, vanillism, yearn, yeuk, yewk
barber's sycosis
comb. araco
remedy antipruritic
weed hellebore
ITCHING hankering, longing, prurient, pruritis, urticant, yewky
ITE See ENTHUSIAST, IST.
ITEM account, agendum, also, article, asset, bit, bulletin, commodity, component, detail, dispatch, element, entry, factor, job, memo(randum), news, novelty, object, paragraph, part(icular), piece, product, scrap, thing, topic, trifle, unit
group of, comb. ana
worthless bean
ITEMIZE calculate, call, detail, list, particularize, recite, recount, rehearse, spell out
ITERATE battologize, ingeminate, repeat, retell, reutter

ITHACA ithake, leukas
head odysseus, penelope, ulysses
ITHAMAR *father* aaron
son daniel, gamael
ITHRA *offspring* amasa
wife abigail
ITHRAN *parent* dishon
ITHREAM *mother* eglah
ITHUNN See IDUN(A).
ITHURIEL'S-SPEAR grassnut
ITINERANT afoot, ambulant, ambulatory, farer, footer, hobo, migrant, migratory, nomad(ic), peregrinator, peripatetic, pilgrim, ranging, roadster, rover, roving, straying, tramp, transient, vagabond, vagrant, viator, wanderer, wandering, wayfarer
ITINERARY circuit, course, directory, gest, guidebook, journey, passage, route, run, schedule, tour, trip, way(bill)
ITONEA athena
ITURAEA *prince* philip
ITYLUS *parent* aedon, zethus
slayer zethus
ITYS *parent* procne, tereus
IULUS ascanius
father aeneas
IVA herb eve, ragweed, yellow-bugle
IVANHOE *author* scott
character athelstan(e), cedric, front de boeuf, gurth, prior aymer, rebecca, rowena, tuck, ulrica
clown wamba
father cedric
IVERNIA See IRELAND.
IVES *partner* currier
IVORIES dice, dominoes, keys, teeth
IVORY bone, creamy, dentin(e), ebur, odontolite, tooth, tush, tusk
-bill campephilus
black abaiser, slave
bull snowbird
carving toreutics
coast cape palmas
coast city abidjan, bouake, gagnoa, sassandra, tabou
coast dam bandama
coast language dioula
coast leader houphouet-boigny
coast people abe, aboure, akan, atle, avikom, koua,

krou, lagoon, malinke, mande, voltaic
coast port abidjan
coast river bandama, cavally, komoe, sassandra
dust eburin, eburite
engraving scrimshaw
nut anta, jarina, tagua
palm corojo, corozo, tagua
pert. dentine, eburnean, eburneoid, eburnous
plum snowberry, wintergreen
raspings scobs
scource tusk
synthetic ivoride
tower dream, retreat
tree palay, wrightia
walrus rib(a)zuba
yellow rose de nymphe
IVY aaron's beard, alehoof, aralia(d), arbutus, bindweed, climber, creeper, foalfoot, gill, hedera, hib-

bin, hove, ivywort, jill, kenilworth, laurel, overgrow, plant, vine
berry wintergreen
bush mountain laurel
chickweed speedwell
clump tod
crowned with hederated
finger tendril
flower hepatica
ground ahartalau, alehoof, creeping-charlie, foalfoot, hove(a)
kenilworth aaron's beard, cymbalaria
league brown, columbia, cornell, dartmouth, harvard, pennsylvania, princeton, yale
pert. hederaceous, hederal, hederic
poison climath, mercury, rhus, sumac(h)

vine virginia creeper
IVYWORT araliaceae
IWIS certainly, indeed, truly
I W W *man* wobbly
symbol sabcat
IXELLES elsene
IXIA corn-lily, sparaxis
IXION *consort* dia, hera, nephele
father phlegyas
jailer tartarus
kingdom lapith
punishment wheel
sister coronis
son centaurus, pirithous
stone rotator
IYNX *parent* echo, pan
IZMIR smyrna
IZRAHIAH *son* isshiah, joel, michael, obadiah
IZZARD end
IZZAT credit, honor, prestige, reputation

J

JAAL beden, goat, ibex
JAALAM *father* esau
JAALIN bedouin
JAAZANIAH *kin* jeremiah
JAB attempt, blow, buck, bump, bunt, dig, pinch, poke, punch, push, stab, strike, taunt, thrust
JABAL *father* lamech
JABBAR alcindor
JABBER babble, burble, cackle, chackle, chat(ter), gab(ble), gibber(ish), jargon, javer, jaw, patter, prate, prattle, talk, yabber
JABBERWOCKY jargon, nonsense, rigmarole
feature noncewords
paths mome
word brillig, gyre, slithy, tove
JABBLE agitate, confuse, confusion, ripple, splash
JABIRU bird, cicondiid, ibis, stork
JABNEEL jabneh, jamnia
JABORANDI pilocarpus
JABOT ruffle
JACAL See HUT.
JACAMAR galbula
JACANA parra
JACARANDA carob(tree), cybistax, rosewood, tallyho
JACARE alligator, caiman, cayman

JACCHUS callithrix, marmoset
J'ACCUSE *author* zola
cause dreyfus
JACHIN *father* simeon
JACINTH hyacinth, ligure, tawny, zircon
zodiac sign libra
JACK banner, bat, bauer, beater, blende, boor, bower, bowl, bube, can, card, carnation, cavalla, clown, coat, coin, color, creel, crick, dib, dicky, ensign, farthing, fellow, flag, hoist, hood, increase, john, jug, kathal, knave, laborer, male, man, mariner, money, mule, nanca, nob, noddy, opener, pam, pennant, pennon, pickerel, pigeon, pike, pitcher, playboy, pool, polignal, rabbit, raise, rockfish, ruin, sailor, sawhorse, squaw, standard, streamer, tankard, tool, toy, tree, turnspit, uplifter, valet, wenzel, winch
around kid, rib, tease
-at-a-pinch friend, helper
bean canavalia, overlook
bean globulin canavalin
cards bower, knape, knave, knight, nob, pam, pur, varlet(to), wenzel

cheese monterey
clubs bragger, matador, noddy, pam
crevalle toro
fairy tale beanstalk, giant killer, sprat
fruit jaca, kathal, sourjack
-full-of-money capitalist
giant blunderbore
group quatorze
in bowls baby, kitty, mark, master, mistress
-in-office incumbent, official
-in-the-box cheat, cuckoopint, firework, gear, hermit crab, peddler, screw, sharper, swindler
-in-the-pulpit arad, arisaema, aroid, arum, brown dragon, carob, figwort, flower, herb, love-in-a-mist, plant, indian turnip, wakerobin
johnson black maria, coalbox, shell
-jump-about angelica, bird's-foot, trefoil, goutweed
-ketch hangman
ladder bull chain, gangway
milieu beanstalk, steeple
nasty bounder, cad, sloven, sneak
nicker goldfinch
-of-all-trades dogsbody, gimcrack, handyman, tinker
of dover hake, stockfish

~o-lantern ignis fatuus, luminescence, st elmo's fire, watchman, will-o-the-wisp
pine bank's, cypress, jeffrey, loblolly, lodgepole
pot all, award, bonanza, fund, pool, stakes, windfall
pudding buffoon, fool, merry-andrew, zany
rabbit hare, lepus
rose avens
salmon wall-eyed perch
spaniard wasp
sprat charles
stickler busybody
tar sailor
tree jacka, nangka
trumps nob
up add, boost, increase, raise, rebuke
JACKAL agent, animal, bied(s), canid, canine, canis, diebs, dragon, henchman, instrument, kola, menial, siacalle, sycophant, thooid, thos, toady
cry pheal
-headed god anubis, apuat, duamutef, upuaut
JACKANAPES ape, animal, beau, coxcomb, dandy, fop, monkey, prig
JACKAROO ringneck, tyro
JACKASS dolt, donkey, dunce, fool, nitwit, witling
clover alkali mustard
comb. ono
deer kob-antelope
fish morwong, terakhi
JACKDAW baj, blackbird, caddow, cadesse, chough, coe, crow, daw(cock), dawish, grackle, kadder, kae, nuisance, titmouse
symbol of conceit
JACKER slipman, torcher
JACKET acton, anorak, baju, bania, benjamin, benny, bietle, binding, blazer, blouse, bolero, camisole, cardigan, carmagnole, casing, chaqueta, cleading, cover(ing), dick(e)y, doublet, dolman, dustwrapper, envelope, eton, fecket, gansy, greatcoat, grego, hanselin, hull, jerkin, jersey, jumper, jupon, norfolk, overcoat, paletot, parker, peacoat, peel, reefer, rind, sacque, shrug, skin, spencer, tabard, temiak, topcoat, topper, tunic, vest, wamus, wrap(per)

armor-covered acton, truss
army blouse
box-pleated norfolk
bright blazer
crocheted sontag
dressing camisole
heavy chaqueta, parka
hooded anorak, grego, grieko, parka
kind dinner, dressing, lounging, mess, norfolk, pea, pilot, shell, shooting, ski, smoking, sports, tuxedo
knitted jersey, sontag
leather jerkin
light blazer
-like camisole
mail acton, aketoun, habergeon
old-time doublet
overlapping double-breasted
part lapel
short bolero, eisenhower, eton, jerkin, kabaya, reefer, spencer
short-flapped coatee
sleeveless bolero, penelope, tabard, vest
steel-lined placcate
woman's jupe, jupon, spencer, zouave
work pawneen, blouse
JACKHAMMER plugger, sinker
JACKKNIFE barlow, dive, pika
trick mumble-the-peg, mumblety-peg
JACKLEG scab, sharper, strikebreaker
JACKMAN shellman
JACKSAW goosander, titmouse
JACKSCREW tick
JACKSMELT peixery
JACKSNIPE chorook, creaker, jed, judcock, peert, sandpiper, scape, snight, squatter, tailor
JACKSON, ANDREW old hickory
advisors kitchen cabinet
burial place hermitage
party democratic
profession lawyer
vice president calhoun, van buren
JACKSON, HELEN HUNT *novel* ramona
JACKSON, STONEWALL *courier* belle boyd
JACKSON, THOMAS J. *nickname* stonewall

JACKSTAY horse, parrel, railway, rope, staff
JACKSTONES dibs
JACKSTRAW(S) blackcap, effigy, figure, game, nonentity, spi(l)likin, warbler, whitethroat
JACOB, JACOB'S israel
altar el bethel
brother edom, esau
burial site machpelah
chariot monkshood
daughter dinah
descendant israelite, levite
father-in-law laban
ladder belladonna, butter-and-eggs, bittersweet, carrion-flower, celandine, celastrus, hyacinth, larkspur, orpine, phlox, solomon's-seal
mountain gilead
parent isaac, rebecca
rod asphodel
son as(h)er, benjamin, benoni, dan, gad, gershon, issachar, joseph, judah, levi, naphtali, reuben, sarasadae, simeon, zebulun
staff mullein
sword iris
well nablus
wife bilhah, leah, rachel, zilpah
JACOBIN demagogue, dominican, hummingbird, pigeon, plotter, radical, revolutionary
church lord mar
irish wild goose
JACONET cloth, fabric, nainsook
JACQUARD faconne
JACQUES See PEASANT.
JACTANCE, JACTATION bluster, boasting, bragging, ostentation
JACU bird, guan
JACULATE dart, hurl, project, throw
JADA *son* jether, jonathan
JADAPATI See VARUNA.
JADE axstone, befool, bother, cloy, depress, drab, dun, enervate, exhaust, fag, fatigue, glut, green, hack, harass, harlot, hilding, horse, hussy, huzzy, jezebel, mineral, minx, nag, nephrite, pall, plug, pounamu, quean, rannel, rosinante, sate, satiate, shrew, slaister, slut, surfeit, tantalize, tease, tire, tit, trash,

tremolite, trollop, tucker, wanton, weary, wench, woman, wreck
lady touwan
white alabaster
JADED blase, disjaskit, dulled, exhausted, fed up, forjesket, spent, surfeited, tired, wearied, weary, worn
JADEITE feitsui
JADOO, JADU jinx, magic
JAEGER allan, boatswain(bird), bonxie, bosun, dirtbird, dungbird, gull, hunter, lari(d), rifleman, shooi, skua, SOLDIER, teaser, trumpie, tuliac
JAEL *kin* heber, shua(h)
victim heber, sisera
JAFFA joppa
JAG awn, bag, barb, bristle, bun, burden, calk, cargo, carry, cleft, dag, denticulation, dovetail, freight, hair, indent, jab, load, mess, notch, orgy, part, pendant, pike, pink, point, portion, prick(et), projection, protuberance, saturnalia, scrap, shred, slash, sosh, spree, stab, tatter, thrust, toot, tooth, transport, wallet
JAGANNATH *festival* rathayatra, snanayatra
JAGGED cutting, drunk, erose, hackly, indented, lacerated, laciniate, notched, pinked, pointed, ragged, rough, rugged, serrate(d), shagged, sharp, slashed, snagged, uneven
line zigzag
JAGGER rolling stone
JAGGERY goor, gour, gur, khajur, khaur, kittul
JAGUA genipap, tree
JAGUAR cat, o(u)nce, panther, tiger, uturuncu
prey capybara, tapir
JAH See HEBREW *god.*
JAHANGIR *father* akbar
JAHANNAN See HELL.
JAHATH *father* shimei
leader josiah
JAHAZIEL *parent* bilhah, naphtali, zechariah
JAHDAI *son* ephah, geshan, jotham, pelet, regem, shaaph
JAI ALAI pelota
basket cesta, chistera
court cancha, fronton
player pelotari

racquet cesta
term quante, rebote
JAIL asylum, bagne, bagnio, bailey, barracoon, bars, big house, black hole, bocardo, booby hatch, bridewell, brig, bullpen, cage, calaboose, calabozo, can, carcel, carcer, cell, chauki, choky, clink, cooler, coop, crib, death house, donjon, dump, dungeon, freezer, gaol, gehenna, gib, grate, guardhouse, hell, hold, hole, hoosegow, immure, imprison, incarcerate, intern, jug, keep, kidcote, kitty, limbo, lock-up, lodge, manacle, milldoll, mure, oubliette, panopticon, pen (itentiary), poky, pound, prison, quod, rattle, reformatory, rock, shackle, slammer, stalag, stir, thana, tol(l)booth, tolzey, tower, tronk
famous alcatraz, bastille, butyrka, curragh, dartmoor, folsom, kilmainham, leavenworth, lubyanka, ludgate, marshalsea, newgate, old bailey, san quentin, singsing, spandau, sugamo, sukhanovka, tullianum
fever typhus
in behind bars, serving time, up the river
navy brig
sentence, unfair bum rap
temporary barracoon, holding tank
term rap, sentence, verdict
JAILBIRD See CRIMINAL, HOODLUM.
JAILBREAK blastout
JAILER alcaide, alcayde, custodian, gaoler, guard, keeper, screw, turnkey, warden, warder
JAIN *doctrine* ajiva
founder mahavira
initiation diksha
sect ajivika, dhundia, digambara, lunka, svetambara
teacher vardhamana
JAIR *parent* manasseh, shimei
son mordecai
JAKAN *parent* ezer
JAKE cash, dally, dandy, fine, first-rate, ginger, great, green-horn, hick, jacob, money, okay, peasant, rube,

rustic, satisfactory, trifle, yokel
JAKEL *son* agur
JAKIM *father* shimei
JAKO parrot
JALAP mechoacan, turpeth
JALAPATI See VARUNA.
JALAUN *capital* orai
JALISCO *indian* cora
JALON *father* ezra
JALOPY aircraft, auto, car, clunker, crate, flivver, hotrod
JALOUSE surmise, suspect
JALOUSIE blind, envy, shutter
JAM bind, block(age), bruise, congestion, conserve, corner, cram, crowd, crush, dilemma, fix, frock, gorge, interfere, jelly, mass, mess, mob, multitude, obstruction, pack, pickle, pinch, plight, predicament, preserve, press(ure), push, quandary, scrape, session, squeeze, stop(page), strait, tamp, throng, thrust, tighten, wedge
through legislate, railroad
JAMAI *father* tola
JAMAICA bullhoof, capparis, passion-flower
apple cherimoya
bark princewood
bay montego, st ann's
birch gumbo-limbo
bird tody
buckthorn cherokee rose
cactus turk's-head
capital kingston
cherry fig
city kingston, port antonio, port maria
cobnut pignut, quabe
coin quattie
cult rastafarians
dish guango, patois
dogwood ba(r)basco, fishwood, jack-in-a-box, joewood, wild cinnamon
ebony cocuswood
gecko woodslave
grackle tinkling
hair style dreadlocks
honeysuckle passionflower
island cayman
leader marcus garvey
liquor jake, rum, tia maria
mart straw market
mesquite cashaw
mignonette henna
pepper allspice
plant akee

premier manley
rainbird hunter, tomfool
resort montego bay
river black, minho
rosewood amyris
saltwort batis
shrub broomtree
snapdragon manyroot
sorrel roselle
spiderwort frenchweed
sugar cane caledonian queen
sumac poisonwood
termite duck-ant
thistle prickly poppy
thrust hopping dick
tree black guava, breadnut, garlic pear, lagetto, licca, plantain
vervain gervao
wood uassi
wood sorrel begonia
wood thrush maybird
JAMB alette, corner, gamb, pillar, post, turn, wing
JAMBEE calamus, cane, palm, walking stick
JAMBOREE carousal, festival, frolic, spree
JAMES chauffeur, diego, jemmy, jimmy, seamas, shamus, sovereign
JAMES I *jester* archie armstrong, thomas derrie
kingdom england, ireland, scotland
nickname pieman
parent darnley, mary stuart
queen consort anne
JAMES II *father* charles i
kingdom england, ireland, scotland
JAMES, HENRY *novel* daisy miller, portrait of a lady, princess casamassima, roderick hudson, the ambassadors, the american, the aspern papers, the bostonians, the golden bowl, the turn of the screw, the wings of the dove, washington square, what maisie knew
JAMES, SAINT *burial site* rome
brother john
daughter anne
parent alphaeus, salome, zebedee
symbol cockles, gourd-bottle, pole, scallop-shell, staff
JAMIN *father* simeon
JAMMED crowded, crushed, massed, stuck

JAMON bacon, guitar, ham
JAMSHID *kingdom* peris
JANACEK *opera* jenufa
JANE EYRE *author* charlotte bronte
character rochester
JANGADA catamaran
JANGAR raft
JANGLE altercate, babble, blare, bray, burr, buzz, caw, chatter, clam, clang(or), clank, clash, contention, croak, differ, discord, fight, gossip, groan, growl, grumble, irritate, jar, noise, prate, quarrel, saw, screech, snarl, snore, squabble, stridulate, twang, twank, wrangle
JANGLING ajar, altercation, babble, bickering, clashing, discord(ant), dissonant, harsh, quarreling, wrangling
JANISSARY See JANIZARY.
JANITOR caretaker, cleaner, concierge, custodian, doorkeeper, durwan, gatekeeper, guardian, mehtar, porter, sexton, super, usher
JANIZARY conscript, creole, mercenary, rabirubia, slave, solach, solak, soldier
chief dey
JANN demon, eblis, genii, jinn
JANNAI *father* joseph
son melchi
JANUARY *birthstone* garnet
6th epiphany, twelfth night
JANUS deceiver, divanus, matutinous, pater, portunus
daughter canens
-faced deceitful, falsehearted
JAPAN, JAPANESE cipango, dai nippon, enamel, kingdom of suicide, lacquer, nihon, nippon, paint, varnish, yamato, zipangu
abacus soroban
abalone awabi
aborigine aino, ainu
adam, eve izanagi, izanami
admiral ito, togo
advertising agency dentsu
agricultural union nokyo
air base chitose
aircraft zero
alcove tokonoma
alloy mokum, shibuichi
allspice chimonanthus
-american ainoko, issei, kibei, nisei, sansei

amusement hall pachinko parlor
annals nihongi, nihon shoki
annals, compiler ono yasumaro, prince toneri
annals, 1st part findaiki, jindaiki
annals, memorizer hieda-no-are
anthem kimigayo
apartment danchi
apricot ansu, ume
arborvitae thujopsis
army reserve hoju, kobi
aroid konjak
art design notan
art figure haniwa, hobird
auto datsun, mazda, prince, skylark, toyopet, toyota
bacteriologist kitasata
badge kirimon, mon
barbecue (naga)hibachi
bards katari-be
baron daimio, daimyo, han
bath onsen
battle cry banzai
battlefield pilgrimage senseki, jumpai
bay amort, ariake, atsumi, ise, miku, mutsu, osaka, otaru, senda, suruga, tokyo, toso, toyama, uchiura, wakasa, yedo
bean a(d)zuki
beer biiru
beetle popillia
beni blue spiraea, red, rouge
beverage sake, saki
book, ancient (See also annals, above.) engilshiki, fudoki, kogoshui, kojiki, manyoshu, shojiroku, tango-fudoki
boxes, set of inro
brake warabi
brazier hibachi
bream tai
brocade nishiki
broth osuimo(no)
brothel shinjuku
buddha aizen-myoo, amida, amita, apis, ashuku nyorai, bato kannon, daibutsu, daiitaku-myoo, dainichi nyorai, fudo-myoo, fugen bosatsu, fuku-kensaku kannon, gozanze-myoo, gundari-myoo, hosho nyorai, jizo bosatsu, ju-ichimen kannon, jundei kannon, kannon bosatsu, kokuzo bosatsu, kongo-yasha-myoo, kujaku-myoo, maitreya, mida, miroku bosatsu,

monju bosatsu, nyorai, senju kannon, sho kannon, yakushi nyorai
buddha, disciple arhat, binzuru
buddhism amidism, zen
buddhism proclaimed by prince regent shotoku
buddhist doctrine shingon, tendai
buddhist festival bon
buddhist 1st emperor yomei
buddhist 1st empress suiko
buddhist 1st family soga
buddhist form world taizokai
buddhist gods' souls ara-mitama (violent), nigi-mitama (gentle)
buddhist idea world kongokai
buddhist monk dengo daishi, kobo daishi, nichiren, shinran, shonin
buddhist organization komeito, soka-gakkai
buddhist sect hosso, jodoshinshu, jodo-shu, kegon, saddharma, sanron, shinshu, zen
buddhist-shinto unity ryobushinto
bureaucrat zaikai
bush clover hagi
business term ringi
cabinet wood kiri
cake kashi, koji, okashi
calamities god yaso-magabu-bi
calculator abacus, soroban
calisthenics judo
cape ashizuri, daio, erimo, esan, iro, jizo, kyoga, mela, mino, muroto nojima, noma, nomo, oki, oma, rurui, sada, sawa, shakotan, shio, shiriya, soya, suzu, todoga, toi
capital edo, kyoto, miyako, nara, saikio, tokio, tokyo, yedo
carp koi
carriage kago, sados
case inro
cedar cryptomeria, sugi
champagne shampen
chant nam myo ho renge kyo
character hibunci
cherry sakura
chess shogi
chevrotain napu
chief advisor kwampaku
chivalry bushido
chopsticks (o)hashi

church (o)tera
circle maru
city akita, amagasaki, aomori, arao, asahogawa, ashaikawa, atami, chiba, choshi, fukui, fukuoka, fuse, gifu, hagi, hakodate, hamamatsu, himeji, hirosaki, hiroshima, hitachi, hofu, ichinoseki, kagoshima, kamakura, kanazawa, kawasaki, kioto, kobe, kochi, kofu, kokura, kumamoto, kure, kyoto, lida, matsue, matsuyama, mito, moji, muya, nagano, nagasaki, nagoya, nara, niigata, nikko, ogaki, oita, okayama, okazaki, omutu, osaka, otaru, otsu, saga, sakai, sapporo, sasebo, sendai, shizuoka, suita, takada, tokio, tokyo, toyama, toyohashi, ueda, ueno, ujina, wakayama, yawata, yedo, yokohama, yokosuka
clan gen, hei, satsuma
class eta, heimin, kwazoku, roi, samurai, shizoku
clogs geta
cloisonne shippo
clover hagi, lespedeza
coat mino
coin cash, cobang, ichebu, ichibu, itzeboo, itzebu, itziboo, koban(g), mon, nibu, oban(g), rin, rio, sen, shu, tempo, yen
commoner heimin
commune dessa
company iwasaki, mitsubishi, mitsui, sumitomo, yasuda
composition haikai
confection ame
conglomerate zaibatsu
constellation deities nijuhachi bushu
conveyance jinrikisha, kago, ricksha(w)
cooking vessel hibachi, wok
councillor karo
court da(i)ri
courtier kuge
crepe chirimen
crest kikumon, mon
crow, sacred yata-garasu
cult zen
cup sakazuki
current black stream, kurosiwo, kyroshio
cushion zabuton
dagger tanto
dance bugaku, chonchina, kagura, san-gaku, saru-gaku

dancing girl geisha
date plum persimmon
deer s(h)ika
deity See *god, goddess,* below.
department kori
dependence amae(ru)
dictator oda nobunaga, tojo, toyotomi hideyoshi
diplomat aoki, homura, kurusu, nomura, togo
dish kombu, motsu, omaka sai, sukiyaki, sushi, tempura, teriyaki, yaki, yakitori
district ken
divine force kami
dog akira, akita, tanate
doll festival hina matsuri
door fusuma
drama kabuki, masakado, nogaku, noh
drawing mandala
drink biiru, cherry blossoms, green tea, rice wine, sake, shampen, uisukki
drum taiko
duty giri(ninjo)
dwarf kappa
dye process yuzen
dynasty meiji
earthenware banko, raku
economic federation keidanren
economist akita, shimomura
emblem rising sun
emperor akihito, antoku, chuai, edo, go-daigo, gotoba, hachiman daibosatsu, hirohito, ieyasu, junnin, juntoku, kammu, keiko, meiji, mikado, mutsuhito ojin, okam, seiwa, sutoku, taisho, tenno, tosho-daigongen, tsuchi-mikado, yomei temmu, yoshihito
emperor, 1st jimmu tenno
emperor's throne shinza
empress gemmyo, jingo, koken, nagako, nagamiya, suike
ethics bushido
evergreen akeki, sciapopitys
exclamation banzai
explosive shimose
fabric birodi, chirimen, habutai, habutaye, nishiki, silk
family fujiwara, hojo, minamoto
family registration koseki
fan ogi
farewell sayonara
feast (o)bon, (o)matsuri, tanabata, utas

fencing kendo
fern ball, bamboo, coniogramme, davallia, squirrel's-foot
fertility god susanoo
festival hina matsuri, obon
fetish obe
financial clique zaibatsu
fish aburabozu, ayu, fugu, funa, koi, masu, porgy, ryukin, sashimi, shubunkin, tai, tho
floor bed futon
flower nelumbium, udo
flower arrangement ikebana, ikenobo, ohara, ononoimoko, sogetsu
flower festival hana-matsuri
flute fuye
food kombu, miso, rice
footwear geta, tabi
foreigners gaijin
foreign ministry gaimusho
form world taizokai
game gimmi, gobang, gomoku, igo, ken, pachinko, sugoruku, wei-chi
garment haori, kimono, mino, mompei
gateway toran, torii
gelatin agalloch, agar(agar), isinglass
general iyeyasu, kuroki, oyama, tojo, yamashita
gentry shizoku
giant daidarabotchi
girdle obi
girdle box inro
girl geisha, musume
god (See also *buddha; happiness, 7 gods of; road god; sea god.*) aji-suki-takahikone, amatsukami, amatsumikaboshi, ame-no-hohi, ame-no-kagaseo, ame-no-oshido-mimi, ame-no-wakahiko, amida, amita, atago-gongen, benten, bishamon, daibot, daikoku, ebis(h)u, fukurokuju, funado, gozu-tenno, hachiman(daibosatsu), hamori, hariti, hayaji, haya-tsu-muji-no-kami, hiruko, homasubi, hotei, inari, izanagi, jurojin, kagazuchi, kaguzuchi, kamadonokami, kami, kaminari, kamunahobi, kantokinoki, kashiwanokami, kishimojin, kompira, kukunochi, kunado, kunitsukami, kuraokami, kuvera, marici-deva, marishiten, mii-nokami,

minato-nokami, myoken, nainokami, nigihayahi, ninigi, oiwa daimyojin, okitsuhiko, okitsuhime, okuninushi, oyamatsumi, sengensama, sha, shinatobe, shinatsu-hiko, shiozuki, sukunabikona, susanoo, takaminusubi, takamu-musubi, takemikazuchi, takitsuhiko, tatsutahiko, tatsutahime, tsukiyomi, wakahiru-me, yasomago-tsu-bi
goddess amano-uzume, amaterasu, hani-yasuno-kami, hariti, izanami, kamimusubi, kariteimo, kono-hanasakuya-hime, nuzichi, sengen-sama, shinatobe, shitateru-hime, takami-musubi, tatsuta-hime, toyo-ukehime, tsukiyomi, ukemochinokami, wakahirume, yakami
god souls aramitama (violent), nigimitama (gentle)
goldfish funa, koi
goodbye sayonara
governor shogun, taikun, tycoon
greeting banzai, irasshaimase, konban wa, konnichi wa, mokari-makka, ohayogozaimasu
guts hara
happiness, 7 gods of benzaiten, bishamonten, daikoku, ebisu, fukurouju, hotei osho, jurojin, pusa
harp koto
head, decapitated kagu-hana, miru-me
healer binzuru
heaven ama, gokuraku
heaven, bridge ama-no-hashidate
heavenly punishment tempatsu
heavenly river ama-no-gawa
herb acorus, featherfern, toad-lily, udo
hero saigo takamori, yamato takeru
hippies bozuoki, futen, gaijin
history kojiki
holding company zaibatsu
honor code bushido
horseradish wasabi
hot springs onsen
idea world kongokai
immigrant to u s issei
ink sumi
ink painting sumie

inlay zogan
inn ryokan
iris shadow
isinglass See *gelatin,* above.
island bonin, cipango, hokkaido, hondo, honshu, iki(shima), izu, kiushu, kiusiu, kuril(e), kyushu, loochu, oita, okigunto, okinawa, okushiri, rebun, rishiri, riukiu, ryukyu, sado, shikoko, shikoku, sikok, tsushima, yakujima
ivy ampelopsis, geranium creeper
jacket haori
kelp kombu
killifish medaka
kingmaker kuromaku
kings, heavenly guards bishamon, jikoku, komoku, lokapala, shitenno, tamon, zocho
knife aikuchi, kwaiken
korean war orders divine aid
labor offensive shunto
lacquer urushi
lake biwa, kutchawa, shikotsu, suwa, towada, toya
landscape art bonsai
legislature diet
lesbian resubian
light-skinned ainu
lily auratum
litter cango, kago, norimono
liturgical prayers norito
loincloth fundoshi
loquat biwa
lord daimio, daimyo, hatamoto
lovers' hotels abekku hoteru
lyric haiku, hokku
magnolia yulan
maple fullmoon, momiji
marital art See *self-defense,* below.
massage shiatsu
mats tatami
meaning haragei
measure boo, carat, catty, cho, djo, fun, go(go), hiro, hiyak-hiro, hiyak-kin, inc, isse, issho, ittan, kati, ken, kin, koku, komma-ichida, kon, kujira-shaku, kwamme, momme, niyo, picul, rin, shaku, shi, sho(o), sun, tan
medicine case etui, inro
medicine god okuninushi
meditation nembutsu
medlar loquat
mercenary ninja

metal work bori, guri-bori, jimigaki, mazegane, shibui-chidoshi, zogan
mikado dairi
mile, nautical kairi
military code bushido
military government shogun
military police kempeitai
military service yobi
millet (barn)(cockspur) grass
mime san-gaku
ministers turned into gods fujiwara kamatari, suga-wara michizane, tenjin
mist bai
monastery tera
monk (See also buddhist monk.) sesshu
monopoly zaibatsu
moon deity tsukiyomi
moon, full mochi-zuki
mulberry kozo, kuwa
musical instrument aoi-tsuba, fuye, koto, samisen, taiko, t(su)ruyume
music and dancing san-gaku, saru-gaku
national anthem kimigayo
national park aso
nature forces kami
naval base kure, sasebo, truk
naval officer yamamoto
naval victory tsushima
news agency domei
newspaper asahi, komei-shin-bun, mainichi, yomiuri
niche tokonoma
noble daimio, daimyo, ha-tamoto, kami, kuge, kwa-zoku, samurai
non-people hinin
novel tale of genji
novelist murasaki
numbers (1–9) ichi, ni, san, shi, go, roku, shichi, hachi, ku
oak shirakashi
occupation group scap
officer shikken
orchid snakemouth
ornament inro, netsuke
outcast burakumin, eta, hinin, ronin, yeta
outlaw ronin
pagoda taa
painter baiitsu, foujita, harunobu, hiroshige, hoku-sai, korin, mitsunobu, rei-sai, sanraku, sotatsu, uta-maro
painting style kano, nanga, rimpa, sesshu, shijo, tosa, ukiyo(y)e, yamatoe

palanquin kago, norimono
paper-folding art origami
parent-child relationship oyabun-kobun
peak asahi, asama, asosan, enasan, fuji(san), fujiyama, hakusan, hiuchi, hondo, ku-jusan, tokachi, uso, yariga, yesso, zao
pearl mikimoto
peninsula izu
people aino, ainu, cipango, issei, nippon(ese), nisei, sansei
persimmon hyakume, kaki, triumph
physician noguchi
physicist tomonage
pillbox inro
pinball pachinko
pine matsu
plane zero
plant aucuba, cydonia, kudzu, sugamo, tea, udo
plum kelsey
poem haikai, haiku, hokku, tanka, waka
poem collection manyoshu
poet basho, matsuo, mura-saki
poison barb shuriken
police boxes koban
political leader togo
political party komeito, min-seito, seirankai, seiyuhonto, seiyukai
population decline kaso
porcelain hirado, hizen, imari, nabeshima
porgy tai
port akita, akkad, aomori, hakodate, hiogo, hiroshima, kanazawa, kobe, koche, kure, matsuyama, moji, nii-gata, oita, omuta, osaka, otaru, sakai, sakata, sasebo, shimonoseki, shizuoka, ta-kamatsu, tokio, tokushima, tokyo, toyohashi, tsu, ube, wakayama, yokohama
porter akabo
pottery awaji, awata, banko, binkozan, bizen, mimpei
prayers norito
prefecture ken, kin, kori, mino, oita, owari, yamagu-chi
prime minister ashida, fu-kuda, hatoyama, ikeda, ishibashi, ito, katayama, kishi, konoye, miki, sato, tanaka, tojo, yoshida
prince akihito
print urushiye

print maker sharaku
prison sugamo
province, ise, iwaki, kai, sat-suma, yamato
quince japonica, loquat
racers' circuit sahkittozoku
radish daikon
railroad new tokaido line, shinkansen
raincoat mino
raisin tree cock's-claw
recess tokonoma
reciters katari-be
recreation site pachinko par-lor
regent shikken
regime meiji restoration, to-kugawa shogunate
region karafuto
relief carving nikubori
religion buddhism, shinto(ism), sokagakki
religious leader kagawa
rice gohan, kome, mochi-gome
rice product ame, sake, saki
rifle arisaka
river tonegawa, yalu
road god chimata-nokami, dosojin, funado, kunado, saenokami, yachimatahiko
robe kimono
rose aino, bara
rubdown shiatsu
rug crazy quilt, solitaire, ta-tami
ruler shogun, son of heaven, taikun, tenno, tycoon
ruler, 1st ninigi
salad herb udo
salmon masu
samurai ronin
sandal geta, zori
sash obi
sash fixture netsuke
sauce iyu, udo, unagi
school juku, yobiko
screen shoji, tagasode
script kana(majiri)
scriptures engishiki, fudoki, jindaiki, kogoshui, kojiki, nihongi, nihonshoki, sho-jiroku
scroll emaki, gohonzon, ka-kemono, makimono
sculptor noguchi
sea amakusa, inland, suo, tsushima
seafood, cooked tempura
sea god hohodemi, kompira, kuvera, owata-tsumi, ryobu-shinto, shiozuchi, suitengo
seal, personal hanko
seaweed nori

sect ryobu, sokogakkai

self-defense aikido, j(i)jutsu, j(i)ujitsu, judo, karate, kungfu, sumo

shinto with 2 faces ryobu-shinto

ship name maro, maru

shitenno See *kings, heavenly guards,* above.

shoe geta, zori

shogun family ashikaga, tokugawa

shoot udo

shrine jingu, jinja

shrub aburachan, aucuba, cydonia, g(o)umi, hortensia, japonica, kerria, mitsumata, nandina, quince, retinispora, sas(s)anqua, stewartia, tea-of-heaven, tobira

silk chirimen, habutai, habutaye

silk worm kaiko, uamamai

silk worm disease uji

sock tabi

soldier heitai, joju

soldier's pay sen

song tanka, uta

spruce yeddo

spurge pachysandra

statesman genro, hara, hiranuma, ito, matsuoka, mori, saionji, yamagata

stockmarket kabutocho

storm monsoon, taifu, tengu, tsunami, typhoon

storm god susanoo

stove hibachi

strait bungo, kii, nemuro, osumi, tanega, tokara, tsugaru, tsushima

straw coat mino

straw hat ballibuntl

student group chukakuha, kakumaruha, zengakuren

suicide harakiri, harikari, seppuku, shinju

sun goddess amaterasu

sun tree hinoki

sword cat(t)an, daisho, kamashimo, katana, tachi, wacadash, wakizashi, zashi

sword alloy shakudo

sword decoration fushi, menuki, mitokoromono

sword guard tsuba

sword mounts kanamono, kodogu

sword pommel kabuzuchi, kashira

syllabary iroha

symbol shintai

tea ceremony chanoyu

tea girl musume

tea house chaya

tea shop chashitsu, kissaten

tea whisk chasen

temple isegrand, sengakuji, sha, tera

"thank you" arigato, domoarigato

theatre kabuki, shingeki

throne shinza

thumb therapy shiatsu

tidal wave tsunami

title kami, mikado, okami, shogun, tenno

tortoise shell bekko

towel oshibori

tower pagoda, tope

town machi, mura, toi

trade organization jetro

trade union domei, sohyo

tradition bonsai, bushido, harikari, judo, kabuki, karate, sand painting, seppuku, shinju, tea ceremony

train bullet, shinkansen

tree akamatsu, akeki, camphor, castoralia, cycas, epaullette, full-moon maple, ginkgo, hinoki, kiaki, kiri, kozo, matsu, nikko fir, paulownia, pine, sakalin fir, shirasashi, sugi, upas urushi, yeddo

tree, sacred hinoki, sakaki, sakura (nomiya)

troubador basho

underworld jigoku, neno kuni, sokono kuni, yakuza, yomi-tsu-kuni

underworld ruler emma-hoo, yama raja

union federation sohyo

university doshisha, keio, kyoto, sophia, tokyo, waseda

untouchables burakumin

varnish tree urushi

vegetable daikon, gobo, udo

vehicle jinrikisha, ricksha(w)

velvet birodo

view shakkei

village bustee, busti, mura

vine akebi(a), bignonia, kudzu, tecoma

volcano asama(yama), aso(san), fuji(yama), mihara

wall shoji

war cry banzai, tora

war god hachiman daibosatsu, ojin

warrior class bunbury odo, ronin, samurai

warrior class code bushido

wasp tiphia

wax tree sumac

weight carat, catty, fun, hiyakkin, kati, kin, kon, kwamme, kwan, momme, niyo, picul, rin, rjoo, shi

welcome irasshaimase

wild orange tachibana

wine akadama, sake, saki

winged being tengu

wisteria fuji

wood tamo

wooden clog geta

workers' confederation domei

wrestler sumotori

wrestling See *self-defense,* above.

writer akutagawa, fujiwara nokisaki, futabatei, hironari, koboabe, mishima, motoori norinaga, sakyo komatsu, shimazaki

writing jana, janki

yeast koji

yeoman goshi

zither koto

JAPAPURA hollandia

JAPE banter, crack, deceive, deride, fool, gag, gaud, insult, jeer, jest, joke, mock, quip, taunt, trick, wisecrack, witticism

JAPETUS *moon of* saturn

JAPHETH *father* noah

son gomer, javan, madai, magog, mesech, shem, tiras, tubal

JAPHIA *father* david

JAPHLET *father* heber

son ashvath, bimhal, pasach

JAPONICA astilbe, bush, camellia, crape myrtle, quince, shrub, steen

JAQUES *father* roland de boys

JAR agitate, amphora, askos, banga, beaker, brunt, cadus, can, cell, clash, clatter, concussion, conflict, container, crock, cruse, differ, discord, dolium, drill, ewer, fight, grate, grind, hydria, impact, irritate, jangle, jerk, jog, jolt, jounce, juer, jug, kalpis, martaban, offend, olla, outrage, package, pelike, pinata, pitcher, pithos, preserve, pykter, quake, rattle, rock, shake, shock, tamnos, start(le), stinkpot, succussion, terrine, tick, tinaja, toby, upset, urn, vessel, vibrate

bell cloche
coarse crock, terrine
earthenware crock, gallipot, gamla, olla, pankin, pithos, tarro, terrine
fly cicada
fruit mason
large cadus, dolium, situla
leyden condenser
long-necked goglet, gurglet
loose wrest
majolica albarello
opening anthesteria, pithoigia
-owl goatsucker
porous gurglet
ring lute, rubber
squat koro
stone croppa, steen
2-handled amphora
water banga, chatti, chattu, goglet, gumlah, gurglet, hydria
wide-mouthed ewer

JARAH *son* alemeth, azmoth, zimri

JARBIRD nuthatch

JARBLE bemire, moisten, wet

JARDINIERE bowl, pot, soup, stand, urn, vase

JARED *son* enoch

JARGON abracadabra, argot, bafflegab, baragouin, barrikin, beach-la-mar, beche-de-mer, cant, chatter, chinook, choctaw, dialect, dog latin, doubledutch, drivel, enigma, flash tongue, gibberish, gobbledegook, greek, hep talk, idiom, jabber(wocky), jive, kedgeree, koine, lingo, lingua franca, nonsense, patois, patter, pidgin, pigeon english, pig latin, polyglot, rane, rigmarole, schmooze, shelta, shop talk, siwash, slang(uage), speech, talk, talkee-talky, talky-talky, twitter, vernacular, zircon
senseless balderdash
technical grimgribber
thieves' flash

JARHA *son* attai

JARIB *father* simeon

JARL chieftain, earl, headman, quarrel

JARLEY, MRS *friend* little nell

JARMUTH *king* priam

JARRING clashing, discord(ant), dissonant, lute, shaking

JARRY *farce* ubi roi

JARV(E)Y, JARVIE coach, driver, hackney

JASIONE bellflower, sheep's-bit

JASMINE bela, cestrum, clematis, gelsemium, jessamine, jessamy, malati, matrimony vine, papaw, perfume, pikake, sampaquita, woodbine
cape katjepiering
red frangipani

JASON *companion* coronus, paul
consort creusa, glauce, medea
men argonauts
parent aeson, alcimede, eleazar
quest golden fleece
ship argo
son alcimedes, antipater, euneus, thessalus, thoas
teacher chiron
uncle pelias

JASPER biotite, bloodstone, chalcedony, creolite, diasper, mica, morlop, murra, quartz, rube, ruby
zodiac sign pisces

JASS pinochle

JASSY iasi, yassy
coin leu, ley

JATEORHIZA moonseed
root calombo, calumba, colombo, columbo

JAUNDER gabble, prattle

JAUNDICE aurigo, bias, envy, gulsach, hepatikos, hepatitis, icterus, jealousy, prejudice, yellows
blue cyanosis
complication kernicterus
pert. icteric, icterode
preventive rhogam
remedy anti-icteric, bilirubin, celandine

JAUNDICED bigoted, bitter, envious, grudging, intolerant, jealous, sallow, unfair, yellow

JAUNT cruise, excursion, expedition, gad, gallivant, hike, jolt, jounce, journey, ramble, run, sally, shake, stroll, tour, tramp, travel, trek, trip, voyage, walk, wander

JAUNTY airy, animated, careless, chic, chipper, cocky, dapper, dashing, debonair, easy, fine, finical, gay, genteel, lively, modish,

natty, nonchalant, perk(y), shanty, showy, smart, sporty, sprightly, spruce, stylish, swaggering, unconcerned

JAUP bespatter, dregs, spatter, splash, spurt

JAVA (see also EAST INDIES, INDONESIA.) coffee, fowl, tji
aboriginal kalang
almond canarium, kanari, pili, talisay
animal banteng, napu, teledu
arrow poison upas
badger ratel, teledu
berry cubeb
bird beo, thrush-tit
buddhist temple boro budur
canvas ada
capital jakarta
carriage sado(o)
chevrotain napu
city bandoeng, bandung, bantam, batavia, bogor, dessa, djakarta, jakarta, jogjakarta, kediri, madioen, malang, semarang, serang, soerakarta, surabaya
civet dedes, rasse
commune dessa
condiment ajowan
cotton kapok
dance serimpi
dancers bedoyo
deer napu
delinquent kalang
drama topeng
dutchman blanda
fabric ikat
fig tree gondang
fruit gondang, lomboy
grackle beo
island bali, lombok, madura
island group sunda
language balinese, kavi, kawi, madurese, sassak, sudanese
lomboy plum
man pithecanthropus
measure kan, paal, palen, rand
medicine ajowan
midday meal rice table
musical instrument bonang, gambang, gamelan(g), gender, saron
orchestra gamelan(g)
ox banteng
peak amat, gede, lawoe, murjo, prahu, raoeng, semeroe, slamet(a), soembing

people krama, kromo, sudanese
pepper cubeb
plateau ijen
plum duhat, jaman, jambo(o)l, jambos(a), jambul, lomboy
port batavia, surabaya, tegal, tjirebon
puppet show wajang, wayang
rice field sawah
ruler rajah, susuhunan
seed ajava, ajowan
skunk teledu
sparrow munia, paddybird, ricebird, weaverbird
speech krama, ngoko
squirrel jelerang
steak sushi
strait sunda
straw peanit
sumac fuyang
temple boro budur, c(h)andi, thandi
theater kabuki
tree antiar, gondang, upas
village bantam, dessa
volcano bromo, gede, kelut, merapi, raung, semeru, slamet
weight amat, po(u)nd, soekel, tali
wild dog adjag
xylophone gambang
zither galempong, galempung
JAVAN *son* dodanim, elishah, kittim, tarshish
JAVELIN aclys, acontium, angon, assagai, dart, gavelock, handstaff, hurlbat, jereed, jerid, lance, pike, pile, pilum, pole, shaft, spear
game jereed, jerid
point sagaie
thrower meleager
JAW, JAWS bawl out, berate, bill, bite, blame, censure, chaft, chap, chat(ter), chaw(le), chin, choke, chop(s), clack, condemn, criticize, dash, fauces, gab(ble), gonia, gossip, jabber, jowl, mandible, maw, maxilla, mouth, muzzle, nag, pour, rail, rate, reprove, revile, scold, snout, speech, talk, tonguelash, upbraid, vise, vituperate, wang, wave, wig, yak
big actinomycosis
comb. gnath(o)
false clamp

forceps beak
having short hemignathous
having wide eurygnathic
hole cesspool, sewer
lower chin, mandible
muscle masseter, temporal
part ramus
pert. gnathal, gnathic, malar
point gonion
projection prognathism
tissue gum
tumor adamantinomia
undershot layback
upper maxilla
without agnathic, agnathous
JAWBONE articular(e), credit, jowl, maxilla, talk, trust, wang
part mesognathion
JAWFOOT maxilliped
JAWSMITH demagogue, dentist, orator, speaker, talker
JAY aphelocoma, blue(coat), chatterbird, chatterer, dupe, gae, garrulus, magpie, meatbird, motmot, piet, roadmonkey, sirgang, xanthoura
JAYHAWK *state* kansas
JAYHAWKER guerrilla, kansan, raider, spider, tarantula
JAY, JOHN *pseud.* publius
JAZERANT armor, gesseron
JAZZ bebop, blues, boogie woogie, bop, bossa nova, dance, jitterbug, jive, liveliness, megillah, music, rag (time), rubato, shimmy, stomp, syncopation, talk
band date gig
barrelhouse gutbucket
beat bebop
blues-based funk
count basie
fan cat, hepcat, ragtimer, swinger, syncopator
group combo, spasm band
improvize fake
jargon jive
-like music calypso
loud barrelhouse
opening intro
singing scat
style barrelhouse, bebop, dixieland, mainstream, new orleans, swing
theme riff
up accelerate, animate, boost, enliven, increase, speed, spruce, syncopate
JAZZY active, lively, sporty, wild

JEALOUS apprehensive, covetous, desirous, distrustful, doubtful, envious, green (eyed), grudging, jaundiced, lustful, suspicious, vehement, vigilant, watchful, wrathful, yellow(eyed)
JEALOUSY apprehension, envy, green-eyed monster, heartburn, mistrust, resentment, suspicion, yellows
incarnate othello
symbolic color yellow
JEANS levis, PANTS
fabric chino, denim
JEBERECHIAH *son* zechariah
JECOLIAH *son* uzziah
JECONIAH *son* hoshama, jekamiah, malchiram, nedabiah, pedaiah, shealtiel, shenazzar
JEDIDAH *kin* adaiah, amon, josiah
JEDUTHUN *son* galal, gedaliah, hashabiah, jeshaiah, mattithiah, shemaiah, uzziel, zeri
JEEL damage, jelly, mischief
son jechonias
JEEP carryall, pickup, truck
amphibious seep
JEER barrack, bob, boo, chiack, deride, derision, fleer, flout, flute, frump, gibe, gird, glaik, hoot, insult, jape, jibe, laugh at, mob, mock(ery), rally, ridicule, scoff, scomm, sneer, taunt, twit
JEERING bird, derisive, flout, mocking, sceptical
JEEVES butler
JEFE chief, commander, head, leader
JEFFERSON, THOMAS
birthplace shadwell, virginia
burial site monticello
daughter martha, mary
home monticello
love sally hemings
party republican
profession lawyer
territory colorado
vice president aaron burr, george clinton
JEHALELE(E)L *son* asareel, azariah, tiria, ziph (ah)
JEHIADA *wife* jehoshabeath, jehosheba
JEHIEL *parent* jehoshaphat
son abdon, ahio, baal, gedar,

kish, mikloth, nadab, ner, shechaniah, zacher, zechariah, zur
wife maacah
JEHIZKIAH *father* shallum
JEHOAHAZ *parent* hemutal, jehoram, jehu
son joash
JEHOHANAN *captain for* jehoshaphat
son ishmael
JEHOIACHIN *successor* salathiel
JEHOIADA *enemy* athalia
son benaiah, zechariah
wife jehoshabeath
JEHOIAKIM *son* coniah, jeconiah, zedekian
JEHONATHAN *father* uzziah
JEHORAM *offspring* ahaziah, jehoahaz, jehoshabeath
JEHOSHAPHAT *captain* adnah, amasiah, ednas, eliada, jehohanan, jehozabad
leader solomon
parent asa, azubah, nimshi
son azariah, jehiel, j(eh)oram, jehu, michael, shaphatiah, zechariah
wife athaliah
JEHOVAH almighty, elohim, god. have(h), jah, lord, yahveh, yahweh, yhva, yhwa
gift of, name meaning matthew
is god, name meaning elijah
witness pioneer
JEHOZABAD *leader* jehoshaphat
JEHOZADAK *son* joshua
JEHU coachman, drive(r), speeder
father jehoshaphat, obed
son azariah, jehoahaz
JEIEL *scribe of* uzziah
son banaiah
JEJUNE arid, banal, bare, barren, diluted, dry, dull, empty, flat, hungry, inane, insipid, meager, skimpy, slight, stale, sterile, thin, uninteresting, unproductive, vapid, wishywashy
JEKAMIAH *father* shallum
son elishama
JELL clot, congeal, crystallize, firm, gelatinate, stiffen, thicken
JELLY alcogel, aspic, colloid, conserve, emulsion, fisnoga, flummery, gelatin, gelee,

jam, jeel, pectin, poha, preserve, quiddany, rhob
animal gelatin(e)
base pectin
calf's foot fisnoga, sulze
-like gelatinous
nut coconut
plant kei-apple, seaweed
JELLYFISH acaleph, aurelia, carvel, coward, cyanea, medusa, pacifica, pelagia, quarl, salp, scyphozoan, scyphula, slobber, strobila, sunfish, velella, weakling
body umbrella
comb. cetene
group acrespeda, discophora
larva ephyra
part exumbrella, pileus, tentacle, umbrella
stinging sea-nettle
umbrella pileus
JEMIMA *father* job
JEMMY boot, crowbar, dandy, greatcoat, handy, jimmy, lever, neat, spruce
JEMUEL *father* simeon
JENNA See PARADISE.
JENNET ass, donkey, horse, mule
JENNY airplane, ass, crane, female, jane, spinner, wren
JEOPARDIZE endanger, expose, hazard, risk
JEOPARDY chance, danger, dilemma, hap, hazard, insecurity, liability, menace, peril, problem, risk, threat, trick, venture
JEPHUNNEH *son* caleb, kenaz
JEQUIRITY black-eyed susan, guinea-pea, indian licorice
bean angolaseed, eyen, ruttee
JERAHMEEL *son* achia, ahijah, bunah, onam, oren, ozem, ram
JERBA lotus land
JERBOA allactaga, dipus, gerbil, jaculus, jumper, rodent
kangaroo bettong
JEREED javelin, jerrid, tzirid
JEREMIAD complaint, cry, lament(ation), plaint, tale, tirade, tragedy, woe
JEREMIAH *friend* baruch
offspring ezekiel, hamutal, jaazaniah
parent habaziniah
JEREMOTH *parent* elam

JERICHO *despoiler* achan
publican zacchaeus
rebuilder hiel
woman rahab
JERIEL *father* tola
JERIOTH *husband* caleb
JERK biltong(ue), bob, budzat, chap, charqui, chump, diddle, dolt, dope, drip, dullard, firk, flick, flip, flirt, flounce, fool, frump, gird, grab, hitch, jerque, jibe, jig, jigger, jigget, jiggle, jog(gle), jolt, jouk, melamed, nerd, nidge, pluck, preserve, pull, push, putz, reflex, sad sack, schlep(per), schmo, s(c)hmuck, shake, snake, snap, sneer, snig, spang (hew), spasm, start, surge, switch, thrill, throw, tic, tweak, twist, twitch, vellicate, whip, wiggle, wrench, yank, yerk
JERKLINE harness
JERKS chorea, convulsions
JERKWATER hick, insignificant, small-time
JERKY biltong(ue), bultong, charqui, elboic, fidgety, flicky, flingy, hitchy, jiggety, joggly, jolty, jouncy, jumpy, palmodic, ratchety, saccadic, sharp, tasajo, twitchety, twitchy, vellicative
JEROHAM *parent* elihu
son adaiah, athaliah, azariah, eliah, elkanah, jaresiah, shamsherai, sherariah, zichri
JEROME *brother* napoleon
JEROME, SAINT hieronymus
emblem lion
pert. hieronymic
JEROMIN don juan
JERRY aware, conscious, german, knowing, kraut, soldier
-built cheap, flimsy, frail
shop See SALOON.
sneak dastard, rogue
JERSEY camisole, cloth, fabric, frock, gansey, guernsey, jacket, maillot, shirt, singlet, sweater, tricot, wool, zephyr
capital st helier
cudweed everlasting
fir scrub-pine
lightning applejack
livelong cudweed, enaena

police officer centenier
port st helier
red swine
tea checkerberry, winter-green
thistle centaury
JERUBBAAL See GIDEON.
JERUSALEM aholibah, ariel, celestial city, city of david, hephzibah, oholibah, sion, solyma, urusalima, zion
artichoke ball-thistle, canada(potato), earthapple, girasol(e), helianthus, herb, sunflower, topinambou, tuber
cherry solanum
conqueror omar
corn durra
cowslip lungwort
cross lychnis
cucumber gherkin
date bauhinia, butterfly-flower, schizanthus
delivered, author tasso
garden gethsemane
going to musical chairs
haddock opah
hill moriah, olivet, sion, zion
king adonizedec, baldwin
lamentation site wailing wall
mosque omar
name, old ariel, jebus, salem
oak ambrose, chenopodium, goosefoot, mexican tea
pea gram
pert. hierosolymitan
pickle gherkin
pony ass, donkey
pool bethesda, dihon, siloam
prophetess anna, anne
ridge olivet
sage phlomis, sageleaf
section meashearim, perea
sheep market bethesda
shrine dome of the rock, holy sepulcher, wailing wall
spring See *pool,* above.
star aaron's-beard, salsify, snow-in-harvest
temple solomon's cloister
temple treasury corban
thorn or tree ambrose, cascol, catechu, parkinsonia, retama
willow oleaster
JERUSHA *father* zadok
husband uzziah
JESHER *father* caleb
JESHUA *ruler of* mizpah
son ezer, jeddu, josabdus, jozabad
JESIAH *father* uzziel

JESPERSON *language* ido
JESS leash, ribbon, strap
JESSAMINE See JASMINE.
JESSE *daughter* abigail, zeruiah
father obed
son abinadab, david, eliab, nethaneel, ozem, raddai, shammah, shimma
JESSICA *father* shylock
lover lorenzo
JESSUR daboia, reptile, snake, viper
JEST act, badinage, banter, bob, bourd, butt, chaff, clown, cog, crack, deed, derision, droll, fool, fun, gag, game, gammock, gaud, geste, gleek, jape(ry), jeer, jibe, joke, jollity, jolly, kid, laugh, mask, merriment, mock, mot, nothing, pageant, persiflage, play, prank, quip, raillery, ridicule, scoff, spoof, sport, tale, taunt, trifle, twit, waggery, wisecrack, wit(ticism)
JESTER antic, badchen, boor, bourder, buffo(on), clown, comedian, comic, disour, fool, goliard, harlequin, idiot, insult, japer, joker, juggler, larker, merryandrew, mime, motley, owlglass, pantaloon, picador, prankster, quipster, railleur, scoffer, stooge, trinculo, wamba, wisecracker, wit, zany
headdress cap and bells
staff bauble
JESTING banter, drowl, funny, sceptical, waggish
JESUIT, JESUIT'S ignatian, loyolite, paulist, tertian
bark cinchona, marsh-elder
drops friar's balsam
founder loyola
head black pope
motto amdg
nut water chestnut
resin balsam-capivi, copaiba
saint francis xavier, ignatius loyola, regis
tea mate
JESUITISM equivocation, quibble, sophistry
JESUS See CHRIST.
bug water-strider
JET aircraft, airliner, artifice, black(amber), blast, boast, bolt, carouse, coal, dart, disgorge, douche, dummy, ebony, emit, essence, essen-

tial, fantail, fashion, flush, font, fount(ain), gagate, geyser, gist, gush, jerk, jolt, jut, ladle, manner, mig, nozzle, parade, plane, pour, project, raven, roll, rush, sabre, sally, scorpion, shoot, soffione, spout, spray, spring, spurt(le), squirt, stream, stroll, stupa, surge, walk, well
black bugle
lag dysrhythmia
liner concorde, sst
propulsion unit jato
-setter gadabout, goer
stream squirt
JETHER *kin* amasa, ara, ephunneh, ezra, pispah
JETHRO *son-in-law* moses
JETSAM flotsam, jettison
JETTISON abandon, cast off, discard, dump, jetsam, relinquish
JETTY breakwater, bridge, buttress, dock, groin, groyne, mole, pier, starling, wall, wharf
JETUR *kin* ishmael
JEU amusement, game, play
de main horseplay
de mots pun
d'esprit quip, witticism
JEUSH *father* esau, rehoboam, shimel
JEUZ *father* shaharaim
JEW, JEW'S, JEWISH (See also HEBREW, ISRAELI.) judaic, semitic
apple egg plant
autonomous region city birobijan, tikhona, valgeim
-baiting anti-semitism
bird ani
central and eastern europe ashkenazim
community aljama, kehillah, kolel, shtetel, shtetl, synagog(ue)
crow chough
harp crembalum, flamfew, gewgaw, guimbard, trangam, trillium, trump
homeland paper balfour declaration
mallow desi, jute
monkey macaque, saki
myrtle butcher's-broom
of malta barabas
pitch asphalt, bitumen
quarter ghetto, mellah
school aljama
spain and portugal sephardim

state israel, jewish autonomous region
stone marcasite
wandering inchplant, lakedion, salathiel
JEWEL (See also JEWELRY.) baguette, bauble, bead, bearing, bespangle, bijou, brilliant, brooch, cameo, chatelaine, darling, diamond, drop, enchase, gem, incrust, intaglio, ornament, pin, prize, stone, treasure, trinket
box casket, casquet
case tye
connoisseur lapidarist, lapidary
fabulous draconites, serpentstone
facet bezel, lozenge, quoin
kind See GEM *stone, kind.*
name meaning cameo, opal, pearl, ruby
parcel of bag, bulse, purse
phoney paste
setting bezel, dop, ouch, pave
weight carat, karat
JEWELER gemmary, gemologist, glyptographer, glyptologist, lapidarist, lapidary
cup dop(p)
glass loupe
rouge colcothar
JEWELRY (See also *piece*, below.) bijou(terie), bangle, beads, brilliant, bulse, gaud, gems, ice, junk, loot, parure, perrie, rocks, stones, trinket
adorn with begem, bespangle
alloy oreide, oroide
costume junk
cutting device dop(p)
false glass, logie, oroide, paste, strass
piece bead(s), birthstone, bracelet, brooch, cameo, chain, choker, circlet, clip, eardrop, earring, lavaliere, locket, necklace, pearls, pendant, pin, ring, solitaire, stickpin, tiepin, torque
set of parure
setting pave
JEWELWEED ballistic fruit, celandine, ceroline, garden balsam, herb, impatiens, kick-colt, quick-in-the-hand, solentine, snapweed, touch-me-not
JEWFISH abura-bozu, erilepis, grouper, guasa,

junefish, mero, mulloway, percoid, promicrops, sea bass, serrand, warsaw
JEZEBEL courtesan, drab, fury, gorgon, harlot, jade, mallow, trollop, virago, witch
father ethbaal, ithobal
husband naboth
niece dido
offspring athaliah, jehoram
victim elijah, naboth
JEZELUS *son* abadias, sechenias
JEZER *mother* naphtali
JEZLIAH *parent* elpaal
JEZREEL *parent* etam, hosea
plain of esdraelon
JIB arm, balk, boggle, boom, chore, crane, demur, derrick, face, gib(bet), gigue, prow, retreat, sail, scruple, shift, shy, sinecure, spitfire, standstill, stick(le), strain, tack
boom spar
JIBE accord, agree, comport, conform, correspond, fit, fling, flird, gaff, gibe, harmonize, sarcasm, scoff, shift, square, tack, tally, taunt
JIBSAM *father* tola
JIFFY flash, instant, minute, moment, (split)second, trice, twinkling, whiff
JIG ballad, buck, cajole, dance, delude, drill, jerk, jolt, prank, shake, ship, song, squid, trap, trick
fishing pilk
ore-washing hutch
JIGGER bicycle, bridge, boost, cart, chigger, chigoe, chigre, contraption, device, door, dram, dray, drink, escalate, gadget, guy, hike, imprison, jerk, mask, object, prison, raise, shot, streetcar, support, tackle, thingumbob, vatman, vessel
fluid rel
JIGGERY-POKERY humbug(gery), jugglery, juggling, sham
JIGGLE bob, dance, diddle, jerk, jog, rock, shake, shimmy, sway, teeter, twitch, vellicate, wiggle
JILL beloved, girl, sweetheart, woman
companion jack
JILLION many, numerous
JILT abandon, begowk, be-

gunk, cast off, cheat, deceive, discard, gunk, hoax, kick, mau, mitten, reject
JIMDANDY ace, admirable, fine, great, oner, topnotcher
JIMJAM(S) creeps, gadget, gimcrack, horrors, shakes, trepidation
JIMMY bar, betty, coalcar, crowbar, dexterous, james, lever, open, pry, smart, spoil, spruce
JIMNAH *parent* asher
JIMP neat, slender, spruce, trim, scant, skimp
JIMPRICUTE elegant, handsome, neat
JIMSON *weed* apple of peru, datura, dewtry, fireweed, physalis, stinkweed, stramonium, stramony, thorn apple
JINGLE car, chime, chink, clink, confuse, ding(dong), doggerel, jangle, poem, rhyme, rickle, ring, sinkle, song, verse
shell anomia
JINGOISM chauvinism, militarism, patriotism, warmongering
JINGOIST chauvinist, flagwaver, militarist, spreadeagleist, warmonger
JINK, JINKS caper, cheat, chink, defeat, dodge, frolic, prank(s), trick(s)
JINNEE, JINNI afreet, afrit, alukah, bottle-imp, demon, eblis, genie, genii, jenniyer, shaitan, spirit, yaksha
powerful marid
JINRIKISHA carriage, gocart, kuruma, rickshaw
man kurumaya
JINX, JYNX bedevil, charm, hex, hoodoo, jadu, jonah, ill wind, magic, oppress, sign, spell, whammy, witch
JIPIJAPA chidra, palmilla, panama(hat), toquilla
JIPPER baste, cook, gravy, juice
JITNEY car, five cents, motorist, nickel, vehicle
JITTER fidget, jerk, jump, twitch
JITTERBUG dance, truck
JITTERS collywobbles, dithers, fidgets, heebiejeebies, nerves, nervousness, shakes, willies
JITTERY agitated, creepy,

edgy, feverish, fidgety, hectic, impatient, jumpy, nervous, perturbed, restive, restless, shaky, skittish, uneasy, upset
JIVARO palto, shuara, xibaro
JIVATMA atman, ego, self, soul, spirit
JIVE banter, dance, jargon, jazz, kid, lingo, syncopate, tease
JO beloved, darling, dear, joy, pleasure, sweetheart
JOAB *armor-bearer* naharai
kin amasa, david
victim absalom
JOACHIM *wife* anne
JOAH *son* eden
JOAHAZ *son* joaz
JOAKIM *wife* susanna
JOAN *husband* edward
son richard ii
JOANNA *husband* chuza
JOANNES *parent* hecatan
JOAN OF ARC maid of orleans, pucelle
battle orleans
execution site rouen
JOASH *son* achaz, amaziah, gideon
successor amaziah
JOB, JOB'S act, affair, assignment, berth, billet, burglary, business, buy, capacity, cartload, char(e), chore, concern, craft, crime, duty, employment, enterprise, factor, fraud, function, hire, hold-up, jab, lump, market, matter, metier, office, peck, piece, place, position, post, profession, project, province, pursuit, robbery, sell, situation, shift, stab, stint, strike, stump, task, theft, thrust, trade, work, undertaking
affliction boils
comforter bildad, elihu, eliphaz, pessimist, zophar
daughter jemima, kerenhappuch, kezia
-holder incumbent, worker
holding 2 moonlighting
on the alert, attentive, with it
pond bridewell, prison
soft sinecure, snap
tears adlai, adlay, coix, corn beads, crysolite, grass
wife makhir, rahmat, sitis
JOBAB *parent* elpaal
JOBATION rebuke, reproof, scolding

JOBBER brogger, hack, middleman, pieceworker, wholesaler, worker
JOBBERY chicanery, corruption, graft
JOBE lecture, reprove, scold
JOBO gumbo-limbo, hog plum
JOCASTA *consort* laius, oedipus
father creon
offspring antigone, eteocles, ismene, oedipus, polynices
JOCHEBED *father* levi
husband amram
offspring aaron, miriam, moses
JOCK athlete, food, john, provisions, rustic, scot, soldier
JOCKEY blackleg, cavalier, chanter, cheat, cushion, deceive, equestrian, equison, horseman, knave, maneuver, manipulate, minstrel, outwit, pad, rider, rogue, roper, saddle, sharper, skipjack, speeder, swindler, trick, turfite, turfman, vagabond, waster
apparel silks
disk arranger, deejay, impresario
weight allowance bug
whip bat
JOCONIAH *father* josiah
JOCOSE blithe, comic(al), droll, dry, facetious, frolicsome, funny, hilarious, humorous, JOCULAR, jocund, jolly, jovial, laughable, lepid, ludicrous, merry, playful, roguish, sportive, waggish, witty
JOCOTE DE MICO barbas
JOCULAR animated, blithe, cheerful, convivial, debonair, droll, facetious, festive, funny, gay, gladsome, gleeful, humorous, jesting, JOCOSE, joking, loco, merry, playful, sportive, vivacious, waggish, witty
JOCUND airy, blithe, cheerful, gay, glad, hilarious, jolly, jovial, merry, playful
JOD yodh
JODA *son* josech
JODDUS *wife* obdia
JODHPURS See PANTS.
JODO See PARADISE.
deity amida, amita, amitabha
JOE fellow, guy, joseph

-pyeweed boneset, eupatory, gravelroot
JOEL samuel, shemaiah
JOEWOOD barbasco, ironwood, joebush, wild cinnamon
JOEY clown, coin, kangaroo
JOG(GLE) bob, diddle, dunch, exercise, hod, hotch, jar, jerk, jolt, jostle, jounce, jundie, mog, move, notch, notify, nudge, pace, poke, press, prod, push, remind, rock, run, shake, shove, stir, suggest, thrust, trot, trudge, turn, tweak, walk, warn
-trot monotonous, tedious, walk
JOHANAN *parent* eliashib, ellioenai, josiah
son azariah, joda
JOHN coin, eoin, evan, giovanni, hans, ian, ivan, jack, jean, johan(nes), juan, man, policeman, seaghan, sean
barleycorn whiskey
birch society founder welch
brown's body, author benet
bull britannia, england
crow turkey-buzzard
doc nonentity
dory boarfish
down fulmar
go-to-bed-at-noon goatsbeard
hancock signature
mother salome
of gaunt family lancaster
of gaunt father edward
of gaunt protege chaucer
saint, burial site ephesus
saint, father simon
saint, island patmos
saint, symbol eagle
son eupolemus, mattathias
the baptist elijah
the baptist, parent elizabeth, zachariah, zacharias, zachary
the baptist, symbol cross, lamb
the baptist, victim of salome
JOHNNY, JOHNNIE chaser, dude, englishman, fellow, hanger-on, lover, male, penguin, person, sculpin, soldier, stage-door-man
appleseed john chapman
cake corncake, hoecake, pone
-come-lately tyro

darter blind simon, boleosoma
-jump-up violet, wild pansy
on the spot attentive, prepared, prompt, ready
reb confederate
JOHNSON, ANDREW
birthplace raleigh, north carolina
burial site greenville, tennessee
party republican
profession tailor
JOHNSON, DR SAMUEL
birthplace lichfield
friend bathurst, james boswell
hero rasselas
periodical rambler
romance rasselas
JOHNSON, ESTHER stella
JOHORAM *mother* jezebel
JOIADA *kin* eliashib, jonathan
JOIARIB *kin* adaiah, eliashib, zechariah
JOIN abut, add, adject, affiliate, affix, affy, annex, append, articulate, assemble, associate, attach, belong, bind, bond, border, cantle, cement, coalesce, coapt, combine, compound, concur, connect, consolidate, cooperate, couple, dovetail, engage, englue, enlist, enroll, enter, fasten, glue, graft, hitch, incorporate, integrate, junction, knit, league, line up, link, lock, marry, mate, meet, merge, mingle, miter, mitre, mix, oop, pair, rabbet, relate, seam, sign on, solder, splice, stitch, suture, tag, tie, touch, unite, wed, weld, yoke
battle engage, joust
hands ally
in participate, take part
in marriage couple, hitch, splice, wed
issue argue, challenge, collide, engage, fight
sewing stitch, suture, tack
up enlist
JOINED accolle, akin, allied, combined, emboite, kindred, related, seamed, united
JOINER carpenter, extrovert, framer, member, woodworker
JOINING accession, addi-

tament, addition, additive, additory, combination, compacture, connection, encounter, JOINT, junction, meeting, rencontre, rencounter, synectic
bar yoke
JOINT ankle, arthrodia, arthron, articulation, bipartite, bond, brothel, butt, closure, collective, combined, common, connection, coupling, den, dive, dual, dump, elbow, ginglymus, hangout, hinge, hip, hock, internode, junction, knuckle, link, lithe, lock, miter, mortise, mutual, nexus, node, part, pivot, rabbet, saloon, seal, seam, shared, sink, spald, splice, suture, tenon, tuck, undivided, union, united, wrist
ailment sprain
ankle coot
articulated hinge
basal cardo
carpenter's shiplap
cavity bursa
comb. anc(h)ylo, ankylo, arthr(o), condylo
covering flashing
crural knee
effort cooperation, teamwork
elbow noop
excision arthrectomy
fir ephedra
flexible hinge
gliding arthropodia, diarthrosis
grass bedstraw, culm, equisetum, paspalum
grooved rabbet
having many polyarticular
hip coxa, thurl
lubricator synovia
make tight stem
oil synovia
out of dislocated, inauspicious
pain arthralgia, arthritis, arthrosia, bursitis, gout, rheumatism
part mortise, tenon
pert. arthral, arthrous, articular, nodal
plant wandering jew
put out of dislocate, displace, luxate, sprain
right angle elbow, ell, knee, tee
rust cattail-fungus
sac bursa
stem node

stiffness anchylosis, ankylosis, rheumatism
study of arthrology
surgery arthrectomy, arthroplasty
turned outward valgus
universal cardan
venture pool
vertical build
wheel-like trochite
wing flexure
without acondylose, acondylous, anarthrous
JOINTED arthral, arthrous, articulated, knotty
charlock kraut, runch
JOINTWEED equisetum, mare's-tail
JOINTWOOD cassia
JOIST beam, scantling, stud, timber
JOJOBA pignut, sheepnut
JOKE anecdote, antic, april fool, banter, ba(u)r, butt, caper, chaff, crack, dido, double-entendre, fool, frolic, fun, gag, gaud, gegg, gleek, grind, hoax, humor, jape(ry), jest, josh, kib(b)itz, kid, laughingstock, mot, nothing, play, plisky, prank, pun, quip, rally, rib, sally, scintillate, shaggy-dog, sparkle, sport, story, trick, trifle, twit, waggery, wisecrack, wheeze, witticism, yarn
off color blue
old chestnut, platitude
political squib
practical gag, hoax, hotfoot, plisky, shavie, shortsheet
JOKER boarder, bragger, buffoon, bug, card, catch, clown, creature, dor, farceur, fellow, flaw, fool, humorist, jester, josher, kibitzer, man, mistigri(s), punster, quipster, snoozer, tickler, wag, wild card, wit
JOKSHAN *kin* abraham, dedan, sheba
JOKTAN *father* eber
son abimael, almodad, diklah, ebal, hadoram, havilah, hazarmaveth, jerah, jobab, obal, ophir, sheba, sheleph, uzal
JOLL jowl, knock, lurch, roll over
JOLLITY festivity, frolic, fun, gaiety, gambol, gayness, glee, hilarity, jest, joviality, merriment, mirth,

play, pleasure, romp, splendor, sport

JOLLY arrogant, banter, blandish, blithe, bold, boon, brave, buxom, cajole, chaff, cheer(ful), cheery, chubby, convivial, crouse, excellent, flatter, gawsy, gay, great, guy, happy, hilarious, intoxicated, jocose, jocund, jovial, joyful, joyous, kid, large, larking, laughing, lively, lusty, marine, merry, playful, pleasant, plump, quiz, rag, rally, red-cheeked, rib, roguish, sailor, splendid, sportive, strong, very, waggish, witty
boat dandy, yawl
jumper sail
roger flag, skull and crossbones

JOLT agitate, blow, bounce, bump, churn, clash, concussion, convulse, dird, dirl, drink, impact, jar, jerk, jog(gle), jostle, jounce, jut, pace, rock, shake, shock, start(le), succussion, thrust

JOLTERHEAD dunce, porgy

JOLTING bouncy, bumpy, choppy, jarring, jerky, joggl(et)y, jolty, rough

JONAH crab, hoodoo, jinx
father amittai, saul
son andrew, cephas, peter, simon
swallower whale

JONAM *son* joseph

JONATHAN *friend* david
parent ahinoam, saul
son: jadua, mephibosheth, obeth, peleth, zaza, zechariah
victory site geba

JONES, CASEY *railroad* illinois central
train cannonball special

JONES, EMPEROR robeson

JONES, HENRY cavendish

JONES, JOHN PAUL *flagship* bonhomme richard
hero under richard dale

JONES, TOM *benefactor and uncle* squire allworthy
sweetheart sophia western

JONGLEUR bard, gleeman, minstrel, poet(aster), rhymer, scald, scop, troubadour, trouvere

JONQUIL daffodil, jonk, lily, narcissus

JONSON, BEN *nickname* bricklayer

play alchemist, bartholomew fair, cynthia's revels, every man in his humor, sejanus, volpone
tavern mermaid

JOPPA *woman of* dorcas

JORAM *officer of* josiah
son ahaziah, ozias

JORD *husband* odin

JORDAN *archeological site* khirbet-qumran
capital amman, rabbath-ammon
city amman, aqaba, ariha, bethany, bethel, bethlehem, el kerak, hebron, irbid, jarash, jerash, karak, kerak, kirmoab, krak, nablus, petra, sarqa, zerke
coin dinar
king hussein
peak ataiba, bukka, dabab, gilead, hor, mubrak, nebo, pisgah
port aqaba
ravine kedro
region bashan, moab, per(a)ea
ridge mount of olives, olivet
river jordan, yarmuk
valley ghor

JORIM *son* eliezer

JORTH *husband* odin
son thor

JOSAPHIAS *son* assalimoth

JOSECH *son* semein

JOSEDECH *son* cadoel, jeshua, joakim, joshua

JOSEPH, JOSEPH'S barnabas, barnaby, barsabbas, giuseppe
brother (See also JACOB *son.*) napoleon
buyer potiphar
coat amaranth, coleus
father-in-law potipherah
flower goat's-beard
nephew tola
offspring ephraim, igal, james, jannai, jesus, judah, jude, manasseh
parent jacob, rachel
walking-stick jacob's-ladder
wife asenath, mary

JOSEPHINE blush, pheny

JOSH banter, chaff, guy, jolly, kid, quiz, rag, rally, rib, ridicule, string, TEASE, twit

JOSHUA *altar* ebal
ancestor telah
associate caleb
burial site gaash, mount ephraim, timnath-serah

camp gilgal
conquest adullam, aphek, arad, bethel, debir, eglon, geder, gezer, hebron, hepher, hormah, jarmuth, jericho, jerusalem, lachish, lasharon, libnah, makkeday, tappuah
general for moses
parent eliezer, nun
succeeded moses
tree cactus, redbud, yucca
valley aijalon

JOSIAH *courtier* asaph, eddinous, zacharias
father amon, jedidah
governor maaseiah
messenger achbor, ahikam, asahiah
officer jachonias, jahath, jechonias, joram, mechonias, nathanael, obadiah, ozielus, sabias, samaeas, zechariah
priest hilkiah, jehiel, zechariah
recorder joahaz
scribe shaphan
servant asaiah
son jeconiah, jechonias, jehoahaz, jehoiakim, joachaz, johanan, shallum, zedekiah
wife hamutal

JOSKIN boor, bumpkin, rustic

JOSS chance, crowd, divinity, employer, jolt, jostle, idol, image, master, overseer
house temple
stick incense

JOSTLE buffet, bump, collide, collision, crowd, differ, discord, elbow, fight, hogshouter, hurtle, hustle, interference, jab, jar, JOG(GLE), jolt, maul, push, rush, shake, shock, shoulder, shove, thrust

JOT ace, atom, bit, chore, grain, gram, iota, item, jog, jolt, mark, minim, mite, mote, note, particle, point, scintilla, scrap, scruple, smidgen, smitch, speck, tare, tittle, whit, wight
down note, record, write

JOTHAM *parent* gideon, jahdai, jerubbaal

JOTTING entry, memo(randum), notation, note

JOULE *part* erg

JOUNCE bob, bounce, bump, jar, jog, jolt, jostle, rock, shake

JOURNAL annals, bulletin, cahier, cashbook, chronicle, daybook, diary, diurnal, ephemeris, gazette, gudgeon, hotbox, ledger, log(book), magazine, minutes, newspaper, periodical, pictorial, pulp, record, register, review, slick, trunnion
bearing rhoding
keeper diarist
sea logbook
JOURNALISM fourth estate, press
JOURNALIST author, columnist, editor, newsman, reporter, writer
woman sobsister
JOURNEY campaign, circuit, comino, course, cruise, drive, errand, excursion, expedition, eyre, fare, flight, gait, gate, globe-trot, hadj, hegira, hejira, hike, hop, iter, jaunt, jump, junket, odyssey, outing, passage, peregrination, progress, ramble, ride, roam, rove, run, safari, sally, siege, sightsee, sithe, tour, traik, trail, travel, trek, trip, turn, voyage, wayfare, wend, whirl
day's diet, jornada
desert jornada
division lap, leg
long odyssey, pilgrimage, trek
pert. itinerant, peripatetic, viatic
plan itinerary
stupid idiodyssey
upward anabasis
JOURNEYMAN apprentice, assistant, helper, subordinate, yeoman
JOUST bout, box, break a lance, combat, contest, fight, spar, tilt, tournament, tourney
field list
ready to atilt
JOVE, JOVE'S (See also ZEUS.) jupiter
fruit persimmon, spicebush
hound eagle
nut acorn
JOVIAL affable, amiable, blithe, boon, bully, companionable, congenial, convivial, cordial, festal, festive, gay, genial, goodnatured, jocund, jolly, mellow, merry, risible, sociable

companion bon-vivant
feast carousal
JOVIALITY festivity, hilarity, jollity, mirth
JOWL chap, chaule, cheek, chops, dewlap, jaw, maxilla, wattle
JOY beatitude, blessedness, bliss, cheer, delectation, delight, dream, ecstasy, elation, enchantment, euphoria, euphrosyne, exult (ation), felicity, gaiety, gladness, glee, grace, happiness, heaven, hilarity, intoxication, jubilance, mechaieh, mirth, paradise, pleasure, rapture, ravishment, rejoice, rejoicing, seventh-heaven, sunshine, transport, utopia, zest
cry of lullilloo
exclamation boy, goody, hot dog, hot ziggety, man, oh boy, oo-la-la, whee, wow
god See HAPPINESS *god.*
goddess hathor
leaf rattlesnake-root
muse tara
name meaning aine
-of-the-ground periwinkle
-of-the-mountain arbutus, marjoram
ride spin
song of p(a)ean
water See LIQUOR.
JOYCE, JAMES *work* dubliners, finnegan's wake, ulysses
JOYFUL beamy, blessed, blithe, enjoyable, gay, glad, gladsome, gleeful, happy, jocund, jolly, merry, pleasurable, rapturous
name meaning festus
JOYLESS cheerless, desolate, dismal, dour, melancholy, miserable, unblithe, unhappy
JOYOUS blithe, buoyant, cheer(ful), delighted, ecstatic, elated, exultant, frolic, gay, gioioso, glad, gleeful, happy, jocund, merry, mirthful, rapturous, transported, vestal, youse
JOZADAK *son* jeshua
JUBAL *parent* adah, lamech
JUBE rood, loft, screen
JUBEROUS doubting, dubious, hesitating
JUBILANT elated, exultant, gleeful, gleesome, happy, rapturous

JUBILATION celebration, cheer, elation, exultation, festivity, joy(ance), jubilee, laughing, laughter, merriment, rejoicing, triumph
JUCA cassava, manioc
JUDAEA See JUDEA.
JUDAH (See also JUDEA.) rehoboam, roboam
capital jerusalem
city adar, ain, aman, azem, eder, enam, hazor, shema, telem, ziph
consort tamar
daughter-in-law tamar
descendant anub, jerahmeel, maaz, oren
governor gedaliah, sheshbazzar, tatnai, zerubbabel
king abijah, ahaz(iah), amasias, amaziah, amon, asa, athaliah, azariah, david, degaliah, eliakim, hezekiah, jeconiah, jehoahaz, jehoiachin, jehoiakim, jehoram, jehoshaphat, joachaz, joakim, joash, josiah, jotham, manasseh, mattaniah, ochozias, uzziah, zedekiah
lion of haile selassie
parent jacob, leah
queen athlaiah
son carmi, hezron, hur, onan, perez, pharex, shelah, shobal, simeon, zara(h), zerah
JUDAISM See HEBREW.
JUDAS *betrayer* quisling, traitor
father jacob, simon
replacement matthias
suicide field aceldama, akeldama
surname iscariot
symbol money bag
tree cercis, redbud
JUDEA See also JUDAH.
district apherema, hamath, lydda, ramathaim
governor gedaliah, pontius pilate, sanabassar, zerubbabel
king ahaz, amon, antigonus, archelaus, aristobulus, asa, herod, jehoiachin, jehoshaphat, johoram
town bethlehem
JUDGE 3 try, ump 4 beak, cadi, caid, call, cazi, cazy, deem, doom, dope, find, foud, imam, juez, kadi, kazi, kazy, rank, rate, rule 5 allow, award, bench, count, court, dayan, edile, fancy, hakim, infer, judex,

opine, trier, tryer, value 6
assess, critic, decide, decree,
deduce, deemer, esteem, expert, gather, jurist, keeper,
puisne, regard, settle, umpire 7 account, alcalde, arbiter, bencher, censure,
condemn, discern, examine,
imagine, justice, mediate,
munsiff, podesta, presume,
referee, resolve, scabine,
shamgar, suppose, surmise
8 centenar, conclude, consider, doomsman, doomster,
estimate, his honor, min-
ister, mittimus, quaestor,
reviewer, sentence 9 arbitrate, authority, criticize,
determine, judicator, moderator, pronounce, surro-
gate 10 adjudicate, arbitrator, chancellor, magistrate
11 adjudicator, cognos-
cente, connoisseur
aide assessor
before the sub judice
bench banc(us)
chamber camera
chamber, pert. cameral
circuit eyre, iter
favorably approve
gavel mace
group bench, judiciary,
 magistracy
junior puisne
kind assessor, barmaster,
 chancellor, circuit, deputy,
 jurat, linesman, master of
 the rolls, probate
name meaning dan
office camera, chambers
rigorous rhadamanthus
robe toga
rule of kritarchy
seat banc(us), bench
JUDGMENT account, acu-
 men, advice, appraisal,
 arret, assessment, assize(s),
 award, belief, call, censure,
 circumspection, conclusion,
 condemnation, conviction,
 criticism, decision, decree,
 determination, discernment,
 doom, estimate, finding,
 gate, gumption, horse sense,
 intelligence, mandate, opinion, order, sachel, sagacity,
 sens(e), sentence, steven,
 taste, thinking, verdict,
 view, wisdom, witting, writ
day doomsday
doctrine of apophantic
good common sense
immediate apercu

lack acrisy, aphronia
last doom, great assize
left to one's discretionary
place of court, tribunal, tribune
seat bench
settled conviction
standard of barometer,
 canon, criterion, gauge,
 measure, norm, touchstone,
 yardstick
JUDICIAL critical, forensic,
 juridic(al), legal
examination inquest
JUDICIARY bench, court
document cape, decision,
 writ
JUDICIOUS astute, calcu-
 lating, careful, cautious, circumspect, considerate, cool,
 critical, discreet, discretionary, discriminating,
 enlightened, equitable, expedient, fair, just, objective,
 politic, provident, pru-
 dent(ial), rational, reasonable, reflecting, sagacious,
 sage, sane, sapient, sensible,
 shrewd, sober, sound,
 thoughtful, well-advised,
 wise
JUDITH *father* beeri, merari
husband esau, manasses
offspring korah
victim holophernes
JUDO jujitsu, kata
award black belt, blue belt
player kudoka
practice randori
term shodan
JUDY sweetheart
partner punch
JUG aiguiere, amphora,
 askos, beaker, bellarmine,
 boggle, buire, can, con-
 tainer, cooler, coop, crouke,
 cruisken, cruse, ewer,
 flagon, gaol, goglet, gotch,
 hydria, imprison, jail, jar,
 lecythus, lekythos, lockup,
 lota(h), mug, oenochoe,
 olpe, pitcher, prison, prochoos, ranter, schnabel-
 kanne, stew, toby, vase,
 vessel, urn
bulging gotch
handled buire
leather bombard, jack
man-shaped toby
1-handled urceus
room for ewery
spouted buire, dollin
spoutless olpe
stoneware bellarmine

JUGGERNAUT idol, jagan-
 nath(a), krishna, vishnu
idol kesora
JUGGLE alter, baffle, be-
 guile, bobble, cheat, conjure, deceive, imposture,
 magic, prestidigitate,
 shuffle, trick
JUGGLER buffoon, cheat,
 conjuror, deceiver, jester,
 jongleur, magician, prestidigitator
box tranca
JUGGLERY conjuration, es-
 camotage, hankypanky, hocuspocus, hokeypokey,
 imposture, jiggery-pokery,
 legerdemain, prestidigitation, sleight of hand, trickery
JUGLANS black oak, butternut, carya, hickory, walnut
JUGLARES carapus,
 fierasfer, pearlfish
JUGOSLAVIA See YUGO-
 SLAVIA.
JUGULATE kill, strangle
JUGURTHA *captor* sulla
JUICE abstract, aguamiel,
 anima, blood, bree, broo,
 casiri, cremor, current,
 drink, electricity, essence,
 flow, fluid, gas(oline),
 gravy, humor, jus, latex, liquid, lymph, milk, moisten,
 money, must, ooze, pep,
 resin, rhob, sap(a), stum,
 succus, suck, sura, water,
 wet
apple cider
comb. opo
concentrated sirup, syrup
dried aloe, kino
fruit ade, casiri, cider, must,
 omphacy, rob, rohob, stum,
 vinegar, wine
full of succous, succulent
intoxicating soma
-pear shadbush
plant achete, latex, milk, sap
poisonous hebenon
tobacco ambeer, ambier
JUICED See DRUNK.
JUICELESS arid, dry
JUICY fat, frim, fruity, frum,
 interesting, luscious, mellow, naish, nesh, oozing,
 pulpy, sappy, scandalous,
 succose, succulent, waterish
JUJITSU judo, self-defense
JUJU amulet, charm, fetish,
 magic, sorcery
JUJUBE ber, chinese date,

elb, lotebush, lozenge, tsao, zizyphus
JUKE *box* nickelodeon, phonograph, piccolo
house brothel, stew
joint cabaret
predecessor pianola
JULIA *brother* caesar
consort agrippa, marius, pompey, proteus, tiberius
friend paul
nephew caesar
offspring agrippina, antonius, caesar
servant lucetta
JULIAN *emperor* augustus, caligula, claudius, nero, tiberius
JULIANA *house* orange
kingdom holland, netherlands
JULIET *betrothed* paris
cousin tybalt
family capulet
father capulet
lover romeo
servant gregory, peter, sampson
JULIUS CAESAR See also CAESAR.
author shakespeare
character artemidorus, brutus, calpurnia, casca, cassius, cato, cicero, cinna, claudius, clitus, dardanius, flavius, lepidus, ligarius, lucilius, lucius, marc antony, marullus, messala, metellus cimber, octavius, pindarus, popilius lena, portia, publius, strato, titinius, trebonius, varro, volumnius
conspirator brutus, casca, cassius, cinna, decius brutus, ligarius, metellus cimber, trebonius
slayer brutus, casca
tribune casca, flavius, marullus
triumvir lepidus, marc antony, octavius
wife calpurnia
JULY *birthstone* cornelian, onyx, ruby, turquoise
14th bastille day
26th st anne's day
JUMBLE agitate, blend, botch, chaos, clutter, confuse, confusion, disarray, disorder, gallimaufry, garble, hash, hodgepodge, huggermugger, jolting, litter, medley, melange, mess, mishmash, mix(ture), mom-

ble, muddle, muss, olio, pie, raff, raft, ride, rog, shake, smachrie, snarl, stir, tangle, welter, wuzzle
of sounds lurry
JUMBLED crazy, hashy, huddling, jolted, macaronic
JUMBO elephant, enormous, giant, huge, windmill, whopper
JUMP advance, advantage, bail out, balestra, ballonne, bob, bounce, bound, breach, buck, canter, caper, capriole, ciseaux, curvet, escape, evade, flee, flight, gambade, halma, hop, hurdle, hurry, increase, jerk, journey, leap(frog), lollop, loup, lutz, miss, pace, parachute, prance, saltation, salto, sault, skip, spang, spring, start, stend, stoit, twitch, vault, wallop
aboard join
all over rebuke, reprimand, scold
long halma
on assail, nag, rebuke, reproach
ship desert
the gun anticipate, prejudge, presume
JUMPER barker, blouse, bucking bronco, coat, coupler, drill, handyman, hopper, jacket, jersey, jumble, lammy, leaper, plowshare, quitter, rompers, sled, slip-on, sunfisher, swage, timber-topper
JUMPING busy, hot, saltant, teeming
bean sapium
betty garden balsam
disease lata(h), palmus
fish mudskipper
frog county calaveras
hare pedetes
off-place boonies, outpost, outskirts, sticks
plant louse psylla
rodent jerboa
stick pogo, pole
JUMPY creepy, edgy, feverish, fidgety, frisky, hectic, impatient, irritable, itchy, jittery, nervous, restive, restless, shaky, skittish, timid, uneasy
JUNCO bird, finch, snowbird
JUNCTION adjacency, alliance, apposition, bond, carrefour, coalition, combina-

tion, combine, concurrence, confluence, connection, contact, crossroads, hookup, joining, joint, link, meeting, mortise, railroad, reunion, roundabout, seam, suture, union
line suture
point bregma, lambda
JUNCTURE articulation, bracket, combination, condition, connection, coupling, crisis, emergency, exigency, joint(age), JUNCTION, linking, ophryon, pass, pinch, plight, predicament, quandary, seam, situation, state, status, strait, suture, union
JUNCUS black grass, bogrush, camel's-straw, candlerush, rush, schoenus
JUNE *beetle* dorbug, figeater
berry serviceberry, shadbush, tree
bug buzzard, cotinus, dor(r), dumclock, figeater, may beetle, phyllophaga
14th flag day
gem agate, alexandrite, emerald, moonstone, pearl
grass koeleria, poa
pink swamp azalea
2nd sunday children's day
JUNG *pupil* brill
JUNGLE boondock, botch, bush, camp, chaparral, entanglement, forest, rukh, shola, tangle, thicket, undergrowth, wasteland, wilderness
bendy weenong
book author kipling
clearing milpa
dweller beast, savage, snake
ox gaur, gayal
plant cohoba
sheep muntjac
vine liana
wood saj
JUNIAS *friend* paul
JUNIOR after, bud, cadet, fils, immature, inferior, lower, minor, puisne, puny, secondary, son, subordinate, younger, youthful
JUNIPER cade, cedar, evergreen, ezel, gorse, hackberry, larch, retem, sabine, savin(e)
berry gaylussica
creeping savin(e)
fruit sloeberry

gall cedar apple
gum tree sandarac
JUNK boat, cable, cast(off), chunk, debris, discard, dreck, drug(s), exuviate, gear, gook, HEROIN, lump, molt, narcotics, reed, refuse, rope, RUBBISH, rubble, rummage, rush, schlock, scrap, sculch, shed, shmatte, shmotte, slough, slum, soma, stuff, tongkang, trash, waste
dealer chiffonier, ragman, ragpicker, scavenger, scrapman, stumpdigger, tatter
merchandise borax
yard dump
JUNKER aristocrat, conservative, german, noble, prussian, squire
JUNKET basket, banquet, delicacy, dish, entertain(ment), excursion, feast, journey, outing, picnic, play, pudding, tour, trip
JUNKIE See ADDICT.
JUNO, JUNO'S (See also HERA.) asteroid, curitis, moneta, pronuba, sospita, uni
bird peacock
festival matronalia
name caprotina, cinxia, domiduca, lucetia, lucina, martialis, matronalia, moneta, nuxia, ossipago, populonia, pronuba, regina, rumina, sospita
tears vervain
JUNONIA carthage
JUNTA, JUNTO bloc, cabal, clique, combination, combine, confederacy, coterie, council, faction, gang, group, meeting, party, ring, set, tribunal
JUPE(S) bodice, coat, corset, dress, jacket, shirt, skirt, stays, tunic
JUPITER (See also ZEUS.) jove, mushtari, planet, pluvius, stator, thunderer, ultor, victor
angel zadkiel
beard anthyllis, fungus, houseleek, hydnum, joubarb
festival feria
fulgur lightning
gem cornelian
island hobe sound
metal tin

moon amalthea, callisto, europa, ganymede
name conservator, dapalis, elicius, feretrius, liber, lucetius, optimus maximus, pistor, propugnator, stator, terminus, victor
pert. jovian
pluvius rain
study of surface zenology
tree oak
JURE See LAW.
JUREL buffalo-jack, caranx, crevalle, fish, hardtail, mackerel, runner
JURGEN'S *country* poictesme
JURIDIC(AL) See LEGAL.
JURISDICTION abbacy, ambit, authority, bail(iery), bailiage, bailiffry, bailiwick, beylik, bounds, circuit, command, compass, confines, control, county, diocese, diwani, domain, domination, drostdy, duty, emirate, field, foujdary, fuero, function, judicature, khanate, law, ligeance, limits, obedience, office, parish, pashalic, power, province, range, reach, realm, right, rule, scope, see, soc, soke, sovereignty, sphere, supervision, sway, territory, venue
comb. ric
ecclesiastical deanery, diocese, parish, see
supreme jus gladii
JURISPRUDENCE law, nomology
JURISPRUDENT criminologic, forensic, legalistic, nomistic, nomothetic(al)
JURIST brehon, dicast, judge, justice, lawyer, legalist, magistrate, mufti, talesman
JUROR assizer, centumvir, dicast, recognitor, talesman, venireman
group jury, panel
list tales
JURY assize, committee, dicast, judices, jurata, panel, peers, twelve, venire(men)
additions tales(man)
attempt to influence embracery
choose impanel
county visne
enclosure box

member dicast, talesman, venireman
summons venire
JUS gravy, juice, justice, law, principle, right
JUST about, accurate, almost, barely, but, candid, condign, conscientious, correct, decent, deserved, due, equitable, ethical, even (handed), exact(ly), fair, giusto, honest, honorable, impartial, lawful, leesome, liefsome, logical, merciful, merely, merited, moderate, moral, noble, objective, only, precisely, proper, reliable, right(eous)(ful), scrupulous, simply, square, strict, tried, true, trustworthy, unbiased, uncorrupt, upright, valid, virtuous, zadoc
about almost, nearly
as after, similarly
deserts due
in time opportunely, promptly, sonica
now recently, suddenly
only barely, hardly, scarcely
out fresh, new, novel
right bang on, perfect
the same nevertheless
JUSTICE artegal, deserts, dharma, doom, equity, fairness, fairplay, hora, judge, magistrate, penalty, reason, reward, right, validity
chief burger, chase, ellsworth, fuller, hughes, jay, marshall, rutledge, stone, taft, taite, taney, vinson, waite, warren, white
deity astraea, dice, dike, fides, forseti, forsite, maat, mitra, nemesis, paideia, ramman, rhadamanthus, themis
fugitive from runagate, runaway, skedaddler
goddess themis
of peace jaypee, squire
pert. juridical
seat banc(us), bench, court, tribunal
symbolic color purple
JUSTIFIABLE defensible, excusable, fair, lawful, legitimate, logical, pardonable, reasonable, right(ful), warranted
JUSTIFICATION alibi, apologia, apology, authority,

composition, consecration, defense, excuse, reason, vindication, warrant

JUSTIFY absolve, acquit, adjust, allow, apologize, approve, assert, authorize, back, clear, condone, confirm, defend, demonstrate, exculpate, excuse, exonerate, explain, gloss, gloze, maintain, mitigate, palliate, permit, prove, rationalize, sanction, support, uphold, vindicate, warrant

JUSTINIAN *consort* theodora
general belisarius

JUSTLE bolt, bump, cog, jolt

JUT beetle, bulge, butt, jolt, knock, overhang, project (ion), protrude, shoot out, shove, stick out, topple

JUTE ambary, aramina, bagging, baline, bast, burlap, chingma, corchorus, desi, fiber, flax, gunny, hemp, pat, phloem, plant, ramie, sacking, tat, tow
chief hengist, horsa
fabric baline
opener bale-breaker

JUTLAND See DENMARK.
native dane, german, heruli, jute
strait kattegat

JUTTING bulbous, bulgy, extrusive, hanging, outstanding, hanging, projecting, salient

JUTTY See JETTY.

JUTURNA *brother* turnus
lover jupiter, zeus

JUVENILE actor, boyish, callow, child(ish), childlike, girlish, green, immature, infantile, ingenue, kid, maiden, puerile, puisne, soubrette, sprig, undeveloped, unfledged, vernat, young(ster), youth (ful)
delinquent bodgie

JUXTAPOSE abut, adjoin, appose, compare, neighbor, put with

JUXTAPOSED abreast, abutting, adjacent, adjoining, conterminous, contiguous, side by side, tangent

JUXTAPOSITION additament, addition, additory, adjacency, application, apposition, balance, contiguity, contact, nearness, proximity, touch

JYNX charm, spell, woodpecker, wryneck

K

KAAMA hartebeest

KAAN inn, kaun, kawa, khan, lord, prince, resthouse

KABALA, KABBALA See CABALA.

KABAYA badju, baju, cabie, surcoat, tunic

KABOB shashlik

KABUL *bazaar* charchatta
greeting salaam
title amir

KABYLE berber, riff

KACHIN chingpaw, singfo, singpo

KADAR *foe* nagy

KADDISH doxology, hymn, prayer

KADMIEL *son* jeshua

KAE jackdaw, oblige, serve

KAFFIR bantu, caffre, fingo, infidel, kati, tambuki, tembu, waiguli, xosa
beer homebrew
boy umfaan
bread encephalartos
corn grain, millet, sorghum
language xosa
lily clivia
thorn tea-tree
tribe pondo, temby, xosa, zulu
warrior impi
weapon keri, kiri, knobkerrie

KAFKA *work* metamorphosis, the castle, the trial

KAGO litter, palanquin

KAIF See MARIJUANA.

KAIL cole, ibex, KALE

KAIN sarong, tribute

KAINGIN swidden

KAISER caesar, emperor, ruler
last residence doorn
tartuffe wilhelm, william i

KAKA nestor, parrot

KAKATOE abacay, calangay, cockatoo

KAKORTOKITE agpaite

KALADI See CALADIUM.

KALAPOOLIAN *indian* ahantchuyuk, atfalati, yamel

KALE borecole, brassica, broccoli, cabbage, cash, cole(wort), collard, kail, malanga, sprouts

KALEIDOSCOPIC changeable, psychedelic, variegated, varying

KALEVALA *character* aino, ilmarinen, joukahrinen, kullervo, lemminkainen, louhi, pohja
deity ahti, ahto, akka, ilma, jumala, kuu, luonnotar, mielikki, nyyrikki, paiva, pellervoinen, rauni, tapio, tuulikki, ukko, vellamo
editor lonnrot
hero wainamoinen

KALI alkali, carpet, demon, glasswort, plant, saltwort, yuga
festival dewali
husband siva

KALIMANTAN borneo

KALININGRAD konigsberg

KALINITE alum

KALIUM potassium

KALLSTROEMIA caltrap, caltrop, tribulus, zygophyllaca

KALMIA calfkill, calicobush, laurel

KALMUCK eleut(h), khosha, mongol, ta(r)tar, uirad
god of dead abida

KALONG flying-fox, fruitbat

KAMA cupid, desire, love, lust, passion, pleasure

KAMACHATKAN *aborigine* kamchadal
codfish wachna
hut balagan
salmon mykiss

KAME comb, esker, fort, hill(ock), ridge

KAMICHI screamer

KAMPYLITE campylite, mimetite

KANA irofa, iroha

KANAKA blackbird, hawaiian, melanesian, polynesian
KANDH khond, kui, kuy
KANGAROO australian, bandicoot, bettonga, bilbi, boomer, boongary, dendrolagus, didelph, euro, filander, gin, macropus, marsupial, paddymelon, potoroo, roo, tungo, wallaby, wallaroo, woilie
apple gunyang, poroporo
female doe, gin, roo
group troop
male boomer
rat bilbi, bilby, jerboa, potoroo
young joey
KANSAS *capital* topeka
city abilene, atchison, belleville, chanute, coffeeville, colby, dodge city, emporia, great bend, hays, hutchinson, iola, junction city, lawrence, leavenworth, liberal, salina, topeka, wichita
college baker, bethany, sterling, tabor, washburn
county atchison, elk, gove, nemaha, ness, reno, trego
fort riley, scott
indian comanche, kansa, kaw, kickapoo, kiowa, osage, pani, pawnee, wichita
lake cheney, kirwin, milford, neosho
motto ad astra per aspera
native jayhawk(er)
nickname garden of the west, sunflower state
peak sunflower
president eisenhower
river arkansas, missouri, republican, smoky hill
state bird meadowlark
state flower sunflower
state tree cottonwood
KANT *categories* modality, quality, quantity, relation
KAOLIANG broomcorn, challu, plant, sorghum
KAPEK *drama* rur
subject robot
KAPOK ceiba, fiber, floss, oil, tree
source deba
KAPU taboo
KAPUT broken, defeated, destroyed, doomed, fallen, finished, ruined
KARAISM ananism
KARAITE hebrew

KARA KIRGHIZ bourout, burut
KARAKUL astrakhan, fur, lamb, llama, sheep
KARATE self-defense
belt black, blue, brown, purple, white, yellow
blow chop
kick roundhouse
teacher seinsi
yell kee-hop
KAREAH *son* johanan
KARELIAN *lake* onega
KARITE shea-tree
KARMA destiny, duty, fate, rite
bad demerit
stories avadana
KARNAK thebes
KASA glaga, grass, talthib
KASHA cereal, fabric, grain, mush
KASHMIR *alphabet* sarada
beer chang
capital srinigar
city leh
deer hangul
fabric shatush
garment choga
language burushaski, shina
official pundit
peak nanga-parbat
people pakhpuluk
rug namda, numda(h), soumak
shepherd caste gaddi
state jammu
KAT catha, celastra, kafta, khat, quat, shrub, staff-tree
KATABASIS retreat, troparion
KATANGA *ruler* msiri
KATE bird, brambling, hawfinch, KATHARINE, kitty
KATH astringent, cashoo, catechu, cutch, gambier
KATHARINE, KATE shrew
attendant alice
parent baptista, charles, isabel
sister bianca
suitor petruchio
KATMANDU *country* nepal
principality bhadgaon, patan
KATUKA russell's viper, snake
KATUKINA *indian* canamary
KATYDID grasshopper, insect
KATZENJAMMER anguish, clamor, hangover, uneasiness, uproar

KAU auk-auklet
KAURI agathis, berairou, cowrie, resin, tree
KAVA ava, awa, drink, kawaka, pepper, resin, root, shrub, yanggona, yaqona
KAW akha, indian, sioux
KAY islet, key, left
brother king arthur
father ector
KAYAK canoe
KAYO deaden, end, flatten, floor, great, knockout
KAZACHOK *step* prisiadka
KAZAKSTAN *capital* alma-ata
city kustanai
people bukeyet, inner horde
salt lake balkhash
KAZOO bazoo, braggadocio, hewgag, mirliton, zarah
KEACH ladle, scoop, sip
KEATS, JOHN *poem* endymion, eve of st agnes, hyperion, isabella, lamia
elegy to adonais
KEB See GEB.
KECK belch, heave, queasiness, recoil, retch, spew, vomit
KECKLE cackle, chuckle, giggle
KEDAR *kin* isaac, ishmael
KEDEMAH *kin* ishmael
KEDGEREE hodgepodge, jargon, medley, rice
ingredient curry
KEEF See MARIJUANA.
KEEL barge, capsize, careen, carina, carinula, cool, crista, fin, fowl, incline, kale, kiln, lighter, list, ocher, ruddle, serrula, ship, tilt, timber, turn over, upset, vat
angle steeve, steeving
block templet
even balance
hole ruffle
-like carinal, carinated
on even apoised, poised, trim
over capsize, overturn, seel, swoon
part skag, skeg
right angle to abeam
-shaped carinate
strake garboard
wedge templet
without ecarinate, ratite
KEELBILL ani, ano, bird
KEELHAUL torture
KEEN acrid, acrimonious, acute, agog, alert, angry,

anxious, ardent, argus-eyed, astute, avid, biting, bitter, blubber, bright, brisk, canine, caustic, clear, clever, cold, cry, cunning, cutting, dirge, discerning, eager, earnest, enthusiastic, exquisite, fervent, fine, fired, fly, funny, gare, great, incisive, inflamed, intelligent, intense, knowing, mordant, mourn, nifty, on the ball, penetrating, piercing, piquant, poignant, probing, profound, pungent, sensitive, sharp, shrewd, shrill, smart, snell, tart, trenchant, vehement, violent, vivid, wail, weep, whimper, with it, zealous

-edged vorpal

KEENER howler, mourner, rascal

KEENING lamentation, wailing

KEENLY acutely, dearly, deeply

KEENNESS acidity, acies, acrimony, acumen, ardor, asperity, edge, pungency, rigor, sharpness, zest

KEEP accommodation, behave, board, bread, care, carry, case, castle, celebrate, charge, cherish, clasp, commemorate, conceal, conduct, confine, conserve, continue, control, custody, desire, detain, direct, donjon, feed, fishpond, fort(ress), guard, harbor, have, heed, hide, hoard, hold(back), husband, inhabit, jail, livelihood, living, maintain, manage, obey, observe, own, perform, possess, practice, preserve, prison, protect, provide, provision, reserve, restrain, retain, rocca, salt, save, secure, shelter, solemnize, stet, stronghold, support, sustain, sustenance, tend, watch, withhold, witie

abreast follow

account of calculate, follow, record, tab

alive maintain, persevere, preserve, sustain

an eye on care for, guard, observe, scrutinize, supervise, watch

apart isolate, quarantine, separate, space

at arms length avoid, hold off, repulse

at it apply, bulldog, hustle, persevere, persist, work

away from abhor, absent, avoid, dodge, eschew, shun

back abstain, arrest, bar, check, conceal, contain, dam, delay, detain, hap, harness, hide, hinder, reserve, restrain, retard, save, secrete, slow, stay, stop

busy apply, bustle, hustle, labor, occupy, toil, work

calm cool down, go slow, relax, subside, take it easy

clear of avoid, elude, shun, skip

close to cling

company associate, consort, date, escort, gang, go together

dark hide, hush, secrete

down control, discipline, dominate, domineer, hold in, influence, repress, restrain, subject, suppress

from abstain, avoid, control, deny, prevent, refrain, restrain

going continue, drive, endure, hustle, persevere, proceed, run on, survive, sustain, try

hidden hoard, secrete

in cage, confine, detain, imprison, inhibit, repress, restrain, retain, shut(in)(up), suppress, withhold

in line control, discipline, manage, regulate, rein, restrain, supervise

in mind remember, retain

in step conform, synchronize

in stock carry, merchandise, offer

in the background hibernate, hide, retreat, shrink

off fend, shield, shoo

on continue, endure, hustle, persevere, plod

on course cape, head

on hand accumulate, reserve, stock, store

one's fingers crossed anticipate, expect, hope

one's head cool it, relax, settle down, subside, take it easy

one's word deliver, fulfill, level(with), perform

out banish, bar, debar, except, exclude, exile, reserve,

restrict, retain, save, shut out, withhold

quiet button up, hush, shut up, silence

the faith See GOOD-BYE.

under subject, suppress

up carry on, continue, endure, go on, maintain, subsist, support, sustain

your shirt on calm down, cool it, delay, relax, settle down, subside, take it easy

KEEPER alcaide, attendant, bailiff, cowherd, curator, custodian, gaoler, guardian, herder, jailer, nurse, rahdar, ranger, screw, traiteur, ward(en), warrener, yemer

KEEPERS finders

KEEPING board, care(taking), confinement, conformity, congruity, custody, feed, guard(ianship), harmony, holding, maintenance, observance, possession, provision, reservation, retention, retentive, support, symmetry, tutelage, ward

room parlor

KEEPSAKE bibelot, curio, druery, giftbook, memento, relic, souvenir, token

KEEST marrow, sap, substance

KEEVE cistern, kier, kiver, tub, vat

KEF keef, kief, languor, MARIJUANA

KEG anker, bareca, bareka, barrel, barrico, butt, cade, cag, cask, costrel, drum, firkin, tub, tun, vat

-fig kaki, persimmon

open broach, tap, unhead

KEIJO seoul

KELD fountain, spring

KELL caul, chrysalis, cocoon, net

KELLER, HELEN *teacher* anne sullivan

KELLY derby, hat, topsoil

KELP agarum, ash, badderlocks, barilla, bellware, black ash, cuvy, girdle, kobu, seagirdle, seaweed, varic, ware, wrack

and fish flakes dashi

edible alaria, badderlocks, henware, honeyware, murlin, seaweed

fish ephipus, gunnel, poronotus

food from kombu, seatron

hen weka
pigeon sheathbill
pigment phycophaein
plover dowitcher
product algin, iodine, soda
KELPIE barb, nick, sheepdog
KELPWARE bladderwrack
KELT celt, cloth, mixture, salmon, slat, trout
KELTER condition, kilter, money, order, rubbish, undulate
KEMP athlete, boor, champion, contend, contest, fighter, hair, warrior
KEN admit, cognizance, compass, descry, discern, domain, field, gamut, grasp, grip, horizon, house, insight, instruct, know (ledge), look, lore, mastery, orbit, perception, prescience, province, purview, radius, range, reach, recognition, recognize, scope, see, sight, sphere, sweep, understanding, view, vision
seneschal to king arthur
KENAF ambari, ambary, gombo, hibiscus, mesta, papoula, stokroos
KENAZ *brother* caleb
parent elah, eliphaz
son othneil, seraiah
KENILWORTH *author* scott
character amy robsart
ivy basket-plant, pedlar's-basket
KENNEBEC *river into* androscoggin
KENNEDY *cape* canaveral
compound hyannisport
john f, principles new frontier
KENNEL canel, c(h)annel, den, doghouse, drain, gutter, lair, watercourse
KENO *successor* bingo
KENT *borough* erith, penge
fair maid of joan
founder hengist, hortha
freedman laet
king esingae
leader king lear
nightingale blackcap
tribal law laes
unit yoke
KENTUCKY *bluegrass* poa
capital frankfort
cave mammoth
city ashland, berea, bowling green, corbin, covington, danville, frankfort, glasgow, hazard, henderson, hopkins-

ville, lexington, louisville, madisonville, newport, owensboro, paducah, shively
coffee tree bonduc, chicot
college ashbury, berea, brescia, centre, ursuline
county adair, estil, fayette, magoffin, menifee, trigg
derby site churchill downs, louisville
drink bourbon, mint julep
hemp wood-nettle
honoree colonel
horse race derby
hunter bindweed
indian cherokee, iroquois, shawnee
lake cumberland
moss portulaca
native corncracker
nickname bluegrass state, corncracker state
peak big black mountain
port louisville
range cumberland
region blue grass
river barren, cumberland, dix, ohio, salt, tennessee
specialty bourbon, fried chicken
state bird cardinal
state flower goldenrod
state tree tulip-poplar
title colonel
KENYA *bay* formosa
capital nairobi
city eldoret, gedi, kipni, kisumu, kitui, lamy, malindi, meru, mombasa, moyale, nairobi, nakur, narok, nayuki
coin shilling
game area amboselli, arusha, manyara, nakuru, nyeri, rift valley, samburu
garment kanga, kitenge
island manda
lake magadi, naivasha, rudolf, victoria
language kikuyu, luo, swahili
leader kenyatta, mboya
measure wari
national park tsavo
peak kenya, kulai, logonot, matian, nyiru
people baluhya, bantu, dorobo, giriama, hamitic, hilotic, kamba, kikuyu, kipsigis, kisii, luhya, luo, masai, meru, nandi, ogaden, suk, turkana
pygmy wandorobo
reserve masai
river athi, lak, tana, turkwell

tree ayieke
volcano elgou
wine tembo
KEOS *native* cean
KEP catch, haul, intercept, keep, meet
KER death, fate, ghost, spirit
KERAK *ancient* kir-moab
KERALA *capital* trivandrum
KERATIN albuminoid, epidermose
KERATOID horny
KERB See CURB.
KERCHIEF analav, babushka, bandan(n)a, curch, cypress, cyprus, handkerchief, hankie, headdress, kaffiyeh, kingomak, madras, napkin, neckcloth, panuelo, peplum, romal, rumal, therese
3-cornered fichu
KERCHOO sneeze
answer to gesundheit, god bless you, salute
KERESAN *indian* acoma, pueblo, sia
KERF cut(ting), groove, notch, skaff, slit, undercut
KERMANSHAH brownstone, carpet, chestnut, coconut, rug, sandstone
KERMES dyestuff, grain, oak, pigment, scarlet, vulcanizer
KERMESS, KERMIS carnival, celebration, fair, festival
KERN boor, churn, corn, galloglass, grain, granulate, mill, peasant, quern, rustic, salt, soldier
river indian bankalachi
KERNEL battlement, berry, cause, center, core, corn, crenel(ate), essence, gist, grain, heart, hub, keynote, meat, nub, nucleus, nut, pit(h), seed, tonsil
comb. cary(o), kary(o)
edible nut
having nucleate
unhusked capes
KEROSENE coal-oil, paraffin
KESTREL bird, falcon, fanner, hawk, keelie, kite, sparrowhawk, stanchel, stannel, stonegall, windhover
KET carrion, filth, good-for-nothing
KETCH boat, catch, jack, saic, sailboat, ship
KETONE acetone, acridin-

ium, acridone, adrenalone, butanone, butyrone, camphor, carone, chromone, civetone, deguelin, haptanone, irone, menthone, muscone, phorone, pulegone, shogaol, thienone, thujone, valeron

alcohol anisoin

colorless anthrone, thujone

crystalline anthrone, rotenone, thienone, xanthone, zingerone

liquid acetol, pinacolin, propione

oily carone, irone, thujone

unsaturated pulegone

KETTLE billycan, boiler, calabash, ca(u)ldron, canner, container, dixie, fessel, flambeau, lebes, marmit, maslin, pail, pot, setpot, sirop, stewpot, teapot, tripod

covered canner, steamer

handle bail, kilp

hook hangle, kilp, trammel

large ca(u)ldron

nose spout

of fish mess, muddle, picnic

KETTLEDRUM anacara, at(t)abal, festival, nagara, naker, party, tabo(u)r, timbal(e), timpano, tympano, tympany

KETURAN *husband* abraham

KEVEL bar, bit, bollard, cleat, cudgel, gag, gambol, hammer, kick, peg, staff, timber

KEWPIE *doll originator* rose o'neil

KEY answer, atoll, attune, basic, bolt, cay, chord, cipher, clamp, clavicin, clavis, clef, clew, clicket, close, clue, code, combination, cotter, crib, digital, essential, explanation, fundamental, gamut, guide, harbor, island, isle(t), lever, linchpin, manual, material, opener, pin, pitch, pony, primary, reef, scale, solution, spanner, spline, style, tapper, tasto, tonality, tone, tune, vital, wedge, winder

arithmetical additive

art alembroth

ash pigeon

chain chatelaine

-cold apathetic, dead, indifferent

comb. cleid(o)

crib pony

false glut, picklock

filler uller

fruit lime, samara

guitar or harp dital

keeper chatelaine, claviger, steward

man boss, chief, leader, pianist

member phi beta kappa

musical instrument button, dital, tasto

notch ward

of life ankh

of mediterranean gibraltar

of russia smolensk

part bit, bow, collar, loop, pin, stem, ward, web

pattern meander

pitch-raising dital

pert. tonal, tonic

position anchor

-pounder pianist, steno

-shaped cleche, urde, urdy

skeleton betty, gilt, screw, twirl(er)

specialist locksmith, screwsman

telegraph bug, tapper

way slot, spline

west native conch

KEYBOARD claviature, clavier, digitorium, manual, pedalier

instrument See MUSICAL INSTRUMENT *keyboard.*

KEYED *up* agog, eager, taut, tense, tuned

KEYHOLE groove, slot

-shaped clithridiate

KEYNOTE basis, core, cornerstone, feature, gist, kernel, nub, principal, tonic

KEYNOTER boss, orator

KEYSTONE arch, base, essential, integral, principle, quoin, sagitta, second base, support, vertex, voussoir, wedge

state pennsylvania

KEZIA *father* job

KHADIJA *husband* mohammed

KHAFRE *brother* cheops

KHAKASS *capital* abakan

KHAKI(S) biscuit, olive-drab, regimentals, tan, uniform

KHAN caravansary, cham, chief, dignitary, hawn, inn, kaun, kawa, khakan, lord, prince, resthouse, shere, sovereign, tacon, tavern, title

genghis, dynasty yuan

keeper khanjee

residence xanadu

KHANDA See SWORD.

KHASI nicobarese, palaung

KHAYA cail-cedra, mahoganytree

KHAYYAM, OMAR *birthplace* nishapur

poem rubaiyat

translator fitzgerald

KHEDIVE governor, quiteve, suzerain, viceroy

estate daira

KHENTI See OSIRIS.

KHMER cambodian

ruins angkor(wat)

KHNEMU, KHNUM *consort* anquet, anuket, satet, sati

KHOIKHOI hottentots

KHONSU *parent* amen, nut

temple builder raamses, rameses, ramses

temple site karnak

KHOR gorge, ravine, watercourse

KHOT contractor, farmer

KHUPU cheops

KHUSKHUS cuscus, vetiver

KHYBER *pass tribe* afridi

KIANG chigetai, hemionus, onager

KIBE chap, chilblain, crack, frostbite, lesion, sore, ulcer

KIBITZ advise, comment, criticize, gibe, joke, meddle, needle, second-guess, tease, wisecrack

KIBITZER adviser, beholder, bystander, counsel, daubitzer, dorbitzer, dormitzer, joker, lapwing, meddler, observer, onlooker, plover, punster, second-guesser, spectator, tsitser, witness

KIBOSH defeat, deny, destroy, disable, end, jinx, kill, negate, nonsense, silence, suppress, veto

KICK backlash, bang, blow, boot, borrow, bunch, calcitrate, calcitration, charge, complain(t), curse, drive, dun, excitement, fling, foot, funk, grievance, gripe, grouch, growl, grumble, hack, heel, impel, kevel, moan, object(ion), oppose, pocket, porr, pote, protest(ation), punt, reaction, rebound, recoil, reject, remonstrate, resist, rise, shin, sixpence, spur(n), stingo,

thrill, vim, volley, withstand, yerk
against resist
around consider, discuss, mistreat
ballet brush
downstairs demote, downgrade, expel
in ante(up), contribute, die
low brush
off begin(ning), die, initiate, open(ing)
out dismiss, eject, expel
over the traces rebel, revolt
the beam tamper, weight
the bucket die, expire
up a row anger, bluster, brawl, rampage, storm
upstairs advance, promote
KICKBACK atone, bribe, rebate, recoil, refund, response
KICKER booter, complainer, foot, malcontent, protester, punter, rebel, tedder
KICKISH irritable
KICKS excitement, PANTS, thrills, trousers
KICKSHAW appetizer, bauble, delicacy, gadget, gewgaw, hors d'oeuvre, tidbit, toy, trifle, trinket
KICKUP disturbance, row, steamboat, water-thrush
KID baby, banter, box, chaff, child, cod, deceive, eanling, fagot, flatter, fledgling, fool, goat, guy, harry, hoax, humbug, infant, jape, jest, jolly, josh, juvenile, lad, little one, pen, pester, plague, pod, rag, rally, rib, spoof, sport, sprig, squirt, suede, taunt, tease, teenager, tichen, tot, tub, twit, worry, youngster, youth
-glove fastidious
meat capretto
out of dissuade
skin chevrette
undressed suede
KIDCOTE See JAIL.
KIDDER banterer, chaffer, guyer, josher, persifleur, ragger, ribber, tease
KIDNAP abduct, blackbird, panyar, ravish, seize, shanghai, snatch, steal, take
KIDNAPPER abductor, blackbirder, snatcher, spiriter
KIDNEY character, class, description, disposition, ilk, kind, nature, neer, nephros,

nier, organ, rein, rognon, sort, stripe, temperament, type, waiter
artificial hemodialyzer
bean bon, frijole, phasel, scarletrunner
bean tree wisteria
comb. nephr(o), reni
deposit gravel, stone
disease bright's, nephria, nephritis, nephropathy, nephrosis, ripple, uremia
disease treatment dialysis
liverleaf hepatica
of the same congenial, identical
part calyx, capsule, glomerulus, hilum, nephron, tubule
pert. adrenal, nephric, renal, suprarenal
-shaped reniform
-stone gravel, jade, nephrite
vetch anthyllis, cat's-claw
KIDNEYROOT baccharis, joe-pye-weed
KIDNEYWORT navelwort, star-saxifrage
KIEV *street* krechatik, shevchenko
KIFF See MARIJUANA.
KIKU chrysanthemum
KILAUEA *crater goddess* pele
KILIMANJARO *peak* kibo
KILL achieve, asphyxiate, assassinate, astonish, astound, bag, bayonet, beat, blast, blot out, brain, bump off, burke, butcher, cancel, cell, channel, chloroform, choke, church, consume, creek, croak, cut down, deaden, decimate, defeat, destroy, diddle, disapprove, dispatch, dispose of, do away with, do in, drain, drown, electrocute, eliminate, end, erase, execute, exhaust, exterminate, extinguish, fell, finish, fix, ganch, garrot(t)e, gas, get, hang, hurt, immolate, impress, jugulate, lapidate, lay out, liquidate, massacre, misdo, mortify, muffle, murder, neutralize, noyade, overwhelm, poison, polish off, punish, purge, put(away), quarry, remove, river, ruin, settle, shoot, silence, slaughter, slay, smite, smother, snuff, spifflicate, starve, stifle, stone,

stonker, stop, strangle, stream, strike dead, stymie, suffocate, suppress, throttle, veto, victimize, waterway, wind up, wipe out
by inches torment, torture
-calf butcher
comb. cide
-cow bully, personage, spikerush
-joy antithalian, brooder, crapehanger, damper, lemon, moper, nark, sourpuss, spoilsport, wetblanket
time goof, idle, play
KILLCROP changeling
KILLDEER plover
KILLED skittled, slain, winged, zapped
KILLER apache, assassin, bluebeard, bravo, burker, burkite, butcher, cain, cannibal, cretacean, cutthroat, decapitator, executioner, exterminator, gorilla, gun(man), gunner, hangman, hatchetman, headhunter, highbinder, hitman, immolator, insecticide, keeler, manslayer, murderer, pesticide, poison, shark, slayer, thug, torpedo, triggerman
tub vermicide
-diller See THING *big*.
whale grampus, orca
KILLIFISH cobbler, fundulus, gudgeon, mayfish, minnow, mudfish, mummichog, panchax, pursyminnow, rockfish, sacalait, studfish, swampine
KILLING amusing, captivating, cleanup, euthanasia, exhausting, funny, homicide, mort, murder, quell, slaughter, success, tuant
blow coup de grace
of birds avicide
of children infanticide, prolicide
of relative filicide, fratricide, matricide, parricide, patricide, sororicide
of self suicide
of wolf lupicide
KILLWEED loosestrife
KILLIWORT celandine
KILMER *poem* trees
KILN bake, calciner, cutte, drier, dry, furnace, leer, lehr, o(a)st, oven, stove, tiler(y)

for hops cockle, oast
scum whitewash
KILOGRAM *50* centner
100 quintal
KILOWATT *hour* kelvin
KILT fasten, filibeg, hang,
philabeg, philibeg, piupiu,
plait, pleat, skirt, tartan, tie
up, tuck up
pouch sporran
printed lavalava, pareu
KILTER condition, kelter,
order, pelter, skeet, state
off agee
KILTIE scot(sman)
KIMBERLITE blue-earth,
blue-ground, yellow-ground
KIM kimball o'hara
author kipling
home india, lahore
KIMONO dressing gown,
duster, gown, housecoat,
robe, yukata
sash obi
KIN (See also KINSHIP.)
affinity, allied, analogue,
chasm, clan, class, cognate,
connections, consanguinity,
crack, descent, family,
folks, germane, homologue,
kind(red), kith, koto,
offspring, parallel, progeny,
race, related, rela-
tion(ship), relative(s), sept,
sib, sibling(s), slit, sort,
tribe, zither
KIND affable, affectionate,
amene, amiable, benevo-
lent, benign, big(hearted),
boon, brand, breed, brood,
cast, character, charitable,
class, clement, color, compassionate, denomination,
description, designation, division, family, feather,
form, friendly, generous,
genial, genos, genre, gentle,
genus, goodhearted, gra-
cious, grain, group, hu-
mane, ilk, indulgent, kidney, kosher, lenient,
loving, make, manner,
merciful, mild, mister,
mode, mold, nature, num-
ber, obliging, persuasion,
pleasant, race, seely, sort,
spece, species, stamp,
strain, stripe, style, sweet,
tender, tribe, type, variety
name meaning agatha
of quasi, rather, similarly,
somewhat
similar homogeneous
KINDLE animate, arouse,

beet, bete, blaze, burn, emblaze, excite, fire, flame,
flare, foment, ignite, illume,
incite, inflame, instigate,
light, provoke, rouse, solicit, start, stimulate, stir,
tend, tind, tine, turn on,
whet
KINDLING brood, firing, ignition, inflammation, issue,
lighting, litter, offspring,
sticks, tinder, wood
KINDLY agreeable,
beneficent, benign, big,
blithe, charitable, clement,
congenial, considerate, favorable, fitly, genial, gentle,
gracious, hende, hereditary,
humane, KIND, lawful,
legitimate, mild, naish,
native, natural(ly), pleasant,
properly, readily, rightful,
soft, sympathetic, thoroughly, thoughtful
KINDNESS affection, aloha,
altruism, benefaction, bene-
fice(nce), benefit, benevolence, benignity, bonhomie,
bonte, boon, bounty, can-
do(u)r, charity, clemency,
compassion, consideration,
favor, fondness, friendship,
generosity, gentleness, goodness, grace, hospitality,
humanity, indulgence,
lenity, love, mercy, philanthropy, tenderness
lacking cruel, mean, selfish
KINDRED affinity, akin, allied, analogous, blood, clan,
cognate, congenial, consanguinity, corresponding,
family, flesh, joined, kin,
kith, kobong, parallel, race,
related, relationship, relatives, sib(ship), tie, united
group siol
pert. co(n)generic
KINE beast, cattle, cows
KINEMATOGRAPH tachy-
scope
KINESIS activity, motion,
movement
KINETIC active
KING, KING'S (See also
KING ARTHUR, KING
LEAR, and under individ-
ual names, e.g., HENRY,
JAMES, etc.) ariki, authority, baginda, bali, basileus,
cacique, card, checker,
chief, czar, dam, emperor,
jehu, kral, leader, leir, majesty, monarch, nudd, numa,

padishah, peg, personage,
pin, potentate, prince,
reges, regulus, rex, rey, rial,
roi, roy, ruler, sophy, sovereign, supreme, tsar, tzar
agent missus
ass-eared midas
auk dovekie
beadsman beggar, blue-gown
blue cobalt, smalt
bodyguard thane
chamber camarilla
changed to wolf lycaon
child prince, princess
clover melilot
crab aglaspis, limulid, lumulus, maia, panfish, trilobite
crab, body cephaletron
crab, pert. limuloid
crab, relative aglaspis
crow buchanga, drongo
crown guelder-rose, melilot
devil hawkweed
evil scrofula
fairy oberon
family dynasty, house, line
fruit mangosteen
fur vair
garment armil(la)
greedy croesus, midas
hunter laughing jackass
legendary bran, hogni,
l(1)ud, midas, minos,
oberon, prester john, shesha
letter brief
-like regal, royal
mackerel cero
-maker boss, campaigner,
politician, warwick
monkey bodhisattva,
guereza, mahakapi-jataka
mullet goatfish
murder of regicide
name meaning basil, cyrus,
elroy, eric, leroy, rex, roy
of arms garter, norroy
of bath beau nash
of beasts lion
of birds eagle
of dwarfs alberich
of kings haile selassie
of knots bowline
of men agamemnon, jupiter,
odin, zeus
of metals gold
of rivers amazon
of rome napoleon ii
of terrors death
of the forest oak
of the herrings chimaera,
oarfish, opah
of the hill champ
of the jungle tiger

of the mullets apogon, bass
of the salmon ribbonfish
of the sea herring
of trumps honor
of waters amazon
parakeet wellat
peace grith
personnel aven(u)er, bailiff,
dapifer, palatine, thane,
viceroy
pert. regal, regnal, royal
petty regulus, royalet
plover dulwilly
ransom fortune
rights regalia
secretary chancellor
share prisage
-size big, decuman, gross,
huge, large, mammoth
snake ophibolus
spear asphodel
steward dapifer
symbol crown, mace,
scepter, sceptre
title basileus, highness, majesty, sir(e)
topper ace
tyrant kingbird
vulture catharta, fal-
coniformis, pap(a)
wealthy croesus, midas
wheel-bound ixion
yellow orpiment, pigment
KING ALFRED *city* lon
scholars asser, ethelstan,
grimbald, plegmund, wer-
frith, werwulf
KING ARTHUR *abode*
aval(l)on, caerleon, cam-
elot
and knights round table
battle badon, camlann
birthplace tintagel
brother kay
brother-in-law loth
burial site avalon, glastonbury
butler bedivere, bedver,
lucas
chamberlain ulphius
chaplain pyramus
consort garwen, guendolen,
guinevere, gwyl, indec
constable badouin
court astolat, avalon, caerleon, camelot
crowner dubric
dagger carnwenhau
daughter gyneth
dog cavall
enemy lucius, mo(r)dred,
morgan le fay, nero, royns
father-in-law leodogra(u)nce
fool dagonet, daguenet

forest calydon
foster-father ector
half-sister bellicent
hall ehangwen
historian gildas
history easter annals
horse spumador
knight 3 kay 4 bors, ider 5
arrok, balan, balin, bryan,
cador, dynas, edyrn, harry,
hebes, helwn, ywain 6 an-
dret, boarte, bohort, clegis,
darras, edward, ermyne,
fergus, gareth, gauter, gawain, lybius, lyonel, ma-
dore, marrok, melyas,
melyon, melyot, modred,
ozanna, playne, sadoke,
ulfius, ywaine 7 brewnor,
caradoc, cardoke, cradock,
degrave, dinadan, dodynas,
gaheris, galahad, geraint,
grummor, gwyarte, hervyse,
lamorak, lamyell, launfal,
lavayne, mordred, paladin,
pelleas, pyramus, selyses,
tristan, valence 8 ascamour,
bedivere, bleheris, brastias,
clarryus, cloddrus, craddock,
dryaunte, eglamore, gal-
leron, gryfflet, ironside, lam-
begus, lancelot, meriadoc,
neroveus, parsifal, percival,
petipace, sagramor, tristram
9 alexander, brandiles,
epynogres, hectymere,
launcelot, morganous, palomides, persaunte, pertolepe,
perymones, pharamond,
plenoryus, sagramore, sen-
trayle, severause 10 bel-
lyaunce, crosseleme, degre-
vaunt 11 bellengerus, constantyne
lady elain(e), enid
lampoonist dinadan
lance ron(e)
legend matter of britain
magician merlin
mare lamri, llamrei
nephew gareth, gawain, hoel,
mo(r)dred
parent igerna, igraine, uther,
ygerne
queen ganor, gineura, guene-
vere, guinevere
roman name ambrosius
aurelianus
romance morte d'arthur
seneschal kay, ken, queux
shield pridwin, priwen
ship prydwen
sister anna, morgain, morgana, morgan le fay

slayer mo(r)dred
son bors
spear rhongomyant, ron(e)
steward launfal
sword caledvwich, caliburn,
excalibur
tale alai
twin balan, balin
victim galapas, rython
warden brastius
KING AUGEAS *brother*
actor
KING BOMBA ferdinand ii
KING CANUTE *consort*
emma
KING CYMBELINE *daughter* imogen
son arviragus, guiderius
KING EGBERT bretwalda
KING ETHELRED the
unready
KING FERDINAND bomba
KING GATH achish
KING JOHN lackland
author shakespeare
character arthur, bigot,
blanch, chatillon, con-
stance, de burgh, elinor,
essex, gurney, henry,
lady faulconbridge, lewis,
lymoges, melun, pandulph,
pembroke, peter, philip the
bastard, salisbury
mother eleanor, elinor
nephew arthur
nickname soft-sword
niece blanch
son henry
KING LEAR *author* shakespeare
character albany, burgundy,
cordelia, cornwall, curan,
doctor, edgar, edmund,
fool, gloucester, goneril,
kent, king of france, os-
wald, regan
daughter cordelia, goneril,
regan
dog tray
father bladud
friend kent
KING MALTRAIEN *son*
clarien, clarifan
KING MARSILE *wife* bramimonde
KING PELEUS acastus
KINGBIRD bee-eater, bee-
martin, flycatcher, petchary,
pipiri, tyrannus
KINGBOLT mainpin
KINGCUP butter-cress,
crowfoot, gold cup, lemonade, ranunculus
KINGDOM classification, do-

main, dominion, empire, estate, hereafter, monarchy, paradise, realm, sovereignty, sphere, state, supremacy, universe
ancient elam, moab
animal fauna
come death, execution, grave, paradise, utopia
three shu, wei, wy
vegetable blora
KINGFISH bagara, barb(el), cero, chenfish, chief, hake, haku, mink, opah, pintado, sciaenid, sierra, threadfin, tomcod, tommycod
KINGFISHER alcedo, alcyones, ceyx, dacelo, halcyon, poditti, torotoro
turned into alcyone, ceyx
KINGHEAD ragweed
KINGLET goldcrest, lionet, regulus, wren
KINGLY august, basil(ic), basilican, dignified, imperial, leonine, princely, regal, regnant, royal, sovereign
KINGPIN big wheel, chief, leader, top, vip
KINGSHIP devaraja, royalty, sovereignty
KINGSLEY, CHARLES
pseud. parson lot
work alton locke, hypatia, water babies, westward ho
KINGU *consort* tiamat
father apsu
slayer marduk
KINK bend, buckle, burl, caprice, charley horse, coil, cough, cramp, crick, crotchet, eccentricity, entanglement, expedient, foible, gasp, knot, loop, mat, pain, quirk, snarl, snick, spasm, stitch, turn, twist, whim
KINKAJOU animal, aporoso, heyrat, potos, potto
KINKY capricious, crotchety, curled, curly, eccentric, egregious, encomic, knotted, matted, twisted
KINO bija(sal), catechu, dye, gum
tree bija
KINSHASA leopoldville
KINSHIP affinity, bearing, blood, cognation, connection, consanguinity, filiation, likeness, nasab, relation(ship), sibness, sibrede

father's side agnation
mother's side enation
KINSMAN affine, ally, bandhava, blood(brother), cousin, gotraja, relation, relative, sibling, winemay
group ahl
maternal enate
paternal agnate
KIO ngaio
KIOSK bandstand, booth, newsstand, pavilion, summerhouse
KIP bed(room), brothel, grasser, hide, hill, inn, lodging, sleep, tern, tilt, weight
KIPCHAK *language* coman
KIPLING, RUDYARD *character* akela, gunga din, kaa, kim, lew, mowgli
elephant guj-moti
poem barrack-room ballads, fuzzywuzzy, gunga din, mandalay, recessional
tiger shere-khan
wolf akela
work captains courageous, jungle book, just-so stories
KIRGHIZ *capital* frunze
people bourout, burut, kassak, kazak
range alai
tent yurt
KIRI knobkerrie, paulownia
KIRK See CHURCH.
master church-warden
KIRMAN *carpet* lavehr
KIRTLE coat, dress, gown, petticoat, skirt, tunic
KISAEUS *son* semeius
KISH basket, gabion, powder
kin abiel, ner, saul, shimei
KISMET destiny, doom, fate, lot, portion
KISS baccio, basiate, basio, beso, bill and coo, brush, buss, caress, glance, graze, greet(ing), honi, lallygag, lip, neb, osculate, osculation, peck, pree, salute, shave, smack, smooch, sweetmeat, touch, woo
-me-quick bonnet, heartsease, london-pride, ringlet, wild pansy
off s(c)hloomp, s(c)hlump
of peace pax
pert. oscular
stolen smoorich
study philematology
the rod bow, submit, yield
up fawn, sycophant, teacher's-pet, toady
KISSER face, mouth

KISSING lipwork, smicksmack
bug conenose
disease mono(nucleosis)
KIST basket, caphite, chest, cistvaen, coffin, counter, installment, pit, treasure, trunk
KIT bag, basket, box, bungey, caboodle, carson, cat, chit, collection, container, duffel, equipment, gear, kitten, lot, milk-float, outfit, pack, pail, pochette, toolbox, tub, violin
KITCHEN ben, but, caboose, calan, camboose, chil(la), cookery, cookhouse, cuisine, galley, sculley
appliance broiler, dishwasher, freezer, mixer, oven, refrigerator, stove, toaster
article utensil
bob wood louse
garden olitory
handle lifter
utensil beater, blender, bowl, canopener, cooker, grater, knife, pan, pitter, pot, ricer, roaster, rolling pin, sieve, sifter, spatula, spoon, strainer
work surface counter
KITE belly, bird, chil(la), counterfeit, cyte, drache, drag(on), elanet, elanus, elevate, falcon, fin, flier, forktail, fraud, glede, glide, hawk, milan, milvine, pigeon, puddock, puttock, raise, rascal, rogue, sentry, sharper, soar, toy
kind box, hargrave
-like accipital, accipitrine
KITH, KYTH acquaintance, appear, confess, country, declare, fatherland, kin (dred), kinsmen, knowledge, manifest, recognize, region, show
and kin family, relations, relatives
KITHLESS alone, desolate
KITTEN catling, child, fledgling, kitling, pussy
group kindle, litter
symbol of playfulness
KITTENISH coy, infantile, playful
KITTIM *king* perseus
KITTIWAKE annet, bird, pickup, ressa, rissa, sea gull, tarrock, tirrlie, waeg

KITTLE arise, clever, dangerous, difficult, enliven, fickle, fidgety, generate, perilous, perplex, please, puzzle, quick, smart, tickle, ticklish, touchy

KITTLEPINS skittles

KITTY ante, badrons, baudrons, bowl, CAT, pool, pot, receptacle, stakes, widow

-cornered catawamptious, catawamp(o)us, diagonal

KIVA estufa

floor hole sipapu

KIWI apteryx, bird, moa, penguin, wraf

fruit chinese-gooseberry

KLAMATH *indian food* wokas

weed amber, goatweed, st john's-wort

KLAP blab, blow, hit, klop, yak, yammer

KLAXON alarm, blare, honk, horn

KLEPTOMANIAC filcher, pilferer, robber, thief

KLONDIKE canfield, fascination, game, solitaire

KLOOF glen, gorge, ravine, valley

KLUTZ blockhead, dummy

KNAB nibble

KNACK ability, adroitness, aptitude, aptness, art, bent, break, capacity, catch, chink, conceit, contrivance, crack, delicacy, dexterity, ease, facility, faculty, feat, feel, flair, forte, genius, gibe, gift, hang, junket, mock, repartee, skill, sleight, snap, strike, talent, toy, trick, trinket, turn

KNACKER castanet, clapper, horse, nag

KNACKY clever, ingenious

KNAG knot, prong, snag, spur

KNAP bite, break, button, chip, crest, crop, cut, hill(top), knock, knoll, nibble, rap, snap, strike, summit, talk

KNAPSACK bag, case, kit, mochila, musette, pack, pouch

KNAPWEED ballweed, bellweed, black soap, bluet, bluetop, boleweed, bullweed, bundweed, buttonweed, centaury, clubweed, cow parsnip, crop-

weed, drumstick, flattop, hardhead, harebottle, harshweed, ironhead, ironweed, knotweed, matfelon, ragwort, rhapontic, scabious, sweep

KNARL See GNARL.

KNAVE bower, camooch, cheat, coquin, cost, custrel, eques, jack, knight, lorel, losel, menial, miscreant, nob(s), noddy, pam, peasant, picaro(on), rascal, rautener, rogue, scamp, scoundrel, servant, sharper, slipstring, swindler, tom, trickster, varlet(to), villain, wenzel

and queen intrigo, intrigue

clubs pam

cribbage nob

KNAVERY catzerie, chicanery, dishonesty, patchery, rascality, villainy

KNAVISH blackguardly, corrupt, dishonest, felonious, rascally, recreant, reprobate, roguish, scampish, scoundrelly, villainous

KNEAD elt, fashion, form, malax(ate), manipulate, massage, mix, mold, petrie, press, rub, squeeze

KNEE angle, beg, bow, genu, ginglymus, implore, joint, kneel, sleeper, suffrago, supplicate

armor genouillere

bend genuflect, kneel, plie

bone cap, dip, hock, houghbone, paletta, rotula, sesamoid

breeches breekums, knickers, pants, small-clothes, trousers

cap patella, sesamoid

comb. genu, gon

curvature gonycampsis

-deep shallow

drill prayer

flexure genu

gout gonagra, gonitis

-high low

-hole desk

hollow ham

joint hock, toggle

-like rotular

muscle subcrureus

on bended deferential, humbly, obeisant, obsequious, solicitous

ornament canion

part See KNEE *bone.*

pert. carpal, genual, patellar

-pine krummholz

-slapper joke, whopper

KNEEL appeal, beg, bow, fawn, genuflect, grovel, kowtow, salaam

KNEELER penitent, pew, priedieu, springer

KNEELING shiko

KNEEPAN patella, rotula

KNELL passing bell, ring, tailer, toll, warn

KNEW kenned, learned, understood, wist, wot

KNICKERS bloomers, pants, plusfours

KNICKKNACK artifice, bauble, clattertrap, gewgaw, gimcrack, kickshaw, notions, toy, trick, trifle, trinket, virtu

KNIFE balarao, barong, bistoury, blade, bolo, bowie, bread, butcher, campit, carver, catlin(g), chiv(e), corer, couteau, coutel, creese, cut, dah, dao, defeat, dirk, dow, facao, gully, itac, kiotome, kukri, lancet, machet(e)(te), parang, patu, scalpel, serpette, shiv, skean, snicker(snee), spattle, spokeshave, stab, switchblade, sword, trevat, trevet, trivet, ulu, whittle

blade grain, tang

case sheath

comb. dori

currier's beam(ing), cleaner

curved ulu

-edged sharp

handle bolster

hunting bowie

large bolo, snee

long porker

maker cutler

1-bladed barlow

painter's spatula

part blade, bolster, choil

-pleated kilted

pocket bolo, snee, switchblade

sharpener hone, steel, stone, whetstone

sheath bowie

shoemaker's butt

short spud, sundang

street switchblade

surgical See SURGEON *instrument.*

switchblade flickknife, shiv

symbol of st bartholomew

the surgery

wallpaper casing

KNIGHT accolade, adub, attendant, bachelor, banneret, baronet, bevis, cabal(lero), cavalier, champion, chevalier, childe, dub, eques, equite, equity, errant, esquire, gallant, hippeus, horseman, lord, lover, paladin, promote, ritter, ruggiers, sir, springer, templar, tulk

armor-bearer armiger
attendant page, squire, varlet
badge cognizance, cordon bleu
banner gonfalon, gonfanon
carpet dammeret, lover
champion paladin
chess chevalier, horse
cloak tabard
ensign pennon, star
-errant amadis, paladin
-errantry chivalry, magnanimity
famous (See also KING ARTHUR *knight.*) almanzor, arviragus, bayard, caradoc, cradock, harold, lohengrin
fight joust, tilt, tournament
garment armor, mail, tabard
hospitaler knight of malta, knight of st john of jerusalem
lady bradamante, britomartis
make accolade, dub
of handcuffs constable, policeman
of la mancha don quixote
of malta hospital(l)er, knight of st john of jerusalem
of st crispin cobbler, shoemaker
of the cloak raleigh
of the pestle apothecary, druggist
of the road drummer, footpad, hobo, tramp, vagabond
of the round table See KING ARTHUR *knight.*
of the shears tailor
page See KNIGHT *attendant.*
plumed james blaine
service escuage
templar mason, shriner
templar idol baphomet
templar religious house preceptory
templar standard beauseant
title sir
virgin bradamante
wife dame, lady

without fear chevalier bayard
wreath orle
KNIGHTHEAD apostle, bollard
KNIGHTHOOD caballeria, cavalry, chivalry, nobility
confer accolade, dub
rules chivalry
KNIGHTLY brave, chivalrous, courteous, courtly, gallant, noble, quixotic
KNIT braid, cement, compact, compaginate, compress, conjoin, connect, consolidate, contract, couple, cure, fasten, heal, interlace, interlock, join, link, plait, pucker, purl, purse, seam, spin, unite, weave, wrinkle
one's brow scowl
KNITTER legger
demon madame defarge
KNITTING affairs, brocade, business, contraction, craft, crochet, fastening, handiwork, network, purling, union, weaving
direction cast on, purl
loop steek
machine loom, weaver
needle wire
pattern argyle
rod needle
row course
stitch cable, purl
term cast off, gauge, purl, sley, stitch
KNOB bellpull, berry, blow, boss, buhr, bulge, bulla, bull's eye, bump, burr, button, capitulum, caput, club, croche, dune, emboss, finial, handle, head, hill, hump, knoll, knop, knurl, lever, lump, nob, node, nub, nurl, omphalos, opener, ornament, pluke, pommel, protuberance, skiffle, sphere, stud, swelling, trigger, tubercule, umbo
celery celeriac
comb. tyl(o)
conical bot(t)
-like capitellate, capitulate, nodal
ornamental boss, stud
pert. nodal, nodose, orlet, torose, tuberous, tylotate
pointed finial
wooden burl, knur(l)
KNOBBY hard, hilly, lumpy,

nodal, nodose, torose, tuberous, tylotate
KNOBKERRIE club, kiri, missile, weapon
KNOBSTICK blackleg, cane, club, rat, scab, snob
KNOBWEED horse balm
KNOCK bang, bash, blame, blow, box, buffet, bump, bustle, call, canvass, chap, check, chop, clash, collide, crack, criticism, criticize, cuff, dash, daud, decry, ding, discredit, disparage, dunt(le), end, hill, hit, jolt, kayo, knap, knatch, knoit, move, pass, polt, pound, punch, rap, rattle, rout, shop, slap, smear, stoter, strike, tank, tap, thump, tirl, wap, win, wound
about abuse, actor, canvass, handyman, rough, sloop, travel, wander, yacht
down bowl over, demoralize, depress, drop, dump, fell, floor, introduce, level, lower, name, overthrow, prostrate, raze, souse, take apart, unpile, vanquish
in the head defeat, destroy, kill
it off cut it out, stop
-knee baker's leg, deformity, inknee, valgus, varus
off accomplish, author, deduct, get out, improvise, leave, quit, reduce, secure, stop, write
out anesthetize, bash, beauty, blockbuster, coldcock, conk, deaden, destroy, disable, dope, down, drug, end, flatten, floor, form, kayo, narcotize, nobbler, paralyse, peach, sockdolager, stun, terrific, topnotcher, vanquish, victory, wow
-out button chin
under submit, succumb, yield
up arouse, awake(n), destroy, fatigue, lift, ruin, tire out
KNOCKER crow, hammer, peddler, risp, whacker
KNOLL down, dune, elevation, hill(ock), holt, hummock, knap, knob, lump, mesa, mound, toll
wooded hurst
KNOP boss, bud, bunch, button, capitulum, finial, knob,

pinnacle, projection, stud, tub

KNOT (See also *kind, below.*) amoret, ascot, beach-robin, bend, bob, bond, bow, braid, bulge, bur(l), burr, cluster, complication, congeal, connection, coterie, difference, difficulty, distort(ion), enigma, entanglement, gathering, granny, group, halch, hank, harl, hitch, joint, kink, knag, knar, knor, knur(l), laniard, lanyard, loop, lump, marriage, mat, maybird, mile, morass, nep, node, nodule, nodus, noil, noyl, perplexity, problem, puzzle, sandpiper, snag, snipe, snub, swarm, tangle, tat, tie, tuft, union, wart, wrinkle

ball-like monkey's fist
builder's clove-hitch
cutter alexander
fiber noil, noyl
fibrous nep
gordian complexity, dilemma
hair bun, chignon, knurl, noil, noyl
kind anchor, becket, bend, bowline, builder's, carrick bend, cat's-paw, clinch, clove hitch, croche, cuckold's-neck, diamond, figure-of-eight, flat, flemish, french shroud, german, gordian, granny, halfcrown, hitch, lanyard, loop, manrope, marling hitch, mascle, matthew walker, mesh, netting, open-hand, over-hand, prolonge, reef, running, sheepshank, sheetbend, shroud, single slide, slipknot, square, stevedore's, stopper, surgeon's, timber, truckman's, turk's-head, wall, weaver's
lace tat(t)
looped bow
loose nowed
love amoret
nautical spanish reef
on rope sheepshank
ornamental bow
pert. See KNOTTED.
remove enodate, enode, unravel
rope end back-splice
rope-shortening sheepshank
running noose, slip
thread burl

wood burl, burr, gnarl, knag, kna(u)r, knur(l), nur, snub
KNOTGRASS bindweed, birdweed, blackstrap, doorweed, hogweed, horsebalm, knotweed, knotwort, lignum, paspalum, pigweed, pinkweed, polygony, wireweed
KNOTHOLE elfbore
KNOTTED, KNOTTY clotted, complex, complicated, craggy, difficult, gnarled, gnarly, gordian, intricate, involved, nodal, nodated, nodose, nodous, nowed, perplexing, puzzling, reticular, rough, rugged, scabrous, tangled
KNOTWEED allseed, dodder, hogweed, jumpseed, knawel, polygony, spurry, tickseed
KNOTWORT knawel
KNOW appreciate, apprehend, ascertain, can, cognize, comprehend, con, conceive, confess, discern, disclose, distinguish, experience, fathom, guard, intuit, ken, knoll, make out, mound, perceive, realize, recognize, regard, reveal, savvy, see, sense, trow, understand, weet, wis(t), wit, wot(h)
-how ability, craftsmanship, knowledge, professionalism, savvy, skill, talent, wit
-it-all boaster, braggart, conceited, showoff, smarty, wiseacre
-nothing agnostic, ignoramus, sam, scissorbill
-thyself nosce te ipsum
KNOWING acute, alert, artful, astute, aware, bright, brilliant, canny, clever, cognition, conversant, cunning, discerning, gnostic, hep, informed, intelligent, intentional, learned, observant, percipient, quickwitted, realization, sage, sapient, scient, scious, sharp, shrewd, smart, spack, stylish, vigilant, wise, with it, worldly
KNOWINGLY cannily, pointedly, purposely, scienter, willfully, witterly, wittingly
KNOWLEDGE accomplishment, acquaintance, aparavidya, avidya, capac-

ity, cognition, cunning, dianoia, episteme, erudition, experience, fact, familiarity, gnosis, information, insight, intelligence, jnana, ken, kith, know-how, learning, lettrure, lore, notition, omniscience, prescience, privity, sapience, scholarship, science, scientia, skill, vidya, wisdom, witting
branch ology
by experience empiricism
capacity for brains, intellect, smarts
comb. ology
esoteric guptavidya
highest noesis
intellectual aparavidya
lack ignorance, nescience
means to organon
mysterious arcanum
mystical gnosis
object of cognitum, scibile
occult cabala, clairvoyance, telegnosis
profound pansophy
seeker philonoist, scholar, student
slight inkling, sciolism, smatter(ing)
source of organon
study of apodictic
summary encyclop(a)edia
superficial sciolism
supreme prajma
systematized science
theory kenlore
transcendental paravidya
universal omniscience, pantology
without atechnic
KNOWLEDGEABLE au fait, aware, informed, intelligent, sciental, skilled
KNOWN beken, common, conscious, couth, distinguished, eminent, exoteric, famed, familiar, famous, leaked, noted, notorious, out, proverbial, released, stated
become kithe, kythe
KNOX, JOHN the big spider
KNUB nudge, thump
KNUCKLE jarret, joint, node, resist
-bone(s) cockal, dib, dolos(se), shackle, tail, talus
down to bow, exert, strike, submit, yield
-head blockhead, boor, cad, clod

KNUR(L) bead, bulge, dwarf, gnarl, knob, knot, mill, null, ridge, snarl, tangle

KO deaden, destroy, flatten, floor, knock out, prostrate

KOALA baalu, baloo, bear, carbora, koolah, monkey-bear, phalanger, phascolarctos, teddybear, wombat

KOBOLD brownie, demon, dwarf, fairy, gnome, goblin, hobgoblin, hodeken, hutchen, nis(se), nissespire, spirit, sprite

KOCHLEFFL activist, busybody, gadabout, go-getter, livewire, organizer, promoter, spoon

KODALY *opera* hary janos

KOEL rainbird

KOHATH *father* levi

son amram, hebron, izhar, uriel, uzziel

KOHINOOR diamond

KOHL antimony, eye shadow

KOHOUTEK comet

KOJAH animal, fur, mink

KOKAM(A) gemsbok, kukan, loris

KOKLASS bird, fowl, pheasant, pucras, pukras

KOKO bird, executioner, lebbek, palm, parson-bird, rail, siris, taro

KOKOON antelope, gnu

KOL *native* bhar, bhilo, dravidian, larka, munsa, santal

dialect See MUNDA.

KOLA bichy, gooranut, jackal, nut

KOLAIAH *son* ahab

KOLARIAN See KOL.

KONIGSBERG kaliningrad

KOOK fool, nut, tsedoodelteh, tsedrayteh

KOOKY bizarre, crazy, insane, kinky, nutty, strange

KOP hill, mountain

KOPECK *1–½* para

15 auksinas

100 ruble

KORADJI bo(o)yla, sorcerer, witch-doctor

KORAH *conspired against* moses

father esau

KORAN *angel* azrael, azrafil, el khidr, gabriel, israfil, michael, rushvan, sijil(l)

compiler's son ali

division alcoran, sura(h), suro

division, 1st al-fatiha

heaven-hell boundary alaraf

lade al cauther

limbo alarf

niche for mihrab

pert. alcoranic

register sijil(l)

teacher alfaki, alfaqui(n), ulema

verse ayah, iya

wall alaraf

watchdog al rakim

KORE chaos, damia, desponia, persephone

lover hades

parent demeter, zeus

KOREA chosen, kingdom of silla

bay kanghwa

capital pyongyang, seoul

carrier ehige

city andong, anju, antung, capyong, chinju, chinnampe, chongjin, chonju, chuminjun, chunchon, fusan, gunzan, haeju, hamhung, heijo, huichon, hungnam, inchon, iri, jushin, kaeson(g), kanko, keijo, keishu, kenjiho, kunsan, kwangjo, kwanju, mason, mokpo, moonsan, moppo, pochon, pusan, riri, samchok, seishin, seoul, shingishu, sinuiju, suan, suwon, taegu, taejon, uiju, wonju, wonsan

coin hwan, kwan, woh

community panmunjon

dinner kaesang

dish kimchee, kimchi

founder, legendary chi-tse, chi-tzu, ki-tse

game ho-hpai, ke-pouk-hpai, kko-ri-pouk-tchi-ki, kol-ye-si, o-koan, ryong-hpai, sang-ryouk, sin-syo-tyen, tjak-ma-tchi-ki

kingdom paikche

leader park chung hee, rhee

meeting place kaesong

peak chiri

peninsula ongjin

port chemulpo, gensan, hungnam, inchon, jinsen, mokpo, pusan, wonsan, yosu

president park, rhee

regent ito

reservoir fusan, pujon

river amnok, han, imjin, kin, kum, kun, lobk, naktong, nam, pukhan, somjin, taedong, tumen, yalu, youngsan

self-defense tae-kwon-do

shrub tea-of-heaven

soldier rok

stockade koje

tree pagoda

weight won

KORI bustard, weaver

KOSHER appropriate, authentic, clean, conforming, devout, ethical, fair, fit, kashruth, kind, lawful, legal, legitimate, proper, pure, real mccoy, reliable, sympathetic, trustworthy, understanding

hindu style halal

laws kashruth

meat-maker porger

not tref

KOSIMO *indian* klaskino, koprino, quatsino

KOSO panamint

KOTO zither-harp

KOULAN gour

KOWHAI goai, locust, pelu, sophora, tree

KOWTOW bow(and scrape), fawn, flatter, genuflect, kneel, salaam, shiko

KOWTOWER sycophant, toady

KOZ *son* urijah

KRA(A)L boma, community, corral, crawl, enclosure, hut, manyatta, pen, stad, stockade, village, zimbabwe

KRAIT adder, bungarum, korait, snake

KRAKOW *astronomer* copernicus

castle wawel

concentration camp auschwitz, oswiecim

market place rynek glowny

river wisla

university jagiellonian

KRAS goat, tahr

KRATER kelebe

KRATOS *captive* prometheus

mother styx

KRAUT cabbage, charlock, soldier

KRENK illness, nothing

KRETZCH complain, croak, fuss, groan, grunt, moan, wheeze

KRI kere, kthibh

KRIEMHILD *brother* gunther

husband etzel, siegfried

mother uta

victim gunther, hagen

KRILL plankton

KRIMMER fur, lambskin, skin

KRIS See SWORD.

KRISHNA (See also

VISHNU.) juggernaut, vasudeva
biography bhagavata-purana
birthplace mathura, vrindavan
brother balarama
grandson aniruddha
idol jagannath, juggernaut
life harivansha
moral treatise bhagavadgita
paradise goloka
parent devaki
race yadava
sister subhadra
KRISS KRINGLE saint nicholas, santa claus
KRONOS See CRONUS.
KRUNG THEP bangkok
KRUPSKAYA *husband* lenin
KRYPTON *source* atmosphere
KTHIBH kere, kri
KUA makua, makwa
KUALA LUMPUR muddymouth
KUBA bushongo, kabistan
KUBLA KHAN *author* coleridge
city xanadu
grandfather genghis khan
river alph
KUDOS fame, glory, praise, renown
KUDZU pueraria
KUI kandh, khondi, lolo
KUIBYSHEV samara
KUKLA *pal* ollie
KU KLUX KLAN *member* klansman, klucker, kluxer
official grand dragon, imperial wizard, kleagle
unit klavern

KUKURUKU ikpere
KULAK agriculturalist, farmer, fist, peasant, usurer
KULANAPAN *indian* pomo
KULM bird, crane, heron
KUMISS drink, omeiris
-*like* kefir, kephir
source camel's milk
KUMMEL allasch
flavor anise, caraway
KUMQUAT nagami
KUNG CHIU confucius
KUOMINTANG council
yuan
KURD persian
ancestors gordyaean
carpet mosul
country iran, iraq, russia, syria, turkey
dish skyr
guerrilla army pesh merga
language kermanji
leader mulla mustafa barzani
KURIL(E) *island* chishima, etoro, iturup
volcano fuyo
KURLAND *inhabitant* lett
KURRAJONG bottletree, calool, lacebark, sourgourd, sterculia
KURTOSIS arc, curvature
KURUMA cart, jinrikisha, wheel
KURVEH See PROSTITUTE.
KUSA dharba
KUSH *capital* merde, napata
father ham
KUSHA darbha
KUST nep, node
KUSUM safflower

KUTCHA crude, makeshift, raw
opposite pucka
KUTENAI *indian* akamnik, akanekunik, akiskemikinik, akiyenik
KUWAIT *city* abdullah, ahmadi, fahaheel, hawalli
island bubiyan, warba
KVAS beer, cider, quass
KVETCH alibier, complain, eke out, exert, fret, fuss, gripe, grunt, pinch, push, shrug, sigh, squeeze, wetblanket
KWAKIUTL *indian* awaitlala, guavaenok
KWANGCHOW canton
KWANGSI-CHUANG *capital* nanning
city kweilin
KWANGTUNG *capital* canton
port dairen
KWAN-YIN avalokiteshvara, bodhisattva
KWATPAI See DOMINOES.
KWEICHOW *capital* kweiyang
KYAH bird, partridge
KYLE channel, farmer, sore, ulcer
KYOTO saikyo
KYPHOSIS curvature, deformity, humpback, hunchback
KYURIN lesghin, lezghian
KYUSHU *base* sasebo
city kumamoto, nogata
port kokura, oita
volcano aso

L

L eleventh, extension, fifty, lambda, lamedh, twelfth, wing
LAADAN *son* jehiel, joel, zetham
LAAGER camp, fortification
LAB blab, gulp LABORATORY, rennet
LABAN *daughter* leah, rachel
kin bethuel, jacob
sister rebecca, rebekah
LABBER daub, splash
LABDACUS *enemy* pandion
grandson oedipus
kingdom thebes

parent nycteis, polydorus
son laius
LABEFY impair, weaken
LABEL appellation, band, bookplate, brand, call, card, classify, codicil, decal, describe, designate, designation, docket, earmark, epithet, fiche, fillet, flap, hallmark, identification, infula, lambeau, lappet, mark, name, nomenclature, paster, rider, seal, slip, stamp, sticker, strip, tag, tally, tassel, ticket, title
point lambeau
LA BELLE LUCIE alex-

ander the great, game, midnight oil, solitaire
LABELLUM border, lip, petal
part hypochil
LABIATE horehound, lipped, mint
LABILE adaptable, plastic, unstable
LABIUM border, deutomala, lip, metastoma, pedipalps
LA BOHEME *composer* puccini
dance musetta's waltz
heroine mimi
LABOR begar, birth, bullock, business, cark, chore, cor-

vee, delve, drudge(ry), effort, endeavor, exertion, fag, flounder, grind, heave, industry, lucubrate, manuary, moil, overwork, pains, parturition, service, strain, stress, strive, struggle, suffer, sweat, swink, task, tave, teave, toil, travail, tread, trouble, turmoil, turn to, WORK, yakka
compulsory begar
device strike, walkout
difficult dystocia
foreign aperu
hired togt
-saving automatic, mechanical
severe agon
symbol blue shirt, hard hat
union afl, artel, cio, guild, ilgwu, iww, umw
unpaid corvee

LABORATORY officina, operatory, prosectorium, workroom, workshop
gear beaker, bunsen burner, etna, petri, pipet, retort, test tube, vial

LABORED difficult, fancy, forced, heavy, operose, ornate, painstaking, stiff, strained

LABORER artisan, bagdi, bhar, bijwoner, blue-shirt, bohunk, bracero, coolie, craftsman, esne, fellah, flunky, guaso, hand, hardhat, holeya, mechanic, mozo, navvy, operative, operator, peasant, peon, pieceworker, proletarian, roustabout, sandhog, seggon, servant, spalpeen, toty, worker, workhand, workman
canal navvy
forced begari
group crew, gang
hired togt
inferior seggon
unskilled bohunk, coolie, cooly

LABORIOUS arduous, assiduous, busy, difficult, diligent, hard, heavy, herculean, industrious, onerous, operose, strenuous, sweaty, toilful, toilsome, uphill

LABRADOR *indian* nascapee, nascapi
product iron ore
retriever newfoundland
strait belle isle

tea evergreen, gowiddie, ledum
violet butterwort

LABRADORITE anorthosite, feldspar

LABRUS ballan, cunner, tautog, wrasse

LABURNUM base-tree, cytisus, goai, golden-chain

LABYRINTH confusion, enigma, intricacy, maze, meander, perplexity, puzzle
builder daedalus
fish anabantid
inhabitant minataur
owner minos
site crete

LABYRINTHINE circuitous, daedal, tortuous

LAC dye, LAKH, milk, resin, scarlet

LACE (See, also *kind*, below.) adorn, baldric, beat, brace, braid, broach, compress, cord, edging, embroider, ensnare, entwine, fasten, fibula, filigree, flavor, fortify, gin, intertwine, lash, mix, net(tin), noose, plat, pleach, raddle, snare, spike, string, thrash, throw, tie, trim, twine, unite, weave
barred grille(e)
bobbin-made antwerp, blond(e), bone, chantilly, honiton, torchon
bug tingis, tingitid
cape mantilla
center alencon
coarse macrame
collar ruche
edge picot, puntilla
end a(i)glet
flower wild carrot
front jabot
goffered ruche, ruching
gold biliment, cannetille, orris
heavy guipure, tatting
kind alencon, allover, aloe, alost, argentan, argentella, aurillac, biliment, blond(e), bobbin(e), bone, breton, bridal, bruges, brussels, bullion, burano, buratto, cannetille, carnival, carrickmacross, chantilly, cluny, colberteen, colbertine, dentelle, duchess, fichu, filet, filigree, galloon, galon, gold-thread, grille(e), grospoint, guipure, honiton, illusion, lacis, limerick, lisle,

macrame, maline(s), mechlin, milan, nanduti, needle (point), pillow, point, potlace, reticella, rosepoint, tambour, tatting, torchon, val(enciennes), venetian, venise, ypres
knotted macrame, tatting
lizard monitor, varanus
make crochet, tat
-maker twisthand
mechlin maline(s)
metallic bullion
needlepoint argenton, reticella, teneriffe
net breton, regeau
opening eyelet
pattern cascade, larme, toile
point argentella, aurillac, aurragh, brussels, greek, milan, roman, rose, venetian
shuttle tat(ting)
silver cannetille, orris
square hole filet
stitches jours
string thong
strip ruche
tag or tip a(i)glet(te)
trimming gard, jabot
veil mantilla
work dentelle

LACEBARK akaroa, daguilla, kurrajong, lacewood, lagetta, ribbonwood, tree

LACED decorated, fastened, fortified, intoxicated, streaked, tied, tightened

LACEDAEMON *descendant* castor, clytemnestra, dioscuri, helen, hippocoon, icarius, tyndareus
founded sparta
parent taygete, zeus
son amyclas
wife sparta

LACERATE afflict, break, claw, cut, fracture, harrow, hurt, lance, lancinate, laniate, maim, mangle, notched, puncture, rend, rip, sever, shred, tear, torment, wound

LACERATED distracted, jagged, mangled, torn

LACERATION cut, rip, tear, wound

LACERT lizard, muscle

LACEWOOD sycamore

LACHE coward, letch, pond

LACHES carelessness, delay, lapse, laxness, lewd, neglect, negligence, slight, wanton

LACHESIS bothrops, bushmaster, fate, pit-viper, snake

LACHISH *king* japhia

LACHRYMALS doldrums

LACHRYMATORY handkerchief, tear-bottle, vase

LACHRYMOSE crying, sad, tearful, weepy

LACING beating, braid, rope, shoestring, thong, thrashing, trimming, weaving

LACK absence, blemish, crime, dearth, defect, deficiency, depreciate, destitution, disgrace, disparage, fail, faute, miss, need, offense, paucity, require, scarcity, shortage, want

LACKADAISICAL bathetic, blase, enervated, faineant, idle, improvident, indifferent, indolent, inert, languorous, languid, lazy, listless, nonchalant, perfunctory, slothful, slow, supine, unconcerned

LACKEY butler, employee, flunky, follower, footman, henchman, menial, servant, slave, stooge, sycophant, toady, valet

LACKING absent, bankrupt, barren, bereft, blank, but, desolate, devoid, gnede, imperfect, indigent, minus, missing, needed, short, shy, wanting, without
comb. lipo

LACKLUSTER cloudy, cold, colorless, dead(ened), drab, dull, dun, flat, glassy, glazed, leaden, lifeless, mat, somber, vacant

LACONIA *capital* sparta
king myles
people obe
ruling class spartiate
serf helot

LACONIC breviloquent, brief, brusque, compact, concise, curt, epigrammatic, pithy, pointed, sententious, short, succinct, summary, taciturn, terse, to the point

LA COSA NOSTRA lcn, mafia, syndicate

LACQUER chaton, duco, enamel, japan, lac, paint, urushi, varnish
ingredient balsam, capivi, copaiba
tree bihar

LACROSSE *forerunner* bagataway
stick crosse

LACTEAL, LACTROUS galactic, milky
circle galaxy, milky way

LACTONE bergaptene, campholide, cumarin, diketene, limonin, meconin

LACTUCA butterweed, lettuce

LACUNA break, cavity, depression, gap, hiatus, interval, lack, pit, space

LACUSTRINE abyssal, aquatic, bathybic, bathysmal, fluvial, fluviatile, marine, neritic, oceanic, pelagic, thalassic

LACY delicate, fragile, weblike

LAD(DIE) billy, boy(o), bucko, bugger, bursch, caddie, caddy, callan(t), carl, chap, chiel, dick, fellow, gossoon, lover, mate, muchacho, nipper, shaveling, shaver, springer, stripling, youngster, younker, youth
awkward gromet, grummet
mischievous gamin
my avick
on call bellboy, messenger, page
serving coistrel, coistril, gillie, gossoon

LADAKH *animal* ammon, antelope, ibex, markhor, red bear, snow leopard, wild horse
language oldi
range himalaya, karakoram, zaskar
stove bukhari

LADDER escalade, gangway, puleyn, run, scalade, scale, stee, steps, styp, trap
ascend by climb, escalade
fireman's pompier
fort-scaling escalade
jacob's charity
-like scalar(iform)
part hook, ratline, rime, rondle, rundle, rung, stave
pert. scalar, scalose

LADE bail, burden, charge, dip, drain, draw, fraught, load, lode, millrace, pack, ship, watercourse

LA-DE-DA, LA-DI-DAH affected, dandyish, foppish, pretentious

LADEN burdened, charged, cumbered, encumbered, expecting, fraught, freighted, hampered, loaded, oppressed, weighted

LADING bailing, burden, cargo, freight, load, placement

LADINO horse, mestizo, mixture, spaniol

LADLE bail, bowl, box, bucket, clath, cup, cyath(us), dip(per), dish(out), flatboard, keach, kyathos, lade, potstick, scoop, shovel, spade, spoon, stoop
handled cyath(us), kyathos, shank
large scoop
out soup sleech
spout geat

LADON *guarded* apples of hesperides
offspring daphne, syrinx
parent phorcys
slayer hercules

LADRONE blackguard, brigand, highwayman, latherin, marauder, robber, rogue, slattern, thief, tulisan
island guajan, guam, marianas, saipan

LADY, LADY'S archduchess, baroness, beebee, begum, belle, beloved, bibi, burd, countess, dame, devi, domina, don(n)a, duchess, female, frau, gentlewoman, khanum, madam, madonna, marchioness, margravine, matron, mistress, noblewoman, peeress, ranee, sahiba, sen(h)ora, signora, spouse, viscountess, wife, WOMAN
black hearts, poplar, queen of spades
book founder godey
chained andromeda
comb beggar's-needle, groundenell, herb, needlechervil, scandix
curious pandora
day annunciation, assumption
delight pansy
eardrop fuchsia, jewelweed, touch-me-not
fern backache-brake
glove bird's-foot trefoil, fleawort, foxglove, lungwort
godiva's village netherwallop
gossipy old yenta
gracious gnadige frau
in the chair cassiopeia

in waiting See *maid*, below.
-*killer* carpet knight, carpet-monger, casanova, dandy, donjuan, gallant, lothario, philanderer, rake, sheik, wolf, womanizer
knight bradamente, britomartis
-*like* chic, dainty, demure, fastidious, feminine, genteel, noble, polite, refined, seemly, tender, wellbred
-*lint* stitchwort
love amore, amour, belamour, delia, mistress, sweetheart
maid abigail, bower may, cameriera, duena, tirewoman
man beau, courtier
mantle dewcup, pedelion
needlewort hedge-parsley
nicotine tobacco
nightcap anemone, canterbury bell, hedge-bindweed
noble countess, duchess, marchioness, princess, queen, viscountess
of babylon catholic church
of the lake ellen, nimue, nymph, vivian
of the lake author scott
of the lake character alice brand, dhu, ellen, lord richard, urgan
percy's brother mortimer
percy's husband hotspur
pincushion saxifrage, thrift
pocket jewelweed
psalter rosary
seal black bryony
shoe bottekin, bottine, columbine
silk habit pelisse
slipper columbine, cypripedium, duck, nerveroot, nervine, orchid, umbilroot, valerian, venus's-cup, yellows
smock cuckooflower, hedge-bindweed, toothwort
stately grande dame
thumb peachwort, persicary, smartweed
with lamp florence nightingale
young damozel, demoiselle, jeune fille, signorina

LADYBIRD, LADYBUG beetle, burnie-bee, cardinalis, coccinella, epilachna, hippodamia, insect, novius, vedalia
prey aphid, bollworm, corn-ear worm, flea-hopper, fruit-scale, leaf-hopper, leaf-worm, mealy-bug

LADYFINGER banana, cuckoopint, effeminate, kidney vetch, red pepper, spongecake, weakling

LADYFISH albula chiro, bonefish, doncella, elops, grubber, menhaden, oio, pudiano, wrasse

LAEL *offspring* gershonite
parent eliaspath

LAERTES *consort* anticlea
daughter-in-law penelope
father acrisius, arcesius, polonius
kingdom ithaca
mother chalcomedusa
sister ophelia
son odysseus, ulysses
victim hamlet

LAFAYETTE *marquis de* marie joseph paul yves roch gilbert du motier
wife adrienne

LAG apprehend, arrest, banish, belated, commit, dally, dawdle, delay, dillydally, drag, fall behind, hang back, hindermost, idle, insulate, jailbird, last, late, linger, loiter, procrastinate, retard(ation), saunter, slacken, slow, sluggish, soil, stave, stay, steal, tardy, tarry, trail, wait, wash(ing), wet

LAGAN flotsam, jetsam

LAGARTO alligator, galliwasp, lizard-fish

LAGASH *king* gudea

LAGENA bottle, flask

LAGENARIA bottle-gourd, calabash, plant

LAGER See BEER.

LAGGARD backward, comatose, dawdle(r), dilatory, drone, impassive, indolent, leisurely, lethargic, lingerer, loiterer, poke, reluctant, slow(coach), slowpoke, sluggard, sluggish, snail, stick-in-the-mud, stiff, straggler, tarrier, tortoise

LAGGING cleading, drawling, forepole, insulation, sentence, tardy

LA GIOCONDA mona lisa

LAGNIAPPE bit, bonus, gift, gratuity, handsel, memento, pilon, present, tip, trifle

LAGOMORPH animal, con(e)y, hare, paca, pika, rabbit

LAGOON atoll, bar, basin, bayou, coral reef, cove, haff, laguna, liman, pond, pool
islands ellice

LAGWORT coltsfoot

LAHMI *brother* goliath

LAHORE *gardens* shalimar

LAIC borrel, civil, lay(man), secular, temporal

LAID *down* posed, prescribed, thetic, traditional
low exhausted, killed, sick, slain, wounded
off canned, fired, sacked, unemployed, unoccupied
up ill, sick
waste bare, devastated

LAIDLY loathsome, repulsive, ugly

LAIN concealment, disguise, layer, stratum

LAINER lash, strap, thong

LAIR bed, burrow, cave(rn), couch, covert, den, earth, ewer, form, grave, hold, hole, holt, layer, lie, lodge, lore, meuse, mew, mire, mud, pen, pipe, quagmire, rest, retreat, run, shed, trap, tunnel

LAIRY earthly, filthy, miry

LAIS courtesan, hetaera, wanton
rival phryne

LAISH *son* phalti(el)

LAISSEZ-FAIRE do-nothing, free enterprise, indifference, individualism, mercantilism, unconcern

LAIT examine, flash, immature, lightning, milk, pollack, search

LAITY congregation, dilettantism, flock, fold, laymen, people

LAIUS *father* labdacus
kingdom thebes
slayer oedipus
son oedipus
wife jocasta

LAKE brook, chott, contest, dana, den, fight, fun, game, jhil, lago(on), laguana, llyn, loch, mere, mough, pit, play, pond, prison, reservoir, salina, shat, shott, sluice, sport, stream, taal, tank, tarn, van, vlei; vley
albert people luri
artificial, largest mead
carp drum, laker
chad people buduma, maba, shari

chad river shari
champlain, river into ausable
como breeze breva
constance bodensee
constance, city on bregenz
deepest baikal
deposit trona
dweller lacustrian
dwelling cottage, crannog, palafitte
erie, city on buffalo, cleveland, lackawanna, sandusky, toledo
fenny broad
fever malaria
geneva breeze bornan, rebat
george horicon
goddess artemis
great erie, huron, michigan, ontario, superior
herring blueback, cisco, grayback, kiyi, sockeye
hiawatha's shining big sea water
highest titicaca
indian erie
inhabiting lacustral
island ait
lady of the ellen
largest superior
lawyer burbot, lota
longest dead sea
man-made mead
marshy liman
michigan, city on chicago
michigan, river into chicago, grand
mother naal
mountain tarn
mythical tritonis
nymph limniad, naiad
of the cat erie
ontario, river into genesee
outlet bayou
pert. lacustral, lacustrine, limnal
plover sanderling
poet coleridge, southey, wordsworth
refuge crannog
salmon namaycush
salt chott, salina, shot(t)
shallow lagoon, lagun(a)
sheepshead drumfish
small gurges, pond, pool
state michigan
superior fish siscowet
superior, hiawatha's shining big sea water
superior indian basket bokark
temporary pinag
trout namaycush, waha
whitefish pollan

world's highest titicaca
world's largest superior
LAKH 100 crore
LAKME composer delibes
LAKSHMI shree, sri
consort vishnu
festival dewali
LALLYGAG idle, kiss, loaf
LAM beat, escape, flee, hit, run, strike
LAMA alpaca, auchenia, brown, candlenut, ecclesiastic, guanaco, monk, priest, teshu
highest dalai
home tibet
2nd highest teshu
LAMAIST dignitary hutukhtu
monastery lamasery
priest gelong, getsul
sacred city lassa, lhasa
stupa chorten
LA MANCHA gentleman don quixote
LAMB, LAMB'S agneau, agnello, agnus, astrakhan, baahling, broadtail, cade, chilver, cosset, ean(ling), fledgling, fur, hogling, innocent, karakul, mutton, paschal, pet, poddy, twagger, yean(ling)
abandoned by mother cade
and wheat kibbe
breast of carre
cry baa, maaba
disease swayback
female ewe, gimmerhog, tup
foot plantain
fur astrakhan, broadtail, budge, galyac, galyak
give birth to (y)ean
hand-raised hob
holy agnus
-kill staggerbush
leg of gigot, wabbler, wobbler
-like gentle, meek
male hieder, ram
noses shootingstar
of god agnus dei, christ
pet cade, cosset
quarters baconweed, frostblite, goosefoot, muckweed, orach
rack sedlo
slice target
swayback warfa
symbol of innocence, sacrifice, st agnus
toes black medic, kidneyvetch

tongue corn-mint, mullein, plantain
unshorn gimmer-hog
wool wassail
year-old chilver
young cosset, (y)eanling
LAMB, CHARLES dog dash
pert. elian
pseud. elia
sister mary
work essays of elia, tales from shakespeare
LAMBASTE beat, chide, clobber, fan, pound, punish, rebuke, ribroast, thrash, towel
LAMBENT beaming, beamy, bright, brilliant, effulgent, flickering, gleaming, glowing, lucent, luminous, lustrous, radiant, refulgent, shimmering, wavering
LAMBREQUIN curtain, decoration, mantling, valence
LAMBSKIN apron, bag(h), dad, beat, blow, budge, cape, fabric, galyak, krimmer, salzfelle, suede, thrash
LAME abortive, bum, claudicant, cojo, cripple(d), defective, disable(d), feeble, flabby, flimsy, gammy, gimpy, gravel, halt(ing), hobbling, hurt, ineffectual, inefficient, infirm, insufficient, limphault, limping, loam, maim(ed), paralyzed, spavined, unconvincing, unpersuasive, unsatisfactory, unsuitable, weak
-brain dolt, dunce, fool
LAMECH ancestor cain
father methuselah
offspring jabal, jubal, naamah, noah, tubalcain
wife adah, zillah
LAMELLA folium, fornix, gill, lamina, plate, plica, scale
LAMENT bemoan, bewail, beweep, care, complain, coranach, croon, cry(out), deplore, dirge, elegize, elegy, epicedium, grieve, hone, jeremiad, keen, kinah, kommos, moan, mourn, ochone, pine, plange, plangor, regret, repine, rue, sorrow, threap, threnody, wail, weep, wey, yammer
expression of wirri
for dead keening
musical dumka

LAMENTABLE deplorable, distressing, grievous, pitiable, pitiful, regrettable, rueful, sad, terrible, tragic, unfortunate, woeful yammerly, yemer

LAMENTATION anguish, bemoaning, bewailing, cry, dirge, dole, dolor, elegy, grieving, jeremiad, keening, mourning, plaint, plangor, regret, sigh(ing), sorrow, tangi, tears, threne, ululation, wail(ing), weeping
exclamation ah me, alack (aday), alas, lackadaisy, lackaday, o dear, welladay, wellaway, wirri, woe's me

LAMIA demon, monster, vampire, witch

LAMINA blade, coat, collop, cut, disc, film, flake, flap, foil, fold, lametta, lap, layer, leaf, membrane, obex, pane(l), peel, pellicle, plait, plate, plating, ply, rasher, scale, scum, sheet, shell, shim, skin, slab, slat, slice, table(t), veneer, wafer

LAMINATE coat, foil, layer, plate

LAMINATED fissile, flaky, foliate(d), lamellar, scaled, spathic, tabular
rock shale

LAMMERGEIER arend, bone-breaker, fulmar, gypaetus, osprey, vulture

LAMMERMOOR *bride* lucia

LAMMOCK lounge, slough

LAMP aeolight, aldis, argand, bull's-eye, crusie, davy, etna, eye, flash, geordie, helion, lamina, lantern, light, look, lucerne, lucigen, luminary, moon, see, star, sun, torch(ere)
alcohol etna
arc monophote
black aspergillin, link, pigment, soot
condensing ring cric
18th-century buillotte
fireplace kyle
flashing strobotron
4-cornered chill
fuel coal-oil, kerosene, oil, paraffin, supa
holder husk
incandescent bulb
inspector ager
iron cresset, crusie

-lighter match, spill, taper, torch
makeshift bitch
miner's davy
of heaven moon
of phoebus sun
oil kerosene, supa
ornament epi
pert. lucernal
ring cric
safety cluster, davy, geordie
shade blinker, fin, globe, gobo
shade hoop harp
sperm oil sinumbra
spirit etna
stand candelabrum, chandelier
waving of arati
youth with aladdin

LAMPEDUSA *book* the leopard

LAMPERN lamprey, seveneyes, seven-holes

LAMPETIA *parent* apollo, helius, neaera

LAMPING brilliant, flashing, luminous, shining

LAMPOON abuse, berhyme, burlesque, caricature, cockalan, geste, libel, parody, pasquil, pasquinade, pastiche, ridicule, roorback, satire, satirize, skit, squib, travesty

LAMPREY agnatha, eel, hagfish, lampern, myzont, petromyzon, rock-sucker, say-nay, seven-eyes, seven-holes
larva ammoc(o)ete
migration eelfare

LAMPWICK match, mint, phlomis, plant

LAMUS *parent* hercules, omphale

LANA flannel, genipap, wood, wool

LANAI enclosure, porch, veranda

LANATE(D) hairy, wooly

LANCASHIRE *section* eccles

LANCASTER *house of,* founder john of gaunt
house of, symbol (red)rose

LANCE blade, broach, cane, cut, dart, fling, glaive, gleave, hurl, javelin, joust, launce, launch, open, perforate, pierce, puncture, shaft, spear, spiculum, spike, stab, throw, weapon
comb. lonch(o)
guard vamplate

head morne, mourne, socket
-headed snake fer-de-lance
-knight lansquenet
mythical ron
rest faucre, fewter, queue
ring burr
sergeant corporal

LANCELET acrania, amphioxus, branchiostoma, cephalochorda

LANCELOT *beloved* elaine, guinevere, lily maid
castle joyeuse garde, joyous gard
father ban
friend arthur, bellengerus, blamoure, bleobris, bors, clarrus, clegis, dynas, ector, gahalantyne, galyhoden, galyhud, harry, hebes, lavayne, lyonel, melyas, menaduke, neroveus, palomides, plenoryus, sadoke, safere, selyses, urry, valyaunte, vyllyars
nephew bohort, bort
son galahad, hawain
sword aroundight, aroundite
uncle bors

LANCER cavalryman, hussar, soldier, sowar, spearer, trooper, u(h)lan

LANCET fish, fleam, instrument, knife, scalpel, serra, window
fish surgeonfish
point neb

LANCEWOOD canela, cigua, copa, oxandra, yariyari, yaya

LANCINATE lacerate, pierce, rend, stab, tear, torment

LAND 3 erd, lot, sod, win 4 acre, area, doab, duab, farm, gain, gish, gore, odal, odel, padi, plat, plot, soil, turf, udal, wold 5 arada, arado, arder, catch, earth, field, glebe, heath, laine, light, paddy, patch, perch, reach, realm, roost, shore, solum, terra, terre, tilth, tract, twait, weald 6 alight, arrive, assart, attain, cantle, debark, domain, estate, ground, meadow, medina, nation, region, secure 7 achieve, advance, capture, country, deplane, descend, detrain, holding, pasture, quillet, terrain, terrene, thwaite 8 allodial, dismount, pomerium, prae-

dium, property 9 continent, disembark, territory, touch down 10 settle down
alluvial batture, bottoms, carse, delta
ancestral ethel
and water-living amphibian, amphibious
arable laine, lea, ley
arid or barren badlands, desert, gall, steppe, usar, waste
arm panhandle, peninsula, spit
attached to pr(a)edial
barter excambion
between furrows selion
between two rivers doab, duab
block forty
body continent, island
book terrier
border rand
bottom callow, cross, haugh, slash, strath
breeze coromell, terral
church abadengo, glebe, termon
clear acre, al(l)odium, al(l)ody, assart, brush, cure, deaden, field, odal, sart, slash, udal
clearing kaingin
common ejido, exido, stray
connection ne(c)k, reach
cultivated arable, arada, arado, fallow, farm, feering, field, furrow, lamorage, metairie, orchard, ranch, thwaite, tillage, tilth, twaite, wainage
dealer realtor
depressed graben
description topography
diked polder
division canton, district, konohiki, laine
east of eden nod
elevated alp, hill, mesa, mound, mountain, plateau, ridge
enclosed intake
end, guardian bellerus
extension cape, peninsula
fallow arder, lea
fertile carse
feudal benefice, feod, odal
flat mesa
form cuesta, cusp
freehold mulk
furrowed feering
government-owned public domain
grant casate, enam(dar), feu, gale, inam, pata, sasan

gravelly geest, graves
grazing field, hirsel, hirsle, meadow, pasture, plain, range
growth on vesture
heathy rosland
held in fee simple See *clear,* above.
heritable al(l)od(ium), al(l)ody, fief, odal, odel, udal
hilly down
householder's barton, casate, demesne
hypothetical lemuria
imaginary cockayne, faerie, lilliput
in foreign territory enclave
law solum
leased tack
living on terrestrial
low bog, bottoms, carse, fen, gall, holm, intervale, polder, vale, valley
management agronomics, agronomy
manager bailiff, overseer, reeve, steward
marshy swale
mass asia, bulge, CONTINENT
mass, hypothetical gondwana
mass, largest eurasia
meadow lea
measure acre, are, arpent, bovate, caballeria, carucate, chain, decare, deciare, dessiatine, devach, hectare, hektare, hide, kiliare, kipuka, manzana, mecate, meter, mile, morgen, perch, ploughland, plowland, rig, ro(o)d, sulung, virgate, wist
mythical See PARADISE; UTOPIA.
narrow isthmus, neck, peninsula, spit, strake
native birthdom, blighty, home
north, farthest ultima thule
obdurate till
of beulah See PARADISE; UTOPIA.
of bliss gokuraku
of bondage egypt
of cakes scotland
of giants utgarthar
of magicians glubdubdrib
of midnight sun arctic, finland, norway, sweden
of milk and honey israel, utopia
of myrrh azab, saba

of nod bed, sleep
of opportunity arkansas
of philosophers balnibarbi
of plenty goshen
of regrets india
of rising sun japan, nippon
of steady habits connecticut
of the leal See HEAVEN; PARADISE.
of the rose england
of the shamrock eire, erin, ireland
of the thistle scotland
of the thousand lakes finland
of the white elephant siam, thai
of wealth el dorado
on aground, ashore, punish, rebuke, shoreward
open heath, moor, slash, vega, weald, wold
ownership, pert. odal, udal
parcel (See also *cultivated,* above.) acre, arado, clearing, erf, estate, few, field, gore, laine, lot, mock, patch, piece, plat, plot, ranch, range, solum, spong, trace
pasture alp, feed, hoga, leason, veldt
pert. agrarian, agro, continental, geoponic, real, terrestrial
pirate claim-jumper, squatter, swindler, thief
plowed arable, fallow, furrow, thwaite, twaite
plowed in a day jornada
point cape, ness, ras, spit
prepare for seed harrow, plow, till
profit crop, esplees, rent(e)
promised canaan, palestine
public ager, commons, parc, park, preserve, reserve
pure amida, amitabha, jodo, sukhavati
rail corn-crake
-raker footpad
rat marauder, thief
reclaimed novalia, polder
reeve bailiff, overseer, steward
resown hookland
reverting to state escheat
river-drained basin
rock-covered brule
rough brake, bush
sandy dene, dune, shore
savannah lalang
science geodynamics, geognosy, geography, geology, geomorphology, geophysics,

geoscopy, mineralogy, physiography
scrubby scrog(s)
scurvy purpura
sea, recovered from innings, intake, polder
shard linchet
share dher
ship tank
shrub-covered brule, roughet
-slater sow bug, wood louse
small parcel suerte
snail bubble shell, bulimoid, bulimus, bulla, physa
snow-covered savanna(h)
-spring lavant
strip cape, doab, duab, head (land), isthmus, peninsula, promontory, rap, screed, slang, spit, spong, tongue
swampy bog, woodsere
tax cess, hidage, terrage
taxes, valued for cadastre
tenure feu, fief, leasehold, serjeanty, sorhon
tilled See *cultivated, plowed,* above.
timber acres, novalia, sticks, sucken, woods
tongue doab, duab
treeless llano, pampas, plain, prairie, savanna(h), steppe, tundra, wold
triangular delta, gore
uncultivated barefallow, brule, b(r)ush, desert, forest
urchin hedgehog
waste barrens, desert, heath, moor, wilderness, wilds
waterlocked ile, island, isle
watery bayou, bog, flow, maremma, marina, marsh, moor, morass, swamp, woodsere
western hesperia
wet soak, swamp, swang
LANDHOLDER coscet, laird, talukdar, thane, thegn, yeoman, zamindar
LANDHOLDING barony
LANDING (See also *kind,* below.) arrivage, arrival, beachhead, debarkation, disembarkation, dock, gaut, ghat, jetty, key, landfall, levee, level, perch, pier, quay, splashdown, stor(e)y, tarmac, wharf
kind crash, dead-stick, fishtail, half-pace, nose-over, nose-up, pancake, sideslip, three-point, two-point

place airdrome, airfield, airport, airstrip, dock, harbor, key, levee, quai, quay, runway, wharf
strip runway
LANDLADY concierge, duena, goodwife, hostess, mistress, padrona, wife
LANDLOPER adventurer, nomad, vagabond, vagrant, wanderer
LANDLORD boniface, freeholder, goodman, host, hote, innkeeper, lessor, master, owner, padrone, proprietor, squire, zamindar
LANDLUBBER *farmer* grass-comber
LANDMARK baken, bound(ary), cairn, cippus, copa, dole, dool, guide, hoarstone, march, mearstone, meith, mere, mere(stone), milestone, senal, waypost
LANDOWNER bhumidar, bonder, cacique, effendi, franklin, freeholder, gamori, gentry, geomoroi, landlord, latifundista, squire, squirling, zamindar
LANDSCAPE decorate, depiction, description, epitome, painting, paysage, picture, plan(t), prospect, scene(ry), view
art bonsai
LANDSLIDE avalanche, eboulement, lahar, slip, victory
LANDTAG assembly, council, diet, legislature
LANDVOGT bailiff, governor
LANDWARD agrarian, country, inland, rural, rustic
LANE alley(way), byway, chare, court, drang, drive, loke, pass, passage(way), path(way), road, route, street, tewer, track, vennel
narrow boreen, char(e), tewer
LANGLAND *allegory* piers, plowman
LANGLE fetter, hobble
LANGO *tribe* latuka
LANGOBARD *king* alboin
LANGOSTA grasshopper, locust
LANGOUSTE crawfish, lobster
LANGUAGE abuse, accent, argot, cant, censure, chib,

dialect, diction, expression, gobbledegook, idiom, jargon, jive, lede, leed, lingo, lingua, lip, parlance, patois, patter, phrasing, profanity, rhetoric, rune, slang, speech, style, talk, tongue, ursprache, utterance, vernacular, vocabulary
affected euphuism
algorithmic algol
ancient aryan, chinese, greek, hebrew, latin, pali, sanskrit
aramaic syriac
artificial See *international,* below.
bureaucratic gobbledegook
change interpret, misquote, paraphrase, translate
classical attic, greek, latin
comb. gloss(o), glot(to)
common chinese, english, french, german, italian, japanese, russian, spanish
confusion babel
dead archaism, latin
dirty filth, obscenity, ordure, smut
elegant rhetoric
extinct raetic, rhaetian, yana
figurative imagery, trope
florid sillabub
foolish flummery, stuff
form idiom
having two bilingual, diglot
hybrid bamboo-english, beach-la-mar, beche-le-mer, chinook, hausa, hindustani, kiswahili, kitchen-kaffir, koine, linguafranca, pidgin, savir, swahili, talk-boy, talkee-talkee, talky-talky
indic assamese, hindi
inflectionless, pert. anaptocic
informal argot, patois, slang
international anglic, antido, arulo, esperanto, europan, ido, interlingua, kosmos, latinesce, latino, linguafranca, linguageral, lingualumina, monario, mondolingue, myrana, nov-esperanto, novial, novlatin, occidental, optez, pasigraphy, pasilaly, romanal, shona, solresol, spelin, universala, volapuk
know-all pantoglot, polyglot
letters alphabet
loss aphasia, aphemia
monosyllabic monkhmer
nonmetrical prose
nonsensical gibberish
origin, pert. glottogonic

parent ursprache
pattern speechway
pert. lingual, semantic(al)
pidgin caviteno, fanakalo, sabir
pompous bombast, bull, oratory, rhetoric, wind
poor barbarism, slang
pretentious claptrap
romance catalan, french, italian, latin, portuguese, spanish
rules grammar, syntax
sacred pali
secret argot, code, cryptology, openglopish
semitic arabic, canaanite, chaldean, hebrew
showy flubdub
spoken diction, pronunciation
strange argot, cant, dialect, jargon, lingo
study etymology, glossology, glottology, grammar, lexicology, linguistics, morphology, paleography, philology, phonemics, phonetics, rhetoric, semantics, syntactics, syntax
synthetic See *international,* above.
terse telegraphese
to incite exhortation
ungrammatical abusage, abusion, barbarism, catachresis
unintelligible gibberish, gobbledegook
universal See *international,* above.
LANGUID apathetic, dead, dopey, droop(y), enervated, exanimate, heavy, hebetudinous, idle, impassive, inactive, inert, lackadaisical, leaden, lethargic, lifeless, listless, lumpish, lymphatic, ourie, pepless, phlegmatic, sleepy, slow, sluggish, spiritless, supine, torpid, unhurried, weak, weary
LANGUISH brood, decline, decrease, despond, droop, dry up, dwine, fade, fail, faint, flag, pine, sear, shrivel, sicken, sigh, sink, snivel, spoil, wane, waste, weaken, wilt, wither, wiz(z)en
LANGUISHING downcast, enervated, indolent, inert, infirm, lasting, listless, long-

ing, pining, sick, supine, weakened, yearning
LANGUOR blues, debility, depression, doldrums, drowsiness, dullness, dumps, ennui, exhaustion, fatigue, feebleness, hebetude, inanition, indolence, kaif, ke(e)f, kief, kiff, lassitude, laxity, lethargy, listlessness, oscitance, sluggishness, stagnation, stupefaction, stupor, tedium, torpidity, torpor, vapors, weakness, weariness
LANGUOROUS dilatory, indolent, indulged, lax, leaden, loose, pampered, passive
LANGUR animal, douc, entellus, lotong, lutong, maha, monkey, presbytis, simpai, wanderoo
LANK(Y) angular, drooping, gangling, gaunt, lean, limp, meager, rangy, rawboned, scrawny, shrunken, skinny, slabsided, slender, slight, slim, slunken, spare, stringy, tall, thin
LANNES *commander* napoleon
LANSEH ayer-ayer, duku, fruit, lanzon
LANTANA oregano, verbena
LANTERN (See also LAMP.) absconce, bowet, buat, bull's-eye, cimboric, cupola, femereil, flashlight, illumination, jacklight, lamp, light(house), luminary, pharos, sconce, signal, tholus, window
cloth haitsai
dark absconce, absonsa
festival bon
fish iniome
flounder megrim
fly fulgorid
-jack ignis-fatuus
-jawed lean, underhung, undershot
lily daffodil
magic epidiascope, megascope, sciopticon, stereopticon
optical episcope
pinion rundle, trundle
wheel trundle
LANYARD cord, gilguy, laniard, rope, thong, wapp
LAOCOON *slayer* serpents
son antiphas, persis, thymbraeus

LAODAMAS *father* alcinous, eteocles
slayer alcamaeon
victim aegialeus
LAODAMIA *consort* protesilaus, zeus
parent acastus, hippolyte
son sarpedon
LAODICE electra
husband helicaon, phoroneus
parent agamemnon, clytemnestra, hecuba, priam
son munitus
LAODICEAN indifferent, irresolute
LAODOCUS *parent* apollo, phthia
slayer aetolus
LAOMEDON *consort* strymo
father ilus
kingdom troy
offspring bucolion. hesione, priam, themiste, tithonus
servant apollo, poseidon
slayer hercules
LAOS tai
capital luang prabang, vientiane
city luang prabang, nape, paklay, pakse, savannakhet, thakhek, xieng
coin att, kip
communist group pathet lao
leader souvanna phouma
measure bak
peak atwat, bia, copi, khat, khoung, lai, loi, san, tiubia
river done, khong, mekong, noi, se bang
tribe hmong, kha, lao, meo, miao, thai, yao, yun
LAOTHOE *consort* priam
son lycaon, polydorus
LAO-TZU *disciple* yin hsi
founded taoism
gift tao te ching
incarnation celestial master of the first origin
mount green ox
LAP adjunct, barm, beat, bind, bosom, circuit, cuddle, cut, drink, entangle, fold, imbrication, include, involve, lamina, leg, lick, overlay(er), overlie, phase, polish, ripple, slash, tie, touch, wash, wind, wrap
board panel
dog messan, messet, peke, pet, pom, shough
jointed clinch
pert. gremial
robe afghan, blanket, coverlet, rug, throw

LA PASIONARIA dolores ibaruri

LAPEL facing, flap, fold, lappet, revere, revers

LAPHRIA artemis

LAPIDARY engraver, jeweler, stonecutter, *instrument* dial, dop, pewtermill

LAPIDATE kill, pelt, stone

LAPIDEOUS hard, rocky, solid, stony

LAPIDOTH *wife* deborah

LAPIN coney, fur, hare, rabbit

LAPIS LAZULI azure, blue, cobalt, lazulite, lazurite, sapphire, smalt, stone, ultramarine

LAPITH *enemy* centaurs *king* ixion phlegyas, pirithous

LAPLAND *city* kola *god* jumula, rot *magic drum* quodba *people* sami *santa claus* yule swain *sled* pulk(a)

LAPPET barbe, cornet, ear, fanon, flap, fold, infula, lap(el), lobe, moth, pan, streamer, wattle

LAPSE apostasy, backslide, blunder, boner, breach, break, bull, course, crime, decline, decrease, descend, deteriorate, deviate, die, end, error, expire, failing, false-step, fault, faux pas, floater, foible, frailty, inadvertence, indiscretion, interval, miscue, misstep, mistake, offense, omission, oversight, pass(age), pause, progress, recede, recidivism, return, reversion, revert, run out, shortcoming, sin, sink, slide, slip, stumble, surrection, tardy, trip, violation *pert.* caducous

LAPUTA *inhabitants* philosophers *kingdom* lagado

LAPUTAN absurd, fanciful, preposterous

LAPWING bird, flopwing, hoopoe, hornpie, pee(s)weep, pewit, piewipe, plover, teewhaap, tewit, teruter, teuchit, tirwit, tuit, vanellus, weep, wype

LARCENER See THIEF.

LARCENOUS brigandish, light-fingered, piratic, piraty,

priggish, stealy, sticky-fingered, thieving, thievish

LARCENY banditry, burglary, felony, robbery, stealing, theft

LARCH epinette, juniper, larix, tamarack, tree

LARD adeps, adipose, axunge, bedeck, blubber, enarm, enrich, fat(ten), flare, fleck, garnish, grease, improve, laird, line, lord, marrow, saindoux, strew, suet, tallow *and wax* cerates *source* fat-back

LARDER buttery, cave, dairy(house), pantry, provisions, spence, stillroom, store(room)

LARDY unctuous

LARDYDARDY affected, dandyish

LARGE ample, astronomical, big(gish), blown up, bold, broad, bulky, bull, bumper, burly, capacious, colossal, comprehensive, considerable, copious, enormous, excessive, exorbitant, extensive, extreme, fat, free, generous, gigantic, goodly, grand, great, heroic, huge, hulky, immense, inordinate, liberal, mammoth, man-sized, massive, obese, prodigious, renky, sizable, sollicker, spacious, substantial, swacking, tall, tidy, titanic, tremendous, vast, wal(l)y, weighty, wide *amount* bushels, heaps, scads *comb.* macr(o), meg(a), megal(o) *-eared* macrotous *extremely* astronomical, giant, gigantic, goliath, huge, immense, jumbo, swacking, whacking *-footed* megapod *-hearted* charitable, generous, liberal, sympathetic *-nosed* nasute *-skulled* macrocephalic *-toothed* macrodont(ic), megadont(ic) *-winged* macropterous

LARGENESS bigness, breadth, bulk, liberality, magnitude, prolixity, range, scope

LARGESS benefaction, boon, bounty, contribution, donation, fairing, favor, free-

dom, generosity, gift, grant, gratuity, largition, liberality, present, sportula, subvention

LARGEST maximum

LARIAT cabestro, lasso, lazo, noose, reata, riata, rope, trap *loop* honda, hondo(o), hondou

LARK adventure, alauda, alouette, bird, calander, calandre, canter, caper, escapade, frolic, gambol, jape(ry), laverock, mischief, parchment, peewee, pipit, play, prank, revel, singer, spree, sturnella, trick, wagtail *bunting* finch, longspur *butty* meadow-pippit *group* bevy, exaltation *plover* seed-snipe *sparrow* quàilhead *symbol of* cheerfulness *white* snow-bunting

LARKSPUR delphinium, locoweed, staggerweed, stavesacre

LARRIKIN clown, disorderly, hoodlum, loafer, rough, rowdy, street arab

LARRUP beat, flog, HIT, pound, thrash, wallop, whip

LARRY confusion, excitement, grout, hoe, mortar, noise

LARVA atrocha, aurelia, caterpillar, chrysalis, cocoon, embryo, ghost, grub, nymph, pupa, redia, slug, spector, spirit, wiggler, worm, wriggler *aquatic* hellgrammite *beetle* grub *early stage* pupa, redia *eye* loa, pseudocellus *final stage* chrysalis *fly* bot(t) *footless* maggot *free-swimming* trochophore *pert.* nepionic *wingless* creeper, maggot

LARVATE concealed, hidden, masked, obscure

LARYNX adam's apple, gullet, throat, voicebox *disorder* alalia, croup *opening* glottis

LASCAR boatman, mariner, sailor, serang, soldier

LASCIVIOUS amoral, bawdy, blissom, carnal, coarse, concupiscent, erotic,

fleshly, goatish, gross, immoral, indecent, lecherous, lewd, libertine, libidinous, licentious, lickerish, lubric(i)ous, lustful, obscene, prurient, salacious, satyric(al), sensual, wanton
LASCIVIOUSNESS aselgeia, lechery
LASER *weapon* death-ray
LASERWORT silphium
LASH abuse, anchor, assail, baste, batter, BEAT, belabor, belt, berate, bind, blister, buffet, cane, canvass, careless, cartwhip, castigate, chastise, chilly, comb, dash, drive, fasten, flabby, flagellate, flash, flay, flog, goad, impel, lace, lavish, loose, negligent, pommel, pour, prod, push, quirt, rate, raw, relaxed, scold, scourge, secure, slap, smite, spank, squander, stripe, stroke, switch, thong, THRASH, tie, trice, urge, wet, ship, yerk
mark welt
out at attack
LASS(IE) beloved, colleen, damozel, damsel, filly, gill, girl, petticoat, sweetheart, tendrel, trull, wench
LASSITUDE blues, dumps, ennui, exhaustion, languor, lethargy, sluggishness, stupor, torpor, vapors, weakness, weariness
LASSO cabestro, catch, circle, hook, lariat, lash, noose, reata, riata, rope, trap
LAST abide, aby, aftermath, block, cellar, cling, closing, coda, concluding, continue, darrein, dernier, dure, end, endure, eventual, extend, extreme, final, finish, following, hindmost, hold, latest, linger, loser, losing, lowest, newest, omega, outlive, pattern, persist, reach, remain, stand, stay, supreme, survive, swansong, tail(end), terminal, trailing, ultimate, utmost, wear
but 1 penult(imate)
but 2 antepenult(imate)
days of pompeii, character ione, nydia
lap end, finish
long outwear, perendure
man charles i

of the fathers bernard
of the goths roderick
of the greeks philopeomen
of the mohicans uncas
of the romanovs anastasia
of the romans aetius, brutus, stilicho
of the tribunes cola di rienzi
place prize booby, consolation, sop
supper cena, coena, communion, eucharist, maundy
supper room cenacle
supper vessel hanap, holy grail, sangreal
LASTING abiding, chronic, constant, continuing, daylong, diuturnal, dragged, durable, enduring, eternal, extended, fixed, languishing, lasty, lengthened, lifetime, lingering, livelong, long drawn out, long-lived, longstanding, macrobiotic, overlong, perdurable, perennial, permanent, perpetual, persistent, persisting, prolonged, protracted, remaining, remembered, solid, spunout, stable, standing, staying, steadfast, strong, sturdy
briefly ephemeral, temporary
for many years plurennial
LASTLY conclusively, finally, in conclusion, in fine, recently
LATAKIA tobacco
LATCH alight, anoint, belay, bolt, catch, clicket, clink, close, comprehend, fastener, get, grasp, haggaday, hook, lasket, lock, moisten, receive, seize, shack, shut, snare, sneck, snick, take
on to cling, get
LATCHET gurnard, loop, strap, thong
LATCHKEY clicket, passkey
LATE back(ward), behind(time), belated, dead, deceased, deep, delayed, departed, detained, dilatory, dillydallying, easygoing, eleventh-hour, far on, held up, lackadaisical, lagging, latrede, lax, lingering, loitering, micawberish, moratory, neoteric, new, overdue, past, recent(ly), remiss, serotine, slack, slow, sluggish, sometime, tardy, tedious, umquhile, umwhile,

unpunctual, unready, untimely
comb. neo
LATELY latterly, not long ago, recent(ly), slowly
LATEMOST final, last
LATENT abeyant, asleep, concealed, delitescent, dormant, hidden, idle, immature, inactive, inert, larval, latescent, lurking, obscure, possible, potential, quiescent, rudimentary, secret, smoldering, suspended, underlying, undeveloped, unrevealed, unripe, veiled, virtual
LATER after(while), anon, behind, by and by, elder, following, future, hereafter, neozoic, newer, posterior, presently, proximate, puisne, soon, subsequently, ulterior
LATERAL flank(ing), indirect, pass, side(ward), skirting
LATERALLY aside, askance, asquint, edgeways, edgewise, right and left, sidewards, sideways, sidewise
LATEST craze, fad, farthest, final, last, latter, modern, newest, novelty, present, rage, terminal
LATEX fluid, gutta, juice, milk, rubber, sorva
coagulant achete
containing laticiferous
LATH face, scantling, slat, spale, splent, splint, stave, stooth, strip, swale
backing furring
house nursery
-legged spindly, thin
LATHE barn, beater, capstan, chuck, granary, mandrel, potter's wheel, sley, throw, tool, turn, turret, wisket
capacity swing
copying blanchard
holder monitor
operator turner
part apron, bed, chuck, faceplate, feedrod, mandrel, poppethead, pulley, setover, tailstock, toolpost
primitive pole
turning throw
LATHER beat, cream, flog, foam, freath, frenzy, froth, fume, head, impatience, scum, soap, suds, spume,

strike, sweat, thrash, wallop, wash, yeast

LATHYRUS beach-pea, bitter-vetch, camp-pea, pride-of-california

LATIFOLIA bladder-campion

LATIN (See also ROMAN.) chicano, cuban, italian, mexican, south american, spaniard
dance mambo
dictionarist calepino
grammar donat, donet
grammatical case ablative, accusative, dative, genitive, nominative, vocative
pronoun ego, hic, ille, ipse, iste

LATIN AMERICA See SOUTH AMERICA.

LATINUS *daughter* lavinia
father faunus
kingdom latium
son-in-law aeneas
wife amata

LATITUDE amplitude, breadth, compass, deviation, elbowroom, extent, freedom, laxity, leeway, locality, margin, play, range, reach, region, room, rope, scope, space, sweep, swing, way, width, zone
complement colatitude
difference in southing
measure degree, parallel
zero degrees equator

LATITUDINARIAN freethinker, liberal

LATIUM *city* alba longa
tribe aequi

LATONA See LETO.

LA TOSCA floria

LATRANT barking, complaining, snarling

LATRINE boggard, privy, toilet

LATRON brigand

LATTER last, later, latest, modern, past, recent, second
day saint irvingite, mormon

LATTICE cancelli, cancels, confines, espalier, filigree, frame(work), fret(work), grating, grill(e), herse, limits, pinjra, tracery, treillage, trellis, umbrel, window
-like cancellate(d), cancellous, clathrate
plant cape asparagus, laceleaf

-work grate, grating, tukutuku

LATVIA *capital* riga
city cesis, dunaberg, dvinsk, jelgava, libau, libava, rezekne, riga, tukums, valmiera
coin kapeika, lat(u), rublis, santims
measure arshin, deciatine, kanne, krouchka, kroushka, kulmet, let, lofstelle, pourvette, sagene, stof(f), stoof, tonnseteel, verchoc, verchok
native balt, lett
parliament sacima
part courland, kurland
port riga
river gauja, lielupe, ogre, salaca
weight liespfund

LAUD acclaim, adore, anthem, antiphon, applaud, canon, canticle, celebrate, cittern, commend, compliment, eulogize, exalt, extol, glorify, hymn, lute, macarize, magnify, panegyric, praise, psalm, revere(nce), sing, song, worship, venerate

LAUDABLE allowable, commendable, exemplary, praiseworthy

LAUDATIOUS sumptuous

LAUDATORY acclamatory, applausive, approbative, epenitic, eulogy, praising

LAUFEY *son* loki

LAUGH boff, boffo(la), cachinnate, cachinnation, cackle, checkle, chortle, chuckle, convulsion, crow, deride, fleer, gaff, giggle, grizzle, guffaw, ha(w)-ha(w), hee-hee, jeer, jubilate, mirth, nicker, rejoice, rire, ris, risibility, roar, scoff, shake, shout, shriek, smile, smudge, snicker, snigger, sniggle, snort, split, tee-hee, titter
at deride, flout, hoot, insult, mock, ridicule
comb. gelo(to)
disposed to risible
incipient grin, smile
loud gauster
off dismiss
pert. gelastic, gelogemic

LAUGHABLE absurd, amusing, asinine, comic(al), convulsing, droll, facetious,

farcical, funny, inane, jocose, jocular, ludicrous, ridiculous, risible, risorial, sidesplitting, tickling, waggish, witty

LAUGHER hyena

LAUGHING cheerful, derisive, derisory, gay, gibbly, gleeful, hysterical, merry, mirthful, riant, rident, risible
bird gull, loon, pewit, woodpecker
buddha maitreya
crow thrush
gas nitrous oxide
gull blackcap, pewit
jackass arethusa, clockbird, kingfisher, orchid
owl wekau, whekau

LAUGHINGSTOCK butt, guy, joke, ridicule, sport

LAUGHTER cachinnation, cackle, chuckles, gales, hilarity, hysteria, hysterics, irrition, jubilation, merriment, mirth, risibility, risus, snirt
comb. gelo(to)
foolish abderian
-loving jolly, merry
name meaning isaac
-pert. risorial
-prone ridibund
-provoking gelogenic
rude heehaw

LAUNCE *dog* crab
master proteus

LAUNCH actify, activate, activize, baptize, barrage, begin, boat, bombard, cast, catapult, dart, descant, fire, float, hurl, institute, jump, lance, leap, pierce, plunge, prick, project, propel, release, send(up), shoot, shove off, skip, start, throw, wound
upon undertake

LAUNCHING blast-off, count-down, inauguration, lift-off, opening, start
instrument bazooka, pad
time d-day

LAUNDER lave, rinse, sluice, trough, type, wash

LAUNDERER, LAUNDRESS trilby, washerwoman

LAUNDRY blanchisserie, laundromat, lavatory, wash(ing)
liquid bluing
service rough-dry

LAUNFAL *abode* oleron
beloved tryamour
leader king arthur
LAURA *author* caspary
beloved petrarch
LAUREATE crown(ed), distinguished, honor(ed), poet
LAUREL aniba, aucuba, award, bay(berry), brewster, cajeput, cajuput, calfkill, cassytha, cordia, crown, daphne, distinction, fame, garland, honor, ivy(wood), kalmia, madrona, mallet, myrtle, oleander, palm, persea, petterwood, pittospor(um), reward, rhipsalis, salmon, shrub, sweetwood, tarairi, tarata, tree, trophy, wicky, woevine, wreath
bank, medicinal coto
bay magnolia
big-leaf rhododendron
black loblolly bay
butter bayberry oil
changed to daphne
comb. lauro
crowned with laureate
fresh water salmon
great spoonhutch
ground arbutus
hawthorn toyon
mountain calicobush
oak acajou
wood madrona
wreath eiresione, honor
LAURENCE, St *emblem* gridiron
LAURUSTINE viburnum
LAUSUS *father* mezentius, numitor
sister ilia
slayer aeneas, amulius
LAVA (See also *kind*, below.) asperite, basalt, bomb, cinders, clinker, lapillus, magma, pahoehoe, scoria, slag, verite
basaltic malpais
block aphrolite
cinder scoria
coarse puglianite
extrusive gaussbergite
field pedregal
fragment ash, favilla, lapillos
hole fumerole
kind asperite, dacite, latite, malpais, orendite, pantellerite, taxite, venanzite, verite
mass bomb, coulee
pulverized ashes
solidified coulee

source pyrosphere
stream coulee
LAVABO basin, cleansing, lavatory, trough, washbowl
LAVACRE bathtub
LAVALAVA kilt, sulu
LAVALIERE jewelry, ornament, pendant
LAVANDULA See LAVENDER.
LAVATORY bagnio, balneum, basin, bath(house), bowl, cabana, caldarium, sauna, sudatorium, sweatroom, tepidarium, trough, tub, vaporarium, washbowl, washroom
LAVE asperge, bail, bathe, clean, deterge, dip, droop(ing), lade, leave, pour, remainder, rest, rinse, sea, soak, wash
LAVENDER amethyst, aspic, behen, cassidony, color, flower, inkroot, laundress, mint, perfume, perse, plant, purple, spick, stechados, stichado(s), washer
cotton santolina
great aspic
pert. violaceous
LAVENGRO *author* borrow
heroine isopel berners
LAVER amanori, basin, cistern, font, phiale, porphyra, sealettuce, seaweed, ulva, washbasin, washbowl
LAVINIA *betrothed* turnus
brother lucius, martius, mutius, quintus
husband aeneas, bassianus
lover bassianus
parent amata, latinus, titus andronicus
tormentor chiron, demetrius
LAVISH abundant, bestow, bountiful, copious, dissipate, dote, excessive, extravagant, exuberant, flush, free, generous, give, handsome, heap upon, improvident, inordinate, liberal, lush, luxuriant, luxurious, munificent, opulent, ornate, prodigal, profligate, profuse, sport, squander, sumptuous, thriftless, unstinted, wanton, waste(ful), wild
LAW act, adat, authority, axiom, bill, canon, code, command(ment), constitution, decalog(ue), decree, derecho, dharma, dictate, doom, droit, edict, enact-

ment, fas, form(ality), formula, jure, jurisprudence, jus, justice, legislation, lex, litigation, mandate, measure, nomos, order, ordinance, precept, prescript(ion), principle, reglement, regulation, rogation, rubric, rule, ruling, statute, sutra(h), talion, talmud, theorem, tora(h)
-abiding obedient
abstract jus
action See *suit*, below.
advocate of new neonomian
and order (See also ORDER.) enforcement, peace
and order, lacking, comb. anomy
biblical decalog(us), pentateuch, tora(h)
body code, constitution
case, famous cause-celebre
case, postponed remanet
claim hakh, lien
client, female domina litis
client, male dominus litis
comb. leg(i), nomo
compilation codex, corpus juris
contrary to illegal, illicit, unconstitutional, unlawful
court clerk prothonotary
court official amala(h), judge
decree edict, fiat, finding, nisi
degree llb, lld
deity maat, misharu, zeus
dietary kashruth
divine fas
document capias, deed, elegit, summons, writ
enforcer police, sheriff
evil privilege
expounder of jurist
fictitious name in doe, roe
formed by corporate
-giver moses, solon, thesmothete
kind blue, canon, chancery, civil, common, criminal, curfew, dharma, equity, maritime, pandect, sutra, sutta
manu sutra, sutta
marriage levirate
matter tort
moral, god of varuna
mosaic See *biblical*, above.
offense crime, delict, error, malum, sin, tort
of nations droit des gens

of the land lex terrae
opposer anarchist, criminal
opposition to antilegalism, antinomy
oral noncupative, parol
order writ
permitted by See *within the,* below.
pert. canonic(al), forensic, judicial, legal, legislative
philosophy jurisprudence
points gonia, lis, res
proceedings action
proposed bill
prosecution See LAWSUIT.
religious fas, halakha
responsible in age of discretion
science of nomology
student stagiary
term abandum, abate, abator, ademption, amise, backberend, certiorari, constat, defendant, delict, detinue, droit, estreat, ex jure, forprise, intestate, ivisi, jus, laches, malum, mora, nisi, nolo-contendere, res, seizin, subpoena, tort, trover, venue
treatise nomography
versed in legist
volume codex
warning caveat
within the canonic, due, ennomic, just, legal, legitimate, licit, right, valid
without, comb. anomy
writ allocatur, warrant
written lex scripta
LAWBREAKER criminal, desperado, felon, hoodlum, hougher, nogoodnik, offender, sinner, transgressor, violator, wrongdoer
LAWFUL allowable, allowed, condign, constitutional, due, ennomic, just(ifiable), justified, leesome, legal, legitimate, licit, liefsome, permitted, right(ful), valid, warranted
LAWLESS anarchic, disobedient, illegal, illegitimate, lewd, ruffian, unlawful, unruly
LAWLESSNESS anarchy, anomie, anomy, disorder, insurrection, license, mob rule, riot(ing), unruliness, vice
LAWMAKER assemblyman, congressman, delegate, legifer, legislator, nomog-

rapher, representative, senator, solon
LAWMAKING constitutive, enactive, legislation, nomothetic
LAWMAN judge, justice, LAWYER.
LAWN arbor, batiste, cambric, cloth, cotton, cyprus, fabric, glade, grass, green(sward), linon, quintin, sieve, sod, sward, terrace, tiffany, turf, umple, yard
billiards troco
bowling bocci(e), boule
disease brown patch
pest bermuda grass, crab grass, dandelion, devil grass, fleabane, golden rod, orchard grass, oxalis, plantain, prairie grass, spurge, weeds
LAWRENCE, D. H. *novel* kangaroo, lady chatterley's lover, sons and lovers, the rainbow, women in love
LAWRENCE, St *tears* meteor, shooting star
LAWRENCE, T. E. *alias* shaw
LAWSUIT action, assumpsit, brabble, case, lege, lis, litigation, prosecution, replevin, truebill
continuance imparlance
engaged in appellant, defendant, litigant, plaintiff, suitor
subject of res
LAWYER abogado, advocate, agent, amicus curiae, attorney(at law), avocato, avoue, barrister, bencher, brehon, commoner, conveyancer, counsel(lor), deputy, green bag, hirst, intercessor, jurist, legist, mouthpiece, pettifogger, pleader, proctor, procurator, prosecutor, scrutator, shark, solicitor, templar, trampler, vakeel, vakil
creeping blackberry
dishonest ambulance-chaser, pettifogger, shyster
fee retainer
fictional perry mason, tutt
gangster's mouthpiece
inferior leguleian
-like leguleian
patron saint ives, yves
robe silk
woman portia

LAX backward, careless, derelict, dissolute, dull, flabby, flaccid, free, improvident, indolent, lenient, licentious, limp, loose, neglectful, negligent, open, relaxed, remiss, salmon, slack, slow, soft(en), swag, tardy, unrestrained, vague, wanton, weak
LAXATIVE aperient, hydromel, lapactic, relaxant, solutive
LAXITY freedom, laschety, latitude, looseness, neglect, negligence, relaxation, remissness, slack
LAY aim, air, apply, ascribe, attach, ballad, bet, bury, business, carol, chanty, civil, congregational, cover, creed, deposit, direct(ion), ditty, drop, exorcise, faith, heap, impose, impute, inter, laic(al), law, level, lie, locate, lyric, melody, moderate, pave, place, plant, poem, point, popular, position, profane, price, put, quiet, reclined, relieve, repose, rest, row, secular(ist), set, settle, smooth, song, spread, stratum, superimpose, tune, wager
about attack, hustle, struggle, try
anchor moor
an egg bomb, fail, flop
aside or away abandon, cashier, delay, deposit, discard, dismiss, doff, dump, neglect, pigeonhole, prepare, remove, save, shelve, shuck, store, table
back dog, goldbrick, shirk
bare confess, denude, detect, disclose, expose, open, reveal, strip, uncover
by accumulate, amass, cache, deposit, hive, hoard, husband, reposit, save, store, stow, treasure
crosswise cob
down abdicate, affirm, ante(up), bet, careen, establish, plant, posit, postulate, prescribe, relinquish, rest, set, stipulate, store, surrender, yield
down the law dogmatize, insist, proscribe, reprimand
eggs ledge, oviposit, warp
for ambush, intercept
forth display, exhibit, show

hands on acquire, attack, bless, catch, grab, impose, maul, ordain, seize
hold of affect, apprehend, arrest, catch, fang, grip(e), latch, seize, take
in See *by*, above.
into attack, beat
it on thick coat, exaggerate, flatter, lavish, overcharge, overdo, smalm, smarm
low fell, kill, slay, strew, strike, weaken
money on back, bank on, bet on, rely on, support
off cashier, cease, circumscribe, desist, discharge, dismiss(al), don't, drop, explain, fire, furlough, hedge, jettison, measure, reduce, refrain, removal, respite, shutdown, silence, stop, unburden
on administer, apply, attack, beat, cover, impose, inflict, paste, spread, strike
oneself out exert, strive, try
open break, expose, reveal, unmask
out cast, chart, deaden, diagram, disburse, disperse, display, dummy, establishment, exercise, exert, exhibit, expend, extend, fell, invest, kill, map, mise, outline, plan, plot, purpose, scheme, seek, set-up, spend, spread, tableau, wardrobe
over cover, delay, excel, postpone, sojourn, stay, surpass, whip
siege beset, court, woo
to assault, attack, attribute, blame, press, try
to rest bury, inhume, inter
up afflict, bestow, confine, disable, excel, heap, hive, hoard, hospitalize, put by, reserve, save, shelve, stock, store, treasure
waste depredate, desolate, destroy, devastate, harass, peel, pillage, ravage, ruin
LAYBOY jogger
LAYER bed(ding), belt, blanket, carpet, chess, coat, coping, couch, course, crust, deck, delaminate, desquamate, dess, exfoliate, fascia, film, flag, flake, hen, lamina, lap, level, lissom, measure, patina, ply, provine, scale, seam, shelf, skin, slab, stage, story,

strata, stratify, stratum, streak, table, tier, veneer, zone
bottom bedding
leaflike folium
LAYERED filmy, flaky, foliaceous, foliated, lamellate, laminate(d), leafy, membranous, deacon, gauche, stratified, stratose, tabloid, tabular, tiered
LAYLOCK lilac
LAYMAN amateur, catechumen, deacon, gauche, laic, nonprofessional, parishioner, secular, stranger
group cofradia
LAYNE conceal, disguise, hide
LAZAR leper, outcast
LAZARET(TO) hospital, leprosarium, leprosary, spital
LAZARUS *home* bethany
sister martha, mary
LAZE idle(ness), estivate, lop, lounge, malinger, otiose, sloth, soldier
LAZINESS accidie, acedia, apathy, feverlurden, indifference, oisivity, sloth, springfever, torpor
LAZULITE azure(stone), blue spar, lapis-lazuli
LAZY clumpst, clumse, comatose, droghlin, faineant, feckless, idle, inactive indolent, inert, languid, lax, lethargic, limpsy, listless, lither, lurdan, luther, negligent, otiose, passive, relaxed, remiss, slack, sliving, sloan, slothful, slouchy, slow, sluggard, sluggish, supine, sweert, torpid, traily, vicious, wicked
susan turntable
LAZYBONES bum, drone, idler, indolent, loafer, lusk, slouch, sluggard
LAZZARONE bum, vagabond
LEA fallow, grassland, lay, mead(ow), pasture, prairie, scythe, unplowed
LEACH dissolve, letch, lixiviate, melt, moisten, percolate, refine, slice, soften, wet
LEACHY pervious, porous
LEAD actor, advance, allure, avant-garde, ballast, bear, beckon, begin, blaze, bring, bullets, captain, carry, cart, chief, clew, clue, command,

conduct, control, convey, counsel, dade, direct, dominate, drag, element, engineer, entice, escort, excel, first, fix, front, graphite, gravitate, guide, head, hero, induce, influence, instruct, manage, manuduce, marshall, mayne, metal, outstrip, persuade, pilot, pioneer, plumbago, plumbum, point, precede, precent, presa, prevail on, set, shepherd, sinker, solder, spearhead, spend, star(t), steer, surpass, tee, tend, top, tote, van, wad, weight
alloy calin, frary metal, pewter, terne
ash litharge
astray allure, betray, deceive, delude, entice, inveigle, lure, mang, mislead, pervert, seduce, tempt
black graphite, plumbago, wad(d)
blue galena
carbonate ceruse, cerussite
chromate crocoite
color dull, gray, livid, olive, plomb, wan
comb. molybdo, plumb(i), plumbo
compound aikinite, bayldonite, bellite, cesarolite, coronadite, penfieldite, plattnerite, pyromorphite, ramdohrite, rathite
deep sea dipsey, dipsy
glass strass
hot clew, clue
impure base-bullion
mineral fiedlerite
mock blende, plummet, sphalerite
monoxide litharge, massicot
musical presa
ocher massicot
on decoy, inveigle
ore anglesite, galena, pyromorphite
paste strass
pellet bullet, shot
pencil graphite
pig fother
pipe cinch certainty
planet saturn
plumbing bluex
poisoning millreek, painter's colic, plumbism
red corcoite, minium
red ore crocoite
silicate barysilite
singleton sneak

sounding plummet
sulphate anglesite, caracolite
sulphide galena, gergronite
telluride altaite
the way pace
-tin calin, solder
tin coat terne
to advance, entail, precede
tungstate raspite
white blanc d'argent, ceruse, cerussite, krems
work plumbage, plumbing

LEADEN base, cheap, cumbrous, dull, dun, gloomy, heavy, inert, lackluster, languid, listless, massive, oppressive, plumbean, plumbeous, plumbic, saturnine, sluggish, unfeeling, unwieldy

LEADER 3 ace, cid, dux, yan 4 boss, cock, datu, duce, duke, jefe, king, naik, omda, tyee 5 akela, baron, chief, doyen, first, guide, mahdi, omdeh, pacer, pilot, ruler, scout, seyid, titan 6 archon, caliph, cantor, despot, fuhrer, master, opener, sachem, sayyid, tendon, topdog, tycoon, victor 7 article, bellcow, captain, drungar, ellider, foreman, head man, manager, marshal, officer, prophet, skipper, supremo, viceroy 8 bellmare, caudillo, chairman, coxswain, director, ethnarch, favorite, governor, shepherd 9 chieftain, commander, conductor, editorial, forehorse, gauleiter, headliner, pacemaker, precentor, president, strategos, topbanana 10 avantgarde, bellwether, controller, coryphaeus, headhoncho, pacesetter, 11 frontrunner, predecessor 14 standardbearer
black abernathy, bradley, brooke, brown, carmichael, chisholm, cleaver, jackson, king, malcolm x, marshall, muhammad ali, newton, powell, randolph, seale, stokes, wilkins, young
comb. agog(ue)
name meaning guy
without acephalous

LEADERSHIP aegis, authority, bal(e)batim, charisma, chiefdom, conduct, direction, establishment, guidance, hegemony, manage-

ment, mastery, power structure
pert. ducal

LEADING ahead, banner, big, capital, central, chief, direction, dominant, eminent, example, favorite, first, foremost, governing, guidance, guiding, head, hint, important, in front, main, on top, paramount, preceding, principal, prominent, ruling, stellar, suggestion, supreme, tending, van
comb. agog(ue)
two ways bivious

LEADWORT crowtoe, plumbago

LEAF blade, bract(eole)(let), buyo, cadjan, carpel, coca, cotyledon, flap, foliage, folio(le), folium, frond, fulyie, fulzie, gluma, glume, grass, involucre, involucrum, lamina, leave, lemma, membrane, needle, ola(y), olla, page, paillette, pa(u)n, petal, pile, scale, sepal, sheet, spathe, spear, spire, stipule, tepal
angle axil
aperture stoma
appendage bract(eole)(let), glume, ligula, spathe, stipel, stipule
aromatic See HERB.
arrangement phyllotaxy
base fovea, pericladium
-bearing foliaceous
blade lamina, limb, pagina
bud gemma
circle corolla
comb. phyll(o)
curvature epinasty
disease erinea, mosaic
eater koala
edge crenation
excess of pleiophylly
extra insert
exudate honeydew
floating lilypad, pad
gland lenticel
grass blade
green chlorophyll
gum tragacanth
having foliar, foliated
having rough asperifoliate
heddles gear
hinged alap
hollow phyllode
hopper dikrella, dodger, homopter, jassid, thrips
kind calyx, corolla, petal, sepal

large frond
louse aphid
manna lerp
medicinal bucha, senna
mid-rib penna
miner ant, hispa
modified bract, bracteole, bractlet
mold kolinsky
-nosed phyllorhine
part areola, angle, axil, blade, bract, corolla, costa, crenation, folium, lenticel, ligule, lobe, lobule, midrib, nervure, pagina, pen, petal, petiole, pore, rib, sepal, stalk, stem, stipel, stipule, stoma(ta), vein
pert. foliar, peltate, phylline, sinuate
pinnate jugate
point mucro
pointed apiculate
pores stoma(ta)
-producing phyllogenetic
rudimentary cataphyll(um)
scorch mellisiose
-shaped acuminate, acute, acerose, cordate, crenate, cuneate, deltoid, dentate, ensiform, linear, obovate, obtuse, ovate, palmate, pinnate, reniform, serrate, spatulate
small frondlet
spot frogeye
stalk angle, axil, celery, petiole, stem
stem, pert. petriolar
stemmed caulescent
strip of defoliate
thin lamella
vein costa, nervure, rib
vein arrangement venation
wasp sawfly
without aphyllose, aphyllous

LEAFLET bill, brochure, catalog(ue), circular, dodger, folder, handbill, literature, pamphlet, pinna, tract

LEAFY green, foliate, foliose, frondose

LEAGUE agreement, alliance, ally, amalgamate, association, band, bloc(k), bond, bund, coalition, combination, combine, compact, company, confederacy, confederation, conjoin, convenant, federation, fusion, group, hansa, hanse, join, length, partnership, party, pool, set, society, systasis, treaty, union

baseball american, national
merchants hansa, hanse
of nations city geneva
pert. federal
LEAGUER besiege, camp, siege
LEAH *burial site* machpelah
father laban
husband jacob
offspring dinah, issachar, levi, simeon
sister rachel
LEAK betray, chink, cleft, crack, crevice, disclose, distil, divulge, dribble, drip (ping), drop, escape, exude, fissure, hole, loss, ooze, perforation, pit, puncture, reveal, screeve, seep, sigger, spill, tell, trickle, trill, ullage, waste, weep, zigger
-proof impervious, secure
repair calk
LEAL accurate, constant, correct, faithful, genuine, just, lawful, legal, loyal, real, resolute, sta(u)nch, steadfast, true, trustworthy
LEAM beam, blaze, flash, gleam, glimmer, husk, shell
LEAN angular, bare, bear, bend, bony, cant, careen, confide, curve, depend, deviate, divert, emaciated, fleshless, gangling, gangly, gaunt(ed)(y), gawkward, gawky, gravitate, haggard, heel, incline, lank(y), lantern-jawed, lathy, list, meager, pinched, poor, rangy, rattleboned, rawboned, rely, rest, ribby, rigwiddie, rigwiddy, scanty, scraggy, scrannel, scranny, scrawny, sheer, skeletal, skinny, slabsided, slank, slant, slender, slight, slim, slink(y), slope, slunken, spare, spindling, spindly, svelte, sway, sylphlike, tend, thin(faced)(set), thrawn, tilt, tip, toom, underweight, unproductive, weedy, willowy
as a beanpole, rake
minded unintelligent
on depend on, rely, straddle
-to hut, linter, outshot, shack, shed, shelter, skillion
toward prefer
LEANDER *beloved* hero
river hellespont
LEANING acclinal, accumbent, affection, anaclisis,

aptitude, bent, bias, decubitis, dependency, disposition, faculty, flair, gift, inclination, inclinatory, incumbent, lopsided, partiality, penchant, preference, prejudice, proclivity, propensity, reclining, relying, tendency, tending, turn
tower city pisa
LEAP ballone, ballotade, bounce, bound, buck (jump), caper, capriole, clear, curvet, dance, dart, demivolt, dive, entrechat, fly, frisk, gambol, hippetyhop, hop, hurdle, increase, jump, loup, lowp, lowr, lunge, negotiate, pole vault, pounce, pulse, ramp, salto, sault, scoup, skip, spang (hew), sprent, spring, sprunt, start, stend, throb, vault
suicidal brodie
year bissextile
LEAPING bouncing, bounding, caprizant, hopping, hurdling, salience, salient, saltant, saltation, springing, steeplechase, vaulting, timber-topping
upon supersalient
LEAR (See also KING LEAR.) doctrine, gravy, lair, learning, lere, lesson, lore, sauce, tape
LEARCHUS *brother* glaucus, melicerta
parent athamas, ino
slayer athamas
LEARN ascertain, con, determine, discover, divine, edify, find out, glean, have, hear of, get(on to)(wise to), hear, lear, lere, master, realize, see, study, teach, unearth
by heart memorize
LEARNED academic, abstruse, bookish, cultured, doctus, educated, erudite, esoteric, expert, grounded, informed, lettered, literate, mastered, pedantic, polymathic, profound, recondite, sage, scholarly, versed, wise
class clerisy, intelligentsia, literati
person academician, acharya, bhat, bleu, bluestocking, bookman, bookworm, brahman, egghead, erudite, high-

brow, inkhorn, intellectual, minerva, ollav, pedant, philomath, polyhistor, pundit, sage, savant, scholar, seer, teacher
LEARNER abecedarian, abecedary, apprentice, autodidact, beginner, catechumen, coed, collegian, disciple, initiate, matriculant, neophyte, novice, plebe, prentice, probationer, pupil, schoolboy, schoolgirl, student, trainee, tyro
LEARNING accomplishments, acquirements, art, attainments, booklore, culture, doctorship, education, enlightenment, erudition, information, insight, instruction, ken, knowledge, lear, lore, mathesis, pedantry, philomath, scholarship, science, skill, wisdom, wit
ancient center alexandria
deity quetzalcoatl, sarasvati, seshat
display of pedantry
encyclopedic polyhistor, polymathy
in old age opsimathy
love of philology
pert. palladian
place academe, academy, athenaeum, college, school, seminary, university
LEASE assedat, backtack, charter, common, contract, convey, cowle, demise, engage, glean, hire, let, lie, lisse, lying, pasture, patta, pick, pottah, remise, rent(al), sublet, tenure, untrue
bind by thirl
-hold homestead
-holder ijaradar, livier, renter, tenant
prepayment foregift
LEASH bind, bridle, cord, curb, deterrent, harl, hold, jess, lead, line, lish, lune, lyam, noose, rein, restrain(t), secure, shackle, snare, strap, string, swinge, tether, thone, three, tierce, trap, trash, whip
hound limer
ring terret
LEASING falsehood, lies, lying, renting
LEAST fewest, little, lowest, minimal, minimum, shortest, slightest, smallest

bit rap
flycatcher chebec
sandpiper oxeye, peep, stint
LEASTWAYS merely
LEATHER (See also *kind*, below.) baseball, beat, belting, castigate, cuir, hides, peau, shell, skin, skiver, strap, thrash, work, yuft
alum-dressed aluta
apron barmskin
artificial See *substitute*, below.
bag alforja
baseball cowhide, horsehide
bottle borachio, girba, matara, olpe
-colored alutaceous
comb. scyt(o)
convert into tan, taw
cordovan cordwain
crushed ecrase
cutter clicker
deposit on bloom
dressing dubbin(g), neatsfoot oil, shoepolish
dry(ing) sam(m), sammy
fine canepin, kid, suede, vellum
finish buff
fish foolfish, lija
flask See *bottle*, above.
flower clematis, viorna
form crimp
glove capeskin, kid, napa, pigskin, suede
hamper buffalo
hides jufty
imperfection, frieze
inspector sealer
kind aluta, antelope, balat, bark, basil, bock, broigne, buckskin, buff(alo), bulgar, bullneck, cabretta, calf (skin), canepin, cape(skin), castor, chammy, chamois, cheverel, cheveril, cordovan, cow(hide)(skin), dongola, doze, elk, goatskin, hogskin, jufti, kangaroo, kid, kip, korova, lambskin, levant, lizard, maroquin, mocha, morocco, napa, niger, oriole, oxhide, patent, pigskin, roan, russia, saddle, saffian, sealskin, shagreen, sheepskin, skiver, suede, trank, vellum, yuft
leaf cassandra
-like coriaceous, tough
machine edgekey, edger
moccasin loafer, weejun
moisten sam
mouse bat

napped suede
oil neatsfoot
pare skive
patch clout
pert. tooled
piece clout, latigo, thong, welt
piercer awl
pouch kit, sporran
prepare tan, taw
press pad, crimp
refuse spetch
sheepskin bock, buck, cabretta, roan, skiver
sheet buffing
shoe calf, pigskin, suede
shreds moslings
soft aluta, chamois, cordovan, doeskin, napa, suede
stocking character natty bumppo
strip belt, latugo, rand, thong, welt
strong buckskin, cowhide
substitute corfam, dermatine, keratol, vinyl
tool skiver
untanned shagreen
wash losh(e)
waste tanite
whip blacksnake
worker barker, bedder, chamar, chuckler, cordwainer, currier, fluffer, madiga, saddler, skinner, tanner, tawer
workshop grindery, tannery
LEATHERBACK luth, ruddy-duck, turtle
LEATHERHEAD dolt, dummy, friarbird
LEATHERJACKET alphitonia, black beech, cupania, filefish, grub, johnnycake, pancake, zapatero
LEATHERNECK gyrene, marine
LEAVE abandon, absence, adieu, allow(ance), approval, away, bequeath, bunk, buzz off, cede, concede, confide, conge, consent, cut out, decamp, demise, departure, desert, devise, endorsement, endow, entrust, escape, evacuate, exeat, exeunt, exit, farewell, flee, fly, forgo, forleit, forsake, furlough, grace, grant, largesse, let, levy, liberty, license, lief, permission, permit, quit, raise, relegate, relinquish, renounce, resign, retire, sabbatical, sacrifice, sanction, scram, sign out,

strand, suffer(ance), surrender, tolerance, vacate, vacation, vade, vamoose, waive, will, withdraw(al), yield
alone abandon, desolate, ditch, forbear, shun
behind abandon, beat, outdistance
destitute strand
hurriedly blow, bug out, bugger off, bundle off, flee, scat, scram, screw, scur, skip, skirr, take the air, vamoose
in the lurch abandon, desert, dismiss, maroon, slight, strand
of absence absit, exeat, furlough, sabbatical, vacation
off abbreviate, cease, desist, deval, don't, elide, forgear, forsake, halt, peter, quit, relinquish, stay, stop, surcease
out bate, elide, eliminate, omit, skip
permission to conge, exeat
-taking adieu, apopemptic, conge(e), departure, farewell, parting, valedictory, waygang
unauthorized awol
LEAVEN alloy, baking powder, barm, enliven, enzyme, ferment, imbue, impregnate, infuse, ingrain, inoculate, lighten, permeate, pervade, soda, suffuse, taint, temper, yeast, zyme
comb. zymo
LEAVENING barmy, diastatic, emptings, enzymic, fermentative, fermenting, peptic(al), raising, working, yeasty, zymic
LEAVES foliage, frondescence, leafage, pages, patrin, tea
boiled chard
dried bucco, bucho, buka, lauhala
handful patrin
having large macrophyllous
having narrow stenophyllous
medicinal bucco, bucku, coca, file, farfara, fumaria
styptic matico
withered induviae
LEAVINGS ash(es), balance, carry-over, chaff, culls, draff, dregs, dust, fragments, hash, junk, leftovers, odds and ends, orts, pieces,

refuse, relics, remainder, remains, remnants, residue, rest, scraps, waste

LEBAN *daughter* leah

LEBANON *capital* beirut, beyrouth

castle beaufort, saida, sidon, toron

city arca, baalbek, beirut, beyrouth, broummana, ehden, heliopolis, hermel, merjuyun, saida, sidon, sur, tripoli, tyre, sahle, zahla

coin livre, piastre

dance dabkeh, dabkey

drink arak, arrack

fort byblos

leader malik

peak aruba, hermon, ka-discha, kennisseh, mzar, sannine

people arab(ian), druse

plain elbika

poet kahlil gibran

port beirut, saida, sidon, sur, tripoli, tyre

prime minister karami

river damour, kasemieh, leontes, litani, lycos

tree cedar

valley beqaa

LEBBEK kok(k)o, siris

LEBENSRAUM space, territory

LECANIUM saissetia, scale

LECH capstone, monument, river, slab, stone

LECHEATES zeus

LECHER debauchee, don juan, erotic, goat, libertine, luxur, palliard, satyr, sensualist

LECHEROUS abandoned, boarish, carnal, dissolute, immoral, lascivious, lewd, libertine, libidinous, lustful, scabrous, wanton

LECHERY delight, pleasure, profligacy, salaciousness, salacity, satyriasis, satyrism

LECTERN ambo, analogion, dais, desk, eagle, escritoire, lateran, latterin, pulpit(um), stand

LECTOR anagnost, churchman, ecclesiastic, reader

LECTURE address, admonition, advice, censure, chide, declaim, discourse, earbash, expound, exprobate, flay, harangue, hearing, homily, jobe, moralize, oration, preach(ment), prelect(ion), rate, rebuke, recite, reproof,

scold, sermon(ize), speak, speech, talk

illustrated chalk-talk, slide show

LECTURER chalk-talker, discourser, docent, expositor, expounder, lector, preacher, prelector, prof(essor), prolocutor, reader, sermoner, sermonist, sermonizer, speaker, teacher

LEDA *consort* tyndareus, zeus

father thestius

lover swan

offspring castor, clytemnestra, dioscuri, helen, pollux

LEDE language, leed, nation, people, person

LEDEN language, noise, speech, voice

LEDGE altar, apron, bank, banquette, bead, bench, berm(e), border, bracket, cay, channel, cleat, clint, console, frame, hobb, lay, lode, offset, projection, reef, retable, ridge, settle, shelf, sill, snout, stance, stratum, vein

LEDGEMAN breaker

LEDGER account book, ambassador, antiphony, breviary, journal, lieger, log, millstone, register, resident, slab, stationary, tombstone

board ribbon

check audit

entry credit, debit, item

page folio

LEE cover, peace, protection, river, shelter(ed), side, tranquility

opposite stoss

LEECH annelid, apodan, bdella, bdelloid, bleed, bloodletter, bloodsucker, branchellion, cupper, drone, egel, extortioner, extortionist, favorite, gill, glossiphonia, hanger-on, helminth, hirudine, hookworm, lickspittle, parasite, sail, sangsue, sponge(r), sycophant, toady, usurer, worm

comb. bdell(a)(o)

-craft medicine

-like bdello(id), hirudinoid

-man physician

sucker acetabulum

LEED language, song, speech, tale, tune

LEEK allium, green onion,

plant, porret, rocambole, scallion

colored prasine

emblem of wales

green porraceous

LEEP boil, scald, toast

LEER appearance, aspect, cheek, complexion, empty, eye, flank, gaze, goggle, hungry, loin, look, ogle, oven, pintlekeek, scoff, signal, skime, slink, smirk, sneak, sneer, stare, twire, unladen, void

LEERFISH garrick

LEERY, LEARY alert, cunning, distrustful, empty, faint, knowing, suspicious, wary

LEES addle, amurca, bottoms, draff, dregs, dross, dunder, emptings, grounds, grout, mother, odds and ends, ort, refuse, remainder, remains, residue, sediment, settlings, slag, ullage, winedraf

LEET court, crossroads, light, list, nominate, pile, stack

LEEWAN couch, divan, sofa

LEEWARD *island* antigua, barbuda, dominica, guadeloupe, montserrat, nevis, saba, st kitts, windward

LEEWAY elbowroom, headroom, latitude, room, space

LEFT abandoned, aguache, cack, car, cast, clicky, coochy, counterclockwise, cuddy, departed, deserted, forsaken, gauche, gawk, gospel-side, haw, kay, larboard, liberal, marooned, near side, port, quit, radical, remaining, residual, sinister, sinistral, southpaw, unorthodox, verso, went

comb. l(a)evo, sinistro

-handed ambisinister, awkward, buckfisted, cack(y), caggy, cank(fisted), car (pawed), cawky, click(y), clumsy, coochy(gammy), cow(ey)-pawed, devious, doll(y)-pawed, gammy (fisted) (palmed), gauche, gawky, gibblefisted, insincere, insolent, kayfist, kaypawed, keck(y)fisted, keggy, kithogue, kittaghy, left-cooch, lyft, malicious, mancino, sc(r)ootchy, sinister, skiffy, southpaw,

squiffy, superficial, unskillful, watted, watty
-*handedness* mancinism
toward aport, haw, herring,
levorotatory, sinistrad
undone neglected
LEFTIST comrade, pinko,
progressive, radical, revolutionary
LEFTOVER hash, hoddle,
manavelins, morsel, ort, refuse, remainder, surplus,
undone
LEG bough, bow, cheesecake,
circuit, course, crus, extremity, forelimb, gam,
gamb(e), gambon, gam-
mon, gangleshank,
jamb(e), lap, limb, long-
shank, moggan, oviger,
part, peg, pestle, pile, pin,
planta, podite, pole, pony,
post, prop, run, scrape,
shank(s mare), spindle-
shank, stem, stilt, stump,
support, tack, tram, trestle,
trotter, underpinning, voyage, walk
armor jambe
bail escape, flight
band strapple
bone femur, fibula, ilium,
shin, tibia
chain slang
comb. scel(o)
covering hose, pedule, sox,
stocking
curvature rh(a)ebosis
having short breviped
it depart, escape, flee, walk
joint ankle, hock, knee
joint covering kneelet
muscle gastrocnemius, per-
on(a)eus, plantaris, soleus
muscle disease acnemia
of lamb gigot
of mutton sleeve gigot
ornament anklet
part ankle, anticnemion,
calf, crus, drumstick,
femur, fibula, gambrel,
ham, haunch, hip, hock,
knee, peronaeus, shank,
shin, tibia, thigh
pert. crural, sural
piece jambeau
pull hoax, joke
style cabriole
tendon achilles
up advantage, assist, boost,
edge, help
wooden peg, prop, stump,
timber-toe
LEGACY bequest, devise, en-

tail, estate, heritage, inheritance, windfall, zchuss
failure ademption
hunting heredipety
inheritor beneficiary, heir,
legatee
LEGAL (See also LAW.) authorized, constitutional, judicial, jural, juridic(al),
kosher, lawful, leal, legit-
(imate), licit, official, permitted, rightful, sanctioned,
sound, statutable, statutory,
valid
aid organization aclu
order capias, caveat, mandamus, mittimus, precept,
warrant, writ
paper contract, deed, lease,
summons, writ
process caveat, detinet, detinue
profession bar, law
remedy See LAW *suit.*
right droit
site venue
status caput
tender See MONEY.
term See LAW *term.*
LEGALISM scribism, strictness
LEGALIZE authorize, codify,
constitute, decree, enact,
formulate, legislate, ordain,
regulate, sanction, validate
LEGALLY by law, de jure
competent capax, sane
LEGATE ambassador, bequeath, consul, delegate,
deputy, envoy, governor,
messenger, minister, pan-
dolph
LEGATEE beneficiary, heir
joint coheir, collegatary
LEGEND adage, anecdote,
caption, edda, epigraph, epitaph, fable, fiction, haggada, head(ing), inscription,
lectionary, list, motto,
myth(ology), narrate, narrative, passional, proverb,
record, roll, rubric, saga,
story, tale, tell, threap, title,
tradition
devotion to philomythia
interpretation solarism
of sleepy hollow author
washington irving
of sleepy hollow character
brom bones, ichabod crane,
katrina van tassel
LEGENDARY doubtful, dubious, fabulous, fancied,
fictional, fictitious, imagi-

nary, imagined, invented,
mythical, questionable, traditional
LEGER book, fine, light,
ledger, slab, trivial
LEGER, ALEXIS S. *pseud.*
st john perse
LEGERDEMAIN con-
juration, deception, jug-
glery, juggling, sleight of
hand, trick
LEGERITY agility, alacrity,
briskness, celerity, dexterity, dispatch, lightness, nimbleness, speed, swiftness
LEGGING(S) bootikin, bottine, brogues, chaps, chivarra, cocker, coggers,
gaiter, galligaskin, gamash,
gambado, gaskin, gogger,
leathers, puttee, shanks,
spat(terdash), strad
furnished with oreate
waterproof antigropelos
LEGHORN hat, hen, livorno
LEGIBLE clean, clear, deci-
pherable, distinct, plain,
readable, recognizable
LEGION army, group, host,
multitude, number, quan-
tity, soldiers, terz(i)o
division cohort, hastati, maniple, principes, triarii
thundering twelfth
LEGIONNAIRE See SOL-
DIER.
LEGISLATE authorize, constitute, enact, legalize, make
laws, ordain, pass, put
through
LEGISLATION act, constitution, dysnomy, enaction,
enactment, law(making),
sanction
bad asynomy, dysnomy
deity eunomia
LEGISLATOR alderman,
congressman, councilman,
delegate, deputy, draco,
lawgiver, lawmaker, mem-
ber, minos, moses, par-
liamentarian, peer, politician, representative, senator, solon, speaker, whip
group See LEGISLATURE.
LEGISLATURE assembly,
board, boule, bundesrat(h),
camera, chamber(s), com-
mons, congress, cortes,
council, court, dail, diet,
douma, duma, folkmoot
forum, house, junta, knesset, lagting, landrath, landtag, moot, parliament, raad,

reichsrat, reichstag, rigsraad, rigstag, riksdag, seim, sejm, senate, session, seym, storting, thing, tinewald, tynwald, yuan, zemstova
procedure closure, filibuster, guillotine, lobby, logroll, pigeonhole, pocket, smother, table, talkathon, vote
one-house unicameral
two-house bicameral

LEGITIMATE appropriate, cogent, fair, genuine, just(ified), kosher, lawful, legal, licit, logical, natural, normal, official, orthodox, proper, reasonable, recognized, regular, sound, typical, usual, valid, warranted

LEGMAN errandboy, messenger, reporter

LEGREE, SIMON slavedriver, taskmaster, tyrant, villain

LEGUME alfalfa, bean, clover, fasel, guar, lentil, loment, medic, pea, pod(der), podware, soybean, strombus, uva, vegetable

LEGUMIN casein, clot, conglutin, globulin

LEI bouquet, flowers, garland, wreath
flower frangipani, plumeria
-making hanalei

LEIPOA bird, lowan, mallee, megapod(e), pheasant

LEISTER gig, SPEAR, waster

LEISURE chance, comfort, convenience, ease, freedom, idle(hours), opportunity, otium, relaxation, repose, respite, rest, retirement, sparetime, time, toom, unemployment, unoccupied, vacation

LEISURED free, otiose

LEISURELY comfortable, delayed, deliberate(ly), dilatory, easy, free, gradual, laggard, languid, lax, relaxed, restful, slack (ened), slow(ly), tardily, unhurried
personification roger bontemps

LEITMOTIF argument, matter, motive, subject, text, theme, topic

LELEGES *king* altes

LEMAN lover, mistress, paramour, sweetheart

LEMMA argument, bract, glume, leaf, premise, theme, title

LEMMING dicrostonyx, mouse, myodes, rodent, vole

LEMNISCUS band, fillet, laqueus, ribbon

LE MOKO pepe

LEMON cedra(te), chlor, citrus, failure, fruit, killjoy, kumquat, tree
cucumber mango-melon
disease blackpit, peteca
grass roosa, rusa, siri, tanglad
lobelia balm
peel twist, zest
seed pip, putamen
sole carter, flatfish, flounder, marysole, smear-dab
verbena aloysia
vine barbados-gooseberry
-wood dagame, tatara
-yellow citrean, citreous, citrine

LEMONADE *and beer* shandy

LEMUR adapid, ampongue, anaptomorphus, angwantibo, animal, arctocebus, avahi, ayeaye, babacoote, babakoto, bushbaby, cobengo, colugo, galago, indri, kinkajou, kokam, kuban, kubong, lori(s), macaco, maholi, maki, microcebus, mongoose, monkey, nattock, potto, primate, semiape, sifak(a) tarsier, tarsioid, vari
flying colugo
fossil adapis
large indri
long-tailed avahi
nocturnal ayeaye
relative tarsier
ring-tailed macaco
ruffed vari
small angwantibo

LEMURES ghosts, spirits

LEMURIA See UTOPIA.

LENAEUS bacchus, dionysus

LENAPE *indian* algonquian, delaware

LEND abide, accommodate, advance, afford, alight, arrive, devote, expend, furnish, give, grant, import, lease, let, loan, loin, occer, prest, settle, stay, support
an ear hearken, heed, listen
at interest gavel

LENGTH compass, distance, duration, extent, footage, fluidity, line, longitude, longness, measure, mileage, oblongness, pace, part, period, piece, portion, range, reach, roll, run, sidth, size, span, stretch, string, strip(e), term, yardage
athwartship aburton
comb. longi, mec(o)
continuous stretch
measure agate, angstrom, archeen, arpent, arshin(e), aune, block, boardfoot, braza, cable, centimeter, chain, chih, circumference, covid, cuadra, cubit, decimeter, dha, diameter, diget, dra, ell, fathom, fermi, finger, foot, furlong, gaz, gez, guz, hand(breadth), hatt, hectometer, inch, kilometer, knot, league, lightyear, line, link, mecometer, meter, micron, mil(e), millimeter, millimicron, minute, nail, pace, palm, parsec, perch, pied, pik, point, quadrant, radius, ro(o)d, second, span, step, stride, toise, yard
times width area

LENGTHEN augment, continue, distend, draw out, elongate, expand, extend, increase, let out, pad, produce, prolong(ate), protract, spin out, stretch, sustain, wiredraw

LENGTHWISE along, endlong, endways, endwise, longitudinally, longways, plankways

LENGTHY diffuse, drawn out, extended, extensive, farflung, far-reaching, interminable, long(ish), padded, prolix, prolonged, protracted, tall, tedious, tiresome, verbose, wearisome, windy, wordy

LENIATE alleviate, soften

LENIENCE, LENIENCY benignancy, charity, clemency, easiness, easygoingness, gentleness, grace, indulgence, kindness, mercy, mildness, moderateness, patience, pity, softness, tolerance

LENIENT agreeable, assuasive, balm(y), benign, bland, clement, complacent, demulcent, easy(going), emollient, gentle, grateful, gratifying, indulgent, lax, merciful, mild, moderate, palliative, patient, pleasant, pleasing, relaxing, soft(en-ing), soothing, sparing, spoiling, tender, tolerant

LENIFY alleviate, assuage, mitigate, soften

LENIN *name* ulyanov
party bolshevik
wife krupskaya

LENINGRAD petrograd, st petersburg, window on the west
ballet kirov
founder peter the great
river neva
street nevsky prospect

LENIS bland, gentle, smooth, soft

LENITIVE anodyne, as-suasive, balmy, emollient, gentle, laxative, lenient, mild, palliative, softening, soothing

LENITY benevolence, char-ity, clemency, compassion, gentleness, grace, humanity, indulgence, kindness, laxity, mercy, tolerance

LENS (See also *kind*, below.) adon, bull's eye, eyepiece, glass(es), lenticle, lunettes, meniscus, toric
absence aphakia
adjustable zoom
aplanatic euryscope
comb. phac(o)
combination barlow
corrected rectigraph, rectilin-ear
flat plano
flattened aplanation
hand reader
hood sunshade
kind anamorphic, bifocal, hypergon, lenticular, menis-cus, pantoscope, telephoto, toric, unar, wide-angle, zoom
measurement ligne
measuring instrument diopter
-shaped lentoid, phacoid
shield gobo
telephoto adon
wide-angle pantoscope
without aphakia

LENT careme, fast, gentle, imprest, loaned, mild, quad-ragesima, slow, springtime
cake hotcross bun
color black, violet

day before pancake day, shrove tuesday
days before carnival, mardi gras
fast xerophagia, xerophagy
1st day ash wednesday
1st sunday invocabit
1st sunday before quinqua-gesima
2nd sunday before sex-agesima
4th sunday bragget, laetare
5th sunday carlin(g), judica
lily daffodil

LENTEN fasting, meager, meatless, plain, somber

LENTIGINOUS flaky, freck-led, scurfy, speckled

LENTIGO blemish, freckle, mark

LENTIL dhal, duckweed, ervum, legume
meal revalenta
wafer popadam, poppercake

LENTOUS gradual, sluggish, viscid, viscous

L'ENVOI farewell, postscript, stanza, verse

LEO lion
gem sapphire

LEOGADAN *son-in-law* king arthur

LEONARDO *master* bassanio
masterpiece mona lisa

LEONATO *brother* antonio
consort imogen
daughter hero
niece beatrice

LEONCAVALLO *opera* i pagliacci, zaza

LEONIDAS *daughter* chi-lonis
house agiadae
parent cleonymus
patron seleucus
rival agis
son-in-law cleombrotus

LEONINE lionlike, powerful, savage
mistress dionyza

LEONTES *daughter* perdita
friend polixenes
kingdom sicilia, sicily
wife hermione

LEONTEUS *beloved* helen

LEONTOCEBUS midas

LEOPARD cat, cat-amount(ain), cheetah, jag-uar, libbard, ocelot, ounce, panther, pard(al), tree-tiger, wagati
author lampedusa
group leap
-like pardine

lily sansevieria
-man magician, weretiger
-marmot gopher, sper-mophile
snow irbis, ounce
symbol of sin
toadfish sapo

LEOPOLD *mistress* tres belle
wife astrid

LEOPOLDVILLE kinshasa

LEOS *father* orpheus

LEPADOID barnacle, lepa

LEPANTO navpaktos
battle, loser ali pasha, turks
strait rion
winner don juan, genoa, spain

LEPER cagot, lazar(us), outcast, pariah
house lazarcote, lazaret
island molokai
king uzziah
priest damien

LEPID charming, jocose, pleasant

LEPIDIUM boor's-mustard, canary-grass, peppercress

LEPIDOPTER See BUT-TERFLY; MOTH.
breeder or *collector* aurelian
larva caterpillar

LEPIDOSIREN doko, eel, protopterus

LEPIDOTE flaky, scaly, scurfy

LEPIDUS *brother* paulus
colleague antony, caesar

LEPOMIS bluegill, bluejoe, bream, sunfish

LEPORID hare, pika, rabbit

LEPRECHAUN banshee, brownie, dwarf, elf, fairy, fay, gnome, goblin, luracan, nix, pigmy, pixy, puck, shee, sprite

LEPROSY alphos, han-sen's(disease), lazary, leon-tiasis, lepra, mesel(ry)
remedy chaulmoogra oil, glucosulfone
white leucoderma

LEPROUS lazarly, mesel(y), unclean

LEPUS con(e)y, hare, lep-orid, pika, rabbit

LER *consort* aoife
son manannan

LERNAEA demeter

LESBOS mytilene
boatman phaon
king philomelides
poet alcaeus, arion, sappho, terpander
princess nyctimene

LESION anthrax, chancre, crater, cut, damage, eschar, fissure, gall, gash, hive, hurt, injury, leprid, leproma, leukemid, sore, tertiary, ulcer, wound

LES MISERABLES *author* hugo

character cosette, fantine, gavroche, jean valjean, marius

LESOTHO basutoland

city maseru, teyateyaeng

river caledon

LESS few(er), inferior, lacking, lower, minor, minus, mono, negative, secondary, smaller, without, younger

than under

LESSEE huurder, leaser, renter, tacksman, tenant, termor, transient

LESSEN abase, abate, abridge, alleviate, assuage, bate, belittle, bring down, contract, curtail, cut, decrease, degrade, deplete, depreciate, derogate, dilute, diminish, discount, disparage, dock, dwindle, ease, fade, flag, impair, lighten, lower, mince, minify, minimize, minish, mitigate, moderate, palliate, reduce, relieve, retrench, shorten, shrink, thin, trench, truncate, wane, weaken

effect cushion

LESSER fewer, inferior, minor, minute, smaller

bramble dewberry

celandine pilewort

civet rasse

curlew whimbrel

hemlock fool's parsley

whitethroat babillard

LESSON assignment, censure, class, example, exercise, instruction, lear, lecon, lecture, moral, precept, reading, rebuff, rebuke, recitation, reprimand, reproof, scolding, study, task, warning

LEST anaunter(s), for fear that, in case, that

LESTRIGON cannibal

LET act, allow, behave, cause, charter, consider, delay, discharge, endorse, forbear, hinder, hindrance, hire, impede, lease, leave, license, lose, make, obsta-

cle, omit, permit, pretend, prevent, rent, sanction, suffer, tenant, think, tolerate, yield

alone abe, abstain, and, avoid, miss, notwithstanding, pass, refrain

be leave off, omit, suppose

bygones be bygones forget, forgive, overlook, pass, reconcile

down abatement, anticlimax, blow, calk, chagrin, deceive, deflate, demit, depress, desert, deteriorate, disappoint, disillusion, fail, fall short, forsake, frustration, hangover, humiliate, humiliation, lower, relax(ation), slacken(ing), slow, slump, stand up, stoop, strike, weaken, yield

drop or *fall* avale, betray, divulge, hint, lower, relate, release, remark, sing, slip, snitch, spill, suggest, tattle, tell, vail

fly attack, bolt, detonate, discharge, fire, peg, release, shoot, throw, wing

forth emit

go abandon, acquit, cast off, cede, demit, discard, dismiss, disregard, drop, faik, free, ignore, miss, neglect, refrain, relax, release, spare, surrender, unhand, untie

have it beat, cudgel, lambaste, larrup, overwhelm, punish, strike, thrash, whip

in adhibit, admit, cheat, deceive, enter, immiss, insert, receive

in on divulge, open up, release, reveal, share, tell

it be done fiat

it go abstain, forget it, ignore, neglect, overlook, refrain

it stand sta, stet

know acquaint, inform, tell

loose free, liberate, play, relax, release, slip

off acquit, clear, discharge, erupt, explode, free, release, shoot

on acknowledge, act, admit, betray, emote, heed, hint, play(act), pretend, reveal, sham, tattle

oneself go deteriorate, play, relax

out bleed, breathe out, contract, dismiss, divulge, drain, elongate, emit, enlarge, evacuate, exhaust, expire, extend, give off, hint, hire, lease, lengthen, release, say, throw off, unravel

the buyer beware caveat emptor

up abate(ment), cease, cessation, desist, halt, interrupt(ion), lessen, lull, pause, quit, recess, relaxation, respite, rest, retard(ation), slow, stop

well enough alone accept, avoid, disregard, overlook

LETCH bog, craving, desire, ditch, leach, passion, pond, pool

LETHAL baneful, deadly, destructive, fatal, killing, mortal, necrotic, noxious, pernicious, poisonous, slaying, toxic, virulent

LETHARGIC apathetic(al), comatose, dilatory, drowsy, dull, heavy, idle, impassive, inactive, inert, laggard, languid, listless, oblivious, passive, sleepy, slow, sluggish, stolid, stuporous, supine, torpid

LETHARGY apathy, cataphora, coma, drowsiness, hebetude, idleness, inaction, indifference, indolence, inertia, languor, lassitude, laziness, phlegm, sloth, somnolence, stupor, torpor

LETHE abyss, cataphora, death, forgetfulness, hell, oblivion, river

LETHOLOGICA amnesia

LETITIA paris

grandson napoleon iii

LETO buto, latona

consort zeus

enemy niobe

offspring apollo, artemis, diana

parent coeus, phoebe

rival hera

sister asteria

LETTER agreement, alphabet(ize), answer, billet, breve, brief, bull, cadjan, capitalize, cartel, character, chit, cipher, codicil, communication, consonant, contract, demit, device, dispatch, document, ell, encyclic, epistle, initial, in-

scribe, intelligence, lil, line, literatim, mark, memo(random), message, missile, missive, monogram, note, paraph, pastoral, record, reply, report, rescript, rune, screed, script, sign, stamp, statement, symbol, transliterate, type, vowel, writ (ing)
according to literal
anonymous poison pen
authoritative breve, writ
begging dun, screeve
black gothic
box apartado
capital majuscule, uncial, upper case
carrier correo, footpost, mailman, messenger, postman
challenging cartel
decorate with illuminate, miniate, rubricate
decorated fac, paraph
drop chute, slot
fine line serif
first alif, alpha
formal brief
harmony eutony
introductory systatic
last omega, zed, zee
love billet-doux, poulet
lower case minuscule
of credit circular note
of defiance cartel
of introduction door-opener, endorsement, recommendation
of marque piracy
official breve, brief, bull, document, writ
omission apocope
opener censor, dear, salutation
ornamental fac, illumination, paraph, rubric
-perfect accurate, correct
pope's bull, encyclic(al), tome
runic thorn
seal cachet
short billet, chit(ty), missive, note
silent mute
sloping italic
stroke serif, stem
word logogram
worship grammatolatry
writer correspondent, epistolarian, epist(o)ler, epistolist
LETTERED educated, inscribed, learned, literal, literate, profound, stamped

LETTERHEAD address, stationery, title
LETTERLEAF elixir of love, orchid
LETTERPRESS caption, paperweight, print, text
LETTERS belles-lettres, chronicle, humanities, literature, mail, post, scholarship
man of author, literatus, savant, scholar, writer
LETTRURE knowledge, learning, writing
LETTUCE bib, boston, cos, escarole, fireweed, green, iceberg, karpas, lactuca, milkweed, minion, money, plant, romaine, salad, sallet, ulva, vegetable
bird goldfinch
blue lactuca
disease bottom-rot, stunt
juice thridace, thridacium
-like vegetable celtuce
sea alga, laver, ulva
white cancerweed
LEUCAEUS zeus
LEUCE *changed to* poplar tree
pursuer pluto
LEUCIPPE *offspring* teuthras
parent minyas, thestor
LEUCIPPUS *beloved* daphne
offspring hilaira, phoebe
parent gorgophone, oenomaus, perieres
slayer daphne
wife philodice
LEUCITE amphigene, arkite, batukite, lenad, mineral
LEUCITITE albanite, cecilite, italite, sperone
LEUCOMA walleye
LEUCOPHRYNE artemis
LEUCOTHEA ino, matuta, mother
changed into incense-shrub
husband athamas
parent eurynome, orchamus
slayer orchamus
LEUCUS *companion* odysseus, ulysses
slayer antiphus
LEUD tenant, vassal
LEUKEMIA chloroma, leukosis
LEVANT (See also ASIA MINOR.) decamp, default, east(ern), flee, middle east, morocco, near east, orient, renig, wager, welsh, wind, wormseed

cab araba
caravan cafila
cell serdab
christian melchite
city xanthus
coach araba
coin dinar, fils, luigino, millieme
council divan
country akkad, assyria, babylon, bithynia, elam, lydia, media, sumeria
cup finjan, lingan
fabric aba, barracan, camlet
fiddle rebab
floor, raised leewan
food yog(h)urt
garment caftan, feridgi, gand(o)ura, grego, kaftan
guide dragoman
herb harmel
hound afghan
inn serai
interpreter dragoman
ketch See *ship,* below.
liquor rakee, raki
madder alizari
mantle feridgi
pastry baklava, baklawa
patent berat
people arab(ian), hurri, turk
porter ham(m)al, haumaul, humaul, khamal
potash polverine
river wadi, wady
rug bergama
sheep broadtail, dumba
ship bum, caique, felucca, jerm, ketch, saic, set(t)ee, xebec
shrub poontree
sponge turkey-cup
tip baksheesh, bakshish
valley wadi, wady
veil maharmah
viper cerastes
warrant berat
wind chamsin, etesian, khamsin, seistan, shamal
wormseed aleppo, artemisia
LEVE belief, believe, permission
LEVEE affair, assembly, bank, cheer, dike, ditch, durbar, dyke, embankment, gathering, landing, party, pier, porch, quay, reception, trench, wharf
LEVEL accord, agree, aim, akin, align, alike, aline, beam, bulldoze, clear, demolish, destroy, direct, equal(ize), equate, even, fell, flat(ten), floor, flush,

gallery, grade, homaloidal, horizontal, impartial, just, lay(er), like, lower, niveau, overthrow, pancake, plain(s), plane, plateau, point, position, prairie, press, purpose, rase, raze, reduce, reshape, right, roll, similar, slant, smooth, sphere, station, steady, stor(e)y, stratum, suit, tie(d), tier, tool, topple, train, tunnel, uniform
at aim, attack, concentrate, direct, focus
comb. plani
highest summit, top
lowest basement, floor, rock-bottom
off bulldoze
tool gimbal, plane
up shim
with be frank, equal, speak out
LEVELHEADED balanced, calm, cool, sensible, sound, wise
LEVELHEADEDNESS aplomb, calm
LEVER adjust(ment), bar, beam, boom, cant, clutch, crank, crow(bar), gaffle, gavelock, handspike, helm, helve, jemmy, jimmy, lam, lief, lowder, marlinespike, outrigger, peav(e)y, pedal, prise, prize, pry, pulley, raise, ramhead, tappet, tiller, tool, treadle, tumbler
axis fulcrum
crossbow garrot
lumbering cant, hook, peav(e)y, samson
spokelike bootleg
LEVERAGE advantage, fulcrum(age), influence, power, pressure, prize, pry
LEVERET con(e)y, hare, mistress, rabbit
LEVI *descendant* levite
parent jacob, leah
son gershom, gershon, hebron, jochebed, kohath, lizaphan, matthat, merari, mooli, uzziel
tribe amramites
LEVIATHAN commonwealth, crocodile, dragon, giant, huge, serpent, ship, titanic, whale
author hobbes
LEVIGATE lighten, mix, polish, pulverize, smooth
LEVIS denims, jeans, PANTS

LEVITATE arise, ascend, float, fly, hover, mount, plane, rise, rocket, sail, soar, surge, swim, tower, waft
LEVITE *ancestor* jacob
chief chenaniah
composer asaph
patriarch lael
LEVITY agility, buoyancy, cheerfulness, festivity, flippancy, folly, frivolity, gaiety, giddiness, hilarity, humor, lightness, merriment, mirth, pleasantry, repartee, trifling, whims(e)y, wit
LEVY assess(ment), attach(ment), build, cess, charge, collect(ion), construct, contribution, draft, duty, enroll(ment), entreat, erect, estreat, exact(ion), excise, extent, fine, gathering, gelt, impose, impost, mart, mise, mobilize, muster, payment, raise, rate, seize, stent, tail, tariff, tax, teind, tithe, toll, tribute, wage
LEW coin, lukewarm, mild, shelter(ed), snug, tepid, thin, warm, weak
LEWD bad, base, carnal, coarse, debauched, dirty, dissolute, goatish, gross, hircine, immoral, indecent, indelicate, laches, lascivious, lecherous, libertine, libidinous, licentious, lubricious, lustful, obscene, pornographic, prurient, rude, salacious, scarlet, sensual, vulgar, wanton, whorish
person callet, rep
LEWDNESS bawdry, harlotry, lechery, rakery
LEWIS AND CLARK *indian guide* sacajawea
indian guide's son charbonneau
LEWIS, SINCLAIR *novel* anne vickers, arrowsmith, babbit, cass timberlane, dodsworth, elmer gantry, kingsblood royal, main street
LEWTH shelter, warmth
LEX enactment, jurisprudence, jus, law
LEXICOGRAPHER author, onomastic
LEXICOGRAPHY glossography, glossology, orthoepy, phonology

LEXICON calepin, dictionary, gazetteer, glossary, onomasticon, synonymicon, vocabulary, wordbook
LEY coin, pewter, tax
LEYTE *city* dulag
LEZGHIAN *tribe* budukha, kuri
LHASA *country* tibet
holy man lama, llama
part potala
LIABILITY accountability, amenability, aptitude, arrear(s), blame, burden, chance, charge, contingency, danger, debit, debt, duty, eventuality, incumbency, likelihood, obligation, onus, possibility, probability, proneness, responsibility, tribute
halting of cesser
LIABLE accountable, amenable, answerable, apt, blame(e)able, bound, chargeable, exposed, incident, inclined, likely, obligated, obliged, open, probable, prone, responsible, sensitive, subject, suitable, susceptible, to blame
become incur
to capable of, exposed to, inclined to, likely to, ready for
LIAKOURA parnassus
LIAISON affair, agent, amour, binding, bond, connection, contact, cooperation, intimacy, intrigue, link, relationship
LIANA bejuco, bush rope, cane, cipo, palm, sipo, tael, vine
LIAR ananias, baron munchausen, bouncer, cheat, cracker, crammer, deceiver, equivocator, fabler, fabricator, fabulist, fag, faker, false witness, falsifier, fibber, fibster, fraud, hypocrite, knave, mythomaniac, perjurer, pinto, plant, prevaricator, proctor, pseudologist, pseudologue, romancer, seapin, story-teller, taradiddle(r), tom pepper, untruther, wernard
the al aswad
LIATRIS blazing star, button-snakeroot, gay-feather, trilisa, wild vanilla
LIBATION ambrosia, drink, offering, potation, sacrifice

LIBBET billet, club, flap, rag, stick, strip

LIBEL abuse, accuse, asperse, bill, blacken, calumniate, certificate, circular, defame, degrade, disparage, expose, handbill, invective, lampoon, malign, paper, pasquil, pasquin(ade), request, revile, roorback, skit, slander, smear, squib, traduce, travesty, treatise, vilify

LIBELLER asperser, backbiter, calumniator, defamer, maligner, missayer, slanderer, spatterer, splatterer, traducer, vilifier

LIBERAL abundant, accessible, advanced, ample, benevolent, big(hearted), bleeding heart, broadminded, catholic, charitable, cordial, cosmopolitan, eclectic, exuberant, fair, frank, free(handed)(thinking), generous, greathearted, handsome, indulgent, large(hearted), latitudinarian, lavish, left, lenient, magnanimous, munificent, open(handed), plentiful, princely, prodigal, profuse, progressive, radical, tolerant, unrestricted, unselfish, unsparing, unstinting, whig, wide
arts arithmetic, astronomy, geometry, grammar, history, languages, logic, muses, music, philosophy, quadrivium, rhetoric, trivia

LIBERALITY benevolence, bounty, breadth, catholicity, charity, generosity, gift, gratuity, largesse, magnanimity, plenty

LIBERATE absolve, acquit, affranchise, clear, deliver, detach, discharge, disengage, disenthrall, emancipate, enfranchise, extricate, free, frith, loose, manumit, ransom, redeem, release, remit, rescue, rid, set free, unfetter, ungyve, untie

LIBERATION delivery, escape, freedom, release, rescue, salvation

LIBERATOR bolivar, o'connel, redeemer

LIBERIA *animal* banded duiker
boatman kru
capital monrovia

city bopora, buchanan, garroway, gbanga, greenville, gribo, kakata, marshall, nanakaru, rebbo, sino
coast kru
custom sande
hills bomi
measure kuba
peak niete, nimba, uni
people bassa, gibbi, gissi, gola, grebo, kpelle, kpuesi, kra, krooby, krooman, krou, kru(man), kwa, mandingo, toma, vai, vei
president tubman
range niete
river cavally, cess-cestos, douobe, manna, mano, morro, san pedro, sinoe, st john, st paul

LIBERTINE corrupt, debauchee, dissolute, don juan, erotic, gay dog, immoral, lecher, lewd, lothario, lustful, paillard, panurge, profligate, punker, rake, reprobate, rip, roue, rounder, seducer, sensualist, skirtchaser, smell-smock, stringer, strumpet, wanton, wolf, woman-chaser, womanizer

LIBERTY autonomy, carte blanche, delivery, emancipation, freedom, furlough, immunity, independence, leave, leisure, liberation, license, opportunity, pass, permission, power, privilege, range, scope, sweep, unconstraint, vacation
cap pilleus
statue site bedloe's island

LIBIDINOUS carnal, fleshly, lascivious, lecherous, salacious

LIBIDO desire, drive, energy, force, instinct, motive, striving
arrest fixation

LIBOCEDRUS alerce, alerse, arborvitae, cedar, pine

LIBRA balance, equinox, scales, scorpio's-claws
gem jacinth

LIBRARIAN armarian, bhandari, bibliothec, bookman, custodian, steward

LIBRARY agency, archives, atelier, athenaeum, bhandar, bibliothec(a), bibliotheke, bibliotheque, bookery, bookroom, books, den, gallery, morgue, museum,

office, studio, study, treasury
first public athens
study carrel(1), cubicle

LIBRATE balance, oscillate, vibrate, weigh

LIBRETTIST dramatist, poet, writer

LIBRETTO book, composition, script, testo, text, words

LIBRIUM chlordiazepoxide

LIBYA *alphabet* tifinagh
capital bengasi, benghazi, tripoli
city elmarj, garian, homs, misurata, murzuq, sebha, sidri, tobruk, tripoli, zawia
consort poseidon
gulf bomba, sidra, sirte
king aegyptus, battus, idris
lake, mythical tritonis
leader gaddafi, jalloud, khadafy, qadhsfi
measure barile, bozze, donum, dra, gorraf, jabia, kele, kharouba, mattaro, misura, pik, saa, teman, termino, uckia
moon goddess neith
nomads gaetuli, getulans
oasis kufra, sebha, tazerbo
offspring agenor, belus
peak bette
people, mythical skiapod
port bengasi, benghazi, darna, derrn, homs, khoms, sidri, tobruk, tripoli
province fezzan
queen lamia
weight gorraf, kele, kharouba, termino, uckia

LICE (See also LOUSE.) creepers, nits
fish epizoa
remedy for staresacre

LICENSE abandon, accredit, allow, approbate, authority, authorize, caroome, car(r)oon, carte blanche, certificate, commission, consent, discharge, empower, enable, endorse, exception, exeat, exemption, faculty, familiarity, franchise, freedom, grant, immunity, indulgence, interregnum, irresponsibility, lawlessness, laxity, leave, let, liberty, looseness, mortmain, pass(port), patent, permission, permit, placard, prerogative, presumption, privilege, release, right, sanction, suffer, unconstraint, warrant

LICENSEE agent, broker, dealer, middleman, retailer, salesman

LICENTIOUS abandoned, corrupt, cyprian, dissipated, dissolute, free, gay, immoral, lawless, lax, lewd, libertine, loose, lubric(i)ous, pornerastic, profligate, relaxed, unchaste, wild

LICH body, corpse, like, trunk
bird goatsucker
house mortuary

LICHAS *companion* heracles, hercules
slayer heracles, hercules

LICHEN (See also *genus*, below.) alectoria, archilla, basidiomycete, careweed, cetraria, crottal, crottle, evernia, fungus, lecanora, liverwort, lungwort, manna, moss, oakmoss, parella, parelle, parmelia, rockhair, rocktripe, treehair, wartwort
acid from usnic
comb. bryo
dye from alectoria, archil, cudbear, orchil, orcin(e), orcinol, persis, ratmara
edible iceland moss
genus cladonia, evernia, graphis, gyrophora, lecanora, parmelia, pertusaria, physcia, sticta, usnea
horsetail treehair
outgrowth cephalodium, isidium
pit cyphella, lacuna

LICIT allowed, approved, due, just, lawful, leeful, legal, legitimate, licensed, permitted, regulated, sanctioned

LICK attempt, baffle, beat, bit, blow, conquer, cut, dart, defeat, flog, hit, lap, moisten, osculate, overcome, perplex, punish, puzzle, quantity, rate, reduce, rout, slake, slap, spank, strike, stroke, subdue, suck, taste, thrash, tongue, touch, trace, vanquish, wallop, whip, win, work
into shaped drill, form, train

LICKERISH craving, dainty, desirous, eager, greedy, lascivious, lecherous, lustful, tempting

LICKING beating, defeat, flogging, lapping, thrashing

LICKPENNY miser

LICKSPIT(TLE) favorite, fawn, flatter(er), hanger-on, leech, parasite, sponge, sycophant

LICORICE anise, aniseed, anisum, pimpinella, pomfret, sweetroot
derivative abrin
-flavored drink absinthe, anisette, arak, ouzo, pastis, perroquet, raki, tomate
pill cachou
seed goonch
syrup eclegma

LICYMNIUS *nephew* heracles, hercules
parent electryon, midea
sister alcmena
slayer tlepolemus

LID bred, cap, case, ceiling, check, clapper, clicket, closure, cover, curb, hat, headdress, led, operculum, roof, scuttle, shutter, stopper, tilt, top

LIDLESS sleepless, watchful
teapot cadogan

LIE abide, banger, bask, beguile, blague, bouncer, canard, cheat, cog, covert, cram(mer), crumper, deceit, deceive, deception, delude, deviate, direction, dishonesty, equivocate, exaggerate, exist, extend, fable, fabricate, fairy tale, falsehood, falsification, falsity, feign, fib, fish story, fitten, flam, gab, grabble, half-truth, hide, hoax, howler, inhere, invention, lay, lease, leaze, lige, lodge, loll, mendacity, mislead, palter, position, prevaricate, range, reach, recline, reside, rest, sleep, sojourn, sprawl, story, subsist, tale, tall one, tarradiddle, twister, untruth, whapper, w(h)opper, yarn, yed
-abed idler
along border, skirt
at importune, urge
by adjoin, dally, rest, siding
detector polygraph
down couch, recline, rest, retire, stretch out, submit, yield
in wait ambush, hide, lurk, skulk
low hide, squat

monstrous strammer, w(h)opper
off dally, hold back, rest
on burden, depend on, oppress, shirk, straddle, weigh on
over command, cover, dominate, tower over
prone grabble, streek
quiet snudge

LIEBESTRAUM *composer* listz

LIECHTENSTEIN *capital* vaduz
city balzer, haag, iradug, nendeln, planken, schaan
money rappe
peak rhatikon
river rhine
roman name rhaetia
ruler franz josef
tribe alamanni

LIED lay, lyric, song

LIEF acceptable, agreeable, beloved, dear, desirous, disposed, fain, freely, glad(ly) leave, pleasing, precious, preferable, sweetheart, willing(ly)

LIEGE faithful, lord, loyal, luik
man subject, vassal

LIEN charge, claim, demand, mortgage

LIEU place, room, stead

LIEUTENANT deputy, jaygee, jemadar, kehaya, louey, luff, officer, shavetail, teniente, viceregent, zany

LIFE action, activity, anima(tion), ankh, being, biography, bios(is), biota, blood, breath, career, chronicle, course, days, energy, entity, essence, existence, heart, incarnation, man, personality, sensitivity, snap, soul, spark, spirit, story, survival, viability, vie, vigor, vim, vita (lity), vivacity, years, zest
absence abiosis, death
after death eternity, future, hereafter, immortality, tomorrow
airless anaerobiosis
animal biology, bios, biota, edaphon, fauna
beginning ovule
-belt filling kapok
breath pneuma
buoy float

car ark
chemical See DNA.
comb. bia, bio, vita
cycle anicca
deity bald(e)r, faunus, lub, lucina, mitra, osiris, shu
deprive of disanimate, KILL, murder
desire for tanha
-destroying antibiotic
early childhood, infancy, youth
energy jiva, sakti, shakti
everlasting cudweed
fast rat race
force anima mundi, archeus, atman, bathism, biod, breath, elan vital, heart-blood, jiva(tma), pneuma, prana, shakti, soul
-giver apheta
good things of cakes and ale
guard beltman, protector, rescuer
ideal asrama
in air aerobiosis
insurance tontine
intellectual jivatma
investigation biognosis
jacket mae west
long longevity
master blueprint dna
name meaning eva, eve(lyn), evie, vita, zoe
of ease comfort, prosperity
-of-man honeysuckle, mountain ash, orpine, spikenard
pert. biotic, mortal, vital, zoetic
plant bios, biota, botany, floppers, flora
preserver breeches buoy, float, mae west, neddy, safety belt
principle See *force, above.*
professional career
prolonger elixir, fountain of youth
raft balsa, float
-saving device net
-saving fluid plasma
science anatomy, binomics, biology, ecology, genetics, paleontology, zoology
science term codon, DNA, enzyme, gene, inducer, nucleotide, peptide, psi, represser, rho, scotophobin, sigma, template, virus
scientist agranoff, allfrey, avery, burger, chase, crick, gallo, gamow, haldane, hershey, huebner, kornberg, matthaei, mendel, niren-

berg, petrucci, shettles, temin, watson, wilkins, zamecnik
sea benthos, coral, halibios, plankton
simple amoeba
staff of bread
story (auto)biography, chronicle, history, memoir, vita
substance plasma
such is c'est la vie
symbol ankh, cross, crux ansata, tau
terrestial geobios
tree of arborvitae
unit amoeba, cell, embryo
water of aquavit, visgebaugh
without See LIFELESS.
without oxygen anaerobiosis
LIFELESS abiotic, amort, an(a)emic, arid, azoic, bloodless, boring, brash, breathless, brute, clay, cold, dead, deceased, defunct, dull, exanimate, extinct, flat, heavy, inactive, inanimate, inert, inorganic, insipid, jejune, lackluster, languid, listless, passive, powerless, prosy, rigid, sapless, slothful, sluggish, spiritless, stark, stiff, tame, torpid, vapid, wooden
comb. abio
LIFELIKE animated, eidetic, exact, faithful, photographic, quick, realistic, vive
LIFETIME aeon, age, being, born days, duration, eon, eternity, existence, lasting
LIFT abstract, aid, appropriate, arise, ascend, assist, bear, boost, booty, bucket, carry, cast, cleech, cop, dig, elate, elevate, elevator, erect, exalt, filch, heave, heft, height(en), heist, help, hike, hoist, hold up, hoosh, hove, improve, inspiration, inspire, jack, knock up, leve, levitate, loft, mount, perk, pinch, plagiarize, raise, rear, ride, rise, rocket, settle, set up, sky, snitch, soar, steal, stick up, sublevate, support, surge, swipe, t-bar, theft, thief, thrill, tow, tower, uphoist, upraise, uprear, warp
anchor cat
-off airborne, launch(ing)

-off, time after plus ten
up erect, extol(l), hove, nauntle
valve poppet
LIFTER hoister, hoistman, THIEF
LIGAMENT armilla, band (age), bond, brace, cord, nucha, taenia, tie, tissue, union, zonule
comb. desmo
inflammation desmitis, syndesmitis
kind annular
like desmoid
LIGAN flotsam, jetsam
LIGATE bind
LIGATURE amulet, band (age), bind, bond, cord, digram, digraph, LIGAMENT, plica, pneuma, slur, suture, taenia, thread, tie, wire
LIGGER counterpane, coverlet, creeler, fish(line), footbridge, trimmer
LIGHT (See also *kind, below.*) 3 gay, ray, sun 4 airy, beam, dawn, easy, fair, fine, fire, glim, glow, lamp, land, lume, lunt, puny, rest, soft, star, thin, yang 5 agile, blond, cheap, clear, corky, fanal, flare, flash, foamy, glare, gleam, happy, klieg, leger, loose, lucid, lumen, match, moorn, perch, petty, quick, roost, shiny, small, sunny, taper, torch, truth, vague, white 6 aerial, atonic, bantam, bright, candle, dainty, dilute, facile, fluffy, frothy, gentle, ignite, illume, kindle, little, lucent, luster, pastel, porous, serene, settle, simple, sleazy, slight, smooth, tender, wanton, watery, window 7 buoyant, cresset, descend, fragile, glitter, inflame, lantern, LIGHTEN, lucency, opinion, outlook, radiant, radiate, shallow, smither, sparkle, sunbeam, trivial 8 birdlike, brighten, carefree, daybreak, debonair, delicate, dismount, ethereal, feathery, illumine, luculent, luminary, luminous, pellucid, radiance, sunshine, trifling, volatile 9 cloudless, emanation, frivolous, knowledge, radiation 10 illu-

minate, irradiance, translucid, weightless 11 information, irradiation, superficial, translucent, transparent 12 illumination
amplified device laser, maser
artificial candle, electricity, fluorescent, gas, incandescent, lamp, lantern, mercury lamp, rush, spot, torch, zircon
as air, chaff, day, down, ether, fluff, thistledown
as a bubble, cobweb, cork, feather, straw
beacon fanal, phare
beam chink, gleed, ray(on), shaft, signal, stream, stricture
blurs comae
brigade officer lord lucan, lord raglan
bulb filler argon
bulb part filament
burning cresset, torch
burst of flash, glory
celestial moon, star, sun
circle aura, aureole, corona, glory, halo, nimb(us)
colored blae, blonde, fair
comb. luce, luci, phos, phot(o)
deity adonai, apollo, bald(e)r, baldur, heimdall, lug(h), mithras, nusku, osiris, shu
emit eradiate, glow, luminesce, shine
failure blackout, brownout, deliquium
faint glimmer(ing), scarrow, shimmer(ing), starlight
feast channukah, hanukka(h)
-fingered larcenous, thieving
fixture chandelier, sconce
flood olivette
flux hefner, lumen
globe bulb
heavenly meteor
holder bracket, candelabra, candelabrum, candlestick, chandelier, flambeau, girandole, lamp, pricket, sconce, torch
image spectra
improvised palouser
into attack, punish, set upon, start, undertake
kind abatjour, arc, bude, flash, headlight, incandescent, klieg, lamp, lantern, sconce
let there be fiat lux

making levitation
measure See *unit*, below.
movement toward taxis
name meaning ellen, helen(a), helene, lora, lucia, lucy
of the age maimonides
of the harem nourjehan, nourmahal
of the world jesus, pharaoh
-o'-love inconstant, leveret, wanton
on descend, drop, enter, fall, meet, settle
out depart, start
overpower with dazzle
pert. photic
polar aurora borealis, merrydancers
portable candle, flare, flashlight, lamp, lantern, taper, torch
ray infrared, ultraviolet
ray study actinology
reflected skyme
reflector lens, mirror
refraction halo, photocampsis
refraction, pert. dioptric
refractor prism
science actinology, catoptrics, heliology, heliometry, optics, photics, photology, photometry
spirit mazda, ormazd, ormuzd
spreading halation
traffic blinker
unit candle(hour)(power), carcel, flux, hefner, lumen, lux, ohm, phot(on), pyr, quantum, watt
wavering flicker
waves spectrum
without See LIGHTLESS.
wood acacia, candlewood, fatwood, mangrove, pine

LIGHTEN alleviate, bleach, brighten, comfort, disburden, disencumber, ease, illume, illuminate, illustrate, mitigate, moderate, mollify, leaven, lessen, levigate, levin, reduce, relieve, sweeten, temper, thin
LIGHTER accon, barge, boat, brand, casco, chopboat, congreve, drogher, firebrand, flambeau, flint, fuse(e), fuzee, gabbard, igniter, lucifer, match, mussal, pontoon, portfire, punk, scow, sparker, spill, taper, torch, vesta, vesuvian

LIGHTHEADED barmy, delirious, disordered, dizzy, faint, fickle, flighty, foolish, frivolous, giddy, glaiket, glaikit, heedless, inconstant, indiscreet, reeling, thoughtless, unstable, unsteady, volatile, whirling
person birdbrain
LIGHTHEARTED blithe, buoyant, carefree, cheerful, debonair, frivolous, gay, glad, gleesome, happy, jolly, joyful, joyous, lively, merry, vivacious, volatile
LIGHTHOUSE beacon, fanal, lantern, phare, pharos, seamark
LIGHTLESS aphotic, blind, dark
LIGHTNESS agility, airiness, buoyancy, cheer, delicacy, flippancy, frivolity, gaiety, grace, lambency, legerity, levity, liveliness, lucence, lucency, lucidity, luminosity, translucency
LIGHTNING apamnapat, bolt, eclaire, fireball, firebolt, fireflaught, flash, fouldre, fulmen, fulmination, lait, levin(bolt), thunderball, thunderbolt
antidote bay
bug firefly, glowworm
cyclopes steropes
defier ajax
deity agni, fulgora, jupiter (fulgur), thor, zeus
fear astraphobia
kind ball, chain, forked, globular, heat, sheet
-like fulgurous
pert. fulgural, fulminous
protector arrester, rod
stone sulgurite
war blitz(krieg)
LIGHTS (See also LAMP.) lungs
out taps
LIGHTSOME cheerful, debonair, fickle, frivolous, gay, merry, unsteady
LIGHTWEIGHT bantam, diminutive, nonentity, superficial
LIGNALOES See AGALLOCH.
LIGNEOUS wooden, woody, xyloid
LIGNOSE cellulose, explosive, lignin
LIGNUM VITAE guayacan, pockwood

LIGULAR lorate, stringy, thong

LIGURIAN *capital* genoa

part cinque terre

sea, river into arno

LIGUSTRUM cabbagewood, privet

LIKABLE adorable, enjoyable, pleasant, preferable, sweet, winsome

LIKE admire, affect, akin, allied, analogous, approve, choose, cognate, comparable, copy, cotton to, desire, ditto, dote(on), dupe, duplicate, elect, endorse, enjoy, equal, equivalent, esteem, fancy, favor, hit it off, identical, love, matter, parallel, prefer, regard, related, relish, resemble, resembling, respect, savor, select, semblance, similar, uniform

become, comb. ize

comb. ary, homeo, ical, ine, ish, ist, itic, ode, ody, oid, oil, ose, some

-minded compatible, unanimous

-mindedness accord, agreement, consensus

LIKELIHOOD aptitude, chance, fair shake, liability, outlook, possibility, presumption, probability, prospect, tendency, trend

LIKELY apt, comely, credible, eventual, expedient, fair, feasible, fitly, gradely, imminent, impending, liable, looming, ostensible, plausible, possible, presumable, probable, probably, promising, prone, rational, reasonable, seemly, similar, smittle, specious, suitable, threatening, verisimilar

LIKEN apply, assimilate, collate, compare, match, remene, semble

LIKENESS analogy, aspect, blee, community, copy, counterpart, dead ringer, ditto, dupe, effigy, equality, facsimile, figure, guise, homoiousia, homology, icon, image, parallel, photograph, picture, portrait, representation, resemblance, ringer, semblance, similarity, similitude, spit(ting) image

comb. opsis

LIKESOME agreeable, pleasant

LIKEWISE also, besides, ditto, eke, furthermore, moreover, too

LIKHI *father* shemida(h)

LIKING affection, affinity, appetite, attachment, attraction, fancy, foible, fondness, goo, inclination, palate, partiality, passion, penchant, predilection, preference, relish, smack, stomach, sympathy, taste, theat, tooth

LIL book, letter, little, paper

LILAC blue ash, blue myrtle, ceanothus, china tree, mauve, shrub, syringa

-throat hummingbird

-time place kew

LILITH *husband* adam

successor eve

LILL hole, loll, pin

LILLIPUT *city* mildendo

faction high-heels, low-heels, slamecksan, tramecksan

heretic bigendian

LILLIPUTIAN diminutive, dwarf, midget, SMALL, tiny

LILT cadence, croon, flow, melody, meter, refrain, rejoice, rhythm, sing, swing, trill, tune

LILTING measured, metered, metrical, rhythmic

LILY See *kind,* below.

belladonna amaryllis

black fritillaria, perianth

brown mission belle

butterfly mariposa, sego

calla arum

climbing gloriosa

corn ixia

daffodil narcissus

emblem of florence, france

genus allium, anticlea, bessera, camassia, erythronium, gloriosa, hosta, milla, scilla, zygadenus

gold-banded auratum

iron harpoon

kind adobe, agapanthus, albuca, aloe, amaryllis, annunciation, anthericum, arad, arum, ascension, asphodelus, atamasco, august, avalanche, aztec, barbados, barney-clapper, beaver, belladonna, bengal, bermuda, bessera, blandfordia, bloomeria, bourbon, brandybottle, bullhead, butterfly, ca-

buja, cabuya, cajun, calla, camas(s), cambric, cammas, candlestick, candock, canna, cape, castalia, ceylon, clote, cocuisa, coral drops, day, easter, flag, fleur-de-lis, funkia, hosta, humboldt, iris, ixia, kelp, lis, lotus, lys, madonna, mariposa, martagon, monocot, nenuphar, onion, plantain, pond, sego, tiger, tittree, toi, trumpet, turk's cap, wokas

leaf pad, spathe

-like plant sabadilla, squill, yucca

-livered cowardly

maid of astolat elaine

mariposa star tulip

name meaning susanna(h), suzanne

of france fleur-de-lis

of the valley asparagus, aspidistra, barney-clapper, bead ruby, convallaria, convallily, fetterbush, lilywort, mugget, mugwet, pepperbush, shinleaf, solomon's seal, sourwood

palm toi

plant camas(s), cammas, nerine

pond kelp

sand soaproot

sea crinoid

-shaped crinoid

symbol of purity

tulip-like mariposa

turk's cap martagon

water camalote, candock, castalia, lotos, lotus, nelumbo, nymphaea, wocas, wokas

LIMA bean, haba, mollusk, yam, zapatero

epithet city of kings, ciudad de los reyes

LIMB arm, bough, branch, dismember, extension, extremity, fin, flipper, imp, LEG, lith, manus, member, nectopod, part, podite, process, rogue, scamp, shoot, spald, spaul, tram, wing

absence of amelia, ectromedla

band armlet

bone femur, humerus, propodiale

comb. mel

fetter clip, gyve, handcuff, hobble, manacle, tie

flexion anaclasis
paralysis scelotyrbe
pert. appendicular
swimming-adapted fin, nectopod
thoracic pereiopod
without acolous, anarthrous, apterygial
without use of paraplegic, quadriplegic
LIMBATE bordered
LIMBEC(K) alembic, distill, extract, still
LIMBER agile, athletic, bain, brusher, brutter, carriage, elastic, flaccid, flexibile, graceful, limmock, limp, lissome, lithe(some), plastic, pliable, pliant, resilient, shaft, soften, springy, supple, thill, weak
-pine loblolly, ponderosa
LIMBO alaraf, hell, jail, prison
LIMBUS border, edge
LIME alkali, amber, calce, calcite, calcium, calx, catch, caustic, cedra(t), cement, chunam, citron, citrus, defile, entangle, fruit, fustic, linden, mortar, puna, smear, snare, teil, teyl, trap, tree
bush snare, trap
dark raupenlein
derivative apatite, calcic
formation stalactite, stalagmite
hound lyam
juicer mariner, sailor
linament carron oil
pert. calcareous, calcic, oolitic
phosphate apatite
plant may-apple
powder conite, konite
tree bass, linden, teil, teyl, tilicetum, tupelo
turn into calcify
uranite autunite
wild, fruit colima
yellow amber
LIMELIGHT attention, cynosure, fame, focus, oxycalcium, publicity, spotlight
LIMENIA aphrodite
LIMER bloodhound, mongrel
LIMERICK *land* ireland
LIMESTONE anthraconite, bala, caen, calciphyre, calcrete, caliche, calp, camstane, cauk, chalk, clunch, coquino, dolomite, ganil,

hurlock, kunkur, leith, lias, lyas, malm, marble, oolite, peastone, pisolite, poros, portor, silica, tufa
plateau causse
slab balatte
LIMEWORT dianthus, pink
LIMEY englishman
-land See ENGLAND.
LIMIT abstain, ambit, assign, barrier, border, boundary, bound(s), bourn(e), brim, brink, butt(ing), capacity, check, circumscribe, closure, condition, confine, conscribe, contract, cramp, curb, deadline, define, definition, demarcation, determine, edge, end, fix, frontier, hem in, hinder, line, march, margin, mere, narrow, number, pale, period, point, prescribe, qualification, qualify, range, ration, reduce, regulate, restrain(t), restrict(ion), rim, scant, span, specialize, specify, stent, stint, straiten, stunt, term(ination), termine, terminus, top, utmost, verge
comb. ori
lower floor
upper ceiling
LIMITATION anstoss, bounds, condition, denial, frame, reserve, stint
LIMITED borne, bound, circumscribed, circumscript, conditioned, cramped, exact, few, finite, half-way, little, local, meager, narrow, partial, particular, partway, regional, restrained, restricted, scant, sectional, small, special, stinty, topical
LIMITLESS boundless, illimitable, immeasurable, infinite, unbounded, vast
LIMMER hussy, low, manrope, minx, rascal, rogue, scoundrel, strumpet, worthless
LIMN decorate, delineate, depict, describe, draw, illuminate, paint, portray, sketch
LIMNAEA artemis
LIMON *brother* scephrus
parent maera, tegeates
victim scephrus
LIMONITE bog ore, hematite, iron ore, ocher

LIMONIUM behen, behn, biacuru
LIMOUSINE automobile, berlin(e), brougham, suburban
LIMP clop, clump, debilitated, draggled, drooping, enervated, exhausted, fail, flabby, flaccid, flag, flexible, flimsy, halt, hench, hilch, himp, hirple, hitch, hobble, hoit, hop, lax, limber, limmock, loose, loppy, pace, quaggy, relaxed, scuff, shaffle, slack, slamp, sleazy, sleezy, soft, spent, supple, walk, weak, wilted
as a glove
LIMPET acmaea, chink, flidder, limpin, mollusk, opihi, patella
keyhole fissurella
LIMPID bright, clear, crystal, diaphanous, lucid, luculent, pellucid, pure, sheer, translucent, transparent, transpicuous
LIMPING gimpy, halting, lame, limpy, zoppa
LIMPSY flexible, flimsy, lazy, LIMP, weak
LIN cease, desist, flax, linden, linen, river, stop
LINAGA abaca, bagasse, flax, manila hemp
LINCHPIN center, core, forelock
LINCOLN *assassin* john wilkes booth
biographer herndon, sandburg
birthplace hodgenville, kentucky
burial site springfield, illinois
debater douglas
fiancee ann rutledge
finch sparrow
foe mcclellan
friend speed
law partner herndon
nickname honest abe
party republican
photographer brady
profession lawyer
secretary seward, stanton
son robert todd
vice president andrew johnson, hamlin
wife mary todd
LINDBERGH lone eagle
plane spirit of st louis
LINDEN bass(wood), beetree, daddynut, lime, lin(n), linwood, lyne, teil,

teyl, tiel, tilia, tillet, wood-lind

emblem of prussia

LINE 3 bar, cue, fur, net, pad, row, wad, way 4 arow, band, ceil, clew, cord, dash, draw, edge, face, file, fill, flax, hose, mark, pack, path, pipe, race, rank, road, rope, tape, taum, tome, wire, work, 5 align, array, birth, cable, cover, forte, frame, house, inlay, limit, nerve, order, party, queue, range, ridge, route, score, serif, shell, spiel, stean, stock, stria, strip, stuff, trace, trade, train, trend 6 airway, border, career, cordon, course, crease, family, fettle, furrow, length, metier, parade, patter, policy, secant, series, steene, streak, striae, string, stripe, stroke, trench, vector 7 arrange, babbitt, calling, company, contour, descent, engrave, equator, hachure, incrust, kinship, lineage, marline, marshal, network, pursuit, sheathe, shipper, windrow, wrinkle 8 ancestry, boundary, business, diagonal, division, interest, offering, railroad, striping, vocation 9 direction, inventory, lineament, specialty, striation 10 assortment, occupation, procession, underscore 11 merchandise

barometric isobar

central axis

color streak, stripe

comb. lino, stich(o)

connecting ligature

converting balun

curve-cutting secant

curved arc, bowl, brace, circle, slur, sweep

cut zinco

diagonal bias

dividing edge, frontier, partition

electric wire

fishing backing, boulter, cord, corkline, fleet, leader, ledger, norsel, snell, snood, spiller, spillet, taum, tome, trimmer, trotline

form into align, queue

geographic agonic, equator, isother, latitude, longitude, meridian, tropic

geometric arc, asymptote, cant, ess, parallel, secant, sine, tangent, vector

guide rein

hair ceriph, leger, serif

horizontal level

imaginary agone, axis, capital, hinge, horizon, isobar, isobase, isobath, isobrant, isochasm, isocheim, isochlor, isochore, isogram, isohel, isohyet, isoline, isopag, isophote, isopleth, isostere, isotach, isotherm

in en queue

inclined cant

incomplete hemistich

inside ceil, fur

intersecting secant

island jarvis

junction raphe, seam, suture, synchondrosis, union

longitudinal meridian

measurer campylometer

median raphe

metrical dimeter, sapphic, staff, stich(os)

nautical brail, earing, downhaul, geswarp, hawser, lacing, marline, painter, ratlin(e), roding

of guards cordon

of march parade

of school children crocodile

of sight aim, range

of soldiers column, file, rank

1/10th gry

pert. filar, linear

plotted adiabat

principal axis

radiating beam

raised ridge, weal, welt

starting scratch

straight chord, beeline, as the bird flies

surveying base, chain, wad

thin stria

tow cordelle

transport carrier, feeder

up align, arrange, gather, join, list, plan, queue, schedule

waiting cue, queue

wavy squiggle

with boards wainscot

with bricks revet

with stone pave, stean, steen

LINEAGE ancestry, birth, blood, breed, descension, descent, family, genealogy, heredity, house, kin(dred) (ship), line, pedigree, progenitor, progeny, race,

rank, sib, source, stirp(e)s, stock, strain, succession, trene

noble parage, peerage

LINEAL ancestral, delineated, descended, diphyletic, direct, family, genealogical, genetic, hereditary, inherited, innate, matroclinous, patrimonial, patroclinous, phyletic, phylogenetic, racial, straight

LINEAMENT appearance, aspect, characteristic, face, features, looks, mark, outline, trait

LINEAR long, narrow, running, straight

unit cubit

LINEATE lined, streaked, striped

LINED careworn, creased, lineolate, notate, padded, ruled, striated, wrinkled

LINEMAN center, end, guard, tackle

LINEN (See also FABRIC *linen.*) barandos, barras, batiste, bis(syn), blancard, brabant, brin, buckram, byssus, cambresine, cambric, cloth, clothes, crash, crea, damask, dornick, dowlas, fabric, flax, forfar, gulix, hemp, holland, irish, kompow, lawn, linge(rie), linsey-woolsey, lockram, osnaburg, platilla, raines, scrim, sendal, toile

closet cupboard, ewery, locker

coarse barras, dowlas, galipot, harn, lockram

consecreted antemension

ecclesiastic amice

fabric See FABRIC *linen.*

fiber flax

fine cambric, damask, diaper, lake, lawn, nacarat, raines

flowered damasse

household bedding, napery, napkins, sheets, shirting, tablecloth, tabling

-man clothier, draper

measure cut, heer

merchant draper

officer naperer

sail canvas, duck

scraped langate, lint

sheer toile

source flax

tape inkle

unbleached brown-holland

vestment alb, amice, amit
weaver huri
window shade holland
yarn lea
LINER ball, boat, casing, facing, hit, scriber, shim, SHIP, steamer, steamship, vessel
wrecked andrea doria, lusitania, titanic
LINES contour, figuration, guy, halyards, net(work), outline, reticle, role, script, sheets, style
LING buffalo-cod, burbot, calluna, chestnut, drizzle, eelpout, fish, hake, heath(er), lota, molva, sergeant fish, stokvis
LINGBERRY bilberry, bogstrawberry, comarum, crowberry
LINGBIRD pipit
LINGCOD cultus
LINGE cudgel, flog, thrash
LINGEL lacing, spoon, thong, thread
LINGER abide, cling, continue, crave, creep, dawdle, defer, delay, dillydally, drag, dwell, endure, hang, hanker, haunt, hesitate, hover, lag, last, loiter, postpone, procrastinate, prolong, protract, put off, remain, saunter, stand, stay, tarrow, tarry, trail, wait
LINGERER idler, laggard
LINGERIE frillies, pretties, underclothes, underthings, underwear
LINGO argot, cant, dialect, idiom, jargon, language, patois, patter, slang, speech, tongue
LINGOUM amboina, apalit, bija, bloodwood, dhak, molompi, narra, pampango, rosewood, sandalwood
LINGUA glossa, jargon, language, lingo, proboscis, tongue
LINGUIST classicist, colloquialist, dialectician, eponymist, etymologer, glossarian, glossographer, glottologist, grammarian, grammatist, hebraist, hellenist, interpreter, jargonist, lexicographer, lexicologist, lexiconist, lingster, paleographer, pantoglot, philologer, philologist, phonologist, polyglot, semanticist,

semasiologist, sinologist, vocabularian, vocabulist
LINGUISTICS etymology, grammar, lexicology, philology
LINIMENT arnica, balm, eik, embrocation, embroche, lotion, ointment, opodeldoc
apply embrocate
LINING aligning, brasque, bush(ing), ceiling, coating, contents, doubling, doublure, facing, filling, gasket, inlay(er), insides, insole, insulation, interior, packing, padding, pastedown, sarcenet, sheathing, stuffing, wadding, wainscot(ing)
membrane intima
LINK articulate, associate, association, bind, bond, bracket, catena(te), catenulate, chain, codetta, combine, connect(ion), copula, couple, division, fasten(ing), fetter, gimmal, group, hank, incorporate, integrate, interlock, intermediary, involve, join(t), junction, lax, liaison, lock, loop, lunt, marry, nexus, part, relate, ridge, ring, rik, seam, section, trainer, unite, vinculum, walk, yoke
missing apeman
LINKS fairway, golf course
LINKSMITH chainmaker
LINN cataract, dike, linden, pond, pool, precipice, ravine, waterfall, waterway
LINNET acanthis, chloris, finch, gorsebird, lenard, lintie, redfinch, redpoll, spinus, twite
LINOTYPE *inventor* merganthaler
trigger verge
LINSEY-WOOLSEY cloth, coarse, mixture, uneven, variegated, wincey
LINT bolly, caddice, caddis, carbasus, charpie, cotton, down, dressing, flax, flick, flue, fluff, hemp, lentil, nap, netting, raveling, tilma
knot nib
lump slug
remover canroy
roll dossil, tent
scraped xystus
LINTEL beam, clavel, clavy, darner, hance, platband, squinch, summer, transom

LINTER hut, lean-to
LINUS *parent* amphimarus, apollo, oeagrus, psamathe, urania
slayer apollo, hercules
song dirge
LIOD *husband* volsung
offspring sigmund, signy
LION, LION'S ari, carnivore, cat, celebrity, dignitary, elsa, felis, frasier, hero, king of beasts, leo, llew, magnate, morne, puma, savage, shedu, simba, star, vip
abode den
avatar narasimhavatara
beard pasqueflower
biblical ari
changed to atalanta, melanion
dog peke
-*dragon* openieus
-*eagle* griffin, griffon
ear leonotis, mint
famous elsa, frasier
-*foot* edelweiss, gall-of-the-earth, lady's-mantle
group pride
hair mane, poll
-*headed god* ruti
-*headed goddess* mut
-*heart* dragonhead
-*hearted* brave, courageous
hunter shikari
-*killer* jules gerard
leaf black turnip
-*like* leonine
lizard basilisk
-*monkey* leoncito, tamarin
mountain catamount, cougar, king-cat, painter, panther, puma, screamer
mouth foxglove, snapdragon, toadflax
movie elsa, lahr
mythical griffin, griffon, sphinx
name meaning leo
of god ali
of north pancho villa
pert. leonine
poll mane
slayer hercules
symbol of courage, england, mgm
tail motherwort
tailed monkey macaco, macaque, wanderoo
tamer androcles
tooth dandelion
toothless morne
winged achech, sphinx
young cub, lionet, whelp

LIONHEART richard

LIP, LIPS backtalk, blob, border, chiloma, clip, drip, edge, embouchure, flange, fold, geat, impudence, insolence, kiss, labellum, labium, language, lap, lave, margin, mouth, muffle, murmur, notch, pertness, protuberance, puss, recite, rim, sass, say, shear, sing, sound, speech, spout, trim, tutel, utter, words

comb. cheilo, chilo, chilus, labio

disease perleche

-edged labial

exposed prolabium

flat apron

groove amabile, filtrum, philtrum

having harled, labiate

having broad alate

inflammation ch(e)ilitis, coldsore

lack acheilia

lower fipple, jib

ornament labret, pelele

part cheilion, flews

pert. labial

plug labret, temeta

pretty cupid's bow

reader oralist

-reading labiomancy

service hypocrisy, sanctimony

shaped labelloid

surgery chilotomy

swollen blobber

tumid chiloma

under jib

LIPARI *island* alicudi, eolie, filicudi, panarea, salina, stromboli, vulcano

LIPAROUS fat, obese

LIPID(E) ceride, ester, fat, steride

LIPOMA steatoma

LIQUEFACTION deliquescence, dissolution, eliquation, fluidity, fusion, liquescence, melt, thaw

LIQUEFIED fusil(e), potate

LIQUEFY dissolve, eliquate, fluidify, fluidize, fuse, liquate, melt, run, soften, thaw

LIQUEUR absinth(e), advocaat, alkermes, anesone, angelica, anisette, aurum, benedictine, bols, cassis, chartreuse, chasse, cognac, cointreau, cordial, creme de (cacao)(menthe)(moka)(no-

yau), curacao, dolce vita, drambuie, fior de alpi, fraise, framboise, galliano, genepi, goldwasser, irish mist, kirsch, kumiss, kummel, mandarin, maraschino, marc, menthe, noyau, ouzo, pernod, persico, poussecafe, prunelle, pulque, raki, ratafia, sabra, strega, taffia, tia maria, triple sec, vespetro

anise kummel

apricot persico

aromatic absinthe

brandy and cherry noyau

brandy-based angelica

caraway kummel

cask tun

cherry kirsch(wasser)

coffee creme de caffe, kahlua, tia maria

fruit-flavored ratafia

orange aurum, cointreau, curacao, strega, triple sec

violet creme yvette

LIQUID aqua, aqueous, beverage, broth, cash, clear, DRINK, dulcet, effluent, elixir, flowing, fluid, furfuran, juice, libation, limpid, liquescent, luscious, lymph, mellifluous, melted, molten, musical, nectar, sap(py), serous, slop, smooth, solution, swill, thawed, watery, wet

agitate sparge, whip

alkaloid anabasine, anatabine

ambar bilsted, copalm, sweet-gum

ambar resin storax

colorless acetoin, acetol, alcohol, pyrrol(e), water

comb. elaio

container (See also DRINKING *vessel.*) basin, boiler, bottle, bucket, creamer, cruse, decanter, demijohn, etna, ewer, fiasco, jar, jug, kettle, pan, phial, pitcher, pot, vase, vat, vial

cooking bree, broo, broth, stock

courage liquor

distilled booze, liquor, spirits

fatty olein

film scum

fragrant collen, cologne, ester, perfume

fuming thiophosgene

gaseous steam, vapor

hypnotic paraldehyde

inflammable See *volatile,* below.

insulating askarel

measure aam, ahm, barrel, canada, cup, dram, fifth, gallon, gill, liter, mutchkin, ounce, pint, pottle, rundlet, tenth, tierce

oily aniline, cardanol, chloral, creosol, creosote, octane, olein, picamar

particle form mist, spray

perfumed See *fragrant,* above.

poisonous acetonitrile, anabasine, aniline, cyanogenchloride, pyrrolidine

pressurized aerosol

science of hydraulics, hydrodynamics, hydrokinetics, hydromechanics

sizing glaik

sterilized johnin

sweet honey, molasses, sirup, syrup, treacle

thick dope, tar

thin slurry

viscous shradan, tar

volatile acetone, alcohol, benzine, benzol(e), butane, diluent, ether, gas(oline), kerosene, ligroin, paraffin, toluene

weak blash, slipshop

without aneroid, dry, parched, sere

LIQUIDATE adjust, amortize, clear up, convert, depose, despatch, discharge, eliminate, exterminate, kill, melt, murder, pay(off), purge, sell, settle, sink

LIQUIDATION extinction, homicide, murder, settlement

LIQUOR (See also DRINK alcoholic.) barleybroo, barleybroth, beno, booze, bree, dew, drink, fizz, fogram, hooch, lap, medicine, pengasi

abstinence naphalism, teetotalism

acid verjuice

add to lace, spike

bad balderdash, bug juice, fogram, fogrum, hooch (inoo), moonshine, rotgut, smoke, sneaky pete

bitter tire

bootleg moonshine, sly-grog

bumper carouse

cabinet bar, cellaret, gardevin, tantalus

cane rum, taf(f)ia
cheap plonk, redeye, rotgut, smoke, swill
distilled dew, grappa, phlegm, schnapps, scotch, whiskey
dregs See LIQUOR *residue.*
-drinking bibulous
drink of set-up
drugged hocus, mickey(finn)
fill with skink, tun
fruit applejack, brandy, gin, perrie, perry, ratafia, wherry, wine
glass, small pony
hard booze
homemade bathtub gin, sneaky pete
inspector aleconner
maker abkari, distiller, vintner
malt ale, beer, bock, bub, lager, porter, stout
measure dram, jigger, pony, rouse, snifter
mixture bogus, bragget
mix with lace, spike
mother bittern, hydrol
palm vino
portion jigger, nobbler, pony, shot, slug, snifter, tot
potato mobbie, mobby, vodka
prohibition volsteadism
residue dregs, heeltaps, must, taplash, ullage
rice sake, saki, samshu
sacred ambrosia, haoma, nectar
sale abkari
seller barkeeper, barmaid, barman, bartender, brewer, distiller, publican, rummy, skinker, tapster, vintner
shop bar, pub, SALOON, shebeen, tavern
strong hogan, nippitate, rug, rumbo, stingo, vino
sweet aromatic cordial, liqueur
symbol john barleycorn
tanning layaway, tailing
tax abkari
vat tun
vessel See DRINKING *vessel.*
with wine doctor
LIRA zwanziger
1/20th soldo
LIRIPIPE, LIRIPOOP dotard, hood, lesson, scarf, stratagem, task, tippet, trick
LIRK crease, wrinkle
LIS See FORT.

LISBON crossroads of the world
city center baixa
district alfama, bairro alto
museum gulbenkian
LISH active, agile, nimble, quick
LISS assuage, cease, cessation, peace, release, relieve, remission
LISSOM cleft, layer, platform, strand, stratum
LISSOME agile, flexible, limber, lithe(some), live, nimble, pliable, pliant, slender, supple, svelt(e)
LIST 3 joy, tip 4 albe, band, bill, file, hark, heel, lean, leet, like, menu, name, plow, poll, post, roll, rota, tilt, wish 5 album, arena, bound, brief, cadre, chart, draft, enter, index, limit, panel, score, slant, slate, slope, strip, table, tally 6 active, agenda, ballot, border, choose, column, desire, docket, edging, enroll, fillet, lineup, listen, margin, muster, please, record, roster, screed, scroll, series, stripe 7 agendum, barrace, earlobe, empanel, hearken, impanel, incline, invoice, program, returns, tableau, terrier, waybill 8 boundary, bulletin, cadaster, cadastre, manifest, register, registry, schedule, tabulate 9 blackbook, directory, enclosure, enumerate, inventory, nosecount 10 prospectus, racecourse 11 enumeration, matriculate 12 bibliography
alphabetical index
legal tableau
wine card, carte
LISTEN attend, attention, audit(ion), auscult, bug, ear, eavesdrop, hark(en), hear, heed, list, look, monitor, obey, overhear, oyez, tend, tenez, tention
to dig, ear, hark, hear
LISTENER auditor, ear, eavesdropper, hearer, monitor, otacust
group audience, crowd, gate, house
LISTENING attention, audient, audition, auscultation, bugging, hearing, wiretapping

device audiometer, ausculator, bug, dictograph, ear trumpet, hearing aid, phone, sonometer, stethoscope, telephone
LISTER friar, lector, plow, preacher, reader, ridger, sulky
LISTING billing, edge, enlistment, enrollment, frame, lashing, leaning, registration, registry, sapwood, selvage, tabulation, tipping
individual entry, item
LISTLESS apathetic, donsie, donsy, dull, enervated, heavy, heedless, idle, impassive, inactive, indifferent, inert, lackadaisical, languid, leaden, lethargic, passive, phlegmatic, poppied, supine, unfeeling
LISTLESSNESS acedia, apathy, calmness, coolness, disinterest, dispassion, doldrums, ennui, enough, indifference, languor, melancholia, sluggishness, stoicism, torpor, unconcern
LISTS arena, circus, court, diamond, field, racecourse, ring, rink, tournament
LIT bed, burning, drunk, dye(stuff), ignited, intoxicated, stain(ed)
LITAE *father* zeus
LITANY aitesis, collect, ectene, ektene, orapronobis, orison, prayer, rogation, service, supplication
LITCH langsat, lanzon, longan, rambutan
LITE delay, expect, few, little, rely on, small, trust, wait
LITERACY cultivation, education, scholarship
LITERAL abecedarian, accurate, alphabetic(al), bald, capital(ized), close, dull, exact, factual, faithful, lettered, orthodox, precise, prosaic, real, servile, strict, textual, true, unembellished, unicia, unvarnished, verbal, verbatim, word-for-word
LITERARY belletristic, bookish, classical, cultural, erudite, learned, lettered, literate, pedantic, scholarly, stilted, versed
association atheneum

criticism epicrisis, irony, satire
hack grub
sketch cameo
thought pense
work See LITERATURE form.

LITERATE bookish, educated, instructed, learned, lettered, profound, reader, scholar, schooled, well-read, writer

LITERATURE belles-lettres, book, broad(sheet), broadside, circular, classics, dodger, encyclical, flier, folder, handbill, humanities, leaflet, letters, program
collection ana(lecta)
extracts anthology
form article, cento, essay, fiction, non-fiction, novel(la), play, poem, poetry, satire, theme
fragments catalecta
study of philology
unpublished inedita

LITH division, joint, limb, member, segment

LITHE agile, bain, brisk, calm, gentle, graceful, lightsome, limber, lissome, listen, mild, nimble, palliate, plastic, pliable, pliant, relieve, serene, shelter, slender, slight, slim, smooth, soften, spare, spry, supple, svelte, swack, thicken, wandle

LITHER agile, bad, false, flexible, lazy, slothful, supple, wicked, worthless

LITHOGRAPH aquatone, chromo, print, reproduction

LITHOGRAPHY *ink pad* dabber, tompion

LITHOID hard, rocky, solid, stony

LITHOSPERMUM alkanet, bloodroot, gromwell, hoary puccoon

LITHUANIA lietuva, litva
assembly seimas
capital kaunas, kovno
city aesti, balt, jelgava, kapsukas, kaunas, klaipeda, kovnac, kovno, lett, memel, siauliai, vilna, vilnius
coin auksinas, centas, fennig, lit, litas, marka, ostmark, skatikas, skatiku
dialect zmudz
god perkun
jew litvak

people balt, lett, litvak, samogitian, yatvyag, zhmud
port memel
river dubysa, nemunas, neris, progolya, rusne

LITIGATE accuse, appeal, arraign, bring suit, cite, contest, defend, implead, indict, plead, prosecute, subpoena, sue, summon

LITIGATION (See also LAWSUIT.) action, argument, case, contest, dispute, law, lis, moot, pleading, pleaship, suit

LITIGIOUS aggressive, assertive, bellicose, belligerent, contentious, militant, pugnacious, quarrelsome

LITTER (See also *kind,* below.) ambulance, bed (ding), bier, brood, cabin, clutter, coffin, couch, disorder, dool(e)y, dooli(e), duff, farrow, hay, jumble, kindle, louster, mahmal, mess, mulch, muncheel, offspring, palanquin, raff, redd, refuse, rubbish, rummage, scatter, stretcher, strew, trash, untidiness, young
bearer stretcherman
bug despoiler, slattern, slob
kind brancard, cacolet, dandy, dooli(e), dooly, go-cart, handbarrow, horimon, jampan, kajawah, lectica, norimon, palanquin, panier, polki, sedan(chair), smytrie, stretcher, talabon, tonjon

LITTLE bantam, base, bitsy, brief, contemptible, cramped, crumb, dapper, darling, diminutive, dinky, dwarf, exiguous, feeble, half-pint, illiberal, inconsiderable, insignificant, light, lilliputian, limited, meager, mean, miniature, miniscule, minute, modicum, not much, paltry, petite, petty, peu, piddling, pint-sized, poco, poky, puny, runty, scanty, selfish, short, skimpy, slight, slim, sma, small(ish), somewhat, thin, tiny, trifling, trivial, two-by-four, unimportant, weak, wee
america site bay of whales
betty blue queen elizabeth
bit bittock
bo-peep mary queen of scots

boy blue cardinal wolsey
britain armorica, benwic, brittany
by little edgingly, inchmeal, peuapeu
comb. cle, ette, micr(o), steno, ule
corporal napoleon
dorrit, mate arthur clennam
john, alias reynold greenleaf
john's leader robin hood
-known obscure, orphic, recondite
miss muffet mary queen of scots
name meaning erica, etta
one child, kid(die), snip, sprig
paris brussels
toe minimus
tom tucker cardinal wolsey
women author alcott
women character amy, beth, jo, laurie, meg
women's surname march

LITTLENESS atomity, bigotry, meanness, selfishness

LITTORAL bank, beach, coast(al), foreshore, region, ripa, seaside, shore, strand

LITTURGY abodah, ceremonial, ceremony, eucharist, form, hierurgy, maarib, mass, minchah, minhag, neilah, prayer, rite, ritual, service, shaharit, synapte, worship
basin lavabo
part anaphora
sign selah
singer cantor

LITUUS spiral, staff, trumpet

LITYERSES *father* midas

LIVE abide, active, alert, animated, breathe, continue, dwell, dynamic, eager, effective, efficient, endure, energetic, exist, fare, forceful, glowing, green, inhabit, last, leeve, lively, lodge, lusty, persist, potent, remain, reside, room, settle, sojourn, stay, stop, strenuous, subsist, survive, vigorous, vital, vivid
alone ba(t)ch
and let live tolerate
-box car
down atone
-ever crassula, edelweiss, strawflower
-forever everlasting, lulang, orpine, sedum

high indulge, spend, squander, thrive

in inhabit, occupy, reside

in luxury batten

in the country rusticate

it up indulge, luxuriate, play, spend

oak encina

off drone, leach, sponge

passively vegetate

permit to reprieve, spare

through endure, survive, triumph

-wire activist, baelboosteh, berrieh, dynamo, go-getter, hustler, kochleffl, organizer, promoter, tummler

LIVELIHOOD being, bread (and butter), income, job, keep, living, maintenance, means, pay, profession, revenue, salary, subsistence, support, wage(s)

LIVELINESS activity, animation, bounce, briskness, celerity, effervescence, fire, fizz, glee, lilt, pep, rapidity, sparkle, speed, spirit, spunk, vitality, vivacity

LIVELONG enduring, entire, lasting, tedious, whole

LIVELY active, agile, airy, alert, amusing, animated, audacious, blithe, bonny, bright, brilliant, brisk, buckish, buoyant, cadent, cant, cheerful, chirpy, cobby, cosh, crouse, dapper, dashing, desto, energetic, exciting, foppish, fresh, frolicsome, gai, gay, gleeful, grig, impetuous, intense, interesting, jolly, keen, kinky, lighthearted, merry, nimble, peart, perk(y), pert, piquant, quick, ruddy, semmit, sparkling, speedy, spirited, sportive, sprack, sprightly, spry, swinging, tait, tid, tittupy, trotty, vif, vigorous, vir, vivacious, vivant, vivid, volatile, wimble, yare

person dynamo, grig

LIVEN animate, cheer, encourage, rouse

LIVER fegato, foi, hepar, maw, viscera, vitals

atrophy lupinosis

brown autumn oak

comb. hepat(o)

disease cirrhosis, hepatitis, jaundice

enzyme glycogenase

extract acanthine

-like hepatoid

lily flag, iris

pert. hepatic, jecoral, visceral

rot fascioliasis

sausage braunschweiger

sausage tree etua

scientist hepatologist

secretion bile

LIVERISH bilious

LIVERPOOL *dish* lobscouse

native liverpudlian

native, famous ringo

singers beatles

LIVERWORT acrogen, agrimony, anthocerote, archegoniate, blasium, bryophyte, cryptogram, fern, hepatica, jungermannia, marchantia, moss(wort), plagiochila, porella, riccia

lettuce false wintergreen, pyrola

LIVERWURST braunschweiger, sausage

LIVERY appearance, clothing, dress, habit, insignia, lodging, quarters, stable, uniform, wardrobe

LIVESTOCK bestials, chattel, flock, herd, store, stuff

disease bloat, bottle-jaw, bracken sickness, hoven

migration transhumance

roughage stover

LIVIA *husband* augustus, cato, tiberius

offspring drusus, servilia, tiberius

LIVID angry, ashen, ashy, blae, blea(k), blue, discolored, dusky, ghastly, gloomy, haw, murky, opaque, pale, pallid, wan

LIVING active, alive, animate(d), being, benefice, breathing, current, existing, extant, flowing, ignited, keep, life, maintenance, native, operative, quick, resident, subsistence, support, sustenance, very, viable, vital, vivid, whick, zoetic

again redivivus

comb. bio, vivi

-dead ghost, phantom, spirit, zombi

ecclesiastical benefice

near the ground epigean

off others entozoic, parasitic, symbiotic

on land or water amphibious

on shore ripal, riparian

together consorting in syndasmos, quasi-conjugal diads, shacking up

LIVONIAN esth, lett, liv

LIVORNO leghorn

LIXIVIATE alkali(ne), leach, refine, wash

LIXIVIUM lye

LIZA mullet

LIZARD ablepharus, adda, agama, agamid, ambryhynchus, ameiva, amphisbaenid, anguid, anguis, anniellid, anole, anoliss, arbalo, ascalabota, autarchoblossa, basiliscus, basilisk, bloodsucker, bluey, bummajo, calotes, caudate, chameleon, checcha, dab(b), d(h)ab(b), diapsid, draco, dragon, dubb, eft, galliwasp, gecko, geitjie, gekkote, gila(monster), goanna, guana, hardim, ibid, ibit, iguana, kakariki, lacert, laguan, mokomoko, moloch, monitor, newt, reptile, rhiptogosse, saurian, saurus, sauvegarde, scorpion, seincid, seps, skink, tegu(exin), teiid, teioid, teju, tuatara, tucktoo, uma, uran, uta, varan, whiptail, worral, zonure, zonuroid

beaded gila monster

blue-tailed scorpion, tiliqua

burrowing chirotes

changed to ascalabus

climbing iguana

color-changing anole, anoli(s), chameleon

comb. saur(a)(o)

croaking gecko

extinct mosasaur

fabulous basilisk, dragon

family teiidae, xenosauridae

fish bombay duck, bummalo, galliwasp, harpadon, iniome, saury, soapfish, spearing, synodus, ulae

genus ablepharus, acontias, agama, ameiva, callisaurus, celustus, diploglossus, dipsosaurus, lacerta, lanthanotus, megalania, uta

gridiron-tailed callisaurus

iguanid anole, anoli(s), conolophus, tuatara, tuatera, uta

insectivorous anole, anoli(s)

large arbalo, gila monster, komodo, leguan, teju

-like iguanoid, lacertine, saurian

-*like mammal* salamander
limbless anguid, anguis, blindworm, glass-snake, rhineura, thunderworm
monitor anoli, uran, varan(us), worral
pert. iguanoid, saurian
poisonous gila monster
sand adda, skink
serpent seps
shaped lacertiform
small cheecha
spiny dabb, mastigure, sceloporus
starred agama, hardim
state alabama
-*tail* anemopsis, ass's-foot
veranoid griscus, waran
wall gecko, tarente
winged basilisk, dragon
wormlike anniellid
LLAMA alpaca, guanaco, kechua, paco, vicuna
habitat andes
relative camel
LLAMREI *master* king arthur
LLANO lowland, plain(s), prairie
LLOYD *friend* gwawl
enemy pryderi
LLUD, LLYR *kingdom* britain
offspring bran(wen), gwyn(n), manawyddan
LLYN lake, pool
LO behold, look, observe, see
LOACH beardie, carp, cobitis, dojo, mudfish, thunderfish
LOAD adulterate, afflict(ion), aggravate, alter, backpack, bale, burden, bushel, cargo, cark, carriage, charge, clog, cost, cram, cumber, deacon, doctor, dope, drug, encumber, expense, fill, fraught, freight, goods, hamper, haul, heap up, impediment, incubus, jagg, lade, lading, lot, onerate, onus, oppress, pack, pile up, pitch, pressure, price, prime, quantity, shipment, stack, steeve, stow, succubus, supply, surfeit, tote, truss, weight
kind pay, peak
of coal keel
-*pulling capacity* draft, draught
small hurry, jag(g), jobble
to excess comble, encumber
LOADED adulterated, burdened, charged, coated,

drunk, furred, laden, weighted
LOADER bucker, charger, longshoreman, stevedore
LOADSTONE adamantine, attraction, magnet(ite), siderite, terrella
planet mercury
LOAF bange, bap, bread, caddle, dally, dawdle, dillydally, drone, goof off, howff, idle, lallygag, loiter, lounge, lump, manchet, mass, mike, mooch, mouch, piece, rest, shammock, slim, slive, sorn
LOAFER abbey-lubber, beggar, bum, coberger, faitour, flaneur, hood, hooligan, idler, indolent, larrikin, lazybones, lounger, sandal, slipper, slouch, soldier, vagabond
LOAM clay, cledge, dirt, earth, lame, loess, rab, regur, silt, soil
LOAMMI *father* hosea
LOAN accommodation, advance, credit, dhan, imprest, lend, mutuum, prest
interest usance
shark usurer
LOANBLEND hybrid
LOANER moneylender, pawnbroker, shark, shylock, usurer
LOATH a(d)verse, backward, dainty, disinclined, hesitant, indisposed, laith, loth, reluctant, unwilling
LOATHE abhor, abominate, agrise, despise, detest, disdain, dislike, flinch, hate, quail, refuse, reject, repudiate, scorn, scunder, scunner, spurn
LOATHING abhorrent, aversion, disgust, distaste, hate, hatred, repulsion, revolt, revulsion
LOATHSOME abhorrent, abominable, anathematic, carrion, cloying, damned, detestable, disgusting, foul, hateful, laidly, nasty, nauseous, obnoxious, obscene, odious, offensive, repellent, repulsive, revolting, ugly, unlief, vile, wlatful, wlatsome
LOB bat, bowl, box, chandelle, cob, cop, droop, dullard, fire, hang, hit, loft,

lugworm, pitch, pollack, project, propel, puck, stair, step, strike, throw, till, toss, whack
LOBBY advocate, agency, agent, anteroom, corridor, coulisse, entrance, entry (hall), entryway, foyer, gateway, hall(way), influence, lounge, narthex, persuade, pressure, solicit, tambour, third house, urge, vestibule
LOBBYIST advocate, promoter, propagandist
LOBE ala, alula, arolium, auricle, axis, earflap, earlap, epichile, exite, fiber, fibre, fillet, fin, flap, fluke, galea, glabella, glossa, hemapod, labellum, lap(pet), ligule, list, lobing, lobule, lobulus, mala, mantle, palpifer, phylloid, projection, squamule, tooth, vannus, vermis
ornament eardrop, earring
pert. lomatine
LOBELIA bladderpod, deathcamass
LOBLOLLY bay, clown, gruel, laurel, lodgepole, lout, medicine, mudhole, mush, pine, ponderosa, puddle, tree
LOBO boxcar, wolf
LOBSTER crawfish, crayfish, crustacean, decapod, homard, homarus, langosta, langouste, lubber, macruran, palinurus, shedder
boat peapod
claw chela, nipper
color bittersweet
eggs coral, roe
enclosure crawl
female hen
liver tomalley
part chela, claw, coral, nipper, pincer, telson, thorax, uropod
pert. macruran
pot coy, crail, creel, fishpot, trunk
roe coral
small joe, nancy, pawk
spiny crawfish, crayfish, palinurid
trap bownet, car, corf, creel, pot
LOCAL branch, bucolic, chapter, confined, edaphic, endemic, epichoric, home (grown), insular, limited, narrow, native, neighbor-

hood, parochial, particular, provincial, regional, restricted, rural, sectional, specific, topical, train, union, vernacular, vicunal

LOCALE, LOCALITY area, belt, district, domain, environs, field, habitat, locus, neighborhood, part, place, position, province, purlieu, region, scene, section, sector, site, situs, sphere, spot, stead, territory, tract, venew, venue, vicinage, vicinity, zone

pert. endemic, grass-roots

LOCALIZE bound, delimit(ate), limit, position, situate

LOCATE allocate, anchor, assign, billet, camp, consign, deposit, discover, dispose, embed, emplace, ensconce, establish, find, identify, install, lodge, moor, pinpoint, pitch, place, post, put, quarter, repose, root, seat, set(tle), site, situate, spearhead, spot, stand, station, stow, tether

LOCATING *system* sofar

LOCATION address, base, bearings, emplacement, farm, home, installation, locale, locus, lodg(e)ment, place(ment), point, position, region, scene, settlement, site, situation, spot, standing, station, stead, ubiety

comb. topy
geographic seat
natural habitat

LOCH bay, creek, inlet, lake, lin(ctus), lough, mere, ness, pond

LOCHIA artemis

LOCHINVAR *bride* ellen
river eske

LOCH KATRINE *lady* ellen

LOCHLIN dane, scandinavian

LOCH NESS *monster* nessie

LOCK, LOCKS berger, bind, bolt, button, clasp, clinch, close, cotter, cowlick, curl, dag, debbeh, detent, ecluse, embrace, engage, fasten(er), feak, fence, floodgate, frib, grapple, hair, hank, hasp, hide, hobble, hold, hug, jam, join, latch, mane, mop, obstruct, padlock, ringlet, sasse, secure,

shackle, shut out, sluice, stang, steckle, strand, tag, tate, tie, tress(es), trick, trim, tuft, unite, yale
control headgate
cylinder yale
horns dispute, fight
keeper nab, risp
nut jamnut, keeper
part bolt, cam, cylinder, nab, strike, stump, talon, tumbler, ward
-stepper convict
stock and barrel all, altogether, entirely, utterly, whole
-up calaboose, choky, cooker, coop, gaol, hoosegow, imprison, jail, jug, limbo, PRISON, tronk

LOCKE, DAVID R. *pseud.* petroleum v. nasby

LOCKER ascham, box, closet, clothespress, treasury, wardrobe

LOCKERMAN nibbler, scotcher, snibbler

LOCKET chain, lavaliere, pendant

LOCKJAW amasesis, ankylostoma, tetanus, trismus

LOCKSMAN turnkey, warden

LOCO crazy, insane, loon(e)y, luny, mad, weed
weed marijuana, peavine

LOCOMOTION motion, movement, stir, travel

LOCOMOTIVE (See also *kind*, below.) bigboy, choochoo, diesel, dilly, engine, iron horse, moving, switcher, traveling
extra helper
fireman tallowpot
front cowcatcher, pilot
heavy mogul
inventor stephenson
kind atlantic, bogie, calliope, centipede, columbia, decapod, diesel, dinky, doctor, dollie, donkey, dummy, eight-wheeler, forney, loader, mallet, mikado, mogul, mountain, pilot, pusher, shunter, tenwheeler, yarder
repair shop roundhouse
service car coalcar, tender
small dinkey

LOCRI *father* zeus

LOCRINE *daughter* sabrina
father brut

LOCUM TENENS alternate, deputy, doctor, double, lieutenant, pinch hitter, stand-in, substitute, supply

LOCUS area, axode, conchoid, dose, drug, locality, place, point, rank, site, surface

LOCUST See also *insect*, below.
berry glamberry, nance
bird grackle, pratincole, starling, stork, wattled-stare
clammy robinia, rose-acacia
compound acacetin, acacin
eater acridophagus, dialbird, starling
group plague, swarm
insect atlas moth, attacus, bangalay, bay-bay, bellbearer, bruke, cicad(a), cicala, cigala, cricket, grasshopper, harvest fly, mantis, quaker, sawyer, skipper, tetrigid, weta
larva bruke
noise stridulation
plant senna
pod carob-bean, cleva
tree acacia, algar(r)oba, carob, clammy, courbaril, honey, kowhai, robinia, silverchain

LOCUTION collocation, diction, expression, idiom, language, phrase, term, voice

LODE canal, course, deposit, drain, fissure, lead, ledge, load, mine, path, reef, rider, road, scrin, source, vein, waterway
cavity voog, vug(g), vugh

LODESTAR center, cynosure, focus

LODESTONE See LOADSTONE.

LODGE abide, accept, accommodate, address, alight, barracks, bed, bestow, billet, board, branch, burrow, cabin, camp, catch, cavern, contain, cottage, couch, den, deposit, dorm, dwell, encamp, entertain, establish, fix, harbor, hold, hostel, hotel, house, howff, hut, inhabit, inn, install, lair, lie, live, luge, place, plant, put up, quarter, receive, remain, reside, room, roost, settle, shelter, society, sojourn, station, stay, stop, store, stow, take, tarry, tavern *and eat* board and room, cosher

doorkeeper tiler

LODGEPOLE *pine* jeffrey, loblolly, tamarack

LODGER boarder, roomer, tenant, transient

LODGING(S) accommodation, apartment, bed, billet, board, camp, diggings, digs, dwelling, flat, gist, gite, habitation, haft, hostel, hotel, housing, INN, kip, libken, libkin, nest, pad, quarters, residence, rooms

LODOVICO *kin* brabantia

LOEGRIA england

LOFT air, attic, balk, bat, ceiling, garret, hit, lift, lob, proud, scaffold, sky, sol(1)ar, whack

hay tallet, tallit

LOFTINESS affectation, altitude, dignity, eminence, height, highness, importance, grandeur, magnanimity, majesty, nobility, ostentation, pride

LOFTING, HUGH dr. doolittle

LOFTY aerie, airy, alpine, andean, arresting, arrogant, assuming, dignified, distant, elevated, eminent, exalted, eyrie, eyry, formal, glorious, grandiloquent, great, haughty, hifalutin(g), high (flown)(minded), imposing, magnified, majestic, noble, olympian, ostentatious, proud, raised, splendid, steep, striking, sublime, superb, TALL, topful, towering, upward, wingy

name meaning bridget, brigid

LOG account book, bankbook, billet, block, cashbook, chuck, clog, daybook, diary, journal, ledger, lumber, passbook, puncheon, record, register, stump, timber, viga, wood

anchor dead man

carrier bummer, bunk, skidder, sloop, tode

contest birling, roleo

fixer rosser

haul handbank, siwash, sloop, swamp, tode

house tilt

hut isba

gin jammer

group boom, deck, drive, raft, rollway

kind puncheon, slab, spalt

load-holder dutchman

manipulator cattyman

measure scalage

mine-supporting nog

-noser sniper

perch darter, hogfish, rockfish

platform machan

raft-binding swifter

rafter viga

revolve or *roll* birl, logroll

road corduroy

roller birler, canter, dealer, decker, politician

roller's sled godevil

rolling birling

rolling tournament roleo

run sluiceway

sawed boule

skid tode

slabbed cant

spiked deadener

split puncheon

splitter wedge

sunken deadhead

tool cant, hook, peav(e)y, tode

truck bummer

LOGARITHM *base* ten

inventor napier, neper

unit bel

LOGE booth, box, room, stall

LOGGER ballhooter, cutter, girdler, heavy, lumberjack, rosser, sawyer, scorer, sniper, stupid, timberer, topper, woodchopper, woodcutter

boot pac(k)

boss bully

contest roleo

device buckingboard, springboard

hook See LOGGER *tool.*

platform apron

rod canary

shoe larigan, pac

sled alligator, tode, travois, wynn

tool cart, peav(e)y, pe(e)vy, nigger, scorer, tode

trousers tin pants

trunk wanigan

wheels, pair katydid

LOGGERHEAD blockhead, caretta, clodpole, clodpoll, knapweed, numskull, shrike, thickskull, turtle

LOGGIA arcade, balcony,

gallery, lanai, piazza, porch, portico

LOGI *defeated* loki

LOGIC ars artium, dialectics, nyaya, rationality, reasoning, sanity, sense, syllogistics

aristotelian organon

assumption premise

baconian induction

branch alethiology

distinguishing mark differentia

fallacy idol, idolum

inductive epagoge

method analysis, deduction, dialectic, epagoge, generalization, induction, inference, syllogism, synthesis

mode darii

omission of step saltus

pert. heuretic

premise lemma

specious sophism

syllogisms sorites

term apodictic, apophantic, apriori, ferio, ferison, lemma, organon, premise, proposition, subaltern, syllogism

LOGICIAN dialectician, dialector, reasoner, syllogist

LOGICAL admissible, analytic(al), clear, cogent, coherent, consistent, credible, dialectic(al), just(ifiable), legitimate, likely, lucid, plausible, rational, reasonable, sane, sensible, sound, subtle, syllogistic, telling, valid, well-founded

LOGOGRIPH anagram, riddle

LOGORRHEA talkativeness, wordiness

LOGWOOD admiral, bluewood, brazil, campeachy, campecha, dyewood, hypernic, mangrove

LOGY dull, heavy, inert, sluggish

LOHENGRIN *character* elsa, parsifal, telramund

composer wagner

LOIN(S) aloyau, back, flank, flitch, hand, leer, lunyie, reins, side, wing, withers

-cloth breechcloth, breechclout, dho(o)ti, diaper, girdle, g-string, izar, lungi, malo, maro, pagne, panung, parue, pata

muscle psoas

pert. lumbar, lumbo

LOIRE *city on* st nazaire
tributary allier
valley region anjou

LOIS *offspring* eunice, timothy

LOITER coose, dally, dawdle, delay, dillydally, drawl, dringle, hawm, haze, hove, idle, lag, linger, lollygag, poke, procrastinate, saunter, shaffle, slug, slummock, strake, taigle, tarry, trail, wait

LOITERER drone, idler, laggard, layabout, lurcher

LOKA sphere, universe, world

LOKE alley, lane, lawk, road

LOKI *companion* aesir
conqueror thor
consort angerboda, angerbotha, angrbodha, angurboda, grid, siguna, sigyn
imprisoned by geirrod, thjazi
offspring asvidar, fenrir, fenris, hel(a), jormungand, midgard, nare
parent farbauti, laufey, naal
seer utgardaloki
slayer heimdall
uninvited guest of aesir
usurped seat of vidar
victim balder, bragi, idun, sif
wagered with brokki, sindri
wandering   companion hoenir, odin

LOLIGO calamary, octopus, squid

LOLITA nymphet
bewitched humbert humbert
creator nabokov, sirin

LOLL dangle, droop, frowst, idle, lie, lill, lounge, recline, rest, scamble, sprawl

LOLLIPOP candy, suckabob, sucker

LOLLOP bound, curvet, hop, loll, lope, lounge, ricochet, skip

LOLLY bribe, candy, ice, lollipop, loot, money, snow, treat

LOLO kui, nosu

LOMBARD banker, cannon, moneylender, pawnshop
governor catapan
king alboin
lake como, garda, maggiore
language langobardic
poplar black lady
steward gastaldo

LOMILOMI massage, press, rub, shampoo

LONDON *accent* cockney

airport croydon, gatwick, heathrow
almshouse spitalfields
ancient agusta, trinovant(um)
apprentice square-cap
art gallery british museum, burlington house, courtauld, dulwich, kenwood, national, sloane, tate, v and a, victoria and albert, wallace
barrister templar
bathhouse dummums
bohemian section chelsea, soho
borough (See also *district*, below.) battersea, bethnal green, chelsea, deptford, greenwich, hammersmith, hampstead, islington, kensington, marylebone, paddington, stepney, wandsworth
bridal path the row
bridge albert, chelsea, putney, tower, waterloo, westminster
brown carbuncle
bus conductor clippy
cafe district soho
cart license caroon
cathedral st paul's
cattle market smithfields
circus astley's
clock big ben
club almack, atheneum, boodles, brooks, carlton, conservative, kit-cat, macaroni, reform, union, whig, whites
coffee house will's
commercial street threadneedle
criminal court old bailey
criminal refuge alsatia, whitefriars
department store harrod's, selfridge's
district (See also *borough*, above.) acton, adelphi, alsatia, bankside, belgravia, billingsgate, blackfriars, bloomsbury, brixton, camberwell, camden town, charing cross, chelsea, ealing, east end, haymarket, holborn, lambeth, limehouse, mayfair, pimlico, pye corner, soho, strand, vauxhall, west end, westminster, whitechapel
execution site tyburn
fashionable area belgravia, mayfair, west end

feature fog
financial district the city
fishmarket billingsgate
flower market covent garden
fortress tower
founder brut, lud(d)
gambling club crockford's, white's
guildhall statue gog, magog
hack-writers' section grub street
hawker coster, mun
horsepath rotten row
insurance company lloyd's
landmark big ben, st pauls, tower
lord mayor dick whittington
market covent garden
monument cenotaph, gog, magog, marble arch, nelson, tower, victoria
native cockney, flatcap
newspaper district fleet street
night brawler nicker
official remembrancer
opera house covent garden
palace buckingham, kensington, savoy, st james
plague year annus mirabilis
police court bow street
police headquarters scotland yard
porter george, georgina
prison bridewell, fleta, marshalsea, newgate, old bailey, tower
promenade embankment, mall
quarter billingsgate, charing cross, covent garden, hyde park, kew gardens, knightsbridge, mall, petticoat lane, piccadilly circus, portobello, smithfield, soho, st giles, strand, west end, whitefriars
roisterer mun
society mayfair
square bedford, belgrave, bloomsbury, cadogan, carlyle, eaton, euston, finsbury, fitzroy, leicester, onslow, piccadilly, russell, sloane, soho, tavistock, trafalgar, trinity
stables mews
state barge galley foist
stock exchange gorgonzola hall
street bond, bow, cannon, cheapside, downing, drury lane, fleet, harley, haymarket, grub, kingsrow, oxford, pall mall, park lane,

paternoster row, piccadilly, regent, savile row, strand, wardour

suburb ealing, finchley, kew, twickenham

subway tube

tavern boar's head, pub

theater adelphi, aldwych, drury lane, fortune, garrick, globe, haymarket, hippodrome, old vic, royal court, sadler's wells, saville, savoy, strand, winter garden

LONDON, JACK *novel* call of the wild, seawolf

LONE isolated, LONELY, one, only, particular, separate, single, sole, solitary, unique

eagle charles lindbergh

ranger aide tonto

star state texas

LONELINESS dejection, depression, solitude, vacancy

fear of autophobia

LONELY, LONESOME abandoned, alone, deavely, depressed, deserted, desolate, dreary, forlorn, forsaken, isolated, lorn, remote, secluded, solitary, unfrequented, unket, unkid

LONER hermit, misanthrope, stag

LONG ache, arigue, aspire, beg, covet, crave, desire, distant, dree, extended, far, fluid, hanker, hone, hunger, itch, lathy, lengthen, lengthy, pine, prolix, prolong(ed), protracted, sesquipedalian, slow, tall, tedious, thirst, want, wiln, wish, wordy, worry, yearn, yet

ago eld, langsyne, past, yesterday, yore

and slender elongated, lathy, linear, reedy, spindly, squinny

arm rifle

-billed curlew smoker

boat sloop

bow battle crecy

comb. dolich(o), macro

-drawn out extended, interminable, longspun, padded, prolix, verbose

-faced sad, solemn

for care, covet, crave, desire, hone, miss, want, wish

-hair dryball, hippie, intellectual, oldster, surfer

-headed clever, farsighted, sage, shrewd, smart, wise

home grave

island city brentwood, east meadow, elmont, southampton, uniondale

island, end montauk point

island indian rockaway

island oyster bluepoint

island sound, river into connecticut

-legged spauldrochy

live evviva, viva

-lived durable, lasting, macrobian

-nose gar

shot improbability, odds

-suffering endurance, forbearing, fortitude, grit, meek(ness), patience, patient, resignation, tolerance, tolerant

suit forte, skill, specialty, talent

time age, blue moon, born days, coon's age, donkey's years, eternity, forever

to aspire

tom gun, skipper

water kawaiola

-winded garrulous, lengthy, prolix, prosaic, tedious, tiresome, verbose, windy, wordy

LONGANIMITY forbearance, forgiveness, patience, tolerance

LONGBEAK dowitcher

LONGBEARD bellarmine, old man

LONGE exercise, guide, lunge, namaycush, rein, rope, strap, thrust, trout

LONGERON spar

LONGEVITY durability, macrobiosis

goddess anna perenna

symbol agate, crow, tortoise

LONGFELLOW *character* evangeline, hiawatha, john alden, miles standish, nakomis, priscilla

junction excelsior

poem evangeline, excelsior, psalm of life, village blacksmith, wreck of the hesperus

LONGHORN cattle, native, steer, veteran

LONGING ache, ambition, appetite, aspiration, athirst, craving, cupidity, desiderium, desire, envy, itch, lust, need, nostalgia, pas-

sion, thirsty, willing, wishful, yet

LONGITUDINALLY endlong, lengthwise

LONGJAW billfish, cisco, needlefish

LONGLEGS stilt(bird)

LONGLICK molasses

LONGSHANKS edward i, stilt(bird)

LONGSHOREMAN docker, dockhand, dockwalloper, hobbler, loader, lumper, roustabout, stevedore, stower, wharfhand, wharfie

LONICERA bindweed, honeysuckle, twinberry

LOO cardgame, dreiblatt, eltomate, napoleon, pam, sechsern, shweck, sixte, tippen, zwicken

term bold stand, miss, mistigri

LOOBY bounder, fool, lubber, rustic

LOOF luff(a), luif, palm, paw

LOOK air, appear(ance), aspect, bearing, behold, bode, browse, cast, con(template), deek, dekko, examine, expect, expression, eye, eyeful, eyeshot, face, gander, gape, gawk, gaze, glance, glare, glime, glimpse, glom, glower, goggle, heed, hist, inspect, ken, leer, manner, mien, moon, observe, ogle, oversee, peek, peep, peer, pipe, pore, pose, posture, preview, pry, regard, scan, scrutinize, search, see, seek, seem, semblance, sight, skew, snoop, spy, stare, supervise, survey, view, visage, vision, voila, watch, witness, wlite, yawp

-alike double, twin

after attend, care for, procure, serve, supervise, tend

ahead anticipate, envision, envisage, foresee, prepare, ready

amorous leer, ogle, smicker

askance gledge, glent, glim, leer, skew, sklent

at behold, consider, eyeball, glom, pipe, regard, spectate

back recall, relive, remember, rethink, retrospect, review

brief glimpse

closely pry, scan, scrutinize

cross-eyed sheyle
daggers glare, glower, scowl
down one's nose condescend, sneer, snub, upstage
down on despise, scorn, snub
everywhere ransack, search
favorably smile
for anticipate, await, expect, foresee, quest, search, seek
forward prospice
here heed, hist, listen
into examine, inspect, investigate, observe, sound, study
lecherous leer
like favor, resemble
loving belgard
obliquely glime, goggle, skew, squint
on attend, consider, esteem, observe, regard, think of, view, watch
out beware, fend, jiggers, warning, watch
over browse, disregard, examine, ignore, inspect, overlook, reconnoiter, reconnotre, scan, scrutinize, survey, toise
pryingly keek, peek, peep, snoop, spy
quick glent, scry
sharp beware, dress, excel, primp, watch
sidelong glee, glime
slyly glance, glink, leer, peep, ogle
sullen frown, glare, gloom, glunch, lour, lower, scowl
to avail, count on, expect, prepare, tend, watch
toward face
up aspire, call, improve, meet, rise, search, seek, visit
upon contemplate, think
up to admire, honor, regard, respect
wildly glop, waul, whawl
LOOKER bailiff, beauty, herdsman, inspector, keeper, searcher, steward
-on audience, beholder, bystander, eyewitness, kibitzer, observer, spectator, witness
LOOKING examination, inspection, observation, scansion, scrutiny, supervision, surveillance
glass mirror, reflector
glass plant karamu
up encouraging, improving, propitious

LOOKOUT atalaya, bantay(an), bartizan, belvedere, cockatoo, crow's nest, kykuit, observatory, patrol, picket, prospect, scout, sentinel, spotter, tout, tower, view, vigil, watch, widow's-walk
LOOKS appearance, countenance, face, features, lineaments, lines, phiz(og), physiognomy, visage
LOOM appear, approach, auk, await, beam, beetle, bird, bulk, dobbie, dobby, draw, emerge, frame, gentle, gloom, guillemot, hover, hulk, imminence, impend, implement, jacquard, leem, loon, menace, moderate, overhang, overpick, portend, puffin, receptacle, rise, schiffli, seem, threaten, tool, vessel, weave(r), weaving
adjust gate
attachment lappet
axle rocktree
bar dagger, easer, sword
fixer tackler
harness caam, headle, heddle, leaf, mounting, simblot
head jacquard
inventor cartwright, jacquard
large bulk
lever lam
part backstay, bar, batten, beam, caam, easer, feeler, griff, hanger, harness, heald, heddle, lam, lathe, leaf, lingoe, reed, shed, shuttle, sley, sword, temple, treadle, warp, weft
rod shaft
LOON auk, bird, boy, cobble, diver, dolt, ducker, fellow, gavia, grebe, guillemot, gunner, harlot, hoodlum, imber, lad, lout, lubber, lunatic, menial, mistress, oaf, pygopod, rascal, rogue, simpleton, wabby, whabby
red throated cobble
LOONY, LUNY crazy, daft, foolish, insane, lunatic, wild
LOOP ambit, ansa, arch, beat, bend, bight, billet, bow, bride, buckle, buttonhole, circle, circuit, coil, cringle, crook, crupper, curve, embrasure, eye(let), fake, fold, frog, grommet, honda, hook, hoop, keeper, kink, knot, latchet, link,

lug, mat, noose, opening, pearl, picot, purl, ring, round, shank, slink, slip, sneak, spiral, staple, stitch, surround, tab, terry, turn (around), u-turn, weave, wind, withy
and thimbles clew, clue
edging picot
fabric terry
-forming brochidodromous
hanging festoon
heddle doup
knitting purl, steek
lace picot
lariat honda, hondoo
ornamental picot
rope bight, slug
running noose
-shaped fundiform
steel oolly, wootz
tight kink(le)
LOOPER inchworm
LOOPHOLE alibi, aperture, chink, eyelet, escape, evasion, excuse, fort, m(e)use, oillet, opening, out(let), plea, porthole, pretext, slit, weakness, wicket
LOOPY cunning, deceitful, insane, sly
LOOSE absolve, apart, asunder, at large, baggy, careless, casual, coarse, corrupt, detach, disengage, disentangle, disjoin, dissolute, drooping, droopy, easy, escaped, extricate, flabby, flaccid, flimsy, frank, free, haphazard, hit-or-miss, immoral, improvident, incompact, independent, insecure, lax, lewd, liberate, licentious, light, limber, limp, loppy, movable, negligent, open, profligate, rambling, random, relax(ed), release, remiss, separate, slack(en), soft, unbind, unconfined, undo, unfasten, unfetter, ungirt, unlock, unshackle, unstable, untie, untight, vague, wanton, wild, wobbly
at---ends bored, dags, restless, tagrag
-jointed lanky, ramshackle, rangy, rickety, shackly, wobbly
-tongued garrulous, gossiping, loquacious, talkative, voluble
LOOSEN break, detach, dissolve, ease, free, laxate, lib-

erate, open, relax, resolve, slack(en), unbend, undo, unscrew, unstring, untie

LOOSENESS laxity, relaxation, slack

LOOSENING abatement, softening
comb. lys(i)

LOOSESTRIFE crosswort, killweed, lysimachia, lythrum, moneywort, peatweed, peatwood, primwort

LOOT bag, boodle, booty, burglarize, gut, haul, lolly, money, pillage, plunder, prize, ransack, ravage, rifle, rob, sack, snaffle, spoils, STEAL, swag, thieve
receipt theftbote

LOOTER See THIEF.

LOP amputate, crop, curtail, cut(off), deduct, detach, dock, dodd, droop, hang, obtruncate, oche, poll, prune, snag, snathe, sned, snig, snip, stump, trash, truncate, twine
-eared drooping
seed phryma

LOPE amble, bound, canter, curvet, gallop, hop, lollop, pace, pad, race, rack, ricochet, run, scamper, scoot, singlefoot, skip, trot, walk

LOPPER clabber, clot, congeal, curdle(d), slush

LOPPY baggy, drooping, flabby, flaccid, lax, limp, loose, relaxed, slack, sleasy

LOPSIDED alist, alop, askew, crooked, unbalanced

LOQUACIOUS articulate, babblative, babbling, blithering, chattering, chatty, eloquent, fluent, gabby, garrulous, glib, talkative, vocal, voluble

LOQUACITY cackle, chat (ter), effusion, facility, fluency, gab, garrulity, garrulousness, gassiness, glibness, gush(iness), multiloquence, prating, prattle, slush, talkativeness, volubility, windiness
excessive leresis

LOQUAT biwa, nispero

LORCA *drama* blood wedding, bodas de sangre

LORD, LORD'S aire, almighty, baron, bel, bey, captain, ceremon, chan, commander, county, deity, dominator, domine, domi-

neer, duke, earl, god, governor, grandee, kaan, kaun, kawn, khan, knight, laird, lauk, liege, luddy, magnate, marquis, master, noble, paladin, palatine, peer, potentate, ruler, seid, seigneur, seignior, superior, suzerain, swami, thakur, vavasor, viscount
-and-ladies cuckoopint, duck, jack-in-the-pulpit
attendant thane
chancellor woolpack
chancellor's seat woolsack
day sabbath, sunday
group aristocracy, peerage, society
have mercy kyrie eleison
haw-haw william joyce
jim's ship patna
messenger malachi
of darkness hyle
of heaven tien chu
of hosts elohim
of misrule abbot of unreason
of the dance balmarcodes
of the flies beelzebub
of the world lokindra
prayer paternoster
protector nejus
supper eucharist, nachtmaal
supper cup chalice
table altar
territory banat
wife lady

LORDLY arrogant, despotic, dictatorial, dignified, disdainful, grand, haughty, imperious, insolent, lofty, magisterial, majestic, masterful, noble, overbearing, pompous, proud, superb, supercilious, uppish
name meaning adon, cyril, frey, lars

LORDSHIP allegiance, authority, dynasty, manor, mastery, possession, seigniory, signoria

LORE advice, counsel, doctrine, erudition, information, instruction, knowledge, learning, legend, mastax, mythology, rune, scholarship, science, superstition, tradition, wisdom
comb. ology

LORELEI charmer, siren

LORENZO *beloved* jessica
friend bassanio

LORETTE prostitute, trollop, wanton

LORGNETTE opera glass, starer

LORGNON eyeglass, pincenez

LORICA breastplate, corselet, covering, cuirass, lute, sheath, shell, shield, testa

LORIKEET corella, parrot, warrin, weroole

LORIOT oriole

LORIS animal, kokam, lemur(oid), sloth

LORN alone, bereft, desolate, forlorn, forsaken, lone(ly), lonesome, solitary

LORNA DOONE *author* blackmore
hero john ridd
locale exmoor

LORRAINE *capital* metz
invader stanislas
king charles the bald
river saar

LORRY flatcar, rolley, rully, truck, wagon

LORUHAMAH *father* hosea

LORY corella, loory, lorikeet, parrot, touraco

LOSE amit, blunder, bury, cast, disappear, drop, estrange, fail, fall, forfeit, forlese, lapse, lease, mislay, misplace, miss, release, sacrifice, slatter, spill, squander, succumb, waste
color bleach, fade
consciousness black out, faint, swoon
control blow, crack
courage break down, falter, fear, flee
deliberately throw
freshness fade, wilt, wither
ground fall(back)(short), slip, slow
heart faint, jade, quail
heat chill, cool
hope despair, despond, give up
interest fag, flag, tire
luster dim, dull, tarnish
nerve chicken
one's head break down, panic, rattle
out fail, miss
patience chafe
sight of disappear, forget, neglect, overlook
strength fade, fail, languish, sicken, weaken
weight enseam, reduce, slenderize, slim, thin down

LOSEL good-for-nothing,

LOSER, vagabond, worthless, wretch

LOSER also-ran, booby, cellar-dweller, defeatee, goner, last, LOSEL, mediocrity, neb(b)ech, neb(b)ish, prey, s(c)hlemie(h)l, schlimazel, shlemihl, shlimazl, tailender, underdog, victim, wretch

LOSH alteration, elk, hide, splash

LOSS affliction, bereavement, breakage, casualty, cost, damage, damnum, decrease, decrement, defeat, deperdition, deprivation, destruction, detriment, disappearance, downfall, expense, failure, forfeit(ure), hurt, injury, lapse, leak (age), misfortune, miss, penalty, perdition, privation, qualm, ruin, sacrifice, toll, trouble, undoing, waste

LOST abandoned, absent, absorbed, asea, astray, bewildered, bushed, confused, damned, defeated, deperdite, destroyed, dissipated, engrossed, farblondjet, forfeit(ed), forlorn, gone, hidden, hopeless, incorrigible, irreclaimable, irredeemable, lorn, mislaid, misplaced, missed, missing, obdurate, overthrown, perplexed, rapt, reprobate, ruined, strayed, subverted, tinsel, unregenerate, vanished, wasted, wrecked

in absorbed, engrossed, hidden, merged, oblivious
to inaccessible

LOT (See also LOTS.) assortment, backyard, batch, boodle, bunch, bundle, caboodle, chance, choise, collection, destiny, dicker, doom, fate, fortune, grist, group, hap, hazard, land, luck, much, oodles, parcel, part, patch, plat, plot, portion, quantity, rimption, scad(s), share, sum, teems, tichel, troop
building erf
burial lair, plot
by proportionately
-casting sortition
kin abraham, benammi, gareth, gawain, haran, milcah, moab

kingdom lothian, norway, orkney
of people boodle, crowd, multitude
ordeal sodom
vacant common(s)
wife bellicent, eavesdropper

LOTA burbot, fish, waterpot

LOTAN *kin* homam, hori, seir, timna

LOTH See also LOATH.
brother-in-law king arthur
son gawain, mordred

LOTHARIO casanova, gigolo, lover, rake, roue, seducer
beloved calista

LOTI, PIERRE louis viaud
rival zola

LOTION ablution, balm, eyewash, lenitive, liniment, loture, ointment, salve, unguent, wash
fragrant bay rum
rub with embrocate

LOTS bushel, gobs, great deal, heaps, loads, many, much, multitude, myriads, numbers, numerous, plenty, quantity, reams, scads, scores, slews
divination by sortilege
feast of purim
sacred urim

LOTTE *de mer* angler fish, monk fish

LOTTERY ambo, bingo, biribi, blanque, draw, gamble, grab bag, hona, keno, lotto, pool, raffle, sweepstakes, terno, tombola, turkey draw
choice gig
prize benefit, purse, tern

LOTTO bingo, game, keno, lottery, tombola

LOTUS chinquapin, lote, melilot, narcotic, plant, trefoil, wankapin
bird jacana
eater dreamer, utopian, visionary
eater land jerba
enzyme lotase
grass butterjags, cat-clover, melilot, nelumbo, trefoil
indian rose lily
land See UTOPIA.
lily water-chinquapin
personification ptah
tree celtis, date plum, jujube, lote, nettle-tree, nitraria, persimmon, sadr, zyzyphus

LOUD big, blatant, bluster-

ing, boisterous, bold, booming, brassy, brazen, buckeye, clamorous, clangorous, clarion, coarse, criant, deafening, earrending, earsplitting, flashy, flaunting, forte, fortissimo, full, gaudy, impudent, intense, noisy, obtrusive, pealing, powerful, reboant, resounding, ringing, showy, slambang, sonorous, splashy, stentorian, strepent, striking, vehement, violent, vulgar, wight
as thunder
-mouthed blatant, boisterous, scurrilous, thersitical, vociferous, vulgar
-speaker bullhorn, megaphone, squawker, tweeter, woofer
-spoken randy

LOUDLY crescendo, forte (mente), fortissimo, lustily, noisily, viva voce

LOUDNESS bang, bedlam, clamor, clash, din, hubbub, hurlyburly, intensity, noise, power, racket, sonority, tumult, uproar, volume, zoon
unit sone

LOUGH lake, loch, mere, pool, sea, water
diver gull

LOUHI *conqueror* vainamoinen
consort pohjola
enemy finns

LOUIS BONAPARTE *wife* hortense

LOUIS XI *daughter* anne

LOUIS XII *jester* triboulet

LOUIS XIII *adviser* richelieu
consort anne of austria
jester longely

LOUIS XIV roi soleil, the sun king
art rococo
confessor la chaise
consort maintenon, montespan
financial adviser tonti
jester angeli
nickname grand monarque
reign of siecle d'or
saying l'etat c'est moi

LOUIS XV bien aime
consort dubarry, pompadour
saying after me the deluge, apres moi le deluge

LOUIS XVI *epithet* veto
wife marie antoinette

LOUISIANA *account book* bilan

bayou teche
boat bateau
bouillabaise gumbo
canvas back horse-duck
capital baton rouge
city bastrop, baton rouge, bogalusa, bunkie, gretna, houma, kenner, lafayette, lake charles, monroe, new orleans, opelousas, ruston, shreveport
college dillard, grambling, lsu, tulane
county acadia, caddo, lafourche, parish, tensas
creek bayou
culture tchefuncte
decree arret
dialect cajun, creole
drumfish gaspergou
festival mardi gras
french founder iberville
governor bienville
grass bena, carpet, vetiver
heron demoiselle
indian adai, andarko, arikara, atakapa, bayogoula, caddo, eyeish, haini, ioni, nachitoch, ovachita, pawnee, rees, waco, washa
island avery
lake borgne, clear, darbonne, iatt, larto, maurepas, pontchartrain, saline
native acadian, cajun, creole, pelican
nickname pelican state
patois creole
plover papabot(e)
river amite, bayou, mississippi, ouachita, red, tensas
state bird pelican
state flower magnolia
state tree bald cypress
territory capital st louis
tobacco perique

LOUISVILLE *founder* george rogers clark

LOUK blow, close, lock, pull up, thrash, uproot, weed, whip

LOUNGE anteroom, bange, bar, dawdle, divan, froust, frowst, glider, hawm, idle, lammock, laze, loaf, lobby, loiter, loll(up), loppet, perch, recline, rest, rizzle, room, roost, saunter, settee, slinge, sofa, sorn, soss, sozzle, sprawl, traik
lizard idler

LOUNGER boulevardier, idler

LOUP fish, flee, jump, leap, mask, pawnee, skidi

LOUP-GAROU lycanthrope, werewolf

LOUR frown, impend, LOWER, money, scowl, threaten

LOURD dull, lout, rather, sluggish, sot

LOURING gloomy, morose, threatening

LOUSE anoplura, ant cattle, beggar-tick, blister mite, bob, booger, braula, cootie, crab, creeper, crumb, gisler, grayback, mite, morpion, palmer, parasite, pediculid, pediculus, pou, puce(ron), sisten, slater, sow, tick
berry spindletree
-eating phthirophagous
egg nit
fish gisler
fly sheep-tick
plant aphid, aphis
up botch, queer, spoil
wood slater, sow
young nit

LOUSEWORT cockscomb, coxcomb, hellebore, rattle, snaffles, stavesacre, woodbetony

LOUSTER bustle, confusion, litter, scramble, work

LOUSY awful, bad, bum, crappy, crummy, disgusting, execrable, horrible, mean, miserable, outrageous, punk, seedy, terrible

LOUT bend, blunderbuss, boeotian, bohunk, boor, bounder, bow, bumpkin, churl, clodhopper, clown, clunch, cuif, flout, gaum, gawk, grobian, hit, hob, loblolly, loiter, loll, looby, loon, loun, lown, lubber, lummox, lurk, lusk, oaf, rube, rustic, slangrell, slouch, sneak, stare, stoop, thrum, tripal, whaup, yahoo, yokel
lanky slangrell

LOUTISH awkward, boeotian, burly, callow, clumsy, crude, gauche, green, inept, maladroit, raw, rough, rude

LOUVER abatvent, chimney, diffuser, dovecote, femerell, luffer, shutter, slat, slit, turret

LOVABLE adorable, alluring, amabel, amiable, angelic, attractive, bewitching, captivating, charming, cuddly, enchanting, engaging, fascinating, sweet, winning, winsome
name meaning amabel

LOVE admiration, admire, adoration, adore, affection, agape, aimer, allegiance, amo(u)r, appreciate, ardor, attachment, bhalobasha, care for, charity, cherish, clemency, compassion, cupid, darling, dear, desire, devotion, dilection, doat, dote(on), drury, enamo(u)r, enjoy, eros, fancy, fervor, fidelity, fire, flame, fondness, goodwill, gra, heart, idolatry, idolize, infatuation, kama, like, liking, loo, loyalty, minne, paramour, passion, pet, piety, popularity, regard(s), relish, shine, solidarity, spark, spoon, sweetheart, sympathy, treasure, understanding, value, woo, worship, zeal, zero,
affair amorette, amour, flirtation, intrigue, romance, tryst
apple eggplant, tomato
bird parrot, turtledove
brotherly agape, charity
bug march-fly
charm philter
comb. amat, eroto, phil(o)
curl bow-catcher
emblem myrtle
-entangle stonecrop, virgin's-bower
feast agape, banquet, gathering
-flower agapanthus
full of amative, besotted, doting, erotic, fond, infatuated
gift amatorio
god aengus, amor, angus, apollo, ares, baal, bhaga, cama(deva), camdeo, cupid, dagda, eros, frey(r), kama, oengus, pothos
goddess aphhrodite, as(h)tarte, ashtoreth, athor, freya, freyja, hathor, inanna, is(h)tar, urania, venus
in-a-mist bishopswort, passion flower, snow-in-harvest
-in-idleness heartsease, pansy
-in-winter pipsissewa
knot amoret, memento
-lass sweetheart

letter billet-doux, poulet

-lies-bleeding amaranth, bleeding-heart, pheasant's-eye, thrumwort

lock candenette, curl, earlock, heartbreaker, tress

muse erato

name meaning lief

natural storge

nest chalet, demesne, gazebo, harem, kiosk, rendezvous, tryst

of beauty aesthetica

of children pedophilia

of country chauvinism, patriotism

of diety bhakti

of fine arts virtu

of god for mankind agape

of marvelous teratism

of offspring philoprogeneity, storge

of self amour propre, autophilia, narcissism

pact shinju

personified amoret, cupid

pert. amatory, erotic

plant blue creeper

poem amoretto

potion aphrodisiac, charm, philter, philtre

science erotology

seat causeuse

self-giving agape

-sick enamored, fond, infatuated, languishing, pining, stricken

-smitten man-keen

song amoret, ballad, canso, canzo, minnelied, serenade, strephonade

spiritual agape

story fiction, novel, romance

symbol emerald, hippogriff

token amoret

trick amoretto

unlawful lemanry

village of saronno

vine dodder

worthy of, name meaning erasmus

LOVED adored, cherished, darling, dear, idolized, pet, precious, prized, treasured

LOVEL *father* gawain

LOVELORN fond, forlorn, forsaken

LOVELY adorable, alluring, amiable, amorous, beautiful, bonny, charming, comely, delicate, delightful, fair, graceful, handsome, rare, sweet, taking

name meaning angelica

LOVEMAN cleavers

LOVER, LOVER'S admirer, adorer, amant(e), armorist, amoroso, beau, beloved, bon ami, bonne amie, boy friend, caballero, casanova, cavalier, celadon, cicisbeo, corydon, courter, don juan, enamorato, esquire, fellow, flame, gallant, inamorato, infatuate, johnnie, leman, lothario, minion, paramour, pursuer, rato, romeo, spark(er), spoon(er), sprunny, squire, strephon, suitor, swain, sweetheart, valentine, womanizer, wooer

comb. phil(e)

famous pairs abelard-heloise, antony-cleopatra, aucassin-nicolette, daphnis-chloe, pelleas-melisande, romeo-juliet

knot dodder

leap cape ducato

patron saint valentine

pride persicary

LOVE'S LABOR LOST *author* shakespeare

character armado, biron, boyet, catherine, costard, dull, dumain, ferdinand, holofernes, jaquenetta, katharine, longaville, maria, mercade, moth, nathaniel, rosaline

LOVING adoring, affection(ate), amative, amatorian, amatory, amorous, ardent, brotherly, constant, devoted, doting, erotic, faithful, fervent, fond, idolatrous, impassioned, kind, leal, reverent(ial), romantic, tender, true, uxorious, warmhearted

comb. phil(ia), philo

cup award, bratina, tig, tyg

LOW abject, abysmal, bad, bas(e), beggarly, bestial, blaze, blore, blue, cheap, coarse, common, croon, crouched, debased, decumbent, deep, deficient, dejected, depressed, devious, downcast, evil, faint, feeble, flame, flat, glow, gross, hill, humble, ignoble, inferior, knee-high, level, light, limmer, mean, meek, melancholy, menial, moo, mound, neap, obscene, orra, plain, plebian, prostrate,

raffish, rascal, ribald, sad, scrubby, scurvy, short, sick, small, soft, sordid, sorry, squat(ty), submiss, tasteless, turpid, unelevated, unfavorable, vile, vulgar, weak

-brow barbarian, ignoramus, ignorant, philistine, plebeian, proletarian, raw, savage, vulgarian

comb. chamae, tapin(o)

cornel bunchberry

country belgium, holland, luxemburg, netherlands

-cut decollete, plunging

-down base, buckass, confidential, dope, gully, inside, mean, ravine, tip

grade inferior

-lived base, common, contemptible, despicable, mean

person beggar, blackguard, blighter, bugger, cur, dregs, nogoodnik, riffraff, scum, sneak, subordinate, worm, wretch

-pitched base, deep, faint, gentle, gruff, inaudible, muffled, murmurous, piano, soft, subdued, throaty, weak, whispery

-priced bargain, cheap, cutrate, nominal

tide ebb, neap

LOWAN bird, leipoa, mallee

LOWBORN waff

LOWBOY dressing-table

LOWBRED bastard, coarse, crude, ill-mannered, plebeian, rude, vulgar

LOWELL, JAMES R. *pseud.* biglow

work biglow papers

LOWER abase, adown, avale, below, couch, cower, cut, debase, decrease, degrade, demean, demit, demote, depress, dim(inish), dip, disgrace, douse, down, dro(o)p, duck, earlier, embase, excavate, frown, glare, gloom, glower, humble, humiliate, impend, inferior, knock down, less(en), let down, loom, lour, minor, moderate, modify, nether, plunge, portend, reduce, resign, scowl, sink, smaller, strike, subjacent, threat, tumble, under, vail, weaken, wile

banner vail

class baseborn, proletarian

oneself demean, descend, sink

LOWERING beetle, dark, dip, duck, gloomy, heavy, imminent, morose, overcast, sinister, sullen, threatening
of body fondu
of land ablation

LOWEST bedrock, bottom(most), extreme, last, least, nadir, nethermost, rockbottom, undermost
part basement, cellar, floor, nadir, perigee

LOWLAND bottoms, glen, holm, laich, lalland, plain, polder, spit, valley
barren landes
riverside inks

LOWLANDER sassenach, saxon, zhmud
language lallan(d)

LOWLANDS belgium, brabant, flanders, holland, the netherlands

LOWLY base, howe, humble, ignoble, mean, meek, menial, modest, poorly, retiring, slightly, subdued, submissive, tame, unpretending, unpretentious

LOWN calm, lubber, oaf, quiet, rogue

LOX fish, salmon

LOXIA crossbill, wryneck

LOXIAS apollo

LOY slick, spade, tool

LOYAL ardent, constant, dedicated, dependable, devoted, devout, faithful, feal, firm, hold, leal, liege, obedient, resolute, scrupulous, sta(u)nch, steadfast, steady, true(blue), unfailing, yeomanly
be---to adhere, back, defend, idolize, support, worship

LOYALIST tory

LOYALTY allegiance, constancy, devotion, faith, fealty, fidelity, homage, honor, lewty, pietas, troth, truth
island lifu, uea, uvea
religious pietas

LOZENGE cachou, catechu, coign, cremule, diamond, jube, jujube, mascle, pastil(e), pastille, pill, quarry, quoin, rhomb, rosedrop, rotula, rustre, tablet, tabule, troche
medicated tabella

of cement wafer
-shaped mascled

LSD acid, cubes, mescaline, pearly gates, peyote, psilocybin, sunshine
effect backlash, depression, hallucination
experience bad trip, freakout
source ergot, rye-fungus

LUBBER blubber, bohunk, boor, bungler, calf, chucklehead, churl, clod(hopper) (poll), clown, clumsy, colt, dolt, donkey, drone, dub, duffer, fool, galoot, gawk(y), gowk, hulk, idler, lilburne, looby, loon, lout, lown, lummox, lump, lunkhead, oaf, rube, slob, slouch, stick, swab, thick, yokel
fiend brownie, elf

LUBBERLAND cockaigne, utopia

LUBRICANT antifriction, aquadag, beeswax, black lead, dope, graphite, grease, lard, mucilage, mucus, oil, plumbago, synovia, tallow, unguent, wax

LUBRICATE anoint, cream, dope, dress, embrocate, glycerinate, glycerinize, grease, inunct, liquor(up), moisten, oil, pinguefy, pomade, pomatum, salve, slick(on), smooth, soap, unguent, wax

LUBRIC(I)OUS antic, elusive, lascivious, lewd, shifty, slippery, tricky, unstable, wanton

LUBYANKA *prison* gosstrakh, gosuzhas

LUCAN *slayer* nero

LUCANIA basilicata

LUCAS *butler to* king arthur

LUCCA *coin* barbone
saint anselm

LUCE fish, fleur-de-lis, pike
claire booth, play the women
mistress adriana

LUCENT beaming, brilliant, effulgent, glowing, lambent, LUCID, splendid

LUCENTIO *beloved* bianca
father vicentio
servant biondello, tranio

LUCERNE alfalfa, clover, dog, fodder, legume, lynx, medic(ago), trefoil

LUCETTA *mistress* julia

LUCIANA *brother-in-law* antipholus
sister adriana

LUCID bright, clear, crystal, diaphanous, distinct, evident, gauzy, intelligible, light, limpid, lucent, luculent, luminous, manifest, normal, obvious, pellucid, plain, radiant, rational, resplendent, sane, sheer, shining, transparent, vivid

LUCIEN *brother* napoleon

LUCIFER abaddon, ahriman, apollyon, asmodeus, azazel, beelzebub, belial, demon, devil, eblis, evil, lighter, match, mephisto(pheles), phosphor(us), sammael, satan, shaitan, venus
consort philonis
offspring ceyx, daedalion, hesperides
parent astraeus, atlas, aurora, cephalus, eos

LUCILIUS *master* timon

LUCINA diana, midwife, mollusk, moon

LUCITE acrylic, plexiglas, resin

LUCIUS *brother* martius, mutius, quintus
father titus andronicus

LUCK accident, adventure, break, cess, chance, destiny, eure, fate, fortune, gamble, hail, haminga, handsel, hap(pen), hazard, issue, kidney-vetch, lot, mazel, omen, portent, portion, prosperity, success, theedom, venture
bad ace, ambsace, cess, deuce, dirdum, dole, doom, evileye, hoodoo, jinx, ylahayll
bad, bringer jonah
bad, symbol black cat, raven
charm See LUCKY *piece.*
god See HAPPINESS *god.*
good fortune, hap, theedom
lady fate
pert. aleatory, LUCKY
stroke of fluke
unexpected bunce

LUCKLESS sad, unfortunate

LUCKY aleatory, ample, auspicious, beneficial, benign, blessed, canny, chanceful, chancy, favorable, felicitous, fortunate, full, generously, gracious, grandmother, happy, meet, midwife, profitable, promising, propitious, providential, sonsie, sonsy, successful, timely, too, wife

piece alectorian, amulet, charm, clover, grigri, horseshoe, mascot, periapt, rabbit-foot, shamrock, swastika, talisman, toadstool
strike fluke, fortune
LUCRATIVE advantageous, avaricious, beneficial, fat, gainful, greedy, paying, productive, profitable, remunerative, rewarding, well-paying, worthwhile
LUCRE acquisition, emolument, gain, greed, MONEY, pelf, profit, riches, swag, wealth
filthy See MONEY
LUCTIFEROUS mournful, sorry
LUCTUAL saddening, sorrowful
LUCUBRATION article, composition, deliberation, manuscript, meditation, study, thought, work
LUCULLUS *ally* artemidorus, damagoras
brother marcus
brother-in-law appius, cato
colleague cotta
deputy sextilius, sornatius
enemy cethequs, lucius
father servilius
foe memmius, mithridates, tigranes
freedman callisthenes
friend cato, praecia
grammarian tyrannion
lieutenant fabius, murena, pomponius, triarius, voconius
messenger demonax
mother caecilia
philosopher antiochus, strabo
rival cassius, pompey
superior sylla
uncle metellus
victim neoptolemus, vettius
wife clodia, servilia
LUCY, ST *symbol* palm branch
LUD *father* shem
kingdom britain
LUDICROUS absurd, amusing, antic, burlesque, comic(al), diverting, droll, farcical, foolish, funny, grotesque, hideous, jesting, laughable, mad, queer, ridiculous, risible, silly
LUFF borrow, lieutenant, tackle
LUFFA sponge

LUFTWAFFE *plane* heinkel, junker, messerschmitt, stuka
LUG bait, blockhead, bow, box, burden, cargo, carry, drag, draw, ear, freight, hale, handle, haul, hug, lamfhada, load, loop, lout, patch, pole, pull, rake, rod, sail, samildanach, tote, transport, trawl, tug, worm, worry, zulu
battle mag tuireadh
victim balor, fomorians
worm annelid, arenicola, lob(worm), sandworm
LUGDUNUM lyons
LUGE lodge, sled
LUGGAGE baggage, freight, impedimenta, imperial, swag, trappings, traps, trunk
hand bag, case, flight bag, gladstone, grip, imperial, satchel, suitcase
roll swag
LUGGAR jaggar, jugger, laggar
LUGS affectations, airs, ostentation
LUGUBRIOUS depressing, dismal, doleful, dolorous, dour, gloomy, glum, melancholy, morose, mournful, oppressing, plaintive, rueful, sad, saturnine, sorrowful, sullen, teary, woeful
LUKE, ST *aide to* paul
profession doctor, medicine
symbol calf, ox
LUKEWARM cool, indifferent, irresolute, lew, tepid, uninterested, wlach
make tepify
LULL abate, allay, assuage, break, breather, calm(ness), cease, cessation, compose, croon, halt, hiatus, hush, interval, letup, mitigate, pause, respite, rest, rock, silence, soothe, still, stop, subside, tranquilize
LULLABY baloo, balow, berceuse, cradlesong, hushaby, husheen, lullay, schlummerlied, song
LULU ace, allowance, daisy, darb, owl, pip, top-notcher
LUM chimney, pond, pool, sink
LUMBER balata, blunder, board, clog, cordwood, driftwood, dunnage, encumber, firewood, hamper,

impediment, log(s), lombard, mess, pace, pawn (shop), plank, pledge, plod, refuse, rubbish, rumble, shake, shingle, slab, stock, stovewood, strip, timber, trash, trudge, walk, wood
along clump, lob(b)
bend in sny
camp office wanigan
decay redheart
inferior saps, scoot
state maine
LUMBERER blunderer, moneylender, pawnbroker, swindler
LUMBERING awkward, clumsy, rumbling
LUMBERJACK See LOGGER.
hero paul bunyan
LUMBERMAN axeman, feller, hewer, railsplitter, sawyer, whittler
boots cruisers, overs
LUMBUMBASHI elizabethville
LUMINARY actinic, bulb, candle, catoptric(al), celebrity, fire, glim, heliographic, illuminant, illumination, intellectual, lamp, lantern, light, luster, lustre, moon, notable, orb, personage, photic, photoactinic, planet, radiant, star(s), sun, taper, torch, vip
LUMINESCENCE corposant, ectoplasm, fata morgana, fluorescence, foxfire, ignis fatuus, jack-o'-lantern, phosphorescence, st elmo's fire, will-o-the-wisp, wisp
LUMINOUS aglow, beaming, beamy, blazing, bright, brilliant, burning, candescent, clear, effulgent, flashing, gleaming, glinting, glorious, glowing, incandescent, irradiative, lambent, lamping, light, lucent, luminant, luminiferous, lustrous, orient, radiant, refulgent, rutilant, shimmering, shining, shiny, splendid, starry, streaming, sunshiny, sunny
LUMMOX blunderbuss, boor, bungler, gawk, lobster, lout, lubber, oaf, yahoo
LUMP accumulation, bar(ge), batch, beat, bit, blob, block, bloom, bolus,

bulge, bulk, bull's eye, bump, bunch, burl, cake, chump, chunk, clag, claut, clod, clot, clump, clunk, clunter, cluster, cob, congeal, cut, dollop, endure, glebe, gob(bet), group, hank, hubble, hunch, hunk, knob, knot, knurl, loaf, lob, lot, lubber, mass, mouse, node, nodule, nub(ble), nugget, part, pat, piece, protuberance, solid, stump, swad, swelling, thresh, thump, tumor, wad, wart, whang, wodge
large doll, hunk
metal slug
off calculate
rubber thimble
small knobble, nodule, wart
soft plastic clam
together amass, combine, group
yeast bee

LUMPER longshoreman, middleman, militiaman, potato, stevedore, stimble, worker

LUMPFISH cockpaddle, sucker

LUMPISH awkward, boorish, bulky, dull, heavy, inactive, inert, languid, ponderous, sluggish, stodgy, stolid, stupid

LUMPY bumpy, chunky, clunch, cobbly, knobby, nodous, nodular, swollen
-*jaw* actinomycosis

LUNA argent, SELENE, silver

LUNACY aberration, craziness, delirium, dementia, derangement, folly, foolishness, frenzy, hysteria, insanity, madness, mania, moon, psychosis

LUNAR (See also MOON.) celestial, crescent, orbed
vehicle lem

LUNARIA satinpod

LUNARY volvelle

LUNATIC absurd, aliene, bat, bedlamite, coot, crackbrain, crackpot, crazed, crazy, demented, demoniac, deranged, fanatic, frenetic, gelt, goofy, insane, loon(y), madcap, madman, maniac, moonling, moonstruck, ninny, noddy, noncompos, nut, phrenetic, psychotic, screwball, tom o' bedlam,

tsedoodelt(er), tsedrayt(eh), zany
asylum bedlam, bethlehem, madhouse, nuthouse
saint avertin

LUNCH(EON) bagging, bever, brunch, dejeuner, eat, elevens, feed, nacket, noonmeat, piece, repast, snack, tea, tiff(in), undern
laborer's elevener
room cafe, grill
time noon

LUNETTE blinder, crescent, fieldwork, fort, horseshoe, lens, moon, outwork, satellite, spectacles

LUNG(S) bellows, dragon, gill, light(s), longue
collapse atelectasis
collier's anthracosis
comb. pneum(a)(o), pneumo(n), pulmo
description pneumography
disease anthracosis, calcicosis, chalicosis, consumption, emphysema, phthisis, pneumonia, siderosis, tuberculosis
excision pneumonectomy
having pulmonate
membrane pleura
part alveolus, pleura
pert. pneumonic, pulmonary, pulmonic
sound bruit, rale, rattle
without apulmonic

LUNGE barge, foin, jab, leap, longe, lurch, namaycush, pace, pitch, plunge, push, stab, thrust

LUNGEOUS mischievous, rough

LUNGFISH barramunda, ceratodus, cycloid, dipnoid, mudfish, sirenoid

LUNGFLOWER marsh-gentian

LUNGWORT bluebell, cowslip, hawkweed, hellebore, lichen, mullein, pulmonaria

LUNT kindle, light, smoke, vapor

LUNULE albedo, halfmoon

LUNY See LOONY.

LUPINE bluebonnet, fierce, rapacious, ravenous, sundial, wolfish

LUPIS abaca, hemp

LURCH bilk, careen, cheat, deceive, disadvantage, disappoint, dodge, duck, embarrassment, fall, filch, flounder, jolt, monopolize,

oscillate, pitch, prowl, reel, rob, roll, scend, shift, slide, slip, sneak, stagger, steal, stoit, swag(ger), sway, swindle, swing, teeter, toss

LURCHER betrayer, mongrel, poacher

LURE allure, ambush, attract (ion), attrahent, bag, bait, beguile, bewitch, bucktail, call, capture, charm, coax, come-on, decoy, draw, ensnare, entice, entrap, fascinate, gudgeon, inveigle, invite, pitfall, rope in, seduce, slock, snare, stoolpigeon, tempt, tice, tole, toll, trap, trumpet

LURER bait, enticer, siren, tempter, trapper

LURID ashen, ashy, crimson, dark, deathly, dim, dismal, ghastly, gloomy, grim, grisly, gruesome, livid, macabre, malign, obscene, pale, pallid, purple, racy, red, risque, rufous, sallow, sensational, shocking, sinister, startling, terrible, vivid, wan, yellow

LURK ambush, couch, creep, dare, dodge, gumshoe, hide, miche, prowl, pussyfoot, secrete, skulk, slink, sneak, steal, surprise, trick, underlie, waylay

LURKING grassant, latent

LURRY confusion, drag, hurry, jumble, tumult, worry

LUSCINIA bluebreast, bluethroat, bulbul, nightingale

LUSCIOUS delectable, delicious, delightful, dulcet, juicy, mellow, palatable, pleasing, sapid, savory, succulent, sweet, tasty, toothsome, voluptuous

LUSH abundant, alcoholic, beat, blow, dash, drink, drunk(ard), expensive, exuberant, fertile, flexible, fresh, intoxicated, juicy, lavish, limber, liquor, luxuriant, luxurious, mellow, opulent, prodigal, profuse, rich, rush, savory, soft, sot, splash, splendid, strike, swarming, teeming, thriving, wild

LUSIA demeter

LUST animalism, appetite, avarice, blood, choose, concupiscence, coveting, cove-

tise, craving, desire, greed, gusto, hankering, hircosity, hunger, kama, libido, liking, passion, pleasure, sensualism, thirst, urge, yearning, yen, zest
god chemos(h)
personification argante, corflambo, malecasta
symbol goat
LUSTER beauty, brightness, brilliance, burnish, chandelier, distinction, effulgence, fame, glare, glister, glory, gloss, iridescence, luminary, naif, polish, radiance, schiller, sheen, shimmer, shine, splendor
LUSTERLESS dead, dim, dull, faded, flat, mat(t) (te), tarnished, vacant, wan
LUSTFUL animal, cadgy, carnal, cyprian, fleshly, goaty, gross, hircine, jealous, lascivious, lecherous, lewd, rammish, randy, ruffian, ruttish, satyrical, sensual, wanton
LUSTRATION abhiseka, ablution, cleansing, inspection, penance, purification, review, rinsing, survey, washing
LUSTROUS adularescent, bright, brilliant, burnished, effulgent, glace, glorious, glossy, glowing, illustrious, lambent, lucent, luminous, naif, nitid, oriental, polished, radiant, refulgent, resplendent, rising, shining, shiny, silky, silvery, splendid, waxen, waxy
LUSTY athletic, bouncing, brag, cant, energetic, gawsie, hale, healthy, hearty, husky, muscular, physical, rugged, sound, sportive, stalwart, stout, strenuous, strong, sturdy, tough, vigorous
LUTE adhere, angelica, asor, biwa, cement, citole, clay, dicord, domra, dyphone, instrument, lyre, mandore, minikin, nabia, nable, penorcan, rake, rebec(k), ring, sarod, screed, seal, smooth, spread, tamboura, tar, template, theorbo, trichord, vihuela
double dyphone
-like instrument angelot, arch(i)lute, bandore, ban-

durria, banjer, banjo(rine), banjo-uke, banjuke, banjulele, cittern, guitar, luth, mandobass, mandola, mandolin, mandolute, mandore, pandora, pandore, tamb-(o)ura, tanbur, teorbe, theorbo, uke, ukulele, zither
LUTECIUM cassiopeium, metal, yttrium
LUTER dauber, paster
LUTETIA paris
LUTHER, MARTIN *antagonist* tetzel
condemnation site worms
home wartburg, wittenberg
opponent eck
LUTIANUS cabellerote, snapper
LUTJANID jewfish
LUTOSE miry, muddy
LUTUAMIAN *indian* modoc
LUXATE dislocate, displace, remove
LUXEMBOURG *city* capellen, diekirch, echternach, ettlebruck, petange, remich, roodt, vianden, wiltz
lowland bonpays, gutland
measure fuder
peak burgplatz
plateau ardennes
range ardennes
river alzette, moselle, our, sauer, sure
LUXOR thebes
LUXURIANCE abundance, affluence, elegance, fertility
LUXURIANT abundant, exuberant, fancy, fertile, florid, flourishing, fruitful, jungly, lavish, lush, opulent, ornate, overgrown, overrun, plenteous, plentiful, prodigal, productive, profuse, prolific, proud, rank, rich, teeming, uberous
LUXURIATE bask, delight, enjoy, flourish, glory, grow, indulge, revel, spend, thrive, wallow, wanton
LUXURIOUS babylonian, babylonish, capuan, comfortable, deluxe, epicurean, expensive, gaudy, gilded, grand, lavish, lucullan, lush, majestic, mollitious, opulent, palatial, pleasurable, plush, posh, precious, regalado, rich, sensual, sensuous, showy, silken, splendid, sumptuous, swanky, sybaritic, tryphena, tryphosa, voluptuous

LUXURY abundance, affluence, amenity, bed of roses, cornucopia, delight, ease, elegance, extravagance, finery, frill, gratification, joy, magnificence, means, opulence, pleasance, pleasure, prosperity, richness, sensuality, superfluity, wealth
lover sybarite, voluptuary
LUZON See PHILIPPINES.
LYAEUS dionysus
LYCAEUS zeus
LYAM bloodhound, leash, lyme
LYCANTHROPE werewolf
LYCAON *changed to* wolf
kingdom arcadia
offspring callisto, caucon, maenalus, nyctimus, tegeates
parent loathoe, pelasgus, priam
slayer zeus
LYCEE academy, college, ecole, gymnasium, institute, school
LYCEUM chautauqua, hall, platform
walk peripatus
LYCIA *capital* antiphellus
chieftain glaucus, sarpedon
LYCIUM box(thorn), bursaria, matrimony-vine, teak
LYCOMEDES *guest* achilles
kingdom scyrus
victim theseus
LYCON *slayer* peneleus
teacher straton
LYCOPHRON *slayer* hector
LYCOPODIUM buckgrass, buckhorn, club-moss, crowfoot, foxtail, moss, staghorn
LYCOPUS ajuga, bugle(weed), bugloss
LYCURGUS *adversary* dionysus
brother polydectes
father aleus, dryas, eunomus
kingdom thrace
son ancaeus
victim dryas
LYCUS *consort* dirce
kingdom cilicia, mysia, thebes
parent pandion, poseidon, pylia
rescued antiope
slayer amphion, zethus
victim creon
LYDIA maeonia
capital sardis
flute magadis

king alyattes, candaules, croesus, gyges, iardanus, tmolus
mountain tmolus
plain hermus
queen omphale
river cayster, pactolus
LYDIAN effeminate, gentle, sensual, soft, voluptuous
LYE alkali, bouk, buck, lessive, lixivium, soaplees, strake
pert. lixivial
spent soaplees
LYGODESMA artemis
LYING abed, accumbent, awald, awalt, couchant, cretism, deceitful, deceptive, decumbent, delitescent, delusory, dishonest, dormant, equivocating, false (hood), lease, leasing, leaze, mendacious, mentery, misleading, passive, reclining, recumbency, recumbent, supine, untruthful, wrong
apart dissite
close quat
in accouchement, birth, childbed, confinement
on back supine
on face prone
over jacent, jessant
struck dead for ananias
LYKEIOS apollo
LYME See LYAM.
LYMPH casein, chyle, liquid, plasma, sap, serum, spring, virus, water
channel cisterna
disease cat-scratch, elephantiasis
gland bubonic
gland degeneration scrofula
gland description angiography

gland study angiology
gland swelling bubo
tumor angioma
LYMPHATIC aquatic, enthusiast(ic), frantic, languid, lunatic, plasmic, sluggish
LYNCEUS *brother* aphareus, idas
consort hympermnestra
foe danaus
kingdom argos
opponent castor, danaus, pollux
parent aegyptus, aphareus, arene
slayer pollux
victim danaus
LYNCH dewitt, gibbet, hang, murder
LYNETTE *knight* gareth
LYNGI *slayer* sigurd
victim sigmund
LYNX badger, bobcat, caracal, carcajou, cat, catamount(ain), gorkun, losse, lucern(e), lucivee, pishu, syagush, wildcat
-eyed oxyopia
rufus bobcat, wildcat
LYON lugdunum
LYRA glockenspiel, turtle
star in vega
LYRE asor, barbiton, chelys, cithara, cither, harp, instrument, kinnor, kissar, kithara, lute, phormix, rebec(k), sackbut, shell, testudo, trigon, zither
inventor jubal
turtle leatherback
LYREBIRD bullen-bullen, menura, pheasant
LYREMAN dogday-cicada
LYRIC alba, cancion, cantabile, canzone, choral, descourt, dithyramb, g(h)azel,

hokku, lai, lay, madrigal, melic, melodious, musical, ode, operatic, poem, rondel, song, tenson, tuneful, vocal
ancient alcaic
love alba
muse erato, polyhymnia, polymnia
pert. catullian
poem canzone, epode, lay, melic, song
poet odist
13-line rondeau
LYRIST composer, poet, singer
LYRUS *parent* anchises, aphrodite
LYSANDER *ally* cyrus, tisaphernes
beloved hermia
critic eteocles
father aristoclitus, heraclidae, libys
friend agesilaus, thorax
historian ephorus, theopompous
slayer neochorus
victim pharnabazus
LYSIMACHUS *captor* dromichaetes
consort arsinoe, penelope
father-in-law ptolemy
kin agathocles, ptolemaeus, simon
kingdom macedonia, thrace
leader alexander
opponent antigonus, demetrius
parent antia, proetus
slayer hera
son agathocles, aristides
LYSSA hydrophobia, rabies
LYTTA blister-beetle, cantharis, worm
LYTTON, BULWAR *pseud.* owen meredith

M

M *wrong use of* mytacism
MA bellona, but, maat, mamma, MOTHER, mum (my)
MAACAH *consort* caleb, david, rehoboam
offspring abijah, absolom, asa, nahor
parent absalom, reumah, talmai
MAASEIAH *father* shallum
governor for josiah

son azariah, neriah, zedekiah, zephaniah
MAAT *husband* thoth
son naggai
symbol feather
MABOLO camagon, fruit, plum
MACABRE daunting, deathly, ghastly, grim, grisly, gruesome, horrible, horrid, horrific, horrifying, lurid, sick

MACACA, MACACO See MACAQUE.
MACADAM pavement, roadway
MACANA axe, club, sword, weapon
MACAO *chinese name* aomen
coin avo, pataco
island coloane, taipa
MACAQUE ape, broh, bruh, kra, lemur, macaca, ma-

caco, machin, monkey, rhesus, simi, zati

MACAREUS *daughter* isse
father aeolus
sister canace

MACARIA *parent* deianira, hercules

MACARIZE felicitate, laud

MACARONI beau, buck, buffoon, coxcomb, dandy, duck, dude, elegant, exquisite, fool, fop, nob, PASTA, paste, spark, swell, toff
type elbow

MACARONIC burlesque, confused, doggerel, jumble(d), mixed, skew

MACAULAY, THOMAS *work* history of england, horatius, lays of ancient rome

MACAW aracanga, ara(ra), ararauna, arra, bird, cockatoo, maracan, parrot
pert. arine

MACBETH *character* angus, banquo, caithness, donalbain, duncan, fleance, hecate, lady macbeth, lady macduff, lennox, macduff, malcolm, menteith, ross, seyton, siward, witches
domain glamis
ghost banquo
officer seyton
slayer macduff
title thane
victim banquo, duncan

MACCABEES hasmoneans, john, jonathan, josephus, judas, mattathias, simon

MACCABEUS, JUDAS *conquest* acrabattene, apollonius, dathema, jazer, seron
village modin

MACE blade, cattail, club, croc, gas, gavel, mallet, rod, sceptre, sparth, spice, staff, stick, swindle, swindling, symbol, weapon
-bearer bailiff, beadle, marshal, sergeant-at-arms, verger
nutmeg aril(lode)
reed dod(d)
royal scepter, sceptre, staff

MACEDONIA *army unit* phalanx
city ber(o)ea, edessa, pella, pydna, thessalonica, thessalonike
coin stater

district paeonia
dynasty ptolemies
general antipater, seleucus
king abgar, aeropus, alexander, amyntas, archelaus, cassander, demetrius, philip, pierus,
madman alexander
palace aigri, pella
peak athos, olympiad, olympus
people albanian, bulgarian, greek, serbian, servian
pike sarissa
royal line founder archelaus
shrine pearl mosque
statesman antipater
turk konariot(e)
weapon sarissa

MACERATE decompose, delay, mortify, oppress, pine, pulp, ret, soak, soften, sour, steep, torment, vex, waste, wear away, wet

MACHAON *brother* podalirius
parent asclepius, coronis

MACHETE bolo, curtaxe, cutlass, guitar, guloc, knife, parang, tarpon

MACHIAVELLI *work* il principe, the prince

MACHIAVELLIAN crafty, cunning, deceitful, falsehearted, guileful, jobber, politician, rascal, schemer, treacherous, wily

MACHICOLATION battlement, fort, gallery, parapet

MACHINATE cabal, contrive, design, devise, maneuver, plan, plot, scheme, trick

MACHINATION artifice, cabal, conspiracy, device, intrigue, plot, scheme, stratagem

MACHINE (See also DEVICE, and *kind*, below.) apparatus, appliance, association, automaton, auto(mobile), barker, bloc, breaker, cabal, car(rier), caster, contraption, contrivance, create, device, engine, gadget, gear, implement, instrument, make, mill, motor, organization, party, system, tool, utensil, vehicle
adding totalizer
clay-softening malaxator
cloth-shearing cropper
coding key-punch

dredging couloir
finishing edger
glazing calender
grain-cleaning awner
grinding mill
gun chauchat, gatling, hotchkiss, lewis, maxim, sten, stinger, strafe, tata
gunner strafer
gun place nest, pillbox
heavy bulldozer, steamroller
kind automobile, baler, beetle, bulldozer, calendar, carryall, collator, compressor, crab, crane, derrick, dredge(r), edger, forklift, gin, grader, hercules, hoist, hydraulic press, lawnmower, motor(cycle), mower, navvy, pile-driver, power shovel, press, pusher, roller, scraper, sewer, shredder, slubber, snowplow, spaller, spinner, stamp, steamroller, steamshovel, tractor, trone, typewriter, water-wheel, windlass, winnower
lifting See *raising*, below.
-made manufactured, stereotyped
ore-separating vanner
parimutual totalizator, totalizer
part cam, gear, pawl, piston, rotor, tappet, wheel
parts assembly
pile-driving gin
pistol burp-gun
political bloc, party, system
raising crane, elevator, hoist, lift
rubber extruder
self-moving automoton, robot
shaping edger, lathe, swage
shop turnery
surfacing facer
talking gramophone, victrola
threshing combine
war See ENGINE *war*.
works block
wrapping baler

MACHINERY (See also MACHINE.) agency, agent, apparatus, asset(s), channel, engine, equipment, factory, gear, hardware, materiel, means, medium, organ, outfit, paraphernalia, plant, tackle, works

MACHIR *offspring* gilead

MACILENT emaciated, lean, marasmic, marcor, thin

MACKENZIE *range* ogilvie
MACKEREL akule, atkafish, bawd, blinker, bloater, bluefish, bonito, cero, chad, chub, cisco, coelho, escolar, hardhead, herring, jurel, opelu, pentado, peto, pimp, pintado, saurel, scad, scomber, scombr(o)id, seerfish, sierra, spike, tassard, tink(er), tunny, wahoo
banded pilotfish, rudderfish, seriola
-bird kittiwake, wryneck
bony slink(er)
chub tinker
gaff gambeer
-goose phalarope
group shoal
-gull tern
horse bluefish, jurel, saurel, scad, tunny
inferior slink(er)
large cero, peto, pintado, wahoo
-like bonito, scad, scombroid
net spiller
pickled scalpeen
shark carcharias
yellow cavalla, crevalle
young blinker, spike, tinker
MACKINAW raincoat
MACKLE blemish, blot(ch), blur, double, macula, mark, print, spot, stain
MACRAME *work* knot
MACROBIOTIC lasting, long-lived
MACROCOSM world, universe
MACROERGATE ant
MACROSCOPIC gross, huge, large
MACROZAMIA banga, boyar palm, burrawang, cycad
MACULA, MACULE See MACKLE.
MACULAR, MACULATE blotched, defiled, impure, pollute(ed), spotted, stain, variegate
MAD absurd, anger, angry, ardent, berserk, bonkers, brainsick, crazy, dangerous, dazed, demented, deranged, dippy, distracted, distraught, doting, eager, earthworm, eccentric, enraged, excited, fey, foolish, frantic, frenetic, frenzied, furious, gay, gite, gyte, hilarious, hysterical,

hyte, imbecile, indignant, infatuated, inflamed, infuriated, INSANE, irate, loco, loon(e)y, lunatic, luny, maggot, maniac(al), mindless, non compos mentis, nonsensical, psychotic, rabid, raging, rash, ravening, reckless, senseless, teed off, turbulent, unwise, vain, vexed, violent, wild, witless, wood, wrathful, yond
about ardent, eager, enthusiastic
apple eggplant
doctor alienist
-dog skullcap anagallis, herb, hoodwort, madweed, pimpernel
get blow one's top, boil, burn, erupt, fly off the handle, foam at the mouth, forget one's self, get one's irish up, have a conniption, infuriate, lose one's temper, see red, sizzle, throw a fit
-tom catfish, tadpole
MADAGASCAR malagasy
animal ayeaye, babacoote, fo(u)ssa, indri(s), lemur, temee, tendrac, tenrec, vansire, viverrine
bird ground-roller, kirombo, philepitta
capital tananarive
city antisirabe, atananarivo, majanga, manakara, mananjory, nossibe, tamatave, tananarive, tulear
civet fossa(ne), foussa
deity angatch, ataokoloinona, ndriananahary, rabefihaza, razanes
district imerina
fabric rabanna
forest people tanala
island group aldabra
lake alaotra
lemur avahi, ayeaye, babacoote, indri(s), mongoose
measure gantang
monkey lemur
oil ylangylang
palm raffia
people antaiva, antanandro, avaradrano, bara, betsileos, betsimisaraka, cotier, hova, lemurian, malagasy, marina, merina, sakalava, tsirinana, vazimba
periwinkle vinca-rosea
plant lace-leaf

port diego-suarez, majunga, morondava, tamatave
president tsiranana
prison antinamora
range ankaratra
river ikopa, mangoky, mangoro, mania, onylahy, sofia
shawl lamba
shrub anthospermum, assonia
silk spider spinder
snake langaha
spurge crown of thorns
tree assonia, clove-nutmeg, flamboyant, poinciana, raffia, ravensara, voavanga
MADAM bawd, courtesan, dame, don(n)a, frau, frow, goodwife, hussy, lady, maam, missus, mistress, mrs, mum, nun, pani, senora, signora, sinebada, wench, wife, woman
butterfly chocho(san)
butterfly composer puccini
butterfly lover pinkerton
butterfly marriage broker goro
tussaud's museum, waxworks
MADCAP adventurous, audacious, daredevil, fiery, hotheaded, hotspur, impulsive, lunatic, rash, reckless, wild, wit
MADDEN agitate, anger, annoy, antagonize, craze, dement, derange, distract, enrage, exasperate, excite, frenzy, incense, inflame, infuriate, irk, irritate, loco, pixilate, possess, provoke, rile, roil, shatter, unbalance, unhinge, vex
MADDENING enraging, infuriating, irritating, vexatious
MADDER aal, alizarin, anthospermum, asperula, borreria, bouvardia, casasia, coprosoma, dyestuff, evea, garance, mether, plant, rubis, spurwort, woodruff
dried gamene
family bedstraw, cinchona, coffee, evea, gardenia, houstonia, ipecac, lizary, munjeet, rubiaceae, tanagra
genus catesbaeae, cinchona, exostema, morinda, richardsonia, rondeletia, rubia
preparation garancine, garanceaux, pincoffin
root pigment alizarin, mull
tree bangcal

wild infant's-breath
yellow dutch-pink
MADE artificial, built, invented, manufactured, prepared, set, successful, trained
-*beaver* castor, skin
fast bound, tied
of whole cloth coined, fabricated, invented
public announced, delated, issued, released
short abridged, curtailed, docked
to order bespoke, custom
-*up* accrete, artificial, coined, complete, fabricated, invented, painted, perfect
MADEIRA bual, mahogany, malmsey, wine, wood
capital funchal
city funchal, monte
discoverer gonzalez marco, teieira
famous lovers anna d'arfet, robert machin
island dezerte, grande
shrub carrot tree
vine bridalwreath, maiden's-wreath, spiraea
wind leste
wine bual, canary, gomera, malmsey, marsala, sercial, tinta, tinto, verdelho
wine-making estufado
MADEMOISELLE fraulein, girl, miss, mistress, mlle, senorita, signorina, woman
MADHOUSE asylum, babel, bedlam, bughouse, chaos, maelstrom, row, shamble
MADISON, JAMES *birthplace* pt conway, virginia
burial site montpelier, virginia
home montpelier
profession lawyer
pseud. publius
vice president elbridge gerry, george clinton
MADMAN frenetic, furioso, lunatic, maniac, phrenetic, psychotic
MADNESS aberration, agitation, anger, delirium, dementia, derangement, dewanee, disturbance, ecstasy, enthusiasm, excitement, folly, frenzy, furor, ire, lunacy, mania, mishegaas, mishegoss, moonery, piblokto, widdrim
comb. lysso
MADON *king* johab

MADONNA blessed virgin, dei mater, (holy)mary, mater dolorosa, mother of god, notre dame, our lady, queen of heaven, star of the sea, stella-maris, virgin (mary)
little evita peron
MADRAS *city* adoni, arcot, calicut
district malabar, nellore
hemp sunn
measure cawn(e)y, manei, mercal, para, par(r)ah, puddee
weight cash, chinnam, fanam, mangelin, pagoda, pollam, powe, seer, varahan
MADREPORE acropora, coral, fungid
glass millefiori
MADRID *market* rastro
museum prado
park prado
MADRIGAL ballett, canzon(e), glee, lyric, ode, poem, round(elay), song, verse
MADRONA laurel, manzanita
MADWORT bugloss, cress, gold-of-pleasure, lobularia
MAE WEST lifebelt, lifepreserver
MAECENAS patron, supporter
friend augustus
protege horace, virgil
MAELSTROM agitation, current, eddy, swirl, turmoil, whirling, whirlpool
MAENAD(S) bacchae, bacchante, bassara, bassar(i)d, frow
attendant to dione, dionysus
MAENALUS *father* lycaon
MAEON *ambushed* tudeus
MAERA See HECUBA.
blinded polymnestor
father atlas
husband tegeates
master icarius
MAESTRO musician, teacher
di cappella choirmaster, kapellmeister
MAETERLINCK *heroine* monna vanna
work ariane and bluebeard, monna vanna, the blue bird
MAFFLE bewilder, blunder, confuse, muddle, mumble, squander, stammer
MAFIA la cosa nostra, lcn,

refuge, syndicate, the mob, the outfit
actor marlon brando
ancillary gang black guerrilla army
boss of bosses capo di tutti capi
chief consigliere, godfather
chronicler mario puzo
code maranzano, omerta
convention apalachin
counsellor consigliere
fight for control castellammarese war
group regime, squad
leader accardo, aiuppa, alderisio, anastasia, bonanno, bonpensiero, bruno, cain, corallo, dalitz, decurtis, dellacroce, dibella, dragna, fratianno, galante, gambino, giancana, godfather, marcello, nicoletti, pappadio, rastelli, rizzitello, salerno, spilotro, tieri, torello
lieutenant capo(regime)
meeting sitdown
member button-man, hit man, picciotto
members mafiosi
official capo(regime), consigliere, don sottocapo, soldier, superdon
rulers commission
specialist enforcer, hitman
MAFURRA elcaja, roka, tree
MAG bird, chat, chatter(box), halfpenny, magneto, magpie, margaret, titmouse
MAGADIS dulcimer, flute, monochord
MAGAZINE armory, arsenal, book, cassette, chamber, depot, drum, ephemeris, journal, organ, periodical, publication, pulp, repertory, repository, reservoir, retort, review, shop, slick, store(house), tabloid, warehouse
MAGDALEN convertite, penitent
MAGE See MAGICIAN.
MAGELLAN *destination* spice islands
page juan vicaya
ship concepcion, san antonio, trinidad, victoria
starting point san lucar de barrameda
strait of alikuluf
MAGENTA fuchsin(e), roseine

MAGGED fretted, worn

MAGGOT caprice, earthbob, gentle, grub, larva, mad(dock), mathe, mawk, muckworm, skipper, warble, whim, wormil
bait gentle
case puparium
-pated crotchety, whimsical

MAGGOTY blighted, capricious, eccentric, wormy

MAGI balthasar, gaspar, melchior, sages, wise men
feast of epiphany
gift frankincense, gold, myrrh

MAGIC alchemy, apotropaism, art, brujeria, cantrip, conjuration, conjury, craft, demonology, devil(t)ry, diablerie, diabolism, divination, enchantment, fairy, fetish(ism), goetic, goety, hocuspocus, hoodoo, hypnotism, jadoo, jadu, juju, legerdemain, mana, maya, necromancy, obeah, phylacteric, power, rite, rune, shamanism, show, sorcery, sortilege, spell, supernatural, talismanic, thaumaturgy, theurgy, trick, voodoo(ism), weird, witchcraft, witchery, wizardry
black goetic, goety, malefice, satanism, sorcery, witchcraft
bullet miracle drug
charm amulet, fetich, fetish, mascot, merrythought, periapt, phylactery, rabbit's foot, scarab, talisman, wishbone
city miami
comb. thaumat(o)
formula sesame
goddess circe, hecate
island catalina
pert. See MAGICAL.
power mana
practice conjuration, conjury
ring king gyges
rod aaron's rod, caduceus, divining rod, rhabdos, wand, witch hazel
symbol abraxas, caract, charm, pentacle, rune
transform, as if by aladdinize
white theurgy, turgy
word abracadabra, hocuspocus, incantation, presto, selah, sesame

MAGICAL bewitching, charming, circean, goetic, hermetic, necromantic, numinous, occult, thaumaturgic, theurgic, wizard, wonder

MAGICIAN archimage, charlatan, circe, conjurer, cunjah, dunninger, goetic, gwydion, houdini, isangoma, juggler, koschei, mage, magi(an), magus, mandrake, medicineman, merlin, mundunugu, necromancer, obeah-doctor, obeahman, prestidigitator, shaman, sorcerer, thaumaturge, theurgist, trollman, uther, voodooist, wabeno, wangateur, witch(doctor), wizard
assistant famulus
command presto-chango
device craft, fake, feke
manual grimoire
motion pass
phrase See MAGIC *word*.
pocket profonde
staff See MAGIC *rod*.

MAGINDANAO moro

MAGIRIST See COOK.

MAGISTERIAL arrogant, august, authoritative, controlling, dictatorial, dignified, directing, doctrinaire, dogmatic, domineering, haughty, imperious, lofty, lordly, masterful, official, oracular, overbearing, proud, stately, weighty

MAGISTRAL dogmatic, effectual, guiding, MAGISTERIAL, principal, sovereign

MAGISTRATE aedile, ag(h)a, alabarch, alcalde, alderman, amtman, archon, avoyer, bailie, bailiff, bailli, beak, burgomaster, cadi, cady, censor, chief, consul, counsel, dictator, doge, echevin, edile, ephor, foud, governor, hakim, judge, jurist, justice, justiciary, kadi, mayor, mollah, mufti, nomarch, phylarch, praetor, prefect, president, pretor, prytanis, puisne, stradico, strategos, suffete, syndic, tribune, ulama, ulema
collar gollila
group bench
petty agoranome

MAGMA dregs, ichor, mixture, sediment
and clay buchite
basalt limburgite

MAGNA grand, great
carta signer king john
carta site runnymede
graeca colonists sybarites
graecia ideal republic, sicily
mater (See also RHEA.) atargatis, cybele, great mother, ops

MAGNANIMITY big heart, bigness, chivalry, elevation, exaltation, forgiveness, fortitude, generosity, greatness, heroism, liberality, loftiness, nobleness, sublimity

MAGNANIMOUS big, broadhearted, charitable, exalted, forgiving, free, generous, heroic, highminded, honorable, large, liberal, lofty, noble, unselfish

MAGNATE ace, baron, bashaw, big cheese, bigshot, bigwig, brass, celebrity, cob, fat cat, grandee, head, high roller, leader, lion, lord, millionaire, mogul, nabob, name, nawab, noble, personage, power, ruler, shogun, somebody, star, titan, tycoon, vip, wheel

MAGNESIA amalgam, bitter-earth, periclase, pulvil

MAGNESITE brown spar, dolomite

MAGNESIUM *borate* borocite, pinakiolite, pinnoite, priceite
compound angarlite, artinite, bischofite, bobierite, brucite, carnallite, dolomite, epsomite, selliate, spinel
silicate cerolite, enstatite, olivine, serpentine, talc
source magnesite
sulphate esomite, loweite

MAGNET adamas, attraction, attrahent, charmer, loadstone, lodestar, lodestone, pole(star), solenoid, stylenoid, terrella
electro solenoid
kind artificial, bar, horseshoe
part armature, keeper

MAGNETIC attractive, charming, compelling, powerful
unit biot-savart, gauss, gilbert, kapp, maxwell, oested, weber

MAGNETISM attraction, charm, drawing power, influence, pull
animal biod, charisma, mesmerism
unit gauss

MAGNATITE iron ore, loadstone, lodestone

MAGNETIZE attract, captivate, draw, influence, pull, saturate, touch

MAGNIFIC eulogistic, generous, grandiloquent, honorific, illustrious, imposing, MAGNIFICENT, munificent, pompous, renowned, sublime

MAGNIFICAT cantic(le), rhapsody

MAGNIFICENCE aureole, bravery, brilliance, flare, gite, glory, grandeur, halo, liberality, luster, luxury, majesty, nimbus, nobility, parade, pomp, splendor, state, sublimity

MAGNIFICENT august, babylonian, brilliant, dignified, eulogistic, extraordinary, glorious, gorgious, grand (iose), great, honorific, illustrious, imperial, imposing, impressive, lavish, lofty, loquent, lustrous, luxurious, majestic, munificent, noble, opulent, palatial, pompous, princely, regal, resplendent, rial, royal, showy, splendent, splendid, stately, sublime, sumptuous, superb, vast

MAGNIFY acclaim, aggrandize, aggravate, amplify, augment, dilate, distend, enlarge, exaggerate, exalt, expand, extol, glorify, greaten, increase, inflate, laud, maximize, multiply, overstate, praise, swell

MAGNILOQUENCE bombast, rhetoric

MAGNILOQUENT aureate, boastful, bombastic, dramatic, euphuistic, flowery, grandiloquent, histrionic, loquacious, pompous, rhetorical, tumid, turgid

MAGNITUDE area, bigness, bouk, bulk, compass, dimension, expanse, extent, greatness, importance, infinite, level, mass, quantity, range, reach, size, spread, stretch, volume

MAGNOLIA battree, beavertree, bigbloom, bullbay, champac, cucumber-tree, elk bark, hackberry, mauricio, michelia, sweet bay, umbrella tree, yulan
state mississippi

MAGNUM bottle
double jeroboam
opus achievement, book, masterpiece, work

MAGNUS *hitch* knot
son cnut, knut

MAGPIE babbler, bird, bishop, chatterer, cissa, crow-shrike, daw, ha(g)-gister, kotri, madge, magg, margaret, marget, nanpie, ninut, pheasant, pian(n)et, piat, pica, piemag, pienanny, piet, pigeon, piot, pyat, pyet, scold, shrike, smew, talker
changed to arne, pierides
diver smew
lark grallina, peewee
robin dayal, dhyal
shrike tanager

MAGSMAN sharper, swindler

MAGUEY agave, aloe, cantala, centuryplant, furcraea, mescal
drink pulque

MAGURO albacore, fish, tuna

MAGYAR (See also HUNGARY.) szekel, szekler
water spirit viz-anya, vizi-ember, vizi-leany

MAHA langur, monkey, samba-deer

MAHABHARATA *battle* kurukshetra
hero pandu
heroine savitri
part bhagavadgita
rivals kauravas, pandavas
villain duryodhana
wife draupad

MAHALALEEL *son* jared, shephatiah

MAHARAJAH gaekwar, nizam, rajah, ruler

MAHARANI empress, princess, queen

MAHARASHI bhrigu, rishi, sage

MAHAT consciousness, intellect, intelligence

MAHATMA adept, ar(a)hat, arant, gandhi, master, monk, mystic, sage, saint

MAHAYANA buddhism, hinayana

MAHIMAHI dolphin, dorado, fish

MAH JONG ma cheuk, ma chiang, ma chiao, mo tsiah, pung chow
piece tile
term bambec, bouquet, character, charleston, crack, dog(ging), dragon, east wind, flower, honor, kong, pung, quint, quong, season, sextet, simple, stack, stick, suit

MAHLI *son* eleazar, kish

MAHLON *mother* naomi

MAHOGANY acajou, albarco, almon, andiroba, avodire, bagtikan, bangalay, baywood, caju, caoba, carapa, cedar, crabwood, gunnung, hardtack, jarrah, khaya, madeira, raton(ia), ratteen, sapele, sipo, swietenia, tabasco, tanguile, thitka, toon(a), totara, tree, woolybull, yellowwood
bastard bangalay
burl roe
flat bedbug
gum jarrah
-like sabicu
-pine totara
white primavera

MAHOMET See MOHAMMED.

MAHONIA agarita, agrito, algerita, ashberry, odostemon, oregon grape
root extract barberry, berberis

MAHORI *language* See POLYNESIA *language.*

MAHSEIAH *father* zedekiah
son neriah

MAHU demon, devil, eccentric, left-hander, queer

MAHUA fulwa, illipe, illupi, madhuca, mowha, mowra, phulwara
fat fulwa, illipe-butter, phulwa

MAIA crab, goddess, nymph, star
consort hephaestus, vulcan, zeus
parent atlas, pleione
son hermes, mercury

MAID abigail, ama(h), ayah, bedmaker, biddy, bonne, bonnie, char(woman), child, cinderella, damsel, domestic, eyah, femme de

chambre, girl, hired girl, iya, lady-help, lassie, **MAIDEN**, matranee, meisje, miss, servant(girl), servitrix, slavey, soubrette, spinster, tweenie, tweeny, virgin, waiting-woman, wench
blue-eyed minerva
in waiting abigail, damozel, damsel, suivante
kitchen scogie
lady's abigail, tirewoman
mythical nymph
nurse amah, ayah, bonne
of all work factotum, slavey
of astolot elaine
of athens macri
of orleans joan, pucelle
old spinster, tabby
servant ancilla, biddy, bonne, domestic, hired girl, lisette, tweeny
MAIDEN (See also MAID.) bird, celibate, colleen, dalaga, dame, damozel, dolly, earliest, early, first, fraulein, fresh, froken, gal, initial, juvenile, lass(ie), madchen, may, miss(y), new, purile, senorita, signorina, untried, unused, virgin, youthful
basket on head canephor
blush pink poplar
changed to spider arachne
changed to tree carya
duck shoveler
name nee
name meaning corinna
oak durmast
pink dianthus, spink
wreath francoa, spiraea, vine
MAIDENHAIR *fern* adiantum, bermuda, brittle, california, capillaire, farley
tree ginkgo
MAIDENHOOD chastity, freshness, newness, purity
MAIDENLY celibate, feminine, gentle, girlish, modest, virgin(al)
MAIGRE sciaenid, weakfish
MAIL (See also ARMOR.) bag, buckler, consign, correspond(ence), da(u)k, dawk, express, frank, letters, mall, mole, parcelpost, payment, post(age), postbag, protect, rent, send, shield, special delivery, spot, tappall, tax, transmit, tribute, wallet
bag postbag, pouch

boat aviso, packet
box drop, letterdrop, pillarbox, postbox
carrier courier, postman
coat See ARMOR.
shell chiton
shirt privy coat
system pony express
to be held poste restante
undeliverable dead letter, nix(y)
MAILED posted, protected, speckled, spotted
MAILLOT bathingsuit, pullover, sweater
MAIM batter, blemish, cripple, crush, damage, defect, demolish, disable, disfigure, dismember, harm, hurt, impair, injure, lacerate, lack, mangle, mar, mayhem, mutilate, spoil, trunk, wound
MAIMON ape, baboon, mandrill
MAIN body, broad, bulky, capital, cardinal, central, chief, conduit, direct, duct, essential, expanse, first, force, foremost, fundamental, great, head, huge, important, key, leading, line, might(y), ocean, paramount, pipe, potent, power, primary, prime, principal, pure, sea, sheer, stellar, strength, utmost
course blue plate, entree
drag artery, avenue, boulevard, heart, street
gauche dagger, left hand
point essential, gist, jet, kernel, nub, pith
street author lewis
street town gopher prairie, sauk center
MAINE down east
bay casco, passamaquoddy, penobscot
bird chickadee
capital augusta
city auburn, augusta, bangor, bar harbor, bath, biddeford, boothbay, brunswick, kittery, ogunquit, orono, portland, presque isle, skowhegan, waterville
college bates, bowdoin, colby
county aroostook, kennebec, knox, waldo
herring quoddies
indian abnaki, wewenoc
island orrs

lake moose(head), rangeley, schoodic, sebago, sebec
lobster center monahigan, monhegan
national park acadia
native down-easter, maniac
nickname pine tree state, wonderland
peak bigelow, cadillac, katahdin
port bangor, bath, portland
resort bar harbor
river androscoggin, aroostook, kennebago, kennebec, penobscot, saco
ship down-easter
state flower pine cone, thistle
state tree pine
MAINLAND continent, europe
MAINLINER See ADDICT.
MAINLY chiefly, exceedingly, forcibly, greatly, mostly, powerfully, principally, strongly, very, violently
MAINPRISE bail, pledge, surety
MAINSPRING motive, source, start
MAINSTAY anchorman, backbone, basis, element(al), fundamental, hope, key, pillar, prop, reliance, sinew, staff, supporter
MAINTAIN advocate, affirm, aid, allege, argue, assert, aver, avouch, avow, bear, carry(on), claim, conduct, contend, continue, declare, defend, dispute, endure, fight, have, hold, insist, justify, keep, nourish, persist, possess, preserve, protest, provide for, retain, state, support, sustain, threap, uphold, upkeep, vindicate
again reassert
MAINTENANCE aid, alimony, bearing, behavior, conservation, custody, defense, keep, livelihood, living, preservation, provision(s), retention, service, status quo, subsistence, support, sustenance, upkeep, vindication
MAISON See HOUSE.
de sante asylum, hospital, sanatorium
dieu hospital
MAITRE *d'hotel* headwaiter, major-domo, manager, steward

MAITREYA See BUDDHA.

MAIZE atole, cereal, corn, djagoong, grain, jagong, mealies, staple, zea
bread piki
malady ear-rot

MAJAGUA algodoncillo, balibago, baru, bola, burao, corkwood, emajagua, guana, hau, huamaga, maho(e), mohoe, mojo, purau, tree

MAJESTIC august, dignified, elevated, formal, glorious, grand(iose), grave, great, high, imperial, imposing, impressive, kingly, lofty, maestoso, magnificent, monumental, noble, olympian, regal, royal, sovereign, splendid, stately, statuesque, sublime, superb, tremendous

MAJESTY augustus, dignity, grandeur, king(ship), magnificence, monarch, nobility, potentate, power, ruler, sovereign(ty), stateliness, sublimity
symbol crown, eagle, scepter

MAJOLICA delft, earthenware, faience, pottery
jar albarello

MAJOR capital, chief, dignitary, dur(um), essential, grandee, greater, higher, important, leading, maggiore, magnifico, officer, senior, specialize, specialty, strut, superior
-domo agent, bailiff, butler, emcee, factor, oeconomus, reeve, seneschal, steward
-league big-time, important
third ditone

MAJORATE augment, increase

MAJORCA *capital* palma

MAJORITY age, body, bulk, excess, feck, greater, mass, maturity, most, plurality, preponderance, quorum, seniority, substance, superiority

MAKAIRA aguja, agujon, gar, marlin

MAKE accomplish, achieve, acquire, appoint, arrange, bear, brand, bring about, build, cause, cobble, coerce, compel, compose, composition, constitute, constrain, construct, contrive, create, design, earn, effect, estab-lish, estimate, execute, fabricate, fashion, finish, force, forge, form(ulate), frame, fulfill, gain, generate, get, graith, grow, halfpenny, identify, income, induce, iwurch, kind, manage, model, mo(u)ld, name, oblige, perform, prepare, pretend, produce, realize, receive, recognize, render, score, seduce, settle, shape, shuffle, steal, structure, style, synthesize, sustain, train, turn out, type, win, yield
a fool of begowk, deceive, dolt, doodle, dor(re), dupe, humiliate
a fortune prosper, score, succeed, thrive
a go of it accomplish, achieve, succeed
a hit please, score, succeed
a killing prevail, profit, score, succeed, triumph, win
a leg salaam
a living earn, eke out, get by, make out, manage, scrape along, work
a man of benefit, discipline, drill, educate, encourage, mature, raise, train
a mess botch, confuse, pie, spoil
a splash splurge, succeed, win
acquainted introduce, present
active energize, stimulate
advances approach, court, cultivate, influence, proposition, woo
allowance for consider, discount, excuse, extenuate
all square avenge, even, remedy, revenge, settle, tie
amends abegge, abye, answer, atone, expiate, redeem, redress, repair
an end of despatch, destroy, dispatch, kill, polish off, stop
angry gramy, ire, wrath
as if act, dissemble, pretend, put on
available lend
away with abolish, destroy, dump, embezzle, jettison, murder, squander, steal, take
bare denude, strip
beer brew

believe act, assumed, borak, dissimulate, dramatic, dummy, fake(ry), feign(ed), feint, fiction, foal, magic, play-act(ing), pretend, pretense, pretext, put on, sham, shimsham, show(y), simulate, simulation, spurious
better ameliorate, amend, beat, beet, heighten
bold challenge, dare, undertake, venture
bones about scruple, stickle
book bet, wager
bright clarify, engild, illume, lighten
brisk perk
brown tan
bulky mass
by stamping mint
certain assure, certify, ensure, insure, promise
cheerful buck up, perk up, solace
choice choose, opt, select
clammy engleim
clear argue, clarify, declare, describe, develop, disclose, discover, discuss, emphasize, exhibit, explain, expound, lighten, reveal, specify, stress, untangle
cognizant acquaint
column ploy
comb. ate, ify, ize
complete finish, sphere
compulsory bind, demand, require
concise edit, prune
cultivatable empolder
dark blacken
destitute bereave
different alter, change, modify
dirty bedabble, (be)grime, moil, muddy, soil
display of affect, discover
do eke, get by, improvise, manage
drunk befuddle, besot, fox, fuddle, intoxicate, souse, sozzle, stupify
dry haz(z)le, parch
earlier advance
easier alleviate, ameliorate
effervescent aeriate
effigy guy
end of fetch, snib
enduring anneal
even glaze, level, smooth, square, weigh
eyes flirt

faces gimble, grimace, murgeon
fair weather flatter
false pretences masquerade, sham
familiar accustom, acquaint, inform
famous eternize
fast bail, batten, belay, bind, buckle, fasten, fix, gird, hitch, knit, nail down, secure, stop, tie
fat batten
firm brace, fasten, fix
fit adjust, aptate, arm, drill, exercise
foolish daff, freen, nugify, stultify
footsore surbate
full farce, fulfill, stuff
fun of droll, gaff, glaik, guy, jest, joke, josh, kid, quip, rib, ridicule, scoff, scout, smoke
fuss over nothing faff
glad fain
glass found
glossy polish, shine, sleek, wax
golden aureate, endore, gild
good accomplish, approve, atone, compensate, complete, perform, recoup, redeem, remedy, succeed, thrive, win
grinding noise grinch
happy beatify, bless, elate, felicify, gladden, please, satisfy
hard endure, hornify, steel, taw
hash of botch, confuse, scramble, spoil
haste dash, hurry, rush, scurry
headway advance, enforce, improve, progress, prosper, stem, walk
hesitate stagger
hollow cave
holy bless, consecrate, hallow, sacre, sanctify, venerate
ill ail, morbify, sicken
impact assail, impress
impure adulterate, contaminate, poison
incursion harry
indistinct bedim, blur, confuse, obscure
insignificant micrify
into bundle fardel
invalid damask
it arrive, succeed, triumph

jagged indent
joyful rejoice
known acknowledge, admit, advertise, advise, air, announce, avow, beken, bewray, bid, blaze, blazen, blow, break, broach, bruit, bulletin, celebrate, confess, couthe, decipher, declare, delate, descry, disclose, discover, divulge, expose, give out, impart, indicate, inform, kithe, noise, proclaim, promote, promulgate, promulge, publicize, publish, relate, reveal, signify, sound, speak, spread, tell, uncover, wise
lace crochet, tat
larger add to, augment, increase
law enact, legalize, legislate
leather tan
less dense rarefy, thin
less severe mitigate
level even, true
light leaven
like act, assimilate, compare, pretend, resemble
love bill and coo, bundle, court, cuddle, gallant, ricky-chow, smooch, spoon, sweet-talk, trifle, woo
manifest evince, explain
melancholy hyp, sadden
melodious attune
mention speak
merry celebrate, cheer, disport, enjoy, frolic, gaud, jet, play, rehayte, shrove, sport
metallic sound bong, chink, clang
milder assuage
mincemeat beat, decimate, demolish, destroy, grind, hurt, overwhelm, rout
mistake boob, err, fluff, goof
monotonous noise drone, hum
mountain of molehill exaggerate, overdo
moral ethicize
much of dandle, dawt, emphasize, exaggerate, exalt, praise, stress
neat care for, feat, groom, redd, smug, straighten, tidy
nest timber
nonmagnetic degauss
numb an(a)esthetize, daze, etherize
off annex, bag, bolt, depart, embark, flee, go away,

heist, hook, leave, scamper, spirit
old age, antiquate, void
one join, marry, une, unite
oneself scarce flee, scram, vamoose
one's way airt, bore, trade
open air, patefy
out accomplish, achieve, complete, decipher, delineate, descry, detect, discern, draw up, escape, espy, establish, execute, fare, feign, fill, finish, get along, glean, know, manage, notice, observe, perceive, pretend, prove, record, remark, score, see, solve, spot, succeed, thrive, write
over alien(ate), assign, change, convert, deliver, esteem, praise, recoct, recreate, redo, refashion, reforge, reform, renovate, repair, restore, revamp, transfer, turn
pale blanch, bleach, chalk
peace appease, bury the hatchet, conciliate, pacify, settle
plain See *clear*, above.
pleasant sweeten
pretentious buckram
progress advance, gain, gather, improve, prosper, stem
public See *known*, above.
quiet allay, appease, calm, sooth
rattling noise tirl
ready address, apparel, belay, boun, busk, dispose, dress, fettle, graith, prepare, prest, prime, yark
reference mention
resistence mutiny, rebel, revolt
resolute steel
rich freight, imburse
right adjust, atone, correct, emend, remedy
rosy flush
rough asperate
rustling sound fissle, fistle
rutting cry fream
sharp cacuminate
short abbreviate, abridge, cut, dock, epitomize, reduce, shorten
sign of the cross bless
slender attenuate
small belittle, micrify, minimize
smaller compress, minify

smooth gentle, glaze, hammer, levigate, scrape, sleek, slick

soft gentle, nesh

soggy sop

sore rankle

sour fox, wind

sport of lark

spotted dapple, stipple

spruce perk, smarten

stab at attempt, endeavor, try

strong fasten, fortify, steel, strengthen

stupid moider, stultify

suitable adapt

sure See INSURE.

terms bargain, capitulate, mediate, surrender

tipsy fluster

torpid benumb

tracks depart, escape, flee, hare, hurry, run, speed

transition to modulate

turgid bloat

uneasy begruntle, unsettle

unfit denature, ruin, spoil

up analyze, anatomy, arrange, assemble, coif, combination, compensate, compile, complete, compose, composition, compound, compute, concoct, confect, consistency, contents, cook, cosmetics, create, fabric(ate), fashion, form(at), getup, grease-paint, improvise, indite, lay-out, lipstick, mix(ture), nature, organization, originate, pacify, paint, prepare, reconcile, settle, structure, synthesize, texture, travesty, weave

up for atone, compensate

up one's mind ascertain, decide, determine, settle

up to accost, address, court, cultivate, flatter, influence

use of adopt, apply, appropriate, avail, employ, exploit

vain bloat

vibrant sound chirr

void abate, abolish, annul, cancel, erase, erose, nullify, repeal

war battle, challenge, fight, warray

well cure, heal

wet draggle, drench, soak, souse

worse aggravate, impair, intensify, pejorate

wry face blench, shrink, wince

MAKER architect, author, creator, declarer, designer, doer, factor, father, forger, generator, inventor, manufacturer, mover, operator, originator, parent, prime mover, producer, progenitor, sire, smith, writer

comb. fex

MAKESHIFT apology, bewith, contrivance, ersatz, expedient, improvised, jackleg, jerry(built), kutcha, manage, pis aller, pretext, provisional, resort, rude, scamble, stopgap, substitute, surrogate, temporary, tentative, tousy

MAKI lemur

MAKING batch, composition, material, structure

comb. fic(ation)

MAKO blue-pointer, shark

MAKONNEN, RAS TAFARI haile selassie

MAL bad, evil, rotten

apropos inappropriate, inexpedient, inopportune, unseasonal, untimely

de mer seasickness

du pays homesickness

MALABAR bay, handkerchief

almond almendro(n), kamani

bark ochna

canoe ballam, tonee

monkey wanderoo

nightshade basella

nutmeg bombay-mace

palm talipot

rat bandicoot

wind elephanta

MALACCA *island* penang

language sakai, semang

people sakai, semang

weight asta, kip

MALACHITE azurite, bice, bremen, mineral

pseudo prasine

MALADJUSTED neurasthenic, neurotic, psycho, sick

MALADJUSTMENT *emotional* parataxis

MALADROIT awkward, bungling, clumsy, gaffe, gauche, inept, shmegegge, unhandy, unskillful

MALADVENTURE escapade, mishap

MALADY affection, afflic-

tion, ailment, amok, cause, complaint, disease, disorder, distemper, illness, indisposition, mischief, morbidity, oncome, sickness

MALAGA grape, wine

MALAGASY See MADAGASCAR.

MALAHACK carve, cut, deface

MALAISE discomfort, distress, dysphoria, pain

MALAK *kingdom* taro

MALAPERT bold, flippant, forward, impertinent, impudent, insolent, rude, sassy, saucy

MALAPROP(ISM) bulbenik, slipslop, solecism

MALARIA ague, blackwater fever, chill, lake fever, miasma, paludism, shakes, vapor

carrier anopheles, plasmodium, vivax

pert. paludose, paludous

remedy atabrine, ma pien tsao, quinacrine, quinine, thaline, verbena

symptom ague, shakes

MALARKEY bunk(um), hot air, megillah, nonsense

MALAWI nyasaland

capital zomba

city blantyre, lilongwe, mzuzu

coin kwacha

highlands shire

lake nyas(s)a

language cewa, ngoni, nyanja, tonga, tumbuka, yao

leader kamuzu banda

peak mlanje

people bantu, chewa, nyanja, yao

prime minister banda

valley rift

MALAY, MALAYSIA See also INDONESIA; POLYNESIA.

adam tiki

address tuan

almond kanari

alphabet tagal

animal anoa, arna, banteng, chevrotain, gaur, lar, plandok, saladang, seladang, sladang, tapir, tiger

apple jambo, kawika, ohia

archipelago See *country* and *island,* below.

arum aglaonema

backgammon tabal

banana fei
beefwood belah, toa, tooa
bird poe, tue, tui; weka
boat ballam, caracoa, caracora, caracore, catamaran, cougnar, moguey, moki, outrigger, pindjaap, praam, prah(am), praho, prao, prau, proa, tongkang, toup, waka
buffalo carabao, seladang
burial place ahu
camphor borneol
canoe See *boat,* above.
capital kuala lumpur
charm keitiki
chief ariki, dato, datto, datu
christian abaca, ague, ilokano
citizen baba
city davao, iloilo, ipoh, johore, kuching, kupang, malacca, manado, sandakan, singapore
clan ati, hapu, ringatu
cloth batik, malo, pareu, tapa
club marree, mere, patu, rata
coin tampang, taro, tra(h)
communal house morong
condiment sambal, sambel
council hall balai
country indonesia, polynesia, sabah, sarawak, singapore
crane sarus
creator maui, tiki
crocodile gharial
dagger barong, crees(e), cris(e), krees(e), kris, parang, patu
dance haka, hula
deer plandok, thameng
demon akua, atua
disease amok, amuck, lata(h)
district malacca
dress or garment cabaya, kabaya, malo, pareu, sarong
drink kava
emperor baginda
fern tara, uluhi
first man tiki
fowl asil
fruit rambutan
fruit tree hevi
game sepakraga
gecko tokay
gentleman tuan
gibbon lar
god See POLYNESIA god.
goddess pele
gomuti ejoo
government kompeni
hardwood resak

headhunter italone
head man dat(t)o, datu, pangerang, penghulu
herb entada, pia, taro
house whare(wananga)
island alor, amboina, ambon, arroe, arrou, aru, bali, banda, bangka, belitong, billiton, boefon, boeroe, bohol, borneo, buru, buton, butung, celebes, ceram, djailolo, figi, flores, gaga, goa, halmahera, hawaii, jamdena, java, jilolo, kai, lombok, luzon, madura, mindoro, misol, morotai, muna, muru, musool, new guinea, obi, oma, palawan, panay, peleng, penang, rapa, salajar, salwati, sandwich, sangi, sangir, singapore, soemba(wa), sulu, sumatra, sumba(wa), tahiti, talaur, tanimbar, timor(laut), tokelal, ton, uea, uvea, waigeu, wetar
island group society
isthmus kra
jacket ba(d)ju
jumping disease lata
killing frenzy amok
king ariki, baginda
knife See *dagger,* above.
language achinese, battok, bugi, dyak, javanese, lampong, makassar, niasese, rejang
law adat
loin cloth malo, pareu
loria tiria
lugger toup
magic nana
marriage ambilanak, ambilian
measure chupak, gantang, para, parah, parrah, pau, pipe, tael, tun, wang
memorial See *statue,* below.
money mace
moslem kadayan, moro
mound ahu
mountain gunong, gunung, tahan
mouse-deer plandok
mulberry bark tapa
musical instrument anklong
native abongo, apayao, aripas, ata, ati, bajau, bicol, bikol, bilaan, bisayan, bobongo, bugi(nese), d(a)-yak, futunan, hapu, hawaiian, ilokano, ita, jakun, kanaka, mahori, malacca, malay(an), maori, marque-

san, negrite, nesogaean, nivean, obongo, polynesian, rejang, sakai, samal(laut), samoan, semang, semelai, tagakaolo, tagal(og), tahitian, tongan, vicol, visayan
neuralgia lata
orangutan mias
oven imu, umu
ox banteng, tsine
palm areca, areng(a), atap, ejoo, gebang, gomuti, nibong, nibung, nipa(h), sago, talipot, tara
parrot lories, lory, tui
part dindings
peak binaija, bulu, gunong, gunung, leuser, murjo, niapa, niut, raja, rindjani, slamet, tahan
pepper avas, siri(h)
pheasant argus
pigeon lupe
pine ara, hala
pit umu
plant kanaka, taro, ube, uvi
play wayang kulit
political leader rahman
port georgetown, jesselton, jucking, kotabahru, kotabharu, kuantan, malacca, penang
power mana
priest tohunga
public square alunalun
rajah panglima
rice field sawah
river barito, kutai, pahang, perak
ruler faipule
sauce sambal
saying auwe
servant taio
shrine ahurewa
skirt sarong
spirit atua
state johore, kedah, kelantan, negri, pahang, penang, perak, perlis, selangor, sungei, trengganu, ujong
statue ahu, tiki, zogo
store pataka
sword parang
tatooing moko
teak djati
tic lata(h)
title tuan
tree ahia, akaroa, akia, ara, benkulen, canangium, duku, durian, ilangilang, ipil, jelutong, kajugaru, kapur, lanseh, narra, niepa, ohia, rata, santalum, shorea, tanehakas, terap, upas

tunic kabaya
verse form pantun
village campong, kaika, kainga, kampong, pah
vine zanonia
volcano gunongapi
wages utu
weight chee, mace, tael, tampang, wang
woman vahine, wahine
yam ube, uvi
yam bean wayaka

MALCHISHUA *father* saul
MALCHUS *ear severed by* peter
MALCOM *father* duncan
MALCONTENT agitator, bellyacher, complainant, complainer, crab, crank, croaker, discontented, dissatisfied, faultfinder, finian, frondeur, griper, grouch, grouser, growler, grumbler, insurgent, kicker, murmurer, mutterer, reactionary, rebel(lious), restless, sniveler, uneasy, unhappy
MALDIVE *capital* male
MALDUCK fulmar, nelly
MALE boy, fellow, gent(leman), jack, lalaqui, MAN, manly, mannish, mascle, masculine, purusha, strong, stud, tup, vigorous, virile
comb. andr(o), androus, andry
descent, pert. patrilineal
dominated by androcentric
gelded barrow, eunuch, galt, gelding, steer
hormone drug androgen
offspring brother, sib(ling), son
orchis bloodybutchers, bloodyfingers, crowfoot, crowtoes, cuckoo, cullion, foxglove, nosebleed, purples, ragwort, trillium
primal purusha
traits, lack of anandria
MALEDICTION abuse, anathema, attack, ban, blasphemy, curse, damn(ation), darn, denunciation, diatribe, execration, expletive, imprecation, malison, oath, profanation, profanity, slander, swearword, threat
MALEDICTORY blasphemous, execrative, impious, imprecatory, profane
MALEFACTION crime, mal-

feasance, offense, wrongdoing
MALEFACTOR baddie, baddy, convict, criminal, culprit, evildoer, felon, hoodlum, malfeasant, malfeasor, offender, outlaw, sinner, wrongdoer
MALEFIC baneful, evil, harmful, hurtful, malicious, malign, mischievous, sinister, wicked
MALEVOLENCE despite, evil(eye), hate, hatred, illwill, malice, malignity, grudge, hostility, spite, spleen
MALEVOLENT bad, baleful, black-hearted, cruel, despiteful, despiteous, envious, evil, fell, grudging, harmful, hating, hostile, illdisposed, illwilled, malefic, malicious, malign, rancorous, sinister, spiteful, wicked
MALFEASANCE error, malversation, misconduct, misprision, sin
MALFEASANT See MALEFACTOR.
MALFORMED deformed
MALI french sudan
capital bamako
city gao, kayes, mopti, san degou, sikasso, timbuktu
emperor mansa musa
lake debo, garou, korarou
language dogon, dyula, malinke, mande, marka, peul(h), senoufo, songhai
peak manding, mina
people bambara, fellata, fula(h), fulani, malinke, moor, peul(h), senoulfo, songhai, tuareg
president keita
river azaouak, bagoe, bakoy, bani, baoule, niger, senegal
MALICE animosity, animus, antipathy, bitterness, despite, enmity, envy, evil, grudge, hain, hatred, illwill, jealousy, malevolence, malignance, meanness, pique, poison, rancor, spite, spleen, venom
MALICIOUS bitter, cankered, cantankerous, catty, cruel, despiteful, despiteous, dogged, envious, harmful, hateful, heinous, invidious, jealous, malefic(ent), malevolent, malign(ant), mean,

noxious, ornery, pernicious, rancorous, resentful, sinister, spiteful
action arson, sabotage, vandalism
intention animus
MALIGN abuse, asperse, assail, baleful, begrudge, bewray, blacken, blaspheme, calumniate, decry, defame, defile, deprave, depreciate, disparage, evil, harmful, hostile, hurtful, inimical, libel, malefic, MALICIOUS, MALIGNANT, slur, smear, traduce, venomous, vilify, virulent
MALIGNANCY cancer
MALIGNANT attern, attery, bad, baneful, cancerous, cankered, dangerous, deleterious, diabolical, evil, felonious, fiendish, harmful, hateful, heinous, hellish, ill, inauspicious, inimical, malefic, malicious, mean, noxious, pernicious, poisonous, sinful, spiteful, swart, venomous, vicious, virulent, wicked, wrathful
MALIGNITY animosity, deadliness, fatality, grudge, hate, hatred, hostility, liver, malice, malignancy, spite, spleen, vengefulness, venom, violence, virulence, virus
MALIK owner, proprietor, zaminda
MALINGER avoid, evade, goldbrick, laze, shirk, skulk, soldier
MALINGERER galleystoker, goldbrick(er), leadswinger, sconcer, shamabram, shirker, slacker, sojer, soldier
MALISON anathema, curse, execration, imprecation, malediction, torment
MALKIN cat, dowdy, drab, effigy, guy, hare, maid, mawkin, mop, puppet, scarecrow, servant, slattern
MALL allee, game, gull, mallet, maul, promenade, strip, walk
MALLARD anas, drake, duck, greenhead, moss duck, puddleduck, twister
flock sord, sute
MALLEABLE adaptable,

amenable, docile, ductile, plastic, pliable, pliant, soft, tensile, tractable, tractile, yielding

MALLEE bird, brushwood, eucalyptus, rowan, thicket, tree

bird leipoa

MALLEMUCK albatross, bird, fulmar, malmarsh, mollie, petrel

MALLET beat(er), beetle, bungstarter, club, dresser, driver, engine, flogger, gavel, hammer, locomotive, mace, mall, maul, mell, plowmell, sledge, splatcher, tup

clod-breaking bilder

currier's mace

hatter's beater

leaden madge

paver's reel, tup

MALLEUS ambos, equinia, glanders, hammer, ossicle

MALLOW abelmoschus, abutilon, altea, escoba, ge-mauve, hock, kokio, malva, mauve, pieprint, plant, sida

dwarf cheese, pellas

false moss-rose

family cotton, hollyhock, okra

flowered pavonia

fruit frog-cheese, piemarker, pieprint

genus abutilon, pavonia, plagianthus, thespesia, thruberia

MALLUCA *parent* harim

MALM clay, limestone, marl, soil

MALMESBURY *philosopher* hobbes

MALMSEY grape, madeira, malvasia, wine

MALNUTRITION cachexia, cachexy

remedy amigen

MALO girdle, loincloth

MALODOROUS f(o)etid, fusty, gamy, high, mephitic, musty, noisome, obnoxious, olid, putrid, rancid, rank, smelly, stenchy, stinking, stinky, virose

MALORY *work* morte d'arthur

MALPRACTICE malefaction, misconduct, misuse

MALPRAMIS *father* beligant

slayer duke naimes

MALRAUX *novel* man's fate

MALT *brewing* browst

crushed mash

drink ale, beer, bock, brew, lager, porter, stout, zythum

froth barm, suds

ground grist, smeddum

infusion wort

mixture maltate, zythum

pert. aly

refuse coom(b), draff

sugar maltose

-tasting corny

vinegar alegar, wort

worm tippler, toper

MALTA *boat* dghaisa

capital mdina, val(l)etta

city mdeina, mellieha, mosta, rabat, sliema, valletta, zeibrun, zurrieg

coin grain, grano

fever brucellosis

goddess calypso

gondola dghaisa

hamlet casal(e)

headdress faldetta

island near gozo

jew of barabas

measure artal, caffiso, canna, kantar, parto, ratel, rotl, salm(a)

point delimara

priest kappillan

suburb florian

wind gregale, levanter

MALTESE *cross* fireball, lychnis

-mushroom cynomorium

MALTHA asphalt, bitumen, brea, tar

MALTOSE amylon, sugar

MALTREAT abuse, beat, bedevil, defoul, demean, hespil, huspel, mistreat, misuse, mohock, outrage

MALUM evil, offense, wrong

MALUS angophora, apple, crabapple, tree

MALVA dock, mallow

MALVERSATION corruption, extortion, fraud, misbehavior

MALVINA *islands* falkland, les malouines

MALVOLIO *steward to* olivia

MAMELUKE servant, slave, soldier

MAMMA See MOTHER.

MAMMAL See also kind, below.

amphibious otter

antlered caribou, deer, elk, moose, reindeer

aquatic baleen, beaver, beluga, cetacea, coypu, des-

man, DOLPHIN, dugong, gibbar, grampus, halicore, hippo(potamus), humpback, huse, inia, kreng, manatee, morse, orca, otary, otter, pinniped, poggy, PORPOISE, rorqual, rytina, scrag, seacow, seal, sea-lion, shark, sirenian, WALRUS, WHALE, yungan

arboreal banxring, fisher, glutton, kinkajou, lemur, monkey, opossum, orang-outang, orangutan, raccoon, sloth, tarsier, tree-shrew

armored apara, armadillo

badger-like balisaur, pahmi, ratel

bovine bison, bos, bull, calf, cow, longhorn, steer, taurine, zebu

burrowing aardvark, armadillo, badger, gopher, groundhog, mole, rabbit, squirrel, suricate, wombat

camel-like guanaco

canine coyote, dog, fox, wolf

caprine goat

carnivorous coyote, dasyure, glutton, ichneumon, mongoose, mustelid, panda, procyonid, raccoon, teledu, tiger, wolf, wolverine

cat-like cheetah, jaguar, lion, mongoose, ocelot, panther, serval, tiger

cetacean dolphin, porpoise, whale

civet-like genet

coat fur, hide, nutria, pelage, pelt, skin

cud-chewing ruminant

deer-like chevrotain

domestic cat(tle), cow, dog, goat, horse, sheep

edentate aardvark, antbear, anteater, armadillo, pangolin, sloth, tamandua, tamanoit

embryo sac amnion

equine ass, colt, filly, foal, horse, mare, pony, stallion, zebra

even-toed artiodactyl

extinct amblypod, brontops, creodont, ganodont, glyptodont, machairodus, mastodon, paleoparadoxia, pantodont, rytina, titanotherium

feline cat, cheetah, cougar, jaguar, leopard, lion, lynx,

ocelot, panther, polecat, puma, serval, tiger, wildcat

fish-eating otter

fleet antelope, deer, hare

flying bat

giraffe-like okapi

gnawing mole, mouse, rat, rodent, vole

herbivorous (See also *bovine* and *equine*, above.) daman, dugong, hippo, manatee, orangutan, rhinoceros, ruminant

hoofed artiodactyl

horned antelope, bison, buffalo, cow, gaur, goat, oxen, reem, reindeer, rhinoceros, unicorn

hornless anoplotherium, anoplotheroid

insectivorous banxring, bat, desman, hedgehog, mole, tendrac, tenrec

kind anthropoid, apara, aswail, bhalu, canine, carnivore, cat, cetacean, coati, daman, dhole, dugong, edentate, eutheria, feline, hathi, hatty, herbivore, insectivore, kiang, lagomorph, lemuroid, loper, loxodon, marsupial, marten, mataco, metatheria, monotreme, mungo, nodiak, okapi, ounce, peccora, peludo, pholidota, placental, poyou, primate, protitheria, rodent, ruminant, ruminate, tamandu, tatou, tayra, theria, toxodon, ungulate, zebu

lagomorph rabbit

large behemoth, elephant, hippopotamus, mammoth, mastodon, rhinoceros, whale

largest whale

lemurine potto

leopard-like cougar, jaguar, lion, lynx, ocelot, pard, polecat, puma, tiger, wildcat

llama-like vicuna

marine See *aquatic*, above.

marsupial anteater, ariel, bandicoot, bilbi, boomah, boomer, coala, cuscus, dasyure, diprotodon, forester, jerboa, joey, kangaroo, kapoune, koala, macropus, marmosa, moncat, mongan, mulgara, numbat, opossum, pademelon, petaurist, phalanger, phascogale, phi-

lander, possum, quica, selva, silva, tait, tapoa, tarsipes, thill, thylacine, tungo, wallaby, wallaroo, wombat, yapok

meat-eating carnivore

mole-like desman

monkey-like lemur, loris

mouse-like shrew

nocturnal bat, coon, coyote, hyena, kinkajou, lemur, macaco, opossum, platypus, possum, raccoon, ratel, tapir, tarsier

omniverous hog, pig, swine

order, highest primate

order, lowest marsupial

perissodactyl horse, rhinoceros, tapir

placental monodelphia

plantigrade bear, coon, panda, raccoon

porcine boar, hog, peccary, pig, swine

prehistoric See *extinct*, above.

primitive amblypod(a), condylarth

raccoon-like coati

retentive elephant

rhinocerous-like baluchitherium, tapir

ringtailed coon, lemur, macaco, rac(c)oon

ruminant alpaca, antelope, bison, buffalo, camel, cattle, chewer, cow, deer, giraffe, goat, llama, moose, okapi, sheep, steer, vicuna

scaled pangolin

shelled armadillo

short-tailed bobtail, rabbit

skunk-like zoril

slow-moving loris, sloth

small genet

smallest shrew

snake-eating mongoose

spiny porcupine, tendrac, tenrec

thick-skinned elephant, hippopotamus, pachyderm, rhinoceros

toothless edentate

tropical coati, peccary, rhino(ceros)

tusked elephant, mammoth, mastodon, walrus

ungulate daman, horse, swine, tapir

ursine bear, panda

viverrine falanaka, galidia

vulpine fox, wolf

web-footed otter, platypus

winged bat

wing-footed aliped

wolf-like coyote

zebra-like quagga

MAMMEE apricot, marmalade-tree, sapodilla

MAMMOCK break, chunk, cut, divide, fragment, hill, piece, scrap, tear

MAMMON cupidity, riches, wealth

MAMMOTH colossal, colossus, cumbrous, elephant, enormous, giant, gigantic, great, herculean, huge, large, mastodon, monster, monstrous, mountainous, titan(ic), weighty

MAMMULA papilla, spinneret

MAMMY (See also MOTHER.) nurse, stoneroller

-coot gallinule

MAMO bird, drepanis, iiwi

MAMORE tributary guapore

MAN 3 boy, don, guy, him, lad, mug, run, sir, tao, vir, wer, wow 4 babu, bird, body, bozo, buck, chal, chap, cove, dick, duck, gent, hand, herr, jack, john, kane, male, mate, rule, sire, soul, tulk, uomo 5 adult, baboo, being, bimbo, biped, bloke, brace, churl, equip, freke, groom, homme, human, joker, lover, party, sahib, segge, senor, swain, swipe, valet, wight 6 beggar, bugger, butler, feller, FELLOW, garcon, hombre, johnny, kimmie, manage, mantzu, master, meneer, mister, mortal, PERSON, player, sailor, signor, sirrah, vassal, wallah 7 bleeder, esquire, fortify, homonid, husband, mynheer, neshoma, neshuma, operate, servant, signore, soldier 8 creature, customer, employee, garrison, monsieur, neshamah, populate, seignior 9 anthropos, caballero, earthling, gentleman, worldling 10 humanbeing 11 homosapiens

able ace, whiz(z)

about town corinthian, dandy, flaneur

age of pleistocene

ages of bronze, golden, heroic, iron, silver

aggressive birkle

alone solus
among men paragon
artificial golem, robot
as one unanimously
-at-arms knight, soldier
bad CRIMINAL, rotter, villain
bad-tempered bodach, curmudgeon, grouch
bald pil(l)garlic
best brideman
big bruiser, cob, giant
bird aviator, flyer
brass talos, talus
brave hero, lion
-bull bucentaur, minotaur
castrated eunuch, spado
clumsy misfit, oaf
coarse bodach, boor churl, knave, oaf, ruffian
comb. andr(o), androus, anthrop(o), viri
common homo vulgaris, yeoman
con barnard, buncosteerer, capper, decoy, imposter, shill, steerer, tipster, tout(er)
conceited coxcomb
cruel beast, brute, monster, ogre, ruffian, turk, villain
cunning montebank, rogue, shyster, trickster
degenerate cur
difficult momzer
disagreeable gleyde
dislike of misandry
dissolute rake, roue
docile milktoast, milquetoast, throttlebottom
dread of androphobia
dressed as woman berdache, bessy, malinche
early proanthropus
-eater cannibal, lamia, requin
-eating androphagous, cannibalism
-eating monster lamia
eccentric codger, geezer, weirdo
effeminate androgyn(e), cockney, dildo, fairy, meacock, milksop, miss nancy
enlisted private, rating, sailor, sergeant, soldier
epitome micranthropos
extinct See *prehistoric*, below.
extra stag
fancy ponce
fashionable beau brummel, blood, boulevardier,

corinthian, dandy, dude, fop, toff
fastest thialfi
fat butterball, fatso, filo, gordo
first adam, adapa, alalcomeneus, ask(r), bure, buri, iapetus, izanagi, tiki, yama
-fish merman
friday assistant, henchman, servant
-fungus earthstar
genus archencephala
great vavasor
group archontia, fraternity, host, lodge, multitude, rabble, society
handsome adonis, apollo, beau, fop
hard-headed boche
hard-hearted knark
hard-pressed job
hater misanthrope
henpecked hoddy-doddy, milquetoast, socrates
holy sadhu, saint, sannyasi
honest truepenny
-horse apsara, centaur, gandharva
immoral rep(robate)
impetuous hotspur
important grandee, hero, lord, magnate, nabob, name, vip
insane furioso
iron stayer, talos, talus
isle of, native manx
isle of, pert. manx
isle of, point ayre
-jack asphalt, cordia, pitch, tree
-keen fond, love-smitten, savage
-keeper newt
ladies' beau(x), carpet knight, dammaret, gallant, romeo
lame bacach
lazy idler
learned bhat, doctor, erudite, lamdan, literati, literatus, ollamh, philologist, professor, pundit, savant, scholar, sophist, teacher, ulema
-like object android, automaton, robot
little bantam, cockalorum, homuncio, homunculus, pygmy, runt, shortie, shrimp
-machine cyborg
-made artificial, ersatz, manufactured, synthetic

married benedict, bridegroom, consort, groom, hubbie, husband, mate, partner, spouse, yokemate
medicine angakok, doctor, peal, priest, shaman
midwife accoucheur
military prussian, soldier, spartan
miniature micranthropos
money paymaster
mother of cybele, eve
name meaning enos
newly rich nouveau riche
of action dynamo
of all work factotum, handyman, joey, mozo
of authority agha, seignior
of blood charles i, david
of blood and iron bismarck
of destiny napoleon bonaparte
of galilee jesus christ
of god ascetic, bethuel, ecclesiastic, minister, pastor, preacher, prelate, priest, prophet, rabbi, saint
of god, name meaning gabriel
of horus ashur
of letters author, literatus, litterateur, writer, savant, scholar
of motley fool
of ross kyrle
of silence napoleon iii
of sorrows jesus christ
of straw figure, nonentity
of taste aesthete, connoisseur
of the earth manroot, morning glory, potato
of the hour hero, lion, star
of the moon yue-laou
of the woods orangutan
of the world cosmopolite, layman, secularist, sophisticate
of war andrew, battleship, big red, bird, caravel, fish, frigate, nautilus, soldier, warrior
of war bird albatross, skuagull
of war fish pastor
old back-number, bodach, boss, centenarian, codger, crone, cuff, dean, dodo, dotard, doyen, duffer, eckehart, emeritus, father, fogram, fogy, forgrum, fuddy-duddy, gaffer, geezer, general, geronte, governor, grandfather, grandpa, grandpop, grandsire, gray-

beard, husband, longbeard, methuselah, mossback, nestor, nonagenarian, octogenarian, patriarch, retiree, senex, senior, sire, square, stager, starets, superior, uncle, velyarde, warhorse
old clothes poco
1-eyed arimasp, cyclops, monoculus
100-eyed argus
on horseback boulanger, savior
outdoor athlete, camper, fisherman, hunter, trapper
outstanding ace, adept, crackerjack, magnifico, marvel, nonpareil, oner, outstander, pastmaster, pip(pin), prodigy, ripper, shark, stemwinder, topper, tops, trump, whiz, wizard
personifying anthropomorphic
pert. anthropoid, human(e), mortal, virile
piltdown eoanthropus
polished smoothie
prehistoric africanthropus, aurignacian, cro-magnon, folsom, furfooz, grenelle, grimaldi, hominid, java, neanderthal, peking, piltdown, rhodesian, steinheim, stone age, swanscombe, tepexpan
primitive aborigine, savage, urmensch
prototype cro-magnon
resembling android, anthropoid
rich astor, baruch, billionaire, capitalist, croesus, daddy warbucks, dives, dupont, ford, getty, gotrocks, have, hughes, maecenas, magnate, midas, millionaire, moneybags, morgan, mr gotrocks, nabob, nawab, plutocrat, rockefeller, rothschild, tycoon, vanderbilt
righteous saddik
righthand aide, henchman
science of anthropology, ethnology
sea gob, merman, sailor, tar
second-story cat burglar
self-important cockalorum
shadowless ascian
short, thick grub
single bachelor, celibate, stag, widower
-sized big, large
sly fox

spirited ball of fire, sparkplug, stemwinder
spiritless meacock
spirit of akh
stalwart spartan
-stealing kidnapping
straight stooge
strong atlas, hercules, kwasind, paul bunyan, powerhouse, samson
tenacious bulldog
-tiger werewolf
-trap siren
undercover agent, detective, investigator, spy
unemployed batlan, batlon
well dressed barbermonger, beau brummel, buck, dandy, dude, exquisite, fop, jackadandy, macaroni, puppy, spark, swell, toff
white buckra, cachila, kabluna, pakeha, paleface
wicked rascal, scoundrel, villain
wise hakam, nestor, owl, sabio, sage, savant, seer, solomon, solon, tohunga, wizard
without a country nolan
without a country, author hale
young bachelor, bahur, beau, bochur, bouchal, boy, buck(een), caddie, caddy, ephebe, fiance, lad, springal, suitor, sweetheart, varlet, younker, youth
MANACLE band, bind, bond, chain, check, clog, cuff, darby, fetter, hamper, handcuff, hinder, hog-tie, impede, irons, obstruct, restraint, shackle, snaffle, tirret, trammel
MANAEAN *courtier to* herod
MANAGE accomplish, administer, afford, arrange, bear, behave, carry on, conduct, contrive, control, cultivate, curb, deal with, devise, dight, direct, engineer, fare, finagle, get along, get on, govern, guide, handle, husband, lead, make do, man, maneuver, manipulate, negotiate, operate, order, pilot, ply, regulate, rule, run, steer, succeed, superintend, swing, tend, treat, use, wangle, wield, work

frugally economize, eke out, husband
hard to balky, fractious, incorrigible, ornery, unruly
MANAGEABLE acquiescent, amenable, compliant, controllable, convenient, corrigible, docile, domitable, easy, flexible, governable, handy, orderly, pliant, restrainable, ruly, toward(ly), tractable, wieldy, yare
MANAGEMENT administration, agency, care, carriage, charge, conduct, control, demeanor, direction, directorate, disposal, economy, gestion, government, heel, leadership, operation, practice, prudence, regulation, running, steerage, work
domestic husbandry, menage
good eutaxia, eutaxy
poor cacoeconomy
MANAGER administrator, agent, aumildar, baleboosteh, baleboss, boss, captain, cellarer, curator, daroga, director, engineer, entrepreneur, executive, foreman, gerent, governor, grieve, herenaca, master, operator, overseer, principal, purser, reeve, schemer, steward, straw-boss, superintendent
assistant caporal
political fugleman
MANAKIN bird, manacus, MANIKIN, pipra
MANANA before long, future, tomorrow
MANANNAN *father* ler
MANAS ego, mind, rationality, sensorium
MANASSA *mauler* jack dempsey
MANASSEH *city* aner
kingdom judah
parent hashum, joseph
son amon, jair
MANASSES *father* ezekias
wife judith
MANAT *father* allah
personified fortune
MANATEE cowfish, dugong, hagfish, hogfish, lamantin, mermaid, sirenian
MANAVELINS hoddle, leftovers, odds and ends, pan, pot
MANAWYDDAN *brother* bran(wen), evnissyen

father lludd, llyr
rescued pryderi
MANCALA ahanbah, bau, bohnenspiel, chanka, chongkak, chungcajon, gabata, game, kale, kpo, madji, mbau, mungala, naranj, poo, wari, wawee
MANCHESTER cottonopolis
resident mancunian
MANCHURIA *army division* banner
city aigun, anshan, harbin, hulan, kirin, mukden, niuchwang, penki
dynasty ta ching
military ruler chang-tso-lin
people daur(i)
port antung
province jehol, kirin
river amur, liao, yalu
MANCIPIUM slave, subject
MANCIPLE bondman, purveyor, servant, slave, steward
MANCO CAPAC *father* inti, sun
wife mama ocllo
MANDARIN aex, bureaucrat, chinese duck, fruit, governor, kuan, official, orange, red, towkay
orange satsuma, tangerine
residence yamen, yamun
MANDATE approval, authority, behest, bidding, breve, brief, charge, colony, command, commission, decree, dictate, direction, dominion, edict, endorsement, fiat, injunction, instruction, law, order, possession, precept, prescript, process, protectorate, referendum, rescript, ruling, sanction, territory, warranty, writ
MANDATORY binding, commanding, compulsory, conclusive, decisive, final, imperative, irrevocable, necessary, obligatory, peremptory, preceptive, required, requisite
MANDIBLE beak, bone, chop(s), gnathite, jaw(bone), jowl, maxilla, operculum, seta
part mala, molar
MANDOLIN lute, mandora, oud
MANDRAKE (See also MAGICIAN.) alraun, alruna, arum, bryony, dudaim,

mandragora, may-apple, poppy, tamus
MANDREL arbor, axis, axle, ball, bobbin, chemise, lathe, pick, sleeve, spindle, stud, triblet
MANDRILL ape, baboon, hog-ape, maimon, morman, papio
MANDUCATE chew, eat, masticate
MANE brush, crine, fringe, hair, juba, locks, mop, roach, ruff, shag, stubble, tresses
-liked crined, jubate
MANEGE gait, horsemanship, lope, pace, trot, volt
exponent rider
MANEUVER act(ion), angle, artifice, battle, conduct, demonstration, device, encirclement, engineer, fainague, feint, finagle, finesse, flank, gerrymander, handle, intrigue, jockey, kriegspiel, machinate, manage, manipulate, mission, movement, operate, operation, outwit, pesade, plan, plot, resort, ruse, scheme, shift, stratagem, strategy, tactic(s), trick, turn, vrille, wangle, wile
aviation barrelroll, chandelle, fishtail, flathat, immelmann, loop, spin, wingover
gently ease
military tactic
MANFUL bold, brave, courageous, male, masculine, resolute, stalwart, sta(u)nch, stout, strong, sturdy, tough, virile
MANGANESE *black* pyrolusite
brown bister, bistre, burntumber
compound alabandite, allactite, apjohnite, armangite, asbolite, backstromite, braunite
garnet spessartite
mica alurgite
ore psilomelane
silicate bementite, caryopilite, errite, graunite, partschinite, peckhamite
source pyrolusite
wad asbolane
MANGE canker, dartars, fodder, itch, meal, reef, scab(ies), scurvy

cause acarid, demodex, mite
MANGER bin, box, bunker, compartment, cratch, creche, crib, heck, praesepe, rack, stall, trough
MANGLE batter, botch, break, bruise, butcher, calender, cripple, crush, cut, damage, deface, demolish, destroy, disfigure, flatiron, flatten, garble, hack, harm, hurt, injure, iron, lacerate, magg, maim, mammock, mangrove, mar, maul, murder, mutilate, press, ruin, sadiron, slash, smooth, spoil, tear
MANGO amchoor, amhar, amini, anacardium, anchovy-pear, bauno, bird, carabao, dika, drupe, fruit, gadung, gedong, grias, madu, melon, ndeei, pahutan, pepper, pico, tree
bird carabao, hummingbird, oriole
dried amchoor, amhar
fish threadfin
grove tope
point nak
squash chayote
tree amra, mangifera
MANGROVE aegiceras, avicennia, bacao, bacauan, catechu, ceriops, courida, goran, hangalai, langarai, logwood, mangle, myrtal, rhizophora, shrub, tree
bark extract cutch
pole bority
MANGY base, contemptible, mean, ronion, ronyon, scabby, scabetic, scurvy, seedy, shabby, squalid
MANHANDLE abuse, maul, paw, remove, rough up
MANHATTAN See NEW YORK.
MANHOOD adamhood, bravery, courage, humanity, maturity, resolution, virility
MANIA aberration, bug, coethes, complex, compulsion, craze, delirium, dementia, enthusiasm, excitement, fad, fascination, fixation, folie de toucher, frenzy, furor, hysteria, infatuation, insanity, lunacy, madness, monomania, obsession, passion, perversion, phrenitis, phrenzy, psychosis, rage, transport
buying oniomania

comb. itis
dancing tarantism
stealing kleptomania
MANIABLE   manageable,
palpable, tractable, workable
MANIAC(AL) crazed, crazy,
demented,   demoniac,
deranged, fanatic, frantic,
hysterical, insane, irrational, lunatic, mad(man),
non compos mentis, psychotic, raving, violent,
wood
MANICARIA bussu, palm,
troolie
MANICURE   clip,   cut,
groom, pare, polish, trim
MANIFEST apert, apparent,
appear, argue, arrant,
attest, bare, betray, bill,
bold, bring out, clear,
couth, declaration, definite,
demonstrate, develop, discernible, disclose, display,
distinct, evidence, evident,
evince, exhibit, explicit, express, extant, frank, graith,
gross, indicate, indubitable,
invoice, list, naked, noticeable, obvious, open, ostend,
ostensible, overt, palpable,
patent, perceivable, perceptible, perspicuous, phanic,
plain, present, produce,
prominent, prove, public,
represent, reveal, seeable, self-evident, shew,
show(n), signify, suggest,
token, unfold, visible, waybill
MANIFESTATION act, appearance, aura, avatar,
coming, demonstration, disclosure, display, effect,
epiphany, exhibition, glint,
ostent, revelation, showing
divine lila, shekinah, shekinali, spirit
frightening chimaera
vague glimmer, glint
MANIFESTO announcement,
declaration, decree, edict,
evidence, fiat, order, ostent,
placard, rescript, statement,
writ
MANIFOLD allotropic(al),
copy, different, disparate,
divergent, divers(e), heteromorphic, many, multifarious, multiple(x), multiply, numerous, polymorphous, protean, replicate,
several, sundry, various

MANIHOT See **MANIOC.**
MANIKIN   doll,   dummy,
dwarf, ecorche, figure, homunculus, midget, model,
pantine, phantom, pygmy,
runt
winged ker
MANILA *airfield* clark
bay boat bilalo
creek estero
hemp abaca, cebu, linaga
hero dewey
river pasig
MANILKARA almique, balata, bully-tree, sapodilla,
star-apple
MANIOC cassava, catella,
juca, manihot, tapioca, yuca
MANIPLE band, company,
fano(n), fanum, handful,
handkerchief, orale, sudarium, vestment
MANIPULATE alter, boom,
brandish, chivvy, coax, control, corner, engross, fake,
falsify, feel, finger, flourish,
handle, humor, jockey, juggle, knead, manage, maneuver, monopolize, operate,
pilot, ply, raid, rig, shape,
shuffle, swing, touch, use,
wave, wield
fraudently rig
MANIPULATION intrigue,
jugglery, operation, pass,
stratagem
MANIS anteater, pangolin
MANITOBA *indian* cree
MANKIND adam, anthropos,
flesh, folk, humanity, people, primates, race, society,
species, universe, world
division clan, people, race,
tribe
hatred of misanthropy
king of yima
parent adam, eve, iapetus
pert. anthropic(al), common
seed of adapa
MANLINESS arete, dignity,
heroism, intrepidity, manship, virility, virtus
MANLY bold, brave, daring,
hardy, male, masculine,
mature, noble, resolute,
stalwart, stout, strong,
sturdy, upright, virile
name meaning andrew
MANN,   THOMAS *work*
buddenbrooks, death in
venice, magic mountain
MANNA ambrosia, amrita,
exudate, food, ganzangabin,

juice, laap, lerp, nectar, trehala
-croup semolina
grass glyceria
gum eucalyptus, lerp
sugar mannitol
MANNEQUIN See **MANIKIN.**
MANNER(S) accent, action,
address, air, appearance, aspect, attitude, aura, bearing,
behavior, breeding, carriage, conduct, cost, custom, decorum, demeanor,
deportment, dignity, etiquette, facture, fashion,
form, front, guise, habit,
havance, kind, look,
method, mien, mode,
modus, mores, nature,
poise, practice, presence, p's
and q's, savoir-faire, sort,
species, style, system, tact,
taste, thew, trick, type,
usage, use, way, wont
affected air
amusing drollery
arrogant brag, hauteur
flamboyant bravura, dash,
panache
forbidding shell
formal starch
outward facade, front
swaggering side
usual habit
MANNERED affected, airy,
artificial, campy, chichi,
cute, formal, morate, stiff,
thewed, unnatural
well bal(a)batish, polite
MANNERISM affectation,
air, eccentricity, habit,
idiasm, idiosyncrasy, minauderie, oddness, peculiarity, pose, quirk, trick
MANOAH *son* samson
MANOR   abode,   acreage,
bury, castle, deme(s)ne, estate, hall, ham, house, mansion, property, township
land barton, deme(s)ne
lord patron
MANROOT   bigroot,   ipomoea, morning-glory, wild
potato
MANROPE limmer
MANSARD roof
MANSE dwelling, house, parsonage
MANSERVANT   andrew,
butler, factotum, garcon,
gilley, gillie, groom, help,
moso, mozo, syce, valet

MANSHIP courage, courtesy, homage, honor, humanity

MANSION abode, castle, chateau, court, dome, dwelling, hotel, house, palace, palais, palazzo, residence, tower, villa, yamen
of the moon alnath

MANSLAUGHTER barbarity, blood, butchery, carnage, felony, homicide, massacre, murder

MANSLAYER androphonos

MANSUETE gentle, kind, mild, tame

MANTA blanket, cloth, mantelet, ray, shelter

MANTEL beam, clavel, filament, ledge, lintel, parel, shelf, slab
ornament bibelot
tree lintel

MANTIC divination, prophetic

MANTILLA cape, cloak, scarf, veil, yashmak

MANTIS cagu, camel-locust, crab, rearhorse
crab squilla

MANTIUS *father* melampus
son clitus

MANTLE balandrana, barracan, blanket, blush, camail, camlet, capa, cape, capote, chlamys, chrisom, chrysome, chuddar, cloak, coat, conceal, cope, cover, disguise, envelope, feridji, filament, flare, flush, foam, form, frock, gather, hood, jabul, khirka, lamba, manteau, ocrea, pall(ium), penstock, ricinium, robe, screen, shelter, slavin, spread, tabard, whittle, wrapper
hooded burnoose
rock regolith

MANTLING blushing, covering, envelope, lambrequin

MANTO *father* hercules, tiresias
son mopsus

MANTRA charm, dharani, fetish, gayatri, hymn, savitri, spell
collection atharva-veda

MANU *father* brahma
laws of sutra, sutta

MANUAL baedeker, bombarde, book, bowditch, breviary, cambist, canon, catechism, cembalo, clavier, coach, dial, didache, direc-

tory, eucholog(ion), farse, formulary, grimoire, guide, handbook, keyboard, litany, missal, ordinal, ordinary, portas, porthors, prayerbook, reference, rubric, schoolbook, synopsis, text-(book), tutor, vady, virginal
art craft, handicraft, trade
laborer carl
training sloid, slojd, sloyd

MANUAO bird, honey-eater, iao

MANUFACTURE assemble, build, coin, concoct, construct, create, fabricate, fashion, forge, form, invent, make, produce, product(ion), shape, synthesize, turn out, yield

MANUFACTURED built, constructed, created, fabricated, fashioned, formed, machine-made, made, ready-made

MANUFACTURER diskery, maker, producer, spinner, supplier, wright

MANUMIT deliver, discharge, emancipate, enfranchise, free, liberate, release

MANURE compost, cultivation, dressing, droppings, dung, fertilizer, folding, fulzie, gooding, laetation, mig, muck, ordure, poudret, saur, sleech, stercorate, tath, tillage, worthing
pile dunghill, hott, mixen

MANUSCRIPT article, book, codex, composition, copy, document, draft, essay, exemplar, flimsy, folio, holograph, mss, opus, original, palimpsest, pandect, pintura, scrive, scroll, text, thesis, uncial, work, writing
back dorso
copier scribe
decoration rubric
hieroglyphic pintura
mark obelus
page folio
preservative cedrium
unpublished inedita

MANX cat, rumpy
goblin boagane, bogle
-man celt, gael
shearwater crew, puffin, scrabe(r)
speech gaelic

MANY bags, bales, bushels, countless, different, divers,

endless, galore, gobs, heaps, jillion, loads, lots, maint, manifold, moult, much, multiferious, multiplied, multitude, myriad, numerous, oodles, piles, plenty, plurality, reams, rife, scads, sere, several, sundry, ten, tons, various
-chambered polythalamous
-colored motley, pied, pinto, variegated
-columned polystyle
comb. multi, poly, vari
-eyed polyommatous
-footed multiped
good hantle
great mort, QUANTITY, raff, raft, swith
-handed briarean
-scaled polylepidous
-sided changeable, manifold, multilateral, polyhedral, various, versatile
times again and again, often, recurrent, repeatedly
-tined polycladine

MANYPLIES belly, omasum, psalterium, stomach

MANYROOT ruellia, spirit-leaf

MANZANILLA apple, bidens, olive, quercus, sherry, tree, weed

MAOCH *kingdom* gath
son achish

MAORI arawa, ati, fish, polynesian
ancestor tiki, tupuna
bird hula, poe, tue, tui
canoe waka
chaos kore
charm heitiki
chief ariki, rangatira
clan ati, hapu, ringatu
club marree, merai, mere, patu, rata
community kaik(a)
compensation utu
creator maui
dance haka
demon atua
fish moki
food kai
foreigner paheha
forever ake
fort pah
fuel tree mapau
god atua
hen weka
hero maui
house whare(kai), wharewananga, wherekura
image tiki

knife patu
law utu
meeting house wharepuni
monster taniwha
oven umu
parrot bird tui
priest tohunga
raft catamaran, moguey, moki
ribbon tree akaroa
rootstock roi
sacred place ahurewa
storehouse pataka, rua, whata
tattoo moko
theological college wharekura, wharewananga
tree akaroa, manuka, mapau, rata, tanehakas
tribe arawa, ati, hapu
village kaik(a), kainga, pah
wages utu
weapon marree, mere, patu, rata
white man pakeha
wood rata
MAO TSE-TUNG *birthplace* shaoshan
event long march
niece wang hai-jung
program cultural revolution, great leap forward
wife chiang-ching
MAP atlas, card, carte, cartogram, cento, chard, chart, delineate, design, diagram, directions, draft, draught, drawing, elevation, explore, face, globe, graph, hachure, image, lay out, mercator, outline, plan, plat(e), plot, projection, scheme, sketch, survey, topography, view
collection atlas
copier pantograph
line cotidal, isothere
maker cartographer, charter, chorographer, mercator, topographist
making astrography, cartography, chorography, topography
out arrange, chart, outline, plan, plot, prepare
townsite plat
world mappemonde
MAPAU See MAPLE.
MAPLE carpodetus, dogwood, escalloniace, matipo, mazer, piripiri, sycamore, tarata, wingseed
ash box-elder
cup mazer
derivative aceric

flowering abutilon, mallow
fruit samara
genus abutilon, acer, asarum, flindersia
grove camp, sapbush
kind amur, ash-leaved, bird's-tongue, black, boxelder, broad-leaved, b(r)ush, curly, fullmoon, mapau, mazer, mountain, norway, silver, striped, sugar, swamp, tapa
leaf, emblem of canada
sap spout spile
scale pulvinaria
seed key, samara, wing
striped moosewood
syrup, boiled humbo
MAQUEREAU prostitute, wanton
MAR blemish, blot, botch, damage, deface, deform, disfigure, flaw, harm, hurt, impair, injure, misguggle, ruin, scar, scratch, shend, spoil, sully, warp, wreck
MARA demon, evil, kama, naomi, nightmare
MARABOU adjutant, argala, bird, morabit, silk, stork
MARABOUT hermit, mohammedan, saint
house kouba
MARACA gourd, rattle
MARANTA ararao, araru, arrowroot
MARASMUS athrepsia, emaciation, malnutrition, marcor, wasting
MARAT *assassin* charlotte corday
MARATHON contest, race
father epopeus
opponents greece, persia
runner pheidippides
son corinthus
victor miltiades
MARAUD attack, dacoit, despoil, foray, invade, harry, pickeer, pillage, plunder, raid, ravage, rob, rove, sack
MARAUDER bandit, brigand, cateran, footpad, highwayman, hun, ladrone, looter, lootie, pillager, pirate, plunderer, ravager, robber, thief, vandal, viti
MARBLE(S) (See also *kind* and *playing*, below.) cold, game, hard, inflexible, lasting, limestone, marl, marmor, rigid, sculpture, shooter, smooth, stone, taw, unfeeling, variegated, white

black anthraconite, jet
city cemetery
defect terrace, terras(se)
famous arundel, elgin
faun, author hawthorne
faun character donatello, hilda
foul fulk
game bonce, bowl, gully, keeps, knucks, miggles
green serpentine
-hearted callous, unfeeling
imitation marezzo, scagliola
kind anthraconite, basalt, brocatel(le), carrara, cipolin, dolomite, marl, palombino, parian, pavonazzo, pentelic, purbeck, rance, ranse, serpentine, travertine
large bullock(er), shooter, taw
-like hard, solid, variegated
marked rance
mosaic tessera
move fulk
mover elgin
ornamental brocatel(le), giallo-antico
pert. marmoric
picture mosaic
playing agate, aggie, alay, alley, bonce, bowl, cat's-eye, commie, commy, dobie, doby, duck, glassie, glassy, immie, knicker, knuckler, mealie, mib, mig(g), nicker, pea, peewee, plumps, ringers, shooter, steely, taw
polish ayrstone, snakestone
polishing ganosis
quarry site carrara
red griotte, rance, ranse, rosso-antico
shooter taw
slab dalle, stele
small peewee
streak vein
toning genosis
tool boucharde
white carrara, dolomite
wood albizzia, olive
MARBLED marmorate, marmoreal, mirly, mottled, veined
MARBLEHEAD fulmar
MARC ANTONY See ANTONY, MARC.
MARCELLUS *aide* bantius
brother otacilius
colleague capitolinus, crispinus
mother octavia

son marcus
uncle augustus
MARCH adjoin, advance, anabasis, attack, border, boundary, country, debouch, defile, file, frontier, hike, landmark, month, pace, parade, proceed, procession, progress, rank, route, step, stretch, territory, tramp, tread, trine, troop, walk
birthstone aquamarine, bloodstone, jasper
dates ides, nones
day's etape, jornada
horsemen cavalcade
in front lead
king sousa
-land borderland, frontier
out of time break step
-past parade
sisters amy, beth, jo, meg
spirited two-step
step double-quick, goosestep, quick-step, slow-time
25th annunciation, lady day
MARCIA *father* philippus
husband cato
MARCO POLO *island* cipango
peiping cambalu(c)
title messer
MARCUS *brother* titus
son publius
MARCUS AURELIUS *virtues* fortitude, justice, moderation, wisdom
work meditations
MARDI GRAS carnival, fat tuesday, festival, shrove tuesday
king rex
MARDOCHAEUS *cousin* esther
predecessor haman
uncle aminadab
MARDUK bel-marduk, merodach
abode duku
attribute marru, spade
command anunnaki
consort erua, sarpanitu, zarpanit, zirbanit
dignity anutu
enemy tiamat
feast zagmuk
offspring nabu
omnipotence symbol tablets of fate
parent enki, ninigiku
rebel against adad, anu, ishtar, shamash

temple akitu, esagil
victim kingu
MARE, MARE'S blues, dam, equine, filly, gillie, gillot, goblin, grasni, hag, horse, incubus, meare, melancholy, moon plain, nightmare, sea, specter, spirit, trestle, witch, yad(e), yaud
changed to thea
group stud
milk, fermented k(o)umiss
nest hoax, trick
nostrum mediterranean
on shanks afoot, walking
tail cirrus, cloud, equisitum, hippurid
young filly
MAREMMA marsh, miasma
MAREROTH *son* ezias
MARESHAH *father* caleb
MARGARELON *father* priam
MARGARET gretchen, maggie, magpie, pearl, peggy, sailor's-choice
attendant to hero
brother valentine
seducer faust
MARGARINE butterine, spread
MARGATE porgy
MARGIN area, bank, border, boundary, bourn, brim, brink, collateral, compass, confine, deposit, edge, end, field, fringe, hem, labrum, latitude, limit, lip, profit, range, rim, room, scope, selvage, side, spread, term, verge
narrow hair
notched erose
note in annotation, apostil(e), scholium
purchaser bull
reading kere, kri
slope cess
up speculate
MARGOSA azadirachta, melie, neem(ba), nim, tree
MARGRAVE markgraf, rudiger
MARGUERITE chrysanthemum, daisy
MARIAN *lover* robin hood
MARIANA *betrothed* angelo
island agrihan, alamagan, anatahan, asuncion, guam, guguan, maug, pagan, rota, saipan, sarigan, tinian
island capital jaluit, saipan
language chamorro
people chamorro

port apra
rain squall shurada
MARIB *queen* sheba
sailor sinbad
MARIE DE MEDICI *husband* henry iv
MARIGOLD aster, baclin, boots, buddle, calendula, caper, catchop, cowslip, flower, golland, helio, kingcup, marybud, orange, sunflower, tagetes, thistle
fig carpetweed, samh
marsh mareblob
wild pineapple-weed
MARIJUANA acapulco gold, b(h)ang, bleu de hue, boo, broccoli, cannabis, charas, churrus, dope, drug, ganja, gigglesmoke, goofweed, grass, green(dragon), greenies, griffo, hallucinogen, hashish, hay, hemp, joysmoke, kaif, kif(f), locoweed, moocah, narcotic, panama red, park lane number two, pleiku-pink, pot, rope, tea, weed
cigarette bambalacha, butt, gigglesmoke, goof, greefa, griffo, indian hay, joint, mary jane, mary warner, mary weaver, mohasky, moocah, mooter, muggle, reefer, smoke stick
exporter coyote, martha, painter, possum
holder crutch
user mugglehead, pothead
MARIMBA akalimba, xylophone
MARIMOTH *son* aziah
MARINA basin, dock, esplanade, harbor
nurse lychorida
parent pericles, thaisa
MARINADE, MARINATE brine, pickle, preserve, soak
MARINE aquatic, bathybic, devildog, fighter, fleet, fluvial, gyrene, lacustrine, leatherneck, maritime, nautical, naval, neritic, oceanic, pelagic, saline, seadog, seascape, soldier, thalassic, topman
comb. thalass(i)(o)
contract bottomry
detection device loran
instrument aba, pelorus, radar, sextant
isopod slater
motto semper fidelis

science oceanography, oceanology
skeleton coral
slogan gung ho
training center parris island, pendleton, quantico
MARINER (See also NAVY man.) barnacleback, bluejacket, buscarl(e), flying dutchman, gob, hearty, jack (tar), jacky, lascar, limejuicer, limey, lobscouser, matelot, matlow, navigator, old salt, pirate, rating, SAILOR, salt, seadog, seafarer, seaman, shellback, shipman, tar, warrener, water dog, windjammer
ancient, cry asail
ancient, torment albatross
compass card rose
compass point rhumb
MARION,   FRANCIS swamp-fox
MARIONETTE bufflehead, duck, figure, judy, poppet, punch, puppet
famous charlie mccarthy, mortimer snerd, punch and judy
maker sarg
MARIPOSA *lily* calochortus, flower, hedychium
MARIS *companion* sarpedon
MARITAL conjugal, connubial, epithalmic, hymeneal, married, matrimonial, nuptial, spousal, wedded
MARITIME See also MARINE, NAUTICAL.
court admiralty
provinces new brunswick, nova scotia, prince edward island
MARIUS *admirer* julius caesar
ally sulpicius
assassin catiline
beloved cosette
colleague aquilius, catulus, lutatius
conquest ambrones, cimbro, norici, teutones
cousin caesar
diviner bataces, martha
enemy geminius, metellus, rutilius, silo, sylla
father-in-law mucius
friend jean valjean, munerius, sabaco
lieutenant claudius
mother fulcinia
nephew caius-lusius
officer scipio-africanus

rival jugurtha
supporter carbo, lampanius, telesinus
wife julia caesar
MARJORAM herb, mint, oregano, origanum
MARK 3 aim, bar, cut, die, dot, dye, end, eye, jot, mar, tag 4 band, blot, coda, coin, dash, dent, dupe, flaw, gash, goal, hack, hash, heed, line, mole, note, rack, scar, seal, sign, spot, tick 5 blaze, brand, breve, buist, cairn, chalk, check, fleck, flick, frank, gauge, hatch, label, limit, nevus, notch, patch, point, price, print, proof, score, smear, speck, spoil, spoor, stain, stamp, tally, title, token, trace, track, trait, watch 6 blotch, caract, dapple, device, dogear, emblem, emboss, figure, gospel, letter, macron, macula, menhir, mottle, notate, notice, obelus, pharos, pimple, regard, scotch, scrive, splash, stigma, streak, stripe, stroke, symbol, target, tilaka 7 bestick, betoken, blemish, engrave, feature, freckle, impress, imprint, jotting, lentigo, measure, observe, purpose, scratch, speckle, striate, symptom, vestige 8 annotate, boundary, catstone, cicatrix, discolor, evidence, identify, indicate, inscribe, memorial, milepost, monument, standard, stigmata 9 celebrate, character, criterion, designate, emphasize, milestone, objective, signature, underline 10 evangelist, importance, impression, stigmatize, touchstone, underscore 11 distinguish 12 characterize 14 characteristic
angular hook
bad demerit
cadency brisure
comb. lineo
crescent-shaped lunule
crosswise crank
curved slur
diacritical accent, apex, breve, cedilla, di(a)eresis, dot, hacek, modifier, tilde, tittle, umlaut
disgrace stain, stigma
distinctive attribute, badge,

cachet, insigne, insignia, sign(ation), stamp, stigma
double dagger diesis
down bargain, depreciate, lower, record, reduce
heraldry avol
identification colophon, crest, dagger, earmark, fingerprint, ken, lug, mole, scar, signet, split, tattoo
kingdom cornwall
meridian mire
nephew tristram
of extraordinary, great
off allot, circumscribe, demarcate, scribe
omission caret, dele
⅛th ure
ornamental bottu
out appoint, cancel, define, delete, measure, obliterate, prescribe
paragraph pilcrow
parenthetical bracket
possessive apostrophe
printing or punctuation accent, acute, ampersand, apostrophe, asterisk, brace, bracket, breve, caesura, caret, cedilla, circumflex, colon, comma, dagger, dash, dele, di(a)eresis, diesis, dot, ellipse, ellipsis, erotema, exclamation, finger, fist, grave, guillemet, hamza(h), hand, hyphen, index, interrogation, leader, macron, obelisk, obelus, paragraph, parallel, paren (thesis), period, point, prime, question, quotation, semicolon, serif, slant, solidus, space, star, stet, stigme, tilde, tittle, umlaut, virgule
question erotema, eroteme
quotation guillemet
reference See *printing*, above.
ringlike annulus
saint, animal lion
saint, companion paul
sectarian bottu, tilaka
signature cross
striped strake
surveyor's bench
time await, be still, delay, do nothing, procrastinate, stall, wait
tiny dot
white blaze, rache, ratch
wife iseult, isolde
MARK ANTONY See ANTONY, MARK.

MARKED big, celebrated, clear, conspicuous, destined, eminent, emphasized, emphatic, extraordinary, great, noticeable, pelleted, pointed, scarred, scored, severe, spotted, spotty
comb. ulose
extremely intense
with lines gyrose, linear, notate, ruled
with spots notate
MARKER ahu, chip, counter, dan, flag, hobble, iou, MEMORIAL, meta, monitor, MONUMENT, pointer, post, pylon, recorder, scorekeeper, scorer, sign, stela, stele, tab(ber), tablet, token, typer
croquet clip
floating buoy
perforated stencil
traffic button
MARKET agora, baza(a)r, bourse, boutique, business, buy, chain store, cheaping, clientage, clientele, close out, commerce, commissary, co-op(erative), cross, curb, custom, deal, debouche, dispose of, dump, emporium, establishment, exchange, exposition, fair, five-and-ten, forum, granary, grocery, gunge, gunj, halle, house, job, macellum, magasin, mart, mercato, merchandise, move, parian, pasar, patronage, post(exchange), realize, rialto, sacrifice, sale, scalp, sell, shop, sook, souk, staples, store, suq, tolbooth, trade, trading post, trone, vend, warehouse
building clothhall
cattle triste
common euromart
day nundine
financial over the counter, stock exchange, wall street
meat shambles
overseer aedile
pert. nundinal
place agora, pit, stalls, street, trone
place god agoraios, hermes, mercury
public pasar
shelf gondola
town bourg(ade), village
MARKETABLE commercia-

ble, purchasable, salable, vendible
MARKETING hawking, huckstering, merchandising, peddling, salesmanship, selling
MARKKA finmark
MARKSMAN archer, artilleryman, bersagliere, bowman, carbineer, crack shot, gun(ner), hunter, musketeer, nimrod, pluffer, rifleman, saimer, sharpshooter, shooter, shootist, shot, sniper, toxophilite, trapshooter
legendary freischutz
poor bolo
MARL clay, earth, fertilizer, greensand, malm, marble, marlite, soil
MARLBOROUGH battle blenheim
enemy french, marsin, tallard
palace blenheim
MARLEY *partner* scrooge
MARLIN aguja, agujon, alligator-gar, curlew, gar, godwit, makaira, needlefish, spearfish
-sucker remora
MARLINSPIKE fid, grenadier, jaeger, lever, pricker, skua-gull, stabber
MARLOWE *play* doctor faustus, edward ii, jew of malta
MARLY adobe, clayey, gumbo, loamy, marbled, spotted
MARM maam, woman
MARMALADE codiniac, confection, jam, preserve(s), spread, squish
tree achras, chico(mamey), mamie, mammee, sapodilla, sapote, zapote
MARATHI *father* uri
MARMAX *beloved* hippodamia
slayer oenomaus
MARMION *horse* bevis
MARMITE bomb, kettle, pot
MARMONT *commander* napoleon
MARMOSET animal, callithrix, jacchus, mico, monkey, orabassu, quircal, sagoin, saimiri, tamarin, titi, wistiti
MARMOT animal, arctomys, bobac(k), gopher, groundhog, hyrax, pahmi, pia,

prairie dog, rodent, sciurid, siffleur, spermophile, suslik, whistler, woodchuck
flying taguan
pouched spermophile, squirrel
MARNE *hero* joffre
MARNER, SILAS *foster child* eppie
MAROON abandon, aztec, beach, camp, chestnut, cimarron, copper, desert, enisle, firework, isolate, marone, picnic, slave, strand, terra cotta
MAROONER buccaneer, pirate
MARPESSA *consort* idas
father evenus
MARQUAND *detective* moto
MARQUE letter, license, reprisal, seizure
MARQUEE awning, canopy, shelter, sign, tent
MARQUETRY buhl, inlay, intarsia
material ivory, nacre, shell, wood
MARQUIS See LORD.
MARRAKECH *district* gueliz, medina
park l'hivernage
MARRIAGE alliance, bridebed, buckle, conubium, daiva, espousal, exogamy, karao, knot, levirate, match, matrimony, mota, muta, nuptials, opsigamy, punalua, splice, sponsal, spousal, union, vow(s), wedding, wedlock
absence agamy
abstainer bachelor, celibate
agreement ambilanak, ambilian, betrothal, engagement
arrange for betroth
banns spurrings
before antenuptial
below position hypogamy
broker matchmaker, proxenete, schatchen, shadchan(im)
comb. gamo, hymen(o)
common law free union
complex polygamy
contract ketubah, sponsalia
deity cama, demeter, frey, frigg(a), gaea, hera, hulda, hymen, jugatinous, juno, mutunus, pronuba, sif, teleia, tellus, vor
fear of gamophobia
4th tetragamy
hater misogamist

hatred of misogamy
kind bigamy, common-law, companionate, deuterogamy, digamy, endogamy, levirate, leviration, monandry, monogamy, monogyny, morganatic, polyandry, polygamy, polygyny, trial
notice banns, spurrings
of aged opsigamy
of gods theogamy
of slaves contubernium
outside the tribe exogamy
pert. conjugal, connubial, endogamic, hymeneal, marital, spousal
plural polygamy
portion tocher
2nd deuterogamy, digamy
secret elopement
settlement dos, dot(e), dow(e)ry, mahr
single monogamy
song callithump, charivari, epithalamium, hymen, prothalamion
symbol sardonyx
terms tenaim
to lower class woman anuloma
to promise affiance, betroth
to several husbands polyandry
to 2 people bigamy
trial sirvinacuy
vows troth
wife, multiple polygamy, polygyny
within the clan endogamy

MARRIAGEABLE adult, concubitous, eligible, nubile, viripotent

MARRIED conjugate, connubial, hitched, marital, matrimonial, spliced, wed (ded)
couple darby and joan, man and wife, newlyweds, philemon and baucis
5 times pentagamist

MARROT auk, guillemot, puffin

MARROW adipose, associate, center, companion, core, essence, gist, glut, join, keest, lard, lover, marie, marry, match, mate, medulla, merch, pith, pulp, sap, spouse, squash, substance, suet, tallow, vitality
bone fist, gist, knee, pith
bone cell plasmacyte
cabbage chou moellier

inflammation medullitis
-like medullary, pithy
without weak

MARROWSKY spoonerism

MARRY buckle, catch, couple, elope, ensure, espouse, hitch, indeed, in truth, join, make one, marrow, match, mate, nuptial, pair off, splice, take to wife, team, tie(the knot), unite, wed, weld, wive, yoke

MARS (See also ARES.) mamers, marmar, maspiter, mavors, quirinus, silvanus, teutates
area aeria, amazonis, hellas, hellespontus, iapigia, juventa-fons, lacussolis, memmonia, panchaia, pandoraefretum
band or belt libya
comb. areo
consort rhea-silvia
day tuesday
description aerography
discoverer hall
escort bellona, honos, pallow, pavor, vacuna, virtus
festival quinquatrus
gem emerald
inhabitant martian, mavortian
marking canal, mare, oasis
metal iron
moon deimos, phobos
parent juno, jupiter
pert. arean, areo, mamertine, martian, mavortian
precinct rome
red colcothar, totem
sacred animal horse, wolf, woodpecker
son remus, romulus
study of areology
symbol ancilia

MARSEILLAISE *composer* rouget de lisle

MARSH baygall, bayou, bog, bottom(lands), carr, cienaga, corcass, cricksand, everglade, fell, fen(land), flam, glade, holm, j(h)eel, jhil, lerna, liman, maremma, mere, mire, moor(land), morass, mud, muskeg, ngaio, ooze, palude, peat bog, pinsk, pocosin, pontine, pripet, quag(mire), quicksand, salina, slew, slough, slue, strother, sump, swale, swamp(land), turlough, vlei, vley, wash

beetle cattail
bellflower bedstraw, campanula
blue-bill scaup duck
buck sitatunga
chickweed bog-stitchwort
cinquefoil comarum
clover buck-bean
comb. helo, limmo, paludi
crocodile goa
daisy thrift
elder guelder-rose, iva, jacko
fever helodes, malaria, traidenum
fire will-'o-the-wisp
fleabane plowman's-wort, pluchea
gas firedamp, methane, miasma
goddess marica
goose graylag
grass See *plant*, below.
harrier bog glede, puddock, puttock
hawk bog glede, harpy, harrier
hen bittern, coot, moorhen, rail
inhabitant limnophile
land broads, fell, fen, maremma, muskeg, pontine, slew, slue, sough, swale
living in helobious, limnophilous
mallow althea, confection, hibiscus, hollyhock, plant, rose of sharon, sweet, wymote
marigold boots, bullflower, bull's-eye, buttercup, caltha, caper, cowlily, cowslip, crazy, dragon, drunkard, elkslip, gamond, goldcup, gools, gowlan, kingcup, matybud
parsley tapegrass, wild celery
pennywort watercup
pert. miasmic, paludal, paludine, quaggy, quashy, spewy, uliginous, uvid
pink sabbatia
plant bulrush, caltha, catchfly, cattail, elatine, fescue, iva, reed, sedge, spart, tule
plover sandpiper, woodcock
quail meadowlark
rabbit muskrat
robin chewink, towhee
rush spart
salt corcass, salina
sedge bulrush
spirit jack-o-lantern

tea ledum
trefoil bitterworm, bog-bean, buck-bean
violet butterwort
wren longbill
MARSHAL align, aline, arrange, array, assemble, collect, commander, convoke, direct, dispose, escort, farrier, gather, general, groom, guide, jeronimo, lead, line, marechal, official, order, organize, range, systematize, usher
MARSHALL ISLAND ebon, mill, namur, ralik, wake
atoll eniwetok
fiber adad
MARSHY boggy, callow, fenny, lutose, miry, muddy, oozy, paludal, paludine, plashy, poachy, quaggy, quashy, sloppy, sloughy, soft, spewy, spongy, sposhy, squashy, squelchy, swampy, uliginose, uliginous, uvid, waterlogged, wet
lake liman
MARSILE *followers* blancandrin, clarin, estamarin, eudropin, jouner, machiner, malbien, priamun, quarlan
MARSOON beluga
MARSUPIAL See MAMMAL *marsupial.*
ancestor pantothere
feature pouch
MARSYAS *competitor* apollo
instrument flute
killed by flaying
slayer apollo
MART See MARKET.
MARTEL See CHARLES MARTEL, HAMMER.
MARTELLO stronghold, tower
MARTEN animal, fisher, foin, martrix, mustela, phascogale, sable, sobol
group richesse
MARTENSITE sorbite
MARTHA *brother* lazarus
emblem dragon, keys
sister mary
MARTIAL aggressive, army, bellicose, belligerent, brave, hostile, mettlesome, militant, military, warlike, warrior
art See SELF-*defense.*
MARTIN ape, monkey, progne, swallow, swift
chuzzlewitt character peck-

sniff, sairey gamp, tapley
MARTINET disciplinarian, drill, tyrant
MARTINEZ-ZUVIRIA *pseud.* hugo wast
MARTINIQUE *capital* ile de france
cigar bout
garment jupee
volcano pelee
MARTIUS, CAIUS coriolanus
brother lucius, mutius
father titus-andronicus
MARTYR afflict, agonize, anastasia, kill, mutilate, persecute, prey, sacrifice, saint, sufferer, torment, torture, victim, wound
child agnes
early crispin, polycarp, stephen
4th century blaise
royal charles i
MARTYRDOM affliction, butchery, death, distress, killing, mortification, passion, torment, torture
place of golgotha
MARTYRIZE crucify, excruciate, rack
MARVEL admiration, admire, amazement, astonishment, curiosity, exception, ferly, gazingstock, magnale, marl, miracle, nonesuch, phenomenon, portent, prodigy, rara avis, rarity, selcouth, selly, sensation, sight, spectacle, stunner, surprise, wonder
MARVELOUS amazing, bang on, extraordinary, fabulous, improbable, miraculous, mirific, outstanding, prime, prodigious, remarkable, spectacular, splendid, strange, striking, superb, unique, wonderful, wondrous
MARX, KARL *bible* communist manifesto
collaborator engels
MARY mamie, marilla, maura, moll(y), poll(y)
MARY I bloody mary, mary tudor
father henry viii
husband philip
mother catherine of aragon
MARY II *father* james ii
husband william iii

MARY MAGDALEN *symbol* ointment jar
MARY, QUEEN *husband* george
MARY, QUEEN OF SCOTS bopeep, little miss muffet, moppet
disease cholorosis, porphyria
consort bothwell, darnley, francois ii
cousin elizabeth
execution site fatheringhay
horse black agnes, rosabelle
parent james v, mary of guise
secretary riccio, rizzio
MARY, SAINT madonna, maris stella, mother of sorrows, regina coeli, theotocos, theotokos, virgin
brother lazarus
feast candlemass
house loretto
husband cleophas, clopas, joseph
hymn ave regina coelorum
parent anna, anne, joachim
sister martha
son jesus, john, mark
MARYLAND *battlesite* antietam
bay chesapeake
capital annapolis
city annapolis, baltimore, bethesda, catonsville, college park, cumberland, easton, essex, frederick, hagerstown, laurel, ocean city, pikesville, pocomoke, rockville, towson
college goucher, hood, st johns
county allegany, cecil, somerset, talbot
flower black-eyed susan, coneflower, daisy, goldenrod
founder calvert
indian conoy, nanticoke
lake pretty boy
native crawthumper, terrapin
nickname cockade state, free state, old line state
peak backbone
port baltimore
race track bowie
river chester, choptank, patuxent, potomac, susquehanna
soldier macaroni
state bird oriole
state flower black-eyed susan
state tree oak
swamp pocoson

MARYSOLE carter, fish, leader, smear-dab

MARZIPAN *ingredient* almond

MASADA *builder* king herod *commander* eliezer ben yair *defenders* zealots *enemy* roma, silva, titus *historian* josephus flavius

MASAI *country* kenya, tanganyika *farmers* wakwafi, wakwavi

MASCAGNI *opera* cavalleria rusticana, iris

MASCLE lozenge, male, mesh, net, scale, spot

MASCOT billiken, charm, good luck, talisman *blue* romany

MASCULINE energetic, lalaqui, lusty, male, manly, mas, powerful, robust, sound, strenuous, strong, vigorous, virile *appearing* andromorphous *comb.* andro *to make* virify *woman* amazon, androgyne, hoyden, romp, tomboy

MASH beat, beer, brew, cereal, champ, chap, creem, crumble, crush, feed, flail, flirt(ation), grain, hammer, infatuation, infuse, lover, malt, mass, meal, mesh, mess, mix(ture), muddle, ogle, press, pulp, pulverize, slop, smash, smush, soften, squash, squelch, steep, sweetheart, triturate, trouble, wort *father* aram

MASHER beetle, dandy, flirt, goat, lecher, lump, philanderer, pulverizer, satyr

MASJID mosk, mosque, temple

MASK camouflage, cloak, conceal, cover(ing)(up), curtain, dance, defilade, disguise, dissemble, dissimulate, domino, drama, effigy, evasion, falseface, hide, icon, image, loup, masque(rade), mesh, mum, mumm(ery), party, portrait, pretend, pretext, protect, relief, respirator, safeguard, screen, shield, shroud, simulacrum, statue, subterfuge, veil, visor, vizard *concealed by* larvate *crest* onkos

designer benda *half* areito, domino, loup *topknot on* onkos

MASKANONGE fish, longe, muskellunge, pike

MASKED concealed, covered, disguised, hidden, larvate(d), obscure, personate, vizarded

MASKER domino, guisard, masquer(ader), mummer

MASKING synergistic

MASOCHISM algolagnia, algophilia

MASON bee, bricklayer, builder, comacine, knobbler, lammikin, lapicide, scutcher, stonecutter, wasp *assistant* goujat *cord* skirreh *door* tile *doorkeeper* tiler, tyler *gear* hod *officer* grand master *order* blue lodge, demolay, knight-templar, shriner *regalia* apron *symbol* trowel *tool* float, gurlet, hawk, hock, level, rab, scotch, scutch, shim, trowel *year of light* anno lucis

MASONRY abutment, adobe, arch, ashlar, ashler, blocage, brickwork, dome, revetment, rubble, spandrell, stonework, vault *groove* raggle *joint* joggle *unit* block, brick, stone *wedge* shim

MASQUERADE act, ball, camouflage, carnival, conceal, costume, cover, dance, disguise, drama, guise, hide, impersonation, imposture, mardi, maskery, mum(m), party, pass for, pose, pretense, revel, sham *cloak* domino

MASQUERADER domino, masker, masquer, mummer, ragshag

MASS accumulation, aggregate, amount, assemblage, assemble, bank, batch, blend, block, body, bolus, bulk, cake, ceremony, clot(ure), clump, cob, collect(ion), congeries, congregate, drift, eucharist, extent, fuse, gather, gob(bet), group, heap, hoard, horde,

hotchpotch, jam, liturgy, lump, magnitude, majority, matter, meet, merge, missa, mob, multitude, muster, node, pack, piece, pile, plebians, plurality, proletariat, quantity, requiem, rite, ritual, ruck, sacrament, service, shock, size, skein, solid, stack, store, substance, sum, swarm, total, tumor, unify, volume, wad, whole *addition to* farce, farse *amorphous* hodgepodge, jumble, symplasm *basin* aquamanale, aquamanile *book* kyriale, missal *comb.* cumulo *confused* chaos, clot, clutter, hotchpotch, imbroglio, jumble, jungle, mess, rummage, shuffle, snarl, tangle, welter *directory* ordo *for the dead* black mass, requiem *form into* wad *glassy* slag *globular* moorball *granular* kryptol *indistinct* smudge *kind* dirge, high, low, requiem, rosary *living* blastema *low* missa bassa, missa privata *meeting* rally *-monger* priest *mountain* orogen *musical* See *part,* below. *of particulars* aggregate *overhanging* boss, cornice *part* agnus dei, alleluja, allelulia(h), anamnesis, blessing, canon, collect, communion, consecration, credo, dismissal, elevation of the host, epistle, fraction, gloria, gospel, gradual, introit, kyrie(eleison), lavabo, offertory, paternoster, pax, preface, sanctus, secreta, tersanctus, tract *pert.* missal, missatical, molar *produce* clone *requiem* month's-mind *rounded* bolus, cob, knob, nob, nodule, rondle *small* dab, floc, pat, speck, wad *soft* mash, moxa, mummy *sung* missa cantata

tangled knurl, mop, shag, snarl
thick soft goo, mush
unit dalton
utensil See EUCHARIST
vessel.
vestment See VESTMENT
religious.
MASSA *father* ishmael
MASSACHUSETTS *bay* buzzard's
cape ann, cod
capital boston
city agawam, arlington, athol, attleboro, ayer, barre, belmont, beverly, boston, braintree, brockton, brookline, cambridge, chicopee, cohasset, concord, danvers, dedham, everett, gloucester, groton, holyoke, ipswich, lawrence, lenox, lexington, lynn, malden, marlboro, medford, melrose, methuen, nahant, natick, needham, newton, northampton, norwood, otis, peabody, pittsfield, randolph, reading, revere, salem, saugus, scituate, taunton, uxbridge, waltham, wellesley, westfield, winchester, winthrop, worcester, yarmouth
college amherst, radcliffe, simmons, smith, wellesley, wheaton, williams
early commune brook farm
governor, colonial bradley, endecott, endicott, winthrop
indian nauset, pocomtue
island chappaquidick, dukes, martha's vineyard, nantucket
lake onota, quabbin, webster
nickname bay state
oyster cotuit
peak alander, brodie, everett, greylock, potter
peninsula cape ann, cape cod
pond walden
port boston, gloucester, new bedford, salem
range berkshires, taconic
resort cape cod, marblehead, nahant, nantucket, swampscott
river blackstone, charles, chicopee, concord, connecticut, deerfield, nashua, taunton
school andover, groton
state bird chickadee

state flower arbutus, mayflower
state tree elm
university brandeis, clark, harvard, mit, tufts
MASSACRE barbarity, battue, bloodbath, butcher(y), carnage, decimate, genocide, havoc, kill(ing), manslaughter, murder, pogrom, scupper, septembrize, shambles, slaughter, slay(ing)
MASSAGE anatripsis, bindegawelve, chirapsia, facial, knead(ing), lomilomi, malaxation, pat, rolfing, rub(bing), rubdown, shiatsu, stroke, stroking, therapy, treat, tripsis
device vibrator
motion effleurage
MASSAGER masseur, masseuse, rubber, vibrator
MASSEBAH baal
MASSECUITE fillmass, goor, gur, sugar
MASSENA *quail* coppy
MASSENET *opera* don quichotte, don quixote, herodiade, le cid, le jongleur de notre dame, manon, sappho, thais, werther
MASSES hoi polloi, plebes, populace, proletariat, vulgus
MASSIVE beamy, big, bulky, clumsy, cumbersome, cumbrous, dense, enormous, firm, gigantic, great, gross, hard, heavy, huge, hulking, impressive, large, leaden, monumental, obese, ponderous, solid, sound, stately, sturdy, substantial, thick, unwieldy, weighty
MAST acorns, beech(nuts), billiard cue, brown, buck, cue, fruit, nuts, pannage, pillar, pole, post, spar, sprit, staff, structure, stuff, support
4th bonaventure
6th driver
against aback
chain tye
comb. malus
crosspiece fid
fallen shack
inclination rake
middle mainmast
part bibb
platform manitop
support bibb, step
tree akak, akok(a), asak

wood for ash, kamani, poon
MASTER 3 rab 4 baas, beak, boss, cock, head, host, jack, lord, mian, rule, sire, tame, tuan, whiz 5 adept, break, bwana, chief, inkos, laird, learn, owner, prime, rabbi, saheb, sahib, shark, swami, tutor 6 artist, bridle, buckra, defeat, expert, genius, leader, maitre, mentor, patron, sircar, subdue, victor, winner, wizard 7 captain, conquer, control, dominie, excel in, maestro, mahatma, manager, nakhoda, officer, padrone, prodigy, skipper, teacher 8 cardinal, champion, director, dominate, educator, employer, governor, hotelier, landlord, overcome, overseer, seigneur, seignior, skillful, vanquish 9 authority, commander, conqueror, innkeeper, patriarch, preceptor, principal, subjugate 10 controller, instructor, proprietor 11 crackerjack, gain command, householder 13 paterfamilias, 14 superintendent
at arms jauntie, jaunty
card ace, king, trump
comb. arch(i)
cruel simon legree
eton beak
fencing lanista
harbor havener, havenor
hard despot, simon legree
-key passe-partout
of ceremonies abbott of unreason, caeremoniarius, chairman, emcee, lord of misrule, marshal, official, toastmaster
of craft kahuna
of household balabos, goodman, hospodar, paterfamilias
of revels alytarch
pert. herile
single sloop
stroke coup
studio bottega
MASTERFUL absolute, arbitrary, arrogant, authoritative, despotic, dogmatic, domineering, imperative, imperious, lordly, overweening, peremptory, selfwilled, violent, virile
MASTERLY expert, skillful, superior

MASTERMIND control, direct, expert, make, manage, plan, plot, produce, sage, wiseacre

MASTERPIECE chef d'oeuvre, magnum opus, monument, production, triumph, trump

MASTERWORT angelica, cow-parsnip, goutweed, sanicle

MASTERY ability, ascendancy, authority, cleverness, command, conquest, control, defeat, dexterity, dominion, expertise, expertness, grasp, gree, grip, hegemony, influence, ken, leadership, lordship, overcoming, proficiency, skill, subdual, subjugation, supremacy, sway, triumph, understanding, victory, virtuosity, wizardry

MASTHEAD flag, hightop

MASTIC adhesive, cement, confusion, disorder, gum(my), liquor, resin, sabotage, tree, viscid
bully jocum(a)
plant cat-thyme
tree acoma, ausubo, cocullo, cocuyo, gumbo-limbo, pistacia

MASTICATE chaw, chew, crush, cut, grind, gum, knead, manducate, pulp
inability amasesis

MASTIFF alan, aland(t), bandog, burly, massive, tie-dog

MASTODON behemoth, brevirostrine, giant, huge, mammoth, mammut, phiomi

MAT banig, bedding, bolster, cloth, coaster, cotter, dim, doily, drugget, dull, entangle, footer, guardnap, interweave, kaitaka, kilim, knot, lackluster, lauhala, matrix, mattoir, moss, pad, petate, rug, snarl, spandrel, twist, weave, webbing, yapa
border taniko
fiber bass
-grass fogfruit, lippia, marram, nard
-man wrestler
palm-leaf yapa
reed cattail
rice-straw tatami

MATA HARI siren, spy

MATACAN *indian* ashluslay, vejoz

MATACO apar, armadillo, coronado

MATADOR (See also BULLFIGHTER.) capeador, espada, toreador, torero
assistant chulo
sword estoque

MATCH accord, adapt, agree, allumette, balance, bonspiel, bout, bracket, call, cap, companion, compare, compete, competition, conform, congreve, contest, copy, correspond, counterpart, couple, ditto, double, equal, even, fellow, fight, fit, fuse(e), fuzee, game, harmonize, imitate, kippeen, light(er), locofoco, lucifer, marriage, marry, mate, measure up, oppose, pair, paragon, parallel(ize), pattern, peer, pit against, repay, rival, size, sort, square, suit, tally, touch, trial, twin, two, union, vesta, vesuvius, vie, yoke
box veneer squelette
king kreuger
shooting bir
wax vesta
wooden fusee, fuzee

MATCHLESS alone, best, consummate, exquisite, incomparable, inimitable, makeless, nonesuch, peerless, unapproached, unequaled, unique, unlike, unpaired, unrivaled

MATCHLOCK gun, musket
man buxberry

MATCHMAKER See MARRIAGE *broker*.

MATE, MATES abash, aid(e), assistant, associate, baffle, brace, breed, brother, buddy, bully, bunkie, cawk, chap, chum, companion, compeer, comrade, confound, consort, couple, cully, double, equal, exhaust, fellow, fere, gear, helper, husband, mariner, marry, match, matey, officer, pair, pal, pareil, partner, pirraura, salt, servant, spouse, tea, teamworker, twin, two, wife, yerba
gunner's armorer
source yerba

MATELOT gob, mariner, matlow, sailor, seaman, tar

MATER mom, MOTHER, mum(my)
dolorosa virgin mary
turrita cybele

MATERIAL actual, apposite, apropos, batch, bodily, bolt, brief, carnal, CLOTH, concrete, constituents, corpor(e)al, corporeous, data, drap, element, essence, FABRIC, facts, fleshly, fundamental, germane, goods, graith, grist, hyle, hylic, important, incarnate, intrinsic, key, matter, metal, momentous, necessary, nonspiritual, objective, palpable, pertinent, phenomenal, physical, pise, pith, plasma, primary, profane, quiddity, quintessence, real, relevant, salient, sensual, sensuous, somatic(al), staple, stuff, subject, substance, substantial, swatch, tangible, temporal, textile, thingy, true, venal, vital, weighty
basic body
coloring tinction
comb. hylo
combustible kindling, tinder
discard junk, refuse, rubbish, scrap, slag, trash, waste
eliminated cullage, culls
foundation underlay
group batch
loose detritus, gravel, sand
raw ore, staple, stock
sedimentary silt
slimy swarf
synthetic nylon, orlon, plastic, rayon

MATERIALISM animalism, atomism, diamat, earthliness, hylonism, hylotheism, mechanism, monism, naturalism, panpsychism, physicalism, positivism, rationalism, somatism, worldliness

MATERIALISTIC banaustic, bourgeoise, practical, profane, sensual, worldly

MATERIALIZE actualize, appear, come to light, corporealize, corporify, embody, incarnate, incorporate, objectify, personify, realize, reify, reincarnate, show up, substantiate, turn up, visualize

MATERIALLY considerably, substantially

MATERIEL ammunition, apparatus, equipment, gear, machinery, outfit, tackle, weapons

MATERNAL affectionate, kind, loving, motherly, parental

relationship enation

MATERNITY maternology, motherhood

goddess apet

ward natuary

MATEY buddy, chum, companionable, friendly, MATE

MATH arithmetic, crop, exact, MATHEMATICS, monastery, mowing

MATHE grub, maggot, moth, worm

MATHEMATICIAN abacist, actuary, adder, algebraist, arithmetician, calculist, figurer, geodesist, geometer, geometrician, trigonometrician

famous albiruni, alkashi, boole, carroll, cremona, descartes, euclid, euler, fermat, gauss, huygens, kelvin, laplace, leibnitz, napier, newton, pascal, ptolemy, russell, vernier, vieta, wiener

medieval algorist

MATHEMATICS arithmetic, methesis, numbers

abbreviation ged

aggregate field, sequence

arbitrary number radix

books bourbaki

branch algebra, algorism, analysis, arithmetic, calculus, geodesy, geometry, logarithm, quadratics, topology, trigonometry

constant parameter

curve genic

deduction analysis

diagram graph

element antcedent, base, coefficient, complement, consequent, cube(root), decimal, denominator, differential, dividend, divisor, exponent, factor, fluent, fluxion, formula, fraction, increment, index, integral, logarithm, minuend, modulus, multiple, multiplicand, multiplicator, multiplier, numerator, power, quotient, racix, reciprocal, repetend, root,

square root, subtrahend, totient, variable

entity vector

equation surd

exercise problem

expert cpa

factor quaternion

function cosine, sine, tangent

game See GAME *mathematical.*

instrument abacus, adding machine, arbalest, compass, computer, quipu, sector, sliderule, vernier

invariant comitant

irrational number surd

line tangent, vector

number digit

perpendicular apothem

proposition theorem

pure number scalar

quantity operand, scalar, sine

ratio cosine, derivate, sine

symbol digit, equal, faciend, figure, minus, number, operand, plus

term abelian, abscissa, acnode, addend, affine, aliquant, aliquot, analysis, arbalest, cardinal, constant, cosh, cosine, facient, log, mobius strip, nappe, nome, quadrant, secant, sech, surd, tensor, times, variable, vextor

variable pronumeral

writer, anonymous bourbaki

MATHOLWYCH *wife* branwen

MATIN(S) call, matutinal, morning, prayer, service, song, watchdog

MATINEE affair, afternoon, entertainment, gown, levee, negligee, party, play, reception, salon, show

idol actor, darling, lion, star

MATING breeding, homogamy, matching, pairing, panmixia

MATLOW See MATELOT, SAILOR.

MATRASS bolt(head), bottle, carafe, cucurbit, flask, tube, vessel

MATRIARCH mother, woman

control momism

MATRICULATE admit, adopt, enroll, enter, list, record, register

MATRIMONIAL conjugal, connubial, hymeneal, marital, married, nuptial, spousal, wedded

go-between blackfoot

MATRIMONY alliance, espousal, marriage, nuptials, rite, sacrament, spousal, union, wedding, wedlock

vine box(thorn), bursaria, cestrum, jasmine, jessamy, lycium

MATRIX bed, calymma, cast, dyadic, form, foundation, gangue, groundmass, mat, mine, mold, mother, mould, pattern, protoplasm, shape, stroma, venter

plate stereo

MATRON dame, dowager, housekeeper, lady, mistress, mother, widow, wife, woman

MATRONAL feminine, grave, sedate

MATTAN *son* shephatiah

MATTANIAH *father* elam

son hashabiah, jeiel, shemaiah, zaccur

MATTATHA *son* menna

MATTATHIAH *son* joseph, math

MATTATHIAS *father* simon

son apphus, avaran, eleazar, gaddis, john, jonathan, judas, maccabaeus, maccabee, simon, thassis

MATTED cespitose, disorderly, dull, felted, felty, pinny, snarled, stringy, tangled, tauted, unburnished, waukit

mass batt

MATTER affair, ail, amount, argue, argument, body, business, cause, comether, concern, constituent, content, copy, count, difficulty, elements, event, field, frist, gear, ground(s), hyle, import(ance), interest, item, like, manuscript, material, means, mind, moment, motive, object, pith, portion, purulence, pus, quantity, reck, res, sense, significance, signify, space, stuff, subject, substance, suppurate, tell, text, theme, thing, topic, trouble, value, weigh

business shauri

disputed issue

essential gist, point

foreign dross

indeterminate apeiron
it doesn't nichevo
-of-fact arid, downright, dry, forthright, literal, naked, ordinary, phlegmatic, plain, pragmatic, prosaic, prosy, realistic, simple, stolid, utilitarian
particle atom
pert. hylic
potential prakriti
primordial chaos
property inertia, mass
pulverized attritus
rarefied fog, gas, miasma, mist, vapor
small minutia, trivia
subject content, scope, theme, thesis
worthless garbage, rubbish, slag, trash
MATTHAN *father* eleazar
son jacob
MATTHAT *father* livi
son heli, jorim
MATTHEW apostle, disciple
burial place salerno
symbol halbert, lance, purse
MATTHIAS *burial place* rome
symbol battle-axe, hatchet
MATTHIOLA flower, gilliflower, shrub, stock
MATTING bump, rabanna, sawali, sirki, tangling, tatami, tatty
MATTOCK adz(e), axe, bill, grubber, hoe, pickaxe, tubbal, twibil
MATTRESS bed(ding), pallet, razai, resai, tick
cover tick(ing)
straw paillasse
stuffing feathers, fiber, foam rubber, hair, pulu, seawrack, straw
MATURATION completion, development, incubation
MATURE accrue, adult, age(d), autumn, come of age, complete, develop, digest, due, feather, fledge, form, full-blown, full-fledged, grow(up), grown, harden, inure, mellow, old, payable, perfect, ready, ripe(n), season(ed)
MATURITY adulthood, age, development, full bloom, majority, manhood, maturation, obligation, ripeness, seasoning, womanhood
legal age of consent

MATUTA leucothea, mother
MATZOTH *piece* afikomen
MAUD hag, mule, plaid, rug, shawl
MAUDLIN bathetic, beery, costmary, emotional, foolish, fuddled, fuddly, gushy, intoxicated, mawkish, moist, muddled, mushy, romantic, sentimental, silly, slushy, soppy, tearful, tipsy, yarrow
MAUGHAM *work* cakes and ale, east of suez, moon and sixpence, of human bondage, our betters, rain
MAUI *capital* lahaina
resort hana, kaanapali
MAUL abuse, beat, beetle, bruise, club, damage, deform, gavel, hammer, hit, hurt, injure, mace, mallet, mangle, moth, muzzle, pound, rough up, split, staff
MAU MAU *country* kenya
originators kikuyu
MAUMET doll, figure, god, guy, idol, image, pigeon, puppet, scarecrow
MAUN(D) basket, beg(ging), hamper, measure, weight
MAUNDER beg, digress, growl, grumble, mutter, ramble, wander
MAUPASSANT *novel* bel ami, boule de suif, pierre et jean
MAURITANIA *capital* nouakchott
king atlas
neighbor senegal
president daddah
MAURITIUS *capital* port louis
coin rupee
extinct bird dodo
hemp cabuja, fique
tree colophane
MAUSOLEUM baradari, mole, monument, tomb, turbeh
famous taj mahal
MAUVE dye, lilac, mallow, plum(colored), purple, violaceous, violet
taupe copra
MAVERICK calf, dissenter, dogie, eccentric, nonconformist, stray, tyro, yearling
MAVIS missel-bird, thrush
MAW appetite, belly, craw, crop(py), gorge, gullet, liver, maa, mallow, mother,

mow, seagull, stomach, throat
-worm hypocrite
MAWKISH banal, disgusting, drippy, flat, inane, insipid, jejune, maudlin, mawmish, mushy, nasty, nauseous, offensive, romantic, sentimental, sickly, slushy, soppy, squeamish, stale, vapid
MAXILLA gnathite, jaw(bone), mala, mouth, seta
MAXIM adage, aphorism, apothegm, axiom, barb, belief, brocard, byword, canon, cliche, device, dict(um), doctrine, epigram, formula, gallicism, gibe, gnome, logium, moral, motto, precept, principle, protasis, proverb, rule, sarcasm, saw, saying, slogan, truism, truth
MAXIMILIAN *wife* anne of brittany, carlota
MAXIMUM all, capacity, ceiling, crest, extreme, greatest, highest, largest, limit, most, outside, peak, record, supreme, top, ultimate, utmost
MAY can, hawthorn, heyday, liberty, mai(den), make, might, mote, possibility, prime, shall, spiraea, springtime, sycamore, syringa, viburnum
apple barberry, cohosh, mandrake
bird bobolink, knot, thrush, whimbrel
birthstone agate, emerald
blob cuckooflower
bloom hawthorn
blossom lily of the valley
bug cockchafer, june beetle, ladybird, ladybug, ladyfly
bush hawthorn
cock maypop, melon, plover
curlew whimbrel
day be(a)ltane, signal, sos
day eve walpurgis night
festival ambarvalia, be(a)ltane
fish bass billy, killifish, rockfish
flower anemone, arbutus, callalily, cowslip, cuckooflower, hawthorne, hepatica, marigold, spring beauty, stitchwort
fly dayfly, drake, dun,

ephermerid, green drake, naiad, spinner
fowl whimbrel
goddess maia
gowen daisy
haw applehaw
magic weaverbird
pear shadbush
2nd sunday mother's day
sucker cutlips
3rd of rudmasday
tree hawthorn
MAYA (See also MAYAN.) devi, magic, nature, power, prakriti
son buddha
MAYAN cocom
calendar decoder seler
calendar period uayeb, uinal
city, ruined akumal, calakmul, chichen itza, coba, izamal, palenque, tulum, uxmal
day uayeb
deity acat, akanchob, akna, bacabs, backlum-chaam, chaac, chac mo(o)l, chin, cukulcan, echua, hapikern, hunab-ku, itzamna, ixazaluoh, kinebahan, kisin, kulkulkan, nohochacyum, usukun, uyitzin, xamaniquinqu, yantho, yuncemil
figure, grotesque maximon
history chilam balam
indian aguacateca, cakchikel, chanabal, chol, chontal, chorti, chuje, ixil, jacalteca, kekchi, mam, motozintleca, peten, pokomam, pokonchi, quiche, tzental, tzotzil, uspanteca, yucatan, yucatec
month uninal
rain god chac mo(o)l
serpent, feathered kulkulcan
source book popul-vuh
time period baktun, haab, katun, tun
well cenote
year-end days uayeb
MAYBE happen, perchance, perhaps, possibly, probably, uncertainty
yes, maybe no comme ci comme ca
MAYENCE *count* ganelon
MAYFLOWER *landing* plymouth rock
sister ship speedwell
MAYHEM battery
MAYONNAISE dressing
sauce remo(u)lade
MAYOR alcalde, bur-

gomeister, kmet, magistrate, maire, official, provost, sindaco
MAYPOP apricot vine, maracock, maycock, passionflower
MAYWEED anthemis, balder('sbrae), composit, cotula, dillweed, hogweed, ma(y)thes
MAZAMA brocket, coassus, goat, pampas deer, pronghorn
MAZARIN *predecessor* richelieu
MAZDA (See AHURA-MAZDA.) medha, ormazd
MAZE bewilderment, confusion, deception, delirium, delusion, fancy, labyrinth, perplex(ity), stupify
maker daedalus
MAZED bewildered, lost, meandered, muddled, perplexed, snarled, stupefied, tangled
MAZUMA See MONEY.
MAZY circuitous, complex, labyrinthian, labyrinthine
MC COY (See GENUINE.) quill
MC CUTCHEN *character* beverly
novel graustark
MC KINLEY, WILLIAM
birthplace niles, ohio
burial site canton, ohio
party republican
profession lawyer
vice president hobart, roosevelt
MEAD hydromel, meadow, melicratum, mercedes, metheglin
MEADOW abel, arado, baan, bog, callow, chinampa, field, grassland, haugh, ing, lawn, lea, mead, paramo, pasture, potrero, prairie, saeter, swale, thwaite, vega, wong
anemone pasqueflower
barley rie
beauty bertolonia, deer grass
bird bobolink
brook bottle-green
bur sweet-gale
campion ragged robin
chicken rail
cress cuckooflower
crowfoot buttercup, frogwort
cup pitcherplant
flower bluets, harebell

grass glyceria, kentucky bluegrass, mannagrass, poa, redtop
growing in pratal
hen bittern, clapper, coot, rail
mouse arvicole, vole
mushroom champignon
nymph limoniad
of dead heroes asphodel fields
parsnip alexanders
pea angleberry, cowpea
pert. pratal
piece of swale
pink ragged-robin
pippit buttylark, cheeper, furzelark, lingbird, tietick, titling, twitlark, wekeen
rue poor-rhubarb
saffron colchicum, crocus, naked lady, upstart
saxifrage seseli
scabish cocash
sorrel sourdock
MEADOWLAND alp, mowing, mowland
MEADOWLARK medlar, sturnella
MEADOWSWEET brideweed, bridewort, meadwort, spiraea, toadflax
MEAGER arid, bare, barren, deficient, destitute, emaciated, exiguous, flimsy, frugal, gaunt, impoverished, inadequate, jejune, lank, lean, leepit, lenten, limited, naked, narrow, penurious, poor, puny, rare, scant(y), scratchy, scrimpy, skimpy, skinny, slender, slight, slim, small, spare, sparse, starved, sterile, stingy, stinted, straitened, tenuous, thin, trivial, wanting
MEAL almuerzo, amyl, at(t)a, bait, banquet, bever, bite, blowout, bran, breakfast, brunch, bub, buffet, cena, cereal, chow, coena, collation, comida, cornmeal, cribble, dejeuner, dinner, eats, evenmete, farina, feast, feed, festa, flour, food, graddan, grain, grout, gurgeons, lunch(eon), mange(r), masa, meat, melder, mess, mush, picnic, pinola, pinole, powder, pulverize, ration, refection, refreshment, repast, sago, salep, scoff, semolina, snack, spread, supper, syssition,

tea, tiffin, trencher, tuck(er)

army chow, mess

at parting voidee

boiled mush

coarse cribble, grout, gurgeons, kibble

common mess, syssition

fine farina, semolina

fixed price table d'hote

ground atole, graddan, massa, melder

impromptu bite, snack

informal buffet, potluck

irregular scambling

light bever, bite, elevener, lunch(eon), snack, tea, tiffin

outdoor barbecue, clambake, cookout, picnic

part course

pert. farinacious, farinose, floury

self-service buffet

test ewald

-ticket breadwinner, forte, job, patron, patsy, skill, talent

with milk sturoch

MEALTIDE chow, meltith

MEALY dry, farinaceous, floury, friable, pale, peronate, powdery, soft-spoken, spotty

back cicada

-bug coccid, pest, pseudococcus, scale

-mouthed adulatory, affected, bland, false, hypocritical, plausible, suave, unctious

tree arrowwood

MEAN 3 aim, bad, low, par, say, tin 4 base, clam, norm, poor, rule, talk, tell, vile, ween 5 cheap, imply, mezzo, mingy, nasty, petty, runty, seedy, small, snide, snivy, sorry, speak, spell, tight, venal 6 abject, aspire, common, convey, denote, design, desire, dirten, frugal, humble, import, intend, lament, little, measly, medial, medium, menial, middle, narrow, paltry, resent, scurvy, shabby, sordid, STINGY, vulgar 7 average, bespeak, betoken, caitiff, connote, doggish, express, ignoble, miserly, plebian, purport, purpose, resolve, selfish, signify, suggest, vicious 8 beggarly, churlish, degraded, grudging, indi-

cate, inferior, mediator, middling, ordinary, paskudne, pitiable, recreant, shameful, stand for, tightwad, wretched 9 determine, irascible, malicious, mercenary, miserable, paskudneh, penurious, symbolize 10 ungenerous 11 contemplate 12 cheeseparing, contemptible, intermediary, parsimonious

fellow churl, squib

golden juste milieu

MEANDER extravagate, fret, gad, gallivant, labryinth, peregrinate, prowl, ramble, range, roam, rove, stray, traipse, turn, twist, wander, wind

MEANING acceptation, aim, argument, bearing, burden, case, connotation, construction, content, definition, denotation, design, drift, effect, essence, explicans, expression, force, gist, hang, idea, impact, implication, import, innuendo, intention, interpretation, matter, meat, mention, object, pith, point, purport, purpose, sense, significance, signification, spirit, subject, substance, suggestion, tenor, text, value

basic unit of sememe

comb. iatro, iatry

diverse polysemy

full of eloquent, explicit, expressive, meaty, ominous, pithy, pointed, predictive, pregnant, sappy, sententious, significant, succinct, suggestive

new trope

opposite antonym

pert. literal, semantic

science of hermeneutics, semantics, semasiology, sematology, significs

MEANINGLESS absurd, aimless, inane, insignificant, null, pointless, purportless, purposeless, senseless, stupid

MEANNESS bigotry, cattiness, devilment, devil(t)ry, egotism, evil, hatefulness, ignobility, lowness, malice, maliciousness, malignance, orneriness, pusillanimity, spite

MEANS affluence, agency, agent, apparatus, assets,

capital, cash, channel, currency, device, effects, expedient, faculty, funds, gimmick, income, instrument, measure, media, medium, mesne, method, mode, modus operandi, money, moyen, oppulence, possessions, power, resources, revenue, riches, securities, steps, supply, tactics, technique, tool, vehicle, way(s), wealth, wherewithal

of access approach, avenue

of defense bulwark, hedge, moat, shield, wall

of livelihood job, labor, profession, trade, vocation, work

of support aliment, alimony, income, maintenance

provide aid, allow, arm, assist, enable, help, implement, permit

MEANT aforethought, implied, intended, intentional

MEANWHILE ad interim, at the same time, for a time, for the nonce, interim, interval, meantime, nevertheless, recess, whilst

MEASLES esca, morbilli, rash, roseola, rubella, rubeola

MEASLY base, cheap, contemptible, insignificant, MEAN, mingy, miserly, paltry, petty, picayune, pitiful, puny, sorry, stingy, trifling, trivial, valueless, worthless

MEASURE (See also country involved or object measured, e.g. LAND, LENGTH.) account, act(ion), adjust, aid, allot, amount, appraise, assess, balance, bar, cadence, calculate, calibrate, caliper, canon, capacity, cess, check, compare, compute, criterion, degree, dimension, divide, dose, estimate, expedient, extent, fathom, ga(u)ge, girth, length, limit, mark, melody, met(age), mete(r), methe, model, norm, pace, part, pittance, plumb, poise, portion, probe, procedure, provision, quantify, quantity, rate, regulate, rhythm, rule, scan, share, size, sound,

space, span, standard, step(off), survey, tape, tempo, test, time, touchstone, tune, volume, weigh(t), width, yardstick
across breadth
angular arc, mil, radian
antique baluster
astronomical azimuth
biblical aphah, cab, cubit, epha, hin, homer, kor, log
circular degree, minute, second
comb. meter, metro
cubic cord, faden, gareh, hectostare, liter, peck, perch, pint, quart, shaku, stack, stere, stero, tchast, volume(try)
depth plumb, sound
dry bale, bushel, cup, epha(h), liter, peck, pint, quart, spoon, stere
established standard
fish cot, cran, draft, draught, hamper, last
flexible tape(line)
for measure equity, interchange, revenge
for measure character abhorson, angelo, barnardine, claudio, elbow, escalus, francisca, froth, isabella, juliet, lucio, mariana, mistress overdone, peter, pompey, thomas, varrius, vincentio
hardness mohs
liquid aam, arroba, barrel, chop(p)in, cup, dram, drop, fifth, firkin, flagon, gallon, gill, hectoliter, hin, hogshead, jigger, keg, kiloliter, lagen, liter, log, magnum, minim, ounce, pint, pipe, pony, quart, run(d)let, saa, spoon, tenth, tierce, tun
medicinal grain, gram, gutta, minim, ounce
metric angstrom, are, carat, centiare, centiliter, centimeter, centistere, decaliter, decameter, dec(i)are, decastere, deciliter, decimeter, decistere, dekadrachm, dekagram, dekaliter, dekameter, dekiare, dekistere, gram(me), hectar(e), hectoliter, hectometer, hectostere, kiliare, kilo, kiloliter, kilometer, kilostere, liter, manzana, megameter, meter, microliter, micromillimeter, micron, miglio,

milliare, milliliter, millimeter, millistere, myrialiter, myriameter, sat, sen, shih, stere, tanan
nautical fathom, knot
off lay out, mark, pace, rule, step
official standard
out apportion
rough rule of thumb
short ullage
small barleycorn, grain, micron, millimicron, mite
space parsec
2-quart pottle
up qualify
MEASURED balanced, cadenced, calculated, deliberate(d), disciplined, graduated, metrical, ordered, paced, rhythmical, stated, studied, temperate, uniform, weighed
MEASURELESS boundless, endless, illimitable, immense, infinite, limitless, unbounded, unlimited, vast
MEASUREMENT amount, bulk, capacity, computation, depth, dimension, distance, extent, gauge, level, limit, mensuration, metage, meterage, quantity, size, sounding, survey, volume
mental psychometry
official metage
pert. dimensional, metric
MEASURING *comb.* metry
instrument alidade, caliper, cochain, compass, divider, farinometer, ga(u)ge, jacob's staff, level, meter, odometer, pedometer, perambulator, plumb(bob) (rule), plummet, rod, rule(r), scaler, scales, speedometer, square, stadia, tachymeter, tape(line), telemeter, yardstick
worm autographa, cabbagelooper, geometrid, spanworm
MEAT (See also *cut,* below.) aliment, atta, barbecue, beef, board, brawn, cagmag, dinner, dish, entree, essence, feed, flaysh(ed)ig, flesh, food, game, gist, joint, kernel, lamb, matter, meal, meaning, mete, morsel, muscle, nutriment, pith, point, pork, principle, quarry, roast, staple, sub-

stance, support, sustenance, vifda, vivda
and cabbage bubble and squeak
and fish laulau
and vegetables goulash, mulligan stew
ball croquette, dumpling, fricandel(le), pinda, ravioli, rissole
barbecued kebab, sate
boiled bouilli, sod(den)
bony scrag, spareribs
broiled grillade, griskin
canned bullamacow, spam
chopped burger
cube cabob, dice, kebob
cured bacon, biltong(ue), flitch, ham, pastrami, pemmican, prosciutto, salami, sausage
curer bathman
cut aiguillette, aitchbone, arm, baron, breast, brisket, butt, chine, chop, chuck, clod, cube, cutlet, edgebone, fil(l)et, flank, ham, hock, icebone, knuckle, leg, loin, porterhouse, rack, rasher, rib, roast, round, rump, saddle, sey, shank, shin, shortribs, shoulder, side, sirloin, steak, tenderloin
dealer butcher
dish bubble and squeak, croquette, curry, fricandeau, fricando, goulash, hachis, haricot, hash, haslet, lobscouse, mulligan, pasty, pelmeni, potpie, potroast, ragout, ravioli, roast, salmi, sauerbraten, scrapple, shas(h)lick, shishkebab, stew, toad-in-the-hole
dried biltong(ue), bultong, charqui, jerky, mummy, pem(m)ican, vifda, vivda
-eater carnivore, omophagist
fat blubber, speck, suet
forbidden terepha, tref
frozen frigo
ground hamburger, mince, rissole, sausage
hook gambrel
inferior cagmag, sticking
inspection bedikah
jelly aspic
jerked See *dried;* above.
juice blond, gravy
lean muscle
leftover emince, hash
market shambles

minced chuet, hamburger, jigote, rissole, sanders

minced with curry bobooti, bobotee, bobotie

outdoor cooked barbecue

peppered prosciutto

pickled pastrami, souse

pie bakemeat, crustade, pasty, pirogen, piroshki, rissole

pin skewer

potted rillett(e)

preserve corn, cure, dry, freeze, pickle, salt, smoke

pudding haggis

ragout haricot

raw steak tartar(e)

raw-eating omophagia

roasted brede, cabob, kebob

salted junk, mart

sauce a-one, caper, gravy, horseradish, worcestershire

server dapifer

side sowbelly

slice aguillette, chop, collop, colp, cutlet

smoked bacon, buccan, ham, pastrami

smoking place buc(c)an

stewed bouilli, daube, haricot, goulash, ragout, slumgullion

stock blond, bouillon

unwholesome cagmag

works abattoir, slaughterhouse

MEATBIRD jay, nutcracker

MEATLESS fasting, lenten, maigre, pareve, parve

MEATUS alveary, bur(r), canal, channel, duct, foramen, opening, passage

MEATY pithy, pointed, pregnant, sappy, significant, solid, substantial, substantive, weighty

MECCA *caliph, first* abubekr

deity hobal, hubal

emigrant from companion

governor shereef, sherif

holy well zem

inhabitant meccawee

pert. meccawee

pilgrimage hadj, hegira, hejira

pilgrim garb ihram

shrine caaba, kaaba, kaabeh, mosque

MECHAIEH enjoyment, joy, pleasure

MECHANEUS zeus

MECHANIC artificer, artisan, cardcheat, cardsharp,

cheater, craftsman, feltman, grease monkey, hand, joiner, laborer, machinist, mender, operative, operator, repairer, roustabout, tooler, toolman, worker, workman, wrench

inferior butcher

MECHANICAL automatic, banausic, dull, dumb, extemporaneous, frozen, hackneyed, impromptu, impulsive, inhuman, instinctive, involuntary, laborsaving, machinal, pavlovian, spontaneous, stereotyped, trite, useful

man automaton, golem, robot

not hormic

part cam, gear, rotor, stator, tappet

MECHANICS dynamics, engineering, hydraulics, kinematics, kinetics, physics, pneumatics, statics

MECHANISM action, apparatus, agency, channel, control, device, gear, implement, instrument, machine (ry), materialism, means, rigging, system, tackle, technics, wheels, workings, works

driving engine, motor, propeller

eccentric cam

self-moving automaton

MECHLIN *lace* malines

MECHLIZINE antivert

MEDAL award, badge, coin, decoration, honor, medaille, medallion, oscella, plaque, prize, reward, ribbon, star

kind bronze star, calabash, carnegie, congressional, croix de guerre, cross of merit, distinguished flying cross, iron cross, navy cross, purple cross, purple heart, silver star, victoria cross

MEDALLION cameo, coin, contorniate, decoration, medal, paduan, panel, panhagia, patera, plaque, portrait, relief, tablet, tondo

MEDAN *father* abraham

MEDB *queen* mab

consort ailill, conchobor, conor

country connacht

MEDDLE associate, butt in, combine, dabble, discom-

mode, entermete, fiddle, fight, fool with, fuss, heckle, inconvenience, interfere, interlope, interpose, interrupt, intervene, intrude, mell, mess, mingle, mix, molest, monkey, obtrude, potter, pry, putter, snoop, tamper, tangle, tinker, trouble

MEDDLER backseat driver, busybody, buttinsky, cagmag, interferer, kibitzer, snoop(er), pry

MEDDLESOME busy, curious, fresh, handersome, impertinent, interfering, intrusive, nebby, officious, pragmatic(al)

MEDE See MEDIA, PERSIA.

MEDEA *consort* aegeus, jason

kin absyrtus, apsyrtus, chalciope, circe

parent aeetes, idyia

rival creusa, glauce

son medeus, thessalus

spell site caucasus, colchis

victim creusa

MEDEUS *parent* aegeus, medea

MEDIA *city* ecbatana, phraata, rages

caste magi

emperor deioces

founder arbaces

inhabitant aryan, mesne, mede, parthian, PERSIAN

king ahasuerus, arphaxad, astyages, cyaxares, darius, deioces, evi, phraortes, reba

part atropatene

range zagros

MEDIAN average, intermediate, mean, medium, mesial, mesne, middle, norm, par

line raphe

plane meson

strip mall, terrace

MEDIATE adjudge, adjudicate, appease, arbitrate, bargain, conciliate, halve, harmonize, help, intend, intercede, interfere, interpose, intervene, judge, middle, moderate, negotiate, opine, pacify, plan, propitiate, purpose, reconcile, referee, settle, step in, treat with, umpire

MEDIATION agency, arbitrament, arbitration, bisection, conciliation, decision, halving, hearing, intervention

MEDIATOR advocate, agent, amboceptor, arbiter, arbitrator, daysman, diplomatist, go-between, interagent, intercessor, intermediary, judge, means, medium, middler, moderator, muser, negotiator, omber, peacemaker, referee, umpire

MEDIC clover, doctor, hop, intern(e), medicago, nonesuch, physician, resident, student, surgeon
false medicaster
purple alfalfa, lucern(e)

MEDICAGO alfalfa, baby's-slippers, bird's-foot-clover, bur clover, burgundy trefoil, butter jags, (button)(calvary)clover, caterpillars, lotus, lucerne, spanish trefoil

MEDICAL, MEDICINAL (See also MEDICINE, SURGEON.) aesculapian, alleviative, curative, healing, iatric, paeonian, physic(al), remedial, salutary, therapeutic, therial, therical
capsule cachet
comb. algia, haemia, hemat, iatric, iatro, itis, oma
compound hepar, iodin(e), pill, serum, turpeth
file See *history,* below.
fruit See PLANT *medicinal.*
group ama
herb See PLANT *medicinal.*
history case, catamnesis, chart, file
institution clinic, hospital, rest home, sanitarium
instrument See SURGEON *instrument.*
insurance bluecross, blueshield, medicaid, medicare
literature materia medica
lore armamentarium
man See DOCTOR, HEALER, MEDICINE *man,* SURGEON.
officer coroner
pioneer aesculapius, aristotle, bernard, descartes, galen, harvey, hippocrates, imhotep, lister, pare, pasteur, vesalius
remedy antibiotic, antidote, elixir, pill, shot, tonic

science See MEDICINE.
school, inferior diploma mill
stoppage stasis
student extern(e), intern(e), resident
tablet lozenge, pellet, pill, pilula, pilule, troche
therapy cobalt, radium, x-ray
treatment, comb. iatria, iatry
MEDICAMENT See MEDICATION
MEDICASTER charlatan, quack
MEDICATE anoint, cure, doctor, dope, dose, drug, embrocate, heal, oil, physic, salve, treat
MEDICATION cure, dosage, remedy, smegma, specific, treatment
MEDICI *balls* palle
MEDICINAL See MEDICAL.
MEDICINE (See also *kind,* below.) amulet, anodyne, antidote, balm, charm, cure, dose, drink, DRUG, eclegm, elixir, emulgent, healer, lenitive, liquor, medicament, pharmaceutical, pharmacy, physic, punishment, remedy, science, therapy, trade, treatment
amount dosage, dose
brewed tisane
children's pediatrics
comb. iatric, iatro
dropper pipette
god aesculapius, ascelepius, asklepios, diancecht, hermes, hippocrates, mercury, ningishzida, okuninushi
hormone acth
inactive placebo
kind (See also ANTIBIOTIC.) adrenaline, alkaseltzer, anacin, aspirin, atabrine, atebrin, balm, betaine, bismuth, bromoseltzer, boric acid, cascara, castor oil, cordial, cortisone, digitalis, drops, eardrops, electuary, ergot, histamine, hormone, insulin, iodine, ipecac, laxative, menthal, mepacrine, merthiolate, pectoral, pepsin, physic, quinine, salts, sassafras, stomatic, sulfa, sulphur, vichy water, vitamin
-like pilular
man angakok, angekok,

basir, curandero, DOCTOR, doser, healer, intern, kahuna, leech, lutern, magician, peai, peay, physician, piache, piay, priest, rainmaker, resident, shaman, sorcerer, SURGEON, tohunga, voodoo, witchdoctor, wizard
measurement dosimetry
mild tisane
noncuring ptisan
patent nostrum
pert. aesculapian, iatric(al)
quack embrocation, javapepper, lydia pinkham's, nostrum, peruna, sarsaparilla, snuff, swamp oil, tigerfat
senior geriatrics
soothing abirritant, arnica, balm, camphor, glycerin, glycerol(e), lanolin, menthol, petrolatum
specialty acology, allopathy, anesthesiology, audiology, cardiology, chiropathy, chiropractics, dentistry, dermatology, diagnostics, embryology, endocrinology, etiology, fluorscopy, geriatrics, gerontology, gynecology, hematology, homeopathy, hygiene, immunology, midwifery, mycology, naturopathy, neurology, nosogeny, nosology, obstetrics, opthalmology, optometry, orthopedics, otology, pathology, pediatrics, physiology, podiatry, psychiatry, psychology, radiology, serology, surgery, teratology, therapeutics, tocology, toxicology, traumatology, urology, virology
technician anesthesiologist, anesthetist, dresser, orderly, radiographer, x-rayist
system ayurveda
universal panacea
veterinary theriatrics
watery ptisan
MEDIETY half, moderation, moiety, temperance
MEDIEVAL antiquated, conservative, gothic, middle ages, old-fashioned, primitive
attendant comes
beast epic reynard the fox
beauty heloise
calculator abacus

chattels farleu
cloak courtepy, surcoat
coin bracteate, tari
dagger anlace
dandelion mix taraxacum
drama auto sacramental, miracle play
estate feod
ewer aquamanale, aquamanile
fabric acca, baldacchino, baldaquin, baudekin, brocade, samite
fiddle giga
fort carcassonne
galley aesc, bireme, galiot, unireme
garment chiton, cotehardie, cyclas
giant ferumbras, fierabras
glassware waldglas
guild hanse(atic league)
helmet armet, chapel de fer, heaume
hero rinaldo
husbandman acreman
king's fur vair
leg covering pedule
liberal arts quadrivium
lyric alba
market building cloth hall
military engine catapult, cat(house)
money farleu
monster werewolf
musical instrument clavichord, rebec, rote
navigation chart portolano, rutter
officer bailli, constable, seneschal, vogt
order, chivalric knights templar
prayer book portass
prince's champion paladin
receptacle bahut
religious exhibition processus
satire sotie
shield ecu, pavis, rondache
shirt bleaunt
society g(u)ild
stone-thrower perrier
tale lai, lay
title comes
tribunal vehm
trust commenda
vessel dromon, galley, nef
warden castellan
weapon crossbow, gisarme, lance, mace, oncin, ranseur, SWORD
MEDINA *arab* aus
citizen ansar

moslem ansar, ansarian
ruler shereef, sherif
MEDIOCRE amateur, average, below par, bush-league, characterless, colorless, comme ci comme ca, common(place), couci-couci, fair, hack, indifferent, inferior, lala, mean, medium, middling, moderate, neuter, neutral, ordinary, passable, poor, second-rate, so-so, tolerable, vulgar
MEDIOCRITY also-ran, loser, nobody, non-entity, second-rater, so-so
MEDIOLANUM milan
MEDITATE brood, chew, cogitate, concoct, consider, contemplate, contrive, deliberate, devise, examine, inspect, intend, mull, muse, plan, ponder, pore, prepend, propose, purpense, purpose, puzzle, reason, reflect, revolve, ruminate, speculate, study, think, watch, weigh
MEDITATION contemplation, deliberation, devotion, dhyana, discourse, higgaion, moyen, musing, omphaloskepsis, reflection, rumination, study, thought, yoga, za-zen
and exercise yoga
hall zendo
muse melete
MEDITATIVE contemplative, pensive, reflective, speculative, thoughtful
MEDITERRANEAN interior, middle, midland, mittelmeer
boat accon, felucca, galliot, mistic(o), nef, polacre, saic, settee, tartan, xebac, zebac(k)
chaparral macchie, maqui
chicken ancona, minorca
coast riviera
cordial rosolio
dish octopus, squid
eastern See LEVANT.
falcon lanner
fever brucellosis
fish aco, cabrilla, mackerel, remora, sargo(n), tripletail, tunny, umbra
fish seine madraque
fruit azarole, grape, olive
fruit fly ceratitis
galley galiot
goddess eurynome
grass diss

gulf antalya, catania, gabes, hammamet, iskenderon, lions, sidra, taranto, tunis
herb acanthus, ammi, anacyclus, anise, bellium, bessera, borago, catananche, chicory, cichoria, cornflag, crocus, satureia, savory, silversage
island antikythera, candia, capri, corsica, crete, cyprus, djerba, ebusus, elba, gozo, ibiza, ischia, iviza, lampedusa, lesbos, majorca, mallorca, malta, minorca, panaria, pantelleria, rhodes, rodi, sardinia, sicily, stromboli
island group aegadean, aegadian, balearic, dodecanese, lipari
language sabir
liqueur alkermes
parrot fish scarus
plant acanthus, aizoon, arbutus, asphodel, cactus, cardoon, eucalyptus, euphorbia, fig, lentisc, medlar, mimosa, myrtle, prickly pear, thapsia
resort cannes, capri, costa brava, cote d'azur, nice, riviera, taormina
river to aude, ebro, jucar, nile, rhone, varo
sea adriatic, aegean, ionian, ligurian, tyrrhenian
ship See *boat,* above.
shrub azarole, caper, tamarisk
sponge zimocca
storm borasca, borasco, borasque
thistle scolymus
tree azarole, cade, carob, ceratonia, mastic, olea, olive, senna
wind contraste, etesian, euroclydon, gregale, levanter, mistral, otesan, ptesian, siroc(co), solano, tramontana
MEDIUM agency, agent, average, balian, bath, bister, channel, clairvoyant, color, common, continuum, doer, fair, go-between, golden mean, indifferent, instrument(ality), intermediary, mean(s), measure, median, mediator, mediocre, middle, middling, moderate, oracle, ordinary, organ, par, psychic, second-rate, seer,

showcase, so-so, spiritualist, vehicle

communication bulletin, cable, journal, letter, magazine, mail, newspaper, note, periodical, phone, press, radio, telegraph, telephone, television, tellie

culture agar, broth, hyrax

of exchange currency, money

transmission air(wave), radio, television

MEDLAR fruit, lazarole, meadowlark, mespil, tree

wood myrtus

MEDLEY air, assemblage, babel, bariolage, brouhaha, cento, chivari, clangor, collectanea, fantasia, farrago, gallimaufrey, goulash, hash, hodgepodge, jumble, kedgeree, macaroni, macedoine, melange, miscellany, mishmash, mix(ture), olio, pasticcio, pastiche, phantasmagoria, potpourri, rhapsody, rondo, salmagundi, slampamp, song, variety

race relay

MEDOC *wine* lafite, latour, margaux, mouton-rothschild, pauillac, saint estephe, saint julien

MEDON *parent* codrus, oileus, rhene

slayer aeneas

warned penelope

MEDREGAL amber-fish, bonito, seriola

MEDRICK bird, gull, tern

MEDULLA center, compendium, cord, essence, marrow, pith, summary, tissue

oblongata bulb

oblongata stripe oblex

MEDUSA acaleph, blubber, geryonid, gorgon, jelly(fish), monster, quarl, sea nettle, witch

consort poseidon

offspring chrysaor, pegasus

parent ceto, phorcys

representation gorgoneum

sister euryale, stheno

slayer perseus

MEED award, bonus, bounty, bribe(ry), compensation, desert, deserve, gift, guerdon, hire, metir, praise, premium, prize, recompense, repay, requital, reward, satisfaction, share, wages, worth

MEEK calm, compliant, daft,

deft, docile, forbearing, gentle, humble, indulgent, kind, lamb-like, lenient, long-suffering, lowly, manageable, mild, milky, moderate, modest, mure, orderly, pacific, passive, patient, pitiful, quiet, resigned, soft, subdued, submissive, tame, tolerant, weak-kneed, yielding

person lamb

MEEKNESS humility, resignation

MEERSCHAUM gravel, kiefekil, pipe, seafoam, sepiolite

color gravel

MEET (See also MEETING.) abut, adapted, adjoin, answer, appear, approach, appropriate, apt, assemble, battle, border, brave, bump into, butt, chance on, collide, combat, come(across), come together, concur, conform, confront, congregate, content, contest, convene, converge, cope, cross, discharge, encounter, equal, event, execute, face, fair, felicitous, find, fit(ting), flock, fulfill, game, gather, good, gratify, greet, happy, hit upon, intersect, join, just, match, mild, muster, observe, pay, perform, please, proper, qualified, right, run(across), satisfy, seemly, stumble(on), suffice, suitable, timely, touch, transect

athletic game, gymkhana, tournament

boldly brave, breast

casually rencontre, rencounter

face to face affront, confront

forcibly rencounter

halfway mediate

needs suffice

requirements pass

MEETING adjacent, assemblage, assembly, audience, body, cabal, caucus, collision, company, conclave, confab, conference, conflux, congress, connection, consultation, conventicle, convention, convergence, convocation, council, counsel, discussion, duel, encounter, fight, gam, gath-

ering, get together, group, hearing, huddle, indaba, interview, joining, joint, junction, juncture, mall, moot, palaver, rally, reception, rencontre, rencounter, rendezvous, reunion, revival, seance, session, slam, synod, tertulia, tribunal, tryst, union, wardmote

casual rencounter

house morada

mafia sitdown

of minds agreement, consensus, unanimity

of neighbors husking

place ambalam, tinwald

political caucus

secret cabal

site amphitheatre, auditorium, hall, hotel, resort, room

social bee, club, hobnob, jolly

town tunmoot

MEGALITH dolmen, memorial, monument

MEGAMEDE *husband* thespius

MEGAPENTHES *father* menelaus, proteus

MEGAPHONE vamphorn

electric bullhorn, loudspeaker

MEGAPODE brush-turkey, leipoa, maleo, mound-bird

MEGARA *father* creon

founder car

king nisus, pylas

lover hercules

native euclid

slayer hercules

MEGAREUS *daughter* euaechme

MEGARUS *father* zeus

MEGATHERIUM sloth

MEGES *uncle* odysseus, ulysses

MEGIDDO armageddon

MEGILLAH baloney, detail, jazz, malarkey, nonsense, rigmarole, scroll

MEGRIM(S) ache, blues, caprice, dizziness, doldrums, dullness, fad, fancy, flounder, freak, headache, hypochondria, melancholia, migraine, staggers, vertigo, whiff, whim

MEHABEEL *son* delaiah

MEHTAR bhungi(ni), bungy, groom, janitor, stableboy

MEHUJAEL *kin* irad, methuselah

MEILICHIUS zeus

MEIOSIS abatement, belittling, litotes

MEKONG *delta* cochin-china *river site* asia, indochina, vietnam

MELAENIS aphrodite

MELALEUCA cajeput, cajuput, kaheput, myrtle, paperbark, paperbush, punk tree

MELAMED drip, jerk, schlemiel, teacher

MELAMPUS *kin* amythaon, antiphates, bios, idomene

MELANCHOLIA athymia, barythymia, cyclothymia, depression, despondency, hyp, hypochondria, hyps, psycolepsy, sadness

MELANCHOLIC depressed, hyppish, sad

MELANCHOLY atrabile, atrabiliar, atrabilious, black-blooded, black-dog, blues, cheerless, chill, cold, contemptuous, dearn, dejected, depressing, depression, depressive, desperate, despondency, despondent, disconsolate, discouraging, dismal, dispirit(ed), doleful, dolor, dowie, downcast, downhearted, dreamy, drear(y), dumpish, dumps, ennui, forlorn, gloom(y), hypochondria(c), hypped, hysteria, irascible, joyless, lugubrious, mare, melodramatic, mirthless, misery, misogynic, moody, mournfulness, oorie, oppressive, pathetic, penseroso, pensive(ness), pessimistic, poignant, rueful, sad, serious, sombre, sorrowful, spleeny, sullen, thought-(ful), tristesse, tristful(ness), unhappy, vapors, wistful(ness)

MELANESIA(N) *deity* adaro, qat

language fijian, kiriwina, misima, tagula, tarapon

native dobuan, efatese, fiji, kanaga, kanaka, papuan, santo

MELANEUS *son* eurytus

MELANGE gumbo, medley, mix(ture), olio

MELANION See HIPPOMENES.

MELANIPPE *consort* poseidon

parent ares, chiron

son aeolus

MELANIPPUS *beloved* comaetho

parent hicetaon, perigune, theseus

slayer amphiaraus, antilochus

son ioxus

victim tydeus

MELANITE andradite, garnet

MELANOMA cancer, tumor

MELANOSIS black canker, ink disease

MELANOUS brunette, dark, melanic

MELANTERITE inkstone

MELANTHIUS *master* odysseus, ulysses

MELANTHO *mistress* penelope

MELANTIUS *sister* evadne

MELAS *parent* chalciope, phrixus

MELCHI *son* levi, neri

MELCHIAH *kin* harim, pashur

MELCHIEL *son* charmis

MELD announce, blend, bolivia, declare, expose, merge, play, samba, show(down), spread, unite

MELE ballad, chant, song, verse

MELEA *son* eliakim

MELEAGER *beloved* atalanta

half-brother tydeus

parent althea, oeneus

victim calydonian boar

wife cleopatra

MELECH *parent* micah

MELEE affray, altercation, brawl, broil, combat, confusion, contest, diamond, disorder, dogfight, encounter, fight, fracas, fray, quarrel, riot, row, rumpus, scrap, scuffle, set-to, skirmish, squabble, stour, tourney, uproar, wrangle

MELIA, MELIE *abductor* apollo

consort inachus, poseidon

kin amycus, caanthus, oceanus, phoroneus

MELIADUS *son* tristram

MELIBOEA *consort* alexis

MELICERTES See PALAEMON.

MELICHTHYS durgon, triggerfish

MELIE See MELIA.

MELILOT(US) clover, trigonella

MELIORATE better, improve, mitigate, soften

MELIPONA angelito, honey bee

MELISMA cadenza, jubilus, melody, plainsong, tune

MELISSA balm, bee, mint, plant

nourished zeus

sister amalthea

MELISSEUS *consort* amaltheia

daughter adrasteia, ida

MELKARTH baal, moloch

MELL beat, hammer, harvest, home, honey, kirn, maul, meddle, mingle, mix

MELLIFLUENT, MELLIFLUOUS dulcet, honeyed, hyblaean, mellow, melodious, smooth, sweet

MELLOW adult, age(d), amiable, aromatic, develop, dulcet, genial, golden, grown-up, improve, intoxicated, jovial, juicy, lush, malm, mature(d), mellifluous, milden, mollify, old, resonant, responsive, rich, ripe(n), sapid, savory, seasoned, smooth, soft(en), soothing, succulent, sweet, sympathetic, tender, warm (hearted)

MELODEON accordian, organ

MELODIOUS agreeable, arioso, canorous, cantabile, dulcet, euphonious, happy, harmonious, lyric(al), melic, mellifluous, mellifluent, mellisonant, mellow, musical, orphean, orphic, pleasant, resonant, rich, ringing, silver(toned), silvery, sirenic, soft, songful, sonorous, sweet, tuneful, tuny

MELODIST composer, harmonist, singer, vocalist

MELODRAMA bathos, blood and thunder, emotionalism, excitement, ham, passion, sensationalism

MELODRAMATIC bryonesque, bryonic, dramaturgic, emotional, energetic, exaggerated, gaudy, grand, histrionic, maudlin, mawkish, melancholy, pretentious, romantic, sensational, showy, theatrical

MELODY air, aria, cabaletta, cantilena, canto, cantus,

canzon(e), cavatina, chant, chazanut, chime, chorale, descant, diapason, ditty, dulcetness, euphony, harmony, hum, lay, measure, melisma, mellifluence, melos, music, raga, rhythm, rosalia, song, strain, sweetness, theme, tone, tune
altered musica ficta
compass ambitus
counter descant
in sequence melos, rosalia, round
pert. ariose, arioso, plagal
plaintive dump
plural counterpoint
simple cantilena
unaccompanied monody, solo
MELOID blister-beetle, cantharid, insect
MELON (See also *kind*, below.) amphisarca, blubber, bombe, bonus, dividend, fruit, patrimony, pepo, profit, sponspeck, winnings
inedible cucurbit, dudaim
kind cantalo(u)pe, casaba, citron, cucurbit, gourd, honeydew, mango, maycock, peponida, persian, pumpkin
-like ornament amalaka
mold bombe
pear pepino
rock cantaloup(e), muskmelon
tree papaya
MELOS melody, song, tune
MELPOMENE *lover* achelous
muse of tragedy
offspring See SIRENS.
MELT affect, blend, blow, colliquate, convert, defrost, de-ice, deliquesce, diminish, disappear, discandy, disintegrate, disperse, dissipate, dissolve, droze, dwindle, flow, flux, fuse, liquefy, move, percolate, perspire, render, rind, run, smelt, soften, spleen, squander, subdue, swale, sweal, sweeten, thaw, touch, unfreeze, vanish, waste
partly frit
water outwash
MELTED contrite, fused, fusile, liquified, molten, runny, soft, thawed
MELTON box-cloth

MELURSUS aswail, sloth-bear
MELUS *changed to* apple tree
father cinyras
friend adonis
MELUSINA *parent* elinas, pressina
MELVILLE *character* ahab, moby dick
work benito cereno, billy budd, mardi, moby dick, omoo, pierre, typee
MELZAR *master* nebuchadnezzar
MEMBER arm, associate, belonger, branch, brother, capitular, cardholder, clause, component, constituent, detail, district, division, element, enlistee, enrollee, fellow, fraction, fragment, guildsman, insider, joiner, leg, limb, mention, organ, parcel, part, participant, pledge, portion, section, sector, segment, shoot, sister, socius, unit
group of association, club, fraternity, lodge, society, sodality, sorority
new apprentice, entrant, initiate, neophyte, novice, pledge
oldest dean
staff attache
subordinate associate
MEMBRANE allantois, amnion, aponeurosis, axilemma, blype, capsule, caul, chorion, coat, conjunctiva, cuticle, diaphragm, dura, eardrum, envelope, fascia, film, fold, galea, labellum, lamina, layer, leaf, lemme, loma, mater, meninges, meninx, mucosa, oolemma, pellicle, pericardium, peritoneum, pia, pleura, retina, sac, serosa, skeet, skin, stratum, striffen, tela, timbal, tympanum, vela, velum, web
comb. amnio
corti tectorium
diffusion osmosis
divided by septate
fold plica
fringe loma
lining intima
spore endosporium, intine
web-like tela
MEMBRANOUS husky, hy-

menoid, pliable, scariose, skinny, thin
MEMENTO bibelot, curio, favor, keepsake, loveknot, memorial, relic, remembrance, reminder, souvenir, token, trophy
MEMNON *ally* priam
armor-maker hephaestus
colossi location thebes
founder of babylon walls, susa
grandfather hyperion
kingdom ethiopia
parent aurora, eos, tithonus
slayer achilles
uncle priam
victim antilochus
MEMO agenda, agendum, aide-memoire, annotate, annotation, bordereau, brief, bumf, chit, commonplace, dispatch, docket, entry, footnote, iou, item, jotting, letter, memoir, memorial, minute(s), missive, notation, note, record, reminder, report, statement, ticket
book agenda, calendar, diary, tickler
legal jurat
MEMOETIUS *father* iapetus
MEMOIR ana, anthology, autobiography, article, biography, chronicle, essay, history, memorial, note, record, report
MEMORABILIA See MEMOIR.
MEMORABLE distinguished, extraordinary, marked, notable, pronounced, remarkable, remembered, reminiscent, signal
MEMORANDUM See MEMO.
MEMORIA chapel, church, memory, reliquary, shrine, tomb
MEMORIAL abstract, agalma, ahu, arch(ive), bauta, ca(i)rn, cenotaph, chronicle, column, cromlech, cross, cyclolith, dolmen, ebenezer, footstone, gravestone, hoarstone, marker, megalith, memento, memoir, memo(randum), memory, monolith, monument, needle, note, obelisk, pillar, pyramid, recollection, record, relic, reliquary, remembrance,

shaft, shrine, slab, stone, stupa, tablet, testimonial, token, tomb(stone), tope, trophy
carved totem
park cemetery
post totem
stone cairn, mausoleum, statue
MEMORIALIZE address, celebrate, commemorate, petition
MEMORIST prompter
MEMORIZE learn(by heart), parrot, remember
MEMORY anamnesis, crypt-amnesia, honor, image, immortality, mind, mneme, recall, recognition, recollection, record, remembrance, reminiscence, retention, retrospection, rote, storage
aid acetycholine, anemnestic, mnemonic, petite madelaine, reminder, rna, tickler
art of improving mnemonics
basis engram
book album, diary, scrapbook
comb. mnem, mnesia, mnesis
complete pantomnesia
device mnemonic(on)
from by heart, by rote
goddess mnemosyne
injurious to antimnemonic
lapse parapraxis
-losing amnemonic, manesic
loss amnesia, aphasia, blackout, blank, forgetfulness, lethe, paramnesia
muse mneme
pattern engram
person with visual eidetic
pert. con, mnemonic, mnes(t)ic
pleasant afterglow
practice mnemonism
principle mneme
pseudo paramnesia
quirk deja-vu
routine rote
unit, computer buffer
MEMPHIS *builder* epaphus
bull apis
chief evi
deity dor, imhotep, nefertum, ptah, sekhmet
dominoes dice
MEN humanity, mankind, party, people, sons
at arms chivalry

dread of androphobia
group archontia, army, assembly, band, brotherhood, committee, crew, force, fraternity, gang, horde, host, lodge, navy, order, outfit, party, people, posse, staff, team, troops
learned clerisy
party smoker, stag
quarters andron, selamlik
wise See MAGI.
MENACE alarm, bandersnatch, boast, commination, cow, forebode, forecast, frighten, fulminate, impend, intimidate, intimidation, jeopardy, overhang, peril, portend, presage, problem, scare, threat(en), thunder, villain
MENACING fierce, formidable, imminent, minacious, minatory, sinister, threatening
MENAGE club, establishment, house(hold)(keeping), husbandry, residence, society
MENAGERIE collection, tiergarten, zoo
MENANDER *comedy* arbitration, samia
friend epicurus
teacher theophrastus
MEND accommodate, ameliorate, amend, beet(e), better, botch, clout, cobble, convalesce, correct, cure, darn, doctor, emend, excel, fix, get well, heal, help, improve, knit, moise, overhawl, patch, ranter, readjust, rebuild, reconcile, rectify, redress, reform, refurbish, regulate, remedy, remodel, renew, renovate, repair, restore, retouch, rightle, sew, solder, spetch, suture
fences pacify, politick
one's ways reform
poorly botch
MENDACIOUS deceitful, dishonest, false, fibbing, lying, paltering, prevaricating, untruthful, wrong
MENDACITY deceit, deception, duplicity, falsehood, falsity, fib, lie, lying, untruth
MENDER beatster, cobbler, darner, doctor, fixer, mechanic, renovator, repairer,

repairman, tinker(er), trouble-shooter
MENDICANT ajivika, almsman, avadhuta, bairagi, baul, beggar(man), begging, bhikkshu, bhikku, bhikky, breviger, carmelite, dandi, dandy, euchite, fakeer, fakir, friar, gaberlunzie, gosain, monk, naga, pandaram, pauper, sannyasi, servite, solicitor, solicitous
MENDOLE cackerel
MENE See SELENE.
MENELAUS *brother* agamemnon, simon
captive adrastus
host antenor
offspring hermione, megapenthes
parent aerope, atreus, plisthenes
rival paris
steersman canopus
victim deiphobus, scamandrius
wife helen
MENESTHEUS *father* areithous, peteus
kin erechtheus, orneus
son appollonius
MENFRA minerva
MENHADEN albula, alewife, bonyfish, bugfish, bughead, bunker, chebog, chiro, clupeid, ellfish, elops, fatback, hardhead, ladyfish, mossbunker, oldwife, pogie, po(r)gy, sardine, savelha, shadine, shiner
MENHIR bauta, catstone, gorsedo, hagiolith, mark(er), monolith, peulvain, stone
MENIAL abject, attendant, base(born), blackguard, domestic, fag, fawning, flunky, groveling, hireling, ignoble, knave, lackey, low(ly), mean, minion, obsequious, page, retainer, scullion, serf, SERVANT, servile, slavish, sordid, subservient, varlet, vile, wallowing, worker
MENINGES arachnoid, dura mater, pia mater
MENIPPE *father* orion
sister metioche
MENISCUS cartilage, crescent, disc, lens
MENNA *son* melea
MENNONITE amish, am-

manite, hooker, huterite, wisler
bishop amman
founder menno simons
MENODICE *offspring* hylas
MENOECEUS *father* creon
offspring creon, hippomene, jocasta
MENOETIUS *brother* atlas, empietheus, prometheus
parent actor, aegina
son patroclus
MENOMINEE black-back, chivey, prosopium, whitefish
MENORAH candelabrum
MENSURATION See MEASUREMENT.
MENTAL cerebral, daft, endopsychic, ideal, intellectual, intelligent, inward, mindly, phrenic, phrenologic(al), psychic(al), psychologic(al), rational, reasoning, spiritual, subjective, thinking
activity brainwork, cerebration, cogitation, imagination, skull-practice, thought
discipline yoga
disorder amentia, anoesia, anoia, aphasia, ataxia, brainstorm, dementia, idiocy, insanity, madness, mania, megalomania, melomania, mongolism, moria, neurosis, paranoia, paranomia, paraphrenia, psychosis, schizophrenia, thymopathy
force afflatus
healing psychotherapy
health tool ect, electroshock
hygiene psychiatry
picture See IMAGE *mental.*
specialist psychiatrist, psycholoy
suffering calvary
MENTALITY acumen, endowment, intellect, intelligence, mind, rationality, reason, sanity, sense, spirit, wits
MENTALLY *deficient* arrested, babbling, backward, crazy, defective, halfbaked, half-witted, imbecile, insane, loony, moronic, nit-witted, simple(minded), subnormal, wanting
MENTIFEROUS telepathic
MENTION allude, allusion, announcement, broach, call,

citation, cite, clepe, comment, discuss, drop, enumerate, indicate, information, mind, mint, name, nod, notice, observation, observe, plug, remark, speak, specify, statement, talk, trace, utterance, vestige
by name nemme, nemn, nempne
implied connotation
privately tip
MENTOR cicerone, counsel (or), guru, instructor, nestor, sage, teacher
companion odysseus, ulysses
father alcimus
pupil telemachus
MENTUM See CHIN.
MENTZALIA bartonia, blazing star, gentian
MENU bill(of fare), card, carte(du jour), cuisine, fare, list, meal, schedule, table
part appetizer, blue plate, dessert, entree, salad, soup, special
special plat du jour
MENYANTHES bittertrefoil, bitter-worm, bogbean, bog-myrtle, buckbean
MEPERIDINE demerol
MEPHIBOSHETH *kin* jonathan, saul
MEPHISTO(PHELES) devil, fiend, lucifer, satan
MEPHITIC baneful, deadly, fetid, foul, loathsome, malodorous, miasmatic, miasmic, noxious, offensive, pestilent(ial), poisonous, putrid, repugnant, toxic
MEPHITIS miasma, skunk, smell, stench, stink, vapor
MEPROBAMATE equinil, miltown, tranquilizer
MERA *consort* zeus
MERAB *husband* adriel
parent ahinoam, saul
MERAIOTH *son* azariah, zadok
MERARI *kin* judith, levi, mahli, mushi
MERCANTILE commercial, trading
MERCATOR chart, map
enlargement inset
MERCENARY abject, acquisitive, armatoles, avaricious, brabanter, condottiere, covetous, employee, gallo(w)glass, grasping,

greedy, hack(ney), hessian, hired, hireling, ignoble, janizary, mean, myrimidon, paid, pindari, sepoy, sordid, truculent, venal, vendible
MERCHANDISE articles, artware, buy, cargo, chaffer, commodities, effects, furniture, goods, hardware, line, market, notions, sell, staples, stock, store, stuff, trade, trading, traffic, ven(ibles), wares
cheap borax, brack, camelot
pert. emporeutic
MERCHANT chandler, chapman, coster, dealer, distributor, draper, exporter, goladar, hansard, howadji, huckster, kitely, marcantant, mercer, monger, nepman, povindah, purveyor, retailer, seller, seth, shopkeeper, soudagur, storekeeper, sutler, taipan, tallyman, trader, tradesman, trafficker, vender, vendor, vintner, walla, wholesaler
caste bania(n), banyan, teli
group cartel, guild, hansa
of venice antonio
of venice character antonio, bassanio, gobbo, gratiano, jessica, leonardo, lorenzo, nerissa, portia, salanio, salarino, salerio, shylock, stephano, tubal
of venice heroine portia
rich fugger
soldier povindah
vessel argosy, bilander, fluyt, holcad, indiaman
wholesale packer
MERCIA *king* offa
MERCIFUL benign(ant), charitable, clement, compassionate, condoning, forbearing, forgiving, kind(ly), humane, indulgent, lenient, mild, misericordious, pardoning, pitiful, sparing, tender, tolerant
MERCILESS adamant(ine), barbarous, bloody, brutal, callous, cruel, fell, feral, ferocious, fierce, graceless, gratuitous, grim, hard, heartless, implacable, inexorable, inhuman, obdurate, pitiless, relentless, remorseless, ruthless, savage, unfeeling, unrelenting, unsparing, wanton
MERCURIAL active, buoy-

ant, capricious, changeable, clever, commercial, effervescent, elastic, elegant, eloquent, erratic, fast, fickle, frivolous, inconstant, ingenious, mobile, mutable, protean, quick, resilient, shrewd, spirited, swift, thievish, unstable, variable, volatile
ointment blue-butter
MERCURY (See also HERMES.) azoth, chibrit, dragon, god, guide, herma, messenger, planet, poison ivy, quicksilver, spirit, teutates, thief
alchemic azoth
alloy amalgam, ammiolite, calomel, coloradoite, eglestonite, moseite
black poison ivy
compound ammiolite
gem loadstone, lodestone
parent jupiter, maia
source cinnabar, granza
MERCUTIO *friend* romeo
kinsman escalus
slayer tybalt
MERCY amercement, benevolence, blessing, blithe(ness), charity, clemency, commiseration, compassion, favor, forbearance, forgiveness, grace, grith, humanity, indulgence, leniency, lenity, misericord(e), pardon, passion, pity, quarter, ruth, tenderness, thanks, tolerance, yearning
angel of nurse
goddess kwannon
having See MERCIFUL.
killing euthanasia
seat bench, propitiation, throne of god
show condone, forgive, indulge, pardon, reprieve, spare
stroke coup de grace
sword curteen
without See MERCILESS.
MERE absolute, bald, bare, beautiful, blunt, border, bound(ary), club, divide, entire, famous, fen, few, glorious, lake, landmark, limit, marsh, mother, ocean, only, pond, pool, pure, scarce, sea, sheer, simple, single, small, sole, stark, such, unadorned, undiluted, unmixed, unqualified, utter

comb. psil(o)
handful few, sprinkling, wisp
nothing trifle
MERED *father* ezra
MEREDITH *work* beauchamp's career, egoist, modern love, shaving of shagpat
MERELY absolutely, also, anerly, at least, barely, but, entirely, exclusively, in part, just, leastways, leastwise, only, purely, quite, scarcely, simply, singly, solely, utterly, wholly
MERENRA *servant* herkhuf
MERETRICIOUS blatant, cheap, coarse, deceptive, delusory, false, flashy, gaudy, pretentious, punkish, sham, tawdry, vulgar, wanton
MERETRIX prostitute
MERGANSER becscie, bird, bracket, diver, earlduck, garbill, goosander, harle, herald, jacksaw, mergus, nun, rantock, sawneb, sheldrake, smee, smew, snowl, spike, tadpole, towhead, tweezer, weaser, wheezer
female dun-diver
hooded cock robin, sheldrake, strawbill, towhead
red-breasted earl-duck
MERGE amalgamate, articulate, blend, cement, change, coalesce, combine, compact, compose, concentrate, consolidate, convert, fuse, immerse, integrate, join, marry, meld, mingle, mix, sink, unify, unite, wed, weld
MERGER absorption, amalgamation, blend, cartel, combination, consolidation, enosis, enterprise, fusion, marriage, mixture, trust, union
MERGING alliance, amphimixis, anastomosis
MERIDIAN acme, apex, apogee, circle, climax, culmination, grade, midday, noon, peak, pinnacle, plane, siesta, south, summit, top, zenith, zone
MERINO delaine, fabric, sheep, wool, yarn
MERIT badge, brownie point, caliber, credit, desert, deserve, dignity, due, earn (ings), excellence, feather

in cap, guerdon, honor, mark, meed, perfection, quality, rate, reward, thank, value, virtue, worth(iness)
name meaning moira
MERITORIOUS creditable, deserving, laudable, praiseworthy, valid, worthy
MERL blackbird, blackie
MERLIN falcon, magician, pigeon-hawk
grass quillwort
magician to king arthur
mistress vivian, vivien
pupil morgana, morgan le fay
son vanoc
wood broceliande
MERLON battlement, cop, fort
MERMAID harlot, lorelei, lurlei, merrow, naiad, nereid, nixie, siren, swimmer
false floerkea
tavern frequenter beaumont, ben jonson, fletcher, selden, shakespeare
MERMAN manfish, marmenill, seaman
MERMERUS *parent* jason, medea
MERO grouper, guasa, rock hind
MERODACH See MARDUK.
MEROPE *brother* helios, phaethon
consort cresphontes, sisyphus
offspring aepytus, glaucus
parent atlas, cresphontes, cypselus, oenopion
MEROPS *consort* clymene
kingdom ethiopia
son adrestus, phaethon
MEROSTOME See ARTHROPOD.
MEROVINGIAN *coin* siaga
king dagobert
MEROZOITE agamete, enhemospore, spore
MERRILY gayly, joyously, lustick
MERRIMENT daffery, daffing, festivity, frolic, fun, gaiety, glee, hilarity, jocularity, jollity, jovialty, joy, jubilation, laughter, levity, mirth, sport(iveness), whoopdedoo
MERRY animated, blithe, boisterous, bonny, boon, bully, buxom, cadgy, cant, cheerful, convivial, droll,

feastly, festive, frolicsome, fun-loving, gai, gay, glad, gleeful, gleesome, happy, hilarious, intoxicated, jocose, jocular, jocund, jolly, jovial, joyful, joyous, larking, lively, lustick, mirthful, raffing, riant, riotous, risible, rollicking, sportive, sprightly, sunny, uproarious, vivacious, vogie, winsome

andrew acrobat, antic, aper, boor, buffo(on), clown, comedian, comic, droll, fool, harlequin, jester, joker, jokester, merryman, mime, mountebank, pantaloon, pickleherring, scaramouch, stooge, zany

as a cricket, grig

dancers aurora borealis, corona, northern lights

-go-round calso, car(r)ousel, flying horses, kellys goats, little war, maneges de chevaux de bois, roundabout, spinning jenny, turnabout, whirlabout, whirligig

-go-round prize brass ring

let us be gaudeamus igitur

-man See *andrew,* above.

monarch charles ii

person grig

widow composer lehar

wives of windsor, character bardolph, caius, evans, falstaff, fenton, ford, mistress, nym, page, pistol, quickly, robin, rugby, shallow, simple, slender

MERRYMAKER birkie, caperer, cavorter, frolicker, grig, reveller, rollicker, romp, skylarker, trojan

MERRYMAKING ale, carnival, conviviality, festive, festivity, gaiety, gossiping, jolly, kirn, merriment, rag, reel, revel(ry), splore, sport(ance), wassail

MERRYTHOUGHT furcula, talisman, wishbone

MERRYTROTTER seesaw, swing

MERRYWING bufflehead, duck, goldeneye

MERSE dip, immerse, marsh, plunge

MERTENSIA bluebell, cowslip, lungwort, plan, pneumaria

MERTON *college postmaster* portionist

MESA bench, cartouch, hill, mount(ain), oakwood, peak, plain. plateau, table(land), terrace

edge ceja

small mesilla

MESACH mishael

MESCAL cactus, challote, maguey, mexical, peyote, peyotl, plant, shrub, sotol, wokowi, yucca

MESCALERO apache, faraon

MESEL leper, leprous

MESELRY leprosy

MESH areola, catch, engage, entangle, gear, interlock, lace, macula, mask, mease, mitome, moke, net(ting), network, plait, reticulate, screen, snare, tissue, trap, web

fabric net(ting), skipdent, tiffany

MESHA *father* caleb

MESHECH *companion* daniel, shadrach

father japheth, shem

MESHED engaged, netlike, netted, reticulate, tangled

MESHELEMIAH *son* elam, elioenai, jathniel, jediael, jehohanan, zebadiah, zechariah

MESHES booby trap, noose, pitfall, quicksand, snare, toils, trap

MESHEZABEEL *son* berechiah

MESHUGGE absurd, crazy, extravagant, nuts, wild

MESHULIAM *kin* elpaal, hilkiah, zadok, zerubbabel

MESIAL median, middle

MESMERIC fascinating, irresistible, spellbinding

MESMERISM hypnosis, hypnotism, magnetism

MESMERIZE entrance, fascinate, hypnotize, spellbind

MESOPOTAMIA See also IRAQ for contemporary references.

boat gufa, kufa

capital bag(h)dad

captives' place halah

city arbela, arbil, amara, ana, babylon, bag(h)dad, basra, edessa, erbil, hilla(h), hit(is), karbala,

kerbela, kirkuk, kish, kufa, mosul, najaf, nippur, samarra, seleucia

civilization akkadian, assyrian, babylonian, eblan, sumarian

coin dinar

district basra, kurdistan

diviner balaam

general kassem

king chushanrishathaim

kingdom mitanni

leader saddam hussein takriti

oasis maniya

people arab, aramean, babylonian, chaldean, iraki, iraqi, kurd, mitanni

port basra, busra(h)

raft kelek

range kurdistan, zargos

regime baathist

river euphrates, shatal-arab, tigris, zab

tree homa

wind shamal

MESOZOIC *period* comanchean, cretaceous, jurassic, triassic

MESQUITE algar(r)oba, buffalo grass, bush, carob, cashaw, cushaw, honey (pod), ironwood, keawe, mosquito, pacay, prosopis, shrub

bean flour pinole

MESS ashtunk, batch, befoul, blunder, botch, bumble, bungle, cauch, chow, clat, clutter, commotion, confuse, confusion, course, dabble, defile, disarray, dishevel, disorder, error, farrago, feed, fiasco, food, fright, gaum, hash, higgledy-piggledy, hodgepodge, hotchpotch, imbroglio, jumble, limber, litter, mash, meal, meddle, mishmash, misup, mix(ture), modicum, muck, mullock, muss, mux, olla-podrida, omnium-gatherum, picklement, pittance, predicament, putter, rummage, rumple, salmagundi, scramble, shambles, share, slaister, soil, soss, squabble, stew, strew, swill, table, tousle, tumble, untidiness

around juke, meddle, potchkee, potchkeh, trifle

-mate associate, companion, eucalyptus, yuba

-up melee, muddle

MESSAGE bode, bodword, brevet, cable, call, card, communication, communique, correspondence, depeche, dispatch, embassage, embassy, epistle, evangel, express, gospel, letter, memo(randum), mission, missive, note, report, rumor, signal, sond, telegram, tidings, wire, word
coded cryptogram, scytale
good news evangel
of respect commendation, recado
spirit psychogram
MESSALINA courtesan, profligate, prostitute, wanton
husband claudius
modern catherine ii
son brittanicus
MESSENE *husband* polycaon
king amarynceus
parent triopas
MESSENGER ambassador, angel, apostle, ariel, beadle, bearer, bellboy, bellhop, bunene, carrier(pigeon), chiaus, chuprassy, commissionaire, courier, crier, dak, delegate, emissary, envoy, estafet(te), express, facteur, forerunner, go-between, harbinger, herald, hermes, hircarra, intermediary, iris, malachi, mercury, minister, mummu, nunciate, nuncio, omen, page, paul revere, peon, pigeon, post(boy), poster, postrider, precursor, prophet, revere, runner, sand, send, toty(man), vaux
biblical angel, apostle, gabriel
gods ariel, bhrugi, gnas, hebe, hermes, iris, mercury, namtaru, valkyrie
magazine pacolet
mounted cossid, courier, estafet(te), paul revere, pony express
name meaning malachi
rna ribonucleic acid
special express
MESSIAH conservator, deliverer, jesus christ, savior, wovoka
composer handel
MESSINA *builder* dionysus
governor leonato
people mamertini, samians
strait, mirage fata morgana

strait, rock scilla, scylla
strait, whirlpool charybdis, galofalo, galofaro, garofaro
tyrant agathocles
MESSUAGE farm, haw, homestead, meese, midstead
MESSY augean, blowzy, collied, difficult, dirty, disordered, embarrassing, every which way, frowzy, gooey, grimy, grubby, sloppy, sozzly, sticky, unclean, untidy
MESTIZO cholo, cross, curiboca, griffe, ladino, mameluco, metis
MESTOR *parent* andromeda, perseus
MESTRA *consort* poseidon
parent erysichthon
MET agreed, bushel, equaled, measure(ment), new yorker, opera, opposed, trysted
METABOLISM anaboaism, assimilation, catabolism, metamorphosis, metastasis
test bmr
METABUS *daughter* camilla
METAGNOMY See DIVINATION.
METAL (See also *kind,* below.) alloy, ballast, bullion, element, macadamize, material, mettle, mine(ral), ore, pave, rails, shale, spirit, stuff, substance, type
alloy aich, babbit, brass, bronze, ceramel, cermet, gallium, matte, monel, niello, pewter, solder, steel
arch hoop
babbitt lining
band bail
bar gad, i-beam, ingot, risp
base alloy, dross, matte, sprue
blue basalt
bolt rivet
bonding cladding
box canister
cake slag
capping calotte
casting ingot, pig
clippings scissel
coarse matte, regulus
coat armature, enamel, patina, plate, rust, tarnish, terne
-containing metalliferous, ory
cross asteriscus
crude matte, ore, slug

cutter acetylene, ethine, ethyne
decorate engrave, etch
decorated niello, ormolu
decorative chrome
defect snake
deposit lode
disk badge, medal(lion), paten, tag
divalent calcium
dross See *refuse,* below.
ductile nickel
fastener bolt, brad, cotter, nail, pin, rivet, screw, snap, solder, zipper
filings lemel
film See *coat,* above.
fissure lode
gilded ormolu
grayish chromium, manganese, steel
guard bumper
hard iron, nickel, steel
hardness measure mohs
hardness tester brinnell
heavy lead, osmium, uranium
impure alloy, matte, regulus
inflammable rubidium
ingot bar, gad, pig
kind aluminum, americium, barium, beryllium, bismuth, brass, bronze, bullion, cadmium, calcium, cerium, cesium, chromium, cobalt, copper, cuprum, dysprosium, gadolinium, gallium, germanium, gold, hafnium, holmium, indium, iridium, iron, lanthanum, lead, lithium, lutecium, magnesium, manganese, mercury, molybdenum, neodynium, nickel, niobium, ore, osmium, palladium, pewter, phosphorus, platinum, polonium, potassium, promethium, quicksilver, radium, rhenium, rubidium, ruthenium, samarium, scandium, silver, sodium, steel, strontium, tantalum, technetium, terbium, thallium, throium, thulium, tin, tingsten, titanium, uranium, vanadium, ytterbium, yttrium, zinc, zirconium
layer seam, stope
leaf foil
lightest lithium
lining bushing
liquid mercury
lump nugget, ore, pig, regulus, slug

magnetized electromagnet
mass bullion, ingot
mixture alloy
molten squirt, tap
nonexpanding invar
perforated stencil
piece jack, slug
plate ampyx, apron, dod, gib, lame, lamina, latten, shim
porous sponge
precious gold, platinum, silver
rare acmite, derium, didymium, erbium, europium, iridium, lutecium, terbium, thulium, uranium, yttrium
reddish copper
refuse dross, gate, matte, recrement, scoria, shrug, slag
royal gold
scrap filing
shaper swage
sheet (See also *plate*, above.) doubles, kalamein, tagger
silvery calcium, cobalt, titanium
sleeve bushing
source ore
spacer slug
spike gad
stannic tin
strip spline
suit armo(u)r, mail
surface niello
tag a(i)glet
test assay
thread lame
tin-like cadmium
unrefined ore
vein lode
ware grayware, lormery, pontypool, revere, tole
waste See *refuse*, above.
wedge shim
white calcium, silver, tin
work bori, repousse, zogan
-work god hephaestus, vulcan
worker armorer, aurifex, barman, bellcaster, blacksmith, braz(i)er, burnisher, coppersmith, fooner, forger, forkman, founder, foundryman, gilder, goldsmith, ironsmith, metallurgist, plater, puddler, riveter, silversmith, smelter, solderer, steelworker, sudsman, tinner, tinsmith, vulcan, welder
works anvil, bloomery, forge, foundry, smeltery, smithery, smithy

METALLIC (See also METAL.) brazen, hard, harsh, inorganic, mineral, tinny
METAMERE merosome, segment, somatome, somite
METAMORPHOSE alter, change, convert, develop, mature, modify, shape, transfigure, transform, transmew, transmogrify, transmute, transubstantiate, vary
METAMORPHOSIS alteration, anamorphism, change, degeneration, metabole, modification, mutation, permutation, petalody, phyllody, sepalody, transfiguration, transformation, transmutation, variation
comb. ody
floral petalody
METANIRA *husband* celeus
offspring abas, demophoon, triptolemus
METAPHOR allegory, analogy, comparison, figure of speech, image, metonymy, simile, translation, trop(h)e
faulty catachresis
prolonged allegory
METAPHORICAL figurative, translatitious
METAPHRASE construe, paraphrase, translation, version
METAPHRAST interpreter, translator
METAPHYSICAL abstract, abstruse, jesuitic, occult, supernatural
being ens
poet cowley, crashaw, donne, herbert
METAPHYSICS cosmology, ontology
METAPSYCHOSIS esp
METASTASIS anastrophe, change, chiasmus, hypallage, hysteron, metabolism, metathesis, palindrome, parenthesis, synchysis, tmesis, transfer, transformation, transition
METASTROPHE interchange
METATHESIS interversion
METATROPIC saprophytic
METE allocate, allot, apportion, assign, award, bound (ary), deal, dispense, distribute, dole, dream, give,

goal, limit, measure, meat, parcel, post, serve, stake
METELLUS *enemy* marius
friend turpillus
lieutenant rutilius
rival jugurtha
METEMPSYCHOSIS change, samsara, transformation
METEOR aerolite, argid, bolide, bolis, comet, cosmic dust, falling star, fireball, rainbow, shooting star, shot star, whirlwind
august perseid
-exploding bolide, bolis, fireball, meteorite
mark crater
name andromede, andromid, antlid, aquarid, aquilid, argid, arietid, aurigid, bielid, bootid, camelid, cancrid, cepheid, columbid, coronid, draconid, dragon, leonid, lyncid, lyraid, orionid, pegasid, piscid, taurid, toucanid
november leonid
shower andromede, leonid, virginid
streak trail
METEORIC brilliant, celestial, ephemeral, flashing, rapid
METEORITE (See also METEOR *name*.) aerolite, aerolith, aerosiderite, argid, asiderite, baetulus, baetyl(us), bolide, cloud stone, diogenite, eucrite, pallasite, skystone
metallic siderite
pit pezograph
science aerolitics
stony achondrite, aerolite, chondrite
worshipped baetulus, baetyl(us)
METEOROLOGICAL *balloon* kytoon, sonde
instrument barometer, barothermograph, bolide, thermometer
layer stratopause
METEOROLOGIST forecaster, weatherman
METER accent(uation), alexandrine, anapest, antispast, arsis, athena, beat, cadence, caesura, dactyl, diaeresis, dipody, ell, emphasis, euphony, foot, gauge, gayatre, iamb(us), ictus, lilt, measure, mora, movement, numbers, pulse,

rhyme, rhythm, spondee, stress, swing, tetraseme, thesis, time, triseme, trochee, verse
10th decimeter
100th centimeter
1000th millimeter
10 decameter
100 hectometer
1000 kilometer
10,000 grex, myriameter
cubic liter, litre, stere
halting scazon
millionth micron
reader gamsman
square cent(i)are
100 square are
1000 square decare
unit matra, mora(e)

METHAMPHETAMINE
speed

METHANE formene, marsh gas, paraffin
and metal alkid
pert. formenic
radical alkyl

METHOD approach, arrangement, art, course, fashion, form(ula), gate, manner, mean(s), mode, modus operandi, order, plan, procedure, process, receipt, recipe, rede, regularity, route, routine, rubric, rule, rut, scheme, sort, strategy, style, system, tack, tactics, technic, technique, theory, usage, way
clever kink(le)
customary course, habit, practice, routine, rut
fixed formula, rule
specialized technique

METHODICAL analytical, business-like, careful, efficient, exact, formal, logical, orderly, organized, punctilious, regular, systematic, trig

METHODISM *founder* wesley

METHUSELAH old man, oldster
kin duryl, enoch, lamech, noah

METHYL *compound* acetol, acetonitrile, anisole, anserine, butanone, carbinyl, carbonium, cres(s)ol, helianthin, nitrile, toluene

METICULOUS accurate, attentive, careful, close, conscientious, correct, critical, curious, delicate, demand-

ing, detailed, exact(ing), fastidious, fine, finical, finicking, finicky, fussy, minute, narrow, nice, observant, painstaking, particular, precise, punctilious, punctual, refined, rigid, rigorous, scrupulous, scrutinizing, sticky, strict, subtle
person purist

METIER art, business, calling, craft, forte, game, labor, line, occupation, profession, pursuit, speciality, sphere, thing, toil, trade, vocation, work

METIOCHE *father* orion

METION *parent* erechtheus, praxithea

METIS *consort* zeus
daughter athena
parent oceanus, tethys

METISSE half-breed, mixture, mulatto, octoroon

METOPE *consort* asopus
offspring aegina, salamis, thebe

METRIC(AL) (See also METER.) measured
beat ictus
comb. centi, deci, deka, giga, kilo, mega, micro, milli, nano, pico, tera
foot anapest, arsis, bacchius, choriamb, dacytl, dipody, iamb(us), ionic, spondee, syzygy, tribrach, trochee
length meter
mass gram
measure See MEASURE
metric.
stress ictus
unit matra, mora
volume liter
weight gram, kilogram

METRO subway, tube, underground

METRONOME *part* pendulum

METROPOLIS capital, center, complex, city, megalopolis, municipality, seat, town

METROPOLITAN archbishop, bishop, ecclesiastic, eparch, municipal, ordinary, primate, principal, urban

METTLE ardor, audacity, backbone, bravery, courage, fortitude, ginger, grit, guts, heroism, nerve, pluck, pride, resolution, sand,

spirit, spunk, temerity, tenacity, valor

METTLESOME bold, fiery, flighty, gingery, gritty, high-strung, impatient, peppery, plucky, proud, restless, skeigh, skittish, spirited, spunky

MEUSE gap, (loop)hole, maas
tributary waal

MEW(S) barn, bird, cage, cast, caterwaul, change, cob, cog, conceal, confine, coop, cry, den, enclose, garage, gull, hay(mow), meow, mia(o)u, mia(o)w, molt, retreat, seagull, shed, shut up, spicknel, stable

MEWL cry, squall, whimper

MEXICAN-AMERICAN chicano, cholo, gringo, pachuco, pinto, wetback
battle alamo, buena vista
defector agringada, malinchistra, tio taco, vendido
district barrio

MEXICAN, MEXICO (See also AZTEC.) bracero, cholo, lepero, wetback
agave century-plant, datil, mescal, zapupe
american chicano, pachuco
animal boati, cacomistle, cenepate, javelina, tayra, tejon
annuity censo
antelope pronghorn
archeological site mitla, monte alban, palenque, uxmal
asphalt chapapote
attorney coyote
avocado chinin, coyo
bakery panaderia
basket grass otate
bean frejol, frijol(e)
bedbug conenose
beer cervesa
beetle bookworm
beverage chia, damiana, margarita, mescal, octli, pulque, sotol, tepache, tequila
bird jacamar, jacana, potoo, tinamou, towhee, verdin, zopilote
blanket serape
bread pan, tortilla
bribe mordida
brigand ladrona, villa
buggy arana
bull toro
bulrush tule

cactus agave, alfilerillo, alicoche, bavoso, cacanapa, carden, chaute, chende, chichipe, cholla, echinocereus, indian fig, maguey, mescal, pitahaya, rattail, santa marta, squero
candlewood ocotillo
carriage arana
cat eyra, margay
century plant agave, mescal, tequila
check point aduana
christmas bonus aguinaldo
church bell ringer campanero
city acapulco, aguas calientas, arizpe, buena vista, cananea, colima, cuernavaca, culiacan, durango, guadalajara, guanajuato, guaymas, jalapa, juarez, leon, mazatlan, merida, mexicali, monclova, monterrey, morelia, oaxaca, obregon, orizaba, pachuca, parral, patzcuaro, potosi, puebla, puerto vallarta, saltillo, san luis potose, san miguel, tampico, taxco, tenochtitlan, tepic, ti(a)juana, tlalpan, toluca, torreon, tula, tuxtla, uxmal, veracruz, victoria, zacatecas
city center jardin, plaza
city ruins teotihuacan
city section pink zone, tacubaya
city slums vecindades
city subway metro, stc
cloak manta, narica, serape
clover coca
coat poncho
coati tejon
cockroach cucaracha
coin adobe, azteca, centavo, claco, cuarto, dinero, dollar, onza, peso, piaster, tlac(o)
communal farm ejidero(s)
conqueror alvarado, cortes, cortez
coral drops bessera
corn callo, cereal, grano, maiz, teosinte
corn on the cob elote
cottonwood alamo
cowboy charro, gaucho, vaquero
culture mazapan
dance hat dance, huapango, jarabe, macehualixtli, raspa, sandunga
defeat cerro gordo

dictator pancho villa, santa an(n)a
dish ahuatle, ajos, albondigas, atole, bunuelos, burrito, cahuama, camerone, canadero, chilaquille, chili(relleno)(verde), chimichanga, chorizo, empanada, enchilada, fly eggs, frontera, guacamole, huachinango, hueva, machacado, manacata, manacha, menuda, mixiote, mole, pollo, puchepo, quesadilla, sopapilla, steak picado, taco, tamale, taquito, tortilla, tortita de coco, tostada, tostadita, tostado
dollar peso
dove inca
drink cervesa, damiana, margarita, mescal, pulque, tepache, tequila
drug damiana, jalap, peyote
early dweller aztec, maya(n), olmec, toltec
egg nog rompope
elm mezcal, olmo
emperor augustin, maximillian
empress carlotta
estate estancia, finca rural, hacienda, latifundio
fan palm erythea
farm, communal ejido
farm laborer bracero, campesino, peon
fascist sinarquist
fern bird's-nest moss
fiber catena, civil, datil, istle, ixtle, pita, sisal
fire plant painted-leaf
fish aboma, awa, bobo, garlopa, goby, lisita, menudo, salema, totuava
flavorer adobo, chili, cilantro, jalapeno, pasilla, salsa, tomatillo
foreigner gringo
fox zorro
fruit ahuacatl, avocado, papaya, sapodilla, sapota, toranja, tuna
garment chirapa, huipel, manga, serape
general arista, cardenas, santa an(n)a
ghetto barrio
giant salmeron
goat mixiote
goby aboma de rio, emerald fish
god See AZTEC *deity.*

gopher quachil, thomoys, tucan, tuza
gourd chicayote
grapefruit toronja
grass broomroot, deer, epicampes, euchlaena, hanequin, otate, sacaton, teosinte, zacaton
greeting buenas dias, buena suerte
groundsel geranium, senecio
gruel atole
guardian spirit nagual
guavina aboma de mar
gulf tehuantepec
gulf islet cay
gulf, river to apalachicola, brazos, colorado, pearl, rio grande, suwannee
herb arracacia, aztec marigold, bird-plant, cactusdahlia, cigar-plant, crown-of-jewels, cyclobothra, marigold, ragwort, tagetes, tomatillo, tronador, tuberose
hero diaz, juarez, miguel hidalgo
historian See CORTEZ *historian.*
hog peccary
holiday cinco de mayo, fiesta
holy night noche buena, tamale night
hors d'oeuvres antojitos
house casa(de campo), jacal(ucho)
hymn alabado
immigrant bracero, wetback
independence city dolores hidalgo, queretaro
independence cry el grito
independence day cinco de mayo
indian 3 ixe, mam, mie, ova, ser 4 chol, cora, jova, maya, meco, mixe, pame, roto, seri, teca, teco, xova 5 aztec, chizo, chora, huabi, huave, jonaz, kamia, lipan, mayan, nahua, olmec, opata, otomi, pinto, seria, yakui, yaqui, zoque 6 acaxee, apache, cahita, chocho, concho, cucapa, eudeve, kiliwi, mixtec, nevome, otonia, paipai, pakawa, pueblo, toboso, toltec, zotzil 7 acolhua, akwaala, amishgo, chatino, chincha, chinipa, chontal, cotonam, couhimi, guasave, huastec, huaxtec, huichoi, kumeyal, mazatec, misteca, mixteca, nahuatl, nayarit,

sinaloa, teguima, tehuana, tehueco, tepanec, totonac, tzental, tzotzil, zacatec 8 chanabal, chaponec, chuchona, colotlan, comanito, conicari, guasapar, huasteco, hulchole, irritila, jacaltec, janamare, lacandon, lagunero, mazateca, popoloco, tarascan, tarumari, tepacano, tepehuan, tezcucan, totonaco, tzapotec, yucateco, zapoteca 9 attacapan, campesino, comecrudo, tlascalan 10 coahuiltec, cuitlateca, tarahumara 12 motozintleca

influence mordida

insect corixa, cucaracha, turicata

island san esteban, san lorenzo, tiburon

isthmus tehuantepec

ivy cobaea

lake chapala

land breeze coromell

landmark senal

land owner ranchero

land reformer zapata

laurel madrona

lava field pedregal

liquor kahlua, tequila

lizard basilisk, gila(monster), uta

masonry adobe

mat petate

measure adarme, alma, almud(e), arroba, bag, baril, caballeria, carega, carga, cuarteron, cuartillo, fanega, jarra, labor, legua, libra, linea, marco, ochaua, onza, pie, pulgada, quintal, sitio, terceo, vara

medicinal plant acapulco

medicine man curandero

migrant worker bracero, wetback

milkweed romerillo

mixed blood mestizo, saltatras

mullet agonostomus, bobo, lisita

mush atole

musical instrument cabacas, chiapanecas, clarin, maracas, quiros

musician mariachi

noah coxcox

noble tzin

nomad raramuri, tarahumara

novelist azuela

oak emory, encina, roble

octaroon albino

onyx alabaster, tecali

orange choisya, naranja

pack saddle aparejo

painter castellanos, covarrubias, orozco, rivera, siqueiros, tamayo

palmetto big thatch

pancake arepa, tortilla

papier-mache figure pinata

peak blanco, bufa, citlaltepetl, cupula, ixtaccihuatl, orizaba, perote, popocatepetl

peasant campesino

peccary javelina

peninsula baja, yucatan

people See *indian*, above.

pepper chili, jalepena

persimmon chapote

pine ayacahuite, ocote, okote, pinon

plant acapulco, agave, agrito, amole, amolilla, cardon, cassia, chaute, chia, coyotillo, datil, istle, ixtle, izote, jalap, jicama, maguey, ocotillo, pita, sabadilla, salvia, sisal, sotol, talap, tequila, yucca

plantation hacienda

poet balbuena, diaz-miron, gutierrez-najera, torresbodet

policeman chota, mordito, rurale

policemen federales

poppy argemone, chicalote

porridge atole

port acapulco, campeche, ensenada, guaymas, matamoros, mazatlan, tampico, veracruz

porter tamen

prehistoric mound cuicuilco

president aleman, alvarez, arista, avila, calles, cardenas, carranza, diaz, echevveria, el tapado, gil, huerta, juarez, lopez-mateos, lopez-portillo, madero, obregon, ordaz, portillo, santa an(n)a

proprietor ranchero

pullman accommodation alcoba

pyramid teccallis, teopanzalco, teotihuacan, tepoztlan

ranch hacienda

range sierra madre

reed otate

resin tree drago

resort acapulco, baja, can-

cun, costa de oro, guaymas, la paz, manzanillo, mazatlan, merida, mismaloya, pichilingue, puerto navidad, puerto vallarta, san blas, sayulita, teacapan, tepic, zihuatanejo

revolutionist carranza, iturbide, madero, pancho villa, santa an(n)a, zapata

rice arroz

river balsus, bravo, conchos, fuerte, gila, grande, grijalva, lerma, panuco, rio grande, salado, santiago, tabasco, tonto, yaqui

robe manga

rodent tucan

rubber tree ule

sacred book popul-vuh

saddle aparejo

sage cuauhtitlan

salamander axolotl

saloon cantina

salvia chia

sandal guaracho, huarache

sauce jalapena, salsa, salsera, tabasco

sausage chorizo

scorpion vinegarroon

seed jumping bean

shawl reboso, rebozo, serape, tapalo

shrub agarita, agrito, algerita, aliso, allthorn, amoreuxia, anagua, anama, anaqua, apache plume, arrayan, arrowwood, azafran, cachimilla, ceiba, choisya, colima, cupflower, escobeda, granjeno, guayule, karwinskia, mejorana, ocotillo, quailbush, ramona, tarbush, texas-jujube

silver center guanajuato, taxco

silver discoverer juan de rayas

silvermine mina de valenciana

skunk conepate

slave peon

slum barrio, vecindade

soap plant amole

squatter paracaidista

state aguascalientes, campeche, chiapas, chihuahua, coahuila, colima, durango, guanajuato, guerrero, hidalgo, jalisco, leon, michoacan, morelos, nayarit, nuevo leon, oaxaca, puebla, quintana, san luis potosi, sinaloa, sonora, tabasco, ta-

maulipas, tlaxcala, vera-cruz, yucatan, zacatexas
statesman calles, torres-bodet
stew pecadillo
stirrup tajoader
stirrup cover tapadera
sugar panocha, penuche
tea alpasotes, apasote, ba-sote, chenopodium, fish-weed, wormseed
temple teocalli
thong romal
throwing stick atlatl
tick turicata
titmouse verdin
tour gira
tree abeto, acxoyatl, ahue-huete, aliso, alnus, amapa, anacahuite, archipin, ar-rayan, ayacahuite, boojum, canadulce, capulin, cardon, cascalote, chacte, chaparro, cholla, cirio, cochil-sapota, colima, colorin, condakia, copalcocote, coral-bean, coyo, drago, ebano, eboe, elephant, fustic, goa-cedar, guamachil, gum, huamu-chil, logwood, madras-thorn, mahogany, man-zanilla, mezcal, ocote, okote, palto, parahancornia, pinon, pitayaya, purple haw, retama, sabino, sero, tabebuis, tamarind, ule, ul-maceae
tripe menudo
turtle cahuama, cooter
typhus tabardillo
vegetable chili, jicama, to-matillo
vest chaleco
village ejido, tecali
volcano colima, ixtaccihuatl, jorullo, jurullo, paricutin, popocatepetl, toluca, tuxtla
vulture zopilote
war battlefield palo alto
weapon maquahuit
weasel tayra
weight adarme, arroba, bag, carga, libra, marco, ochava, onza, quintal, tercio
wildcat eyra
wood ebano
worker bracero, majado, peon, wetback
yucca izote
MEYERBEER *opera* din-orah, l'africana, le pro-phete, les huguenots, ro-berto il diavolo, the prophet

MEZENTIUS *ally* turnus
slayer aeneas
son lausus
MEZEREON aquilaria, ca-mellia, daphne, shrub
MEZHACH *governor for* neb-uchadnezzar
MEZZANINE balcony, en-tresol, floor, gallery, story
MEZZO half, middle, moder-ate
MIAS orangutan
MIASMA blackdamp, choke-damp, contagion, effluvium, gas, infection, malaria, maremma, mephitis, reek, steam, stench, toxin, vapor
MIASMIC fetid, mephitic, noxious, pestilential, poi-sonous, toxic, venomous
MIBSAM *kin* ishmael
MICA alurgite, anomite, as-tite, biotite, cat-silver, da-mourite, daze, diorite, fuch-site, glimmer, glist, isin-glass, lepidolite, muscovite, nacrite, paragonite, phlogo-pite, roscoelite, silicate, slude, talc
aggregate book
son ozias
trap minette
MICAH *father* uzziel
son abdon, ahaz, melech, pithon, tahrea
MICHAEL michel, micky, miguel, mike
father jehoshaphat, saul
son zaraeas
symbol scales
MICHAELMAS *daisy* aster
blackbird ring-ouzel
spring indian summer
MICHAIAH *father* zaccur
son mattaniah
MICHAL *consort* david, phalti
parent ahinoam, saul
MICHE hide, skulk, sneak
MICHELANGELO *work* david, pieta, sistine chapel
last name buonarroti
MICHER pander, sneak, thief, truant
MICHIGAN *airport* willow run
bay keweenaw, saginaw, sturgeon, thunder
capital lansing
city adrian, alpena, ann arbor, bad axe, battle creek, bay city, benton harbor, birmingham, cadillac, caro, cheboygan, dearborn, de-

troit, escanaba, flint, grand rapids, hillsdale, jackson, kalamazoo, lansing, manis-tee, midland, monroe, mus-kegon, niles, owosso, pe-toskey, pontiac, port huron, river rouge, roseville, royal oak, saginaw, trenton, troy, warren, wassar, wayne, wyandotte, wyoming
college adrian, albion, alma, calvin, hillsdale, oakland, olivet, owosso, wayne
county alcona, ionia, iosco, kalkaska, osceola, tuscola
indian ottawa, potawatomi
island mackinaw
lake austin, bawbees, burt, clear, devils, erie, hough-ton, moline, round, st clair, torch
motto i will defend, tuebor
native wolverine
nickname wolverine state
peak porcupine
port bay city, manitowoc
river cass, detroit, escanaba, huron, saginaw, st clair, st marys
state bird robin
state flower apple blossom
strait mackinaw
tree white pine
MICKEY knockout, potato
MICKLE big, great, large, many, much, size
MICO callithrix, marmoset
MICOMICON utopia
MICONIA camacey, goose-berry, plant, tamonea
MICROBE bacillus, bac-terium, bug, germ, microor-ganism, organism, patho-gen, speck, virus
absence asepsis
MICROBIC amoebic, bac-terial, embryonic, germinal, incipient, microzoic, rudi-mental, rudimentary
MICROCOSM atom, bit, body, cell, community, man, miniature, monad, town, village, world
MICROLINE amazonite, an-orthoclase, feldspar
MICROMORPH See DWARF.
MICRONESIA *islands* bikini, carolines, ellice, gilbert, guam, kwajalein, majuro, makin, marianas, marshalls, nauru, nui, ponape, rota, saipan, truk, wake, wotho, yap

drug sakau
greeting kaselehlia
native kanaga, nauruan
MICROORGANISM amoeba, animalcule, arthrospor, azofier, bacillus, bacteria, butyric, diatom, dyad, entozoa, foraminifer, germ, gonidium, gregarine, infusoria, mastigopod, microbe, microphyte, microspore, microzoa, monad, moner(on), paramecium, phytozoa, protozoa, rhizopod, rotifer, schizomycete, tetrad, triad, virus, zoospore, zygote
MICROPERDIX bush-quail, perdicula, turnix
MICROPHONE transmitter
hidden bug
shield gobo
MICROSCOPE *measuring*
lens aperometer
part camera lucida, condenser, eyepiece, lens, mirror, nosepiece, stage, tube
reflecting engyscope
MICROSCOPIC fine, infinitesimal, little, miniature, minute, petite, small, teeny, tiny, wee(ny)
MICROTIS campagnol, vole
MICROWAVE *amplifier*
maser
MID between, middle
point basion, gnathion, porion, stomion
-victorian antiquated, bourgeois, hidebound, illiberal, oldster
MIDAS leontocebus
benefactor dionysus
kingdom phrygia
misfortune ass's ears
parent cybele, gordius
river pactolus
son lityerses
touch philosopher's stone
MIDBRAIN mesencephalon
MIDDAY noon(tide)(time)
intermission lunch, noon hour, nooning
pert. meridian
MIDDEN basurale, dunghill, fragment, refuse, sherd
MIDDLE amidship, atween, between, bisection, center, central, centroid, centrum, centry, core, diameter, equator(ial), equidistant, focus, halfway, heart, hub, interior, intermediary, intermediate, intervening, mean,

medial, median, mediating, mediterranean, medium, mes(i)al, mesne, mezzo, midland, midriff, midst, omphalos, waist(line)
ages moyen age
ages, pert. medieval
buster lister
class bourgeoisie
-class man babbitt, bourgeois
comb. medi, mes(o)
course compromise, fifty-fifty, golden mean, half-measure, halfway, medium, midway, moderation, via media
ear tympanum
earth midgard
east See LEVANT.
english poem pearl
march character garth
of the road center, moderation
principles axiomata media
-rate mediocre
-splitter lister
toward centrad, mes(i)ad
way See *course*, above.
MIDDLEMAN agent, broker, bumaree, butty, dealer, go-between, huckster, interlocutor, intermediary, jobber, licensee, retailer, salesman, trader
MIDDLING average, decent, fair, indifferent, intermediate, mean, mediocre, moderate(ly), ordinary, passable, poor, rather, second-rate, so-so, tolerably
comb. mes(o)
MIDDLINGS betweens, dunst, feed, semolina, shorts
MIDDY blouse, cadet, midshipman
MIDEA *consort* electryon
offspring licymnius
MIDGARD mithgarth(r)
bridge bifrost
neighboring land asgard
origin ymir
serpent jormungandr
serpent's parent angerboda, loki
serpent's slayer thor
serpent's victim thor
MIDGE bit, dwarf, fish, fly, gnat, hackney, punkie, speck, stout
MIDGET dandiprat, dwarf, homunculus, manikin, peewee, pygmy, runt, shrimp
MIDIAN *king* evi, hur, reba, zalmunna, zebah, zur

parent abraham, keturah
prince oreb
son abida(h), eldaah, ephah, epher, hanoch, henoch
MIDLOTHIAN edinburgh
MIDMOST central, intimate
comb. mesati, meso
MIDNIGHT bull's noon, witching hour
MIDRIB costa, midwein, shaft
MIDRIFF apron, diaphragm, middle, partition, septum, skirt
MIDSHIPMAN cadet, middy, oldster, plebe, reefer, smottie, snotty, toadfish, wart
MIDST burden, MIDDLE, setting, surrounding, thick
MIDSUMMER *day* johnsmas
men live-long, orpine, sedum, stonecrop
MIDSUMMER NIGHT'S DREAM *character* bottom, cobweb, demetrius, egeus, flute, helena, hermia, hippolyta, lysander, moth, mustardseed, oberon, peaseblossom, philostrate, puck, quince, robin goodfellow, snout, snug, starveling, theseus, thisbe, titania
fairy puck
hero demetrius
heroine helena
MIDWAY carnival, fair, gayway, halfway, mediating, medio, medium, moderate
MIDWEST *indian* chippewa, fox, illinois, kaskasia, kickapoo, menominee, miami, munsee, omaha, oneida, osage, peoria, piankashaw, potawatomi, sauk, wea, winnebago
MIDWIFE accoucheuse, baba, cummer, dhai, dholl, gamp, gracewife, granny, hebamme, howdie, howdy, kimmer, lucina, luckie, nurse, obstetrician, obstetrix, partera
MIDWIFERY obstetrics
MIDWISE moderately
MIELIKKI *husband* tapio
MIEN air, aspect, bearing, behavior, brow, carriage, countenance, demeanor, deportment, front, guise, look, manner, ostent, poise, port, pose, position, presence, semblance, way
expressionless poker face

MIFF aggravate, anger, displease, dudgeon, fight, offend, pet, provoke, put out, quarrel, take offense, tiff, wither

MIFFED, MIFFY hurt, sensitive, touchy

MIG agate, duck, manure, marble, plane

MIGHT ability, arm, bulk, capability, efficacy, energy, force, intensity, lustiness, may, potency, power, puissance, quantity, strength, vigor, vim
-be possibility

MIGHTY able, athletic, authoritative, big, bold, efficacious, enormous, extensive, extremely, fell, great, huge, immense, important, influential, intense, momentous, monumental, omnipotent, potent, powerful, prodigious, puissant, remarkable, robust, samsonic, sizable, strong, stupendous, sturdy, tremendous, valiant, vast, very, vigorous, violent, wonderful
in war armipotent, bellipotent
in war, name meaning ptolemy
like similar

MIGNON dainty, delicate, graceful, petite, pretty, small
beloved wilhelm

MIGNONETTE flower, green, lace, luteola, reseda, weld, wo(a)ld, would
green reseda
tree henna
vine madeira, madia, tarweed

MIGNONITIS aphrodite

MIGRAINE ache, cephalgia, headache, hemicrania, megrim

MIGRANT emigree, evacuee, expatriate, migrator, mover, trekker, vackie
worker arkie, bracero, okie, wetback

MIGRATE colonize, flit, move, resettle, run, transfer, treck

MIGRATION diaspora, exodus, flight, hadj, passage, pilgrimage, run, swarm(ing), tour, travel, trek

MIGRATORY gypsy, no-

mad(ic), roving, strolling, vagabond, vagrant, wandering

MIHRAB chamber, niche, slab

MIKADO dairi, emperor, ruler, sovereign, tenno
character katisha, koko, nankipoo, poohbah, yumyum
composer gilbert, sullivan
court dairi, dari
executioner koko
office mikadoate

MIKE gobo, loaf(ing), loiter, michael, mick, microphone, speaker, transmitter

MIL thousand

MILAN *coin* ambrosin
museum brera
old name mediolanum
opera la scala
ruling family sforza, visconti

MILCAH *husband* nahor
kin haran, huz, rebekah

MILD affable, amiable, assuasive, balmy, benign, bland, calm, clement, compassionate, complacent, considerate, delicate, easy(going), forbearing, genial, gentle, gracious, humane, indulgent, insipid, kind(ly), lenient, meek, melch, merciful, milky, moderate, mollifying, moy, naish, pacific, patient, placid, pleasant, quiet, serene, shy, smooth, soft, soothing, suave, submissive, summery, tame, temperate, tender, tolerant, tranquil, unassuming, vapid, warm
as milk, moses

MILDEW blight, decay, fungus, mo(u)ld, must, odium, rot
downy bremia, phycomycetes
genus erysibe, erysiphe, peronospora, plasmopara, podosphaera, sphaerotheca
powdery erysiphe

MILDNESS amiability, clemency, compassion, favor, humanity, indulgence, leniency, lenity, mercy, moderation, quarter, tolerance, toleration

MILE *1 to 3* coss
3 league
19.2 trillion parsec
-high city denver
nautical kairi, knot, naut

part block, foot, furlong, pole, rod, verst, yard

MILEAH *son* buz

MILED *son* eber, ith

MILEPOST marker, stela, stele

MILESTONE essential, event, landmark, league, marker, mil(l)iarium, occasion, waypost

MILETUS *offspring* byblis, caunus
parent apollo, aria, delone

MILFOIL achillea, ahartalav, bloodwort, herb, plant, yarrow

MILIEU ambience, background, climate, element, environ(ment)(s), medium, mise-en-scene, purlieu, setting, sphere, surroundings, terrain

MILITANT aggressive, antagonistic, assertive, bellicose, belligerent, combative, contending, contentious, edgy, extremist, fighter, martial, opposing, pugnacious, pushing, soldier, warlike, warring, warrish

MILITARISM boulangism, jingoism, prussianism, warmongering

MILITARIST chauvin(ist), jingo(ist), rajput, warlover, warmonger

MILITARISTIC belligerent, chauvinistic, jingoish, jingoist(ic)

MILITARY (See also ARMY.) martial, militia, soldiery, troops, war-like
academy annapolis, ground school, royal naval college, sandhurst, st cyr, west point, woolwich
advance See *drive*, below.
adventurer filibuster
alliance cento, nato, seato
area sector
array fyrd(ung)
assistant adjutant, aide
barracks casern(e)
base barracks, billets, camp, depot, encampment, field, quarters, stockade
braid a(i)glet, aiguillette
cloak sagum
coat buff(y)
command about face, achtung, at ease, attention, halt
commission brevet
company decury, peloton, venlin, vexillum, watch

compulsory service draft, selective service, sss

decoration blue max, croix de guerre, cross of merit, dfc, distinguished conduct medal, distinguished flying cross, distinguished service cross, distinguished service medal, dsc, dsm, dso, fourragere, iron cross, medaille militaire, medal for valor, medal of french recognition, medal of honor, military cross, navy cross, purple heart, silver star, victoria cross

draft compulsory service, selective service, sss

drive advance, anabasis, big push, breakthrough, penetration

drumbeat berloque, breloque

engine See ENGINE *war.*

entertainment tattoo

equipment arsenal, materiel

expedition anabasis, crusade, harka, katabasis, warpath

force army, array, corps, fleet, guard, legion, navy, reserve, troops

formation block, echelon, file, line

hat busby, helmet, kepi, shako

hat covering havelock

horsemen cavalry, cossacks, hussars

informer spy

inspection drill, parade, review

jacket buffcoat, eisenhower, shell

landing point beachhead

lodging See *quarters,* below.

machine basilisk, camion, jeep, tank

man See SOLDIER.

maneuver tactic

mine fougade, fougasse

obstruction abat(t)is

operations campaign, strategy

order command

pit trou-de-loup

police constabulary, gendarmes, mp's, shore patrol

post thana

quarters barracks, billets, camp, casern(e), garrison, presidio

road agger

salute salvo

science logistics

signal chamade

storehouse arsenal, etape

toehold airhead, beachhead

training, universal draft

unit artillery, auxiliary, beefeaters, bugle corps, cavalry, cohort, coldstream guards, column, commandos, detachment, detail, file, foot, gendarmes, grenadiers, ground troops, gunners, home defense, horse guards, infantry, landwehr, militia, minutemen, national guard, regulars, reserves, rifles, sabaoth, shock troops, signal corps, storm troops, wa(a)c, waaf, wam, wasp, wave, wrac, wraf, wren

volunteer force foreign legion

MILITATE conflict, contend, debate, fight, make (for), operate, tell

against contest, counteract

MILITIA array, fyrd, milice, national guard, reserves, soldiery, troops, warfare

-man See SOLDIER.

MILIUM grass, millet, nodule

MILK beverage, bleed, clabber, drain, draw(out), drink, elicit, exhaust, exploit, extract, fluid, food, lac, lait, latex, leban, leben, manipulate, milch, mulct, nurse, rammel, secretion, skyr, strip, suckle, tayir, tyre, white

and honey fertility, prosperity

-and-water flat, indifferent, insipid, pap, silly, weak, wishywashy

and wine sillabub, sillibub, syllabub

breast diddy, suck

bush rauwolfia, shrub, wrightia

cart bungey, kit, pram

clabbered slip-cheese

coagulated curd

coagulator rennet

comb. lact(i)(o)

cow's mess

crust eczema

curd casein, cheese, tayir, tyre, zeiga

curdled clabber, lopper, skyr, tatmjolk, tayer, tyre, yogh(o)urt, yog(o)urt

curdler rennet, rennin, ruen

deodorizer aerator

derived from lactic

drink (See also *fermented,* below.) cocoa, malt, shake

duct galactophore

fat butter

fat measurer butyrometer

fermented airan, kefir, kisselo, k(o)umys, koumiss, kumiss, lacto, matzoon, mleko, yog(h)urt

fever cerebral anemia

first beastings, beestings, biestings, colostrum

-fish anged, awa, bandeng, bangos, chanos, sabalo(te), savola

float bungey

fluid plasma

food lacticinia

formation galactopoiesis

gland udder

glass opaline

hot saloop

leg phlegmasia alba dolens, weed

-like lactiform

mouse spurge

new rammel

of almonds amygdalate

of human kindness compassion, sympathy

of the aged claret, red wine

out drain, emulge

pail bowie, eshin, kit, leglen, soa, soe, trug

part casein, lactose, plasma, serum, whey

pert. (See also MILKY.) lactary, lacteal, lactic

plant creamery, creeper, euphorbia

preparation lactarene, lactarine

protein casein(ogen)

raw rammel

sap latex

secretion of lactation

separator creamer

shake float, frappe

shop creamery, dairy, lactarium

sickness alkali disease, slows, tires, trembles

sickness plant snakeroot

skimmed lanital

-snake kingsnake, spotted adder

-sop See *-toast,* below.

sour bleeze, blinky, bonnyclabber, curd, jocoque, skyr, whey, whig

stone galactite

strainer milsey, milsie
sugar lactose
test babcock
-toast ineffectual, mild, namby-pamby, spineless, timid soul, wishy-washy
vetch astragalus, bird-egg pea, homalabus, phaca
watery blash, blue john
watery part whey
whey serum
MILKLESS agalactia, barren, eild, par(e)ve, yeld
MILKMAID bindweed, cuckooflower, holly, oxlip, trefoil
MILKMAN chalker, dairyman, vendor
MILKSOP cockney, cotquean, coward, drip, effeminate, milquetoast, molly(coddle), sissy, weakling
MILKWEED acerates, araujia, asclepias, butterflyweed, chervil, dogbane, hoya, lactuca, periploca, romerillo, sandvine, secamone, sow thistle, spurge, stapelia, swallowwort
butterfly monarch
down silk
fluid latex
tuft coma
MILKWOOD melkhout, paperbark
MILKWORT babies-feet, bachelor's button, bird-on-the-wing, campanula, centaury, crossflower, gangflower, gaywings, polygala, rogation, senega
MILKY adularescent, chalky, effeminate, filmy, frosted, galactic, gentle, lacteal, lacteous, lactescent, lactic, lactiferous, meek, mild, namby-pamby obscure, opalescent, opaline, opaloid, pearly, soft, spawning, spiritless, tame, timid, timorous, white, wishy-washy
become lactesce
mangrove blind-your-eyes
way galaxy, nebula, via lactea
way, black space coalsack
way, constellation monoceros
way, pert. galactic
MILL arrastra, awe, beat, bloomer, box, clow, comminute, create, crush(er), factory, fight, game, grater,

grind(er)(stone), knurl, machine, molinet, morelles, muhle, nine men's morris, notch, nurl, plant, press, pulverize, quern, roller, seethe, shape, shop, smutter, snuffbox, spinnery, steal, thrash, trapiche, vanquish
adjunct stream
around seethe
beetle cockroach
bill adz
clapper chatterbox
course millrace
dam weir
-end remnant
-foil ahartalav
hand cropman
pert. molinary
pond atlantic, binnacle, binocle, dam, dike, ditch, ocean, sea
primitive quern
run average, common, flow, ordinary
sail vane
stream fleam
wheel part awe, lade
worker batterman, dogger
MILLENNIUM chiliad, good times, PARADISE, UTOPIA
MILLEPEDE chilognatha, diplopod, galleyworm, myriapod, pillbug, woodlouse
MILLER baker, boxer, eagleray, flycatcher, harrier, millward, moth, multurer, pugilist, white-throat
dusty auricula, bear's-ear, centauria, corncockle, mullein pink, rose campion, wormwood
thumb bird, blob, bullhead, cabot, chabot, cott(o)id, cottus, fish, goldcrest, muddler, titmouse, warbler
MILLET arzun, bajra, bajree, birdseed, buda, cenchrine, cereal, chena, cumbu, dagassa, dhoor, dhurra, dukhn, durr(a), emu, grain, grass, hirse, hureek, joar, jond(r)a, jowar(i), juar, kadikane, koda, kodra, kous, milium, milly, moha(r), panicle, panicum, proso, tenai, whisk, zaburro
broom-corn hirse, kadikane
painting the angelus, the gleaners
pearl bajra, bajree, bajri

pert. miliary
seed drink bosa, boza(h)
shama cocksfoot
MILLIMETER 1/1000th micron
MILLION conto, fortune, many, multitude, pile, quent
comb. meg(a)
elephants, land of laos
millions trega, trillion
10 crore
1000 billion, milliard
MILLIONAIRE capitalist, croesus, dives, magnate, midas, nabob
MILLIPEDE diplopod, julid, pillworm, polypod, ringworm, wireworm
MLLISECOND sigma
MILLITHRUM titmouse
MILLRACE binnacle, binocle, flow, forebay, lade, lead, leat, tailrace
MILLRIND moline
MILLS *bomb* grenade
MILLSTONE affliction, albatross, bedder, buhr(stone), burr(stone), cumber, grinder, impediment, ledger, load, pulverizer
bar rynd
depression bosom
designation nether, upper
socket cockeye
support rind, rynd
MILPA ladang
MILQUETOAST, CASPAR the timid soul
creator webster
traits See MILK-*toast.*
MILREIS *1000* conto
MILT spleen
MILTON, JOHN *prince of darkness* belial
rebel angel ariel
work areopagitica, comus, il penseroso, l'allegro, lycidas, paradise lost, paradise regained, samson agonistes
MILVAGO caracara, chimachima, chimango, hawk
MIM demure, modest, prim, quiet, shy
MIMAS *companion* aeneas
moon of saturn
parent amycus, theano
slayer ares, hercules, mezentius
MIME act(or), ape(r), buffoon, clown, copy, drama, farce, imitate, imitator, impersonator, jester, marceau, mimic, mummer, play(er), trouper

helper of siegfried
smith to nebelung
MIMESIS imitation, mimicry
MIMETITE campylite
MIMI *beloved* rodolfo
MIMIC ape(r), copy(cat), counterfeit, feign, hit off, imitate, imitator, impersonate, mime(tic), mock(er), monkey, parrot, pretend, pseudo, quasi, sham, simulate, take off
thrush mockingbird
MIMICRY apery, apism, burlesque, camouflage, echo, imitation, mimesis, parrotry, trick
MIMIR *abode* jotunnheim
decapitator vanir
reared sigurd
recipient of head odin
sword miming
MIMOSA acacia, acuan, albizzia, aroma, cassie, cat's-claw, desmanthus, gama, huisache, inga, sensitive-plant, siris, tree, turmeric, wattle-bark, yellow
MIMUSOPS baku, balata, bully-tree, sapodilla
MIN bethink, man, memory, mention, prince, remember, remembrance, remind, ruler
MINA coin, maneh, money, myna, watchman, weight
MINACIOUS menacing, minatory, threatening
MINAEAN *sun god* athtar
MINAHASSA celebes
MINARET spire, steeple, tower, turret
MINCE affect, blanquette, bridle, chop, cube, cut, dice, diminish, extenuate, hash, lessen, minimize, pace, pie, pose, prink, ragout, restrain, sashay, shred, simper, slash, smirk, tiptoe, walk
MINCEMEAT gigot
MINCING finical, migniard, minikin, niminy, skipjack
MIND animus, attend, bent, beware, brain(s), care(for), chit, complain, desire, faculty, gray matter, hear, heed, impulse, inclination, intellect, intelligence, intend, intent(ion), listen, memory, mens, mention, mood, note, notice, nous, obey, object, observe, opinion, psyche, reason, recall, reck, recollection, regard,

remember, remembrance, sense, soul, souvenir, spirit, tend(ancy), think, watch, will, wisdom, wish, wit(s)
closed bigotry
comb. menti, noo, psych(o)
conscious sentient
cure psychotherapy
elevation anagogue
keep in entertain, remember
of one accordant, agreed, unanimous
open tolerance
origin and development psychogenesis
peace of ataraxia
pert. mental, noetic, phrenic, psychological
reading esp, telepathy
-set obstinate, stubborn
split schizophrenic
state of mood, morale, temper, tune
wandering evagation
MINDANAO See PHILIPPINES.
MINDED biased, disposed, inclined, partial, predisposed, prone, recollecting, remembering, willing
MINDFUL alert, attentive, aware, careful, considerate, heedful, heedly, observant, regardful, solicitous
MINDLESS careless, heedless, inattentive, indifferent, mad, stupid, stupified, unintelligent
MINE amoi, bal, bank, bargh, blow up, bomb, bonanza, burrow, caisson, camouflet, cavity, chimney, colliery, delf, deposit, dig(gings), dike, eldorado, entrenchment, excavate, excavation, explosive, fortify, gallery, gangue, golconda, gopher, lode, matrix, meum, mineral, ore, pan, pay dirt, pit, placer (deposit), prospect, quarry, resue, rib, ruin, sap, shaft, shoot, source, stock, stope, store, vein, wheal, workings
air passage brattice, brattishing
anti-personnel button
area washery
basket corf
boss shifter, shiftman
bucket kibble
car barney, buggy, giraffe, gunboat, larry, lorry, skip, tram

cavity bag
ceiling astel, nog
coal colliery, pit, rob
crossbar stempel, stemple
deposit lode, nest, placer, vein
disease See MINER *disease.*
engine barney
entrance adit, footrill, pithead, portal, stopping, stulm
equipment sinking pump
excavation spale, stope
explosive acoustic, aerial, anti-personnel, booby trap, contact, fougade, fougasse, grisounite, grisoutine, ground, land, magnetic, oyster, pressure, sonic, submarine
fire gas afterdamp
floor sill
gallery bord, brow, slovan
goblin knocker
god trolis
gold homestead
guardian gnome
military See *explosive, above.*
old gwag
open loggia
partition sollar, soller
passage adit, airway, brattice, drift, drive, head, level, roof, run, shaft, sill, slant, slum, stenton, stope, stulm, undercast, winze
passage corner arrage
prop nog, sprag, stull
pump rod spear
railroad coalroad
refuse attle, goaf, gob, slag, tailings
reservoir standage, sump
rich bonanza, golconda, jack pot, lode
rock-breaker alligator
roof support astel, cog, nog
-run average, common, ordinary, unassorted
shack coe
shaft groove, gruff, heuch, heugh, incline, pit, slope, staple, winning
shaft drain sump
shaft opening eye
shaft platform angleset, sollar, soller
shaft step stempel, stemple
sifter lue
support sollar, soller
surface placer
surveyor dialer
sweeper algerine, paravane
tender trapper

thrower minenwerfer, minnie
timber browpiece, pitwood,
stull
trough buddle
tub corf
tunnel See *passage,* above.
underground hypogee, hypogeum
unproductive borasca, shicer
unsystematically gopher
vein lode
wagon rolley, tram
wall astel
worker See MINER.

MINER argonaut, bal, barer,
butty, byeman, cageman,
cager, canary, collier, crut-
ter, dammer, desert rat,
digger, doggie, drawman,
excavator, forty-niner,
geordie, hagger, hutcher,
leadman, onsetter, panner,
pickman, prospector,
sapper, snubber, sourdough,
stripper, trapper, winzeman
basket corf, dan
court barmote
disease ancylostomiasis,
anthracosis, black lung, collier's lung, phthisis
judge barmaster
lamp davy, geordie
nail brad, spad
pickaxe bede, flang, mandrel
rope loop slug
shovel banjo
surveying instrument dial
tool gad
worm hookworm

MINERAL inorganic,
METAL, ore, rock, vein
adamantine diamond
aggregate ballas, saussurite
alkaline trona
amorphous pinite
apatite wilkeite
black allanite, cerine, coal,
coffinite, euxenite, geet,
grahamite, graphite, hematite, hielmite, ilmenite, irite,
jet, keilhauite, knopite, min-
guetite, niobite, onofrite,
polybasite, riebeckite, tanta-
lite, tennantite, thorianite,
thorite, tourmalin(e), uranite, wad, yenite
blue beryl, cordierite, covellite, cyanite, iolite, turquoise
blue-gray galena
brass-yellow pyrite
bright blende
brittle euclase, seybarite

brown cerine, egeran, elaterite, guildite, jarosite, lederite, paco, pitticite,
pyrochlore, rutile
carbonate ankerite, calcite,
chalk
cerium koppite
chlorite clinochlore,
griffithite, moravite, pen-
ninite
clay-like almerite, mont-
morillonite
coke carbonite
comb. ite, lite, lyte
common quartz
conglomerate banket
crystalline anglesite, apatite,
azurite, balljasper, boracite,
calcite, diamond, dolomite,
elaterin, feldspar, felsik,
felspath, galena, garnet,
knopite, mica, pyrite,
quartz, spar, topaz, yenite
deposit carbona, flat, gulf,
lode, nest, placer, sinter,
vein
deposit cavity voog, vug(g),
vugh
earth-like glebe
enclosing another perimorph
epidote withamite
explosive exrasite
fibrous asbestos, carpholie,
oakenite
finding device doodlebug
flaky mica
flesh-colored sarcoline
formation dendrite, geode
gem tourmaline
glassy mica, quartz
gray chromium, crookesite,
edenite, forbesite, franc-
keite, frieseite, hopeite,
pyrosmalite, smaltite, tetrahedrite, trona
green alalite, amesite, annabergite, apatite, baikalite,
demantoid, erinite, gahnite,
ilesite, libethenite, malachite, pimelite, prasine,
prehnite, slavikite, smarag-
dite, smectite, torbernite,
uralian, uralite
gunpowder niter
hard adamant, alalite, corundum, diamond, ruby, spinel
hardness scale mohs
jelly vaseline
kind actinolite, absolite, calcite, cawk, coal, danalite,
furnacite, jamesonite, nose-
lite, pimelite, quartz, spalt,
spar, talc, ulexite, uranite,

urao, wadd, witherite, wulfenite, ziolite
liquid mercury, water
lustrous blende, chalcocite,
gieseckite, glance, rutile,
smaltine, smaltite, spar, tetrahedrite
magnetic jacobsite, lodestone
medical pharmacite
micaceous biotite, chlorite,
muscovite, pyrophyllite,
torbernite, vermiculite
mixture magma
monoclinic pearceite, pectolite, pharmacolite
native ore
non-combustible asbestos,
mica
non-metallic boron, gangue,
iodine, spar
oil See OIL *mineral.*
olivine monticellite
orange sandix
organic asphalt, coal, tar
pitch alchitran, asphalt(um),
bitumen, tar
pyroelectric boracite
quartzlike opal
radiated asteoite
radio-active clarkelite, curite
rare alabandite, amalgum,
barylite, cymrite, dechenite,
erbium, euclase, gaylussite,
seamanite, sinhalite, spur-
rite, thorite, tychite
red balas, balljasper, fluo-
cerite, friedelite, garnet,
kottigite, rhodochrosite,
rhodonite, rutile, zincite
resinous amber, opal
salt alum
scale mohs
scapolite wernerite
seam vein
sectile argentite
silicate allanite, babingtonite,
mica
silver-white calaverite, wol-
fachite
soft gypsum, kernes, mica,
salt, talc
spot macle
spring aqua, bath, spa, well
sulfate langite
tallow harchettine
tar asphalt, brea, maltha,
pitch
transparent crystal, fluor,
mica, pollux, quartz, sanidine, sodalite
vermiculite philadelphite
vitreous apatite, phenacite,
quartz, spar

water evian, pullna, seltzer, vichy

wax baikerite, ozocerite, petrostearin

white barite, chalk, howlite, silver, smaltine, smaltite, spalt, stilbite, talc, trona, urao

yellow balljasper, carnotite, dimorphite, ecdemite, epidote, helvite, iron, lagonite, monimolite, pyrite(s), sulfur, sulphur, topaz

zeolite gonnardite, phillipsite, thomsonite

MINERVA (See ATHENA.) azalea, cardinal, menfra, rhododendron, wisdom

feast quinquatrus

MINESTRONE See SOUP.

MING mention, recount, remember, remind

capital nanking, peking

MINGLE admix, amalgamate, associate, blend, card, coalesce, combine, commix, compound, concentrate, concoct, confound, confuse, conjoin, connect, consolidate, felter, fraternize, fuse, hobnob, huddle, integrate, intermix, join, medly, meld, merge, mix-(ture), pool, stir, unify, unite, weave

-mangle hodgepodge, medley, mixture

MINGWORT wormwood

MINGY mean, stingy, tight

MINIATE decorate, illuminate, paint, rubricate

MINIATURE baby, diminutive, doll, dwarf(ish), elzevir, image, little, microcosmo(os), midget, minikin, minny, minute, petite, pocket, portrait, puppet, reduce, rubrication, small, teeny, tiny, toy, wee(ny)

MINIFY decrease, lessen

MINIKIN affected, baize, dainty, darling, delicate, diminutive, dwarf, elegant, favorite, mincing, miniature, minion, shrill, small, tiny, treble

MINIM ant, bit, dash, drop, friar, gutta, halfnote, halfrest, jot, minnow, minute, mite, smallest, speck, tittle, whit

MINIMAL least, smallest

MINIMIZE belittle, cheapen, decrease, decry, depreciate,

derogate, detract from, disparage

MINIMUM jot, least, lowest, nadir, slightest, smallest, tittle

MINING (See also MINE, MINER.) grooving, spatter

bed division cleave

chair dog

chute pass, telegraph

fault check, coup, hitch, leap

gutter bottom, hassing

joint cleat, sline

patron saint barbara

tool gad, pick, trepan

MINION creature, dainty, dependent, favorite, follower, hanger-on, henchman, idol, myrmidon, parasite, servant, subordinate, vassal

MINISTER aid, ambassador, angel, atabeg, attend, care(for), cater(to), clergyman, cleric, curage, deacon, deputy, dewan, diplomat, dominie, ecclesiastic, elder, envoy, executive, father, foster, furnish, gallah, haman, help, legate, nuncio, nurse, officer, officiate, padre, palatine, parson, pastor, peshkar, peshwa, plenipotentiary, preacher, prefect, premier, priest, secretary, serve, succor, tend, treat, vizi(e)r

home consulate, embassy, manse, parsonage

prime taoiseach

MINISTRY agency, aid, bureaucracy, cabinet, clergy, department, office, service

MINIUM red, vermillion

MINIVER ermine, fur, vair

MINK animal, ermine, fur, huron, jackdash, kojah, kolinsky, lutreola, mustela, sable, vison

-fish drum

MINNEHAHA *husband* hiawatha

MINNESINGER bard, jongleur, minstrel, musician, poet, rhymer, scald, scop, troubadour, trouvere, vocalist

MINNESOTA *capital* st paul

city ada, albertlea, austin, babbitt, bemidji, bloomington, blue earth, brainerd, duluth, edina, ely, fosston, hibbing, mankato, minneapolis, minnetonka, moorhead, mora, richfield, rob-

binsdale, rochester, st cloud, st paul, winona

college augsburg, bemidji, bethel, carleton, hamline, macalester, st olaf, winona

county anoka, hennepin, isanti, roseau, wabasha, waseca

flower lady's-slipper, moccasin flower

indian chippewa, dakota, menominee, ojibwa, santee, sioux

iron range cuyuna, mesabi, vermilion

lake bemidji, itasca, leech, minnewaska, red, superior, winniboshish

native gopher

nickname gopher, north star state

peak eagle, misquah

range cuyuna, mesabi, misquah

river desmoines, rainy, st croix

river, city on mankato

state bird loon

state flower moccasin

state tree (norway)(red) pine

MINNOW baggie, bonytail, cyprinid, diminutive, dogfish, fathead, fish, gambusia, gularis, guppy, hitch, inanga, killifish, menise, mennom, minim, moonfish, penk, phantom, pinhead, pinkeen, redfin, satinfin, silverfin, splittail, squawfish, stickleback

MINOAN *capital* cnossos, knossos

native cretan

pottery kamares

site phaistos

MINOR accessory, adolescent, boy, child, friar, girl, infant, inferior, junior, less(er), lower, petty, secondary, second-string, small(er), subordinate, subsidiary, teen-ager, teener, trivial, under age, unimportant, youth

details trivia

MINORATE curtail, diminish, lessen

MINORCA *port* mahound

MINORITY few, immaturity, infancy, nonage, pupilage, teens

MINOS *brother* rhadamanthys, sarpedon
builder daedalus
consort britomartis, paria, pasiphae, scylla
construction labyrinth
grandson alcaeus
kingdom crete
monster minotaur
offspring androgeus, ariadne, catreus, creteus, deucalion, phaedra
parent europa, jupiter, lycastus, zeus
slayer cocalus
stepfather asterius
victim scylla
MINOTAUR asterius
home labyrinth
owner minos
parent bull, pasiphae
slayer theseus
MINSTER cathedral, chadband, church, monastery
MINSTREL badchan, badhan, balladier, ballad singer, bard, bhat, entertainer, gleeman, harper, harpist, interlocutor, jongleur, moke, musician, pardhan, pierrot, poet, rhapsodist, rhymester, rimer, scald, scop, serenader, singer, skald, songman, tambo(urine), troubadour, trouvere
border walter scott
show performer bones, endman
society areoi, arioi
13th century goliard
MINT (See also *genus*, below.) address, aim, ajuga, albahaca, allheal, ballota, balm, balsam, basil, bergamot, blephilia, blow, bonanza, bugle, candy, catnip, chia, clare, clar(r)y, coin, counterfeit, dittany, fabricate, feign, feint, fine, forge, form, fortune, fresh, herb, hint, horehound, horseweed, hyssop, insinuate, intend, invent, ironwort, issue, labiate, lampwick, lavender, make, marjoram, menthol, money, nana, olitory, oregano, original, penny-royal, perilla, phlomis, pile, plant, potherb, produce, purpose, sage(leaf), savory, selfheal, sideritis, source, stachys,

stamp, storehouse, suggest, think, thyme, unmarred, unused, venture
camphor menthol
family balm, basil, calamint, hyssop, lamiaceae
genus agastache, anisomeles, ballota, bettonica, blephilia, coleus, collinsonia, marrubium, melissa, mentha, micromeria, monarda, nepeta, perilla, phlomis, ramona, rosemarinus, scutellaria, thymus
geranium costmary
levy brassage, seigniorage
liqueur creme de menthe
medicinal bengal-sage
MINTHE *lover* hades
MINUET basse danse, dance, scherzo
MINUS absent, bereft, concave, deduct(ion), deficiency, deprived, lack(ing), less, loss, lost, negative, subtract, wanting, without
MINUSCULE diminutive, insignificant, lower case, petty, small, tiny
MINUTE accurate, atomic, careful, circumstantial, correct, detail(ed), diminutive, entry, exact, fine, flash, insignificant, instant, item(ized), jiffy, little, meticulous, miniature, minim(al), miniscule, moment, nice, particular, period, petty, precise, right, scrupulous, second, short, slight, small, teeny, time, tiny, trice, trifling, twinkling, wee(ny)
-jack timeserver
24 ghurry
women, leader prudence wright
MINUTELY continual, exactly, fully, in detail, smally, unceasing
MINUTEMAN defender, missile, pioneer, revolutionist, sentinel, sentry
air base grand forks, malmstrom, whiteman
MINUTES acta, annals, chronicle, diary, entry, item, journal, memo(random), note, record, report
MINUTIAE details, particulars, trivia
MINX baggage, brat(ling), colleen, doll, filly, giglet,

girl, hussy, jade, midinette, miss, quean, rogue, wench, witch
MINYADES *father* minyas
MINYAE, MINYAN *capital* orchomenus
country boeotia, thessaly
king alcis, athamas
leader ascalaphus
MINYAS *daughter* alcithoe, arsippe, clymene, leucippe, minyei(a)s
MIPHKAD mir, myrrh
MIQUELET bandit, partisan, soldier
MIRACLE anomy, marvel, play, prodigy, rarity, surprise, theurgy, wonder (work)
comb. thaumat(o)
drug antibiotic, aureomycin, bacitracin, chloromycetin, cure, gramicidin, magic bullet, mycomycin, penicillin, remedy, streptomycin, subtilin, sulfa (diazine)(nilamide)(thiazole)
play guary
site cana, fatima, lourdes
wheat poulard
worker ba(a)lshem, magician, thaumaturge, wizard
MIRACULOUS extraordinary, incomprehensible, magical, marvelous, phenomenal, prodigious, supernatural, thaumaturgic, wonderful, wonder-working
MIRADOR argentina, balcony, bay window, brown, loggia, tower, turret
MIRAGE chimera, deception, delusion, dream, fata morgana, flyaway, hallucination, illusion, phenomenon, serab, vision, will-o-the-wisp
MIRANDA *father* prospero
planet uranus
suitor ferdinand
MIRANHAN *indian* boro, maranha, mariana, mirana, miranha
MIRE addle, bog, clabber, clart, dirty, entangle, fen, glar, glaur, involve, marsh, moil, muck, mud, ooze, seugh, slake, slime, slosh, slough, slub, slud(der), sludge, sluit, slush, slutch, stick, swamp, wet, worthing
drum bittern
duck mallard

MIRIAM *brother* aaron, moses
husband hur
MIRIT *palm* moriche
MIRLIGO dizziness, vertigo
MIRLITON chayote, kazoo, pipe
MIRMAH *father* shaharaim
MIRO bendy-tree, bird, wood-robin
MIROKU See BUDDHA.
MIRON neptune
MIRROR catopter, copy, crystal, exemplar, glass, ideal, image, imitate, looking glass, model, paradigm, paragon, pattern, reflect(or), reflex, simulate, speculum, tain
backing tain
foil tain
iron spiegeleisen
large pier-glass
of the wicked nieh-ching-tai
ornamental bilbao glass, bull's-eye
pert. cataptric(al), specular
MIRTH baudery, cheer, delight, festivity, fun, gaiety, gladness, glee, hilarity, hysterics, jollity, joviality, joy(fulness), laugh(ter), levity, merriment, pleasure, risibility, sport
god cosmos, komos
MIRTHFUL amusing, blithe, cadgy, gay, gleeful, jocular, joyous, laughful, merry, risible
MIRTHLESS gloomy, glum, melancholy, miserable, SAD, unhappy
MIRY boggy, claggy, clashy, dirty, filthy, guttery, lutose, muddy, oozy, slaky, slimy, swampy
MISADVENTURE accident, calamity, casualty, catastrophe, disaster, grief, misfortune, mishap
MISANTHROPE cynic, diogenes, hater, introvert, loner, miser, misogynist, timon(ist)
author moliere
hero alceste
MISANTHROPIC antisocial, cynical, misogynic, misogynous, pessimistic
MISAPPLY abuse, crook, disuse, misuse
MISAPPROPRIATION defalcation, embezzlement, peculation, stealing, theft, thievery
MISBEGOTTEN bastard, deformed, illegitimate
MISBEHAVE act up, carry on, cut up, disobey, horse around, misbear, misfare, misguide, mislead, roughhouse
MISBEHAVIOR horseplay, immorality, impropriety, mischief, misconduct, misdemeanor, naughtiness, rowdiness, ruffianism, sin
MISBELIEF delusion, fallacy, heresy, idolism, illusion, misconception, miscreed
MISBELIEVER heretic, infidel, miscreant
MISCALCULATE err, miscast, miscount, misreckon, overshoot, underestimate
MISCALL abuse, misname, misnomer, mispronounce, revile, slander
MISCARRIAGE abortion, error, failure, lapse, misdeed, misdemeanor, misfire, mishap, mistake
MISCARRY abort, backfire, die, err, fail, fizzle, founder, go amiss, go astray, go wrong, misgo, perish
MISCELLANEOUS assorted, chow(chow), different, disparate, divergent, divers(e), heterogenous, indiscriminate, manifold, many, motley, orra, promiscuous, sundry, varied, variegated, various
quantity job-lot
MISCELLANY ana(lects), assortment, collectanea, collection, compilation, conglomerate, excerpts, farrago, medley, mishmash, mixture, mob, oddments, odds and ends, olio, omnium-gatherum, pasticcio, salmagundi, selections, sundries, variety
MISCHANCE accident, adversity, calamity, casualty, cataclysm, catastrophe, contretemps, disaster, misadventure, misfortune, mishap, reverse
MISCHIEF antic, bale, bane, cantrip, caper, damage, devilment, devil(t)ry, dido, disservice, elfishness, espieglerie, evil, harm,

havoc, hob, hurt, ill, impishness, injury, knavery, misbehavior, misfortune, murchy, prank(ishness), puckishness, rascality, roguery, shenanigans, stunt, trick(ery), trouble, waggery, waggishness, wonder, wrack
deity ate, eris, loke, loki
-maker devil, elf, firebrand, gremlin, hellion, hoyden, imp, instigator, knave, prankster, puck, rascal, rogue, scamp, tike, trickster, troublemaker, tyke, villain, wag
malicious sabotage, vandalism
spirit imp, puck
MISCHIEVOUS arch, elfin, elfish, foxy, harmful, hempie, hempy, ill, impish, knavish, larkish, misleared, misleered, mocking, naughty, parlish, playful, pliskie, puckish, rascal(ly), roguish, sly, sportive, teasing, tricky, waggish, wanton, wicked
MISCONCEPTION delusion, illusion, misconstruction, mistake, misunderstanding
MISCONDUCT culpa, delinquency, dolus, immorality, malfeasance, malpractice, misbehavior, mismanage, offense, shtik(eleh), shtickl(ech), doing
mark of demerit
MISCREANT criminal, heretical, infidel, knave, misbeliever, rascal, rat, reprobate, scoundrel, thief, unbeliever, unbelieving, unscrupulous, villain, wretch
MISCUE blunder, error, lapse, miss, mistake, slip
MISDEED crime, default, forfeit, malefaction, offense, sin, slip, transgression, unwork, violation, wrong
MISDEMEANOR champerty, crime, delict, delinquency, fault, misbehavior, misdeed, offense, sin, tort, transgression
MISDIRECT lie, misguide, mislead, mystify, pervert
MISDO botch, destroy, illtreat, injure, kill, offend
MISDOUBT fear, mistrust, suspect, suspicion

MISE bargain, compact, contract, convention, covenant, entente, indenture, levy, pact, stake, tax, treaty

en scene backdrop, background, environment, milieu, setting

MISENUS *companion* aeneas

father aeolus

MISER avare(l), carl, cheese parer, churl, clusterfist, codger, cuff, curmudgeon, dryfist, euclio, flayflint, harpagon, hetty green, hoarder, holdfast, huckster, hunks, lickpenny, mammonist, moneygrub(ber), muckworm, nabal, niggard, nipcheese, pinchfist, pinchgut, pinchpenny, save-all, scrapepenny, scraper, scrat, screw, scrimp, scrooge, sharepenny, shylock, silas marner, skinflint, snudge, tightwad, uriah heep, wretch

preoccupation numismatics

MISERABLE abject, afflicted, bad, base, calamitous, chetif, contemptible, crummy, dawny, deeny, dejected, desolate, despicable, despondent, disconsolate, distressed, doleful, dusty, forlorn, forsaken, hopeless, low, meager, mean, melancholy, paltry, pathetic, piteable, pitiful, poor, sad, sick, sordid, sorry, tragic, unhappy, unpleasant, unthende, vile, wansome, woeful, worthless, wretched, yemer

MISERLINESS snudgery

MISERLY avaricious, cheap, chinche, churlish, close, covetous, gnede, greedy, grippy, mean, moneyscrubbing, niggardly, parsimonious, penny-pinching, penurious, pinching, save-all, scrimping, sordid, stingy, tight(fisted), wansith

MISERY ache, adversity, affliction, agony, anguish, bale, blues, calamity, chagrin, cheerlessness, dejection, depression, desolation, despondency, displeasure, distress, doldrums, dolor, gloom, grame, grief, headache, heartache, hell, hurt, infelicity, melancholia, mel-

ancholy, misease, misfortune, oppression, pain, penury, privation, ruth, sorrow, squalor, suffering, torment, tragedy, trial, tribulation, unhappiness, woe, wretchedness

valley baca

MISFEASANCE offense, trespass, wrong

MISFIRE fail, fizzle, go wrong, miscarry, skip, snap

MISFIT batlan(im), boggler, duffer, eccentric, fumbler, galoot, gawk, hobbledehoy, lobcock, loobie, lout, lummox, oaf, s(c)hlemiel, shlemi(e)hl, slob, square peg, stiff, swab, tchotchke (leh), tsatske(leh)

MISFORTUNE accident, adversity, affliction, ambsace, bad luck, blight, blow, calamity, casualty, cataclysm, catastrophe, collision, contretemps, crack-up, crash, cross, curse, damage, debacle, dirdum, disaster, disgrace, dole, grief, hardship, harm, ill-luck, malheur, misadventure, mischance, mishap, pile-up, reverse, scath, scourge, shock, smash, tragedy, traik, trial, tribulation, trouble, unluck, unselth, whammy, wreck

MISGIVING alarm, allovers, anxiety, anxious, apprehension, apprehensive, distrust, doubt, dread, fear, foreboding, fright, hesitation, mistrust, premonition, presage, qualm, scruple, skepticism, suspicion, uncertainty

MISGUIDE abuse, injure, maltreat, misgovern, mislead, spoil

MISGUIDED foolish, ill-advised, indiscreet, injudicious

MISHAEL mesach

MISHAM *parent* elpaal

MISHANDLE botch, bungle

MISHAP accident, affliction, blow, calamity, casualty, catastrophe, chance, debacle, hap, hazard, maladventure, misadventure, mischief, misfortune, mistide, unhap, wanhap

MISHMA *kin* ishmael

MISHMASH botch, goulash, hash, hodgepodge, hotchpotch, jumble, medley,

mess, mix-up, olio, olla-podrida

MISHNA(H) doctrine, scripture, talmud

companion baraithas, gemara

festivals moed

pert. mishnaic, mishnic(al), tannaic

section abot(h), halakoth, kodashim, moed, nashim, nezikin, perakim, sedarim, tohoroth, zeraim

supplement tosephta

MISHRAITES *ancestor* caleb

MISINFORM lie, mislead, mizzle, pervert

MISINTERPRET belie, confuse, distort, err, garble, gloss, misapprehend, misconceive, misconstrue, misjudge, misread, misrender, misunderstand, obscure, pervert, twist, warp, writhe

MISJUDGE err, miscalculate, misdeem, miswern, overestimate, underestimate

MISLAY displace, lose, misplace, miss

MISLE drizzle, mist, mizzle

MISLEAD bamboozle, beguile, betray, blear, bluff, cheat, confuse, deceive, decoy, delude, double-cross, dupe, fair, fool, gull, hoax, hoodwink, humbug, inveigle, lure, misdirect, misguide, misinform, mismanage, outwit, pervert, seduce, take in, wilder

MISLEADING blind, bum, catchy, crooked, deceptive, delusive, fallacious, false, fraudulent, illusory, puzzling, sophistical, tortious, wrong

thing red herring

MISLIKE aversion, disagreement, disapprove, disease, displease, dissension, distaste, wasting

MISMANAGE blunder, blunk, botch, bungle, err, fumble, misconduct, misrule

MISOGYNIST celibate, cynic, misanthrope, pessimist, woman-hater

MISPAY displease, dissatisfy

MISPICKEL arsenopyrite

MISPLACE disarrange, lose, mislay, miss(et)

MISPLAY blow, bobble, bumble, duff, err(or), fluff,

fumble, mismove, mistake, muff, renege, renig

MISPRINT corrigendum, mistake, typo

MISPRISION contempt, depreciation, despite, misconduct, misdemeanor, misprize, neglect, scorn, sin, slight

MISPRONUNCIATION cacoepy, cacology, solecism

MISQUOTE adulterate, color, falsify, misinterpret, misrepresent, misstate

MISREPRESENT abuse, angle, belie, camouflage, cloak, color, contort, counterfeit, disguise, dissemble, distort, exaggerate, falsify, feign, garble, mask, miscolor, mislead, overstate, pervert, simulate, skew, slander, slant, stretch, trump up, twist, understate, warp, wrench

MISREPRESENTATION bunco, bunko, calumny, caricature, dishonesty, distortion, falsehood, falsification, fib, fraud, garbling, lie, mendacity, parody, perversion, story, swindle, twist

MISRULE *lord of* abbot of unreason

MISS abandon, avoid, cut, damsel, disregard, elude, err(or), escape, evade, fail-(ure), fall short, forbear, forgo, fraulein, girl, jump, lack, lady, leave, lose, loss, mademoiselle, maiden, miscarry, mistake, mistress, muff, neglect, omission, omit, oversight, pass (over)(up), pretermit, procrastinate, require, senorita, signorina, skip, slip(up), spinster, virgin, want

MISSAY abuse, slander, vilify

MISSEL mistletoe
bird chercock, draine, jaypie, mavis, shrite, sycock, thrush

MISSHAPEN blown, clumsy, deformed, distorted, ill-made, malformed, monstrous, thrawn, ugly

MISSILE ammo, ammunition, arrow, assegrai, ball, bola, bolt, bomb, bullet, cannonball, cartridge, dart, dingbat, fobs, galosh, grenade, knobkerrie, lance, outcast, pellet, projectile, ROCKET, scrag, shaft, shell, shot, sinker, spear, stone, weapon
anti-missile auntie, aunty
ballistic See ROCKET names.
ball-rope bola(s)
defective dud
defense dew line
destroyer egads button
final check count-down
guidance system azusa
guided See ROCKET names.
housing silo
pert. ballistic
pointed arrow, dart, javelin, spear, sword
satellite launch blue scout
science ballistics
spotter dew, msr, par
struck with pelted
tapered base boat tail
target-striking bull's-eye
thrower espringal, spring-al(d)
tip cone

MISSING absent, away, awol, gone, lacking, lost, mislaid, misplaced, truant, wanting, without

MISSION aim, assignment, bombing, business, charge, church, commission, committee, crusade, delegation, deputation, end, errand, goal, maneuver, message, object(ive), post, purpose, sortie, task

MISSIONARY agent, apostle, emissary, evangelist, revivalist

MISSISSIPPI big muddy, father of waters
barge periauger, piragua, pirogue
capital jackson
city biloxi, bogalusa, clarksdale, columbus, corinth, grenada, helena, kosciusko, laurel, meridian, natchez, pascagoula, tupelo, vicksburg, winona
city on clinton, memphis, minneapolis, new orleans, st louis
college alcorn, belhaven, millsaps, rust, tougaloo
county attala, hinds, itawamba, neshoba, noxubee, panola, tippah, yazoo

discoverer-explorer desoto, joliet, marquette
fish crapet, crappie, deerhorn, eelcat
flatboat ark
indian biloxi, chicksaw, chocktaw, mandan, natchez, sac, tious, tonikan, tunica
lake barnett, enid, grenada, okatibbee, sardis
marbles dice
motto virtute et armis
mussel deerhorn
native mudcat, tadpole
nickname bayou, magnolia, mudcat state
peak woodall
port natchez
river big black, leaf, pearl, tombigbee, yazoo
source itasca
state bird mockingbird
state flower magnolia
state tree magnolia
tributary arkansas, des moines, illinois, missouri, red, st croix, white, yazoo

MISSIVE billet, communication, correspondence, dispatch, epistle, letter, line, memo(randum), message, note, record, report
love valentine

MISSOURI *capital* jefferson city
city berkeley, bethany, bolivar, bonne terre, cameron, cape girardeau, clayton, columbia, eldon, hannibal, hayti, independence, inkster, joplin, kansas city, kirkwood, lamar, lebanon, macon, mexico, moberly, rolla, sedalia, sikeston, st louis, warrensburg, webster groves
civil war hero quantrill
college avila, drury, lincoln, stephens, tarkio, webster
county davies, iron, macon, pettis, ray, taney
dam osage
gourd calabazilla, cucurbita, wild squash
grape catbird
hummingbird ass, donkey
indian osage, sac
lake ozark, tablerock
native piker, puke
nickname bullion state, ozark, show me
peak taumsauk
plateau ozark
president truman

river osage
state bird bluebird
state flower hawthorn
state tree dogwood
tributary platte
MISSPELLING cacography, pseudography
MISSPENT lost, squandered, wasted
MISSTATE See MISQUOTE.
MISSTEP error, faux pas, slip, stumble, trip
MIST babies'-breath, bewilderment, blur, brume, cloud, dag, dew, dim, drisk, drizzle, drow, fog, harr, haze, humidity, misle, moisture, nebula, obscurity, precipitation, rack, rag, rain, roke, scud, serein, smaze, smeeth, smirr, smog, smur(r), sprinkle, steam, uncertainty, ure, vapor
cold berber, drow
flower ageratum, blue boneset, eupatory, hempagrimony
goddess nephele
sweeping brume
white fog, hag
yellow bai
MISTAKE addle, balk, barney, blooper, blunder, bobble, boner, boob, booboo, bull, confuse, corrigendum, default, erratum, error, fallacy, fault, faute, flaw, floater, fluff, gaffe, howler, inaccuracy, lapse, mess, miscalculation, misconception, miscue, misplay, misprint, misprize, miss, muddle, oversight, sin, slip(up), stumer, stumour, typo
date anachronism
linguistic malapropism, solecism, spoonerism
loss by leakage
printing errata
sport foul
MISTAKEN all wet, astray, at fault, deceived, deceptive, delusive, erroneous, false, faulty, improper, inaccurate, inexact, misconceived, off base, unsound, untrue, wrong
MISTER art, baboo, babu, class, craft, don, function, goodman, herr, husband, kind, man, master, messieurs, mian, monsieur, mynheer, necessity, need, occu-

pation, office, pan, reb, require, saheb, sahib, senhor, senor, signor, sir(e), skill, sort, trade, want
MISTIGRI jack, joker, pam
MISTIMED anachronous, antedated, outdated, overdue, postdated
MISTLETOE allheal, flametree, gadbush, loranthus, nuytsia, viscum
bird flower-pecker
sap substance viscin
MISTREAT abuse, ill-use, misuse, outrage, violate
MISTRESS amie, beebe, belle amie, beloved, bibi, campaspe, dame, delilah, demeter, demimondaine, despoina, doll, doxy, dulcinea, first lady, frau(lein), goodwife, governess, hetaera, homemaker, housewife, instructress, kept woman, kittock, lady-love, madame, mademoiselle, matron, metreza, migniard, minion, missis, mothersuperior, mrs, neaera, paramour, parnel, patroness, rectoress, sahiba, senhora, senora, senorita, signora, sinebara, sweetheart, tackle, teacher, timandra, wahine, woman
name meaning mart(h)a, mattie, zita
of adriatic venice
of night tuberose
of seas great britain
of world rome
quickly's husband pistol
quickly's tavern boar's head
MISTRUST apprehension, disbelief, disbelieve, doubt, dubiety, dubiosity, foreboding, misdoubt, misgiving, skepticism, suspect, suspicion, uncertainty
MISTY blurry, brumous, cloudy, confused, daggy, dark, dewy, filmy, foggy, hazy, indistinct, mochy, moist, mooth, murky, mystical, nebular, obscure, shadowy, spiritual, uncertain, unclear, vague, vaporous, wet
MISUNDERSTANDING breach, clash, difference, difficulty, disagreement, discord, error, fight, imbroglio, misconception, mistake, quarrel, rift, rupture

MISUSE abuse, corrupt, damage, desecrate, exploit, harm, hurt, ill-treat, impair, injure, malpractice, maltreat, mar, misapply, misdirect, misemploy, mishandle, mismanage, mistreat, outrage, overwork, perversion, pervert, proface, prostitute, spoil, squander, waste
MITE acarapis, acarid(a), acarina, aleurobius, analgesid, arachnid, atom(y), bdellid, bdelloid, bicho, bit, blister, chigoe, child, coin, demodex, dite, dram, farthing, handworm, insect, iota, jot, leptus, louse, minim, minute, modicum, molecule, monad, mote, mucuim, particle, peewee, small, smidgen, smitch, sou, speck, tick, tittle, tot, trifle, weight, whit
comb. acaro
fear of acarophobia
genus acarus, psoroptes, sarcoptes, tetranychus, tyroglyphus
infestation acariasis
itch sarcoptid
-killer acaricide
-like acaroid
poison miticide
predatory anystid
study acarology
web-spinning red spider
MITELLA See MITERWORT.
MITER belt, bishopric, cap, cidaris, cowl, fillet, girdle, gusset, hat, headband, headdress, join, junction, tavern, tiara, timber, timbre, turban
flower cyclamen
lappet infula
ornament petalon
MITERPHORUS dionysus
MITERWORT bishop's-cap, coolwort, fairy cup, foamflower, mitella, tiarella
MITHRAS tauroctonus
beast bull
ceremony mithriac, taurobolium
MITHRIDATE alexipharmic, antidote, electuary
MITHRIDATES *admiral* dorylaus
aide callistratus
brother cosis
castle inora

conqueror sylla
consort berenice, hypsicratia, monime, stratonice
daughter cleopatra
deputy taxiles
eunuch bacchides
favorite metrodorus
foe bruttius-sura
foster-brother gaius
general archelaus, cosis, taxiles
lieutenant adrianus, callimachus, dorylaus, menander, menemachus, myro, olthacus, sornatius
parent ariobarzanes
priest hermaeus
rival pompey
sister nyassa, roxana, statira
son ariarathes, machares, pharnaces
son-in-law tigranes
MITIGATE abate, allay, alleviate, assuage, attemper, balm, bate, beat, cool, decrease, delay, diminish, ease, extenuate, justify, lenify, lessen, lighten, mease, meliorate, moderate, mollify, pacify, palliate, qualify, quell, reduce, relax, relieve, remit, salve, slake, soften, soothe, succor, sweeten, temper, tone, weaken
MITIGATION abatement, alleviation, diminution, moderation, mollification, palliation, propitiation, relief
MITOSIS *stage* anaphase, prophase, telophase
MITT(EN) cuff, gauntlet, glove, hand(s), jilt, loofie, mousquetaire, muff(le), nipper
MITTIMUS commitment, discharge, dismissal, magistrate, mudge, notice, quietus, warrant, writ
MITTY petrel
MITU curassow
MIX addle, adulterate, alloy, amalgamate, associate, beat, blend, box, brew, broil, bulk, card, caudle, coalesce, combine, commingle, compound, confound, conjoin, consort, cross, fight, formula, fraternize, fray, fuse, garble, hobnob, imbue, integrate, interlard, join, jumble, knead, mass, meddle, mell, merge, mess, mingle, mong, muddle, predica-

ment, scramble, shuffle, stir, swizzle, toss, twine, unite, whip, wuzzle
drink bitter lemon, bitters, seltzer, soda, tonic
up affray, ball-up, boner, conflict, confuse, confusion, contest, derange, error, fight, hash, intermingle, jumble, melee, mess, miscue, mishmash, muddle, snafu, tangle
with water blunge, dilute, doctor, slake, weaken
MIXED assorted, blended, carded, chow(chow), composite, farraginous, half-and-half, heterogeneous, hybrid, impure, indiscriminate, macaronic, medley, miscellaneous, mongrel, motley, piebald, streaky, varied, variegated, various
blood baluga, griffe, griqua, halfbreed, ladino, marabou(t), mestee, mestizo, metis(se), mulatto, mustee, octoroon, quadroon, quintroon
capable of being misceability
not pure, sincere
up arsy-varsy, chaotic, crazy, farblondjet, haywire, tsedoodelt(eh), tsedrayt(eh)
MIXER bartender, beater, blender, muddler, party, paver, setup, shaker
MIXTURE (See also MIXED *blood*.) adulteration, alloy, amalgam, assortment, babel, blend, cacophony, cafuso, cholo, chowchow, citrange, coalescence, combination, combo, composite, composition, compost, compound, conglomeration, crazy quilt, cross(breed), cur, custard, dustee, farrago, fusion, fustee, gallimayfry, griffe, griqua, half-breed, half-caste, hash, hodgepodge, hotchpotch, hybrid, infusion, jumble, junction, kogasin, ladino, magma, mash, maslin, medley, melange, merger, mess(tee), mestizo, mingle-mangle, miscellany, mixty-maxty, mong, mongrel, mosaic, motley, mulatto, mustee, octoroon, olio, olla-podrida, pasticcio, pastiche, patchwork, pot-

pourri, quadroon, quintroon, sacatra, salad, saltcat, sambo, scramble, stew, union, variety, zambo
animal cattalo, crossbreed, cur, griffin, griffon, mule, zebrass, zebrule
caulking blare, grout, putty
combustible explosive
confused botch, chaos, fuddle, jumble, sozzle
cooking batter, filling, roux, stuffing
crumbly streusel
explosive firedamp
freezing cryogen
fruit citrange, plumcot, pomato, tangelo
gilding assiette
thickening roux
unpalatable drammock
watery slurry
MIZPAH *ruler* colhozeh, jeshua
MIZRAIM *father* ham
son anamin, caluhim, caphthorim, lehabim, ludim, naphtuhim, pathrusim
MIZZAH *father* reuel
MIZZLE confuse, decamp, depart, disappear, drizzle, flee, give up, misinform, mist, rain, speckle, spit, spot
MIZZONITE dipyre
MNEMON *companion* achilles
slayer achilles
MNEMONIC eidetic, mnesic, mnestic
MNEMOSYNE *consort* zeus
offspring See MUSES.
parent gaea, uranus
MO bit, book, flash, further, instant, MOMENT, more, other, second, volume
MOA apteryx, bird, dinornis, dinornithid, kiwi, ratite
MOAB *city* arnon, aroer, baalmeon, bethjeshimoth, bethmeon, bozrah, dibon, elealeh, heshbon, holon, horonaim, kerioth, kirheres, kiriathaim, luhith, mephaath, misgab, nebo, sihon, zoar
giant emin, etym, zuzim
god chemosh
king balak, eglon, malak, mesha
mountain nebo
people emim
woman naomi, ruth
MOAN bewail, complain(t),

deplore, grieve, groan, keen, kvetch, lament (ation), mourn, munge(r), pity, reem, sigh, sob, sorrow, sough, suffer, suum, wail, whine

MOAT canal, dike, ditch, entrenchment, foss(e), graff(e), gutter, rundel, trench, trough

MOB army, assembly, barney, canaille, cattle, clique, cohue, crowd, crush, doggery, drove, flock, gang, group, herd, hoi polloi, horde, host, jam, legion, mafia, mass, miscellany, multitude, people, populace, press, rabble, riffraff, rout, ruck, set, swarm, throng, underworld, varletry, voulge

cap dormeuse

impersonation blatant beast

law or rule anarchy, disorder, lawlessness, mobocracy, ochlocracy, violence

member lyncher, rioter

worship mobolatry

MOBILE ambulatory, capricious, changeable, changeful, fickle, fluid, inconstant, liquid, locomotive, mercurial, motile, movable, populace, protean, unstable, variable, versatile, wandering

river tributary tombigbee

MOBILIZE activate, animate, assemble, call to arms, catalyze, cry havoc, draft, enlist, enroll, gather, levy, muster, organize, rally, recruit, start

MOBSTER butcher, demagogue, gangster, hoodlum, rabbler

MOBY DICK peleg, whale

author melville

pursuer ahab

ship pequod

MOCCASIN boot(ee), brown, congo, copperhead, cottonmouth, footwear, larrigan, loafer, makak, pac(k), pampootie, pit viper, shoe(pack), shuffler, slipper, snake, tegua

flower camel's-foot, cypripedium, fissipes, lady's-slipper, nervine

with legs larrigan, shanks

MOCHA bark, coffee, leather

stone moss agate

MOCHILA knapsack, rucksack

MOCHY damp, misty, moist, muggy

MOCK adopt, affect, ape, apish, banter, bob, burlesque, caricature, chaff, cheat, copy, counterfeit, deceive, defy, deride, disappoint, disregard, dor(re), dupe, fake, false, feigned, fleer, flout, fool, forged, fraudulent, gibe, gird, hoot, imitate, imitation, imitative, imp, insult, jape, jeer, jibe, make-believe, mimic, murgeon, niggle, parody, pretend(ed), rally, ridicule, scoff, scorn, sham, sleer, sneer, spurious, stick, taunt, tease, travesty, twit

-bird blackcap, warbler

blow feint

chervil lady's-comb

cucumber balsam apple

cypress artillery plant, belvedere, burning-bush, dittany, fraxinella, gas-plant, kochia, wahoo

-heroic burlesque, comic(al)

moon paraselene

nightingale blackcap, warbler

orange seringa, syringa

plane sycamore

-up model

MOCKER bird, bourder, deceiver, flauter, girder, mimic, mockingbird, railleur, scoffer, scorner

MOCKERNUT black walnut, bullnut, hickory, pignut

MOCKERY bismer, borak, bourd, burlesque, contempt, delusion, derision, dor, farce, futility, glaik, hething, imitation, irony, ludibry, mimicry, ridicule, ruse, sarcasm, satire, scorn, sham, sport, travesty

god momus

MOCKING acid, gab, ludibrious, sport(ive)

bird mimus, mower

MOCTEZUMA See AZTEC, MONTEZUMA.

MOD craze, fad(dy), garish, gauche, modern, neo, offbeat, outre, weird

MODE bamalip, category, condition, conduct, course, craze, cry, custom, cut, decor, dernier cri, drift, fad, fakofo, fashion, ferio,

fesapo, flair, form, kind, manner, method, mood, order, popularity, posture, rage, situation, stance, state, style, system, tenor, trend, variety, vogue, way

MODEL archetype, copy, criterion, diorama, drawing, dummy, example, exemplar, exemplum, figure, form, fugleman, gauge, ideal, image, manikin, mannequin, maquette, matrix, measure, mock-up, mold, norm, original, paradigm, paragon, pattern, perfect, plan, portrait, pose(r), praiseworthy, praxis, protoplasm, prototype, rule, sculpture, shape, sit(ter), specimen, standard, subject, touchstone, type

after copy, emulate

comb. typ(o)

full-sized gabari(t)

preliminary proplasm

-t flivver, old(fashioned), tin lizzy

working praxis

MODERATE 4 bate, calm, cool, curb, damp, dull, even, fair, just, mild, slow, soft, tame 5 abate, allay, bland, blunt, cheap, check, lower, mezzo, quiet, remit, slake, small, sober, swage 6 center, common, dampen, deaden, decent, direct, frugal, gentle, lessen, modest, modify, obtund, pacify, reduce, soften, steady, stifle, subdue, temper, weaken 7 appease, ascetic, assuage, average, chasten, control, lenient, lighten, mediate, mollify, preside, qualify, relieve, smother, sparing 8 attemper, decrease, diminish, economic, meeterly, mitigate, modulate, palliate, regulate, restrain, suppress, tone down 9 abstinent, alleviate, arbitrate, constrain, indulgent, judicious, temperate, tolerable 10 abstemious, economical, reasonable 11 indifferent 12 conservative, intermediate 13 dispassionate

MODERATELY fair, gey, in reason, meetly, middling, midwise, pretty, rather, soberly, temperately, within bound

MODERATION abatement, abstinence, catharsis, conservatism, constraint, control, diminution, gentleness, golden mean, happy medium, mean, methe, mildness, mitigation, modesty, reason, restraint, slackening, sobriety, sophrosyne, temperance

MODERATOR arbiter, arbitrator, chairman, conductor, judge, mediator, president, referee, umpire

MODERN advanced, contemporary, fresh, futuristic, groovy, last, late(st), neologist, neoteric, new(est), new-fangled, novel, original, present, progressive, recent, streamlined, ultra-ultra, up-to-date
comb. neo
movement dada, hippie, pop-drug

MODERNIZE refurbish, remodel, renew, renovate, streamline, update

MODEST bashful, becoming, chary, chaste, civil, coy, decent, deft, demure, deprecative, diffident, douce, edel, good, homely, humble, lowly, maidenly, mean, meek, moderate, moral, mure, plain, prim, proper, prudish, pudent, pudibund, queasy, quiet, reasonable, reserved, reticent, retiring, seemly, self-effacing, sheepish, shrinking, shy, simple, small, squeamish, temperate, timid, timorous, unassuming, unobtrusive, unostentatious, unpretentious, verecund, virtuous

MODESTY chastity, decency, diffidence, humility, nicety, propriety, prudery, pudency, pudicity, reserve, shyness, simplicity, victorianism
deified pudicitia

MODICUM bit, drop, little, mess, pittance, share, smidgen, speck

MODIFICATION adjustment, alteration, bob, change, ecad, engram(ma), mutation, qualification, sandhi, transformation, variation

MODIFY adapt, adjust, affect, alter, amend, ara-

bize, attemper, change, compare, convert, diversify, doctor, emend, faucalize, graft, improve, increase, limit, lower, master, metamorphose, moderate, modulate, qualify, reduce, reform, restrict, revise, shape, soften, temper, tone, touch, transfigure, transform, transmogrify, vary

MODILLION ancon, bracket, cartouche, truss

MODISH braw, chic, dapper, dashing, faddish, faddy, fashionable, natty, nifty, nobby, popular, posh, smart, soigne, stylish, trendy

MODRED, MORDRED *father* loth
uncle king arthur
victim king arthur

MODULATE adapt, adjust, attune, change, harmonize, inflect, intone, merge, moderate, qualify, regulate, sing, soften, sound, temper, tune, vary

MODULATION abatement, accent, cadence, change, harmonization, inflection, intonation, passagio, pitch, tone, transition

MODULE capacity, compass, diameter, exemplar, measure, model, pattern, size, standard

MODULUS norm, quantity, snail, standard

MODUS manner, means, method, mode, procedure, way

MOED festival, mishnah

MOERAE *mother* themis

MOERAGETES apollo

MOG decamp, depart, go off, jog, move, travel

MOGGY calf, cat, pet, scarecrow, slattern

MOGUL autocrat, babob, baron, big cheese, biggie, biggun, biggy, bigshot, bigwig, locomotive, lord, magnate, mongolian, padishah, personage, potentate, ruler, sachem, vip
capital agra
ruler akbar, aurangzeb, babar, baber, babur, shahjehan
tent yurt

MOHAIR angora, astrachan, astrakhan, broadtail, cam-

let, civilian, fur, moire, wool

MOHAMMED mahomet, mahoud, mahound, mahund, maliom, mohomet, mudejar, muhammad, prophet
associate ansar, ashab, muhajirun, sahib
birthplace mecca
bow catum
camel al adha, al kaswa
concubine mariyeh
cuirass fadha
descendant ali, ashraf, emir, hasan, hosein, husain, ibrahim, said, say(y)id, seid, shereef, sherif, zaid
father-in-law abubekr
flight from mecca hadj, hegira, hejira
follower ansar, wahabee, wah(h)abi, wahabit(e)
grandfather abd-el-mutallib
helmet al mawashah
horse alborak
journey hadj, hegira, hejira, miraj
mule daldah, fadda
offspring ali, fatima
opponent abu sofian
parent abdall(ah), amina
sayings hadit
skirmish battle of the moat
standard bajura
successor calif, caliph, diadochi, iman
sword al battaa, fakar, hatef, medham, monthawi, saadia
title ali, imam
tomb medina
tribe koreish
uncle abbas, abu-talib
wife aisha, ayesha(h), barra, hafsa, k(h)adidja, maimuna, omm-habiba, rehana, safiya, sauda, zeinab

MOHAMMEDAN abadite, abbadide, abdal, ag(h)a, alaouite, alim, arain, ayyubid, bagirmi, bashkir, dervish, hadji, hafiz, hanif, ibadhi(te), islam(ic), kazakh, khaksar, mahometan, mahound, mahund, malay, MOORISH, morisco, moro, moslem, motazilite, mudejar, muslim, mussulman, paynim, qadarite, salar, sangil, sanguile, saracen, sart, shiah, shiite, sidi, sifatite, sufi, sunnite, swat(i), turban, turk

ablution abdest, widu, wudu, wuzu

almsgiving sadaqat

angel abou jahai, azazel, azrael, gabriel, israfil, isrefel, monkir, mordad, munkar, nakir

ascetic dervish, fakeer, fakir, SUFI

bazaar sook

beggar fakeer, fakir

belt zon(nar)

berber dynasty hafsid, safsite

bier tabut

bird, fabulous aboulomri, ak-baba, kerkes

blacksmith lohar

blood-relationship nasab

branch sunni

breakfast iftar

brotherhood tariqa

building, religious caaba, ima(u)mbarah, kaaba, kaabeh

calendar jumada, muharram, rabia, rajab, ramadan, safar, shaban, shawwal, zulhijah, zulkadah

caliph almohades, ovar

camp mahala

cap kofia, taj

caravansary imaret

carpet, holy kiswa(h)

caste mopla(h)

charm agave

chief See *ruler*, below.

city, sacred kairou(w)an, mecca, medina

cloak aibornoz, burnoose, burnous, jubbah

coin altun, denar, dinar, dirhem

college or council ulema

compass kebla-noma

compilation alsahih

convert ansar, mured

country See *nation*, below.

court divan, diwan

covenant ark tabut

creed kelima, sunna

crown taj

crusade jehad, jihad

dagger khanjar

decree irade

demon afreet, afrit, eblis, genie, jann, jinnee, jinni, shaitan, sheitan

dervish calendar, isawa, kadris, sadite, santon

dervish meeting dhikr

devil See *demon*, above.

devotions raka(h)

devout mumin

disbeliever giaour

disciple murid

divorce ahsan, hasan, mubarat, talak

doctrine tawhid

drinking cup lotah

dynasty abbasid, almohad, almoravid, ayubid, ayubite, bahmanid, fatimid, ghaznevid

easter eed

emblem crescent

fairy peri

fast ashura, ramadan

fate kismet

festival bairam, eed, muharram

finance minister dewan

flute nay

foundation wakf, waqf

freethinker aladinist

garment bourkha, buibui, burga, burk(h)a, burnoose, burnous, ihram, isar, izar, jama(h), jubbah, jupon, kamis, shintiyan

gentile raia

god allah, eblis, jann

guide pir

headdress fez, kul(l)ah, taj, tarbooch, tarboosh, tarbouche, tarbush, turban

heaven alfardaws, alicon, assama, falak-al-aflak, faradis, jenna

heaven and hell boundary alaraf

heirarchy ulema

hell adhab-al-cabr, hawiyah, hutamah, jahannam, jahim, jehennam, latha, sair, sakar

heretics shiites

hermit marabout

holiday ramadan

holy man ima(u)m, marabout

holy war jehad, jihad

horse, winged buraq

hotel imaret

house selamlik

imams, 13 abdallah hasan, ali, alian-naqi, ali-ar-riza, haidar, hasan, hosein, jafer, mohammed al-mahdi, mohammed el-bagir, murteza, musa al-kazhim, zein el abidin

infidel kaf(f)er, paynim, rayan

judge cadi, caid, cazi, cazy, hajib, hakim, ima(u)m, kadi, kazi, kazy, mufti, qaid

kinship nasab

knife staghan, yatag(h)an

lady begum, tola

language hindustani, pali, urdu

law adat, bai, fikh, fiqh, halal, sharia(h), sheri(at), sheriyat, sunna

law expert mauli, mo(o)lvi, moolvee, moulvi, mufti

leader See *chief*, above.

malay sassak

market sook

marriage mota, muta

marriage settlement mahr

meal iftar

mendicant fakeer, fakir

men's quarters selamlik

messiah mahdi

minaret crier muezzin

monastery khankah, tekke, tekya

monk fakir

mosque masjid

mountain caf

musical instrument rebab

mystic mahdi, sufi

mysticism sufism

mythical creature dabba

nation afghanistan, algeria, arabia, bahrain, bangladesh, cameroon, chad, egypt, gabon, gambia, guinea, indonesia, iran, iraq, jordan, kuwait, lebanon, libya, mauritania, morocco, niger, oman, pakistan, qatar, saudi-arabia, senegal, sierra leone, somalia, sudan, syria, united arab emirates, upper volta, yemen

noble ameer, amir, emeer, emir, sa(y)id, sharif, sherif

non giaour, kaffir, raia, raya, rayah, zendik

nymph houri

official See *ruler*, below.

opinion futwa

orthodox hanif, sunnite

peddler bora

people bag(h)irmi, bashkir, bazigar, dehgan, egyptian, hanif, isawa, laz(i), maba, moor, moro, salar, samal, saracen, sart, senousi, senus(s)i, senussian, sufi, sunni, swat(i), turk

physician hakeem, hakim

pilgrim ha(d)ji, hajji

pilgrim dress ihram

pilgrimage hadj

pilgrimage place caaba, kaaba, kaabeh, kufa, mecca

plan tazia

platform mastaba

practice purdah

prayer nafl, namaz, salah, salat
prayer call adan, azan
prayer direction kiblah
prayer place idgah, masjid, mosque
priest ima(u)m, khatib, talisman, wahabi
prince See *ruler,* below.
princess begum, tola
principle ijma, taqiya
property grant wakf, waqj, wukf
prophecy shahada
prophet mahd, shair
pulpit mimbar, minbar
purification abdest, widu, wudu, wuzu
puritan form wahhabism
queen begum
reformer wahabee, wah-(h)abi
relative mahram
religion bahaism, islam
religious observance din, ibada
religious teacher alim
rest house khankah
rosary comboloio
rug, prayer asan(a)
ruler ag(h)a, ameer, amir, begum, cadi, caid, calif, caliph, dat(t)o, dewan, emeer, emir, hakeem, hakim, imam, kalif, kaliph, khalif, khan, mahdi, mian, mir(za), mufti, nawab, nazir, nizam, qadi, rais, reis, said, say(y)id, se(y)id, sharif, sheik, shereef, sherif, sidi, soldan, sultan, syed, tola, vali, vizi(e)r, wali, wazir
sabbath friday
saber scimitar, scimiter, yatag(h)an
sacred book alcoran, coran, KORAN
sacred well zemzem
saint abdal, kederli, marabout, pir, santon
salutation sala(a)m
scholar ulema
school hanafi, hanbali, kubba, kuttab, madras(s)a(h), madrasseh, qubba, shafti, ulema
scripture See *sacred book,* above, and KORAN.
sect abadite, ahmadi(ya), almohades, almoravides, dervish, ibadite, imamite, isawa, ismailiya, jabarite,

kadarite, kharijite, motazilite, murjiite, senussi, shiah, sifatite, sunnite, wahabee, wah(h)abi
shirt kamis
shrine dome of the rock, kaaba, kaabeh, masjid, mosk, mosque, qubba, ziara(t)
slave mameluke
soldier ghazi
son-in-law ali
spirit genie, genii, ginn, jin, jinn(ee)(i), jinnyeh
spiritual adviser pir
stone, sacred sakhrat
student softa, ulema
sultan mahmud
sword seif
tax jezia(h), zakah
teacher alfaki, alfaqui(n), alim, coja, hodja, imam, khoja(h), molla(h), mujtahid, mulla(h), murshid, pir
temple See *shrine,* above.
title See *judge, ruler, teacher,* above.
tomb pir, taboot, tabut
tomb dome weli
tree tuba
trees shia(h), sunni
tunic jama(h)
unbeliever kaf(f)ir
uncle abbas, abu, talib
veil izar, iz(z)ar, tagilmust, yashmak
viceroy nabob, nawab
war, religious jahad, jihad
warrior g(h)azi, saracen
weight artal, miskal, rotl
women's quarters harem
women's seclusion purdah
MOHANDAS the mahatma
MOHAWK *indian* caughnawaga
chief brant, thayendanegea
MOHICANS *last of* uncas
author cooper
MOHO bird, gallinule, honey-eater, notornis, rail
MOHOCK apache, attack, desperado, gangster, maltreat, ruffian, thug
MOHR bezoar, gazelle
MOHS *scale, hardness degrees* (1) talc, (2) gypsum, (3) calcite, (4) fluorite, (5) apatite, (6) feldspar, (7) quartz, (8) topaz, (9) sapphire, (10) diamond
MOHURI ahmadi, ahmedi, dinar
MOIDER bother, confuse, crowd, distract, encumber,

perplex, prattle, smother, toil, wander, worry
MOIETY half, mediety, middle, part, portion, share
MOIL agitation, bespatter, confusion, daub, defile, dirty, drudge(ry), furrow, hornless, labor, meddle, mire, moisten, mule, seethe, spill, spot, stain, taint, tire, toil, torment, trouble, turmoil, vexation, wallow, weary, wet, work, worry
MOILING carking, daubing, dirtying, wetting
MOIST clammy, dabby, damp(ish), dank, dewy, drippy, drizzly, foggy, humid, irriguous, juicy, marshy, mesic, misty, mochy, muculent, muggy, nesh, oozy, rainy, roral, roric, rorulent, rory, sammy, sloppy, soaky, soppy, sticky, swack, swampy, tearful, teary, uvid, watery, weepy, wet(tish)
MOISTEN anoint, asperge, baptize, baste, bathe, bedew, bespatter, besprinkle, dabble, damp(en), dash, dew, dip, hose, humectate, humidify, imbrue, irrigate, latch, leach, madefy, moil, paddle, ret, sam, slobber, slop, slosh, soak, sparge, splash, sp(l)atter, sponge, spray, sprinkle, swash, syringe, water, wet, wokie
MOISTURE aquasity, bree, damp(ness), dank, dew, drip, drop, fog, humidity, humo(u)r, liquid, rain, roke, wet(ness)
excess edema
expose to ret
goddess tefnut
-laden sodden, soggy
pert. hygric
remove blot, dehydrate, dry, wipe, wring
without arid, burned, dehydrated, desiccated, dry, parched, scorched
MOJARRA fish, patao, shad, silver-jenny
MOJO amulet, charm, fetish, majagua, moxo
MOKE dolt, donkey, fog, horse, mesh, minstrel, mist, musician, network

MOKI fish, moguey, mokihi, raft, trumpeter

MOLA sunfish

MOLAR chopper, crunching, fang, grinder, grinding, tooth
having crowned bunodont
without agomphiasis

MOLASSES blackstrap, claggam, longlick, sirup, sorghum, syrup, theriac(a), treacle
and sugar meladda
drink swanky, switchel
rum tafia

MOLAVE hardwood, puriri, teak, tree, vitex

MOLD, MOULD ame, bend, blight, block, body, build, cast, decay, die, earth, fashion, fen, fontanel, form, frame, fungus, gabari, humus, impression, intaglio, kind, knead, last, matrice, matrix, mildew, mix, model, moulage, must, nature, negative, pattern, pig, plasm, print, protoplasm, rot, rust, seal, shape, soil, sow, stain, stale, stamp, template, wither
aspic dariole
blue fungus, penicillium
board reest
bread mucorales, thamnidium
channel geat, git, spray
core matrix, nowel
filling machine bumper
frozen bombe
hole sprue
in wax ceroplast
melon bombe
metal skillet, sow
opening ingate
part ame, gate, geat, git, nowel, sprue
pert. humic
round bombe
slime acrasia, acrasid
small pariole
sooty fumagine

MOLDABLE docile, patient, plastic, pliable, pliant

MOLDAU vltava

MOLDAVIA See also RUMANIA.
republic bessarabia

MOLDER crumble, dwindle, figurer, mangle, mosker, plaster, plastic
tool flange

MOLDING ame, aaron's rod, astragal, baguet, band-

elet(te), baston, bead(ing), beak, boot-jack, cable, casement, cavetto, chain, chaplet, conge(e), cyma, dado, echinus, eyebrow, fascia, fillet, gula, knurling, linget, listel, lozenge, nailhead, necking, ogee, ovolo, reed(ing), reglet, regula, rose, scotia, scroll, splay, split, talon, thumb, tondino, torus, tringle, trochilus
box babbitting-jig
case chape
classical cyma
comb. plasty
combination ledgement
concave cavetto, conge(e), cove, coving, gorge, gula, oxeye, scotia
convex astragal, baguette, baston, boltel, boutel(l), bowtel(l), cable, fusarole, gadroon, knulling, knurling, ovolo, reed(ing), rudenture, shaft, thumb, tore, torus
curved cyma, nebule, ogee
dart anchor
decorative egg and dart, ovolo
disk-ornamented bezantee
echinus thumb
edge ar(r)is
egg-shaped ovolo, ovulo
flat fillet
flat narrow reglet
hollow casement, scotia
narrow fillet, listel, reglet, tringle
ogee cyma, gola, gula, talon
ornament dancette
ovolo thumb
projection coving
raised bilection, bolection
rounded billet, fusarole, ovolo, torus
rule for screed
semicircular edgeroll
square architrave, listel
s-shaped ogee
wavelike cyma, nebule, ogee

MOLDY, MOULDY foisty, foughty, fusty, gamy, high, mucid, muggy, musty, old, putrid, stale, timeworn, vinny
become finew, fust, moul, spoil

MOLE an(n)icut, barrier, beauty spot, blemish, bles, breakwater, bulge, bulk, burrow, buttress, cake,

chrysochlore, cob(b), excavate, fault, fortification, harbor, hydatid, imperfection, jetty, mark, mass, mausoleum, mooncalf, moudie, mound, n(a)evus, oont, pier, quay, rodent, soricoid, starnose, talpa, talpoid, tape, taupe, tomb, tower, uropsile, want, wen, wont, zandmole
-cast molehill
-catcher king-snake
comb. talpi
cricket changa, churrworm, earth-crab
genus bathyergus, sapanus, scalopus, talpa
hill heap, hoyle, trifle, tump
kind chrysochlore, starnose
-like mammal desman, talpa, tape
plant caper-spurge
rat nesokia, semni, slepez, spala, zemmi, zokor
symbol of blindness

MOLECULE ammine, atom, biogen, bit, corpuscle, dipole, hydrone, ligand, mite, monad, particle, speck, trifle
component anion, atom, ion
genetic dna
pile reactor

MOLESKIN fustian, taupe

MOLEST abuse, annoy, assail, attack, bother, discommode, disquiet, disturb, harass, harry, heckle, hector, infest, interfere, intrude, irk, meddle, mislest, obtrude, persecute, perturb, pester, plague, pursue, tamper, tease, torment, trouble, vex

MOLIERE *character* alceste, argan, elmire, jourdain, orgon, sganerelle, tartuf(f)e
comedy georges dandin, la malade imaginaire, l'avare, le bourgeois gentilhomme, le misanthrope, les precieuses ridicules, tartuffe, the miser
residence auteuil

MOLIONE *consort* actor, poseidon
offspring cteatus, eurytus

MOLIONES cteatus, eurytus
aided augeas
competitor nestor
father actor, poseidon
slayer hercules

MOLL mary, prostitute, sweetheart, wench
blood gallows
MOLLIFICATION abatement, mitigation, relief
MOLLIFY abate, allay, appease, assuage, bate, calm, compose, conciliate, decrease, dulcify, ease, lessen, lighten, mellow, milden, mitigate, moderate, pacify, placate, propitiate, qualify, quiet, reduce, relax, relent, relieve, sleek, soften, soothe, sweeten, temper, unruffle
MOLLIPILOSE downy, fluffy, hairy
MOLLITIOUS luxurious, sensuous, softening
MOLLUGO airoacea, carpetweed
MOLLUSK (See also *genus*, below.) 3 ark, mya 4 clam, cone, leda, pipi, pupa, slug, spat, umbo, unio 5 awabi, blunt, borer, chama, chank, chink, clamp, cohog, conch, cowry, doris, drill, helix, limax, nacre, naiad, pearl, pinna, polyp, shell, snail, squid, squin, thais, turbo, varix, venus, whelk 6 aeolid, atrypa, bailer, bubble, cerion, cockle, courie, dolium, elysia, gueduc, jingle, lepton, limpet, mussel, oyster, pecten, pholad, quahog, semele, stromb, tellin, triton, winkle 7 abalone, aglossa, athyris, bioherm, biolite, bivalve, blubber, cardita, decapod, flidder, inkfish, junonia, octopus, piddock, polypod, quahaug, rissoid, scallop, slobber, toheroa, trepang, trophon, venerid 8 argonaut, atremata, brechite, bullnose, calamary, ceratite, duckfoot, figshell, haliotis, nautilus, pteropod, saxicava, strombus, univalve, vermetus 9 bluepoint, carinaria, cephalata, cercomona, gastropod, heteropod, lampshell 10 ampullaria, applesnail, cuttlefish, gossophora 11 bellerophon, bubbleshell
bivalve anomia, arca(cea), chama, clam, cockle, conch, fistulana, leda, macoma, monomyaria, mussel, oyster, piddock, razorclam,

scallop, spat, spondylus, unio, venerid
blood pigment pinnaglobin
class amphineura, argonaut, brachiopod, cephalopod, gastropod, pelecypod, pteropod, scaphopod, tunicate
double-shelled clam, limpet, oyster
edible abalone, asi, clam, mussel, oyster, quahog, snail, squid, whelk
8-armed octopus
embyronic shell prodisoconch, protoconch
extinct ammonoid
filament byssus
fossil ammonite, heligmus
fresh water chiton, etheria, mussel
gastropod abalone, pulmonatum, slug, snail, taenioglossa, w(h)elk
genus aeolis, arca, astarte, buccinum, bullidae, chiton, donax, dreissensia, eolis, firoloida, ledum, murex, nerita, oliva, pectunculus, petricola, pyrula, waldheimia
gills cerata, ctenidium
heteropod atlanta
hinge articulus
large part mantle
largest chama
larval veliger
marine abalone, amphineura, asi, astarte, calico clam, cuttlefish, epitonium, murex, nautilus, salp, scallop, tooth-shell
muscle adductor
1-shell See *univalve,* below.
part metasoma
shell cowrie, cowry, protegulum, testa
shell concretion pearl
shell-less slug
small limax
study malacology
teeth radula
10-armed squid
tribe naiades
2-shell See *bivalve,* above.
univalve cowrie, cowry, snail
wrinkled shell cockle
young spat
MOLLY basket, mali, mallemuck, milksop
captain margaret cochran corbin
MOLLYCODDLE baby, cotquean, effeminate, humor,

indulge, milksop, milquetoast, pamper, pantywaist, sissy, spoil, wanton, weakling
MOLOCH baal, lizard, melkarth, milcom
MOLOKAI *priest* damien
MOLOSSUS *parent* andromache, neoptolemus, pyrrhus
MOLT cast, discard, ecdysis, exuviate, intermew, junk, mew, mute, scrap, shed, slough
MOLTEN fused, fusible, liquid, liquified, meltable, melted, thawed
MOLUCCA balm, bells of ireland, mint, molucella, shellflower, spice island
bean bonduc-nut, guilandina nicker-nut
island amboina, banda, ceram, maluku
port ambon
tribe alfuro
MOLUS *offspring* meriones
parent ares, demonice
MOMBIN fruit, hog-plum, jocote, spondias
MOME blockhead, fool
MOMENT advantage, avail, bit, blink, breathing, clink, consequence, consideration, date, fillip, flash, gird, gliff, glisk, gravity, import (ance), impulse, influence, instant, jiff(y), juncture, matter, minute, particle, period, point, prestige, profit, sec(ond), significance, spurt, stage, tick, trice, twinkle, twinkling, use, value, weight, worth
critical corner, crisis
decisive crisis, nick
odd spare time
of the impromptu
of truth anagnorisis, crisis, denouement, epiphany, recognition
on the spur of impromptu, inspired, now, today
opportune kairos
particular then, when
MOMENTARILY briefly, periodic(al)(ally)
MOMENTARY brief, ephemeral, fleeting, fugitive, immediate, instantaneous, passing, short(-lived), transient, transitory
MOMENTLY briefly, instantly, suddenly

MOMENTOUS authoritative, bustling, critical, crucial, decisive, epochal, eventful, fateful, fell, grave, important, influential, memorable, notable, outstanding, phenomenal, pivotal, serious, stirring, vital, weighty

MOMENTUM force, headway, impetus, impulse, pace, push, speed, velocity
unit bole

MOMISH foolish

MOMUS critic, faultfinder, ridicule, scold

MOMZER bastard, illegitimate, impudent, scalawag

MONACHAL celibate, cenobitic, claustral, monastic, monkish

MONACO *city* monte carlo
dynasty grimaldi
language french
people monegasques
prince albert, antoine, charles, florestan, honore, louis, rainier
princess grace kelly
river vesubie
section lacondamine, monacoville, monte carlo

MONAD animalcule, atom, bit, deity, element, entity, henad, individual, jiva, molecule, one, organism, part (icle), protozoan, radical, speck, unit, univalent, zoospore

MONADNOCK baraboo, hill, mountain

MONA LISA la gioconda
artist leonardo da vinci

MONARCH anosia, autocrat, butterfly, cepheus, chief, czar(ina), despot, diadem, dictator, emperor, empress, kaiser, king, leader, majesty, potentate, queen, ruler, sachem, shah, sovereign, sultan, tsar, tzar
greedy midas

MONARCHAL imperial, kingly, regal, sovereign

MONARCHY kingdom, sovereignty, state

MONARD bee-balm, bergamot, flower, horsemint, mint, oswego-tea, plant

MONASTERY abbey, badia, bonzery, cell, cenoby, certosa, church, cloister, convent, friary, hospice, khankah, kyaung, lamasery, laura, mandra, math, minster, nunnery, priorate, priory, ribat, sanctuary, tekke, tekya, tera, vihara, wat
apartment calefactory
carthusian certosa, la grande chartreuse
church minster
dormitory dorter
dweller cenobite, monk
eastern laurel
head abbott, amma, archimandrite, hegumen, prior
hospital fermery
layman oblate
librarian armarian
manuscript room scriptorium
pert. celibate, cenobitic
republic athos
room cell, lavabo, misericord(e)
stall stasidion
steward manciple
title dom, fra
visitor definitor

MONASTIC anchoritic, ascetic, celibate, cenobitic(al), claustral, hermitlike, monachal, monk(ish), monkly, oblate, order, recluse, secluded, solitary

MONETA juno

MONETARY bursal, financial, fiscal, pecuniary

MONEY (See also .COIN, SHELL *money*.) 3 ice, oil, oof, sap, tin, wad 4 ante, cash, coin, crap, cush, dibs, dump, dust, gate, gelt, gilt, gold, jack, jake, kale, lari, loot, mina, mint, moss, muck, peag, pelf, roll, salt, swag, ullo 5 beans, bills, blunt, bones, bonus, booty, brass, bread, bucks, bunce, check, chink, chips, clink, dough, draft, funds, grigs, ichor, juice, larin, lolly, lucre, means, mopus, notes, ochre, paper, peage, rhino, rocks, salve, sauce, scrip, sewan, sugar, token, uhllo 6 actual, boodle, change, cheque, dinero, do-re-me, grease, larree, mazuma, moolah, plunks, remedy, seawan, silver, specie, spense, stakes, steven, talent, tender, wampum, wealth 7 ballast, berries, bullets, cabbage, capital, chattel, coinage, dollars, finance, lettuce, marbles, mintage, nest egg, ooftish, shekels 8 bankroll, clinkers, currency, ointment, potatoes, proceeds, property, sterling, treasure 9 exchequer, greenback, principle, simoleons, wherewith 10 greenstuff, root of evil, spondulics 11 certificate, filthy lucre, gingerbread, legal tender, spondulicks, wherewithal
additional bonus
ancient aes
available capital
bag fels, follis, purse
bags capitalist
bar bonk, tang
base shice
belt zone
blood breaghe, cro, wergild
box arca, brazier, chest, drawer, pirlie, register, safe, till
bribe boodle, payola, soap
bronze aes
bug economist
certificate bill, bond, check, cheque, note, scrip, warrant
-changer argentarius, banker, broker, cambist, cashier, saraf, serar, shroff
-changing agio
coinage mint
coined specie
container cash register, safe, strong box
copper aes
counterfeit bogus, boodle, duffer, queer, slither
cowrie shells
depreciation agio, inflation
down arles, cash, cod, deposit
drawer cash register, shuttle, till
due debt, devoirs
earnest arles, arrha, deposit, handgeld, handsel, hansel, token
exchange fee agio
false See *counterfeit*, above.
found treasure, trove
gambler's barato
gift alms, bequest, charity, donation, endowment
given to lord farleu, farley
gold crown, doubloon, ducat, eagle, guinea, louis d'or, mohur, moidore, napoleon, ned, slug, sovereign, yellowboy
-grubber fortune-hunter, gold-digger, huckster, mam-

monist, mercenary, MISER, philistine
hard specie
hat tampang
hearth fumage
held deposit, escrow
hook-shaped lari(n), larree
invested stock
-lender banker, banya, broker, cambist, chetty, creditor, loan-shark, lombard, lumberer, mahajan, marwari, pawnbroker, portgager, shylock, uriah heep, usurer
machine john jacob astor
-maker breadwinner, coiner, counterfeiter, earner, minter, moneyer, provider
making banausic, profitable
manual cambist
maxim gresham's law
medieval ora
metal change, coin(age), specie
overdue arrears, debt
oversupply inflation
paid down cash, deposit, downpayment
paper bill, currency, flimsy, frogskin, green(back), kale, lettuce, scrip
plant honesty, moneywort
plastic chargeaplate, credit card
premium agio
prize pewter
provided with heeled, loaded, RICH
push spiff
quantity bankroll, barrel, bundle, fortune, heap, mint, nest egg, pile, pot, pretty penny, purse, scads, wad
ready alcontado, asset, cash, darby, stuff, stumpy
roll rouleau, wad
sent remittance
shell See SHELL *money.*
silver sycee
small amount change, chicken feed, mite, peanuts, pittance, spill
soft paper
sorter saraf, shroff, teller
standard banco, gold, specie
stone fei
subsistence batta
transactions banking, finance
traveling viaticum
unit crown, cruzeiro, dollar, drachma, franc, guilder, krona, krone, lira, maneh, mark, milreis, mina, mite,

ora, peso, piaster, pound, rial, ruble, rupee, tael, talent, unitas, yen
without bankrupt, broke, busted, destitute, flat, hungry, hurting, impecunious, impoverished, pauperized, penniless, pinched, poor, poverty-stricken, strapped
MONEYED flush, loaded, rich, wealthy, well-to-do
MONEYWORT creeping-charlie, creeping-jenny, honesty, mang, myrtle, primwort, satinpod, virgin's-bower
MONG barter, crowd, mingle, mingling, traffic
MONGER dealer, mercer, merchant, trader, vender, vendor
MONGKUT *tutor* anna
MONGOLIA(N) *animal* napu
ass chigetai
buddhist leader bodgo gegen
capital karakorum, ulan bator, urga
caravan leader bashi
city kirqhiz, kobdo, kweisui, ulan bator, urga
coin mungo, tugrik
conjuror shaman
conqueror batu-khan, genghis khan, jenghis, jenghiz, tamerlane, timourguragen
desert gobi, ordos
dwelling yurt
dynasty yuan
dynasty founder kublai khan
emporer jahangir, jehangir
fuel argal, argol, argul
kingdom dzungaria
language khalka
liquor chi
monk lama
people aimak, annamese, aymak, balkar, berberi, buriat, buryat, chud, daghur, durban, eleut(h), garo, hun, indonesian, kalka, kalmuck, karakalpak, khalkha, kirghiz, lai, lapp, lepsha, manchu, mishmi, pareoean, rai, shan, sharra, silingal, soyot, ta(r)tar, torgot, torgut, tungus, yacoot
priest lama, shaman
province chahar
religion confucianism, lamaism, shamanism, shintoism
river onon, pei(ho)

ruler czar, dua, hutuktu, mogul, tsar
tent yurt
tree supa
warrior tartar, tatar
weight lan
MONGOOSE civet, herpestes, ichneumon, lemur, meerkat, mung(o), urva, vansire
kipling's rikki-tikki-tavi
MONGREL cross(breed), cur, dog(gerel), feist, fice, fist, hybrid, limer, mixed, mixture, mutt, piebold, reprobate, sandpiper, scrub, tasteless
collie beardie
skate angelfish
whitefish tullibee
MONICKER (knick)name
MONITION advice, caution, indication, information, instruction, notice, order, summons, tuition, warning
MONITOR admonish, adviser, catamaran, check(er), conscience, counsel(lor), director, eavesdrop(per), ibid, informant, instructor, lantern, listen(er), lizard, mentor, overseer, pr(a)epositer, prefect, reminder, ship, teacher, watchdog
bug conenose
lizard anoli, goanna, ibid, uran, varan(us), waral, worral
MONK, MONK'S abbacomes, abbate, abbe, abbott, ajivika, anchorite, ar(a)hat, ascetic, baeda, bairagi, baldicoot, beadsman, bede(sman), bonze, brother, bullfinch, caloyer, celibate, cenobite, cluniac, conventual, culdee, dervish, dom, eremite, fakir, ferret, fish, fra, friar, gallach, goyin, hermit, hieromonach, lama, lohan, maro, mendicant, monastic, oblate, padre, palmer, pilgrim, pilarist, poong(hee), poonghie, prior, recluse, religieux, religious, saki, sannyasi, santon, shorling, starets, stylite, sufi, talapoin, trappist, yahan
benedictine cluniac
black benedictine
cap kul(l)ah

cell kil(l)
cloak analabos, analav, melote
community cloister, kellion, lamasery, monastery, priorate, priory, scete, skete
fish angel shark, angler, butterfly fish, lophius, spadefish, squatina
flower catasetum, orchid
franciscan capuchin, st anthony
gun harquebus
habit analabos
haircut tonsure
head abbot, dandelion
hood aconite, amice, atees, atis, bearbane, capouch, cowl, mousebane, napellus, wolfsbane, woodbane
idle abbey-lubber
lay conversus
legendary prester john
librarian armarian
order See ORDER *religious.*
parrot loro
pepper tree agnus castus
robe ependytes, habit
scapular cuculla
silent trappist
wandering gyrovague
white cistercian

MONKEY, MONKEY'S 3
ape, sai 4 bali, bega, bimi, broh, bruh, butt, douc, dupe, fool, kaha, lori, maha, maki, mona, mono, saki, sime, titi, tota, waag, zati 5 acari, aotus, araba, cebid, diana, drill, jacko, jocko, kahau, lemur, mimic, munga, oatus, papio, patas, puggy, sajou, tetee, toque, ungka, vitoe 6 ateles, baboon, bandar, bavian, cebide, chacma, coaita, couxia, gibbon, grison, grivet, guenon, hapale, howler, langur, macaca, machin, meddle, miriki, monach, nisnas, oubari, pinche, rhesus, rilawa, rillow, saguin, samiri, simian, simpai, spider, tamper, teetee, teeter, temper, trifle, vervet, warine, weeper, wistit, wouwou 7 babuina, bhundar, cacajao, colobin, colobus, gorilla, guariba, guereza, hanuman, kalasle, lungoor, macaque, meercat, moustoc, ouakari, primate, quakari, roloway, saimari, saimiri, sapajou, siamang,

stentor, tamarin, tarsier 8 alouatte, araguato, caiarara, capuchin, durukuli, entellus, leoncito, mandrill, mangabey, marmoset, martinet, mustache, orabassu, talapoin, tchincou, wanderoo 9 barrigudo, beelzebub, belzebuth, brachyure, lagothrix, malbrouch, marimonda, orangutan, proboscis 10 angwantibo, anthropoid, arctocebus, callicebus, callithrix, cercocebus, cercopithe, chimpanzee, douricouli, orangutano 11 douroucouli
arboreal grivet, potto, teetee, titi
bear koala
bearded entellus
beautiful guereza, mona
bonnet toque, zati
bread baobab
bridge catwalk
broad-nosed platyrrhine
business See MONKEY-SHINES.
capuchin cebus, sai, sapajou
cebine sai
cry chatter, gibber
-cup pitcherplant
diana roloway
dog affenpinscher
dog-headed aani
entellus hanuman, hoonoomaun
flower figwort, mimulus, musk, toadflax
genus aotus, ateles, cebus, colobus, macaca
god hanuman
grivet tota, waag
guenon mona, nisnas, talapoin, vervet
hand ass's-foot, coltsfoot
howling alouatte, araba, araguato, guariba, mono, stentor
jar goglet
king bali, ramayana
large sajou
long-tailed entellus, guenon, hanuman, kaha, langur, maha, patas, sai, talapoin, wanderoo
macaque rhesus
nocturnal aotus
nut peanut
pert. simian
pod rain-tree
proboscis kaha, noseape
purple-faced wanderoo

puzzle pinon, tree
race bandarlog
red pata
rhesus bandar
-rigged trimmed
saki couxia, couxio
sapajou sai
small apelet, apeling, grivet, lemur, marmoset, sime, tarsier, teetee, titi, toto
spider ateles, beelzebub, belzebuth, coaita
squirrel See SQUIRREL *monkey.*
suit uniform
symbol of tricks
tailless ape
tamarin pinche
togue rilawa
trial *character* darrow, scopes
tufted toque, zati
vine morning glory, pomea
with interfere, meddle, tamper
wrench spanner
MONKEYPOT goglet, kararali, lecyth(is), sapucaia
MONKEYSHINES antics, aperies, buffoonery, capers, didos, horseplay, pranks, singerie, tricks
MON-KHMER *language* jakun, khmer, mon
MONOCEROS sawfish, swordfish, unicorn
MONOCHORD agreement, clavichord, concord, harmony, magadis, magas, sonometer
MONODY dirge, homophony, lament, melody, ode, poem
MONOGRAM character, chrismon, cipher, design, initial, letter, name, outline, sign(ature), sketch
MONOGRAPH article, bulletin, description, discourse, pamphlet, piece, sketch, study, treatise, vignette
MONOLITH column, memorial, menhir, monument, obelisk, pillar, shaft, statue, stone
circle cromlech, stonehenge
MONOLOGUE apostrophe, aside, descant, discourse, disquisition, soliloquy, speech, talk
MONOMANIAC crank, enthusiast, fanatic, paranoic, zealot

MONONGAHELA *city on* clarksburg, duquesne, pittsburgh

MONOPOLIZE absorb, appropriate, consume, control, corner, engross, forestall, hog, hold, impropriate, manage, manipulate, own, possess, regrate, sew up, take over, usucapt

MONOPOLY absorption, appalto, appropriation, cartel, coemption, conglomerate, copyright, corner, enterprise, forestallment, oligopoly, patent, pool, possession, prescription, syndicate, synergism, trust, usucapion, zaibatsu

MONOTONOUS boresome, boring, changeless, dead, dingdong, dreary, dull, harping, humdrum, insipid, irksome, prosaic, redundant, samely, samesome, singsong, sodden, tedious, tiresome, toneless, treadmill, uniform, uninteresting, unrelieved, unvaried, wearisome

MONOTONY dullness, sameness, uniformity

MONOTREME duckbill, echidna

MONROE, JAMES *birthplace* virginia
burial site richmond, virginia
party republican
profession lawyer
vice president daniel tompkins

MONSOON kaskaz, rainstorm, varsha

MONSTER afreet, afrit, bilsh, brute, bugaboo, colossus, demon, devil, didymus, dipygus, dragon, enormity, enormous, fiend, freak, fright, ghoul, GIANT, gila, goul, gowl, grotesque, hellhound, hippogriff, hoodlum, horror, huge, janiceps, marvel, ogre, prodigy, sight, teras, vampire, warlock
bull-man minotaur
comb. terat(o)
dog scylla
double anadidymus, didymous, dipygus
dragon-fowl cockatrice
fabulous or famed abominable snowman, acephal(us), argus, bagwyn, basilisk, big

foot, bucentaur, centaur, cerberus, charybdis, chichicache, chimera, cockatrice, cyclops, dipsas, echidna, ellops, geryon, gorgon, grendel, griffin, harpy, hydra, kraken, lamassu, lamia, leviathan, loch ness, manticore, medusa, minotaur, pegasus, pistrix, rahab, sagittary, sasquatch, satyr, scylla, shaitan, sileni, sphinx, taniwha, tarasque, titan, typhon, unicorn, vampire, yeti
female gorgon, harpy, lamia, medusa, mormo, scylla, vampire
fire-breathing chimera, dragon
green-eyed envy, jealousy
handless acheirus
headless acephal(us)
heraldic opinicus
human teras, terata
100-eyed argus
100-handed aegaeon, briareus, gyges
100-headed typhoeus, typhon
legless api, apus
-like teratoid
lion-eagle griffon
lion-goat chimera
lion-headed chimera
man-bull bucentaur, minotaur
man-eating empusae, lamia, ogre, vampire
man-goat satyr
man-horse centaur, ghandharva, sileni
man-lion manticour
misshapen paracephalus
mythical See *fabulous or famed*, above.
9-headed hydra
pert. taratoid
sea belue, cetus, kraken, pistrix
serpent ellops, hydra
shark-tiger pongo
short-limbed nanomelus
single autosite
snake-haired gorgon, medusa
super-human grendel
supernatural larva
2-bodied disomus
3-bodied geryon
2-headed dicephalus, janiceps
water nicker
winged harpy, pegasus, sphinx
woman-bird siren

woman-lion sphinx
woman-serpent echidna, lamia
youth-eating minotaur

MONSTROUS aberrant, abnormal, absurd, atrocious, bad, base, big, black, colossal, corrupt, deformed, enormous, evil, exorbitant, fantastic, flagrant, foul, freakish, gigantic, glaring, great, gross, grotesque, gruesome, hateful, heinous, hideous, horrible, horrid, huge, ill-made, ill-shaped, immense, infamous, large, macabre, misshapen, monumental, odd, outrageous, overwhelming, perverted, prodigious, pythonic, rank, scandalous, slapping, teratoid, titanic, tremendous, ugly, unshapely

MONTAGUE *enemy* capulet
nephew benvolio
servant abraham
son romeo

MONTAIGNE *mistress* marie de gournay

MONTANA *capital* helena
city anaconda, billings, bozeman, butte, chinook, choteau, forsyth, glasgow, hardin, haure, helena, kalispell, kipp, malta, missoula, roundup
country fergus, hill, missoula, pondera, teton, wibaux
indian arapaho, assinaboine, atsima, bannock, blackfoot, cree, crow, flatfoot, flathead, hohe, kutenai, salish, shoshone, siksika
lake flathead, fort peck, hebgen, medicine
national park glacier, yellowstone
nickname big sky country, bonanza state, mountain state, stubtoe, treasure state
peak ajax, baldy, cowan, gallatin, granite, hilgard, pentagon, snowshoe, sphinx, torrey, trapper
range absaroka, big belt, crazy, lewis, purcell, rocky
river kootenai, madison, milk, missouri, powder, shields, sun, teton, tongue, willow, yellowstone
state bird meadowlark
state flower bitterroot
state tree ponderosa pine

MONTANIST (cata)phrygian
sect artotyrite
MONTANO *friend* othello
MONTE CRISTO *author* dumas
 count dantes
MONTEITH handkerchief, punch bowl
MONTENEGRO *capital* cetinje
 city cetinje, niksic, podgorica, titograd
 coin florin, para, perpera
 lake scutari, shkoder
 peak durmitor
 port antivari, bar, dulcigno, ulcinj
 river moraca, zeta
 ruler vladlika
MONTERO cap, forester, hunter, mountain, ranger
MONTEZUMA *ambush* chblula
 capital tenochtitlan
 conqueror cortez
 cypress ahuehuete
 daughter isabel
 downfall tenochtitlan
 enemy cortes
 father axayacatl
 kin cacama, cuitluhuac, don carlos
 lieutenant cualpopoca
 people aztecs
 revenge diarrh(o)ea, turista
 sacrifice xiuhtlamin
 successor cuautemoc, cuitlahuac
MONTH measure, mensis, mes(e), mois, monat
 2 dimester
 3 quarter, trimester
 6 semester
 calendar excess epact
 comb. meno
 1st day calends, kalends
 following proximo
 half fortnight
 next proximo
 of sundays eternity, never
 pert. mensal
 preceding ult(imo)
 present inst(ant)
MONTICLE cone, hill(ock), knob, knoll
MONTREAL *airport* mirabel
MONUMENT arch(ive), bilith(on), ca(i)rn, cenotaph, chaitya, chhatri, column, cromlech, denkmal, dolmen, gravestone, lech, marker, masterpiece, mausole(um), memorial, men-

hir, obelisk, pillar, plaque, pyramid, record, shaft, slab, statue, stela, stele, stone, tabut, testimonial, tomb (stone), tower, trilith, tropaion, trophy, wat, work
 confederate stone mountain
 prehistoric dolmen, stonehenge
MONUMENTAL august, big, bulky, colossal, enormous, gigantic, great, high, huge, imposing, impressive, large, majestic, mammoth, massive, moving, stately
MONZONITE appinite, banatite
MOOCH(ER) beg(gar), bum, cadge, dependent, dupe, freeloader, guest, idle, leech, loaf, loiter, parasite, pilfer, roam, s(c)hnorrer, skulk, sneak, sponge(r), steal, vagrant
MOOCHA breech-cloth, girdle, loin-cloth
MOOD anger, caprice, character, courage, disposition, due, fit, freak, grief, heart, humor, manner, mind, soul, spirit, streak, stripe, style, talent, temper, thought, tid, tone, vein, whim, zeal
 assumed pose
 cross frumps, grizzle, pet
 grammatical conditional, imperative, indicative, obligative, permissive, potential, subjunctive
 pert. modal
 recollective retrospection
 sullen strunt, sulks
MOODY angry, arrogant, atrabilious, brave, broody, capricious, contemplative, dejected, gloomy, glum, melancholy, mopish, mopy, morose, pensive, sad, saturnine, sulky, sullen, temperamental, thoughtful, vapory
MOOL bury, crumple, earth, grave, mingle, mould
MOOLI *father* levi
MOON artemis, astarte, buat, chandra, crescent, cynthia, daydream, diana, fogeater, gape, gaze, goldcrest, hecate, hekate, idle, lamp, languish, lewanna, look, lucina, luminary, luna(r), lunette, mahi, meniscus, month, moonlet, muse, phoebe, roam, satellite,

selene, selenic, stare, wander
 above superlunar
 age on jan. 1 epact
 angel mah(i)
 apogee apsis
 area barrow, boothill, diamondback, mare, mount marilyn, sea of serenity, sea of storms, sidewinder
 aspect phase
 basin mare
 beyond translunary
 -blind lunatic
 -blindness nyctalopia
 circle around corona, halo
 circular area walled plain
 color blue, silver
 comb. selen(o)
 course, part mansion
 crater euler, linne, plana
 creeper See MOONFLOWER, MOONSEED.
 crescent apogee, cusp, horn, isis, meniscus, perigee
 dark area mare
 dark period interlunation
 daughter nakomis, nokomis
 descending node catabibazon
 dog halo, paraselene
 -eye bloater, cisco, hiodon
 fern See MOONWORT.
 festival calends, kalends, neomenia
 festival goddess chang wu
 flight See MOON *shot.*
 full mochi-zuki, plenilune
 gem crystal
 geographer selenographer
 god aah, chandra, ensu, khensu, khons, kuu, meztli, nanna, sin t(h)oth, tsuki-yomi
 goddess artemis, ashtaroth, astarte, belisarna, bendis, chango, chang wu, cynthia, diana, hecate, hekate, hengo, isis, lucina, luna, men, neith, ngame, orthia, phoebe, selena, selene, sin, tanit(h)
 gorge alpine valley
 half lune
 halo bur(r)
 horn cusp
 inhabitant selenite
 january 1st epact
 jellyfish aurelia, chrysalis
 landing vehicle eagle
 lights baily's beads
 lily moonflower
 -mad insane, lunatic
 man gipsy, robber
 mansion alnath, cancer

measurer diopter
metal silver
module columbia, eagle, intrepid
mountains altai, apennine, carpathian, caucasus, dorfel, haemus, jura, massif
observing instrument selenoscope
orbit phase anabibazon, apsis
perigee apsis
personified selena, selene
pert. lunar(ian), lunary, luniform, phasic, selenian, selenic
phase full, gibbous, horning, new
picture selenograph
point cusp, horn
point farthest from earth apogee
point nearest earth perigee
position octant
-raking daydreaming, woolgathering
rat gymnure
ring capuanus, caramuel, raurich, vaisala ·
rocks grapefruit
sea mare-spumans
-shaped cynthian, lunar, lunate, lunular
shot See ASTRONAUT references.
shot term alsep, aristarchus, ascent, boot hill, censorinus, copernicus, diamondback, fra munro, impact, lrl, magnetometer, mount marilyn, ocean of storms, sea of storms, sea of tranquility, seismometer, serenity, spectometer, surveyor, tycho, vulcanism
-sick insane, lunatic, mad
site st albans
spots baily's beads
station botein
-struck See -sick, above.
traveler spaceman
trefoil tree-medic
valley cleft, rill(e), sonoma, taurus
vehicle lem
walker astronaut
walking eva, extra vehicular activity
waning waniand
MOONACK woodchuck
MOONCALF dolt, dunce, fool, imbecile, mole, monster, monstrosity
MOONFISH harvest-fish,

jorobada, minnow, opah, spadefish, sunfish
MOONFLOWER achete, anemone, calonyction, daisy, datura, evening glory, morning glory, oxeye, quamoclit
MOONLIGHTING adventure, bootlegging, expedition, extra work, night job, racket, raid
MOONSEED anamirta, arbuta, calycocarpum, cissampelos, cupseed, menispermum
MOONSHINE (See also DRINK *alcoholic.*) balsamweed, bootleg, busthead, empty, flummery, fustian, hooch, humbug(gery), idle, liquor, nocturnal, nonsense, rubbish, sauce, shinny, trivial, whiskey
MOONSTONE adularia, albite, feldspar, hecatolite, orthoclase
author wilkie collins
MOONWORT botrychium, grapefern, honesty, lunary, ophio
MOONY dreamy, listless, round, silly
MOOR (See also MOHAM-MEDAN, MOORISH.)
affix, algerian, algerine, anchor, arab, attach, bedouin, bent, berber, berth, bind, chain, commoty, comonte, dock, fasten, fen, fix, goldfish, heath, hill, land, lash, marrano, marsh, mograbi, morisco, moroccan, moslem, othello, peat, plain, riff, rivet, root, saracen, secure, settle, steady, tether, tie, trim, turco, waste
berry bog-bilberry, cranberry, vaccinium
besom heather
bird grouse
blackbird ouzel
buzzard harpy, harrier
cock blackcock, gorcock, grouse, muircock
evil dysentery
flower buck-bean
foundation peat
fowl or game gorhen, grouse
grass bog-asphodel, nard, sundew
hawk harpy, harrier
hen coot, gallinule, gorhen, rail

infertile lande
land fen, outfield
monkey macaque
myrtle sweet-gale
palm carex, catkin, sedge
pout grouse
stone granite
whin needle-furze
MOORAGE anchorage, buoyage, fee
MOORBURN anger, fight, quarrel, temper
MOORE *work* alciphron, corruption and intolerance, evenings in greece, history of ireland, irish melodies, lalla rookh, loves of the angels, sacred songs, the blue stocking, the sceptic
MOORING anchorage, berth, dock, harbor(age), marina, port, quay, slip
mast hangar
MOORISH See also MOHAMMEDAN.
cloak albornoz
cymbal zel
dance morisco
drum at(t)abal, kettledrum, tabor
fabric tiraz
family abencerrages
garment albornoz, burnoose, burnous, jupon
god tervagant
horse barb
judge cadi
king of granada boabdil
opiate ke(e)f, kief
palace alcazar, alhambra
pirate salleeman
princess galiana
ship caramoussal, sapit
MOORTETTER pipit, stonechat
MOORUP cassowary
MOORWORT andromeda, bog rosemary
MOOSE alces, cervid, eland, elk
berry hobblebush
bird canada jay
dewlap bell
ear pickerelweed
flower trillium
horn antler
lips muffle
milk whiskey
MOOSEWOOD dirca, hobblebush, leatherwood
MOOT argue(ment), assembly, complain, contestable, controversial, debatable, debate, dig, discuss(ion), dis-

putable, disputed, dubious, encounter, grub, litigation, meeting, molt, plead, postulate, propound, root, speak, stir, tell, utter

MOOTER bolt, disputer, multure, spike, treenail

MOP blindfold, clean(se), grimace, hair, hoodwink, locks, malkin, mane, mawkin, merkin, muffle, mute, polish, pout, scovel, scrub, sop, sponge, swab, swob, tousle, towel, tresses, tuft, wash, wipe, wrap

of hair tousle

oven-cleaning scovel

threads thrum

up complete, dispose of, drink, finish, sop

MOPANE ironwood

MOPE agonize, brood, despond, droop, fool, fret, gloom, idle, kill-joy, mump, pout, sag, sulk, walk

-eyed purblind, shortsighted, stupid

MOPES dods, doldrums, dorts, dumps, frumps, glooming, mulligrubs, mumps, pouts, sulks, sullens

MOPING, MOPISH confused, foolish, fusty, gloomy, glum, morose

MOPPET baby, child, darling, dog, doll, girl, sponge, tike, toddler, tot, tyke

MOPSUS *parent* ampycus, ampyx, apollo, chloris, manto

rival calchas

slayer amphilochus

MOPSY prostitute, slattern, son, trollop, wanton

MOPUS See MONEY.

MORA default, delay, footstool, fustic, game, limma, love, meter, postponement, semeion, stool, tree

MORAL adage, allegory, austere, blue, chaste, conscientious, decent, epimyth, ethic(al), faithful, gnome, good, honest, honorable, incorrupt(ible), just, lesson, maxim, mental, noble, pious, point, precept, pure, puritanic(al), right(eous), scrupulous, story, straight, strict, tag, true, upright, virtuous

character ethos

fable apologue

lapse sin, venality, vice

law code, decalogue

rearmament founder buchman

teaching apologue, edification, lesson, maxim, preaching, preachment, precept, sermon

MORALE confidence, cooperation, esprit de corps, hope, mood, spirit, zeal

MORALISTIC didactic, strict

MORALITY bushido, dharma, ethics, goodness, honesty, honor, merit, nomism, principles, probity, rectitude, standards, virtue

MORALIZE expound, lecture, pontificate, preach, sermonize

MORALS See MORALITY.

description ethography

MORASS bog, fen, flow, flush, marsh, mess, quag (mire), rattrap, slack, slough, sump, swamp, tangle

weed hornwort

MORATORIUM cancellation, delay, write-off

MORAVIAN See CZECHOSLOVAKIA.

bishop comenius

capital brno, brunn

MORAY conger-eel, elgin, gymnothorax, hamlet, muraena, muraenid, pusi

MORBID apprehensive, dark, deadly, deathly, diseased, disordered, frightful, gloomy, grisly, gruesome, hideous, horrible, infected, insane, macabre, pathological, peccant, sick, terrible, unhealthy, unwholesome

sensation cac(a)esthesia

MORCEAU bit, composition, morsel, piece

MORDACIOUS See MORDANT.

MORDANCY acrimony, asperity

MORDANT (See also *kind,* below.) acid, acrid, acrimonious, acute, biting, burning, caustic, cauterant, chape, clear-cut, corrosive, crisp, cutting, erosive, incisive, keen, piquant, pungent, racy, sarcastic, satiric (al), scathing, sharp, snappy, spicy, spirit, trenchant

kind acid, argal, argol, bauxite, diaspore, gibbsite, nitrate, vitriol

MORDECAI *benefactor* ahasuerus, artaxerxes, xerxes

enemy haman

kin abihail, esther, hadassah, jair

MORDRED See MODRED.

MORE additional, again, also, anew, besides, better, beyond, bis, boot, custom, elder, else, encore, excess, extra, further, greater, helder, increase, mae, mair, mas, noch, other, over, piu, plant, plus, root, stump, super, too, uproot

and more increasingly

comb. ple(i)o, plio

or less approximately, somewhat

than above, beyond, but, exceeding, over, plusquam, rising

than enough abundant, ample, excess(ive), extra, prodigality, sufficient, too

than one couple, few, many, plural(ity), several

than one, comb. multi

MORE, THOMAS *jester* patison

work utopia

MOREL blackish, carrionflower, cherry, fungus, helvella, morchella, moriglio, mushroom, nightshade, slanum, wonderberry

MORELLES game, mill, nine men's morris

MORELLO griotte, mulberry

MOREOVER additionally, again, also, and, besides, beyond, eke, else, further (more), likewise, mairatour, then, thereto, too

MOREPORK bird, boobook, mopehawk, mopoke, nightjar, ninox, owl, peho, podargus, ruru

MORES conventions, customs, etiquette, folkways, lares, manners, penates, usage

MORGA(I)N LE FAY argante, fata morgana

brother king arthur

foundling passelyon

husband ogier, uriens

mother igrayne

MORGUE deadhouse, haughtiness, impassivity, library, mortuary, stolidity

MORIBUND acherontic, dead, decadent, decaying, dying, effete, sick, terminated

MORINGA horseradish-tree
oil ben

MORION cabasset, helmet, quartz
blade comb

MORISCO moor

MORMO bugbear, she-monster

MORMON danite, josephite, laman, latter-day saint, lds
angel moroni
cricket grasshopper
destroying angel danite
emblem bee
founder joseph smith
heaven (celestial) (telestial) (terrestial) glory
holy city nauvoo, salt lake city
leader brigham young
officer apostle, deacon, elder
pioneer solomon spalding
priesthood aaronic, melchizedek
prophet joseph smith, moroni
sacred instrument urim
secret order danite
state deseret, utah
temple tabernacle
theory lamanite
tree black poplar
weed mallow, velvetleaf

MORNING ack emma, antemeridian, aurora, beginning, cockcrow, dawn, daybreak, eos, forenoon, matin(al), matutinal, morn, sunrise, sunup, underne
coat cutaway
concert aubade
drink antifogomatic, coffee, orange juice
-glory aguinaldo, alomovine, bindweed, campanilla, convolvulus, gaybine, ipomoea, koali, manroot, merganser, monkeyvine, pilikai, scammony, twiner, vine
land east, orient
meal breakfast, elevenses
noon and night always, ceaselessly, constantly, eternally, long, unceasingly
performance matinee
pert. matin(al), matutinal
prayer aubade, matins
reception levee
song aubade, matins
star bartonia, daystar, ju-

piter, lucifer, mars, mentzelia, mercury, phosphor, saturn, venus

MORO *chief* dat(t)o, datu, dyak, iban
dialect lanao, sulu
island mindanao, philippines
knife barong
mantle jabul
people doloano, illano, lanao, lutao, malanao, samal, sulu, yakan
priest atli, pandita, sarip
sword campilan

MOROCCO maroquin, mauritania
berber moor, riff(ian), shluh
cape n(o)un
capital rabat
chief abd-el-krim
city agadir, casablanca, fes, fez, ifni, marrakech, meknes, porte, rabat, safi, tangier, tetuan
coast riff
coin dirham, floos, flue, miskal, mouzouna, okia, okieh, ounce, rial
district errif, ifni, riff, sus
dynasty almoravide
emperor miramolin, miramamolin
enclave ifni
general kaid
government maghzen, makhzan
gown djellaba, jelab, jellab(a), jel(l)ib
hat fez
-head merganser
island madeira
-jaw surf-scoter
jewish quarter il-millah
king hassan
leather levant, maroquin
measure artal, cadee, covado, dirhem, fanega, gerbe, izenbi, kala, kintar, muhd, quintral, ratel, rotl, saah, sahh, tangin, tomini, ueba
military expedition harka
millet johnson grass
oasis tafilelt
official calif, caliph(a), kalif, khalif, khaliph
peak abyla, jebel-musa, toubkal
people berber, glaoua, kabyle, maghzen, makhzan, moor, moslem, muslem, shilha, shilluh, shlu(h)
port agadir, casablanca, ceuta, elarish, ifni,

lara(i)che, mazagan, mililla, mogador, rab(b)at, saf(f)i, sale, sali, sla, tangier, tetuan
province ceuta, melilla
public land gish
range rif
red ca(u)ldron
resident general lyautey
river dra, moulouya
ruler shereef, sherif, sultan
ruler's wife sherifa
soldier askar
tree alerse, arar, argan, sandarac
troops mehella
weight artal, artel, dirhem, gerbe, kintar, quintal, ratel, rotl
wind charqui, leste

MORON ament, cretin, fool, halfwit, idiot, imbecile, natural, olive, simpleton

MORONIC dull, idiotic, insane, sluggish, stupid

MOROSE acerb, angry, blue, broody, brusque, choleric, churlish, clumse, crabbed, crabby, cross, crusty, dark, dour, dumpish, frowning, gloomy, glowering, glum, gruff, grum, irascible, lingering, louring, lowering, mad, moodish, moody, moping, mopish, mopy, mumpish, particular, peevish, perverse, rusty, saturnine, scowling, snappish, sour, spleeny, splenetic, stuffy, sulky, sullen, surly, testy, waspish
become sour

MOROSENESS asperity, dumpishness, gloom, glumness, grumness, misery, moodiness, mopiness, mumpishness, sullenness

MORPHINE *derivative* heroin

MORRIGAN, **MORRIGU** *consort* nudd

MORRIS, WILLIAM *press* kelmscott

MORRO bluff, castle, dune, fort, headland, hill(ock), mole, point
castle site habana, havana

MORS *brother* sleep, somnus
parent night, nox

MORSE brooch, clasp, code, walrus
signal dah, dit, dot

MORSEL bit(e), cate, drop, fragment, gobbet, morceau,

mouthful, nig, noisette, ort, part(icle), piece, pitsel(eh), sample, scrap, skerrick, snack, snap, sop, taste, tidbit, titbit

MORT abundance, corpse, dead(ly), death, dummy, fatal, female, kill, lard, many, quantity, salmon, skeleton, whist, woman
cloth pall

MORTAL bad, baneful, being, brittle, capital, deadly, deathling, deathly, destructive, dire, dying, earthling, earth(l)y, ephemeral, fatal, great, grievous, grim, human, individual, lethal, man, mundane, person, poisonous, relentless, severe, soul, sublunary, terrene, terrestrial, venial, venomous, virulent, worldly
body khet

MORTALITY death, flesh, humanity, impermanence, loss, murrein, pestilence

MORTALLY deadly, extremely, fatally, greatly, grievously, severely

MORTAR bedding, binder, bowl, bumicky, cannon, cap, cement, coehorn, compo, grout, gun, hobit, holmos, lime, minnie, nightlight, petard, plaster, pugging, putty, so(o)rkee, so(o)rki, so(o)rky, vessel
and pestle dollie, dolly
beater rab
boat palander
coarse pugging
finish depeter
inferior slime
ingredient cement, gypsum, lime
instrument brayer, hod, pestle, rab
rocket trombe
small hobit, royal, tinker
straw bauge
thin grout, larry

MORTARBOARD catercap, hawk, squarecap, trencher
part tassel

MORT D'ARTHUR *author* malory

MORTGAGE antichresis, bond, bottomry, deed, encumbrance, engage, hypothecation, lien, monkey, oblige, pawn, pledge, plight, promise, security, thirlage,

trust-deed, vadium-vivum, wadset, weddeed
giver lienor, moneylender
receivor debtor, lienee

MORTICIAN undertaker

MORTIFICATION asceticism, chagrin, death, embarrassment, envy, gangrene, hair shirt, humiliation, martyrdom, necrosis, penance, rot, sackcloth, shame, spite, vexation

MORTIFIED abas(h)ed, annoyed, ashamed, chagrined, diseased, embarrassed, harassed, harried, humbled, humiliated, rotten, worried

MORTIFY abase, abash, chagrin, crucify, crush, deaden, decay, deflate, deny, disgrace, embarrass, humble, humiliate, offend, punish, put out, shame, sphacelate, spite, subdue

MORTISE amortize, cavity, cocket, fasten, fit, foundation, hole, join, notch, slip, slot, tool
and tenon joint
insert tenon
machine slotter
side cheek

MORTON, FERDINAND *nickname* jelly roll

MORTUARY charnal, cinerarium, corsepresent, deadhouse, deathly, funeral, funerary, graveyard, lichhouse, morgue, necropolis, ossarium, sawlshot, sepulcher, soulscot, soulshot
car hearse

MOSAIC aucuba, check (ed)(ered), frisolee, intarsia, musive, parquet(ry), picture, terrazzo, tessellate(d), tiled, tiles, variegated
apply incrust, inlay
flooring terrazzo
glass smalto
gold ormolu
inlay certosina, certosino, smalto
-like tessellated
pavement asarotum
piece smalto, tessera
potato crinkle
tile abaciscus, abaculus, tessara

MOSCHATEL adoxa

MOSCOW muscovy
airport domadedovo, sheremetyevo, vmukovo

cathedral arkhangelsky, uspensky
citadel kremlin
feature arsenal, kremlin, oruzheinaya, soborny
guard strelitz
native muscovite
pert. muscovite

MOSES *basket* bassinet
brother aaron
competitor jambres, jannes, mambres, yambres, yanos
conspirator against abiram, dathan, korah
emissary caleb
escape route pi-ha-khiroth, sea of passage
father-in-law jethro
general caleb, joshua
helper ahiezer
hiding place bulrushes
law pentateuch, tora(h)
mountain ebal, gerizim, horeb, nebo, sinai
offspring eliezer, gershon
parent amram, jochebed
pert. mosaic
rescuer bathia
sister miriam
spy caleb, gaddiel, igal, nahbi
successor joshua
wife zipporah

MOSEY amble, depart, ramble, shuffle, stroll, walk, wander

MOSK See MOSQUE.

MOSLEM See MOHAMMEDAN.

MOSQUE caaba, dargah, durgah, jami, kaaba, kaabeh, kiblah, masjid, mesquita, mosk, omar, shrine, temple
arcade liwan
gallery, women's tecassir
official ahong, ima(u)m, nazir
part jami, mihrab, mimbah, minaret
student softa, ulema
tower minaret

MOSQUITO aedes, anopheles, culicid, dipteran, gallinipper, gambiae, gnat, imago, insect, pest
bee angelito, karbi, melipona, trigona
-bill shooting star
blight helopeltis
-borne disease encephalitis, malaria
comb. culici
fish gambusia

genus aedes, anopheles, culex, mansonia, megarhinus, psorophora, stegamyia
hawk dragonfly, nighthawk
house culex-pipiens
killer culicide, spray
kind pothole, water-tiger
larva wiggler
order diptera
plant mint, pennyroyal
repellant citronella, culicifuge
state new jersey
yellow fever aedes
MOSS (See also *genus,* below.) acrocarpus, acrogen, agar, archidium, archil, arthrodont, banga, barbula, bartramia, bog, bryace, bryophyte, carrageen, crowfoot, cryptogram, fern, foxfeet, fungus, gulaman, haircap, hypnum, lichen, liverwort, marsh, meese, mnium, money, morass, musci, muskeg, parella, peat-bog, pleurocarpus, portulaca, pulu, ranunculus, seaweed, sedum, sphagnum, staghorn, stonecrop, swamp, tortula, turk's-cap, usnea
agate dendrachate
alpine andreaea
animalcule bryozoan
-back conservative, fog(e)y, oldster
-backed aged, antiquated, oldfashioned, passe, sluggish, stale
basal lobe ala
-bound hidebound, rigid
capsule theca
cheeper bunting, pipit
club lycoped
comb. bry(o), musci
coral bryozoan
corn silverweed
duck mallard
edible agar(agar)
fern thudidium
flowering portulaca, pyxie, widow's-cress
fruit sporogonium
gametophyte protonema
genus bryum, buxbaumia, dawsonia, fissidens, mnium, phascum, polytrichum, rhacomitrium, splachnum
group acrocarpi, pleurocarpi
growing on muscicolous
-grown See *backed,* above.
hag peat bog, pit, slough

hammer bittern
-head merganser
-hood calyptra
life bryology
-like hepatic, mnioid, muscoid
-like plant baby tears
mat bear's bed
pert. aploperistomatous, hepatic, mnioid
pink phlox
plant heath
polyp bryozoan
rose false mallow
science bryology
tooth blephara
tree-hanging weeper
water fontinalis
MOSSBUNKER fish, menhaden, pogy
MOSSTROOPER bogtrotter, freebooter, marauder, r(a)ider, refugee
MOSSWORT bryophyte
MOSSY boggy, downy, dull, grassy, green, marshy, muscose, overgrown, stupid, turfy, verdant
MOST almost, best, chief(ly), general, greatest, highest, il piu, majority, maximum, nearly, plurality, preponderance, ultimate, utmost
MOSTLY chiefly, feckly, largely
MOT butt, chachma, device, epigram, gag, hachma, jest, khaukhma, mark, moat, motto, pun, quip, vitz, word, zinger
MOTE atom(y), barrow, bit, dot, eminence, fescue, fleck, height, hill, iota, match, may, might, moathill, motion, particle, seed, speck, spot, squib, stalk, straw, trifle, tumulus
MOTEL autocourt, hotel, inn, motor-inn
MOTH acrea, aegeriid, agaristid, agrotis, anaphe, antler, apatela, arctida, arrinda, atlas, attacus, bagworm, bee, bell, black witch, bogong, bombycid, bombyx, brown-tail, bucculatrix, buff-tipped, bumblebee-hawk, burnet, canace, catocala, cepropia, cochylis, codling, convolvulus, dermestes, egger, emperor, eudemis, fly weevil, geometer, gypsy, hawk, herald,

heterocera, hummer, insect, lackey, lappet, lepidoptera, luna, micro, miller, muga, noctuid, notchwing, pegasus, poplar-hawk, quaker, regal, royal, sphingid, sphinx, tent-maker, thisbe, tinean, tortrix, tussah, tussur, urania, wainscot, wax, yucca
acrea estigmene, tiger moth
aloeus canace
ball ingredient camphor, naphthalene
black grapeleaf-folder
breeder aurelian
buff-tipped phalera-bucephala
cabbage mamestra, noctuida
carpenter prinoxysus
carpet larentiid, trichophaga
cecropis silkworm
clearwing aegerid, sesia, sesiid
clothes larentiid, tinea, tineid, tineina
codling carpocapsa, tortricida
day-flying pyromorphida
diamondback mamestra, noctuida
-eaten aged, blighted, decayed, decrepit, hackneyed, out-dated, stale, trite, worn
family aegeridae, agaristidae, arctiidae, geometridae, tineina, tortricidae
genus bucculatrix, coleophora, crambus, endromis, gelechia, graptolithe, plusia, plutella, prodenia, pyrausta, sesia, tinea, tryris, tortrix, urania
goat prinoxystus
grain-eating angoumois
green luna
gypsy liparian
hawk goatsucker, morningglory sphinx, phalus
hunter goatsucker
larva armyworm, bagworm, bean-cutworm, caterpillar, fruitworm, grassworm, leafminer, ogodonta, palmerworm, webworm
liparian goldtail
mullein verbascum
noctuid agrotis, underwing
patch chloasma
polyphemus silkworm
-proof tree cedar
pyralid corn-borer, pickleworm, pine pest
repellant camphor

silkworm anthera, cecropia, eria, muga
small micro
spots chloasma, fenestra
spotted acrea, forester
suborder heterocera
tapestry trichophaga
tiger apantesis, euprepia
tussock euproctis
MOTHER abbess, adopt, amma, ancestress, arene, author, care for, dam, dregs, foster, generate, genetrix, hysteria, ina, lees, leucothea, madre, mam (ma), mammy, mater, matriarch, matuta, maw (ther), mere, mither, modur, mom(my), mulier, mum(my), mumsy, native, nurture, origin, parent, producer, source, starter, vat, venter, vernacular
carey's chickens omens, stormy-petrel
carey's goose fulmar, petrel
comb. matri, metro
country homeland
divine matrigan
earth gaia
-gate bord, tramway
goddess allat, amman, arene, devi, erua, hera, kali, matris, rhea
goose author perrault
goose character (See also NURSERY *rhyme character.*) baker's man, betty blue, big bad wolf, bobby shaftoe, bopeep, boy blue, cross patch, curly locks, daffy down dilly, georgey porgey, goosey-gander, handy spandy, jack-a-dandy, jack and jill, jack horner, jack sprat, jennie wren, kitty fisher, little bo-peep, little boy blue, little miss muffet, lucy locket, mistress mary, mother hubbard, old king cole, old mother hubbard, peter piper, polly flinders, pumpkin eater, pussy, queen of hearts, taffy, tattle-tale-tit, tommy trot, wee willie winkie, willie wanbeard
government by matriarchy, metrocracy
great agdistis, cybele, rhea
heart shepherd's purse
hubbard dress, gown
-in-law backseat driver,

bellemere, eldmother, ersatz mother, shviger
-in-law plant dieffenbachia
-killing matricide
lode fraternity clampers, e clampus vitus
of believers aisha, ayeshah
of cities balkh
of day and night nox, nyx
of god madonna, mary
of gods ana, anu, brigantia, brigit, cybele, frigga, rhea
of graces aegle
of man cybele
of millions kenilworth ivy
of months moon
of one unipara
of parliaments england
of pearl abalone, conchiolin, iridescent, nacre, oyster, river-mussel
of presidents virginia
of revolutions paris
of sorrows mater dolorosa, virgin mary
of states virginia
of the family materfamilias
of thousands daisy, kenilworth ivy, saxifrage
pert. maternal, spindle
-related enate, enatic
slayer orestes
spiritual amma
-spot birthmark
superior abbess, mistress, nun, prioress
turned to stone niobe
MOTHERED coddled, thick, viscid
MOTHERGATE bord, tramway
MOTHERLY caring, loving, maternal, matronal
MOTHERWORT feverfew, joe-pye weed, leonurus
MOTIF applique, border, design, device, edging, figure, motive, pattern, theme, topic
MOTILE mobile, motive, movable
MOTION action, activity, advance, aestus, agitation, ambulation, beckon, bob, circuit, clip, course, current, direct(ion), drift, flow, flux, gait, geste, gesticulate, gesture, guide, impetus, impulse, kinesis, life, mobility, mobilization, momentum, move, movement, moving, nod, pace, port, procedure, progress, proposal, rate, request, set, sign, speed, step,

stimulation, stir, stream, suggestion, sweep, tendency, travel, trend, velocity, wave
abrupt chop, jerk
around axis eddy, gyre, revolution
body, pert. gestic
capable of spontaneous automatic
circular compass, gyre
comb. cin, kinesi
convulsive jerk, shakes, twitch, vellication
dizzy swimbel
energetic appulse
expressive gesture
forward headway, thrust
gliding skitter, slide, slip, swim
imparting kinetic
impetuous bensaill, bensall, bensell, bensill
inability to originate akinesia
in constant motatorious
involuntary dyskinesia, tic
jerky bob, jiggle, lipe, swag
line, main axis
make a move, offer, propose, recommend, suggest
pert. gestic, kinematic(al), kinetic, motile, motive
picture See MOVIE.
producing motific, motile
quantity momentum
rate rpm, speed, tempo, time
reverse backrun
rotary backspin, seesaw, sidespin, sway
science ballistics, dynamics, kinematics, kinetics, physics
sideways crab, crawfish
slow crawl
spinning english
spontaneous autokinesis
suspended particles pedesis
swimming flutter
transmitter belt, cog, gear
upward heave, lift, scend, upthrust
viewing device strobe
MOTIONLESS anchored, asleep, becalmed, breathless, calm, dead, fixed, immobile, inactive, inert, numb(ed), paralyzed, petrified, quiet, rigid, sedentary, sessile, spellbound, stable, stagnant, stagnate, stalled, standing, static, stationary, statue-like, steadfast, still, stirless, stockstill, torpid, transfixed
MOTIVATE activate, actu-

ate, advance, animate, arouse, compel, dispose, drive, egg on, encourage, excite, fire, foment, force, forward, foster, further, goad, impel, incite, induce, influence, inspire, inveigle, jog, lead, move, persuade, predispose, prevail, prod, promote, prompt, propel, provoke, push, quicken, rouse, spur, start, stimulate, stir, suggest, sway, urge

MOTIVATION actuation, allurement, animation, arousal, catalysis, coaxing, disposition, encouragement, excitement, impulsion, inclination, inducement, inspiration, instigation, lure, persuasion, provocation, stimulation, stimulus, suggestion, wheedling

MOTIVE account, active, aim, aria, basis, bias, cause, consideration, design, drive, dynamic, end, force, foundation, goad, ground, idea, impulse, incentive, inducement, influence, intent (ion), lure, mobile, motif, movable, moving, occasion, pattern, press, pretext, purpose, reason, rinceau, root, sake, spring, spur, stimulus, stirring, subject, text, theme, topic, urge
musical attacco
ostensible pretext

MOTLEY assorted, buffoon, costume, different, diverse, heterogeneous, incongruous, medley, miscellaneous, mixed, mottled, piebald, pied, promiscuous, ragtag, skewbald, varied, variegate(d), various
man of fool, jester, pierrot

MOTMOT bird, houtou, huhu, picarian, sawbill

MOTOR apparatus, auto (mobile), car, drive, efferent, engine, generator, instrument, kinetic, machine, mover, power, propel, ride, rotator, transport, travel, turbine, vehicle
additive antifreeze, antiknock
agraphia anorthography
aphasia alalia
bike motorcycle
bike cushion pillion
city detroit, motown

coach bus, greyhound, omnibus
court inn, motel
electric dynamo
fuel benzine, diesel, gas (oline), petrol
function motricity
hand-powered baromotor
inn auto court, motel
irregularity parakinesia
part cam, capacitor, carburetor, coil, piston, rotor, stator
rotary turbine
speed control rheocrat
speed up gun, rev
truck bobtail, camion, dray, flatbed, lorry

MOTORBOAT palander, runabout

MOTORCYCLE autoette, honda, moped, tricar, tricycle, vespa

MOTORIST autoist, busman, chauffeur, chauffeuse, driver, james, jitneur, road hog, trucker

MOTORMAN carman, driver, engineer, mechanic, trollyman, wattman

MOTOWN detroit

MOTTLE bespot, blotch, check, marble, speck(le), sponge, spot, stain, tabby

MOTTLED blotched, brocked, calico, checkered, clouded, dapple(d), marbled, marked, motley, pepper-and-salt, piebald, pied, pinto, roed, roey, scroddled, skewbald, splashed, spotted, stained, variegated

MOTTO adage, aphorism, apothegm, axiom, byword, cachet, empresa, epigram, epigraph, eureka, gnome, impresa, maxim, mot, posy, proverb, reason, saw, saying, shibboleth, slogan, thought, title, watchword

MOUCHARD detective, informer, police-spy

MOUE face, grimace, pout

MOULD, MOULDY See MOLD, MOLDY.

MOUND agger, ahu, bank, barbette, barrier, barrow, berry, boundary, bounds, bourock, bulwark, bunker, butt, causey, cop, dam, dher(i), dune, embankment, enclose, escalade, eskar, fort, heap, hill(ock),

hummock, hump, knoll, mole, monticle, morro, motte, pile, pingo, pome, rampart, rise, sandtrap, step, stupa, tee, tell, teocalli, terp, terrace, tomb, tump, tumulus
ancient motte, tell, terp
bird leipoa, megapod(e)
burial barrow, berry, guaca, huaca, kurgan, law, low, tola, tor, tumulus
fortified dun
glacial kame
historic cahokia, elephant, etowah, serpent
lily spanish dagger, yucca
military barbette
of light kohinoor
palisaded motte
pert. tumular
pitcher's box, hill, slab
turkey megapode
volcanic hornito

MOUNT alp, arise, arrange, ascend, aspire, back, bestraddle, bestride, block, board, charger, climb, colline, escalade, fasten, fix, get on, glue, go up, harness, heave, hill, horse, increase, jump, levitate, mesa, moriah, palfrey, paste, peak, pile, place, rise, rocket, scale, seat, set, soar, steed, surge, swarm, tower, vault, volcano
etna mongibel
etna city catania
everest chomolongma
everest peak lhotse
guard watch
helicon fountain aganippe
holyoke founder lyon
horse fork, light
ida psiloriti
ida magician dactyl, daktyl
ida nymph oenone
of olives olivet
parallel bars kip(p)
parnassus fountain castalia
rushmore sculptor gutzon borglum
rushmore subject jefferson, lincoln, roosevelt, washington
2-legged bipod
3-legged tripod
up to cost, total

MOUNTAIN aiguille, alp, amba, barrow, ben, berg, bundoc(ks), butte, crest, dagh, djebel, elevation, fell, great, heap, heights, hill (top), hump, jebel, kaf, kop, mass, mauna(lani), meru, mesa, mont, ord, peak, pike, pinnacle, pisgah, point, quantity, sierra, summit, tor, vast

andromeda fetterbush

antelope chamois

ash dogberry, eucalyptus, mozemize, rountree, rowan, sorb(us), winetree

badger marmot

balm oswego tea, yerba santa

banana fei

barometer orometer

base foothill, piedmont

basin hoya

beaver boomer, rodent, sewellel

beyond tramontine, transalpine

biblical See BIBLE *mountain.*

blackbird ring ouzel

bluet centaury

bobcat lynx

box bearberry

bracken fern

bramble cloudberry

burning volcano

canary ass, donkey

cap scalp

carboniferous altaid

cat bobcat, cacomistle, cougar, lynx

chain cordillera, range

cherry chickasaw-plum

climber alpestrian, alpinist, cragsman, hillary

climbing alpinism

climbing gear carabiner, cleat, crampon, piton

cock capercaillie

comb. ore(o), oro, mont(i)

cowslip auricula

cranberry foxberry

crest arete, cumbre, peak, tor

curassow oreophasis

damson marupa, paradise tree

deity oread(e)s, troll

depression col

descent abseil

devil moloch

dew bootleg, moonshine, whiskey

duck harlequin, sheldrake

dweller highlander, hillbilly, montagnard, tramontane, ultramontane

finch brambling

flat mesa

flax amianthus, centaury, corn-spurry, quaking-grass, snakeroot

flower crane's-bill, edelweiss, gentian

formation orogenesis, orogeny

fringe fumitory, wormwood

gap col, corrie, defile, pass

goat ibex, mazame

god atlas, olympus, tmolus

gully chimney

herb brook-saxifrage

high alp

highest everest, mckinley

hollow in side cirque, coomb, corrie, cwm

holly brick-timber, catberry, gooseberry, nempanthus

ivy laurel

lake tarn

laurel calfkill, calicobush, ericad, heath, ivy(wood), kalmia

laurel thicket slick

laurelroot briarroot

leather asbestos, palygorskite

leatherwood flannelbush

legendary See *mythical,* below.

-like etiolin

lily turk's-cap

linnet twite

lion See LION *mountain.*

low butte, mesa

magpie butcherbird, woodpecker

mahoe emajagua

mahogany quail b(r)ush

-making process orogeny, upheaval

marmot whistler

mass massif, orogen

mint basil, bezel, calamint, ocimum, oswego tea, sheepskin

misery bearmat, tarweed

movable ossa

muses' helicon

mythical candy, glass, helicon, kaf, meru, olympus, ossa, parnassus, pelion, qaf

nymph dryad, oenone, oread

panther cougar, leopard, ounce

parrot kea

parsley fluellen

partridge dove, quail

pass bealach, bernard, brenner, cenis, clove, col, cut, defile, donner, duar, gap, gate, gha(u)t, gorge, kloot, kotal, poort, sag,

st got(t)hard, simplon, slip, swire, swirl, tioga

pasture alp, s(a)eter

peach yerba santa

peak acme, aiguille, alp, apex, cima, cone, man, pico, summit

pert. montane, MOUNTAINOUS, orological

pink arbutus

pool tarn

quail partridge

railroad cogway

range alaska, allegheny, alpid, alps, altai, andes, apennine, appalachian, atlas, blue ridge, brooks, byrannga, cascade, catskill, cherskogo, chukotskoye, coast, dindymus, dolomite, gha(u)t, himalaya, hump, kaf, kamchatka, kolymskiy, koryakskiy, kunlun shan, pamir, putorana, pyrenees, qaf, rockies, rocky, sawback, sayany, shenandoah, sierra, sikhote-alin, tetons, tien shan, ural, verkhoyansky, yablonovy

range summit divide

raspberry cloudberry

ridge arete, crest, peak, sawbuck, s(i)erra, spur, summit

road ess

rocky nunatak, teton

rose laurel

round reek

sacred om(e)i

sage artemesia, germander

science orogeny, orography, orology, volcanology

sheep bighorn

shelter gite

sickness puna, soroche, veta

side, sunny adret

small butte, dagh, hill(ock), knob, mesa, nob

snow jokul, neve

soap halloysite

spinach orach(e)

state arizona, colorado, idaho, montana, nevada, new mexico, utah, west virginia, wyoming

study orography

submarine guyot

sunny slope adret

sunset reflection alpenglow

tallow hatchettine

tatar tauli

tea wintergreen

thrush ring-ouzel

top See *peak,* above.

trail marker cairn, karn
witch quail-dove
with 5 peaks pancasika, pancasirsa
wood rockwood
MOUNTAINEER aaron, climber, frontiersman, hayduck, heiduc, hillbilly, hillman, montesco, orestes, tiersman, wasir, wazir
song yodel
staff alpenstock
MOUNTAINOUS alpen, alpestrine, alpigene, alpine, colossal, elevated, giant, high, hilly, huge, mammoth, monticuline, monticulous, montiform, montigeneous, orological, rangy
MOUNTEBANK buffoon, charlatan, chest, clown, empiric, faker, fraud, gracioso, imposter, mime(r), operator, phony, pitchman, pretender, quack, trickster, zany
MOUNTIE patroller, policeman, ranger
MOUNTING ascending, ascent, embellishment, equipment, flight, incabloc, montant, scape, setting, standard, support
shockproof incabloc
style setting
MOURN agonize, bemoan, bewail, croon, cry, deplore, dole, droop, elegize, grieve, grizzle, keen, lament, long, moan, murmur, pine, repine, rue, sigh, sorrow, wail, weep
MOURNER *bench* anxious seat
group cortege
hired dismal, keener, saulie
MOURNFUL black, careful, dejected, dire, dirgeful, distressing, doleful, dreary, elegiac, elegious, funereal, gloomy, lamentable, lugubrious, maestive, melancholy, mestful, mestive, pitiful, plaintive, rueful, sad, somber, sorrowful, sorry, threnodic, woeful, yearnful
MOURNFULNESS dolefulness, grief, grievousness, lugubriousness, misery, plaintiveness, ruefulness, sadness, sorrowfulness
MOURNING black, dolor, keening, lament(ation),

sad, shiva, sorrow(ing), widowed
bride plant, scabious
cloak butterfly, camberwell-beauty
dress alma, blacks, crape, crepe, dismal, sables, weeds
fabric bombasine, bombazeen, bombazine, crepe, cypress, radzimer
group cortege
heavy widow's weeds
widow geranium, scabious
MOUSE animalcule, arvicole, bankvole, bruise, contusion, cricetid, diminutive, lerot, loir, mur(ine), mus, migale, myomorph, prowl, rodent, shiner, swelling, vermin, vole, wale, weight
around prowl, pursue, search
bird coly, shrike
blind shrew, sorex
breeding place murarium
comb. mys
deer chevrotain, napu, plandok
-ear chickweed, forget-me-not, hawkweed
-ear cress crucifer
field harvest, metad, migale, mus, vole
flying glider
gray boulevard
group nest
hare pika
hound weasel
leaping jerboa
-like drab, muriform, murine, nugale, quiet, retiring, shy, timid
-like animal erdshrew, lemming, vole
male buck
meadow vole
milk sun-spurge
over study
pox extromelia
shrew erd, hyrax, migale, sorex
striped kusu
tiny harvest-mouse
trap lure, tipe
web cobweb, gossamer, phlegm
MOUSEBANE monkshood
MOUSSORGSKY *opera* boris(godounow)(godunov), khowantchina
MOUSY bashful, colorless, diffident, drab, modest, noiseless, quiet, shy, silent, timid, timorous

MOUTAN flower, peony, plant
MOUTH abra, adit, bazoo, beal, bocca, bouche, cavity, chaps, cheeks, chew, chops, clapper, codon, declaim, delta, dupe, eater, embouchement, embouchure, empty, entrance, estuary, express, firth, flummer, frith, gab, gebbie, gob, grimace, impudence, influx, inlet, jaw(s), jib, jowls, kiss(er), lade, lick, lips, lorriker, mandible, maw, maxilla, mow, mug, mumble, mun, mush, muss, muzzle, neb, nozzle, opening, ora, orifice, oro, ostiole, outlet, premaxilla, rictus, scotia, speak, speech, stoma, talk, taphole, trap, utter, verbal, voice, yap
away from aborad, abroral
by oral(ly)
canker stomacace
comb. bucco, ori, stom(o)
crooked wapperjaw
deformity harelip
disease aptha, canker, ecthyma, noma, stomatitis, thrush
down in the chapfallen, dejected, depressed, disheartened
embryonic stomodeum
foaming at the frantic, furious, rabid, raging
foulness saburra
furnace bocca
having distinct eustomatous
having none astomia
having small microstomatous
having 2 distomatous
-like orificial
muscle caninus
narrowing stenostomia
off blah blah, chatter, jabber, talk
open agape, slack-jawed
organ crembalum, harmonica, pandean, panpipe
part gum, labia, lips, palate, pharynx, roof, uvula
people without astomoi
pert. cibarian, oral, orificial, oscular, palatal, rictal, stomat(ic)
projecting spout
river delta, firth, lade
roof palate
surgery stomatoplasty
through peroral
tissue gum

toward orad

-watering alluring, appetizing, desirable, salivant

wide rictus

without astomatous, astomous

MOUTHFUL bit, bite, drop, gag, gob(bet), lot, morsel, sample, sip, snack, sup, taste

MOUTHPIECE agent, attorney, bar, beak, fipple, go-between, informant, interlocutor, interlocutrix, lawyer, microphone, mike, muse, prolocutor, prophet, reed, representative, respirator, speaker, spokesman, stem, syrinx

MOUTHWASH collutory, collutorium, gargle, lavoris, listerine, prophylactic

MOUTHY bombastic, loquacious, ranting, talkative

MOVABLE changeable, fickle, flexible, free, inconstant, loose, mobile, motile, mutable, portable, variable

MOVABLES appurtenances, furniture, goods, mobiles, moble, wares

MOVE 3 act, bob, cam, gee 4 bear, birl, blow, boom, draw, goad, lead, melt, pass, play, push, rock, send, spur, stir, turn, work 5 barge, bound, brush, budge, carry, cater, cause, drive, force, impel, kedge, mudge, power, rouse, shift, skirr, slink, sneak, speed, touch 6 affect, arouse, canter, career, change, convey, deploy, enjoin, excite, hustle, incite, induce, kelter, kindle, MOTION, prende, prompt, propel, remble, sashay, strake, strike, travel 7 actuate, advance, agitate, animate, attempt, disturb, impress, inspire, migrate, proceed, propose, provoke, quicken, suggest, trundle 8 ambulate, dislodge, displace, locomote, motivate, persuade, transfer, transmit 9 advantage, influence, instigate, introduce, prevail on, recommend, stimulate, transport, transpose, variation

about float, ocomote, shuffle, stir, wander, wend

across thwart, traverse

ahead advance, forge, proceed

aimlessly bogue, shuffle

along bounce, bowl, depart, hurry, maunder, mog, mosey, progress, shog, travel

aside skew, swivel

away decamp, depart, ebb, emigrate, recede, retreat, shy

back retreat

back and forth dartle, diddle, dodge, falter, flap, oscillate, rock, seesaw, shuffle, shuttle, sway, teeter, wabble, waffle, wag, wiggle, wigwag, zigzag

backward arsle

behind fall back, follow

by force muscle

by jerks buck, flirt, hitch, jigget, jiggle, jinkle, twitch

camera pan

clumsily flob, joll

comb. kinesi

down decline, descend, drop, fall, stoop

energetically bustle, rustle, scurry

false balk, feint, misstep

fast frick, frike, frisk, scur(ry), skirr, squirt

first advantage, initiative

forward advance, drive, edge, forge, prograde, progress, surge

furtively glide, skulk, slink, slive, sneak, steal

gradually edge

heaven and earth persevere, try

heavily flump, lug, lumber, trudge

here and there browse, dart

inability to appraxia

in circles eddy, gyrate, mill, purl, spin, spiral, swirl, twirl, writhe

in water float, squelch, swim, wade

leisurely amble, maunder

nervously dither, fidget, kelter, tic, twitch

noiselessly creep, glide, pussyfoot, skulk, slink, slip, sneak, steal, tiptoe

noisily bustle, clatter, clump, rollick

obliquely edge, joll, sidle, skew, slue

off depart, firk, recede, rynt

on advance, succeed

on the active, advancing, busy, energetic

on wheels roll, trundle

over budge, joll, lurch, nudge

quickly bicker, boom, bound, buzz, cannonball, career, course, dart, dash, duck, firk, flit, fly, gallop, hightail, hurry, hurtle, jump, leap, run, scat, scoot, scud, scur(ry), skate, skeet, skim, skirr, skite, spank, speed, spring, squib, start, stour, sweep, thud, wallop, whew, yank

rhythmically bob, dance, goosestep, jig, jog, march

round and round eddy, swirl, twirl

sidewise crab(sidle), crawfish, edge, sidle, slue, wag, wigwag

sinuously snake, wiggle, writhe

slowly bogue, crawl, creep, drawl, drumble, edge, fudge, hag, inch, las, linger, mog, pant, sloom, snail, trintle, worm

smoothly drift, float, glide, skate, skim, slide, slip

steadily forge, trudge

sudden gambade

suddenly bolt, flounce, startle, yerk

to greet, salaam

to and fro agitate, fan, flap, flop, seesaw, shake, shuttle, sway, wag, wigwag

together converge, join, unite

unsteadily blunder, bumble, falter, hobble, stagger, stumble, wamble, wobble

up and down seesaw, teeter-totter

upward arise, ascend, rise

MOVED affected, impressed, penetrated, sensitive, stirred, touched

MOVEMENT act(ion), activity, cadence, carry, cause, change, circulation, crusade, current, deed, drive, eddy, flow, gambado, gesture, impulse, incident, kinesis, locomotion, maneuver, meter, MOTION, motor, mudge, operation, organization, rhythm, stir, stroke, style, taxis, tempo, theme, travel, trend

backward backlash, backwash

biological taxis
brownian pedesis
capable of mobile, motile
comb. kinesi
cure by motorpathy
deceptive feint
downward decline, descent, fall
final coda
forward advance, progress, sweep
humanist renaissance
impairment akinesia
independence swadeshi
involuntary reflex, tic
mass stampede
measured rhythm
musical burla, dumka, entree, finale, saraband
reflex allokinesis
reverse reaction, retraction
rocking howd
skilled suerte
spasmodic hiccough, hiccup, sprunt
surface seiche
turning caracole
upward ascent, climb, rise, scend, surge
voluntary autokinesis
zigzag tack

MOVER author, doer, instigator, motor, producer, prompter, proposer

MOVIE biopic, cartoon, celluloid, cine(ma), documentary, drive-in, feature, film, flick(er), motion picture, newsreel, nickelodeon, photoplay, preview, screen, silent, silverscreen, talkie, trailer, travelogue
art cinematics
award emmy, oscar
comb. cine
cowboy horse opera, oater, western
end fade-out
fan cineaste
land hollywood
machine animatograph, cinematograph, kinetoscope, projector
maker cinematographer, director, producer
outline scenario, script
pathetic tearjerker
pert. cinematic, cinematographic
pioneer de mille, goldwyn, ince, lasky, mayer, selznick, zanuck
projector animatograph, bio-

graph, cinematograph, kinematograph
term boom-shot, close-up, fader, pan, reel, retake, shot, take, wide-screen
3-dimension cinerama
writer scenarist

MOVING active, affecting, afloat, agitation, agoing, alive, animate, astir, distressing, emotional, exciting, going, heartbreaking, impelling, impressive, influential, inspiring, mobile, motile, nomadic, pathetic, persuading, persuasive, pitiful, poignant, progressive, provoking, quick (ening), rallying, rousing, stimulating, stirring, thrilling, touching
about ambulant, ambulatory
backward cancrizans, crab
comb. kino, plano
forward advance
part cam, cog, rotor, wheel
rapidly dashing, skelping, speeding, stickle
up and down anaseismic

MOW barb, can, cradle, cornfield, cut(down), dess, goaf, granary, grimace, harvest, hayrick, haystack, heap, jest, loft, math, may, mew, mock(ery), mouth, must, ought, pile, pout, scythe, sheaf, shorten, should, sickle, skim, smooth, stack
down cut, fell
storage toss

MOWER meader, mocker

MOWGLI *friend* akela, baloo, balu
elephant hathi
python kaa

MOWLAND meadow, mowlot

MOXIE chutzpah, confidence, nerve

MOZA *father* caleb

MOZAMBIQUE *cape* delgado
capital beira
city beira, chemba, lourenco-marques, nampula, pafuri, tete, zumbo
district niassa
lake chuali, nhavarre, nyas(s)a
leader chissano, dos santos, machel
native yao
party frelimo

port beira, porto amelia, inhambane
river lugenda, msalu, save, zambezi

MOZART *opera* bastien et bastienne, cosi fan tutti, don giovanni, idomeneo, magic flute, marriage of figaro, nozze di figaro, re pastore, zauberflote

MOZZETTA camail, hood, cape

MR heer, herr(en), master, monsieur, senhor, senor, ser, signor(e)

MRS bibi, devi, dona, frau, goodwife, hanoum, madam(e), missus, mistress, mme, pani, senhora, senora, signora, wife, woman

MUCH abundant, almost, approximately, awful, bagful, bags, big, bundles, caress, considerable, far, fele, gobs, great, heaps, high, indeed, large, loads, lots, many, mickle, mighty, molto, nearly, oodles, plenteous, plentiful, plenty, quantity, reams, scads, slosh, trust, very
ado about nothing character antonio, balthasar, beatrice, benedick, borachio, claudio, conrade, dogberry, don juan, don pedro, friar francis, hero, leonato, margaret, ursala, verges
comb. eri, multi, poly
in little multum in parvo
too trop(po)
very awfu, geylies, greatly

MUCHACHA girl, lass, senorita, signorina

MUCHACHO boy, lad, ragazzo, youth

MUCID, MUCULENT clammy, moldy, mucous, musty, pituitous, sammy, slimy, slithery, snotty

MUCILAGE adhesive, cement, glue, gum, lubricant, mucago, mucus, paste, plaster

MUCILAGINOUS adhesive, gluey, glutinous, gummy, malacoid, sticky, thick, viscid

MUCK bungle, cack, dirt, dirty, dung, earth, fertilizer, filth, glop, manure, mess, mire, money, ooze, potter, ruin, slime, soil, toil, waste, wealth

about idle, loiter, potter
-midden dunghill
MUCKER boor, bounder, bungler, confusion, disorder, fall, hoard, mess, muddle, wretch
MUCKLE bother, club, fret, great, mickle, much, putter, size
MUCKMENT dirt, filth, trash
MUCKRAKE expose, smear
MUCKWEED lamb's-quarters
MUCKWORM miser, niggard
MUCKY contemptible, dirty, disgusting, filthy, muddy, sordid, vile
MUCOUS blennoid, moist, mucoid, muculent, slimy, viscous
MUCUS lubricant, phlegm, pituite, rheum, secretion
comb. blenn(o)
MUD clabber, clart, dirt, dregs, fango, glar, glaur, gobbet, goo, gore, gutters, libel, marsh, mire, moil, muck, murgeon, ooze, salse, saur, silt, slander, slime, slob, slodder, slop, slosh, slubber, sludder, sludge, slush, slutch, sluther, squad, sullage, sump
bass sunfish
bath illulation, pelotherapy
cat catfish, flathead
cat state mississippi
clear of slutch
clot clart
comb. pel(o), telmat(o)
-covered belute
dab flounder
dabbler killifish
dauber wasp
deposit silt
devil hellbender
dipper ruddy-duck
eel siren
enclosure bawn
fever scratches
flat corcass, slob
flow lahar
hen coot, gallinule, rail
hole loblolly, pan, pulk, quagmire, sloo, slough, slue, wallow
hut adobe, jacal
lacustrine gyttja
lark gamin, meadowlark, pipit, shoveler, urchin, vagabond
-like luteous

living in limicolous
mark mudflow
minnow dogfish, mudfish
peep sandpiper
pert. luteous
pike saury
puddle chuckhole, chughole, hogwallow, loblolly, slap, slop, wallow
puppy dogfish, hellbender, necturus, salamander
purslane elatine
rake claut
rich gyttja
-skipper climbing fish, goby
sling abuse, attack, defame, discredit, slander, smear
slimy ooze
snipe woodcock
stuck in bemired
sunfish bass, warmouth
teal greenwing
volcano salse
worm ipo
MUDAR akmuddar, akund, mador, yercum
MUDDLE addle, agitate, ball up, befog, becloud, befuddle, bewilder, blunder, botch, bumble, chaos, cloud, clutter, confound, confusion, daze, disarray, discomfit, discompose, disorder, distract, dum(b) found, embarrass, err, faze, fiasco, flurry, fluster, fog, fuddle, haze, intoxicate, jumble, maffle, mess, mix (up), mystify, nonplus, perplex, pie, POTTER, puzzle, rattle, snafu, snarl, soss, squander, stagger, stir, stumble, stupefy, upset
MUDDLED addled, addle-headed, addle-pated, at sixes and sevens, beery, befuddled, bemazed, bemused, blear-witted, blundering, burbled, capernoited, chaotic, cockamamy, confused, dopey, dizzy, drumly, foggy, groggy, hazy, intoxicated, lutulent, mazed, muzzy, ree, slimed
MUDDY besmeared, claggy, clarty, clashy, cloudy, confused, dark, dirty, dreggy, drovy, drubly, drumly, druvy, dubby, dull, glet, gloomy, indistinct, limous, lutose, miry, moist, muck(s)y, muddled, murky, nasty, obscure, oozy, opaque, plashy, pud-

dle, roil(ed)(y), slab(by), slaky, slimy, sloppy, sloshy, sloughy, slubby, sludgy, slushy, sozzly, splashy, squashy, squelchy, soft, turbid, uliginose, uliginous, unclear, vague
river mouth kuala lumpur
MUDFISH amia, bowfin, dalag, goby, grindle, killifish, komtok, loach, mudminnow, mummichog, parrotfish
MUDGUARD cuttoo, fender, splasher, wing
MUDWEED crosswort, limosella
MUEZZIN crier
call adan, azan
MUFF beard, blunder, bobble, bungle(r), duffer, effeminate, fail(ure), mitten, whitethroat
MUFFED crested, irritated, vexed
MUFFET *frightener* spider
MUFFIN biscuit, bread, brioche, bun, cake, cob, crumpet, gem, hazel, manchet, quick bread, scone, sinker
MUFFLE blindfold, bumble, camouflage, choke, conceal, cover, cushion, damp(en), deaden, deafen, dress, drown, dull, envelop, gag, kill, mute, muzzle, nose, protect, repress, shroud, silence, smother, soften, soft-pedal, squelch, stifle, stop, subdue, suppress, throttle, tone down, tongue-tied, wind, wrap
MUFFLED deadened, deaf, flat, hollow, mute, silenced, sordine, sordo, sourdine, subdued, wrapped
MUFFLER bandage, bandana, boxing glove, comforter, exhaust-box, ruff, scarf, silencer, tippet
MUFTI assessor, cits, civilian, civvies, expounder, magistrate, officer
MUG assault, attack, countenance, cram, cup, drizzle, dupe, emote, face, fool, grimace, gun, hoodlum, jug, man, map, mouth, mungo, nog, noggin, overact, physiognomy, pot, pulse, puss, ruffian, schooner, schoppen, seidel, sheep, shot, stein,

study, tankard, thug, toby, treat, vessel, visage

shot photo, picture

small noggin

MUGA caterpillar, moth, silk

MUGGER assailant, criminal, crocodile, goa, peddler, tinker

MUGGET entrails, lily-of-the-valley, woodruff

MUGGINS all fives, all threes, dominoes, fool, game, simpleton, sniff

MUGGY clammy, close, damp, dank, humid, misty, moist, moldy, puthery, sticky, stuffy, sultry, warm, whitethroat

MUGHOUSE saloon, tavern

MUGIN *crow of* odin

MUGWORT artemesia, bastard-feverfew, bulwand, galium, mugweed, wormwood

MUGWUMP apostate, bolter, chief, individualist, objector, personage, pharisee

MUHAMMAD See MOHAMMED.

MUKDEN shenyang

MULATTO griffe, griqua, metis, mixture, octoroon, quadroon, quintroon, pardo, terceron

-jack yellow fever

MULBERRY aal, ach, alroot, antiaris, artocarpad, artocarpus, aute, awl, blackberry, breadfruit, breadnut, brosimum, castillo, caucho, cecropia, cow-tree, dodder, dorstenia, fruit, kozo, leopardwood, more, morello, morus, murrey, rubra, sourbush, sycamine, thimbleberry, treculia, tree, wauke, whitebeam

bark kapa, tap(p)a

beverage morat

bird starling

cloth tap(p)a

family moraceae

fig sycamore

-shaped moriform

MULCH cover, cultivate, litter, manure, sawdust, straw

MULCIBER hephaestus, vulcan

MULCT amerce(ment), blemish, cheat, claim, defect, demand, exact, fine, forfeit (ure), penalize, penalty, punish, require, sconce, scot, sentence, steal

MULE acemila, ass, bigener, bucker, bullhead, burro, bury, cencerro, chilblain, crumple, donkey, hardtail, hinny, hybrid, intransigent, ironman, jarhead, jenny, jughead, maud, mewl, mixture, mongrel, mool, mute, pump, quadroon, quateron, rattail, sandal, scuff, shoe, slipper, spinning jenny, sumpter, tractor

armadillo mulita

chair cacolet

-deer blacktail, dassie, godwit, ruffe

disease murrina

driver muleteer, skinner

goddess epona

group atajo, drove, mulada

killer mantis, scorpion, walking-stick, wheelbug

leading cencerro

-like asinine, MULISH

male jack

parent ass, horse, mare, stallion

shoe planch(e)

skinner See MULETEER.

spinning ironman

symbol of obstinacy

untrained shavetail

MULETEER almocrebe, arriero, assman, driver, peon, skinner

MULISH dogged, firm, fixed, headstrong, hybrid, intractable, obdurate, obstinate, pigheaded, recalcitrant, refractory, set, sterile, stiffnecked, stubborn, stupid, sullen, unruly

MULL blunt, bustle, chaw, cloth, cogitate, cow, crag, crumble, crush, dull, dust, err, failure, fettle, fiasco, grind, heat, humus, mess, mulmul, muslin, ointment, point, ponder, powder, pulverize, reflect, rubbish, ruminate, snuffbox, spice, steatin, study, sweeten, think

over brood, pore, study, think

MULLAH See TEACHER.

MULLEIN aaron's-rod, adam's-flannel, agleaf, beggar's-blanket, breadplant, candlewick, doveweed, feltwort, flannelleaf, foxglove, hagtaper, iceleaf, lungwort, torch, velvetdock, velvetleaf, verbasco, verbaseum

MULLET bobo, bouri, garau, goatfish, harder, joturus, kanae, lebrancho, lisita, liza, molet, mugil(o)id, mull(o)id, puffin, redhorse, springer, spurrowel, sucker, tallegalane

hawk osprey

heraldic spurrowel, star

king apogon, bass, cardinalfish

MULLIGATAWNY soup

MULLIGRUBS blues, colic, doldrums, grumpiness, mopes, sulks

MULLOCK dirt, litter, mess, refuse, rubbish, spoil, waste

MULLOWAY jewfish, kingfish, sciaenid

MULTICOLORED calico, dappled, pied, spotted, variegated

MULTIFARIOUS different, discordant, discrepant, disparate, divergent, divers(e), incompatible, manifold, many, numerous, several, sundry, varied, various

MULTIFOLD copied, duplicated, iterated, MANIFOLD, repeated, various

MULTIFORM diverse, polymorphic, polymorphous, varied

MULTIPLE decuple, faciend, factor, manifold, many, numerous, plural, ratio, septuple

MULTIPLY amplify, appreciate, augment, balloon, breed, calculate, engender, enlarge, expand, generate, increase, magnify, procreate, proliferate, propagate, pullulate, reproduce, spread, stretch, teem

by 5 quintuple

by 6 sextuple

by 8 octuple

by 10 decuple

MULTITUDE army, assemble, bevy, body, bunch, cohue, collection, covey, cram, crowd, crush, drove, flight, flock, force, galaxy, gathering, GROUP, heap, herd, hirsel, hive, hoi polloi, horde, host, hotter, huddle, jam, knot, legion, loads, lots, majority, mampus, many, mass(es), meinie, meiny, millions, mob, multiplicity, much, myriad, nest, number, ocean, pack, people, plurality, populace, press, push, quantity, rabble, raft, ruck, sea, score, shoal, sight, slew, slue, superabundance, swarm, throng

MUM ale, beer, CHRYSANTHEMUM, clum, dark, dumb, hush, madam, mask, mother, mute, quiet, silence, silent, speechless, still, taciturn, voiceless

MUMBLE brock, chavel, chew, drumble, faffle, flummer, grumble, hummer, maffle, moffle, mump, murmur, mussitate, mutter, palter, patter, stammer, whisper

MUMBO JUMBO abracadabra, bugaboo, bugbear, charm, demon, fetish, hocuspocus, idol, incantation, mummery, nonsense, rigmarole

MUMCHANCE hazard, masking, merrymaking, mummer

MUMMER actor, buffoon, disguiser, guisard, guiser, masker, mime, pantomimist, performer, player

MUMMERY acting, ceremony, disguise, gibberish, hocuspocus, hodening, hypocrisy, mask, morris, puppetry

MUMMIFY dry(up), embalm, preserve, shrivel

MUMMIUS achaicus

MUMMU *parent* apsu, tiamat

MUMMY cadaver, carcass, congo, corpse, mom, MOTHER, mummio, relic, remains, skelet
apple papaya
-brown bay, snuff, tamarack
case sledge
cloth byssus
-like figure ushabati

MUMP beg, cheat, deceive, displeasure, grimace, grin, mope, mumble, mutter, sulk(s), sullenness

MUMPER beggar, imposter, sulker

MUMPISH dull, glum, morose, sulky, sullen

MUMPS branks, doldrums, mopes, parotitis
pert. parotitic

MUN him, man, may, mouth,

must, river, roisterer, shall, them

MUNCH bite, champ, chew, chomp, crunch, eat, growse, growze, mange, masticate, munge

MUND grith, right

MUNDA *language* asuri, bhumij, gadaba, kharia, kherwari, kol, kolarian, korwa, kurki, mundari, santali, savara

MUNDANE animal, carnal, cosmic, earthen, earth(l)y, fleshly, global, mortal, ordinary, planetary, profane, secular, sublunary, temporal, terrene, terrestrial, unspiritual, worldly

MUNG *bean* balatong, gram, mongoe, mug

MUNGA macaque, monkey, muga, zati

MUNGO (See also MUNG *bean.*) mongoose, mug, shoddy, waste, wool

MUNICH *airport* riem
festival fasching, oktoberfest

MUNICIPAL civic, civil, metropolitan, politics, town, urban
building broletto, city hall, signoria, town hall
corporation barrio, borough
officer alcalde, bailie, burgermeister, burgomaster, maire, mayor, sindaco

MUNICIPALITY cabildo, city, metropolis, municipium, town(ship)

MUNIFICENT altruistic, benevolent, bounteous, bountiful, charitable, generous, handsome, lavish, liberal, philanthropic, princely, prodigal, profuse, royal

MUNIMENT archive, deed, defense, document, fort, protection, record, stronghold, support

MUNIPPUS *parent* cilla, thymoetes
slayer priam

MUNITIONS armament, arms, artillery, materiel, ordnance, store, weapons

MUNRO, H.H. *pseud.* saki

MUNSHI interpreter, secretary, teacher, writer

MUNTJAC animal, deer, kakar, kidang, muntiacus, ratwa

MUNYCHUS *parent* demophon, laodice

raised by aethra

MURAD IV amurath

MURAL fresco, painting, partitioned, picture, septal, topia, wall(ed)

MURALIST benton, cimabue, da vinci, giotto, orozco, rivera, sargent

MURAT *beau* sabreur
commander napoleon

MURCIA *city* lorca, mula, totana
river segura

MURDER assassinate, assassination, bane, barbarity, blood, botch, bump off, burke, butcher(y), carnage, death, destroy, dispatch, execute, felony, homicide, kill, liquidate, mangle, manslaughter, mar, massacre, murther, rub out, ruin, scrag, slaughter, slay(ing), spoil, thuggery
comb. cide
fine bloodwite, cro, wer(e)gild
of brother fratricide
of father parricide, patricide
of friend amicide
of king parricide, regicide
of mother matricide, parricide
of offspring filicide, prolicide
of parent parricide
of relative parricide
of sister sororicide
of sovereign parricide
of spouse mariticide
of wife uxoricide
of woman femicide
payment for cro, eric
secret murdrum

MURDERER assassin, bravo, butcher, cain, cutthroat, felon, gunman, hitman, killer, slayer, thug
famous bluebeard, dracula, jack the ripper, vlad tepes
fee blood money
-of women bluebeard, boston strangler, chevalier raoul, jack the ripper, son of sam

MURDEROUS blood-guilty, blood-thirsty, bloody, brutal, cruel, dangerous, deadly, destructive, difficult, fell, felon, ferocious, gory, homicidal, sanguinary, savage, sicarious, trying

MURE demure, gentle, immure, imprison, jail, meek, modest, moor, soft, squeeze, thrust, wall

MURGELEIS *owner* ganelon
MURID disciple, mouse, pupil, rat, rodent
MURK cloud, darken, darkness, dusk, overcast, soil
MURKY black, cheerless, cloudy, dark, dejected, dim, dull, dusky, gloomy, glowering, hazy, lowering, lurid, misty, muddy, obscure, opaque, puddly, roiled, roily, smoky, turbid
MURL crumb(le), molder
MURMUR aspirate, babble, breath(e), brool, brum, buzz, chirm, clum, complain, complaint, coo, cry, curr, fret, grank, grouse, grumble, gurgle, hum, inkle, lip, mumble, murgeon, mutter, pipple, purl, purr, repine, rumble, rumor, rustle, sigh, soo, souffle, sough, susurrate, susurration, susurrus, trickle, undertone, whimper, whisper
MURPHY *bridey* ruth simmons
furniture wall-bed
MURRAIN anthrax, fever, mortality, pestilence, plague, plaguy, texas-fever
MURRE arrie, auk(let), bacalao-bird, guillemot, lungie, rockbird, strany, tink(er), uria
MURVA hemp, ifa, pangane, plant, sansevieria
MUS animal, mouse, rat, rodent
MUSA banana, manila-hemp, plantain
MUSAGETES apollo
MUSANG polecat, powcat
MUSCADINE bull-ace, bullgrape, bully tree, damson, grape, prunus, scuppernong, vitis
relative bird-grape
MUSCAT See OMAN.
MUSCLE abductor, adductor, agonist, ambiens, biceps, biventer, brachialis, brawn, caninus, clout, coraco, dilator, erector, extensor, flesh, flexor, force, gemellus, gluteus, incisor, lacert, levator, masseter, myon, psoa, scalenus, sinew, sphincter, strength, temporal, tendon, tensor, teres, thew(s), triceps
atrophy amytrophy

balm liniment
band taenia
column sarcostyle
comb. my(o)
contracting agonist, constrictor
contraction, pert. metachronal
control technique biofeedback
cramp fibromyositis
derived from inosic
disorder abasia, achalasia, amyosthenia, amyotaxia, amyotinia, amyotrophy, ataxia, crick, dysergia
displacement myectopia, myectopy
drawing in retractor
elevating levator
expansion dilator
extending protractor
fiber rhabdium, tenia
flexor bender, biceps, brachialis
in intrude
irritant veratrin(e)
lack ataxia
lifting erector, levator
-like myoid
limb-straightening extensor
man atlas, bully, hoodlum, powerhouse, stalwart
ossification sarcostosis
outward-turning evertor
pain myalgia
pert. myoid, sarcous, scalene, torose
poison albopannin, veratrine
protein actin, actomyosin
reinforcing accessorius
rigidity catalepsy
ring-like sphincter
rotating evertor
round teres
science myology
segment myocomma
sensory end spingle
spasm convulsion, cramp, crick, tic, tonus
stiffness charley horse
straight rectus
straightening extensor
sugar inosital, inosite
trapezius cucullaris
triangular deltoid
tumor myoma
turning evertor, rotator
2-headed biceps
type smooth, striated
weakness atony, dystrophy
MUSCOVITE mica, red russian
MUSCOVY *duck* pato, scovy

MUSCULAR athletic, brawny, burly, hale, herculean, husky, mighty, robust, ropy, sinewy, sound, stalwart, stout, strong, thewy, torose, vigorous
MUSE(S) bragi, castalides, cogitate, complain, consider, contemplate, creator, day-dream, deliberate, dream, dump, excogitate, genius, inspiration, marvel, meditate, mneme, moon, mull, murmur, pierides, pipe-dream, poet, ponder, reason, reflect, remark, reve, revolve, ruminate, rune, study, think, trifle, weigh, wonder, woolgather
astronomy urania
attic xenophon
beloved cretheus
birthplace piera
chief calliope
comedy thalia
companion crotus
dancing terpsichore
eloquence calliope
fountain aganippe, hippocrene
group pierides
history clio
home aolea, aonia, helicon, parnassus, piera
horse pegasus
meditation melete
mountain helicon, parnassus
music euterpe, polyhymnia
9 calliope, clio, erato, euterpe, melpomene, polyhymnia, polymnia, terpsichore, thalia, urania
parent jupiter, mnemosyne, zeus
pert. castalian, pierian
poetry calliope, erato, thalia
sacred lyric polyhymnia, polymnia
sacred spring castalia, castaly
shelterer pyreneus
shrine aolea, aonia, piera
song aoede, aoide
tragedy melpomene
MUSEUM archives, gallery, glyptotheca, musee, pinacot(h)eca, pinakotheke, salon, thesaurus, treasury
director curator
famous ashmolean, bargello, berlin, british, dresden, frick, hermitage, louvre, madame tussaud's, metro-

politan, munich, tate, uffizi, vatican, vienna
volunteer docent

MUSH atole, confuse, crumble, crush, cut, face, flattery, gruel, hasty pudding, indent, journey, kasha, march, meal, mouth, notch, pap, polenta, porridge, proceed, pudding, pulp, sagamite, scrapple, sentimentality, sepon, slush, sofkee, supawn, travel, umbrella, walk

MUSHI *son* eder, jeremoth, mahli

MUSHROOM agaric, basidiomycete, beaver, blewits, boletus, boom, button, cepe, champignon, chanterelle, death-cup, develop, fungus, hat, lepiota, marasmius, misy, mitra, morchella, morel, moril(le), parvenu, pixy-stool, puffball, shaggy-mane, toadstool, truffle, umbrella, upstart, whitecap
cap mitra, pileus
capped pileate
color beaver-brown, camel
cooked with a la boitelle
disease flock
eating mycophagy
edible champignon, chanterelle, morel, truffle
fairy-ring champignon
gill surface comb
hallucinogenic amanita
-like fungous
part annulus, basidiospore, basidium, comb, gill, hymenium, mitra, pileus, sterigma, stipe, trama, volva
poisoning mycetism
poisonous amanita, death-cup, toadstool
seed spore
-shaped agariciform
stem stipe
wild lepiata
young button

MUSHY gooey, maudlin, mawkish, pulpy, romantic, sentimental, slushy, soft, soppy, thick, wishy-washy, yielding

MUSIC (See also MUSICAL references.) air, attunement, chime, concord, dream, dreher, euphony, gimel, gymel, harmony, mellifluence, melodics, mel-

ody, minstrelsy, motet, rag, rhythm, score, sound, strain, swing, symphony, synchronism, timbre, tone, tune, unison
abridgement ridotto
accompaniment backing
aid baton, diapason, metronome, monochord, pitchpipe, sonometer, tuningfork
angel israfe(e)l, israfil
assembly eisteddfod
beat battuta, ictus, moto, pulse, rhythm, takt, tempo
beat prolonged buole
between acts entracte
book antiphonal, hymnal
cadence clausula, deceptive, half, imperfect, perfect, plagal
calypso goombay
change of key modulation, transposition
chapel-style a cappella, oratorio
character accent, bar, brace, breve, clef, dot, flat, key, ligature, natural, note, presa, rest, segno, signature, sharp, slur, staff, stave, swell, tie, trill, vinculum
chord triad
church See *sacred*, below.
closing coda, postlude, stretta
composition See MUSICAL COMPOSITION.
computer moog synthesizer
concert site alhambra, bandshell, bandstand, bijou, carnegie hall, gaff, hippodrome, la scala, melodeon, odea, odeon, odeum, palladium, theatre, windmill
contest eisteddfod
count basie
cue presa
dance-style da ballo
deafness to amusia
direction See MUSICAL DIRECTION.
disc cymbal, record(ing)
discordant charivari, scordato
district tin pan alley
drama ballet, dance, opera, operetta, oratorio, revue
effect oompah
embellishment acciaccatura, agremens, appoggiatura, arpeggio, cadence, cadenza, fioritura, grace note, mor-

dent, ornament(ation), passaggio, roulade, trill
entertainment See *event*, below.
evening abendmusik, dream, serena
event ballet, ceilidh, choral, comic opera, concert, dance, eisteddfod, festival, grand opera, jam session, minstrelsy, musicale, opera
exercise czerny, gradus, scales, sol-fa, solfeggio
extra encore
festival eisteddfod, feis
figuration expert notator
finale coda
florid bravura, coloratura
flourish See *embellishment*, above.
form See MUSICAL COMPOSITION.
frozen architecture
gliding slur
god apollo, bes, tezcatlipoca
goddess sarasvati
group See MUSICIAN *group*.
hall See *concert site*, above.
hodgepodge medley
ignorance amusia
improvise vamp
instrument See MUSICAL INSTRUMENT.
interval diatesseron, microtone, quint, settima, tritone
introduction intrada, overture
jazz skiffle
key tasto, tonality
key, major ditone, dur
key, minor moll(e)
lament dumka
language italian
leader See CONDUCTOR.
leap salto
libretto testo
link codetta
lively furlana, galop
lover cat, hepcat, jitterbug, melomane, musicmonger, philharmonic
machine gramophone, jukebox, musicbox, phonograph, pianola, radio, victrola
mania melomania
mark slur
measure bar
medley cento, olio, pasticcio, potpourri, rondo
mode aeolian, dorian, lydian, mixolydian, phrygian
modern atonal, bebop, bop,

electronic, jazz, ragtime, rock
morning aubade
muffler mute
muse euterpe, polyhymnia
notation See *character*, above.
notation system neume, tablature
note breve, crotchet, mese, meson, minim, nete, neume, pneuma, quaver, ray, soh, sol, trite
note, guido's alamire, alt, are, befa, bemi, cefaut, cesolfaut, delasol(re), doh, ela(mi), fefaut, gammaut, gesolreut
note stem filum
note sustained fermata
of the spheres planeting
ornament agrement, cambiata, fioritura
ornate quality floridity
overtone harmonic, klang
passage alla breve, bourdon, break, bridge, burden, cadence, cadenza, chorus, coda, codetta, cue, falderal, falderol, fanfare, flourish, interlude, intermezzo, link, measure, movement, phrase, refrain, repeat, reprise, response, ritornel(le), roulade, stanza, strain, stretta, stretto
passion for melomania
patron apollo, erato, euterpe, muses, notre dame de dusen, orpheus, pierides, polyhymnia, polymnia, terpsichore
patron saint cecilia
pause c(a)esura, fermata
performer virtuoso
pert. euterpean, harmonic, orphic
phrase leitmotif, motif
pick plectron, plectrum
polyphonic counterpoint
popular calypso, jazz, ragtime, rock(-n-roll)
progression scale
publisher tinpan alley
refrain burden, derry, epode, fal(l)a, ludden, repetend, response
repeat replica, reprise, round
repeat sign segno
response answer, antiphon(on), antiphony, offertory
resounding higgaion

rhythm beat, ictus, meter, pulse, swing, tempo, time
rough charivari
round rondo
run glissando, volata
sacred agnus dei, anthem, cantata, canticle, chant, chorale, doxology, hymn, laud, mass, missa, motet, oratorio, paean, psalm, recessional, spiritual
sad dirge, mesto
scale gamut
scale system czerny
school conservatory
score, full partitura
sentimental schmal(t)z
set to arrange
shake tremolo, trill
sharps and flats accidentals
sign (See also *character*, above.) segno, slur
silence rest
solo arioso, cadenza, recitive
spirit neck, stromkarl
staccato secco
stress accent, arsis
string catgut, chord, snare
style expression, fingering, glissando, legato, pizzicato, slur, spiccato, staccato
symbol See *character*, above.
syncopated jazz
tempo agoge, grave, lento, presto, takt
term accent, agage, alamire, arpeggio, arsis, bar, bridge, chord, chorus, chromatic, ecbole, flat, flourish, gamut, grace note, harmonic, key, major, measure, melody, minor, mordent, motif, movement, ossia, overtone, pitch, run, scale, score, sharp, testo, theme, tone, tremolo, triad
theme leitmotif, leitmotiv, motif, tema
theory agogics
3 b's bach, beethoven, brahms
timing device metronome
title maestro
transition segue
tremble tremolo, trill, vibrato
triplet tercet, triole
turn gruppetto, volto
unaccompanied a cappella
upbeat anacrusis, arsis
vibrato bebung
virtuoso bravura
vocal gimel, gymel
voice alto, baritone, base,

bass, canto, cantus, contralto, descant, soprano, tenor, treble
MUSICAL (See also MUSIC references.) dulcet, harmonic, harmonious, liquid, lyric(al), melodic, melodious, orotund, review, rhythmic(al), show, sweet, tonal, tuneful
comedy hit, musical, review, revue, show
MUSICAL COMPOSITION
3 air, duo, jig, lay 4 alba, aria, ayre, duet, gato, glee, hymn, idyl, juba, lied, mass, noel, nome, opus, raga, reel, solo, trio 5 blues, canon, carol, catch, cento, chant, derry, dirge, ditty, epode, etude, fancy, fugue, gavot, gigue, march, motet, murky, nonet, octet, opera, polka, rondo, round, score, suite, troll, valse, waltz 6 anthem, arioso, aubade, ballad, ballet, bolero, branle, burden, cantus, chanty, chaser, lieder, minuet, monody, septet, serena, sextet, shanty, sonata, tiento 7 arietta, ars nova, ballade, ballata, bourree, boutade, bransle, cadenza, calypso, cantata, canzone, caprice, chacona, chantie, descant, discant, forlane, furlana, gavotte, lullaby, mazurka, partita, pibroch, prelude, quartet, quintet, requiem, romance, romanza, rondeau, rondino, scherzo, toccata, virelai, ziganka 8 accentus, airvarie, berceuse, brindisi, cachucha, canticle, cavatina, chaconne, concerto, courante, entracte, fantasia, galliard, guaracha, habanera, hymeneal, nocturne, operetta, oratorio, overture, pastoral, rhapsody, ricercar, saraband, serenade, serenata, sinfonia, sonatina, symphony, terzetto, vorspiel 9 allemande, arabesque, bagatelle, barcarole, brautleid, cabaletta, capriccio, gailliard, malaguena, monophony, passepied, pastorale, plain song, polonaise, preghiera, quartette, quintette, ricercare, roundelay, seleccion, selection,

volkslied 10 abendmusik, canzonette, concertino, humoresque, intermezzo, recitative, rondoletto, tarantella, tarantelle 11 arrangement, concertante, passacaglia, recessional 12 cantus firmus, cantus planus, konzertstuck, schlummerlied, transcription, zigeunerlied 13 divertissement

aria-like arioso

dance. See DANCE *music.*

dancer's ballet, boutade, gymnopedie

dawn aubade

declamatory recitative

ending coda, finale, postlude

exercise etude, scales, study

free form caprice, capriccetto, capriccio

impromptu boutade

interlude verset

jazz bebop, blues, boogiewoogie, jive, rag(time), rock(-n-roll)

light divertimento

movement adagio, allegro, andante, cantabile, fugue, largo, march, minuet, rondeau, rondo, scherzo

night nachtmusik, nocturne, serenade

nocturne serenade

note breve, eighth, ela, half, nete, punctus, quadruple(t), quaver, whole

operatic scena

religious See MUSIC *sacred.*

round canon, fuge, troll

stop rest

theme leitmotif, leitmotiv, motif, tema

voice aria, song

work opus

MUSICAL DIRECTION

above sopra

abruptly secco, spiccato

accented marcato, martellato, sforzando, sforzato

actively allegretto, allegro

again bis, da capo, dal segno

agitated agitato, concitato

agreeable amabile

airy sfogato

all tutti, tutto

alone arioso, solus

alternate ossia

always sempre

animated animando, animato, anime, animoso, con animo, con moto, spiritoso

as usual al solito

as written alloco, sta

augmentation accrescimento

backwards cancrizans

begin now attacca

below sotto

bitter amarevole

bold audace

bowed arco

bright anime

brisk vivace

clear chiara, chiaro

cold freddo

compassionate pietoso

contrary a rovescio

cut vide

cut time alla breve

dance style da ballo

despairing disparato

devout divoto

dignified maestoso

diminishing calando, decrescendo

disconnected staccato

distorted rubato

double doppio

dying calendo, morendo, perd(endosi), smorzando, smorzato

emotional appassionato

emphatic marcato, sforzando

end fine

energetic animato, anime, animoso

enough basta

evenly egualmente

everyone tutti

exceedingly molto, tres

excited agitato, spiritoso

fading away See *dying,* above.

fast accelerando, affrettando, allegretto, allegro, animato, animoso, con anima, con brio, desto, mosso, moto, prestissimo, presto, schnell, spiritoso, stretto, tostamente, tosto, veloce, visto, vite, vivace, vivacissimo, vivo

faster accelerando, affrettando, stretto

fast, less meno mosso

fast, rather poco allegro

fearlessly con bravura

first primo

flowing andante, andantino, legato

fluctuating rubato

following segue, seguendo

freely ad libitum, capriccioso, sciolto

from the beginning da capo

full pieno

furious furioso

gay brillante, giocoso

gentle amabile, dolce

graceful allegretto

gravely serioso

gypsy style alla zingara

held tenuto

hurried agitato

immediately subito

in like manner simile

in time a tempo

in unison a due, all'unisono

irregular rubàto

joyous giocoso

lead in presa

left hand main gauche, sinistra

less meno

let it stand sta

light allegretto, sfogato, volante

little poco

little by little poco a poco

lively See *fast,* above.

loud forte, fortissimo, stark

lovingly amabile, amoroso

low sotto

majestic grandioso, maestoso

march-like alla marcia

melodious arioso

moderately andante, mezzo, moderato, modesto

more piu

more lively piu allegro

much molto

murmuring mormorando

muted sordino, sordo

noisy strepitoso

not too much non troppo

omitted vide

1 string a una corda

1 voice asoluto, solo

otherwise ossia

passionate appassionato

passionless freddo

performer's pleasure a capriccio

perform what follows segue

plaintive dolente, doloroso, lacrimando, lacrimoso, piangendo

playful giocoso, scherzando

pleasant piacevole

plucked pizzicato

poignant amarevole

pulsating vibrato

quaver tremolo

quick See *fast,* above.

quickening alla breve, affrettando, strengendo

quiet tacet

rapid succession arpeggiando

repeat al segno, ancora, bis, di nuovo, volta

required obbligato

restless agitato
resume speed a tempo
retarding lentando
reticently heimlich
right hand destra mano, main droite
sad amarevole, con dolore, dolente, dolentissimo, doloroso, mesto
sentimental affettuoso
sharp sforzando, staccato
silence tacet
simple semplice
singing cantabile
skip salto
skipping saltato
sliding glissando
slow adagietto, adagio, allargando, andante, andantino, a poco, grave, larghetto, largo, lento, tardo
slower allentando, calando, rall, retenuto, ritardando
slower and louder allargando
slower and softer smorzando, smorzato
smooth legato, piacevole
soft dolce, mezza-voce, pianissimo, piano, soave
softer decrescendo, diminuendo, mancando
soft pedal, with a una corda
solemn grave
solo a cappella, arioso
somewhat poco
so much tanto
sorrowful See *mournful,* above.
sparkling scintillante
spirited animato, con brio, spiritoso, vigoroso
stately maestoso
stop basta
sublime elevato
sustained sustenuto, tenuto
sweet dolce, soave
syncopated alla zoppa
tastefully gustoso
tender affettuoso, amabile, amoroso, con affetto, con amore
then poi
thrice ter
throughout sempre
together a due, ensemble
too much tanto, troppo
to the end al fine
tranquil calmato
transition segue
turn the page volti
2 strings due corde
2 times due volte
vanishing diluendo
very assai, molto, tres

very little pochettino
very much molto
vibrate tremolo
vivaciously con brio
whole tutto
with con
with affection affettuoso
with dignity maestoso
with feeling con affetto, con espressione
with force con forza
without accompaniment a cappella
with spirit con brio
with the bow coll' arco
with the mute con sordino

MUSICAL INSTRUMENT

bamboo anklung
bass cello, helicon, serpent, tuba, violoncello
biblical sabeca, tabret
brass althorn, altohorn, baroxyton, basson russe, bugle, clarion, cornet, corno di caccia, cornopean, cymbals, euphonium, flugelhorn, french horn, helicon, horn, lituus, lure, mellophone, ophicleide, sackbut, sax-cornet, saxophone, sliphorn, sousaphone, tromba, trombone, trumpet, tuba
electronic theremin
gourd guiro
iron bowl gum-gum
keyboard accordion, adiaphon, aeolharmonica, autophon, baby grand, bandonion, calliope, calliophon, celesta, cembalo, choralcello, choraleon, clavicembalo, clavichord, clavicithern, clavicymbal, clavier, claviharp, concertina, grindorgan, harmonica, harmonichord, harmonium, harpsichord, hurdy-gurdy, klavier, lyrechord, manichord(on), melodeon, melodica, monochord, mouth organ, orchestrina, organ, panmelodion, pianino, piano (forte), pianola, pipe organ, regal, seraphine, spinet, symphonion, telharmonium, terpodion, tetrachordon, upright, uranion, vielle, virginal, vocalion
keyboard-wind aeolodicon, aeolomelodicon, aeolopantalon, aeosklavier, choraleon
machine-played bellonion
old arch(i)lute, asor, ban-

dore, barbiton, bassanello, buccina celesta, chrotta, cithara, cittern, cornemuse, cromorne, crowd, crumhorn, dulcimer, gigue, gittern, harpsichord, lute, lyre, marimba, nabla, pandura, pantaleon, pibcorn, psaltery, rappel, rebab, rebec, rocta, sabeca, sambuca, sambuke, serpent, spinet, trumpet-marine, vina, virginal
percussion anacara, atabal, balafo, becken, bells, block, bones, carillon, castanets, celesta, chime, clappers, cymbals, drum, glockenspiel, gong, idiophone, jingle stick, lyra, maraca, marimba, naker, pulsatile, rappel, rattle(bones), sistrum, tabor(et), tabret, tambour(ine), timpani, tonitruone, trap(s), triangle, tympani, vibes, vibraharp, vibraphone, xylophone
pert. fidicinal
reed aulos, bagpipe, bassoon, batyphone, bombardon, cervalet, cervelat, clarinet, cromorne, crumhorn, english horn, gora(h), heckelphone, kayamba, krum(m)horn, musette, oboe, rackett, rankett, saxaphone, seraphine, shawm
stringed 3 gue, tar, uke 4 arpa, asor, bass, gora, harp, koto, lute, lyre, rota, turr, vina 5 banjo, cello, crowd, gorah, goura, jamon, nabla, nanga, rebab, rebec, rocta, ruana, sarod, sitar, tarau, viola 6 cither, fiddle, guitar, kissar, rebeck, rubeba, sabeca, sancho, santir, urheen, violin, zither 7 bandore, bandure, baryton, cembalo, cithara, cithern, cittern, claviol, cythera, dichord, dyphone, gittern, kithara, mandola, mandore, pandura, samisen, sarangi, sarinda, tambour, theorbo, ukelele, violone 8 autoharp, barbiton, bass viol, claviole, dulcimer, electrum, fidicula, mandolin, melodion, octavina, pandoura, tamboura, violotta 9 archilute, balalaika, bandurria, mandolute, pantaleon, polychord, polyphone, taro-

patch, tripodian 10 bull fiddle, calascione, contrabass, mandocello 11 aeolian harp, harpsichord, violoncello 12 viola da gamba
stringed, curved side ribs
stringed, face belly
supplementary ripieno
2-necked theorbo
wind aeoline, aerophone, alpenhorn, althorn, arghool, aulos, bagpipe, basaree, bassanello, bassethorn, bassoon, bignou, bin, biniou, bombardon, buccina, bugle, cervalet, cervelat, cheng, clarinet, clarion, cornet, dolcian, doucet, english horn, eunuch flute, fife, flageolet, flugelhorn, flute, french horn, galoubet, harmonica, helicon, horn, jug, monaulos, mouth organ, musette, nehiloth, nose flute, oboe, ocarina, octobass, ophicleide, panpipe, phonikon, pibcorn, piccolo, rackett, recorder, reed, sang, sarusphone, sax (ophone)(horn), serpent, shawm, sheng, taragato, theorbo, trombone, trumpet, tuba, zampogna
wind mouthpiece beak, reed
wind stopper fipple
MUSICIAN artist, asaph, bandman, bard, bopster, bower, cellist, gambist, guido, harmonist, instrumentalist, korahite, linos, maestro, mariachi, minstrel, orpheus, performer, player, recitist, scald, skald, soloist, thrummer, tunester, twang-(l)er, violinist, violist, virtuoso, symphonist
group band, choir, chorus, duet, ensemble, glee club, klezmer, orchestra, nonet(to), quartet(te), septet(te), sextet(te), symphony, trio
progenitor jubal
title maestro
MUSING absentminded, abstracted, contemplation, deliberation, dreamy, meditation, meditative, musardry, pensive, reflection, oblivious, thoughtful
MUSK ambrette, cattail, deer, monkey-flower, perfume, plant
beaver muskrat

cat civet
cavy hutia
cod fop
crowfoot moschatel
cucumber casabanana
deer cervid, chevrotain, kastura, moschus
hog peccary
lorikeet parakeet
mallow abelmosk
okra abelmosk
ox ovibos
polyp octopus
shrew desman, sondeli
thistle carduus, cirsium
turtle stinker, stinkpot
weasel civet
MUSKELLUNGE esox, fish, longe, muskie, pike
MUSKET bandhook, biscayen, blunderbuss, bundook, carbine, culverin, dragon, escopeta, falcon, firearm, fusil, gingall gun, hawk, jingal, rifle, snaphaan, tophaike
ball goli
fork gaffle
lock rowet
rest croc, gaffle
MUSKETEER aramis, athos, fusileer, marksman, porthos, soldier, strelitz
author dumas
friend d'artagnan
MUSKHOGEAN, MUSKOGEE *indian* acolapissa, apalachee, apalachi, bayogoula, chickasaw, choctaw, creek, hitchiti, koasati, mikasuki, natchez, seminole, tohome, tuskegee, yamasi
MUSKMELON atimon, cantaloupe, casaba, crenshaw, mango, rock melon, rockyford, spanspek, wungee
MUSKRAT desman, musquash, ondatra, rodent, shrew, squash
fur musquash
MUSKROOT moschatel, nard, sumbul
MUSKWOOD caoba, guarea, olearia, pameroon-bark
MUSKY aromatic, fragrant, moschate
MUSLIM See MOHAMMEDAN.
MUSLIN adati, ban, beteela, charkhana, cloth, cossas, cotton, dorea, doria, gurrah, fabric, jamdani, jamlanee, madras, mosal, mull, mulmul, nainsook, organdy,

plumetis, seerhand, shalee, sheeting, shela, shilla, stenter, swiss, tanjib, tarlatan
bag tillot
lace carrickmacross
striped dorea, doria
transparent tarlatan
MUSNUD council, cushion
MUSS chaos, clutter, commotion, conflict, confuse, confusion, disarrange, dishevel, disorder, fuffle, glommox, jumble, litter, mess, mouth, muddle, row, rubbish, rumple, scramble, squabble
MUSSAL lighter, torch
MUSSEL anodon, bivalve, bullhead, clam, cozza, deerhorn, glochid, lacert, mollusk, moule, mucket, mytilid, naiad, nerita, parlour, unionid
cracker biskop
duck scoter
fresh water anodon(ta), naiad, pimpleback, quadrula, wartyback, yellowback
genus lampsilis, modiolus, mytilus, unio
large horse
part byssus
pearly unio
sea nerita, modiolus
MUSSULMAN See MOHAMMEDAN.
MUSSY dirty, disordered, messy, rumpled, slovenly, smeared, soiled, untidy
MUST blight, bood, dulce, duty, essential, frenzied, frenzy, fustiness, have to, imperative, juice, maun, may, mildew, mold, mun, musk, necessary, need, obligation, ought, powder, required, sapa, shall, should, stum, wine
liquor arrope
not maunna
MUSTACHE beard, burnsides, handlebars, soupstrainer, valance, whisker
cover bigothero
monkey guenon, moustoc
MUSTANG broncho, bronco, cayuse, horse, pony
color sphinx
MUSTARD armoricia, aubrietia, awlwort, barbarea, berteroa, brassica, cadlock, cakile, chadlock, charlock, condiment, cress, flixweed,

kedlock, nigra, plant, poultice, seasoning, senvy, sinapis, woad
beetle blackjack
black brassica, cadlock, nigra, raphanus, wild radish
gas yperite
genus aethionema, barbarea, brassica, erysimum, sinapis
hedge flixweed, fluxweed
plant aethionema, alyssum, anastatica, arabidopsis, arabis, camelina, cole, cress, gold-of-pleasure, kale, radish
plaster capsicum, dressing, poultice, sinapism
pod silicle
sprinkle with sinapize
wild charlock
MUSTELID animal, badger, ferret, marten, mink, otter, ratel, skunk, weasel
MUSTER align, arrange, array, assemble, assembly, call, cite, collect, comprise, congregate, convene, convoke, display, drum up, enlist, enroll(ment), exhibit, flock, gather, group, levy, list, marshal, mobilize, order, organize, range, report, schedule, show, summon
out disband, discharge, release
MUSTY apathetic, blighted, dirty, dull, fetid, fogyish, foisty, foughty, foul, frowsty, fusty, gloomy, hackneyed, hoar(y), listless, malodorous, moldy, noisome, obsolete, putrid, rafty, rancid, rank, raunchy, sour, spiritless, stale, stinking, testy, trite
MUT *husband* amen, amon
offspring chon, chunsu, khonsu
MUTABLE alterable, changeable, changeful, erratic, fickle, fitful, inconstant, protean, swaying, swinging, unsettled, unstable, unsteady, vacillating, variable, wavering
MUTATE alter, break, change, modify, mutant, sport, vary
MUTATION adaptation, albino, alternation, change, freak, modification, move, posthouse, remove, revolt, revolution, shift, sport,

transformation, umlaut, variation
MUTCHE harass, nag, struggle, torment
MUTE aphasiac, aphonic, aphonous, breathless, damper, deaden, drown, dumb, inarticulate, laloplegic, lene, muffle(d), mum, quiet, silenced, silent, so(u)rdine, speechless, stifle, still, surd, taciturn, tongue-tied, unpronounced, voiceless
trumpet derby
MUTILATE batter, castrate, concise, cripple, crush, damage, deface, deform, delete, demolish, disfeature, disfigure, dismember, expunge, garble, geld, hack, hamstring, hurt, injure, maim, mangle, mar, martyr, ruin, scar, spoil
crime mayhem
MUTINOUS contumacious, disaffected, disobedient, factious, insubordinate, intractable, rebellious, recalcitrant, refractory, riotous, seditious, unruly
MUTINY agitation, coup, insubordination, insurrection, perfidy, putsch, rebellion, revolt, revolution, sedition, strife, treason, uprising
MUTIUS *brother* lucius, martius, quintus
father titus andronicus
MUTT chump, cur, dog, dolt, mongrel, simpleton
MUTTER bark, channer, chunter, complain, crool, cry, growl, grumble, maunder, mumble, mump, murmur, mussitate, patter, threaten, tootmoot
MUTTON agneau, braxies, braxy, cabob, candle, gigot, jimmy, kabob, mouton, prostitute, sheep, vifpa, vivpa
bird oii, petrel, puffinus, shearwater
chops beard, burnsides, whiskers
diseased braxy
dried vifda, vivda
leg cabob, gigot, wabbler, wobbler
stew navarin
tops cleavers, goosefoot
MUTTONFISH abalone, diapterus, eelpot, haliotis,

mojarra, pargo, porgy, sama
MUTTONHEAD blockhead, dimwit, dolt, dunce, fool, screwball, simpleton
MUTUAL collective, common, correlative, give-and-take, joined, joint, public, reciprocal, related, respective, shared, symbion, united
help gotong-royong, teamwork
MUX botch, mess, mixture
up disarrange
MUZHIK See PEASANT.
MUZZ grind, muddle, student, study
MUZZLE bind, censure, chops, cope, clevis, dartars, disable, face, foreface, gag, grub, jaws, maul, mouth, muffle, nose, paralyse, respirator, restrain, shackle, sheathe, silence, snout, squelch, suppress, stifle, thrash, tongue-tie
loader caplock, carronade
wood black sally
MUZZY befuddled, blurred, confused, dazed, dull, fuzzy, hazy, muddled, stupid, tipsy
MYALL acacia, boree, warrigal, wattle tree, yarran
MYCENAE *attacker* argos
ceramic ring kernos
city ialysos, ialysus
feature lion gate(s), tholos, tombs
founder perseus
king agamemnon, aletes, atreus, electryon, eurystheus, sthenelus
tomb tholos
vase bugelkanne, pseudamphora
war leader agamemnon
MYELIN *component* glialcell, oligodendroglia
MYGALE bird-spider, shrewmouse
MYGDON *son* coroebus
MYNA grackle, mina
MYNHEER See MAN.
MYOO See BUDDHA.
MYRIAPOD centipede, chilopod
MYOPIC ametropic, nearsighted, purblind, shortsighted
MYOPORUM acacia, amulla, blueberry, boobyalla, supplejack, wattle, willow

MYRIAD countless, host, many, multitude, numberless, numerous, uncounted

MYRIAPOD antennatum, arthropod, centipede

MYRICA arrayan, bayberry, wax-myrtle

MYRMICID See ANT.

MYRMIDON henchman, mercenary, minion, servant, vassal
father zeus
king achilles, agabus, agacles
leader achilles, eudoris
son actor

MYRO *statue* discobolus

MYROBALAN bahera, belleric, cherry-plum, emblic, fruit

MYRRH commiphora, gum, miphkad, perfume, resin, shrub, stacte

MYRRHA *kin* adonis, cinyras

MYRTLE amomis, arrayan, astromeda, baltic, bay, bearberry, brush-cherry, callistemon, condiment, eugenia, guava, japonica, jarool, laurel, moneywort, pepperwood, periwinkle, ramarama, shrub, tree, vinci, vine
creeping periwinkle
-green baltic
-like cajeput, cajuput

MYSELF masel, numero uno

MYSIAN *ally* trojans
general apollonius
king telephus
spring pegae

MYSORE *capital* bangalore
coin ahmadi, ahmedi, dinar, mohur
state soorg

MYSTERIOUS abstruse, ambiguous, arcane, baffling, bottomless, cabalistic, carking, confusing, cryptic, dark, deep, delphic, eerie, enigmatic, esoteric, exotic, hidden, incomprehensible, inexplicable, inscrutable, mystic(al), obscure, occult, oracular, perplexing, puckish, puzzling, recondite, runic, secret, sphinxian, subtle, supernatural, uncanny, unknown, wakon, weird

MYSTERY arcana, arcanum, cabala, ceremony, conundrum, craft, cryptogram, drama, enigma, esotery, eucharist, guild, kabala, mass, mist, novel, play, problem, puzzle, riddle, rite, rune, sacrament, secret, sphinx, story, subtlety
comb. crypto
initiate epopt
writer agatha christie, eric ambler, graham greene, ian fleming
writing award edgar

MYSTIC(AL) adept, anagogic, ascetic, cabalic, cabalist, covert, cryptic, dark, epoptic, esoteric, hierophant, idealistic, magical, mahatma, mystagogue, occult, oracular, orphic, runic, secret, spiritual, sufi(st), symbolic, taoist, telestic, yogin, yogish
art cab(b)ala, kab(b)ala
cry evoe
pagan gnostic
word abracadabra, abraxas, evoe, presto, sesame
writing cipher, code, rune

MYSTICISM anagoge, anagogics, anthroposophy, asceticism, cab(b)alism, esoterics, esoterism, esotery, kab(b)alism, occultism, theosophy, yoga, yogism

MYSTIFY agitate, baffle, bamboozle, beat, becloud, befog, bewilder, bother, buffalo, confound, confuse, discompose, dumfound, faze, hoax, muddle, nonplus, obfuscate, perplex, perturb, puzzle, rattle, stump, upset

MYTH allegory, apologue, creation, fable, fabrication, fiction, figment, folktale, imagination, invention, legend, parable, saga, story, tradition

MYTHICAL apocryphal, created, fabled, fabulous, fanciful, fantastic, fictional, fictitious, imaginary, invented, legendary, visionary
creature apepi, basilisk, centaur, cerberus, chimera, cockatrice, cyclops, dipsas, dragon, drake, garuda, gorgon, griffin, harpy, hippocampus, hippogriff, hirocervus, hydra, kraken, lorelei, manticora, mermaid, merman, minotaur, ogre, ogress, phoenix, python, roc, sagitary, salamander, satyr, simurgh, siren, sphinx, unicorn, wivern, xiphopagus, zombi
land lemuria
mountain kaf

MYTHOLOGY fable, fairylore, folklore, legend, lore

MYTILENE lesbos
governor lysimachus

MYXINE hagfish

N

NAAL *child* loki

NAAM distrain(t)
father caleb

NAAMAH *offspring* rehoboam
parent lamech

NAAMAN *cured by* elisha
disease leprosy
parent elud

NAAR, NARR buffoon, clown, fool

NAASON *son* salma, salmon

NAB ambush, apprehend, arrest, capture, catch, clutch, cop, detain, ensnare, entrap, grab, grasp, nibble, pinch, seize, snare, snatch, take

NABAL churl, miser
home maon
wife abigail

NABK anabo, anabong, christ's-thorn, nabbuk, nabo, neback, nebbuck, nebuk, nubk, shrub

NABOB capitalist, croesus, deputy, dives, governor, lord, magnate, midas, millionaire, personality, plutocrat, viceroy
deputy nawab

NABOKOV *novel* lolita, pnin, speak memory
pseud. v sinin

NABONIDUS *son* belshazzar

NABOTH *slayer* jezebel

NACE ashamed, destitute

NACELLE basket, boat, car, chassis, cockpit

NACKET boy, caddie, cake, lunch

NACRE conchiolin, iridescence, mother-of-pearl, pearl, shellfish

NACREOUS iridescent, lustrous, pearly

NACRITE kaolin(e), mica, mineral

NADAB *kin* aaron, appaim, seled

NADIR base, bathos, bedrock, bottom, depth
opposite zenith

NAEVUS See NEVUS.

NAG abash, ache, annoy (ance), badger, baleboosteh, berate(r), bother, browbeat, bully, carp(er), caviler, censurer, cheppeh, clapperclaw (er), cobra, complain, criticize, dingdong, disapprove, disconcert, dobbin, domineer, frab, fret, fuss, garran, gee-gee, gleyde, gnaw, hack(ney), haggle, harass, harp, heckle, hector, henpeck, horse, intimidate, irritate, jade, jaw, mutche, nudni(c)k, nuisance, padnag, paramous, pest(er), pick on, plague, plater, plug, pony, rail(er), ranter, rebuke, rosinante, scold, shrew, slater, snake, snark, tcheppeh, tease, torment, twit, upbraid(er), utz, wanton, xanthippe, yap

NAGA cobra, kabui, lhota, mendicant, narra, sema, serpent, snake
ruler shesha, vasuki, vishnu

NAGGAI *son* esli

NAGGING annoying, complaining, critical, criticism, faultfinding, petulant, teasing, unrelenting

NAGGLE dispute, haggle, pettiness

NAGOR antelope, bohor, redunca, reedbuck, reitbok, tohi

NAHATH *father* reuel

NAHBI *spied on* moses

NAHOOR bharal, oorial, sha, sheep, sna, urial

NAHOR *brother* abraham
father serug
offspring huz, maacah, terah
wife milcah

NAHSHON *son* salma, salmon

NAHUATLAN *indian* aztec, cazcan, mexica, nicaro, pipil, tepanec, tezcucan, tlasca(la)n, toltec

NAHUM *son* amos

NAIAD hydriad, mussel, nymph

NAIL (See also *kind*, below.) arrest, boss, brad, brag, bullen, catch, cheat, claw, clench, clinch, clou, dowel, drive, dump, expose, fasten, fix, garron, hammer, hit, hoof, pin, plate, recognize, scale, secure, see, seize, shell, spad, specie, spike, sprig, steal, strike, stud, tack(et), talon, tenter, tingle, ungual, unguis
absence anonychia
-biting onychophagia, phaneromania
broad-headed roofing nail
cloth-holder tenterhook
comb. helo, ungui
down bag, button up, capture, contract for, fasten, obtain, settle, sew up, sign
drive at slant toe
epidermis perionychium
growth onychauxis
having acronychous
hob tacket
holder nog
hooked tenter(hook)
horseshoe stub
inflammation onychia
ingrowing acronyx, onyxis
kind barbed, boat, box, chair, clout, cooler, finishing, flooring, fourpenny, hinge, horseshoe, roofing, tenpenny, threepenny, upholsterer's, wire
loss piptonychia
marking lunule, spad, speed
mining spad
of crucifixion sagitta
ornamental stud
overgrowth onychauxis
polish enamel
set brad punch
shoemaker's brad, sparable
size ninepenny, penny, tenpenny
small brad, tack, tingle
-studded cloue
toed toshnail
under subungual
wooden dowel, fid, peg

NAILROD herring, stickweed, tobacco

NAINSOOK cotton, fabric, jaconet, muslin

NAISSANCE birth, growth, issue, origin

NAIVE artless, babe, candid, credulous, frank, fresh, green, guileless, gullible, ingenuous, innocent, instinctive, natural, open, original, plain, simple, sincere, trusting, unaffected, unfeigned, unsophisticated, unsuspecting, untaught, unworldly
person babe, ingenue, matmid, yeshiva-bucher

NAIVETE greenness, gullibility, ingenuousness, simplicity

NAJA cobra, serpent, snake

NAKED au naturel, bald, bare, barren, blunt, clear, clothesless, cuerpo, denuded, desert, direct, disclosed, discovered, dry, evident, exact, exposed, indecent, literal, manifest, matter-of-fact, mere, nude, obvious, open, outspoken, plain, pure, raw, revealed, scuddy, sheer, simple, stripped, unclad, unclothed, uncolored, uncovered, undisguised, undressed, unguarded, unprotected, without a stitch
comb. gymno
lady colchicum, meadowsaffron
oat pilcorn, pilkins, pillas

NAKEDWOOD colubrina, mabi, snakebark, snakewood

NAMAYCUSH cree, cristivomer, fish, laker, longe, longue, lunge, siscowet, togue, trout

NAMBY-PAMBY coddle(d),

NAKEDWOOD colubrina, inane, indecisive, indifferent, insipid, overnice, pretty-pretty, sentimental, silly, vapid, weak(ling), wishy-washy

NAMDA horseblanket, numda(h), rug, saddlecloth

NAME address, adduce, alias, announce, appellation, appellative, appoint, assign, autograph, baptize, benight, call, category, celebrity, choose, christen, cite, clepe, cognomen, credit, declare, define, delegate, denominate, describe, designate, designation, distinction, dub, elect, eminence, enti-

tle, enumerate, epithet, eponym, estimation, fame, glory, handle, identify, indicate, label, make, mention, moni(c)ker, naam, nemel, neven, nom, nomen(clature), nominate, note, noun, opt, patronym, personage, personality, pseudonym, renown, reputation, repute, select, set, signature, sobriquet, specify, symbol, tab, tag, term, title, toponym
additional agname, agnomen
ancestors eponym
assumed alias, allonym, anonym, incognito, nom de plume, onomastie, pseudonym, so(u)briquet
backwards ananym
bad caconym
-bearing onymous
big See MAGNATE.
-call berascal
city-derived eponym
comb. aria, nym, onomato, onym
consisting of onomastic
derivation eponymy
diversity of polyonomy
family agnomen, cognomen, eponymy, sirname, surname
father-derived patronym(ic)
fictitious jane doe, john-a-no(a)kes, john-a-stiles, john doe, richard roe
1st forename, praenomen
good credit, honor, standing
inability to anomia
last cognomen, patronymic, surname
list onomasticon
maiden nee
mother-derived matronym(ic), metronym(ic)
original protonym
pert. onomastic
pet hypocorism(a), nickname, sobriquet
place-derived toponym
secondary byname, cognomen, nickname, sobriquet, surname
study of terminology, toponymics, toponymy
substitution allography
tablet facia
technical onym
thing noun
unknown anonymous
well-suited euonym
without anomia
with 2 terms dionym
wrong misnomer

NAMED appointed, called, chosen, cited, designated, dubbed, elected, hight, known as, nominal, nominated, styled, titular, ycleped, yclept
NAMELESS allonymous, anonymous, bastard, illegitimate, incognito, indescribable, ineffable, inexpressible, innominate, obscure, pseudonymous, undistinguished, unknown
city rome
NAMELY explicitly, for, id est, in other words, scilicet, specifically, that is, to wit, videlicet, viz
NAMEPLATE facia, masthead, plaque
NAMESAKE eponym, homonym, junior
NAMIBIA southwest africa
NAMTARU *messenger to* hades
NANA *hero* nata
NANAI ishtar
parent anat, anu
NANDU rhea
NANKING *pagoda* porcelain tower
NANNA *father-in-law* odin
husband balder, bald(u)r
NANNY amah, goat, nurse (maid)
plum sheepberry
NANOID dwarf(ish)
NANOISE *father* usnech
slayer conchobar
wife deirdre
NAOMI mara
daughter-in-law ruth
husband elimelech
land settled in moab
son chilion, mahlon
NAOS adytum, cella, sekos, shrine, star, temple
NAP beauty sleep, bite, blow, bur(r), ca(u)lk, crap, down, doze, drowse, fiber, fluff, forty winks, fuzz, grain, grasp, knock, lint, nibble, pile, ruff, seize, shut-eye, siesta, sleep, slumber, snap, snooze, steal, strike, texture
coarse pile, ras, shag
-like cloth duffel, ras
midday siesta
raise card, tease
raising device gig, teasel, teasle, teazle
NAPE neck, niddick, nucha, nuque, scrag, scruff, turnip

NAPERY doilies, drygoods, linens, napkins, tablecloth
material damask, linen
NAPHISH *kin* ishmael
NAPHTALI *census-taker* ahira
parent bilhah, jacob
son guni, jahziel, jezer, shallum
NAPHTHALENE camphorball, camphylene, mothball
NAPKIN cloth, diaper, doilie, hankerchief, kerchief, napery, neckerchief, serviette, sudatory, towel
NAPLES neapolis
beggar lazzarone
biscuit ladyfinger
coin carlin(e), oncetta, oncia
dance tarantella
house spirit little monk, monaciello
king joseph bonaparte, murat
patron saint san gennaro, san januarius
royalty bourbon
secret society camorra
yellow nanking
NAPLESS bald, hard, threadbare
NAPOLEON boot, cherry, coin, color, pastry, spurge
battle acre, auerstadt, austerlitz, bautzen, beresina, borodino, dresden, eckmulh, elchingen, eylau, friedland, jena, leipzig, ligny, lodi, lutzen, marengo, pultusk, sedan, ulm, wagram, waterloo
birthplace ajaccio, corsica
brother jerome, joseph, louis, lucien
brother-in-law murat
emblem violet
exile elba, st helena
game like pam
horse marengo
idolator chauvin
isle corsica, elba, st helena
marshal augereau, bernadotte, davout, lannes, marmont, massena, murat, ney, soult, vandamme
mentor jomini
mother hortense
nickname boney, jupiter scapin, little corporal
sister elsa, pauline
spy karl schulmeister
vanquisher blucher, kutuzov, nelson, russians, wellington
wife josephine, marie louise

wine favorite chambertin
NAPOLEON III badinguet, boustrapa, louis, rantipole, verhuel
defeat sedan
friend fialin
grandmother letitia
mother hortense
uncle joseph
wife eugenie
NAPOO(H) all gone, annihilate, dead, die, finished, kill(ed)
NAPPY bib, diaper, dish, fluffy, heady, hearty, intoxicated, napkin, pily, shaggy, sleepy, strong, tipsy, velutinous, velvety, villous, wooly
NARAKA See HELL.
NARCISSUS amaryllis, crinium, daffodil, ego(t)ist, flower, herb, jonquil, lily, nancy, plant, polyanthus
beloved echo
disease smo(u)lder
parent cephiscus, liriope
punisher nemesis
trumpet daffodil
NARCOSIS coma, drowsiness, insensibility, sleep, stupefaction, stupor, torpor, unconsciousness
NARCOTIC (See also DRUG and DRUG *addictive*.) addictive, anesthesia, anesthetic, anodyne, bromide, dope, drug, hallucinogen, hypnotic, intoxicant, junk, lenitive, nepenthe, opiate, painkiller, sedative, somnifacient, soporific, stuff, stupefacient, tranquilizer
addict See ADDICT.
agent gazer, nark
dose locus
kind (See also DRUG *addictive*.) alcohol, AMPHETAMINE, bang, barbiturate, belladonna, benj, bhang, cannabis, charas, cocaine, codeine, dagga, datura, diacodion, ether, fagine, ganja, ghow, gow, hasheesh, hashish, hemp, heroin, hops, horse, hyoscyamus, kef, kief, kif, laudanum, lotus, LSD, mandrake, marihuana, MARIJUANA, mescaline, mickey finn, morphine, pellotine, peyote, pot, reefer, scopolamine, snow, stramonium, takouri

package bindle, deck
plant cannabis, coca, cuca, darnel, dutra, hemp, kaat, ket, khat, mandrake, marijuana, poppy
seller connection, dealer, peddler, pusher
shot fix
synthetic methadone
traffic racket
NARD balm, matgrass, muskroot, ointment, rhizome, spice
NARDOO, NARDU ardoo, clover, matgrass, spikenard
NARES nose, nostrils
NARGHILE hooka(h), pipe
NARIAL See NASAL.
NARK annoy, blab, informer, irritate, killjoy, note, observe, spoilsport, spy, stoolpigeon, tease, vex
NARR growl, snarl
NARRA apalit, asana, lingoum, naga
NARRAGANSET algonquian, horse, indian, turkey
NARRATE bruit, depict, descant, describe, detail, disclose, discourse, recite, recount, rehearse, relate, report, reveal, spin, state, tell, yarn
NARRATIVE account, anecdote, apologue, ballad, book, chronicle, conte, drama, epic, episode, epos, fable, fabrication, fiction (al), fictive, figment, history, homeric, jataka, novel(la), parable, recital, recountal, rehearsal, relation, report, review, saga, story, tale, yarn
poem epic, epos, saga
prose novel, story
short anecdote
NARRATOR anecdotist, bidpai, chronicler, novelist, pilpay, raconteur, reciter, recounter, relater, relator, sagamon, storyteller, teller, writer
NARROW bare, beloid, bigoted, borne, circumscribe(d), close, closefitting, compress, condense, confine(d), constrict(ed), contract(ed), cramp(ed), decrease, exiguous, fine, hairbreadth, incapacious, incommodious, lanceolate, lean, limit(ed), lineal, linear, little, meager, mean, meticu-

lous, near, necessitous, parsimonious, pent, poky, poor, prejudiced, prudish, reduce(d), restrict(ed), rigid, rigorous, scant(y), slender, slim, small, strait, strict, stringent, taper, thin, thrifty, tight
blue flag boston iris
comb. angusti, dolich(o), sten(o)
down confine, restrict
-hearted mean, parsimonious, ungenerous
-leaved angustifoliate
-minded biased, bigoted, borne, confined, hidebound, illiberal, insular, intolerant, local(istic), parochial, pedantic, petty, prejudiced, provincial, sectarian, victorian
-mindedness bias, bigotry, provinciality
not big, broad, catholic
NARROWNESS bias, bigotry, compression, constriction, contraction, exiguity, hairsbreadth, stricture
NARROWS canal, channel, defile, ghat, isthmus, neck, pass(age), sound, strait(s)
NARTHEX anteroom, entry (way), foyer, hall, lobby, passage, porch, portico, pronaos, stoa, vestibule
NARWHAL monodon, unie
horn tusk
NASAL (See also NOSE.) narial, narine, nosy, ozaena, ozena, rhinal, stringy, twangy
eminence glabella
NASBY, PETROLEUM david locke
NASCENCY beginning, birth, genesis, origin
NASCENT beginning, developing, emerging, growing
NASEBERRY sapodilla
NASH, RICHARD beau ideal
NASHON *grandson* david
NASHVILLE *music event* grand ole opry
music event site ryman auditorium
warbler calaveras
NASICORN rhinoceros
NASTROND See HELL.
NASTURTIUM capucine, flower, nosewort, radicula,

roripa, sturshum, sturtion, tropaeolum

NASTY abhorrent, bad, brackish, coarse, dangerous, defiled, dirty, disgusting, filthy, foul, fulsome, gross, harmful, horrid, icky, improper, inclement, indecent, indelicate, loathsome, malicious, mawkish, mean, mucky, nauseant, nauseating, nauseous, noisesome, noxious, obnoxious, obscene, odious, offensive, pah, paskudne(h), polluted, pornographic, rank, repellent, repugnant, repulsive, revolting, ribald, sickening, smutty, sordid, squalid, stormy, strong, tainted, ugly, unclean, unpleasant, unseemly, vile, vulgar, waspish

person brock, cow, meanie

NAT demon, hornless, spirit

NATA *wife* nana

NATAL beginning, congenital, connate, gluteal, inborn, indigenous, innate, native

city ladysmith, pietermaritzburg

people zulu

plum amatungula, carissa

port durban

NATANT afloat, aquatic, floating, swimming

NATARAJA See SIVA.

NATATION aquatics, bathing, floating, swimming

NATATORIUM bath, pool, tank

NATCHEZ stinkard, stinker

NATHAN *kin* david, mattatha, zabad

NATHANAEL *son* eliab

NATION commonwealth, community, country, ethnos, geat, host, kingdom, land, lede, multitude, people, power, race, realm, society, state, tribe, volk

at war belligerent

comb. ethno

group alliance, axis, bloc, coalition, entente, league, nato, seato

pert. national, statal

symbol crest, flag

NATIONAL citizen, federal, general, gentilic, gentilitian, NATIVE, public, subject, vernacular

guard heimwehr, militia

park See under individual states.

urban league director young

NATIONALISM chauvinism, jingoism, patriotism, phyletism

NATIVE aboriginal, aborigine, all-american, artless, atta, autochthon(al), autochthonous, binghi, citizen, congenital, corn, denizen, domestic, enchorial, endemic, free, fuzzy-wuzzy, genuine, gugu, habitual, homebred, homemade, inborn, inbred, indigenous, inhabitant, inherited, inner, intrinsic, living, nair, natal, natural, neif, normal, old-timer, original, primeval, primitive, pristine, raw, real, resident, rightful, simple, son, sourdough, unaffected, vernacular

comb. ist, ite, ote

free timawa

states bundelkand

wit intelligence, smarts

NATIVITY beginning, birth, creche, geniture

NATO *commander* haig, lemnitzer, norstad

headquarters brussels, mons, shape

NATRON anatron, glassgall, saltpeter, sandiver

NATTER chat(ter), complain, faultfind, gossip, grumble

NATTERJACK newt, toad

NATTY brave, braw, chic, dapper, dashing, fashionable, foppish, jaunty, modish, neat, nifty, nobby, posh, prim, smart, spruce, stylish, tidy, toffish, trig, trim

NATURAL accustomed, artless, bare, belonging, built-in, carnal, casual, common, constitutional, cretin, crude, customary, easy, existing, expert, familiar, fool, habitual, home, idiot, illegitimate, impulsive, inborn, incorporate, informal, ingenuous, ingrained, inherent, innate, instinctive, in the blood, lifelike, moron, naive, normal, open, ordinary, physical, plain, primitive, raw, real(istic), regular, simple, spontaneous, typical, unaffected, uncul-

tivated, unenfeigned, unforced, unlabored, unpretentious, unregenerate, unstudied, usual, wholesome, wild, wonted

condition norm

force anima mundi

gift dower, flair, talent

principle guna

NATURALIST akeley, andrews, animist, audubon, biologist, botanist, brehm, burbank, carver, darwin, devries, fresia, gray, jordan, lamarck, lindley, linnaeus, linne, mendel, muir, pliny, sars, thoreau, zoologist

NATURALIZE acclimate, accustom, adapt, adopt, domesticate, enfranchise, familiarize, habituate, matriculate

NATURALLY consequently, genially, kindly, normally, physically, plainly, spontaneously

NATURALNESS ease, elegance, inherence, innocence, naivete, spontaneity, unconstraint

NATURE anatomy, aspect, bent, brand, cast, character(istic), color, cosmos, crasis, creation, dharma, disposition, essence, feather, figure, form, ilk, kidney, kind, make-up, mood, ousia, personality, physis, prakriti, quality, range, shape, sort, species, stripe, structure, temperament, tenor, type, universe, way

boy eden ahbez

by born

daughter luonnotar

deity artemis, cybele, indra, isis, marsyas, nymph, pan, thor

demon genius

having the same homogeneal, homogeneous, uniform

human flesh, mankind

inherent genius, talent

mastery eutechnics

moral ethnos

of, comb. acean, aceous, ative, dry

organic bios

pert. cosmic, cosmo, natural, real

preservation science ecology

print phytograph

spirit nat

state of naked, nude

ultimate essence
way of tac
worship pantheism, physiolatry, physitism

NAUGHT aught, cipher, destruction, evil, lost, nihil, nil, nothing, ought, ruin (ed), trifle, useless, wicked, worthless, zero, zilch
set at disdain

NAUGHTY bad, balky, contrary, destitute, disagreeable, disobedient, evil, froward, ill(behaved), impish, improper, mischievous, obscene, perverse, rascally, restive, roguish, unhealthy, wayward, wicked, worthless, wrong

NAUJAITE agpaite

NAUPLIUS *consort* clymene
father poseidon
kingdom euboea
son oeax, palamedes

NAUSEA antipathy, aversion, disgust, dizziness, heaves, loathing, mal de mer, pall, qualm, queasiness, repugnance, seasickness, squeamishness, vomit, weewows

NAUSEATE appall, disgust, loathe, revolt, sicken, stomach, turn, twist, ulate

NAUSEATED airsick, carsick, disgusted, qualmish, qualmy, queasy, revolted, seasick, sick(ish), squeamish, weewowy

NAUSEATING, NAUSEOUS abhorrent, bilious, brackish, despicable, detestable, disgusting, fulsome, loathsome, mawkish, mawmish, nasty, offensive, repellent, repulsive, revolting, sickening, strawsome

NAUSICAA *quest* odysseus, ulysses
parent alcinous, arete

NAUTCH dance, entertainment

NAUTICAL marine, maritime, naval, navigational, oceanic, seafaring, seagoing, seamanlike, tarrish, water-borne
call ahoy, avast, belay, ohoy
equipment becket, binnacle, bobstay, capstan, compass, decca, derm, earing, fid, grapnel, grommet, helm, loran, marline, marling,

pelorus, sextant, skeet, sonar, toggle, tye, wapp
flag cornet, pennon
hazard fog, mine, reef, sub (marine)
measure cable's length, fathom, knot, sea-mile, ton
order aboard, about ship, ahead, ahoy, aloft, anchorsaweigh, astern, avast, back, belay, clear the decks, down helm, dowse sail, full speed, go about, hard alee, hard over, heave(ho), helm alee, hold fast, larboard, port, reef, slow ahead, slow astern, starboard, steady, trim up, up helm
ornament acroterium, billethead, scrollhead
pin fid
rope tye
sounding system asdic, sofar, sonar
symbol anchor, trident
term abast, abeam, abox, aburton, afore, ahoy, alee, alist, alow, atrip, atry, aweigh, avast, batten, bring to, haul off, heave to, lash, leeward, luff, pay off, ply, stow, tack, trice, unreeve, uphelm, windward

NAUTILUS argonaut(a), mollusk
commander captain nemo

NAUVOO See UTOPIA.

NAVAHO, NAVAJO *conqueror* kit carson
hut hogan
people anasazi, athapascan

NAVAL (See also NAVY.) marine, maritime, nautical

NAVARRE *king* ferdinand
queen margaret, margot, marguerite
queen's parent catherine de medici, henry ii

NAVE aisle, apse, axis, axle, center, fist, hall, hob, hub, nathe, nef, nieve, pace

NAVEL belly-button, center, dimple, middle, nombril, omphalos, umbilicus
abnormality acromphalus
center acromphalus
comb. omphalo
having none anomphalous
of the world cuzco
pert. omphalic

NAVELWORT blue-eyed mary, collinsia, innocence, pennycake, pennyhat, pennyleaf, spiderwort

NAVIGABLE accessible, passable, portable

NAVIGATE boat, conduct, cross, cruise, direct, guide, journey, keel, manage, operate, ply, sail, seafare, steam, steer, travel, traverse, voyage
in air aviate, fly, glide, soar
in outer space astrogate

NAVIGATION boating, cabotage, cruising, nautics, periplus, sailing, seafaring, seamanship, shipping, voyaging
chart medieval portolan(o), rutter
coastal cabotage
god janus-portunus
instrument compass, pelorus, sextant
manual bowditch
measure fathom, knot, seam, ton
system asdic, loran, oboe, sofar, sonar, telerans
warning buoy, lighthouse, vigia

NAVIGATOR aeronaut, aviator, baffin, bering, cabot, columbus, cook, copilot, da gamma, dias, drake, eric, flyer, leif eric(s)son, mariner, pilot, raleigh, ross, sailor, tasman
island samoa

NAVVY bearer, digger, excavate, hand, laborer, navigator, operative, roustabout, steamshovel, worker

NAVY armada, fleet, flotilla
cadet midshipman
cannon carronade
captain fourstriper
commander admiral
construction group seabees
high command admiralty
jail brig
man blue(jacket), cadet, devil dog, galiongee, gob, gyrene, jolly, leatherneck, marine, middy, midshipman, sailor, salt, seabee, seadog, swab, tar, toty
officer admiral, armo(u)rer, boatswain, bosun, captain, chief, commander, commodore, cop, ensign, lieutenant, mater, navarch, quartermaster, rear admiral, skipper, striper
officer, petty yeoman
punishment colt
radio operator sparks

shirker coberger

signal flag cornet

stores pitch, tar, turpentine

transport flute

unit argosy, armada, coast guard, escadrille, fleet, flotilla, gyrenes, jollies, leathernecks, marines, merchant marine, mosquito fleet, seabees

vessel battleship, blockship, boyer, caravel, car(r)ack, carrier, chaser, corsair, corvette, crash boat, cruiser, cutter, destroyer, dreadnaught, flagship, flattop, frigate, galleass, galleon, gunboat, ironclad, ironsides, lantcha, lst, man of war, mine-layer, monitor, pt-boat, ram, scout, snorkel, sub(marine), sweeper, tanker, tender, tincan, transport, troopship, u-boat, warship

wireless operator sparks

writer mahan

NAWAB deputy, magnate, nabob, prince, ruler, viceroy

NAY blackball, but also, denial, deny, flute, negative, never, nyet, prohibition, refusal, refuse

NAYWORD byword, proberb, reproach, watchword

NAZE headland, point, promontory

NAZI fascist, hitlerite, rightist

collaborator quisling

concentration camp auschwitz, belsen, belzec, buchenwald, chelmno, dachau, maidaneck, mauthausen, nordhausen, oswiecim, ravensbruck, sachsenhausen, schirmeck, sobibor, stalag, theresienstadt, treblinka

elite guard schutzstaffe

leader gauleiter, goebels, hess, himmler, hitler

militia sturmabteilung

police gestapo

propagandist lord haw haw

song horstwessel

symbol flyfot, swastika

victim anne frank

war trials nuremberg

NEADAB *father* aaron

NEAERA *consort* aleus, helios, strymon, zeus

father pereus

offspring aegle, evadne, lampetia, phaet(h)usa

NEANDERTHAL *site* krapina

NEAP flow, low, shaft, tide, tongue

NEAPOLIS naples

NEAR about, abut, adjacent, adjoin, against, akin, almost, anigh, approach, approximate, around, aside, at hand, beside, border(ing), circa, close(by), contiguous, converge, dear, equal, familiar, fast by, forby(e), hairbreadth, hard by, hend(e), hot, immediate, imminent, impend, inby, intimate, like, match, narrow, neighbor(ing), next, nigh, parsimonious, pres, propinque, proximal, proximate, ready, round, short, similar, stingy, touch, trench on, upon, verging on, vicinal, warm, within

by adjacent, anent, around, at hand, beside, convenient, gin, handly, hard by, local, next, nigh, thereabouts

comb. cis, juxta, par(a), pros

east See LEVANT.

-go close shave

NEARIAH *son* azrikam, elioenai, hezekiah

NEARLY about, all but, almost, as good as, barely, closely, close to, generally, most, nar, nigh, not quite, roughly, roundly, stingily, thereabouts, well-nigh

NEARNESS adjacency, approach, approximation, closeness, contiguity, earshot, hair(s)breath, immediacy, propinquity, proximity, span, spell, step, stone's throw, vicinity

NEARSIGHTED amblyopic, blind, myopic, purblind, shortsighted

person myope

NEAT adroit, appropriate, bos, bovine, bulls, cattle, clean, clear, clever, concise, correct, cosh, cows, crisp, dainty, dapper, deft, dinky, douce, exact, expert, featy, feil, fine, finical, finished, good, great, groomed, heppen, jimp, mack, methodical, natty, net, nice, orderly, oxen, plain, precise, prim, pure, refined, repair, sequence, seriatim, series,

shapely, shipshape, sleek, smart, smug, snug, spick-and-span, spruce, straight, succession, systematic, tasteful, taut, terse, tidy, tight, to rights, tosh(y), trig, trim, turn, unadulterated, uncut, undiluted, unmixed, wonderful

as a new pin, wax

cattle nowt

NEATHERD cowherd, stockman

NEATNESS apple-pie order, fine fettle

NEB beak, bean, bill, end, face, kiss, mouth, nib, nose, penpoint, point, scab, snout, tip

NEBAJOTH *kin* ishmael

NEBAT *son* jeroboam

NEBBECH, NEBBISH alas, loser, nonentity, sad sack, shlemiel, shmendrick, unfortunately

NEBBY impertinent, sharp, spiteful

NEBO *mountain* pisgah

son benaiah, jadau, jeiel, joel, mattathiah, zabad, zebina

NEBRASKA *capital* lincoln

city beatrice, broken bow, cozad, gering, grand island, hastings, kearney, lincoln, north platte, omaha, scottsbluff

college dana, doane, duchesne, hastings

county colfax, deuel, loup, nemaha, otoe, sarpy

indian kiowa, omaha, oto(e), pawnee, ponca, sioux

nickname antelope, blackwater, cornhusker, treeplanters

region badlands

river dismal, elkhorn, logan, niobrara, platte, republican

state bird meadowlark

state flower goldenrod

state tree elm

university creighton

NEBUCHADNEZZAR *general* holophernes

god destroyed by bethshemesh

guard arioch, nebuzaradan

jewish governor abednego, azariah, hananiah, meshach, mishal, shadrach

magician belteshazzar, daniel

persecutor of abednego, meshach, shadrach
servant ashkenaz, melzar
son belshazzar
NEBULA andromeda, cloud, coalsack, crab, galaxy, lyra, orion
kind anagalactic, dark, diffuse, galactic, planetary, spiral
NEBULOUS clouded, cloudy, dim, evasive, hazy, indistinct, misty, muddy, nebular, obscure, shadowy, uncertain, unclear, vague
envelope chevelure, coma
light counterglow, gegenschein
NECESSARILY certainly, come what may, consequently, indispensably, needs must, of course, perforce, surely, unavoidably, willy-nilly
NECESSARY apodictic, basic, binding, called for, certain, compelled, compelling, compulsive, compulsory, critical, essential, exigent, friend, fundamental, imperative, important, importunate, indispensible, inevitable, integral, irreplaceable, irresistible, key, kinsman, mandatory, momentous, must, need(ed), needful, obligatory, organic, prerequisite, pressing, required, requisite, significant, strategic, unavoidable, urgent, vital, wanted
NECESSITATE behoove, cause, compel, constrain, demand, drive, entail, force, impel, oblige, postulate, require
NECESSITOUS destitute, indigent, narrow, needy, pinched, pinching, poor
NECESSITY aliment, besoin, business, compulsion, constraint, demand, destiny, destitution, essential, exigency, fate, godsend, indigence, lack, mister, muscle, must, need(i)ness, obligation, postulate, poverty, prerequisite, qua non, requirement, requisite, requisition, sine, urgency, want
of life aliment, bread, food, water
NECK caress, channel, choke, collum, crag, crane, cuddle,

fondle, hang, isthmus, nape, narrow, nucha, nuque, pet, point, scruff, smooch, spit, strait, strake, swire, tongue, woo
ailment torticollis, whiplash
and crop bodily, entirely, summarily, utterly
and neck close, even, indeterminate, tie
armor gorget
artery carotid
back cervix, nape, niddick, nucha, nuque, scruff
cloth See NECKPIECE.
coat george
comb. cervic(o), der(o), trachel(o)
frill jabot, ruche, ruff
guard camail, mozzetta
hair mane
injury whiplash
muscle paxwax, scalene, scalenus, splenius, trapezius
muscle, pert. scalene
nape nucha, nuque
of the woods neighborhood
ornament See NECKLACE.
pain nuchalgia
part gula, throat, withers
pert. cervical, jugular, nuchal, wattled
plumage hackle
ruff fraise, quellio
-shaped colliform, vee
thin scrag
vein jugular
NECKING fondling, gorgerin, kissing, molding
NECKLACE baldric(k), band, beads, carcan(et), chain, chaplet, choker, collar, cravat, esclavage, gorget, grivna, haltern, hiaqua, jewelry, lavalier(e), lavalliere, locket, noose, pearls, riviere, rope, sankha, sautoir, tie, torc, torque
part tutt
poplar cottonwood
NECKLINE bateau, boat, cowl, crew, sabrina, scoop, vee
NECKPIECE amice, ascot, bandana, barb(e), barcelona, belcher, bertha, bib, boa, burdash, chemisette, choke(r), collar, collet, comforter, cravat, crumpler, dickey, fichu, four-in-hand, fur, guimpe, gules, jabot, kerchief, muffler, neckerchief, pannelo, rabat, rebato, ruche, ruff, scarf, soli-

taire, stock, stole, tie, tippet, tucker
NECKTIE ascot, bow, cravat, four-in-hand, overlay, scarf
fabric mogadore, silk
party hanging, lynching
ready-made teck
NECKWEED hemp, speedwell
NECROMANCER conjurer, diviner, enchanter, exorcist, magician, psychagogos, soothsayer, sorcerer, witch, wizard
NECROMANCY black art, conjuration, divination, enchantment, goety, magic, prognostication, sorcery, spell, witchcraft
pert. goetic
NECROPOLIS cemetery, graveyard
NECROPSY autopsy, postmortem
NECROSIS death, mortification, rot, spacelus
NECTANDRA bebeeru, bibiri, bibiru, cinnamon, evergreen, laurel, sassafras
NECTAR ambrosia, amrita, beewine, honey(dew), manna, meglio, wine
bird eater, honey, sunbird
NEDDA *husband* canio
NEDDER adder, snake
NEDDY ass, donkey, horse
NEED absence, ask, behoove, call for, claim, compulsion, covet, crave, cry for, defect, demand, desideratum, desire, destitution, distress, duty, egence, essential, exact, exigency, extremity, hunger, imperative, indigence, indispensible, lack, mister, must, necessary, necessity, need, obligation, penury, poverty, prerequisite, privation, require (ment), requisite, shortfall, straits, stress, thar(f), thirst, urgency, want, wish
fire wildfire
NEEDLE (See also *kind,* below.) annoy, badger, bait, bodkin, bother, embroider, eyeletter, frond, heckle, hector, hound, hypo, indicator, irritate, kib(b)utz, leaf, memorial, obelisk, perforate, pierce, pique, pointer, prick (er), prod, quil, ride, scold, sew, spike, spine, spur, sting,

stylus, taunt, tease, thorn, twit, urge, vex, yen
adam's yucca
bath shower
bug nepa, nepid, ranatra
bush pinbush, ury
case etui, etwee
chervil lady's-comb
comb. acu
etching drypoint
finisher eyer
furze moor-whin
gun dreyse, rifle
hole eye
kind blunt, bodkin, darner, hypodermic, knitting, phonograph, sail, style, stylus, tacking, upholstery
man tailor
pine spill
short blunt
sorter hander
surgical acus, acusector

NEEDLEFISH agujon, belone, belonid, earl, gar, longjaw, pipefish, sailfish, saury, shook, spearfish, timucu, tylosurus

NEEDLELIKE acerate, acerose, acerous, acicular, aciform, acuate, aculeate, acuminate, belonoid, pointed, spicular, styloid

NEEDLEPOINT angleterre, argentan, argentella, bargello, lace, petitpoint, stitchery

NEEDLESS gratuitous, superfluous, uncalled-for, unessential, unnecessary, useless, worthless

NEEDLEWOMAN couturiere, dressmaker, seamstress

NEEDLEWOOD hakea

NEEDLEWORK basting, brocade, buttonholing, crochet, cross-stitching, edging, embroidery, hemming, hemstitch(ing), knitting, netting, picot, purling, quilting, sampler, sewing, tacking, tatting
loop bride
pattern sampler
piece petit point

NEEDY beggared, destitute, down-and-out, indigent, necessitous, penniless, poor

NEEM margosa, tree

NE'ER-DO-WELL black sheep, bum, cur, duffer, good-for-nothing, incompetent, indolent, ineffectual,

loafer, losel, loser, schlemiel, shiftless, slouch, worthless, wretch

NEF clock, nave, navicula

NEFARIOUS abominable, atrocious, base, black, corrupt, degenerate, detestable, evil, execrable, flagitious, flagrant, gross, heinous, horrible, impious, infamous, iniquitous, monstrous, outrageous, rank, terrible, vicious, vile, villainous, wicked

NEFERTITI, NEFRETETE
capital tel-el-amarna
husband akhanaton, akhenaten, amenhotep
sculptor thutmose

NEFERTUM *father* ptah

NEGATE abnegate, abrogate, annul, avow, controvert, counteract, deny, disaffirm, disavow, disprove, dispute, invalidate, negative, neutralize, nullify, rebut, refuse, refute, thumbs down, veto

NEGATION annihilation, annulment, denial, disclaimer, nay, not, nullity, nyet, obliteration, refusal, veto

NEGATIVE apophatic, balky, blackball, contradict(ion), contrary, contravene, denial, deny, film, gainsay, impugn, indifferent, minus, nae, nay, nein, neither, neutral(ize), never, nix, no how, non, nope, nor, not a bit, not at all, no way, nullify, nyet, repugnant, resistive, traverse, unh-unh, veto, x-ray
comb. dis, non
principle yin
proposition apophasis, paraleipsis
slangy nary, naw, nihil, nix, nope, zilch

NEGISTHUS *victim* atreus

NEGLECT bypass, culpa, default, delinquency, dereliction, despise, disregard, failure, gloss over, ignore, inadvertence, inattention, laches, laxity, laxness, let slip, limbo, loiter, miss, NEGLIGENCE, nonperformance, omission, omit, overlook, oversight, pass over, prevade, procrastinate, remissness, shirk, skip, slight

NEGLECTED abandoned, dilapidated, disregarded, shelved, unheeded, unkempt

NEGLECTFUL careless, delinquent, derelict, disregardful, heedless, inattentive, lax, negligent, remiss, slack, thoughtless
of duty breach, defection, misprision, nonfeasance

NEGLIGEE bathrobe, dishabille, dressing gown, kimono, matinee, nightgown, peignoir, robe, wrapper

NEGLIGENCE carelessness, culpa, disregard, inadvertence, inattention, indifference, laches, laxness, NEGLECT, oversight, remissness, sloppiness

NEGLIGENT careless, derelict, heedless, improvident, indifferent, lash, lax, neglectful, offhand, remiss, slack, slipshod, slovenly, soft, thoughtless, unconcerned, yemeless

NEGLIGIBLE insignificant, little, slight, small, trifling

NEGOTIABLE assignable, practicable, practical, saleable, transferable, transmissible, vendible

NEGOTIATE accomplish, advise, arrange, assign, bargain, barter, broke(r), chaffer, concert, conclude, conduct, confer, consult, deal, dicker, direct, entreat, haggle, intercede, leap, manage, mediate, parley, sell, stipulate, temporize, transact, transfer, treat, troke, truck

NEGOTIATION arbitration, bargaining, chaffer(ing), deal, dicker(ing), haggle, haggling, higgling, parley, trade, treaty

NEGOTIATOR interagent, intermediary, mediator, merchant, proxenete, trader

NEGRILLO abongo, babonbo, bushman, dwarf, obongo, pygmy

NEGRITO abenlen, aeta, akka, akra, andamese, ata, ati, atta, australoid, baluga, bambute, batak, battak, batwa, black, bushman, dwarf, eboe, gumbo-limbo, inkra, ita, karon, melanesian, papuan, pygmy, sakai, semang, tapiro, toma

NEGRO See BLACK.

NEGUS beverage, drink, emperor, ruler, sovereign, wine

NEHELAMITE shemaiah

NEHEMIAH *brother* hanani

parent hachaliah

NEHMAUIT *husband* thoth

NEIF fist, native, serf, servant

NEIGH almost, hinny, near, nicker, snort, whicker, whinny

NEIGHBOR abutter, accolent, adjacent, adjoin, approach, bor, border(er), bystander, donstairsikeh, fellow(man), friend, joiner, juxtapose, mate, neiper, nexdoorekeh, nexdooreker, opstairsikeh, opstairsiker, perihelion, tangent, ucalegon

NEIGHBORHOOD area, bailiwick, barrio, block, community, district, environment, environs, local(e), locality, nearness, precincts, propinquity, proximity, purlieu, region, section, surroundings, territory, venue, vicinage, vicinity

pert. vicinal

NEIGHBORING accolent, adjacent, approximant, bordering, contiguous, local, nearby, nigh, vicinal, vicine

NEIGHBORLY amicable, cordial, folks(e)y, friendly, generous, gracious, hospitable, kind(ly), pacific, peaceable, sociable, social

NEITHER nather, nither, nor yet, not any, not either

comb. neutro

hot nor cold indifferent, irresolute

more nor less equal, exactly

right nor wrong adiaphorous

NEJDI arab

NELEUS *brother* pelias

consort chloris

daughter pero

kingdom pylus

parent poseidon, tyro

son nestor

NELSON *aide* captain hardy

home paradise merton

mistress lady emma hamilton

victory trafalgar

NELUMBO chinquapin, lotus, water lily

NEMATODE ascarid, eelworm, filament, mononch, pinworm, roundworm, storngyle, trichina, worm

NEMBUTAL downer, pentobarbital, yellow-jacket

NEMEA *parent* selene, zeus

NEMESIS adrastia, agent, alastor, ate, avenger, bane, fate, penalty, retribution, rhamnusia, upis

NEMOPHILIA baby-blue-eyes, bird's-eye

NEMUEL *father* simeon

NEOFORMATION cancer, tumor

NEOLATRY novelty

NEOLITHIC *period* campignian, carnacian, halafian

pottery bandkeramic

site skarabrae

NEOPHYTE amateur, beginner, catechumen, convert, devotee, novice, proselyte, tyro

NEOPTOLEMUS phyyhus

NEOTERIC fresh, late, modern, new, novel, original, recent

NEP bryony, catnip, knot

NEPAL shangri-la

capital kat(h)mandu

city bhadgaon, bhaktapur, bhatgaon, birgunj, kat(h)mandu, lalitpur, patan

coin anna, mohar, rupee

district terai

dynasty malla

ethnic group indo-aryan

goddess chomolongma

hindu gurkha

king birendra bir bikram shah dev(a), mahendra, tribhuyan

language khas-kura

mountain climber hillary, tenzing

peak See HIMALAYA *peak.*

people aoul, bhotia, bokra, gorkhali, gurkha, hindu, kha, kiranti, lepcha, limbu, mangar, murmi, newar, rai(s), tharu

river babai, bheri, gandak, kali, karnali, kosi, mugu, narayani, rapti, sarda, seti, tamur

ruler rana

scimitar khukri

sheep bharal, nahoor, nayaur

shrine bodnath, pagoda, stupa, swayambhunath

soldier gurkha

temple swayambhu

title mukhtiyar, rana

tree sal, sisoo, toon

warrior gurkha

wild pig pygmy-hog

NEPENTHE anodyne, drug, hashish, heroin, monkey-cup, narcotic, opiate, opium, pitcher-plant

NEPETA catmint, catnip

NEPHEG *father* david

NEPHELE *consort* athamas, athamus, ixion

offspring helle, phrixos, phrixus

NEPHELITE eleolite, lenad, mineral, sommite

compound analcimite, analcitite, buchonite, canadite

NEPHESH See SOUL.

NEPHEW benvolio, nepote, neve, plemenik, vasu

pert. nepotal

NEPHRITE actinolite, amphibole, amphibolite, axstone, jade, pounam(u), tremolite

NEPHTHYS aphrodite, nebthet, nike

consort osiris, set(h)

kin isis, osiris, set

son anubis

NEPOTISM bias, favoritism, patronage

NEPTUNE (See POSEIDON.) ler, miron, ocean, sea(god)

brother jupiter, pluto

consort galacia

discoverer galle

emblem trident

parent rhea, saturn

satellite nereid

NER *kin* abiel, kish, saul

NEREIDS amphitrite, arethusa, cymodoce, galatea, limnoria, nymph, psamathe, thalia, thetis

parent doris, nereus

NEREUS *consort* doris

daughter See NEREIDS.

parent gaea, pontus

son nerites

NERGAL allatu

kingdom hades, hell, underworld

NERI *son* shealtiel

NERIAH *kin* baruch, mahseiah, seraiah

NERISSA *mistress* portia

NERITA bleeding-tooth, gastropod, snail

NERITIC abyssal, aquatic, bathybic, bathysmal, fluvial, fluviatile, lacustrine, marine, oceanic, pelagix, thalassic

NERO emperor, fiddler, tyrant
consort octavia, poppaea
crown crape-jasmine
eunuch sporus
parent agrippina, claudius
successor galba
victim lucan, seneca
NERVE assumption, audacity, backbone, brass, bravery, brazenness, cheek, composure, conduit, conveyor, coolness, cord, courage, crust, effrontery, encourage, endurance, energy, fiber, firmness, force, fortify, fortitude, gall, grit, guts, hardihood, heart, impertinence, impudence, insolence, intrepidity, invigorate, machismo, macho, mettle, might, pith, pluck, power, presumption, resilience, resolution, sand, sensitivity, sinew, source, spirit, spunk, stamina, steadiness, steel, strength, temerity, tenon, tissue, vein, vigor, vitality, wire
ailment amok, amuck, aneuria, aphasia, apraxia, athetosis, beriberi, brachialgia, chorea, epilepsy, floccillation, huntington's(chorea) (disease), hysteria, ischialgia, lata, neuralgia, neuritis, neuropathy, palsy, paresthesia, parkinson's disease, pseudoangina, pseudotabes, sciatica, shaking palsy, st vitus dance, subsultus, tic
band taenis
branch ramus
cell anaxon, cyton(e), dendraxon, diaxone, inaxon, neuron
cell extension axon(e), dendrite, neurite
cell framework stroma
center brain, cortex, ganglion, plexus
chemical dopamine
comb. neur(o)
cranial optic, vagus
fiber pons
fiber layer alveus
inflammation neuralgia, neuritis
ingredient lecithin
irritant veratrin(e)
layer alveus
motor efferent
network plexus, rete, retia
operation neurolysis

pathway ganglion, hilium, rete
pert. neural, neurotic
poison veratrin(e)
protector myelin
-racking irritating, trying
root radix
science neurology
sensory afferent
stimulant bahnung, spermine
tissue cinerea, endoneurium, neurine
tonic cimicifugin
tumor gliomo, neurinoma, neurocytoma, neuroma, neuromatosis
NERVELESS brave, calm, courageous, dead, foolhardy, inert, powerless, unnerved, weak
NERVES buck fever, budge, butterflies, collywobbles, excitability, fidgets, fluster, funiculi, heebie-jeebies, jactation, jitters, shakes, stagefright, strain, stress, tension, trepidation, uneasiness, vellication
NERVOUS anxious, apprehensive, atwitter, bothered, creepy, disturbed, edgy, energetic, excitable, fearful, fidgety, fitful, flurried, flustered, forceful, fretful, fussy, goosy, high-strung, irritable, jerky, jittery, jumpy, lusty, on edge, overstrung, overwrought, restive, restless, sensitive, shaky, sinewy, skittish, spirited, strenuous, strong, taut, tense, timid, timorous, tittupy, touchy, twitchy, twitterly, uneasy, unstrung, upset, vigorous
disorder See NERVE *ailment.*
system center brain
system chemical norepinephrine
system description neurography
system disease neuropathy
system nomenclature neuronymy
NERVY assured, bold, brash, brazen, courageous, excitable, game, gutty, impatient, impudent, insolent, jerky, NERVOUS, on edge, plucky, presumptuous, pushy, sinewy, strong, unsteady, vigorous
NESCIENT agnostic, aloof, ignorant, illiterate, indiffer-

ent, unconcerned, uneducated, unlearned, unlettered, untaught
NESH dainty, delicate, fastidious, funk, juicy, kingly, mild, moist, slack, soft(en), squeamish, tender, timid, weak, yielding
NESOKIA badger, bandicoot, rodent
NESS cape, headland, point, promontory, ras, suffix
NESSUS centaur
river evenus
slayer hercules
NEST abode, aerie, aery, airport, aviary, birthplace, brink, brood, cletch, clutch, colony, cuddle, den, dray, drey, eyrie, eyry, haunt, hotbed, house, inhabit, lair, larvarium, nid(e), nidi, nidus, resort, retreat, settle, swarm, vespiary, web, withy pot
build nidificate nidify
builder ant, bee, bird, hornet, wasp
comb. oeca
egg decoy, funds, inducement, money, rainy day fund, reserve, savings
of boxes inro
of eggs clutch
pert. cubilose, nidic
science of caliology
NESTLE bundle, burrow, cherish, cuddle, fidget, lie, nuzzle, pet(tle), protect, settle, shelter, snudge, snuggle, snuzzle, spoon
NESTLING baby, bird, child, eyas, fledgling, nidulate, poult, retreat, squab
NESTOR counselor, nelides, oldster, patriarch, sage, solon
kin anaxibia, antilochus, neleus, thrasymedes
kingdom pylos
victim amarynceus
NET acquire, bait, basket, bright, buckstall, capture, catch, caul, clean, clear, entangle, fabric, flan, flew, flue, fyke, gain, gin, haaf, income, kell, lacis, lasso, mesh, moke, neat, profit, pure, reticule, reticulum, rinse, sagene, salambao, seine, serien, snare, snood, spiller, stent, take, toil, trammel, trap, trawl, trim,

tulle, value, wash, weave, web, weight
bag fyke, reticule
comb. dicty(o)
dip scaffnet
fabric bobbinet, lace, malines
fine tulle
fishing flue, fyke, grab-all, lam, raffle, sagene, seine, stent, trammel, trawl, trink
fowling trammel
hair snood
interstice hole, mesh
-leaf plantain
-like cancellate(d), crossbarred, grated, gridded, laced, lacy, latticed, meshed, meshy, plexiform, retiary, reticular, reticulate(d), retiform
silk malines, reticle
small reticle
-winged neuropteroid
NETHANEE *parent* jesse
NETHANIAH *son* ishmael, jehudi
NETHER below, beneath, blast, debase, down, humiliate, inferior, infernal, lower nedder, under
NETHERLANDS (See HOLLAND.) batavia, friesland
NETHERMOST bottom, lowest
NETHERWORLD See HADES, HELL.
NETTED interwoven, retiary, reticulate
NETTING caul, deeping, footing, lace, ling, mesh, screen, wirework
NETTLE abrade, affront, aggravate, agitate, anger, annoy, bluetop, bother, chafe, clown heel, disturb, exasperate, fret, gall, glidewort, henbit, herb, incite, irk, irritate, knittle, offend, peeve, perturb, pique, plant, provoke, ramie, richweed, rile, roil, rouse, ruffle, shrub, smartweed, sting, taunt, tree, trompillo, trouble, upset, vex
cell nematocyst
creeper blackcap, whitethroat
dead archangel, henbit, lamium, richweed, weaslesnout
genus boehmeria, lamium, parietaria, pileaurtica
geranium coleus
potato queenroot
rash hives, uredo, urticaria

tree gympie, lotus
NETTLESOME irritable, irritating
NETWORK abc, cbs, complex, fret, group, mesh, moke, nbc, plexus, reseau, rete, reticle, reticulum, sagene, scheme, system, tessellation, tissue, vas, web (bing)
forminto plex, reticulate
NEUME climacus, clivis, pes, pneuma, podatus, punctum, quilisma, scandicus, sequence, torculus, virga, virgula
NEURAL dorsal, neuric, posterial, verval
recording engram
NEURALGIA causalgia, costalgia, lata, neuritis, sciatica
remedy agathin, tonga
NEURASTHENIA aneuria, neurosis
NEUROGLIA astroglia, glia
NEUROLOGICAL *test* agpar
NEURON nervure
appendage axon(e), neurite
space synapse
NEUROPTERA ant-lion, caddice fly, lace-winged fly, planipennia
NEUROSIS breakdown, crackup, hysteria, maladjustment, neurasthenia, psychasthenia, psychopathy, psychosis
NEUROTIC hypochondriac, hysterical, masochistic, nervous, neurasthenic, neuropath, parapathic, psychasthenic, psychopath(ic), psychotic, sadistic, sick, sociopath
condition latah
NEUTER asexual, castrate, epicine, impartial, intransitive, NEUTRAL, sexless, sterile
NEUTRAL achromatic, adiaphorous, colorless, dispassionate, even, fair-minded, impartial, indefinite, independent, indifferent, individualist, mediocre, negative, nonbelligerent, noncombatant, nonpartison, pacifistic, unaligned, unbiased, undecided
color beige, grey
spirits alcohol
NEUTRALIZE annul, blunt, cancel, conquer, counteract, counterbalance, countervail, defeat, frustrate, negative,

nullify, offset, overcome, saturate, subdue, undo, vitiate, void
comb. ant(i)
NEUTRALIZER antidote, buffer, counteractant
NEUTRINO lepton
NEUTRON particle
discoverer chadwick
star pulsar
NEVADA *capital* carson city
city carson city, elko, ely, fallon, hawthorne, henderson, las vegas, nellis, reno, sparks, virginia city
county elko, nye, storey, washoe
fish killifish, pupfish
indian achomawi, atsugewi, digger, klamath, modoc, mohave, p(a)iute, shoshone, washo
lake mead, pyramid, ruby, tahoe, walker
nickname sagebrush state, silver state
peak east
river humboldt, peese, truckee
state bird bluebird, sagehen
state flower sagebrush
state tree pinon
volcanic rock koipato
NEVE firn, glacier, ice, nephew, snow
NEVER at no time, narra, nary, nay, ne'er, nie, not ever
-ending amaranthine, continuous, deathless, endless, eternal, everlasting, immortal, infinite, interminable, lasting, perdurable, permanent, perpetual, sempiternal, stable, unceasing
-never dreamland, illusory, imaginary, unreal, untrue
say die continue, endure, persevere, resist
NEVERTHELESS after all, but, how-be-it, however, howsoever, howsomever, natheless, notwithstanding, still, yet
NEVUS birthmark, blemish, bulge, freckle, lentigo, mark, mole, spiloma, spilus
NEW additional, another, beginning, fresh, green, just out, late(st), modern(istic), neoteric, neue, nouveau, nova, novel, original, recent, recreated, regenerated, renovated, spic-and-span, un-

accustomed, unused, young, youthful
aversion to misogamy
brand See FRESH.
comb. caen(o), cen(o), neo, nov(o)
deal agency ccc, nra, nya, tva, wpa
rich belgravia, nouveau riche
testament antilegomena, apocalypse, epistles, evangels, gospels
testament, authorative homolog(o)umena
testament book See BIBLE book.
testament coin denarius
year rosh hashanah
year's day nauruz, noroose, nowroze
year's eve hagmena, hogmannay
year's food haggis, hopping john
NEW AMSTERDAM new york
governor peter stuyvesant
NEWBORN infantile, neonate, yeanling
NEW BRITAIN *capital* rabaul
port rabaul
secret society dukduk
NEW BRUNSWICK *capital* fredericton
island campobello
river miramashee, miramichi
NEW CALEDONIA *bird* kagu
capital noumea
island belep, depins, huon, loyalty, walpole
port noumea
tree bastard-box
NEWCOMER cheechaco, cheechako, comeling, deb, greenhorn, immigrant, johnny-come-lately, kimberlin, malihini, novice, outsider, ringneck, settler, tyro
NEW DELHI *hotel* oberoi
NEW ENGLAND *aristocrat* brahman, brahmin
chair brewster, carver, windsor
clock acorn clock
federalists essex junto
fish cod, hake
flower bluets, rue
heroine hannah duston
indian abnaki, malecite, massachuset, micmac, montauk, narraganset, nauset, niantic, nipmuc, pasama-

quoddy, pennacook, penobscot, pequot, possepatuck, seneca, setauket, shinnecock, wampanoag
music festival tanglewood
native down-easter, jonathan, yank(ee)
of the west minnesota
pert. novanglican
settler pilgrim, puritan
ship down-easter
theology calvinism, puritanism
NEWFOUNDLAND *airport* gander
cape race, ray, st john's
capital st john's
discoverer john cabot
fisherman banker
house tilt
indian micmac
lane drung
native newfie, outporter
port st john's
seal ranger, swile
shoal grand banks
NEW GUINEA papua
animal bene, echidna, nodiak
bay geelvink, milne, oro
bird cassowary, mudlark
capital port moresby
city aitape, daru, kikori, kitbadi, lae, port moresby, rabaul, soron, wau, wewak
eastern papua
echidna nodiak
export copra
gulf huon, papua
harbor lae
hog bene
island a(r)roe(s), aru, buka, ceram, jobie, manus, mussau, papua
island group cretin, kiriwina, ninigo, sainson, solomons, trobriands
kangaroo dorcopsis
kingfisher torotoro
lady sinebada
net bag bilum
parrot korikeet, lory
peak albert-edward, carstensz, victoria, wilhelmina
people arapesh, arau, karon, kebar, koiari, koitapu, kukukuku, melawei, papuan, parambli, tapiro, trobriander
port buna, daru, duan, madang, port moresby, wewak
range orange, owen-stanley
river amberno, degul, fly, hamy, sepik
sea arafura, bismarck, coral

shrub bitter-king
strait torres
victory gona
west irian
NEW HAMPSHIRE *academy* exeter
capital concord
city berlin, claremont, concord, exeter, hanover, keene, laconia, manchester, nashua, rochester, sandwich
college dartmouth
county belknap, coos
lake ossipee, squam, sunapee, umbagog, winnipesaukee
nickname granite state
notch crawford, franconia
peak chocorua, flume, monadnock, moriah, paugus, washington, waumbek
port portsmouth
president pierce
range white
river androscoggin, bellamy, connecticut, israel, merrimack, saco, souhegen
state bird finch
state flower lilac
state tree birch
NEW HEBRIDES *capital* noumea, vila
island, api, efate, epi, mabrim, maewo, malekula, tan(n)a, vate
port vila
volcano lopevi
NEW JERSEY *capital* trenton
city asbury park, atlantic city, bayonne, belleville, bergenfield, bridgeton, camden, cape may, carteret, clifton, collingswood, cranford, dumont, elizabeth, englewood, ewing, fort lee, freehold, garfield, hackensack, haddon, hawthorne, hillside, hoboken, hohokus, irvington, kearny, keyport, linden, livingston, lodi, long-branch, madison, maplewood, matawan, metuchen, middletown, millburn, millville, montclair, morristown, neptune, newark, nutley, oradell, orange, paramus, passaic, paterson, pennsauken, plainfield, pleasantville, princeton, rahway, raritan, ridgewood, roselle, sayreville, secaucus, summit, teaneck, tenafly, totawa, trenton, union city, wallington, watch-

ung, wayne, westfield, woodbridge, wyckoff
cliffs palisades
college upsala
county bergen, camden, essex, monmouth, morris, passaic, union
flower violet
indian delaware
nickname garden state, mosquito state
peak highpoint
peninsula sandy hook
port bayonne, camden, hoboken, perth amboy
president cleveland
resort asbury park, atlantic city
river cohansey, dennis, haynes, mantua, mullica, passaic, ramapo, raritan, toms, tuckahoe
state bird goldfinch
state flower violet
state tree red oak
university princeton, rutgers
NEW JERUSALEM utopia, zion
foundation jasper
NEWLY afresh, again, anew, lately, quickly, recently, soon
NEWLYWED benedick, benedict, bride(groom), groom, honeymooner
NEWMAN, J. H. *autobiography* apologia pro vita sua
NEWMARKET cloak, coat, game, grabouche, michigan, saratoga, stops
horse race cesarewitch
NEW MEXICO *art colony* taos
capital san juan, santa fe
cavern carlsbad
ceremony corn dance
city alamogordo, albuquerque, artesia, aztec, bananea, carlsbad, clovis, deming, gallup, hobbs, las cruces, los alamos, piedras-negras, roswell, santa fe, socorro, taos, torreon
colonizer onate
county catron, chaves, hidalgo, luna, mora, otero, quay, taos
culture mimbres
dam elephant butte
explorer onate
fish spikedace
indian acoma, anasazi, hano, isleta, jemez, keres, laguna,

manso, mescalero, navaho, navajo, pecos, picuris, piro, pueblo, santa ana, santo domingo, sia, tano, taos, tewa, tigua, tiwa, tonoa, zuni
indian lands cibola
indian musical instrument ollabumba
motto crescit eundo
name, old cibola
national park carlsbad
nickname land of enchantment, sunshine
peak truchas
pueblo nambe, picuris, pojoaque, san ildefonso, san juan, santo domingo, sia, taso
range guadalupe, sangre de cristo
river gila, pecos, rio grande, san jose, ute
shrub agrito
state bird roadrunner
state flower yucca
state tree pin(yon), taranta(h), velvet ash
turpentine tree taranta(h)
uranium district ambrosia lake
NEWNESS freshness, modernity, novelty, originality
NEW ORLEANS crescent city
festival mardi gras
jazz district storyville
native creole
section latin quarter
street bourbon
NEWS advice, aviso, courier, dope, evangel, ferly, gospel, information, intelligence, khubber, knowledge, message, notice, report, speerings, tidings, witting, word
agency aneta, associated press, dnb, domei, ins, international, reuters, tass, united press, upi
beat scoop
gatherer cub, reporter
good evangel
item article, column, flash, local
media journal, magazine, newspaper, periodical, press, radio, television, telly
NEWSBOY camelot, carrier, vendor
NEWSCASTER anchorman, announcer, commentator, herald, reporter
NEWSMONGER busybody, gossip, reporter, tattler

NEW SOUTH WALES See AUSTRALIA.
NEWSPAPER courant, daily, diurnal, extra, gazette, herald, journal, mercury, news, organ, periodical, publication, rag, review, roto(gravure), sheet, tabloid, tattler, times, tribune, weekly
article column, item, leader
communist pravda, tass
employee compositor, editor, linotyper, pressman, printer, reporter
falangist arriba
file morgue
hoax canard
man cartoonist, columnist, commentator, copyreader, correspondent, editor, gazeteer, journalist, legman, paragrapher, photographer, redactor, reporter, rewriteman
measurement column-inch
section agony column, business, comics, editorial, family, financial, funnies, magazine, news, obit(uary), opinion, real estate, roto(gravure), society, sports, travel, weather, women's
sensational hate sheet, smear sheet, tabloid
underground See PRESS *underground.*
NEWSSTAND booth, canterbury, kiosk, stall
NEWSY advisory, informative, instructive
NEWT amphibian, axolotl, ebbet, effet, eft, evat, evet, lizard, mankeeper, reptile, salamander, triton, triturus
-like ake, esk
NEWTON, ISAAC *dog* diamond
treatise principia
NEW YORK big apple, empire city, father knickerbocker, fun city, gotham, new amsterdam, nieuw amsterdam, sin city
advertising center madison avenue
airport jfk, kennedy, la guardia
avenue fifth, flatbush, madison, park
bay jamaica, moriches, peconic
bohemian district bowery, chelsea, coenties slip, greenwich village, soho
bond big mac

borough bronx, brooklyn, kings, manhattan, queens, richmond, staten island
building chrysler, empire state, flatiron, panam, rca, rockefeller center
canal erie, gowanus
capital albany
city 3 rye 4 rome, troy 5 ilion, islip, nyack, olean, utica 6 albany, attica, auburn, cohoes, elmira, geneva, goshen, ithaca, oneida, tappan 7 babylon, batavia, buffalo, congers, corning, dunkirk, geneseo, hewlett, kenmore, mahopac, massena, merrick, mineola, montauk, oneonta, pennyan, potsdam, suffern, syosset, wantagh, yonkers 8 bethpage, catskill, cortland, deerpark, endicott, herkimer, kingston, lockport, lynbrook, newburgh, ossining, syracuse, tuckahoe 9 amsterdam, brockport, glencover, hempstead, jamestown, levittown, oceanside, peekskill, plainview, rochester, rotterdam, scarsdale, tarrytown, tonawanda, 10 amityville, binghamton, bronxville, floral park, hicksville, lackawanna, long island, mamaroneck, massapequa, ogdensburg, saugerties, watervliet 11 canandaigua, lindenhurst, mount vernon, new rochelle, plattsburgh, white plains 12 gloversville, niagara falls, poughkeepsie
college adelphi, bard, barnard, canisius, cony, elmira, finch, hamilton, hobart, hofstra, hunter, iona, pace, skidmore, union, vassar, wagner
county broome, cayuga, chemung, chenango, duchess, erie, genesee, herkimer, kings, nassau, niagara, oneida, onondaga, oswego, otsego, putnam, queens, richmond, rockland, saratoga, schuyler, seneca, steuben, suffolk, tioga, ulster, yates
democrat, radical barnburner, locofoco
district battery, bowery, bowling green, central, eastside, greenwich village, harlem, hell's kitchen

district, corrupt tenderloin
division borough
dutch settler knickerbocker
early landowner patroon
fern bear's-paw
governor clinton, harriman, lehman, rockefeller, roosevelt
harbor entrance ambrose channel
harbor island ellis, staten
honky-tonk bowery
immigration station ellis island
indian cayuga, erie, iroquois, manhattan, mohawk, montauk, oneida, onondaga, seneca, shinnecock, tuscarora
intersection, famous times square
island bedloes, blackwells, ellis, fire, fishers, governors, liberty, long, manhattan, shelter, staten, welfare
lake cayuga, conesus, erie, finger, george, honeoye, oneida, ontario, otisco, otsego, owasco, placid, saranac, saratoga, schroon, seneca, skaneateles, success
mayor beame, la guardia, lindsay, wagner, walker
military academy westpoint
monastery new skete
museum frick
nickname empire state, excelsior state
parade feature ticker tape
park battery, bronx, central, prospect
peak bear, marcy, slide
political organization tammany hall
port buffalo, oswego
president fillmore, roosevelt, van buren
prison attica, sing sing, tombs
race track belmont, saratoga
range adirondacks, catskills, taconic
reservoir ashekan
resort catskills, coney island, lake placid, poconos, saranac
river ausable, delaware, east, genesee, harlem, hoosic, hudson, mohawk, niagara, oswego, st lawrence, susquehanna, tioga
slum hell's kitchen
society four hundred

square herald, madison, times, union, washington
state bird bluebird
state flower rose
state tree sugar maple
stock exchange amex, big board, wall street
street bowery, broadway, fifth avenue, forty second, madison avenue, park avenue, wall
subway bmt, ind, irt, lex
symbol eustace tilley, gotham, knickerbocker
tennis city forest hills
theater anta, rialto, rko
times founder raymond
university alfred, colgate, columbia, cornell, cuny, fordham, liu, nyu, suny, syracuse, yeshiva
waterfall niagara
NEW ZEALAND antipodes, aoteaorta, aotearoa
airport mangere
ancestor tupuna
anteater echidna
bay awarua, cloudy, fitzroy, golden, hawke, lyall, ohua, pegasus, poverty, rangaunu
beach orewa
bellbird mako
biddybid mapau, piripiri
bird apterix, apteryx, bellbird, blightbird, bush canary, bush wren, fernbird, honeyeater, huia, kaka(po), kaki, kea, kiwi, kokako, koko, kuku(pa), kulu, lowan, mako(mako), moa, mohua, morepark, notornis, oii, pardelotte, peho, poe, roa, rockwren, ruru, titi, tui, weka, wrybill, xenicus
bird, wingless apteryx, weka
blackberry creeping-lawyer
bramble busy-laywer
cape egmont, farewell, palliser
capital wellington
caterpillar aweto, weri
cattail raupo
city auckland, clatha, dunedin, foxton, hamilton, invercargill, kawakawa, oamaru, oreti, otaki, picton, raetihi, rotorua, taupo, timaru
clan ati, hapu
clay papa
cloak kaitaka
commemorative song waiata
compensation utu
corn kanga

cowtree karaka
crow kokako
dance haka
demon taipo
dessert pavlova
evergreen tarata(h), tawa, toatoa
falcon quail-hawk
fern pitau, pteris, tara, weki, wheki
fern root roi
fiord isse, milford sound
fish barraconta, barracuda, halfbeak, hiku, hiwihiwi, ihi, inanga, mako, rockling, skipper, snock, terakihi, trumpeter, warhou, whapuku, yellowbelly
flax harakeke, korari
flower kotukutuku
food kai
fort pah, pau
fruit chinese gooseberry, kangaroo-apple, kiwi
fruit pigeon kuku
fuschia kotukutuku
gallinule pukeko
glacier franz joseph, tasman
grass toetoe
gulf hauraki
gun tupara
harbor otago
herb breadplant, daisy, euphrasia, eyebright
heron kotuku
holly olearia
honey-eater parsonbird, tui
hopbush akeake
hut whare
island niue, north, otea, puketutu, south, steward
island group antipodes, cook
kangaroo apple poroporo
kiwi apteryx, moa, roa
laburnum goai
lake ada, brunner, diamond, gunn, hawea, kanieri, manapouri, ohau, okareka, okataina, paradise, pukaki, pupuke rerewhakaitu, rotoaira, rotokawau, rotoma (hana), rotora, rotorua, tarawera, taupo, teanau, tekapo, waikaremoana, wakatipu, wanaka
liquor waipiro
lizard mokomoko
locust weta
madder coprosma
mahogany totara
mollusk pipi
morepork ruru
mountain climber hillary
muttonbird oii, petrel

myrtle ramarama
national bird apteryx, kiwi
native anzac, maori
ostrich moa
oven kohua
owl ruru
palm nikau
parrot kaka(po), kea, lorikeet, lory, nestor, rosella, tarapo
parson bird koko
peak aorangi, aspiring, blackburn, chope, cook, coronet, earnslaw, egmont, flat, lyall, messenger, mitre, ngongotaha, ohope, otari, owen, pihanga, ruapehu, stokes, tapuaenuka, tarawera, tauhera, tauranga, tongariro, tutamoe, tyndall
penguin rockhopper
peninsula mahia, otago
people arawa, ati, kiwi, maori, mori, ringatu, totara, tutu
peppertree horopito
pigeon kuku
pigment kokowai
pine kahikatea, kauri, matai, rimu, totara
piripiri biddybird
plant angelica, blandfordia, blatti, burrawang, karo, macrozamia, parrot's-bill, saltbush
port auckland, dunedin, gisborne, lae, lapier, nelson, new plymouth, otago, timaru, waitemata, wellington, westport
prime minister atkinson, coates, domett, forbes, fraser, massey, savage, seddon, stout, ward
race track biga
raft moti
railbird koko, weka
range remarkables, southern alps
reef great barrier, oteo
reptile tuatara, tuatera
resort rotorua
ribbonwood houhere
river clutha, manawatu, mokau, rangitikei, shotover, tamaki, taramarkau, tongariro, waihou, waikato, waimakariri, waipa, wairoa, wanganui, whakapapa
robin miro
rumor furphy
sailor kiwi
scabbardfish hiku
sedge toetoe

settlement pah, pau
settler shagroon
shark mako
sheep corriedale
shrub goai, grama, houhere, karamu, karo, kiekie, kowhai, matagouri, muttonweed, pimelea, ramarama, ribbonwood, tumatakuru, tutu, waivatua, wild-irishman
smelt inanga
soldier anzac
song waiata
spa aroha, rotorua, tearoha
statesman ballance, braser, seddon, vogel
stingray wairepo
stockade pah, pau
storehouse pataka
teak puriri
tree ake(ake), akepiro, alectryon, cedar, dodonaea, goai, hinau, hin(o)u, hopbush, horopito, houhere, imou-pine, kahikatea, kaikaka, kaikawaka, kaiwhiria, kapuka, karaka, karamu, kauri, kaury, kawaka, kio, knightia, kopi, kowhai, laceback, maho, maire, mako(mako), mangeao, manuka, mapau, miro, naio, ngaio, nikau, olearia, pelo, pelu, pohutukawa, puka, pukatea, puriri, ramarama, rata, rewarewa, ribbonwood, rimu, tarairi, tarata(h), tarwood, tawa, titoki, toatoa, toro, toru, totara, tumatakuru, wahahen, whau
vine aka
volcano egmont, ngauruhoe, ruapehu, tongariro
wages hoot, utu
warbler riroriro
waterfall sutherland
weapon mere, meri, patu
welcome haeremai
wineberry mako(mako)
woman wahine
woodhen weka
wren xenicus
NEXT abutting, adjacent, adjoining, after, beside, closest, contiguous, dray, ensuing, ewest, following, immediate, intimate, later, near(est), neist, prochain, prochein, shortest, succeeding, then, touching, wise
in order eka
of kin goel

to almost, nearly
to last penult
NEXUS bond, chain, connection, link, tie
NEZ PERCE *chief* joseph
NGAI mana, orenda
NGAIO kaio, kio, naio, tree
NIAGARA avalanche, cascade, flood, grape, torrent, vine
falls boat maid of the mist
NIAM-NIAM azande(h), babungera, zande(h)
NIB beak, bill, end, kink, nose, point, prong, shaft, teat
NIBBLE bit, bite, browse, carp, champ, chew, chimble, criticize, crop, eat, fidget, gnabble, gnaw, graze, knab(ble), knap, morsel, moup, nab, nag, nattle, nip, peck, pick, pilfer, shank, shear, snaggle
NIBELUNGENLIED *character* andarvi, brun(ne)hilde, brynhild, erda, etzel, fafnir, gunther, hagen, kriemhild, mime
dwarf alberich
hero siegfried, sigurd, theodorick
king agnar, gunther, nibelung, schilbung
villain hagen
NIBS big shot, personage, vip
NICAEA *council date* easter
NICARAGUA *capital* managua
city granada, jinotega, leon, managua, masaya, matagalpa
coin centavo, cordoba, peso
god chiquinau, ciaga, ecalchot, mictanteot, misca, quiateot, tamagostad, vizetot
indian cukra, diria, lenca, mangue, matagalpa, mico, mixe, mosquito, rama, sambo, smoo, toaca, ulva
lake managua
measure cabelleria, cahiz, cajuela, estadal, manzana, milla, suerte, tercia, vara
peak madera, mogoton
poet dario
port bluefields, corinto
president somoza
river coco, escondido, grande, tuma, wanks
volcano leon, managua, momotombo, negro, telica
weight bag, caha, tonelada

NICCOLITE arite, mineral
NICE accurate, acute, agreeable, amiable, canny, careful, chaste, clean, commendable, conscientious, considerate, critical, dainty, decent, decorous, delicate, delightful, demure, discerning, discriminate, discriminating, elegant, exact(ing), excellent, exquisite, fastidious, fine, finical, finicky, fit, friendly, fussy, genteel, good, gracious, hairsplitting, kind, lovely, meager, meticulous, mincing, modest, neat, particular, per(s)nickety, pleasant, pleasing, polite, proper, prudish, pure, queasy, rare, refined, reserved, respectable, right, rigid, savory, scrupulous, seemly, spare, squeamish, strict, subtle, suitable, sweet, tactful, thoughtful, trivial, virtuous, weak, well-behaved, well-mannered
affectedly niminy-piminy
NICETIES amenities, civilities, courtesy, etiquette, minutiae, perjinkities, trivia
NICETY accuracy, correctness, delicacy, discernment, discrimination, judgment, justness, precision, taste
NICHE aedicule, alcove, ancona, apse, bay, cant, carol, carrell, compartment, corner, covert, cranny, cubicle, edicule embrasure, habitacle, hole, indentation, mihrab, nestle, nook, position, recess(ion), retreat, roundel, tabernacle, tokonoma, wro
ornamental tabernacle
NICHOLAS *daughter* anastasia
saint father christmas, kriss kringle, santa claus
NICHOLAS NICKLEBY
character cherryble, crummles, gride, kate, madeline bray, miss belvawney, mulberry, noggs, smike, squeers, vincent
school dotheboys hall
NICIAS *aide* hiero
colleague demosthenes, menander
deceiver hermocrates
enemy alcibiadies, cleon, eurycles, gonglus, hyperbolus

father niceratus
lieutenant callippus, lamachus
patron demostratus, pericles
NICIPPE *brother* atreus
NICK arrest, charge, cheat, chip, cut, defraud, dent, dint, gamble, gouge, groove, hack, hit, incise, indentation, indenture, instant, jag, mar, mill, nack, nitch, notch, prison, record, rob, score, snick, steal, touch, trick
NICKEL blip, coin, five cents, jit(ney), nimbus
alloy alfenide, annabergite, argenton, awaruite, beyrichite, bunsenite, calorite, elinvar, invar, kamacite, konar, konel, millerite, monel, niccolite, nichrome, pentlandite, taenite
containing niccolic
ore garnierite
NICKELODEON jukebox, movie
NICKER brawler, laugh, marble, money, neigh, nix, nymph, pound, sprite
tree bonduc, coffee-tree
NICKNAME agname, agnomen, alias, byword, cognomen, diminutive, handle, hypocorism, monarcho, monica, moni(c)ker, sobriquet
NICKNAMING prosonomasia
NICOBAR ISLANDS *capital* port blair
NICOMACHUS *son* aristotle
NICOSTRATUS *brother* megapenthes
parent helen, menelaus
NICTATE blink, connive, twink(le), wink
NIDANA *chief* avidya
NIDDERING base, cowardly, infamous
NIDE brood, inhabit, litter, nest
NIDOR aroma, odor, savor, scent, smell
NIDUS birthplace, core, nest, nucleus, oritin, repository, source
NIECE nepote, oye
NIELLO inlay, tula
NIEPA *bark* niota
NIETZSCHE *work* beyond good and evil, birth of tragedy, thus spake zarathustra
man superman

NIEUW AMSTERDAM new york city

NIEVE fist, hand, neif

NIFELHEIM bjarmaland, hell

ruler hel

serpent nidhogg, nidhug

NIFTY attractive, brave, braw, chic, clever, dapper, dashing, excellent, fashionable, fine, great, modish, natty, nobby, posh, smart, spruce, stylish, toffish

NIGER joliba, kworra, ramtil

capital niamey

city maradi, tahoua, zinder

language mande, mandingo

mouth nun

native djerma, fulani, hausa, idjo, idyo, idzo, peul, songha, toubou, tuareg, warri

oasis kaouar

river dillia

warrior aro

NIGERIA *capital* lagos

city aba, abeokuta, ado, benin, bida, buea, calabar, ede, enugu, ibidan, ilesha, ilorin, isa, iwo, jos, kachia, kaduna, kano, lagos, maiduguri, mushin, offa, ogbomosho onitsha, oshogbo, oyo, takoba, yola, zaria

general gowon

language efik

leader balewa gowon, schick

people abo, angas, aro, benin, bini, djo, ebo(e), edo, efik, egba, ejam, ekoi, fulani, gwari, hausa, ibibio, ibo, idyo, ijaw, ijo, nupe, vai, yoruba

port calabar, harcourt, lagos

province adamawa, bornu, ijebu, isa, kano, nupe, ogoja, ondo, owerri, oyo, sokoto, warri

region air, asben, benin, calabar, oil rivers, yorubaland

river benin, benue, calabar, gana, gongola, kadunu, komadugu, niger, oli, sokoto, yobe

secessionist state biafra

secret society egbo

spirit juju

statesman awolowo, azikine, azikiwe, balewa

tree afara, terminalia

walled city kano

NIGGARD chinche, churl, MISER, nither, nithing,

pinchbeck, puckfish, scrimper, scrunt

NIGGARDLY avaricious, carking, cheeseparing cheapskate, chintzy, churlish, close(fisted), covetous, curmudgeonly, economical, frugal, grasping, greedy, ignoble, mean, miserly, paltry, parsimonious, pennypinching, penurious, scanty, skinflint, small, sordid, sparing, stingy, strait, thrifty, tight(fisted)

NIGGERFISH coney, cony, grouper, guativere, hind

NIGGLE cheat, criticize, deceive, fidget, overelaborate, potter, taunt, trifle

NIGH adjacent, almost, anear, approach, close, contiguous, direct, near(ly), neighboring, often, short

side left

NIGHT (See also NYX.) adversity, bedtime, belated, curfew, dark(ness), darky, death, eleventh hour, eve (ning) gabe, gabi, nacht, natt, noche, nott, nox, NYX, obscurity, sera

air snelly

and day constantly, continually, nychthemeron, tirelessly, unceasingly

animal coon, lemur, opossum, possum, raccoon, ratel

ape aotus, durukuli

attack camisado

bird bat, moorhen, nightingale, owl, shearwater

blindness hemeralopia, nyctalopia

chair closestool

churr goatsucker

comb. noct(i), nyct(i)(o)

crawler bait, dewworm, earthworm

depth holl

division watch

dress nightgown, slop, wilycoat, wyliecoat

emerald crysolite, olivine

fish cod

flit woodcock

flyer bat, moth, owl

god hod(er), hodur, somnus, tezatupoca

goddess artemis, hecate, leda, leto, natt, nott, nox, NYX

lamp veilleuse

last yestreen

letter telegram, wire

offspring See NYX *offspring.*

owl dissipater, roue

pain nyctalgia

parrot kakapo

peck woodcock

person noctambule

personification nox, nyx

pert. nocturnal

queen moon

rail negligee, robe, wrapper

sergeant damselfish

signs zodiac

spot nitery

stay out all pernoctate

stick billy, espantoon, truncheon

table somnoe

-walker angleworm, footpad, prostitute, somnambulist, thief

-walking noctambulation, noctambulism, noctivagant, noctivagous, noctivigation, sleepwalking, somnambulation, somnambulism

-walking spirit lemures

watch pervigilium

watchman guard, sentinel, sentry, sereno

wear gown, jammies, nightie, pajamas, pj's, pyjamas

NIGHTCAP anemone, biggin, boil, brawler, bully, clockmutch, cowl, doremeuse, dowd, drink, houve, mutch, one for the road, pillowcup, pirnie, sporific, sundowner

NIGHTCLUB bistro, boite (de nuit), cabaret, cafe, dive, hotspot, restaurant

NIGHTFALL acronycal, acronychal, candlelight, dusk, een, eve, evening, gloaming, occurring at acronical, twilight

NIGHTGOWN (See also NIGHT *dress.*) bedgown, pajamas, toosh, wyliecoat

NIGHTHAWK bullbat, cuiejo, dissipater, goatsucker, morepark, nightjar, petral, pisk, taxi, vehicle

NIGHTINGALE atticbird, barleybird, blackcap, bulbul, florence, jenny lind, luscinia, philomel(a), procne, progne, siskin, thrush, wagtail, wryneck

group watch

turned into aedon

NIGHTJAR caprimulgus, evejar, goatsucker, icebird,

morepark, nighthawk, potoo, spinner, wheeler

NIGHTMARE alp, cacod(a)emon, cauchemar, demon, dream, elf, ephialtes, fiend, hallucination, incubus, mara, ordeal, succubus, terror, torment, trial, tribulation, vision, witch
preventive antephialtic

NIGHTSHADE alkekengi, basella, belladonna, bittersweet, brunfelsia, datura, duscle, dwale, henbane, herb, houndsberry, morel(le), pokeweed, prairieberry, rivinia, sandbur, solanales, solanum, stonecrop, trillium, trompillo, weed, wonderberry

NIHILISM anarchy, destructiveness, skepticism, terrorism

NIHILIST anarchist, bolshevist, communist, socialist, terrorist
art movement dada, pop surrealism

NIK believer, cultist, devotee, enthusiast, fan(atic), follower, lover

NIKE apteros, athena, victory
parent pallas, styx
sister bia

NIL dye, indigo, ipomoea, naught, nilgai, nothing, zero, zilch

NILE (See also EGYPT references.) alawy
as god hapi
bird ibis, wryneck
blue, lake tsana
blue, part abbai
blue, people bertat
blue, region abbai
blue, source dambea, dembea, ethiopia
boat baris, cangia, dahabeah, felucca, gaiassa, nuggar, sandal
captain rais, reis
cataract catadupe
catfish bagare, docmac
city abri, alexandria, argo, asyut, cairo, el mansura, idfu, isna, luxor, mansura, qina, qus, rojaf, rosetta, saite, tanis, tanta
crocodile mugger
dam aswan
debris sudd
falls ripon
fish bagre, bichir, binny,

bolti, docmac, erse, mormyr(o)id, saide
floating vegetation sudd
god hapi, khnemu, khnum
grass umsuff
headwater lake edward
houseboat dahabeah
island philae, roda
lizard adda
nomad beja
people bari, beja, golo, jur, luo(h), lwo, madi, nilot, nuo, suk
pert. nilotic
plant lotus, sudd
region nubia
reptile croc(odile)
river gauge nilometer
ruins miroe
source kagera, lake albert, lake victoria, tsana
star sirius
tree ambash, ambatch
tributary atbara, kagera
white, people luo, lwo, shilluk

NILGAI antelope, boselaphus, neelghaw, nylgau

NILGIRI *tribesman* badaga

NILOTIC *language* dinka, shilluk
people golo, jur, luo, lwo, nuo, suk

NILUS *daughter* anchinoe

NIM margosa, neem, pilfer, steal, thieve

NIMBLE active, acute, adroit, agile, alert, bright, brisk, clever, deft, dext(e)rous, fast, flippant, flit, funny, gleg, light, limber, lish, lissome, lithe, lively, prompt, quick, rapid, responsive, sensitive, smart, sprighty, spry, supple, swack, swift, swipper, tripping, vigilant, volant, watchful
kate bur, cucumber
will grass, muhlenbergia

NIMBLENESS agility, dexterity, haste, legerity, lightness, sleight

NIMBOSE cloudy, stormy

NIMBUS agnus dei, aura, aureole, cloud, gloria, glory, halo, vapor

NIMIETY excess, redundancy, superabundance, surfeit

NIMMER See THIEF.

NIMROD chasseur, despot, gunner, hunter, marksman, orion, ruler, tyrant

city accad, achad, akkad
kin cush, noah
kingdom babel
son bel

NINCOMPOOP ass, blockhead, dolt, dunce, fool, ninny, simpleton, witling

NINE ball team, neuf, neun, nove, nueve, quinine, team
a.m. midmorn, undern
-angled figure nonagon
comb. enne(a), nona
days' devotion novena
days' wonder ephemerid, ephemeron
-eyes eel, gunnel, lamprey
group of ennead, nonary, nonet
-headed monster hydra
holes bumble-puppy
hundred sampi, san
inches span
instruments nonet
-killer shrike
men's morris game, mill, morelles, muhle
of clubs comet
of diamonds bragger
of trumps dix, menel, sancho
pert. enneatic, nonary
worlds alfheim, asgard, hel, jotunnheim, midgard, muspellsheim, niflheim, ninheim, svartalfaheim, vanaheim
worthies alexander, arthur, caesar, charlemagne, david, godefroy, godfrey, hector, joshua, judas maccabaeus

NINEBARK physocarpus, rosacean, sevenbark

NINEFOLD nonuple

NINEPINS kayles, keels, skittles, squail

NINETY koppa
year-old nonagenarion

NINEVEH *founder* ninus
king sardanapalus
rival babylon

NINGAL *husband* sin

NINIGIKU enki

NINKHURSAG belil
consort bel, enlil

NINNY blockhead, booby, dolt, dunce, fool, goose, idiot, lout, niddycock, noodle, patch, peakgoose, sammy, simp(leton)
-hammer ass

NINOX boobook, morepark, owl

NINURTA *consort* gula
father bel(us)

NINUS *city* nineveh

consort semiramis
NIOBE funkia, herb, hosta, plant
consort amphion, zeus
enemy apollo, artemis, leto
kin aedon, apis, pelops, phoroneus
offspring amyclas, argus, chloris
parent tantalus
sister-in-law aedon
NIORD, NJORD *enemy* aesir
home noatum
offspring frey, frey(j)a
people vanir
NIP benumb, bit, bite, blast, blight, catch, check, chill, chip, cold, compress, cut, deduct, depart, destroy, dram, draught, drink, freeze, frost, gibe, hold, pain, pang, peck, pinch, pressure, sarcasm, seize, sever, sip, snatch, snip, squeeze, steal, swallow, tang, taut, tuck, tweak, twinge, twitch, vex, wither
and tuck close, equal
-cheese miser, purser
in the bud check, stop
NIPA at(t)ap, drink, mat, palm, thatch, tree
product tuba
NIPPER biter, boy, brakeman, chela, claw, costermonger, crab, cunner, drink, grab, gripper, hand, incisor, lad, miser, rack, thief, urchin
NIPPERS dog, forceps, handcuffs, pince-nez, pincers, pliers, tongs, tweezers
NIPPING, NIPPY biting, bitter, bleak, cold, grasping, vigorous, zestful, zesty
NIPPLE bean, bud, diddy, dug, dummy, mamilla, nibble, pap(illa), spean, teat, thelium
NIPPLEWORT ballogan, wartweed, wartwort
NIPPON See JAPAN.
NIRVANA composure, ecstasy, emancipation, emptiness, extinction, nibbana, oblivion, paradise, reunion, serenity, tranquility
attainment moksha
practice paramita
triple fire dosa, moha, raga
NISAN abib
NISI if not, unless
NIS(SE) banshee, brownie, dwarf, fairy, gnome, goblin,

kobold, nix, puck, shee, spirit, sprite
NISUS desire, effort, endeavor, impulse, power, striving
daughter scylla
friend aeneas, euryalus
kingdom megara
parent hytarcus, ida, pandion
NIT egg, hazelnut, insect, louse, neet, nut
NITCH alcove, bundle, connect, fagot, join, niche, nick, notch
NITER natron, peter, petre, potash, saltpeter
NITHER blast, debase, humiliate, neither, oppress, shiver
NITHING coward, dastard, niggard
NITID bright, gay, glossy, lustrous, radiant, shining, spruce
NITRATE azotate, ester, gerhardtite, salt
cellulose guncotton
rock caliche
NITROBENZENE mirbane
derivative benzidine
NITROGEN alkaligen, azo, azote, element, explosive, fertilizer, gas, quinoline
comb. azi, azo, azot(o)
combine with azotize
compound ammonia, azine, azole, azolitmin, azomethine, betainogen, triazane, triazine, uramil, urea, xanthine
measurer azotometer
pert. azotic, azotous
ring, pert. azycyclic
NITROGLYCERINE dynamite, explosive, glonoin, sirup, soup, tnt, trinitrate, trinitrin, vasodilator
discoverer sobrero
NITWIT boob, dizzard, dope, dunce, fool, gaby, goose, halfwit, jackass, muddlehead, simpleton
NIVAL, NIVEOUS snowy, white
NIX don't, dwarf, negative, NISSE, nobody, nothing, prohibit, spirit, stop, veto
NIXON RICHARD *dog* checkers, king timahoe
downfall watergate
friend abplanalp, rebozo
physician tkach
valet sanchez
wife pat

NIZAM ruler, soldier, sovereign
NIZY fool, noodle
NJORD, NJORTH *child* frey(a), freyja, freyr
father-in-law thiatsi, thiazi, thjazi
home noatun
wife skadi, skathi
NKVD *forerunner* ogpu
NO baal, bail, bale, declination, denial, drop dead, nae, napoo(h), naw, nay, negative, nein, nix, nogaku, none, nor, not(hing), noway, nowise, nyet, refusal, thumbs down, veto
account good-for-nothing, no good, shmendrick, trifling, worthless
doubt probably
-go bust, failure, fiasco, futile, hopeless, useless
-good bum, cheat, drifter, lowlife, parech, trickster, wastrel, wretch
great shakes nonentity, ordinary, small, unimportant
more dead, gone, napoo, past, phut
-show absentee
thanks moichel
NOACHIAN ancient, antiquated, old
NOAH, NOAH'S atrahasis, coxcox, xisuthras
babylonian utnapishtim
dove columba
father lamech
follower arkite
grandfather methuselah
grandson aram, gilgamesh
great-grandson hul
mountain ararat
pert. noachian, noetic
raven corvus
refuge ark
son ham, japheth, sem, shem
wife noraida
wine cup crater
NOB beau, blow, buck, coxcomb, dandy, dude, elegant, fop, handle, head, hump, jack, knave, knob, lump, macaroni, nave, noble, personage, spark, swell, take, toff
NOBBUT also, except, just, only, unless
NOBBY fine, great, smart
NOBEL PRIZE *biochemistry* northrop, stanley, synge
chemistry alder, arrhenius, aston, baeyer, boschbuch-

ner, burgius, butenandt, calvin, curie, debye, diels, fischer, giauque, grignard, haber, hahn, harden, haworth, hevesy, heyrovsky, hinshelwood, hodgkin, hoff, joliot, karrer, kendrew, kuhn, langmuir, libby, martin, mcmillan, moissan, monod, mullikan, natta, nernst, northrop, ostwald, pauling, perutz, pregl, richards, robinson, rutherford, ruzicka, sabatier, sanger, seaborg, semenov, soddy, standinger, stanley, sumner, svedberg, synge, tiselius, todd, urey, vigneaud, virtanen, wallach, werner, wieland, wilkinson, windaus, woodward, ziegler, zsigmondy

economics arrow, kuznets, leontief, samuelson

literature agnon, andric, benevente, bergson, bjornsen, buck, bunin, camus, carducci, churchill, deledda, dugard, echegaray, eliot, eucken, faulkner, france, galsworthy, gide, gjellerup, hamsun, hauptmann, heidenstam, hemingway, hesse, heyse, jensen, jimenez karlfeldt, kipling, lagerkvist, lagerlof, laxness, leger, lewis, maeterlinck, mann, martindu-gard, mauriac, mistral, mommsen, o'neill, pasternak, pirandello, pontoppidan, prudhomme, quasimodo, reymont, rolland, russel, sachs, sartre, seferiades, shaw, sholokhov, sillampaa, spitteler, steinbeck, st john-perse, tagore, undset, white, yeats

medicine 3 dam 4 cori, dale, hess, hill, koch, ross 5 bloch, bovet, cajal, crick, doisy, golgi, hench, jacob, krebs, krogh, loewi, lwoff, lynen, minot, moniz, monod, ochoa, tatum 6 adrian, barany, beadle, bekesy, bordet, burnet, carrel, domagk, eccles, enders, finsen, florey, frisch, gasser, huxley, kocher, kossel, lorenz, morgan, muller, murphy, pavlov, richet, watson, weller 7 banting, behring, ehrlich, eijkman, fibiger, fleming, heymans,

hodgkin, hopkins, houssay, huggins, jauregg, kendall, laveran, lipmann, macleod, medawar, nicolle, robbins, spemann, theiler, waksman, warburg, shipple, wilkins 8 cournand, erlanger, forssman, kornberg, meyerhof, richards, siegbahn, theorell 9 einthoven, lederberg, tinbergen 10 gullstrand, lansteiner, reichstein 11 sherrington 12 szentgyorgyi

peace addams, angell, arnoldson, asser, bajer, balch, bardeen, barkla, basov, beernaert, branting, briand, buisson, bunche, butler, cecil, chamberlain, cremer, dawes, ducommun, dunant, fried, gobat, guidde, hammarskjold, henderson, hull, jouhaux, kellogg, king, kissinger, la fontaine, lamas, lange, le duc tho, luthuli, marshall, moneta, mott, nansen, noel-baker, orr, ossietsky, passy, pauling, pearson, pire, renault, roosevelt, root, schweitzer, soderblom, stresemann, suttner, unicef, wilson

physics appleton, bardeen, barkla, bason, blackett, bloch, bohr, born, bothe, bragg, brattain, braun, chadwick, c(h)erenkov, compton, curie, dalen, davisson, debroglie, dirac, einstein, esaki, fermi, feynman, fran(c)k, giaever, glaser, guillaume, heisenberg, hertz, hess, jensen, josephson, kastler, lamb, landau, laue, lawrence, lee, lenard, lippmann, lorentz, marconi, mayer, michelson, millikan, mossbauer, pauli, perrin, planck, powell, purcell, rabi, raman, rayleigh, richardson, roentgen, schwinger, segre, shockley, stark, stern, tamm, thomson, tomonaga, townes, waals, walton, wien, wigner, wilson, yang, yukawa, zeeman

NOBILITY aristocracy, county, dignity, elevation, elite, eminence, generosity, gentility, gentry, glamor, grandeur, honor, importance, kwazoku, loftiness, magnificence, magnitude,

majesty, peerage, probity, quality, rank, station, status, superiority, szlachta

emblem llautu

name meaning adelaide, adelbert, adelina

rank See NOBLEMAN.

NOBLE aristocrat(ic), armigerous, august, blueblood(ed), burly, chivalrous, dignified, ducal, elevated, eminent, empyreal, epical, estimable, ethel, ethical, exalted, excellent, famed, famous, fine, gallant, generous, genteel, gentlemanly, good, grand(iose), great(hearted), handsome, haught, heroic, highborn, highminded, honest, honorable, illustrious, imperial, important, imposing, impressive, just, khass, kingly, liberal, lofty, lordly, magnanimous, magnificent, majestic, manly, moral, patrician, princely, pure, queenly, renowned, righteous, splendid, stately, sublime, superb, swell, thoroughbred, titled, upright, virtuous, whole-souled, worthy

friend, name meaning alvin

-minded whole-souled

name meaning arthur, earl(e), eli, elsa, elza, ethel, hiram, ilsa

pine pipsissewa

savage indian

NOBLEMAN acerbas, adeliger, almaviva, ariki, aristocrat, ashraf, athel, barin, baron, bashaw, belarius, brahman, brahmin, cacique, chevalier, count, daimio, damoiseau, dige, don, duke, earl, edel, emir, fidalgo, flaith, furst, gentilhomme, gentleman, gesith, graf, grandee, herzog, hidalgo, jarl, junker, kame, king, knight, kuge, laird, landgrave, lord, lucumo, magnate, magnifico, maharajah, marchese, marquess, marquis, milord, murza, optimate, orloff, orlov, panglima, paris, pasha, patrician, peer, prince, raja(h), rial, ritter, seigneur, seignior, senor, signor(e), sirdar, starost, tha-

kur, tzin, viscount, volpone, yo(u)nker
NOBLENESS See NOBILITY.
of birth eugeny
NOBLEWOMAN baroness, contessa, countess, duchess, lady, marchesa, marchioness, marquise, marquisina, milady, peeress, princess, queen
NOBODY also-ran, chaimyankel, chotchke(leh), cipher, jackstraw, kabtzen, kabtzonim, milchedig, milchik, nadie, nemo, nix, none, nonentity, nothing, scarab, scrub, tchotchke(leh), tsatske(leh)
NOBS darling, dear, jack, knave
NOCENT criminal, guilty, harmful, hurtful, injurious
NOCTUID armyworm moth, catocala, cutworm-moth, prodenia, worm
NOCTURNAL (See also NIGHT.) astrolabe, moonshine, night(ly), nightwalker, streetwalker, tenebrous
NOCTURNE barcarol(l)e, lullaby, painting, serenade, uhtsong
NOD affirmative, approval, assent, beck(on), bend, blunder, bob, bow, doddle, doze, droop, drowse, err, greeting, incline, nap, nid, niddlenoddle, nip, noddle, nutate, salaam, salutation, salute, sign(al) signify, sleep, slip, summons, sway, tend, wink
land of, dweller cain
NODDING annuent, cernuous, drooping, drowsy, nutant, pendent, tottering
NODDLE beat, brain, capernoite, capernutie, head, nape, noodle, pate, strike
NODDY drowsy, fool(ish), fulmar, hackney, jack, knave, noio, noodle, simpleton, sleepy, tern
tern anous, auk, fulmar, noio, ruddy-duck
NODE articulation, complication, connection, difficulty, dilemma, entanglement, joint, knob, knot, knur(l), kust, nodosity nodus, point, protuberance, swelling, tumor
NODULE amydale, auge,

blister, bump, cathead, geode, granule, knot, leproma, lump, mass, milium, node, phyma, sarcoid, tubercule, tumor, whitehead
stone geode
NOE *son* ham
NOEL carol, christmas, natalis, song, xmas, yule(tide)
NOG ale, block, drink, peg, pin, treenail
NOGAH *father* david
NOGGIN brain, cup, drink, gill, head, mug, nob, noodle, pate
NOISE ado, air, alarm, babel, ballyhoo, bedlam, bellow, blare, blast, blat, bluster, boom, brawl, bruit, cackle, cacophony, call, chang, charivari, chirm, chortle, clamor, clang(or), clap, clatter, clitter, confusion, din, discord, disquiet, dream, fracas, gossip, hell, hubub, hullabaloo, jangle, outcry, pandemonium, racket, rantan, rattle, riot, roar, rowdydow, ruckus, ruction, rumor, rumpus, sass, scandal, shivaree, sonance, sound, strepor, stridor, talk, thunder, tummel, tumult, uproar
abater earplug
about air, bruit, peal, publish, report, tell
comb. caco
dull klop, thud
-maker bell, calliope, clacker, clapper, horn, klaxon, rattle, razzledazzle, siren, snapper, ticktack, whistle
rushing whoosh
whining zing
NOISELESS aphonic, catlike, hushed, quiet, silent, soundless, still(y), tacit, unvoiced, voiceless
NOISOME baneful, destructive, dirty, disgusting, fetid, filthy, foul, fusty, harmful, injurious, insalubrious, loathsome, malodorous, mephitic, musty, nasty, noxious, obnoxious, offensive, pernicious, putrid, rancid, rank, revolting, rotten, squalid, stinking, terrible
NOISY babylonian, blatant, blusterous, boisterous, brassy, brawly, brazen, clamorous, clangorous, clashy, creaky, dinsome,

fremescent, impudent, loud, obstreperous, rackety, strepent, streperous, strepitant, strepitoso, strident, tumultuous, turbulent, uproarious, vociferous
NOKOMIS *grandson* hiawatha
NOMA canker, ulcer
NOMAD alany, amalekite, apache, arab, bazigar, bedouin, beja, bushman, gypsy, kababish, luri, migrant, pilgrim, romany, rover, saka, saracen, scenite, semite, shinwari, shua, shukria, sleb, slubbi, solubbi, tramp, traveler, tuareg, vagabond, wanderer, zingero
NOMADIC ambulant, ambulatory, itinerant, migratory, peripatetic, roaming, roving, vagrant, wandering
NOM DE PLUME alias, aloym, incognito, pen name, pseudonym
NOMENCLATURE antonomasia, appellation, designation, dictionary, glossary, glossology, list, name, naming, onomatology, onymy, orismology, phraseology, register, term(inology), toponymy
NOMINAL basic, cheap, honorary, inexpensive, lowpriced, negative, nuncupative, ostensible, quasi, selfstyled, slight, so-called, soidisant, titular, token, topical, trifling, trivial, unreal
value par
NOMINATE appoint, assign, call, designate, elect, entitle, intend, name, offer, present, proffer, propose, put up, run, select, specify, tender
NOMINEE applicant, aspirant, candidate
NOMOLOGY See LAW.
NON negative, not, prohibition
compos mentis See INSANE.
-iron drip-dry
-living inanimate
-material spiritual
-payment default
-spiritual aphneumatic, carnal, material
NONAGE immaturity, infancy, minority, pupilage
NONAGENARIAN See MAN *old.*

NONCE nanes, nones, occasion, present, purpose
for the temporarily

NONCHALANCE abandon, casualness, composure, easygoingness, indifference, insouciance, offhandedness, unconcern

NONCHALANT aloof, blase, calm, careless, casual, collected, composed, cool, detached, easy, glib, imperturbable, indifferent, insouciant, jaunty, pococurante, smooth, unalarmed, unconcerned, unperturbed, unruffled

NONCONFORMING anomalous, out-of-step

NONCONFORMIST beatnik, bohemian, deviationist, dissenter, eccentric, heretic, hippie, maverick, oddball, rebel, recusant, revisionist, schismatic, screwball, secesh, sectarian, sectary, sulphite

NONCONFORMITY adharma, disagreement, dissent(ion), heresy, neglect recusance, refusal

NONDESCRIPT bland, colorless, common(place), indefinite, indescribable, indeterminable, unclassifiable

NONE nae, nane, nary, neen, nin, nobody, not any, nothing
comb. nulli
the less however, nevertheless, notwithstanding

NONENTITY cipher, dud, dummy, insignificance, jackstraw, john doe, lightweight, mary roe, mediocrity, neb(b)ech, neb(b)ish, nihility, nil, nobody, nothing(ness), nullity, obscurity, picayune, puppet, res-nihili, richard roe, runt, scrub, small beer, trifle, whiffet, zero

NONESSENTIAL accessory, accidental, accidentary, adscititious, adventitious, appendage, appurtenance, ascititious, casual, contingent, extra(neous), extrinsic, frill, subsidiary, supervenient, unnecessary, unneeded

NONESUCH apotheosis, apple, best, marvel, matchless, model, nonpareil, oddity, paradigm, paragon, pattern,

perfection, phoenix, rara avis, tops, unequaled, unrivaled

NONEXISTENCE nihility, nothingness, nullity, vacuum, void

NONEXISTENT absent, blank, dead, defunct, empty, flimsy, missing, napooh, negative, nonbeing, nought, null, quenched, ungrounded, vacant, void

NONLICET illegal, unlawful

NONNY See FOOL.

NONOBSERVANT casual, elusive, evasive, inattentive, lawless, lax, slippery

NONPAREIL apotheosis, best, nonesuch, paragon, peerless, phoenix, supreme, type, unrivaled

NONPARTISAN impartial, independent, individualist, neutral, objective

NONPLUS baffle, balk, bewilder, confound, confuse, daze, disconcert, distract, dum(b)found, embarrass, faze, floor, frustrate, impasse, muddle, mystify, perplex(ity), poser, puzzle, quandary, rattle, stump, thwart

NONRESISTANCE passivity, resignation, submission

NONSENSE 3 gas, rot 4 blah, bosh, bull, bunk, crap, crud, flam, fuff, gash, guff, jazz, pish, pugh, rats, tosh 5 bilge, blash, clack, drool, folly, fudge, gabby, haver, hokum, hooey, prate, pshaw, stite, stuff, trash, tripe 6 babble, bunkum, drivel, faddle, fidfad, gabble, gammon, gibber, hot air, humbug, jabber, jargon, kibosh, parody, rattle, shtuss, slaver, trifle, trivia 7 baloney, blabber, blather, bushwah, dribble, eyewash, farrago, fustian, hogwash, prattle, rubbish, twaddle, twattle, whoopla 8 blah-blah, blathery, buncombe, claptrap, falderal, flummery, folderol, malarkey, megillah, mishigas, morology, pishpash, tommyrot, trimtram, trumpery 9 absurdity, baragouin, bavardage, frivolity, gibberish, moonshine, phillilew, poppycock, shmegegge, silli-

ness 10 applesauce, babblement, balderdash, bobbemyseh, double-talk, flapdoodle, hocuspocus, mumbojumbo, rigamarole 11 jabberwocky, tarradiddle 12 bibblebabble, blatherskite, bletheration, fiddledeedee, fiddlefaddle, gibblegabble, gobbledegook 13 horsefeathers
creature gaboon, gazook, gollywog, goluk, goof, goop, gyascutus, hoofenpoofer, oink, prock, quangle-wangle-quee, smoo, snark, splintercat, tree-squeak, wampus, whangdoodle, whifflebird
expression of chut, pah, phooey, piffle, poof
flattering flummery
poem jabberwocky
pretentious flubdub, tarradiddle
talk pseudolalia
verse amphigo(u)ry

NONSENSICAL absurd, foolish, gibberish, moronic, preposterous, skimbleskamble

NONVIOLENCE ahimsa, satyagraha

NOODLE blockhead, brain, clodpole, clodpoll, dolt, fool, head, loksh, ninny, simpleton, thickskull
dish kreplach, pansit, ravioli

NOODLES farfel, ferfel, fettucini, lakshen, lasagne, lokshen, mein, pasta, ravioli

NOOK alcove, angle, bay, cant(le), carol, carrell, compartment, corner, cove, cranny, cubicle, embrasure, headland, herne, hideaway, hole, niche, quoin, recess, retreat, wro

NOON acme, apex, culmination, dine, dinner, high, lunchtime, meridian, midday, midi, top, undern
after postperidian
before morning, premeridian
flower fig-marigold, goatsbeard
rest siesta

NOOSE bight, bond, catch, caudle, cho(c)ker, circle, ensnare, entrap, grin, halter, hang, hitch, honda, kinch, laniard, lasso(o), leash, loop, naik, necklace, rope, snare, springe, tether,

tie, toils, trap, twitchel, weave, widdy
fishing dull
hangman's squeezer
hangman's, pert. hempen
NOOTKA *indian* ahousaht, aht, clayoquot, ehatisaht, moatcaht, mooachaht, wakashan
NORFOLK *duke of* mowbray
NORM average, canon, gauge, integer, mean, measure, medium, model, modulus, norma, par, pattern, rule, standard, template, templet, test, touchstone, type, typical, yardstick
NORMA *composer* bellini
NORMAL accustomed, afebrile, analogical, average, common, cool, customary, familiar, feverless, general, habitual, just, lucid, mean, median, natural, neutral, ordinary, par, perpendicular, rational, regular, sane, school, standard, typical, usual, vertical, wonted
variation from acatastasia
NORMALLY as a rule, as usual, commonly, customarily, frequently, generally, naturally, ordinarily, regularly, usually
NORMAN(DY) *bagpipe* loure
banner gonfanon
beach omaha
capital caen, rouen
cheese angelot
conqueror eisenhower, guiscard, rollo, william
department calvados, eure, manche, orne
drink calvados
goblin lubin
river eure, orne, seine
sword spatha
NORN fate, skuld, urd, urdhr, urdth(a), verd(h) andi, verthandi, weird sisters, wurd, wyrd
horse doomstead
NORRIS *novel* mcteague, octopus
NORSE See also NORWAY.
abode of gods asgard, valhalla
adam ask(r), bure, buri, mannus
apple custodian ithun
archer egil
archery god uller
assembly ting

bard sagaman, scald, skald
blood and honey hydromel, odrerir
bridge bifrost, rainbow
chaos ginnungagap
chief jarl, rollo, yarl
chronicle heimskringla
cow audhumbla, audumla
crow, mythical hugin, munin
day of doom ragnarok
deity, triple haenir, lodur, odin
demon fylgja, fylgjur, hatto, nidhogg, surt(r), wode
destiny goddess See NORN.
dialect norn
dragon fafner, fafnir
drink, sacred hydromel, odrerir
dwarf alviss, brokk, ivaldir, sindri
earth goddess jorth
epic edda, saga
explorer eric(sson), erikson, leif
fates See NORN.
fire, land of muspellsheim
fountain, mythical hvergelmir
galley aesc, drake
game hnefatafl
genii alfar
giant aegir, atli, baugi, bergelmir, eggther, fafnir, geirrod, gunnlod, gymir, harbard, hler, hrungnir, hrym, hugi, hymer, hymir, jotun(n), junner, logi, loki, mimir, mymir, skrymir, surt, suttung, thjazi, thrym, troll, utgardaloki, utgartha, wade, wate, ymir
giantess angerboda, gerda, grid, groa, gunnlod, natt, norn, nott, ran, sittung, skadi, skrymir, skuld, thjazi, thock, thok(k), thrym, urd(ar), urth, utgardaloki, wyrd, ymir
giant land jotunheim, utgard, utgarthar
giants, father of ymir
giant's ship naglfar
goat heidrun
god or goddess See AESIR.
gods, father of bor
gods, mother of bestla
gods, nurse of heidrun
gods, race of aesir, vanir
guardian spirit fylgja
heaven asgard, bilskirnir, breithablik, folkvang, glathsheim, glitnir, himinbjorg, hlithskjalf, noatum, ses-

srymnir, sokkvabekk, thruthheim, thruthvang, valaskjalf, valhalla, vingolf; vithi, ydalir
heaven guardian heimdall(r)
hell See NORSE *underworld.*
hero egil(l), siegfried, sigurd
horse alsvinn, alsvith, arvak, goldfax
kelpie nick
king atli, nibelung, nidung, schilbung, stolaf
land scandinavia
letter rune
life force lif
light god balder, heimdall
liquor akavit, aquavit
maiden valkyrie
mariner eric the red
minstrel bard, scald, skald
mist, world niflheim, niflhel
monster fenrir, garm, kraken, midgard, serpent
nobleman jarl
oak branstock
palace gladsheim
people hyperboreans
plateau fjeld
poem edda, rune, saga
poet scald, skald
poetry god bragi
ring draupnir
ring guardian andvari
river gjoll
saint olaf, olaus
sea devil nicor
sea god aegir, niord
seeress volva
serpent jormungard, kraken, midgard, nidhogg
ship drake, drakkar, naglfar, skidbladnir
sky god tiu, tiw, tyr, zio, ziu
spear gungnir
sun god balder
toast skal, skoal
tree yggdrasil
twilight of the gods gotterdammerung, ragnarok(kr)
underworld niflheim, niflhel, utgarthar
warrior berserker
watchdog garm(r)
wisdom god odin
wolf fenrir, freki, geri
woman embla, idun
NORSEMAN dane, finn, scandinavian, swede, viking
fastest thialfi
NORTH arctic, boreal, polar, septentrional
comb. arct(o)

-easter blow, gale, storm, wind
lion of pancho villa
-men norse
pole discoverer peary
star cynosure, loadstar, lodestar, polaris, polestar, tramontane
star state minnesota
NORTH AFRICA(N) algerian, berber, moor
air conditioner climatiseur
animal arui, dieb(s), fennec, gundi, leucoryx, udad
antelope addax, gazelle, leucoryx
bread abret, kisra
caliph fatimid
city, ancient carthage, zama
coast barbary
country algeria, egypt, morocco, sudan, tripoli(tania), tunisia
country, ancient numidia
dialect sabir
dish couscous
dynasty aghlabid, aglabite
finch moro
fox fennec
fruit date, fig
garment burnoose, burnous, haik
gnome owl
gown See AFRICA *garment.*
grass alfa, teff
herb mother-of-thyme
hill djebel, jebel
inn fonda
jackal dieb(s)
language berber
lyre kissar
market sook
measure rotl
oasis wadi, wady
olive barouni
people arabian, berber, egyptian, hamite, ibadhi, ibadite, kharijite, moor, moroccan, nilot
port sfax
rodent gundi
roman colony leptis magna, lixus, mauritania, numidia, timgad, zaghawa
sheep aoudad, arui, udad
valley wadi, wady
viper echis
warehouse fonduk
wind hamseen
NORTH AMERICA See also AMERICA, CANADA and MEXICO references.
animal badger, muskox, raccoon

badger braireau, brairo
bat corynorhinus
beetle searcher
bird bluejay, bufflehead, cardinal, catbird, cedarwaxwing, coot, crow, fulmar, grackle, grossbeak, killdeer, kingrail, murrelet, pisobia, plover, sandpiper, warbler
bog muskeg
butterfly comma, junonia, ursula
cactus cacanapa, opuntia
cat cougar, mountain-lion, panther, puma
catfish bullhead
cedar red, savine, waxwing
clam quahog
cod coalfish
constrictor bullsnake, gophersnake, pituophis
cudweed enaena
deer caribou, elk, moose, wapiti
discoverer cabot, columbus, erics(s)on
duck aix, bucephala, bufflehead, butterback, butterball, canvasback, charitonetta, glaucionetta, teal
elk wapiti
evergreen cedar, cypress, festoon-pine
falcon anatum
fern flowercup, osmunda, spleenwort, woodsia
finch siskin
fish alewife, bream, bullhead, candlefish, eulachon, fantail, maskalonge, maskanonge, muskellunge, ronquil, sandroller, sauger, tullibee
fleabane skevish
goose blackbrant
grass andropogon, bent, bouteloua, turkeyfoot, uniola
herb abronia, agastache, aletris, alkanet, alumroot, anemone(lla), anise, anogea, anticlea, arbutus, aster, basilbalm, basilmint, bellwort, bergamot, brookline, camass, catgut, cerastium, chickweed, chocolate flower, cocash, colicweed, cow-vetch, dogbane, falsedaisy, featherfoil, fireweed, foamflower, frasera, gerardia, gilia, goldenpert, goldenrod, gromwell, heuchera, kneiffia, kuhnia, lachnanthes, lewisia, lily, lithospermum, loosestrife, milkweed, nailrod, pine-

drops, purslane, richweed, sandverbena, sandwort, sego, selfheal, squawroot, sundrop, verbena, verbesina, veronica, yerba buena
highest point mt mckinley
honeysuckle twinberry
indian See ALASKA, AMERICA, CANADA, and MEXICO *indian;* see also under individual states.
lizard anole, anoli
lowest point death valley
maple box elder
marmoset tamarin
marmot whistler
mint blephilia
moslem sect sanusi
newt red-eft
northernmost part boothia
orchid arethusa, fissipes, pogonia, ram's-head, snakemouth
owl wapacut
peak See MEXICO *peak,* UNITED STATES *peak.*
people american, canadian, mexican
pike dore, muskellunge
plant abronia, arethusa, artemisia, beach-heather, bloodroot, bloodwort, blueflag, bullbrier, camas(s), fontainea, garrya, penstemon, ragwort, redroot, rosinweed, saururus
pondweed creekgrass
puccoon bloodroot
rail sora
range See CANADA *range,* MEXICO *range,* UNITED STATES *range.*
reindeer caribou
rodent muskrat
shorebird gull, willet
shrew blarina
shrub antelope-bush, arbutus, arrowwood, azalea, beak-plum, buttonbush, cephalanthus, chokeberry, dogwood, fothergilla, gravelweed, groundsel, honeysuckle, hydrangea, jojoba, jove's-fruit, lonicera, osier, persimmon, rhodora, rodinia, salix, spicebush, viburnum
skate barndoor
snake cowsucker, rubberboa
spruce engelmann, epinette
succulent purslane
sucker redhorse
sunfish lepomis
thistle euthamia

thorn sockspur
thrush robin
towhee chewink
tree alder, arborvitae, aspen, balm of gilead, balsam, basswood, bladdernut, buckeye, buttonwood, carpinus, catalpa, hemlock, hickory, hornbeam, larch, larix, linden, mabi, oneberry, pa(w)-paw, redbud, robinia, sassafras, sorb, staphylea, sweetsop, tarmarac(k), titi, tuliptree, tupelo
trout namaycush, steelhead
turtle terrapin
vine chinaroot, honeysuckle, smilax, virginia creeper
wake-robin snakebite
warbler blackburnian, blackpoll
weed cuckold, groundsel, pellitory, senecia
wolf coyote
wolverine cougar, indian-devil
NORTH ATLANTIC *alga* furcellaria
cod rockling
fish capelin, frigate, mackerel
island aran, britain, faroes, iceland, ireland, manhattan
seagull skua
NORTH BRITAIN (See also SCOTLAND.) caledonia
NORTH CAROLINA *cape* fear, hatteras, lookout
capital raleigh
city albemarle, asheville, chapel hill, charlotte, durham, edenton, gastonia, goldsboro, greensboro, greenville, henderson, hickory, jacksonville, kannapolis, kinston, lenoir, lumberton, new bern, roxboro, shelby, statesville, tarboro, thomasville, williamston, wilson, winston-salem
college catawba, davidson, elon
county ashe, bertie, bladen, catawba, dare, hoke, onslow, pamlico, wake, yadkin, yancey
indian buffalo, cheraw, chowanoc, coree, eno, hatteras, moratok, pamlico, tuscarora
island roanoke
native buffalo, tarheel
nickname tarheel state, turpentine state

peak clingman's dome, harris, mitchell
port wilmington
president johnson, polk
range black
river chowan, fear, haw, lumber, neuse, peedee, roanoke, tar, wateree, yadkin
sound bogue, core, croatan, pamlico
state bird cardinal
state flower dogwood, goldenrod
state tree pine
university duke
NORTH, CHRISTOPHER john wilson
NORTH DAKOTA *capital* bismarck
city bismarck, bottineau, fargo, grand forks, jamestown, minot, williston
college jamestown
county eddy, pembina, traill
indian arikara, hidatsa, mandan
nickname flickertail, sioux
peak black butte
river cannonball, cedar, deslacs, heart, james, missouri, rush, sheyenne, souris
state bird meadowlark
state flower prairie rose
state tree elm
NORTHERN *artic*, boread, boreal, borean, hyperborean, polar, septentrional
bear russia
cross cygnus
fruit cloudberry
lights aurora borealis, merry dancers
-most land thule, ultima thule
region arctic
seas arctalia
spy apply
sucker stone roller
waggoner charles' wain, ursa major
NORTH KOREA See KOREA.
NORTH PACIFIC See PACIFIC.
NORTH SEA *arm* firth of forth, moray firth, skagerrak, zuider zee
bay the wash
boat coble
canal kiel
duck scoter
islands frisian
port bergen, bremen, emden, hamburg, hull

river to aller, dee, eider, elbe, ems, escant, maas, meuse, rhine, schelde, scheldt, tees, thames, tweed, tyn, weser
NORTHUMBERLAND *king* clarivaunce
retainer morton, travers
son henry percy, hotspur
NORTH VIETNAM (See also VIETNAM.) *capital* hanoi
city bacninh, caobang, donghoi, haiphoang, namdinh, thanhhoa, viettri
coin dong
communist party viet cong
forces communsi, cosvn, viet cong, viet minh
gulf tonkin(g)
newspaper nhandan
peak fansipan
port benthuy, haiphong, honggai
president ho chi minh
river chay, chu, gam, koi, nhiha
NORTHWEST *indian* chinook, cree, pathan, sherani
NORWAY, NORWEGIAN See also NORSE references.
bird ptarmigan, rype
boat praam, praham, pram
cape naze, nordkapp, nordkyn, lindesnes
capital christiania, oslo
cart stolkjaerre
cheese gammelost, gjetost, ost
chieftain jarl
church stave
city alesund, arendal, bergen, bjort, bodo, drammen, floro, gol, hamar, horton, larvik, molde, moss, narvik, nes, odda, oslo, rena, sandnes, skien, skjak, stavanger, voss
coin krone, ore
composer grieg
constitution grundlov
converter olaf tryggvason
counties amter
county amt, bergen, finmark, fylke, hedmark, letemark, nordland, opland, oslo, ostfold, rogaland, troms(o), vestfold
dance gangar, halling, spingleik, springar
dialect See *language,* below.
dish skyr
district ruler hersir

division amt
dog elkhound
dramatist ibsen
drink aquavit
embroidery hardanger
ethnologist heyerdahl
explorer amundsen, eric, leif, mohn, nansen, sars
giant brusted, hardrada, osen
goblin kobold, nisse
god, goddess See AESIR.
governor amtman(d)
haddock rosefish
historian lange
house spirit nis(se)
inlet alst, ands, bjorna, bokn, fiord, fjord, folda, hadsel, hortens, kob, lakse, nord, ofot, ran, salt, sogne, sunn, trondheim, tyri, vest
island alsten, averoy, bomlo, bouvet, donna, froya, gurskoy, hinnoy, hitra, hopen, janmayen, karmoy, lofoten, mageroy, seiland, senja, smola, solund, soroy, svalbard, vannoy, vega
king haakon, olaf, olav(e), oscar
lake alte, femund, ister, mjosa, rostavn, snasa, tunnsjo
land divisions fylkis
language landsma(a)l, norse, nynorsk
lobster nephrops
mathematician abel, lie
measure alen, fathom, fot, kande, korntonde, ma(a)l, pot, skieppe
musical spirit stromkarl
musician bull
mythological See NORSE references.
naturalist asbjornsen
needlework hardanger
noble jarl
opera singer flagstad
parliament lagt(h)ing, odelsting, stort(h)ing
peak blodfjel, galdhoepig, glitretind, hallingskarvet, hardangerjokul, harteigen, kjolen, myrdalfjell, numedal, ramnanosi, skagastolstind, snohetta, sogne, telemark, ustetind, vibmesnosi
plateau doure, dovre, fjeld, hardanger
port a(a)lesund, bodo, hammerfest, harstad, kirkenes, kristiansand, moss, narvik, oslo, stavanger, tromso, trondheim, vadso
range kjolen

river alta, bardu, begna, ena, glomma, klar, lagen, lougen, namsen, orkla, otra, otter, pasvik, rana, rauma, reisa, tana, teno
rock barkevikite, farisite, fenite, gabro, greyalite, norite
ruler See NORWAY *king.*
saint odes, olaf
spirit fylgja, neck, nis(se), stromkarl
statesman lie
timber dram
toast sk(o)al
traitor quisling
violinist ole bull
warship wasa
weight bismerpund, lod, mark, pund, skaalpund
whirlpool maelstrom
writer bojer, hamsun, ibsen, undset

NOSE antlia, beak, beezer, bill, boko, bow, bugle, cap, cheat, confront, conk, cyrano, detect(ive), gnomon, individual, inform(er), lorum, meddle, muffle, muzzle, nares, nasus, neb, nese, nez, nib, nostrils, nozzle, odor, olfactor, oppose, pecker, perfume, person, proboscis, prow, pry, pug, reproach, rhinarium, rub, scent, schnoz(zle), search, smell(er), sniff, snitch, snoop, snoot, snout, socket, spy, thrust, touch, trace, trunk
absence of arrhinia
ailment adenoids, catarrh, cold, coryza, nasitis, ozena, rheum, rhinitis, roup, sniffles
aquiline roman
bag morral
band bosal, cavesson, musrol
bandage accipiter, ligator
blunt snub
bone ethmoid, vomer
cartilage septum
cavity cavum
comb. nasi, rhin(e)(o), rhinous
count census, list, rollcall
disease coryza, oz(o)ena, rhinitis
dive collapse, drop, fall, plunge, vrille
drip gleet, rheum
drops collunarium
elongated proboscis
examination rhinoscopy

flat camus(e), pug, simous, snub
flatness simity
flute bin, poogye, pungi, upanga, vina
glasses pince-nez
having large nasute
hitch bozal
into collide, meddle, pry, snoop
lead by control, dominate
long snout
look down condescend, disdain
medicine drops, errhine
muscle nasalio
on the correctly, precisely
opening nares, nostril
out defeat, discover, ferret, scent
pain rhinalgia
paint liquor
part. agger, bridgelnares, nostril, septum, vomer
partition septum, vomer
pert. narial, narine, nasal, rhinal
-piece nasal, noseband, nozzle
-pinch pince-nez
pincher barnacle
ridge agger
ring band, cattle-leader, pirn
ruby wellington
science rhinology
snub pug, simous
speak through nasilate
study nasology
surgery rhinoplasty
turned up retrousse
NOSEBLEED bloody butchers, epistaxis, herb, orchis, painted-cup, rhinorrhagia, trillium, yarrow
NOSEGAY bob, bouquet, corsage, odor, perfume, posy, scent, tutty
NOSESMART watercress
NOSHEN bite, snack, tidbit
NOSTALGIA desire, heimweh, homesickness, languishment, longing, mal du pays, melancholia, sentiment, yearning, yen
NOSTALGIC elegiac(al), homesick, sentimental
NOSTOLOGY geriatrics
NOSTRADAMUS astrologer, prophet, seer
NOSTRIL(S) blowhole, nares, naris, nose, snuffers, thirl, thrill
having paired dirhinous
having small hyporhined

pert. narial, naric, narine
-*shaped* nariform
NOSTRUM panacea, patent medicine, remedy, tonic
NOSY beaky, curious, fetid, fragrant, impertinent, inquisitive, intrusive, meddlesome, naric, nasal, personal, probing, prying, pushy, searching, snoopy
ole wellington
-*parker* bluenose, busybody, snoop
NOT awnless, baal, bail, bale, beardless, hornless, nae, nary, nay, negation, negative, neither, nicht, none, nor, nought, pas, poll(ed), shaven, shear, shorn, smooth, sorra
a little greatly, much
all there crazy, insane, loony, oblivious
any nairy, nane, nary, nil, nokin, none, nul, stead
at all never, nohow, noway(s), nowhit, nowise, pas du tout
bad bearable, tolerable
budge persevere, persist
comb. dis, non
cricket foul, unfair
divided unitary, united, whole
easy difficult
enough insufficient
ever neer
final interlocutory, nisi
for publication confidential, restricted, secret
fully, comb. semi
genuine artificial, fake, false, tin
hard to take pleasant
infrequently often, unseldom
in style de mode, out, passe
involved aloof, bystander, innocent
likely improbable
long ago lately, recently
moving inert, static, stationary
odd even
often infrequently, seldom
one nary, none
permanent acting, interim, pro-tem, temporary
shortened unabridged
so false, untrue
so dumb intelligent
the same another, different, dissimilar, other
unlike similar

wanted de trop, superfluous, unnecessary, useless
NOTABLE big, celebrated, celebrity, considerable, conspicuous, distinguished, eminent, extraordinary, famous, gifted, great, historic, important, kingpin, luminary, magnate, memorable, noted, noticeable, notorious, observable, outstanding, perceptible, personage, prominent, remarkable, uncommon, unusual, vip
NOTABLY especially, greatly, principally
NOTARIZE acknowledge, attest, certify, ratify
NOTARY graffer, notable, notar, notebook, noter, notorious, observer, official, recorder, scrivener
public tabellion
NOTATION entry, explanation, memo(randum), note, observation, segno
phonetic romic
NOTCH blaze, boot-jack, carf, chop, cleft, concave, cope, crena(te), crenel(ate), crimp, cut, dap, defile, degree, dent, depress(ion), dimple, dint, escallop, gab, gain, gap, gash, gorge, groove, gudgeon, gully, hack, hag, hila, hilum, hollow(out), impress, imprint, incise, incision, incisura, indent(ation), indenture, jab, jag, jog(gle), kerf, mark, mill, nick, nitch, nock, pass, peg, pink, pit, pock, rabbet, recess, rut, scallop, scarify, score, scotch, serra(te), step, tooth, vandyke
bar rotch
pert. erose
NOTCHED castellated, crenate(d), dentate, erose, lacerate(d), machiolated, palmate, ragule, raguly, serrate(d), serriform, serrulate(d), toothed
NOTCHING cockscomb, crenation, crenelation, crest, denticulation, picot, rickrack, saw(teeth), serration
NOTE annotation, apostil(le), asset, attend, attention, behold, betoken, billet, bordereau, call, certificate, character, check, chit, comment(ary), correspond(ence), descry, discern, discover,

dispatch, distinction, emience, entry, epistle, espy, explain, explanation, fame, glory, gloss, greenback, heed, importance, indicate, iou, item, jot, label, letter, line, loan, marginal(ia), mark, memo(randum), message, mind, minute, missive, money, notice, observation, observe, postil, promise, quality, record, regard, remark, renown, report, reputation, scholium, see, set down, sign, signify, statement, symbol, symptom, token, tone, tune, view, write
accompanying overtone
bank finnip, flimsy, frogskin
bugle mot
case billfold, pocketbook, wallet
double breve
8th quaver, unca
escape echappee
explanatory annotation, gloss, scholium
grace nachschlag
guarantee aval
guido's See MUSIC *note, guido's.*
half minim
highest ela
highpitched beep
long breve, brevis
love poulet
marginal annotation, apostil(le), postil, scholium, tot
middle mese
musical See MUSIC *note.*
nonharmonic cambiata
promissory bon, exchequer bill, good, hundi, iou
quarter crotchet, semiminim
sequence cadence, meter
sharpening ecbole
short chit(ty), memo
16th demiquaver, semiquaver
64th hemidemi-semiquaver
succession gamut, strain, tiralee
tail filum
32nd demisemiquaver, subsemifusa
tuning accordatura
well nota bene
whole semibreve
writer annotator
NOTEBOOK adversaria, cahier, diary, journal, log, notary, record
NOTED celebrated, couth,

distinguished, eminent, famed, famous, great, illustrious, important, insigne, notable, notorious, outstanding, prominent, remarkable, renowned, salient, signal

NOTEWORTHY See NOTED.

NOTHING bagatelle, blank, boffo, cipher, clean slate, goose egg, joke, luke, naught, nawt, nichts, nihil, nil, nix, nobody, nonentity, not, nought, nowt, nul(l), nulla, rien, trifle, vacuum, void, zero, zilch
at all tinker's dam(n)
but mere, only
doing napoo(h)
else but certainly, defacto, in fact, ipso facto, really
from de nihilo
like dissimilar
to it See EASY.

NOTHINGNESS blank, emptiness, insignificance, nada, nihility, nonexistence, nullity, triviality, void, worthlessness, zero

NOTICE acknowledge, admonition, advertisement, advice, allude, announcement, attention, await, behold, bill(board), bulletin, call, care, caveat, circular, cognizance, comment(ary), count, criticism, critique, descry, detect, discern, discover, distinguish, espy, favor, handbill, heed, idea, information, intelligence, knowledge, make out, mark, mention, mind, news, note, notification, notion, observation, observe, order, perceive, perception, placard, poster, proclamation, quote, recognize, regard, remark, reminder, respect, review, see, sign, spy, survey, view, warning
book blurb
death obit(uary)
favorable rave
honorable citation
legal caveat
marriage ban(n)s
official bulletin, citation, edict, proclamation, summons, warrant
paid advertisement
patent office caveat

public affiche, ban(n)s, programma, sign
refuse to cut, ignore, snub
take nota bene
take no disdain, disregard
to leave mittimus

NOTICEABLE arresting, conspicuous, evident, flashy, manifest, marked, notable, noteworthy, obvious, open, outstanding, palpable, patent, pointed, prominent, remarkable, salient, signal, significant, striking

NOTIFY acquaint, admonish, advertise, advise, announce, apprise, broadcast, caution, cite, declare, disclose, divulge, inform, jog, proclaim, promulgate, publicize, publish, remind, reveal, tell, warn

NOTION apprehension, bee, begriff, belief, bromide, caprice, conceit, concept (ion), contrivance, conviction, curio, desire, device, fancy, fondness, gadget, humor, idea, image, imagination, impression, impulse, inclination, inkling, invention, kink, model, omen, opinion, persuasion, sentiment, supposal, supposition, theory, thought, vagary, view, whim(wham)
fantastic pipe dream
fixed tick
foolish nonsense, vapo(u)r

NOTIONAL fanciful, ideal, ideational, imaginary, unreal, visionary, whimsical

NOTIONATE fanciful, headstrong, strong-willed, stubborn

NOTIONS buttons, giftware, goods, knickknacks, merchandise, novelties, sundries, thread, toiletries, wares

NOTONECTID backswimmer, boatbug, insect

NOTORIETY ballyhoo, celebrity, disgrace, eclat, fame, glory, honor, notoriousness, publicity, renown, reputation, repute

NOTORIOUS apparent, arrant, big, celebrated, conspicuous, disreputable, egregious, eminent, evident, famed, famous, flagrant, glaring, gross, illustrious, infamous, known, manifest,

noted, questionable, rank, scandalous, shady, shameful, strong

NOTRE DAME mary, our lady
actor charles laughton
character esmeralda
founder edward gorin
hunchback quasimodo

NOTT *horse* hrimfaxi
son dag

NOTUS auster
parent eos

NOTWITHSTANDING against, albeit, algate(s), all the same, altho(ugh), but, conditionally, despite, even (so), for all that, howbeit, however, in any event, in spite of, irrespective, mauger, maugre, natheless, nevertheless, none the less, non obstante, regardless, tho(ugh), whatreck, yet

NOUGAT candy, confection, nut

NOUGHT annihilate, aught, bad(ly), base, cipher, lost, naught, naughty, nil, nonentity, nothing(ness), null, ruined, unfit, useless, vile, wickedness, worthless, wrecked, wrong(ly), zero, zilch

NOUGHTS *and crosses* game, go bang, ticktacktoe, tic-tac-toe, tittattoe

NOUMEA new caledonia, new scotland

NOUMENAL ontal, ontic, real

NOUN appellative, aptote, gerund, name, nominal, supine, thing
comb. ana, ance, arian, ary, ata, ation, ator(y), atrix, eer, ence, ent, ery, fer, ial, ien, ility, ing, ion, ior, ise, ist, orium, tion
form case, gender
indeclinable aptote
kind aptote, common, diptote, monoptote, proper, regular, triptote
quotation hypostasis
verbal gerund, supine

NOURISH advance, aid, breed, cherish, cultivate, develop, eat, educate, encourage, feed, foison, goster, graze, grow, help, lactate, maintain, norice, nurse, nurture, nutrify, pasture, provide, rear, stimulate, strengthen, succor, suckle, supply, support, sustain, train

NOURISHER altrice

NOURISHING alible, aliment(ary), alma, alms, healthful, hearty, invigorating, nutrient, nutritious, nutritive, rich, strengthening, wholesome

NOURISHMENT aliment, foisoil, food(stuff), keep, living, manna, meat, nutrient, nutriment, pabulum, support, sustenance

NOUS alertness, cleverness, god, intellect, mind, reason, understanding, wit

NOUVEAU RICHE arriviste, parvenu, upstart, vulgarian

NOUVELLE fiction, news, novelette

NOVA new, star, temporary

NOVALIS friedrich von hardenberg

NOVA SCOTIA acadia, acadie
bay fundy
cape breton, canso, george, sable
city annapolis, grand pre, halifax, port royal, royal
giantess anne swann
lake bras d'or
mineral acadialite
mountain ash dogberry
people acadian, bluenose
port halifax, sidney, truro, yarmouth
ship bluenose

NOVEL atypical, book, brand new, daring, different, fiction, fresh, hot, modern, narrative, neo(teric), new(fangled) (fashioned), off-beat, original, paperback, prose, rare, recent, romance, serial, singular, story, strange, tale, thriller, uncommon, unique, unusual
boys' tom swift
cut abridgement, condensation
first tale of genji
first, author lady murasaki
lurid yellowback
picaresque gil blas
sensational penny-dreadful, yellowback
short conte, novelette, novella

NOVELTY change, curiosity, dernier cri, fad, freshness, innovation, newness, originality, recency, the last word, uncommonness, uniqueness, wrinkle
advocate of neo
aversion to neophobia
cult of neolatry
desire for neophilism

NOVEMBER *1st* all hallows, all saints day, all souls day, samhain, samuin
5th guy fawkes day
birthstone topaz
meteor leonid

NOVICE abecedarian, alphabetarian, amateur, apprentice, archarios, beginner, blancbec, catechumen, chela, convert, dabbler, deb(utante), dilettante, dub, entrant, fledgling, freshman, frosh, gosling, greener, greenhorn, ham, ignoramus, infant, initiate, learner, neophyte, newcomer, novitiate, nun, postulant, probationer, punk, puny, pupil, recruit, rhasophore, rookie, rooky, starter, student, tenderfoot, tiro, tyro(ne), youngling, younker
in arms bachelor

NOVITIATE fuchs, novice (ry), postulant, probation

NOVOBIOCIN albamycin, cathomycin

NOW anymore, ar(r)ah, at once, at present, current (ly), existing, extant, forthwith, here, immediately, instant, nonce, noo, present, since, suddenly, today, yet
and then anon, occasionally, sometimes
just enow, erstwhile, fresh

NOWHERE naegait, naegate, no place, nowhither, obscurity

NOWT blockhead, bullock, cattle, lout, naught, nothing, nought, oxen

NOX See NYX.

NOXIOUS baneful, corrupting, dampish, deadly, deleterious, destructive, detrimental, evil, fetid, guilty, harmful, hateful, hurtful, injurious, miasmatic, miasmic, nasty, nocent, nocuous, noisome, offensive, pernicious, pestiferous, pestilent, poisonous, putrid, scaddle, stinking, toxic, unhealthy, unwholesome, venomous, vicious, virulent
atmosphere malaria

NOZZLE adjutage, beak, bib(b), cock, faucet, giant, grovel, jet, mouth, nose, nuzzle, outlet, snout, socket, spout, tap, tube, tuyere, vent, vermorel
blast furnace tuyere
fire-fighting niagara
mining giant
perforated rose

NTH degree, extreme, maximum, power

NUANCE difference, finesse, gradation, nicety, shade, variation

NUB core, crux, ear, essence, essential, gallows, gist, hang, heart, hub, jab, jag, kernal, key, knob, knot, knub, lump, neck, nob, nudge, pith, point, protuberance, snag, tachlis

NUBBIN bulge, diminutive, ear, saddle, stub, stump, tomtit

NUBBLES *love* little nell

NUBIA cloud, scarf, wrap

NUBIAN barabra, hadendoa, nuba
harp nanga, sistrum
palm doom, doum, dum
snake regulus

NUBILOUS cloudy, dim, foggy, indefinite, indistinct, misty, obscure, opaque, vague

NUCHA nape, neck, spinal cord

NUCLEAR elementary
carrier cvan
chemistry atomics
cloud mushroom
cross section unit barn
element proton
energy, peaceful use project plowshare
event a-test
fission term atom-smasher, bombardment, breeding, bullet, chain reaction, cleavage, critical mass, disintegration, fusion, ionization, target
fuel uranium
fusion fission
machine betatron
network fiber linin
physics atomics
reactor breeder
reactor moderator boroncarbide
technique beta ray backscat-

tering, moss bauer effect measurement, neutron activation analysis

NUCLEIC *acid molecule* dna, enzyme, rna

NUCLEON *group* shell *product* peptone

NUCLEOSIDE adenosine, cytidine, inosine, vicine

NUCLEUS cadre, cell, center, centriole, centrosome, centrosphere, colony, core, deuteron, deuton, focus, heart, hub, isotope, karyon, karyosome, kern(el), meat, merocyte, mesoplast, middle, midst, nidulus, pith, plasmosome, plastosome, principle, root, seed, source, sperm, umbra
cell hemikaryon, karyon, syncaryon
cell, comb. cary(o), kary(o)
diploid amphikaryon
pert. nucleate
resting stage interkinesis
starch hilum
sunspot umbra

NUDD *consort* morrigu

NUDE bald, bare, barren, exposed, manifest, mere, naked, painting, picture, plain, sculpture, seasan, statue, stripped, unclothed, undraped, undressed
color seasan
walking streaking

NUDGE chuck, dunch, elbow, goad, job, jolt, knub, nog, poke, prod, push, remind, shove, signal, thrust, touch

NUDIBRANCH conch, gastropod, mollusk, snail

NUDISM gymnosophy, naturism

NUDIST adamite, gymnosophist

NUDNI(C)K annoyer, bore, nag, pest

NUGAE jests, trifles

NUGATORY bootless, empty, fruitless, futile, hollow, idle, ineffective, ineffectual, inoperative, insignificant, invalid, null, otiose, petty, trifling, trivial, useless, vain, worthless

NUGGET asset, gold, hunk, lob, lump, mass, piece, plum, prill, slug, treasure, value, yellow

NUISANCE abomination, annoyance, bandersnatch,

bane, bore, evil, gadfly, hurt, inconvenience, injury, pain, pest, plague, sting, terror, trial, vexation
remover abator

NULL annul, boss, empty, insignificant, invalid, irrite, knurl, nil, nonexistent, nugatory, unavailing, useless, vacuous, void

NULLAH channel, gap, gorge, gulley, ravine, watercourse

NULLENSPIEL game, spiderweb

NULLIFIDAN agnostic, atheist, disbeliever, infidel, skeptic

NULLIFY abolish, abrogate, annihilate, annul, beat, cancel, compensate, counter (act), flaw, frustrate, invalidate, lame, lapse, negate, negative, neutralize, offset, repeal, revoke, stultify, undo, veto, void

NULLITY cipher, nonentity, nothing, trifle

NUMB asleep, blunt, chill, clumse, clumsy, dazed, deaden(ed), drug(ged), dull, funny, hebetate, helpless, incapable, inert, insensible, obtund, rigescent, senseless, stun, stupefy, stupid, stuporous, tabetless, torpid

NUMBAT anteater

NUMBER act, address, aggregate, allot, amount, apportion, augend, bit, calculate, call off, cardinal, census, character, chiffer, cipher, collection, comprise, compute, contain, copy, count, decimal, destine, digit, edition, enumerate, estimate, factor, figger, figure, foliate, group, herd, hirsel, host, integer, kind, lac, lakh, limit, measure, multitude, myriad, numeral, numerate, numero, ordinal, page, paginate, part, prime, quantity, reckon, scalar, slew, steen, sum, surd, symbol, tally, tell, total, unit, whole
added to augend
added to another addend
among include
broken fraction
cardinal alefnull, alephzero, one, two, three, four, five, six, etc.

comb. arithm(o), decieth, pent(a), quad(ro), tri, uni
describable by scalar
dice sise
excessive deluge, spate
extra encore
fanciful googol
indefinite jillion, lac, lakh, several, steen, sundry, tharve, threave, um(p)steen, zillion
irrational surd
kind arabic, roman
large army, crowd, googol, heaps, horde, host, lac, lakh, legion, lots, many, multiplicity, multitude, myriad(s), nonillion, octillion, plenty, quantity, scads, score(s), slew, stacks, store, um(p)steen, vigintillion, wheen, world
least whole unit
natural integer
obsession arithmomania
odd impair
one ego, first-rate, self
ordinal first, second, third, fourth, etc.
ordinal, comb. eth
perfect three
prime one, two, three, five, seven, eleven, thirteen
pure scalar
small few, curn, curran, handful, paucity, spatter, sprinkling
10, under digit
2 avis, second fiddle
whole digit, integer

NUMBERLESS See NUMEROUS.

NUMBFISH electric-ray, torpedo

NUMBLES entrails, heart, innards, inwards, lights, liver

NUMBNESS apathy, obdormition, stupidity, stupor
comb. narc(o)

NUMEN deity, divinity, force, genius, spirit, vestal

NUMERAL See NUMBER.

NUMERATION adding, calculation, computation, counting, dactylonomy, estimation, foliation, mathematics, pagination, reckoning, telling, total(ing)

NUMEROUS abundant, big, considerable, copious, countless, crowded, divers, endless, extensive, fertile, frequent, galore, great, innu-

merable, jillion, large, legion, lots, main, manifold, many, multiple, multitudinal, multitudinous, myriad(s), no end, numberful, plentiful, profuse, rank, rife, several, stour, sundry, teeming, thronged, ump(s), teen, umteen, unride, zillion
comb. multi
very excessive, extensive
NUMIDIA *bird* crane, demoiselle
city hippo
king bocchus, hiempsal, jugurtha, masinissa
NUMINOUS awe(inspiring), mysterious, spiritual, supernatural
NUMITOR *brother* amulius
grandson remus, romulus
kingdom alba longa
NUMSKULL blockhead, cabbagehead, daff, dodo, dolt, dunce, FOOL, lackwit, loggerhead, squarehead, stupid, twit
NUN abbess, bhikkuni, canoness, clare, clarisse, clergywoman, cloistress, conventual, lorettine, minchen, minoress, monial, monkess, moth, novice, pigeon, postulant, priestess, prioress, recluse, religieuse, sister, smew, superioress, teresa, theatin, titmouse, ursuline, vestal, votaress, votary
bird monasa, titmouse
chief abbess, amma, domina, mother(superior)
community convent
dress habit, wimple
dress part analav, barb(e), faille, gimp, kerchief
franciscan clare
headdress wimple
hood faille
moth tussock
order dominican, lorettine, marist, poor clares, trappistine, ursuline
roman vesta
son joshua
NUNCIO ambassador, diplomat, envoy, legate, messenger, minister, representative
NUNCUPATIVE circumstantial, designative, nominal, oral, so-called, spoken, unwritten
NUNNERY abbey, cell, cloister, convent, minchery, monastery

founder of 1st eabald
head abbess, domina, mother(superior)
NUNNI antelope, blesbok
NUPHAR brandy-bottle, candock, flower, herb, nymphaea, pond-lily, spatterdock
NUPSON fool, simpleton
NUPTIAL bridal, conjugal, connubial, hymeneal, marital, matrimonial, spousal
NUPTIALS espousal, hymeneals, marriage, matrimony, spousal, wedding, wedlock, wifething
NUQUE nape, neck
NURLY cross(grained), ill-tempered, surly
NURSE ama(h), attend, ayah, baba, baby-sitter, bonne, care for, cherish, cradle, cultivate, encourage, eyah, feed, foster, fostress, further, granny, guard, indulge, iya, lactate, mammy, medic, midwife, nana, nanny, norice, nourish, nurture, nutrice, pamper, probationer, probe, promote, rear, sister, sitter, suckle, tend, treat, umfaan
bottle biberon
child's ama(h), aya(h), nana, nanny
famous edith cavell, florence nightingale, sister elizabeth kenny
headgear wimple
monastic infirmarian
needle igitur
shark gata
wet dhai, dholl
NURSEHOUND dogfish
NURSEMAID amah, bonne, hamai
NURSERY arboretum, birthplace, brooder, conservatory, creche, fosterage, greenhouse, hothouse, lathhouse, race
rhyme character (See also MOTHER *goose character.*) betty blue, blue ben, boggen, bopeep, boldero, colin, dame trot, dandyprat, daw, dun, etticoat, faustus, finikin, flinders, foster, giles, griggs, grundy, horner, jack sprat, jennie, jenny, jill, judy, king cole, kitty, mackey, mc diddler, miss muffet, morey, mother hubbard, polly, polt, porgie,

punch, redbreast, rose, shaftoe, simon, taffy, terence, tom thumb, tommy trot, tonsey, tucker, warley, wee willie winkie
NURTURE breed(ing), care for, cherish, cultivate, discipline, educate, education, feed, food, foster, nourish (ment), nurse, raise, rear(ing), school, support, sustain, tend, train(ing), tutelage, upbringing, uphold
NUT (See also *kind*, below.) buff, bully, burr, cob, core, cow goddess, crank, dolt, eccentric, enthusiast, expense, fanatic, fool, fruit, head, kernel, kook, lunatic, noix, oddball, pancreas, pith, problem, seed, sky goddess, tsedoodelt(eh), tsedrayt(er)
almond-like pili
-bearing nuciferous
beverage cola, kola
bitter hickory, pignut
breaker nutcracker
-brown chestnut, hazel, walnut
cashew sedge
coal anthracite
collective mast, shack
comb. cary(o), kary(o), nuci
companion bolt
confection marchpane, marzipan, nougat
consort geb, keb, seb
fallen shack
father shu
grass cyperis, scleria, sedge
group mastage
hickory carya, filbert
hook beadle, constable
house asylum, boobyhatch, madhouse
husk shack, shell
ivory anta
kind acorn, almond, anta, beechnut, betel, bonduc, brazil, breadnut, butternut, buyo, cashew, chestnut, chincapin, chinkapin, chinquapin, cobnut, coco(a)nut, cola, corozo, cumara, dika, filbert, gooranut, groundnut, grugru, hazel, hickory, kola, lichee, li(t)chi, lychee, macadamia, peanut, pecan, physicnut, pili, pinon, pistachio, sassafras, souari, suwarrow, tuba, walnut
kola bichy, gourou
-like drupe tryma

off one's confused, crazy, erroneous, insane, mad, unreasonable, wrong
offspring aah, haroeris, horus, isis, khensu, khonsu, nephthys, osiris, set(h), thoth
palm betel, coco(a)nut, cycad, lichee, li(t)chi, lychee
pert. nucal
physic tuba
pine pinon
pine seed pignolia
ripe leamer
rush chufa
shaped nuciform
shell abridge, bit, trifle
shell, in a briefly, concisely
sister, twin geb, keb, seb
stimulating betel, cola, kola
tanning bomah
NUTCRACKER meatbird, nuthatch, nutpecker, pillory, xenops
NUTGALL *product* ink
NUTHATCH jarbird, nutjobber, sitta, titmouse, tomtit, treemouse, xenops
NUTLET gyrolith, nucule, pyrene
NUTMEG calabash, mace, melon, myristica, spice, tree
bird cowry, finch
color beaver
covering mace
geranium pelargonium
hickory waternut
husk mace
-like fruit camara(n)
state connecticut
NUTRIA coypu, fur, grege, ragondin
NUTRIENT, NUTRIMENT aliment, diet, food, keep, nourishment, nurture, nutrition, pabulum, provender, refection, refreshment, starter, subsistence, support, sustenance, viands
NUTRITION alimentation, assimilation, eutrophy, ingestion, trophism
comb. troph(o)(y)
faulty dystrophia, dystrophy
pert. trophic
science biochemics, biochemy, dietetics, enzymology, sitology, threpsology, vitaminology
NUTRITIOUS, NUTRITIVE alible, battel, battle, healthful, nourishing, nutrient, salubrious, salutary, strengthening, trophic, wholesome

NUTTY amorous, buggy, bughouse, bugs, crackbrained, cracked, **CRAZY**, demented, eccentric, fascinating, flavorful, foolish, fruity, gaga, insane, loco, loving, mad, piquant, pleasant, potty, queer, racy, ridiculous, silty, smart, spicy, swagger, tetched, touched, zany, zestful
about enthusiastic, fervent
NUX VOMICA brucin, snakewood, tetanic
NUZZLE bundle, burrow, caress, cuddle, dig, embrace, fondle, foster, nestle, nuddle, nurture, pet, root, rub, snoozle, snuff, snuggle, snuzzle
NYASA See **MALAWI**.
NYDIA *rival* ione
NYE brood, eyas, flock, group, nest, nide
NYLON *fabric* cire
hosiery no-run
inventor carothers
NYM *companion* bardolf, falstaff, pistol
NYMPH abarbarea, aegle, aetna, albunea, alphesiboea, amalthaea, anchiale, antevorta, apsaras, arethusa, argiope, argyra, aria, asterodia, atlantid, batia, brome, butterfly, byblis, callisto, calypso, camena, circe, corycia, cynosura, cyrene, damsel, daphne, dryad, echo, egeria, embryo, erythea, eurydice, galatea, hamadryad, helice, hespera, hestia, houri, hyad, hydriad, iache, kelpie, larva, liriope, maenad, maia, maiden, mais, marpessa, muse, naiad, nais, napaea, nereid, nixie, oceanid, oenone, ondine, oread, pitana, pixy, pleiad, prosopon, pupa, sprite, stream, styx, sylph, syrinx, undine
causacian asterodia
cave oread
celestial apsaras
changed to bear callisto
changed to tree daphne
city poliad
cretan cynosura
dancer apsaras
flower limoniad
fountain abarbarea, albunea, camena, egeria, naiad, salmacis

glen napaea
grove See **NYMPH** *wood*.
hills oread
immortal nereid, oceanid
knowledge of future antevorta
knowledge of past postvorta
lake limniad, naiad
law-making egeria
meadow limoniad
moslem houri
mountain oread
mount ida oenone
prophetic antevorta, thriae, thriai
pursued by apollo arethusa, daphne, syrinx
queen mab
river naiad, nais
sea argyra, callirrhoe, calypso, clymene, clytie, cymodoce, galatea, mermaid, merrow, nereid, oceanid, ondine, scylla, siren, symaethis, undine
spring arethusa, argyra, telphusa
tree dryad, hamadryad, nereid
water apsaras, arethusa, ariel, clytie, crena, doto, egeria, ephydriad, galatea, hydriad, juturna, kelpie, limniad, lorelei, lurlei, nai-(a)d, nais, neda, nerine, nix(ie), nyse, ondine, pegal, rusalki, sprite, undine
wood alsa(e)id, arethusa, auloniad, camenae, dryad, grayling, hamadryad, hyads, hyloeorae, napae(a)e
NYMPHAEA aphrodite, candock, castalia, castaly, lotus, plant, thriai, waterlily
NYMPHOMANIA andromania, lust
NYORAI See **BUDDHA**.
NYROSA aytha
NYSSA pepperidge, sourgum, tupelo
NYSTAGMUS tic, wink
NYX *brother* erebus
father chaos
home hades
offspring aether, air, atropos, charon, clotho, day, death, doom, dreams, eris, fates, fraud, gaiety, hemera, hesperides, ker, lachesis, light, misery, moera, momus, moros, nemesis, oizus, oizys, old age, sleep, somnus, strife, thanatos
NYYRIKKI *father* tapio

O

O cipher, circle, och, omicron, zero

OAF blockhead, blunderbuss, boob, boor, bulbenik, bulvan, bulvon, changeling, clod(hopper), clown, dolt, dunce, dzhlob, fool, galoot, gawk(y), gowk, idiot, loon, lout, lubber, lummox, nincompoop, ouph(e), palooka, peasant, pompion, rube, sawney, schlemiel, slob, swab, yokel

OAFISH awkward, simple, stupid

OAHU See HAWAII.

OAK acajou, admiral, aik, ambrose, balsam, barberry, barren, bear, beefwood, belotta, bitter, black(jack), bluejack, brash, brave, briar, brier, brown, bull, bur, canyon, cerris, champion, chaparro, chestnut, chinkapin, club, cork, durmast, egilops, emory, encina, flittern, holly, holm, ilex, kellog(g), kermes, kusam, lea, live, palayan, pin, post, quercitron, quercus, red, roble, robur, scarlet, scrub, silk, swamp, tanbark, toumey, turkey, turtosa, valonia, wainscot
apple gall, shickshack
bark cork, crut, emory, mill
bark product quercin, tannin
beauty amphidasis, moth
bitter cerris
black quercitron
blight anoecia, louse
chestnut tanbark
comb. dryo, querci
decay piped-rot
evergreen holm
family fagaceae
fern dryopteris, polypody
fruit acorn, bellote, camata, mast
fungus armillaria
genus lithocarpus, quercus
grove encinal, oakenshaw
holm holly, ilex
jerusalem ambrose
male durmast
moss evernia, lichen
pert. quercine, roboreous
plantation quercetum
seed See OAK *fruit.*
tannin quercinic, queric
thicket chaparral
toad bufo
turkey cerris
web cockchafer
white roble
wood cartouch(e), durango, mesa
young flittern

OAKEN hard, strong

OAKUM *stuff with* calk, caulk, seal
thread pledget

OAR blade, paddle, pallet, ply, pole, propel, row, rower, scull, spoon, sweep
blade palm, peel, wash
boss button
bow gouger
comb. remi
fulcrum axis, oarlock, rowlock, thole
handle grasp
part blade, handle, loom, palm, peel
pin thole
-shaped remiform, remiped
short scull
wood ash

OARSMAN bencher, bostanji, bowman, remex, rower, sculler, stroke, waterman

OASIS aguada, bar, dakhla, gafsa, merv, ojo, refuge, siwa, spa, spring, wadi, wady
tree palm

OAST cockle, host, kiln, oven

OAT(S) ait, angora, aucht, avena(ge), avoine, cereal, egiops, feed, food, grain, grouts, haver(grass), pipe, provender, whitecorn
and barley dredge
cake caper, havercake, sourbread
disease grayleaf, grayspeck, take-all
ear wagtail
edible portion groats
feeling one's gay, healthy, sprightly
-fowl snow bunting
glutenin avenin
head panicle
husks shealing, shude
kernel groats
-like avenaceous
naked pilcorn, pilkins, pillas
paid as rent avenage
pert. avenaceous
sour flummery
unthreshed oathay
wild escapade, indiscretion, peccadillo

OATER horse-opera, western(er)

OATH affidavit, affirmation, aith, anathema, attestation, ban, blasphemy, bond, curse, cuss(word), damn, epithet, execration, expletive, imprecation, invective, malediction, pledge, profession, promise, rapper, sanction, serment, swear(word), vow, word
administer adjure
archaic lackaday
god of dius fidius, hercules, horcus, sancus
helper compurgator
knight's egad
mild all-fired, arrah, beans, bedad, begad, begorra, begorry, behear, bejab(b)ers, blame(d), blast, blessed, blimy, bloody, by cracky, by jove, confounded, consarn, creeps, crickey, crikey, cripes, crumbs, dadblame(d), dadblast(ed), dadburn(ed), daddrat, dadrot, dagnab, dang(ed), darn(ed), dash, dern, deuced, dickens, doggone(d), drat, egad, gad, gadsbod(i)kins, gadswoons, gadzooks, gee(whizz), goldang(ed), goldarn(ed), golly, gosh(darn), hang it, heck, hell-fire(d), infernal, jabers, jeepers, jimminy, judas priest, lud, mack, mackins, mafey, odsbod(i)kins, parbleu, pardy, ruddy, sblood, sdeath, sfoot, slid, slife, snails, swounds, thunder, zooks
take depose, pledge, promise, swear
-taker jurant
witness's voirdire

OATMEAL brewis, brochan, brose, browis, burgoo, burgout, drammock, porridge, pottage, stodge, yellow

and water drammach, drammock, drummock, drummock
bad man's chervil, hemlock
bread anack, jannack
cake pone, scone

OAXACA *indian* amishgo, zapotec(a)

OB *river tributary* irtish

OBADIAH abdias, prophet, quaker
commander josiah

OBBLIGATO accompaniment, escort, indispensible, require

OBCONICAL pear-like, pear-shaped, pyriform

OBDUCTION See AUTOPSY.

OBDURACY callousness, hardheartedness, hardness, heartlessness, insensitivity

OBDURATE abandoned, adamant(ine), balky, callous, casehardened, dogged, firm, hard(bitten)(headed), hardened, harsh, immobile, impassive, impenitent, indurated, inexorable, inflexible, insensible, intractable, mulish, obstinate, perverse, refractory, rough, rugged, set, severe, stiff-necked, stony, stubborn, sullen, tough, unbending, unyielding

OBEAH bewitch, charm, fetish, magic, sorcery, voodoo
doctor magician

OBED *grandson* david
parent boaz, ephlal, ruth, shemaiah
son azariah, jehu, jesse

OBEDEDOM *son* ammiel, issachar, jehozabad, joah, nethaneel, peulthai, sacar, shemaiah

OBEDIENCE accordance, allegiance, bow, compliance, conformance, conformity, control, curtsy, docility, dutifulness, fealty, jurisdiction, obeisance, observance, resignation, rule, servility, subjection, submission, submissiveness, subservience, tameness
one who demands authoritarian, boss, disciplinarian, martinet
passive nonresistance

OBEDIENT acquiescent, amenable, biddable, bridlewise, compliant, deferential, devoted, disciplined, docile, duteous, dutiful, faithful,

law-abiding, loyal, manageable, meek, obeisant, orderly, pliable, pliant, quiet, resigned, respectful, responsive, servile, subject, submissive, subservient, tall, tame, tractable, well-behaved, yielding
plant dragonhead

OBEISANCE abaisance, allegiance, binge, bow, congee, curts(e)y, deference, esteem, fealty, fidelity, homage, honor, humblesso, jouk, loyalty, regard, respect, reverence, salaam, salutation, veneration

OBEISANT deferential, obsequious

OBELISK aguglia, column, dagger, guglia, hagiolith, mark, memorial, monument, needle, obelus, pillar, pylon, shaft, tower

OBERON abode, aval(l)on, ghalal, mommur
planet uranus
wife titania

OBESE adipose, beefy, bloated, chubby, chumpy, chunky, corpulent, fat(tish), fleshy, gross, heavy-set, imposing, liparous, paunchy, plump, podgy, portly, puffy, pursy, pyknic, rolypoly, rotund, stocky, stodgy, stout, thickset, tubby, turgid

OBESITY adiposity, corpulence, overweight, polysarcia, rotundity
disease diabetes, heart attack, high blood pressure, hypertension, liver disease, osteoarthritis

OBETH *father* jonathan

OBEY acquiesce, behave, comply, conform, defer, ear, follow, hear, heed, keep, listen to, mind, observe, regard, salute, submit, toe the line, yield

OBFUSCATE becloud, befog, bewilder, cloud, confuse, darken, dim, fog, muddle, mystify, obfusk, obscure, opaque, perplex, stupefy

OBI charm, fetish, girdle, obeah, sash
accessory inro

OBIT death, decease, item, mass, necrology, OBITUARY, obsequies, release, requiem, rest, service

OBITER DICTUM comment, opinion, reflection, remark

OBITUARY biography, chronicle, necrologue, necrology

OBJECT affair, agent, aim, article, balk, bar, boggle, buck, butt, care, carp, cavil, censure, challenge, commodity, complain, concern, criticize, demur, denounce, design, dingus, disapprove, dissent, dohickey, doodad, end, expostulate, figure, form, GADGET, gimmick, gismo, goal, hickey, idea, incentive, inducement, intent(ion), interpose, jib, jigger, kick, matter, mind, mission, motive, oppose, particular, phenomenon, point, protest, purpose, reality, rebuke, remonstrate, reprobate, scope, scruple, shy, sight, something, stick, substance, thing(umabob) (umajig)(gummy), widgit
beloved darling, minion, mistress, sweetheart
conspicuous landmark
incorrect naming of paranomia
lesson example
man-made artifact
of dislike aversion
of dread bogey, bog(g)ie, bogy, bugbear
rare antique, curio
sacred churinga, guaca, huaca, shrine, thummim, urim, zogo
small atom, bit, mite, pirlie
tilted at quintain
ultimate telos

OBJECTIFY actualize, embody, envisage, envision, externalize, incarnate, materialize, realize, reify

OBJECTION bar, beef, but, cavil, censure, criticism, defense, demur(ral), deprecation, disapprobation, disapproval, disfavor, dislike, doubt, exception, hatred, mislike, opposition, opposure, protest, quarrel, question, quibble, rejection, remonstrance, scruple, thumbs down
legal demur
trivial cavil, hairsplitting

OBJECTIONABLE awful, displeasing, exceptionable, frightful, ghastly, horrid, illaudable, inexpedient, obnoxious, offensive, opprobrious, terrible, unpleasant, unsavory

OBJECTIVE actual, aim, aspiration, bull's eye, butt, concrete, corporeal, design, desire, destination, detached, direction, end, equitable, external, fair, goal, impartial, impersonal, intent(ion), just, mark, material, mission, OBJECT, palpable, physical, point, purpose, pursuit, quintain, raison d'etre, sake, sensible, tangible, target, ultimatum, unbiased, unprejudiced

OBJET D'ART bibelot, curio, figurine, vase, virtu

OBJURGATE abuse, ban, berate, castigate, chide, condemn, criticize, curse, damn, denounce, execrate, jaw, rate, rebuke, reprehend, reprobate, reprove, revile, SCOLD, upbraid, vilify, vituperate

OBJURGATORY abusive, critical

OBLATE dedicated, depressed, devoted, flattened, monastic, monk, offer(ed)
spheroid oval

OBLATION anaphora, charity, corban, devotion, offering, sacred, sacrifice

OBLIGATE astrict, bind, commit, indebt, OBLIGE

OBLIGATION agreement, annuity, assignment, bond, burden, charge, check, compulsion, condition, constraint, contract, debt, due(s), duty, favor, fealty, indebtedness, iou, liability, load, must, necessity, need, oath, onus, ought, owed, pledge, promise, responsibility, score, tie, tribute, vow

OBLIGATORY binding, bounden, compulsory, enforced, forcible, imperative, imposing, incumbent, mandatory, necessary, required
not ad libitum, voluntary

OBLIGE accommodate, aid, assist, avail, back, benefit, bind, coerce, compel, constrain, demand, engage, exact, favor, force, gratify, help, kae, make, necessitate, OBLIGATE, please, pledge,

press(ure), profit, require, support, tie, uphold

OBLIGED beholden, bound (en), constrained, debtful, fain, favored, grateful, obligated, obstricted, pleased, pledged

OBLIGING accommodating, amiable, civil, compliant, considerate, favorable, helpful, hospitable, indulgent, kind, officious, polite, thoughtful

OBLIQUE askance, askew, aslant, awry, backhand(ed), bent, bevelled, bias, cant, circuitous, crooked, deviate, devious, diagonal, embelif, ·evasive, inclined, indirect, left-handed, louche, obscure, roundabout, scalene, sidelong, sidewise, sinister, slant(ed), slope, sloping, squint, thwart, tilted, tortuous, transverse, underhand
comb. lox(o), plagi(o)
render splay
stroke slash, solidus
surface cant

OBLIQUELY agee, aglede, akimbo, aside, askance, askew, asquint, awry, biaswise, cater, crosswise, sidelong, sideways, sidewise

OBLITERATE abolish, abrogate, annihilate, annul, blot out, cancel, cover, dele, delete, destroy, efface, erase, expunge, exterpate, extinguish, negate, nullify, obscure, rase, raze, rub out, rule out, scratch out, smear, sponge, strike out

OBLIVION amnesty, disregard, forgetfulness, insensitivity, lethe, limbo, nirvana, oubliance, pardon, silence, unconcern,
brother mihuntang
producer drug, narcotic, nepenthe

OBLIVIOUS absent-minded, abstracted, amnesic, amort, asleep, bemused, deaf, dreaming, dreamy, faraway, forgetful, heedless, lost, museful, musing, preoccupied, unconscious, undiscerning, unfeeling, unmindful, unobservant, woolgathering

OBLONG avelonge, elliptical, elongate(d), quadrangular, rectangular

rounded ellipse

OBLOQUY abuse, backbiting, detraction, billingsgate, blame, brand, calumny, censure, contempt, criticism, disapproval, disgrace, dishonor, disrepute, infamy, invective, odium, opprobrium, reproach, reproof, scandal, scurrility, shame, slander, smear, stain, stigma, stricture, vitriol, vituperation

OBNOXIOUS abhorrent, base, blameworthy, culpable, curst, detestable, distasteful, faulty, hateful, horrid, invidious, liable, loathsome, nasty, noisome, objectionable, odious, offensive, rancid, repellent, repugnant, repulsive, revolting, terrible, vile

OBOE aulos, chalumeau, chanter, chirimia, cor, hautboy, musette, piffero, reed, schalmei, shawm, surnai, surnay, szopelka
bass heckelphone, rackett
comb. aulo
di caccia fagottino, tenoroon
early shawn

OBSCENE bad, bawdy, blue, brazen, coarse, dirty, fescennine, filthy, foul(mouthed), fulsome, gross, immodest, immoral, improper, impure, indecent, indelicate, lascivious, lewd, licentious, loathsome, low, lurid, nasty, offcolor, offensive, pornographic, racy, raw, repulsive, ribald, risque, salacious, scabrous, scatological, scurrile, scurrilous, sexy, shameful, smutty, sultry, unclean, unprintable, vile, vulgar, wanton

OBSCENITY bawdry, dirt, filth(iness), indecency, lubricity, pornography, ribaldry, salacity, scatology, smut, vulgarity
cult aischrolatreia

OBSCURANTIST barbarian, philistine

OBSCURE abstruse, adumbrate, ambiguous, becloud, bedarken, bedim, bewilder, black(en), blank(et), blear, blind, blot, blotch, blur(ry), caliginous, cloud(ed)(y), conceal, cover, cryptic, dark (en), darkle, darkling, deep,

delphic, delude, difficulty, dim, disguise, doubtful, dubious, dusky, enigmatic, envelop, equivocal, esoteric, film, fog, gloom(y), gray, hard, hidden, hide, humble, indefinite, indistinct, inky, intricate, involved, latent, lowly, misty, murk(y), mysterious, mystic(al), nameless, nubilate, obfuscate, occulate, occult, opaque, orphic, overcast, oversile, recondite, remote, screen, secret, shade, shadow(y), shady, smear, undefined, unknown, vague
comb. adelo, aphan(o)
OBSCURED clouded, disguised, hazy, hidden, infuscate
OBSCURITY ambiguity, cloudiness, dark(ness), dimness, fog, gloom, mist, nonentity, obscuration, privacy, seclusion, shadow, silence, tenebres
OBSECRATE appeal, beg, beseech, entreat, petition, pray, supplicate
OBSEQUIES ceremony, funeral, mass, obit, pyre, rites, ritual, service, wake
OBSEQUIOUS abject, adulatory, assiduous, attentive, beggarly, bootlicking, compliant, courtly, cowering, crawling, cringing, deferential, devoted, dutiful, fawning, flattering, footlicking, funereal, groveling, hangdog, ingratiating, leechlike, menial, obedient, obeisant, parasitic, prostrate, servile, slavish, slick, sniveling, sponging, submissive, subservient, sycophantic, timeserving, toadying, truckling, vernile
agreement assentation
person limberham, toady
OBSERVABLE discernable, evident, manifest, notable, noticeable, perceivable, remarkable, visible
OBSERVANCE adherence, aquittal, aquittance, attention, behavior, ceremony, compliance, custom, discharge, execution, festivity, fidelity, form, freet, freit, fulfil(l)ment, honor, keeping, obedience, ordinance, performance, practice, re-

gard, rite, rule, satisfaction, solemnity
religious communion, novena, sacrament
superstitious freet, freit
OBSERVANT alert, atten (tive), aware, careful, eyeful, faithful, heedful, mindful, perceptive, regardful, respectful, scrupulous, seeing, vigilant, watchful
person argus
OBSERVATION assertion, attention, auspice, autopsy, belief, comment, criticism, critique, descant, espial, espionage, examination, eye (sight), gloss, idea, image, lookout, note, notice, opinion, pronouncement, reflection, remark, spying, statement, supervision, surveillance, viewing, watch(ing)
post beacon, belvedere, bleachers, crow's nest, gallery, grandstand, lighthouse, lookout, observatory, outlook, peephole, pharos, watchtower
preliminary proem
reasoning from aposteriori
OBSERVATORY agassiz, cordoba, dunlap, eidouranion, hale, hooker, lick, lookout, palomar, planetarium, mt wilson, tower, yerkes
OBSERVE abide by, adhere(to), athold, attend, behold, carry out, celebrate, comment, conform, contemplate, descry, detect, discern, discharge, discover, espy, esteem, examine, execute, express, eye, follow, fulfill, heed, hold, inspect, keep, look, mark, meet, mention, mind, nota, notice, obey, perceive, perform, profess, redeem, regard, remark, respect, revere, satisfy, say, scan, see, sherlock, solemnize, spot, survey, tent, tout, twig, view, utter, watch, witness
OBSERVER audience, beholder, bystander, eyewitness, informer, kibitzer, looker-on, onlooker, spectator, watcher, witness
OBSESS beset, besiege, bewitch, compel, drive, grip, hagride, harass, haunt, hold, impel, infatuate, in-

fluence, invest, possess, preoccupy
OBSESSED crazy, dippy, dotty, hipped, hung up, possessed, spellbound
OBSESSION bug, compulsion, craze, drive, entrancement, fascination, fixation, idee fixe, hang-up, maggot, mania, monomania, passion, possession, siege, tic
OBSIDIAN iztle, iztli, lapis, lava
OBSOLETE ancient, antiquated, antique, archaic, bygone, dated, dead, discarded, disused, effete, musty, old(fashioned), outdated, outmoded, outworn, passe, past, unfashionable, venerable
OBSTACLE anstoss, bar, barricade, barrier, block(ade), bunker, catch, curb, dam, determent, deterrent, difficulty, dike, drag, discouragement, drawback, fence, fraise, hedgehog, hindrance, hitch, hurdle, impediment, let, obex, obstruction, opposition, pillbox, restraint, retard, roadblock, rub, sandtrap, sawyer, snag, stile, traverse
insurmountable impasse
military abatis
OBSTETRICIAN accoucheur, accoucheuse, granny-doctor, midwife
OBSTETRICS maieutics, midwifery, tocology
OBSTINANCY resistance, resolution, stubbornness
symbol mule, pig
OBSTINATE asinine, assish, balky, bullheaded, bulldogged, contrary, crabbed, crotched, cussed, determined, dogged, dour, entete, faithful, firm, fixed, froward, hard, headstrong, heady, inflexible, intractable, mulish, obdurate, opinionated, persevering, persistent, pertinacious, perverse, pigheaded, prefract, recalcitrant, recusant, refractory, renitent, resolute, rowdy, self-willed, set, sot, stancy, steadfast, stern, stiffnecked, stomachy, strict, strong(willed), stubborn, sulky, sullen, tenacious, un-

bending, unruly, unyielding, willful

as a mule, pig

not amenable, supple

OBSTREPEROUS blatant, boisterous, clamorous, effervescent, headstrong, loud, noisy, rackety, refractory, strident, uncontrolled, unruly, vociferous

OBSTRINGE bind, constrain

OBSTRUCT arrest, avert, balk, bar, barricade, blanket, block(ade), bolt, bottleneck, check, choke, clog, close, cumber, curb, dam, debar, delay, dit(t), embarrass, foil, hamper, hinder, hobble, impede, incommode, inhibit, lock, obviate, occlude, oppose, plug, preclude, prevent, restrain, retard, shut off, slow, stay, stifle, stop, throttle, thwart, trip

OBSTRUCTION bar, barricade, barrier, block(ade), blockage, bottleneck, bung, cavil, choke, clog, congestion, cork, dam, embolism, embolus, gag, gasket, gorge, hang up, hedgehog, hindrance, hitch, impediment, infract(ion), interruption, jam, let, obstacle, obstipation, occlusion, padding, plug, snag, spile, spill, stay, stop(gap), stopper, stopple, stuffing, tap, wadding

OBTAIN accomplish, achieve, acquire, areche, arrive, attain, bag, borrow, buy, cadge, capture, carry, catch, chevise, come, contract for, earn, effect, elicit, ettle, exist, extract, fang, fasten, fetch, find, fulfill, gain, get, hent, hold, induce, keep, lead, occupy, possess, prevail, procure, purchase, reach, reap, receive, scrounge, secure, settle, sew up, succeed, win

by threat blackmail, extort

dishonestly cheat, crook, extort, fleece, nobble, skelder, steal

with difficulty eke, inch

OBTEST appeal, beg, beseech, invoke, protest, supplicate

OBTRUDE butt in, eject, expel, flaunt, force, give, glare, impose, interfere, in-

terlope, intervene, intrude, jet, meddle, mediate, press, presume, push, ram, shove, sorn, thrust

OBTRUNCATE behead, decapitate, hew, lop, retrench, shorten

OBTRUSIVE blatant, bumptious, curious, forward, insolent, meddlesome, nosy, officious, pert, prying, pushing, self-assertive, snoopy

OBTUND blunt, deaden, dull, moderate, quell

OBTUSE blind, blunt, boorish, callous, crass, dense, dim, dull, gauche, heavy, hebetudinous, impassive, imperceptive, insensible, insensitive, phlegmatic, slow, sluggish, stolid, stupid, tactless, thick, unfeeling, unobservant, wooden

comb. ambly

OBUMBRATE cloud, darken, shade

OBVERSE converse, counterpart, face, front, opposite

of coin head

OBVIATE anticipate, avert, avoid, escape, forestall, intervene, oppose, preclude, prevent, ward off

OBVIOUS apparent, arrant, banal, blatant, bold, broad, certain, clear, common, conspicuous, distinct, evident, exposed, gross, hackneyed, intelligible, liable, loud, manifest, open, palpable, patent, plain, prominent, salient, signal, slick, stark, striking, subject, visible

not arcane, deep, esoteric, hidden, masked, profound, secret, subtle

OBVOLUTION fold, twist

OCA oxalis, plant, sorrel, soursop, tuber

OCARINA camote, sweet potato

OCCASION affair, basis, break, call, cause, ceremony, chance, circumstance, condition, engender, episode, event, exigency, function, habituate, happening, inception, incident, induce(ment), inspire, instant, juncture, moment, motive, need, nonce, occurrence, opportunity, origin, pass, pretext, produce,

prompt, provoke, purpose, reason, sele, sith, situation, source, subject, state, stound, tide, time, topic

festive celebration, fete, gala, holiday, shindig, utas

social coffee, party, soiree, tea

OCCASIONAL accidental, antrin, by-the-way, casual, contingent, daimen, desultory, extra, incidental, infrequent, irregular, odd, off, orra, parenthetical, part-time, random, rare, scarce, spare(time), sporadic, uncommon

OCCASIONALLY anon, at times, betimes, now and then, once in awhile, sometimes

OCCIDENT europe, hesperia, sunset, west

OCCLUDE absorb, choke, close, leave out, obstruct, shut(in)(out), take in, throttle

OCCULT abstruse, anagogic(al), arcane, cabalic, cabalistic, canny, conceal(ed), cryptic, eclipse, esoteric, hidden, latent, magic(al), metaphysical, metapsychial, mysterious, mystic(al), obscure, psychic, recondite, rosicrucian, secret, shrouded, sibyllic, sibylline, supernatural, theosophic(al), transmundane, unknown, unrevealed, veiled, voodoo, weird

science alchemy, esoterics, necromancy

symbol cryptogram

OCCULTISM cab(b)ala, kab(b)ala, magic, mystery, mysticism

OCCUPANCY control, habitation, possession, retention, tenancy

OCCUPANT addressee, dweller, householder, incumbent, indweller, inhabitant, inmate, occupier, possessor, renter, resident, tenant

OCCUPATION absorption, activity, art, berth, business, call(ing), career, control, craft, employment, function, game, habitation, industry, job, line, manurance, metier, occupancy, position, possession, presence, profession, pursuit, service, sphere, tenancy, tenure, toil, trade, use, vocation, work

subordinate avocation, hobby

OCCUPIED absorbed, active, busy, captured, employed, engrossed, held, intent, kept, peopled, populated, populous, rapt, settled, taken, took

OCCUPY absorb, amuse, arrest, beset, busy, capture, contain, employ, engage, engross, expend, fill, follow, garrison, have, hold, include, inhabit, interest, keep, lie, live in, own, permeate, pervade, possess, pourprise, reside in, seize, take, use

illegally jump, sit in, squat

OCCUR appear, arise, arrive, befall, betide, break, chance, come(about)(to pass), crop up, develop, emanate, encounter, ensue, eventuate, exist, fall, follow, hap(pen), issue, light, materialize, oppose, pass, proceed, result, rise, succeed, take place, transpire, turn up

again recur, repeat

OCCURRENCE affair, accident, adventure, appearance, case, casualty, circumstance, contingency, encounter, episode, event (uality), exigency, experience, happening, incident, item, juncture, melting, occasion, pass, situation

chance adventure

supernatural miracle

unfortunate casualty

unusual oddity

OCEAN antarctic, arctic, atlantic, blue, brine, briny, deep, drink, expanse, fishpond, hyaline, indian, kai, main, mere, millpond, pacific, pond, SEA, tide, waters

bottom bed

bug halobates

depth measurement bathymetry

depth measurer echograph

depth, pert. bathyal, bathybic, bathysmal

floating matter algae, flotsam, lagan

god, goddess See SEA *god, goddess.*

-going nautical, sea-faring

mammal whale

nymph galatea, oceanid, siren

perch redfish

periodic motion tide

pert. neptunian, OCEANIC

ripple twine

route lane

spray arrowwood, creamcups, ironwood

student of thalassographer

swell sea

OCEANA See UTOPIA.

OCEANIA australasia, MALAYSIA, melanesia, micronesia, polynesia

sacred object zogo

OCEANIC abyssal, aequoreal, aquatic, bathybic, bathysmal, briny, dips(e)y, fluvial, lacustrine, large, marine, maritime, nautical, naval, neritic, pelagic, seaborn, thalassic, vast

bonito sardasarda, skipjack

tunicate salp

OCEANID aethra, clymene, pluto

parent oceanus, tethys

OCEANUS *consort* tethys

offspring (See also NYMPH *sea.*) aegia, argia, caanthus, clytie, dione, doris, electra, eurynome, metis, oceanid, persa, proteus, styx, tyche

parent gaea, gaia, ouranos, uranus

OCELLUS eye(let), spot, stemma

OCELOT cat, juagatirica, leopard, tiger, wildcat

OCHER, OCHRE almagra, doubloon, gold, hematite, kiel, limonite, money, ore, pigment, raddle, sil, tangier, tungstite, wad(d)

burnt tangier

color with raddle

red abraum, keel, kiel, kokowai, raddle, reddle, rubric, rud(dle), sinopis, tiver

source dakhla

yellow sil, spruce

OCHIMUS *father* helius

kingdom rhodes

offspring cydippe

wife hegetoria

OCHOZATH See ASHUZZATH.

OCHUS *kin* artaxerxes, darius

slayer bagoas

son arses

OCIMUM amyris, basil, bezel, bush tea, mint, pycanthemum, sheepskin, trigonella

OCNUS *founder of* mantua

mother manto

OCOTEA canela, stinkwood, sweetwood, til-tree

OCOTILLO candlewood, coachwhip, fouquieria, gochnatia

OCRISIA *consort* lar, vulcan

master tanaquil, tarquin

son servius-tullius

OCTAVE cask, diapason, eight(h), huitain, interval, key, ottava, parry, series, sheminith, stanza, tone, utas, verse

flute flautino, piccolo

high alt

singing magadize

2 disdiapason

OCTAVIA *brother* augustus

husband marcellus, mark antony, nero

offspring marcellus

parent claudius, messalina

rival cleopatra

OCTAVIAN augustus

rival mark antony

OCTAVIUS *slayer* cinna

OCTOBER *birthstone* aquamarine, beryl, opal, rozircon, tourmaline

brew ale

31st halloween

OCTOPUS calamaretti, catfish, cephalopod, cuttle (fish), devilfish, hee, inkfish, kalamaria mollusk, polypus, poulp(e), preko, scuttle, squid

arm tentacle

secretion ink

10-armed decapod

OCTOROON mestee, mestizo, metis, mustee

OCTROI, OCTROY command, concede, concession, dictate, grant, privilege, tax

OCULAR eye(piece), ophthelmic, optic(al), orbital, seeing, seen, visual

OCULIST ophthalmologist, optician, optometrist

ODALISK concubine, slave

ODD anomalous, auk, awk, azygous, bastard, bizarre, burlesque, choice, comical, curious, droll, eccentric, erratic, extra(ordinary), fantastic, funny, gauche, grotesque, individual, irregular, laughable, left, lone, occasional, off, orra, out(land-ish), outre, quaint, queer, peculiar, rare, rum(my), secluded, single, singular, solitary, strange, surplus, uncommon, unearthly, unique, unitary, unket, unkid, unmatched, unnatural, unpaired, unusual, weird, whimsical

assortment cats-and-dogs
jobber caddie, caddy, factotum, handyman, joey, swamper, workman
-toed perissodactyl

ODDBALL See ECCENTRIC, ODDITY.

ODDITY abnormality, anomaly, bizarrerie, card, caution, character, codger, coot, curiosity, duck, duffer, eccentric(ity), exception, galoot, geezer, geke, gig, gink, goof, goop, guy, idiosyncrasy, kink, monstrosity, nonesuch, peculiarity, prodigy, quaintness, queerness, quirk, quizzity, rara avis, rarity, rumness, singularity, spook, strangeness, rummy

ODDMAN arbiter, referee, umpire

ODDS advantage, allowance, bet, bisque, chance, degree, difference, discord, disparity, dispute, dissension, edge, handicap, inequality, likelihood, morning line, price, probability, quarrel, ratio, tossup, variance
and ends bits(and pieces), brott, carry-over, fewtrils, fragments, hash, leavings, leftovers, miscellany, mixture, orts, raggle-taggle, refuse, remainder, remnants, rest, scraps, seconds, shakings
favoring the house vigorish
long improbability

ODE canticle, canzone, epicede, epicedium, epinicion, hymn, lyric, melody, monody, paean, palinode, parabasis, pindaric, poem, psalm, song, stasimon
birthday genethiliacon
nuptial epithalamium
part epode, strophe
victory epinicion, epinikion

ODEON, ODEUM gallery, hall, theater

ODER *city on* breslau
tributary neisse, oppa, warta

ODIN alfadir, nickar, othin, sigge, wodan, woden, wotan
brother vili
conqueror fenrir, fenris
country svithiod, swithiod
court valhalla
created by ask, embla
crow hugin, mugin
daughter-in-law nanna
descendant scyld
disguise harbard
disobeyed by brynhild
favorite family aesir, volsungs
grandfather buri
hall einherian, valhalla
horse sleipner
kin nanna, vile, vili, volsung
maiden valkyie
messenger hermod, valkyrie
palace gladsheim, syn
pantheon See AESIR.
parent bestla, bor(r)
protege hadding, volsung
raven hugin, munin
ring drahpner, draupnir, drupnir
rival hrungnir
seat valaskjalf
ship naglfar, skidbladnir
skald bragi
son balder, bladr, bragi, donar, hermod, thor, tor, tyr, vali, vidar, vithar(r)
spear gugner, gungnir
steed sleipnir
sword gram
throne hlidskjalf
victim bergelmir, giants, ymir
wife frea, freya, freyja, fria, frigg(a), jord, rind(r)
wolf freki, gere, geri

ODIOUS abhorrent, abominable, base, damnable, detestable, disgusting, distasteful, foul, hateful, heinous, hideous, loathsome, nasty, obnoxious, offensive, paskudne(h), repellent, repugnant, repulsive, revolting, terrible, ugly, unlovable, vile

ODIUM abhorrence, antipathy, aversion, censure, detestation, disfavor, disgrace, dishonor, dislike, disrepute, hate, hatred, ignominy, infamy, loathing, ob-

loquy, opprobrium, scandal, shame

ODOR aroma, balm, bouquet, breath, effluvium, efflux, emanation, empyreuma, essence, ewder, exhalation, fetor, flavor, foetor, fragrance, frowst, fume(t), hodure, incense, musk, nidor, nose(gay), perfume, pungency, redolence, reek, repute, savor, scent, smell, sniff, snuff, stench, tang, tincture, tinge, trail, verdure, waff, waft, whiff
comb. osma, osmo
cooking fumet, nidor
emit offensive reek
floral fume
foul ewder, fetor, fist, frowst, mephitis, must, reek, stench, stink
fresh balm, ymur
pungent spice
study osmics
sweet suaveolent
without aosmic, scentless, unscented

ODORIFEROUS, ODOROUS aromatic, balmy, effluvious, fetid, fragrant, musky, nidorose, olent, perfumed, pungent, redolent, scented, scentful, smellful, smelly, tangy

ODUM iroko

ODYSSEUS outis, laertiades, ulixes, ulysses, ulyxes
adversary ajax, cyclops
antagonist irus
bay afales
beggar irus
captive hecuba
captor calypso, polyphemus
chronicler homer
companion antiphus, elpenor, eurybated, eurylochus, leucus, mentor, perimedes, polites
consort calypso, circe
cowherd philoetius
dog argos, argus
enchantress circe
enemy polyphemus, poseidon, irus, lotus eaters
friend See *companion*, above.
grandfather arcesius, autolycus
hazard bosporus, scylla and charybdis, sirens, wandering rocks
home ithaca

host aeolus, alcinous, antenor
lotus island djerba
nurse euryclea
parent anticlea, laertes, sisyphus
plant moly
protector athena
rescuer leucothea, nausicaa
rival ajax
slayer telegonus
son auson, polyporthis, romanus, telegonus, telemachus
swineherd eumaeus
temptress circe, lotus eaters, sirens
village vathi
victim antinous, prytanis
voyage odyssey
wife callidice, penelope
wrestling opponent philomelides

ODYSSEY (See also ODYSSEUS.) travel, wandering
author homer
bard demodocus, phemius
beggar armaeus, irus
character achilles, ajax, alcinous, anticlea, antiphates, arete, athena, calypso, cicones, cimmerians, circe, cyclops, demodocus, eumaeus, hermes, laertes, lamus, leucothea, lotophagi, nausicaa, penelope, polyphemus, poseidon, telemachus, tiresias, zeus
herald peisenor
island aeaea, ogygia, phaeacia, scheria, thrinacia
river oceanus
sorceress circe, sirens
spring artacia

OEAGRUS *consort* calliope
kingdom thrace
son linus, orpheus

OEAX *parent* clymene, nauplius

OEBALUS *father* telon
kingdom sparta
son hippocoon, icarius, tyndareus

OECONOMUS agent, bailiff, bursar, factor, major-domo, manager, reeve, seneschal, steward

OECUS apartment, hall, room

OEDIPUS *complex* momism
consort jocasta
foster parent perioboea, polybus
kin creon, labdacus

kingdom thebes
mountain cithaeron
offspring antigone, eteocles, ismene, polyn(e)ices
parent jocasta, laius
refuge attica, colonus
trilogy author sophocles
victim laius, sphinx

OENEUS *kin* agrius, andraemon, diomedes
kingdom calydon, pleuron
offspring deianira, gorge, meleager, toxeus, tydeus
wife althaea

OENOCHOE jug, olpe, pitcher, prochoos

OENOMAUS *charioteer* myrtilus
daughter hippodameia
father ares
kingdom pisa

OENONE *husband* paris
rival helen

OENOPION *daughter* merope
father dionysus
kingdom chios
victim orion
wife helice

OENUS *kin* hercules
victim toxeus

OESTRUS desire, frenzy, fury, heat, impulse, passion, rut, stimulus, sting

OF (For definitions beginning OF, see following word: e.g., OF air, see AIR: *pert.*; OF service, see SERVICE: *of.* Under OF here are conventional phrases, e.g., OF *course*, OF *age*.) about, anent, before, concerning, for, from, in re, off, van, von, with
age adult, arrived, mature, ripe, seasoned
a kind comparable, mediocre, similar
all ava
a truth certainly
comb. ory
course absolutely, bien entendu, certainly, consequently, de cursu, for sure, natch, necessarily, no doubt, to be sure
each ana, per
late recently
necessity consequently, needs
note celebrated, extraordinary, famous, outstanding
old erstwhile, whilom
2 minds irresolute

OFF abnormal, absent, afar, aff, agee, apart, aside, away, begone, crazy, delirious, depart, discontinued, distant, divergent, doff, erring, far, from, further, gone, hence, inaccurate, inferior, insane, launched, occasional, odd, opposite, postpone, rancid, remote, remove(d), reverse, slack, slight, swallow, tainted, wet, wrong
and on alternately, changeably, irregularly, now and then, occasionally
base mistaken, wrong
-center eccentric, excentric
-color blue, campy, clashing, discordant, dubious, harsh, incongruous, improper, risque, sick, suggestive, tasteless, unhealthy, vulgar
comb. aph, apo
-glide detente, vocule
guard tardy, unaware, unprepared, unready
-key discordant
one's feed bad, ill, low, sick
-side foul, right, violation
the beaten track astray, extraordinary, novel, uncommon, unusual
the cuff extemporaneously, impromptu, improvising, spontaneous(ly)
the record confidential(ly), entre nous, unofficial

OFFAL bran, carrion, draff, filth, furfur, garbage, gralloch, gurry, hogwash, offscourings, offscum, refuse, riffraff, rubbish, scum, scurf, sewage, slop(s), slough, swill

OFFBEAT eccentric, fresh, mod, nonconforming, novel, odd, unconventional, unusual

OFFBREAK googly

OFFENBACH *opera* la belle helene, la vie parisienne, tales of hoffman

OFFEND affront, agrieve, anger, annoy, appal(l), bother, bruise, cag, chafe, displease, distaste, err, exasperate, excite, fret, gall, grate, grieve, harm, horrify, huff, hurt, insult, irk, irritate, jar, miff, mortify, nettle, outrage, pique, provoke, rasp, rass, shock, sin, slight, slur, snub, sting, stumble, transgress, trespass, vex, violate, wound

OFFENDER malefactor, misdoer, sinner, transgressor, wrongdoer

OFFENSE abuse, affront, aggression, assault, attack (ers), breach, crime, default, delict(um), delit, dudgeon, displeasure, enemy, evil, fault, felony, foe, grief, grievance, harm, huff, hurt, illegality, indignity, infraction, iniquity, injury, injustice, insult, larceny, malum, misconduct, misdeed, misdemeanor, misfeasance, onset, onslaught, outrage, peccancy, pique, resentment, scandal, sin, strunt, theftbote, tort, transgression, trespass, umbrage, vice, violation, wrath, wrong

against law crime, delict (um), delit, felony, misdemeanor

civil stellionate, tort

give See OFFEND.

heinous piacle

mild delict, delit

moral evil

OFFENSIVE abhorrent, abominable, abusive, aggression, aggressive, anger, assault, attack(ing), bad, beastly, biting, coarse, contemptible, crude, cutting, despicable, detestable, dirty, disagreeable, disgusting, displeasing, distasteful, dreadful, execrable, fetid, forbidding, foul, fulsome, gross, hateful, hideous, insolent, invading, loathsome, mawkish, misbeholden, nasty, nauseant, nauseous, noisome, noxious, obnoxious, obscene, odious, opprobrious, outrageous, provocation, repellent, repugnant, repulsive, revolting, ribald, rotten, sarcastic, scurrilous, shocking, sickening, stinging, tasteless, ugly, unpleasant, unsavory, vile, vulgar, warlike, wicked

OFFER adduce, advance, advertise, allege, approach, assign, attempt, auction, bequeath, bestow, bid, bode, cap, carry, confer, defer, delate, design, exhibit, extend, give, hand, hold out,

intend, issue, motion, move, oblate, overture, ply, prefer, present(ation), press, proffer, promise, propine, proposal, propose, proposition, propound, purpose, render, rendition, sacrifice, sell, show, submission, submit, suggestion, supply, take, tender, tendry, threaten, volunteer

excuse alibi

last ultimatum

oneself volunteer

proof verify

publicly jactitate

resistance defy

solemn pledge, promise, vow

OFFERING bali, bhut-bali, bid, contribution, corban, dali, dolly, donation, gift, libation, line, nuzzer, oblation, piacle, present, sacrifice, tribute, wares

burnt sacrifice

religious deodate, oblate, oblation, tithe

sacrificial hiera, sphagion

OFFERTORY anthem, collection, donation, hymn

OFFHAND abrupt, ad-lib, blase, breezy, brusque, careless, casual(ly), cavalier, curt, easygoing, extemporaneous(ly), extempore, glancing, glib, hasty, impromptu, improvised, informal, nonchalant, readily, unpremediated, unstudied

OFFICE advice, agency, appointment, bailiwick, berth, billet, branch, bureau, business, calling, camarin, capacity, ceremony, chair, chambers, charge, chore, closet, commission, daftar, dataria, department, discharge, diwani, drostdy, dufter, duty, edility, favor, function, headquarters, job, metier, operation, place, position, post, pystery, room, service, shop, situation, station, stint, studio, study, task, trust, warning, wike(n), work

boy chokra

chief boss, manager

clerical cassock

comb. acy, ate

deprive of depose, impeach

divine akoluthia, breviary

ecclesiastic benefice, frock,

matins, service, sext, vespers

help clerk, duftery, secretary, staff, stenographer, typist

machine addressograph, calculator, comptometer, computer, copier, dictaphone, stenotype, typewriter, xerox

morning matins, orthron, orthros

politics backstabbing

priestly sacerdocy

public archeion, bureau, government

purchase or *sale* barratry

put in again reelect, reinstate, reseat

remove from impeach, unseat

-seeker candidate, nominee, pol

stamp dater, meter, sealer

symbol of mace, verge

timekeepers pennyhole

whispering confessional

OFFICEHOLDER bureaucrat, incumbent, official, placeman, winner

OFFICER adjutant, agent, alcade, alderman, alnager, ameen, amin, apparitor, avener, bailie, bailiff, beadle, binbashi, bulldog, captain, cashier, command, conduct, constable, controller, cop, deputy, dewan, direct, diwan, exon, fang, feodary, functionary, general, governor, jailor, jemadar, kleagle, leader, lictor, macer, manager, mate, minister, mustang, parnas, policeman, sanctum, schepen, seneschal, sheriff, shikken, steward, tahsildar, tindal, tipstaff, voght

assistant aide, deputy, yeoman

bardic druid

chief daroga, dewan, diwan, nasi, parnas

church See CHURCHMAN.

college beadle, bursar, dean

customs douanier, gager, gauger, jerquer, shark, tidesman

future cadet

group brass, cadre, corps, elite

judicial assessor, comptroller, recorder, treasurer

law bailiff, bobby, constable, cop, coroner, detective, flic,

gendarme, marshal, patrolman, policeman, sheriff, trooper
local alderman, bailie, burgess, grieve
military See ARMY *officer*, NAVY *officer*.
minor chinovnik
petty beadle, bureaucrat, yeoman
police alytarch, captain, detective, javert, kotwal, runner, sbirro, searcher, thanadar
presiding archon, auditor, chairman, emcee, moderator, president, speaker
public alderman, burgomaster, commissar, congressman, councilman, judge, maire, mayor, minister, notary, podesta, selectman, vizier, warden
ship's See SHIP *officer*.
stable avener
staff adjutant, aide, redtab, tab
state ambassador, consul, minister, secretary
subordinate exon
warrant boatswain, bosun
youngest boots
OFFICIAL (See also OFFICER.) aedile, ag(h)a, almoner, amlah, approved, archon, atabeg, authoritative, bashaw, blimp, bureaucratic, burgomaster, calapha, canonical, cathedral, censor, ceremonious, certain, chamberlain, chancellor, clerk, dignitary, doge, edile, eponym, executive, fonctionaire, formal, functionary, governor, hajib, hazzan, herald, jurat, kuan, kwan, legitimate, lord, magistrate, magnate, mandarin, marshal, mayor, minister, missus, nazir, orthodox, panjandrum, placeman, premier, president, prevot, prexy, prime minister, pristaw, proctor, professional, prytanis, rabmag, referee, rightful, sahib, sanctioned, satrap, secretary, selectman, syndic, taotai, taoyin, tribune, true, verger, vip, wedana
administrative executive, gerega, reeve
assistant aid(e), deputy
blundering dogberry

city alderman, councilman, crier, manager, marshal, mayor
civil bailiff, constable, governor, judge, marshal, mayor, patrolman, policeman, president
corrupt grafter
decree fiat, ukase, writ
despotic satrap
excise revenooer, revenuer
minor amala, satrap
permit visa, vise
OFFICIATE act, administer, anoint, celebrate, chrism, confirm, function, impose, minister, perform, preside, serve, supply
OFFICIOUS aggressive, arrogant, assertive, busy, cool, demanding, dutiful, formal, forthy, forward, impertinent, impudent, interfering, intrusive, kind, meddlesome, meddling, obliging, obtrusive, pert, pompous, pushy, pragmatic, saucy, tampering
OFFING aftertime, distance, future, futurity, horizon
OFFISH clammy, reticent, rude, stiff, unapproachable, upstage
OFFSCOURINGS dregs, filth, garbage, leftovers, mud, offal, refuse, remainders, riff-raff, rubbish, scurf, wretch
OFFSET adjust, antidote, balance, cancel, compensate, complement, contra, counter(act), counterpoise, counterweight, cushion, equalize, negate, negative, neutralize, nullify, offshoot, poise, print, propagule, recompense, redeem, slab, split, start, step
OFFSHOOT adjunct, apophysiary, bough, branch, byproduct, descendant, effect, filiation, get, issue, limb, member, outgrowth, part, progeny, prong, pup, ramification, result, rod, scion, sion, son, sprig, sprout
OFFSPRING bairnteam, brat, brood, child(ren), chit, daughter, descendant, dustee, effect, foster, fruit, fry, generation, geniture, griqua, heir, imp, increase, issue, junior, kid, kin, line-

age, monisco, mustafina, nishada, origin, outcome, posterity, produce, product, progeny, result, scion, seed, son, source, spawn, youngster
comb. proli
OFTEN common(ly), customarily, frequent(ly), generally, ordinarily, recurrently, repeatedly, unseldom, usually
OG thomas shadwell
OGASAWARA *island* bonin
OGEE cyma, gula, molding, talon
OGGANITION growl, snarl
OGIER *enemy* saracens
OGLE coquetry, examine, eye, flirt, gaze, glance, goggle, leer, look, marlock, mash, scrutinize, see, smicker, stare
OGPU *successor* nkvd
OGRE afreet, afrit, bogey, bogie, bogle, bogy, brute, bugaboo, bugbear, demon, devil, dwarf, ghoul, giant, goblin, hobgoblin, hugon, lamkin, lamminin, linkin, monster, scarecrow, specter, spectre, spirit, terror, windigo, yaksha
shout fee-faw-fum
OGYGES *father* boeotus, poseidon
kingdom attica, boeotia, thebes
OGYIAN aged, ancient, primeval
sea nymph calypso
OHAD *father* simeon
O'HARA, JOHN *novel* appointment in sammara, butterfield eight
O'HARA, SCARLETT *home* tara
lover rhett butler
OHEL *father* zerubbabel
O. HENRY *william* porter
OHIO *capital* columbus
city akron, alliance, ashland, ashtabula, athens, berea, bluffton, cadiz, canton, cincinnati, cleveland, columbus, dayton, elyria, findlay, fostoria, fremont, huntington, kent, kettering, lakewood, lancaster, lima, lorain, marietta, marion, massillon, newark, niles, norwood, painesville, parma, piqua, portsmouth, rocky river, sandusky, steu-

benville, struthers, tiffin, toledo, vermilion, warren, willoughby, willowick, wooster, xenia, youngstown, zanesville
college antioch, bowling green, defiance, dennison, hiram, kent, kenyon, oberlin, marietta, wittenberg, wooster, xavier
county cuyahoga, erie, hamilton, lucas, miami, ross, seneca, stark, summit
indian erie, wyandot
lake erie
native buckeye
nickname buckeye state
peak campbell hill
port cleveland, lorain, toledo
president garfield, grant, harding, harrison, hayes, mckinley, taft
river cuyahoga, maumee, miami, muskingum, scioto
river, city on cincinnati, east liverpool, henderson, marietta, owensboro
river tributary cumberland, monongahela, tennessee, wabash
sandstone bereagrit
section western reserve
state bird cardinal
state flower carnation
state tree buckeye
OHM *millionth* microhm
OIDEMIA butterbill, butternose, coot, scoter
OIL (See also *kind,* below.) aceite, anele, anoint, balm, ben, bergamot, blubber, bribe(ry), cardol, carvacrol, cedrium, chrism, coumaran, cream, crude, erigeron, essence, eupion, fat, flatter(ry), fuel, ghee, gingerol, grease, inunct, lanolin, lard, lube, lubricate, medicate, myrrhol, oleo, oleum, olium, painting, petrol(eum), phlorol, phthalan, pinguefy, pomade, pomatum, pthhalan, retinol, sdravets, sebum, shortening, smear, smooth, suet, tallow, tetralin, ulyie, ulzie, unction, unguent, vetiver, zachun
almond-odored benzonitrile
animal blubber, butter, castor, cod-liver, doegling, dripping, fat, ghee, halibut-liver, haliver, lanolin, lard, margarine, menhaden,

neatsfoot, oleo, shortening, sperm, suet, tallow, whale
apply anoint
aromatic balm, nard
beetle meloe, meloid
berry olive
blasting nitroglycerine
bone olanin
bottle ampulla, cruce, cruet, cruize, cruse
butter ghee, oleo (margarine)
can bomb, oiler
cask rier
cedar alchitran, alkitran
city dhahran
coal kerosene, paraffin, photogen
coating cambouis
colorless anthranil, cetane
comb. elaio, oleo
consecrated chrism
derived from oleic
discoverer edwin drake
edible aceite, olive, peanut, sesame
exporting country abu dhabi, algeria, indonesia, iran, iraq, kuwait, nigeria, qatar, saudi arabia, venezuela
exporting group opec
field baku, ploesti
film alick
fish escolar, gurry
fixed cocum, kokum
flask olpe
flax linseed
fragrant attar, caffeol, caffeone, cedar, geraniol, irone, ottar
fuel kerosene, paraffin, photogen
gas blaugas
herb sesame
holy chrism
illuminating See *lamp,* below.
jar See *vessel,* below.
juniper alchitran, alkitran
kind aceite, ajowan, arachis, argan, asarum, attar, babassu, bambok, bay, behen, ben(ne), bito, buchu, cade, cajaput, carapa, cassia, castor, cerate, cetene, chia, coal, coconut, cohune, corn, costus, curcas, dika, eboe, ester, estragon, hop, kapok, kerosene, labdanum, lanolin, lard, linseed, mace, madia, mafura, myricia, neroli, njave, olive, orris, palm, paraffin, patchouli, peanut, perilla, ravison, rue,

rusa, safflower, soybean, sperm, tallow, tansy, til, train, tung, tunny, whale, xylitone, ylang-ylang
lamp argand, coal-oil, kerosene, lucigen, paraffin, photogen, pyronaphtha
linseed carron, linoleum
liquid olein
market teli
medicinal castor, mineral
mineral anthracene, benzine, carbolic, cetane, coal, colza, creosote, cresol, gasoline, kerosene, naphtha(lene), paraffin(e), petrolatum, petroleum
nut butternut, coconut, peanut, pyrularia, rabbitwood, virola
odoriferous ericinol
ointment oleamen
painting canvas
paint source linseed
palm oilberry
palms bribe, pay off, tip
pan sump
pert. oleic
pine frother
plant sesame
poisonous anemonol
poor middling
producing olifiant
prospector wildcatter
refuse shode
rock limestone, shale
rub with anoint, grease
salt bittern
scented balm
seed castor bean, cottonseed, linseed, ramtil, rapeseed, sapseed, sesame, teel, til
seed tree roka
shale torbanite
skin sebum
solid kikuel
source shale
torch lucigen
tree eboe, mahwa, poon, tung
turpentine camphene, camphine
vegetable absinthe, almond, anise(ed), avocado, bay, beechnut, camphor, candlenut, carapa, castor, citronella, clove, cocoabutter, colza, copaiba, copra, corn, cottonseed, croton, eucalyptus, flaxseed, fusel, kekuna, kokum-butter, lemon, linseed, macassar, maize, oleoresin, olive, peanut, pine-

tar, resin, sesame, spikenard, turpentine, walnut
vessel alabastos, alabastron, ampulla, aryballos, askos, cresset, cruce, cruet, cruize, cruse, drum, lekythos, olpe, rier, tanker
vulcanized factice
water fennel androl
well duster, gasser, gusher, wildcat
well, dry duster, gasser
well, 1st u s titusville
whale sperm
OILBIRD fatbird, guacharo
OILCLOTH linoleum
OILED anointed, drunk, stewed, tanked
OILEUS *kingdom* locris
son ajax, medon
OILSKIN raincoat, slicker, squam
OILSTONE hone, shale, whetstone
OILY adulatory, bland, blubbery, buttery, compliant, creamy, diplomatic, fat(ty), fawning, flattering, glib, greasy, hypocritical, ingratiating, insinuating, lardy, lubricative, lubricous, oleaginous, oleic, oleose, oleous, pinguid, plausible, sebaceous, servile, slick, slippery, smooth, soapy, suave, subservient, sycophantic, unctuous, unguinous
comb. lipar(o)
liquid aniline, bupleurol, octane, picamar, tar
OIME alas
OINTMENT balm, balsam, basilicon, benzocaine, carron, cerate, ceroma, chrism, cold cream, grease, lenitive, linament, money, mull, nard, oleate, paste, populeon, remedy, remolade, salve, spikenard, unction, unguent, vaseline, whitfield
application embrocation
base beeswax, petrolatum
biblical spikenard
dry xeromyron, xeromyrum
fragrant nard, valerian
hair pomade, pomatum
mercurial blue-butter
of gods ambrosia
oil carron, cerate, oleamen
veterinary remolade, remoulade
wax cerate
OISE *city on* compiegne
OISIN See OSSIAN.

OJIBWAY chippewa, saulteur
hero hiawatha
sage jessakeed
secret order meda, mide
OJO oasis, spring
OKAPI giraffine
OK(AY) acceptable, accurate, affirmative, agreement, all right, approval, approve, assent, correct, great, groovy, jake, okeh, ratify, right, roger, sanction, yes
OKINAWA *capital* naha
city shuri
OKLAHOMA arlington, game, rummy
capital guthrie, oklahoma city
city ada, ardmore, bartlesville, blackwell, duncan, enid, fort sill, guthrie, guymon, hugo, idabel, lawton, mcalester, miami, muskogee, ponca city, salupa, shawnee, stillwater, tulsa
college cameron, langston, phillips
county alfalfa, atoka, caddo, kay, okfuskee, okmulgee
indian apache, arapahoe, caddo, cherokee, chickasaw, choctaw, creek, delaware, iowa(y), kansa, kaw, kiowa, loup, osage, oto(e), ottawa, pawnee, ponca, quapaw, seminole, shawnee, tawakoni, waco, wichita
lake atoka, eufaula, fort gibson, heyburn, hulah, keystone, markham ferry, oologah, pensacola, tenkiller, thunderbird, wister
national park platt
native okie, sooner
nickname boomer, sooner
oil field, early glenn pool, redfork
peak black mesa
range ouachita, ozark
region cimarron
reservoir See *lake,* above.
river arkansas, canadian, cimarron, grand, red, washita
state bird flycatcher
state flower mistletoe
state tree redbud
university norman, stillwater
OKRA bamia, bandicoy, bandikai, bendee, bendy, gob(b), gombo, gubbo, gumbo, mallow, ochra, portia tree, soup
OLAM eternity, infinity, perpetuity, universe

OLD aeonian, aged, alt, ancient, anile, antediluvean, antiquated, antique, archaic, auld, back-number, dated, decrepit, doddering, doting, eild, eld(erly), erst, experienced, feeble, former, fossil, fusty, gray, has-been, hoary, infirm, matriarchal, mature, medieval, model-t, moldering, mo(u)ldy, mucid, musty, obsolete, ogygian, ole, patriarchal, primal, primeval, primitive, quondam, rancid, seedy, senectuous, senescent, senile, shabby, stale, superannuated, trite, umwhile, venerable, weak, wintry, worn
abe lincoln
adam evil, original sin, wickedness
age anility, antiquity, autumn, codgerhood, debility, decline, decrepitude, dotage, infirmity, longevity, senect(i)tude, senescence, senility, winter
age, pert. elderly, geratic, gerontal, gerontic, senile
age study geriatrics, nostology
age symbol grasshopper
as methuselah, the hills
bailey court, gaol, jail, prisson
bay state massachusetts
blood and guts patton
boy alumnus, devil, fellow, man
bullion thomas hart benson
campaigner politician, veteran
cedar brown madder, tanagra
clothesman poco
clootie devil
comb. palae(o), pale(o)
curiosity shop character brass, codlin, fred, garland, jarley, little nell, nubbles, quilp, sally, sampson, short, swiveller, trent
dominion state virginia
english black-letter
english brown bronc(h)o
faithful geyser
-fashioned ancient, antiquated, antique, archaic, back number, corny, crinoline, dated, dowdy, fogram, fogrum, fusty, has-been, horse-and-buggy, intelligent, model-t, moldy, moth-

eaten, musty, obsolescent, obsolete, offbeat, old-hat, outmoded, out of date, passe, precocious, primitive, quaint, seedy, stale, timeworn, tintype, vintage
fogy conservative, dotard, stodgy
franklin state tennessee
glory flag, stars and stripes
goat lecher
gooseberry demon, devil, satan
growing senescent
hand vet(eran)
harry devil, satan
hat banal, hackneyed, passe, platitude, threadbare, trite
hickory andrew jackson
ironsides constitution
ironsides adversary hms guerriere
ironsides captain isaac hull
ironsides commodore edward preble
ironsides hero john hogan, steven decatur
ironsides sister ship philadelphia
ironsides supplier paul revere
kinderhook van buren
king cole preceder asclepoid
lady of threadneedle street bank of england
-line conservative, established
line state maryland
maid celibate, lapwing, periwinkle, prude, skate, spinster, spinstress, thornback, zinnia
maid's-bonnet lupine
maid's-nightcap geranium
maid's-pink corn-cockle, soapwort
man (See also MAN *old*.) cuckoo, kangaroo, rosemary, southernwood, whitebeard
man-and-woman houseleek
man cactus cephalocerus, pilocereus
man's-beard clematis, equisetum, fringe-tree, saxifrage, traveler's-joy
man's-eyebrow sundew
man's-flannel mullein
man's-head cactus, carnation
man's-root spikenard
nick devil, satan
noll oliver cromwell
north state north carolina
poker devil, satan
pretender james iii

rough and ready zachary taylor
rowley charles ii
salt mariner, sailor, tar
scratch devil
sledge all-fours, game, highlow jack, pitch, seven-up
sod eire, erin, ireland
soldier butt, veteran
squaw calloo, callow, clangula, cockawee, coween, diver, ducker, hound, longtail, mommy, quandy, seaduck, sharptail, southerly
story platitude
testament book See Bible book.
testament division apocrypha, hagiographa, hexateuch, kethubhim, ketubim, nebiim, octateuch, pentateuch, prophets, septuagint
first 5 books pentateuch
first 8 books octateuch
testament geneologies begats
testament giants anak(im)
3-stars ulysses grant
-timer kamaaina, native, veteran
-time(s) ago, eld, former, late, quondam, past, yore
wives tale lore, superstition
woman See WOMAN *old*.
woman's bitter fiddlewood
woman's tree quiina
OLDEN ancient, bygone, former, medieval
OLDER alder, ancestor, elder, forefather, precessor, prior, senior, staler
OLDEST dean, eldest, firstborn, primogenital
OLDWIFE alewife, balistes, bream, duck, fish, menhaden, parrotfish, pompany, scarus, spot, squaw, triggerfish
OLD WORLD *animal* genet, antelope
ape baboon, catarrhina
bird coot, coucal, cuckooshrike, curlew, demoiselle, glareola, grackle, greenshank, grignet, myna, roller, scoter, teal, terek, thickhead, thickknee, wagtail, wall-creeper, whistler
crane demoiselle
cuckoo coucal
curlew bustard, marlin
dish tansy
falcon saker
fern ceterach
figwort iceplant

finch brambling
flycatacher grignet, parisoma
garganay teal
goat ibex
grass alang, imperata
herb aconite, alliaria, anchusa, anthemis, arctium, armoracia, asperugo, asperula, butterbur, centaury, coriander, galeopsis, glory-of-the-snow, henbane, horseradish, isatis, madder, madwort, reseda, sabatia, tansy, urginea
lizard agama, chalcides, chameleon, seps
mint melissa, phlomis
orchid arachnite, cordula
partridge alectoris, caccabis
pear pyrus
pert. gerontogeous
plant anthyllis, asperugo, axseed, coronilia, crownvetch, kidney-vetch, madwort, ragwort, tarragon
plantain ispaghul
sandpiper redshank
shrub alangium, arrimby, cotoneaster, genista, pavena, peabush, wild pepper, withania, zelkova
squill wood-hyacinth
swift apus
thrush chat, redstart, whinehat
tree balanite
vine balsam apple
warbler chiffchaff, trochilus, willow-wren
weed candlewick, flannelleaf, mullein, velvet-plant
OLE acclaim, bravo, cheer, huzzah, old, yell
OLEA ironwood, maire, olive, tree
OLEAGINOUS bland, fawning, OILY, sanctimonious, sleek, soapy, unctuous
OLEANDER bay, ceylonrose, dogbane, laurel, nerium, rhododendrum, rosebay, shrub
OLEARIA ake-ake, sandalwood, starwort
OLENT fragrant, odorous, scented
OLENUS trilobite
father zeus
wife lethaea
OLEO (MARGARINE) butterine, marge, spread
OLEORESIN anime, apiol, balsam, copaiba, elemi, galipot, gurjun, iridin, lab-

danum, tacamahac, tolu(s), turpentine

OLFACT See SMELL.

OLFACTION esphresis, osmesis, smelling

OLFACTORY *organ* nose

OLIBANUM *perfume* cense

OLID fetid, malodorous, reeky, smelly

OLIGARCHY aristocracy, plutocracy

OLIGIST hematite

OLIO chowchow, collection, hash, hodgepodge, medley, melange, mishmash, mixture, ollapodrida, pasticcio, potpourri, show, stew, vaudeville

OLIPRANCE jollity, merrymaking, romp

OLIVE barouni, brunet, button, citrine, devilwood, drupe, escutcheon, fruit, lierre, morillon, olea(aster), oxhorn, pimola, reseda, tree
branch child, descendant, eiresione, irenicon, overture
brown bronze-nude
color drab
eye pimiento
fly dacus
freestone manzanilla
fruit drupe
inferior moron
oil, comb. elaio
oil lees amurca
oil substitute argan
pert. oleaceous
residue sanza
stuffed pimola
wild oleaster
wood brun-dore

OLIVER hammer, holliper, noll
bark black sassafras
beloved celia
brother orlando
father fenier, rowland de boys
friend roland
leader charlemagne
servant adam, dennis
sword hauteclaire
twist character artful dodger, bill sikes, brownlow, bumble, dawkins, fagin, fang, mrs maylie, monks, nancy rose

OLIVIA *brother* sebastian
clown feste
servant fabian, maria
steward malvolio
suitor sir andrew aguecheek
uncle sir toby belch

OLLA document, jar, jug, olio, ollapodrida, palmleaf, pot, puchera, puchero
-podrida hash, hodgepodge, medley, mixture, olio, potpourri

OLLIE *friend* kukla

OLM proteus, salamander

OLSZTYN east prussia

OLYMPIA *husband* bireno

OLYMPIAN aloof, god, goddess, heavenly, majestic, splendid

OLYMPIC GAMES *police officer* alytarch
sacred grove altis
site elis
sled luge
statue zan
symbol torch

OLYMPICIST athlete

OLYMPIO victor hugo

OLYMPUS heaven, paradise, sky, valhalla
cupbearer ganymede
god, goddess See GREEK god, goddess.
hindu meru
huntress artemis
king zeus
pert. celestial, exalted, godlike, heavenly, majestic, olympic
physician paeon
queen hera
sacred grove altis
scandinavian asgard
site macedonia
vale tempe

OMAN *canal* fallaj
cape madraka
capital masqat, muscat
city ashkhara, fida, marbat, masqat, matrah, nigwa, salala(h), suwaih, tinouf, wazit
coin gaj, ghazi, goz, mahmudi
dynasty albusaid
island masera
language arabic, baluchi
leader tarek
peak akhdar, hafit, harim, nakhl, sham, tayin
people adnan, baluchi, qahtan
port dubai
ruler bin-taimur, gaboos, iman, said, seyyid
well qarani

OMAR KHAYYAM *country* iran, persia
quatrain rubai
translator fitzgerald

work rubaiyat

OMASUM belly, bouk, fardel, manyplies, psalterium, stomach

OMBER, OMBRE calabrasella, game, hombre, la mouch, mediator, quadrille, quintelle, roi rendu, solo, psitzeln, tresillo
card basto
term charivary, chicoree, codillio, consolation, contentment, degout, devole, discord, estrapade, fanatique, forcee, gano, guinguette, hazard, miliro, remise, repuesto, yeux

OMEGA end, last

OMELET egg foo yong, frittata

OMEN abode, adumbration, augur(y), auspice, black cat, bode(r), divination, divine, forbode, foreshadow, foretoken, forewarn(ing), freet, freit, handsel, harbinger, indication, intimation, iya, mark, messenger, misgiving, portent, prediction, premonition, presage, prognostic(ation), promise, prophecy, rainbow, sign, soothsay, token, symptom, warning, weird, whate
interpretation conjecture

OMENTUM caul, epiploon, web, zirbus

OMER sheaf, umber
10 epha(h)

OMINOUS baleful, baneful, boding, direful, doomful, fateful, foreboding, illomened, inauspicious, malefic, malign, menacing, portentous, prediction, premonitory, prognostic, prophetic, shvartz(er), sinister, threatening

OMISSION balk, cut, default, disregard, elision, ellipsis, error, exclusion, failure, guilt, lapse, miss, neglect, oversight, preterition, sin, syncope, want
mark apostrophe, caret, dele, ellipse
pretended paralepsis, paralipsis
tacit silence

OMIT bate, bypass, cancel, cut(out), dele, delete, discard, disregard, drop, efface, elide, eliminate, erase, evade, exclude, expunge, forget, ignore, kill, let go, miss, neglect, overlook, pass, pretermit, skip, slight, spare, want

OMNI all, everywhere, omniscient

OMNIBUS barge, busboy, carrier, collection, comprehensive, herdic, jogger, kittereen, public vehicle

OMNIPEN ampicillin

OMNIPOTENCE might, power

OMNIPOTENT almighty, arrant, divine, mighty, omnipresent, omniscient, powerful, unlimited

OMNIPRESENT all over, everywhere, infinite, pervasive, prevalent, ubiquitary, ubiquitous

OMNISCIENCE god, knowledge, pansophy

OMNISCIENT all-knowing, all-wise, learned, pansophic(al), powerful, smart, wise

OMNITUDE allness, totality, universality

OMNIUM-GATHERUM dance, hodgepodge, mess, miscellany, mixture

OMNIVOROUS devouring, gluttonous, greedy, pamphagous

OMOO *sequel* typee

OMPHALE *consort* hercules, tmolus
father iardanus
kingdom lydia
son agelaus, lamus

OMPHALOS altar, boss, center, core, focus, heart, hub, middle, midst, navel, nob, nucleus, umbilicus

OMRI *offspring* ahad, athaliah
successor ahab

ON above, ahead, along, anenst, anent, atop, attached, away, concerning, forth, forward, near, onward, toward, upon, willing
account of because, for, over
all counts utterly, wholly
all sides about, around, everywhere, extensively
and off changeably, irregularly, now and then, occasionally, sporadically
and on constantly, continually, continuously, ever, forever, increasingly, tedious

a par equal
board agreeing, associated, joined, here, present, with
call handy, payable, ready
comb. epi
condition that provided, providing
dit gossip, report, rumor, they say
easy street comfortable, prosperous
edge anxious, apprehensive, bothered, critical, nervous, upset
end continually, continuously, vertically
fire ablaze, ardent, burning, emotional, gleaming, hot, zealous
guard careful, cautious, suspicious, vigilant, watchful
hand along, here, in stock, present
high aloft, risen
ice absolute, actual, assured
pins and needles anxious, concerned, nervous
purpose deliberately, intentionally
that account hence, therefore
the ball active, alert, alive, all there, bright, concentrating, nimble, observant, operating, prepared, prompt, quick, ready, trying, with it
the beam groovy, hep, straight, with it
the blink ailing, busted, broken, disabled, indisposed, out of order
the contrary but, instead, per contra, rather
the dot now, punctually, suddenly, today
the double fast, quickly, swiftly
the fence neutral, uncommitted, undecided, wavering
the go busy, enroute, moving, nomadic, roaming, roving, traveling, wandering
the house free, gratis
the lam fugitive
the level candid, fair, honest, reliable, square, true
the lookout after, alert, observant, vigilant, watchful
the march aggressive, attacking, invading, prowling, wandering, warring
the nose accurate, precise, punctual
the other hand again, al-

though, but, contrarily, contrariwise, contrary, however, laterally, nevertheless, nonetheless, rather
the other side across, over
the road abroad, active, away, bumming, busy, enroute, forwards, selling, toward, traveling, wandering
the rocks aground, bankrupt, destitute, high and dry, iced, stranded
the run active, busy, fleeing, frantic, fugitive, overworked, wandering
the side beside, bonus, broadside, clandestine, extra, moonlighting, secret
the spot dangerous, embarrassed, here, promptly, suddenly, today, trapped
the square or *up and up* fair, honest, open, true
the verge about, approximate(ly), imminent, near
the wagon abstaining, abstemious, bone-dry, dry, non-drinking
the whole altogether, by and large, generally, substantially
time prompt, punctual, ready
tiptoe anxious, eager, edgy, quietly, sneaky, stealthy
to aboard, atop, aware, hep
top of above, ahead, aloft
your way begone, git, scram

ONAGER alacran, ass, catapult, gour, kiang, k(o)ulam, scorpion, sling

ONAM *son* jada, shammai

ONAN tsonecan
consort tamar
father judah

ONASSIS *consort* jaqueline kennedy, maria callas
nickname ari, daddy-o, telis

ONCE ago, aince, anes, anew, ene, erst(while), ever, former(ly), immediately, in short, past, quondam, semel(l), sometime, together, umquhile, umwhile, une fois, whenever, whensoever, whilom, yance
around cycle
in a while now and then, occasionally, sometimes
more again, and, anew, bis, echo, encore, iterum, newly, repeat(edly), yet
-over scrutiny

ONCOMING advancing, approach(ing), beginning, forward, progressive

ONDE ondoyant, ondy, wavy

ONDINE *lover* hans, palemon

ONE absolute, ace, ain, alone, alpha, ane, anybody, assimilate, common, eins, entity, first, ichi, individual, integer, ite, man, monad, only, person, same, single (ton), singular, sole, solitary, tae, tane, tene, this, together, una, unbroken, undivided, une, unit, unite (d), unity, unmarried, uno, whole, yae, yan, yen, yin, you

after another alternately, consecutively, serially, seriatim, successively, tandem

and ½, comb. sesqui

become merge

behind another tandem

berry hackberry

by one apiece, each, indianfile, separately, single-file, singly

-celled elocular

-chambered monothalamous, unicameral

-colored monochroic, monochromatic

comb. ehno, idio, mon(o), uni

evil devil, satan, shaitan, sheitan, wond

-eye diamond king, heart jack, spade jack

-eyed monocular, monophtalmic, monoptic(al)

-eyed man arimasp

-footed monopode, uniped

for the book marvel, wonder

-gilled monobranchiate

-horse inferior, little, petty, second-rate, small

-hoss shay deacon's masterpiece

hoss shay author holmes

hundred and 44 gross

hundred percent all, pure, total

hundred-year-old centenarian

-liner gag, jest

-master sloop

more another

more than plural

name meaning mona, una

-night stand gig

out of many e pluribus unum

-sided askew, biased, big-

oted, eccentric, excentric, ex parte, partial, prejudiced, unbalanced, unilateral, unjust

spot ace, buck, dollar

tenth tithe

-time erstwhile, former(ly), past, quondam

thousand grand, mil, mille

to-one biunique

24th carat, karat

up ahead, winning

-winged monopterous

year old annotine, annotinous

year record annal

ONEFOLD guileless, linear, simple, sincere, single

ONEGITE amethyst, gem (stone)

ONEIDA *founder* noyes

O'NEILL, EUGENE *drama* ah wilderness, all god's chillun got wings, anna christie, bound east for cardiff, emperor jones, great god brown, hairy ape, strange interlude, the iceman cometh

O'NEILL, ROSE *drawing* kewpie doll

ONENESS agreement, aloneness, concord, constancy, identity, sameness, singularity, uniformity, union, unity

ONER ace, best, expert, lalapaloosa, topnotcher, unicum

ONEROUS arduous, burdensome, cumbersome, cumbrous, difficult, distressing, dull, exacting, grievous, hard, heavy, hefty, irksome, laborious, oppressive, ponderous, troublesome, vexing, weighty

ONFALL attack, onset

ONIAS *kin* jason, simon

ONION allium, ayegreen, bermuda, boll, bulb, cepa, chibol, cibol, cipa, eschalot(e), holleke, leek, lily, pearl, pickler, plant, porrett, scallion, shallot, spanish, valencia, vegetable

bulb button, set

bulbless scallion

cooked with lyonnaise

disease bulb rot, smudge, yellow dwarf

group rope

-like cepaceous, chive, leek, shallot

roll bialy

sauce lyonnaise, soubise

set button

small eschalot(te), pearl, scallion, shallot

string reeve, trace

strong skunk-egg

wild crow-garlic, rush-garlic

ONIONSKIN india-paper

ONLEPY only, sole, solitary, unmarried

ONLOOKER audience, beholder, bystander, eyewitness, gazer, kibitzer, rubberneck, spectator, tsitser, viewer, watcher, witness

ONLY afald, allenarly, alone, anerly, arrah, barely, best, but, chief, entirely, excepting, exclusively, extremely, finest, lone, lonely, mere(ly), nob(b)ut, onlepy, save, simple, simply, singly, sole(ly), solitary, uniquely, wholly

just barely, hardly

ONNOPHRIS osiris

ONO yoko

ONOMASTICON dictionary, glossary, lexicon, list, vocabulary, wordbook

ONRUSH attack, birr, course, flow, tide(way)

ONSET, ONSLAUGHT assault, attack, attempt, beginning, blast, blitz, braid, brattle, brunt, charge, commencement, dash, dint, encounter, faird, fard, frush, incursion, insult, invasion, lash, offense, offensive, onfall, outbreak, raid, rese, rush, siserara, start, storm, stour, thrust, venue

ONSTEAD farmhouse, homestead, offices, steading

ONTARIO See also CANADA.

canal rideau, trent

capital toronto

city galt, hamilton, kingston, kitchener, london, ottawa, windsor

lake simcoe

river st lawrence

ONTO aboard, atop

ONUPHIS osiris

ONUS blame, burden, charge, duty, encumbrance, impediment, incubus, load, obligation, oppression, responsibility, task, weight

ONWARD advancing, ahead, ake, along, away, charge,

en avant, forth, forward, future, march, progressing, progressive
comb. proso
ONYCHOPHOR See ARTHROPOD.
ONYX chalcedony, gem, jasponyx, mineral, nicol(l)o, onix, onycha, onychin, pus, quartz, sardonyx, tecali
marble alabaster
pert. onychin
use cameo
zodiac sign aquarius
OOCYTE egg, gamete, gametocyte, progamete
OODLES abundance, barrelful, gobs, heap(s), lashings, lots, much, plenty, quantity, scads, slithers
OOF money
OOFLESS broke
OOFY rich, wealthy
OOLAK boat, wollock
OONT camel, mole
OOP bind, join, unite
OOZE bog, drip, escape, exudate, exudation, exude, filter, gleet, gook, leak, marsh, mire, muck, mud, percolate, perspire, seep, sipe, sleech, slew, slime, slue, sop, squdge, strain, sweat, swelter, transude, trickle, weeze, wese
OOZING seepage, spewing, squdgy, weeping, weepy
OOZY miry, muddy, quaggy, seepy, sleechy, spongy, washy
OPAH cravo, fish, kingfish, lamprid, mariposa, moonfish, soko, sunfish
OPAL ceraunium, fiorite, gem, geyserite, girasole, hyalite, isopyre, jaspopal, menilite, stone
colorless hyalite
-eye greenfish
fire girasol
impure isopyre, menilite
symbol of hope
variety cacholong, fire, harlequin, lechosos, menilite, noble, pitch, resin
OPALESCENT chatoyant, cymophanous, iridescent, irisated, opaline, pearly, prismatic
OPALIA *festival of* ops
OPAQUE abstruse, adiaphonous, becloud, bemist, cloud (ed), crass, dark(en), darkling, dense, dim, dirty, dull,

dusk(y), eyeshade, film, fog, fuliginous, gloomy, haze, imperceptive, impervious, intransparent, mist, muddy, murk(y), nubilous, obfuscate, obscure, obtuse, opacate, opacous, purblind, roiled, roily, smoke, smoky, stupid, thick, turbid, unintelligible, vague
OPATA endeve, jova, piman, xova
OPEN 3 cut, dup, pop, rip, tap 4 ajay, bald, bare, fair, free, part, rent, rift, rive, show, slit, tear, undo, vent 5 agape, alert, apert, begin, blank, bluff, break, broad, burst, chink, clear, crack, empty, frank, lance, loose, naive, naked, overt, plain, spald, split, start, unbar, untie, widen 6 actify, breach, broach, candid, cleave, divide, expand, expose, extend, gaping, honest, liable, patent, porous, public, reveal, rimose, simple, spread, uncase, uncork, unfold, unlock, unseal, untied, unwrap, vacant 7 artless, blossom, cordial, develop, dispart, display, enlarge, evident, exhibit, explain, exposed, liberal, natural, obvious, rupture, sincere, subject, unblock, unclasp, unclose, unravel, visible, yawning 8 absolute, activate, amenable, apparent, commence, disclose, dispread, generous, initiate, manifest, patulous, separate, telltale, unfasten, unsealed 9 available, dehiscent, disclosed, impartial, ingenuous, outspoken, sensitive, uncertain, undecided, unfeigned, unguarded 10 aboveaboard, accessible, divaricate, forthright, liberalize, responsive, unreserved 11 transparent, unprotected 12 unobstructed, unrestricted
air alfresco, outdoor
air, pert. subdial
-and-shut assured, certain, manifest, obvious, simple
-bill anastomus, bird, stork
bursting dehiscence
cloth scutch
country campagna, cham-

paign, outdoors, plains, veldt, weald, wold
-door access, generosity, hospitality, liberality, public, welcome
-eyed alert, attentive, awake, curious, discerning, expectant, receptive, staring, vigilant, watchful
fire attack, begin, invade, start
gape dehisce
-handed free, generous, indulgent, liberal, munificent, receptive, unstinting
-hearted artless, candid, cordial, frank, generous, indulgent, ingenuous, liberal
-minded accessible, amenable, interested, persuadable, receptive, recipient, responsive, tolerant
-mouthed agape, aghast, attentive, breathless, clamorous, curious, expectant, gaping, greedy, ravenous, spellbound, thunderstruck, vociferous
out disclose, enlarge, ream, reveal
partly ajar
-sesame foothold, incantation, ingress, password, toehold
sky, pert. subdial
slightly ajar
the door admit, begin, facilitate, induce, initiate, prepare, receive
to question doubtful, dubious, unsure
up attack, begin, confess, crack, develop, disclose, reveal, start, speed, yawn
wide agape, dehiscent, fullblown, yawn(ing)
OPENER aperient, clavis, corkscrew, debut, inauguration, key, knob, latch (string), passepartout, screw, starter
OPENING 3 bay, bur, cut, eye, gap, job, yat 4 arch, bung, burr, cave, dawn, door, drop, flaw, gape, gate, gulf, hole, loop, pass, pore, rent, rift, rima, slit, slot, tear, vent, void, yawn, yeat 5 brack, break, canal, chasm, chink, cleft, crack, first, hatch, inlet, intro, mouth, sinus, space, split, start, stoma 6 access, areole, breach, cavity,

chance, cranny, eyelet, fusuma, gambit, hiatus, meatus, nozzle, outlet, recess, sluice, socket, wicket, window **7** apopyle, crevice, fissure, foramen, keyhole, loculus, orifice, passage, scupper, scuttle, stomata, vacancy **8** aperture, bull's eye, entrance, fenestra, fontanel, hatchway, loophole, porthole, position **9** beginning **10** initiation, interstice **11** development, opportunity, perforation **12** commencement, introduction

anatomical antrum, atrium, bur(r), canal, cardia, fossicle, mouth, nares, nostril, ostiol, pore, pylorus, sinus, stoma(ta), ventricle, vesicle
arched alcove, arcade
crescent-shaped lunette
enlarge drill, ream
erosional fenster
escape meuse, muse
full of small porous
funnel-like choana
having fenestrate
having narrow stenopaic
having 2 biporose, biporous
small alveolus, chink, cranny, eyelet, forament, pinhole, pore, slit
wide dehiscent

OPENLY aboveboard, directly, en plein jour, face to face, frankly, freely, publicly, straight

OPENNESS candor, exposure, frankness, overtness, simplicity, susceptibility

OPENWORK ajour, bratticing, filigree, lace, net, tracery

OPERA africaine, aida, ballo in maschera, barber of seville, bartered bride, boheme, boris godounow, carmen, cavalleria rusticana, cid, coq d'or, cosi fan tutti, don giovanni, don quixote, elektra, ernani, euryanthe, falstaff, faust, favorita, fedora, fidelio, flying dutchman, forza del destino, fra diavolo, gioconda, gotterdammerung, hamlet, herodiade, lakme, lohengrin, louise, lucia de lammermoor, lucrezia borgia, madama butterfly, magic flute, manon lescaut, marriage of figaro, masked ball, meis-

tersinger, mignon, mikado, norma, orfeo, ot(h)ello, pagliacci, parsifal, prince igor, rheingold, rienzi, rigoletto, rondine, rosenkavalier, sadko, samson et dalila, siegfried, singspiel, sonnambula, tales of hoffmann, tannhauser, thais, tosca, traviata, tristan and isolde, trovatore, turandot, walkure, werther, william tell, wozzeck, zauberflote
cheer viva
comedian buffa, buffo
composer alfano, auber, beethoven, bellini, berlioz, bizet, boito, borodin, britten, charpentier, debussy, delibes, donizetti, dukas, flotow, gilbert, giordano, glinka, gluck, gounod, halevy, handel, humperdinck, krenek, leoncavallo, mascagni, massenet, menotti, meyerbeer, monteverdi, m(o)ussorgsky, mozart, offenbach, prokofieff, puccini, purcell, rimsky-korsakow, rossini, sabina, saint-saens, smetana, spontini, strauss, taylor, thomas, verdi, wagner, weber, wolf-ferrari
daytime soap(er)
division scena
early burletta
glass binocle, binoculars, jumelle, lorgnet(te)
hat See HAT *opera.*
horse western
house covent garden, la fenice, la scala, met, theatre
kind burletta, comic, horse, light, soap
part aria, recitative
singer alda, bori, callas, caruso, curci, diva, eames, farrar, flagstad, gigli, melba, moffo, patti, pons, steber, sutherland
16th century pastorale
song aria, cabaletta, cavatina, sortita
star diva
words libretto

OPERATE accomplish, act, affect, behave, carry on, conduct, deal, drive, effect, function, man(age), maneuver, manipulate, militate, order, perform, perk, pilot, play, proceed, push,

react, run, speculate, steer, tick, use, work
by hand manipulate

OPERATION action, affair (s), agency, conduct, deal, efficacy, execution, exercise, function, management, maneuver, manipulation, office, performance, plant, play, potency, practice, process, running, steering, surgery, transaction, work(ings)
comb. ectomy, stomy, tomy

OPERATIVE active, agent, artisan, artist, craftsman, detective, dynamic, effective, efficacious, efficient, fecund, fertile, fruitful, live, means, mechanic, worker, working, workman
beyond itself transeunt
for past retroactive

OPERATOR actor, agent, broker, cheat, conductor, creator, dealer, dentist, director, doctor, doer, driver, engineer, facient, handler, helmsman, jockey, macher, maker, manager, manipulator, mechanic, mountebank, performer, physician, pilot, player, quack, runner, schemer, speculator, steersman, success, surgeon, swinger, tooler, trader
poor plug

OPERCULUM aptychus, cover, eyestone, flap, fold, lid, mandible, onycha, opercle, plate

OPEROSE busy, diligent, laborious, painstaking, troublesome

OPHELIA *beloved* hamlet
brother laertes
father polonius

OPHELTES archemorus
father lycurgus
slayer serpent

OPHIDIAN See SNAKE.

OPHIO adder's-tongue, botrychium, fern, moonwort

OPHION *companion* cadmust
creator eurynome
offspring amycus

OPHIR *father* joktan

OPHIUCHUS aesculapius, serpentarius
parent apollo, coronis
star in delta, epsilon, yedposterior, yed-prior

OPHTHALMITIS athena

OPIATE (See also DRUG *addictive.*) anesthetic, anodyne, calmative, deaden, dope, dwale, hypnotic, narcotic, nepenthe, sedative, soporific, tranquilizer

OPINE account, adjudge, appraise, believe, conclude, consider, deem, estimate, hold, judge, reckon, remark, suppose, think

OPINION apprehension, assumption, attitude, avis, belief, censure, concept(ion), consideration, conviction, credo, decision, dictum, doctrine, dogma, doom, doxie, doxy, esteem, estimate, estimation, eye, feeling, idea, impression, judgment, light, mind, notion, observation, outlook, persuasion, point of view, prejudice, presumption, pulse, reaction, resolution, sense, sentiment, slant, tenet, theory, thesis, thinking, thought, trowing, vardi, vardy, view, voice, ween (ing)
erroneous misconception
expression of vote
false pseudodox
favorable esteem
fixed conviction
form judge
good broo
group anthology, symposium
having same homodox
pert. doxastic
preconceived bias, partipris, prejudice
professed credo, creed
religious credo, creed, doxy
sampling gallup poll, harris, neilsen
united unanimity
unorthodox heresy

OPINIONATED arbitrary, assertive, assured, certain, cocksure, dogmatic, highhanded, intransigent, obdurate, oracular, peremptory, positive, pragmatic, sanguine, stubborn, sure, uncompromising

OPIS *companion* artemis

OPIUM black king, chandoo, chandu, drug, heroin, hop, karakhan, mecon(ium), morphine, mud, opie, thebaine, toxicant
addiction thebaism
alkaloid codein(e), morphine, narcotin(e), papaverine

camphorate paregoric
comb. mecono
concentrate heroin
derivative meconic
extract chandoo, chandu
poppy papaver
seed maw
source poppy
tincture laudanum, paregoric

OPOSSUM didelphis, marsupial, oyapock, phalanger, quica, sarigue, tacuacine, vulpine, yapo(c)k
mouse marmosa, marmo(u)se, tacuicine
shrimp mysid, mysoid
water yapock, yapok

OPPIDAN civic, etonian, townsman, urban

OPPILATE block, clog, fill, obstruct, stop up

OPPONENT adversary, antagonist, anti, assailant, competitor, enemy, foe, rival
imaginary windmill

OPPORTUNE appropriate, apropos, apt, auspicious, convenient, expedient, favorable, felicitous, fitting, fortunate, happy, lucky, pat, prompt, propitious, quick, ready seasonable, suitable, timely, well-timed

OPPORTUNIST chameleon, creeper, early bird, operator, politician, sharp(er), timeserver, trimmer

OPPORTUNITY advantage, angle, audience, break, chance, facility, freedom, hent, hint, juncture, leisure, liberty, occasion, opening, place, room, scope, season, sele, shot, show, slant, tide, time

OPPOSAL examination, opposition, posing, puzzle

OPPOSE antagonize, assail, attack, balk, bar, battle, beard, block, buck, challenge, clash, combat, compare, compete, conflict, confront, contend, contest, contradict, contrair, contrapose, contrast, contravene, cope, counter(act), cross, defend, defy, deny, disapprove, discountenance, encounter, expose, face, fight, front, gainsay, go against, impugn, lock horns, match, mate, meet, occur, offer, offset, oppugn, pit,

polarize, protest, rebel, rebut, repel, repugn, repulse, resist, stickle, storm, subtend, take issue, thwart, traverse, violate, withstand
stubbornly calcitrate, kick

OPPOSED adverse, against, alien, anti, antipathetic, antithetic, averse, balky, con, contradictory, contrary, counter, fronted, hostile, inimical, met, nay, negative, opposite, pitted, renitent, rival

OPPOSITE abreast, absonant, adverse, against, anti, antilogy, antipodal, antipole, antithetic(al), antonym, confronting, contra, contradictory, contrary, contrast, converse, counter, crosswise, diametric, face to face, facing, fornent, fronting, hostile, incompatible, inverse, negative, obverse, other, paradox, perverse, polar(ic), repugnant, reverse, toward, versus, vis-a-vis
comb. ant(i), contra, enantio
exact antipode, antithesis, counterpole
extremities antipodes, poles
number counterpart, duplicate, obverse
to abreast, subtend

OPPOSITION animosity, antagonism, antipathy, antithesis, argument, challenge, clash, collision, competition, conflict, confrontation, contradiction, contrariety, contrast, contravention, counteraction, defiance, demur(ral), discord, disobedience, dissent, facing, fronting, friction, hate, hostility, interference, objection, obstacle, oppugnance, polarity, polarization, protest, reluctance, renitence, renitency, repugnance, repulsion, resistance, rivalry, static, violation

OPPOSITENESS antilogy, antithesis, contrariety, negativism, perversity, polarity

OPPRESS abuse, afflict, agrieve, annoy, burden, confront, constrain, crush, depress, domineer, dragoon, extinguish, extort, hagride, harass, harry, hoodoo, jinx, jonah, load, macerate, maltreat, mistreat, nither, outrage, overpower, overwhelm, persecute, press, rack, ravish, reduce, ride, squeeze, subdue, suppress, sway, task, tax, thew, torment, torture, trample, tyrannize, weigh, worry, wrong

OPPRESSED downtrodden, laden, servile, weighted (down)

OPPRESSION affliction, burden, dejection, depression, despondence, dullness, extortion, grievance, lassitude, lowness, misery, mizraim, repression, thrall, tyranny

OPPRESSIVE airless, bitter, burdensome, carking, close, coercing, compelling, despotic, dire, domineering, dowie, exacting, grinding, heavy, hot, imperious, leaden, melancholy, onerous, overbearing, ponderous, rigorous, severe, suffocating, sultry, torrid, tyrannical, unpleasant, weighty

OPPRESSOR bull of bashan, csar, czar, despot, dictator, incubus, nero, tyrant, tsar, tzar

OPPROBRIOUS abusive, despised, disgraceful, ignominious, insulting, malevolent, malicious, malign, offensive, railing, reproachful, scurrile, scurrilous, shameful

OPPROBRIUM abuse, calumny, catcall, censure, contempt, contumely, criticism, disapproval, disdain, disgrace, dishonor, disrepute, ignominy, infamy, invective, obloquy, odium, outrage, reproach, scandal, shame, stricture, vitriol

OPPUGN assail, attack, combat, contend, contradict, controvert, counteract, criticize, dispute, fight, oppose, resist, thwart, withstand

OPS See also RHEA.
associate consus
consort saturn
festival opalia
personification fauna, tellus, terra

OPT adopt, choose, cull, decide, elect, espouse, pick, prefer, select, vote, will, wish

OPTIC(AL) eye, ocular, visual
illusion mirage
instrument alidad(e), barnacles, bifocals, bombsight, bull's-eye, camera lucida, chromatrope, condenser, eriometer, eyeglasses, finder, focometer, glass(es), glims, goggles, laser, lens, lorgnette, lorgnon, magnifier, meniscus, microscope, mirror, monacle, optometer, panopticon, periscope, pincenez, prism, reflector, scope, sight, skiascope, spectacles, spectrograph, spectroscope, speculum, stauroscope, teinoscope, telescope, thaumatrope, viewer
instrument part reticle
organ eye
toy kaleidoscope, zoetrope
science gastroscopy, microscopy, optics, optology, optometry, photology, spectrometry, stereoscopy, telescopy
specialist oculist, ophthamologist, optometrist

OPTIMISM buoyancy, cheerfulness, hope(fulness), pollyannaism

OPTIMIST dr pangloss, pollyanna, utopianist

OPTIMISTIC auspicious, bullish, cheerful, eupeptic, expectant, glad, hopeful, joyous, lighthearted, panglossian, roseate, rosy, sanguine, sunny

OPTIMUM best, capital, superlative

OPTION alternative, call, choice, choosing, discretion, election, future, preference, prerogative, privilege, right, selection, spread, wish(ing)
play tournee

OPTIONAL and-or, discretionary, elective, permissive, spontaneous, voluntary

OPULENCE affluence, amplitude, plenty, profusion, riches, wealth

OPULENT abundant, affluent, baronial, copious, flush, gorgeous, lavish, lush, luxuriant, luxurious, moneyed, ostentatious, plentiful, plush(y), pretentious, prodigal, profuse, prosperous, rich, showy, splendid, sumptuous, wealthy

OPUNS *father* zeus

OPUNTIA barbary-fig, cacanapa, cactus, tuna

OPUS book, composition, embroidery, etude, labor, manuscript, product(ion), study, work
overlabored lucubration

OR alternative, aut, before, eer, either, ere, optionally, sooner than, than, topaz, until
heraldic gold, yellow
so thereabouts

ORACHE atriplex, greasewood, saltbush

ORACLE augur, authority, axiom, diviner, medium, mentor, predictor, prophet, pythia, responsory, revelation, sage, seer, sibyl, soothsayer, sphinx, tripos
board ouija
guardians bessi
pert. erudite, pythonic, vatic
seat adytum, aphaca, arcadia, athens, colchis, delos, delphi, dodona, mycenae, paphos, tripod
spontaneous autophone

ORACULAR ambiguous, authoritative, cabalistic, delphic, dictatorial, doctrinaire, dogmatic, equivocal, magisterial, magistral, mysterious, mystical, orphic, otic, portentous, prophetic, pythonic, vatic(al) wise

ORAGE See STORM.

ORAL acroamatic, actinal, aloud, articulate(d) buccal, enunciated, examination, mouthed, nuncupative, orificial, oscular, outspoken, parle, parol(e), phonetic, phonic, pronounced, said, sounded, spoken, stomatic, unwritten, uttered, verbal, vocal, voiced
instruction catechesis, catechism

ORALE fanon

ORALLY verbally, vivavoce, vocally

ORANGE (See also *kind*, below.) aurora, bergamot, bigarade, brazil, buccaneer, carnelian, ceres, chile, claybank, copper, cowslip, flame, flamingo, genip, hedge, honeydew, jacinthe, leather, maclura, marathon, mikado, morocco, navaho, paprika, persimmon, pomander, pon-

ceau, pumpkin, rangpur, suntan, tangelo, titian
berry cranberry, limeberry
bird tanager
bitter curacao
blight quick decline
brownish spice, terracotta
color apricot, copper, peach, tangerine, tenne, titian
disease leprosis
extract neroli
flower choisya
gourd cucurbita
grass bastard gentian, knitweed, pine-tassel, pineweed, sarothra
hawkweed fireweed, hieracium
heraldic tenne
kind bergamot, bitter, blood, bodock, calamondin, chino, chinotti, citrange, florida, jaffa, king, mandarin, mock, navel, osage, seville, styrax, temple, valencia
large king
leaf karamu
light apricot
-like bel, osage, tangelo, tangerine
liqueur curacao
mandarin rangpur, satsuma, tangerine
membrane zest
milkweed asclepias, butterfly-weed, candyweed
milkwort candyweed
mock syringa
oil neroli
osage bodock, hedge, maclura
peel aurantiicortex, zest
pert. aurantiaceous
quit honeycreeper
-red coral, henna, saffron
-red dyestuff alga
rockfish flioma
root bittersweet, goldenseal
section lith
seed pip
seedless navel
seville chinotti
-shaped oblate
small calamondin, satsuma
sour bigarade, chinotto, curacao
spring styrax
sulphur alfalfa butterfly, colias
sweet china, chino
tawny tenne
virus tristezza
wood osage
ORANGUTANG ape, bimi, mias, pongo, primate, saltier, satury, satyr, wood(s) man
ORATE address, declaim, discourse, harangue, lecture, plead, speak, speechify, spellbind, spiel, spout, spruik
ORATION address, concion, declamation, discourse, harangue, hesped, homily, lecture, olynthiac, panegyric, philippic, prelection, sermon, speech, suasoria, talk
funeral elogy, encomium, monody
ORATOR advocate, boanerges, demagogue, discourser, elocutionist, perorator, petitioner, plaintiff, preacher, prolocutor, rhetor(ician), sermonizer, soapboxer, speaker, spellbinder, spokesman, stumper, talker
famous bryan, burke, cato, churchill, cicero, demosthenes, douglas, fox, lysias, otis, webster
ORATORIANS *founder* st philip neri
ORATORICAL articulate, eloquent, rhetorical, soulful
ORATORIO *coda* stretto
handel's messiah, semele
haydn's seasons
ORATORY bethel, chantry, chapel, elocution, eloquence, expression, faldstool, oraculum, oriel, proseuche, rhetoric, sacrary, talk
fathers founder philip neri
ORB ball, bereft, circle, earth, encircle, enclose, eye, firmament, globe, moon, planet, sphere, star, station, sun, surround, world
ORBED globate, lunar, round, spherial
ORBICULAR annular, circular, discoid, globular, rotund, round, spherical
ORBIT ambit, arc, auge, ball, circle, circuit, compass, cycle, domain, ellipse, expanse, eye(hole), field, gamut, horizon, ken, locus, path, province, purview, radius, range, reach, realm, region, route, scope, sphere, spiral, sweep, track, trajectory
point aphelion, apogee, apsis, nadir, node, perigee, perihelion, syzygy, zenith
ORC(A) dolphin, dragon, giant, grampus, monster, ogre, whale
ORCHARD arbor, arbustum, coppice, copse, garden, grove, huerta, plantation, pomarium, sugarbush, tope
creator johnny appleseed
grass cocksfoot, dogfoot
ORCHESTRA band, capelle, ensemble, gamelan, kapelle, symphony
bells glockenspiel
circle parquet, parterre
seat balcony, parquet, parterre, pit
section brass, percussion, strings, timpani, winds, woods, wood(winds)
ORCHID acineta, addersmouth, aerides, amethyst, angraecum, anguloa, arethusa, baldbaby, baldberry, birdsnest, fletia, bloody-fingers, boatlip, brassavola, brassia, calanthe, calopogon, calypso, catasetum, cattleya, coeloglossum, coralroot, cordula, crakefeet, crowfoot, crowtoe, cullion, cymbid(ium), cypripedium, cytherea, dendrobium, disa, dufoil, epidedrum, fa(u)am, flywort, gymadenia, gynander, habenaria, heleborine, hellebore, isotria, labellum lady(s) slipper, laelia, lavender, limodorum, listera, malaxis, monkflower, oncidium, peramium, perse, perularia, petal, phajus, pogonia, purple(lips), ramshead, san sebastian, satyrion, tipularia, tongueflower, triphora, twayblade, vanda, vanilla
appendage caudicle
drug from salop
edible salep
egg oosphere
food salep, vanilla
leaves faham
lip slipper
male chillion, crowtoe, drakesfeet, giddy-gander, standelwelks, standelwort
man georges carpentier
part anther, labellum
pod derivative vanilla
root scullion(s)
tea faham
terrestrial spiranthes
tuber cullion, salep
tuberous nodding-cap
ORCHIS See ORCHID.

ORCHOMENUS *father* zeus
king erginus
people minyans
river cephissus
ORCUS (See also HELL.)
hades, pluto
ORDAIN allot, appoint, arrange, authorize, benight, call, canonize, command, commission, consecrate, constitute, decree, deem, destine, dictate, enact, establish, frock, install, institute, invest, legislate, order, predestine, prepare, pronounce, saint, send, shape, will, wite
ORDAINED destined, due, legal, prescript
ORDEAL calvary, crucible, fire, gaff, gauntlet, gethsemane, nightmare, test, torment, torture, trial, tribulation, wringer
bean calabar-bean, poison
tree acocanthera, akazga, strychnos, tanghin, tanguin
ORDER 3 ban, bid, law, row, run, way 4 call, case, club, fiat, hest, hire, kind, line, rank, rule, sect, trim, type, will, writ 5 align, aline, array, caste, class, edict, enact, genre, group, guide, lodge, peace, range, taxis, ukase 6 adjust, assign, behest, charge, choose, cosmos, degree, direct, engage, enjoin, govern, graith, manage, method, ordain, school, select, summon, system 7 arrange, bidding, command, concord, control, dictate, dispose, harmony, mandate, marshal, operate, pattern, reserve, verdict 8 instruct, organize, regulate, sequence, syntaxis, tidiness 9 authority, community, direction, pronounce 10 ceremonial, fraternity, injunction, regulation, sisterhood 11 appointment, arrangement, association, brotherhood, certificate, instruction, requisition 12 prescription, tranquillity 14 classification, pronunciamento
angelic choir, dominions, quire, thrones
architectural corinthian, doric, ionic, tuscan
back recommit, remand
civil eunomy

comb. ini, taxis, taxo
connected seriatim
cosmic rita, tao
educational benedictine, ursaline
follow obey
form scop
garter, symbol blue ribbon
goddess dice, dike, irene
good eutaxie, eutaxy
lacking amiss, chaotic, cluttered, confused, disarrayed, messy, mussy, rough, unkempt, untidy
legal daywrit, nisi, precipe, sentence, sist, subpoena, summons, vacatur, writ
merit albert, aviz, bath, garter, leopold, st louis, st olaf, vasa
military hospitaller, templar, teutonic
official billet
out of broken, busted, forebackwardly
personification eunomia
religious acoemeti, acoimetae, alcantara, alexian, ambrosian, augustinian, austin, barnabite, benedictine, bernardine, black friar, bonhomme, capuchin, carmelite, carthusian, cistercian, clare, claretian, cluniac, columbanian, cordelier, dominican, essene, franciscan, friar, gilbertine, hospitaler, jesuit, lorettine, loyolite, marist, maturine, minorite, oblate, poor clares, recollet, samgha, sangha, sulpician, templar, trappist, urbanist, ursaline, valliscaulian
reverse viceversa
separate a la carte
sequential chronology
written billet, draft, draught
ORDERED bespoke, coherent, regular
ORDERLY aide, attendant, batman, businesslike, conventional, decorous, docile, formal, graithly, messenger, methodical, neat, obedient, pacific, peaceable, peaceful, proper, punctilious, quiet, regular, servant, shipshape, snod, sowar, spick-and-span, suwar, systematic, tidy, trig, trim, uncluttered
ORDINAL book, number, regular
comb. eth
ORDINANCE appointment,

array, assize(s), canon, capitulary, ceremony, command, decree, decreta (l), direction, dispensation, edict, enactment, fiat, LAW, mandate, order, plan, precept, prescript, rank, regulation, rite, rule, station, statute
ORDINARY accustomed, archbishop, average, banal, bare, bishop, book, common (place), customary, everyday, familiar, general, habitual, homely, homespun, household, inexpert, judge, lay, low, matter-of-fact, mean, mediocre, metropolitan, natural, nomic, normal, plain, plebeian, popular, primate, prosaic, prosy, public, pure, quotidian, recurrent, regular, ruck, rumtytoo, simple, tavern, trivial, ugly, usual, vulgar, vulgate, wonted, workaday
ORDINATION appointment, arrangement, disposition, installation, order
pert. inthronistic
ORDNANCE ammunition, arbalest, armor, arms, artillery, cannon, catapult, firearm, gun, materiel, mine, mortar, munitions, orgue, petard, peterero, rabinet, stores, supplies, torpedo
ORDO almanac, booklet, calendar, directory, mass, order
ORDONNANCE arrangement, decree, law, ORDER
ORDURE dung, filth, manure
comb. scat(o)
ORE augury, clemency, coin, craze, crude, favor, glory, grace, hematite, honor, iron, lode, mercy, metal, MINERAL, paco, paydirt, respect, reverence, rock, seaweed, smeddum, tin, vein, wool
aggregate kidney
box flosh
broken dirt
bucket hoop clevis
cleaning vanning
crude heads
crusher dolly
cube siderite
deposit bank, bonanza, flat, lode, mine, scrin, seam, stope, vein
dressing machine vanner

excavation pit, stope
extraction exploitation
fusing smelting
fusing place smeltery
impure halvans, speiss
layer seam, stope
loading platform plat
lump hardhead
mass squat
receptacle mortar
refuse scoria, tailings
screen grate, trommel
separator vanner
sluice trunk
treat for smelting beneficiate
vein See ORE *deposit*.
washing trough strake
worthless dress, matte, slag
OREAD fairy, nymph, peri, seamaid
OREB *son and slayer* gideon
OREGON *bay* coos
box pachystima
capital salem
city albany, ashland, astoria, corvallis, eugene, grants pass, medford, nyssa, pendleton, portland, roseburg, salem, willamette
coin beaver
college reed
county clatsop, klamath, linn, malheur, umatilla, wasco, yamhill
crabapple powitch
explorer feno
grape barberry, mahonia
hydroelectric plant dalles, swift
indian alsea, bannock, cayuse, chetco, chinoo, clackama, clatsop, coos, kalapooian, kalapuyan, klamath, klikitat, kuitsh, kusan, modoc, molala, sahaptin, sastean, shastan, siletz, taklema, tenino, tillamook, umatilla, umpqua, wallawalla, walpapi, wasco, yanan, yaquina, yunca
lake crater, harney, kalmath, malheur, waldo
landmark mt hood
motto alis volat propriis
national park crater lake
nickname beaver state, webfoot state
peak grizzly, hood, jackass, mazama, rainier, tacoma, tidbits, walker, wilson
port astoria, portland
range blue coast, cascades
river blitzen, columbia, deschutes, imnaha, klamath,

owyhee, powder, rogue, willamette, silvies, umpqua
state bird meadowlark
state flower mahonia, grape
state tree fir
trail fort boise, casper, kearney, laramie
trail origin independence
university eugene
wind chinook
ORELLIN achiote, annatto, bixa, bixin
ORESTES *friend* pylades
nurse arsinoe, cilissa
parent agamemnon, clytemnestra
pursuers erinnyes, furies
sister electra, iphigenia
victim aegisthus, clytemnestra
wife hermione
OREXIS appetite, desire
ORGAN agency, agent, branch, calliope, cheng, harmonium, instrument, journal, magazine, means, medium, melodica, member, newspaper, part, periodical, pointel, publication, spokesman, voice
absence aplasia
adjust registrate, voice
anatomical appendix, bladder, diaphragm, ear, esophagus, eye, heart, kidney, larynx, liver, pancreas, pleura, spleen, stomach, thymus, thyroid, tonsil, windpipe
algaic procarp
auricular ear
barrel autophon
base fundus
bird crow-shrike
bristle-like seta
cactus saguaro
comblike pecten
covering adventitia
death of necrosis
desk See *keyboard*, below.
device coupler, tremolo
displacement ectopia, exstrophy, heteropia
examining device autoscope, probe, speculum
fish drumfish
flutter device tremolo
footlike pes
full grand-choeur
funnel-shaped infundibulum
gallery loft
hand hurdy-gurdy, organistrum, serinette
hearing ear

interlude verset
internal viscera
inventor st cecilia
key digital, tasto
keyboard claviature, clavier, console
kind accordion, harmonium, melodian
-like instrument autophon, calliope, calliophone, choralcelo, harmonica, hurdygurdy, melodeon, melodica, music box, orchestrina, orchestrion, seraphina, seraphine, spinet, symphonion, vielle, vocalion
lymphoid tonsil
motion muscle
note tremolent
olfactory nares, nose
opening ora
optical eye
original syrinx
part action, airchest, backfall, bellows, box, console, coupler, diapason, drawknob, feeder, key, manual, pallet, pedal, pipe, piston, pulldown, rackboard, reed, roller, shutter, slider, soundboard, sticker, stop, swellbox, tracker, windchest
pert. afferent
pipe flue, flute, mixture, montre, reed, schwegel, tremolant
pipe tuner toner, voicer
portable regal
prehensile chelae, claw, clutch, digit, duke, finger, fist, hand, hook, manus, nail, nipper, palm, paw, pincer, pounce, talon, tentacle, ungula
prelude verset
reed harmonium, physharmonica, regal
respiratory lung
saw-like serra
secreting gland
seed-bearing pistil
sense sensilla
sensory ear, eye, nose
small melodeon, melodica, portative, regal
speech lip, mouth, throat, tongue
stop 4 echo, harp, oboe, reed, sext, terz, tuba, viol 5 acuta, dolce, flute, gamba, nasat, orage, quint, tibia, viola 6 bifara, bifero, curtal, cymbal, decima, dolcan, dulcet, fugara, gadekt, mas-

ard, montre, octave, scharf, tierce, tromba 7 aeoline, bassoon, bourdon, celeste, clarion, cremona, dolcian, doublet, euphone, fagotto, larigot, melodia, mixture, piccolo, piffara, posaune, rankett, subbass, tertian, tremolo, trumpet, violina 8 bombarde, carillon, clarinet, cromorna, diapason, dulciana, gemshorn, prestant, register, tenoroon, trombone 9 bellgamba, celestina, cornopean, doublette, harmonica, hohlflote, krummhorn, melopiano, nachthorn, principal, rohrflute, saxophone, undamaris, waldflote 10 clarabella, cornoflute, quindecima, spitzflote, subbourdon 11 voix celeste 12 vox caelestis

stop, delicate vox angelica

stop, storm-initiating orage

stop, string gamba

stop, voicelike vox humana

tactile feeler

taste tongue

transplanted isograft

tune voice

vibrato tremolo

waste kidney

ORGANIC constitutional, essential, fundamental, inborn, inherent, natural, organized, structural, vital

body zooid

compound amine, imid(e), ketol

extract cardaissin

nature bios

radical ethyl

unit monad

ORGANISM amoeba, anaerobe, animal, bacteria, being, benthos, bion, biota, body, complex, creature, ecad, fauna, flora, germ, idorgan, mesophile, monad, monas, morphon, nekton, pathogen, person, plankton, plant, scheme, spore, suscept, system, virus, zooid

air, not requiring anaerobe

air-requiring aerobe

bacterial germ, microbe

body soma(ta)

dark-thriving photophobe

development ontogeny

disease-producing bacteria, germ, microbe, pathogen, virus

elementary alga, am(o)eba,

diatom, monad, monas, protist, spore

modified ecad

pelagic nekton

plant spore

potential idorgan

process m(e)iosis

science of autecology, synecology

sea nekton, plankton

small amoeba, germ, monad, spore

vegetable plant, tree

ORGANIZATION agency, army, arrangement, array, association, business, cadre, character, church, classification, club, company, composition, constitution, corps, disposition, enterprise, establishment, firm, foundation, frame, fraternity, group(ing), institute, institution, lodge, morim, outfit, schema, sect, setup, skeleton, society, sorority, structure, system

auxiliary synodical

business company, cooperative, corporation, establishment, firm, guild, partnership

college alumni, frat(ernity), sorority

criminal cosa nostra, maf(f)ia, mob, syndicate

hierarchy peck(ing) order

labor guild, union

musical band, chorale, chorus, combo, ensemble, orchestra

patriotic dar, sar

political apparatus, bloc, hetaeria, hetairia, party

secret apache, bpoe, elks, foresters, frat(ernity), free masons, ioof, kkk, kop, kuklux-klan, lodge, maccabees, maf(f)ia, masons, midewin, moose, peo, shriners, sorority, underground, wow

skeleton cadre

social circle, club, forum, lodge

veterans american legion, amvets, avc, dav, fidac, gar, sar, veterans of foreign wars, vfw

without amorphous

women's dar, now, peo, sorority, waf, wctu, wrc

ORGANIZE actify, activate, activize, adjust, architect, arrange, begin, constitute,

construct, coordinate, design, dispose, embody, establish, fashion, form, found, frame, initiate, institute, integrate, order, plan, produce, project, rally, regiment, regulate, scheme, set up, shape, start, structure, systematize, systemize, unionize

ORGANIZER author, designer, kochleffl, planner, producer

ORGIASTIC dionysian, dissipated, drunken, saturnalian, turbulent

revel bacchanalia, carousal

ORGON *creator* moliere

enemy tartuffe

wife elmire

ORGULOUS haughty, proud, showy, splendid

ORGY bacchanal(lia), binge, bout, bum, carousal, debauch, dissipation, frolic, jag, lark, merrymaking, revel(ry), rite, romp, saturnalia, shindy, spree, wassail

ORIANA *father* lisuarte

lover amadis

ORIBI antelope, bleekbok, ourebi, palebuck

ORIEL bay(window), casement, chapel, dormer, mirador, portico, recess, window

seat carol

ORIENT (See also ORIENTAL.) accommodate, adapt, adjust, arrange, asia, blue, bright, dawn(ing), east(ern), glowing, indogaea, levant, locate, luminous, luster, lustrous, morning land, pearl, pellucid, red, resplendent, rising, sheen, shining, sparkling, sunrise

express king of trains, train of kings

express destination istanbul

express origin paris

express stop belgrade, lausanne, milan, sofia, trieste, zagreb

pink cherub

red vermilion

ORIENTAL (See also ASIA, CHINA, JAPAN.) almond-eyed, asian, bright, brilliant, eastern, levantine, lustrous, ortive, pearl, pellucid, precious, rising, shining

animal zebu

apricot ume

archangel uriel
bazaar bezesteen
bearer hama
beverage arrack, rakee, raki, sake, soma, tea
bird bush-robin, ianthia, tarsiger
bird, fabulous huma
bow salaam
calculator abacus
cap calpac(k), fez, turban
caravansary imaret, khan, serai
carriage jinricksha(w), ricksha(w), sado
cart araba
cheese beancurd
christian abba, uniat
cockroach blackbeetle
coin dinar, para, rin, sapek, sen, yen
combat karate, kung fu
commander ameer, amir, emeer, emir, ra(i)s, reis
corn para
cosmetic kohl
council divan
cuckoo coel, koel
cymbal tal, zel
dance coo(t)ch, hootchy-kootchy, nautch
deity bel
destiny kismet
disease beriberi
dish pilaf, pilau, pilaw
drug hashish, hemp, heroin, opium
drum anacara, tomtom
dulcimer santir
dwelling dar
eating utensil chopsticks
emperor sultan
exercise aikido, jiujitsu, judo, karate, sumo, tai chi chuan, yoga
fabric alacha(h), cambresine, silk
factotum comprador
fan ogi, punka(h)
fate kismet
fish koi, tai
fishnet salamboa
food beancurd, pilaf, pilau, pilaw, rice, salep
foreign enclosure compound
game fantan, hei, mahjong(g)
gate dar
gelatin agar-agar
gem eye-agate, pearl
giant dondasch
guitar sitar
homer firdusi
inn imaret, serai

interpreter dragoman
knife bolo, dah
litter doolee, dooley, doolie
lute tar
maid See ORIENTAL *nursemaid.*
mansion yamen
musical instrument anacara, samisen, santir, sitar, suray, surna, tar
name ali
nomad ta(r)tar
note chit
nursemaid ama(h), aya(h), eyah, hamai, iya
oboe suray, surna
outlaw dacoit, ronin
palanquin See ORIENTAL *litter.*
panacea acupuncture
patent berat
people asian, chinese, eastern(er), indian, japanese, korean, levantine, mohammedan, moslem, muslim, sere, tai, ta(r)tar, tho
pine matsu
pipe narg(h)ile, nargileh
plane tree cheenar, chinar, sycamore
poem kasida
porgy tai
porter hamal
potentate aga
priest fakir
prince aga, khan
punishment bastinado
rest house khan, serai
rice dish pilaf, pilau, pilaw
rice paste ame
rug (See also PERSIA *rug.*) afshah, afshar, akhissar, amritsar, baku, baluch(istan), bergama, bergamee, bergamot, bokhara, bukhara, chinese, ferahan, giordes, hamadan, hazak, herat, herez, isfahan, ispahan, juruk, kali, karajas, kaross, kashan, kerman (shah), khila, kirman, konia, kula, kumeh, kurdistan, ladik, lerestan, mahal, mecca, melas, mesh(h)ed, nammad, pamiri, saraband, sarouk, sedjadeh, senna, serabend, shiraz, shirvan, smyrna, soumak, tabriz, tekke, tilpah, tuzla, ushak, yuruk, zofra
rug, imitation axminster
rug pattern ainaleh
rug variation abrash
ruler ameer, amir, calif, ca-

liph, emeer, emir, khan, shah, sultan
saber scimitar, tulwa(u)r
sailor calash, lascar
salutation kowtow, saheb, sahib, sala(a)m
sash obi
sauce soy
servant See ORIENTAL *nursemaid.*
ship dhow, saic
ship captain rais
shirt camise, kamis
shoe baboosh, babouche, cobcab, go-ahead, sandal
shrub henna, tea, wineberry
silkworm tussah, tusseh, tusser, tussore
skipper rais, reis
snake acrochordina
sword scimitar
tale ali baba, arabian nights
tamarisk atle(e)
tambourine daira
title aga, amir, baba, huzoor, khan, pasha, sahib, sirdar, sri
tower pagoda
tradesman bakal
tree atle(e)
wagon araba
water pipe hooka(h), hubble-bubble, narghile, nargile(h)
weapon adaga
weight abbas, bhaar, cantar, catty, kantar, kati, miskal, picul, rotl, shi(h), tael
whip chab(o)uk
wind monsoon
worker coolie, cooly
ORIENTATION aspect, attitude, bearings, briefing, introduction, locality, position
ORIFICE aperture, bung (hole), cavity, chimney, entrance, foramen, fumarole, hole, interstice, lura, mouth, opening, osculum, ostiole, outlet, perforation, pore, porule, rictus, spiracle, stoma, throat, vent
small pore, stoma
volcanic blower, fumarole
ORIFICIAL mandibular, maxiliary, mouthlike, oral
ORIFLAMME banderol, banner, ensign, flag, standard
ORIGAN dittany, marjoram, mint
ORIGIN alpha, ancestry, beginning, birth, bottom, bud, cause, commencement, cosmogony, dawn, derivation,

descent, etymology, father, font, foundation, fount(ain), genesis, germ, inception, initiation, lineage, nas, nature, nee, occasion, offspring, outset, parentage, provenance, provenience, rise, root, seed, source, spring, start, stock

comb. ese, geny, ite

common isogenic

foreign ecdemic

mental psychogenesis

native endemic

on earth epigene

racial, pert. phenogenetic

ORIGINAL aborigine, archetype, audacious, basal, basic, creation, creative, eccentric, elemental, elementary, embryonic, ethnic, exemplar, first, fontal, fresh, fundamental, genetic, genuine, germinal, independent, initial, in ovo, invention, inventive, model, native, neoteric, novel(ty), parentage, pattern, primal, primary, prime(val), primitive, primordial, pristine, protogenic, prototype, radical, rudimentary, sample, seminal, source, stock, unique

comb. arch(i), prot(o)

ORIGINALITY authenticity, creativity, independence, ingenuity, invention, novelty

ORIGINALLY first, inherently, initially, primarily

ORIGINATE arise, author, begin, birth, breed, causate, cause, coin, commence, compose, conceive, concoct, contrive, create, derive, design, devise, discover, dream up, emanate, embark, fabricate, father, flow, found, frame, hatch, improvise, initiate, institute, invent, issue, occasion, proceed, produce, propagage, rise, sire, source, spring, start, stem, think up

ORIGINATIVE causal, creative, productive

ORIGINATOR author, creator, father, generator, inventor

ORINOCO *indian* achagua, chiriana, guaharibo, guahibo, piaroa

river fish electric eel

river tributary apure

ORIOLE bananabird, bunyah, cacique, figbind, firebird, gold bird, hangbird, hangnest, icterus, loriot, mimeta, peabird, pirol, troupial

color tan

golden baltimore, loriot, pirol

ORION algebar, hunter, nimrod, rigel, samson

belt ellwand, golden yardarm

blinded by oenopion

consort eos, merope, side

dog aratus, canis major, dirius

guide cedalion

parent earth, euryale, hyrieus, poseidon

slayer artemis, diana, scorpion

ORISON prayer, praying, request, speech

ORITHYIA *abductor* boreas

offspring calais, chione, cleopatra, zetes

parent erechtheus, praxithea

ORKNEY ISLANDS flotta, hoy, mainland, pomona, ronaldsay, rousay, sanday, shapinsay, stronsay

bay scapa flow, voe

capital kirkwall

excavation skarabrae

firth pentland

fishing bank haaf

freehold odal, udal

gull trumpie

hut skeo, skio

land odal, udal

landholder odalar, odalman, udaler, udalman

magistrate foud

promontory noup

queen bellicent

tower broch

water sprite tangie

ORLANDO *Beloved* rosalind

brother jaques, oliver

father rowland de bois

steed vegliantino, veillantif

uncle charlemagne

ORLE bearing, border, chaplet, fillet, tressure, wreath

ORMAZD See AHURA MAZDA.

ORMENIUM *king* amyntor

ORMER abalone, ear-shell, haliotis

ORMOLU alloy, brass, gilding, gilt, gold, varnish

ORNAMENT (See also *ar-*

chitectural and *kind*, below.) 3 dub, epi, fob, pin 4 deck, etch, gaud, gild, knob, ouch, ring, seme, stud, tool, trim 5 adorn, array, badge, beset, braid, bulla, cameo, chase, color, decor, dress, frill, grace, gutta, honor, jewel, mensk, paint, prink 6 amulet, armlet, bangle, bedeck, blazon, brooch, buckle, carcan, emboss, enrich, polish, scroll, sequin, tassel, tinsel 7 agremen, amenity, bedizen, bejewel, bibelot, bracket, bucrane, display, epergne, furbish, garnish, miniate, netsuke, rosette, schmuck, smarten, spangle, trinket, varnish 8 anaglyph, beakhead, beautify, biliment, bracelet, carcanet, decorate, emblazon, frippery, gimcrack, nicknack, trimming 9 accessory, adornment, amazonite, bric-a-brac, cartouche, clinquant, embellish, enthemion, hobilment, microline, rubricate 10 decoration, knickknack 13 embellishment

ancient palmette

apex finial

architectural acanthus, acroterium, amalaka, antefix, anthemion, apophyge, archivolt, astragal, beading, beak, billet, boss, cartouche, cavetto, cinquefoil, conge, cornice, cusp, cyma, dado, dancette, dentil, encarpus, fascia, fillet, finial, fret, frieze, gutta, list(el), MOLDING, ogee, ovo(lo), patera, pendant, quatrefoil, reed, rosace, rosette, scotia, scroll, splay, strigil, strix, supercilium, torus, trefoil, volute

bas relief patera

bell-shaped clochette

biblical urim

boat-shaped nef

budlike knosp

cheap agremens, bauble, figgery, geegaw, gingerbread

circular patera, rosette

clawlike griff(e), spur

crescent-shaped lunette, lunula

crystal prism

curly scroll

delicate tracery
diamond-shaped epigonation
dress bar-pin, chequeen, embroidery, frog, jabot, lace, ruffle, sequin, spangle, zecchino
floral anthemion, rosette
god adiel
gold lace bull's-eye
grotesque babery, baboon, gargoyl
hanging anadem, bangle, bob, bulla, earring, fringe, lavaliere, pendant, tassel
head temple, tiara
inlaid emblema
jewelled biliment
kind aglet, aiglet, aigrette, applique, arabesque, arras, batik, bouquet, boutonniere, bow, bugle, chaplet, corsage, drapery, egret, embroidery, epaulet, festoon, filigree, fleuron, foliage, garland, griffito, inlay, niello, orphrey, panache, parquetry, plume, pompom, ruffle, snood, tracery, wreath
magical amulet, FETISH
pert. chased
protuberant boss
rococo rocaille
scroll-like cartouche, volute
sculptured acrosolium, acroterium, aphlaston, aplustre, bucrane, bucranium, corbel
set of parure
shoulder epaulet
6-lobed sexfoil
spiral epi, helix
tufted pompom, rosette, tassel
urn-like soupiere
vine-leaf pampre
ORNAMENTAL artistic, chichi, decorative, fancy festooned, frilly
ORNATE adorned, aureate, baroque, begilt, busy, decorated, elaborate, elegant, embellished, fanciful, fancy, figured, flamboyant, flashy, florid, flossy, flowery, garish, gay, gilded, labored, lavish, luxurious, opulent, ornamented, ostentatious, pretentious, rhetorical, rich, rococo, showy, sumptuous, taffeta, tawdry, wordy
ORNERY base, common, contrary, crabbed, crabby, insignificant, irascible, low,

malicious, mean, ordinary, perverse, refractory, stubborn, unmanageable
ORNEUS *brother* cecrops, metion
father erechtheus
ORNITHOLOGIST audubon, birdman, birdwatcher
ORNYTUS beuthis
ORO gold, mouth
OROBANCHE anoplanthus, beechdrop, broomrape, broomwort, cancerroot, indian pipe, squawroot, water-betony
ORONTES *city on* hama
ORONTIUM arum, bog torch, golden-club, plant
OROTUND bombastic, clear, full, mellow, musical, pompous, resonant, rising, smooth, strong
OROZCO *specialty* mural
ORP fret, weep
ORPAH *husband* chilion
ORPHAN annie, bereft, derelict, foundling, stepchild, ward
ORPHANAGE asylum, creche, home
ORPHEUS *birthplace* pieria
burial site libethra
destination hades
18th century handel
instrument lyre
parent apollo, calliope, oeagrus
slayers maenads
son musaeus
wife eurydice
ORPHIC dionysiac, enchanting, entrancing, esoteric, mystic, oracular
goddess baubo, iambo
ORPHNE *son* ascalaphus
ORPHREY band, border, embroidery
ORPIMENT arsenic, harta(i)l, orange, red, yellow
ORPINE bagleaves, evergreen, live-forever, pryophyllum, sedum, stonecrop
ORRA chores, good-for-nothing, idle, miscellaneous, occasional, oddly, unemployed, unmatched, worthless
ORRERY cosmoscope, eidouranion, observatory, planetarium
ORRIS braid, galloon, gimp, iris, lace
ORSINO *attendant* curio, valentine

beloved olivia
page viola
ORSON *brother* valentine
ORT bit, crumb, end, fragment, leaving, leftover, morsel, refuse, reject, remnant, scrap, select, trible
ORTHIA artemis
ORTHODOX acceptable, accepted, approved, authentic, authoritative, believer, bienpensant, canonical, canonist, catholic, christian, conventional, correct, customary, devout, evangelical, faithful, firm, fundamental(ist), legitimate, literal, official, pious, prim, proper, punctilious, received, right(ful), scriptural, sound, standard, textual(ist), traditional, true, usual
ORTHOGONAL perpendicular, quadrangular, rectangular, right-angled, vertical
ORTHOGRAPHY elevation, spelling, writing
ORTHOPHYRE atatschite, porphyry
ORTHOS *mother* echidna
ORTHRUS *slayer* hercules
ORTIGA nettle
ORTOLAN bird, bobolink, bunting, emberiza, gallinule, rail, sora, wheatear
ORTSTEIN hardpan
ORWELL *character* prole
satire animal farm
ORYX antelope, beatrix, beisa, gazelle, gemsbok, kookoom, leucoryx, pasang, paseng
OS bone, esker, mouth, opening, ora, orifice
magnum capitatum
OSAGE sioux
orange or *apple* bodock, bois d'arc, bowwood, hedge, maclura, tree
OSAKA *bay port* kobe
old name naniwa
OSCAN *language* safine
OSCILLATE bob(le), change, coggle, dangle, falter, flap, flicker, flop, fluctuate, flutter, hesitate, liberate, lurch, pendulate, pitch, pivot, pussyfoot, quaver, quiver, reel, rock, roll, seesaw, shake, shillyshally, shimmy, sway, swing, switch, swivel, teeter, toss, totter, tremble, undulate, vacillate, vary, vibrate,

wabble, waddle, waffle, wag(gle), wamble, waver, weave, whirl, wiggle, wobble
OSCILLATING floppy, fluctuant, libratory, pendulant, pendulous, tottery, undulant, vibrant, wavy, whirligig, whirly, wiggly, wobbly
OSCILLATION change, fluctuation, flutter, howl, liberation, pendulation, shimmy, squeal, swing, switch, trepidation, undulation, vacillation, variation, vibration, wave(ring), wobble
transformer tesla
OSCITANT apathetic, careless, drowsy, dull, gaping, sleepy, sluggish, stupid, yawning
OSCULATE buss, contact, kiss, touch
OSIER basket, dogwood, edder, redbrush, rod, salix, sallow, skein, split, twig (withy), want, wilgers, willow, withe
cage tumbrel
grove holt, osiery
OSIRIS amenti, arsaphes, bennu, dionysus, djed, hades, hershef, khenti (-amenti), mendes, nature god, onnophris, onuphis, ousir, serapis, unnefer
birthplace thebes
crown atef
god of fertility, nature, underworld
grand vizer thoth
incarnation bennu, bird, bull, onuphis, sacred son of mendes
kin isis, nephthys, set(h), typhon
lieutenant anubis, upuaut
parent geb, keb, nut, seb
sacred plant ivy
servant thoth
sister isis
slayer set(h), typhon
son anubis, horus
successor to andjeti
symbol crook, whip
temple site abydos
title lord of the westerners, universal lord
wife isis
OSLO christiana
OSMESIS olfaction, smelling
OSMOSIS absorption, dialysis, diffusion, interaction, interchange, penetration, transudation

get by absorb
OSPREY bird, buzzard, enr(e), feather, gled(e), hawk, ossifrage, pandion, sea eagle
OSSE attempt, dare, presage, promise, recommend, utterance, venture
OSSEOUS bony, hard, lithic, ossiferous, osteal, solid, spiny
OSSET caucasian
OSSETE *hero band* narts
leader batradz
OSSIAN *father* finn, fion
kingdom morven
OSSIANIC bombastic, flowery, pompous
OSSICLE adoral, alveole, ambos, bone(let), incus, malleus, scutella, stapes
OSSIFIED callous, conservative, conventional, fixed, hardened
OSSIFY calcify, harden
OSSUARY See BURIAL *place*.
OSTENSIBLE affected, alleged, apparent, assumed, avowed, clear, conspicuous, declared, exhibited, feigned, illusory, manifest, obvious, open, plausible, pretended, professed, purported, quasi, seeming, simulated, specious
OSTENSORIUM pyx
OSTENTATION affectation, airiness, airs, array, blare, boast, ceremony, clinquant, dash, display, eclat, exhibit(ion), fanfare, flare, flash, flourish, foppery, frippery, front, gaudery, glitter, grandeur, loftiness pageant(ry), parade, pomp(osity), pompousness, pretense, pretension, show(iness), spectacle, splash, splendor, splurge, strut, swagger, swank, swash, tinsel, vainglory, vaunting, veneer
OSTENTATIOUS airy, ambitious, arty, blatant, boasting, brummagen, catchpenny, classy, dashing, dramatic, elaborate, fancy, fandandle, flamboyant, flashy, flossy, fussy, garish, gaudy, gay, gewgaw, gimcrack, glittering, grandiloquent, grandiose, high-falutin(g), high-toned, jaunty, lofty, loud, pompous, pretentious,

proud, ritzy, showy, spectacular, splashy, splendid, sporty, stagy, swank(ing), swanky, swashbuckling, tall, tawdry, tinhorn, toplofty, vain
OSTEOPATHY *founder* still
OSTERREICH See AUSTRIA.
OSTIARY doorkeeper, porter
OSTIOLE aperture, mouth, opening, orifice, pore, stoma
OSTLER groom, stableman, stockman
OSTRACISM ban(ishment), boycott, coventry, exclusion, expelling, taboo, tabu
OSTRACIZE ban(ish), bar, blackball, blacklist, boycott, censure, cut, deport, exclude, excommunicate, exile, expatriate, expel, extradite, outlaw, proscribe, punish, reject, snub, transport
OSTRACON ballot, fragment, potsherd, shard, shell
OSTRICH brevipen, camelbird, emu, nandu, rhea, strucion, struthio
extinct moa
feather boa, boo, plume
jerked biltong
-like self-deluded, struthious
-like bird em(e)u, ratite, rhea
symbol of stupidity
OSTROGOTH *king* ermanrich, theodoric
OSTRYA bois de fer, bumelia, hop-hornbeam, ironwood
OSWEGO *tea* balm, beebalm, butterflyweed, indian-plume, mint, monarda
OTAHEITE See TAHITI.
apple hevi, macupi
OTALGIA earache
OTARY seal
OTATE eared
OTHELLO *character* bianca, brabantio, cassio, desdemona, emilia, gratiano, iago, lodovico, montano, roderigo
courtesan bianca
father-in-law brabantio
friend cassio, montano
gentleman roderigo
heroine desdemona
predecessor montano
villain iago
wife desdemona

OTHER additional, alternate, alternative, different, distinct, either, else, former, fresh, further, ither, left, more, opposite, remaining, rest, second, tidder, tother
comb. all(o), heter(o)
-directed conformable
self friend
side across, obverse, reverse, verso
than besides, but, contrary
OTHERNESS alterity, diversity
OTHERWHERE elsewhere, elsewhither
OTHERWHILE(S) occasionally, sometimes
OTHERWISE alias, aliter, alternative(ly), besides, contrarily, different(ly), els(e), ense, except, or else, ossia, secus
OTHERWORLDLY extraterrestrial, fey, heavenly, imaginary, spiritual, supernatural
OTHNI *father* shemaiah
OTHNIEL *father* kenaz
son hathath, meonathai
wife achsah
OTIANT idle, resting, unemployed
OTIC auditory, aural, auricular
OTIONIA *father* erechtheus
OTIOSE aloof, bootless, dull, empty, faineant, fruitless, futile, heavy, hollow, idle, inactive, indolent, ineffectual, lazy, leisured, nugatory, pointless, redundant, remote, slothful, sterile, superfluous, surplus, unemployed, useless, vain, worthless
OTIS bustard
OTOLOGIST aurist
OTTAWA bytown
OTTER annatto, huron, loutre, lutra, mampalon, mustelin, paravane, tarka
brown loutre
burrow couch
den holt
dung spraints
father hreidmar
sea enhydra, kalan
sheep ancon
slayer loki
tail pole
track spoor, spur
OTTOMAN (See TURKEY.)
couch, divan, fabric, footstool, othman, pouf(fe), seat, squab, stool, sultane
dynasty founder osman
government porte
OTUS *brother* ephialtes
parent iphimedia, poseidon
slayer apollo
OUAKARI acari, monkey, u(a)kari
OUBLIETTE See JAIL.
OUCH adorn, bezel, bracelet, brooch, clasp, exclamation, fibula, jewel, necklace, ornament, sore
OUDH kosala
OUGHT anything, befit, behoove, bit, bood, boot, bore, bud, cipher, duty, entertained, had best, had better, have, mote, mow, must, naught, nought, obligation, owe(d), own, should, zero
OUIDA louise de la ramee
OUIJA *board* planchette
OUNCE cat, cheetah, jaguar, leopard, oket, okia, okieh, once, onka, snow-leopard, tael, uncia, ure, wildcat
1/4th blanquillo
1/8th or *1/16th* dram
1/20th easterling, pennyweight
8 cupful
10 miskal
16 pound
64 inch
OUR hore, nos(tro), notre, nous, possessive, pronoun, wer, wir
OURICURY cabecudo, licuri, licury
OUSE *tributary* cam
OUSEL dipper
OUST bar, bounce, bump, cashier, debar, debout, depose, deprive, disbar, discard, discharge, dislodge, dismiss, displace, dispossess, eject, eliminate, evict, exclude, fire, forejudge, remove, sack
OUSTER dismissal, ejection, eviction, expulsion, firing, suspension
OUT abroad, absent, along, at a loss, away, beaten, begone, departed, disclosed, dissimilar, done, down, drawback, eccentric, eject, evil, excuse, exit, expel, exterior, external, extinguish(ed), forth, from, hence, hors, in the red, issued, odd, on strike, oot, passe, public, published, result, revealed, scat, scram, senseless, taboo, uit, unconscious, unfashionable, unprofitably, without, wrong
and out absolute(ly), arrant, by far, complete(ly), crashing, direct, errant, great, gross, incomparable, rank, sheer, sworn, thorough, unqualified, utter, wholly
at elbows indigent, seedy, shaggy, slovenly
comb. ect(o), exo
for after
of among, aus, bereft, beside, dehors, forth, from, hors de, lacking, without
of bounds exorbitant, forbidden, prohibited
of breath blown, breathless, bushed, excided, exhausted, panting, spent
of character alien, foreign, inappropriate, inexpedient
of, comb. exo, ext(o)
of commission broken, bung, busted, crank
of date antiquated, back number, belated, by-gone, dated, dowdy, gone by, obsolete, old-fashioned, passe, past, tacky, timeworn, unfashionable
of doors al fresco, foreign
of gear See OUT *of order.*
of hand impromptu, refractory, through, uncontrollable
of harness retired
of humor angry, disturbed, unhappy
of joint angry, broken, disorderly, edgy, upset
of kilter See OUT *of order*
of line aberrant, askew, bias(ed), disagreeing, dissimilar, erring, erroneous, unconventional
of one's mind daft, deleerit, fey, insane
of order alop, amiss, askew, awry, broken, bung, busted, collapsed, crank, deficient, disorderly, faulty, haywire, infirm, invalid, kaput, on the blink, shattered
of place amiss, inept, lost
of play dead, foul
of pocket broke, expenses, poor
of practice green, rusty, soft
of range beyond, distant, impossible, inaccessible

of sight absent, beyond, costly, dear, doggo, exorbitant, extreme, gone, invisible, superlative, utter(ly)

of sorts angry, cranky, crook, cross, grumpy, indisposed, peevish, sick, unhappy

of the blue sudden(ly), unexpected(ly)

of the depths de profundis

of the ordinary bizarre, different, novel, odd, peculiar, strange, uncommon, unique, unusual

of the question absurd, hopeless

of-the-way abroad, afield, aside, beyond, circuitous, deviative, distant, farfetched, improper, lonely, occasional, offensive, remote, secluded, unusual

of this world great, superb

of tune discordant, disorderly, false, inappropriate, scordato, tense, uptight

of whack See OUT *of order.*

with it confess, disclose, divulge, tell

OUTBACK bush, country, hinterland, sticks

OUTBEAR bear, lead, outcarry, sustain

OUTBEARING arrogance, demeanor, projection

OUTBID bargain, exceed, overrate, surpass

OUTBIRTH product, progeny

OUTBRAID draw, eject, extract, UPBRAID

OUTBRAVE excel, outdare, surpass

OUTBREAK attack, bout (ade), burst, bust-up, caprice, conflict, emeute, eruption, explosion, fit, insurrection, invasion, outburst, outcrop, rash, rebellion, revolt, riot, row, ruckus, ruction, sally, sortie, tumult, uprising, violence, whim

emotional hysteria

new recrudescence

sudden spate, spurt

OUTBUILDING backhouse, barn, barton, garage, hemmel, outhouse, privy, shed, skeeling, skilling, steading

OUTBURST agony, anger, blast, blaze, blowout, blowup, bout, brunt, burst, con-

vulsion, ebullition, eructation, eruption, excitement, explosion, flare(up), flash, fume, gale, gere, gust, outflare, gale, gere, gust, outbreak, outpouring, passion, rage, revolt, rush, sally, scene, shout, spate, storm, strain, stream, tantrum, tear, tempest, tiff, tirade, tornado, torrent, upheaval, violence, volcano, whiff

OUTCAST abandoned, cagot, castaway, castoff, chandala, declasse, degraded, deported, deportee, derelict, disowned, displaced, eta, evacuee, exile(d), expatriate, expellee, fingo, fingu, forsaken, ishmael, leper, outlaw, outlet, outwale, oysvorf, pariah, proscript, reject(ed), reprobate, ronin, untouchable, vagabond, yeta

social cagot, eta

OUTCLASS beat, excel, outwit, surpass

OUTCOME aftermath, browst, conclusion, consequence, denouement, destiny, effect, emanate, emanation, end, event, exitus, exodus, fate, issue, lot, product, progeny, proof, result, sequel, solution, success, term, upset, upshot

OUTCROP appear, basset, blossom, blowout, ledge, outburst

OUTCROPPING bult, scabrock

OUTCRY alarm, auction, ballyhoo, bawl, bellow, boast, bray, bruit, call, caw, clamor, complaint, cry, dite, exclaim, gaff, howl, hubbub, hue, lamentation, noise, objection, phillilew, pother, proclaim, protest, racket, roar, scream, screech, scry, shilloo, shout, shriek, steven, tumult, vociferation, wail, yarm, yell, yip

public scandal, stink

OUTDATE age, antiquate, archaize, obsolete, outmode

OUTDATED anachronous, obsolete, old-fashioned, outmoded, passe

OUTDISTANCE beat, best, cap, conquer, cop, cow, defeat, exceed, excel, flog,

nonplus, outside, outstrip, overcome, pass, surpass, tap, transcend, trump, win, worse

OUTDOOR(S) abroad, alfresco, exterior, forth, open-air, outside

lore bushcraft, woodmancraft, woodmanship

OUTER alien, ectad, ectal, exterior, external, extraneous, foreign, outside, outward, upper, utter

comb. ect(o), exo

OUTERMOST extreme(st), farthest, final, outward, remotest, utmost, utter

OUTFACE confront, defy, overcome, resist, subdue

OUTFALL mouth, sallie, sortie, vent

OUTFIELD garden, moorland, pasture

OUTFIELDER gardener

OUTFIT accouter(ments), apparatus, appoint, arm, attire, business, caparison, clothes, costume, dress, endow(ment), ensemble, equip(ment), fitout, furnish(ings), furniture, gang, garb, gear, get-up, group, grubstake, kit, layout, materiel, office, organization, paraphernalia, prepare, provision, ready, regalia, rig(gings), suit, supply, tackle, team, troop(s), troup, unit, wardrobe

infant's layette

OUTFITTER clothier, haberdasher

OUTFLOW drain, effluence, efflux, escape, flux, issue, outpour

OUTGO circumvent, cost, drain, efflux, egress, exceed, excel, exit, exodus, expenditure, issue, outcome, outdistance, outdo, outflow, outlay, outlet, outrun, outstrip, product, surpass

OUTGOING departing, effluence, effluvium, emanation, extroverted, limit, migratory, responsive, sociable

OUTGROWING enate

OUTGROWTH apophyge, apophysis, appendix, byproduct, carbuncle, cockle, consequence, effect, emergence, enation, epiderme, evolution, excrescence, offshoot, product, result, scale, side-issue, spine

oophytic pseudobulbil

OUTHOUSE biggin(g), bog(s), latrine, linhay, privy, shed, skeeling, skeo, skillion, toilet

OUTING airing, cookout, ejection, excursion, holiday, journey, junket, trip, vacation, waygoose

cloth flannel(ette)

OUTISH See ECCENTRIC.

OUTKNEE bowleg

OUTLANDER alien, emigre, foreigner, immigrant, outsider, pardesi, stranger, tramontane

OUTLANDISH absurd, alien, barbarian, barbaric, barbarous, bizarre, brutal, campy, curious, droll, eccentric, erratic, exotic, fantastic, foreign, freakish, gauche, grotesque, irregular, odd, outre, peculiar, quaint, queer, remote, ridiculous, singular, strange, tasteless, tramontane, uncouth, unique

OUTLAST abide, continue, elapse, endure, outlive, outwear, overbide, persist, resist, surpass, survive

OUTLAW arrant, babaylan, ban, bandido, bandit, banish, bar, caco, criminal, dacoit, dhu, disqualify, embargo, exile, exlex, expatriate, fleme, fugitate, fugitive, highwayman, hooligan, illegal, illicit, interdict, ishmael, ostracize, outcast, prohibit, proscribe, ronin, taboo, tabu, tory, woodkern

famous belle starr, black bart, dillinger, jessie james, robin hood

group manzas, nest

OUTLAY cost, disbursement, expenditure, expense, outgo

OUTLET avenue, avoidance, bayou, catharsis, channel, debouche, debouchment, door, egress, emunctory, escape, exit(us), faucet, gate, hole, issue, loophole, market, mouth, nozzle, opening, orifice, outcast, outcome, outgate, passage (way), pore, port, release, relief, sale, sallyport, sinkhole, socket, spout, stream,

tap, vent, ventage, venthole, vomitory

for air grill(e), vent

OUTLINE abbreviation, abrege, abridge(ment), adumbrate, agenda, agendum, analysis, apercu, block, blueprint, brief, capsule, chart, compend(ium), condensation, configuration, conformation, conspectus, contents, contour, define, delineate, delineation, describe, design, diagram, digest, draft, draught, edge, epitome, features, figuration, figure, form, frame (work), galbe, guideline, lineaments, lineature, map, model, pandect, perimeter, plan, plot, precis, profile, relief, scenario, scheme, shape, silhouette, skeleton, sketch, summarize, summary, survey, syllabus, synopsis, tournure, trace, tracing, treatment

vague ghost

OUTLIVE See OUTLAST.

OUTLOOK angle, anticipation, aspect, attitude, expectation, eye, forecast, foretaste, framework, frontage, ground, inspect, light, likelihood, lookout, opinion, outstare, perception, perspective, position, possibility, posture, prediction, presage, probability, prognosis, prophecy, prospect, purview, range, regard, respect, scope, select, sentinel, sight, slant, standpoint, tower, view(point), vista, watch

medical prognosis

OUTLYING exterior, extraneous, extrinsic, frontier, remote, suburban

area environ(s), purlieu, suburb

OUTMODED antiquated, antique, dated, obsolete, old, outdated, passe, unfashionable, used

OUTPOST country, forepost, purlieu, sentry, settlement, station, suburb, vanguard, warden

defensive barbacan, barbican

OUTPOUR disgorge, flow, outburst, outflow

OUTPOURING effluence,

flood, gale, gush, lavish, onding, river, stream

OUTPUT crop, cut, energy, expel, get, grist, harvest, net, power, proceeds, produce, production, result, turnout, upcome, yield

OUTRAGE abuse, abusion, affront, atrocity, chagrin, crime, debase, deprave, evil, ill-treat, indignity, injury, insult, jar, malefaction, maltreat, mistreat, misuse, offend, offense, oppress, persecute, pervert, rape, rapine, ravish, scandalize, shock, violation, violate, violence, wrong

OUTRAGEOUS absurd, atrocious, damned, excessive, exorbitant, extreme, flagrant, glaring, great, gross, heinous, immoderate, infernal, inordinate, monstrous, nefarious, notorious, preposterous, rank, shameful, shocking, terrible, undue, ungodly, vicious

OUTRANK prefer, surpass

OUTRAY emanate, insult, outshine, overcome, surpass, vanquish

OUTRE absurd, bizarre, eccentric, exaggerated, exorbitant, extravagant, odd, strange, weird

OUTREACH cheat, deceive, exceed, extend, outwit, overreach, project, protrude, search, surpass

OUTRIDER forager, hayduk, heiduk, heyduck, highwayman, servant

OUTRIGGER boat, boom, canoe, lever, pahi, praho, prahu, prau, proa, spider

OUTRIGHT absolute, arrant, clean, complete, direct(ly), downright, entire(ly), great, openly, straightforward, thorough, total, unmitigated, unqualified, whole, wholly

OUTRIVAL defeat, eclipse, excel, outvie, surpass, win

OUTROOT See UPROOT.

OUTRUN beat, cote, elude, exceed, expire, forerun, forespeed, outgo, prevent, spend

OUTSET beginning, first, go-off, outlay, set-off, setout, start, take-off

OUTSHINE blind, dazzle, deface, distain, excel, outdo, surpass

OUTSIDE alien, bout, but, exterior, external, extrinsic, foreign, free, outdoors, outer, surface, utter
comb. ect(o), exo, extro
of beyond

OUTSIDER alien, bounder, emigre, exoteric, extranean, foreigner, ishmael, stranger

OUTSKIRTS border, boundary, bounds, environment, fringes, limits, purlieu, suburbs

OUTSMART circumvent, defeat, outwit

OUTSPOKEN apert, artless, bluff, blunt, bold, broad, candid, direct, explicit, express, frank, free, loud, naked, open, oral, plain, round, square, straightforward, truthful, unreserved, unrestrained

OUTSTANDING ace, a-one, arch, arresting, big, bluechip, conspicuous, distinguished, due, eminent, excellent, exceptional, extrusive, fabulous, famed, famous, heroic, important, jutting, marked, marvelous, momentous, noted, owing, phenomenal, pre-eminent, principal, projecting, prominent, pronounced, rare, remaining, remarkable, salient, signal, snazzy, standout, star, stellar, striking, sublime, superior, supreme, uncollected, unfulfilled, unpaid, unsettled, well-known

OUTSTAY linger, tarry

OUTSTRETCH broaden, expand, extend, spread, strain

OUTSTRETCHED expanded, extended, stent

OUTSTRIP best, cap, cote, devance, distance, exceed, excel, lead, lose, outdo, outrun, overhaul, overtake, surpass, top, transcend, win

OUTWARD alien, apparent, bodily, dermad, dissipated, ectad, exterior, external, extrinsic, foreign, formal, outer, outside, overt, patent, physical, superficial, visible, wild
facing extrorse, extroversion
most exine, extine
turn evert

OUTWEAR consume, destroy, exhaust, outgrow, outlast, outlive

OUTWEIGH outpoise, overbalance, overshadow, preponderate

OUTWEIGHING dominant, preponderant

OUTWIT avert, baffle, balk, best, cheat, checkmate, circumvent, cozen, cross(bite), deceive, defeat, defraud, dupe, euchre, foil, fox, frustrate, gull, jockey, maneuver, mislead, obviate, outsmart, overcome, overreach, preclude, prevent, stonker, surmount, swindle, take-in, thwart, victimize, worst

OUTWORK bawn, best, bray, complete, defense, fleche, fortification, jetty, lunette, outdo, revelin, tenail(le)

OUTWORN bygone, fusty, mildewed, moldly, obsolete, passe, wappened

OUZEL amsel, bird, blackbird, colly, dipper, piet, thrush, whistler

OVAL amphitheater, arena, eggshaped, ellipse, ellipsoid, elliptic(al), nummular, oblate, oblong, obovate, obovoid, ovate, ovoid, ovule, prolate, spheroid, stadium, vesical, vulvate, vulviform
figure cartouche

OVATION acclaim, applause, cheer(s), exultation, festivity, hand, homage, salvo, testimonial, tribute

OVEN baker, caboose, calcar, cookstove, furnace, hangi, hibachi, imu, kiln, kohua, leer, lehr, o(a)st, oon, range, stove, tanur, tiler, umu
annealing lehr
clay tandoor
fork fruggan, fruggin
goddess fornax
implement peel
mop scovel
poker fruggan
underground beanhole

OVENBIRD accentor, baker, furnarius, furner, hornero, seiurus, teacher, titmouse, warbler

OVER about, above, across, addition, afresh, after, again, aloft, also, anew, aside, at an end, athwart, atop, atour, before, besides,

beyond, completed, concluded, covering, dead, decided, done, during, encore, end(ed), excess(ive), extra, finish(ed), gone, here and there, higher, mas, more, oer, owre, past, plus, pre-eminent, recovered, remaining, repeatedly, resuscitated, revived, roundabout, settled, stopped, super(ior), surplus, through(out), thru, to boot, too, twice, undue, upper, upside-down, upturned, yonder
again afresh, anew, bis, encore, once more
against compared, fornent, near
-all also, comprehensive, especially, everywhere, general, napoo(h), surtout, throughout, utterly
and above atop, atour, beside(s), best, beyond, exceeding, forby(e), remaining, therewithal
and over repeatedly
comb. hyper, super, supra, sur, tra(ns)
much excess(ive), exorbitant, surplus, too
the hill exhausted, fallen, finished, old, passe, through, wornout
there yon(der)

OVERABUNDANCE excess, glut, nimiety, plethora, surplus, too much, waste

OVERACT burlesque, caricature, emote, exaggerate, grimace, ham, mug, outdo, rant, spout

OVERAGE excess, older, retarded, surplus, work(manship)

OVERALLS butternuts, chaparajos, chapar(r)eras, chaps, denims, pants, sherryvallies, tongs, trousers

OVERASSUMING bold

OVERAWE abash, browbeat, buffalo, cow, daunt, domineer, frighten, intimidate, subdue, sway

OVERBALANCE dominate, outweigh, weight

OVERBEAR carry, domineer, outweigh, surpass

OVERBEARING absolute, aggressive, arrogant, autocratic, bullying, cavalier, despotic, dictatorial, disdainful, domineering, haughty, high-handed, imperious, insolent, lordly, magisterial, masterful, oppressive, overpowering, proud, scornful, snobbish, subduing, supercilious, tyrannical

OVERBLOUSE tunic

OVERBLOWN exsufflicate

OVERBURDEN encumber, overlade, overtax, plethora, surcharge, task

OVERBUSY fussy, gaudy

OVERCAST accloud, becloud, bind, clouded, cloudy, dark(en), dim, dull, fog, gloomy, glum, haze, heavy, lowery, nebulous, obscure, sew, smog

OVERCHARGE bleed, cathexis, cheat, excise, exploit(ation), extort(ion), fleece, gouge, gyp, holdup, inflation, overassess, overpay(ment), overtax, plethora, profiteer(ing), skin, soak, stick, sting, surcharge, surfeit, usury

OVERCLOUD See OVERCAST.

OVERCOAT abolla, abrigo, aquascutum, balmacaan, benjamin, benny, burberry, burnoose, bursattee, byrrus, camail, capote, chesterfield, coonskin, cothamore, fearnought, greatcoat, grego, inverness, joseph, loden, mac(kintosh), mantle, mino, mozzetta, oilskin, paletot, pardessus, parka, pelisse, poncho, raglan, raincoat, redingote, robe, shuba, slicker, slipon, spencer, taglioni, tarpaulin, trenchcoat, ulster, waterproof, wraparound, wraprascal

close-fitting surtout

hooded capote, parka

light siphonia

loose balmacaan, mantle, paletot, raglan, wraprascal

material boyleslaw, duffle

sleeveless inverness, mantle

straw mino

wooden bier, coffin

OVERCOME accomplish, appall, awe, beat(en), best, brokenhearted, bushed, catch, charm, complete, confute, conquer, convince, craven, crush(ed), daunt, defeat(ed), demoralize, des-

olated, discomfit, domineer, encumber, exceed, fordo, happen, heartbroken, hurdle, master, mate, outdo, outstrip, overbear, overpower, overthrow, overturn, persuade, prevail, prostrate, rout, rule, shock, stricken, subdue, subjugate, suppress, surmount, surplus, triumph, undone, unhappy, upset, vanquish, win

by heat sunstruck, sweltering

we shall venceremos

OVERCROWD deluge, flood, swamp

OVERDO burlesque, caricature, exaggerate, exceed, excel, exhaust, fatigue, inflate, overcook, overtax, overwork, percoct, strain, stretch, supererogate, surpass

OVERDONE artificial, burned, charred, exaggerated, extreme, exuberant, fustian, gauche, gaudy, grandiloquent, grotesque, hackneyed, well-done

OVERDUE anachronism, arrear(s), behindhand, belated, deferred, delayed, delinquent, detained, late, outstanding, owing, postponed, remiss, retarded, slackened, slow(ed), tardy, unpaid, unsettled

OVEREAGER feverish

OVEREAT cram, devour, gorge, satiate, stuff

OVERESTIMATE boost, eulogize, extol, glorify, inflate, magnify, overrate, overvalue, panegyrize, puff, strain, stretch

OVEREXERT overtax, strain, torfel, torfle

OVERFED bursting, fulsome, rank, rotund, stuffed

OVERFLOW abound, abundance, alluvion, brim over, bubble over, cascade, cataclysm, cataract, debord, deluge, ebullience, engulf, excess, exundate, float, flood, gush, inundate, outlet, overbrim, overrun, plenty, plethora, profusion, redundance, rest, run over, slop, slosh, spate, spew, spill, spue, submerge, superabound, superabundance, surplus, swamp,

swarm, teem, vent, well over, whelm

OVERFLOWING awash, big, brimful, brimming, bursting, copious, deluge, exuberance, freshet, inundation, profuse

OVERGARMENT blouse, cloak, duster, smock, tabard

OVERGO cover, discover, exceed, excel, outwit, overpower, overrun, pass, surmount, transgress

OVERGROWN bushy, fozy, fulsome, rank, sedgy, spratty, spreading, spritty, thick

OVERHAND advantage, mastery, whip

OVERHANG beetle, beetling, brew, bulge, eaves, fantail, impend(ence), jut, loom, menace, portend, project (ion), rake, shelve, stick out, suspend

OVERHANGING beetling, imminent, impending, suspended, threatening

OVERHAUL beat, check, examine, fix, forereach, inspect, inventory, mend, outstrip, overtake, pass, reach, renovate, repair, restore

OVERHEAD above, aloft, average, burden, cost, expense, maintenance, oncost, severally, tilt, upkeep, upward

OVERINDULGENT intemperate, lenient

OVERISSUE inflation

OVERJOYED delighted, elated, enraptured, happy, JOYOUS, jubilant, rapturous, ravished, transported

OVERLAPPING equitant, imbricate(d), jugate, lapstreak, obvolute, shingled

OVERLAY applique, cap, ceil, coat, couch, cover (ing), cravat, debruise, encrust, glaze, hide, imbrication, lap, obscure, oppress, overburden, overlie, patch, plate, smother, spread, stucco, superimpose, superpose, veneer

OVERLIE bridge, cap, command, dominate, imbricate, lap, oppress, override, shingle, span

OVERLOAD burden, charge, encumber, glut, ornament, plethora, sate, surcharge

OVERLOOK absolve, acquit, balk, bewitch, blink, condone, contemplate, dismiss, dominate, examine, excuse, forego, forget, forgive, free, front on, ignore, inspect, let go, manage, misknow, miss, neglect, omit, pardon, pass, read, regard, scan, scrutinate, scrutinize, skip, slight, spare, superintend, supervise, surmount, survey, tolerate, tower, wink at

OVERLORD despot, domineer, liege, master, potentate, satrap, suzerain, tyrannize

OVERLY carelessly, exceedingly, excessively, negligent, too superficial

OVERLYING bridging, brochant, equitant, imbricate(d), incumbent, lapping, shingled, spanning, superimposed

OVERMAN arbiter, chief, foreman, leader, overpower, overseer, referee

OVERMATCH beat, best, crush, defeat, exceed, subdue, surpass, vanquish

OVERMODEST See OVERNICE.

OVERMUCH excess(ive), surplus, too

OVERNICE affected, dentical, euphemistic(al), euphuistic(al), exquisite, fastidious, finical, finicky, fussy, goody-goody, mincing, namby-pamby, precieuse, precious, precise, priggish, prim, prudish, simpering, squeamish

OVERPASS bridge, exceed, overrun, passage(way), span

OVERPLUS advantage, cornucopia, excess, plenty, plethora, rest, superfluity, surplus

OVERPOWER awe, benight, dazzle, engulf, enrapture, entrance, OVERCOME, OVERWHELM, quell, stimulate, subdue, swamp, whelm, wrixle

OVERPOWERING dazzling, dire, fierce, killing, monstrous, stunning

OVERREACH cheat, circumvent, cozen, deceive, defraud, dupe, exaggerate, exceed, grease, nobble, out-

wit, overrun, pass, strain, swindle

OVERRIPE mushy, soft, squashy

OVERRULE abrogate, govern, influence, master, overcome, persuade, repeal, reverse, veto

OVERRUN abound, beat, beset, bespread, crush, desert, despoil, destroy, devastate, eclipse, exceed, excel, grow over, infest, luxuriate, outdistance, outdo, outrace, outstrip, overflow, OVERWHELM, pass, permeate, pervade, ravage, spread, surmount, surpass, surplus, swarm, teem, tower, trample

OVERSEAS abroad, away, transatlantic, transoceanic, transpacific

OVERSEE administer, blunder, check, deceive, delude, direct, disregard, err, examine, eye, handle, inspect, manage, neglect, overlook, scan, superintend, supervise, survey, view, watch

OVERSEER acequiador, bailiff, banksman, bishop, boss, caporal, cesnor, chaprasi, cork, curator, driver, ephor, foreman, gaffer, grave, grieve, head(man), inspector, kangani, leader, manager, martinet, master, principal, pristow, superintendent, supervisor, surveyor, tapsman, tentor, warden
agricultural agronome
spiritual bishop, pastor, priest

OVERSHADOW adumbrate, beat, beshade, cloud, cover, darken, dim, dominate, dwarf, eclipse, obscure, outdo, outweigh, overcast, preponderate, shade, shelter

OVERSHOE arctic, boot, flapper, foothold, gaiter, galosh(e), goloe, golosh, goloshoe, gum(boot), pantafle, patten, rubber

OVERSIGHT blunder, care, charge, control, direction, disregard, error, examination, failure, fault, gaffe, inattention, inspection, jeofail, lapse, management, mistake, neglect, negligence, omission, scrutiny, superintendance, supervise, super-

vision, surveillance, tutelage, watch

OVERSIZED gross, hulking, large, lubberly, lumpish

OVERSKIRT pan(n)ier, peplum

OVERSLIP escape, neglect, omit, pass, slipover, transgress

OVERSPREAD See SPREAD.

OVERSTATE exaggerate, hyperbolize, magnify, misrepresent

OVERSTEP encroach, exceed, impinge, overrun, transgress, trespass

OVERSTRAINED epitonic

OVERSTUFF fatten, gorge, sate, satiate, upholster

OVERSUPPLY deluge, excess, glut, surplus

OVERSWARM See OVERRUN.

OVERT above-aboard, apparent, candid, evident, expanded, frank, manifest, observable, obvious, open, patent, public, unconcealed, uncovered, undeceiving

OVERTAKE apprehend, attain, beat, captivate, catch, detect, ensnare, forehent, gain, involve, outstrip, overget, overhaul, pass, reach, rejoin, seize

OVERTAX burden, exceed, overwork, strain, stress

OVERTHROW afflict, allay, best, capsize, checkmate, confound, dash, defeasance, defeat, deject, demolish, depose, derange, destroy, destruction, devolve, discomfit(ure), dislodge, down, evert, fell, fling, foil, fold, hurl, level, OVERCOME, OVERWHELM, prostrate, quash, raze, refute, reversal, reverse, revolution, rout, ruin(ate), rush, subvert, supplant, tip, topple, tumble, unhorse, unseat, upset, vanquish, worst, wrack, wreck

OVERTHWART across, adverse, antagonistic, crossways, crosswise, indirect, opposing, opposite, perversely, rebuss, slanting, transverse

OVERTIME bonus, excess, extended

OVERTIRE fatigue, tax

OVERTOP cow, dwarf, eclipse, exceed, excel, overreach, surpass, tower, transcend

OVERTURE advance, approach, beginning, bid, calumet, exordium, music offer(ing), olive branch, opening, placation, preamble, preface, prelude, prelusion, presentation, proem, proffer, prologue, proposal, proposition, request, ritornel, tender, vorspiel, white flag

opera sinfonia

OVERTURN capsize, cartwheel, cave, coup, culbut, defeat, destroy, fell, invert, keel over, knock down, overcome, overset, OVERTHROW, overwhelm, pervert, refute, reverse, revolution, slight, somersault, somerset, spill, subversal, subvert, terve, throw, tilt, tip, tipple, topple, transpose, upend, upset, walt, welt(er), whalm, whelm

OVERWEENING arrogant, confident, exaggerated, insolent, presumptuous, pretentious, selfimportant, vain

OVERWEIGHT fat, gross, heavy, obese, outgang, plethora, polysarcia, ponderous, rotundity, stout(ness)

OVERWHELM astonish, astound, avalanche, blanket, bury, conquer, cover, crush, cumber, defeat, deluge, destroy, distress, drouk, drown, flatten, flood, floor, immerse, inundate, oppress, overpower, overthrow, quell, reduce, refute, rout, shut out, smash, snow, stun, subdue, submerge, surprise, swamp, upset, vanquish, whitewash, worst

OVERWHELMING catastrophe, conclusive, dazzling, dire, fierce, formidable, stunning

OVERWORK burden, exhaust, grind, hoin, labor, sweat, task, tax, tire, toil, wear out

OVERWORN exhausted, obsolete, spent, stale

OVERWROUGHT edgy, elaborated, excited, fancy, grandiloquent, nervous, overdone, upset

OVID *burial site* tomi
surname naso
work amores, ars amandi, ars amatoria, fasti, heroides, medea, metamorphoses, tristia

OVILLUS hercules

OVINE ewe, lamb, ram, sheep(like)

OVIS aoudad, argali, auri, bighorn, sheep

OVOID egglike, obovoid, ovate, oviform, ovule

OVOLO boltel, molding, oval, thumb

OVULE egg, embryo, gemmule, germ, nit, seed(let)
integument primine

OVUM cell, egg(cell), germ, oosphere, seed, spore
comb. ova

OWALA *tree* bobo, mimosac(eae)

OWE attribute, aught, bear, claim, due, ewe, hence, lamb, own, possess, shall

OWED awn

OWEN, ROBERT *community* new harmony

OWER debtor, ewer, oar, over, pitcher

OWING ascribable, attributable, because, behind, beholden, due, indebted, matured, obliged, outstanding, owed, payable, resulting, unpaid, unsettled

OWL (See also *kind*, below.) aziola, billywix, boobook, bubo, cue, eal, gnome, harfang, hawk, hooter, howlet, jenny, katogle, ketupa, lulu, madge, momo, mucard, ninox, padge, pouie, prowl, pry, raptor, ruru, scops, snory, stare, strix, surn, tyto, ule, ullet, utum, wapacut, wekau, whekau, woolert
barn lulu, madge, pouie, tyto
barred strix, syrnium
burrowing speotyto
call hoot, screech, ululation
changed to ascalaphus
clover butter-and-eggs, orthocarpus
eagle bubo, katogle
ensign of athens
eye area disk
family strigidae
genus bubo, ninox, strix, syrnium, tyto
group parliament
hawk surn
-head plover

horned aziola, bubo
kind acadian, arctic, barn, barred, billy, screech, tawny
laughing w(h)ekau
-like strigine
parrot kakapo, tarapo
short-eared momo
small aziola, glaucidium, howlet, richardson's, snowy, utum
snowy harfang
stomach contents cast
swallow nightjar
symbol of wisdom
young owlet, utum

OWLGLASS buffoon, jester, tyl(l) eulenspiegel

OWN acknowledge, acquire, admit, ain, allow, ane, appropriate, assent, aught, avow, awn, claim, concede, conduct, confess, control, direct, disclose, divulge, enjoy, grant, have, hold, howe, keep, manage, master, nain, ought, possess, profess, recognize, retain, reveal, tell
comb. idio
up confess

OWNER baleboosteh, baleboss, bourgeois, capitalist, freeholder, landholder, landlord, malik, master, padrone, partner, possessor, proprietor, squire, walla

OWNERLESS castoff, derelict, deserted

OWNERSHIP capital, dominium, lordship, monopoly, occupation, possession, property, proprietary, seignoralty, seignory, seizin, seizure, tenancy, tenure, title
joint community property, coparcen(ar)y
pert. odal

OX, OXEN aiver, anoa, arna, arnee, aurochs, banteng, banting, beef, beeve, bibos, bison, bos, bovine, buffalo, bugle, bull(ock), cattle, gaur, gayal, kine, kouprey, mithan, musk, neat, nowt, owse, reems, sanga, seladang, steer, stot, tallower, tolly, tsine, twinter, yak, zebu
comb. bovi
driver bullwhacker
dumb thomas aquinas
extinct aurochs, urus
-eyed boopis

-god apis
group span, team, yoke
grunting yak
guider forelooper
harness span, yoke
hidethong riem
hornless moil
-like bovine, dull, patient, slow, sluggish, stolid
meat, cured biltong, bugloss
musk ovibos
sacrifice chiliomb
shoe cul
skull bucrane, burcanium
small runt
sole whiff
son merari
stall boose, boosy
stomach tripe
strap reim, rein, riem
symbol of patience, pride, strength
-tongue anchusa, bugloss, picris, weed
tumor clyer, wen
wild anoa, aurochs, banting, bibos, buff(alo), bugle, gaur, reem, seladang, urus, yak
working aver
young stot
OXALINE humboltine
OXALIS oca, plant, shamrock-pea, sorrel
OXAYL carbonyl, carboxyl
OXBERRY bryony, cuckoo-pint
OXBIRD dunlin, oxpecker, sanderling, sandpiper, weaverbird
OXBITER cowbird
OXBLOOD coptic, kazak(h), red
OXBOT warble-fly
OXCART ar(a)ba, rut
carry in kurvey
tongue cope
OXEYE aster, bird, black-eyed-susan, boce, bogue, camomile, cloud, daisy, dunlin, fish, flower, heliopsis, megalops, plover, sandpiper, titmouse
OXFORD cloth, fabric, shoe, university
academic term See ENGLISH *academic term.*
alumni, famous archbishop laud, arnold, charles lutwidge dodgson, sir christopher wren, jude the obscure, keble, lewis carroll, newman, pusey, tolkien, sir william blackstone

bell great tom
bibliophile sir thomas bodley
boat race torpid
bridge folly, magdalen
center carfax
ceremony encaenia
church saint mary the virgin
club hide-and-seek
college all souls, balliol, christ church, jesus, magdalen, merton, new, oriel, pembroke, queens, st catherines, st johns, the house, trinity, university, wadham, worcester
earl of asquith, harley
examination great-go, greats, mods, smalls
examination suit subfusc
humorist spooner
library bodleian
main street broad, cornmarket, high, queen
market high and covered
medical discovery penicillin
movement moral rearmament, puseyism, tractarian (ism)
movement founder buchman
museum aldate's, (old)ashmolean
officer beadle, bedel(l), chancellor, don, master, proctor, warden
oldest quadrangle mob quad
overseer queen elizabeth ii, visitor
patroness frideswide
priory studley
reading room radcliffe camera
religious movement methodism, moral rearmament
river cherwell, isis, thames
scholar commoner, demy, fellow
scholarship rhodes
tutor don
university seat clarendon building
visitor overseer, queen elizabeth ii
OXGANG bovate, osken, plowgang
OXHEAD blockhead, dolt, fool
OXHEART cabbage, cherry, napoleon
OXIDATE See OXIDIZE.
OXIDATION burning, decay
by exposure to air autocodation
gradual eremacausis
OXIDE cadmia, calx, earth,

floss, limonite, moiles, rust, zaffer
barium baryta
calcium lime
cobalt saffer, zaffre
hydrocarbon radical ether
iron colcothar, magnetite, rust
mercurous montroydite, turpeth
radioactive thoria
sodium soda
strontium strontia
zinc cadmia
OXIDIZE boil, burn, calcine, corrode, rust
OXLIP milkmaid, pa(i)gle, primrose, primula, primwort
OXPECKER beefeater, starling
OXTER armpit, elbow, embrace, enarm, hug
OXUS amu-darya
OXWORT butterbur
OXYDERCES athena
OXYGEN element, gas, oxygenium, ozone
acid chloric, sulphuric
allotropic ozone
comb. oxa
compound oxid(e)
deficiency anoxemia, anoxia, asphyxia
excess maderisation
form ozone
pert. hyperbaric
producer plankton
radical oxyl
removal reduction
source air, atmosphere
OXYGENATE aerate, air, carbonate, oxidize, ventilate
OXYNEURINE betain(e)
OXYRHYNCH crab, fish, mormyrus
OXYSALT sulphate
OXYTETRACYCLINE terramycin
OXYTOCIN pitocin
OXYTROPIS aragallus
OYER court, hearing, pleading, trial
OYEZ attend, attention, hear, listen
OYSTER avicula, bivalve, bluepoint, box, chincoteague, copis, cotuit, count, croquette, greengill, huitre, lynnhaven, malpeque, mollusk, native, new orleans, ostrea, pinna, plant, powldoody, rattler, reefer, sharper, shell, wellfleet

bed bank, claire, layer, laying, oysterage, parc, park, scalfe, scalp, stew
bed material culch, cultch, cutch
bird sanderling
catcher bird, krocket, olive, piannet, pilwillet, pynot, scolder, shelder, skeldrake, tirma, trillachan, trittichan
comb. ostreo
crab pinnotere
cut tidbit
drill borer
eggs spawn
enemy starfish
farm See OYSTER *bed.*

fish tautog, toadfish
fossil ostracite
gatherer tongman
grass kelp, sea-lettuce
measure wash
pearl silverlip
pest boring-sponge, cliona
plant lungwort, rhoeo, salsify
rake tongs
rock chama
seed pearl
-shaped ostreiform
shell cul(t)ch, husk, shuck, test
small blister, cherrystone
sold by pound count

spawn culch, cultch, cutch
tree mangrove
2, 3 or 4 warp
uncultivated reefer
vegetable salsify
young set, spat
OYSVORF bum, outcast, scoundrel
OZ *book author* baum
character dorothy, scarecrow, tinman
OZARK *state* arkansas, missouri
OZEM *kin* david, jesse
OZIELUS *commander* josiah
OZONE air, atmosphere, ether, gas, oxygen

P

PA, PAH dad(dy), father, fort, pap(a), pappy, paw, pop, settlement, stockade, stronghold, village
PAAW bustard
PABULUM aliment, cereal, food, fuel, manna, nourishment, nutriment, prog, support, sustenance
PAC boot, moccasin, shoe
PACA agouti, capa, cavy, cuniculus, labba, lava, rodent
PACE advance, amble, bema, bundle, canter, canto, chapter, clip, clop, clump, course, easter, flounce, footstep, gait, gallop, hitch, hobble, hoofbeat, hop, impetus, jog, jolt, jump, limp, lock-step, lope, lumber, lunge, march, measure, mince, nave, paddle, pasch, passage, passo, passus, peace, piaffe(r), platform, prance, precede, proceed, rack, rate, sashay, scuttle, single-foot, skip, slog, slouch, speed, stagger, stalk, stamp, step, stomp, stride, strut, stump, swagger, swing, tempo, toddle, totter, trace, tread, trip, trot, velocity, walk, wamble, way
PACER ambler, horse, leader, pacemaker, spanker, trippler
PACESETTER leader, model
PACHISI game, ludo, uckers
PACHUCO zootsuiter

PACHYCEREUS cactus, cardon(a)
PACHYDERM elephant, hathi, hippo(potamus), jumbo, mammoth, mastodon, rhino (ceros)
PACHYDERMIA elephantiasis
PACHYSANDRA box(wood), spurge, tricera
PACIFIC calm, conciliatory, eirenic(al), halcyon, irenic(al), irenicon, meek, mild, ocean, orderly, peaceable, peaceful, quiet, serene, tranquil, untroubled
aborigine amphinesian
atoll see PACIFIC *island.*
barracuda scooter
bonita victorfish
clam gweduc
coast bird turnstone, wandering-tatler
coast herb barrenwort, campanula, elkclover, elkgrass, pink, silene
coast hurricane cordonazo
coast range cascades, cordilleras, sierra nevadas
coast shrub bayberry, ceanothus, myrica, salal, toyon
coast state california, oregon, washington
coast tree chincapin, chinquapin
fish aburabozu, albacore, barracuda, beshow, bonito, candlefish, corbina, dolphin, halibut, machete, mackerel, marlin, moorish-idol, ron-

cador, sculpin, seabass, skate, skipjack, smelt, surffish, swordfish, tambor, tubesnout, tuna, victorfish, yellowtail
highway camino real
indian chinook, nootka, siwash
island 3 aru, hao, yap 4 anaa, bali, buka, fiji, guam, lifu, maui, oahu, rapa, reao, truk, uapu, uvea, wake 5 amanu, atoll, baker, bonin, ducie, katsu, kuril, mauru, munga, papua, samoa, tahaa, tikei 6 ahunui, hatutu, hawaii, hivada, kodiak, komodo, levant, makemo, manihi, midway, moorea, morane, pinaki, rurutu, ryukyu, saipan, savage, tahiti, taiwan, takume, tepoto, tubuai, tureia 7 aratika, huahine, marokau, marutea, mehetia, mururoa, okinawa, phoenix, raiatea 8 borabora, eniwetok, fakarava, fatuhiva, johnston, matahiva, nukuhiva, pitcairn, pukapuka, raivavae, rangiroa, rimatara, tasmania, vanavana 9 mangareva, new guinea, raratonga, tematangi 10 fangataufa, nengonengo, new britain 12 bougainville
island bird kagu, murrelet, thickhead, whistler
island cloth tapa
island fern palapalai
island grass neti

island group actaeon, admiralty, caroline, cook, ellice, friendly, gilbert, hawaii, indonesia, mariana, marquesas, marshall, midway, new caledonia, new hebrides, oceania, palay, pelew, phillipines, samoa, sandwich, society, solomon, sula, tonga, tuamotu, tubuai
island pine ieie, kou, lehua
island plant copperleaf, eulalia, neti, salal, taro
island region oceania, polynesia
island shrub salal, tiara
island tree candlenut, dasheen, eddyroot, hala, ipil, kou, lehua, madrona, taro
military base guam
morning glory pilikai
ocean archipelago aru, malay, samoa, sulu
ocean current blackstream, el nino, japan(ese), kuroshio
ocean discoverer balboa
ocean inlet monterey bay, papagayo gulf, puget sound
ocean part arafua sea, banda sea, bering sea, celebes sea, coral sea, east china sea, philippine sea, sea of japan, south china sea, sulu, tasman sea, timor sea
ocean, river into biobio, columbia, fraser
rockfish tambor
sea See *ocean part*, above.
shark mako
shrub salal
smelt smoothtongue
stepping stones aleutians
strait formosa, taiwan
tarpon machete
tree hala, ipil
PACIFICATION abatement, armistice, conciliation, truce
PACIFIER comforter, dummy, lenitive, mitigative, nipple, ring, sedative, soother, sop
PACIFIST bolo, conchie, conscientious objector, irenic, neutral, peaceable
PACIFY abate, allay, alleviate, appease, assuage, becalm, calm, come to terms, conciliate, lull, make up, mitigate, moderate, mollify, pease, placate, propitiate, qualify, quell, reconcile, relieve, soothe, stickle, still, temper, tranquil(l)ize

PACK 3 bag, box, can, jam, lot, ram, set, wad 4 bale, bevy, cade, cram, deck, doup, fill, gang, heap, jamb, lade, load, mass, pile, plot, sack, ship, stow, tame, tamp, tote, tuck 5 bunch, carry, covey, crame, crate, crowd, drove, flock, GROUP, horde, press, shook, skulk, somer, stack, steve, stive, store, stuff, swarm, truss 6 barrel, begone, bottle, bundle, burden, carton, depart, duffel, duffle, embale, encase, fardel, gaggle, hamper, number, parcel, pocket, steeve, throng 7 arrange, besiege, compact, freight, PACKAGE, pannier, portage, prepare, process, rummage, squeeze, sumpter 8 assemble, compress, conspire, contrive, knapsack, quantity, wrapping 9 multitude, transport 10 collection, congregate, impediment, manipulate
animal ass, burro, camel, donkey, llama, mule, somer, sumpter
builder gobber
horse driver sumpter
leader akela
off begone, dismiss, repulse, shank, turse, wag
-rat collector, hoarder, neotoma, prospector, rodent, saver
the deal cheat, conspire
tightly cram, stive, wedge
PACKAGE (See also PACK.) all-expense, bag, bale, ball of wax, barrel, basket, bindle, bolt, box, budget, bundle, capsule, cargo, carton, cartridge, case, cask, ceroon, container, crate, dorlach, encase, enclose, encyst, fadge, fagot, fardel, fascine, hamper, incase, jar, packet, pad, parcel, pot, robbin, roll, rouleau, sack, seroon, sheaf, tank, tin, truss
hide-covered ceroon, seroon
PACKED bristling, compact, crammed, crawling, crowded, dense, firm, jammed, loaded, populous, replete, serried, stuck, swarming, teeming, tumid, weighted
PACKER baler, canner, car-

rier, cheat(er), conspirator, dealer, jar, plotter, roper
PACKET boat, book, bundle, deck, PACKAGE, parcel, roll, sachet
PACKHORSE jagger, somer, sumpter
PACKING content(s), filling, gasket, gauze, grommet, lading, lining, obstruction, paper, placement, rags, stowage, stuffing, waste
clay lute
hammer sheep's-foot
house abattoir, meatworks
material baline, excelsior, gasket, gauze, straw
plant cannery
water-tight gasket, washer
PACKMAN cadger, hawker, peddler
PACKSACK duffelbag, kyack
PACKSADDLE aparejo, bardel(le), bat
PACT accord, agreement, bargain, cartel, compact, concordat, contract, covenant, deal, entente, indenture, mise, treaty, truce
PACTION See PACT.
PACTOLIAN golden
PAD amplify, apartment, bed(ding), block, bolster, bombast, boot, boss, buffer, bulk, burr, bustle, cover, cram, cushion, dabber, diggings, digs, enlarge, expand, follow, foot(fall), footpad, frog, home, horse, house, increase, inker, mat, numnah, pace, pack(age), padnag, pallet, pannier, path, pat(ter), perch, pillion, pillow, pitterpatter, place, print, puff, pulvillus, quilt, quire, ream, residence, road, robber, sashoon, slab, socket, sponge, starfish, stuff(ing), tablet, thicken, thud, toad, track, tramp(le), tread, trudge, velure, wad, walk, way
straw sunk, wase, wisp
PADCLOTH housing, saddlecloth
PADDED endless, longspun, prolix, verbose
PADDER footpad, highwayman
PADDING bombast, bushing, caddis, fill(er), lining, mahoitre, packing, redundancy, softening, stuffing, superfluity, wadding

PADDLE agitate, battel, battle(dore), beater, blade, bucket, canoe, dabble, discipline, flipper, lumpfish, oar, pace, palm, punish, row, scoop, scull, spank(er), spoon, spud, squander, stroke, sweep, toddle, trample, tread, trifle, wade, wallop, waste
box wheelhouse

PADDLEFISH duckbill, ganoid, polyodon(t), shovelfish, spadefish, spoonbill, sturgeon

PADDOCK close, enclosure, field, frog, garston, lot, park, pasture, sledge, toad, yard
-pipe horsetail
-stone greenstone
-stool toadstool

PADDY almanac, batty, cushiony, field, irishman, rice, soft
lucern escoba, sida

PADDYBIRD heron, ruddyduck, sheathbill, sparrow

PADDYMELON quokka, wallaby

PADDYWHACK beat, irishman, passion, pet, rage, spanking, temper, thrashing

PADFOOT barghest

PADISHAH emperor, king, mogul, potshaw, ruler, sovereign, sultan

PADIUS birdcherry, buckthorn, dogwood

PADLOCK close, closing, fasten(er), lock, seal, secure, shackle

PADNAG amble, horse, trot

PADRE chaplain, cleric, father, friar, monk, priest

PADRONE boss, chief, innkeeper, landlord, master, owner, patron

PADUA *coin* aquilino
lord benedick
native patavian

PAEAN apollo, celebrate, hymn, ode, praise, song, triumphal

PAEON *son* agastrophus

PAGAN agnostic, alangan, apayao, ata, bagobo, bangon, bilaan, bontoc, buid, bukid, dumagat, ethnic, gentile, harlot, heathen, idolater, idolatrous, infidel, irreligious, paynim, sabian, subanun, unbeliever, ungodly

god baal, idol
land barbary
pert. gnostic

PAGE(S) attendant, bellboy, bellhop, boy, buttons, cahier, call, child, donzel, equerry, foliate, folio, henchboy, henchman, ichoglan, leaf, menial, messenger, number, paginate, paviser, record, recto, rubric, servant, sheet, squire, summon, varlet, verso, youth
book cahier, folio
bottom tail
facing spread
1st flyleaf, frontmatter
lady's escudero
left-hand verso
number folio, paginate
paper sheet
right-hand outpage, recto
size quarto
space between gutter
title rubric, unwan

PAGEANT aquacade, carnival, cavalcade, display, drama, exposition, imitate, mimic, parade, platform, play, pomp, procession, scene, show, spectacle, stage, tableau, tamasha, theatrical

PAGEANTRY display, heraldry, magnificence, ostentation, parade, pomp, splendor

PAGINATION enumeration, foliation, numeration

PAGLIACCI *character* beppo, canio, nedda, silvio, tonio
composer leoncavallo

PAGLIAIO See HUT.

PAGNE breechcloth, loincloth, petticoat

PAGODA coin, gazebo, hoon, josshouse, kryailteyo, pon, summerhouse, taa, temple, tower, varella, wat(t)
ornament epi, finial, tee
stone agalmatolite, pagodite
tree banyan, frangipani, plumeria

PAGOSCOPE hygrodeik, hygrometer

PAGRUS besugo, braise, porgy, roach, rutilus, seabream, tai

PAH bah, disgusting, fort, improper, nasty, nonsense, stockade, village

PAHATHMOAB *son* adna, bezaleel, binnui, chelal, ha-

shub, maaseiah, manasseh, mattaniah

PAHI canoe, ship

PAHLAVI *country* iran, persia
text bundahish

PAHMI bobac, helictis, mustelid

PAID cashed, content, discharged, drunk, even, hired, mercenary, satisfied, settled, spent, squared
in full satisfied

PAIDEUTICS pedagogy

PAIGLE cowslip, crowfoot, cuckooflower, oxlip, stitchwort

PAIK beat, blow, hit, pommel, strike, stroke, thump

PAIL attack, blicky, bouk, bowk, brazier, bucket, can, cog(gie), cogue, collock, container, dandy, eimer, eshin, harass, hod, milk, noggin, piggin, scuttle, situla, skeel, soe, thrash, trug, vessel
handle bail
pottery seal
small blickie, blicky, eshin
wooden cog(ue), luggie, piggin

PAILLASSE bed(ding), mattress, pallet

PAILLETTE paillon, sequin, spangle

PAIN 3 ail, nip, woe 4 ache, agra, bale, bite, blow, bore, burn, care, cark, gall, gout, hell, hurt, kink, pang, rack, stab, teen, tine 5 agony, bread, chafe, cramp, crick, dolor, grate, grief, gripe, labor, prick, scald, shock, smart, spasm, steek, sting, thraw, throb, throe, trial, wound, wring 6 aching, appall, bother, bruise, grieve, harrow, injury, misery, pierce, punish, sorrow, stitch, strain, stroke, suffer, throes, tingle, twinge, twitch, wrench 7 afflict, agonize, algesis, anguish, anxiety, lumbago, malaise, myalgia, otalgia, penalty, prickle, pyrosis, scourge, torment, torture, travail, trouble 8 aggrieve, backache, convulse, distress, otodynia, sciatica 9 aggravate, dysphoria, suffering, toothache 10 affliction, difficulty, discomfort, excruciate, punishment 11 algesthesis

abdominal colic, cramps, gastralgia, gripe(s), stomach-ache, tormina

absence analgesia, an(a)esthesia, anodynia

back notalgia, sciatica

bridge of kuchu chiao

burning smart

-causing algetic

comb. agra, algia, alg(i)o, algy, odynia

darting twinge

fear of algophobia

heat-caused thermalgesia

insensitive to anesthetic, anesthetized, impassible

in the neck See BORE, PEST.

measurer algometer

measuring unit dol

of mind agony, torment

personification oizys

pert. algetic

producing algogenic

relayer nerve

relieve allay, alleviate, analgize, assuage, deaden, dull, ease, lessen, palliate, quiet, salve, soften, soothe

reliever ascriptin, aspirin, bufferin, cope, coricidin, darvon, empirin, excedrin, percodan, phenaphen, vanquish

sensation of algesis

sensitivity to algesia, hyperalgesia

wrenching torsion

PAINE, THOMAS *work* age of reason, common sense, rights of man

PAINFUL algetic, angry, bitter, careful, cruel, difficult, diligent, dire, distressing, excruciating, grueling, hurtful, intolerable, irksome, laborious, punishing, racking, sharp, sore, splitting, terrible, thorny, throbbing, troublesome, unbearable

comb. mogi

PAIN-KILLER acesodyne, acetophenetide, acupuncture, analgesic, analgetic, an(a)esthetic, anodyne, aspirin, atropine, balm, bufferin, caffeine, coca, codeine, darvon, drug, heroin, lenitive, meperidine, morphine, narcotic, opiate, paregoric, phenacetin, reliever, sedative

PAINLESS indolent

PAINLESSNESS analgesia, anodynia, aponia

PAINS care, diligence, effort, exertion, industry, labor, toil, travail, trouble, work

PAINSTAKING assiduity, assiduous, busy, care(ful), cark, diligence, diligent, effort, elaborate, exertion, fussy, labored, meticulous, operose, particular, punctilious, scrupulous, studied, thorough(ness)

PAINT adorn, beautify, bedaub, begild, besmear, blot, blush, brush, calcimine, coat, color, cosmetics, cover, dab, daub, decorate, delineate, depict, describe, distemper, elemi, email, enamel, engild, fard, feign, figure, gaud, gild, gilt, glaze, gloss, gloze, image, impaste, japan, lac (quer), limn, lipstick, miniate, parget, picture, pigment, portray, prime, represent, rouge, shellac, shmeer, sketch, slapdash, slick, smear, stain, stipple, tinge, urfirnis, varnish, wash, watercolor, whitewash

comb. picto

disguised with fucate

egg and water tempera

face eyeshadow, fard, fucus, lipstick, parget, powder, rouge

finish, dull flat, matte

finish, glossy enamel

1st coat clearcole, primer, size, sizing

glossy dominie, enamel

ingredient banana-oil, bivinyl, butadiene, drier, lac, megilp(h), meguilp, oil, pigment, turpentine

pattern stencil

red chica, lake, roset

solvent acetone, thinner, turpentine

sprayer airbrush

spreader brush, roller, spatula

the town red carouse, frolic, play

thinner solvent, turpentine

PAINTBRUSH castilleja, figwort, hawkweed, nosebleed, painted-cup, st-john's-wort, wickawee

PAINTED artificial, colored, disguised, enameled, feigned, fucate, goffered, pastose, pinto, rouged, variegated

beauty butterfly, vanessa

bunting finch, longspur, nonpareil, pape, passerina, pop

cup bloody-noses, bloody-warrior, castilleja, wickawee

hyena cape hunting dog

lady pink, pyrethrum, thistle-butterfly

leaf fireplant

partridge francolin

snipe rostratula

PAINTER artist, brushman, cougar, dauber, decorator, limner, muralist, panther, pictor, puma, rope, sternfast

animal landseer

bird audubon

botanical bauer

famous bellini, bellows, blake, bonnard, botticelli, braque, bruegel, cezanne, chagall, constable, copley, corot, correggio, dali, daumier, david, da vinci, degas, duchamp, dufy, durer, eakins, el greco, fra angelico, fragonard, gainsborough, gauguin, giotto, goya, gris, hals, hogarth, holbein, ingres, kandinsky, kent, klee, leger, leonardo, manet, masaccio, matisse, michelangelo, millet, modigliani, mondrian, monet, munch, murillo, opie, orozco, picasso, pissarro, raphael, rembrandt, renoir, reynolds, rivera, romney, rousseau, rubens, sargent, seurat, signac, sisley, stuart, tintoretto, titian, toulouse-lautrec, turner, utrillo, vandyke, van gogh, velasquez, vermeer, vlaminck, vuillard, watteau, whistler

finger dauber

paste gesso

PAINTING art, bodegon, camaieu, canvas, cartoon, croute, daubing, draft, encaustic, fresco, gouache, gradino, grisaille, illustration, mural, oil, pata, picture, portrait, predella, still-life, tempera

canvas pata

circular tondo

colloidal tempera

equipment amasette, brush, easel, oils, paint, palette, pallet

exhibit salon, vernissage

foliage boscage
genre bambacciata, bambocciade, bambochade
medium acrylic, casein, oil, tempera
method alla-prima, distemper, fresco, gouache, grisaille, impasto, scumble, secco, tempera, watercolor
mixture magilp, megilp(h), meguilp
1-color monochrome, monotint
on plaster fresco, mural, secco
opaque gouache
plant corn-gromwell
round tondo
sacred pieta, tanka
scenic landscape, pastoral, scape, seascape
still-life bodegon, natura morta
style abstract, action, bolognese, classic, cubism, dadaist, expressionism, fauvism, futurism, genre, gouache, idealist, intimism, kano, mannerism, realism, spray, suprematism, surrealism, synthetism, tempera, tenebrism
technique See PAINTING method.
the town red on a binge, on a tear
3-paneled triptych
unskilled daubery
wall fresco, mural, panel
PAIR brace, bracket, case, combine, couple(t), diad, doublet, duad, duet, duo, dyad, gemini, jumelle, marry, match, mate(s), rig, span, team, twain, twin(s), two(some), unite, wed, yoke
comb. zygo
having 2 bigeminate
royal paraial, triplet
PAIRED bigeminal, binal, binary, binate, didymous, double, gemel, geminate, hitched, jugate, matched, mated, teamed, twin, wedded, zygous
PAISANO buddy, compatriot, comrade, countryman, pal, peasant, roadrunner
PAISLEY design, fabric, pattern, print, shawl, tie
PAIUTE *indian* digger, paviotso, shoshone
PAJAMAS drawers, jammies,

nightwear, pants, shalwar, sleeper, trousers
trousers bottoms
PAKAWAN *indian* pinto
PAKISTAN *archeological site* mohenjo-daro
bay soymiani
canal nara, rohri
cape fasta, jaddi, jiwani
capital islamabad, rawalpindi
city chalna, dacca, dir, gujranwala, hyderabad, islamabad, jamalpur, kalat, karachi, khulna, lahore, larkana, lyallpur, multan, peshawar, quetta, rawalpindi, sargodha, sialkot, sidi
coin anna, paisa, pice, rupee
dam tarbella
delta char-manpura, ganges
desert sind, thar
language baluchi, bengali, punjabi, pushtu, sindhi, urdu
leader ayub khan, bhutto, jinnah, khan, mujib, rahman, yahyakhan
mountain pass bolan
peak tirichmir
people afridi, baluchi, bengal, khattack, mahsud, mohammedzai, pathan, puktuns, punjabi, pushtuns, sherani, shinwari, sind(h)i, sini, wazir, yusefzai
poet igbal
port chalna, karachi
prince aly khan
province hunza
range himalaya, karakoram, kirthar, makran, sulaiman
river bado, chenab, dasht, ganges, indus, jamunna, jhelum, kabul, kundar, nal, porali, ravi, zhob
saint shashams, sunking
state bahawalpur, baluchistan, bengal, chitral, dir, kalat, khairpur, kharan, peshawar, sind(h), swat, waziristan
weight maund, seer, tola
PAKTONG tutenag
PAL accomplice, ally, associate, billy, buddy, chum, cobber, companion, comrade, confederate, copain, crony, dad, digger, friend, jack, louke, mate, pard, partner
PALA antelope, impala, pallah, plantain, rice, vine
PALACE alcazar, belvedere, castle, cellar, chateau, chigi, court, edifice, elysee, kra-

ton, louvre, mansion, palais, palate, palazzo, praetorium, pretorium, seraglio, serai, stead, storehouse, trianon, vatican, zwinger
fairy shee, sidhe
officer equerry, paladin, palatine
papal lateran
PALADIN anseis, astolf, champion, douzeper, hero, knight, lord, peer, roland
PALAEMON glaucus, melicertes, portu(m)nus
parent athamas, ino
PALAEOPHILE antiquarian
PALAESTRA arena, athletics, exercise, gym(nasium), school, wrestling
PALAESTRIAN athlete, gymnast
PALAL *father* uzal
PALAMON *rival* arcite
wife emelye, emilia
PALANQUIN chair, conveyance, dandi, doolee, dooley, doolie, juan, kago, litter, palkee, palki, sedan, stretcher, tonjou
bearer boy, hamal, musahar, sirdar
PALAS butea, dhak, tree
product gum, kino
PALATABLE acceptable, agreeable, appetizing, delectable, delicious, gustable, luscious, mellow, piquant, pleasant, pungent, relishable, sapid, saporous, savory, spicy, tasty, toothsome
make flavor, salt, season, spice
PALATAL front, gutteral, soft, velar
PALATE appetite, epipharynx, gourmet, gustation, gusto, relish, taste, tooth, uraniscus, uvula, velum, zest
pert. uvular, velar
soft cion, uvula, velum
PALATIAL corinthian, large, luxurious, magnificent, ornate, plush, silken, splendid, stately
PALATINE cape, governor, minister, officer, paladin, palatial, royal, tippet
PALAU *city* koror
meetinghouse abai
religion modeknge
PALAVER balderdash, cajole(ry), chat, chatter, colloquy, confabulate, confer (ence), conversation, con-

verse, debate, discuss(ion), flatter(y), flummery, gash, glaver, jargon, palabra, parley, rigmarole, speech, talk, twaddle, wheedle

PALCH mend, patch, tiptoe, walk

PALE anemic, ashen, ashy, barrier, biscuit, blake, blanch(ed), blank, blate, blench, bloodless, boundary, bounds, chlorotic, colorless, deathly, defense, dim, district, doughy, drained, drawn, enclosure, etiolated, fade, faint, fallow, feeble, fence, ghastly, gray, haggard, inadequate, inane, indistinct, ineffective, ineffectual, infirm, insipid, insufficient, lessen, limit(s), livid, lurid, mealy, obscure, pallid, pallor, pastel, pasty, picket, region, sallow, scoop, sickly, slat, stake, stick, stripe, take fright, vague, wan, watery, waxen, waxy, weak, white, whiten, whitish, wishywashy, worn
-belly plover
-buck oribi
deadly ashen
horse death
in haurient

PALEA bract, chaff, dewlap, fold, ramentum, scale, squamella, wattle

PALED enclosed, fenced, striped

PALEFACE caucasian, white (man)

PALENESS achroma, bleach, pallor

PALEOLITHIC *man* caveman, cro-magnon, heidelberg, neanderthal, piltdown
period abbevilean, abbevilian, acheulean, acheulian, chellean, gravettian, primaldian, solutrean, stone-age
tool microlith

PALEONTOLOGIST fossilist, geologist

PALEONTOLOGY ichnolithology, ichnology

PALEOZOIC *era* cambrian, carboniferous, devonian, ordovician, permian, silurian
land mass cascadia
plant bothrodendron, calamarian, calamite, lepidodendron, lycopodium, sigillaria

PALERMO panormus

PALESTINE (See also HE-

BREW and ISRAEL references.) canaan, erets, eretz, filastin, israel, philistia, zion
animal daman
capital jerusalem
city abelmeholah, aceldamo, acre, akeldama, akir, arimathaea, ashdod, bire, cana, dan, endor, gath, gaza, ghazze, hebron, jabneel, jabneth, jamnia, jericho, jerusalem, nazareth, rama, safad, salem, samaria, shechem, shiloh, tob
conqueror arabs, assyrians, babylonians, crusaders, egyptians, greeks, hebrews, mallabaeans, mamelukes, persians, romans, turks
country canaan, edom, erets, moab, philistia, samaria, yisroel
former name canaan
giants anak(im)
god baal
guerrillas al fatah, al saiqa, arab liberation front, black september, fedayeen, plo, popular democratic front
jewish erets, eretz, ysrael, ysroel
king abimelech
lake galilee, hule(h), merom, tiberius
landmark dan
language aramaic, hebrew
leader habash, yasser arafat
meadow abel
measure See ISRAEL *measure.*
peak ebal, gerizim, gilead, hermon, jebel, moriah, nebo, olives, pisgah, ramon, seir, tabor, tur, zion
people, ancient amahaarez, amorites, ephraim, philistines
plain ono, sharon
port ashkelon
province galilee
rabbi hillel
river See ISRAEL *river.*
roman capital caesarea
sect essene, pharisee, sadducee
shrub christ's-thorn
weight talent, zuzu

PALETOT cloak, coat, cover, garment, greatcoat, jacket, overcoat

PALETTE *knife* spatula

PALEWISE vertically

PALFREY See HORSE.

PALGRAVE *anthology* golden treasury

PALICI *parent* thalia, zeus

PALIKAR See SOLDIER.

PALIMPSEST brass, manuscript, paper, parchment, rewritten, tablet

PALINDROME hannah, madam, oro, otto

PALING enclosure, fence, fencing, limit, pale, picket, stake

PALINGENESIS baptism, metamorphosis, metempsychosis, rebirth, recreation, regeneration, renaissance, revival

PALINODE ode, poem, recant, retract(ion), song

PALIO *opening signal* campanone
site siena

PALISADE barrier, boma, cippus, cliff, defense, enclose, enclosure, espalier, fence, fortification, fortify, hurdi(e)s, impalement, pale, paling, picket, precipice, rimer, stake, stockade, tambour

PALISANDER dalbergia, rosewood, tree

PALL animetta, casket, censorship, cloak, cloth, cloy, coffin, cover(ing), dim, dishearten, disspirit, dull, fabric, fail, faint, fog, glut, gorge, jade, mantle, nausea, pale, pawl, qualm, sate, satiate, satiety, shroud, smoke, stuff, surcharge, surfeit, tire, weaken
funeral mortcloth

PALLA garment, impala, mantle, pallium, tunic

PALLANTIDS *slayer* theseus

PALLAS asteroid, athena, giant, titan
ally aeneas
consort styx
offspring cratus, kratos, nike
parent crius, eurybia, evander, lycaon, pandion, triton
sand grouse attagen
slayer athena

PALLET beater, bed(ding), blanket, brush, click, cot, couch, disk, hawk, headpiece, lip, mattress, pad (dle), paillasse, pate, pawl, piston, plancher, quilt, shovel, valve

PALLIARD beggar, bum,

lecher, rascal, vagabond, vagrant

PALLIATE abate, allay, alleviate, cloak, conceal, condone, cover, cushion, diminish, disguise, dissemble, ease, exculpate, excuse, extenuate, forgive, gloss, gloze, hide, justify, lessen, lighten, mask, mitigate, moderate, please, qualify, reduce, relieve, satisfy, shelter, smooth, soften, temper, veil, whiten, whitewash

PALLIATION abatement, disguise, excuse, extenuation, relief

PALLIATIVE alleviative, anaphrodisiac, anodyne, assuager, assuasive, calmant, calmative, demulcent, lenient, lenitive, remedy, sedative

PALLID ashen, ashy, bloodless, colorless, drained, ghastly, gray, livid, PALE, pasty, thin, wan, washy, waxen

PALLION bit, nodule, pall, pellet, piece

PALLOR anemia, kurtosis, pastiness, sallowness, wanness
deathly ash

PALLU *father* reuben

PALM (See also *kind*, below.) blade, bribe, conceal, crown, fluke, fob, foist, garland, guerdon, hand, handle, impose, kudos, laurel, manipulate, obtrude, paddle, plume, prize, reward, steal, stroke, thenar, tip, touch, tree, trick, trophy, vola
acuyari grugru
assai manicole
bast piassava
betel areca, bonga, pinang, pugua
book taliera, tara
branch lulab
bussu troolie, trooly
cabbage assai, palmetto
civet bondar, musang, paguma
climbing calamus, rat(t)an
cloth medrinaque
cockatoo arara
coconut niog
disease koleruga
drink assai, beno, bino, milk, nipa, sagwire, sura, taree, toddy, tuba

dwarf sabal
fabric bassine
fanleaf carnauba, copernicia, corypha, erythea, gebang, inodes, palmetto, pritchardia, rhapis, sabal, silverthatch, talipot, thrinax, trachycarpus, washingtonia, yaray
feather cabbage, gomuti, howea, nibong, nibung, palmiste, royal, urucuri, urucury
fern ponja
fiber atap, buri(ti), coquita, corozo, coyol, datil, eruc, gebanga, gomuti, iyo, lif, medrinaque, raffia, tal, tucum(a)
food assai, coco(nut), date, nipa, nut, sago, sura, taree, toddy
fruit coconut, date, fatpork, nipa, punatoo, salak, seaapple
fungus graphiola
gingerbread doom, doum, dum
hand loof, thenar, vola
hut barasti
juice, fermented sura
kind 3 dum, eng, fan, ita, pal, saw, tal 4 arak, atap, bast, book, brab, buri, bush, coco, date, doom, doum, ejoo, ikmo, irok, jara, kath, koko, loof, niog, nipa, olay, sago, tara 5 arara, areca, areng, assai, betel, bonga, boyer, bunga, bussu, cocoa, coyol, curua, cutch, cycad, datil, howea, inaja, ivory, jagua, katha, loulu, merus, nikau, ratan, royal, sabal, salak, tacum, tecum, toddy, tucum, unamu, yagua, yaray 6 anahao, arenga, assahy, auburn, bacaba, barrel, baytop, bottle, buriti, cachou, cashod, cayota, chonta, cohune, contar, corojo, corozo, coyure, gebang, gomuti, grigri, grugru, inodes, jambee, jupati, kentia, kittul, musang, nibong, nibung, pacaya, raffia, raphia, rattan, rotang, tooroo, trooly, tucuma, ubusso 7 acuyari, apricot, attalea, babassu, bactris, bombaje, bourbon, cabbage, calamus, caranda, caryota, catechu, coquito, corypha, erythea, feather, gambier, geonoma,

jaggery, moriche, palmyra, phoenix, pupunha, sagwire, serenoa, taliera, talipot, tokopat, troolie, urucury 8 bangalow, carnauba, coquilla, cyanthus, fishtail, jacitara, jipijapa, latanier, locoicea, palmetto, piassaua, umbrella 9 acrocomia, alexandra, manicaria, roystonia 10 cashcuttee
leaf atap, bussu, ca(d)jan, chip, fan, frond, latanier, ola(y), ole, olla
leaf mat nipa, petate, yapa
lily t(o)i
low bussu, troolie, trooly, ubussu
nipa at(t)ap
of hand flat, loof, table, thenar, vola
off on fob, foist, impose, shab, trump
out appaume
palmyra brab, ola(y), ole, olla, ronier, tal(a), talipot
part thenar
pert. frondous, palmaceous, palmar, pinnate
pinnate alexandra, inaja, jupati, nikau, paxiuba, pupunha
pith sago
-play handball, tennis
product coconut, copra, date, fiber, oil, wax
rattan calamus, jambee
reader See PALMIST.
resin dragon's-blood
sago areng, gomuti, irok
sap beno, toddy, tuba
seed corozo
spiny acrocomia, acuyari, grigri, grugru, tucuma
springs indian cahuilla
starch sago, talipot
stem cane, rat(t)an
stemless curua, pacaya, pindova
sugar gur, jaggery
symbol of victory
thatch barriguda, cadjan, nipa
tree, name meaning tamar
trimmer skinner
wax carnauba, ceroxyl
wine beno, bino, sagwire, sura, toddy
wing-leaved cohune

PALMATE broad, flat, lobed, webbed

PALMER ferule, louse, monk, pilgrim, prestidigitator, traveler, votary, wood-louse

PALMETTO andropogon, big

thatch, grass, sabal, saw, serenos, thrinax
cabbage pond-thatch
state south carolina
PALMIST chiromancer, fortuneteller, oracle, predictor, prophet
PALMISTRY chirognomy, chiromancy, divinition, fortune-telling
PALMY bright, flourishing, prosperous
PALMYRA bassine, brab, lontar, palm, ronier, tadmor, tal(a), talipot, tree
biblical name tadmor
builder solomon
destroyer aurelian
fabric bassine
fruit punatoo
leaf ola(y), ole, olla
queen zenobia
PALOOKA fool
PALP antenna, cajole, coax, feel, flatter, palpus, pat, praise, tentacle, touch
PALPABLE apparent, appreciable, audible, corporeal, credible, evident, maniable, manifest, obvious, open, ostensible, patent, perceptible, plain, ponderable, seeming, sensible, tactile, tangible, touchable
PALPATE examine, feel, touch
PALPEBRA eyelid
PALPITATE beat, drum, fluctuate, flutter, oscillate, pulsate, pulse, thrill, throb, vibrate
PALPITATION beat, fluctuation, flutter, oscillation, palmus, pulsation, pulse, quiver(ing), throb(bing), tirl, tremble, vibrate
PALSY apoplexy, deaden, paralysis, paralytic, paralyze, parkinsons disease, shake, shaking, shock, stroke
PALTER babble, bargain, chaffer, chatter, corrupt, dally, dodge, elude, equivocate, escape, evade, falsehood, fib, haggle, jumble, lie, mumble, parley, prevaricate, quibble, snaffle, shift, squander, traffic, trick, trifle, vacillate
PALTI *father* raphu
PALTRY abject, base, beggarly, catch-penny, cheap, cheesy, childish, claptrap, common, contemptible, des-

picable, flimsy, gimcracky, insignificant, lacking, low, mean, measly, minor, miserable, niggardly, orra, petty, picayune, piddling, pitiful, poor, puny, sad, scrubby, scummy, scurvy, shabby, shoddy, small, sorry, tinpot, trashy, trifling, trivial, unimportant, vile, waff, worthless, wretched
PALU escolar
PALUDAL fenny, malarial, marshy, swampy
fever malaria
PAMIR galcha
PAMPA(S) plain(s), puelche
cat kodkod, pajero
deer mazame
grass cortaderia
weapon bolo
PAMPER baby, caress, cherish, cocker, coddle, cosher, cosset, cram, cuddle, dandle, feed, fondle, forwean, glut, gratify, humor, indulge, maunge, mollycoddle, pet, please, posset, regale, saginate, smoodge, spoil, tickle, tiddle, tutor, wally
PAMPERED crammed, fed, indulged, lucuriant, spoiled, spoon-fed
PAMPHLET booklet, brochure, catalog(ue), chapbook, circular, dodger, essay, folder, leaflet, propaganda, tract(ate), treatise, workbook
PAMPHLETEER author, propagandist, writer
PAMPOTTEE moccasin, sandal, shoe
PAMUKKALE hierapolis
PAN aegipan, agree, all, ape, attack, basin, betel, brasier, braizer, broil, broiler, cake, cook, cranium, criticize, disapprove, dish, face, faunus, fry, harden, hollow, inuus, join, kettle, lappet, mine, pannikin, part, photo (graph), portion, pot, result, ridicule, roaster, simia, sir, skillet, slate, spider, subsoil, tab, tub, unite, vessel, vley, vly, wash, wok
attendant panisc, panisk
beloved autonoe, eurydice, pitys, selene, syrinx
coal-burning brazier, grill
-cook fry

evaporating cover, saltpan, tache
frying skillet, spider
god faunus
gold-washing batea, tina
home arcadia
instrument flute, pipe, reed, syrinx, zampogna
iron frache, skillet, yet
kind boiler, bowl, broiler, grill, posnet, roaster, saucepan, scalepan, skillet, spider, tache
long-handled pingle
mountain maenalus
oil sump
oracle site arcadia
parent hermes, penelope, zeus
pipe antara, quill, sicu, siku, syrinx, zampogna
shallow baker-sheet, batea, cookie-sheet
son crotus, seilenos, silenus
3-footed posnet
PANACEA allheal, catholicon, care(all), elixir(vitae), heal-all, nepenthe, panchreston, panpharmacon, polychrest, remedy, solace
PANACHE feathers, flare, manner, ornament, plume, style, surface, swagger, tuft, verve
PANAMA darien, hat, tree
canal big ditch
canal engineer de lesseps, goethals
canal lake gatun
canal locks gatun, miraflores
capital panama
city ancon, azuero, balboa, colon, david, panama, penonome, santiago
coin balboa, cent
crop abaca, cacao
culture, prehistoric cocle
cut culebra
dam gatun
disease banana-wilt
fish berrugate, verrugato
governor goethals
gulf chiriqui, darien
gum tree copa, yaya
hat carludovica, jipijapa
hat source cyclanthus, jipijapa, toquilla
indian carien, choco, cueva, cuna, guaymi(e)
island rey
lake gatun
measure celemin
peak chico, columan, gandi, santiago

port balboa, colon, cristobal, portobello

province chiriqui, cocle, colon, veraguas

range veragua

-red See MARIJUANA.

river bayano, chagres, chepo, panugo, sambu, tuira

shell oliva

tree alfaje, balata, cativo, copa, fabace, maria, quira, trichilia, yaya

wood quillai-bark

PANAMINT *indian* koso, shoshone

peak telescope

PANAX ginseng

PANAY See PHILIPPINES.

capital iloilo

PANCAKE arepa, blintz(e), chapatty, corncake, crepe, crumpet, fadge, flam, flapjack, flapper, flawn, flipper, fraise, fritter, froise, griddlecake, hotcake, kisra, latke, lefse, overturn, pikelet, round-robin, slapjack, tourt

day shrove tuesday

group stack

PANCREAS bur, gland, nut, sweetbread

digestive juice chyme

enzyme amylase, lipase, trypsin

product insulin

PANDA ailurus, arctictus, bear(cat), binturong, civet, wah

giant ailuropoda, coonbear

PANDANUS alasas, artocarpus, baroi, breadfruit, candelabrum-tree, chandelier-tree, fruit, grewia, kahala, pterospermum, screwpine, treculia

PANDAREUS *daughter* aedon, cleothera

parent merops

PANDARUS *companion* aeneas

kin alcanor, bitias, lycaon

PANDECT apercu, code, compendium, digest, outline, precis, sketch, survey, syllabus

PANDEMIC carnal, contagious, cosmopolitan, disease, epidemic, general, sensual, universal, vulgar, widespread

PANDEMONIUM babel, bedlam, bluster, chaos, commotion, confusion, din,

disorder, hell, hubbub, hullabaloo, lawlessness, noise, racket, riot, rumpus, tumult, turmoil, uproar

PANDEMOS aphrodite

PANDER(ER) bawd(strot), cater, cringe, fawn, go-between, gratify, micher, pimp, please, procure(r), purvey, regale, ruffian, serve, tickle, toady, truckle, wait on, whiskin

PANDIA *parent* selene, zeus

PANDION ally, tereus

consort boreas

enemy labdacus

kin idaea, itys, plexippus, theseus

offspring aegeus, butes, erechtheus, philomela, procne

parent cecrops, cleopatra, erichthonius, phineus

PANDORA bandore, bivalve, guitar, lute

box epidemic, evils, troubles, woes

brother-in-law prometheus

consort epimetheus

creator hephaestus

PANDOWDY cobbler, grunt, pie, pudding

PANDROSOS *kin* aglauros, cecrops, herse

PANDU *son* arjuna, bhima, nakula, sahadeva, yudhishthira

uncle bhishma

wife draupadi

PANE brick, coverlet, division, facet, glass, glaze, lamina, light, lozen, panel, part, peen, piece, portlight, quarry, quirk, section, sheet, slash, surface, window

PANEGYRIC acclaim, citation, commendation, compliment, eloge, encomium, eulogy, extollation, extolling, laudation, praise, tribute

PANEGYRIST booster, claque(r), commender, encomiast, eulogist, eulogizer, praiser, proneur, puffer

PANEL abacus, board, brain trust, caisson, coffer, cushion, group, indict, inlay, inquest, insert, inset, jury, lacunar, light, list, mandorla, pad(dle), pane, partition, plaque, rosace, round-table, saddle pad, schedule, sec-

tion, session, slab, tympan, venire

circular roundel

-den brothel

fence loop

flush bead-and-butt

framing stile

gauze scrim

glazed laylight

hinged polyptych, triptych

member discussant

recessed coffer, lacunar, orb

sculptured boiserie

strip splat

sunken caisson, cassoon

3-part triptych

PANFISH crab, horseshoe, king-crab, scup

PANG ache, agony, anguish, attack, bite, compunction, cram(med), cramp, crick, distress, fill, fit, full, gird, gnawing, grief, heartache, hitch, kink, lancination, nip, pain, pinch, prick, prong, rack, sorrow, spasm, stab, stitch, stoun, stuff(ed), suffering, throe, torment, torture, travail, tweak, twinge, twitch, wrench

PANGANE bowstring-hemp, ifa, murva, plant, sansevieria

PANGIM *native* goan

PANGLOSS *pupil* candide

PANGOLIN animal, anteater, armadillo, edentate, manid, manis, pholidota, smutsia, tangilin

PANGUINGUI *term* foot, head, non-comoquers, stringer, valle

PANHANDLE beg, cadge, schnorren, skelb, skilder

state oklahoma, west virginia

PANHANDLER beggar, s(c)hnorrer, shnorer

PANIC agitation, alarm, consternation, crash, crisis, dismay, disquiet, dread, fear, fray, fright(en), funk, overwhelm, scare, schrik, sensation, stampede, startle, success, swither, terror, upset, wild, worry, wow

bent munro-grass

PANICLE anthela, cluster, juba, raceme, whisk

PANICUM arzum, broomcorn, cereal, digitaria, guinea-grass, millet, witchgrass

PANJANDRUM big-shot,

magnate, official, personage, poohbah, vip
PANNICLE brainpan, skull
PANNIER basket, cajava, corbeil, curagh, currack, dorsel, dossal, dosser, drapery, framework, kajawah, kedjave, overskirt, pack, pantry, ped, seron, waiter
horse's curagh, currach, currack, curragh, currock
-man hawker
PANOAN *indian* amahuaca, caripuna, cashibo, chamicuro, doraskean, mayoruna, pacaguara, senci, setibo, sipibo
PANOCOCO ironwood, swartzia, wamara
PANOPEUS *companion,* amphitryon
parent asteria, phocus
twin crisus
PANOPLY arms, array, covering, defend, protect(ion), uniform
PANOPOLIS *god* min
PANORAMA painting, scene, spectacle, sweep, view, vista
PANORAMIC bird's-eye, comprehensive, sweeping
PANORMUS palermo
PANSY african violet, bellflower, cat's-face, fancy, fantaque, flower, pense(e), trinity, viola, violet
wild heartsease
PANT ache, aim, anhele, aspire, blow, breathe, breathing, cistern, covet, crave, desire, fountain, friese, fuff, gasp, heave, hech, huff, hunger, long, need, palpitate, pech, pegh, pine, pool, puddle, puff, pulsate, snort, sugge, thirst, thrill, throb, tift, want, weary, well, whiff, wish, yearn
PANTAGRUEL *author* rabelais
companion panurge
grandfather grangousier
island medamothi
parent badebec, gargantua
PANTALOON buffoon, butt, clown, comedian, dotard, fool, harlequin, jester, stooge, zany
daughter columbine
PANTALOONS breeches, PANTS, trousers
PANTELLERIA *old name* cosyra
PANTHEON aesir, deities,

gods, immortals, olympians, shrine, temple, theogony, vanir
builder hadrian
PANTHER animal, cat, cougar, jaguar, leopard, ocelot, painter, pard, puma
wood sandarac
PANTHINO *master* antonio
PANTHUS *mother* agave
son euphorbus
PANTIES bikini, briefs, drawers, scanties, shorts, step-in, underdrawers, underpants
PANTILE biscuit, hardtack, imbrex, tile
PANTOCRATOR all-ruler, christ
PANTODON butterfly-fish
PANTOFLE chopine, patten, slipper
PANTOGRAPH eidegraph, polygraph
PANTOMIME act, burlesque, drama, dumbshow, gesticulation, gesture, mimicry, play, show
act in mumm
character clown, columbine, harlequin, pantaloon, pierrot, scaramouch
PANTRY ambry, armariolum, armarium, armary, butlery, buttery, cave, closet, covey, cuddy, cupboard, ewery, larder, pannier, spence(r), spicery, storeroom, stue
servant pantler
PANTS bags, bloomers, breeches, britches, capris, chinos, cords, culottes, denims, drawers, ducks, duffs, galligaskins, jeans, jodhpurs, kicks(ies), knickers, levis, overalls, pajamas, pantaloons, rompers, shakseer, shalwar, shintiyan, shorts, slacks, snuggies, tights, trews, trousers, trunks
band boyang
cycling pedal-pushers
hangers galluses, hips, suspenders
leather calzoneras, chaparajos, chaparejos, chapar(r) eras, chaperajos, chaps, lederhosen
opening fly
padded bombards
short bermudas, lederhosen, trunks
strap bowyang

tartan trews
PANTY See PANTIES.
PANTYWAIST cowardly, effeminate, sissy, weakling
PANUELO collar, kerchief, neckcloth, ruffle
PANURGE *companion* pantagruel
PANZER armor, armous, tank
PAOLO *beloved* francesca
PAP barb(el), barbus, dad (dy), diet, dug, emulsion, FATHER, favors, flummery, food, nipple, nonsense, nourishment, pappy, paste, patronage, paw, pimple, pop, porridge, potato, pulp, teat, tumor, vulture
of the hass uvula
PAPA baboon, clay, daddy, ecclesiastic, FATHER, padre, patriarch, pope, potato, priest, sire, vulture
doc duvalier
doc's land haiti
PAPACY apostolic-see, pontificate, popedom, vatican
dread of papaphobia
PAPAGO *ceremony* bat dance
farm milpa
indian bean people, pima
PAPAL (See also POPE.) apostolic, catholic, papane, pontifical, popal
retreat castel gandolfo
state latium, marches, romagna, umbria, vatican
state coin baiocco, bajocco, paolo
PAPAVER See POPPY.
PAPAVERINE pavabid
PAPAW asimin(a), bushwhacker, corazon, jasmine, papaio, PAPAYA
PAPAYA carica, fruit, lechosa, melon tree, pa(w)paw
enzyme papain
extract carpaine
juice caroid
PAPER (See also *kind,* below.) article, blank, card (board), certificate, composition, credential, document, essay, instrument, journal, lil, manuscript, money, monograph, papier, papyrus, pelure, periodical, precis, pulp, sheet, stationery, tapa, theme, tract, treatise, vellum
absorbent blotter, towelling

artist's torchon
birch spoolwood
bits confetti
blemish fisheye
box carton(ier)
brown kraft
building felt
bush See PAPERBARK.
case binder, file, folio
chewed spitball
cloth-like tapa
commercial certificate
crisp, thin pelure
currency scrip
cutter scissors, shears, slitter
damaged casse, cassie, re-tree, salle
decorative gift-wrapping
detachable coupon, stub, tab
dispose of shred
dye auramine
fabric barkcloth
festive confetti, streamer, ticker-tape
fine bond, linen, vellum
finish calendar
folded airplane, folio, saddle
folder stroker
folding art origami
guazy tissue
gloss gill
group corpus, dossier, file
gummed label, paster, seal, stamp, sticker, tape
hard pelure
imperfect casse, heavy-felt
imprint watermark
kind bagasse, blotting, bond, butcher, carbon, crepe, drawing, flimsy, fly, fools-cap, letter, manila, news-print, note, onionskin, pa-pier-mache, parchment, pasteboard, rice, roofing, sand, sheathing, sheet, tar, tissue, tracing, vellum, wall, waste, wax, wrapping, writing
large-size atlas
legal binder, contract, deed, lease, summons, warrant, will, writ
-like chartaceous
lighter spill
-making machine fourdrinier
masking frisket
measure bundle, page, quire, ream, sheet
medicinal powders charta
money assignat, bill, blue-back, cash, certificate, cur-rency, dollar, fiat, folding-stuff, frogskin, greenback,

lettuce, note, rags, scrip, shinplaster
mulberry aute, kozo
mulberrybark tapa
nautilus argonaut
official document, hookum, targe, white
pad block, tablet
parchment papyrin, perga-myn, vellum
photographic sepia
piece leaf, page, scrap, scrip, sheet
plant papyrus
postage stamp pelure
pulp ulla, waterleaf
roll spill, stomp, stump
roofing rag-felt
rough torchon
scroll gohonzon, parchment
semi-transparent glassine
6 sheets of sextern
size albert, antiquarian, at-las, bag-cap, bastard, bil-let, cabinet, cap, casing, co-lumbier, copy, crown, demi, demy, elephant, emperor, flatcap, flat-letter, folio, foolscap, gentlemen's, ha-vencap, imperial, kentcap, legal, letter, medium, note, octavo, peerless, post, pott, prince of wales, quad-remy, royal, short-demy, sixmo, superroyal, theorem, thirds, town
source acaroid gum, acaroid resin, aspen wood
spoiled salle
streamer serpentine
strip tape
strong kraft
thickness caliper
thin bible, india, onionskin, pelure, tissue
toilet bumf, tissue
transparent cellophane
24 sheets quire
uncut bolt, roll
unfolded sheet fine
untrimmed edge deckle
wall tenture
watermarked batonne
web ply
wrapping kraft, manila, screening, sealing, skip
writing linen, stationery
writing size cap, foolscap
PAPERBACK book, cahier, reprint
PAPERBARK cajeput, caju-put, callistemon, kajeput, melaleuca, milkwood, pa-perbush, punktree

used in mitsumata
PAPERBOARD bender, card-board, chipboard, paste-board, pulpboard, veneer
PAPERY chartaceous, flimsy, frail, sleazy, unsubstantial
PAPHIAN prostitute, wanton
goddess aphrodite
PAPHOS *parent* galatea, pyg-malion
PAPILLA ceras, cerata, dei-rid, mammula, nipple, pap-ula, thelium
PAPILLOMA angleberry, corn, wart
PAPIO (See also BABOON.) cynocephalus, mormon
PAPIST catholic
PAPOOSE baby, child, infant
carrier cradleboard
-root blueberry, cohosh, gin-seng, squawroot
PAPPOSE bearded, downy
PAPPUS awn, beard, bristle, down, scale, thistledown, tuft
PAPPY father, mushy, soft, succulent, tender
PAPUA See also NEW GUINEA.
bay acland, dyke, holnicote, milne
capital port moresby
city buna, daru, kikori, sa-marai
gulf, river into fly
islands flyspeck
kangaroo dorcopsis
people arapesh, arau, bain-ing, baitsi, banaro, biak, buang, ekari, hula, iatmul, kate, kerewa, kiwai, koiari, kwoma, melanesians, sivai, sulka
river fly, kikori, purari
PAPYRUS biblos, biblus, bul-rush, glumal, manuscript, paper, reed, scroll, sedge
repository capsa
strip orihon
PAR average, enclose, enclo-sure, equal(ity), equiva-lence, fish, level, median, mean, normal, parity, pen, salmon, standard, through, value
1 over bogey, bogie
1 under birdie
2 under eagle
PARA coin, fodda, parrah, perau, RUBBER
40 piaster
100 dinar, perper
rubber borracha

rubber cake biscuit
rubber tree hevea
PARABEMA diaconicon, prothesis
PARABLE adage, allegory, apolog(ue), bestiary, byspell, byword, comparison, exemplar, fable, fiction, forbysen, mashal, myth, procurable, proverb, similitude, story, tale, type
objective moral, proverb
PARABOLA antenna, arc, curve
PARABOLICAL allegorical, fictional, figurative
PARACELSUS *remedy* azoth
solvent alkahest
PARACHUTE achene, bail out, brolly, chute, descend, drop, escape, fall, jump, patagium, seed, umbrella
descent airdrop, bailout, brollyhop, jump, skydive
formation paracel
inventor lenormand
material nylon, silk
part basket, canopy, car, harness, pack, ripcord, safety-loop, shroud-line
release pulloff, ripcord
troops geronimo boys
PARACHUTIST aerialist, chuter, chutist, jumper, jumpmaster, paradoctor, paratrooper
group stick
PARACLETE advocate, aider, comforter, consoler, helper, pleader, servant
PARADE advertise, air, array, assemble, autocade, boast, brag, callithump, cavalcade, cortege, disclose, display, etalage, event, exercise, exhibit(ion), expose, file, flaunt, flourish, grandeur, march(past), marshal, motorcade, ostentation, pageant(ry), parry, path, pomp, prance, pretension, procession, promenade, publish, reveal, review, show(iness), spectacle, splendor, stalk, strut, swagger, sweep, top, vaunt, vent, walk
boisterous callithump
feature ticker tape
ground broadway, maidan, place d'armes
PARADIGM example, exemplar, grammar, ideal, mirror, model, pattern, standard
PARADISE (See also NORSE *heaven.*) aalu, aaru, above, abraham's bosom, afterlife, aidenn, amitabha, ananda, arcadia, avalokitesvara, avalon, beulah (land), bliss, canaan, ciel, eden, elysian fields, elysium, empyrean, eternity, ether, firmament, gallery, garden (of eden), glory, gokuraku, goloka, great white throne, happiness, happy hunting grounds, HEAVEN, hereafter, ialu, jenna, jodo, joy, kingdom-come, mahasthamaprapta, nirvana, olympus, park, perfection, plumage, promised land, seventh heaven, shangri-la, sky, svarga, swarga, UTOPIA, valhalla, welkin, wonderland, yaru, zion
bird of apus, emerald, lyrebird, manucode
bird of, flower strelitzia
bridge alsirat
comb. urano
fish macropodus
flower cat's-claw, devil's-claw
fool's limbo
grosbeak cutthroat
lost, angel ariel, arioch, gabriel, ithuriel, uriel, uzziel, zophiel
lost, author milton
lost, seraph abdiel
nut sapauaia
on earth shangri-la
pert. edenic
plant mezereon
river fahfah, geon, gihon, zulal
tree aceituna, bitterwood, quassia, stavewood, tuba
PARADISIAC blissful, delightful, edenic, elysian, heavenly
PARADOX absurdity, anomaly, antinomy, contradiction, dilemma, inconsistency, koan, puzzle, reverse
PARADOXICAL antilogical, contradictory, illogical
PARAFFIN alkane, alkannin, kerosene
PARAGE birth, equality, family, lineage, rank
PARAGON ace, acme, apersee, apotheosis, beauty, compare, competition, consort, equal, exemplar, gem, ideal, masterpiece, match, mate, mirror, model, nonesuch, nonpareil, paladin, parallel, pattern, perfection, peropus, phoenix, rival(ry), standard, surpass
PARAGONITE mica
PARAGRAM pun
PARAGRAPH article, caput, clause, indent, item, material, part, passage, pause, peelcrow, phrase, plank, rubric, section, theme, verse
mark peelcrow, pilcrow
PARAGUAY *capital* asuncion
city asuncion, belen, caacupe, caazapa, concepcion, ita, luque, pilar, trinidad, villa rica, yuty
coin guarani, peso
department boqueron, caazapa, guaira, itapua, olimpo
fiber plant caraguata
indian abipon, guarani, guayaqui, moskoi
lake vera, ypacarai, ypoe
language guarani
measure cordel, cuadra, cuarta, fanega, legua, line (a), lino
palm pindo
plain chaco
river acaray, apa, confuso, parana, tibiquare, ypane
river tributary pilco-mayo
tea mate, yerba
weight quintal
PARAIBA *capital* joao-pessoa
PARAKEET aratinga, budgereegah, budgerigar, budgerygah, budgie, conure, greenleek, kakariki, lovebird, palaeornis, parrot, popinjay, puffin, rosehill, rosella, wellat
PARALEIPSIS apophasis, preterition
PARALLEL abreast, akin, aligned, alike, along(side), analog(ous), analogue, coextend, collateral, comparable, comparative, compare, concurrent, copy, correlate, correlative, correspond(ing), counterpart, entrench, equal, equidistant, equispaced, even, homologue, identical, imitate, like, lined up, match, multiple, quantity, resemblance, resemble, same, similar(ity), uniform

PARALLELISM agreement, analog(ue), analogy, comparison, correspondence, evenness, regularity, uniformity

PARALLELIZE align, collimate, collineate, compare, correspond, equate, follow, line up, match

PARALLELOGRAM oblong, rectangle, rhomb(oid)(us), square

PARALOGISM casuistry, fallacy, sophism, sophistry

PARALYSIS abepithimia, apoplexy, cramp, diplegia, hemiplegia, holoplexia, inaction, inertia, monoparesis, monoplegia, palsy, paraplegia, paresis, shock, stagnation, stroke, torpor
comb. plegia, plegy, plexia
extremities panplegia
4 limbs quadriplegia
general holoplexia
infantile poliomyelitis
lower body paraparesis, paraplegia
1 extremity monoplegia
partial paresis
with paralytic, paretic

PARALYZE alarm, anesthetize, astonish, awe, cripple, dare, deaden, disable, immobilize, incapacitate, knock out, numb, palsy, scare, scram, shock, stun, terrify, unnerve, weaken

PARALYZED benumbed, crippled, numb, palsied, scared

PARAMORPHINE thebaine

PARAMOUNT above, all-absorbing, capital, cardinal, chief, commanding, controlling, dominant, foremost, important, leading, main, master, overall, overruling, personage, potentate, predominant, preeminent, premier, preponderant, primary, prime, principal, ruler, ruling, sovereign, superior, superlative, supreme, surpassing, suzerain, top

PARAMOUR amoret, boyfriend, concubine, courtesan, doxy, franion, gallant, hetaera, hetaira, kept woman, leman, lover, mistress, sweetheart, sweetie, wanton, woman

PARANA *city on* rosario
tributary iguassu, paraguay, rio grande

PARANG knife, sword

PARANYMPH advocate, bestman, bridesmaid

PARAPET bahut, balustrade, barbet(te), barrier, bastion, breastwork, bulwark, butt, earthwork, epaulement, footpath, fortification, pluteus, railing, rampart, redan, sidewalk, support, wall
low balustrade
part crete, merlon
v-shaped redan

PARAPHERNALIA apparatus, appurtenances, armentaria, armentarium, badges, belongings, effects, equipage, equipment, furnishings, gear, insignia, machinery, materiel, outfit, possessions, regalia, tackle, trappings

PARAPHRASE amplification, construe, expand, interpret, recapitulate, rehash, rendering, rephrase, restate (ment), reword, transcription, translate, translation, version

PARAPRAXIS blunder, lapse, slip

PARASHAR *father* shakt

PARASITA anoplura, arachnid, epizoa, lice, mite, PARASITE, tick

PARASITE aphid, autophyte, baggage, barnacle, bleeder, bootlick(er), bug, bur(r), cadge, cephalina, chark, cringer, deadbeat, deadhead, dicyemid, drone, ectoza, entozoon, epizoon, favorite, fawner, feeder, flatterer, flea, flunky, fly, free-loader, fungus, gnatho, gregarine, hanger-on, leech, lickspittle, louse, moss, pothunter, rust, sacculina, shadow, slaverer, smellfeast, smut, sparganum, spiv, sponge(r), sucker, sycophant, tagtail, toady, trencher, truckler, tryp, tubhunter, virus
animal babesia, cowbird, cuckoo, entozoan, flea, louse, mite, tick, trypanosome
blood fluke, tryp
climbing cassytha

disease flagellosis, malaria, trichinosis
external dodder, ectozoa, epizoon, flea, lice, louse
fungus lichen
-infested mity, wormy
internal bacteria, entorganism, entozoa, fungus, germ, hookworm, worm
intestinal roundworm, strongyl(e), tapeworm
malarial cryptozoite
marine remora, rhopalura, sponge
1-host, pert. monoxenous
pert. symbiotic
plant agaric, aphid, aphis, dodder, entophyte, fungus, lichen, mistletoe, moss, rust, smut, thrips
protozoan bakesia, proteosoma
worm trichina

PARASITIC biophilous, cytozoic, ectozoan, ectozoic, entozoan, entozoic, obsequious, rapacious, supercrescent, sycophantic, trencher

PARASOL aogiri, brollie, bumbershoot, kittysol, shade, sunshade, tiresol, umbrella
ant sauba
land of white laos
mushroom lepiota
tree aogiri

PARASSUS liakura

PARATORIUM sacristy, vestry

PARATROOPER *cry* geronimo
uniform jumpsuit

PARAVANE otter, torpedo

PARBOIL blanch, cook, overheat

PARCA fate, moira
goddess of childbirth

PARCEL accord, allocate, allot, apportion, assign, award, bale, batch, bulse, bunch, bundle, collection, conacre, deal, detail, distribute, divide, division, dole, fardel, fraction, fragment, grant, group, land, lot, member, mete, pack (age), packet, part(ly), passel, piece, plat, plot, portion, property, prorate, ration, section, sector, segment, wisp, wrap
of ground close, conacre, lot, pendicle, solum, suerte
post bang(h)y, mail

PARCH bake, bristle, brustle, burn, char, cook, crackle, dehydrate, dessicate, dry, gizzen, graddan, rizzar, roast, scorch, sear, shrink, shrivel, stale, toast, torrefy, wither

PARCHED adust, arid, burned, burnt, dried, dry, fiery, gizzen, sere, thirsty, torrid

PARCHEESI game, ludo

PARCHMENT charta, document, drumhead, forel, lambskin, lark, mezuzah, palimpsest, papyrin, scytale, skin, vellum
bark karo
book cover for(r)el
constituent amyloid
fine vellum
-like pergameneous
manuscript palimpsest
paper docket, pergamyn
piece membrane
reused palimpsest
roll pell, scroll
worm chaetopterus

PARD camelopard, chum, companion, friend, LEOPARD, pal, panther, partner, tiger

PARDALOTE diamond-bird, forty-spot

PARDESI foreigner, outlander

PARDI(E) certainly, indeed, parbleu, surely, verily

PARDON absolution, absolve, acquit(tal), amnesty, assoil, condone, exculpate, excuse, exonerate, forego, forget, forgive(ness), free, indulgence, liberate, mercy, release, remission, remit, reprieve, shrive, spare, tolerate, waive
general amnesty
me sorry
plea for venie
stall confessional

PARDONABLE defensible, excusable, justifiable, veniable, venial

PARE abate, chip, curry, curtail, cut(off), decorticate, decrease, deduct, depreciate, diminish, divest, form, lessen, pair, peel, prepare, prune, reduce, remove, resect, scrape, shave, skin, skive, strip, thin, uncover, undress, whittle
leather skive
stone boast

PARECH no-good, pariah, rascal

PAREIRA caapeba, curare, velvetleaf, vine

PARELLA dock, lichen, rumex

PARENESIS advice, counsel

PARENT ancestor, ancestry, author, begetter, beginning, breeder, cause, dad(dy), elder, father, for(e)bear, genitor, guardian, mater, mother, origin, pater, producer, progenitor, sire, source
female dam, mama, mater, mom(my), MOTHER, mum(my)
killing matricide, parricide, patricide
male dad(dy), FATHER, papa, pappy, pater, pop, sire
undivided holethnos

PARENTAGE birth, brood, descent, extraction, family, kindred, kinship, origin, progeny

PARENTAL ancestral, fatherly, maternal, motherly, paternal
affection philoprogenitiveness, storge

PARENTHESIS aside, brace, bracket, curve, hook, innuendo, insertion, interlude, interval

PARENTHETICAL accidental, bandy, bowed, by-the-way, casual, incidental, occasional

PAREU loincloth, sarong, skirt

PARFAIT biscuit, dessert

PARFLECHE box, case, pouch, rawhide, saddlebag, strap

PARGET coat, decorate, gild, gypsum, make-up, paint, plaster, roughcast, whitewash

PARGO fish, lutianus, muttonfish, pagrus, porgy, snapper

PARHELION mocksun, sundog

PARIAH cagot, exile, ishmael, leper, outcast, parech, proletarian

PARIAN china, marble, market, porcelain

PARIDA bushtit, titmouse, verdin

PARIETAL resident, somal, somatic

PARIETARIA nettle, pellitory

PARI-MUTUEL *machine* totalizator, totalizer, tote

PARING flake, gubbin, leftover, part, peel, piece, refuse, remainder, scrap, shred, speck

PARIS lutetia
adversary menelaus, philoctetes
airport charles de gaulle, le bourget, orly, roissy
art exhibit salon, vernissage
bishop denis, lombard
botanical garden jardin des plantes
boulevard champs elysees, rue de la paix, st honore
captive clymene, helen
cathedral notre dame
cemetery pere la chaise
consort helen, oenone
dance apache, valse
district See PARIS *section.*
division arrondissement
friend romeo
garden luxembourg, tuileries
green acetosenite, insecticide
hat belltopper
historic site champs de mars
host menelaus
kin cassandra, escalus, troilus
landmark arc de triomphe, champs elysees, eiffel tower, notre dame, pantheon
latin quarter left bank, rive gauche
market les halles
newspaper le figaro
palace elysee, louvre, luxembourg, tuileries
parent hecuba, priam
park bois de boulogne, luxembourg garden
patroness st genevieve
planner haussmann
plaster gesso
police flics, gendarme(rie), surete
police chief prefet
protectress aphrodite
quarter latin
race track auteuil, longchamp
raised by agelaus
red minium
revolutionaries communards
revolutionary government commune
river seine
section left bank, mont-

martre, montparnasse, right bank, st germain-des-pres
section, artists left bank, montmartre, rive gauche
sepulcre pantheon
shop girl midinette
singer edith piaf
slayer philoctetes, pyrrhus
son aganus
square place pigalle
stock exchange bourse
suburb aubervilliers, auteuil, clichy, issy, le bourget, montreuil, neuilly, orly, passy, sevres, st denis, st ouen
subway metro
theatre comedie francaise, grand guignol
thug apache
university sorbonne
victim achilles
PARISH bethel, charge, congregation, county, cure, diocese, flock, fold
church rectory
farmland glebe
feast clerk-ale
head minister, pastor, priest, rector, vicar
lantern moon
meeting vestry
officer beadle, borsholder, meresman, vestryman
PARITY analogy, equality, equivalence, evenness, level, likeness, owelty, par, price, sameness
PARK arsenal, basin, claire, common(s), deposit, enclosure, establish, field, green, grove, hay, leave, paddock, paradise, pasture, place, playground, prater, promenade, put, seat, settle, stand, station, store, valley, zoo
area green belt
custodian keeper, ranger
fixture bench, settee
lane, number 2 See MARIJUANA.
PARKA anorak
PARKINSON'S *disease* palsy, paralysis
disease cure l-dopa, sinemet
side effect dyskinesia
symptom akinesia
PARKLEAVES tutsan
PARKWAY avenue, boulevard, drive, highroad, highway, road, street, terrace, throughway
PARLANCE conversation, diction, discourse, idiom,

language, phraseology, speech, talk
PARLAY double, increase
PARLEY address, advise, argue, arbitration, chat, commune, confer(ence), consult, converse, debate, discuss(ion), dispute, dodge, indaba, negotiate, negotiation, palaver, palter, parlance, parling, powwow, speak, talk, temporize, treat, utter
PARLIAMENT assembly, conference, congress, council, dail, diet, estates, fantan, game, lasting, legislature, majlis, saeima, senate, sevens, storting, thing, volksraad
member lord
official black rod
publication blue-book, hansard, white-paper
PARLIAMENTARY congressional, legislative
PARLOR ben, drawing room, living room, locutory, sala, salle, salo(o)n, salotto, sitting room, snuggery, solarium
-house brothel
ivy hampweed
milking bail
moss baby's-tears
palm aspidistra
pert. boor
PARLOUS awful, critical, dangerous, exceedingly, excessively, hazardous, keen, mischievous, perilous, risky, shocking, shrewd, surprising, terrible
PARMA *cheese* parmigiano
duke farnese
PARMENIO *friend* alexander
prisoner antigone
son philotas
PARNAHIBA *city on* teresina
PARNASSUS liakoura
deity apollo, dionysus, muses
nymphs thriai
spring castalia, castaly
summit lycorea, tithorea
PAROCHIAL cathedral, conservative, ecclesiastic, insular, limited, local, narrow(minded), petty, prejudiced, sectarian, synagogical
PARODY amphigory, amphigouri, burlesque, caricature, copy, imitation, lampoon,

nonsense, pastiche, rib, ridicule, rigamarole, satire, satirize, skit, spoof, squib, takeoff, travesty
nonsensical amphigory, amphigour
PAROL noncupative, oral, pleading, unwritten, utterance, verbal, word
PAROLE discharge, faith, freedom, pledge, probation, promise, release, speech, watchword, word
PAROLLES *leader* bertram
PARONYCHIA felon, nailwort, panaris, whitlow
PAROSH *son* benaiah, eleazar, jeziah, malchiah, malchijah, miamin, pedaiah, ramiah
PAROTITIS mumps
PAROUSIA advent, coming
PAROXYSM access(ion), agitation, agony, anger, attack, colic, convulsion, emotion, epitasis, exacerbation, fit, frenzy, outburst, pain, pang, rapture, raptus, seizure, shower, spasm, storm, stour, tantrum, throe
PAROXYSMAL convulsive, spasmodic, spastic, upheaving
PARQUET checkerwork, flooring, inlay, mosaic
circle orchestra, parterre
PARR brandlin(g), fish, salmon, samlet, scegger, skegger
PARROT, PARROT'S (See also *kind,* below.) ape, bird, chatter, copy, echo, imitate, imitator, memorize, mime, mimic, repeat
-beak or -bill clianthus, glory-pea
bill membrane cere
blue-bellied lorrikin, warrin
bulfinch paradoxornis
family psittacidae
feather milfoil
fever psittacosis
finch crossbill
fish bluefish, cotoro, labroid, lauia, loro, mudfish, oldwife, pseudocarus, scarid, scarus, sparisoma, vieja
gray jako
green amazona, cagit
hawk hia
kind abacay, agapornis, amazona, ara, aracanga, aracari, arara, ararauana, bluebonnet, borbeta, broadtail,

budgereegah, budgerigar, budgerygah, budgie, cagit, cockateel, cockatiel, cockatoo, conuropsis, conurus, coracopsis, corella, grassie, hia, jako, kaka(po), kea, lorie, lorikeet, lorilet, loro, lory, lovebird, macaw, nestor, parakeet, picarian, platycercus, poll(y), popinjay, psittacus, rosella, tarapo, tiriba, toucan, touraco, vasa, vaza, warrin
large nestor
-like psittaceous
long-tailed conure, macaw
monk loro
owl kaka(po)
red borbeta
PARRY avert, avoid, bypass, counter, defend, deflect, dodge, elude, evade, evasion, fence, fend, prevent, quibble, quinte, refute, repartee, reply, resist, retort, sixte, thwart, tierce, ward off
PARSE analyse, anatomize, construe, diagram, dissect
PARSI, PARSEE zoroastrian
funeral tower dokhma
girdle kusti
holy fire adaran, behram
prayer ahuna, vairya
priest dastur, destour, dustoor, dustour, mobed
scripture avesta, bundahish, pahlavi, sadda
sect shenshai
PARSIFAL *castle* monsalvat
character amfortas, klingsor, kundry
composer wagner
healing implement spear
PARSIMONIOUS avaricious, cheeseparing, close(fisted), frugal, grasping, greedy, illiberal, mean, mercenary, miserly, narrow, niggardly, pennypinching, pennywise, penurious, poor, prudent, scant, skimpy, sordid, spare, sparing, stingy, thrifty, tight(fisted), wretched
PARSIMONY avarice, frugality, prudence
PARSLEY ache, caucalis, chervil, cicely, cilantro, conium, coriander, cumin, eltrot, eringo, eryngo, fennel, fluellin, hemlock, herb, hogweed, karpas, sanicle, selinum, umbel
beaked chervil

bit sprig
camphor apiol(e), ether
derivative apiin, apiol(e), ether
fern rock-brake, tansy
piert bowel-hive grass, breakstone, heath, knawel, pearlwort, saxifrage
relative anise, celery
PARSNIP bundweed, cadweed, conium, harts-eye, heart's-eye, hogweed, madnep, pastinaca, queenweed
water sium
PARSON clergyman, ecclesiastic, guidepost, minister, preacher, rector, shepherd, vicar
bird fey, gull, honey-eater, koko, poe(bird), poybird, rook, tue, tui, tuwi
country rum
PARSONAGE benefice, church, clergy, deanery, glebe, manse, pastorate, pastorium, presbytery, rectory, vicary
PART (See also PARTS.) 3 any, bit, cut, leg, lot, mix 4 area, book, butt, chip, clip, duty, half, hunk, item, limb, link, lobe, lump, open, pass, quit, rend, role, shed, slab, slat, snip, some, tear, twig, twin, unit, ward, wing 5 allot, break, chunk, crumb, joint, leave, organ, patch, piece, quota, scion, scrap, sever, shard, share, shred, slice, snack, space, split, spray, sprig, strip, stump, tithe, verse, whack, whang 6 aspect, branch, cantle, clause, cleave, column, depart, detach, detail, differ, divide, factor, length, member, moiety, morsel, number, parcel, paring, phrase, pinion, rasher, region, sample, sector, shiver, snatch, stitch, sunder, switch, tatter, unyoke 7 article, cantlet, chapter, cutting, disjoin, diverge, divorce, element, faction, flinder, flitter, helping, passage, portion, quarter, remnant, section, segment, shaving, smither, tendril 8 clipping, dissever, district, disunite, division, fascicle, fraction, fragment, interest, offshoot, particle, separate, shtickle, splinter, syllable 9 appor-

tion, component, intervene, paragraph, partition, shivereen 10 contingent, detachment, distribute, particular, smithereen 11 constituent, installment, subdivision
1/12th uncia(1)
1/5th quintus
1/4th fardel, ferling, quarter
accompanying burden, obbligato
artificial prosthesis
baglike sac
best See PART *important.*
bristlelike seta
choice cream, elite, essence, marrow, stardom
coarse dregs
comb. demi, hemi, mere, meri, mero, semi
company differ, divorce, separate
distinct article, unit
duplicate spare
essential See PART *important.*
final epilog, last, shank
1st beginning, front, initial, onset, prime, start
highest apex, crest, crop, crown, height, summit, top
hundredth centesm
important base, basis, body, core, crux, element, essence, focus, fundamental, gist, heart, hub, kernel, keynote, marrow, meat, nub, nucleus, pith, principle, substance
inmost center, core, heart
latter heel
lower secondo
main body, trunk
middle center, midst
minor bit, cog
missing lacuna
moving gear, rotor, wheel
narrow neck
principal body, gross
projecting apse, arm, buttress, jag, jet, jog, leg, lobe, spur(n)
remaining butt, dregs, heel, tailings
revolving cam, cylinder, orb, rotator, rotor
root-like radicle
rounded boss, bulb
small (See also PARTICLE.) atom, bit, detail, jot, iota, minim, mite, moiety, smidge(n), snippet, speck, tithe, whit
suddenly rend, snap

surface break
tenth tithe
time occasional
uppermost chief, peak, top (side), upside
with abandon, cast, cede, discard, distribute, donate, give, leave, lose, relinquish, sell, share, trade
PARTAKE accept, bestow, bite, eat, enjoy, get, inform, obtain, parten, participate, procure, receive, sample, savor, share, sip, tell
of share, taste, use
PARTED apart, cleft, cloven, deceased, divided, partite, separated, shared
from bereft
PARTHAON *parent* agenor, epicaste
son oeneus
wife euryte
PARTHENIUM feverfew, guayule
PARTHENOGENESIS ampherotoky, apogamy, apomixis, arr(h)enotoky, deuterotoky, reproduction
PARTHENON *builder* callicrates, ictinus, phidias
entrance propylaea
marble pentelic
part cella, frieze, metope, posticum, prodomus, pronaos
sculptor phidias
statue ilissus
PARTHENOS athena
PARTHIA(N) *concubines* sybaris
emperor alexander, arsaces
general pharnapates, sillaces, surena
hall iwan
king hydrodes
official arsaces
prince pacorus, phraates, vagisas
shot taunt
PARTIAL biased, colored, disposed, favorable, fractional, fragmentary, halfway, imperfect, predisposed, prejudiced, sectional, semi, swayed, unequal, unfinished, warped
comb. demi, meso, semi
to make semify
PARTIALITY approval, bent, bias, favor(itism), fondness, inclination, partisanship, predilection, prejudice
PARTIALLY half(way), in-

completely, partly, some (what)
PARTICIPANT accessory, actor, cotenant, member, partaker, partisan, partner, party, shareholder, sharer, sharing
PARTICIPATE chip in, compete, contribute, cooperate, divide, enlist, enter into, join, partake, share
PARTICIPATION association, cahoots, companionship, contribution, fellowship, interest, partaking, partnership, plot, sharing
PARTICIPATOR accomplice, attendant, celebrant, partaker
PARTICLE alpha, amicron, amount, article, atom, beta, bit, boson, cantlet, clause, conjunction, corn, corpuscle, crot, crumb, dot, drop, fermion, fig, filing, flake, geiger, gemmule, ghost, grain, granule, gru(e), heat, ion, iota, jot, knit, lepton, meson, mesotron, mite, modicum, molecule, moment, mote, nucleus, PART, piece, point, portion, positrino, prefix, preposition, psychon, ray, rizzom, scintilla, scrap, seed, shred, smidge(n), smitch(in), spark, speck, starn, stime, stitch, styme, suffix, thrum, tittle, twint, whit
affirmative yes
atomic electron, ion
burnt cinder
chaff palea
component quark
cosmic meson
electric anion, ion, proton, thermion
elementary boson, neutrino, neutron
hypothetical magneton
icy sleet
incandescent spark
jagged splinter
minute amicron, atom(y), bleb, corn, crumb(le), dust, grain, granule, iota, jot, mite, molecule, mote, ort, rament(um), ray, scintilla, speck, submicron
negative nor, not
pluvial drop(let)
positive cation, kation
ultimate psychon

uncharged neutrino, neutron
unstable pion
PARTI-COLORED harlequin, motley, piebald, pied, variegated
PARTICULAR accurate, appropriate, article, careful, certain, characteristic, choosy, circumstance, concrete, conscientious, dainty, detail(ed), discriminate, discriminating, distinct(ive), especial, event, exact, exclusive, express, fact, fastidious, feature, finical, fussy, individual, instance, intimate, intrinsic, item, limited, local, lone, meticulous, minute, nice, odd, part, peculiar, pernickety, personal, picky, precise, private, punctilious, respect(ive), rigid, rigorous, scrupulous, separate, single, singular, sole, solitary, special, specific, squeamish, sticky, strict, technicality, topical, unique, unusual
PARTICULARIZED accurate, correct, detailed, exact, individualized, itemized, minute, precise, specialized, specified
PARTICULARLY especially, expressly, extra, familiarly, fully, intimately, notably, only, personally, principally, severally, specially, specifically, unusually
PARTING adieu, adios, break, death, departure, disjunction, dispersion, dividing, division, dying, farewell, final, godspeed, goodbye, leave(taking), sendoff, separating, separation, sharing, valediction, valedictory
of the ways crossroads
PARTISAN adherent, ally, backer, champion, defender, denominational, devotee, disciple, factional, favorite, follower, friend, guerrilla, halberd, helper, interested, partial, partner, pike, satellite, sectarian, sectary, sectional, sectionary, sider, staff, supporter, sympathizer, terrorist, truncheon, zealot
comb. crat
group bloc, camp, claque, clique

unwavering stalwart, zealot
PARTITE *comb.* merous
PARTITION allot, apportion(ment), baffle, bail, barrier, brattice, brattish, bulkhead, cabin, casing, cloison, dam, diaphragm, disconnection, dissepiment, divide, division, enclose, fence, hallan, iconostas, interseptum, midriff, panel, paries, scantle, screen, separate, separation, sept(a), septulate, septulum, septum, set apart, severance, shoji, speer, stoothing, wall
mining sollar, stopping
PARTITIONED mural, septal, walled
PARTLET band, biddy, chemisette, collar, hen, pertelot, ruff, woman
PARTNER accomplice, ally, associate, auxiliary, butty, camarada, chum, coadjutor, collaborator, colleague, companion, comrade, confederate, confrere, consort, co-worker, half, husband, join, kamerad, mate, pal, pard(ner), participant, partisan, sharer, sidekick, spouse, teammate, wife, yokemate
comedian's stooge
paid gigolo
PARTNERSHIP alliance, association, axis, business, cahoot(s), comates, community, compagnieschap, company, connection, firm, hoey, hui, participation, union
PARTRIDGE alectoris, bird, bobwhite, caccabis, cheeper, chukar, francolin, frenchman, grouse, kyah, lerwa, patrick, perdix, quail, redleg, rudge, seesee, tetraonid, tinamou, titar, yutu
berry boxberry, cowberry, eyeberry, oneberry, snowberry, twinberry
black francolin
call churr, juck, juke
changed to perdix
group covey
plant wintergreen
sand seesee, tehoo
snow lerwa
white ptarmigan
wood acapu, andira, granadilla
young cheeper, squealer

PARTS (See also **PART.**)
brains, gifts, talent, wits
break into diffract
having distinct apophyllous
having 2 binary, dimerous
innermost core, heart, penetralia
joined adnexa
repetition of merism
totality of unity
PARTURITION accouchement, birth, childbirth, delivery, dystocia, eutocia, labor, lying-in, travail
PARTY affair, association, ball, bal masque, bash, blowout, body, bust-up, cabal, cantico, circle, clique, comite, company, coterie, dance, detachment, drum, entertainment, faction, faid, festivity, fete, gala, gathering, gettogether, group, hoedown, hop, housewarming, infare, interest, junto, league, masquerade, opponent, participant, person, play, potlatch, prom, ring, scrum, sect, shindig, shindy, shower, smoker, sociable, social, soiree, squantum, stag, tea, tertulia, troop, wingding
afternoon reception, tea
beach clambake
bridal shower
dancing cantico, fandango, german, hoedown, hop, prom
drinking binge, blast, blow (out), cocktail party, soiree, tasting
evening ball, gregory, rout, soiree, tertulia
farewell sendoff
favor cracker
fishing hukilau
good wingding
guilty culprit
hunting faid
man partisan
masquerade guise
men's smoker, stag
organization caucus
political caucus, fronde, junto, kenseikai, minseito, side, swaraj, zentrum
-pooper killjoy, spoilsport
reconnaissance patrol
seashore clambake, picnic
switcher mugwump
tea drum
3rd stranger
to in on

PARULIS abscess, gumboil
PARURE apparel, jewels, ornament, paring, peeling
PARUS See TITMOUSE.
PARVATI *consort* siva
father himavat
son ganesha
PARVENU arriviste, capitalist, nouveau-riche, snob, upstart
PARVIS colonnade, conference, court, disputation, porch, portico
PASANG bezoar-goat
PASCAL *essays* pensees
PASCH(AL) easter, good friday, passover
lamb agnus-dei
sacrifice passover
PASE farol, natural, veronica
PASEAH *son* jehoiada
PASH blow, crush, dash, fall, head, hurl, infatuation, poll, rain, rush, smash, snowfall, strike, throw
PASHA ali, bashaw, bem, dey, dowlah, emir, noble, officer, personage
territory pachalic, pashalic, pashalik
PASHUR *son* elasah, elioenai, gedaliah, ishmael, jozabad, maaseiah, nethaneel
PASIDICE *son* actor
PASIPHAE *consort* minos
offspring androgeos, ariadne, asterius, catreus, minotaur, phaedra
parent creta, helios, perseis
PASKUDNE(H) contemptible, dirty, mean, nasty, odious, sloppy, unkind
PASQUEFLOWER anemone, aprilfool, badgerweed, crocus, pulsatilla
PASQUINADE lampoon, libel, pasquil, satire, satirize, skit, squib
PASS 3 act, bet, col, cut, die, gap, way, win 4 by me, comp, dree, duar, fade, flit, flow, foin, gaut, ghat, hand, mess, move, pace, path, road, slip, stab, step, visa, walk, wend 5 alley, bandy, canto, elide, enact, excel, ghaut, glide, gorge, kotal, lapse, notch, pinch, poort, punta, range, reeve, relay, route, sally, spend, state, throw, utter, while 6 arroyo, avenue, billet, bridge, carnet, convey, course, cri-

sis, defile, elapse, exceed, expire, extend, happen, overgo, perish, permit, pierce, plight, ratify, strait, thrust, ticket, travel, twofer, vanish 7 absolve, advance, allonge, decease, deliver, devolve, excrete, freebie, license, narrows, outrace, proceed, promote, protect, put over, skitter, succeed, warrant 8 approach, beallach, exigency, graduate, juncture, overhaul, overstep, overtake, surmount, transfer, traverse 9 circulate, clearance, condition, disappear, emergency, legislate, offensive, purwannah, situation 10 difficulty, get through, permission, protection 11 annie oakley, predicament, safe conduct

along derive, hand down

around detour, skirt

away blow over, cease, depart, die, disappear, elapse, end, expire, forfare, forthgo, perish, spend, surrender, transfer, vanish

back and forth crisscross

bad checks kite

boat punt

by bygo, clear, cote, disregard, elapse, forego, go by, ignore, intermit, omit, overgo, overlook, skip, slight, snub, vade, wend

dangerous plight

football flare, forward, hook, lateral, spiral

for ape, imitate, impersonate, masquerade, mimic

free annie oakley, freebie, paper

gradually dim, fade

law approve, decree, enact, establish, legislate, ordain, ratify, sanction

lightly brush, foist, skate, skitter

muster conform, satisfy, suffice

narrow abra, beal, belt, notch, slype

off cease, con, disappear, foist, impose, masquerade, palm off, parry, sham

on advance, affect, bequeath, continue, decide, devolve, die, elapse, endow, hand down, leak, lunge, proceed, ratify, relay, tell, thrust, transfer, vote

out administer, conk, deal, debouch, disappear, disburse, distribute, exhaust, exit, faint, swoon

over (See also PASS-OVER.) balk, bridge, condone, cross, die, disregard, elapse, elide, examine, excuse, expire, ford, free, ignore, intersect, miss, neglect, omission, omit, overlook, progress, scour, skip, slight, sweep, transfer, traverse

over lightly scan, scud, skim, sweep

over slowly drag

over smoothly elide

quickly flit, scurry, speed, spin, strike

slowly drag, lag

sudden lunge, thrust

the hat beg, collect, solicit

through cross, endure, enter, experience, override, penetrate, permeate, pervade, pierce, progress, reeve, suffer, transit, traverse, undergo

up decline, disdain, disregard, evade, jump, miss, reject, skip, slight

PASSABLE acceptable, accessible, adequate, admissible, current, fair, mediocre, middling, moderate, ordinary, small, soso, tolerable

PASSAGE 3 act, gap, gut, way, wro 4 adit, door, duct, exit, fare, gate, hall, iter, lane, open, part, path, pore, ramp, slip, text, walk 5 aisle, allee, alley, alure, bogue, canal, chute, gorge, inlet, route, slype, smoot, sound, stope, stulm 6 andron, arcade, artery, atrium, avenue, bridge, burrow, course, cruise, defile, egress, flight, meatus, motion, outlet, strait, travel, voyage 7 areaway, balteus, channel, diazoma, excerpt, gallery, gangway, hallway, ingress, journey, narrows, opening, straits, transit 8 aperture, approach, approval, aqueduct, baltheus, cloister, corridor, crossing, entrance, movement, overpass, progress, transfer 9 breathing, breezeway, colonnade, enactment, migra-

tion, paragraph, underpass 10 ambulatory, bottleneck, connection, transition 12 thoroughfare 13 accommodation, communication

abnormal fistula

air flue, vent(iduct)

between 2 walls slype

biblical capitulum, pericope, text

comb. pora

covered arcade, cloister, cryptoporticus, pawn, portecochere, slype

hawk tartaret

literary chapter, citation, excerpt, paragraph, pericope, quotation, snippet, text, verse

musical bar, break, cadenza, coda, cue, fanfare, flourish, link, measure, obbligato, phrase, repeat, roulade, run, spiccato, stave, stretta

narrow aisle, alley, bottleneck, defile, gorge, hass, jetty, neck, notch, slip, slype, smoot, strait

one outlet blind-alley, close, cul-de-sac, dead end, impasse

out egress, exit

secret alure

swift flight

underground burrow, cuniculus, gallery, mine, postern, sottopassaggio, souterrain, stope, subway, tunnel

PASSAGEWAY See PASSAGE.

PASSE aged, antiquated, archaic, dead, disused, extinct, faded, obsolete, outmoded, outworn, past, worn

-partout frame, key, spandrel, tape

PASSENGER fare, ferryman, itinerant, pilgrim, rider, tourist, traveler, voyager, wayfarer

non-paying stowaway

pigeon ectopistes

seat pillion

space cabin

unbooked cad

PASSER-BY ambler, passant, pedestrian, saunterer, spectator, stroller, traveler, witness

PASSERINE See SONGBIRD.

pert. cardueline

PASSIFLORA bull-hoof,

granadilla, jamaica, may-pop, passionflower, tacso, vine

PASSIM everywhere, here and there, repeatedly

PASSING beyond, crossing, cursory, death, departing, departure, devolution, elapsing, ephemeral, evanescent, examining, exceeding(ly), excessive(ly), fleeting, fugitive, happening, hasty, momentary, preeminent, preterition, satisfactory, short-lived, sliding, surpassing, temporary, transient, very
bell knell
by cote
duck king-eider
fancy caprice, craze, fad, infatuation
slowly lag
strange extraordinary, odd

PASSION affect(ion), anger, aphrodisia, appetite, ardency, ardor, blood, calenture, cordiality, craving, craze, crush, desire, devotion, distress, dolor, ecstasy, emotion, empressement, enthusiasm, eroticism, excitement, experience, fancy, feeling(s), fervency, fervidity, fervor, fire, flame, frenzy, furor, fury, gusto, heart, heat, infatuation, inspiration, interest, ire, letch, longing, love, lust, mania, melodrama, oestrus, rage, rapture, sattva, sensation, sensitivity, sentiment, spirit, suffering, sympathy, tenderness, thirst, torment, transport, trial, unction, urge, urging, vehemence, verve, violence, warmth, wrath, yearning, yen, zeal
animal kama
flower bull-hoof, granadilla, jamaica, maracock, maypop, tacsonia, vine
for, comb. mania
play site oberammergau
without calm, cold, freddo, painless, unemotional

PASSIONATE amorous, angry, ardent, boiling, burning, desirous, dionysian, ebullient, excited, febrile, feeling, fervent, fervid, feverish, fierce, fiery, flaming, flushed, fond, frantic, glowing, gutsy, headlong, hectic,

hetup, highstrung, hot(headed), impetuous, inflamed, intense, irascible, peppery, perfervid, perturbed, provoked, quickened, red-hot, restless, seething, splenitive, stormy, sultry, torrid, turbulent, upset, vehement, warm, zealous

PASSIVE acquiescent, apathetic, compliant, cool, dull, emotionless, idle, impassive, inactive, indifferent, inert, languid, lifeless, meek, obedient, pathic, patient, phlegmatic, pliable, pliant, quiet, resigned, static, stoic, stolid, submissive, suffering, supine, uncomplaining, unconcerned, unemotional, unfeeling, uninterested, unresisting, yielding

PASSIVITY inactivity, inertia, resignation, stagnation, submission

PASSOVER feast, pasch(a), pasque, pesa(c)h
bread afikomen, matzah, matzo(s), matzoth
commencement nisan
feast seder
food banned chametz
pert. paschal
songs hallel
story haggada(h)

PASSPORT conge(e), dustu(c)k, furlough, laisser-passer, license, permit, safe-conduct, tescaria, tezkirah
endorsement visa

PASSWORD countersign, dustu(c)k, mot de passe, open-sesame, shibboleth, tessera, token, watchword

PAST above, accomplished, aforetime, after, ago, agone, ancient, antecedent, antiquity, aorist(ic), archaic, aside, auld langsyne, away, back(ward), before, behind, beyond, bygone, dead, departed, earlier, early, elapsed, eld, ended, erst(while), expired, extinct, finished, foregoing, foretime, forgotten, former(ly), gone, heretofore, history, hitherto, langsyne, last, late, long ago, obsolete, old(en) times, once, out-of-date, over, passe, preceding, preter(it), previous(ly), prior, quondam, recent, retrospective, since, sometime, spent,

then, through, timeless, ultimo, urth, was, whilom, yesterday, yesteryear, yond, yore
due delinquent
immediate yesterday
master adept, expert
meridian elderly
pert. historic
tense preterit(e)

PASTA bavetti, bucatini, cannelloni, cappelletti, ditali, fedelini, fettucine, fusilli, lasagne, linguine, macaroni, mafalde, manicotti, melone, mezzani, noodles, pappardelle, pastini, ravioli, rigati, rigatoni, rotelle, spaghetti (ni), tagliarini, tagliatelle, tortellini, trenette, vermicelli, ziti
ingredient semolina

PASTE adhere, adhesive, badigeon, barbotine, batter, bond, brasque, cement, defeat, dika, dough, fake, fasten, finery, gesso, glue, goiabade, goracco, guarana, gum, imitation, miso, mixture, mucilage, ointment, panada, pap, plaster, pulp, punch, shmeer, slurry, stick(um), strass, strike, wallop
aromatic pastil(e)
calking blare, grout
clay barbotine
colored pastel
dried guarana
fish bagoong
hearth-lining brasque
holder tube
hole-filling badigeon
plastic-repair slurry
potter's barbotine
rice ame
soft pate-tendre
tobacco goracco
-up collage, decoupage, layout, montage
weaver's buckety

PASTEBOARD bandbox, card(board), cartonnage, flimsy, frail, sham, ticket

PASTEL crayon, delicate, drawing, fair, light, pale, sketch, tint, whitish, woad

PASTERN fetter, foot, hopple, shackle, tether

PASTERNAK *heroine* lara
novel dr zhivago

PASTICCIO hodgepodge, jumble, medley, mixture,

olio, pastiche, patchwork, potpourri

PASTICHE caricature, hodgepodge

PASTIL(LE) cachou, candle, crayon, incense, lozenge, perfume, scent, troche

PASTIME amuse(ment), diversion, divert, fun, game, hobby, interval, oleary, period, pleasure, recreation, sport

PASTOR clergyman, dominie, ecclesiastic, guardian, keeper, minister, musset, PREACHER, priest, rabbi, rector, shepherd, starling, vicar

PASTORAL agrestic, agricultural, arcadian, bucolic, clerical, crosier, drama, ecclesiastical, georgic, herdsman, idyll, picture, poem, priestly, rural, rustic, shepherd, song, sylvan, villatic
god pan
place arcadia

PASTRY bakemeat, baklava, baklawa, barquette, biscuit, bouchee, cake, carcake, cornet, creampuff, danish, doucet, dowdy, eclair, empanada, flan, food, kercake, napoleon, pandowdy, pasty, pate, pattycake, pattyshell, pie, puff, savarin, scone, strudel, sweet, tart, timbale, torte, trifle, tuck, turnover
cook pastler
filled creampuff, eclair, frangipane, pie, rissole, talmouse, tart, turnover
garnish cream, fruit, meringue
ring-shaped gimbal
shell barquette, bouchee, croustade, crust, dariole, incrustation, talmouse, timbale
shop patisserie
spicy banbury-tart
strips lattice
undercrust abaisse
wheel jagger

PASTURAGE See PASTURE.

PASTURE agist, browse, colp, cowgate, eat, ejido, ewelease, feed, food, forage, gang, gate, gise, gist, grass(land), graze, grazing, haft, half, ham, hay, heaf, herbage, herdwick, hoga, ing(e), keep, lea(land),

lease, leasow, meadow, nourish, park, potrero, range, seter, sheepwalk, shieling, soil(age), soum, vaccary, veldt
bird plover, vesper-sparrow
god dumuzi, pan
grass alfalfa, clover, grama, rye, tore
land bent, leasow, rake, soum, tack
rights agist, commonage, cowgate, eatage, horsegate, stint
summer agostadero
unused frith
wet slink

PASTY argillaceous, ashen, ashy, clayey, colorless, doughy, drained, gray, loamy, pale, pallid, pulpy, sambouse, soft, sticky, thick, wan, waxen, white

PAT apposite, appropriate, apropos, apt, auspicious, blow, butter, caress, chuck, clod, dab, felicitous, fit (ting), fixed, flatten, foot, form, glib, happy, immovable, impel, irishman, jute, lump, massage, mold, opportune, palp, paw, pertinent, pet, piece, plug, primed, propitious, put-up, rap, rehearsed, seasonable, shape, smooth, soothe, stroke, suitable, tap, throw, thud, tick, tig, timely, tip, touch
-ball rounders
on the back advocate, boost, comfort, congratulate, encourage(ment)

PATA canvas, painting, puttee, sword, turban

PATAGONIA *cattle* niatas
cavy mara
deity setebos
indian tehuelche
people onas, tehuelche
plant azorella, balsam-bog
rodent capybara, cavy, mara
tree alerce, alerse, maniu

PATAMAR boat, courier, messenger, vessel

PATAND base, plinth, sill

PATCH adjunct, adjust, amend, area, beam, bit, blemish, blotch, bodge, botch, bout, clobber, clout, clown, cobble, correct, cover, darn, deceive, dollop, dolt, eke, emblem, excerpt, field, fix, fool, garden, jest-

er, join, knave, lot, mark, mend, mouche, ninny, parcel, passage, piece, plaster, plot, portion, reconcile, regulate, remnant, repair, restore, revamp, scrap, settle, sew, slat, speck, spetch, splat, spot, stain, strip, swatch, tract, vamp
clumsily botch, clamper, clout
livid pelioma
shoulder flash, insignia
together rhapsodize
word expletive

PATCHER mender, sartor, sewer, tailor

PATCHHEAD scoter, surfer

PATCHWORK botch, cento(n), crazy-quilt, fragments, hodgepodge, jumble, medley, mixture, montage, mosaic, quilt, pasticcio, scraps, variegation
literary cento

PATCHY cross, irascible, spotted, spotty, testy, tetchy, uneven

PATE badger, brain, costard, crown, foie ₌ gras, head, paste, pasty, patty, pie

PATELLA dish, kneecap, kneepan, limpet, pan, rotula, sesamoid, whirlbone

PATEN arca, disc, dish, disk, plate, vessel

PATENT apparent, available, berat, brevet, certificate, charter, clear, conspicuous, copyright, distinct, evident, expanded, flagrant, franchise, glaring, grant, gross, indulgence, instrument, license, manifest, notorious, obvious, open, palpable, patulous, permission, plain, privilege, prominent, proprietary, rank, right, salient, spreading, unconcealed, unobstructed
cutch catechu
medicine nostrum
notice caveat

PATER dad(dy), FATHER, master, pap(p)a, pop, priest

PATERNAL fatherly, parental

PATERNITY fatherhood, fathership
determine affiliate, filiate

PATH access, alameda, alle·, ambate, berm(e), boardwalk, byway, camino, casaun, course, direction,

esplanade, footway, gate, groove, lane, line, locus, orbit, parade, passage, pave, pist(e), prado, promenade, rack, rake, road (way), roddin(g), route, run(way), rut, senda, sidewalk, swath(e), tariqat, track, trail(way), trajectory, trod, trottoir, trundle, twitchel, walk(way), way
animal's pist(e)
bridle rotten row, spurway
mathematical locus
narrow berm, rack, roddin(g), trig, trocha
planet's orbit
sheep's roddin(g)
steep borstal(l)
stone steen
PATHAN *city* islamabad, peshawar
law paktunwali
militia khyber rifles, waxiristan scouts
people afghan, afridi, bajouri, bangash, dangarik, khattak, mahsud, paythan, puktun, sherani, shinawari, sivati, turi, wazirs, yusefzai
PATHETIC affecting, distressing, doleful, emotional, forlorn, melancholy, miserable, moving, passionate, pitiable, pitiful, plaintive, poignant, rueful, sad, stirring, tearful, teary, tender, touching, wretched
PATHFINDER fremont, natty bumppo, scout
author cooper
PATHIC catamite, diseased, passive, suffering, victim
PATHOGEN bacillus, bacterium, germ, microbe, organism, virus
PATHOLOGICAL diseased, infected, morbid
comb. oma
PATHOS affliction, emotion, poignancy, s(c)hmaltz, snivel, suffering
insincere bathos
PATIENCE acceptance, backbone, bigness, charity, composure, condonation, dock, endurance, forbearance, fortitude, grit, indulgence, leave, lenience, leniency, longanimity, longsuffering, permission, persistence, pluck, resignation, stoicism, submission, suffer-

ance, sympathy, tolerance, toleration, understanding
symbol job
PATIENT bovine, calm, case, dull, endurant, enduring, forbearing, game, indulgent, invalid, lenient, longanimous, longsuffering, meek, ox-like, passive, persevering, self-controlled, shut-in, sluggish, sober, spartan, stoic(al), stolid, sufferer, tolerant, tolerative
be bear, endure, tolerate
PATINA dish, film, pan, paten, polish, sheen
PATIO atrium, court(yard), enclosure, lanai, piazza, porch, terrace, veranda
PATOIS argot, cant, creole, dialect, gossip, gumbo, jargon, lingo, patter, provincialism, slang, speech, vernacular
PATRIARCH alder(man), ancestor, despot, ecclesiastic, elder, exarch, father, head, master, nasi, oldster, pater(familias), pitri, senior, sire, venerable, veteran
biblical abraham, asher, benjamin, cain(an), dan, eber, enoch, enos, esau, gad, ham, heth, irad, isaac, ishmael, israel, jacob, japheth, jared, job, jocktan, joseph, judah, kenan, lamech, levi, mahaled, methuselah, nahor, naphtali, noah, peleg, reuben, serug, seth, shem, simeon, terah, zebulun
of ferney voltaire
PATRICIAN aristocrat, blueblood, emperor, gentleman, lord, magnate, master, noble, oligarch, overlord, patroon, plutocrat, silkstocking, squire, suzeraine, upperclass, wellborn
group landed gentry
PATRIMONY ancestry, birthright, heritage, inheritance, longacre, portion
PATRIOT allen, chauvinist, compatriate, countryman, flagwaver, hale, jingo(ist), lover, loyalist, nationalist, otis, revere
PATRIOTISM amor patriae, chauvinism, flaggery, jingoism, nationalism, spreadeagle(ism)
lack incivism
PATROBAS *friend* paul

PATROCLUS *friend* achilles
parent menoetius, menoitios, periapis, periopis, sthenele
slayer hector
troops myrmidons
victim sarpedon, sthenelaus, thrasydemus, thrasymelus
PATROL detachment, guard, lookout, picket, police, protect, scout, spotter, spy, stooge, watch(man)
car black-and-white, black maria, carryall, cruiser, paddy-wagon, prowl-car, squadcar, wagon
man bluecoat, bobby, cop, guard, officer, policeman, watch
PATRON advocate, angel, applauder, attendant, audience, backer, benefactor, boss, buyer, cartridge, champion, clapper, claquer, client, contributor, customer, defender, enthusiast, fan, fautor, financer, follower, frequenter, goer, guarantor, guardian, habitue, master, meal-ticket, pleader, preferrer, promoter, proprietor, protector, purchaser, saint, spectator, sponsor, staker, supporter, surety, theatergoer, visitor
group claque, following
of arts angel, maecenas, sponsor
stock exchange buyer, seller, trader
wealthy carriage-trade
PATRONAGE advocacy, advowson, aegis, aid, assistance, auspices, backing, booty, business, condescension, countenance, custom(ers), egis, encouragement, favor(s), gravy, gravy-train, guardianship, guidance, hearing, help, influence, market, melon, moolah, mordida, padroado, pap, payola, plum, pork, protection, sponsorship, support, trade
corrupt simony
support from pap
to relatives nepotism
PATRONIZE aid, condescend, defend, deign, father, finance, frequent, justify, promote, sponsor, stoop, take up, trade(with), use, vindicate

PATRONIZING hoitytoity

PATRONYMIC *comb.* idae

PATROON captain, proprietor, supporter
land manor

PATROUS apollo

PATSY fall-guy, sap, s(c)hnook, shnuk, stooge, sucker

PATTEN base, chopin, cioppino, clog, creeper, foot, overshoe, sill, skate, snowshoe, stand, stilt, support

PATTER argot, babble, blather, blatter, cant, chatter, dialect, drum, gab(ble), gibber, harangue, jabber, jargon, jive, language, lingo, mutter, nonsense, pad, patois, pound, prate, prattle, slang, spatter, speak, speech, talk, tirl, vernacular, walk

PATTERN apotheosis, archetype, behavior, bysen, cast, characteristic, configuration, conformation, copy, cut, design, device, devise, draft, ensample(r), example, exemplar, figure, form(at), gestalt, guide, habit, herringbone, ideal, imitate, impression, likeness, map, match, matrix, meaning, measure, method, mirror, model, module, mold, motif, motive, moulage, norm, original, outline, paradigm, paragon, parallel, picture, plan, precedent, predisposition, prototype, sample, scale, seme, set(t), shape, specimen, standard, stencil, stereotype, stripes, syndrome, template, tendency, type
cross-barred check, plaid, tartan
crude roughcast
elaborate faconne
fish-scale papelonne
hat block
shoe last
striped barre
watered moire

PATTON *nickname* old blood and guts

PATTY bouchee, praline, tablet, vol au vent
shell croustade, dariole, talmouse, timbale

PATULOUS diffuse, distended, expanded, gaping, open, spread(ing)

PAUCITY dearth, exiguity, famine, fewness, insufficiency, lack, poverty, scantiness, scantity, scarcity, smallness

PAUL saint, saul, tentmaker
affliction thorn
aide apollos, archippus, aristarchus, artemas, barnabas, demas, epaphras, erastus, gaius, luke, mark, nason, onesimus, secundus, silas, sopater, sylvanus, timothy, titus, trophimus, tychicus
birthplace tarsus
clerk barnabite
convert apollos, crispus, damaris, dionysius, gaius, stephanas, titius-justus
correspondent apphia, archippus, colossians, corinthians, demas, epaphras, ephesians, galatians, hebrews, philemon, philippians, romans, thessalonians, timothy, titus
crown tiara
enemy alexander, hymenaeus
friend ampliatus, andronicus, apelles, apollos, aquila, artemas, asyncritus, barnabus, claudia, epaenetus, erastus, eubulus, hermas, hermes, herodion, jason, julia, junias, linus, nereus, nympha(s), olympas, onesiphorus, patrobas, persis, philologus, phlegon, phoebe, prisca, priscilla, pudens, rufus, silas, stachys, titus, trophimus, tryphaena, tryphosa, urban, zenas
host gaius
prosecutor tertullus
silversmith demetrius
symbol book, sword
woman baptized by lydia

PAUL VI montini

PAULDRON epaulet(te), paleron, poldron, pollet(te)

PAULINA *husband* antigonus

PAULUS aemilius
antagonist perseus
consort papiria
daughter tertia
enemy servius-galba
son fabius, scipio
son-in-law cato

PAUNCH abdomen, bay-window, belly, bouk, corporation, disembowel, entrails, glut, gulp, gut, potbelly, rumen, stomach, stuff, tripe

PAUNCHY abdominous, obese, potbellied, swag-bellied, thick-girthed, ventricose

PAUPER almsman, bankrupt, beggar, casual, down-and-outer, have-not, indigent, mendicant, poorling, roundsman, starveling

PAUSANIUS *enemy* mardonius
father cleombrotus
kin leonidas, plistarchus
slayer amyntas
son plistonax
victory plataea

PAUSE abeyance, break, breather, breathing, c(a)esura, cease, cessation, check, delay, deliberate, demur, deval, dwell, halt, hem, hesitate, hesitation, inaction, interim, interlude, intermission, intermit, interruption, interval, kick, lapse, letup, limma, linger, lull, recess, remission, repose, respite, rest, scruple, selah, stance, stand, stay, stop, suspense, suspension, swell, tarry, truce, wait, waver
musical c(a)esura, fermata

PAUT clump, finger, paw, poke, stamp

PAVABID papaverine

PAVAKA *father* agni

PAVAMANA *father* agni

PAVE asphalt, brick, cobble, cover, floor, lay, prepare, road, ruderate, setting, smooth, surface, tile
the way clear, ease, facilitate, prepare

PAVEMENT asphalt, blacktop, bouldering, bricks, causeway, causey, cement, cobbles(tones), concrete, curbing, edgestone, flagging, flags(tones), floor(ing), gabbatha, kerb(stone), macadam, road, sidewalk, stone, tar, tile(stones)
block cube, sett, stone, wheeler
material asphalt(um), brick, concrete, macadam, tarmac
mending cold-patch
painted asarotum

PAVID fearful, timid

PAVILLION arbor, arena, auricle, banner, canopy, cover(ing), ensign, flag, gloriette, house, howdah, kiosk, litter, marquee, pandal, pawl, pinna, royal, tabernacle, teld, tent

PAVING *material* asphalt, cobble, flagstone, slurry, tar
square mitchel
stone flag

PAW claw, clutch, crubeen, dad, dupe, feel, flipper, fondle, foot, fumble, gaum, grope, hand(le), hoof, manhandle, maul, obscene, pad, patte, paut, port, pud, stroke, tool, touch, trick
ground paut
part claw

PAWK impertinence, trick, wile

PAWKY arch, bold, canny, cunning, forward, lively, saucy, shrewd, sly, squeamish

PAWL bolt, catch, click, cog, detent, hand, ratchet, sear, stop, tent, tongue, trip

PAWN agent, bauer, borrow, cat's-paw, chessman, counter, deposit, dupe, earnest, forfeit, gage, gallery, gambit, guaranty, hazard, hock, hostage, instrument, lend, man, peacock, pignus, pledge, promise, puppet, risk, security, soak, stake, token, tool, victim, wadset, wager
above value moskeneer
chess pon, poune
disposition of skeleton
take from redeem

PAWNBROKER avuncular, lender, lumberer, moneylender, uncle, usurer

PAWNEE almond, caddo, chaui, indian, kitkehahki, loup, panee, pani, pitahauret, pledgee, skidi, water
color biscuit
deity arch of heaven, atira, morning star bride, soatsaki, tirawa
rite hako
sun shakuru

PAWNSHOP lombard, montde-piete, my uncle's

PAWPAW fruit, immoral, indecent, naughty, papaw, papaya, tree

PAX friend(ship), hush, peace, quiet, silence, truce
dei armistice

PAY acquit, amortize, ante, appease, atone, award, cash, compensate, compensation, content, defray, deposit, disburse, discharge, earning(s), emolument, expend, fee,

gratify, guerdon, halvans, hire, income, indemnify, indemnity, liquidate, lolly, pacify, pension, pingle, pittance, please, ransom, rebate, recompense, redeem, redress, refund, reimburse, remit, remunerate, remuneration, render, requite, return, reward, salary, satisfy, sawdee, screw, settle(ment), shepe, soud, souldie, sowd, spend, square, stipend(ium), subsidize, support, tender, tip, treat, tribute, wage(s), yield
attention advert, come, court, dig, gaum, get with it, heed, listen, look out, regard, take care, tent, watch out
back avenge, get even, interchange, rebate, refund, reimburse, retaliate, revenge, settle
court cultivate, flatter, gallant, propose, solicit, sue, woo
dirt gold, mine, ore, profit
extra batta, bonus, cumshaw, douceur, gratuity, honorarium, kickback, pourboire, premium, tip
fixed salary, stipend, wages
for abegge, absorb, aby(e), buy, bye, cover, finance, purchase, rent, stand, treat, underwrite
homage adore, attorn, chefe, cheve, chive, honor, salaam, salute, worship
load burden, cargo, freight, pack(age)
no attention disobey, disregard, ignore, neglect, overlook, slight, snub
off acquit, bribe, climax, compensate, conclusion, denouement, discharge, end, finish, fix, free, get even, mordida, profit, punish, reckoning, requite, result, retaliate, retribution, reward, settlement, sink, slacken, the bite, unwind
out bleed, disburse, discharge, dispend, distribute, expend, punish, slacken, spend
small lolly, screw
taxes gild
the penalty abegge, aby(e), atone
up ante, liquidate, quit, settle

PAYABLE due, matured, on call, owing

PAYAGUA *indian* agaz, sarigue

PAYING gainful, lucrative, profitable, remunerative
guest boarder, tenant, transient

PAYMASTER bakshi, bu(c)kshee, bukshi, buxy, cashier, officer, pagador, purser, treasurer

PAYMENT acquittal, acquittance, aid, allowance, amortization, annat, annuity, award, benefit, bounty, cens, clearance, compensation, consideration, contribution, cro, defrayal, deposit, dole, earnest, eric, expenditure, fee, gale, gild, grant, headpenny, honorarium, kain, kist, levy, liquidation, lobola, mail, mense, offer, pension, pledge, quittance, ransom, rebate, reckoning, recompense, remittance, remuneration, rent, requital, resolute, reward, satisfaction, scot, settlement, stipend, subsidy, subvention, support, tack, tax, toll, trewage, woodgeld
deferred arrears
demand for bill, dun
due cens
evade bilk, default
fixed canon, kist
for offence enach, fine
for release loosing, ransom
guarantee aval
illegal bribe, kickback, payola
initial ante, deposit, down
method cost plus, installment plan, never-never
on delivery cod
periodic gale, gavel, installment
promise iou
received credit
regular gale
without free, gratis

PAYNIM ethnic, gentile, heathen, infidel, pagan, panime

PAYOLA bribe(ry), kickback

PCP angel dust, phencyclidine

PDQ See FAST.

PEA anthyllis, arhar, aspalathus, bill, butea, carmele, catjang, chick, cicer, dal, dhal, erebinthos, fragment,

gandul, garbanzo, garvanzo, gram, khesari, lang, legume, marble, pigeon, plant, podder, powdare, pulse, roe, seed, senna, soja, split, tangier, tur, vegetable, vetchling
berry coffeeberry
bird oriole, wryneck
chick cicer, garbanzo, garvanzo, gram
crab pinnotere
disease black-pit
dove zenaida
early hastings
family fabaceae
family plant senna, vetch
finch chaffinch
flour erbswurst
flower petal vexillum
fowl pavo, PEACOCK, peahen
genus aeschynomene, clitoria, dalea, lathyrus, oxytropis, parosela, phaca, tephrosia
grit pisolite
heath carmele
herb aeschynomene, amorpha, astragalus, baptisia, cajanus
large telephone
marrowfat ronceval
-mouth minnow
parched carl(ing)
petal keel, vexillum
picker viner
pigeon cajan, catjang, tur
pod boat, cob, pescod, pyse, quash, squash
sausage erbswurst
seeds pulse
-shaped pisiform
shrub anagyris
soup fog, smaze, smog
soup ingredient hambone
split d(h)al, dhall
trailing groundnut
tree agati, baphia, bowdichia, butea, caragana, katurai, laburnum, sandalwood, sesbania
PEACE accord, amity, armistice, calm, composure, concord, contentment, detente, ease, frith, goal, grith, harmony, hope, law-and-order, liss(e), nirvana, order(liness), pacifism, pax, quiet, quietude, repose, requiem, salem, serenity, shalom, sholem, sholom, silence, tranquillity, truce
be with you pax-vobiscum

bird dove, paloma
corps head shriver
god bald(e)r, eir, forseti, forsette, frey, ing
goddess concordia, dice, dike, eir(ene), freda, irene, minerva, nerthus, pax, selene
king of jesus, melchizedek
name meaning erin(a), irene, irina, nola, olga, olive
offering calumet, dove, gift, irenicon, olive-branch, overture, pipe
officer See POLICEMAN.
of mind ataraxia, composure, nirvana, satisfaction, serenity, tranquillity
passionate nirvana
path to detente
pipe calumet, overture
pledge fritherbor(g)h
symbol calumet, dove, olive(branch), pax, pipe, white flag
to you aleichem shalom
uneasy pax romana
PEACEABLE amicable, complacent, friendly, gentle, henotic, irenic, neighborly, orderly, pacific, PEACEFUL, placid, still
name meaning solomon
PEACEFUL amicable, bloodless, calm, comfortable, composed, concordant, cool, friendly, gentle, halcyon, happy, harmonious, homelike, irenic(al), kind, mild, neutral, pacific, placid, quiet, restful, serene, shy, silent, silver, smooth, sober, soft, steady, still(ly), tranquil, undisturbed, untroubled
PEACEMAKER conciliator, intercessor, mediator, pacifist, propitiator, reconciler
PEACH (See also *kind*, below.) accuse, ace, amygdalus, beauty, betray, blab, doll, foster, fruit, indict, inform, padus, rosewort, snitch, squeal, tattle, tell, top-notcher, tree
brandy boof
clingstone pavy
family amygdalaceae
freestone crawford, elberta, foster
grafted on quince melocoton
kind carman, cling(stone), crawford, crosby, elberta,

emu-apple, foster, freestone, hale, isabella, orejon, pavie, pavy, peento, persian, pientao, quadang, quadong, quantong, russelet, salwey
-like fruit apricot, nectarine
myrtle hypocalymma
origin almond, china, persia
relative apricot
state georgia
stone pit, putamen
weevil curculio
PEACHBLOW fakir
PEACHES benzedrine
PEACHWORT lady's-thumb, persicary
PEACHY fine, great, splendid, wonderful
PEACOCK fowl, mao, pajock, paon, pavo(ne), pawn, phasianid, poo, pose, pownie, strut, swagger
bittern sun
-blue paon
butterfly kiho, vanessa
constellation pavo
eyes argus
fan flabellum
feather fiber mari
female hen, peahen
fish wrasse
flower adenanthera, barbados-pride, bear-tree, flambeau, poinciana, sandalwood
group muster
heron bittern
-like conceited, pavonine, vain
markings ocelli
ore bornite, chalcopyrite, erubescite
-pheasant polyplectron
symbol of pride
tail alga, padina
tail spot eye, ocellus
PEAG(E) money, pedage, tax, toll, wampum
PEAK acme, alp, apex, apogee, arete, ben, butte, cima, climax, cone, crag, crown, culmination, cupula, cusp, dolt, dwindle, fail, headland, height, hill, icecap, maximum, meridian, mesa, mount(ain), pico, pike, pinnacle, pique, pitch, piton, promontory, simpleton, spire, steal, summit, tip, tolt, top, tor, vertex, volcano, zenith
comb. acr(o), apic(o)
ice berg, cap, serac
isolated tolt

needle-shaped aiguille
ornament epi, finial
rocky alp, arete, crag, tor
snow-capped calotte, dome
volcanic cone
PEAKED bilious, drawn, emaciated, haggard, infirm, pale, pointed, poor, sickly, slimpsy, thin, tired, wan, worn
PEAL assail, blare, boom, carillon, change, chime, clap, clash, din, echo, fish, grilse, resound, ring, roar, salmon, shovel, strike, summons, thunder, toll, touch, trout
PEAN ermine, sable
PEANUT arachis, beennut, bit, bur, earthalmond, earthnut, earthpea, goober, grassnut, groundnut, katchung, mani, mean, monkeynut, petty, pinda(l), small, trifle, valencia
color flax
disease tikka
oil arachis
worm sipunculid
PEAR alligator, ambrette, anjou, bartlett, bergamot, beurre, bon chretien, bosc, brandywine, burrel, chaumontel, comice, diego, fruit, kieffer, muscadine, nopal, panini, poire, prickly, pyrus, sabra, seckel, sickle, tasajillo, tree, tuna, warden, winter
autumn bosc
bartlett bon chretien
black chokeberry
blight mealy-bug
cider perrie, perry
disease blackend, brownblotch, bull's-eye-rot, stonypit
haw blackthorn, crataegus, sloe, thorn
hybrid keiffer
prickly cactus, nopal, opuntia, pinpillow, tuna
-shaped apioidal, bulbous, obconic(al), pyriform, rounded
shell pyrula
small seckel
squash chayote, perry
stony knots in calculary
winter warden
PEARL argent, baroque, bdelium, blister, bouton, capsule, cataract, dewdrop, drop, gem, luster, mabe, margaret, margarite, mar-

gery, moonbeam, nacre, nacr(e)ous, olivet, onion, purl, seed, tear, tern, ticot, tooth, treasure
artificial alburnus, blay, bleak, olivet, seed
bird barbet, guinea-fowl
blue gray, metal, moonbeam
blush rosetan
bush exochorda
chain rope
diabase variolite
disease tuberculosis
essence blanc d' ablette
-eye cataract
fish carapus, fierasfer
flat bouton, butter-pearl
generating perliginous
gray griseous
harbor attack tora tora
imitation argentine, olivet
irregular slug
-like nacre, olivet
millet bajra, bajri, buzzardgrass, cattail, cumbu, dagassa, duchin, dukhn, jondla, kous(e), pennisetum, sorghum
mosque home agra, macedonia
moss carrageen
name meaning gogo, gret(t)a, margaret, margery, margot, peg, rita
of great luster orient
of the antilles cuba
of the east zenobia
opal cacholong
oyster black-lip, mollusk
pierced widow
plant gromwell
seed aliofar
smoked mitraille
source abalone, argenteum, blanc d'ablette, oyster
spar dolomite
weight tank
PEARLSIDES argentin
PEARLWEED poverty, sagina, sealwort
PEARLY clear, fair, frosted, iridescent, limpid, milky, nacreaous, nacrous, nacry, opalescent, opaline, opaloid, pellucid, precious, rosetan, translucent
everlasting cudweed, everwhite, livelong, moonshine
gates heaven
PEASANT agricole, agriculturalist, appleknocker, arkie, billjim, bogtrotter, bonhomme, boor, bracero, bucolic, bumpkin, campe-

sino, carl(ot), ceorl, chawbacon, churl, clod(hopper), clown, cocker, commoner, coolie, cottar, cotter, countryman, cullion, esne, farmer, fellah, fellow, fool, fouter, frieze-coat, hayseed, helot, hick, hind, hob(inol), jacques, jasper, kern(e), kisan, kulak, laborer, litus, moujik, muzhik, okie, paisano, peon, plebeian, provincial, rascal, rayat, reuben, rube, russet, rustic, ryot, servant, slave, smatchet, sodbuster, swain, tao, tike, tiller, truffe, tyke, vulgar, wetback, yahoo, yap, yokel
bard robert burns
class jacquerie
crusade leader peter the hermit, walter the penniless
dress dirndle
freeholder bonder
holding cotland, full-land, virgate, yardland
landholder coscet, cotset
painters barbizon school
rebel jack-straw, john ball, wat tyler
tenant collibert
turned to stone battus
PEASE appease, pacify, quiet, reconcile
crow tern
pert. pulse
PEASEBROSE porridge, pottage
PEASHOOTER beanblower, beanshooter, blower, blowgun, pistol, puttyblower, slingshot
PEAT coom(b), darling, favorite, fuel, ger, gor, lawyer, minion, moor, muck, mull, pet, sod, turf, yarpha
bog cess, moss, yarpha
cutter piner
dig sheugh
fuel vag
layer flaw
reek whiskey
shovel slade, slane, spade, tuskar, twiscar
substance dopplerite
PEATWOOD loosestrife
PEAU hide, skin
d'ange angelskin, fabric, finish
de soie fabric, silk
PEAVEY canthook, hook, lever
PEBBLE bantam, chuck(ie), crystal, dib(stone), drake-

stone, dreikanter, finger-stone, flax, gibber, grain, gravel, jack(stone), plum, quartz, riprap, scree, shilla, slingstone, stane, stanner, stone, sycite
-*shaped* calciform, calculiform
PEBBLY beachy, rocky
PECAN carya, hickory, nogal, nut, pacane, tree, wood
PECCADILLO error, fault, flaw, mischief, offense, sin
PECCANT bad, corrupt, diseased, erroneous, evil, faulty, guilty, incorrect, insalubrious, morbid, offender, rotten, sinner, sinning, unhealthy
PECCARY javali, javelina, musk-hog, tagassu, tajacu, tayassu(id), warree
PECH breath(e), pant, sigh
PECHT fairy, gnome, pict, pygmy
PECK beak, bite, carp, chimble, dab, dot, eat, fall, food, hole, jerk, kiss, knip, many, measure, nag, nibble, nip, pant, peggle, pick, pitch, prick, pyke, strike, stumble, tap, tease, throw, twit
1/8th quart
1/4th forpet, forpit, lippie, lippy
4 bushel
at attack, carp, harass, nag, tease, twit
PECKER beak, bill, courage, eater, feeder, nose, resolution, spirits
PECKSNIFF hypocrite
PECORA antelope, deer, giraffe, goat, oxen, sheep
PECOS *law west of* judge roy bean
PECULATE appropriate, confiscate, defalcate, embezzle, filch, loot, misuse, pilfer, plunder, pre-empt, purloin, rifle, rob, steal, usurp
PECULATOR See THIEF.
PECULIAR aberrant, anomalous, atypic, bizarre, buggy, bughouse, bugs, characteristic, curious, different, distinct(ive), distinguishing, eccentric, erratic, especial, exceptional, exclusive, extraordinary, fantastic, grotesque, independent, individual, intrinsic, nutty, odd, off, outlandish, particular, personal, proper, quaint,

queer, rare, separate, single, singular, special, specific, squirrelly, strange, typical, uncommon, unique, unusual, weird
comb. idio
PECULIARITY attribute, characteristic, crotchet, distinction, distinctiveness, eccentricity, feature, fike, foible, idiasm, idiom, idiosyncrasy, individuality, kink, mannerism, oddity, partiality, particularity, quirk, singularity, trait, trick, twist
PECUNIARY bursal, financial, fiscal, monetary
PECUNIOUS moneymad, RICH
PEDAGOGIC pedantic, preceptoral, professorial, teacherish, teacherly, tuitional, tutorial
PEDAGOGUE dominie, inkhorn, PEDANT, scholar, schoolmaster, squeers, teacher, thwackum
PEDAGOGY didactics, discipline, instruction, school, teaching
PEDAIAH *son* shimei, zerubbabel
PEDAL celeste, footfeed, lever, propel(ler), swell, throttle, treadle
coupler tirasse
extremity foot, pad, paw
piano celeste
pushers slacks
PEDANT academe, conformist, dunce, formalist, gamaliel, olofernes, pangloss, pedagogue, precisionist, prig, purist, scholar, schoolmaster, tassel, teacher, tutor
female bluestocking
PEDANTIC abstruse, academic, bibliophagic, bibliophilic, bookish, donnish, dry-as-dust, erudite, formal, inkhorn, learned, literary, pedagogic(al), purist, recondite, scholarly, scholastic, stilted, stodgy, yekke
PEDASUS *kin* abarbarea, aesepus
slayer euryalus
PEDDLE bend, cadge, canvass, colport, dally, haggle, hawk, higgle, meddle, piddle, retail, sell, solicit, tout trant, trifle, vend
PEDDLER arab, badger

boxwallah, broker, camelot, chapman, coster, dustyfoot, faker, fogger, footgoer, hawker, huckster, jagger, jowter, juggler, merchant, mugger, niggler, roadman, sandboy, seller, smous(er), swadder, trader, tranter, trogger, trucker, vendor
accomplice shill
of fish ripier, ripper
of religious books colporteur
pack wallet
wares troggan
PEDDLING hawking, insignificant, marketing, petty, piddling, trifling
PEDESTAL acropodium, acroter(ium), akroter, anta, base, bearing, block, foot, foundation, gaine, leg, padmasana, podium, postament, support
lotus-shaped padmasana
low socle
part base, dado, die, orlo, plinth, quadra, socle, surbase
put on elevate, enshrine, exalt, idolize, worship
small piedouche
PEDESTRIAN afoot, ambler, commonplace, dull, hiker, hitch-hiker, hoofer, jaywalker, passerby, peripatetic, plodding, prosaic, slow, tramp(er), unimaginative, walker
PEDIATRICS *specialty* neonatology
PEDICEL foot(stalk), peduncle, stalk, stem
umbel ray
PEDICULARIS betony, figwort, lousewort
PEDIGREE ancestry, bloodline, breed, credentials, derivation, descent, genealogy, kind, line(age), model, purebred, roots, stemma, strain
PEDIMENT base, fastigium, fronton, pavement, support
PEDLAR See PEDDLER.
PEDUNCLE crus, eyestalk, hypocarp, knot, pedicel, petiole, scape, stalk, stem, stipes
PEEK blink, chirp, glance, glimpse, look, peep, peer, pry, see, sight spy, squint, view
PEEKABOO bopeep, game peepbo, peepeye
PEEL bark, castle, cork, cor-

tex, cut off, decorticate, deduct, delaminate, dermatogen, desquamate, epicarp, equal, excoriate, exfoliate, extort, fell, flake, flay, fort, harl, hide, hull, husk, lamina, layer, match, orangeado, pail, palisade, pare, pellicle, pelt, periderm, peridium, phelloderm, phellum, pile, pillage, pillow, rind, rob, scale, scalp, shave, shed, shovel, shuck, skin, skive, slipe, spade, stake, stockade, strip, stronghold, tower, uncover, undress

candied orangeado

grated zest

off craze, flake, harl, shed, shuck, skin

PEELED alert, beggared, threadbare, tonsured, worn

PEELER bailiff, bobby, bull, catchpole, constable, cop (per), corer, crab, gendarme, hustler, officer, pillager, policeman, shedder, spudder, storm, stripper

PEELING paring, parure, rind, skin

PEEP appear, chatter, cheep, chirp, chuck, churr, coo, crevice, cry, dekko, emerge, glance, glimpse, glint, look, peek, peer, pipit, pry, pule, reconnoiter, sandpiper, skeg, snoop, spy, squeak, squeal, squinny, teet, toot, tote, view

-eye peekaboo

hawk kestrel

show raree, spectacle

PEEPER eye, frog, keek, spy, toad, tom, voyeur

PEEPHOLE aperture, crevice, eyelet, judas-window, opening

PEER archduke, aristocrat, armiger, associate, baron (et), coequal, companion, compeer, comrade, contemporary, count, daimio, duke, earl, equal, esquire, examine, feere, fellow, fere, gape, gaze, glance, glare, glint, gloze, landgrave, look, lord, make, margrave, marquis, match, mate, noble(man), paladin, palsgrave, peek, peep, pry, rival, seigneur, seignior, squire, stare, thane, twire, viscount, waldgrave

wife of See LADY.

PEERAGE aristocracy, baronage, dignity, nobility, rank

PEERESS See LADY.

PEER GYNT *author* ibsen

composer grieg

parent ase

role anitra, solveig

PEERLESS banner, best, incomparable, matchless, nonpareil, superlative, supreme, top, transcendent, unequalled, unique, unmatched, unrivaled, unsurpassed

PEES(E)WEEP bird, finch, greenfinch, lapwing, pewit

PEEVE aggravate, annoy, bother, chafe, exasperate, fret, gall, grudge, irk, irritate, nettle, provoke, roil, vex

PEEVISH acerb, bilious, cantankerous, capernoited, capricious, captious, carping, choleric, churlish, contemptible, contentious, contrary, crabbed, cranky, critical, cross, crusty, faultfinding, fractious, fratchy, frecket, fretful, froward, gruff, huffy, irascible, irritable, morose, nettled, obstinate, pensy, perverse, pettish, petty, petulant, pindling, querulous, sanshach, snappish, sour, spiteful, spleeny, splenetic, stubborn, sulky, sullen, tatter, teaty, techy, teeny, testy, thrawart, thrawn, tiffish, touchy, twanky, twarly, twitty, uppity, waspish, wemod

person attercop, crosspatch, schlack, schlag, s(c)hlock

PEEVISHNESS bile, petulance, protervity

PEEWEE bird, diminutive, dwarf, infinitesimal, lapwing, lark, marble, phoebe, runt, small, tiny

PEG bind, blow, bolt, claw, cleat, confine, crink, degree, dowel, drudge, fastener, figure, foot, grade, hammer, hasten, hit, hob(b), hurry, knag, leg, marker, nob, nog, notch, obstruction, perch, pierce, pin, piton, plod, plug, point, pretext, prong, reason, recognize, restrict, run, scob, scollop, see, sperket, spike, spile, spill, stake, step, strike, support, tapoun, tee, thole, throw, tip-

cat, tooth, tre(e)nail, trunnel, walk, work

along drudge, persevere, plod

iron piton

out bind, cease, die, fail, perish, weaken, weary

square misfit

thatch scob

top peerie, peery, piry

wooden dowel(l), fid, nog, skeg, spile, spill, thole

PEGA(DOR) remora

PEGALL basket, packall

PEGASUS hypostome, quaviver

ensign of corinth

rider bellerophon

son aquarius

source medusa, perseus

star in andromeda

PEGGOTTY *niece* emily

PEGMATITE perthite

PEGROOTS setterwort

PEGU *catechu* kath(a)

ironwood acle

native mon

PEIGNOIR dressing-sack, gown, kimono, negligee, robe, wrapper

PEIPING cambalu(c), PEKING, tatu

PEIRITHOUS *friend* theseus

PEISE balance, blow, force, impact, oppress, poise, poize, weigh(t)

PEJORATIVE depreciatory, derogatory, disparaging

PEKAN wejack

PEKING, PEIPING cambaluc, tatu

dialect mandarin

landmark great hall of the people

newspaper peoples' daily

PELAGIAN, PELAGIC abyssal, aquatic, bathysmal, celestine, fluvial, lacustrine, marine, neritic, oceanic, sealer, thalassic

phenomenon tide

PELARGOMORPH heron, ibis, stork

PELASGUS corynetes

son lycaon

PELECANIFORMES cormorant, frigatebird, gannet, pelican, snakebird

PELEG *kin* eber, reu

PELET *father* jahdai

PELETH *father* jonathan

PELEUS *accuser* astydamia

armor-bearer crantor

brother phocus, telamon

consort antigone, thetis
descendant pelides
horse balios
parent aeacus, endeis
purifier acastus, eurytion
son achilles, pelides
subjects myrmidons
teacher chiron
victim cretheis, eurytion, phocus
PELEW See PALAU.
PELF booty, despoil, gain, loot, lucre, money, pilfer, refuse, riches, rob, rubbish, spoils, trash, wealth
PELIAS *kingdom* iolcus
nephew jason
offspring acastus, alcestis, amphinome, ampyx, evadne
parent poseidon, tyro
twin neleus
PELICAN alcatras, culvern, frigatebird, onocrotal, retort
flower gooseflower, snakeroot
-like bird solan
state louisiana
PELIDES achilles, neoptolemus
father peleus
PELIDNA brant-snipe, dunlin, plover, sandpiper
PELLES *daughter* elaine
PELLET ball, bead, beebee, bolus, buckshot, bullet, cast, disk, doli, fecula, granule, hailstone, marble, missile, ogress, pallion, pea, pearl, pebble, pill, pilule, shot, sphere, stone, trattle
snow graupel
PELLICLE coating, crust, cuticle, epistasis, film, lamina, layer, membrane, periplast, scum, skin
PELLINORE *son* agglovale, durnor, gawain, lamerok, percivale, tor(e)
PELLITORY agrimony, bertram, feverfew, masterwort, sneezewort, wallwort, yarrow
PELL-MELL confusion, disorderly, full-tilt, hastily, headlong, helterskelter, melee, posthaste, uproar, vehemently
PELLUCID bright, brilliant, clear, crystal, diaphanous, light, limpid, lucent, lucid, luminous, pure, radiant, sheer, translucent, transparent

PELOPIA *kin* aegisthus, atreus, thyestes
PELOPIDAS *consort* thebe
enemy spartans
friend epaminondas
PELOPONNESUS apia, argos, morea
city argos, corinth, sparta
conquerors aetolians, dorians, spartans
gulf argolic, laconian, messenian
isthmus corinth
king epeus
peak erymanthus
people achaean, ionian, moreote, pelasgian
province achaia, arcadia, corinthia, laconia, messenia
river god alpheus
war battle aegospotami
PELOPS *charioteer* cillus
consort hippodamia
kin niobe, tantalus, zeus
slayer hermes
son alcathous, atreus, chrysippus, pittheus, thyestes, troezen
PELORUS *slayer* ares
PELOTA See JAI ALAI.
PELT bark, beat, bethump, blow, bombard, bowl, calarer, caracal, dash, epidermis, fall, fell, fitch, fur, hail, hair, hide, hurl, lapidate, pace, peel, pellet, pepper, pluck, pound, prize, push, rack, rage, rate, refuse, rind, rubbish, sable, sculp, shoot, skin, slash, slough, stone, strike, throw, trophy, woolfell
dealer furrier
PELTER horse, kilter, miner, miser, passion, rage, shower, skeet, skinflint
PELUDO armadillo, dasypus
PELVIS *bone* ilium, ischium, pubes
diameter conjugata
pert. iliac
PEN ballpoint, bolt, bought, box, bught, cage, case, compose, confine, COOP, corral, cot(e), crawl, creep, crib, cub(by), dam, enclose, enclosure, engross, farm, fasten, faud, feather, fold, head(land), homestead, hutch, imprison, incarcerate, incase, indite, jail, kraal, paddock, pasture, penitentiary, pinfeather, plantation, prison,

quill, restrain, script, shut in, stall, sty, style, stylograph, stylus, swan, volume, warkloom, write, yard
case poppet
fold prison
kind ballpoint, felt, fountain, ink, marking, stick, stylograph
-like stylar, styloid
name alias, allonym, anonym, incognito, nom de plume, pseudonym
pal correspondent
point neb, nib, stub
reed calamus
up stive
PENAL corrective, disciplinary, punitive, punitory
PENALIZE abuse, amerce, chasten, check, condemn, correct, discipline, fine, handicap, mulct, punish, restrict, sconce, sentence
PENALTY amend(e), amerce, bete, bloodwit, cain, chastisement, compensation, cost, damages, disadvantage, doom, fine, forfeit (ure), hardship, impediment, praemunire, price, punishment, retribution, sentence, solace, subpoena, sursize, verdict
pay aby(e)
PENANCE atonement, contrition, distress, flagellation, lustration, maceration, mortification, pain, punishment, purgation, purgatory, repentance, shrift, sorrow
symbol ashes, hair-shirt, sackcloth
PENBRITIN ampicillin
PENCE 20 ora
100 pound
PENCHANT attraction, bent, bias, flair, fondness, genius, gift, knack, leaning, liking, partiality, pennon, prejudice, proclivity, propensity, talent, taste, tendency, turn
PENCIL blue, brush, charcoal, crayon, cymograph, eversharp, lead, liner, mechanical, pointel, red, sketch, stick, stylus, tuft, wad(d)
cedar juniper
pert. desmic
point apicula
pusher author, writer
slate skaillie
stone pyrophyllite

wood mordore
worn down stub

PEND arch(way), confine, dangle, depend, emergency, flap, hang(fire), incline, lean, PEN, pressure, swing, trail, vault

PENDANT addition, adjunct, aglet, aiglet, analog(ue), appendix, bagged, bob, bulla, counterpart, drape, drop, eardrop, flag, hanger, hanging, jag(g), languet, lappet, lobation, lobe, lobule, luster, ornament, palaoa, pendeloque, pendle, pendulum, pennant, slope, tabard, tag, tail, tassel
cloud tuba
kind chain, drop, earring, flap, lavaliere, liripipe, lobe, locket, pigtail, queue, tail, tassel, tippet, tossel, train, wattle

PENDENNIS *author* thackeray
character arthur, blanche amory, helen, laura, miss fotheringay, warrington

PENDENT appended, cernuous, dangling, dependent, depending, downhill, flowing, hanging, hung, icicle, impending, jutting, lop, nodding, overhanging, pendular, pendulous, pensile, promiss, sloping, suspended, swinging, undecided, weeping

PENDENTIVE squinch, trompe

PENDING at hand, doubtful, dubious, during, hanging, open, pendent, pensile, problematical, unassured, undecided, undetermined, unsettled, until, waiting

PENDULATE change, fluctuate, oscillate, sway, swing, undulate, vacillate, vibrate, waver

PENDULOUS cernuous, droopy, flabby, hanging, overhanging, sagging, saggy, slouch, suspended, swinging, vacillating, wavering

PENDULUM swing(el), swingle, vibratile
inverted noddy
kind compensation, compound, gravity, gridiron, mathematical, mercurial, motor, physical, riefler, sec-

onds, short-free, simple, torsion
weight bob

PENELOPE guan, jacket, weaver
ancestor lacedaemon
consort hermes, odysseus, telegonus, ulysses
father-in-law laertes
parent icarius, periboea
sister iphthime
slave dolius
son pan, telemachus
suiter agelaus, amphinomus, antinous, eurymachus

PENETRABLE accessible, comprehensible, pervious, vulnerable

PENETRATE affect, bore, break, burrow, carry, comprehend, cut, delve, detect, diffuse, dip, discern, discriminate, drench, drill, encroach, enter, entrench, filter, gimlet, imbue, impale, impress, infiltrate, insert, invade, move, pass, perceive, percolate, perforate, permeate, pervade, pierce, prick, probe, puncture, reach, register, saturate, sink(in), soak, spread, stab, steep, trespass, understand

PENETRATING acute, astute, biting, caustic, chilly, cold, deep, discerning, ingoing, intelligent, intrant, knowing, perceptive, percipient, piercing, profound, pungent, sagacious, sharp, shrewd, shrill, subtle, trenchant

PENETRATION acuity, acument, discernment, discrimination, entrance, fathom, inroad, insight, intuition, judg(e)ment, knowing, perception, perceptivity, perforation, sagacity, sharpness, understanding, wit

PENEUS *offspring* atrax, cyrene, daphne
parent oceanus, tethys

PENGUIN adelie, aptenodyte, auk, bird, breviped, dipper, diver, eudyptes, gentoo, gentu, johnny, macaroni, pinwing
family spheniscidae
home penguinery, pole, rookery
kind adelie, emperor, jackass,

king, rockhopper, spheniscus

PENICILLIN pentids, penveek, v-cillin-k
discoverer alexander fleming

PENINSULA byland, chersonese, demi-island, demiisle, mull, neck, penile, point, tongue

PENINSULAR deltaic, deltal, isthmian, isthmic
state florida

PENITENCE anguish, attrition, compunction, contrition, penance, regret, remorse, repentance, rue, selfreproach, shame, sorrow
garment hair shirt, samarra, san-benito
place canossa
saint mary magdalene
season lent
symbolic color violet

PENITENT audient, confessor, contrite, humble, magdalen, prodigal son, regretful, remorseful, repentant, ruer, sorry, weeper
3rd stage kneeler

PENITENTIARY big house, JAIL, jug, priest, prison, stir, tench

PENK fish, minnow, pink, tap, try

PENMAN amanuensis, author, calligrapher, chirographer, clerk, composer, scribe, writer

PENMANSHIP cacography, calligraphy, chirography, hand(writing), longhand, manuscript, script, writing

PENNACOOK *indian* agawam

PENNANT award, banderole, banner, bunting, burgee, color(s), cornet, ensign, fane, flag, guidon, jack, pencel, pennon, pensil, pinion, prize, roger, standard, streamer, wheft, whip
pirate's (jolly)roger
yacht burgee

PENNATE feathered, penniform, winged

PENNILESS bankrupt, broke, busted, destitute, flat, impecunious, indigent, needy, poor, strapped

PENNON banner, feather, flag, PENNANT, pinion, streamer, wing

PENNSYLVANIA *borough*

media, pottstown, shamokin, shenandoah
capital harrisburg
city abington, aliquippa, allentown, altoona, baden, baldwin, beaver, bethel, bethlehem, braddock, bradford, bristol, bryn mawr, butler, carbondale, carlisle, charleroi, chester, clairton, duquesne, easton, emmaus, ephrata, erie, etna, gettysburg, hanover, harrisburg, harrison, haverford, hazelton, hershey, jeannette, johnstown, lancaster, lebanon, mckeesport, meadville, mill creek, monessen, newcastle, norristown, philadelphia, pittsburgh, plum, pottsville, radnor, reading, ridley, scranton, shamokin, sharon, springfield, swissvale, uniontown, whitehall, wilkesbarre, williamsport, york
college haverford, juniata, lycoming, ursinus
county berks, bucks, cambria, juniata, lycoming, tioga, venango, wyoming
-dutch dish shoofly-pie
-dutch folk art fraktur
-dutch sect amish, dunker, mennonite
-dutch sign hex
flood johnstown
founder william penn
insurrection whiskey rebellion
lake erie
mountainman coker
native amish, dutch
nickname keystone state
president buchanan
range alleghenies, pocono
river allegheny, caldwell, clarion, delaware, genesee, juniata, lehigh, licking, monongahela, ohio, schrader, schuylkill, susquehanna, towanda
sect, communistic harmonist
state bird grouse
state flower mountain laurel
state tree hemlock
university bucknell, carnegie tech, drexel, duquesne, lehigh, pitt, temple, villanova
PENNY bit, bristly, broon, brown, cent, coin, copper, denarius, follis, groat, meg, money, oulap, pence, red, saltee, sou, stiver, turner

1/16th cee
1/2 halflin, hapenny, make, obolus
10 dime
12 shilling
100 dollar, pound
-a-line cheap, hack, inferior
ante poker
bird dabchick
cake navelwort
-dreadful dime novel, horrible
father See MISER.
flower honesty, lunaria
grass navelwort, rattle
pies navelwort
-pinching cheeseparing, close (fisted), mean, miserly, niggardly, parsimonious, penurious, poor, stingy, tight (fisted)
stone quoit
weight dwt, sterling
whistle fipple-flute
PENNYCRESS boor's-mustard, fanweed, stinkweed, thlaspi
PENNYROYAL bluecurls, brotherwort, fleabane, hedeoma, hillwort, mentha, mint, pudding-grass, selfheal, squawweed, tickweed, wild thyme
PENNYWORT centella, cotyledon, ivy, sibthorpia
PENNYWORTH bargain, cheap, modicum, value
PENSION aid, alimony, allowance, annuity, boardinghouse, boardingschool, dues, expenditure, gratuity, income, inn, installment, lodging, malikana, outlay, retire(ment), room and board, salary, stipend, subsidy, support, tax, tribute, wages
custodian concierge
planner townsend
PENSIONARY beneficiary, endowed, hireling, magistrate, statesman
PENSIVE attentive, dreamy, grave, meditative, melancholic, musing, pencey, pensy, pondering, reflective, sad, serious, sober, solemn, speculative, thoughtful, thoughty, wistful
PENSY conceited, fretful, peevish, proud, squeamish
PENT caged, confined, enclosed, paint, reservoir, shut up, suppressed

PENTACLE hexagram, medal, pentagram, pentalpha, solomon's-seal, star, symbol, talisman
PENTAD quintad
PENTATEUCH bible, law, torah
book deuteronomy, exodus, genesis, leviticus, numbers
PENTECOST shabuoth, whitsunday
PENTHESILEA *parent* ares, ortrera
slayer achilles
subjects amazons
PENTHEUS *death site* cithaeron, parnassus
grandfather cadmus
kingdom thebes
parent agave, echion
slayer agave, autonoe, ino
PENTHOUSE aerie, annex, apartment, appentice, bulkhead, dwelling, hangar, leanto, lookum, pentice, pentis, pluteus, roof, shed, skeeling, skillion, suite, treehouse
PENTIDS penicillin
PENTOBARBITOL nembutal
PENTOPOLIS *king* simonides
PENTOSE apiose, arabinose, ribose, xylose
acid pna
PENTYL amyl, starch
PENUEL *parent* etam
PENUMBRA adumbration, shade, shadow, umbrage
PENURIOUS avaricious, barren, cheeseparing, close (fisted), curmudgeonly, destitute, grasping, illiberal, indigent, mean, miserly, niggardly, parsimonious, penny-pinching, poor, prudent, scanty, stingy, tight (fisted), wanting
PENURY avarice, beggary, borasco, destitution, exigency, indigence, necessity, need, pinch, poverty, privation, scantiness, scarcity, strait, want
PEON attendant, bond(s)man, constable, footman, hand, helot, laborer, messenger, pawn, peasant, pelado, policeman, prole, serf, slave, soldier, thrall, vassal, villein
PEONY burmese-ruby, flower, moutan, paeonia, piny, plant, red
PEOPLE ancestry, beings, ca-

naille, cattle, clan, daoine, demos, family, fold, folk(s), gens, gente, gentry, humanity, individuals, inhabit(ants), kin, lede, mankind, men, mob, multitude, persons, populace, population, race, rank-and-file, settle, society, state, stock, them, they, throng, tillicum, tribe, volk, world

ancient assyrians, cara, cham, dardani, egyptians, elymi, etruscans, falisci, firbolg, getae, grecians, greeks, hurri, itali, jakun, jung, khmer, kipchak, kodagu, medes, romans, sabines, sacae, seba, sekhwan, sequani, seres, siculi, silures

ape-shaped skull prognathi

cave-dwelling horite

comb. demo, ethno

common bourgeoisie, canaille, demos, hoi polloi, masses, mob, peons, plebe(ian), proles, proletarian, rabble, rednecks, tilikum, unwashed, vulgus

common, pert. democratic

curly-haired euplocomi

extinct chango, chatot, chono, cofan, coree, guinau, hibito, kot, saponi, shirino

foe of demophobe

forest sakai, saora, saura

friend of demophil

group army, assembly, association, band, batch, body, bunch, chorus, citizenry, city, clan, clique, comitia, committee, community, company, concourse, congregation, convention, corps, coterie, crew, crowd, family, flock, fold, herd, horde, host, knot, lot, mass, meeting, mob, multitude, nation, orchestra, organization, party, posse, press, push, queue, RABBLE, race, ring, school, set, shoal, society, swarm, team, tribe, troupe

headless acephali

insignificant nonentities, pipsqueaks

lowest canaille

mouthless astomoi

nomadic gypsy, igdyr, ihlat, saracen, shagia, shammar, shortzy, shukria, shuwa

1-eyed cyclops

ordinary folks

plain amish, mennonite

primitive chenchu, dafla, irula, kadir, kurukh

primitive, pert. proethnic

related clan, family, folk, kin, tribe, volk

small fairies

well-bred gentility, gentry

PEP activity, animation, dash, energy, force, ginger, initiative, punch, spirit, vigor, vim

pill amphetamine, drug, narcotic, upper

without apathetic, languid, listless

PEPE le moko

PEPIN *nickname* the short

son charlemagne

PEPINELLA chayote

PEPINO cucumber, philesia

PEPO cucumber, gourd, melon, pumpkin, squash

PEPPER (See also *kind*, below.) attack, ava, beat, betel, bomb, capsicum, cava, cayen(ne), condiment, cubeb, flavor, ikmo, itmo, kava(kava), mango, matico, paprika, pelt, pim(i)ento, piper, rain, relieno, shoot, shower, siri(h), spice, sprinkle, strew, strike, thrash, variegate, vim

-and-salt gray, jasper, mottled

betel kava(kava)

beverage kava(kava)

black pimenta, pipernigrum

cress boor's-mustard

extract capsicin

family piperaceae

hot cayenne, chili, jalapeno, poblano, serrano, tabasco

java cubeb

kind ava, betel, capsicum, cava, cayenne, chili, cubeb, ikmo, itmo, jalapeno, kavakava, paprika, pim(i)ento, siri(h), topepo

package robbin

part piperine

picker peter piper

plant ava, betel, capsicum, chile, chil(1)i, kava(kava), piper

pot ingredient cassareep, tripe

red chile, chil(1)i, ladyfinger

root dentaria, toothwort

sauce ajilimojili, pepper vinegar, pineapple piquant, poor man's sauce, romesco,

rouille-marseillaise, seafood gumbo, tabasco

shrub ava, cava, kava, kawa

tree drimys, horopito, molle, pim(i)ento, schinus

PEPPERBOX pistol, spitfire, tower, turret

PEPPERCORN trifle, trivial

PEPPERGRASS anounou, canarygrass, cockweed, cress, cubeb, lepidium, pillwort, shepherd's-purse

extract benzyl-cyanide

PEPPERIDGE bayberry, nyssa, sourgum, tree, tupelo

PEPPERMINT blackmitcham, labiate, menthe

camphor menthol

flavored liquid alantol

synthetic anisyl

PEPPERWOOD ash, clovecassia, laurel

PEPPERWORT dittander

PEPPERY abrupt, angry, excitable, fiery, gingery, hasty, headlong, hot(headed), impetuous, irritable, mettlesome, passionate, piquant, pungent, racy, sharp, snappish, snappy, spicy, spirited, spunky, stinging, waspish, zestful, zesty

PEPPY active, bouncy, energetic, gingery, lively, perky, sparkling, vigorous

PEPSIN enzyme

vegetable caroid

PEPTIC digestive, leavening, tonic

PEPYS *surgeon* hollier

PEQUOD *captain* ahab

quest moby dick

sailor ishmael

PER each, for, through, via

se basically, directly, essentially, intrinsically, itself

PERADVENTURE chance, doubt, hap, happily, maybe, mayhap, perhaps, possible, possibly, uncertainty

PERAMBULATE amble, promenade, ramble, stroll, traverse, walk

PERAMBULATOR baby-carriage, bassinet, buggy, carriage, cart, pedometer, pram, pushwainling, stroller, viameter, waywiser

PERAMELES badger, bandicoot, marsupial

PERCALE cotton, fabric, penang, sheet

PERCEIVABLE apparent, discernible, evident, manifest, observable, patent, perceptible

PERCEIVE appreciate, apprehend, behold, cognize, comprehend, contemplate, cotton, descry, detect, discern, discover, discriminate, distinguish, divine, espy, feel, figure, get, grasp, know, make(out), note, notice, observe, penetration, pierce, probe, realize, recognize, remark, see, sensate, sense, spot, survey, take, taste, understand, view

PERCENTAGE advantage, agio, allowance, bonus, commission, cut, discount, fee, odds, part, portion, profit, quota, rake-off, ratio, share
mining ley

PERCEPT concept, idea, image, notion, recognition, sensation

PERCEPTIBLE appreciable, clear, conspicuous, evident, lucid, manifest, notable, noted, noticeable, obvious, palpable, patent, ponderable, sensible, signal, tangible, traceable, visible
hardly faint, shadowy, vague

PERCEPTION acumen, appreciation, apprehension, awareness, bearings, clairvoyance, cognition, comprehension, consciousness, discernment, ear, esp, gaum, idea, insight, judgment, knowledge, penetration, recognition, seeing, sensation, sense, sharpness, tact, understanding, vision
capable of sentient
impaired acatamathesia
pert. sensory

PERCEPTIVE alert, apprehensive, astute, aware, discerning, observant, penetrating, percipient, sensitive, sharp

PERCH (See also *kind,* below.) aerie, alfione, alight, aviary, bar(se), bas(s), begti, bekti, block, bugara, callop, fish, height, hogfish, inhabit, jook, jouk, land, light, lounge, lug, mado, marteniko, nest, okow, peg, perca, perk, pike, pole, prop, reach, rest, rockfish, rod, roost, ruff(e), sauger,

seat, settle, shaft, sit, slumber, squat, staff, station, straddle, trumpeter, weapon, zander, zingel
kind barse, crappie, cunner, embiotoca, lobotes, rockfish, rosefish, ruff(e), tripletail, zingel
-like fish anabas, darter, surffish
2-year-old egling

PERCHANCE haply, maybe, perhaps, possibly

PERCHITA berchta

PERCOLATE brew, drain, drip, exhale, exude, filter, leach, melt, ooze, operate, permeate, refine, run, seep, sift, silt, sipe, soak, strain, transude, weep

PERCOLATOR biggin, cafetiere, coffeepot, displacer, dripolator, filter, siper

PERCUSSION blow, brunt, clash, collision, concussion, detonation, hitting, impact, jar, jolt, repercussion, shock

PERCY effeminate, hotspur, sissy
work reliques

PERDICULA microperdix, quail, turnix

PERDITA *helper* camillo
lover florizel, polixenes
parent hermione, leontes

PERDITION annihilation, ballyhack, bally(w)rack, bowwows, damnation, death, demolition, destruction, discreation, downfall, extermination, fall, hell, loss, misery, ruin, wreck

PERDIX (See also PARTRIDGE.) polycaste
invention chisel, compass, saw
kin daedalus

PERDU(E) concealed, exposed, hidden, lost, obscured, reckless, soldier, spy

PERDURABLE abiding, continuing, endless, enduring, eternal, everlasting, lasting, permanent, perpetual, persisting, stable

PEREGRINATE journey, roam, sojourn, travel, traverse, walk, wander

PEREGRINATION discussion, journey, pilgrimage, sojourn, travel, trip, wandering

PEREGRINE alien, bird, exotic, falcon, foreign(er),

hawk, pilgrim, roving, strange
falcon saker, tassel, tercel

PEREMPT beat, defeat, destroy, quash

PEREMPTORY absolute, arbitrary, arrogant, authoritative, certain, compulsive, conclusive, decided, decisive, destructive, dictatorial, dogmatic, domineering, express, final, fixed, flat, imperative, imperious, magisterial, mandatory, masterful, positive, resolute, ruinous, unqualified

PERENNIAL annual, constant, continuous, enduring, eternal, everlasting, herb, lasting, neverending, perdurable, permanent, perpetual, recurrent, seasonal, stable, unceasing, yearlong, yearly

PERENNIALLY See FOREVER.

PERESTRELLO, FELIPA
husband columbus

PEREUS *daughter* neaera
father elatus
mother laodice

PEREZ *kin* hezron, judah

PERFECT absolute, accomplish, accurate, aok, best, blameless, certain, choice, complete, consummate, content, correct, crown, develop, entire, expert, faultless, finish(ed), flawless, gemlike, great, happy, holy, hotsytotsy, ideal, idealize, immaculate, impeccable, improve, infallible, intact, integral, inviolate, irreproachable, made-up, model, paradisiac, praiseworthy, precise, prime, pristine, pure, refine, righteous, satisfying, sheer, simple, sinless, sole, sound, spheral, spotless, stainless, sublime, sure, taintless, thorough, transcend, true, unblemished, undefiled, unequaled, unflawed, unqualified, untainted, utopian, utter, whole
comb. teleo

PERFECTI cathari, manichaeans

PERFECTION accomplishment, acme, beauty, bloom, completion, consummation, correctness, excellence, faultlessness, finish, ideal,

maturity, merit, ne plus ultra, nonesuch, paragon, pattern, pink, purity, ripeness, sublimity, virtue
attainer siddha
realm of paradise, utopia
PERFECTIONIST fussbudget, precisionist, purist, stickler
PERFECTLY altogether, completely, correctly, exactly, fitly, greatly, ideally, just, quite, rightly, thoroughly, to a tee, utterly
PERFERVID ardent, fervent, glowing, impassioned, intense, intensified, passionate, vehement
PERFIDIOUS deceitful, dishonest, disleal, disloyal, faithless, false(hearted), forsworn, mercenary, perjured, snaky, spiteful, traitorous, treacherous, unfaithful, venal
PERFIDY apostasy, corruption, deceit, defection, disaffection, disloyalty, double-dealing, duplicity, faithlessness, falseness, foul-play, infidelity, treachery, treason
PERFORATE augur, bite, bore, broach, cancel, cut, dock, drill, eat, enter, erode, gouge, hole, honeycomb, impale, lance, needle, penetrate, permeate, pierce, pinhole, pink, prick, probe, punch, puncture, ream, riddle, rime, sieve, spear, spike, spit, stab, stick, tap, terebrate, transfix, trepan, trephine
PERFORATION aperture, bore, broach, diabrosis, drillhole, eyelet, foramen, hole, impalement, leak, opening, orifice, penetration, piercing, pinhole, puncture, septula, stencil, terebration, thirl, toret, transfixion, tresis
ornamental punching
PERFORCE compulsion, constrain, necessarily, necessity
PERFORM accomplish, achieve, acquit, act, administer, appear, attain, behave, broadcast, build, carry out, cast, celebrate, char(e), complete, conclude, dight, discharge, dispatch, dispose of, effect, enact, end, exe-

cute, exert, exhibit, exploit, fill, finish, fulfill, function, furnish, gain, make, meet, observe, operate, perpetrate, play, practice, present, produce, reach, render, show, solemnize, stage, transact, work
again re-enact
duty office, officiate
hastily scamp, skimp
inadequately boggle, bollix, botch, bungle, mess up
well sparkle, star
with ceremony solemnise, solemnize
PERFORMANCE accomplishment, achievement, act(ing), action, administration, affair, benefit, booking, ceremony, commission, completion, concert, custom, deed, discharge, dispatch, doing, effectuation, execution, exercise, exploit, feat, fulfil(l)ment, function, masque, matinee, mummery, observance, operation, opus, perpetration, play, practice, pursuance, pursuit, rehearsal, rendition, rite, show, stunt, success, test, transaction, triumph, work
brilliant bravura, coup
daytime matinee
dramatic topeng
1st debut, premiere
individual solo
no relache
shortened john robinson
standard bogey
theatrical benefit, bill, bow, entertainment, matinee, pantomime, pitch, premiere, presentation, production, rehearsal, show, variety
trial audition, tryout
PERFORMER acroama, actor, agent, artist(e), dancer, doer, entertainer, executant, executor, freak, gambist, headliner, impersonator, mime, mummer, musician, operator, player, pretender, soloist, thespian, trouper, star, virtuoso
aquatic dolphin, seal
burlesque grinder
circus leaper
company cast, troupe
diligent drudge, plugger

low-grade ham(fatter)
supplementary ripieno
top-notch ace, diva, star
PERFUME agallochum, agallock, agalwood, agar, agilawood, aloes, ambergris, ambrette, ambrosia, aquilawood, aroma, aromatize, atar, athar, attar, attargul, balm, balsam, bergamot, bouquet, carvol, cense, chypre, civet, cologne, diapasm, embalm, essence, ester, floressence, fragrance, frangipani, frankincense, fumigate, heliotrope, incense, irone, jasmine, lavender, lignaloes, marechal, musk, myrrh, nose(gay), odor(ize), orangery, ottar, otto, pastil(le), patchouli, redolence, rosewater, sachet, savor, scent, smell, spice, thurify, toiletwater, vaporize
artist nez veritables, nose
bag sachet
base See *source,* below.
center grasse
container See PERFUMER.
extraction enfleurage
fixitive skatole
kitten skunk
medicated pastile, pastil(le), troche
musky civet
oil neroli
powdery pulvil
source abelmost, acetaldol, acetophenone, aldol, ambergris, ambrain, anethole, anisole, anisyl, benzoin, bergamiol, bergamot, borneol, bornyl, cassia, civet, galbanum, hypnone, khuskhus, labdanum, ladanum, linalool, musk, myrrh, neroli, onycha, orris(root), patchouli, spikenard, vetiver, whale, ylangylang
watery eau(x)
PERFUMER atomizer, breathseller, censer, fumigator, incensory, odorizer, phial, pomander, potpourri, pouncet-box, sachet, scentbag, thurible, vial, vinaigrette
PERFUNCTORY apathetic, careless, casual, cursory, disinterested, formal, halfhearted, indifferent, lackadaisical, mechanical, superficial, token, unconcerned

PERGAMUM bergama
coin cistophorus
dynasty attalid
king attalus, eumenes
PERGAMUS *parent* andromache, neoptolemus
PERGOLA arbo(u)r, balcony, bower, colonnade, gazebo, ramada, summerhouse, trellis
PERHAPS ablin(g)s, belike, conceivably, doubtful, haply, happen, haps, mappen, maybe, peradventure, perchance, possibly, probably
PERI dwarf, elf, fairy, houri, spirit, sprite
king jamshid, jamshyd, yima
PERIAPT amulet, charm, fetish, talisman
PERICARP berry, bladder, boll, bur, nut, pod, shell
PERICLES *author* shakespeare
brother ariphron
character antiochus, boult, cerimon, cleon, dionyze, escanes, gower, helicanus, leonine, lychorida, lysimachus, marina, philemon, simonides, thaisa, thaliard
consort aspasia, thaisa
daughter marina
disciple alcibiades
enemy anaxagorus, cleon, diopithes, dracontides, epitimus, hagnon, hermippus, menon, protagoras
father xanthippus
friend anaxagoras, ephialtes, menippus, phidias, pyrilampes
general sophocles
lieutenant phidias
nickname schinocephalos
opponent cleon
rival thucydides
servant evangelus
son eupolis, paralus, xanthippus
teacher anaxagoras, aristotle, damon, zeno
ward alcibiades
PERICLINE albite
PERICLYMENUS *brother* nestor
father neleus, poseidon
slayer heracles, hercules
PERICRANIUM brain, head, skull
PERICU indian, waicuri
god niparaya
goddess amayicoyondi

gods' children acaragui, quaayayp
gods' enemy tupuran, wac
moon creator cucumunk
star creator purutabui
PERICULUM danger, peril, risk
PERIDOT chrysolite, mineral, olivine
PERIDOTITE anabohitsite, buchnerite, eulysite, josefite, picrite, saxonite, scyelite, wehrlite
PERIERES *kingdom* messenia
son aphareus, leucippus
wife gorgophone
PERIGUNE *consort* theseus
PERIL adventure, crisis, danger, exposure, hazard, insecurity, jeopardy, liability, menace, risk, scylla, threat, throng, trance
PERILAUS *cousin* clytemnestra
PERILOUS chancy, dangerous, desperate, dreadful, forlorn, hazardous, hopeless, icarian, insecure, kittle, precarious, risky
PERIMETER ambit, border, boundary, bounds, circuit, circumference, compass, edge, limit, margin, outline, periphery, rim
PERIOD 3 age, bit, day, dot, end, eon, era, lag 4 aeon, bout, butt, date, goal, hour, life, moon, span, stop, term, time, tour, turn, week, year, yuga 5 annum, avail, bound, break, cycle, epact, epoch, hitch, kalpa, limit, month, pause, phase, point, round, shift, space, spell, stage, track, trick, watch, whack, while 6 chance, decade, ghurry, hemera, inning, minute, moment, relief, season, second, tenure 7 century, interim, lustrum, manhour, outcome, quarter, respite, stretch 8 division, duration, interval, juncture, lunation, occasion, semester, sentence 9 cessation, fortnight, interlude 10 completion, conclusion, enlistment, generation, manvantara, millennium 11 continuance, culmination, interregnum 12 intermission, interruption
crucial crisis

dull slack
festive holiday, vacation
holding tenure
infinite eternity
lengthy aeon, eon, eternity, siege
mourning shibah, shiva
occasional snatch
of an earlier ancient, archaic
penitential lent
playing chukkar, chukker, frame, half, hand, inning, quarter, round, set
service administration, hitch, term
short blink, fit, shake, snatch, spell, spurt
sleep godown, hibernation
time century, day, decade, eon, fortnight, hour, minute, month, second, week, year
work shift, spell, stint, trick
PERIODIC alternate, annual, cyclic(al), daily, diurnal, epochal, etesian, fitful, hebdomadal, intermittent, isochronal, momentarily, occasional, quarterly, quotidian, recurrent, recurring, regular, repeated, rhythmic(al), routine, seasonable, seasonal, serial, spasmodic, sporadic, weekly, yearly
PERIODICAL annual, bulletin, daily, digest, ephemeris, etesian, gazette, house organ, journal, magazine, monthly, organ, paper, publication, pulp, quarterly, review, serial, sheet, slick, tabloid, weekly, yearbook
single issue number
PERIPATETIC ambulant, ambulatory, aristotelian, itinerant, nomad(ic), pedestrian, rambling, roving, vagrant, walker, wanderer, wandering
PERIPHERAL confined, deep, distal, distant, exterior, external, marginal, outer
PERIPHERY ambit(us), areole, border, bound(ary), bounds, circuit, circumference, compass, confine, edge, end, environs, fringe, frontier, limit, lip, march, outside, perimeter, skirt, space, suburbs, surface
PERIPHETES corynetes
parent hephaestus

slayer theseus
weapon mace

PERIPHRASIS circumlocution, pleonasm, redundancy, verbiage

PERIPHRASTIC circumlocutory, devious

PERISCOPE altiscope, hyposcope, omniscope
wake feather

PERISH cease, crumble, decay, decease, depart, destroy, die, disintegrate, end, expire, fade(away), forfare, go under, miscarry, pass, rot, ruin, shrivel, squander, starve, succumb, swelt, tyne, vanish, waste, wither
slowly fade, wane

PERISHABLE brittle, caducous, caduke, dying, ephemeral, evanescent, soft, transitory

PERISOREUS jay, moosebird, whisky-jack

PERISSODACTYL horse, rhinoceros, tapir

PERISTOME fringe, teeth

PERISTYLE arcade, arcature, colonnade, court, hall (way), peripteral, portico, quadriporticus

PERITHECIUM alveola, alveolus, ascocarp, cavity, pit, pore, socket

PERITONEUM *fold* omentum
membrane siphac

PERITROCH embryo, larva

PERIVISCERAL extraenteric

PERIWIG galera, peruke, perwick, perwinkle, shellfish, toupee

PERIWINKLE blue, blueblossom, bluebottle, bluebutton, cutfinger, dogbane, girl, lirotina, maid, mussel, myrtle, paragon, periwig, pinpatch, sengreen, shell, shrub, snail, thais, turbo, vinca, whelk

PERJURE cheat, deceive, delude, forswear, lie, mislead, prevaricate, violate

PERJURY *induce to* suborn

PERK animated, brisk, cocky, condescend, freshen, jaunty, lift, operate, perch, percolate, PERQUISITE, preen, prink, privilege, proud, smarten, spruce, stand up, thrust
up cheer up, freshen, im-

prove, lift, prune, recuperate, refresh

PERKY chipper, cocky, conceited, debonair, gay, jaunty, lively, neat, smart, sprightly, tidy, trig, trim

PERMANENCE durability, duration, endurance, perpetuity, stability

PERMANENT abiding, ageless, all-time, changeless, coiffure, constant, continuing, continuous, durable, endless, enduring, eonian, everlasting, fixed, hairdo, immutable, indelible, intact, invariable, lasting, perdurable, perennial, perpetual, persistent, remaining, solid, stable, standing, stative, staying, steadfast, timeless, unchanging, unfading, unvarying
condition hexis, status

PERMANENTLY See FOREVER.

PERMEABLE accessible, passible, penetrable, pervious, porous, pory

PERMEATE animate, bespread, diffuse, dominate, drench, fill, filter, honeycomb, imbue, impregnate, infiltrate, inform, infuse, ingrain, insinuate, invade, leaven, occupy, overrun, overspread, overswarm, penetrate, pervade, pierce, saturate, soak, spread, stab, steep, suffuse, transfuse

PERMISSABLE admissible, allowable, allowed, free, lawful, legal, legitimate, licit

PERMISSION acceptance, allowance, approval, assent, authorization, carteblanche, concession, condonation, consent, darst, endorsement, go-ahead, grace, grant, green-light, indulgence, leave, leve, liberty, license, okay, pass, patent, permit, privilege, sanction, sufferance, support, tolerance, warrant
request by-your-leave
with pace

PERMISSIVE concessory, indulgent, tolerant

PERMIT accede, accord, admit, allow, approve, authorize, beteem, brevet, cedula, charter, concur, condone,

conge, consent, dustu(c)k, empower, endorse, endure, exeat, favor, fiat, franchise, furlough, grant, green-light, humor, imprimatur, indulge, leave, let, license, pass, patent, permission, sanction, suffer, ticket, tolerate, visa, vouchsafe, yield

PERMITTED allowed, free, innocent, legal, licet, licit
not illicit

PERMUTATION alternation, barter, change, conversion, exchange, metamorphosis, move, shift, transformation

PERMUTE alter, barter, change, exchange, interchange, transfer, transform, transmute

PERNICIOUS bad, baleful, baneful, deadly, deleterious, destructive, detrimental, evil, fatal, harmful, hurtful, injurious, malefic, malign, mischievous, nefarious, noisome, noxious, pesky, pestilent, pesty, poisonous, quick, ruinous, sinister, swift, toxic, venomous, vicious, vile, villainous, wicked

PERNICKETY, PERSNICKETY dainty, fastidious, finical, finicky, fussy, meticulous, neat, nice, particular, squeamish

PERNOD *drink* suisette

PERON *wife* evita, isabelita

PERONATE mealy, wooly

PERORATE address, declaim, harangue, orate, protract, speak

PERORATION argument, conclusion, discourse, purlicue, sequel, speech, summary

PEROXIDE bleach, decolor

PERPENDICULAR abrupt, apothem, bluff, cathetus, erect, evendown, immediate, on end, orthodiagonal, orthogonal, plumb, precipitous, rampant, rectitude, right-angled, sheer, steep, upright, vertical
elevation altitude

PERPER *1/100th* para

PERPETRATE achieve, commit, effect, perform

PERPETUAL abiding, ceaseless, continual, continuous, durable, endless, enduring, eternal, everlasting, fixed, immortal, incessant, infinite, lasting, neverending, perdurable, perennial, permanent, sempiternal, set, settled, stable

motion solitaire

PERPETUALLY ad infinitum, always, constantly, endlessly, ever, forever

PERPETUATE continue, eternize, immortalize, maintain, preserve

PERPETUITY athanasy, endlessness, eternity, immortality, imperishability, infinity, olam, permanence, sempiternity, serial

PERPLEX amaze, astound, baffle, bamboozle, barbulyie, beat, bedevil, beset, bewilder, blaik, boggle, bother, buffalo, bumbaze, cap, complicate, confound, confuse, corner, crux, cumber, diffuse, discompose, distract, disturb, doze, dumbfound, elude, embarrass, embroil, entangle, floor, fool, gravel, hamper, harass, hobble, involve, kittle, lick, mammer, mither, moider, muddle, mystify, nonplus, perturb, plague, pose, pother, putter, puzzle, riddle, snarl, stagger, stick, stump, surprise, tangle, thwart, torment, twitch, upset, wrixle

PERPLEXED anxious, asea, confused, difficult, distraught, doubtful, entangled, intricate, involved, knotted, puzzled, troubled

PERPLEXING baffling, carking, crabbed, crabby, difficult, equivocal, knotty, mazy, puzzling

PERPLEXITY anxiety, care, complexity, complication, concern, confusion, difficulty, dilemma, disorder, doubt, enigma, entanglement, fog, foiter, intricacy, pickle, plight, predicament, problem, puzzle, question, riddle, stalemate, strait, uncertainty, were

PERQUISITE(S) accessory, adjunct, appanage, appurtenance, benefice, birthright, bonus, booty, bribe, fee, gain, goupin, gowpen, gratuity, income, lucre, perk(s), pickings, preroga-

tive, privilege, profit, purchase, right, salary, tip, zchuss

presidential veto

PERRAULT bluebeard

PERRON base, platform, stairs, steps

PERSECUTE abuse, afflict, aggrieve, badger, bait, beset, bother, grill, harass, harry, hound, oppress, martyr, molest, plague, pursue, rack, ride, torment, torture, worry, wrong

PERSECUTION *complex* paranoia

victim refugee

PERSEPHASSA *father* zeus

PERSEPHONE brimo, carpophorus, cora, despoina, kore, pher(s)ephatta, praxidike, proserpina, proserpine

abductor hades, pluto

companion iache

consort hades, pluto

daughter artemis, cora, kore

parent ceres, demeter, poseidon, zeus

PERSES *brother* aeetes, circe

consort asteria

offspring hecate

parent crius, eurybia, hilios

PERSEUS aurigena, champion, eurymedon, hero, rescuer

consort andromeda

cutlass harpe

grandfather acrisius

grandson aphareus

guide athena, hermes

parent danae, jupiter, zeus

son cynurus, electryon, sthenelus

star algol, atik

victim acrisius, medusa, polydectes

PERSEVERANCE constancy, determination, diligence, endurance, grit, insistence, patience, persistence, pertinacity, resolution, stamina, steadfastness, steadiness, strength, tenacity, tolerance

PERSEVERE abide, bear up, carry on, continue, endure, hang in there, hold (on) (out), last, persist, plod, plug along, remain, stay, stick, tore, tough it out

PERSEVERING assiduous, bulldog, busy, constant, dauntless, diligent, dogged, enduring, insistent, patient,

persistent, pertinacious, relentless, resolute, sedulous, solid, staying, steadfast, steady, stick-to-itive, strong, stubborn, tenacious, tireless, undaunted, undiscouraged, unfaltering, unflagging, unflinching, unrelenting, unswerving, untiring, unwavering, unwearying

PERSHING *nickname* black jack

PERSIA, PERSIAN See also IRAN.

abbey badia

adam and eve mahlya and mahlyanag, mashya and mashyoi, masya and masyanag

admiral ariamenes

alexander sanjar

almond badam

ancient aryan, bactrian, dahan, elamite, hyksos, mede, parthian, tat

angel feroher, mah, morded

apple citron, peach

archangel asha-vahishta

ascetics safi, sophi

assembly majilis, meklis

attacker alexander the great, ghuz

automobile paykan

battle marathon, thermopylae

beverage haoma, soma

bird bulbul, nightingale, rhyntaces

bird, fabulous kerkes

blind fish carp, loach, whitefish

boat garookuh

book of kings shah-nameh

bug miana

builder shah abbas

cape halileh

capital isfahan, pasargadae, persepolis, shiraz, suza, teheran, tehran

castle warden disdar, dizdar

cat angora

deity See PERSIA *god, goddess*

demon aeshma, ahriman, ako-mano, akuman, angramainya, apaosha, ariman, asmodeus, azidahaka, daeva, druj, ized, jahi, karapan, kavi, naonhaithya, nasatya, nasu, pairaka, rudrashiva, sauru, taurvi, yatu, zairi(sha), zohak

desert dashtikavir, dashtilut, kerman, lut

dessert baklava
dish ashe, borani badenjon, chelo kebab, djoudje, dolme barg, grape leaves, khoreshe gheim, khoreshe ghormesabzi, mast-vakhiar, mazeh
doctrine babi(i)sm
door jar
drink doughe, haoma, soma
dyestuff indigo
dynasty achmaemenid, arsacid, buyid, kaianian, parthian, safavid, safawid, samanid, sassanid, seljuk, sophis
dynasty founder agha
educator jamalud-in
elf peri
epic shah-namah
evergreen olax
fabric ardassine, ormuzine
fairy deev, elf, fay, peri
fanatic abdal
festival salam
fire festival shebseze
fire god atar
fire-maker fratakara
fire-worshipper ateshperest, fratakara, gabar, gheber, mazadaian, parsee, parsi
1st king haoshyangha, hoshang, husheng
1st man gayomart, mashya
1st woman mashyoi
fish, mythological mah
flower kerz(e)reh
founder cyrus
game asnas
gardens paradeisoi
garment candys, chador, chedar
gate dar
gazelle cora
general artabanus, mardonius, pisuthnes, roxanes
genii fravashis, yazatas
giant akuan
glory khwareno
goat bezoar, pasang
god, goddess abracax, ahriman, ahura-mazda, anahita, angra-mainyu, apo, apsu, ariman(es), artaxerxesmnemon, assara-mazaas, asura, atar, deva, haoma, hvare-khshaeta, indra, mah, mazda, mithra(s), mitra, nasatyas, ochus, ormazd, oromasdes, spenta-armaiti, tishtriya, tremanius, varuna, vivanhvat, yima
governor khan, satrap
grass millet
gratuity baksheesh, bakshish

guardian angels fravashis
gulf city abadan
gulf island bahrain, bahrein
gulf kingdom chaldea
gulf port bushire, dubai
gulf province fars
gulf, river into shattal-arab
gulf wind shamal, sharki, shimal, shurgee
gum tragacanth
gypsy sisech
hall apadana
harp sang
headdress fez, tiara, turban
hemp bang
hercules rustam
hero feridum, irej, minucher, rotastahm, rustam, rustem, rustum, tahmuras the glorious, thraetona, yima, zal
hook money lari(n)
immortal ameretat, ameshas spenta, amshaspends, arbidihist, ashavahishta, bahman, haurvatat, khordadh, khshathra-vairya, mourdad, shah river, spenta-armaiti, vohu-mano
island bahrain, bahrein, kishm, qishm
javelin jereed, jerid
king achaemenes, ahasuerus, arsakes, artaxerxes, assuerrus, beder, cambyses, cyaxares, cyrus, dahak, darius, feridun, giamschid, haoshyangha, hoshang, husheng, jam(shyd), jemshid, khusrow, minucher, mohammed, reza, pahlavi, rustem, rustum, sha(h) (of shahs), tahmurus, tamerlane, tamnuras, xerxes, yazdegerd, yima, zal, zohak
koran student hafix
lake maharly, nemekser, niris, niriz, sahweh, sistan, tasht, tuzlu, urmia, urumiah, urumiyeh
lamb astrakhan, karakul
language aryan, avestan, farsi, gathic, kurdish, medic, pahlavi, pahlevi, pashto, zend
legislature majlis
light god mithra, ormazd
lord kaan, kaun, kawn, khan, saman
lynx caracal
measure arasni, artaba, cane, capicha, charac, chebell, chenica, farsakh, farsang, foot, gareh, gariba, gasab, gaz, gez, ghalva, gireh, guz,

jerib, kafix, makuk, mansion, mishara, mou, ouroub, parasang, piamaneh, sabbitha, stathmos, yava, zar, zer
messiah saoshyant
monk dervish
monster azhidahaka
monument sahyad
moon mahi
mystic sufi
new year's day nowroze
nightingale bulbul, luscinia
noble family barmecide
nomads beluchi
non-mortality ameretat, amritatvam
official mehmander
oil center abadan
painter bihzad, manes, mani (chaeus)
palace shushan
pantheist babist
parliament majlis, mejlis
party rastakhiz, tudeh
peak ararat, binalud, cush, demavend, hamunt, hindu, khormuj, kush, sabalan, zard(eh)kuh
people bactria, bakhtiari, bartangi, beluchi, belucki, durzada, farsi, galcha, gheber, gilaki, guebre, hadjemi, ihlat, iranian, iranic, kajar, kizilbash, kurd, lur, mazanderani, mede, memnonian, mukri, nomad, parsi, sart, susian, tadjik, tajik, tat, tudah, turkoman
philosopher abou-ebn-sina
physician avicenna
pipe calean, hookah, kalain, narghile
plant opium, poppy
plaster gatch
poem ghazal
poet ferdosi, firdusi, hafez, hafiz, jalal-uddin-rumi, jami, omar-khayyam, sa(a)di
port bandar-abbas, basra, bushire, jask, pahlevi
pottery gombroon
priest archimage, atharvan, magi, nadab
prime minister mossadegh
primitive bull gosh
prince arimanes, cyrus, mirza
prince, biblical admatha, carshena, marsena, memucan, meres, shethar, tarshish
prophet manes, zarathustra, zoroaster

province azerbaidzhan, azerbaijan, carmania, elam, fars, hyrcania, khuzistan, luristan, sogdiana, susiana, yezd
punishment chab(o)uk
queen astin, farah, shahbanou
range elburz, jagatal, siahan, zagros
red vermilion
red deer maral
religion ateshperest, babism, bahaism, fire-worship, manichaeism, mazdaism, mithraism, mohammedanism, zoroastrianism
religious leader ali-muhammad, bab-eddin, baha-ullah, zarathustra, zoroaster
revolt leader bardiya, magnus gaumata
river araks, aras, bampur, bendemer, euphrates, gorgan, haliri, jagin, karkheh, karum, kizil-uzen, mand, mashkel, safid(rud), shur, tab, tigris, zab, zuhreh. zyendeh
robe chador
rose gul
royal residence niavaram palace
rug afshar, ardebil, bakshaish, baluchi, bergama, bokhara, feraghan, ferahan, gorevan, hamadan, isfahan, ispahan, kali, kashan, kermanshah, khorassan, kilim, kirman, namda, nammad, pergam, sarouk, sedjadeh, senna, serabend, sheeraz, shiraz, smyrna, teheran, tilpah, yarkand
ruler ameer, amir, atabek, attabeg, ismail, king of kings, mir(za), samanid, satrap, shah, sophi, sultan
sacred cord kusti
sacred formula ahuna vairya
saint safavi(d), safawi(d)
salt swamp kavir
satan dahak
satrap cyrus, tisaphernes
screen purdah
script shikasta
scripture avesta, gathas, koran, vendidad, vispered, yashts, zend-avesta
secret police savak
sect babi, ithnasheri, shiah, shiite, sunnee, sunni(te), yez(i)di, zoroastrian

shah abbas, ismail, mohammed-riza-pahlevi
slave dehwar
soup ashe, djoudje
spirit, good amshapends, fravashis, yazatas
sprite peri
strait hormuz
sun mihr
sword acinaces, shamshir
talisman mantra
tapestry susanee
tax collector tahsildar
tentmaker omar
throne peacock
throne room aiwan
tiara cidaris
tick miana bug
tiger sher, shir
tile kas(h)i
title aryamehr, atabeg, atabek, azam, baba, darius, great king, khan, mir(za), shah, shahanshah, sophi, sophy
tobacco shiraz, tumbak(i), tumbek(i)
torture scaphism
town-dweller lur, sart
trumpet ker(r)ana
turk sart
underworld ruler yima
universal law asha
utopia bashdi, ghaon, haroju, muru, nissa
viceroy satrap
victory genius verethraghna
water goddess anahita
water pipe kalian
water system aquifer, qanat
water vessel aftaba
water wheel noria, tympana, tympanum
weight abbas(si), artal, batman, danar, dang, dirhem, dola, dram, dung, gandum, karwar, lot, maund, miscal, miskal, nakhod, nimman, pinar, ratel, rik, rotl, saddingham, sang, se(e)r, sir, tcheirek, una
wheel noria, tympanum
wind badisadobistroz, barih, samoor, shamal, shemaal, shimal, shumal
wine red hermitage, shiraz
wisdom, spirit of vohu-mano
woman persis
woman's apartment zenana
writing cuneiform
writing, sacred book of tobit, zend-avesta
zoroastrian gabar, gheber

PERSICARY heartsease, heartweed, lady's-thumb, peachwort, redleg(s), redshank
PERSIFLAGE badinage, banter, chaff(ing), flippancy, kidding, mockery, pleasantry, quip, raillery, rally(ing), ridicule, twitting
PERSIMMON chapote diospyros, ebony, ga(u)b, hyakume, kaki, possumwood, simon, triumph, zapote
family ebenaceae, ebony
tree gab, gaub, lotus
PERSIS *father* laocoon
friend paul
PERSIST abide, adhere, bore(in), carry through, continue, endure, hang(in), hold, insist, last, persevere, plod, prevail, recur, remain, repeat, stay, stick, urge, wear
PERSISTENT assiduous, bulldogged, continuing, continuous, dree(ch), durable, firm, gritty, hard, lasting, obdurate, obstinate, persevering, regular, relentless, resolute, stick-to-itive, stout, stubborn, tenacious
PERSNICKETY See PERNICKETY.
PERSON (See also FELLOW.) animal, article, baby, being, bod(y), bugger, cat, chap, character, child, cog, cooky, cuss, duck, ego, entity, fish, galoot, gazabo, gink, guy, head, heart, homunculus, human, individual, johnny, life, lion, man, manikin, nibs, number, one, party, piece, role, self, sinner, sister, soul, specimen, spirit, sprite, thing, tillicum, wagtail, wight, woman
abject slave
absent-minded musard
accursed anathema
accused appellee
acting in place of proxy
addressed you
aggressive hotshot
angry sourhead
aloof cold fish
arrogant huff, snob, tengu
attractive knockout, stunner
bald skinhead
baptized illuminato, illuminatus, member

base cad, caitiff, puttock, rascal

beatified beatus

beloved enamorata, enamorato

betrothed finance(e)

boorish goop, oaf

brachycephalic shorthead

brilliant genius, mastermind

bringing luck mascot

canonized saint

cheery optimist

coarse boor, cow, mucker, stirk

comb. ade, ado, ego, idio

conceited coxcomb, huff, stuckup

contemptible bauchle, cad, scoundrel

cowardly craven, sissy, squib

crazy beehead, lunatic, nut, psycopath

cringing flunky, snake, snool, spaniel

cruel fiend, sadist

dainty mimmock

dedicated ascetic, saint

deformed caliban, cripple, hodmadod, hunchback

dishonest bezonian, blackguard, crook, knave, racketeer, rapscallion, rascal, rascallion, reprobate, rogue, rotter, scamp, scapegrace, scoundrel, snollygoster, thief, varlet, villain

dull bore, clunk, dope, droud, goon, goop, grub, lump, mome, mope, slob, stick

extraordinary ace, buster, corker, humdinger, oner

fat blimp, gurk, lump, squab

foolish boob(y), doodle, dotard, gosling, gubbins, gump, hoit, jerk

good-for-nothing jackeen, waster

greedy grasper, yisser

group See PEOPLE.

half-grown haflin, hafling, stripling

held as pledge hostage

high-ranking eminence, magnate, vip

holy saint

horned cornute

ignorant See *stupid*, below.

ill-mannered boor, churl, clown, grub, skunk

ill-tempered crab, crosspatch, ettercap, grouch, taistrel

indefinite anybody, anyone, so and so, somebody, someone

indifferent to pain stoic

inexperienced babe, beginner, ingenue, novice

injured casualty, victim

insignificant ablach, creep, nonentity, peanut, pettitoes, pinkeen, shurf, sprat

large chunk, skelper, strapper

lazy bum, daw, hoit, idler, lordan, lurdan, slouch, sluggard

lean bag of bones, barebones, gangerel, ribe, tangle, thingut

learned acharya, egghead, intellectual, literatus, polyhistor, professor, pundit, savant, scholar, wiseacre

left-handed kithogue, kitthoge, portsider, southpaw

living near neighbor

low beast, rascal, scum

lusty bilch, bilsh

mad bedlamite, loony, nut

mangy ronyon

married husband, spouse, wife

mean bastard, bezonian, churl, hound, scab, shicer, skate, smatchet, sneak, stinker

mechanical automaton, robot

middle-class bourgeois(ie)

mixed-blood creole, halfbreed, mestee, mestizo, metis, mulatto, octoroon

named after another namesake

narrowminded mrs grundy

nervous auldwife

non-jewish gentile

odd gig, quiz(z)y, ratbag

old graybeard, grayhead, senior

old-fashioned fog(e)y

1-legged uniped

perfidious serpent, snake, traitor

plump bilsh

powerful agent, authority, autocrat, baron, bearcat, behemoth, captain, commander, csar, czar, delegate, deputy, despot, dictator, emperor, hercules, leviathan, mogul, official, plutocrat, potentate, proxy, regent, sachem, samson, surrogate, titan, tyrant

prejudiced bigot, nativist, partisan, racist, sectarian, segregationist, xenophobe, zealot

primitive troglodyte

proposed for office candidate, nominee

puny scart, shilp, shrimp

quarrlesome brabbler, brangler, bickerer, fire-eater, squabbler, wrangler

ragged gamin, guttersnipe, mudlark, ragamuffin, slorp, sloven, slubberdegullion, tatterdemalion

reckless careless, madcap, ramstam

representing another agent, alternate, mimic, proxy, stand-in, substitute

resembling another double, sosia, twin

reticent clam

returning remigrant

rustic coon, hayseed, homespun, kern(e)

saucy piet, smartypants

scornful barracker, fleerer, flouter, girder, jeerer, jiber, scouter, sneerer

second thou, you

self-righteous pharisee

sick aegrotant, ailer, invalid, patient

silly cuckoo, dobby, goose, gump, liripoop, nimshi, softhead, softie, spoon

small dwarf, midget, poppet, runt, smolt, smout, sprat

sponsored by another protege, ward

strange wampus

stray waif

stubborn ass, buckie, stout

studious grind

stunted urf

stupid blinkard, bonehead, boob, dimwit, dodo, dolt, duffer, dunce, fathead, idiot, jackass, jerk, lummox, moron, nitwit, noodle, sap(head), schnook, sheep, stunpoll, stupe, thickhead, thickwit

tiresome pillbore

ungrateful ingrate

unique oner

unknown inconnu, stranger

unmarried bachelor, celibate, maiden, spinster

unpleasant goop, pill, skite, sorehead

unscrupulous catso, knave

wealthy capitalist, millionaire, nabob, nob, plutocrat

white abiculi, albino, fay, haole, ofay, paleface

wounded blesse

young blade, boy, callant, chap, child, chipling, cub, junior, juvenile, kid, lambkin, smolt, sprig, stripling, teenager, whippersnapper, yonke, younker, youth

PERSONABLE attractive, comely, fair, good-looking, handsome, shapely, well-favored

PERSONAGE baron, bashaw, bigshot, bigwig, bloke, celebrity, chief, dignitary, dignity, figure, grandee, heavyweight, high-muck-a-muck, his nibs, individual, king, luminary, magnate, mugwump, nabob, name, nibs, nob, notable, panjandrum, pasha, peer, person, pillar, portrait, principal, rajah, sole, sachem, shogun, somebody, sophee, sophi, star, suffee, tycoon, vip, worthy

PERSONAL bodily, corpor-(e)al, direct, exclusive, individual, inquisitive, intimate, nosy, notice, particular, peculiar, physical, private, probing, prying, snoopy

PERSONALITY character, charisma, complexion, disposition, ego(ity), figure, hubris, individuality, machismo, makeup, particularity, presence, selfhood, soul, style, temper(ament), vedette

aggressive somatotonia

cult fuhrerprinzip

disorder anxiety, apathy, crack-up, delirium, delusion, depression, euphoria, hostility, hysteria, immaturity, inferiority, lethargy, maladjustment, melancholia, mendacity, neurasthenia, neurosis, psychosis, shellshock

dual jekyll and hyde

split schizophrenia

study psychodynamics

type ambivert, ectomorph, endomorph, extrovert, introvert, mesomorph, phlegmatic, syntone

PERSONATE See IMPERSONATE.

PERSONIFICATION em-

bodiment, incarnation, prosopopoeia, representation

PERSONIFY embody, figure, humanify, impersonate, incarnate, materialize

PERSONNEL crew, employees, faculty, force, hands, men, roster, squad, stable, staff, team, troupe

officer adjutant

PERSPECTIVE angle, composition, configuration, distance, expectation, optical, optics, proportion, prospect, range, scale, scene, scope, slant, telescope, view, vista

PERSPICACIOUS acute, astute, clear, discerning, keen, lucid, penetrating, piercing, probing, sagacious, sharp, shrewd

PERSPICACITY acumen, discernment, insight, intelligence, keenness, vision, wit

PERSPICUOUS clear, conspicuous, definite, explicit, express, lucid, manifest, open, patent, plain, precise, specific, translucent, transparent, visible

PERSPIRATION audor, dew, diaphoresis, exudate, exudation, hidrosis, ooze, sudor, sudoresis, SWEAT, swelter, transpiration, transudation, yolk

deficiency oligidria

excessive ephidrosis, hidrosis, polyhidrosis

induced diaphoresis

lack adiaphoresis, anhidrosis

offensive cacidrosis

pert. sudoric

reducing adiaphoretic

sheep suint, yolk

stopper agaricin

PERSPIRE brean, cook, egest, excrete, exude, melt, ooze, pug, SWEAT, swelter, transpire, transude, wilt

PERSPIRER shvitzer, sweater

PERSTRINGE censure, criticize, dazzle, dull, faultfind, glance

PERSUADABLE exorable, gullible, open-minded

PERSUADE accuate, affect, align, allure, argue, argufy, assure, blandish, blarney, bounce, brainwash, bring over, bring round, cajole, canoodle, coax, convert, convince, drive, engage, en-

list, entice, entreat, gain, get, hook, impel, impress, incite, induce, influence, inveigle, land, lead, move, overcome, prevail, proselyte, proselytize, rule, seduce, sell, soften up, suborn, sway, talk into, touch, urge, wangle, weise, wheedle, win, woo

PERSUADED believing, credulous, gullible, pliable, resolved

PERSUASION alignment, authority, belief, bias, brainwashing, church, conversion, conviction, creed, cult, doctrine, dogma, enlistment, faith, jawboning, judgment, kind, opinion, prejudice, propagandism, religion, school, sect, seduction, sort, tenet, view

method blandishment, blarney, cajolery, propaganda, taffy

personified peitho, suada, suadela

PERSUASIVE coaxy, cogent, compelling, conclusive, conviction, convictive, convincing, eloquent, impelling, missionary, seductive, stringent, unctuous

PERT active, alert, alive, arch, bird, blooming, bold, brash, brisk, canty, chipper, chirk, chirpy, chirrupy, clever, cocket, cocky, comely, conceited, dapper, daring, discourteous, expert, exquisite, flip(pant), flourishing, forward, fresh, frisky, gay, impertinent, impudent, insolent, live(ly), malapert, nimble, obnoxious, officious, open, perky, petulant, presuming, presumptuous, quick, sandpiper, sassy, saucy, skillful, smart(y), snippy, sprightly, volatile

PERTAIN affect, appertain, apply, attach, bear, befall, belie, belong, come, concern, connect, fit, inhere in, refer, regard, relate, touch

PERTAINING For clues using this phrase, see under main word: e.g. FAMILY, *pert.;* IRISH, *pert.*

to anent, concerning, germane, in re, pertinent

comb. aceous, age, arious, ary, ery, ese, ile, orious, ose, ous

PERTINACIOUS bullheaded, determined, dogged, firm, headstrong, inflexible, mulish, obdurate, obstinate, persevering, persistent, pigheaded, resolute, stanch, stiffnecked, strong, stubborn, tenacious, tough, unyielding, willful

PERTINACITY firmness, obstinacy, persistency

symbol bulldog

PERTINENCE applicability, bearing, connection, relevance, timeliness

PERTINENT about, adapted, ad rem, anent, applicable, apposite, appropriate, apropos, apt, bearing on, belonging to, cogent, congruous, connected, fit, fitting, germane, happy, material, opportune, pat, proper, related, relative, relevant, right, suitable, telling, timely, to the point, well-adapted

not inapposite, inappropriate, irrelevant

PERTNESS cheek, conceit, lip

PERTURB addle, agitate, alarm, annoy, bewilder, confound, confuse, derange, discompose, disconcert, disorder, disquiet, distress, disturb, dum(b)found, flurry, fluster, flutter, harass, irk, muddle, nonplus, ruffle, trouble, upset, vex

PERTURBATION agitation, alarm, anxiety, commotion, dismay, irregularity, plight, pother, trepidation, trouble, turmoil, uneasiness, variation, violation

PERTURBED agitated, anxious, bothered, concerned, discomposed, disquieted, distressed, disturbed, excited, exercised, flustered, irked, passionate, ruffled, shaken, tremulant, tremulous, troubled, vexed

PERU, PERUVIAN (See also INCA.) biru

altitude sickness soroche

animal alpaca, atoc, llama, paco, taruco

apple jimsonweed

archeological site machu-picchu

bark cinchona

bird guanay, lindo, yeni, yutu

bird, sacred cuntur

brandy pisco

burial chamber huaca

capital lima

carrot arracach

chief cacique

city arequipa, callao, cuzco, huanuco, ica, iquitos, lima, paita, pisco, puno, trujillo

coin centavo, dinero, libra, peseta, sol

community ayllu, comunidad

cormorant guanay

creeper pito

culture, ancient mochica, nasca, nazca, pucara

current el nino

dance cachua, cueca, kaswa

deer alpaca, taruco

deity (See also INCA *deity*.) huaco, mama, pachacomac, pachamama

department ancach, cusco, cuzco, ica, junin, lima, loreto, piura, puno, tacna, tumbes

desert atacama, nazca

dog alco

dress sayamanto

drink aguardiente, pisco

drug cocaine

empire, early inca, yunca

fertility goddess mama

fertility rite chiaraje

fog garua

fox atoc

fruit cherimoya, sugar-apple

halfbreed cholo

headband wincha

hemp agave

herb fittonia

hill loma, medano

historian garcilaso de la vega

indian amahuaca, ande(s), atalan, aymara, boro, callawaya, campa, cana, canchi, carib, chan(c)a, changos, chanka, chimu, chincha, chumpivilca, chuncho, cocama, colan, colla, inca, inka, jibaro, jivaro, kechua, lama(no), mayoruma, mochica, nasca, omagua, pano, peba, piro, quechua, quiche, quolla, senci, setibo, sipibo, tiahuanaca, tiatinagua, yagua, yunca, yutu

inn tambo

island chincha

king (See also INCA *king*.) cacique

kingdom chimor

kingly title inca

lake titicaca

language See PERU *indian*.

leader odria

liberator bolivar

liquor pisco

llama alpaca, paco

marriage, trial sirvinacuy

measure celemin, fanegada, galon, topo, vara

mineral quisqueite

mnemonic device quipu

mountain sickness soroche

mummified nobles chimus

nobility emblem llautu

partridge yutu

peak coropuna, huamina, huascaran

people See PERU *indian*.

plant kramaria, learco, massua, oca, pigweed, pito, rhatany, ulluco

plateau tablazo

poet vallejo

political party apra

port callao, ilo, mollendo, pisco, trujillo, tumbes, ylo

president belaunde, castilla, leguida

prickly pear polarbear-cactus

prince cacique

province See PERU *department*.

rain garua

relic huaco

river amazon(as), apurimac, curaray, ene, huallaga, ica, ilo, madre de dios, maranon, napu, oroton, pampas, pastaza, paucartambo, piura, rimac, sama, santa, tigre, ucayali, urubamba, yaguas, yavari

rodent chinchilla

ruin huaca, machu-picchu

shrub chilca, matico, ratanhia, rhatany, shansa

skin disease uta, verruga

soup criolla, sopa

spirit huaca

statesman belaunde

tableland puna

tanager lindo, yeni

tavern tambo

tinamou yutu

tobacco sana

tower, prehistoric chulpa

tree algarroba, bucare, cinchona, erythrina, pacay, vichaya

trial marriage sirvinacuy

tuber oca
viceroy toledo
volcano el misti
wart verruga
weight libra, quintal
wind puna, puno, sures
writer vallejo
PERUKE flash, galera, galerum, hair, periwig, toupee, wig
PERUSAL scrutiny, sight
PERUSE con, examine, extend, handle, inspect, read, scan, study, supervise, survey, use up, wander, wear out
PERVADE animate, bathe, diffuse, extend, fill, fire, imbue, impenetrate, impregnate, inform, infuse, ingrain, interfuse, leaven, occupy, penetrate, perfuse, permeate, saturate, traverse
PERVADING prevalent, profound, universal, widespread
PERVASION diffusion, imbuement, overrunning, penetration, permeation, suffusion, transfusion
PERVERSE adamant(ine), awk(ward), awry, backward, balky, cam, camshach, camsteary, camsteery, cantankerous, car, churlish, contentious, contrary, cranky, cross(grained), cussed, difficult, disobedient, distorted, divers, dogged, erring, forward, fractious, froward, gammy, headstrong, insubordinate, intractable, irascible, louch, mulish, naughty, obdurate, obstinate, ornery, peevish, petulant, pigheaded, refractory, restive, self-willed, sinister, snivy, stiffnecked, stubborn, stuffy, sulky, sullen, thrawn, thwart, troublesome, uncooperative, unhelpful, unreasonable, unruly, untoward, unyielding, wayward, wicked, wil(l)ful, wogh, wraist, wraw, wrongheaded, wroth
PERVERSION aberrance, aberration, abnormality, apostasy, corruption, depravity, distortion, diversion, error, falsification, immorality, maladjustment, mania, misconstruction, misdirection, misuse, sophistry

kind fetishism, hypochondria, malacia, masochism, narcissism, paraphia, sadism
PERVERT abuse, apostate, backslider, color, contort, corrupt, crook, debase, debauch(ee), deceive, degenerate, degrade, deprave, desecrate, deviate, distort, divert, falsify, garble, heretic, ill-treat, invert, maltreat, misconstrue, misdirect, misinterpret, misrepresent, mistreat, misturn, misuse, outrage, poison, recreant, renegade, reprobate, seduce, skew, spoil, traduce, turncoat, twist, upset, varnish, vitiate, warp, yahoo
PERVERTED abandoned, abnormal, abused, bad, contorted, corrupt, depraved, distorted, grotesque, misapplied, misdirected, misguided, monstrous, outraged, turned, twisted, unnatural, vicious, warped, wicked
comb. alltri(o)
PERVICACIOUS obstinate, refractory, stubborn, willful
PERVIGILIUM insomnia, night-watch, wakefulness
PERVIOUS accessible, intelligible, leachy, open, penetrable, perforate, permeable, transparent
PESACH lamb, passover, pesah
PESCADORES boko-gunto, bokoto, hoko-gunto, hokoto, pengu-penghutao
part hoko, mako
PESHKAR accountant, agent, minister, steward
PESHKOV *pseud.* maxim (gorki)(gorky)
PESKY annoying, disagreeable, irksome, nettlesome, pestering, plaguey, troublesome, very, vexatious, vexing
PESO carolus, coin, conant, cordoba, dollar, duro, patacao
PESS footstool, hassock
PESSIMISM cynicism, despair, dyspepsia, gloom, weltschmerz
PESSIMIST alarmist, bear, cynic, defeatist, grouch, jeremiah, malist, seek-sorrow, worrier, worrycarl, worrywart
PESSIMISTIC alarmed, black,

cowardly, cynical, dark, depressed, downbeat, foreboding, gloomy, misanthropic, misogynic, morose, negative, oppressed, weighed down
PEST affliction, annoyance, annoyer, ant, bane, blast, blight, bore, bully, buttinski, contagion, curse, epidemic, flea, fly, harasser, harrier, heckler, infliction, insect, moth, nag, nudni(c)k, nuisance, pestilence, plague, schelm, scourge, tease, tick, torment(or), trouble, vermin, weed
control insect lacewing, ladybug, praying mantis
household ant, cockroach, fly, mosquito, moth, mouse, rat, rodent, termite
PESTER afflict, aggravate, annoy(ance), badger, bait, bedevil, bore, bother, bug, chafe, chevy, crowd, disturb, dun, entangle, fret, gall, harass, harry, heckle, hector, hex, hox, impede, importune, infest, molest, nag, obstruct, perturb, plague, rib, scold, tantalize, tease, torment, trouble, upset, worry
PESTHOUSE hospital, lazaret(to)
PESTICIDE arsenical, biocide, chlordane, ddt, debugger, fumigant, poison
PESTIFEROUS, PESTILENT (IAL) annoying, baneful, catching, contagious, deadly, deleterious, evil, fatal, infectious, miasmic, mischievous, noxious, pernicious, plagu(e)y, poisonous, toxic, troublesome, venomous, vexing, virulent
PESTILENCE bane, calamity, contagion, curse, death, disease, epidemic, hydra, plague, qualm, scourge
deity irra
weed butterbur
PESTILENT See PESTIFEROUS.
PESTLE beetle, bray(er), grind, ham, masher, mix, muller, pilum, pistil, pound (er), pulverize(r), shank, stamper
vessel mortar
wooden beetle
PET anger, animal, annoyance, baby, beastie, beloved,

boil, cade, canoodle, cant, caress, cat, cherish, chuck, coddle, cosset, cuddle, dandle, darling, daut(ie), dawt(ie), dear, displeasure, dither, dog, dudgeon, endearing, faddle, fantad, favor(ite), fit, fondle, gentle, hamster, huff, humor, indulge, love, miff, mollycoddle, neck, offend, offense, pamper, pat, peeve, petkin, pique, popular, precious, quiet, rage, smooch, snit, sore, spark, special, spoil, spoon, stroke, sulk(iness), sweetheart, temper, tetch, tiddling, tizzy
lost estray
PETAIN *exile* ile d'yeu
PETAL bract, helm, hood, labellum, leaf, plate, segment, sepal, vexillum
-bearing petalous
extract attar
having narrow stenopetalous
oil attar
part calcar, claw
pert. ala, corolla, whorl
without apetalous
PETALITE castorite
PETARD firecracker, firework
PETASITES butterbur, coltsfoot, dock, herb
PETASUS cap, cupalo, hat
owner hermes, mercury
PETCOCK faucet, spigot, valve
PETE safe, strongbox
PETEMAN burglar, cracksman, safeblower, thief
PETER bag, bundle, cease, cosmetic, diminish, dwindle, end, exhaust, fade, fail, fisherman, niter, pedro, pierre, piers, rock, run out, simon, slump, trunk, tsar, wane, weaken, weary, wine
animal cock
brother andrew
burial place rome
cut off ear of malchus
follower cornelius
friend heidi
funk by-bidder, decoy
maid announcing rhoda
pan author barrie
pan character hook, nana, smee, wendy
pence rome-penny, tax, tribute
restored by aeneas, dorcas, tabitha
staff mullein

sword malchus
symbol keys, sword
the great's wife catherine
PETERMAN burglar, fisherman, PETEMAN, thief
PETHUEL *son* joel
PETIOLE leafstalk, mesopodium, peduncle, phyllode, podeon, stalk, stem, stipe
sheath ocrea
PETIT insignificant, little, mean, minor, petty, small, tiny
mal epilepsy, seizure
pain bun, roll
PETITE baby, diminutive, dwarf, little, mignon(ne), miniature, minikin, minute, small, teeny, tiny, trim, wee(ny)
noblesse gentry
PETITION address, appeal, apply, ask, beg, beseech, bill, boon, entreat(y), impetrate, implore, invoke, memorialize, orate, oration, plea, plead, pray, prayer, request, rogation, solicit(ation), steven, sue, suit, supplicate, supplication, wish
circular roundrobin
PETITIONER applicant, asker, beadsman, bedesman, beggar, candidate, orator, plaintiff, requestor, seeker, solicitor, suitor
chancery relator
PETN peritrate
PETO fish, mackerel, wahoo
PETRARCH *beloved* laura
PETREL albatross, allamonti, allamoth, allamotti, assilag, bill, blue-billy, cahow, diablotin, fulmar, glutton, kaeding, mallemuck, mitty, muttonbird, nelly, nighthawk, prion, seabird, seafowl, shearwater, spency, stinker, stinkpot, stormbird, stormcock, teetee, titi, witch
blue-footed titi
diving teetee
genus hydrobates, oestrelata, pachyptila, pelecanoides
nocturnal cahow
stormy allamoth, assilag, mitty, mother carey's chicken, tom-tailor
PETRIFIED calcified, frightened, petrous, scared, spellbound, stony, terrified, transfixed
PETRIFY affright, alarm, astonish, astound, awe, be-

numb, calcify, daze, deaden, dum(b)found, fossilize, freeze, frighten, harden, lapidify, mineralize, paralyze, scare, shock, stonify, stun, stupefy
PETRIFYING deadening, hardening, numbing, petrescent, stony, terrifying
PETROCHEMICAL cyclohexane, ethylene, isobutylene, orthoxylene, polypropylene
PETROGRAD See LENINGRAD.
PETROLEUM ethane, ethyl, gas(olene)(oline), illuminant, lubricant, lubricator, octane, oil, oleum
hydrocarbon pseudocumene
product alcohol, asphalt, butane, canadol, coke, cymogene, diesel, ethyl, gasoline, kerosene, mineral oil, naptha, paraffin, petrol, petrolatum, propane, propylene, vaseline, wax
refining process cracking
residue masut, mazut
PETRONIUS *character* trimalchio
companion nero
novel satyricon
PETROUS hard, rocky, stony
PETRUCHIO *city* verona
servant curtis, grumio, joseph, nathaniel, nicholas, peter, philip
wife kate, katharine
PE-TSAI brassica, chinese-cabbage, pechay
PETTED cade, dandy, piqued, spoiled
PETTICOAT apron, bajo, balmoral, basquine, benjy, bustle, cotte, crinoline, dick(e)y, feminine, fustanella, girl, gore, green, jupe, jupon, kilt, kirtle, lass(y), luhinga, placket, skirt, slip, sous(e), underskirt, vasquine, vest, whittle, wilycoat, woman(ish)(ly)
extender farthingale
short half-slip
tails shortcake, teacake
PETTIFOG argue, bicker, cavil, pilfer
PETTIFOGGER knave, lawyer, leguleian, quack, shyster, tyro
PETTIFOGGERY chicane(ry), trickery, tricks

PETTINESS naggle, parvinimity, triviality

PETTISH fretful, huffy, irascible, irritable, obstinate, peevish, peewee, petulant, plaintive, querulous, snappish, testy, waspish

PETTLE cherish, cuddle, indulge, nestle, paddle, potter, spade, spud

PETTY base, childish, confined, diminutive, fiddling, frivolous, inconsiderable, inferior, insignificant, jerkwater, little, mean, measly, minor, minuscule, minute, niggling, nugatory, one-horse, orra, paltry, peddling, petit, pettifogging, picayune, picayunish, piddling, pindling, pok(e)y, provincial, puny, schoolboy, small(fry) (minded)(time), tinhorn, trifling, trivial, twattle, unimportant

captain centurion

constable borsholder

dancers aurora borealis, northern lights

matter fidfad

morel nightshade, spikenard

mugget woodruff

mullein cowslip

rice quinoa

spurge devil's-milk

whin needlefurze, restharrow

PETULANT angry, captious, choleric, crabbed, crabby, cranky, cross, displeased, fidgety, fractious, grouchy, grouty, grumbly, grumpy, huffy, ill-humored, immodest, impatient, insolent, irritable, nagging, naggy, peevish, pert, pettish, plaintive, querulous, restive, saucy, shrewish, skittish, snappish, sulky, sullen, surly, testy, touchy, vixenish, vixenly, wanton, waspish, whiny, willful

PETWOOD halmalille

PEUMUS boldo, boldu, evergreen

PEW amen corner, bench, bought, box, bught, cheep, chirp, cry, compartment, congregation, lot, pfui, prong, pugh, rostrum, seat, sedilia, stall, station, stream

ornament poppyhead

square bought, bught

PEWEE, PEWIT bird, flycatcher, gull, lapwing, PEE-WEE, phoebe, woodcock

PEWTER bid(d)ery, bidree, bidri, gray, ley, mug, prize, sadware, tankard, tutenag

coin tra

dishes sadware

ingredient antimony, bismuth, copper, lead, tin

PEYOTE cactus, drug, hikuli, mescal, peyotl, plant

PHACELIA bluebell, waterleaf

PHACELITE chabazite

PHAEA *slayer* theseus

PHAEACIA corfu

ancestor phaeax

king alcinous, nausithous

princess nausicaa

visitor odysseus, ulysses

PHAEDRA *consort* theseus

parent minos, pasiphae

sister ariadne

son acamas

stepson hippolytus

PHAETHON *bird* swan

parent clymene, helios

sisters heliadae

slayer zeus

PHAETON automobile, carriage, duke, spider, stanhope

butterfly baltimore

PHAGEDENA bulimia, gangrene, ulcer

PHALANGER animal, ariel, cuscus, koala, marsupial, opossum, pentail, possum, squirrel, tapoa

flying acrobates, petaurina, petaurus, pygmy-glider, squirrel

PHALANGIDA arachnid, daddy-longlegs

PHALANX formation, group, infantry, phalanstery, troops

ungual phalangette

PHALAROPE bowhead, cootfoot, lobefoot, seagoose, whalebird

PHALERA bead, boss, cameo, disk, moth, stud

PHANEROGAM carpophyte, plant, spermatophyte

PHANTASM apparition, bogle, deception, delusion, dream, eidolon, fancy, fetch, hallucination, haunt, idolon, idolum, illusion, image, imposter, PHANTOM, phenomenon, pipedream, revenant, shade, shadow, specter, spirit, spook, vision, wraith

PHANTASMAL chimerical, illusory, transitory, unreal

PHANTASY fancy, fiction, imagination, PHANTASM

PHANTOM adamastor, airdrawn, appearance, bogey, bogie, bugbear, delusion, demon, devil, double, eidolon, elusive, falsehood, ghost, idolon, illusion, image, manikin, model, PHANTASM, shade, shadow, specter, spectral, spirit, umbra

hideous adamastor

menace boogeyman

ship flying dutchman

PHANUEL *daughter* anna

PHAON *consort* sappho

passenger aphrodite

PHARAOH (See also EGYPT.) ale, beer, busiris, king, ruler, tyrant

daughter bathia

fig sycamore

hen vulture

magician jambres, jannes

mouse ichneumon

name (See also EGYPT *king*.) apries, cephrenes, cheops, hophra, memnon, mencheres, meneptah, necho, osorkon, osorthon, phuoris, rameses, sethos, seti, shabakok, shishak, suphis, thuoris, tirhakah

rat ichneumon

PHARE lighthouse, pharos, strait

PHAREZ *kin* david, esrom, hamul, hezron

PHARISAICAL canting, false, formal, hypocritical, sanctimonious, self-righteous

PHARISEE hebrew, hypocrite, impostor, mugwump, nicodemus

PHARMACEUTICAL (See also DRUG.) materia-medica, medicinal, simple

PHARMACIST apothecary, chemist, dispenser, druggist, gallipot, pharmacopolist, posologist

mate bayman

PHARMACON drug, medicine, poison

PHARMACY apothecary's, chemist's, dispensary, drugstore, remedy, store

honey mel

weight obole, obolus

PHAROS beacon, chandelier, cloak, lantern, lighthouse, mark(er), torch

PHARYNX mastax, throat

PHASE angle, appearance, aspect, caprice, chapter, condition, end, facet, faze, form, guise, instar, look, part, perturb, posture, semblance, shape, side, situation, stage, state, step, transition
initial bud
PHASEOLUS See BEAN.
PHEASANT (See also *kind*, below.) argus, argusianus, bird, cheer, chir, fireback, fowl, grouse, guan, ithagine, kalij, kallege, leipoa, macartney, magpie, monal, monaul, moonal, phasianus, pukras, ringneck, tragopan
breeding place stew
brood bevy, eye, nid(e), nye
cuckoo coucal
duck merganser, pintail
eye adonis, buttercup, rosaruby
finch waxbill
firebacked macartney
flight bouquet
kind argus, blood, golden, kallege, lady amherst's, mongolian, ring-necked, silver
like-bird francolin, grouse, guan, leipoa, lyrebird, magpie
nest nide
-tailed warbler emu-wren
PHEGEUS *daughter* alphesiboea, arsinoe
kingdom psophis
purified alcmaeon
son-in-law alcmaeon
PHENCYCLYDINE angeldust, pcp
PHENE *beloved* hermes, mercury
PHENOBARBITOL luminal
PHENOL aloesol, chavicol, creosol, durenol, eugenol, laccol, orcinol, resorcin, thymol
alcohol catechol
crystalline ammoresinol, apionol
derivative aloesol, ammoresinol, anol, cresol, orcin, salol, thymol
PHENOMENAL actual, big, bustling, corporeal, eventful, extraordinary, factual, great, marvelous, material, miraculous, momentous, objective, outstanding, physical, preternatural, prodigious, real, remarkable, sen-

sible, splendid, stirring, substantial, unusual, valid
PHENOMENON anomy, apparition, appearance, asterism, curiosity, effect, event, ghost, image, manifestation, marvel, matter, miracle, object, paradox, phantasm, phantom, portent, prodigy, rara-avis, rarity, shade, shadow, siderism, sight, specter, spirit, substance, symptom, wonder, wraith
PHENYL aryl, salol, tolyl
benzene biphenyl, diphenyl
cyanide benzonitrile
hydrate phenol
isocyanate carbonil
mercaptan thiophenol
methane toluene
methyl ketone acetophenone, hypnone, scent
salicylate salol
PHERECIUS harmonides
PHERES *offspring* admetus, idomene, lucurgus, periapis
parent cretheus, tyro
PHIAL bottle, cup, vessel, vial
PHIALE bowl, fountain, laver, saucer
PHIDIAS *patron* pericles
work athena, jupiter, parthenon, propylaea, zeus
PHILABEG filabeg, kilt
PHILADELPHIA quaker city
building independence hall
district mainline
fleabane skevish
husband ptolemy
lawyer rascal, shyster
park fairmount
PHILAMMON *offspring* eumolpus, thamyris
parent apollo, chione
PHILANDER coquette, dally, flirt, lover, opossum, smock, trifle, wolf
PHILANDERER chaser, don juan, flirt, heartbreaker, ladies'-man, ladykiller, masher, wolf, woman-chaser
PHILANTHROPIC altruistic, benevolent, charitable, humane, humanitarian, magnanimous, unselfish
PHILANTHROPIST almoner, almsgiver, altruist, benefactor, benevolist, do-gooder, donor, good samaritan, humanitarian, robin hood, well-doer

PHILANTHROPY alms, altruism, benevolence, charity, goodwill
universal omnibenevolence
PHILAO *father* alcimedes
PHILARIO *friend* iachimo, leonatus, posthumus
PHILATELY deltiology, timbrology
PHILEMON *guest* hermes, jupiter, mercury, zeus
master cerimon
wife baucis
PHILIP *assassin* pausanias
brother herod
captain taurion
city stagira
courtier apelles, megaleas
father dionysius
friend aratus
mediator demaratus, pixodorus
son alexander, arrhidaeus
uncle-in-law attalus
wife cleopatra, eurydice, olympias, philinna
PHILIP II *fleet* armada
wife maria, mary-tudor
PHILIPPA OF HAINAUT *consort* edward iii
PHILIPPIC declamation, diatribe, invective, oration, screed, tirade
speaker cicero, demosthenes
PHILIPPINES *animal* carabao, civet, lemur, tarsier, timarau
ant anai, anay
archipelago sulu
armlet calombigas
aroid pungapung
artillery lantaca, lantaka
aunt caca
bamboo batakan
bamboo, woven sawali
banana lacatan, lakatan, saguing
bandit tulisan
bark agamid
barracks cuartel
bay manila, subic
beer pangasi
bird abacay, calangay, maya
blind-your-eyes alipata
boat balangay, banca, banka, barangay, baroto, bilalo, casco, pontin, vinta
breadfruit camansi
brigand ladrone
buffalo carabao, timarau
cagayan ibaneg
calash See *carriage*, below.
canoe banca

capital baguio, cabecera, manila, quezon

carriage calash, calesa, calesin, carretela, carromata

cedar calantas

century plant maguey

ceremony cassicassi

charm anting-anting

chief cabeza, dat(t)o, datu, ilocano, iloco, ilokano, panglima

child anax, bata

cigar bunco

city agoa, albay, aparri, baguio, basilan, bogo, cabanutuan, calocan, cavite, cebu, cotabato, dagupan, davao, dumaguette, gapan, iba, ilagan, iloilo, iriga, lanao, laoag, manila, naga, palo, pasay, tarlac, vigan

cockatoo calangay

coin centavo, conant, peseta, peso

conqueror lopez de legazpe

coral tree dapdap

cyclone bag(u)io

dagger balarao, itac, itak

deity bat(h)ala, dagon

dialect bamboo-english

diplomat romulo

discoverer magellan

dish buro

district lepanto

division ato

dogwood tua

drink beno, bubud, pangasi, tampoy, vino

duck egg balut

dwarf aeta, negrito

evergreen kapok

fabric bandala, canamo, meddrinaque, pina(yusa), rengue, sinamay

family group barangay

fanatic pulahan

farmer lao, tao

fern nito

fetish anito

fiber abaca, baroi, buntal, camansi, castuli, eruc, grewia, husi, jusi, pandanus, pineapple, pterospermum, saba, sabutan

fig agamid, balete

fish dalag, langaray

fish, climbing martinico

fish poison tuba

food baha, balut, poi, saba, taro

forest dita, gubat

fort corregidor, cota, cotta, gota, kota

fowl manoc

galley calan

game panguingui

garment saya

grass boho, bojo, cogon

guerrilla huk

gulf davao, lingayen, ragay

gun baril

hardwood acle, aranga, ipil, makassar ebony, narra

hat salacot

head cloth potong

hemp abaca, manila, ramie, sinawa

hemp cloth pinayusa

herb bamban, donax

hill-dweller babaylan

house bahay, camalig

idol anito

insurrectionist aguinaldo

island babuyan, batan, bohol, cebu, corregidor, culion, cuyo, jolo, leyte, lubang, luzon, marinduque, masbate, mindanao, negros, palawan, panay, paragua, poro, samar, sulu, ticao

island group batanes, sulu, visayan

jar banga

kerchief panuelo

killer juramentado

knife balarao, barong, bolo, campit, itac, itak, machet(e)(te)

language See *people*, below.

leader aguinaldo, marcos

leather balat

leper colony culion

lighthouse faro

liquor See *drink*, above.

litter talabon

lizard ibid, ibit

mahogany almon, bagtikan, shorea

malayan daggau, gaddang, italone, lanao, sulu, visayan

mango bauno, carabao, pahutan

mangrove hangalai, langrai

market parian

market-day tiangue

massacre belangiga

measure apatan, balita, braza, caban, catty, cavan, chinanta, chupa, fardo, ganta, lachsa, loan, picul, punto, quilate, quinon

monitor ibid

monkey douc, langur, macaque, machin

moslem lanao, moro, sanggil, sulu

mother ina

mountaineer mentesco

mudfish dalag

muskmelon atimon

naval base cavite

non-christian infiel

nut pili

orange calamondin

outlaw babaylan

pagan bontok, ibilao, ilonget, italon, kalinga, montes(co)

palm ahahao, anahau, bejuco, calmus, niog, nipa

palm fiber eruc

palm wine beno, bino

parrot cagit

patriot rizal

peak (See also *volcano*, below.) apo, banahao, iba, mayon, pagsan, pulog

peasant lao, tao

peninsula bataan

people abaca, aeta, apayao, aripa, arupaat(t)a, ati, babaylan, bagobo, baluga, batak, batan, bicol, bikol, bilaan, bisayan, biscol, bontoc, bontok, bukidono, busao(s), cagayan, catalangane, dulangane, eta, filipino, ibanag, ibilao, ifil, ifugao, igalot, igorot(te), illano, ilocano, isinai, ita (nega), lanao, lutao, lutayo, macajambo, magindanao, malanao, manabo, manguian, mangyan, manobo, montes, moro, mundo, naboloi, negrito, pampanga(o), pangasinan, sambal, sinay, sulu, tagal(a), tagalog, tao, timaua, timawa, tinguiane, tino, tirurai, vicol, visayan, yakan, zambal

pepper betel

pigeon bleeding-heart

plant abaca, acapulco, aga (mid), alasas, alem, baroi, batad, campanilla, ficus, pandanus

plum duhat, duhr, lansa, lanseh, mabolo, sapote, sirvelas

political party independista

port aparri, bacolod, batangas, calapan, cavite, davao, debu, iloilo, laoag, legaspi, manila, tacloban, zamboanga

president macapagal, magsaysay, quezon, roxas

priest aglipay, babaylan, pandita, pandito, sarip

prince cachil

province abra, agusan, aklan, albay, bataan, bohol, capiz, cavite, cebu, davao, iloilo, isabela, laguna, lanao, leyte, quezon, rizal, samar, surigao, tarlac
raft balsa
rebel aguinaldo, huk
reptile python
rice aga, barit, bigas, canin, macan, paga
rice beer pangasi
rice grass zacate
rice polishings darac
river abra, agno, agusan, cagayan, laoang, magat, mindanao, pampanga, pasig
road daan
robbery bandolerismo
rope anabo, nabo
sack bayon
salute salamat
sapodilla chico
sarong padadion
sash tapis
sea sulu
seasoning alpasotes
secret society katipunan
sentinel bantay
servant alila, alipin, bata
shawl slendang
shirt baro
shrine virgin of antipolo
shrub abroma, alem, anabo, anilau, comumbia, fatsia, nabo, saging
silk alcaiceria
skirt saya
slave alipin
slipper chinela
soapvine gogo
soldier gugu, ladrone, moro
spirit anito
springs tibi
statesman roxas
stream ilog
sugar mill central, trapiche
sumac anam, anan
summer capital baguio
sweetheart querida
sweetsop ates
sword barong, campilan
tax cedula
termite anai, anay
thatch nipa
timber cahuy
town bayan
townhall tribunal
tree 3 dao, iba, tua, tui 4 acle, alba, alle, anam, ates, bogo, cabo, dita, ipil, niog, paho, pili, poon, supa, tuwi, yate, ypil 5 agoho, almon, amaga, anabo, balao, balau,

bayok, betis, bulak, cahuy, cebur, guijo, lauan, lebur, ligas, narra, tabog, vitex, yacal 6 alagao, alagau, alupag, amuyon, anagap, anahao, anahau, apalit, aranga, banaba, bancal, banuyo, bataan, batino, botong, dapdap, dungon, katmon, lanete, mambog, marang, molave, sapote 7 agathis, amboina, amuguis, amuyong, anabong, anonang, apitong, banilad, binukau, camagon, danglin, gumihan, hapiton, katurai, mambong, mancono, mayapis, pahutan, tindalo 8 almaciga, ampalaya, balibago, bauhinia, bitanhol, calantas, camuning, kalipaya, lumbayao, malapaho, siruelas, tanguile 9 alintatad, batikulin, batitinan, maccaasim, marakapas, palomaria, palosapis 10 bansalague, batikuling, calamondin 11 alibangbang, balinghasay, malaanonang 12 aclangparang, kalamansanai 13 makassar ebony
tree bark aga(mid)
trepang balate
u s general black jack pershing, hell-roaring smith, macarthur
u s headquarters zamboanga
vehicle carromata
vine amlong, gogo, iyo
volcano albay, apo, askja, canlaon, hibok, mayo, taal
warehouse godown
warrior magani, moro
watchtower atalaya, bantayan
water tubig
water buffalo carabao
water jar bango
weapon barong, bolo, campilan
weaverbird maya
weight catty, chinanta, fardo, lachsa, picul, punto, quilate
wharf pantalan
white man cachil(a)
wind colla
wine alac, beno, bino
wood acle, ebony, mahogany, narra, sandal, teak
writer riza
yam lima(lima), tugui, ube, uve
yam bean singhamas
PHILIPPUS *daughter* marcia
son-in-law cato

PHILISTINE babbitt, barbarian, boeotian, boob, boor, bourgeois, caphtorim, conformist, cretan, debauchee, drunkard, dull, enemy, gigman, hypocrite, ignorant, mammonish, mucker, obtuse, prosaic, pulesati, purasati, reactionary, standpat, uncultured
army unit mashhith
capture ark of the covenant
city ascalon, ashdod, ekron, esdud, gath, gaza, geth
foe david, samson
giant goliath
god baal, beelzebub, dagan, dagon
home caphtor
king abimelech, achish
oppressor samuel
victory shiloh
PHILOCTETES *father* poeas
friend hercules
suitor of helen
victim paris
PHILOLOGUS *friend* paul
PHILOLOGY etymology, linguistics, semantics, speechlore
PHILOMATH astrologer, mathematician, scholar, student
PHILOMELA nightingale
consort tereus
kin butes, itys, pandion, procne
slayer itys
PHILOPOEMEN *avenger* lycortas
battle mantinea
city megalopolis
father craugis
foe cleomenes, dinocrates, machanidas
friend polyaenus, simmias
teacher cleander, demophanes, ecdemus
PHILOSOPHER (See also *famous*, below.) pundit, sage, solon, thinker
atom monad
cynic antisthenes, crates, diogenes, hipparchia, menippos, metrocles, monimos
cyreniac aristippus
disciples school, sect
egg panacea
eleatic democritus, melissus, parmenides, protagoras, tarsus, zeno
ephetic epochist
famous abelard, anaxogoras, anselm, aristippus, aristotle,

augustine, averroes, bacon, bentham, bergson, berkeley, bruno, cicero, comte, confucius, croce, democritus, descartes, dewey, duns-scotus, empedocles, engels, epictetus, epicurus, fichte, frege, grotius, hegel, heidegger, heraclitus, hobbes, hume, husserl, james, jaspers, joad, kant, kierkegaard, leibniz, locke, lucretius, mach, maimonides, maritain, mill, moti, nestor, nietzsche, parmenides, philo, pierce, plato, plotinus, protagoras, rousseau, russell, santayana, schelling, schopenhauer, seneca, socrates, solon, spencer, spinoza, thales, theophrastus, thomas-aquinas, whitehead, wittgenstein, wundt, xenophanes, zeno, zoroaster

game chess

kind cynic, eleatic, empiricist, eristic, idealist, logical-positivist, phenomenologist, realist, skeptic, stoic, zetetic

land balnibarbi

laughing democritus

of ferney voltaire

of malmsbury hobbes

of samosata lucan

of sans souci frederick the great

of syracuse dion

of wimbledon took

sceptic pyrrho, timon

scholastic aquinas

socratic cebes, crito, glauco, simmias, simon, socrates, xenophon

stoic chrysippus, cleanthes, diogenes, posidonius, zeno

stone adrop, elixir, microcosm, panacea, ruby

stone substance carmot

weeping heraclitus

PHILOSOPHICAL calm, collected, cool, enduring, erudite, impassive, imperturbable, rational, reasonable, relaxed, sage, sapient, sedate, sensible, serene, stoical, temperate, thoughtful, tranquil, unruffled, wise

element rect

pleiad See GREECE *sages, seven.*

unit monad

PHILOSOPHY agnosticism, animalism, animism, atom-

ism, casuistry, comtism, cosmology, cynicism, cyrenaicism, deism, DOCTRINE, dualism, eclecticism, egoism, eleaticism, empiricism, epicureanism, epistemology, esoterics, esthetics, ethics, existentialism, gnosticism, gospel, hedonism, hinduism, humanism, hylism, idealism, identism, ideology, logic, manichaeism, materialism, mechanism, megarianism, metaphysics, mimamasa, monism, mysticism, naturalism, nominalism, noumenalism, nyaya, occamism, ontology, panlogism, pantheism, phenomenology, platonism, pluralism, positivism, pragmatism, rationalism, realism, sankhya, scepsis, scholasticism, sensism, skepticism, somatism, sophism, stoicism, syncretism, system, taoism, theism, thomism, transcendentalism, vedantism, vitalism, wisdom, yoga

ancient cynic, stoic

first metaphysics

moral ethics

natural physics

of the garden epicureanism

PHILOTELIC *unit* stamp

PHILOTRIA elodea, pondweed, waterweed

PHILOTUS *master* timon

PHILTER, PHILTRE amatory, aphrodisiac, charm, drug, potion, wanga

PHILYRA *consort* cronus

father oceanus

son chiron

PHIMEDEIA *consort* poseidon

PHINEAS *brother* hophni

parent eleazar, eli

son abishua, ahijah, eleazar, gershom, ichabod

victim cozbi, zimri

PHINEIS *beloved* enalus

PHINEUS *beloved* andromeda

brother cadmus, cepheus

consort idaea

parent agenor, auchinoe, belus

rescuer calais, zetes

rival perseus

sister europa

slayer perseus

PHINTIAS *friend* damon

PHIZ(OG) face, looks, mug

PHLEBOTOMIST bleeder, bloodletter, hemophiliac, surgeon

PHLEBOTOMIZE bleed, venesect

PHLEBOTOMY bleeding, bloodletting, lancet

PHLEGM apathy, calm, composure, coolness, dullness, equanimity, fleume, gleet, impassivity, indifference, moisture, mucus, pituite, rheum, sangfroid, serenity, stoicism, stolidity, water

PHLEGMATIC aloof, apathetic, calm, chilly, cold, composed, cool, dull, emotionless, frigid, impassive, imperturbable, indifferent, inert, languid, lethargic, marble, mucoid, nonchalant, passionless, passive, slow, sluggish, stoic(al), stolid, unconcerned, unemotional, unfeeling, uninterested, viscous, watery

PHLEGON *friend* paul

PHLEGYAS *kingdom* lapith, orchomenos

offspring coronis, ixion

parent ares, chryse

slayer apollo

PHLOEM bark, bast, flax, hemp, jute, leptome, ramie, tissue

PHLOGISTIC burning, fiery, flaming, heated, impassioned, inflammatory

PHLOX albion, blossomwithy, blue-hill, camla, cobaea, cyme, flox, jacob's-ladder, sweet-william

genus cobaea, collomia, linanthus, polemonium

PHOBIA (For specific phobia, see under noun: e.g., HEIGHT *fear of.*) apprehension, awe, dread, fear

PHOBOS *father* ares

PHOCIS *conqueror* philip

king strophius

peak parnassus

river cephissus

PHOCUS *half-brother* peleus

parent aeacus, ornytion, psamathe

slayer peleus, telamon

wife antiope

PHOEBAD prophetess, seeress

PHOEBE artemis, bird, bridgebird, diana, flycatcher, moon, peewee, pewee, pewit, sayornis, selene

daughter asteria, leto
friend paul
husband coeus
parent gaea, leda, leucippus, tyndareus, uranus
sister clytemnestra
PHOEBUS (See APOLLO.) bright, light, pure, sol, sun
PHOENICIA *adam and eve* genos and genea
capital tyre
chronicler damascius, mochus, philo
city accho, acre, aradis, ashdod, ashkelon, berytus, byblos, debir, gaza, gebal, ghineh, gubla, jebel, joppa, kadesh, nega, sarepta, sidon, simyra, tyre, tyrus, ugarit
colony carthage
dialect punic
empire achaemenian
flute gingras
giant antilebanon, brathy, cassios, lebanon
god adod, adonis, aeon, aleyin, amurru, amynos, asclepius, atlas, baal, balmacodes, batau, beelsamin, cabeiri, cronos, dagon, danel, demarus, djezzin, elagabalus, elioun, eros, eshmo(u)n, eshmun, etrah, genos, hadad, haytau, hiylon, hypsistos, hypsouranios, keret, kolpia, kusor, latpon, magos, melkart, misor, mot-and-shur, mouth, ousoos, pothos, protogonos, qadesh, reshef, ruti, sahar, salem, sibani, sidon, sutekh, sydyk, taautos, terah, trismegistus, uranus
goddess anat, asherah, asherat, ashtoreth, astart(e), baalat, baau, baltis, dione, elat, genea, oadesh, rhea, sapas, tanit(h)
governor, biblical sisinnes
king agenor
people curetes, semites, sidonians
pert. punic
philosopher eudemus
poet panyasis
port byblos, sidon
princess europa
ruin limassol
sacred writings ras shamrah
ship golah
stela yehawmelek
writer sanchuniathon
PHOENIX apotheosis, beauty,

ben(n)u, feng-huang, nonesuch, nonpareil, paragon, rara avis
daughter europa
host peleus
parent amyntor, cleobule, hippodamia
pupil achilles
tree palm
PHONE buckywalter, call (up), communicate, klang, receiver, ring(up), talk, telephone
book directory
call buzz
PHONEME laryngal, morph, toneme
PHONETIC lingual, oral, vocal, voiced
notation romic
system palaeotype
PHONOGRAPH gramophone, graphophone, hi-fi, jukebox, nickelodeon, record-player, stereo, talking-machine, turntable, victrola
coin-operated jukebox, nickelodeon
head pickup
inventor edison
needle stylet, stylus
record disc, disk, phonogram, platter, release
PHONOGRAPHY shorthand, stenography
inventor pitman
PHONY bastard, bogus, brummy, bunyip, charlatan, counterfeit, fake(d), fictitious, fraud, hypocrite, imposter, sham, spurious, tromben(y)ik
PHORCYDES See GORGONS.
PHORCYS *consort* ceto, crataeis, hecate
offspring GORGONS, HESPERIDES, ladon
parent gaea, pontus
PHORONEUS *consort* cedo, laodice
kingdom argos
offspring apis, car, niobe
parent inachus, melia
PHOSPHATE apatite, arrojadite, attacolite, cabocle, cacoxene, ehlite, fertilizer, floats, goyazite, griphite, koninckite, palaite, uranite, wavellite
aluminum attacolite, paravauxite, peganite
calcium podolite
center nauru, pleasant island

compound autunite, barrandite, bassetite, borickite, cabocle
hydrous andrewsite, weinschenkite
lead parsonsite
lime apatite
manganese palaite
zinc parahopeite
PHOSPHOR lucifer, venus
PHOSPHORESCENCE afterglow, briming, luminescence
sea marfire
PHOSPHORESCENT gleaming, luminous, noctilucous, scintillating
PHOSPHOROS artemis, hecate
PHOTOENGRAVING aquatone, halftone, heliotypography, lithography, rotogravure, zincography
PHOTO(GRAPH) (See also *kind*, below.) art, candid, cheesecake, film, flash, glossy, heliochrome, heliograph, image, kodak, likeness, montage, mug(shot), pan(el), pic(ture), pinup, print, shoot, shot, simulacrum, snap(shot), still, tintype
bath developer, fixer, reducer, toner
book album
colored kodachrome
color process pinachromy
copy photolith, print, stat, xerox
description caption
developer adurol, amidol, aminophenol, dope, eikonogen, hypo, metol, ortol, paraaminophenol, pyrogallol, revelator, rodinal, soup, toner
development place darkroom
finish nose, tie
fixing agent hypo
improve retouch
instantaneous pistolgram, polaroid
instrument enlarger
kind ambrotype, cabinet, calbotype, carte de visite, composograph, daguerreotype, diamond, ferrotype, imperial, motion, passport, photostat, portrait, still, talbotype, tintype, x-ray
large blow-up
negative film

old-fashioned daguerreotype, tintype
on glass vitrotype
printing aristotype, artotype, ozotype
2nd retake
solution emulsion, hypo
subject cheesecake
x-ray skiagram

PHOTOGRAPHER calotypist, cameraman, camerist, cinematographer, daguerreotypist, kodaker, lensman, portraitist, radiographer, skiagrapher, snapshooter, talbot-typist

PHOTOGRAPHIC exact, faithful, lifelike

PHOTOGRAPHY *inventor* daguerre, niepce, talbot
instrument actinograph, diaphragm, dryer, easel, enlarger, filter, finder, flash, lens, light-meter, photometer, range-finder, reflector, shutter, timer, tripod, viewer, view-finder

PHOTOLOGY optics, photics

PHOTOMETRIC *unit* lumen, lux, pyr, rad

PHOTOSTAT copy, dupe, duplicate, xerox

PHRADMON *son* agelaus

PHRA INDRA *golden carpet* erawan

PHRASE adage, bar, catchword, clause, collocation, commation, conceive, couch, describe, epigram, epithet, express(ion), flatter(y), formularize, formulate, fuss, gush, idiom, idiotism, indite, locution, maxim, measure, motto, part, passage, present, sentence, slogan, statement, style, term(inology), utterance, verbalism, vocalize, voice, work(age)
important punch line
musical attacco, subject
redundant cheville
rhythmical commation
stock bromide, cant, cliche

PHRASEOLOGY cant, diction, expression, jargon, language, nomenclature, parlance, style, vocabulary, wording

PHRATRY clan, curia, phyle, tribe

PHRENETIC avid, crazy, delirious, excited, fanatic, frantic, insane, lunatic,

mad, passionate, pythian, rabid, violent, zealous

PHRENOLOGY bumpology

PHRIXOS, PHRIXUS *consort* chalciope
parent athamas, nephele
sacrifice golden fleece
sister helle
son phrontis
stepmother ino

PHRYGIA *city* colossae, ipsus
conqueror croesus
converter montanist
cybele magna-mater
flute-player marsyas
goddess cybele
gods attis, atys, cab(e)iri, kab(e)iri, men, sabazios
king gordius, midas, otreus
moon god men
peasant baucis
river meander, sangarious
sect cataphrygian, montanist

PHRYNE courtesan, hetaera, prostitute, wanton

PHRYNIA *consort* alcibiades

PHTHIA *consort* amyntor, apollo, zeus
seducer phoenix
son dorus, laodocus, polypoetes

PHTHISIS asthma, consumption, decay, tuberculosis
remedy aseptolin

PHURAH *master* gideon, jeribbaal

PHUT *father* ham

PHYLACTERIC magic

PHYLACTERIES tefillin, tephillin, tfillin

PHYLACTERY amulet, charm, infula, record, reminder, scroll, spell, talisman

PHYLETIC lineal, phylogenetic, racial

PHYLEUS *kin* astyocheia, augeas

PHYLLIS *changed to* tree
father sithon
lover demophoon

PHYLOMACHE *kin* acastus, alcestis, pelias

PHYLUM annelata, annelida, bryozoa, chordata, class, division, hoka(n), lignosae, nadene

PHYMA nodule, tumor

PHYSALIS cape-gooseberry, capulin, chinese-lantern, condalia, ground-cherry, hardwood, jimsonweed, pop(per), tomatillo, tree

PHYSARIA bladderpod

PHYSIC aperient, aperitive, cathartic, cure, drug, heal, laxative, medicament, medicate, medicine, natural, pill, purgative, purge, relieve, remedy, specific, therapeutics, treatment
nut curcas, pignon, pulghereseed, tartago, tuba

PHYSICAL animal(istic), bodily, carnal, corpor(e)al, curative, elemental, elementary, exam(ination), external, fleshly, material, natural, objective, personal, phenomenal, real, sensible, somal, somatic, substantial, true
universe anima-mundi

PHYSICIAN (See also DOCTOR, MEDICAL, MEDICINE and SURGEON references.) consultant, curer, medic, practitioner, restorer, sawbones
beloved st luke
chief archiater
comb. iatro, ician
famous aesculapius, barnard, carrel, colles, dooley, finlay, finsen, galen, haller, harvey, jenner, laveran, lister, maimonides, mayo, mesmer, morton, osler, paget, pare, parran, perera, pott, reed, rhazes, roux, rusk, sabin, salk, white
ignorant medicaster
name meaning asa, jason
prince of avicenna
symbol caduceus

PHYSICIST abee, ampere, boyle, bunsen, curie, erman, faraday, galvani, goddard, hahn, hylozoist, mach, marconi, materialist, naturalist, ohm, rossi, teller, volta
atomic bohr, compton, einstein, fermi, meitner, millikan, pauli, rabi, urey

PHYSICS *branch* ceraunics, dynamics, mechanics, pneumatics, statics
comb. geo
unit erg

PHYSIOGNOMY countenance, expression, face, features, looks, mien, mug, portrait, puss, visage
study phrenology

PHYSIOLOGY biology, bionomics, bionomy

PHYSIQUE anatomy, appearance, body, build, constitution, figure, frame, strength
PHYSIS nature
PHYSOSTIGMINE esere, eserin(e)
PHYSOSTOME carp, catfish, herring, salmon
PHYTEUS apollo
PHYTOLOGY See BOTANY.
PIA gabgab, marmot
PIACLE crime, guilt, offense, sin
PIAN frambesia, tumor, yaws
PIANISSIMO soft(ly)
PIANIST anda, arrau, bachaus, busoni, cliburn, curzon, fisher, gould, hess, hofmann, horowitz, · iturbi, kempf, levant, lhevinne, liszt, pachmann, paderewski, richter, rosen, rubenstein, schumann, serkin, solomon
PIANNET chatterer, magpie, oyster-catcher, woodpecker
PIANO anemochord, babygrand, box, concert-grand, floor, flugel, low, soft(ly), story, upright
dumb digitoria, digitorium, fingerboard
early clavichord, harpsichord, spinet
jack hopper, sticker
key digital, ivory, natural
keyboard claviature, clavier
part backfall, backstop, bellyrail, bolster, butt, check, damper, hammer, ivories, jack, key, pedal, prolong, roller, sounding-board, string, wippen
pedal celeste
pedal keyboard pedalier
player pianola
small spinet, virginal
street hurdygurdy
tuning temperament
upright clavial, spinet
white key natural
PIARIST escolapio
PIASSAVA attalea, bahia, bast-palm, cohune, coquillanut, iyo, jara, leopoldinia, palm, piacaba, raphia
PIASTER dollar, dong, peso
1/40th para
120th asper
PIAUI *capital* teresina
PIAZZA balcony, campo, canopy, gallery, loggia,

place, porch, portico, square, stoop, veranda
PIBROCH *player* piper
PICADOR bullfighter, debater, jester, wit
PICARO(ON) adventurer, bandit, brigand, corsair, knave, pirate, prey, rascal, rogue, sharper, thief, tramp, vagabond
PICASSO *painting* guernica
style cubism
PICAYUNE mean, measly, paltry, peddling, petty, piddling, puny, pusillanimous, small-minded, trifle, trifling, trivial
PICCOLO flautino, flute, ottavino
PICEA evergreen, spruce
PICHICIAGO armadillo, chlamyphore
PICI barbet, bee-eater, honeyguide, jacamar, kingfisher, nuthatch, puffbird, toucan, woodpecker, wryneck
PICK adorn, bargain, beele, best, bit, cast, cavil, cheat, choice, choose, cleanse, collect, cream, criticize, cull, decide, detach, determine, diamond, discover, draw, eat, elect, elite, fling, gaff, gather, glean, gnaw, gore, grasp, harvest, indent, infer, lease, mandrel, nibble, opt, peck, penetrate, pierce, pike, pilch, pilfer, pitch(fork), plectrum, pluck, point, preen, prefer, pride, provoke, push, quarrel, remove, rob, scrap, scratch, seek, seize, select(ion), separate, settle, sift, single out, spade, spike, steal, strum, take, throw, thrust, tool, trim, twitch, wale, warp, winnow
a bone with argue, dispute, fight, quarrel
at nag, scratch, worry
knot burl
-me-up bracer, kittiwake, restorative, stimulant, tonic
miner's mandrel, mandril
off pluck, shoot, snipe
on abuse, annoy, bother, bully, censure, choose, criticize, harass, nag, pester, scold, select, tease
out assort, choose, cull, eliminate, extract, garble, glean, select, sort, spot, take

to pieces analyze, censure, dismantle, macerate, tear apart
up acceleration, acquaintance, acquire, anacrusis, arrest, bargain, bracer, call for, carrier, cartridge, chippy, collect, draw up, dredge, fish up, gain, gather, hitchhiker, improve(ment), increase, pilfer, prostitute, recover(y), recuperate, regain, restorative, retrieve, revival, ride, stimulant, stimulation, take up, tidy, tonic, trollop, truck, wanton
up again resume
up the tab pay, settle, treat
PICKABACK astraddle, astride
PICKAX bede, bill, gurlet, mattock, pike, tool, tubber, twibil(l)
PICKED adorned, choice, chosen, cleared, dainty, elect, exclusive, fastidious, peaked, piked, plucked, pointed, select(ed), spiny, spruce, stripped, trim
PICKEER bicker, flirt, maraud, pillage, pirate, privateer, quarrel, skirmish, wrangle
PICKEREL dunlin, esox, fish, jack, pickering, pike, sauger, slinker, walleye
weed alligator-wampee, moose-ear, pontederia, potamogeton, tule, wampee
PICKET bind, bullet, enclose, fasten, fence, fortify, goonsquad, guard, lookout, marker, moor, outguard, outpost, pale, paling, palisade, panel, patrol, peg, piquet, post, rail, scout, sentinel, sentry, shackle, slat, spotter, stake, strike, tern, tether, torture, watchman
PICKINGS booty, brick, earnings, fragment, gains, loot, perks, perquisites, scrap
PICKLE achar, alec, atsana, bind, bit, box, brine, capers, condite, confect, corn, cornichon, cure, dawdle, dilemma, dill, few, fix, gherkin, glean, grain, higdon, hot water, intoxicate, jam, kernel, kimchi, little, mango, marinade, marinate, mess, muddle, nibble, peck, piddle, pilfer, plight, predic-

ament, preserve, problem, quandary, scrape, serve, soak, steep, stew, strait, trifle, trouble, vinegar, vitriol
factory cia
fish alec
grass glasswort
herring buffoon, merry-andrew
mixed higdon
solution brine
spiced piccalilli
sweet relish
PICKLED drunk, marinated, sour, soused
PICKLEWEED glasswort, greasewood
PICKMAW gull
PICKPOCKET bung, buzzer, buzzgloak, cannon, clyfaker, cutpurse, dip(per), diver, fig(boy), file(r), fingersmith, foist(er), ganef, gun, hook(er), knuckler, larcenous, mobsman, pursesnatcher, ratero, rob(ber), shepherd's-purse, spurry, stealer, thief, weed, wire
PICKSOME fastidious, particular
PICKTHANK flatterer, informer, sycophant, talebearer
PICKTOOTH indolent, lazy, slothful
PICKWICK PAPERS *author* dickens
borough eatanswill
character arabella allen, dowler, jingle, magnus, mrs bardell, mrs hunter, nupkins, sam weller, sawyer, snodgrass, stiggins, trotter, tupman, wardle, weller, winkle
landlady mrs bardell
lawyer pell
manservant sam weller
squire wardle
PICKY choosy, conscientious, dainty, fastidious, finical, finicky, fussy, per(s)nickety, pitchy
PICNIC al fresco, barbecue, burgoo, cinch, clambake, cookout, ease, eat, entertainment, excursion, festival, fun, outing, snap, squantum
game baseball, horseshoes
spot bois, country, park, woods
PICOSECOND psec

PICOT edging, loop, notching, pearl, perle
PICOTAH pacota, sweep
PICRIS aralia, chicory, oxtongue, weed
PICT briton, paint, scot
PICTOGRAPH glyph, hieroglyph(ics), ideogram, ideograph
PICTORIAL graphic, journal, magazine, picturesque, publication, vivid
PICTURE abstract(ion), ancona, batik, canvas, cartoon, chalk, charcoal, chromo, collage, copy, crayon, cyclorama, daub, decal, delineate, depict, describe, description, design, diagram, diorama, doodle, draught, draw(ing), emblem, engraving, envisage, envision, epitome, etching, fresco, gouache, icon, illumination, illustration, image, landscape, likeness, limn, makimono, miniature, model, montage, mosaic, movie, mural, nude, painting, panorama, pastel, pastoral, pattern, pencil, photo(graph), pinup, portrait(ure), portray, print, profile, represent(ation), reproduction, ritratto, scene(ry), sketch, snapshot, study, tableau, tapestry, triptych, view, vignette, vision, watercolor
border frame, mat
comb. pinaco
composite collage, montage
exact sponimage
gallery (art)museum, salon
gem cameo
group album, ancona
landscape pastoral, paysage
mat spandrel
moving cinema, film, flick, movie
on glass crystograph
pert. iconic
puzzle jigsaw, rebus
religious tanka
rolled kakemono, makimono
round tondo
section gravure, roto(gravure)
small cameo, microphotograph, miniature
stand easel
stereoscope anaglyph
3-dimensioned stereograph
3-paneled triptych

transfer decal
viewer alethoscope, projector, stereoscope
wall fresco, mural
PICTURESQUE alluring, artistic, attractive, beautiful, charming, colorful, eloquent, graphic, pictorial, quaint, salient, scenic, strange, striking, vivid
PIDDLE dally, dawdle, field, pick, pightle, play, putter, toy, trifle
PIDDLING dawdling, footling, jerkwater, paltry, petty, picayune, trifling, trivial, unimportant, useless
PIE bakemeat, blackbird, chaos, clutter, cobbler, coin, compose, confusion, crustade, dessert, disarrange, disarray, disorder, dowdy, flan, flawn, heap, jumble, magpie, mess, mixture, muddle, pandowdy, past(r)y, patty, pile, quiche, snarl, tart, torta, torte, tourte, turnover
apple stuckling
chart circlegraph
cheese quiche
crust abaisse, coffin, huff, paste, shell
dish cobbler, coffin
-eyed drunk, intoxicated, smashed, soused
meat past(r)y, rissole
mutton kitcat
nanny magpie
part crust, slice, wedge
trimmer edger
with ice cream a la mode
PIEBALD calico, dappled, heterogeneous, horse, mixed, mongrel, motley, mottled, parti-colored, patched, pied, pintado, pinto, piotty, pyot, spotted, varicolored, varied, variegated
PIECE 3 bit, cob, cut, eat, eke, GUN, log 4 bone, chip, gare, hunk, item, join, lump, mend, part, pawn, role, slab, slat, snip, stub, tate, tile, tune, unit, work 5 block, chunk, crumb, dagon, drama, ivory, lunch, paper, patch, pezzo, renew, rifle, scrap, share, shred, shtik, slice, steek, stone, unite 6 cantle, castle, collop, detail, flitch, gobbet, length, member, nibble, parcel, repair, sector,

sketch, specie, wanton 7 adjunct, article, cantlet, checker, compose, counter, driblet, firearm, flinder, flitter, morceau, portion, section, segment, shtickl, snippet, trollop 8 assemble, distance, division, fortress, fraction, fragment, nearness, quantity, treatise, vignette 9 shtikeleh 10 manuscript, production, prostitute, stronghold 11 composition

all of a intact

broken brack, fraction, shard

de resistance acme, best, entree

group of 60 shock

irregular snag

large dollop, hunk, mole, stull

matched set, suite

musical See MUSICAL COMPOSITION.

of a consistent, plain, similar, simple

of eight escudo, peso, real

out assemble, cantle, complete, eke, jigsaw, supplement

pivotal sear

rotating cam, rotor, spindle, wheel

sample swatch

small bit, chip, crumb, driblet, fig, flitter, gigot, kip, morceau, morsel, patch, pea, prill, snip(pet), speck, splinter, tate

split off splint(er)

tapering gare, gore, gusset, shim, wedge

thick hunk, slab

thin flake, slat, slice

twisted curl, wisp

wedge-shaped glut, shim

PIECEMEAL bit-by-bit, inch-by-inch, in snatches, little-by-little, step-by-step

PIED bird, blotchy, dappled, foot, motley, mottled, particolored, piebald, pintado, pinto, skewbald, variegated

antelope bontebok

-a-terre apartment, flat, lodging

dishwasher wagtail

diver smew

finch bunting, chaffinch

monk bernardine, cistercian

piper of hamlin author browning

piper of hamlin charmed children, rats

wagtail cob(b), peer, pile, pillar, seedbird, waggie, washdish, washtail, waterie

widgeon garganey, golden-eye, goosander

PIEDFORD patagon

PIELUS *descendant* alexander

parent andromache, neoptolemus

PIEPLANT rhapontic, rhubarb

PIER abutment, anta, berth, breakwater, bunder, buttress, cob(b), dam, dock, gatepost, groin, haven, jetty, key, landing, mole, moor(ing), pilaster, pile, pillar, post, quai, quay, shaft, stagion, stelling, stilt, support, tilt, wall, wharf

base socle

float bridge

glass mirror

part alette, apron, pile, socle

support pile, piling

PIERCE abroach, affect, bore, broach, brob, brod, chill, cleave, cloy, comprehend, cut, dirl, discern, drill, empale, enter, ficche, gore, gouge, gride, hole, hurt, impale, lance, lancinate, pain, penetrate, perforate, pike, plow, poniard, prick, pritch, probe, puncture, rend, riddle, rit, rive, rove, skewer, smite, spear, spiculate, spike, split, stab, steek, stick, sting, stob, strike, tang, tear, thrill, thring, thrust, tunnel

PIERCE, FRANKLIN *birthplace* hillsboro, new hampshire

burial site concord, new hampshire

party democratic

profession lawyer

vice president william king

PIERCED ajoure, cribral, cribrose, perforate(d)

PIERCER auger, awl, eye, gimlet, ovipostor, stiletto, sting(er)

PIERCING acerb, acrimonious, astringent, astute, biting, bitter, bleak, brisk, caustic, cold, cutting, deafening, earsplitting, fell, high, keen, loud, nipping, penetrating, perforation, piteous, poignant, profound, pungent, raw, searching, sharp, shrill, snell, stabbing, stimulating, stinging, tart, thin, thorn(y), violent

PIERIDES See MUSES.

PIERUS *consort* clio

son hyacinthus

PIET bird, chatterbox, chattering, dipper, magpie, ouzel, pyot

PIETISM *leader* francke, spener

PIETISTIC(AL) adoring, devout, fervid, perfervid, religious, reverential, sanctimonious, venerating, worship(p)ing

PIETY ardor, belief, compassion, devotion, faith, fealty, fervor, godliness, holiness, loyalty, obedience, piousness, pity, religion, religiosity, reverence, sanctity, tartuf(f)ery, tartuf(f)ism, zeal

false sanctimony

symbolic color blue

PIEWIPE lapwing

PIFFERO fife, oboe

PIFFLE folderol, nonsense, twaddle

PIG, PIG'S aperea, bacon, bar, barrow, boar, bonav, bonham, brock, casting, cochon, cormorant, crock, cushion, dogboat, farrow, flask, gilt, glutton, gourmandizer, grice, grumphy, gussie, ham, hog, ingot, jar, litter, mold, omnivore, pitcher, policeman, pork(er), porkin, pot, pressman, roadhog, shoat, shote, sixpence, slattern, sled, slob, sow, stoolpigeon, sucker, swine, weaner

bed See PIG sty.

-boat submarine, u-boat

breed duroc

brood litter, team

bush boschvark

call sooey

comb. choerus

deer babiroussa, babirus(s)a

8 fodder

eye trillium

fat axunge, lard

feed swill

feet crubeen, pettitoes, souse

female gilt, sow

fish grunt, sailor's-choice, wrasse

flesh bacon, ham, pork

flower groundsel
foot fish, scorpaena, trotter
group farrow, fodder, litter, swine, team
guinea See GUINEA *pig.*
iron grundy
iron ballast kentledge
iron, 8 fodder
latin See ARGOT.
lead fother
-like suiform, suiline
-like animal aardvark, peccary
litter far(row)
male barrow, boar, hog
metal bar, ingot
nut black walnut, carya, hickory, hognut, jojoba
pen See PIG *sty.*
pert. porcine
potato cowbane, groundnut
rat bandicoot
red duroc
smallest of litter anothony, dilling, tantany, titman
sound oink, wee
stomach jaudie
sty hoggery, hovel, mess, piggery, poke, reeve, slum, swinecote, swinehull, swinery
suckling roaster
symbol of dirt, greed, obstinacy
tail braid, candle, cleavers, coleta, cue, plait, queue, rope
-tailed macaque bruh, macaco
trotter crubeen
wild boar, javelina, peccary
yoke quadrant, sextant
young bonav, boneen, bonham, farrow, gilt, grice, gruntling, gurry, piggie, piggy, piglet, runt, shoat, shote, slip, snork, squeaker, teatman

PIGEON (See also *kind,* below.) bird, cheat, coward, deceive, dove, dupe, fleece, girl, gull, kuku, paloma, pidgin, pluck, squeaker, sucker, sweetheart, taube
-berry buckthorn, coffeeberry, dogwood, elder, juneberry, pokeweed
blood garnet, red
blue coracina, cuckoo-shrike
brown bister
call coo
carrier homer, horseman, scandaroon

clay gyro(pigeon), skeet, target
crowned goura
domestic baldhead, barb, nun, pouter, ruff, runt, satinette, trumpeter
dwarfed runt
extinct dodo
fancy jacobin
food saltcat
french gombo
frilled satinette
fruit kuku, lupe, treron
genus columba, goura, macrophygia, zenaida
grass bristlegrass, crabgrass, foxtail
hawk falcon, merlin
-hearted chickenhearted, cowardly, timid
homing scandaroon
house aviary, columbary, cote, dovecote, rook(ery)
kind antwerp, baldhead, bandtailed, barb, bleedingheart, blue, bronzewing, brushwing, capuchin, carneau, carrier, crowned, cushat, dodlet, dove, fantail(ed), finikin(g), frillback, fruit, goura, homer, homing, horntail, isabel, jacobin, kuku, lupe, magpie, maltese, manuma, manutagi, maumet, mourningdove, nun, partridge, passenger, pintado, piper, pouter, priest, ringdove, rock, roller, ruff, squabbler, squatter, tippler, toothbill, treron, trumpeter, tumbler, turbit, turner, turtledove, wonga
-like columboid
-livered gentle, meek, mild, timid
long-tailed cuckoo-dove, namaqua
man messenger
pea angola, arhar, cajan(us), catjang, dahll, dal, gandul, seed, tare, tur(ner)
pert. columboid, peristeronic
pouter cropper
shooting skeet
short-beaked barb(ed)
squab squealer
stool nark, pig, singer, spy
symbol of cowardice
tooth-billed didunculus, dodlet
tumbler roller
wild bandtailed
wood kuku
woodpecker flicker

young piper, squealer
PIGEONHOLE analyse, arrange, assort, box, cache, cellule, classify, compartment, corner, cubbyhole, cubicle, defer, delay, file, ignore, label, list, lose, niche, order, organize, recess, shelf, shelve, slot, sort, store, stow, systematize, table
PIGGIN dipper, handy, pail, pipkin, tub
PIGHEADED contrary, contumacious, determined, dogged, headstrong, mulish, obdurate, obstinate, pertinacious, perverse, recalcitrant, refractory, stiffnecked, stubborn, willful
PIGMENT (See also DYE.) color(ing), dye(stuff), imbue, paint, stain, tincture, tint
black abaiser, aspergillin, charcoal, india ink, melanin, sepia, tar, veriter
blood hemoglobin
blue azurite, bice, bilicyanin, biliverdin, ceruleum, cholecyanin, cyanin, iolite, marennin, phaeophytin, pyocyanin, smalt, ultramarine, verditer
blue-green leucocyan
board palette
brown asterin, bilifuscin, bister, bistre, burnt ocher, fuscin, melanin, mummy, sepia, sienna, umber
brownish-yellow sienna
calico printing canarin(e)
carotinoid arumin
coal tar aniline
colorless extender
copper borate bolley's green
crinoid antedonin
crystalline cyanin
cuttlefish sepia
dark melanin
earth ocher, umber
green bice, biliprasin, biliverdin, verditer, veriter
hollyhock alth(a)ein
inert talc
kind aniline, massicot, rubiate
lack achromia, albinism, alphosis, tacheture
lead ceruse, cerussite, massicot
madder-root alizarin(e), rubiate
on canvas impasto
orange realgar

oyster marennin
pepper capsumin
poisonous naples-yellow
red actiniochrome, alizarin, amatito, arumin, bilirubin, cappa(g)h, carmine, carotene, carotin(oid), chica, haem, hematin, heme, kokowai, lake, madder, patise, puccoon, realgar, rosemallow, russian calf, sandyx, scarlet, sinopia, turacin, urorubin, urrhodin, vermilion
water-soluble anthocyanidin, cyanidin, pelargonidin
white anatase, baryta, blancfixe, ceruse, lead, lithopone
woodwork kokowai
yellow anthochlor, anthoxanthin, aureolin, carotinoid, diatomin, etiolin, fisetin, flavin, galangin, gamboge, gentisin, giallolino, ocher, orpiment, phthiocoll, phylloxanthin, retinene, uranidine, urobilin
yellow-brown sienna
PIGMENTATION color, jaundice, lentigo, lentil
PIGMY See PYGMY.
PIGNUS lien, pawn, pledge
PIGROOT blue-eyed grass
PIGSCONCE pighead
PIGSKIN football, glove, saddle, sphere
PIGSTICKER butcher, pocketknife, sled, sword
PIGWASH hogwash, swill
PIGWEED amaranth(us), beetroot, careless, chenopodium, frostblite, goatfoot, goosefoot, herb, quinoa
PIGWIGGEN dwarf, elf
PIKA cony, hare, lagomorph, leporid, ochotona, rodent
PIKE barracuda, beacon, begone, bet, cairn, cock, dive, dore, esox, farmer, fid, fish, gade, gamble, ged(d), gore, hayfork, haystack, highway, hilltop, jack(knife), jag, javelin, lucy, mountain, muskellunge, peak, pick(ax), pickerel, pierce, pitchfork, point, pole, poulaine, pricket, road, rod, sarissa, sauger, shaft, shirk, spear, spike, spine, squawfish, staff, tang, thorn, thrust, tong, tower, tuck, vouge, walleye, weapon
-like fish arapaima, blowfish,

glasseye, jackfish, luce(t), robalo, sauger
perch brasse, dore, dory, percid, sander, sauger, walleye, zander
squirrel chinchilla
walleyed dore, dory
PIKEMAN miner, soldier, wattleboy
PIKER cheapskate, coward, gambler, quitter, shirker, smallbore, speculator, telltale, thief, third-rater, tightwad, tinhorn, tramp, vagabond, vagrant
PIKESTAFF stave, walkingstick
PILASTER a(i)lette, anta, canton, column, fust, pier, pillar, ridge, telamon, tower
PILATE *prisoner released by* barabbas
prisoner condemned jesus
wife claudia, justicia, procla
PILCH filch, pad, pick, pilfer, pluck, saddle
PILCHARD alewife, fumado, herring, menhaden, sardine, sardinella, sprat
PILE accumulate, amass, assemble, awn, bale, bank, battery, beam, beard, bing, blade, brash, breakwater, building, bulk, burr, cache, canch, cock, collect(ion), cop, dart, dass, dess, down, edifice, fabric, fagot, fiber, fill, fortune, fur, gather, glume, grain, hack, hair, heap, hoard, hot(t), javelin, leaf, load, lot, mass, money, mound, mow, nail, nap, pack, pelage, pier, pillar, pole, post, quantity, rick, ruck(le), sess, shaft, shag, shock, spike, spile, spindle, spine, stack, stake, stilt, store, structure, timber, tower
arranged in cocked, stacked
body barrel
driver beetle, fistuca, gin, hercules, impacter, oliver, ram, tup
driver's dolly follower
driver's weight monkey, ram, tup
funeral mound, pyre
hay cock, doodle, rick, shock, stack
it on exaggerate, overdo
little hot(t)
loose rickle
of bones regina
of logs cord, deck

of sheaves sess
rubbish dump
small canch, cock
up accident, accumulate, amass, coacervate, crash, exaggerate, gather, hoard, increase, mass, misfortune, save, store
PILEWORT celandine, crain, crane, ficaria, ficary, figwort, fireweed, prince's-feather
fiber adad
PILFER cabbage, cop, crib, filch, finger, grab, hook, loot, manavel, pelf, pinch, plunder, purloin, rifle, rob, scrounge, seize, slock, snatch, sneak, snitch, STEAL, swipe, take
PILGARLIC wretch
PILGRIM caravanist, crusader, hadji, journeyer, migrant, migrator, monk, palmer, pelerin, peregrinator, peregrine, pioneer, traveler, wanderer, wayfarer
bottle ampulla, costrel
garb ihram
holy land palmer
leader bradshaw, brewster
monument site plymouth rock, provincetown
saint alexius
settler alden, brewster
ship mayflower, speedwell
staff cane, courdon
PILGRIMAGE crusade, excursion, expedition, hadj, journey, quest, tour, trip, voyage
shrine assisi, canterbury, cologne, compostella, genetsano, guadalupe, loretto, lourdes, montserrat, oetting, puy, rome, st denis, trier, walsingham, zell
PILGRIM'S PROGRESS *author* bunyan
character apollyon, christian(a), faithful, greatheart, hopeful, interpreter, matthew, mercy, pliable, timorous, worldly-wiseman
fiend apollyon
giant despair, grim, maul
goal celestial city
place beulah, delectable mountains, house beautiful, slough of despond, vanity fair
PILL ball, baseball, blackball, bolus, capsule, cigarette,

creek, decorticate, despoil, dope, dose, extort, goli, goofball, granule, impoverish, jerk, lozenge, medicine, pare, parvule, peel, pellet, pillage, pilula, pilule, pitcher, placebo, pluck, plunder, pool, remedy, rind, rob, shell, skin, strip, tablet, tear, troche
aromatic cachou
beetle byrrhus
headache aspirin
inert ingredient excipient
pep See DRUG and NARCOTIC.
pert. pilular
phoney placebo
small parvule

PILLAGE appropriate, booty, confiscate, depredate, depredation, despoil, devastate, direption, expilate, flay, fleece, forage, foraging, foray, gut, harry, invade, loot (ing), maraud(ing), pickeer, plunder, prey, prize, raid, ransack, rape, rapine, ravage(ment), raven, ravish, razzia, reave, rifle, rifling, rob(bery), sack(ing), spoil, spoliate, spoliation, steal, strip, swag, sweep, theft, usurp, waste

PILLAGER freebóoter, peeler, plunderer, predator, robber, sacker, snapchance
band skinners
of rome alaric

PILLAR arcade, atlas, beam, bedpost, bilith, caryatid, colonnette, columella, column, cylinder, herma, jamb, massebah, memorial, newel, obelisk, osiride, pedestal, peristyle, personage, pier, pilaster, pilastrade, pile, portico, post, prop, protector, pylon, shaft, stanchion, stela, stele, support, totem-pole, tower
capital chapiter
carved stela, stele, totempole
changed to olenus
coal spurn, stook, stoop
comb. stylo
doorway trumeau
earth hoodoo
engaged respond
figured osiride
figure for telamon
4-sided obelisk
group crura

head-surmounting hermes
-like stelar
mine stook, stump
of society paragon
quadrilateral gaine
sacred asherah
saint stylite
series of colonnade, peristyle, portico
slab-capped bilith
stone cippus, cornerstone, memorial, monument, needle, obelisk, shaft, stela, stele
tapering obelisk
temporary deadman
top chapiter, pommel, wreath
without astyler

PILLARIST monk, recluse, stylite

PILLARS atlantes
of hercules abila, calpe, gibraltar
of islam din, ibadat

PILLBOX brougham, cap, emplacement, fort(ification), hat, inro, obstacle, scatula, shelter, stronghold

PILLBUG armadillid, cheeselip, isopod, keeslip, milliped, woodlouse

PILLED bald, bare, barked, beggarly, decorticated, meager, mean, peeled, pillaged, poor, shaven, threadbare, tonsured, wretched

PILLION cap, cushion, pad, saddle

PILLORY brand, cangue, crucify, frame, halsfang, jougs, juggs, punish, ridicule, stock, stretchneck, thew, trone, yoke

PILLOW bedding, bolster, cod, cushion, float, fustian, oreiller, pad, pillion, softening, support, wanger
case or *cover* bere, flanerie, linen, pilliver, sham, slip, tye
cup nightcap
stuffing dacron, down, eider, feathers, kapok

PILLWORT pilularia

PILON bonus, gift, gratuity, lagn(i)appe, present

PILOSE hairy

PILOT ace, airman, burner, captain, cicerone, cond, conduct, conn, control, cowcatcher, coxswain, crewman, direct(or), driver, engineer, fly(er), guide, handle, head, helm(sman), herd,

lead(er), manage, manipulate, operate, operator, palinurus, preacher, run, safeguard, shepherd, solo, steer (sman), thamus, wheelsman, wingman
bird plover
biscuit hardtack
boat pontin
coat pea-jacket
computer airlog
fish amberfish, jackfish, mackerel, remora, romero, seriola, whitefish
grounded kiwi
snake copperhead
speaking tube gosport
whale blackfish

PILOTWEED compassplant, rosinweed, silphium

PILPUL argument, disputation, investigation

PILUM javelin, pestle

PIMA *indian* cahita, cora, eudeve, jova, mayo, nevome, opata, ova, papago, xova, yaqui

PIMENTO, PIMIENTO allspice(tree), bayberry, myrtle, paprika, pepper(tree), schinus, vermilion

PIMLICO cloth, fabric, friarbird, glass, shearwater

PIMP bawd, bully, cadet, fagot, fontionnaire, informer, kindling, mackerel, macrio, maquereau, pander(er), peachum, procurer, ruffian, scoundrel, sneak, stoolpigeon, whiteslaver

PIMPERNEL anagallis, burnet, chaffweed, eyebright, mad-dog-skullcap, poterium, prunella, sanguisorba, selfheal, speedwell, waywort, wincopipe
scarlet margeline
yellow taenidia

PIMPINELLA anise, aniseed, anisum, licorice

PIMPING insignificant, paltry, petty, puny, sickly, weak

PIMPLE beal, bladder, blob, boil, bubukle, bump, burble, burl, carbuncle, elevation, eruption, fester, flaw, hickey, lesion, papule, plouk, pluke, pustule, quat, spot, sty, swelling, tetter, tumor, wheyworm

PIMPLEBACK mussel, quadrula, wartyback

PIN acus(ector), affix, apex,

attach, axle, badge, bobbin, bolt, broach, brooch, caligo, callus, center, clasp, coag, coak, confine, cotter, curler, dowel, enclose, fasten, feather, fibula, fid, fine, fix, forelock, gudgeon, handle, hobb, hold, jewel, join, kayle, knot, latch, lill, linchpin, nail, needle, nog, obstruction, ornament, peen, peg, pen, piece, pinnacle, pintle, point, preen, rivet, secure, skewer, skittle, small, spill, spil(l)ikin, spindle, stake, stud, tampion, thole, tige, toggle, transfix, trifle, tumbler

belaying bit, bollard, cleat, kevel

blocks dowel, nog

bowling duckpin, headpin, kingpin, sleeper

case poppet

clover alfilaria

coupling drawbolt

culinary skewer

cushion everlasting, guelderrose, scabious

grass alfilaria, erodium

hair barrette

headed rivot

hook horse trainer, yearling trainer

jackstraw spilikin

jane curds and whey

machine cotter

main kingbolt

meat-fastening skewer

metal piton

money allowance, cash

nautical fid

oar thole

on attach, attribute, charge

ornamental a(i)glet(te), broach, cameo

pillow pimplo

pivot pintle

plant tacca

prick annoyance, irritation

rifle tige

small lill, minikin, peg

split cotter, forelock

tapered drift

tirling risp

weed alfilaria, lechea

wooden coag, coak, dowel, fid, nog, peg, spile, thole, trenail

wrench spanner, spanule

PINABEL *friend* ganelon

PINACOTHECA See MUSEUM.

PINAFORE apron, daidly, ga-

berdine, girl, saveall, slip (per), smock, sundress, tidy, tier, tyer

character hebe

PINAX catalogue, dish, picture, plaque, scheme, table(t)

PINBALL bagatelle, flipper

machine pachinko

machine site pachinko parlor

PINCE-NEZ eyeglasses, glasses, lorgnon, nosepinch, specs, spectacles

PINCERS caliper, chela, forceps, forcipate, mullets, nippers, pliers, tenail(le), tew, tongs, tuarn, tweezers

PINCH afflict, apprehend, arrest, bit, cabbage, clutch, compress, confine, constrict, cop, cramp, crib, crimp, crisis, crux, dash, difficulty, drop, emergency, extort, fix, gripe, hardship, hinch, iota, kvetch(er), lift, limit, nab, nip, pain, pang, pass, pilfer, plight, predicament, press(ure), pugil, purloin, rob, scrimp, scrinch, shortage, snape, snitch, snuff, splash, splatter, squat, squeeze, STEAL, stint, strain, strait(s), stress, swipe, theft, tuck, tweak, twinge, vellicate

-back coat, miser, niggard

bar lever, pry

bug stag-beetle

cock clamp

hitter alternate, double, replacement, stand-in, substitute, supplanter, supply, understudy

PINCHBECK alloy, cheap, counterfeit, fake, false, pretended, sham, spurious

PINCHED arrested, careworn, chitty, compressed, contracted, distressed, drawn, gaunt, haggard, poor, scrawny, skinny, squeezed, starved, stolen, straitened, underfed, urled, wasted, worn

PINCHING cold, distressing, griping, miserly, narrowing, nipping

PINCHPENNY carl, MISER, niggard(ly), stingy, tightwad

PINDARIC alexandrine, irregular, ode, unrestrained, verse

PINDARUS *master* cassius

PINDLING delicate, frail, little, peevish, petty, puny, sickly, small

PINE (See also *kind*, below.) ache, afflict, agonize, conifer, consume, covet, crave, cry, deal, desire, difficulty, droop, dwindle, enervate, evergreen, exhaust, fade, fail, flag, fret, grieve, hanker, hone, hunger, lament, languish, long(ing), mourn, pain, punishment, saddle, shrink, sorrow, starve, suffer (ing), thirst, torment, torture, trouble, want, waste, weaken, wither, woe, wood, yearn

away droop, dwine, snurp, wanze, winder

bark aphid aldeges, chermes, phylloxera

beverage pina

black callitris, camphorwood, corsican, jack, jeffrey, loblolly, lodgepole, matai, podocarpus, rimu

blue lim

board deal

casagha beefwood, casuarina

celery-topped tanekaha

cheer chil, chir

cone clog, strobile

disease blister-rust

exudation resin, rosin

family pinaceae

finch siskin

fremont's pinon

fruit cone

fruit-like conic

genus abies, araucaria, callitris, larix, libocedrus, podocarpus

ground foxtail

grove pinetum

gum sandarac

kind aleppo, balfours, balsam, beefwood, camphorwood, casagha, cedar, cheer, chil, chir, cypress, fir, foxtail, georgia, gray-leaf, hala, hemlock, huon, imou, jack, jeffrey, kauri, kaury, larch, loblolly, lodgepole, matsu, northern, norwegian, ocote, pandan, parana, pinon, pitch, red, rimu, sabine, screw, slash, soledad, spruce, table-mountain, torrey, totara, vaco(u)a, white

jeffrey blackbark, bull, jack, loblolly, lodgepole, ponderosa

knot dovekie

leaf needle
lodgepole tamarack
mahogany totara
marten sable
mouse vole
needle alfilaria, shat, spill, twinkles
pert. warryn
pitch thyme
plant bromeliaci
product resin, rosin, tar, turpentine
red rimu
sap bino, hypopit(h)ys, monotropa
screw hala
scrub shorts(c)hat
seed pignon
shore hackmetack
siskin finch
slash loblolly
snake bull snake, constrictor, gopher snake, pituophis
soledad torrey
sugar pinitol
tar retene
textile screw ara, pandan
tree See PINE *kind*, TREE *evergreen*.
tree, changed to pitys
tree state idaho, maine, montana, new mexico
tulip pipsissewa
wood candlewood
PINEAPPLE abacaxi, ananas, bomb, decoration, grenade, nana, ornament, pina, pinguin, pita, puya
disease blackeye, tangleroot
family bromeliaceae
island hawaii, lanai
segment pip
weed marigold
PINFEATHER pen, plume, stipule, stump
PINFISH chub, diplodus, jimmy, porgy, sailor's-choice, sargo, spot, stickleback
PINFOLD confine, enclose, faction, JAIL, pound
PING knock, prick, push, strike, urge
pong paddle bat
PINGLE effort, enclosure, pan, pot, strive, struggle, trifle
PINGUEFY enrich, fatten, lubricate
PINGUID adipose, bland, fat(ty), fertile, obese, oily, rich, unctuous
PINHEAD clown, dolt, dummy, fool, minnow, trifle
PINION aile, arm, battle-

ment, bind, cogwheel, confine, disable, feather, gable, gear, lantern, noil, plume, plumule, quill, restrain, shackle, wallower, wheel, wing
wheel mobile
PINK acme, adorn, agrostemma, aurore, bisque, blink, bloom, boat, carnation, caryophyllus, cherub, coat, color, condition, coral, cut, damask, deck, decorate, dianthus, diminish, drip, eyelet, fade, flower, fuschia, gleam, grayling, gulliver, health, hit, hole, incarnadine, minnow, notch, paragon, pastel, peep, penetrate, perforate, pierce, polycarpon, pounce, prick, prime, puncture, ragged robin, red, rose, rosy, salmon, scallop, scarlet, ship, shrimp, silene, small, smart, stab, strike, stylish, swell, toff, trim, tussore, vessel, wink, wound
curlew spoonbill
deep guimpe
disease corticium, rubellosis
eye conjunctivitis, duck, influenza, syndesmites
fish blind-goby
needle alfilaria
pearl azalea, hermosa
pill cure-all
poplar maiden's-blush
purplish peachblow
-root redroot, spigelia, starbloom, wormweed
vivid solferino
wild silene
wine rose
-wood wallaby-bush
PINKED jagged
PINKIE, PINKY boat, finger, pirlie, schooner, small
PINKS seconal, silene
PINKWEED knotgrass
PINNA aphlebia, auricula, auricule, bivalve, earflap, feather, fin, leaflet, mollusk, wing
PINNACE boat, launch, procuress, prostitute, ship, tender, vessel, woman
PINNACLE acme, apex, apogee, climax, crest, crown, culmination, finial, height, meridian, mountain, peak, serac, spire, summit, top, tor, tower, turret, zenith
glacial serac

rocky aiguille, gendarme, hoodoo, scar, tor
PINNIPED seal
PINNOCK bridge, conduit, culvert, drain, sparrow, titmouse
PINOCHLE goulash, marriage, penuchle, pollack, wipe-off
-like game bezique
low card nine
score dix, meld
source jass
term bete, bonus, dix, flush, flux, kitty, meld, open, roundhouse, roundtrip, widow
PINPOINT aim, exact, fix, isolate, locate, speck, trifle
PINT octarius, pinnet, swigger
1/4 gill, jack
1/2 cup, little, midget, nip (perkin), puny, small, split
9/10 mutchkin
2 quart
-size puny, pygmy, sawed-off
PINTADO bird, cero, chintz, fish, guinea-fowl, kingfish, pied, pigeon, pinto, sierra, spotted
PINTAIL cracker, duck, grouse, ladybird, longneck, piketail, smee, smew, spike, sprig
PINTLE bolt, dowel, hinge, hook, pin
PINTO bean, calico, horse, indian, mottled, piebald, pied, pintado, pony, speckled, spotted
bean rosillo
indian pakawan
PINWHEEL catherine-wheel, gear, windmill
PINWING penguin, pinion
PINWORM ascarid, nema (tode), oxyurid
infestation enterobiasis
PIONEER apostle, begin, blaze, boyscout, bushman, chalutz(im), colonist, digger, discover, earliest, emigrant, excavator, explore(r), first, forerunner, guide, halutz(im), laborer, lead, miner, nomad, open up, original, piner, preparatory, rawhider, rustic, settle(r), trailblaze(r), wood(s)man
PIOUS canting, devout, divine, dutiful, excellent, faithful, false, fervent, froom, godly, good, holy, hypocriti-

cal, loyal, orthodox, pietistic, religious, reverent(ial), sacred, sainted, saintly, sanctimonious, worthy

PIP ace, apple, beat, bit, blackball, blossom, break, cheep, chi(r)p, cough, crack, cry, defeat, degree, die, dilly, dyspepsia, echo, hit, kill, lulu, one, paip, peep, peevishness, pink, pippin, root, roup, scrap, seed, segment, speck, speed, spot, star, step

-squeak nonentity, s(c)hlemiel, shell, shlemi(e)hl, shmendrick, twerp

PIPAL bo-tree, fig, toad

PIPE (See also *kind*, below.) blare, blowtube, boiler, boom, briar, brier, bruyere, burrow, calumet, canal, candle, cane, can(n)el, cask, certainty, channel, chibouk, chibouque, chimney, cinch, conduit, corncob, cry, downcomer, downspout, drain, duct, dudeen, fife, fistula, flageolet, flue, flute, hayburner, hewgag, hooka(h), hose, hub(b), hulve, lair, lampoon, larigot, lead(er), main, meerschaum, mirliton, narg(h)ile, nargileh, note, oat, oboe, outlet, pant, pasquinade, phone, pibroch, pungi, reed, riser, scan, screech, see, sing, sough, sound, spout, stack, straw, tee, telephone, trachea, trowel, trunk, tube, tubule, tunnel, uptake, watch, weeper

angle elbow, ell, tee

bending device hickey

body barrel

bowl stummel

bowl interior heel

ceremonial calumet

clamming brail

clay camstane, camstone, churchwarden, dudeen, straw, tile

closer valve

connecting hogger

dance jig

down dismiss, quiet, shut up, silence

draw on shaugh, shooh

dream chimera, fantasy, illusion, muse

end bell, hub(b), taft

fish earl, longjaw, snacot, syrictes

flue labial

4 lengths fourble

furnace or *heating* caliduct, riser, tuyere

hole lill

joint calepin, coupling, cross, elbow, ell, nipple, tee, turnout, wye

kind bent, briar, bulldog, calabash, calumet, chillum, churchwarden, clay, freehand, hookah, meerschaum, narg(h)ile, straight grain, water, wellington

-layer politician, schemer, yarner

-laying graft, intrigue

lighter fidibus

-like tubate

line channel, grapevine

musical fife, fistula, flute, gewgaw, hornpipe, reed, schwegel, sordine

off depart, die, imitate, leave

organ (See also ORGAN.) erzahler, flute, kinura, labial, schwegel, tremolant

part bowl, ferrule, heel, shank, stem, stummel

pastoral larigot, oat, reed

peace calumet

pert. tubate

player fifer, flautist, flutist, pan, piper, shepherd

privet lilac, syringa

reed mirliton

residue dottle

-shaped fistuliform, tubular

shepherd's larigot, reed

short cutty, dudeen, nosewarmer

small tubule

smoke tewel, tuyere

snake-charmer's pungi

source briar(root), brier (wood)

spiral coil

steam riser

stem stoppel, stopple

stone catlinite

stove chimney, flue, tewel, top-hat

support cradle

terracotta bleeder

toy hewgag

tree catalpa, elder, lilac, mock-orange

vertical lamphole, stack

water calean, hookah, hubble-bubble, narg(h)ile, nargileh

wrench stillson

PIPER bird, dog, gurnard, halfbeak, pepper, pigeon, worm

dance for jig

follower children, rats

kind pied

river weser

son tom

PIPETTE baster, dropper, taster, tube

measuring stactometer

PIPEWOOD fetterbush

PIPEWORT hatpin, woolweed

PIPING cording, crying, cutting, fluting, rouleau, shrill, soft, tranquil, trimming, tubing, weeping, whistling

crow cassican, flutebird

hare pika

hot burning, novel, scalding, sizzling, torrid

PIPIRI flycatcher, kingbird

PIPISTRELLE bat, noctule

PIPIT anthus, bird, cheeper, lingbird, mosscheeper, motacilla, teetan, tietick, titlark, titling, twitlark, wagtail, wekeen

PIPPIN apple, seed

PIPSISSEWA chimaphila, evergreen, wintergreen

PIQUANCY flavor, ginger, keenness, pungency, raciness, salt, sauciness, spice, spirit, tartness, zest

PIQUANT acerb, aphoristic, appealing, appetizing, attractive, biting, bold, challenging, charming, concise, cutting, interesting, peppery, provocative, pungent, racy, salty, sharp, snappy, spicy, stimulating, stinging, taking, tangy, tart, tasty, winsome, zestful, zesty

PIQUE absorb, aggravate, agitate, anger, annoyance, arouse, attract, chafe, cut, displeasure, dive, dudgeon, entertain, enthrall, exasperate, excite, fret, goad, grudge, huff, ignite, inflame, interest, irk, irritate, irritation, kindle, nettle, offend, offense, pain, peeve, pet, plume, preen, prick, pride, pritch, provocation, provoke, punch, pyke, quarrel, quicken, resentment, rouse, spite, stimulate, sting, stir, strife, strunt, umbrage, vex (ation)

PIQUET cientos, hoc, impe-

rial, le cent, picket, ronfle, sa(u)nt, talon, tatteln
score pic
slam capot
term capot, fredon, pic, quatorze, quin, repic, rubicon, sink, tierce
PIRACY appropriation, buccaneering, capture, conveyance, freebootery, larceny, plagiarism, privateering, theft
PIRAEUS *builder* themistocles
PIRAGUA canoe, dugout, pettiagua, pirogue
PIRANHA caribe, fish, pirai, piraya, serrasalmo
PIRATE algerine, appropriate, brigand, buccaneer, corsair, filibuster, freeboot(er), hijack(er), hook, marauder, mariner, marooner, nutt, picaroon, pickeer, plagiarist, plagiarize, predator, privateer, rob(ber), rover, scummer, seadog, seawolf, steal, thief, viking
bird jaeger-gull
coast trucial-oman
famous barbarossa brothers, blackbeard, captain kidd, captain william, edward teach, henry morgan, lafitte, long john silver, pew, sir john hawkins
flag blackjack, (jolly)roger
gallows yardarm
loot booty
ship brigantine, corsair, rover, xebec
weapon snee
woman anne bonny, mary read
PIREN *kin* bellerophon, glaucus
PIRENE *changed to* fountain
consort poseidon
parent achelous, asopus
son cenchrias
spring site acrocorinth
PIRIPIRI biddybid(dy), birch, birk, herb, mapau, weed
PIRITHOUS *captor* pluto
consort deidamia, hippodamia
friend theseus
parent dia, ixion, zeus
subjects lapithae
PIRL fumble, move, purl, spin, twine, twist
PIRN bobbin, quill, reed, ring, spindle, spool, twitch, yarn

PIRO arawakan, tanoan
PIROGUE boat, canoe, perioque
PIROUETTE circle, eddy, gyrate, revolve, rotate, spin, swirl, turn, twirl, wheel, whirl
PIRR flurry, gull, gust, speed, tern, whiz, wind
PISA *cemetery* campo santo
wonder campanile, leaning tower
PISANIO *master* posthumusleonatus
PISCARY fishery
PISCATION fishing
PISCATOR angler, fisherman
PISCES fish(es)
gem jasper
PISCINA basin, bath, drain, fishpond, lavatory, pool, reservoir, sacrary, swimming pool, tank
PISCINE bath, ichthyic
appendage fin
PISGAH *summit* nebo
PISH dismiss, nonsense, reject
PISISTRATUS *consort* timonassa
enemy lycurgus, megacles
father hippocrates
son hipparchus, hippias, iophon, thessalus
PISMIRE ant, emmet, insect
PISTACHIO anacardium, fistic, green(almond), nut, pistick, witchhazel
PISTE path, print, racecourse, ring, spoor, track, trail
PISTIL chive, gynecium, pointel, umbone
part carpel, sorema, stigma, style
PISTLE epistle, story, tale
PISTOL automatic, barker, buffer, bulder, buller, colt, dag(g), derringer, dungeon, firearm, fluke, gat, gun, heater, iron, joker, luger, mauser, potgun, reporter, revolver, rod, saturday night special, shoot, shooting-iron, sidearm, tack, wag, weapon
case holster
friend bardolph, falstaff, nym
lock rowet
self-loading mannlicher
toy sparkler
PISTON disk, knob, pallet,

plug, plunger, roller, sucker, valve
hydraulic ram
PIT abaddon, abysm, abyss, alveola, arena, audience, barathron, bothros, bury, cave, cavern, cavity, chasm, core, crater, cyphella, delf(t), dell, delve, dent, depression, diggings, dint, ditch, downfall, dungeon, endocarp, excavate, excavation, faveolus, fenestra, fossa, fovea, foxhole, grave, groove, gulf, hades, hell, hole, hollow, indentation, jail, kernel, lacuna, leach, lesion, match, megaron, mine, notch, oppose, peritheceum, pock(et), pockmark, pool, puncture, raddle, scar, seed, shaft, sink, slough, sluice, snare, stone, sump, tomb, umu, variole, vat, wallow, weem, well, workings
against compare, oppose
baking imu, oven, umu
bitter stippen
bottomless abaddon, abyss, barathron, barathrum, dungeon, hades, hell
coal heuch, heugh
medical fossa
miry slough, sluig
mouth bank-head
peach putamen, seed
rifle sangar
river indian palaihnihan
roofed cist, kist
sacrificial bothros
shallow variole
small alveolus, fovea, foveola, lacuna, staple
tanning handler, layer, leach, lime, suspender
viper agkistrodon, bothrops, bushmaster, copperhead, ferde-lance, habu, lachesis, rattlesnake, snake, water-moccasin
PITA arghan, brocket, deer, fiber, flax, hemp, istle, karatas, pineapple, yucca
PITANE *daughter* evadne
PITCH accent, alchitran, alkitran, altitude, ascertain, asphalt, ballyhoo, bicker, bitumen, bowl, cant, careen, cast, decline, declivity, degree, depth, descend, descent, determine, dip, dive, drop, elevation, encamp, erect, establish, fall, fix,

fling, flounder, game, grade, hard, heave, height, hoist, hurl, incline, inflection, intonation, key, light, lob, lurch, maltha, manjak, modulation, move, oscillate, patter, pave, performance, plant, plunge, raise, rear, reel, regulate, relate, resin, rock, roll, rosin, sap, scale, scend, scope, send, set, settle, shy, sledge, sling, slope, spiel, story, sway, swing, talk, tar, tell, throw, tone, top, toss, totter, tumble, twirl, wallow, welter, yarn, yaw

above sharp

apple copei, cupay

below flat

coal lignite

coat with pay

cobbler's code

color piceous

deviation anomaly

difference in interval

full volley

game all-fives, all-fours, bunch, cinch, dom-pedro, holding, old sledge, pedro (sanchez), razzle-dazzle, sellout, set-back, seven-up

glance manjack, manjak

high alt(issimo), blooper

illegal balk

indicator clef

instrument pipe, tonometer, tuning-fork

into attack, begin, eat, start, undertake

musical tone

off discordant

pert. piceous

pine loblolly, lodgepole

pipe epitonion, tuner

symbol neume

tuning to lower anesis

unit mel

PITCHBLENDE radium, uranium

PITCHER aftaba, aiguiere, amphora, ascidium, beaker, boggle, buire, canette, carafe, container, creamer, crock, crowbar, cruet, cruiske(e)n, ewer, flask, gorge, gotch, heaver, hurler, jar, jug, marble, moundsman, oenochoe, olla, olpe, pourie, prochoos, reliefer, righthander, southpaw, stacker, stone, thrower, toby, tosser, twirler, urceole, urceus, urn, vase, vendor, vessel

bulging gotch

earthenware g(e)orge

error balk

handle ear

left-handed southpaw

lip beak

molly mary hays

motion windup

mound box, hill, slab

plant adam's cup, biscuit, cephalotus, chrysamphora, darlingtonia, eve's-cup, fevercup, flytrap, foxglove, huntsman's cup, monkeycup, nepenthe, sarracenia, skunkweed, watercup

relief fireman

-shaped ascidiform, urceolate

warm-up area bull-pen

PITCHFORK pick, pikel, pikle, sheppeck, sheppick, throw, thrust, toss

PITCHHOLE cahot, pothole, recess

PITCHMAN salesman, solicitor, vendor

PITCHPOLL flip, somersault

PITCHY black, defiling, intense, profound, wicked

PITEOUS compassionate, devout, doleful, dolorous, entreating, imploring, mean, melancholy, merciful, paltry, pious, pitiable, PITIFUL, plaintive, poignant, tender

PITFALL ambush, boobytrap, danger, decoy, difficulty, entrap, gin, lure, meshes, quicksand, snare, springe, temptation, toils, trap

PITH ambash, ambatch, center, core, distillation, essence, essential, force, gist, importance, jet, kernel, marrow, meaning, meat, medulla, nerve, nub, nucleus, papyrus, pluck, point, principle, pulp, quiddity, quintessence, sap, strength, substance, vigor

full of See PITHY.

helmet topee, topi

-like medullose

tree ambatch

PITHECANTHROPUS apeman, java-man

PITHECOLOBIUM breakaxe, cat's-claw, quebracho, sloanea, tamarind

PITHLESS weak

PITHOM *builders* israelites

pharaoh rameses

PITHON *parent* micah

PITHY aphoristic, brief, cogent, compact, concise, corky, forceful, forcible, heady, hearty, laconic, meaty, pulpy, sententious, short, significant, spongy, strong, substantial, succinct, summary, terse, vigorous

plant sola

PITIABLE cheap, contemptible, dejected, deplorable, depressed, despairing, desperate, despondent, distressing, forlorn, heart-rending, hopeless, melancholy, miserable, PITIFUL, rueful, sad, scurvy, seely, sorry, terrible, woeful, wretched

PITIFUL abject, affecting, bad, base, compassionate, contemptible, despicable, lamentable, mean, measly, meek, moving, paltry, pathetic, rueful, ruth(ful), sad, shameful, silly, sorry, tender, touching, woeful

PITILESS brutal, cruel, dispiteous, ferocious, grim, hard (hearted), implacable, inexorable, mean, merciless, relentless, revengeful, ruthless, savage, stony, unfeeling, unrelenting

PITPIT guitguit

PITSEL(EH) babe, baby, bit, infant, morsel, piece

PITTACUS *enemy* alcaeus

victim phrynon

PITTANCE allowance, alms, bit, carfare, charity, dole, donation, gift, mess, mite, modicum, ration, scant (ling), share, song, trifle

PITTED cuppy, etched, faced, foveate, foveola(te), foviate, matched, notched, opposed, pockmarked, punctate, punctured, scarred, stoned

PITTER-PATTER drum, flutter, trepidation

PITTHEUS *daughter* aethra

parent hippodamia, pelops

pupil theseus

PITTOSPORUM butterbush, laurel, mapau, tarata(h), tree

PITUITARY *dysfunction* acromegaly

product acth, tethelin

PITY charity, clemency, commiserate, commiseration, compassion, condolence, empathy, favor, feeling, forbearance, grace, grief, humanity, lament, lenience, leniency, lenity, mercy, moan, passion, pathos, quarter, regret, relent, remorse, rew, rue, ruth, shame, spare, sympathy, waesuck, yearn(ing)

PITYING clement, forbearing, humane, lenient, merciful, soft(hearted), sorry, sympathetic, tender, touched, warm

PITYS *lover* pan

PIUS XI ratti

PIVOT about-face, axis, axle, center, come about, dowel, evener, focus, fulcrum, gudgeon, heel, hinge, joint, junction, rotate, slew, slue, swing, swivel, toe, travel, traverse, trunnion, turn, veer, volte-face, wheel, wordle
  pin kingbolt, pintle
  stand pedestal

PIVOTAL cardinal, central, crucial, decisive, depending, polar

PIXIE, PIXY banshee, brownie, dwarf, elf, faery, fairy, fay, gnome, goblin, leprechaun, nix, prankish, puck, rascal, rogue, shee, sprite
  stool mushroom, toadstool

PIXILATED confused, crazy, daffy, dotty, eccentric, impish, prankish, touched

PIZARRO *ambush site* cajamarca
  brother gonzalo, hernando, juan
  captain almagro, de solo, hernando, huascar
  chronicler cieza de leon, garcilaso, xeres, zarate
  friend diego de almagro
  half-brother francisco martin de alcantara
  interpreter felipillo
  lieutenant alcon, briceno, de candia, de carrion, de cuellar, de jaren, de luque, de molina de paz, de peralty, de rivera, de soraluce
  missionary valverde
  order santiago
  secretary francisco xeres
  successor almagro
  title adulantado, alquacilmayor
  treasurer nicolas de rivera
  victim atahualpa

wife inez yupanqui

PIZE curse, oath

PIZZA fugazza, fugazzetta

PLACARD advertise(ment), affiche, announce(ment), bill, broadside, document, flyer, handbill, notice, post(er), proclamation, redline, stomacher, tag, ticket

PLACATE appease, calm, conciliate, forgive, gentle, mollify, pacify, please, propitiate, reconcile, satisfy, smooth, soothe

PLACE 3 fix, job, lay, pad, put, set 4 area, base, book, cask, cast, city, digs, dive, duty, farm, hire, home, lair, lieu, park, pose, post, rank, rest, road, role, room, seat, site, situ, spot, stop, town, vest, work, yard 5 abode, array, birth, clime, haunt, haven, house, inset, joint, locus, lodge, order, patio, platz, plaza, plotz, point, posit, scene, setup, situs, space, stand, stead, stell, stick, tract, venue, where 6 assign, assort, bestow, billet, employ, engage, ground, impose, insert, invest, locale, office, piazza, plotst, region, repose, roomth, settle, spread, square, status, street, ubiety 7 appoint, arrange, ascribe, calling, deposit, dispose, hangout, install, marshal, opening, pursuit, station, village 8 district, function, identify, locality, location, organize, position, premises, province, schedule 9 attribute, establish, homestead, situation 10 employment, occupation 11 opportunity, recognition
  again reseat, restore
  allotted assignment, berth, station
  alternately stagger
  apart enisle, isolate, segregate, separate
  at the ad loc
  before anterior, appose, confront, prefix, present
  beneath infrapose
  between insert, interpose
  boggy slump, swamp
  burial ahu, catacomb, cemetery, grave, kil(1), lair, laystall
  business office, plant, store

camping etape
  comb. age, arium, chor(o), ery, gaea, gea, orium, topo
  crosswise thwart
  distant thule, timbuktu
  enclosed hay, worth
  end for end reverse
  familiar slait
  fear of a particular topophobia
  1st supremacy, supreme, tops
  fortified castle, fastness, keep, lis(s)
  fortified, comb. boro(ugh)
  frequented dive, hangout, haunt, resort
  from which whence
  hiding cave, covert, hiddels, mew, niche, retreat, stowaway
  hollow alberca, gulf, hole, holl, scoop, sinkhole
  holy See SACRED *place.*
  imaginary never-never
  in a row align, aline
  in its original in situ
  intermediate limbo
  in the in loco
  in the 1st imprimis
  in the sun fame, glory, recognition
  last also-ran, booby prize
  lodging billet, camp, libken, logis
  lurking hulster
  market agora, forum, mart, rialto, trone
  meeting rendezvous, tryst
  name toponym
  nesting nidary
  of lieu, stead
  of action venue
  of refuge ark, asylum, bast, hideout, hold
  one inside another nest
  out of inept
  perfect heaven, paradise, utopia
  poetic clime
  quiet dell, den, nook
  rocky rocher
  rowdy bear-garden
  sacred See SACRED *place.*
  secret corner, cranny, hideaway, lair
  shady frescade, gloom, swale, umbracle, umbrage
  sheltered gite, haven, nook, scug
  side by side appose, collocate, juxtapose
  snug cosy-corner, cubby(hole), inglenook
  swampy sough

PLACEBO
3rd show
tight jam, pickle
to place, comb. loco
trial venue
worship of topolatry

PLACEBO parasite, toady, vespers

PLACEMENT allocation, appointment, assignment, attribution, classification, collocation, deposit(ion), disposition, distribution, employment, hire, installation, lading, loading, location, packing, putting, reposition, situation, storage, stowage

PLACERVILLE hangtown

PLACID bonny, calm, collected, composed, constant, cool, equable, even, gentle, halcyon, lenient, meek, mild, nonchalant, pacific, peaceful, quiet, restful, serene, smooth, steady, suant, tranquil, undisturbed, unruffled

PLACKET fent, hole, opening, petticoat, pocket, slit, spare, woman

PLAGIARISM crib(bing), piracy, plagium, stealing, theft

PLAGIARIST borrower, copyist, pirate, taker, thief

PLAGIARIZE crib, lift, pirate, purloin, steal

PLAGUE afflict(ion), annoy, badger, bait, bane, beset, blast, blight, bother, calamity, cancer, catastrophe, chafe, contagion, curse, disease, dun, epidemic, frab, fret, gall, hamper, harass, harry, hector, hound, hurt, imp, importune, infest, molest, murrain, nuisance, pain, persecute, pest(e), pester, pestilence, pursue, ride, scourge, smite, stroke, tantalize, tease, torment, trial, trouble, try, twit, weary, worry, wound
bubonic black-death
carrier flea, fly, germ, rat, virus
comb. loimo, pesti
pert. loimic

PLAICE flatfish, flounder, fluke, worm

PLAID bracken, check(ed) (ered), cloth, fabric, garment, maud, mosaic, patchwork, shawl, stole, tartan, tessellate(d)

PLAIDMAN highlander, scot

PLAIN(S) 3 dry, lea, low 4 bald, bare, bush, cama, chol, down, easy, even, fell, flat, full, mere, mesa, moor, neat, open, plat, plot, pure, ugly, vega, wold 5 attic, basin, blair, blank, bluff, blunt, broad, campo, clean, clear, corah, delta, downs, flats, flush, frank, heath, homey, level, llano, lucid, overt, pampa, playa, quiet, solid, veldt, vocal, weald 6 bemoan, bewail, candid, chaste, coarse, desert, entire, graith, homely, humble, modest, pampas, patent, salada, sebkha, simple, square, steppe, tundra, whinny 7 artless, ascetic, audible, certain, evident, expanse, express, legible, lowland, mesilla, obvious, plateau, prairie, prosaic, quamash, regular, saltpan, savanna, sincere, spartan, unmixed, visible 8 apparent, campagna, campaign, complain, complete, definite, distinct, explicit, homelike, informal, ithavoll, manifest, moorland, ordinary, palpable, piedmont, platform, plebeian, savannah, semplice, specific, straight 9 camestral, champaign, downright, dunstable, ingenuous, outspoken, primitive, simonpure, tableland, unadorned, undiluted 10 forthright, restrained, unassuming 11 campestrian, perspicuous, transparent 12 matter of fact, unmistakable 13 unembellished
alkali usar
alluvial apron, bajada, haugh
among trees laund
as a pikestaff
barren llano
dealing candor
depression swale
-dweller llanero, pedionomite
elevated mesa, plateau, tableland
goddess maia, majesta
grassy camas(s), quamash, savanna(h)
indian algonquian, arapaho(e), arikara, assiniboine, athapascan, caddo, cheyenne, comanche, cree, creek, dakota, fox, hidatsa, iowa, kaw, kickapoo, kiowa, mandan, omaha, oneida, oto(e), ottawa, pawnee, ponca, potawatomi, sac, sauk, shawnee, sioux, teton, yankton
low-lying macha(i)r
marshy blair
people amish, dunkers, mennonites
salt flats, salada, sebk(h)a
sloping conoplain, cuesta, hope
song cantus firmus, ground, melisma
-spoken blunt, unreserved
stone flagstone, paving
treeless llano, pampas, prairie, savanna(h), steppe, tundra
wanderer plover-quail

PLAINCLOTHESMAN detective, flycop, split, spy, stool

PLAINLY broadly, commonly, de plano, directly, frankly, naturally, ordinarily, point-blank, prosaically, simply, unaffectedly

PLAINSMAN llanero

PLAINT complaint, lament, wail

PLAINTIFF accusant, accuser, appellant, claimant, complainant, complainer, delator, demandant, dolente, incriminator, indicter, indictor, informer, libelant, litigant, prosecutor, querent, suer, suitor

PLAINTIVE complaining, cross, crying, discontented, doleful, doloroso, dolorous, elegiac, fretful, lamentive, lugubrious, mangendo, melancholy, moanful, mournful, peevish, pensive, pettish, petulant, piteous, pitiful, puling, querulous, repining, rueful, sad, sorrowful, thoughtful, ululant, wailful, whimpering, whining, whiny, wistful, woeful

PLAIT basketweave, braid, brede, coil, complect, crease, crimp, cue, fetch, fitch, fold, frounce, gather, goffer, hoy, interweave, knit, lamina, mat, mesh, pigtail, plat, pleat, plex, plicate, plication, ply, queue, quill, quirk, raddle, ravel, ruff, rumple, scallom, trace, tuscan, twist, wattle, weave, wimple, writhe

series kilting
straw milan, trace
PLAITED artful, braided, browden, corrugated, devious, folded, interwoven, involved, kilted, knitted, plicate, plisse
PLAN agenda, agendum, aim, architecture, arrange-(ment), block(out), blueprint, brew, brief, budget, cabal, calculate, card, cast, chart, cogitate, concept(ion), conspiracy, conspire, contemplate, contrivance, contrive, coup, deal, decoct, delineate, delineation, design, device, devise, diagram, disposition, draft, draught, draw(ing), drift, ebauche, epure, ettle, figure, forecast, form, frame, graph, hang, idea, image, intend, intent(ion), intrigue, itinerary, layout, line up, maneuver, map, meditate, method, model, module, notion, outline, pattern, plat, plot, policy, prearrange, premeditate, prepare, procedure, profile, program, proje(c)t, proposal, propose, proposition, prospectus, purpose, racket, rough, schema, scheme, set up, shape, skeleton, sketch, strategy, system, theory, way
ahead anticipate, forecast
architectural blueprint, epure
5-year piatiletka
insubstantial house of cards
together concert, cooperate
without aimless, casual
PLANCHER bed, board, ceiling, floor, pallet, plank(ing), platform, slab, soffit
PLANCHETTE automatograph, circumferentor, plank
PLANE aequor, AIRCRAFT, beader, courier, even, explain, face, facet, flat, flush, glide, grade, horizontal, level, levitate, ply, shave, smooth, snibel, soar, surface, tool, traverse, tree, trowel, unwrinkled
block stock
boundary perimeter
chart mercator
curve ellipse
handle toat, tote
inclined chute, ramp, shute, slide, slip

iron bit, blade
kind bench, block, grooving, iron, jack, router, tonguing
median meson
molding holl(ow), houle
on same coplanar
perspective table
point cone
sloping cuesta
tree buttonbush, buttonwood, cheenar, chinar, cotonier, plantain, platan(us), sycamore
tree fruit monkeyball
PLANER *tree* hornbeam, sycamore, zelkova
PLANET almuten, asteroid, earth, globe, jupiter, mars, mercury, moon, neptune, pluto, saturn, sphere, star, terrella, terrene, uranus, venus, world
aspect biquintile, cusp, decil(e), trine
between intercosmic
brightest venus
conjunction alictisal
course orbit
death-dealing anareta
hypothetical vulcan
influence atazir, hyleg
malevolent anareta, infortune
minor asteroid
nativity-influencing almuten
newest pluto
orbit ellipse
orbit point apastron, aphelion, apogee, apojove, apop, apsis, auge, nadir, node, perigee, syzygy, zenith
position alichel, alictisal, aspect
red mars
relation conjunction, opposition, sextile, trine
relative position orrery
ringed saturn
ruling dominator
-ruling period alfridary
satellite moon
science of astrogeology
shadow umbra
small asteroid, iris, terrella
-stricken siderated
-sun representation orrery, planetarium
treatise planetography
PLANETARIUM eidouranion, observatory, orrery
PLANETARY astrologer, earthly, erratic, terrestrial, wandering, worldwide
PLANGENT clangorous, me-

tallic, plaintive, reverberating, thrilling
PLANISPHERE astrolabe, meteorscope
PLANK article, bend, board, brattice, chess, claim, clapboard, clause, deck, face, flitch, forepole, garboard, gravestone, lumber, madrier, patta, pay, pole, post, ribband, sag, shide, shole, shore, slab, slam, slate, splice, stealer, stone, stringer, stud, swale, theal, ticket, timber, two-by-four
breadth strake
curved sny(ing)
down advance, ante, deposit, pay, shell out
drag rubber
end butt, stub
facing campshedding, campshot
PLANKING brattice, ceiling, garboard, hatch, lagging, swale, waterway
ship strake
PLANKTON alga, diatom, krill, organism, protozoa
collector d-net
PLANT affix, agency, annual, attach, bios, bolt, broadcast, bury, bush, cannery, colonize, company, conceal, concern, corporation, crop, cutting, decoy, deposit, desert, detective, dibble, drill, engender, establish(ment), factory, firm, fix, flower, forge, gasworks, herb, hide, hoax, insert, install, inter, introduce, lodge, manufactory, mill, packinghouse, place, plot, populate, pose, position, pottery, provide, put, raise, refinery, sapling, scheme, secrete, seed, seminate, set(tle), shop, shrub, slip, sow, spy, station, stock, store, swindle, transplant, tree, vegetable, vine, workshop
abnormal ecad
acid-juice knotweed, nettle, ribes, smartweed
aconite bikh
ailment chlorosis
air-directed aerotropic
air pore stoma
alismaceous alismad
alliaceous chive, garlic, leek, onion, scallion, shallot
alternate-leaved allogophyllous

ammoniac oshac
ancestor ortet
and animal life biota
-animal zoophyte
annual mousetail
apiaceous ache, anise, cumin
appendage ascidium, awn, stipule
aquatic aldrovanda, alga, alisma, aquatile, arrowhead, awlwort, bilder, brasenia, callitriche, castally, duckweed, frog(s)bit, glyceria, hydrophyte, isoetes, laceleaf, limi, lotus, nelumbo, nitella, nuphar, nymphaea, pickerelweed, pondlily, pondweed, sagittaria, saltwort, spatterdock, starfruit, starwort, sudd, trapa, tule, utricularia, waterlily
araceous or aromatic abrotanum, albahaca, angelica, anise, anthurium, arum, cabbage, caladium, carum, clary, dill, dittany, lavender, lily, mint, nard, nondo, nutmeg, ocimum, sage, southernwood, spikenard, tansy, tarragon, waterlily
arrowhead wapatoo
astringent alder, avens, matico, sumac
axis stalk, stem, trunk
base alkaloid, caudex
bayonet datil
bearing once monocarp
benthonic enalid
bignoniaceous catalpa
bitter colicroot, ers, rue, tansy, vetch
blue-blossomed ageratum, cornflower, lupine
body cormus
bog abama, narthecium
boraginaceous borage, bugloss, forget-me-not, heliotrope, puccoon
bramble briar, brier, furze, gorse, wait-a-bit, zilla
branched bush, shrub, tree
brassicaceous candytuft, cole, iberis, kale, mustard, radish, rape, turnip, watercress
breathing organ stoma(ta)
bristly cactus, teasel
bromeliaceous pineapple, pinguin
bruise-healing daisy, soapwort
bryophitic moss
bulbous allium, amaryllis, antholyza, camas(s), cam-

mas, chive, daffodil, galtonia, garlic, jonquil, leek, lily, narcissus, nerine, onion, quamash, royal-crown, sego, shallot, tritonia, tuberose, tulip
calyx-lacking achlamydeous
capsule boll, pod, silique
carnivorous bladderwort, dionaea, drosera, heliamphora, pitcher plant, venus' flytrap
cast-iron aspidistra
castor oil palmcrist, ricinus
caustic moxa
celery-like alexanders, udo
cell gamete
cereal pigweed
chlorophyll-lacking albino
chlorophyll rich alga
climbing bine, bryony, creeper, ivy, lawyer, liana, liane, morning-glory, philodendron, ulluco, vetch, vine
clover-like calomba, medic
cluster cyme
coiling organ tendril
cold-thriving psychrophyte
color chlorophyll, endochrome, kaempferol
comb. botano, phyto
composite ageratum, artemisia, aster, coreopsis, cornflower, cosmos, hawkweed, ragweed, ragwort, rosinweed, succory, tansy, tarweed, thistle, tidytips
composite feature floret
cone strobil(e)
cone-bearing brachyphyllum, conifer
consecrated haoma
covering bark, velumen
creeping ipecac, kareao, kareau
crossbred hybrid
cross-fertilization allogamy
cruciferous alga, alyssum, awlwort, cabbage, fern, moss, rockcress, rutabaga, turnip, wall-rocket, wasabi
cryptogamous alga, fern, moss
cultivation in liquid hydroponics
cuticle cutin
cutting phyton, slip
cyperaceous sedge
decay wet-rot
decorative bush, fern, flower, ivy, shrub
deeply heel
desert agave, alhagi, brittlebush, cactus, candle-

wood, ephedra, ocotillo, xerophyte, yucca
developing upward acropetal
dicotyledonous apetala, exogen, geranium, papaverales
dipsacus teasel
disease anthracnose, aucuba, bacteriosis, blackheart, blackstem, blast, blight, blister, blotch, blueing, brindle, brunissure, bunt, cabbage-top, calico, canker, clubroot, coleur, crownwart, drop, edema, ergot, erinose, fen, fireblight, flock, frogeye, fruitspot, fungus, gall, gout, kermes, knot, mold, peteca, pox, rot, rust, scab, scald, scale, scurf, smudge, smut, speck, spike, stemrot, stenosis, stigmonose, timber-rot, tipburn, tukra, twist, walloon, wilt
dried hortus-siccus
dye-yielding angolaweed, archil, henna, kamala, orselle, wad(e), weld, woad, woald, would, wurras, wurrus
edible (See also VEGETABLE *kind*.) 3 cos, dal, fei, hoi, nep, oca, rye, soy, ube, urd, wot 4 aipi, anay, anet, anta, arum, baga, baho, bene, bigg, biwa, bole, bosc, buyo, cane, cepa, chit, chow, corn, coyo, dhal, dill, eddo, eker, fard, fuji, gean, gobo, guar, hevi, ikmo, jobo, kers, lint, mani, meum, nape, neep, olax, paga, pasa, peco, pepo, ragi, sith, skeg, sloe, sorb, tare, teff, yamp, yuca 5 adlai, ahava, anise, arzun, avena, badam, bahoo, bendy, benny, betel, bichy, broma, camas, carum, chaya, choco, cibol, clary, cubeb, dholl, doora, emmer, eruca, fardh, gourd, gubbo, haver, jaman, jawar, kafir, loofa, maize, mebos, morel, nogal, ochro, oopak, osage, paddy, pagle, pangi, pulse, ragee, sitao, spelt, sprue, swede, tonka, tulsi, wheat, yampa, yucca 6 aralia, atimon, barley, batata, borage, cereal, citron, colane, durian, dushaw, garlic, goober, hyssop, kanari, legume, peanut,

pomelo, rennet, salvia 7 chervil, chicory, collard, oxheart, pommelo, popcorn, potherb, ricinus, tapioca, tarragon
embryo plantule
enzyme cytase, cytochrome, myrosine
epiphytic imbe, tillandsia
ericaceous azalea, cardinal, cranberry, kurume, minerva, rhododendron
etiolated albino
euphorbiaceous castor-oil, poinsettia, spurge
everlasting immortelle, orpine, strawflower
exudate gum, latex, milk, resin, rosin, sap
fabaceous axseed, baby's-slipper, butter-jag, coronilla, ers, pea, vetch
fernlike filicoid
fertilization porogamy
fertilization agent pollen
fiber aloe, caraguata, ehuawa, hemp, istle, ixtle, jute, pita, ramie, sida, sisal
firmly brace
floating frogbit, lotus, sudd, waterlily
flowering (See also FLOWER.) acanthus, ageratum, angiosperm, arum, avens, azalea, bar(r)eta, calla, candytuft, canna, comos, coreopsis, damewort, gentian, geranium, gerardia, gloxinias, goldenrod, hollyhock, lobelia, marigold, monkshood, orpin, oxalis, pavonia, petunia, phlox, pulsatilla, rhodora, rose, snapdragon, spir(a)ea, tamarix, teasel, torenia, valerian, yucca, zamia
flowerless acrogen, fern, lichen, moss, thalogen
fodder amil, vetch
forage alfalfa, clover, daincha, guar, rape, sorghum, sweet clover, trifolium
forgetfulness-causing lotus
fossil annularia, aptiana, calamite, dendrolite, gristhorpia, jeanpaulia
funereal amaranth, cypress, laurel, myrtle, oak, olive, rosemary
gall acarocecidium
generating powerhouse
grain barley, corn, oat, rye, teff, wheat
grass cloth ramee, ramie

grassland bacc(h)ar
grass-like sedge
group association, batch, cluster, family, genus, order, thicket
growing from inside endogenic
growing from outside exogenic
growing in another endophyte
growing in heaps acervate
growing on another aulophyte, parasite
growth gall
growth layer cambium
growth measurer auxanometer
growth regulator auxin
habitat ecad
habitat adjustment ecesis
hair villus
head blossom, bud, bur(r), flower, fruit
healing achillea, aloe, dock, milfoil, sanicle, yarrow
heath-like crakeberry
herbaceous anise(ed), anisum, artichoke, celery, coriander, ebulus, inula, licorice, pimpinella, ranal
hollow-stemmed bamboo, cane, reed, rush
hybridization xenia
imprint autophytograph
infection phytosis
insect-devouring pitcher plant, venus' flytrap
irradaceous crocus, freesia, gladiolus, iris, ixia, lily
joined to another graft
joint node
juice See PLANT *exudate.*
labiate calamint, motherwort, satureja
leaf blade, frond, needle, phyllome
leafless dodder, restiad, triurid, ulex
leguminous alfalfa, arachis, bean, clover, cube, lentil, medic, pea, senna, soy (bean)
lesion canker
lice aphid
life bios, flora, vegetation
-like vegetable, vegetal, vegetarian, vegetative
liliaceous allium, aloe, asphodel, beargrass, bellwort, birthroot, camas(s), cammas, campanula, chive, daffodil, garlic, greenbrier, iris, leek, lotus, onion,

paradisia, rocambole, sabadilla, scilla, sego, shallot, sotol, squill, tulip, uvularia, yucca
lipless achilary
long-rooted phreatophyte
louse alderblight, aphid, aphis, apple-blight, homopter, phylloxera, psyllid, puceron
louse secretion laa(r)p, lerp
low aizoon
male androgametophore, macrander, mas
malvaceous abelmosk, algalia, altea, althaea, cotton, escoba, hibiscus, mallow, okra
manufacturing factory, mill, shop
marine alga(e), amphipleura, bacillaria, benthos, biddulphia, enalid, ditchgrass, kelp, plankton, rockweed, samphire, sealace, seapink, tangle, thrift, wrack, zostera
marsh bitterbloom, bulrush, cattail, centaury, fern, juncus, reed, sabatica
medicinal 3 hop, oak, rue 4 agar, alem, aloe, cola, dill, flax, herb, kino, lime, nard, sage, uixi 5 ajava, ajova, anise, artar, buchu, cubeb, elder, ergot, erica, guaco, jalap, orris, peony, poppy, senna, tansy 6 arnica, carrot, catnep, catnip, cohosh, croton, fennel, garlic, ipecac, kousso, laurel, nettle, seneca, senega, simple, spurge, squill, tisane, yarrow 7 aconite, boneset, calamus, camphor, caraway, catechu, chirata, copaiba, ephedra, gentian, hemlock, henbane, juniper, lobelia, mullein, mustard, parsley, rhubarb, saffron 8 acapulco, barberry, camomile, crowfoot, foxglove, licorice, plantain, rosemary, silphium, valerian, wormwood 9 asparagus, bearberry, buckthorn, colchicum, coltsfoot, dandelion, feverweed, liquorice, monkshead, sassafras 11 assafoetida, bittersweet
menthaceous balm, basil, catmint, catnip, lavender, mint, peppermint, sage, thyme

minute microphyte, spore
modified ecad
mottled leaf ralsbane
multicellular metaphyte
native indigene
non-flowering fern
not native adventive
noxious tare, weed
nursery seedling
oil tube vitta
oil-yielding odal, peanut, sesame
1-seeded olacaceae
ornamental See *flowering* above, and FLOWER.
packing cannery
painful to touch briar, brier, knotweed, nettle, smartweed, thorn
papaveraceous celandine, creamcups, poppy
parasite fungus, moss, phytosis
parasitic dodder, mistletoe, rafflesia
part axil, blossom, branch, carpel, leaf, petal, pistil, pod, raceme, raphe, root, stamen, stipel, stipule, stoma(ta), strobile, tendril, trunk
pepper ara
perennial carex, daisy, golden-stars, sedum, tomato, tree
perfume source attar, myrtle, ottar, otto
pert. agamic, botanic, floral, phytic, vegetal, vegetative
pest cankerworm, cutworm, red-spider
pigment anthochlor, anthocyan(in), carotene, carotinoid
pod boll, lentile
poisonous aconite, aconitum, akee, amanita, atis, banewort, belladonna, black nightshade, buttercup, caladium, calfkill, castor oil, conium, cowbane, crocus, curare, daffodil, datura, deathcup, dieffenbachia, elephant's ear, foxglove, greyana, hellebore, hemlock, hemp, henbane, jasmine, jequirity beans, jimsonweed, kalmia, kentucky coffee tree, lily-of-the-valley, loco(weed), mescal, monkshood, moonseed, mother-in-law plant, mountain laurel, mushroom, nightshade, nux-vomica,

oleander, opium-poppy, philodendron, pikeweed, poison ivy, poison oak, rhododendron, rhus, sheeplaurel, snakeroot, snow-on-the-mountain, spurge, stavesacre, swainsona, thornapple, upas, water hemlock, yucuchu
pore lenticel, stoma
potted bonsai
potting material sphagnum (moss)
prickly acanthaceous, aspalanthus, briar, brier, cactus, cardon, nabk, nettle, nopal, nubk, prickfoot, rose, tearthumb, teasel, teazel, thistle, thorn, trefoil
protector cold frame
pungent pepper
raising agriculture, floriculture, hydroponics
reedy sprit
refuse scroff
rendering knackery
reproducer archegonium, bulb, grain, nut, pip, putamen, seed, spore, stolon, stone
reproduction acervulus, agamogenesis
resinous tarweed
rock lichen, moss
root amole
rope hemp
runner stolon
salad cabbage, celery, chicory, cress, endive, greens, lettuce, purslane, romaine, watercress
saprophytic indian pipe
savanna psilophyte
scented musk-tree
science agrobiology, botany, ecology
sea alga, alimon, enalid
2nd crop etch
secretion nectar, sap
seed nut, pip, putamen, stone
seedless fern
self-feeding autophyte
sensitive dormilona, mimosa
shoot bine, cion, rod, runner, scion, spring, stolon, sucker, vimen
silk floss
skin-irritating nettle, poison ivy, smartweed
snake-bite-curing blazingstar, bugbane, cankerweed, false-aloe, gay-feather, guaco, senega, snakeroot

solanaceous capsicum, tobacco, tomato
sour sor(r)el
spinachy orache
spinous cactus, kantiara
spiny-headed caltrap, caltrop, tribulus
sprout, 1st acrospire
staminate husband
starch-yielding arum, cassava, corn, pia, taro, wheat
stem axis, bine, birn, caulis, corm, culm, haulm, pedicel, peduncle, petiole, risp, shaft, stalk
stemjoint node, payton
stemless acaulescent, awlwort, moss, thallus, yautia
stem sheath ocrea, vaginant
stem tissue pith
stinging nettle
submerged enalid
succulent agave, aloe(s), century-plant, gasteria, haworthia, herb, houseleek, maguey, tambac, toadflower
sucker soboles
tanning sumac(h)
tendril bine
thallophytic lichen
thistle-like artichoke, teasel
thorny See PLANT *bramble* and *prickly.*
3-leaved clover, shamrock, trifolium
tissue pith, stereome, tapetum
trailing arbutus, buyo
tropical See TROPICAL *plant.*
tufted dryas
twining bindweed, climber, honeysuckle, rhynchosia, scammony, tinet, wisteria
umbelliferous angelica
uncultivated weed, wilding
unicellular protophyte
unidentified hordock
urticaceous nettle
verbenaceous lantana
wall creeper, ivy
water See PLANT *aquatic.*
weedy dock, knawel, spurge
woody acacia, bush, coontie, rockbrush, shrub, tree, vine
xyloid tree
yellowing flavedo
young cion, scion, seedling, set, shoot, springer, sprout, vinelet
PLANTAGENET angevin
badge broom
founder geoffrey

king edward, henry, john, richard

pert. angevin

PLANTAGO See PLANTAIN.

PLANTAIN adam's fig, adder's-violet, alisma, balisier, banana, benting, buckhorn, cock, finger, fireweed, fleawort, goodyera, herbeve, isphagul, lambsfoot, mudweed, musa, netleaf, pala, pantano pisang, plane tree, plantago, pussy's-toes, ratsbane, ribwort, roadweed, sitfast, thrumwort, tree, wabron(leaf), waybread, weed

dough foofoo

eater splitbeak, touraco

lily funkia, hosta

PLANTATION arbustum, bosket, bowery, cafetal, colonization, colony, estate, farm, fazenda, finca, fishery, foundation, grange, grove, hacienda, holt, installation, peopling, pinetum, quercetum, ranch, shamba, spring, thicket, trapiche, vineyard, wood, yerbal

coffee cafetal, fazenda, finca

osier holt, osiery

sugar trapiche

trees forest, orchard

willow holt, osiery

PLANTER agriculturalist, colon(ist), farmer, grower, machine, pioneer, seeder, settler, snag, sower, thief

decorative lavabo

government by plantocracy

PLANTING *device* dibble, footdrop

PLAQUE bother, broach, brooch, disc, disk, meda, pin(ax), plate(au), platelet, relief, sarcoid, slab, tablet

PLASH bespatter, blash, entwine, flop, intertwine, lip, lop, pleach, plop, pool, puddle, rain(fall), ripple, spatter, speckle, splash, wash, weave

PLASHY marshy, muddy, watery, wet

PLASM matrix, mold

PLASMA blood, lymph, protoplasm, quartz, serum, whey

PLASTER adhesive, adobe, affix, blister, cake, cast, ceil, cement, cerate, chunam, clay, cleam, compen-sate, compo, conceal, concrete, cover, daub, diaculum, diapalma, dressing, gatch, gesso, glue, grout, gum, gypsum, harl, hypocritical, malagma, maul, mortar, mucilage, parge(t), paste, roughcast, salve, scagliola, sham, sinapism, slick, smalm, smear, smooth, soothe, spread, stucco, teer, treat, vesicant

adhesive bandage, bandaid, diachylon, emplastrum

block batter

clover melilot

coarse grout, parget, stucco

coat arriciato, arricio, cat

ingredient fiber, hair, lime, quickline, sand, water

medical blister, charge, sparadrap, topic, treat

mustard sinapism

of paris cement, gesso, gypsum

patch spackle

2nd coat arricciato, arriccio

stone gypsum

2 coats renderset

wax cerate

PLASTERBILL surf-scoter

PLASTERBOARD cellotex, gypsum, lath, sheetrock

PLASTERED drunk, intoxicated, soused, swacked

PLASTERER dauber, daubster, pargeter

glue size

tool darby, float, spatula, trowel

PLASTIC (See also *kind,* below.) adaptable, amenable, catalin, changeable, creative, docile, ductile, elastic, fictile, flexible, formative, impressionable, labile, laminate, malleable, molder, morphotic, organic, pliable, pliant, putty, resilient, soft, supple, tractable, tractile, unctuous, yielding

art sculpture

base styrene

cement mixture cloy

coating krylon

component ester, polymer

cotton-sizing viscose

dentist's cement

ingredient urea

kind acetate, acrylic, albolite, alkyd, bakelite, buna, casein, cellophane, celluloid, formica, furan(e), laminate, lignin, lucite, melamine, neoprene, nylon, parylene, plexiglas, polymer, resinoid, tectonic, terpene, vinyl(ite)

lump gob

sealer pliofilm

surgery anaplasty, anaplerosis

PLASTRON breastplate, calipee, dickey, trimming

PLAT absolute(ly), arrange, bluntly, boat, braid, buffet, chart, dish, flat(ten), fold, hasten, hurry, layout, level, locality, map, outline, place, plain, PLAIT, plan, plateau, plot, quadrat, quite, scheme, slap, straightforward, strike, surface, tableland, wattle, weave

4-sided quadrat

PLATAEA *battle* marathon

enemy thebes

founder androcrates

general arimnestus

victor pausani

PLATANUS See PLANE tree.

PLATBAND border, epistyle, fillet, impost, lintel, list, molding

PLATE aglet, anode, argent, armor, assiette, baffle, bague, base, board, bolt, bowl, bridge, buttstrap, card, case, caster, caul, coat, course, cup, denture, dial, disc(us), dish, disk, epistome, facia, flake, foil, food, galvanize, gib, glass, gloss, grid, hammer, home, illustration, impression, lamel(la), lamina, layer, leaf, lithograph, meal, paillete, paillon, paten, patera, piece, plaque, platter, print, receptacle, rubber, scale, score, screen, scute, shale, sheath(e), sheet, shell, sill, silver, slab, spangle, stove, tagger, tain, teeth, tegmen, tile, timber

armor ailette

battery grid

boiler spud

bone scapula

border marli

circular disc, disk

communion paten, patina

cooking grid

cover cloche

deep mazarine

dorsal alinotum

ear-covering tegmen

earthen muffin
fireplace ironback
flat apron
from matrix stereo(type)
gelatin bat
glass slide
holder cassette
home dish, rubber
horny scale, scute
hot grill(e)
iron lapstone, latten, marver, moldboard, skewback, stave, turnsheet
large doubler
-like lamelliform, placoid
lock selvedge
mark hallmark
metal See METAL *sheet.*
name facia
organ pipe languet
perforated dog, grid, pinnule, stencil
pile of bung
pitcher's mound, rubber, slab
rack creel
reptile carapace, scute, shell
rimless coupe
steam boiler dasher, sput
stereotype cliche
thin bractea, lame(lla), lamina, leaf, paten, shim, tagger, tain, tegmen, tile, wedge
throwing discus
wooden trencher
PLATEAU anasazi, bench, causse, dish, downs, fjeld, hamada, hat, highland, karoo, karroo, level, mesa, niveau, paramo, plain(s), plaque, platform, sabana, salver, sila, stage, summit, tablazo, table(land), upland
high sabana
rocky scabland
PLATEMAN middler
PLATFORM 3 map, top 4 base, bema, bima, dais, deck, dock, kang, plan, shoe, site 5 apron, arena, basis, bench, bimah, block, chart, dolly, flake, float, floor, forum, heiau, porch, shelf, solea, speak, stage, stand, stoop, stull, stump 6 azotea, bridge, design, gantry, ground, hurdle, lyceum, machan, paepae, perron, pillar, podium, policy, pulpit, scheme, sledge, sollar, soller 7 almemar, balcony, battery, chaflet, estrade, gallery, landing, loge-

ion, maintop, paddock, pattern, program, rostrum, skidway, soapbox, support, terrace, tribune 8 barbette, footpace, hustings, scaffold, stallage, tribunal 9 bandshell, bandstand, banquette, beamboard, blueprint 10 catafalque, foundation 11 emplacement 12 landing-stage, presentation
altar predella
church pulpit, solea
fish-drying flake
food-storing whata
fort barbette
gun barbet(te), sponson
mining sollar, soller, stull
movable dolly, skid, sledge
ore buddle
raised dais, lissom, pantalan, podium, pyal, rostrum, skid, solea, stand, stoep, stoop, tribune
reloading staith
rock stance
ship's foretop, gangplank, maintop
sleeping kang
temple dukan
theater logeion, stage, theologium
wheeled dolly, float, skid
wood plancher
PLATINUM element, gray, metal, platina
blond towhead
comb. platin(o)
compound sperrylite
crude platina
pert. osmic
source alluvial, rustenberg
wire oese
PLATITUDE banality, bromide, chestnut, cliche, commonplace, corn, dullness, inanity, old saw, prosaicism, rechauffe, reiteration, staleness, truism
PLATITUDINOUS aphoristic, bromidic, dull, tiresome, trite
PLATO *birthplace* aegina, athens
dialogues apology, crito, gorgias, laws, parmenides, phaedo, phaedrus, philebus, republic, sophist, symposium, theaetetus, timaeus
disciple brutus, dion, helicon
followers academics
friend aristides
grove academe, academy
idea eide, eidos

jewish philo judaeus
knowledge moesis
mythical land atlantis
parent ariston, perictione, potone
pupil aristotle
rival philistus
school academy
teacher socrates
work (See also *dialogues,* above.) crito, dialogues, menexenus, republic
PLATONIC idealistic, impractical, nominal, spiritual, theoretical, visionary
body cube, dodecahedron, hexahedron, icosahedron, octahedron, tetrahedron
PLATOON company, coterie, formation, group, peleton, set, squad, subdivision, team, unit, volley
commander lieutenant
PLATTER ashet, base, disc, dish, disk, lanx, plate, record(ing), release, salver, server, trencher
-shaped scutellate
PLATY moon(fish)
PLATYCERCUS broadtail, parakeet, parrot, rosella
PLATYHELMINTH cestoda, fluke, nemertinean, planarian, tapeworm
PLATYPUS duckbill, duckmole, mallagong
PLATYSTEMON creamcup, poppy
PLATZ burst, explode, piazza, place, plaza, plotst, plotz, seat, split, square
PLAUDIT acclaim, applause, approval, cheer, encomium, hurrah, huzzah, praise, rooting
PLAUSIBLE affable, apparent, believable, ben-trovato, bland, colorable, conceivable, credible, delusive, diplomatic, fulsome, illusory, logical, oily, ostensible, politic, popular, possible, probable, sleek, smooth, snod, sound, valid, well-founded, well-grounded
PLAUTUS *comedy* amphitruo, baccides, casina, curculio, menaechmi, miles, persa, pseudolus, stichus
PLAY 3 act, bet, bow, dub, fun, run, rux, toy, use 4 blow, game, jest, joke, lark, mock, move, romp, sham, show, skip, tuck, tune,

work 5 amuse, antic, caper, charm, cutup, dally, drama, enact, farce, feign, fence, flirt, frisk, jolly, joust, opera, prank, range, revel, scope, slack, sound, spiel, sport, spree, stake, strum, sweep, swing, wager 6 action, assist, assume, cavort, dabble, fiddle, finger, frolic, gamble, gambol, masque, musery, render, rollix, trifle, wanton 7 carouse, carry on, contend, contest, debauch, disport, execute, flounce, freedom, guignol, miracle, mystery, operate, pageant, pastime, perform, pretend, roister, rollick, skylark, tragedy, twiddle 8 latitude, ridicule, scenario, simulate 9 accompany, amusement, celebrate, dalliance, diversion, looseness, melodrama, operation, pantomime, personate, speculate, syncopate 10 concertize, masquerade, recreation, symphonize 11 counterfeit, disportment, horse around, impersonate

act affect, dramatize, fool, pretend, sham
a part act, gammon, guizard, pretend
around flirt, philander, trifle
badly bobble, err, miff, muff, strum, thrum
ball begin, cooperate, open, start
bill program
boisterous horseplay
boy buffoon, clown, fool, idler, jack, loafer, madcap, man-about-town, sport, swinger
boy's girl bunny
by ear improvise
-by-play detailed
character persona
day holiday
division act, scene
down depreciate
fair square deal
false betray, deceive, mislead
farcical sotie
-fellow comrade, pal
festival festspiel
for accompany, court, try, woo
for a sucker exploit, fool
for reading closet-drama
for time delay, filibuster, procrastinate, put off, stall

funny burletta, comedy, farce
girl bunny, chotchke(leh), tchotchke(leh), tsatske(leh)
-goer first-nighter
havoc botch, ruin, spoil
hooky awol, bug out, jouk, leave, miche, mooch, mouch, plunk, run away, stray, trone, wag
introduction prologue
kind burletta, comedy, curtain-raiser, farce, melodrama, musical, one-act, pantomime, soaper, tragedy
long speech in tirade
morality everyman
musical burletta, opera, operetta
nervously fidget
-off championship, contest, deceive, feign, game, imitate, impose, perform, practice, pretend, showdown
on words acronym, carriwitchet, carwitchet, pun
out complete, exhaust, finish, tire, weaken, weary, wind up
outline scenario, script
part act, aside, bit, curtain, epilogue, epitasis, exode, finale, prelude, prologue, prop, role, scena, scene, walk-on
place arena, bowl, casino, coliseum, colosseum, commons, course, court, diamond, fairway, field, forum, gridiron, links, oval, park, ring, rink, stadium, stage, stand(s), theater, track
placebo agree, toady
possum act, ambush, camouflage, deceive, disregard, pretend, sham
put on produce, stage
silent pantomime
sponsor angel, backer
time recess
tricks jape, jink
truant See PLAY *hooky.*
up buck, dramatize, emphasize, promote, rear
up to court, cultivate, fawn, flatter, support, woo
used in lusory
with fire chance, dare, gamble, risk

PLAYA beach, salina, sebk(h)a
PLAYED *out* ended, ex-

hausted, finished, spent, tired, used, worn
PLAYER acrobat, actor, actress, athlete, barnstormer, busker, card, carouser, comedian, comedienne, competitor, contestant, cricketer, cutup, diva, dub, frisker, frolicker, gambler, gamboler, gamester, ham, hand, harpist, juggler, merrymaker, mime, mummer, musician, performer, pianist, reveler, skylarker, speculator, sport, stager, star (let), stroller, teammate, thespian, trifler, tragedienne, trouper
card bidder, dealer, eldest, pone
fundless lumber
group cast, squad, team, troupe
leading star
list cast
low-score booby
piano pianola
poor dub, dud, ham, scrub, second-string, sub
rugby hooker, scrum
strolling barnstormer, serenader, troubado(u)r
with lowest score booby
PLAYFUL blithe, elfin, frisky, frolicsome, gay, hilarious, jocund, jolly, jovial, kittenish, larksome, lively, lusory, merry, mirthful, mischievous, prankish, pranksome, pranky, roguish, sportive, sprightly, toysome, trickish, tricksy, tricky, waggish, wanton
as a kitten
PLAYGROUND close, commons, diamond, field, grid (iron), oval, parc, park, stadium, yard
PLAYHOUSE casino, cinema, movie, theater
PLAYMATE comrade, fellow, friend, pal
PLAYROOM bar, den, gym, nursery, studio
PLAYTHING bauble, chotchke(leh), plaik, sport, sucker, tchotchke(leh), TOY, trifle, tsatske(leh)
PLAYWRIGHT author, dramatist, scenarist, writer
PLAZA carrefour, green, park, piazza, platz, plein, square, zocalo
PLEA abater, alibi, allega-

tion, answer, apology, appeal, argue(ment), claim, contend, contention, defense, demurrer, dilatory, entreaty, excuse, guilty, justification, lawsuit, nolo, not-guilty, offer, petition, prayer, pretext, proposal, quarrel, request, strife, suit, supplication
to end abater
PLEACH interlace, interweave, plait, plash
PLEAD adduce, advocate, allege, apologize, appeal, appear, argue, assert, beg, beseech, champion, claim, defend, dispute, entreat, implore, intercede, intervene, mediate, moot, petition, playte, pray, press, pursue, reason, rejoin, solicit, sue, suit, supplicate, urge, wrangle
PLEADER advocate, suitor, vakeel, vakil
PLEADING advocacy, answer, argument, defense, demurrer, entreaty, intercession, litigation, oyer, parol(e), suppliant
PLEASANCE amenity, courtesy, gauze, luxury, PLEASURE, veiling
PLEASANT acceptable, affable, agreeable, alluring, amenable, amiable, amusing, attractive, balmy, bien, bright, buffoon, canny, catchy, charming, cheerful, cheery, congenial, cordial, delicious, delightful, desirable, diverting, douce, drunk, enchanting, enjoyable, farrand, fine, friendly, gay, genial, gentle, good(humored), gracious, grateful, gratifying, hende, hoddy, humorous, jocular, kind (ly), laughable, leesome, lepid, liefsome, likable, lovely, melodious, merry, mild, nice, obliging, playful, pleasing, queme, satisfying, seemly, soft, sportive, sprightly, sweet, wally, welcome, weme, wethe, winsome
comb. hedy
island nauru
it is not non libet
trip See GOOD-BYE.
PLEASANTNESS affability,

amenity, amiability, charm, compliancy, gaiety, suavity
PLEASANTRY banter, fun, humor, jest, jocularity, joke, levity, quip, sally, squib, waggery, witticism
PLEASE agree, amuse, arride, bewitch, bitte, charm, choose, content, delectate, delight, dulcify, elate, enchant, exalt, fancy, fullfil(l), gladden, gratify, hit (the spot), humor, indulge, kittle, per favore, prefer, queme, regale, satisfy, send, s'il vous plait, suffice, suit, sweeten, tickle
exclamation pray, prithee, s'il vous plait
PLEASED apaid, cheerful, content, delighted, fain, fond, fulfilled, glad(some), grateful, gratified, happy, proud, suited, willing
PLEASING acceptable, agreeable, alluring, amene, amiable, attractive, becoming, bonny, charming, comely, corking, delectable, desirable, drooly, dulcet, eesome, enchanting, fetching, glad, gracious, grateful, gratifying, indulgent, lief, likesome, liking, luscious, nice, palatable, placable, pleasant, roseate, savory, soothing, sweet, welcome, winning
very snazzy
PLEASURE amusement, bang, bliss, boot, charm, choice, delectation, delight, desire, diversion, divertisement, enjoyment, entertainment, este, felicity, fruition, fun, gaiety, gladness, glee, grace, gratification, gratify, gree, gusto, happiness, joie de vivre, jollies, jollity, joy, kama, kicks, liking, lust, mechaieh, mirth, nicety, passe-temps, pastime, preference, recreation, regalement, relaxation, relish, satisfaction, savor, simche, spice, sport, thrill, titillation, will, zest
and pain, science of algedonics
at one's ad lib(itum)
deity bes(a), comus, voluptas
dome site xanadu
ground park, pleasance

in pain algolagnia, masochism, sadism
insensitiveness to anhedronia
-loving apolaustic, hedonic (al), hedonistic
material cakes and ale
pert. apolaustic, epicurean, hedonic(al), sybaritic
philosophy of hedonism
-seeker cake-eater, epicure, epicurean, franion, hedonist, playboy, player, sport
stolen forbidden fruit, stouth, stowth
PLEAT braid, crimp, flute, fold, frill, goffer, gusset, kilt, knife, PLAIT, plicate, ruck sunray, tuck, wrinkle
PLEATED folded, plaited, plicate, plisse, shirred, sunburst
PLEBE cadet, freshman, midshipman, mob
PLEBEIAN banal, base (born), coarse, cockney, common(place), crude, homely, homespun, humble, ignoble, ill-bred, inferior, low(ly), lowborn, lowbred, mass, mean, ordinary, peasant, pedestrian, plain, popular, proletarian, rude, ruptuary, ungenteel, vulgar
PLEBISCITE ballot, decree, franchise, initiative, mandate, referendum, vote
PLECK enclosure, lot, plot, speck, spot, stain
PLECTOGNATH filefish, globefish, sunfish, triggerfish, trunkfish
PLECTRUM fescue, malleus, pick, pointel, quill, tongue, uvula
PLEDGE affiance, affirm, bail, bet, betrothal, bind, bond, borrow, bottomry, caution, certainty, chattel, collateral, commitment, consign, contract, covenant, deposit, earnest, engage, entrust, espouse, fest, gage, guarantee, handsel, health, hest, hock, hostage, hypothecate, impawn, impignorate, mainprise, mortgage, oath, obligation, oblige, parol(e), pawn, pignus, plevin, plight, post, promise, replevin, replevy, security, si(c)ker, sponsion, stake, surety, swear, tie, toast, token,

troth, truth, undertake, vadimony, vadium, vas, vow, wad, wage, word

drinking brince, brindisi, propine, toast

formal sponsion

security for bond, gager, marker

PLEDGED engaged, hight, sworn

PLEDGET bandage, compress, dossil, dressing, oakum, plug, stopper, swab, wad

PLEDGING propination

PLEGADIS curlew, ibis

PLEIAD *of alexandria* apollonius, aratus, callimachus, homer, lycophron, nicander, theocritus

PLEIADES alcyone, asterope, celaeno, electra, maia, merope, sterope, taygeta

companion artemis

constellation taurus

lost electra, merope

lover ares, poseidon, sisyphus, zeus

parent aethra, atlas, pleione

pursuer orion

PLEIKU pink See MARIJUANA.

PLEIONE *consort* atlas

daughters See PLEIADES.

PLEISTHENES *father* atreus

mother aerope

son agamemnon, menelaus

PLENARY absolute, complete, entire, full, perfect, replete, unqualified

PLENIPOTENTIARY absolute, agent, ambassador, commission, diplomat, envoy, minister

PLENISH equip, fill, furnish, outfit, refill, stock

PLENITUDE See PLENTY.

PLENTEOUS abounding, affluent, copious, fertile, fruitful, generous, PLENTIFUL, rich

PLENTIFUL abundant, ample, bounteous, bountiful, copious, enough, exuberant, fertile, fruitful, full, galore, generous, gobs, lavish, liberal, luxurious, many, numerous, opulent, plenteous, prodigal, productive, profuse, prolific, rich, sonsie, sonsy, spareless, sufficient, teeming

PLENTY abundance, abundant, adequacy, affluence,

agogo, ample, amplitude, appreciable, bags, barrels, bounty, competence, copiousness, enough, enow, extravagance, exuberance, fat(of the land), flood, foison, fortune, full(ness), galore, generosity, generous (ness), lavishness, liberality, luxuriance, luxury, opulence, overflow, perfection, plenitude, plethora, prevalence, prodigality, profuseness, profusion, quantity, repletion, richness, routh, satisfaction, scouth, slew, sonse, store, sufficiency, superabundance, surfeit, teems, uberty, wealth

father of abiathar

goddess abundantia, annapurna, ops, rhea

horn of achelous, cornucopia

illusion of barmecide

personification abundantia

PLEON abdomen, telson

PLEONASM circumlocution, fullness, iteration, macrology, periphrasis, redundancy, tautology, verbiage

PLEONASTE ceylonite, spinel

PLESSIS richelieu

PLETHORA congestion, deluge, engorgement, excess, flood, fullness, glut, overburden, overflow, overload, plenty, pleurisy, polyemia, prodigality, redundancy, repletion, satiety, saturation, superabundance, superfluity, surfeit, surplus

PLETHORIC bombastic, bursting, distended, inflated, overfull, overloaded, swollen, tumid, turgid

PLEURISY empyema, plethora

root asclepias, butterflyweed

PLEURON *parent* aetolus, promoe

PLEURONECTID dab, flatfish, flounder, halibut, plaice

PLEXIFORM complex, complicated, intricate, netlike, rete

PLEXIGLASS acrylic, lucite, polymer, resin

PLEXIPPUS *kin* althaea, meleager

PLEXUS entanglement, geniplex, glomus, network, proplex, rete, tangle

PLIABLE, PLIANT adapta-

ble, amenable, bendable, bendsome, compliant, docile, ductile, elastic, extensible, extensile, fictile, fingent, flexible, flexile, formable, formative, giving, impressible, impressionable, irresolute, limber, lissome, lithe(some), malleable, moldable, obedient, openminded, plastic, receptive, resilient, responsive, sensitive, sequacious, soft, springy, submissive, suitable, supple, susceptible, tractable, tractile, yielding, waxy, willowy, winding, workable, yielding

PLICA bend, fold, gill, lamella, ligature, plait, pleat

PLIERS bender, flector, flexor, forceps, nippers, pinc(h)ers, tweezers

PLIGHT affiance, attire, betroth(al), bind, blame, braid, case, condition, contract, covenant, danger, defect, difficulty, dilemma, dress, embrace, engage (ment), fix, fold, guilt, hardship, jam, mood, pawn, pickle, pinch, plait, pledge, plisky, predicament, promise, quandary, risk, scrape, sin, situation, state, straits, want

PLIM enlarge, fill(ed), grow, inflate, plump, swell, swollen

PLINTH abacus, base (board), block, couch, orlo, patand, quadra, scamillus, skirting, socle, subbase, table

PLISKIE, PLISKY frolic, mischievous, plight, trick

PLOD dig, drudge, grub, labor, lag, lumber, mog, peg, persevere, plaid, plodge, plug, slog, slough, stump, thud, toil, tore, tramp, trudge, vamp, walk, work

through mud slough

PLODDING dull, lumpish, pedestrian, stodgy

PLOP bubble, clap, dive, drop, fall, plump, sink, squarely, throw

down deposit, pay

PLOSHER gossip, shvitzer

PLOT 3 lot, map, peg 4 acre, area, brew, burn, cast, draw, pack, plan, plat, ruse, site 5 block, cabal, chart, close, croft, draft, field, forge, glebe, graph, hatch, patch, plain, pleck, press, scald, splat, story, trace, tract, trick 6 brigue, casate, clique, cook up, create, design, device, devise, garden, intend, malign, my.hos, parcel, scheme, scorch, script, shamba, sketch, square, tamper, wangle 7 collude, compact, complot, concoct, conject, connive, diagram, fashion, finagle, frameup, machine, outline, prepare, project, purpose, section 8 artifice, conspire, engineer, fainague, intrigue, maneuver, scenario 9 collusion, delineate, fabricate, machinate, stratagem 10 conspiracy

garden allotment, bed, parterre, patch, quarter, quinta
grass lawn, meadow, sonk
inventor scenarist, schemist
of land common, erf, forty, grave, haggard, lazybed, lot, patch, pleck, scherm, shamba, terrain

PLOTINUS *work* enneads
PLOTTER hatcher, jacobin, schemer
PLOUGH See PLOW.
PLOUK, PLOOK knob, pimple
PLOUNCE flounder, plunge
PLOUT burn, dash, plash, scald, scorch, splash
PLOUTER dabble, potter, wade
PLOVER bird, bullhead, charadrius, collier, courser, courtesan, dotterel, drome, dulwilly, dupe, hillbird, killdee(r), kolea, lapwing, maycock, owlhead, oxeye, papabot, pilot, piping, quaily, ringneck, sandpiper, sandy, spurwing, squatarola, squealer, stilt, stonehutch, strandlooper, toadhead, turnix, turnstone, whistler, wirebird, wrybill
black-bellied beetlehead, bottlehead, bullseye, maycock, pilotbird
blackheart dunlin
golden fieldbird, hawk's-eye
group congregation
-page dunlin, sandpiper
-quail plain-wanderer
ruddy sanderling

spur-winged blacksmith
3-toed thick-knee
wilson's collier
PLOW (See also *kind* below.) arado, break, buster, cart, charles'-wain, cleave, cultivate, dig, dipper, farm, flunk, furrow(er), groove, harrow, land, lister, plane, plod, plough, pluck, rabbet, reinvest, rive, rove, scaut, scratch, split, stir, sulk, sull(ow), till, trench, ursamajor, wagon
back reinvest
blade colter, coulter, share
boy yokel
cotton bull-tongue, scooter
crosswise thorter
handle hale, staff, start, stilt
head beam, clevis, frame
in the fall backset
inventor bootes, triptolemus
kind breaker, bull-ditcher, disk, drill, gang, gopher, lister, moldboard, prairiebreaker, rotary, scooter, shovel, snow, stirring, sulky, turnplow, walking
lightly riffle, skim
part beam, bottom, buck, chip, clevis, co(u)lter, disk, flay, hale, jointer, handside, moldboard, pinhead, share (beam), she(a)th, slade, sole, stilt, throck
slice flag
sole hardpan, share, slade
staff spattle(hoe)
tax carucage
PLOWFISH ray, rhina
PLOWGANG area, bovate, land, oxgang
8 carucate, hide
PLOWING aration, arder, caruage, stirring
ridge hack, selion
PLOWLAND arado, carucate, hide, measure, tilth
PLOWMAN acreman, cincinnatus, clodhopper, farmer, husband, rustic, tiller
command gee, haw
spikenard co(u)lter
PLOWSHARE blade, co(u)lter, laver, lay, reest, share, slip, sock
bone pygostyle, vomer
PLOY action, affair, bend, carousal, coup, escapade, frolic, joke, maneuver, merrymaking, move, pastime, plan, play, revelry, sport, strategy, tactic

PLUCK avulse, backbone, beard, bout, bravery, cheat, cheek, courage, cull, daring, deplume, determination, drag, draw, endurance, fleece, flunk, fortitude, game(ness), garner, gather, grit, guts, hardihood, harvest, jerk, mettle, nerve, pick, pith, plunder, plunk, pug, pull, reject, resolution, rob, sand, singe, snatch, spirit, spunk, stamina, steal, strip, strum, tear, temerity, tenacity, tug, twang, twitch, valor, will
a crow settle
down humble
feathers stub
out exterminate, extract
string tirl
up eradicate, summon
wool roo
PLUCKLESS apathetic, indifferent
PLUCKY adhesive, bold, brave, courageous, daring, distinct, flint, game, gamy, gritty, mettlesome, nervy, obsidian, resolute, sandy, sharp, spirited, spunky, sticky
PLUFF explode, fire, puff, rise, shoot, shot, swell
PLUG advertise, advocate, barricade, beat, blank, block(ade), blow, bone, boost, bott, bouchon, boxing, buckle, build-up, bung, ca(u)lk, close, clot, commendation, cork, dook, dossil, dottle, drudge, embolus, estop, ferrule, fid, fill, horse, jade, knock, mention, nag, obstruction, occlude, occlusion, peg, persevere, pledget, plod, praise, publicity, publicize, puff, punch, quid, recommend, shoot, slog, spigot, spile, stop(per), stopple, stopwater, strike, sweat, swot, tamp(i)on, tap, toil, try, wad, wedge
bib faucet, spigot
bloodstream clot, embolism, embolus
cannon bod, bott, tampion
clay bott
cock spigot
fishing bug
grenade bouchon
hat gibus, tile, topper
-in jack

nose tembeta(ra)
oakum fid
organ stopple, tampion
surgical pledget, tampon
-ugly criminal, gangster, hoodlum, rowdy, ruffian, thug, tough
volcano core

PLUGBOARD control-panel, switchboard

PLUGGER booster, jack-hammer, publicist, rooter, tout(er)

PLUM (See also *kind* below.) asset, beauty, cinch, damsel, damson, dividend, drupe, fruit, gravy, light, mild, nugget, patronage, perquisite, plim, plump, prize, prune, prunus, raisin, rise, shake, skeg, soft, swell, treasure, trophy, windfall
bun leas
cake baba, barmbrack, bramback
coco icaco
-colored mauve, puce, purple, violaceous
comb. pruni
curculio turk, weevil
dried prune
duff pudding
family amygdalaceae
green gage
kind amatungula, amra, bullace, burbank, cheney, cheston, damson, duhat, duhr, gage, greengage, icaco, islay, jaman, jambool, jambosa, jambul, jobo, kelsey, lansa, lanseh, lomboy, mabolo, orleans, prunello, prunus, quetsch, rosacean, rosewort, sapote, sirvelas, skeg, sloe, victoria
pocket fool
red burbank
sapodilla chinco, lanzon, nispero
seed pit, putamen
tree disease black-knot, fool
-violet canyon
weevil curculio
wild brushapple, islay, skeg, sloe

PLUMAGE adornment, down, dress, feathers, floccus, fluff, hackle, ornament, pennage, ptilosis, remiges, robe, ruff, tuft
1st floccus

PLUMB absolute(ly), bung, close, complete(ly), delve, directly, downright, entire-

ly, exactly, explore, fathom, gage, investigate, lead, measure, perpendicular, plummet, plunge, pool, probe, sheer, sinker, solve, sound, squarely, straight(en), thorough, understand, unravel, vertical(ly), weight
bob plummet
line merkhet

PLUMBAGO graphite, herb, lead(wort), lubricant, lustre, ore, plant

PLUMBLESS abysmal, abyssal

PLUMBUM lead

PLUME adorn, aigret(te), appreciate, crest, culgee, deprive, despoil, egret, feather, figure, groom, guerdon, hackle, palm, panache, pappas, pinion, pinna, pique, pluck, plumicorn, plumule, preen, pride, quill, reward, rob, scapular, strip, topknot, trophy, tuft, value, vibrissa
nutmeg sassafras
-poppy bocconia, macleaya

PLUMERIA frangipani, jasmine

PLUMMET criterion, dive, drop, fall, fathom, float, lead, plumb, pommel, sound, test, weight

PLUMP adipose, ample, blunt(ly), bonnie, bonny, burly, buxom, chesty, chubby, clap, clump, cluster, corpulent, crowd, crummy, dilate, direct(ly), distend, downright, drop, dull, dumpy, fall, fat(ten), fleshy, flock, fubsy, fulsome, gawsie, gross, group, obese, plop, plunge, plunk, portly, rich, rolypoly, rotund, rounded, rude, say, shower, sink, soss, squab, squarely, stout, straight, suddenly, support, throddy, throw, thud, tidy, tubby, tubsy, utter, vertically, vote, zaftig
as a partridge
down deposit, pay
out plim

PLUMPER blow, cropper, fall, lie

PLUMULE acrospire, androconium, bud, feather, gemmula, geoblast, pinion

PLUNDER baggage, bezzle, boodle, booty, brigandage,

cheat, creach, creagh, dacoit, denude, depredate, despoil, devastate, fleece, forage, gains, gut, harrow, harry, loot, makings, maraud, panyar, pelf, perplex, pilfer, pillage, pirate, pluck, poach, prede, prey, profit, raid, ransack, rape, rapine, ravage, raven, ravin(e), reave, reif, rifle, ripe, rob, sack, spoils, spoliate, spulzie, steal, strip, swag

PLUNDERER bandit, brigand, depredator, despoiler, falcon, filibuster, freebooter, harpy, hawk, hoodlum, looter, marauder, pillager, pirate, predator, preyer, raider, raptor, ravager, ravisher, rifler, routier, sacker, spoiler, spoliator, thief, vampire, vandal, viking, wrecker

PLUNGE absorb, baptize, bet, brainge, bury, cave, clap, descend, difficulty, dip, dive, douse, drive, duck, dump, dunk, embarrass, enter, fall, flounder, gamble, hurry, immerge, immerse, leap, lunge, merse, overcome, overwhelm, penetrate, pitch, plump, pool, predicament, run, rush, sink, soss, sound, souse, speculate, speculation, submerge, submersion, swoop, tank, thrust
into begin, engulf, immerge, study, undertake, volunteer

PLUNGER cavalryman, diver, frogman, gambler, gamester, piston, ram, risker, skin-diver, speculator, striker, swab

PLUNK blow, clap, croak, deposit, dive, dollar, drop, flop, money, pluck, plump, pull, push, sink, squarely, strike, strum, suddenly, support, throw, thud, toss, twang

PLURALITY bulk, majority, many, mass, most, multitude, number, preponderance, quantity

PLUS add, addition(al), adjunct, also, and, excess, gain, increase, more, over, positive, supplemental, too
-fours knickerbockers, knickers

PLUSH beaver, corinthian, fabric, flatten, grand, luxurious, palatial, posh, silken, splendid, swank(y), velour

PLUTARCH *ancestor* nicharchus
work lives

PLUTO dis, hades, orcus, planet
brother jupiter, neptune
discoverer tombaugh
favorite nymph minthe
horse abaster, abatos, aeton, nonion
kingdom hades, hell
mother-in-law demeter
parent saturn
tree cypress, maiden's-hair
wife persephone, proserpine, prosperpina

PLUTOCRACY aristocracy, bourgeoisie, obligarchy, society, timocracy, villadom

PLUTOCRAT capitalist, croesus, moneybags, nabob

PLUTONIC anogentic, hellish, igneous

PLUTONIUM *product* curium
source pitchblende

PLUTUS *associate* eirene, tyche
blinded by zeus
parent demeter, iasion

PLY adapt, beat, bend, bent, bias, comply, condition, conduct, double, drill, employ, exercise, exert, fold, follow, function, handle, importune, inclination, lamina, layer, manage, manipulate, mold, navigate, operate, perform, plait, pleat, plight, practice, quirk, rande, run, sail, shape, sheet, state, steer, strand, supply, swing, tack, thickness, touch, travel, twist, urge, use, warp, web, wield, work, yield
with drink birle

PLYMOUTH *brethren* darbyites
colony leader bradshaw, brewster, standish
colony festival thanksgiving
rock fowl, hen

PNEUMA breath(ing), ligature, neume, soul, spirit

PNEUMATIC airy, spiritual, tire

PNEUMONIA dolar de costado, pulmonitis

kind bronchial, croupous, lobar, virus

PO eridanus
on northern side transpadane
on southern side cispadane
tributary adda, oglio, trebbia

POA bluegrass, meadowgrass, tussock, wiregrass

POACH bleach, boil, cook, cut, dig, drive, encroach, force, interfere, intrude, mix, pierce, poche, poke, potch, push, ram, shirr, simmer, soak, spear, stab, stamp, steal, stir, thrust, trample, trespass

POACHER baldpate, bullhead, lurcher, pogge, spoach, stalker, thief, widgeon
salmon rebecca, rebekah

POBS pap, porridge

POCAHONTAS *baptismal name* rebecca
father powhatan
rescued john smith
spouse rolfe

POCHARD bird, diver, duck, dunair, dunbird, dunker, fowl, goldhead, nyroca, poker, redhead, scaup, smee, whinger, whinyard

POCK bag, blemish, gouge, hollow, mark, notch, pit, poke, pox, pustule, scar, spot
mark pithole
-marked foveate, pitted, scarred, variolar, variolous

POCKET accept, appropriate, bag, bight, billet, camouflet, cavity, chamber, cly, conceal, confine, cul-de-sac, diminutive, enclose, envelope, fob, fund(s), glen, hole, hollow, keep, lode, miniature, money, pack, pecuniary, pit, poche, poke, pouch, prat, private, profonde, purse, receive, sac(k), secret, small, socket, steal, suppress, swallow, take, vacuum, void, wealth
billiard hazard, hole, pot
billiards pool
bird scarlet tanager
-burner money
gopher camass-rat, quachil, sand-rat, thomomys, tuza
knife pigsticker
money peculium
mouse perognathus
ore bonanza, churn, lode
-picking figging

shape u-cut
small fob
trouser becket, fob, prat
water alberca, tinaja

POCKETBOOK bag, billfold, clutch, fob, handbag, income, kick, lil, money, mussel, notecase, poke, portemonnaie, pouch, purse, resources, reticule, skin, wallet

POCKY bag(gy), contemptible, loathsome, pitted, vile

POCO little, slightly, somewhat

POCOCURANTE apathetic, careless, indifferent, nonchalant, trifler

POD aril, bag, belly, boll, bur, capsule, carob, case, cocoon, covering, envelope, flock, group, herd, hull, husk, kid, legume, loment, pipi, podocarp, potbelly, pouch, rind, sac, schaup, school, seedcase, sheath (ing), shell, shuck, silicle, silique, sunt, swad, swell, tamarind, whaup
explosive sandbox
frame replum
subterranean earthnut
tanning pipi

PODAGRA gout

PODARGE *consort* zephyr

PODDY calf, lamb, potbellied, stout

PODESTA governor, judge, magistrate, mayor

PODGY See PUDGY.

PODIUM balcony, base, dais, foot(stalk), foundation, lectern, pedestal, phytomer, platform, pulpit, rostrum, soapbox, stump, support, wall

PODOCARPUS evergreen, kahikatea, miro, pine, yacca, yellowwood, yew

POE *beetle* gold bug
bird raven
character mr pym
detective dupin
foster father allan
house usher
poem annabel lee, bells, raven, ulalume
story cask of amontillado, gold bug, ligeia, purloined letter

POEM alba, amhran, amoebaeum, amphigory, amphigouri, ballad(e), bucolic, cantara, cantata, cantic(le), canto, carmen, cento, couplet, dit, dithyramb, ditty, doggerel, duan, eclogue, elegy, epic, epigram, epode, epopee, epopoea, epos, gazel, georgic, haiku, iambic, idyl(l), jingle, lai, lay, limerick, lyric, macaronic, madrigal, monody, ode(let), palinode, parody, pastoral, piyyut, poesy, psalm, quatrain, raff(e), rann, rhapsody, rhyme, rime, romance, rondeau, rondel(et), roundel (ay), rune, saga, sestet, sestina, soliloquy, song, sonnet, telestich, tercet, triolet, VERSE, versicle, virelay, vision

4-line quatrain, tetrastich
6-line hexastich
7-line heptastich
8-line triolet
10-line decastich, dizain(e)
13-line rondeau
14-line rondel, sonnet
1-verse monostich
6-verse sestina
amatory amoretto, sonnet
break in rhythm c(a)esura
collection anthology, cancionera, divan, parnassus, sylva
dawn aubade
epic epopee, epopoea, epos, lusiad, ode, rhapsody, saga, thebaid
foot anapest, iamb(us), spondee, trochee
heroic See POEM *epic.*
lamentation elegy
liturgical selihoth, viddui, vidduy
lyric alba, canzona, epode, ghazel, lai, lay, partimen, rondel
medieval alba, lai
melodic lyric
moral dit
mournful dirge, elegy
narrative ballad, cantata, epic, epos, lai, lay
nonsensical cramboclink, doggerel, limerick
nuptial epithalamion
ottava rima cantare
part anacrusis, antistrophe, book, burden, canto, chorus, envoy, epilogue, fit, foot, l'envoi, line, measure, passus, refrain, sestiad, stanza, stave, strain, strophe, verse

pastoral bucolic, eclogue, georgic, idyl(l)
pert. odic
religious hymn, psalm, yigdal
rural See *pastoral,* above.
satirical dit, iambic, kasida, parody
set to music cantata
shepherd's eclogue
short dit(ty), epigram, epilog(ue), epyllion, odelet, rondelet, sonnet, versicle
tone ballade
POESY bouquet, motto, nosegay, poem, POETRY, sentiment, verse
POET author, ballader, balladmonger, bard, bucoliast, creator, dreamer, elegiast, elegist, epopoeist, feramorz, heliconist, idyllist, imagist, laureate, lyrist, metrist, minstrel, muse, odist, palinodist, parnassian, rhapsodist, rhymer, rhymester, rimer, rimester, rishi, scald, scop, singer, skald, songsmith, sonneteer, troubadour, versemonger, versifiaster, versifier, writer
blind homer
fleshy morris, rossetti, swinburne
lyric odist
medieval trouvere, trouveur
of haslemere tennyson
of the poor crabbe
pastoral bucoliast
poets' spencer
poor See POETASTER.
realm cloud-land
saved by fish arion
POETASTER balladmonger, bardlet, bardling, bavian, bavius, dabbler, gleeman, jongleur, minnesinger, poeticule, poetito, rhymer, rhymster, rimer, rimester, scop, versifier
POETIC beautiful, dreamy, elegiac, epic, fanciful, idealized, imaginative, lyric(al), odic, romantic, visionary
foot See FOOT *metrical.*
form See POEM.
talent poesy
POETRY creation, epos, melic, poesy, prosody, rhyme, rime, scansion, song, soniou, verse
deity apollo, brage, bragi, muse, odin, ogma

inferior doggerel
line of stich
muse calliope, erato, euterpe, thalia
pert. elegiac, iambic, melic, musal, odic, peirian
popular gwerziou, soniou
rhymeless blank verse
symbol cicada
POGO *creator* kelly
figure porky
POGROM attack, butchery, carnage, genocide, massacre, pillage, riot, slaughter
POGY menhaden, perch, spadefish, trout
POI *source* taro
POIGNANCY acrimony, bathos, pathos, pungency, spirit
POIGNANT acrid, acrimonious, acute, affecting, amarevole, biting, bitter, cutting, disturbing, incisive, intense, keen, moving, pathetic, penetrating, piercing, piquant, pointed, pressing, pricking, probing, profound, pungent, racy, sensitive, severe, sharp, smart, snappy, spicy, stimulating, stinging, tart, touching, trenchant, urgent
POIKILE porch, stoa
POILU See SOLDIER.
POINCIANA barbados-pride, bird-of-paradise, delonix, flambeau, flamboyer, gulmohar
POINSETTIA banner, fireflower
POINT 3 aim, bit, dot, end, jag, jet, jot, lay, neb, nib, nub, ord, pen, pin, tip, top 4 apex, barb, beam, bear, bill, cape, cast, cusp, edge, fork, gaff, gist, goal, head, hint, horn, item, lead, mark, mull, nail, name, naze, neck, ness, node, peak, pike, pith, show, spit, spot, spur, step, stub, tack, tail, tend, tine, whit 5 angle, delta, digit, focus, guide, issue, lance, level, prick, prong, punct, punta, punto, quill, refer, score, slant, spear, speck, spike, spine, spire, sprig, stage, state, steer, taper, theme, topic, train, trial 6 allude, antler, apogee, bisque, bodkin, burden, center, course, crisis, decree, degree, detail, direct, gimlet, locale, mark-

er, moment, needle, object, period, plight, skewer, tittle, tongue, trifle, vertex, zygion 7 barbule, essence, feature, instant, isthmus, meaning, pricket, prickle, project, scruple, sharpen, spicule 8 apiculus, decision, foreland, headland, indicate, juncture, locality, location, particle, salience, sandspit 9 attribute, direction, gravitate, objective, peninsula 10 accusation, conclusion, particular, projection, promontory, resolution

at issue crux

-blank bang, blunt(ly), completely, direct(ly), exact(ly), express, perfect(ly), plainly, precise(ly), range, reach, squarely, unqualified, wholly

blunt mornette

cardinal east, north, south, west

central pivot

come to a concentrate, focus, taper, zero in

compass airt(h), course, ene, ese, nne, nnw, rhumb, sse, ssw, wnw, wsw

contact focus

coupe cutwork

crowning capsheaf, capstone

curve acnode, crunode, node

d'appui fulcrum

-device completely, correct, exact, faultless, nice, particular, perfection, perfectly, precise

exclamation bang, screamer

farthest ultima thule

fencing lunge, thrust

final end, outcome, upcome

fine nicety, technicality

finishing goal, tape

focal epicenter, epicentre

for point punctatim

highest acme, apex, apogee, auge, climax, crest, everest, flood, maxima, maximum, meridian, ne-plus-ultra, noon(tide), peak, pinnacle, solstice, summit, vertex, zenith

junction bregma, lambda

lateral alare

lowest bedrock, bottom, nadir, perigee, zero

main bottomline, crux, essence, essential, gist, jet, kernel, meat, nub, pith, sum

marker punctator

median hormion

moon's cusp

of departure base, basis, port, post, start, takeoff

of honor conscience, pundonor

of reference stylion

of view angle, attitude, belief, bias, eye, ground, opinion, outlook, position, respect, sight, slant, stand

on a atip

out assign, designate, digit, direct, emphasize, evidence, finger, imply, indicate, infer, muster, notify, presage, remind, show

pedal drone

pert. apical, cacuminal, focal

scoring ace, goal, punto, run, trick

-shaped punctiform

sharp prick(le)

stationary spinode

striking salience

strong forte, skill

supporting fulcrum, pivot

tapering acumen

the finger blame, charge

to the ad rem, apposite, cogent, concise, germane, pertinent, relevant

turning cardo, crisis, epoch, tide

up emphasize

utmost extreme, extremity

vantage pousto, tower

vibration node

vital crux, nub

weak blot, fault, flaw, foible

POINTED acicular, acid, acuate, aculeate, acuminate, acute, aimed, angular, apiculate, aristate, barbed, brief, concise, conical, conspicuous, corniculate, cornified, cornute(d), cuspate, cusped, cuspidate, definite, emphatic, fastigate, horned, horny, lanceolate, marked, meaty, needlelike, noticeable, ogival, pertinent, piercing, piked, piquant, pithy, poignant, pregnant, pungent, purposeful, sharp, significant, speary, spiculate, spiked, spiky, spined, spinous, spiny, stellate, stinging, tapered, tapering, terse, tined, trained, vitriolic

comb. oxy, stylo

end cusp

object, fear of aichmophobia

upward acockbill

POINTEDLY knowingly, on purpose, willfully, wittingly

POINTEL organ, pencil, pistil, plectrum, pontil, punty, stiletto, stylus, tool

POINTER advice, almury, arrow, blaze, clew, clue, cue, direction, dog, dubhe, fescue, finger(post), forefinger, guide(board)(post), gundog, hand, hint, idea, index, lead, rod, sign(board) (post), snakepiece, stag, stick, stylus, tip, wand, yad

POINTLESS absurd, blunt, dry, dull, dumb, flat, idle, inane, insipid, meaningless, obtuse, otiose, remote, senseless, silly, stupid, vapid, witless

POISE address, aplomb, assault, attack, balance, ballast, bearing, bias, blow, calmness, carriage, composure, confidence, dignity, equanimity, equilibrium, grace, hover, impact, importance, inclination, indecision, librate, measure, neutralize, oppress, pause, rest, savoir-faire, self-assurance, self-confidence, serenity, stability, stabilize, stand, steady, suspend, suspense, tact, trim, weigh(t)

POISON (See also *kind,* below.) bane, contaminate, corrupt, diliriant, envenom, fester, infect, kill, liquor, pervert, pesticide, pollute, potion, rankle, taint, toxic (ant), toxicum, toxify, toxin, venin, venom, virus, vitiate

ant formicide

antidote alexipharmic, mithridate, ruby

arrow aconite, antiar, antjar, curare, curari, derris, haya, inee, sumpit, urare, urari, wagogo, woorali

ash sumac, torchwood

auto carbon-monoxide

bay star-anise

-bearing veneniferous

berry bittersweet

berry tree butterbush, pittosporum

bush gastrolobium, oleander, trema

comb. arseno, toxi(c)(co), toxo

daisy feverfew, mayweed

detector aladdin's-ring, gun-doforus, opal, peacock, rhinoceros-horn

dogwood sumac(h)

extract urari

fear of toxiphobia

fish akia, babasco, barbasco, fugu, haiari, mad-tom, scorpion, tinosa, toadfish, weever

flag iris

flower bittersweet, oleander

fungus amanita

hemlock bunk, cash, chicory, cicuta, coniine, conium, wild-chervil

ivy black mercury, climath, climbing-sumac, laurel, markery, markweed, mercury, rhus(toxicodenron)

kill by venene, venin

kind abrin, aconite, aconotin(e), acquetta, amarin(e), antiar, antimony, arsenic, ascaron, atropine, atter, babasco, belladonna, bikh, bito, brucia, brucine, cacodyl, carbon dioxide, carbon monoxide, chlorine, coninine, curare, curari, cyanide, datura, ddt, derris, etter, flybane, formaldehyde, gall, hemlock, hemp, henbane, jimsonweed, lead, loco, mescal, miasma, morphine, nabee, nicotine, nightshade, nitrogen, nux-vomica, paris-green, pesticide, phallin, phenol, prussic-acid, ptomaine, ratsbane, ricin(e), strychnine, sumac, tanghin, tannin, tutu, upas, urare, urari

-like toxicoid

nut nux-vomica

oak rhus, sumac, yeara

pert. arsenious, toxic

plant See PLANT *poisonous.*

producing toxigenic

protein ricin(e)

rat antu, squill

remedy treacle

rhubarb butterbur

science of toxicology

snake venom

sumac boartree, burtree, dogwood

tobacco henbane

tree blind-your-eyes, gift-balsam, milky-mangrove, upas

weed loco

POISONING botulism, ichthyism, intoxication, jim-mies, lathyrism, mycetism, plumbism, ptomaine, pyemia, sepsis, septicemia, toxemia

POISONOUS attern, attery, baneful, corrupting, deadly, deletery, destructive, detrimental, fatal, lethal, loco, malign(ant), mephitic, miasmal, miasmatic, miasmic, mortal, noisome, noxious, pernicious, pestilent, septic, toxic(ant), toxiferous, venene, venenose, venomous, virose, virulent

POISONWOOD bumwood, crabwood, manchineel, metopium, sumac

POISSON fish

-bleu blue-cat, catfish, grayling

d'avril mackerel

POKE attack, bag, blow, bore, brim, core, cowboy, dally, dawdle(r), drag, elbow, goiter, gore, grope, harness, heap, hellebore, hook, intrude, jab, jog, jostle, laggard, loafer, loiter, look, meddle, nudge, peep, pocket, pook, porr, potter, pouch, prod, proddle, project, pry, puggle, punch, purse, push, putter, rauk, rot, sack, search, shoulder, shove, sleeve, sock, spear, stir, strike, thrust, tobacco, urge, wallet

about roke, root, scrounge, search

berry cancer-jalap

fun at banter, kid, ridicule

-in strander

off stray, travel, wander

out protrude

pudding titmouse

POKER (See also *game*, below.) beadle, bugbear, duck, game, hobgoblin, pochard, poit, rod, staff, stick, stir, stoker

call look, see

chip bone, check, counter, fish, jet(t)on

chip group kitty, pile, pot

double straddle

drawing pyrography

fund kitty, pot

game acepots, anaconda, cross-cards, dealer's-choice, declarations, draw, dutch straight, mistigri, pennyante, poque, strip, table-stake

game, draw acepots, ambigu, asnas, bluff, bobtail-to-open, bouillotte, brag, brelan, cold-hands, commerce, contract, deuces-wild, english, gile, gil(l)et, gleek, jackpot, jacks-back, kingsback, lamebrain(pete), limits, mike, monte, my bird sings, my ship sails, poch (en), pot-limit, progressive, round-the-world, schnautz, shotgun, southern-cross, spit-in-the-ocean, stormy weather

game, stud baseball, beat-your-neighbor, butcherboy, double-barreled-shotgun, down-the-river, dr pepper, eight-card, flip, football, four-of-a-kind, heinz, high-low, hi-lo, joker, kankakee, peek, peep and turn, pistol-pete, red-dog, rickey de lait, seven-toed pete, shifting-sands, shove-em-along, take it or leave it, texas tech, wild widow, woolworth

game, wild baseball, bed-spring, cincinnati(liz), criss-cross, deuces-wild, eight-card, football, hurricane, joker, lowball, mistigri, pig-in-the-poke, showdown, spit-in-the-ocean

hand bicycle, blaze, bobtail-flush, flush, jackpot, kilter, pelter, roodle, skeet, skip (per), straight(flush), three-of-a-kind, tiger, two-pair

-like game bouillote

stake ante, chips, kitty, pot

term ante, back-to-back, bluff, buy in, call, check, feed the kitty, flush, fold, hole-card, inside straight, in the hole, kitty, limit, open (ers), pass, pat hand, raise, see, showdown, side-bet, stake, stay, sweeten the pot

POKEWEED coakum, ditch-stonecrop, foxglove, garget, inkberry, nightshade, phytolacca, pocan, redberry, scoke

POKY, POKEY base, bovine, cramped, dowdy, dull, jail, little, mangy, mean, narrow, petty, ratty, seedy, shabby, slovenly, slow, small, stodgy, stuffy, tedious, trifling, untidy

POLAND, POLISH polonia, polska, sarmatia
actress modjeska
anthropologist malinowski
assembly diet, seim, sejm, senat, seym
astronomer copernicus
auto exchange gieldy samochodowe
cake baba
capital cracow, krakow, warsaw
carriage britska, droshky
checkers quebec-draughts
china hog, pig, swine
city auschwitz, beuthen, bialogard, bialystok, breslau, brest, bytom, chelm, chorzow, cracow, danzig, dukla, frombork, garocin, gdansk, gdynia, gleiwitz, gliwice, gnesen, grodno, kalisz, katowice, kielce, kolo, kracow, krakow, lida, lidzbark, liegnitz, litousk, litovsk, lodz, lublin, lvov, lwo, lyck, lyublin, narev, nysa, oels, oleztyn, opole, oswiecim, pila, posen, poznan, przemysl, radom, sosnowiec, sroda, szcezecin, tarnopol, tarnow, torun, vilna, walbrzych, warsaw, wroclaw, zabrze
coin abia, dalar, ducat, fennig, groschen, grosz, gulden, halerz, korona, marka, zloty
commander anders, bor
commune kutno, plock, radom, ruda, sopot
communist leader gomulka
composer chopin, leschetizky, moszkowski, paderewski, szymanowski
concentration camp auschwitz, chelmno, oswiecim
dance cracovienne, krakowiak, kujawiak, mazurka, polka, polonaise
deity datan, kremara, kurwaichin, lankapatim, marzanna, modeina, priparchis, siliniets, tanals, walgino
dollar dalar
drink krupnik, vodka
dynasty jagello, piast
exclamation psiakrew
game palant
gauleiter hans fran(c)k
gentry szlachta
harpsichordist landowska
hero copernicus, pulaski, tadeusz kosciuszko

housewife pani
idol baba-yaga
island wolin
jew galitzianer
jewish mystic frankist
kerchief babushka
king augustus, boleslav, casimir, conti, sigismund, sobjeski, stanislaus
lady dziedziczka, pani
lagoon frischeshaff
lake goplo, mamry, sniardwy
lancer uhlan
legislature See *assembly,* above.
marshes pripet
measure cal, cwierc, cwierk, garniec, korzec, kwarta, kwarterka, linja, lokiec, mila, morg(a), pret, sazen, stopa, vloka, wloka
militia pospolite
miss panna
nobility szlachta
nobleman pan, starost
novelist reymont, sienkiewicz
patriot kosciusko, pulaski
peak sudeten, tatra
people mazur, silesian, slav
pianist chopin, leschetizsky, paderewski
poet mickiewics
police slinas
political leader gomulka
port elblag, gdynia, stettin
posen poznan
president, 1st pilsudski
province pomerania
ragout borsch
range carpathian, tatra
region masuria, silesia
river alle, biala, brda, bug, dniester, drana, dwina, gwda, lyna, narev, narew, neisse, nemunas, niemen, notec, nyeman, nysa, oder, pilica, podra, pripet, prosna, san, seret, styr(pa), vistula, warta, wieprz, wista, wistoka
sausage kielbasa
scientist curie
sect, mystical hasid
szlachta gentry, landowner, nobility
tenor kiepura, reszke
title dziedziczka, pan(i), pann
weight centner, funt, kamian, lut, skrupul, uncya
writer peretz
POLAR (See also ANTARCTIC, ARCTIC.) emanent, guiding, opposite, pivotal

body apoblast, polocyte
explorer byrd
flora and fauna cryoplankton
formation icecap
lights aurora australis, aurora borealis, merry-dancers, northern-lights
plant rosinweed
study arcticology
whale bowhead
POLARIS alrucaba, missile, northstar
base holyloch
POLARITY *therapy* See MASSAGE.
POLE axis, axle, bar(ling), beam, boom, brog, caber, column, crotch, extremity, firmament, focus, hub, impose, juffer, kilhig, mast, mazur, nader, neap, oar, palo, perch, pike, pile, pivot, poll, post, poy, prop, propel, punt, quant, reach, ricker, rissle, rod, shaft, sky, slav, spar, spoke, sponge, sprit, staff, stalk, standard, stave, stick, stilt, stud, tail, terminal, thill, tongue, totem, ufer, xat
bean scarlet-runner
bird-decoy stool
electric anode, cathode, electrode, kathode
fishing cane, gaff, pew, rod
flattened at oblate
-fluke flounder, sole
forked crotch
having axiality
horse wheeler
logging janker, kilhig, killig
mangrove bority
memorial totem, xat
mine lagging
nautical mast, sprit
negative cathode
piked pickaroon
positive anode
rope-dancer's poy
sacred asherah
shepherd's kent
star cynosure, focus, guide, lodestar, polaris, principle, stella, tramontane
strip template
thatch-roof wattle
-to-pole ax(i)al
tossing caber, kabar
totem xat
vault jump, leap
vehicle cope, neap, thill
walking ashplant, cane, stilt
POLECAT ferret, fitch(et),

fitchew, fou(1)mart, marriput, musang, perwitsky, putorius, reprobate, sarmatier, skunk, weasel, zoril(la)
pelt fitch
tree buckthorn
POLEHEAD tadpole
POLEMIC(S) argument, controversy, debate, disputant, dispute
POLEMICAL apologetic, contentious, controversial, disputatious, eristic
POLIAS athena
POLICE check, civilization, clean(up), condition, control, cops, craft, examine, govern, guard, order, patrol, protect, regulate, regulation, tidy, toxotae, watch
badge buzzer, shield, star
call apb
capture haul up, run in
car black maria, paddy wagon
club billy(club), blackjack, espantoon, nightstick, pantoon, sap, spontoon, truncheon
dog german shepherd
force blue knights, carabinieri, cheka, chekists, cid, city's finest, constabulary, fbi, force, fuzz, gendarmerie, gestapo, glinas, interpol, kgb, mounties, mps, mvd, nkvd, ogpu, policia, polizei, posse, surete, vopos
headquarters bargello, barracks, booby-hatch, kotwalee, marshalcy, station, tan(n)a, thanah
line cordon
office prefecture
raid bust
spy mouchard
station See POLICE *headquarters.*
trap dragnet
weapon (See also POLICE *club.*) mace, tear gas
POLICEMAN alytarch, askari, bailiff, bangbeggar, bargello, beagle, beetlecrusher, biter, bluebottle, bluecoat, blueknight, bobbie, bobby, bulky, bull, bumbailiff, burkundauze, burkundaz, burly, carabiniere, catchpole, commissioner, constable, cop(per), crusher, deputy, detective, dick, esclop, flatfoot, flic, fuzz, gendarme, ghaffir,

g-man, grasshopper, guard, gumshoe, heat, inspector, javert, john, kotwal, law, leatherhead, marshall, officer, peeler, pig, plainclothesman, private-eye, roundsman, rural, sbirro, sepoy, sergeant, shamus, sheriff, shoofly, shrieve, smokey, speed-cop, spruce, thanadar, tipstaff, watch(man), zaptiah, zarp
traffic pointsman
POLICY administration, artifice, contract, contrivance, course, device, government, line, method, order, plan, platform, principles, procedure, program, sagacity, scheme, shrewdness, state, strategem, ticket, tontine, trick, voucher, wisdom, wit
aggressive big stick, blood and iron
maker boss, chief, head
statement white paper
POLIGNAC hearts, nojacks, quatre-valets, slobberhannes, sotas, stay-away
POLIO *foundation site* warm springs
therapist sister kenny
vaccine pioneer sabin, salk
POLISH (See also POLAND.) abrasive, amend, breeding, brighten, brush, buff, burnish, chamois, civilize, cultivation, culture, develop, eclat, elegance, embellish, fad, finish, furbish, gentility, gentleness, glance, glaze, gloss, grace, improve, lap, levigate, luster, lustre, patina, perfect, planish, punish, rabat, refine(ment), renew, restore, rub, sand, scour, shammy, shine, simonize, sleek, slick, slight, smooth, style, taste, touch up, urbanity, wax
off accomplish, despatch, dispatch, dispose of, end, finish, kill, knock out, liquidate, slay
POLISHED bright, buffed, civil, compt, cultivated, cultured, elegant, fine, gallant, genteel, glossy, lustrous, POLITE, refined, shiny, sleek, slick, smooth, terse, urbane
POLISHER brush, buffer, emery, pumice, rabat, rouge, sand, waxer

POLISHING friction, frottage, limation, sanding, waxing
POLITE accommodating, affable, attent(ive), bland, ceremonious, chivalrous, civil, complacent, complaisant, considerate, correct, cortes, courteous, courtly, cultured, debonaire, deferential, diplomatic, fair, gallant, genteel, gentle(manly), graceful, gracious, mannerable, neat, obliging, polished, politic, refined, respectful, smooth, suave, tactful, thoughtful, tidy, urbane, well-bred, well-kept
POLITENESS attention, civility, courtesy, politesse
POLITES *parent* hecuba, priam
POLITIC advisable, artful, astute, bland, careful, cautious, clever, crafty, cunning, diplomatic, discreet, discriminate, expedient, feasible, hardheaded, ingratiating, judicious, oily, possible, practical, provident, prudent, sagacious, shrewd, sleek, smart, smooth, suave, tactful, unctuous, urbane, wary, wise
POLITICAL (See also POLITICS.) civic, civil, governmental
association synomosy, verein
booty barrel, boodle, graft, jackpot, jobbery, melon, pap, patronage, pipelaying, plum, plunderbund, pork barrel, slush, soap, spoils
division borough, city, community, county, department, district, hundred, kingdom, nome, palatinate, parish, province, shire, state, sultanate, ward
economy catallactics
gathering caucus, convention, rally
group bloc, cabal, cadre, caucus, cell, cenacle, clan, faction, junta, machine, party, ring
hack or *hanger-on* (ward) heeler
incumbents ins
influence lobby
party black-shirt, communist, conservative, democratic, dixiecrat, farmerlabor, fascist, federalist,

gop, independent, labor, liberal, mugwump, nazi, prohibition, republican, socialist, tammany hall, tory, whig
party list slate
party principles plank, platform
power clout
symbol bandwagon
POLITICIAN administrator, boodler, boss, campaigner, candidate, carpetbagger, conniver, diplomat, grafter, heeler, henchman, incumbent, lawmaker, legislator, logroller, machiavellian, officeholder, officeseeker, opportunist, pipelayer, politico, reformer, ruler, runner, senator, spoilsman, statesman, strategist, trimmer, warhorse, wheelhorse, wirepuller
group caucus, committee, convention, junta, party, soviet
POLITICK campaign, caucus, gerrymander, wheel and deal
POLITICS discretion, expedience, government, kingcraft, prudence, realpolitik, statecraft, statesmanship, strategy
language of bafflegab, buncombe, doubletalk, gobbledegook, officialese, washingtonese
term ballot, candidacy, canvass, carpetbagger, caucus, coalition, crusade, election(eer), franchise, gerrymander, grassroots, hustings, landslide, lobbyist, logroller, muckraking, mudslinging, nominate, nomination, petition, pipelaying, plebiscite, poll(s), pressure group, primary, public opinion, referendum, returns, roorback, runoff, slate, stump, suffrage, ticket, vote, whistle-stop
POLK, JAMES *birthplace* mecklenburg, north carolina
burial site nashville, tennessee
party democratic
profession lawyer
vice president george dallas
POLKA dance, jacket
step galop
POLL ballot, canvass, clip,

coll, count, cow, cut(off), deduct, despoil, dodd, enumerate, fleece, head, list, mane, nape, number, parrot, plunder, record, register, schedule, shave, shear, skull, survey, tax, trim, vote
-taker gallup, harris, nielson, psephologist
tax capitation, census
watcher scrutinizer
POLLACK baddock, billet, bluefish, coalfish, gade, gadid, grayfish, lait(he), lob, loricate, lythe, moulrush, pollachius, saithe, sey, sillock, theragra, walleye
POLLARD abbreviate, awnless, beardless, bran, chevan, cow, dehorn, doddle, dotard, loppard, prune, tree, wheat, woosere
tree dotard, runnel
POLLED hornless, pollarded, shaved, shaven, shorn
POLLEN beebread, dust, farina, fertilizer, flour, meal, microspores, powder, spores
basket corbicula
-bearer anther
brush sarothrum, scopa
catarrh hay-fever
effect on seed xenia
grain mass pollinia, pollinium
sac theca
tube spermary
POLLER barber, extortioner, plunderer, pollster, registrar, taxgatherer, voter
POLLEX dactylopodite, digit, finger, phalange, thumb
POLLINATE fecundate, fecundize, fertilize
POLLINATION geitonogamy
artificial caprification
by water hydrophily
self cleistogamy
POLLIWOG amphibian, fledgling, tadpole
POLLUTE adulterate, alloy, attaint, befoul, contaminate, corrupt, debase, debauch, defile, deprave, desecrate, dirty, foil, foul, infect, intoxicate, maculate, muddle, pervert, profane, ravish, smear, soil, stain, sully, taint, violate, vitiate
POLLUTED corrupt, DRUNK, foul, turbid, unclean, unsafe
POLLUTION defilement, desecration, filth, foulness,

impurity, infection, stain, sullage, uncleanness
POLLUX (See also DIOSCURI.) polydeuces
brother castor
mother leda
opponent idas, lynceus
star beta
POLLYANNA glad-girl, optimist
author porter
POLO *division* chucker, chukka(r), chukker
mount horse, pony
stick mallet
POLONAISE carpet, dance, fackeltanz, garment, overcoat, polacca, polony, rug
POLONIUM radium
discoverer curie
source pitchblende
POLONIUS corambis
chamberlain to hamlet
king claudius
offspring laertes, ophelia
servant reynaldo
POLONY polish, polonaise, sausage
POLT blow, club, knock, thump
POLTERGEIST ghost, spirit, spook
POLTROON abject, cad, contemptible, coward(ly), craven, dastard(ly), idle, ignoble, lazy, mean, milksop, pusillanimous, recreant, scaramouch, scurvy, sluggard, sneak, sop, sorry, wretch
POLY herb, many, teucrium
POLYANDRIC monothelious
POLYANDRIST nair, tibetan
POLYBORUS caracara, hawk
POLYBUS *foster son* oedipus
kingdom corinth
wife alcandre
POLYBUTES *slayer* poseidon
POLYCASTE See PERDIX.
POLYCILLIN ampicillin
POLYDECTES *guest* danae, perseus
slayer perseus
POLYDORUS great-grandson oedipus
offspring labdacus
parent cadmus, harmonia, hecuba, hermes, laothoe, priam
sister iliona
slayer achilles, polym(n)estor
POLYGALA centaury, gaywings, herb, milkwort

POLYGAMY polyandry, polygyny

POLYGLOT bible, book, dictionary, jargon, linguist, multilingual

POLYGON *6-sided* hexagon
8-sided octagon
9-sided nonagon
equal-angled isagon

POLYGONIA anglewing, butterfly, vanessa

POLYGONUM adderwort, bearbine, bindweed, bistort, blackheart, blueweed, bryony, snakeweed

POLYGRAPH author, copier, keeler, lie-detector, myograph

POLYHEDRON bead, prismatoid
summit pentace

POLYHYMNIA *sisters* muses
son triptolemus

POLYIDUS *revived* glaucus
son euchenor

POLYMATHIC erudite, learned, scholarly

POLYMELA *consort* echecles, hermes, peleus
offspring endorus
parent actor, phylas

POLYMELUS *slayer* patroclus

POLYNESIA (See also HAWAII, MALAYSIA.)
battlefield tahua
beefwood belah, to(o)a
beverage ava, kava, kawa
chestnut rata
chieftain ariki
dance siva
deity aitu, atua, dok, hina, kanaloa, kapo, konori, laulaati, lono, mana, mauitikitiki, morogrog, nareau, nepelle, ngendei, nobu, papa, pele, ponape, qat, raki, rigi, rona, rongala, rongo, ruahatu, taaroa, tabu-eriki, tamakaia, tane, tangaroa, tawhaki, vatea, wyungare
dove goddess tangaroa
dragon ati
exclamation aue
fish isda, tagalog
food kai, poi, taro
garment lavalava, pareu, sarong
god See *deity,* above.
heaven havaiki, langi
herb pia, taro
hero maui
homeland havaiki

image ahu, tiki, zogo
island cook, easter, ellice, fiji, line, motu, phoenix, rapa, samoa, tokelau, tonga
island group society
king alii, arii, ariki, baginda, tit
language (See also *people,* below.) austral, maori, niue, tokelau, uvea
magic power mana
marker ahu
mat lauhala
meat laulau
mound ahu
people aitukakian, ati, batonga, futunan, hawaiian, kanaka, malaysian, maori, marquesan, nesogaean, niuan, nivean, samoan, sawaiori, tagalog, tahitian, tongan, tuamotu
pigeon lupe
pine hala
plant antidote-lily, kanaka, rafflesia, tara
power, supernatural mana
shrub alstonia, dogbane
sky langi
song himene
stone god tiki
temple enclosure marae
tree alstonia, dogbane
woman vahine, wahine

POLYNICES *brother* eteocles
parent jocasta, oedipus
sister antigone, ismene
uncle creon
wife argia

POLYP coral, hydra, hydroid, hydrula, isopod, octopus, polyzoan, sea-anemone, seapen, tumor, zooid
feather-shaped seapen
larva actinula
skeleton coral

POLYPEMON *slayer* theseus

POLYPHEMUS cyclops, monster, powerhouse, stalwart
aided hephaestus
beloved galatea
father poseidon
victim acis, antiphus
wounded by odysseus, ulysses

POLYPHONY counterpoint

POLYPODY anchista, asplenium, athyrium, camptosorus, fern

POLYPOETES *parent* apollo, callidiee, hippodamia, odysseus, phthia, pirithous, ulysses

POLYSACCHARIDE amylose, dextran, fucosan, galactan, gelose, glycan, glycogen, hexosan, inulin, irisin, levan, lichenin, mannan, polyose, secalose, sinistrin

POLYSPAST(ON) joist, pulley

POLYTRICHUM bear's-bed, haircap-moss

POLYXENA *betrothed* achilles
parent hecuba, priam

POLYXO *nurse to* hysipyle
slayer helen

POLYZOAN cestode, merozoan, polyp, radiate

POMACE cheese, must, rape, stock, stosh

POMADASYS burrito, burro, fish, grunt, rhoniscus

POMADE anoint, balm, cider, cream, fat, grease, inunct, lipstick, lubricate, lubrication, oil, ointment, pomatum, unguent

POMATO tomato

POME apple, azarole, ball, fruit, globe, head, juneberry, pear, quince

POMEGRANATE balausta, grenade
emblem of spain
family punicaceae
flower balaustine
rind granatum, malicorium
syrup grenadine
tree balaustine

POMELO grapefruit, shaddock

POMERANIA *capital* stettin
city anklam, thorn, torun
island rugen, usedom
province pomorze
river oder

POMERANIAN spitz
ancestor samoyed

POMFRET bully, henfish

POMME *blanche* breadroot
de terre potato

POMMEL bascabel, bat, beat, bob, bruise, buffet, chisel, crutch, finial, flail, flap, flat, flog, hit, horn, knob, nevel, paik, pake, plummet, pound, protuberance, tore
bag cantina

POMOLOBUS alewife, blackbelly, herring

POMONA hamadryad
consort vertumnus
courtier pan, sylvanus

POMP array, bobance, bravado, ceremony, circumstance, cortege, display, equipage, form(ality), gala, glory, grandeur, liturgy, magnificence, ostentation, pageant, parade, pompousness, pride, procession, ritual, show(iness), solemnity, spectacle, splendor, sprunk, state, strut, vainglory, vanity

POMPADOUR chatterer, coiffure, updo, upsweep

POMPANO alewife, allice, caranx, cobbler(fish), dart, jurel, mackerel, oldwife, palometa, poppyfish, saurel
clam coquina

POMPEIA *betrothed* marcellus
consort caesar, sulla
parent cornelia, mucia, pompey, scribonia

POMPEII *heroine* ione
mountain vesuvius
neighbor herculaneum

POMPELMOUS shaddock

POMPEY *ally* afranius, caesar, crassus
backer domitius, marcellinus
consort aemilia, antistia, cornelia, flora, julia, mucia
deceiver clodius
father strabo
father-in-law caesar, metellus
friend brutus, canidius, cicero, demetrius, domitius, jubius, labienus, manilius, mark antony, memmius, menas, mumerius, scipio, tidius, varrius, varro
patron antistius, sulpicius
rival bibulus, brutus, carinna, cinna, cloelius, domitius, geminius, lucullus, mithridates, piso, scipio, terentius, valerius, ventidius
servant alexander, demetrius
slayer achillas, calvius, pothinus, septimius, theodotus
son cnaeus, sextus
supporter gabinius, servilius, sylla, trebonius, vatinius
victim brutus, carbo, perpenna, vindius

POMPION *golden* pumpkin

POMPON ball, cabbage-rose, chrysanthemum, dahlia, fish, grunt, margate; ornament, tuft

POMPOSITY beadledom, beadlery, bighead, bumbledom, inflation, orotundity, ostentation, podsnappery, stuffiness, tumor

POMPOUS altisonant, antiloquent, august, bewigged, bigwigged, bloated, bombastic, budge, dictatorial, flatulent, formal, fustian, gassy, grandiloquent, grandiose, high-sounding, important, imposing, inflated, magniloquent, orotund, ostentatious, pontifical, pretentious, self-important, showy, solemn, stilted, stilty, stuffy, swollen, toplofty, tumid, turgent, turgid, vain, wiggy

PONCHIELLI *opera* la gioconda

PONCHO cloak, manga, raincoat, ruana, serape

POND aquarium, basin, canal, dam, delf, dike, lache, lagoon, lake, linn, llyn, lochan, lum, mere, moat, ocean, POOL, slough, stagne, tarn, vlei, vley
artificial aquarium
crow coot, fulica
dirty soal
dogwood buttonbush
duck mallard
fish aquarium, bluegill, bream, gurges, piscina, sunfish
fish-storing stew
flower alligator-bonnets, cambric-leaf, lily, lis, water lily
frog ranarium
grass potamogeton, potatomoss
hen coot, fulica
lily cambric-leaf, clote, spatterdock
man jacker
oyster claire
pine jeffrey, limber, loblolly, ponderosa
scum alga
small khal
snail coret, khal
stagnant dub

PONDER appraise, brood, cast, cogitate, consider, contemplate, deliberate, evaluate, examine, meditate, mull, muse, pore, reflect(ion), remord, reverie, revolve, ruminate, speculate, study, think, turn, weigh

PONDERABLE appreciable, grave, important, momentous, palpable, perceptible, sensible, significant, tangible, weighable, weighty

PONDEROUS awkward, big, bulky, burdensome, clumsy, cumbersome, cumbrous, dull, fat, great, heavy, hefty, important, labored, lumpish, maladroit, massive, massy, momentous, onerous, oppressive, overweight, soggy, stiff, substantial, thoughtful, unwieldy, vast, weighty

PONDWEED batterdock, butterbur, creekgrass, potamogeton

PONE bread, cake, cornbread, johnnycake, loaf, lump, paune, swelling, turf, writ

PONGEE fabric, paunche, shantung, silk, tussah

PONIARD bodkin, dagger, dirk, pierce, poignado, stab, stylet

PONT bridge, ferry(boat), float, pontoon

PONTIFF bishop, ecclesiastic, pontifex, pope, priest
pert. papal, sistine

PONTIFICAL dignified, edict, papal, POMPOUS, prelate

PONTIFICATE bombast, swank

PONTOON bateau, batel, boat, bridge, caisson, dhow, dock, float, lighter, rhino, scow, skipjack, vessel, vingt-et-un
plank chess

PONTUS *consort* baea
daughter ceto, eurybia
euxinus black sea, the hospitable sea
king mithridates
parent baea, uranus
son aegaeon, briareus, nereus, phorcys, thaumas

PONY ante, basuto, bhutia, bidet, bronc(h)o, cab, cavy, cayuse, crib, dales, diminutive, dram, exmoor, forester, galloway, garran, glass, griff, hackney, horse, manipur, mount, mustang, nag(gy), paint, piebald, pinto, portion, ride, sheltie, shelty, shetland, small, tacky, tangun, tat, tattoo, translation, trick, trot, welch, welsh, yaboo, yabu
group drove, string
piebald tangun

POOCH bulge, dog, POUCH

POODLE barbet, clip, dog, hunter, pet, retriever, shock
POOH(-POOH) bah, boo, deride, disdain, hoot, ignore, nonsense, pish, pshaw, slight, sneeze at, taunt
creator milne
POOHBAH panjandrum, vip
POOK heap, pick, pile, pluck, PUCK, pull, shock, shook, stack
POOKA hobgoblin, PUCK, specter, spirit, sprite
POOL ante, basin, billiards, carr, cartel, combine, contribute, corner, dib, dike, dub, enterprise, fund, game, group, jeel, jheel, jhil, kitty, lagoon, lagune, lake, linn, llyn, lock, lough, marsh, meare, mere, monopoly, natatorium, plash(et), plunge, POND, pot, puddle, reservoir, slew, stable, stake(s), syndicate, tank, tarn, trust, undercut, undermine
artificial cushion
auction calcutta
ball cue, eight, ringer, spot
closed stagnum
comb. limn(o)
dirty letch, sipe
fish stewpond, trunk
game eightball, pin, rotation, snooker, straight
mountain tarn
muddy letch
relative bagatelle
small flashet
snipe redshank
stick cue
swimming bath, lido, natatory, plunge
POOLWORT snakeroot
POON beat, calophyllum, dilo, domba, keena, laurel, mastwood, peon, pound, puna, tamanu, telugu, tree
POONGHIE priest, pungyi, rahan, talapoin
POOP cheat, cozen, deceive, deck, dickey, exhaust, fire, fool, gulp, hinddeck, information, low-down, nincompoop, puppis, seat, stern, tire, toot, weary
out fail, fatigue, tire, weaken, weary
POOR 3 bad, bum, low, sad 4 base, bunk, down, lean, mean, puny, sick, thin, vile, weak 5 badly, broke, dinky, needy, petty, plain, seedy,

seely, short, sorry, wrong 6 bad off, barren, feeble, flimsy, hard up, humble, infirm, meager, measly, paltry, rabble, ragtag, scanty, shabby, sickly, simple, slight, sordid 7 codfish, obolary, pinched, reduced, scrawny, squalid, trivial, unhappy, unlucky, unsound 8 bankrupt, deprived, indigent, inferior, mediocre, scrannel, stranded, strapped, trifling 9 defective, deficient, destitute, emaciated, imperfect, miserable, unmoneyed 10 inadequate, straitened 11 embarrassed, impecunious, indifferent, nondescript, out of pocket, unfavorable, unfortunate 12 impoverished, inauspicious, insufficient 13 disadvantaged 14 underprivileged, unsatisfactory
as churchmouse, job
creature indigent, pauper, pilgarlic, wretch
-do scrapple
farm county-house
fist blunder, error, failure
-jan's-leaf houseleek
joe bird, heron
john cod, fish, hake
man's cabbage winter-cress
man's geranium saxifrage
man's herb gratiola, hedge-hyssop
man's mustard hedge-garlic
man's pepper lepidium, peppergrass, stonecrop
man's remedy valerian
man's soap brake, hardhack, spiraea
man's weatherglass anagallis, pimpernel
patron saint of anthony
rhubarb meadow-rue
richard benjamin franklin, richard saunders
robin almanac, campion, cleavers
soap hardhack
soldier friarbird
-spirited base, cowardly, mean
POORHOUSE almshouse, asylum, measondue, workhouse
POORLY abjectly, ailing, badly, barely, ill(disposed), indisposed, shabbily, sick
POORTITH poverty
POP ask, backfire, beverage,

blast, blister, blow, boss, bubble, bulge, bunting, burst, clap, cola, concert, crack, dad(dy), dart, detonation, drink, explode, FATHER, fire, instant, knock, leap, pawn, pistol, protrude, report, shoot, shot, snap, soda, strike, stroke, thrush, thrust
dock digitalis, foxglove
-eyed exophthalmus
in call, insert, visit
off die, sleep
the question propose
POPADAM poppercake, wafer
POPE, POPE'S (See also *name*, below.) bird, bishop, bullfinch, holy father, metropolitan, papa, patriarch, pontifex, pontiff, priest, primate, puffin, ruff, shrike, weevil
address allocution
agent qu(a)estor
cap camauro, mitre
cape fannel, fano(n), fanum, mozzetta, mozzetta, orale, phano
chamberlain camerlengo, camerlingo
church lateran
court curia, dataria, datary, rota, see
crown tiara, triregnum
deputy cardinal
document brief, bull, decretal, encyclical
document collection bullarium, bullary
domain papacy
envoy ablegate, legate, nuncio, nuntius
epistle decretal
exile avignon, babylonian captivity
eye noix, nux
fan flabellum, flabrum
fanon orale
fictitious female joan
governor legate
headdress miter, mitre, tiara
huguenot mornay
name adrian, agapetus, alexander, anacletus, anicetus, benedict, boniface, caius, calixtus, callistus, celestine, clement, cletus, constantine, cornelius, damasus, dionysius, donus, eugenius, eutychianus, gaius, giovanni, gregory, hadrian, hilar(i)us, honorius, hormisdas, hyginus, innocent, john, julius,

lando, landus, leo, liberius, linus, lucius, marcellinus, marcus, marinus, martin, melchiades, montini, mornay, nicholas, pacelli, paschal, paul, pelagius, peter, pius, pontian, ratti, romanus, roncalli, sabinianus, sergius, severinus, silverius, simon, simplicius, siricius, sisinnius, sixtus, soter, stephen, sylvester, symmachus, telesphorus, urban, victor, vigilius, vitalian, zachary
of geneva calvin
palace See POPE *residence.*
pert. papal, papane, pontifical
publication acta sanctae sedis
reformer gregory
residence avignon, castel gandolfo, rome, vatican
scarf fannel, fanon, orale
seal bulla
secretary apocrisiary
title holiness, holy father
tribunal See POPE *court.*
POPE, ALEXANDER *friend* addison
nickname wasp of twickenham
poem dunciad, essay on man, rape of the lock
POPEYE *baby* swee pea
creator segar
girl olive oyl
POPGUN cap pistol, pengun, pluffer, potgun, scoot
POPINJAY bird, chatterbox, coxcomb, dandy, fop, macaroni, papingo, parrot, woodpecker
POPLAR abbey, abela, abeltree, alamo, aspen, bahan, balsam, baumier, cottonwood, garab, liar, lombardy, people, populus, tulip-tree, whitebark
black liar, lombardy, mormontree
white abele, bolle(s), rattlertree
POPLIN cake, cotton, fabric, tabinet
POPPAEA *husband* nero
POPPET child, doll, idol, pencilbox, puppet, valve
POPPIED drooping, drowsy, drugged
POPPLE bob, bubble, corncockle, heave, poplar, toss
POPPY argemone, balewort, blaver, blood-drops, boc-

conia, canker, cardosanto, coprose, coquelicot, creamcups, dannebrog, earache, foxglove, headache, papaver, plant, ponceau, redweed, romneya, squatmore
corn ponceau, soldier
drug heroin, morphine, opium
extract passewa
family papaveraceae
field canker
fish pompano
juice chick
mallow callirrhoe
name meaning rhea
pert. papaverous
prickly chicalote
red granate
seed maw, mohn
syrup diacodion, diacodium
POPPYCOCK bosh, folly, havers, nonsense, rot, stuff, trash
POPULACE commonalty, country, crowd, demos, great unwashed, hoi-polloi, humanity, mass(es), mob(ile), people, plebs, population, proletariat, public, rabble, world
POPULAR accepted, all the rage, approved, being done, celebrated, cheap, common, current, democratic, demotic, easy, epidemic, familiar, fashionable, favorite, general, inferior, lay, liked, modern, ordinary, pleasant, pleasing, plebeian, populous, praised, prevailing, prevalent, proletarian, public, simple, smart, standard, staple, stylish, traditional, up to date, usual, vulgar, well-known, well-liked
POPULARITY boom, celebrity, currency, fame, fashion, favor, glory, heyday, mode, prevalence, repute, vogue
POPULARIZE democratize, explain, push, restore, resurrect, revive
POPULATE inhabit, man, occupy, people(d), propagate, settle(d)
POPULATION colony, commonwealth, community, flotsam, folk, inhabitants, kindred, people, populace, public, society, universe, voters
count census

division syntagma
study demography, larithmics
POPULOUS abounding, crowded, filled, jammed, numerous, packed, settled, swarming, teeming
POPULUS See POPLAR.
POPWEED bladderwort
POQUELIN moliere
PORBEAGLE lamna, lamn(o)id, shark
PORCELAIN (See also *kind,* below.) china(ware), enamel(ware)
clay kaolin(e)
decoration rice-grain
furnace hovel
ingredient bone-ash, borax, clay, gypsum, kaolin, pegmatite, petuntse
kind amstel, arita, belleek, blanc de chine, budweis, caen, celadon, chantilly, derby, dresden, gombroon, haviland, imari, kakiemon, kuan, kyoto, lenox, limoges, mandarin, meissen, ming, murra, nankeen, nankin, sevres, spode, swansea, wedgewood
manufacturing city limoges, meissen
mould ramekin
paste pate
unglazed biscuit, bisque
PORCH anta, backstoop, balcony, colonnade, dingle, entrance, galilee, gallery, lanai, levee, loggia, narthex, parvis, passage, patio, piazza, poecile, porte-cochere, portico, pronaos, ramada, solarium, stoa, stoop, terrace, veranda(h), vestibule
church galilee, narthex
front anticum, veranda(h)
sun solarium
swing glider
west galilee
PORCIA *brother* cassius
father cato
husband bibulus, brutus
son bibulus
PORCUPINE animal, cawquaw, coendou, erethizon, ericus, hedgehog, hedgepig, hystrix, porkpen, porky, rodent, urson
-anteater echinda
brush-tail atherurus
coat quill, spine
disease ichthyosis
fish atinga, balloonfish,

bur(r)fish, dicdon(t), erizo, globefish

grass spinifex, stipa

quill pen, spine

PORCUS bagre, catfish

PORE alveola, alveolus, bajonado, cavity, cell, cinclis, cram, depression, duct, examine, foramen, gaze, gloze, inspect, interstice, lenticel, look, meditate, opening, orifice, ostiole, outlet, passage, peritheceum, pit, ponder, poor, porr, read, reflect, socket, stare, stir, stoma(ta), study, thrust

over contemplate, read, regard, scan, study

plant alveola, lenticel, ostiole

without eporose

PORGY besugo, bream, fish, jolthead, mamamu, margate, menhaden, pagrus, pargo, pinfish, pluma, scup, spadefish, sparid, tai

PORK bacon, baldrib, brawn, cracklings, croak, fat, favor, flitch, gammon, gravy, ham, hog, jambon, lard (oon), obesity, patronage, pig, swine

and salmon laulau

barrel booty, graft, gravy, spoil

chop griskin, thumbnail

cut bald-rib, chop, ham, pigs' feet, side-meat, sparerib, trotter

fish catalineta, grunt, sisi

intestine, fried chitterling(s)

loin griskin

pie hat

-rice dish tonkatsu

salt bacon, sowbelly, speck

sausage banger

strip bacon, lardoon, sidemeat

PORKY fat, greasy, pig, porcupine

PORNOGRAPHIC dirty, lewd, licentious, obscene, salacious, sexy, smutty

PORNOGRAPHY curiosa, erotica, esoterica, rhyparography, scatology, smut

symbol phi

PORONOTUS butterfish, dollarfish, ephipus, gunnel, kelpfish

POROUS absorbent, apertured, cancellous, cavernous, cellular, cribriform, honeycombed, leachy,

letchy, penetrable, permeable, pervious, pory, riddled, sievelike, slotted, spongy

PORPHYRIO gallinule, sultana

PORPHYRITE palatinite

PORPHYRY elvan(ite), eurite, grorudite, paisanite, phenocryst, pilandite, rock, wennebergite

PORPOISE cetacean, cowfish, dolphin, gairfish, hogfish, inia, palach, pellock, phocaena, puffer, puffing-pig, snuffer, whale

PORR cram, kick, poke(r), push, stir, thrust

PORRECT extend, present, tender

PORRET garlic, leek, onion, scallion

PORREX *kin* ferrex, gorboduc

PORRIDGE atole, brochan, brose, broth, burgoo, burgout, crowdie, crowdy, flummery, grout, gruel, hodgepodge, kasheh, khir, mush, oatmeal, pease, pob(s), pobbies, polenta, pottage, pudding, sagamite, samp, skillagalee, skilly, soup, sowens, stirabout, tartan

dish for bicker, porringer

-like pultaceous

PORSENA *hostage* cloelia

kingdom etruria

PORT air, anchorage, bearing, behavior, carriage, carry, cove, demeanor, deportment, destination, end, front, gate, goal, harbor, haven, hithe, income, inlet, larboard, left, manner, market, meaning, mien, opening, portal, pose, position, presence, purport, refuge, rental, sea town, transport, tribute, tune, wine

bear to tack

charge ballastage, wharfage

-fire lighter

natal durban

wine ruby, tawny, vintage

wine stain birthmark, hemangioma, nevus

PORTABLE bearable, mobile, movable

PORTAGE cargo, freight, pack, tarbet, tonnage

PORTAL archway, barway, bulkhead, dingle, door (way), entrance, entry,

gate(way), hatch(way), ingress, mouth, opening, passage(way), porch, portecochere, postern, pylon, stile, threshold, tollgate, trap(door), turnstile, vestibule

PORTAMENTO demilegato, drag, glide, glissade, scoop, slide

PORTCULLIS bar(rier), cataract, close, door, gate, grating, halfpenny, herse, lattice, orgue, pursuivant, shut

PORTEND adumbrate, attest, augur, auspicate, betoken, bode, denote, divine, extend, forebode, forecast, foreshadow, foretell, forewarn, import, indicate, lower, mean, menace, omen, phenomenon, predict, premonish, presage, prognosticate, prophesy, signify, threaten, warn

PORTENT apprehension, ayah, barghest, caution, ceremony, disaster, event, foreboding, foretoken, marvel, misgiving, omen, ostent, precaution, premonition, presage, prodigy, prognostic, sign, token, warning

PORTENTOUS fateful, menacing, monstrous, ominous, threatening

PORTER akabo, ale, attendant, badger, bearer, beer, bellboy, berman, bock, cargador, carrier, chaprasi, chokidar, concierge, coolie, darwan, doorman, drogher, durwaun, gatekeeper, guard, hamal, hummaul, janitor, khamal, lager, lever, mozo, ostiary, redcap, servant, stout, suisse, tamen, tiler, tyler, usher

and stout cooper

PORTER, K. A. *work* flowering judas, ship of fools

PORTER, WILLIAM S. *pseud.* o henry

PORTFOLIO assets, attachecase, blad, briefcase, holdings, investments, scepter, securities, shares, stocks, valise

PORTHOS *companion* d'artagnan

PORTIA *alias* balthazar

husband brutus

lawyer for antonio

servant balthazar, nerissa, stephano
suitor bassanio, morochus
tree bendy, maho(e)
PORTICO ambulatory, arcade, atrium, colonnade, loggia, narthex, parvis, peridrome, peristyle, piazza, porch, pteroma, stoa, veranda(h), vestibule, xyst (us)
circular cyrtostyle
covered xyst(us)
enclosed peridrome
long veranda(h), xyst(us)
wing pteron
PORTION allocate, allot-(ment), allowance, amount, apportion, assign, bit, block, cant(le), canton, chance, cut, dab, deal, destiny, detail, dispense, distribute, divide(nd), division, dole, doom, dose, dot, dowry, dunt, endowment, excerpt, extract, fate, fortune, fraction, fragment, gobbet, helping, inheritance, length, lot, luck, member, mete, morsel, parcel, part, piece, prorate, quantity, quota(tion), ration, scrap, section, sector, segment, selection, serving, share, some, tot, whack
additional rasher
allotted moira, scantling
blood, clotted cruor
bride's dowry
coarser boltings
food helping serving
marriage dot(e), tocher
perceptible kenning
representative sample
sizable dad, dunt, hunk
small bit, chack, dab, dollop, dram, drop, grain, gram, heeltap, modicum, remnant, scantle, scantlet, shadow, smack, smidgen, sosh, soupcon, spice, spunk
PORTLY chubby, chunky, corpulent, dignified, fat, fleshy, husky, impressive, obese, plump, rotund, stately, stout, tubby
PORTMANTEAU bag, clothes-rack, pockmanky, suitcase, valise
PORTOLAN(O) navigation chart, rutter
PORTRAIT description, effigy, figure, head, icon, ikon, image, imago, likeness,

mask, miniature, painting, picture, portrayal, profile, retrait, silhouette, simulacrum, statue
pert. iconic
sitting seance
PORTRAY act, character (ize), delineate, depaint, depict, describe, draw, enact, form, illustrate, imitate, impersonate, limn, paint, picture, represent, symbolize
PORTUGAL, PORTUGUESE *africa* angola, cabinda
bay setubal
boat caravel, moleta
brandy aguardiente
cape espichel, mondego, roca, st vincent
capital lisbon, lusitania
city beja, braga(nca), coimbra, evora, faro, funchal, guarda, lisbon, lusitania, oporto, ovar, porto, sebutal, viseu
coin angolar, avo, centavo, conto, coroa, crown, crusado, dobra(o), equipaga, escudo, indio, joe, johannes, justo, macuta, milreis, moidore, octave, real, rei(s), rupia, testao, testone, tostao, vintem
colony angola, damao, diu, goa, guinea, macao, mozambique, principe, timor
commander alcaide, alcayde
commune braga
crown jewel braganza diamond
dance fado
district evora, loanda, tete
dollar pataca
dynasty braganza
east indian castice
epic lusiad
explorer cabral, cao, da gama, dias, diaz, magellan, prince henry
festival chamarita
folksong fado
giant ferragus
grape crushers pisadores
guinea capital bissau
guitar machete
historian barros
iliad lusiad
india daman, diu, goa
india-born feringi
island angola, azores, madeira, principe, st thomas, sao t(h)ome, terceira, timor

jailer alcaide, alcayde
jews sephardim
king diniz
lady don(n)a
leader caetano, gomes, niniz, salazar, spinola
legislator cortes
man dom
measure alma, almud(e), alqueire, alquier, bota, braca, canada, covado, estadio, fanga, ferrado, geira, legoa, linha, meio, milha, moio, onca, palmo, pipa, pollegada, quartilho, quarto, selamin, tonelada, vara
navigator See *explorer*, above.
native castice, iberian
nobleman fidalgo, grandee
parliament congresso
peak acor, estrella, gerez, marao, monchique, mousa, peneda, serra d'estrella
people iberians
poet camoens, deus-ramos
port faro, lisbon, oporto
premier salazar
province alemteho, algarve, azores, beira, estremadura, evora, madeira, minho, rebatejo, tejo, tete
queen elizabeth of aragon, isabella
resort algarve, cascaes, estoril, sintra
revolutionary septembrist
river cavado, chanca, douro, duero, guadiana, legoa, lima, linha, milha, min(h)o, mira, moio, mondego, quarto, sabar, sado, seda, selamin, sor, tagus, tajo, tamega, teja, tonelada, tua, vara, vouga, zatas, zezere
saint sao
sausage linguica
shrine fatima
skirt abada
song fado
sugar mountain pao de acucar
"thank you" obrigado
title dom, dona, donna, senhor(a), senhorita
university coimbra
vessel mulet
village aldeament, aldeia
weight arratel, arroba, excropulo, grao, libra, marco, oitava, onca, once, quintal
wind colla
wine bucellas, calcavella,

carcavelhos, carcavellos, port

woman senhora

PORTULACA bitterroot, moss, purslane, rose-moss

POSADA hotel, inn

POSE affect(ation), air, assert, assume, attitude, attitudinize, baffle, bewilder, carriage, catarrh, cold, feign, guise, hoard, impersonate, mannerism, masquerade, mien, mince, model, mystify, nonplus, peacock, perplex, place, poise, port, position, posture, posy, pretend, pretense, propose, propound, puzzle, question, quiz, role, sham, simper, simulate, sit, stance, stand, suppose, symbolize

POSEIDON asphalius, earthshaker, enosichthon, genethlios, hippias, neptune, prosclystius

brother hades, zeus

celtic ler

consort aethra, alcyone, alope, amphithemis, amphitrite, amymone,, anippe, arne, caemos, calyce, canace, celaeno, chione, corcyra, demeter, ephialtes, europa, gaea, harpale, iphimedeia, medusa, melia, mestra, molione, phimedeia, pirene, pitana, salacia, salamis, theophane, thoosa, tyro

enemy trojans

horse hippocampes, scyphius

island calauria

master laomedon

offspring aeolus, aethusa, agenor, al(e)bion, aloadae, aloeus, amphimarus, amycus, amymone, ancaeus, antaeus, antaios, anthas, arion, belus, benthesicyme, boeotus, busiris, byzas, caucon, cenchrias, cercyon, charybdis, chrysaor, cychreus, cycnus, despoena, ephialtes, eumolpus, euphemus, euriphylus, eurypylus, evadne, hippothous, lotis, lycus, nauplius, nausithous, neleus, ogyges, ogygus, otus, pelias, polyphemus, rhode, rhodos, scylla, sinis, theseus, triton, zetes

parent cronos, ops, rhea

priest butes

sceptre triton

servant proteus

symbol dolphin, trident, triton

temple sounion

victim polybutes

worship site helice

POSER enigma, facer, hypocrite, model, posturer, pretender, problem, puzzle, question, sticker, stickler, stumper, twister

POSH brave, braw, chic, dapper, dashing, elegant, fashionable, luxurious, modish, natty, nifty, nobby, plush, slush, smart, spruce, stylish, swagger, swanky, toffish

POSIT affirm, assert, assume, dispose, establish, place, postulate, premise, presume, presuppose, put, set

POSITION action, angle, appointment, aspect, assertion, assignment, assumption, attitude, bearing, berth, billet, billing, calling, capacity, cense, charge, circumstance, coign(e), demeanor, duty, employment, engagement, exposure, frontage, function, hang, hypothesis, job, incumbency, lay, level, lie, locality, location, locus, mien, office, opening, orient, outlook, place, point, port, pose, post, postulate, posture, premise, presence, presumption, proposition, rank, set, site, situation, situs, slant, sphere, spot, stance, stand(ing), statement, station, status, tenet, thesis, ubiety, vacancy, viewpoint, work

advantageous ground floor

change move, shift, veer

comb. thesis, topy

defensive bridgehead, fort

dominating upper-hand

embarrassing corner, fix, hole, spot

having the same homologous

in in situ

inconspicuous back-seat

initial anlaut

medial inlaut

pert. situal

put in practical instate

relative footing, grade, rank, standing

report white paper

social caste, state, valour

suitable niche

symbolic hasta

POSITIVE absolute, active, actual, affirmative, assured, authoritative, basic, believing, certain, cocksure, concrete, confident, constant, decided, decisive, definite, doctrinaire, dogmatic, downright, effective, emphatic, exact, explicit, firm, flat, genuine, imperious, indisputable, material, oracular, peremptory, photo, plus, practical, prescribed, print, pure, real, sanguine, sure, thetic, true, unqualified

pole anode

3 kromogram

POSITIVELY absolutely, actually, certainly, definitely, extremely, greatly, indubitably, obviously, really, truly

POSITIVISM *founder* comte

POSITRON *discoverer* anderson

POSNET pot, saucepan

POSS beat, dash, drive, knock, pound, push, stamp, thrust

POSSE band, crowd, detachment, force, group, partisans, throng, volunteers

POSSESS acquaint, bear, bewitch, boast, command, control, convince, direct, dominate, enjoy, familiarize, fill, gain, get, haunt, have, hold, impart, influence, inform, inhabit, inherit, install, instruct, keep, madden, maintain, manage, master, monopolize, obsess, obtain, occupy, own, persuade, reserve, secure, seduce, seize, take, win

POSSESSED bedeviled, calm, cool, crazed, crazy, demoniac, demonized, eccentric, had(st), hanted, haunted, insane, mad(dened), obsessed, pixilated, poised, spellbound, spooked, spooky

name meaning jerush(h)

POSSESSION acquisition, aplomb, appropriation, asset, attachment, aught, aver, belonging, colony, control, custody, demesne, dependency, dewanee, discipline, entrancement, gavelkind, grasp, hold(ing), keeping, mandate, mastery, money,

monopoly, obsession, occupancy, occupation, ownership, property, reception, retention, sasine, seisni, seizin, seizure, socage, state, taking, tenancy, tenantry, tenure, territory, villeinhold, villenage, wealth
burdensome elephant
family heirloom
landed estate
of found goods trover
take seize
temporary lend, loan
POSSESSIONS assets, belongings, capital, domain, effects, estate, fortune, goods, graith, havings, means, property, resources, stuff, wealth, wrack
POSSESSIVE genitive, greedy, jealous, retentive, tenacious
POSSESSOR holder, occupant, occupier, owner, proprietor, tenant
POSSET balductum, beverage, coagulate, cosset, curdle, merrybush, pamper, powsowdy, turn, vomit
POSSIBILITY capacity, chance, contingency, eventuality, feasibility, liability, likelihood, maybe, mightbe, perhaps, potential(ity), power, tossup
POSSIBLE able, attainable, best, conceivable, contingent, credible, doable, eligible, eventual, expedient, feasible, latent, likely, obtainable, plausible, potential, practical, probable, thinkable, utmost, workable
POSSIBLY haply, maybe, mayhap, peradventure, perchance, perhaps
POSSUM animal, camouflage, coon, pogo, tait
haw bearberry, viburnum, witherod
play deceive, feign, pretend
POSSUMWOOD persimmon, sandbox-tree
POST 3 dak, job, leg, pay, set, tie 4 ante, base, bitt, camp, dawk, fort, jamb, mail, pier, pole, prop, rail, rush, send, sham, site, stob, stud 5 affix, after, berth, enter, haste, knead, later, locus, newel, opium, place, speed, stake, stand, stile, stilt 6 anteup, assign, billet,

cippus, column, gibbet, hasten, marker, office, picket, pillar, pledge, record, runner, stooth, stower, timber, trunch 7 asherah, bollard, capstan, chapter, courier, garetta, mullion, placard, publish, quarter, station, studdle, support 8 announce, baluster, banister, deadhead, dispatch, doorjamb, legpiece, position, puncheon, quintain, register, stanchel, stancher, standard 9 advertise, bannister, messenger, situation, stanchion 10 assignment, correspond, stronghold 11 appointment
and lintel trabeation
carved totem
chaise carriage, coach, jack, po(s)chay
chimney speer
-croaker drumfish, leiostomus, pinfish, spot
customs chokey, dogana, douane
desirable plum
easy pipe, sinecure, snap
exchange canteen, commissary, market, store
fence dropper
gate durn
-meridiem afternoon, midday
mooring buoy, dolphin
-mortem autopsy
nautical bitt, bollard
observatory cupola
office box apartado
race marker meta
sacred asherah
side jamb
sign parson
support crowfoot
trader sutler
turning meta
POSTAGE stamp(age)
design burelage, burele, spandrel
free frank
POSTAL *abbreviation* apo, pob, ppi, rfd, rte
machine dater, dealer, stamper
POSTBOX mailbox, pillarbox
POSTBOY courier, horseman, messenger, postilion, yams(tch)ik, yemschik
POSTER advertise, affiche, banner, bill(board), broadside, card, clap, courier, dodger, handbill, hoarding,

messenger, placard, sheet, sign(board), sticker
POSTERIAL dorsal, gluteal, lumbar, occipital, tergal
POSTERIOR after, back, behind, bum, caudal, dorsal, hind(er), later, posticous, rear, rump, subsequent, superior, wheerikins
POSTERITY breed, brood, children, descent, descendants, family, fruit, generation, heirs, issue, offspring, progeny, seed, sequel, sons, stock, succession
POSTERN back, clocket, door(way), entrance, exit, gate(way), inferior, klicket, lesser, opening, passage, posticum, private, portal, rear, side
POSTFIX add, annex, append, suffix
POSTHASTE express, fulltilt, headlong, hurry, immediate(ly), pellmell, quickly, speed(ily), swiftly
POSTHOLE *digger* loy
POSTHOUSE inn, mutation, yam
POSTHUMUS *friend* philario
servant pisanio
wife imogen
POSTICHE artificial, counterfeit(ing), imitation, pretense, sham, spurious, switch, toupee, wig
POSTICUM backdoor, epinaos, opisthodomos, postern
POSTIL annotate, comment(ary), gloss, homily, note
POSTILION See POSTBOY.
POSTLUDE epilog(ue), sortie, sortita, voluntary
POSTMAN courier, correo, letter-carrier, mailman
POSTMARK backstamp, cancellation
POSTPONE adjourn, arrest, carry(over), continue, defer, delay, fabianize, intermit, linger, nol-pros, pigeonhole, procrastinate, prolong, prorogue, put off, refer, remand, remit, reprieve, retard, shelf, shelve, slacken, slow, stay, subordinate, suspend, table, wait
POSTRIDER courier, messenger, postilion
POSTSCRIPT addendum, adjunct, afterthought, codicil, eke, ender, envoy, footnote, sequel

POSTULANT applicant, apprentice, candidate, neophyte, novice, novitiate, nun, petitioner, probationer

POSTULATE advance, affirm, ask, assert, assume, assumption, aver, axiom, claim, condition, demand, enunciate, fundamental, hypothesis, law, moot, nominate, posit(ion), predicate, prelude, premise, presume, presumption, principle, propose, proposition, propound, require, sanction, state, stipulate, submit, suppose, supposition, theorem, theory, thesis

POSTURE affectation, air, attitude, bearing, carriage, demeanor, deportment, form, guise, image, lounge, mien, mood, orant, outlook, peacock, place, port, pose, position, pretend, role, sham, shape, situation, slouch, squat, stance, stand, stature
erect orthostatic
kneeling shiko

POSY anthology, bouquet, compliment, corsage, flower, legend, motto, nosegay, poem

POT abyss, ante, basin, basket, bet, bowl, chytra, crock, crucible, cruse, cup, cuvette, drink, drug, favorite, fishtrap, grimace, jug, helmet, hole, jackshea, kettle, kitty, liquor, lota(h), loto, MARIJUANA, maslin, money, narcotic, olla, outdo, outwit, overreach, pan, pile, pingle, pit, plant, pocket, pool, posnet, preserve, rake-off, reward, saucepan, sausage, shoot, shot, stack, stake(s), takeout, tipple, vade, vessel, wager, win(nings)
ale wort
arch kiln
au feu stew
ball dumpling
-bank pottery
-bearer potifer
brass maslin
build ante
bulging olla
bushman's jackshay, jackshea
campfire billy
chamber commode, jeroboam, jerry, jordan
chemical aludel

chimney can, tun
clay buckpot, chatty, chytra, crock, cruse, olla, pipkin
drink shant
handle bool
hanger hale
hat bowler, derby
lead graphite
leather gispin
liquor brewis
lobster coy, trunk
long-handled pindle
marigold sunflower
measuring tappit-hen
melting crucible
metal potin
pear-shaped aludel
pie fricassee, stew
rustler cook
soup marmit(e)
stick ladle
stone ca(u)ldron, steatite
tea track
3-legged crock, posnet
12-gallon dixie, dixy
-walloper dishwasher, domestic, drinker, drunk(ard), scullion, servant
-ware crockery, pottery
wheel noria
-whisky poteen

POTABLE ale, beer, beverage, drink(able), liquor, water

POTAGE See SOUP.

POTAMOGETON batterdock, butterbur, pondgrass, pondweed

POTASH alkali, kali, niter, nitre, pearlash, polverine, salin(e)
crude salin(e)
factory ashery
feldspar orthoclase

POTASSIUM kalium
carbonate pearlash, potash
chloride muriate, sylvin(e), sylvite
compound alum, alunite, apophyllite, arcanite, avogadrite, carnallite, chrome, kalite, muriate, potash
nitrate grough, niter, saltpeter
salt alkali
sulphate alum, misenite

POTATION bender, beverage, drink, liquor, spree, symposium

POTATO batata, bluenose, browallia, brunfelsia, burbank, camote, chat, idaho, ima, imo, kumara, lumper, manroot, mickey, murphy,

oca, pap(a), pomme de terre, pratey, rural, russet, skerry, solanum, spud, tuber, vegetable, yam(p)
and cabbage colcannon
ball noisette
basket skeough
bean groundnut
beetle hardtack
-bogle scarecrow
bread boxty
chip crisp
disease blackdot, blackleg, blight, brown-ring, canker, curl, dartrose, giant-hill, haywire, murrein, powdery-scab, pox, rhizoctonia, ring-rot, silver-scurf, yellow-dwarf
dish au gratin, lyonnaise, salad, scalloped
family solanaceae
french fried chip, gauffrette
genus browallia, brunfelsia
inferior chat
kind burbank, early-rose, epicure, green-mountain, idaho, irish, rural, russet, sweet, yam(p)
made with parmentier
masher chapper, ricer
moss pondgrass
planting ridge ruck
slices lattice
soil otto
starch farina
state idaho, maine
stewed stovies
substitute sunchoke
sweet batata, camote, oca (rina), patata, yam
tule wapatoo
wart black-scab

POTBELLIED abdominous, distended, fat, paunchy, poddy, stomachy, tubby, ventricose

POTBELLY corporation, paunch, ventricosity

POTBOILER book, manuscript, painting, potwaller

POTBOY cupbearer, ganymede

POTCH bleach, hit, insult, poach, reverse, setback, slap, smack, smash, strike

POTE crimp, kick, mote, nudge, plate, poit, poke(r), push, shove, stick, stir, thrust

POTENCY efficacy, elan, energy, force, influence, intensity, might, power, puissance, strength, vigor, vis, vitality

POTENT able, absolute, almighty, authoritative, cogent, convincing, crozier, crutch, dynamic, effective, effectual, energetic, forceful, forcible, great, highgeared, influential, lusty, mighty, powerful, puissant, stay, stiff, strenuous, striking, strong, sturdy, support, telling, tenacious, trenchant, unlimited, vigorous, virulent, warrant

POTENTATE aga, ameer, amir, baron, chief(tain), dynast, emeer, emir, emperor, imperator, king, liege (lord), lord, majesty, mog(h)ul, monarch, overking, overlord, prince, royalty, ruler, sachem, sovereign, suzerain

POTENTIAL abeyant, aptitude, conceivable, dormant, inactive, inchoate, influential, latent, latescent, mighty, open, possibility, possible, quiescent, undeveloped, unrealized

energy engal

POTENTILLA bloodroot, bloodwort, indian-paint, puccoon, redroot, tellerwort, tormentil, turmeric

POTERIUM burnet, pimpernel, sanguisorba, woodwort

POTGUN braggart, cannon, mortar, pistol, rumor

POTHEAD addict, blackfish, dullard, user

POTHER ado, agitation, beset, bewilder, bother, bustle, commotion, confuse, confusion, dispatch, disturbance, dither, excitement, fluster, flutter, fuss, harass, haste, hurry, muddle, perplex, perturbation, puzzle, row, speed, stir, to-do, trouble, tumult, turmoil, uproar, upset, vex, worry

POTHERB chard, costmary, greens, kale, mint, mustard, olitory, quelite, spinach, tampala, werte, wort

POTHOLE cahot, kettle, tinaja

POTHOOK bail, cleek, collar, cotterel, crook, dracken, hake, hangle, nine, rackan, rod, scrawl, slowrie, trammel

POTHOS amlong, anthurium, arum, eros

POTHOUSE alehouse, low, mughouse, saloon, tavern, vulgar

POTION beverage, dose, draft, dram, draught, drink, drug, medicine, mixture, philter, philtre, poison

sleeping belladonna, dwale, narcotic, opiate, sedative, soporific

POTIPHAR *wife* rail, zuleika

POTLATCH ceremony, feast, festival, gift

POTLUCK chance, haphazard, meal, random

POTOMAC *city on* cumberland, washington

tributary antietam, shenandoah

POTPOURRI admixture, anthology, fantasia, farrago, gallimaufry, hash, hodgepodge, jambalaya, jar, jumble, maslin, medley, melange, mishmash, mix(ture), olio, ollapodrida, pasticcio, pastiche, patchwork, potpie, ragout, salmagundi, stew

POTSHERD bit, chip, fragment, ostracon, panshard, piece, shard, teste

POTSHOT aimless, assail, attack, casual, chance, criticism, drunk(ard), intoxicated

POTTAGE brewis, brose, broth, bruet, oatmeal, porridge, pulment, soup, sowl, stew

POTTED drunk, planted, preserved

meat rillett

POTTER, POTTER'S annoy, bother, ceramist, chat(ter), cloamer, dabble, dacker, daiker, daker, dally, dawdle, diddle, disher, dodder, drinker, fiddle, footle, fossick, fotter, handler, idle, jotter, kumhar, loiter, meddle, mess, muck, muddle, nantle, niggle, perplex, pettle, piddle, plowter, poke, pouter, pry, push, putter, saunter, tamper, terrapin, tiddle, tinker, toper, trifle, truck

asthma dyspnea, phthisis

clay alumina, argil

clay slab bat

field blood acre, cemetery

machine jolly

paste barbotine

wheel disk, jigger, kick, lathe, pallet, throw

POTTERY (See also *kind,* below.) ceramics, china, crockery, dishes, earthenware, factory, plant, porcelain, stoneware, ware

-bark tree cayenne-rose, sassafras

black basalt

city stoke-on-trent

civilization minyan

clay alumina, argil, kaolin, slip

colored majolica

culture pucara

decor mishima

decorated sigillate

decorating brush putois

decoration barbotine, broderie, canalatura

enameled majolica

firing box saggar(d), sagger

fragment shard, sherd

glass-like vitreous

glazed faience

kind agateware, aretine, astbury, awaji, basalt, belleek, biscuit, bisque, bizen, blanc, boccaro, bristol, bucchero (nero), celadon, champleve, china, chun, cloisone, crouch, delft, dipware, faience, figuline, grayware, ironstone, ironware, jasper, kamares, kashan, keramos, kuan, leeds, lusterware, majolica, mimpei, satsuma, sigillate, slipware, terracotta, tickney, ting, tung, tzuchou, uda, vitreous, yueh

mineral feldspar

pert. ceramic

piece figuline

prehistoric bandkeramik, grayware

products ceramics

speckled graniteware

statuette figuline, figurine, tanagra

terracotta albertware

tree caraipa, caraipe, caraipi

unfired greenware

unglazed bizen, boccaro

variegated agateware

wheel See POTTER *wheel.*

POTTING drinking, planting, shooting, tippling

POTTO aposoro, bush-dog, icticyon, kinkajou, lemur

POTTY crazy, daffy, dotty, eccentric, foolish, haughty,

insane, petty, supercilious, trivial

POUCH alfarga, alforja, bag, budget, bulge, bursa, burse, bursicle, caecum, cod, crumen(a), cyst, gipser(e), mailbag, ovicyst, pocket(book), pod, pok(k)e, purse(t), sac (cule), sachet, sack, silicle, socket, spleuchan, spleughan, sporran, swallow, vesicle
abdominal marsupium
bone marsupial
comb. cyst(is)(o)
furry sporran
girdle gipse(e)
rawhide parfleche
-shaped bursiform, saccate, sacculate

POUDRETTE fertilizer, manure

POUF bang, hairdress, ottoman, puff

POUGHKEEPSIE *college* vassar

POULARD chicken, pullet

POULE See PROSTITUTE.

POULTICE cataplasm, dressing, epitheme, malagma, quilt, relieve, sinapism, spongiopilin, stupa, stupe, treat
emollient malagma

POULTRY bantam, biddy, bird, broiler, brooder, capon, chanticleer, chick (abiddy), chicken, chicky, cock-a-doodle(doo), drake, duck, fowl, fryer, ganger, gobbler, goose, guinea-fowl, hen, partlet, pheasant, pigeon, poulard, pullaile, pullet, rooster, rock-hen, tom, turkey, volaille
breed ancona, andalusian, australorps, brahma, campine, cochin, cornish, dorking, faverolle, hamburg, houdan, langshan, leghorn, minorca, orpington, plymouth-rock, rhode island red, sumatra, sussex, wyandotte
disease coryza, gapes, limberneck, pip, pox, roup
fat schmal(t)z
fattening gavage
yard barton, hennery

POUNAMU greenstone, jade, nephrite

POUNCE adorn, attack, bruise, claw, comminute, decorate, dive, dust, em-

boss, grasp, jump, leap, perforate, pierce, pink, poke, pound, powder, prick, pummel, punamu, punch, sandarac, seize, smooth, spring, stab, stamp, swoop, talon, tattoo, thrust
game canfield, china, solitaire
upon ambush, attack, grab, nab, seize, swoop

POUND assail, bang, baste, batter, beat, belabor, blackjack, blow, bray, bruise, buffet, cage, chap, club, comminute, confine, cudgel, dam, drub, drudge, enclosure, flail, flap, frail, hammer, hit, jail, knock, lambaste, larrup, livre, nicker, patter, pelt, pen, pestle, pinfold, pommel, pond, prison, pulp, pulverize, pummel, quid, ram, rap, sandbag, shelter, slug, smite, spank, strike, tamp, thrash, thresh, thud, thump, triturate, tund, wallop, weight, whip
1/100th pence
1/20th shilling
1/16th ounce
1/8th handful
1/5th ora
1 quid
12 gaun
14 stone
25 pon(e)y
100 central, century
500 monkey
2000 avourdupois short ton
2240 avourdupois long ton
away drudge, persevere, work
ezra, poems cantos personae
fine bray, pulverize
fish kelp, madrague
keeper pinder, pinner, ponder
note nicker, quid

POUNDING *instrument* jackhammer, mallet, pestle

POUNDMASTER pinder, pinner, ponder

POUR abound, birle, bucket, cascade, decant, diffuse, discharge, drain, drench, emit, empty, fall, flood, flow, flush, gush, hail, hale, heald, hield, issue, jet, lave, libate, outflow, radiate, rain, river, roll, run, shed, shower, sluice, spew, spout, storm, stream, superfuse, surge, swarm, swill, teem,

tide, toom, torrent, vent, vomit, well
down descend, dump, rain, shower
down the drain squander, waste
forth chatter, declaim, disgorge, orate, overflow, say, shed, spew, spout, tide, utter, vent, well
it on hustle, labor, speed, strive, try
off decant, sluice
out diffuse, empty, libate, shed, skink, spill, stour, utter

POURBOIRE douceur, fee, gift, gratuity, handout, tip, trinkgeld

POURPARLER conference, discussion

POURPOINT bedquilt, doublet, gipon, jupon, quilt, tunk

POUT bib, boody, bulge, bullhead, catfish, eelpout, fish, grimace, groin, grouch, maid, mop(e), moue, pique, protrude, scowl, sulk, swell
horned bullhead, catfish

POUTER pigeon, poke, potter, stir, teemer

POUTING bouderie, moping, piqued, protruded

POVERTY adversity, bankruptcy, beggary, dearth, deficiency, destitution, distress, exigency, illth, impecuniosity, impecuniousness, impoverishment, indigence, insolvency, insufficiency, lack, leanness, need, pass, paucity, pauperage, pauperism, pearlweed, penury, pinch, poorness, rags, rarity, scarcity, straits, tenuity, wandreth, want
plant beach-heather, fieldpine, hudsonia, lingwort
program vista
-stricken See POOR.
weed buttonweed, cowwheat, pearly-everlasting, spurry

POW blow, discharge, head, hit, poll, pool, pull

POWDER abir, algaroth, bestrew, bir, bray, cataplasm, cement, chalk, charge, chinol, comminute, cosmetic, craunch, crumble, crunch, crush, curry, debris, dermal, detritus, disintegrate, dose, dust, emplasm, erbia, escape, explosive, farina,

flight, flour, flumerin, gerate, granulate, grate, grind, hemal, hurry, impetuosity, kamala, kermes, kish, kosin, kumkum, levigate, lupulin, meal, medicine, mellon, mill, molder, mull, onset, palegold, peyton, picra, pinole, pollen, pounce, pound, pulverize, rachel, rasp(ings), runout, rush, sand, scatter, scobs, smeddum, smeeth, soot, spackle, stour, strew, sprinkle, talc(um), triturate, yttria
abrasive emery
aloes picra
anthelmintic kosin
antimony kohl
antiseptic aristol, borax, boron
astringent boral
base orris root
beater sinterer
bitter adonidin
bleaching chemic
bronzing brocade
brownish lignin
case bandoleer, bandolier
cathartic kamala
container arsenal, cartridge, compact, horn, magazine
crystalline anthracene, arsphenamine, barbital, barbitone, ethinamate, guaiasanol, nalorphine, palmitin, thimerosal
disinfectant paraform
dusting eepastic
fluorescent flumerin
goa araroba
gold venturine
graphitic kish
gray antu
hair must
ingredient talc
make bray, calcine, grind, pulverize, triturate
malt smeddum
medicinal cataplasm
paper charta
perfumed abir, sachet
pert. floury, seme, semee
pink calamine
poisonous antu, robin
polishing corindon, corundum, cuttlebone, emery, sandarac
post dryrot
puff bellows, effeminate, feminine, fop, gull
reddish abir, kumkum, simmon
rose-colored erbia

sachet pulvil
scented sachet, talcum
shield gerate
siliceous silex
skin boral, rachel, talcum
smokeless amberite, cordite, filite, indurite, peyton, poudre, solenite
stencil-making pounce
sublimation flowers
sweat-masking empasm(a)
take a depart, escape, flee, git, run out, scram
white ammelide, ammeline, chinol, halazone, hyporit, lanthana, paraform, scandia, yttria
yellow adonidin, dermol, kosin, lupulin, malarin, mellon, samaria, tannigen

POWDERY arenose, branny, chalky, detrital, disintegrated, dusty, explosive, farinaceous, fine, floury, friable, furaceous, granulate(d), gritty, impalpable, mealy, pulvereous, pulverized, pulverulent, sabulous, sandy, scurfy

POWER 3 arm, gas, jet, use, vim, vis 4 arms, beef, boss, bulk, dint, gift, grip, heat, hold, host, iron, kami, king, main, mana, maya, move, odyl, push, rule, soup, sway, will, work 5 atoms, cloud, force, huaca, hydro, might, odyle, reign, right, ruler, skill, state, steam, thews, vigor, wakon, yarak 6 baraka, brahma, effect, empire, energy, foison, genius, impact, moloch, nation, regime, sinews, spirit, stroil, talent, virtue 7 ability, cogence, command, control, country, demesne, faculty, kingdom, license, magnate, operate, potency, stamina, voltage, wakonda, warrant 8 autonomy, capacity, coercion, dominion, dynamics, efficacy, function, leverage, potestas, strength, virility 9 abundance, authority, influence, multitude, puissance 10 attraction, capability, competence, efficiency, government, resolution 11 electricity, omnipotence, prerogative, sovereignty 12 jurisdiction, potentiality
boat cruiser, glider, motorboat, skiff, stinkpot, yacht

breakdown blackout, outage
civil caesar
comb. dyna, dynami(a), mega
company trust, utility
deprive of deparliament, dethrone, impeach, maim
discretionary carte blanche
divine afflatus, charisma, moira
divine, having deipotent
extraphysical mana
failure blackout, outage
5th sursolid
focal dioptry
formative plastodynamia
growth bathmism
impersonal wakan(da), wakon
intellectual brain(s), genius, wit
kingly diadem
knowledge jnanashakti
lack atony
legal jus
magic orenda
manifestation maya
measurer cratometer
mighty armipotence, omnipotence
natural odyl(e)
nature's mana
of attorney agency, blank check, carte-blanche, commission
output capacitance, capacity
partnership champerty
personal baraka
personality charisma, macho
personification aditya, asura, danava
persuasive rhetoric
political dominion
provide with endow, endue
ratio bel
reflective albedo
royal rialty
sacred kami
sea motion yarage
2nd square
source coal, electricity, engine, fuel, gas, geothermal, hydro, nuclear-fission, oil, petroleum, solar, steam, sun, thermal, water
spiritual ngai
structure establishment, leadership, society
supernatural alchera, alcheringa, arado, magic, mana, ngai, orenda, wakan
supreme heaven, imperium
symbol baton, iron, mace, orb, scepter, sceptre, sword

3rd cube
unit bel, rpm, watt
unlimited omnipotence
POWERFUL able, almighty, amain, authoritative, bold, brawny, capable, cogent, competent, considerable, convincing, drastic, effective, efficacious, efficient, fat, feckful, forceful, great, herculean, heroic, husky, influential, leonine, loud, lusty, mighty, muscular, omnipotent, potent, prepotent, puissant, severe, sinewy, skookum, strenuous, strong, sturdy, substantious, telling, valiant, vigorous, weighty, wight, wilde
comb. mega
name meaning frederi(c)k, richard
POWERHOUSE antaeus, atlas, briareus, buck, colossus, cyclops, dynamo, giant, goliath, hercules, husky, ironside, moose, polyphemus, samson, snoozer, stalwart, strongman, tarzan, titan
POWERLESS decrepit, feeble, helpless, impotent, impuissant, inactive, incapable, inert, infirm, lifeless, prostrate, rudderless, tillerless, unable, weak
POWHATAN wahunsonacock
daughter pocahontas
indian matchotic
tribe algonquin
POWWOW assembly, caucus, ceremony, confer(ence), congress, conjurer, convention, gathering, huddle, medicineman, meeting, priest
POX chickenpox, canker, cowpox, erysipelas, plague, smallpox, variola, vericella
POY gallery, pole, terrace
POYOU armadillo, pelou, peludo
PRABBLE chatter, quarrel, shout, squabble
PRACTIC artful, cunning, difficult, experienced, PRACTICAL, shrewd, skilled
PRACTICABLE achievable, actable, applicable, attainable, beneficial, doable, feasible, negotiable, operable, performable, pliable, possi-

ble, superable, surmountable, usable, workable
PRACTICAL able, active, actual, applied, banausic, businesslike, busy, capable, concise, efficacious, efficient, experienced, homespun, ordered, orderly, possible, potent, pragmatic, proficient, prompt, prosaic, realistic, sane, skilled, skillful, systematic, thorough, unromantic, unscrupulous, usable, useful, utile, utilitarian, versed, workable, work(a)
day, working, worldly
arts crafts, handicraft
joke booby-trap, hoax, humbug, jape(ry), lark, prank, trick
PRACTICE act(ion), art (ifice), background, behavior, brushup, business, calling, canon, carry on, ceremony, compass, conduct, custom, deed, dexterity, drill, effect, employ, engage (in), execute, exercise, experiment, fashion, follow, frequent, fulfill, habit(ude), handling, influence, intrigue, iterate, labor, management, manner, method, mode, observance, operate, operation, perform, plan, plot, ply, praxis, procedure, proceed (ing), process, prosecute, pursue, pursuit, rehearse, repeat, routine, rule, rut, scheme, seasoning, stratagem, system, train(ing), treat(ment), try(out), undertake, usage, usance, use, wage, way, wont, work
ceremonial rite
communal sunna(h)
exercise etude, scales
magic conjure
on corrupt, deceive, exploit, impose on, tamper with, trick
pert. pragmatic
religious cult(us)
sharp chicanery, deceit, dodge, fraud, game, trickery, usury
unscientific empiricism
PRACTICED adept, conversant, disciplined, exercent, experienced, old, seasoned, skilled, skillful, trained, veteran
PRACTITIONER, agent, artist, assistant, civilian, doc-

tor, doer, feldsher, healer, homeopath, lawyer, learner, novice, physician, plotter, professional, schemer
comb. ician
PRAD horse
PRAENESTE *founder* caeculus, telegonus
PRAENOMEN aulus, name
PRAEPOSITUS abbot, prior, provost
PRAESEPE beehive
PRAETOR judge, magistrate
attendant lictor
PRAETUS *daughter* mera
PRAGMATIC(AL) businesslike, busy, conceited, curious, disturbed, dogmatic, energetic, forward, intrusive, matter-of-fact, meddlesome, meddling, obtrusive, officious, practical, prying, realistic, sedulous, skilled
PRAGUE golden city, praha
beer plzen prazdroj
castle hradcany ,
cathedral st vitus
church loretto
feature cernin palace, karlstejn, wenceslas square
king wenceslas
martyr st john nepomuk
monastery strahov
palace belvedere, cernin
quarter hradcany, malastrana
river vltava
theater tyl
university carolinum, charles
PRAIRIE camass, cam(m)as, flatland, grassland, lea, meadow, mesa, plain, plateau, quamash, tract
anemone pasqueflower
antelope pronghorn
apple breadroot
berry nightshade, trompillo
breaker plow
chicken grouse
clover petalostemon
crabapple bechtel's crab
crocus pasqueflower
dock feverfew
dog barking squirrel, cynomys, gopher, marmot
dogweed marigold
dweller plainsman
fire castilleja, painted-cup
grub hop-tree
herb anemone, boebera, dyssodia
in forest camass, cam(m)as, quamash

lotus compassplant, hosackia
mallow moss-rose
moneywort loosestrife
mud gumbo
pigeon plover, sandpiper
pine gayfeather, liatris
plant butterflyweed, gaura, ground-plum
poppy primrose
potato breadroot
rose baltimore belle
sage mugwort
schooner ark, covered wagon
small prairillon
smoke torchflower
state illinois
tree clump motte
turnip breadroot
wake-robin brown bess, trillium
weed cinquefoil
wolf coyote
PRAISE acclaim, accolade, adore, advertise, aggrandize, alose, applaud, applause, apple polish, approbation, approval, approve, belaud, bhajan, bless(ing), blow up, blurb, boost, brag on, build up, carol, celebrate, celebration, cheers, cite, commend(ation), compliment, cry up, doxologize, eclat, eloge, elogy, emblazon, encomium, esteem, eulogize, eulogy, exalt (ation), extol, fawn, flatter(y), glorify, glory, gratitude, hery, honor, hosanna, hymn, kudize, kudos, laud (ation), macarism, magnify, meed, paean, panegyric, panegyrize, pat on the back, plaudit, plug, prize, puff (ery), reward, roose, salaam, salute, tout, trade-last, tribute, value, worship
bestowal of accolade
exaggerated flattery, fuss
exclamation hosanna
hunger for esurience
insincere clart, daubing
name meaing hillel
song anthem, bhajan, hymn, paean, psalm
to god adscription, alleluia, ascription, hallelujah, laus deo
with cum laude
with great(est) (magna) (summa) cum laude
PRAISEWORTHY admirable, commendable, complimentary, creditable, deserv-

ing, estimable, exemplary, laudable, meritorious, model, palmary, splendid
PRALINE confection
pert. nutty
PRAM See BABY *carriage.*
PRANCE bound, brank, canter, caper, cavort, dance, frolic, gambol, pace, parade, pesade, ride, romp, spring, stalk, stir, strut, swagger, swank, sweep, tittup
PRANK adorn, antic, beautify, bedeck, bedizen, boutade, brogue, caper, capriccio, caprice, curvet, deck, decorate, dido, dress, embellish, escapade, fegary, figary, fold, freak, frolic, gambol, game, humor, jest, jig, jink, jog, joke, lark, marlock, monkeyshine, nipup, ornament, perk up, play, pleat, prance, prat, preen, primp, prink, quiz, rigwiddie, rigwiddy, rollick, shavie, shenanigan, shine, shtickl (ech), shtik(eleh), smart, spangle, spoof, sport, trick, vagary
PRANKER caperer, dancer, horse
PRANKSTER gonef, gonif, gonov, wit
PRASE chalcedony, mineral, quartz
PRASINE chrysoberyl, emerald, mineral, pseudomalachite
PRAT beat, bum, buttock, nudge, pocket, prank, push, rump, spank, trick
PRATE babble, blate, blatter, bleat, boast, brag, buck, bukh, carp, chat(ter), gab (ble), gibber, gossip, jabber, loquacity, nonsense, patter, prattle, rant, scold, talk, twaddle, yap
PRATFALL blunder, defeat, error, tumble
PRATINCOLE glareola
PRATTLE argot, babblement, bavardage, blather, blether, cackle, chavish, clack, clatter, confabulate, gaff, jaunder, lisp, PRATE, smalltalk, speech
PRAVITY crookedness, deformity, DEPRAVITY
PRAWN carid(oid), crevette, crustacean, macruran, nipper, palaemon, pandalus, pe-

neus, scampi, SHRIMP, squilla
comb. caris
PRAXIS action, custom, example, exercise, grammar, habit, model, practice
PRAXITELES *model* phryne *statue* aphrodite, hermes
PRAXITHEA *husband* erechtheus
PRAY adjure, appeal, ask, beg, beseech, bid, bless, conjure, daven, effect, entreat, implore, importune, invite, invocate, invoke, petition, plead, please, praise, request, sue, supplicate, thank, vouch
let us oremus
PRAYER abodah, agnus dei, alenu, anaphora, angelus, antiphon(y), apolysis, appeal, ave(maria), beadroll, bene(diction), beseechment, cathisma, chaplet, collect, complin, credo, ectene, entreaty, fatihah, gayatri, geullah, grace, hail mary, imploration, importunity, imprecation, intercession, invocation, kaddish, kyrie, litany, mantra, matin(s), miserere, namaz, novena, obsecration, obtestation, orison, pater-noster, petition, plea, preghiera, request, rogation, rosary, salah, salat, service, suit, supplication, tahanun, tehinnah, thanks(giving), vesper, yizkor
bead(s) ave, rosary
book breviary, euchology, hora(e), mahzor, missal, ordo, portas(s), porthors, porthouse, ritual, siddur
call adan, azan, bell, chime, ezan, oremus
canonical breviary
comb. ora
confession confiteor
consecration anaphora, epanaphora
desk prie-dieu
dismissal apolysis
eucharist anamnesis, anaphora
evening vespers
fervor kavvanah, kawwanah
for dead requiescat
for mercy miserere
form chant, litany
hours for horae canonicae
joint knee
last complin(e)

leader imam

liturgical amidah

long cathisma

morning aubade, matin

9-day novena

personification litae

place church, idgah, mihrab, mosque, synagogue, temple

recital geulah, hamotzi, kedusha

rug kulah, melas, meles, namazlik

say backward blaspheme, curse

season advent

set aitesis, akoluthia, book of hours, comprecation, irenica

shawl tallith

short benediction, collect, grace, invocation

stick baho(o), paho, pajo

tower minaret

wheel-user lama

PREACH advocate, announce, deliver, discourse, edify, enjoin, evangelize, exhort, expound, homilize, inculcate, inform, instruct, lecture, moralize, predicate, proclaim, pronounce, pulpiteer, sermonize, s(o)ugh, speak, talk, teach

down decry, humiliate, oppose, repress, silence, threaten

up commend, exalt, extoll

PREACHER churchman, circuit-rider, clergyman, darshan(im), ecclesiastic, evangel(ist)(izer), exhorter, friar, homilist, khatib, lecturer, lollard, maggid, minister, orator, padre, pardoner, parson, pastor, predicant, priest, prophet, pulpiteer, rabbi, sermoner, sermonist, sermonizer, shepherd, speaker, spintext, teacher, tubbist, tubster

blundering martext

patron saint paul

PREACHING evangelism, hearing, homiletics, kerugma, kerygma, prophecy, pulpiteering, pulpitism, sermon (izing)

PREACHMENT See SERMON.

PREAMBLE avant-propos, beginning, exordium, foreword, introduction, overture, preface, preliminary, prelude, proem, prologue, prolusion, protasis, whereas

PREARRANGE forecast, foresee, plan, premeditate

PREBEND allowance, benefice, stipend, tithe

PRECARIOUS assumed, begging, casual, chancy, contingent, critical, dangerous, delicate, doubtful, dubious, haphazard, hazardous, importunate, insecure, insubstantial, perilous, risky, rocky, shaky, slippery, slippy, supplicant, uncertain, undependable, unfounded, unreliable, unsound, unstable, unsure, unwarranted

PRECAUTION care, cautel, caveat, forewarn, guard against, portent, preadmonish, warn

take insure

PRECEDE antecede, antedate, anticipate, exceed, forerun, forestall, guide, head, introduce, lead, outrank, pace, pioneer, preamble, precurse, preface, prelude rank, spearhead, surpass, usher

PRECEDENCE antecedence, lead(ing), order, primacy, priority, rank, right(of way), rule, superiority, supremacy, tradition

comb. ante

right of pas

PRECEDENT antecedent, anterior, authority, decision, draft, example, forerunner, instance, model, original, pattern, prognostic, rule, sign, specimen, standard, token, usage

PRECEDING above, aforesaid, antecedent, anterior, before, earlier, first, foregoing, foremost, former, front, head(ing), in advance, lead(ing), past, pioneer(ing), precedent, precessional, precursory, preliminary, prevenient, previous, prior, proambient, prodromal, van

PRECENTOR canon, cantor, chaplain, choirdirector, coryphaeus, ecclesiastic, leader, psalmist

PRECEPT act, adage, axiom, behest, belief, breve, brief, canon, caution, charge, code, command, dictate, dictum, direction, doctrine, dogma, formula, idea, injunction, instruction, law, mandate, maxim, motto, order, ordinance, prescript(ion), principle, regulation, rule, statute, sutra, sutta, tenet, torah, warrant, writ

PRECEPTIVE dictated, didactic, didascalic, educational, formulary, instructive, mandatory, prescribed, prescript(ive), regulation, standard

PRECEPTOR instructor, master, principal, teacher, tutor

PRECINCT ambit, bound (ary), close, district, domain, enclosure, environs, hieron, sphere, temenos

leader captain

PRECIOSITY affectation, elegance, refinement

PRECIOUS admired, adorable, adored, affected, arrant, beloved, cherished, choice, complete, costly, darling, dear, egregious, elegant, esteemed, expensive, extremely, fastidious, favorite, golden, great, invaluable, overnice, overrefined, particular, perfect, pet, precise, priceless, prized, rare, silver, stagy, thorough, treasured, valuable, very, wellliked

little few

stone See GEM.

PRECIPICE bluff, cliff, clogwyn, crag, craig, declivity, descent, downfall, drop, height, heuch, heugh, khud, krans, krantz, linn, pali, palisade(s), pena, scar(p), scree, sheer, steep, wall

PRECIPITATE, PRECIPITANT abrupt, accelerate, breakneck, clarify, coerce, condense, constrain, destroy, dew, disorder, dispatch, drive, expedite, fall, force, free, gravitate, hasten, hasty, headlong, headstrong, heady, hurried, hurry, impel, impetuous, impulsive, liberate, lycopin, materialize, overthrow, plunge, premature, quicken, rain, rash, reckless, refractory, remainder, result, rushing, separate, slapdash, snow, speed, steep, sudden, tumble, willful

PRECIPITATELY abruptly, headfirst, suddenly

PRECIPITATION acceleration, deposit, descent, dew, downpour, fall, hail, haste, impetuosity, mist, precipitate, prematurity, rain(fall), remainder, rush, sleet, snow, virga

PRECIPITIN coagulin

PRECIPITOUS abrupt, bluff, bold, brant, hasty, headlong, hurried, perpendicular, rapid, rash, rising, sheer, soaring, steep, sudden, towering

PRECIS abstract, apercu, blueprint, brief, compendium, digest, epitome, junonia, outline, pandect, sketch, summary, survey, syllabus

PRECISE absolute, accurate, articulate, buckram, categorical, ceremonial, ceremonious, certain, clear, conscientious, correct, definite, distinct, even, exact, explicit, express, fastidious, finicky, formal, literal, meticulous, minute, nice, overnice, painstaking, particular, priggish, prim, punctilious, right, rigid, rigorous, scrupulous, specific, starchy, stiff, strict, stringent, tidy, trig, true

PRECISELY definitely, exactly, expressly, finely, formally, justly, prim(ly), punctually, sharp, squarely, strait, to a tee

PRECISIAN(IST) conformist, formalist, pedant, perfectionist, prig, puritan

PRECISION abstraction, accuracy, clarity, definiteness, definition, delicacy, exactness, formality, justness, nicety, reservation, strictness

PRECLUDE avert, bar, block, close, debar, deter, discontinue, eliminate, estop, forbid, forestall, hinder, impeded, obstruct, obviate, prevent, prohibit, quit, restrain, shut out, silence, stop, ward off

PRECOCIOUS advanced, beforehand, forward, precox, premature, unripe

PRECONCEIVE dream, fore-

know, ideate, plan, scheme, think

PRECONCEPTION bias, prejudgment, prejudice

PRECURSOR antecedent, cause, crier, forefather, foregoer, forerunner, harbinger, john the baptist, herald, mark, messenger, predecessor, prodrome, reason, sign, symptom, token

PREDATOR destroyer, hawk, owl, robber

PREDATORY consumptive, destructive, harmful, hungry, injurious, looting, marauding, pillaging, piratical, plundering, predacious, rapacious, raptorial, ravenous, spoliative

PREDECESSOR ancestor, elder, forefather, foregoer, guide, leader, PRECURSOR, progenitor

PREDELLA altar(step), footpace, gradin, platform, retable, shelf

PREDESTINATION *believer* particularist

PREDESTINE decree, destinate, determine, doom, foredoom, foreordain, forepoint, foretell, foretoken, ordain, predetermine, predoom, preordain

PREDETERMINE bias, destine, forecast, predict, PREDESTINE, prejudice, preordain, prepossess

PREDETERMINATION See DESTINY.

PREDICAMENT box, complication, condition, corner, difficulty, dilemma, emergency, exigency, extremity, fix, hobble, hole, hot water, imbroglio, impasse, jam, mess, mix, muddle, pass, pickle, pinch, plight, plunge, pretty pass, problem, quagmire, quandary, scramble, scrape, situation, slough, spot, state, stew, strait(s), tight spot

PREDICATE adumbrate, affirm, assert, aver, avouch, avow, base, commend, declare, found, imply, postulate, praise, preach, predict, proclaim, protest, state, warrant

PREDICT adumbrate, anticipate, augur, auspicate, betoken, bode, call, croak, di-

vine, dope, forecast, foresee, forespeak, foretell, halsen, hariolate, omen, portend, presage, prognosticate, prophesy, pythonize, soothsay, vaticinate, warn, weird

PREDICTION anticipation, augury, auspice, bod(e) word, boding, divinition, foreboding, forecasting, foresight, foretelling, hariolation, horoscope, manticism, omen, palmistry, portent, presage(ment), prognosis, prognostication, promise, prophesy, vaticination, vaticine

basis zodiac

PREDICTIVE divinatory, fatidic, mantic, mantistic, prognostic, prophetic

PREDICTOR aeromancer, augur, auspex, chaldean, chiromancer, clairvoyant, divinator, diviner, forecaster, foreseer, fortuneteller, haruspex, presager, prophet, sage, seer(ess), soothsayer, sortileger

PREDILECTION aptitude, bent, bias, choice, disposition, flair, gift, hang, inclination, knack, leaning, liking, partiality, penchant, preference, propensity, relish, turn

PREDISPOSE affect, govern, impress, incline, influence, prejudice, sway, tend

PREDISPOSED biased, capable, inclined, minded, partial, prone, sold, tending

PREDISPOSITION bent, bias, inclination, itch, pattern, predilection, propensity, susceptibility

PREDOMINANCE ascendancy, dominion, influence, superiority

PREDOMINANT ascendant, chief, controlling, directing, foremost, great, influential, leading, main, obtaining, paramount, powerful, preponderant, prevailing, prevalent, principal, reigning, ruling, sovereign, superior

PREDOMINATE control, exceed, preponderate, prevail, rule

PREEMINENCE brilliance, distinction, precedence, superiority

PREEMINENT banner, big, capital, cardinal, celebrated, chief, consummate, distinguished, dominant, excellent, excelling, finished, foremost, grand, great, outdoing, outstanding, palmary, paramount, peerless, prominent, ranking, splendid, star, stellar, superior, superlative, supreme, surpassing, top, transcendent, unequalled

PREEMINENTLY par excellence

PREEMPT appropriate, arrogate, collar, confiscate, coopt, debar, eliminate, exclude, grab, grasp, seize, take, usurp

PREEN adorn, bodkin, brooch, clasp, congratulate, decorate, doll up, dress, gloat, groom, hook, ornament, perk up, pierce, pin, pique, plume, prank, press, prick, pride, primp, prink, prune, sew, sleek, smooth, spruce, stitch, swell, trifle, trim

PREFABRICATE create, form, make, manufacture

PREFACE avant-propos, beginning, blessing, exordium, foretalk, foreword, front, herald, induction, introduce, introduction, isagoge, open, overture, prayer, preamble, preliminary, prelude, proem, prologue, prologuize, prolusion, protasis, usher

PREFECT chief, chi-fu, dean, director, executive, head, magistrate, minister, monitor, official, prefer, prepositor, president, promote, student, wali

PREFECTURE district, eparchy, jong, ken, province

PREFER advance, affect, approve, attribute, bring, care, choose, cull, desire, elect, endorse, exalt, fancy, favor, handpick, introduce, like, offer, opt, outrank, pick, present, proffer, promote, raise, recommend, refer, regard, select, single out, submit, surpass, tender

charges arraign

PREFERABLE better, lief, rather, superior

PREFERENCE bias, choice,

countenance, darling, desire, election, favor(ite), liking, option, partiality, pick, predilection, priority, privilege, promotion, propensity, say, selection, superiority, taste

PREFERENTIAL choosy, chosen

PREFERMENT advancement, ascent, benefice, countenance, elevation, favor, partiality, priority, progress, promotion, rise, seniority

PREFIGURE augur, foresee, foreshadow, foretell, ideate, imagine, indicate, predict, shadow, symbolize, type

PREFIX adjunct, affix, before, doon, dun, prelude, purpose, resolve, title

PREGNABLE assailable, vulnerable

PREGNANT abundant, big, breeding, cogent, concise, eloquent, enceinte, expressive, fertile, forcible, fruitful, gestant, gravid, important, inventive, meaningful, meaty, obvious, pithy, pointed, potential, pressing, productive, promising, ready, redolent, sententious, significant, suggestive, swelling, teeming, weighty

PREHALLUX calcar, toe

PREHALTER squama

PREHENSILE clawed, digital, digitate(d), fingered, grasping, raptorial, retentive, taloned

PREHENSION (See also APPREHENSION.) arrest, seizure

PREJUDICE bent, bias, bigotry, blind spot, damage, detriment, disadvantage, discrimination, expectation, favoritism, harm, hurt, ignorance, incline, indoctrinate, influence, injure, injury, intolerance, jaundice, kink, leaning, mischief, narrowness, partiality, preconception, predilection, prepossess(ion), presumption, racism, scunder, scunner, slant, soothsay, twist, unfairness, warp

appealing to ad hominem

racial apartheid, discrimination, racism, xenophobia

without big, broad-minded, fair, liberal, tolerant

PREJUDICED biased, bigoted, colored, discriminatory, distorted, illiberal, intolerant, jaundiced, narrowminded, partial, sectarian, slanted, subjective, unfair

PREJUDICIAL biased, contrary, damaging, deleterious, detrimental, harmful, hurtful, injurious, sinister

PRELATE abbess, abbot, archbishop, bishop, cardinal, chief, cleric, deacon, dignitary, ecclesiastic, head, hierarch, leader, monsignor, ordinary, pontiff, pope, priest, primate, superior

PRELECT discourse, lecture, speak

PRELECTION address, allocution, discourse, harangue, homily, lecture, oration, reading, sermon, speech, talk

PRELIMINARY ahead, antecedent, exordial, first, introductory, liminary, opening, preamble, preceding, precursory, prefatory, prelude, preparatory, previous, prior, proemial, rough draft

PRELUDE avant-propos, beginning, borspiel, descant, exordium, foreword, induction, intrada, introduction, overture, preamble, preface, prefix, prelim(inary), premise, presupposition, proem (ium), prolegomenon, prolepsis, prologue, prolusion, protasis, overture, ritornel (le), verset, voluntary, vorspiel

PRELUDIN See AMPHETAMINE.

PREMARIN estrogen

PREMATURE abrupt, advanced, early, forward, fruitless, halfbaked, halfcocked, hasty, oversoon, precipitate, precocious, previous, sudden, unprepared, unripe, unseasonable, untimely

PREMEDITATED advised, calculated, conscious, considered, deliberate, designed, intended, intentional, meant, planned, purposed, set, studied, voluntary, willful

PREMIER acme, best, chief, earliest, first, foremost, head, leading, oldest, primary, prime minister, principal, ruler, supreme

PREMIERE first night, open(ing), performance, star *danseuse* coryphee

PREMISE affirmation, apriorism, assertion, assumption, basis, condition, foundation, ground, hypothesis, lemma, philosopheme, position, postulate, prelude, presumption, presupposition, proposal, reason, stipulation, sumption, supposal, supposition, term, theorem, theory, thesis

PREMISES area, building(s), data, digs, grounds, home, house, land, property

PREMIUM agio(tage), allowance, award, batta, bonus, bounty, contango, extra, favor, fee, gift, giveaway, gratuity, guerdon, lagniappe, payment, present, price, prize, quality, rate, recompense, remuneration, special, state, usury
at a rare, scarce

PREMONITION apprehension, bodword, esp, feeling, foreboding, forefeeling, forescent, forewarning, hunch, impression, information, intimation, notice, omen, portent, presage, presentiment, suspicion, warning

PREMONITORY foreboding, forewarning, ominous

PREOCCUPATE anticipate, forestall, surprise

PREOCCUPATION absent-mindedness, absorption, appropriation, assimilation, attention, attentiveness, brown study, detachment, engrossment, fixation, hangup, incorporation, insight, prolepsis, reverie, woolgathering, worry

PREOCCUPIED absent(minded), absorbed, abstracted, busy, crazy, distrait, distraught, dreaming, engrossed, fascinated, filled, forgetful, immersed, inattentive, intent, lost, musing, oblivious, rapt, spellbound, unmindful, unobservant

PREOCCUPY absorb, appropriate, bias, engage, engross, obsess, prepossess

PREP (See **PREPARE.**) school, student
school grade form

PREPARATION accomplishment, adaptation, anticipation, arrangement, base, basis, bath, blend, brew, concoction, confection, decoction, dope, equipment, extract, fitness, fitting, formation, foundation, groundwork, makeready, manufacture, medication, mix, precaution, preface, production, provision, qualification, readiness, ready, rehearsal, scaffold(ing), simple, study(hour), training
place of laboratory, paratorium
sweet dolce
unctuous cerate
without ad lib, careless, extemporaneous, extempore, impromptu, improvised, spontaneous

PREPARE accommodate, accouter, accustom, adapt, address, adjust, alert, apparel, appoint, arm, arrange, array, author, betake, block out, brew, busk, calculate, clear, compose, compound, concoct, condition, cook, create, cultivate, decoct, develop, devise, dight, draft, dress, edit, equip, ettle, fit, fix, forearm, furnish, get(ready), gibe, gird, graith, groom, ground, hatch, instruct, insure, lay by, make(ready), man, marinate, outfit, pave, plan, prime, process, procure, produce, provide, qualify, ready, redact, rehearse, repair, revise, roughhew, set(tle), supply, taw, train, treat, unlimber, write
hastily rash
oneself address, anticipate, await, buckle, expect, foresee, practice, rehearse, train, unlimber

PREPARED alert, apt, available, boun(d), equipped, fit, forehanded, girt, graith, groomed, handy, made, on guard, prest, primed, readied, ready, ripe, set, skilled, yare
in advance canned

PREPENSE aforethought, deliberate, design, fore-

thought, preconceive(d), precontrive, premeditate(d)

PREPOLLENT influential, predominant, prevailing, superior

PREPONDERANCE ascendancy, dominance, dominion, influence, majority, plurality, prevalence, weight

PREPONDERANT dominant, influential, outstanding, paramount, predominant, predominating, preeminent, salient, signal, sovereign, supreme, surpassing

PREPONDERATE decide, descend, dispose, dominate, exceed, gravitate, incline, overbalance, outweigh, persuade, prevail, surpass

PREPOSITION about, across, after, all(a), alongside, before, but, con, cum, des, except, for, from, in(to), of(f), on(to), out, over, per, prefix, sans, tae, through, till, until, unto, up(on), with(out)

PREPOSSESS appropriate, bias, influence, prejudice, preoccupation, turn

PREPOSTEROUS absurd, bizarre, crazy, exorbitant, fanciful, fantastic, foolish, grotesque, inept, irrational, outlandish, outrageous, ridiculous, screwy, senseless, silly, unbelievable, undue, unreasonable

PREREQUISITE condition, essential, exigency, necessary, necessity, need, postulate, qualification, requirement

PREROGATIVE advantage, ap(p)anage, authority, birthright, claim, due, faculty, honor, leading, perquisite, precedence, preeminence, privilege, right, superiority

PRERUPT abrupt, precipitous, steep, sudden

PRESAGE announce, augur(y), betide, betoken, bode, boding, divine, forebode, foreboding, forecast, foreshadow, foretell, harbinger, herald, import, mean, omen, ominate, osse, ostent, portend, portent, predict(ion), premonition, prescience, presentiment, prognostic(ate), prophecy, prophesy, prophet, show, sign(ify), soothsay, symptom, token, warning

PRESBYTER antistes, clergyman, ecclesiastic, elder, minister, prester, priest

PRESBYTINAE guereza, langur, monkey

PRESCIENCE foreknowledge, foresight, omniscience, prenotion, presage, prevision

PRESCIND abstract, cut short, detach, disengage, isolate, separate, sever

PRESCRIBE act, advise, advocate, allot, appoint, assign, authorize, command, confine, control, define, designate, dictate, direct, enjoin, establish, fix, foretell, guide, indite, instruct, invalidate, lay down, limit, ordain, order, outlaw, prophesy, set(tle), tax, urge

PRESCRIBED allotted, appointed, assigned, basic, destined, fixed, ordained, ordered, prescriptive, ruled, set(tled), thetic(al)

PRESCRIPT command, direction, law, mandate, order, precept, rule

PRESCRIPTION axiom, bill, custom, direction, forescript, form(ula), instruction, law, limitation, medicine, monopoly, precept, receipt, recipe, remedy, restraint, right

PRESCRIPTIVE customary, traditional, usual

PRESENCE air, apparition, appearance, aspect, assembly, attendance, bearing, behavior, being, carriage, company, demeanor, existence, front, ghost, look, manner, mien, person(ality), port, position, potentiality, sovereign, specter, spirit, ubiety, ubiquity, whereabouts

of mind aplomb, composure, poise, self-possession

PRESENT 3 act, aim, gie, now, put, say 4 boon, gift, give, here, open, show, star, tell 5 adsum, award, being, bonus, bound, favor, grant, issue, nonce, offer, raise, ready, stage, today, yield 6 accord, actual, adduce, allege, at hand, bestow, confer, convey, direct, donate, extant, intent, khilat,

latent, latest, modern, prefer, reward, submit, supply, tender, xenium 7 advance, cumshaw, current, deliver, display, douceur, exhibit, expound, fairing, feature, furnish, handsel, instant, located, porrect, premier, produce, proffer, provide, situate, tashrif, topical, trot out 8 acquaint, approach, backshis, describe, donation, existent, existing, gratuity, largesse, manifest, situated, uptodate 9 attendant, attentive, available, baksheesh, dramatize, favorable, immediate, introduce, lagniappe, putacross, verthandi 10 ubiquitous 11 benefaction 12 contemporary, contribution 13 participating

again rerun

always chronic

-day contemporary, current, faddish, mod(ern), up-to-the-minute

everywhere ubiquitous

era cenozoic

in detail discuss

to guest xenium

with another collocal

PRESENTABLE fair, suitable, tolerable

PRESENTATION act, analysis, appearance, argument, bestowal, billing, debut, delivery, display, donation, image, muster, overture, performance, proposal, proposition, schema, show, spectacle

1st debut, premiere

PRESENTIMENT alarm, anticipation, apprehension, dread, fear, foreboding, forefeel, misgiving, premonition, prenotion, prospect, terror

PRESENTLY anon, before long, by and by, directly, enow, forthwith, immediately, now, shortly, soon

PRESERVATION conservation, keeping, maintenance, retention, safekeeping, salvation, saving

PRESERVATIVE abrastol, alcohol, borax, brine, conservative, creosote, formaldehyde, marinade, medicine, pickle, salt, spice, sugar, vinegar

PRESERVE anhydrate, ath-

old, bless, brine, bottle, can(dy), confiture, conservation, conserve, continue, corn, cure, defend, dehydrate, deliver, dessicate, dry, embalm, enshrine, ensilage, evaporate, freeze, fume, guard, jam, jar, jelly, jerk, keep, kipper, maintain, marinade, marinate, marmalade, mothball, mummify, park, perpetuate, pickle, pot, protect, put up, redeem, refrigerate, rescue, reservation, reserve, retain, retreat, safeguard, salt, sanctuary, save, season, secure, shelter, shield, shikargah, smoke, souse, spare, store, support, sustain, tan, tin, uphold

in brine corn, cure, pickle, salt

in oil marinate

in sugar candy, crystallize

PRESIDE administer, chair, conduct, control, direct, guide, moderate, operate, regulate, rule, run, superintend

PRESIDENT administrator, boss, commander, damask, executive, governor, guardian, head, officer, protector, ruler, sovereign

nickname abe, cal, fdr, gerry, ike, jack, jimmy, teddy

PRESIDIO fort, garrison, post, settlement

PRESS 3 dun, hug, jam, mob, ram, wad 4 bear, cram, goad, host, iron, mash, pack, prod, push, roll, rout, seek, spur, tamp, urge 5 argue, brize, brizz, chirt, clamp, clasp, crimp, crowd, crush, exact, force, group, horde, hurry, knead, level, media, order, pinch, print, serry, smash, stamp, stomp, stuff, tread, tweak, wedge 6 assert, attach, attack, burden, charge, closet, compel, crease, crunch, cumber, enroll, exhort, harass, hasten, hustle, insist, legion, mangle, oblige, smooth, squash, strain, stress, strive, thrimp, thring, throng, thrust, weight 7 advance, concise, contend, embrace, entreat, flatten, obtrude, oppress, solicit, squeeze, squelch, straits,

thrutch, trample, urgency 8 astringe, beardown, busyness, calendar, compress, cupboard, distress, persuade, throttle 9 constrain, emphasize, importune, influence, multitude 10 commandeer, compulsion, difficulty, newspapers 12 fourth estate
-agent advertise, ballyhoo, flack, huckster, publicist
between rollers calender
corrector proofreader
critic censor
famous aldine, elzev(i)er, kelmscott
in enter, interfere, intrude
in ranks serry
kind cylinder, electrotype, letterpress, platen, punch, rotary, web
notice publicity
out render, sieve, stamp, strain, tread
release advance, blurb, handout, publicity
syndicated wire service
together bale, bind, serry
underground berkeley barb, east village other, fifth estate, freep, free press, good times, village voice
PRESSED coarctate, compacted, cooked, dense, harassed, hurried, molded, serried, squeezed, urged
PRESSER baler, ironer, mangle
of skins sammier
PRESSING critical, crying, demanding, exacting, exigent, imperative, important, importunate, insistent, persistent, rushing, urgent
PRESSMAN pig, printer, prover
PRESSURE bearing, blast, brunt, build-up, burden, busyness, coercion, compression, constraint, cramp, crush, dispatch, distress, exaction, exigency, force, heat, hurry, impression, influence, instancy, nip, oblige, oppression, pinch, push(ing), shear, squeeze, stamp, strain, stress, tension, thrust, torsion, tweak, urge(ncy), weight
comb. bar(o)
cooker autoclave, steamer
difference in draft, draught
equal isobaric
gauge algometer, barograph,

barometer, baroscope, bourdon tube, manometer, manoscope, piezometer, tonometer
group lobby
manual taxis
perception baresthesia
principle boyle's law
unit bar(ad), barie, barye, decibar, dyne, mesobar, microbar, micron, torr
PREST advance, duty, hasten, lend, loan, neat, prompt, proper, quick, readily, ready, soon
PRESTER hurricane, presbyter, priest, serpent, snake, vein, whirlwind
PRESTIDIGITATION jugglery, juggling, legerdemain, MAGIC, sleight of hand, trick
PRESTIDIGITATOR conjuror, juggler, MAGICIAN, palmer, pythonic
PRESTIGE authority, cachet, caste, consequence, credit, deception, dignity, dominion, eclat, eminence, esteem, face, fame, glory, honor, illusion, influence, kudos, moment, note, position, power, pressure, prominence, rank, renown, reputation, repute, sorcery, standing, station, stature, status, sway, trick, weight, yiches, yichus, yihus
PRESTO at once, immediate(ly), in haste, instantaneous, passing, quickly, rapid(ly), suddenly
PRESUMABLY hypothetically, probably, theoretically
PRESUME anticipate, arrogate, assume, conclude, conjecture, dare(say), deduce, expect, gather, grant, guess, hope, imply, impose, infer, judge, posit, postulate, predicate, prejudge, premise, presuppose, pretend, profess, suppose, surmise, think, usurp, venture
on deceive, encroach, exploit, impose
PRESUMPTION assumption, audacity, brass, cheek, conjecture, contumely, conviction, crust, hypothesis, implication, insolence, license, likelihood, nerve, opinion, outrage, position, postulate, premise, succudry, sup-

posal, surmise, surquidry, view
PRESUMPTIVE a priori, arrogant, assumed, brash, circumstantial, due, icarian, inferred, plausible, probable, supposed
PRESUMPTUOUS arrogant, assuming, assumptive, audacious, bold, brash, brassy, cheeky, familiar, foolhardy, forward, fresh, haughty, icarian, impudent, insolent, overweening, pert, PRESUMPTIVE, proud, sassy, saucy, wil(l)ful
PRESUPPOSE assume, conjecture, deduce, gather, guess, imply, infer, judge, posit, postulate, premise, surmise
PRESUPPOSITION belief, cause, deduction, guess, implication, inference, judgment, opinion, prelude, premise, position, surmise, view
PRETEND act, affect, aim, allege, arrogate, aspire, assert, assume, attempt, beguile, bluff, boggle, claim, cloak, counterfeit, deceive, delude, design, disguise, dissemble, dissimulate, extend, fake, feign, fool, forebode, impersonate, import, intend, let on, make believe, malinger, mask, masquerade, mislead, offer, play-act, plot, portend, pose, possum, pretext, proceed, profess, purport, put on, represent, seem, sham, signify, simulate, try, undertake
PRETENDED alleged, assumed, avowed, fake, false, feigned, proposed, pseudo, seeming, sham, so-called, unreal
PRETENDER actor, attitudinarian, attitudinizer, bluffer, braggart, charlatan, claimant, deceiver, euphemist, euphuist, fake(r), fourflusher, fraud, hypocrite, imposter, mountebank, pose(u)r, posurist, pseudo, punk, quack, seemer, shoddy, swaggerer, tinhorn
religious tartuf(f)e
PRETENSE act, affectation, air(s), allegation, artifice, bravado, camouflage, cant, claim, cloak, color, cover,

deceit, deception, dissimulation, excuse, fabrication, fake(ry), falsehood, feint, fraud, gloss, gloze, humbug(gery), imposture, intent(ion), makebelieve, makeshift, ostentation, playacting, plea, pose, postiche, pretext, purpose, put-on, right, ruse, semblance, sham, show, side, simulation, subterfuge, swank, title, wile
at aim, attempt
PRETENSION ambition, aspiration, claim, dream, duplicity, expectation, fancy, guile, hope, hypocrisy, intention, prerogative, PRETENSE, PRETEXT, privilege, right, title, vanity
PRETENTIOUS affected, ambitious, apish, artificial, arty, assuming, bombastic, braggy, conceited, conspicuous, flashy, florid, garish, gaudy, grandiloquent, grandiose, haughty, highfalutin(g), inflated, ostentatious, pompous, presuming, puffed(up), self-important, shoddy, showy, sidy, strained, swollen, tawdry, toplofty, unnatural, vain
PRETERMIT break off, disregard, ignore, intermit, interrupt, miss, neglect, omit, pass, suspend
PRETERNATURAL abnormal, atypic, gousty, irregular, miraculous, remarkable, strange, superhuman, uncommon
PRETEXT apology, blind, bluff, claim, cloak, color, cover, escape, excuse, feint, gesture, gloss, guise, handle, makeshift, mask, peg, plea, pretend, PRETENSE, pretension, put-off, refuge, semblance, sham, shift, show, stall, stratagem, subterfuge, trick, umbrage, varnish, veil
PRETORIA *homeland* bantustan
PRETTIKIN feat, trick
PRETTY attractive, beauteous, beautiful, betcheri, bonita, bonnie, bonny, budgeree, canny, clever, comely, considerable, cunning, cute, dainty, deft, excellent, fair, fine, finical, foppish, gay, gey, good, handsome,

ingenious, interesting, intrepid, joli(e), knickknack, lovely, mignon, moderately, petite, pleasing, pooty, pure, rather, sharp, stout, strong, tolerably, toy, trim, winsome, wonderful
pass predicament
-pretty keepsake, knickknack, nambypamby
PREVAIL abound, actuate, conquer, dominate, drive, endure, exist, fold, impell, master, move, obtain, overcome, persist, persuade, predominate, reign, rule, succeed, sway, triumph, win
against better, resist, weather, withstand
upon allure, convince, entice, entreat, impress, induce, influence, lead, persuade, sway, urge, win
PREVAILING current, dominant, efficacious, epidemic, extensive, frequent, general, going, happening, influential, moving, ordinary, present, prevalent, rife, universal, usual, widespread
PREVALENT about, accustomed, brief, catholic, common, current, customary, dominant, efficacious, epidemic, extant, familiar, general, happening, indigenous, influential, popular, potent, powerful, predominant, raging, rampant, recurrent, rife, successful, usual, victorious, widespread, wonted
PREVARICATE belie, cavil, deviate, dodge, elude, equivocate, evade, fabricate, invent, LIE, misrepresent, palter, pettifog, quibble, shuffle
PREVENE anticipate, forestall, overtake, precede, prevent, take
PREVENT anticipate, arrest, avert, avoid, baffle, balk, bar, block, check, circumvent, dam, debar, deflect, deter, discourage, disenable, dispose of, estop, exclude, fend(off), foil, forbid, foreclose, forestall, forlet, frustrate, halt, hasten, help, hinder, impede, inhibit, intercept, interdict, interrupt, obstruct, obviate, outrun, precede, preclude, prepossess, prohibit, remove, repel,

restrain, rule out, save, stave off, stay, stop, thwart, ward (off), warn, withhold
PREVENTION anticipation, avoidance, deterrence, discouragement, estoppel, hindrance, obstacle, obstruction, precaution, preclusion, preface, prejudice, prohibition, prolepsis
comb. ant(i)
PREVIOUS antecedaneous, antecedent, anterior, before, done, earlier, erst, first, foregoing, former, inopportune, over, past, preceding, premature, prior, untimely
PREXY See PRESIDENT.
PREY booty, capture, chase, depredation, feed(on), fleece, loot, loser, martyr, oppress, pillage, plunder, prize, quarry, quest, raid, rapine, ravage, raven, ravin, rob, seizure, spoil, victim, wretch
living on predatory
PRIACANTHUS catalufa, catfish
PRIAM *consort* arisba, hecuba, laothoe
counselor antenor, panthous, thymoetes, ucalegon
daughter cassandra, creusa, ilione, laodice, polyxena
father laomedon
grandfather ilus, tithonus
herdsman agelaus
nephew memnon
sister aeghylla, cilla, hesione
slayer neoptolemus, pyrrhus
son aesacus, agathon, antiphus, aretus, corythus, deiphobus, gorgythian, hector, hektor, helenus, isus, laocoon, margarelon, paris, polydorus, troilus
victim munippus
PRIAPISM tentigo
PRIAPUS *parent* aphrodite, dionysus
symbol cornucopia, sickle
worship site lampsacus
PRICE amount, ante, appraise, apprise, apprize, assess, award, bid, bribe, charge, carriage, cheap, compensation, consideration, cost, damage, esteem, estimation, evaluate, excellence, expenditure, expense, fame, fare, fee, fiar, fier, figure, freight, han(d)sel, hire, lay, odds, outlay, par (ity), penalty, praise, pre-

mium, pretium, prize, quotation, ransom, rate, reward, sacrifice, score, sum, superiority, tab, tariff, terms, toll, valorize, valuate, value, victory, worth
asking quotation
determination preciation
low bargain, wanworth
maintain peg
per dish a la carte
proper value
reduced bargain, sale
rise advance, appreciation, boom, inflation
PRICELESS absurd, amusing, cherished, costly, dear, expensive, funny, humorous, inestimable, invaluable, precious, prized, rare, unique, valuable, witty
PRICK adorn, aim, bore, briar, broach, brod, brog, choose, cloy, cut, degree, dot, dress, drill, drob, end, enter, footprint, gad, gallop, goad, hole, impel, incite, intent, jag(g), mark, needle, nettle, nick, note, pain, pang, particle, penetrate, perforate, pierce, ping, pink, pique, point, prickle, prink, pritch, probe, punch, puncture, qualm, remorse, skewer, slash, slit, smart, sour, spine, spur, stab, stick, sting, tang, target, thorn, thrust, tingle, turn, urge, wound
song descant
PRICKER horseman, needle, rider, spine, stabber, thorn
PRICKET buck, candle(stick), dag, finial, pike, spire
PRICKLE acantha, aculeus, barb, basket, briar, brier, bur(r), PRICK, prod, seta, sieve, spear, spicula, spiculum, spine, sting, thistle, thorn, thrill, tingle
-back cock's-comb
grass burdock, tragus
PRICKLOUSE tailor
PRICKLY acanaceous, barbed, brambly, briery, burred, burry, echinate(d), horrent, muricate, rough, scabrous, scratchy, sensitive, spicular, spiny, stinging, thistly, thorny, vexatious
ash hercules'-club, ruewort
cedar cade
comb. echino
heat acne, lichen, rash

nightshade sandbur
pear barbary-fig, cactus, nopal, opuntia, pinpillow, sabra, tun(a)
pine leopard-tree
poppy argemone, argemony, bird-in-the-bush, cockscomb
samphire parsnip
PRICKMADAM stonecrop
PRICKTIMBER dogwood, spindletree
PRIDE adorn(ment), airs, arrogance, band, beauty, boast(fulness), brag, bravado, complacency, conceit, condescension, congratulate, crow, decoration, dignity, disdain, display, ego(t)ism, elation, excess, exuberance, flock, gasconade, glorify, glory, group, haughtiness, hauteur, hubris, hybris, immodesty, insolence, loftiness, lordliness, lust, mettle, ostentation, patronage, pick, pique, plume, pomp, preen, prime, respect, self-esteem, self-respect, show, smugness, snottism, spirit, superiority, surquidy, swagger, treasure, vainglory, vanity, vaunt, wlonk(hede)
and prejudice author jane austen
and prejudice character bingley, collins, darcy, elizabeth bennet, lady catherine, wickham
fill with bloat, boast, exalt, inflate, peacock, puff up, vaunt
-of-india chinatree, varnishtree
-of the desert camel
self amour propre, conceit, ego(tism), tympany
symbol peacock
PRIDWIN *shield of* king arthur
PRIEST aaron, abbe, abuna, asiarch, amauta, babaylan, bhikkru, bhikshu, calchas, caserdos, cassock, chaplain, clergyman, cleric, confessor, cure, deacon, divine, druid, ecclesiastic, eli, epulo, fakir, father, flamen, fra, gosain, hierophant, kashyapa, lama, maga, marist, massmonger, minister, mobed, mystagogue, oblate, orator(ian), padre, pandita, papa, papaloi, parson, pas-

tor, patrico, pontiff, poongee, presbyter, prester, rabbi, sarip, shaman, tohunga, vicar, zadok
agricultural arval
army chaplain, padre
assistant acolyte
cap biretta, galerum
caste magus
chief syriarch
doctor shaman, wabeno
eunuch gallus
fish cherna, cod, rockfish, sebastodes
garment See VESTMENT *religious.*
group clergy, magi, ministry, sacerdocy, sacerdotage, salii
handwarmer calefactory
headdress saghavert
high aaron, caiaphas, cohen, dastur, destour, eli, hierarch, jehoiada, kahuna, phineas, pontifex, pontiff
in-the-pulpit cuckoopint
king patesi
mendicant fakir
outlaw babaylan
pagan babaylan
pert. aaronic(al), clerical, levitic(al), sacerdotal
voodoo gangang, hungan, mambu
PRIESTESS auge, bacbuc, entum, horse, mamaloi, mambo, mambu, phitones, phoibad, pythia, vesta
voodoo horse
PRIG bargain, beg, bluenose, buck, coxcomb, dandy, entreat, filch, fop, haggle, pan, pedant, pickpocket, pilfer, pitcher, plead, precisianist, prim, prink, prude, purist, puritan, quibble, ride, sharp, smug, snob, steal, thief, tinker
vulgar jackanapes
PRIGGISH complacent, conceited, egotistic, larcenous, prim, prudish, righteous, self-satisfied, smug, snobbish, snobby, thievish
PRIM ceremonial, dapper, decorous, demure, fastidious, formal, groom, mimsey, natty, neat, nice, paramour, precise, prig(gish), primp, prissy, privet, proper, proud, prudish, sedate, sleek, smart, smelt, smug, spruce, square-toed, stiff, strait-laced, stuffy

PRIMA DONNA diva, lead, singer, star, vocalist
famous flagstad, lind, patti, ponsel, russell, schumann-heink

PRIMA FACIE apparently, obvious, self-evident

PRIMAL absolute, basic, chief, first, fresh, new, original, prime(val), primitive, pristine, ultimate
chaos abyss

PRIMARY abecedarian, abecedary, aboriginal, basic, beginning, capital, cardinal, caucus, central, chief, earliest, election, elemental, elementary, essential, first, fundamental, hypogene, initial, key, leading, main, original, paramount, prime, primeval, primitive, primordial, principal, pristine

PRIMATE ape, archbishop, bishop, catarrhina, churchman, ecclesiastic, elder, exarch, katholikos, lemur, man, marmoset, monkey, patriarchy, prelate, sime

PRIMAVERA mahogany, spring, tabebuia

PRIME beginning, best, bloom(ing), blue-ribbon, central, charge, chief, choice, coach, copacetic, dawn, dew, excellent, finest, first, fresh, front, fundamental, heyday, leading, lewd, load, lustful, main, marvelous, master, may, paint, original, pink, prepare, pride, primal, primary, principal, prune, service, splendid, spring (time), superb, tonic, trim, tutor, virility, vitality, wind(up), youth(ful)
comb. arch(i)
minister atabeg, chancellor, premier, ruler
mover author, origin, producer, root, source
of life bloom, heyday, spring, youth

PRIMED cocked, prepared, ready, set, skilled

PRIMER abecedarium, abecedary, cap, detonator, first, hornbook, original, prayerbook, textbook, wafer

PRIMEVAL ancient, early, first, native, ogygian, old, original, PRIMARY, pristine

PRIMING *iron* drift
wire picker

PRIMITIVE aboriginal, ancient, antediluvean, antiquated, archaic, austere, barbarian, barbaric, basic, beginning, brutal, crude, dark, earliest, elemental, first, fundamental, gothic, ignorant, larval, naive, native, old, original, persistent, prehistoric, primary, primeval, primordial, priscan, pristine, protopathic, quaint, radical, rough, rudimentary, savage, simple, spartan, tribal, uncivilized, unsophisticated, wild
comb. archae(o), arche(o), arch(i)
friends quakers

PRIMOGENITOR ancestor, forefather

PRIMORDIAL archical, cambrian, crude, first, fundamental, original, primary, PRIME, PRIMEVAL, primitive

PRIMORDIUM anlage, beginning, bud, commencement, origin, rudiment, start

PRIMP adorn, beautify, deck, decorate, doll up, dress, perk up, prank, preen, prink, prune, purse, spruce, titivate

PRIMROSE afterglow, auricula, bird's-eye, circaea, clarkia, cowslip, fairycup, flower, gay, glaux, herb, innocent, onagra, oxlip, pimpernel, plumrock, polyanthus, primula, scabish, scurvish, spink, suncup
dwarf mistassini
evening scurvish
family primulaceae
family herb anagallis, anrosace
willow clovestrip

PRIMULA cowslip, oxlip, polyanthus, primrose, primwort

PRINCE, PRINCE'S adeling, aetheling, ahluwalia, alder (man), ameer, amir, archduke, atheling, bharata, chief, czarevitch, dauphin, duke, dynast, elector, emeer, emir, furst, gaekwar, heir-apparent, heir-presumptive, iman, imaum, khan, king, knez, lord, magnate, maharaja(h), mirza, mon-

arch, nasi, nawab, noble, peer, prinz, raja(h), rana, ras, rial, ruler, said, satrap, say(y)id, shahzada, sheik(h), shereef, sherif, sovereign, toparch, tsarevitch, wang, worthy, zerbino
allowance appanage
black edward
ecclesiastical cardinal
fairy tale frog
falstaff's hal
father atabeg, atabek, king
feather amaranth, lilac, pilewort, syringa
hal's brother clarence, humphrey, john, lancaster
hal's father henry iv
legendary gebir
of apostles st peter
of artists durer
of darkness ahriman, beelzebub, devil, satan
of demons asmodeus, beelzebub
of destruction tamerlane, timour
of enchanters merlin
of evil spirits sammael
of gossips pepys
of liars ananias, pinto
of peace jesus christ, messiah
of poets ronsard
of the sonnet joachim du bellay
of spanish poetry vega
of wales' motto ich dien
operatic igor
petty satrap, tetrarch, vergobret
pine pipsissewa
rupert macaroni, yankee doodle
rupert metal brass
sold into slavery oroonoko
title serene
val's father aguar

PRINCELY bountiful, dignified, generous, imperial, kingly, liberal, luxurious, munificent, noble, opulent, regal, royal, sovereign, splendid, stately

PRINCESS antiope, begum, creusa, czarevna, dido, empress, glauke, ildico, infanta, kumari, maharanee, maharani, malikzadi, noblewoman, palla, peeress, psyche, raj-kumari, ranee, rani, sara(h), shahzadi
changed into crow coronis
loved by cupid psyche

loved by zeus europa
margaret's husband armstrong-jones, earl of snowden
mythological atalanta
name meaning sara(h), sari, zadi, zara
turned to stone anaxarete
PRINCETON *symbol* tiger
PRINCEWOOD *tree* baria, canalete, cerillo, cyp(re), salmwood
PRINCIPAL acme, arch, auctor, author, backer, capital, captain, cardinal, central, chattel, chief, dominant, essential, first, foremost, fundamental, great, head(master), high(est), important, leader, leading, main, major, master, metropolitan, outstanding, palmary, paramount, person, preceptor, predominant, preeminent, premier, primary, prime, protagonist, soloist, staple, star, stellar, superintendent, superlative, supreme, top, trumpet, vital
comb. arch(i)
embodiment avatar
PRINCIPEN ampicellin
PRINCIPLE agent, axiom, base, basis, beginning, belief, canon, category, cause, character, component, convention, criterion, dictum, doctrine, element, elixir, endowment, essence, faculty, form, foundation, fundamental, gospel, ground, ingredient, integrity, law, logos, maxim, meat, nucleus, origin, pith, postulate, prana, precept, prescript, regulation, rudiment, rule, seed, source, spark, specific, tenet, theorem, truth, usage, yang, yin
cosmic heaven, prajapati, urgrund
elementary brocard
female sakti, yin
1st abc, arche, basis, cause, fundamentum, rudiment, seed
fundamental groundsel
germinal stamen
guiding polestar
life ghost, prana, soul
male purusha, yang
narcotic fagine
ontologic dharma
primal apeiron

rational logos
reincarnation manas
7 hindu atman, buddhi, kama, linga-sharira, manas, prana, sthula-sharira
summary creed
theorem truth, yang, yin
vital anima, archaeus, soul, spirit, stamen
without amoral
PRINCIPLES abc's, code, creed, ethics, policy, probity, rudiments
mixture euonymian
without amoral
PRINCOX coxcomb, fop, youth
PRINE goodwit
PRINK bedeck, caper, deck, decorate, dress, glance, mince, preen, primp, prune, smudge, wink
PRINT calico, copy, dent, design, develop, dint, edition, engrave, enlarge(ment), enstamp, etching, fabric, fix, footstep, image, impress(ion), indent(ation), issue, letterpress, mark, newspaper, paisley, picture, positive, press, proof, publish, pug, reissue, run(off), seal, setoff, sign, slide, stamp, stat, strike off, token, trace, type, vestige
brown rotogravure, sepia
colored ivorytype
kind aquatone, cyanotype, dactylogram, engraving, etching, leimtype, lithograph, microcopy, monotype, negative, photo(copy), photograph, photostat, positive, woodcut, xerox
lover of typophile
shop chapel
silk-screen serigraph
PRINTER compositor, devil, linotyper, pressman, stereotypist, typesetter, typographer
devil fly
emblem colophon
famous aldus, caxton, elzev(i)er, fust, gutenberg, jenson, morris, nuthead, plantin, rogers, short, thomas, tory
festival wayzgoose
helper devil, fly
pad inker
stick shooter
tray composing-stick

union label bug
PRINTING *blind* braille
block cut, linoleum, quad, quat, quod, riser, wood
blurred mackle, macule
color chromolithography
cross stroke ceriph, serif
direction cut, dele(te), stet
equipment bank, bed, bevel, biron, blanket, boss, brayer, burr, case, chase, composing stick, dabber, dauber, footstick, form, frame, frisket, galley, gauge, gripper, gutter, inker, make-ready, matrix, mold, overlay, platen, quoin, ratchet, reglet, roller, rounce, shooter, slur, stick, turtle, tympan, underlay
error erratum, pie, typo
form cut, die, frame, frisket, matrix
frame chase, frisket, galley
goddess papyra
incorrect pseudography
ink spreader brayer
mark See MARK *printing.*
measure agate, empen, empica, pica
metal block quad
photoengraving heliotype
plate anastatic, electro, stereo(type)
plate defect hick(e)y
press stamp
press inventor hoe
press part See PRINTING *equipment.*
press, small multigraph
process aristotype, autogravure, benday, braille, copperplate, electrotype, flexography, letterpress, linotype, lithography, monotype, offset, photoengraving, photolitho, phototypy, roto(gravure), stenotype, stereotype, typeset, typography, zincotype
proof vandyke
script ronde
2nd reissue
spacer quad, slug
term backmatter, colophon, dedication, errata, folio, flyleaf, frontmatter, galley, imprint, index, inscription, introduction, page, proof, recto, reverso, revise, table, title, verso
type mixed pie
type style See TYPE *style.*

PRIODONTES armadillo, cabalassou

PRIOR afore, ahead, already, antecedent, anterior, archaic, before, cidevant, cleric, coadjutor, earlier, elder, ere(now), farther, fore(going), former, forward, head, hitherto, lead(ing), monk, past; precedent, preceding, precursory, previous, priest, superior
comb. ante, pre

PRIORITY ascendancy, position, precedence, preference, privilege, rank, superiority

PRIORY abbey, cloister, convent, monastery, nunnery

PRIPET *tributary* styr

PRISCILLA *friend* paul
husband aquila
suitor john alden, miles standish

PRISM block, cylinder, nicol, spectrum, wernicke
color range spectra
device iriscope
pair porro
6-sided parallelepiped

PRISMATIC angular, brilliant, chromatic, iridescent, opalescent, opaline, variegated

PRISON asylum, bagne, bagnio, bailey, barracoon, bars, bastille, big-house, black hole, bocardo, bondage, boobyhatch, bridewell, brig, bullpen, cage, calaboose, can, carcer, cell, chauki, choky, clink, confine, cooler, coop, concentration camp, deathhouse, donjon, dump, dungeon, enclosure, freezer, gaol, gehenna, gib, grate, hell, hold, hole, hoosegow, JAIL, jug, keep, kidcote, limbo, lockup, mure, oubliette, panopticon, pen(itentiary), pinfold, pound, quod, ratel, rattle, reformatory, rock, stir, tench, thana, tolbooth, workhouse
camp See NAZI *concentration camp.*
famous See JAIL *famous.*
grounds spike-park
gruel skilly
guard screw
keeper gaoler, guard, jailer, jailor, turnkey, warden
military andersonville, black hole, stalag

naval brig, hulks
pert. carceral
room cell, dungeon, hole, solitary, sweatbox, tank
sentence rap
spy mouton

PRISONER cageling, caitiff, captive, con(vict), defendant, detenue, felon, gaolbird, inmate, intern(ee), jailbird, lag(ger), lifer, parolee, stirbird, termer, trusty
base chevy, chivy
camp oflag
exchange agreement cartel
fee chummage
group (chain)gang
of chillon bon(n)ivard
of the vatican pope
of war kriegie, pow
of zenda rudolf rassendyl

PRISSY effeminate, finicky, fussy, nice, precise, priggish, prim, prudish, puritanical, sissified

PRISTINE early, first, fresh, new, original, primary, prime(val), primitive, pure, unspoiled, untouched

PRITCH beer, offense, pierce, pique, prick, spike, staff

PRITTLE-PRATTLE chat (ter)(erer), talk(er)

PRIVACY darkness, huggermugger, intimacy, isolation, privity, quiet, retirement, retreat, seclusion, secrecy, secret, sequestration, solitude
in aside
place without goldfish bowl

PRIVATE alone, cabinet, civilian, closet, confidential, covert, doughboy, esoteric, hidden, homefelt, hushhush, infantryman, inmost, internal, intimate, inward, isolated, khass, personal, pocket, privy, quite, remote, retired, secluded, secret, separate, sequestered, singular, snug, soldier, solitary, special, stanch, unofficial, withdrawn
chamber sanctum(sanctorum)
comb. idio
enterprise capitalism, commerce, entrepreneurism
eye detective, gumshoe, investigator, operative, shamus, tailer, tec

PRIVATEER caper, corsair,

drum(b)ler, dunkirk, kidd, pirate, vessel

PRIVATELY alone, apart, aside, inwardly, sotto-voce, sub rosa, tete-a-tete

PRIVATION absence, defect, depletion, deprivation, destitution, exigency, hardship, indigence, lack, loss, misery, need, negation, pinch, poverty, strait, want

PRIVET alatern, cabbagewood, forestiera, hedge, ibolium, ibota, ligustrum, prim(p), primprint, primwort, print, shrub, skedge (with)
border hedge

PRIVILEGE advantage, allow(ance), appanage, authorize, berat, birthright, boon, charter, claim, clear, concession, copyright, due, entitle, entry, exemption, faldage, favor, franchise, freedom, grace, grandeza, grant, honor, immunity, indulgence, liberty, license, munity, octroi, option, patent, perk, permission, perquisite, power, prerogative, qualify, right, sanction, soc, soke, theam, title, use, vouchsafe
commercial octroi
war-time angary

PRIVILEGED allowed, authorized, chartered, eligible, entitled, excused, exempt, favored, franchised, immune, licensed, palatine, qualified, restricted, special

PRIVITY confidence, knowledge, privacy, seclusion, secrecy, secret

PRIVY backhouse, backstairs, chic sale, clandestine, concealed, confidant, covert, donicker, familiar, furtive, hidden, intimate, john, latrine, outhouse, personal, petty, private, secret, stealthy, surreptitious, toilet, watercloset
coat armor, mail, shirt

PRIZE accolade, acme, admire, appraise, appreciate, award, bacon, benefit, best, blue-ribbon, bonus, booty, bounty, brass ring, caption, cherish, cup, emption, enshrine, esteem, estimate, evaluate, force, garland, glaive, gree, guerdon, honor, laurels, lever, loot, love, measure, medal, meed, palm, plum, plunder, praise, premio, premium, price, prime, prix, PRY, rate, regard, respect, reward, scalp, spoils, stake, swag, tern, token, treasure, trophy, value, winning(s)

actors' emmy, oscar, tony

capture all sweep

fight barney, bout, contest, match, mill, scrap

fight demand knock-out

fighter boxer, bruiser, pugilist, slugger, stumblebum

1st blue ribbon

gag zonk

lottery tern

money award, gunnage, purse, reward, stake

mystery writers' edgar

time bank night

PRIZED chary, dear, treasured

PRO advocate, affirmative, aye, expert, favoring, for, professional, yes

PROA canoe, caracoa, caracore, outrigger, paro(o), pra(h)u, prow

PROBABILITY chance, credibility, expectation, favor, liability, likelihood, odds, presumption, prospect, vantage

PROBABLE apt, credible, feasible, hopeful, liable, likely, plausible, possible, presumable, presumptive, promising, rational, reasonable, verisimilar

PROBABLY apparently, belike, credibly, doubtless, likely, no doubt, presumably, seemingly, ten-to-one

PROBATE court, evidence, evident, proof, proved, tried

PROBATION discharge, examination, investigation, novitiate, parole, proof, proving, test, trial, tryout

PROBATIONER apprentice, delinquent, intern(e), neophyte, novice, novitiate, nurse, postulant, stibbler, student

PROBE acus, analyze, ankylomele, dig, enter, examination, exam(ine), exploration, explore, fathom, feel (er), fish, grope, gyromele, inquest, inquiry, inspect, instrument, investigate, inves-

tigation, measure, penetrate, pierce, prod, prove, research, scrutinize, search, see, seek, sound, stab, stylet, test, tracer, trial, try

curved ankylomele

surgical acus, stylet, tent

PROBER explorer, seeker, tracer

PROBITY cando(u)r, character, conscience, fidelity, goodness, honesty, honor, integrity, justness, nobility, principles, rectitude, reliability, reputability, strength, truth, uprightness, veracity, virtue, worthiness

PROBLEM bugbear, case, conundrum, crux, dilemma, disputation, enigma, exercise, flaw, hangup, headache, hitch, hydra, issue, knot, matter, mystery, nut, perplexity, plight, poser, predicament, proposition, puzzle, quandary, question, riddle, situation, topic, trouble

-solving method algorism, algorithm, arithmetic, calculation

PROBLEMATIC(AL) ambiguous, cryptic, doubtful, dubious, enigmatic, equivocal, puzzling, questionable, suspicious, uncertain, undecided, unsettled, vague

PROBOSCIGER arara, cockatoo, macaw, parrot

PROBOSCIS antlia, beak, haustellum, neb, nib, nose, promuscis, rostrum, snout, syphon, tongue, trunk

insect antlia

monkey kaha(u), nasalis, nose-ape

section lore, lorum, nares, nostril

PROCACIOUS impudent, insolent, pert, petulant

PROCAS *son* amulius, numitor

PROCAVIA cony, daman, hyrax

PROCEDURE agenda, agendum, behavior, ceremonial, conduct, course, derivation, issue, management, manner, method, order, plan, policy, practice, process, produce, program, progress, rite, rote, routine, rule, step, system, tactic(s), way

complicated rigmarole

habitual rote

legislative See LEGISLATURE *procedure.*

PROCEED act, advance, aggress, arise, bear, become, begin, come, continue, derive, devolve, elapse, emanate, ensue, extend, fand, fare, flow, follow, fond, forthgo, frame, issue, move, occur, operate, originate, pass, process, progress, prosper, pursue, rise, roam, seek, spring, start, stem, step, succeed, wend

laboriously barge, mog, plod, plow, slog, trudge, wade

rapidly breeze, gallop, haste, run, scurry, speed

PROCEEDING(S) act(ion), activity, affair, afflux(ion), business, conduct, course, deed, doings, event, measure, minutes, operation, PROCEDURE, process, progressing, report, step, transaction, trial, warrant

PROCEEDS avails, cash, fee, gate, income, money, prevenue, profit, returns, revenue, take, vail, yield

PROCELARIA albatross, petrel, shearwater

PROCESS account, act(ion), activity, advance, can, change, control, cook, course, develop(ment), direction, drift, edict, emanation, extension, injunction, issuance, mandate, manner, measure, mechanism, meiosis, method, operation, order, outgrowth, prepare, procedure, proceeding, progress, projection, step, sterilize, story, summons, treat, warrant, working, writ

abrupt mucro

comb. ance, ancy, ence, ency, ese, iasis

destructive deperition

legal bail, caveat, detinet, detinue, instance, suit

organism meiosis

plant energesis

pointed awn, languet, spine, stylus

PROCESSION autocade, caravan, cavalcade, ceremony, charivari, column, cortege, course, crocodile, file, formation, funeral, line, litany, march, motorcade, move-

ment, parade, pomp, progress, promenade, retinue, review, skimmington, string, train, trionfo, triumph
comb. cade
flower polygala
rowdy skimmity
PROCIPHILUS alder-blight, aphid, aphis, louse
PROCLAIM acclaim, advertise, announce, apprise, bid, blare, blast, blaze, boast, broadcast, call, celebrate, claim, cry(out), declare, deem, denounce, disclose, discover, divulge, enounce, enunciate, expound, forespeak, grede, harbinger, herald, inform, knell, manifest, notify, outcry, preach, predicate, promulgate, protest, publish, renounce, reveal, scry, sing, state, tell, toot, tout, trumpet, utter, vent, voice
PROCLAMATION announcement, annunciation, avowal, ban, bando, banns, bidding, blaze, blazon, broadcast, declaration, decree, edict, fiat, hue, law, manifestation, manifesto, notice, notification, order, promulgation, publication, rerd(e), sign, ukase
of marriage banns
PROCLES *father* aristodemus
twin eurysthenes
PROCLIVITY anlage, aptitude, aptness, bent, bias, disposition, faculty, flair, gift, inclination, knack, leaning, penchant, predilection, prejudice, proneness, propensity, tendency, turn
PROCNE *consort* tereus
kin butes, pandion, philomela
son itys
PROCRASTINATE dally, dawdle, defer, delay, dillydally, fiddlefaddle, filibuster, hang back, hesitate, hold off, lag, linger, loiter, miss, postpone, prolong, prorogue, protract, put off, stall, temporize, vacillate
PROCRASTINATION cunctation, deferment, delay, dilatoriness, inactivity, neglect, postponement, stall, vacillation
PROCREANT fruitful, generating, producing

PROCREATE bear, beget, breed, engender, generate, get, multiply, produce, propagate, reproduce, sire
PROCREATION begetting, breeding, generation, offspring, production, proliferation, propagation, reproduction, virility
PROCREATOR ancestor, author, generator, parent
PROCRIS *consort* cephalus, eos
dog laelaps
father erectheus
slayer cephalus
PROCRUSTES damastes, polypemon, stretcher
equipment bed
slayer theseus
PROCTOR advocate, agent, attorney, beggar, counsel, imposter, invigilator, lawyer, patron, procurator, prog, proxy, rector, solicitor, steward
assistant bulldog
PROCURATION acquisition, care, commission, management, proxy
PROCURATOR administrator, agent, bursar, manager, proctor, steward
PROCURE achieve, acquire, arrange, attain, attract, borrow, breed, bring, buy, cater, cause, conquer, contrive, earn, effect, elicit, entreat, fetch, gain, get, hire, induce, labor, lead, obtain, plead, pray, prevail, purchase, reach, secure, solicit, try, win
PROCURER cadet, pander(er), pimp, proxenet, purveyor
PROCURESS bawd, commode, hack, lena, madam, pander
PROD awl, brod, brog, crossbow, dabber, dig, drive, egg, goad, horse, hurry, impel, incite, jab, jog, jostle, lash, motivate, nudge, poke, press, prick(er), probe, prompt, puncture, push, remind(er), reproof, shove, skewer, spur, stimulate, thrust, urge, whip
PRODDLE fumble, poke, potter, stir up
PRODIGAL abundant, ample, copious, extravagant, exuberant, flush, improvi-

dent, incontinent, intemperate, lavish, liberal, lush, luxuriant, munificent, plentiful, profligate, profuse, reckless, spendall, spender, spendthrift, squanderer, unrestrained, wanton, wasteful, waster, wastrel, wastrie, wastrife
PRODIGALITY abundance, excess, extravagance, liberality, plenty, plethora, profusion, superabundance, superfluity, surplus, vice, waste
PRODIGIOUS abnormal, amazing, astonishing, colossal, enormous, extraordinary, gigantic, great, herculean, huge, immense, mammoth, marvelous, mighty, miraculous, monstrous, monumental, phenomenal, portentous, strange, stupendous, tremendous, unique, vast, wonderful
PRODIGY ace, brain, genius, intellect, marvel, master, miracle, monster, oddity, omen, ostent, portent, rarity, sign, top-notcher, wizard, wonder
PRODITION betrayal, treason
PRODROME(S) forerunner, precursor, warning, wind gods
names boreades, calais, chione, cleopatra, zetes
parent boreas, oreithyia
PRODUCE accomplish, achieve, act, adduce, advance, ante, author, bear, beget, bloom, blossom, breed, bring about, cause, coin, compose, conceive, contrive, create, devise, effect(uate), engender, execute, exhibit, extend, fabricate, facture, fashion, form, fruit(s), furnish, generate, get, goods, grow, hatch, introduce, invent, inwork, make, manifest, manufacture, merchandise, object, occasion, offer, offspring, originate, output, outturn, perform, present, proceeds, procreate, product(ion), prolong, promote, propagate, provide, raise, rear, result, return, shape, show, stage, start, stock, submit,

supply, teem, wage, work, yield

agricultural crops, fruit, harvest, husbandry, podware, vegetables

-man coster, greengrocer, peddler, truck-farmer, truck-gardener

PRODUCED artificial, made, staged, synthetic, wrought

from without exogenous

independently autogenous, endogenous

PRODUCER artificer, author, backer, begetter, breeder, builder, creator, designer, deviser, director, doer, entrepreneur, executor, farmer, father, founder, generator, grower, initiator, inventor, maker, manufacturer, mother, mover, organizer, originator, parent, provider, sire

PRODUCT article, artifact, blend, brain-child, brand, brew, child, coinage, commodity, composition, compound, concoction, confection, consequence, creation, crop(s), decoction, device, end, fruit, gain(s), growth, handiwork, invention, issue, item, manufacture, object, oeuvre, offspring, opus (cule), outcome, outgrowth, output, proceeds, PRODUCE, PRODUCTION, progeny, result, returns, sum, thing, total, turnout, work, yield

comb. ade

secondary congener

waste dregs, REFUSE, residue(nt), tailings

PRODUCTION accomplishment, composition, creation, effectuation, effort, elaboration, execution, extension, fabrication, film, formation, fruit, fulfillment, generation, handicraft, handiwork, manufacture, manuscript, movie, origination, output, performance, preparation, PRODUCT, work

measure man-year

slackening cacanny

successful hit, smash

PRODUCTIVE abundant, active, battel, battle, bearing, bountiful, causative, clever, copious, creative, exuberant, fat, fecund, fertile,

fruitful, gainful, generative, generous, inventive, loamy, lucrative, luxuriant, original, originative, parous, plenteous, plentiful, pregnant, prolific, rich, teeming, uberous, yielding

PROEM foreword, introduction, overture, preface, prelude

PROETUS *brother* acrisius

consort antea, stheneboea

daughter hysippe, iphianassa, iphinoe

invention shield

parent abas, ocalea

PROFANATION blasphemy, corruption, debasement, desecration, irreverence, perversion, pollution, sacrilege, transgression, violation, violence, vitiation

PROFANE abuse, abusive, blasphemous, calumnious, carnal, contaminate, debase, defile, defoil, defoul, desecrate, dishallow, dishonor, earth(l)y, evil, foul, godless, heathen, heretic, impious, imprecatory, impure, irreligious, irreverent, lay, maledictory, material(istic), misuse, mundane, noa, pervert, pollute, sacrilegious, scurrile, scurrilous, secular, smear, temporal, terrestrial, ungodly, unhallow(ed), unholy, unsacred, unsanctified, unspiritual, violate, vulgarize, wicked, worldly

PROFANITY abuse, billingsgate, blasphemy, chillulhashem, curse, cursing, cussing, damning, impiety, imprecation, malediction, malison, oath, swearing

PROFESS acknowledge, admit, affect, affirm, allege, assert, avouch, avow, claim, confess, declare, edge, follow, observe, own, practice, pretend, proclaim, protest, purport, state, teach

PROFESSED apparent, expert, hypocritical, ostensible, pretended, purported

PROFESSION art, assumption, avowal, business, calling, career, craft, declaration, employment, faculty, faith, forte, function, game, job, line, metier, occupation, protestation, pursuit,

religion, service, specialty, testimony, thing, trade, vocation, work

PROFESSIONAL ace, authority, expert, finished, functional, hired, official, paid, pro, skilled, technical, trained

non amateur, laic, lay

PROFESSOR doctor, don, educator, fly, hanif, instructor, teacher, tutor

rank below adjunct, assistant, associate, instructor, lecturer

PROFFER attempt, bestow, bid, confer, design, essay, extend, give, hand, indication, intend, offer, prefer, present, propose, tender, tent, volunteer

PROFICIENCY ability, accomplishment, aplomb, aptness, capability, competence, maitrise, mastery, skill

PROFICIENT able, accomplished, actual, adept, apt, capable, competent, conversant, dext(e)rous, drilled, effective, efficient, expert, finished, practiced, qualified, skilled, skillful, versed

PROFILE biography, chronicle, contour, curve, drawing, figure, form, graph, likeness, outline, plan, portrait, shape, silhouette, size, skyline, vita

board template

PROFIT acquire, advance, advantage, avail, behoof, benefit, bestead, boot, clean up, clear, earn, edify, fee, fruit, further, gain, get, good, guerdon, harvest, improve, income, increase, interest, lucre, meed, melon, mend, move, net, realize, reap, return(s), reward, scalp, service, take, use, utility, vail, value, vantage, winnings, yield

illegitimately exploit

maker quaestuary

receiving pernancy

taker pernor

undercover booty, loot, payola

without fruitless, unprofitable

PROFITABLE advantageous, auspicious, beneficial, economic, expedient, fat, favorable, fruitful, gainful, golden, good, helpful, lucrative, paying, productive, propitious, remunerative, repaying, rewarding, salutary, useful, utile, vailable, valuable, worthy

PROFITEER bleed, cheat, exploit, gouge, overcharge

PROFLIGACY dissipation, extravagance, lechery, libertinage, libertinism, prodigality, turpitude, venery, wenching, whoring

PROFLIGATE abandoned, beaten, corrupt, debauched, depraved, dissipated, dissolute, extravagant, fast, free, immoral, indecent, lavish, lax, lecher, libertine, licentious, loose, overthrown, prodigal, promiscuous, rake(hell), rakish, reprobate, roue, routed, slack, spender, spendthrift, vicious, wasteful, waster, wastrel, wild

PROFOUND absorbing, abstruse, abysmal, acroamatic, acute, buried, cultured, deep(seated), depth, difficult, educated, erudite, exhaustive, great, hard, heartfelt, heavy, homefelt, indelible, intense, keen, learned, lettered, literate, mysterious, occult, ocean, penetrating, pervading, piercing, poignant, probing, recondite, sagacious, sage, scholarly scholastic, sharp, shrewd, strong, studious, thick, thorough, unfathomable, wise

PROFUSE abundant, bountiful, copious, diffuse, excessive, extravagant, exuberant, free, generous, hearty, immoderate, lavish, liberal, lush, luxuriant, munificent, overflowing, plentiful, plenty, prodigal, spreading, sumptuous, teeming, wasteful

PROFUSION abundance, affluence, extravagance, exuberance, fluency, liberality, opulence, plenty, prodigality, quantity

PROG beggar, food, forage, gibe, goad, poke, prick, proctor, prod, provender, prowl, search, steal, stir up, supplies, taunt, tramp, vagrant, victuals

PROGENITOR ancestor, author, forebear, forefather, manu, original, parent, pitri, precursor, sire, stock

PROGENY breed, brood, child(ren), descendants, descent, family, generation, increase, issue, kin(dred), lineage, offshoot, offspring, outcome, parentage, posterity, product, race, resultant, scion, seed, shoot, son, strain

insect society

PROGNOSIS forecast, interpretation, prediction, prognostication, sign, symptom

science of proleptics

PROGNOSTIC augury, boding, foreboding, forecast, foretelling, foretoken, interpretive, omen, ominous, portent, predicting, predictive, presage, prophecy, sign, symptom, token

PROGNOSTICATE anticipate, apprehend, augur, bespeak, betoken, bode, divine, forebode, forecast, foresee, foreshow, hariolate, omen, portend, predict, prenote, presage, prophesy

PROGNOSTICATOR augur(er), divine(r), haruspex, predictor, prophet, seer, soothsayer

PROGRAM action, activity, advance, agenda, agendum, bill, blueprint, broadcast, budget, calendar, card, catalog(ue), draft, edict, index, list, menu, notice, outline, plan, platform, playbill, policy, procedure, proclamation, prospectus, schedule, syllabus, timetable

PROGRESS advance(ment), advancing, boom, career, circuit, course, current, dash, dent, develop(ment), drive, expedition, fare, forward, furtherance, gain (ground), get on, go ahead, grow(th), headway, impel, impetus, improve(ment), journey, lunge, march, mature, motion, move(forward), movement, ongo (ing), passage, proceed, process(ion), prosper, rate, rise, speed, succeed, tour, travel, way

feebly dodder, shuffle

opposed to bourgeois, diehard, hidebound, old-line, philistine, reactionary, square-toed, standpat

planned telesia, telesis

slowly crawl, creep, dally, loiter

PROGRESSION advance, chain, course, movement, passage, sequence, series, set, stage, string, succession, suite, swing, train

PROGRESSIVE active, advanced, antegrade, ascensive, enterprising, forward, go-ahead, gradual, graduated, improver, increasing, left, liberal, modern, moving, oncoming, ongoing, onward, proceeding, radical, reformer, up-to-date

party bull moose

party founder la follette, roosevelt, wallace

PROHIBIT ban, bar, check, countermand, curb, debar, deny, disallow, embargo, enjoin, estop, exclude, forbid, forfend, hinder, impede, inhibit, interdict, obviate, outlaw, preclude, prevent, proscribe, restrain, shut(out), stop, taboo, tabu, veto, withhold

PROHIBITED contraband, forbidden, hot, illegal, illicit, taboo, tabu, unlawful, verboten

PROHIBITING vetitive

PROHIBITION ban, bar, declaration, don't, embargo, estoppel, forebode, frustration, injunction, interdiction, law, nay, veto, volstead act

legislators sheppard, volstead

organization anti-saloon league, wctu

pioneer carry nation

product bathtub gin, nearbeer

sacred taboo, tabu

PROJECT affair, aim, beetle, bulge, business, butt, cast, contemplate, contrive, design, devise, draft, enterprise, hurl, idea, imagine, intend, intention, jet, jut, launch, outline, overhang, pattern, pitch, plan, plot, problem, propel, proposal, propose, proposition, protrude, purpose, scheme, task, throw, undertaking, venture, work

wasteful boondoggle

PROJECTILE ammo, ammunition, arrow, ball, bomb, bullet, cartridge, dart, discus, jaculatory, missile, pellet, quoit, rock(et), shell, shot, shrapnel, sinker, spear, torpedo, trajectile

curve parabola

explosive part warhead, warnose

pert. ballistic

science of ballistics

submarine torpedo

PROJECTION ajutment, angle, apse, arm, barb, block, boss, bracket, bragger, bulge, bump, calk, cam, cascabel, caulk, cog, contrivance, corbel, cornice, crena(tion), croc, denticle, dentil, design, dormer, ear, ell, eminence, fang, fin, firing, flange, gunnery, hob(b), hub, hump, hurling, jaculation, jag, jut(ty), knob, knop, knuckle, ledge, lee, lobe, lug, node, nose, overhang, plan(ning), prediction, prominence, prong, protrusion, protuberance, ratchet, rim, salient, sawtooth, scale, scheme, scheming, shooting, shoulder, snag(gle), socle, sprocket, spud, spur, tenon, toe, tooth, transference

rounded bulge, crena, lobate, lobe, tooth, umbo

rounded, pert. lobar

sharp barb, fang, spur

PROJECTOR alchemist, analemma, balopticon, biograph, bioscope, cinematograph, kino, magic-lantern, megascope, planner, promoter, schemer, stereopticon, vitascope

PROKE incite, POKE, stir, thrust

PROKOFIEV *opera* love for three oranges

PROLAMIN gliadin, hordein, kafarin, secalin, seine, zein

PROLATE elongated, extended, oval, stretched

PROLEGOMENON foreword, induction, introduction, overture, preamble, preface, prelude, proem, prologue

PROLETARIAN coarse, commoner, common man, laborer, lower-class, mean, pariah, peasant, pleb(eian), poor, roturier, rude, vulgar, wage-earner, worker, working

PROLETARIAT commonage, commonal(i)ty, hoi, masses, peasantry, polloi, poor, public, rabble, rank and file, riffraff, third estate

PROLIFERATE generate, grow, increase, multiply, pullulate, reproduce, swarm, teem

PROLIFIC abounding, abundant, birthy, breedy, broody, creative, fecund, fertile, fruitful, generating, generative, plentiful, productive, profuse, proliferous, propagative, reproductive, spawning, teeming

PROLIFICATE fertilize, generate, increase, spread, teem

PROLIX boring, diffuse, diffusive, dull, extended, irksome, lengthy, long(winded), pleonastic, prolonged, prosaic, protracted, redundant, tautological, tedious, tiresome, uninteresting, verbose, wearisome, windy, wordy

PROLOCUTOR advocate, chairman, lecturer, mouthpiece, orator, speaker, spokesman

PROLOGUE avant-propos, exordium, preamble, preface, prelude, proem, protasis

PROLONG amplify, continue, delay, deter, dilate, drag out, draw(out), dree, elongate, endure, enlarge, expand, extend, increase, last, lengthen, persist, postpone, procrastinate, protract, spin out, spread, strain, stretch, string out, sustain, twine

PROLONGED chronic, continued, delayed, dilated, extended, lasting, lengthy, prolix, sostenuto, sustained

PROM ball, bash, dance, party, promenade

PROMACHOS athena

PROMENADE alameda, avenue, ball, boardwalk, dance, deck, display, drive, esplan-

ade, exhibit, gallery, hall, mall, march, marina, parade, pasear, paseo, path, prado, procession, ride, saunter, stroll, traipse, walk

PROMETHAZINE pheneran

PROMETHEUS *brother* atlas, epimetheus, menoetius

captor bia, haphaestus, kratos

chained on kazbek, mt caucasus

daughter-in-law pyrrha

liberator heracles, hercules

parent clymene, gaea, iapetus, themis

sister-in-law pandora

son deucalion

tormentor eagle, vulture, zeus

PROMINENCE agger, altitude, amygdala, bulla, calcar, celebrity, colliculus, condyle, conspicuousness, cusp, distinction, eminence, fame, fashion, glory, hamulus, honor, importance, lingula, oliva, prestige, projection, promontory, protuberance, salience, salient, tragus, tubercle, umbo

PROMINENT beetle, big, blatant, bold, capital, celebrated, chief, conspicuous, distinct(ive), distinguished, famous, great, high, important, jutting, leading, main, manifest, marked, notable, noticeable, obvious, outstanding, principal, projecting, protrusive, protuberant, remarkable, salient, signal, steep, wellknown

PROMISCUITY derangement, disharmony, disorder, immorality

PROMISCUOUS aimless, blended, careless, casual, epicene, haphazard, immoral, indiscriminate, irregular, lewd, licentious, light, loose, merged, mingled, miscellaneous, mixed, motley, random, slipshod, undiscriminating, wanton

PROMISE affiance, agree (ment), assumpsit, assurance, assure, augur, avouch, avow(al), avowance, behest, behight, betroth(al), bid, bond, commit(ment), compact, consent, contract, convenable, convenant, dec-

laration, declare, earnest, ensure, fair, fiance, foretoken, guarantee, halsen, hest, hete, hope, insurance, insure, iou, jure, mortgage, note, oath, obligation, offer, omen, osse, parole, pawn, plea, pledge, plight, prediction, profession, stipulation, suggest, swear, troth, trust, truth, undertaking, vow, warrant(y), word (of honor)
oral stipulation cautio
person of comer
PROMISED *land* canaan, heaven, paradise, utopia
land fountain ain
PROMISING assuring, auspicious, bright, encouraging, fair, favorable, flattering, happy, hopeful, likely, lucky, probable, propitious, toward(ly)
PROMISSORY contractual, covenantal, stipulating, votary, votive
note bill, certificate, check, hoondi, hundi, iou, obligation, pledge, ticket
PROMOE *husband* aetolus
son calydon, pleuron
PROMONTORY bill, cape, cliff, elbow, eminence, headland, highland, hoe, jutland, mount, nase, naze, ness, noup, point, projection, prominence, rise, salient, scaw, skaw, snout, spit, tor, upland
PROMOTE abet, advance, aggrandize, aid, assist, avail, betray, better, boom, boost, brevet, cultivate, dignify, elevate, encourage, ennoble, exalt, exploit, extend, finance, foment, forward, foster, further, get behind, graduate, hasten, help, hurry, improve, increase, knight, motivate, nurse, pass, patronize, prefer, publicize, push, quicken, raise, speed, support, upgrade
PROMOTER abettor, activist, agent, angel, backer, booster, broacher, bubbler, friend, gogetter, hustler, kochleffl, lobbyist, organizer, patron, publicist, pusher, supporter
PROMOTION advance (ment), advertising, back-

ing, brevet, build-up, bump, commission, elevation, exploitation, financing, furtherance, graduation, grubstake, hype, irenics, lift, patronization, preferment, progress(ion), publicity, raise, sponsorship, stake, subsidy, support
PROMPT abrupt, active, advise, alert, animate, apt, assist, bring about, cause, cue, clue, eager, early, easy, elicit, enjoin, evoke, excite, expeditious, given, hint, immediate, impel, incite, inclined, induce, influence, inspire, instant, instigate, jog, keen, move, nimble, occasion, practical, prod, pronto, provoke, punctual, quick, ready, remind(er), soon, speedy, suggest, summary, swift, tell, twit, urge, vigilant, watchful, willing, yare, yeder
PROMPTER aid, cuer, mover, readier, reminder, souffleur
PROMPTLY apace, at once, directly, forthright, forthwith, immediately, in good time, instanter, instantly, on time, precisely, pronto, punctually, quickly, right away, right off, soon, speedily, straight(a)way, swiftly, tid, tite, tyt(e)
PROMPTNESS alacrity, celerity, dispatch, expedition, immediacy, punctuality, quickness, speed, swiftness
PROMULGATE advertize, announce, blazen, broadcast, communicate, declare, disclose, impart, proclaim, pronounce, publish, reveal
PRONAOS anticum, narthex, portico, vestibule
PRONE abed, accustomed, addicted, agroof, agrufe, agruif, apt, bent, couchant, declivous, decubitus, disposed, dormant, downward, easy, exposed, fell, flat, groof, gruf, habituated, headlong, homily, horizontal, inclined, lain, level, liable, likely, minded, open, passive, predisposed, procumbent, pronate, propense, prostrate, ready, reclining, recumbent, sensi-

tive, sermon, subject, supine, susceptible, tending, willing
face down fell, prostrate
face up decubitus, passive, supine
PRONENESS bent, liability, tendency
PRONEUR eulogist, panegyrist
PRONG antler, bill, branch, crotch, fang, fold, fork, fourche, furcula, furculum, horn, nib, offshoot, peg, pew, point, pugh, ramification, spean, spire, spur, stem, tang, teng, tine, ting, tip, tooth, tusk
buck pronghorn, springbok
hooked pew, pugh
key spanner
sharp nib
PRONGHORN antilocapra, ber(r)endo, cabree, cabret, cabrie, cabrit, deer, mazame, prairie-antelope, ruminant
PRONOUN all, any, both, ces, each, ella, elle, her(s), herself, him(self), his, ich, ils, its, itself, lei, loro, lui, mes, mia, mine, myself, none, one(self), our(s), ourself, ourselves, she, some, sua, that, thee, their, them(selves), these, they, thine, this, those, thou, thy, toi, tua, una, une, usted, voi, vostra, what, which, who(ever), whom, whose, you, your(s), yourself
demonstrative that, this, whom
indefinite all, any, both, each, none, one, some
interrogative what, which, who(m), whose
personal she, they, you
possessive her(s), his, its, mine, one's, our(s), their(s), thine, your(s)
substantive whoever, whosoever
PRONOUNCE accent, affirm, announce, articulate, aspirate, assert, assibilate, assign, award, behight, censure, declaim, declare, decree, deliver, display, enounce, enunciate, judge, manifest, ordain, order, recite, report, rule, say, sentence, slur, sound, speak,

specify, state, stress, tell, utter
fail to elide, slur
free absolve
guilty condemn, sentence
PRONOUNCED arresting, conspicuous, decided, evident, great, high, intense, manifest, marked, obvious, oral, outstanding, patent, striking, unmistakable
PRONOUNCEMENT announcement, declaration, decree, dicta, dictum, fiat, judgment, manifesto, observation, opinion, order, remark, statement, utterance, verdict
PRONTO fast, immediately, prompt(ly), quick(ly)
PRONUNCIATION accent, articulation, burr, delivery, diction, drawl, enunciation, etacism, lam(b)dacism, lisp, slur, twang
broad plateasm, plateiasmus
correct orthoepy, phonology
incorrect cacoepy, lam(b)dacism, lisp, psellism
mark See MARK *printing.*
rough bur(r)
symbol agma, eng
PROOF adminicle, analysis, argument, assay, attempt, certification, corroboration, credentials, demonstration, document, evidence, exhibit, experience, galley, ground, impenetrable, impregnable, ordeal, outcome, pull, reason, repro, result, revise, safe, showing, slip, strength, substance, test (imony), thoroughly, token, trial, utterly, validation, verification, voucher, witness
against callous, impervious, resistant, secure
PROOFREAD copy-edit, correct, revise
PROOFREADER *mark* cap, caret, dele, space, stet
PROP bolster, brace, bridge, brob, buttress, column, crutch, encourage, fortify, foundation, fulcrum, gib, help, hold, leg, mainstay, nog, perch, pierce, pin, pole, post, rance, scotch, shore, spike, sprag, spurn, staff, stake, stanchion, stay, stell, stilt, strengthen, strut, support, sustain, timber,

truss, underlay, underpinning, uphold, upright
-like fluciform
up cushion, sustain
PROPAGANDA agitation, ballyhoo, brainwashing, doctrine, ideas, inculcation, indoctrination, promotion, publicity, rumors, scheme, school, system
agency agitprop, agitpunkt
pacifist boloism
PROPAGANDIZE advertise, brainwash, evangelize, indoctrinate, preach, publicize, sell
PROPAGATE abroach, advance, bear, beget, breed, diffuse, disseminate, engender, extend, further, gemmate, generate, increase, multiply, populate, procreate, produce, promote, publish, reproduce, scatter, sire, spread, transmit
by seed proseminate
PROPAGATION breed(ing), diffusion, dissemination, distribution, extension, generation, increase, offspring, procreation
sexual amphigony
PROPEL boom, bowl, bunt, bushwack, butt, carry, compel, constrain, drive, flick, force, forward, gun, haul, hurtle, impel, kent, launch, motivate, move, oar, oblige, pedal, pole, prick, project, push, range, rev, roll, row, scull, send, shove, shunt, start, throw, thrust, treadle, troll, trundle, urge
PROPELLER airscrew, driver, fan, fin, game, oar, paddle, pedal, poy, propellant, propulsor, rotor, screw, solitaire, treadle, turbine, windmill
arm blade, vane
jet hydromotor
race slipstream
PROPEND hang, incline, tend, tilt
PROPENSE deliberate, disposed, favorable, inclined, leaning, partial, prone
PROPENSITY affection, aptitude, bent, bias, disposition, flair, forte, gift, inclination, knack, leaning, liking, metier, partiality, penchant, predilection, predisposition,

proclivity, tendency, thing, turn, yen
PROPER accurate, adapted, advisable, applicable, appropriate, apt, attribute, becoming, befitting, ceremonious, chaste, comely, comme il faut, compatible, complete, condign, congenial, congruous, conventional, correct, cricket, decent, decorous, demure, distinct(ive), due, exact, excellent, fine, fit(ting), formal, germane, goodly, handsome, happy, honest, identical, individual, inherent, legitimate, meet, modest, moral, nice, orthodox, peculiar, pertinent, prim, relevant, respectable, right(ful), sedate, seemly, separate, suitable, suited, thoroughly, unmistaken, veritable, very, virtuous, well
PROPERLY aptly, aright, duly, extremely, featly, fitly, gladly, gradely, inherently, intrinsically, meetly, rightly, strictly, suitable, utterly, well
PROPERNESS decency, decorum
PROPERTY acquest, addle, allodial, al(l)od(ium), appropriate, appurtenance(s), asset(s), attribute, aught, aver, baggage, bona, building(s), capital, catallum, characteristic, chattel(s), dhan, effects, equity, essence, estate, exploit, fitness, freehold, gear, glebe, having(s), holding(s), land(s), means, money, ownership, peculiarity, possession(s), power, production, proprietage, propriety, quality, real estate, realty, resource(s), stock, substance, thing, tool, trait, warison, wealth, worth
act to regain replevin
bride to husband dos, dot, dowry
charge against lien, mortgage
clear al(l)od(ium), al(l)ody
dead wife to husband courtesy
destruction arson, sabotage, vandalism

enemy herem
landed desmesne, domain, estate, hacienda, praedium, real estate
landed, pert. cadastral
movable catallum, chattel(s), effects, gear
personal bona, chattel(s), goods, lares and penates, peculium, stuff
receiver alienee
register cadaster, cadastre
reversion escheat
right dominium, easement, lien, title
rural farm, finca, podere
seizure right angary
settle entail
settlement bride-price, dos, dot, dowry
stolen booty, loot, lucre, pelf, stealth
suit for trover
transfer alienation
transferring party alienor
woman's stridhan

PROPHECY augury, bodement, declaration, exhortation, forecast, foretelling, oracle, preaching, prediction, presage, prognosis, pythonism, revelation, sibyllism, spae, utterance, vaticination, vaticine, vision, weird
god apollo

PROPHESY anticipate, aread, areed, ariolate, augur, declare, divine, dope, exhort, forebode, forecast, foreshow, foretell, indicate, ominate, osse, portend, preach, predict, preindicate, presage, prognosticate, spae, vaticinate

PROPHET (See also *famous,* below.) andron, andrus, angel, astrologer, augur, auruspex, chiromancer, clairvoyant, crystal-gazer, divinator, divine(r), druid, ecclesiastic, extispex, forecaster, foreknower, foreteller, fortuneteller, geomancer, haruspex, haruspices, leader, mantis, necromancer, oracle, palmist, predictor, presager, prognosticator, psychic, python, sage, seer, sibyl, soothsayer, sphinx, teacher, vates, vaticinator
brother tecumseh
famous amos, antevorta, asa-

hiah, azur, balaam, cassandra, cehi, daniel, elias, elijah, elisha, ezekiel, ezra, gad, habakkuk, haggai, hosea, iddo, isaiah, jehu, jeremiah, joel, john, jonah, joseph, joshua, malachi, micah, mohammed, moses, nahum, nathan, nostradamus, obadiah, pythia, samuel, shemaiah, sibyl, silas, silvanus, smith (joseph), spyne, syrus, tiresias, zechariah
female See PROPHETESS.
fiery elijah
holy sacer, vates
murder of vaticide
pert. delphian, delphic, fatidic(al), sibyllic, vatic(al) (inal)

PROPHETESS anna, anne, antevorta, cassandra, deborah, huldah, phoibad, pythia, pythoness, seeress, sibyl, spaewife, voluspa

PROPHETIC delphian, delphic, divinatory, fateful, faticid(al), interpretative, mantic, ominous, oracular, portentous, predictive, presageful, prescient, vatic(al)
comb. mantic

PROPHYLACTIC antidotal, antidote, antisepsis, antiseptic, aseptic, bactericide, dentifrice, disinfectant, fumigant, fumigator, gargle, germicide, medicine, prevent(at)ive, protective, remedy, sanitary, toothpaste

PROPINE disposal, gift, give, offer, pledge, present, proffer, propose, tip, toast

PROPINQUITY adjacency, affinity, approximation, closeness, contiguity, kindred, kinship, likeness, nearness, neighborhood, proximity, relationship, vicinity

PROPITIATE accord, adapt, adjust, appease, atone, calm, conciliate, content, gentle, immolate, mediate, mild, mollify, pacify, placate, reconcile, sacrifice, satisfy, soothe

PROPITIOUS advantageous, auspicious, beneficial, benevolent, benign(ant), cheering, encouraging, favorable, fortunate, good, gracious, happy, helpful, kind(ly), lucky, merciful,

opportune, pat, promising, prosperous, providential, reassuring, rosy, timely, toward

PROPONENT advocate, agent, backer, champion, exponent, second(er), supporter

PROPONTIS *island* marmara

PROPORTION allotment, amount, analogy, apportion, balance, compare, compass, degree, dividend, division, dose, equation, eurythmy, extent, form(at), harmony, lot, part, portion, pro rata, prorate, quantity, quota, ratio, ration, scale, shape, share, size, space, symmetry
given stent, stint
harmonious eurythmics, eurythmy, symmetry
lack of asymmetry

PROPORTIONAL, PROPORTIONATE accordant, according, adequate, answerable, balanced, commensurate, comparable, comparative, competent, consonant, corresponding, even, harmonious, in ratio, in scale, reciprocal, relative, respective, spatial, sufficient, uniform

PROPOSAL bid, blueprint, feeler, grace, hypothesis, idea, instance, intention, motion, motive, move, offer, overture, plan, plea, presentation, project, proposition, prospectus, resolution, statement, suggestion, terms

PROPOSE advance, aim, allege, anticipate, approach, aspire, bring up, broach, confront, contemplate, converse, design, exhibit, face, fancy, image, imagine, intend, intention, introduce, mean, meditate, moot, move, nominate, offer, plan, plot, postulate, project, proposition, propound, purpose, scheme, show, start, state, submit, suppose, talk, wish

PROPOSITION adage, ask, axiom, corollary, deal, empirema, hypothesis, legislation, modal, offer, overture, plan, porism, premise, problem, project, PRO-

POSAL, propose, protasis, question, seduce, supposal, theorem, theory, thesis, topic, undertaking
antecedent prejacent, premise
assumed true axion, corollary, lemma
empirical emp(e)irema
logical termal
mathematical theorem
preliminary lemma
PROPOUND advance, invoke, moot, pose, posit, postulate, propose, question, start, state
PROPOXYPHENE darvon
PROPRIETARY estate, medicine, owner(ship), possessor, property, PROPRIETOR
PROPRIETOR amo, boniface, laird(ie), lord, malik, master, owner, padrone, patroon, talukdar, tanist, yeoman
PROPRIETY civility, code, convention, decency, decorum, dignity, elegance, etiquette, fitness, form, grace, idiom, manners, mense, morality, morals, ownership, politesse, property, prudery, rectitude, respectability, rule, standard, usage
lacking in bohemian, unconventional
personified emily post, mrs grundy
PROPULSION bunt, butt, drift, ejection, expulsion, pulsion, push, shove, shunt
PROPULSIVE ballistic, driving, impellent, propellant, propelling, propulsory, protrusile, pulsive, pushing, shoving, urging
PROPYLAEA *designer* mnesicles
PROPYLAEUM entrance, vestibule
PRORATE allot, apportion, assess, charge, distribute, divide, parcel, portion, proportion, ration
PROROGUE adjourn, defer, dissolve, extend, postpone, procrastinate, prolong, protract
PROSAIC arid, barren, boring, bread-and-butter, common(place), dry, dull, factual, flat, foot, humdrum,

insipid, irksome, jejune, lengthy, literal, longwinded, matter-of-fact, monotonous, ordinary, pedestrian, plain, platitudinous, plebian, practical, prolix, prosy, sober, staid, stolid, stuffy, stupid, tedious, tiresome, trite, unembellished, unexciting, unimaginative, uninteresting, unpoetic, unromantic, usual, vapid, workaday
PROSCENIUM foreground, front, stage
front area apron
PROSCRIBE attaint, ban(ish), black-list, condemn, curse, damn, denounce, doom, embargo, forbid, interdict, ostracize, outlaw, prevent, prohibit, reject, sentence, tabu
PROSCRIPT criminal, hoodlum, outlaw
PROSCRIPTION ban, exile, interdiction, outlaw(ry), prohibition, restraint, restriction, taboo, tabu
PROSE chat, composition, language, literature, narrative, ordinary, parlance, platitude, prosaic, story, text, tongue
art of rhetoric
form biography, essay, fiction, history, nonfiction, novel, romance, story, tract, treatise
PROSECUTE accuse, arraign, carry(on), charge, chase, continue, engage in, execute, finish, follow, hound, implead, indict, indite, intend, litigate, practice, proceed, pursue, seek, sue, wage
PROSECUTION arraignment, proceeding, process, suit, undertaking
PROSECUTOR attorney, plaintiff, pursuer, quaestor, sakeber, suer
special cox, jaworski
PROSELYTE convert, devotee, disciple, ger, neophyte, newcomer, novice, novitiate, pursuant
PROSELYTIZE brainwash, convert, persuade
PROSODY meter, metrics, poetics, POETRY, scansion, versification
meter See POETRY *meter.*
study poetics

PROSOPIS algar(r)oba, cashaw, cushaw, mesquite
PROSPECT anticipate, anticipation, aspect, avenue, chance, command, customer, examination, examine, expectation, exploration, explore, exposure, face, forecast, foresee, foresight, future, futurity, gopher, hope, hunt, landscape, likelihood, look (out), mine, offscape, outlook, probability, promise, range, result, scene, search, street, survey, view, vista
for gold speck
glass telescope
PROSPECTIVE anticipated, anticipatory, coming, eminent, expected, foreseen, foresighted, future, impending, provident
PROSPECTOR fossicker, miner, sourdough
PROSPECTUS announcement, approach, bulletin, catalog(ue), compendium, outline, plan, precis, presentation, program, schedule, scheme, sketch
PROSPER advance, batten, bloom, blossom, burgeon, cheve, chive, cotton, dow, edify, fare, favor, fay, flourish, flower, grow, hie, progress, rise, speed, succeed, thrive, wax
PROSPERITY affluence, boom, clover, comfort, ease, fleshpots, flourish, fortune, gain, hap, happiness, ikbal, luxury, opulence, plenty, progress, seel, sele, sons(e), success, thrift, ups, velvet, weal(th), welfare, well-being
deity frey, hygeia, ing, salus
symbol pumpkin, turquoise
PROSPERO *brother* antonio
daughter miranda
friend gonzalo
helper ariel
slave caliban
sprite ariel
PROSPEROUS affluent, auspicious, bien, blooming, booming, boon, comfortable, fat, favorable, flourishing, flush, fortunate, golden, halcyon, happy, lucky, lush, opulent, palmy, plush, rich, rosy, sonsie, sonsy, successful, thriven,

thriving, weirdly, well-off, well-to-do
make secundate
name meaning felix, zada
PROSPERPINA See PERSEPHONE.
PROSS boast, chat, gossip, vaunt
PROSTITUTE baggage, bat, bawd, berdache, boom-boom, broad, callet, call-girl, canidia, cat(amite), chippie, cocotte, corrupt, courtesan, courtisane, croshabell, cyprian, debase, delilah, demimondaine, demirep, doxy, drab, fille de joie, floozy, fricatrice, harlot, harridan, heta(e)ra, hetaira, hobbyhorse, hooker, kurveh, licentious, lorette, maquereau, meretrix, messalina, misuse, mopsy, mrs warren, nafka, paphian, phryne, play-for-pay girl, poule(de luxe), pucelle, pug, punk, putain, quail, quean, rannel, sadie thompson, scarlet woman, seduce, slammock, slattern, sloven, slubberdegullion, slummock, slut, spoil, stew, streetwalker, strumpet, swine, tart, thais, traipse, trollop, trug, trull, twist, venal, wanton, white slave, whore
boss bully, pander(er), pimp, procurer
customer kangourou
house bagne, bordel(lo), brothel, chabanais, maison de tolerance, one-two-two, sphinx, stew
male berdache
place of correction spinning house
protector bully
reformed convertite, magdalen
PROSTRATE abase, abject, bow, collapse(d), couchant, deferential, demolish, demoralize(d), depress(ed), disable, dormant, exhaust(ed), fallen, fatigue(d), fell, flat(tened), fling, grief-stricken, grieve, helpless, horizontal, hurkle, impotent, level, low, mean, obeisant, obsequious, overcome, overthrow, over-tire(d), paralyze, powerless, procumbent, prone,

raze, recumbent, repent(ant), sick, spent, stoop, submissive, supine, throw, tired, trailing, tucker out, upset, weary, worn
oneself couch, fawn, grovel, hurkle, salaam
PROSTRATION anguish, bow, cave-in, collapse, deflation, dejection, downcast, downthrow, exhaustion, fall, humility, impotence, kowtow, overthrow, overturn, precipitation, recumbency, reverence, shock
PROSY banal, commonplace, dry, dull, flat, heavy, humdrum, inane, insipid, irksome, jejune, lifeless, PROSAIC, stupid, tedious, tiresome, uninteresting, weary
PROTAGONIST actor, advocate, agent, champion, character, competitor, contender, defender, enemy, foe, hero(ine), leader, paladin, participant, principal, spokesman, star, supporter
PROTASIS foreword, introduction, maxim, overture, preamble, preface, prelude, proem, prologue, proposition
PROTEAN actor, changeable, changeful, dramatic, edestan, manifold, mutable, variable
PROTECT arm(or), assure, barricade, bestride, bield, bind, bless, bulwark, champion, cherish, cloak, conserve, convoy, copyright, cover, cushion, defend, ensconce, ensure, escort, fence, forfend, fortify, foster, guard, harbor, haven, hedge, house, insulate, insure, nestle, panoply, patent, patrol, police, preserve, safeguard, save, screen, seclude, secure, sentinel, shade, shelter, shend, shepherd, shield, shroud, treasure, ward, watch, wear
with coating barff
PROTECTED anchored, armored, covered, guarded, housed, immune, impregnable, inviolable, invulnerable, locked, safe, secure, shady, shielded, snug, walled
PROTECTION aegis, amulet, apron, armature, armor,

asylum, bib, buffer, bulwark, care, conservation, cover, cowcatcher, custody, defense, defilade, egis, fender, frith, guard(ianship), indemnity, influence, insurance, lee, moat, parapet, pass(port), patrocinium, preservation, safeguard, safekeeping, safety, security, shell, shelter, shield, smock, targe, tutelage, umbrage, umbrella, vaccination, vaccine, wardship, warrant
right girth, grith, mund
PROTECTIVE conservative, custodial, defensive, guardian, prophylactic, tutelar(y)
coloration mimesis, mimicry
PROTECTOR bib, bodyguard, champion, convoy, cordon, defender, fautor, guard(ian), keeper, lookout, padishah, paladin, patrol(man), picket, regent, safekeeper, sentry, shah, vedette, warden, watchdog, watchman
name meaning edgar, edmund, raymond
PROTECTORATE colony, condominium, dependency, mandate, possession, state, territory
PROTEGE charge, client, dependent, pensioner, protectee, pupil, smike, ward
PROTEIDA *family* necturus, olm, proteus, salamander, typhlomolge
PROTEIN abrin, actin, albumen, albumin, aleurone, amandin, amigen, amine, amino acid, apoferritin, arbacin, avidin, bynin, casein, chlorophyll, clupeine, collagen, creatine, edestin, elastin, ferritin, fibrin, gelatin, gliadin, globin, globulin, glutelin, glutin, gorgonin, hemoglobin, histone, hordein, ichthulin, ipomoein, keratin, lactalbumin, lecithin, legumin, linin, lipide, livetin, meat, mucedin, mucin, myogen, ordein, oryzenin, ovalbumin, ovoglobulin, peptide, peptone, prolamin(e), protamine, proteose, ricin, rna, salmine, sericin, sozin, sturine, tendomucin, vitellin, zein
acid proline

basic arbacin, histone
blood fibrin, globulin
colorless achroglobin
conjugated ichthulin
defensive sozin
deficiency disease kwashiorkor
egg albumen, albumin, avidin
granular aleuron(e)
group globulin
indigestible fibroin
insoluble albuminoid, fibrin, gelatin, keratin
milk casein
mixture crotin
poisonous abrin, ricin(e)
seeds aleurone, prolamin
silver argerol
simple prolamin
source bean, egg, fish, lentil, meat, soy(bean)
vegetable glutelin, phytonitellin
PRO TEM acting, ephemeral, temporarily, temporary
PROTEROGLYPHA coalsnake, cobra, seasnake
PROTESILAUS *parent* astyoche, iphiclus
slayer hector
wife laodamia
PROTEST affirm, assert, asseverate, assure, aver, avouch, avow(al), bark, beef, boggle, call, challenge, clamor, complain, contest, croak, cry, declare, default, demur, deny, deprecate, dispute, dissent, exception, expostulate, haro, holler, howl, inveigh, kick, object(ion), obtest, oppose, plaint, predicate, proclaim, profess, promise, publish, raise hell, refusal, refuse, reject, remonstrate, repudiate, resist, revolt, rhubarb, scruple, sit-in, snarl, squawk, squeal, stipulate, testify, vow, warrant, yell
in vain bark at the moon
literature samizdat
PROTESTANT alascan, anglican, calvinist, dissenter, huguenot, lutheran, methodist, presbyterian, puritan, swaddler
doctrine social gospel
movement reformation
sect anabaptist, mennonite, orangeist
PROTEUS amoeba, beanleafroller, olm

consort antia, julia, silvia
daughter idothea, iphianassa, lysippe, theonoe
friend valentine
master poseidon
parent aglaia, antonio, oceanus, tethys
servant launce
son telegonus, tmolus
PROTOCOL agreement, compact, convention, document, etiquette, memorandum, rule, usage, wont
PROTOGENIA *consort* zeus
parent deucalion, pyrrha
PROTOGONIA *parent* erechtheus, praxithea
sister otionia
PROTOMARTYR stephen
PROTON *accelerator* cosmotron
PROTOPINE fumarine
PROTOPLASM amoeba, cytoplast, ovoplasm, periplast, plasma, plasson, sarcode, spore
movement cyclosis
outer layer extoplasm
substance gel
tissue blastema
unit pangen
PROTOPLAST cell, energid
PROTOTYPE ancestor, antetype, archetype, example, exemplar, ideal, image, model, original, pattern, source
PROTOZOAN actinopod, actipylea, adelea, adinida, agamete, aggregata, am(o)eba, antinophrys, arcella, babesia, bodonid, ciliate, foliculina, foram, heliozoan, hypozoan, infusoria, lobosa, monad, moner, paramecium, piroplasma, radiate, radiolaria, rhizopod, sarcodina, stentor
flagellate adinida, polymastiga
fresh-water am(o)eba, arcella, paramecium
inner part endosarc
mouth cytostome
outer layer ectoplasm, ectosarc
parasitic ameobida am(o)eba
PROTRACT continue, defer, delay, detract, dilate, drag on, draw out, eke, elongate, extend, lengthen, linger, perorate, plot, postpone, prolong, protrude, run on,

slacken, slow, spread, stay, stretch, string out, suspend, sustain, trail, train
PROTRACTED dragging, drawn out, dreich, extended, fabian, lasting, lengthy, long(ish), prolix, verbose
PROTRUDE beetle, blear, bristle, bulge, bunch, extend, herniate, interfere, jut, obtrude, outreach, poke out, pout, project, protuberate, shoot, stand out, stick out, strut, swell, thrust
PROTRUDING bold, bulging, eminent, excrescent, extruding, gibbose, gibbous, humped, jutting, outstanding, prognathous, projecting, prominent, protrudent, protrusile, protuberant, salient, steep
PROTRUSION hernia, PROTUBERANCE
PROTUBERANCE bean, boll, boss, bud, bulb, bulge, bump, bunch, buttress, callus, capitellum, capitulum, caput, eminence, excrescence, extrusion, flange, flankard, gibbosity, gnarl, heel, hump, hunch, inion, jag, jog(gle), knob, knot, knurl, lip, lobe, lump, nob, node, nodosity, nub, papilla, pimple, pommel, projection, prominence, protrusion, puff, salience, salient, scab, shoulder, snag, swelling, torus, tuberosity, tumor, umbo, wart, wen, withers
ragged jag(g)
PROTUBERANT blubbery, bottled, bulgy, bumpy, bunchy, convex, gibbous, strut(ting), swelling, swollen, torose, tumid
PROUD admirable, aristocratic, arrogant, boastful, brant, chesty, chuff, cockhorse, conceited, condescending, contented, copped, dignified, disdainful, ego(t)istic(al), elated, exalted, fierce, flooding, glad, grand, happy, haughty, high, ikey, immodest, imperious, imposing, impressive, independent, inflated, insolent, loft(y), lordly, orgul(ous), overbearing, pleased, pom-

pous, presumptuous, pretentious, prideful, pursy, saucy, scornful, self-esteeming, self-respecting, smug, snobbish, snobby, snooty, splendid, stately, stomachy, superbious, supercilious, superior, swollen, uppish, uppity, vain(glorious), valiant, vaunty
as lucifer

PROUDLY excellently, high, successful

PROUST *cake* madeleine
character albertine, swann

PROVE argify, argue, argufy, ascertain, assay, assess, attempt, attest, authenticate, aver, become, bespeak, betoken, bring off, check, cinch, clinch, conclude, confess, confirm, convince, corroborate, demonstrate, deraign, determine, essay, establish, evidence, evince, experience, experiment, fatten, fix, grow, hold water, indicate, justify, make good, manifest, pree, prive, reason, settle, show, substantiate, succeed, suffer, taste, tempt, test, thrive, try, validate, verify, warrant
false belie, betray, refute
guilty attaint, convict
valid defend

PROVENANCE beginning, derivation, inception, origin, root, source, start(ing)

PROVENCE, PROVENCAL languedoc, romanesque
ballad singer musar
cupboard panetiere
dance tambourin
drum tambourin
ideal love domnei
literary group felibrige
poem canzone, estrif, planh
poet mistral
singer troubadour
song alba, canso, canzo, sirvente
wind mistral
wine bandol, bellet, cassis

PROVENDER cater, chow, corn, eats, feed, fodder, food, forage, grain, grub, hay, meat, oats, provide, provision(s), straw, viands

PROVERB adage, allegory, aphorism, apothegm, axiom, barb, brocard, byspell, byword, enigma, epi-

gram, forbysen, gallicism, gnome, maxim, motto, nayword, parable, paroemia, saw, saying, soothsay, truth, wheeze
collector paramiographer, paroemilogist
writer paroemiographer

PROVERBIAL aphoristic, common, familiar, sententious, well-known

PROVIDE accommodate, accouter, afford, agree, appoint, arm, arrange, bequeath, cater, chevise, clothe, contribute, deliver, destine, endow, endue, equip, feed, fill(up), finance, find, foison, foresee, fund, furnish, gird, give, grant, insure, invest, look after, prepare, present, procure, produce, provision, purvey, ration, ready, recruit, reinforce, replenish, stimulate, stock, store, supply, support, yield
food cater, grub, scaff
for cheveys, chevise, consider, fend, finance, furnish, insure, keep, maintain, prepare, reserve, support, sustain
funds bankroll, endow, finance
with besee

PROVIDED boden, but, conditionally, equipped, furnished, on condition, prepared, ready, sobeit, subject to, supplied, whether (or not)

PROVIDENCE care, caution, concern, discretion, economy, fate, foresight, god, heaven, prudence, thoughtfulness, thrift

PROVIDENT careful, cautious, discreet, economical, farseeing, foresighted, frugal, judicious, prudent, saving, sparing, thoughtful, thrifty, wise

PROVIDENTIAL auspicious, benign, favorable, fortunate, given, happy, kind(ly), lucky, miraculous, opportune, prudent, timely

PROVINCE area, arena, bailiwick, beat, business, calling, canton, charge, circuit, colony, country, county, demesne, department, dependency, diocese, district,

division, domain, dominion, duty, emirate, empire, eparchy, field, forte, function, job, jurisdiction, limit, metier, mudiria, nomarchy, nome, office, orbit, prefecture, pursuit, realm, region, sheng, shire, sircar, sphere, state, syssel, task, territory, tract, vilayet, work, yamato
pert. nomic

PROVINCIAL bucolic, countrified, crude, hick, homely, homespun, insular, limited, local, narrow, parochial, peasant, petty, regional, restrained, rural, rustic, sectional, stuffy, suburban, unpolished, unsophisticated, vulgar

PROVISION (See also PROVISIONS.) administer, armament, arrangement, arrayal, board, cater, chow, clause, condition, equip, fare, feed, foresight, foundation, grist, groundwork, keeping, outfit, preparation, provide, proviso, purveyance, replenishment, scran, serve, sleeper, stock, store, supply, unless, viands, victual, wraith
buyer achatour, purveyor
seller sutler, vivandier
-tree seed sabadilla, sabanut, sapota

PROVISIONAL acting, conditional, contingent, dependent, experimental, iffy, makeshift, special, substitute, temporary, tentative

PROVISIONS acatery, annona, board, bouge, cates, chevisance, chow, commissariat, commons, eats, equipment, fare, fodder, food, forage, groceries, grub, larder, provender, rations, scran, stocks, stores, supplies, terms, viands, viaticum, victuals, vivres
search for forage
stock of acatery, larder, magazine

PROVISO article, caution, caveat, clause, condition, fast, salvo, stipulation, term

PROVOCATION affront, anger, appeal, casus-belli, chafe, challenge, discomfort, excitement, fret, gall, incentive, irritant, irritation, offense, torment, trial

PROVOCATIVE agacant(e), aggressive, annoying, appealing, appetizing, desirable, exciting, heady, influential, interesting, intoxicating, irritant, provoking, stimulant, stimulating, suggestive, zaftig

PROVOKE affront, aggravate, agitate, anger, annoy, antagonize, arouse, bait, bog, bristle, chafe, challenge, cheppeh, embitter, evoke, exacerbate, exasperate, excite, fire, foment, forthcall, frump, galvanize, goad, harass, huff, incense, incite, induce, inflame, inspire, instigate, insult, invite, invoke, ire, irk, irritate, madden, miff, move, needle, nettle, offend, outrage, peeve, perturb, pique, prompt, quicken, rile, roil, rouse, ruffle, spur, stir, summon, tar(r), tcheppeh, tease, teen, tempt, thrill, upset, urge, vex, vrother

PROVOKED angry, cross, furious, irate, mad

PROVOST administrator, bailiff, chief, dean, director, executive, head, jailer, judge, keeper, magistrate, mayor, officer, official, praepositus, prefect, prior, proconsul, reeve, steward, superintendent, viceroy, warden
office prepositure

PROW beak, benefit, boom, bow(sprit), brave, courage, duty, ferro, gallant, good, honor, job, nose, outrigger, proa, prore, PROWESS, rostrum, speron, stem, steven, valiant, vessel
pert. prorean
-shaped carinate

PROWESS ability, audacity, boldness, bravery, courage, excellence, gallantry, heroism, ingenuity, mettle, might, power, puissance, skill, spirit, strength, valor

PROWL brevit, cruise, gad, gallivant, lookout, lurk, meander, mooch, mouse, pace, pilfer, prole, pursue, ramble, range, raven, roam, rob, rove, seek, slink, steal, stealth, stray, stroll, traipse, tramp, wander

PROWLER burglar, peeper, robber, slasher, thief, tomcat, voyeur, walker

PROXIMAL, PROXIMATE close(st), coterminous, direct, immediate, imminent, nearest, next

PROXIMITY adjacency, approach, closeness, contiguity, juxtaposition, nearness, presence, propinquity, vicinage, vicinity

PROXY agent, alternate, authority, ballot, commission, deputy, election, factor, locum-tenens, pinch-hitter, proctor, procurator, representative, stand-in, sub(stitute), surrogate, vicar, vice, vote

PRUDE bluenose, comstock, goodygoody, grundyite, hypocrite, nice-nelly, prig, purist, puritan, victorian

PRUDENCE austerity, calculation, canniness, care, cautel, caution, chariness, circumspection, discretion, economy, expedience, forehandedness, foresight, frugality, frugalness, husbandry, judgment, management, parsimony, providence, sagacity, skill, sleight, sophrosyne, thrift, wisdom
symbol ant

PRUDENT advisable, alert, astute, canny, careful, cautelous, cautious, circumspect, discreet, discriminating, doose, douce, economical, expedient, farsighted, foresighted, frugal, judicious, politic, provident, quaint, sage, sane, sapient, sensible, shrewd, si(c)ker, solid, sparing, thrifty, thriven, verty, wise

PRUDERY grundyism, priggishness, primness, primosity, propriety, pudency, puritanism, rigidity

PRUDISH barkbound, blue, demure, hidebound, mimsey, mimzy, narrow, nice, old-maidish, overmodest, priggish, prim, prissy, puritanical, quakerish, smug, squeamish, stiffnecked, straitlaced, stuffy, victorian

PRUNE amputate, castrate, clear, clip, coll, coul, cow, crop, cultivate, cut, deduct, dehorn, doll up, dress, drip, geld, lop, perk up, plum(e), preen, prime, primp, prink, purge, razee, reduce, remove, retrench, shape, shave, shear, shorten, simpleton, simplify, smooth, snathe, sned, switch, thin, tonsure, top, trifle, trim
inferior frog
wild pappea

PRUNELLA angina, fabric, heal-all, hedge-sparrow, herb, selfheal, thrush, twill, weed

PRUNING abscission, cutting, shaping, trimming
hook calabozo, sarpe
implement billhook, dhaw, serpette
shears secateur

PRUNUS almond, amarelle, ansu, apricot, bullace, bully-tree, capulin, cereza, cherry, damson, fruit, peach, plant, plum, sloe, tree

PRURIENT bad, desiring, dirty, evil, itching, itchy, lascivious, lewd, longing, lustful, sensual

PRURITIS hives, itch(ing)

PRUSSIA(N) (See also GERMANY.) borussian, prutenic
aristocracy junker(s)
brown gold-pheasant
coin achtehalber, friedrichsdor
drink spruce-beer
emblem linden
general scharnhorst
goose embden
knight noachite
lancer junker, u(h)lan
leather spruce
measure fuder, fuss, meile, morgen, oxhoft, rute, scheffel, zoll
military science authority karl von clausewitz
official landrat(h)
red colcothar
victory sadowa
weight mark, quentchen

PRY ask, browbar, busybody, elevate, elicit, enquire, examine, extract, ferret, gaze, grope, inquire, inspect(ion), investigate, jimmy, lever(age), lift, look, meddle(r), mouse, move, nose, open, peep(er), peer, piggle, poke, potter, prise,

prize, probe, pull, putter, raise, scringe, scrounge, scrutinize, search, seek, snoop, spy, tear, teet, wrest, wring
into brevit, snoop
PRYDERI *abductor* gwawl
parent pwyll, rhiannon
PRYING busy, curious, impertinent, inquisitive, intrusive, meddlesome, nos(e)y, peeping, personal, snoopy
PRYTANIA See HECATE.
PSALM anabathmos, anthem, antiphon(y), canon, cantate, canticle, chant, chorale, gatha, hymn, introit, laud, miserere, ode, poem, praise, song, verse
46th alamoth
51st miserere
95th venite
98th cantate
100th jubilate
130th de profundis
book breviary, hallel, psalter
kind cantate, hallel, introit, lauds, miserere, venite
musical sign selah
part cathisma
processional introit
writer david
PSALTERIUM belly, bouk, lyra, manyplies, omasum, stomach
PSALTERY gusla, sautree, zither
PSAMATHE *consort* aeacus, proteus
son phocus, theoclymenus
PSEUDO bogus, counterfeit, fake, false, feigned, imitation, mock, pretended, sham, simulated, spurious
PSEUDOCARP anthocarpous, apple, fig, hip, pineapple, strawberry
PSEUDOGRAPH forgery
PSEUDOLOGUE liar
PSEUDOMEMORY paramnesia
PSEUDOMORPHOUS epigene
PSEUDONYM alias, allonym, anonym(e), incognito, nom de guerre, nom de plume, pen-name, so(u)briquet
PSHAW nonsense, poof, pooh, pugh, shucks, sugar
PSIDIUM arrayan, guava, myrtle
PSITTACINE macaw, parakeet, parrot
PSYCHE brain, censor, con-

science, desire, ego, instinct, intellect, intelligence, libido, mind, pneuma, self, soul, spirit, subconscious, superego, unconscious, urge, wit(s)
consort cupid, eros
persecutor aphrodite, venus
pert. idic
PSYCHEDELIC colorful, hallucinogenic, kaleidoscopic
prophet leary
PSYCHIATRIST alienist, analyst, head-candler, neurologist, nut-doctor, shrink(er), somatist
famous adler, binet, breuer, brill, charcot, freud, horney, james, janet, jung, mesmer, meyer, rank, reik, ward, wundt
PSYCHIATRY alienism, analysis, psychoanalysis, psychodometry, therapy
case history anamnesis
PSYCHIC animastic, cerebral, clairsentient, clairvoyant, extrasensory, immaterial, medium, mental, metaphysical, occult, preternatural, prophet, seer, spectral, spiritist, spiritualist, supernatural, supersensible, telekinetic, transmundane, unworldly
emanation aura
energizer antidepressant
seizure epilepsy
PSYCHOANALYSIS psychiatry, psychognosis, psychognosy
of children pedanalysis
patient analysand
PSYCHOLOGICAL mental, subjective
healing therapy
illusion deja-vu
lift abreaction, build-up, catharsis
moment crisis
school behaviorism, gestalt
test alpha, apperception, aptitude, association, aussage, babcock-levy, beta, binet, brown, cattell, gesell, goldstein, ink-blot, oseretsky, rorschach, stanford-binet, tat, wechsler
theory associationism, gestalt
PSYCHOLOGIST See PSYCHIATRIST.
PSYCHOPATH See PSYCHOTIC.

PSYCHOPOMP charon, hermes
PSYCHOSIS amentia, dementia, dipsomania, fugue, hallucinosis, hypomania, insanity, lycanthropy, neurosis, paralogy, paranomia, pathomania, senility
PSYCHOTIC alcoholic, catatonic, crackpot, crazy, cycloid, dipsomaniac, hebephreniac, hypochondriac, insane, kleptomaniac, lunatic, mad(man), manicdepressive, megalomaniac, neurotic, odd, off, paranoiac, paranoid, psychopath, schizo(id), schizophrenic
PSYLLIUM fleawort
PTAH *associated with* sekhet
embodiment apis
son imhotep, nefertum
wife sekh(m)et
PTARMIC sternutative
PTARMIGAN bird, grouse, lagopode, lagopus, ripa, rype
PTERIC alar, alate, winglike
PTERIS bracken, brake, fern
rootstock roi
PTERODACTYL ornithosaur, pterosaur
PTEROGLOSSUS aracari, toucan
PTEROPOD clione, mollusk, wing-snail
organ cephalocone
PTEROSPERMUM baroi, grewia, pandanus
PTISAN barley, coddle, decoction, tea, tisane
PTOLEMAEUS See PTOLEMY.
PTOLEMAIS See PTOLEMY.
PTOLEMY epiphanes, euergetes, lathyrus, philadelphus, philometor, philopator, physcon, soter
brother menelaus
consort berenice, cleopatra, philadelphia, thais
coronation anacleteria
daughter cleopatra, sabra
general cleonides
parent abubus, arsinoe, chrysermas, dorymenes, dositheus, lagus, philip
son lysimachus, memphitis, philadelphus
steward nicias
teacher aristobulus
work almagest, centiloquy
PTOMAINE amylamine, cadaverine, gadinin(e), neu-

rine, poison, putrescine, saprin(e), sepsin(e)

from cheese tyrotoxine

PUAH *son* tola

PUB bar, boozer, inn, saloon, tavern

crawl barhop

room snug

vessel mug, stein, toby

weapon dart

PUBBLE chubby, fat, full, plump

PUBLIC accessible, audience, civic, civil, clientele, common, communal, community, commutual, conjoint, cooperative, demos, external, following, free, general, humanity, inn, international, known, kung, mankind, masses, mutual, national, open, overt, people, populace, popular, population, proletariat, rabble, social, society, state, universal, vulgar, widespread

house bar, bistro, pub, saloon

persuasion jawboning

service electricity, gas, railway, telegraph, telephone, utility, waterworks

speaker orator, oratrix

square piazza, platz, plaza, zocalo

way alley, boulevard, bridge, freeway, highway, road, street, throughway, tunnel, turnpike

PUBLICAN catchpole, catchpoll, farmer, keeper, peasant, tax-collector, zaccheus

PUBLICATION advertisement, airing, almanac, annals, announcement, annual, book(let), bulletin, digest, edition, elziver, ephemeris, evulgation, gazette, handbill, issuance, issue, journal, leaflet, magazine, monthly, pamphlet, paper, periodical, piece, printing, prodrome, promulgation, pulp, slick, tabloid, weekly

examiner censor

make-up format

permit release

preliminary prodromus

prepare for edit, redact, revise

regular periodical

PUBLICIST adman, advertiser, agent, ballyhooer, bannerman, billposter,

blurbist, booster, commentator, copywriter, flack, huckster, journalist, plugger, pressagent, promoter, sandwichman, skywriter, solon, spieler, writer

PUBLICITY advertisement, airing, announcement, ballyhoo, billing, blurb, brouhaha, build-up, currency, daylight, exploitation, exposure, fame, heraldry, hoopla, information, ink, limelight, notice, notoriety, plug, press-notice, promotion, propaganda, puff(ery), reclame, space, spotlight, write-up

agent (See also PUBLICIST.) beater, flack, pressagent, promoter

avoidance privacity

PUBLICIZE advertise, air, announce, ballyhoo, blaze, blazon, break, bruit, build-up, cry, delate, emblazon, herald, immortalize, promote, tout

PUBLICOLA john quincy adams

PUBLISH advertise, air, announce, blaze, blazon, blow, bring out, broach, broadcast, bruit, carry, circularize, circulate, communicate, confiscate, declare, delate, diffuse, disclose, discover, disseminate, divulgate, divulge, edit, evulgate, expose, express, hawk, impart, introduce, issue, print, proclaim, promulgate, propagate, put out, report, reveal, spread, syndicate, tell, utter, vend, vent(ilate)

without authority pirate, plagiarize

PUBLISHER broacher, editor, issuer, journalist, printer

copy announcement, blurb

inscription colophon

PUBLIUS *father* marcus andronicus

PUCA See POOKA.

PUCCINI *heroine* mimi

opera gianni schicchi, girl of the golden west, la boheme, la tosca, madam(a) butterfly, manon lescaut, turandot

PUCCOON alkanet, bloodroot, bloodwort, goldenseal, gromwell, gromyl, po-

tentilla, sanguinaria, tellerwort, tormentil, turmeric

PUCE brown, eureka-red, flea, red, uda, victoria-lake

PUCELLE courtesan, damsel, joan of arc, maid, PROSTITUTE, virgin

PUCK blow, brat(ling), butt, disk, dwarf, elf, faery, fairy, fay, gnome, goatsucker, goblin, hobgoblin, imp, lob, nix, pixy, robingoodfellow, rogue, rubber, spirit, sprite

PUCKA, PUKKA authentic, complete, fixed, genuine, good, lasting, real, substantial, superior, sure, thoroughgoing, valid

PUCKER agitation, anxiety, astringe, bewilderment, bind, bulge, cockle, compress, constrict, contract, corrugate, cotter, crease, dither, draw, dudgeon, fold, furrow, gather, good, knit, lucken, perplexity, purse, real, ruck, ruffle, shirr, solid, wrinkle

bush wax-myrtle

-mouth flounder

PUCKERED bullate, bulliform, cockled, drawn, gathered, sour, wrinkled

PUCKFIST braggart, niggard, puffball

PUCKISH annoying, elfin, impish, mischievous, mysterious, whimsical

PUCKNEEDLE alfilaria, corn-cockle, lady's-comb

PUD foot, forefoot, hand, paw, pood, pudding

PUDDER (See POTHER.) uproar

PUDDING blanc-mange, brown-betty, burgoo, cabinet, charlotte(russe), cottage, custard, dessert, dowdy, duff, dumpling, fender, floating-island, gain, hackin(g), haggis, haupia, jaudie, jello, junket, kugel, mush, nesselrode, pad, panada, pandowdy, pease, plum, reward, rolypoly, sago, sausage, sponge, stirabout, suet, tansy, tapioca, tartan, yorkshire

black bloodsausage

boiled hoy

deep-dish dowdy

fruit hedgehog

grass pennyroyal

hasty mush, sepon, supawn
ingredient farina, tapioca
meat haggis
pipe canafistulo, cassia, drumstick-tree
sausage hackin(g)
steamed hedgehog, rolypoly
stick thivel
white sausage, whitehass
PUDDINGHEAD dimwit, fathead, simpleton
PUDDINGHOUSE belly
PUDDINGWIFE bluefish, doncella, gluefish, pudiano, wrasse
PUDDLE befoul, bungler, charco, clay, dabble, dib, dub, flodge, loam, marsh, mess, muddle(r), pick, plash(et), plud, pollute, pool, putter, quagmire, sink, slab, slodder, slump, spot, stir(up), swamp, tamper, trample, wallow, wash
duck mallard
jumper helicopter
PUDDOCK buzzard, kite, toad
PUDGY big, bulging, chubby, chunky, dumpy, fat, heavy, obese, puddy, rolypoly, spuddy, squat, stuffy, thickset, tubby
PUDIC chaste, decent, modest
PUDU venada
PUEBLO town, village
assembly room estufa, kiva
headdress maskette
indian acoma, anasazi, hopi, keres, moki, moqui, piro, puelche, tanoa, taos, walpi, zuni
kiva hole sipapu
PUELCHE pampa, tehuelet
PUERILE babyish, boyish, callow, childish, feeble, foolish, green, idle, immature, infantile, juvenile, maiden, raw, rude, silly, sophomoric, trivial, unfledged, unripe, unthinking, virgin(al), weak, young, youthful
PUERTO PRINCIPE camaguey
PUERTO RICO *bark* mabi
bay aquadilla, boqueron, rincon, sucia
bird rola, yeguita
breadfruit castana, chestnut
capital san juan
celery apio, arracacha

chayote tallote
city aguadilla, arecibo, bayamon, caguas, cayey, coamo, dorado, fajardo, guanica, guayama, humacao, manati, mayaguez, ponce, san juan
crape myrtle astromeda
drink anis-golila
fish sama, sisi
island culebra, mona, vieques
measure caballeria, cuerdo
muttonfish sama
native borinqueno, gibaro
palm coyure, yagua, yaray
plant aguinaldo, apio
politician albizu-campos, munoz-marin
porkfish sisi
port aguadilla, arecibo, mayaguez, ponce, san juan
river anasco, camuy, canas, fajardo, tanama, yauco
shrub chamiso, encinillo
switch-sorrel chamiso
tree emajagua, guaraguao, guayroto, mora, yafua, yaray
vine farolito
PUFF advertise, ballyhoo, bedspread, billow, blanket, blast, bloat, blow, blurb, boast, bouillone, brag(gart), breath(ing), burst, chug, cloud, comforter, commendation, cover, criticism, decoy, distend, distension, drag, eiderdown, elate, emit, enlarge, erupt, exalt, exhale, expand, expel, extol, flam, flatus, fluff, fuff, gust, huff, inflate, inhale, pant, pastry, pegh, pooh, pop, pouf, praise, publicity, publicize, review, sham, smoke, spread, suck, swell, waff, waft, weary, whiff, wind, wisp
adder bitis, viper
-cheek bomba, windbag
cream duchesse
fish See PUFFER.
-leg hummingbird
out bell, blub(ber), efflate, effume, exhale, inflate
paste dough, pate a choux
sudden gust
up bloat, blow, distend, elate, heave, inflate, swell, tumefy
PUFFBACK dryoscopus, shrike
PUFFBALL basidiomycete, bullfice, bullfist, calvatia,

earthstar, fist, fungus, fuzz (ball), geaster, mushroom, puckfist, smoke, snuffbox
fungus calvatia
PUFFBIRD barbacou, barbet, barbican, barbion, bucconid, capitonid, dreamer, monasa, monase, nunbird, nunlet
PUFFED blew, bombe, cocky, inflated, pretentious, souffle
out baggy, ballooned, bellied, bouffant
up arrogant, astrut, billowed, bloated, blown, bombastic, bouffant, carried, conceited, elated, imposing, inflated, large, pretentious, souffle, strutting, swollen
PUFFER atinga, baller, blowfish, burfish, bybidder, dabchick, eggfish, engine, globefish, kier, panegyrist, pike, porpoise, slimer, swellfish, tambor, tetradon, titmouse, toadfish, triodon
PUFFIN apple, auk, bird, cockandy, coulterneb, fratercula, marrock, marrot, mullet, pape, parakeet, pope, puffball, shearwater, tomnoddy, tomnorry, willock
PUFFING *pig* porpoise
snake hognose-adder
PUFFY billowy, bloated, bombastic, bouffant, bulgy, chubby, distended, distent, dropsical, flabby, gusty, inflated, pretentious, pursy, short-winded, soft, swollen
PUG bargeman, boxer, camois, camuse, chaff, churn, clay, dog, dwarf, elf, fighter, footprint, goblin, gouge, grind, harlot, hobgoblin, knead, mistress, monkey, nose, perspire, pluck, plug, poach, poke, print, prostitute, puck, pugilist, pull, rebuke, refuse, retrousse, servant, slight, snub, sprite, tamp, temper, thrust, trade, trample, uptilted, upturned
moth eupithecia
-nosed camous, camus(e), simous
PUGET SOUND *city on* bremerton, seattle, tacoma
indian snohomish
PUGGY beloved, monkey, muggy, perspiring, sweaty

PUGH pew, pish, prong, pshaw

PUGILIST battler, boxer, bruiser, champion, fighter, prizefighter, pug, slogger *assistant* handler, second

PUGNACIOUS aggressive, assertive, bellicose, belligerent, combative, contentious, litigious, militant, pushing, quarrelsome, scrappy, warlike

PUISNE associate, feeble, inferior, junior, later, petty, puny, student, subordinate, subsequent, unskilled, younger

PUISSANCE arm(y), control, energy, force, host, might, potency, power, prowess, strength

PUISSANT authoritative, forceful, forcible, formidable, great, masterful, mighty, potent, powerful, strong

PUKE cloth, emetic, spew, upchuck, vomit

PUKKA See PUCKA.

PULCHRITUDE beauty, comeliness, excellence, grace, loveliness

PULCHRITUDINOUS beauteous, beautiful, bonny, comely, fair, goodlooking, handsome, lovely, pretty

PULE cheep, chirp, complain, cry, peep, pipe, pool, repine, snivel, whimper, whine

PULEX See FLEA.

PULING spindly, whining

PULK pool, puddle, regiment

PULL allure, arrest, ascent, attract(ion), bouse, bout, chug, clout, contest, draft, drag(gle), draught, draw, drink, duct, extract, favor, gather, graft, hale, handle, haul, heave, hitch, hook, influence, jerk, lug, magnetism, pluck, power, puff, reduce, remove, rend, repossess, rive, rog, rug(gle), s(c)hlep, shlepper, snatch, sool, strain, stretch, struggle, suck, tear, throe, tit, tousle, tow, trail, train, trawl, trek, trice, trick, troll, try, tug, turn, twinge, twitch, uproot, weight, wrench, yank
about mousle, sool, tew, toze
apart criticize, discerp, di-

vulse, rend, rip, separate, tear
away avel(l), remove, withdraw, wrest
back remove, restraint, retract, retreat, scruple, withdraw, yield
bell set
-devil scrodgill, scrouger
down demolish, depress, destroy, disassemble, draw, earn, fell, lower, prostrate, raze, receive, reduce
ears sole, sowl
foot depart, flee
for cheer, encourage, root
in absorb, appear, arrest, arrive, check, end, rein, resorb, restrain, retract, stop, suck, windlass
nose snite
off accomplish, achieve, avulse, manage, strip, succeed
one's freight beat it, depart, escape, leave
one's leg or nose deceive, flatter, hoax, hoodwink, joke, josh, kid, ridicule
out depart, deracinate, desert, exterminate, extirpate, extract, flee, leave, outbraid, withdraw
over (See also PULLOVER.) arrest, cite, maillot, shirt, stop, ticket
strings control, influence, rule
suddenly trice
through emerge, recover, resuscitate, revive, surmount, survive
together attract, cooperate, knot
up arraign, arrest, check, disestablish, elate, extirpate, extract, halt, hoist, louk, pluck, rein, reprove, rouse, stop, trice, uplift, uproot, weed

PULLBACK drawback, hindrance

PULLET chick(en), child, earock, eerock, fowl, frier, fryer, hen, pollard, poulaine, poullard

PULLEY block, capstan, caster, cone, crane, drum, ferrule, fuzee, jockey, lever, rope, sheave, shiver, tackle, trochlea, truckle, wharrow, wheel
block crawl
block bottom arse

case block
groove gorge
part arse, drum, gudgeon, rigger
wheel sheave, truckle

PULLMAN berth, car, coach, diner, sleeper

PULLOVER jersey, maillot, shirt, slipon, sweater, t-shirt

PULLULATE bud, develop, germinate, grow, multiply, produce, proliferate, sprout, swarm, teem

PULMONARIA adam-and-eve, cowslip, lungwort, scorpion, spider

PULMONARY lungwort
collapse atelectasis
disease pneumonia, tuberculosis

PULMONATA gastropod, slug, snail

PULP bagasse, chyme, coagulate, crush, curd, flesh, grume, journal, macerate, magazine, marc, marrow, mash, mass, masticate, mush, pap, paste, periodical, pith, pomace, publication, sauce, slush, smash, sponge, squash, squeeze, squelch, squish, tissue, whey
fruit butter
machine blender, macerator
mining slime
wood aspen, spruce

PULPIT ambo, analogion, bema, clergy, cloth, dais, desk, lectern, mimbar, minbar, ministry, platform, podium, preachers, priesthood, rail, rostrum, scaffold, soapbox, stage, stand, stump, tribune
address from khutba(h)
board type
canopy tester
choir books analogion
sounding-board abat-voix

PULPITEER preach, sermonize

PULPY baccate, crass, doughy, flabby, fleshy, gelatinous, grumous, mashy, mushy, pappy, pasty, pithy, pulpous, sidder, siddow, soft, spewy, spongy, squashy, squdgy, squelchy, squishy, succulent, thick

PULQUE drink, liquor, mescal, stimulant
god tepozteco
source agave, maguey

PULSATE beat, drum, fluctuate, move, oscillate, palpitate, pant, quiver, strike, thrill, throb, thump, tremble, vibrate, waver
PULSATION beat(ing), drumming, heartbeat, heartthrob, lifeblood, palpitation, pitter-patter
in artery ictus
PULSE accent, artery, attack, battuta, bean, beat, cadence, dahll, dal, drive, fluctuate, impact, impel, legume, lentil, meter, oscillate, palpitate, pea, pulsate, pulsidge, quiver, rhythm, sphygmus, spurt, stroke, throb, vibrate, vibration, wave
beat battuta
comb. sphygmo
failure acrotism
having slow bradycrotic
measurer pulsimeter, sphygmograph, sphygmometer, sphygmophone
pert. ictic, sphygmic, sphygmoid
split dahll, dal
tracing sphygmogram
PULVERABLE chalky, crimp, crisp, crumbly, friable, shivery, short, triturable
PULVERIZATION abrasion, atomization, comminution, mashing, pounding, smashing, thrashing, threshing, tripsis
PULVERIZE abrade, atomize, beat, bray, bruise, buck, comminute, contriturate, craunch, crumb(le), crush, demolish, destroy, disintegrate, flour, grain, granulate, grate, grind, levigate, mash, meal, micronize, mill, mollicrush, mull, pound, powder, press, scranch, scrunch, smash, squash, thrash, thresh, triturate
PULVERIZER blender, comminutor, disintegrator, granulator, grater, grinder, harrow, kern, levigator, masher, mill(stone), muller, pestle, quern(stone), roller, steamroller, triturator
PULVERULENT crumbly, dusty, powdered, powdery
PULVILLUS plantula

PULVINAR couch, cushion, seat
PULVINO dosseret
PULY complaining, puling, whining
PUMA carnivore, cat (amount), cougar, kechua, painter, panther
PUME yarura
PUMICE abrasive, clean, glass, grind, lava, smooth, stone
powdered talc
rock trass
source lava
PUMMEL baste, batter, BEAT, belabor, bethump, buffet, drub, fib, hammer, hit, maul, paik, pounce, pound, punch, SLUG, smite, strike, thrash, thresh, thump
PUMP (See also *kind,* below.) ask, blow up, booster, court shoe, distend, drain, elicit, expand, extract, footwear, gin, grill, heart, inflate, interrogate, jack, lift, probe, pulsate, pulsometer, question, quiz, racker, raise, ram, shoe, slipper, sludger, spurt, stirrup, swell, syringe, throb, toepler
constellation antlia
-doctor grather
handle seep, swipe
kind air, aspirator, bicycle, bucket, centrifugal, chain, donkey, forcer, hydraulic, jet, lift, piston, pulsometer, rotary, sand, shell, sling, suction, turbine, vacuum
medical syringe
part barrel, handle, plunger, ram, spear, sweep, swipe
rod spear
vacuum pulsometer
PUMPKIN chump, citrul, cucurb(ita), cushaw, gourd, melon, pepo(n), peponida, pompion, quash(ey), squash, vegetable, vine
-head blockhead, dolt, fool, puritan
seed bluegill, butterfish, flatfish, flounder, pepo, redbelly, sailboat, sunfish, sunny
wild buffalo-gourd, calabazilla
yam sweet potato
PUN ambiguity, assonance, beat, calembour, double-entendre, equivoque, jeu de

mots, joke, knock, mot, nick, paragram, paronomasia, pestle, plat, pound, quibble, quip, ram, whim, witticism, wordplay
PUNA plateau, poon, sickness, soroche, wind
PUNCH ade, awl, backhander, baste, beat, beverage, biff, bishop, blow, bore, box, buffoon, bust, clout, clown, couse, cuff, die, dowse, drill, drink, energy, england, force, gad, glog, grounder, herd, HIT, horse, jab, jester, kick, magazine, mattoir, mountebank, negus, paste, perforate, perloir, pierce, poke, pound, press, prick, pritchel, prod, prop, pummel, puncture, shaper, short, slap, slosh, slug, smite, sock, spirit, stamp, stout, strike, swat, thickset, thrust, tool, vigor, vim, zetz
and judy england and france
and judy character swatchel
and judy dog toby
board pushcard
bowl sneaker
chasing tracer
etcher's mattoir
1st editor lemon
horseshoe pritchel
house boarding-house, inn, tavern
in arrive
knockout haymaker, kayo
out depart
oval plaisher
press bear, drop
spiced bishop, glog, negus
steel perloir
PUNCHEON awl, cask, dagger, die, log, post, pule, snap, stamp, stud, timber, tool
PUNCHER bodkin, cowboy, horseman, perforator, socker, stockman
PUNCHINELLO buffoon, clown
PUNCHY befuddled, dazed, farchadat, fat, forceful, stubby
PUNCTILIO apex, conscience, detail, etiquette, exactness, finesse, instant, mark, meticulosity, point, strictness, technicality
PUNCTILIOUS attentive, careful, ceremonial, conscientious, conventional, cor-

rect, exact(ing), fastidious, formal, fussy, methodical, meticulous, nice, observant, orderly, particular, pointed, precise, precisian, proper, regular, scrupulous, squeamish, strict, systematic

PUNCTUAL accurate, concentrated, explicit, formal, indivisible, infinitesimal, meticulous, on time, pointed, precise, prompt, quick, ready, right, sharp, small

PUNCTUALLY exactly, on the dot, on the nose, on time, precisely, promptly, sharp

PUNCTUATE accent(uate), break, distinguish, divide, dotted, emphasize, interrupt, intersect, mark, point out, spotted, stop, stress

PUNCTUATION See also MARK *printing.*

mark accent, apostrophe, brace, bracket, breve, caesura, colon, comma, dash, diacritic, dot, ellipsis, hyphen, parens, parenthesis, period, point, prick, question mark, quotation mark, quotes, semicolon, slash, stigme, stop, virgule

PUNCTURE blowout, bore, centesis, collapse, cut, deflate, depression, destroy, disprove, drill, flat, hole, hurt, knife, lacerate, lance, leak, needle, open(ing), penetrate, perforate, perforation, pierce, pink, piqure, point, prick, prod, punch, stab, stick, sting, wound

comb. stixis

vine or weed caltrap, caltrop, tribulus

PUNDIT authority, brahman, brahmin, clerk, expert, learned, learner, literatus, nestor, official, philosopher, polyhistor, sage, scholar, solon, svami, swami, teacher, thinker

PUNG sled, sleigh

PUNGENT acid, acrid, acute, aromatic, biting, bitter, bold, caustic, cutting, effluvious, escharotic, expressive, funny, hot, incisive, irritating, keen, mordant, painful, penetrating, peppery, piercing, piquant, poignant, pointed, pricking, probing, racy, rough, sar-

castic, severe, sharp, snappy, sour, spicy, stabbing, stimulating, stinging, tangy, tart, telling, tez, trenchant, zestful

PUNGI bin, flute, pipe

PUNIC carthaginian, faithless, false, perfidious, treacherous

apple pomegranate

faith infidelity

war battle zama

war combatant carthage, rome

war general fabius, hannibal, scipio

PUNISH abuse, amerce, avenge, banish, bastinado, beat, birch, blister, cane, cartwhip, castigate, chasten, chastise, correct, corrige, crucify, deport, disbar, disciple, discipline, dismiss, distrain, execute, exile, ferule, fine, fix, flog, frap, handicap, hang, immure, impale, imprison, keelhaul, lambaste, lash, lick, mulct, ostracize, pain, penalize, pillory, pommel, rebuke, requite, revenge, rusticate, scold, scourge, sentence, shend, slate, smite, spank, strappado, torment, torture, trounce, twink, unfrock, whip, wreak

PUNISHMENT amende, assessment, castigation, correction, damnation, dirdum, discipline, execution, exile, expulsion, ferule, fine, gig, gruel, herisson, infliction, jankers, judgment, lash, loss, mulct(ation), pain, payment, p(e)ine, penalty, penance, punition, purgatory, rack, retribution, revenge, sack, sentence, smart, stocks, suffering, supplice, wrack

agent of nemesis

capital See EXECUTION.

freedom from impunity

instrument azote, bastinado, belt, birch, bitter pill, branks, bullwhack, bullwhip, cane, cat(o-ninetails), club, cowhide, crop, cucking-stool, ducking, ferule, flagellum, galley, gallows, horsewhip, knout, kurbash, lash, paddle, pillory, quirt, rattan, rawhide, razorstrap, rod, ruler,

scaffold, scourge, sjambok, stick, stocks, strap, switch, thong, treadmill, trebuchet, triangle, whip(lash), wrack

military jankers

personification poena

pert. penal, punative

spare absolve, acquit, clear, exculpate, exonerate, free

study penology

PUNITIVE corrective, grueling, penal, punishing, punitory, retributory, revengeful, tortuous, vengeful, vindictive

PUNJAB See also INDIA.

capital lahore

caste jat

hindu jat

state bagul

warrior sikh

PUNK amador, bad, beginner, bum, cheesy, child, conch, crumby, elephant, fuel, gangster, goshawful, grim, hoodlum, inferior, jerk, lighter, lousy, miserable, novice, poor, prostitute, pung, putrid, rotten, snide, stinking, strumpet, tinder, touchwood, tramp, tyro, worthless

source agaric

tree cajeput, cajuput, kajeput, melaleuca, paperbark, paperbush

PUNKIE fly, gnat, midge

PUNT boat, boot, drive, gamble, garvey, hit, kent, kick, pole, propel, skerry, wagon

pole kent, poy, quant

PUNTER bidder, gambler, scalper, servitor

PUNY feeble, frail, inexperienced, infirm, junior, little, manikin, meager, measly, novice, paltry, petty, picayune, pint-size, puisne, pygmy, recent, sawed-off, shilpit, slight, small, sproty, subordinate, subsequent, tiny, trifling, trivial, unskilled, weak, younger

PUP boy, dog, fledgling, fop, offshoot, offspring, seal, stream, tributary, whelp

group litter

PUPA chrysalis, egg, flaxseed, instar, nymph, puppet, tumbler, w(r)iggler

-bearing pupigerous

case cerion, cocoon, larva, theca

PUPIL cadet, chela, child,

disciple, ecolier, eleve, eye-ball, freshman, junior, learner, minor, neophyte, norry, plebe, scholar, schoolboy, schoolgirl, senior, sophomore, student, tutee, tyro, youth
absence acorea
comb. cor
contraction hippus, miosis
defect aniscoria
diameter aperture
dilator atropine
-monger tutor
narrowing stenocoriasis

PUPPET actor, agent, cat's-paw, charlie mccarthy, creature, doll, dupe, effigy, figure(head), guignol, guy, image, instrument, jack-o-lent, judy, marionette, maumet, miniature, mortimer snerd, nonentity, ollie, pawn, punch, snerd, stooge, tool, vassal
head aunt sally
maker sarg
show guignol, punch and judy, shadow-play, vertep, wajang, wayang

PUPPY boy, dandy, dog, dough, fledgling, fop, puppet, sapling, shark, whelp, young
female gyp
fish squatina
foot ace of clubs
love infatuation

PUR *brother* abel, cain

PURBLIND bigoted, bisme, bisson, blind, myopic, obtuse, shortsighted, sightless, stupid

PURCELL *opera* dido and aeneas

PURCHASABLE asale, available, corrupt, for sale, marketable, salable, venal

PURCHASE ac(h)ate, acquire, acquisition, advantage, attempt, bargain, barratry, booty, bribe(ry), buy, chase, cheap(en), contrive, employ, emptio(n), endeavor, foothold, footing, gain, get, grasp, grip, haul, hire, hold, influence, koop, leverage, market, obtain, procure, property, provide, pulley, resource, secure, shop, strive, tackle, truck, yield
back redeem, regain

PURCHASER(S) buyer, cli-

ent(ele), clientry, customer, dealer, mercenary, patron (age), shopper, trader, trafficker, vendee

PURDAH curtain, harem, screen, seclusion

PURDY disagreeable, self-important, surly

PURE absolute, abstract, angelic, authentic, blank, candid, cast, chaste, clean, clear, complete, decent, devout, downright, ethered, ethical, excellent, faultless, fine, fresh, genuine, good, guiltless, holy, immaculate, impeccable, innocent, intemerate, inviolate, irreproachable, lily-white, limpid, lucid, main, mere, mistress, modest, moral, neat, net, noble, paramour, perfect, pious, pristine, pute, real, seraphic, sheer, simple, sincere, spiritous, spotless, stainless, taintless, theoretic, thorough, true, unadulterated, unalloyed, undefiled, unimpeachable, unmixed, unsoiled, unsullied, untainted, untarnished, utter, virgin(al), virtuous, white
and simple downright, mere, ordinary, plain, spic-and-span
blooded thoroughbred
name meaning agnes

PUREE bisk, bisque, pulp, sieve, soup

PURELY barely, chastely, completely, merely, only, simply, solely, very, wholly

PURFLE border, decorate, edge, hem, ornament, outline, purl, trim

PURGATION ablution, catharsis, cleansing, lustration, penance, purification

PURGATIVE abstergent, aloedary, aloes, aloin, aperient, aperitive, barbaloin, calomel, cathartic, citrullin, cleanser, diasene, emetic, evacuant, jalap, lapactic, laxative, nataloin, physic, purge, senna, turpeth

PURGATORY chasm, cleft, erebus, hell, limbo, misery, pain, swamp, torment

PURGE absolve, absterge, acquit, atone, clarify, clean(se), clear, depose, depurate, deterge, discharge,

eliminate, emit, exonerate, exterminate, extinction, fire, flush, kill, laxative, mundify, physic, prune, purify, remove, rub out, scour, seethe, shrive, treat, trim, wash
political epuration

PURI *home* jaggannath

PURIFICATION abdest, ablution, baptism, catharsis, consecration, depuration, distillation, elution, lustration, lustrum, purge, sanctification, vastation, wudu
feast candlemas
flower galanthus, snowdrop
pert. lustral

PURIFIER alembic, catharsis, cleanser, depurator, refiner

PURIFY aerate, baptize, bleach, bless, catharize, chasten, chastise, clarify, clean(se), decontaminate, depurate, distill, epurate, expurgate, exorcise, fine, fumigate, launder, lustrate, oxygenate, purge, rarefy, refine, render, sanctify, snuff, sprinkle, spurge, try, wash
by smoke fumigate
ore dilve

PURIM feast of lots
chronicler dositheus, lysimachus, ptolemaeus
meal seudah

PURINE adenine

PURIRI bulreedy, ironwood, teak

PURISM correctness, pedantism, pedantry, precisianism

PURITAN admonishioner, admonitionist, ascetic, bluenose, canter, catharan, croppy, gospeler, pilgrim, prude, roundhead, stuffed shirt, wowser
city boston
garment mandillion
last adams
statesman cromwell

PURITANICAL austere, blue, dogmatic, genteel, precise, priggish, prim, prissy, proper, prudish, rigorous, strait-laced, strict

PURITANISM asceticism, austerity, dogmatism, hyperorthodoxy

PURITY candor, chastity, cleanness, finesse, honor,

immaculacy, innocence, sattva, virginity, virtue, white
symbol lily, unicorn
symbolic color silver, white
PURL ale, beer, border, capsize, cropper, curl, eddy, embroider, fall, frill, knit, murmur, outline, plunge, purfle, rib, ripple, run, spill, spin, stitch, swirl, tern, tip over, tottle, trickle, unhorse, upset, wheel, whirl
PURLHOUSE tavern
PURLIEU(S) area, bounds, confines, district, environ (ment), haunt, locality, neighborhood, resort, suburb
PURLOIN abstract, burglarize, cab(bage), cop, crib, defalcate, embezzle, filch, finger, lift, peculate, pilfer, pirate, plagiarize, snitch, STEAL, swipe
PURLOINER See THIEF.
PURPLE amaranth, amethyst, ardoise, blatta, brilliant, burgundy, cardinalate, cassius, crocus, dye, eggplant, eveque, flamboyant, flaunting, fuchsia, furious, gridelin, heliotrope, imperial, lavender, lilac, logwood, lurid, luxuriant, magenta, mauve(tte), modena, orchid, ornate, orotund, perse, pigment, plum, pontiff, power, prophyrous, prosperity, puce, purpure, racy, rank, regal, rhetorical, risque, royalty, showy, solferino, sovereign, station, tyrian, uda, violet, wealth, wistaria
band clavus
blackish sloe
brown puce
deep eveque, modena, perse
dye cassius, murex
fish murex
gallinule hyacinth, sultana
grackle blackbird, quiscalus
heart amaranth, award, copaiva, medal, order, peltogyne, tree, wood
land of tyre
loosestrife killweed
-navy marine
pale mauve, violet
ragwort jacoby
sandpiper redleg(s), rockbird
seller of lydia

-top grass, triodia
visual erythropsin, rhodopsin
PURPORT allege, bearing, convey, design, disguise, drift, effect, feck, gist, impart, imply, import, intent(ion), mean(ing), object, pretense, profess, PURPOSE, sense, signify, substance, tendency, tenor
PURPORTED ostensible, pretended, self-styled, so-called, soi-disant
PURPOSE aim, ambition, artha, aspiration, bourn, cause, consider, crusade, decide, decision, design, determination, determine, end, ettle, function, goal, hang, heart, hent, intend, intent (ion), main, mark, mean (ing), mecca, mission, motive, object(ive), obtent, plan, plot, ponder, predesign, project, propose, proposition, purport, pursue, reason, relevance, resolution, resolve, sake, scheme, scope, study, target, tend, terminus, think, try, use, wish
alleged excuse, pretext
answer the apply, avail, serve
for this ad hoc
having telic
in nature teleology
not to the irrelevant
on advisedly, calculated, consciously, deliberately, designedly, intentionally, knowingly, pointedly, voluntarily, willfully, wittingly
pert. teleological, telic
to the ad rem
ulterior ax(e) to grind
without aimless, desultory, driftless, lazy, meaningless, needless, random, useless
PURPOSEFUL aimful, bound, calculated, decided, determined, firm, intent(ional), pointed, resolute, resolved, stalwart, steadfast, steady, telic
PURR dunlin, thrum, whurl
PURRONE euxanthone
PURSE almoner, ante, award, bag, billfold, bourse, buckskin, bulse, bung, burse, carryall, cl(a)y, cloy, clutch, cockle, cradle, crease, crumenal, dummy, finances, funds, gipsire, handbag, jan,

knit, means, moneybag, pocket(book), poke, portemonnaie, pouch, prize, pucker, reticule, reward, ruffle, spark, sporran, spung, stake, treasury, wallet, wrinkle
-bearer bursar, treasurer
crab ayuyu, birgus, pagurid
kilt sporran
-like bursiculate, bursiform
net seine
-rat pocket-gopher
snatcher pickpocket, thief
tassel hyacinth
PURSER boucher, bursar, cashier, clerk, nipcheese, paymaster, pinchgut, teller, treasurer
PURSHIA antelopebrush, bitterbrush, buckbush, ceanothus, coralberry, wolfberry,
PURSING mimp, prim
PURSLANE calandrina, claytonia, montia, pigweed, portulaca, pussly, rosemoss, spekboom, spurge
PURSUANT according(to), agreeable(to), conformable, following, prosecutor, pursuer
PURSUE badger, bait, carry on, chase, chevy, chiv(e)y, continue, court, cultivate, desire, dog, ensue, exercise, follow, gallop, harass, hotfoot, hound, hunt, maintain, oppress, persecute, persevere, persist, plead, plod, practice, proceed, prosecute, ride, run, search, seek, shack, shadow, shag, specialize, stalk, sue, tag, tail, trace, track, trade, trail
PURSUER chaser, follower, hunter, lover, persecutor, plaintiff, prosecutor, shadow, skiptracer, tail
PURSUIT activity, affliction, assault, attack, avocation, business, calling, career, cause, chase, employment, end, entreaty, excercise, fad, forte, hobby, hunt, job, metier, objective, occupation, persecution, practice, profession, prosecution, quest, scent, search, specialty, stalk, suit, target, trade, undertaking, venture, vocation, work
with hounds hot-trod(e)
PURSUIVANT antelope, at-

tendant, dingwall, falcon, follower, march, squire

PURSY asthmatic, baggy, corpulent, fat, fleshy, monied, obese, pampered, plump, puckered, pudgy, puffy, pursed, stout, swollen, wealthy
minnow killifish

PURULENT attern, attery, pyic

PURVEY arrange, assessment, assist, cater, equip, foresee, furnish, get, obtain, order, outfit, pander, procure, provide, provision, supply, tax

PURVEYANCE foresight, preparation, prevision, providence, provision, supplies

PURVEYOR bawd, pimp, procurer, proveditor, supplier

PURVIEW authority, compass, field, gamut, horizon, ken, limit, orbit, province, radius, range, reach, scope, sweep

PURWANNAH grant, order, pass, permit

PUS amper, corruption, fester(ing), humor, ichor, matter, maturation, purulence, rankling, sanies, suppuration, weeping, worsum
collection abscess
containing mattery
-like puriform
pert. pyoid

PUSH accelerate, action, advance, attack, back, bear, bevel, birr, blitz, blow, boil, boom, boost, bore, bunch, bunt, butt, cant, clique, compel, constrain, crisis, crowd, ding, drive, dush, elbow, emergency, energy, enterprise, extend, extremity, force, gang, goad, group, hunch, hurtle, hustle, impel, impetus, importune, impulse, influence, jostle, knock, kvetch(er), mass, move, nub, nudge, oblige, obtrude, offense, offensive, pelt, ping, poke, porr, poss, pote, press(ure), prod, promote, propel, propulsion, prosecute, set, shove, shtoop, shtup, shunt, speed, sponsor, stress, support, thring, throng, thrust, tush, urge, vigor, vim

apart separate, spread
back rebuff, repel, repulse, rout
button pressel
cart barrow, pram, stroller, trolley
down depress, detrude
forward advance
in crush, enter, intrude, invade, stove
off begin, depart, leave, start
on continue, press, proceed, yerk
open dup
out debout, expel, extrude, launch
rake hay-sweep
through accelerate, end, expedite, finish, force, wind up

PUSHER booster, connection, engine, locomotive, plunger, trailer, trammer
airplane canard

PUSHING aggressive, assertive, assured, confident, energetic, enterprising, forward, intrusive, militant, obtrusive, officious, vigorous

PUSHKIN *work* boris godunov, captain's daughter, eugene, onegin

PUSHOVER child's play, cinch, dupe, gull, snap, weakling

PUSHPIN inanity, triviality

PUSILLANIMOUS afraid, cowardly, craven, dastardly, destitute, faint-hearted, feeble, irresolute, mean-spirited, poltroon, poor, recreant, scurvy, sorry, tame, timid, timorous, weak

PUSS baudrons, CAT, cheet, child, countenance, face, girl, hare, lip, mouth, mug, physiognomy, pout, purse, rabbit, skunk, visage

PUSSY abscessed, CAT, catkin, clover, feline, hare, purulent, pyic, tabby, tipcat

PUSSYFOOT cautious, creep, dodge, evade, guarded, hedge, lurk, oscillate, prohibitionist, quibble

PUSSYTOE cat's-ear

PUSTULE achor, agria, amper, beal, blain, bleb, blister, blotch, bubble, bulla, burl, carbuncle, eruption, pimple, swelling, tetter, wart, wheal

PUT affirm, apply, assert, as-

sign, assume, attach, attribute, bestow, bet, bring, butt, buy, cast, connect, constrain, convey, deduce, deposit, devote, dismiss, drive, establish, express, fix, flow, force, formulate, give, impel, impose, incite, inflict, invest, laid, launch, lay, locate, make, move, oblige, offer, option, ordain, phrase, place, plant, provide, push, remove, render, repose, set, shoot, spew, sprout, stall, state, steek, stick, subject, suppose, surrender, throw, thrust, translate, urge, vomit, wager
about agitate, annoy, circulate, disconcert, disturb, incite, jib(e), pivot, publish, tack, turn
across accomplish, clarify, finish, impose, score, sell, succeed, transport
and take instrument teetotum
an end to abate, abolish, abrogate, break up, call, demolish, destroy, expiate, finish, kill, nullify, ruin, slay, snuff, spike, still, stop, surcease, terminate, void, wreck
aside bank, cache, can, daff, defer, delay, dismiss, hain, pigeonhole, postpone, preserve, reserve, save, shelve, shuffle, shunt, stash, store, table
at assail, attack, charge, chatter, dun, prosecute, throw
at rest allay, calm, hush
away accomplish, bank, bury, cache, consume, devour, discard, dispose of, divorce, eat, expel, hide, keep, kill, murder, renounce, repudiate, reserve, save, shed, shelve, stash, store, stow
back defeat, delay, demote, deny, hinder, impair, refuse, reinsert, reinstate, reject, remit, replace, repulse, restore, retain, return, rout, save, tack
before appose, face, offer, present, profer, propose, tell
beside compare
between interpose
by deprive, disappoint, neg-

lect, refuse, reject, reserve, save, store

down ante, arrest, ascribe, attribute, belittle, crush, defeat, deflate, degrade, denigrate, depose, deposit(ed), depress, discontinue, drink, drop, estimate, extinguish, humble, kill, laid, lain, list, oppress, quell, record, reduce, repress, reprimand, silence, sink, snub, squash, stop, subdue, subscribe, suppress, write

forth act, apply, busy, cast, circulate, develop, discharge, dismiss, exert, expel, extend, extrude, give (out), invest, issue, moot, offer, present, profer, propose, propound, publish, reach, set out, show, sprout, start, thrust

forward act, advance, assert, bourgeon, burgeon, carry, offer, prepose, propone, propose, provoke, urge

heads together confer, conspire, plan, plot, scheme

in ante, baffle, bottle, call, case, deposit, disembark, divert, elude, enclose, enter, establish, frustrate, insert, interpose, interrupt, intervene, intromit, land, plant, seat, set, sheathe, spend

in for apply, ask, claim, request, solicit

in force accomplish, authorize, effect, enact, execute, legislate

in motion activate, actuate, arouse, begin, carry out, impel, instigate, launch, start, undertake

in order adjust, arrange, clarify, daiker, fix, mend, neat(en), redd, remedy, repair, settle, sort, tidy

into effect execute, sanction

into practice attempt, carry out, effect, exercise, plot

into service activate, use

into shape practice, prepare, repair, restore, tidy(up), train

into words enunciate, express, phrase, say, speak, state, utter

in with agree, join, merge

it up to confront, propose, proposition, propound, suggest

off adjourn, baffle, defer

(red), delay, demur, discard, disconcert, dismiss, divert, divest, dodge, doff, elude, evade, evasion, excuse, fabianize, fob, foist, frustrate, haft, hinder, leave, parry, postpone, procrastinate, reject, remove, repel, retard, sail, shelve, stall, table, uncover

on accelerate, act, add, address, administer, adorn, advance, affect(ation), apply, assign, assume(d), bother, cover, deceive, don, employ, endue, exaggerate, fake(d), feign(ed), impose, impute, incite, indue, inflict, instigate, intrude, load, mount, overload, perform, present, pretend, pretense, produce, promote, rouse, sham, show, spurious, stage, stake, superpose, swank, trick, use, wager

on airs affect, promenade, show off, strut, swank

one's cards on the table disclose, level

one's foot in it blunder, err

one's nose out of joint beat, bother, deflate, irritate

on ice See PUT *off.*

on the dog decorate, dress, ornament, preen, prink, swagger, swank

onto tip

out anger, annoy, banish, bewilder, bother, cashier, chagrin, comply, conform, confuse, deport, destroy, disappoint, discompose, disconcert(ed), discountenance, dislocate, dismay, dismiss, displace, display, displease, dispossess, distress, douse, eject, eliminate, end, evict, exert, exile, expatriate, expel, extend, extinguish, fire, hurt, invest, irate, irk, issue, loan, mad, make an effort, miff(ed), mortify, offend, ostracize, oust, overcome, perform, plant, print, protrude, publish, retire, sack, sail, shoot, slake, snuff, spend, spout, start, trouble, try, use, vex

out of face disconcert, embarrass, shame

out of joint dislocate

over accomplish, assign, bilk, cheat, clarify, deceive, defer, impose, manage,

postpone, score, sell, succeed, trick

-put motorboat, motorcar

right or straight address, amend, correct, disillusion, emend, inform, level, relate, remedy, tell

the bite on beg, borrow, solicit

through accomplish, bring off, carry out, channel, complete, effect, enact, execute, legislate, manage, prepare, realize, succeed

to add, administer, apply, attach, close, compel, consign, entrust, exercise, force, join, petition, practice, send, shut, unite, use

together add, aggregate, annex, assemble, attach, build, coalesce, collect, combine, compose, congregate, construct, create, gather, join, knit, muster, organize, piece, set, sew(ed), unite(d)

to rights arrange, correct, neat(en), redd, remedy, sort, straighten, tidy

to shame abash, dash, discomfit, dishonor, humiliate, mortify, shame

under bury, inter

up accomodate, ante, billet, build, bundle, can, conspire, create, dwell, endure, entertain, erect, establish, expose, hang(up), hoard, host(age), increase, lay by, lift, live, lodge, name, nominate, offer, pack, pay, pledge, plot(ted), post, prepare(d), present, preserve, primed, raise, rehearsed, reside, sling, sojourn, stake, stay, stop, store, suspend

upon abuse(d), attack, bother(ed), impose(d), intrude, oppress, tease, torment, victimize

up with abide, bear, bide, brook, endure, stand, stomach, submit, suffer, swallow, take, tolerate

PUTAIN See PROSTITUTE.

PUTAMEN endocarp, membrane, pit, seed, stone

PUTATIVE alleged, assumed, attributable, attributed, conjectural, deemed, hypothetical, reputed, simulated, supposed, supposititious

PUTREFACTION decay, decomposition, disintegration, rot

PUTREFY corrupt, crumble, debase, decay, decompose, deprave, disintegrate, fester, pollute, rot, spoil, sweat

PUTRID bad, corrupt, decayed, decomposed, depraved, dirty, disagreeable, displeasing, fetid, foul, friable, fusty, immoral, lousy, malodorous, musty, noisome, obscene, offensive, punk, putrescent, rancid, rank, rotten, septic, stinking, tainted, vicious, vile

PUTSCH rebellion, revolt, take-over, uprising

PUTTEE bandage, gaiter, legging, pata, spat

PUTTER caddle, dally, dawdle, fool(around), friggle, fuss, golf club, idle, iron, loiter, mucker, muckle, potter, tinker, trammer, trifle

-on feeder, handler, instigator

-out depositor, lender, supplanter

-up backer, inciter, instigator, proposer

PUTTOCK bailiff, buzzard, catchpole, hanger-on, harrier, kite, makeweight

PUTTY cement, mud

-blower peashooter

ingredient silicone

-like amenable, docile, pliable

PUTTYROOT adam and eve, crawfoot, orchid

PUTZ ass, creche, easy-mark, fool, jerk, simpleton, yokel

PUXY cross, difficulty, ill-tempered, miry, puckish, quagmire, quandary, snappish, swamp(y)

PUZZLE acrostic, addle, amaze, anagram, astonish, astound, baffle, beat, befog, befuddle, bemuddle, bemuse, bewilder, bother, charade, confound, confuse, confusion, conundrum, crossword, crux, difficulty, discomfit, disconcert, distract, dum(b)found, embarrass, enigma, entangle, fickle, flabbergast, foiter, glaik(s), grip, intrigue, jigsaw, kittle, muddle, muse, mystery, mystify, nonplus, palindrome, paradox, per-

plex, pose(r), problem, puxy, quandary, queer, rebus, riddle, stick, sticker, stop, taissle, tangram, think, trangam, trouble

PUZZLING ambiguous, bewildering, confusing, knotty, paradoxical, riddling

PWYLL *consort* rhiannon

son pryderi

PYCANTHEMUM basil, bezel, koellia, mountain-mint, ocimum

PYCNONOTID bulbul, luscinia, nightingale

PYEMIA bloodpoisoning, septicemia, toxemia

PYGARG addax, animal, antelope, osprey, sea-eagle

PYGMALION *beloved* galatea, statue

father agenor, belus, mutgo

helper aphrodite

kingdom cyprus, tyre

sister dido

son paphus

statue galatea

victim sichaeus

PYGMY achango, achua, afify, akka, amba, ashango, atomy, batwa, dandyprat, doko, dwarf(ish), elf, gnome, homunculus, manikin, midget, minim, negrillo, peewee, pigmy, pixy, runt, short, shrimp, small, teeny, tiny, vaalpens, wee, wochua

goose cotton-teal, goslet, nettapus

island blefuscu, france

musk deer chevrotain

owl glaucidium

rattlesnake massasauga, sistrurus

PYIC purulent, pussy, superating

PYKNIC fat, obese, paunchy, squat, sthenic, stout

PYLADES *friend* orestes

parent anaxibia, strophius

wife electra

PYLON gateway, marker, meta, monument, portal, post, stake, tower

PYLOS *king* nestor

PYRAMID enlarge, increase, memorial, parlay, pile, point, speculate, tomb, tower

builder cephren(es), cheops, k(h)afre, khufu, mencheres, menkure, mycerinus, pharaoh, suphis

crayfish buisson

double twin, zirconoid

inverted hopper

ruins benares

-shaped stone ben-ben

site cholula, egypt, el giza, gizeh, mexico, teocalli, tepoztlan

swindle ponzi

PYRAMIDAL big, enormous, great, huge, imposing, tapered

PYRAMUS *lover* thisbe

PYRARGYRITE argyrythrose

PYRAZINE aldine, diazine, piazin

PYRE bale, bier, bonfire, fire, heap, pile, suttee, tophet

PYRENEES *bandit* miquelet

chamois izard

city tarbes

marble griotte

pass perche, somport

peak aneto, nethou

people basques

republic andorra

resort pau

PYRETIC febrile, feverish

PYRITE bale, brazil, firestone, magistral, marcasite, mundic, stannite

PYROLA limonium, shinleaf, wintergreen

PYROMANIAC arsonist, firebug, incendiary

PYRONYXIS ignipuncture

PYROPE cape-ruby, garnet, gem

PYROPHONE harmonicon

PYROSIS brash, heartburn

PYROTECHNICS fireworks

PYROXENE acmite, augit-(it)e, coccolite, diallage, diopside, hedenbergite, jade (ite), pectolite, rhodonite, sa(h)lite, schefferite, silicate

PYRRHA titania

consort deucalion

father epimetheus

PYRRHONISM doubt, incredulity, skepticism

PYRRHULOXIA blood-alp, bullfinch, finch, grosbeak, olp

PYRRHUS neoptolemus

brother demetrius

city berenicis

conqueror manius-curius

friend oplacus

kidnapper androclides, angelus

kingdom epirus

nephew demetrius
nickname eagle
parent aecides, glaucias, phthia
rescuer hippias, neander
son ptolemy, sopater
victim neoptolemus
wife antigone, bardyllis, bircemio, lanassa
PYTHAGORAS *birthplace* samos
daughter camo

disciple empedocles
symbol hexagram
PYTHIAN ecstatic, phrenetic
games, 1st phemonoe
games site delphi
PYTHIAS *friend* damon
PYTHIUS apollo
PYTHON adjiger, anaconda, boa(constrictor), boid, carpetsnake, daemon, dragon, kaa, peropod, prophet, rocksnake, seer, serpent, snake

female phitones, witch
god zombi
slayer apollo
PYTHONIC huge, inspired, monstrous, oracular
PYX artophorion, binnacle, box, capsa, casket, chest, ciborium, coffer, container, pix, tabernacle, vessel
PZAZZ ardor, elan, style, zest, zip

Q

Q cue, queen, queue
QATAR *city* doha, uumsaid
people baluchi, pushtu, yemeni
product oil
ruler khalifa
ruling family thani
QEBHSNUF *father* horus
QED quod erat demonstrandum
QIANA fabric, fiber
QUA bird, heron, quagmire
QUAB eelpout, fish, gudgeon
QUACK charlatan, circulator, crocus, cry, empiric, fake(r), gabble, gobble, hoarseness, honk, horsedoctor, humbug, imposter, medecin-tant-pis, medicaster, mountebank, pretender, punk, quake, saltimbanco, salver, sangrado
grass couch
remedy nostrum
QUACKERY bluff, charlatanism, charlatanry, cunning, deceit, duplicity, empiricism, four-flushing, guile, humbug(gery), imposture
QUACKLE choke, suffocate
QUAD block, campus, court (yard), horse, imprison, jail, park, quod, quoth, sibling, type
QUADRA border, fillet, frame, listel, plinth, socle
trunk barrel
QUADRAGESIMA(L) fasting, forty, lenten, sermon
QUADRANGLE campus, cheesebox, close, court, enclosure, parallelogram, quadrate, rectangle, rhomboid, square, tessara, tetragon, tetragram, tetrahedron, tract, trapezia

QUADRANT altimeter, arc, bow, conformable, farthing, fourth, gill, quarter, radial, section, semicircle, square, tetrant
QUADRATE adapt, adjust, agree, balanced, bone, conform, correspond(ent), cube, dovetail, ideal, perfect, quader, quarter, quartile, rectangle, square(d), suit
QUADRIC conicoid, ellipsoid, hyperboloid, sphere, spheroid
QUADRIFORM perfect, square
QUADRIGA car, chariot, horses
QUADRILATERAL See QUADRANGLE.
QUADRILLE allemande, cards, contredanse, cotillion, dance, lancers, music, squared
term cavalier seul, lete, pantalon, poule
QUADROON metis, mixture, quateron, terceron
QUADRULA mussel, pimpleback, wartyback
QUADRUMANE ape(let), chimpanzee, gorilla, lemur, marmoset, monkey, primate
QUADRUPED animal, fourfooted, mammal
QUADRUPLET cycle, fourling, quartole
QUAERE ask, inquire, inquiry, query, question, seek
QUAFF carouse, draft, drink, guzzle, imbibe, partake, swallow, swill
QUAG bog, marsh, quake, quiver, shake
QUAGGA animal, ass, zebra

QUAGGY boggy, fenny, flabby, marshy, miry, muddy, queachy, soft, spongy, wet, yielding
QUAGMIRE bog, difficulty, ensnare, fen, hag, impasse, lair, marsh, mizzy, morass, ooze, predicament, pucksey, puddle, puxy, quaw, swamp, trap
QUAHOG blunt, bullnose, clam, cyprina, venus
QUAIL bird, blench, bobwhite, coagulate, coil, colin, coturnix, courtesan, cow-(er), cringe, crough, curdle, daunt, decline, destroy, die, duraquara, edishhen, fade, fail, falter, fawn, flinch, hemipod, impair, lophortyx, iowa, massena, oreortyx, partridge, perish, prostitute, quake, quaver, quell, recoil, retreat, shrink, shudder, skulk, slink, sneak, spoil, subdue, succomb, tinamou, tremble, turnix, waste, waver, weet, wet-my-lip, wince, wither
bush iowa, perdicula
button hemipode, turnicid
dove pigeon
group bevy, covey, flock
hawk bush-hawk, cooper's, falcon, nesierax
snipe dowitcher
young cheeper, squealer
QUAINT adorn, affected, antique, archaic, artful, attractive, beautify, crafty, curious, droll, dry, eccentric, elaborate, elegant, erratic, expert, fanciful, fastidious, graceful, haughty, ingenious, naive, neat, nice, odd, old-fashioned, outlandish,

overnice, peculiar, pleasing, pretty, proper, proud, prudent, queer, refined, singular, skilled, spiderish, squeamish, strange, uncouth, unique, unusual, whimsical, wily, wise

QUAKE agitate, didder, dither, falter, hesitate, oscillate, quack, quail, quaver, quiver, seism, shake, shimmy, shiver, shock, shudder, teeter, temblor, thrill, tremble, tremor, upheaval, vibrate, waver, wobble

QUAKER albatross, aminadab, aspen, beaconite, bird, broadbrim, fox(ite), friend, grasshopper, gun, heron, hicksite, locust, moth, obadiah, rachel, shadbelly, tremble(r), whacker
blue gray
bonnet bluet
city philadelphia
colored drab, dull, gray, inconspicuous, neutral
founder george fox
gray acier
group friends
ladies bluet, meadowsweet
liberal hicksite
poet barton, whittier
state pennsylvania

QUAKING ash, aspen, shaking, shivering, timorous, trembling, tremor, tremulant, trepid(ation)
grass birds-eyes, briza, cowquake, cuckoo-flower, wagwants

QUALIFICATION ability, allowance, aptitude, attainment, attribute, capability, capacity, cession, change, character, coloring, competence, concession, condition, consideration, discount, endowment, essential, exemption, extenuation, grant, habilitation, knowledge, limit(ation), modification, nature, prerequisite, provision, requisite, reservation, restriction, skill, stipulation, talent, trait

QUALIFIED able, accomplished, apt, authentic, authorized, capable, capacious, competent, conditional, conditioned, eligible, experienced, fit(ted), guard-

ed, leavened, licensed, likely, limited, mitigated, modified, modulated, proved, quizzed, ready, restricted, seasoned, skilled, softened, suitable, tempered, tested, trained, tried, warranted

QUALIFY abate, able, absolve, adapt, adjust, alter, assuage, capacitate, certify, change, characterize, contemper, describe, empower, enable, entitle, equip, fit, limit, measure up, mitigate, moderate, modify, name, pass, prepare, reconcile, restrain, restrict, soften, suffice, temper, train, vary, weaken

QUALIFYING assuasive, exceptional, extenuating, lenitive, palliative
term but, even so, except (ing), gif, gin, however, if so, less'n, so long as, so that, unless, without

QUALITY accomplishment, aristocracy, art, aspect, atmosphere, attribute, brand, brilliance, caliber, capacity, characteristic, chop, class, cost, difference, distinction, excellence, excellent, fashion, feature, form, gentry, goodness, grade, kind, manner, mark, mettle, mold, nature, nobility, occupation, part(icular), position, profession, property, quale, rank, rate, skill, society, standard, strain, style, superiority, timber, timbre, trait, virtue, worth
artistic virtu
comb. acity, acy, ance, ancy, ence, ency, ice, icity, ness
distinctive atmosphere, attribute, aura, personality
excellent corker, thew
highest best
inherent in universe guna, rajas, sattva, tamas
mark cachet
natural tarage
primal guna
subtle bouquet, shade
symbol grademark, hallmark

QUALM anxiety, apprehension, calm, compunction, conscience, croak, demur, disbelief, doubt, drow, faintness, fear, foreboding, hesitation, melancholy, misdoubt, misgiving,

mistrust, nausea, pain, pall, pang, regret, scruple, seasickness, squeam, suspicion, throe, uncertainty

QUAMASIA camass(ia), herb, plant

QUANDARY bewilderment, canary, contingency, difficulty, dilemma, exigency, fix, hardship, impasse, jam, juncture, mess, mire, nonplus, pass, perplexity, pickle, plight, predicament, problem, puzzle, scrape, strait, swither, upset, vicissitude

QUANT cane, pole, propel, punt

QUANTITATIVE mensural, mensurative

QUANTITY 3 all, bag, bit, box, lac, pot, sum, ton, wad **4** bags, body, bulk, case, deal, dose, feck, gobs, heap, host, lakh, load, lots, many, mass, mess, mise, much, pail, peck, pile, raft, sack, size, slew, some, swad **5** acres, array, aught, batch, bunch, crate, flask, flood, grist, group, kitty, loads, ocean, plate, reams, scads, sight, spate, stack, store, total, troop, whole **6** amount, armful, barrel, basket, boxful, budget, bundle, bushel, extent, figure, galaxy, galore, hantle, number, oceans, oodles, pocket, potful, supply, thrave, vector, volume, weight, yaffle **7** content, fortune, handful, measure, myriads, pailful, portion, quantum, roomful, sackful, surfeit, tankful **8** bellyful, mountain, mouthful, plateful, slathers, spoonful, strength **9** abundance, aggregate, amplitude, barrelful, basketful, great deal, magnitude, pocketful, profusion **10** cornucopia
consumed intake
directionless scalar
electrical capacitance, capacity
estimated wey
excessive glut, spate
fixed constant
full complement
indeterminate some
irrational surd
large acre, barrage, bar-

rel(ful), bucket(s), bushel, cluster, dollop, flood, forest, hirsel, mass, melder, mint, multitude, myriad(s), oodles, peck, pile(s), quantum, reams, scads, skinful, slather, tons

math scalar, vector

measure cup, spoon, tablespoon, teacup

per unit rate

prescribed dosage, dose

small bit, curn, dab, dollop, dram, dribble, driblet, drop, grain, hair, iota, jobble, modicum, morsel, nip, particle, pennorth, quantulum, screw, scruple, shade, smicket, smidgen, smitch, songle, soupcon, spot, tot, touch, trace

QUANTUM allotment, amount, body, part, phonon, phonton, quantity, share, unit

QUAP heave, palpitate, palpitation, quaver, throb

QUAPAW *indian* arkansas, kwapa, ozark

QUAR block, choke, curdle, fill, quarter, sour

QUARANTINE ban, confine, cordon, detain, exclude, fast, interdict(ion), isolate, isolation, penance, restrain(t), sanction, seclusion, segregate, segregation, separation, sequestration, yellow-jack

station lazaret(to)

QUARL(E) brick, coagulate, curdle, jellyfish, medusa, tile

QUARLY jasper

QUARNERO *city on* rieka, rijeka

QUARREL affray, altercation, argue, barney, battle, bicker(ing), bolt, brabble, brack, brawl, breach, breeze, brigue, broil, cangle, cavil, chisel, clash, collieshangie, complaint, conflict, contention, contest, controversy, diamond, differ, disagree, discord, dispute, dissension, distance, disturbance, fall out, feud, fight, flite, flusk, flyte, fracas, fray, fuss, gruff, hassle, imbroglio, jangle, melee, miff, misunderstanding, odds, prabble, quarry, reason, rippet, row, rumpus,

run-in, scene, scrap, spat, sputter, squabble, squeal, stashie, strife, strike, struggle, threap, tiff, tuilyie, tuilzie, tumult, upscuddle, variance, wrangle

QUARRELSOME adverse, antagonistic, argument(at)-ive, battlesome, bellicose, belligerent, brawling, cantankerous, choleric, combative, contentious, counter, discordant, disputatious, dissentious, feisty, fractious, frampold, fratchy, hostile, inimical, irascible, irritable, litigious, petulant, phrampel, pugnacious, rancorous, rowty, rumgumptious, scrappy, ugly

person bantam, brabbler, brangler, breedbate, catamaran, troublemaker

talking backslanging

QUARRY chase, delf(t), delve, dig, excavate, excavation, game, heugh, hunt (ed), kill, latomia, latomy, mine, object, prey, quest, raven, ravin, source, victim

close to hot

man scabbler, scappler

stone latomia, latomy

term tirr

QUART *1/8th* gill

1/4th cup

1/2 pint

1.0567 liter

2 cab, flagon, kab, magnum

4 gallon

8 peck

QUARTER accommodate, allot, apportion, area, barrio, bed, bestow, billet, board, canton, cleave, clemency, coin, colony, contrada, direction, dismember, district, division, domain, fardel, farthing, faubourg, forbearance, fourth, grace, harbo(u)r, haven, lenience, lenity, locality, location, lodge, lodging, mercy, mildness, part, period, pity, place, plot, poblacion, portion, post, quadrature, raith, region, residence, room, ruth, section, shelter, side, skirt, span, station, stud, suburb, term, territory, twenty-five cents, two-bits

1/2 bit

2 half-dollar

note crotchet

rest sospiro

QUARTERING bona(u)ght, division, housing, lodging

QUARTERLY magazine, periodical, review, trimestr(i)al

QUARTERMASTER caterer, steward, supplier, victualer

QUARTERS abode, apartment, barracks, berth, billet, bivouac, bothy, cabin, camp, cantonment, chambers, chummery, commons, diggings, digs, dorm(atory), dwelling, etape, flat, gite, house, housing, lodgement, lodgings, raith, room, roost, shelter, tenement

men's selamlik

nautical cabin, focsle, forecastle, gunroom, steerage, wardroom

winter hibernacle

women's harem

QUARTET foursome, quadruplet

QUARTZ agate, alencon, amethyst, amydaloid, aventurine, basanite, birkremite, bloodstone, carnelian, chalcedony, citrine, crystal, flint, heliotrope, hornstone, jasper, leopardite, mineral, morion, onyx, prase, rubasse, sard(onyx), siderite, silica, sinopole, tarso, topaz, touchstone, yentnite

-albite adinole

conglomerate banket

crystal cairngor(u)m

crystalline amethyst, citrine, rubasse, smokey

-diorite banatite, tonalite

dull flint

flint silex

green chrysoprase, hawk's-eye, plasma, prase

-monzonite adamelite

pert. agatine

polymorph tridymite

-porphyry beresite

pulverized potter's flint

red birkremite, carnelian, jasper, rubasse, sard, sinople

silica silex

smoky cairngorm

syenite akerite, birkremite

-tourmaline carvoeira

transparent aventurine, goldstone, rock crystal

variegated agate

waxy chalcedony

yellow topaz

QUARTZITE ganister, itabarite, sandstone, silcrete

QUAS beer, cider

QUASAR *explorer* schmidt

QUASH abate, abolish, abrogate, avoid, cancel, cass (are), conceal, crush, destroy, dismiss, drop, extinguish, overthrow, peapod, pumpkin, quell, shake, shatter, sopite, spike, splash, squash, squelch, stop, subdue, suppress, tremble, vacate, veto, void

QUASI almost, as if, as though, nominal, resembling, seeming(ly), similar, spurious, supposedly

QUASIMODO *rescued* esmeralda

QUASISTELLAR quasar

QUASKY oquassa

QUASSIA bitter-ash, bitters, bitterwood, drug, paradise tree, tonic

QUAT blister, boil, collapsed, glut(ted), pimple, press, pustule, quit, satiate, squash, squat, sty, upstart

QUATCH betray, deceive, flat, move, shake, speak, squat, stir, tattle, twitch, wince, word

QUATRAIN poem, rubai, stanza, verse

rhyme scheme abab

QUAVER brandish, didder, dither, falter, fear, flourish, fluctuate, freddon, hesitate, quake, quap, quiver, shake, shimmy, shiver, shudder, sway, teeter, thrill, totter, tremble, tremolo, trepidate, trill, twitter, vacillate, vibrate, vibration, wabble, waver, wobble, wrible

QUAY breakwater, bunder, dock, harbor, kay, key, landing, levee, mole, pier, quell, subdue, wharf

dues wharfage

QUEACHY boggy, bushy, feeble, fenny, marshy, small, swampy, weak, woodsy

QUEAN girl, harlot, hussy, jade, prostitute, shrew, slut, trollop, wench, woman

QUEASY delicate, fastidious, hazardous, nauseated, qualmish, risky, sick, squeamish, squeezy, swampy, ticklish, troubled,

uncertain, uncomfortable, unhealthy, unsettled

feeling, butterflies

QUEBEC (See also CANADA.) stadacona

cape gaspe

carriage caleche

city levis, montreal, quebec

draughts polish checkers

founder champlain

island anticosti

leader maurice duplessis, rene levesque

nickname gibraltar of america

party liberal, parti quebecois

patron saint anne, jean baptiste

QUEBRACHO axbreaker, axmaster, breakax, ironwood

bark derivative antipyretic, aspidospermin(e), febrifuge, macaglia, yohimbine

QUECHUAN *indian* aymara, calchaquian, chola, cuzceno, inca, kichua, nasca, quiteno, quitu, runasimi, yunca

QUED bad, DEVIL, evil

QUEECHY feeble, puny, sickly, small, weak

QUEEN, QUEEN'S ant, basta, bee, begum, belle, bess, card, cat, czarina, dame, empress, fers, flirt, goddess, intrigo, intrigue, lady, maharani, monarch, ober, ranee, rani, rank, regina, reine, ruler, sovereign, termite

anne's lace plant, umbel, wild carrot

anne's leg style cabriole

anne's melon dudaim

arm musket

balm alyssum

camel camelot

charlotte indian haida

chess fers, fiers, phearse

city buffalo, cincinnati

conch cameo, cassis, helmit, mollusk, strombus

delight herb, oil, perennial, queenroot

dick richard cromwell

elizabeth bess, cynthia, diana, oriana

fairy See FAIRY *queen.*

famous anne, argante, athalia, atossa, brunhild, candace, cassiopeia, catherine, dido, elena, elizabeth, ena, gertrude, gloriana, guin-

ever(e), hecuba, jocasta, juno, mab, marie, mary, medb, omphale, oriana, roxana, sheba, statira, tamara, tamora, titania, victoria, zenobia

fish croaker, drumfish, wahoo

flower bloodwood, myrtle

gili-flower damewort

herb tobacco

husband king, prince-consort

legendary calafia

-like dignified, gracious, noble, regal, reginal, royal, sovereign

mother of cities london

needlework meadowsweet

of See under place: e.g., ENGLAND *queen,* HEAVEN *queen.*

of adriatic venice

of antilles cuba

of hearts elizabeth

of isles albion

of night moon

of north edinburgh

of northern seas elizabeth

of spades basta, card, lizzie, lizzy

pawn fers

pert. reginal

root stillingia, yawshrub

weed wild parsnip

QUEENLY haughty, majestic, noble, reginal, royal

QUEENSLAND (See also AUSTRALIA.) bananaland

capital brisbane

hemp jelly-leaf, lucern, paddy-lucern, sida

kangaroo boongarry

river barcoo

sorrel hibiscus

tribe goa, koko, waggumbura

tulip waratah

tulipwood harpullia

QUEER abnormal, banter, bizarre, comic(al), counterfeit, crab, crimp, curious, dippy, disconcert, dishonest, dotty, doubtful, droll, drunk, dubious, eccentric, erratic, extraordinary, faint, fanciful, fantastic, foul up, fruity, funny, gay, giddy, grotesque, gum(up), hinder, humorous, insane, intoxicated, louse up, nutty, obsessed, odd, outlandish, peculiar, quaint, qualmish, questionable, quisby, rally, ridicule, ruin, rum, shady, sham, singular, snafu, spoil, spurious, strange, suspicious, touched, unique, unusual, unwell

person coot, nut, oddball

QUEET ankle, coot

QUEEVE bend, turn, twist

QUELL abate, allay, assuage, beat, calm, check, crush, damp(en), dash, destroy, ease, end, extinguish, flow, fountain, kill, moderate, obtund, overpower, overwhelm, pacify, perish, put down, quail, quash, QUENCH, quiet, reduce, repress, slaughter, soothe, spring, squelch, stanch, stifle, still, subdue, suppress, well

QUEME agreeable, comely, fit(ting), handy, neat, pleasant, please, quiet, satisfy, snug, suit(able), tidy

QUEMOY *sorghum wine* kaoliang

QUENCH allay, assuage, check, cool, damp(en), delay, destroy, deter, end, extinguish, go out, gratify, quash, QUELL, quiet, sate, satisfy, slake, slock, stanch, stifle, still, subdue, subside, suppress

QUENCHLESS greedy, indestructible, insatiable

QUENELLE dumpling, entree, forcemeat, meatball

QUENTIN DURWARD *author* walter scott

patron louis xi

uncle le balafre

QUERBRACHO breakax(e), pithecolobium, sloanea, tree

QUERCITRON blackjack, dyestuff, oak, quercus, sheoak, yellow

QUERCUS See OAK.

QUERENT complainant, complaining, inquirer, plaintiff

QUERIMAN mugil, mullet

QUERKEN choke, stifle

QUERL coil, twirl, twist

QUERN grinder, kern, metate, mill(stone)

QUERULOUS carping, complaining, cranky, cross, fastidious, faultfinding, fractious, fretful, grouchy, grumbly, huffy, irritable, peevish, pettish, petulant, plaintive, snappish, tetch,

touchy, wailing, waspish, whining, whiny

QUERY ask, catechize, challenge, doubt, examine, impugn, inquire, interrogate, pump, QUESTION, quiz, speer

QUEST adventure, ask, bay, demand, desire, emprise, enterprise, examine, expedition, exploit, goal, hunt, inquire, journey, probe, problem, pursue, pursuit, search, seek(ing), solicitation, test, urging, venture

QUESTION accuse, argue, ask, backspier, buzz, catechize, cause, challenge, charge, contention, converse, crux, debate, demand, dilemma, discuss(ion), dispute, doubt, dread, dubiety, enigma, examine, grill, impeach, impugn, inquire, inquiry, interpellate, interrogate, interview, investigation, issue, legislation, moot point, nut, objection, pose(r), problem, proposition, pump, puzzle, quaere, query, quiz, riddle, scout, scruple, shrive, speech, speer, stickler, stumper, talk, targe, test, topic, try, waver

absurd car(ri)witchet

difficult poser, stumper

mark butterfly, eroteme, quaere, query, violet-tip

of rules point of order

rhetorical eperotesis, erotesis

unresolved crux

QUESTIONABLE ambiguous, controversial, corrupt, debatable, deceptive, disputable, disreputable, doubtful, dubious, equivocal, fishy, improbable, incredible, moot, obscure, open, suspect, suspicious, unbelievable, uncertain, undecided, vague

QUESTIONNAIRE canvass, feeler, form, inquiry, inventory, poll

QUETCH move, shake, speak, stir, twitch, wince

QUETHE bequeath, call, clamor, cry, say, tell, testament, will

QUETZAL bird, quezal, trogon

worshipper aztec, mayan

QUETZALCOATL gucumatz, kulkulcan

QUEUE braid, breadline, coil, crocodile, cue, file, group, line(up), pigtail, plait, rank, row, stem, tail (piece)

QUIBBLE altercate, ambage, ambiguity, argue, bicker, boggle, brabble, caption, carp, cavil, chicane, cog, dodge, equivocate, equivocation, evade, evasion, fence, haffle, hedge, jesuitism, lie, palter, paralogize, parry, prevaricate, pun, pussyfoot, quiddity, quillet, quip, quirk, quodilibet, scold, shift, shuffle, shy, sidestep, sophism, sophisticate, subtilize, tergiversate

QUICA opossum, sarigue

QUICK abrupt, accelerated, active, acute, adroit, agile, alert, alive, animate(d), apace, apt, birdlike, brisk, burn(ing), busy, celeritous, center, clever, deft, ephemeral, expeditious, expert, express, fast, fiery, fleet, flit, fly, gay, hasty, headlong, heart, immediate, impatient, impetuous, impulsive, instant, intelligent, intense, keen, kindle, light, lish, live(ly), living, moving, nimble, passionate, pronto, rapid, ready, rushing, sharp, shifting, smart, snappy, speedy, sprightly, spry, sudden, swift, swipper, tall, tosto, vigorous, vital, vivid, volant, yare, yarry, yeder, yielding

bread biscuit, cornbread, muffin, pone, scone

comb. tachy

-in-the-hand impatiens, jewelweed

-selling leeftail

-tempered doncy, donsy, excitable, hotheaded, inflammable, irascible

to the acutely, deeply, veraciously

-witted acute, alert, all there, apt, bright, brilliant, clever, funny, humorous, intelligent, keen(-minded), knowing, nimble, ready, sharp, witty

QUICKBEAM rowan-tree

QUICKEN accelerate, activate, actuate, advance, animate, arouse, bestir, energize, enliven, excite, expedite, facilitate, feed, ferment, fire, flash, foment, further, galvanize, goad, hasten, hurry, induce, inspire, inspirit, kindle, light, motivate, pique, precipitate, provoke, refresh, resuscitate, revive, rouse, sharpen, speed, spur, stimulate, stir, vitalize, vivify, whet

QUICKHATCH glutton, wolverine

QUICKLIME calcium-oxide, rusma

QUICKLY anon, apace, belive, briefly, cito, deftly, directly, fast, forthwith, hastily, immediately, instanter, instantly, licketysplit, lively, presto, promptly, pronto, rapidly, rath, soon, speedily, vite

QUICKNESS acidity, activity, acumen, alacrity, alertness, animation, celerity, dexterity, dispatch, expedition, haste, life, liveliness, perspicacity, progress, promptitude, promptness, pungency, rapidity, sagacity, sharpness, skill, speed, swiftness, velocity, vigor, wit
symbol greased lightning

QUICKSAND ambush, bog, booby trap, danger, flow, marsh, pitfall, snare, syrt (is), toils, trap, treachery

QUICKSET hawthorn, hedge, thicket

QUICKSILVER active, elusive, heautarit, mercurial, mercury, oremix, tierras
planet mercury

QUID barter, bite, chaw, chew, cud, essence, exchange, fid, guinea, pound, return, something, sovereign, wad
pro quo equivalent, interchange, tit-for-tat

QUIDDANY codiniac, jelly, syrup

QUIDDITY cavil, distinction, essence, nature, peculiarity, quibble, subtlety, trifle, whatness

QUIDDLE bit, dawdle, quiver, shiver, trifle

QUIDNUNC busybody, frump, gossip, politician, snoop, tattler

QUIESCENT abeyant, arrested, asleep, calm, dormant, immobile, inactive, inert, latent, motionless, passive, placid, potential

QUIET serene, silent, sleeping, static, still, supine

QUIET 3 coy, mum, pet, tut 4 calm, cool, cosh, ease, hush, lown, lull, meek, mild, mute, psst, rapt, rest, rock, slow, tame, weme 5 accoy, allay, canny, daunt, dry up, fixed, happy, mousy, order, peace, privy, resty, shush, slack, sober, still 6 docile, gentle, hushed, merely, modest, pacify, placid, remote, repose, secret, sedate, serene, settle, shut up, silent, simple, smooth, soothe, stable, stilly, subdue 7 compose, halcyon, leisure, orderly, passive, private, relieve, repress, restful, retired, settled, silence 8 calmness, composed, decorous, inaction, inactive, inertion, isolated, peaceful, secluded, security, serenity, stagnant 9 alleviate, balbatish, composure, contented, noiseless, peaceable, placidity, quiescent, repressed, soundless, stillness, unruffled 10 balabatish, motionless, unmolested 11 clandestine, tranquility, tranquilize, undisturbed
down hush, settle

QUIETENER sedative

QUIETISM molinism, mysticism, passiveness, passivity, resignation

QUIETLY on the qt

QUIETUDE See QUIET.

QUIETUS acquittal, acquittance, death, defeat, discharge, end, mittimus, mort, obit, release, repose, rest, settlement

QUIFF forelock, girl, puff, whiff

QUILEUTE *indian* chimakua, hoh

QUILKIN frog, toad

QUILL barb(icel)(ule), barrel, bobbin, bristle, calamus, cannon, cilium, cop,

feather, feeler, fescue, filament(ule), fold, fuse, needle, pen, pierce, pinion, pipe, plait, plume, porcupine, remex, remiges, shaft, sleeve, spina, spindle, spine, spur, toothpick, trundle, tube, vibrissa
-driver clerk, writer
-pig porcupine

QUILLAI, QUILLAJA soapbark

QUILLBACK buffalofish, carpoides, carpsucker, catostomida, sailfish, skimback

QUILLWORT fernwort, isoetes, joe-pye-weed

QUILT beat, bedcover, bedspread, blanket, caddow, chalon, comfort(er), counterpane, cover(let), duvet, eider(down), flog, gulp, mattress, pallet, patchwork, poultice, pourpoint, seam, sew, stitch, swallow, thrash, throw, welt, whip
down duvet, eider(down), puff
material batts

QUIMBOISEUR fetish, magician, voodoo, wizard

QUINACRINE atabrine

QUINCE angers, b(h)el, bitterbark, coyne, cydonia, japonica, squinch
jelly codiniac, quiddany
seed cydonium

QUINCEWORT squinancy

QUININE bitters, febrifuge, kina, loja, loxa, quina, tonic
bush bear-brush, garrya
comb. chin(o)
plant jojoba
source cinchona-bark
substitute bebeerine, javanine, pereirine, quina
tree bitterbark, hop-tree, horseradish tree

QUINK brant, goose

QUINOA cereal, petty-rice, pigweed

QUINONE embelin

QUINSY angina, cynanche, squinancy, strangullion, tonsilitis
remedy black currant, squinancy

QUINTA countyseat, estate, garden, house

QUINTAIN objective, target

QUINTESSENCE acme, apex, attar, best, clyssus, core, cream, distillation, elixir, essence, ether, extract, gist, heart, osmazome, pith, quiddity, substance

QUINTET cinquain, pentad

QUINTILIAN *teacher* after

QUINTUPLE five(fold), pentamerous, quinary, quintet

QUINTUS *brother* lucius, martius, mutius
father titus andronicus

QUIP bon mot, caprice, comeback, conceit, crack, crank, epigram, equivocation, facetiae, gag, gibe, gimcrack, humor, jape, jest, jeu-d'esprit, jib, joke, mot, oddity, persiflage, plaisanterie, pleasantry, pun, quibble, quirk, repartee, retort, ripost(e), sally, saying, scoff, spoof, taunt, turn, vagary, whimsey, wisecrack, witticism

QUIRA caoba, hormigo, macawood, redwood, roble, vencola

QUIRE book, choir, fold, inquire, pamphlet, paper, quere, sextern
20 ream

QUIRK angle, bead, caprice, channel, clock, conceit, crotchet, curl(icue), curve, deviation, distortion, eccentricity, epigram, equivocation, evasion, fillet, fit, flourish, foible, gibe, groove, jerk, knack, mannerism, mot, paroxysm, peculiarity, ply, quibble, quip, shift, singularity, subterfuge, taunt, trait, trick, turn, twist, warp

QUIRL bend, coil, curl, scraper, twist

QUIRT block(up), romal, strike, whip

QUISBY bankrupt, broke, down and out, idler, queer

QUISLE betray

QUISLING collaborator, rat, traitor

QUIT abandon, abdicate, abscond, absolved, abstain, acquit, ankle, avoid, behave, belay, bereft, bolt, bow out, cease, clear(out), comport, conduct, coot, deliver, demean, demit, depart, deport, desert, desist, destitute, die, discharge, discontinue, disuse, drop out, escape, evacuate, exit,

flee, fold, forgo, forsake, free, give up, leave, liberate, release, relieve(d), relinquish, remove, renounce, repay, resign, retire, retreat, rid, run, scram, settle, shirk, stop, surrender, vacate, whit(e), withdraw, yield

QUITCLAIM acquit, discharge, release, relinquish (ment)

QUITE actually, altogether, braw, but, clever, completely, enough, entirely, exactly, fair, greatly, perfectly, positively, pretty, rather, really, substantial, totally, truly, very, wholly
so also, exactly, precisely, very true
some many, numerous

QUITS cleared, equal, even, recompense, released, retaliation
call it abandon, end, give up

QUITTANCE acquitance, atonement, compensation, departure, discharge, give up, recompense, release, repay(ment), reprisal, requite, return, revenge, settlement

QUITTER coward, defeatist, dropout, matter, piker, pus, quiver, seal, shirker, slag, suppurate, turnback, twitter, welsher, yielder

QUIVER active, array, arrows, beat, bever, bicker, case, cocker, didder, dindle, dirl, dither, flichter, flicker, flitter, flutter, frisson, group, hoster, lively, nidga, nimble, palpitate, pulsate, pulse, quag, quail, quake, quaver, quod, shake, sheath, shimmy, shiver, shudder, teeter, thirl, thrill, throb, tirl, totter, tremble, tremor, tressilate, trill, twiddle, twitter, vibrate, wobble
-leaf aspen
tree aloe, kokerboom

QUIXOTE See DON QUIXOTE.
of the north charles xii

QUIXOTIC abstract, chimerical, eccentric, fanciful, fantastic, idealistic, imaginary, impracticable, impractical, mad, queer, rash, roman-

tic, sentimental, unpractical, utopian, visionary

QUIZ ask, bandalore, banter, busybody, butt, chaff, coach, enigma, exam(ination), examine, guy, hiss, hoax, inquire, jest, joke, jolly, josh, kid, mock, peer, poser, prank, probe, puzzle, query, question(ing), quip, rag, rally, rib, ridicule, speer, taunt, test, whiz

QUIZZICAL amusing, bantering, curious, eccentric, erratic, funny, incredulous, odd, quaint, queer, skeptical, teasing, unbelieving

QUOD See JAIL.

QUODLIBET debate, fantasia, medley, question, quibble, subtlety

QUOIN angle, base, coin, corner, keystone, lozenge, voussoir, wedge

QUOIT(S) cromlech, disc (us), disk, hobber, jukskei, liner, penny-stone, ring, throw
mark mot, tee
pin bob
shot leaner, ringer
target hob, peg, pin

QUONDAM erst, former(ly), old, once, onetime, past, sometime

QUORUM assembly, body, council, group, house, majority, minyan

QUOTA allowance, contingent, divide, dividend, part, percentage, portion, proportion, quotient, ratio, share

QUOTATION attribution, authority, bid, chria, cital, citation, epigraph, excerpt, extract, memo(randum), motto, note, passage, price, reference, selection, snippet
mark guillemet

QUOTE adduce, allege, cite, copy, examine, excerpt, extract, mention, name, note, observe, paraphrase, parrot, recite, repeat, report

QUOTH quad, quod, said, spoke, uttered

QUOTHA forsooth, indeed

QUOTIDIAN commonplace, daily, diurnal, everyday, ordinary, periodic(al), recurring, routine, trivial

QUOTIENT fraction

QUOTITY collection, group

QUTAR *capital* doha

R

R rho
RA aten, atmu, atum, bacis, chepera, harakhte, harmachis, horus, iokaris, khepera, mentu, mnevis, phra, shu, sokaris, sun, tem, tum
chronicle litanies of the sun
consort eusos, iusaas, m(o)ut, nebhet-hotep, rat, reddedet, uerthekeu
embodiment bennu, bird, bull, hawk, merwer, mnevis, phoenix
enemy apepi, great serpent
home heliopolis, prince's palace
obelisk benben
offspring athor, geb, isis, ma(a)t, nephthys, nut, osiris, pharaohs, selket, selquet, set, shu, tefnut, thoth
parent geb, keb, neith, nut, seb
scribe weneg
serpent apepi
symbol benben, cat, falcon, lion, sacred asp, uraeus
weapon divine eye, hathor
RAAD assembly, catfish, council, raash
RAAMAH *son* dedan, sheba
RABAT victoria
RABATO, REBATO collar, piccidill, ruff
RABBET backjoint, channel, check, filleter, fillister, groove, joint, plough, plow, rabat, rebate, recess
RABBI amora, cacam, clergyman, ecclesiastic, gamaliel, gaon, hakam, khakham, lord, master, sabora(im), scholar, tana, tanna(im), teacher
assistant cantor
1st salaried duran
group amoraim, tannaim
robe ephod
rod yad
school yeshibah, yeshiva(h), yeshivoth
wife rebbetsan, rebbetzin
RABBIT adapis, astrex, beljeek, beveren, bunny, capon, coneen, con(e)y, cottontail, coward, cunny, hare, jack, lagomorph, lapin, leporid, lepus, leveret, novice, pole, rex, rodent, snowshoe, tapeti, tyro, warrener, wat(t), wooler
berry beef-suet tree, buffalobush, shepherdia
breed angora, belgian, dutch, flemish, havana, lagotis, oarlop, tan
brush broom-sage
burrow clapper
disease snuffles
ear aerial, antenna, cactus, toadflax
famous brer, cottontail, flopsy, mopsy, peter
female doe
fever tularemia
fish chimaera, globefish, puffer, siganid, spiny
flower foxglove, toadflax
foot charm, clover, fetish, talisman
footprint prick
fur arctic seal, beaverette, con(e)y, flick, flitch, french seal, hatter, lapin, rack, scut, sealine
group flick, nest, warren
home burrow, cage, clapper, hutch, warren
-like animal agouti, marmot, perameles, pika
male buck
meat archangel, lapan
mouth cutlips, harelip, snapdragon, sucker
net flan, hay
pea catgut, goat's-rue
pert. leporine
peter, creator beatrix potter
peter, kin cottontail, flopsy, mopsy
peter, source hilltop farm, sawrsy, windermere
root sarsaparilla
silky-haired angora
skin rack
stew hasenpfeffer
swamp tapeti
symbol of fecundity
tail fud, scut
tobacco balsamweed
trap tipe
vine groundnut
warren conyger, tenement
wood buffalo nut, elk nut, pyrularia, tree
young bunny, gazabo, gazebo, kitten, leveret, starter
RABBLE bobtail, braggery, canaglia, canaille, cattle, clamjamfry, coarse, commonalty, confusion, crowd, disorderly, doggery, dregs, frape, gabble, gang, ging, herd, hoi-polloi, horde, hubbleshow, masses, meinie, meiny, mob, mouth, multitude, people, populace, proletariat, raddle, raff, ragab(r)ash, ragtag, rangale, rascal, refuse, riffraff, rigmarole, roughscuff, rout, ruck, scaffraff, scum, shovel, skim, sordes, stir, swarm, tag, trash, tummult, unwashed, varletry, vulgar
-rouse agitate, stir
-rouser agitator, demagog(ue), instigator, ragtag
RABELAIS *character* bacbuc, badebec, bridlegoose, bridone, pantagruel, panurge, picrochole, triboulet, trippa
birthplace chinon
giant chalbroth, gargantua, widenostrils
pseudonym alcofribas
work gargantua, pantagruel
RABELAISIAN bawdy, coarse, dirty, profane, sarcastic, satirical
RABI crop, harvest
RABID babbling, desperate, distracted, distraught, eager, extreme, fanatic(al), fiery, frantic, frenetic(al), frenzied, furious, incoherent, insane, intolerant, mad, madding, maniac(al), phrenetic(al), radical, raging, rampant, ranting, raving, ultraistic, violent, virulent, wild, zealous
RABIES hydrophobia, lyssa, madness, piblokto, rage
pert. lyssic
RABINOWITZ, S. *pseudonym* shalom aleichem
RABSHAKEH *commander* sennacherib
RACCOON ag(o)uara, alaska sable, arctoid, crabeater, guara, mapach(e), procyon, rattoon, tejon, treebear, washer
berry may-apple
crab-eating agouara
fox cacomistle

-like animal coati, panda
RACE (See also *kind*, below.) accelerate, ancestry, birth, bloodstrain, breed, brood, career, carry silk, caste, channel, chase, chiv(v)y, clan, class, compete, competition, conduit, contest, course, current, dash, drag, family, flow, flume, free-for-all, gallop, geste, groove, group, haste, heat, hie, holethnos, house, hurry, lane, line(age), mankind, nation, pace, path, pedigree, people, pluck, progeny, progress, regatta, relay, rod, root, run, rush, scamper, scratch, slash, slit, sluice, snatch, sort, span, speed, sprint, stirp(s), stock, strain, stream, stud, team, tear, track, tribe, trot, turf, waterway
-about roadster, sloop
apex period hemera
auto five hundred, grand prix, indy, lemans, mille miglie, rally(e)
board gangplank
boat gig, regatta, shell
classification adriatic, alpine, black, brown, caucasian, caucasoid, malayan, mediterranean, mongolian, negroid, nordic, prehistoric, teutonic, vistulian, white, xanthochroid, yellow
colors silks
comb. ethn(o), gen(o)
consciousness ethnicity
course career, circus, corso, dragstrip, dromos, furlong, gymkhana, oval, ring, speedway, stadium, stretch, track, turf
course, comb. drome
course, famous aqueduct, ascot, bowie, craven, doncaster, epsom downs, gold meadows, goodwood, hardwicke, hialeah, hollywood park, houghton, indianapolis, jamaica, laurel, newmarket, nurburgring, oaks, pimlico, santa anita, saratoga, st leger, tropic
course hustler tout
cross-country point-to-point
evolution of phylogeny
exhausting grueller
expert dopester, tipster, tout
extermination genocide
finale home-stretch

gait gallop, pace, run, trot
genesis of ethogeny
gods aesir, olympians, vanir
gondola regatta
group clan, family, tribe
hairy aino, ainu
harness trot
horse bangtail, maiden, mantis, mudder, pacer, plater, sleeper, trotter
horse, inferior hayburner, plater, ruck
horse ridge riva
human breed, ilk, man (kind), species, stirps
human, study of anthropogenesis, anthropology
jumping scurry
kind broose, brouse, brouze, claiming, cross-country, derby, futurity, handicap, harness, hundred yard, hurdle, marathon, mile, obstacle, plate, potato, purse, relay, sack, slalom, sprint, steeplechase, sweepstake, three-legged, torch, torpids, walkover
long marathon
marker meta, pylon, tape
mill channel, flume, lade
mythical centaur(s)
obstacle steeplechase
official starter, timer
paleolithic cro-magnon
part heat, lap, length
pert. ethnic
prehistoric furfooz
preliminary heat
relay medley
rowing henley, poughkeepsie, regatta, sculls, torpids
rule ethnocracy
runner lizard
science ethnogeny, ethnology
series regatta
short bicker, dash, scurry, sprint
smooth-haired leiotrichi
starting line scratch
tipster tout
torch lampededromy, lampedephoria
track See RACE *course*.
undivided holethnos
wedding broose, brouze
yellow-skinned xanthoderm
RACEME bunch, cluster, spike, strig
RACER blacksnake, cinderman, coluber, courser, crab, fish, jehu, miler, runner, serpent, snake, speeder, sprinter, turntable

RACEWAY arroyo, canal, channel, fishway, flume, groove, millrace
RACHEL *father* laban
husband jacob
sister leah
son benjamin, joseph
RACHIS backbone, chine, spindle, spine, strig
RACIAL clannish, ethnic, gentile, lineal, phyletic, phylogenetic, tribal
RACINE *work* andromaque, athalie, berenice, britannicus, esther, phedre
RACIST bigot, sectarian
RACK afflict, agony, amble, anguish, annoy, bar, bink, bottleholder, brake, buc(c)an, buck, canter, cloud, comb, course, crash, cratch, creel, crib, destruction, drier, drive, excruciate, flake, fly, foresaddle, frame (work), gait, gallop, gantry, gin, grating, grill, hack, harass, harry, heck, jib, lope, oppress, pace, pain, path, persecute, pervert, pottaro, route, run, rush, scud, shock, singlefoot, skin, spreader, strain, stretch(er), suffering, tear, torment, torture, trace, track, treble, trot, try, vestige, walk, worry, wrench, wring, wrong
and ruin decay, decline, destruction
dish bink, creel
display easel
wooden buc(c)an
RACKET agitation, babel, bandy, bat, black market, blow, bootlegging, bustle, clamor, clangor, clatter, crosse, din, discord, disturbance, dodge, excitement, extortion, fraud, fuss, gamble, game, hubbub, hullabaloo, hurly-burly, hustle, imposture, knock, moonshining, noise, outcry, paddle, patten, pelota, raquet, rattle, razoo, revel(ing), rumpus, scheme, shakedown, smuggling, snowshoe, spat, stramash, trick, tumult, uproar
light battledore
pouched crosse
tennis scufe
RACKETEER bagman, bandit, criminal, extortionist,

gangster, hood(lum), mafioso

RACKETY boisterous, dissipated, exciting, gay, noisy, turbulent

RACKING agonizing, chastening, cruel, excruciating, fierce, grueling, inhuman, intense, pacing, punishing, savage, vehement

RACKLE clank, clatter, headstrong, noise, rash, rattle, reckless

RACY brazen, breezy, brisk, colorful, exciting, fiery, fresh, gamy, gingery, interesting, lively, lurid, naive, natural, peppy, piquant, pungent, purple, rich, risque, salty, sexy, smart, snappy, spicy, spirited, stimulating, stirring, strong, suggestive, unspoiled, vigorous, zestful, zesty

RAD afraid, eager, elated, exhilerated, quick, ready

RADAMES *beloved* aida

RADAR locator, loran, microwave, shoran, teleran

beacon racon, ramark, transponder

countermeasure chaff, dueppel, jamming, spoofing, tinfoil

defection clutter, refraction

direction finder compass, goniometer huffduff, sniffer, superduper

image blip

kind agca, asv, cca, dewline, dme, dvop, gca, gci, ground, iff, law, mad, mew, mti, navaglobe, oboe, par, rawin, sarah, scr, search, surface, surveillance, taxi, trw, volscan

navigation system lanac

part altimeter, amplifier, analyzer, detector, magnetron, mixer, modulator, oscillator, pulser, receiver, screen, tracker, tr-box, trigatron, tr-switch

pulse echo, high-frequency, trigger

receive home on, identify, lock on, map, paint, pick up, pinpoint, scan, spot, sweep, trigger, tune in

screen scope

sound blip

RADDAI *parent* jesse

RADDLE beat, branch,

cheat, fence, hedge, hurdle, interweave, ravel, red ochre, reed, rod, rouge, ruddle, scar, separator, stick, thrash, twig, twist, wattle, weave, wheedle

RADIAL actiniform, actinoid, artery, bar, quadrant, ray(ed), round, spreading

RADIANCE aureola, beauty, brightness, brilliance, effulgence, glare, gleam, glint, glitter, glory, lambency, light, luminosity, luster, refulgence, sheen, splendor, vividness

RADIANT agleam, aglow, auroral, axis, beamful, beaming, beamy, bright, brilliant, cheerful, ecstatic, effulgent, flashing, gleaming, glittering, glorious, glowing, gorgeous, happy, illustrious, lambent, line, livid, lucent, lucid, luminous, lustrous, pleased, refulgent, reluctant, resplendent, scintillating, sheen, shining, sparkling, splendid, vivid

RADIATE actinoid, beam, bush, diffuse, disperse, disseminate, effulge, effuse, emanate, emit, gleam, glitter, glow, illuminate, irradiate, project, proliferate, ramble, ramify, ray, scatter, shed, shine, spread, yield

comb. actino

RADIATING casting, centrifugal, emanant, stellate

RADIATION actinism, aura, beam, diffusion, dispersion, emanation, light, ray

comb. actino

detector geiger

measure millirem

ratio absorptance

science actinism, actinology

source cesium, plutonium, strontium

unit langley, megarad, rad, rem, rep, roentgen

RADIATOR calefactor, emanater, furnace, heater, register, transmitter

RADICAL advanced, atom, auxotox, basal, base, basic, capital, cardinal, complete, drastic, essential, excessive, extreme, extremist, fanatical, foundation, full, fundamental, heretic, heroic, inherent, innate, intrinsic,

left(ist), leftwing, liberal, original, progressive, rabid, rebel, red, revolutionary, revolutionist, root, rouge, sign, substratal, support, surd, thorough, ultra(istic), underlying, violent, vital, whole

aliphatic alkylene, alkylidene

bivalent amylidene, benzal

chemical acetyl, adenyl, adipyl, aluminyl, amyl, aryl, capr(o)yl, carbamyl, caryl, cetyl, halogen, ion, linalyl, phenyl, phytyl, tartryl

political anarchist, bolshevik, bolshie, commie, communist, extremist, fellow-traveler, jacobin, left(wing), locofoco, marxist, menshevik, nihilist, pink(ie)(o), red, revolutionary, revolutionist, sympathizer, ultraist

toxic auxotox

univalent benzoxyl, benzyl, indyl

RADICATE establish, fix, plant, root

RADICLE come, etymon, fiber, hypocotyl, radix, root(let), stemlet

RADIO blooper, broadcast, receiver, set, transmit(ter), wireless

advertisement commercial, plug, spot

aerial antenna, mast, rabbit-ears, tower, yagi

cabinet console

compliance wilco

detector radar

energy source quasar, quasi-stellar object

frequency audio, band, channel, kilocycle, kilohertz, megacycle, short-wave

-guided bomb azon

hams cbs

interference atmospherics, beep, crosstalk, drift, fading, hashing, hum, squeal, static

inventor de forest, marconi

kind am-fm, heterodyne, hi-fi, high-fi, intercom, neutrodyne, portable, short-wave, superheterodyne, transceiver, transistor, two-way, walkie-talkie

man announcer, broadcaster, commentator, disk-jockey, ham, mixer, monitor, sparks

part amplifier, antenna,

baffle, chasis, condenser, crystal, detector, dial, diode, filter, knob, rheostat, selector, speaker, transformer, tube
portable walkie-talkie
program broadcast, newscast, rerun, serial, soaper, soap-opera
rating hooper, nielsen
receiver neutrodyne
signal check monitor
signal device beeper
speaker amplifier, bullhorn, cone, diaphragm, horn, tweeter, woofer
station group network
tube grid
tubeless crystal set, transistor
wave measurer ondometer
wave source pulsar
wire litz

RADIOACTIVE hot
element actinium, americium, astatine, berkelium, californium, curium, einsteinium, fermium, francium, mendelevium, neptunium, nobelium, plutonium, polonium, promethium, radium, radon, thorium, uranium

RADIOACTIVITY contamination, fallout
comb. actino
unit curie

RADIOGRAPH exograph, skiagram, x-ray

RADISH cadlock, charlock, cradlock, crossweed, crucifer, daekon, daikon, raphanistrum, raphanus, rifart, runch

RADIUM *discoverer* curie
emanation niton, radon
source carnotite, pitchblende, uranite, uranium
unit curie

RADIUS circle, compass, diameter, extent, field, ken, length, limit, orbit, purview, radix, range, reach, scope, spoke, sweep, throw, width

RADIX base, cause, etymon, radical, root, source, support

RADON actinon, niton, thoron
source radium

RAFF common, dregs, heap, huddle, idle, jumble, leavings, litter, low, lumber, plenty, rabble, refuse, riffraff, rubbish, scum,

store, supply, sweep, timber, trash

RAFFIA fiber, hood, palm
fabric rabanna

RAFFISH bad, boorish, cheap, common, disgraceful, disreputable, flashy, frowsy, infamous, low, offbeat, rakish, tawdry, unkempt, vulgar(ian), worthless

RAFFLE chance, confuse, crumple, drawing, entangle, gamble, game, jumble, lottery, net, perplex, rabble, refuse, rifle, rubbish, serrate, tangle

RAFT balsa, barge, carrier, catamaran, collection, cow, crib, dingey, dinghy, float, flow, gharnao, heap(s), jangada, jangar, kelek, lot(s), mass, moguey, moki(hi), numbers, pipery, plenty, quantity, radeau, rakit, spar, transport(ation), viga, zattare
bamboo rakit
dog raker
duck bird, bluebill, redhead, scaup
log boom, brail, crib, pipery
rider huck finn, jim
rubber lilo
wood balsa

RAFTER blade, bougar, caber, carline, flock, number, plow, timber, viga
angle heel
bird flycatcher
curved compass
notch mortige

RAG annoy, banter, berate, billet, bit, catkin, chaff, cloth, dance, dress, farthing, fog, fragment, garment, guy, harass, hoarfrost, jolly, josh, kid, lichen, limestone, mist, mock, quiz, rally, remnant, rib, rumpus, scold, scrap, shale, shamtte, shmotte, shred, slate, straggle, syncopate, tatter, taunt, tear, tease, torment, tune, wiper, wrangle
beer-soaked dyile
fish icosteid
gourd lufa
picker See RAGMAN.
-shag masquerader
-tag (and bobtail) mob, rabble, raff, riffraff
wool mungo, shoddy

RAGAMUFFIN clown,

scarecrow, shabroon, tatterdemalion, titmouse, vagabond

RAGE acrimony, amentia, anger, asperity, beef, birse, blow, bluster, boil, breth, caprice, chafe, craze, cry, desire, eagerness, enthusiasm, excite(ment), explode, fad, fashion, fervor, flare, folly, frenzy, fret, fume, furor(e), fury, haste, heat, huff, hysteria, indignation, insanity, ire, madness, mania, mode, outburst, passion, raillery, ramp(age), rant, rashness, rave, rese, reverie, spleen, sport, spread, storm, style, tantrum, tave, tear, teave, tevel, turbulence, tyauve, vehemence, violence, vogue, wanton, wax, whim, wrath
all the craze, cri, dernier, fad, modish, popular, stylish, trendy

RAGGED bare, broken, deepworn, defective, dilapidated, discordant, duddie, duddy, erose, exhausted, frayed, harsh, irregular, jagged, mean, poor, raguly, rent, rough, ruffled, rugged, scoury, scraggly, seedy, shabby, shaggy, shopworn, shreddy, straggling, strident, tattered, threadbare, timeworn, uneven, unfinished, unkempt, wellworn, worn (to shreds)
edge border, brink, verge
jacket harp-seal
lady guara, love-in-a-mist
robin cuckoo
sailor bluebottle, cornflower, prince's-feather

RAGGEE, RAGGY cereal, eleusine, grass, korakan, mand(ua), marua, millet

RAGGING bantering, rebuke, reproof, scolding

RAGING ferocious, fervent, fierce, flagrant, frantic, furibund, furious, grim, incensed, infuriated, insane, livid, mad, rabid, rampant, turbulent, violent, wild, wrathful, yond

RAGLAN overcoat, sleeve

RAGMAN bunter, catalogue, clothier, devil, haberdasher, hobo, junkman, list, oldclothesman, tatter, tramp, vagabond, vagrant

RAGOUT blanquette, borscht, borst, bortsch, capilotade, chipolata, civet, fricasse, gallimaufry, goulash, haricot, hash, mince, patoun, pulpatone, salmi(s), salpicon, stew, terrine, tucket
RAGTIME jazz, jive, music, rhythm, syncopation
RAGUEL *offspring* raphael, sarah
wife edna
RAGUSA dubrovnik
RAGWEED ambrosia, bitterweed, franseria, hayweed, helenium, hogweed, horseweed, ironweed, iva, kinghead, kingweed, plant, richweed, sneezeweed
RAGWORT benweed, bundweed, butterweed, cammock, cankerweed, coughweed, cow parsnip, cushag, groundsel, jacoby, knapweed, liferoot, scabious, seggrom, senecio
RAH bravo, cheer, hurrah, huzza, ole
RAHAB dragon, harlot, monster
home jericho
husband salmon
son boaz, booz
RAHAM *son* jorkoam
RAHU *tail* ketu
RAID assault, attack, blitz, board, bodrage, bordrag, breach, chappow, chevachie, commando, creach, creagh, despoil, escalade, forage, foray, harass, hership, incursion, inroad, invade, invasion, irruption, manipulate, maraud, onset, onslaught, panyar, pillage, piracy, razzia, reise, reive, roadstead, sally, scale, siege, sortie, spreagh, spreath, steal, storm, tala
narcotics bust
RAIDER bushwhack(er), commando, green beret
RAIL abuse, array, arunt, banter, bar, berate, betongue, bird, blast, bull, callet, censure, cloak, complain, coot, courlan, crake, decorate, denounce, dress, enclose, fence, fender, flout, flow, garment, guard, gush, jaw, jest, limit, moho, neckerchief, objurgate, ortolan, picket, plank, post, rant, rate, rebuke, reproach, re-

vile, scoff, scold, sedge, septum, skitty, sora, swear, taunt, thripple, timber, tonguelash, track, tringle, upbraid, weka
altar septum
arched hoopstick
at curse, rattle, revile, scoff
bird or coot bilcock, clocker, coot, cornbird, courlan, crake, koko, marshhen, moho, oarcock, ortolan, sedge, sora, spectator, weka
chair ledge
fence rider
genus creciscus, porzana, rallus, sora
layer gandydancer
pert. ralline
power-supplying conductor, third
safety easer
splitter lincoln, mauler
support crosstie
RAILHEAD depot, vanguard
RAILING balconet(e), balustrade, banister, bar, barrier, fence, fender, gallery, gitter, grate, parapet, parclose, rabulous, traverse, vedika
RAILLERY asteism, banter, chaff, fun, irony, jest, persiflage, play, pleasantry, rally, ridicule, sarcasm, satire, sport
RAILROAD accelerate, arterial, branch, carrier, ceinture, coaler, elevated, expedite, force, hasten, herd, hurry, interurban, jam through, legislate, line, monorail, push, ramrod, runway, rush, send, sidetrack, siding, speed, subway, track, tram(way), transport, trunkline, tube, underground, way
bedroom berth, couchette, drawing-room, lower, pullman, roomette, upper
branch feeder, spur, stub
bridge tressel, trestle
bumper buffer
car boxcar, brake van, buggy, caboose, chaircar, clubcar, coach, coalcar, day coach, diner, dinghy, dolly, flatcar, giraffe, gondola, hog, hopper, mail, parlor, piggyback, pullman, rattler, reefer, refrigerator, sleeper, smoker, tank, tender, truck, waggon, wagon-lit

center depot, gare, roundhouse, station, stazione, terminal, terminus
chair ledge, saddle
crossrail frog
engine diesel, dolly, dummy, hog, locomotive, mogul
engineer, famous casey jones
financiers tin plate millionaires
intersection crosspoint
light flare, fusee, signal
man brakeman, brakie, conductor, dispatcher, engineer, fireman, guard, lineman, motorman, porter, redcap, stoker, switchman, trainman, yardman, yardmaster
mountain funicular
passenger line amtrak, railpax
safety device banjo-signal
signal flare, fusee, fuzee, semaphore, trimmer
switch frog, shunt
term crosstie, crow, gauge, pedestal, semaphore, sleeper, tie, timber
ticket eurail pass
tie sleeper
timetable bradshaw
track right of way
track worker gandydancer
underground bart, ind, irt, metro, mta, subway, tube
RAILWAY ascensor, cogroad, cogway, elevated, funicular, incline, jackstay, monorail, RAILROAD, subway, train, tranvia, tube
RAIMENT apparel, array, attire, cloth, clothes, clothing, costume, dress, garb, garment, habiliments, tog(s), vesture
RAIN abound, bestorm, bestow, chirrimirri, cloudburst, dag, deluge, downpour, drisk, drizzle, drop, fall, flood, flurry, furrow, give, hurl, jupiter-pluvius, misle, mist, mizzle, monsoon, perel, plash, pour, precipitation, ridge, rine, serein, shed, shower, spate, spit, sprinkle, storm, stream, teem, thundershower, torrent, weep, wet, yield
author somerset maugham
barrel cistern
bringer kachina
chart hyetograph
check postponement, stub

cloud nimbus
comb. hyeto, ombro
evening serein
fine drizzle, misle, mist, mizzle, serein
forest selva
fowl channelbill, cuckoo, woodpecker
gauge hytegraph, ombrometer, pluvioscope, udometer, udomograph
glass barometer
god agne, esus, frey, indra, ing, jupiter-pluvius, parjanya, thor, tlaloc, zeus
goddess tefnut
gutter eave(s), rone
heavy See RAINSTORM.
heroine sadie thompson
icy hail, sleet, snow
leader downspout
light dribble, drizzle, heatdrops
-loving ombrophilous
maker magician, seeder, sorcerer
measure inch
measure line isohyet
or shine certainly, earnestly, in any event, without fail
pert. hyetal, iridal, pluvial
serpent naga
setting pago pago, samoa
tree algar(r)oba, genisaro, guango, mesquite, monkeypod, saman, zaman(g), zamia
worm earthworm, nematode, nightcrawler
RAINBIRD cuckoo, koel, plover, stormbird, tomfool, woodpecker
RAINBOW arc(h), hummingbird, iris, omen, sunbow, trout, variegate
bridge bifrost
broken winddog, windgall
chaser doctrinaire, idealist, visionary
darter blue-johnny
description phantasmatography
fish guppy, maori, parrotfish, wrasse
goddess iris
-like iridal, iridescent, iridian, opalescent, prismatic
lunar moonbow
maker prism
measurer spectrometer
name meaning iris
pert. iridal
runner shoemaker, skipjack
trout steelhead

weed loosestrife
RAINCOAT aquascutum, burberry, bursati, mac(k), mac(k)intosh, mino, oilskin, pliofilm, poncho, slicker, tarpaulin, trenchcoat, ulster, waterproof
RAINFALL onding, plout, skiff, stemplow
RAINSPOUT cloudburst, rone
RAINSTORM brash, cloudburst, deluge, downpour, drencher, flood, gullywasher, monsoon, pelter, plash, scud, shower, soaker, spate, spout, teem, thundersquall, wet
RAINY cluttery, damp, drippy, drizzling, drizzly, flooded, misty, mizzly, moist, pluvial, pluvious, pouring, showery, slattery, streaming, weeping, wet
day hard times
day need nest egg, raincoat, resources
season monsoon, varsha
RAISE 3 hob, sow 4 boss, bump, buoy, grow, hect, hike, hove, jack, kite, levy, lift, rear, RISE, sing, soar, stir 5 arear, arise, bonus, boost, breed, build, cairn, crane, enrol, erect, exalt, hance, heave, hoist, mound, mount, plant, rouse, start, tower, train, utter 6 arouse, awaken, cantle, create, emboss, enroll, excite, gather, incite, leaven, loosen, muster, nantle, pull up, remove, reward, uplift 7 address, advance, amplify, animate, augment, bring up, collect, conjure, elevate, enhance, enlarge, forward, further, lighten, magnify, nurture, produce, promote, recruit, relieve 8 assemble, heighten, increase 9 conjure up, construct, cultivate, elevation, intensify, originate, promotion, sublevate, transcend 10 invigorate
by hand nob
cain complain, cry, rage, rampage, rave
hell anger, brawl, cry, play, protest
hopes cheer, encourage
nap brush, row, tease(l), teazle

objection boggle, cavil, nitpick
up arear, buoy, elate, elevate, exalt, extol
RAISED arrect, bold, bred, convex, cultivated, elevated, embossed, enleve, erect, exalted, grew, grown, hefted, high, hove, leavened, levered, lifted, mountant, pried, rampant, reared, stilted, sublimated, upcast, upflung, uplifted, upraught, upreared
in a barn boorish, hick
RAISIN grape, lexia, muscatel, pasa, plum, reyson, sultana, zibeb
cordial rosolio
fresh grape
quantity frail
seedless currant
tree cock's-claw, currantbush
RAISING erection, leaven(ing), rearing, yeast
device crane, derrick, elevator, gru, hoist, jack, pulley
RAJ reign, rule
RAJA(H) chief, gaekwar, guicowar, king, nizam, noble, personage, prince, ruler, silk
wife ranee, rani
RAJMAHAL *creeper* bowstring, chiti, je(e)tee, jiti, marsdania, vine
RAJPUT gahrwal, razbooch, samma, sumra
RAKAN arhat, lohan
RAKE bank, bevel, blood, bomb(ard), bury, card, casanova, claut, clear, collect, comb, cover, cultivate, debauchee, dissipate, don juan, draw, enfilade, finecomb, gather, groove, gulley, inclination, incline, lecher, libertine, load, lothario, path, pepper, pitch, profligate, raff, range, ransack, rasp, reach, roue, rove, rub, rubiator, ruck, run, rut, satyr, scour, scrape, scrapple, scratch, search, shell, slope, sweep, tool, track, trip
grain gavel
horsedrawn gleaner
-off commission, dividend, kickback, percentage, portion, profit, rebate, share, take
symbol of st barnabas

RAKEHELL dashing, debauched, debauchee, dissolute, immoral, jaunty, lewd, libertine, profligate, rascal, smart

RAKISH dashing, devilish, jaunty, rantepole, sporty, wanton

RALLY advance, arouse, assemble, assembly, attack, awaken, banter, bully, chaff, clambake, collect, concentrate, convene, convention, convocation, deride, drag, encourage, event, excite, fire, flout, gather(ing), gibe, harass, improve, jeer, joke, jolly, josh, kid, meet(ing), mobilize, mock, muster, noise, organize, provoke, quicken, race, rag, raillery, recover, recuperate, refresh, rejuvenate, resurrect, revive, rib, ridicule, rise, rouse, scoff, stimulate, stir, strengthen, summon, tantalize, taunt, tease, twit, unite, waken, worry

RAM, RAM'S aries, batter, beak, beetle, buck, bulldoze(r), butt, charge, choke, collide, cram, crash, crowd, fill, force, hit, ovine, pack, piston, plunger, poke, press, prow, push, rancid, rostrum, schooner, sheep, slide, stamp, stop up, strike, stuff, tamp, teap, thrust, tup, wad, warship, wedge, weight, wether(teg)
battering aries, corvus, terebra
cat male, tom
grandson david
-headed god amen, am (m)on, khnemu, khnum
horn cat's-claw, shofar, shophar
-like arietine, arietinous
son amminadab, eker, jamin, maaz
tongue ribwort

RAMA(CHANDRA) melchora
consort sita
half-brother bharata
priest kashyapa

RAMADES *beloved* aida

RAMAGE boughs, branches, frenzied, hawk, rough, unruly, untamed, wild(ness)
hawk braucher

RAMASS collect, gather

RAMBLE bush, chatter, digress, excursion, gad, gallivant, haze, hike, meander, peregrinate, proliferate, prowl, radiate, ramify, range, roam, rove, saunter, spread, sprogue, straggle, stray, stroll, tour, trace, traipse, travel, walk, wander

RAMBLER gadabout, gallivanter, roamer, rose, rover

RAMBLING aimless, circuitous, cursory, desultory, deviative, devious, digressive, disconnected, discursive, distraught, episodic, inconstant, loose, maundering, peripatetic, pointless, roving, wandering

RAMBUNCTIOUS active, boisterous, noisy, rampageous, rude, uncontrolled, unruly, untamed, violent, wild

RAMBUTAN soapwort

RAME branch, cry, demand, limb, question, repeat, scram, skeleton, wail

RAMEE, DE LA *pseudonym* ouida

RAMEKIN dish, hash, mixture, pan

RAMENTUM palea, palet, particle, scale, scraping, shaving

RAMESES See RAMSES.

RAMHEAD arm, clodpate, cuckold, hook, lever

RAMIE bast, boehmeria, fiber, flax, hemp, jute, ortega, phloem, rhea

RAMIFICATION arm, branch(ing), consequence, divergence, division, fork(ing), implication, offshoot, outgrowth, part, prong, ramus, separation

RAMIFY branch, extend, sprangle, spread

RAMILLIE hat, wig

RAMMACK clamber, gawk, romp, scamp

RAMMEL brushwood, crumble, earth, milk, refuse, rubbish, rummle, slash, trash, undergrowth

RAMMISH lewd, lustful, ramage, rank, rush, smelly, untamed, violent

RAMONA elm, sage
author helen hunt jackson

RAMOSE branched, branching, cladose, forking

RAMP access, adit, approach, bank, bound, caper, cheat, climb, clutch, crawl, creep, cuckoopint, dupery, erect, exit, footpad, fraud, gangplank, gradient, helicline, incline, passage, platform, rage, rampage, ramson, read(ing), rob, romp, rush, scud, seize, slip, slope, snatch, stair, steal, storm, swindle, unruly, uprear, walk
curved helicline

RAMPAGE agitate, anger, binge, carry on, cry, cut loose, rage, riot, romp, roughhouse, row, run amuck, run riot, spree, storm

RAMPAGEOUS boisterous, harumscarum, rambunctious, rambustious, roisterous, rollicking, rough, rowdy, rumbustious, unruly, violent, wild

RAMPANT abandoned, blustery, brutal, climant, excessive, extravagant, exuberant, feral, fierce, flourishing, furious, illtempered, lavish, lush, luxuriant, perpendicular, plentiful, plenty, prevalent, profuse, raging, rampageous, rank, reared up, rife, salient, stormy, teeming, unbridled, unchecked, unruly, violent, wanton, widespread, wild
and winged segreant

RAMPART agger, argin, barbette, barbican, barricade, barrier, bastion, breastwork, bulwark, buttress, defense, escarp, line, mole, mound, munition, parapet, ravelin, redan, vallation, vallum, wall
detached ravelin
earthen bray
ground around escarp
-like defilade, wall
palisaded vallum
part agger, spur

RAMPIKE raunpick, rounspik, snag, stump

RAMPION bellflower, campanula

RAMPIRE dam, embankment, footpath, highway, road, strengthen

RAMROD discipline, formal, gunstick, martinet, push through

RAMRODDY formal, rigid, stiff, unbending

RAMSES *city* pithom
son menephtah
wife nefertari

RAMSHACKLE dilapidated, disorderly, dissipated, loose, rickety, rude, shaky, tumbledown, unfirm, unruly, unstable, unsteady

RAMSON bear's-garlic, buckram, garlic

RAMSTAM headlong, headstrong, reckless(ly), thoughtless

RAMTIL guizotia, niger, sesame

RAMUS branch, division, fork, process, projection, ramification

RAN *consort* aegir, hler

RANA bullfrog, bulltoad, callula, frog, prince, ruler, toad

RANCE marble, prop, shore, stone, support

RANCEL ransack, search

RANCELMAN constable, policeman

RANCH acreage, casa, chacra, estancia, estantion, farm(stead), finca, grange, hacienda, plantation, pluck, podere, range, scratch, spread, station, tear, wrench
worker (See also COWBOY.) cattleman, cowpoke, estanciero, farmer, grazier, herdsman, rancher(o), sheepman, stockman

RANCID acerb, blinky, curdled, decayed, fetid, frowsty, frowzy, fusty, high, musty, noisome, obnoxious, off(ensive), putrid, ram, rank, reas(t)y, reechy, reest, repulsive, resty, rotten, rusty, sour(ed), spoiled, stale, stinking, strong, tainted, touched, turned, unclean, unpleasant

RANCOR animosity, animus, antagonism, antipathy, bitterness, choler, enmity, gall, grudge, hate, hatred, hostility, malevolence, malice, malignity, spite, spleen, venom, virulence

RAND border, coin, edge, highland, margin, rant, ridge, roon, rund, storm, strip

RANDAN boat, rampage, randy, revel, spree, uproar

RANDIA boxbrier, indigoberry, inkberry

RANDOM accidental, aimless, casual, chance, chancy, desultory, force, fortuitous, haphazard, hit-or-miss, impetuosity, incidental, irregular, potluck, purposeless, rush, spurt, stray, stream, vagabond, vagrant, violence
at hobnob, irregularly

RANDY aggressive, bad, beggar, canvass, carousal, carouse, coarse, crude, dirty, disorderly, festivity, frolic, ill-mannered, lascivious, lecherous, lewd, loud-spoken, revel, riotous, rough, rude, shrew, spree, unmanageable, virago, vulgar, wild

RANGE 3 gad, ken, ply, row, way 4 area, beat, ghat, hike, kind, line, oven, play, rank, roam, rove, scan, shot, size, sort, span, tier, view, walk 5 align, array, carry, class, drift, field, foray, fraze, gamut, ghaut, orbit, order, prowl, ranch, reach, scale, scene, scope, space, start, stove, stray, sweep, tramp, vista 6 course, extent, forage, length, radius, ramble, region, series, sphere, spread, stroll, survey, wander 7 arrange, command, compass, dispose, expanse, explore, habitat, horizon, marshal, meander, outlook, purview, station, stretch, traipse 8 ballpark, classify, diapason, distance, latitude, prospect, province, spectrum 9 cookstove, direction, gallivant, grassland, mountains, territory 10 calefactor, cordillera, domination 11 environment, perspective, systematize
archer's bowshot, butts, green
finder mekometer, sight, stadia, telemeter, trekometer
mountain chain, cordillera, gaut, gha(u)t, sawback, tier
pole picket
shooting gallery

RANGER commando, montero, policeman, rover, sat-

ellite, soldier, wanderer, warden

RANGIFER caribou, reindeer

RANGLE entangle, gravel, straggle, stray, tana, wander, wrangle

RANGY lean, long-limbed, mountainous, reedy, roomy, skinny, slender, specious, spindly, tall, thin, weedy

RANI, RANEE lady, princess, queen, wife
husband rajah

RANK 3 bad, row 4 base, dank, evil, file, foul, gamy, line, lush, rate, rich, size, sour, tier, wild 5 align, array, berth, cense, class, dense, dirty, fetid, glory, grade, gross, humid, musty, nasty, order, power, proud, range, sheer, thick, utter, wrong 6 affair, arrant, coarse, degree, estate, esteem, fester, figure, mighty, putrid, rancid, rating, rotten, series, status, strong, uneven, vulgar, wanton 7 arrange, caliber, calibre, calling, copious, corrupt, dignity, echelon, extreme, fertile, froward, glaring, haughty, lustful, noisome, overfed, ruttish, spoiled, station, violent 8 abundant, altitude, complete, estimate, flagrant, headlong, indecent, palpable, position, prestige, standing, stinking, terrible, vigorous 9 character, downright, excessive, exuberant, formation, hierarchy, luxuriant, offensive, overgrown, plentiful, privilege, repellent, repulsive 10 perquisite 11 aristocracy, distinction
advance in ascend, promote, rise, skip, upgrade
and file commonal(i)ty, hoi polloi, masses, proletariat, rabble, rangale
confer brevet, commission
deprive of break, bust, cashier, depose
high aristocracy, dignity, eminence, gentry
highest chief, first-string, major, premier, prime, senior, sovereign, supreme, top crust, top dog, top drawer
lower in inferior, junior, minor, second-string, subordinate, under

lowest cellar

mark of stripe

military See ARMY *officer.*

reduce in abase, degrade, demote, descend, downgrade, drop, fall

social class, estate, position, standing

RANKLE chafe, decay, fester, fret, gall, hurt, inflame, injure, irritate, pain, poison, sore, suppurate, ulcerate

RANSACK comb, dacker, drag, explore, gut, look, loot, pillage, plunder, rake, ravage, rifle, ripe, ruin, rummage, sack, scour, search, steal, strip

RANSOM acquit, atone, buy, deliver(ance), expiate, fine, forfeit, free, liberate, liberation, manumit, penalty, raim, rame, reclaim, recover(y), redeem, release, rescue, save

money redemptory

RANSTEAD toadflax

RANT anger, bluster, boast, bombast, carouse, carry on, cry, dance, declaim, discourse, emote, explode, flatulence, frolic, froth, fume, fustian, inflation, merrymaking, objurgate, overact, rage, rail, rand, rave, rebuke, revel, riot, rodomontade, scold, scout, song, speak, speech, spout, steven, storm, talk, tune, turgidity, vociferate

and rave faunch

RANTAN See RANDAN.

RANTING frantic, furious, hysterical, insane, mad, rabid, tearcat

RANTIPOLE daredevil, imp, rakish, termagant, unruly, wild

RANUNCULUS blisterweed, bolt, buttercress, buttercup, crowfoot, goldcup, golland, guiltycup, hedgehog, kingcup

RAP bang, betrayal, bit, blame, blow, bop, box, censure, charge, clap, clout, complaint, condemnation, converse, crack, criticism, criticize, cuff, exchange, grab, halfpenny, hasten, hurry, knap, knock, pound, rascal, rebuke, scoundrel, seize, sentence, skein, smite, snatch, steal, strike, swear,

talk, tap, taunt, term, thump, thwack, tirl. trifle, tunk, whack

RAPACIOUS aggressive, avaricious, covetous, cruel, extortionate, ferocious, fierce, gluttonous, grabby, grasping, greedy, leonine, lupine, parasitic(al), predaceous, predatory, preying, ravening, ravenous, taking, voracious, vulturous, wolfish

RAPACITY appetite, avarice, cupidity, edacity, exaction, extortion, greed(iness), ravin

symbol hawk

RAPE abuse, assault, brassica, coleseed, colewort, defile, despoil, dishonor, file, filter, hash, hasten, hastily, herb, hurry, navet(te), navew, oppress, pillage, plant, plunder, pomace, rapine, rasp, ravish, robbery, rope, ruin, scratch, seduce, seize, seizure, stuprate, stupration, transport, turnip, violate, violation, wine

seed colsa, colza, ravison

RAPHAEL angel, azarias

companion tobias

son raguel

RAPHE joint, line, seam, suture, union

RAPHIA bamboo, palm, pissava

RAPID abrupt, agile, apace, brisk, chute, expeditious, fast, fleet, hasty, hurried, mosso, moving, nimble, quick(ened), riffle, schnell, skelpin, speedy, steep, stickle, swift, tantivy, wingy

RAPIDITY celerity, fleetness haste, quickness, radeur, speed, velocity

RAPIDLY apace, fast, fleetly, quickly, skelp, speedily

RAPIDS chute, dalles, riff(le), rift, rip(ple), ripraps, shoot, soo

RAPIER bilbo, blade, estoc, sword, toaster, verdun

part cupguard, quillon, ricasso

thrust stoccado, stoccata

RAPINE force, pillage, plunder, rape, ravishment, seizure, spoilation, transport, violence

symbol vulture, wolf

RAPPAREE creaght, freebooter, plunderer, robber, vagabond

RAPPEE snoose, snuff

RAPPER knocker, lie, oath

RAPPORT accord, affinity, agreement, confidence, connection, favor, good terms, harmony, relation(ship), understanding

RAPSCALLION blackguard, good-for-nothing, ne'er-dowell, rascal(ly), rogue, scamp, villain, wretch

RAPT abducted, absorbed, captivated, carried, deep, ecstasy, ecstatic, enchanted, engrossed, enraptured, entranced, fascinated, gripped, happy, intent, lifted, lost, preoccupied, rapine, ravish, snatch, tense, trance, transport(ed)

RAPTORES bird, eagle, hawk, owl, vulture

RAPTORIAL accipital, accipitrine, hawklike, predatory, prehensile

RAPTURE beatitude, bliss, dharana, dhyana, ecstasy, elation, enthusiasm, exultation, felicity, happiness, joy, paroxysm, passion, ravishment, rhapsody, samadhi, spell, trance, transport

RAPTUROUS carried away, ecstatic, elated, enchanted, exalted, exultant, flushed, glad, happy, joyful, jubilant, overjoyed, transported

RARE airy, antrin, attenuated, capital, choice, curious, delicate, dispersed, distinctive, early, elegant, ethereal, excellent, exceptional, exclusive, extraordinary, fine, flimsy, gaseous, good, incomparable, infrequent, inimitable, occasional, odd, precious, rarified, recherche, refined, scarce, seenil, seldom, seldseen, sindle, singular, slender, slight, slim, sodden, sparse, special, sporadic, strange, subt(i)le, surpassing, tenuous, thin, transcendent, uncommon, undercooked, underdone, unique, unlikely, unsubstantial, unusual, vaporous, very, windy

ben ben jonson

bird rara avis
comb. mano
RAREFIED airy, attenuated, diluted, ethereal, refined, spiritual, thin
RAREFY attenuate, dilute, diminish, distend, ex‚ tenuate, inflate, reduce, refine, thin
RARELY hardly, infrequently, scarcely, selden, seldom
RARITY curio(sity), marvel, miracle, oddity, phenomenon, prodigy, rara avis, tenuity, thinness, wonder
RAS cape, commander, fabric, fascist, headland, leader, prince, vizier
RASA amrita, essence, flavor, fluid, sap, taste, water
RASCAL ablach, base, bezonian, blackguard, blighter, budza(r)t, bugger, camooch, catso, churl, coon, coquin, dodger, fox, ganef, hosebird, imp, intriguer, keener, kite, knave, limmer, loon, low, mean, miscreant, mob, palliard, parech, peasant, picaroon, rabble, raggil, rakehell, rapscallion, raptril, rogue, rubiator, scalawag, scamp, scapegrace, scapin, scoundrel, shag, skalawag, skeesicks, skellum, slicker, sly dog, smoothie, spalpeen, taistrel, taistril, thief, trickster, varlet, villain, widdifow
RASCALLY base, dishonest, false, knavish, limmer, mean, rooky, shagrag, trickish, tricky, unprincipled, worthless
RASE alter, cut, demolish, erase, graze, growl, incise, level, rage, rise, rub out‚ scrape, scratch, snatch, tear(down)
RASH abrupt, active, adventurous, audacious, blight, blind(fold), brash, brisk, careless, cut, daring, dash, desperate, eczema, erase, eruption, exanthema, foolhardy, forlorn, giddy, hasty, headlong, headstrong, heedless, hives, icarian, impetuous, improvident, imprudent, impulsive, incautious, indiscreet, injudicious, mad (brain), overconfident, over-

hasty, pour, precipitate, pressing, ratch(et), reckless, roseola, rush, rustle, scamp, slash, spots, sudden, temeritous, thoughtless, unchary, unwary, urgent, venturesome, venturous, vigorous, wanton, wild
man hotspur
RASHER bacon, collop, coloppe, piece, portion, rockfish, serving, slice
RASHNESS acrisy, folly, impulse, rage, rese, temerity
RASORIAL gallinaceous, gnawing
RASP abrade, annoy, belch, bray, denticle, eruct, file, grate, irk, irritate, offend, pound, raze, riffler, rub, scrape, tooth, vex
palm paxiuba
pod flindosa
RASPBERRY akpek, arnberry, avarin, bazoo, bird, blackcap, bogberry, boo, bronx cheer, cuthbert, fruit, molka, plumbog, respasse, rosacean, rubus, st regis
brandy framboise
dwarf bogberry, cranberry, plumbog
streak bluestem
RASPING, RASPY clangorous, grating, guttural, harsh, hoarse, irritating, offensive, raucous, rough, scraping, screaky, strident
RASPINGS leftovers, powder, refuse, remainder, scobs
RASSE civet, weasel
RASSELAS *author* samuel johnson
prison happy valley
RAT adviser, apostate, bandicoot, betrayer, blab, blackleg, buck, councilor, counselor, craber, cushion, desert(er), drat, fink, gnawer, hairpiece, informer, knobstick, louse, myomorph, pad, quisling, quitter, renegade, renege, reprobate, rodent, rottan, rut, scab, scoundrel, scratch, snob, squeal(er), stoolpigeon, switch, track, traitor, vermin, vole, wart, yellowbelly
-bite fever sodoku
catcher pied piper
chinchilla abrocome
field metad
fish chimaera

genus mus, spalax
goose brant
hare pika
kangaroo bilbi, bilby, potoroo, squeaker, tungo
kind hamster, kok, metad, mole, mouse, mus, noki, spalax, tosher, zemmi, zemni
-like muriform, tapoatafa
nest confusion, jumble, mess
pineapple pinguin
poison antu, arsenic, ratsbane
pouched pocket-gopher
smell a suspect
spiny echimys, heteromys, longcheres, proechimys
RATAFIA, RATAFEE biscuit, cordial, curacao, liqueur, macaroon, noyau
RATCH bar, board, dog, reach, rend, rotche, stretch, turn
RATCHET catch, click, detent, dog, pawl, projection
RATE 3 bat, jaw, ret, tax 4 agio, cast, cess, cost, duty, gait, kind, levy, pace, pelt, rail, soak, step, toll 5 abuse, allot, batta, chide, curve, merit, price, ratio, scold, speed, style, teind, tempo, tithe, value, weigh, worth 6 amount, assess, assize, BERATE, charge, degree, esteem, excise, figure, impost, manner, rebuke, reckon, regard, revile, settle, stride, tariff, vilify 7 analyze, assizes, censure, compute, deserve, measure, premium, reproof, REPROVE, tribute, upbraid 8 admonish, appraise, consider, denounce, estimate, evaluate, handicap, progress, quantify, reproach, standing, velocity 9 apportion, calculate, criticize, objurgate, quotation, REPRIMAND, valuation 10 assessment, proportion, tonguelash, vituperate
RATEL animal, badger, mellivora, musteline
RATHE betimes, content, eager, early, quick(ly), soon, speedily, speedy, willing
RATHER astite, before, choice, comparatively, druther, earlier, ere(r), first, former, gey, helder,

indeed, instead, kindly, liefer, liever, precious, preferably, preference, prior, quickly, ruther, somewhat, sooner than, tidder, titter

RATHSKELLER beerhall, restaurant, saloon

RATIFICATION authorization, confirmation, sanction, sigil, signature, signet, stamp

RATIFY accept, accredit, affirm, amen, approve, authenticate, authorize, autograph, bless, certify, confirm, corroborate, cosign, countersign, endorse, establish, homologate, indorse, initial, license, notarize, obsignate, okay, okeh, pass, roborate, rubberstamp, sanction, seal, settle, sign, subscribe to, substantiate, undersign, underwrite, validate, verify

RATING appraisal, assessment, bluejacket, cense, class(ification), credit, estimate, evaluation, gob, grade, mariner, matlow, rank, rebuke, reprimand, sailor, scolding, seaman, standing

high aaa, a-plus, triple-a

RATIO average, contrast, degree, equation, index, part, percentage, portion, proportion, quota, quotum, rank, rate, ration, relation, secant, share

RATIOCINATION argument, illation, inference, logic, reason(ing), thinking, thought

RATION allot(ment), allowance, apportion, budget, deal, dispense, distribute, divide, dole, food, limit, mete, parcel, part(ake), pittance, portion, prorate, relation, share, supply, tucker

extra buckshee

RATIONAL cool, discoursive, enlightened, equitable, fair, fit, intellectual, intelligent, judicious, just, logical, lucid, mental, normal, philosophical, proper, reasonable, reasoning, right, sagacious, sane, sensible, sober, sound, thinking, thoughtful, wise

RATIONALE explanation,

exposition, ground, logos, reason(s)

RATIONALIZATION alibi, defense, excuse, explanation, plea

RATIONALIZE defend, excuse, explain, justify, reason, simplify, thob, vindicate

RATITE apteryx, cassowary, diornis, em(e)u, kiwi, moa, ostrich, rhea, struthian, unkeeled

RATOON shoot, spring, sprout, sucker

RATTAIL braid, comb, file, fish, grenadier, mule, ribwort, spoon, tapering

fescue capon's-grass

serpent fer-de-lance

RATTAN bejuco, cane, lash, noose, palm, rattoon, rotang, sega, switch, thong, whip, wicker

palm bejuco, calamus, cane, liana

vine berchemia, supple-jack

RATTEN crib, filch, molest, poach, spoil, steal

RATTLE abash, addle, agitate, beat, bewilder, birl, brattle, burl, caixinha, calabash, castanet, chackle, chase, chatter, chocalho, clack(er), clangor, clapper, clatter, clitter(clattle), clutter, confuse, cowwheat, crotal, daze, discomfit, disconcert, disturb, embarrass, faze, flurry, fluster, gab, grogger, jail, lousewort, maraca, muddle, noise, nonplus, nonsense, perplex, prattle, prison, racket, rail, rale, rappel, rebuke, rick, rickle, rouse, ruckle, scold(ing), shail, shake, signal, sistrum, skellat, talk(er), tirl, toy, trouble, uproar, upset

bronchial rale, rhoncus

yellow cockscomb, coxcomb

RATTLEBAG bladder-campion, noisy, rackety

RATTLEBONED lean, skinny

RATTLEBRAIN ass, clown, fool, simpleton

RATTLEBRAINED emptyheaded, flighty, foolish, frivolous, giddy, hairbrained, scatterbrained

RATTLEBUSH baptisia, crotalaria, indigo

RATTLEHEAD cavalier, scatterbrain

RATTLEMOUSE bat

RATTLENUT chinquapin

RATTLEROOT bugbane

RATTLESNAKE belltail, canebrake, cascabel, cascavel, crotalus, diamondback, massasauga, sidewinder, sistrurus

bean cedron

bite meadow-rue

herb baneberry

master blazing-star, falsealoe, gay-feather, liatris, snakeroot

pert. crotaline

pilot copperhead

plaintain adder's-violet, netleaf, networt, orchid, ratsbane

rattle button, crepitaculum

root birdbell, bugbane, cankerweed, joyleaf, senega

venom neurotoxin

RATTLETOP bugbane

RATTLETRAP geegaw, knickknack, morass, mouth, pitfall, quagmire, ramshackle, rickety, trifle, vehicle, wreck

RATTOON raccoon, RATOON, RATTAN

RATTY angry, dilapidated, mean, motheaten, nasty, pitiable, shabby, unkempt, worn, worthless, wretched

RATWA muntjac

RAUCOUS braying, cacaphonous, dry, grating, harsh, hoarse, husky, rasping, rough, scrannel, squawky, strident

RAUK poke, roke, scratch, stir, vapor

RAUN fish, herring, roe, rown, salmon, spawn

RAUNCHY careless, dirty, obscene, slovenly, smelly, smutty

RAUWOLFIA *extract* reserpine

RAVAGE abuse, corrode, decimate, desolate, despoil, destroy, destruction, devastate, dilapidate, eat, erode, foray, gut, harry, havoc, infest, invade, lay waste, loot, obliterate, overrun, overthrow, pillage, plunder, prostrate, ransack, rape, raven, raze, rob, ruin, sack, seduce, spoil, spoliate, subvert, violate, waste, wrack, wreck

RAVANA *consort* sita

RAVE anger, berate, blurb, bluster, bombast, bubble, crush, cry, declaim, effervesce, enthuse, explode, fume, harangue, infatuation, prate, prattle, pry, puff, rage, rail, rake, rant, rathe, roam, rouse, storm, stray, tear, wander

RAVEL break, comb, crumble, disentangle, fracture, fray, fret, involve, ladder, plait, raddle, run(ner), separate, sleave, slough, snarl, tangle, undo, untangle, untwist, unweave, unwide, wattle
composition bolero, la valse

RAVELIN demilune, fort(ification), halfmoon, outwork, rablin

RAVELOE *weaver* silas marner

RAVEN alala, bertram, bird, black, chough, consume, corbel, corbie, corbin, corvus, croaker, crow, desire, devour, forage, plunder, prey, prowl, quarry, ralph, seize, victi, waybird
author poe
comb. corax
cry caw, croak, pork, qualm
ensign of denmark
heroine lenore
of battle badb-catha
symbol of bad luck

RAVENING, RAVENOUS acquisitive, catawamp(o)us, cormorant, craving, famished, fierce, gluttonous, grasping, greedy, hollow, hungry, lupine, mad, predatory, preying, rabid, rapacious, starved, turbulent, voracious

RAVENNA *tomb* dante

RAVINE arroyo, barranca, canon, canyon, chasm, chine, cleuch, cleugh, clough, clove, coulee, dale, dell, dimble, dingle, ditch, donga, flume, gap, ghyll, glack, gorge, grike, gulch, gully, heugh, impetuous, khor, khud, lin(n), lynn, notch, nullah, quebrada, rambla, raven, rush, sheugh, vale, valley, wadi, wady
dry rambla

narrow flume

RAVING bombast, delirament, deliration, delirious, extraordinary, frantic, frenzied, furious, gorgeous, incoherent, irrational, rabid, remarkable, superlative

RAVISH abduct, abuse, afforce, annihilate, captivate, charm, corrupt, defile, deflower, delight, despoil, enrapture, entrance, force, harrow, harry, kidnap, outrage, plunder, rape, remove, rob, seize, shanghai, snatch, stuprate, suppress, transport, violate

RAVISHING delightful, enchanting, gorgeous

RAVISHMENT ecstasy, joy, rapture, transport

RAW abraded, artless, bare, biting, bitter, bleak, callow, chafed, chill(y), coarse, cold, crude, cutcha, cutting, damp, dazy, elementary, exposed, fresh, galled, green, half-cooked, ignorant, immature, inclement, indelicate, inexperienced, kutcha, lash, lean, naked, native, natural, neat, nude, obscene, rare, rough, rude, sore, spun, straight, uncooked, uncultivated, undiluted, unprepared, unrefined, unripe, unseasoned, unskilled, untaught, untrained, untried, verdant, virginal, visceral, vulgar, weerish, wet, windy

RAWBONED angular, gaunt, lank, lean, scrag, scrawny, skinny, spare

RAWHIDE beat, cowhide, greenhide, knout, parfleche, pelt, quirt, skin, thong, whang, WHIP
thong babiche
thread shaganappi

RAX become, grow, pull, reach, strain, stretch

RAY alpha, anode, arrange, array, batfish, batoid, beam(let), beta, brachium, canal, cathode, cheer, chucho, cosmic, cowfish, darnel, dewbeam, diameter, dorn, dress, drilvis, emanation, equip, fish, gamma, glance, gleam, glimmer, guitarfish, homely, lenard, light, line, manta, mobula, moonbeam, numbfish, obi-

spo, order, particle, placoid, plowfish, pylstert, radiance, radiation, rank, roker, rye, sawfish, seapurse, sephon, shaft, shine, sight, skate, spark, stingaree, streak, stream, stripe, thornback, torpedo, trygon, vision, wairepo
cluster aigrette
comb. actin(o), aene
cow-nosed rhinoptera
female maid
fin spine
having 2 diactinal
-like actinic, actinoid, radial, radiate
measurer actinometer
particle mesotron
spotted obispo
starry skate
surrounded by en soleil
thornback dorn

RAYON acetate, bemberg, celanese, cloth, duchess, fabric, faille, fiber, moire, ninon, pongee, radius, taffeta, textile, tulle, viscose
yarn size denier, drammage

RAZE abolish, abrade, annihilate, break down, chop down, cut, demolish, destroy, devastate, efface, eradicate, erase, exterpate, extinguish, fell, graze, incise, knock down, level, obliterate, overthrow, prostrate, pull down, remove, ruin, scrape, scratch, shave, subvert, wound, wreck

RAZEE abridge, prune, reduce, retrench

RAZOR blade, clam, mussel, rattler, scrape, shave(r), tusk
clam pirot, raso(i)r, solen, spout
fish chopa-blanca
grinder goatsucker
kind electric, rattler, safety, straight-edge
sharpen hone, strop
stone novaculite
thin-bladed rattler

RAZORBACK finback, hog, ridge, rorqual, roustabout, whale
state arkansas

RAZORBILL alca, auk, falk, murre, noddy, rockbird, scoot, scout, skimmer, tink(er), willock

RAZZ banter, boo, chaff, deride, raspberry, ridicule, tease, torment

RAZZIA foray, incursion, pillage, raid

RAZZLE-DAZZLE car(r)ousel, cinch, commotion, confuse, confusion, hilarity, noisemaker, spree, uproar

RE (See also RA.) about, anent, concerning, regarding

REACH accomplish, achieve, advene, affect, area, arrive, attain, brace, bribe, carry, catch, come(to), compass, cover, deliver, distance, expanse, extend, extent, fathom, fulfill, gain, get (to), grasp, hawk, hit, impress, influence, ken, length, lie, magnitude, make, obtain, orbit, outstretch, overtake, perch, perform, plain, play, pole, possess, proceed, promontory, radius, range, reik, retch, run, ryke, scheme, scope, seize, shaft, span, sphere, spit, spread, stretch, strike, suffice, sweep, thrust, touch, understand, vista, vomit
across span
forth extend
-me-down cheap, readymade, second-hand
out spread, stretch, utter
under subtend

REACHING aspiration, captation, effort, endeavor, grasping, penetrating, profound

REACT answer, behave, buck, function, operate, resist, respond, reverberate, work

REACTION answer, backlash, behavior, blowoff, change, emotion, exchange, feeling, impact, impression, influence, kickback, kneejerk, opinion, rebound, recoil, reflection, reflex, refluence, repercussion, response, return, revulsion, rise, start, swingback, sympathy, taxis, tendency, tropism
delayed double-take
involuntary reflex

REACTIONARY apostate, bircher, bourbon, conservative, diehard, dodo, malcontent, philistine, rightist, rightwing, standpat(ter), tory

REACTOR agent, choker, conductor, furnace, pile, reagent

READ abomasum, advise, attribute, browse, con, construe, counsel, decipher, declare, describe, discern, discover, drone, estimate, expound, foresee, foretell, guess, indicate, infer, instruct, interpret, kere, keri, kri, learn, measure, note, peruse, pore, predict, prelect, recite, register, relate, retinize, scan, skim, solve, speak, stomach, study, suppose, teach, tell, think, understand
ability to literacy
aloud deacon
carefully pore, study
fast gobble, scan, skim
inability to alexia, dyslexia, paralexia, strephosymbolia
metrically scan
off dictate
out of depose, dismiss, expel, oust
publicly lecture, pr(a)lect, recite
well bookish, dog-eared, learned, literate, scholarly, studious, thumbed

READER anagnost, bibliophage, book(worm), censor, dipper, editor, elocutionist, instructor, lector, lectrice, lecturer, lens, lister, maftir, peruser, pocketbook, pr(a)elector, primer, reciter, textbook
elementary primer, tenpenny

READILY cheerfully, eagerly, easily, freely, gladly, happily, probably, promptly, quickly, willingly

READINESS address, alacrity, aptitude, aptness, art, capacity, dexterity, ease, facility, fluency, gift, graith, inclination, promptitude, promptness, quickness, skill, tendency, willingness

READING bookwork, calling, capitulum, interpretation, kere, keri, kethib, kri, lection, perusal, qri, queri, rendition, scholarship, translation, version
desk ambo, escritoire, lectern, pulpit
difficulty alexia, dyslexia, paralexia, strephosymbolia
room athenaeum

READY active, acute, adept, adroit, alert, amenable, apert, apt, arm(ed), arrange, available, bain, boun(d), cheerful, clever, convenient, dext(e)rous, disposed, docile, eager, equip(ped), expedite, expert, facile, fit, fluent, forward, free, game, glad, glib, graith, handy, happy, hearty, here, inclined, keen, liable, likely, live, loaded, mature, near, nimble, on tap, on time, open, opportune, plan, point, prepare(d), present, pret, prime(d), proficient, prompt, provide, quick, repair, rife, ripe, set, sharp, skilled, skil(l)ful, supplied, there, train, unhesitating, willing, yare
-made bought, manufactured
money cash

REAL actual, authentic, being, certain, concrete, cordial, essential, existent, factual, faithful, genuine, gradely, greatly, heartfelt, hearty, important, intrinsic, literal, loyal, material, much, palpable, physical, positive, pure, regal, royal, sensible, sincere, solid, substantial, substantive, sure, tangible, thingy, true, unaffected, unfaked, unfeigned, valid, veritable, very, vrai
being, pert. ontal
estate acquest, acreage, acres, asset, chattels, demesne, domain, freehold, ground, hereditament, holding, house, land(s), lot, manor, messuage, parcel, plot, premises, property, realty, tenement, toft, zamindari
estate claim encumbrance, lien, mortgage, tax, trustdeed
estate, clear al(l)od(y), alodium
estate register cadaster, cadastre
mccoy genuine, kosher, true
100 isabella
property bona

REALGAR arsenic, rosaker, sandarac

REALISTIC accurate, authentic, basic, businesslike,

concise, down-to-earth, efficient, factual, hard (headed), lifelike, literal, matter-of-fact, practical, pragmatic, probable, rational, reasonable, sane, scientific, sensible, sober, sound, thorough, unromantic, usual, vivid

REALITY actuality, being, corporeality, dasein, entity, fact, identity, matter, objectivity, oversoul, truth, verity
believer in cartesian
doctrine actualism
science of metaphysics, ontology, philosophy
treat as hypostatize
ultimate brahma, divinity, god, source

REALIZATION accomplishment, achievement, awakening, being, fruition, knowledge, recognition, sense

REALIZE accomplish, achieve, acquire, actualize, appreciate, apprehend, bring, capture, comprehend, conceive, effect, embody, execute, experience, fulfil(l), gain, get, imagine, incarnate, know, make, market, materialize, objectify, obtain, perceive, perform, profit, receive, recognize, reify, sell for, sense, think, understand, win

REALLY absolutely, actually, aroo, arrah, aru, certainly, de facto, fancy, genuinely, indeed, just, positively, sooth, surely, truly, verily, wis(ha), you don't say
and truly honor-bright, scout's-honor

REALM area, bourn(e), circle, clime, country, demesne, department, district, domain, dominion, empire, gaeldom, ground, jurisdiction, ken, kingdom, land, notalia, orbit, place, property, province, region, reign, riche, sphere, state, terrene, territory, turf, zone
comb. ric
eastern emirate
fabulous el dorado

REALTY honesty, loyalty, possession, property, realm, reaute, regality, royalty

REAM bevel, bore, broaden, countersink, cream, draw, enlarge, expand, foam, fraise, froth, perforate, quantity, scum, skim, stretch, top, widen

REAMER borer, broach, burr, cherry, chisel, drill, rancer, rhymer, rimmer, squeezer, tool, widener

REANIMATE cheer, encourage, liven, pep, rally, recreate, regenerate, reinvigorate, renew, restore, resuscitate, revive, revivify, wake

REANIMATION anabiosis, reincarnation, renewal, resurrection, resuscitation, revival

REAP acquire, collect, crop, cut, derive, garner, gather, get, glean, harvest, mow, rake, realize, receive, rip, rope, sheaf, shear, sickle

REAPER cocker, cradler, death, gleaner, sickler, stibblerig, tasker
tool crotchet, rake, sickle, twibil

REAR aback, abaff, abaft, after, appear, arise, arriere, astern, back, behind, boost, breed, bring up, build, butt(ocks), collect, construct, create, derriere, dorsal, dorsum, drag, duff, educate, elevate, erect, establish, exalt, farm, forthbring, foster, gather, heave, heel, hind, hinder, hindmost, instruct, introduce, jump, leap, lift, nurse, nurture, occiput, originate, pesade, pitch, poop, posterior, produce, propagate, raise, ramp, rare, reverse, rise, rouse, rump, stend, stern, tail(piece), teach, tergal, tower, train, vomit, wake, withers, wrest
-horse mantis
in the atergo
to the abaft, aft, astern, posterior, postern

REARING elevation, erection, forcene, fresne, rampant
horse's pesade

REARRANGE adjust, change, jigger, readjust, reorder

REARWARD aft, backward, caudad, caudal, retrograde

REASON account, aim, alibi,

analyze, antecedent, a priori, argue(ment), basis, brain, cause, conclude, consider, debate, deduce, deliberate, discuss, end, explain, explanation, foundation, generalize, ground(s), hoti, hypothesize, incentive, inducement, intellect(ualize), justification, logic, logos, matter, meaning, mind, motive, nous, object(ive), occasion, particularize, peg, ponder, proof, prove, purpose, question, ratiocinate, rationale, rationalize, root, sake, sanity, sense, solution, subject, support, syllogize, theorize, think, understanding, warrant, wherefore, wisdom
alleged pretext
contrary to absurd, crazy, illogical, stupid
deprive of dement
exercise of moesis
for being raison d'etre
hatred of misology
lack amentia, dementia, folie, insanity, madness, mania
pert. noetic
to believe evidence

REASONABLE acceptable, agreeable, cheap, economical, equitable, fair(minded), feasible, inexpensive, intelligent, judicious, just (ifiable), legitimate, logical, moderate, pervious, plausible, proper, prudent, rational, realistic, sane, sensible, sound, temperate, valid, wise

REASONING analysis, a priori, argument(ation), conclusion, deduction, dialectic, induction, logic, philosophy, proof, ratiocination, thinking, thought
basis of premise
clumsy argal
discursive dianoia
equivocal casuistry
false sophistry
hatred of misology
pert. dianoetic

REASSURE cheer, comfort, convince, embolden, encourage, hearten, inspire, inspirit

REAS(T)Y fetid, rancid, spoiled

REATA lariat, lasso, lazo, riata, rope

REAVE break, burst, deprive, despoil, divest, pillage, plunder, rave, remove, rend, rob, seize, split, steal, tear, unravel

REBATE blunt, check, deduct(ion), diminish, discount, dull, groove, kickback, pay-back, rabbet, recess, reduce, refund, reimburse, remission, restore, return, ribbet, weaken

REBEC fiddle, lyre, rebab, ribibe, sarod, viol(in)

REBECCA, REBEKAH *beloved* ivanhoe
brother laban
burial site machpelah
father bethuel, isaac
husband isaac
offspring esau, jacob, leah, rachel

REBEL agitator, anarch(ist), arise, brawler, cade, croppie, defiant, defy, disobey, fauve, frondeur, iconoclast, insubordinate, insurgent, insurrectionist, malcontent, mutineer, mutinous, oppose, protest(er), red, reluct, renegade, resist(er), revolt, revolutionist, rise, traitor, turncoat

REBELLION agitation, anarchy, contumacy, insurgency, insurrection, mutiny, opposition, putsch, revolt, revolution, sedition, treason, uprising, war
famous civil war, jack straw's, sepoy, tyler's

REBELLIOUS anarchic, audacious, contumacious, defiant, disobedient, insubordinant, insurgent, mutinous, refractory, revolutionary, seditious

REBIRTH recreation, regeneration, renaissance, renascence, revival
doctrine amidism, amitabha

REBOANT aroar, reverberating

REBOUND backfire, backlash, boomerang, bounce, bound, car(r)om, dap, echo, kick, react(ion), recoil, redound, reflect, repercuss(ion), resile, resilience, reverberate, ricochet, skip, snapback, spring, stite, stot
clip retainer

REBUFF brush off, censure, check, chide, cow, deny, high-hat, push back, rebuke, recall, refuse, reject (ion), repel, repudiate, repulse, rout, scat, scold, slap, snub, spurn

REBUKE admonish, admonition, assail, bawl-out, beat, berate, blame, blast, blister, blow, call down, castigate, castigation, censure, check, chew out, chide, correct(ion), criticize, cuss out, dirdum, disgrace, downset, dress down, eat out, exprobate, gansel, increpation, jobation, jump on, keelhaul, lambaste, lecture, lesson, nag, nip, object(ion), objurgate, punish, put down, rag(ging), rap, rate, rebuff, rehete, remord, reprehend, reprehension, repress, reprimand, reproach, reprobate, reproof, **REPROVE**, restrain, riddle, roast, SCOLD, scorcher, sermon, setdown, sit on, slap, sneb, snib, take down, trim(ming), tut, upbraid(ing), what-for, wig(ging)

REBUS enigma, puzzle, riddle

REBUT check, confute, contradict, controvert, countercharge, counterclaim, disprove, negate, negative, oppose, rate, recoil, refute, rejoin, repel, repulse, retire, revile, surrebut, surrejoin

REBUTTAL answer, argument, countercharge, counterclaim, rejoinder, surrejoinder

RECALCITRANT adamant, defiant, disobedient, factious, hard, headstrong, insubmissive, intractable, obstinate, opposed, ornery, perverse, rebel(lious), refractory, renitent, resistant, stubborn, sullen, unruly, wayward, willful

RECALL abnegate, annul, applause, bethink, call back, cancel, cite, countermand, educe, elicit, encore, evoke, memory, mind, recant, rechate, recollect(ion), remember, remind, reminisce, renew, repeal, rescind, restore, retract, revival, revive, revoke, rouse,

stir, summon(s), think, unlook, waken, withdraw

RECANT abandon, abjure, back down, backtrack, call back, crawfish, crawl, deny, disavow, disclaim, disown, foreswear, recall, renounce, repudiate, rescind, retract, revoke, swallow, take back, unsay, withdraw

RECAPITULATE calculate, describe, paraphrase, recite, recount, rehearse, reiterate, repeat, rephrase, restate, review, reword, sum(marize), sum up

RECAPITULATION anacephalaeosis, repetition, review, summary

RECAPTURE recall, recover(y), regain, remember, retake

RECAST change, reconstruct, reform, remodel, remold, reshape

RECEDE back, contract, decline, depart, diminish, dwindle, ebb, fade, go away, regress, retire, retract, retreat, retrocede, retrograde, shrink, sink, surrender, wane, withdraw

RECEIPT acceptance, acquit(tance), answer, apocha, binder, expedient, formula, prescription, receptacle, RECEPTION, recipe, recu, remedy, reset, snapout, stub, voucher

RECEIPTS accounts, box office, cash, earnings, entrada, gain, gate, house, income, payments, revenue, royalty, sales, take

RECEIVE absorb, accept, accommodate, acquire, admit, adopt, assent, assume, bear, cash, catch, come by, contain, derive, draw, embrace, entertain, experience, fang, gain, get, grasp, greet, hold, immit, import, inaugurate, include, ingest, inherit, initiate, install, instate, intromit, let in, obtain, pocket, realize, secure, shelve, support, sustain, take, undergo, welcome

RECEIVED accepted, orthodox, traditional

RECEIVER alienee, bailee, beneficiary, collector, cymaphen, devotee, donatary, donee, fence, grantee, greeter, heir(ess), host, inheritor, pernor, receptacle, receptionist, recipient, sindico, teller, treasurer, trustee

comb. ceptor

RECENSION censure, critique, enumeration, examination, review(ing), revision, survey

RECENT current, fresh, green, holocene, last, late(r), latest, latter(day), modern, neoteric, new, novel, past, young

comb. cene, ceno, neo

RECEPTACLE 3 ark, bag, bin, box, can, cup, jar, pan, pot, urn, vet 4 bath, boat, boot, bowl, cage, case, crib, dish, etui, ewer, font, inro, pail, roll, sack, safe, tank, tray, vase, well 5 apron, banga, basin billy, burse, caddy, chest, crate, creel, crock, etwee, kiosk, stoup, torus, vault 6 acerra, ashcan, basket, bottle, bucket, carton, cellar, hamper, holder, hopper, patera, pitchi, pipkin, pittin, robbin, ruskin, saucer, trough, vessel 7 bladder, brazier, capcase, carrier, cistern, compote, corbula, hanaper, humidor, parison, pitcher, platter, scuttle, sebilla, utensil 8 canister, carryall, catchall, gallipot, gynobase, magazine, ossarium, receiver, trencher 9 autoclave, container, porringer, recipient, reservoir 10 repository

comb. angium, clinal, cline, clinic

wooden pitchi, sebilla

RECEPTION acceptance, accoil, accueil, admission, adoption, affair, at home, capacity, collation, conference, couchee, crush, diffa, durbar, entertainment, entrance, feast, fete, gathering, greeting, infare, intuition, levee, ovation, party, possession, receipt, recipience, recovery, recueil, ruelle, salon, soiree, tea, welcome

crowded crush, hurricane, squash

favorable bel-accoil

place anteroom, atrium,

foyer, hall, parlo(u)r, salon, vestibule

wedding infare

RECEPTIVE admissive, cordial, docile, interested, open-minded, pliable, pliant, sensitive

RECESS adjourn, ala, alcove, ambry, apse, bay, break, carol, carrell, cave, cleft, closet, concave, cranny, crevice, crypt, cubicle, embrasure, grotto, halt, haustrum, indentation, inlet, interlude, intermission, interruption, interval, lull, niche, nook, pause, rabbet, receding, respite, retire, retreat, seclude, seclusion, sinus, slot, socket, suspension, tokonoma, vacation

RECESSED sunk(en)

RECESSION deflation, depression, hard times, recedence, retirement, retraction, retreat, setback, slump, surrender, withdrawal

RECESSIVE backward, ebbing, modest, receding, reserved, retiring, shrinking, shy, unsocial, withdrawn

RECHAB *kin* jonadab, malchiah, rimmon

RECHAUFFE chestnut, hash, platitude, rehash, warmed up

RECHERCHE arcane, choice, curious, elegant, exclusive, exotic, exquisite, farfetched, fine, fresh, good, new, novel, obscure, original, precious, rare, refined, select, smart, uncommon, unusual

RECIDIVATE backslide, decline, deteriorate, fall back, lapse, relapse

RECIDIVISM apostasy, backsliding, decline, devolution, lapse, relapse, repeat, repetition

RECIPE axiom, dish, formula, instructions, pattern, prescription, procedure, receipt, remedy, rule

RECIPIENT beneficiary, donatee, donee, heir, laureate, receiver, receptacle

RECIPROCAL analagous, changeable, coequal, common, commutual, complemental, complementary, convertible, correlative, correspondent, corresponding,

cross, dependent, equiparrant, equipollent, equivalent, give-and-take, homologous, interchangeable, joint, linked, mutual, numeric(al), reciprocative, related, secant, seesaw, shared, united

comb. allelo

RECIPROCATE accord, alternate, bandy, exchange, interchange, repay, requite, retaliate, retroact, return, revenge, share

RECIPROCATION agreement, archilowe, correspondence, equivalence, exchange, give-and-take, revenge

RECIPROCITY cooperation, give-and-take, interchange, repayment, requital, revenge

RECITAL account, concert, description, enumeration, litany, musical(e), narration, narrative, program, reading, rehearsal, relation, repetition, report, saga, statement, story, tale, tikkun

RECITATION dhikr, exercise, lecture, reading, RECITAL, rhapsody

RECITATIVE arioso, scena

RECITE cantillate, carp, chant, count, declaim, describe, detail, enumerate, itemize, narrate, number, parrot, quote, read, recapitulate, recount, rehearse, relate, render, repeat, rhapsodize, say, scan, speak, state, tell

RECITER anteri, conteur, diseur, diseuse, elocutionist, narrator, raconteur, scald, skald

RECK care, concern, deem, estimate, heed, matter, mind, nevertheless, regard, rick

RECKLESS adventurous, audacious, banzai, bayardly, blind, bodacious, brash, breakneck, careless, daredevil, daring, desperate, devil-may-care, dissolute, foolhardy, furious, harumscarum, hasty, headlong, heedless, hotheaded, hotspur, hurried, impetuous, imprudent, incautious, inconsiderate, indifferent, irresponsible, mad, neglectful, negligent, perdu(e), precipitate, ramstam, rash, regardless, slapdash, thoughtless, unwary, venturesome, venturous, wanton, wild

RECKON account, add, adjudge, allot, aret(te), assign, audit, bank, believe, calculate, call, cast, cipher, claim, class, compute, conclude, consider, count, deem, depend, enumerate, estimate, evaluate, expect, explain, figure, foot, guess, impute, include, intend, judge, name, number, numerate, opine, pretend, racken, rate, recite, recount, regard, rely, repute, ret(te), settle, specify, sum, suppose, tally, tell, think, total, tote, tottle, trust

with anticipate, consider, contend with, deal with, remember, settle

RECKONING account, bill, calculation, check, compot, count(ing), date, enumeration, esteem, estimation, fee, numeration, payment, penalty, result, reward, score, scot, settlement, shot, tab, tale, tally, verdict

machine abacus, adder, brain, calculator, computer, ibm, tabulator

RECLAIM amend, check, correct, deliver, domesticate, embolden, gainsay, object, protest, ransom, recall, recover, rectify, redeem, reform, regain, regenerate, remedy, renew, renovate, repair, rescue, restore, restrain, retrieve, revoke, salvage, save, tame, train

RECLINE accumb, couch, incline, lean, lie, loll, lounge, repose, rest, sprawl, straddle

RECLINING abed, accumbent, bending, couchant, curving, dormant, leaning, prone, prostrate, recumbent, relaxing, reposing, resting, supine

RECLUSE anchoret, anchorite, ascetic, cenobite, cloistered, cloisterer, convent, eremite, eremitic, hermit(age), hidden, hierony-

mite, inclusa, inclusus, marabout, monk, nun, pillarist, santon, seclude(d), secret, sequestered, shut-in, solitaire, solitary, stay-at-home, stylite, umbratile

RECOGNITION acceptance, acknowledgment, anagnorisis, appreciation, award, cognizance, discernment, glory, identification, perception, place in the sun, realization, sensibility

RECOGNIZABLE clear, evident, manifest, patent

RECOGNIZANCE avowal, badge, bond, contract, obligation, pledge, profession, rank, symbol, token

RECOGNIZE accept, accredit, acknowledge, admit, agnize, apprehend, beknow, comprehend, correct, crown, detect, discover, distinguish, greet, identify, keeth, ken, kithe, know, nail, note, notice, observe, own, peg, realize, recall, remark, review, revise, salute, see, spot, tell, understand

RECOIL back(lash), balk, blench, boomerang, bounce (back), contrecoup, defy, demur, dodge, falter, flinch, funk, hesitate, kick, quail, react(ion), rebound, rebuff, recalcitrate, rejounce, repercuss(ion), repulse, resile, resilience, retract, retreat, reverse, revert, ricochet, scruple, shrink, shuck, shudder, shy, spring(back), stick(le), stram, wince, withdraw

RECOLLECT bethink, mind, recall, record, recover, remember, remind, reminisce, retain, think

RECOLLECTION anamnesis, concentration, meditation, memoir, memorial, memory, mind, rally, recall, recovery, remembrance, reminiscence, souvenir

RECOMMENCE begin again, continue, renew, reopen, reprise, resume

RECOMMEND acclaim, advise, advocate, applaud, approve, condone, consign, counsel, endorse, entrust, exhort, extol, introduce, praise, sanction, suggest, tout, urge

RECOMMENDATION ad-

vocacy, advocation, approval, certificate, character, chit, credential, reference, testimonial, tribute, voucher

RECOMPENSE amende, amends, atone(ment), award, balance, compensate, compensation, eric, expiate, expiation, guerdon, income, indemnify, meed, mense, offset, pay(ment), recoup, recovery, redeem, redemption, redress, reimburse, remunerate, reparation, repay, requite, retrieval, return, revenge, reward, satisfaction, satisfy, square, wage

without free, gratis

RECONCILE absolve, accept, accommodate, accord, adapt, adjust, agree, amend, appease, atone, attune, balance, compose, conciliate, conform, correct, gree, harmonize, mend, pacify, patch, placate, propitiate, rectify, restore, reunite, revise, satisfy, settle, shrive, square, wean

RECONCILED fain, resigned, saught, submissive, vain

RECONCILIATION accommodation, accord, atonement, harmony, irenicon, repair, reunion

RECONDITE abstract, abstruse, academic, cabalistic, concealed, cryptic, dark, deep, erudite, esoteric, hidden, learned, mysterious, mystical, obscure, occult, pedantic, polymathic, profound, scholarly, scholastic, secret

RECONDITION furbish, reform, refurbish, rehabilitate, renovate, repair, restore

RECONNAISSANCE espial, espionage, examination, intelligence, observation, recce, recco, reccy, recognition, recon(noiter), scouting, search, survey

unit pony-patrol

RECONNOITER discover, examine, explore, inquire, inspect, observe, pickeer, recall, recognize, remember, scan, scout, spy, survey, tout

RECONSIDER forthink, rethink, review

RECONSTRUCT rebuild, recast, reconstitute, recreate, remodel, reorganize, repair

RECORD 3 act, cut, log, tab 4 acta, book, date, disc, disk, dope, file, list, memo, note, poll, post, roll, sing, tape 5 actum, album, annal, chart, diary, enter, entry, fasti, graph, hadit, learn, quipo, quipu, relic, score, sijil, trace, write 6 agenda, annals, attest, docket, enroll, insert, ledger, legend, memoir, memory, minute, notate, ponder, recite, report, repute, ring up, scroll 7 account, almanac, blotter, calends, catalog, declare, dossier, estreat, hansard, history, jot down, journal, kalends, lexicon, mediate, mention, minutes, narrate, platter, reflect, rotulet, set down, tickler, vestige, witness 8 annotate, archives, calendar, cashbook, cassette, document, evidence, inscribe, inscroll, memorial, monument, muniment, notebook, register, registry, remember, schedule, tabulate, yearbook 9 catalogue, chronicle, recollect, scrapbook, testimony 10 enrollment, memorandum, reputation, surpassing, transcript 11 matriculate 13 transcription

court eyre

envelope sleeve

holder binder, cabinet, file

keeper recorder, registrar

official actum

personal diary

phonograph disc, disk, platter, single

police blotter

public archives

ship's log

RECORDER accountant, biographer, c(h)artulary, fipple-flute, flaute, flute, galoubet, greffier, judge, magistrate, notator, register, registrar, witness

RECORDING album, disc, label, memory, platter, recollection, tape, wire

instrument anemograph, auxograph, barograph, dic-tagraph, dictaphone, ergograph, gramophone, log, melograph, myograph, oscillograph, pari-mutuel, phonograph, pluviograph, radiograph, register, scoreboard, seismograph, seismometer, seismoscope, tape recorder, telegraphone, teletype, telltale, thermograph, ticker, time clock, totalizator, turnstile, votograph

RECOUNT calculate, deem, describe, detail, enumerate, itemize, narrate, number, particularize, recite, rehearse, relate, repeat, report, specify, spread, state, tell

RECOUP balance, compensate, deduct, indemnify, offset, recompense, recover, recruit, redeem, refund, regain, reimburse, remunerate, restore, retrieve

RECOURSE access, admittance, asylum, flow, gathering, recur, refuge, rescue, resort, resource, restaur, return, revert, stand-by, subterfuge, tide, use

have appeal, avail, betake, move, react, refer

RECOVER bounce back, come back, compensate, convalesce, cour, cowr, cure, get well, heal, mend, offset, overcome, rally, recapture, reclaim, recruit, recuperate, redeem, reform, regain, repossess, rescue, restore, resume, retake, retop, retrieve, salve, survive, upset

health convalesce, recuperate

possession replevin, replevy

RECOVERY anastasis, comeback, convalescence, cure, ransom, recapture, reclamation, recoup, recuperation, redemption, reformation, remedy, replevin, replevy, repossession, restoration, resumption, retake, retrieval, return, salvage, snapback, trover

of possession replevin, replevy

sudden snapback

RECREANT abject, apostate, backslider, base, betrayer, coward(ly), craven, dastard(ly), deserter, disloyal, faithless, false, ignoble, knave, knavish, pervert, poltroon, pusilanimous, renegade, reprobate, subdued, submissive, tame, timid, timorous, traitor (ous), treacherous, turncoat, unfaithful, untrue, wretch, yellow, yielding

RECREATE amuse, animate, divert, enliven, entertain, quicken, refresh, rejuvenate, renew, restore

RECREATION activity, amusement, diversion, divertisement, ease, entertainment, frolic, pastime, play, pleasure, rebirth, refreshment, regeneration, relaxation, repose, sport

time break, holiday, recess, vacation, weekend

RECREMENT dregs, dross, refuse, remainder, saliva, scoria, scum, secretion, slag, spume

RECRIMINATE accuse, backslang, countercharge, retort

RECRUDESCENCE reappearance, recurrence, relapse, renewal, restoration, return, reversion, revival

RECRUIT add, assemble, bezonian, bleu, boot, buck private, conscript, draft(ee), enlist, enroll(ment), fresh, gather, induct, jawan, learner, levy, mobilize, muster, novice, provide, raise, rally, recoup, recover, recuperate, refresh, regain, reinforce, renew, repair, replenish, restore, revive, rookie, rooky, sailor, soldier, supply, train (ee), tyro

RECTANGLE box, huipil, oblong, parallelogram, quadrangle, square, tessera

RECTIFY adjust, align, ameliorate, amend, better, clarify, correct, cure, distill, emend(ate), fix, help, improve, justify, mend, purify, rebuild, redress, refine, reform, regulate, remedy, repair, restore, revise, right, salvage, straighten

RECTITUDE correctness, goodness, honesty, honor, integrity, justice, morality, nobility, probity, righteousness, straightness, uprightness, virtue

RECTOR chief, clergyman,

ecclesiastic, head(master), leader, proproctor, ruler *assistant* curate

RECTORY benefice, manse, parsonage

RECUMBENT couchant, couche, cubatory, dormant, idle, inactive, leaning, lolling, lying, prone, prostrate, reclining, reposing, resting, sprawling, supine

RECUPERATE convalesce, cure, get better, get well, heal, improve, mend, perk up, pick up, rally, recoup, recover, recruit, redeem, reimburse, rest(ore), resuscitate, retrieve

RECUPERATION convalescence, lysis, recovery, rest(oration)

RECUR advert, alternate, come again, come back, cure, cycle, heal, intermit, iterate, reappear, recede, recover(y), recrudesce, refer, remedy, repair, repeat, resort, restore, retrieve, return, revert, revolve, rotate

RECURRENCE atavism, iterance, repeat, reprise

RECURRENT, RECURRING alternate, common, continual, cyclic, fitful, frequent, intermittent, mnemic, oftentime, ordinary, periodic, persymmetric, prevalent, regular, repeated, returning, reverting, rhythmic, spasmodic, usual

RECURVIROSTRA avocet, avoset, stilt

RECUSANT apostate, dissenter, dissentient, nonconformist

RED archil, aubusson, azalea, begonia, bismarck, bloodshot, bloody, blushing, bokhara, bolshevik, bordeaux, bukhara, burgundy, canna, cardinal, carmine, carnation, catawba, cerise, cherry, chestnut, choleric, color(ado), communist, coral, crimson, eric, erubescent, flushed, fulgid, garnet, goya, gules, hebe, indian, inflamed, lake, lurid, magenta, mandarin, morocain, murray, nacarat, orchil, pim(i)ento, pink(o), pompeii, puce, puniceous, radical, revolutionist, rojo, rosso, rosy, rouge, rozet, rubelle,

rubescent, rubicund, rubious, rubric, ruby, ruddy, rufescent, ruf(o)us, sanguine, scarlet, stammel, titian, tomato, toreador, tuly, vermilion, vivid, wine

adder copperhead,

admiral atalanta, butterfly, pyrameis, vanessa

antique canna

as blood, rose

astrachan apple

-backed mouse bank-vole, evotomys

-backed sandpiper dunlin

-backed shrike pope

baneberry redberry, toadroot

bay persea

bead vine licorice

bean pencil-cedar

beard barbarossa, sponge

bell columbine

-bellied snipe dowitcher

bellied terrapin skilpot, slider

bellied woodpecker chab

belly char, grouper, terrapin

benjamin birthroot

-bill oyster-catcher, waxbill, whiday

bird bullfinch, cardinal, tanager

blindness protanopia

-blooded courageous, vigorous, viril, vital

blotch adustiosis

-blue amaranth, anemone, ardoise, burgundy, claret, gridelin, heliotrope, lilac, magenta, mauve(tte), purple, raisin, solferino

-box bureaucratic, eucalyptus, official

brazil roset

-breast bream, dowitcher, knot, robin, ruddock, sandpiper, sunfish

-breasted bream flatfish, flounder

-breasted knot grayback, greyback

-breasted plover knot, sandpiper

-breasted snipe brownback, dowitcher

bright cerise, cherry, crimson, ponceau, scarlet, tuly, vermilion

-brown auburn, bay, cappa(g)h, crotal, rubiginus, rufous, russet, sepia, sienna, sorrel, terracotta, umber

-brush cornel, osier

-buck impala

campion robin, soldier

castilian cochineal

cedar juniper, sabina, savin

cent bit, copper, trifle

clover sapling, trefoil, trifoly

coloring anchusin, carthame, carthamin

comb. erythro, rhod, rufi

commander atalanta, butterfly

cross founder barton, dunant

cross knight george

cross knight's wife una

currant goya, rizzle, tizzar

dark burgundy, claret

deep carmine, murrey, ruby

deer hart, hind, olen, stag

dog banker and broker, banknote, high-card pool, slippery-sam

drum redfish, spot

dull rufous, tawny

dye aal, alkanet, an(n)atto, annoto, arnatto, aurin(e), bordeaux, brazil(ein), chay, choy, eosin, lac, morindin, orcein, orseilline, puccoon, rubin(e), scarlet

dyewood barwood, camwood

eureka puce

-eyed vireo grasset, preacher

-faced blowzed, blushing, crimson, embarrassed, florid, flushed, flushing, glowing, rosy, rubescent, rubicund, ruddy, scarlet

fear of erythrophobia

fever erysipelas

fiery minium

flag provocation, stop, warning

-foot booby(bird)

glowing rutilant

goosefoot pigweed, sowbane

-green blindness daltonism

greyish azalea, phenicious

grouper mero, negre, redbelly

grouse gorcock, gorhen, lagopode, moorbird, muirfowl

gum eucalyptus, jarrah, liquidambar, strophulus

gurnard cur, elleck, rochet, soldier

-haired auburn, carroty, chestnut, sandy, titian

haired, name meaning rufus

-handed flagrante delicto, guilty

-hat cardinal

heraldic gules

herring artifice, capon, diversion

hind cabrilla, graysby, grouper

horse sucker

-hot ardent, burning, eager, excited, fiery, frankfurter, furious, new, passionate, ready, torrid, violent

ink plonk, wine

in the bankrupt(ed), broke, flat, out

iron oxide agate, tarragona

kauri berairou

-knees smartweed

lane esophagus, throat

laver sloke

-letter important, indelible, memorable, unforgettable

letter day holiday

light carnation, carnelian, coral, peach, pink, rose, salmon

-light district tenderloin, yashiwara

man indian

marked with rubric(ate)

medium adrianople, levant, turkey

morocco pheasant's eye

-mouth fish, grunt

ocher abraum, raddle, ruddle, tiver

-orange henna

osier cornel, redbrush, willow

-pencil abridge, censor, correct, delete

pepper capsicum, cayenne, chile, chil(l)i

pigment actiniochrome, arumin, astacene, astacin, roset, sandix

planet mars

powder abir, alkannin

purplish burgundy, claret, dahlia, fuschia, hyacinth, lake, lilac, magenta, mallow, murex, puniceous

rag provocation, tongue

raspberry cuthbert

river republican riel

river tributary ouachiat

rockfish tambor

-root alkanet, amaranth, bloodwort, gromwell, indian-paint, pigweed, potentilla, puccoon, sanguinaria, tellerwort, tormentil, turmeric

rot rust

sage lantana

sandalwood chandam

sea erythra, erythrean, thalassa

sea fish angler, badia, crocodilefish, fridmani, lionfish, nudicranch, scorpionfish, seeing-eye-fish, stonefish, triggerfish

sea gulf aqaba, suez

sea island perim

sea peninsula sinai

sea port suakin

sea principality asir

sea script preserver essene

sea stingray sephen

shirt anarchist, camicia rossa, reserve, revolutionary, revolutionist, substitute

snapper cachucho, etelis, fish, huachinango

square feature kremlin, lenin's tomb

stopper eugenia, ironwood

-tailed phoenicurous

-tailed bird koae

tape bureaucracy, delay, fabianism, inaction, routine

tapism beadledom

tapist bureaucrat, official

-throated loon wabby

-tinged flammulated, rufescent, rufous

titi leatherwood

-top agrostis, bluejoint, bonnetgrass, couch, finebent, finetop, fiorin, furzetop

turkey adrianople

tuscan mascara

venetian siena, sierra

vermilion vermeil

vitriol bieberite, botryogen, colcothar

wax copper

white and blue flag, stars and stripes, union jack

-yellow agate, alabaster, alesan, alomba, amber, argentina, ascot, auburn, beaver, bisk, bismark, bisque, brazil, burnt sienna, burnt umber, cafe au lait, caramel, carrot, castor, chestnut, coconut, corn, cranberry, doubloon, gypsy, kermanshah, lama, marathon, maroon, mirador, nutria, ochre, orange, peachblow, saffron, sandstone, saravan, sudan, tangier, tenne, titian, white jade

REDACT amend, draft, edit, frame, pen, reduce, revise

REDAN breastwork, fort(ification), fortress, rampart

REDBUD cercis, judastree, junebud

REDCAP bonnet rouge, extremist, goldfinch, policeman, porter, radical, spectre, tarboosh, trainman

REDCOAT bloody-back, britisher, soldier

REDD clean, clear, counsel, deliver, end, extinguish, free, litter, nest, rebuke, refuse, rescue, rid, scold, separate, settle, spawn, tidy, unravel

REDDEN blush, burn, color, crimson, flush, glow, incarnadine, light, mangle, rubric(ate), ruddle

REDE advice, advise, agree, aid, clear, control, council, counsel, decide, decree, explain, govern, guard, guess, guide, hap, imagine, interpret(ation), judgment, lot, narrate, occurrence, plan, predict, protect, proverb, reason, relate, remedy, saw, saying, scheme, speech, stomach, story, tale

REDEEM atone, buy, compensate, convert, deliver, free, fulfill, liberate, offset, ransom, reclaim, recoup, recover, recuperate, reform, regain, regenerate, reinstate, release, replevin, replevy, repurchase, rescue, restore, retake, retrieve, salvage, salve, save, settle, substitute

REDEEMER deliverer, emancipator, goel, liberator, manumitter, messiah, redemptor, rescuer, savio(u)r

REDEMPTION adoption, atonement, conversion, deliverance, ransom, rebirth, recompense, recovery, reformation, regeneration, release, repurchase, rescue, restoration, salvation

REDEYE bass, catsup, cicada, copperhead, fish, rockbass, rudd, sunfish, vireo, whiskey

REDFIN dace, redhorse, shiner, yellowfin

REDFISH drum, fathead, grouper, ocean-perch, rockfish, rosefish, salmon, sheephead

REDHEAD bloodflower, carrot-top, diver, duck, finch,

kizilbash, pochard, woodpecker

REDHEADED *lizard* blue-tailed skink, scorpion

REDINTEGRATE reconcile, reestablish, renew, restore, reunite

REDNESS erubescence, glow, heat, rubedinous, rubedity

REDOLENCE aroma, balm, bouquet, fragrance, odor, perfume, scent, smell, sweetness

REDOLENT aromatic, balmy, fragrant, imbued, impregnated, odoriferous, odorous, recollective, remindful, reminiscent, rich, scented, smelling, spicy, suggestive, sweet

REDOUBLE echo, increase, ingeminate, reduplicate, re-echo, reflect, reiterate, repeat, reprise, reproduce, resound, retrace

REDOUBT fort(ification), schanz, sconce

REDOUBTABLE awful, brave, doughty, dread(ful), fearful, fearsome, formidable, frightful, intrepid, obstinate, strong, terrible, valiant

REDOUND abound, accrue, advance, conduce, flow, issue, overflow, proceed, recoil, reflect, render, resound, result, return, reverberate, rise, roll back

REDPOLL bird, finch, linnet, warbler

REDRESS allay, alleviate, amend(s), assuage, atone (ment), compensation, correct, heal, help, improvement, indemnity, rectify, reform, relief, relieve, remedy, repair, reparation, restitution, restoration, retribution, revenge, satisfaction, vengeance

REDSHANK bird, cardinal, clee, duck, fieldfare, gambet, pellile, persicary, poolsnipe, redleg, sandpiper, shake, tattler, teuk, yelper

REDSKIN indian, rojo, tawny

REDSTART brantail, fireflirt, firetail, thrush, warbler, whitecap, yelper

REDUCE 3 cut, dim 4 beat, buff, bust, diet, pare, raze, reef, rend, rout, slim, slow, thin 5 abase, abate, adapt, allay, annul, break, level, lower, slash, smelt 6 appall, debase, deduct, defeat, demote, depose, derate, dilute, humble, impair, lessen, rebate, recall, refine, settle, shrink, subdue, temper, weaken 7 abridge, afflict, analyse, analyze, assuage, cashier, conquer, cripple, curtail, cutback, cutdown, degrade, depress, deprive, destroy, disable, dwindle, rescind, restore, shorten 8 compress, condense, contract, decrease, diminish, discount, mark down, minimize, moderate, overcome, pull down, retrench, vanquish 9 breakdown, bring down, deoxidize, overpower, overthrow, subjugate, undermine 10 abbreviate, depreciate, impoverish, slenderize 11 fletcherize

purity adulterate, alloy, doctor, water

sail reef

speed slow, throttle

tension blow off, relax, unwind

to ashes burn, raze, sack

to half dimidiate

to nothing annul, void

to powder calcine, crush, grind, pulverize

REDUCED broken, degraded, dwarfed, imperfect, infirm, poor, sunk, vestigial, weakened

REDUCTIO AD ABSURDUM apagoge, argument, disproof, logic, proof, rebuttle, refutation, result

REDUCTION abridgment, analysis, contraction, copy, cut(back), decrease, discount, dockage, emaciation, meiosis, rebate, relief, shaving, shrinkage, slash, weakening

in cost concession, discount, saving

REDUNCA antelope, bohor, cervi, nagor, reedbuck, reitbok

REDUNDANCY battology, bombast, circumlocution, diffuseness, dilogy, dingdong, excess, harping, macrology, monotony, nimiety, padding, periphrasis, pleonasm, plethora, prolixity, repetition, superfluity, tautology, tautophony, tedium, turgidity, verbiage, verbosity, wordiness

REDUNDANT abundant, diffuse, excessive, expletive, extra, exuberant, otiose, pleonastic, plethoric, prolix, repetitive, superabundant, superfluous, surplus, tautological, useless, verbose, wordy

REDWING blackbird, francolin, gadwall, pop, swinepipe, thrush, windle, winnard

REDWOOD bastard-tree, buckthorn, cedar, dyewood, mahogany, rohan, sandalwood, santalin, sequoia, snakebark

REE arikara, bird, channel, crazy, dam, drunk, enclosure, fuddled, harbor, reeve, riddle, right, river, ruff, sandpiper, sheepcote, sheepfold, sift, wild

REECHY fetid, rancid, reeky

REED arrow, arundinaria, arundo, bennel, bulrush, calamus, cattail, culm, dart, dent, donax, fistula, grass, junk, molding, otate, phragmite, pipe, pirn, raddle, rix, rood, rush, sag(gon), sley, spear, stalk, stem, stomach, thatch, tube, tule, twill, whistle, winding

-bearing arundiferous

bent carrizo

-bird bobolink, warbler

buck antelope, bohor, koba, nagor, redunca, reedbuck, reitbok, waterbuck

bunting black bonnet, ring-bird

canary grass daggert, spire

carriers cannophori

comb. calam(i)(o)

ditch bennel

end tongue

foxtail dod

giant donax

grass arundo, carrizo

instrument See MUSICAL INSTRUMENT *reed.*

-like arundinaceous, arundineous

mace cattail, clubgrass, cooper's-flag, flaxtail, matreed, raupo

organ harmonium, melodeon
pen calamus
pipe mirliton
warbler pitbird
REEDLING titmouse
REEDY arundinaceous, long, shrill, skinny, slender, small, soft, splindly, think, weak
REEF atoll, balance, bank, bar, bioherm, boiler, cay(o), eruption, furl, island, itch, kay, key, ledge, lode, makatea, mange, ridge, ryft, saddle, sandbar, shelf, shoal, shorten, skerry, slow, spit, stick, swift, tombolo, vein
builder coral
sail furl, shorten
REEFER cigarette, coat, eton, fumer, jacket, midshipman, miner, muggles, oyster, refrigerator, smoke
REEK cloud, emit, equip, exhalation, exhale, exude, fester, fog, fug, fume, haze, heap, mist, mountain, nidor, pile, reach, rig, seaweed, smeek, smell, smoke, steam, stench, stink, vapor(ize)
REEKY burning, fetid, olid, smelly
REEL bobbin, dance, dash, drum, eddy, falter, flounder, hammer, lurch, noise, oscillate, peal, pirn, pitch, rock, roll, scribe, scrieve, spin, spool, stagger, swabble, sway, swift, swim, swing, teeter, titubate, totter, turn, waggle, walter, waver, wheel, whirl, wince, winch, winder, wind(lass), wintle
back retreat
dyeing wince
fishing pirn, troll, trow, trull, winch
in pull back, retract, windlass
silk-drawing filature
warp-drying balloon
yarn crib, pirn, swift
REELING dizzy, giddy, intoxicated, lightheaded, staggering, swimming, wambling, whirling
REELRALL confusion, disturbance, topsy-turvy
REEM moan, unicorn, urus, wild ox
RE-ENLIST re-up

REESHIE beat, clatter, rustle
REEST bacon, balk, cure, moldboard, plowshare, rancid, smoke(house)
RE-ESTABLISH reinstate, replace, restore
REEVE agent, bailiff, enclosure, factor, fasten, official, overseer, pass, pen, pucker, ruff, sheepfold, steward, strip, superintendent, thread, twist, wind, wrinkle
REFECTORY dining hall, frater, fratry, table
REFEL discredit, disprove, refute, reject, repulse
REFER accredit, address, advert, allude, appeal, appertain, apply, arbitrate, ascribe, assign, associate, attribute, belong, charge, cite, commit, concern, connect, consign, consult, credit, designate, direct, harp, impute, introduce, mention, pertain, point, quote, recur, regard, relate, resort, send, turn
REFEREE arbiter, arbitrator, auditor, brehon, decide, go-between, judge, mediator, moderator, ump(ire)
decision nod, out, safe, score
REFERENCE allusion, appeal, approval, attribution, bearing, book, certificate, citation, concern, connection, consideration, direction, endorsement, note, pertinence, quote, recommendation, regard, relation(ship), relevance, renvoi, respect, sign, tribute
book almanac, atlas, bibliography, calepin, catalogue, concordance, cyclopedia, dictionary, directory, encyclopedia, gazetteer, handbook, index, lexicon, syllabus
mark See MARK *printing.*
point bench mark, stylion
ready promptuary
REFERENDUM ballot, initiative, mandate, plebescite, vote
REFINE bolt, chasten, chastise, clarify, clean(se), clear, concoct, cultivate, cupel, decoct, decrassify, depurate, develop, distill, elaborate, elevate, elutriate, exalt, filter, filtrate, finish, improve, leach, lixiviate,

perculate, perfect, polish, purify, rarefy, rectify, riddle, screen, separate, sharpen, sieve, sift, slick, smelt, spiritualize, strain, sublimate, sublime, subtilize, test
REFINED aesthetic, attic, chaste, civil(ized), clarified, courteous, courtly, cultivated, cultured, delicate, discriminate, distilled, elegant, exact, exquisite, fastidious, genteel, gentlemanly, graceful, highbred, ladylike, meticulous, nice, niminy, perfected, polished, polite, precise, purified, quaint, rare, spirituous, subtle, tasteful, terse, urbane, well-bred
REFINEMENT breeding, civility, courtesy, cultivation, culture, delicacy, depuration, dignity, discrimination, distillation, elegance, finesse, finish, gentility, grace, judgment, polish, politeness, purification, quality, style, suavity, subtlety, taste, urbanity
lacking boorish, crass, crude, rude, wild and wooly
REFINER alembic, colander, colatorium, cradle, cribble, purifier, rocker, sieve
REFLECT attend, bethink, cogitate, consider, contemplate, copy, debate, deflect, deliberate, direct, discredit, divert, echo, glance, imitate, look, manifest, mediate, mirror, muse, ponder, pore, reason, redound, refract, remark, return, reverse, revert, revolve, ruminate, shimmer, shine, simulate, slur, speculate, study, think, turn(back), weigh
REFLECTION afterthought, anacampsis, animadversion, ascription, aspersion, assault, attack, bend, blame, blink, censure, cogitation, concentration, connection, consideration, contemplation, counterpart, criticism, deliberation, derogation, disparagement, echo, eyeshine, glare, idea, image, imputation, iridescence, likeness, mediation, musing, relation, reproach. return, reverberation, rumination, shadow,

simulacrum, slur, snow-blink, statement, stricture, study, thinking, thought
measurer albedograph
pert. catadioptric
REFLECTIVE analytical, logical, meditative, pensive, speculative, subtle, thoughtful
REFLECTOR abatjour, critic, looking glass, mirror, skylight, speculum
REFLEX bend, copy, curve, fold, image, introspection, involuntary, reaction, RE-FLECTION, reversed, spontaneous, tropism, turn
measurer anacamptometer
REFLUX ebb(ing), euripus, flow, refluence, return(ing)
REFORM amelioration, amend, better(ment), censure, change, convert, correct(ion), direct, disband, emend, help, improve, instruct, make over, mend, modify, prune, punish, rebuild, rebuke, recast, reclaim, recondition, rectify, redeem, redress, reduce, re-educate, refashion, regenerate, regeneration, rehabilitate, remedy, remodel, renew, repair, repatriate, repent, reprove, reshape, restore, revise, trim
REFORMATION betterment, correction, improvement, redemption, regeneration, repentance, resipiscence
leader calvin, luther
REFORMATORY See JAIL.
REFORMER amender, apostle, do-gooder, luther, progressive, reviser, utopian, utopiast
unpractical utopian
REFRACT break down, deflect, divide, impair, reflect, refringe
REFRACTION deflection, diaclasis, distortion, rebate, rebound
device lens, prism, telescope
pert. anaclastic, dioptric
REFRACTORY abrasive, adamant(ine), alundum, balky, breachy, camsteary, camstery, cantankerous, contrary, contumacious, defiant, disobedient, fractious, froward, headstrong, immune, incorrigible, indocile, indomitable, intrac-

table, irrepressible, mulish, mutinous, obdurate, obstinate, obstreperous, ornery, perverse, rebellious, recalcitrant, reesty, restive, stubborn, sullen, ungovernable, unmanageable, unresponsive, unruly, unyielding, wayward, wild, willful
REFRAIN abstain, aria, avoid, bob(wheel), burden, cease, check, chorus, curb, derry, desist, epistrophe, epode, fala, falderal, forbear, forego, give up, govern, hold, inhibit, keep from, lilt, ludden, lullaby, nonny-nonny, pass, quit, repeat, repetend, response, restrain, ritornel(le), shun, song, spare, stop, tag, tornada, undersong, withhold, wonde
from avoid, forego, spare, waive
from use abjure, boycott, reject
part lala, tra(la)
REFRESH animate, bathe, brace(up), brisk(en), caudle, cheer, chirk up, comfort, cool, divert, drink, enliven, exhilerate, fan, fortify, invigorate, perk up, quicken, rally, reanimate, recover, recreate, refete, refurbish, regale, regenerate, rehete, rejuvenate, remind, renew, renovate, repair, rest, restore, retouch, revive, revivify, slake, stimulate, strengthen, vivify
REFRESHING balmy, cool(ing), dewy, exhilerating, fresh, heartening, stimulating, tonic
REFRESHMENT bait, collation, drink, elevens, food, healing, lunch, refresco, restoration
REFRIGERANT ammonia, antipyretic, carbon-dioxide, coolant, cooling, cryogen, dry-ice, febrifuge, freon, ice, liquid-air, refreshing
REFRIGERATE air-condition, chill, cool, freeze, freshen, ice, infrigidate, preserve, refresh, ventilate
REFRIGERATION chilling, congealment, congelation, cooling, cryogeny, freezing, glaciation
science cryogenics

REFRIGERATOR condenser, cooler, deep-freeze, freezer, fridge, frigidaire, icebox, reefer
REFT bereaved, cleft, divested, divided
REFUGE abri, adullum, ark, asylum, bield, bilbie, burrow, cache, closet, corner, cove, cover, covert(ure), crannog(e), crypt, cubby (hole), den, doorn, dugout, fort(ress), funkhole, harbor, haven, hide-away, hidiehole, hidlin(g), hole, home, hospital, lair, pillbox, plea, port, preserve, pretext, protect(ion), recess, recourse, reset, resort, resource, retreat, rock, safehold, safety, sanctuary, sanctum, security, shed, shelter, spital, stash, stronghold, subterfuge, umbrage, vault
REFUGEE cowboy, deserter, emigre(e), escapee, exile, fugitive, fuidhir, maroon, mosstrooper, runaway
REFULGENCE brightness, brilliance, radiance, splendor
REFULGENT beamy, bright, brilliant, glistening, glowing, lambent, lucent, luminous, lustrous, radiant, relucent, resplendent, shining, splendid
REFUND kickback, rebate, recoup(ment), reimburse(ment), repay(ment), restitute, restitution, restore, return
REFURBISH brighten, buff, dust, freshen, modernize, recondition, refresh, rehabilitate, renew, renovate, repair, restore, shine
REFUSAL bolt, declension, declination, denial, mitten, nay(say), rejection, repulse, thumbsdown, vee
affected accismus
REFUSE 3 cot, pob 4 balk, coom, culm, deny, dirt, dust, junk, kemp, lees, marc, nill, orts, pelf, pelt, raff, rags, scum, slag, smut, veto 5 ashes, bavin, bones, chaff, coomb, crawm, demur, draff, drast, dregs, drest, dross, expel, griff, hurds, renig, repel, scobs, scorn, scrap, scree, scurf, shard, slops, sprue, spurn,

stent, straw, stump, swill, tares, trash, waste, weeds 6 baffle, colder, debris, embers, garble, litter, lumber, naysay, negate, recuse, reject, renege, revoke, rubble, scoria, scruff, sculch, shoddy, shrink, sinter, triage 7 abandon, bagasse, brockle, cinders, decline, disavow, filings, garbage, grounds, gubbins, hogwash, hold out, offscum, parings, relicts, remains, residue, rubbish, stubble, sullage, surplus, useless, wastage 8 abnegate, alluvium, clinkers, deadwood, denegate, detritus, diluvium, disallow, leavings, nonsense, oddments, raspings, renounce, riffraff, rinsings, shavings, withhold 9 colluvies, effluvium, leftovers, mundungus, repudiate, scourings, settlings, sweepings, worthless 10 wastements 11 odds and ends

craft scow

fish chum, gubbins

food garbage, swill

metal dross, scoria, slag

mine tailings

pert. colluvial

pile basurale, cesspit, cesspool, dump, midden

threshing colder, husk

whale gurry

REFUTATION argument, defense, denial, disproof, elenchus, hypobole

REFUTE answer, avoid, confound, confute, contradict, contravene, controvert, convince, crush, defeat, deny, discredit, dismiss, dispose of, disprove, dispute, explode, finish, floor, gainsay, impugn, infringe, negate, negative, oppose, overthrow, parry, rebut, redargue, reject, reprove, retund, settle, squash, squelch, subvert, traverse, upset

serving to elenctic(al)

REGAIN get back, recoup, recover, recruit, redeem, renew, restore, retrieve

REGAL august, channel, dignified, grand, groove, imperial, imposing, kingly, majestic, noble, princely, queenly, resplendent, rigole,

royal, sovereign, splendid, stately, sublime

name meaning erica

REGALE amuse, arride, delight, dine, divert, eat, entertain, feast, feed, fete, gladden, gratify, please, refresh, rejoice, repast, satisfy, tickle, treat

REGALIA badges, cigar, costume, crown, decorations, dress, emblem, ensigns, finery, insignia, paraphernalia, rights, rod, royalty, sceptor, sovereignty, symbol

REGAN *husband* cornwall

father king lear

sister cordelia, goneril

REGARD account, admire, adore, affection, appear, appraise, appreciate, approbation, aspect, attachment, attend, attention, attitude, attribute, behold, call, care, cherish, concern, consider(ation), contemplate, count, deem, deliberate, esteem, estimation, eye, face, favor, gaze, glance, heed, hold, homage, honor, interest, judge, keep, look, love, mark, mind, note, notice, obey, observation, observe, ogle, outlook, particular, pertain, prefer, prize, prospect, rate, reckon, relation, remark, repute, respect, revere(nce), scan, see(m), survey, think, thoughtfulness, touch, treasure, treat, value, veneration, view, worship, worth

highly admire, revere, venerate, worship

REGARDFUL attentive, careful, considerate, courteous, heedful, mindful, observant, thoughtful

REGARDING about, anent, apropos, as to, concerning, in re, respecting

REGARDLESS careless, deaf, heedless, in any case, inattentive, indifferent, neglectful, negligent, nevertheless, notwithstanding, unconcerned, unmindful

REGARDS best wishes, compliments, devoirs, greetings, love, remembrance, respects

REGATTA contest, fabric, liberty, race

town cowes, henley, poughkeepsie

REGEM *parent* jahdai

REGENCY dominion, government, office, rule

REGENERATE convert(ed), devout, holy, newborn, reanimate, reclaim, reconstitute, recreate(d), redeem(ed), reform(ed), refresh, rejuvenate, renovate(d), revive(d), revivify, save(d)

REGENERATION amendment, change of heart, conversion, conviction, rebirth, reclamation, recreation, redemption, reform(ation), regrowth, reproduction, restoration, revival

REGENERATOR s(h)iva

REGENT deputy, director, governor, headmaster, kubera, kuvera, master, minister, officer, official, protector, ruler, superintendent, teacher, vicar, viceroy

bird bird of paradise, bowerbird

diamond pitt

of the sun uriel

REGIME administration, dynasty, government, incumbency, period, reign, rule, tenure

REGIMEN administration, class, control, course, cure, diet, drill, government, hygiene, kind, regulation, remedy, rule, system, treatment

REGIMENT alai, company, control, cossack, discipline, governance, guidance, infantry, management, order, ordinance, organize, polk, pulk, pulton, pultun, reign, rule(rship), tercio, unit

cossack pulk

flag colors

member grenadier

nucleus cadre

officer boots, colonel

part battalion, company, squadron

REGINA See QUEEN.

REGIN(N) *brother* fafnir

slayer sigurd

ward siegfried, sigurd

REGION area, bailiwick, beat, belt, climate, clime, country, demesne, department, district, division, domain, enclave, erd, field,

frontier, ground, heavens, kingdom, land, locale, locality, location, neighborhood, part, place, plage, portion, province, purlieu, quarter, realm, scene, section, sector, segment, shire, site, sky, space, sphere, spot, terrain, territory, tract, vicinity, zone
celestial langi, shangri-la
comb. nesia, ric
cultivated garden
description periegesis
desolate hamada, puna, waste
enclosed enclave
infernal See HELL.
limestone karst
nearctic anglogaea
pert. areal, local, provincial
physical characteristics fundament
remote strand, thule
undisturbed kratogen
upper ether, heaven
warm tropics
wooded montana, taiga
woodless desert, highmoor, llano, meadow, pasture, plain, savanna(h), steppe, weald, wold
REGIONAL insular, local, parochial, provincial, sectional, territorial, topographic(al), zonal
REGISTER adjust, annals, archive(s), book, calendar, calends, canon, catalog(ue), chronicle, compass, correspond, demonstrate, docket, enrol(l), enter, entry, enumeration, evince, greffier, impress, index, inscribe, inventory, kalends, ledger, list, log, matriculate, muster, pedigree, penetrate, poll, punch, range, record, represent, ring up, roll, roster, rota, rotulet, schedule, scroll, show, sign up, subscribe, table, tally, telltale, thermometer, vent
cash damper
death necrology
family genealogy
historic rotulet
legal agenda, docket
official cadaster
social almanach de gotha, bluebook
REGISTRAR accountant, actuary, clerk, guard, pat-

wari, putwari, recorder, secretary
REGISTRATION booking, cataloguing, census, enrol(l)ment, entry, insertion, list(ing), matriculation, recording, tabulation
REGLE govern(ing), groove, regulation, rule
REGNANT dominant, influential, predominant, prevalent, regent, reigning, ruling, widespread
REGORGE gush, rush(back), swallow, vomit
REGRATE buy, lament, monopolize, offend, regret, retail, sell, sorrow
REGRATER huckster
REGRESS backslide, recourse, re-entry, relapse, retrograde, retrogress(ion), return, revert, withdrawal
REGRESSION fixation, reentry, relapse, return, reversion, setback, withdrawal
REGRESSIVE backward, retroactive
REGRET anguish, apologize, apology, arue, aversion, bemoan, bethink, bewail, complain, compunction, contrition, demur, deplore, disappointment, dislike, distress, dole, forthink, grief, grieve, heartache, lament(ation), misgivings, miss, mourn, ochone, penitence, qualm, remorse, repent(ance), repine, repining, rue, ruth, scruple, selfreproach, sorrow, spurn, woe
exclamation of och, pity, sorry, too bad, what a shame
REGRETFUL apologetic, bad, contrite, dirty, penitent, repentant, repining, rueful, sad, sorry
REGRETTABLE deplorable, lamentable, sad, terrible, unfortunate
REGULAR amiable, analytic, besetting, clockwork, common, complete, consistent, constant, conventional, customary, decorous, established, even, fixed, frequent, habitual, harmonious, isometric, legal, methodic(al), normal, ordered, orderly, ordinary, ordinate, periodic, persistent, plain,

punctilious, recurrent, recurring, repeated, repetitive, rhythmic, right, routine, seasonal, serial, set(tled), smooth, sober, soldier, standard, stated, steady, stock, suant, symmetrical, systematic, thorough, typical, uniform, usual, utter, well-trodden
REGULARITY method, sameness, smoothness, symmetry, system
lack acatastasia
REGULARLY constantly, correctly, daily, day by day, duly, even, hourly, lawfully, normally, officially, orderly, properly, recurrently, seasonally, statedly
REGULATE adjust, arrange, authorize, conduct, control, correct, determine, direct, discipline, dispose, establish, fix, frame, govern, guide, manage, master, measure, methodize, moderate, modulate, order, pace, raddle, rectify, remedy, rule, run, set, square, standardize, systematize, temper, time, true
REGULATION adjustment, administration, bylaw, canon, control, curfew, customary, direction, disposition, government, instruction, law, management, normal, order, ordinance, ordinary, precept, prescript(ion), principle, provision, regle, restriction, rule, statute, usual
REGULATOR control, governor, guide, rheometer, rheostat, thermostat, valve
REGULUS cast(ing), globule, kinglet, matte, metal, ruler, slurry, snake
REGURGITATE flow, gush, spew, throw up, vomit
REHABILITATE furbish, reable, recondition, reestablish, reform, refurbish, reinstall, renew, restore
REHASH paraphrase, recast, rechauffe, repeat, rephrase, restate, revamp, review, revise
REHEARSAL account, drill, dry run, hearsal, hersall, practice, preview, recital, repetition, training, tryout
REHEARSE calculate, cite,

coach, delineate, describe, detail, drill, enumerate, go over, instruct, itemize, iterate, mention, narrate, portray, practice, prepare, quote, recap(itulation), recite, recount, reiterate, relate, repeat, say, speak, state, tell, train

REHOBOAM, ROBOAM *father* solomon
son abia, abijah, attai, jeush, shelomith, shemariah, zaham, ziza
wife abihail, maacah, mahalath

REIF booty, loot, plunder, robbery

REIFY actualize, embody, materialize, objectify, realize

REIGN authority, control, dominate, dominion, dynasty, empire, flourish, govern(ment), incumbency, influence, kingdom, period, power, predominate, prevail, prevalence, raj, realm, regime, riche, rule, sovereignty, suzerainty, sway, tenure, term
of st swithin rain
of terror anarchy, despotism
pert. regnal, regnant, royal
year of anno regni

REIMBURSE compensate, indemnify, offset, pay, rebate, recompense, recoup, redress, refund, remunerate, repay, replace, requite, restore, satisfy

REIMKENNAR prophet, sage, sorcerer, sorceress

REIN bridle, check, command, control, curb, deterrent, direct, govern, guide, harness, haunch, hindrance, influence, kidney, leash, loin, repress, restrain(t), shackle, slow, stop, strap, thong, turn

REINCARNATION anabiosis, palingenesis, reanimation, rebirth, resuscitation, transmigration
principle buddhi, manas

REINDEER caribou, cervid, cervine, cervoid, rednosed, rengifer, rudolph, tarant
moss sward

REINFORCE add, augment, back, bolster, brace, double, guy, increase, provide, stay,

stiffen, strengthen, supply, support

REINSTATE establish, refresh, rehire, reinstall, replace, restore, revest, set

REIT seaweed, sedge

REITBOK antelope, bohor, nagor, redunca, reedbuck

REITERATE drum, echo, harp, ingeminate, recapitulate, rehash, rehearse, repeat, restate, resume

REJECT abandon, abhor, abjure, athetize, ban, blackball, bump, cashier, castaway, cast off, cull, debar, decline, delete, deny, desert, disallow, disapprove, disbelieve, discard, discharge, discount, discredit, disdain, dismiss, disobey, disown, eject, eliminate, evict, exclude, expel, forsake, forswear, jettison, jilt, ort, oust, pish, put by, rebuff, refuse, relegate, renounce, repel, reprobate, repudiate, repulse, respue, scorn, scout, scrap, second, shed, shut out, snub, spew, spurn, substandard, throw out, vomit, waive, wastements

REJECTAMENTA discard, refuse, rubbish, wrack

REJECTED banished, banned, castaway, dumped, exiled, offcast, outcast, spurned, superfluous, unloved

REJECTION brush, defiance, denial, mitten, objection, protest, rebuff, refusal, spurn

REJOICE arride, carol, cheer, chirrup, dance, delight, elate, enchant, enjoy, enrapture, exhilerate, exult, fain, frisk, gladden, glory, gratify, hauoli, joy, jubilate, laugh, lilt, please, regale, revel, rollick, sing, skip, smile, tickle, tripudiate
in have, own

REJOICING cheer, festivity, glee, jubilation, mirth
exclamation cheerio, glory be, hail, hallelujah, hoopee, hooray, hurrah, hurray, huzza, praise be, rah, ray, three cheers, whoopee, whoops, wow, wowee, yippes

REJOINDER answer, comeback, rebuttal, replication,

reply, reprisal, response, return, reversion

REJUVENATE freshen, redintegrate, refresh, refurbish, regenerate, reinvigorate, renew, restore, revive, unold

REKEM *son* shammai

RELAPSE apostasy, atavism, backslide, decline, degenerate, deteriorate, deterioration, fall, hypostrophe, lapse, recidivate, recidivation, recidivism, recrudescence, recurrence, regress (ion), repetition, return, reversion, revert, sink, slide, slip, subside, withdraw

RELATE account, allude, ally, appertain, apply, ascribe, assert, associate, attach, blend, combine, compare, concern, connect, correlate, delineate, depend, describe, detail, disclose, enumerate, integrate, involve, join, link, narrate, pertain, recite, recount, refer, rehearse, repeat, report, restore, reveal, say, state, tell, unite

RELATED affiliate(d), agnate, akin, alike, allied, analogous, appropriate, associated, attendant, avuncular, cognate, concerning, connected, consanguineous, correlative, dependent, enate, enatic, foster, germane, kin(dred), mutual, narrated, of a kind, of a sort, pertinent, proportional, reciprocal, recounted, RELATIVE, said, sib, united
comb. ary, ative, istic, ory, ular
through father agnate, patrilateral
through mother cognate, enate, enatic

RELATION account, bearing, blood, capacity, chronicle, connection, description, friendship, function, history, kin(dred), kinship, kinsman, link, narration, narrative, pertinence, ratio, recital, recitation, reference, rehearsal, RELATIVE, report, respect, sib, story, tale, telling, tie
between species affinity
local ubiety

mutual correlation
proportional ratio
severing of diffidation
RELATIONSHIP affair, affiliation, affinity, agency, agnation, alliance, association, bearing, bond, brotherhood, cognation, connection, consanguinity, correlation, dependence, equation, filiation, fraternity, homology, intimacy, juxtaposition, kindred, kinship, liaison, pertinence, rapport, reciprocity, reference, sibrede, sibship, sympathy, tie-in, union, unity
close belonging, intimacy, proxysm
familiar habitude
lack of diffinity
RELATIVE about, agnate, allied, analogous, apposite, approximate, aunt(ie), aunty, brer, brethren, brother, bub, bud(dy), comparable, comparative, compared, correspondent, dad(dy), daughter, eme, father, foster, frater, germane, grandchild, grandfather, grandmother, granny, in-law, kin(dred), kinsman, mom, mother, mum(my), nephew, niece, nuncle, nunks, nunky, parallel, parent, pertaining, pertinent, pop, proportionate, relation, relevant, sib(ling), sis(ter), son, suitable, twin, uncle
favoritism to nepotism
group clan, family, line, sept, tribe
through marriage in-law
through mother's side bandhu, cognate, enate
through remarriage, comb. step
RELAX abate, amuse, bask, bate, bend, cool it, divert, drift, ease, give, go easy, let down, loose(n), mitigate, moderate, modify, modulate, mollify, relent, relieve, remit, slack, slow(up), soften, stop, take it easy, thaw, unbend, unbrace, unlax, unstrain, unwind, weaken, yield
RELAXATION abatement, amusement, breather, comfort, detente, diversion, ease, entertainment, joy, lei-

sure, let-up, loosening, mitigation, pleasure, recreation, relache, relief, repose, rest, slackening, slow-up, solace, yoga
RELAXED calm, flaccid, flexuous, gentle, informal, lash, lax, lenient, loose, mild, mitigated, remiss, sinuous, slack, soft, sonsie, unbraced
RELAXER anesthetic, sedative, tranquil(l)izer, valium
RELAXING comfortable, restful, softening
RELAY agent, da(w)k, pass on, race, relief, remuda, reserve, satellite, servometer, spell, supply, transfer
horses remuda
hounds avantlay
post da(w)k
race medley
system angaria
RELEASE absolve, acquit(tance), alleviate, assoil, break, catch, catharsis, death, deliver(ance), detach, detente, discard, discharge, disengage, dismiss, dispense, disperse, dispersion, distribute, drop, emancipate, escape, excuse, exempt, exonerate, extricate, forgive, free(dom), hand out, launch, let go, liberate, liberation, license, liss, loose, manumit, mitigate, mokska, mukti, parole, permit, publish, relax, relent, relieve, relinquish, remise, remit, removal, remove, reprieve, rescue, rest, slake, spring, statement, story, tell, trip, turn loose, unbind, unburden, undo, unfasten, unhand, unloose, unpen, untie, voucher, yield
conditional parole
from debt freith
from slavery emancipate, manumit
press handout
written quitantie
RELEGATE assign, banish, charge, commit, confide, consign, credit, delegate, demote, deport, discard, dismiss, doom, entrust, exile, refer, reject, remove, submit
RELENT abandon, abate, acquiesce, bend, bow, capitulate, comply, defer, dis-

solve, ease, ebb, forbear, give(in), melt, moderate, modify, mollify, refrain, regret, relax, slacken, soften, submit, subside, succumb, thaw, wane, yield
RELENTLESS adamant(ine), austere, bitter, cruel, ferocious, fierce, firm, grim, hard, harsh, immovable, implacable, inexorable, inflexible, merciless, obdurate, persevering, persistent, pitiless, remorseless, rigid, rigorous, ruthless, severe, stern, stiff, stony, strict, stringent, stubborn tenacious, unbending, undying, unforgiving, unmerciful, unremitting, unyielding
RELEVANT ad rem, allied, applicable, apposite, appropriate, apropos, apt, cognate, congruous, fit(ting), german(e), important, material, pertinent, proper, related, relative, right, significant, suitable, well-adapted
RELIABILITY credence, dependability, probity, responsibility, stability, steel, sureness, trustworthiness
RELIABLE authentic, authoritative, believable, calculable, certain, cogent, consistent, convincing, dependable, dinkum, established, faithful, fast, firm, incorruptible, inerrant, infallible, inviolable, kosher, predictable, responsible, safe, secure, solid, sound, stable, sta(u)nch, steadfast, steady, straight, substantial, sure, telling, tried, true, trustworthy, trusty, truthful, unfailing, upright, valid, veracious, well-founded
RELIANCE affiance, anchor, assurance, belief, certitude, confidence, credence, credit, dependence, expectation, faith, hope, mainstay, support(er), trust
RELIC(S) antique, archaism, artifact, corpse, curio, eolith, fossil, fragment, halidom, huaco, keepsake, memento, memorial, microlith, monument, paleolith, record, remainder, remains, remnant, residue, ruin(s),

souvenir, survival, token, trace, vestige
holder etagere, feretory, lipsanotheca, reliquary, whatnot
pert. reliquary
student of archaeologist
vender calmierer
RELICT left, monadnock, remains, remnant, residual, survivor, widow(ed)(er)
RELIEF acquit, aid, allayment, alleviation, anaglyph, assistance, assuagement, balm, boot, boss, bot(e), cameo, catharsis, comfort, cure, deadening, deliverance, dole, dulling, ease(ment), embossment, escape, fret, glyph, help, intaglio, lax, lessening, mitigation, moderation, mollification, outline, palliation, plaque, redress, reduction, relaxation, release, relievo, remainder, remains, remedy, remission, replacement, repousse, reprieve, rescue, rilievo, softening, solace, soothing, spell, substitute, succor, support, truce, welfare
high alto-rilievo
hollow intaglio
low basso-relievo, stiacciato
organization care, red crescent, red cross, unicef
ornament adorno, cameo, fret
pitcher fireman
sculptural agraf(f)e
RELIEVE abate, aid, allay, alleviate, alternate, appease, assist, assuage, beet, bete, boot, comfort, confess, console, cure, deaden, debarrass, decrease, deliver, diminish, disembarrass, dull, ease, freshen, heal, help, improve, indemnify, lessen, lighten, liss(e), mitigate, moderate, mollify, palliate, poultice, qualify, rally, redress, reduce, relax, remedy, remit, remove, respite, return, rob, salve, slacken, slake, soften, soothe, spare, spell, strengthen, subdue, succor, support, sustain, temper, weaken
of deprive, seize
RELIGIEUX See CHURCHMAN, MONK.

RELIGION (See also *kind,* below.) belief, church, communion, creed, cult, denomination, devotion, devoutness, doctrine, faith, godliness, persuasion, piety, sanctity, sect, system, teaching, theology
kind bahaism, bon, buddhism, christianity, confucianism, gnosticism, hanifya, hinduism, islam, jainism, judaism, lamaism, mazdaism, mohammedanism, moslemism, obeah, orphism, shinto, sikhism, sufism, taoism, yoga, zen, zoroastrianism
primitive hecastotheism
study theology
system of faith
RELIGIOUS ascetic, believing, blue, canonic(al), conscientious, devotional, devout, divine, doctrinal, doctrinary, faithful, fervent, godly, holy, literal, meticulous, monastic, orthodox, pietistic, pious, reverent, rigid, sacral, sacred, saintly, scrupulous, sectarian, spiritual, theologic(al), zealous
belief credo, creed
brotherhood sodality
community ashram, cell, cenoby, cloister, congregation, convent, hermitage, lamasery, monastery, nunnery, parish, priorate, priory
formally orthodox, pharasaic, rigid, strict
group church, cult(us), denomination, sect
house kellion
instruction catechism
offering oblation, tithe
official See CHURCHMAN.
opinion doxy
order See ORDER *religious.*
overly bigoted, fanatic(al)
purification februation
sayings logia
science apotropaism
war crusade
RELINQUISH abandon, abdicate, abjure, abnegate, cancel, cast, cease, cede, deliver, demit, desert, desist, discard, disclaim, disgorge, dispose of, divorce, drop, extradite, forbear, forgo, forsake, forswear, give, grant, jettison, leave,

let, part with, quit, recant, release, render, renege, renounce, resign, retire, sacrifice, shed, spar, submit, surrender, throw over, vacate, waive, withdraw, yield
RELIQUARY apse, arca, box, casket, chasse, chest, chorten, feretory, halidom, memorial, scrine, shrine, steepa, tomb
RELISH (See also *kind,* below.) achar, appetite, appetizer, appreciate, approve, botargo, condiment, dash, degust(ate), delight, dote on, enjoy, fancy, flavor, gratification, gusto, inclination, leaning, like, liking, love, palate, partiality, pleasure, sapidity, sauce, savor, seasoning, sing, sowl(e), stomach, tang, taste, warble, zest
kind achar, botargo, cats(h)up, caviar, chutney, curry, garum, ketchup, mustard, piccalilli
mental palate
RELUCENT bright, gleaming, light, radiant, refulgent, shining
RELUCT fight, rebel, resist, revolt, struggle
RELUCTANCE antipathy, aversion, disinclination, grudge, indisposition, opposition, resistance
unit oerstad, rel
RELUCTANT afraid, ashamed, averse, backward, chary, disinclined, forced, grudging, halting, hesitant, indisposed, laggard, lo(a)th, loathful, obstinate, remiss, renitent, resisting, sweer, thwart, uneager, unwilling, wary
RELUME ignite, light, reillumine, rekindle
RELY allot, await, bank, base, belong, bet on, cleave, commit, confide, consist, count, depend, entrust, expect, gather, hold, hope, lean, lippen, rally, reassemble, reckon, repose, rest on, stand on, subsist, trust
REMAIN abide, bide, bivouac, cling, continue, dwell, endure, exist, halt, inhabit, last, lie, linger, live, lodge, loiter, manent, persist, reside, rest, roost, sojourn,

stand, stay(put), stop, subsist, survive, tarry, thole, wait
comb. meno
still stagnate

REMAINDER arrear(s), ash(es), balance, butt, carcass, carry-over, chaff, cinder(s), debris, decay, deposit, detritus, draff, dregs, dross, effluvium, embers, end, excess, filings, fossil, fragments, ghost, grounds, heeltap, leavings, lees, leftover(s), loess, oddments, odds and ends, offscourings, offscum, orts, overage, parings, precipitate, rags, raspings, rear, REFUSE, relics, remanence, remnant, residual, residue, rest, rump, scobs, scoria, scourings, scrap(s), scum, sediment, settlings, shard, shavings, sherd, silt, sinter, slag, smut, soot, sordes, stay, stump, sublimate, surplus, survivor, trace, vestige, waste

REMAINING another, biding, fossil, lasting, le(d)ger, left(over), neat, net, odd, outlying, outstanding, over (and above), permanent, remanent, resident, residual, residuary, sedimental, spare, surplus, surviving, vestigial, vestigiary

REMAINS antiquity, bones, carcass, corpse, fossils, fragment, relic(s), remainder, remnant, residue, rest, ruins, spoilment, trace, vestige

REMALIAH *son* pekah

REMAND commit(ment), recall, recommit, remit, return

REMANENCE See REMAINDER.

REMARK animadvert, annotation, assertion, behold, characteristic, comment(ary), commentate, crack, descry, discern, distinguish, espy, gloss, heed, indication, interjection, mark, mention, mot, muse, note, notice, obiter dictum, observation, observe, opine, perceive, reflect, regard, sally, say, see, sign, state (ment), survey, token, utter(ance), view

amiable douceur
appended epilegomenon
censorious animadversion, criticism, reproof
concluding envoi
cutting crack, dig, put-down, rub, taunt
embarrassing blooper, boner, booboo, break, faux pas, gaff
explanatory scholion, scholium
funny gag, jest
light banter, chaff
pointed barb
stupid betise
trite bromide, platitude
unfavorable brickbat, reflection, slur
unpleasant jeer, jest, slur, stinger
witty bon mot, gag, jest, mot, quip, sally, sarcasm, witticism

REMARKABLE bonzer, considerate, curious, discernable, egregious, exceptional, extraordinary, fabulous, great, notable, noteworthy, observable, outstanding, phenomenal, prominent, salient, signal, singular, sollicker, spanking, strange, striking, strong, uncommon, unprecedented, unusual, wizard, wonderful
thing beaut, caution

REMBLE move, remove, stir

REMBRANDT *painting* anatomy lesson, night watch
pupil dou(w), dow

REME scream, shout

REMEDY action, adjust, aid, alleviate, amend, analeptic, anesthetic, anodyne, antacid, antidote, assuage, balm, balsam, boot, bot(e), catholicon, correct(ive), counteractant, cure(all), doctor, dose, drug, elixir, emend(ate), emetic, fix, gain, hale, heal, help, lighten, make good, maturant, medicament, medication, medicine, mitigate, narcotic, nostrum, palliative, panacea, patch, physic, pill, placebo, prescription, prophylactic, recipe, rectify, redress, reduce, reform, regulate, relief, relieve, repair, reparation, restorative, restore, revise, right, salve, sedative, shot, snake oil,

sop, specific, tonic, treat, unction, vaccine, vesicant
comb. ant(i)
favorite nostrum
fever febrifuge
imaginary elixir, panacea, placebo
jaundice icteric
modification tinction
poison treacle
quack nostrum
secret arcanum
susceptible to curable, sanable, tractable
universal azoth, catholicon, panacea

REMEMBER bethink, call up, commemorate, ideate, look back, mean, mem, memorize, mention, mind, ming, recall, recollect, rememorate, remind, reminisce, renew, retain, retrace, retrospect, review, reward, think back

REMEMBRANCE allusion, anamnesis, consideration, discourse, gift, inscription, keepsake, memento, memo (randum), memorial, memory, mention, mind, minning, monument, notice, recall, recollection, reference, regards, reminder, reminiscence, retrospect, reward, souvenir, token, trophy
comb. mnesis
name meaning minnie
symbol rosemary

REMIND admonish, advise, alert, bring back, cue, hint, jog, mention, notify, nudge, point out, prod, recall, recollect, remember, rememorate, suggest, warn

REMINDER admonishment, admonition, advice, cue, hint, jogger, memento, memo(randum), mnemonic, note, nudge, phylactery, prod, prompt(er), remembrance, souvenir, string, suggestion, tickler, tip, twit, warning

REMINISCE bethink, look back, muse, recall, recollect, remember, remind, retrospect, review

REMINISCENCE anamnesis, anecdote, memoir, memorabilia, memory, recall, recollection, remembrance, reminder, souvenir, tale

REMINISCENT redolent, remindful, suggestive

REMISE carriage(house), free, giving, granting, release, remission, remit(tance), replace, respite, return, send back, surrender, thrust

REMISS backward, careless, delinquent, derelict, dilatory, diluted, dissolved, faineant, faint, forgetful, gentle, heedless, idle, improvident, inattentive, indolent, languid, lax, lazy, lenient, liquified, loose, mild, moderate, neglectful, negligent, relaxed, reluctant, remise, remit, shiftless, slack, slothful, slow, tardy, thoughtless, unmindful

REMISSION abatement, absolution, amnesty, cancellation, cessation, deliverance, diminution, forgiveness, hiatus, interruption, lessening, liss(e), pardon, pause, relaxation, release, remise, remittal, remittance, respite, rest, return, subsidence, suspension

REMIT abandon, abate, abrogate, absolve, allot, annul, assign, bate, cancel, commit, condone, decrease, defer, desist, diminish, direct, excuse, forgive, forward, free, give up, insert, liberate, mitigate, moderate, modify, modulate, overlook, pardon, pay, postpone, put off, readmit, recommit, refer, relax, release, reprieve, resign, respite, restore, return, send, settle, shrive, slack(en), square, submit, surrender, suspend, transfer, transmit, vindicate

REMITTANCE allowance, payment, settlement, transmittal

REMNANT balance, butt, crumb, crust, dreg(s), end, fent, fragment, klip(pe), leaving, left(over), oddment, ort, part, piece, portion, rag, relic(s), remainder, remains, residue, residuum, rest, scissel, scoria, scrag, scrap, section, segment, shred, slag, stub, suggestion, trace, vestige, wrack

REMODEL convert, improve, patch, rebuild, recast, reclaim, reconstruct, recreate, reform, refresh, remold, renew, renovate, repair, restore

REMONSTRANCE advice, benedicite, counsel, demonstration, evidence, expostulation, likeness, proof, protest, representation, reproof

REMONSTRATE argue, combat, complain, criticize, declare, demonstrate, demur, denounce, dissuade, enjoin, expostulate, kick, object, oppose, plead, point out, protest, reprobate, reprove, resist, withstand

REMORA clog, curb, delay, drag, echeneid, fish, guaican, hindrance, lootsman, obstacle, obstruction, pega(dor), stayship, stopship, sucker(fish), suckstone, whalesucker

REMORD afflict, censure, ponder, rebuke, regret, remember, REMORSE, taint

REMORSE anguish, apology, attrition, ayenbite, compassion, compunction, contrition, demur, distress, grief, guilt, pain, penance, penitence, pity, prick, qualm, regret, remord, repentance, rue, ruth, scruple, sorrow

REMORSEFUL compassionate, contrite, guiltsick, penitent, pitiable, pitiful, regretful, repentant, sorry

REMORSELESS cruel, implacable, inexorable, merciless, pitiless, relentless, ruthless, unmerciful, unrelenting, unrepentant

REMOTE abditive, abstracted, alenge, alien, aloof, apart, backwater, behind, cool, desolate, detached, distant, divergent, far(away)(fetched), forane, foreign, forlorn, hidden, hiding, impersonal, inaccessible, inconsiderable, indirect, insular, interior, irrelevant, isolated, nemo, off, otiose, out of the way, past, pointless, private, quiet, removed, reticent, retired, secluded, secret, separate(d), sequestered, slight, solitary, standoff, strange,

ulterior, unfrequented, unfriendly, unlikely, unrelated, uttermost, withdrawn
more endmost, farther, further, ulterior
most diametric, extreme, ultimate, ultima thule
possibility improbability

REMOUNT *string* remuda

REMOVAL ablation, abstraction, amotion, axe, carriage, cartage, cleanup, deduction, departure, deprivation, detachment, dislodgment, dismissal, erasion, excision, exile, ousting, release, relegation, stripping, surgery, transference, withdrawal
comb. ectomy
surgical exeresis

REMOVE 3 cut, gut, rid, top 4 bail, bark, blot, dele, doff, fire, kill, oust, part, sack, skim, step, stir, take, undo 5 avoid, brush, class, clear, cream, douse, eloin, erase, expel, heave, hoist, sever, shift, shuck, shunt, slipe, space, steal, stone, strip 6 ablate, banish, cancel, change, convey, deduct, degree, delete, depart, depose, disbar, divest, efface, eloign, excise, export, murder, recall, remble, unpack, unwrap, uproot 7 abolish, absence, bail out, cashier, cast off, destroy, discard, dismiss, disroot, divorce, extract, prevent, purloin, release, replace, rescind, subduct, sublate 8 abstract, amputate, aspirate, carry off, dislodge, displace, estrange, lay aside, persuade, relegate, subtract, transfer, withdraw 9 disappear, dislocate, eliminate, eradicate, extirpate, promotion, translate, transport, transpose 10 extinguish, transplant 11 assassinate, exterminate
bark ross
color bleach
dirt clean, garble, scour, swob
fluid aspirate
hair depilate, shave
impurities boil off, filter
legally disbar, eloign, eloin, impeach, oust
roots grub

skin hull, husk, pare, peel, shell, shuck

REMOVED abstract(ed), afar, alien, aloof, apart, away, distant, far(away) (off), off, remote

REMUDA cavayard, cavy-(yard), horses, relay, remounts

REMUNERATE avail, award, compensate, grant, gratify, indemnify, pay, recompense, reimburse, remit, repay, requite, reward, satisfy

REMUNERATION bounty, compensation, emolument, fee, honorarium, income, pay(ment), recompense, reimbursement, requital, reward, salary, satisfaction, stipend, wages

REMUNERATIVE beneficial, compensating, compensative, compensatory, gainful, lucrative, profitable, retributory, rewarding, valuable

REMUS *birth place* alba longa
brother romulus
discoverer faustulus
founder of rome
grandfather numitor
parent aemilia, aeneas, dexithea, ilia, latinus, mars, rhea-silvia, roma
slayer romulus

RENABLE eloquent, fluent, glib, ready

RENAISSANCE nara, palingenesis, rebirth, renascence, renewal, revival
artist botticelli, cellini, della robbia, del sarto, donatello, ghirlandaio, rosselli, verrocchio
cannon aspic
chest cassapanca
glassware waldglas
idyll pastourelle
poem cantare

RENCOUNTER action, battle, clash, collide, collision, combat, conflict, contest, debate, duel, ENCOUNTER, fight, joining, meet-(ing), rencontre, repartee

REND abscind, bark, breach, break, burst, chop, cleave, discerp, disintegrate, dismember, dispart, disrupt, divel(icate), divide, enrive, fracture, hurt, lacerate, open, pierce, pull, remove,

rent, rip, rive, rupture, screed, seam, separate, sever, slit, split, sunder, tear, uproot, wrend, wrest
from extort

RENDER accomplish, account, achieve, acquit, afford, bear, bestow, cede, clarify, coil, concentrate, confess, construe, contribute, convert, decoct, defat, deliver, depict, distill, emit, execute, explain, express, extract, furnish, give, impart, inflict, interpret, make, melt(down), part with, pay, perform, play, precary, present, press, provide, put, recite, relinquish, repeat, represent, requite, restore, return, reward, soak, squeeze, statement, steep, submit, supply, surrender, tallage, tell, translate, transmit, treat, try, yield
homage attorn, venerate
verdict judge, pass
void annul, cass, defeat

RENDERING account, delivery, depiction, expression, interpretation, performance, rendition, representation, return, version

RENDEZVOUS affair, appointment, assemble, assembly, assignation, date, engagement, gathering, hangout, lovenest, meet(ing), place, refuge, resort, retreat, tryst

RENDITION account, conduct, delivery, performance, surrender, translation

RENDROCK dynamite

RENEGADE agnostic, apostate, backslider, changeling, cocklorel, deserter, dorax, forsaker, fugitive, heretic, iconoclast, pervert, rat, rebel, recreant, runagate, traitor(ous), turncoat

RENEGE abandon, cheat, deceive, decline, deny, desert, err, fainaigue, rat, refuse, renig, renounce, repeal, retract, revoke, shirk, welch, welsh

RENEW beet(e), continue, correct, enliven, invigorate, mend, modernize, rally, reassume, rebuild, recover, recreate, rectify, reform, refresh, refurbish, regenerate,

reinstate, rejuvenate, remember, renovate, repair, replenish, restock, restore, resume, revamp, revise, revitalize, revive, streamline, transfigure

RENIER *son* oliver

RENIG See RENEGE.

RENISH furious, uncouth, wild

RENITENCE elasticity, opposition, reluctance, resistance

RENITENT elastic, obstinate, opposed, opposing, recalcitrant, reluctant, resistant, rigid

RENKY lanky, large, robust

RENNET abomasum, apple, cheeselep, cheeselip, coagulate, curdle(r), earning(s), ferment, membrane, powder, rennin, ruen, steep, vell
ferment enzyme, rennin
substitute steepgrass

RENOIR *masterpiece* les grandes baigneuses

RENOUNCE abandon, abdicate, abjure, abnegate, abstain, announce, cede, cut off, declare, decline, deny, disavow, disclaim, discontinue, disown, eschew, forbear, forfeit, forgo, forsake, forspeak, forswear, give up, leave, manswear, proclaim, quit, recant, refuse, reject, relinquish, remit, renay, renege, repudiate, resign, retract, revoke, sacrifice, spurn, stop, surrender, waive, withsay, yield

RENOVATE clean(se), fix, furbish, invigorate, mend, moloker, patch, polish, prune, recondition, redintegrate, redo, refresh, refurbish, regenerate, rejuvenate, remodel, renew, repair, restore, revive, shine

RENOWN acclaim, authority, brilliance, celebrity, distinction, eclat, eminence, fame, glory, honor, influence, kudos, luster, name, note, notoriety, prestige, report, reputation, repute, rumor, swagger, weight

RENOWNED acclaimed, celebrated, celebrious, distinguished, eminent, extolled, famed, famous, illustrious, magnific, noble, noted, notorious, outstanding, prominent, redoubted, signal

RENT apartment, avenge, breach, break, broken, cain, champart, charter, cleft, cuddy, custom, division, endow, engage, fee, fissure, fracture, gaunch, hire, hole, income, landgafol, lease, let, onstand, pay(ment), rend(er), revenue, reward, rift, rip(ped), rupture, schism, separation, shabby, share, slit, split, stallage, tack, tatter(ed), tax, tear, tenement, toll, tore, torn, tribute, wage
feudal prestation
ground censo, census
high rackrent
paid in produce avenage, cain, kain

RENTER fine-draw, lessee, occupant, repair, roomer, sew, stockholder, tenant, transient

RENUNCIATION abandonment, abjuration, abnegation, apostasy, denial, disavowal, disclaimer, forgoing, rejection, relinquishment, renouncement, repudiation, sacrifice, surrender, temperance

REP fabric, reap, silk, wool

REPAIR accommodate, amend, atone, beet(e), betake, bete, boot, bot, botch, bote, bushel, calk, careen, cobble, commission, compensate, condition, correct, darn, doctor, emend, fettle, fix, haunt, heal, imp(rove), mend, overhaul, patch, piece, ready, rebuild, recane, recap, recoup, rectify, redress, reheel, remedy, remodel, renew, renovate, resort, restore, retinue, retouch, retread, retrieve, return, right, service, sew, splice, tine, tinker, train, upkeep, vamp(up)
badly botch
garment bushel, patch
man mechanic, mender, tinker
shop dockyard, garage, roundhouse, shipyard

REPAIRMAN cobbler, mechanic, mender, tinker, woffler

REPAND bent, crooked, undulating, uneven, wavy

REPARATION amende, amends, atonement, balm, bot(e), compensation, correction, damages, expiation, indemnity, recompense, redemption, redress, remedy, remuneration, repair, requital, restitution, restoration, revenge, reward, satisfaction

REPARTEE answer, backchat, badinage, banter, comeback, conversation, fencing, humor, irony, levity, persiflage, pleasantry, quip, raillery, rejoinder, reply, retort, ripost(e), sally, sarcasm, satire, sparing, wit

REPAST bait, banquet, bever, brunch, collation, dinner, entertainment, feast, feed, food, lunch, meal(time), snack, spread, supper, tiffin, treat, viands, victuals, void(ee)
light collation
pert. prandial

REPATRIATE reform, restore, return

REPAY answer, appay, avenge, cap, compensate, indemnify, match, meed, offset, quit, rebate, recompense, refund, reimburse, remunerate, requite, restore, retaliate, return, revenge, reward, satisfy, yield

REPEAL abandon, abolish (ment), abolition, abrogate, amend, annul(ment), avoid, cancel(lation), countermand, counterorder, emend, forgo, invalidate, nullification, nullify, obrogate, override, overrule, recall, renege, renig, renounce, rescind, rescission, retract(ion), reversal, reverse, revocation, revoke, take back, vacate, vacatur, void, withdraw(al)

REPEAT account, again, battologize, bis, cite, din(g), dingdong, ditto, divulge, do again, duplicate, echo, elaborate, encore, harp, imitate, ingeminate, insist, iterate, memorize, mime, mimic, parrot, perseverate, persist, quote, rame, reaffirm, reassert, recapitulate, recidive,

recital, recite, recount, recrudesce, recur, redo, redouble, refrain, rehash, rehearse, reiterate, relate, repetition, replica, reprise, reproduce, resay, restate, resume, retail, retell, review, reword, segno, strike, summarize, tautologize, thrum
from memory recite
in cadence chant, chime
mark segno

REPEATEDLY ad infinitum, afresh, again, anew, continually, continuously, day after day, de novo, frequently, many times, oft(en), over(again), time after time, year after year

REPEATER backslider, echo, firearm, gun, holdover, parrot, pistol, recidivist, rifle, veteran, watch

REPEL appall, beat, check, combat, debar, decline, disgust, extinguish, force, nauseate, oppose, parry, pellate, prevent, push back, rebuff, rebut, refuse, reject, remove, repudiate, repulse, resist, restrain, revolt, rout, shut out, sicken, stop, vanquish, ward off, withstand

REPELLENT abhorent, apocrustic, distasteful, grim, harsh, hateful, hedgehoggy, hideous, invidious, loathsome, nasty, obnoxious, offensive, rebarbative, repugnant, repulsive, resistent, revolting, squalid

REPENT amend, atone, beet, bete, bewail, complain, forthink, grieve, lament, mourn, reform, regret, reptant, rue

REPENTANCE attrition, compunction, confession, contrition, penance, penitance, pity, reformation, regret, remorse, rew, rue, ruth, shame, sorrow

REPENTANT contrite, penitent, sorry

REPERCUSSION backwash, concussion, detonation, echo, impact, percussion, rebound, recoil, re-echo, reflection, repulse, return, reverberation, shock
unexpected afterclap

REPERTOIRE See REPERTORY.

REPERTORY accumulation,

arsenal, calendar, catalog(ue), collection, index, line, list, magazine, offerings, repertoire, show, stock, store(house), treasury

REPETITION again, battology, bis, copy, dilogy, dupe, duplicate, echo, encore, iterance, iteration, merism, over, palilogy, parrotry, ploce, recapitulation, recidivism, redundancy, rehearsal, reiteration, replica, report, reprise, reproduction, restatement, rote, tautology, troll
constant cataphasia
emphatic epizeuxis, ploce
of idea tautology
of others echolalia, echolia, mimicry
of word ploce
reverse epanodos
rhetorical anadiplosis, anaphora, antimetabole, antistrophe, epanalepsis, epanaphora, epanodos, ploce

REPETITIVE alliterative, echoic, iterant, pleonastic, reboant, redundant, regular

REPHAEL *father* shemaiah

REPHAH *father* ephraim

REPHAIAH *parent* hur, miriam

REPINE complain(t), fail, fret, grieve, gripe, grumble, lament, languish, mope, mourn, regret, rue, wane, weaken

REPLACE change, dismiss, displace, follow, put back, recoup, recover, refund, regain, reimburse, reinstate, relieve, remise, renew, repay, repone, reset, restore, return, stead, stet, substitute, succeed, supersede, supplant, swap, swop

REPLACEMENT ersatz, pinch-hitter, substitute, successor, supplanter, transfer, transposition, understudy

REPLENISH complete, feed, fill, nourish, provide, refill, reinforce, renew, restore, store, suffice, supply

REPLETE abounding, abundant, bloated, chockfull, complete, crammed, fat, fill(ed), flush, full, glutted, gorged, overfed, perfect, plenary, plentiful, plenty,

replenish, rife, sated, satiated, satisfied, stock, stout, stuffed, supply, surfeited

REPLETION fullness, fulth, plenty, plethora, profusion, satiation, satiety, saturity, surfeit

REPLEVIN attach, pledge, recovery, redeem, return, writ

REPLICA bis, carbon, copy, duplicate, ectype, facsimile, image, imitation, likeness, reflection, repeat, repetition, reproduction, revie, transcript, xerox

REPLY acknowledge, answer, defense, echo, jawab, mot, react(ion), rebut, rejoin, rejoinder, repartee, replique, resound, respond, response, retort, retract, return, riposte, rsvp, sass

REPORT 3 air, cry, pop, say 4 bang, buzz, card, clap, fame, note, shot, tale, talk, tell 5 brief, bruit, crack, glory, noise, relay, rumor, speak, state, story, voice 6 accuse, advise, answer, breeze, canard, charge, delete, dilate, expose, finger, gossip, impart, inform, muster, recite, record, relate, retort, reveal, review, spread, threap 7 account, comment, crackle, declare, divulge, hansard, hearsay, inkling, message, minutes, narrate, opinion, process, publish, recount, returns, riposte, summary, verdict, version, whisper, write up 8 announce, bulletin, critique, describe, disclose, dispatch, rehearse 9 broadcast, chronicle, criticism, delineate, explosion, pronounce, statement 10 commentary, detonation, reputation 11 communicate, information, proceedings 13 communication
detailed play-by-play
false canard, fib, fish story, furphy, libel, lie, misstatement, shave, slander, tall tale
final wrap-up
law case
legislative cahier, hansard
news flash, scoop
official archive, hansard, minutes, record

order to call-up
popular rumo(u)r

REPORTER(S) columnist, cub, informant, journalist, legman, newshawk, newshen, newsman, pistol, press, scoop(er), writer
symbol thirty
woman newshen, sob sister

REPOSE calm(ness), comfort, compose, composure, confide, depend, deposit, ease, lay, leisure, lie, peace, place, placidity poise, quiescence, quiet(ude), recline, refresh, relaxation, relief, rely, replace, rest, seat, serenity, set(tle), sit, sleep, slumber, tranquil(l)ity, trust

REPOSEFUL calm, cozy, peaceful, placid, quiet, restful, serene, silent, snug, still, tranquil

REPOSIT deposit, place, replace, store

REPOSITORY archive, box, cabinet, capsa, capsule, chapel, closet, cupboard, depot, granary, hanaper, lode, magazine, museum, repertory, sepulcher, storehouse, treasury, vault, vein, warehouse

REPREHEND admonish, berate, blame, censure, chide, condemn, criticize, denounce, disprove, rate, rebuke, reprimand, reprise, reproach, reprobate, reprove, SCOLD, upbraid, warn

REPREHENSIBLE accusable, amiss, blameable, blameworthy, censurable, criminal, culpable, ill, imputable, indictable, reproachable, reprovable, scabrous

REPRESENT act, adumbrate, answer for, betoken, characterize, delineate, denote, depict, describe, designate, display, draw, enact, exemplify, exhibit, feature, front for, illustrate, imitate, impersonate, limn, manifest, object, paint, personate, picture, play, portray, present, produce, profess, protest, register, render, serve as, show, simulate, stage, state, symbolize, typify

REPRESENTATION act-(ing), art, avowal, chart, delineation, demonstration, depiction, description, drama, draught, drawing, effigy, embodiment, epitome, example, exemplification, exhibition, exponent, expression, extract, icon, idea, idol, ikon, illustration, image(ry), likeness, make-believe, model, picture, portraiture, portrayal, protest, remonstrance, reproduction, sample, schema, scheme, sham, show, similitude, simulation, sketch, spectacle, symbol, tableau, type
facsimile typorama
mental fancy, image

REPRESENTATIVE adumbrative, advocate, agent, ambassador, assemblyman, characteristic, congressman, consul, delegate, depictive, deputy, emissary, envoy, executor, exponent, factor, figurative, heir, illustrative, legate, legislator, nuncio, observer, proxy, salesman, sample, senator, specimen, substitute, tribune, typical, vakeel, vakil, vicar

REPRESS blunt, bottle up, bridle, bury, censor, check, choke, conceal, constrain, crub, crush, daunt, deaden, depress, drown, hush, inhibit, muffle, overpower, put down, quash, quell, reduce, rein, reprime, restrain, restrict, silence, stifle, stop, strangle, subdue, suppress, withhold

REPRESSION inhibition, rejection, reserve, sublimation, supression

REPRIEVE amnesty, delay, forgive(ness), grace, parole, postpone, preserve, release, relief, relieve, remand, remit, respite, suspend, truce

REPRIMAND admonish, bawl out, berate, blame, call down, cashier, censure, chide, come down on, condemn(ation), criticize, denounce, lecture, punish, put down, rate, rebuke, reprehend, reproach, reprobate, reproof, reprove, SCOLD, score, skate, slate, slo(a)n, sneb, snib, upbraid

REPRIME repress, subdue
REPRINT copy, facsimile, paperback, reproduction, tauchnitz
REPRISAL eye-for-eye, prize, recapture, redress, requital, retaliation, retribution, revenge, tit-for-tat, vengeance
REPRISE charge, compensate, cost, deduction, encore, loss, reassume, recapitulation, recapture, recommence, recover, renewal, repeat, repetition, reprehend, reprieve, withdraw, withhold
REPROACH abuse, accuse, admonish, animadversion, berate, bismer, blame, blot, censure, charge, chide, condemn, correption, criticism, criticize, disapproval, discredit, disgrace, dishonor, ignominy, obloquy, odium, opprobrium, rate, rebuke, reprehend, reprehension, reprimand, reproof, reprove, revile, scold(ing), scorn, shame, slander, stigma, taunt, upbraid, warn, wite, withnim
term of for shame, raca
REPROACHFUL abusive, bitter, blameworthy, critical, opprobrius, shameful
REPROBATE abandon(ed), bad egg, blame, bounder, bugger, cad, censure, condemn(ed), corrupt, culpable, cur, cuss, degenerate, denounce, depraved, disapprove, disown, dissolute, dog, evil, guilty, hardened, heel, immoral, iniquitous, knave, knavish, louse, miscreant, mongrel, outcast, pariah, pervert, polisson, profligate, rascal, rat, rebuke, recreant, refuse, reject, reprehend, reprehensible, reptile, repudiate, rip, rogue, rotter, scalawag, scamp, scapegrace, scoundrel, serpent, sinner, skalawag, skunk, snake, stinker, swine, unprincipled, unregenerate, varmint, vicious, villain, viper, wastrel, wicked, worm, wretch
REPRODUCE bear, beget, breed, copy, duplicate, engender, generate, get, manifold, multiply, portray, pro-

create, produce, propagate, recite, reconstitute, reconstruct, redo, repeat, sire, trace, xerox, yield
asexually clone
REPRODUCTION amphimixis, anagenesis, apogamy, apomixis, carbon, cast, copy, counterpart, duplicate, ectype, edition, exogamy, facsimile, gamogenesis, generation, image, likeness, metagenesis, monogenesis, parthenogenesis, photo(graph), photostat, picture, print, propagation, recall, replica, syngamy, tape, transcript
pert. genesic
REPRODUCTIVE progenitive
body auxospore, azygospore, cell, egg, gamete, sperm, spore
REPROGRAPH copy, stat
REPROOF admonition, animadversion, blame, censure, chiding, contumely, correption, disgrace, lecture, obloquy, prod, rebuke, reprehension, reprimand, REPROACH, reproval, scolding, set down, snub
REPROVE abuse, admonish, berate, blame, blister, call down, castigate, censure, chaste(n), chastise, chew out, chide, convict, convince, criticize, disprove, objurgate, punish, rate, rebuke, refute, reject, remonstrate, reprimand, REPROACH, reprobate, scold, snib, trim, undernim, upbraid, vilify, vituperate, withtake
REPTILE (See also *kind*, below.) crawling, creeper, creeping, despicable, diapsid, groveling, knave, low, malignant, reprobate, reptant, saurian, snake, synapsid
age mesozoic
aquatic clidastes, crocodile, hellbender, ichthyosaur, mugger, proganosaur, salamander, seasnake, turtle, waterdog
carnivorous pelycosaur
comb. herpeto
edible turtle
extinct aetosaurus, anomodont, baptonodon, cotylo-

saur, cynognathus, dinosaur, diplodocus, galesaur(us), gordonia, mesosaur, microconadon, mixosaur, mosasaur, nothosaurus, parasuchia, pelycosauria, phytosaur, placodont, plesiosaur, pliosaur, protorosaur, pteranodon, pterosaur, pythonomorpha, teleosaur

flying pteranodon, pterodactyl

group sauria

kind aboma, adder, alligator, asp(ic), boa, chameleon, coachwhip, cobra, cribo, croc(odile), d(h)abb, dinosaur, diplodocus, dragon, dubb, eft, elaps, frog, galliwasp, gator, gavial, gecko, geikia, gharial, gilamonster, goa, guana, hellbender, ichthyosaur, iguana, jacare, jessur, krait, lacert, lizard, mamba, moccasin, mudpuppy, muggar, mugger, muggur, nakoo, newt, puff adder, racer, scorpion, serpent, skink, snake, sneck, squamata, stegomus, synapsid, terrapin, toad, tortoise, tortuga, tuatara, tucktoo, turtle, tweeg, varan, viper, waterdog, whiptail, worm, worral, yacare

-like herpetiform

marine See REPTILE *aquatic.*

membrane allantois

mythical basilisk, dragon

pert. herpetic, ophidian, saurian

scale podotheca, scute, scutum

student of herpetologist

study herpetology

vertebra proatlas

REPTILIAN bad, base, contemptible, crawling, creeping, debased, despicable, evil, groveling, harmful, herpetic, knavish, low, malignant, mean, obsequious, ophidian, reptant, saurian, snaky, sneaky, treacherous

REPUBLIC commonweal (th), democracy, government, poblacht, state

author plato

ideal atlantis, icaria, oceana, utopia

of letters literature

of monasteries athos

of south africa See SOUTH AFRICA.

world's smallest nauru

REPUBLICAN conservative, sansculot(te), stalwart, swallow, weaverbird

river tributary smoky hill

southern lily-white

REPUDIATE abandon, abjure, abrogate, condemn, decline, default, defy, deny, disaffirm, disapprove, disavow, discard, disclaim, disdain, dishonor, disown, divorce, eschew, exclude, forbear, forgo, forswear, rebuff, recant, refuse, reject, renounce, repel, repulse, sacrifice, scorn, scout, spurn

REPUESTO codill(e), codillo, defeat

REPUGN fight, oppose, repel, resist, strive

REPUGNANCE abhorrence, antagonism, antipathy, aversion, disgust, dislike, displeasure, distaste, hate, hatred, horror, hostility, loathing, opposition, reluctance, repulsion

REPUGNANT abhorrent, adverse, alien, antagonistic, antipathetic, averse, base, contradictory, dirty, disagreeable, distasteful, extraneous, foreign, foul, hateful, hideous, hostile, inimical, invidious, loathsome, low, nasty, noisome, odious, offensive, opposed, repellant, repulsive, resistant, revolting, uncongenial, vile

REPULSE beat, canvas(s), chase, check, defeat, denial, deny, drive off, exclude, foil, push back, rebuff, rebut, recoil, refel, refusal, refuse, reject(ion), repel, repudiate, resist, rout, snub, thrust back, ward off

REPULSION antipathy, aversion, disgust, dislike, distaste, divorce, loathing, rebuff, repellency, repugnance, repulse, revolt, revulsion

REPULSIVE abhorent, bad, dain, disgusting, evil, fetid, forbidding, greasy, hateful, hideous, loath(some), loth, nasty, noisome, obnoxious, offensive, repellent, repugnant, resistant, revolting,

scabrous, squalid, toady, ugly, unsavory, unsightly

REPUTABLE credible, creditable, esteemed, estimable, fine, good, honest, honorable, honored, redoubted, respectable, standard, upright, worthy

REPUTATION account, celebrity, character, distinction, esteem, estimation, fame, glory, honor, izzat, memory, name, opinion, position, rank, record, REPUTE, respect, savor, standing, worship

bad black eye, infamy

good respect, standing

loss of scandal

REPUTE account, ascription, attribute, celebrity, character, credit, deem, distinction, eclat, esteem, estimation, fame, favor, glory, hold, honor, image, impute, judgment, mark, name, note, notoriety, odor, opinion, prestige, prominence, rank, reckon, regard, renown, report, reputation, respect, status, suppose, think, weight, word

REPUTED accounted, assumed, conjectural, deemed, dit, gossiped, hypothetical, noised, putative, renowned, said, supposed, supposititious

REQUEST address, appeal, apply, ask, beg, behest, beseech, bespeak, call, claim, demand, desire, entreat(y), implore, importune, importunity, instance, invitation, invite, order, petition, plea, pray(er), requisition, rogation, solicit, sue, suit, supplicate, supplication, touch, wish, yearn

strong command, demand, dun

REQUESTOR applicant, candidate, petitioner, seeker

REQUIEM coronach, dirge, funeral, hymn, introit, mass, peace, quiet, repose, rest, service, trental

REQUIN maneater, shark, tommy

REQUIRE ask, assign, beho(o)ve, bid, call for, charge, claim, compel, crave, demand, dictate, enjoin, entail, exact, expect,

force, inquire, involve, justify, lack, mister, necessitate, need, obligate, oblige, prescribe, request, search, seek, solicit, want, warrant
payment charge

REQUIRED compulsory, de rigueur, due, inperative, mandatory, necessary, needed, obligatory, requisite, set

REQUIREMENT call, command, demand, duty, necessity, need, prerequisite, prescription, requisite, sine qua non

REQUISITE condition, essential, indispensable, necessary, need(ed), needful, needy, request, required, REQUIREMENT, vital

REQUISITION application, billet, call, demand, draft, order, request, requirement

REQUITAL amends, antapodosis, compensation, foryield, gratify, guerdon, repayment, reprisal, retaliation, retribution, revenge, reward, tally, vengeance, war, yield

REQUITE acquit, atone, avenge, compensate, defray, deserve, interchange, pay back, punish, reciprocate, recompense, recover, regain, reimburse, remunerate, repay, retaliate, retrieve, return, revenge, reward, satisfy

REREBRACE armor, cannon

REREDOS backplate, brazier, drapery, fireback, partition, retablo, screen

RERIR *grandson* sigmund

RES matter, object, point, subject, thing
publica commonweal(th), republic, state

RESCIND abolish, abrogate, annul, cancel, countermand, cut, invalidate, nullify, recall, recant, remove, repeal, retract, retreat, revoke, vacate, veto, void, withdraw

RESCRIPT annotation, answer, counterpart, decree, edict, epistle, injunction, letter, order, rewriting, subnotation, subscription

RESCUE aid, au secours, conserve, deliver(ance), disentangle, emancipate, extricate, free, help, liberate,

liberation, manumit, preserve, ransom, reclaim, recover(y), redd, redeem, redemption, regain, release, retrieve, salvage, salvation, save, set free, succor

RESCUER perseus, redeemer, savior

RESE hurry, impulse, onset, quake, rage, rashness, rush, shake, tremble

RESEARCH analysis, arbeit, bookwork, data, enquiry, examination, examine, experiment(ation), exploration, explore, facts, inquest, inquire, inquiry, investigate, investigation, probe, scrutiny, study, test, thought
rocket aerobee

RESEDA bladder-green, leek, mennuet, mignonette, rocket, verd-vessie

RESEMBLANCE accord, affinity, agreement, analogy, assonance, comparison, conformity, correspondence, facsimile, harmony, image, imitation, likeness, parallel, picture, ringer, similarity, similitude

RESEMBLE agree, appear, assemble, assimilate, collect, compare, copy, counterfeit, depict, favor, imitate, liken, look like, portray, represent, seem like, symbolize, take after
cause to assimilate

RESEMBLING after, alike, approximate, like, same, semblant, similar
comb. esque, ick, ish, ive, oid, phane

RESENT anger, begrudge, bristle, complain, feel, hate, malign, perceive, recognize, regret, remember, repent, savor, smell, snap, suggest, take amiss, take ill, take offense, take umbrage

RESENTFUL angry, bitter, cross, envious, hurt, indignant, jealous, malicious, offended, piqued, stomachy, umbrageous

RESENTMENT acrimony, aggravation, anger, animosity, aninus, annoyance, antagonism, antipathy, bad blood, bitterness, choler, disdain, displeasure, dudgeon, exasperation, gall, grudge, hate, hatred, hostil-

ity, huff, ill will, indignation, ire, irritation, jealousy, malice, offense, pique, rancor, spite, spleen, umbrage, vexation

RESERPINE serpasil
source rauwolfia, snakeroot

RESERVATION booking, caution, condition, dibs, engagement, exception, forprise, limitation, preservation, proviso, qualification, retention, saving, scruple, space, tract

RESERVE abstain, allot, backlog, bespeak, book, buffer, cash, caution, cave, coldness, composure, conserve, constraint, control, delay, deposit, detain, diffidence, discretion, distance, engage, fallback, forprise, fund, hay in the barn, hoard, hold, inhibition, keep, limitation, modesty, nest egg, pre-empt, preserve, put aside, refuge, relay, repression, reservoir, restraint, retain, retention, reticence, save, savings, schedule, self-restraint, sepone, sepose, set aside, shyness, silence, spare, stock(pile), store, supply, surplus, taciturnity, tenenue, withhold
financial cushion, nest egg

RESERVED aloof, apart, bashful, booked, close(lipped)(mouthed), cold, composed, constrained, controlled, cool, costive, coy, demure, detached, diffident, distant, except(ed), formal, indifferent, inhibited, kept, modest, preserved, recessive, removed, restrained, reticent, retiring, save(d), secretive, shy, silent, spared, stand off(ish), taciturn, unco, uncommunicative, undemonstrative, unsociable, withdrawn, withheld

RESERVOIR basin, boss, caisson, catchbasin, catchment, cavity, cenote, cistern, favissa, fund, lake, piscina, pond, reserve, siphon, standage, stock, store(house), sump, supply, syphon, tank, tarn, weir
discharge hushing
underground cenote

RESET abode, alter, harbor, help, plant, receipt, receiving, receptacle, reform, refuge, replace, replant, resort, secrete, sharpen, shelter, succor

RESETTLE migrate, move

RESHAPE recast, reform, remodel

RESIDE abide, bide, big(g), continue, depart, dwell, endure, habitate, howff, inhabit, inhere, leave, lie, live, lodge, occupy, put up, remain, room, settle, sink, sojourn, stay, stop, subside
temporarily bunk, camp, visit

RESIDENCE abode, address, apartment, biding, castle, convent, deanery, domicile, doon, dormatory, drostdy, dwelling, embassy, fireside, habitat(ion), hearth, home (stead), hostel, house (hold), hut, inglenook, ingleside, legation, lodging, mahal, manor, manse, mansion, menage, palace, persistence, residuum, seat, sediment, seraglio, shed, stay, tata, villa, yamen, yamun
brief stay, visit
legal domicile

RESIDENT abiding, beneficiary, burgess, cit(izen), commorant, denizen, doctor, dweller, dwelling, firm, fixed, governor, incumbent, inhabitant, inherent, inmate, intern(e), lessee, living, lodging, minister, occupant, present, remaining, residing, resting, stable
comb. ite, ote
foreign alien, metic

RESIDUE ash(es), balance, calx, cinders, dreg(s), dross, excess, exudate, grounds, gunk, lafe, leavings, lees, leftovers, marc, ort(s), relic(s), REMAINDER, remains, remanent, remnant, rest, sediment, silt, slag, sludge, slumgum, sordes, surplus, tailings
leave adsorb
pulpy pomace

RESIGN abandon, abdicate, abnegate, cede, consign, deliver, demit, eschew, forgo, give up, leave, quit, relinquish, renounce, retire,

sacrifice, secede, submit, surrender, vacate, waive, withdraw, yield

RESIGNATION abdication, acceptance, acquiescence, compliance, deference, demission, endurance, forbearance, fortitude, humility, meekness, modesty, nonresistance, passiveness, passivity, patience, pluck, quietism, renunciation, submission, surrender, tolerance, toleration, withdrawal
letter demit

RESIGNED acquiescent, adjusted, complaint, passive, reconciled, subdued, submissive, unassertive, uncomplaining

RESILE rebound, recede, recoil, repercuss, retract, retreat, return, reverberate, shrink, withdraw

RESILIENCE bounce, buoyance, elasticity, energy, force, give, life, power, rebound, recoil, recovery, spring, tone

RESILIENT buoyant, debonair, elastic, expansive, flexible, rebounding, recoiling, spirited, springy, supple, volatile

RESIN 3 alk, gum, lac, tar 4 batu, brea, kava, kawa, kino, tolu 5 alkyd, amber, anime, butea, copal, cumar, elemi, epoxy, gugal, gugul, jalap, kauri, lacca, matti, myrrh, pitch, rosel, rosin 6 amyrin, antiar, asarum, balsam, binder, charas, conima, damnar, eserin, googul, guacin, guaiac, hartin, mastic, storax, tamanu 7 acaroid, acouchi, acrylic, alouchi, ambrite, aroiera, asphalt, benzoin, bisabol, catalin, copaiba, derride, exudate, fluavil, galipot, gamboge, herabol, lacquer, megilph, retinol, sagapen, seedlac, shellac 8 alkitran, almaciga, archipin, bakelite, bdellium, benjamin, cachibou, cannabin, colophan, copaline, euosmite, formvail, galagala, galbanum, gallipot, gedanite, glessite, guaiacum, labdanum, malapaho, melamine, olibanum, opopanax, phenolic,

retinite, sandarac, scammony, urethane 9 alchitran, ambergris, ambrosine, asafetida, colophane, colophony, elaterite, krantzite, sagapenum, sandarach, stabelite, tacamahac 10 euphorbium, guttagamba, terebrinth 11 guttapercha, liquidamber 12 frankincense
aromatic myrrh
balsamic acaroid, bdellium, benzoin
brown elaterite
calibar bean eserin
cerate basilicon
composition alkyd
dammar almaciga
fossil amber, ambrite, gedanite, glessite, hartite, retinasphalt, retinite, rumanite
fragrant ammoniac, cachibou, elemi, frankincense, myrrh, sandarac
gingerroot asarum
green ramanu
gum ammoniac, antiar, asaf(o)etida, assaf(o)etida, bdellium, bengal-kino, bis(s)abol, butea-kino, copal, dammar, gamboge, googul, gugal, gugul, laser, mastic
guttagum gamboge
kauri amboina-pitch
-like resinoid, retinoid
medicinal argeira
mineral caoutchouc, elaterite
narcotic charas, churus
pepper-tree mastic
plant prairie-dock
poisonous cannabin, derrid(e)
purified shellac
rockrose labdanum
shrub blisterbush
source angico, apalit, arar, aroeira, boswellia, camansi, canarium, clusia, commiphora, courbaril, doon, protium, rockrose, salai
synthetic acrylic, amb(e)-roid, bakelite, catalin, lucite, plexiglas, silicone
turpentine alk, gal(l)ipot

RESINOID alnuin, asclepidin, cerasin, chelonin, helonin, juglandin, lobelin, trillin

RESINOUS asphaltic, bituminous, gummose, gummous, gummy, pitchy, roset(t)y, rosiny, tarry, waxed

RESIST antagonize, assail, assault, attack, balk, beat off, buck, combat, confront, contest, counteract, defeat, defend, defy, disobey, dispute, face, fend, fight, foil, forbear, forgo, frustrate, gainstand, hold(off)(out), impugn, meet, oppose, parry, prevent, protest, rebel, rebuff, recalcitrate, refrain, refuse, reluct, repel, repugn, repulse, rest, stand(fast)(up to), stave off, stay, stem, stick, strive, struggle, thwart, ward off, weather, withset, withstand

RESISTANCE blockage, defence, defense, drag, friction, front, hostility, impedance, obstacle, opposition, rebuff, reluctance, renitence, sedition, stand, suppression

armed guer(r)illa, underground

box rheostat

passive satyagraha

to change inertia

unit begohm, megohm, microhm, milliohm, ohm, stratohm

RESISTANT defiant, hard, hostile, negative, obstinate, recalcitrant, renitent, repellent, stout, stubborn, tenacious, tough, unyielding, withstanding

RESISTOR bleeder, r(h)eostat

RESOLUTE animose, bent, bold, brave, constant, courageous, decided, desperado, determined, dogged, doughty, earnest, faithful, fast, feeble, firm, fixed, friable, game, grim, gritty, hard, infirm, inflexible, intrepid, leal, loyal, manful, obstinate, paid, payment, persevering, plucky, positive, resolved, rigid, set, stanch, steadfast, steady, stout, stubborn, true, undaunted, unshaken, valiant, weak

RESOLUTION acuerdo, analysis, anatomy, backbone, breakdown, censure, courage, decision, definiteness, deliberation, determination, disentanglement,

dissection, division, end, firmness, fortitude, grit, guts, harmonization, heart, legislation, manhood, mettle, motion, nerve, obstinacy, perseverance, pluck, power, proposal, proposition, purpose, resolve, scheme, settlement, solution, spirit, stamina, staunchness, steadfastness, strength, tenacity, thew, topic, verdict, vigor, will (power)

RESOLVE acquaint, act, analyse, anatomize, assoil, assure, bethink, conclude, confirm, consult, convince, decide, declare, decree, deliberate, determine, diminish, disentangle, dispel, disperse, dispose, dissect, dissipate, dissolve, divide, free, fuse, inform, intend, lapse, loosen, melt, part, plan, project, propose, purpose, reduce, relax, resolution, rule, scatter, scheme, separate, settle, solve, steven, think, unravel, unriddle, untangle, vouch, weaken, will

RESOLVED bent, bound, certain, convinced, decided, deliberate, determined, firm, intense, intent, liquified, melted, persuaded, relaxed, RESOLUTE, separated, settled

RESONANCE body, boom, clang(or), intensification, rapport, reflection, resound, reverberation, ringing, roar, roll, rumble, syntony, tintinnabulation, tympany, vibration

pert. syntonic, syntony

RESONANT booming, deep, full, mellow, plangent, pulsing, resounding, reverberant, rich, ringing, sonorous, throbbing, thunderous, vibrant, vibrating

RESORT abode, address, apply, assemblage, baths, betake, casino, cause, company, concourse, crowd, devote, direct, dive, employ, expedient, frequent, hangout, haunt, hotel, howf(f), inn, makeshift, meet(ing place), purlieu, recourse, recur, refer, refuge, reissue, rendezvous, repair, reset,

resource, retreat, return, revert, shift, shore, source, spa, springs, stopgap, substitute, throng, tryst, turn, use, utilize, visit, watering place

health sanatorium, sanitarium, spa

hot spring spatel

RESOUND beat, boom, celebrate, chime, chink, clang, clink, din, dun, echo, explode, extol(l), jingle, murmur, peal, proclaim, reverberate, ring, roar, roll, rumble, thunder, tinkle, tintinnabulate, utter, vibrate

RESOUNDING impressive, loud, RESONANT

RESOURCE(S) ability, asset(s), bankroll, belongings, capital, contrivance, device(s), estate, expedient, funds, ingenuity, means, method, money, power, recourse, reserve(s), resort, riches, savings, shift, skill, stocks, stratagem, substance, substitute, supply, support, value, wealth, worth

guardian conservationist, conservator, ecologist, environmentalist

hidden ace in the hole

RESOURCEFUL apt, clever, expert, facile, fendy, fertile, ingenious, resilient, sharp, shifty, smart

RESPECT acknowledge, admiration, admire, adoration, adore, aim, anticipate, appreciate, appreciation, aspect, attention, attitude, awe, care, cherish, concern, consider(ation), courtesy, deem, defer(ence), detail, dignity, duty, esteem, estimation, face, favor, fear, front, heed, homage, honor, idolize, interest, look, notice, obeisance, observe, outlook, ovation, overawe, particular, point, postpone, prize, reference, regard, relation(ship), repute, respite, revere(nce), tashrif, testimonial, toast, tribute, value, venerate, veneration, worship

act of devoir

pay bow, curts(e)y, genuflect, greet, kneel, ko(w)tow, pledge, sala(a)m, salute, scrape, toast

RESPECTABILITY babbittry, consequence, decency, probity

RESPECTABLE august, bal(a)batish, conventional, decent, douce, estimable, fausant, good, honest, honorable, proper, redoubted, reputable, reverent, sublime, tolerable, upright, venerable

RESPECTFUL careful, ceremonious, civil, considerate, courteous, decorous, deferent(ial), duteous, dutiful, heedful, honorific, obeisant, obsequious, observant, polite, reverent(ial)

RESPECTING about, anent, concerning, pertaining to, regarding

RESPECTIVE attentive, careful, concrete, correspondent, corresponding, distributive, heedful, individual, own, partial, particular, proper, proportional, proportionate, relative, separate, several, special, specific, suitable, sundry

RESPECTIVELY apiece, each, individually, particularly, proportionately, severally, singly, successively

RESPECTS compliments, devoirs, greetings, regards

RESPIRATION anapnea, aspiration, breath, breathing, dyspnea, eupn(o)ea, exhalation, expiration, inhalation, inspiration, sigh

comb. spiro

difficulty asthma, cough, dyspn(o)ea, emphysema, rale

disease bronchitis, catarrh, cold, cough, flu, influenza, ondine's curse, pneumonia, tuberculosis

failure apnea, apnoea, asphyxia

normal eupn(o)ea

rapid tachypnea

recorder anapnograph, atmograph, respirometer

test agpar

RESPIRATOR aspirator, gasmask, inhalator, inspirator, iron-lung, lungmotor, muzzle, oxygen mask, pulmotor, resuscitator

RESPIRE blow, breathe, ex-

hale, expire, inhale, inspire, live, revive, sign, snuffle

RESPITE alleviate, break, breath(er), breathing space, cessation, delay, desist, extension, forbear(ance), frist, halt, hiatus, interlude, intermission, interval, layoff, leisure, opportunity, pause, period, postponement, prolong, recess, regard, relief, reprieve, respect, rest, spell, stay, stop, surcease, suspend, suspension, time out, truce, withhold

RESPLENDENT aureate, blazing, bright, brilliant, dazzling, effulgent, flaming, glittering, glorious, glowing, gorgeous, grand, illustrious, luminous, lustrous, magnificent, outstanding, radiant, refulgent, shining, silver, splendid, sublime, superb

RESPOND accept, accord, act, answer, anthem, behave, corbel, correspond, echo, feel, match, pilaster, pillar, react, rejoin, reply, response, responsory, retort, return, rise, rsvp, satisfy, sense, write

RESPONDENT answerer, answering, corresponding, defendant

RESPONSE accord, amen, answer, anthem, antiphon(y), chorus, earful, echo, letter, reaction, refrain, rejoinder, reply, retort, sensation, sympathy, verse

choral introit

involuntary reflex

RESPONSIBILITY accountability, blame, burden, care, charge, duty, encumbrance, guilt, incubus, liability, obligation, onus, reliability, trust(worthiness), wite

evade pass the buck, shirk, soldier

RESPONSIBLE accountable, amenable, answerable, bal(a)batish, blam(e)able, capable, chargeable, competent, culpable, dependable, good, honest, liable, reliable, respectable, solid, solvent, stable, subject, trustworthy

RESPONSION(S) answer,

disputation, exam(ination), little-go, smalls

RESPONSIVE answering, aware, bitwise, bridlewise, compassionate, corresponding, docile, elastic, hypophonic, lenient, obedient, openminded, passible, pliable, pliant, prone, reactional, replying, responsible, sensitive, sentient, supple, susceptible, sympathetic, tender, warmhearted

REST 3 fix, lay, lie, nap, put, set, sit 4 base, calm, crap, ease, halt, idle, lean, loaf, loll, lull, rely, seat, stop 5 abide, abode, break, cease, couch, death, found, hinge, light, pause, peace, perch, place, quiet, relax, renew, roost, stand, trust 6 alight, anchor, bottom, depend, desist, excess, fewter, gaffle, ground, linger, lounge, recess, refuse, relics, repose, settle, siesta, sprawl, unbend 7 balance, bivouac, breathe, caesura, comfort, consist, deposit, holiday, leisure, lie down, lodging, recline, refresh, remains, remnant, residue, respite, shelter, silence, slumber, support, surfeit, surplus 8 breather, inaction, interval, leavings, quietude, reposure, residuum, serenity, take five, vacation 9 cessation, establish, remainder, stillness 10 inactivity, relaxation 11 odds and ends, tranquility 12 intermission

bring to bottom, bury, land, light

day sabbath, sunday

harrow cammock, ononis, weed

house ambalam, chan, chhatri, dak-bungalow, dharmsala, hostel, hotel, inn, kaan, kaun, kawn, khan, khankah, serai, tavern

musical sospiro

musket croc, gaffle

noonday nap, siesta

on one's oars gold-brick, idle, relax, shirk, soldier

period break, coffeebreak, smoke-o(h)

poetic caesura

principle adharma

RESTATE paraphrase, recapitulate, rehash, repeat, rephrase, reword

RESTAURANT automat, beanery, beanstop, bistro, boite, brasserie, buffet, buttery, cabaret, cafe(teria), chophouse, deli(catessen), diner, drive-in, eatery, estiminet, filling station, foodery, grill, grubbery, hashhouse, hotel, inn, lunchroom, mess(hall), night club, onearm, pizzeria, pub, rathskeller, rotisserie, steakhouse, tavern, teahouse, tearoom, trattoria, wineshop

fee cover-charge

meal blue plate, table d'hote

unsanitary greasy spoon

RESTFUL comfortable, peaceful, placid, quiet, relaxed, relaxing, reposeful, soft, tranquil

RESTING abed, asleep, dormant, latent, quiescent, sleeping

place bed, camp, gist, gite, halfpace, landing, quarterpace, quarters, stage, stop

RESTITUTION amends, apocatastasis, atonement, compensation, indemnity, payment, rebate, recompense, recovery, redress, refund, reimbursement, reinstatement, reparation, repayment, requital, restoration, return

RESTIVE balky, contrary, disobedient, fidgeting, froward, impatient, inactive, inflexible, mulish, obstinate, persistent, perverse, pigheaded, recalcitrant, refractory, RESTLESS, sluggish, stubborn, uneasy, unmanageable, unruly

RESTIVENESS anxiety, impatience

RESTLESS agitated, antsy, anxious, changeful, discontented, feverish, fickle, fidgety, fikie, fitful, flighty, fluttery, fretful, fussy, haunty, hectic, impatient, inquiet, itchy, jittery, jumpy, inconstant, nervous, perturbed, rampler, RESTIVE, roving, sleepless, spasmodic, twitch(et)y, unceasing, uneasy, unquiet, unresty, unsettled, wandering

RESTLESSNESS disquiet, fidgets, jactation, unrest

RESTORATION anaplerosis, apocatastasis, exchange, improvement, instauration, reconstruction, recovery, reinstatement, remodeling, renewal, renovation, repair, reparation, replacement, restitution, resurrection, return, revival

of war spoils postliminy

RESTORATIVE acopon, alterative, analeptic, anodyne, corrective, curative, invigorating, remedial, remedy, renewer, reparatory, reviver, salutary, sanative, tonic

RESTORE calm, convert, convey, cure, doctor, fix, give back, heal, mend, put back, readjust, rebuild, recall, reclaim, recompense, reconstruct, recover, recuperate, redeem, reestablish, refresh, refund, refurbish, rehabilitate, reinstall, reinstate, rejuvenate, remedy, renew, renovate, repair, repay, replace, rescue, restitute, retrieve, return, revive, save, stet

confidence reassure

deletion stet

to consciousness bring round, revive

to health cure, doctor, heal, mend

vigor rejuvenate

RESTORER balsam, cobbler, curer, furbisher, healer, medicine, mender, ointment, patcher, repairman, soother, tinker(er)

RESTRAIN abridge, abstain, arrest, awe, bar, bate, bind, block, bridle, calm, catch, chain, chasten, check(mate), clog, compesce, confine, constrain, contain, control, cork up, cramp, curb, dam, deter, dissuade, enjoin, fetter, forbear, forbid, govern, guard, halter, hamper, handcuff, hinder, hold back, impede, imprison, inhibit, interrupt, keep back, leash, limit, moderate, muzzle, obstruct, prevent, refrain, rein, reserve, restrict, rule, shackle, simplify, snaffle, snub, stay, stem, stint, stop, strangle, stymie, subdue,

suppress, temper, tether, tie, trammel, trash, withdraw, withhold

RESTRAINED bated, captive, chaste, disciplined, discreet, hidebound, pent, plain, reserved, reticent, selfcontrolled, severe, simple, sober, temperate, unadorned

RESTRAINER band, bit, bonds, bridle, curb, deterrent, fetter, gag, handcuffs, harness, leash, muzzle, rein, shackle, stay, stranglehold

RESTRAINT aplomb, arrest, aweband, barrier, bit, bondage, check, coercion, commitment, confinement, compulsion, constraint, control, curb, decency, deterrence, discipline, duress, economy, force, incarceration, inhibition, law, leash, limitation, manacle, moderation, order, prevention, prohibition, quietness, repression, reserve, restriction, reticence, shackle, simplicity, stayer, stop(page), suppression, taboo, tabu, temperance, trammel, unobtrusiveness

burdensome ball and chain

free from extricate, unbind, unshackle, untie

without ad libitum

RESTRICT abridge, abstain, ban, bind, bound, censor, check, circumscribe, coerce, confine, constrict, contract, corral, cramp, curb, diminish, entail, hamper, hinder, impede, keep(in bounds), limit, mancipate, modify, narrow, prohibit, qualify, repress, restrain, scantle, shrink, stint, swaddle, thirl, tie(down), trammel

RESTRICTED classified, confined, exclusive, finite, held down, insular, limited, local, narrow, secret, strait, strict

RESTRICTION burden, but, condition, confinement, constriction, denial, limitation, qualification, regulation, reservation, restraint, stent, stint, tightening

RESTRICTIVE astringent, binding, cliquish, determinative, exclusive, limiting, select, severe, styptic

RESTRINGE bind, confine, restrict

RESTY inactive, lazy, quiet, rancid, reasty, restive, sluggish

RESULT accrue, act, additament, addition, additive, aftermath, answer, apotelesm, arise, attend, close, come about, conclusion, consequence, corollary, decision, derivative, development, devolve, effect, end (ing), ensue, event(uate), fall out, fare, finish, follow, fruit, happen, harvest, issue, offshoot, offspring, outcome, pan out, payoff, proceed, product, prove, rebound, recoil, resolution, revert, rise, score, sequel(a), sequence, solution, spawn, spring, succeed, success, sum, terminate, total, turn out, upcome, upshot, yield

comb. ade, ado, tion, tious, ure

favorable success

in afford, beget, cause, determine, effect(uate), entail, fulfill, produce, realize

remote repercussion

unfortunate backfire

RESUME abridgment, abstract, assume, begin again, bio, biog, biography, continue, dossier, epitome, epitomize, go on, recommence, re-enter, reiterate, renew, reoccupy, reopen, repeat, repossess, return to, roundup, summarize, summary, synopsis, vita

march break camp

RESUPINE apathetic, lying, prostrate, recumbent

RESURRECT disinter, exhume, rally, reanimate, restore, resuscitate, revive, revivify

RESURRECTION anastasimon, anodos, ascension, easter, rebirth, restoration, revival, rise, rist

plant fernwort

symbol grape, holly

symbolic color green

RESUSCITATE bring to, quicken, rally, renew, restore, resurrect, revive, revivify

RESUSCITATION anabiosis,

katsu, reanimation, reincarnation, renewal, revival

RET ascribe, dampen, drench, impregnate, impute, moisten, rait, rate, reckon, rot, saturate, soak, sog, sop, steep, waterlog

RETABLE altar, gradin, ledge, predella, shelf

RETAIL barter, commercial, distribute, hawk, market, peddle, regrate, relate, repeat, sale, sell, trade, vend

RETAILER agent, broker, chandler, dealer, huckster, merchant, middleman, salesman

RETAIN athold, behold, belong, conserve, detain, employ, engage, enjoy, entertain, forbear, have, hire, hold(back), host, husband, keep, maintain, own, possess, preserve, prevent, recollect, refrain, remember, reserve, restrain, save, stet, sustain, withhold

RETAINER(S) adherent, attendant, bodyguard, burkunda(u)ze, cortege, dependent, employment, engagement, fee, henchman, hewe, huscarl, income, menial, myrmidon, pandour, retinue, servant, train

RETAKE recapture, recover(y), redeem, rephotograph

RETALIATE avenge, counter, get even, hit back, pay (back), punish, reciprocate, repay, requite, retort, return, revenge, strike back, turn on

RETALIATION punishment, recompense, recrimination, repayment, reprisal, requital, retorsion, retort(ion), retribution, revenge, talion, tit-for-tat, vengeance

RETARD arrest, backen, baffle, balk, belate, brake, catch, check, clog, decelerate, decrease, defer, delay, detain, encumber, fetter, hamper, hinder, hold up, impede, interrupt, laten, lessen, obstruct, postpone, procrastinate, reduce, restrain, slacken, slow, stem, stop, stunt, tarry

RETARDATION arrest, backwardness, check, deceleration, decrease, delay, detention, drag, ease-off, hin-

drance, holdup, lag, mongolism, obstruction, setback, slackening, slowdown, slowness

RETARDED backward, behind, defective, feebleminded, overage, simple, slow, stupid, subnormal

RETCH expand, extend, gag, keck(le), hawk, heave, reach, recche, recoil, spew, strain, stretch, vomit

RETE net(work), plexus, scale, web

RETENTION holding, keeping, lien, maintenance, memory, possession, prehension, preservation, recall, recollection, remembrance, restraint, retainment, self-control, tenacity

RETENTIVE clinging, grasping, gripping, holding, keeping, parsimonious, prehensile, restrained, restraint, reticent, stick-to-itive, tenacious, viselike

RETENUE discretion, reserve, selfcontrol, selfrestraint

RETHE ardent, cruel, fierce, severe

RETHENESS cruelty, ferocity, rage, uproar

RETIARY meshed, netlike, spider(y), telar

RETICENCE reserve, restraint, secretiveness, shyness, silence

RETICENT aloof, backward, bashful, close(mouthed), cold, constrained, cool, curbed, dark, detached, discreet, distant, frigid, inaccessible, inhibited, introverted, mysterious, offish, prudent, quiet, remote, removed, repressed, reserved, restrained, retiring, secretive, shrinking, shy, silent, snug, sparing, stand-offish, suppressed, taciturn, tightlipped, undemonstrative

RETICULAR, RETICULATED cancellate, cancellous, entangled, intercrossed, intricate, meshed, netlike, netted, retiary, retiform, weblike

RETICULE bag, basket, bonnet, cabas, carryall, etui, etwee, handbag, pocket, purse, satchel, workbag

RETICULUM bag, belly,

mattulla, meshwork, mitome, net(work), neuroglia, stomach, tissue

RETIFORM See RETICULAR.

RETINA *afterimage* photogene
cell rod
fatigue minuthesis
part color zone, cone, rod, yellow-spot
pigment chlorophane, chromophane, rhodophane, rhodopsin

RETINACULUM band, frenum, funicle, gland, muscle

RETINON codol

RETINUE attendants, company, cortege, court, crew, entourage, escort, family, followers, following, ging, harem, meiny, retainers, retention, rout, service, sowarry, suite, tail, train, troop

RETIRE abdicate, back, bed(down), crawl in, depart, depose, disappear, dismiss, dissuade, flop, hit the hay, leave, pension, quit, recede, recoil, recover, remove, resign, resile, retract, retreat, retrocede, return, rusticate, sack down, scram, settle, turn in, vanish, withdraw

RETIRED abed, devious, emeritus, gone, hidden, inactive, inmost, isolated, lone, otiose, outgone, private, quiet, remote, removed, reserved, secluded, secret, sequestered, shadowy, solitary, superannuated, withdrawn

RETIREMENT departure, dismissal, isolation, leisure, privacy, recession, retreat, secess, seclusion, settlement, solitude, withdrawal

RETIRING backward, bashful, concave, diffident, fugient, gentle, introverted, modest, nesh, quiet, recessive, reserved, reticent, shy, timid, umbratic, unobtrusive, unsociable, withdrawn

RETORT alembic, answer, backword, blizzard, boiler, bombola, comeback, countercharge, crucible, mot, pelican, quip, rebut, recoil,

recriminate, reflect, reject, rejoinder, repartee, repay, reply, response, retaliate, retaliation, riposte, rise, sally, set-down, squelch, sterilizer, tube, turn, vessel, vial, wisecrack

RETOUCH amend, correct, improve, repair, rework

RETRACE backtrack, recall, reinspect, remember, return

RETRACT abandon, abjure, abrogate, annul, back down, bend, crawfish, deny, disavow, disown, draw back, forswear, nullify, prevent, pull in, recall, recant, recede, remove, renounce, repeal, repudiate, rescind, resile, retire, retreat, retrograde, revoke, withdraw

RETRACTION palinode, recantation, recession, withdrawal

RETREAD recap, repair, tire, vet(eran)

RETREAT 3 ark, den, ebb, jib, mew, run, shy, spa **4** abri, cave, duck, flee, lair, nest, nook, port, quit, rest, rout, spot, turn **5** arbor, blink, bower, cover, crawl, crypt, dodge, haven, ingle, leave, quail, wince, yield **6** adytum, alcove, asylum, back up, blench, bug out, burrow, castle, cop out, corner, cringe, depart, escape, flinch, go back, harbor, recede, recess, recoil, reduce, refuge, resile, retire, return, revolt, safety, shrink, studio, swerve **7** cenacle, hideout, privacy, rescind, respite, retrace, retract, sanctum, shelter **8** anabasis, back down, cloister, crawfish, draw back, fall back, hang back, hideaway, preserve, pull back, security, sidestep, solitude, stampede, turntail, withdraw **9** anchorage, departure, hermitage, isolation, katabasis, recession, rusticate, sanctuary, seclusion **10** give ground, ivory tower, retirement, withdrawal **11** anacleticum
military katabasis
religious as(h)ram

RETRENCH abbreviate, abridge, bate, clip, curtail, cut(back)(down), decrease,

deduct, diminish, economize, excise, intercept, lessen, omit, pare, reduce, remove, repress, roll back, save, shorten

RETRENCHMENT breastwork, cut, deduction, diminution, ditch, lessening, parapet, rampart, traverse

RETRIBUTION affliction, amends, compensation, mannaia, nemesis, pay, penalty, punishment, recompense, redress, reparation, repayment, reprisal, requital, restitution, retaliation, return, revenge, reward, trial, vengeance
goddess ara, ate
law karma

RETRIEVE correct, fetch, find, get back, mend, rally, rebuild, recall, reclaim, recoup, recover, recruit, recuperate, redeem, regain, remedy, repair, rescue, restore, revive, salvage, save, shack

RETROGRADATION decline, deterioration, reversion

RETROGRADE backslide, backward, catabolic, contrary, crawfish, decadent, decline, declining, degenerate, deteriorate, ebb, inverse, invert(ed), lapse, opposed, rearward, recede, recidivate, regressive, relapse, retiring, retrace, retract, retreat(ing), retrocede, retrogression, return, reverse(ly), revert, slow, withdraw(ing), worsen

RETROGRESS See RETROGRADE.

RETROGRESSION atrophy, degeneration, fallback, retreat, retroaction, reversion, setback

RETROSPECT look back, recall, recollect, refer, reflect, remember, reminisce, review

RETROSPECTION recollection, review

RETROVERSION annulment, reversal, reversion

RETUND attenuate, beat back, blunt, dull, refute, subdue, turn

RETURN advert, answer, backtrack, bring(back), come back, compensate,

compensation, dividend, elect, exchange, gain, give back, homecoming, income, indemnify, interchange, make amends, net, pay, put back, reaction, realization, reappear, rebate, rebound, reciprocate, recommit(ment), recompense, recourse, recovery, recrudesce, recur(rence), reddition, reelect, reentrance, reentry, refund, regress(ion), rejoin, remand, remigrate, remigration, remit, render, rendition, renew, repatriate, repay, replace, reply, report, requite, respond, restitution, restoration, restore, retaliate, retort, retract, revenue, reverse, reversion, revert, revisit, revolve, reward, ripost(e), rotate, send back, setback, take, turn, wind, yield
evil for evil retaliate
not yielding nonprofit, unprofitable
to relapse, resume
RETURNS gain, gate, income, proceeds, receipts, report, votes
RETZ, DE bluebeard
REUBEN *parent* jacob, leah
REUEL *father* esau
son mizzah, nahath, shammah, zerah
REUMAH *offspring* gaham, maachah, tebah, thahash
REUNION affair, assembly, convention, event, gathering, meeting, reconciliation
island city st pierre, st denis
REUNITE rally, reconcile, rejoin, reune
REVAL riga
REVAMP change, redo, reform, renovate, revise, update
REVEAL advise, air, announce, babble, bare, betray, bewray, bid, blab, blare, bring out, clarify, communicate, confide, decipher, descry, develop, disbosom, disclose, discover, disembosom, display, divulge, evidence, exhibit, expose, impart, indicate, inform, introduce, jamb, manifest, offer, open, ostend, present, proclaim, publish, show, speak, tell,

unburden, uncover, unhele, unmask, unravel, unveil, unwrap, wray
REVEALING anacalypsis, apocalyptic(al), disclosure, OPEN
REVEILLE call, dian(a), levet, rouse, signal, travally
REVEL bezzle, bizle, carnival, carouse, celebration, conviviality, delight, disorder, domineer, entertainment, feast, festival, gala, gavall, high-go, indulge, merrymaking, orgy, play, randy, riot, roist(er), splore, spree, tresche, wake, wassail, withdraw
REVELANT clear, intelligible, revealing
REVELATION afflatus, apocalypse, appearance, bathkol, bible, disclosure, discovery, dream, giveaway, gospel, inspiration, manifestation, oracle, prophecy, showing, theophania, theophany, theopneustia, theopneusty, tora(h), vision
discreditable expose
symbol pale horse
REVELER bacchanal, bacchante, buster, carouser, franion, pierrot, player, roisterer
REVELRY bacchanal(ia), carnival, carousal, carouse, festival, joy, orgy, merrymaking, REVEL, soiree, spree, wassail
cry evoe
god comus
indulge in roist(er)
REVENANT apparition, demon, eidolon, fetch, ghost, haunt, phantasm, phantom, shade, specter, spirit, spook, wraith
REVENGE amends, avenge (ment), boulangism, comeuppance, expiate, get even, justify, punish(ment), quittance, reciprocation, recompense, redress, reparation, repay(ment), reprisal, requital, requite, retaliate, retaliation, retribution, revanche, satisfaction, tit for tat, ultion, vengeance, vindicate, wreak, wroik
goddess nemesis
REVENGEFUL grim, inexorable, obdurate, relentless, vindictive

REVENUE annat(es), assets, benefice, earnings, entrada, fruits, funds, income, interest, jagir, money, proceeds, produce, profit, receipts, rent(al), rente, return, tax(es), yield
collecting right dewannee, dewanny, diwani, jagheer, jaghir(e), jagir
collector aumil(dar), irs, talukdar, taxgatherer, zamindar
farmer firmarius
1st year's annat
pope's annat(es)
source amani, apanage, capital, interest, taxes
state hacienda
water jalkar
REVERBERATE answer, bounce, echo, react, rebound, recoil, redound, reecho, reflect, repeat, repel, repercuss, resile, resound, return, revert
REVERBERATING echoing, reboant(ic), repercussive, resonant, resounding, ringing, sonorous, vibrant
REVERBERATION boom, echo, plangency, reboation, rebound, reflection, repercussion, resound(ing)
without anechoic
REVERE admire, adore, apotheosize, appreciate, bless, cherish, defer, deify, esteem, hallow, honor, love, prize, regard, repute, respect, treasure, value, venerate, worship
REVERENCE adoration, apotheosis, awe, bow, curtsy, deference, devotion, dignity, dread, esteem, fealty, fear, fidelity, homage, loyalty, mensk, obeisance, piety, regard, REVERE, veneration, worship, wurth, zeal
gesture of genuflection, genuflexion, kneeling
REVEREND abuna, churchman, holy, revered, sacred, sri, venerable, venerated
REVERENT awesome, awful, deferential, devout, dutiful, respectful, solemn, strong, venerational, venerative
REVERIE absentmindedness, brown-study, daydream, dream, dump, dwam, fancy,

fantasy, inattention, joy, mooning, musing, notion, pensiveness, phantasy, pipedream, preoccupation, rage, rejoicing, revelry, rumor, vision, wantonness, woolgathering

REVERS lapel

REVERSAL backcast, backflip, blow, cassation, change, double, inversion, overthrow, overturn, regression, retoflexion, retroversion, reversion, rout, switch, tergiversation, turnabout, volte-face
comb. all(o), dis
dramatic peripateia

REVERSE about-face, across, adverse, adversity, affliction, annul, back(off) (up), butt, calamity, catastrophe, check, contradict, contrary, converse, convert, countermand, countermarch, defeat, descent, disaffirm, disaster, discouragement, down, evert, flop, fold, invert, mischance, misfortune, mishap, obverse, opposite, overthrow, overturn, paradox, rear, recoil, relapse, repeal, rescind, retrace, retract, return, reversion, revoke, right about, rout, setback, subvert, tail, tergiversation, tragedy, transpose, trial, turn(about) (around), undo, upend, upset, vacate, verso, veto, void, volte-face
comb. ant(i)
direction back(pedal) (track) (water) (up)
page verso
rotation backspin

REVERSION atavism, birthright, cast-back, cataplasia, escheat, feedback, lapse, recidivism, reconversion, regression, relapse, remainder, remains, residue, retrocession, retrogression, retroversion, return(ing), reversal, reverse, revulsion, scraps, throwback, turn (about)
cells anaplasia, anaplasis
to primitive cataplasia

REVERT advert, annul, antistrophe, back(slide), escheat, go back, lapse, recede, recidivate, recover, recur, regress, relapse, re-

store, retreat, retrocede, retrograde, retrogress, return, reverse, revest, revive, revoke, turn back, undo

REVERTING atavistic, recessive, refluent, reflux, regressive

REVEST attire, clothe, dress, put on, reinstate, revert, robe

REVETMENT facing, retaining wall

REVIEW advise, analyze, article, canvass, comment(ary), criticism, criticize, critique, discuss, dissertate, drama, examine, handle, inspection, journal, magazine, narrative, notice, parade, periodical, procession, puff, reconsider, reexamine, remember, repeat, repetition, resume, retrospect, revise, scrutiny, show, study, summarize, summary, survey, tell, ventilate, write up

REVIEWER author, censor, censurer, critic(aster), commentator, commenter, reviser, writer

REVILE abuse, asperse, assail, bawl out, berate, blackguard, blaspheme, calumniate, curse, debase, defame, denigrate, disgrace, disparage, execrate, hate, jaw, libel, malign, objurgate, rail, rate, reproach, scold, shend, shent, slander, smear, taunt, tonguelash, traduce, upbraid, vilify, vituperate, wig

REVINCE See REFUTE.

REVISE alter, amend, better, blue-pencil, castigate, change, correct, edit, emend(ate), improve, look over, modify, patch, readjust, rearrange, recast, rectify, redact, redress, reexamine, reflect, remedy, renew, revamp, review, rework, rewrite, update, work over

REVISION correction, recension, review, survey, version

REVIVAL palingenesis, rebirth, renaissance, renascence, restoration, service

REVIVALIST apostle, evangelist, missionary

REVIVE activate, bring back, come to, cheer, daw, en-

liven, perk(up), popularize, quicken, rally, reanimate, recall, recover, recuperate, refresh, regenerate, reinspirit, reinvigorate, rejuvenate, rekindle, relive, remember, renew, renovate, respire, restore, resurrect, resuscitate, revitalize, revivify, rouse, wake
fermentation stum
fire chunk

REVOCATION ademption, annulment, nullification, recall, recantation, repeal, retraction, reversal, withdrawal

REVOKE abjure, abolish, abrogate, adeem, annul, cancel, check, commute, countermand, enact, enforce, execute, finagle, lift, nig, nullify, prevent, recall, recant, recover, renege, renig, repeal, rescind, restrain, retract, reverse, revive, vacate, void, withdraw
at cards fainague, finagle

REVOLT agitation, appall, arise, aversion, contumacy, desert, disgust, disobey, displease, distaste, emeute, insurgence, insurrection, loathing, mutiny, nausea(te), offend, outbreak, putsch, rebel(lion), recoil, reluct, repel, repugnance, repulsion, revolution, riot, rise, rising, sedition, sicken, strike, uprising, uproar

REVOLTING abhorrent, abominable, disgusting, fearful, hateful, hideous, horrid, loathsome, nasty, nauseating, obnoxious, odious, offensive, repellent, repulsive, shocking, ugly

REVOLUTION alteration, anarchism, anarchy, bend, bolshevism, breakdown, cataclysm, castastrophe, change, circuit, convulsion, coup(d'etat), cycle, debacle, epoch, gyration, gyre, insurrection, mutiny, orbit, overthrow, overturn, putsch, rebellion, recurrence, revolt, revulsion, rotation, subversion, turn, twist, uprising, upset, war, wheel
american See AMERICA *revolution.*
french See FRANCE *revolution.*

rate revs, rpm

REVOLUTIONARY, REVOLUTIONIST anarch(ist), bolshevik, bolshevist, bolshie, bonnet-rouge, carbonarist, carbonaro, castro, extremist, fenian, insurrectionary, lenin, marat, pestel, radical, reb(el), red(cap), sans-culot(te), septembrist, settimo, sinnfeiner, subversive

REVOLVE agitate, birl, cant, circle, circulate, cogitate, consider, contemplate, deliberate, eddy, excogitate, gyrate, meditate, muse, orbit, oscillate, pirl, pirouette, ponder, reason, recur, reflect, restore, return, roll, rotate, ruminate, speculate, spin, study, swing, swirl, think, trundle, turn, twirl, weight, wheel, whirl

REVOLVER bulldog, colt, dungeon, firearm, gat, gun, hogleg, pistol, repeater, rifle, rod, sidearm, weapon

REVUE burlesque, entertainment, follies, musical, parody, show
skit blackout

REVULSION aversion, disgust, dislike, distaste, fear, inversion, loathing, reaction, repugnance, repulsion, reversion, revolt, revolution, transformation, withdrawal

REWARD accolade, agree, ameed, award, badge, bonus, bounty, bribe, compensate, compensation, consider, crown, cup, decide, decorate, decoration, desert, fee, garland, gersum, gratuity, guerdon, heed, honor(arium), income, indemnity, laureate, laurel, look, medal, meed, merit, notice, observe, oscar, pay, plume, praise, premium, present, prize, profit, quarry, recognize, recompense, regard, remunerate, remuneration, repay, requite, return, tip, token, trophy, utu, wages, warison, yield

REWARDING fat, premiant, satisfying

REZIA *father* ulla

RHADAMANTHUS *brother* aeacus, minos

parent europa, jupiter, zeus
wife alcmene

RHAMNUS bearberry, bogbirch, buckthorn, chittamwood, coffeeberry, dogwood, holly, rheinberry
product cascara, lokao

RHAPONTIC knapweed, pieplant, rhubarb

RHAPSODIC effusive, enthusiastic, rapturous

RHAPSODIST anthologist, enthusiast, reciter, visionary

RHAPSODY bombast, composition, fustian, jumble, medley, miscellany, poem, rant, rapture, recitation, rodomontade, series, song, string
section lassu

RHEA agdistis, antaea, avestruz, bird, cybele, dindymene, em(e)u, fiber, grass, moon, nandow, nandu, ops, ostrich, ramie, ratite, satellite
attendants atys, corybantes, curetes, galli
consort cronus, kronos, saturn
moon of saturn
offspring ceres, demeter, hades, hera, hestia, juno, pluto, poseidon, vesta, zeus
parent gaea, uranus
priest curete

RHEA SILVIA *consort* mars
father numitor
son remus, romulus

RHEBOK antelope, peele, pelea, roebuck

RHEIMS *river* vesle

RHEMA term, verb, word

RHENE *consort* oileus
son medon

RHENIUM *source* molybdenite

RHEOSTAT dimmer, regulator, resister

RHESA *kin* johanan, zerubbabel

RHESUS bandar, bhunder, bundar, macaque, monkey
parent eioneus, euterpe, oceanus, tethys
slayer diomedes, odysseus, ulysses

RHETOR master, orator, speaker, talker, teacher

RHETORIC antiloquence, bombast, diction, elegance, elocution, eloquence, floridity, flourish, floweriness, grammar, grandiloquence,

hyperbole, magniloquence, oratory, ornateness, speech, syntax

RHETORICAL articulate, aureate, bombastic, declamatory, eloquent, figured, flamboyant, flatulent, florid, flowery, fluent, forensic, grammatical, grandiloquent, inflated, magniloquent, oratorical, ornate, swelling, tumid, turgid
device alliteration, anadiplosis, anaphora, anastrophe, antiphrasis, antistrophe, antithesis, apagoge, apophasis, aporia, apostrophe, asyndeton, epandos, litotes, metaphor, onomatopoeia, personification, simile, synchoresis
digression ecbole
plus grammar and logic trivia

RHEUM catarrh, chole, cold, discharge, rhinitis, rhubarb, tears

RHEUMATISM *muscular* myalgia
remedy agathin, alphol, analgen, mezerium, salacetol, salol, steroid
root twinleaf, wild yam, wintergreen
weed dogbane, pipsissewa

RHEXIA deer-grass, meadow-beauty

RHIANNON *consort* manawyddan, pwyll
offspring pryderi

RHINAL narial, nasal

RHINE ditch, drain, hemp, rijn, runnel
city on bingen, bonn, dusseldorf, mannheim, speyer, spires
magic hoard rheingold, rhinegold
nymph lorelei
pert. rhenish
rock trass
tributary aar(e), ijssel, ill, lahn, main, moselle, ruhr, waal
wine affentaler, bacharach, forst, geisenheimer, hock, johannisberger, leister, liebfraumilch, marcobrunner, moselle, niersteiner, rauentaler, riesling, rudesheimer, rulander, scharlachberger, stein(berger), sylvaner, traminer

RHINESTONE dewdrop

RHINO cash, money, pontoon

RHINOCEROUS abada, abath, badak, baluchitherium, borele, ceratorhine, diceros, keitloa, nasicorn, reem, topan, unhofo, unicorn, upeygan
beetle scarab(aeid), uang
bird beefeater, hornbill, topau
cousin tapir
extinct aphelops, baluchitherium, elasmotherium, teleocerus
woolly tichorhine

RHIPIDION fan, flabellum, whisk

RHIPSALIS cactus, cassytha, woevine

RHIZOCTONIA *disease* black dot, dartrose, rosette, russet-scab, scurf, stemcanker

RHIZOID rootcell, rootlet

RHIZOME aralia, arnica, aruke, asarum, bulb, caapi, calams, corm, culvers, gentian, ginger, ipecac, kava(kava), nard, scopola, stolon, taro, trillium, tritcum, zedoary

RHIZOPOD amoeba, arcella, diffugia, foraminifera, pelomyxa, testacean

RHODE *consort* helius
parent amphitrite, aphrodite, helia, helios, poseidon
son actis

RHODE ISLAND *bay* narraganset
bent agrostis, couch grass, foxtail, furzetop, redtop
capital providence
city bristol, cranston, kingston, newport, pawtucket, providence
college brown, bryant, pembroke
founder roger williams
greening apple
indian narraganset, niantic, wampanoag
insurrectionist dorr
island block
motto hope
native gunflint
nickname little rhody
peak durfee hill
red chicken, fowl
river blackstone, pawtuxet
state flower violet
state tree maple

RHODES *city* ialysos

conqueror artemisia
festival chelidonia
knight hospitaler
magicians telchines
peak atabyrian
statue abaton, colossus
tyrant cleobulus
wonder colossus

RHODESIA zimbabwe
army school bulawayo, gwelo
capital salisbury
city bulawayo, gwelo, ndola, salisbury, umtali
language bantu, ila
leader ian smith, muzorewa, nkomo, sithole
nationalist movement anc, zanu, zapu
northern zambia
people balokwakwa, bantu, barotse, bemba, ila, mashoma, matabele
people's army zipa
river limpopo, sabi, zambezi
ruins zimbabwe

RHODEUS bitterling, fish

RHODODENDRON azalea, big-leaf laurel, bouquet de flore, caractacus, cardinal, laurel, minerva, nerium, oleander, rosebay, spoonhutch
root briarroot, brierroot
thicket slick

RHODOS See RHODE.

RHOMB(US) circle, diamond, lozenge, parallelogram, rhombohedron, wheel

RHONCHUS croaking, rale, snoring, whistling

RHONE eridanus
city on arles, avignon
tributary ain, arly, arve, drome, gard, isere, saone

RHONGUMYANT *owner* king arthur

RHONISCUS brachydeuterus, burrito, burro, grunt, pomadasys

RHUBARB argument, citrine, dispute, disturbance, error, fight, hassel, pieplant, rheum, sh(l)emozzl, shtuss, yaweed
acid rhein
bog butterbur
cousin aloe

RHUS bihar, cedar, sumac, varnish tree, wax tree

RHYME, RIME clink, crambo, doggerel, jingle, measure, poem, poesy, po-

etry, rhythm, slant, stanza, triolet, verse, versify
4-line quatrain
game crambo
inferior crambo, doggerel
royal rimur, troilus
3-line tercet
without blank verse

RHYMER, RHYMESTER bard, jongleur, minstrel, poet(aster), reamer, rimer, scald, scop, troubadour, trouvere, versifier

RHYTHM accent, beat, cadence, eurythmy, foot, ictus, lilt, measure, melody, meter, metre, movement, pulse, swing, tempo, throb, thump
break in caesura
instrument anklong, anklung, cymbals, drum, tamborine, triangle
monotonous singsong
pause caesura
regulator metronome
syncopated jazz, ragtime

RHYTHMICAL cadenced, cadent, lilting, measured, metered, metrical, periodic(al), pulsating, recurrent, rhymed, vibrant, vibratory

RIA creek, inlet

RIAL coin, excellent, great, king, magnificent, noble, prince, royal, splendid
1/100th dinar

RIALTO bridge, exchange, island, market, mart, theater, theatre

RIALTY ceremonial, grandeur, pomp, state

RIANT airy, blithe, bright, cheerful, gay, laughing, mirthful, smiling

RIATA lariat, lasso, lazo, reata, rope

RIB bait, banter, batten, bone, branch, bristle, bulge, chaff, costa, ctenophore, devil, dike, furrow, girder, guy, hair, hoop, jolly, josh, kid, nervure, pleural, purl(in), quill, rag, rally, ridge, ripple, scroll, stratum, support, tease, timber, varix, vein, vitta, wife
below infracostal, subcostal
between intercostal
comb. cost(o)
grass buckthorn, hardhead, plantain, RIBWORT, windles
having costate

outside extracostal
pain costalgia, intercostal-neuralgia
pert. costal, costate
surgery costectomy
vaulting lierne
without decostate, ecostate

RIBALD abusive, atellan, blasphemous, bounder, coarse, filthy, good-for-nothing, gross, harlot, indecent, irreverent, jocular, lewd, loose, low, obscene, offensive, rabelaisian, rascal, raw, retainer, salty, scabrous, scurrilous, servant, vile, vulgar

RIBALDRY harlotry, indecency, obscenity, profanity

RIBAND decoration, RIBBON, scroll

RIBAT See MONASTERY.

RIBBAND bar, plank, scantling, spar, timber

RIBBED costate, furrowed, joshed, ridged, supported

RIBBLE-ROW rigamarole, string

RIBBON band(erole), bannerol, bend, binding, bow, braid, came, coque, cordon, decoration, fil(l)et, lisere, ornament, radula, rib(b)and, shred, sliver, strip(e), tawdry, tissue, torsade, tressure
-back chair, chippendale
badge cordon
binding lisere
border lisere
bush centipede-plant
colored divisa
decoration medal, rosette
ends fattrels
fern adder's-tongue, pteris
fish aguavina, bandfish, cutlass, dealfish, garfish, guapena, oarfish
garters caddice, caddis
grass bride's-laces, dodder, gardener's-garters, phalaris
gum eucalypt(us)
headdress tressour, tressure
honor cordon
inscribed banderol(e)
-like cestoid, taeniate, taenioid
silk corse, padou, tape, taste
tree akaroa, hoihere, houhere, lacebark
worm nemertean, nemertine
worsted caddice, caddis

RIBBONWOOD hoheria, houhere

RIBES cassis, currant

RIBONUCLEIC ACID messenger rna

RIBROAST beat(ing), lambaste, thrash(ing)

RIBWORT bottlebrush, cat's-cradle, chimneysweep, curldoddy, hardhead, headsman, klops, plantago, plantain, rattail, windles

RICCIO *secretary to* mary

RICE aman, amelcorn, angkhak, batty, bigas, boro, branch(es), brushwood, canin, cereal, chit(s), congee, darac, grain, grass, macan, manomin, oryza, paddy, padi, paga, pala(y), reis, risotto, sela, siddha, staple, stick, twig(s)
and meat doulma
ball croquette, pinda
boiled canin, kanin, pilau
brandy woogapai
coarse grits
cooked with meat jambalaya, pilaf, risotto
crop aghanee
disease blast, speck
dish pilaf, pilau, pilaw, risotto
drink apong, bubud, pangasi, sake, samshu
feeding on oryzivorous
field batty, ladang, paddy, padi, sawah
field embankment pilapil
-fish dish riasi-goring
flower pimelea
glucose ame
grass barit, broomroot, leersia, zacate
hen gallinule
husk palay, shood, shud(e)
inferior aga, chits, paga
land of denjong, sikkim
long-stemmed aman
milk gruel, porridge, pudding
mountain smilo
-paper tree pithplant, tetrapanax
paste ame
-pea dish hopping john
polish extract tikitiki
polishings darac
rail sora
refuse shood, shud(e)
shell olivella, truncatella
short-stemmed aus
soft congee
spring boro
sticky suman
uncooked bigas
unmilled pad(dy)

weevil calandra
wild manomin, reed

RICEBIRD bobolink, bunting, cacique, emeriza, gallinule, sparrow

RICH able, abounding, absurd, abundant, affluent, ample, amusing, aromatic, bounteous, bountiful, canch, canorous, colorful, comfortable, costly, daedal, dear, elaborate, expensive, fancy, fat, fecund, fertile, flush, fragrant, fruitful, full, funny, generous, greasy, hearty, heeled, high-priced, independent, laughable, loaded, loamy, lush, luxuriant, luxurious, magnificent, mellow, melodious, money-eyed, oofy, optime, opulent, ornate, orotund, pecunious, pinguid, plentiful, plummy, plush(y), posh, precious, productive, prolific, prosperous, resonant, rolling, savory, set up, spicy, sumptuous, superb, thriving, tinny, valuable, vibrant, vivid, wealthy, well-off, well-to-do
man See MAN *rich.*
name meaning alda, edie, edith, otha, otto, ulrica
newly arriviste, belgravia, nouveau-riche, parvenu, upstart
symbol el dorado
the plutocracy, society

RICHARD I coeur de lion, lionheart
brother king john
father henry ii
mother eleanor of aquitaine
prison durnstein

RICHARD II *character* aumerle, bagot, berkeley, bolingbroke, bushy, edmund, fitzwater, green, henry, hotspur, john of gaunt, lancaster, mowbray, norfolk, northumberland, pierce, ross, salisbury, scroop, surry, willoughby, york
cousin henry bolingbroke, henry iv
dog mathe
father edward
horse roan-barbary
queen anne of bohemia
servant bagot, bushy, green
uncle edmund, john of gaunt, lancaster, york

RICHARD III humpty dumpty
brother clarence, george, gloucester
character anne, berkeley, blount, bourchier, brackenbury, buckingham, catesby, clarence, derby, edward, elizabeth, gloucester, hastings, henry, herbert, lovel, margaret, morton, norfolk, ratcliff, richmond, rotherham, stanley, surrey, tressel, tyrrell, urswick, vaughan
horse white surrey
queen anne
slain at bosworth field
slayer henry vii
victim clarence
RICHARDSON, S. *work* charles grandison, clarissa harlow, pamela
RICHELIEU armand du plessis
successor mazarin
RICHES assets, bundle, fortune, gold, lucre, means, opulence, pelf, pile, possessions, resources, substance, treasure, weal(th), worth
demon of mammon
region of el dorado
worship of plutomania
RICHLY amply, dearly, fully, thoroughly
RICHNESS body, elegance, luxury, sumen
RICHTERITE amphibole, amphibolite
RICHTHOFEN *squadron* jagstaffel
RICHWEED bugbane, coolweed, horsebalm, pilea, ragweed, snakeroot
RICK canch, chatter, cord, goaf, gofe, granary, heap, jingle, noise, pile, rattle, reke, richard, rickle, ruck, scold, smoke, sprain, stack, twist, wrench
cloth tarpaulin
RICKETS rachitis
RICKETY crazy, feeble, frail, imperfect, rachitic, ramshackle, rocky, sensile, shackly, shaky, tottering, tottery, tumbledown, unsound, unstable, unsteady, wavery, weak
RICKRACK braid, edging, insertion, notching, ribbon, trimming

RICKSHAW carriage, jinrikisha, samlor
RICOCHET bounce, bound, carom, curvet, deflect, glance, hop, rebound, recoil, skip, staccato
RICTUS cleft, fissure, gape, grimace, grin, mouth, throat
RID clear, counsel, deliver, destroy, disburden, discard, disembarrass, disencumber, dispatch, dispose (of), doff, eject, eliminate, expel, free, kill, liberate, loose, purge, redd, rede, relieve, relinquish, remove, rescue, scour, shut, spawn, tidy, unload
RIDDANCE cleaning, deliverance, escape, freeing, relief, shut
RIDDLE ambiguity, blaik, bolt, bore, charade, conundrum, criticize, crux, cryptogram, disprove, enigma, explain, foiter, impair, logogram, logogriph(us), mystery, penetrate, perforate, permeate, perplex, pierce, pit, poser, problem, pun, puncture, puzzle, question, rebus, refine, refute, ruddle, separate, shoot, sieve, sift(er), solve, sphinx, sticker, winnow
RIDDLING divining, enigmatic, puzzling
RIDE annoy, auto, badger, bait, banter, bother, canter, cast, cavalcade, chauffeur, chevy, coast, continue, control, criticize, dominate, drive, endure, excursion, float, gallop, harass, heckle, hector, hound, journey, lift, manage, mistreat, motor, mount, move, overlap, pickup, prance, ridicule, road, roll, rollercoaster, score, spin, straddle, survive, tool, torment, tour, transport, trip, tyrannize, worry
at anchor dally, rest
bike pedal
ceremonial dosa
coattails coast
down overtake, overthrow, overturn, trample
hard busket, hurry, speed
herd on control, discipline, guide, manage, shepherd

jolting jumble
moocher schnorrer
out endure, last, survive
roughshod over discipline, domineer, overbear, override, overrun
shanks' mare walk
without power coast, glide, parachute, sail
RIDER addition, adjunct, agent, allonge, amendment, annex, bogier, buckaroo, cavalier, clause, codicil, cowboy, endorsement, equestrian, freebooter, highwayman, horseman, jockey, knight, label, mosstrooper, passenger, revision, salesman, traveler, trainer
RIDGE arete, arris, asar, back, balk, bank, bar(gh), bilo, boss, bridge, brow, bulge, bult, burr, butt(e), carina, catoctin, chain, chine, comb, cordillera, corrugation, crest, crown, cuesta, dorsum, downs, drum, elevation, eschar, esker, fret, gold, gyrus, hause, hill, hogback, inthrow, kame, linch(et), loma, mountain, osar, parma, plume, prominence, rafter, rand, range, raphe, rib, rideau, ruck, ruga, saddle(back), sastrugi, serac, serra, shin, sierra, spine, spur, stria, top, tor, wale, welt, w(h)eal, wrinkle, yardang, zastrugi
anatomical carina
buster cultivator
chewing endite
clay dowle
cloth wale, welt
connecting hause
convoluted gyrus
drainage breaker
earth balk
flesh collop
glacial eschar, eskar, esker, kame, osar, paha
glumes carina
hairlike lira
hickory shellbark
ice serac
isolated bargh
land bult, hogback, selion, stitch
level lande
long rand
low cuesta, parma, rand
mark wale, weal, welt, wheal, whelk

mountain backbone, comb, sierra

myrtle ironwood

narrow drum, razorback

notch gabel

oak blackjack

plowing bouting

pole rooftree

projecting scout

protecting camp rideau

residual catoctin

runner frontiersman

sandy dene, dune, lande, osar, wavemark

seashore stanner

sharp-crested arete

shell pilae, varices, varix

skin wale, welt, w(h)eal

slight ponticulus, propons

sloping cuesta

small rideau

snow sastrugi, zastrugi

unplowed ba(u)lk, linch(et)

wooded chenier, knurling

RIDGED carinate, sharp

RIDICULE assail, asteism, banter, borak, buffoon, burlesque, caricature, chaff, deride, derision, expose, flout, fool, gibe, guy, hoot, irony, jeer(ing), jibe, lampoon(ery), laugh at, leer, make fun of, mimic, mock(age) mockery, pan, parody, pasquile, pasquinade, pastiche, pillory, quiz, raillery, rally, raspberry, razz, rib, ride, roast, sarcasm, satire, satirize, scoff, scout, smirk, sneer, snicker at, snigger at, sport, squib, taunt, twit

exclamation come off it, fiddledeedee, fiddlesticks, nuts, phooey, pish(pash), poo(h), pshaw, pugh, tut(tut)

god momos, momus

object of butt, laughingstock, sport, target, victim

RIDICULOUS absurd, amusing, antic, bizarre, cockamamy, comic(al), derisive, droll, farcical, foolish, funny, grotesque, incredible, indecent, insane, ironic(al), irrational, laughable, ludicrous, nonsensical, outrageous, preposterous, risible, silly, trifling, trivial, unbelievable, waggish

thing jigamaree, thingumbob

RIDING anchorage, avenue, chevachie, clearing, divi-

sion, equitation, jurisdiction, overlapping, pageant, road, section, shivaree, subdivision, trithing

administrator reeve

costume breeches, habit, jodhpurs, levis, pants

school academy, manage, manege

school ring piste

shoe solleret

whip crop, quirt, rod

RIDOTTO abridgment, ball, dance, entertainment, gathering, masquerade, redoubt, resort, retreat

RIEKA fiume

RIEM oxhide, strap, strip, thong

RIF, RIFF berber, diaphragm, kabyle, midriff, moroccan, riffle, ripple

revolutionary abdel-krim

RIFE abounding, abundant, brief, clear, common, copious, current, customary, easy, epidemic, famed, familiar, inclined, manifest, numerous, ordinary, pandemic, plain, plentiful, plenty, possible, prevalent, ready, replete, reported, teeming, universal, usual, widespread

RIFFIAN arab(ian)

RIFFLE flutter, groove, hopper, plow, rapid, rattle, ripple, shallow, shuffle, waterfall, wave

RIFFLER file, rasp, trough

RIFFRAFF canaille, cattle, chaff, dregs, mob, offal, offscourings, offscum, populace, proletariat, rabble, raff, ragabash, refuse, rubbish, scum, sordes, sweepings, trash, vermin

RIFLE (See also *kind*, below.) arisaka, bandhook, bullpup, bund(h)ook, burglarize, carbine, chassepot, despoil, devastate, escopet(te), filch, firearm, furrow, gamble, groove, gun, ja(e)ger, jezail, juzail, krag, longarm, mauser, musket, pilfer, pillage, plunder, propel, purloin, raffle, ransack, ravage, reeve, repeater, rob, snider, soldier, spoliate, sporter, steal, strip, thieve, weapon, yager

accessory bayonet, ramrod

ball minie

breach loader chassepot, snider

case boot

contest bisley

kind bazooka, browning automatic, carbin(e), enfield, flintlock, garand, hawken, kentucky, lancaster, martini, mauser, minie, m-one, ninety mm recoilless, remington, snider, springfield, whitworth, winchester

magazine mauser

pin tige

scope starlight

RIFLEMAN bersagliere, ja(e)ger, marksman, shot, sniper, soldier, yager

RIFT belch, blemish, breach, break, burst, chasm, chink, clash, cleave, cleft, cranny, crevasse, crevice, divide, division, fault, fissure, flaw, gap, lag, misunderstanding, open(ing), penetrate, rapid, rent, rima, rive, rupture, schism, separation, shallow, split, tear

RIG adjust, apparatus, ardri, assemble, backstay, banter, bedizen, cheat, clothe, clothing, coach, derrick, dress, equip, equipage, equipment, fig, fit, fix, fool, four-in-hand, fourup, frolic, furnish, gear, gig, gunter, hoax, lateen, manipulate, outfit, pair, prepare, random, ransack, reek, ridge, rifle, romp, row, ship, span, spike(team), spudder, storm, swindle, tackle, tandem, team, tempest, trick, turnout, unicorn, wanton, wardrobe, wind, wriggle

-out appearance, outfit, wardrobe

part brace, mast, sail, shroud, spar

RIGA balsam, reval

island oesel, saare

native latvian, lett

RIGGED trimmed

fully ataunt

lightly monkey-sparred

RIGGING cable, gear, ridge, roof, ropes, spar, tackle, tackling, wardrobe

sled dogboat

RIGHT 3 due, fee, fit, gee, ius, pat, yes 4 bang, cure, fair, good, jus·, meet, nice, okay, okeh, pure, real, reet, rule, sane, soke, tory, true, very 5 amend, check, claim, droit, emend, exact, legal, level, licit, moral, recto, roger, sound, title, truth 6 actual, adjust, adroit, avenge, decent, demand, dexter, equity, honest, kosher, lawful, proper, remedy, revise, seemly, settle, square, strict, zchuss 7 correct, dextral, faculty, fitting, freedom, genuine, germane, liberty, license, merited, obverse, perfect, precise, rectify, redress, warrant 8 accurate, appanage, balanced, decorous, deserved, directly, inerrant, interest, orthodox, regulate, relevant, sporting, squarely, straight, suitable, usufruct 9 authentic, authority, clockwise, desirable, equitable, expedient, faultless, hunkydory, impartial, integrity, pertinent, precisely, privilege, rectitude, starboard, vindicate 10 applicable, birthright, evenhanded, infallible, legitimate, perquisite, scrupulous, unmistaken 11 appropriate, comme il faut, dextropedal, entitlement, prerogative, reactionary 12 conservative, conventional 16 according to hoyle

about face pivot, reverse, tergiversation

all hunky(dory), jake, okay, okeh

angle, 100th grad(e)

-angled orthogonal, perpendicular, rectangled

away anon, at once, directly, forthwith, immediately, instantly, now, promptly, straightway, suddenly

belligerent's angary

by de jure

comb. dextro, rect(i)

confer authorize, entitle, legalize, name, ordain, qualify, sanction

exclamation amen, aok, c'est ca, i'll say, okay, quite, rather, roger, that's for sure

exclusive concession, patent(s), prerogative

feudal thirl(age)

free quarters corody

hand greeting, welcome

handed clockwise, dextral, dextrous

-hand man aide, assistant, henchman

handwise deasil, deiseal, dessil

hereditary udal

in one's own suo jure

inquiry soken

legal droit, ex jure, hak(h), hypothec, ius, jure, jus

-minded honest, sane, upright

mining gale

off See *away*, above.

of presentation advowson

of protection mund

of succession reversion

of way lane, path, precedence, street, track

on bull's eye, to a tee

pasturage commanage, cowage, eatage, feed, horsegate, stint

royal regalia

side dexter

time tid

to control authority

to seize property angary

to the a droite

to vote ballot, franchise, suffrage

toward dextrad

turn gee

twining to dextrose

-up honest, steep

whale balaenid, bowhead, mysticete, nordcaper

widow's terce, tierce

wife's property curtesy

-winger bircher, conservative, extremist, reactionary, tory

wood-cutting greenhew, vert

RIGHTEOUS blameless, blue, devout, equitable, ethical, fair, godly, good, guiltless, holy, honest, honorable, innocent, just, moral, noble, pious, right, sainted, saintly, upright, virtuous, worthy, zadoc, zadok *man* tzaddik

RIGHTEOUSNESS dharma, equity, justice, rectitude, sanctity, tsadaka, tzedaka

RIGHTFUL canonical, condign, due, equitable, fair, genuine, honest, impartial, just, lawful, legal, legitimate, official, orthodox, proper, true

RIGHTIST See **RIGHT** *-winger*.

RIGID accurate, adamant (ine), ascetic, austere, brassbound, brittle, castiron, changeless, close, compact, consistent, exact(ing), firm, fixed, formal, hard(shell), harsh, inflexible, ironclad, meticulous, precise, renitent, rigorous, rodlike, set, severe, solid, starched, starchy, stark, static, stern, stiff, stout, straitlaced, strict, stringent, strong, stubborn, taut, tenacious, tense, thorough, tight, tough, unbending, unchanging, unpliant, unrelaxed, unyielding, virgate, wooden, yekke

RIGIDITY rigor, severity, stiffness, strictness *muscular* catalepsy

RIGMAROLE amphigory, amphigouri, chatter, megillah, nominy, nonsense, rabble, rane, slampamp, slampant

RIGOLETTO *role* borsa, ceprano, gilda, marullo

RIGOR affliction, asperity, austerity, chill, cold, cruelty, difficulty, fury, hardness, hardship, harshness, inflexibility, rigidity, roughness, severity, sternness, stiffness, strictness, stringency, toughness, trial, tribulation, tyranny, vicissitude, violence

RIGOROUS accurate, ascetic, astringent, austere, bitter, close, cold, draconic, drastic, exact(ing), finical, firm, hard, harsh, inflexible, onerous, oppressive, precise, punctilious, rigid, scrupulous, severe, spartan, stern, stiff, stoic(al), strict, stringent, violent

RIGSBY hoyden, wanton

RIG-VEDA See **VEDA**.

RIJEKA fiume

RILE acerbate, aggravate, agitate, anger, annoy, dirty, disturb, exasperate, irk, irritate, offend, provoke, roil, turbidity, upset, vex

RILKE *work* duino elegies

RILL arroyuelo, brook(let), course, creek, crick, ditch, furrow, groove, narrow, purl, rillock, rivulet, runnel, shallow, sike, stream(let), trench, tricklet *stone* ventifact

RIM basil, bezel, bezil, border, boundary, brim, brink, edge, enclose, felloe, felly, fillet, flange, frame, limit, lip, margin, membrane, orle, perimeter, peritoneum, rimrock, somma, tire, verge
ash hackberry
basket hoop
crater somma
external flange
horseshoe web
protective bank, frame
raised boss
shield orle
wheel felloe, felly, tire
RIMA apperture, breadfruit, chink, cleft, fissure
RIMBAUD *poem* season in hell
RIME apperture, chink, cleft, congeal, crack, cranreuch, fissure, freeze, frost, hoar (frost), ice, perforate, poem, poetry, rent, RHYME, rung, verse
book edda
giant ymer, ymir
RIMMAN copyreader
RIMMON *son* baanah, rechab
RIMPLE crease, crumple, fold, ripple, rumple, wrinkle
RIMSKY-KORSAKOV *opera* czar's bride, le coq d'or, sadka, snegourotchka
RIMU imou, red pine
RINALDO *steed* bajardo, bayard
RIND bark, body, clarify, coat, cortex, crust, epicarp, fell, hoarfrost, hull, husk, integument, melt, peel, pellicle, pelt, shell, skin, sward, swarth
comb. lepo
RIND(R) *husband* odin
offspring vali
RINDLE brook, flow, rivulet, runnel, stream
RING 3 bee, cut, orb, RIM, set 4 bail, band, belt, bloc, burr, cric, ding, dirl, echo, gang, gird, gyre, halo, hank, hoop, link, loop, nimb, peal, pirn, rink, tang, toll 5 arena, bague, bezel, bezil, bingo, cabal, chime, clank, clink, court, group, junto, knell, lunet, party, phone, quoit, rigol, sound 6 anklet, border, brough, circle, circus, clique, collar, corona,

gasket, ginnal, girdle, jingle, nimbus, repeat, signet, spiral, strike, terret, territ, tinkle 7 annulet, annulus, armilla, aureole, circlet, combine, coterie, curette, faction, ferrule, grommet, inclose, resound, rowlock, vibrate 8 cincture, cingulum, encircle, proclaim, resonate, surround 9 archivolt, encompass 10 annulation, racecourse 11 association, reverberate 14 tintinnabulate
bird reed-bunting, vervel
boiler strake
boxing arena
bracelet bangle
bright halation, halo
carrier best-man, go-between
cinch larigo
colored areola, areole
column bague
comb. cycl, dactylio, gyro
curtain eye
dance carol
disease brown rot
down conclude, end, lower
finger annulary, hoop, jing, third
fleshy annulus
game carom, quoit(s)
gauge moot
harness button, dee, larigo, terret, torret, turret
hooped gemel, gimmal
in arrive, begin, clock in, foist, introduce, punch in, start, substitute
interlocking gemel, gimmal
joined gimmer, gimmor
kind boxing, teething, wedding
lamp flame cric
-like annulate
little annulet, circlet
luminous aureole, brough, halo
magic talisman
money manilla
moon agatharchides, bode, bond, broch
nautical grommet
-neck jackaroo, newcomer, pheasant
-necked torquate
-necked duck blackie, blackjack, bullneck, bunty, canvasback, dogy, moonbill, nyroca, ringbill, scaup
nose pirn
off end, hang up, silence
of the nibelung composer wagner

of the nibelung maker alberich
of the nibelung role alberich, brunhild, etzel, giselher, gunther, hagen, hernot, hildebrand, kriemhild, siegfried, sieglind, sigurd
ornamental bee, bracelet, leglet
out depart, leave, resound
ouzel amsel, thrush, turdus, whistler
packing lute
part arc, chaton
plaited rush, wisp
plover collier, dulwilly, ringneck, sandy
reins terret, territ
rope grommet
seal signet
series coil
setting bezel, bezil, chaton, tiffany
-shaped annular(y), annulate, circinate, circular, orbed
stone voussoir
surgical curette
tapering belcher
target sous(e)
toothed iron harrow
top of bezel, bezil
tree frill
valve wafer
vibrating dirl
wedding band
RINGDOVE cowshot, cowshut, cushat, cushie, pigeon, queest, quist, toozoo, turtledove
RINGED annular(y), annulate, annulose, circular, encircled, engraved, gyrate, married, surrounded, wedded, zonate
snake colubrid
RINGER bell, cowboy, crowbar, dummy, fraud, likeness, quoit, sharp(er), stand-in, stockman, substitute, swindler
RINGING bright, chiming, clam, dingdong, dinging, jingling, knelling, loud, orotund, pealing, resonant, resounding, rolling, sonorous, sounding, tinkling, tintinnabulation
RINGLEADER enterpriser, entrepreneur, instigator, sparkplug
RINGLET circle(t), crisp, curl, frizz, lock, tendril, tress

RINGTAIL bassarisk, cacomistle, cacomixle, godwit, harrier, lemur, raccoon, studding-sail

RINGWORM annelid, barber's-itch, kerion, millepede, serpigo, tetter, tinea
bush acapulco, candlestick, cassia, guava, senna, shrub

RINK arena, circle, course, encounter, glaciarium, hero, man, race, ring, skate, warrior

RINNAH *father* shimon

RINSE absterge, bluing, clean(se), henna, lave, rench, rensh, ringe, scind, sind, sluice, wash(ing)

RINSING(S) dregs, refuse, residue, sind

RINUCCINI *opera* dafne, daphne, eurydice

RIO canal, coffee, river, stream, watercourse

RIO DE JANEIRO *bay* botafogo
girl rita
landmark sugar loaf
native carioca
old name santa lucia
resort buzios, copacabana, ipanema, petropolis
slums ravelas

RIO GRANDE *city on* el paso, juarez
dam elephant butte
tributary pecos

RIOT acclaim, agitation, arise, brawl, broil, carousal, clamor, clem, commotion, confusion, debauch, demonstration, despoil, din, disorder, dissent, dissipation, disturbance, emeute, eruption, excess, fight, fracas, fray, hit, hubbub, jumble, melee, mutiny, noise, pandemonium, peasant, pogrom, racket, raid, rantan, revel(ry), revolt, rollick, row, ruckus, rumpus, ryot, score, sensation, shindig, skylark, spree, success, tear, triumph, tumult, turbulence, upheaval, uproar, upset
bloody bloodwite

RIOTOUS abandoned, boisterous, disorderly, dissipated, loose, loud, luxuriant, profligate, roid, saturnalian, seditious, tumultous, turbulent, unrestrained, unrestricted, unruly, wanton

RIP basket, blast, break, cheat, cleave, coop, cut, debauchee, disclose, discover, divide, flow, fray, frazzle, hag, harridan, horse, laceration, libertine, nag, open, pace, part, rend, rent, reprobate, rive, rush, saw, scamp, sever, shred, slit, speed, split, strop, sunder, tear, unseam, whetstone
current undertow
off deceit, fraud, steal, take, theft
-roaring boisterous, exciting, hilarious, lively, noisy, riotous, turbulent, uproarious
tide undertow

RIPA bank, beach, coast, foreshore, litoral, shore, strand

RIPE accomplished, addled, adult, aged, august, auspicious, bank, clean, clear, complete, consummate, developed, drunk, empty, examine, experienced, finished, fit, fullfledged, fullgrown, grown-up, intoxicated, investigate, mature(d), mellow (ed), perfected, plunder, prepared, ransack, ready, rifle, riverbank, rob, search, seashore, seasonable, seasoned, sidder, siddow, timely
comb. hadr(o)

RIPEN addle, age, better, bloom, blossom, complete, develop, digest, enhance, evolve, fatten, fit, grow, heighten, improve, maturate, mature, mellow, perfect, prepare, season, suppurate, unfold

RIPHATH *father* gomer

RIPOSTE answer, counterstroke, quip, reaction, rejoinder, repartee, reply, response, retaliate, retort, return, thrust

RIPPER bar, blade, bobsled, bobsleigh, humdinger, peddler, ripsaw, thief

RIPPET quarrel, romp, uproar

RIPPING admirable, capital, excellent, fine, grand, great, remarkable, splendid, swell, wizard

RIPPLE acker, agitate, babble, billow, bubble, burble, cockle, comb, curl, cut, dimple, eagre, fraze, fret,

guggle, gurgle, lap, oscillate, plash, purl, riff(le), rip, roller, ruffle, rumble, scratch, slosh, splash, surge, swash, swell, tear, trickle, trill, undulate, undulation, vibrate, wash, wave(let), wrinkle
cloth zibeline
grass ribwort

RIPPLY undulant, undulating, wavy

RIPRAP base, foundation, wall

RIPSACK whale

RIPSNORTER braggart, humdinger, snifter

RIP VAN WINKLE *prototype* peter klaus

RISE acclivity, advance, appear, ascend, ascent, aspire, awake, begin(ning), billow, boost, bound, break, bulge, buoy, canch, clamber, climb, derive, develop (ment), dome, elevate, elevation, emanate, emerge, eminence, enlarge, exsurge, flow, gain, grade, grow(th), heave, highland, hill, hoist, hove, hulk, incline, increase, issue, leap, levitate, lift, loom, mount, occur, originate, proceed, progress, promontory, prosper, raise, reaction, rear, rebel, resurge, retort, revolt, riot, rocket, rouse, slope, soar, source, sourd, spring, start, stem, succeed, surface, surge, swell, thrive, tower, triumph, upland, uprear, upsurge, wake
above accept, conquer, tower, triumph
again resurge, resurrect
and fall billow, heave, surge, tide, undulate, welter
gradually loom
price bulge, inflation
rapidly kite, mushroom, skyrocket
suddenly boom
to apex culminate
up ascend, fume, insurrect, rear, rebel

RISIBLE absurd, amusing, comic(al), diverting, droll, funny, gelastic, humorous, laughable, ludicrous, merry, ridiculous

RISING abscess, acclivity, advancing, approaching, arist,

ascendant, ascending, ascensive, assurgent, boil, booming, bull, elevated, exceeding, gradient, growing, insurrection, montant, more than, nearing, orient, ortive, revolt, rist, rousant, steep, strake, surgent, surging, swelling, tumor, upwith, yeast
high aerial
pert. ortive
sharply abrupt
RISK adventure, chance, crackle, danger, dare, endanger, expose, fortune, gage, gamble, hazard, imperil, invest, investment, jeopardize, jeopardy, liability, luck, peril, plight, plunge, speculate, speculation, stake, venture, wager
RISKY chanceful, chancy, critical, dangerous, haphazard, hazardous, jeopardus, perilous, precarious, random, techous, ticklish, touch and go, touchy, venturesome, venturous
RISP bulrush, file, grass, rasp, rub, scratch, stalk, stem, tirl, wisp
RISQUE blue, brazen, broad, gross, hazardous, improper, indecent, lurid, obscene, offcolor, purple, racy, ribald, risky, salty, scabrous, spicy, suggestive
RIST ascent, engrave, increase, insurrection, resurrection, rising, scratch, source, wound
RIT cut, pierce, rip, scratch, slit, split, tear
RITE abdest, accolade, agape, asperges, aspersion, augury, baptism, bora, celebration, ceremonial, ceremony, communion, confession, confirmation, cult, custom, exequy, fitly, form(ality), funeral, hako, initiation, litany, liturgy, lustration, novena, obe(ah), obsequy, observance, ordinance, orgy, patriarchate, pax, prayer, procedure, rightly, RITUAL, sacra(ment), sacrum, service, solemnity, spell, sraddha, usage, well, worship
last extreme unction
penitential exomologesis
purification abdest, lustration

RITORNEL(LE) interlude, prelude, refrain
RITTER cavalier, knight
RITUAL ceremonial, ceremony, feast, form, haggada, liturgy, ordeal, RITE, sacrifice, service, solemn, tashlik, visparad, vispered
evil-preventing apotropaism
meaningless mumbojumbo
meat-inspection bedikah
personified brihaspati
prayer salat
site altar
RITZY elegant, expensive, fashionable, haughty, modish, ostentatious, posh, snobbish, swanky
RIVAL adversary, antagonist, approach, compete, competitive, competitor, contend, contestant, cope, cutthroat, emulate, emulous, enemy, equal, even, excel, fight, foe, match, opponent, oppose, opposing, outdo, outshine, peer, struggle, vie
RIVALRY antagonism, champerty, competition, contention, envy, game, jealousy, opposition, striving
comb. ant(i)
RIVALS *author* sheridan
character anthony absolute, faulkland, lydia languish
RIVE arrive, bank, bite, burst, cleave, cleft, disembark, distress, fracture, harrow, lacerate, open, pierce, plow, pull, reave, rend, rent, rift, rob, sever, shore, slit, split, stab, steal, sunder, tear, thieve, thrust, tug, wedge
droit right bank
gauche left bank
RIVEL shrink, shrivel, wither, wizen, wrinkle
RIVEN cleft, rent, split
RIVER abundance, affluence, affluent, arterial, bahr, bourn(e), bow, branch, channel, creek, diamond, estuary, flood, flow, fume, hawking, headwaters, ilog, inlet, kill, millstream, plenty, ree, rio, riviere, run, strait, stream, tji, torrent, tributary, wadi, wady, watercourse
arm estuary, fork, tributary
bank levee, rand, ripa, ripe, strand, wharf
bank path berm

bed batture, bottom, channel, laagte, wadi, wady
bed, dry arroyo, canada
bed, elevated batture
birch betula
black oak beefwood
boat ark, barge, baulea(h), cabin boat, canoe, felucca, flatboat, foist, houseboat, pulwar, punt, robroy, rowboat, shallop, tow
bottom See *bed,* above.
branch billabong, fork, tributary
changed into acis, alpheius
channel alveus, banco
comb. fluvio, potamo
current eddy, rapids
dam weir
deity achelous, alpheus, artemis, asopus, axius, belisama, cayster, eridanus, inachus, selinus, simois
deposit alluvial fan, alluvium, delta, silt
dog hellbender
dolphin bouto, inia
dragon croc(odile)
duck greenwing, mallard, teal, widgeon
father of mississippi
gauge nilometer
grass millet
head source
horse hippo(potamus), rhino
ice embacle, glacier
inhabiting fluvicoline
inlet bayou, slew, slough
island ait, eyot, holm
king of amazon
kubla khan's alph
lake formed by oxbow
land bottom, carse, flat(s), holm
land formed from batture
landing ghat
large bahr
largest amazon
living in amphibian, rheophile
log run sluiceway
mouth beal, boca, delta, estuary, lade
mussel unio
mythical alph, styx
nymph naiad, nais, sabrina
obstruction gorce, snag
ocean outlet sea-reach
of fire phlegethon
of forgetfulness lethe
of hate styx
of heaven milky way
of sorrows acheron
passage bridge, estuary, ford

pert. amnic, fluminose, fluminous, fluvial, fluviatile, potamic, riparian, riverine
pool cathole
rapids riffle, rift, stickle
ridge bar
sacred alph, ganga, ganges, nile
science of potamology
shoal towhead
side bank, embankment, shore
siren lorelei
small bache, bayou, bourn(e), branch, brook, burn, creek, ria, rill(et), rindle, rivulet, run(nel), stream(let), stripe, strype, tchai
song afton, old man river, rio grande, suwannee, swanee, wabash
stairs gaut, ghat
thief ackman, riverrat
underworld acheron, cocytus, flegeton, lethe, phlegethon, styx
valley strath
weed podostemace, podostemon, waterweed
winding ess
RIVET affix, anchor, arrest, attach, bolt, brad, clinch, connect, fasten, fix, join, moor, roove, secure, tie, unite
RIVIERE necklace
RIVULET See RIVER *small.*
RIX reed, rush
RIXATRIX scold, virago
RIYAL *1/22th* girsh, gursh
RIZPAH *kin* aiah, saul
RIZZAR currant, haddock
RIZZOM bit, ear, particle, stalk, straw
ROACH azurine, blattid, braise, brush, butt, cockroach, coiffure, cut(ting), cut off, cyprinid, fish, hill, hog, insect, leiostomus, rock, roll, rutilus, soil, spot, stone, sunfish
ROACHBACK grizzly bear
ROAD agger, alley(way), approach, arterial, artery, autobahn, autostrada, avenue, bargh, beallach, belt, boulevard, byway, calzada, camino, career, causeway, causey, chaussee, chemin, concourse, course, court, dike, drag, drang, drive(way), drun, embankment, estrada, expressway, follow,

freeway, gangway, harbor, highway, iter, lane, leg, main drag, motorway, pad, parkway, passage, path, pike, place, praya, raid, railway, route, slab, speedway, strada, street, tao, tarmac, telford, thoroughfare, thruway, toby, track, trail, turnpike, vennel, via, way
agent footpad, highwayman, thief, toby
bend ess, hairpin
cement slab
cliff corniche
country boreen, driftway, lane
crossing, fear of dromophobia
cul-de-sac impasse
descending bahada, bajada
edge berm, shoulder, verge
gods chimata nokami, dosojin, funado, kunado, saenokami, yachimatahiko
goose brant
gypsy drun
hog egotist, motorist
house cabaret, inn, nightclub, saloon, tavern
improvised cash
knight hobo, tramp, vagabond
lacking invious
logging crosshaul, skidway
main highway
maker bulldozer, caterpillar, grader, harl, paver, steamroller
middle of the moderate
military agger
monkey blue jay
narrow drang, drung, roddin
on the on the go, touring
paved calzada, chaussee
paving asphalt, bricks, concrete, gravel, macadam, sand, stones, tar(mac), telford
pert. viatic
principal arterial, artery
private drive(way)
raised agger, causeway, rampire
runner bird, chaparra, cock, cuckoo, geococcyx, paisano
scraper harl(e)
shoreline praya
shoulder berm
side shun-pike
-side inn albergue, motel
steep bargh, path, sprunt
surface See *paving,* above.

temporary detour, shoofly
test experiment, try
turnout layby
under layer subcrust
unimproved drove
weed plantain
zigzag switchback
ROADBED ballast, bitumen
ROADBLOCK barricade, barrier, obstruction
ROADBOOK atlas, directory, gazetteer, guide, itinerary, map, michelin
ROADMAN canvasser, drummer, peddler, salesman
ROADMASTER overseer
ROADSTEAD downs, raid
ROADSTER auto, bicycle, buggy, car, horse, raceabout, runabout, speedster, tricycle, vehicle
ROAM bangle, drift, err, gad, gallivant, meander, mooch, nomadize, peregrinate, proceed, prowl, ramble, range, roil, rove, scamp, straggle, stray, stroll, swerve, ta(i)ver, traipse, tramp, travel, vagabondize, vagary, walk, wander, waver
ROAMER fugitive, gadabout, gallivanter, gipsy, gypsy, hobo, nomad, peregrinator, rambler, rover, tramp, traveler, vagabond
ROAN antelope, bull, cow, grizzle, horse, sheepskin
antelope bastard, bemsbok, egoceros
barbary owner richard
ROANOKE big lick, money, wampum
bell cowslip
ROAR bark, bawl, bell(ow), bere, blare, blart, bluster, boom, brawl, bray, brool, buller, clamor, crash, cry, din, fream, guffaw, holler, howl, laugh, noise, outcry, peal, rair, rant, rare, rerd, resound, roll, rome, root, rote, rout, rumble, rummes, rummish, scream, shout, shriek, sough, steven, storm, thunder, trumpet, ululate, yell
low brool
ROARER cobberer, devil, madman, powerhouse, stalwart
ROARING boisterous, boom, brisk, busy, disorderly, great, howling, loud, riot-

ous, sensational, successful, thriving

boy twibil(l)

game curling

meg cannon

ROAST asado, assail, assate, attack, bake, banter, barbecue, brede, broil, burn, calcine, cook, criticism, criticize, decrepitate, grill, heat, kalua, parch, razz, rebuke, ridicule, roti(sserie), swelter, torrefy, torrify, warm

-beef plant iris

ROASTING assation, burning, hot, sweltering, torrid

jack turnspit

rod skewer, (turn)spit

ROB bereave, burglarize, burgle, cheat, cop, defalcate, deflower, defraud, despoil, embezzle, etiolate, filch, fleece, fob, harry, highjack, hijack, hold up, lift, loot, peculate, pelf, pilfer, pillage, pinch, plagiarize, pluck, plunder, purloin, ravage, ravish, reave, reive, rifle, roll, rumpade, sack, snaffle, snatch, snitch, spoil, spoliate, spung, STEAL, stick up, strip, strub, swindle, take, thieve, toby, touch(up), unpurse

roy canoe

ROBALO centropomus, fish, sergeant, serranid, snook, snowk

ROBBER bandit, bandolero, baraggas, brigand, buccaneer, burglar, corsair, dacoit, depradator, despoiler, ebonite, fomor(ian), footpad, g(h)oul, heister, highwayman, holdup(nik), hoodlum, ladrone, la(t)ron, moonman, pad, pillager, pirate, privateer, rabiator, ravener, reave, rifler, spoiler, thief, tobyman, yegg(man)

famous cacus, gilderoy

fly asilid, brachyera

frog barking frog

mountain choar

wandering routier

ROBBERY bandolerismo, burglary, depredation, felony, heist, holdup, housebreaking, ladronism, larceny, pickpocketing, pillage, piracy, plagiarism, plunder, reavery, reif, safe-cracking, screw, spoliation, stealing, stickup, theft, thievery

highway latrocinium, toby

sea piracy

ROBE aba, apparel, arisaid, array, attire, buffalo, caftan, camis, camus, candys, chimer(e), cloak, clothe, costume, coverlet, cymar, dolman, dress, frock, galabia, garment, gown, invest, kanzu, kimono, kittle, manga, mantle, purple, revest, sack, simar, sticharion, stola, talar, throw, tire, toga, tunic, vest(ment), vesture, wolfskin, wrap, yukata

actor's syrma

ankle-length syrma, talar

baggy bakkhu

baptismal chrisom

bishop's chimer(e)

camelhair aba

coronation colobium, dalmatic

de chambre neglige(e)

de nuit nightdress, nightgown

funeral sable

gift khalat, khilat

light camis, camus

loose burnoose, burnous, camis, camus, cymar, kimono, mant(eau), mantua, peignoir, sack, simar, symar

masquerade venetian

monk's ependytes, haploma

outer jama

royal dalmatic, purple

wearing togate

woman's caftan, cymar, kimono, negligee, simar

ROBERT bloodwort, dobbin, herb, popkin

o'lincoln bobolink

ROBESPIERRE *epithet* the incorruptible

ROBIN bird, bumpkin, campion, chewink, erithacus, lout, merula, miro, pinfish, redbreast, reddock, ruddock, thrush, tody, tootler, trimming, turdus, wingfish

bluestring robert walpole

bush ianthia, tarsiger

christopher, father milne

friend batman

goodfellow dwarf, elf, fairy, hobgoblin, puck, sprite

master falstaff

round petition

-runaway dewdrop, ivy

sandpiper or *snipe* dowitcher, knot

the bobbin henry viii

wake See WAKE -robin.

wood miro

ROBIN HOOD bandit, outlaw, wearer of the green

admirer richard coeur de lion

assumed name locksley

beloved marian

betrayer prioress of kirklees

chaplain friar tuck

foe sheriff of nottingham

follower allan-a-dale, friar tuck, little john, marian, merry men, tinker, will scarlet, will stutely

friar tuck

friend allan-a-dale

home sherwood forest

larder oak tree

livery kendal green

minstrel allan-a-dale

right-hand man little john

victim guy of gisbourne

ROBINSON CRUSOE *author* defoe

boy xury

character friday

home york

prototype selkirk

ROBLE beech, oak, quira, tree, umbarana

ROBORANT drug, strengthening, tonic

ROBOT android, automaton, gelem, golem, televox

blitz bombardment

bomb ntwe, v-bomb, vone

play rur

ROBUST athletic, boisterous, brawny, coarse, energetic, hale, hard(y), healthy, hearty, husky, iron, lusty, muscular, pithsome, powerful, renky, rich, rough, rude, rugged, rumbustious, sinewy, sound, stalwart, stiff, stour, stout, strapping, strong, sturdy, swacking, valiant, vigorous, wally, well, wholesome

ROBUSTNESS pith, strength, vigor

ROC bird, roque, rukh, simurg(h)

ROCCA donjon, fortress, hold, keep

ROCCELLA angolaweed, archil, canarymoss, capeweed, lichen

ROCHET alb, bishop, camisia, cloak, frock, gurnard, smock, vestment

ROCK boulder, brack, candy, careen, chert, cliff, coin, cooky, crag, cromlich, dag, daze, defense, diamond, dolmen, dornick, falter, flounder, gibraltar, gravel, gruss, ice, jail, jostle, jounce, klip, lava, ledge, lull, megolith, menhir, mineral, money, monolith, music, oscillate, pebble, pitch, promontory, quake, quiet, reel, refuge, roach, roll, scarth, scoria, scylla, shake, shog, sima, skarn, specie, stagger, stone, stun, support, sway, swing, teeter, toph, tor, totter, trap, trass, tremble, undulate, whin
aggregate auge
artificial granolith
badger cony, hyrax
bare scarth
basaltic ankaramite, basanite, fourchite, greenstone, miharaite, tephrite, whinstone, wichtisite
basin bullan, keeve, kieve
bass cabrilla, redeye
bed cap, plum
bell columbine, flower
bird murre, sandpiper
blackbird ring-ouzel
boring tool trepan
-bottom base, cheapest, foundation, lowest
-bound rugged
brake bird's-foot-fern, polypody
broken attle, gravel, sand
cavity geode, voog, vug(g), vugh
cedar sabino
chain reef
chip spall
chunk knuckle
classification petrography
clay ganister, pelite, slate
cleavage, pert. metataxic
coarse psephite, varnsingite
cod priest-fish
comb. ite, lite, petro, saxi, yte
composite capel
concretions oolite
cook wrasse
-covered area brul(e)
crab cancer
cress arabis, bishop's-wig, molewort, sicklepod
crushed greet
crystal bohemian ruby, bristol stone, quartz, rose quartz, rubasse

crystalline diorite, franomerite, greisen, schist
dangerous scylla
debris attle, detritus, drift, eluvium, gravel, head, scree, talus
decayed clay, geest, gossan, gozzan, iron-hat, laterite, sand, saprolite, wacke
deep-seated plutonite
dense adinole
deposit moraine
development anamorphism
dike absarolite, bahiaite, banakite, beerbachite, bekinkinite, damkjernite, dancalite, gauteite, hamrongite, helsingkite, heronite, heumite, inninmorite, issite, lestiwarite, odinite, ouachitite, pawdite, polzenite, prowersite, sovite, stavrite, windsorite
dove god, guillemot, pigeon
drill borebit, bullpoint
eel gunnel
extrusive absarokite, andesite, ciminite, cumbraite, dacite, dellenite, spilite, toscanite
falcon merlin
fever brucellosis
fine-grained clay, sand, shale, trap
fissile shale, shaul, shoal
flint-like chert, clint, quartz
fluid lava
fold anticline
foliated gneiss
-forming, pert. petrogenic
fracture leptoclase
fragment pebble
fragmental bressia, psephite
garden alpinery
geranium alumbroot
glassy buchite
goat ibex
grains mica, sand
granitoid diorite, dunite, gneiss, quartz, unakite
granular diorite, gabbro, griquaite, gruss, ijolite, koswite, oolite
green prase
grooves lapies
group combo, trio
grouse ptarmigan
gunnel butterfish, dollarfish, ephipus, kelpfish, poronotus
gurnet fortescue
hard chatoyant, chert, flint, granite, quartz, whin
hare kliphaas

hind agauji, cabramora, grouper, mero
hopper eudyptes, macaroni, penguin
igneus (See also *volcanic*, below.) agglomerate, amygdaloid, anorthosite, aphanite, basalt, bill, borolanite, boss, chrysolite, dacite, diabase, diorite, dolerite, domite, dunite, essexite, felsite, flint, gabbro, granite, granodiorite, granolite, granophyre, ijolite, ijussite, kodurite, laccolith, latite, lava, macromerite, melanocrate, metabasite, minette, missourite, orthosite, peridot, phanerite, picrite, pitchstone, polymere, porphyry, pulaskite, quartz, rhyolite, shonkinite, sial, silexite, sima, syenite, taxite, tephrite, teschenite, tinguaite, tonalite, trachybasalt, trachite, trap, trass, tufa, tuff, urtite, variolite
igneus, pert. athrogenic
impure chert
in another rock xenolith
in magma xenocryst
insulated skerry
intrusive dacite, diorite, gabbro, granite, hortite, maenaite, pegmatite, runite
iron-bearing gal
isolated scar(r), scaur
jasmine androsace
jutting See *peak*, below.
kangaroo wallaby
kind adindle, agate, banakite, basalt, flagstone, flint, gneiss, granite, igneous, limestone, lytta, marble, metamorphic, perthite, porphyry, quartz, rhyolite, sandstone, schist, sedimentary, shale, shaul, slate, spilite, tufa, tuff, volcanic
knob buhr, burr, knuckle
laminated gneiss, mica, shale, shaul, shoal, slate
layer blister, folium, septum, shelf, shell, skullcap, slate
layered bedding, strata
ledge sipe
-like hard, solid
lily orchid
living among rupestrine, rupiculous
mass aiguille, batholite, batholith, lopolith, mountain, nappe, peak

melanocratic lherzite, vibetoite, vogesite
melon cantaloupe, muskmelon
melting process anatexis
metamorphic adinole, amphibolite, buchite, collobrierite, eclogite, epidiorite, glaucophanite, gneiss, gondite, granulite, hornfels, lavialite, leptite, limurite, nebulite, phtanite, schist, skarn, zobtenite
mica-bearing dolomite, glimmerite
mine capping
molten lava, magma
moss grimmia, lichen, widow's-cross
music syncopation
mythical scylla
name meaning lias, peter
native snapper
nodule geode
on the bankrupt, destitute, ruined, shattered, wrecked
opening grike
organic bioherm, biolite, biolith
painting petrogram, pictograph
peak arete, crag, kip, needle, ridge, scar, tor
performer freak
pert. petrean, petric, saxatile
phonolitic apachite
pigeon sand-grouse
pile hoodoo, jail
pipit tietick
pit quarry
plant lichen, moss, sedum
plover sandpiper, turnstone
plutonic abyssal, allivalite, covite, granobaggro, harrisite, hollaite, lakarpite, mangerite, mariupolite, melteigite, monmouthite, monzodiorite, tawite, turjaite, yamaskite
point See *peak*, above.
porous arsoite, gibelite, toph, tufa, tuff
proterozoic animikean
protruding clint, scar
pulverized flour
rabbit hyrax, pika
rare alnoite
-ribbed confirmed, uncompromising, unyielding
rose cistus, dayflower, hibertia, hudsonia, rockcist, sagerose, sunflower
rough crag, knar, scarth
rounded rognon, sheepback

salmon amberfish, coalfish
salt amole, emol, halite
sandwort cyme
schistose epidosite, porphyroid
science geology, petrography, petrology
sedimentary arkose, conglomerate, gypsum, ironstone, limestone, medina, sandstone, shale
sedimentary, pert. holoclastic
sharp crag
siliceous ganister, graybilly, hornfels, malmstone, sial
slaty phyllite, schalstein, shilf
slide avalanche
smooth slickenside
snake krait, python
snipe sandpiper
solid gibber
splitting mica, schist
starling ouzel
stratum anticline, lenticle, syncline
study lithology
submerged shelf
sucker lamprey
surface karren
tar petroleum
the alcatraz, gibraltar
thin shale, slate
tripe gyrophora, lichen
trout bodieron, boregat, greenling, hexagrammos
upthrust mass nappe
volcanic (See also *igneus*, above.) andesite, ashstone, basalt, domite, eutaxite, koipato, latite, lava, nephelinite, peperino, phonolite, pyroclastic, rhyolite, sanukite
warbler cataract-bird, origma
whetstone novaculite
whiting fish, kelpfish, odax, stranger
worthless gangue, slag
wren bird, turco
ROCKAWAY carriage
ROCKBRUSH colubrina, rosilla
ROCKER chair, cradle, oscillator, pedestal, pigeon, refiner, seat, shoofly, skate
ROCKET (See also ASTRONAUT, MISSILE, SPACE.) arise, ascend, brassica, charlock, dash, firedrake, firework, lance, levitate, missile, mount, projectile, repulsor, rise, satellite, signal, skylight,

soar, spaceship, starship, surge, tower, weapon, weld, wo(a)ld, would
balloon-launched rockoon
blue delphinium, monkshood
bomb bumblebomb, buzzbomb, chase-me-charlie, doodlebug, robomb, robot bomb, vergeltungswaffe
booster agena, atlas, saturn
combustion end burnout
control system bangbang
defense abm(is), sabmis, safeguard, sage, spartan, sprint
drag reducer boattail
flight bouquet
forward section nosecone, warhead, warnose
fuel See *propellant*, below.
glider sailplane
kind (See also *names*, below.) aam, antimissile, asm, ata, atg, atom, aum, bazooka, cruise missile, demolition, flare, fufo, gapa, gta, gtg, harpoon, homing, hvar, icbm, irbm, lance, liquid, loon, mirv, neutron, piggyback, ram, retro, sam, smoke, solidfuel, spinner, srbm, ssm, sts, supersonic, winged, xaam, xasm, xsam, xssm
landing reentry, splashdown
launcher bazooka, calliope, hedgehog, mark-ten, meilewagon, mousetrap, projector
launching airburst, blast-off, brennschluss, flight, propulsion, shoot, shot
low altitude satelloid
names, american 3 abm, asm, asp, ram, tow, ulm 4 able, dart, dove, fobs, fufo, hawk, icbm, irbm, jato, juno, lark, loki, loon, mace, mirv, nike, pofo, slam, thor, vone, vtwo, zuni 5 agena, asroc, astor, atlas, cajun, delta, genie, golem, komet, mirve, nativ, quail, scout, snark, talos, titan 6 bomarc, corvus, deacon, dragon, falcon, lobber, mauler, navaho, petrel, rascal, redeye, sabmis, saturn, sprint, subroc, tartar, viking 7 aerobee, aerojet, bullpup, centaur, firebee, jupiter, mariner, matador, neutron, polaris, regulus, skybolt,

sparrow, spartan, terrier, tiny tim, trident, wagtail 8 ablestar, astrobee, corporal, crossboy, dingdong, explorer, hound dog, lacrosse, maverick, pershing, poseidon, redstone, sentinel, sergeant, tomahawk, vanguard 9 bold orion, holy moses, minuteman, safeguard 10 copperhead, honest john, little john, shillelagh, sidewinder 11 minnie mouse 12 davy crockett, lance missile 13 cruise missile

names, russian belyayev, bikovsky, blackie, breezie, feoktistov, frog, gagarin, galosh, komarov, kubasov, laika, leonov, lunik, mikolayev, popovitch, salyut, sam, scud, shatalov, shohin, soyuz, sputnik, strela, talinn, terechkova, titov, yegorov, zeus

nozzle jetavator

part capsule

personnel **headquarters** blockhouse

pert. ballistic

pioneer goddard, von braun, von karman

propellant ballistite, bromine-pentafluoride, liquid hydrogen, liquid oxygen, lox, polyurethane

propulsion backflash, blast, charge, jet blast, retrorocket, thrust

reconnaisance samos

research aerobee, astrobee, delta, vanguard

salad roquette

sensing device seeker

stage agena, delta

underwater nixie, polaris, poseidon, torpedo, ulms

unit stage

upper stage agena

vapor loss boil-off

warhead measurement kiloton, megatonnage

world war ii buzzbomb, v-bomb

ROCKFISH bass, bocaccio, chilipepper, chinafish, corsair, flathead, flioma, garrupa, greenling, grouper, jack, killifish, lionfish, perch, priestfish, rasher, redfish, redsnapper, reina, rena, scorpaneid, sculpin, sebastodes, tambor, viuva

ROCKLING baud, gade, roker, sorghe, whistler

ROCKWEED alga, bladderkelp, fucus, fungus, lichen, moss, pelvetia, seatang, seaweed, wrack

ROCKY adamantine, bouldery, calcified, chancy, cliffy, coarse, craggy, daft, difficult, dizzy, firm, flinty, granitic, gravelly, gritty, hard, lapideous, lithoid(al), marbly, monolithic, obdurate, obstinate, pebbly, petrean, petrous, rough, rugged, rupellary, shaky, shingly, sick, slaty, solid, steadfast, stony, stubborn, tottering, tottery, uncertain, unfeeling, unsteady, wavery, weak, wobbly

ford cantaloupe, melon

ROCKY MOUNTAIN *fern* athyrium

fever cause rickettsia

fever tick dermacentor

fir alpine fir, balsam-spruce

garrot goldeneye

goat antelope, mazame

herb anemone, aster, beardtongue, bronzebell, forget-me-not, queencup, saxifrage, springbeauty, stenanthella

park estes, glacier, yellowstone

plant bitterroot, gentian, goldenrod, solidago

range absaroka, big belt, big horn, bitterroot, sangre de cristo, san juan, sawatch, teton, uinta, wasatch

resort aspen, breckenridge, crested butte, fraser valley, jackson hole, park city, snowmass, steamboat, sun valley, vail

sedge carex

sheep bighorn

tree hemlock, pine, tsuga

wind chinook

ROCOCO antiquated, arty, baroque, bizarre, fantastic, flamboyant, florid, gauche, ornate, outdated

ROD authority, axle, bacterium, baculus, bar, baton, bolt, broach, brochette, caduceus, came, cane, crook, crop, crosier, crozier, discipline, distaff, fishpole, gat, gun, guy, lance, lath, lytta, mace, offshoot, oppression, osier, perch, pikestaff, pistol, pointer, pole, power, punish-

ment, race, raddle, revolver, rib, rule, scepter, sceptre, scion, scob, shaft, shoot, skewer, spear, spit, spoke, sprag, staff, stake, stave, stem, stick, stock, tribe, tringle, tube, tyranny, wand, whip, wire

axial axostyle, virgula

barbecue spit

basketry osier

billiard cue

bundle driver, fasces

cartilaginous columella, lytta

clamming brail

comb. rhabd(o)

connecting pitman

disciplinary ferula, ferule

divination by dowsing, rhabdomancy

divining dowser, twig

fibrous lytta

flexible raddle, wattle

forked crutch

40 furlong

graduated stadium

100 square acre

iron snap

key tommy

lead came

lightning, point aigrette

-like rigid, virgate

l-shaped gagger

measuring ellwand, judge, metestick, metewand, meteyard, spile, stadia, yardstick

metal t-iron

movable piston

official baculus, mace, scepter, sceptre, verge

pert. baculine

pointed skewer

-shaped bacillary, bacilliform, baculiform, rhabdoid, virgate, virgulate

small lance

square perch

supple swabble

tethering stake

thatch fastening, spelk, springle

thin scallom, teyne

tie anchor

umbrella rib

whip ferule, gad, plet

withe bilberry

wood scob

RODENT 3 bun, rat, tan 4 bawd, caby, cony, degu, glis, hare, loir, mara, mole, paca, pica, pika, tana, tawn, tuan, tuza, utia, vole, want, watt, wont 5 aguti, bawty, bobac, bunny, cavia, coney, coypu, cutty, daman, dassy, ganam, gundi, hirax, hutia, hyrax, jutia, labba, lepus, lerot, metad, moudy, mouse, porky, ranny, shrew, sisel, sorex, talpa, urson, xerus, zapus, zemmi, zokor 6 agouti, agouty, bawtie, beaver, boback, chippy, coypou, craker, cururo, dassie, gerbil, gnawer, gopher, jerboa, jumper, malkin, marmot, mawkin, murine, muroid, mygale, nutria, oarlap, oarlop, parker, rabbit, rattan, rotton, sokher, suslik, taguan, talpid, tapeti, wabber, warner 7 assapan, blesmol, chincha, chippie, dipodid, geomyid, hamster, lemming, leporid, leveret, muskrat, potoroo, rathare, sandrat, sleeper, sondeli 8 capibara, capybara, chipmunk, dormouse, hedgehog, leporide, octodont, sewellel, spalacid, squirrel, tucotuco, viscacha, vizcacha, water rat 9 groundhog, guinea pig, porcupine, woodchuck 10 anomalarus, chinchilla, cottontail, jack rabbit, prairie dog

aquatic beaver, coypu, muskrat, water rat

burrowing gopher, groundhog, mole, nesokia, pocket mouse, prairie dog, sewellel, tucotuco

bushy-tailed marmot, packrat

disease tular(a)emia

gnawing beaver, mole, mouse, rat

jumping dipus, jerboa

largest capibara, capybara

migratory lemming

murine abrocome, anomalurus, capromys, dinomys, dipus, geomys, gerbillus, glires, lepus, mouse, mus, myodes, myoxus, rat, rattus, sigmodontes, tamias, tupaia, xerus, zapus

nocturnal sewellel

pert. glirene, rosorial

prehistoric stenofiber

rabbit-like pica, pika

rat-like abrocome, vole

short-tailed gundi

small cururo, mouse

RODEO enclosure, exhibition, roundup, show, spectacle

horse buck-jumper

rider cowboy

RODERIGO *beloved* desdemona

duped by iago

RODGE gadwall

RODIN *consort* camille claudel, rose beuret

home meudon

sculpture balzac, burghers of calais, dante, thinker

RODMAN chainman, clashee, clashy, hoodlum, surveyer

RODNEY good-for-nothing, idler, shirk(er), vagabond

RODOLFO *beloved* mimi

RODOMONT boaster, braggadocio, braggart

RODOMONTADE bluster, boast(ful), boasting, bombast, braggart, brag(ging), fustian, pretentious, pride, rant, rhapsody, vainglory, vanity, vaunting

ROE capret, caviar, doe, eggs, hind, milt, spawn, trubu

deer capreolus

source shad, sturgeon

ROEBUCK chevreuil, girl

group bevy

ROENTGEN *invention* x-ray

ROESTONE oolite

ROG jumble, pull, shake, stir

ROGATION appeal, litany, petition, prayer, request, supplication, worship

ROGER See YES.

ROGUE bait, beggar, blackguard, cad, caitiff, canter, catso, cheat, coquin, criminal, cutup, decry, demon, devil, drole, elephant, elf, enfant-terrible, foister, gipsy, gue, gypsy, hellion, hemp(seed), hempy, imp, kemp, kite, knave, ladron, loon, mazik, minx, mountebank, panurge, picaro(on), pixy, puck, quack, rap(scallion), rascal(lion), reprobate, rowdy, ruffian, scalawag, scamp, scoundrel, scum, sharper, shelm, shyster, sinner, skeesicks, skellum, sneak, sport, swindler, swinger, thief, tinker, tramp, trickster, vagabond, vagrant, varlet, villain, wag, wander, whipjack

pert. picaresque, sly, wanton

ROGUERY cheating, fraud, knavery, mischief, patchery, rascality, trickery, tricks, truantry, villainy

ROGUISH arch, dishonest, espiegle, frolicsome, funloving, impish, kittenish, knavish, mischievous, pawky, playful, puckish, sly, sportive, unscrupulous, vagrant, waggish, wanton

ROID frolicsome, riotous, rough, severe, unmanageable

ROIL aggravate, agitate, agitation, anger, annoy, bewilder, bother, dirty, disorder, disturb, enrage, exasperate, fidget, foul, horse, incense, infuriate, irk, irritate, madden, nettle, peeve, provoke, roam, romp, ruffle, steed, vex, wander

ROILED muddy, RILED, turbid, vexed

ROISIN DUBH See IRELAND.

ROI SOLEIL louis xiv, sun king

ROISTER bluster, brag, bully, carouse, galravage, galravitch, gilravage, play, revel, scour, spree, swagger

ROISTERER buster, ephesian, hoodlum, mum, reveler, scourer, twibill

ROISTERING boisterous, hoiden, hoyden, rampageous, uproarious

ROKA See MAFURA.

ROKE fog, mist, moisture, poke, rowk, smoke, steam, stir, vapor

ROKER ray, rockling, thornback

ROKY See ROUKY.

ROLAND warden of the breton march

avenger thierry

beloved belle aude

chanson author turoldus

defeat roncesvalles, roncevaux, rouncival

foe ferragus, ganelon, gan(o), saracens

friend florismart, oliver

horn olivant

horse veillantif

parent bertha, milo

stepfather ganelon

sword durandal, durindana

uncle charlemagne

victim angoulaffre

ROLE bit, business, cameo,

cast, character, duty, feeder, function, guise, heavy, impersonation, ingenue, lead, lines, office, part, person(age), personification, piece, pose, posture, pretense, relief, walk-on

leading star

ROLFE, JOHN *wife* pocahontas

ROLL (See also *kind,* below.) billow, bolt, bombinate, boom, bowl, bread, bundle, cadre, carotte, catalog(ue), coast, coil, curl, cylinder, document, dough, file, flounder, frisk, funds, furl, grovel, gyrate, infold, inventory, inwrap, jibe, list, lurch, money, move, package, pitch, pivot, propel, record, register, reverberate, revolve, roam, roar, rob, roster, rota(te), rotulet, rumble, schedule, scroll, slate, spindle, stagger, sway, swing, tattoo, thunder, tilt, toss, trill, trindle, troll, trundle, turn, undulate, utter, wad, wallow, wamble, wander, wheel, whirl, wind, wrap, yaw

back cam, decrease, defeat, reject, retreat, retrench, setback

blanket bindle, shiralee

-call assemble, muster, solitaire

cloth bolt, wreath

coins rouleau

dust kitten

eyes goggle, waul, whawl

glass marver

hard bagel

hollow cannelon

in arrive, retire, wallow

into ball clew, clue

into one combine

kind bagel, bap, bialy, biscuit, brioche, bun, cannelon, croissant, crumpet, kaiser, muffin, parker house, popover, rissole, rusk, scone, sesame, vienna

logs birl

long flute

military cadre, roster

onion-flavored bialy

onward devolve

out arise, get up, rise

over comb, joll, reverse, welter

padded burlet

paper cartouch(e), scroll, spill

penny tommy

sleeves reeve

sweet danish, schnecken

together convolve

top desk, tambour

up accumulate, amass, collar, collect, congregate, furl, increase, stow

whip backrest

wool carding, rove, roving, slub

ROLLAND, ROMAIN *novel* jean christophe

ROLLER bandage, barrel, billow, bowl, brayer, breaker, canary, caster, comber, curler, cylinder, dandy, dressing, fillet, fly, mangle, pigeon, pin, platen, presser, pulverizer, rotator, sirgang, smoother, surcingle, tumbler, undulation, wave, wheel, winch

coaster bobsled, chute-the-chute, shoot-the-shoots, switchback

skate pedomotor

ROLLEYWAY gangway, road, track, tramway

ROLLICK bluster, brag, disport, frolic, gaiety, gambol, joviality, lark, play, rejoice, riot, rollix, romp, skylark, sport

ROLLICKING careless, gay, hilarious, jovial, lively, merry, rampageous, riproaring, wild

ROLLING bumpy, coiling, fold, leveling, lurching, shifting, spiral, surging, swaying, variable, wavy, wheely

descent by devolution

stock caboose, car, coach, engine, locomotive, pullman, sleeper, train

stone enfle, game, rotator, schwellen, wanderer

weed roly-poly, tumbleweed

ROLLMOP herring

ROLYPOLY dumpy, fat(ty), game, obese, portly, pudding, pudgy, rascal(ly), rogue, rotund, round, saltwort, tumbler, tumbleweed, worthless

ROMAINE cos, fabric, lettuce, plant, vegetable

ROMAN (For city references, see ROME.) antiqua, brave, bream, catholic, distinguished, fiction, frugal, goose, gownsman, honest, italian, latin, noble, novel, papal, severe, simple, stern, upright

abbot abbas

actor roscius

administrator brutus

adviser to kings egeria

album albe

alcove ala

allies aedui

ancestral hero aeneas

and world urbi et orbi

apartment decus, insula

apostle neri, paul

arch abutment alette

armor cataphract, corium

army insigne eagle

army troops alares, marius' mules

army unit ala, century, cohort, curia, legion, maniple

asiatic battle masada

assembly centuriata, comitia, curiata, forum, senate, tributa

attendant aleiptes, aliptes

augur auspex, tolumnius

authority symbol fasces

awning velarium

axe dolabra

baggage cart carrus

banner labarum

barbarian onion-eater

barracks can(n)aba

basket cist

baths balneae, caldarium, frigidarium, thermae

bathtub labrum

battle array acies

battle site baduhenna

birth goddess carmenta, nicostrata, parca, postverta, prorsa

book cover diptych

booth liber, taberna

bottle amphora

boundary limes

bowl patina

bowman sagittarius

box capsa, cist

boxing glove cestos, cestus

boy camillus, puer

breeze ora

bronze aes

brooch fibula

brothel lupanare

brothers remus, romulus

building aedes, aedile, insula

burial site catacomb

cake, sacrifical mole

calendar ephemeris

calendar, fixed point calends, ides, kalends, nones

camp castrum

candle firework, signal

cap pileus

cape byrrus, sagum

capital city urbs

captain centurion

carriage See *chariot,* below.

cart birota, carrus

catholic calotin, papist, popist, romist

cavalry cataphracti

cavalry division turma

ceiling lacunar

cell naos

censor flaminius

census lustrum

chair, official's curule

chariot biga, esseda, essede, quadriga

children's goddess adeona

circus, part carcer, meta, spina

cistern impluvium

citadel arx

citizen aerarian, casca, civis, plebian, quirite

civil war battle actium

clan gens, gentes

class, lower plebs

class, lowest aerian

cloak See *garment,* below.

clock solarium

cohort insigne dragon

coin aes, antoninianus, asses, aureus, decussis, denarius, dinder, dupondius, follis, libra, miliarensis, quadrigatus, quinarius, quincunx, semis, sesterce, sestertium, sextans, siliqua, solidus, tremissis, uncia, vallar, victoriatus

collar rabat

colony kanem, leptis magna, lixus, mauritania, numidia, timgad, zaghawa

colosseum signal jugula, mitte

comedy atellanae, exode

commander centurion

command post praetorium

companion comes

conqueror alaric, gaiseric

conspirator casca, cassius, catiline

consul brutus, cinna, marius, scipio

contract nexum, vadimonium

copper aes

couch accubitum, accubitus,

biclinium, pulvinar, triclinium

council decemvir, triumvirate

court atrium, comitium, curia, forum, rota, tribunal

courtesan lalage

crossroads compitum, trivia

cry ave, hoc

cuirass lorica

cup acetabulum, cotula, cylix, kylix, patera, skyphos

custodian neocorates

custom ritus

dagger sica

dance, religious tripudium

date calends, ides, kalends, nones

day breeze ora

dead, abode of orcus

dead spirits larvae, lemures, manes

death mors

decree decrete

defeat site cannae

dictator caesar, camillus, sulla

dining room oecus

dinner cena

disease bulimia

dish lanx, patera, patina

district pagus

divine law fas

diviner augur, auspex

divinities appiades

division, military century

doctor aesculapius, archiater

dog maltese, melita

door janna

drain cloaca maxima, cuniculus

drill terebra

earth goddess ceres, terra

earthwork agger

emperor adrian, aemilianus, alexander, antonine, augustus, aurelian, balbinus, caesar, caligula, caracalla, carinus, carus, claudius, commodus, constantine, constantius, decius, didius, diocletian, domitian, elagabulus, eugenius, florianus, galba, galerius, gallienus, gallus, geta, glycerius, gordian, gratian, hadrian, heliogabalus, honorius, hostilianus, jovian, julian, julius, libius, licinius, lucius-verus, macrinus, magnentius, majorian, marcian(us), marcus aurelius, maxentius, maximian, maximinus, nepos, nero, nerva,

numerianus, octavian, olybrius, otho, otto, pertinax, petronius, philip the arab, probus, pupienus, saturninus, septimus-severus, sigismund, theodosius, tiberius, titus, trajan, valentinian, valerian, vespesian, vitellius, volusanius

emperor, eastern arcadius, justinian, leo, marcian, theodosius

emperor's physician archiater

emperor's standard labarum

emperor's title augustus, caesar

emperor's worshippers augustales

empire, eastern byzantium

empress athenais, eudocia, theodora

enclosure aedicula

enemy alaric, attila, carthage, cimbri, hannibal, huns

ensign boar, eagle, horse, wolf

entrance atrium

epic aeneid

epicure apicius, lucullus

epigrammatist martial

estate latifundium

ewer aquaemanale, aquamanile

families annibaldi, barberini, cenci, colonna, doria, farnese, frangipani, orsini, savelli

family gens

farmer agricola, colonus

fate ananke, decuma, morta, nona, parca(e)

fertility god picumnus, pilumnus

festival agonium, ambarvalia, equiria, feralia, feria, floralia, fontinalia, fordicidia, fornacalia, larentalia, lemuralia, liberalia, lupercalia, matralia, matronalia, negalesia, opalia, paganalia, parentalia, parilia, robigalia, sigillaria, terminalia, vota

fever malaria

field campus

fighter gladiator

fire god vulcan

flag draco, vexillum

flask alabastrum, ampulla

fleuve saga

flower goddess flora

fortress castrum, san angelo

fruit goddess pomona

furies dirae

galley bireme, quadrireme, trireme, unireme

gambling cube talus, tessera

game(s) ludi, munera, munus, prolusio(nes), quinquennalia, venatio(nes)

garden god vertumnus

garland corona

garment abolla, alicula, amictus, byrrys, cyclas, lacerna, paenula, palla, paludamentum, planeta, ricinium, sagum, stola, synthesis, talar, toga, trabea, tunic

gate decumana

general agricola, agrippa, antony, belisarius, caesar, camillus, capitolinus, cassius, cominius, crassus, cunctator, dolabella, drusus, fabius, flaminus, lartius, lucullus, mancinus, marius, metellus, narses, pompey, regulus, scipio, sertorius, stilicho, sulla, sylla, titus, varro

geographer mela

-german battle baduhenna

ghost lemur, mane, retiarius

giant caca, cacus, eleazer, maximinus

gift sportula

girdle balt(h)eus, cestus

girl camilla, puella

gladiators andabatae, dimachaeri, essedarii, laquerii, mymillones, retiarii, samnite, secutores, velites

goal post meta

god adranus, aesculapius, amor, apollo, auster, bacchus, bonus eventus, boreas, comus, consus, cronus, cupid, deus, dis(pater), eurus, fabulinus, faun(us), februus, genius, invus, janus, jove, jupiter, lar(es), liber(pater), lupercus, manes, mars, mercury, momus, morpheus, mors, neptune, orcus, pales, penates, phoebus, picumnus, picus, pilumnis, pluto, portunus, quirinus, robigus, saturn, semosancus, silvanus, sol, somnus, sylvanus, tiber(inus), vagitanus, vatican, vediovis, veduis, vejovis, vertumnus, virbius, vulcan

goddess abeona, abundantia, acca-larentia, adeona, adrastea, aestas, angerona, anna-perenna, annona, ara, astrea, aurora, bellona, bona-dea, caca, cardea, carmenta, carmentis, ceres, concordia, damia, decuma, diana, discordia, dubona, egeria, epona, fauna, felicitas, feronia, fides, flora, fornax, fortuna, hestia, iris, juno, lara, libitina, lua (mater), lucina, luna, maia, mania, matuta, minerva, moneta, morta, muta, nilostrada, nona, nox, nyx, ops, pales, parca(e), pax, pomona, postvorta, pronuba, proserpina, proserpine, regina, rhea-silvia, rumina, salacia, salus, selena, selene, spes, suada, tacita, tellus(mater), terra, trivia, urania, vacuna, venus, vesta, victoria

god of gods janus-pater

gods, domestic lares, penates

gods, minor sondergotter

gods, queen of juno

gourmand apicius

governor legatus, proconsul, procurator, tetrarch

governor of britain agricola

graces gratiae

grain, free annona

grain speculator dardanarius

grammarian donatus, priscian

gravestone cippus

greeting ave

guard(s) lictor, usipetes

hairpin acus

hall odeum, oecus

hangman carnifex

harvest festival opalia

harvest goddess ops

hat or helmet galea, petasos, petasus

healer fabiola, marcella, paul

hearth goddess hestia

hell ade, eita, orcus

herald's staff caduceus

hero aeneas, coriolanus, fabricius, horatius, pollux, remus, romulus, scaevola

highway See *road*, below.

historian fannius, heraclides, josephus, justin, livy, nepos, piso, polybius, ponticus, posidonius, procopius, sallust, suetonius, tacitus

holiday (See also *festival*, above.) feria, ides

holy empire See HOLY ROMAN EMPIRE.

hood cucullus

horn buccina

hut tegurium

incense jar acerra

insignia spqr

jar cadus, dolium, hydria, oinochoe, olla

javelin aclys, pile, pilum

judge aedile, edile, judex, qu(a)estor, triumvir

jurist caius, gaius, justinian, papinian

justice of the peace irenarch

king alaric, ancus-marcius, nemi, numa, romulus, servius, tarquin(ius), tullius, tullus-hostilius

king's advisor egeria

lace reticella

land fundus

landscape mural topia

language latin

law fas, jus, lex, mos, rubric, twelve tables

law court comitium

leader dux

legion insigne eagle, spqr

legionnaire manipular

legion, part See *army unit*, above.

list(s) albe, album

litter lectica

lyre trigon

magistrate aedile, apparitor, archon, augur, censor, comes, consul, edile, irenarch, lictor, nestorian, politarch, pr(a)etor, prefect, qu(a)estor, septemvir, tribune, triumvir

maiden, mythical cloetia

marble cipolin

market emporium, forum

market day nundine

marriage proclamation talasio

martyr agnes, cecilia, sebastian

masonry diamicton

matron cornelia

meal cena

measure acetabulum, actus, amphora, asses, bes, centuria, clima, congius, cotyle, cubit(us), culeus, cyanthus, decempeda, deunx, digitus, dodrans, dolium, duella, gradus, hemina, heredium, juger, leuga, libra, ligula, medimnus, mile, millarium, modius, obolus, palmipes, palmus, passus, pes, pollex, quadrant, quartarius, rasta, saltus, scruplus, semis, septus, sexis, sextans, sex-

tarius, sextula, sicilium, solidus, stadion, stadium, triens, uncia, urn(a), versus
metal aerarian
military formation ala, phalanx
military insigne phalera, spqr
military machine tenebra
military sandal caliga
military unit See *army unit*, above.
military vessel bireme, trireme
missionary paulinus
money chest brasier, brazier
money-dealers argentari
month aprilis, augustus, december, februarius, januarius, junius, maius, martius, november, october, quintilis, sextilis
month, 1st day calends, kalends
mother mater, matuta
mound agger
name praenomen
naturalist pliny
needle acus
niche aedicula
nobility optimates
noble ramnes
noncitizen peregrinus
notary tachygrapher
nymph albun(e)a, antevorta, camenae, carmenta, egeria, postvorta
ocher doubloon
official See *magistrate*, above.
oil jar alabastron, alabastrum
orator brutus, caecilius, cato, cicero, diophanes, hortensius, rienzi, sicinnius
ornament bulla, patera
palace troops palatines
palladium ancile
patriot cato, cincinnatus, cinna
pavement asarotum
peace irene, pax
peasant colona, colonus
pen calamus
penny peter's-pence
people atestene, etruscans, laeti, latins, patricians, plebians, sabines
performance acroama
pert. classical
pestle pilum
philosopher apollonides, apuleius, blossius, boethius, cato, dellius, demetrius, plotinus, seneca, theophrastus

physician aesculapius, archiater
pillar cippus
plain compagna
plant good-king-henry
platter lanx, paterna
pledge pignus, vas
poetaster bavius
politician lepidus, sejanus
porcelain murr(h)a
port god portunus
praenomen appius, aulus, caius, gaius, manius, marcus, quintus, servius, sextus, spurius, tiberius, titus
priest(s) arval(es), bellonarii, epulo, fecial, lupercus, pastophorus, pontifex, salii
priestess vestal
priests' group quindecemvir, quindecimvir
priests, pert. arval
procurator felix, pilate
province armenia, assyria, cilicia, dacia, dalmatia, gallia, gaul, illyricum, lycaonia, numidia, pannonia, paphlagonia, pontus, thrace
provisions annona
purification lustrum
purification feast lupercalia
queen, legendary tanaquil
rampart agger, vallum
rebel spartacus, spuriusmaelius
reformer gracchus
regulator censor
religious ceremony See *festival*, above.
religious law fas
reservoir favissa
resort herculaneum
rhetorician quintilian
road agger, appian, iter, itinera, via
rocker cuna
roof opening compluvium
room aedicula, ala, atrium, ceroma, coenaculum, exedra, fumarium, oecus, tablinium
room, anointing alipterion, elaeothesium, unctuarium
ruins site besancon, evora, fano
sacred box cist, kist
sacred cow taura
sailor nauta
saint neri
savior marius
scholar atticus, varro
school scola
scourge alaric

scrivener tabellion
scroll stemma
scroll box scrinium
sea monster pistrix
seat bisellium, sella
seer augur
senate and people spqr
senate emblem laticlave
senate house curia
senator cato, decurion
sentry box excubitorium
serf colona, servus
share-cropping laetic
shelter taberna
shepherd faustulus
shield ancile, clipeus, clypeus, parma, pelta, scutum, testudo
ship navis
ship ornament aplustre
shoe caliga
show place circus
shrine aedicula, sacrarium, tegurium
slave androcles, mancipium
slinger funditor
smoking room fumarium
soap sapo
sock udo
soldier class vexillary
soldier(s) buccellarius, cataphract, hastatus, veles, velites
soldiers' shelter testudo
spa capri
spear verutum
spirit numen
sports official asiarch
staff lituus
stage logeion
standard aquila, labarum, signum, vexillum
standard bearer vexillary
statesman agrippa, boethius, caesar, cassiodorus, cato, cicero, cincinnatus, maecenas, pliny, seneca, sertorius, stilicho
storage place horreum, penaria
street corso, iter, platea, strada, via(veneto)
sun god janus, sol
supper room cenaculum
sweating room laconicum
sword dolo, ensis, falx, gladius, lorica, rudis
symbol fasces
table diptych
tablet album
tax annona, indiction
tax-gatherer publican
temple cella, naos, pantheon
tenement insula

tent praetorium
theatre odeum
ticket tessera
tile imbrex
title augustus, comes
toga praetexta
towel mappa
treasurer quaestor
treasury aerarian, aerarium, fiscus
trial quaestio
tribal division curia
tribune cola di rienzi
triumvirate member caesar, crassus, lepidus, mark antony, octavius, pompey
trumpet bunnin(a), lituus, tuba
trumpeter tubicen
tunic palla
tunic stripes laticlave
undertaker pollinctor
underworld orcus
underworld gods inferi
vase See *vessel*, below.
vehicle carrus, cisium, claburlarium
vessel alabastrum, amphora, capanna, lanx, lebes, murr(h)ine, quadrantal
vestibule fauces
veteran emeritus
victory monument tropaeum
victory procession triumph
vintner ausonius
votive statue sigillum
wall builder hadrian
war flags labara
war garb patera
warrior, virgin camilla
warship trireme
water channel specus
weight See *measure*, above.
well curb puteal
willow favonius
wine frascati
wine bottle amphora, ampulla
wine region atripalda, campania-felix
wine shop taberna
woe eheu
wonder colosseum
wormwood corydalis, ragweed
wrestler's unguent ceroma
writer accius, apuleius, attius, avianus, boethius, caesar, cato, catullus, cicero, cinna, ennius, flaccus, gaius, horace, juvenal, livy, lucan, lucillius, lucretius, martial(is), minucius, naso, nepos, ovid, perseus, pe-

tronius, phaedrus, plautus, pliny, propertius, sallust, seneca, silius, statius, suetonius, tacitus, terence, tibullus, varro, vergil, virgil
writing tablet diptych
yearly crop annona
youth ephebus
ROMANCE affair, amour, court, fable, fabrication, falsehood, fancy, fantasy, fiction, flirtation, gest(e), idealism, idealize, love, novel, poem, story, tale, tell, utopia, woo
isle bali, capri
language catalan, french, italian, latin, portuguese, provencal, rumanian, spanish
ROMANIA See RUMANIA.
ROMANOV *last* anastasia
ROMANSH ladin
ROMANTIC amorous, erotic, exaggerated, extravagant, fabulous, fanciful, fantastic, fictional, fond, idealistic, imaginary, imaginative, improbable, invented, lover, maudlin, mawkish, mushy, passionate, quixotic, sentimental, slushy, soppy, unreal, utopian, visionary, wild
ROMANTICIST (day)dreamer, idealist
ROMANTICIZE color, dramatize, embroider, exaggerate, glamorize, heighten, idealize
ROMANY gipsy, gypsy, nomad
ROME (See also ROMAN, for classical references.)
eternal city
airport ciampino, fiumicino, leonardo da vinci
amphitheater circus maximus, colosseum, flavium
amphitheater part spoilarium, spoilary
amphitheater seat sella
aqueduct pont du gard
basilica lateran, st peter's
betrayer tarpeia
biographer See ROMAN *writer*.
bishop pope
burial site catacomb
cathedral lateran, st peter's
chapel sistine
church ara coeli, basilica, lateran, san paolo, santa maria maggiore

families annibaldi, barberini, cenci, colonna, doria, farnese, frangipani, orsini, savelli
founder aeneas, remus, romulus
fountain trevi
hill aventine, caelian, capitoline, esquiline, janiculum, palatine, pincian, quirinal, saturnian, viminal
insignia spqr
lake albano, nemi
marshes pontine
museum campideglio, vatican
palace borghese, chigi, corsini, doria, farnese, lateran, madama, odescalchi, palatium, torlonia, venezia
peak arx, tarpeian rock
piazza barberini, colonna, del popolo, di spagna, esedra, lateran, minerva, montecitorio, navona, pia, venezia
prison regina coeli, tullianum
river tevere, tiber
section ostia, parioli, trastevere
street corso, iter, platea, strada, via(veneto)
ROMEO casanova, don juan, lothario, lover, slipper
beloved juliet
family montague
friend benvolio, mercutio
rival paris
servant balthasar
victim tybalt
ROMEO AND JULIET *author* shakespeare
character abraham, balthasar, benvolio, capulet, escalus, friar john, friar laurence, gregory, juliet, mercutio, montague, paris, peter, queen mab, romeo, sampson, tybalt
families capulet, montague
setting verona
ROMP antic, caper, carousal, carouse, chit, courant(e), disport, escapade, frisk, frolic, gambol, gammock, girl, hoiden, hoit, hoyden, lark, play, prance, rammack, roil, rollick, rommack, shirl, skylark, sport, tomboy
ROMULUS See REMUS.
ROMUS *father* aeneas, ascanius

RONCADOR croaker, grunt, haemulon, sciaenid, umbrina

ROND border, marsh, rand, shred

RONDEAU (See RONDO.) lyric, poem, song, verse

RONDEL(LE) bead, circle, diamond, gem, lyric, poem, tower

RONDO lyric, poem, song, verse

RONDURE circle, plumpness, roundness, sphere

RONE brake, brushwood, bush, gutter, rainspout, thicket

lance of king arthur

RONIN outcast, outlaw

ROOD cross, crucifix, measure, reed, rud, spawn, stang
1/8th yard
4 acre
goose brant
tree beam, cross

ROOF (See also *kind,* below.) at(t)ap, bonnet, ceiling, cover(ing), cupola, deck, dome, dwelling, house(top), plafond, planchment, riser, shell, shelter, summit, tectum, thack, top
angle fastigium, hip
arched camera
boards abatvent
cloth chutt
comb. stego, tecto
covering epi
edge eave(s)
false cricket
finial epi
flat azotea, leads, terrace
kind barrel(vault), chopper, composition, cricket, cupola, dirt, flat, french, gable, gambrel, hammerbeam, hip, jerkinhead, leanto, pantile, penthouse, pitched, pyramidal, sark, shake, shed, shingle, spire, straw, tar, thatched, tile, wagon(vault), wood(en)
-like tectiform
line ridge
material composition, copper, gravel, pantile, paper, scraw, shake, shingle, slate, straw, tar, terne, thatch, tile, tin, turf
opening bull's-eye, scuttle, skylight
ornament antefix, epi
part bargeboard, bargecou-

ple, cleat, comb, eave, epi, fillet, gable, joist, kingpost, monitor, purlin, queenpost, rafter, ridge(pole), shingles, strut, timber, truss, valley
rounded cupola, dome
sloping abatvent
small lookum
structure on cupola, dormer, penthouse
support cruck
tapering spire
thatched at(t)ap, chopper, dak, thack
tile imbrex
timber rafter
top comb, ridge(pole)
truncated hip
truss fink
vaulted dome

ROOFTREE dwelling, home, ridgepole

ROOK blacky, castillo, castle, cheat, corvus, crake, crouch, crow, cub, defraud, dupe, fleece, game, judge, raven, roc, roke, ruck, ruddy-duck, rukh, sharper, steal, swindle(r), vapor
cry cawk
group clamor

ROOKERY confusion, disturbance, rumpus, slum, tenement

ROOKIE beginner, colt, drongo, freshman, neo, novice, recruit, scrub, trainee, tiro, tyro

ROOKY damp, disheveled, foggy, hoarse, misty, rascally, recruit, roky, smoky, swindling, untidy

ROOL crumple, ruffle

ROOM accommodation, ada, aedicule, ala, alcove, apartment, atrium, attic, auditorium, aula, bath, board, boudoir, cabin(et), camarin, camera, capacity, cell, chamber, chambre, class, compartment, compass, cubicle, cuddy, den, enlarge, estufa, ew(e)ry, exedra, expanse, extent, farm, field, form, gallery, grade, holding, ida, inhabit, kiva, latitude, leeway, lieu, live, lobby, lodge, loft, lounge, margin, oecus, office, opportunity, parvis, place, position, post, quarters, range, rank, rotunda,

sala, salle, scope, scouth, seat, shack, space, stall, stanza, station, stead, studio, tablinum, thalamus
assembly chamber, kashga
at bottom basement
at top attic, garret
bath hammam
circular rotunda
cliff hypogeum
comb. atrio
conversation drawing room, exedra, salo(o)n
decoration parament, wainscot
dining cenacle, dinette, kitchen, nook, refectory
dirty rathole, rat's nest
drawing salo(o)n
dressing apothesis, boudoir, camarin, tirehouse, vestuary, wardrobe
food larder, pantry
group suite
hot caldarium, stew
inner inbye, spence
linens ewery
living lanai, serdab, solarium, voorhuis
narrow crib
octagonal tribuna
outer but
paintings gallery
portable camper, tent, trailer
prayer oratory
private boudoir, garderobe, schola, snug
reading atelier, atheneum, den, library, study
reception divan, mandarah, parlor, salon, salotto
recess alcove, niche
record tablinum
refrigerated cooler
retiring recamera
round rotunda
sea berth
sleeping barrack, bedroom, boudoir, dormer, dormitory, lodge, roomette
small cell, closet, cubicle, cuddy, snug(gery), stew
smoking divan, diwan, tabagie
storage attic, buttery, camarin, cellar, cupboard, ew(e)ry, larder, loft, magazine, pantry, shed, storehouse, thalamus
subterranean basement, undercroft
sweating laconicum, sudarium, sudatory
temple epinaos

throne aiwan
together chum, shack up
tower belfry
upper solar
waiting antechamber
ROOMER boarder, guest, lodger, tenant, transient
ROOMMATE chum, roomie, roomy
ROOMS apartment, digs, flat, layout, lodging, pad, quarters, suite
ROOMY airy, ample, big, broad, capable, capacious, comfortable, commodious, extensive, large, rangy, spacious, spacy, vast, wide
ROON border, darling, rand, round, shred, treasure
ROORBACK canard, falsehood, fiction, gossip, lampoon, lie, rumor, smear
ROOSE boast, extoll, flatter, praise, vaunt
ROOSEVELT, F. D. *advisers* brain trust
burial site hyde park
conference casablanca, teheran, yalta
economic program new deal
home campobello, hyde park
retreat shangri-la, warm springs
ROOSEVELT, THEODORE
battle kettle hill, san juan hill
birthplace new york city
burial site oyster bay
follower bull moose
home oyster bay, sagamore hill
party progressive, republican
policy big stick
profession publicist
troops rough riders
vice president fairbanks
ROOST abode, alight, aviary, bauk, bed, cage, garret, harbor, inhabit, jouk, lair, land, light, lodging, lounge, nest, perch, pole, quarters, rest, rookery, roust, rust, shelter, sit, sleep, squat, support, tide
ROOSTER(S) adderstongue, capon, cock, coupler, gallo, gamecock, gooseneck, hook, manoc, strutter, viola, violet
fish papagallo
horse hippalectryon
strut lak
ROOT ancestor, applaud, barrack, base, basis, begin-

ning, bottom, bulb(il), burrow, cause, cheer, core, derivation, dig, earthnut, encourage, eradicate, establish, fawn, fix, foundation, fountainhead, ground, grub, holler, hurrah, huzzah, imbed, implant, inception, jalap, more, motive, origin, orris, parent, place, plant, poke, provenance, pry, radical, radicle, radix, rahrah, reason, remove, rhizome, rhyzome, rise, roar, rout, rummage, rut, search, set (tle), source, spur, start, stem, stock, support, tuber (cle), unearth, watap
and branch completely, entirely, throughout, utterly, wholly
astringent rhatany
branch tapoun
canal therapy endodontics
candied eryngo
cap calyptra, calyptrogen, pileorhiza, spongiole
comb. radici, rhiz(a)(o)
deeply screw
disease anaberoga
dried althea, bryonia, capoorcutchery, inula, ipecac, jalap, krameria, licorice, scammony, seneca, veratrum
dyeing chay(a), choy, madder
edible apio, arracach(a), beet, carrot, cassava, celeriac, cous, cowish, eddo, ginger, oca, parsnip, potato, radish, roi, rutabaga, sassafras, sweet potato, tania, taro, tubercle, turnip, wasabi, yam
end butt
farinaceous breadroot
fibrous sponge
for acclaim, applaud, cheer, encourage, rahrah
fragrant orris, vetiver
growing on epirhizous
insane hemlock, henbane
medicinal artar, calombo, calumbo, colombo, columbo, gentian, ginseng, jalap, jena, lappa, licorice, orris, poke, rhatany, sassafras, seneca, senega
orchid cullion
out deracinate, disclose, discover, displant, eliminate, eradicate, everse, evulse, exterminate, extirpate, ex-

tract, grub, stock, stub, supplant, withdraw
outer layer exoderm
parasite balanophorace, broomrape, orobancha, rabbitwood
pert. radical
plant amole
poisonous poke
primary radicle, taproot
-producing rhizogenic
projecting spur
pungent crinkleroot, ginger, taro
sewing watap
shoot ratoon
small radicel, radicle
starch koonti
tonic See *medicinal,* above.
tree spurn, tang
tubercle clog
up See *out,* above.
without arrhizal, parasite
word etym(on)
ROOTED chronic, deepseated, established, fixed, implanted, inveterate, set, traditional
ROOTER buffalofish, enthusiast, fan, follower, plow, plugger, supporter
ROOTLE burrow, grub
ROOTLET crampon, radicel, radicle
ROOTS *author* alex haley
source ancestor kunta kinte
source country gambia
source village juffure
ROOTSTOCK biscuit, casava, dannum, ginger, origin, orris, pannum, pip, rhizome, source, stolon, taro, tumeric
ROOVE bur(r), rivet
ROPE aga(l), bight, bind, bobstay, brace, brail, breeching, cable, catch, cigar, cord(age), curb, ensnare, fasten, gad, guy, halter, halyard, hawser, hemp, inveigle, jeff, lacing, lariat, lasso(o), latitude, lazo, line, longe, lure, marline, noose, painter, pazaree, pinion, prolonge, reata, reeve, restrain, riata, rood, scope, secure, snotter, soam, stay, strap, string, strop, tack, taum, tether, tie, toggle, tow, trace, trammel, twine, tye, vang, widdy, withe
anchor rode, tieout, viol, voyal
animal's halter, tether

auxiliary preventer
band raband
bell hanger, tyall
bridle hackamore
cable keckling
cattle aweband, ceel, seal
circus jeff
collar parral, parrel
covering quilting
dancer acrobat, funambulist, funambulo
derrick telegraf
draft soam
drag guss
ends feazings
fasten reeve
fiber abaca, allaeanthus, anabo, bast, caroa, coir, cotton, feru, flax, grass, hemp, imbe, istle, ixtle, manila hemp, mung, munj, oakum, rhea, sisal
fish stringer
fishing pinion, seaming
flag-raising halyard
foot horse
gallows See *hangman's*, below.
gate cringle
grass soga
grip sally
guide dragline, fairlead, wapp
guy cable, stay, vang
hair braid, cabestro, lariat, lasso
handle becket, fettle, shackle
handmade fox
hangman's hemp, necktie, tippet, widdy
harness halter, trace
harpoon foregoer
holder becket, bollard, grommet
horse-training longe
in deceive, inveigle, lure, secure, string along
join splice
joint tuck
knob mouse
knot bend
ladder rung ratline
lead longe, rein
length bridle, course, drift, stopper
light ratlin(e)
loop becket, bight, fake, flake, frap, kinch, noose, parral, parrel, snorter, snotter
maker follower, ratliner
nautical backbone, backstay, bobstay, bowline, brace, brail, bridle, buntline, cat-

fall, colt, downhaul, earing, fang, fast, foretack, fox, gasket, geswarp, gilguy, guesswarp, guy, halyard, hawser, inhaul, jackstay, jibstay, lacing, laniard, lanyard, leefang(e), lift, line, mainsheet, marline, martingale, messenger, outhaul, painter, parral, parrel, pazaree, pendant, pigtail, raband, ratlin(e), roband, robbin, rode, rounding, selvagee, sennit, sheet, shroud, sling, snorter, snotter, span, stay, stirrup, stopper, strap, strop, swifter, tack, timenoguy, tye, vang, wapp, woolding
off circumscribe, divide, partition, separate
onions reeve
ornamentation torsade
part slatch
pass through reeve
plaited sennit
raft brail
restraining tether
rigging cordage
ring becket, garland, grommet, hank, snorter, snotter
secure belay
short monkeytail, shank, wanty
size grist
slack slatch
small marline
smuggler's lingtow
source abroma, agamid, amuyong, balete, hemp
stay guy
steer heel
stolen rumbo
straw fettle, gad, sime, sim(m)on, soogan, sugan, vine
tallowed gasket
thread reeve
throwing lariat, lasso, reata, riata
tie with hobble, lash, tether
tight high-wire
tighten frap
tow cordelle
walker funambulo
walk on funambulate
whip colt
winder drum
wire haulback, jackstay
work cordage, rigging
yarn fox, trifle
ROPER cowboy, decoy, jockey, packer

ROPERY roguery, trickery, tricks
ROPY glutinous, muscular, sinewy, stringy, tenacious, thick, threadlike, tough, viscid, viscous
ROQUE croquet
RORAL dewy, moist, roric, rory
RORQUAL finback, sei, sibbaldus, sulphurbottom, whale
RORTY fine, gay, sporty
ROSALIND *beloved* orlando
ROSARY beading, beadroll, beads, bede, chaplet, corona, devotion, garland, prayer(beads), rosebed, tasbih
bead ave(maria), gaud(y), gloria patri, paternoster
5 mysteries corona
section decade
ROSCOE gat, gun, pistol, revolver
ROSE (See also *kind*, below.) briar, erysipelas, flower, flush, nozzle, pink, shrub, vine
acacia prickly-locust, robinia
apple brushcherry, eugenia, jambool, jambo(sa), pomarosa
bay oleander, rhododendron, willow-herb
bed rosary
beetle chafer
bog arethusa
box cotoneaster
-breasted cockatoo galah
bud debutante
burnt pompeii
bush balwarra
bush fruit hip
campion corncockle, dusty miller, lychnis, mullein-pink
city pasadena, portland
climbing baltimore belle, dorothy perkins, lady banks, rambler
clump of roan, rone
-colored alluring, coral, favorable, hopeful, optimistic, pink, pleasing, pollyanna
-colored starling pastor, tilyer
comb. rhod(in), rhodo
cotton cudweed
disease brown canker
dog canker, wild brier
emblem of england, lancaster, york
essence See *oil*, below.

fruit button, cathip, cynorrhodon, haw, hep, hip, hypanthium
gall bedeg(u)ar
genus acaena, comarum
herb goats-beard
hip berry, choop, choup, pseudocarp, shoop
honey rhodomel
hybrid american beauty, columbia, ophelia, polyantha
kind agrimony, althea, american beauty, ard's rover, banks(ia), bedegar, bengal, bon selene, bourbon, boursault, bramble, briar, bride, brier, bucky, burbank, burnet, cabbage, columbia, crocus, dog(berry), eglantine, flush, glaieul, guelder, gul, hugonis, lady banks, lokelani, lozenge, manetti, moss, musk, noisette, ophelia, peace, pedelion, pompon, ramanas, rambler, rhoda, rois, saffron, talisman, wild
-like plant avens
madder casino-pink
mallow hibiscus, hollyhock
moss portulaca, purselane
name meaning rhoda
of jericho resurrection-plant
of sharon aaron's-beard, alth(a)ea, crocus, hollyhock, lotus, marshmallow, saffron, st-john's-wort
of the world camellia
oil atar, athar, attar(gul), ottar, otto
ouzel starling
parakeet rosella
pink centaury
pogonia snakemouth
quartz bohemian ruby, rock-crystal
red american beauty, ramanas
tangle alga
temple cereamium, red alga
tickseed coreopsis
tree medlar
wild briar, eglantine
window catherine-wheel
yellow austrian, brier, marechal niel
ROSEATE auspicious, hopeful, optimistic, pleasing, sanguine
spoonbill ajaja
ROSEFISH bergall, bergylt, bream, brim, cunner, haddock, redfish, snapper
ROSELLE sabdariffa, sorrel

ROSEMARY costmary, moorwort, rosmarine, sundew
ROSEOLA measles, rash, rubella, rubeola
ROSETTE badge, chou, cockade, knot, ornament
-like rosular
ROSEWOOD bubinga, jacaranda, molompi
ROSH *father* benjamin
ROSICRUCIAN *master* apollonius
ROSIN (See also RESIN.) colophony, flux
rose st-john's-wort
spirit pinolin
ROSINANTE horse, jade, nag, plug, steed
owner don quixote
ROSSINI *heroine* rosina
opera barber of seville, barbiere di siviglia, william tell
ROSTAND *play* chantecler, cyrano de bergerac, l'aiglon
ROSTER agenda, canon, catalog(ue), inventory, list, register, roll, rota, schedule, scroll, slate, table, tally
ROSTRATE beaked
ROSTRUM acroter, beak, capitulum, dais, pew, platform, proboscis, prow, pulpit, ram, snout, stage, tribune
ROSY angry, auroral, auspicious, blooming, blushing, bright, cheerful, dandy, favorable, fine, flattering, florid, flushed, healthy, hopeful, incarnidine, optimistic, pink, promising, red, rosaceous, rubicund, ruddy, sanguine
bush hardhack
the wine
ROT banter, blight, bosh, caries, cariosity, chaff, corrupt(ion), crumble, decay, decompose, die, disease, disintegrate, dote, doze, fester, filth, foul(ness), gangrene, guff, hoofrot, joke, mold(er), mortification, mortify, necrosis, nonsense, pollute, poppycock, putrefaction, putrefy, putresce(nce), putridity, refuse, ret, rox, rubbish, sour, sphacelation, sphacelus, spoil, stagnate, taint, tease, trash, twaddle, vitiate, waste, wrox
apple frogeye
foot foul

fruit leak
grape slipskin
-grass butterwort, flukewort
noble botrytis-cinerea, edelfaule
ROTA court, curia, hurdy-gurdy, list, register, roll, roster, rotula, round, table, tribunal
ROTARY circle, circumgyratory, circumvolutory, crossway, gyral, gyrational, gyroscopic, gyrotory, swirly, trochilic, vertiginous, vortical, vorticular, whirlabout, whirligig, whirly
ROTATE alternate, bandy, beat, birl, circle, circulate, circumvolve, eddy, exchange, gyrate, gyre, interchange, oscillate, pirouette, pivot, pronate, rabatte, recur, revolve, rock, roll, rote, slue, spin, swap, swirl, swivel, tirl, troll, trundle, turn, twiddle, twirl, wheel, whirl(igig), whirr, whiz
ROTATION change, circulation, circumgyration, circumvolution, eddy, gyration, reeling, revolution, rolling, spin(ning), swinging, swirling, swiveling, torque, trolling, turn(ing), twirl, vertigo, vortex, wheeling
part arbor, axis, axle, bobbin, cam, gear, mandrel, propeller, reel, rotor, spindle, spit, spool, wheel
speed measurer strobe
ROTCHE alle-alle, bull(bird), dovekie, ratch, rotge
ROTE crowd, heart, memorization, repeat, repetition, routine
ROTGUT See LIQUOR.
ROTIFER animancule, bdelloid, floscularia, lipopod, loricate, philodina, ploima (te)
ROTOR impeller, spinner
ROTORCRAFT helicopter
ROTTEN ampery, bad, cankered, carrion, contemptible, corrupt, decayed, decomposed, depraved, despicable, dirty, diseased, disgusting, druxy, evil, fetid, foul, gangrenous, immoral, miserable, moosey, mortified, nasty, offensive, peccant, punk, putrescent, putrid, putrified, rank, roxy,

sour, sphacelate, spoiled, tainted, treacherous, ulcerated, unsound, venal, wicked, wrong
comb. sapr(o)
ROTTENNESS carrion, turpitude
ROTTENSTONE tripoli
ROTTER blackguard, bounder, cad, paskudn(y)ak, reprobate, shirker, slacker
ROTUND big, chubby, corpulent, fat, fleshy, flowing, full, large, obese, overweight, plump, portly, round(ed), spheroid, stout
ROTUNDITY curvature, cylindricality, entirety, fullness, plumpness, roundness, sphericality, spheroidity
ROUE casanova, debauchee, don juan, lecher, libertine, lothario, rake
ROUGE blush, cosmetic, flush, fucate, paint, polish, raddle, radicle, red(den), ruddle, scrimmage, touchdown
animal carmine
ROUGH 3 raw 4 curt, hard, rank, rude, wild 5 abuse, acrid, bluff, blunt, brusk, bumpy, burly, burry, crude, gross, gruff, harsh, noisy, raggy, raspy, rocky, rowdy, scaly, seamy, stark, stern, tousy, vague 6 abrupt, bitter, borrel, broken, brutal, burred, callow, choppy, coarse, craggy, crusty, hackly, hoarse, hobbly, horrid, hubbly, jagged, knotty, ragged, ruffle, rugged, rustic, severe, shaggy, sketch, sticky, stormy, uneven, unfele, unkind 7 austere, boorish, bristly, brusque, chapped, cragged, gnarled, hoodlum, jarring, knotted, prickly, raucous, ruffian, uncivil, unequal, unlevel, violent 8 agrestic, asperate, corduroy, formless, impolite, indecent, nodulose, scabrous, scraggly, squarose, wrinkled 9 barbarian, difficult, irregular, splintery, temptuous, turbulent, unlearned, unrefined 10 boisterous, corrugated, incomplete, indelicate, knockabout, rampageous, unfinished, unpolished 11 acrimonious, approximate, rudi-

mentary 12 discourteous 13 unceremonious
and ready brutal, burly, crude, effective, makeshift, rude, towsy, towzie, unpolished
and ready, old zachary taylor
and tumble bare-fisted, rampageous, uproar, violent
as a cob, nutmeg grater
-bent fool-hay
comb. trachy
edges fash
going difficulty, trouble
-hob gash
-it siwash
-leg hawk
-mill gash
out draft, sketch
rider commander roosevelt, wood
slightly asperulous
stuff obscenity, undercoat, violence, vulgarity
weed hedge-nettle
ROUGHCAST form, model, panget, pattern, plaster, slapdash, sparg, spatterdash
ROUGHEN agitate, chap, coarsen, corrugate, crinkle, crumple, engrail, feaze, fray, fret, frost, gnarl, gnaw, gnurl, granulate, nurl, rumple, scratch, shag, splinter, stiver, wrinkle
ROUGHHEWN brutal, churlish, coarse, crude, uncultivated, uneven, unpolished
ROUGHLY about, approximately, coarsely, cruelly, generally, harshly, incompletely, more or less, rudely, severely
ROUGHNECK bangster, boor(ish), bounder, bully, cad, hoodlum, mucker, peasant, rowdy, tough, uncouth
ROUGHNESS acrimony, asperity, bumpiness, choppiness, crudity, granulation, hispidity, inequality, irregularity, rugosity, severity, stubble, tooth, unevenness
ROUGHROOT gayfeather
ROUGHSCUFF boor, rabble
ROUGHSHOD *ride* dominate, trample, tyrannize
ROUGHSLANT lean-to
ROUKY damp, foggy, hoarse, misty, roky, smokey
ROULADE arpeggio, embellishment, flourish, volata

ROULETTE *term* bas, carre, dernier, enplein, impair, manque, martingale, milieu, noir, pair, passe, prison, rouge, skillo, tourneur
ROUND about, beady, beat, brisk, bulbous, bulging, catch, circle, circuit, circular, clockwise, complete, course, curve(d), cycle, cycloid, cylinder, cylindrical, dance, discoid, encircle, encompass, fair, finished, full, giro, globate, globe, globose, globular, group, honest, inform, just, large, liberal, nearly, orbed, orbiculate, perfect, plump, polished, rapid, revolution, ring, ronda, rota(tion), rotula, rotund, route, routine, rundle, rung, salvo, series, shotty, sing, song, sphere, spherical, spheroid, succession, surround(ing), swollen, tour, traverse, troll, unbroken, unqualified, veer, wheel, whirl, whisper, whole
about approximately, circling
angle perigon
as a ball, orange
a turn corner
bass sunfish
chair baluster, rung
clam bullnose, quahog.
dance bran(s)le, hay, polka, ray, roundel(ay), schottische, schottish, waltz
-headed brachycephalic, cropped
herring shadine, stradine
log end snipe
lot board lot, hundred shares
musical troll
off crown, fillet, top, trim
on assail, betray, desert, reproach
out belly, bulge, complete, fatten, fill, finish, fulfill, integrate, orb
pompano palometa, permit
robin angler, cigarfish, cuttoo, document, letter, pancake, petition, sequence, series, tournament
-shouldered bible-backed, deformed, stooped
table (See also KING ARTHUR *knights.*) conference, deliberation, discussion, forum
the bend crazy, insane, mad

-*the-clock* continually, continuous

timber edges beard

up amass, assemble, collect, corral, gather, herd, muster, resume, scrounge, wrangle

ROUNDABOUT ambagious, ambient, ambigatory, ambiguous, blique, circuitous, circular, circumlocution, comprehensive, dance, detour, devious, encircling, exterior, farfetched, indirect, jacket, merry-go-round, oatcake, plump, prolix, rotary, spiral, tortuous, traffic-circle, turning, winding, wordy

ROUNDED blunt, bombe, bowly, bunting, circular, complete, dumpy, finished, gibbous, ovate, plump, polished, shapely, sonorous, spheroid, stocky

and notched retuse

comb. gyro

ROUNDEL circle, fountain, guze, heurt, niche, pellet, plate, pomme, rondeau, RONDEL, shield, tray, trencher

azure hurt

gules torteau(x)

or bezant, byzant

purpure golp(e)

sable gunstone

sanguine guze

vert pomey

ROUNDELAY glee, madrigal, poem, song

ROUNDER blow, criminal, dissipater, drunkard, informer, libertine, preacher, roue, spendthrift, sport, wastrel

ROUNDHEAD croppy, puritan, swede, weakfish

enemy cavaliers, prince rupert

statesman pym

ROUNDHOUSE coach, lockup, poop, prison, repair shop, watchhouse

ROUNDLY approximately, bitterly, boldly, briskly, completely, fully, generally, openly, outspokenly, severely, sharply, thoroughly, unsparingly, vigorously, wholly

ROUNDNESS boldness, directness, openness, orbicularity, plainness, rotundity,

severity, sharpness, symmetry, vigor

ROUNDS assignment, beat, route, territory

ROUNDUP assembly, camber, gathering, herd, meeting, rodeo, summary

ROUNDWORM ascarid, eelworm, gordian, gordium, helminth, nema(tod), pinworm, strongyl, toxocara

infestation strongylosis

ROUP auction, call, clamor, cold, croak, hoarseness, rolp, roop, sale, sell, shout(ing)

ROUPY harsh, hoarse

ROUSE agitate, anger, animate, arouse, awake, awaken, bestir, call, carouse, elicit, enliven, excite, fire, foment, goad, hearten, hie, incite, inflame, instigate, kindle, provoke, quicken, raise, rally, rise, roust, ruffle, start, stimulate, stir, surprise, upset, vivify, wake(up), waken, wecche, whet

to action alar(u)m, bestir

ROUSING active, brisk, exciting, great, lively, rising, stirring, vigorous

ROUSSEAU *hero* emile

work confessions, contrat social, emile, social contract

ROUST bellowing, current, roaring, rouse, stir, tide, tumult

ROUSTABOUT deckhand, floorman, hand(yman), laborer, loader, longshoreman, razorback, worker, workman

ROUT agitation, assembly, balk, band, beat, bellow, brant, bray, chase, check (mate), clamor, clobber, company, conquer, crowd, crush, dart, debacle, defeat, discomfit(ure), disorder, distress, drive back, drum, foil, frustration, fuss, knock, lick, mob, noise, overcome, overpower, overthrow, overwhelm, press, push back, rabble, rebuff, reduce, repel, repulse, retinue, reversal, reverse, riot, roar, root, route, rummage, rush, scatter, scoop, search, setback, shellac(king), shutout, slumber, smear, snore, snow, strike, subdue, sub-

jugate, swarm, throng, troop, trouble, tumult, turn out, uproar, vanquish

out clean, discover, locate, uncover

ROUTE artery, beat, circuit, corridor, course, cutoff, direct(ion), gest(e), itinerary, journey, lane, line, march, orbit, pass(age), path, road, round, routine, run, send, shortcut, tack, trace, track, trail, trajectory, trip, walk, way

circuitous detour

direct beeline

ROUTH abundance, abundant, plentiful, plenty

ROUTINE beat, course, custom(ary), cut and dried, daily grind, everyday, formula, general, grind, groove, habit(ual), harness, humdrum, method, periodic(al), practice, procedure, rat race, regular, rote, round, rule, run, rut, system, tack, technique, track, treadmill, troll, uniform, usage, usual, wont

exhausting daily grind, rat race, treadmill

ROVE arroba, card, conjecture, draw out, gad, gallivant, maraud, meander, part, pass, pierce, plow, prowl, ramble, range, roam, roof, space, spatiate, straggle, stray, stroll, swerve, traipse, tramp, traverse, wander, washer

ROVER bandid, boy scout, coloradan, dog, flirt, freebooter, gadabout, gallivanter, gangrel, gipsy, gypsy, hobo, hoyle, ishmael, itinerant, masher, migrant, nomad, pilgrim, pirate, rambler, roamer, sailor, scummer, straggler, traveler, tripper, vagrant, waif, wanderer

ROVING cursory, devious, discursive, errant, inconstant, rambling, restless, slub(bing), vagrant, wandering

ROW abuse, affray, altercation, argument, bank, barney, brawl, broil, canoe, clamor, combat, conflict, contest, dispute, fight, file, fracas, fray, fuss, garray, line, list, melee, muss, navi-

gate, noise, oar, order, paddle, pother, propel, pull, quarrel, queue, range, rank, remigate, rough, ruction, rumpus, scold, scrap, scull, series, shindy, squabble, string, swath, tier, upbraid, uproar, wrangle
comb. sticho(us)
form in align, aline
not arranged in astichous
of beans trifle
of grain hack, swathe
of houses block, crescent, terrace, tract
of seed hill
poorly catch a crab
ROWAN ash, quicken, ran, rantree, roddin, rountree, service, sorb(us), whitten, wicken, wiggen, witchen, witchwood
ROWBOAT baris, bark, barque, caique, canoe, cobil, coble, cog, dinghy, dory, funny, galley, gig, kobil, lurker, randan, rumboat, scull(er), skiff, skift, wherry
stern transom
ROWDY barrater, barrator, bear, bhoy, blusterer, boisterous, boorish, bounder, bully, disorderly, fighter, hoodlum, hooligan, larrikin, noisy, obstinate, plug-ugly, rampageous, rogue, roguis, roisterer, rough(neck), ruffian, thug, tough, tricky, uproarious, vicious, vulgar, yahoo
ROWDYDOW hubbub, noise, rumpus, uproar
ROWDYDOWDY boisterous, noisy, uproarious
ROWEL circle, goad, prick, spur, urge, wheel
ROWEN aftermath, crop, field, sequel, stubble
ROWENA *ancestor* king alfred
beloved ivanhoe
father hengist
guardian cedric
husband vortigern
rival rebecca
suitor athelstan(e)
ROWER blade, boatman, caiquejee, crewman, galiot, oar(sman), paddler, sternman, stroke
bench bank, thoft, thwart, zyga, zygon
group bank, crew, eight

match regatta
outermost thalamite
2nd level zygite
ROWLAND DE BOYS *son* jaques, oliver, orlando
ROWLOCK crutch, fulcrum, poppet, rullock, stirrup, tholepin
ROWY streaked, streaky, striped
ROX decay, rot
ROXANA *husband* alexander
rival statira
ROXY decayed, rotten, softened
ROYAL august, basilic(al), basilican, coin, courtly, dignified, excellent, good, imperial, imposing, kingly, magnificent, majestic, mortar, munificent, noble, potentate, princely, queenly, regal, regius, resplendent, rial, sovereign, splendid, stag, stately, superb
academy's 1st president reynolds
academy founder george iii
agaric mushroom
antelope kleeneboc, madoqua
blue hathor, smalt
-born porphyrogene
canadian mounted police mountie(s)
court, pert. aulic
crown diadem, tiara
edict arret
fern osmond, osmund
name meaning basil
officer palatine
palm coyal
power rialty
purple crimson
red vermil(l)ion
road camino real
spouse consort
standard banner, emblem, flag
stole armil(l)(la)
symbol baton, crown, mace, ora, orb, scepter, sceptre
title highness, majesty, regent, sire
treasury fisc, fisk
ROYALE custard, grosgrain
ROYALIST carlist, cavalier, monarchist, tory
ROYALTY alii, aristocracy, bonus, dividend, duty, fee, gale, income, kingdom, kingship, nobility, percentage, pomp, realm, realty,

receipts, regalia, return(s), revenue, share, sovereignty
symbol crown, ermine, mace, purple, regalia, scepter, sceptre
ROYET mischievous, romping, unruly, wild
ROYSTONEA cabbage palm, cabbage tree, palmiste
RSVP acknowledge, answer, reply, respondez s'il vous plait
RUANDA-URUNDI See BURUNDI and RWANDA.
RUB abrade, anoint, bark, bray, brighten, bruise, brush, buff, burnish, caress, chafe, check, contact, crisis, crux, difficulty, dilemma, dub, embrocate, excoriate, fault, feeze, file, flaw, fray, fret, friction, fridge, frush, furbish, gall, gibe, grate, graze, hindrance, hurry, impediment, imperfection, irritate, knead, massage, mop, nuzzle, obstacle, obstruction, plaster, polish, rasp, raze, run, rush, scour, scrape, scrub, scuff, shine, sleek, smear, smooth, sponge, spread, stimulate, stroke, swab, touch, towel, treat, triturate, wax, wear, whetstone, wipe
down chirapsia, comb, curry, groom, massage, search, shiatsu, wipe
elbows associate, fraternize, jostle, justle
gently caress, graze, stroke
hard scour, scrub
in apply, emphasize, harp on, insist, smear
off abrade, bark, erade, erase, erode, obliterate, transfer, wear
out annihilate, cancel, deduct, dout, efface, elide, erase, erode, expunge, kill, murder, obliterate
the wrong way annoy, antagonize, displease, grate, irritate, offend, ruffle
together fiddle
up burnish, furbish, polish, recall, renew, revive
with oil anoint, lubricate
RUBAIYAT *author* omar khayyam
translator fitzgerald
RUBBED abraded, worn
RUBBER arctic, band, borracha, buna, burucha,

caoutchouc, caucho, ceara, crepe, dapicho, dapico, dishcloth, ebonite, elastic, eraser, ficus, file, foam, galosh, guayule, gum, home-plate, lastex, latex, massager, masseur, masseuse, neoprene, overshoe, para, rambong, raser, rubstone, sernamby, soveprene, swipe, tires, vulcanite, wheels, whetstone
adulterant almeidina
black ebonite
boa ball-python, charina
boat lcr
cake biscuit
cement butanal, butyraldehyde
city akron
compound factice, kerite
constituent polyprene
crude borracha, burucha, latex
fruit jar lute
hard ceara, ebonite, vulcanite
inferior sernamby
juice achete
-like substance gutta
lining gasket
lump thimble
native See *para*, below.
-nose sturgeon
-off fettler
oil caoutchoucine
para balata, borracha, ceara, mangabeira, sorva
plant guayule, landolphia
plant berry abolifruit
raft lilo
reclaimed shoddy
sap latex
-stamp approve, endorse, ratify
substitute factice
synthetic buna, butadiene, butyl, elastomer, neoprene, perbunan, sovprene, vinylite
tree caoutchouc, castilla, caucho, ficus, hevea, hule, landolphia, milker, para, rambong, seringa, tuno, tunu, ule
tree disease black stripe, black thread, brown bast
vulcanized ebonite
wild borracha, ceara
RUBBERNECK candlepins, game, gape, gawk, gaze, sightsee(r), spectator, tourist, traveler, voyeur

RUBBERS disease, ray, scab, shab
RUBBERY elastic, tough
RUBBING abrasion, chafing, frication, friction, frottage
RUBBISH attle, baggage, blah, brockle, bushwa(h), cagmag, chaff, clamjamfry, clutter, colder, crap, crawm, cul(t)ch, debris, dross, dust, eyewash, flam, flum, foolishness, garble, junk, kelter, ket, litter, lumber, mull (ock), nonsense, offal, pelf, pelt, raff(le), REFUSE, riffraff, ross, rot, rubble, rummage, scoria, scrap, scree, scruff, slag, spilth, stent, stuff, taffike, trash(y), tripe, trivia, trooslach, truck, trumpery, waste, worthless, wrack
container dustbin
growing in ruderal
heap dump
mining slag, stent, tailings
vegetable wrack
RUBBLE brash, chalk, RUBBISH, slither, stent, stone, talus
RUBE boor, bumpkin, clodhopper, clown, countryman, fural, hayseed, hick, jake, jerk, lout, lubber, oaf, peasant, rustic, yokel
RUBEFACTION redness
RUBELLA measles, roseola, roteln, rubeola
RUBELLITE tourmaline
RUBESCENT flushing, reddening, ruddy
RUBICOLA bogsucker, woodcock
RUBICON *words* anerriphtho, kubos, the die is cast
RUBICUND erubescent, florid, flushed, glowing, red (dish), rosy, rubescent, ruddy
RUBIDIUM *source* pollucite
RUBIGINOUS brown, reddish, rufous, rustcolored, rusty, tawny
RUBLE *1/100th* kapeika, kopek
1/2 poltina, polti(n)nik
10 chervonets, chervonetz
RUBRIC canon, category, class, flourish, form, group, head(ing), law, paraph, red(chalk)(ocher), redden, title
book ordines, ordo

RUBUS akala, arnberry, blackberry, bramble, bumble, dewberry, dog-rose
RUBY agate, anthrax, carbuncle, carmine, crimson, gem, hummingbird, pyrope, red(den), rubasse, rubin, scarlet, spinel, stone, vermeil
arsenic realgar
blende sphalerite
copper cuprite
quartz rubasse
spinel almandine, almandite, balas(s), rubicelle
sulphur realgar
wasp cuckoo-fly
wood sandalwood, shea
zodiac sign aries
RUCK(LE) average, cower, crease, crouch, crowd, crumple, draw, fold, furrow, group, heap, huddle, mass, multitude, ordinary, pile, pucker, rabble, rake, rick, rut, sit, squat, stack, wrinkle
RUCKSEY bend, stoop, yield
RUCKUS ado, commotion, confusion, disturbance, fracas, noise, quarrel, row, ruction, rumpus, storm, tarrarom, terrarom, uproar
RUCTION disturbance, fight, fracas, fraction, fray, melee, noise, outbreak, quarrel, row, RUCKUS, uproar
RUDBECKIA black-eyed-susan, coneflower, cornflower, daisy, gaillardia, goldenglow
RUDD azurine, carp, fish
RUDDER governor, guide, hellim, helm, steer(age), stern, timon
back talon
bushing pintle
control helm, tiller
diving hydrovane
edge bearding
fish black pilot, chopa (blanca) cockeye pilot, kyphosid, opaleye
gudgeon brace
part gudgeon, pintle, stock, talon, yoke
post stern
RUDDERLESS impotent, powerless, tillerless, weak
RUDDLE bole, flush, keel, kiel, redden, rouge, smit
RUDDY bloody, blousy, blowsy, blowzy, blush, contemptible, execrable, florid,

flushed, fresh, glowing, infamous, lively, red(dish), redden, rode, rubicose, rubicund, rude, sanguine, tanned

duck blackjack, blatherskite, blue-bill, bobber, booby, bristletail, bullneck, bumblebee-coot, canvasback, dunbird, greaser, hardhead, hickoryhead, noddy, paddy, pintail, scaup, sleeper, spatter, sprig, widgeon, wiretail

plover sanderling

RUDE abusive, artless, barbarian, barbarous, bloody, bluff, boisterous, bold, boorish, borrel, brusque, brutal, callow, carlish, churlish, clumsy, coarse, crude, crusty, curt, discordant, discourteous, disrespectful, ferocious, fierce, flippant, formless, fresh, green, gruff, harsh, homespun, ignorant, ill-bred, impertinent, impolite, impudent, inclement, inexpert, insolent, insulting, jarring, loutish, makeshift, pert, plebeian, primitive, raw, rough, rowdy, rugged, rural, rustic, sassy, saucy, savage, severe, simple, stormy, sturdy, surly, tasteless, tumultous, turbulent, uncouth, unkempt, unpolished, unpolite, unrefined, untrained, vigorous, violent, vulgar, wild

person bear, boor, churl

RUDENESS barbarism, discourtesy, disrespect, ferity, gaff, rudity

RUDIMENT anlage, base, basic, beginning, element, embryo, fundamental, germ, principle, remains, root, seed, source, start, vestige

pert. inchoate

RUDIMENTARY abecedarian, abortive, basic, causal, elemental, elementary, embryonic, fundamental, germinal, immature, initial, larval, microbic, original, primary, primitive, undeveloped, vestigial

RUE afflict, agathosma, amyris, bemoan, bewail, bitterness, boronia, casimiroa, compassion, deplore, disappoint(ment), dolor, grief,

grieve, harmel, herb, lament, mourn, pity, plant, regret, remorse, repent(ance), rewe, ruta, sorrow, street, suffer, tentwort

bargain forfeit

genus evodia, phellodendron, pilocarpus, ptelea, ruta, thalictrum

wild isfand

RUEFUL contrite, depressed, despondent, dismal, distressing, doleful, dolorous, hopeless, lamentable, lugubrious, melancholy, mournful, oppressed, penitent, piteous, pitiable, plaintive, regretful, remorseful, sad, somber, sorrowful, sorry, woeful

RUFF applaud, bird, choker, collar, dickey, disorder, drumbeat, fish, fraise, fringe, hackle, mane, nap, neckpiece, perch, philomachus, pigeon, plait, plumage, pride, ree(ve), roof, ruche, RUFFLE, sandpiper, stamp, stechen, sunfish, tippet, trump, vainglory, zenith

female reeve

support rabato

RUFFE blacktail, dassie, deer, godwit

RUFFED *bustard* houbara

lemur vari

RUFFIAN apache, bear, boor, bounder, bravo, brutal, bully(boy), cruel, cutter, cutthroat, cuttle, desperado, devil, gangster, gunman, hackster, hessian, hoodlum, hooligan, lawless, licentious, lustful, mohock, murderous, pander, paramour, pimp, rage, rogue, roughneck, rowdy, stormy, thug, tough, violent

RUFFLE aggravate, agitate, annoy(ance), border, brandish, brawl, bridle, bristle, bully, commotion, confuse, confusion, crimp, crumple, derange, disarrange, disconcert, dishevel, disorder, display, disturb, drum, edging, excite, exhibit, expedient, fold, flaunt, flounce, flurry, flutter, fret, frill, furbelow, gather, irritate, jabot, mesentary, muss, nettle, parade, perturbation, provoke, pucker, riffle, ripple, roil, rool, ruche, ruching, ruff,

shake, show, shuffle, strut, swagger, tumult, undulation, upset, vex, wrinkle

dust balayeuse, skirt

edge heading

neck dickey, fraise, jabot, ruche, ruff

RUFFLED agitated, dishevel(l)ed, disorderly, perturbed, rough, tousled, uneven, unkempt, wavy, winding

RUFOUS reddish, rubicose, rubiginous, rusty, sanguine, tawny

RUFUS *friend* paul

RUG (See also *kind,* below.) bargain, blanket, CARPET, comfortable, covering, coverlet, cozy, dog, drugget, footpace, frieze, haul, kanara, liquor, mat, maud, petate, pull, robe, runner, rya, senna, shag, snug, tear, tug, wrap, wrench

edge serging

embroidered felt namda, nammad, numda(h)

gown watchman

grass petate

handwoven turkoman

kind (See also ORIENTAL *rug,* PERSIA *rug.*) agra, aubusson, axminster, bergama, bergamo(ot), drugget, oriental, persian, plush, rya, shag, throw, wilton

modern rya

namad kazak

oriental See ORIENTAL *rug.*

persian See PERSIA *rug.*

plaid maud

prayer ghiordes, namazlik

reversible kilim

skins kaross

RUGATE rugose, wrinkled

RUGBY football, rugger

formation scrum(mage)

headmaster dr arnold

play scrum

servant to doctor caius

term fives, heeling, knockon, mark, maul, noside, pitch, scrum(mage), tackle, touch, try

RUGEN ISLAND *cape* arkona

town bergen

RUGGED arduous, asperse, austere, brawny, burly, coarse, crabbed, cragged, craggy, crude, difficult, energetic, fierce, gnarled, hale, hard(y), harsh, healthy, homely, ironbound, irregular, jagged, lusty, muscular, plain, ragged, rank, robust, rockbound, rocky, rough, rude, savage, scabrous, scragged, scraggy, seamed, shaggy, snagged, snaggy, solid, sour, stern, stony, stormy, strict, strong, sturdy, surly, tempestuous, tough, turbulent, uncivil, uneven, unflagging, ungracious, unkempt, unpolished, unrefined, vigorous, wrinkled

RUGGEDNESS roughness, strength, vigor

RUHR *city* bottrop, dusseldorf, essen, stuttgart
river eder

RUIN annihilate, ballyhack, ballyw(r)ack, bane, bankrupt, beggar, blast, blight, break, bust, butch, calamity, catastrophe, chaos, collapse, cook, cooper, crash, damage, debris, decay, deface, defeat, demolish, demolition, despoil, destroy, destruction, devastate, devastation, diddle, dilapidate, dilapidation, disaster, disfigure, doom, downfall, fail (ure), fall, fate, foredo, havoc, hurt, impair, injure, injury, leese, loss, maim, mangle, mutilate, overthrow, perdition, pervert, rack, ravage, raze, relic, rend, sabotage, seduce, shatter, shend, smash, spoil, subvert, thwart, tumble, undo, vandalize, violate, wrack, wreck(age)

RUINED bankrupt, blasted, blown, broken, decayed, desolate, destroyed, dilapidated, fallen, forlorn, gone, hopeless, spoiled, wrecked

RUINOUS baneful, cutthroat, deadly, decayed, destructive, dilapidated, disastrous, shendful, subversive, tragic (al), tumbledown

RUKH bird, forest, jungle, roc, simurg(h)

RULE 3 law, raj, row, run, way 4 code, deem, form, lead, line, norm, sway 5 adage, axiom, basis, bylaw, canon, guide, habit, judge, logos, maxim, model, order, power, regle, reign, riche, right, sutta, tenet 6 belief,

custom, decide, decree, direct, domine, govern, manage, master, method, regnum, settle, system 7 command, conduct, control, counsel, dictate, execute, formula, mandate, mastery, measure, precept, prevail, regimen, resolve, routine, theorem 8 behavior, doctrine, domineer, dominion, keystone, moderate, ornament, persuade, practice, regiment, standard 9 authority, criterion, determine, direction, enactment, formality, influence, postulate, precedent, prescript, principia, principle, procedure, pronounce 10 administer, convention, government, regulation 11 commandment, fundamental 12 jurisdiction, prescription 14 administration
absolute autarchy
according to de regle
by all pantarchy
by best people aristarchy
by children paedarchy
by judges kritarchy
by men androcacy, patriarchy
by people democracy
by women matriarchy
codifier hoyle, roberts
comb. archy, cracy, cratic, ocracy
exception to fallency
infraction cheating, foul
joint synarchy
of coss algebra
of 3 birthroot, trillium
out bar, blackball, block, debar, deduct, disbar, eliminate, exclude, forbid, obliterate, obviate, preclude, prevent, prohibit, refuse, scratch, suspend
over control, dominate, manage, oversee, superintend. tyrannize
universal panarchy
unjust despotism, tyranny
unjustly tyrannize

RULER 3 aga, bey, dey, min, oba 4 amir, boss, cham, czar, doge, duce, emir, kaid, khan, king, lord, raja, shah, tsar, tzar 5 akbar, alder, ameer, calif, chief, emeer, imaum, mogul, mwami, nabob, nagid, nawab, negus, nizam, pacha, queen,

rajah, sheik, sophy, tenno 6 archon, bashaw, caesar, caliph, curaca, despot, dynast, eparch, exarch, ferule, fuhrer, gerent, hersir, induna, iswara, kaiser, leader, mikado, prince, regent, sachem, satrap, sheikh, sherif, shogun, sirdar, suffee, sultan, tycoon, tyrant 7 cacique, effendi, elector, emperor, empress, faipule, fuehrer, hutuktu, infanta, khedive, magnate, monarch, pharaoh, shereef, viceroy, wielder 8 alderman, autocrat, dictator, drighten, drightin, governor, hospodar, interrex, mandarin, margrave, padishah, phylarch, premier, princess, sagamore, seigneur, subahdar, suzerain, tetrarch 9 authority, commander, dalai lama, dominator, imperator, landamman, landgrave, pendragon, potentate, president, sovereign, werowance, yardstick 10 chancellor, margravine 11 grand visier(vizier) 12 straightedge 13 prime minister
absolute autarch, autocrat, czar, despot, dictator, tsar, tyrant
benevolent c(h)akravartin
comb. arch, crat
curved sweep
family dynasty
former alexander, batista, caesar, czar, diem, fu(e)hrer, hitler, lenin, leopold, mussolini, napoleon, nhu, nicholas, stalin, tsar, tzar
group decemvirate, duarchy, pentarchy, petrarchy, tetrarchy, triarchy, triumvirate
hereditary dynast
name meaning alaric, henry, reginald
1 of 2 duarch
1 of 3 triarch, triumvir
religious hierarch, pope
secret cryptarch
wife begum, czarina, empress, infanta, maharani, queen, ranee, rani, sultana, tsarina, tzarina

RULING authoritative, average, current, decision, dominant, governing, hegemonic, influential, law, mandate, paramount, predominant, predominating, prevailing, prevalent, regle, regnant, reigning, sovereign, statute, verdict

comb. archy

RULL trundle, wheel

RUM bacardi, bad, cachaca, chap, dangerous, dye, eccentric, excellent, fine, good, great, grog, jamaica, liquor, ocuby, odd, peculiar, poor, queer, rome, serious, strange, switchel, tafia, tough

and cola cuba-libre

and molasses bogus

and spruce beer calibogus

and water grog

cheap tafia

distillate arrack

drink bombo, bumbo, daiquiri, grog, tom and jerry

shop bar(room), drunkery, saloon, taproom, tavern

RUMANIA(N) dacia, moldavia

airline tarom

artist brancusi, grigorescu

bacteriologist babes

canal bega

capital bucharest

city aiud, arad, bacau, bacav, balta, bendery, braila, brasov, brasso, bucharest, cerna(vti), chisinau, cluj, craiova, czernowitz, deva, focsani, galati, galatz, iasi, irongate, jassy, kishinev, klausenberg, kolosvar, lasi, lvpeni, neamt, oradea, ploesti, satumare, severin, sibiu, sighet, temesvar, timisoara, torda, turnu, yassy

coin ban, lei, leu, lev, ley, triens, uncia

composer enesco

conductor perlea

conservative boyar

district See *region, below.*

folk song doina

founder dracul, vlad

hebraist schechter

hero vlad tepes, vlad the impaler

inventor poenaru

king carol, dracul, hospodar, michael, stephen, vayvode, vlad, waywode

king's consort magda, marie

lake sinoe

leader ceausescu

measure faltche

monastery voronet

musician enesco

oil center ploesti

oppressor phanariot

pass rosu(l)

peak bihor, caliman, codrul, negoi, pietrosu, rodnei

people dacians

poet eminescu

port braila, constanta, galati, galatz

province ardeal, moldavia, walachia

queen elizabeth, marie

queen's pen name carmen sylva

region alba, banat, bihor, bucovina, bukovina, dobrogea, dobruja, iasi, jassy, maramures, moldavia, transylvania, walachia

river alt, aluta, arges(ul), bistrita, buzdu, crasna, danube, dniester, ialomita, jiu, moros, mures, olt(ul), prut, schyl, siret, vedea

ruler See *king,* above.

sculptor brancusi

steel center hunedoara

title domn

travel service carpati

violinist enesco

wind crivetz

wine carbonet

RUMBA carioca, dance

king cugat

RUMBLE boom, borborygmus, complaint, disturbance, fight, grumble, hotter, murmur, ramble, report, ripple, roar, roll, rumor, seat, snore, thunder, uproar

-bumble hodgepodge, jumble, miscellany, mixture

RUMBUMPTIOUS overbearing, rambunctious, rampageous

RUMDUM drunk, intoxicated, reeling

RUMEN belly, cud, gullet, paunch, stomach, tripe

RUMEX bloodwort, canaigre, cankerroot, dock, sorrel

RUMINANT alpaca, antelope, bison, bos, bovida, buffalo, camel(opard), capra, cattle, cavicorina, cervida, chevrotain, chewing, cow, deer, elk, ewe, giraffe, goat, llama, mazame, meditative, moose, musk-ox, napu, okapi, oxen, quidder, reindeer, sheep, steer, thoughtful, tu-

bicorn, ungulate, vicuna, yak, zebu

female cow, doe, ewe, nanny

male buck, bull, ram

stomach abamasum, abamasus, bonnet, omasum, paunch, read, reed, reticulum, rumen

RUMINATE chaw, chew, cogitate, consider, deliberate, excogitate, meditate, mull, muse, ponder, reflect, regurgitate, revolve, speculate, think, weigh

RUMINATION cogitation, deliberation, merycism, reflection, regurgitation, thought

RUMMAGE confuse, confusion, derange(ment), disarrange, examine, forage, fossick, gather, grub, junk, litter, mess, ransack, rommack, rout, rubbish, search, seek, stir, stow(age), tousel, turmoil, upheaval, uproar

sale jumble

RUMMY canasta, chap, drunk(ard), game, odd, queer, sot

game arlington, boathouse, canasta, colonel, conquian, conquien, cooncan, eights, gin, kaluki, liverpool, michigan, oklahoma, pan(guine), persian, zioncheck

term bait, blitz, block, box, break, come-on, crack, deadwood, discard, feed, gin, hit, knock, reduce, rope, run, salt, schneider, set, split, undercut, unload, upcard, wildflower

2-player conquian

RUMOR breeze, bruit, bushtelegraph, buzz, canard, clamor, clatter, complain, cry, fame, flak, furphy, gossip, grapevine, hearsay, hoax, inkling, message, murmur, noise, norate, notoriety, on-dit, oui-dire, report, reputation, repute, reverie, roorback, rumble, scandal, scuttlebutt, story, sugh, tale, talk, tattle, tidings, tittletattle, towntalk, uproar, voice, whisper, word

personified fama

repeat noise

RUMORMONGER blazer, busybody, gossip, quidnunc, talebearer, tattler, tattletale, telltale, tittletattle, yenta, yente

RUMP backside, bankrupt, beam, breech, buttocks, croup, crupper, dock, doub, haunch, hip, hunkers, insult, plunder, podex, posterior, rear, remainder, remnant, roast, sacrum, stern, tail
comb. pygal, pygo
feathers brail

RUMPAD highway

RUMPELSTILTSKIN See DWARF.

RUMPLE bedraggle, cockle, crease, crinkle, crumple, crush, dishevel, fold, frowse, muss, plait, rool, ruffle, seam, tail, touse, tousle, tumble, wrinkle

RUMPLED disheveled, disorderly, tousled, uncombed, unkempt, untidy

RUMPUS barney, brawl, commotion, confusion, controversy, disturbance, fracas, hubbub, hurlyburly, nitty, noise, pandemonium, racket, rag, riot, row, rowdydow, ruckus, touse, towrow, tumult, uproar

RUMRUNNER bootlegger, smuggler

RUN 3 bye, gad, get, git, hie, hop, jog, leg, peg, ply, rin 4 bolt, dart, dash, emit, flee, flow, fuse, gait, gush, hunt, lair, lead, leak, lope, melt, mold, move, pace, pass, race, rack, rule, rush, sail, scat, scud, tear, tend, tour, trip, trot, turn, type, weep, work 5 assay, bleed, blend, bound, brash, break, brook, burst, drive, elope, guide, haste, hurry, incur, jaunt, leg it, order, panic, point, pring, range, ravel, reach, route, scoot, score, scoup, scram, speed, spurt, stand, start, swell, trace, track, trail, trend 6 accrue, branch, canter, career, course, demand, direct, elapse, endure, escape, extend, flight, gallop, govern, hasten, ladder, length, manage, plunge, propel, pursue, rotate, scurry, series, spread, sprent, spring, sprint, stream, strear, thrust, travel, voyage 7 analyze, average, conduct, con-

tend, contest, control, diffuse, dogtrot, flutter, freedom, hotfoot, jogtrot, liquefy, migrate, operate, proceed, rivulet, roulade, routine, scamper, scuddle, scuttle, spurtle, stretch, vamoose 8 continue, dissolve, dominate, function, sequence, stampede, traverse 9 direction, discharge, migration, skedaddle, suppurate 10 accelerate, prevalence, succession 11 watercourse
about auto, car, discurre, fisk, gad(der), motorboat, roadster, roam, tig, vagabond, vehicle, wagon, wander(er)
across encounter, find, meet, strike, traverse
after chase, court, cultivate, fetch, flatter, follow, pursue, search for, woo
against attack, bump, contend, counteract, jostle, oppose, take on, thrust, vie
aground beach, founder, hurtle, sink, strand, suffer
along away, beat it, begone, depart, get, git, scram, shoo, vamoose
amok, amuck assail, attack, cut loose, rage, rampage, riot
around deception, evasion, felon, whitlow
away bolt, decamp, depart, desert, elope, escape, flee, fly, leave, maroon, scamper, scud, skedaddle, stampede, vamoose
away with abduct, abscond, decamp, elope, kidnap, steal, take off
brief flutter, flyer
counter to cross, oppose, transverse
down abuse, brief, capture, chase, collide, creaky, crush, decline, decry, depreciate, derelict, dilapidated, disparage, exhausted, fail, find, hit, ill, infirm, kill, overbear, overrun, overthrow, precis, pursue, report, sick, sink, spent, squalid, stop, summary, trace, track, traduce, unwound, weakened, wear out, worn out
-down condition disrepair, irrepair

fast haste(n), scorch, scour, scud, scurry, skirr, split, sprint
for office campaign, contend, name, nominate, stand
-in altercation, argument, arrest, capture, collide, collision, contest, disagreement, fight, insert(ion), interpose, merge, quarrel, tiff, transform
into add up, collide, cost, meet
its course conk out, die, elapse, end, expire, finish, lapse, terminate
off bolt, bunk, contest, depart, depreciate, desert, drain, drool, effluence, elope, election, flee, flow, impress, pipe, print, tiebreaker, waste
off at the mouth babble, blabber, chatter, drool, slobber
off with See *away with*, above.
of the mill average, common(place), mediocre, normal, ordinary, par, so-so, unexceptional
on chatter, continue, endure, spill(over)
out consume, desert, elapse, empty, end, exhaust, expatriate, expel, expire, extend, flight, flow, issue, jut, lapse, peter, pour, protract(ed), spent, spill, spilt, spread, squander, waste, weary
over browse, examine, exceed, number, overflow, overspread, rehearse, repeat, review, strike
ragged exhausted, fagged, spent, tired
riot dissipate, exaggerate, overrun, rampage
through consume, examine, impale, inspect(ion), perforate, permeate, pervade, pierce, rehearse, repeat, review, spend, squander, stab, summary, transfix, waste
together converge
trial maiden voyage
up accumulate, ascend, charge, construct, enlarge, erect, grow, increase, rise
up against collide, encounter, experience, meet
wild See *amok*, above.

RUNAGATE apostate, deserter, fugitive, refugee,

RENEGADE, runaway, vagabond, wanderer

RUNAWAY apostate, decisive, deserter, escapee, escaper, express, fugitive, landslide, overwhelming, refugee, RUNAGATE

RUNCH charlock, radish

RUNDLE ball, circle, coil, pin, rotator, round, rung, runnel, stream, trundle

RUNDLET barrel, cask, tun

RUNE character, charm, conversation, counsel, hieroglyph, language, magic, mystery, poem, secret, song, sorcery, speech, verse, wen, wyn(n)
inventor dvalin

RUNESMITH bard

RUNG cudgel, girdled, handle, hooped, range, rim, round, rundle, spoke, staff, stair, stakes, stave, step, stick, timber, tread, trundle

RUNIC *alphabet* futhark, futhorc
letter thorn

RUNLET, RUNNEL barrel, brook, channel, creek, rivulet, rush, stream(let)

RUNNER agent, amberfish, bawd, branch, candidate, carpet, channel, collector, conduit, courier, cursor, detective, drummer, duck, fault(slip), fish, gate, goer, heeler, horse, impeller, intelligencer, jurel, ladder, leatherjack, mat, messenger, miler, operator, part, racer, ravel, rocker, roller, rug, salesman, scarf, scuttler, skee, ski, sled, smuggle, solicitor, speeder, sprinter, sprue, stall, stolo(n), supervisor, tackle, throwrug, touter, vagabond, waterrail, whippet
blue caranx, hardtail, jurel
famous adrastos, atalanta, camilla, ladas, pheidippides
flume herder
pair sloop
race scuttler
sledge slipes

RUNNING abroach, advancing, assault, attack, care, career(ing), casual, charge, consecutively, continuous (ly), courant, course, current, cursive, cursorial, discharge, easy, fleeing, flowing, fluid, footing, linear, melting, operating, operation, passing, present, prevalent, procursive, pussy, quick, race, sailing, skirmish, smuggling, spreading, successive, sustained, trip
about courant, cursory
across diagonal
away, comb. drapeto
birch snowberry
board footboard
comb. drome, dromous
forward procurrent
gear mobile
head title
myrtle periwinkle
shed roundhouse
toad natterjack
toward appulse

RUNT chit, diminutive, durgan, durgen, dwarf, elf, hag, manikin, midget, nonentity, peewee, pigeon, pigmy, pygmy, shargar, shortie, shorty, shrimp, slink(er), titman, urling, wrig

RUNTY boorish, churlish, contemptible, diminutive, mean, puny, scrub(by), small, stunted, tiny, undersized

RUNWAY airstrip, apron, bridge, channel, chute, clearway, duct, fairway, flight strip, groove, island, passageway, path, platform, ramp, road, strip, tarmac, track, trail, trough

RUPEE *1/10th* tanga
1/16th anna
100,000 lac, lakh
10,000,000 crore

RUPERT'S *drop* tear

RUPIA *1/2* pard(a)o, xerafin

RUPTURE breach, break, burst, clash, cleft, disrupt(ion), erupt(ion), feud, fracture, hernia, hostility, hurt, misunderstanding, quarrel, rend, rent, rhexis, rift, separation, shatter, split

RUR *character* robot

RURAL agrarian, agrestic, agricultural, arcadian, bucolic, chinwhisker, countrified, COUNTRY, geoponic, georgic, hayseed, hick, hoosier, pastoral, policeman, provincial, rough, rube, rustic(al), sylvan, upland, villatic
area backwoods, boondocks, boonies, bush, country (side), sticks
deity faunus, pan
poem georgic, idyl(l)

RURITANIA *castle* zenda
hero rassendyll

RUSCUS butcher's-broom, holly

RUSE artifice, blind, boast, chicane(ry), deceit, dodge, fall, feint, fraud, hoax, humbug, makeshift, maneuver, praise, resort, roose, shift, slip, stratagem, subterfuge, trick, vaunt, wile

RUSH (See also *kind,* below.) 3 hie, jet, rip, rix, run, sag, woo, zip 4 birr, bolt, dart, dash, flow, herb, hump, post, race, rash, reed, scud, scut, take, tear 5 blout, brook, brush, chase, chevy, court, feeze, fling, grass, haste, hurry, onset, press, sally, scoot, scour, sedge, shoot, spade, spark, speed, sprit, spurt, straw, surge 6 attack, barrel, career, charge, combat, course, defeat, demand, fescue, hasten, hurtle, hustle, runlet, runnel, scurry, sortie, stream, thrash, trifle 7 assault, brattle, cattail, contest, destroy, impetus, repulse, scamper, scuddle, scuttle, swither 8 cataract, eruption, outburst, overcome, picayune, scramble, stampede, step on it 9 attention, entertain, make haste, overthrow, skedaddle 10 accelerate 11 undergrowth 12 precipitation
around bustle, charge
away bolt, dash, flee
basket canister, frail
clump rashbuss
coarse goosecorn
common floss
edible chufa
family junaceae
flat shalder
fossil juncite
headlong boil, stampede
hour peak
kind bulrush, camel's-straw, cattail, chufa, esparto, fescue, frail, juncus, spart, sprat, sprit, reed-mace
light candle, seave
load barth, gavel
noisy scutter
nut chufa

onward birr, surge
plant, pert. junaceous
scouring equisetum, gunbright, pewterwort
toad natterjack
wheat couch-grass
RUSK biscuit, bread, cake, toast, zwieback
RUSKIN *home* brantwood, coniston water
RUSSELL *countess, pseudonym* elizabeth
viper daboia, daboya, jessur, katuka
RUSSETT apple, brown, cloth, coat, fabric, homespun, peasant, potato, rustic
RUSSIA, RUSSIAN bear, byzantine, cossack, ersar, ivan, muscovite, muscovy, red, ros, rossiya, rus(sine), SIBERIA, ussr
actor stanislavski, stanislavsky
actress nazimova
admiral kolchak
airline aeroflot
airplane mig, sukhoi, tupolev
alphabet cyrillic
anarchist bakunin, kropotkin
animal alan, borzoi, chamois, corsac, desman, karagan, orloff, owtchah, saiga, samoyed(e), zokor
antelope chamois, saiga
apple astrachan
aristocrat boyar(d), knez, kniaz, knyaz
assembly See *legislature,* below.
astronaut See ASTRONAUT *russian.*
authorities nachalstvo
auto lada, moskyitch, pobeda, zhiguli, zis
badge znak
ballet See *dance,* below.
ballet producer diaghilev
bank crappette
barrow kurgan
battle inkerman, pultowa, stalingrad
bay kola
beatnik slilyaga
beer kvas(s)
beverage heater samovar
biologist lysenko
boat baidak, ballatoon, bratina
bondman serf
boots valenki
botanist besser
braid soutache
byron pushkin

cabbage soup shchee
cabin izba
cabinet member commissar
cactus thistle
calendar julian
calf brown, cappa(g)h, caroubier, fudge, india-tan
cap aska, balaklava
cape chelyuskin, chita, dezhnev
capital kiev, leningrad, moscow, petrograd, st petersburg
carriage ar(a)ba, dros(h)ky, kibitka, tarantas(s), telega, troika
castle starosty
cathedral sobor
caviar ikary, ikra
celebrity pakhan
cellist piatigorsky, rostropovich
chemist mendeleev, semenov
chess master alekhine, botvinnik, spassky
chief pakhan
choreographer fokine, moiseyev, petipa
cider kvas(s)
citadel kremlin
city 3 aka, osa, ude, ufa 4 baku, eisk, gori, iosh, kien, lida, lvov, lwow, omsk, orel, orsk, perm, riga, sumy, tula, ulan, uman 5 batum, biisk, biysk, chita, gomel, gorki, isker, kasan, kazan, kerki, kirov, kovel, kursk, kyzyl, lutsk, lysva, miass, minsk, orsha, pensa, penza, pinsk, pskov, rovno, rzhev, serov, shuya, tomsk, ukhta, vilna 6 belovo, grodno, grozny, igarka, kaluga, kertch, kovrov, kurgan, moscow, odessa, perovo, rostov, sartov, syzran, tambov, tiflis, tyumen, uralsk, vyborg 7 alma ata, angarsk, armavir, barnaul, bataisk, bryansk, bukhara, donetsk, irkutsk, ivanovo, izhevsk, kalinin, kopeish, lipetsk, lugansk, mogilev, nalchik, norilsk, pololsk, poltava, rybinsk, shakhty, sovetsk, tobolsk, vitebsk, vologda, yaktusk 8 andizhan, cernauti, gorlovka, kemerovo, kostroma, kuntsevo, murmansk, namangan, novgorod, orenburg, pavlodar, smolensk, taganrog, tashkent, vladimir, voronezh,

yaroslav 9 akmolinsk, archangel, ashkhabad, astrakhan, babushkin, berezniki, dyushambe, karaganda, kiselevsk, kuibishev, leninakan, leningrad, lyubertsy, makeyevka, melitopol, rubtsovsk, samarkand, serpukhov, ulyanovsk, volgograd, yaroslavl, zaporozhe 10 chernovtsy, daugavpils, ioshkarola, khabarovsk, komsomolsk, pyatigorsk, samarkhand, sebastopol, simferopol 11 kaliningrad, pervouralsk, stanislavov 12 brestlitovsk
clover orel
coachman yams(tc)hik, yemschik
coal area donbas, donets
coin abassi, altin(inink), auksinas, bisti, chervonets, copec(k), deneshka, genga, grivna, grosh, imperial, kopec(k), piatak, poltina, poltinnik, poluska, rouble, ruble, shaur, valiuta
committee collegium, politburo, presidium, tsik
commune kolkhoz
composer arensky, balakirev, borodin, cui, glazunov, gliere, glinka, kabalevsky, khachaturian, markevich, moussorgsky, prokofiev, rachmaninoff, rimsky-korsakov, rubinstein, scriabin, shostakovitch, stravinsky, tchaikovsky, tcherpnin
comrade tovarich, tovaris(c)h
conductor koussevitsky, markevich, smallens
conspirator decembrist
convention rada
coop amtorg, arcos, artel, centrosoyus
cosmonaut, woman tereshkova
cossack ta(r)tar
council duma, rada, soviet
country house dacha
coupon shop beriozka
criminal class shoblayobla, urki
croquette krometski, krometsky
cup bratina, chark
currency store berioska, kashtan
czar alexander, alexis, go-

dunov, ivan, nicholas, paul, peter, tsar, tzar

dance cosaque, cossac, gopak, hopak, kolo, kozachok, saber, trepak, tzazatski, ziganka

dancer baryshnikov, danilova, karsavina, lifar, makarova, moiseyev, nijinsky, nureyev, pavlova, plisetskaya, ulanova

decree ukase

defence minister malinovsky

delicacy caviar(e)

desert kyzylkum, steppe, tundra

designer bakst

devil chort

diplomat dobrynin, gorchakov, gromyko, kuznetzov, malenkov, malik, molotov, nesselrode, scherbakov, sobolev, stalin, tsarapkin, vishinsky

director dovzhenko, pudovkin, stanislavski, stanislavsky

dish pelmeni, pelmeny, sedlo

dissident kulak

district guberniya, karelia, stanitsa, stanitza, steppe, volost

dog alan, beltir, borzoi, owtchah, psovie, samoyed(e), wolfhound

domain starosty

dress sarafan

drink brick-tea, chacha, kumiss, kvas(s), mare's milk, obarne, obarni, quas(s), slivovitz, vodka, vodki

driver izvozchik

dumpling pelmeni

dynasty romanov

efficiency method stakhovism

elite nachalstvo

emperor See *czar*, above.

empress aleksandra, alexandra, anna-ivanovna, autocatrix, catherine, czarina, elizabeth

endearment term kiska, kroshka, ponchik

engineer tupolev

exclamation nichevo, nitchevo

expansionism hegemonism

expert kremlinologist

far east amur, kamchatka, khabarovsk, magadan, primoriya, sakhalin, yakutia

farm collective, kochenev-

---

sky, kolkhoz, sovkhos(e), sovkhov

farmer kulak

farm machine niva

fiddle gudok

field marshal kutuzov, suvorov

fish beluga, sterlet, sturgeon

fish soup solianka

5-year plan piatiletka

flax hank bobbin

fleet escadra

folksong bylina

food black bread, borsch, borsht, bortsch, caviar, pelemo, pirau, pirozhki, sturgeon, zabuski

forest taiga, tundra, urman

fort etape

fortress kremlin

founder ivan, lenin

fox corsac, karagan

fuel oil astatki

funeral feast pominki

fur karakul

fur coat shuba

fur trader baranov

gambling game coocoo

garden dvor

general bagramyan, buddyonny, budenny, chuikov, de tolly, golikov, hetman, ivanov, konev, kuropatkin, moskalenko, nicholas, rokossovsky, suvorov, timoshenko, totleben, vasilevsky, vatutin, voronov, voroshilov, yepishev, yeremenko, zhukov

geographer kropotkin

georgian inghilois

giant louishkin

goldsmith faberge

good bye proshchai

government group comintern, duma, kommandature, politbureau, politburo, pr(a)esidium, rada, soviet, tsik, zemstvo

government official mazurov, rashidov, rudikov, suslov, titov

government seat kremlin

grain durum, emmer

grandduchess anastasia

grandmother babushka

grassland steppe

great velika

guild See *coop*, above.

gulf azov, mezen

gun kruka

hat, fur shapka

head man starosta

hemp konopel, rine

---

herb sacaline

hero igor, ivan, lenin, nevski, stalin

hills valdai

hippie bichi

historian ponomarev

holy mother of moscow

holy picture icon, ikon(o)

hood bashlik, bashlyk

hors d'oeuvre zakuska

horse orloff, tarpan

horseman cossack

house balagan, barabara, dacha, isba

hut isba

hydroelectric plant bratsk, inguri, kuibyshev, nurek, volograd

image icon, ikon(o)

imperial order ukase

iron sable

island hiiumaa, saaremaa, sakhalin

island group andreanof

"it doesn't matter" ni(t)-chevo

-japanese war battle mukden, sea of japan, tsushima

journalist ehrenburg, polyakov, simonov

kerchief analav

labor association artel

labor camp gulag

lagoon liman

lake aral, azof, azov, baikal, balkash, byelo, chany, elton, erara, ilmen, kola, lacha, ladoga, neva, onega, peipus, pskov, seg(o), selety, taymyr, tengiz, topo, vigo, vozhe, zaysan

landlord khozyain

landowner boyar(d), pomeshchik

leader beria, brezhnev, bukamin, bukharin, efremov, grishin, gromyko, khrushchev, kirilenko, kosygin, kozlov, kulakov, kunayev, kuznetzov, lenin, litvinov, malenkov, malik, mazurov, molotov, podgorny, polianshi, shcherbakov, shcherbitsky, shelepin, sobolov, stalin, suslov, tsarapkin, vishinsky, voronov, zorin

leather bulgar, juchten, jufti, shagreen, yuft

legislature duma, rada, zemstvo

liberation osvobozhdeniye

little russene, ruthene, ukranian

marsh liman, pripet

marshal zhukov

massacre pogrom

mathematician kovalevsky, lobachevsky

measure archine, arsheen, botchka, boutylka, charka, chetverik, chetvert, chkalik, dessiatine, duim(e), fass, foute, fut, garnetz, korec, korek, krouchka, kroushka, ligne, liniya, lo(o)f, osmin(a), pajak, paletz, polugarnetz, pood, quar, sagene, stekar, stof(f), tchast, tsarki, vedro, verchoc, verchok, verst(a)(e)

medical assistant feldsher

meteorological station wrangel

mile verst(e)

millet proso

ministry commissariat

missile See ROCKET *names, russian.*

mister gospodin

monarchy founder rurik, ryurik

monk rasputin, starets

museum hermitage

mush kasha

musical instrument balalaika, gudok, gusle

musician balakirev

musketeer strelitz

muskrat desman

name aki, igor, ivan, olga, peter, sonya

naval academy frunze

negative nyet

neurologist bechterew

"never mind" nichevo

news agency novosti, tass

newspaper izvestia, pravda, trud

nobleman barin, satrost

northernmost town kola

oil center baku

olive oleaster

opera boris godounov, boris godunoff, boris godunov, eugen onegin

overseer pristav

pail parasha

painter bakst, chagall, cozens, kandinsky, roerich, vereshchagin

pancakes blini

party ketcherinka

peak belukha, elbrus, lenin, pobedy

peasant kulak, m(o)ujik, muzhik, muzjuk, slav

peninsula crimea, kamcha-

tka, karelia, kola, taimyr, yamal

people byelorussian, cossack, ersar, kulak, muscovite, red, siberian, slav, soviet, tatak, ukranian, velika

philosopher berdyaev, ouspensky, plekhanov

physician voronoff

physicist basov, cereknov, cherenkov, frank, landau, prochorov, tamm

physiologist pavlov

pianist balakirev, brailovsky, gabrilowitsch, gilels, goedicke, horowitz, lhevinne, pachman, rachmaninoff, rachmaninov, richter, scriabin, tcherpnin

plain steppe, tundra

planning organization gosplan

poachers brankonieri

poet annenski, annensky, asegev, bagritski, balmont, blok, bunin, dzyubin, lermontov, mayakovski, pushkin, yesenin, yevtushenko

police cheka, chekists, gpu, kgb, mgb, mvd, nkvd, ochrana, ogpu, organi

police briefing room spetsodel

police chief beria, shelepin

police embassy referentura

police headquarters lubianka

policy nep

political party black hundred, maximalist, menshevik, octobrist

pool carline

port anapa, archangel, balabkava, batum(i), derbent, лisk, krons(h)tadt, kuibyshev, leningrad, liepaja, livonia, makhachkala, memel, murmansk, odessa, okha, pechenga, petsamo, rostov, samara, sevastopol, sochi, taganrog, vladivostok, yeisk

porter dvornik

post boy yams(tch)ik

premier bulganin, kosygin, khrushchev, lenin, malenkov, stalin

president mikoyan, podgorny, shvernik, voroshilov

presidium member andropov, demichev, ilyichev, titov

prince knais, knez, knyaz, vladimir

prison butyrka, etape, lefor-

tovo, lubyanka, sremskamitrovica, sukhanovka

prison carriage carette

prison regime spetz

prison telegraph parasha

propaganda agency agitprop

province See *republic,* below.

publication krokodil

radical bolshevik, menshevik, nihilist, red

range alai, altai, anadyr, caucasus, sayan, stanovi, tien-shan, urals, yablonoi

rank tchin

region (See also *republic,* below.) abkhazia, adygei, altai, altay, bashkir, carpatho-ukraine, caucasia, caucasus, circassia, iberia, inkerman, kamchatka, karelia, krasnodar, krasnoyarsk, mordzin, ossetia, stavropol, steppe, ruva, uzbek, yakut

region, industrial kuznetsk basin

republic or state abasia, abkhasia, abkhazia, amur, armenia, azerbaijan, belorussia, bughdan, bukhara, buriat, buryat, byelorussia, chuvash, estonia, galicia, georgia, guria, ingush, kabardia, karelia, karthli, kartili(a), kavkaz, kazakstan, kirghizia, kirgiz, lapland, latvia, lithuania, moldau, osetiya, pamir, polesia, siberia, sogdiana, tula, turkmenistan, ukraine, uzbekistan

revolutionary breshkovsky, kalinin, kerenski, lenin, rykov, stalin, tomsky, trotski, trotsky

revolutionary group narodniki, nihilists

river abakan, aka, aldan, amga, amur, angara, berezina, bug, dnieper, dniester, don(ets), dvina, ili, irtysh, kama, kara, ket, kolyma, kuban, lena, lovat, memel, mezen, nadym, ner, neva, niemen, oka, onega, orel, pechora, pripet, ros, selenga, styr, sura, svir, syrdarya, taz, terek, tobol, tom, tym, ufa, ural, volga, yana, yenisei, zeya

ruler See *czar, leader* and *premier,* above.

sable sobol

saint nicholas, olga, vladimir
satellite cosmos, elektron, luna, lunik, mars, molniya, polyot, proton, sputnik, voskhod, vostok, yantar, zond
savant afanasiev
scientist blagonravov, grindel, sakharov
sculptor archipenko, neizvestny, zadkine
sea aral, azov, baikal, black, kara, okhotsk
secret police chief lebedev
sect d(o)ukhobor, molokan, popovets, raskolnik, stundist
sheepdog owtchah
shelter etape, isba
shops, privileged beriozka
singer chaliapin, kipnis
sleigh piatnitza
soup borsch, borst, bortsch, shchi, shtchee, stchi
space leader tsiolkovsky
spy abel, blake, hayhanen, sorge
spy agency kgb
state See *republic*, above.
state farm kochenevsky
statesman brezhnev, molotov, potemkin, vishinsky, witte
stockade etape
symbol bear, hammer and sickle
synod sobor
tavern caback, kabak
tax obrok
tea chifir
teacher starets
tea urn samovar
tent kibitka
"thank you" spaseba
theatrical group member blueblouse
theologian berdyaev
theosophist blavatsky
thistle saltwort, tumbleweed
tightwad fist
title autocatrix, beriya, boyar(d), czar(evitch)(ina), starosta, tsar(evitch)(itza), tzar(evitch)
toast nazdorovya
trade union artel
trading agency amtorg
travel agency intourist
trusty prisoner naryadchik
turnip rutabaga
vehicle See *carriage*, above.
vigilantes druzhiniki
villa dacha

village mir, stanitza
village council selsoviet
village elder starosta
violinist elman, heifetz, kogan, milstein, oistrakh
vodka samogon
volcano aragats
wagon telega
warehouse etape
war orphans besprizorni
weight dol(i)a, funt, lana, last, lo(o)f, lot(h), once, pood, poud
wheat durum, emmer
whip knout, plet(e)
whist biritch
white bielorouss
wolfhound alan, borzoi, psovie
worker dvornik, prole, stakhanovite
writer (See also *poet*, above.) aleichem, aleksandr, andreyev, annenski, artsybashev, artzybashev, asegev, babel, bagritski, balmont, bely, blok, bukharin, bunin, chokhov, chukovskaya, dostoevsky, fadeyev, fedin, gogol, goncharov, gorki, gorky, ivanov, jehuda, katayev, kaverin, kryukov, kuprin, leonov, mandelstam, medvedev, nabokov, nekrasov, pasternak, pushkin, rabinowitz, roerich, sergyeevich, sholokhov, simonov, sokolov, solzhenitsyn, tolstoi, tolstoy, turgenev, ustinov, voinovich, voznesensky, yesenin
youth stilyagi
youth group comsomol, komsomol
RUSSUD forage, grain
RUST aerugo, blight, canker, color, corrode, corrosion, decay, decline, degenerate, deteriorate, eat, erode, ferrugo, fungus, idleness, impair, inaction, inertia, mold, oxidate, oxidation, oxidize, patina, stale, uredo, verdigris, weaken, wither
-colored ferruginous
genus caeoma, coleosporium, endophyllum, gymnoconia, kuenneola, peridermium, phragmidium, puccinia, uredo
knot tubercule
-mite disease buckskin

plant blight, ferrugo, fungus, hemiform, leptoform
-proofing metal cadmium, zinc
RUSTAM, RUSTEM, RUSTUM *dragon* asdeev
epic shah-hamah
father zal
father-in-law mihrab
horse reksh
kin rudabah
monarch kai-kaus, kai-khosrau, kai-qobad
opponent isfendiar
son sohrab
steed raksh
victim akuan, sohrab
wife rudabeh
RUSTIC agrestic, agriculturist, arcadian, artless, austere, awkward, backwoods(man), boor(ish), bucolic, bum(p)kin, bushman, campesino, carl(e), chawbacon, chuff, churl, clod(hopper), clown, coarse, contadino, corydon, crude, damoetas, damon, daphnis, doric, farmer, gaffer, geoponic, georgic, hayseed, hick, hob(binoll), hobnail, hodge, homely, homespun, honest, hoosier, jake, joskin, looby, lout, lumpkin, mossback, pastoral, peasant, pioneer, plain, plowboy, plowman, primitive, provincial, put, reub, rough(hewn), rube, rude, rural, silvester, simple, spartan, sturdy, swain, sylvan, thyrsis, unadorned, unaffected, uncouth, unpolished, villatic, woodsman, yokel
dance bergamasca, bergamask, bobbing-joan, tarantella
RUSTICATE banish, isolate, retire, suspend
RUSTICITY agrarianism, artlessness, awkwardness, boorishness, ignorance, inurbanity, provincialism, simplicity, stupidity, yokelism
RUSTLE brush, brustle, crinkle, fissle, fistle, flow, froufrou, hirstel, hum, hurry, hustle, murmur, reesle, scroop, skitter, steal, stir, sweep, swish, whir, whish, whisk, whistle
of silk scroop
up snaffle, snavvle
RUSTLER abactor, abigeus,

cattlethief, duffer, dynamo, hustler, thief, waddy

RUSTLING crinkly, froufrou, gentle, murmuring, soft, soughing, susurr(o)us, whispering

RUSTUM See RUSTAM.

RUSTY aged, cankery, clumsy, cross, dirty, discolored, faded, foul, green, impaired, inexperienced, informer, morose, obstinate, out of practice, rancid, reasty, rebellious, restive, rubiginous, shabby, stained, stale, stiff, stubborn, sullen, surly, traitor, uncivil, unpracticed, vile

RUT channel, ditch, furrow, groove, habit, heat, impasse, oestruate, oestrus, oxcart, path, pity, rabbet, raik, rat, roaring, root, routine, strake, track, tread, uproar, wrinkle

RUTABAGA brassica, swede, tuber, turnip, vegetable

RUTH commiseration, compassion, condolence, cruelty, empathy, grief, mercy, misery, pitiful, pity, regret, remorse, repentance, sad-

ness, sorrow, sympathy, tenderness, woe

husband boaz, booz, mahlon
mother-in-law naomi
son jesse, obed

RUTH, BABE bambino, mahatma, sultan of swat

RUTHENIAN *country* ung
division boiko

RUTHENIUM *source* iridosmine

RUTHFUL lenient, pitiful, sorrowful, tender, woeful

RUTHLESS adamant, barbarous, bitter, bloody, brutal, cruel, fell, feral, ferocious, grim, hard, harsh, heartless, inclement, inhuman, insensitive, merciless, pitiless, relentless, remorseless, sadistic, savage, unmerciful

RUTILATE glitter, glow, shine

RUTILUS braise, bream, fish, pagrus, roach

RUTTER chart, dragoon, gallant, horseman, plow, portolan(o), trooper

RUTTISH, RUTTY lustful, rank, salacious

RUTULIAN *chief* rhamnes

RUX play, sport, worry
RUY DIAZ DE BIVAR el cid
RWANDA *capital* kigali
lake kivu
language kirundi, swahili
peak karisimbi
people bahutu, batutsi, batwa, hutu, tutsi, twa, watusi
president kayibanda
range mitumba
river akanyaru, kagera, luvironza
RYA rug
RYBINSK shcherbakov
RYE bread, eray, flour, gentleman, grain, grass, ree, reye, rie, secale, spelt, whisk(e)y
and wheat triticale
beard awn
disease blindseed, ergot, fungus, rust, take-all
grass darnel, eaver, marcite, ray
poison darnel
RYOT peasant, raiyat, servant, slave, tenant, tiller
RYTINA hydromalis
RYUKYU *island* okinawa

S

S *-shaped* ogee(d), sigmate, sigmoid

SAAR sarre

SAAREMMA *island* osel

SABA fiber, musa, sheba
nut false-sapota

SABADILLA *seed extract* cevadilline, cevadine, cevin(e), sabadinine, veratria, veratridine, veratrina

SABAH north borneo

SABAL erythea, fan palm, palm(etto)

SABALO milk-fish, tarpon

SABANNA See SAVANNA.

SABANNUS *son* moeth

SABAOTH armies, hosts, sabbath

SABBATARIAN seventh-day adventist

SABBATH day of rest, dies non, fast(day), friday, hallowday, holyday, lord's day, sabaoth, saturday, shabbat; shabbos, sunday
dinner cholent

SABBATIA centaury, herb, marsh-pink, sea-pink

SABBATICAL leave(of absence), rest, vacation

SABBATON boot, shoe, solleret

SABELLAN gritty, sandy

SABELLIAN italian, italic, sabine, samnite
dialect marrucinian, paelignion

SABER, SABRE acinaces, ataghan, bancal, cutlas(s), kukri, rapier, scimitar, stab, staghan, sword, tulwa(u)r, yatagan
part blade, grip, guard, plate, pommel, sable, shamshir, tang
rattling militarism

SABERTOOTH cat, tiger

SABERWING hummingbird, pampa

SABIAS *leader* josiah

SABINE *capital* reate
goddess vacuna

king tatius, titus
maiden tarpeia
resident horace
people vestini
SABLE antelope, black, brush, dark(ened), dismal, dusky, ebon(y), fish, gloomy, marten, mustela, mysterious, pellet, saber, sabre, sad, sobol, sombre, threatening, zibeline
antelope black-buck
fur zibel(l)ine
SABLEFISH beshow, candlefish, cod, eulachon, mustela
SABORA rabbi
SABOT clog, geta, shoe
SABOTAGE damage, destroy, destruction, injury, mischief, undermine, vandalism, wreckage
SABOTEUR subversive
SABRA *father* ptolemy
rescuer st george
son alexander, david, guy

SABRE See SABER.

SABRINA *parent* estrildis, locrine
river severn

SABUJA *indian* cariri(an)

SABULOSE, SABULINE arenaceous, dusty, floury, granular, gritty, sandy

SAC amnion, ampulla, ascus, bag, bladder, bursa, cavity, cistern, cyst, follicle, hygroma, membrane, pocket, pod, pouch, sacculus, sack, sake, theca, utricle, venter, vesicle
comb. asco, burs
fungus blood-cup, peziza
spore ascus, askos

SACALAIT killifish, warmouth

SACAR *child* ahiam

SACATON grass, hay

SACCATE bursiform, encysted, pouched, pouch-shaped

SACCHARIN(E) glucose, gluside, honeyed, lactone, sticky, sugary, sweet(ening)
derivative agavose, maltwort
source coal-tar

SACERDOTAL clerical, hieratic, priestly

SACHEM boss, chief, personage, ruler, sagamore

SACHET bag, pad, perfume, reticule, scent(bag)

SACK bag, base, bayon, bed, budget, cashier, catch, demolish, despoil, destroy, destruction, devastate, discharge, dismiss(al), drop, fire, goose, gown, gunny, harry, havoc, jacket, jilt, loot, overdress, pack(age), peignoir, pillage, plunder, poke, pouch, ransack, ravage, raze, rifle, rob, robe, sacque, sherry, spoil, spoliate, spoliation, strip, waste, wine
cloth and ashes penance, remorse, retribution
coarse bayon, gunny
in retire
mail bum
material burlap, gunny, hemp, hessian, jute
palm-leaf bayon

SACKBUT sambuke, trombone

SACKLESS bashful, dispirited, guiltless, harmless, innocent, peaceable, unmolested, weak

SACRAMENT baptism, ceremony, communion, confirmation, covenant, eucharist, host, lord's supper, mass, matrimony, mystery, oath, orders, penance, pledge, promise, rite, service, sign, symbol, token, unction
vessel See **EUCHARIST** *vessel.*

SACRARIUM chancel, chapel, oratory, piscina, sacristy, sanctuary, shrine, synsacrum, tabernacle, vestry

SACRED anointed, awful, blessed, cherished, consecrated, dedicated, divine, enshrined, geistlich, hallowed, heavenly, hieratic, holy, huaca, ineffable, inviolable, inviolate, pious, pure, religious, respected, revered, reverenced, sacrosanct, sainted, sanctified, santa, santo, solemn, spiritual, taboo, tabu, treasured, unutterable, valued, venerable, venerated
comb. hagio, hier(o)
fig pipal
fish kannume
force kami
make anoint, beatify, bless, canonize, consecrate, enshrine, hallow, sanctify
most sacrosanct
object sacrum
place abaton, ahuwara, altar, altis, bethel, chaitya, chapel, church, fane, harem, hiera, hieron, sanctuary, sanctum(sanctorum), shrine, synagogue, temple

SACREDNESS inviolability, sanctity, solemnity, spiritualism, spirituality, tjurunga, venerability

SACRIFICE abdicate, abnegate, abstinence, atone(ment), bunt, chagigah, chiliomb, corban, eschew, forbear, forfeit(ure), for(e)go, gambit, give(up), hagigah, hecatomb, holocaust, host, idolothyte, immolate, immolation, kapparah, korban, litation, lose, loss, mactation, martyrdom, oblation, offering, offertory, pawn, privation, propitiate, relinquish, renounce, resign, rite, scapegoat, self-denial, self-renun-

ciation, sell, sphagion, surrender, suttee(ism), victim, yajna, yield
animal guilt-offering, sphagion
god agni
horse ashvamedha
men of fedayeen
offering hiera, sphagion
of 100 oxen hecatomb
of 1,000 oxen chiliomb
of women gynethusia
place altar
propitiatory hiera, sphagion
symbol lamb

SACRIFICIAL piacular

SACRILEGE blasphemy, defilement, desecration, pollution, profanation, profanity, sin, transgression, trespass, violation

SACRILEGIOUS blasphemous, impious, profanatory, profane

SACRISTAN ecclesiastic, sexton, verger

SACRISTY diaconicon, paratory, sacrary, sextry, vergery, vestry
pert. vestral

SACROSANCT See SACRED.

SAD 3 bad, wan 4 blue, dark, deep, dire, dowy, dram, dull, evil, poor 5 adust, black, dense, dusky, fixed, grave, heavy, mesto, moody, sated, sober, soggy, solid, sorry, stiff, stout, tired, weary 6 broody, dismal, dolent, donsie, dreary, gloomy, paltry, rueful, scanty, solemn, somber, steady, tragic, triste, wicked, woeful 7 doleful, dumpish, forlorn, hapless, naughty, painful, pensive, pitiful, serious, unhappy, unlucky, valiant, wistful 8 dejected, desolate, dolorous, downcast, grievous, luckless, mournful, pathetic, pitiable, shameful, subtrist, terrible, wretched 9 afflicted, cheerless, depressed, long-faced, mirthless, plaintive, sorrowful, steadfast, surfeited 10 calamitous, deplorable, despondent, distressed, illstarred, lamentable, lugubrious, melancholy 11 distressing, heartbroken, unfortunate 12 disconsolate, heavyhearted, inauspicious, inconsolable 13 broken-hearted

comb. tragi(c)

-looking friday-faced

sack ass, bolo, idiot, jerk, mooch, moron, neb(b)ech, neb(b)ish, s(c)hnook, shnuk, twerp, weakling, wretch

-tree hursinghar

SADDEN attrist, darken, deplore, depress, desolate, distress, dull, dump, grieve, lament

SADDLE aparejo, burden, chine, clitellum, col, control, cricket, encumber, ephippium, howdah, load, loins, pilch, pillion, recado, ride, ridge, seat, selle, stick, straddle, tag

belt surcingle

blanket apishamore, corona, tilpah

boot gambado

bow arson, cantle, cinch

cloth See *pad*, below.

cover housing, mochila, pilch

18th century demipique

flap jockey, skirt

horn pommel

horse bidet, mount, palfrey, pony, remuda

kind cavalry, cowboy, english, mcclellan, pack, pilch, pillion, riding, side, western

knob pommel, tore

light pilch, pillion

maker See SADDLER.

mat flet

motorcycle pillion

1-legged rider somerset

pack aparejo, bardel(le)

pad blanket, housing, namda, panel, pillion, shabrack, shabraque

part bellyband, bolster, cantle, cinch, corona, croup, crutch, girth, horn, jockey, latigo, lorimer, mochila, pad, panel, pilch, pommel, safe, skirt, stirrup, strap, sudadero, tore

pommel crutch, forebow, horn, knob, tore

rock oyster

strap cinch, girth, latigo, lorimer, loriner

straw sods, suggan, sunk

tree maker fuster

with charge, hamper, impose, oblige, stick

without asellate, bareback, unhorsed

wooden panel

SADDLEBACK caterpillar, concave, harp-seal, hill, hooded-crow, jack(bird), oyster, ridge

SADDLEBAG alforja, cantina, jag(g), pannier, sumpter, teetsook

SADDLER cobbler, codder, cozier, fuster, knacker, lorimer, loriner, seal, shoemaker, whittaw

SADDUCEE priest, renegade, secular, unconventional

opponent pharisee

SADISM algolagnia, algophilia, cruelty

SADNESS anguish, bathos, blues, dejection, depression, desolation, despair, distress, dolor, dumps, gloom, grief, grieving, heartache, heartbreak, melancholy, misery, mourning, pathos, regret, sorrow, tribulation, tristesse, unhappiness, vapors, woe

SADO carriage, dos-a-dos

SAFARI caravan, excursion, expedition, hunt, journey, trek

servant bearer

vehicle land-rover

SAFE all right, arca, bank, cache, careful, chest, coffer, cozy, cupboard, dependable, firm, guarded, okay, pete, protected, reliable, sane, scot free, seaworthy, secure, shielded, si(c)ker, snug, sound, stable, steady, strongbox, sure, sykerly, tame, tried, trustworthy, unharmed, unhazardous, unhurt, vault, well

as the bank of england

conduct bodyguard, convoy, cowle, escort, grith, guard, pass(port), permission, protection

cracker boxman, burglar, cracksman, pete(r)man, raffles, screwsman, thief, torchman, yegg(man)

name meaning salva, titus

SAFEGUARD aegis, bastion, bodyguard, buffer, bulwark, bumper, conserve, convoy, cowcatcher, dashboard, defend, defense, ensure, escort, fender, guard, hand-

rail, insure, pass(port), preserve, protect(ion), safety, save, screen, secure, shield

SAFEHOLD refuge

SAFEKEEPING care, conservation, custody, preservation, protection, salvation, storage

SAFELY siccar, sicker, surely

SAFETY assurance, asylum, custody, deliverance, protection, redemption, safeguard, salvation, security, shelter, surety, warrant

belt life-preserver

god hercules, sancus

lamp dav(e)y

pin clasp, fubula

place of ark, asylum, haven, port, refuge, retreat, sanctum

rail easer, guardrail

zone island, refuge, shelter

SAFFLOWER alazor, kusum, saffron

SAFFRON azafran, colcothar, crocus, ditaxis, kamala, kusum, safflower, satinleaf, sensational, thistle, yellow, zedoary

SAG bag, bend, bow, bulge, bunt, curve, decline, decrease, deflate, depreciate, dip, drift, dro(o)p, fall, flag, flop, hang, languish, lean, lull, reed, rush, saw, saying, sedge, settle, sink, slouch, slump, sny, weaken, wilt, yield

SAGA edda, epic, gest, history, legend, myth, narrative, poem, recital, rimur, seeress, story, tale, witch

SAGACIATE fare, thrive

SAGACIOUS acute, argute, astute, canny, discerning, farsighted, hardheaded, intelligent, judicious, keen, knowing, penetrating, perceptive, perspicacious, piercing, prophetic, prudent, sage, sane, sapient, sensible, sharp, shrewd, wise, witty

SAGACITY acumen, acuteness, apperception, astuteness, discernment, flair, gumption, insight, judgment, ken, penetration, perception, percipience, perspicacity, perspicuity, policy, quickness, sapience, wisdom, yephede

symbol elephant

SAGAMORE chief, ruler, sachem

SAGE abaris, abstruse, acute, adept, argute, authority, brilliant, buddha, canny, clary, confucius, counsel(l)or, deep, devarshi, discerning, erudite, eyeseed, gnostic, grave, herb, intellect, intelligent, judicious, katha, keen, knowing, learned, longhead, maharshi, mahatma, master (mind), mentor, mint, nestor, oracle, owlish, perceptive, philosophic, plato, profound, prophet, prudent, pundit, SAGACIOUS, salvia, sane, sapient, savant, scholar, seasoning, seer, sensible, sharp, shrewd, smart, sober, socrates, solemn, solomon, solon, swami, thinker, tohunga, venerable, wise, wiseman, witan, wite, wizard
annual chia
aquinian juvenal
cheese cheddar
cheronean plutarch
clammy clary
cock grouse
greek See GREEK *sage.*
hen grouse, nevadan
of bethlehem lungwort, spearmint
of chelsea carlyle
of concord ralph waldo emerson
of ferney voltaire
of monticello jefferson
of pylus nestor
prairie mugwort
7 See GREECE *sages, 7.*

SAGEBRUSH absinthe, artemisia, hyssop
drama oater, western
state nevada

SAGGY baggy, drooping, droopy, flabby, hanging, pendulous

SAGITTA arrow(worm), chaetognatha, constellation, keystone, otolith, worm

SAGITTARIUS archer, bowman, constellation
gem amethyst

SAGO arrowroot, palm, pudding, starch
palm coontie, cycas, gebang, gomuti, jaggery, metroxylon, palmyra, phoenix, sagwire

plant cuckoopint
source cycas

SAGRADA cascara

SAGUARO cactus, cereus, pitahaya, suwarro

SAHAPTIN *indian* nez-perce

SAHARA cocoa, desert, waste(land)
people arab, berber, nomad, tuareg
plateau hammada
region air, asben, erg, samen
valley samen
wind gibleh, leste

SAHIB gentleman, man, mister

SAHIBAH lady, mistress, woman

SAID above, dit, oral, quoth, related, repeated, spoken, stated, uttered
ancestor mohammed

SAIDA sidon

SAIGA ahu, animal, antelope, coin

SAIGON *airbase* bienhoa

SAIL (See also *kind,* below.) assail, awn, boat, canvas, coast, craft, cross, cruise, dance, dart, duck, embark, fan, fin, float, fly, glide, haul, luff, muslin, navigate, passage, rig, rush in, sally, scoon, scud, sheet, ship, shoot, skim, soar, tentacle, travel, van, vessel, wing, yacht
balance atry
before the wind prosper, succeed
border doubling
briskly spank
cloth canvas, duck
corner clew, clue, goosewing, tack
creeping saxifrage, stonecrop
down avale, awale
edge foot, head, leach, leech, luff
fast gale, ramp, scur, skirr
fastener clew, clue, jackstay
fluke whiff
fore-and-aft trysail
4-sided lug(sail)
fragment hullock
furl reef
group kites, linens, outfit, vela
height hoist
hoisted atrip
into attack, berate, collide, rebuke, take on, undertake
kind balloon(jib), cheater, crossjack, foreroyal, forestay, gunt(h)er, jamie-green,

jib, lateen, lug, main, mizzen, royal, skysail, spanker, spencer, spinnaker, spitfire, square, stay(sl), studding, stunsail, topgallant, topsail, trysail
light shadow
lowest course
nearer wind luff
part bunt, clew, footband, foreleech, leech, luff, sheet, slab, yardarm
pert. velic
prepare to trim
rope earing, halyard, inhaul, leefang(e)
shorten reef
slack part slab
small royal
square crossjack, driver, lug
studding ringtail
take in reef
throw water on skeet
tie trice
top sky-raker
to windward thrash
triangular bentinck, jib, lateen, marabuto, raff(e), raffie, trinket
wind badgir
with wind abeam lask
yard rae, spar

SAILBOAT See VESSEL *sailing.*

SAILFISH aguja, bannerfish, billfish, boho, boohoo, gar, guebucu, istiophorus, longjaw, needlefish, saury, spearfish, sucker, voilier, volador, woohoo

SAILING afloat, afluking, boating, cruising, departure, floating, fluking, navigation, sea-faring, trip, voyage, yachting

SAILOR, SAILOR'S billy budd, blue(jacket), bowswain, calash, canotier, clashy, coalpasser, coxswain, deckhand, fishhead, gob, harpooner, hearty, jack(tar), jacky, kiwi, klosh, lascar, leatherneck, limey, lithsman, marinal, marine, mariner, mate(lot), matlow, middy, midshipman, navigator, old salt, salt, seabee, seadog, seafarer, seaman, searover, shellback, shipman, shipmate, shoaler, stoker, swab, tar(pot), tierer, toty, traveler, waterdog, windjammer, yardsman

albatross cape-sheep
amusement scrimshaw
assent aye
associate messmate
awkward landlubber
blessing oath
blouse middy
blue chicory
call ahoy
chant yo-heave-ho
chapel bethel
choice bream, grunt, lagodon, pigfish, pinfish, porgy, whiting
coat monkeyjacket, peajacket, reefer
fare hardtack
fictional ralph rackstraw
furlough leave
game ablewhackets
gloves haling hands
goddess britomartis, brizo
group crew, hands
housewife ditty bag
jumper lammie, lammy
king william iv
knot wild geranium
mess tub kid
nap calk
novice (land)lubber
paradise fiddler's green
potion grog
protector mother car(e)y
quarters focsle
saint brendan, elmo, eulalia, nic(h)olas
song barcarole, chant(e)y, shant(e)y
tobacco mugwort
SAILPLANE floater, glider
SAIN bless, consecrate, cross, heal, sanctify
SAINT abdal, alvar, anba, angel, apostle, ar(a)hat, beatify, bhagat, bless, canonize, cherub, devotee, enshrine, hallow, holy, marabout, mormon, ordain, pir, puritan, sacred, sanctified, santa, santo, seraph
agnes's flower snowflake
albans verulamium
andrew's cross saltier, saltire
anthony's cross ankh, tace, tau
anthony's fire ergotism, erysipelas, herpes, shingles
anthony's pig runt
anthony's turnip meadowcrowfoot
augustine's rival pelagius
barnabas' prayer ave maria
barnabas' thistle knapweed
basil monk caloyer

biographies acta sanctorum, hagiography, hagiology, menology
calendar of menology
catalog diptych
catherine's home siena
catherine's symbol wheel
christopher st kitts
comb. hagi
create canonize, sanctify
david's bloom leek(s)
elmo's fire castor-and-pollux, corposant, flame, furole, helena, hermo, luminescence
emilion's owner ausonius
francis's birthplace assisi
francis's legends fioretti
francis's nickname poverello
george's duck sheldrake
george's herb valerian
george's prize una
george saved sabra
george's sword ascalon, askelon
invocation of hagiolatry
jacob's dipper pitcherplant, sarracenia
james's weed shepherd's-purse
john's bread aglar(r)oba, carob
john's evil epilepsy
john's-wort aaron's-beard, amber, androseme, ascyrum, broombrush, bushbroom, cammock, hypericum, rosin-rose, tutsan
kitts capital basse-terre
lawrence tributary richelieu
louis blues composer handy
louis feature gateway arch
louis founder laclede
louis name gateway city
lucie cherry mahaleb
martin's bird harrier
martin's evil drunkenness
mary's herb costmary
nicholas kris(s) kringle, santa claus
patrick's breastplate lorica
paul's architect wren
paul's birthplace tarsus
paul's clerk barnabite
paul's companion luke
paul's epistle corinthians, philemon, phillippians
peter simon
petersburg leningrad, petrograd
peter's corn einkorn
peter's sword malchus
peter's treasure pieta

peter's-wort cowslip, primula, snowberry
peter's wreath francoa, spiraea
philip's birthplace neri
pierre island oleron
records of hierology
regis ranere, raspberry
relic box chasse
relic chapel feretory
stephen's loaves stones
study of hagiography
symbol (See also under name of saint.) halo
theresa's town avila
veronica's handkerchief sudarium
vitus's dance chorea
weeping swithin
worship of dulia, hagiolatry, hierolatry
SAINTED, SAINTLY angelic(al), beatific, devout, godly, holy, pious, righteous, sanctimonious, virtuous
SAINTHOOD sanctity
SAKE account, advantage, behalf, benefit, beverage, blame, cause, concern, consideration, dispute, drink, end, fault, good, guilt, imperfection, interest, lawsuit, motive, objective, purpose, regard, safety, score, welfare, wellbeing, wine
SAKHALIN *gulf river* amur
SAKI bisa, couxia, h h munro, monkey, yarke(e)
monkey pithecia, yarke(e)
SAKRA indra
SAKYAMUNI See BUDDHA.
SAL rock, salt, sarah, shorea, sial, tamarisk
SALAAM bend, bob, bow, compliment, conge, curts(e)y, genuflect, greeting, kneel, kowtow, nod, obeisance, prostrate, salutation, salute, scrape
SALABLE marketable, merchantable, negotiable, purchasable, sellable, suitable, venal, vendible
SALACIA *consort* neptune, poseidon
SALACIOUS dirty, lascivious, lecherous, lewd, lustful, obscene, pornographic, ruttish, scabrous
SALAD (See also *kind, below.*) aspic, mixture, sallet, slaw

bowl saladier
cabbage coleslaw
corn fetticus, maches
days immaturity, puerility, verdancy, youth
dressing ingredient blue cheese, cream, eggs, herbs, lemon, mayonnaise, oil, pepper, salt, sour cream, soy sauce, spices, thousand island, vinaigrette, vinegar
ingredient avocado, beans, cabbage, celery, costmary, cress(e), endive, escarole, greens, kerse, lettuce, onion, parsley, potato, romaine, scallion, spinach, tomato, udo, watercress
kind avocado, caesar, cobb, coleslaw, egg, fruit, louis, macaroni, marine, meat, mixed green, nicoise, palace-court, slaw, tossed, vegetable
make toss
tree redbud
years teens, youth
SALADIN *dynasty* ayubite, ayyubid
SALAH *son* eber
SALAMANDER ambystoma, amphibian, amphiuma, axolotl, brasier, caudate, crawler, creeper, dogfish, eft, fire-eater, gopher, hellbender, incinerator, lizard, mecodont, newt, olm, plethodon, poker, reptile, salamich, shadrach, stove, triton, urodele
aquatic necturus, triton, triturus
blind haideotriton
eel-like amphiuma
fossil andrias
larval axolotl
wool asbestos
SALAMIEL *son* nathanael
SALAMIS *consort* poseidon
king ajax, cychreus, nicocreon, telamon
parent asopus, metope
son cychreus
victor themistocles
SALANIO *friend* antonio, bassanio
SALARY allowance, compensation, consideration, earnings, emolument, fee, hire, honorarium, pay, pension, pittance, recompense, remuneration, screw, stipend, wage(s)

SALATHIEL ezra
son zerubbabel
SALE auction, barter, cant, chamber, clearance, corned, deal, demand, disposal, exchange, hall, handsel, market, mongery, palace, outlet, reclame, rummage, salte(d), sellout, simony, trade, transaction, vend(ition), vendue, willow
auction block, cant
bargain red tag
made for quick catchpenny
public auction
rummage jumble
talk build-up, pitch
tax alcabala
SALEM *jurist* sewall
king melchizedek
SALEMUS *kin* chelkias, zadok
SALEP eulopia, orchid
SALERIO *friend* antonio, bassanio
SALERNO *prince* tancred
SALESMAN agent, bagman, broker, chapman, clerk, dealer, drummer, hawker, hustler, middleman, peddler, pitchman, representative, retailer, seller, solicitor, sutler, vender, vendor
SALESWOMAN clerk, shopgirl, vendeuse
SALICYLIC *acid derivative* aspirin
SALIENT bounding, bulge, conspicuous, german(e), important, jetting, jumping, leaping, manifest, material, noticeable, projecting, prominent, pronounced, protruding, rampant, redan, signal, significant, springing, spur, striking, trench, weighty
angle arris, cant
point beginning, detail, essential, feature, gist, heart, nub, source
SALIENTIA aglossa, amphibia, anura, costata, frogs, linguata, toads
SALINE brackish, brine, briny, marinal, potash, salar, saliferous, salty, tear
lake shat
solution brine
SALISBURY *old* sarum
steak hamburger
SALISHAN *indian* atnah, bellacoola, chehalis, clal-

lam, coeur d'alene, colcine, comox, cowichan, cowlitz, dwamish, flathead, nanaimo, nisqualli, okinagan, pishquow, puntlatsh, puyallup, quinaielt, quinault, samish, semiahmoo, shuswap, siletz, sinkiuse, skokomish, songeesh, songish, sooke, spokan(e), squawmish, squawtits, squaxon, sumass, tillamook, tulalip, twana
SALIVA dribble, drivel, drool, expectoration, ptyalism, rheum, slabber, slaver, slobber, spit(tle), sputum
absence aptyalism
comb. sialo
excessive hygrostomia, ptyalism
pert. sialic, sialoid
resembling sialoid
SALIVAN *indian* maku, piaroa
SALIVARY salivant, salivous, sialagogic
glands parotids
SALIX catkin, itea, osier, sallow, tree, willow
SALLET (See aso HELMET.) salade
SALLOW adust, anemic, ashen, bloodless, colorless, gray, muddy, osier, pale (faced), pallid, pasty, salix, sallee, saugh, shoot, sick, twig, wan, wattle, willow, yellowish
SALLY attack, burst, dance, dash, debouch, demarche, digression, emerge, erupt, escapade, escape, excursion, foray, fray, frolic, gambade, issuance, issue, jaunt, jerk, jest, joke, journey, leap, outburst, outrush, pleasantry, projection, quip, quirk, raid, ripost(e), rush, sortie, spring, squib, start, trip, wattle, willow, witticism, wren
in our alley composer carey
lunn bun, teacake
-picker chiffchaff, warbler, wren
port gateway, military passage, postern
SALLYMAN velella
SALMA *descendants* ataroth, beth-joab, bethlehem, boaz, booz, manahethites, netophathites, zorites

wife rachab, rahab

SALMAGUNDI farrago, gallimaufry, hash, hodgepodge, jumble, medley, melange, mishmash, mixture, olio, potpourri

SALMON anadrom, ayu, baggit, barramunda, blueback, bluecap, botcher, brandlin(g), burnett, ceratodua, chinook, chum, coho(e), count, dog(fish), epiceratodus, gib, gilling, goldfish, grilse, haddo, holia, humpback, kahawai, kelt, keta, kipper, kokanee, laspring, laurel, lax, lox, lungfish, masy, mort, mykiss, neoceratodus, nerka, newfish, parr, pike, pink, quinnat, raun, redfish, runfish, samlet, saumon(t), sauqui, sawmon(t), schoodic, sewen, shedder, slat, smolt, smoot, sockeye, springer, sprod, taimen, tecon, tyee, weakfish
adult gilling, nerka
after spawning kelt, shedder
baby alevin, pink
beaked sandfish
before spawning gilling, girling
blueback nerka, sauqui, sockeye
color an(n)atto, arnatto, roucou
cured gravlaks, kipper
disease furunculosis
dog chum, keta
enclosure weir, yair, yare
female baggit, blackfish, hen, raun, shedder
giant taimen
herring milkfish
humpbacked haddo, holia
landlocked kipper, ouananiche, schoodic, sebago
louse gisler
male buck, cock, gib(fish), kipper
measurement bind
milter eke
net maud
1-year-old bluecap
pool stell
quinnat tyee
shark porbeagle
silver coho, quisutsch
small peal, skirling
smoked lox
son boaz
soup pistou
spent judy, runfish, slat

3-year-old mort, pug, smolt
trap putcher, yair, yare
trap opening slap
trout sewin
2-year-old gilling, hepper, smolt, sprod
wife rahab
young alevin, bluecap, botcher, brandling, essling, fog, graveling, grilse, hepper, jerkin, laspring, parr, peal, pink, samlet, skegger, smolt, sprag

SALMONEUS *brother* sisyphus
daughter tyro
death by lightning
parent aeolus, enarete
wife alcidice, sidero

SALOME *husband* zebedee
mother herodias
son james, john
stepfather herod-antipas
victim john the baptist

SALON affair, apartment, assemblage, assembly, drawingroom, exhibition, gallery, hall, levee, museum, parlor, party, reception, room, salotto

SALOON alehouse, bar, barrelhouse, beergarden, bierstube, bistro, blind pig, brasserie, cabaret, cafe, cantina, cocktail lounge, cuddy, dive, dramshop, drawingroom, faro, ginmill, groggery, grogship, honkytonk, jerry shop, joint, lounge, mughouse, oasis, parlor, pitstop, pothouse, pub, rathskeller, rumshop, speakeasy, taproom, tavern
illegal blind pig, blind tiger, speakeasy

SALOOP salep, sassafras

SALSIFY goatsbear(d), oyster plant, sanicle, scorzonera

SALT abietate, adipate, alkali, allowance, alum, amidol, anisate, antiseptic, aurate, bitter, borax, brine, briny, condiment, corn, corrective, costly, cure, dear, deduction, doctor, emol, ester, expensive, flavor(ing), gammon, gob, halite, humor, ite, kainite, kern, lactate, lustful, mal(e)ate, mariner, mate, money, nacl, niobate, oleate, orach, osmate, phytate, piquancy, plumbite,

powder, preservative, preserve, pungency, pungent, reh, reserve, sailor, sal(ic), saline, savor, seaman, season(ing), sel, sense, sharp, smack, sodium chloride, souse, spice, tar, taste, tropate, uranin, usar, veteran, wit, zest, ziram
alkaline borax
astringent alum
attic wit
away invest, preserve, save, store
bismuth benzobis
boiler weller
bush acacia, atriplex, bluebush, wattle
cedar tamarisk
comb. ate, ite, hali, halo, sali
container cellar, sea, shaker
crystalline acerdol, analgene, borax
deposit salina, saline
divination by halomancy
double alum
duty gabelle, granage
efflorescence reh, usar
epsom salamandrum
gauge salinometer
glauber's sal mirabile, mirabilite
hair alunogen
lake caspian, chott, shor
lake, river into bear
-like halid(e), haloid, saline
lump saltcat
maker waller
-making solution bittern
marsh lick, salina
metal silicate
mixture reh, soyate
name of, comb. ate
of opium narcotine
of the earth acme, best, paragon
of wisdom alembroth
pan playa
pert. haloid
pit pezograph, vat, wich, wych
pork sowbelly
preserve with corn
relish achar
residue bittern
rheum eczema
river dam roosevelt
rock halite, pig, salgemmae
solution brack, brine, saline
source deerlick, sea
tax See *duty,* above.
tree atle(e), tamarisk
water brack, brine, ocean, sea, tears

water, growing in halophilous
-*water tailor* bluefish
-*water trout* weakfish
with grain of askance, cum grano salis
working halurgy
works salina, saltpans
works pond sump
SALTANT dancing, jumping, leaping, salient
SALTCELLAR saltfat, saltfoot, seller, shaker
SALTED corned, cured, doctored, experienced, hardened, immune, marinated, planted, proficient, sale, seasoned
SALTPETER anatron, natron, niter, nitre, prunella
SALTWEED samphire, toadrush
SALTWORT barilla, glasswort, glaux, kali, kelpwort, salsola, thistle
SALTY brackish, breezy, briny, funny, halinous, muriated, piquant, pungent, racy, ribald, risque, saline, sharp, spicy, witty, zestful
SALU *son* zimri
SALUBRIOUS advantageous, beneficial, benign, bright, favorable, healthful, healthy, hygienic, invigorating, SALUTARY, sanitary, warm, wholesome
SALUTARY advantageous, beneficial, benign, corrective, curative, healing, healthful, healthy, helpful, hygienic, immune, medicinal, profitable, remedial, restorative, SALUBRIOUS, sanitary, tonic, useful, wholesome
SALUTATION achara, address, aloha, ave, bel accoil, bayete, bow, chinchin, ciao, compellation, dieugard, eminence, excellency, grace, GREETING, haeremai, hail, HELLO, highness, honor(able), howdy, kowtow, lady(ship), lord(ship), majesty, mizpah, mizpeh, noble, prosit, reverend, sahep, sahib, salaam, SALUTE, sir, slainte, toast, welcome, worthy
SALUTE acclaim, accost, address, affect, bow, compliment, congratulate, curts(e)y, dip, excite, festivity,

firework, greet(ing), hail(se), halch, halse, health, honor, impress, influence, kiss, nod, safety, SALUTATION, salvo, signal, toast, visit, viva, vive, welcome, welfare
military present arms
SALVADOR See EL SALVADOR.
SALVAGE compensation, discount, reclaim, recover(y), redeem, redemption, rescue, save, scrounge
SALVATION bodai, delivery, enlightenment, kaivalya, liberation, moksha, nirvana, preservation, redemption, rescue, salvage, save, soulheal
army founder general booth
attaining by self autosoteric.
name meaning hosea, isaiah
pert. soterial, soterical, soteriological
SALVE allay, anoint, assuage, balm, cerate, cure, demulcent, embrocation, emollient, excuse, flatter(y), gratuity, hail, heal, justify, lenitive, liniment, lotion, lubricate, medicate, money, nerval, ointment, plaster, quiet, relieve, remedy, resolve, safeguard, save, smear, solve, soothe, support, tar, treat, unguent, welcome, wheedle
SALVELINUS char(r), oquassa, trout
SALVER bowl, coaster, dish, plateau, tray, waiter
SALVIA artemisia, cancerweed, chia, clary, mejorana, mint(weed), plant, sage(brush)
SALVO broadside, cheers, discharge, exception, excuse, explanation, festivity, fusillade, pretext, proviso, quibble, reservation, salute, shot, shout, tribute, volley
SAM assemble, collect, curdle, moisten, unite
SAMA audition, muttonfish, tripletail
SAMADH cremation, immolation, shrine, tomb
SAMAN baggage, equipage, furniture, raintree, stores
SAMARIA, SAMARITAN cuthean, cuthite
alphabet alaf, bith, dalat, gaman, goph, jud, kaph,

labad, min, nun, phi, rish, sadi, sen, shan, simcat, tav, tit
center schechem
deity nibhaz, tartak
people assyrian, israelite
personified aholah, aholibah, oholah
SAMARKAND *ruler* tamburlaine, tamerlane, tim(o)ur
SAMBA carioca, dance
SAMBAR cervus, deer, elk, maha, rusa
SAMBUCUS bloodwort, bush, elder(berry)
SAME akin, alike, all one, cognate, ditto, duplicate, egal, equal(ly), equivalent, even, ibid(em), idem, identic(al), ilk, invariable, just, like(wise), meme, one, parallel, selfsame, similar, stesso, tantamount, twin, unchanged, uniform
always the semper idem
comb. aut(o), equi, hom(o), iso, tauto
make equalize, equate
SAMENESS analogy, consistency, constancy, correspondence, equability, evenness, homogeneity, identity, likeness, monotony, oneness, parity, regularity, resemblance, respondence, similarity, steadiness, uniformity
SAMHAIN *eve* halloween
SAMIAN See SAMOS.
SAMLET parr, salmon
SAMMAEL See DEVIL.
SAMMY clammy, moist(en), ninny, simpleton, sodden, soldier, watery
SAMOA See *aso* MALAYSIA, POLYNESIA.
airport tafuna
barn owl lulu
bird iao, lulu, lupe, manuali, manuao, manum(e)a, manusina, manutagi, maomao
bowl tanoa
capital apia
city apia, fagatogo, pagopago, pangopango, utulei
cloth para, tapa
coin tala
council fono
dance siva
deity tagaloa
fish ataata, salele, sesele
garment lavalava, pareu
honey-eater iao

hostess taupo(u)
island manua, ofu, olosega, rose, savaii, tau, tutuila, upolu
maiden taupo(u)
meeting aumaga
mollusk asi
mudworm ipo
organization aumaga
owl lulu
peak alava, fito, matafao, rainmaker mountain, savaii, vaea
port apia, pagopago, pangopango
spirit atua
warrior toa
SAMOS *philosopher* melissus, pythagoras
tyrant polycrates
SAMOSATA *philosopher* lucan
SAMOTHRACE *statue* winged victory
SAMOYED *people* beltir, kaibal, kamassin, koiba, nentsi, tuba, yurak
SAMP cereal, hominy, maize, meal, mush, porridge, soup
SAMPAN boat, skiff
SAMPHIRE saltweed
SAMPLE bite, case, cast, compare, cross-section, essay, examine, example, excerpt, experiment, fragment, illustration, instance, match, morsel, parable, parcel, part, pattern, piece, portion, pree, savor, segment, sip, slip, specimen, swatch, taste(r), test, token, trial, try, warning
room See SALOON.
SAMPLEMAN demonstrator, taster
SAMPLER archetype, example, model, needlework, original, pattern, specimen
SAMSON, SAMPSON nimrod, orion
beloved and *betrayer* delilah
birthplace zorah
black coneflower, echinacea
father manoah
fish arripis, salmon
master capulet
spring enhakkore
weapon jawbone
SAMUCAN *indian* satieno, ugarono
SAMUEL *ancestor* zuph
home ramah
offspring abiah, joel
parent elkanah, hannah, tola

teacher eli
tomb nebi samwil
victim agag, agog
SAMURAI bushi, soldier, vassel, warrior
class shizoku
code bushido
number seven
outcast ronin
SAN bushmen, hemp, sunn
SAN ANTONIO *landmark* alamo
SANATORIUM (See also HOSPITAL.) resort, rest home, retreat, SANITARIUM, spa, station
SANATORY curative, healing, healthful
SAN BENITO samarra
SAN BLAS tule
SAN CARLOS arivaipa
SANCHO PANZO *home* barataria
master don quixote
mule dapple
steed ass
wife teresa
SANCTIFICATION beatification, canonization, consecration, holiness
SANCTIFY anoint, bless, canonize, cleanse, consecrate, dedicate, enshrine, hallow, purify, venerate
SANCTIMONIOUS canting, devout, false, fanatic(al), feigned, holy, hypocritical, moralistic, pharisaical, pietistical, pious, preachy, sacred, saintly, self-righteous
SANCTIMONY affectation, cant, devoutness, falseness, fanaticism, goodiness, goody-goodiness, holiness, hypocrisy, insincerity, lip service, mummery, pharisaism, pietism, piety, piousness, pretense, religiosity, sanctity, self-righteousness, tartuffery, unctuousness, zealotry
SANCTION abet, accredit, allow(ance), amen, approbate, approbation, approval, approve, assent, authority, authorization, authorize, canonize, commission, confirm(ation), consent, countenance, countersign, decree, empower, enactment, encourage, endorse(ment), enforce, fiat, imprimatur, justify, legal-

ize, let, license, oath, okay, okeh, penalty, permission, permit, punishment, ratification, ratify, recognition, subscribe, suffrage, support
SANCTITY awesomeness, awfulness, divinity, godliness, goodness, halidom(e), hallowedness, holiness, inviolability, pureness, purity, righteousness, sacredness, sacrosanctity, sainthood, saintliness, saintship, solemnity, spirituality, unworldliness, venerability
SANCTUARY, SANCTUM adyt(um), altar, ark, asylum, athen(a)eum, bamah, bast, bema, bethel, cabirion, cella, chancel, church (yard), cloister, cover, delubrum, fane, grith, haikal, halidom(e), harbor, haven, heaven, holy of holies, home, monastery, naos, preserve, priory, protection, refuge, retreat, sacrarium, sacrary, safety, security, sekos, shelter, shrine, temple
inner penetralia
lawbreaker's alsatia
wall peribolos
SAND abrade, arena, beach, courage, desert, embassy, gift, grain, gravel, grit, guts, iserine, iserite, message, messenger, mettle, mission, nerve, order, paar, pluck, powder, present, shore, silica, smooth, spirit, tailing, victuals
and clay loam
and gravel dobbin, gard
and stone chad
bank or *bar* barra, batch, beach, char, den(e), dune, flat, hurst, hyrst, reef, shelf, shoal, spit, towhead
bath treatment ammotherapy
boil blowout, spring
borer smelt
brain acervulus, sabulum
brier horse-nettle
-bur nightshade, weed
cherry butter-plum, prunus
cock redshank
colic saburra
colored smalt
comb. amm(o), psamm(o)
dab flounder
darter speck
deauville stucco
deposit beach-cusp
ditch wadi, wady

drift esker, kame

dune areg, barchan, bark(h)an, den(e), drab, medano, seif, towan

eel grig, hornel, launce, sandfish

fine ammochryse, wharp

fish beaked salmon, sea bass

flea amphipod, chigger, chigoe, jigger, screw, scrow

flounder fluke, windowpane

fly phlebotomus

fly bush turmeric

full of arenose

gravel dobbin, gard

grouse attagen, ganga, pintail, pterocles, rocker

hill See *dune*, above.

hog digger, tunnel worker

hole bunker

hopper amphipod, beach-flea

inhabiting arenicolous

in kidney arena

iron-ore iserine

lark plover, sanderling

launce ammodyte, hornel, lant, sandling, scriggle, smelt, wriggle

layer binding

-like arenoid

lily leucocrinum, soaproot

lizard race-runner

lob lugworm

-loving ammophilus

martin bank-swallow

mineral iserine

mist bai

mouse dunlin

myrtle sleekleaf

particles grains, silt

partridge seesee

pear pyrus

pert. See SANDY.

pig badger

pit bunker, point

quartz-containing silex

quick See QUICKSAND.

rat gopher

ridge osar

rocket cressweed, flixweed

sea bottom paar

shark blue dog, bone dog, dogfish

smelt atherine, silversides

snake eryx

spurry tissa

sucker whiting

tableland karoo

trap bunker, mound, obstacle

verbena abronia, chickweed

widgeon gadwall

SAND, GEORGE amandine

lucile aurore dupin, madame dudevant

amours balzac, chopin, de musset, flaubert, heine, liszt, merimee, sandeau

heroine helen, lelia

home nohant

novel consuelo, elle et lui, indiana, jacques, spiridion

offspring maurice, solange

SANDAL alpargata, baxa, buskin, caliga, charuk, clog, espadrille, flat, flipflop, foothold, geta, go-ahead, guaracha, guarache, huarache, huaracho, loafer, moccasin, patten, romeo, rullion, scuff(er), shoe, slipper, talaria, tatbeb, tegua, weejun, zori

episcopal campagus

part thong

tree See SANDALWOOD.

winged talaria

SANDALWOOD adenanthera, akeake, algum, almug, bucida, buckleya, camwood, chandam, chandana, comandra, fawn, flowerfence, iliahi, maire, necklace-tree, olearia, santal, santol, saunders, zelkova

SANDARAC arar, realgar, resin, sindura, tree

pert. thyine

powder pounce

resin tears

tree alerse, arar, callitris, lignum

tree wood alerce, alerse, arar, citron, lignum vitae, thuja, thyine

SANDBAG ambush, attack, ballast, blackjack, coerce, cudgel, hit, set upon, stun, weapon, weight

SANDBAGGER bandit, thief

SANDBLAST clean, depaint, grind, resurface

SANDBLASTER froster

SANDBOX *tree* assacu, hura

tree capsule regma

SANDERLING oxbird

SANDMAN dustman, sleep

SANDPAPER finish, grind, polish, shine, smooth

tree chaparro

SANDPIPER beachrobin, bird, brownie, bullpeep, charook, creaker, curlew, dunlin, fatbird, fiddler, gambet, grayback, haybird, jack(snipe), knot, krieker, leadback, mongler, oxbird,

oxeye, peep, peetweet, pert, philomachus, plover, pume, redleg, redshank, reeve, rockbird, ruff, sanderling, sandpeep, shadbird, snipe, squatter, stib, stint, sweeswee(t), tattler, teeter, telltale, terek, tilter, ti(l)tup, tiptail, triddler, tringa, wader, weet

female reeve

group fling

pectoral brownie, chorook, creaker, fatbird, fernbird, grassbird, grass-snipe, haybird, jacksnipe, pe(e)rt, pisobia, squatter, triddler, warbler

pectoral, pert. tringine, tringoid

small pume, sanderling, stint

spotted peetweet, sweeswee(t), teeter(tail), ti(l)tup, tiptail, tipup

stilt drumstick, frostsnipe

swimming phalarope

SANDSTONE arkose, articulite, berea grit, bluejack, blue-vitriol, braystone, carstone, coconino, coconut, fake, flag, gaize, ganister, graywacke, grit(stone), hazel, itacolumite, kermanshah, medina, psammite, rubstone

block sarsen

flexible articulite, itacolumite

pert. arenilitic

slab comal

SANDSTORM buran, habo(o)b, hab(b)ub, samum, simoom, simoon, tebbad

SANDWICH club, grinder, hero, ho(a)gie, hot dog, insert, interpose, poor boy, submarine, torpedo

hero poor boy

islands hawaii, kanaka

islands discoverer cook

SANDWORT arenaria, longroot, sandweed

SANDY arenaceous, arenarious, arenose, arenous, desert, dusty, eremic, granular, gritty, plucky, psammous, sabuline, sabulous, scot(sman), shifting, shifty, unstable, xanthochroid

SANE adjusted, all there, cogent, compos mentis, cure, good, healthy, judicious, logical, lucid, normal, prudent, rational, realistic, reasonable, right(minded), sage, sain, sapient, sensible, sober, sound, wholesome, wise

SANFORIZE preshrink

SANFORIZED preshrunk, shrunken

SAN FRANCISCO yerba buena

bay island alcatraz, mare, treasure

big 4 crocker, hopkins, huntington, stanford

feature alcatraz, bay(bridge), chinatown, coit tower, fisherman's wharf, fog, golden gate(bridge), lombard street, seven hills

founder juan batista de anza

madam mammy pleasant, sally stanford

nickname frisco

section barbary coast, embarcadero, haight-ashbury, nob hill, north beach, russian hill, telegraph hill

SANG blood, ginseng, herb, panax, sheng, weight

SANGA zebu

SANG-FROID aloofness, aplomb, composure, confidence, cool(ness), detachment, equanimity, indifference, insouciance, nonchalance, phlegm, self-possession, unconcern

SANGUINARIA bloodroot, bloodwort, puccoon, redroot, tellerwort, turmeric, yarrow

SANGUINARY bloodthirsty, bloody, crimson, cruel, gory, murderous, SANGUINE

SANGUINE ardent, assured, bloodred, bloodstone, bloodthirsty, bloody, bright, buoyant, certain, cheerful, confident, crayon, cruel, expectant, ferocious, fond, gory, guze, hematic, hematite, hopeful, murrey, optimistic, plethoric, positive, red, roseate, rosecolored, rosy, ruddy, sardonyx, savage, sunny, sure, warm

SANGUISORBA burnet, pimpernel, poterium

SANGUISUGE bloodsucker, leech

SANHEDRIN assembly, council, court, gerousia

chief abbet(h)din, nasi, rabban

SANICLE allheal, astrantia, bugbane, cohosh, hellebore, lungwort, masterwort, salsify, sanicula, self-heal, snakeroot, snakeweed, wild ginger

SANITARIUM clinic, hospital, resthome, retreat, SANATORIUM, spa

SANITARY beneficial, clean, curative, healing, healthful, hygienic, prophylactic, sterile, uninfected, wholesome

cordon quarantine

SANITATION antisepsis, disinfection, fumigation, hygiene, hygienics, hygiology, sterilization

SANITIZE boil, chlorinate, clean, decontaminate, disinfect, fumigate, hygienize, pasteurize, sterilize, whitewash

SANITY balance, competence, intelligence, lucidity, normalcy, normalness, rationality, reason, saneness, sobriety, soundness, wholesomeness

SANJAK *lord* bey

SAN JUAN *hill hero* pershing, roosevelt

SANKHYA *elements* ether, sky, space

term akasa, guna, prakriti, purusha

SAN MARINO *church* pieve

districts castelli

peak titano

suburb borgo

SANNYASI ascetic, beggar, mendicant, wanderer

SANS without

-culotte jacobin, radical, revolutionary

souci carefree, content, indifferent, nonchalant

SANSEVIERIA bow string hemp, ifa, murva, pangane

SANSKRIT *alphabet* devanagari, kalekah

breath sound visarga

compound words bahuvrihi

deity aditi, aditya, devi, indra, kama, manu, uma, vasu, vayu

dialect pali, prakrit, vedic

dictionary amara-kosha

drama s(h)akuntala

early vedic

epic ramayana

epic character hanuman, sita, yayu

fables panchatantra

grammarian panini

heroine s(h)akuntala, sita

knowledge vidya

language marathi, panjabi

literature s(h)ruti

precept sutra, sutta

scholar saussure

school tol

song gita

soul atman

verse sloka

word mantra

SANTA BARBARA *island* catalina

SANTA CLAUS kris(s) kringle, saint nicholas

helper elf

reindeer blitzen, comet, cupid, dancer, dasher, donder, prancer, vixen

SANTA FE *trail origin* independence

SANTA LUCIA rio de janeiro

SANTA MARIA *tree* balsam, birma, calaba, galba

SANTEE *tributary* wateree

SANTIAGO *airport* pudahuel

founder de valdivia

SANTO holy, sacred, saint

SANTO DOMINGO *leader* dessalines, toussaint l'ouverture

slave leader bugjargal

SANTON dervish, hermit, recluse, saint

SANTORINI atlantis, thera

city akrotiri

SAON *father* hermes

SAO PAULO *resident* paulista

SAO SALVADOR bahia

SAP alveloz, blood, chump, cripple, debilitate, deplete, destroy, disable, dolt, drain, dupe, elan vitale, empty, energy, enervate, enfeeble, entrenchment, essence, excavate, exhaust, fluid, fluxure, fool, humbo, impair, impoverish, juice, keest, latex, lymph, mine, moisture, money, ooze, patsy, rasa, ruin, seve, simpleton, sparkle, substance, trench, tunnel, undermine, unsettle, vigor, vitality, weaken, wreck

beverage tuba

black melaxuma

cavity vacuole

chafer cetonia, euphoria

dried gum, resin, rosin

lose bleed, ooze

poisonous upas

spout spile
sugar maple humbo
SAPAJOU cebus, grison, monkey, sajou, warine
SAPHIE amulet, charm, saffi, safie, talisman
SAPID, SAPOROUS agreeable, appetizing, engaging, flavorful, palatable, relishing, savory, tasty, toothsome, zestful
SAPIDITY flavor, relish, savor, smack, tang, taste
SAPIENCE astuteness, intelligence, judgment, knowledge, sagacity, sense, taste, wisdom
SAPIENT discerning, erudite, judicious, knowing, learned, perspicacious, prudent, sagacious, sage, sane, scholarly, sensible, shrewd, smart, wise
SAPINDALE celastrace, staff-tree, vine
SAPIUTAN animal, anoa, bovine, buffalo, cow
SAPLESS devitalized, dry, exsuccous, feeble, flaccid, insipid, weak, withered, worthless
SAPLING ashplant, greyhound, saple, scob, seedling, shillala, spring(er), staddle, tiller, tunnel, youth
cup tankard
SAPO soap, toadfish
SAPODILLA achras, balata, black-bully, bumelia, chico, chiku, chipozapote, dilly, fruit, gum, mammee, manilkara, naseberry, nisberry, nispero, palaquium, sapota, sapote, sawo, star-apple, tree, zapote
juice chicle
SAPONITE piotine
SAPOR flavor, gusto, relish, savor, taste
SAPOTA matasano, sapodilla
SAPPER digger, engineer, soldier
SAPPHIRA *husband* ananias
SAPPHIRE adamas, astrion, blue, corundum, hummingbird, hyacinth, safir, topaz
berry sweetleaf
gurnard tub
yellow topaz
zodiac sign leo
SAPPHO *consort* bilitis, phaon
home lesbos
SAPPY dumb, feeble, flabby,

fluid, foolish, frim, frum, juicy, luscious, lush, moist, pithy, plump, rainy, sentimental, SILLY, sodden, stupid, succulent, tainted, vital, weak
SAPROPHYTIC metatropic
SAPSAGO cheese, fromage-vert
SAPSAP peperek
SAPSUCKER woodpecker
SAPUCAIA coco(a), kakaral
SAPWOOD alburnum, blea, guayabi, listing, splent, splint
SARACA asak, asok(a), mast-tree
SARACEN arab, corsair, heathen, infidel, MOHAMMEDAN, moor, moslem, nomad, pagan, vandal
battle tours
comfrey ragwort
corn buckwheat
emir balan
king marsiglio, marsilius
knight rogero, ruggiero
leader saladin
SARACENIA adam's-cup, pitcher-plant
SARAEAS *parent* ezerias
son ezra, josedech
SARAGOSSA zaragoza
SARAH *burial site* machpelah
father raguel
husband abraham
maid hagar
son isaac
SARASADAE *father* jacob
son salamiel
SARASVATI benten, shakti, vac(h)
consort brahma
SARATOGA game, michigan, newmarket, springs, trunk
SARAWAK *rajah* james brooke
2nd son tuan-muda
tribe bakatan, murut
SARCASM asteism, attack, banter, borak, brocard, bywipe, censure, criticism, cut, derision, detraction, gibe, irony, jeers, mockery, mordancy, rebuke, reproach, ridicule, satire, taunt, wit
pert. ironical
SARCASTIC acerb(ic), acid, backhanded, biting, bitter, caustic, cutting, cynical, dry, ironic, malicious, mor-

dacious, mordant, sardonic, satiric(al), sharp, witty
SARCLE hoe, weed
SARCOMA cancer, disk, growth, tumor
SARCOPHAGUS casket, coffin, gravestone, limestone, tomb, wine-cooler
roof tegurium
SARD carnelian, chalcedony, sardine, sardious
SARDA bone-eater, bonito, mackeral, skipjack
SARDINE anchovy, bang, clupeid, fish, herring, lile, lour, pilchard, sild
SARDINIA *cheese* pecorino, romano
city alghero, bono(rva), cagliari, iglesias, nuoro, oristano, sassari, thatari
coin carline
greek colony olbia
gulf asinara, cagliari, oristano, orosei, palmas
island maddalena, tavolara
peak gallura, limbara, linas, rasu, serpeddi, vittoria
plant baby-tears
port alghero, bosa, cagliari
prehistoric tower noraghe, nuraghe, nuraghi
province cagliari, nuoro, sassari
river coghinas, lascia, mannu, tirso
wind bentu de soli
SARDONIC acrid, biting, bitter, cynical, deriding, derisive, dry, ironical, jaundiced, malign, mocking, morose, ridiculing, sarcastic, satirical, scornful, sinister, taunting
SARDOU *drama* fedora
heroine tosca
SARGASSO gulfweed, seaweed
SARGON *capital* akkad
SARMENT(UM) branch, cion, cutting, runner, stem, twig
SARONG comboy, kain, kikepa, padadion, pareu
SAROYAN *hero* aram
SARPANITU zirbanit
consort marduk
SARPE girdle, pruner, torque
SARPEDON *ally* pelagon
brother clarus, minos, rhadamanthus, themon
companion atymnius
kingdom lycia

parent deidamia, europa, evander, laodamia, zeus

slayer patroclus

squire thrasymelus

victim alcamaon, tlepolemus

SARPLE bag, bale, cloth, covering, weight, wrapper

SARSAPARILLA dutchman's-pipe, nunnari, shotbush

beverage mead

SARTRE *philosophy* existentialism

work huis clos, nausea, nausee, no exit

SARUM salisbury

SASH band, belt, benn, burdash, casement, casing, chassis, corset, cummerbund, fascia, frame, framing, gate, girdle, obi, saree, sari, scarf, tapis, tobe, tubbeck, waistband, window

bar astragal, muntin(g)

silk benn, obi

weight mouse

SASHAY mince, move, skip, travel

along depart, leave

SASKATCHEWAN *capital* regina

indian cree

river assiniboine

SASS backchat, backtalk, guff(y), lip, sauce

SASSAFRAS cayenne rose, cinnamonwood, daphnandra, laurel, plume-nutmeg, salo(o)p, satinwood, saxifrax

drink saloop

laurel See CALIFORNIA laurel.

leaves gombo-ashish

nut pichurim

oil safrol(e)

tree ague

SASSANID *ruler* ardashir, chosroes, yazdegerd

SASSY See SAUCY.

SATAN (See also DEMON, DEVIL.) eblis, fiend, old nick, shrew, tempter

SATANG *100* bhat

SATANIC bad, cruel, devilish, diabolic, evil, fiendish, hellish, infernal, malevolent, malicious, vicious, wicked

SATARUPA *husband* brahma

SATCHEL bag, cabas, case, etui, etwee, gladstone, grip, keester, reticule, sack, suitcase, valise

SATE appease, assuage, cloy, content, cram, fill, glut, gorge, gratify, indulge, jade, overdose, pall, pamper, SATIATE, satisfy, saturate, slake, stuff, surfeit

SATELLITE (See also ROCKET references.) adherent, appendage, attendant, companion, courtier, dependent, disciple, echo, fan, follower, hanger-on, heeler, henchman, luna, lunet, MOON, orb, partisan, planet, retainer, ROCKET, sectary, shadow, tagtail, trabant, umbriel, underling, votary, wardheeler

communications anik, comsat, domsat, westar

early-warning midas

instrumented ranger

man-made alouette, anna, apollo, ariel, atlas, cosmos, courier, discoverer, early bird, echo, elektron, essa, explorer, faith, friendship, gemini, greb, injun, lanibird, luna, lunik, mariner, mars, mercury, midas, molniya, nimbus, oso, pageos, pioneer, polyot, proton, ranger, relay, samos, snap, sputnik, surveyor, syncom, telstar, tiros, topsi, traac, transit, vanguard, vela-hotel, voskhod, vostok, yantar

path ellipse, solar orbit

series vostok

television tiros

SATI *husband* khnemu, khnum, siva

SATIATE cloy, dawl, glut (ted), gorge, overfill, pall, quat, replete, sade, sate(d), satisfy, saturate, stall, stodge, surfeit

SATIATING fulsome, rich, stodgy

SATIETY abundance, bellyful, dislike, fill, full, ful(l)ness, glut, plethora, repletion, skinful, surfeit

SATIN atlas, camlet(een), charmeuse, coothay, cypress, cyprus, damask, duchess, etoile, fabric, mushru, pekin, silk

bower bird bird of paradise

bush podalyria, saffron

cotton-backed mushru

fin minnow

flower chickweed, honesty, lunaria, saffron, sulla

imitation lustrine, sateen, satinet(te)

pod See *flower,* above.

silk duchess

spar calcite, gypsum

sparrow flycatcher

striped coothay

-weave fabric camlet(een)

SATINLEAF alumroot, caimitillo, tree

SATINWOOD harewood

SATINY fine, glossy, silky, sleek, smooth

SATIRE burlesque, calumniation, caricature, coup de plume, derision, diatribe, farce, grind, humor, imitation, invective, irony, lampoon, mockery, parody, pasquinade, philippic, ridicule, sarcasm, spoof, squib, take-off

SATIRIC(AL) abusive, aristophonic, atellan, biting, bitter, burlesque, caustic, censorious, cutting, cynical, dry, figurative, hudibrastic, ironic(al), mordacious, mordant, poignant, pungent, reproachful, sarcastic, sardonic, scathing, slashing, taunting, wry

SATIRIST burlesquer, caricaturist, juvenal, lampooner, parodist, pasquin(ader), sillograph(er)

SATIRIZE abuse, attack, caricature, censure, criticize, denounce, detract, expose, grind, lampoon, parody, pasquin, ridicule

SATISFACTION amends, apology, assythment, atonement, blood-money, boot, bot(e), comfort, compensation, complacence, complacency, content(ment), delight, duel, ease, fulfillment, gratification, gree, happiness, indemnity, manbote, payment, pleasure, plenty, recompense, redress, remuneration, reparation, requital, resolution, revenge, satiety, selfcomplacence, settlement, smugness, treat, utu

exact avenge, get even

SATISFACTORY acceptable, adequate, all right, ample, appeasing, assuaging, atoning, conclusive, contenting, decent, delightful, delighting, ducky, enough, expiatory, fine, fulfilling, good, gratifying, hunky(dory), jake, neat, nice, okay, pat, satisfying, sufficient, suitable, tolerable

SATISFIED apaid, appeased, believing, certain, chuff, complacent, content(ed), fed, glad(dened), gratified, pacified, paid, pleased, proud, replete, smug, vain, willing

SATISFY acquit, adjust, allay, answer, appay, appease, assuage, assure, atone, cloy, compensate, confirm, content, convince, corroborate, defray, delight, discharge, feast, feed, fulfill, gladden, glut, gratify, gruntle, indemnify, indulge, match, meet, observe, pacify, pay, please, prove, queme, quench, recompense, regale, reimburse, remunerate, repay, requite, reward, sair, sate, satiate, serve, settle, slake, substantiate, suffice, suit, verify

SATRAP despot, governor, mir, official, overlord, prelate, prince, ruler, sultan, tyrant, viceroy

SATTVA goodness, tranquillity, truth

SATURATE absorb, deep, dip, douse, drawk, drench, drunken, fill(ed), imbibe, imbue, immerse, impregnate, infuse, intense, penetrate, permeate, pervade, ret, sate, satiate, satisfy, seethe, slocken, soak(ed), sog, sop, souse, steep, submerge, suffuse, surfeit, waterlog, wet

SATURATED bursting, drunk(en), soaked, sodden, soggy, soppy, spongy, wet

SATURDAY sabbath
night special hand gun
pert. sabbatine

SATUREJA calamint

SATURN cronus, planet, stercutius, vitisator
consort ops
festival consualia, larentalia, paganalia, saturnalia, sementivae feriae
gem turquoise
host janus

metal lead
moon dione, enceladus, hyperion, iapetus, japetus, mimas, phoebe, rhea, tethys, themis, titan
offspring juno, jupiter, neptune, pluto
parent gaea, uranus
rings ansa, moonlets
spirit agiel, bohel, casziel, dacdel, uuchathon
temple treasury aerarium
wife cybele, ops

SATURNALIA carnival, confusion, dissipation, feast, festival, orgy, revel, riot

SATURNINE crabbed, dismal, dour, dull, gloomy, glum, grave, heavy, morose, reserved, serious, silent, sluggish, somber, staid, sulky, sullen, surly, taciturn

SATURNINUS *brother* bassianus
general titus andronicus

SATYAGRAHA gandhism, non-violence

SATYR ampelos, ape, butterfly, capripede, centaur, deity, demigod, faun, lecher, letch, libertine, minotaur, orangutan, panisc, panisk, silenus, woodwose
dance sikinnis
god of dionysus
parent hermes, iphthima

SATYRUS orthagoras

SAUCE (See also *kind, below.*) baste, booze, condiment, crayon, dip, dressing, drink, flavor, flog, gravy, insolence, money, pickle, pulp, rebuke, relish, sass, season(ing), sowl(e), temper
brown bordelaise, espagnole
curry sambal
dish gravyboat
fish alec, bagoong, garum, tartare
garlic gansel, pesto
kind alec, anchovy, a-one, barbecue, bearnaise, bechamel, bercy, bourdelaise, catchup, catsup, chawdron, chili, cream, curry, daube, espagnole, gansel, garum, gascony, genevoise, gravy, hollandaise, ketchup, lear, macedoine, marengo, marinara, matelote, mayonnaise, melba, meuniere, mornay, mustard, nesselrode, newburg, nicoise,

pesto, piquante, ravigote, remo(u)lade, robert, soubise, soy, supreme, tabasco, tartare, tomato, veloute, veloutine, vinaigrette, worcester(shire)
peppery poivrade
thick panada
thickening lear, roux
tomato marinara
white bechamel

SAUCEPAN basin, boiler, posnet, pot, skillet, stewpot

SAUCER caisson, dish, patera, phiale, plate
flying ufo
-shaped acetabuliform

SAUCY airy, arch, audacious, bantam, bold, brash, cavalier, chic, cocket, cocky, copped, coxy, discourteous, disrespectful, donsy, dorty, flip(pant), forward, fresh, frivolous, impertinent, impudent, insolent, intrusive, lippy, malapert, officious, pawky, pert, piet, piquant, pokey, rakish, rude, sanshach, sassy, smart(y), snappy, snippy, sprightly, thwart, volatile

SAUDI ARABIA *capital* riyadh
city alhofuf, damman, dhahran, hail, hofuf, hufuf, jedda, jidda, jubail, mecca, medina, taif, yenbo
coin girsh, gursh, pound, riyal
desert alnafud, dahana, nafud, nefud, nufud, red
gulf aqaba
king abdulaziz, faisal, ibnsaud, khalid
plateau nejd
port jedda, jidda
prince abdullah, fahd, muhammad, sudeiri-seven
region asir, dahna, nejd
weight oke

SAUGER cynoperca, fish, horsefish, perchpike, stizostedion

SAUGHT ease, peace, quiet, reconciliation

SAUK CENTER gopher prairie

SAUL *consort* ahinoam, rizpah
cousin abner
death site bet shean, gilboa
deserted by adnah, ednas

divining woman witch of endor
father hillel, kish, simeon
general abner
ghost elohim
herdsman doeg
kin abiel, azan, ner
offspring abinadab, eshbaal, ishui, jonathan, malchishua, merab, michal
of tarsus paul
sight-restorer ananias
successor david
sword saadia
victim achimelech, ahimelech
SAULT fall, jump, leap, rapid
SAUNA bath(house)
SAUNDERS, RICHARD benjamin franklin
SAUNTER amble, bummel, dacker, dander, dawdle, faffle, idle, lag, linger, loiter, lounge, mog, potter, promenade, ramble, range, roam, rove, ruminate, shool, sidle, snaffle, sta(i)ver, stray, streel, stroll, toddle, toit, traipse, walk, wander
SAUREL bluefish, fish, gascon, mackerel, pompano, scad, skipjack, trachurus, xurel
SAURIAN crocodile, dinosaur, ichthyosaur, lizard, reptile
SAURY billfish, bluefish, gar, gowdnook, longjaw, needlefish, sailfish, scombresox, skipjack, skipper, spearfish
SAUSAGE andouillet(te), balloon, baloney, banger, beagle, blackpot, bologna, boloney, boudin, bratwurst, braunschweiger, cervelat, chorizo, coppa, drisheen, frank(furter), gigot, hotdog, kielbasa, liverwurst, mortadella, pepperoni, polony, rollejee, rollich(i)e, salame, salami, saucisson, sausinger, saveloy, thuringer, wiener, wurst
casing bung
comb. allant(o)
dried cervelat, saveloy
poisoning allantiasis, botulism
pork chorizo
pudding hackin
-shaped allantoid(al), potuliform

SAUTE brown, cook, fry
SAUTERNE sauvignon blanc, semillon, wine
SAUTOIR chain, ribbon
SAVA *tributary* drina
SAVAGE animal, anthropophagite, atrocious, barbarian, barbaric, barbarous, beast, bestial, bloody, brutal, brute, brutish, butcherly, cannibal, cruel, fell, feral, ferine, ferocious, fierce, furious, grim, harsh, hoodlum, hyena(ish), inhuman, intrepid, leonine, lupine, man-eater, mankeen, merciless, pitiless, primeval, primitive, rapacious, ravenous, reckless, relentless, rough, rude, rugged, rustic, solitary, tiger(ish), truculent, uncivilized, uncultivated, unpolished, unrestrained, untamed, untaught, vicious, violent, voracious, war-like, warragal, wild, wilroun, yahoo
as a bear, tiger
comb. agrio
island niue
island people niuan
noble indian
SAVAGERY barbarism, brutality, cruelty, ferocity, fierceness, fury, sadism, violence, wildness
SAVANNA campo, grassland, plain, sabana
bird seriema
blackbird ani
lands lalang
wattle fiddlewood
SAVANT bhat, bookman, pedant, pundit, sage, scholar, solon, wiseman
SAVE accumulate, avoid, bank, bar, but, can, conserve, cure, deliver, dry, economize, except, exclude, free, freeze, have, heal, hoard, hold, hooverize, husband, keep, last, liberate, maintain, prepare, preserve, prevent, protect, ransom, reclaim, recover, redeem, release, rescue, reserve, retain, retrench, safeguard, salvage, satisfy, scrape, scrimp, shield, skimp, spare, stint, stockpile, store, tin, unless, warrant
SAVED redeemed, regenerate, rescued, unspent

SAVIN(E) cedar, evergreen, heath, juniper, sabine, tree
SAVING careful, chary, compensating, economic(al), economizing, economy, except(ing), frugal, offsetting, preservation, redeeming, rescue, reserving, sparing, thrift(y)
plan christmas club, menage
tree savin
SAVINGS account, addlin(g)s, fat, nest-egg, reserve, stockpile
SAVIOUR christ, jesus, lord, messiah, nazarene, redeemer, soter
SAVITRI *husband,* brahma
SAVOIR-FAIRE address, adroitness, aplomb, cleverness, confidence, courtesy, dignity, discrimination, ease, experience, facility, grace, nonchalance, poise, readiness, self-possession, skill, sophistication, tact, worldliness
SAVOIRE-VIVRE breeding, manners
SAVOLA cutlass, fish, milkfish
SAVOR appreciate, atmosphere, aura, character (istic), degust(ate), delight, enjoy(ment), experience, feeling, flavor, gout, gratification, gratify, gusto, learn, like, odor, perceive, perception, please, pleasure, quality, relish, reputation, repute, sample, sapidity, scent, season, sip, smack, smell, spice, stamp, suit, tang, taste, tinge, tone, understand, zest
SAVORLESS flat, insipid
SAVORY agreeable, ambrosial, appetizing, aromatic, delectable, delicious, delightful, flavorful, flavorsome, good, gustable, gusty, likable, luscious, mellow, merry, mint, nectareous, nice, palatable, piquant, pleasing, relishing, rich, salty, sapid, saporous, scrumptious, sipid, smervy, tasty, toothsome, yummy
SAVOY *family castle* chillon
SAVVY comprehension, intelligence, know, skill, understand(ing), wisdom
SAW (See also *kind,* below.) adage, aphorism, apothegm,

axiom, bow, buck, bur(r), byword, cliche, command, cut(ter), decree, dictate, discourse, epigram, fiddle, gnome, jangle, maxim, motto, proverb, rede, rend, rumor, salve, saying, scear, slice, slogan, speech, statement, tale, talk, tool, word
blade web
circular bur(r), buzzsaw, dapper, edger, trimmer
comb. serri
crosscut briar
cut kerf
cyclindrical crown, trepan, trephine
edge safe
fern bungwall, dygal, hardfern
gate frame
groove kerf
kerf skaff
kind back, briar, buck, edger, fret, jig, pit, rip, scroll, serra, stadda, trepan, trephine, trimmer, whip
-like serrated
logs snore
part redan, serra, tine, tooth
surgical trepan, trephine
-toothed serrate(d)
2-bladed stadda
SAWAIORI *language* See POLYNESIA *language*.
SAWBACK sierra
SAWBELLY alewife
SAWBILL merganser, motmot
SAWBONES doctor, surgeon
SAWBUCK ten dollars, tenspot
SAWDUST coom(b), dregs, filings, scobs
SAWFISH batoid(es), combfish, pristis, ray, sier
SAWFLY cephid
SAWHORSE buck, jack, rack, trestle
SAWMILL rasper
SAWNEY foolish, oaf, scot (sman), silly, vacillating, weak, zany
SAWWHET bird, owl
SAWYER beetle, logger, logman, lumberman, pitman, weta, woodcutter
SAWYER, TOM *brother* sid
friend huckleberry finn
girl friend becky thatcher
SAX dagger, horn, scimitar, sword, tool
horn althorn, alto, baritone, barytone, tuba

SAXIFRAGE astilbe, badan, bauera, bennet, breakstone, burnet, pearlwort, rockfoil, self-heal, sengreen, seseli, stonebreak
SAXON sassenach
chief horsa
coin sceat
deity ear, frea, hermensul, hertha, odin, thor, tiu, tiwaz, tuesco, woden
earl godwin
epic heliand
giant miller
idol termagant
king alfred, egbert, harold, horsa, ina, ine, otto
lady godiva, rowena
language plattdeutsch
pert. ingveonic
serf esne
swineherd gurth
warrior thane, thegn
SAXONY cloth, flannel, wool, yarn
native sorb, wend
SAXOPHONE alto, sopranino, tenor
base tuba
SAY advise, affirm, allege, allow, announce, answer, articulate, assay, assert, asseverate, assume, attempt, aver, bid, blabber, bucket, call, carp, check, cite, communicate, declare, deem, deliver, direct, emit, enunciate, express(ion), fabric, impart, import, indicate, lip, mantle, present, pronounce, quethe, recite, relate, remark, repeat, report, signify, silk, sound, speak, speech, state(ment), suppose, taste, tell, test, utter, verbalize, vocalize, voice, wool, word
again rehash, reiterate, repeat
casually remark
no deny, negate, nick, nix, prohibit, refuse
repeatedly decantate
-so assertion, assurance, authority, command, dictum, discretion, order
uncle surrender
under oath depose, swear
yes agree, consent
SAYING(S) adage, aphorism, apothegm, agrapha, assertion, axiom, byword, declaration, dit, epigram, logia, maxim, mot(to), proverb,

quip, rede, saw, statement, tag, utterance, word
apt bon mot
clever mot, quip, sally
collection ana, gnomology
concise epigram
distinguishing shibboleth
dogmatic dictum, levitism
jesus agrapha
obscure enigma, puzzle
trite bromide, cliche, platitude, saw
SAYONARA See GOODBYE.
SCAB apostate, blackleg, blackneb, blemish, crust, eschar, fink, incrustation, mange, rascal, rat(ter), roin, schab, scissorbill, scoundrel, strikebreaker
SCABBARD holster, integument, pilcher, quiver, scaleboard, sheath, tsubas
-fish cutlassfish, frostfish, hiku, para
put in sheathe
tip boterol(l), crampit
trimming chape
SCABBY bad, base, blotched, contemptible, flaky, low, mangy, mean, paltry, roinish, scald, shabby, spotty, stingy, worthless
-head hedge-parsley
SCABIES itch, mange, psora, tinea
SCABIOUS blacksoap, bluecap, bundweed, cow parsnip, flaky, fleabane, horseweed, knapweed, premorse, ragwort, scabby
SCABROUS asperous, difficult, flaky, harsh, knotty, lecherous, risque, rough, rugged, salacious, scabby, scaly, scurfy, sultry, uneven, unmusical
SCAD akule, cigarfish, goggle-eye, goggler, peat, quiaquia, saurel, scald, skate, sod, xurel
SCADDLE confusion, cruel, depart, fierce, injury, mischief, mischievous, nervous, noxious, skittish, thievish, timid, wild
SCADS gobs, heaps, masses, money, lots, oodles, oodlins, plenty, quantity, tons
SCAFF beg, food, provide, rabble, riffraff, sponge
SCAFFOLD(ING) bridge, cage, catasta, dais, dock,

easel, gallery, gallows, gibbet, hayloft, hoarding, loft, pegma, platform, stage, staging

SCALAWAG imp, momzer, pony, rascal, rogue, runt, scamp, scapegrace, sculpin
ally carpetbagger

SCALD bard, blanch, burn, contemptible, cook, dodder, excite, gleeman, inflame, jongleur, leep, minnesinger, minstrel, poet(aster), rhymer, rhymester, scabby, scad, scop, scorch, scurf(y), scurvy, sear, shabby, singe, steam, torment, troubadour, trouvere, vex, worry

SCALDING boiling, burning, hot, torrid

SCALE (See also SCALES.) 3 cup, hut 4 bowl, brix, coat, film, husk, leaf, marc, pale, pare, part, peel, port, rule, rung, scab, shed, size, soar 5 bract, clean, climb, flake, gamut, gauge, layer, lepis, mount, palea, palet, pelog, pelta, piece, plate, range, ratio, scurf, scute, shive, spill, weigh 6 ascend, attack, caudal, dander, extent, fornix, imbrex, ladder, lamina, perule, putnam, rament, reduce, rustre, series, slough, spread, squama, tartar, weight 7 balance, clamber, coating, compare, elytron, humeral, lamella, landing, measure, paleola, reaumur, scatter 8 analemma, covering, disperse, escalade, lecanium, lodicule, ramentum, separate, squamate, standard, urostege 9 exfoliate 10 desquamate, proportion 12 incrustation
balance pan
beetle tiger
black lecanium, oleae, saissetia
board scabbard
bony scutum
comb. lepido, lepis, pholido, pholis, squami
covered with leprose, scutate, scutellate, squamose, squamous
down decrease, reduce
duck merganser, sheldrake
fern ceterach
1st degree tonic

fish ganoid, haddock, hake, pollack
graduated rete, vernier
insect bark louse, coccid
insect study coccidology
leaves induviae
-like leprose, scurfy
major gamut
measuring See SCALES.
moss hepatica, liverwort
note See MUSIC *note.*
pan basin
small squamella
without alepidote, esquamate

SCALES balance, dander, libra, ramenta, scorpio's claws, trone, vernier, weigher
pan basin

SCALETAIL squirrel

SCALLOP bivalve, coquille, crena, dag, doughboy, indent, mollusk, notch, pecten, pectinid, pink, queen, quin, squash, squin
-edged crenate, invected

SCALP cheat, cut, defeat, denude, head, market, peel, profit, rob, scabble, scrape, sieve, sift, skull, speculate, toupee, trophy, wig
disease alopecia, dandruff, favus, porrigo, scurf
doily toupee, wig

SCALPEL arthrotome, blade, dissect, knife, lancet

SCALPER agent, scauper, speculator, ticket-broker, trader

SCALPLESS bald

SCALY base, despicable, flaky, horny, lamellar, lamelliform, laminar, lepidote, leprose, low, mean, paleate, perulate, pityroid, scabrous, scutate, squamate, squamose, squamous, stingy, tegular

SCAM scorch, spot, stain

SCAMANDER meander, menderes, wander, xanthus
consort idaea
offspring callirrhoe, teucer
parent oceanus, tethys

SCAMANDRIUS astyanax
parent andromache, hector, strophius
slayer menelaus

SCAMBLE botch, collect, litter, mess, remove, scramble, seize, shamble, shove, snatch, trample

SCAMBLING brawling, dis-

orderly, irregular, makeshift, quarrelsome, scattered

SCAMELL godwit

SCAMP bacalao, blackguard, booger, bugger, dart, deserter, goodfornothing, graze, hallion, hessian, highwayman, imp, knave, nickum, offscouring, peasant, rammack, rascal, rip, roam, rogue, scal(l)awag, scant, scapegrace, scoundrel, scubber, sharper, skellum, skimp, slight, snoozer, sorrel, spalpeen, stint, swindler, thief, touch, tyke, vagabond, varlet, villain, wander, widdifow

SCAMPER brattle, chevy, chivvy, depart, flight, fly, frolic, hasten, hie, hurry, race, run, rush, scoot, scud, scurry, skedaddle, skitter, speed, trot

SCAN apprehend, audit, browse, consider, contemplate, criticize, examine, glance, inspect, judge, look(at), metricize, notice, observe, overlook, perceive, peruse, pore over, regard, remark, scrutinize, skim, skip over, study, survey

SCANCE blame, comment, glance, glitter, shine

SCANDAL affair, affront, backbiting, calumny, clash, crime, defamation, defame, detraction, discredit, disgrace, dishonor, disrepute, gossip, ignominy, indignity, infamy, insult, odium, offense, opprobrium, outrage, rumor, scanmag, shame, sin, slander, talk, vice, wrong
political teapot dome, watergate, xyz affair

SCANDALIZE defame, disgrace, malign, offend, revile, shock, slander, traduce, vilify

SCANDALMONGER busybody, clat, gossip, meddler, tattle-tale

SCANDALOUS derogatory, disgraceful, dishonorable, evil, furciferous, ignominious, infamous, libelous, low, notorious, offensive, opprobrious, shameful, shocking, terrible, ugly, unholy

SCANDENT climbing

SCANDINAVIA(N) dane, finn, geat, lapp, lochlin, norse(man), northman, norwegian, ostman, ros, rus, swede, varangian, viking
airline sas
alphabetical character rune
apollo balder, baldur
bard sagaman, scald, skald
bay fiord, fjord
boar, mythological saehrimnir
buffet smorgasbord
chief jarl
coin krona, skilling
division amt
drink aquavit, glog
dwarf troll
earth mother hertha
elf norn, verdandi
explorer eric
fairy ellefolk, ellemaid, nis(se)
fertility god njord
freedman hauld, leysing
fruit cloudberry, lingonberry
giant jotum, mimir, troll, ymer, ymir
giantess skuld, urth, wyrd
goblin nis(se)
gods See AESIR and NORSE references.
grin fleer
heaven asgard
heritable land odal, odel
hero's home valhalla
inlet fjord
king atli
land odal
language norse
legend edda, saga
legendary creature kraken, nis(se), troll
legislature thin(g)
liquor akvavit, aquavit
magistrate amtman
measure alen, ass, bismerpund, carat, centner, last, lisp(o)und, lod, mark, mylast, ort, pund, shippound, ska(a)lpund, skeppund, skibslast, skieppe, skippund, sten, untz, vog
mock fleer
money krone
musician scald, skald
mythical hero volund
narrator sagaman
navigator eric, lief
nobleman jarl
norn skuld, urd, verdandi
official amtman
olympus asgard
pert. norse

pirate viking
plateau fjeld
poem edda, saga
poet scald, skald
prince rurik
prophetess vala
range kjolen
rulers ros, rus, varangians
sailor klosh
sea monster kraken
ship aese
strife god loki
sun god frey, ing
thunder god thor
trumpet lure
venus frey(j)a
weight (See also *measure*, above.) lisp(o)und, lod
wisdom god mimir
SCANDIUM *source* monazite, thortveitite, wiikite
SCANNING analysis, audit, examination, inspection, scrutiny, study, surveillance
pattern grid
SCANSORES cuckoos, parrots, toucans, trogons, woodpeckers
SCANT brief, chary, cut down, distress, fail, few, geason, hardly, inadequate, infrequent, insufficient, jimp, lacking, lean, little, meager, meagre, meet, narrow, niggardly, parsimonious, poor, reduce, scamp, scantle, SCANTY, scarce(ly), scarcity, short, shy, skimp(y), skinny, slight, small, sparing, sparse, stingy, stint, straiten, thin, wanting, weak, without
comb. oligo
SCANTLE fail, gauge, lessen, partition, reduce, restrict, SCANT, slate, stint
SCANTLING abridgment, bolster, caliber, draft, fil(l)et, grade, joist, lath, limit, lumber, measure (ment), modicum, outline, portion, remnant, ribband, sample, SCANT, size, sketch, specimen, standard, stud(ding), trestle
SCANTY bare, deficient, exiguous, frugal, gnede, lacking, lank, lean, meager, narrow, parsimonious, poor, rare, SCANT, scranny, scrimp(y), skimp(y), slender, slim, spare, sparse, thin
SCAPE escapade, fault,

freak, peduncle, scene, shaft, slip, snipe, stem, view
SCAPEGOAT aunt sally, azazel, dupe, fall guy, goat, gull, patsy, sacrifice, substitute, victim, whipping-boy
SCAPEGRACE black-sheep, goodfornothing, incorrigible, madcap, profligate, rascal, reprobate, rogue, scal(l)awag, scamp, varlet, villain
SCAPEL caulicle
SCAPOLITE dipyre, ekebergite, marialite, sarcolite
SCAPULA blade(bone), omoplate, platebone, shoulderblade, tegula
part acromion, fossa
SCAR arr, blemish, catface, chink, cicatrice, cicatrix, cinder, cliff, clinker, crack, crag, defect, disfigure (ment), fester, flaw, hurt, injury, keloid, mar(k), parrotfish, pockmark, raddle, rock, seam, shard, shore, shy, slag, slit, stigma, wild, wound
-bearing cicatricose, hiliferous
-like cicatricial, uloid
ornamental keloid
tissue acestoma, uloid
SCARAB(AEUS) ateuches, beetle, cetonia, charm, fetish, nobody, sap-chafer
symbol of khepera
SCARAMOUCH buffoon, clown, fool, ne'er-do-well, poltroon
SCARCE bare(ly), close, dear, deficient, exiguous, frugal, geason, infrequent, insufficient, occasional, parsimonious, rare, scant(y), scrimp(y), shott, skimp(y), slack, sparing, sparse, sporadic, stingy, uncommon, unusual, wanting
comb. spano
SCARCELY barely, hardly, imperceptible, infrequently, jimp, merely, only just, rarely, scant(ly), seldom, slightly, uneaths, unnethe, vix, weneth
SCARCITY dearth, famine, inadequacy, infrequency, insufficiency, lack, need, parsimony, paucity, penury, poverty, rareness, rarity, want(ing)
SCARE affray, affright,

alarm, appall, awe, boof, bree, cow, crisis, daunt, dismay, dread, faze, fear, fleg, flig, fright(en), gliff, gloff, intimidate, panic, scarify, shock, shoo, shy, spook, startle, terrify, terror(ize)
up collect, discover, find, locate
SCARECROW bogeyman, boggard, boggart, bogglebo, bogle, bogy, bugaboo, bugbear, deadman, dudder, dudman, effigy, ghost, goblin, guy, hobgoblin, hodmandod, jackstraw, malkin, maumet, moggy, ogre, shail, shawfowl, shewel, specter, spectre, tattiebogle, terror
SCARED afeary, afraid, frightened, goosey, spooked, terrified, upset
SCAREMONGER alarmist
SCARF abnet, ascot, babushka, band(anna), barbe, benefice, boa, burdash, cabaan, claudent, cointise, cormorant, cravat, cymar, dopatta, fascinator, fichu, flense, foulard, liripipe, liripoop, lungi, mantilla, muffetee, muffler, neckerchief, necktie, nubia, overlay, puggree, reboso, rebozo, saree, sari, sash, sautoir, screen, shawl, slendang, stole, tapalo, tie, tippet, turban, unite, uparna, veil, wrap
bird cormorant, shag
clerical abnet, maniple, rabat, stole
feather boa
fur stole
joint boxing
lace barbe
long abnet
military sash
prayer tallis, tallith
triangular fichu
SCARFSKIN cuticle, epidermis
SCARIFY assail, cut, flay, frighten, lacerate, notch, scar(e), scratch, torment
SCARLET bawdy, crimson, flagrant, kermes, lewd, offensive, pink, red, ruby, salacious, tuly, unchaste, whorish
balm oswego tea
-berry bittersweet
dye tuly

fever canker-rash
haw hawthorn
ibis guara
letter, author hawthorne
letter, character arthur dimmesdale, hester prynne, pearl, roger chillingworth
lychnis fireball, nonesuch
pimpernel bird's-tongue, eyebright
tanager firebird, redbird
will, friend robin hood
SCARP cliff, cut, declivity, descent, incline, precipice, slope
SCARPIA *slayer* tosca
SCART cormorant, mark, niggard, puff, scrap(e), scratch
SCARTH rock, scar, sherd
SCARY alarming, anxious, eerie, eery, frightening, frightful, ghostly, spooky, timid, uncanny, weird
SCAT away, beat it, begone, blow, buffet, burst, get away, git, out, rain, scatter, scoot, scram, shower, smash, tax, tribute, vamoose
SCATHE assail, blast, cost, damage, denounce, harm, hurt, injure, injury, misfortune, scorch, sear, wither
SCATHEFUL harmful, hurtful, pernicious
SCATHING acerb(ic), acrid, acrimonious, biting, blistering, burning, caustic, cutting, ferocious, fierce, incisive, injuring, mordacious, mordant, savage, scorching, searing, severe, tonguelashing, trenchant, truculent, wounding
SCATTER begone, bespatter, bestrew, broadcast, cast, circulate, circumfuse, deal(out), defeat, derange, diffuse, disband, discard, disgregate, disject, disparple, dispel, dispense, disperse, disseminate, dissipate, distract, distribute, divide, flee, fling, fritter, issue, litter, propagate, rout, scamble, scoad, separate, shed, shower, skail, sow, sparple, spray, spread, spreng, sprinkle, squander, strew, strow, swatter, ted, throw, toss, waste, winnow
SCATTERBRAIN addlepate, clown, featherbrain, feath-

erpate, flibbertigibbet, fool, giddyhead, harebrain, shatterpate
SCATTERBRAINED barmy, dizzy, emptyheaded, flighty, frivolous, frothy, gaga, giddy, rattlepated, shuttlewitted, thoughtless, throughother, volatile, witless
SCATTERED chaotic, diffuse, disconnected, disheveled, dispersed, disrupted, distracted, divided, erratic, fugitive, infrequent, irregular, isolated, open, rambling, seme, separated, sparse, sparsile, sporadic, spotted, straggling
comb. laxi
SCATTERING dash, diaspora, few, sprinkle, sprinkling, strewing
SCATTERLING vagrant, wastrel
SCAUP *duck* blackhead, bluebill, cannonball, diver, ducker, dunbird, grayback, myroca, pochard, shuffler, widgeon
SCAUT push, scrape, shove, trample
SCAVAGE duty, scavenge(r), scewing, tax, toll
SCAVENGER bhangi, bhungi, bungy, corydora, halalcor, mehtar, rat, saprophyte, scaffie, streetcleaner, sweep, vulture
SCAW headland, promontory, scall, scurf(y)
SCENARIO libretto, outline, play, plot, script, synopsis
SCEND heave, lift, pitch
SCENE act(ion), arena, background, curtain, diorama, display, drama, drapery, episode, event, exhibition, exterior, interior, landscape, locale, locality, outburst, painting, panorama, photo, picture, place, prospect, quarrel, representation, scape, seascape, setting, show, sight, site, spectacle, sphere, spot, stage, surroundings, tableau, theater, view, vista
active beehive
behind backstage
last curtain, epilogue, finale
part take
-shifter grip
SCENERY decor, display,

drop, flat, landscape, panorama, set(ting), show, surroundings, view

piece backcloth, drop, flat

SCENIC dramatic, graphic, panoramic, picturesque, theatrical

view scape

SCENT air, aroma, aura, bouquet, breath, clew, clue, detect, effluvium, emanation, essence, flair, flavor, fragrance, fumigate, hint, incense, inkling, intimation, marechal, nidor, nose, odor, pastille, perceive, perfume, redolence, savor, sign, smell, sniff, snuff, spoor, stench, tang, track, trail

artificial drag

-bag perfumer, sachet

scale androconium

scatter cense

SCENTED aromatic, fragrant, musky, perfumed, odorate, odorous, olent, redolent, smelling, spicy, tangy

SCEPHRUS *brother* limon

father tegeates

slayer limon

SCEPTER, SCEPTRE authority, baton, emblem, ferula, mace, rod, sovereignty, staff, verge, wand

SCHAFKOPF game, sheepshead

term spadilla, spadille

SCHEDIUS *beloved* helen

parent hippolyte, iphitus

SCHEDULE action, activity, agenda, agendum, bill, blueprint, book, budget, calendar, canon, card, catalog(ue), cedula, docket, engage, inventory, line-up, list, menu, muster, panel, plan, poll, program(me), prospectus, register, roll, roster, rota, routine, schema, set, slate, table, tabulate, tariff, time(table)

SCHELLY gwyniad, skelly

SCHELM rascal, rogue

SCHEMA diagram, form, outline, plan, representation, SCHEME

SCHEME aim, angle, arrangement, artifice, aspire, cabal, cadre, cast, chart, complex(ity), complot, concoct(ion), conspiracy, conspire, contrivance, con-

trive, design, device, devise, diagram, diversion, draft, enterprise, epitome, expedient, figure, form, hookup, imagine, intend, intrigue, knavery, lark, machination, manipulate, method, network, ordering, outline, plan, plot, policy, practice, program, project, proposal, propose, proposition, purpose, rede, semblance, shift, sketch, stratagem, strategy, system, table, tactics, tamper, theory, trick, web

delusive bubble

dishonest bamboozle, cozen, hoax, shift

SCHEMER artist, conniver, conspirator, conspirer, designer, engineer, fainaiguer, figaro, finagler, intriguer, machiavellian, machinator, maneuverer, plotter, projector, wirepuller

SCHEMING artful, calculating, crafty, deceitful, designing, fetching, intriguing, planful, tricky

SCHILLER *work* die rauber, don carlos, joan of arc, maria stuart, piccolomini, the robbers, wallenstein, wilhelm tell

SCHISM breach, break, clique, disagreement, discord, dissent, disunion, division, faction, rent, rift, scission, sect, separation, split

SCHISMATIC apostate, dissenter, heretic, nonconformist, sectarian, sectary

SCHIST ampelite, hornblende, itabarite, mica, mineral, mylonite, ollenite, phyllite, slate, stone

opal porodine

SCHISTOSOME bilharzia, blood-fluke, trematode

SCHIZOCARP achenodium, cremocarp, fruit, regma

parts cocci

SCHIZOPHRENIA catatony, insanity, psychosis, split personality

having schizoid

syndrome catatonia

SCHIZOPHRENIC insane, psychotic

SCHLACK, SCHLAG shrew, slob, yenta

SCHLEMIE(H)L caspar milquetoast, chump, fall-guy, fool, gull, loser, melamed,

misfit, patsy, pipsqueak, s(c)hmo, s(c)hnook, shnuk, simpleton

S(C)HLEP, SHLEPPER beggar, drag, drip, jerk, pull, thief, unkempt

SCHLESWIG-HOLSTEIN *capital* kiel

SCHLOCK cheap, inferior, junk, trash(y)

SCHLOOMP drag, drip, kiss off, shlump, shuffle, slattern

SCHMALTZ banality, butter, corn, emotionalism, fat, good luck, luxury, pathos, sentimentality, wealth

S(C)HMO, S(C)HMUCK booby, butt, cad, dope, fallguy, goat, jerk, oaf, ornament, schlemiel, slob, sob

SCHNEIDER beat, blank, overwhelm, shut out, tailor

S(C)HNOOK, SHNUK See SCHLEMIE(H)L.

SCHNORREN beg, borrow, panhandle

SCHNORRER bargainer, beggar, bum, cheapskate, chiseler, drifter, indigent, mooch(er), panhandler

SCHNOZZLE nose, proboscis

SCHOLAR academician, beauclerc, bhat, bibliosoph, bookman, classicist, clerk, disciple, gaon, humanist, illuminate, imam, lamdem, latinist, learner, literate, litterateur, lituratus, master, maulana, pandit, pedagogue, pedant, precisionist, pundit, pupil, sabora, sage, savant, schoolboy, student, taberdar, thaumaste

group academy, college, ulema, university

-poet goliard

servant femulus

SCHOLARLY abstruse, academic, bookish, collegiate, educated, educational, erudite, exact, learned, literary, literate, pedagogic(al), philomathic, precise, profound, recondite, scholastic, schooled, studious

SCHOLARSHIP aid, allowance, award, bibliomania, bibliophilism, bibliotry, bookiness, bookishness, bursary, burse, culture, education, erudition, fellowship, grant, information, instruction, intellectualism, knowledge, learning, letters, literacy, lore, pedantry, stipend

SCHOLASTIC academic, classical, collegiate, conventional, curricular, educational, formal(ist), learned, liberal, pedant(ic), schoolman, student, studious, versed

SCHOLIAST annotator, commentator

SCHOLIUM annotation, axiom, comment, explanation, note, remark

SCHOOL academy, adherents, alma mater, association, athenaeum, belief, bevy, cheder, circle, class, coach, college, company, covey, cultivate, debate, direct, disciples, discipline, doctrine, drill, drove, ecole, educate, escuela, exercise, faculty, flock, followers, form, gaggle, gallery, gam, gang, group, guide, gymnasium, heder, herd, institute, institution, instruct, ism, lead, lycee, lyceum, manege, multitude, order, pack, palaestra, persuasion, phrontistery, portico, practice, prep, punish, reprove, schule, scuola, sect, seminary, shoal, style, swarm, tame, teach, tol, train, tutor, university, varsity, yeshibah, yeshiva(h)

absence hooky
bench form
boys' prep
elementary grades, primary
fee tuition
-fellow comrade, condisciple
grounds campus, quad
group nea, pta
hall aula
honor society arista, ephebian
kind elementary, finishing, grade, gymnasium, high, lycee, military, prep(aratory), primary, secondary, trade, vocational
marine gam, shoal
military academy
official dean, headmaster, preceptor, principal, scholarch, superintendent
orthodox hanafi
pert. academic, pedantic
reform borstal

religious aljama, parochial, seminary, yeshiva
riding academy, manege
secondary academy, colegio, gymnasium, high, lycee, lyceum, prep, realschule, vocational
shark tope(r)
task assignment, composition, homework, lesson, pensum, prep, problem
term quarter, semester, trimester
vedanta advaita

SCHOOLBOOK abc, atlas, cocker, geography, grammar, hornbook, manual, primer, reader, reciter, speller, text

SCHOOLBOY clergion, fag, scug

SCHOOLED educated, lettered, literate, taught, trained

SCHOOLING breeding, culture, discipline, education, grounding, instruction, reprimand, reproof, tuition

SCHOOLMAN classicist, divine, scholastic, student

SCHOOLMASTER akhoond, akhun(d), beak, birchman, caji, caxi, dominie, dux, head, instructor, kho(d)ja, orbilius, pedagog(ue), pedant, professor, scholarch, teacher, tutor

SCHOONER ballahoo, ballahou, boat, glass, jack, measure, mug, pinky, pungey, ship, tern, vessel
builder andrew robinson
3-masted ram, tern
5-masted quint

SCHOPENHAUER *philosophy* pantheism

SCHRIK fright, panic

SCHUBERT *song cycle* die winterreise

SCHUMAN *songs* dichterliebe

SCIATICA boneshave, boneshaw, ischialgia, neuralgia, neuritis

SCIENCE ability, art, canon, knowledge, learning, lore, mathesis, ology, proficiency, scholarship, skill, study, technics, technology, trade, vocation
comb. ancy, aphy, echny, emy, ery, etry, graphy, ics, ion, ography, ology, omy,

onomy, opy, phy, sophy, try, ure
dismal economics
domestic cooking, home economics
fiction award hugo
god nebo, t(h)oth
group thinktank
industrial technology
legal law
military strategy
moral ethics
natural biology, botany, physics
occult alchemy, astrology, magic
physical astronomy, chemistry, geology, meteorology, minerology, petrology, physics
political metapolitics
principle logic
religious theology
social civics, economics, sociology

SCIENT(IAL) able, capable, competent, knowing, skilled, skillful

SCIENTIFIC accurate, efficient, exact, objective, realistic, skillful, sound, technical, thorough
advance breakthrough
term, comb. alis, anum, anus, aris

SCIENTIST authority, expert, polemicist, researcher, savant

SCILICET namely, to wit, videlicet, viz

SCILLA bluebell, bluebottle, jacinth, sea-onion, squill, wood-hyacinth

SCIMITAR billhook, foil, khepesh, rapier, saber, s(e)ax, sword, tulwaur, turk, weapon
-shaped acinaciform

SCIND cleave, cut, part, rinse, sunder

SCINTILLA atom, bit, glimmer, glitter, iota, jot, particle, ray, scrap, shadow, spark, tittle, trace, whit

SCINTILLATE coruscate, flash, glance, gleam, glint, glisten, glister, glitter, joke, shimmer, snap, spark(le), twinkle

SCINTILLATION flash, gleam, glitter, quip, spark (le), twinkle, twinkling

SCION branch, bud, child, cion, clave, cutting, cyon,

descendant, graft, heir, imp, offshoot, offspring, part, rod, root, shoot, slip, son, sprig, strout, twig

SCIPIO africanus
consort aemilia
enemy fulvius, hannibal
friend caius-laelius

SCIRON *consort* chariclo
daughter endeis
grandson peleus, telamon
kin aeacus, cychereus
slayer theseus

SCIRPUS akaakai, bulrush, sedge

SCISSION cutting, dissension, dividing, division, split(ting)

SCISSOR clip, cut, shear, trim
-tooth carnassial

SCISSORBILL know-nothing, scab, skimmer

SCISSORS blades, clipper, secateur, shears, snips
blade bill
grinder goatsucker
pruning secateurs
-shaped forficiform

SCISSURE break, cleft, cut, division, opening, split

SCIURUS See SQUIRREL.

SCLAFF blow, fall, shoe, slap, slipper

SCLATCH botch, daub, splash

SCLERITE axillary, epimeron, labium, plagula, planta, torma

SCLEROSIS hardening, induration

SCOB box, chest, desk, gag, peg, rod, sapling, splint

SCOBS leftovers, powder, raspings, remainder

SCOFF carp, curse, deride, disbelieve, discount, discredit, disdain, doubt, eat, fleer, flout, food, gibe, gird, gleek, gybe, jeer, jibe, leer, meal, mock(ery), plunder, rail, ridicule, scorn, scout, sneer, steal, taunt, twit
-law See CRIMINAL.

SCOFFER abderite, clown, hickscorner, jester, mocker, skeptic

SCOLD abuse, admonish, barge, bawl out, beat, berate, betongue, blame, brawl, bullyrag, call(down), callet, camp(le), cant, carp (er), castigate, catamaran, cavil(er), censor, censure, channer, chastise, chide, criticize(r), ding, execrate,

exprobate, faultfind(er), fight, flay, frab, frondeur, fuss, harpy, harridan, hazen, jaw, lecture, momus, nag, objurgate, rag, rail, rally, rant, rate, rebuke, redd, reprimand, reproach, reprove, revile, rixatrix, shrew, skin, slate, targe, tatter, tax, termagant, threap, threep, trimmer, trounce, twit, upbraid, vilify, virago, vituperate, vixen, wig, wrangle, xanthippe, yap

SCOLDING admonishment, admonition, backslanging, blessing, calling, carritch, castigation, censure, chiding, comeuppance, dirdum, dressing, exprobration, hell, jobation, lecture, rag(ging), raking, rebuke, reprimand, reproach, reproof, reproval, tongue-lashing, twit, upbraiding, wigging

SCOLOG monk, rustic, scholar, servant, student

SCOMBER See MACKEREL.

SCOMBRESOX bluefish, halfbeak, saury

SCONCE amerce, applique, bracket, box, brains, bulwark, candlestick, cover, entrench, excuse, fine, fort, head, lantern, mulct, partition, penalize, pretext, redoubt, screen, seat, sense, shelf, shelter, skull, swape, top, trick

SCONE biscuit, bonnet, farl(e), teacake

SCOON sail, skim, skip

SCOOP bail, beat, bucket, cavity, chisel, chistera, curet(te), didle, dig, dip(per), dish, dredge, excavate, exclusive, gather, gouge, hollow, keach, lade, ladle, net, news, shaul, shovel, skeet, skimmer, skippet, spade, spoon, story, trowel, wimble
up gather, lap, lave

SCOOT away, begone, blow, dart, decamp, depart, dray, flow, gush, hurry, out, rush, schuit, scoter, scout, scram, scud, scurry, shoot(er), skeet, skite, skyt, sled, slide, sloop, squirt(er), vamoose

SCOOTER barracuda, boat, coot, duck, glider, plow, sailboat, squirt, syringe, toy

SCOP bard, minnesinger, minstrel, poet, rhymer, scald, troubadour, versifier

SCOPE aim, ambit, area, circle, compass, domain, expanse, extent, field, freedom, gamut, horizon, ken, latitude, leeway, length, liberty, margin, opportunity, orbit, play, province, purview, radius, range, reach, room, scouth, size, space, span, sphere, spread, stretch, sweep, tether, tract, vent
full purview
having comprehensive put in same coextend

SCOPTICAL jeering, jesting, scoffing

SCORCH assail, barbecue, birsle, blister, bristle, broil, brown, burn, char, cook, cut, dry, frizzle, grill, heat, hurt, parch, rivel, roast, ruin, run, scald, score, scowder, scratch, sear, sere, shrivel, singe, slash, sotter, speed, stain, stale, sweal, swelt(er), swinge, swithe(n), swither, torrify, wither

SCORCHING burning, caustic, fiery, hot, parching, shriveling, speeding, torrid, withering

SCORE (See also SCORING *point.*) abrade, account, ace, acquire, arrange, assail, behalf, berate, bill, break out, bull's-eye, calculate, chalk, charge, compose, composition, count, crease, criticize, cut, debt, enumerate, excoriate, furrow, gash, grade, grievance, groove, ground, grudge, homer, incision, judge, knock, lash, list, mark, mill, motive, music, nick, notch, number, obligation, orchestrate, point, price, rate, rating, reason, reckon(ing), record, register, run, sake, scold, scratch, script, shear, slash, strike, success, tab, tally, taw, tick(et), total, twenty, upbraid
½ ten
low booby
tie deadlock

SCORIA cinder, dross, lava, refuse, remainder, scum, slag, sullage

SCORIFY burn, reduce, smelt

SCORING *point* ace, basket, down, gin, goal, grand slam, hit, hole(in one), homer, home run, run, slam, tally, touchdown, trick

SCORN arrogance, bismer, contemn, contempt, contumely, deride, derision, despise, despite, disdain, disgrace, disgust, disprize, disregard, dor(re), flout, geck, gibe, hoker, ignore, indignity, insolence, jeer, look down on, misprisal, misprize, mock(ery), reject-(ion), repudiate, ridicule, scoff, scout, slight, sneer, sniff, snub, sport, spurn, taunt

gesture of geck

SCORNFUL aloof, arrogant, bitter, contemptuous, disdainful, dismissive, fastidious, haughty, insolent, stuck-up

SCORPENE hogfish

SCORPER chisel, scauper

SCORPIO *claws* libra, scales

gem agate

neighbor ara

star in antares

SCORPION alacran, arachnid, catapult, cobbler, eumeces, fortescue, lizard, nepa, onager, pedipalp, scourge, skink, stinger, uropygi, vinegarroon, whip (tail)

appendage pedipalp(us)

fish hogfish, lapon, loricate, rascacio, rascasse, rosefish, sculpin, serran, toadfish

-fly panorpa

stinger telson

water nepa, nepid

SCOT bluebonnet, bluecap, bonnetman, caledonian, celt, clansman, gael, gluneamie, highlander, jock, kelt, kiltie, lallans, lowlander, mac, pict, sandy, sawnie, sawn(e)y, scotchman, scottie, tartan

-free clear, safe, unhurt, untaxed

SCOTCH (See also SCOTLAND for geographical and other references.) block, check, chock, crush, curb, cut, fee, frustrate, gash, haggle, help, hesitate, hinder, humorous, hurt, impediment, injure, line, liquor, mark, notch, parsimonious, prop, score, scote, scruple, scutch, stamp out, stop, support, thrifty, thwart, wedge, whisk(e)y

abode howff

abundance scouth

accent birr, bur(r)

addition eik, eke

affair hypothec

ailing unweel

alas waesucks

almost freckly

aloof abiegh

and drambuie rusty nail

ankle queet

anything oughtlins

argue arglebargle, argybargy

argument clamper

arrange ettle

ascent upcome

atom haet, hate

attack onfall

attempt mint

awry agl(e)y

balk reest

bankrupt dyvour

bark yaff(le), youff

baste flamb

bee sting forebroad

bite chack

blame dirdum

blessing rebuke, scolding

bloody redwat

blow baff, clamehewit, da(u)d, dird, gowf(f), paik

bold bardy, forritsome

booty spreaghery, spuilzie

brain harn

brat gaitt, gett, nacket

brawl habble

buffet scuff

bump on head clour

bunch cluther

burden clag

chance dint

cheerful cadgy

chilly leepit

clamber scrauchle, sprauchle

claw cloof, clufe, clutch

clothe clead

commotion kippage

companion marrow

complaint molligrant

confusion jabble

coot bell kite, beltie, queet

cough hoast

covetous gair

cranky fifish

creaking jarg

crowd meiny

crumb murl

crush scrunge

cuddy draper, peddler

curdle lopper

curlies kale

dally jauk

damp wack

darling dautie

deformed unmackly

delirious gyte

demure mim

despise forhoo(y), forhow

despoil spuilzie

dew dag

dismal oorie

disturbance brulyie

dolt steg

don't dinna

each ilka

else ense

ember grieshoch, izle

empty toom

endure dree

enemy unfriend

-englishman southron

entangle frankle

entrails harigald, jaudie

excellent braw

extra orra

eyebrow bree, eebree

eyes een, ees, nie

faint dwaim

faithful leal

fall cloit

fat fodgel

fatal unsonsy

fatigue traik

few wheen

fiddle itch, scab

fidgeting fissle

fine braw

fingering wool, yarn

firebrand bleery

fit exies

flag blue saltire

flattery whillywha

flinch blunk

folly dafting

forward forrit

frighten fley

frightful ugsome

frown glunch

ghastly grugous

glide scrieve

good-humored crouse

gorge with food stech

graze scuff

great unco

grief dree

haggle argle-bargle, argy-bargy

handful claucht, claught, claut, gowpen

headstrong rackle, ramstam

healthy feirie, grushie
heap dass, dess
heavy tharf
help heeze, heize
hesitation sussy
horny waukit
hysterics exies
ignorant unkenning
iliad epigoniad
ill-humored crouse
indeed awat
insane redwood
insolence snash
intend ettle
-irish erse
jaded forjesket
jilt gunk
jump loup, stend
just leesome
lie yed
lithe wandle
long-legged spauldrochy
makeshift bewith
meager leepit
mercury foxglove
merry raffing, vogie
mischief barnsbreaking
miser scrat
mismanage blunk
mist drow, ure
misty mooth
mockery glaik
muddled ree
nauseating stawsome
near inby
negative dinna, nae
next ewest
nibble nab
nimble gleb
nonsense bletheration, haver
noon dine
nose nese
now noo
odd orra
of all ava
once aince, ane(s), anis
one ain, aine, tae, yae
other ither
our wir
outstretched stent
own ain, ane, awn, nain
pain steek, thraw
pant pech
pleasant farrand, leesome
poverty poortith
powerful feckful
prattle jaunder
preposition tae
price fiar, fier
prompt yare
promptly tite
prove pree, prive
purpose ettle
quarrelsome frampold

relieve liss
remarkable unco
rend screed
restless fidge
rob reive, spung
scream skelloch
secrete reset
shabby scuffy
sharp snell
shivering oorie, ourie
shout scroinoch, scroinogh
shred blype
shuffle jank
slender jimp
slice skelb
smoke smeek
smoky smuisty
sorrow sorra, wae
spank scud
spiteful nebby
splash jaup
spot mail
stain smot
steal condiddle
stiff tharf
strange unkenned
strength maught
stupid staumrel
surely atweel
surly gurl
taste pree
tasteless waugh
teal bufflehead(duck)
terrier aberdeen, cairn, die-
    hard, scottie, verminer
terror dreddour
thin scrank
tipsy nappy
topaz cairngorm, tassel
touch tig
trouble fash, kiaugh
trust lippen
unbending tharf
uncover tirr
undergo dree
unlatch unsneck
unsafe unsicker
vagary flagarie
value feck
vanish sant
very much awfu
vigor vir
weary forjesket
when fan
wild ree
woo splunt
work darg(ue)
worry fash
wrangle yed
SCOTER basque, bird, butter-
    bill, butterboat, butter-
    nose, coot, diver, duck(er),
    filk, fowl, fulica, melanitta,
    oidemia, pishaug, scoot(er),

skunktop, surfduck, surfer,
    whilk
SCOTIA See SCOTLAND.
SCOTLAND (See SCOTCH
    for expressions and vocabu-
    lary.) alba, albain(n), al-
    bany, albion, albyn, cale-
    donia, ecosse, land of
    cakes, lothian, scotia
adventurer admirable crich-
    ton
airport prestwick
alder arn
alderman bailie
ale yill
ale cup yill-caup
alimony aliment
ancestor fore-elder
animal, dwarfed wallydrag
animal pen cruive
anthropologist frazer, keith
architect campbell, gibbs
artist nicol, raeburn
attendant gillie, gilly
attorney aralie, clusia
awl elsen
baby weanie
bacteriologist fleming
bag mail
bagpipe doodlesack
bagpipe music pibroch
bailiff reeve
balladeer sir harry lauder
bank brae
barge gabbard, gabbart
barrow carry
basket crane, murl(a)in,
    scull
bat backiebird
bay scapa
beef mart, sey
beetle golach, goloch
beggar dyvour, hallanshaker
bell skellat
bellringer clinkum
biologist geddes
bird bae, grouse, hern, jack-
    daw, kae, muir, smeu(th),
    snabby, swinepipe, throstle,
    whaup
bishop primus
blood-money cro
boat coracle, filfil, scaffy,
    sexern, skaffie, zulu
bonfire tandle
borough brugh
botanist brown, fortune
boundary landimere, loup,
    mear, mere, stend
boy callan(t), mannie,
    nacket
brand smot
brandy athole
brat gaitt, gett, nacket

bread bannock, briar, clod, mealock, saps, tammie
breakfast disjune
briar rose
bribe cuddy
brook sike
broth bree
brownie urisk, uruisg
bucket say
bull stot
bullfinch nope
bully bangster
bun cookie, cooky
burial mound tor
bushel fou
cabbage bowkail
cake bap, barmbrack, barnbrack, bramback, farl(e), nacket, scone
calamity oncome
camp follower gudget
canal caledonian
candidate slate leet
candle end doub
cannon carronade
cap balmoral, blackcap, bluebonnet, braidbonnet, glengarry, how, salmonberry, sowback, tam(o'shanter)
cap tassel toorie
cape wrath
capital edina, edinburgh
carpenter squareman
carpet kidderminstor
carriage shandrydan
cascade force, lin(n)
castle balmoral, cawdor
cattle angus, aryshire, galloway
cattle raid spreagh, spreath
cattle shed hammel
cave fingal's
chafing dish choffer
chair regal
chalk cauk
channel kyle, minch
checkerboard dambrod
cheekbone haffet
cheese dunlop
cheese vat chessart
chemise sark
chemist black, dewar, graham, todd, ure
chest kist
chief thane, thegn, toisech
child bairn, dalt, gaitt, gett, scuddy, smatchet
child, naked scuddy
church kirk, kurk
cinder smithydander
city aberdeen, airdrie, alloa, alloway, ayr, banff, brora, burgh, clydebank, coatbridge, cupar, dumfries,

dundee, dunfermline, dunkeld, duns, edinburgh, ellon, falkirk, frunock, girvan, glasgow, greenlock, hamilton, hawick, inverness, kilmarnock, kirkcaldy, kirkwall, leith, oban, paisley, perth, renfrew, rothesay, salen, st andrews, stirling, troon
clan chief thane, thegn
clergyman drummond
cloak cleading, jupe, plaid
cloth forfar, kelt, tartan, tweed
clothing cleading, trog(g)s
club kebbie
coastal water scapa flow
codfish droud, glashan
coif how
coin atchison, bawbee, bodle, bonnetpiece, broad, demy, doit, ecu, folles, groat, halfpenny, hardhead, lion, mark, plack, rial, rider, ryal, turner, unicorn
colt stag
companion marrow
composer lauder
confusion jabble
congress mod
constitution sett
coot bell kite, beltie, queet
coronation site stone of scone
corpse lich
cotter mailer
counsel rede, reed
county aberdeen, angus, argyle, ayr(shire), banff, berwick, bute(shire), caithness, clackmannan, cromarty, dumbarton, dumfries, fife, kincardine, kinross, kircudbright, lanark, lothian(s), midlothian, moray, nairn, orkney, peebles, perth, renfrew(shire), ross, roxburgh, selkirk, shetland, stirling (shire), sutherland, wigtown
court lyon, markmoot
court officer doomster, macer
covenanter cameron
cow crummie, crummy, quey
cracker bake
cross crantara, crostaire
crowd meiny
cup quaich, tass(ie)
curlew whaup
dagger dirk, skean(dhu) (ockle)
daisy gowan

dance bob, ecossaise, gilliecallum, highland fling, petronella, reel, strathspey, walloch
darling dautie
day's journey diet
demon deil
designer mackintosh
devil auld clootie, cloot, deil, hornie, mahound
diaper hippen, hipping
diningroom spence
direction airt(h)
dirge coronach
dish bassie, brose, choffer, coleannon, haggis, scaff
dismal oorie
district coila
disturbance brulyie
dog bawtie, bawty, cairn terrier, collie, messan, scottie, sealyham, terrier
dolt steg
dovecote dooket
drapery pand
drink catlap, meridian, tass, toddy
drinking bout screed
duck bufflehead
dunce dobby
dungeon massymore
dwarf ablach, blastie, droich, knurl, urf, wally
dwelling, ancient crannog
earnest money arles
ear of corn icker
economist smith
editor dyce
elm wych
ember grieshoch, izle
emblem thistle
epiphany uphelya
essayist carlyle
estuary See *firth*, below.
expletive behear
explorer diorkeney, fortune, glooscap, livingston, park, rae, sinclair, zichmni
eye, evil drochuil
fabric blunks, crea, harris tweed, tartan, tweed
faggot fagaid
fairy boggart, brownie, certie, certy, fain, fane, nis(se)
family ilk
farm mains
farmer cotter, crofter
farm house onstead, steading
farm lease tack
farm, rented mailing
farmstead town
fashion scotice
feast, funeral dirgie, dirgy
fellow, mean smatchet

ferrule virl
festival beltane mod uphelya
financier law
firebrand bleery
fireplace chimla-lug, chimley-lug, ingle
firth clyde, cromarty, forth, kyle, linnhe, loch, lorn, moray, pentland, solway, tay
fish baddock, codfish, glashan, salmon, sile, sillock, spalding, vendace
fish, dried spelder
fish haul drave
fish measure cran(e)
fish trap ya(i)re
fisticuff nevel(l)
flag blue saltire
flock hirsel
flour smeddum
flower bluebell, harebell
fog haar
food scaff, vivers
fool ceck, haverer
foray hership
fort dune, roundabout
foster child dalt
fox todlowrie
freckle ferntickle
freedom symbol black rain
friend eme
frieze kelt
fuel elding, shirrel
gait bat
game barley-break, shinny, shinty
game bird grouse
garment arisard, fecket, kilt, maud, tartan, toosh
garter wooer-bab
general campbell
genius ingine
gentleman duniewassal
geologist geikie
ghost taisch
giant big sam, macdonald
giant hag nickheven
gift boondoggle
girl cummer, deem, kimmer, lass(ie), meg, quean, tawpie, tawpy, towdie, winklot
glanders mortersheen
glutton draffsack
gnome pecht
goblet tass(ie)
godmother cummer, kimmer
goldsmith ged
good-for-nothing keffel
gossip claver, clishmaclaver, trattle
granary girnal, girnel
grandchild nepote, oy(e)

grandparent gudame, gudesire
granite gowan
grouse muirfowl
gruel crowdy
guide gilly
gull popeler
gutter siver
hag nickneven
hamlet clachan
hammer mell
hamper rusky
hands paddling
hare bawd
harness trace theat
harp clarsach
hawk allan
haystack trampcock
hazelnut nit
heater choffer
hedgehog hurcheon
heir teind
heron herle
herring matie
highlander bluebonnet, cateran, gael, plaidman, trewsman
highland fling walloch
hill brae, snab, strone
historian buchan, hume, skene
hoar-frost cranreuch
hobgoblin boggart
hock hough
hoe padle
hoist heeze, heize
hole howe
home haft
homespun kelt
hoof cloof, clufe
horse clydesdale, cooser, fittielan, furrahin, galloway
household goods inspreith
house spirit brownie
hut crew, crue
icicle shoggle, tangle
infantry black watch, ladies from hell
inheritance law annat
inlet See *firth,* above.
intermission devall
intestine tharm
inventor macintosh, watt
island ar(r)an, barra, bute, harris, inch, iona, islay, jura, lewis, mull, orkney, rhum, shetland, skye, staffa
island group hebrides, orkney, shetland
island, rocky skerry
isthmus tarbet
jackdaw kae
jacket cleading
jail quod, tol(l)booth

jaundice gulsach
jelly jeel
joke bar
jump loup, stend
jurist haldane, jeffrey
kale borecole, curlies
kerchief curch, napkin
killing pay cro
kilt filibeg
kin sib
king baliol, bruce, carados, duncan, macbeth, robert bruce
king's burial place iona, st oran's
kiss smoorich
kitchen but
knife skean-dhu, whittle
labor, day's darg
ladder trap
lake awe, dee, fyne, gair, gare, katrine, laggan, leven, lin(n), linnhe, loch, lomond, lough, maree, morar, ness, nevis, oich, rannoch, ryan, sloy, tay
lament ochone
land, alluvial carse
land, bottom haugh
land tax cess
land tenure feu
lane vennel
language celtic, erse, keltic, lallan(d)
leader of revels abbot of unreason, lord of misrule
leaf fulyie, fulzie
leap loup, scoup, stend
leave-taking waygang
leg moggan, tram
lessee tacksman
lexicographer craigie, murray, ogilvie
liberator robert bruce
lightning fireflaught
limb lith
limestone cauk
linen crea
liqueur drambuie
liquor athole, barley(bree) (broo)(broth), scour, whittier
litter smytrie
lord laird, thane, thegn
lout tripal
love loes
lowlander sassenach
lowlands, pert. lallan(d)
lullaby baloo, balow
lumpfish cockpaddle
lunch nacket
maggot mawk
magistrate bailie
malt smeddum

marauder cateran
market trone
marriage portion dos, dote
mate fere
mathematician gregory, maclaurin, napier, neper
measure auchlet, boll, chalder, choppin, cop, cran(e), davach, fall, firlot, lippie, lippy, mile, mutchkin, noggin, particate, peck, pint, rood, rope, shaftment, shathmont, span, stimpart, stimpert
meat dish scousa
meat pudding haggis
mendicant gaberlunzie
merchant lipton, roupingwife
midwife howdie, howdy
military leader douglas
milk utensil leglen, milsey, milsie
millrace lade
miner dammer, geordie
mineshaft heuch, heugh
miner's lamp geordie
minnow mennom
mire glaur
miser scrat
money arles, cro, siller
monk culdee
monkey puggy
mood tid
mortgage wadset
mountain pass killiecrankie
mountain region highlands, trossachs
mud rake claut
murder fine cro
music pibroch
musical instrument bagpipes
music festival mod
mystic brahan, seer
name prefix mac
national symbol thistle
native See SCOT.
neck crag
nephew nepote
newt mankeeper
new year's eve hogmanay
noble angus, cathness, lennox, macduff, menteth, rial, ross
noose widdy
northern pictland
northern tip john o'groat's
novelist barrie, buchan, cronin, lockhart, macdonald, munro, oliphant, scott, stevenson
number curn
oak eik
oat ait

oatmeal and water drammach, drammock, drummock
officer bailie
ogre lamkin, lamminin, linkin
order thistle
outlaw cateran, dhu, rob roy
outsider extranean
overcoat slipon
ox nowt
package dorlach
pail cog(gie), cogue
pancake flawn
pantry spence
parish wemyss
party ceilidh
passageway alley, trance
pastry carcake, scone
patron saint andrew
peak attow, ben lomond, ben nevis, cheviot, dearg, hope, macdhui, nevis, tinto, wyvis
peat yarpha
peat spade tuskar
peddler jagger
peeper keek
peer thane, thegn
peerage thanage
penny folles, turner
person, lean ribe
person, stubborn buckie
pew desk
philologist craigie
philosopher bain, caird, hamilton, hume, stewart
physician arbuthnot, black, cronin, jameson, manson
physicist dewar, maxwell, watt, wilson
physiologist haldane, macleod
pickpocket ratero
piece tate
pig crock, grice, grumphie, grumphy
pike ged(d)
pile dass, dess
pillory jougs, juggs
pinafore daidly
pine riga, speyside
pine flowers bay lambs
pipe cutty
pirate kidd
pitcher cruisken
plague traik
plaid tartan
plain machar
plan ettle
plant heather
plaything die
pledge wad
plowgang bovate
plunder creach, creagh, reif

poet See *writer*, below.
polaris base holy loch
pole caber
political party squadrone
pool carr, linn
porridge brose, crowdy, oatmeal
port aberdeen, alloa, banff, campbeltown, dundee, glasgow, greenock, largs, leith, leven, oban, st andrews, sterling
portion, large dad, dunt
potato masher chapper
pouch spleuchan, spleughan, spor(r)an
prank rigwiddie, rigwiddy, shavie
precipice heuch, heugh
pretender cowan
prince zerbino
prize gree
prodigy admirable crichton
prop stell
property aught
proprietor laird
propriety mense
psychologist bain
pudding haggis, tartanpurry
puddle dib, dub
puffin cockandy
pullet earock
purse spor(r)an, spung
quantity hirsel, mask
quarrel collieshangie, tuilyie, tuilzie
quarter day beltane
queen mary stuart
question backspier
quiver dorlach
rabble clamjamfry
race broose, ilk
rain dag, dribble
rake claut
range grampians
rascal ablach, taistrel
raven corbie
ravine cleuch, cleugh
rebellion sherramoor
reformer knox
regiment black watch
region galloway, trossachs
resort craignure, howff, oban, prestonpans, st andrews
ridge drum, run
river affric, afton, annam, ayr, clyde, dee, deveron, don, doon, esk, findhorn, forth, garry, glen, nith, norn, north, spey, tay, teviot, tummel, tweed, ythan
river land carse
river mouth beal

rivet roove
rivulet burn, rindle
robbery reif
rogue hallion
roof thack
roof turf scraw
rope soam, taum, wanty
royal family stewart, stuart
rubbish trooshlach
rumor reverie
run scoup
rustic landward
sailor selkirk
sailyard rae
saint columba, cuthbert
satirist arbuthnot
sausage whitehass, white-
  hawse
scales trone
scarecrow tattiebogle
scholar admirable crichton,
  jebb
schoolmaster dominie, dux
scientist boyd-orr, dewar,
  ure, watt
scone farl(e)
scoundrel whaup
scratch rauk, scart
scurvy grass sea bells
scythe handle snead
sect berean, buchanite, glas
servant deem, gillie, gilly,
  thane
sewer jawhole
shade scug
shawl maud, tozie
sheep fronter, thrinter
sheepfold crew, crue, ree
shelter scug, sheal
shipbuilder clydesider
shovel sheel
shower ding-on
shrew targer
singer lauder
sirloin backsey
skull harnpan
slap skeeg
slattern daw
slope downset, slent
slum backlands
snack chack
snap chack
snare grin
snipe heather-bleat
snowflake flag
snuff beggar's-brown
sod delf
soldier cateran, lady from
  hell
son mac
song annie laurie, ballad,
  ballant, stroud, stowd
sore sair
soup broo, cockaleekie

sparrow spurdie
spirit banshee, kelpie
spring voar
squall drow
stack scroo
staff kent, nibby
stair, spiral turnpike
steward mormaor
stocking maggan
stomach crappin, kite, kyte
stonecutter squareman
stormy petrel assilag
street rew
strip tirr
student bejan(t), semibe-
  jan(t)
stunted person urf
summit dod(d)
swamp wham
sword claymore, ferrara
talon clutch
tangle fank
tantrum tirrivee
tartan set(t)
tax assessor stentmaster
tenant cotter, crofter
tenure feu, sorehon, sorren
tern tarret
test pree
tether baikie
textile design plaid, tartan
thistle onopordon
thong whang
thread steek
tie oerlay
tinker caird
tithe teind
title bailie, laird, reeve,
  thane, thegn
titmouse fuffit
toad t(a)ed
tobacco elder
teddy tass
toll darg
tool(s) gibbles, whittle
tooth gam
tower toorock
townhall tol(l)booth
toy wally
trash smachrie
tree camperdown elm, riga
trestle mare
trial pree
trial of strength tossing the
  caber
trickery jookerie
trifle niffnaff, nignay, nignye
trough backet, bakie
trousers trews
truce cry barla, barl(e)y
tub back
tumult dirdum, hubble,
  steery
tumulus burian

tune dra(u)nt
tunic arisard
turbot bannock-fluke
turf flaught
turkeycock bubblyjock
tweed bannockburn, harris
uncle eme
unit ane, yin
valley trossachs
vertigo mirligo
vessel cappie, quaich,
  quaigh, tass(ie)
vest fecket
village bankbar, rew
visit ceilidh
wallet mail
warbler smeu(th)
war cry slogan
warrior kemp
waterfall force, lin(n)
water sprite kelpie, kelpy
wayfarer dustyfoot
weakling ribe, shilp(it)
wealth graith
weapon claymore, skean
  (dhu)
wedding race broose
week ouk
weighing machine trone
weight boll, bushel, drop,
  trone
wheel horral
whimbrel whaup
whirlpool swelchie, swilkie
whiskey athole, barley-bree,
  glenlivat, glenlivit, malt,
  usquebaugh
whiskey and honey drambuie
whiskey, glass of rubdown
whist catch the ten, hearts
whitefish vendace
widow's right terce
wind the hawk
window winnock
winner bangster
witch cummer, gyre-carline,
  kimmer
woman, loose troll
woman, sluttish clatch
work darg(ue)
world warl
wren tope
writer (See also novelist,
  above.) archer, barrie,
  beattie, blind harry,
  boswell, burns, campbell,
  drummond, edina, gra-
  hame, hogg, lang, mac-
  donald, macpherson, moir,
  scott, sharp, skene, stevenson, wilson
yachtsman lipton
yell gowl
youth callan(t), chiel

SCOTT, WALTER *character* amy, anne, athelstan(e), balderstone, balmawhapple, bertram risingham, black douglas, bois-guilbert, bradwardine, dhu, ellen, ivanhoe, lochinvar, lucy ashton, madge, marmion, nigel olifaunt, norna, quentin durward, rebecca, rob, roy, rowena, wayland, wildfire
home abbotsford
work anne of gierstein, antiquar, bride of lammermoor, fortunes of nigel, guy mannering, heart of midlothian, ivanhoe, kenilworth, lady of the lake, marmion, old mortality, quentin durward, rakeby, rob roy, the monastery, the pirate, the talisman, waverly, woodstock

SCOTT, WINFIELD ole fuss 'n feathers

SCOTTISH See SCOTCH, SCOTLAND.

SCOUNDREL base, bezonian, blackguard, bugger, cad, caitiff, cataian, cheat, crook, crumb, cullion, cur, dog, hound, imp, kite, knave, limmer, louse, lown, mean, miscreant, oysvorf, picaro, rapscallion, rascal, rat, reprobate, riffraff, rogue, rotter, scab, scamp, scum, scut, skalawag, skunk, snake, spalpeen, swindler, thief, trash, trickster, varlet, varmint, vermin, villain, warlock, whaup, whayup, worm

SCOUP leap, run, scamper, skip

SCOUR beat, brighten, buff, burnish, clean(se), clear, comb, decamp, draft, drench, free, mop, polish, pumice, punish, purge, pursue, rake, range, ransack, roister, rove, rub, run, rush, sand, scrub, scurry, search, seek, skirr, traverse, wash

SCOURER bloomer, dollier, pickler, sponge

SCOURFISH escolar

SCOURGE afflict(ion), bane, beat, cat, chastise, crop, devastate, exhaust, flagellate, flay, flog, harry, hit, horsewhip, infliction, knout, lash, plague, punish(ment), rawhide, scorpion, shoot, slash,

sucker, swinge, switch, thong, torment, whip(lash)
of god attila
of princes aretino
symbol of st ambrose

SCOURINGS leftovers, refuse, remainder, rubbish

SCOURWEED soapwort

SCOUT agent, auk, cad, cave, chap, deride, detective, disdain, dispise, emissary, explore, fellow, ferret, flout, guide, guillemot, intelligencer, jeer, look(out), messenger, mock, observe, pal, patrol, recon(noiter), reject, repudiate, ridge, ridicule, rock, schuit, scoff, scorn, search, seek, servant, skulk, sleuth, sneak, sneer, spotter, spurn, spy, taunt, watch(man)
founder baden-powell, baron robert stephenson smyth
leader akela, dad, den, sixer
unit den, pack, troop
young cub

SCOUTH plenty, range, room, scope

SCOUTHER confusion, drizzle, SCOWDER, shower, snow(fall)

SCOVY blotchy, muscovy, smeared, streaky

SCOW acon, barge, bateau, batel, boat, coracle, dhow, garvey, lighter, pontoon, skipjack, yacht

SCOWBANK loiter, loll, shirk

SCOWDER burn, bustle, confusion, scorch, shower, singe

SCOWL frown, glare, gloom, glout, glower, grimace, lour, lower, moue, pout, rubbish, scime, stare, venner

SCOWLING beetlebrowed, forbidding, glaring, gloomy, morose

SCRAB grab, scratch, stump

SCRABBLE clamber, climb, drudge, paw, rake, SCRAMBLE, scrape, scratch, scrawl, scribble

SCRAFFLE See SCRAMBLE.

SCRAG garrote, hang, missile, nape, whale

SCRAGGED, SCRAGGY bony, lean, rough, rugged, scrawny, skinny, thin, weedy

SCRAGGLY irregular, jagged, ragged, splintered, unkempt

SCRAGGY bony, dwarf, knotted, lean, meager, rough, rugged, scrawny, thin, weedy

SCRAM aroint, beat it, begone, benumb(ed), blow, bugger, bunk, clear out, clumsy, decamp, depart, elope, escape, flee, get(going)(lost), git, lam, leave, paralyze, puny, quit, retire, run along, scat, shake a leg, vamoose, withdraw, withered

SCRAMBLE clamber, climb, contest, creep(ing), crowd, crush, haste, hurry, hustle, jostle, louster, mess, mix (ture), muss, predicament, push(ing), rush, scale, scatter, scrabble, scraffle, scrape, scrattle, sprachle, sprackle, sprauchle, sprawl, spread, strive, struggle, swarm, toss, traverse, try, uproar, wrangle

SCRAMBLED brouille

SCRAN food, morsel, refuse, scrap(s), victuals

SCRANCH chew, cr(a)unch, gnash, grate, pulverize

SCRANNEL harsh, lean, poor, slight, thin, unmelodious, weak

SCRAP affray, altercation, bit(e), brawl, broil, cast (off), catch, child, combat, contest, crumb, cullet, cutting, demolish, disagreement, discard, driblet, end, extract, exuviate, fight, fracas, fraction, fragment, grain, jagg, jot, junk, leftover, mammock, melee, molt, morsel, oddment, ort, part, piece, quarrel, rag, raze, refuse, reject, remainder, remains, remnant, row, rubbish, rubble, rumpus, scantling, shed, shred, skerrick, slough, snap, snattock, spat, speck, spetch, squabble, tint, trash, waste(ments), wrangle
iron worker busheler
paper scrip
pile boneyard
ragged scart

SCRAPE abrade, bow, bray, comb, contact, corrade, difficulty, dilemma, dredge, eke, embarrassment, engrave, erase, erode, fiddle, file, fix, gall, grate, graze, grind, hurt, jam, kowtow, mess, pare, pickle, pinch, plight, predicament, quandary, rake, rasp, rub, salaam, save, scalp, scant, sclaff, scrabble, scratch, screed, scrimp, scroop, scuff, shave, skimp, skin, stint, touch, trap, triturate, trouble, vicissitude

along harl(e), manage, shool

bottom dredge

out erase, hollow, rake

skins flesh, harass, scud

together assemble, gather, glean, scramble

up collect, gather

SCRAPER barber, curette, fiddler, flint, fresno, godevil, grader, grater, grattoir, gummer, harl, quirl, scrapple, slusher, strigil

SCRAPESHOE sycophant, toady

SCRAPINGS bit, chaff, dregs, dust, earnings, filings, leavings, offscourings, ramenta, refuse, savings, shavings

SCRAPPER boxer, fighter, pugilist

SCRAPPLE mush, panhas, ponhaws, poor-do, rake, scraper

SCRAPPY beligerent, bitty, contentious, fragmentary, inconsistent, irregular, quarrelsome, war-like

SCRAPS dregs, leftovers, orra, ramenta, remainder, scran, scroff

literary ana

SCRAT devil, hobgoblin, miser

SCRATCH abrade, blemish, bruise, cancel, cash, chance, claut, claw, dig, engrave, erase, expunge, feed, fluke, frush, furrow, grate, groove, haphazard, hurt, incise, incision, laceration, line, mar(k), money, nothing, obliterate, pick, picture, pit, rake, rase, rasp, rauk, rist, rit, rub, scar(ify), scart, sclum, scorch, score, scrabble, scrape, scrattle, scrawl, scrawm, scraze, scribble, scrobble, scrout, scrub,

skelp, tear, tease, test, toughen, trial, wherewithall, wig, withdraw, write

hit blooper

not up to inferior, poor

old See DEVIL.

-penny miser, moneygrubber, scrooge

SCRATCHER cider mill, counterfeiter, daybook, forger, raser

SCRATCHES clay fever, mudfever

SCRATCHWEED cleavers

SCRATTLING beggarly, reduced, scanty, scratched

SCRAWK scratch, screech, squeak

SCRAWL crawl, draw, handwriting, penmanship, pothook, scrabble, scratch, scrawm, scribble, scrobble, scroll, sprawl, squiggle, teem, write, writing

SCRAWM climb, scramble, scratch, scrawl

SCRAWNY angular, bon(e)y, exiguous, gaunt, lank(y), lean, meager, poor, rawboned, scraggy, scranny, scrubby, skinny, slender, slim, spare, thin, underweight

SCREAK creak(ing), scream, screech

SCREAM bellow, cry, guffaw, howl, kvitch, laugh, outcry, score, screak, screech, sensation, shrame, shriek, shrill, skelloch, skirl, sough, squall, wail, yammer, yarm, yaup, yawl, yell, yellock, yelp, youp, yowt

SCREAMER anhima, banner, chaja, headline, seriema, swift

SCREAMING blatant, excellent, funny, splendid

SCREE debris, pebble, refuse, stone, talus

SCREECH blast, caterwaul, creak, cry, jangle, outcry, pipe, quark, quawk, screak, SCREAM, screek, screel, shrame, shriek, shrill, skreigh, squawk, squeak, squeal, ululate, wail, whine, whistle, yell

martin swift

owl strich

SCREED article, band, bit, board, breach, diatribe, discourse, drink, fragment,

harangue, land, leveler, list, lute, rend, rent, rip, say, scrape, shred, smooth, strip, tear(ing), tirade

SCREEN arras, backstop, blind, block out, bolt, breakwind, cage, chick, cloak, cloud, conceal, cover(ing), curtain, defend, discriminate, filter, flywire, gauze, gobo, grate, grille, guard, hide, hoard, laun, mask, mesh, movies, netting, paravent, partition, pass, pavis(ade), project, protect(ion), purda(h), refine, reja, reredos, reseau, riddle, safeguard, scarf, sconce, scug, secrete, sept, setting, settle, shade, shelter, shield, shoji, shroud, shutter, sieve, sift, speer, spier, splasher, tatty, testudo, trommel, veil, windbreak, winnow

appear on fade in

architectural spear, spier

auto grill(e)

bamboo cheek, chick

brushwood scherm

bulletproof manta, mantel(et)

canvas pavisade

chancel jube, reredos

ecclesiastic parclose, perclose

fiber tattie, tatty

fire barrage, fender

lattice chancel

ore grate, trommel

paper shoji

play scenario

shielding troops testudo

tapestry arras, ceiling

wind paravent

writer dramatist, scenarist

SCREENINGS culm, slack, sleck

SCREEVE doodle, draw(ing), exude, leak, ooze

SCREW bargainer, bolt, cochlea, coil, contort(ion), crustacean, distort(ion), emolument, exact, extort, fasten(er), fee(ze), flathead, gimlet, helix, hire, hurt, jack, jailer, nag, opener, packet, pay, press, prop(eller), salary, scrimp, scrow, skinflint, spiral, stint, stipend, strain, temper, threading, thumbkin, tightwad, toggle, turn(key), twist, wage, wind, worm, wring *archimedean* cochlea

beam mesquite, screwpod, tornillo

gauge dentin

pine aggag, ara, artocarpus, breadfruit, lauhala, palma, pandanus, vaco(u)a, vacona

pine family pandanaceae

-shaped helical, spiral, spiroid

tree twisty

up confuse, fasten, mess up, muddle, prime, stiffen, strengthen, tangle, tighten

SCREWBALL blockhead, crackbrain, crackpot, crank, crazy, dizzy, dumbbell, ECCENTRIC, fanatic, galloot, goose, insane, lunatic, nut, oddball, queer, sap(head)

SCREWDRIVER compass-key

SCREWED contorted, contracted, drunk, intoxicated, lit, loaded, threaded, twisted

SCREWMAN jackman

SCREWY askew, crazy, ECCENTRIC, foolish, insane, lunatic, mean, niggardly, nutty, oppressive, spiral, tipsy, tortuous, useless, winding, worn out

SCRIBBLE card, doodle, mark, pen, scrabble, scratch, scrawl, squiggle, write

SCRIBE amanuensis, archivist, author, booker, calligraphist, clerk, copier, copyist, cuttlefish, draftsman, ezra, graffer, historian, journalist, masoret, notary, noverint, penman, penner, scrivan(o), scrivener, secretary, sofer, stenographer, teacher, transcriber, write(r)

god nabu, thoth

SCRIBONIA *husband* augustus, octavian, scipio

offspring cornelia, julia, scipio

SCRIGGLE curlecue, squirm, twist, w(r)iggle

SCRIMMAGE battle, bout, brawl, bully, contest, fight, football, joust, melee, play, practice, row, scuffle, search, skirmish, splore, struggle, tussle

SCRIMP deficient, hinch, miser, niggard, retrench, save, scanty, scarcely,

scrape, skimp, sparse, stint, wrinkle

SCRINGE cringe, flinch, flog, glean, net, pry, rub, search, seine, squeeze

SCRIP bag, certificate, list, memo(randum), money, satchel, schedule, scrap, token, wallet

SCRIPT article, bastarda, book, chirography, continuity, dialogue, document, gurmukhi, handwriting, hiragana, kanarese, libretto, longhand, maghribi, maithili, manuscript, meroitic, nastaliq, neskhi, opera, playbook, plot, ronde, scenario, score, serta, sooloos, text, thuluth, treatise, type, writing

angular ronde

cursive serta

writer dramatist, scenarist

SCRIPTURAL biblical, evangelical, gemaric, gospel, inspired, mishnaic, orthodox, revealed, sacred, textual

SCRIPTURE adigranth, agama, alcoran, aranyaka, arcana-caelestia, artharvaveda, avesta, bhagavad-gita, bhagavata purana, bible, book, brahamana, cabala, canon, ching, composition, edda, gemara, granth, grunth, haggada, halakah, holy writ, inscription, itala, koran, masora(h), midrash, mishna(h), motto, purana, rig-veda, sama-veda, shastra, smriti, sruti, sutra, sutta, talmud, tanach, tantra, tenach, testament, text, torah, upanishad, veda, word, writing

interpreter exegete

part lesson

passage text

version douay, itala, vulgate

SCRITHE err, escape, glide, turn

SCRIVE carving, cut, handwriting, inscribe, manuscript, score, scratch, scribe, write, writing

SCRIVELLO tooth, tusk

SCRIVENER amanuensis, moneybroker, notary, scribe, secretary, stenographer, writer

SCROD *parent* cod

SCROFULA evil, figwort, frostweed, inflammation,

king's evil, swelling, tuberculosis

SCROFULOUS contaminated, dirty, evil

SCROG blackthorn, brushwood, crabapple

SCROGGY stunted, thorny

SCROLL amulet, banderol(e), bannerol, bundle, cartouch(e), design, document, draft, engross, flourish, inscribe, list, manuscript, mez(z)uza(h), orihon, outline, papyrus, record, rinceau, roll, schedule, scrow, stemma, streamer, torah, volute

-like turbinal, volute

writing makimono

SCROOGE *visitor* marley

SCROOP creak, crunch, grate, rustle, scrape, squeak

SCROPHULARIA agalinis, antirrhinum, beardtongue, bee-plant, betony, castilleja, digitalis, figwort, flower, herb, mimulus, paulownia, pentstemon, veronica

SCROUGE crowd, press, squeeze

SCROUNGE cadge, pilfer, pry, search, sponge, steal

SCROUNGING calculating, mean, sharp, theft

SCRUB boscage, brake, brighten, brush, bush, clean(se), coppet, drudge, dwarf, inferior, mallee, mean, mongrel, mop, nonentity, paltry, replacement, rub, runt(y), scodgy, scour, shabby, small, stunted, substitute, undersized, wash, work, yannigan

grass scouring-rush

growth bito, burle(e)

land gar(r)igue

turkey leipoa, magapode

SCRUBBY base, bristly, dwarf, inferior, insignificant, low, mean, paltry, shabby, small, stubby, stunted

SCRUFF coating, crust, dandruff, dregs, dross, film, nape, refuse, scum, scurf, surface

SCRUMPTIOUS capital, dandy, delectable, fastidious, fine, great, nice, savory, splendid

SCRUNCH bite, chew, crunch, crush, gnash, gnaw,

grate, huddle, pulverize, squeeze

SCRUPLE anxiety, balk, blench, blink, boggle, coin, compunction, conscience, demur(ral), diffidence, disbelief, doubt, duck, falter, hesitance, hesitancy, hesitate, hesitation, hold off, jib, measure, misgiving, mistrust, object, part, pause, portion, principle, pull back, qualm, question, recoil, reluctance, scotch, shrink, shy, stick(le), stickling, strain, suspicious, swerve, uncertainty, uneasiness, unit, unwillingness, vacillate, waver, weight
1/20th grain
1/2 obole
3 dram
24 uncia
288 juger
1080 hour

SCRUPULOUS careful, cautious, chary, conscientious, constant, delicate, distrustful, doubtful, ethical, exact, faithful, fastidious, finical, finicky, fussy, just, loyal, meticulous, moral, painstaking, particular, precise, principled, punctilious, punctual, reluctant, rigorous, shy, staid, strict, true, upright
to excess fastidious, finical, finicking, finicky, prudish

SCRUTINIZE analyze, audit, canvass, con(sider), contemplate, dissect, examine, explore, eye, inspect, investigate, ogle, penetrate, pierce, probe, pry, resolve, revolve, scan, search, sift, size up, study, survey, weigh

SCRUTINY audit, canvass, contemplation, examination, hawkeye, inquiry, inspection, investigation, observation, once-over, perusal, study, survey, view(ing)

SCRY cry, descry, glance, look, shout, sieve, sift

SCUD ale, beer, blow, cloud, dart, flash, flea, float, fly, foam, gust, rack, rainstorm, ramp, run(ner), rush, sail, scoot, scum, shoot, shower, skim, slap, spank, speed, spoom, spray, wind

SCUFF abrade, blow, bray, buffet, cuff, drag, evade, graze, gust, hit, hurt, mule, rabble, riffraff, rowdy, rub, sandal, scatter, sclaff, scrape, scratch, scruff, shower, shuffle, slight, slipper, touch, tread, wipe off

SCUFFLE amble, brulyie, bustle, clinch, contend, contest, cuff, FIGHT, fray, hoe, melee, scrimmage, scruffle, shamble, shuffle, skirmish, strive, struggle, tussle, walk, wister

SCUFFLER fighter, gummer, wrestler

SCUG pretense, schoolboy, shade, shadow, shelter, squirrel

SCULL basket, boat, bull, oar, paddle, propel, race, row (boat), shoal, spoon, wherry

SCULLERY ewery, pantry

SCULLION base, blackguard, custroon, domestic, fellow, galopin, gippo, menial, peasant, potwalloper, quistron, servant, swiller, washer, wretch

SCULPIN bighead, bullhead, bullpout, cabezon(e), cottus, dragonet, hardhead, loricate, scorpionfish, worthless

SCULPTOR artist, carver, chiseler, figuriste, graver, imager, modeler, molder
famous brancusi, cellini, della robbia, donatello, epstein, ghiberti, maillol, michelangelo, moore, phidias, pisano, praxiteles, rodin
of figurines coroplast
tool caelum, chisel, ebauchoir, gradine, graver, mallet, spatula

SCULPTURE anaglyph, anaglyptics, bronze, bust, cameo, carve, carving, cast, chisel, cut, draft, draught, engrave, figure, form, gisant, gradino, hew, image, marble, mobile, model (ing), mold, mortorio, predella, proplasm, statuary, statue, terracotta, xyloglyphy
art of anaglyptics
base gaine
figure acrolith
framework armature
group mortorio

model proplasm
ornament anaglyph, bucrane, bucranium, cameo
paneling boiserie
part gaine, pillar
pert. glyphic, glyptic(al)
piece bust, head, statue, torso
pre-phidian aeginetan
relief agrafe, agraffe
school attic
slab metope
term alto-relievo, bas-relief, basso-relievo, cavo-relievo

SCUM brat, bubble, bugger, cachaza, coating, cover, cur, dirt, dregs, dross, film, foam, froth, laitance, lamina, offal, offscourings, rabble, raff, refuse, remainder, riddam, riffraff, sandiver, scoria, scour, scruff, scurf, skim, skin, sloak, sloke, spume, sweep, trash, vermin
clear of skim

SCUMFISH choke, discomfit, overpower, suffocate

SCUMMY base, paltry

SCUP bream, fish, mishcup, paugie, porgy, scuppaug, sparid, stenotomus, swing

SCUPPER abandon, drain, massacre

SCURF dander, dandruff, flake, furfur, lamina, offscourings, scale, scruff
covered with lepidote

SCURFY scald, scaly, scruffy
condition buckskin

SCURRILITY abuse, affront, berating, billingsgate, invective, obloquy, scolding, taunt, vituperation

SCURRILOUS abusive, coarse, derogatory, dirty, filthy, foul(mouthed), gross, indecent, insolent, insulting, low, obscene, offensive, opprobrious, profane, ribald, scurrile, thersitical, vile, vulgar

SCURRY beetle, dart, dash, flurry, harry, haste(n), hie, hurry, race, run, rush, scamper, scour, scud, scuffle, scutter, scuttle, sherry, skedaddle, skelter, skice, skirr, skitter, speed, sprint

SCURVY abject, base, beggarly, cheap, contemptible, despicable, discourteous, low, mean, paltry, roynous,

scabby, scald, scorbute, scummy, scurfy, shabby, sorry, vile
grass cress, dayflower, seabells
infantile barlow's disease
pert. scorbutic
preventative antiscorbutic, ascorbic acid, citrus, vitamin c
SCUT boat, dregs, hare, rush, scuttle, tail
SCUTAGE escuage, fine, impost, levy, penalty, tax
SCUTARI shkoder, shkodra, uskudar
SCUTCH fiber, flax, hammer, scotch, swingle, switch, whip
SCUTCHER beater, mason, swingle
SCUTE buckler, coin, elytron, plate, scale, scutella, scutum, shell, shield
SCUTTER See SCURRY, SCUTTLE.
SCUTTLE abandon, airport, basket, beetle, bucket, bustle, capsize, cowl, crab, cuttlefish, destroy, dish, hatchway, hod, hurry, lid, manhole, octopus, opening, place, run, rush, scoot, scud(dle), scurry, scutter, shovel, sink, skep, smash, spad, swamp, top, withdraw, wreck
SCUTTLEBUTT fountain, gossip, rumor
SCUTUM See SCUTE.
SCYLD *ancestor* odin
father sceaf
SCYLLA *beloved* minos
parent crataeis, echidna, nisus, phorcys, poseidon, typhon
partner charybdis
slayer heracles, hercules, minos
SCYTHE blade, cradle, cut, hook, lee, meak, mow, saw, sickle, sye, tool
handle snaith, snath(e), snead, sneath, sneed, sye, tack, thole
sweep swath
SCYTHIA *burial mound* kurgan
diety onga
king colaxais
lamb barometz
people alan, arimaspian, saka
SEA (See also *name*, below.)

aequor, bahr, billow, blue, brim, brine, brin(e)y, channel, deep, float, flood, foam, fret, gulf, holm, hyaline, lake, lave, lough, main, me(e)r, mere, neptune, ocean, pontus, race, strait, strand, swell, tethys, thalassa, tide, water, wave, zee
adder pipefish, stickleback
anemone actinia(n), adamsia, anthozoan, dahlia, edwardsia, metridium, opelet, polyp, vestlet, zoanthid
animal actinarius, coral, rosmarine
approach seagate
arm bay(ou), belt, bight, cove, estuary, euripus, fiord, firth, fjord, flow, frith, gulf, gut, inlet, lagoon, laguna, loch, lough, mouth, narrow(s), reach, ria, roadstead, sinus, sound, strait(s), wash
aster starwort
bar swash
bass bluefish, cabrilla, hanahill, humpback, sandfish, serranid, tallywag
bat devilfish
bath bain de mer
-beach morning glory bayhops, baywinders
beacon lighthouse
bean nickernut
bear otarioid, seal
bent sandsedge
beyond the outre mer, ultra mare
bird albatross, auk, booby, diomedea, duck, ern(e), fulmar, gannet, gull, hagdon, kestrel, mew, pelican, petrel, puffin, scaup, scoter, seagull, shearwater, skua, smew, solan, sula, tern, yager
biscuit bread, champion, galette, hardtack, pantile, racehorse
bladder man-of-war
blite good king henry, goosefoot, strawberry blite, suaeda
blubber jellyfish
bottom bed, benthos, deep, depths
bread (See also *biscuit*, above.) sponge
bream baleen, braise, brama, carp, chad, pagrus, pomfret, porgy, roach, roman,

rutilus, sargus, sparid, tarwhine
breeze virason
bride aphrodite, venus
butterfly pteropod
carp morwong
cat(fish) ariida, chimaera, monkey, seal, walrus, weever, wolf-fish
cave opening gloup
comb. hal(i), halo, mar(i), mer, oceano, thalass(o), thalatto
commander admiral
coot guillemot, scoter
cow dugong, hippopotamus, manatee, rhytina, siren(ian), walrus
creature salp
cress glasswort
crow auk, chough, coot, cormorant, gull, oyster-catcher, skimmer, skua
cucumber balate, beche-demer, holothurian, pedata, synaptid, teat-fish, trepang
current riptide, undertow
cushion thrift
daisy thrift
-death goddess rau
deep, pert. bathic, bathyal, bathymetric, bathysmal, benthal, benthonic, benthopelagic
delicacy nori, roe
demon fomor(ian), wate
depths, comb. abysso
description haliography
dock bear's-breech
dog breaker, dog-fish, fogbow, fog-eater, gob, mariner, navigator, pirate, privateer, sailor, salt, seal, seaman, tar
dotterel plover, turnstone
dragon pegasid, pegasus, quaviver
drake cormorant, eider
duck coot, dipper, diver, ducker, eider, scoter
-dweller paralian
dweller, name meaning morgan
eagle ern(e), osprey, pygarg(us), scaup
-ear abalone, haliotis, snail
eel conger, lamprey
-exploring ship glomar
fan gorgonian
fennel samphire
fig beach-apple
floating on flotsam, jetsam
foam froth, meerschaum, sepiolite, spume

fond of thalassophilous
food abalone, clam, crab, fish, lobster, oyster, roe, scallops, shellfish, shrimp
fox thresher-shark
gate beach, channel, swell
girdle cutweed, cuvy, kelp, laminaria
god aeger, aegeus, aegir, ahti, ahto, apamnapat, atlas, canopus, chaos, cymir, dyaus, dylan, ear, fontus, glaucus, hea, hler, hohodemi, kompira, kuvera, ler, lir, manannan, manawyddan, man-fish, merman, mimir, neptune, nereus, niord, njord, njorth, nun, oceanid, oceanus, owatatsumi, palaemon, proteus, ran, ryobu-shinto, shiozuchi, suitengu, thetis, thriton, van(ir), varuna, ymir
goddess amphitrite, anahita, anaitis, aphrodite, branwen, doris, erua, erue, eurynome, galatea, ino, leucothea, matuta, mermaid, naiads, nana, nereid, nina, rana, salacia, sirens, tethys, thetis
goods sunk at lagan, lagend
goose dolphin, phalarope, solan
grape salsola, saltwort
green celadon
gull annet, cab(be), ern(e), gore, kittiwake, larine, mew, popeler, skua
gypsy bajau, malayan, samallaut, selung
hay eelgrass
heavy popple
hen guillemot, skua
high main
hog porpoise
holly bear's-breech, eryngium
horse hippocampus, scoter, walrus, whitecap
hound dogfish
inhabiting bathybic, holobenthic, pelagic
inland aral, black
inlet See arm, above.
instrument bathysphere
island cotton bolton counts, bourbon
kale cole, crambe
king ler, neptune, pirate, poseidon, viking
lace chorda, thread-tangle, whiplash
land in island, isle(t)

lark dunlin, plover, sanderling, turnstone
lavender beh(e)n, inkroot, statice, thrift
law book mare librum
lawyer gray snapper, grotius, shark
lemon doris
lentil gulfweed
lettuce alga, seaweed, slake, sloke, ulva
level change eustacy
life halibios
lion otaria, seal
-living maricolous, marine, thalassic
maid mermaid, nereid, nymph, siren
mammal See SEAL, WHALE.
mantis squilla
marker beacon, buoy, dan, lighthouse, meith, pharos, searchlight
mew bird, gull, larus
mile knot, naut
milkwort glaux, herb, saltwort
mist gray, quaker
monster cetus, hydra, kraken, leviathan, scylla
motion tide
mount guyot
mouse dunlin, harlequinduck
name adriatic, aegean, arabian, azanian, azov, baltic, banda, barents, bering, black, bosporus, candia, caribbean, caspian, celebes, china, coral, dead, galilee, ionian, irish, japan, kara, laptev, marmara, mediterranean, north, okhotsk, red, ross, sulu, tasman, timor
narrow sound
near maritime
needle garfish
nettle acaleph, blubber, jellyfish, medusa
nymph See NYMPH sea.
oak rockweed
observation equipment bathysphere
of marmara, pert. propontic
old man of phorcus, proteus
onion scilla, squill
open mare librum, midocean
organism nekton, plankton
otter enhydra, kalan, kid
otter cabbage See SEAWEED.
our mare nostrum
owl lumpfish, puffin

oxeye saltweed, samphire
partridge cunner
pen alcyonarian, anthozoan, pennatula
personification davy jones, ler, lir, mermaid, merman, nammu, neptune, oceanid, oceanus, poseidon, siren, thalassa, thetis, triton, varuna
pert. aequoreal, bathymetric, dipsy, haliographic, hydrographic, marinal, marine, maritime, nautical, naval, oceanic, pelagic, thalassic
pheasant pintail, smee, smew, squaw
pig dolphin, dugong, porpoise
pigeon dowitcher, guillemot, rock-dove
pike trident
pink chickweed, sabbatia, thrift
plantain gibbals
poacher alligator-fish, bullhead, pogge
polyp anemone
port groin, harbor
purse or *puss* offset, undertow
quail auklet, turnstone
raven cormorant, sculpin, squaretail
rise and fall ebb, loom
robber buccaneer, corsair, jaeger, pirate, privateer
robin gurnard, merganser, wingfish
rocket beach-sap, cakile
roughness lipper, swell, waves
route lane
rover scummer, viking
saint of elmo
salmon pollack, weakfish
salt producer halogen
scorpion cobbler
serpent elops, hydra
shell clam, conch, scallop, snail, triton
shell cement gulgul
slug cucumber, doto, elysia, glaucus, goniodoris, nudibranch, trepan(g)
smooth hyaline, slatch
snail liparian, triton, w(h)elk, wilk
snake chital, kerril
snipe bellows-fish, phalarope
soldier marine
spider basket-fish, octopus, pycnogonid
spirit mermaid, merrow

spray lipper, spindrift, spoondrift

squirt ascidian, salpa, tunicate

star of isis

starwort aster, camomile

student thalassographer

study thalassography

swallow petrel, tern

swell surf

swine porpoise, wrasse

tangle furbelow, kelp, laminaria

term ahoy, avast, belay, trice

trout bodieron, beregat, herling, hirling, kipper, salter, sewen, smelt, squeteague, weakfish

trout after spawning kelt

trout, young peal

turtle cahuama, chelonia, chelonid, hawksbill, leatherback, loggerhead

unicorn narwhal

urchin arbacia, asternata, cassidulina, cassiduloid, centrechinoid, cidarid, cushionflower, diadematoid, echinid, echinite, echinoderm, echinoid, echinus, radiate, repkie, sand dollar, spatangus, uni, wana

urchin, edible repkie

urchin larvae pluteus

urchin organ sphaeridium

urchin, pert. echinal

urchin's jaws aristotle's lantern

view marinorama

wall boulder head, bulwark, buttress, mole

wall breach gool

water brine, salt

wave, seismic tsunami

-wife wrasse

wolf pirate, privateer, seal(ion), submarine, wolffish

worm annelid, lurg, nereis, sao

wrack eel-grass

wrack, dried alvamarina

SEABEE *motto* can do

SEABOARD coast(land), shore, tidewater

SEACOAST bank, littoral, seaboard, seashore, strand

dweller beachcomber

SEAFARER mariner, navigator, pirate, privateer, sailor, salt, seaman, tar

SEAGOING capable, nautical, naval, seafaring, weatherbeaten

SEAL adhesive, agree, arctocephalus, assent, assurance, attest, authenticate, authenticity, blank, bluesides, bottle, breloque, brown, bull(a), cachet, cap (sule), cauk, close, cocket, confine, confirm(ation), cork, cowroid, determine, die, dotard, enclose, execute, fasten(ing), finish, fix, fob, fur, gasket, guaranty, harp, hood, imprison, jark, label, makluk, mold, obsignate, otarian, otary, padlock, phoca, pinnigrade, pinniped, pledge, pup, ratify, seacat, sealkie, secure, security, seecatch, seetle, shut, sigil(late), signature, signet, stamp, sterrinck, swile, ugrug, ursal, ursuk, validate, wafer, wax, weddell, wig

baby whitecoat

bearded makluk, squareflipper, ugjuk, ursuk

box skippet

breeding ground pribilof islands, rookery

bull beachmaster

coat sealchie, sealkie

colony See *group*, below.

decorated with sigillate

documentary jark

eared otary, zalophus

elephant mirounga

female cow, matka(h)

flower bleedingheart

fur ursal

golden bezel, chrysobull, iceroot

group herd, patch, pod, rookery

harbor dotard, ranger, tangfish

harp bedlamer, bluesides, phoca, saddleback, saddler, whitecoat

hooded clapmatch, cystophora

immature bedlamer

jewel breloque

letter cachet

-like sphragistic

limb flipper

male bachelor, bull, holluschick, quitter, saddler, seecatch

papal bull(a)

personal hanko

pert. phocine, sigillary, sphragistic

polar makluk, otary, phoca,

ross's, seecatch, sterrinch, ursal, ursuk

private secretum

red stone carnelian

ringed floerat

young beater, bedlamer, blueback, bluesides, flipperling, holluschick, hopper, jacket, pup, quitter, saddler, whitecoat

SEALED closed, inaccessible, undisclosed, unknowable, unknown

SEALSKIN matara, sculp, ursal

coat netcha

SEALWORT pearlweed, sagina

SEAM burden, cleft, cloth (ing), crease, crevice, fash, fell, fissure, fold, furrow, groove, hem, horseload, interstice, join(t), juncture, layer, line, load, mark, purl, raphe, ridge, saim, scar, sew, stitch, stratum, streak, strip, suture, tuck, wrinkle

pert. sutural, suturic

tapering dart

SEAMAN calash, gob, jack(y), lubber, mariner, mastman, matlow, merman, nautilus, rating, sailor, salt, seafarer, seasoner, shipman, shipper, smasher, tar

ballad forebitter

chapel bethel

poor hoodlum, paddy-wester, waister, wester, younker

shirt guernsey

take job as ship

SEAMLESS arapho(ro)stic, unsewed, whole

SEAMSTRESS dressmaker, needlewoman, sempstress, sewer, sewster

SEANCE assembly, session, sitting

event trance

holder medium, spiritualist

sound rap

SEAPLANE aeroboat, airboat, amphibian, duck, hydroplane, supermarine, triphibian

SEAR aged, arid, barbecue, blight, braise, brand, burn, callous, catch, cauterize, cere, char, cook, dead(en), dried, dry, effete, exhausted, harden, languish, parch, saw, scar, scorch,

sere, shrink, singe, threadbare, wither(ed), worn
SEARCH ask, beat the bushes, brevit, burrow, cast, chase, comb, court, dacker, delve, dig, dowse, examine, expiscate, exploration, explore, fan, ferret, finecomb, fish, fond, forage, fossick, frisk, grope, hunt, inquest, inquire, inquiry, inspect, investigate, investigation, look, maraud, mouse, nose, penetrate, poke, prequisition, probe, prospect, pry, pursue, pursuit, quest, rake, ransack, rifle, ripe, root, rout, rummage, scan, scour, scringe, scrounge, scrutinize, scrutiny, seek, sift, sleuth, snoop, survey, trace, track, trail, watch
about busk, grope, grub
absurd wild-goose chase
for game ghoom, quest
military reconnaissance
out exquire, ferret
SEARCHER detective, dowser, ferret, hydroscopist, inspector, looker, officer, probe, quidnunc, seeker, sleuth, snoop, tracer
SEARCHING curious, exploratory, groping, hard, inquisitive, investigative, keen, nosy, penetrating, piercing, prying, quizzical, rogatory, sharp, shrewd, snoopy
SEARCHLIGHT flashlight, torch
SEARED burnt, callous, insensible, scorched, tough
SEASHORE beach, cleve, coast, littoral, marine, ripe, seaboard, seacoast, seaside, strand
pert. orarian
SEASICK nauseated, nauseous, queasy
SEASICKNESS hilo, mal de mer, naupathia, nausea
SEASON acclimatize, accustom, age, autumn, beek, budtime, condite, discipline, drill, dry, easter, embalm, equinox, fall, familiarize, flavor, habituate, harden, imbue, interval, inure, lent, mature, moderate, occasion, opportunity, perfect, period, practice, preserve, ripen, salt, savor, school, seedtime, sele, soften, spell,

spice, spring, steven, stound, summer, temper, term, tid, time, tinge, train, weather, winter, zest
dull slack
god vertummus
goddess aestas, dike, eirene, eunomia, HORAE, hyems, ver
highly devil, spice
lenten careme
rainy kharaf, varsha
religious advent, careme, easter, lent, passover
SEASONABLE apposite, convenient, expedient, handy, opportune, pat, relevant, suitable, tideful, timely, towardly, welcome
SEASONED accustomed, experienced, finished, habituated, mature(d), skilled, spicy, veteran, zestful, zesty
SEASONING condiment, flavoring, maturity, relish, salt, sauce, SPICE
SEAT abode, apse, asana, banc, banquette, base, bench, bleacher, bottom, capital, cathedra, chair, chaise, couch, cricket, curule, dais, davenport, derriere, divan, duff, dwelling, establish, fauteuil, foldstool, foundation, fundament, hassock, headquarters, house, howdah, install, locality, location, loge, lounge, mastaba, musnud, ottoman, perch, pew, place, plant, post(ure), put, rear, residence, rocker, roost, rump, saddle, sedile, sedilia, see, sella, session, set, settee, settle, siege, site, sitting, situation, sofa, spot, squab, stall, station, stool, support, tabo(u)ret, throne
baby's lap
backless hassock, ottoman, stool
block cuneus
boat taft, thwart
bone ischium
canopied cosy, cozy
carriage dicky
chimney sconce
country grange, quinta, tower
cushioned pulvinar
draped musnud
driver's dick(e)y(box)
elephant castle, howdah, tower

high perch
individual bucket
long bench, form, settle
of honor bisellium, curule
of justice banc, bench
of power see, throne
on poles horse, litter
reclining dormeuse
reserved box, loge(s)
royal throne
rumble dick(e)y
small toit
straw boss
tier gradin, row, tendido
unreserved bleachers, blues
window banquette
without standee
SEATED assis, established, fixed, located, settled, situated
SEAVER, TOM tom terrific
SEAWAN beads, money, wampum
SEAWARD asea, makai, off
SEAWEED actinia(ria), agar, alaria, alga(e), alimon, badderlocks, barilla, bladder-kelp, bladder-tangle, blindeel, bottle-ore, carrageen, cuvy, delisk, desmid(ian), drift, dulse, enalid, fucoid, fucus, funori, gulfweed, haitsai, hempweed, henware, honeyware, jellyplant, kelp, ko(m)bu, laver, limu, moss, murlin, nori, ooze, oreweed, orewood, ory, redware, reek, reit, rockweed, sargasso, sargassum, seabeard, seatang, seaware, sion, slake, sloke, tang(le), ulva, varec(h), vraic, ware, whipcord, whiplash, wrack
ashes varec(h)
comb. phyceae, phyco
derivative barilla
description phycography
-eating fuciphagous
edible agar, dulse, haitsai, kelp, laver, limu
extract agar
fern hart's-tongue
glue funori
-like fucoid, ory
manure vraic
pert. algous
product agalloch, agar(agar), gelatin, gelose, isinglass
red dulse
sea sargasso
study algology
SEAWORTHY a-one, bold, fit, safe, seakindly, sharp,

shipshape, snug, waterproof, watertight

SEB See GEB.

SEBASTIAN *brother* alonso
friend antonio
sister viola

SEBASTODES bocaccio, priestfish, rockfish

SEBASTOPOL dominoes, fortress

SEBKHA alkali-flat, plain, playa

SEC dry, instant, moment, second

SECEDE abdicate, depart, desert, pull out, quit, resign, retire, splinter, withdraw, yield

SECERN discriminate, distinguish, secrete, separate

SECESSION breakaway, retirement, separation, withdrawal

SECLUDE bar, beleaguer, blockade, boycott, cloister, debar, deny, embargo, enclose, except, exclude, expel, hide, isolate, keep apart, ostracize, prohibit, protect, quarantine, recess, recluse, remove, retire, retreat, screen, secrete, segregate, separate, sequester, withdraw

SECLUDED alone, beleaguered, blockaded, cloistered, cloistral, close, covert, deep, distant, embowered, hidden, hideaway, incommunicado, insular, isolated, lonely, lonesome, lorn, monastic, private, quarantined, remote, removed, retired, screened, secret, segregated, shy, solitary, unfrequented, withdrawn

SECLUSION aloofness, apartheid, blockade, desolation, exclusion, exile, insularity, isolation, loneliness, privacy, privity, quarantine, retirement, retreat, segregation, severance, solitude, withdrawal
desire for agromania
pert. monastic

SECONAL devils, downers, pinks, red devils, reds, secobarbital

SECOND abet, additional, after, aid(e), also-ran, another, assist(ant), attend, back(er), confirm, dupli-

cate, echo, encourage, endorse, exponent, flash, follow, forward, further, handle(r), help(ful), inferior, instant, jiffy, loser, moment, next, other, period, placer, promote, proponant, reinforce, repeat, runner-up, subordinate, support(er), sustain, tick, tidder, time, tother, trice, twinkle, twinkling, uphold, vouch
-best See SECOND-*rate.*
childhood dotage, senility
comb. deuter(o)
-coming sect shakerism, shakers
-coming sect leader ann lee
fiddle subordinate, substitute, underling
growth ratoon, rowen
guess kib(b)itz
-rate average, common, indifferent, inferior, mediocre, medium, middling, moderate, poor, shabby, shoddy, substandard
-rater piker
self alter ego, companion, friend
sight esp, instinct, intuition, myopia
-sighted clairvoyant, fey, intuitive, precognitive, psychic, visionary
60 minute
-story man burglar, thief
team bench-warmers, reserves, scrubs, subs, substitutes, yannigans

SECONDARY accessory, accidental, adventitious, assistant, auxiliary, backfield, by-product, collateral, dependent, deputy, derivative, eventual, following, incidental, indirect, inferior, less, minor, satellite, subject, subordinate, subservient, subsidiary, substitute, succursal, tributary, vicarious
comb. deuter(o)

SECONDHAND borrowed, derived, hand-me-down, old, resold, unoriginal, used, worn

SECRECY concealment, confidence, darkness, dern, hiding, isolation, mystery, privacy, privity, reticence, seclusion, silence, stealth, velation
swear to tile, tyle

SECRET abstruse, arcane, arcanum, backdoor, backstair, blind, clancular, clandestine, classified, cloak-and-dagger, close(t), concealed, confidence, confidential, covert, cryptic, dark, dern, distinct, enigma, esoteric, furtive, hidden, hidling(s), hugger-mugger, hush-hush, incognito, inmost, inscrutable, intimate, key, latent, mysterious, mystery, mystic(al), obscure, occult, oracle, orphic, private, privy, puzzling, recluse, recondite, remote, restricted, reticent, retired, riddle, rune, screened, secluded, separate, shrouded, shy, sinister, snug, stealthy, subrosa, subterranean, surreptitious, uncanny, underground, underhand(ed), under the table, unknown, unseen
agent counterspy, emissary, private-eye, saboteur, scout, spy
comb. crypto
place adytum, blind, cove, crypt, den, haven, hideaway, hideout, recess, refuge, retreat, safe, sanctum
service cia, fbi, intelligence
society black hand, cabal(a), camorra, cosa nostra, egbo, fraternity, junta, junto, kkk, lodge, mafia, masons, ogboni, poro, sorority, syndicate, tong

SECRETARY agent, aide, amanuensis, assistant, clerk, confidant, copier, desk, escritoire, famulus, girl-friday, minister, moonshee, munshi, officer, recorder, scribe, scrivener, stenographer, typist, writer
patriarchal prothonotary

SECRETE bury, cache, cloak, conceal, deposit, disguise, dissemble, embosom, ensconce, excrete, exude, harbor, hide, mask, niche, ooze, plant, produce, remove, reset, salivate, screen, secern, shroud, sink, stash, stow, withdraw

SECRETION autacoid, catarrh, cerumen, chalone, chicle, concealment, drop, emanation, flocoon, gum, hormone, juice, laa(r)p, lactation, larp, latex, lerp,

milk, mucus, resin, rosin, saliva, sap, sebum, secernment, sepia, smegma, spit (tle), sweet, wax
abnormal acatastasia
deficiency asteotosis
fatty sebum
internal autacoid, bile, chalone, endocrine, gall, hormone, incretion, saliva, thyroxin
science of ecrinology, endocrinology, hormonology
SECRETIVE backstair, catlike, cautious, circumspect, close-lipped, covert, dark, feline, insidious, reserved, reticent, silent, sneaky, snug, stealthy, subtle, surreptitious, taciturn, thievish, tight-lipped, uncommunicative, wary
SECRETLY clandestinely, covertly, furtively, inaudibly, inly, in petto, obreptitious, privily, slyly, stealthily, undercover, underhand
SECRETS arcana, byends, curiosa, esoterica
SECT affiliation, babi, bhora, body, church, class, communion, community, creed, crew, cult, denomination, dhundia, faction, faith, fellowship, group, hasidim, isawa, order, organization, party, persuasion, religion, ringatu, schism, school, set, shin, sivaism, society, team, wing, zen
arian anomoean
ascetical abstinent
distinguishing word shibboleth
early christian agnoites, aquarian, nazarene, nestorian
fanatic adamite
flagellant albi
gnostic ebionite, naassene, severian
nudist adamite
ophite cainite
religious abrahamite, albanenses, anabaptist, bahai(sm), mennonite, sabeans, shakers
sunnite shafite
SECTARIAN, SECTARY addict, adherent, bigot, denominationalist, devotee, disciple, dissenter, eclectic, enthusiast, factionalist, fan (atic), follower, hench-

man, heretic, heterodox, narrowminded, nonconformist, partisan, satellite, schismatic, supporter, syncretist, votary, zealot
SECTION agency, area, barrio, belt, block, branch, canton, capitulum, caput, category, chapter, classification, cutting, department, detail, district, division, field, fraction, fragment, length, locality, member, operation, panel, paragraph, parcel, part, piece, plot, portion, region, sector, segment, separate, share, signature, slice, specimen, sphere, subdivision, surgery, territory, tier, township, tract, tranche, unit, vicinity, zone
concluding abgesang, epilogue, finale
conic parabola
dull longueur
hand crewman, laborer, worker
native barrio, casbah, kasba
SECTIONAL imperfect, incomplete, local, partial, regional
SECTOR arc, area, part, quarter, SECTION, segment, zone
SECULAR abiding, aeonian, agelong, carnal, centuried, civil, earthly, enduring, eonian, ignorant, laic(al), lay(man), mundane, periodic(al), permanent, profane, stable, temporal, terrestrial, vulgar, worldly
SECURE acquire, anchor, annex, arrest, assured, at ease, attain, bail, batten, belay, bind, bolt, brace, button(down), capture, carefree, catch, certain, chain, clinch, close, confident, confine, defend, dependable, easy, elicit, engage, ensure, fasten, fetch, firm, fix, foolproof, gain, get, gird, guarantee, guard, hold, invincible, lash, lock, make fast, moor, nail, obtain, padlock, pin, positive, preserve, procure, proof, protect(ed), receive, reliable, restrain, rivet, rope, safe(guarded), seize, shield (ed), sicker, siker, solid, stable, strong, sure, tie

(down), tight(en), trice, trustworthy, undisturbed
SECURELY fast, safe, siccar, sicker, solidly, soundly, surely
SECURIDACA buaze, bwazi, vine
SECURITIES assets, blue chips, bonds, certificates, commodities, convertibles, debentures, futures, holdings, industrials, portfolio, rails, stocks, utilities
dealer broker
pert. interbourse
SECURITY anchorage, assurance, asylum, bail, bond, calm, caution, cedula, certificate, collateral, confidence, covenant, debenture, defense, deposit, earnest, ease, fastness, floater, frith, fund, gage, grith, guarantee, guaranty, guard, hope, hostage, indemnity, insurance, lien, mortgage, obligation, pledge, promise, protection, rente, safety, seal, shelter, stability, stock, strength, surety, token, trust, vadium, warrant(y)
given as gage, pledge
transaction gager
warrant guaranty
SEDAN auto(mobile), brougham, car, chair, conveyance, jampan, litter, palanquin, powerboat, tomjohn, tonjon
SEDATE allay, calm, collected, composed, decorous, demure, dignified, dispassionate, douce, earnest, grave, imperturbable, matronly, placid, proper, quiet, reserved, seemly, serene, serious, settled, sober, solemn, staid, steady, still, thoughtful, tranquil, unobtrusive, unruffled
SEDATIVE aconite, aldol, allonal, amobarbital, amytal, anacin, analgesic, anesthesiant, anesthetic, anodyne, antipyrine, aspirin, atropine, barbital, barbitone, barbiturate, belladonna, bromide, bufferin, calmative, camphor, carbromal, chloral-hydrate, demerol, depressant, dilantin, goofball, hypnotic, ipral, lenitive, metrobamate, miltown, narcotic, nembutal,

opiate, opiatic, pacifier, painkiller, palliative, paregoric, pentobarbital, phenacetin, phenobarbital, pyramidon, quietener, quinine, remedy, reserpine, scopolamine, seconal, serpusil, sodium amytal, sodium bromide, sodium pentothal, somnifacient, soother, soporific, thalidomide, tranquilizer, trional, tuinal, valerian, valium, veronal

SEDENTARY deliberate, inactive, motionless, settled, sitting, slothful, stationary, tranquil

SEDER *food* bitter herbs, charoset(h), haroset(h), matzoth, spring lamb
herb maror
narrative passover-haggadah

SEDGE beachtan, bhabar, bogrush, brood, brown, bulrush, buttongrass, caddisfly, carex, chufa, ehuawa, flag, flock, fly, galingale, glumal, grass, insect, iris, mati, monocot, papyrus, sniddle, sweetflag, thatch, toetoe, toitoi, trichoptera, tussock
button kyllinga
fly granam, grannom
genus andropogan, carex, cyperus, eleocharis, eriophorum, fuirena, scirpus, xyris
hen clapper-rail
root chufa
warbler mockbird, reedbird, wren

SEDIMENT amurca, bottoms, deposit, drast, dregs, drewite, faex, fecula, greaves, grounds, grummel, heeltap, lees, loess, magma, refuse, remainder, residue, sapropel, settling(s), silt (age), slag, sludge, waste
deep-sea blue-mud
iron car(r)

SEDITION commotion, defiance, insurrection, mutiny, putsch, rebellion, revolt, revolution, strife, treason, tumult, turbulence, unrest

SEDITIONARY factitious, inciter, instigator, promoter, seditious, traitor

SEDITIOUS contumacious, disloyal, factious, faithless, insubordinate, mutinous,

perfidious, rebellious, riotous, traitorous, treacherous, treasonable

SEDUCE abuse, allure, beguile, betray, bewitch, blandish, captivate, corrupt, debase, debauch, deceive, decoy, defile, deflower, delude, demoralize, deprave, despoil, entice, force, induce, initiate, inveigle, invite, lead astray, lure, make, mislead, persuade, pervert, ravage, ravish, ruin, soil, sully, tempt, violate, wheedle, wrong

SEDUCEMENT See SEDUCTION.

SEDUCER don juan, enticer, libertine, lothario, rake, romeo, roue, wolf

SEDUCTION attraction, bribe, charm, corruption, enticement, lure, persuasion, stupration, temptation

SEDUCTIVE alluring, attractive, desirable, sexy, tempting

SEDULOUS active, assiduous, busy, constant, diligent, industrious, laborious, persevering, persistent, tireless, unremitting, untiring

SEDUM bird's-bread, moss, orphine, sengreen, stonecrop, wall-pepper

SEE accompany, apprehend, behold, bet, bishopric, call, catch, cathedra(l), chair, consult, contemplate, descry, detect, diocese, discern, discover, distinguish, effect, envisage, envision, escort, espy, examine, eye, gape, gaze, glance, glare, glimpse, glint, guard, inquire, inspect, ken, know, look, meet, note, notice, observe, office, perceive, pipe, provide, recognize, regard, remark, scan, scrutinize, scry, seat, sight, spot, spy, stare, survey, take in, tenez, throne, twig, undergo, understand, vide, view, visit, visualize, watch, witness
above (vide)supra
below (vide)infra
ecclesiastic bishropric, cathedra(l), chair, diocese, seat
eye to eye agree, concur
it through persevere, persist
red rage, rant, storm

through discern, discriminate, penetrate
to attend, care for, fix, take care of

SEED abilla, achene, achiote, achuete, acinus, acorn, alpist(e), ambrette, ancestry, bean, ben, boil, bubble, buckeye, bulb, calinut, carat, caraway, carnel, cokernut, corm, cydonium, decay, descendent, disseminule, drupe, egg, embryo, family, fennel, frijole, germ, grain, inoculate, issue, kernel, milt, nucule, nut, offspring, origin, ovule, pea, pignolin, pignon, pip (pin), pit, plant, pod, posterity, principe, progeny, putamen, pyrene, ream, samara, source, sow, spawn, sperm, spore, start, stock, stone, tare, tuber
apple pip
aromatic anise, anisum, caraway, nutmeg, poppy, sesame
astringent algarrobilla
-bearing organ pistil
beetle bean-weevil
bird mew-gull, pied-wagtail
bread-tree dika
cake wig(g)
capsule silique
carminative anise
case See *covering*, below.
cell cyst
coat, broken bran
comb. angi(o), carpo, sperm(ato), spermi(a)
covering aril(lode), bran, bur(r), carpel, endopleura, hull, husk, integument, legume, loment, peel, pod, shell, shuck, spiricle, teg(u)man, testa, theca
covering, pert. arillary, arillate
distribute drill, sow
-eater finch, grass-quit
edible barley, bean, berry, cereal, corn, endocarp, grain, kernel, legume, nut, oat, pea, pinole, rice, sesame, wheat
feeding on seminivorous
fenugreek helbeh
having small acinaceous
having 2 dispermous
having united synspermous
hot aneth, anise, caraway, mustard, pepper
immature ovule

leaf cotyledon

naked achene, achenium, achenocarp, akene

nut-like pinon

of mankind adapa

oily abilla

1-celled carpel

opening dehiscence

opium poppy paw

organ pistil

part aril, cotyledon, endopleura, endosperm, hilum, hypocotyl, pod, raphe, teg(u)men, testa, turnica

pert. acinaceous, arillary, arillate

plant endogen

pod See *vessel,* below.

poisonous calabar, nux vomica, physostigma

primitive spore

protein aleurone

remove core, gin, picul, pit

scars hila

small pip, seminule

tanning bomah-nut

vessel boll, bur(r), capsule, carpel, cod, follicle, hip, hull, kid, legume, pericarp, pod, shell, silicle, silique, theca, utricle

winged samara

without aspermous

SEEDED arable, dotted, full-grown, inoculated, matured, sown

SEEDLING liner, plant, stechling, steckling

protection cold frame, hothouse

stem caulicle

SEEDY debilitated, dingy, faded, lousy, mangy, miserable, needy, old, poky, poor, ragged, ratty, sc(r)uffy, shabby, shaggy, sick, slovenly, spiritless, squalid, tacky, threadbare, torn, worn, wretched

SEEK apply, ask for, aspire, attempt, beg, beseech, busk, canvass, cast, court, endeavor, ensue, entreat, essay, explore, fand, ferret, fetch, follow, fraist, hunt, importune, inquire, investigate, look(for)(up), probe, prospect, prowl, pursue, quest, ransack, request, research, rummage, scour, scout, search, shop, solicit, sue, try, woo

SEEKER applicant, candidate, petitioner, probe(r), requestor, searcher, tracer, zetetic

knowledge philonist, student

pleasure franion, sybarite

SEEL blind, close, happiness, hoodwink, list, pitch, roll, seal, sele, welfare

SEELY blessed, blissful, feeble, foolish, frail, good, happy, harmless, innocent, kind, poor, silly, simple, timid, weak, wretched

SEEM act, appear, befit, bid, consider, deem, feign, look, manifest, offer, peer, present, pretend, regard, sound

likely bid fair, promise

SEEMING apparent, appearance, aspect, befitting, credible, dissembling, guise, illusory, like(ly), look, masking, opinion, ostensible, plausible, pretended, proper, quasi, semblance, sham, show, specious, suitable

SEEMINGLY apparently, as if, likely, probably, quasi

SEEMLINESS decency, decorum, elegance, grace

SEEMLY appropriate(ly), beauteous, beautiful, becoming(ly), befitting, comely, comme il faut, congruous, consistent, decent(ly), decorous, demure, due, expedient, fair, fit(ting), graceful, handsome, likely, meet, nice, passably, pleasing, proper, rather, right, suitable, suited, tasteful

SEEN considering, learned, soon, versed, visible

already de ja vu

from above bird's-eye

SEENE *husband* endymion

SEEP drain, drip, exude, infiltrate, leak, ooze, percolate, run, sip(e), soak, spring, transude, truckle

SEER amphilochus, augur(er), chaldean, clairvoyant, diviner, forecaster, foreteller, gazer, haruspex, medium, melampus, mopsus, mystic, nostradamus, oracle, predictor, prognosticator, prophet, psychic, sage, scryer, soothsayer, sorcerer, spectator, swami, sybil, vates, visionary

SEERBAND turban

SEERESS al(b)runa, phoebad, prophetess, sybil, volva

SEESAW alternate, change, crossruff, dandle, oscillate, reciprocal, reciprocate, swing, teeter(totter), tiddle, tilter, titter, totter, vacillate, waver

-like bascule

SEETHE agitate, anger, boil, bubble, buller, burn, churn, cook, cree, decoct, digest, elixate, excite, explode, ferment, fizz, foam, fry, fume, hotter, itch, moil, rage, rave, saturate, simmer, soak, sob, sparkle, stew, stir, take offense, wall, walm

SEETHING aboil, boiling, burning, excitement, hot, humming, itching, passionate, scalding, surging, torrid, tumbling

SEG callosity, iris, SEDGE, sink

SEGMENT arc, arthromere, bit, cant(le), chapter, cleave, detail, divide, division, fraction, fragment, isomere, item, length, member, metamere, paragraph, parcel, part, piece, portion, sample, SECTION, sector, separate, somatome, somite, subdivision, syzygy, telson, tmema, tore, verse, ward

heraldic flanch(e)

pert. toric

SEGREGATE apart, classify, discriminate, divide, intern, isolate, part, quarantine, riddle, screen, seclude, select, separate, sequester, set aside, sever, sift, sort, winnow

SEGREGATION apartheid, discrimination, dispersion, distinction, division, insulation, isolation, quarantine, schism, secession, seclusion

SEGUB *son* jair

SEID chief, lord, prince, say(y)id

ancestor mohammed

SEIGNEUR lord, master, noble

SEILENOS *father* pan

SEILUN shiloh

SEINE fish, madrague, net, pocket, river, sagene, spiller, trap, trawl, tuck

city on paris, st cloud, troyes

left bank rive gauche
right bank rive droite
tributary aube, eure, marne, oise
SEINKIEWICZ *novel* quo vadis
SEIR edom, hor
descendant aran
offspring anah, dishan, dishon, ezar, lotan, shobal, timna, zibeon
SEISM earthquake
SEISMIC *sea wave* tsunami
SEIZE annex, apprehend, appropriate, arrest, arrogate, assume, attach, bag, beard, bind, bite, cap(ture), catch, clasp, claw, cleek, clench, clinch, clum, clutch, cly, collar, confiscate, control, cop, corral, deprehend, deprive(of), distrain, embargo, embrace, ensnare, entrap, fascinate, fasten, get(hold of), glom, grab, grant, grapnel, grapple, grasp, grip(e), hap, hent, hold, hook, hug, impound, impress, jump at, keep, nab, nail, nap, occupy, penetrate, pounce, prey, ravish, reave, rob, snare, snatch, spuilzie, steal, strike, take(hold of), throttle, tire, trap, usurp, vang, yoke
by neck collar, scrag, scruff
illegally usurp
the day carpe diem
SEIZURE abduction, access(ion), and(rolepsy, apoplexy, apprehension, appropriation, arrest, assault, attachment, attack, booty, caption, capture, catch, charley-horse, clonos, clonus, confiscation, cramp, dragnet, eclampsia, entasia, epilepsy, epitasis, fit, frenzy, grab, grand mal, grip, hold, holotony, ictus, manucapture, paroxysm, petit mal, possession, prehension, prisal, raptus, retention, seizin, snatch, spasm, spell, stoppage, stroke, taking, tellach, tetanus, throe
comb. lepsy
forcible angaria, angary
legal prisal
SEKH(M)ET hathor
husband ptah
SELADANG buffalo, gaur
SELASSIE, HAILE *name* elect of god, king of kings,

lion of judah, power of the holy trinity, ras-tafarimakonne
SELCOUTH marvel(ous), strange, unusual, wonder(ful)
SELDOM hardly(ever), infrequent(ly), not often, rare(ly), scarcely, sendle, sindle, sparsely, uncommonly, unoften
seen ant(e)rin, occasional, rare, scarce
SELE happiness, occasion, opportunity, season, time, welfare
SELECT adopt, appoint, assign, ballot, best, blue-ribbon, choice, choose, choosy, chosen, clannish, cliquish, cream, cull, decide, delicate, discriminate, discriminating, divide, eclectic, elect, elite, excerpt, exclusive, exempt, eximious, extract, garble, glean, good, handpick, opt, peerless, pick(ed), prefer(red), rare, recherche, restrictive, segregate, separate, set apart, sift, single out, superior, superlative, supreme, take, top-notch, try, unexcelled, vote, wale, winnow
by lot draw
SELECTION(S) alternative, ana(lecta), choice, choosing, collectanea, cull, discrimination, election, excerpt, extract, item, miscellany, option, passage, pick, piece, preference
comb. eclexis
pert. apolegamic
SELECTIVE choos(e)y, conscientious, demanding, discriminate, eclectic
service draft
SELECTOR classer, grader, sorter
SELEMNUS *beloved* argyra
SELENE artemis, hecate, luna, mene, moon
brother helios, sol
consort endymion, pan, zeus
daughter erse, nemea, pandia
parent euryphaessa, hyperion, thea, zeus
SELENIUM *compound* selenid(e)
source clausthalite, sulphur
SELENODONTA camelidae,

cameloidea, camels, llamas, pecora, tylopoda
SELEUCID *country* babylonia, bactria, persia, syria
emperor antiochus
SELEUCUS *ally* perdiccas, ptolemy
consort stratonice
enemy antigonus
father-in-law demetrius
friend antiochus, patrocles
parent antiochus, laodice
son demetrius
SELF absolute, atman, brahma, carnation, daena, ego, entity, identical, inbreed, incarnation, individual, jiva, own, particular, person(al), psyche, same, seity, selfishness, soi, unmixed, very, yours truly
-absorbed autistic, contemplative, introspective, introverted, personal, subjective
-acting automatic, spontaneous
-admiration See *-esteem*, below.
-amputation autotomy
-assertive bumptious, conceited, ego(t)istic, obtrusive, pert, pushy, vain
-assurance aplomb, brass, certainty, cheek, confidence, decision, nerve, poise, presumption, self-confidence, sureness
-assured balanced, calm, complacent, confident
-centered egocentric, independent, introverted, selfish, self-seeking, smug, stable, stationary
comb. aut, auth, auto
command nerve
-complacent priggish, smug, vain
-conceit nosism
-confidence aplomb, assurance, balance, chutzpah, composure, crest, crust, hubris, macho, poise, presence, self-reliance
confidence, lack inferiority complex
-conscious bashful, discomfited, embarrassed, gawky, ill-at-ease, shy, timid, uncomfortable, uneasy
-contained absolute, calm, collected, composed, cool,

independent, reserved, uncommunicative

-*contradictory* absurd, illogical, paradoxical

-*control* abstinence, aplomb, balance, calmness, discipline, encraty, forbearance, patience, restraint, spartanism, stoicism, temperance, tolerance, will

-*defense* aikido, boxing, fencing, fighting, fisticuffs, j(i)ujitsu, j(i)ujutsu, judo, kung fu

-*deification* autotheism

-*denial* abnegation, abstinence, ascesis, asceticism, check, discipline, forbearance, puritanism, renunciation, restraint, sacrifice, temperance

-*denying* ascetic, spartan

-*derived existence* aseity

-*determination* autonomy, freedom, independence

-*determined* independent, spontaneous

-*devouring* authophagous

-*digestion* autolysis, autoproteolysis

-*discipline* ascesis

-*disciplined* austere, spartan, temperate

-*dividing* autotomic

-*effacing* bashful, modest, retiring, shrinking, shy

-*esteem* amour-propre, assurance, complacency, conceit, ego(t)ism, pride, smugness, vainglory, vanity

-*estimation* autometry

-*evident* aphoristic, axiomatic, clear, manifest, obvious, patent, truistic

-*evident truth* axiom, truism

-*examination* introspection

-*existent* increate, ingenerate, innate, uncaused

fear of autophobia, autophoby

feeding on autophagia

-*fertilization* autogamy

-*fulfillment* samadhi

-*generated* autogenous, endogenous, spontaneous

-*government* autonomy, democracy, discipline, independence, restraint, sovereignty, swaraj

-*heal* allheal, blue-curls, brownwort, burnet, figwort, hookheal, hookweed, mint, prunella, sanicle, saxifrage,

tarweed, trichostema, valerian

-*help* coueism

-*identity* egoity, ipseity, proprium

-*importance* exaltation, pomposity, pompousness, pretention, pretentiousness, pride, toploftyness, vanity

-*important* biggety, chesty, consequential, ego(t)istical, pompous, pretentious, proud, purdy, toplofty, vain

-*important person* cockalorum, whippersnapper

-*indulgence* dissipation. freeliving, pleasure, selfishness

inner anima

-*knowledge* anstoss, autognosis, autology, introspection

-*love* amour-propre, autophilia, conceit, narcissism, philauty, self-esteem

-*moving* autokinetic, automatic

-*nourishing* autotropic

other alter ego

own ainsell, nainsel

pert. personal

-*possessed* assured, calm, composed, cool, undisturbed, unperturbed

-*possession* aplomb, assurance, composure, confidence, coolness, discipline, nonchalance, poise, savoirfaire, tact

-*potentate* autocrat

-*produced* autogenous

-*propelling* automotive

-*reliant* bold, courageous, free, independent

-*reproach* contrition, guilt, penitence, regret, remorse, rue

-*restraint* abstinence, ascesis, balance, continence, havlagah, reserve, retenue, temperance

-*righteous* false, pharisaical, pietistical, pious, preachy, sanctimonious, smug, stuffy

-*satisfied* assured, complacent, content, jaunty, priggish, smug, stodgy, vain

second alter ego

-*seeker* gold-digger, hog, sycophant, timeserver, toady, tufthunter

-*styled* soi-disant

-*sufficiency* aseitas, aseity, autarchy

-*sufficient* absolute, aloof,

autotelic, cool, haughty, heterotelic, independent, overbearing, reserved, unfriendly, unsocial

-*taught person* autodidact

-*treatment* autotherapy

universal atman

-*willed* contrary, headstrong, obstinate, perverse, set, unyielding, wayward

-*worship* autholatry, autotheism, egotism

SELFHOOD seity

SELFISH anerly, asocial, base, dissocial, egocentric, egotistic(al), hoggish, illiberal, mean, piggish, possessive, self-centered, small, sordid, stingy

SELFISHNESS calculation, egoism, egomania, egotism, expedience, illiberality, philauty, self-interest, stinginess, suicism

SELFLESS altruistic, charitable, uncalculating, ungrudging, unselfish

SELFSAME alike, equal, equivalent, identical, like, tantamount, uniform, very

SELL auction, bargain, barter, betray, bilk, bootleg, cant, cheat, close out, consign, convert, convey, convince, cover, deal, deceive, deed, deliver, dispose of, dump, exchange, fence, give, gull, hawk, hoax, joke, market, peddle, persuade, retail, scalp, shave, trade, transfer, trick, unload, vend, wholesale, yield

above official rate scalp

at auction roup

at lower price cheapen, discount, dump, undercut, unload

buy and chop

for bring, cost, fetch, get, realize, yield

out betray(al), blab, desert

SELLER agent, auctioneer, bear, boomer, busker, cadger, chapman, colporter, coster(monger), dealer, drummer, factor, fence, hawker, huckster, jobber, marketer, merchant, middleman, peddler, pedlar, salesman, saltcellar, shopkeeper, sutler, trader, tradesman, vender, vendor, wholesaler

SELLY curious, extremely,

marvel(ously), mysterious, seely, self, strangely, wonder(ful)

SELTZER club soda, mineral water, mixer, soda, vichy, water

SELVAGE border, edge, flucan, fringe, gouge, layer, list(ing), sticking, wire

SEM See SHEM.

SEMALEUS zeus

SEMANTICS meaning, semasiology, sematology, semology, significs

SEMAPHORE fishtail, heliogram, signal, wave, wigwag

SEMBLABLE alike, apparent, conformable, like, ostensible, representation, resemblance, resembling, seeming, similar, suitable

SEMBLANCE affectation, affinity, air, analogy, apparition, appearance, aspect, copy, countenance, exterior, face, feint, figure, form, ghost, gloss, guise, image, likelihood, likeness, look, mien, picture, pose, presumption, pretense, pretext, representation, resemblance, seeming, sham, shape, show, similarity, similitude, simulacrum, skerrick, spece, umbrage, visage
false coloring

SEMBLANT air, face, figure, mien, pomp, pretense, SEMBLANCE, show

SEMBLE assemble, collect, compare, cope, dissemble, gather, imitate, like(n), meet, pretend, represent, seem, simulate

SEME bezante, dispersed, fleury, gerated, g(o)uttee, gutty, hurty, sprinkling, strewing
de-lis floretty

SEMEIN *son* mattathiah

SEMEIUS *son* jairus

SEMELE keraunia
consort zeus
nurse beroe
parent cadmus, harmonia
sibling agave, antonoe, ino, polydorus
son bacchus, dionysos, dionysus

SEMELIA *hut* chikee
son ananias, nathan

SEMESTER biannual, course, half, period, term

SEMI half, incomplete, part
(ial), partly, trailer

SEMIAPE lemur

SEMICIRCLE crescent, graphometer, halfcircle, hemicycle, quadrant, sector, sextant

SEMIDOME concha

SEMILIQUID gelatinous, jellied, muddled, r(o)ily, slimy, sloughy, sludgy, slushy, soft, squashy, turbid, uliginose

SEMILLON sauterne, wine

SEMINAL germ(inal), originative, seed, zaftig

SEMINAR class, course, workshop

SEMINARY academy, college, germ, institute, juvenate, school, seedbed, seedsowing, sower, university
rabbinic yeshibah, yeshiva(h)

SEMINATION dispersal, dissemination, inoculation, propagation

SEMINOLE *chief* osceola
indian creek, mikasuki, muskhogean

SEMIPORCELAIN gombroon

SEMIRAMIS astarte
consort ninus
mother derceto

SEMITE, SEMITIC jew(ish)
alphabet brahmi
ancestor shem
demon alukah
god baal(ath), ballat, hadad, moloch, shamash, steraph
goddess allat, anath, asherah, asherim, ashtoreth, astarte, atargatis
language akkadian, amharic, amorite, arabic, aramaic, babylonian, ethiopic, gafat, g(h)eez, ghese, harari, hebraic, hebrew, maltese, sabean, syriac, syrian, talmudic, tigre, tigrina
non kassite
people accadian, akkadian, amhara, ammon, arab, aramaean, assyrian, babylonian, canaanite, caucasian, chaldean, harari, hebrew, jew, moabite, phoenician, sha(i)gia, shaikiyeh, sumerian
pillar massebah
weight gerah, mina, shekel

SEMITONE feint, halfstep, halftone, hemitone, limma

SEMMIT active, feeble, limber, lively, pliable, slender, undershirt, weak

SEMOLINA flour, grain, middlings, semolella, semona, sizings, sujee, suji, wheat

SEMPER See ALWAYS; FOREVER.

SEMPITERNAL boundless, endless, eternal, ever(lasting), illimitable, infinite, lasting, perdurable, perpetual, unceasing

SEMPRONIUS *kinsman* titus andronicus

SEN *1/10th* rin
100 yen

SENATE assembly, body, boule, chamber, council, diet, gerousia, legislature, parliament
and roman people spqr
house curia

SENATOR castellan, congressman, consul, councilor, legislator, representative, solon

SEND address, affect, bestow, broadcast, cast, channel, circulate, commit, consign, convey, delight, deliver, detail, direct, discharge, dismiss, dispatch, drive, eject, embark, emit, expedite, export, express, fling, forward, freight, give, grant, hurl, inflect, issue, mail, move, ordain, pass, post, propel, remand, remit, route, ship, throw, thrust, transfer, transmit, utter, vouchsafe
away banish, cashier, dismiss, dispatch, relegate, repulse, rusticate, ship
back echo, refract, remand, remise, remit, return
by mail drop, post
down demit, rusticate, strike
for call, summon
forth beam, cast, disgorge, effuse, emit, export, fling, mand, publish, yield
in immiss, intromit
into exile banish, relegate
money remit
-off beginning, consignment, dispatch, launching, parting, start, wing
out assign, beam, commission, deport, diffuse, disgorge, dispatch, emit, exile, export, issue, launch, publish, shoot, speed

packing discharge, dismiss, fire, repulse
to jail imprison, lag, mittimus, sentence
to obscurity relegate
up arrest, commit, fly, hoist, imprison, sentence
SENECA *banishment site* corsica
birthplace cordova
consort helvia, julia, paulina
enemy caligula
grandson lucan
pupil domitius, nero
slayer nero
tragedy medea
SENECIO ashwort, bindweed, birdseed, butterweed, cankerweed, cineraria, groundsel, ragwort
SENEGAL *capital* dakar
city dakar, kaolack, kaollak, rufisque, thies
conquerer faideherbe
gazelle korin
language wolof
leader See AFRICA *statesman.*
peak gounou
port dakar
president senghor
river faleme, gambia, saloum, senegal
timber cailcedra
tribe bambara, diola, foula, fulani, laobe, malinke, mandingo, peul, serer(e), soce, tukuler, tukulor, wolof
SENESCENCE age, dotage, senilism, senility
SENESCENT See SENILE.
SENESCHAL bailiff, majordomo, steward
SENGREEN houseleek, periwinkle, saxifrage, sedum, vinca
SENILE aged, ancient, anile, childish, daffle, decrepit, deteriorating, doddering, doddery, doited, dold, dotard(y), doted, doting, dotty, elderly, feeble, grannified, infirm, old, rickety, senescent, superannuated, weak
SENILITY caducity, childishness, decrepitude, dotage, infirmity, old age, progeria, second childhood, senescence, senilism, weakness
premature progeria
symptom alzheimer's disease, pick's disease
SENIOR aine, ancient, chief, dean, doyen, elder(most),

eldest, firstborn, firstling, head, leading, major, master, older, oldest, parent, paterfamilias, patriarch, primogenitary, sire, student, superior, undergraduate
citizen oldster
SENIORITY age, eldership, precedence, priority, quality, rank, state, status, superiority
by birth primogeniture
SENNA bauhinia, brachystegia, caesalpinia, cassia, gymnocladus, purgative, remedy, rug, shrub
infusion assi, blackdrink, ya(u)pon, y(o)upon
SENNACHERIB *father* sargon, shalmaneser
general rabshakeh
grandson asshurbanipal
kingdom assyria
son adrammelech, assarhaddon, esarhaddon, sharezer
SENNAR *native* funj(e), funji
SENNET call, fish, signal, spet, week
SENNIT cord, plait, rope, yarn
SENOR don, gentleman, herr, man, mister, noble, signor(e), sir
SENORA frau, lady, madam, mistress, mrs, signora, woman
SENORITA blenny, girl, iridio, kelpfish, mademoiselle, miss, signorina, srita, srta, woman, young lady
SENSATION appearance, awareness, bomb(shell), coenesthesis, consciousness, eclat, emotion, esthesis, experience, feel(ing), hit, howl, image, impression, marvel, panic, passion, percept(ion), riot, savor, scream, sensibility, smash, success, surprise, taste, tenstrike, thrill, tibbet, tone, triumph, vedana
cold rhigosis
confusion allochinia
deprive of benumb
fright frisson
lacking apathic, numb
loss ap(a)esthesia
prickly pins and needles
subjective aura, psychesthesia
tingling dirl, prickle

visual phose, photoma
warm ardor
without thought anoesis
SENSATIONAL barnumesque, blood-and-thunder, dramatic, emotional, exciting, great, lurid, melodramatic, outstanding, purple, saffron, scandalous, socko, spinechilling, splashy, stimulating, stunning, superb, terrific, thrilling, tremendous, wonderful, yellow
SENSATIONALISM associationism, blare, drama(tics), melodrama, sensism, sensualism
SENSE acumen, analyze, apperceive, appreciation, apprehend, awareness, brains, cognizance, comprehend, consciousness, course, direction, discernment, discretion, drift, estimate, examine, experience, faculty, feel(ing), foresight, gist, grasp, gumption, hearing, import, impression, intelligence, intuit(ion), judgment, know, meaning, mind, opinion, perceive, perception, prudence, purport, realization, realize, reason, respond, sapience, sensation, sensibility, sentience, sight, significance, signification, smell, sound(ness), taste, test, touch, trend, try, understand(ing), view, wisdom, wit(s)
common balance, judgment, prudence
loss of anesthesia
measure ounce
of right and wrong conscience
of sight vision
of smell scent
of touch feel
organ antenna, beneceptor, ear, exteroceptor, eye, nerve, nose, receptor, sensilla, skin, tongue
organ science esthematology
perceived by sentient
seven animation, feeling, hearing, sight, smell(ing), speech, taste, touch
sixth clairvoyance, esp
vital coenesthesis
without foolish, inept
SENSELESS absurd, blind, buzzard, crazy, dull, dumb,

SENSIBILITY fatuitous, fatuous, foolish, futile, halfwitted, idiotic, illogical, inane, inanimate, inept, insane, insensate, insensible, irrational, mad, meaningless, nonsensical, peevish, pointless, purposeless, ridiculous, silly, sottish, stupid, unconscious, unfeeling, unintelligent, unreasonable, unsound, unwise, witless

SENSIBILITY aesthesia, affection, awareness, discernment, discrimination, emotion, esthesia, feeling, heart, impressionability, insight, judgment, perception, preceptivity, receptiveness, receptivity, recognition, responsiveness, sensation, sensitivity, sentiment(ality), susceptibility, susceptivity

SENSIBLE actual, alive, appreciable, astute, awake, aware, cognizant, conscious, considerable, cool, corporeal, delicate, discreet, grateful, impressible, intelligent, judicious, levelheaded, logical, material, palpable, perceptible, persuaded, phenomenal, physical, ponderable, provident, prudent, rational, realistic, reasonable, responsive, sagacious, sage, sane, sapient, satisfied, sensitive, sensual, shrewd, sober, solid, sound, staid, striking, substantial, susceptible, tangible, well-balanced, wise

SENSITIVE acute, affectible, allergic, ardent, artistic, compatible, delicate, discriminate, edel, emotional, exposed, exquisite, huffy, impressible, impressionable, inclined, influenced, intense, irritable, irritated, keen, liable, miffed, miffy, moved, nimble, open, pliable, pliant, poignant, profound, prone, raw, reactive, receptive, responsive, sensible, sentient, sentimental, sharp, skinless, sore, subject, susceptible, susceptive, sympathetic, temperamental, tender, te(t)chy, thinskinned, ticklish, touchy, vivid
brier beshamed-mary
pea honeycup
plant mimosa, oxalis
SENSITIVITY affectibility,

algesia, allergy, delicacy, edelkeit, esthesia, fineness, impressibility, impressionability, irritability, passion, sensibility, sentience, susceptibility, tact, touch
excessive acro(a)esthesia, anaphylaxis
lack blind spot
lacking hebetate
to pain algesia
SENSITIZE cultivate, excite, irritate, quicken, refine, sharpen, stimulate, stir, whet
SENSORY organoleptic, perceptual, sensorial, sensual
SENSUAL animal(istic), bestial, boarish, bodily, brutal, brute, brutish, carnal, coarse, corporeal, cruel, cyprian, epicurean, flesh(l)y, gay, gross, lascivious, lewd, licentious, lustful, mollitious, pandemic, physical, saturnalian, seductive, sensuous, sultry, swinish, sybaritic, voluptuous, vulgar, wanton, worldly
SENSUALIST bon vivant, carpet knight, epicure(an), gourmand, gourmet, hedonist, heliogabulus, sybarite, voluptuary
SENSUALITY animalism, debauchery, flesh, indulgence, intemperance, license, lust, luxury
goddess baubo
SENSUOUS fleshly, luscious, luxurious, satiny, sensual, soft
SENTENCE adage, adjudge, adjudicate, aphorism, attaint, award, axiom, censure, commit, condemn, contents, damn, decide, decision, decree, denounce, determination, doom, futwa, impresa, judge, judgment, juise, juwise, maxim, meaning, opinion, passage, period, phrase, posy, pronounce, proposal, proposition, proscribe, rap, rule, saw, saying, send up, settle, significance, subject, term, trope, verdict, versicle, view
analyze parse
balance parison
concluding apilog(ue), epiphonema
construction syntax
part adjective, adverb, apo-

dosis, clause, noun, object, phrase, predicate, subject, verb, word
prison lag, life, rap, stretch
same backwards and forwards palindrome
short clause
structure error anacoluthon
type complex, compound, simple
SENTENTIOUS aphoristic, ceremonious, compact, concise, conventional, curt, eloquent, energetic, expressive, formal, grandiloquent, laconic, meaningful, moralistic, pithy, pompous, pregnant, proverbial, showy, significant, succinct, taciturn, terse, wise
SENTIENT conscious(ness), feeling, mind, perceiving
SENTIMENT affect, attitude, belief, conviction, emotion, feeling(s), gush, idea, impression, judgment, maxim, motto, notion, opinion, passion, perception, pledge, sensation, sensibility, sentimentality, slant, substance, toast, view
SENTIMENTAL bathetic, corny, dewyeyed, emotional, fond, foolish, gushing, gushy, inane, insipid, lackadaisical, maudlin, mawkish, melodramatic, mushy, nambypamby, nostalgic, romantic, schmaltzy, sensitive, sloppy, slushy, smarmy, sony, soppy, spoony, sticky, sugary, susceptible, syrupy, tender, unctuous
SENTIMENTALITY bathos, goo, hearts and flowers, inanity, mawkishness, mush(iness), nostalgia, nostalgy, s(c)hmal(t)z, slop(piness), slush, smarm, sobstory, syrup
SENTINEL, SENTRY argus, bantay, cockatoo, deino, factionary, guard, keeper, kite, lookout, patrol, pephedro, picket, picquet, soldier, vedette, vigil, wait, warden, warder, watch(er), watchman
box station
mounted graeae, graiae, vedette
pert. perdue
SENTRY See SENTINEL.

SENUAH *son* judah
SEOUL keijo
SEOWAN *indian* oto(e), sioux
SEPAD believe, suppose, think
SEPAL calyx, leaf, petal
part calcar
SEPARATE abscise, alienate, alone, analyze, another, apart, assort, avulse, bisect, break, bust up, canton, classify, cleave, demobilize, detach, different, differentiate, disconnect(ed), discrete, discriminate, disengage, disgregate, disjoin(t), dismiss, dispart, disperse, dissever, dissociate, distinct, distinguish, disunite, diverse, divide, divorce, eliminate, fork, free, independent, individual, intervene, isolate(d), lone, part(icular), partition, peculiar, refine, repudiate, respective, retire, riddle, rive, roulette, scatter, screen, secern, seclude(d), segregate, sejunct, sever, sieve, sift, single, sole, solitary, sort, split, strain, strip, sunder, unique, unscramble, wean, withdraw(n)
comb. abs, dis, idio
fibers hackle
grain fan, thrash, thresh, winnow
ore jig, smelt
threads sleave, sley, unravel
SEPARATED alone, distant, divorced, extracted, free, lone, parted, shredded
comb. dialy
SEPARATELY apart, disjointly, independently, one by one, severally, singly, sunderly, sundry
SEPARATING between, disjunction, disjunctive, schiztic
SEPARATION analysis, apartheid, avulsion, breach, break(away)(up), deduction, diacope, dialysis, disjunction, dispersion, distance, distinction, disunion, divergence, division, divorce, elution, gulf, isolation, parting, partition, quarantine, schism, seclusion, severance, shedding, tmesis, twinning
forcible avulsion

of soul from body psychorrhagy
total diremption
SEPARATIST apostate, bimmeler, dissenter, heretic, nonconformist, pilgrim, schismatic, seceder, secessionist, sectary
SEPARATOR centrifuge, chorizont, creamer, machine, ravel, settler
SEPHARDIC *language* judesmo, ladina
SEPHARVITE *god* anammelech
SEPIA brown, cuttlebone, cuttlefish, dun, ink, pigment, roto(gravure)
SEPOY policeman, soldier, telinga
mutineer pandy
SEPPUKU harakari, harakiri, suicide
SEPS lizard, serpent, snake
SEPT area, clan, class, dog star, family, fine, group, horde, horus, kin, race, railing, screen, seven, sib, tribe
chief flaith
SEPTEMBER *birthstone* chrysolite, sapphire
29th mich(a)elmas
SEPTIC carious, diseased, putrefacient, putrefactive, putrescent, putrid, rotten, saprogenic, saprophilous, saprophytic, spoiled
tank sewer
SEPTICEMIA blood poisoning, pyemia, toxemia
SEPTUM dissepiment, myocomma, myotome, partition, phragma, tabula, vitta, wall
SEPULCHER bier, burial, bury, catacomb, cist, coffin, entomb, grave, monument, repository, tomb, tumulus, urn, vault
SEPULCHRAL charnel, deep, funereal, gloomy, grave, hollow, low, sad, tumulary
SEQUACIOUS attendant, compliant, dependent, ductile, following, malleable, plastic, pliable, pliant, servile
SEQUEL addendum, aftermath, afterthought, appendix, arriere-pensee, arrish, backwash, codicil, colophon, conclusion, consequence, continuance, continuation,

eddish, effect, end(ing), epilogue, finish, follow-up, issue, outcome, postscript, result, rowen, secundines, sequence, suffix, supplement, tailpiece, termination, upshot
SEQUENCE arrangement, chain, course, cycle, ential, following, gamut, gradation, hymn, order, progression, run, scale, sequel, series, set, straight, string, succession, suite, tierce, train
arrange in seriate
SEQUENT attendant, consecutive, consequent, discrete, ensuant, ensuing, follower, following, sequel, serial, succeeding, successive
SEQUENTIAL consecutive, continuous, deducible, discrete, processive, serial, succeeding
SEQUESTER appropriate, attach, cloister, condemn, confiscate, disclaim, enisle, insulate, isolate, mediator, reclude, referee, remove, renounce, retire, seclude, segregate, seize, separate, sequestrate, single, solate, take, umpire, withdraw
SEQUESTERED alone, cloistered, disclaimed, isolated, lonely, private, recluse, removed, renounced, retired, secluded, seized, separated, solitary, unfrequented, withdrawn
SEQUIN basket, chequeen, coin, disk, spang(le), venetian, zecchino, zequin
SEQUOIA big tree, cedar, redwood
largest general sherman
SER gentleman, sir
1/80th tola
1/16th miskal
40 maund
SERAGLIO caravansary, enclosure, harem, inn, khan, oda, palace, resthouse, serai, warehouse, zenana
SERAH *parent* asher
SERAI See SERAGLIO.
SERAIAH *son* ezra
SERAPE blanket, cloak, manta, poncho, shawl
SERAPH angel, archangel, cherub, saint
city nis
SERAPHIC adorable, angelic,

beatific, cherubic, holy, pious, pure, refined, sublime, unworldly, zealot
doctor st bonaventure
SERAPIS See OSIRIS.
SERBIA *ancient* illyria
brigands tchetnitsi, uskoks
coin dinar
dance kolo
dialect shtokavski
district ruler zupan
fairy vila, vily
hero marko
king alexander, peter
legislature skupshtina
measure ralo
nationalist chetnik
native slav
ruler cral
SERE anoint, cere, claw, dessicated, different, diverse, dried, dry, effete, many, SEAR, separate, several, talon, threadbare, various, wax, withered, worn
SEREIN dew, mist, rain
SERENADE alborada, aubade, ballad, court, nocturne, serenata, sing, song, strephonade, woo
mock callithump, charivari, chivari, shivaree
SERENDIP See CEYLON.
SERENE calm, clear, collected, composed, content, cool, dispassionate, easy, halcyon, light, pacific, peaceful, phlegmatic, placid, quiet, sattvic, sedate, serein, shining, smooth, steady, still(y), stoical, tranquil, undisturbed, unperturbed, unruffled
SERENITY balance, calmness, composure, cool, equanimity, peace, quiet (ness), repose, sattva, tranquility
SERF adscript, bondslave, bondsman, chattel, churl, colona, colonus, esne, eta, helot, hireling, litus, menial, neif(e), peasant, penest, peon, praedial, servant, servus, theow, thrall, vassal, villein, yanacona
SERFDOM bondage, captivity, helotism, helotry, serfhood, servitude
SERGE clay, fabric, sagathy, twill, worsted
SERGEANT attendant, chamberlain, chiaus, esquire, nco, noncom, officer,

sarge, servant, surgeon, tenant, topkick
-at-arms bailiff, policeman
-at-law counto(u)r
fish bonito, cabio, coal, cobia, cubbyyew, ling, robalo, snook
major pintano
word hup
SERGESTUS *companion* aeneas
SERIAL consecutive, continual, continuous, discrete, ensuing, following, periodic (al), publication, sequent (ial), successive
SERIATIM consecutively, serially
SERICA See CHINA.
SERICEOUS lustrous, satiny, sericate, silk(y), velvety
SERICULTURE magnanerie
SERIEMA bird, cariama, chunga, gruiform, screamer
SERIES beadroll, cascade, catalogue, category, catena, chain, course, drift, dwyka, gamut, gradation, list, progression, row, run, scale, sequence, set, streak, string, succession, suit(e), system, train
arranged in installment, serial, seriate, seriatim
connected catena
consecutive run, streak
in a en suite
SERINUS canary(bird), dendroica, finch
SERIOLA amberfish, amberjack
SERIOUS acute, ascetic, austere, capital, considerate, contemplative, dangerous, deep, demure, earnest, funereal, grave, great, grievous, grim, heavy, important, keen, meditative, momentous, profound, reflective, rum, sad, sedaté, severe, sober, solemn, somber, staid, stern, sullen, thoughtful, weighty, zealous
SERIOUSLY deeply, earnestly, gravely, sequential, seriatim, soberly
SERMON address, allocution, discourse, dissertation, exhortation, harangue, homily, khutbah, lecture, lesson, pastoral, preach(ment), prelection, reprimand, reproof, scolding, serement, speak, speech, talk

subject text
SERMONIZE admonish, expound, lecture, moralize, speak
SEROLIN coprosterol, koprosterin
SERO(O)N bale, crate, hamper, package, pannier
SEROTINE bat, late
SEROUS fluid, thin, watery
SEROW animal, antelope, goral, jagla
SERPENT aboma, adder, ahi, apepi, apophis, asp, basilisk, boiga, cobra, coil, crocodile, deceiver, dipsass, dragon, elops, entwine, gerard, hydrus, jararaca, krait, monster, naga, ophidian, reprobate, reptile, rope, satan, scytale, seps, SNAKE, toad, train, viper, worm
-bearer ophiuchus
brazen nehushtan
changed to achelous, cadmus, harmonia
comb. ophis
-eater markhor, secretary-bird
elapine naia, naja
fabulous basilisk
feathered gucumatz, kukulkan, quetzalcoatl
garden of eden ophis
god quetzalcoatl
goddess buto
grass bistort
heart of alphard
hooded cobra
king s(h)esha
-like anguine, ophidian
many-headed adissechen, amphisbaena, ananta, azhidahaka, s(h)esha
midgard jormungand(r)
monster ellops
mythological adis(h)esha, amphisbaena, ananta, apepi, apophis, azhidahaka, basilisk, buto, dahak, dipsas, dragon, ellops, hydra, jormungandr, nidhogg, nidhug, s(h)esha
old satan, s(h)esha
pert. anguine
sacred avanyu, awanyu
sky ahi
star alya, ophiuran
stone draconites
symbol of satan, wisdom
tongue dagger, tang
venomous prester, seps
victim laocoon

water hydra
world ananta, s(h)esha
worship ophism
worshipper naassene, ophile, perate
SERPENTINE (See also *kind*, below.) anfractuous, anguiform, anguilliform, anguine, circuitous, crooked, cunning, devious, diabolic, eel-like, flexuous, indirect, insinuate, lumbriciform, meandering, meandrous, metaxite, ophidian, ophioid, ophite, roundabout, sinuous, snake-like, snaky, still, subtle, tortuous, vermiform, wily, wind(ing), worm, zigzag
king antigorite, baltimorite, bowenite, chrysotile, marmolite, metaxite, picrolite, retinalite
motif arabesque
SERPIGO herpes, ringworm, tetter, tinea
SERRAN(A) guapena, sandfish, scorpionfish
SERRANID centromida, centropomus, grouper, robalo, seabass
SERRANO gitanemuk, percoid, squirrelfish
SERRASALMO caribe, charicinida, fish
SERRATE argute, notch(ed), prionodont, raffle, sawed, serried, toothed
SERRATION dentile, notching
SERRIED compact, concise, crowded, dense
SERRY close, crowd, press
SERTORIUS *birthplace* nursia
conspirator antonius, aufidius, manlius, perperna
enemy metellus, pompey, sulla
friend cinna
lieutenant herennius, julius, perperna
mother rhea
officer caepio, didius, marius
slayer perperna
SERUG nahor
SERUM antitoxin, biolog.. (al), fluid, whey
comb. oro
-like serous
SERVANT 3 boy, dey, fag, gyp, man 4 amah, ayah, bata, char, chef, cook, dasi, davy, deem, esne, grub,

help, hind, jurr, leud, maid, maty, mozo, neif, page, peat, peon, serf, syce, taio 5 agent, alila, bacha, bagot, biddy, bonne, boots, boult, chela, davus, gilly, groom, hamal, helot, mammy, neife, nurse, scout, sewer, slave, sosia, valet, wench 6 abdiel, alipin, batman, bearer, bildar, butler, chaker, colona, coolie, cotter, dorine, drudge, fellah, ferash, flunky, garcon, gillie, grumio, haiduk, hamaul, helper, khamal, lackey, menial, minion, porter, potboy, shamus, sircar, slavey, teaboy, teague, tenant, thrall, tranio, tweeny, varlet, vassal, worker 7 abigail, ancilla, bouchal, duftery, equerry, famulus, hackney, hummaul, malchus, pandour, pantler, papelon, peasant, piqueur, pisanio, shammes, shammus, villein 8 bondsman, chaprasi, chasseur, coistrel, coistril, domestic, employee, factotum, follower, handmaid, milkmaid, myrmidon, retainer, scullion, sergeant, servitor, vadelect, wardmain 9 assistant, attendant, charwoman, dependent, housemaid, laundress, maniciple, underling 10 scrubwoman 11 chamberlain, chambermaid, cinderwench, potwalloper, subordinate 12 scullery maid
armed pandour
boy boots, bouchal, chokra, knave
camp bildar
chief sir-rag
college gyp, scout
domestic all-work, hewe, maid, matranee, scullion, sleep-in, tweeny
female ama(h), ancilla, ayah, bonne, dasi, girl, handmaid, lass, maid, mammy, muchacha, nan(ny), nurse, pamela, skivvy, wardmaid, wench
garment apron, livery, uniform
general factotum
group retinue, staff
man andrew, boy, butler, g(h)illie, gilly, jack, khans-

ama, mozo, muchacho, servitor, swain, valet
of god (See also CHURCHMAN, MONK.) abdallah, abdiel
pert. famulary, menial
retired emeritus
tent-pitching clashy
SERVE abet, accommodate, act, administer, advance, aid, answer, apply, assist, attend, avail, await, befit, benefit, beset, bestead, carve, cater to, deal, deliver, distribute, encourage, enlist, enroll, execute, fag, fawn, forward, function, furnish, further, give, help, kae, labor, ladle, look after, maid, mess, minister, obey, oblige, officiate, pander to, permit, pitch, play, promote, provision, satiate, satisfy, settle, stand, succor, suffice, suit, summon, supply, tend, throw, toady, truckle, valet, victual, wait, work
notice admonish, advise, announce, caution, enjoin, exhort, notify, resign, warn
out administer, deal, distribute, mete
tea pour
SERVER acolyte, carhop, caterer, garcon, host, ladle, lazy-susan, salver, spade, steward(ess), tray, urn, waiter, waitress
SERVICE account, advantage, aid, allegiance, assistance, attendance, avail, benefit, business, ceremony, chakari, complin(e), cornage, devoir, devotion(s), duty, employ(ment), equipage, evensong, exercises, favor, fealty, funeral, gain, help, homage, interest, kindness, labor, lauds, liturgy, mass, matins, ministration, ministry, musaf, nones, novena, obsequy, office, position, prayer(s), profit, recompense, repair, retinue, revival, rigging, rite(s), ritual, servitude, sext, tendance, tierce, use(fulness), utility, value, vespers, vigils, wage(s), work, worship, worth, yizkor
charge fee, gratuity, tip
choral matins, vespers

compulsory angaria, angary, conscription, draft, servitude, slavery

domestic chakari

due angaria, angary, boon

evangelistic revival

feudal angaria, avera(ge), bedrip, boon, headward, seaward

50 years jubilarian

for 4 starter-set

for the dead dirge, elegy, funeral, threnody

military airforce, army, conscription, duty, enlistment, escuage, hitch, marines, navy, stretch, term

of beneficial

public electricity, gas, utility, water

religious aha, chapel, church, evensong, lauds, mass, matins, seder, synaxis, vespers

room butlery, buttery, pantry

tree checker, shadbush, sorb(us)

SERVICE, ROBERT *saloon* malamute

SERVICEABLE advantageous, available, beneficial, commodious, durable, friendly, helpful, invaluable, kind, lasting, obliging, steadable, thrifty, useful, valuable

SERVICEBERRY shadbush

SERVICEMAN See SOLDIER.

SERVILE abject, base, bond, caitiff, cowering, crawling, cringing, dependent, enslaved, fawning, ignoble, literal, mean, menial, obsequious, parasitic, sequacious, slavish, subject, submissive, subservient, supine, sycophantic, truckling, vassal

SERVILIUS *master* timon

SERVING course, cover, dishful, fitting, helping, meal, part, plate, portion, smack, tending, whipping

name meaning obed

table buffet, sideboard

SERVITOR apprentice, assistant, attendant, exhibitioner, fag, groom, gyp, page, punter, SERVANT, squire

SERVITUDE apprenticeship, bondage, captivity, depend-

ence, slavery, subjection, theowdom, thirlage, vassalage

SERVOMECHANISM booster, cybernion, hemostat, selsyn, synchro

SESAME ajonjoli, beni(seed), benne, grass, herb, oilseed, password, plant, ramtil, seed, semsem, sergelim, teel, til(seed), tulema, vanglo(e), wangala

grass gama

oil beni, benne

paste taheen, tahin

plant teel, til

seed gingely, gingili, jinjili, tilseed

street denizen puppet

SESELI hartwort, horse-fennel, saxifrage

SESHA *serpent of* vishnu

SESHATA *husband* thoth

SESQUITERPENE caryophyllene, cedrene, cedrol, clovene, copaene, humulene

SESSION acuerdo, assemblage, assembly, assize(s), bout, council, meeting, seance, sederunt, semester, sitdown, sitting, term, vestry, wake

SESTINA lyric, poem, sextain

SET (For references to Egyptian god, SET, see SETH.) 3 bet, dip, fit, fix, gel, lay, let, pit, put 4 band, base, bear, book, cast, firm, form, gang, heal, jell, knit, pack, plat, pose, post, rank, rate, risk, seat, sect, sink, suit, team, tend, wane 5 affix, allot, begin, brood, build, chain, check, class, deter, enter, erect, fixed, group, lease, place, plant, raise, ready, rigid, staid, stake, stand, stick, stiff, suite, trend, trite, upend, usual, value, wager 6 adjust, assess, assign, assume, assure, attach, become, bent on, circle, clique, course, curdle, decree, define, direct, escort, fasten, formal, harden, impose, intent, locate, ordain, phrase, propel, series, settle, string 7 appoint, assured, battery, compose, confirm, congeal, coterie, decided, decline, dispose, implant, inflict, perplex, planted, prepare,

scenery, sharpen, sitfast, station, stiffen, suppose, venture 8 although, attitude, carriage, estimate, incubate, position, regulate, resolute, schedule, sequence, solidify, tendency 9 coagulate, designate, direction, embarrass, establish, obstinate, prescribe 10 assortment, collection, inveterate, succession, unyielding 11 disposition, established, progression

about address, approach, attack, begin, besiege, circulate, fall, fang, gang, report, spread, start, undertake

afloat launch, start

against alienate, antagonize, attack, balance, compare, hostile, oppose

apart allocate, allot, allow, appoint, appropriate, dedicate, destined, devote, differentiate, discriminate, elect, exempt, insulate, isolate, partition, quarantine, reserve, sacred, seclude, segregate, select, separate, sequester, space, taboo

aside abolish, abrogate, allocate, allot, annul, assign, bar, burke, defer, discard, dismiss, dispense, earmark, except, exclude, hain, override, overrule, reject, remove, repeal, reserve, separate, shelve, slip, suspend, table, void

at attack, start

at large free, liberate, release, spring

at naught defy, despise, disregard, flout, override, repudiate, scorn, underestimate, underrate, veto, violate

back check, defeat, hinder, regress(ion), relapse, restrain, retard, retrusion, return, reverse, rollback, rout, slow

before exhibit, present, propose, tell

by accumulate, esteem, reject, reserve, save, shelve, store, value

comb. stat

down abase, alit, appoint, attribute, consider, depose, deposit, descend, determine, encamp, enter, establish, estimate, fix, humiliate, list, note, ordain, place, plop, prescribe, rebuke, reckon, record, regard, register, relate, reprimand, reproof, resolve, retort, score, seat, sit, slacken, upbraid, write

end to end butt

eyes on behold, see

fire to accend, enflame, enkindle, ignify, ignite, inflame, irritate, kindle, light, tind(er), turn on

firmly establish, foundation, plant, posit

forth adorn, announce, arrange, blazon, bring out, commend, decorate, depart, describe, display, enounce, evidence, exhibit, explain, expose, indicate, interpret, lay out, leave, manifest, offer, open, present, promote, promulgate, propone, propose, publish, start, state, translate

forward advance

free See LIBERATE, RELEASE.

fresh relay

in begin, enter, implant, insert, intervene, notch, prevail

in motion begin, impel, initiate, instigate, launch, move, originate, sow, spring, start

in order address, adjust, align, aline, array, daiker, file, frush, line, organize, post, rightle

into inlay

in type compose, print

no store by disbelieve, discount, underestimate, underrate

off (See also SETOFF.) adorn, allot, appear, assign, begin, bundle, compensate, contrast, decorate, depart, discount, discriminate, embellish, emblazon, explode, ignite, measure, print, remove, seem, shoot, show, start

on abet, advance, agitate, assail, attack, bait, begin, beset, browden, incite, instigate, press, urge

on edge annoy, bother, ruffle

on end topsyturvy, upend

one's heart on desire, determine, insist, want

on fire See *fire to*, above.

out (See also SETOUT.) allocate, allot, assign, begin, decorate, describe, display,

embark, embellish, equip, escort, excitement, exhibit, extol, fuss, intend, issue, leave, limit, plan(t), proclaim, project, promulgate, publish, recite, sally, send, start, take off, troop

over assign, convey, transfer

right adjust, align, aline, arrange, correct, direct, disillusion, order(ed), reconcile, redress, remedy, square, systematize, teach

snare tail, till

store by believe, esteem, treasure, trust, value

straight See *right*, above.

thickly stud

-to affix, apply, argument, attach, battle, begin, bout, brangle, combat, conflict, contest, debate, fight, fracas, melee, pluck, quarrel, skirmish, struggle, turn, undertake

up (See also SETUP.) advance, advertise, aid, appoint, arise, arrange, begin, build, built, cause, cinch, compose(d), conceited, create, elate, elevate, erect, establish(ed), exalt, expand, extol, finance, formed, found, glorify, gratify, hoist, install, institute, lift, lodge, oppose, organize, pad, plan, post, prepare, pretentious, propose, provoke, put up, raise, rear, refresh, remedy, repair, restore, rig, serve, snap, spread, upright

upon See *on*, above.

SETA bristle, chaeta, crotchet, hair, plume, podetium, prickle, setula, spine

without achaetous

SETARIA bristlegrass, foxtail, millet

SETBACK check, comedown, dash, defeat, jolt, knock, loss, lurch, offset, relapse, retroaction, retrogression, reverse, throwback

SETH sutekh, typhon

brother abel, cain, horus, osiris

consort nephthys

form black pig

parent adam, eve, geb, nut

slayer horus

son enos, sethite

victim osiris

SETHITE *father* seth

SETOFF compensation, decoration, departure, offset, ornament, outset, start

SETOSE bristly, setacious, setous

SETOUT costume, coterie, display, entertainment, excitement, exhibit, getup, outfit, show, spread, start

SETT bar, block, chisel, hammer, hook, pattern, stone, tartan, tool

SETTEE bench, boat, boudeuse, causeuse, couch, divan, seat, ship, sofa

SETTER dog, gordon, informer, irish, jack, lyricist, sagger, sawhorse, spy

SETTERWORT bear's-foot, pigroots

SETTING atmosphere, backdrop, background, environment, fermail, hardening, insertion, lease, milieu, mise-en-scene, mounting, purlieu, scena, scene, showcase, snare, trap

SETTLE 3 end, fix, pay, put, sag, set, sit, 4 calm, dais, firm, form, haft, lift, live, moor, nail, nest, park, root, rule, seat, sink 5 adapt, agree, bench, clear, close, judge, lodge, lower, order, perch, place, plant, prove, quiet, remit, rivet, shelf, squat, stand, stick 6 accord, acquit, adjust, alight, assign, chip in, choose, clinch, decide, defray, fasten, locate, nestle, pacify, reckon, redeem, refute, repose, reside, secure, shrink, soothe, square, steady 7 appease, arrange, balance, clarify, compose, confirm, conform, depress, descend, destroy, dispose, inhabit, mediate, resolve, satisfy, silence, subside 8 amortize, button up, colonize, conclude, contract, regulate, submerge 9 arbitrate, ascertain, conjobble, designate, determine, discharge, establish, liquidate, terminate 10 adjudicate, administer, capitulate, conciliate, strengthen 11 accommodate, acknowledge, domesticate, tranquilize

accounts avenge, even up, pay off, punish

differences make up, reconcile

down camp, cool it, sink, slump, steady, subside

on bequeath, confer, endow, grant, leave, point

one's hash dispose of, silence, subdue

quarrel reconcile

strike arbitrate, mediate

with avenge, pay, punish, remit

SETTLED alit, assured, calm, certain, colonized, decided, ended, established, fixed, inhabited, inveterate, located, occupied, peopled, populated, populous, range, resolved, seated, sedate, sedentary, serious, smooth, square, stable, staid, sunk

in advance predetermined

SETTLEMENT accommodation, acquittal, adjustment, agreement, amortization, barrio, bundobust, bustee, busti, cash, clearance, cleruchy, colonization, colony, community, compact, compensation, decision, defrayal, demonstration, determination, diktat, discharge, endowment, equity, establishment, fee, fixation, installation, installment, jointure, kevutzah, liquidation, location, maabara, moshav, pact, pah, pau, payment, payoff, peopling, position, presidio, price, quittance, regulation, remainder, remittance, retirement, satisfaction, society, subsidence, town, truce, verdict, village

arrange arbitrate, mediate, negotiate

fortified nahal

legal amise

SETTLER boomer, colonial, colonist, colonizer, emigrant, ender, forehearth, giver, groper, habitant, homesteader, immigrant, mediator, metic, nestor, pilgrim, pioneer, planter, puritan, receptacle, shagroon, siberski, sooner, squatter, trimmer, vessel

group colony

SETUP arrangement, bearing, carriage, disposition, facility, format, home, installation, makeup, organi-

zation, plan, schedule, structure, system, treat, walkaway

SEUGH, SEUCH dirt, ditch, drain, furrow, mire

SEUSS, DR ted geisel

character bartholomew cubbins, grinch, horton, mc elligot

SEVEN hebdomad, heptad(e), PLEIAD(ES), sept, septet(te), septuor, sette, shichi, sieben, siete, zayin, zeta

against thebes adrastus, amphiaraus, caponeus, eteocles, hippomedon, parthenopaeus, polynices, tydeus

against thebes, author aeschylus

-angled heptangular

arts arithmetic, astronomy, geometry, grammar, logic, music, rhetoric

asian churches ephesus, laodicea, pergamus, philadelphia, sardis, smyrna, thyatira

bid (grand)slam

bishops ken, lake, lloyd, sancroft, trelawney, turner, white

bodies (*metals*) copper, gold, iron, lead, quicksilver, silver, tin

bodies (*planets*) jupiter, luna, mars, mercury, saturn, sun, venus

comb. hebdo, hept(a), sept(a)

-day fever septan

days and nights sennight, week

days, every hebdomadal, weekly

deadly sins See SIN 7 *deadly.*

dwarfs bashful, doc, dopey, grumpy, happy, sleepy, sneezy

-eyes lampern

-faced heptahedral

gods of luck See HAPPINESS *gods.*

greek sages bias, chilo, cleobulus, periander, pittacus, solon, thales

group hebdomad, heptad, pleiad, septet

hills See ROME *hills.*

hundred settecento

mothers sapta-matri

of trumps manilla

pert. hebdomadal, septal, septan, septenary

principles See PRINCIPLE

seven.

senses animation, feeling, hearing, sight, smell(ing), speech, taste, touch

-sided solid heptahedron

sisters cactus

sleepers constantine, dionysius, john, malchus, martinian, maximian, serapion

sleepers' guard al-rakim

stars See PLEIADES

virtues See VIRTUE *cardinal.*

-up all-fives, all-fours, drink, game, high-low-jack, pitch, sledge

wonders of world artemesia mausoleum, artemis temple, babylon gardens, catacombs of alexandria, colosseum of rome, great wall of china, leaning tower of pisa, mosque of st sophia, pharaohs, porcelain tower of nankin, pyramids, rhodes colossus, stonehenge, temple of diana, zeus statue

SEVENFOLD septennial, septuple

SEVENS fantan, parliament

SEVENTIETH septuagenary, septuagesimal

SEVENTY *-year-old* septuagenarian

SEVER abscind, breach, break, chop, cleave, cut, deal, depart, detach, discerp, discide, disconnect, discriminate, disengage, disjoin, dismember, dispart, disperse, dissociate, distinguish, disunite, divide, divorce, except, exempt, hack, interpose, lop, outrive, part, prescind, rend, rive, scatter, segregate, separate, shear, slit, split, sunder, tear

comb. temno

from neck behead, decapitate, decollate

SEVERAL apart, different, distinct(ive), divers(e), enclosure, especial, few, individual, manifold, many, multifarious, multiple, numerous, odd, particular, peculiar, private, respective, separate, sere, single, some, special, sundry, various, wheen *comb.* pluri

times repeatedly

SEVERALLY apiece, each, proportionately, respectively, separately, singly, variously

SEVERANCE avulsion, breach, detachment, difference, distinction, division, divulsion, partition, separation, sunder

SEVERE accurate, acerb, acrimonious, acute, arbitrary, arctic, arduous, ascetic, astringent, austere, bad, biting, bitter, blunt, breme, brutal, burdensome, captious, caustic, censorious, chaste, coercive, cold, cruel, difficult, dour, drastic, dure, exact(ing), extreme, forbidding, grievous, grim, grinding, hard(shell), harsh, hetter, imperative, inclement, inexorable, keen, nasty, obdurate, obstinate, onerous, oppressive, peremptory, plain, prussian, pungent, relentless, restrained, rethe, rigid, rigorous, roid, rough, rude, rugged, serious, sharp, simple, spartan, stern, stiff, strict, stringent, strong, taut, trying, tyrannical, uncompromising, unrelenting, unyielding, violent

SEVERELY bad(ly), heavily, roughly, shrewdly, smartly, soundly, stark, stiff(ly), stithly

SEVERITY acerbity, acrimony, asperity, astringency, austerity, bitterness, cold, cruelty, difficulty, exactness, fervency, gravity, grimness, hardness, harshness, inclemency, rigor, roughness, solemnity, sternness, stiffness, stringency, tyranny, violence, virulence

SEVERN *tributary* wye

SEVILLE hispalis

orange chinotti

SEW balk, baste, bind, broth, buttonhole, darn, drain, embroider, fasten, feak, fell, finedraw, hem, hog, knit, mend, needle, ooze, overcast, patch, pottage, preen, purl, quilt, renter, repair, run up, seam, sewer, shirr, smock, sow, steek, stitch, string, sue, suture, tack, tat, whip

loosely baste

up bag, balk, cinch, climax, control, end, finish, monopolize, nail down, nonplus, seam, secure, settle, swindle, tire out

with gathers shirr

SEWAGE affluent, drainage, offal, refuse, soil(age), sullage, waste

SEWAN beads, money, suckauhock, wampum

SEWELLEL aplodontia, beaver, boomer, rodent

SEWEN trout

SEWER cesspool, channel, cloaca, conduit, culvert, ditch, drain, gullion, jawhole, main, piquiere, seamstress, septic tank, servant, shirrer, sink, sough, sump, tailor, vennel

opening manhole

SEWING fancywork, needlework, sempstry, stitchery, suture

case hussy

machine inventor elias howe, lester

machine part bobbin, head, pleater, plicator, treadle, zipperfoot

reinforcement bartack

term gather, hem, pleat, shir

SEX gender, kind, knife, sax, sect

appeal charisma, machismo

cell gamete

comb. geno

common to both epicene

posing as opposite eonism

symbol yin, yang

SEXAGESIMAL sixtieth

SEXANGULAR hexagonal

SEXLESS epicine, neuter

SEXTON beadle, custodian, ecclesiastic, janitor, sacrist(an), shammes, sham(m)us, vesturer, warden

SEXUAL carnal, fleshly, gamic, intimate

propagation amphigony

SEY assay, saithe, say, scye, serge

SEYBERTITE brandisite, mica

SEYCHELLES *island* aldabra, mahe, praslin, silhouette

SEYMOUR, JANE *husband* henry viii

son edward vi

SHAAPH *parent* caleb, jahdai

SHAB herpes, itch, palm off, rid, rubbers, scab, scratch, sneak off, trick

SHABBY base, beggarly, cheesy, contemptible, despicable, deteriorated, dowdy, drab, faded, frayed, frazzled, frowzy, grubby, mangy, mean, old, ourie, outworn, paltry, poky, poor, ragged, ratty, rent, rusty, scabby, scruffy, scuffed, scuffy, scummy, scurvy, seedy, shoddy, small, sneaky, soiled, squalid, stingy, tacky, tagrag, tattered, tatty, threadbare, underhand, unfair, unjust, unkempt, worn

become go to seed, run down, spoil

SHABRAG ragamuffin, urchin

SHACHIA *father* shaharaim

SHACHLE, SHAUCHLE distort, shamble, shuffle, wear out

SHACHLY shambling

SHACK bait, brakeman, cabin, catch, chase, coe, fetch, hibernate, horse, hovel, humpy, husk, hut(ch), lean-to, nag, plug, pursue, retrieve, shag, shanty, shed, shuck, stubble, tramp, vagabond, wander(er)

SHACKLE anklet, band, bilboes, bind, bond, bridle, chain(s), check, circumscribe, clatter, collar, confine, cottage, coupling, cramp, darbies, fetter, gag, garter, gyve, halter, hamper, handcuff, hobble, hogtie, hopple, idle, impede, iron(s), leash, limit, loaf, manacle, muzzle, pastern, picket, rattle, reins, restrain, restrict, ring, secure, shirk, shuffle, stocks, straitjacket, swathe, tether, tie, trammel, trave, yoke

-bone knucklebone, wrist

SHACKLER coupler, coupling, slotter

SHACKLING, SHACKLY idle, lazy, loose, poor, rickety, shaky, shiftless, unimportant, unthrifty, vagrant

SHAD alewife, allice, allis, alosa, alose, anadrom, antonio, bluefish, buck, clupeid, crappie, flatfish, ger-

rid, mojarra, sawbelly, trabu, twaite
scale buckwheat-sage
SHADBELLY quaker
SHADBIRD sandpiper, snipe
SHADBUSH may-pear, dogwood, juneberry, saskatoon, service(berry)
SHADDOCK citrus, fruit, lucban, pomelo, pompelmoose, pompelmous, pompion, pumelo
SHADE adumbration, apparition, awning, baldachino, canopy, clearing, color, conceal, cover, curtain, dark(en), darkness, dash, degree, divide, dull, eclipse, fetch, fresco, ghost, glasses, gloom, hachure, hat, haunt, hue, jalousie, lessen, nuance, obscure, obscurity, ombrage, overshadow, panoply, parasol, part, penumbra, phantasm, phantom, phenomenon, portiere, protect(ion), purdah, revenant, roof, scaum, screen, scug, shadow, shelter, shield, shutter, silhouette, smack, soupcon, specter, spirit, spook, streak, suggestion, sunbonnet, sunhat, suspicion, swail, swale, tent, tinge, tint, tone, touch, trace, umbra(ge), umbrella, veil, venetian-blind, vestige, visor, wraith
brilliant patina
light pastel
-loving photophygous, sciophilous
SHADED dark(ling), drumly, ombre, shady, somber, sombre
SHADETAIL squirrel
SHADFLOWER arbutus
SHADINE herring, menhaden
SHADING fluting, hatching, qualification, variation
SHADOW adumbrate, adumbration, apparition, blot, cleek, cloud, composition, contour, darkness, dim, divine, dog, figure, follow(er), forecast, foretell, form, ghost, gloom, illusion, image, isogyre, moonshade, obscure, obscurity, omen, outline, overspread, penumbra, phantasm, predict, remainder, remnant, satellite, scarrow, scug,

SHADE, shape, shelter, shepherd, shroud, silhouette, specter, spirit, stalk, suggest, symbol, tail, trace, trail, umbra(ge), vestige, yin
-box practice, spar
comb. sci(o), skia
dispelling scialytic
fight with sciamachy
having long macroscian
of death gloom, sheol
outline silhouette
projection of sciagraphy, skiagraphy
without ascian
SHADOWY airy, ethereal, indefinite, obscure, SHADY, spectral, undefined, vague, vaporous
SHADRACH ananias, hananiah
friend abednego, meshach
persecutor nebuchadnezzar
SHADY adumbral, bad, bosky, bowery, bushy, cool, corrupt, dark, deceitful, dishonest, disreputable, doubtful, elmy, equivocal, faint, fishy, hidden, indistinct, infamous, notorious, opaque, questionable, scandalous, shadowy, sheltered, umbrageous, umbrose, umbrous, underhand(ed), unreliable, woody
one gonef, gonif, gonov, nogoodnik
place arbor, frescade
SHAFFLE hobble, limp, loiter, palter, shirk, shuffle, vacillate
SHAFT arrow, axis, bar, blade, bolt, chamber, chimney, column, dagger, dart, deceive, disselboom, excavation, flagpole, flagstaff, fust, gatepost, groove, handle, helve, heuch, heugh, hole, lance, lat, limber, maypole, memorial, midrib, mine, missile, monument, neap, nib, obelisk, opening, passage, perch, pillar, pit, pole, post, quill, ray, reach, rod, scape, shank, spear, spindle, spire, stab, staff, stale, stalk, stave, stele, stem, stick, stilt, stope, support, thill, tiller, tomb, tongue, totem pole, tower, tram, trunk, tunnel, upcast, verge, weapon, well(hole)
blind winze

column fust, scape, tige
convexity entasis
feather scape, scapus
harness heald
hollow cannon
main arbor
mine groove, gruff, heuch, heugh, incline, pit, staple
ornamental verge
part brace, helve, orlo
pointed spire
steeple spire
twisted torso
wagon limber, sharp, stave, thill, tongue
SHAFTED betrayed, hurt, stabbed, undone, wronged
SHAG animal, bait, blackguard, chase, cheat, cormorant, dance, fabric, fetch, follow, hair, jerk, jog, jolt, nap, pile, pursue, rascal, roughness, rug, shack, shake, shog, tangle, texture, tobacco, toss, wool
SHAGBARK carya, hickory
SHAGGY bearded, brush, bushy, confused, disorderly, furry, hairy, hirsute, nappy, ragged, rough, ruffled, rugged, tousy, uneven, unkempt, unpolished, villous
SHAGRAG ragged, rascally, unkempt
SHAGREEN galuchat, leather, sharkskin
SHAGTAIL turtle
SHAH abassi, abaze, padishah, pashah, protector, ruler
SHAHAPTIAN *indian* klikitat, nez perce, tenino, wanapum
SHAHARAIM *son* abitub, elpaal, jeuz, jobab, malcham, mesha, mirmah, shachia, zibia
wife baara, hodesh, mahasham
SHAITAN demon, DEVIL, fiend, storm
SHAKA *half-brother* dingane
patron dingis-wayo
SHAKE 3 bob, jar, jig, jog, rog 4 ague, bump, deal, dirl, fate, halt, jerk, jolt, rese, rock, shed, shog, stir, sway, toze, wave 5 bever, churn, crack, daunt, evade, impel, knock, laugh, nidge, quake, rogle, shock, split, stave, steal, swing, throb, trill 6 arouse, bicker, bobble, bounce, chance, didder,

dither, dodder, falter, hustle, jigger, jigget, jiggle, joggle, jostle, jounce, onrush, quaver, quiver, ruggle, shimmy, shiver, teeter, thrill, totter, tremor, twitch, wabble, wamble, weaken, wiggle, wobble 7 abandon, agitate, brangle, cast off, concuss, derange, dismiss, disturb, flicker, flutter, instant, shimmer, shingle, shudder, stagger, success, tremble, twiddle, twitter, vibrate 8 backlash, brandish, convulse, enfeeble, flourish, frighten, redshank, splinter, unsettle 9 agitation, jactation, oscillate, palpitate 10 convulsion, demoralize, earthquake, succession

a leg bestir, dance, get a move on, get going, hasten, hurry

down bed, blackmail, con-(dition), dance, extort(ion), search, settle, test

off disagree. ditch, doff, dump, escape, excuss, reject, rid, shed

out eliminate, straighten, unfurl

up agitate, agitation, berate, change, chide, disturbance, harass, jar, jumble, mix, rattle, rouse, scold, upset

violently convulse, succuss

with laughter or rage hotter

SHAKEN cracked, perturbed, shook, weakened

SHAKER boaster, dredger, duster, mover, pigeon, sifter, vagrant, vip

founder mother ann lee

SHAKES agitation, ague, all-overs, dithers, heebiejeebies, jimjams, jimmies, jingles, jitters, jumps, nerves, shivers, trembles, trepidation, willies

no great mediocre, nonentity, unimportant, unsuccessful

SHAKESPEARE (See also plays, by title.) immortal bard

actor bernhardt, booth, burbage, burton, craig, garrick, gielgud, irving, kean, kemble, kemp, macready, modjeska, olivier, rehan, siddons, sothern, taylor, terry, tree, ward

alternate author bacon

ambassador capucius

archbishop bourchier, rotherham

assassin brutus

associate burbage

athenian timon

attendant alexas, bardolph, berkeley, charmian, emilia, lucetta, nym, pistol, rosaline, tressel

bachelor benedick

bawd mistress overdone

bellows-mender flute

birthplace stratford-on-avon

bishop beaufort

braggart falstaff, parolles, shallow

butler stephano

cardinal bourchier, campeius, wolsey

carpenter peter quince

character See under titles of individual plays.

clown bottom, costard, feste, gobbo, lavache, touchstone, trinculo

coarse wench doll-tearsheet

collaborator fletcher

comedy all's well that ends well, as you like it, comedy of errors, love's labor lost, measure for measure, merchant of venice, merry wives of windsor, midsummer night's dream, much ado about nothing, taming of the shrew, tempest, twelfth night, two gentlemen of verona, winter's tale

conspirator casca, cassius, trebonius

constable dogberry, dull, elbow

count bertram

countess olivia

country wench audrey, jaquenetta

courtier guildenstern, jachino, osric, osrick, polonius, rosencrantz, voltimand

cupid adam bell

curate See *parson*, below.

cynic apemantus, jaques

deity setabos

deputy escalus

dog crab, tray

drunk borachio

duke antonio, arthur, aumerle, bolingbroke, buckingham, clarence, edmund, exeter, george, gloucester, henry, john of gaunt, lancaster, mowbray, norfolk,

orsino, richard, solinus, suffolk, surrey, theseus, thomas, vincentio, york

earl kent, northumberland, rivers, siward, surrey, warwick, westmoreland

elf puck

emperor saturninus

executioner abhorson

fairy cobweb, moth, mustardseed, peaseblossom, puck

fairy king oberon

fairy queen mab, titania

fantastic lucio

fiend barbason

friar francis, john, laurence, peter, thomas

general agrippa, antenor, antony, aufidius, banquo, canidius, cominius, lucius, macbeth, menenius, othello, silius, taurus, titus andronicus

gentleman baptista, curio, fenton, ford, froth, page, proteus, valentine, vicentio

gentlewoman mistress page, ursula

ghost banquo

governor cleon, leonato, lysimachus

hedge-priest martext

heiress portia

hero bertram, demetrius, hamlet, mark antony, orlando, pericles, petruchio, romeo, titus andronicus

heroine beatrice, cleopatra, desdemona, helena, hermia, isabella, jessica, julia, juliet, kate, katharine, lavinia, ophelia, portia, rosalind, silvia, viola

history play henry(iv, v, vi, viii), king john, richard(ii, iii)

home avon, new place, stratford(on avon)

humorist bardolph, falstaff, page, peto, pistol, poins

idolizer bardolater

island bermoothes

jester See *clown*, above.

joiner snug

justice shallow, silence

king alonso, antiochus, cymbeline, duncan, henry, john, lear, leontes, macbeth, polixenes, richard

knight colville

lady mariana, marina

lawyer portia

lieutenant cassio

lord (See also *nobleman,* below.) abergavenny, adrian, amiens, angelo, angus, antigonus, archidamus, benedick, berkeley, bigot, biron, boyet, camillo, cerimon, claudio, dion, dumain, eros, escalus, escanes, fitzwater, francisco, grandpre, hastings, helicanus, jaques, lafeu, longaville, lovel, lucius, lucullus, ross, sempronius, stanley, thaliard, willoughby

lout cloten

lover bassanio, benedick, claudio, hamlet, lorenzo, romeo

magician prospero

master of revels philostrate

merchant aegeon, antonio

messenger vaux

miser and *moneylender* shylock

moor aaron, othello

mother mary arden

nobleman (See also *lord,* above.) aemilius, angus, belarius, blunt, caithness, lennox, macduff, menteith, mercutio, paris, ross, siward

nun francisca

nurse lychorida

officer bernardo, fang, seyton

page moth, robin

papal legate pandulf

parson evans, martext, nathaniel

philosopher apemantus

physician butts, caius, cornelius, merry-andrew

poem lovers' complaint, passionate pilgrim, phoenix and the turtle, rape of lucrece, sonnets, venus and adonis

priest urswick

prince arragon, don pedro, escalus, florizel, fortinbras, hamlet, humphrey, mamilius, pericles, ulysses

prisoner barnardine

publisher blount, jaggard, pavier, roberts

queen anne, eleanor, elizabeth, gertrude, hermione, hippolyta, mab, margaret, tamora

relative anne, edmund, john, judith, susanna

retainer morton, travers

rhetorician artemidorus

rivals capulet, montague

river avon

rogue autolycus, nym

roman tribune casca

scholar furness, furnivall, kittredge

schoolmaster holofernes

sea captain antonio

senator brabantio

sergeant-at-arms brandon

servant abraham, bagot, balthasar, biondello, borachio, boult, bushy, caphis, cromwell, curtis, davy, fabian, feste, flaminius, gobbo, green, gregory, grumio, hortensius, launce, launcelot, leonardo, leonine, luce, lucilius, lucius, maria, mistress quickly, nerissa, philemon, philotus, pisanio, robin, rugby, sampson, servilius, simple, speed, stephano, titus, tranio, varro

sharper bardolph, nym, pistol

shepherd corin, silvius

shepherdess dorcas, mopsa, perdita, phebe

shrew kate, katharine

simpleton aguecheek

slave caliban

soldier bates, talbot, titus-lartius

spaniard armado

spirit ariel, ceres, iris, juno

steward flavius, malvolio

suitor bassanio, romeo, slender

tailor starveling

tavern mermaid

teacher of rhetoric artemidorus

theater globe, swan

tinker sly, snout

title bard of avon

tragedy antony and cleopatra, coriolanus, cymbeline, hamlet, julius caesar, king lear, macbeth, othello, pericles, romeo and juliet, timon of athens, titus andronicus, troilus and cressida

tribune junius-brutus, sincinius-velutus

twin antipholus

venetian antonio, brabantio, roderigo, shylock

villain aaron, don john, iago

villainess sycorax

weaver bottom

welsh chief glendower

wench audry, doll tearsheet

wife anne hathaway

witch hecate, sycorax

witty man mercutio

SHAKILY by fits and starts, desultorily, fitfully, jerkily, tremulously, unsteadily, waveringly

SHAKING agitated, ague, aguish, aquiver, ballism (us), jac(ti)tation, jarring, quaking, quavery, quivering, quivery, rocking, shivers, shivery, succassation, succussion, succussive, tremor, tremulous

fear of seismophobia

instrument agitator, beater, churn, eggbeater, paddle, shaker, vibrator, whisk

off decussation

pudding whitepot

SHAKO cap, hat, headdress

SHAKTI devi, force, power, prakraiti, tara

husband siva

SHAKY agitated, aguish, all-overish, cas(s)alty, caselty, cazelty, cold, dwaible, dweeble, fidgeting, fidgety, fluttery, groggy, infirm, insecure, irresolute, jerry-built, jittery, jumpy, nervous, palsied, precarious, quivering, quivery, rickety, rocky, shivering, shivery, shook(up), skittery, timid, tittupy, tottering, tottery, totty, trembling, trembly, tremulous, twitchety, twitchy, twitter(l)y, tumbledown, uncertain, unfirm, unreliable, unsafe, unsound, unstable, unsteady, wabbly, wambly, wobbly, wonky, woozy

SHAKYAMUNI See BUDDHA.

SHALE bass, bat, bone, cleave, flag(stone), flake, husk, incrustation, killas, kolm, mesh, metal, mudstone, plate, rock, scale, shamble, shell, shillet, shuck, shuffle, slate, sliggeen, xalle

and magma buchite

and sandstone hazle

black ampelite, cannel-coal

combustible tasmanite

SHALL can, command, may, mun, must, obliged, owe, promise, will, would

not sanna, shanna, shant

SHALLOP boat, dinghy, vessel

SHALLOT allium, cibol, eschalot, onion, scallion, tube

SHALLOW ankle-deep, bank, bar, barmy, basket, bird-brained, cart, cursory, depthless, ebb, empty, featherbrained, flat, fleet, flimsy, flue, foolish, frivolus, frothy, glib, half-baked, hat, hollow, idle, ignorant, inane, light, maga-ziny, paltry, petty, sand-bank, sandbar, shoal, silly, simple, skin-deep, slight, small, superficial, surface, tray, trifling, trivial, unprofound, unsound, volatile, weak

cousin slender

SHALLOWNESS facade, front, inanity, superficiality, triviality, veneer

SHALLOWPATE fool, idiot

SHALLU broomcorn, kaoliang, sorghum, wheat

SHALLUM *parent* josiah, napthali, tikvath, zadok

son hanameel, hilkiah, jehizkiah, jekamiah, maaseiah

wife huldah

SHALMANESER *son* sennacherib

SHALOM farewell, goodbye, greeting, peace

SHALWAR drawers, pajamas, pants, trousers

SHAM act(ing), affect(ation), ape, artificial, assume(d), bluff, bogus, brummagem, bunco, bunko, bunyip, cheat, chemisette, chouse, color(ing), copy, counterfeit, deceit, deception, delude, disguise, dissemblance, dissembling, dissimulation, duffer, dummy, facade, fake(ry), falsefront, farce, feign(ed), feint, forgery, fourflush, fraud(ulent), front, gammon, hoax, humbug, imitate, imitation, imposture, invent, let on, make-believe, masquerade, meritricious, mimic, mock, mummery, plaster, play(act), posture, pretend, pretense, pretension, pretext, profess, pseudo, put on, ruse, seeming, semblance, shoddy, show, simulacrum, simulate, simulation, spurious, stumour, substitute, swin-

dle, trick(ery), trickster, wile

-abraham malingerer

SHAMA See THRUSH.

SHAMAL barih, wind

SHAMAN angakok, angekok, beggar, conjuror, healer, kahuna, machi, magician, medicine man, monk, peai, priest, tohunga, wabeno, witchman

SHAMASH babbar, sun god, utu

coachman aya

consort aya

god of sun

messenger bunene

offspring kittu, misharu

parent ningal, sin

soothsayer baru

temple larsa, sippar

SHAMBLE(S) abattoir, babel, bandy, bauchle, bedlam, bench, butchery, confusion, counter, footstool, hobble, madhouse, mess, sha(u)-chle, shammock, SHUFFLE, slaughterhouse, slog, slouch, stall, stool, walk

SHAME abase(ment), abash(ment), abomination, aidos, attaint, bismer, black eye, blot, chagrin, confusion, contempt, contrition, degrade, disdain, disgrace, dishonesty, dishonor, disrepute, embarrass(ment), fie, guilt, humiliate, humiliation, ignominy, indecency, infamy, mortification, mortify, obloquy, odium, opprobrium, pity, pudency, remorse, repentance, reproach, scandal, scorn, shending, sin, slander, stigma, vergoyne, wrong

exclamation fie(upon), tcktck, tsh-tsh, tst-tst

personification aidos

SHAMED *parent* elpaal

SHAMEFACED abashed, ashamed, bashful, blushing, diffident, discomfited, embarrassed, guilty, humble, modest, self-conscious, sheepish, shy, verecund

SHAMEFUL bad, base, degrading, deplorable, disgraceful, dishonest, dishonorable, disreputable, evil, flagrant, gross, hontous, humiliating, ignoble, ignominous, immoral, improper, indecent, indelicate, infamous, inglorious, mean,

notorious, obscene, offensive, opprobrious, outrageous, pitiful, sad, scandalous, shocking, slanderous, sorry, terrible, unseemly, vile, vituperative

SHAMELESS abandoned, arrant, audacious, barefaced, bold, brash, brazen, browless, callous, dissolute, immodest, immoral, impudent, profligate, sluttish, tough, unblushing, vicious, wanton

SHAMMAH *parent* agee, jesse, revel

SHAMMAI *son* abishur, jada, maon

SHAMMOCK(S) bungle, cheat, dawdle, feet, legs, shamble, shirk, shoes

SHAMMUA *parent* david, galal

son abda

SHAMPOO clean(se), lave, massage, rinse, tripsis, wash

SHAMROCK black medic, black trefoil, hop-clover, seamrog, wood-sorrel

land ireland

pea oxalis

SHAN bashful, kuy, shy, tai, thailand, timid

SHANDY, TRISTRAM *author* sterne

SHANGALLA *tribe* bertat

SHANGHAI abduct, chicken, drug, fowl, intoxicate, kidnap, knock out, ship, slingshot

practitioner larry marr

SHANGRI-LA camp david, paradise, utopia

SHANGY shackle, shangan

SHANK, SHANK'S beam, body, cannon, chain, chank, crop, crura, crus, decay, femur, gam(b), gambe, handle, knot, leg, metacarpus, metatarsus, pack off, pedicel, rope, shaft, shin, stock(ing), support, tang, tarsus, tattler, tibia, walk

mare afoot, legs

pert. crural

pillion pommel

yellow tattler

SHANNY blenny, bully, fish, giddy, shy, silly

SHANTUNG cloth, fabric, pongee, silk, tussah

SHANTY boist, bruise, cabin, chantier, doghouse, groggery, grogshop, hovel, humpy, hut(ch), inn, jaunty, leanto, shack, SHED, showy

SHANTYTOWN bidonville, hooverville, slum

SHAPE adjust, apparition, appearance, appoint, arrange, aspect, axe, being, bend, block, broach, build, cam, cast, center, configuration, conform, construction, contour, contrive, costume, create, cut, decree, design, destine, devise, direct, dress, embodiment, embody, fabricate, fashion, feign, figuration, figure, forge, form(at), frame, gestalt, ghost, guise, hack, impression, incline, likeness, look, make, mint, model, modify, mold, moulage, mould, ordain, outline, pattern, phantom, pink, plan, profile, regulate, semblance, silhouette, stamp, state, structure, suit, swage, torus, trim, whittle
conical beehive, cone
different variform
garden topiary
having identical homochiral
itself crystallize
roughly boast, scabble, scapple
take jell, materialize
taking all pantomorphic
up develop, evolve, improve, straighten out

SHAPEABLE malleable, moldable, plastic, pliable, pliant, viscous

SHAPELESS amorphous, asymmetrical, chaotic, clumpy, contorted, crude, deformed, distorted, dumpy, formless, inchoate, misshapen, monstrous, rough, rude, ugly, unformed, ungraceful, unshapely
comb. amorpho
object blob

SHAPELY becoming, clean (cut), comely, curvaceous, fair, fit, formal, gainly, graceful, morpho, neat, suitable, symmetrical, tight, trim, well-formed

SHAPHAN *son* ahikam, elasah, gemaria, jaazaniah

SHAPHAT *kin* adlai, elisha

SHARD elytrum, fragment, gap, notch, part, piece, pot-

sherd, scale, scaur, shell, sherd, shred

SHARE allot(ment), allowance, ante, apportion(ment), associate, bit, bite, bond, cant, cleave, commission, communicate, contingent, cooperate, cut, dale, deal, dispense, distribute, divide, dividend, division, divvy up, dole, hakh, half, halve, holding, impast, interest, lot, measure, meed, mess, modicum, part, partake, participate, percentage, piece, pittance, portion, proportion, purparty, quantum, quota, rakeoff, ratio(n), shear, slice, snack, stock, whack
ancestral patti
equally halve
greater feck, majority, most
100 board-lot, round-lot
proportional quota
widow's dower(y), dowry, mite, terce, third

SHARECROPPER byowner, farmer, metayer, tenant

SHARED bipartite, collective, common, communal, community, conjoint, dividual, joint, mutual

SHAREHOLDER bondowner, stockowner

SHAREPENNY miser, scrooge

SHAREZER *father* sennacherib

SHARK (See also *genus*, below.) acanthodian, acrodus, angel(fish), bacalao, basking, blacktip, bluedog, bonedog, bonnethead, bramble, bull(head), carcharioid, cestracionte, ceterhinid, cheat, con, dakar, defraud, demoiselle, derschurke, dogfish, dusky, expert, foxfish, galeid, galleus, gata, grayfish, greenland, gummy, hammerhead, haye, hunfish, hybodont, kulp, lawyer, leopard, mako, man-eater, mano, paloma, parasite, placoid, porbeagle, proarthri, requiem, requin, rhina, rip, rogue, rousette, sailfish, saltcod, sandvar, selachoid, sharper, shovelnose, skaamoog, soupfin, spear-eye, sponge, squatina, sunfish, swell, swindler, tear, thrasher, thresher, tiburom,

tiger, tigrone, tope, trick (ery), whitetip
-adhering fish pega(dor), remora
basking sailfish
blue mako
bramble echinorhinus
carpet wobbegong
-eating fish catfish, pega, som
extinct acanthodian, acrodas, hybodes
family squalidae
genus acrodus, alopias, carcharhinus, carcharias, carcharodon, cetorhinus, cladodus, galerohinus, galeus, ginglymostoma, lamna, mitsukurina, selachii, somniosus, sphyrna, squalus
group menaspis
-hunter's weapon bangstick
large mako
-like acanthodian
nurse gata
oil squalene
pilot pega(dor), remora
ray-like angelfish, butterflyfish, monkfish, spadefish, squatinid
sand tiger
-shaped squaliform
small lamia, tope
sucker remora
thresher aliopias, foxfish
viviparous porbeagle
voracious tiburon
whale mhor
young sharklet

SHARKEY, JACK *name* garrulous bob, joseph paul cukoschay, sailor jack

SHARP 3 sly 4 acid, cold, curt, cute, edge, edgy, fine, keen, note, skin, sour, tart, wily 5 acerb, acrid, acute, alert, angry, breme, brisk, cheat, clear, crisp, eager, edged, funny, harsh, quick, rapid, rough, shaft, shark, smart, snell, steal, steep, vivid, witty 6 abrupt, acuate, argute, barbed, biting, bitter, bright, clever, expert, gritty, hispid, jagged, narrow, peaked, pretty, severe, shrewd, shrill, snelly, snithe, stingy, strong, tweaky 7 angular, austere, briskly, bristly, caustic, cunning, cutting, exactly, intense, mordant, nipping, piquant, pointed, prickly, probing, pungent, quickly, slacker, swindle, violent 8 cleancut, dazzling, distinct, incisive, piercing, poignant, profound, promptly, stabbing, vigilant 9 attentive, dishonest, merciless, mucronate, precisely, sagacious, sarcastic, sensitive, trenchant, vitriolic 10 astringent, discerning, knife-edged, mordacious, punctually, razor-edged 11 acrimonious, distressing, double-edged, penetrating 12 rumgumptious, unprincipled, unscrupulous

as a needle, tack
cedar acadia, cade
comb. acet(o), acut(i), oxy
disagreeably edgy
dock sorrel
-edged cultrate
-eyed keen, observant, penetrating
-fanged sarcastic
-pointed acuate, aculeate, mucronic
-sighted argus-eyed, astute, eagle-eyed, lyncean
symbol razor, sword, tack
-tailed grouse pintail
-witted acute, alert, canny, discerning, quick, shrewd, snell

SHARP, BECKY *friend*
amelia sedley
husband rawdon crawley
sheep-dog briggs
SHARPEN acuate, acuminate, barb, cacuminate, cuspidate, edge, enhance, excite, file, grind, heighten, hone, increase, intensify, keen, point, quicken, raise, set, slype, smarten, stimulate, strap, stroke, strop, taper, whet
SHARPENED acuate
SHARPENER carborundum, emery, file, grindstone, hone, novaculite, oilstone, rifle, rip, rubstone, steel, strap, strop(per), whetrock, whetstone
SHARPER barnard, bester, blackleg, bunkoman, carpetbagger, cataian, cheat, cogger, con(fidence)man, deceiver, gamester, gyp, horsetrader, imposter, jackleg, kite, knave, landshark, magsman, nickum, oyster, picaro, ringer, rogue, rooker, shark, spieler,

swindler, thimblerigger, trickster
SHARPNESS acidity, acrimony, acuity, acumen, acumination, acuteness, asperity, bite, discernment, edge, keenness, pointedness, pungency, salt, spinosity, stridor, trenchancy, violence, wit
SHARPSHOOTER bersagliere, boll weevil, crackshot, deadshot, gamester, jager, marksman, sniper, voltigeur
SHASHAK *son* abdon, antothiah, elam, hanan(iah), iphedeiah, ishpan, penuel, zichri
SHASTA *indian* achomawi, astakiwi, atuami, chumaw, hokan, palaihnihan
SHASTRA *class* purana, tantra, smriti, sruti
SHAT tattler
SHATTER blast, blow, break, burst, chatter, chirp, clatter, confuse, crack, crash, craze, creem, crumble, dash, demolish, derange, destroy, disorder, dissipate, dynamite, explode, flinderate, fracture, fragment, impair, madden, rattle, ruin, scatter, shiver, shower, smash, splinter, split, wreck
SHATTERBRAIN See SCATTERBRAIN.
SHATTERED broken, broozled, collapsed, infirm, out of order
SHATTERING devastating, fragment, sprinkling
SHATTERWIT crazy, distracted
SHATTERY breakable, brittle, frail, friable, loose, rickety
SHAUL *father* simeon
SHAUP husk, pod, shell
SHAVE avel, barb, bite, brush, cheat, crop, cut, decorticate, depreciate, discount, extortion, fleece, glance, graze, hoax, pare, peel, plunder, raze, reduce, schawe, scrape, sell, shear, shorten, skin, slice, smooth, spokeshave, steal, strip, swindle, tonse, tonsure, trim
SHAVED polled
SHAVELING friar, hypo-

crite, lad, monk, priest, rookie, strippling, timeserver, youth
SHAVEN bald, beardless, not(t), pilled, tonsured
SHAVER barber, bargainer, boy, chap, cheat, extortioner, fellow, lad, razor, swindler, tonsor, youngster
SHAVETAIL second lieutenant
SHAVIE joke, prank, trick
SHAVING flake, paring, part, piece, rament(um), scrap, shred, slice, spale
SHAVINGS coom(b), dregs, fringetree, leftovers, moslings, refuse, remainder, scobs
SHAW, G. B. *friend* ellen terry
home ayot st lawrence
pert. shavian
play arms and the man, caesar and cleopatra, candida, devil's advocate, heartbreak house, major barbara, man and superman, mrs warren's profession, pygmalion, st joan
SHAW, H. W. *pseud.* josh billings
SHAWL afghan, amilkar, angora, cashmere, chuddar, epiblema, farda, kambal, lamba, manta, mantilla, mantle, maud, nubia, paisley, pashm(ina), pattu, peplus, pushm, puttoo, rebozo, scarf, serape, shoal, slendang, stole, tallith, tapalo, tozie, turnover, whittle, wrap
cashmere amilkar
plaid maud
tasseled tallith
wool pashm, pushm
SHAWNEE *indian chief* tecumseh, tecumtha
salad waterleaf
wood catalpa
SHAY carriage, chaise
SHCHERBAKOV rybinsk
SHE ella, elle, female, feminine, femme, haec, her, lady, woman
character ayesha
-goat alpha aurigae, capella, nanny, star
SHEA buttertree, galam, karite, mandingo
butter bambara, babui, bambuk
tree karite

SHEAF bale, beat, bind, bunch, bundle, bung, cluster, collection, cornbole, gavel, gerbe, glean, hattock, hyperpencil, kern, omer, package, quantity, rick, sheave, stack, swath, thrave, tie
bind into gavel, thrave
grain gait, garb(ace), hose
group sess, thrave
last kirn, neck

SHEALTIEL *son* zerubbabel

SHEAR carve, cleave, clip, cut, defraud, deprive, divide, fleece, fork, gnaw, mince, mow, nibble, nip, nott, part(ing), pierce, plunder, pressure, prune, reap, reduce, rend, sever, shave, shirl, shorten, slide, strain, stress, strip, swindle, thrust, tonsure, torsion, trim
off shirl

SHEARBILL skimmer

SHEARING cutting, groove, harvest, piercing, reaping, tilting
machine cropper

SHEARJASHUB *father* isaiah

SHEARLING alpaca, shearhog

SHEARS forfex, hoist, lewis, pruner, scissors, secateur, snips, snouter
symbol of st agatha

SHEARTAIL hummingbird, tern

SHEARWATER blackhag, cahow, crew, hackbolt, hagdon, haglet, muttonbird, petrel, pimlico, puffin, scrabe(r), seabird, skimmer

SHEATFISH catfish, cilurus, dorad, silurid, waller, wels

SHEATH aglet, axilemma, boondoggle, boot, capsule, case, covering, cyst, dress, envelope, epilemma, etui, for(r)el, holster, hose, hot(t), lorica, myelin, oc(h)rea, pod, quiver, scabbard, sleeve, slough, spathe, theca, torse, tube, wrap (per)
botanical ocred
comb. coleo, lemma
end boterol
pert. ocreate
trimming chape

SHEATHBILL paddy

SHEATHE blunt, case, clad, clothe, conceal, cover, draw in, dress, dull, enclose, face, hide, incase, muzzle, plunge

SHEATHING armor, copper, facing, shiplap, skin, slitwork

SHEAVE gather, hattock, pulley, SHEAF, shive, slice, truckle, wheel
24 thr(e)ave

SHEBA balkis, macqueda, saba
capital marib
father raamah
host solomon

SHEBANG affair, business, concern, contrivance, distillery, dive, establishment, outfit, shack, shanty, shop, structure, thing

SHEBAR *father* caleb

SHECANIAH *son* bariah, hattush, igeal, neariah, shaphat, shemaiah

SHECHEM nablus
father hamor
god baalberith
people samaritans

SHED abri, beam, booth, byre, cabin, cast, clot, cote, cottage, cowbarn, cub, depart, depository, difference, diffuse, dingle, discard, disperse, distinction, divide, doff, drop, dugout, dump, effuse, emit, exuviate, fall (en), fragment, garage, hangar, hemmel, hovel, hull, hut, intersperse, junk, lair, leanto, mew, mo(u)lt, muscule, outbuilding, pandal, part(ing), pour, radiate, refuge, reject, repel, rid, scatter, scrap, seed, separation, shade, shelter, skeeling, skillion, slice, slough, spill(ed), sprinkle, spurn, storehouse, surpass, surprise, throw off, toolhouse, zayat
feathers mew, moult
light on brighten, explain, illuminate
skin ecdysis
tears complain, cry, weep
temporary pandal
weather dingle

SHEDU demon, devil

SHEE banshee, brownie, dwarf, fairy(folk), fay, gnome, nix, pixy, sidhe, sprite
visible on halloween, samhain-eve

SHEEN beautiful, bright (ness), burnish, exalted, fair, glare, glaze, gleam, glitter(ing), gloss, illustrious, light, luster, lustre, machine, polish, radiant, resplendent, shimmer, shine, splendid, splendor

SHEENY See SHINY.

SHEEP, SHEEP'S (See also *kind* and *wild*, below.) bellwether, bleater, congregation, dinmont, ewe, flock, hogg keb, lamb(kin), lonk, mouflon, mouton, mug, mutton, ovine, ovis, pollard, ram, ruminant, sha, shearhog, shearing, tag, tallower, teg, thrinter, tup, wether, woolie, yearling
bighorn argali
black bete-noire, disgrace, karakul, roue
black-faced lonk
blue bharal
brand ruddle, smit
breed See *kind*, below.
coat See *fleece*, below.
cry baa, blat, bleat, maa
dead braxy, traik
difficult cobbler
disease anthrax, bane, belt, big head, black dog, black muzzle, blast, blood, bradsot, braxy, caw, circling, closh, coe, core, coth(e), creeps, crook, daising, dartars, ecthyma, foothalt, footmange, gid, gillar, halt, heartwater, mad, ovinia, pining, rainrot, resp, rinderpest, rot, rubbers, scab, scrapie, shab, sturdy, thwarter, trembles, wildfire, wind
dog bobtail, briard, collie, great pyrenees, huntaway, kelpie, malinois, shelty, shepherd, shetland
dung buttons, scur, treddle, trotters
dysentery moor-evil
feed graze, pasture
female ewe, gimmer, sheder
fleece hogg(erel), hogget, ket, teg(g), wool
flock leader bellwether
fly bot, fag
group flock, herd, mob
hide slat
hornless corriedale, not(t)
hybrid comeback
immersing rod crutch
keeper abel, SHEPHERD

kidney extract venes
-killing ovicide
kind ancon, aoudad, argali, barwal, bharal, bighorn, bikaneri, blackface, braxies, broadtailed, cheviot, churro, columbia, comeback, corriedale, cotswold, criolla, dartmoor, deccan, delaine, dishley, dorper, dorset, down, dumba, exmoor, hampshire, heder, hirsel, hunia, jumbuck, karakul, kerryhill, leicester, lincoln, lonk, lughdoan, masham, merino, nahoor, nayaur, oldenburg, ooriat, oxford (down), panama, paular, pollard, rambouillet, romanov, romney, ryeland, saiga, sha, shropshire, sna, southdown, suffolk, targhee, teeswater, urial, vermont, welshmountain, wensleydale, wiltshire, zenu
laurel calfkill, goldwithy, heath, ivy, kalmia, lambkill, wicky
leather kid, roan, suede
leg hair gare
-like docile, meek, mild, ovine, shy, timid
liniment eik
lost waif
male bellwether, buck, heder, ram, tup, wether
maned aoudad
mange scab
mark brand, smit
merino infantado, paular
mountain bighorn, cheviot, dartmoor, ibex
neck scrag
old gummer
pasture ewe-lease, heaf
path roddin(g)
pen barkary, b(o)ught, cote, crew, crue, fank, fold, kraal, ree(ve), sheepcot, sheppey, stell
pert. aries, ovine, vervecine
pet cosset
plant raoulia
poison lupine, shiverweed, sorrel, staggerweed
pox ovinia, wildfire
rot caw
run station
2nd-year bident, tag(g), teg(g), twinter
shearer gun, ringer
shedding rosella
shelter cote
short-legged ancon

small loaghtan
sorrel spurweed
symbol of timidity
tallow sebum, sevum
tansy fiddleneck
theft abigeat
thick-wooled mug
3rd-year thrinter
tick carapato, fag, gar(r) apata, kade, keb, ked, lousefly
2-year old bident
unshorn heder, hogg
unweaned theave
weaned hoggerel, hogget
white merino
wild aoudad, argal(i), arkar, arui, bharal, bighorn, burrhel, chamois, mouf(f)lon, nahoor, nayaur, oorial, rasse, sestina, sha(poo), sna, thianshan, udad, urial, zenu
wool haslock, tag, teg(g)
wool grease suint
young baahling, bident, eanling, fourtooth, fronter, gimmer, heder, hoggerel, hogg(et), lamb, shearhog, shearling, sheder, tag, teg(g), theave, thrinter, tup, twinter, yeanling
SHEEPBANE pennywort
SHEEPBERRY alisier, blackhorn, hawthorn, honeysuckle, viburnum
SHEEPBINE bindweed
SHEEPCOTE sheppey
SHEEPFACED abashed, awkward, bashful, blate, daffish, embarrassed, meek, shy, silly, timid
SHEEPFOLD See SHEEP *pen.*
SHEEPHEAD jemmy, salema, schafkopf
broth powsowdy
SHEEPHEADED silly, simpleminded, stupid
SHEEPHERDER See SHEPHERD.
SHEEPISH ashamed, bashful, blate, blushing, diffident, embarrassed, guilty, selfconscious, shamefaced, stupid, timid, timorous, verecund
SHEEPSHEAD fathead, james, jemmy, jimmy, pargo, percoid, porgy, sparoid, tautog
SHEEPSKIN basil, bezel, bock, bond, buck, cabretta,

cape(skin), certificate, diploma, dongola, kid, leather, mountain mint, mouton, ocimum, parchment, pelt, pycanthemum, roan, shorling, skiver, slat, soldier, woolfell
cap calpac(k)
dealer fellmonger
layer flesher
pert. vervecine
tanned basan, basil, crust
SHEEPWALK foldcourse, pasture, prison, range, run, slait
SHEEPWEED bog-violet, butterwort, mallow, pinguicula, soapwort
SHEER abrupt, absolute, altogether, arrant, avert, bias, bold, brant, bright, cobwebby, complete(ly), crude, deflect, deviate, deviation, diaphanous, directly, diversion, divert, downright, fair, filmy, fine, frank, gauzy, gazette, gossamer, main, mere, out and out, outright, pellucid, perpendicular, precipice, precipitous, pure, quite, shear, shining, shire, simple, single, sole, stark, steep, swerve, tack, thin, thorough, transparent, unalloyed, undiluted, unmitigated, unmixed, unqualified, upright, utter
off dodge, move away, retreat
SHEET bedding, blanket, board, canvas, card, chain, chudder, cover(ing), daily, expanse, fascia, film, fine, flimsy, flong, folio, frisket, gazette, lamina, layer, leaf(let), linen, membrane, nappe, newspaper, page, pallium, pan(e), paper, papyrus, plate, poster, rope, sail, shroud, sindon, surface, tabloid, wrapper
protective curtain
-rock plasterboard
transparent gelatine
24 quire
winding cerement, shroud, sindon, sudary
SHEETING amerikani, cloth, domestic, fabric, linen, lining, muslin, percale, roofing
stiff beaverboard

SHEIK arab, elder, governor, prince, ruler, shaikh
ritual ride dosa
SHEKEL *1/20th* gerah
 ¼th reba
 ½ bekah
 60 maneh, mina
SHEKELS cash, coin, money
SHELAH *kin* eber, judah
SHELD dappled, pied, speckled, variegated
SHELDRAKE bargoose, burrowduck, casarca, merganser, shelder, skelgoose, stockannet, tadorna
SHELEMIAH *son* hananiah, irijah, jehucal, jucal, nethaniah
SHELF bedrock, bench, berme, bink, bracket, bunning, console, credence, credenza, edge, etagere, gondola, gradin(e), hob, layer, ledge, mantel(piece), predella, reef, retable, sandbank, sconce, settle, shelve, shoal, shoulder, superaltar
altar butsudan, gradino, retable
clock wag-on-the-wall
on the pawned, retired, withdrawn
rock lench(eon)
SHELL ammo, ammunition, arca, armo(u)r, balat, bark, boat, bomb(ard), brachipod, buckie, bullet, bullidae, burgau, burr, cameo, carapace, cartridge, case, casing, cask(et), chank, chitin, coat, cockle, conch(a), conchylium, conker, cortex, cover(ing), cowrie, cowry, crust, dental, ear, epaulet, episperm, exterior, frame, hide, hud, hull, husk, incrustation, lorica (tion), lyre, missile, mollusk, nail, nougat, nucula, obus, ostracon, pericarp, plate, pod, projectile, sack, sankha, scale, scull, scute, scutum, shard, shaup, shield, shock, shot, shrapnel, shuck, skin, spoon, strafe, strip, swad, terbra, test(a), tiara, torpedo, trigonia, triton, troca, tunica, turbinate, turbo, venus, winkle
anti-aircraft flak
apple chaffinch, crossbill
beads peag, wampum
beak umbo
bloom on cuticle

bracelet sankha
button-making troca
cannon black maria, coalbox
casing gaine
cast off exfoliate, exuviate, shed
cavity flue
chambered nautilus
circumference limbus
comb. oeca
cone admiral
covered with loricate
-covering testa
-cracker sunfish
defective dud
diatom frustule
ear abalone, ormer
-eater openbill
edge hinge
embryonic protoconch
explosive bomb, crump, grenade
fossil acrotreta, ammonite, baculite, balamite, conchite, dolite, gryphaea
game flimflammery, fraud, swindle
groove lira, varix
hard lorica
hole crater
ibis openbill
invertebrate test(a)
ivory eburna
marine alectrion, buckie, cassis, conch, cowrie, epitonium, papboat, strombus, triton, turbo, turritella, wentletrap, whelk
mathematical homeoid
measuring device conchometer
mechanism spalter
money allocochick, colcol, cowrie, cowry, hawok, peag(e), se(a)wan, u(h)llo, ulo, wakiki, wampum
opening gape
ornamental runtee
out give, hand over, spend
pastry cornet, dariole, eclair, talmouse, timbale
pear avocado
perfect chambered nautilus
pert. crustaceous
porcelain cowrie
protected by loricate
puff-paste patty
ridge costula
-shaped conchate, conchiform
snail conker, hodmadod
spiral caracol(e), chank, cowrie, cowry, imperforata, nautilus, shankha

study conchology
unexploded dud
vegetable dolma
without oom
SHELLAC beat, defeat, lacquer, paint, resin, rout
SHELLBACK mariner, sailor, salt
SHELLEY, P. B. *alias* ariel
elegy to keats adonais
work alastor, cenci, epipsychidion, prometheus unbound, queen mab
SHELLFISH abalone, bivalve, bluepoint, cigala, clam, cock(le), coquillage, crab, crawfish, crayfish, crevette, crustacean, ecrevisse, hommard, limpet, lobster, mollusk, mussel, nacre, oyster, periwig, periwinkle, pipi, pirot, scallop, shrimp, slug, snail, squill, whelk, wiggle
SHELLFLOWER bells of ireland, mulluca balm, turtlehead
SHELOMITH rehoboam, shimei
SHELTER abri, ark, asylum, awning, balagan, barn, bescreen, bield, bilbie, board, bower, box, burrow, canopy, carport, cave, cloak, cote, cover(t), coverture, defend, defense, dugout, embay, ensconce, garage, gite, hangar, harbor(age), haven, hostel, house, hovel, howf(f), hut(ch), lee, lewth, lithe, lodge, nacelle, pillbox, port, pound, preserve, protect(ion), quarters, quonset, refuge, reset, retreat, roof, safeguard, safety, sanctuary, scog, sconce, screen, scug, security, shade, sheal, shed, sheeling, shield, shieling, skug, sukkah, tent, trench, umbrage, umbrella, wanigan, wickiup, windbreak
animal barth, booly, cot(e), helm, hemmel, stall, stell
bullet-proof abri, mant(e)let, pillbox
fish croy
highway spital
leafy levesel
makeshift breakweather
military pillbox, trench
nautical alee, lee(ward)
portable cabana, manta, tent

temporary bivouac, cabin, hale, hold, tent

SHELVE burke, defer, delay, dish, dismiss, incline, lay aside, ledge, overhang, pigeonhole, postpone, project, put aside, retire, SHELF, store, table, tilt, tip

SHEM *brother* ham
descendant semite
father noah
son aram, arpachsad, arphaxad, asshur, eber, elam, gether, hul, lud, messhech, uzal

SHEMA *son* raham

SHEMAIAH *father* harim
son delaiah, elihu, elzabad, jonathan, obed, othni, rephael, semachiah, urijah

SHEMIDA *son* ahain, aniam, likhi, shechem

SHEMOZZL, SHLEMOZZL abscond, confusion, decamp, fight, rhubarb, uproar

SHENANIGAN buffoonry, evasion, foolery, knavery, nonsense, prank, trick(ery), villainy

SHEND blame, confound, confuse, defend, degrade, destroy, discomfort, disgrace, harm, injure, mar, protect, punish, reproach, revile, ruin, shield, spoil, stupefy, worst

SHENG *1/100th* chao

SHENYANG mukden

SHEOL grave, hades, HELL, underworld

SHEPHATIAH *parent* abital, david
son amariah

SHEPHERD, SHEPHERD'S argus, attend, care for, colin, corin, corydon, daphnis, direct, drafter, drive, escort, follow, gadaria, gaddi, guard(ian), guide, gyges, herd(er), herdsman, hobbler, kurumba, lead(er), melibeus, minister, parson, pastor(al), pilot, shadow, snoozer, strephon, tarbox, tend, thyrsis, tityris, watch
bag scrip
band pastoureau
calendar pimpernel
call ovey
clock pimpernel, salsify
club mullein, plant
companion wagtail-flycatcher

crook See *staff*, below.
dog cebalrai, collie
god pales, pan
hercules' foe antagoras
knot tormentil
needle lady's-comb
of the ocean walter raleigh
pert. pastoral
pipe flageolette, larigot, musette, oat, reed
-purse bindweed, bursa, capsella, caseweed, cocowort, dentaria, mother's-heart, toothwort, toywort
-rod plant, teasel
song madrigal
staff cane, crook, kent, mullein, pedum, teasel
weatherglass pimpernel

SHEPHERDESS amaryllis, bergere, delia, dorcas, galatea, little bopeep, mopsa, pastora, perdita, phebe

SHEPHERDIA beef-suettree, buffaloberry, rabbitberry

SHERBET dessert, drink, glace, granita, ice, sorbet, spoom

SHERD See SHARD.

SHERIDAN, R. *character* absolute, acres, careless, languish, malaprop, puff, surface, whiskerandos
work pizarro, the critic, the duenna, the rivals, the school for scandal

SHERIF, SHEREEF chief, prince, ruler
ancestor fatima, mohammed
realm mecca, morocco

SHERIFF alguacil, bailie, constable, deputy, elisor, grieve, huissier, jailer, officer, reeve, schout, shirra, shreeve, shrieve, tijuana taxi, viscount
jurisdiction bailiwick, shrievalty
men bailiff, catchpoll, deputy, elisor, officer, posse
pert. shrieval, vicontiel

SHERPA climber, tibetan
equipment crampon, piton, rope

SHERRY amontillado, amoroso, hasten, manchu, montilla, oloroso, rangoon, scurry, sherris, solera, wine, xeres
brown doctor
coloring arrope
fine old bristol cream
flavor nutty, rancio

source jerez, xeres

SHERWOOD, R. *work* abe lincoln in illinois, petrified forest

SHESHA ananta, infinity

SHESHAN *son* ahlai

SHETLAND pony, wool
bay voe
boat yole
city lerwick
court justice foud
fishing grounds haaf
freehold udal
harp langspiel
island unst, yell
land odal, udal
landholder odalman, udal (ler), udalman
magistrate foud
measure ure
musical instrument gue
ounce ure
pasture hoga
pony sheltie, shelty
tax scat
viol gue

SHEUGH cover, dig, ditch, furrow, gully, trench

SHEVA *father* caleb

SHEW See SHOW.

SHEYLE grimace, squint

SHIBBOLETH byword, catchword, criterion, password, saying, slogan, test, watchword

SHICER cheat, duffer, jerk, nogoodnik

SHIDDACH marriage, match, wedding

SHIDE billet, board, plank, splinter

SHIELD achievement, aegis, ancile, apothecium, apron, armot, avert, bib, blazon, board, buckler, buffer, canopy, carapace, cartouch(e), casque, clipeus, cloak, clypeus, conceal, conserve, cover, crest, defend(er), defense, defilade, ecu, egis, escutcheon, fender, field, forbid, gobo, guard, gular, gyroma, handle, harbor, hielaman, lorica, lozenge, mail, mulga, palladium, pavis(se), pelta, plate, pridwin, protect(ion), rondache, rondel, rotella, roundel, safeguard, save, scale, sciath, screen, scutcheon, scute, scutum, secure, shade, shell, shelter, shieling, skildfel, sternite, targe(t), testudo, ward off

archer's pannier

area treatment dancette, embattled, engrailed, indented, invected, nebule, unde

band across fess

-bearer escudero, hypaspist, scutifer, squire

bony carpace

border bordure, orle

boss umbo(nal)

bottom base

bullet proof manta, mant-(e)let

cadence marks boar's head couped, boar's head erased, eagle displayed, estoile, garb, lion passant, lion rampant, manche, pheon, stag's head caboshed

circular rotella, roundel, targe(t)

coats of arms, combining dimidiation, escutcheon of pretense, impalement, quartering

color (See also *tincture,* below.) azure, gules, purpure, sable, vert

comb. aspid(o), aspis

crossbowman's pavis(se)

division ente, paly

fern buckler, dryopteris

furs ermine, potent, vair

heraldic blazon, escutcheon, lozenge

hide skildfel

indentation bouche

insect's head clipeus, clypeus

knob umbo

leather chafe

left side sinister

maiden valkyrie

medieval ecu, tilting target

metal argent

notched bouche

oblong pavis(se)

ordinaries (1st son) label, (2nd son) crescent, (3rd son) mullet, (4th son) martlet, (5th son) annulet, (6th son) fleur-de-lis, (7th son) rose, (8th son) crossmoline, (9th son) double quatrefoil

part base, bordure, boss, chief, dexter, ente, fess (point), honor point, impressa, nombril, orle, paly, pointe, sinister, umbo

partition line treatment annulet, bend, billets, bordure, canton, chevron, cross, fess, flanches, fusil, gyron, inescutcheon, loz-

enge, pale, pall, pile, quarter, roundel, saltire

right side dexter

round targe(t)

sacred ancile

-shaped aspidate, clypeate, clypeiform, clypeolar, peltate, scutate, scutiform

small ecu, pelta, scutella, targe(t)

strap bretelle, enarme, guige

subordinaries (See *ordinaries,* above.)

tincture (See also *color,* above.) barry, bendy, checky, chevronny, compony, gyronny, lozengy, paly, party per bend, party per chevron, party per fess, party per pale, party per saltire, quarterly, tierced (per fess)

top chief

SHIELING cottage, hut, pasturage

SHIFT alter, arrange, artifice, avoid, baffle, bestir, camise, change, chemise, contraption, contrivance, contrive, deal, deviate, device, displace, dispose, dodge, dress, effort, evade, evasion, exchange, expedient, feint, fend, fraud, garment, gibe, gybe, haul, jibe, manage, maneuver, move, mutation, order, plea, pretext, quibble, quit, remove, replace, resource, rid, ruse, scheme, shirt, shuffle, shunt, slip, smock, stir, stopgap, stratagem, substitute, subterfuge, surrogate, swerve, tack, tour, transfer, transition, transplant, transposition, trick, turn, vacillate, vary, veer, waist, wend, whiffle, wile

about baffle

boss foreman

ground back-pedal

off defer, delay, dodge, evade, postpone, remove

responsibility pass the buck

SHIFTINESS cunning, deceit, stealth, trickery

SHIFTLESS drifty, feckless, improvident, indolent, inefficient, lazy, slothful, sozzly, thriftless

SHIFTY alert, changeable, changeful, covert, cunning, deceitful, evasive, faithless, fertile, fickle, fly-by-night,

greasy, haft, quick-witted, slippery, treacherous, tricky, unreliable

SHIITE (See also MOHAMMEDAN.) shaikhi, shiah, twelver

center persia, iran

pilgrim site alnajaf, kadhimain, karbala, kum, qum

SHIKKER drunk

SHIKOKU *district* ehime

SHILHI *daughter* azubah

SHILL accomplice, bonnet, capper, cheat, confederate, decoy, dupe, foil, husk, henchman, shell, SHRILL, sonorous

SHILLA beach, gravel, pebble, sand

SHILLELAGH, SHILLALAH club, cudgel, sapling, stick

SHILLIBEER bus, hearse, omnibus

SHILLING bob, coin, deaner, hogg, teviss

1/12th pence, penny

½ sixpence

2 florin

2½ half-crown

5 bull, caroon, crown, decus

20 broadpiece, pound

21 geordie, guinea

SHILLUK *god* juok

SHILLY-SHALLY boggle, foolish, hesitate, hesitation, indecisive, irresolution, pause, trifle, trivial, vacillate, waver

SHILONI *son* zechariah

SHILPIT feeble, flat, insipid, puny, sickly, think, weak, worthless

SHIM glimpse, hoe, image, knife, lamin, level, shadow, shingle, streak, washer, wedge

SHIMEAH *son* jonathan

SHIMEATH *son* zabad

SHIMEI *parent* gera, hashum

son adaiah, beraiah, eliel, elienai, haran, haziel, jahath, jair, jakim, jeush, shelomith, shimrath, zabdi, zichri, zilthai, zina

SHIMEL *father* ela

SHIMMA *parent* jesse

SHIMMER blaze, coruscate, flare, flash, glance, gleam, glimmer, glint, glisten, glister, glitter, gloss, jiggle, light, luster, scintillate, sheen, shimmy, shimper, shine, spark(le), twinkle, wiggle

SHIMMY chemise, dance, quiver, shake, shift, tremble, vibrate, vibration

SHIMON *son* amnon, benhanan, rinnah, tilon

SHIMRATH *father* shimei

SHIN borrow, climb, cnemis, crus, kick, ridge, run, shank, skink, swarm, tibia, walk
pert. cnemial, tibial

SHINAR *city* babel
king amraphel

SHINDIG, SHINDY carousal, commotion, dance, disturbance, fracas, frolic, lark, merrymaking, orgy, party, revel, riot, row, rumpus, shivoo, spree, uproar

SHINE afterglow, beacon, beam, bedazzle, beek, blaze, blink, bloom, bootleg, buff, burn(ish), candescence, caper, coruscate, dawn, daze, dazzle, dido, display, disturbance, excel, fancy, fight, flame, flare, flash, fulgurate, furbish, glaik, glance, glare, glaze, gleam, glint, glisten, glitter, gloss, glow, gloze, illumine, incandesce(nce), liking, luster, meeting, polish, prank, quarrel, radiance, radiate, reflect, rumpus, rutilate, sheen, show, skyre, sleek, sparkle, splendor, star, transluce, trick, twinkle, uproar, wax
faintly blinter, scarrow
up to court

SHINER black-eye, bootblack, bream, bruise, chub, coin, cyprinid, dace, dollarfish, eye, hat, menhaden, minnow, mirror, mouse, notropis, redfin, reflector, roach, silverfish, spawneater, windfish
golden dace

SHINGLE beach, bob, chastise, chesil, clapboard, clip, coiffure, cover, detritus, face, facia, girdle, girth, gravel, haircut, knobble, overlap, overlie, roof(ing), shake, shim, shindie, sign(board) slate, tail, wallop, whip
-back lizard, stumptail
maker clipper
oak blackjack
residue spalt

-splitter prower
wedge-shaped shim

SHINGLES barngun, facia, herpes(zoster), st anthony's fire, zona, zoster

SHINING adazzle, aglow, ardent, blazing, bright, brilliant, burning, clear, effulgent, flashing, fulgent, fulgid, glary, gleaming, glistening, glossy, gorgeous, illustrious, lucid, luminous, lustrous, nitid, radiant, refulgent, reluecent, resplendent, rutilant, sheeny, sparkling, splendent, splendid, starry, sunshiny
comb. pheno
forth profulgent

SHINLEAF pyrola

SHINPLASTER money, scrip

SHINTIYAN trousers

SHINTO See also JAPAN.
deity amaterasu, hachiman, kami
pert. kokka
scriptures kojiki, nihongi, nihonshoki
sect ryobu, shuha
sun goddess amaterasu
temple jinja, jinsha, sha, yashiro
temple gateway torii
2-faced ryobu-shinto

SHINY aglow, argent, bright, burnished, clear, glace, glassy, glossy, gold, luminous, lustrous, money, polished, radiant, sheeny, sleek, slick, sunny, unclouded

SHIP (See also BOAT, NAVY *vessel*, SHIP *kind*, VESSEL *sailing*.) airplane, assume, bark, bottom, consign, craft, embark, export, freight, hulk, sail, send, shift, shoulder, transport, tub, vessel
abandoned derelict
anchorage berth, dock, harbor, slip
ancient galleon, nef
armored carrack, cruiser, destroyer, ironsides, submarine
ascent scend
attendant steward
back aft, skag, skeg, stem, stern
ballast lastage
battens scotchman
beacon fanal
beak speron

biscuit hardtack, patile, pilotbread
boarding device gangplank, ladder
boat barge, ding(e)y, dinghy, dory, gig, jolly, life, pinnace, tender, yawl
body hulk, hull
bottom plank strake
bow stem
bow timber stemson
bracket bibb
breadth of beam
builder boatwright, calker, carver, caulker, joiner, mastmaker, ropemaker, staymaker
building piece bosombar, boss, knee, sny, spale, thwart
building wood angelique
burden cargo
cabin saloon, stateroom
capacity burden, tonnage
capacity unit ton
captain ra(i)s, wafter
carpenter chips
caulking substance berengelite
channel canal, gat, narrow, strait
clean careen, soogee
clean bottom bream
cleaner soogee(moogee), suegee, sujeemujee, sujimuji
clerk purser
coastal bilander, boutre, dhoni, dhow, doni, drog-(h)er, farcost, grab, hoy, lugger, pat(t)amar, shibar, shoaler, tartan, trader
coast guard cutter
codfishing banker, walloper
comb. nau
company of crew, hands
compass housing binnacle
cook slushy
course sealane
cradle slee
crane davit
crew leader bosun
crew member bosun, bungs, cooper, deckhand, engineer, hand, helmsman, mate, navigator, oiler, purser, sailor, steersman, steward, stoker, yeoman
cut down razee
daily record log
dead, built from nails of naglfar
deck See DECK references.
deck drain scupper
deck, lower orlop

deck, remove razee
departure sailing, sortie
depth ga(u)ge
deserter rat
dining room saloon
drinking fountain scuttlebutt
early cog
equipment apparel
escort convoy, corvette
famous aotea, arawa, argo, arizona, birkenhead, bismarck, bonhomme, bounty, clermont, endeavor, fram, gjoa, grafspee, halfmoon, hartford, horouta, lusitania, maine, matatua, mayflower, merrimac, missouri, monitor, nina, olympia, oregon, pelican, pinta, revenge, santa maria, savannah, squalus, tainui, takitunu, titanic, yorktown
fast-sailing clipper
fender skid
fishing hooker, lugger, smack, trawler
flag duster, pennant, jolly roger
flat-bottomed barge, keel
fleet armada
floor deck
frame carcass
framework cradle
front bow, nose
fuel barge, coaler, collier, oiler, tanker
group argosy, armada, fleet, flotilla, navy, squadron, task-force
gutters limbers, scuppers
handrail manrope
hatchway scuttle
hoist boom, camel, capstan, crane, davit
hold hull, thurrock
-holder remora
hospital lazareet, sick bay
hull planking strake
ironclad merrimac, monitor
jail brig, hulk
keel part skeg
kind 3 tow, tug 4 bark, brig, dhow, hulk, junk, koff, mail, mard, maru, pahi, scow, yawl, zulu 5 aviso, barge, drake, ferry, hippo, ketch, liner, oiler, oolak, praam, prore, q-boat, racer, shout, sloop, tramp, yacht, yanky 6 argosy, barque, carack, corvet, cutter, drogen, galiot, galley, launch, lugger, packet, paddle, pontin, puffer, sampan, sealer,

slaver, tanker, tender, tonner, whaler 7 canaler, carrack, carrier, coaster, collier, coracle, cougnar, dredger, drifter, droghen, frigate, gaiassa, galleon, lighter, pinnace, pontoon, shallop, steamer, towboat, trawler, vedette 8 canaller, corvette, dahabeah, indiaman, ironclad, lifeboat, 9 freighter, powerboat, privateer, speedboat, steamboat, steamship, transport, whaleback 10 barkentine, brigantine, sidewinder 11 merchantman, sidewheeler 12 sternwheeler
kitchen caboose, cookhouse, galley
launching track groundway
left side port
line questrope, marline, ratline
lookout conning tower, crow's-nest
medieval asec, bireme, dromon, galiot, knorr, trireme, unireme
merchant argosy, frigate, gal(1)iot, holcad
mid-part amidships, waist
mooring equipment groundtackle
mortgage bottomry
oar-propelled See BOAT.
of desert camel
officer boatswain, bosun, captain, commander, master, mate, navarch, skipper
1-masted sloop
ornament acrostolium, acroterium, aphlaston, aplustre, figurehead
out enlist, export
part 3 aft, bow, fid, nef, rib, sny 4 beak, beam, bibb, bitt, boom, brig, deck, gaff, head, heel, helm, hold, hulk, hull, jack, keel, loof, mast, poop, port, prow, rail, sail, skag, skeg, spar, spir 5 bilge, cabin, davit, hatch, hawse, kevel, orlop, snape, sprit, stern, waist, wheel 6 bridge, bunker, canvas, galley, gunnel, rudder, sheets, steeve, steven, strake, tiller 7 bollard, bulwark, bumpkin, caboose, foretop, futtock, gangway, keelson, killick, knuckle, leeside, scupper, scuttle, sickbay, snorkel, spanker,

spirket, topside, yardarm 8 beakhead, binnacle, bowsprit, bulwarks, camboose, casemate, cutwater, forejack, foreyard, larboard, main mast, porthole, quarters, steerage, wardroom 9 afterbody, crowsnest, gangplank, lazarette, mizzentop, propeller, stanchion 10 pilothouse, roundhouse 11 paddlewheel, scuttlebutt 12 companionway, conningtower 14 superstructure
partition bulkhead
permit to enter port pratique
personnel crew, hands
pert. navicular
pirate gallivat
planking sny, strake
pole mast, spar
privateer brigantine, drumbler
prize capture
prow nose, prore, rostrum, stem
quarantine lazar
quarters focsle, forecastle, steerage
ramming another allision
rear abaft, astern
receiving guardo
record log
remote-controlled drone
repair careen
repair place drydock
rescue ark
rigging tackle
rigging, upper top-hamper
right side starboard
room brig, cabin, caboose, focsle, forecastle, galley, salo(o)n, steerage, wardroom
rope cordage, halyard, hawser, lanyard, line, painter, ratline, shroud, snorter, snotter
route course, lane
sail canvas, cloth, crossjack, fly-by-night, jib, jimbo, jollyjumper, lateen, leech, luff, lug, main, mizzen, moonraker, muslin, rag, reef, royal, spanker, topgallant
sailing See VESSEL *sailing.*
salvager wrecker
shovel skeet
sick bay See *hospital,* above.
sink scuttle
slow bucket
small barkey
speed measurer rhysimeter, silometer
square-masted brig

steps companionway
stern steerage
steward flunk(e)y
supply co(o)per
sweeper topass, topiwala
tackle cat
tender barge, collier, ding-(e)y, gig, pinnace
3-masted lugger, toup
tiller helm
timber apron, bibb, bitt, keel(son), lacepiece, mast, rib, rider, snape, sny, spar, stemson, stick
timber baulk knighthead
timber, curved sny
toll keelage
track wake
trading coaster
twin-hulled catamaran
2-masted brig, snow
unseaworthy baliahoo, ballahou, derelict, hulk, wreck
upward movement scend
war See NAVY *vessel.*
warning device autoalarm, foghorn, siren
windless capstan
window porthole
wood for teak
worm anter, borer, cobra, pileworm, teredo, woodworm
SHIPSHAPE ataunt, first-rate, neat, orderly, snug, sound, taut, tidy, tiptop, trig, trim, uncluttered, yare
SHIPWRECK debacle, destroy, destruction, misfortune, naufrage, naufragie, ruin
causing naufragous
demon alrinach
goods flotsam, jetsam, salvage
SHIPWRIGHT builder, wayman
SHIRAZ afshar, carpet, mecca, rug, wine
SHIRE county, district, horse, province, region, subdivision, territory
SHIRK avoid, blink, bludge, default, desert, dodge, duck, evade, fainaigue, feint, finagle, flee, flunk, fudge, funk, goldbrick, goof(off), lie down, malinger, neglect, pike, rodney, scrimshank, shaffle, shammock, shark, shun, skulk, slack, slink, sneak, soger, sojer, soldier, welsh
SHIRKER bludger, coberger,

embusque, funk(er), loafer, malingerer, quitter, rotter, scowbank, slacker, slinker, truant
SHIRL glide, misselbird, romp, schorl, shear, shrill, slide, slip, trim
SHIRR bake, cook, gather(s), runnings, smock, wrinkle
SHIRT banian, baniya, baro, bleaunt, blouse, bluey, camisa, camiscia, camise, camisia, cilice, clothe, cover, dresser, garment, gipon, guernsey, haire, jersey, jesseraunt, jupe, jupon, kamis, kamleika, middy, palaka, parka, polo, pourpoint, pullover, sark, skivvy, sport, tee, tobe, top, undergarment, underwear, vareuse, waist
bosom plastron
button stud
collar-style button-down
flap labie
frill chitterling, jabot
front, false dick(e)y
hair cilice
linen sarking
loose blouson, camise, kamis
outworn dick(e)y
sleeveless fecket
stuffed blowhard, swaggerer
under singlet, tee
woolen bania(n)
workman's krock
SHIRTLESS poor, poverty-stricken
SHIRTWAIST blouse, garibaldi
SHIRTY angry, cross, huffy, mad, vexed
SHITENNO heavenly guards, lokapala
home mount sumeru
master taishakuten
name bishamon, dhritarashtra, jikoku, komoku, tamon, vaisramana, virudhaka, virupaksha, zocho
trample on demons
SHIVA See SIVA.
SHIVAREE See CHARIVARI.
SHIVE chive, cut, flake, shove, slice
SHIVER bit, break, chitter, chivel, dadder, didder, dodder, dudder, flake, flicker, fragment, freeze, frisson, girl, grue, hotter, nidder, nither, part, piece, pulley, quake, quaver, rend,

shake, shale, shatter, shimmy, shither, shudder, slice, splinter, thrill, totter, tremble, vibrate, wobble
fit ague, chills, goosebumps, goosepimples
SHIVEREENS fragments, smithereens
SHIVERS creeps, fever, shakes, trepidation
SHIVERY aguish, brittle, cold, creepy, oory, ourie, pulverable, shaky, shattery, timid, trembling, tremorous
SHIVOO banquet, entertainment, gathering, shindig
SHKODER scutari
SHLEMIEL neb(b)ech, neb(b)ish, shmendrick, yold
SHLEPPER shmegegge
SHMATTE, SHMOTTE cheap, fawner, junk, rag, shoddy, slattern, sycophant, toady
SHMEER beat, bribe, paint, paste, smear, spread, strike
SHMEGEGGE baloney, cockamamy, drip, hot air, maladroit, nonsense, petty, shlepper, sycophant, whiner
SHMENDRICK casper milquetoast, child, nebech, no-account, pipsqueak, schlemiel
SHMOOS gossip, rumors, shmooz(e), shmues, talk
SHOA *king* menelik
SHOAL assemblage, assemble, bajo, bank, bar(ra), bevy, coralreef, crowd, drave, drove, fill, flat, flote, ford, group, horde, host, ledge, mass, mudflat, multitude, pack, quantity, reef, sandbank, sandbar, school, scull, separate, shallow(s), shelf, silt up, spit, swarm, swash, throng, tideland, towhead
water deposit culm
SHOAT gurry, hog, pig(let), shote
SHOBAL *father* caleb
son alian, ebal, manahah, onam, shephi
SHOCK appall, assail, astonish, astound, awe, baffle, bedazzle, blast, blow, boggle, brunt, buffet, bump, bushy, canvass, catalepsy, cataplexia, clash, cluster, cock, collision, concussion, consternation, convulsion, crash, daunt, daze, disgust,

dismay, disturbance, flabbergast, force, gliff, gloff, heap, horrify, impact, jar, jolt, misfortune, mop, narcosis, numb, offend, outrage, overcome, pain, paralysis, pile, quake, ram, repercussion, rick, scandal(ize), scare, shaggy, sheaves, shock, shuck, stack, start(le), stook, strike, stroke, stun, stupefaction, stupefy, surprise, terrify, trauma, tremor, turn, upset, wonder

absorb decouple

absorber buffer, bungee, cushion, dashpot, snubber

corn stitch, stook, stout

-dog poodle

mental trauma

therapy cst, electronarcosis, ict

to reality sober

SHOCKED aghast, farchadat, scandalized

SHOCKER penny-dreadful, ricker, stooker

SHOCKING abominable, appalling, awful, bad, disgusting, distasteful, dreadful, fearful, frightful, ghastly, grim, hideous, horrible, horrid, horrific, odious, offensive, painful, repellent, repugnant, scandalous, shameful, terrible, ugly, unholy

SHOD booted, calced, dressed, ensoled, muddied, sandaled, shoed, slippered, soled

SHODDY base, cheap, cloth, fabric, fake, false, footy, inferior, paltry, poor, pretentious, refuse, shabby, sham, shmatte, shmotte, sleazy, slovenly, soft(s), spurious, tinpot, vulgar(ity)

article schlack, schlag, s(c)hlock

SHOE(S) anklet, balmoral, beavertop, blake, blucher, boot(ee), brodequin, brogan, brogue, buskin, calceus, caliga, campagus, casing, chopine, clodhopper, clog, cobcab, crakow, derby, dorsey, drag, flat(tie), footgear, footwear, gaiter, galosh, geta, gillie, gilly, go ahead, hushpuppy, maryjane, mckay, moc(c)asin, molding, mule, oxford, pac,

pampootee, patten, planch, pump, romeo, rubber, rullion, sabot, sandal, schone, schoon, schuit, shoon, shune, sling, slipper, sneaker, solleret, stoga, stogy, strap, tie, t-strap, veldschoen, wedgie, zori

aid horn

ankle-high chukka-boot

baby's bootee, cack

blucher creedmore

boy bootblack

brake skate

canvas plimsoll, sneaker

cleat calk(er), calkin, caulk

clog chopine, cobcab, patten, sabot

corrective device arch support

covering gaiter, prunella, rubber, spat

dealer bottier

edge welt

elastic-sided congress boot

15th century poulaine

flexible sollaret

form filler, last, tree

14th century crakow

front vamp

grinding muller

grip cleat

gum plimsoll, sneaker, tennie

heavy brogan

heelless moccasin, pac, zori

heelplate cleat

high boot, brodequin, buskin, cocker, moyle

hobnailed tacket

house moyle, mule, scuff, slipper

lace latc(h)et, string, tie, whang

laced oxford, tennie

lace tip a(i)glet

large gunboat

latchet tab

leather alligator, cabretta, calf, kid, pigskin, suede

leather strip rand, welt

low anklet, auskin, colonial, gilly, pump, sandal, slipper

low-heeled maryjane

makeshift sabotine

metal plate tramp

military caliga

mule planche

old bauchle

ox cue

part archsupport, backstay, calk, cap, caulk, cleat, counter, geta, heel, insole, lace(t), last, lift, lining,

outsole, pull, rand, shank, slipsole, sole, strap, toe, tongue, upper, vamp, welt

party maryjane

paste clobber

piked beaker, cleats, crakow

rawhide himming

repair reheel, resole, retap, stitch

repairer cobbler, jackman

rubber arctic, galosh(e), overshoe

-shaped calceolate

-shiner bootblack, boots

snow racket

soft plimsoll, sneaker, tennie

sole speck

sport gilly, tennie

steel solleret

stiffener counter

stout brogan, brogue

strapped roman-sandal

thick-soled chopine, clog, sabot

thin pinson, sclaff

tie lace, latchet, strap, string, thong, whang

-wearing calced, shod

winged talaria

with gusset congress-boot

wooden clog, geta, klomp, patten, racket, racquet, sabot, secque

worker breaster, cobbler, laster

worn bauchle, scrae

SHOEBILL balaeniceps, bird, stork

SHOELESS *horse* moonwort

SHOEMAKER archer, booter, bottier, chamar, cobbler, codger, cordonnier, cordwainer, corviser, cozier, crispin, farrier, fudger, gouger, laster, snob(ber), snobscat, soler, s(o)uter, stitcher

apprentice snob

awl elsen

bench forme

nail sparable

patron saint crispi(a)n

tool awl, butt, els(h)in, last

SHOEMAKING snobbing

SHOESTRING *weed* poison ivy

SHOFAR cornet, horn, ram's horn, trumpet

note tekiah

SHOG jerk, jog, jolt, jostle, rock, shake

SHOGGIE sway, swing

SHOGGLE dangle, icicle, joggle

SHOGUN chief, governor, magnate, ruler, tycoon

SHOMER *father* heber

son ahi, aram, jehubbah, rohgah

SHOO away, begone, scat, scram, vamoose

-fly hobbyhorse, indigo, pie, rocker, track

SHOOI jaeger, skua

SHOOK See SHOCK.

SHOOL drag, idle, loiter, saunter, scrape, scuffle, shamble, shovel, shuffle, shul

SHOOT 3 bag, bud, fly, gun, hit, jut, pop, pot, udo, zap 4 bang, bine, bolt, chit, cion, dart, dash, drop, emit, fell, film, fire, grow, hunt, kilt, limb, pelt, plug, rush, scud, shot, snap, twig, warp 5 blast, blaze, bough, chute, drill, drive, eject, frond, gemma, hurry, lance, pshaw, range, scion, skirr, snipe, spear, speed, sprig, turio, vimen, whizz, wound 6 attack, branch, extend, flower, ignite, inject, launch, mature, pepper, pierce, propel, ratoon, riddle, sprout, stolon, strike, sucker, thrust, tiller, turion, twinge 7 bombard, budling, burgeon, develop, execute, explode, pick off, project, tendril, tendron, thallus, torpedo 8 catapult, detonate, immunize, protrude 9 discharge, germinate, offspring, variegate 10 photograph

barren apoblast

comb. blast(o)

deer yard

down splash

ducks skag

edible udo

1st braird

flexible bine

from cover snipe

objective bull's eye, target

out contest, fight, protrude, settle, spray

plant bine, cion, frond, gemma, rod, runner, scion, sprig, stolon, sucker, vimen

sound bang, pop, snap, zap

sugarcane lalo

tender flush, sprout

the breeze chat(ter), converse, gossip, talk

up develop, erect, grow, increase, protrude, rocket, skyrocket, upspring, upstart

willow sallow

SHOOTER archer, coat, firearm, GUN, gunner, hunter, marble, marksman, moonlighter, pistol, pluffer, repeater, sagittarius, shot, skeeter, taw

SHOOTING darting, gunplay, hunting, killing, piercing, potting, projection, sprouting

box hunting lodge

gallery tir

iron firearm, gat, gun, pistol, revolver, rod, weapon

match skeet, tir

star comet, cowslip, dodecatheon, fireball, leonid, meteor, primwort

SHOP almacen, apothec, atelier, bodega, bottega, boutique, burse, business, buy, crib, emporium, establishment, exchange, factory, firm, house, imprison, job, market, mart, mercery, mill, office, plant, prison, store, studio, taberna, tendejon, tienda, toko, trade, turnery

blacksmith's forge, smithy

coffee bistro, cafe, estaminet

dairy creamery, cremerie

girl midinette

kind armo(u)ry, grocery, haberdashery, mercery, pharmacy, saddlery, smith(er)y, stith(y)

meat butchershop, charcuterie, rotisserie, shamble

nameplate facia, logo

section bazaar, sook, suq

suttler's canteen

wine bistro, cafe, shebeen, taberna, tavern(a)

SHOPBOARD bench, counter, workbench

SHOPHAR See SHOFAR.

SHOPKEEPER arab, bakal, bourgeoise, businessman, chetty, cit, merchant, retailer, salesman, soudagur, storekeeper, tradesman

SHOPLIFTER booster, thief

SHOPPER buyer, customer

obsessive oniomaniac

SHOPWORN archaic, faded, hackneyed, marred, obsolete, old, ragged, stereotyped, threadbare, trite, wasted

SHOR salina, saltlake

SHORE bank, beach, bench, brink, buttress, coast, dockside, drain, edge, embankment, frighten, hound, land(fall), littoral, marge, offer, playa, prop, ripa, rivage, sand sca(u)r, scold, seaboard, seacoast, sewer, shelve, slope, stay, strand, support, sure, threaten, tidewater, warth, waterfront

adjoining circumlittoral

bird See BIRD *shore.*

crab ochidore

fish dragonet, opaleye

-inhabiting limicoline

leave liberty

pert. littoral

recess bay(ou), cove, firth, inlet

snipe sandpiper

up fortify, support

SHORLING monk, priest, shaveling, shearhog

SHORN not(t), polled, tonsured

SHORT abbreviated, abridge(d), abrupt(ly), bain, bear, bluff, blunt, brief(ly), brittle, brusque, cammed, camus(e), compact(ed), compendious, concise, condensed, cranky, crisp(y), cross, curt(al), curtail(ed), curtate, curtly, cutty, decurtate, deficient, direct, ephemeral, fragile, friable, fubsy, harshly, imperfect, inadequate, incomplete, insufficient, lacking, laconic, lightly, little, low, poor, pulverable, quick, rough, rude, scant(y), scarce, sell, small, snappish, snugly, soon, squidgy, straight, stub(by), succinct, suddenly, sullen, summary, synoptic, terse, tightly, touchy, unceremonious, uncivil, under(sized), undiluted, want, wanting, without

and stout bunty, dumpy, five-by-five, podgy, pudgy, rolypoly, stocky, stodgy, stubby, thickset

and sweet brief, concise, terse

and thick stumpy, trunch(ed)

comb. brachy, brevi

-coupled chuffy

cut compendium, curtail, cutoff

distance bee-line
-eared owl momo
-footed brachypodine
-headed brachycephalic, brachycranic
-legged brachypodus, breviped
-lived brief, ephemeral, fleeting, fragile, fugitive, impermanent, momentary, transient, transitory
-napped ras
-nosed brachystomatous
shrift pause, respite
sighted amblyopic, blind, dull, myopic, nearsighted, obtuse, opportunistic, purblind
-spoken curt, gruff, laconic, terse
-tempered hotheaded, snippy, snuffy, volatile
while bittie
-winded asthmatic, breathless, purfled, purfly, pursive, pursy, wheezy
-winged brachypterous, brevipennate
SHORTAGE deficiency, deficit, inadequacy, insufficiency, lack, need, ullage, want
SHORTCHANGE cheat, defraud, fluff, skimp
SHORTCOMING arrearage, arrears, decline, defalcation, default, defect, deficiency, deficit, delinquency, failure, fault, flaw, imperfection, inadequacy, infirmity, insufficiency, lack, need, shortage, shortfall, slump, ullage, want, weakness
SHORTEN abbreviate, abridge, abstract, apocopate, bob, boil down, check, clip, compress, contract, crop, curtail, cut, decrease, decurt, dele(te), deprive, diminish, dock, economize, elide, epitomize, excerpt, furl, lessen, lop, prune, reduce, reef, retrench, shave, shear, slash, sum up, syncopate, telescope, trim, truncate
SHORTENED abridged, bobtail, curtate, cut, shorn
SHORTENING butter, contraction, fat, grease, lard, oil
SHORTEST least
SHORTFALL deficit, need, shortage

SHORTHAND abbreviating, brachygraphy, eliptical, phonotypy, speedwriting, stenography, tachygraphy
device stenotype
inventor gregg, pitman, tiro
SHORTHANDED undermanned, understaffed
SHORTHORN cattle, durham, tenderfoot, tyro
SHORTLY abruptly, anon, before long, briefly, concisely, curtly, harshly, next, presently, proximately, quickly, soon, succinctly, summarily
SHORTNESS brevity, conciseness, concision, curtness, unlength
SHORTS bermudas, boxers, breeches, briefs, canaille, capris, clippings, deficiencies, drawers, hemp, pants, refuse, scants, toppings, trimmings, trousers, underwear
SHORTSOME amusing, blithe, cheery
SHOSHONE *chief* washakie
god pokunt
indian banak, bannock, cahuilla, comanche, gitanemuck, hopi, moki, mono, moqui, oto(e), otto(e), paiute, pima, piute, utah, ute
SHOT aliipoe, ammo, ammunition, attempt, ball, bet, blank, bracer, bullet, carton, cartridge, chance, changeable, charge, conjecture, contribution, detonation, discharge, drink, flier, fling, fluff, flyer, guess, gunfire, hypo, infused, injection, inoculation, jigger, lead, marksman, missile, pelican, pellet, permeated, photo(graph), plot, pop, portion, pot, projectile, range, reach, salvo, scope, shell, shoat, slug, snort, soldier, spray, upset, vaccination, variegated, welded, worn(out)
archery green
big See MAGNATE.
billiard bricole, carom, drag, follow, safety, scratch, scrow, spread, stab
close-up zoom
kind big, liquor, long, parthian
series burst

star meteor
to pieces dilapidated, disorganized, ruined, upset, wrecked
SHOTGUN double, pepperer, tupara
SHOTTERY *owner* nathaniel hawthorne
SHOULD best had, had better, have (to), mow, must, ought, sud, want
SHOULDER axil(la), axle, bear, bench, berm(e), bough, buttress, clod, coathanger, dod(d), edge, epaule, hump, jostle, nudge, pitch, project(ion), push, raise, ridge, rimbase, roadside, scapula, shelf, spall, spauld, support, thrust
angle epaule
armor epauliere, pauldron
bag musette
ballet position epaulement
beveled gain
blade caracoid, omoplate, scapula, spadebone, spald, speal
blade part acromion
comb. omo
hitter bully, pugilist, rowdy
loop epaulet(te)
muscle deltoid, subclavius, trapezius
ornament epaulet(te), patch, stripe, tab
pad porter's-knot
pain omalgia, omitis, omodynia
pert alar, humeral, scapular
pork hand, picnic
road berm(e), edge, haunch, quarter, rut, verge
strap baldric, bandoleer, bandolier, bretelle, sam browne, sash
to shoulder serried, side by side, together
wrap shawl, stole
yoke bang(h)y
yoke pail cowl, soe
SHOUT acclaim, banzai, bark, barrack, bawl, bellow, bis, boat, boo(hoo), bravo, call, cheer, clamor, clepe, cry, evoe, exclaim, grede, halloo, havoc, holler, hoot, hoy, hue, hurrah, huzzah, laugh, ole, outburst, outcry, oyes, oyez, rah, rejoice, reme, roar, roup, screak, scream, screech, scroinoch, scroinogh, scronach, scry, shilloo, shriek, squall, squawk, steven, summon,

tallyho, treat, tumult, vociferate, whoop, yammer,
yap, yawp, yell, yoicks
approving bravo, cheer, hurrah, hurray, ole
down silence, still
hunting chevy, hallo, holla,
tallyho, view-haloo, yoicks
joyous whoopee
SHOVE abet, aid, banish,
boost, bull, cast, drive,
dunch, eject, elbow, force,
hustle, impel, impulse, jog,
jostle, move, muscle, nudge,
oblige, obtrude, press, prod,
prop, propel, propulsion,
push, put, scamble, shive,
shore up, thrust
aside shunt, sidetrack, switch
off depart, embark, launch,
leave, start
SHOVEL cue, dig(ger),
dredge, hat, intrude, ladle,
loy, pale, peel, rabble,
scoop, scoppit, sheel, shool,
shuffle, skeet, slick, sludger,
spade, spud, strockle, stump-
spud, thrust, tool, van
casting scuttle
perforated skimmer
sand strockle
SHOVELER bluewing, bucker, bufflehead, butterball,
butterbox, duck, fenduck,
scooper, spatula, whinger,
whinyard
SHOVELFISH paddlefish,
spadefish
SHOVELHEAD bonnetshark,
catfish, flathead, hammerhead, shark, sturgeon
SHOW 3 act 4 bear, dash,
fair, give, lead, open, play,
pomp, seem, sham, shew,
tell 5 argue, array, carry,
farce, flair, gloss, guide,
legit, movie, offer, plead,
prove, raree, revue, rodeo,
shine, teach, train, usher 6
action, affect, afford, allege,
appear, aspect, assign, bestow, betray, blazon, circus,
direct, evince, expose,
flaunt, inform, parade, reveal, review, spread, tender,
unfold, unfurl 7 bespeak,
betoken, conduct, declare,
display, divulge, exhibit, explain, perform, present,
pretend, pretext, produce,
proffer, profess, suggest,
theater 8 carnival, disclose,
discover, evidence, indicate,
instruct, intimate, manifest,

pretense 9 barnstorm, burlesque, pageantry, prome-
nade, repertory, represent,
semblance, spectacle 10 appearance, attraction 11
affectation, demonstrate,
opportunity, ostentation,
performance 13 motion picture
approval applaud, cheer, clap
displeasure grouch, grump,
pout
false bubble, tinsel
floor cabaret
forth air, blaze, manifest,
proclaim, publicize, publish
gratitude acknowledge, thank
indecision waffle, waver
-me state missouri
-off act up, cutup, display,
exhibit(ionist), expose,
flaunt, grandstand(er),
knocker, prankster, put on
a front, splurge, swagger
(er), swank, vulgarian
one's hand disclose, divulge,
reveal, tip
puppet droll, guignol, pantomime, wajang, wayang
ring arena, circus
rudimentary satura
street raree
stylized cavalcade, mime,
pageant, pantomime, pa-
rade
superficial gloss, veneer
temporary flash(in the pan)
the way conduct, direct, escort, explain, guide, lead,
usher
up appear, arrive, attend,
beat, disillusion, display,
disprove, expose, materi-
alize, occur, strip, turn up
SHOWCASE counter, etalage, vitrine
SHOWDOWN confrontation,
decision, settlement
SHOWER abound, abun-
dance, attack, barrage,
bath(e), battle, bestow,
bestrew, blash, brash,
cloudburst, combat, com-
morth, conflict, deluge, ding
on, discharge, downpour,
dribble, drizzle, drow, exhibitor, flow, flurry, furnish,
fusillade, indicator, lavish,
misle, mizzle, paroxysm,
party, plash, plump, pour,
rain(fall), rash, rush, scat
(ter), scud, skew, skite,
spate, spray, sprinkle,
squall, sump, sympton,

teem, throe, volley, wash,
water, wet
SHOWERY brashy, clashy,
damp, moist, rainy, scatty,
tearful, wet
SHOWING account, apocalypse, appearance, aspect,
display, exhibition, manifestation, presentation, revelation, sign, vision
1st premiere, vernissage
make a appear, put on a
front
SHOWMAN barker, cos-
tumer, costumiere, designer,
director, exhibitor, impresario, master of cermonies,
producer, prompter, spieler
SHOWY arty, baronial, bediz-
ened, bizarre, bold, brankie, branky, brazen, bril-
lante, brummagem, brum-
my, chichi, claptrap, counterfeit, criant, dashing,
dashy, flamboyant, flashy,
flossy, garish, gaudy, gay,
gimcrack, gorgeous, gran-
diloquent, histrionic, hotshot, inferior, loud, luxurious, magnificent, opulent,
orgulous, ornate, ostentatious, pompous, pretentious.
purple, resplendent, rococo,
spanky, splashy, splendid,
sporty, striking, swanky,
tacky, tawdry, tinselly,
trumpery, worthless
condition bravado
SHPENE titanite
SHRAG lop, trim
SHRAM benumb, shrink,
shrivel
SHRAPNEL ammo, ammunition, projectile, shell
SHRED bit, blype, cantlet,
carve, cut, divide, filament,
floc(cus), flock, fragment,
fray, frazzle, fritter, grate,
hew, lop, mince, part(icle),
piece, prune, rag, ribbon,
rip, rond, roon, screed,
scintilla, scrap, sever, shard,
shatter, sherd, shrip, slice,
sliver, snip, speck, stitch,
string, strip, tag, tailor,
target, tatter, tear, tease,
twig, vestige, wisp
fish scrod
SHREDCOCK fieldfare
SHREW baggage, barge, battle-axe, blarina, brimstone,
callet, cat, curse, erd,
frump, fury, hag, harpy,
harridan, hellcat, hussy,

kate, katharine, malicious, migale, nag, ord, outcast, pentail, randy, schlack, schlag, s(c)hlock, scold, scoundrel, scytale, sinsring, sorex, soricine, spitfire, tana, targer, ta(r)tar, termagant, tupaia, uropsile, virago, vixen, wench, wicked, witch, xant(h)ippe, yachna, yachne, yenta, yente

family soricidae

genus blarina, neosorex, notiosorex, sorex

-like soricine

-mouse hyrax, migale, mygale, scytale, sorex

tree banxring

SHREWD acute, arch, argute, artful, astute, bad, baffling, biting, cagey, calculating, canny, clever, crafty, cunning, cute, dangerous, deep, depraved, discerning, dry, evil, foxy, grievous, harsh, heady, hurtful, injurious, intelligent, keen, knowing, mischievous, parlous, pawky, penetrating, piercing, pokey, politic, practical, prudent, sagacious, sage, sapient, sharp, slick, sly, smart, smooth, sprach, stern, subtle, unfavorable, unsatisfactory, ware, wicked, wily, wise

SHREWDNESS acumen, gumption, policy, sagacity, savvy, slyness

SHREWISH froward, peevish, petulant, vixenish

SHRIEK cry, holler, laugh, outcry, scream, screech, scrike, shout, shright, shrike, spraich, yarm, yell, yip

SHRIEVE sheriff

SHRIFT absolution, confession(al), confessor, disclosure, penance, shrive, shriving

SHRIFTLESS incorrigible, unregenerate

SHRIKE bacbakiri, batara, bellbird, boubou, brubru, butcherbird, campanaro, drongo, dryoscopus, falconet, flasher, flusher, lanius, log(ger)head, migrant, minivet, ninekiller, puffback, squeaker, triller, woodchat, woodthrush

bush antbird

fork-tailed drongo

SHRILL acute, argute, biting, bright, clear, creaking, creaky, earsplitting, hautain, high(pitched), keen, minikin, penetrating, piercing, piping, pipy, poignant, reedy, screaky, scream, screech(ing), screechy, sharp, shriek, squeak(y), strident, stridulate, thin, treble, whistling

SHRILLNESS stridor

SHRIMP apang, artemia, balachan, brownie, camaron, carid(ean), crago, crawfish, crevette, crustacean, decapod, diminutive, dwarf, kid, macruran, midget, mysid, napee, nipper, pandle, parva, peewee, polypott, prawn, pygmy, redtail, runt, scampi, shaver, spectre, stripling

comb. caris

large prawn

opossum schizopod

parasite epicarides

pert. macruran

small krill

SHRINE adyt(um), aedicule, altar, anaktoron, ark, baccheion, box, canonize, case, casket, chaitya, chantry, chapel, chasse, chorten, church, coffin, dagaba, dagoba, dargah, delubrum, durgah, edicule, enclose, entomb, fanacle, feretory, guaca, gurdwara, hallow, hieron, huacm, image, kaaba, lararium, marabout, mausoleum, mazar, memoria(l), naos, pantheon, pir, reliquary, sacrarium, sacrary, samadh, sanctuary, sanctum, sepulcher, stupa, tabernacle, temenos, temple, theseum, tomb, tope, valhalla, ziarat

custodian pheretrer

screen transenna

study naology

SHRINK abbor, abridge, atrophy, blench, blush, boggle, cling, collapse, compress, condense, constrict, contract, cotter, cower, cringe, crumple, curtail, decrease, deflate, demur, depreciate, desert, diminish, dodge, dry up, dwindle, fawn, flinch, funk,

gizzen, huddle, lessen, parch, psychiatrist, quail, recede, recoil, reduce, relax, resile, retire, retract, retreat, retrench, sanforize, scruple, sear, shorten, shrivel, shrug, shuck, shudder, shunt, shy, start, warp, waste, weazen, wince, withdraw, wither, wizen, wrinkle

SHRINKAGE decrease, depreciation, loss, reduction, wastage

SHRINKING afraid, astringent, coy, diffident, recessive, reticent, sensitive, shy, timid, withdrawal

SHRIVE absolve, acquit, confess, disclose, pardon, purge, question, reconcile, rob

SHRIVEL age, buckle, burn, cotter, crine, crozzle, crumple, desiccate, dry, gizzen, languish, parch, rivel, scorch, scrump, sear, shram, shrink, snurp, stale, weazen, wither, wizen, wrinkle

SHRIVELED blasted, corky, haggard, poor, pungled, sere, shirpit, small, starky, svelt, thin, thirl, wede, wizened, wrinkled, wrizzled

SHROFF assort, banker, inspect, moneychanger

SHROUD array, benight, bough, branch, cave, cerecloth, cerement, cloak, clothe, conceal, cowl, cover(ing), crypt, curtain, den, disguise, drape, dress, envelope, foliage, garment, hearse, hide, kell, kittle, lop, mask, muffle, pall, plumage, protect, retreat, rope, screen, shade, shadow, sheet, shelter, trim, vault, veil, windingsheet, wrap

fabric sindon

rope lanyard, ratline, wapp

set rigging

SHROUDED concealed, hidden, occult, veiled

SHROVETIDE carnival, fastmass, guttide

fee cockpenny

food carcake, kercake

tuesday fastens, fasterns, guttide, pancake day

SHRUB beverage, boscage, bush, cudgel, drink, fidget,

foliage, heath, liquor, lop, plant, prune, punch, scratch, tod
aromatic allspice, aralia, batis, boronia, clusia, croton, hogbush, lavender, litsea, mint, rosemary, sage, sassafras, tea, thyme
berry elder, holly, salal
beverage t(h)ea
bushy cade, savin, tod, wahoo, yapon
ceder savin(e)
climbing bignonia, catclaw, cat's-claw, clematis, honeysuckle, jasmine, liana, rubus, smilax, solandra, vitis
collection fruticetum
comb. thamn(o)
creeping pyxie
cruciferous coralwort, cress, leadwort, pepperroot, shepherd's-purse, toothwort
desert afernan, alhagi, camel's-thorn, ocotillo, paloverde, r(a)etem
dwarfed bonsai, coralberry, retinispora
edible deerberry, diddledee
ericaceous arbutus, bearberry, cassiope, gaultheria, heath, rhododendron
euphorbiaceous alem
evergreen abebia, abelmosk, arbutus, ardisia, azara, bago, baretta, bauera, boldo, box, buxus, calfkill, camellia, caraunda, cassiope, ceanothus, christmasberry, cistus, dahoon, erica, evonymus, fatsia, furze, hawthorn, heath, hedera, holly, ilex, jasmine, jujube, juniper, kalmia, kosam, laurel, leatherleaf, madrona, mahonia, mistletoe, moss, myrtle, nandina, oleander, oregon-grape, pepino, privet, pyxie, rhododendron, rosebay, rosemary, ruscus, sakaki, salal, sasanqua, savin, smilax, sugarbush, titi, toyon, widow's-cross, widow-wail, yew
fiber-yielding anilao, anilau
fleshy red-maids
flowering abutilon, azalea, camellia, forsythia, itea, japonica, lantana, laurel, lignonette, lilac, mistletoe, myrtle, oleander, oleaster, privet, quassia, raphiolepis,

rhodora, rose, spir(a)ea, syringa, tiara
fragrant huisache, jasmine, mejorana, mezereon, rosemary
fruit barberry, berberis, blackberry, boysenberry, currant, gooseberry, huckleberry, raspberry, salal, saskatoon
genus abutilon, acaena, alder, aralia, aronia, azalea, bixa, cassiope, erica, fothergilla, genista, inga, itea, ixora, jacobinia, keria, lantana, ledum, olea, rhus, sida, sumac
group boscage, bush
leguminous rhatany
-like bushy, fruticose, fruticulose
low ayapana
medicinal bocca, cubeb, sassafras, soma
narcotic coca, kafta, kat
oil-yielding croton, jojoba
oleaceous forsythia, nightjasmine, privet, pyxie
ornamental acanth(us), andromeda, azalea, camellia, golden-currant, hedge, honeysuckle, hydrangea, ibota, nandin(a), oleander, pearlbush, privet, raphiolepis, retinispora, skimmia, viburnum
parasitic mistletoe
pasture cowberry
pert. fruticose, fruticous
poisonous cube, gif(blaar), ivy, laburnum, lithi, oak, oleander, rhus, sumac(h)
prickly See *spiny*, below.
rosaceous cotoneaster, spirea
rubber guayle
rubiaceous gardenia
rutaceous jaborandi
silk-like fiber anabo, ceiba
spiny acacia, allthorn, aroma, bramble, briar, brier, broom, bumelia, caper, carissa, cat's-claw, colima, cytisus, espino, excambron, furze, genista, goatbush, gorse, granjeno, guajillo, haw(thorn), huajillo, huisache, jujube, junco, loasa, lotebush, rose, tragacanth, turkeybush, ulex, whin, wineberry
spreading toothwort
sticky tarbush
strong-smelling saltwort
stunted scrag, scrog, scrub

tanning sumac(h)
tea-like coca, kat
thorny See *spiny*, above.
tree-like arbuscle
tropical See TROPICAL *shrub*.
tufted cassiope
xerophytic saxaul
SHRUBBERY arboret, boscage, boskage, brake, brush, mogote, plantation, thicket
SHRUFF dregs, dross, rubbish
SHRUG contract, cower, fidget, handshake, hitch(ing), hurkle, jacket, kvetch(er), pull, quiver, recoil, shiver, shudder, sweater, tug
off disdain, dismiss, ignore, negate, slight, underestimate, underrate, veto
SHRUNKEN atrophied, clung, lank, pungled, shriveled, wizened
head tsantsa
SHTIK clowning, gimmick, misconduct, part, piece, prank, trick
SHTOOP, SHTUP press, push
SHTUNK mess, scandal, stink
SHTUSS commotion, contretemps, nonsense, rhubarb, stupidity
SHU *kin* geb, hathor, nut
wife tefnut
SHUAH *parent* abraham, heber, jael
SHUCK covering, discard, hull, husk, peel, pod, recoil, remove, shell, shock, shog, strip
SHUDDER agrise, creep, dither, dodder, frisson, groose, grue, hirtch, hotter, quake, quaver, quiver, shake, shiver, shrug, teeter, totter, tremble, tremor
SHUFFLE artifice, avoidance, change, confuse, dance, deal, derange, disorder, drag(gle), equivocate, equivocation, evade, evasion, huddle, introduce, jank, juggle, jumble, make, milk, mingle, mix, mos(e)y, plod, prevaricate, quibble, riffle, ruffle, ruse, s(c)hloomp, s(c)hlump, sclaff, scuff(le), shamble, shift, shirk, sluther, stir, trick, vacillate
board term block, clean the

board, cross pilot, hammer, hide block, kitchen, tampa pilot, triangle, weight

SHULER gossip, loiterer, stroller, vagabond, vagrant, wayfarer

SHUN attention, avoid, balk, cut, demur, disdain, dodge, elude, escape, eschew, evade, evite, forbear, forsake, hide, loathe, prevent, refrain, refuse, reject, run, scorn, scruple, shove, shrink, shy, steer clear, stick(le)

SHUNT bridge, bypass, conductor, deviate, divert, dodge, ferry, flinch, propel, propulsion, rechannel, remove, shift, shove, shrink, shy, sidetrack, swerve, swing, switch, transfer, turn, veer

SHURTLOFF, ROBERT deborah sampson gannett

SHUT adjust, bar, block (ade), bolt, cease, clear, close(d), confine, cut off, exclude, fasten(ed), fold, free, get rid of, latch, occluse, prohibit, restrain, rid (dance), seal, secure, shoot, slam, steek, stop, upclose, weld

down close, descend, discontinuance, end, layoff, obstruction, restrain, restrict, settle, silence, stop, suppress

-eye acidulous, nap, puckery, sleep

in bar, barricade, bedfast, bedridden, blockade, bottle(d), cage(d), close, confine(d), convalescent, cover, embar, embay, enclave, enclose(d), fence, forbar, hem(med), impound, imprison, intercept, invalid, occlude, patient, pen(t), quarantine, recluse, sick, wall

of clear, free, rid

off beleaguer, block(ade), exclude, hang up, obstruct, screen, seclude, separate, stop(per)

out ban, bar, blackball, blank, blink, block, coup, cut off, debar, defeat, disbar, eliminate, exclude, hinder, interdict, obstruct, obviate, occlude, overcome, preclude, prevent, prohibit,

rout, rule out, schneider, skunk(ed), smother, triumph, victory

together clasp, join

up cage, choke, close, conclude, confine, dam, dummy up, dungeon, enclose, end, gag, hush, immure, impound, imprison, incarcerate, mewed, obstruct, parrock, pen(ned), plug, quiet, recluse, restrict, seclude, shush, silence, still, stive, stop(up), stove, terminate, unite

SHUTHELAH *parent* ephraim

SHUTTER blind(s), buckler, close, cover, diaphragm, flight, gate, jalousie, lid, oscillator, screen, seclude, shade

SHUTTING evening, nightfall

SHUTTLE bar, drawer, flight, flute, inconstant, instrument, lithe, looper, nimble, oscillator, quick, shunt, slide, sliding, slippery, swivel, till, train, unsettled, vacillate, variable, wavering

wield tat, weave

-witted fickle, flighty, scatterbrained

SHUTTLECOCK alternate, bandy, bird(ie), duck, gadwall, peteca, variable, volant

SHVARTZ(ER) black, contraband, gloomy, illstarred, ominous, unfortunate, unhappy, unskilled

SHVITZER braggart, perspirer, plosher, sweater

SHY anerly, attempt, avoid, backward, balk, bashful, blench, boggle, buck, cagey, careful, cautious, chary, coy, daphnean, demur(e), diffident, distrustful, dodge, evasive, experiment, fling, frighten, gawkish, hesitant, hesitate, inadequate, jib, jump, lacking, mim, modest, mousy, needy, quail, quibble, recoil, reluctant, reserved, reticent, retreat, scant(y), scruple, secluded, self-conscious, shamefaced, shanny, sheepish, short, shrink(ing), shun(t), skeigh, skittish, sneer, squab, squeamish, start, stick(le), suspicious, tartle, throw, timid,

timorous, trembly, trial, try, unassuming, unobtrusive, unsocial, wary, waver, withdrawn, without

person shrinking violet, wallflower

SHYLOCK miser, moneylender, usurer

coin ducat

daughter jessica

debtor antonio

friend tubal

servant lancelot-gobbo

SHYNESS coyness, diffidence, modesty, reserve, timidity

SHYSTER ambulance-chaser, crook, pettifogger, rogue

SIALIA bluebird

SIAMANG gibbon

SIAM(ESE) See THAILAND.

cat blue-point

twins chang, eng

SIAN singan

SIB akin, allied, ayllu, brother, calpulli, clan, co-member, congenial, disposed, friendly, inclined, intimate, kin(dred), kinship, kinsman, offspring, related, relation, relative(s), sept, sister, tribe, twin, well-disposed

SIBBALDUS blue-whale, rorqual

SIBELIUS *valse* triste

SIBERIA See also RUSSIA, TARTAR.

animal sable, saiga

antelope saiga

city barnaul, bratsk, chita, igarka, iman, irkutsk, khabarovsk, krasnoyarsk, kurgan, kyzyl, leninsk, listvenichnoye, omsk, samarkand, tashkent, tomsk, uzbekistan, vladivostok, yakutsk

conqueror ermak

cowboy kazakh

dog husky, samoyed(e)

forest taiga, urman

fox corsac

hare flick, tolai

herb candlestick lily, globeflower, golden queen, trollius

hunters and fishers giliak, gilyak, samoyed(e)

hut barabara, barabora, isba, jurt

ibex tek

jumping disease miryachit

lake baikal

language enisei, finno-ugric, ostyak, yenisei

people beltir, chukchi, chuly-matatar, giliak, gilyak, kamas(s)in, kirghiz, koibal, koriak, koryak, orunchun, sagai, soyot, ta(r)tar, tungus, tunguz, yakoot, yakut, yuit, yukag(h)ir
plain steppe, tundra
plant badan, caragana
range alai, anadyr, kolyma
region birobizhan, taiga
river amur, ili, lena, maya, olenek, onon, sobol, tobol, tom
sea aral, kara, laptev, ok-hotsk, nordenskjold, ussuri
squill scilla
squirrel meniver, miniver
squirrel fur calabar, calaber
storm buran, purga
swamp urman
swampy forest taiga
tanning plant badan
tent yurt
tourmaline siberite
village uelen
wild cat manul
wind buran
wool argali

SIBILANCE, SIBILATION hissing, rale, siffle
mark cedilla, legon
SIBILANT hissing, lisping, rustling, wheezy, whispery
SIBILATE aspirate, buzz, fizz(le), hish, hiss, lisp, rustle, siss, sizz(le), spit, sputter, swish, wheeze, whish, whistle, whiz(z)
SIBLING brother, relative, sister
SIBYL fortuneteller, oracle, prophetess, seeress, sorceress, witch
cumaean amalth(a)ea
famous agrippine, babylonian, cimmerian, cumaean, delphian, delphic, egyptian, erythraean, hellespontine, libyan, persian, phrygian, pythian, samian, sardian, tiburtine, trojan
home cumae, delphi
prophecy acrostic
SIC attack, chase, incite, set, sool, such, thus, urge
SICARIAN assassin
SICCA coin, die, rupee, seal, stamp
SICCITY aridity, drought, dryness
SICHAEUS *brother-in-law* pygmalion
SICILY, SICILIAN magna

graecia, trinacria, triquetra, ziz
archer acestus
ash manna
boxer entellus
bull phalaris
cape boeo, faro, passaro
capital palermo
cathedral monreale
city aci, aetna, agrigento, alcamo, bidis, caltanissetta, catania, catanzaro, cefalu, enna, gela, girgenti, hybla, marsala, megana, messina, modica, naro, noto, palermo, ragusa, salaparuta, siracusa, syracuse, taormina, taranto, trapani
coin carlin(e), litra, oncetta, oncia, uncia
composer bellini
conqueror arabs, egyptians, germans, greeks, normans, romans, saracens, vikings
dwarf crachami
evergreen maquis
fountain, truth-revealing acadine
game cottabus
giant lestrigon
god adranus
goddess demeter
gulf catania, noto
gunman, immigrant greenie
ideal republic magna graecia
island egadi, lipari, pantelleria, ustica
king bomba, cocalus, eryx, leontes
lake camarina, pergusa
lord antigonus
measure caffiso, salma
monster pongo
nymph aetna
painter antonello da messina
peak erici, etna, hybla, ibrei, moro, nebrodi
people elymi, sicani, sicel(ior), siculi
philosopher euhemerus
poison aquatofana
port aci, catania, marsala, messina, milazzo, palermo, siracusa, syracuse, trapani
prince mamillius
province enna, catania, messina, palermo, ragusa, siracusa, sutara, trapani
resort enna, taormina
river acis, belice, mazzaro, platani, salso, simeto
rock scylla
saffron crocus
saint agatha

secret society la cosa nostra, maf(f)ia
shepherd daphnis
spa enna
sumac tanner
tyrant phalaris
volcano aetna, etna
whirlpool charybdis
wine corvo, marsala
writer lampadusa, pirandello
youth acis
SICK abed, aeger, afflicted, ailing, all-overish, anemic, apoplectic, bad(ly), bedfast, bedridden, chase, confined, consumptive, corrupted, cothish, cothy, crapulous, cronk, crook, dauncy, depressed, diseased, disgusted, down, dyspeptic, exasperated, faint(ish), fed up, feverish, flattened, ill, incite, indisposed, inform, insane, instigate, invalid(ed), jaded, laid up, languent, mawkish, morbid, mortified, nauseated, nauseous, neurotic, off(color), out of sorts, pale, poorly, prostrate, queasy, rheumatic, rocky, seedy, seek, shut in, sike, stale, such, suffering, surfeited, tired, under the weather, unfit, unhealthy, unproductive, unsound, unwell, urge, wan, weak(ened), weary
as a cat, dog, toad
at heart desolate, sorrowful
bay clinic, dispensary, hospital, infirmary
deathly alamort, amort
headache megrim, migraine
on agitate, incite, sool
person aegrotant, invalid, patient, valetudinaire, valetudinarian
SICKEN affect, afflict, appall, break out, contract, decay, disease, disgust, erupt, fade, fail, fever, impair, incur, languish, nauseate, repel, revolt, surfeit, take ill, tire, turn, upset, weaken, weary
SICKENING disgusting, fulsome, nasty, nauseating, nauseous, offensive, revolting
SI(C)KER assure(d), cautious, certain, confident, dependable, effective, established, fast, firm, fixed, pledge, prudent, safe, secure, stable, sure, trustworthy

SICKLE crook, feather, hook, scythe, sive, spur, tool
grass tearthumb
herb selfheal
-shaped curved, drepanoid, falcate, falciform, hooked
SICKLEBILL bird of paradise, curlew, hummingbird, saberbill, thrasher
SICKLEMAN reaper
SICKLEWORT self-heal, vetch
SICKLY ailing, ampery, bilious, capple(faced), clammy, cothish, cothy, cranky, dauncy, dawny, delicate, diseased, disgusting, doncy, faint, feeble, flue, frail, green, ill, inform, insipid, invalid, languid, maladive, mawkish, pale, peakish, pimping, pindling, puny, queechy, shilpit, unhealthy, wan, wankly, weak(ly)
SICKNESS (See also DISEASE.) affliction, ailment, brash, disease, disgust, distemper, ill health, illness, indisposition, infirmity, mal(ady), nausea, qualmishness, weariness
excuse aeger, aegrotat
feign malinger
motion kinetosis
SICYON *king* epopeus
SIDDHARTHA See BUDDHA.
SIDE agree, ample, arrogance, aspect, bank, beam, behalf, border, cheek, chunk, collateral, conceit, crew, declivity, distant, district, edge, face(t), faction, far, flank(ing), flitch, half, hand, haunch, hypotenuse, incidental, indirect, jamb, join, lateral, latus, lee (ward), margin, match, oblique, occasional, page, part(y), phase, piece, place, pleuron, proud, quarter, rival, sect, severe, shore, sithe, skirting, slope, space, stoss, support, surface, team, verge, width
back behind, rear
bar hound
by side abreast, accole, alongside, beside, cheek by jowl, collaterally, juxtaposed, paradromic, parallel, shoulder to shoulder, tete-a-tete, together

comb. pleura, pleuro
dish entree, entremets
husband orion
issue adjunct, byproduct, offshoot, outgrowth
-kick assistant, associate, buddy, chum, companion, comrade, confederate, follower, friend, mate, pal, pard, partner, satellite
left sinister, verso
-line avocation, byroad, hobby
on the apart
on the same homolateral
pert. costal, lateral
post jamb
right face, front, recto
road bywalk, byway, detour
show attraction freak
show manager grifter
-step avoid, bypass, dodge, duck, evade, parry, quibble, retreat, sidle, slip
to one agee
toward the lateral
with agree, associate, back, encourage, join, subscribe to, support
SIDEARM bayonet, gun, pistol, revolver, sword, weapon
SIDEBOARD buffet, bureau, cellaret, credence, credenza, cupboard, dressoir, server, table
SIDEBURNS burnsides, muttonchops
SIDELONG askance, askew, beside, indirect(ly), lateral(ly), oblique(ly), slanting, sloping, subtle
SIDEPIECE bar, bibb, border, bow, cant, gusset, jamb, landside, rib, wing
SIDEREAL astral, celestial, starlike, starry, stellar
SIDERITE chalybite, horneblend, ironwort, loadstone, meteorite, sparry-iron, spathic-iron
SIDERO *husband* salmoneus
stepdaughter tyro
SIDESADDLE *flower* pitcherplant
stirrup footstall
SIDESLIP digression, drift, drill, skid, slide
SIDESPLITTING funny, hilarious, uproarious
SIDESWIPE carom, collide, glance
SIDETRACK avert, detour,

distract, divert, shunt, spur, switch
SIDEWALK banquette, boardwalk, causey, footpath, path, pavement, trottoir
drawing screeve
edge curb
moving travolator
part crack, curb, kerb, paving
SIDEWARDS See SIDEWAYS.
SIDEWAY bypath, byway, path, postern, sidewalk
SIDEWAYS aside(n), askance, askant, askew, aslant, athwart, crossways, indirect(ly), lateral(ly), obliquely, roundabout, sidewise, sly(ly)
SIDEWHEELER horse, lefthander, southpaw, steamer
SIDEWINDER blow, crotalus, massasauga, rattlesnake, reptile, snake
SIDI *wife* amine
SIDING boards, clapboard, curb, lie-by, sheathing, spur, track
SIDLE cant, crabwalk, deviate, edge, loiter, saunter, skew, skid, skirt, slip, slive, veer
SIDNEY, PHILIP *lady dorothy* sacharissa
work astrophel and stella, shepheardes calendar
SIDON saida
king ethbaal
SIE drip, drop, sift, strain
SIECLE age, century, hundred
SIEGE ableaguer, attack, bench, beset, besiege, blockade, bout, camp, encampment, encirclement, flock, grade, journey, place, rank, seat, situation, station, surround, throne
engine warwolf
pert. obsidional, poliorcetic
-tower mategriffon
SIEGFRIED sigurd
ancestor odin, rerir, sigi
birthplace xanton
cloak of invisibility tarnkappe
daughter swanhild
earth goddess erda
enemy gunther
epic nibelungenlied
followers nib(e)lungs
foster father rebin(n)
grandfather volsung
helper mime

horse grane, grani
parent hiordis, hjordis, sieglinde, sigmund
reared by fafnir, mimir
slayer hagen, hogni
sword balmung, balnunc, gram
tutor regin(n)
victim alberich, fafnir
wife brunhild(e), brynhild, chriemhild(a), gudrun, gutrune, kriemhild
SIEGLINDE *brother* siegmund
father wotan
husband hunding
son siegfried
SIEGMUND See SIGMUND.
SIENA *bell* campanone
district contrada
district symbols dragon, eagle, forest, giraffe, goose, ram, snail, tower, unicorn, wave
marble brocatel(le)
race palio
race site piazza del campo
saint catherine
SIER pintado, sawfish
SIERRA cavalla, cero, fish, kingfish, range, ridge, sawback
SIERRA LEONE *capital* freetown
city henema, kissi
coin leone
language krio, mendi, temne
measure kettle, load
native fulani, gallina, kissi, kono, kuranko, limba, loko, mandingo, mendi, sherbro, susu, temne, vai
peak loma
port bonthe, hepel, sulima
region gold coast, grain coast, ivory coast
river jong, moa, rokkel, scarcy, sewa
secret society poro
SIERRA NEVADA *fog* pogonip
gold deposit blue-lead
peak dana, whitney
SIESTA break, doze, lull, meridian, midday, nap, rest, sleep, snooze
SIEVE basket, bolt(er), boulter, clean, colander, dilluer, drum, gossip, grate, grizzly, laun, prickle, puree, range, refine, rid(der), riddle, screen, scry, searce(r), search, semmet, sift(er), sile, strainer, tamis, tammy,

tattler, tems(e), tiffany, trommel, winnow
-like cribrate, cribriform, ethmoid, porous
SIF *hair-cutter* liki
husband thor
son ull(r)
SIFAKA lemur, propithecus
SIFFLE blow, rale, sibilation, whistle
SIFT analyse, analyze, bolt, bunt, canvass, clean, cribrate, discriminate, discuss, dissect, divide, dredge, dust, examine, inquire, inspect, lue, part, percribrate, probe, ree, refine, resolve, ridder, riddle, scalp, scatter, screen, scrutinize, scry, searce, search, seek, select, separate, sieve, sort, strain, tems(e), test, try, winnow
flour bolt, dress
in infilter
SIFTER bolter, caster, dredger, sieve
SIGH bemoan, bewail, breath, brood, complain, deplore, grieve, groan, heigh-ho, kvetch(er), lament, languish, long, moan, mourn, pech, pine, sife, singult, sithe, snivel, sob, souf, sough, suspiration, suspire, suther, thirst, twank, wheeze, yearn
SIGHT aim, appearance, aspect, bead, behold, catch, chance, descry, discern, display, espy, exhibition, eye, eyeshot, eyesore, finder, fright, gaze, glance, glimpse, guide, inspect(ion), judgment, ken, look(ing), marvel, mirage, opinion, outlook, peek, peep, perception, prospect, quantity, ray, scene, scope, see(ing), sense, show, spectacle, spy, stretch, sum, view, vision, visor, vista, vizzy, witness
and hearing, pert. audiovisual
come into loom
compass vane
defect ano(o)psia, anopia, myopia, paropsis
dimness caliginosity, caligo
gun bead, hausse, peep, scope, visie, vizzy
having keen hawkeyed
imaginary mirage, vision
line of ray

loss amaurosis, blindness
offending eyesore
pert. ocular, visual
prevent blindfold, seel
put out of conceal, hide
second esp, fey, psychic
strange ferlie, ferly
weakness amblyopia
SIGHTING landfall
SIGHTLESS blind, eyeless, invisible, purblind, unseen, unsightly
SIGHTLY beautiful, comely, conspicuous, eyeable, fair, ravishing, stunning
SIGHTS *hater of* misoscopist
SIGHTSEER rubberneck, spectator, tourist, traveler, viewer
SIGHTY farsighted, grand, splendid, visible
SIGIL charm, image, seal, sign(ature), signet
SIGMOID crescent-shaped, curve(d), ess, winding
SIGMUND *grandfather* rerir
opponent hunding
parent liod, volsung, woden, wotan
sister sieglinde, signy
son siegfried, sigurd, sinfiotli
sword gram
wife borghild, hiordis, hjordis, sieglinde
SIGN 4 ayah, bill, clew, clue, eyah, hire, join, mark, note, omen, plus, rune, seal, sein, type 5 badge, charm, cross, forge, index, minus, presa, segno, spoor, stamp, token, trace, track, write 6 attest, augury, banner, caract, cipher, device, effect, effigy, emblem, engage, figure, murmur, notice, paraph, poster, ratify, SIGNAL, signet, symbol, tittle, witter 7 betoken, earmark, endorse, execute, gesture, indorse, initial, meaning, placard, portent, presage, prodigy, shingle, signify, symptom, vestige, witness 8 ceremony, evidence, indicant, inscribe, pretense, telltale 9 autograph, billboard, character, indicator, prognosis, semblance, signature, subscribe, symbolize 10 indication, underwrite 13 constellation, manifestation
again reup
astrological See ZODIAC sign.

away transfer
comb. symbolo
diacritical See MARK *printing.*
direction arrow, fingerpost, guidepost
division obelus
illuminated neon
in this in hoc signo
language dactylology
liturgical selah, shelah
magic rune, sigil
mathematical equal, minus, obelus, plus
musical fermata, forte, segno, swell
off end, out, thirty, withdraw
on or *up* employ, engage, enlist, enroll, enter, hire, inscribe, join, record, register, ship, subscribe
outward evidence, manifestation
over deed, transfer
pert. semantic, semic
seal and deliver bag, button up, capture, execute, nail down, obtain, settle, sew up
up See *on*, above.
zodiac See ZODIAC *sign*.
SIGNAL (See also *device*, below.) alar(u)m, alert, arresting, balefire, beacon, beam, beckon, beep(er), bell, blinker, blip, buzz(er), call, chamade, conspicuous, cue, curfew, distinctive, emblem, eminent, ensign, famous, flag, flash, foghorn, fusee, gesture, glance, glare, greenlight, heliogram, herald, hooter, important, indicate, indication, lantern, leer, marker, memorable, motion, nod, notable, nudge, outstanding, password, pharos, pip, prominent, pronounced, pst, rattle, remarkable, salient, salute, sematrope, SIGN, siren, smoke, sos, speak, striking, symbol, tap, tocsin, token, toll, toot, warning, watchword, wave, whiff, whistle, wigway, wink
device aldislamp, annunciator, buoy, cricket, flare, helio(graph), horn, klaxon, redlight, rocket, semaphore, sematrope, stoplight, teleseme, traffic light
distress flare, fusee, mayday, sos
electric teleseme

fire balefire
flag ensign, wigwag
flare fusee, very light
give false meacon
military flare, turnout
night curfew
radio beam
railroad banjo, fusee, fuzee, highball, target
red vermilion
spirit rap, tap
system code
tower atalaya, bantayan
warning alar(u)m, alert, beacon, blinker, buoy, cue, flare, klaxon, pharos, siren, sos, stop, tocsin
with initials paraph
SIGNALIZE announce, celebrate, display, distinguish, honor, mark, point out
SIGNATURE autograph, birthmark, cipher, countermark, countersign, cross, frank, hand(writing), inscription, john hancock, key, mark, monogram, name, seal, sigil, sign(et), subscription, theme, tughra, visa, vise
flourish paraph
SIGNBOARD shingle
SIGNET authenticate, mark, seal, sigil, signal, signature, stamp
SIGNIFICANCE bearing, body, consequence, content, eloquence, force, gravity, implication, import(ance), influence, meaning, meatiness, merit, moment, purport, sense, strength, stress, suggestiveness, value, virtue, weight, worth
without empty, inane, jejune, stupid
SIGNIFICANT cogent, conclusive, convincing, eloquent, expressive, forcible, important, indicative, meaningful, meaty, momentous, pithy, pointed, portentous, powerful, pregnant, real, serious, sound, striking, substantial, suggestive, symbolic, telling, trenchant, valid, weighty
SIGNIFY allude, announce, argue, augur, betoken, bode, communicate, compare, connote, convey, declare, denote, designate, disclose, evidence, evince, express, foreshow, imply, im-

port, indicate, inform, insinuate, intimate, manifest, matter, mean, portend, say, show, signal, suggest, tell, utter
SIGNORA dame, frau, lady, madam, mistress, mrs, senora, woman
SIGNOR(E) don, gentleman, herr, lord, man, mister, noble, senor, sir
SIGNORINA girl, maiden, miss, senorita
SIGNPOST guide, pointer, waypost
SIGNY *brother* sigmund
consort siggeir, sigmund
offspring sinfiotli
parent hliod, liod, ljod, volsung
victim siggeir
SIGURD *fiance* brynhild
horse grani
parent hiordis, sigmund
reared by reginn
story volsunga saga
victim fafnir, hogni
wife gudrun
SIGYN *consort* loki
daughter hel
SIKE brook, ditch, drain, gully, ravine, rill, sick, sigh, stream, such, trench
SIKER See SICKER.
SIKES *victim* nancy, oliver twist
SIKH (See also INDIA.) akali, mazhabi, singh, udasi
ascetic nirmalin
deity akal
founder nanak
scripture adigranth, granth, grunth
sect akali
temple gurdwara
weapon chakra
writing gurmukhi, panjabi
SIKHARA tower
finial amalaka
SIKKIM (See also INDIA.) denjong
capital gangtok
people bhotia, lepcha, rong
river tista
SIKSIKA *indian* blackfoot
SILAGE ensile, feed, fodder
container silo
SILE beam, betray, cheat, cover, deceive, drip, drop, fall, filter, fish, flow, fry, glide, herring, move, mud, pass, pour, rafter, sieve, sink, skim, soil, spawn, strain(er), stream, subside

SILENCE anarthria, aphasia, aphonia, aphony, calk, calm, caulk, choke, chut, confute, disable, dry up, dumbfound, eliminate, gag, hush, kibosh, kill, lull, muffle, mum, muteness, muzzle, noiselessness, oblivion, obscurity, omerta, oyer, oyez, shush, shut up, soft-pedal, squash, squelch, stifle, still(ness), stun, suppress, tace(t), tush, tut
deity angerona, harpocrates, vidar
man of napoleon iii
martyr of st john nepomuk
SILENCER gavel, muffler, mute, sourdine
SILENE ben, campion, caryophyllus, catchfly, lychnis, pink, plant
SILENT aphonic, calm, closemouthed, conticent, cool, dumb, flat, flavorless, glum, hushed, inarticulate, laconic, mum, mute, noiseless, obmutescent, placid, quiet, reserved, reticent, saturnine, secretive, serene, soundless, speechless, sphinxian, still(y), sullen, tace, tacit(urn), tightlipped, tiptoe, tonguetied, uncommunicative, unrecorded, unresponsive, unspoken, unuttered, unvoiced, voiceless, wordless
person asphasiac, asphonic, clam, mute, laloplegic, sphinx
SILENUS satyr
companion dionysus
invention flute
parent gaea, hermes, pan
victim enceladus
SILEX flint, quartz, silica, urn
SILHOUETTE isotype, likeness, outline, portrait, profile, shade, shadow
SILICA cerite, dioxide, flint, mica, opal, quartz, sand, silex, talc, tridymite, tripoli
rock acidite
SILICATE acmite, aenigmatite, allanite, aloisiite, alvite, amphibole, andalusite, aphrosiderite, augite, autitite, babingtonite, barylite, bazzite, beckelite, bementite, calamine, catapleiite, catoptrite, celadonite, cenosite, cerite, epidote, erion-

ite, euclase, gageite, gehlenite, gnenthite, greenalite, grothine, gyrolite, ilvaite, iolite, johnstrupite, katoptrite, lotrite, mica, mosandrite, opal, phenacite, plancheite, pyroxene, severite, wellsite, woehlerite, zeolite
aluminum andalusite, barylite, pollucite, prehnite
blue bazzite
chlorite moravite
ferric morencite
green epidote, euclase
hydrous cerite, mica, opal, zeolite
magnesium montecellite
SILICON carbide carborundum, silundum
derivative monox
SILIQUA 1/100th contenionalis
24 solidus
2 miliarensis
SILK (See also FABRIC silk.) blossom, cloth, counsel, fabric, gown, soie, thread
brocade baldachin(o), baldaquin, baudekin
brown muga
cocoon bave
comb. seric(i)
corded crin, faille, paduasoy
-cotton tree adansonia, bentang, bombace, bulak, cabbagewood, ceiba, munguba, pochote, semul, simal, yaxche
-cotton tree fiber kapok, kumbi
cover with sericate
crepe georgette
dull gros
embroidery floss
fabric See FABRIC silk.
fiber floss
figured culgee
filament bave, brin, shikii, tram
fine crin, shela, tulle
fineness measure denier
fishline gimp
floss sleave
gauze cypress, cyprus, lisse
gelatin sericin
gland serictery
glossy lute-string, satin, taffeta
gold cloth acca
grass istle, karatas, stipa
gum sericin
handkerchief barcelona
hank hasp

hat beaver, castor, catskin, tile, top hat, topper
heavy armozine, camaca, crin, gros
imitation rayon, satinet
imperfection corkscrew
leavings See waste, below.
light crepe de chine
lining sarcenet, sarsnet
maker seric
measure drammage
medieval sendal
mesh tulle
moth atlas, bombyx, eria, muga, tussah
nodule slub
oak grevillea, lacewood
package moche
pert. seric
plant ramie
purple blatta
quilted matelasse
raw gre(i)ge, marabou(t), sleave, taysaam, tsatlee
raw thread poil
reel filature
ribbed epingle
rustle scroop
satin-backed crepe-meteor
satin finish foulard
shreds noil
soft floss
source cocoon, moth, worm
spider nephila, spinder
-stocking aristocratic, elegant, elite, exclusive, federalist, luxurious, noble, wealthy, whig
stuff tarse
synthetic dacron, nylon, orlon, qiana, rayon
-tail waxwing
tester denierer, scrimeter, serigraph, serimeter
thin alamode, crepe de chine, ninon, tulle
thread bave, brin, douppioni, filoselle, floss, poil, tram
tied and dyed batik
tree albizzia, ceiba, siris
twilled alma, foulard, lousine, surah, tobine
undyed corah
unraveled sleave
upholstery tabaret
viole ninon
waste bur(r), cappadine, floss, frison, knub, noil, schappe, strass
watered moire, tabby
-weed milkweed
wild tussah, tusser, tussor(e), tussur

wood tree calabur, muntingia

work eri

worker throw(st)er

yarn bourette, shap(pe), tram

yarn size denier

SILKEN, SILKY byssine, delicate, fine, gentle, glabrous, glossy, ingratiating, insinuating, lustrous, luxurious, plush, quiet, satiny, seric(eous), sill, sleek, slick, smooth, soft, suave, velvety

cornel redbrush

tamarin marikina

SILKWORM ailanthus, bombycid, bombyx, caterpillar, cecropia, eri(a), muga, promethea, samia, sina, spinner, tussah, tusser, tussore, tussur, univoltine, yamamai

breeder magnanerie

disease calcino, flachery, gattine, grasserie, prebrine, uji

eggs graine

epidemic gattine

leaves alba

organ filator

pert. ailantine, bombic

SILL base, basis, beam, bedplate, bench, edge, foundation, frame, herring, ledge, limen, plate, saddle, seat, shaft, shelf, sile, sole, stone, thill, threshold, timber

SILLA korea

SILLINESS betise, bosh, folly

SILLY absurd, addlebrained, addlepated, anile, anserine, apish, asinine, balmy, barmy, batty, bete, brainless, buggy, bughouse, bugs, childish, confused, cranky, cuckoo, daft, dazed, decipient, dense, dizzy, dotard, dull, dumb, empty, fatuous, feeble, fiddlecome, flighty, foolish, footle, frail, frivolous, funny, goofy, harebrained, halfwitted, helpless, idiotic, idle, ignorant, illogical, imbecile, imprudent, inane, insipid, laughable, ludicrous, mad, nonsensical, paltry, pitiful, pointless, poor, preposterous, puerile, ridiculous, rustic, sawney, senseless, shallow, shanny, sickly, simple(minded), stupid,

thoughtless, tid, trivial, vacuous, weak, witless

billy william iv

SILLYHOW caul

SILT alluvion, alluvium, blue-mud, bull-dust, deposit, diluvium, dirt, dregs, drift, lees, marl, mire, moraine, mud, percolate, remainder, residue, scum, sediment, sleech, sullage, wash

layer varve

up choke, fill, obstruct, shoal

SILUR(O)ID catfish, sheatfish

SILVAN See SYLVAN.

SILVANUS aegipan, faunus, inuus, pan

beloved pomona

SILVENDY dependable, safe

SILVER albata, argent(eous), argentine, argentum, bright, bullion, change, coin(age), coins, costly, eloquent, gentle, luna(r), lustrous, metal, mintage, money, moon, pale, peaceful, pina, plata, plate, precious, resplendent, service, siller, sterling, sweet, sycee, tableware, white

alchemist's diana, luna, moon

alloy albata, asem, billon, pina, platina

and gold ornament orris

antimonide animikite

antiseptic argentamide, argentamine

-back knot(bird)

-bar fish dorab

-bearing argentiferous

bell bellwood, cowlicks, halesia

-bill weaverbird

black stephanite

boom town ouray

bromide bromargyrite, bromyrite

-bush jupiter's-beard, virgin's-bower

carp quillback

citrate itrol

coating argentation

comb. argent(i)(o), argentoic, argentous, argyr(o)

compound acanthite, aguilarite, amalgam, andorite, animikite, aramayoite, argentamine, argentide, argentimide, argyrite, argyrose, bromyrite, canfield-

ite, cerargyrite, embolite, pina, tachiol

cone pina

containing lunar

debased vellon

deposit comstock lode

dollar cartwheel

fir abies, cascade

fox fur platina

gibbon camper, monkey, wou-wou

gilded vermeil

glance argentite

-head chickweed

horn ceragyrite

ingot See ore, below.

instrument argentometer

jenny mojarra

king tarpon

lace filigree, fleeceflower

lactate albata

leaf acacia, boree, hardhack, honesty, hydrangea, jewelweed, myall, poplar, queenroot, wattletree

-like alloy occamy

linden basswood

lunge namaycush

maple globulin acerin

oak flannelbush

official stamp hallmark

ore argentite, bullion, paco, polybasite, stephanite, sycee

perch calico-bass, crappie, grunt, jackassfish, mademoiselle

pert. argental, argenteous, argentic, argentiferous, argentine, argyric, lunar

planet moon

plate sheffield

plover knot

polish almagra

purchase law bland-allison act

-queen gold-dust

rag butterfly

reducing kettle cazo

state colorado, nevada

streak english channel

thaw glaze, ice, rime

thistle acanthus

thread cannetille

-tongue songsparrow

-tongued eloquent, melodious, persuasive

tree black stavewood, ironwood

tree fern pitau

vine catvine

weight mark

worker plater, smith

SILVERFISH cutlassfish,

fishtail, hake, lepisma, savanilla, shiner, slicker, tarpon, woodfish
SILVERIZE plate
SILVERROD asphodel
SILVERSIDES atherine,
brit(t), friar, grunion, iao,
minnow, peixerey, pejerrey,
salmon, skipjack, smelt, tailor, tink(er)
SILVERSMITH bateman, revere, sonar, storr
SILVERTIP grizzly bear
SILVERWARE dishes, flatware, platters, tableware,
vases
ornament gadroon
SILVERWEED argentina,
jewelweed, moss-corn, rue,
tansy
SILVERWING cinder
SILVERY (See also SILVER
pert.) clear, frosted, gray,
lustrous, shining, white
comb. glauco
orach saltweed
SILVESTER rustic
SILVIA *agent* eglamour
beloved valentine
helper eglamore, eglamour
pursuer proteus
SILVIUS *kin* aeneas, ascanius
SILYBUM mariana, thistle
SIMAR chemise, chimer,
cloak, cymar, garment,
robe, soutane, zimarra
SIMBA lion
SIMBALL doughnut
SIMCHA, SIMCHE celebration, pleasure
SIMENON *inspector* maigret
SIMEON *parent* jacob, leah
son jachin, jamin, jarib, jemuel, nemuel, ohad,
s(h)aul, zerah, zohar
SIMIAN See APE, MON-
KEY.
SIMILAR akin, alike, allied,
analogous, approximate,
cognate, companion, com-
parable, congruent, correspondent, equal, equivalent,
even, homogeneous, homo-
taxic, kindred, like, matching, near, of a kind, of a
piece, parallel, quasi, reciprocal, resembling, same,
seemable, sib, such, uni-
form
comb. hom(e)o, homoeo,
homoio
SIMILARITY accordance,
affinity, agreement, analogy,

community, comparison,
conformity, congeneracy,
congruence, correspondence,
harmony, homoiousia, hom-
ology, homotaxy, kinship,
likeness, match, parallel,
reciprocity, resemblance,
sameness, semblance, similitude, unity
SIMILARLY as if, equally,
in like manner, just as, likewise, quasi, siclike, thus(ly)
SIMILE analogy, comparison,
image, metaphor, parabole,
suivez, trope
SIMILITUDE affinity, allegory, analog(ue), analogy,
apograph, assimilation,
comparison, copy, counterpart, ectype, facsimile,
form, image, likelihood,
likeness, parable, pasticcio,
semblance, SIMILARITY,
simulacrum, symbol
SIMILIZE compare, copy,
counterfeit, imitate, liken
SIMLIN See SIMNEL.
SIMMER anger, boil, braise,
brood, bubble, cook, cree,
effervesce, ferment, seethe,
sile, simper, siver, sotter,
stew, tottle
down condense, cool (it)
(off), reduce
SIMMERING angry, boiling,
burning, fiery, furious, hot,
torrid, warm
SIMMON cement, persimmon, rope, sediment
SIMMONS, RUTH bridey
murphy
SIMNEL biscuit, bread, cake,
cracknel, cymling, fruit-
cake, simlin, squash
SIMOLEON dollar, money
SIMON apostle, cephas,
peter, zelotes
brother andrew, jesus, lysimachus, menelaus
burial place rome
pure authentic, genuine,
plain, real, true, unqualified
son john, judas, mattathias
symbol fish, saw
SIMON, NEIL *play* chapter
two, little me, odd couple,
plaza suite, promises promises, sweeney todd, sweet
charity, what's what
SIMONIDES *daughter* thaisa
SIMONY barratry
SIMOON sandstorm, tebbad,
wind
SIMOUS concave, snub

SIMP See FOOL.
SIMPAI langur, monkey
SIMPER bridle, glimmer,
grin, mince, pose, simmer,
smile, smirk, twinkle,
whimper
SIMPLE 4 bald, bare, drug,
dull, dumb, easy, mere,
open, pure, rude, true 5
basic, blank, clear, crass,
dense, green, light, lucid,
naive, plain, quiet, sheer,
silly, stark, thick 6 candid,
chaste, facile, feeble, homely, honest, humble, rus-
tic, severe, single, smooth,
stupid 7 artless, ascetic, asinine, austere, evident, fatuous, foolish, natural, obvious, sincere, spartan, subdued, unmixed 8 absolute,
arcadian, childish, distinct,
explicit, gullible, homelike,
homemade, homespun, ig-
norant, informal, innocent,
manifest, medicine, ordi-
nary, sackless, singular,
trifling 9 childlike, elemental, guileless, ingenuous,
primitive, unadorned, unalloyed 10 effortless, elementary, restrained, unaffected,
unassuming, uncombined
11 unimportant, unob-
trusive 15 straightforward,
unsophisticated
comb. apl(o), hapl(o)
master slender
-minded dumb, foolish, innocent, oligophrenic, seely,
silly, stupid, unsophis-
ticated, unsuspecting
simon clown, dupe, fool,
goose
simon's wish pies
SIMPLETON abderite,
ament, ass, auf, awf, ba-
daud, block, boob(y), cake,
cokes, coot, cow, cretin,
dawcock, dawkin, defective,
dimwit, dolt, dunce, dupe,
fool, gaby, galah, gander,
gaup, gawk, gawney, gawp,
geede, gomeral, gomeril,
goose, gowk, gubbins, gull,
gulpin, gump, halfwit, idiot,
imbecile, innocent, jean-
jean, juggins, lackbrain,
lout, mafflin, mooncalf,
moron, muggins, natural,
nincompoop, nincum, ninny
(hammer), nitwit, noodle,
numskull, oaf, putz, saw-

ney, schlemiel, shlemie(h)l, sillyton, simkin, simp, thickhead, thickwit, tony, widgeon, yokel, yold, zombi

SIMPLICISSIMUS *author* grimmelshausen

SIMPLICITY austerity, chasteness, clearness, elegance, folly, gullibility, humbleness, ignorance, innocence, modesty, naivete, plainness, purity, restraint, rusticity, severity, silliness

SIMPLIFY chasten, clarify, disentangle, disinvolve, ease, elucidate, expound, facilitate, interpret, restrain

SIMPLY absolutely, alone, barely, crudely, easily, entirely, exclusively, foolishly, merely, only, plainly, poorly, purely, quietly, really, solely, stupidly, truly, weakly, wholly

SIMULACRUM cheat, counterfeit, effigy, fake, fraud, humbug, icon, image, imposture, likeness, mask, phantom, photograph, portrait, semblance, sham, similitude, statue, travesty, unreality

SIMULATE act, adopt, affect, ape, approximate, assume, copy, counterfeit, disguise, dissemble, feign (ed), imitate, invent, mask, mimic, mock, pretend(ed), sham

SIMULATED artificial, ersatz, fake(d), fictitious, imitation, mock, pseudo, spurious

SIMULATION act(ing), analogue, appropriation, cant, feint, hypocrisy, makebelieve, pharisaism, pretense, pretension, representation, sanctimony, sham

SIMULTANEOUS coetaneous, coeval, coexistent, coincident(al), coinciding, concomitant, concurrent, conjoint, contemporary, synchronal, synchronous

SIMULTANEOUSLY all together, as one, concurrently, in chorus, in concert, in unison, together

SIMURG(H) roc

SIN acedia, adultery, anger, backslide, blame, covetousness, crime, debt, delinquency, dereliction, degen-

erate, deviate, deviation, envy, enzu, err(or), evil, failing, fall, fault, felony, folly, frailty, gluttony, guilt, hamartia, heresy, idolotry, immorality, iniquity, lapse, lust, misconduct, misdeed, misdemeanor, misprision, murder, nanna(r), nonfeasance, offense, omission, outrage, peccadillo, peccancy, piacle, pride, slip, sloth, transgress(ion), trespass, trip, ungodliness, vice, viciousness, violate, violation, wathe, wickedness, wrong(doing)

assistant zaqar

canonical adultery, heresy, idolatry, murder

city babylon, gomorrah, new york, sodom

consort ningal

offspring adad, ishtar, nusku, shamash

original (old) adam

personification loki

prone to peccable, wayward

7 deadly accidie, acedia, anger, apathy, avarice, covetousness, envy, gluttony, indifference, laziness, lust, pride, sloth, torpor, wrath

symbol dragon, leopard, luminous crescent

title lord of the diadem

without holy, impeccable, innocent, perfect, pure, righteous, uncorrupt(ed)

SINAI horeb

city marib

pass giddi, mitla

SINAPIS charlock, mustard

SINBAD *bird* roc

SINCE after(ward), ago, already, as long as, because, being, considering, continuously, ergo, for, fro, gone, hence, inasmuch, insofar, later, now, past, sith(ins), subsequently, syne, thereupon, when, whereas, yet

SINCERE aboveboard, afald, artless, authentic, bonafide, candid, cordial, correct, earnest, faithful, forthright, frank, genuine, guileless, heartfelt, hearty, honest, honorable, ingenuous, intense, intent, open, outspoken, plain, pure, real, simple, straightforward, true, truthful, unaffected, un-

feigned, upright, veracious, warm, wholehearted, wholesouled, zealous

SINCERITY bonne foi, cando(u)r, faith, genuineness, heart(iness), honesty, integrity, probity, reality, veracity

symbol amethyst, sardonyx

SINCLAIR, UPTON *work* little steel, manassas, sylvia, the flivver king, the jungle, the metropolis, the moneychangers

SIND drench, drink, quench, rinse, rinsing, wash

SINDLE rare, seldom, singular

SINDON cloth, corporal, fabric, indus, linen, tippet, windingsheet

SINE gulf, ratio, sinew, without

prole unproductive, without issue

qua non condition, essential, indispensable, necessity, nonpareil

SINECURE benefice, cinch, easymark, gravy(train), pipe, snap

SINEW fiber, ligament, muscle, nerve, power, snare, strength, string, tendon, thew

SINEWY athletic, brawny, burly, energetic, fibrous, firm, healthy, husky, mighty, muscular, nervous, robust, ropy, sound, stout, stringy, strong, sturdy, tenacious, tendinous, thewy, tough, vigorous, wiry

SINFIOTLI *parent* sigmund, signy

poisoner borghild

SINFUL babylonian, bad, black, criminal, evil, immoral, piacular, ungodly, unregenerate, unrighteous, vicious, vile, wrong

SING announce, betray, blab, cant, carol, carp, celebrate, chant, chirl, chirm, chirp, chirrup, choir, chortle, chorus, confess, croon, descant, ditty, dring, exult, hum, hymn, intonate, intone, jodel, laud, lilt, pipe, praise, proclaim, rejoice, ring, roulade, serenade, solmizate, sough, sowf, tremolo, trill, troll, tweedle, twitter, vocalize, warble, whistle, yodel, yodle

loudly belt, troll(ol)

monotonously dring

out call, gale, peach

praises extol(l), laud

repeatedly decantate

the blues complain, despond, whine

SINGAN sian

SINGAPORE *airport* paya, lebar

flower plumeria

leader lee kwan-yew

river seletar, sungei

strait johore, sembilan

SINGE burn, heat, scorch, sear, sere, stain, sweal

fiber genapp

SINGER alme(h), alto, artist(e), balladeer, bard, baritone, barytone, bass(o), bayadere, buffa, busker, canary, cantabank, cantador, cantatrice, cantor, caroler, chanter, chanteur, chanteuse, chorine, chorister, crooner, descanter, diva, falsetto, griddler, hummer, lark, melodist, minnesinger, minstrel, monodist, poet, prima donna, scald, serenader, soloist, songbird, songster, soprano, tenor, thamyris, troubador, trouvere, vocalist, vocalizer, warbler

comic opera buffo

famous alda, bori, callas, calve, caruso, gigli, gluck, lanza, lehmann, lind, lucca, melba, moffo, nilsson, onegin, patti, pavarotti, pinza, pons, price, ruffo, sills, stevens, tauber, tebaldi, tibbett, traubel

feminine alto, canary, chantress, contralto, diva, songbird, soprano, thrush, warbler

group See SINGING *group*.

mendicant busker

opera diva, prima donna

wandering scald, troubadour, trouvere

SINGHALESE See CEYLON.

SINGING antiphony, calypso, cantation, cantillation, chant, charm, jonglery, lilting, psalmody, serenade

fish midshipman, toadfish

gibbon wouwou

group chanters, choir, chorale, chorus, duet, octet(te), quartet(te), sextet(te), trio

group leader choirmaster, choragus, chorister, coryphaeus, precenter

hinny griddlecake

part voce

pert. cantative, cantatory, choral

style bel canto, coloratura, sprechgesang

suitable for lyric, melic

trio tricinium

voice alto, baritone, bass(o), coloratura, contrabass, contralto, countertenor, falsetto, mezzosoprano, soprano, tenor

SINGLE ace, alone, apart, azygous, bachelor, base-hit, bill, bunt, celibate, char, claw, complete, exclusive, frail, frank, haploid, hit, honest, individual, isolated, lone, mere, mono, odd, one(ply), only, part(icular), plain, pure, separate, sequester, simple(x), sincere, sole, solitary, sound, special, specific, sporadic, true, unadulterated, unalloyed, une, unique, unit, unitary, unlined, unmarried, unmixed, unwed(ded), weak, withdraw

-chamber unicameral

comb. apl(o), hapl(o), mono, uni

file crocodile, procession

-foot amble, bait, gallop, lope, pace, rack, run, trot, walk

-minded artless, guileless, intense, sincere, steadfast, steady, unwavering

out choose, cite, cull, opt, pick, select

whorled monoverticilate

SINGLEHANDED alone, easily, unaided, unassisted

SINGLEHEARTED artless, honest, true

SINGLESTICK backsword, cudgel

SINGLETREE bar, whippletree

SINGLY alone, apart, honestly, individually, kithless, merely, only, particularly, respectively, severally, sincerely, singilatim, solely, solo, unaided, uniquely

SINGSING *site* ossining

warden lawes

SINGSONG chanting, monotonous, redundant, tedious, theatrical

SINGULAR aberrant, abnormal, apart, atypic, bizarre, curious, different, distinguished, diverse, each, eccentric, efficacious, eminent, erratic, excellent, exceptional, extraordinary, fantastic, good, individual, isolated, odd, one, outlandish, particular, peculiar, private, quaint, queer, rare, remarkable, seenil, separate, sindle, sole, strange, striking, superior, surprising, uncommon, unique, unparalleled, unprecedented, unusual, whimsical

SINGULT(US) hic(cup), hiccoughs, sigh, sob

SINIS pityocamptes

parent pemon, polypemon, poseidon, sylea

slayer theseus

SINISTER adverse, augural, bad, baleful, baneful, black, bodeful, boding, car, corrupt, dark, covert, devious, disastrous, dishonest, dismal, doomful, dreary, evil, fateful, fell, foreboding, furtive, gloomy, grim, left(hand), leftward, louche, lowering, malefic, malevolent, malicious, malign(ant), menacing, minacious, ominous, perverse, portending, portentous, secret, somber, spiteful, threatening, ugly, unfortunate, unlucky, unpropitious, vicious

SINISTROUS baneful, erroneous, ill-omened, inauspicious, SINISTER, unfortunate

SINK 3 age, bog, dip, lum, pit, sag, set, sye 4 bore, bowl, drop, fail, fall, flag, flop, hell, hole, lum(b), plop, pool, ruin, slum, sump, sway 5 avale, basin, drain, droop, drown, flump, joint, lapse, lower, merge, plump, quail, sewer, slope, slum(o), swamp, wasel, weary 6 absorb, bottom, cavity, debase, dolina, engulf, finish, hollow, ignore, invest, lessen, recede, reduce, settle, suffer, vanish,

vessel, weaken 7 bog down, capsize, deceive, decline, deepsix, depress, descend, despond, founder, immerse, relapse, scuttle, secrete, subside, swallow 8 collapse, diminish, excavate, hellhole, submerge, suppress 9 domdaniel, gravitate, overwhelm, penetrate 10 degenerate, depression 11 deteriorate, touch bottom
box battery, coffin-boat, float, raft
down avale, bog, decline, kneel, slump, stoop
in bog, bury, impress, penetrate, permeate, soak
of iniquity brothel
room scullery
ship scuttle
well drill
SINKER bagel, bur(r), cesspool, coin, cooler, cruller, deadhead, dollar, donut, doughnut, haustorium, lead, missile, muffin, nail, plumb, plummet, weight
boat catarmaran
fishing dips(ey)(ie)
SINKHOLE cenote, cesspool, drain, ponor, soakaway, uvala
SINKIANG *capital* urumchi
people chinese, kazakh, kirghiz, tadjik, uighur
river tarim
SINLESS See SIN *without.*
SINNER backslider, criminal, culprit, debtor, delinquent, evildoer, malefactor, malfeasor, misfeasor, offender, peccant, penitent, reprobate, rogue, scamp, sinew, transgressor, trespasser, wrongdoer
SINNING errant, erring, offending, peccable, peccant, transgressive, trespassing
SINNIS *daughter* perigune
SINTER cinder, deposit, dross
SINUATE bend, curve, sinuous, tortuous, wavy, wind
SINUOSITY bend, curve, intricacy, winding
SINUOUS anfractuous, bending, circuitous, convoluted, crooked, curved, curving, deviating, devious, erring, flexuous, indirect, intricate, mazy, roundabout, serpen-

tine, sinuate, sly, snaky, spiral, tortile, tortuous, undulating, wavy, winding
SINUS ampulla, antrum, arm, bay, bend, bosom, cavity, channel, curvature, curve, depression, fold, hole, hollow, indentation, loculus, opening, recess, tearpit, tract
arabicus red sea
comb. antro
SIOL clan, group, kin(dred), tribe
SIOUX, SIOUAN abanic, akha, assiniboin, biloxi, boisbrule, brule, catawba, crow, dacotah, dakota, hidatsa, hohe, hunkpapa, iowa, kansa, kaw, mandan, minniconjou, missouri, monacan, oglala, omaha, osage, oto(e), pedee, ponca, quapaw, rosebud, santee, saponi, teton, tutelo, waxhaw, winnebago
force wakan, wakon
god father the sky, great mystery, great spirit, master of life, tirawa, wakonda
rebellion ghost dance
state north dakota
SIP bib, bleb, draft, drink, drop, imbibe, lap, nip, partake, peg, quaff, sample, savor, suck, sup, taste, tipple, toothful, whiff
SIPE drip, ooze, percolate, seep, soak
SIPHON channel, crane, drain, empty, reservoir, siphuncle, skim, thief, tube, valinch
SIPPER bibber, straw, toper, tube
SIR adoni, baronet, cavalier, clergyman, don, effendi, esquire, gentleman, gospodin, governor, herr, knight, lord, man, master, messire, mian, noble, priest, sahib, sayyid, senor(e), sieur, signore, sovereign, title, tuan
SIRCAR accountant, authority, bania(n), government, master, servant, steward
SIRE ancestor, antecedent, beget(ter), breed, cause, engender, father, fellow, forefather, generate, horse, king, lord, male, man, master, parent, procreate, produce(r), progenitor, propagate, stallion, stud

SIREN alarm, alert, alluring, bewitcher, bewitching, charmer, circe, cleo(patra), eel, enchanter, enchantress, enticer, fascinating, fascinator, femme fatale, foghorn, hoot(er), horn, inveigler, lorelei, lurer, lurlei, magnetophone, mantrap, mermaid, parthenope, seducer, seductress, serpent, signal, sorceress, spellbinder, tantalizer, tempter, temptress, vamp(ire), warning, witch
famed circe, cleopatra, lorelei, lurlei
master butes
names aglaophone, molpe, parthenope, peisinoe, thelxepeia
parent achelous, melpomene
resister odysseus, ulysses
symbol double flute, lyre
SIRENIA cetomorphia, dugong, manatee, seacow
SIRIASIS sunstroke
SIRIUS canicula, canismajoris, dogstar, sothis, tishiva
master orion
pert. sothic
SIRLOIN backsey, sey, steak
SIROCCO leste, storm, wind
SIRUP See SYRUP.
SIS girl, SISTER, sweetheart
SISAL agave, cabuya, fiber, hemp, henequin, sizal
SISAMAI *kin* eleasah, shallum
SISEL squirrel, suslik
SISERA *enemy* barak, jael
SISKIN aberdavine, aberdevine, aberduvine, barleybird, finch, nightingale, tarin, wagtail, wryneck
SISSY chicken, cotquean, coward, creampuff, girlish, milksop, mollycoddle, nance, nice, pantywaist, percy, prim, prissy, softy, weakling
SIST cite, delay, desist, stay, stop, summon, suspend, suspension
SISTER girl, kin, nun, nurse, shvester, sib(ling), soeur, sorella, soror, titty, woman
-in-law bellesoeur, femme, shvegerin
-killing sororicide
pert. soror(i)al, sororate
superior abbess

younger cadette

SISTERHOOD order, sorority

SISTERLY affectionate, soror(i)al

SISYPHUS aeolides
consort anticlea, merope
father aeolus, autolycus
grandson bellerophon, hipponous
jailor tartarus
kingdom corinth
son glaucus, halmus, odysseus, ornytion, porphyrion, thersander, ulysses

SIT abide, absquatulate, become, befit, beset, brood, convene, dwell, endure, fit, hatch, incubate, kneel, meet, model, occupy, oppress, perch, pose, press, remain, repose, rest, roost, seat, settle, squat, stand, stay, suit, weigh
back retire, retreat
carelessly loll, sprawl
down besiege, encamp, rest, settle, strike
in attend, participate, protest, take part
on block, conceal, confer, cover, hide, investigate, rebuke, repress, reprimand, snub, squelch, stop, straddle, suppress
on eggs brood, ruck
on the fence straddle
out outstay, remain
tight delay, endure, insist, stand fast
up arise, beg, labor, rise, spring, straighten, upheave, uprear, uprise

SITA *consort* rama(chandra), ravana
father janaka

SITAR guitar

SITARIST ravi-shankar

SITATUNGA animal, antelope, nakong

SITE area, habitat, locality, locate, location, locus, lot, place, plot, position, posture, scene, seat, situation, situs, spot, stand, stance, venue, whereabouts
building steading
excavation dig

SITFAST callosity, crowfoot, fixed, immovable, restbarrow, stationary, stone

SITH afterward, since

SITHE chance, chive, con-

duct, course, journey, lot, mishap, occasion, sigh, time

SITSANG tibet

SITTER dolly, hen, model, nurse, rider, rump, setup

SITTING abode, assembly, assis, astride, brooding, clutch, congress, convocation, dwelling, incubation, meeting, place, pose, posing, seance, seat(ed), sedent(ary), sederunt, sejant, sejaul, sejeant, session, suitable, wake
bull's tribe sioux
bull's victim custer
court assis, assize, session
duck dupe, easy mark, pigeon, pushover, victim
room parlor

SITUATE assign, localize, locate, place, position, set

SITUATED basal, circumstanced, established, fixed, located, lying, marginal, nether, placed, plight, positioned, seated, settled, station

SITUATION aspect, bearings, berth, billet, business, calling, capacity, base, circumstances, climax, condition, crisis, direction, estate, footing, instance, job, locality, location, locus, metier, mode, need, office, pass, perch, place(ment), plight, position, posture, post, predicament, pursuit, seat, settlement, siege, site, situs, spot, standing, state, station, status, stead, strait, surface, whereabouts, work
advantageous catbird-seat
crucial brink, clutch
difficult behind the eightball, box, dilemma, headache, puxy, rattrap, scrape
embarrassing hot-seat
fortunate break

SITULA bucket, pail, vase, urn

SITUS See SITE.

SIVA, SHIVA ardhanari, bhairava, destroyer, isvara, mahadeva, nataraja, regenerator, rudra, sadashiv, samb, shambu
consort devi, durga, kali, parbutta, parvati, sati, shakta, shakti, uma
dancer nataraja
guard bouder, boudon

scripture tantra
snake cobra
son ganesha, skanda
symbol linga(m)
temples kailasa, prambanan
trident trisul(a)
worshipper saiva

SIVER drain, gutter, simmer

SIX digamma, hexad(e), roku, sechs, sei(s), senarius, senary, sise
comb. hex(a), hexo, sex, sise
days hexameron
dice boxcar, sice, size
-eyed senocular
feet under buried, dead
-fingered sexdigital
-footed hexaped, hexapod(al)(an)
group of hexad, senary, sestet, sextet(te)
hundred light brigade
-line stanza sestet, sestina, sextet(te)
nations iroquois
nation(s) members cayugas, mohawks, oneidas, onondagas, senecas, tuscaroras
pert. senary
-pounder cannon
series of hexad
sheets sextern
sheets to the wind drunk, intoxicated, stewed
-shooter firearm, gun, pistol, revolver
-sided hexagonal
-toed sexdigital, sexdigitate

SIXES box-cars, sisters, sixty-days, ssang-ryouk, sugoruku

SIXFOLD hexadic, hexamerous, hexahedral, hexangular, hexatonic, senary, sextuple

SIXPENCE bender, cripple, fiddle(r), kick, sice, simon, sprat, tanner, tester, teston, testril, tizzy

SIXTH sesto
degree, pert. seatic
sense esp, instinct, intuition

SIXTY samech, samekh
pert. sexagesimal
-year-old sexagenarian

SIZABLE ample, big, bulky, capacious, great, large, massive, mighty, spacious, strapping, substantial, thumping, tidy, voluminous, whopping

SIZE adjust, amount, amplitude, area, bigness, bore, bouk, breadth, bulk, buy,

caliber, caliper, candle, capacity, charge, classify, condition, content, dimension(s), expanse, extent, filler, format, gauge, girth, glaze, glue, grade, graduate, group, magnitude. mass, match, measure(ment), mickle, portion, proportion(s), range, rank, scale, scope, sieve, six, sort, space, spread, standard, stiffen, stretch, tonnage, volume, width
book page duodecimo, folio, quarto
change in astogeny
hole bore
indefinite nth
large magnum, super
relative scale
separation device grader, screen, sieve
small nanism, scuddick
up analyze, estimate, examine, judge, measure, scrutinize, test, try
SIZING algin, dressing, glair, glaze, glue, middlings, portion, sealer, shellac, starch, varnish, viscose
SIZY glutinous, thick, viscous
SIZZLE anger, broil, bubble, burn, frizz, fry, hiss, roast, scorch, sear, shrivel, siss, speed, spit
SIZZLING burning, hot, scorching, torrid
SJAMBOK flog, whip
SKADI *father* thjazi
home noatum
husband niord, njorth
offspring frey, frey(j)a
SKAG boat, skeg, split, tear, wound
SKAGERRAK *river into* glomma
SKANDA *father* siva
SKAT bierspiel, frage, frog, grand(o), gucki, nullo, preference, ramsch, rana, revolution, sans prendre, slough, sluff, solo, tapp, widow
term guckser, matador, predict, schwarz, tournee
SKATE barndoor, batoid, bob, chopine, doctor, flair, flapper, flathe, glide, horse, jag, miser, patent, patten, plug, raja, rajid, RAY, rink, rocker, roller, scull, sketch(er), skid, skim,

slide, spree, thornback, tink, tobacco-box, tube
blade runner
jump allegro, axel, salchow
mark cusp
place arena, ice, pond, rink
relative nautilus
SKATHI See SKADI.
SKATIKU *100* auksina
SKATING *contest* rollerderby
figure mohawk, pigeon-wing
SKEDADDLE beat it, bolt, bunk, depart, flee, flit, rush, scamper, scat, scoot, scram, scurry, sneak, spill, vamoose
SKEEG beat, flog, lash, slap
SKEEL bucket, pail, tub
duck sheldrake
SKEELING lean-to, outhouse, penthouse, shed
SKEESICKS good-for-nothing, imp, rascal, rogue, skinflint
SKEET scoop, skate, trapshooting
SKEG glance, oats, peep, plum, tear
SKEGGER fish, parr, salmon
SKEIGH mettlesome, proud, sheich, shy
SKEIN bundle, coil, filament, flight, hank, hasp, mesh, rap, scan, sleave, spireme, thimble, web, wind
SKELDER cheat, panhandle, vagrant
SKELETON anatomy, armature, atomy, body, bones, cadaver, cadre, cage, carcass, coral(lum), draught, frame(work), framing, ilium, loofah, mandible, mort, mummy, ossature, outline, plan, rame, rawbone, remains, scaffolding, scrag, shell, sicula, sketch, spicule, sponge, structure
key gilt, screw, twirler
marine coral, shell, spicule, sponge
SKELL squint, twist, upset
SKELLY chaffinch, chub, reef, rock, skerry, squint
SKELP beat, blow, kick, pare, push, quickly, rainfall, scratch, scuttle, slap, spank, splinter, squall, step, stride, strike, suddenly, thrash, trip
SKELTER hurry, run, scurry
SKEP basket, beehive, hive, ladle, scuttle

SKEPTIC agnostic, apikoros, aporetic, cynic, disbeliever, doubter, ephectic, epicoris, freethinker, humist, infidel, questioner, scoffer, unbeliever
doctrine humism
SKEPTICAL agnostic, aporetic, cynical, doubtful, doubting, dubious, dubitant, ephectic, faithless, incredulous, questioning, quizzical, unbelieving
SKEPTICISM agnosticism, disbelief, doubt, dubiety, mistrust, qualm, scruple, suspicion
SKERRICK bit, morsel, scrap
SKETCH abbozzo, apercu, article, blueprint, cartoon, chart, conspectus, delineation, describe, description, design, diagram, digest, doodle, draft, draw(ing), esquisse, idea, impression, jot, limn, map, maquette, outline, paint, pencil, picture, plan, plot, portrayal, precis, scheme, schizzo, skate, skeleton, skit, study, summarize, survey, syllabus, trace, tracing, vignette
autobiographical vita
preliminary abbozzo, draft, maquette
rough esquisse, pochade
SKEW avoid, awry, bias, blunder, coping, cup, cut, deflect, deviate(d), deviation, distort(ed), drizzle, escape, eschew, fail, flunk, gauche, glance, misrepresent, oblique, pervert, rain, shun, side, slant(ing), slip, squint, swerve, turn, twist
SKEWBACK springer
SKEWER broach, brochette, fasten, hairpin, pierce, pin, prick, skiver, spit, truss
cooked on a la broche, en brochette
SKEWERWOOD spindletree
SKI *acrobatics* hotdogging
brand head
contest biathlon
conveyance chair-lift, t-bar
down slope schuss
fall sitzmark
heel spring amstutz
lift t-bar
maneuver ruade, snowplow

marker sitzmark
part camber, heel, shovel, sole, tip
participant gelandelaufer
position vorlage
race slalom
racing langlauf
resort alta, aspen, blanc, breckenridge, kitzbuhel, mammoth, powderhorn, saalbach, st moritz, steamboat springs, stowe, sun valley, telluride, vail, wolfcreek
run schuss, slalom
salutation heil
shelter hut
term christy, gelandesprung, inrun, langlauf, mogul, passgang, schuss, snowplow, telemark, wedeln
turn christiana, christie, christy, stem, telemark
wax klister
wood ash

SKID brake, check, coast, curb, dog, drag, fender, glide, glissade, platform, rollway, runner, scud, side (slip), skew, slide, slip, slither, slough, snake, swerve, timber, toboggan, travoy, twich, veer

SKIDDOO beat it, begone, clear out, scram, vamo(o)se, via

SKIDI *indian* loup

SKIER snowbird
novice snowbunny

SKIFF boat, caique, canoe, currane, dinghy, flurry, glide, graze, rowboat, sampan, skim, skippet, touch

SKIL beshow, candlefish

SKILL ability, accomplishment, address, adeptness, adroitness, agility, aplomb, aptitude, art(ifice), artistry, can, capability, capacity, cleverness, command, competence, craft, cunning, deftness, dexterity, ease, efficiency, experience, expertise, facility, finesse, forte, handiness, industry, ingeniousness, ingenuity, judgment, knack, knowhow, knowledge, learning, lore, mastership, mastery, metier, proficiency, prowess, quickness, readiness, savvy, science, smartness, talent, technic, technique, touch, vertu, virtu

lack of inertia
special bailiwick, bailliage, domain, forte, virtuosity
without artless, awkward, inapt, inept

SKILLED, SKILLFUL able, accomplished, adept, adroit, apt, artful, artistic, astute, canny, capable, clever, competent, conversant, crafty, cunning, d(a)edal, deft, dexterous, drilled, educated, endowed, expert, finished, fitty, gifted, good, habile, handy, hend(e), hotshot, ingenious, initiate(d), intelligent, just, master, practiced, prepared, primed, proficient, prompt, proper, qualified, quick, ready, reasonable, scient, seasoned, slick, strong, tactical, talented, technical, tidy, trained, tried, up on, versed, wise

SKILLET fryer, frying pan, griddle, pan, pot, prig, spider

SKILLFUL See SKILLED.

SKILLIGALEE broth, oatmeal, porridge

SKIM breeze, browse, brush, contact, cream, dart, despume, film, fleet, flit, float, fly, glide, ream, refuse, remove, rind, scan, schoon, scoop, scud, scum, sile, skiff, skip, skirr, skitter, skive, slide, slight, slubber, speed, summarize, thumb, touch

SKIMBLE-SCAMBER incoherent, nonsense, nonsensical, rambling, senseless, unconnected

SKIMMER cutwater, falk, flicker, flutter, jointer, lari, lingel, rhynchops, scoop, scummer, shimmer, shovel, skep, spoon

SKIMP cheese-pare, economize, meager, scamp, scanty, scrape, scrimp, skinch, stint

SKIMPY chary, exiguous, frugal, meager, mean, parsimonious, poor, scanty, scarce, scrimpy, spare, sparse, stingy, thrifty

SKIN abrade, balat, bark, beat, blype, calf, callus, case, caul, cheat, coat(ing), corium, cuticle, cutis, decorticate, defeat, defraud,

derma, epidermis, exhaust, exuviate, fell, film, flay, fleece, fraud, fur, hide, hild, hull, hurt, husk, integument, jacket, lamina, leather, membrane, overcharge, paraderm, parchment, pare, peel, pellage, pellicle, pelt(ry), plew, purse, rawhide, rebuke, rind, ruin, scalp, scum, sharp(er), shell, slough, sluff, strip, surface, sward, swindle, tegument, trick, urge, vellum

animal coat, coney, fur, hackle, hide, pell(age), pelt(ry), rack, robe, sculp, vair, woolfell
attracted to dermatropic
bare altogether, buff
beetle trox
beneath subcutaneous
blueness cyanochroia, cyanoderma, cyanopathy, cyanosis
boat angeyot, umiak
burned eschar
burning sensation uredo
cast exuviate, shed, slough, spoil
comb. cuti, derm(a), dermis
decoration keloid, tat(t)oo
-deep depthless, shallow, superficial
depression dimple
-devouring dermatophagic
discoloration argyria, chloasma, melasma, sunburn, tan
disease acariasis, acne, anthracia, argyria, barber's-itch, boil, brash, caloris, canker, courap, dartars, dartre, dermatitis, dermatosis, eczema, erysipelas, erytheme, exanthema, exormia, favus, frambesia, herpes, hives, hydroa, ichthyosis, impetigo, itch, keratosis, lepidosis, lepra, lichen, lupus, mange, miliaria, mycetoma, myxedema, pemphigus, pian, pityriasis, prickly heat, psora, psoriasis, purpura, rash, ringworm, rupia, scab(ies), schistomiasis, sclerderma, serpigo, shingles, tetter, tinea, toxicoderma, uredo, urticaria, uta, verruga, vitiligo, xanthoma, xeroderma, xerosis
diver aquanaut, frogman

diver equipment aqualung, compressor, flipper, mask, oxygen, scuba, snorkel, spear

doctor dermatologist

dressed fur

dryness ichthyosis, xerosis

eruption acne, anthema, barngun, blotch, boil, bromism, courap, ecthyma, exanthem, hives, macula, measles, morphea, pimple, rash, rosacea, rubella, rubeola, smallpox, strophulus, uredo

excessive pigment melanism

exudation perspiration, sebum, sudor, sweat

finish tan, taw

fish-like ichthyosis

fissure rhagades

fold dewlap, fourchette, plica

fungus dermatophyte

game bunco, bunko, fraud, swindle

growth corn, mole, wart, wen

hard area callous, corn

hardening of schleroderma, sclerma

inflammation cytitis, dermatitis, ecthyma, erythema, herpes, intertrigo, sunburn, windburn

inner derma

insect cast

itching hydroa

lamb budge

layer blastoderm, corium, cutis, dermis, ecderon, ectoblast, enderon, endoderm, epicarp, epidermis, epithelium, hypodermis, tegument

-like cutaneous, dermatoid, dermoid

mark freckle, scar, strawberry

oil sebum

opening pore

out depart, flee, hurry off, sneak away

outer ecderon, epidermis, husk, peel

over heal

pert. cutaneous, cuticular, deric, dermal, dermoid, epidermal

piece blype

prepare sam(m), sammy, tan, taw

presser sammier

protuberance callosity, callus, mole, verruca, wart, wen

rash See *inflammation*, above.

redness erubescence, erythrosis

roughen chafe

roughness goosebumps, gooseflesh

rough-tanned crust

rug kaross

scraping tool strigil

secretion sebum, smegma, sweat

spot freckle, macula, nevus, petechia, tache

thickening acanthosis

thin striffen

transplant graft

tumor keloid, papilloma

under hypodermal, intercutaneous, subcutaneous

unsheared woolfell

untanned hide, kip, pelt, rawhide, shawgreen

without appellous

without pigment alphosis

yellowed xanthochromia

SKINFLINT cheat, churl, curmudgeon, huddle, miser, niggard, pelter, scraper, screw, skeezix, tightwad

SKINK adda, chalcides, draw, drink, eumeces, hock, liquor, lizard, mabuya, pour, scincus, scorpion, seps, serve, shin, soup

blue-tailed lizard

pert. scincoid

SKINKER tapster

SKINKING thin, watery

SKINKLE glimmer, glitter, scatter, sparkle, sprinkle, strew

SKINNED beaten, cheated, fleeced, stripped, trounced

dark melanic, swarthy

thick pachyderm(ic)

thin sensitive, touchy

SKINNER bet, cheat(er), driver, gyp, swindler, tanner

SKINNY angular, bony, cutaneous, emaciated, gaunt, lank(y), lean, membranous, rawboned, scrawny, spare, scant, slink, stingy, THIN

SKIP abscond, advance, bound, bypass, cad, canter, caper, captain, dance, dap, depart, desert, disregard, ditch, elide, elope, escape, evade, flee, flit, foot(man),

forego, forgo, frisk, gambol, glance, hip, hop, jump, lackey, launch, leap, leave, lope, miss, neglect, omission, omit, pace, pass, play, promote, rejoice, ricochet, salto, scoon, scope, scout, servant, skep, skipper, spring, step, straight, trip, vault

along a surface skitter

over elide, scan, skim, slight

school ditch, tib

SKIPJACK alewife, bateau, batel, bluefish, boat, bonito, butterfish, dhow, elater, fish, fop(pish), jockey, leatherjack, mackerel, mincing, pontoon, runner, sailboat, sarda, saurel, saury, scow, skipper, stripling, upstart

SKIPPER barn, butterfly, captain, chief, command(er), fish, grasshopper, ihi, insect, laodah, leader, locust, lowdah, master, ra(i)s, reis, saury, serang, shed, skipjack

daughters waves, whitecaps

SKIPPET basket, boat, box, ladle, scoop, skift

SKIRL bark, blow, cry, pipe, scream, shriek, whirl, yap

SKIRMISH action, affray, battle, bicker, bout, brawl, brush, buffet, clash, combat, conflict, contest, encounter, engagement, fence, fight, flourish, fray, hassle, melee, ruffle, scout, scrimmage, scuffle, tilt, velitation

SKIRNIR *friend* frey

SKIRR fly, move, run, scour, scurry, skim, tern, whirr

SKIRT abada, adjunct, apron, avoid, bank, base(board), basque, basquine, border, circle, circuit, crinoline, dame, dirndle, dress, edge, edging, engi, environs, evade, filibeg, flank, fringe, fustanella, girl, jumper, jupe, jupon, kilt, kirtle, labie, lavalava, margin, midriff, miss, pannier, pareu, pasin, petticoat, philibeg, pullback, quarter, ramie, rim, sarong, saya, strip, suburb, tamein, trend, tutu, woman

armor base, lamboys, tace, tasse(t)

armor part tonlet

ballet tutu
coat lappet, peplum
divided culotte, harem
feature balayense, dust-ruffle, hem, pleat, slit
grass hula
hoop crinoline, farthingale, krinoline, tubtail
insert gore
length maxi, midi
loop tab
loose bania(n), baniya, banyan
narrow hobble
opening placket
outer peplum, saya
section godet, gore, panel
short bengi, blackout, engi, kilt, kirtle, mini, skirtle, tutu
slit placket
steel lamboys
style a-line
tartan arisaid, kilt
velvet base
SKIRTING baseboard, plinth
SKIT act, asperse, burlesque, caper, dance, flounce, gibe, hoax, jest, jibe, joke, jump, lampoon, leap, parody, pasquinade, play, pound, quip, rain, ridicule, satire, shower, shy, sketch, splash, squib, taunt, trick, wanton
SKITE blow, buffeting, dart, dash, fall, hit, shower, slip, smite, squirt(ing), strike, trick, yellowhammer
SKITTER glide, pass, scamper, scatter, skim, skip, skither, sprinkle
SKITTISH bashful, capricious, coy, excitable, fickle, fidgety, frisky, frivolous, gay, goosy, hectic, highstrung, impatient, irresponsible, jittery, jumpy, lively, nervous, playful, restive, restless, scaddle, shaky, shy, spirited, spooky, timid, tricky, undependable, uneasy, unstable, volatile
SKITTLE(S) enjoyment, game, kayles, ninepins, nonsense, pin, play, squails, squander, trash
ball cheese
SKITTY gallinule, rail
SKIVE cut, dart, pare, run, shave, skim, slide, split, wheel
SKIVER impale, leather, scatter, skewer

SKIVVY undershirt, underwear
SKLENT fib, glance, lie, slant, untruth
SKOAL hail, health, salutation, skal, slainte, toast
SKRYMIR *home* jotun(n)heim, utgard
SKUA bonxie, cape-hen, jaeger, sea-hen, stinkpot, teaser, tuliac, whiptail
SKULDUGGERY fraud, joukery, pawkery, trickery, wickedness
SKULK avoid, dern, conceal, couch, evade, hide, jouk, lurk, malinger, mooch, prowl, quail, scout, skirk, slink, sneak, steal
SKULL bean, brain(box), caput-mortuum, cranium, death's-head, epicranium, harnpan, head, mind, pannicle, pericranium, poll, scalp, scaup, vault
absence acrania
back occiput
bone epactal, epipteric, ethmoid, frontal, inion, mandible, mastoid, maxilla, occipital, parietal, sphenoid, temporal, vomer, zygoma
cavity foramen, fossa, sinus
comb. cephal(o), crania(l), cranio
deformity cymbocephaly, scaphocephaly
dome calvaria
fracture pilation
having long dolichocephalic, dolichocranial
incomplete calvaria
junction bregma, pterion, suture
part asterion, basion, inion, sinciput
pert. cranial, inial
point tylion
pointed acrocephaly
prehistoric cannstatt, talgai
science of craniology
soft spot in fontanel(le)
surgery cranioplasty
the golgotha
upper half sinciput
vault calvarium
without acranial
SKULLCAP beanie, calot(te), calvaria, cap, capeline, chechia, coif(fette), hoodwort, pixie, scutellaria, vault, yamilke, yarmelke, yarmulke, zucchetto

defensive coif(fette)
felt pileus
SKUNK anna, beat, betrayer, cad, chincha, chinche, conepate, defeat, huron, mephitis, mustelid, perfume, kitten, phobycat, polecat, puss, reprobate, seecawk, seganku, smeller, snipe, teledu, woodpussy, zorril(lo)
-bear wolverine
-bird bobolink
black alaska sable
cabbage aracae, collard, pitcherplant, pockweed
egg onion
-head duck, scoter
mushroom death-cup
-like civet, zoril(la)
SKY azure, blue, caelus, canopy, cielo, cope, dyaus, ether, firmament, heaven(s), langi, lift, loft, paradise, summit, tien, top, vault, welkin
belt zodiac
-blue azure, celeste, celestial, cerule(an), lapis-lazuli
clear ether, ozone
comb. scio, uran(o)
god abu, aether, anat, anu, argus, bel, caelus, coel, dyaus, jumala, jupiter, ninurta, odomankoma, tiu, tiw, tyr, ukko, uranus, ymir, zeus, zio, ziu
goddess acrae, astarte, diana, frigg(a), hathor, hecate, hera, iole, isis, jacaste, jocasta, juno, niobe, nut, tienhou, trivia
highest part zenith
line horizon
-man aeronaut, astronaut
mapping astrography
personification aether
pert. celestial, coelar
phenomenon ufo
pilot aviator, chaplain, clergyman, missionary
royal family perseus
serpent ahi
SKYLARK alauda, carouse, frolic, gambol, jump, pipit, play, rollick, run, sport, trick, yerk
SKYLIGHT abatjour, hypaethron, reflector, rocket, window
SKYROCKET girandole, rise, shoot up
SKYWARD aloft
SLAB board, cant, dalle, flag-

stone, flitch, foundation, lamina, lech, ledger, lumber, marver, memorial, mihrab, monument, mud, pavior, piece, plank, plate, portion, profuse, puddle, road, section, slat, slice, slime, stela, stele, stone, table, tablet, thick, tile, viscous, wryneck
column-top abacus
flooring dalle
-like stelar, stelene
of clay bat
of peat scad
printer's table
-sided lean, skinny
stone stela, stele
SLABBER dribble, drivel, drool, gulp, saliva, slaver, slobber
SLABBY miry, muddy, sloppy, thick, viscid, viscous, wet
SLACK abate, baggy, careless, chaff, comb, coom, culm, dell, dilatory, diminished, dormant, dull, easy, extinguish, faineant, feeble, flabby, flaccid, flappy, flimsy, frese, glen, hole, improvident, impudence, inactive, inadequate, indifferent, inert, infirm, insufficient, laggard, lax, laze, lazy, lethargic, loose(n), lull, marsh, moderate, morass, neglectful, negligent, pit, pool, quaggy, quiescent, relax(ed), remiss, shirk, SLACKEN, slake, sleazy, slothful, slow, sluggish, smeddum, soft, tardy, ungirt, unsteady, valley, wanton, warm, weak
off See SLACKEN.
SLACKEN abate, check, curb, decrease, delay, detain, dowse, dwindle, ease, end, hinder, hold back, inhibit, lag, lessen, letup, loose(n), moderate, modify, modulate, reduce, relax, relent, relieve, remit, repose, restrain, retard, SLACK, slag, slake, slow, taper, temper, unbend, wane, weaken
SLACKENING detente, letdown, letup, moderation, retardation
SLACKER drawgate, embusque, goldbrick, goof-off, rotter, sharp(er), shirker, soldier, spiv, welsher

SLACKS See PANTS.
SLADE cave, den, glade, glen, glide, hillside, peat, ravine, sledge, slide, sole, valley
SLAG agglomerate, bottoms, bulldog, cinder(s), clinker, debris, dregs, dross, embers, grounds, lava, lees, recrement, refuse, remainder, remnant(s), residue, scoria, sediment, slacken, slakin, waste
and ore browse, slacken
SLAISTER beat, bedaub, flog, idle, mess, smear
SLAISTERY dirty, garbage, miry, refuse, sloppy
SLAKE abate, allay, appease, assuage, bedaub, besmear, crumble, daub, deaden, disintegrate, drink, flat, free, kiss, lessen, lick, loosen, mire, mitigate, moderate, mud, quench, reduce, relax, release, relieve, sate, satisfy, SLACKEN, slime, smear, stop
SLAM abuse, bang, beat, blow, chelem, clash, close, crack, criticism, criticize, cuff, defeat, flounce, hit, impact, push, rap, ruff, score, shut, stram, strike, taunt, throw, tout, vole, whack, whale
SLAMMOCK dawdle, loiter, slattern, sloven, ungainly
SLAMP limp, supple
SLAMPAMP, SLAMPANT medley, rigmarole, trick
SLANDER abuse, asperse, aspersion, assail, attack, backbite, bedaub, belie, besmear, besmirch, bespatter, blacken, blame, calumniate, calumniation, calumny, cant, charge, damage, decry, defamation, defame, derogate, detraction, discolor, discredit, disgrace, dishonor, distort, gossip, hit, hurt, injure, insult, libel, malign(ation), medisance, misrepresent, missay, obloquy, obtrect, offend, revile, roorback, scandal, smear, soil, tale, traduce, vilification, vilify, vituperation
SLANDERER false witness, famicide, juror
SLANDEROUS derogatory,

disgraceful, libelous, maledicent, shameful
SLANG abuse, argot, cant, chain, cheat, dialect, dupe, jargon, jive, license, lingo, patois, patter, performance, rakish, swindle, vernacular, vulgar
comb. eroo
SLANGWHANG bluster, rant, rave
SLANK lanky, lean, slonk
SLANT acclivity, angle, askew, attitude, bend, bevel, bias, breeze, careen, cock, coloring, declivity, deviate, diagonal, disposition, diverge(nce), facet, flanch, gibe, glance, grade, gradient, heel, inclination, incline, judgment, keel, lean, list, occasion, opinion, opportunity, outlook, position, skew, sklent, slope, splay, stand(point), swerve, taunt, tilt, tip, veer, view(point), virgule
-eyed mongoloid
line slash, virgule
SLANTED arake, askew, atilt, avelonge, awry, bevelled, biased, canted, cock-eyed, crooked, eccentric, oblique, prejudiced, rakish, screwy, sloped, sloping
SLANTING aslope, avelonge, bias, cant, coloring, loxotic, oblique, sidelong, sklent, sloping, squint
SLAP attempt, beat, blad, bleeze, blow, box, breach, buff(et), clap, clout, crack, cuff, cut, flap, frosk, gate, HIT, insult, lap, lash, nick, notch, pass, patch, percuss, plump, potch, punch, punish, rebuff, reprimand, sclaff, scud, skeeg, slam, slight, slug, smack, smite, snub, spank, spat, strike, suddenly, swat, tack, taunt, try, twang, wherret, whip
hard smackeroo
SLAPDASH abrupt(ly), abuse, billingsgate, buckeye, careless(ness), haphazard (ly), hastily, hasty, impetuous(ly), noisily, precipitately, reckless, rough(cast), roughly, suddenly
SLAPE crafty, deceitful, hypocritical, slippery, smooth
SLAPHAPPY befuddled,

dazed, foolish, giddy, irresponsible, punch-drunk
SLAPJACK flapjack, griddlecake, pancake
SLAPPING big, great, huge, monstrous, rapid, rattling, strapping
SLAPSTICK buffoonery, burlesque, comedy, joke, play
SLARE scuff, slur, smear, sneer, taunt
SLART spatter, splash, taunt
SLASH assail, attack, carbonado, carve, censure, chop, cleave, coup, crack, criticize, cut, defeat, depreciate, diagonal, gash, hack, hash, hew, jag, knife, lash, marsh, pierce, race, rammel, reduce, rend, rive, scourge, slice, slish, slit(ter), slosh, splash, p..., stripe, stroke, swale, whip
SLASHER bilhook, dagger, knife, swashbuckler, sword (sman)
SLASK silesia
SLAT bar, batten, beat, blind, blow, board, bow, cast, crack, dab, flap, fragment, hurl, lath, louver, pummel, rib, salmon, sclat, shutter, slab, slap, slate, slot, spline, split, stave, strike, strip, throw, toss, transom
whirled bullroarer, thunderstick
SLATE agenda, bait, blackboard, blae, candidates, censure, chalkboard, chalkstone, criticize, entrants, file, gray, hound, line-up, list, mark, plan, pummel, punish, pursue, rag, rebuke, record, reprimand, rock, roll, roofing, schedule, schist, shale, slab, slattern, stone, thrash, ticket, tile
axe zake
blue shiver, skaillie
break into slabs sculp
clean tabula-rasa
color blae, blue, gray
piece scantle
roofing rag
trimming tool sa(e)x, zax
SLATER critic, crustacean, heler, hellier, skimmity, sowbug, woodlouse
tool stake
SLATHER quantity, slide, slip, slobber, spend, spill, spread
SLATTER clatter, disarrange,

scatter, slater, slop, spill, upset, waste
SLATTERN bitch, bunger, careless, caw, clatch, crone, dollop, dowd(y), drab(bletail), draggletail, faggot, fritter, frow, frump, hag, huckmuck, idler, litterbug, mab, malkin, maux, mawks, moggy, mopsy, pig, prossy, prostitute, s(c)hloomp, s(c)hlump, shmatte, shmotte, slammock, slob, sloppy, sloven(ly), slubberdegullion, slubberer, slummock, slut, swine, traipse, trifler, trollop, trull, waste
SLATTERNLY blousy, blowsy, blowzy, coarse, disheveled, dowdy, fat, filthy, foul, frowzy, ruddy, slipshod, slovenly, squalid, unkempt
SLAUGHTER ab(b)atage, battue, butcher(y), carnage, defeat, homicide, kill(ing), massacre, murder, pogrom, shamble, slay, strage, trounce
of the people pogrom, populicide
pert. internecine
valley of tophet
wanton battue
SLAUGHTERHOUSE abattoir, butchery, frigorifico, matadero, matanza, shambles, stockyard
worker knacker, sider
SLAUGHTERINA she(c)hita
SLAUM daub, smear
SLAV, SLAVIC bohemian, bulgar, croat(ian), czech (oslovak), hunks, hunky, lett, moravian, polabian, pole, russian, serb(ian), servian, sider, silesian, slavonian, slovak(ian), sorb(ian), uskok, vend, vened, wend
alphabet cyrillic, glagolitic
bible ostrog
brotherhood bratsvo
clan zadruga
commander voivod(e)
dance kazachok, kazatshe, kolo
demon babajaga, babayaga
folksong dumka
god svantovit, triglav
governor voivod(e)
gymnast sokol
language bulgar, macedonian, russian
magician koschei

nurse baba
prince knez
ruler czar, samo, tsar
spirit leshy, lesiy
title hospodar, knez
witch babajaga, babayaga
SLAVE addict, agent, alipin, alltud, ame damnee, ardu, bond(s)man, bootlicker, captive, ceile, ceorl, chattel, chela, churl, cumhal, dasi, davus, dehwar, drudge, dupe, esne, forsado, forsar, gallerian, helot, hierodule, hieros, ilot, instrument, labor(er), lascar, lorarius, mameluke, mamluk, manciple, morgiana, neif(e), odalisk, odalisque, praedial, serf, servant, swink, thane, theow(man), thrall, toil(er), uncle tom, vassal, villain, villein, work, wretch
block catasta
caravan coffle
chief bug-jargal
comb. servo
dealer bichy, mango
deformed caliban
driver coach, despot, martinet, simon legree, taskmaster, tyrant
female baubo, bondmaid, broadwife, dasi, iambe, neife, odalisk, odalisque
fighting gladiator, mameluke, mamluk
free emancipate, manumit
fugitive cimmaron, maroon
galley forsado, forsar, sforzato
garment exomis
group chiurm, coffle, gang, helotry, toxotae
harem odalisk, odalisque
legendary baubo, iambe
quarters barracoon, crawl
rule by d(o)ulocracy
runaway androcles, maroon
ship blackbirder
state alabama, arkansas, carolinas, florida, georgia, kentucky, louisiana, maryland, mississippi, missouri, tennessee, texas, virginia
trade center pemba, zanzibar
trade vessel dhow
traffic in mangonize
SLAVER dribble, drivel, drool, fawn, flatter, fondle, froth, kiss, nonsense, saliva, salivate, slabber, slobber, spittle, truckle

SLAVERY bondage, captivity, helotism, helotry, imprisonment, serfage, serfdom, serfhood, mizraim, servility, servitude, subjection, thrall(dom), vassalage, work, yoke
anti jayhawker
debates lincoln-douglas
release from affranchise, emancipate, enfranchise, free, liberate, manumit
SLAVEY drudge, factotum, maid, servant
SLAVIC See SLAV.
SLAVISH abject, base, fawning, ignoble, mean, menial, miserable, obsequious, pliant, servile, sordid, subdued, submissive, subservient, supine, tame, truckling, vernile, wretched
SLAY amuse, annihilate, assassinate, burke, butcher, delight, destroy, dight, dispatch, execute, exterminate, fell, finish, kill, knock, lynch, massacre, murder, slaughter, smite, strangle, strike
SLAYER assassin, bane, criminal, genocide, hitman, hogni, hood, interfector, killer, murderer
comb. ctonus
SLEAVE cleave, divide, floss, separate, silk, sley, tangle
SLEAZY flabby, flaccid, flimsy, frail, limp, loose, loppy, papery, poor, slack, slight, thin, unsubstantial, weak
SLED bobsleigh, cariole, clipper, coast(er), cutter, dogboat, double-ripper, drag, dray, glide, godevil, jumper, luge, monoski, pung, ripper, runner, scoot, skid, SLEDGE, sleigh, slide, toboggan, tode, travois, troika
dog, famous balto
flat-bottomed toboggan
logging sloop, swingdingle, tieboy, tode
wooden catamaran
SLEDGE break, drag, dray, hammer, hurdle, komatik, pulka, seven-up, SLED, sleigh, slipe, smite, strike, trail, train(eau), troll(y), trunk
dog husky

handlebar upstander
runner slipe
SLEECH manure, ooze, silt, slime
SLEEK bland, brush, burnish(ed), conceal, crafty, flatter, freshen, fulsome, furbished, glabrous, glace, glassy, glazed, glide, glossy, groomed, insinuating, lustrous, nap, neat, obsequious, oily, plump, polish (ed), satiny, shiny, silken, silky, SLICK, slippery, sly, smarmy, smart, smooth, snod, soapy, soignee, suave, svelte, tidy, trig, unctuous, urbane
-leaf sand-myrtle
SLEEKIT crafty, deceitful, SLEEK, smooth
SLEEP balmy, bed, bunk, calk, catnap, caulk, death, dorm(ancy), dormition, dorse, doss, doze, drowse, estivate, estivation, flop, hibernate, hibernation, land of nod, lethargy, lib, nap, nod, quiescence, repose, rest, roost, rout, shuteye, siesta, slumber, snooze, snore, snozzle, sommus, somnolence, sopor, stupor, sweven, swoon, unconsciousness
-at-noon goatsbeard
comb. hypn(o), somni, sopor
deep coma, dreamland, sopor, stupor, swoon
-dispelling hypnopompic, somnifugous
frequent need for narcolepsy
drug-induced narcosis
god hypnos, morpheus, soma, somnus
-in domestic, maid, servant
inducer barbiturate, dormitive, dwale, hypnotic, hypnotist, narcotic, opiate, sandman, sedative, somnifacient, sopient, soporific
light catnap, doze, fortywinks, nap, shuteye, siesta, sloom, snooze
like a top
of the soul psychopannychy
on duty ca(u)lk, coop, goldbrick, huddle
outdoors camp
personified hypnos, sandman
pert. morphetic, somnial, soporific
-producing hypnogogic

prolonged sopor
psychotherapy dauerschlaf
put to bore, deaden, entrance, hypnotize, lull, magnetize, mesmerize
science hypnology
semi-conscious predormition
sound snore
talking somniloquy
SLEEPER beam, bet, calf, dormeuse, dormouse, dowitcher, drone, earmark, eliotrid, epimenides, joist, knee, pullman, rafter, rester, shark, slumberer, stringer, stringpiece, support, tie, timber, underdog
20-year rip van winkle
SLEEPING abed, crocard, dormant, dormient, inactive, inert, latent, napping, quiescent, retired, slumbering, snoozing
beauty oxalis, sorrel
car pullman, wagon-lit
pill See SLEEP *inducer.*
place bag, barracks, bed, berth, billet, bunk, cot, couch, cubicle, dormitory, nare, pad, pallet, pullman, quarters
sickness encephalitis, lethargus, nona, trypanosomiasis
sickness cause trypanosome, tsetse-fly
SLEEPLESS alert, assiduous, ceaseless, insomniac, restless, unquiet, vigilant, wakeful, watchful, wide-awake
SLEEPLESSNESS insomnia, insomnolence
SLEEPWALKER noctambule, noctambulist, somnambulist
SLEEPWALKING somnambulism
SLEEPY comatose, dozy, dreamy, drowsy, dull, groggy, heavy, hypnagogic, languid, lethargic, morphic, nappy, noddy, oscitant, phlegmatic, sluggish, slumb(e)rous, slumbery, somniferous, somnific, somnolent, soporiferous, soporific, stuporous, tired, yawning
hollow character headless horseman, ichabod crane, katrina van tassel
staggers hydrocephalus
SLEER mock, sneer
SLEET glaze, ice, rain, storm

SLEEVE arm(let), axel, bushing, cathead, channel, cubital, cylinder, dolman, gigot, housing, manche, mandrel, moggan, pipe, poke, raglan, thimble, tube
badge chevron, stripes
dog pekinese
end cuff
-fish squid
flaring manche, maunch(e)
hanging tab
hole skye
insert gusset
long poke
tapered skein

SLEEVELESS bootless, futile, petty, profitless, shiftless, useless

SLEIGH car(r)iole, cutter, glide, pung, SLED, SLEDGE, sley, slipe, toboggan
bell brelot
runner shoe
sidepiece rave

SLEIGHT agility, artifice, craft(y), cunning, deft(ness), dexterity, dexterous, knack, prudence, quickness, shift, skill, sly, stratagem, trick(ery), wisdom
of hand conjuration, jugglery, juggling, magic, legerdemain, prestidigitation
of hand performer conjurer, mage, magician, prestidigitator

SLEIPNER *owner* odin
SLENDER abstemious, airy, bare, delie, ethereal, faint, feeble, fine, frail, frugal, gaunt, gracile, inadequate, jimp, lank(y), lean, leger, limited, lissom(e), lithe, little, meager, narrow, petit, prim, rare, reedy, scant, semmit, skinny, slight, slim, small, spare, spindling, spinny, spired, spirlie, squinny, stalky, svelt, sylph, tenuous, thin, trim, trivial, waspen, weak, willowy, wispy
beloved anne page
cousin shallow
servant simple

SLENDERIZE bantingize, diet, lose, reduce, slim, thin
SLENT breeze, declivity, glance, jest, rail, slant, slope, split, tear, witticism
SLEUTH cop, detective, dick, ferret, gumshoe, hawkshaw, investigator, operator, path, scout, sloth, snoop, tec, tracer, track(er), trail
famous bond, carter, chan, charles, cool, dupin, fell, freeman, fumanchu, hammer, holmes, justus, lupin, maclain, marple, mason, mayo, mckee, merlini, merrivale, moran, moto, north, poirot, porter, raffles, saint, shayne, valcour, vance, westlake, wimsey, wolfe

SLEUTHDOG bloodhound, talbot
SLEW killed, lot(s), many, marsh, plenty, pond, pool, quantity, raft, slough, SLUE, swamp, turn, twist
SLICE canch, cantle, carve, collop, colp, cut, divide, flitch, gash, jerk, knife, lamina, layer, pare, part, piece, plate, portion, rasher, section, segment, separate, sever, share, shave, shiver, shred, skelb, slab, slipe, sliver, spatula, splinter, strip, stroke, thible, tranche, tray, trench, wedge, whang
SLICK accomplished, alert, chisel, clever, crafty, cunning, daub, expert, first-rate, glib, glistening, glossy, good, greasy, loy, lubric(i)ous, magazine, oily, paddle, paint, periodical, polish, shallow, shiny, shrewd, slippery, sleek, smart, smear, smooth, superficial, trick(il)y, unctuous, urbane
SLICKER cheat, coat, dude, fishmoth, float, gambler, moth, raincoat, rascal, silverfish, sleeker, smoother, trickster
SLICKNESS cunning, oiliness, smoothness, unction
SLIDDER dally, debris, deceitful, depart, instability, leave, slide, slip(pery), slouch, treacherous, unstable
SLIDE avalanche, chute, coast, coule, decline, elapse, fall, glide, glissade, glissando, glitch, incline, print, relapse, retreat, scoot, shear, shirl, sideslip, skate, skid, skim, skip, sled(ge), sleeve, slew, slidder, slip, slither, slue, sluther, toboggan, trough
down slump

fastener zipper
sideways skid
SLIGHT contemn, cut, delicate, diminutive, disdain, disesteem, disregard, faint, feeble, flimsy, flout, foolish, forget, fragile, frail, gauzy, humble, ignore, imperceptible, intangible, level, little, meager, mean, mere, minor, minute, neglect, omit, overlook, paltry, pass by, petty, puny, rare, raze, remote, scamp, scant(y), scoff, scorn, scrannel, shallow, silly, sketchy, skim, skimp, sleek, slender, slim, slur over, small, smooth, snub, superficial, tenuous, thin, thready, trifling, trivial, unimportant, vilipend, wee
SLIGHTEST least, lowest, minimum, smallest
SLIGHTLY carelessly, hardly, imperceptibly, scarcely
comb. sub
SLIM cunning, fine, frail, gaunt, insubstantial, lean, lissome, lithe(some), meager, narrow, rare, remote, scamp, scant(y), skinny, slender(ize), slight, slur, small, spare, sparse, tenuous, thin, weak
SLIME bitumen, crawl, dirt, filth, gleet, glit, gook, gore, guck, ichor, mire, muck, mucous, mud, ooze, schlich, silt, slab, sloak, slop, slosh, slubber, sludge, slush, sluther, sossle, sposh
-eel hagfish
mold acrasia, myxo
SLIMSY flimsy, frail, slight, thin, weak
SLIMY clammy, dirty, disgusting, filthy, gletty, glutinous, limous, mucky, mucous, muculent, offensive, oozy, repulsive, sammy, sleechy, slithery, sticky, vile
SLING arbalest, ballista, bandage, beany, bridle, cannon, cast, catapult, culverin, dangle, drink, fling, halter, hang, harness, hoist, hurl, pitch, slackie, slue, suspend, throw, toss, trebuchet, trebucket, womera
dog crampon
SLINGSHOT beanshooter, catapult, david, shanghai, slappy, tweaker

SLINK couch, coward, crawl, creep, dastard, glide, good-for-nothing, lean, leer, loop, lurk, mackerel, quail, shirk, skinny, skulk, slinge, sly, sneak, steal, thin, weakling, worthless

away flinch, mizzle, shag, shrink, sloke

SLINKY flowing, sinuous, slender, sneaky

SLIP 3 err, pew, sin, tag 4 balk, bull, cast, clay, dock, fall, give, memo, pier, ramp, rein, ruse, shed, skid, skip, skyt, slue, trip, twig 5 berth, boner, break, child, chute, creem, elude, error, fault, gaffe, glide, lapse, leash, loose, lurch, scion, shift, shoot, skate, slide, slump, strap, strip, youth 6 booboo, coupon, elapse, howler, midget, miscue, mishap, slurry, ticket, totter 7 bloomer, blooper, blunder, chemise, cutting, decline, failing, fauxpas, floater, founder, illapse, misstep, mistake, release, scraper, slidder, slither, sluther, stumble 8 accident, camisole, glissade, solecism 9 gaucherie, offspring, oversight 10 memorandum, pillowcase, surrection 11 deteriorate 12 transgression

a cog blunder, err

away absent, depart, escape, flee, leave

baby's gertrude

back relapse

by elapse, pass

draw loper

leather bridle, leash, rein, strap

of the pen lapsus calami

of the tongue lapsus linguae, parapraxis

of wood spill

on don, jersey, overcoat, pullover, sweater, wear

out of doff, flee, shirk

over ignore, slight

pottery barbotine

up blunder, err(or), fail, fumble, miscue, miss, oversight

ware pottery

SLIPCASE for(r)el

SLIPCOVER dustjacket, wrapper

SLIPE blow, glide, innuendo, pare, peel, remove, sledge,

sleigh, slice, sneak, split, strip, sweep off, wool

SLIPKNOT nog, noose, snittle

SLIPPER apron, baboosh, babouche, ballet, bauchle, bootee, campagus, chinela, crakow, everett, fewterer, flat, footwear, glave, go-ahead, juliet, moccasin, moyle, mule, neap, pantofle, panton, pinafore, pinson, pliant, pump, romeo, sandal, sclaffer, scliff, scuff, shoe, shuffle, skeiner, slipshoe, sneaker, spank, step-in, willowy, zori

heelless bauchle

plant bird-cactus

-shaped calceiform, calceolate, soleiform

SLIPPERWORT calceolaria

SLIPPERY crafty, cunning, deceitful, eely, elusive, evasive, fickle, fly-by-night, glassy, glib, glidder, glint, greasy, icy, intangible, lubric(i)ous, oily, precarious, shifty, shuttle, slabbery, slape, sleek, slick(ery), slid(dery), slimy, slithery, sly, smooth, treacherous, tricky, uncertain, unctuous, unreliable, unsafe, unstable, untrustworthy, wanton, wavering

-back skink

-dick doncella, wrasse

root comfry

SLIPSHOD bungling, careless, clumsy, disorderly, dowdy, haphazard, heedless, hit-and-miss, hitty-missy, indifferent, lax, negligent, remiss, shabby, slack, slapdash, slommack, sloppy, slovenly, slummock, tasteless, unkempt, untidy

SLIPSKIN evasive, graperot

SLIPSLOP blunder, gabble, inane, malapropism, nonsense, refuse, slops, twaddle, wishywashy

SLIPSTREAM race

SLIPSTRING halter, knave, prodigal, rascal(ly), slovenly, truant

SLIRT flip, flirt, squirt

SLISH cut, slash

SLIT aperture, breach, buttonhole, carf, chink, chop, cleave, cleft, cloven, crack, cranny, cut, fent, fissure, furrow, gash, groove, hew,

incision, kerf, louver, nag, nick, open(ing), orifice, placket, race, rend, rent, rip, sever(ed), slash(ed), slot(ted), SPLIT, strent, sunder, tear, vent

-like rimal

SLITHER coast, crack, crawl, crook, glide, hasten, hirsel, hurry, meander, rubbish, rubble, sidle, skid, slide, slip, sluther, snake, splinter, wind, zigzag

SLIVE cleave, cut, idle, loaf, slice, slide, slip, sneak, split, stroke, thrust

SLIVER bit, cut, fragment, jacket, piece, rend, shred, skelf, slice, slobber, snip (pet), spelk, spell, splinter, split, stab, strand, wool

SLOAN avaricious, lazy, sly

SLOANEA breakax, carabeen, ironwood, querbracho

SLOB boor, cad, ice, lubber, mire, mud, ooze, schlack, schlag, s(c)hlock, slattern, slommack, sloven, sludge

SLOBBER blubber, beslaver, dribble, drivel, drool, flatter, gush, hawk, jellyfish, kiss, moisten, mud, saliva, salivate, slabber, slaver, slime, slivver, slop, slup, slush, smarm, smear, spew, spit

SLOCK bog, draft, drench, drink, entice, hollow, lure, pilfer, quench

SLOCKEN quench, saturate, slake, suffocate

SLODDER mud, puddle, slush

SLOE blackthorn, gin, haw, plum, prunus, slone, snag

SLOG blow, drive, hit, pace, PLOD, plug, slam, slosh, slug, strike, toil, walk, work

SLOGAN adage, axiom, battlecry, byword, cachet, catchcry, catchword, cry, epigraph, inscription, maxim, motto, phrase, saying, shibboleth, slughorn, watchword

SLOOM decay, doze, drift, slumber, swoon, waste

SLOOP boat, boyer, brig, cutter, dray, raceabout, sailboat, schooner, ship, sled, vessel, warship, yacht

SLOP, SLOPS breeches, cassock, clothing, constable, dregs, garbage, garment, gobble, gush, hogwash, mash, mess, moisten, mud, nonsense, offal, policeman, puddle, refuse, remainder, rubbish, sentimentality, slatter, slime, slobber, slush, smear, smock, sossle, sozzle, spatter, spill, splash, swill, trousers, vinasse, waste

over effuse, emote, gush, sentimentality

pail parasha

SLOPE alp, ascent, bajada, bank, bent, brae, cant, careen, cast, cliff, cuesta, declension, declivity, depart, descent, deviate, dip, diverge, downset, drop, escarp, flee, glacis, grade, gradient, hade, hading, heald, hield, hill, inclination, incline, lean, pali, peak, pendant, pitch, rake, ramp, rise, scarp, shelf, shelve, sklent, slant, slent, splay, stoss, talus, tilt, tip, tumble, veer, versant

angle-measurer clinometer

backward batter

comb. cline, clino

detrital bajada

downward decline, declivity, descent, devall, dip, downgrade, drop, fall, hang, pitch, precipitance, shed

gentle glacis, incline

protective glacis

steep brae, brow, cleve, cliff, scarp

sunny adret

upward acclivity, ascend, ascent, climb, helicline, rise, upgrade, uprise

SLOPING aslant, aslope, bevelled, declive, declivitous, declivous, devex, inclined, inclining, oblique, shelvy, slanted, slanting

backward supine

upward acclinate, acclivitous, acclivity, acclivous

SLOPPINESS blowziness, carelessness, dowdiness, frowsiness, grubbiness, messiness, negligence, seediness, sentimentality, shabbiness, shoddiness, slatterliness, slipshodness, slovenry, sluttishness, sordidness, squalidness, squalor, untidiness

SLOPPY bedraggled, blowzy, careless, dingy, dirty,

dowdy, farpotshket, frowzy, illfitting, lax, loose, maudlin, messy, muddy, neglectful, negligent, paskudne(h), poky, remiss, seedy, sentimental, slabby, slack, slapdash, slattern, slipshod, slovenly, slushy, soppy, sozzly, splashy, tacky, unkempt, untidy, watery, wet

condition swash

-joe sandwich, sweater

SLOSH dowse, hit, ice, loaf, moisten, mud, ripple, slime, slush, spill, splash, splodge, sprinkle, squdge, wallow, wander, wash

SLOT aperture, bar, bolt, cut, deer, depression, groove, guideway, hollow, keyhole, keyway, opening, recess, slat, slit, socket, spline, stab, track, trail, trapdoor

machine hungry tiger, one-armed bandit, vender

machine restaurant automat

SLOTH accidie, acedia, apathy, aswail, brachypod(e), bradypus, choloepus, delay, edentate, idle(ness), ignavy, indifference, inertia, koala, laziness, lazy, lestodon, neglect, pack, pigritia, sin, sleuthhound, slow(ness), sluggish(ness), tardiness, tardo, torpor, unau

animacule tardigrade

bear aswail, bhalu, melursus

extinct megatherium

tree trumpetwood

SLOTHFUL argh, dilatory, faineant, idle, inactive, indolent, inert, lazy, leisurely, lifeless, lither, neglectful, negligent, otiose, passive, remiss, shiftless, slack, sleathy, sluggish, sweer, thokish

SLOTTER dirty, filth, mess, shackler, splash

SLOTTERY dirty, dull, foul, sluggish, wet

SLOUCH bonnet, clown, droop(ing), gait, hat, larrup, laziness, loafer, lollop, louch, lounge, lout, lubber, pace, pendulous, pipe, shammock, slidder, stoop

hat caddie, caddy, smasher

SLOUCHY bent, droopy, inefficient, stooped

SLOUGH bayou, billabong, bog, cast, dejection, despair,

discard, doff, exuviate, husk, inlet, junk, marsh, mire, molt, mud(hole), offal, ooze, plod, predicament, road, scale, scrap, sheath, shed, skin, slew, slonk, sloo, slue, sluff, sluig, spacelus, strike, swamp, waste

-grass bull-grass, spartina, tussock-sedge

of despond depression, despair

of despond victim christian

SLOUGHING ecdysis, exuviation

SLOVEN besom, clart, dray, hallion, loafer, scoundrel, slattern, slob, slouch, slush, trolly, truck, uncultivated, wanton

SLOVENIA *capital* ljubljana

game balinsi

SLOVENLY bedraggled, blousy, blowsy, blowzy, careless, clatchy, clatty, coarse, dingy, DIRTY, disheveled, dowdy(ish), draggletailed, fat, frowzy, frumpish, frumpy, grubby, lax, lazy, messy, mussy, negligent, phlegmatic(al), pok(e)y, ragged, remiss, ruddy, seedy, shabby, shammocking, shoddy, slammocky, slatternly, slipshod, sliving, sloppy, slouchy, slummocky, sluttish, sordid, squalid, tacky, traily, unkempt, untidy

SLOW abate, adagio, arrest, backward, behind, blate, boring, brake, brosy, check, choke, crawling, creeping, curb, decelerate, decrease, delay, detain, dilatory, drag, dull, dummel, ease(off), easy, gentle, gradual, hinder, hold(back), hooly, impede, imperceptible, inactive, inert, languid, languorous, largo, late, leisurely, lent(o), lessen, lingering, moderate, mollify, obstruct, obtuse, phlegmatic, piecemeal, poky, reduce, reef, rein, relax, retard, set back, slack(off), slacken, sluggish, snail-like, stay, stolid, stop, stunt, stupid, tardo, tardy, temper, throttle(down), torpid, trailing, traily, turtlelike, unprogressive, wearisome

as a snail, tortoise, turtle
burning punky
-*coach* See SLOWPOKE.
comb. brady
down arrest, conk out, decelerate, decline, delay, deliberate, idle, lap(se), moderate, relax, retard(ation), seize, stoppage, strike
-*learning* backward, retarded
loris bashful billy, kokam
moderately andante
-*moving* bradykinetic, dormant, sleepy, sluggish
-*paced* tardigrade
tempo adagio, allegretto, andante, andantino, larghetto, largo, lentando, lento
up ease, easing, proo, relax(ation), retard(ation), slack(en)
-*witted* dull, stupid
SLOWNESS delay, lag, lentitude, lentor, sloth, tardity
SLOWPOKE dawdler, gradualist, laggard, loiterer, sloth, slug, snail, tortoise, turtle
SLOWWORM hagworm, pygopodid
SLUBBER botch, darken, daub, dirty, mire, obscure, scamp, skim, slime, slur, stain
SLUBBERDEGULLION boor, slattern, slover, wretch
SLUBBERER botcher, bungler, slattern, slobberer, sloven
SLUDDER See SLUDGE.
SLUDGE deposit, drudge, gook, gunk, ice, mire, mud, ooze, paste, refuse, sediment, settlings, sleet, slime, slob, slosh, sludder, slush, waste
SLUE bias, deviate, lot, number, pivot, quantity, skid, slew, slide, slip, slough, swamp, swing, turn, twist, veer
SLUG bash, bat, beat, blow, bullet, burr, bust, clout, coin, cuff, dawdle(r), delay, drag, dram, draught, drink, drone, hinder, hindrance, HIT, horn, idle(r), knot, laggard, larva, loiter, mollusk, nail, nudibranch, nugget, obstruction, rattle, rest, shot, slap, slow, sluggard, smite, snag, snail,

snifter, spacer, strike, stud, swat, token, trepang
genus arion, doris, doto, elysia, limax
-*horn* slogan, trumpet
-*like* limaciform
pert. limacine
SLUGGARD daw, drone, faineant
SLUGGER batsman, batter, boxer, goon, hitter, mauler, prizefighter
SLUGGISH apathetic(al), bovine, brosy, comatose, dilatory, dopey, dragging, dronish, drony, drowsy, dull, faint, foul, heavy, inactive, indolent, inert, laggard, languid, languorous, lazy, leaden, lentous, lethargic, listless, lourd, lumpish, obtuse, ox-like, patient, pok(e)y, sleepy, sloomy, slothful, slottery, slow, stagnant, stolid, stuporous, sullen, supine, torpid
SLUGGISHNESS apathy, coolness, dispassion, indifference, inertia, insensibility, languor, lead, listlessness, ositancy, phlegm, sloth, stoicism, unconcern, weakness
SLUICE backhatch, breach, cataract, channel, clough, clow, conduit, current, drain, drench, fender, floodgate, flume, flush, gash, gote, gout, launder, opening, passage, penstock, pipe, sasse, scour, sewer, stream, swill, tom, torrent, trough, valve, vent, wash, wastweir, watergate, weir
regulator catpiece
SLUIT ditch, gulch, gully, mire, slough
SLUM alley, barriada, barrio, bidonville, bustee, busti, dump, favela, ghetto, hole, hooverville, jargon, junk, palaver, pigpen, pigsty, rookery, room, shantytown, slime, stable, sty, warren, vecindade
SLUMBER deaden, doze, drowse, jook, jouk, repose, rest, SLEEP, sloom, snooze, stupefy
SLUMBEROUS calm, drowsy, peaceful, sleepy, somnolent
SLUMGULLION drink,

hash, lipperings, servant, stew
SLUMMOCK slattern, sloven
SLUMMY crowded, dirty, sordid, squalid
SLUMP bang, bog, decline, decrease, depreciate, depression, desert, deteriorate, droop, drop, fall, flop, gross, landslide, lump, mass, recession, settle, shakeout, sink, slide, slip, sloom, slouch, soss, trollop
SLUR abase, abuse, asperse, aspersion, blot, blur, brand, calumniate, calumny, cheat, conceal, depreciate, dig, disgrace, disguise, disparage, drag, elide, gloss, impure, imputation, indignity, innuendo, insinuate, insinuation, insult, ligature, mackle, macule, malign, mask, mud, offend, reproach, rush, shuffle, skim, skip, slander, slare, slide, slight, slip, slubber, smear, snub, soil, stain, stigma, sully, traduce, trick, vilify
musical ligature
over miss, neglect, scan, skip, slight, soil, sully
SLURRY besmirch, cement, dirty, indistinct, mixture, mortar, mud, smear, soil
SLUSH drench, drivel, drudge, enamel, fund, grease, grout, ice, lopper, loquacity, melt, mire, mud, mush, posh, refuse, scullion, sentimentality, sleech, slime, slodder, slosh, sloven, sludder, sluice, slutch, swosh, toil, wash
SLUSHY sloppy, sloshy, splashy
SLUT befoul, bitch, candle, cocotte, dowd, dratchell, drossel, girl, harlot, jade, PROSTITUTE, quean, slattern, strumpet, tart, trollop, wanton, woman
SLUTCH See SLUSH.
SLUTHER idle, mud, shuffle, slide, slime, slip
SLUTTISH disorderly, filthy, gross, lewd, SLOPPY, slovenly, sordid
SLY acute, arch, artful, astute, bootleg, cagey, canny, cautelous, clandestine, clever, coony, covert, crafty, crooked, cunning, cute, deceitful, deceptive,

devious, evasive, feline, foxy, furtive, guileful, huggermugger, insidious, loopy, mischievous, oblique, retiary, secret(ive), shrewd, skillful, slee, slink(y), slip, sloan, smart, snaky, sneaky, stealthy, subtle, tricky, underhand, unfrank, vulpine, wary, wily, wink, wise

as fox, old boots

SMACK bang, bit, blow, boat, bracozzo, buss, crack, cutter, dash, delight, flavor, gouff, gusto, heroin, hit, kiss, liking, mouthful, noise, odor, patch, potch, plump, relish, sailboat, sapidity, savor, shade, slap, sloop, smattering, snack, snap, sound, soupcon, spanker, squarely, strain, streak, strike, suddenly, suggestion, tang, taste, tincture, tinge, touch, trace, trow, vein, vestige

-dab directly, squarely
into collide
of resemble

SMACKER blow, buffet, dollar

SMACKING active, brisk, fast, good, large, lively, spanking

SMAIK peasant, rascal, rogue, scamp, scoundrel

SMALL atomic(al), baby, bantam, base, beady, bitty, brief, capsule, chintzy, common, cursory, dab, dawny, diluted, diminutive, dinky, dwarf(ish), fine, gentle, grubby, humble, illiberal, inconsequential, inconsiderable, infinitesimal, lessen, light, lil, lilliputian, limited, lite, little, low, meager, mean, microscopic, miniature, miniscule, minute, moderate, modest, nanitic, narrow, negligible, paltry, peanut, petite, petty, pic(ayune), piccolo, piddling, pink, plain, poky, puny, reedy, scant(y), scrimpy, simple, skimpy, slender, slight, superficial, teen(s)y(ween(s)y), thin, thrifty, thumbnail, tiny, trifling, trivial, unimportant, vest-pocket, weak, wee(ny)

amount See **AMOUNT**
small.

bore insular, parochial
-clothes breeches, shorts, underwear
comb. cule, culum, culus, lepto, micro, mio, olig(o), steno, tapin(o)
cranberry fenberry
extremely minutissimic
-footed micropodal
-fruited microcarpous
fry child(ren), diminutive, kid(s), nonentity, petty, sprat, tot(s), youngster(s), youth
-headed microcephalic
holder toftman
hours dawn, morning
-leaved microphyllous
-minded calculated, mean, narrow, petty, prejudiced, selfish, sordid, stingy, ungenerous, vindictive
portion modicum
scale dwarf, miniature
-skulled microcranous
talk babble, chat, chitchat, gossip, prattle
-time bush(league), insignificant, modest, petty, two-bit
-timer piker
-town provincial
very dwarf(ish), minikin, minute, pygmy, teeny, tiddley
world microcosm
years childhood

SMALLAGE celery, parsley

SMALLER less(er), minor
comb. meio, mio

SMALLEST first, least, minim(us), titman, youngest

SMALLNESS bigotry, exility, fewness, paucity, scarcity

SMALLPOX alastrim, variola
goddess mariamman, shitala
marked with fretten, pitted, pocked, pockmarked

SMALLY finely, minutely, scantily, slenderly

SMALM coddle, flatter, plaster, smear

SMALT asmalte, azure, cobalt-glass, eschel, powder-blue, royal, zaffer

SMARAGD beryl, emerald

SMARM flatter, gush, slobber, smalm

SMARMY bootlicking, flattering, gushing, servile, slobbery, unctious

SMART 3 apt 4 ache, braw, burn, chic, fire, flip, foxy, hurt, keen, neat, pain, pert, pink, posh, smug, tony, trig, trim 5 acute, alert, brave, brisk, clean, elite, grief, heady, jimmy, kippy, large, natty, nifty, nobby, nutty, peert, prick, quick, sassy, saucy, sharp, showy, sleek, slick, spicy, sting, swell, swish, toney, witty 6 active, adroit, astute, bonton, bright, cheesy, chichi, classy, clever, dapper, dressy, expert, flashy, jaunty, modish, shrewd, smooth, snappy, spiffy, sporty, spruce, sprucy, swanky, swishy, tingle 7 alamode, brawlie, brawlys, capable, dashing, elegant, knowing, popular, prickle, pungent, remorse, stylish, toffish, tricksy 8 dextrous, impudent, spirited, stinging, tingling, vogu(e)ish 9 brilliant, competent, dexterous, exclusive, ingenious, recherche 10 affliction, precocious, punishment 11 fashionable, intelligent, quick-witted, resourceful, well-dressed, well-groomed 12 considerable

aleck brazenface, cheeker, flip, hussy, malapert, minx, saucebox, wiseguy
-alecky impudent, sassy, saucy, smarty
set See **SOCIETY.**

SMARTEN brighten, dandify, spruce(up), sprucify, tit(t)ivate

SMARTNESS sass, snap, style, swish

SMARTWEED culerage, persicaria, redknees, redleaf, water-pepper

SMASH annihilate, bang, bankruptcy, bash, batter, beverage, blow, break, bump, cave, clatter, clout, collapse, collide, collision, crash, crush, dash, debacle, defeat, demolish, destroy, drink, hall, hit, mash, misfortune, panic, pash, patch, potch, pound, powder, pulp, pulverize, ruin, sensation, shatter, socko, soften, stampede, stave, stramash, stroke, success, triumph, wreck

-and-grab robbery

up collapse, collide, collision, crash, defeat, failure, impact, ruin, stramash, wreck

SMASHED bung, drunk, intoxicated, lit, stewed, stoned, stoven

SMASHER caddie, caddy, fence, slouch-hat

SMASHING cracking, crushing, effective, extraordinary, fine, great, marvelous, stupendous, successful

SMATCHET boor, imp, jerk, peasant

SMATTER babble, bits, break, chatter, clatter, dabble, defile, fragments, patter, shatter, smut, spatter, spot

SMATTERER dabbler, dilettante, sciolist

SMATTERING bit, sciolism, smack, smatch, superficiality, tincture, tinge, touch

SMEAR 3 hit, lie, mud 4 blob, blot, blur, coat, daub, gaum, glob, gorm, rout, slop, slur, smut, soil, spot 5 abuse, begum, brand, cloud, cover, dirty, glair, glaze, knock, libel, muddy, salve, shame, slare, smalm, smarm, spoil, stain, sully, taint 6 anoint, befoul, beslab, blotch, canard, defame, defeat, defile, macule, malign, revile, shmeer, slurry, smirch, smooch, smudge, smutch, spread, streak, vilify 7 asperse, attaint, begrime, blacken, detract, obscure, pollute, slander, spatter, splotch, tarnish, traduce, whisper 8 besmirch, birdlime, disgrace, maculate, muckrake, mudsling, roorback, slaister, vilipend 9 besmatter, denigrate, disparage, glissando 10 defamation, defilement, obliterate, stigmatize 11 denigration 12 vilification

dab flatfish, marysole

dock good-king-henry

-sheet tabloid

with tar pay

with wax cere

SMEARCASE cottage cheese

SMEARY adhesive, blotchy, blurred, dauby, gaumy, greasy, scovy, smudgy, soiled, sticky, viscous

SMEDDUM clay, dust, ore,

powder, shale, slack, spirit, vigor

SMEE duck, merganser, pochard, smew, widgeon

SMEETH haze, mist, powder, smooth

SMELL aroma, bouquet, breathe, detect, distinguish, emanation, essence, fetor, find, flair, flavo(u)r, fragrance, fume, fust, inhale, nidor, nose, odo(u)r, olfact, perfume, redolence, reek, savor, scent, seek, smack, smeech, sniff, snook, snuff, stench, stink, tang, trace, trail, whiff

acuteness hyperosmia

a rat doubt, scent, suspect

bad reek, stink

comb. brom(o), osma, osmo, ozo

-feast parasite, sponger

having disagreeable fetid, foul, nasty, olid, stinking, stinky

loss anosmia, anosphresia

offensive fetor, mephitis, nidor, reek, stench, stink

out detect, trace

pert. olfactory

science of osmics

sense of olfaction, osmesis, osphresis

-smock anemone, cuckooflower, libertine, roue

strong hogo, stench

SMELLER antenna, bristle, feeler, nose, snoop, whisker

SMELLING aromatic, olfaction, osmesis, scented, **SMELLY**

salts ammonia, hartshorn, sal-volatile

-stick sassafras

SMELLY fetid, foul, fuggy, odorous, offensive, olid, putrid, rank, stinking

SMELT argentina, athreinops, cap(e)lin, decoct, eliquate, eperlan, fish, flux, fuse, gull, hypomesus, icefish, inanga, melt, osmerid, osmerus, peixere, reduce, refine, render, retropinna, salmonid, sand-launce, scorify, silverside, simpleton, smolt, smoothtongue, sparling, sperling, spirinchus, tomcod, trout

-like candlefish

two guinea

young prim

SMELTING *by-product* dregs, dross, refuse, slag

cone pina

mixture matte, speiss

operation campaign

prepare for beneficiate

SMERDIS *brother* cambyses

SMETANA *opera* bartered bride

SMEW diver, duck, merganser, mergus, nun

SMICKER elegant, finical, gay, handsome, smile, smirk(ing), spruce, wanton

SMIDGE(N) atom, bit, dab, iota, mite, particle, smicket, smitch, speck, tittle, trace, whit

SMILAX bamboo-brier, bindweed, briarroot, bullgrip, carrionflower, chinaroot, greenbrier, lilium, lily, sarsa

pert. smilacaceous

product sarsaparilla

SMILE approve, beam, drink, favor, fleer, greet, grin, laugh, rejoice, simper, smicker, smirkle, sneer

affected smirk

SMILING agrin, cheerful, merry, riant, rident, smirky, twinkly

SMINTHEUS apollo

SMIRCH asoil, begrime, blacken, blemish, blot(ch), degrade, discolor, dishonor, smear, smit, smudge, smutch, soil, stain, stigma, sully, tarnish

SMIRK drad, grin, leer, mince, pleasant, quick, ridicule, simper, smart, smile, smiling, smurtle, snort, spruce, trim, yirn

SMIT blow, clay, cut, disgrace, infect, jingle, ruddle, smirch, smut, spot, stain, stroke, tarnish

SMITCH bit, jot, particle, scorch, smidge(n), smither, smoke, smut, spot, whit

SMITE affect, afflict, beat, chasten, collide, cuff, destroy, drive, enamour, gird, hammer, hit, hurl, impress, injure, kill, knock, lay low, pierce, pummel, punish, slap, strike, trouble, visit, wound

SMITH armorer, blacksmith, bosser, farrier, forgeman, forger, glutter, hephaestus, horseshoer, metalist, metalworker, mime, mimit, regin, smug, vulcan

SMITH, ADAM *work* wealth of nations

SMITHEREENS atoms, bits, flinders, fragments, pieces

SMITHSONITE azulite, calamine, monheimite

SMITHY farriery, forge, foundry, smiddy, stithy, studdie

-dander cinder

SMITTEN affected, afflicted, attracted, besotted, drawn, enamo(u)red, epris(e), farchadat, infatuated, stricken, struck

SMITTLE contagious, infect(ious), likely, possess, seize, venomous

SMOCK apron, camise, chemise, dress, garment, jibbah, jumper, philander, robe, shift, shirr, smicket, tunic, woman

SMOG brume, fog, haze, mist, peasoup, poison, pollution, vapor

component fog, ozone, smoke

control device afterburner

disease emphysema

SMOKE anger, baconize, blast, cheroot, cigar(ette), cure, detect, drunk, dry, escape, fag, fireside, flee, floc, fume, fumigate, fumous, funk, gray, havana, haze, hearth, home, inhale, liquor, lunt, mist, notice, obfuscate, observe, perfume, pipe, puff, reek, ridicule, roke, scent, shaugh, signal, smart, smaze, smeek, smell, smitch, smog, smolder, smore, smother, smudge, smush, speed, stain, stive, stogie, suspect, tobacco, trivia, vapor(ize), whiff

and fog smog

and haze smaze

-colored fumous

comb. atmid(o), atmo

cure by reest

giggle See MARIJUANA.

indian kinnikinnick

joy See MARIJUANA.

outlet chimney, flue, fumeduct, fumiduct

pert. fumatory

producing fumiferous

quartz cairngorm

signals bush telegraph

tree chittamwood, cotinus, fustet, fustic, scotino, sumac, zante(wood)

wisp floc

SMOKEHOUSE fumatory

SMOKEJACK brain, flue, funnel, head, stackman

SMOKER auto, car, curlew, funker, party, stag, tobacconist

SMOKESTACK chimney, funnel, pipe, tunnel

SMOKING areek, tux(edo)

apparatus briar, brier, hookah, nargile, pipe, tabagie

mixture charas, churrus

room divan, fumistery, tabagie

SMOKY blackened, dingy, dirty, fumacious, fumid, fumish, fumose, fumy, hazy, reeky, smoldering, smudgy, smuisty, sooty, suspicious, tarnished, thick

city pittsburgh

SMOLDER anger, burn, choke, darken, simmer, smoke, smother, smudge, smush, suffocate

SMOLLET, T. *novel* humphrey clinker, peregrine pickle, roderick random

SMOLT bright, clam, clear, fish, salmon, smelt, smooth, smout, sprod

SMOOCH kiss, lallygag, loaf, lollygag, smear, soil

SMOODGE, SMOOGE fawn, flatter, pamper, pat, wheedle

SMOOTH 3 dab, dub, lay, mow 4 buff, calm, ease, easy, even, fine, flat, glib, iron, lene, mild, oily, pave, sand, soft 5 bland, brant, brent, clear, dress, flush, gloss, gloze, grade, level, light, plain, plane, press, quiet, shave, sleek, slick, soapy, suant, suave 6 creamy, fettle, fluent, glossy, harrow, lubric, mangle, placid, polish, polite, refine, satiny, serene, silken, simple, soften, soothe, svelte, unfret, urbane 7 burnish, cunning, equable, flatten, placate, plaster, politic, regular, settled, sleekit, uniform 8 composed, explicit, friendly, glabrate, glabrous, hairless, levigate, minimize, palliate, pleasant, polished, slippery, unbroken, unctuous 9 courteous, unruffled 10 diplomatic, lu-

bricious, unwrinkled 12 ingratiating 13 uninterrupted

blenny shanny

-chinned beardless

comb. lei(o), leur(o), lio, liss(o)

dogfish blue-dog, carcharias, sand-shark

excessively unctuous

-faced bland(ishing), specious

over appease, calm, glaze, gloss, gloze, minimize

phonetically lene

-spoken or *-tongued* adulatory, flattering, fluent, gentle, glib, hypocritical, ingratiating, persuasive, plausible

the way facilitate, lubricate

-tongue smelt

winterberry canhoop, ilex

SMOOTHER abradant, abrasive, buff(er), calender(er), chamois, drag, flatiron, glazer, loose, grader, harrow, iron, mangle, plane, polisher, press(er), roller, rollingpin, sadiron, sleeker, slicker, sponger, steamroller, trowel

SMOOTHLY easily, evenly, glibly, nicely, politely, regularly, sprousy, sweetly, uniformly

SMOOTHNESS ease, fluency, hypocrisy, levigation, lubrication, lubricity, suavity, urbanity

SMORGASBORD antipasto, aperitif, appetizer, buffet, hors d'oeuvres

SMOT brand, mark, stain

SMOTHER befog, blanket, burke, choke, conceal, daub, deaden, extinguish, fog, hush up, kill, moderate, muffle, overlie, queason, quench, quezen, repress, restrain, smoke, smolder, smore, smudder, smudge, stifle, suffocate, suppress, throttle, welter

SMOUCH cheat, filch, kiss, pilfer, shmooch, smack, smutch, trick

SMUDGE begrime, blot, blur, chuckle, daub, dirt, grime, laugh, macule, prink, smear, smile, smoke, smolder, smother, smug, smut(ch), soil, soot, spatter, spot, stain, stigma, sut, vapor

SMUG affected, blacksmith,

bland, clean, complacent, correct, dig, fresh, grind, neat, pilfer, prig(gish), prudish, sanctimonious, self-satisfied, sleek, smart, smudge, smush, spruce, steal, tidy, trim, vain, well-kept

SMUGGLER bootlegger, contrabandist, rumrunner, spotsman

amateur burro, mule

SMUSH crush, mash, smart, smoke, smolder, smug

SMUT blight, bunt, coom, crock, defile, dirt, filth, fly, fungus, gnat, mark, midge, obscenity, porno(graphy), powder, remainder, scatology, smit, smudge, smutch, soil, soot, stain, sully, taint

genus sorosporium, tilletia, urocystis, ustilago

grass black medic, blackseed, tussock

SMUTCH blacken, defile, dirty, grime, smirch, smitch, smooch, smudge, smut, soil, soot, stain, stigma, sully, taint, tinge, touch, trace

SMUTSIA anteater, armadillo, pangolin

SMUTTY bawdy, dirty, dusky, indecent, obscene, pornographic, salacious, sexy, soiled, sooty, sordid, tainted

SMUZZ ado, stir

SMYRNA izmir, ushak

carpet akhissar

fig eleme, elemi

native smyrniot(e)

SNACK acute, adroit, alert, ball, bever, bit(e), canape, chack, coffee-and, eat, elevenses, grasping, hors d'oeuvre, jibe, latch, lunch, morsel, mouthful, mungey, noshen, nosher, part, piece, portion, quick(ly), repast, share, sharply, sip, smack, snap, snatch, snick, tapa, taste

bar dinette, lunchroom

SNAFFLE bit, bradoon, bridle, bridoon, check, curb, foil, gag, harness, loot, pilfer, restraint, saunter, snuffle, steal

and rein bridoon

SNAFU chaos, chaotic, confusion, disorder(ed), mess, muddle, queer

SNAG bar, block, carp, catch, clog, cut, danger, difficulty, fault, hew, hindrance, impediment, lop, nag, obstacle, obstruction, projection, protuberance, secure, slug, snail, snug, stub, stump, tangle, tear, tie up, tine, tooth, trim, vicissitude

SNAIL (See also *genus,* below.) abalone, achatina, alectrion, amphibola, ampullaria, ancylus, auricula, bittium, cam, cassidid, cerion, chenille, chink, conker, coret, dodman, drill, drone, earshell, escargot, gastropod, haliotis, helicid, helix, hoddydoddy, hodmadod, hua, janthina, laggard, lymnaeid, mollusk, natica, neritoid, nudibranch, periwinkle, physid, pila, purple, ramshorn, slowpoke, slug(gard), snag, solarium, testudo, thais, turbo, unicorn, vertigo, welk, whelk, wilk, winkle, zonitid

carrier xenophora

clam-killing winkle

family pupillidae

flower caracol(e)

flying pteropod

fresh-water planorbis, valvata, viviparus

genus bulimus, clausilia, fusus, latirus, melania, mitra, modulus, nerita, physa, planorbis, triton, truncatella

land achatinid, bulimus, urocoptis, vitrina

-like late, slow, tardy

marine alectrion, amphibola, archetectonica, aspidobranchiate, bittium, busycon, calyptraea, conus, cymbium, eulima, fasciolaria, fusus, marginella, mitra, natica, nerita, nudibranch, pedicularia, phasianella, pleurotoma, pterocera, ranella, stenoglossa, thais, topshell, triton, turbinella, turbo, venus's-comb

shell cochlea, conker, hodmandod, triton

-shell-shaped cochleate, cochleiform

SNAKE (See also *genus* and *kind,* below.) coil, crawl,

crook, drag, draw, filch, ingrate, jerk, meander, ophidian, pull, reptile, serpent, skid, slither, sneak, spiral, spitter, steal, turn, twist, viper, wind, worm, yank

aquatic cerberus

bite bloodroot, trillium, wake-robin

bite remedy cedron, guaco, snakeroot, snakestone

black coluber, hoplocephalus, notechis, ocyophis, quirt, racer, whip, zamenis

-blenny prickleback

blind lizard, typhlops

blunt-tailed rubber boa

boa aboma, epicrates

boat pambanmanche

brown diemenia, potamophis, storeria

burrowing gopher, rainbow

charmer's instrument been, pungi

coil fold

colubrid mussurana, natrix, zamenis

comb. angui, herpet(o), ophi, ophid(io), ophio, ophis, serpenti

constricting anaconda, boa, camoodi(e), camoudie

coral candystick, ilysia

dancer hopi, moqui, taos

deadly See *poisonous,* below.

doctor dragonfly, hellgrammite

-eater markhor, secretary bird

expert herpetologist

eyes aces, ambace, ones, two

fabled yacumama

fear of herpetophobia

flower blueweed, campion, starflower, stitchwort

garter elaps

gentian lion's-foot

genus boa, carphophis, crotalus, elaphe, elaps, eryx, leptophis, mehelya, micrurus, naja, ophidia

god sabazios, zombi

grass forget-me-not, stitchwort

-haired woman eurale, gorgon, medusa, stheno

harmless See *non-poisonous,* below.

hognose chunkhead, puffing adder

hooded cobra

horned cerastes

in the grass ambush, danger, deceiver, threat, traitor

killer mongoose, roadrunner, secretary bird

kind 3 asp, boa, bom, cat, nag 4 boba, boid, jubo, lora, naja, snig 5 aboma, adder, aspic, cobra, congo, coral, cribo, drill, jiboa, krait, mamba, ptyas, racer, tiger, viper 6 bongar, cantil, chital, daboia, elapid, gopher, hisser, ilysia, jessur, katuka, kerril, python, ribbon, roller, runner, taipan, wenona 7 adjiger, aniliid, bokadam, camoodi, coluber, crawler, creeper, culebra, diamond, diapsid, elapine, hagowrm, labaria, langaha, prester, regulus, walpapi 8 anaconda, bonetail, bungarum, cascavel, cerastes, coralito, crotalid, crotalus, eggeater, flathead, hairworm, jararaca, keelback, moccasin, ringhals, viperine 9 boomslang, coachwhip, colubrine, cowsucker, mussurana, rubber boa 10 bandybandy, bushmaster, candystick 11 aesculapius 12 aglyphodonta, proteroglyph

-like anquine, apodal, colubrine, herpetiform, ophidian, serpentine, sinuous, snaky, viperine

lizard seps

mackerel gemphlid

marine chital

-milk spurge

monster ellops

mouth orchid, pogonia

non-poisonous amblycephal(us), boa, coluber, elaphe, garter, musserana

oil liquor, remedy

pert. anguine, colubrine, herpetic, herpetous, ophidian, ophiod, reptilian, serpentine, serpentoid

piece pointer

pipe horsetail

plantain ribwort

poisonous asp, cobra, copperhead, coral, cottonmouth, krait, mamba, proteroglyph, rattler, rattlesnake, tapa, viper

scale gastrostege, scute

-shaped anguiform, serpentine

skin exuvia, hackle, slough, spoil

spitting ringhals

stone ammonite

terrestrial pulmonifera

thousand-headed ananta, sesha, shesha

-tongue moonwort, spearwort

tree boomslang, lora

venomous See *poisonous*, above.

water anaconda

yellow boa

SNAKEBARK colubrina, ironbark, nakedwood

SNAKEBERRY baneberry, bittersweet, byrony, partridgeberry

SNAKEBIRD anhinga, darter, ducklar, plotus, wryneck

SNAKEHEAD figwort, murral, turtlehead

SNAKEROOT asarum, babroot, birthwort, bistort, bitterbush, blazing-star, blolly, bugbane, cohosh, eryngo, gaywings, liatris, poolwort, richweed, sangrel, sanicle, sawwort, seneca, senega, stevia, whitetop, wild ginger

SNAKEWEED See SNAKEROOT.

SNAKEWORM carphiophiops, carphoplis, sciara

SNAKY angry, anguine, meandrous, perfidious, serpentine, sinuous, sly, spiteful, touchy, treacherous, venomous, wavy, wriggly, zigzag

sisters furies

SNAP bargain, bark, biscuit, bit, bite, break, breeze, bubble, capture, catch, center, chack, cheat, cinch, click, close, cloyer, cookie, cozener, crack(le), crepitation, elan, elasticity, energy, facility, fastener, fellow, fillip, flask, flick, flip, fracture, grasp, growl, handcuff, hasty, instant, jiffy, lad, morsel, noise, photo(graph), pop, pounce, puncheon, quick, report, resilience, scintillate, scrap, seize, sharper, sinecure, smack, smart, snack, snarl, snatch, spark, spell, stamp, steal, strike, tap, throw, vigor, vim

at grab, growl, hanch, seize, snarl

back recoil, recover, retort

up bargains snup

SNAPDRAGON antirrhinum, bulldog, buller, bunnymouth, calf's-snout, dogmouth, manyroot, toadflax, tongs

SNAPE bevel, check, disappoint, flinch, nip, rebuke, snub, stint, taper

SNAPJACK stitchwort

SNAPPER biajaiba, bluefish, bream, brim, cabellerote, caji, clipper, cockney, cosaque, countfish, cracker, cubera, error, grouper, jocu, lawyer, lutianus, native, pargo, phainopepla, rosefish, sesi, stitchwort, stringbean, stumble, tamure, uku, ulaula, voraz, whopper, willomai, woodpecker

SNAPPING *beetle* elater(id), skipjack, skipper

turtle loghead, shagtail

SNAPPISH angry, brittle, cranky, crisp, cross, curt, doggish, edgy, fretful, huffy, irascible, ired, irritable, morose, peevish, petulant, puxy, short, snippy, techy, testy, touchy, waspish, waspy

SNAPPY active, acute, brisk, chic, cold, crackling, dashing, fast, keen, lively, modish, piquant, prompt, pungent, quick, racy, ready, sharp, smart, spicy, sudden, zestful, zesty, zippy

SNAPSHOT photo(graph), picture, tintype

SNAPWOOD spicebush

SNARE ambush, bag, bait, beclap, bind, bindlime, booby(trap), brake, capture, catch, cop, deception, decoy, drum, enmesh, entrap, feint, fraud, gin, grin, inveigle, keddah, lime, lure, maneuver, mesh, nab, net, noose, panter, pitfall, ruse, seduce, snarl, snickle, snirl, springe, steal, stratagem, toils, trap(an), trepan, trick(ery), tunnel, web, wile, withe

SNARK boojum, fault, find, missile, nag, snore, snort

SNARL anvil, bark, bowwow, bumble, carl, catch, chaos, clamor, clutter, complicate, complication, confuse, confusion, congestion, disarray, discord, disorder, embrangle, entangle, fight, flare (up), gaunch, gnar(l), gnarr, grizzle, growl, harl, hurr, involve, jam, jangle, jumble, knot, knurl, mess, mucker, muddle, muss, ogganition, pie, protest, quarrel, ravel, scold, snap, snare, sough, strangle, tangle, thunder, twine, twit, venner, waff, yarr, yirr

SNARLED snafu

SNARLY ill-natured, latrant, peevish, surly, tangled

SNARY entangling, insidious

SNASH abuse, gibing, insolence, insult(ing)

SNATCH abduct, bit, capture, catch, clawk, clutch, cop, erept, escape, filch, ganch, get, grab, grasp, grip, hap, kidnap, lift, nab, nip, part, piece, pilfer, pluck, reach, remove, scamble, seize, seizure, snack, snap, snare, steal, swipe, swoop, take, trap, twitch, wrap, wrench, wrest, yerk, yuck

SNATCHY interrupted, irregular, spasmodic

SNEAK ambush, couch, cringe, dastard, escape, filch, lurk, mag, meech, peach, peak, pilfer, pimp, prowl, pry, quail, rogue, shab, shirk, shug, skulk, slink, slounge, sneap, snick, snoop, spy, steal, tattle, thief, thieve, weasel
away slipe, sloke

SNEAKER creeper, gumshoe, plimsoll, shoe, slipper, step-in, tennis-shoe, thief

SNEAKING contemptible, cowardly, craven, creeping, dastardly, furtive, hidden, mean, niggardly, paltry, peaking, poor, secret, sliving, sly, stealthy, surreptitious, underhand

SNEAKY covert, cowardly, deceitful, recreant, secretive, stealthy, yellow
pete liquor, wine

SNEAP check, chide, snape, sneak, spy

SNEB bar, bolt, fasten, rebuke, reprimand, snub

SNECK catch, click, cut, latch, snick, take
-band latchstring
-posset rebuff

SNED lop, prune, snathe

SNEE cut, dagger, dirk, knife, sny

SNEER belittle, deride, disdain, fleer, flird, flout, flurn, gibe, gird, gizzer, gleek, grimace, grin, jaunt, jeer, jibe, mock, ridicule, scoff, scorn, scout, shy, slare, slon, snicker, snort, taunt, wrinkle

SNEEZE dismiss, kerchoo, neese, snuff, sternutate, sternutation
at condemn, despise, disregard, scorn
-causing errhine, pollen, sternutative
pert. errhine, sternutatory
word gesundheit

SNEEZEWEED alant, helenium, ragweed, rosilla, sandyblight

SNEEZEWOOD nieshout

SNEEZEWORT achillea, ball-of-snow, hardhead, hellebore, ptarmica, ptarmite

SNEEZY *friend* See SEVEN *dwarfs.*

SNELL active, acute, biting, caustic, eager, ganging, gut, hard, harsh, keen, piercing, pungent, quick(ly), severe, sharp, snood, swift(ly), tippet, vigorous(ly)

SNIB bar, bolt, capture, catch, check, entrap, fasten (ing), reprimand, reproof, snub, snuff, trap

SNICK bit, cut, latch, nick, part, pierce, portion, share, snack, sneck, snip, strike, tip

SNICKER giggle, laugh, knife, nicker, ridicule, smirkle, snickersnee, snigger, sniggle, teehee, titter, whinny

SNIDE base, counterfeit, dirty, inferior, mean, punk, spurious, supercilious

SNIFF detect, dudgeon, feeler, inhale, inspire, insufflate, nose, perceive, scent, scorn, smell, snaff(le), snivel, snuff, trace, vent, whiff, wind

SNIFFLE(S) cold, rheum, rhinitis, roup, snivel, snotter, snuff(le), whimper

SNIFTER blow, cold, dilemma, drink, inhaler, moment, reverse, slug, sniff, snivel, snort, storm, tot

SNIG chop, drag, eel, jerk, lop, pilfer, snake, sneak

SNIGGLE broggle, catch, eel, ensnare, hook, laugh, sneak, SNICKER, snig, trap

SNIP bit, check, chip, cinch, clip, crewman, crop, curb, cut, filch, fragment, incise, incision, lob, notch, part (icle), piece, share, shorten, shred, snack, snap, snatch, snick, speck, stroke, tailor, thread

SNIPE attack, bird, bleater, blitter, butt, capella, curlew, dowitch(er), duck, ernbleater, fool, gallinago, godwit, heatherbleat, humility, hunt, jack, knot, longbill, nose, sandpiper, sectionhand, shadbird, shoot, skunk, tattler, tool, turnstone, wader, willet
cry scape
eel thread-eel,
fish aulostomi, flutemouth, gar
flock whisp
hawk harrier
painted rostratula
white avocet, sanderling

SNIPEBILL bolt, hinge, plane

SNIPER bushwack, shooter, teaser

SNIPPY blunt, brief, curt, fragmentary, fresh, mean, pert, sassy, saucy, snappish, sniffy, snobbish, snobby, stingy, supercilious, tart

SNIRL gnarl, snarl, tangle, wrinkle

SNIT tizzy

SNITCH betray, blab, cop, filch, inform, lift, nose, particle, peach, pilfer, pinch, purloin, sing, smitch, snatch, sneak, squeal, steal, swipe, tattle, theft

SNIVEL bubble, cant, cry, mucus, pathos, sanctimony, sniff(le), snifter, snotter, snuff(le), weep, whine

SNIVY, SNIVEY contrary, mean, perverse, ugly

SNOB blackleg, bluenose, brahmin, cobbler, commoner, cricket, flunk(e)y, highbrow, high-hatter, knobstick, parvenu, plebian, prig, rat, scab, shoemaker, shoneen, snoot, sob, stuckup, swell, sycophant, toady, townsman

SNOBBISH, SNOBBY arrogant, condescending, dicky, exclusive, highhat, hoity-toity, overbearing, patronizing, priggish, proud, sniffy, snippy, snooty, snotty, sosh, stuckup, superior, uppish, upstage

SNOCKER snore, snort

SNOD cunning, neat, plausible, smooth, snood, snug, trim(med)

SNOGA synagogue

SNOOD fillet, hairnet, snell, snod

SNOOK barracuda, garfish, pry, robalo, scent, search, sergeantfish, smell, sneak, sniff, snoek, snoot

SNOOP brevit, busybody, detective, ferret, gumshoe, look, lurk, meddle(r), peek, peep, piroot, probe, prowl, pry, search, skulk, sneak, spy, thief, voyeur

SNOOPY curious, inquisitive, meddlesome, nosy, obtrusive, prying, sly, sneaky

SNOOSE rappee, SNUFF

SNOOT face, grimace, nose, snout

SNOOTY arrogant, contemptuous, haughty, SNOBBISH, snobby

SNOOZE doze, drowse, nap, siesta, sleep

SNOOZLE cuddle, nuzzle, SNOOZE, snuggle

SNORE jangle, rale, rhonchus, roar, rout, snark, sniff, snocker, snork, snort, snotter, wheeze
pert. stertorous

SNORING rhonchus, stertor

SNORK grunt, snore, snort

SNORT blow, drink, gasp, jeer, laugh, slug, smirk, snark, sneer, sniff, snifter, snore, snorkel, snortle, snur, toot, vent, whoof

SNORTER blow, braggart, powerhouse, rope, snotter, stalwart, wheatear

SNOT blow, mucus, snuff(le), wretch

SNOTTY contemptible, dirty, mean, midshipman, nasty, offensive, offish, slimy, snooty, viscous

SNOUT beak, front, groin, grub, gruntle, jaw, muzzle, nose, nozzle, proboscis,

prow, rostrum, snoot, tobacco, trunk
beetle bollweevil, curculio, platystomid
comb. rhyncho, rhynchus
dig with grout
having pointed oxyrhine
mite bdellid

SNOW cocaine, cover, crystal, defeat, dessert, firn, graupel, grue, heroin, narcotic, neige, neve, nivis, nix, overwhelm, pash, pudding, sleet, sna, sposh, squarerigger, white, winter
and rain sleet
blindness chionablepsia, niphablepsia
-break thaw
bunting oatfowl, snowbird
cock jermonal
comb. chion(o)
depression in sitzmark
drifted windle, yowden
field firn. neve
finch brambling
flea poduran, podurid
flower hepatica
flurry skirl
glacial firn. neve
goose chen. wavy
granular corn. neve
growing in nival
heap drift
house iglo(o), iglu
job flattery
king gustavus adolphus
leopard irbis. ounce
maker frau holle
mass avalanche
melting slob. slush
mound mogul
mountain jokul
mouse pied-lemming, vole
name meaning neva
new-fallen manna
-on-the-mountain ghostweed, spurge
partridge lerwa
pert. nival. niveous
ridge sastrugi. zastrugi
slide avalanche. glissade
study of cryology
under the subniveal
vehicle cariole. coaster. luge, pung. sled(ge). sleigh. toboggan

SNOWBALL cauliflower, guelder-rose, viburnum

SNOWBERRY blolly. moxa, waxberry

SNOWBIRD coaldealer. fieldfare. finch, grouse, junco, ptarmigan

SNOWBUSH ceanothus

SNOWDROP amaryllis, anemone, galanthus, halesia
tree bellwood, cowlicks, tisswood

SNOWFALL flurry, onding, pash, skiff, skift

SNOWFLAKE bunting, crystal, dianthus, finch, flag, flaucht, leucojum, sweetwilliam

SNOWMAN *abominable* yeti
discoverer hodgson

SNOWSHOE bearpaw, pac, patin, patten, racket, racquet, skee, ski, web(foot)
thong babiche

SNOWSTORM blizzard, burga

SNOWY nival, niveous, pure, spotless, white

SNUB abbreviate, avoid, boycott, check, chip, coldshoulder, curb, cut, disdain, highbrow, hinder, humiliate, ignore, neglect, nip, offend, ostracize, pug, putdown, quell, rebuff, rebuke, repress, reprimand, reproof, repulse, restrain, retrousse, scold, scorn, setdown, slap, slight, slur, snag, snib, snool, snoot, snouch, spurn, stumpy, swank, taughten, upbraid, upstage
-nosed simous
-nosed, comb. simo

SNUBBY pug

SNUDGE miser, sneak, sulk

SNUFF aroma, beggar's-brown, bergamot, blackguard, brighten, chafe, clarify, cohoba, copenhagen, disappear, extinguish, heifer-dust, huff, inhale, leavings, lundyfoot, maccaboy, maccoboy, musty, odor, offense, orangery, pinch, pique, pulvil, rappee, remainder, scent, smell, smooth, smutchin, sneesh, sniff, snoose, tabac, umbrage
cheap musty
container See SNUFFBOX.
pinch shmeck, tabac
-taking dipping
up to fine, good

SNUFFBOX mill, mull, puffball, tabatiere, weasand
bean cacoon, entada, liana, mackay

SNUFFLE cant, chafe, fume,

inhale, snaffle, snavel, sniff(le), snivel, twang

SNUFFY annoyed, bad, dirty, disagreeable, displeased, horrid, unattractive, vexed

SNUG bein, bien, canny, close(d), close-fitting, comfortable, comfy, compact, concealed, content, cosh, cosy, couthie, cozy, cuddle, homelike, knob, lew, modest, neat, povie, private, protected, queme, quiet, reticent, safe, seaworthy, secreted, secretive, secure, silent, sizable, slick, snag, snod, snuggle, span, taut, tidy, tight, tosy, trig, trim
down lash, rest, retire

SNUGGERY alcove, den, nest, pub, tavern

SNUGGLE burrow, croodle, cuddle, nest(le), snudge, snuzzle

SNURL snirl, stir up, twist

SO accordingly, ergo, ever, greatly, hence, insomuch, likewise, sae, same, sic, that, then, therefore, thus, true, very
be it amen, okay, okeh, provided
-called alleged, presumed, soi-disant, supposed
far adeo, thus, yet
long goodby, shalom, sholem
-so average, fair, indifferent, intermediate, mediocre, medium, middling, passable, passably, small, tolerable, trifling, unwell

SOAK absorb, alcoholic, bake, bath(e), blow, boil, bowk, bran, brew, charge, cost, dip, douse, drench, drink, drouk, drunk(ard), flush, heat, hit, hurl, imbrue, imbue, immerse, impregnate, inebriate, infiltrate, infuse, inject, insteep, intoxicate, lave, macerate, marinate, overcharge, pawn, penetrate, percolate, permeate, pervade, punch, render, ret, saturate, seethe, sob, sock, sodden, sog, soke, sop, sot, souse, sponge, spree, steep, strike, submerge, surfeit, swamp, swelter, tippler, toper, tosspot, wash, waterlog, weeze, wet
flax rate, ret

in brine corn, cure, marinate, salt

SOAKED draggled, drenched, sodden, sopping, soppy, watery, wet

SOAM chain, rope

SOAP (See also *kind*, below.) abstergent, abstersive, bribe(ry), chips, cleanser, detergent, flatter(y), gogo, lather, money, rub, sapo(ne), saveon, sope, stock, suds, tallate, wash
acid oleic
black knapweed, scabious
comb. sapo
convert into saponify
-frame bar sess
ingredient babassu oil, cetin, fat, lye, palmitin, potash, soda, talc, tallow
kind castile, eschwege, glycerin, green, laundry, liquid, marseilles, saddle, soft, tar
-like compound detergent, saponul
liniment opodeldoc
opera heartstringer, suds, tearjerker
pert. saponaceous
pharmaceutic sapo
plant agave, amole, palmillo, soaproot, soapwort, yucca
plate sess
vine gogo

SOAPBARK quillai, quillaja, soapwood

SOAPBERRY akee, alectryon, allophyllus, blighia, cardiospermum, titoki

SOAPBOX platform, podium, rostrum, stump
center hydepark corner, marble arch, pershing square, union square, washington square

SOAPFISH jabon, synodus

SOAPROOT gypsophila, sand lily

SOAPSTONE alberene, steatite, talc
full of talcose

SOAPSTONER talcer

SOAPSUDS foam, froth, lather

SOAPWORT borith, bouncing bess, bruisewort, cowherb, daisy, floptop, pink, saponary
gentian calathian-violet

SOAPY adulatory, bland, flattering, ingratiating, lathered, oily, oleaginous, sa-

ponaceous, sleek, smooth, soft, suave, sudsy, unctuous

SOAR arise, ascend, aspire, climb, dart, flight, flit, float, fly, glide, hover, kite, levitate, lift, mount, plane, rise, rocket, sail, top, tower, transcend, wing

SOARING essorant, flight, icarian, rising, spiring

SOB blubber, cry, frighten, groan, moan, respite, rest, sab, sigh, simper, sithe, soak, sough, wail, weep, whimper, yex, yoop
-sister journalist
-story alibi, tearjerker

SOBBY damp, soppy, wet

SOBER abstemious, abstinent, ailing, ascetic, austere, calm, chasten, collected, composed, continent, cool, decorous, dignified, dispassionate, dry, earnest, feeble, formal, gentle, grave, heavy, indifferent, moderate, peaceful, pensive, poor, proper, quiet, rational, reasonable, regular, sane, sedate, sensible, serious, settled, solemn, somber, staid, steady, subdue(d), temper(ate), thoughtful, unimpassioned, weighty, wise

SOBK demon, devil

SOBRIETY abstemiousness, abstinence, austerity, continence, dignity, gravity, moderation, restraint, sanity, solemnity, temperance
symbol of ass

SOBRIQUET agname, alias, byname, cognomen, epithet, handle, nickname, title

SOC See DISTRICT.

SOCCER football
player booter, inner, kicker
star pele

SOCIABLE accessible, affable, agreeable, amiable, carriage, chatty, chummy, communicative, companionable, cozy, familiar, folksy, friendly, gregarious, informal, jovial, matey, social, sofa, soiree, tea, tricycle

SOCIAL affable, affair, communal, convivial, cooperative, gathering, gregarious, hospitable, neighborly, party, popular, public, SOCIABLE, supper, tea, tribal

climber parvenu, shtoop, shtup, snob, upstart
disparity inequality
gathering at-home, ball, bee, blowout, cantico, club, dance, party, reception, reunion, smoker, soiree, stag, tea
group caste, clan, class, clique, coterie, estate, family, fraternity, lodge, sept, sorority, tribe
lion big shot, celebrity, magnate
person butterfly, host(ess), mixer
outcast leper, pariah
register blue-book, four-hundred, society
service charity, philanthropy
solidarity asabiyya
standing caste, estate, rank
system feudal, regime, tribal
worker almoner, analyst, clinician, do-gooder, philanthropist
SOCIALISM collectivism, communism, etatism, fabianism, fourierism, guesdism, owenism, phalansterianism, saintsimonianism, syndicalism, utopianism
SOCIALIST anarchist, bolshevik, bolshevist, collectivist, communist, etatist, fabian, manchesterist, marxist, red
famous bellamy, cabet, debs, engels, fourier, jaures, lasalle, marx, mclevy, morris, owen, proudhon, ruskin, saint-simon, shaw, sunyat-sen, thomas
SOCIETY academy, alliance, aristocracy, association, band, beau monde, body, bonton, brotherhood, bund, circle, class, clique, club, college, colony, colorum, community, companionship, company, congregation, coterie, council, county, court, elite, establishment, ethnos, exchange, familistere, familistery, family, fellowship, folk, four-hundred, fraternity, gentlefolk, gentry, group, guild, haut monde, herd, hetaeria, high life, league, lodge, mankind, mayfair, monde, nanigo, nobility, order, party, population, power structure, sabha, salon, samaj, sangh,

smart set, social register, sodality, sokol, sorority, system, the rich, thiasos, tong, union, upper crust, vanity fair, verein
aversion anthropophobia, aphilanthropy, misanthropy
charitable confraternity, sodality
choral choir, glee club
craft artel
division caste, class
entrance debut
gymnastic sokol
high bonton, haut monde, upper crust
island bora bora, tahiti
island capital papeete
island tree aitoa
low rabble, riffraff
membership list blue book, social register
primitive commune
religious amana, brotherhood
secret black hand, camorra, carbonari, egbo, fraternity, hoey, hui, kkk, la cosa nostra, la mano nera, lodge, maf(f)ia, masons, ogboni, poro, purrah, rosicrucian, sorority, syndicate, tong
study of demotics, sociology, socionomy
swell nob, toff
symbol regalia
SOCINIAN *sect* adorantes
SOCIUS associate, fellow, god, individual, member
SOCK anklet, argyle, beat, biff, blow, bootie, bop, buskin, bust, comedy, dainties, drainage, drive, food, footwear, HIT, hose, hurl, indulge, plowshare, punch, sandal, shoe, sigh, slap, slipper, smack, soak, sok(e), stocking, STRIKE, tabi, tabo, treat, udo, vamp, windcone
SOCKDOLAGER answer, argument, blow, clincher, decided, end, facer, oner, rouser
SOCKET alveola, alveolus, box, cavity, cell, chamber, depression, ferrule, futchel, holder, hub, mortise, nose, nozzle, outlet, pit, pocket, pod, pore, receptacle, recess, sconce, shank, shoe, slit, slot, torulus
SOCKEYE blueback, salmon
SOCO bird, bittern, heron

SOCRATES *biographer* plato
consort myrto
death description phaedo
death potion hemlock
dialogue apologia, crito, meno, phaedo
disciple aristippus, ceres, plato, xenophon
escape plotter crito
friend apollodorus
intimate alcibiades, crito
method maieutic
parent phaenarete, sophroniscus
persecutor charicles, critias
wife xant(h)ippe
SOD boiled, clod, clower, delf, divot, earth, fermented, flag, glebe, grass, greensward, ground, land, peat, scraw, seethe, soak, sodden, soggy, soil, sonk. sward, terron, turf
-buster farmer
SODA alkali, barilla, bellywash, beverage, bicarb(onate), pop, sal(eratus), sodium bicarbonate
and claret badminton
-ash plant barilla
baking saleratus
biscuit cracker
mica pragonite
plant atriplex, barilla, salsola, saltbush, saltwort
pop cola, gingerbeer, pepsi, tonic
water seltzer
SODACLASE feldspar
SODDEN bloated, boiled, doughy, draggled, drenched, drunk, dull, intoxicated, moist, pasty, rare, sammy, sappy, saturated, seethed, soaked, soggy, sopping, spirited, spongy, steeped
SODDY adobe
SODI *offspring* daggiel
SODIUM natrium, salt
-alum mendozite
bicarbonate baking powder, baking soda, saleratus
borate borax
carbonate anatron, barilla, borax, natron, pirssonite, salsoda, trona
chloride halite, sal(t), saltcat
comb. natro
compound acmite, aegerite, albite, anatron, antiformin, beryllonite, blankit(e), blodite, borax, brazilianite,

glauberite, mendozite, soda, trona
nitrate niter, nitre, saltpeter
oxide soda
source saltpeter
sulfate glauber's salt, mirabilite, saltcake
thiosulfate hypo
SODOM *king* bera
sister city gomorrah
symbol of corruption, vice
SOE cowl, pail, tub
SOFA bergere, boist, borne, boudeuse, canape, causeuse, chaise-longue, chesterfield, couch, davenport, daybed, divan, dosados, leewan, lounge, loveseat, seat, settee, settle, squab, studio couch
circular borne
18th-century canape
s-shaped tete-a-tete
SOFFIT gather, plancier
SOFT 3 low 4 calm, damp, easy, fell, fine, fond, limp, meek, mild, mure, nesh, waxy, weak 5 balmy, bland, cushy, dabby, dolce, downy, faint, hooly, light, malmy, melch, muddy, pulpy, silky, slack, sleek, slick, soapy, swash, sweet, wethe 6 creamy, doughy, dulcet, feeble, flabby, fleecy, flimsy, fluffy, gentle, mellow, placid, pliant, serene, sidder, siddow, silken, smooth, spongy, spoony, supple, tender 7 amorous, clement, drizzly, ductile, fleshly, flexile, foolish, lenient, melting, plastic, pliable, queachy, relaxed, subdued, velvety 8 delicate, flexible, gullible, moderate, soothing, tolerant, tranquil, yielding 9 indulgent, malleable, negligent, tractable 10 effeminate 11 comfortable, sympathetic
and smooth cottony, flurry, mellow, satiny, silky, soapy, supple
and sweet dolce, dulcet
and wet mushy, squashy, squelchy, squishy
as butter, down, fleece, floss, putty, silk, velvet
chess blubber-grass, bromus
comb. leni, malaco
-cover paperback
drink ade, coke, cola, pepsi, pop, soda, tonic

drink parlor spa
mass pulp, wad
palate cion, uvula, velum
palate, pert. uvular, velar
-pedal muffle, silence, subdue, tone down
-sell low-key
shell barnburner, clam, crab
shelled turtle flapjack, flapper, flipper
-soap adulation, blandish, blarney, brownnose, butter up, con, flatter(y), gush(iness), oil, suavity, unctiousness, wheedle, wheedling
-spoken affable, bland, conciliatory, gentle, ingratiating, mealy(mouthed), mild, smooth, suave
-touch pushover
SOFTEN allay, amollish, appease, assuage, break, calm, conciliate, cushion, dissolve, dulcify, ease, enervate, enfeeble, extenuate, gentle, knead, laxate, leniate, limber, loosen, macerate, malax(ate), mash, meliorate, mellow, melt, milden, mitigate, moisten, mollify, move, muffle, mute, pacify, palliate, relax, relent, relieve, sam(my), smash, soak, sodden, soothe, squash, subdue, supple, sweeten, tame, tan, taw, temper, thaw, tone down, tranquilize, weaken, wokie, yield
by kneading malax
by soaking macerate
up besiege, influence, persuade
SOFTENING abatement, assuasive, bletting, cushion, demulcent, demulsion, emollient, inteneration, lenient, lenitive, loosening, malaxation, mollescent, mollities, molitious, padding, pillow, relaxing, relief, wadding
SOFTHEAD dolt, fool, simpleton
SOFTHEARTED generous, gracious, tender
SOFTLY fairly, foolish(ly), gentle, gently, leise, low, pianissimo, piano, quietly, soave, sotto, spiritless, tenderly, unobtrusively
SOFTNESS ductility, flaccidity, flocculence, gen-

tleness, gullibility, leniency, mollescence, morbidezza, sponginess, tenderness
SOFTY coward, fool, pushover, sissy, weakling
SOG bog, drench, drowse, ret, saturate, soak, sop, steep
SOGGY clammy, damp, dank, doughy, dull, heavy, moist, muggy, soaked, sobby, SODDEN, soft, sopping, spongy, sticky, wet
SOHRAB *father* rustum
SOIE See SILK.
SOIGNE elegant, neat, slick, smooth, tidy, trim, well-groomed
SOIL (See also *kind,* below.) adobe, alluvium, bedaub, bedraggle, befoul, begrime, begum, bemoil, benasty, besmear, besmirch, besmudge, besmut(ch), bespatter, black(en), blot(ch), blur, bole, brand, clay, clunch, corrupt, country, daub, defile, dirt(y), discolor, divot, dub, earth, foul, glebe, grime, groot, ground, humus, lair, land, loam, loess, malm, manure, marl, mool, moss, muck, peat, pedalfer, pedocal, podsol, pollute, realm, refuse, region, residence, seduce, sewage, silt, slander, smear, smirch, smudge, smut(ch), sod, sole, spoil, spot, stain, sward, tash, terra firma, till(age), turf, wallow
above clay kelly
aggregate ped
alkaline solonetz
ash-like podsol, podzol
carbonated pedocal
chalky malm
clayey adobe, bole, galt, malm, marl, maum, rosel, solod, soloth
comb. agro, geo
cultivation tilth
decayed geest
dry groot
erruginous laterite
from rock decay laterite
goddess demeter
gravelly growan, roach
hard rammel
improver ameliorant, compost, fertilizer, manure
infertile gall
kind adobe, alluvium, argil,

bole, clay, clunch, dust, groot, gumbo, humus, kaolin, lair, laterite, loam, loess, malm, marl, mold, mool, moss, peat, pedalfer, pedocal, podsol, silt, snad
layer callow, casing, hardpan, horizon, loess, solum, topsoil
leached latosol
loosen plow, scarify
management agronomy
organic part humus
plumber's smudge
porous sponge
prairie brunizem
rich loam, regur, topsoil
sandy rosel
science agrology, agronomy, edaphology, pedology
silty gumbo
sowing tilth
springy woodsere
sticky gumbo
sweeten lime
wind-deposited eluvium
wornout kapahulu
zonal s(i)erozem
SOILED black(ened), defiled, dingy, dirtied, dirty, filthy, foul, shopworn, smudged, smudgy, smutty, sooty, tarry
SOIREE affair, ball, evening, fete, levee, party, social
SOJA bean, glycine, soybean
SOJOURN abidance, abide, allodge, delay, dwell, howf(f), layover, linger, live, lodge, mansion, reside(nce), rest, station, stay, stop, tarriance, tarry, travel, visit
SOKA   GAKKAI   *leader* ikeda, nichiren
party komeito
term gohonzon-mantra, nam myoho renge kyo, shakubuku, society, value-creation
SOKE district, franchise, jurisdiction, soak
SOKOL falcon
SOL aerosol, coin, gold, helios, hydrosol, phoebus, soh, sou, sun(god)
10 libra, pound
SOLACE abate, allay, alleviate, amuse, assuage, assurance, calm, cheer, comfort, condolement, condolence, consolation, console, diversion, ease, encouragement, gladden, lighten, mitigate,

please, reassurance, recreation, relief, relieve, soothe, sweeten
SOLAN gannet, goose
SOLANUM berengena, bindweed, bittersweet, bluetop, cankerberry, eggplant, horsenettle, jerusalemcherry, morel, nettle, nightshade, potato, wonderberry
SOLAR (See also SUN references.) attic, celestial, chamber, floor, garret, heliac(al), loft, story, tropic
deity See SUN *god, goddess.*
disk aten, aton
plexas paralysis abepithymia
plexus belly, blow, stomach
system member planet
system model orrery, planetarium
term epact
SOLARIUM clock, porch, room, snail, sundial, sunparlor
SOLATIUM   allowance, bonus, compensation
SOLD booked, convinced, taken
illegally bootleg, fenced
SOLDAN *slayer* sir cawline
SOLDER adhere, alloy, braze, cement, float, fuse, join, mend, patch, sowder, spelter, unite, weld
chip link
flux borax, resin, rosin
SOLDERING *iron* copper, doctor
SOLDIER *3* hun, rok, toa, vet *4* bolo, fogy, goum, gugu, impi, ivan, jock, kern, peon, swad, tulk, yank *5* anzac, askar, berne, boche, brave, cadet, fritz, gi joe, guffy, jerry, kerne, khaki, kraut, limey, nizam, perdu, poilu, redif, rifle, spahi, tolke, tommy, whlan *6* amazon, askari, atkins, aussie, batman, bonagh, bummer, digger, gunner, gurkha, haiduk, heinie, jaeger, johnny, lancer, lascar, marine, pieton, ranter, swaddy, thraso, zouave *7* billjim, blighty, brigand, carabin, cateran, corslet, cossack, dogface, draftee, dragoon, fighter, goumier, hobbler, hoplite, matross, palikar, pandour, pavisor, pikeman, poltast, private, recruit, redcoat,

regular, reister, trooper, velites, veteran, warrior *8* arquebus, buckskin, buffcoat, cameleer, cavalier, chasseur,   commando, doughboy, fugleman, fusilier, gendarme, grayback, grognard, ironside, janizary, khandait, malinger, marksman, miquelet, mustache, myrmidon, pioupiou, rapparee, spearman, tolpatch *9* fantassin, goldbrick, grenadier, harquebus, janissary, musketeer *10* basewallah, bloodyback,   carabineer, carmagnole, curiassier, halberdier, militiaman *11* legionnaire, tommy atkins *12* antesignanus, cannonfodder, harquebusier, stormtrooper
ant dinergate
bag haversack, knapsack
brutal cossack, pandour
cap busby
cavalry uhlan
coat capote, tunic
cowardly capitano
detachment file
disease trenchfoot, trenchmouth
encampment bivouac
equipment accouterment, accoutrement
female amazon, aslauga, idisi, valkyrie, wac
flask canteen
foot See SOLDIER *infantry.*
free quartering bonaght, bonaught
group See ARMY *unit* and *infantry.*
guerrilla ranger
herb matico
hired buccellarius, condottiere, feedman, hessian, janizary, landsknecht, mercenary
home-service fencible
infantry almogavar, askar, doughboy, fusileer, fusilier, kern(e), page, peon, pieton, poilu, tolpatch
irregular cateran, jayhawk, miquelet, silladar
jacket eisenhower, jerkin
mercenary See *hired,* above.
model fugleman
mounted cavalier, cavalryman, dragoon, genetor, lancer, lobster, trooper, vedette
native askar(i), gurkha

new bezonian, cadet, chicken, draftee, plebe, recruit, replacement, rooky, trainee
of fortune adventurer
old grognard
pay seh
pensioned commissionaire
pert. military
quarters barracks, billets, bivouac, camp, can(n)aba, casern(e)
revolutionary buckskin, redcoat
shelter foxhole, pillbox, trench
specialized antesignanus, carabineer, carabinier, cuirassier, dragoon, fantassin, fencible, flugelman, fugleman, lancer, sapper, targetter, trooper, velites
trenching tool burgoyne
unknown, tomb arlington
vacation furlough, leave, pass
SOLDIERLY brave, heroic, martial
SOLDIERY horse, military, militia, sebundy, sibbendy
SOLE achirus, allenarly, alone, anacanth, base, bottom, clump, desolate, eopsetta, exclusive, fish, flatfish, floor, foot, foundation, gadoid, halter, hogchoke(r), isolated, lone(ly), mere, one, onlepy, only, particular, pelma, planta, select, separate, single, singular, slade, solea, soleyn, solitary, subsoil, sullen, symphurus, themar, threshold, tonguefish, vola, unique, unmarried, whole, windowsill, yoke
bottom naumk(eag)
broad flatfish, hogchoker
foot pelma, vola
half shoulder
inner rand
leather kelp, laminaria
opposite the antithenar
part shank
pert. plantar
piece girder
shoes speck
strip cleat
SOLECISM anachronism, antiphrasis, barbarism, boner, blunder, error, gaffe, impropriety, lapse, malapropism, misconstruction, misuse, slip

SOLECISTIC(AL) faulty, improper, inaccurate, incongruous, incorrect, inexact, ungrammatic(al), unseemly
SOLELY alone, barely, entirely, exclusively, merely, only, purely, simply, singly, wholly
SOLEMN august, austere, budge, ceremonial, ceremonious, conventional, customary, decorous, demure, devout, dignified, dismal, distinguished, earnest, formal, funereal, gloomy, grave, grim, heavy, important, imposing, impressive, longfaced, majestic, noteworthy, pompous, reverent(ial), ritual, sedate, serious, sober, somber, splendid, staid, stately, sublime, thoughtful, weighty
SOLEMNITY celebration, ceremony, dignity, formality, gloom, gravity, pomp, rite, severity
SOLEMNIZE celebrate, commemorate, dignify, exalt, glorify, honor, keep, marry
SOLENODON agouta, alamiqui, almique, shrew
SOLICIT adjure, appeal, apply, approach, ask, attract, beg, beseech, bid, campaign, canvass, challenge, claim, court, crave, demand, disquiet, drum, educe, elicit, entreat, exact, fish for, hustle, implore, importune, invite, invoke, lure, manage, mooch, plea(d), prosecute, request, seek, sue, supplicate, tempt, tout, urge, woo
SOLICITOR advocate, agent, attorney, ballyhooer, ballyhooman, barker, barrister, canvasser, counsel(or), drummer, lawyer, petitioner, pitchman, proctor, procurator, runner, spieler, tout(er), trampler
SOLICITOUS afraid, anxious, apprehensive, careful, concerned, considerate, desirous, eager, fearful, invocative, jealous, mendicant, prayerful, suppli(c)ant, supplicating, thoughtful, troubled, uneasy, urgent, worried
SOLICITUDE alarm, anxiety, apprehension, assiduity,

attention, care(fulness), concern, desire, fear, foreboding, heart, heed, misgiving, presentiment, thoughtfulness, worry, yeme
SOLID basic, block, body, bulky, cement, close, compact, concrete, concretion, conglomerate, constant, cube, cubic, dense, durable, enduring, entire, fat, firm, genuine, hard, heavy, holosteric, lasting, lump, mass(ive), massy, material, meaty, physical, prism, real, reliable, rugged, secure, sensible, serious, set, sound, stable, stalwart, steady, stiff, stout, strong, sturdy, substantial, thick, tight, true, unanimous, unbroken, uniform, united, valid, vigorous, whole
comb. prism, stereo
5-summited pentacron
geometric cone, cube, cylinder, dodecahedron, frustrum, heptahedron, pentahedron, prism, pyramid, sphere
-horned plenicorn
pert. conic
silver sterling
-toothed pleodont
SOLIDAGO goldenrod
SOLIDIFY cake, candy, cement, coalesce, cohere, compact, compress, concrete, condense, congeal, crystallize, fix, gel, granulate, harden, jell, kern, ossify, petrify, set, stiffen, thicken
SOLIDITY consistency, density, dependability, firmness, hardness, stability, staunchness, substantiality, volume
SOLIDLY firmly, groundly, square, stoutly
SOLIDUNGULATE ass, horse, soliped, zebra
SOLIDUS besant, bez(z)ant, byzant, diagonal, hyperper, nomisma
½ semis
SOLILOQUY apostrophe, aside, discourse, monologue, poem
SOLIPSISM egoism, psychomonism
SOLITAIRE bird, diamond, game, lonely, myadestes, neckcloth, pezophaps, recluse, ring

extinct pezophaps

game 3 fly 4 frog, gaps, harp, hell, olga, shah, star 5 agnes, betty, chico, demon, fanny, louis, lucas, maria, nines, snake, wheel, yukon 6 bisley, carpet, corona, decade, elfern, garden, martha, milton, moojub, nation, nestor, pounce, rumjin, senate, spider, sultan, vienna, xerxes, zodiac 7 amazons, babette, boudoir, bristol, chuckle, citadel, clarino, elevens, emperor, gavotte, glencoe, harvest, montana, newport, octagon, old maid, osmosis, phalanx, pyramid, rainbow, shuttle, terrace, trefoil, zingara 8 assembly, batsford, bullfrog, canfield, canister, colorado, congress, crapette, diplomat, fishbone, klondike, napoleon, necklace, octopode, patience, scorpion, somerset, strategy, triangle, uncle sam, windmill 9 accordion, betsy ross, boomerang, cotillion, financier, gargantua, matrimony, nationale, pike's peak, quadrille, shamrocks, whitehead 10 bethrothal, storehouse 11 desperation, diamond ring, fascination, russian bank 12 perseverance

term build, column, combine, family, fan, foundation, lane, lay out, marriage, matched, natural, reserve, row, space, tableau, talon, wastepile

SOLITARY alone, desert(ed), eremite, forlorn, forsaken, hermetical, hermit, individual, isolated, lone(ly), lonesome, lorn, odd, one, onlepy, only, private, recluse, remote, secluded, separated, simple, single, sole, soleyn, solo, unique, waf, widowed

comb. eremo

SOLITUDE aloneness, dearth, isolation, lack, loneliness, lonesomeness, privacy, retreat, seclusion, uniqueness, wilderness

SOLLAR brattice, gallery, platform, partition

SOLO a cappella, air, alone, aria, arioso, cavatina, flight,

game, lone, omber, perform(ance), piece, pilot, radel, recitative, scena, self, strain, unaccompanied

accompaniment ob(b)ligato

vocal aria, arioso

SOLOMON, SOLOMON'S jedidiah, king, koheleth, sage, sam

ally hiram

bride shulamite

chamberlain ahishar

enemy hadar, jeroboam, rezon

general ahijah, benaiah

gold source ophir

governor ahimaaz, ahinadab, azariah, baana(h), ben abinadab, ben dekar, ben hesed, ben hur, geber, jehoshaphat, shimei

island bougainville, buka, choiseul, gizo, guadalcanal, malaita, new georgia, savo, tulagi

island capital honiara

island gulf huon, kula

island harbor kieta

island tribe telei

island volcano balbi

lily arum, black calla

parent bathsheba, david

pillar boaz, jachin

priest abiathar, zadok

prince azariah

scribe ahiah, elihoreph

seal lily, polygonatum, sealwort, spikenard

secretary of state jehoshaphat

son rehoboam, roboam

song canticle, canzon(et)

successor rehoboam, roboam

superintendent adoniram

temple rebuilder hiram

temple stone shamir

SOLON assemblyman, gnomist, lawmaker, legislator, publicist, sage, senator, statesman, wiseman

SOLUBLE dissoluble, explainable, frim, frum, fusible, liquefiable, meltable, reducible, solute, solvable

SOLUTE arrange, disintegrated, dissolve(d), free, loose, separate, soluble, solve

SOLUTION (See also *kind*, below.) analysis, answer, assoil, blend, breach, brew, clarification, decipherment, decoction, decoding, de-

nouement, determination, discharge, disentanglement, elixir, explanation, eyewash, fluid, issue, key, lacquer, liquid, mixture, outcome, reason, resolution, result, stain, tinct(ure), unraveling, unriddling, untangling

kind brine, eusol, iodin(e), lixivium, lye, phenol, saline, sirup, syrup

medicinal tincture

pickling souse

saline brine

soap nigre

sterile johnin

strength proof, titer, titre

SOLVE answer, ascertain, break, clear up, crack, decipher, decode, detect, determine, discover, disentangle, dissolve, divine, dope out, explain, fathom, figure out, find out, free, get, guess, interpret, make out, pay, plumb, puzzle out, ravel, resolve, set(tle), undo, unfold, unlock, unravel, unscramble, untangle, work

SOLVENT acetone, alcohol, alkahest, aniline, antiformin, benzaldehyde, benzene, butanone, carbon-tetrachloride, chloroform, cumene, detergent, diluent, dilution, dioxane, flux, furfural, fusing, glycerol, glycol, ketone, ligroin(e), liquefacient, liquefier, naphtha, phenol, reliable, resolutive, responsible, solid, solution, sound, stable, substantial, wash, water

universal alkahest

SOMA aruna, aursa, babhru, bhang, drink, grape, haoma, hari, hiranya, honey, mead, mountain-rue, mushroom, pavamana, plant, rhubarb, rue, vine

SOMALILAND punt

antelope beira, beisa

capital berbera, mogadiscio, mogadishu

city berbera, hargeisa, kisimayu, merca

coin besa, somalo

desert aror

division hawiya

gulf aden

measure caba, chela, cubito, darat, parsalah, tabla, top

people asha, danakil, galla, hawiya, isbaak, marehan, rahanwin, shuhali, somali
port berbera, mogadiscio, mogadishu
range guban
river juba, nogal, scebeli
territory afars, issas
weight parsalah

SOMATIC actual, bodily, carnal, corpor(e)al, fleshly, material, parietal, physical

SOMBER austere, black, dark(some), depressing, dern, dingy, dismal, doleful, dreary, dull, funereal, fusc, gloom(y), grave, gray, grim, heavy, lackluster, lenten, melancholy, mournful, rueful, sad, serious, shady, sinister, sober, solemn, sombre, sullen

SOMBRERITE guano, osite

SOME about, any, approximately, certain, des, more or less, number, odd, one, part, piece, portion, several, soever, this

SOMEBODY celebrity, magnate, numero uno, personage, quidam, vip

SOMERSAULT dive, flip, leap, overturn, pitchpoll, reversal, REVERSE, somerset, spotter

SOMERSET *mineral springs* bath

SOMETHING aliquid, beverage, drink, liquid, object, somewhat, whatnot
else aliud

SOMETIME former(ly), late, not always, now and then, occasional(ly), once, past, quondam, somdel, somewhen, whilom

SOMEWHAT aliquid, bit, incompletely, kind of, little, more or less, not much, part (ially), rather, slight, sort of, summat, to a degree

SOMEWHERE *near* about, approximately, around, close

SOMITE cephalomere, gonotome, merosome, metamere, somatome, tergite, zonite

SOMME *city on* amiens, st quentin
tributary ancre

SOMMELIER butler, cellarman, wineserver

SOMNAMBULATE sleepwalk

SOMNAMBULE, SOMNAMBULIST sleepwalker

SOMNIFEROUS hypnotic, opiate, sleep-inducing, soporific

SOMNILOQUY sleep-talking

SOMNOLENCE drowsiness, sleepiness

SOMNOLENT comatose, dozy, drowsy, inert, lethargic, passive, sleepy, sluggish, slumberous, supine

SOMNUS hypnos, sleep
brother death, mors
parent night, nox, nyx

SON bairn, ben, boy, cadet, dauphin, descendent, disciple, epigonus, figlio, filius, fils, fitz, follower, heir, junior, kibei, mac, male, native, offspring, scion, youth, zun
beloved absalom
comb. bar. mac
foster alumnus
4th martlet
illegitimate nephew
-in-law aidem, athum, aydem, beau-fils, gener, mauch, odam
name meaning bar, ben(jamin), bennie
of ben, mac, fitz
of a gun fellow, rogue, wretch
of exhortation barnabas
of god jesus, redeemer, saviour
of man mortal
of perdition judas iscariot
of the right hand benjamin
of the soil farmer, peasant
7th seer
young mopsy
younger lackland
youngest cadet

SONANT intonated, sounding, tonic, vocal, voiced

SONAR asdic

SONATA *movement* adagio, allegro, andante, coda, fugue, largo, minuet, minuetti, presto, rondo, scherzo, trio

SONG 3 air, dit, lay, uta 4 alba, aria, cant, dite, duan, fuss, glee, hymn, leed, lied, lilt, mele, moel, pean, poem, rann, rune, tune 5 blues, canso, canto, canzo, carol, catch, chant, croon, derry, ditty, lyric, matin,

melos, molpe, motet, paean, psalm, rondo, round, siren, troll, verse, vocal 6 anthem, aubade, ballad, branle, cantic, carmen, chanty, clamor, himene, lieder, melody, poetry, serena, shanty, strain, strowd, trifle, vinata, waiata, warble 7 arietta, ballade, ballata, calypso, cancion, cantion, canzone, chanson, chantey, descant, lullaby, melisma, requiem, reverdi, rondeau, rondino, scolion, threnos 8 brindisi, canticle, cantique, canzonet, cavatina, coojine, hymeneal, jubilate, palinode, pittance, serenade, serenata, zortzico 9 barcarole, brautlied, cabaletta, cantilena, kunstlied, mistrelsy, rhapsody, roundelay, volkslied 10 canzonetta, recitative, rondoletto
after epode
art lied(er)
birds' koller, lay, ramage
boat jorram
ceremonial areito
christmas carol, noel, wassail
church villancico
collection anthology, cancionero
college glee
comb. melo
commemorative waiata
cradle berceuse, husho, lullaby
dance ballad, bambuco
division See *part*, below.
drinking bacchic, wassail
edic alvissmal
18th century bergerette
elizabethan eyre
evening evensong, serena(de), serenata, vespers
folk ballad, blues, bylina, cantiga, doina, fado, folk, jubilee
funeral dirge, elegie, elegy, elogium, elogy, epicede, epicedia, lament, monody, requiem, threne, threnody, threnos
girl adeline, betty coed, clementine, daisy, laura, ramona, sal, susanna(h),
group liederkranz
gypsy zingaresca
heroic edda
impromptu scolion
light canzonet

-like ariose, cantabile, lyric (al), melic, melodious

love amoret, aubade, ballad, canso, canzo, fancy, serena(de), serenata

-maker bulbul

medieval conductus

minstrel yedding

monophonic rondeau

monotonous virelay

morning aubade, matin

mountaineer's yodel

mournful dump, endecha, plaint

muse terpsichore

night complin

nuptial See *wedding*, below.

obscure rune

of praise anthem, bhajan, carol, chorale, hymn, magnificat, paean, pean

of solomon cantic(le), canzon(e), canzonet

of solomon, bride shulamite

of the blessed one bhagavadgita

part caccia, canon, canzonet, chace, fala, fit, frottola, gymel, madrigal, melismatic, round, troll

pastoral bergerette, oat

plain ground

refrain aria, chorus, derry, epistrophe, epode, fala, falderal

religious See *sacred*, below.

revolutionary internationale

round troll

sacred anthem, carol, chant, hymn, motet, noel, polymny, psalm, shout, sirvent, villancico

sad See *funeral*, above.

sailor's barcarol(l)e, chant(e)y, rumbelow, shant(e)y

short air, arietta, ode

simple air, ditty, lay, tune

16th century broadside

stupid strowd

thrush mavie, mavis, throstle

toast brindisi

2 voices duet, gymel

vintage vinata

wedding epithalamion, hymen(eal)

work holler

writer ballader, composer, tunesmith

SONGBIRD 3 ani, ano 4 bran, chat, fink, hiat, kala, kate, lark, merl, miro, moho, moro, omao, pape, pope, tutu, wren, yeni 5 ammer, amsel, dayal, finch, hoody, joree, junco, lindo, mavie, mavis, merle, ousel, ouzel, pipit, robin, sabia, serin, shama, spink, twite, veery, vireo 6 alauda, anthus, bulbul, bunyah, burion, canary, citril, corbie, drongo, hoodie, kokako, linnet, loriot, mocker, muffet, oriole, oscine, oxbird, palola, roller, shrike, siskin, thrush, towhee, verdin, winnel 7 babbler, bunting, bushtit, capella, catbird, chewink, chirper, cuckoo, grasset, kinglet, kirombo, maybird, minivet, ortolan, redpoll, redwing, ruddock, scolder, skylark, tanager, titlark, wagtail, warbler, wimbrel 8 bellbird, bengalee, bluebird, bobolink, cardinal, chipchap, grosbeak, hawfinch, lazybird, longspur, philomel, pincpinc, redstart, ringdove, snowbird, thrasher, throstle, titmouse, whinchat 9 goldfinch, stonechat 11 mockingbird, nightingale 12 whippoorwill

genus icterus, irena, lanius, meruca, mimidae, ortalus, oscine, piranga, sialia, sylvia, timalia, turdus

mimicking crow, parsonbird, tue, tui

SONGMAN bard, gleeman, minstrel, singer, skald, troubadour

SONGSTER chanter, lark, philomel, poet, singer, warbler

SONNAMBULA, LA *composer* bellini

role amina, elvino, rodolpho

SONNERATIA blatti, kambala, pagatpat

SONNET octet, poem, seste(t), song, verse

kind italian, miltonic, petrarch(i)an, spenserian

part coda, octet, sestet

prince joachim

rhyme scheme abab, abba, bcbc, cdcd, dcd, efef

SONORA *indian* seri

SONOROUS canorous, deep, full, grandiloquent, loud, melodious, orotund, resonant, resounding, rich, rotund, silvery, sonoric, sounding, vibrant

SONS(E) felicity, fortune, health, prosperity

SONSHIP filiety

SONSY, SONSIE buxom, comely, comfortable, good-natured, handsome, happy, lucky, plentiful, prosperous

SOODLE saunter, stroll

SOOK booth, market, suck, suq

SOOL pull, sick, sowl, tousle

SOON anon, assuredly, at once, beforehand, beforetime, belive, betimes, bientot, by and by, certainly, direct(ly), early, ere long, forthwith, immediate(ly), in due course, in no time, presently, prestly, prompt(ly), pronto, quick(ly), readily, reasonably, short(ly), speedily, speedy, tite, willingly, yern(e)

SOONER before, ere(r), erst, first, preferably, promptly, rather, titter

or later eventually

state oklahoma

than ere

SOONEST rathest

SOONY emotional, sentimental

SOOT bleck, colly, coom(b), crock, dirt, dregs, dust, gentle, grime, melodious, refuse, remainder, smut(ch), soil, sope, sotik, stupp, sweet

-brown bister, bistre

-dew fumago

mercurous stupp

particle aizle, isel, izle, smut

pert. fuliginous

sawdust coom(b)

SOOTH augury, blandishment, cajolery, comfort, delightful, pleasure, proverb, real(ity), soft, soothing, sweet, true, truly, trustworthy, truth(ful)

SOOTHE accoy, allay, alleviate, appease, assuage, becalm, blandish, calm, charm, comfort, compose, console, demulce, dill, dulce, dulcify, extenuate, flatter, gruntle, humor, lull, lullaby, mitigate, mollify, pacify, palliate, pat, pet, placate, plaster, please, quell, quiet, reassure, relieve, salve, satisfy, soften, solace, still, stroke, tranquilize, unriffle, uphold

SOOTHER anodyne, balm, balsam, emollient, lotion, placebo, salve, sedative

SOOTHING abatement, abirritant, anodyne, appeasing, assuasive, balmy, bland, calmative, calming, downy, dreamy, dulcet, easing, gentle, hesychastic, lenitive, relief, sedative
agent abirritant

SOOTHSAY foretell, omen, portent, predict, proverb, sort, spae

SOOTHSAYER ariole, aruspex, astrologer, astromancer, augur(er), auspex, chaldean, divine(r), fortune-teller, hariolizer, haruspex, mantis, oracle, palmist, prognosticator, prophet, python, sage, seer(ess), sortilegus, spaer, telemus, tiresias, vates, weird

SOOTY black(ened), brookie, colly, dirty, dusty, fuliginous, smutted, stained
albatross bluebird, nellie, quaker, stinker, stinkpot
shearwater titi

SOP absorb, blot, bribe, cloud, clown, clump, colly, douceur, drench, dunk, fool, gift, heap, impregnate, lump, mass, mop, ooze, percolate, ret, saturate, soak, sog, sponge, steep, tuft, waterlog, weakling, wet

SOPATER *aid to* paul

SOPHISM argument, casuistry, elench(us), fallacy, fetch, paralogism, shift, subtlety

SOPHIST gorgias, hippias, philosopher, protagoras, quibbler, rhetorician, shuffler, thinker

SOPHISTICATE adulterate, alter, cavil, corrupt, cosmopolitan, cosmopolite, deacon, debase, disillusion, doctor, expert, falsify, garble, load, mondaine, palter, quibble, refine, shift, spoil, varnish, weight, worldling

SOPHISTICATED adulterated, amended, artificial, aware, blase, complicated, hardheaded, knowing, practical, precious, refined, smart, smooth, soigne,

stagy, studied, stylish, svelte, wise, worldly(wise)

SOPHISTICATION adulterant, adulteration, chic, debasement, experience, falsification, quibble, SOPHISM

SOPHISTRY ambiguity, casuistry, deceit, deception, distortion, error, evasion, fallacy, paralogism, paralogy, perversion, quibble, sophism, trickery

SOPHOCLES *birthplace* colonus
son iophon
work ajax, antigone, electra, oedipus at colonus, oedipus the king, philoctetes, trachiniae

SOPHOMORIC adolescent, bombastic, foolish, immature, purile, shallow, superficial, unsophisticated

SOPHONISBA *betrothed* masinissa
father hasdrubal

SOPHORA coral-bean, oak, pagoda-tree, pelu

SOPHROSYNE moderation, prudence

SOPHY personage, philosophy, religion, ruler, sage, science, skill, wisdom, wiseman

SOPITE draft, drooping, droopy, frowsy, quash, quiet, sleep

SOPORIFIC anise(ed), anodyne, catnip, chamomile tea, drowsy, drug, dwale, hypnotic, lady's slipper, lemon-balm tea, lullaby, narcotic, opiate, penny-royal tea, red bergamot, sedative, skullcap, sleep-bringer, somnifacient, somniferous, valerian, wine, woodruff

SOPPING asop, drenched, soaked, soaking, wet

SOPPY juicy, maudlin, mawkish, moist, mushy, romantic, saturated, sentimental, slushy, soaked

SOPRANO canary, canto, coloratura, lyric, singer, treble, voice
famous alda, bori, callas, flagstad, freni, gluck, lind, nilsson, patti, pons, sills, steber, stevens, sutherland, tebaldi

SORA bird, crake, porzana, rail

SORATA *peak* ancohuma, illampu

SORBUS quince, rowan

SORCERER boolya boyla, brujo, conjuror, enchanter, fetishe(e)r, goeta, koradji, mage, magician, medicine man, nagual, reimkennar, shaman, voodoo, warlock, wielare, witchdoctor, wizard

SORCERESS armida, babajaga, bruja, circe, enchantress, gorgon, hecate, hekate, helios, korrigan, lamia, shamaness, siren, usha, witch

SORCERY alchemy, bewitchery, black magic, conjuration, conjurment, demonism, demonology, demonomy, devilry, diablerie, diabolism, divination, enchantment, exorcism, exsufflation, fetishism, gramary(e), hoodoo, incantation, juju(ism), magic, magism, makutu, necromancy, obe, obeah, obi, ouanga, pishogue, rite, rune, shamanism, sortiery, SORTILEGE, spell, thaumaturgia, thaumaturgy, theurgy, vampirism, voodoo(ism), wanga, wigeling, witchcraft, witchery, wizardry

SORDID abject, back-alley, base, cheap, chetif, churlish, contemptible, covetous, despicable, dirty, filthy, foul, gamy, gross, grubby, ignoble, low, mean, mercenary, mesquin, miserable, muddy, nasty, niggardly, poor, riffraff, sad, scurvy, slatternly, slovenly, slummy, sluttish, small, sorry, squalid, venal, vile

SORDINE muffled, mute, trumpet

SORE (See also *kind, below.*) abrasion, aching, afflicted, affliction, anger, angry, annoyed, bitter, contrition, criminal, cross, detriment, difficulty, disease, distressing, evil, extreme, grievous, hurt, indignant, inflamed, irritated, lesion, mad, painful, peeved, penance, resentful, sensitive, severe, sickness, suffering, tender, trouble, vexatious, vexed, violent, wound, wrong

-*eyed pigeon* sheathbill

kind abscess, aposteme, blain, bleb, bouba(s), buba(s), bubo, buck, bulla, bunnion, canker, carbuncle, cethair, chancre, chilblain, eschar, felon, fester(ing), fistula, framb(o)osia, furuncle, gathering, kibe, kyle, lesion, mellit, papule, pet, pimple, polyp, pustule, ruba, scab, sty, ulcer, wale, welt, wheal, whelk, wound

SOREHEAD birdpox, chickenpox, crank, disgruntled, grouch, irritated, pigeonpox

SORGHUM andropogon, batad, broomcorn, cane, chena, cholam, cush, dari, darra, darso, dhurra, dora, doura(h), durr(a), feterita, grain, grass, hegari, imphee, kafir, kaoliang, millet, milo, molasses, shallu, sirup, sorgo, syrup, wheat

SORITE(S) aggregation, collection, enthymeme, heap, mass, quantity, series, syllogism

SORN beg, idle, impose, loaf, lounge, obtrude, scrounge, sponge

SOROBAN abacus

SORORITY club, sisterhood, society

SORREL alezan, alleluia, averrhoa, bread-and-cheese, brown, buck, cankerroot, cuckoo, deer, elktree, elkwood, greensauce, hallelujah, hearts, horse, oca, oka, oxalis, roselle, rubican, rumex, sourock, stabwort,

-*tree* elkwood, hibiscus, sourwood, staggerbush, titi

SORROW ache, afflict(ion), agonize, agony, anguish, attrition, bale, bewail, bitterness, calamity, care, compunction, contrition, cry, damage, dejection, deplore, despair, devil, disillusionment, distress, dole (ance), dolor, drearing, egrimony, grame, grief, grieve, harm, heartache, hurt, keen, lament, melancholy, misery, moan, mourn(ing), pain, penitence, plague, regret(s), remorse, repent(ance), repining, rogue, rue, ruth,

sadness, scamp, sob, sorra, suffering, teen, trial, tribulation, trouble, unhappiness, unwin, wail, weep, weltschmerg, woe

exclamation ewhow, och

over bemoan, bewail, deplore, lament

with comfort, console

SORROWFUL blue, chary, contrite, desolate, dismal, doleful, dolent, doloroso, drear, forgiving, grieved, grievous, lamentable, luctual, melancholy, mournful, pitiable, pitiful, plaintive, ruesome, SAD, sairy, trist(e), unhappy, wan, woeful

tree hursinghar

SORRY apologetic, bad, beggarly, cheap, consciencestricken, contemptible, contrite, dick(e)y, dismal, doleful, evil, gloomy, grieved, grievous, hurt, ignoble, low, luctiferous, mean, melancholy, miserable, mournful, paltry, petty, pitiable, pitiful, poor, regretful, repentant, reproachful, rueful, sad, scabby, scummy, scurvy, shabby, shameful, sordid, straitened, trifling, trivial, unfain, unhappy, vexed, wicked, woe, worthless, wretched

spectacle bysen

SORT, SORTS adapt, adjust, allot, apportion, arrange, associate, assort, attain, beat, befit, blend, brand, breed, cast, character, choose, classify, collection, company, conform, crowd, cull, description, destiny, divide, fashion, fate, file, flock, garble, gathering, gender, grade, group, hump, ilk, join, kidney, KIND, lot, manner, mister, nature, occur, order, pick, pigeonhole, provision, punish, quality, reach, savor, scold, select, separate, set, sift, size, soothsay, species, spice, strain, stripe, suit, swarm, systematize, type, variety, way

merchandise brack

of rather, somewhat

of a mediocre, mixed, poor, so-called

out of cranky, cross, disturbed, ill, sick, vexed

SORTABLE expedient, fitting, proper, suitable, timely

SORTIE attack, foray, issue, mission, raid, sally

SORTILEGE divination, enchantment, lot, magic, SORCERY, witchery

SORVA borracha, couma, latex

SOS alarm, help, mayday, signal

SOSH dash, drunk, intoxicated, jag

SOSS heavily, lap, mess, muddle, plump, plunge, slop, slump, splash, swill, throw, thump

SOSSLE intoxicate, mess, slime, slop

SOT alcoholic, ale-knight, befool, bibber, carouser, child, dipsomaniac, drunk (ard), fixed, fool(ish), guzzle, immovable, inebriate, innocent, lourdy, lush, obstinate, simpleton, soak, squander, stubborn, tipple(r), toper, tosspot

SOTER deliverer, poseidon, ptolemy, savior, sospes, zeus

SOTHO *king* moshesh, sebetwane

SOTOL yucca

SOTTER blister, boil, bubble, crackle, scorch, simmer, sputter

SOTTISH bibulous, doltish, drunken, dull, foolish, senseless, stupid

SOTTO below, beneath, under

portico arcade, passageway

voce aside, privately, whisper

SOU coin, money, trifle

marque stampee

20 franc

SOU, SOWD amount, enlist, pay, quantity, should, strengthen, unite

SOUARI butternut, caryocar, juglans

SOUBRETTE actress, ingenue, juvenile, maid

SOUFFLE fondu(e), puffed, sherbet

SOUGH adit, breathe, channel, chant, complain, cry, die, ditch, drain, groan, growl, howl, moan(ing), murmur(ing), pipe, report, roar, rumor, rustle, scream, sewer, sigh, singsong. snarl, sob, swamp, wail, whine, whisper, whistle, whiz

SOUL alma, ame, anima, atman, atta, being, bore, brain(s), buddhi, courage, dibbuk, discernment, ego, elan, essence, fervor, force, genius, heart, inspirer, intellect, intelligence, jivitma, leader, life, man, marrow, mind, mortal, nature, nephesh, person, pneuma, prana, principle, psyche, purusha, satyagraha, sow(e)l, spirit, sprite, substance, wit(s)
after death bardo
belief in animism
comb. psyche, psycho, thymo
conductor to afterworld psychopompus
conflict with body psychomachy
disembodied ker
essence synderesis
food haslet, manna
greatness megalopsychy
healing psychiasis
individual jiva
liberated kevalin
loss hell, perdition
name meaning alma, enid
nonexistence doctrine anatman, anatta
of the dead lemures
personified alma, psyche
pert. thymetic
2nd degree ruach
-sick dejected, depressed, desolate
-sleep psychopannychism
supreme brahma
transfigured khu
universal hansa
wandering dibbuk, dybbuk
SOULFUL emotional, poetic, sentimental
SOULLESS brute, inanimate, turnipy, unfeeling
SOULT *commander* napoleon
SOUND (See also *kind,* below.) 3 bay, say, try 4 blow, dive, firm, hale, heal, hifi, ring, safe, sane, sing, tape, test, trig, true, well, wise 5 audio, blare, blast, bruit, exact, gliff, grope, inlet, legal, loyal, lusty, noise, plumb, plump, probe, right, rumor, solid, spang,

speak, stout, swash, swoon, utter, valid, vital, voice, whole 6 cogent, entire, fathom, hearty, honest, hubbub, intact, intone, plunge, racket, report, robust, secure, sonant, stable, strait, strong, sturdy, tumult, uproar 7 channel, correct, earshot, examine, explore, healthy, hearing, inflect, logical, meaning, measure, narrows, perfect, phonate, plummet, sonance, sonancy, sputter, straits, vibrant 8 accurate, complete, flawless, intonate, modulate, orthodox, profound, rational, reliable, sensible, stalwart, thorough, vocalize 9 enunciate, faultless, honorable, pronounce, realistic, undamaged, wholesome 10 articulate, convincing, dependable, hullabaloo, scrutinize, unimpaired 11 investigate, substantial
abnormal bruit
absorbent acoustic
absorption unit sabin
adventitious rale
alarm alert, arouse, caution, signal, warn
alike homonym
amorous coo
as a bell, roach
atonic surd, toneless, unheard, voiceless
background undertone
bell-like clang, ding(dong), knell, knoll, peal, ring, tingtang, tinkle
board belly
breathing rale, snore
buzzing whirr, whizz
change anaptyxis
clicking sneck
comb. audio, echo, phon(o), soni
concord of harmony, symphonia, symphony
consonant alveolar
contemptuous snort
contented purr
cooing chirr, turtur
deep bong, rumble
derisive bah, boo, catcall, hiss
detection means hydrophone, radar, sonar
discordant bray, cacophony, jangle, jar
dismal croak, groan, wail

distinctive timber
drum rataplan, ratatatat, roll, tuck
dull clonk, clunk, flump, squelch, thud, thutter
engine chug, ping, purr
explosive bang, bark, blast, boom, clap, pop, puff, report, roar, snort
faint gliff, peep, whisht, whisper
grating gride
gulping glub
guttural burr, grunt
harsh blare, bray, burr, buzz, cacophony, caw, clangor, clank, clash, craunch, creak, croak, crump, crunch, grate, gride, groan, growl, grumble, jangle, jar, rasp, scranch, scrape, scroop, scrunch, stridor, twang
high-pitched ping, screech, shriek, squeak, squeal, stridor, ting, whine, whistle
hissing fizz, siss, sizz(le), swish, zip
hoarse bray, caw, cough, ruckle
humming burr, drone
indistinct blur, mumble, murmur
in doctrine orthodox
initial anlaut
jingling smit, tintinnabulation
kind bang, bark, bawl, bay, beep, bell(ow), birr, bong, boom, bray, cackle, chirp, chirr, clamor, clang(or), clatter, clop, coo, crow, din, ding, dong, glug, growl, grunt, hiss, klop, mumble, murmur, pant, ping, pong, rale, ring, roar, rustle, scream, screech, shriek, sigh, snap, snarl, snort, squawk, squeal, static, thunder, ting, toot(le), wail, warble, whisper, whistle, yap, yell, yelp
light peep, pitapat, swish, whisper
loud bark, bellow, boom, clang(or), clarion, crackle, cry, hubbub, larum, outcry, peal, roar, roll, screak, scream, screech, shout, shriek, squall, squawk, yawp, yell, zing, zoom
low-pitched bass, rumble
low rustling whisp(er)

magnifying device amplifier, bullhorn, loudspeaker, megaphone
measure bel, decibel, mach, sone
measurer audiometer
mentally lucid, normal, sane
metallic chink, clang, clank, clink, ping, ting, tinkle
monotonous drone, hum, moan
mournful groan, sigh, sob, wail
murmuring sough(ing)
musical chime, note, tone
nasal anusvara, snore, stridor, whine
omission ellipsis
out approach, explore, investigate, study
pert. acoustic, audio, auditory, sonal, sonant, sonar, sonic, tonal, vocal
pleasing euphony
producer actinophone
repetition alliteration, echo
respiratory rale
ringing bong, clang, clank, dingdong, peal, tinitus, twang
science acoustics, catacoustics, harmonics, phonetics, phonics, phonography, radiophony, supersonics, telephony
shallow lagoon, laguna, lagune
sharp crack, knack, ping, pop, snap, spang, squirk
shrill screech, screed, skirl, squeak
sibilant hiss, shish, shush, siss
similarity assonance, hom(o)eophony
small chirp, peep, whisper
small, pert. micracoustic
sobbing wail, yoop
solemn peal, toll
splashing lap, splat, swash
sputtering thutter
system audio, hifi, stereo
throat guttural
throbbing thutter
to add dub
transmission, pert. audio
transposition spoonerism
trilled hirrient
unaspirated lene
unit See *measure*, above.
unpleasant bloop, glug, groan, snore, snork
unvaried monotone
vibrant birr

vocal cough, hiccough, hiccup, tone
warning alar(u)m, larum, siren, sos, tocsin
whirring birr
whispering psithurism, susurrus
whizzing ping, swish
yelping bark, yawp, yip
SOUNDBOARD belly
SOUNDER boar, leadman, probe, swine, ticker
SOUNDING(S) depth, echolation, fathomage, inkling, mellisonant, ringing, sonant, sonation
harsh brassy, brazen
instrument bathometer, bathymeter, blue-pigeon, bob, fathomer, fathometer, lead, line, plumb(bob), plumbline, plummet, probe, sonar, sonde
SOUNDLESS abysmal, noiseless, quiet, silent, still, unfathomable
SOUP bisk, bisque, borsch(t), borst, bouillabaise, bouillon, bree, broth, burgoo, chicken, cockalekie, consomme, fog, garbure, gazpacho, gumbo, hoosh, joutes, julienne, kail, kale, lentil, liquid, marmite, minestrone, mock turtle, mortreux, mortrewes, mulligatawny, nitroglycerine, okra, petite-marmite, posol, potage, potato, pottage, power, pozole, puree, shchi, solution, sop, stchi, sup, swoop, tomato, turtle, vegetable, vichyssoise
and fish tuxedo
barley smiggins
base soffrito, stock
beefskin skink
beet borsh(t), borst
-bone arm, knuckle, shin
cabbage shchi, shtchav, shtchee, stchi
clear broth, consomme, julienne
cream vichyssoise
curry mulligatawny
dish bowl, cup, ecuelle, porringer, tureen
-fin shark galeus, tope
fish bouillabaise, chowder, cioppino, solianka
ingredient barley, beans, lalo, noodles, okra, pasta, rice, stock
jellied gazpacho

prune plum-broth
spoon ladle
strainer mustache, mustachio
thick bisque, bumbo, burgoo, chowder, garkure, hoosh, hotchpotch, minestra, minestrone, mortreux, mortrewes, pot(t)age, puree
thickener cornstarch, roux, tapioca
thin broth, consomme
up increase, speed, supe
SOUPCON bit, dash, suggestion, suspicion, taste, trifle
SOUR acerb(ate), acerbic, acescent, acetic, acetify, acetose, acetous, acid(ic), acidify, acidulate, acidulous, acidy, acrid, astringent, austere, bitter, bleeze, caustic, clabber, coarse, cold, crab(bed), cross, cruety, curdle, distasteful, dour, embitter(ed), ferment(ed), flat, foxy, glum, green, grim, gruff, grum (py), hard, harsh, keen, macerate, mean, morose, painful, peevish, pickled, pontic, rancid, sharp, sore, sullen, tart, turn, unkind, unpleasant, unripe, unsweet, vinegarish, vinegary, wry
as verjuice, vinegar
become blink, fox, turn
-belly crosspatch, grouch, killjoy
beginning to bingy, turning
dock sorrel
dough bread, leaven, miner, pioneer, prospector, settler
gourd baobab, cream-of-tartar-tree, kurrajong, sterculia
grass paspalum, pepperidge, sorrel, tree, tupelo, xerophyllumnyssa
gum tree nyssa, tupelo
milk bleeze, clabber, skyr
slightly acescent, acidulous, blinky
turn bleeze
turning acescent, acidulous
SOURCE anlage, ascent, base, beginning, bonanza, bud, cadre, calorie, cause, center, commencement, derivation, edition, egg, embryo, fons, fountain(head), germ, goldmine, grass roots, head(spring), headwater, inception, knop, lode, mainspring, mine, nucleus, offspring, opening,

origin(ator), parent, provenance, quarry, rise, rising, rist, riverhead, root, rudiment, seed, spring, start, stem, stirps, stock, vein, well(head)
accepted authority
authoritative horse's mouth
original spiritual adi-buddhi
primary radix, root
SOURDINE mute(d), silencer, spinet, subdued, trumpet
SOURDOOK buttermilk
SOURING bingy, leaven, vinegar
SOURNESS acerbity, acidity, acor, anger, asperity, crossness, moroseness, rancor, tartness
SOURPUSS See SOUR *belly*.
SOURSOP an(n)ona, annonce, anonol, corresol, custard-apple, fruit, guanabana, sweetsop, tree
SOURTOP blueberry
SOURWEED sorrel
SOURWOOD elkwood, titi
SOUSA *favorite* dixie
SOUSE bathe, blow, cuff, douse, drench, drink, drunk(ard), duck, dunk, ear, fall, immerse, intoxicate, jag, orgy, petticoat, pickle, plunge, pour, prop, soak, sozzle, spree, steep, strike, submerge, swoop, thump, thwack, wash
SOUTANE cassock, simara, zimarra
SOUTER checkers, cobbler, shoemaker
SOUTERLY low, vulgar
SOUTERRAIN grotto, passage
SOUTH (See also SOUTHERN.) auster, dixie, meridian(ale), midi, sough, sud, sur
comb. austro
living in meridional
pole bird penguin, skua
pole continent antarctica
pole explorer byrd
pole tortoise chukwa
wind af(f)er, auster, notus, scirocco, sirocco, squam
wind author norman douglas
SOUTH AFRICA (See also AFRICA.) azania
acacia thornbush
animal blaubok, caama, das, etaac, niare, quagga, sassaby, springbok, spring-

buck, suricate, talapoin, teetee, vervet
animal disease nenta
antelope See AFRICA *antelope*.
armadillo para
arrow poison echugin
ass quagga
assembly raad
aunt tanta
balsam tolu
barracouta snoek
bay algoa, false, walfish, walvis
bird bacbakiri, fink, goaway, hammerkop, kwe, shrike, taha
blaubok etaac
boss baas
brandy cape smoke, dop
bread dika
bream steenbras(s), stumpnose
breastwork scherm
british protectorate basutoland, bechuanaland
british resident uitlander
buffalo niare
bushman kung, qung
bustard gompaauw, paauw
camp la(a)ger
cape agulhas, good hope
capital capetown, pretoria
caterpillar risper
cattle afrikander
cattle disease spirillosis
cattle enclosure kraal
chap kerel
city aus, bloemfontein, bononi, braker, brakpan, capetown, durban, germiston, johannesburg, kaapstad, kimberley, kokstad, krugersdorp, mafeking, mara, modjadji, oudtshoorn, pietermaritzburg, springs, untata, vereeniging
cliff klip
club knobkerrie
coin cent, daalder, florin, krugerand, pond, pound, rand
colonist boer
condiment balachong, blatchang, blatjang
conference indaba, raad
constitution grondwet
cony das
cormorant duiker
corn mealie, mealy
criminal amalaita
cripples lamziekte
current benguella
desert kalahari

dialect kitchen-kaffir, taal
diamond jager, schlenter
diamond mine kimberley
dish bobooti, bobotee, bobotie
district backveld, basutoland
dried meat biltong
drink skokian, sopie
dutch afrikaans, afrikan(d)er, boer, taal
dutch mistress noi
dutch speech afrikaans
eagle berghaan
farmer boer
fastener oxreim
fellow kerel
ferry pont
feverbird roller
fig marigold vetkousie
finch fink
fish bamboo-fish, barracouta, barracuda, box-salpa, snoek, steenbras(s)
flag vierkleur
flower clivia, coral, cowslip, fuchsia, lachenalia, phygelius, protea
fox asse, caama
francolin redwing
game dolos
garment caross, kaross
gazelle springbok, springbuck
"get out" voetsak
gold field benoni, rand
grass danthonia, kikuyo, rhodes
grassbird idle-jack
grassland veld(t)
greenhorn ikona
gulch sluit
gully donga
gun roer, rohr
half-acre erven
harness inspan
heath sparrowwort
herb bear's-paw, bengal lily, bolboxalis, buttercup, cabbagewort, cape-fennel, cape-lily, clivia, crinum, felicia, foeniculum, freesia, gamolepis, gazania, gerbera, gomphocarpus, grappleplant, othonna, pelargonium, pokerplant, restio, vallota, witchweed
hill bult, heuvel, kop(je), spitzkop
hippopotamus zeekoe
hog boschvark
hornbill bromvogel, bucorvus
hut kraal, pondok, rondavel, rondawel, scherm, struis

insect gogga
interior achterveld
iris ixia, moraea
jail tronk
knucklebones dolos
laborer togt
language afrikaans, bantu, bujarati, fanakalo, hindi, khoisan, taal, tamil, telugu, xhosa
legislature raad, staatsraad, volksraad
lily agapanthus, albuca, aloe
liquor vanderhum
lizard geitjie
lord's supper nachtmaal
maiden meisje
maize melie
master baas
measure vara
mole chrysochlore
monarchy lesotho
money, paper riksdaalder
monkey mona, talapoin, tamarin, teetee, vervet
mullet harder
nation angola, botswana, mozambique, rhodesia, zambia
nurse umfaan
outcast fingo, fingu
pass nek, poort
pasture veld(t)
peak aux, injasuti, kathkin, kop
peddler smous(e)
people afrikan(d)er, bantu, basuto, bechuana, boer, damara, hottentot, namas, pondo(misi), tswana, vaalpen, xosa
people's council volksraad
pineapple pina
pioneer voortrekker
plain sebkha, veld(t)
plant aloe, antholyza, aponogeton, avondbloem, bloodlily, cape-cowslip, galtonia, goatsfoot, hesperantha, ixia, king's-flower, kleinia, lachenalia, royal-crown, slangkop, sparaxis, toadflower, tritinia
plateau karroo
platinum rock rustenberg
plot erf
polecat musang
policeman zarp
port capetown, durban, kaapstad, port elizabeth
president oompaul, swart
prime minister hertzog, malan, smuts, verwoerd, vorster

province See *republic*, below.
racial separation apartheid
range drakensberg
ravine donga
redoubt schanz
region kaffraria, zululand
republic botswana, natal, transvaal
reservation bantustan
reunion hereniging
ridge rand, witwatersrand
rifle contest bisley
river kuruman, limpopo, modder, molopo, olifants, orange, vaal
rock kimberlite
rodent ratel
room voorhuis
rue agathosma
sect dopper
settler boer
sharecropper bywoner
shield skildfel
shoe veld(t)shoen
shrike bacbakiri, telephonus
shrub amatungula, ambertree, anchor-plant, aspalathus, assonia, barosoma, brabejum, breath-of-heaven, bush-tea, cyclopia, doornboom, fuchsia, geissoloma, goldenhair, hemp, jasmine, kei-apple, keurboom, lyperia, narras, natal plum, penaea, phygelius, podalyria, purslane, redels, resinbush, rochea, saffron, satinbush, seringa, tambookie, wolveboon
simpleton ikona
snake aboma, black-mamba, boomslang, dendraspis, egg-eater, elaps, mamba, ringhals
soldier springbok
spider, mythological anansi, annancy, nancy
spirit tikolosh
starling spreeuw, sprew
state angola, bamangwato, barotseland, basutoland, bechuanaland, cape-colony, gazaland, griqualand, kaffraria, mashonaland, matabeleland, mozambique, orange free state
statesman botha, hertzog, kruger, malan, smuts, strijdom, verwoerd, vorster
store winkel
stream aar, spruit
sumac karree
swamp vlei, vley

tableland karoo
tick tampan
tortoise hicatee, matama
town See *village*, below.
tract zuurveldt
trader kurveyor, swahili
tree aassagai, akebergia, assegei, bark cloth, beach apple, boxwood, brachystegia, bufflehorn, burchelia, callitris, calodendrum, cape ash, cape ebony, cedar, chestnut, cinchona, ekebergia, elaeodendron, essenhout, gamdeboo, geelhout, kaffirboom, kamassi, karroobush, krugiodendron, ladlewood, lemonwood, marula, olea, ouabaio, spekboom, tenio, wagenboom, wedding-flower
tribal assembly amapakati
umbrette hammerkop
upcountry achterveld(t)
valley laagte, vaal
village kraal, stad(t)
vine cacur, elephant's-foot, honeysuckle, tecomaria, wax-creeper
wagon pole disselboom
warbler grassbird
warrior impi
warthog emgalla
wattle hackthorn
waxbill astrild, estrilda
weapon assagai, assegai
weaverbird taha
weed brass-buttons
whip sjambok
wind cape-doctor
wood sorrel bolboxalis, buttercup
writer cloete, paton
SOUTH AMERICA(N) (See also INCA, LATIN AMERICA, SPANISH, and individual South American countries.) hispanic, ladino, latin(o)
aborigine See *indian*, below.
almond almendra
animal aardvark, afara, agovara, alpaca, antbear, anteater, apar, armadillo, coati, colocola, coypu, eyra, grison, guanaco, jaguar, kinkajou, llama, nutria, paca(rana), peba, poyou, pudu, pyrotheria, quica, sarigue, sloth, tamandua, tamarin, tapir, tatou(ay), vicuna
ant sauba, sauva
anteater tamandua

arbor ramada
armadillo apar, peba, pichiciago, poyou, tatou(ay)
arrow poison curara, curare
balsam copaiba, tolu, umiri
bark agoniada, amalambo
bat desmodus, glossophaga, vampire
bean tonka
beast of burden llama
beaver coypu
beef tasajo
beer chicha
beverage mate
bird agami, ara(cari), arara, aura, baker, barber, barbet, barkingbird, becard, bellbird, boatbill, cacicus, cacique, caracara, cariama, chaja, charo, churga, condor, coscoroba, curassow, flamingo, fruitcrow, guacharo, guan, habia, heron, hoactzin, hoatzin, ibis, jacamar, jacana, jacu, jopin, lindo, mina(h), mitu, myna, oilbird, piririgua, pitta, puffbird, quetzal, rara, screamer, seedsnipe, seriema, spinetail, stairbeak, swordbill, sylph, taha, tanager, tapaculo, terutero, tinamou, tityra, toco, toucan, trumpeter, turco, umbrellabird, warrior, yeni
biscuit panal
blanket serape
boa anaconda
boat cayuco
butterfly borboleta
cactus airampo, borzi
cape horn
cat cougar, eyra, kuichua, mountain lion, panther, puma
catfish aspredo, dorad, pygidid
cattail totora
cattle niata
chaja screamer
chief eldorado
cinnamon ishpingo
cloak or *coat* panolone, poncho, ruana
coffee shop confiteria
coin centavo, medio, peso, tomin
cold region puna
country argentina, bolivia, brazil, chile, colombia, equador, patagonia, peru, venezuela
cowboy gaucho, llanero, planero

cowboy weapon bolas
dance arieto, beguine, bolero, carioca, chacha, conga, criolla, mambo, maxixe, samba, r(h)umba, tango
deer brocket, coassus, guemal, guemul, huemul, mazama, pita, pudu, vanada
desert espinal, hornada
disease espundia
dog agouara, colpeo
dove talpacoti
dye lana
eel carapo
estuary la plata, para
evergreen bebeeru, bibiri, bibiru, nectandra, pino
farm chacra, estancia, estantion, hacienda, ranchero, rancho
fish acapima, acara, acedia, acoupa, aguavina, aimara, arapaima, bloodfin, carib(b)ee, caribe, corbina, gogy, mapo, piranha, piraya, poraque, scalare
flower angel's trumpet
fly pium, tatukira
flycatcher yetapa
fog comanchaca, garua
fox asse
fruit anana, chupachupa, pina
gaiter chaparajo, chaperejo, chivarra, chivarro
game jai alai, pelota
game bird guan, tinamou
garment ruana, serape
gopher quachil
gold oro
gourd abobra
government store tesoreria
grass ichu, quila
grasshopper langosta
grassland campo, pampa(s)
grate babracot
griddlecake arepa
gruel atole
guinea pig cavy
hare tapeti
hawk caracara, carancho, carrion-buzzard, chimango
herb arrowhead, beadplant, biacuru, flaveria, ismene, leonotis, limonium, malanga, pijicapu, romerillo, yareta
herdsman gaucho, llanero
hero bolivar
hummingbird rainbow, swordbill, sylph, topaz, wedgebill
indian abipou, akawai, allentiac, aneto, antesi(an),

aoarau, arawak, arecuna, auca, aymara, aztec, baniva, baniwa, bororoan, caingang, camacan, carib (an), carib(b)ee, cayapo, chavante, chayma, churoya, corabecan, coroado, covarecan, cumanagoto, curavecan, curucanecan, curuminacan, ges, goyana, guahibo, inca, ineri, ite(n), javitero, jivaro, lule, macusi, matacan, moxo, ona, ota, otuquian, oyana, pampean, pampero, patagonian, pioxe, piro, puquina, tama(naco), tapa, tapuyan, timbira, toba, trio, tupi, uro, voto, woyaway, yao
indian hut toldo
island aruba, elobey
jay xanthoura
jungle killer motilone
jungle plant cohoba
knife facao, machete, navaja
lake poopo, titicaca
land measure manzana
language ona, portuguese, spanish
lapwing terutero, teruteru
legislature asamblea
liberator bolivar
lily cocuisa, cucuiza
limestone tosca
liquor chicha
lizard anole, anoli, teju
mahogany caoba
mammal See *animal,* above.
marmoset tamarin
measure manzana, vara
medicine man peai, piay
military leader caudillo
mineral urso
monkey acari, alouatte, aotus, araba, barrigudo, beelzebub, callicebus, callithrix, capuchin, douricouli, douroucouli, grison, lagothrix, marimonda, marmoset, miriki, orabassu, ouakari, pinche, saguin, sai(miri), sajou, saki, samiri, sapajou, tamarin, te(e)tee, titi
moth urania
motmot houtou
musical instrument guiro
nightshade trompillo
northernmost punta-gallinas
opossum quica, sarigue
ostrich nandu, rhea
owl utum
palm acrocomia, assai, babassu, bacaba, bussu,

cocus, cohune, coquito, curua, datil, desmoncus, ita, jara, mauritia, nikau, raphia, tooroo, troly, troolie, tucum, ubussu, unamo, uricuri
parrot macaw
pass la cumbre, uspallata
pastry empanada
peak aconcagua, tupungato
peasant campesino
people anti, campa, inca
physic nut pignon
plague desenvolvimiento
plain llano, pampa(s), vega
plains dweller llanero
plant aji, albuca, alstroemeria, amaryllis, angelon, crassula, curare, espino, eucharis, gum, humenaea, ipecac, tillandsia, yucuchu
plateau region paramo, puna
porcupine coendu
porridge atole
proverb dicho
puffbird monasa
quail duraquara
rabbit tapeti
raft balsa
rancher estanciero
range andes, cordilleras
region amphigaea, gran chaco, guiana, patagonia, puna
resin acouchi
resort ancon, bariloche, buzios, isla margarita, punta del este, santa maria
river amazon, biobio, essequibo, japura, javary, jurua, negro, orinoco, para, paraguay, pilcomayo, plata, purus, rio, ucayali, uruguay
rodent abrocome, agouti, capibara, capybara, chinchilla, coypu, degu, guinea pig, hydrochoerus, mara, moca, paca, tucotuco, viscacha, vizcacha
root oca
rubber dapicho
rubber tree para, ule
ruminant alpaca, llama
saddle recado
sauce aji
scarf manta, rebozo, tapalo
seed abilla
shop joyeria
shrike batara
shrub anchiete, anchorplant, arrayan, bird of paradise, candlewood, ceiba, ceibo, coca, colletia, columellia, erythrina, feijoa, jaborandi,

kapok, mate, matico, pearlberry, pepino, poinciana, remijia, retama, rhatany
sickness soroche
skunk conepate
slaughterhouse frigirifico
snake aboma, anaconda, bom, bushmaster, coralito, ilysia, leptophis, lora
society granfino
sorrel oca
statesman san martin, santander
stork maguari
strait magellan
suspension bridge chimbachaca
tableland paramo(s), puna
tanager habia, lindo, yeni
tapir anta, danta
thicket espinal
tick carapato
tiger chati
tinamou macuca, tataupa
tin king patino
tortoise matamata
toucan aracari, toco
tradewind brisa
tree 3 apa, ebo 4 gama, jume, lana, mora, para, tala, vera 5 balsa, cacao, caoba, carat, carol, cebil, couma, fotui, myrrh, pekea, roble, tenio, umbra, umiri 6 angico, bacury, bibiru, carapa, cenela, chicha, clusia, eperua, lapuna, papaya, piquia, simaba, yachan 7 albarco, aroeira, bebeeru, caranna, copaiua, curupay, guayabi, quayabi, sapucai, urunday 8 algaroba, amarillo, arboloco, bignonia, caracoli, cinnamon, copalche, crabwood, ishpingo 9 algarroba, angelique, araucaria, astronium, balaustre, bethabara, bowdichia, cariniana, ceretonia, couratari, imbirussu, jacaranda, quebracho, tinkabean 10 balaustine, breadfruit, candlewood, cannonball, couroupita, gasparillo, guachamaca, kaneelhart, paddlewood, purplewood, siruaballi 11 chichicaste, sapotizeiro 12 st johns-bread, umbrella tree
tribe campa, motilones, oca
trumpeter agami
tuber oca
turtle matamata

valley hoya
vine abobra, araujia, cacur, cucumis, cushcush, milkweed, passiflora, preira, punya, tacso, yampee
volcano chimborazo, cotopaxi, omate, tolima
vulture condor
walnut conacaste
wasteland patagonia
waterfalls angel, iguassu
weakfish acoupa
weapon bola(s)
weight arroba
wildcat colocola, eyra
wind pampero, puna, puno
wood cesalpinia, curupay, itauba

SOUTH CAROLINA *capital* columbia
city aiken, bamberg, beaufort, belton, camden, charleston, conway, dillon, florence, greenville, greenwood, greer, laurens, manning, newberry, orangeburg, rockhill, seneca, spartenburg, sumter, union, walhalla
college citadel, claflin, clemson, coker, erskine, furman, lander, wofford
county aiken, dillon, horry, jasper, oconee, saluda
dam saluda
fort sumter
indian catawba, congaree, cusabo, pedee, santee, sewee, shawnee, sugeree, wateree, waxhaw, yamasi
lake catawba, hartwell, marion, moultrie, murray, wateree
motto dum spiro spero
native palmetto, weasel
nickname calinky, palmetto state
peak sassafras
plateau piedmont
political group woolhats
president jackson
river ashepoo, broad. edisto, peedee, saluda, santee, savannah
state bird wren
state flower jasmine, jessamine
state tree palmetto
SOUTH CHINA *sea, arm* tonkin gulf
sea island hainan
SOUTH DAKOTA *butte* crow, deersears, finger, mud, saddle, sully, thunder

capital pierre
city aberdeen, brookings, custer, deadwood, eureka, huron, leap, lemmon, miller, rapid city, sioux falls, sisseton, sturgis, vermillion, webster, winner, yankton
college huron, yankton
county brule, custer, day, jerauld, mellette, moody, spink, yankton
dam oahe
indian brule, cheyenne, dakota, sioux, sutaio
lake bigstone, oahe, traverse
monument rushmore
national park wind-cave
nickname blizzard state, coyote state, sunshine state
peak bear, crooks, harney, moreau, sheep, table
range blackhills
region badlands
river cheyenne, james, missouri, moreau
state bird pheasant
state flower pasqueflower
state tree spruce
SOUTHEAST *wind* cape-doctor
wind god eurus
SOUTHEAST AFRICA *deity* kintu, leeyo, minepa, muluku, nenaunir, ngai, nyambi, tilo
SOUTHERN austral, austrine, meridional, sudic, torrid,
breakfast chess pie, grits
buckthorn bumelia
cross crux
cross star acrux, betacrucis, betacrux, crosier
farmer planter
food cornbread, cornpone, fatback, gumbo, hoecake, okra, potlikker
france midi, provence, riviera
fruit pawpaw, scuppernong
illinois egypt
india dravida
indian alabama, apatachee, atakap, calusa, catawba, cherokee, chickahominy, chitimacha, choctaw, creek, hitchiti, lumbee, mattapony, mobile, nanticoke, natchez, powhatan, quapaw, quele, shawnee, seminole, tuscarora, tutelo, upamunkey, yamasee, yuchi
lights aurora australis, aurora polaris

right whale blackfish, eubalaena
states confederacy, dixie
tonic dope
wood abrotanum, appleringie, appleringy, artemisia, boy's-love, wormwood
SOUTH KOREA See KOREA.
SOUTHLAND auster
SOUTH PACIFIC See SOUTH SEAS.
hero emile
SOUTHPAW leftie, lefty, pitcher
SOUTH SEAS See also MALAY references.
arrowroot pia
boat jangada, proa
bubble schemer john law
drink kava
eel tuna
garment pareu, sarong
island aru, atoll, bali, bismarck archipelago, fiji, otaheite, pitcairn, samoa, sulu, tahiti, timor, tonga
islander kanaka, maori, samoan
island group society
island money wakiki
language balinese
product copra
religion cargo-cult
rose oleander
sea coral, tasman, timor
tree candlenut
SOUTH VIETNAM See also VIETNAM.
army arvn
capital saigon
city annhon, binhdinh, danang, hoian, hue, phanrang, quangtri, saigon, songcan, tayninh, vinhloi
delta mekong
general do-cao-tri
guerrilla vietcong
language cham, khmer, rhade
leader le duc tho, nguyen van thieu
massacre my lai, pinkville, quang ngai, song my
peak badinh, knontran, ngoklinh, ninhhoa, tchepone
port danang, nhatrang, quinhon, saigon, tourane
president ngo-dinh-diem
river dongnai, mekong
SOUTHWARK *inn* tabard
SOUTHWEST *indian* anasazi, apache, cree, hopi, na-

vajo, paiute, pima, yuma, zuni
SOUTHWEST AFRICA namibia
SOUTHWESTER gale, hat, squam, storm, wind
SOUVENIR bibelot, curio, keepsake, memento, memory, recollection, relic, remembrance, reminder, token
SOVEREIGN absolute, almighty, autarchic, authoritative, autocrat, autonomous, chagan, chief (tain), coin, controlling, dominant, dynastic, emperor, empress, excellent, extreme, foremost, free, greatest, guinea, head, highest, imperial, imperious, independent, kaiser, king(ly), liege, lord, majestic, mikado, monarch(ial), negus, nizam, paramount, potentate, predominant, prince(ly), principal, queen (ly), quid, regal, royal, ruler, samory, self-governing, skiv, soldan, suffrain, superior, supreme, surpassing, suzerain, transcendent, ultimate, zamorin
advisers privy council
allowance privy purse
authority dominion
decree arret
divinely thearchic
great maharajah
investiture coronation
pardon amnesty
pert. regal, royal
petty tetrarch
power throne
prerogative claim seigniorage
remedy nostrum
SOVEREIGNTY ascendancy, autarchy, autarky, authority, autonomy, caliphate, command, control, demesne, dominion, dynasty, empery, empire, freedom, independence, kingship, majesty, monarchy, power, raj, regalia, regality, regnancy, royalty, rule, scepter, state, sultanate, supremacy, sway, throne
absolute autarchy, despotism, dictatorship, tyranny
emblem crown, kahili
joint condominium
SOVIET See RUSSIA.
SOW broadcast, cast, channel,

disperse, disseminate, ditch, drain, drill, furnish, gilt, grow, grumphy, heap, hog, implant, inoculate, mold, pig, plant, raise, salamander, scatter, seed, seminate, shed, slut, soo, spread, squander, stack, strew, swine, yelt

bug hoglouse, isopod, slater, woodlouse

female gilt

fennel brimstonewort

gelder rogue, scoundrel

grass swine's-cress

thistle dindle, gutweed, hogweed, milkweed, sonchus

-tit frangaria, wood-strawberry

udder suman

wild oats dissipate, play

young elt, gilt, piggy

SOWBACK cap, drumlin, hill, ridge

SOWBANE goosefoot

SOWBELLY bacon, saltpork

SOWBREAD wild cyclamen

SOWENS flummery, paste, porridge, washbrew

SOWER seeder, seedman

of dragon's teeth cadmus

SOWL(E) beat, pottage, relish, sauce, thrash, tousle

SOX *short* anklets

SOY(A) bean, dill, fennel, legume, soi, soja

curd tofu

enzyme urase

pasto miso

tablet torfu

SOZZLY drunk, messy, muddy, shiftless, sloppy

SPA baden, baths, ems, hydro, oasis, pax, resort, sanatorium, saratoga, springs, therma, watering place

SPACE (See also ASTRO-NAUT and ROCKET.) abyss, accommodations, acreage, area, arena, areola, areole, arrange, atmosphere, berth, blank, block, blue, breadth, capacity, chance, cleft, compass, concourse, continuum, course, dimension, dispart, distance, duration, elbowroom, expanse, expansion, extend, extent(ion), field, headroom, hiatus, interval, lacuna, lebensraum, margin, measure, open(ing), opportunity, part, path, period,

place, range, rank, reach, reservation, roam, room(th), rove, scope, separate, sphere, spread, stretch, territory, time, track, tract, universe, void, volume, walk, while

agency nasa

air centrum

architectural metope, pediment, sacellum

between times interim

between triglyphs metope

between 2 points distance, spread

blank lucuna

breathing recess

clear fairway, glade, headway

counter backbar

cramped cubby

empty blank, inane, vacuo, vacuum, void

enclosed area, bowl, chamber, circuit, cloister, closure, compass, confines, hatch, pteroma, verge

fear of agoraphobia

1st man in gagarin

flat homaloid

flight, pert. orbital

for goods storage

full of matter plenum

high point apocynthion

hollowed mortice, mortise

included contents

laboratory mol

level parterre, platea

limitless ether, heavens, immensity, infinite, infinity, olam, plenum, universe, vast(itude), world

mission lunar probe

navigate in astrogate

occupied volume

of time interval

on surface area

open alley, aperture, areaway, court, daylight, fairway, kneehole, laund, lawn, maidan, tahua

open, abnormal desire for agromania

open, comb. agor(a)

outer chaos, ether, void

pert. areal, lacunal, spatial

popliteal ham, hock

portion of place

safekeeping locker, storage, vault

scientist draper, goddard, houbolt, von braun

sheltered killogie

shuttle flying brickyard, orbiter

small areola, areole, cubicle, interstice, pore

station satellite

storage attic, basement, cellar, closet, cupboard, shed, storeroom, warehouse

theory circularism, plenism

traveler astronaut, cosmonaut

triangular spandrel

unfilled breakage, cavity, gap(e), hollow

vehicle rocket, satellite

void abyss, chasm, inanity

wall alcove, niche

white margin

SPACECRAFT (See also ROCKET.) apollo, gemini, mariner, mercury, saturn

brake retrorocket

landing reentry, splashdown

shelter cosmodrome

thrust retrorocket

SPACEMAN See ASTRONAUT.

SPACIOUS ample, boundless, broad, capacious, cavernous, commodious, comprehensive, deep, enormous, expansive, extensive, generous, great, immense, large, limitless, rangy, roomy, vast(y), voluminous, wide (spread)

SPACK forward, intelligent, knowing

SPADASSIN bravo, duelist, swordsman

SPADE burgoyne, card, delve, dig, dredge, excavate, exhume, feck, graff, graft, grub, ladle, loy, paddle, pick, pry, scavel, shovel, slade, slane, spay, spitter, spud, trowel, tuskar, twiscar

ace matador, spadill(a), spadille

bone shoulderblade

depth of graft, spit

deuce little casino

handle tree

long narrow loy

peat slade, slane, tuskar

plasterer's server

queen basta, black lady, black maria, calamity jane, lizzy, slippery anne

-shaped palaceous

sharp spud

small scuppet, trowel

suit digger, espadas, grun, laub, lilies, pick, pique, schippen, schuppen, soldiers, swords

triangular didle
turf slane
SPADEFISH moonfish, paddlefish, porgy, tripletail
SPADEFOOT toad
SPADEWORK drudgery
SPADGER boy, lad, sparrow
SPAHEE, SPAHI See SOLDIER.
SPAIN (See also SPANISH for expressions and vocabulary.) espagna, hesperia, hispania, iberia, sepharad
abbey abadia
abbeylands abadengo
absinthe ajenjo
acrobat volteador
admiral cervera, topete
adventurer almogaver
african province rio muni
alcove alhacena
amulet dije
appetizer tapa
apron delantal
architect churriguerra, gaudi
aunt tia
balcony mirador
ball game pelota
band cobla
bank caja
barracks cuartel
bathtub banera, bano
battle blenheim
bay bahia, biscay, vigo
beach playa
bean frijol, haba
belle maja
blanket manta, serape
boat aviso, balandra, barca, barcolongo
bonnet gorra
booth tienda
boy nino
brandy aguardiente, anisado
breeze, warm cefiro
brigand ladron
brook arroyuelo, quebrada
brotherhood of cities santa hermandad
brunette morena
brush cepillo
bull toro
bullring coso
buyer comprador
cafe tertulia
calico percal, zaraza
canal acequia
canyon cajon, canon
canyon mouth abra
cape ajo, creus, dartuch, espichel, gato, marroqui, moras, nao, ortegal, palos, penas, prior, sacratif, salinas, tortosa, trafalgar

capital cordova, madrid, toledo
card game monte, ombre
cardinal cisneros, mendoza, ximenes
carriage calesa
cart carretela, carret(t)a, carreton
cashew maranon
cashier caja
castle alcazar
castles in dreams, hopes
cathedral city seville
catholic lay organization opus dei
cavalryman ginete
cave altamira
cellist casals
chair silla
champion el cid
channel cano
chant saeta
chaperon duenna
chapter house cabildo
cheer bravo, ole
chest arca, caja
chief adalid, cid, jefe
church iglesia
churchman hosius, osio
city 4 aspe, baza, elda, haro, irun, jaen, lena, leon, loja, lugo, mula, olot, reus, rota, sama *5* alcoy, avaro, avila, baena, bajar, cabra, cadiz, cieza, cueta, ecija, eibar, elche, gijon, ibiza, jerez, jodar, lorca, oliva, palma, ronda, siero, ubeda, urgel, xeres, yecla *6* aviles, azuaga, bilbao, burgos, duenca, gandia, gerona, getafe, guadix, hellin, huelva, huesca, jativa, lerida, lucena, madrid, malaga, mataro, merida, murcia, orense, oviedo, termel, toledo, utrera, zamora *7* almeden, almeria, badajoz, cordoba, cordova, daimiel, granada, jumilla, langreo, linares, logrono, manresa, sagunto, segovia, sevilla, tarrasa, vitoria *8* albacete, alicante, badalona, figueras, pamplona, sabadell, santiago, torrente, valencia, zaragoza *9* algeciras, barcelona, cartagena, salamanca, santander, saragozza *10* hospitalet, vallodolid *12* san ildefonso
city chief alcalde, curaca
civil war heroine ibarruri, la pasionaria

class estado
clerk escribano, escribiente
cloth pina
club basto, tertulia
coastal region costa brava, costa del sol
coat or cloak capa, chaleco, chaqueta, chupa, manta, zamarra, zamarro
cockpit gallera
coffee pot cafetera
coin alfonso, castellan, centavo, centen, centimo, cob, cuartillo, cuartino, cuarto, decima, decimo, dinero, dobla, doblon, doubloon, ducatoon, duro, escudo, excellente, isabelina, maravedi, milesima, peseta, peso, piaster, piastre, pieces of eight, pitsole, real(dor), vellon
collar cuello, gollila
colonial governor bobadilla
colonial labor system repartimiento
colony adrar
commander adalid, alcaide, alcayde, caid, cid
commune alcoy, aliva, ausa, elda, gradu, jaen, lena, lorca, naron, oliva, osuna, reus, rute, siero, sueca, telda, tineo, ubeda, utrera, vich, yecla
composer albeniz, de falla, granados, hidalgo, mompou, pedrell, solar, turina
conqueror alvarado, berbers, carthaginians, conquistador, cortez, de heredia, moors, pizzaro, romans, visigoths
constable alguacil, alguazil
cooperative mesta
cornerstones lastres-piedras
cosmetic angelwater
cotton algodon, bayal
council cabildo, consejo, junta
count conde
court fronton, patio
cowboy ginete, guacho, llanero, vaquero
crate seron
cucumber pepino
cupboard trostera
custom house aduana
dance baile, bolero, bour-(r)ee, caballero, carioca, chaconne, danza(r), fandango, farruca, flamenco, gitana, gitano, guaracha, jaleo, jarabe, jota, malaguena,

pabana, pavan, polo, saraband, sardana, seguidilla, seguiriya, sevillana, tango, zapateado
dancer escudero
day of week (1–7) lunes, martes, miercoles, jueves, viernes, sabado, domingo
defense group somaten
deity dios(sa)
designer castillo
desk vargueno
dialect aragonese, bable, basque, castilian, catalan, euskera, galician, gallego, gascon
dictator francisco franco y bahamonde, primo de rivera
dining room comedor
diplomat alarcon, gondomar
dish arroz con pollo, cigala, comal, gamgas, gazpacho, paella, posole, serrano, zarzuela
district montana, xeres
diva bori
division blue devils
dollar cob, duro, peso, piastre
dramatist alvarez, benavente, calderon, lope de vega, lorca, quintero, tirso de molina
dress traje
drink guarapo, pulque, sangria, verano
driver cochero
duke alba
duty, impost indulto
dynasty omayyad, ommiad
ecclesiastic loyola
emblem pomegranate
emperor ferdinand, fernando
epic poema del cid
estate encomienda, estancia, finca, hacienda
exclamation bravo, carajo, caramba, ole
execution garrot(t)e
explorer adelantado, alarcon, balboa, bruno de heceta, cabeza de vaca, cabrillo, cermeno, colon, coronado, cortes, cortez, de soto, grijalva, mendoza, onate, pizzaro, ponce de leon, ulloa, vizcaino
fabric crea, pano, tiraz
farm hacienda
farmer hacendado, hacendero
farmhouse caserio
fascist falangist

fascist party falange
fashion designer castillo
feastday fiesta
fish cero, pargo, ronco, sesi, sierra
fish stew zarzuela
fleet armada, caraval, flota
food shop cantina
franco follower falangist, franquista
frigate zabra
gambling money barato
game hombre, jai alai, julepe, malilla, monte, muchas-gracias, muerto, nada, omber, ombre, parejas, pedro, pelota, perejila, perro, ramy, ronda, seisillo, solo, sotas, tomate, tresillo, truco, tute
garden alameda
general alba, alva, blas de lezo, franco
gentleman caballero, cavalier, don, grandee, senor
giant eleizegue
giantess giralda
girl chulapa, maja, senorita
goblin duende
government obligation cedula
governor adelanto
greeting hola
griddlecake arepa
grove mata
gruel atole
guerrillas frap
guide practico
guild gremio
guitarist segovia
gun miquelet
gunboat barca
gypsy gitano, zincalo
half-breed ladino
hall sala
hangman's rope mecate
harbor puerto
harbor entrance boca
hat boina, sombrero
hawthorn espino
haze calina
head covering mantilla
headland finisterre
herd manada
herdsman ranchero
hero don juan, durandarte, el cid, montesinos, viriatius
heroine ibarruri, la pasionaria
highway camino real
hill cerro, colina, loma, morro, otero
hillside falda

historian aquilero, maranon, orosius
hogshead almud
holiday fiesta
holy image santo
hoodlum gamberro
hors d'oeuvres tapas
horse cavallo, jennet
hotel albergue, parador, posada
house aldea, casa, casita
house spirit duende
impost indulto
indian cholo, guero, mestizo, trigueno
inlet estero
inn meson, parador
inquisition court triana
inquisition head isabel, torquemada
inquisition stake brasero
inquisitor torquemada
island alboran, ibiza, majorca, mallorca, menorca, minorca, palma, tagomago, tenerife
island group balearic, canary
jailor alcaide, alcayde
jar albarello, bucaro, olla, tarro, tinaja
jew anu im, marrano, sephardim
jewish section aljama
jewish vernacular aljamia
judge alcalde, juez
kettle cazo, olla, tetara
kettledrum atabal, timbal
king alfonso, bonaparte, carlos, charles, ferdinand, geryon, juan carlos de borbon y borbon, phillip, rey, roderick
king, 1st geryon
kingdom aragon, asturias, castile, leon
knife bolo, cuchillo, machete, navaja
knight caballero
lace encaje
lady dama, dona, senora
lake albufera, lago
land solariego
land, common ejido
landmark coto, linde, marca, mojon, senal
land mass isla
land measure or tenure cavalleria
language castilian
lariat reata, riata
leader adolfo suarez gonzales, el caudillo, el cid, jefe, navarro

legion blue devils, sweethearts of death
legislature cortes
letter carrier correo
libertine don giovanni, don juan
linen crea, gaea, hilo, lienzo
lord don
lowland marisma
magistrate corregidor
mahogany caoba
man diego, don, hombre, senor
manager gerente
mantel capa
martyr priscillian, servetus
matador belmonte, manolete
mattress colchon
mausoleum escorial
mayor alcade, alcalde, curaca
meadow arado, prado, vega
measure almud(e), aranzada, arroba, azumbre, braza, caballeria, cafiz, cahiz, cantara, carga, celemin, codo, copa, cordel, cuadra, cuarta, cuarteron, cuartilla, dedo, estadel, estado, fanegada, legua, libra, linea, medio, milla, moyo, palmo, paso, pie, pulgada, racion, sesma, vara, yugada
military academy academia de infanteria, aracoza
missile bolo
missionary junipero serra, las casas
monarchist carlist
monk padre
month mes
month (1– 12) enero, fevrero, marzo, abril, mayo, junio, julio, agosto, septiembre, octubre, noviembre, diciembre
moor morisco
moorish kingdom granada
mosque mezquita
mosque part kiblah, mihrab
motion picture cine
motto empresa
mounts, relay remuda
muffler embozo
muleteer almocrebe, arriero
museum escorial, prado
music chacona, malaguena
musical instrument atabal, bandurria, castanet, vihuela, zambomba
musical offering zarzuela
mystic theresa of avila
national motto plus ultra

national tourist corporation entursa
navigator pinzon
night watchman sereno
nobel prize winner cajal
noble caballero, don, grandee, hidalgo
numbers (1–10) uno, dos, tres, cuatro, cinco, seis, siete, ocho, nueve, diez
nun monja, teresa
official alcalde, alguazil, escriban, regidor
officials the bunker
operetta zarzuela
organist soler
oyster ostra, pinna
painter cano, dali, el greco, genoves, goya, gris, herrera, miro, morales, picasso, ribera, sert, theotokopoulos, velasquez, zuloaga, zurbaran
palace alhambra, escorial, zarzuela
pancake arepa
partisan afrancesado
party democratic center union, eta, falange, frap, junta democratica, movimiento nacional, patriotic front, popular alliance, socialist workers, ucd
patron saint james
peak almonzar, aneto, banuelo, cerredo, estats, gata, guara, montseny, montserrat, mulhacen, nethou, penalara, perdido, pico, rouch, teide, teleno
peasant paisano
peninsula iberia
people cantabri, castilian, catalan, diego, espagna, espana, espanol, gente, iberian, latin, maragato, pict
pert. hispanic, iberian
peso duro
petticoat basquine
philosopher lully
physician servetus
pianist albeniz, granados
pickpocket ratero
plain pampa, sabana
plain dweller llanero
planation finca, hacienda
poet alarcon, aleixandre, alonso, becquer, cernuda, encina, ercilla, espronceda, felipe, guillen, jimenez, lope de vega, unamuno
police benemerita, guardia-

civil, hermandad, policia, rurale
politician blasco ibanez
porcelain alcora
porridge atole
port abdera, adra, algeciras, alicante, almeria, badalona, barcelona, bilbao, cadiz, cartegena, caruna, denia, el ferrol, gades, gadir, gijon, huelva, la coruna, lalita, malaga, mataro, melilla, noya, palos, rota, santander, seville, vigo
porter cargador
post office correo
post office box apartado
pot olla
president azana, zamora
priest cura, dominic, molinos, padre
prime minister arias
princess infanta
proclamation bando
promenade alameda, pasear, prado
province alava, albacete, alicante, almeria, aragon, avila, badajoz, baleares, barcelona basque, burgos, caceres, cadiz, cordoba, coruna, cuenca, galicia, gerona, granada, guadalajara, guipuscoa, huelva, huesca, jaen, leon, lerida, logrono, lugo, madrid, malaga, murcia, navarra, orense, oviedo, palencia, salamanca, santander, segovia, sevilla, soria, tarragona, teruel, toledo, valencia, valladolid, vizcaya, zamora, zaragoza
pruning hook calabozo
queen ena, isabella, maria luisa, regina, reina
raisin pasa
ranch estancia, finca, hacienda, potrero
rancher estanciero, ranchero
range alcaraz, cantabrian, cuenca, demanda, gredos, guadarrama, maladeta, moncayo, monegros, morena, pyrenees, sierra, toledo
rapier See *sword*, below.
ravine quebrada
regent ximenes
regiment tercio
region andalusia, aragon, asturias, basque, castile, castilla, catalonia, comarca, estremadura, la mancha, leon, murcia, navarre, valencia

resort costa brava, costa del sol, torremolinos
revenue officer carabinero
revolutionist descamisado, prim
rice arroz
rider herisson
river adaja, alagon, almeria, almonte, aragon, arlanza, barbate, cabriel, cega, cinca, douro, duero, duraton, ebro, eresmo, esla, gallego, genil, guadalquivir, guadiana, henares, huerva, jalon, jarama, jucar, lima, mijares, minho, mino, odiel, orbego, perales, riaza, rio, segre, segura, sil, tagus, tajo, ter, tinto, torote, turia, ulla
road camino, estrada
robber bandido, bandito, bandolero
robin hood luis candelas
romance caballeria
royal family bourbon
rug alpurjarra
saddle albarda, aparejo
saint dominic, eulalie, james, santiago de compostela, teresa, xavier
sandal alpargata, huarache, huaracho
sausage chorizo
scarf reboso, rebozo, tapalo
scholar vitoria
scorpion alacran
season invierno, otono, primavera, verano
sect alombrados, illuminati
sentinel vedet(te), videt(te)
separatist movement eta
servant criado, mozo
shawl manto, reboso, reboza, serape
sheep infantado, merino
sherry amontillado, amoroso, fino, jeres, manzanilla, oloroso, pedro-ximenez, xeres
sherry pourer venencia
shirt camisa
shoes sabatos, zapatos
shop tienda
shrimp camaron
silk firaz
silver plata
sled narria
snack tapa
soldier almogavar, alvarado, miquelet
song fandango, malagueno, petenara, sequidilla, villancico

soprano bori, de los angeles, tiple
sorcerer brujo
soup gazpacho
spectacle bullfight
spirit duende
spring venero
squirrel ardilla
stanza seguidilla
statesman azana, echegaray, espartero, lopez de ayala, zamora
stew caldera, cocido, zarzuela
stockfarm rancho
street calle
supervisor capataz
swamp cienaga
sword bilbo, colada, espada, espadin, estoque, rapier
swordfish espada
tablecloth mantel(e)
tableland altiplanicie
talk palabra
tax alcabala, alcavala
teacher maestra, maestro
theologian john of the cross, molina, orosius, servetus, suarez
thimble dedal
tidelands las marismas
title dom, don(a), hidalgo, senor(a), senorita
tower atalaya, mirador, torre
townhall cabildo
trail camino
treasure ship atocha
tree espino, pino
trench surcar, tajo
tribunal acuerdo, audiencia
trousers calzoneras
trowel llana
trustee sindico
union official sindicale
union, underground commisiones obreras
valley hoya
vehicle tartana
vessel albarello, balandra, barca, barco, buque, caravel, galleon, nave, zabra
victory cry ole
village aldea, barrio, caserio
vintage vendimia
vulture gallinazo
waistcoat chaleco, chupa
walking stick baston
warehouse almacen
washbasin aljofaina
washer woman lavandera
watch reloj
watercourse arroyo, atarjea
water jar tinaja
watermelon sandia

weight adarme, arienzo, arroba, barril, caracter, castellano, dinero, dracma, escrupulo, frail, grano, libra, marco, ochava, onza, punto, quarto, quilate, quintal, roba, tomin, tonelada
wheat trigo
whip azote
wind brisa, laveche, leveche, solano
window ventana
wine alicant, bastard, bual, garnet, hollock, jerez, malaga, oloroso, rioja, sherry, tinta, tinto, vino, xeres
wine container bota
wine land jerez de la frontera, rioja
wine shop bodega, venta
witch or *wizard* bruja, brujo
witchcraft brujeria
woman dona, maja, senora
writer alarcon, aleman, azorin, barea, baroja, calderon, cela, cervantes, ibanez, lope de vega, lopez de ayala, miguel, miro, montalvo, rojas
SPALACID mole, rat, rodent
SPALATO split
SPALD joint, limb, open, shoulder(blade), splay, splinter, split
SPALE brace, chip, fine, lath, rail, shaving, spall, splinter, timber
SPALL bit, break, chip, crumble, disintegrate, fall, flake, fragment, gallet, hammer, reduce, shoulder, spale, spawl, splinter
SPALPEEN boy, braggart, good-for-nothing, laborer, lad, rascal, rogue, scamp, workman, youngster
SPALT brittle, chip, crisp, split, tear
SPAN arcade, arch, attach, bestride, bridge, cock, completely, confine, connect, cove, cross, distance, encircle, encompass, expanse, extend, extent, fasten, fetter, girder, grasp, hobble, length, link, measure, overlie, pair, perfectly, period, range, reach, rig, roof, rope, seize, space, spread, stretch, subtend, team, two, vault, yoke
iron harpoon
SPANG bang, clasp, crack,

directly, hurl, jump, kick, leap, ornament, spangle, squarely, straight, stride, yoke

SPANGHEW buffet, fling, jerk, leap, spring

SPANGLE aglet, boss, chequeen, gleam, glisten, glitter, ornament, paillette, plate, prank, sequin, shine, sparkle, star, zecchino

-baby fop

SPANIEL clumber, cringing, dog, fawn(ing), sport, sycophant, trasy

breed blenheim, brittany, clumber, cocker, english, field, king charles, norfolk, papillon, ruby, springer, sussex, toy, trasy, water (rug)

toy papillon

SPANISH (including Spanish-American) See SPAIN for geographical entries.

afternoon tarde

america See LATIN AMERICA, SOUTH AMERICA.

article iviza, las, los, una, uno

as como

ashes barilla

bad malo

baroque churriguerresque

bayonet yucca, zote

because porque

bermudas bermoothes

blind ciego

bravo ole

carnation barbados-pride

cat gato

cedar acajou, cedrela

cheap barato

clover lucerne

cold frio

cork bendy-tree

council cabildo, consejo, junta

curlew ibis

dagger yucca

deceit falsedad

documents expediente

earth tierra

elm black sage, ramona

embrace abrazo

entrance entrada

evening tarde

factory oficina

fireplace fogon

firewood lena

fly blister-beetle, cantharides, cantharis, cure, remedy

friend amiga, amigo, compadre

gift aguinaldo, recaldo

girl chulapa, maja, senorita

gold oro

gold and silver oro y plata

golden dorado

goodbye adios, hasta la vista

grass esparto, spart

grass rope soga

grille reja

habeas corpus amparo

hogfish ladyfish

hot calido, caliente

jacinth scilla, squill

james diego, iago

jasmine frangipani, malati

journey, day's jornada

law derecho

leather cordovan

legal affair acto

little poco

mackerel cero, sierra

magic brujeria

main caribbean

measles mildew

miss senorita

mistress amiga

moor morisco

moss tillandsia

mother madre

mouth boca

now ahora

ocher almagra, tangier

old viejo

paprika pimenton

patron padrino

pear avocado

pepper chili, pimento

petrarch de la vega

petticoat basquine

pigeon paloma

plum siruelas

polite cortes

pot olla

pretty bello, bonito, lindo

pronunciation mark tilde

purse bolsa

red rojo

relay remuda

ribbon cinta

rice arroz

right derecho

road camino, estrada

roasted asado

room sala

rooster gallo

sage sabio

school horse lipizzaner, lippizaner

see you tomorrow hasta manana

sesame ajonjoli

shakespeare calderon de la barca

silver plata

sled narria

snack tapa

soap castile

so long hasta luego

state new mexico

stopper ironwood

street calle

thank you gracias

thistle sandbur

tomorrow manana

trefoil alfalfa, lucerne, medicago

trick el mana, treta

trowel llana

tufts rue

very muy

water agua

who knows quien sabe

work labrar, obra, operar

SPANISH AMERICA See LATIN AMERICA, SOUTH AMERICA, SPANISH.

SPANK beat, blister, blow, cane, chastise, crack, dash, drive, flagellate, flog, lash, paddle, pound, prat, punish, scud, skelp, slap, slipper, smack, snap, spang, spat, speed, strike, urge, whip, whop

SPANKER blow, gold, horse, money, pacer, sail, smack, trotter, whopper

SPANKING active, brisk, dashing, fast, fine, fresh, good, great, huge, large, lively, punishment, quick, rapid, remarkable, smacking, stout, strong, vigorous

new fresh, novel

SPANNER firearm, key, lock, tool, wrench

SPAR (See also *kind,* below.) argue, bar, beam, block, bolt, boom, bowsprit, box, caber, charge, close, club, contend, contest, dispute, enclose, fasten, fight, gaff, longeron, lunge, mast, mineral, pole, quarrel, rod, rung, shut, spear, spit, sprit, spurt, steeve, strike, thrust, timber, wrangle, yard

bitter dolomite

blue lazulite

brown dolomite, magnesite

defect shan

diagonal sprit

extremity yardarm

heavy barite, cauk, cawk

hoop bangle

horizontal pudding-boom

kind boom(kin), bowsprit, bum(p)kin, crosstree, dolphin, forejack, foremast, foreyard, gaff, jack, jibboom, mainmast, mast (head), mizzen(mast), pole, sheerpole, spankerboom, spankergaff, sprit, stick, timber, topmast, tree, yard(arm)

-like spathic

up pay, settle

SPARAXIS ixia, wandflower

SPARE abstain, additional, afford, angular, avoid, bare, bear, bony, chary, cheesepare, deprive, desist, dilatory, duplicate, economical, economy, endure, exempt, exigous, extra, fly, forbear, forgive, free, frugal, gaunt, give, lank(y), lean, lenten, meager, occasional, parsimonious, parsimony, placket, preserve, refrain, relent, relieve, relinquish, save, scant(y), scrawny, scrimpy, skimpy, skinny, slender, slight, slim, slit, slow, sparse, stop, stingy, stringy, subsicive, superfluous, surplus, temperate, thin, thrifty, tire, tolerate, withhold

hand cat

time leisure

SPARELESS plentiful

SPARGE bespatter, moisten, plaster, roughcast, spray (ing), sprinkle

pipe weeper

SPARID bamboofish, bream, catalina, porgy, scup, sheepshead

SPARING chary, frugal, gnede, merciful, reticent, scanty, SPARE, stingy, thrifty

SPARK aizle, arc, beam, beau, belle, blade, buck, cause, cavalier, coruscate, court, coxcomb, dandy, date, diamond, dude, ember, escort, esquire, flash, flicker, fop, funk, gallant, glance, gleam, glint, glisten, glister, glitter, grain, ignite, instigate, instigation, interest, iota, izle, jot, knight, love(r), nob, pet, scintillate, shimmer, soil, spatter, spirit, spunkie, squire, start, swain, sweetheart, swell, toff, trace,

twinkle, wit, womanizer, woo

arrester bonnet, cinderframe, cowl

plug igniter distributor, energizer, starter

stream arc

vital ghost

SPARKED spotted, streaked, variegated

SPARKLE animate, animation, blaze, blink, brilliance, brilliant, bubble, coruscate, crackle, diffuse, disperse, effervesce, fire, flash, flicker, glance, gleam, glimmer, glint, glisten, glitter, joke, kindle, liveliness, radiate, scatter, scintillate, shimmer, shine, spirit, splendor, spray, sprinkle, strew, trace, twinkle, vivacity, vivify·

SPARKLING bright, brilliant, bubbly, carbonated, cheerful, crisp, dewy, effervescent, fizzy, funny, gorgeous, lively, micaceous, mousseau, quick, reflecting, shiny, sunny, twinkling, twinkly

SPARLING smelt, tern

fowl merganser

SPARPLE disperse, disseminate, route, scatter, sprinkle

SPARROW accentor, bird, chanter, chippie, chippy, doney, dunnock, fieldie, finch, firetail, hairbird, haysuck, hedgebetty, hempy, isaac, munia, paddy, passer, philip, ricebird, spadger, sparry, sprong, spurdie, titlene, titling, tittlin, towhee, weaverbird, whitecap

chipping hairbird

flock tribe

-grass asparagus

hawk anvil, berigora, falcon, kestrel, musket

hedge accentor, doney, haysuck

house spadger, spug, spurdie

song silver-tongue

white-throated peabody-bird

SPARSE bald, disperse(d), distribute, exiguous, few, infrequent, meager, meagre, occasional, rare, scant(y), scarce, scatter(ed), scrimp (y), skimp(ing), skimpy, slim, spare, sprinkled, thin, thrifty, uncommon

SPART broom, esparto, rush

SPARTA lacedaemon

admiral aracus, callicra, lysander

ancestor hercules

army division mora

battle leuctra

bonds claria

cipher writing scytale

commander anaxilaus, glyippus, lochage lysander, mindarus, pausanias, pharax, pharnabazus

conquerors dorians, thebans

constitution author lycurgus

defeat leuctra, thermopylae

dependents perioeci

dog bloodhound

ephor chilon

father eurotas

festival carnea, carneia

founder lacedaemon

general clearchus, dercyllidas, thimbron

governor harmost

grace phaenna

hero acrotatus

husband lacedaemon

king acrotatus, agesilaus, agesipolis, agis, archidamus, areus, arius, charillus, cleombrotus, cleomenes, euclidas, eudamidas, eurysthenes, leonidas, menelaus, nabis, pausanias, plistoanax, procles

leader lycurgus

magistrate ephor

mountain taygetus

musician phrynis, timotheus

native laconian

parchment scytale

poet alcman, tyrtaeus

prince alopecus, astrabacus

queen helen, leda

rival argos

senate gerousia

slave helot, ilot

tyrant machanidas, nabis

SPARTACUS *lieutenant* cannicius, castus

opponent cassius, clodius, cossinius, crassus, furious, gellilus, mummius, pompey, publius, scrofa, varinus

trainer lentulus

SPARTAN ascetic, austere, courageous, frugal, greek, hardy, laconic, missile, patient, plain, severe, stoic, strict, undaunted

SPARTINA bullgrass, cordgrass, saltgrass, sloughgrass

SPARTLE kick, sprawl

SPARVER canopy, tent, tester

SPASM agitation, attack, chorea, clonus, convulsion, cramp, eclampsia, entasia, epitasis, fit, flutter, grip, ictus, jerk, myotonia, paroxysm, qualm, seizure, stroke, throe, tic
reliever atropia, atropine
tonic holotony
type clonic, tonic

SPASMODIC aberrant, abnormal, changeable, convulsive, erratic, excitable, fitful, inconstant, infrequent, intermittent, irregular, periodic, recurrent, snatchy, spastic, spurtive, sudden, violent
disease tetanus

SPASTIC convulsive, paroxysmal, spasmodic, tetanic

SPAT altercate, altercation, argument, bicker, boothose, bootikin, clop, contention, debate, dispute, fight, gaiter, jower, lay, legging, mollusk, oyster, quarrel, row, seed, set-to, slap, spawn, splash, spot, squabble, strike, tiff, wrangle

SPATE abundance, excess, flood, freshet, gush, outflow, overflow, overwhelm, pond, rain(storm), rush, sluice, torrent, waterspout

SPATHA See SWORD.

SPATHIC foliated, lamellar, sparlike, sparry, spathose

SPATIAL areal, dimensional, proportional, steric(al)

SPATIATE ramble, rove, stroll

SPATTER asperse, besplash, besplatter, besprinkle, broadcast, dabble, dash, defame, dirty, drop, jet, moisten, scatter, slart, slop, slosh, smatter, SMEAR, smudge, spatule, spawn, spirtle, splash, splatter, splutter, spoil, spot, spray, spread, sprinkle, spurt, squirt, stain, strew, sully

SPATTERDASH bonnet, boothose, cutikin, gaiter, legging, roughcast

SPATTERDOCK bonnet, candock, clote, cowlily, duck, hoglily, nuphar, tucky, waterlily, wokas

SPATTLE plowstaff, spatter,

spatula, spawl, spit(tle), sprinkle

SPATULA cestrum, shoveler, slice, spade, spattle, splatter, thible, thivel, tool

SPAWL See SPIT.

SPAWN beget, bulbils, clutch, cormels, deposit, eggs, generate, germ, issue, mycelium, offspring, ova, produce, redd, roe, rud, seed, sile, source, spat, spore, start, todder, yield, young

SPAWNING fertile, milky, prolific
place redd

SPAY alter, caponize, desex, fix, geld, mutilate, spare, sterilize

SPEAK accost, address, articulate, ask, bark, broadcast, bruit, buzz, call, cant, carp, celebrate, chatter, chime, chorus, communicate, converse, declaim, declare, deliver, demagogue, descant, designate, dilate, discourse, elocute, elocutionize, enunciate, exclaim, expatiate, express, extol, gab, hail, harangue, harp, honor, lecture, lisp, manifest, mention, moot, mouth, orate, oration, parle(y), parrall, patter, perorate, pipe up, preach, prelect, proclaim, pronounce, rant, read, recite, request, reveal, say, sermonize, signal, sound, spellbind, spiel, spout, state, stump, talk, tell, term, tongue, utter
affectedly knack, mimp, mince
against accuse, gainsay, oppose
angrily cample, explode, pop off, rouse, splutter
comb. lalo
confusedly clutter, splather
critically carp
curtly bark, birk, snap
disrespectfully abuse, badmouth, snash
evil blaspheme
falsely betray, lie, traduce
favorably approve, commend, praise, recommend
foolishly blather, blither, drivel, drool, gibber, prate
for advocate, engage, push
from memory recite

haltingly stammer, stutter
highly of advocate, approve, praise, recommend
ill detract, disparage, knock
imperfectly lisp, stammer, stutter
inability to aglossia, alalia, alogia, anepia, aphasia, dumbness, mutism
indistinctly jabber, muffle, mumble, murmur, mutter, splutter
loudly rant, rave, thunder
of call, cite, mention, quote, report
offhand extemporize
oracularly orate, pontificate, sermonize
pert. oratorical
playfully banter, joke
profusely dilate, palaver, protract
rapidly chatter, gibber, jabber, patter, splutter, squirt, troll
rhetorically declaim, emote, orate
roughly bur(r)
slightingly backbite, belittle, disparage
slowly drawl, hem and haw
softly murmur, whisper
thoughtlessly blat, splutter
through nose nasillate, snaffle
to accost, address, greet, rebuke, reprove, testify
under breath mumble, mutter
up for advocate, defend, recommend, support

SPEAKEASY blindpig, saloon, shebeen

SPEAKER chairman, declaimer, demagog(ue), drone, elocutionist, haranguer, jawsmith, lecturer, legislator, locutor, mouther, mouthpiece, orator, panelist, prolocutor, ranter, rhetor, speechifier, speechmaker, spellbinder, spieler, spokesman, spouter, talker, tweeter, woofer
hammer gavel
inspired prophet
of many languages linguist, polyglot

SPEAN nipple, prong, teat, wean

SPEAR aclys, amgarn, asj, assagau, assegau, bayonet, bident, blade, bordun, bourdon, branch, broach, catch,

dart, feather, fizgig, fram
(ea), gad, gaff, gave-
lock gidgea, gidgee, gidia,
gidjee, gidya, gidyea, gig,
glaive, gore, grain, har-
poon, impale(r), javelin,
jereed, jerrid, lance(gay),
leaf, leister, missile, part,
perforate, pierce, pike,
poke, reed, rod, sarissa,
shaft, shoot, shut, spar,
speer, spike, sprout, stab,
staff, stalk, stem, stop,
strike, trident, verutum,
walspere, weapon
eel elger, pilger
fishing gaff, gig, grains,
leister, poach, snigger, tren,
trident
flower ardisia
grass aciphylla, agropyron,
ditchreed, foxtail, spaniard
-like hastate, lanciform
part vamplate
play hastilude
point spiculum
salmon waster
shaft truncheon
-shaped hastate
3-pronged leister, trident
thrower atlatl, javelinist,
sling, wom(m)era, woo-
mera(h), woomerang
thrower, name meaning ger-
ald
widgeon goosander, mer-
ganser
SPEARFISH aguja, billfish,
gar, goggle, longjaws, marlin, needlefish, quillback,
sailfish, saury
SPEARHEAD advance, bunt,
coronal, direct, emphasize,
gaff, lead, locate, point, precede, ramrod, spud, van
(guard)
cheek jamb
SPEARMINT labiate, menthe
SPEARWORT banewort, belladonna, crowfoot
SPEARY pointed, slender,
spindling
SPECE drug, kind, semblance, species, SPICE
SPECIAL actual, commodity,
concrete, dear, detailed,
different, distinctive, exceptional, express, extra(ordinary), favorite, individual, intimate, khas(s), limited, local, noteworthy, occasional, paramour, particular, peculiar, personal, pet,
popular, precious, rare, re-

spective, sale, sole, spanking, species, specific, standout, stylish, train, uncommon, unique, unusual
forces green berets
interest lobby
SPECIALIST (See also
DOCTOR.) expert, herald,
master, ologist, surgeon
atomic physicist
city-planning urbanist
comb. ician, ist
ear audiologist, aurist, otologist
eye oculist, opthamologist,
optometrist
medical gynecologist, internist, neurologist, obste-
trician, oculist, orthopedist,
otologist, pediatrician, radiologist, surgeon
mineral mineralogist
money management econo-
mist
SPECIALIZE concentrate,
feature, follow, limit, narrow, particularize, practice,
pursue, restrict
SPECIALTY angle, aptitude,
bailiwick, bailliage, business, career, characteristic,
contract, fondness, forte,
line, long suit, major, metier, partiality, particularity,
profession, pursuit, skill,
talent, vocation, work
SPECIE banger, brad, button,
cash, chinker, chip, clinker,
coin(age), currency, jingler,
legal tender, money, piece,
rock, rouleau, shiner
SPECIES analogue, apomict,
breed, brood, category,
characteristic, class(ification), eidos, espece, exhibition, family, genotype,
genre, genus, humanity, ilk,
image, indigene, king, mankind, phantasm, phantom,
reflection, simple, sort,
spectacle, variety
description protolog
formation speciation
groups genera, genus
kindred cogeneric
modified by environment
ecad
SPECIFIC categorical, clear
(cut), concrete, cure, definite, determinate, especial,
exact, explicit, express, fixed, individual, medicine,
particular, peculiar, physic,
precise, remedy, respective,

restricted, sole, special, tangible, virus
SPECIFICATION blueprint,
condition, description, limit,
process, term
SPECIFY allot, appoint, assign, cite, design(ate), detail, determine, enumerate,
establish, fix, indicate, itemize, limit, mark, mention,
name, particularize, pick,
select, set, state, stipulate
in detail itemize
singly enumerate
SPECIMEN case, cast,
chance, copy, example, ho-
lotype, icotype, illustration,
instance, isotype, mark,
model, part, pattern, person, representation, sample,
slide, swatch, test
SPECIOUS apparent, believable, casuistic, colored, credible, deceitful, deceptive,
delusory, dishonest, empty,
eristic, fair, fallacious,
false, hollow, idle, illusory,
misleading, nugatory, ostensible, plausible, plausive,
pleasing, probable, right,
seeming, showy, spurious,
superficial, tinsel, wain,
weak
SPECK atom, bit, blemish,
blot, crumb, dot, flaw, fleck,
glebe, gnat, grain, iota, jot,
mark, midge, minim, minu-
tia, mite, mote, nit, particle,
pip, point, scrap, snip(pet),
speckle, splotch, spot, sprinkle, stain, tittle, tot, trace,
variegate, whit
black dartrose
SPECKLE bespot, blemish,
blot, dot, fleck, garle, kind,
mark, mizzle, mottle, sort,
spot, sprinkle, stain, stipple,
variegate
-belly gadwall duck, goose
SPECKLED dotted, freckled,
irrorate(d), lentiginous,
mailed, menald, mottled,
patchy, pied, spotted,
stippled, variegated
SPECTACLE attraction, circus, display, drama, example, exhibit(ion), exposition, glass, lens, marvel,
model, pageant(ry), pa-
rade, pattern, pomp, pre-
sentation, representation,
scene, show, sight, spyglass,
steracle, tableau, tamasha,
view

pert. theoric
sorry bysen
structure for arena, coliseum, stadium, theater, theatre
water aquacade
SPECTACLES brills, cheaters, (eye)glasses, goggles, lunets, shades, specs, spex, winkers
part bridge, frame, temple
SPECTACULAR appealing, dramatic, fabulous, marvelous, sensational, striking, wonderful, wondrous
SPECTATOR beholder, bystander, eyewitness, gazer, kib(b)itzer, looker(on), observer, onlooker, overseer, passerby, patron, perceiver, rubberneck, seer, sightseer, slummer, viewer, watcher, witness
author addison, steele
group audience, dedans
SPECTER apparition, bloodybones, bogey, boggle, bogy, boogleboo, bugaboo, bugbear, crab, demon, eidolon, empusa, fetch, ghost, goblin, hant, haunt, hobgoblin, larva, nightmare, ogre, phantasm, phantom, phenomenon, redcowl, revenant, scarecrow, shade, shadow, shrimp, spirit, spook, sprite, taipo, walkingstick, wraith
candle belemnite
evil spoorn
lemur tarsier
SPECTRAL discarnate, disembodied, eerie, eery, ethereal, ghastly, ghostly, incorporeal, insubstantial, phantom, psychic, shadowy, spiritual, spooky, supernatural, weird, wraithlike
SPECTRUM afterimage, apparition, range, specter
color blue, green, indigo, orange, red, violet, yellow
line doublet, ghost, singlet, triplet
part violet ray
SPECULATE cogitate, conjecture, consider, contemplate, dare, deliberate, doctrinize, examine, gamble, guess, hazard, inspect, job, meditate, muse, operate, play(the market), plunge, ponder, pyramid, reason, reflect, revolve, risk, rumi-

nate, scalp, study, suppose, surmise, suspect, theorize, trade, venture, weigh, wonder
SPECULATION adventure, agiotage, arbitrage, bubble, conclusion, conjecture, deliberation, examination, flier, flutter, gamble, gambling, guesswork, ideology, intuition, perception, plunge, surmise, theory, transaction, venture, vision
SPECULATIVE academic, contemplative, curious, hazardous, inquisitive, pensive, prying, reditative, reflective, risky, thoughtful, uncertain
SPECULATOR adventurer, bear, bull, bummaree, gambler, operator, piker, player, plunger, scalper, swinger
SPEECH accent, address, allocution, articulation, chatter, comment, declamation, dialect, diatribe, dilogy, discourse, elocution, exhortation, gab, gaff, gilaki, harangue, homily, idiom, language, lecture, lemosi, lingo, locution, meithei, mention, oration, orison, palaver, parlance, peroration, prattle, preachment, prelection, recital, recitation, report, rhetoric, screed, sermon(et), speaking, spiel, suit, tale, talk, tat, tirade, tone, tongue, travelogue, utterance, valediction, voice, yap
abusive tirade
affected cant
ambiguity amphibology, amphiboly
art of rhetoric
bitter diatribe
boastful bluster, kompology, rodomontade
boldness parrhesia
blunder solecism
change provect
comb. lalo, logo, phrasia
conclusion peroration
contemptuous filippic, frump, philippic, tirade
curt snaphance
disorder (See also *loss,* below.) allolalia, alogia, aphasia, aphonia, balbuties, baryphonia, baryphony, cacoepy, cacology, cataphasia, cluttering, dysarthria, dys-

phasia, dysphemia, dysphonia, echolalia, lallation, lalopathy, lisp, mogilalia, mutism, mytacism, paralalia, paraphasia, pararthria, stammer, stutter, titubation, tongue-tie, traulism, verbigeration
disorder, comb. lalia
element rheme, surd
eloquent fecundity
emotional rhapsody
expert phonetist
figure of See FIGURE *of speech.*
for dead eulogy, threnody
form lexeme
formal allocution, oration
goddess brahmi, devi, sarasvati, vac(h)
hesitation haw, hem, stammer, stutter
impassioned dithyramb, harangue, tirade
inability anarthria, dyslalia
indistinct asaphia, babble, logorrhea
insane bedlamism
internal endophasia
invented idioglossia
lengthy tirade
local dialect, idiom, patois
long spiel
loss alalia, anarthria, anaudia, anepia, aphasia, aphemia, aphrasia, dumbness, laloplegia, muteness
loud lamprophony
ordinary exophasia
part adjective, adverb, article, conjunction, gerund, infinitive, interjection, modifier, noun, object, participle, particle, partitive, person, predicate, preposition, pronoun, qualifier, subject, verb
peculiar argot, idiom, patois
pert. oral, phemic, phonetic
pompous fustian, grandiloquence
provincial argot, dialect, patois
religious homily, preaching, sermon(izing)
repetition battology
repetition rote
repetitive cataphasia, psittacism
set rhesis
slangy slanguage
sound affricate, allophone, apical, arveolar, aspirate,

bilabial, cerebral, consonant, dental, dentilabial, digraph, dipthong, domal, fricative, glide, guna, gutteral, labial, lateral, lingual, liquid, monophthong, mute, nasal, nonsonant, occlusive, palatal, phone(me), sonant, spirant, stop, surd, tenue, tone, triphthong, velar, vocable, vocal, voiced, vowel, vriddhi

soundless endophasia

sparingness parciloquy

ungrammatical apabhramsa

violent kompology, philippic, tirade

wheedling blarney, softsoap

windy aeolistic

SPEECHLESS aphasic, aphemic, aphonic, dumb, inarticulate, mum, mute, silent, taciturn, voiceless

SPEED accelerate, advance, advantage, alacrity, amphetamine, assist, barrel, bat, bolt, boom, bound, bowl, breeze, brush, cannonball, career, celerity, chase, clip, dash, dispatch, equip, exigency, expedite, expedition, fastness, favor, fleet, fly, forward, further, gallop, haste(n), help, hie, highball, hurry, hustle, impetus, momentum, narcotic, pace, post, precipitance, press, progress, promote, quicken, quickness, race, railroad, rapidity, rate, rip, run, rush, scat, scoot, scorch, scud, scurry, skim, spank, step on it, sweep, swiftness, swoop, tear, tempo, velocity, whisk, whiz, zip, zoom

at full amain

comb. tacho

control governor

cop policeman

demon jehu, racer

freak addict

high amain, career, full tilt, haste, posthaste, spurt, zoom

increased freshway

master valentine

measurer accelerometer, cyclometer, dromometer, machmeter, odometer, radar, speedometer, strobe, tachometer, tachymeter, velocimeter

nautical knot

note clock, time

rate pace, rpm, tempo

symbol horse, jehu

unit baud, dyne, gal, mach, rpm, velo

up accelerate, escalate, expedite, gun, hasten, quicken, rev

writing shorthand, stenography

SPEEDER clipper, flier, hotshot, hustler, jehu, jockey, racer, runner, scorcher, sizzler, stepper, turfman

SPEEDFUL efficient, expert, favorable, rapid, successful

SPEEDILY amain, apace, betimes, chopchop, fast, fulltilt, pellmell, presto, promptly, quickly, rapidly, rathe, soon, tantivy

SPEEDWELL catseye, fluellen, gypsyweed, henbit, neckweed, nickwell, veronica, vervain

SPEEDY adept, brisk, expeditious, express, fast, fleet, flying, hasty, hurried, immediate, lively, nimble, quick, rapid(fire), sudden, swift, velocious, volant, winged

SPEEL climb, mount, splinter

SPEER ask, inquire, interrogate, partition, query, quiz, screen, search, seek

SPELDER split, sprawl, spread, stretch

SPELK rod, sliver, splint(er), stick

SPELL abet, abracadabra, alternate; bar, bewitch, bout, brief, cantr(a)ip, charm, compose, curse, decipher, demonifuge, discover, distance, enchantment, entrancement, evil-eye, exorcism, fascination, fit, form, glamor, greegree, grigri, hex, hint, hitch, hoodoo, incantation, interval, jinx, lathe, magic, malefice, mean, mojo, peg, period, pinchhit, pishogue, rapture, relay, relieve, respite, rest, reveal, rung, save, seizure, shift, siege, sign(ify), spare, speak, splinter, substitute, suggest, sway, talk, teach, tell, term, tour, trick, turn, utter, wanga, weird, word, write

brief moment, snatch

fainting drow, dwaim

in another alphabet transliterate

out clarify, define, explain, itemize, particularize

voodoo wanga

SPELLBIND charm, enchant, ensorcell, enthrall, fascinate, orate, spout, transfix

SPELLBINDER orator

SPELLBINDING basilisk

SPELLBOUND agape, aghast, bewitched, breathless, captivated, charmed, enchanted, fascinated, gripped, hypnotized, mesmerized, obsessed, petrified, possessed, transfixed, witched

SPELLING discourse, glossic, nomic, orthography, phonography, preaching, speaking, tale, writing

bad cacography

bee gregory

contest bee, gregory

incorrect pseudography

nonphonetic heteric

phonetic glossic

SPELT ador, cereal, emmer, fitch, grain, thresh, wheat

SPELTER ingot(s), solder, zinc

SPELUNK cave(rn), den, lair

SPENCE buttery, larder, pantry, room

SPENCER butler, coat, jacket, sail, steward, wig

elizabeth gloriana

SPEND apply, attach, beguile, bestow, birl, blow, confer, consume, cost, dash, devote, disburse, dissipate, elapse, emit, employ, exert, exhaust, expend, fasten, fork out, give, grasp, jump, kill, lavish, lay out, lead, lose, manage, outlay, pass, pay, perform, run through, sacrifice, shell out, shop, spring, squander, unpurse, use, waste, weaken, wear, while, wile

extravagantly prodigalize

fruitlessly dawdle, waste

recklessly blow, squander

the summer estivate

time dree, dreie, fool around

SPENDING cash, charge, consumption, cost, expenditure, funds, loss, money

governmental pork-barrelling, pump-priming

SPENDTHRIFT daft, dingthrift, dissipator, fribbler,

fritterer, highflier, locust, panurge, prodigal, profligate, rounder, scattergood, squanderer, wasteful, waster, wastrel

SPENSER, EDMUND poet's poet

character acrasia, alma, amoret, archimago, argante, artegall, arthur, aveugle, belphoebe, braggadocio, britomart(is), calidore, cambell, chymocles, duessa, gloriana, guyon, mercilla, pyrocles, scudamour, triamond, una

name for ireland irena

pseud. immerito

truth una

work amoretti, astrophel, faerie queene, prothalamion

SPENT all in, beat, breathless, burnt, bushed, consumed, dead, debilitated, depleted, dissipated, done (in), drained, enervated, exhausted, fagged, fatigued, footsore, frazzled, gone, impoverished, jaded, limp, played out, pooped, prostrate, tired, toilworn, tuckered, used, washed up, wasted, weak, weary, worn (out)

SPERKET hook, peg

SPERLING herring, smelt, sparling

SPERM *whale* blackfish, cachalot, catodont, physeter

SPERMOPHILE citellus, gopher, ground-squirrel, rodent, suslik

SPET barracuda, signet, sinnet, SPIT

SPETCH mend, paring, patch, refuse

SPEW belch, bog, disgorge, eject, erupt, extrude, gag, heave, regurgitate, reject, retch, scatter, slip, slobber, strew, throw up, upchuck, urp, vomit

SPEWY boggy, foggy, frothy, pulpy, wet

SPHACELATE decay(ed), diseased, gangrenous, mortified, rotten, withered

SPHAGNUM aulocomnium, bogmoss, peatmoss

SPHALERITE blackjack, blende, false-galena, mocklead

SPHENDONE headband, fillet

SPHENE titanite

SPHENISCID See PENGUIN.

SPHENOPHORUS billbug, grasseater, weevil

SPHERE ambit, arena, atmosphere, bailiwick, ball, bead, beat, brahmanda, bulb(il), business, circle, circuit, class, compass, control, demesne, department, district, domain, dominion, duty, earth, expanse, field, function, geoid, globe, globule, heavens, hemisphere, hiranyagarbha, jurisdiction, kingdom, knob, knot, level, locale, lodestar, milieu, office, orb(it), orbicle, order, pale, pellet, planet, position, precinct, province, range, rank, reach, realm, region, scope, space, star, station, stratum, sway, terella, theater, walk, world, zone

celestial colure, cycle, element

comb. sphaer(o)

magnetic earthkin, terella

of influence domain, satrapy

point antapex

small orbicle, spherule

SPHERICAL ampullaceous, bombous, circular, discoid, globate, globose, globular, orbicular, rotund, round

SPHINX bogy, colossus, enigma, hawkmoth, monster, moth, mustang, prophet, puzzle, riddle

-like enigmatic, inscrutable

mother echidna

riddle solver oedipus

site egypt, giza, luxor, thebes

SPHRYNA bonnethead, hammerhead, shark, shovelhead

SPHYGMUS pulse

SPIAL scout, spy, watch

SPICE (See also *kind*, below.) appearance, condiment, embalm, epice, flavor, kind, modicum, mull, odor, perfume, portion, salt, season(ing), sort, soupcon, species, specimen, suggestion, suspicion, tang, taste, touch, variety, zest

ancient stacte

ball fag(g)ot, pomander

biblical balsam, cassia

bush benzoin-tree, calycanthus, snapwood, sweet-shrub

craving malacia

grinder quern

islands grenada, indies, moluccas, ternate

kind allspice, anise, caraway, cassia, cayenne, cinnamon, cloves, coriander, cumin, curry, fennel, ginger, juniper, mace, marjoram, mustard, nutmeg, oregano, paprika, pepper, pim(i)ento, poppyseed, sage, sesameseed, stacte, tamara, thyme, turmeric

mill quern

package robbin

refuse garble

tree sintoc

SPICED ala diable, aromatic, dainty, euchred, flavored, fragrant, nice, scrupulous, squeamish

SPICK blubber, deck, dress up, fat, grease, lavender, titmouse

and span brand-new, clean, fresh, immaculate, neat, new, spotless, tidy, trim

SPICKNEL baldmoney, bearwort, gentian, meu(m), mew, sclere, spignel

SPICULE actine, anchor, aster, barb, caltrop, chela, cymba, desma, diact(in), euaster, hexaster, hexaxon, isochela, monaxon, needle, oxea, oxyaster, prickle, rhab, rod, sclere, sclerite, shell, sigma, spherula, spikelet, spine, sterigma, strongyl, stylus, tetraxon, toxa, triact, trichite, tripod, tylaster, tylote

stellate amphiaster

SPICY active, appetizing, aromatic, balmy, breezy, exciting, flavored, fragrant, natty, off-color, peppery, piquant, pungent, racy, rich, risque, salty, sharp, smart, spirited, suggestive, tangy, witty, zestful, zesty

SPIDER acerata, anansi, arachnid, arain, araneid(an), arrand, attercop, attid, blackwidow, bug, candleholder, cobbe, coppe, drassid, epeira, fryingpan, griddle, karakurt, katipo, knoppie, loppe, mite, nancy, orbitele, pan, pokomoo, retiary, salticid, scorpion, skillet, snare, soldier, solpugid, spinner, telarian,

tripod, trivet, uloborid, venantes
appendage chelicera, pedipalpus
aquatic argyroneta
big john knox
bite poisoning arachnidism, arachnism
black widow pokomoo
bug emesa
burrowing trapdoor
catcher sunbird
cell astrocyte
changed to arachne
comb. arachn(o)
crab maia, maiid, maja, thomisid
family attidae, citigradae, drassidae, pisauridae
fear of arachnephobia
feeding on arachnophagous
flower quaresma
fluid aranein
fly tick
foot hair scopula
genus agalena, aranea, argiope, epeira, eurypelma, latrodectus, mygale, nephila
grass millet
hourglass black widow
hunting pisaurida
leaping saltigrade
-like creature psammead
lily hymenocallis, nerine
long-legged pholcida
monkey ateles, belzebuth, coaita, marimonda, quata, sajou, sapajou
mythological anansi, annancy, nancy
nest nidus, web
net-weaver theridion
orb-weaving aranea, argiope
orchid brassavola, brassia
organ calamistrum, mammula, spinneret
part chelicera, pedipalpus, protarsis
poison neurotoxin
poisonous black widow, solpugida, taint, tarantula
short-legged attid
student arachnologist
study arachnology, araneology
symbol of wiliness
3-legged tripod, trivet
web attercop, nullenspiel
web ingredient fibroin
webless attid
web-spinning retiary, spinneret, telarian
wolf lycosid
SPIDERWORT blue-eyed

mary, collinsia, dayflower, frenchweed, innocence, navelwort, st bruno's-lily, tradescantia, trinity
SPIEL advertise, ballyhoo, cry, game, line, pitch, play, promote, promotion, speak, speech, talk
SPIELER barker, cheater, publicist, sharp(er), solicitor, speaker
SPIER ask, screen, speer, spy
SPIFFY excellent, fine, neat, nifty, smart, splendid, spruce
SPIFLICATE astonish, beat, bewilder, confound, kill, stifle
SPIGOT cock, dossil, dozzle, faucet, nozzle, outlet, peg, plug, spile, spout,. stopcock, tap. valve, vent
SPIKE antler, barb, bayonet, block, brob,. cut, dag; disable, duck, ear, end. finish, fortify, gad, horn, impale, jag, lace, lavender, mackerel, nail, needle, obstruction, perforate, pick, pierce, pike, point, pricket, rig, spadix, spick, spine, stab, strobile, thorn, thwart, tine
-bill godwit, merganser
hole spile
lavender mint
lavender oil aspic
pointed arrow, goad, pike, spear
rush aglethead, eleocharis
-shaped spiciform
SPIKELET alicole, chat, locusta, nail, spicule, spinule
SPIKENARD aralia(d), balm, herb, ivywort, nard, ointment, phu, plant, spignet, spignut, sumbul, valeriana
pert. araliaceous
SPIKETAIL coat, grouse
SPILE decay, forepole, peg, pile, pin, plug, rod, rule, spigot, spill, spout, stake, stop, tap, tube
SPILL brook, bung, chastise, correct, coup, destroy, deteriorate, disclose, downpour, escape, fall, flosh, flow, gratuity, injure, inlay, kill, leaf, leak, let out, lighter, lose, mar, needle, obstruction, overturn, peg, pin, punish, rod, ruin, run, shed, sling, slobber, slop, spile,

spindle, splash, splinter, spoil, spool, squander, stream, strip, tackle, tell, upend, utter, waste
blood kill, war
out pour, spurt, squirt, well
over excess, run, slop
the beans admit, babble, betray, blab, confess, disclose, peach, reveal, sing, tattle
SPILLWAY channel, culvert, dam
SPILOMA birthmark, nevus
SPILTH effusion, refuse, rubbish, shedding, waste
SPIN birl, circle, cut, drive, eddy, fish, gyrate, narrate, pirl, reel, reject, revolve, ride, rotate, screw, speed, spurt, stream, swirl, tell, troll, turbinate, turn, twirl, twist, wamble, weave, wheel, whirl
a yarn narrate
log birl
out extend, prolong, protract, shoot
silk throw
SPINACH epinard, olitory, orach(e), potherb, savoy, vegetable
eater popeye
SPINAL (See also SPINE.) rachidian, vertebral
column axis, axon, backbone, spine, vertebrae
cord alba, axion, medulla, myelon, nucha
cord absence amyelencephalia, amyelia, amyelonic
cord, pert. myelic
formation volute
SPINDLE amphiaster, arbor, axis, axle, baluster, bobbin, broach, cannon, cop, fuseau, fusee, hasp, hydrometer, mandrel, maternal, newel, pin, pipe, pirn, quill, rachis, rod, roll, shaft, slender, spill, spool, stalk, stem, trendle, triblet, wharrow, xeres
center gig
comb. fusi
hollow spool, triblet
lathe sandril
-shanked lean, long-legged, tall
-shaped clostridial, fusee, fusiform, fusoid, fuzee
tree dogwood, evonymus, gaiter, louseberry, pegwood
wheel wharve

SPINDLING attenuated, ineffectual, lean, skinny, slender, tall, weak

SPINE acanthus, acicula, aciculum, arete, axis, axon, back(bone), bristle, bulge, chaeta, chine, courage, fin, glochis, heartwood, illicium, needle, paxilla, pelelith, prickle, quill, rachis, ridge, seta, spicule, spiculum, spur, sward, thorn, turf, vertebra(e)
bone sacrum
comb. acantho, acromio, rachi(o)
curvature cyrtosis, ensellure, kyphosis, lordosis
disease meningitis, myelitis, polio
duplication diplomyelia
end acromion
having acanthoid, acanthous, aristate
having 2 diacanthus
inflammation rachitis, rickets
layer dura
membrane dura
muscle psoas, spinalis
part disc
pert. cervical, dorsal, lumbar, rachidian, sacral
points cakra, chakra
ring coronule
study of acanthology
-tingling eerie, eery, frightening, ghostly, scary
tipped with aristate

SPINEL almandine, balas, candite, chromite, gahnite, hercyrite, inkle, picotite, rubicelle, vermeil, yarn
and iron ceylanite, ceylonite, pleonaste

SPINELESS anacanthous, invertebrate, irresolute, limp, slavish, weak

SPINET clavichord, giraffe, harpsichord, octavina, piano, sourdine, spinney, virginal
key chip
-like instrument autoharp
upright giraffe

SPINETAIL ruddy-duck, swift

SPINK chaffinch, cuckooflower, maidenpink

SPINNER daddy longlegs, fishhook, fly, goatsucker, jenny, mayfly, mule, narrator, nightjar, silkworm, spider, throstle, top

SPINNEY copse, thicket, wood

SPINNING awhirl, fast, lanifice, revolving, speedy, whirling
device distaff
jenny ironman, mule
jenny inventer arkwright, crompton, hargreaves
machine jenny, mule, throstle
mite red spider
rod distaff
term bobbin, flyer, spindle, traveler, wharve, whorl
web telarian
wheel charka, charkha, churruck, turn
wheel part distaff, spindle, treadle, wharve

SPINSTER femme sole, old maid, tabby, vestal
symbol thimble

SPINY, SPINOUS acanthoid, acanthous, barbed, difficult, echinated, hedgehoggy, pointed, prickly, rough, sharp, thorny
comb. acanth(o), acanthus
dog fish sand-shark
-footed acanthopod(ous)
oyster spondyle
rat octodont

SPIRACLE aperture, blowhole, orifice, pore, stigma, stoma, vent

SPIRAEA bridalwreath, francoa, hardhack, may, meadowsweet, rosacean, st peter's-wreath, shrub
blue beni, caryopteris, vervain

SPIRAL acyclic, ambagious, ambagatory, anfractuous, circuitous, cochlear, cochleate, coil(ed), corkscrew, curl(ed), curlicue, curve, curving, galaxy, gyration, gyre, helical, helicine, helicoid, helix, inflation, lituus, screwy, scrolled, spring, tapering, tortile, tortuous, turbinal, turbinate, turning, twirly, twist, volute, whorled, winding
comb. gyro, heli(c), helio, helix
decorated with heliced
motif arabesque
shell caracol(e)
stairs encaracole
twisted in voluted

SPIRE beachgrass, belfry, broach, coil, curl, cusp,

ditchreed, end, fleche, germinate, glade, leaf, peak, pinnacle, point, pricket, prong, pyramid, sapling, shikara, sprout, stag, stalk, steeple, stem, summit, tip, top, tower, twist, whorl
bearer spirifer
cap calotte
final epi
grass reed, sedge
octagonal broach
ornament crocket, epi, final
sweet itea, willow

SPIRIT (See also *evil,* below.) 3 akh, ame, elf, fay, hag, imp, jin, khu, nat, nix, pep, vim 4 aitu, alma, arac, arak, bang, brio, dash, elan, fire, grit, guts, hant, jinn, jiva, kami, kuei, kwei, life, love, mind, pixy, rasa, sand, shee, soul, take, wind, zeal, zemi 5 agiel, angel, anima, ardor, ariel, asuna, atman, dhoul, duffy, duppy, dusio, ethos, force, geist, genie, ghost, gnome, haunt, heart, huaca, igigi, jinni, kelpy, lares, manes, metal, moxie, nerve, numen, oomph, power, punch, ruach, shade, sidhe, spark, spook, spunk, steam, sylph, tangi, verve, vigor 6 afreet, amadan, animus, breath, buddhi, cognac, daring, elixir, energy, esprit, fulgja, genius, ginger, jinnee, kelpie, mettle, morale, nepesh, pneuma, psyche, shadow, sprite, temper, undine, vision, wraith, yaksha, yakshi 7 boggart, bravery, courage, essence, extract, hearten, inspire, jivatma, lemures, manitou, meaning, passion, phantom, purusha, smeddum, sparkle, specter 8 boldness, bonhomie, charisma, chutzpah, katchina, machismo, phantasm, piquancy, pungency, raciness, revenant, strength, vitality, vivacity 7 adamastor, animation, substance 10 apparition, enterprise, enthusiasm, leprechaun, liveliness, salamander 11 disposition, inspiration, poltergeist 12 intelligence, significance
absolute purusha
ancestral anito, katchina, lares, manes, penates

animating anima, animus

appearance pneumatophany

ardent arrack, rack

astral agiel, jophiel, uuchaton

attendant daimon

avenging alastor, alecto, ate, erinys, fury, megaera, nemesis, tisiphine

away abduct, hide, kidnap, secrete

belief in animism

bog will-o-the-wisp

comb. thymo

dead man's akh, chindee, chindi, manes, vampire

death-causing abambou, chulpa

disembodied asuang, ghost, kuei, kwei, larva, shade, soul, spectre

dispossessed fairy

divine is(h)vara, numen

domestic banshee

duck goldeneye

earth erdgeist

effulgent ardors

elemental genie

emancipated muktatma

evil ahriman, ahuramazda, ama(i)mon, amaymon, asmodeus, asuang, asura, ataentsic, ate, baalpeor, baka, banshee, banshie, beng, bhut, bogle, bogy, boko, boll, bugan, buggane, cacod(a)emon, casziel, daemon, daeva, daitya, demon, devil, dibbuk, drow, dybbuk, erynes, fomor, gimp, goric, gyre, hobgoblin, hobomoko, hydra, incubus, jumbie, jumby, kali, kanaima, ker(es), larva, lilith, mara, momus, okee, oki, ormazd, otkon, satan, set, shaitan, sheiten, skookum, troll, trow, warlock, windigo

evil, king of sammael

familiar angel, billy-blind, guardian, guide, numen, totem, tutelary

female anima, ataensic, babajaga, banshee, banshie, belfazor, duppy, dusio, holda, undine

fertility yaks(h)a, yakshi

good calodaemon, eud(a)emon, genie, genus, norn

guardian angel, fylgja, nagual, totem

gum glue

hostile lemures

household lares, penates

human jivatma

inciting armies badb, bodb

jewel azoth

lamp etna

-leaf manyroot

-like ethereal, ghostly

lose despair, despond

loyalty pietas

malevolent See *evil*, above.

malicious dobby

mines knocker

mischievous dusio, kobold, puck, tikolosh

mountain rubezahl

musical brio

noisy poltergeist

phantom (hob)goblin

-raising antidepressant, elating

rapper medium, psychic

refined elixir, soul

sea tangie

sylvan leshy, lesiy

tragedy cothurn

unbaptized babe taran

violent death pisachi

water ariel, kelpy, undine

wrestler doukhobor

writing pneumatography, psychography

SPIRITED active, alert, animated, animato, audacious, avid, bold, con moto, eager, enthusiastic, fell, fervent, fierce, fiery, frampold, game, gam(e)y, gay, gingery, heartsome, hotblooded, kinky, lively, lusty, mercurial, mettlesome, nervy, passionate, peppery, plucky, racy, skeigh, sparkling, spunky, valiant, vivacious, vivid, zealous

SPIRITLESS amort, apathetic, blate, bloodless, cold, cowardly, crass, daviely, dead, dejected, depressed, dispirited, downcast, dreepy, dull, exanimate, faint, feckless, flagging, flat, heatless, hilding, indifferent, languid, leaden, lifeless, listless, meek, milky, mopey, sad, slothful, sodden, soggy, stupid, tame, thewless, unfeeling, vapid, waning, wooden

SPIRITOUS alcoholic, ardent, ethereal, immaterial, pure, refined, SPIRITED

SPIRITS booze, brandy, fet-

tle, firewater, grog, hooch, liquor, pecker

dash of lacer

dwelling place elysium, hades

lift elate, gladden

low blues, depression, despair, dismals, doldrums, dumps, gloom, megrims, spleen

of heartshorn ammonia

of wine alcohol

SPIRITUAL airy, angelic, celestial, devout, divine, ecclesiastic(al), ethereal, good, holy, idealistic, immaterial, incorporeal, inner, mental, mistly, mystical, numinous, otherworldy, pious, pure, refined, sacred, song, spectral, spirited, supernal

apathy acedia

beings angels, seraphs

beings, belief in animism

body sahu

meaning anagoge, anagogics

SPIRITUALIST automatist, medium, psychic

meeting seance

power telekinesis

SPIRITUALITY church, clergy, ethereality, heaven, incorporeality, platonism, rarefaction, sanctity

SPIRITUALIZE dematerialize, discarnate, disembody, disincarnate, dissolve, etherealize, idealize, rarefy, refine, transmigrate

SPIROGYRA alga, frog-spit, green-silk, pond-scum

SPISSATED dense, thickened, viscous

SPIT barbecue, broach, brochette, counterpart, dig, eject, emit, expectorate, flat, froth, fuff, hiss, ignite, image, impale, isthmus, light, likeness, milt, neck, perforate, pierce, point, rain, rod, saliva(te), shoal, sizz, skewer, slaver, slobber, spade, spawl, spindle, spittle, sprinkle, sputter, sputum, stab, stick, sword, tongue

barbecue rotisserie

SPITAL den, dive, hospital, lazaretto, refuge, shelter

SPITBALLING brainstorming

SPITCHCOCK eel

SPITE animosity, animus, annoy, antipathy, begrudge, beset, chagrin, disgrace, dishonor, dislike, disposition, grudge, harass, hate, hatred, hurt, ill will, injury, malevoence, malice, malignity, meanness, mortification, mortify, offend, onde, persecute, pique, rancor, resentment, shame, spleen, thwart, vex(ation)

in— of malgrado, mauger, maugre

SPITEFUL antagonistic, catty, cruel, dispiteous, envious, hostile, malevolent, malicious, malign(ant), mean, nebby, peevish, rangcorous, spleenful, sullen, venemous, vengeful, vicious, vindictive, waspish

SPITFIRE aircraft, angry, brimstone, cacaguego, crank, fiery, hellcat, hot-tempered, imposter, nipper, pepperbox, shrew, staysail, termagant, virago, vixen

SPITTER brock(et), deer, fuse, pricket, spade

SPITTING *snake* ringhals

SPITTLE peel, saliva, slobber, spade, SPIT, sputum

comb. ptyalo

insect cercopid, froghopper

SPITTOON crachoir, cuspidor, garboon, pigdan, target

SPIV criminal, slacker, tout

SPLASH asperse, bathe, bespatter, blash, blot(ch), dabble, dash, daub, excitement, feature, flood, flouse, glob, gout, jaut, labber, lap, lave, losh, mark, moisten, ostentation, pinch, plash, pond, pool, purl, ripple, scatter, skirp, slart, slotter, slunge, spatter, spill, spirtle, splather, splatter, splother, splurge, splutter, spray, sprinkle, stain, strew, swirl, wash, wet

-board fender, flashboard, gate, mudguard, plank, screen, trap

SPLASHY muddy, ostentatious, sensational, showy, sloppy, slushy, sporty, watery, wet

SPLAT blotch, flatten, open, patch, plot, spot, spread

SPLATCHER mallet

SPLATTER besprinkle, dash, hubbub, moisten, rush, spatula, splairge, SPLASH, spot, sprinkle

SPLATTERDASH disturb-

ance, scatter, splutter, uproar

SPLAY adorn, awkward, bevel, carve, clumsy, dislocate, display, expand, expansion, flan, hem, obliquely, open, slant, slope, spread, ungainly

SPLAYFOOT awkward, clumsy, flatfoot, ungainly

SPLEEN anger, antagonism, antipathy, ardor, bile, caprice, cholor, despite, dislike, enmity, fire, fit, freak, grudge, hatred, humor, ill will, impulse, ire, lien, malice, malignity, melancholy, melt, milt, mirth, mood, poison, rancor, spite, temper, venom, virulence, whim

comb. lieno, splen(o)

enlargement splenomegalia, splenomegaly

inflamation lienitis

pain splenalgia

pert. lienal

removal lienectomy, splenectomy

small splenculus

SPLEENFUL,   SPLEENY angry, fiery, fretful, irascible, irritable, melancholy, peevish, splenetic

SPLEENWORT asplenium, athyrium, fern, maidenhair, oakfern, venus's-hair

SPLENDENT beaming, conspicuous, glossy, gorgeous, illustrious, magnificent, shining

SPLENDID aureate, beautiful, bravissimo, bright, brilliant, corinthian, costly, de luxe, distinguished, effulgent, elaborate, elegant, eminent, excellent, extravagant, fine, glorious, gorgeous, grand(iose), great, illustrious, important, imposing, impressive, jolly, luminous, lustrous, luxurious, magnificent majestic, marvelous, nice, noble, olympian, ostentatious, outstanding, palatial, plush, prime, princely, proud, radiant, rattling, regal, rial, rosy, royal, shining, showy, silk stocking, stately, sublime, substantial, sumptuous, superb, superior, supreme, swell, wally, wlonk

SPLENDOR blaze, bravery,

brightness, brilliance, display, eclat, fulgor, gite, gleam, glory, grandeur, luster, luxe, magnificence, parade, pomp, radiance, resplendance, sheen, sumpture

goddess devi, uma

SPLENETIC,   SPLENITIVE choleric, crabby, cranky, cross, depressed, fretful, impetuous, irascible, irritable, malicious, melancholy, peevish, spiteful, sullen, techy, testy, touchy, vapory

SPLICE fix, foot, join, lap, marriage, marry, piece, repair, skelb, union, unite, weave, wed(ding)

SPLINT alburnum, brace, caliper, coal, dressing, junk, lath, match, scob, shiver, spelk, splinter, split, strip, support, tace, tasse, treat

bone fibula

SPLINTER bit, break, burst, calve, chip, flinder, fragment, part, piece, rend, rive, separate, shake, shatter, shide, shive, slither, sliver, spald, speel, spelk, spell, split, truncheon

SPLINTERY brittle, skelvy

SPLINTWOOD alburnum

SPLIT allot, apportion, betray, bifid, bipartite, bisect(ed), bisulcate, blab, breach, break, buck, burst, check, chop, cleave, cleft, cloven, crack, cut, destroy, dilute, divide(d), division, dunt, escape, flaw, flee, flerry, fractured, fragment, halve(d), hew, laugh, leave, maul, open(ing), part, peach, piece, platz, plotst, plotz, rend, rift, rip, rit, rive(n), ruin, run, rupture, schism, separate, sever, share, slipe, smash, snap, spalato, speld, splat, splinter, sunder, tear

comb. schiz(o)

fish scrod

hairs argue, discriminate, paralogize, quibble, sophisticate, subtilize

off screeved, spall, spawl

pea dal, dahl

personality schizophrenia

second flash, instant, jiffy, minute, moment, trice, twinkling

the difference average, share

up divorce, partition, separate, separation

SPLITMOUTH cutlips

SPLITTAIL duck, minnow

SPLITTING apportionment, comical, division, fast, fission, funny, piece, piercing, quick, scission, severe, violent

SPLORE boast, brag, broil, carousal, commotion, debauch, escapade, festivity, frolic, merrymaking, revel, riot, scrimmage

SPLOTCH blob, blot(ch), daub, flick, smear, smudge, SPOT, stain, variegate

SPLUNT court(ing), woo

SPLURGE display, effort, grandstand, indulge, show off, spend, splash, squander, swank

SPLUTTER bluster, bustle, confusion, dispute, flutter, fuff, hurry, noise, nonsense, quarrel, scatter, spatter, splash, splother, sputter, stammer, stuff, stumble, stutter

SPODE china

SPODIUS apollo

SPODOMENE kunzite

SPOFFISH bustling, fussy

SPOIL 3 gum, mar, pet, rob, rot 4 baby, blad, blot, cook, foul, hurt, loot, mank, mess, muss, pelf, ruin, sack, sour, swag, turn, undo, wear 5 blast, booty, botch, break, butch, carve, decay, favor, harry, humor, jimmy, prize, queer, seize, smash, snafu, stain, strip, upset, waste, wreck 6 blight, bruise, coddle, damage, deface, defile, divest, fleece, impair, injure, injury, mangle, pamper, ravage, seduce, slough, thwart 7 blemish, corrode, corrump, corrupt, cripple, crumble, decline, deprive, despoil, destroy, disrupt, indulge, louse up, mullock, pillage, plunder, putrefy, violate 8 collapse, demolish 9 decompose, disfigure, margullie, undermine 11 deteriorate, disorganize, mollycoddle

-paper scribbler, writer

SPOILED bad, blown, blighted, brattish, corrupt, mardy, moldy, musty, rancid, rotten, septic, shent, sour, turned, wasted

SPOILER pillager, plunderer, robber

SPOILFIVE maw

SPOILS bag, booty, graft, loot, pelf, pillage, plunder, prize, swag, theft

SPOILSPORT addleplot, crapehanger, damper, killjoy, marplot, nark, wet blanket

SPOKE bar, check, chock, clog, curb, enchantment, impediment, pin, pole, radius, ray, rod, round, rung, said, saw, saying, spake, speech, spondyl(e), stake, tale, talk

having radial

SPOKEN declaimed, delivered, expressed, oral, parle, parol, phonic, said, told, unwritten, uttered, verbal

imperfectly cacoepistic, gutteral, halting, inarticulate, lisped, mispronounced, mumbled, stammering, stuttering, titubant, twangy

SPOKESMAN go-between, informant, mouthpiece, orator, prolocutor, speaker

SPOLIATION excoriation, injury, pillage, plunder(ing), rapine, robbery, spoil, writ

SPONDIAS amra, ciruela, hogplum, mombin

SPONDULICS cash, funds, MONEY

SPONDYLE joint, shell, spoke, vertebra

SPONGE absorb, ascon, ascula, badiaga, bathe, bleeder, bum, cadge, cancel, clean(se), cosher, deadbeat, dependent, dough, drain, drunk(ard), dry, erase(r), extort, fatten on, feed on, gelfoam, grass, hardhead, hedgehog, leucon, loofa(h), luffa, malkin, mandruka, moisten, mooch, mop(pet), mump, obliterate, olynthus, parasite, porifera, pudding, redbeard, rhagon, scaff, scrunge, shark, silicean, soak, sorn, suberite, suck up, swab, sycon(es), wash, wipe, yellow, zimocca, zoophyte

ascon ascetta, ascula

boring cliona

branching redbeard

calcerous leucon

cavity spongocoel

cell esthacyte

cloth ratine

comb. act, aene

commercial form

cooky ladyfinger

cylindrical grantia

deep-water mandruka

dredge gangava

family aceolomata

fresh-water badiaga, spongilla

genus ascetta, chalina, clathrina, cliona, euplectella, grantia

gourd loof(a), loofah, luffa

-like See SPONGY

on leach, mump, sorn

opening apopyle, osculum, ostiole, pore, prosopyle

pert. poriferal, porous, soft

red microciona

spicule actine, aster, cymba, desma, microrhabdus, oxea, pinulus, rhab(dus), toxa, toxon

tree huisache

young ascon

SPONGECAKE baba(au rhum), babka

small ladyfinger

SPONGER bloodsucker, bum(mer), cadger, deadbeat, extortioner, extortionist, freeloader, hanger-on, leech, lickspit, parasite, sorn, sycophant, toady, tramp, usurer

SPONGEWOOD gastonia, sola

SPONGY absorbent, bibulous, cancellous, elastic, fozy, imbibitory, leechy, light, marshy, moist, oozy, pithy, porous, pulpy, quaggy, rainy, resilient, sodden, soft, soggy, spongoid, weak, wet

SPONSALIA betrothal, contract, engagement, espousal, promise

SPONSION adpromission, platform, pledge, projection, promise

SPONSOR advocate, advocator, answer for, backer, bailsman, bondsman, champion, coach, endorser, finance, guarantee, guarantor, insurer, mainpernor, patron(ize), promoter, support(er), surety, underwriter, vouch for, witness *at christening* godfather, godmother, gossip

SPONSORSHIP aegis, backing, egis

SPONTANEOUS accidental, autogenus, automatic, blind, careless, discretional, ex tempore, free(will), gratuitous, impetuous, impromptu, impulsive, indigenous, instantaneous, instinctive, involuntary, natural, off the cuff, optional, self-acting, simple, unasked, unconscious, unconstrained, unsought, untaught, unthinking unwitting, voluntary, willful

generation abiogenesis

SPONTOON club, espantoon, half-pike, pantoon, truncheon

SPOOF deceive, deception, fool, guy, hoax, jest, joke, kid, prank, quip, swindle, tease, wisecrack

SPOOK apparition, ghost, gyre, hant, haunt, hobgoblin, phantom, plateye, shade, specter, spirit, spy, wraith

SPOOKY eerie, eery, ghostly, haunted, possessed, scary, spectral, uncanny, weird

SPOOL bobbin, broach, coppin, cylinder, reek, spill, spindle, tweel, twill, wharve, whorl, wind

SPOOM run, scud, sherbet

SPOON bail, bill and coo, club, cochlea(r), court, dip(per), dish, feeder, fish, gobstick, golf club, labis, ladle, love, nestle, ninny, oar, pen, scoop, scraper, scupper, shovel, simpleton, student, troll, woo

antique rattail, slip-top

comb. cochleari

cooking kochleffl

eucharistic labis

-fed babied, coddled, pampered, spoiled

fishing troll

river author masters

runcible fork

-shaped cochlear, cochleate, spatular, spatulate

SPOONBILL aiaiai, ajaia, ajaja, bird, ciconiid, curlew, duck, jabiru, paddlefish, platalea, popeler, sandpiper, scaup, spoony

SPOONDRIFT foam, spindrift, spray

SPOONERISM marrowsky

SPOONFLOWER xanthosoma

SPOONFUL bit, cochleare, dab, smitch

SPOONY dull, fond, fool(ish), neat, silly, soft, spic and span, stupid, tidy, trim

SPOOR abature, piste, scent, sign, trace, track, trail

SPOORN hobgoblin, specter

SPORADIC apart, infrequent, irregular, isolated, occasional, rare, scattered, separate, single, uncommon

SPORE aecium, agamete, akinete, antherid, carpel, conidium, fungus, gametophyte, gemmule, germ, gonidium, seed, sori, seminule, swarmer

asexual conidium

case asca, ascus, askos, sporangium, theca

cluster sorus

formation abjunction, abstriction

fruit aecium, ascocarp, telium

-like structure cyst

sac ascus, capsule

SPORONT gamont, oospore, zygote

SPOROPHORE basidium, bracket

SPORRAN pouch, purse

SPORT amuse(ment), athlete, banter, bet, butt, chap, companion, contest, dalliance, dally, dandy, derision, deviate, deviation, display, diversion, divert, entertain(ment), fellow, flash, freak, frolic, fun, gaiety, gamble(r), gambol, game(ster), gaud, hunt(ing), jest(ing), joke, kid, laughing-stock, lavish, mirth, mock(ery), mutation, pastime, play(thing), pleasantry, pleasure, ploy, raillery, recreation, rogue, rollick, romp, rux, scorn, skip, squander, tait, target, toy, trifle, variation, wager, wanton, wear

area amphitheater, amphitheatre, arena, bowl, course, court, diamond, field, forum, green, grid (iron), ground(s), gym (nasium), links, oval, pavil-

ion, ring, rink, stadium, stands, track

event game, match, meet, race

knightly tournament

-minded athletic

official coach, judge, linesman, referee, timekeeper, umpire

of stings croquet

rowdy hijinks

shoes loafers, sneakers

summer diving, fishing, golf, hiking, quoits, rowing, sailing, swimming, tennis, water-skiing

shirt tee

water diving, skiing, surfboarding, surfing, swimming

winter aquatics, hockey, (ice)skating, nautics, skiing, skijoring, sledding, tobogganing

SPORTFUL See SPORTIVE.

SPORTING fair, right, square

house brothel, tavern

lady See PROSTITUTE.

SPORTIVE amusing, coltish, diverting, fay, festive, frisky, frolicsome, gamesome, gay, jesting, jocular, jocund, lecherous, lusory, merry, playful, pleasant, toying, waggish, wanton

SPORTSMAN athlete, fisherman, gambler, gamester, hunter, player, shikaree, shikari

SPORTULA gift, gratuity, largesse, present

SPORTY brave, braw, chichi, daring, dashing, dressy, flashy, flaunting, frothy, gallant, gay, jaunty, jazzy, loud, ostentatious, rakish, rorty, rory(-cum)-tory, saucy, showy, smart, splashy, splurgy

SPOSH mud, slime, slush

SPOT asperse, bespeckle, betray, bit, blame, blaze, blemish, blot(ch), blur, dapple, defect, detect, dirty, discolor, discover, disgrace, dot, drumfish, espy, eye, fault, find, fish, flaw, fleck, freckle, locale, locality, locate, location, macle, macule, mail, male, mark, mascle, mole, monk, mote, mottle, nevus, note, ocellus, pigeon, pinfish, pip, place,

post, predicament, recognize, SEE, sight, site, situation, smit(ch), smudge, speck(le), splatter, splotch, sprinkle, spy, STAIN, station, stigma, stipple, sully, tache, taint, tarnish, trace, track, variegate, wem
brown sprain(g)
decayed blet
drop-like guttula
eye-like ocellus
hallowed bethel, bethesda
on skin birthmark, blister, freckle, lentigo, mole, scab, strawberry
sore bruise, bubu
sun facula, granule
tiny punctule
SPOTLESS blameless, clean, faultless, immaculate, irreproachable, perfect, pure, snowy, stainless, unblemished, unsullied, untarnished, virtuous, wemless
SPOTLIGHT arc, beam, attention, emphasize, illuminate, notice
SPOTRUMP godwit
SPOTTED blemished, blenny, blotched, blotchy, brindled, brooked, calico, damaged, dotted, dotty, espied, figged, flecked, freckled, guttate, macled, macular, maculate(d), maculiferous, maculose, marled, mirled, notate, noted, noticed, observed, patchy, peppered, piebald, pied, pinto, punctuate(d), seen, sparked, specked, speckled, speck(l)y, sprinkled, stippled, streaked, studded, sullied, suspected, tarnished, variegated
eagle ray miller, obispo
fever typhus
flycatcher cobweb, rafter, wallbird
gum eucalypt(us)
jewfish guasa
sandpiper creeker, tiltup, tiptail, tipup
spurge doveweed
wintergreen ratsbane
with white hawked
woodpecker witwall
SPOTTER detective, informer, somersault, spy
SPOTTY defiled, irregular, mealy, patchy, scabby
SPOUCHER bailer, dipper
SPOUSAL marital, marriage,

matrimonial, nuptial(s), wedding, wedlock
SPOUSE affiance, better-half, bride, consort, espousal, fere, fiance(e), groom, helpmate, husband, join, lady, make, marriage, marrow, match, mate, partner, wed(lock), wife, unite, yokemate
having 4 quadrigamist
having several bigamist, polygamist
SPOUT blow(hole), chatter, cock, conduit, declaim, discharge, disgorge, downpour, eject, emit, emote, erupt, expel, exude, faucet, flow, fountain, gargoyle, geat, gush, harangue, jet, jut, lip, mouth, nozzle, orate, pawn (shop), pipe, pledge, pour, rainstorm, rant, recite, riggot, run, shoot, speak, spigot, spile, spill, spume, spurt, stream, strone, tap, tough, tube, utter, vent
grotesque gargoyle
hole nostril
SPOUTER declaimer, speaker, speechifier, whale
SPOW(E) curlew, whimbrel
SPQR senatus populusque romanus, the senate and the people of rome
SPRACK active, alert, deft, lively, nimble, shrewd
SPRADDLE sprawl, spread, straddle
SPRAG billet, check, cod (fish), prop, sprack, timber
SPRAIN chink, hurt, overtax, sprinkle, stave, STRAIN, stremma, tax, thraw, twist, weaken, wramp, wrench, wrest
remedy arnica, linament
SPRAING streak, stripe, tint
SPRANGLE sprawl, spray, spread, straggle, struggle
SPRANK display, showing, sprinkling
SPRAT alfione, bleak, brisling, clupea, fish, garvie, garvock, herring, rush, sixpence, smy, sprit
-borer loom
group drove
young brit
SPRAUCHLE clamber, scramble, sprawl
SPRAWL animation, energy, extend, fall, grabble, lie, loll, lounge, mass, recline,

recumbency, scattering, scramble, spartle, spirit, sprangle, sprauchle, spread, spurl, straggle, stretch, struggle, tave
SPRAY atomize(r), bespread, bough, bouquet, branch, chap, drizzle, flowers, foam, inhalant, issue, jet, lipper, moisten, moisture, scatter, scud, shoot, shot, shower, spindrift, splash, sprangle, spread, spree, sprig, sprinkle, spritz, spume, stour, surf, swish, syringe, twig, vaporize(r), volley
container aerosol-bomb
mash sparge
reduce to nebulize
SPREAD 3 fan, run, sow, ted 4 area, coat, emit, grow, meal, open, size, talk, tell 5 apply, burst, cover, feast, issue, place, range, reach, rivet, rumor, scope, smear, space, splay, strew, widen 6 anoint, branch, delate, deploy, dilate, expand, extend, extent, fanned, gossip, layout, mantle, margin, norate, report, rumour, shmeer, sprawl, spring, unfold, unfurl 7 bedding, blanket, broaden, compass, diffuse, display, expanse, explode, overrun, pervade, prolong, radiate, scatter, splayed, stretch 8 bedcover, coverlet, diaspora, disperse, envelope, increase, multiply, overgrow, permeate, set forth, straggle, transmit 9 amplitude, broadcast, circulate, diffusion, dissipate, expansion, penetrate, propagate, publicize, sprawling, stretched, transfuse 10 difference, distribute, divergence, outstretch, promulgate 12 outstretched 13 advertisement
abroad broadcast, bruit, delate, disseminate, divulge, emanate, libel, noise, norate, publicize, radiate, report, rumo(u)r, spring, toot
apart gape, rhipidate, splay
bread applebutter, butter(ine), jam, jelly, margarine, marmalade, oleo, peanut butter
-eagle boast(ful), bombastic,

exaggerate(d), fall, jingoistic, patriotic, scatter
evenly suant
news gossip, report, rumor
oneself thin diversify
open speld
out bray, brede, deploy, diffuse, expand, extend, fan, flange, flare, lap, mantle, open, span, splay, spraddle, sprawl, straggly, ted, unfold, unroll, widen
plaster teer
rumor buzz, gossip
thin bray, overextended, scanty, sparse
to dry ted
widely eurychoric
SPREADER gambrel
SPREADING bushy, contagious, fanning, flaring, overgrown, patulent, patulous, radial, rhipidate, sprangly, thick
SPREE bacchanal, bat, bender, binge, blowout, bout, buster, bustup, carousal, carouse, debauch, drunk, frolic, fuddle, gell, hellbender, indulgence, jag, jamboree, lark, orgy, play, randan, rantan, revel(ry), shindy, spry, tear, toot
city on berlin, cottbus
SPRENT catch, hasp, leap, run, splash, spring(e), squirt
SPREW spreeuw, sprue, starling, thrush
SPRIG active, bough, brad, branch, duck, eyebolt, fellow, nail, part, piece, pluck, point, scion, shoot, smart, sparrow, spruce, stem, trim, twig, youth
SPRIGHTLY active, agile, airy, alert, animated, blithe, breezy, bright, brisk, fresh, funny, gay, ghostly, incorporeal, jaunty, lively, merry, pe(a)rt, piquant, pleasant, quick, shiny, smart, spanky, sparkly, spirited, spry, tid, vigorous, vivacious, windy
SPRIGTAIL duck, grouse
SPRING (See also *hot*, below.) ain, arise, arouse, bath, begin, bend, bound, braird, budtime, buxton, caper, castalia, cause, charco, coil, come, commence, dart (le), dawn, declare, derive, diffuse, elasticity, emanate,

emerge, energy, explode, fly, font, gambado, grow, hop, impair, increase, intoxicate, issue, jump, keld, lavant, leak, leap, lineage, loom, ojo, origin(ate), primavera, prime, printemps, proceed, punahou, race, recoil, resile, resilience, rise, run, saltation, sapling, seedtime, seep, shoot, source, sourd, sprent, start, stem, stend, vasanta, vault, vigor, voar, walm, well
back bounce, give, rebound, recoil, resile, retort, yield
beauty claytonia, lettuce
beetle elator
boiling tubig
carriage robbin
changed to arethusa
chaplet jammer
comb. creno
eruptive geyser, walm
festival anthesteria, easter, holi
festival ruler may queen
fever indolence, listlessness
goddess aphrodite, venus
gushing charco
harbinger crocus, erigenia, robin, violet
hot balneum, geyser, spa, sprudel, thermae
-like vernal
lily violet
mineral resort, spa
nymph aganippe, argyra, calypso, cassotis, castalia, crenae, hago, pegae, pirene
orange styrax
peeper tree-toad
personification chloris
pert. vernal
sacred hippocrene
salt lick, saline
small font, seep
study of pegology
SPRINGBOARD alcalde, batule, launching pad, opportunity, trampoline, tremplin, wagon
SPRINGBOK antelope, gazelle
SPRINGE agile, ensnare, gin, noose, snare, spry, supple, trap
SPRINGER beater, cow, grampus, kneeler, nachschlag, plant, salmon, skewback, tree
SPRINGFISH miller's-thumb
SPRINGTAIL furcula, podura, skiptail

SPRINGTIME germinal, may, ver, voar, youth
SPRINGWORT fern, mandrake, spurge
SPRINGY bouncy, elastic, flexible, resilient, spongy, wet
SPRINKLE asperge, baptize, bedew, bedrop, cleanse, dag, dart, dash, deg, disperse, dispunge, dot, dredge, drench, drizzle, flour, hose, moisten, mottle, pepper, perfuse, powder, purify, rain, sand, scatter, seed, shower, slosh, sow, sparge, sparple, spatter, speck(le), splash, splatter, spot, spray, sprenge, spurt, squatter, squirt, strew, strinkle, stud, swash, variegate, wet
with flour dredge
with grit sand
with moisture bedew, wet
with mud bespatter
with mustard sinapize
with powder dust
with water deg
SPRINKLER aspergil(lum), aspersorium, atomizer, fountain, shower(bath), sparger, sprayer, strinkle
SPRINKLING aspersion, baptism, bit, distribution, few, scattering, seme, sparge, spattering, spray, spread, stipple
SPRINT bicker, missile, race, run, rush, snare, speed, springe, sprunt, trap
SPRIT branch, bud, germinate, pole, rush, shoot, spar, speck, sprat, sprout
holder becket, cringle, snotter
SPRITE apparition, ariel, brownie, bucca, bugbear, coltpixie, coltpixy, demon, devil(kin), dobby, elf, elve, erlking, fairy, fay, ghost, glaistig, goblin, gremlin, hobgoblin, holda, imp, inspiration, kelpie, kobold, leprechaun, life, mind, mood, naiad, nix(ie), peri, person, pilwiz, pixie, pixy, puck, robin-goodfellow, soul, spirit, spoorn, tokoloshe, umbriel, woodpecker
benevolent kewpie
mischievous goblin, gremlin, puck

water neck, nix(ie), shoopil-tie, undine

SPROCKET cam, chantlate, coin, gear, projection, sprit, tooth, wheel, whelp

SPROD salmon

SPROIL action, activity, agility, energy, force

SPROUT acrospire, branch, brod, bud, burgeon, catch, chit, chun, develop, expand, germinate, grow, offshoot, ratoon, scion, shoot, spear, spire, spout, spr(u)it, spurt(er), sucker, tendron, tiller, upstart, vegetate

comb. blast(ic), blasto, clado

SPRUCE (See also *tree, below*.) braw, chest, coffer, crisp, dapper, dashing, dinky, epinette, evergreen, fashionable, fastidious, finical, foppish, fussy, gim, groom, jemmy, jimmy, leather, natty, neat, nifty, nobby, overnice, posh, primp, prink, prussia, pulpwood, slick, smart, smug, sprug, sprunny, sprunt, stylish, tidy, titivate, toffish, tree, trig, trim

partridge grouse

tree abeto, abies, alcock, balsam, catpine, engelmann, epinette, fir, hemlock, larch, norway, picea, yeddo

SPRUDLE fountain, spring, water

SPRUE asparagus, dross, psilosis, remainder, runner, thrush, waste

SPRUG sparrow, spruce

SPRUIKER announcer, barker

SPRUIT sprout, stream

SPRUNG broken, cracked, drunk(en), released, strained, tipsy

SPRUNNY lover, SPRUCE, sweetheart

SPRUNT active, brisk, hill, leap, spring, spruce, struggle

SPRY active, agile, alive, brisk, clever, energetic, hale, knowing, lithe, nimble, prompt, quick, ready, smart, spruce, strenuous, vigorous

SPUD barker, child, dagger, dig, dough, drill, knife, money, paddle, pile, post, potato, projection, reamer, shovel, spade, tater

hole cellar

SPUDDY chubby, fat, pudgy, stubby

SPUILZIE booty, despoil, seize, spoil

SPUME foam, froth, lather, lava, scum, suds, yeast

SPUNG fob, purse, rob

SPUNK amadou, anger, bravery, courage, enterprise, fire, fortitude, gall, getup, gleam, grit, kindle, match, mettle, nerve, passion, pluck, punk, sand, smeddum, spark, spirit, sprawl, temper, tinder, touchwood

SPUNKLESS apathetic, indifferent

SPUNKY bold, daring, dauntless, fiery, game, gingery, hotheaded, irritable, mettlesome, nervy, peppery, plucky, quick, restive, spirited, touchy

SPUR abet, arete, blockhouse, brace, branch, calcar, calk, clamp, digger, drive, ergot, excite, foment, gad, gaff(le), goad, griffe, hasten, herd, incentive, incite(ment), instigate, knag, lormery, motive, move, point, press, prick, projection, prong, prop, provoke, ram, range, ridge, rip(p)on, rowel, speer, spine, spoor, stimulate, stimulus, strut, tower, track, urge

comb. calcari

having spicate

having 2 bicalcarate

of the moment extempore, impromptu, spontaneous, unplanned

part rowel

railroad siding

-shaped calcarine

wheel rowel

wing gambo, goose

without ecalcarate

SPURGE acalypha, adelia, alchornea, appleroot, balsam, catepuce, doveweed, euphorbia, fluxweed, foam, froth, goquick, hippo, milkbush, milkweed, purge, purify, purslane, snakemilk, sunweed, tithymal, wartweed, wartwort

climbing crown of thorns

-daphne mezereon

genus acalypha, cnidoscolus, excoecaria, gillenia, pachysandra, phyllanthus

-nettle tread-softly

spotted doveweed

-thyme devil's-milk

SPURIOUS adulterated, apocryphal, artificial, assumed, base, bastard, bogus, brummagem, counterfeit, deceptive, dummy, factitious, fake(d), feigned, fictitious, forged, fraudulent, illegitimate, imitation, makebelieve, mock, phony, pseudo, put-on, quasi, queer, sham, shoddy, simulated, snide, so-called, supposititious, synthetic, tin(sel), unreal

SPURN affray, blow, contemn, dash, decline, despise, disdain, disgorge, flout, haste(n), hit, incite, kick, refuse, reject, repel, repudiate, root, rush, scorn, scrape, scratch, slight, snub, strike, stumble, support

SPURRINGS banns

SPURRY beggarweed, cowquake, dodder, frank, knotweed, pinecheat, sandweed, spurgula, tickseed, yarr

SPURT bud, burst, chirt, dart, dash, expel, geyser, gush, haste(n), increase, jet, outbreak, random, rise, run, rush, shoot, speed, splurt, spout, spring, sprout, squirt, stream, surge, trickle, well

SPURTLE (See also SPURT.) stick, sword, trickle

SPURWORT madder

SPUTNIK *dog* laika

SPUTTER ado, bluster, bustle, eject, fizz(le), flutter, fuss, slobber, spatter, spit, sputter, stutter

SPUTUM saliva, spit(tle)

SPY agent, ask, beagle, behold, cloak-and-dagger man, descry, detect, discover, drop, emissary, espy, examine, explore, eye, hircarra(h), informer, inspect, intrigante, look, mouton, peek, peep(er), peer, perdue, pry, question, reconnaisance, reconnoiter(er), scout, scrutinize, search, secret agent, see, setter, shadow, sneap, snoop, spier, spook, spotter,

stooge, stool pigeon, toot, tout, watch(er)
boat vedet(te)
famous abel, andre, angleton, arnold, caleb, cavell, culper, cushman, dulles, eric ambler, gold, greenhow, hale, hnupwan, james bond, mata hari, philbrick, philby, pinkerton, popov, powers, reino hayhanen, rosenberg, sansom, schulmeister, sorge, townsend, van lew, von rintelen, yoshikawa
glass telescope
police setter
racetrack tout
to canaan caleb
SPYRI *herione* heidi
SQUAB bird, callow, chair, coy, crush, curt, cushion, drop, fall, fat, fledgling, flop, fowl, heavy, ottoman, pigeon, piper, plump, sharp, short, shy, slop, sofa, squash, squat, squeaker, squealer, squilgee, stool, stubby, thick, unfledged, upholster
young piper
SQUABBLE argue(ment), bicker, bobbery, brangle, brannigan, brawl, contend, contest, disagreement, dispute, disturbance, fight, hubbub, jangle, melee, muss, quarrel, row, rumpus, set-to, spat, swabble, tiff, tumult, wrangle
SQUAD band, crew, force, group, mud, party, platoon, posse, team, troop
car cruiser
leader corporal
SQUADRON armada, escadrille, fleet, flotilla, regiment, sotnia, square
leader major
SQUAILS ninepins, skittles
SQUALID degraded, dirty, filthy, foul, frowzy, mangy, mean, nasty, poor, repellant, repulsive, scabrous, seedy, shabby, sloppy, slovenly, slummy, sordid, unkempt
SQUALL barat, bawl, bayamo, blast, bleffert, blow, blubber, bluster, borasco, borasque, borrasca, bourrasque, chubasco, cry, dear, dispute, disturbance, drow, flurry, fracas,

fresh, gale, gust, howl, mewl, pet, rain, scream, shower, squawk, storm, tempest, tornado, uproar, wail, waul, weep, windstorm, wretch
violent williwaw
SQUALOR dirt, filth(iness), mire, mud, sloppiness, squalidness, wretchedness
SQUAMA alula, calypter, exopodite, scale, squamosa, tegula
SQUAMOUS flaky, scaly
SQUANDER blow, burn, dispend, disperse, dissipate, lavish, misuse, sack, scatter, spend, sport, swatter, swattle, use up, waste
SQUANTUM festival, party, picnic
SQUARE accord, agora, agree, balance, block, boxy, brawny, bribe, campo, carreau, carrefour, centare, concur, conform, court, dependable, dinkum, direct, discharge, enclosure, even, exact, fair, fit, green, honest, innocent, jerk, jibe, just, market(place), match, mold, park, pattern, pay, piazza, piazzetta, place, plaza, polygon, principle, quadrangular, quadrate, quadrilateral, quarrel, regular, regulate, settle, shape, solid, standard, stout, stuffy, suit, tally, true(up)
and rabbet annulet
-cap apprentice, collegian, mortarboard, student
dance quadrille, reel, tucker
dance number set
from differ, diverge
great pegasus, star
measure acre, centiare, hectar(e)
open piazza, zocalo
public agora, alunalun, common(s), piazza, place, platz, plaza, zocalo
shooting fair, honest, just, right
solid cube
-stem centaury, sabbatia
-toed conservative, oldfashioned, precise, prim
with dovetail
SQUAREHEAD dolt, fool, num(b)skull, screwball, wheat
SQUARELY bung, caplunk, directly, exactly, fair(ly),

flush, full, honestly, openly, plop, plumb, plunk, pointblank, precisely, right, smack, spang, straight
SQUAREMAN carpenter, stonecutter
SQUASH (See also *kind*, below.) blow, conceal, crush, cucurbita, drink, extinguish, flatten, game, gourd, macerate, mash, ooze, plant, press, pulp, pulverize, quash, quell, refute, soften, squeeze, squelch, squish, squ(u)sh, stop, suppress, triturate
-berry dockmackie
bug anasa, stinkbug
kind acorn, banana, cashaw, cocozelle, crookneck, cucurb(it), cushaw, cym(b)ling, gooseneck, gourd, hubbard, italian, marblehead, marrow, pattypan, pepo, peponium, pumpkin, sibley, simmel, summer, turban, zucchini
summer cocozelle, cym(b)ling, zucchini
wild calabazilla
SQUASHY boggy, muddy, pulpy, squelchy, squishy, squdgy, squshy, swash
SQUAT absquatulate, angelfish, bend, blow, broad, bruise, couch, crouch, crush, descend, dumpy, fall, hunker, hurkle, low, perch, pinch, pudgy, quat(ch), quiet, roost, settle, silence, sink, sit, squdgy, squeeze, squ(u)shy, stocky, stoop, stub(by), swot, thickset, wide
SQUATTER bewilder, bywoner, confuse, crouch, flutter, mull, nest(er), paracaidistia, plunge, press, sandpiper, scatter, settler, sprinkle, squander
state kansas
SQUAW coween, female, mahala, mahaly, wife, woman
husband brave, buck, sannup
mint pennyroyal
old scoldenor, scolder
SQUAWBUSH bunchberry, cornel, shoval
SQUAWDUCK cockawee, eider
SQUAWFISH bigmouth, boxhead, chappaul, chub, minnow, yellowbelly

SQUAWFLOWER birthroot, trillium

SQUAWK complain(t), confess, lament, night-heron, protest, scrawk, scream, screech, squall

SQUAWROOT atenia, beechdrops, blueberry, broomrape, cancerroot, clapwort, cohosh, earthclub, elotillo, ginseng, orobancha, papooseroot, yamp

SQUEAK betray, blab, cheep, confess, creak, croak, disturb, inform, peach, peep, screech, scroop, speak, squeal

SQUEAKER beetle, informer, pig, pigeon, shrike, squab

SQUEAKY scrannel

SQUEAL betray, blab, broil, complain, cry, dispute, frail, inform, outcry, pip, protest, quarrel, screak, snitch, sweel, tattle, tell, weary, yell, yelp, yip

SQUEALER canary, duck, fink, grouse, informer, partridge, pigeon, plover, quail, swift, tattler, traitor

SQUEAMISH critical, daunch, dauncy, difficult, fastidious, finical, finicky, finikin, fussy, helo(e), mawkish, modest, nauseated, nauseous, nice, per(s)nickety, pawky, pensy, priggish, proper, prudish, queasy, reluctant, shy, sick, wairch, wambly, wearish

SQUEEZE choke, compress, condense, constrict, contract, crisis, crowd, crush, crux, cuddle, embrace, escape, exact, extort, extract, graft, grip, gripe, hug, influence, jam, kvetch(er), mull, neck, nip, oppress, pinch, press(ure), push, scringe, scrooge, scrunge, scruze, squab, squash, squinch, squiss, strangle, strangulate, thrimble, thrimp, thring, throttle, tweak, twitch, urge, vise, wrest
from sponge
in enter, fudge, intrude
out pinch, render, strain, wring

SQUEEZER juicer, noose, reamer, wringer

SQUEEZY cramped, confined

SQUELCH blow, crush, discomfit, disconcert, extinguish, fall, put down, quash, quell, rebuke, refute, shut off, silence, sit on, squash, squidge, stamp, suppress

SQUELCHY muddy, pulpy, squashy

SQUETEAGUE bluefish, chickwit, drum(mer), squetee, trout, weakfish

SQUIB bomb, detonator, dispute, filler, firecracker, fuse, jet, lampoon, match, missile, mote, pasquil, pasquinade, pastiche, squirt, torpedo

SQUID calamare, calamary, chiperone, cuttlefish, inkfish, kalamaria, loligo, mollusk, octopus, plug, sepia, sleevefish, tantonet
pen quill

SQUIDGY abbreviated, short

SQUIFFY drunk, intoxicated

SQUIGGLE curl(icue), quiver, shake, squirm, turn, twist, wriggle

SQUILL cigala, mantis-crab, scilla, sea-onion, slangkop, urginea

SQUILLA chloridella, crustacean, prawn, shrimp

SQUINCH corbeling, hagioscope, lintel, quince, squeeze, squench, squint, twist, wrench

SQUINT bent, cast, deviate, deviation, esotropia, exotropia, glance, gledge, glee, gleg, glent, gley, goggle, hagioscope, look, peer, scan, sheyle, skell(y), sken, skew, squinch, squinny, strabismus, trend
-eyed envious, gleed, gleyd, malignant, prejudiced

SQUIRE accompany, armiger, armor bearer, attend(ant), beau, donzel, equerry, escort, gallant, gentleman, henchman, landjunker, landowner, lover, page, scutiger, servitor, shield bearer, spark, square, swain, timias, younker
petty squireen, squireling

SQUIRM agonize, bend, curl, flinch, recoil, scriggle, shrink, skew, squiggle, turn, twist, wince, wind, wriggle, writhe

SQUIRREL ardilla, assapan, boomer, bun(t), calabar,

calaber, chickeree, chipmunk, chippy, copperhead, eggeater, gopher, grayback, jelerang, pteromis, ratatosk, rodent, scaletail, schillu, sciurus, scug, shadetail, sisel, taguan, xerus
cage routine, rut
cup hepatica
flying polatouche, taguan
food camass, nuts
ground gopher, sisel, suslik, tamias
-like sciuroid
monkey marmoset, saimiri, titi
nest dray, drey
pelt calabar, calaber, vair
pert. sciuroid
pike chinchilla
plague tularemia
red chickaree, eggeater
shrew pentail, tana, tupaia
small striped chipmunk
tail brush

SQUIRRELFISH alaiki, marian, matajuelo, mojarra, sailor's-choice, sandfish, serrano, soldier, welshman

SQUIRRELLY eccentric, funny, nutty, peculiar

SQUIRT chirt, dart, disgorge, eject, flow, jet, outburst, pour, prate, salp(a), scoot, skite, slirt, spatter, splash, spout, spray, sprent, sprinkle, spritz, spurt, squib, stream, syringe, whippersnapper

SQUISH marmalade, nonsense, pulp, squash

SRAMANA See BUDDHA.

SRI fortunate, glorious, holy, lakshmi, reverend
husband vishnu
lanka See CEYLON.

S-SHAPED agee, sigmate, sigmoid

STAB attack, attempt, bayonet, cleave, confecture, cris, cut, dagger, gore, hurt, impale, injure, kill, knife, knive, lance, pain, pang, paunch, penetrate, perforate, pierce, pink, plunge in, poniard, prick, prickado, puncture, saber, skewer, sliver, spear, spike, spit, stake, stick, stiletto, stitch, stoccado, stump, sword, thrust, transfix, trial, try, tusk, wound
in the back betray(al), shaft, slander, smear

STABBER assassin, awl, bayonet, marlinespike, pricker
STABILITY anchor, aplomb, balance, constancy, endurance, equilibrium, fastness, firmness, immutability, permanence, purpose, reliability, resolution, security, solidity, soundness, staunchness, steadfastness, steadiness, strength, substantiality
STABILIZE adjust, balance, ballast, brace, establish, firm(up), fix, freeze, hold, immobilize, poise, regulate, set, settle, steady, stiffen, support, transfix, trim
STABILIZER acardite, balance(r), ballast, counterweight, gyroscope, mordant, pendulum, shockabsorber, springs
STABLE barn, byre, changeless, confirmed, constant, durable, equerry, fast, fiducial, firm, fixed, hemel, immobile, immutable, kennel, lasting, livery, mews, permanent, reliable, resolute, safe, secure, shed, slum, solid, sound, stall, stalwart, standing, static, staunch, steadfast, steady, stout, strong, sturdy, substantial, tambo, tough, trustworthy, unvarying
boy jockboy, jostler, lad, mafoo, mafu, mehtar
compartment stall
drain groop
officer avener
royal or group mews
STABLEMAN avener, groom, hostler, ostler, stockman
STACCATO abrupt, detached, disconnected, jerky, ricochet, saltato, secco, sharp
mark aspiration
not tenuto
STACHYS betony, hedge-nettle
friend paul
STACK assemble, bank, brash, canch, chimney, clamp, cock, collect, flue, funnel, gather, goave, group, heap, hoard, kitty, leet, load, pack, pile, pipe, poak, pook, pot, quantity, rick(le), ruck, scintle, scroo, set, shock, stalk, tump

small canch, cob, rickle
support for staddle
up progress, stand, tier, total
up with compare, correspond, equal, match, progress, stand
STACKYARD haggard, mowhay mowie, stackgarth
STACTE cinnamon, myrrh, spice, storax
STAD kraal, town, village
STADACOMA quebec
STADDLE cane, crutch, frame(work), sapling, staff, stain, support, swath, tree
STADIUM amphitheater, amphitheatre, arena, astrodome, bowl, coin, coliseum, course, dromos, field, furlong, stage, stands, theater, track
indoor astrodome
STAFF advisers, aides, alpenstock, ankus, associates, baculus, ballow, band, baston, bat(on), bodyguard, bourdon, caduceus, cambuca, cane, catchpole, club, committee, company, crew, croche, crook, crosier, cross, crozier, crummie, crutch, cudgel, distaff, employees, entourage, equip, faculty, fasces, filch, following, force, gang, group, hands, kent, kuerr, lathee, limb, line, lituus, mace, man, muleta, mullein, paterissa, pedum, personnel, piton, pole, retinue, rhabdos, rissle, rod, rung, scepter, servants, shaft, spear, squad, stable, stanza, stave, stick, suite, support, team, thyrsus, wand
bacchante's thyrsus
bearer macer
bishop's baculus, bagle, crosier, crozier, pastoral, rod
forked linstock
graduated limb
herald's caduceus
hooked nibby
ivy-twined thyrsus
magic caduceus, rhabdos, wand
mountain-climbing alpenstock, ballow, piton, pole
of office caduceus, mace, rod, scepter, vare, verge
pastoral cane, crosier, crozier, pedum
pointed pike, pritch
royal baton, scepter, sceptre

shepherd's ankus, crook, kent, mullein
spiked ankus
symbol of st alexis
teaching faculty
tree catha, celestra(ce), kat, sapindale
vine bittersweet
STAG (See also ANIMAL *male.*) betray, buck, bull, caribou, cervus, cock, colt, deer, drake, gander, hart, horse, inform(er), male, man, party, pointer, pollard, royal, segg, shorten, single, smoker, spade, staig, stallion, stride, unattached, wren
antlers attire
bearded tragelaph
beetle lucanus, pinch(ing) bug
bush black haw, honeysuckle
changed to actaeon
gold-antlered cerynea
hercules' arcadian hind, cerynean hind
horn antler, bezantler, rial, sumac, tine
horn point broach
hornless hummel, pollard
-horn sumac dividivi
symbol of cuckold(om)
3 years or more royal, spade, spire
STAGE age, arena, boards, broadway, catasta, coach, dais, degree, display, dock, enact, exhibit, floor, footlights, forum, grade, hemmel, juncture, layer, legit, perform, period, phase, platform, point, prescenium, present, pulpit, rostrum, scaffold, scene, shelf, span, station, step, story, theater, theatre, theatron
center of limelight
cupola lantern
curtain drop, scrim
dance black bottom, cakewalk, tap
direction alarums and excursions, all, aside, enter, exeunt, exit, mane(n)t, remain, sennet, sola, solus
-door man johnnie
ensemble cast, crew
equipment See *part,* below.
extra supe, super(numerary)
flood crest
front part apron
hay hemmel

landing bridge, staith, stelling

manager regisseur

movable pegma

on en scene

part apron, backdrop, boards, cloth, coulisse, curtain, drop, flat, flies, flipper, float, footlights, grid(iron), loft, oleo, paradus, prop(s), rag, ring, scenery, scruto, set(ting), skenai, skene, spot, tab, teaser, tormentor, wing

pert. scenic, theatrical

pulley sloat

raised dais, estrade

scenery props, set

side wing

slant rake

summons act-call

thunder device bronteum

trapdoor scruto, slot

trumpet call sennet

whisper aside

STAGECOACH diligence, dilly, tallyho, VEHICLE

crew coachman, driver, flunky, footman, forerunner, guard, harbinger, hostler, linkboy, linkman, man-on-the-box, outrider, outrunner, porter, postillion, precursor, rifleman, shotgun, whip

STAGEHAND callboy, chips, dayman, flunky, flyman, gaffer, grip, juicer, machinist, pitman, sceneshifter, scenist

STAGGER agitate, alternate, attempt, bewilder, blunder, boggle, botch, bumble, bungle, consternate, daver, dodge, doubt, falter, flounder, frighten, hesitate, hobble, lurch, megrims, pace, reel, stammer, startle, stite, stoit(er), stot(ter), stumble, stun, surprise, sway, titubate, totter, try, unsettle, vacillate, vibrate, wauchle, waver, wobble

STAGGERBUSH lambkill, neopieris

STAGGERING areel, incredible

STAGGERS dunt, stavers, vertigo

STAGGERWEED larkspur, shiverweed

STAGNANT dead, dull, foul, inactive, inert, motionless,

quiet, slow, sluggish, standing, static, still

STAGNATE hibernate, stall, stand, vegetate

STAGNATION abeyance, backwater, doldrum(s), dormancy, dullness, inertia, languor, latency, passivity, standstill, stasis, suspense, torpor, vegetation

STAGY artificial, assumed, dramatic, melodramatic, theatrical

STAID calm, complacent, composed, cool, decent, decorous, demure, earnest, grave, priggish, prosaic, sedate, seemly, sensible, serious, set(tled), smug, sober, solemn, steadfast, steady

STAIN abuse, attaint, besmear, besmoke, blacken, blemish, blot(ch), blur, brand, buff, carmalum, cloud, color, corrupt, dab, darken, daub, defect, defile, dirty, discolor, disgrace, dishonor, dye, eclipse, fleck, flick, foil, foul, fox, giemsa, imb(r)ue, infamy, macula(te), macule, mark, mole, paint, pigment, pleck, pollution, scorch, singe, slubber, slur(ry), smear, smirch, smot, smudge, smut(ch), soil, spatter, speck(le), splash, splotch, spoil, spot, stigma, suddle, sully, taint, tarnish, tash, tincture, tinge, tint, varnish, vilify, wem(my)

black ebonize

brick scumming

linen mell

remove bleach

STAINED dirty, doaty, foxy, smudged, smutchy

STAINLESS clean, faultless, immaculate, perfect, pure, spotless

STAIR(S) advance, ascend, companionway, degree, escalier, flight, ladder, perron, pitch, ramp, rung, stage, step(s), stile, sty

curved sweep

edge noser, nosing

holy scala santa

moving escalator

outdoor perron, stoop

part balustrade, bridgeboard, landing, newel, nosing, riser, rung, step, string (course), tread

platform landing, quarterpace

portable ladder

post newel

river bank ghat

series flight

ship's companionway, ladder

spindle speel

winding caracol(e), cochlea, turnpike, vice

STAIRCASE caracol(e), escalator, escalier, grece, grice, griece, ladder, perron

STAIRWAY escalier, perron, stoop

STAITH dock, embankment, wharf

STAKE ante, anvil, back, baikie, balk, bet, brasero, chance, commit, corner, deposit, equity, finance, gage, gamble, hazard, interest, kitty, loggat, logget, mark, mise, money, pale, paling, palisade, palus, pawn, peel, peg, pel, picket, pile, pledge, pole, post, pot, prize, promise, purse, risk, share, spile, spoke, sprag, staff, stalk, stick, stoater, stob, support, trunch, venture, wager

at implicated, involved

-driver bittern

fence palisade

-like palar

-out ambush, surveillance, trap

pointed sowel

-shaped palar, sudiform

symbol of st anastasia

STAKEHOLDER banker

STALAG jail, prison

STALE ambush, banal, cheapen, common, crumbling, decoy, dull, dry, dusty, effete, fallow, flat, flavorless, frow(z)y, fusty, hackneyed, handle, insipid, lifeless, lure, mildewed, moldering, moldy, motheaten, mouldy, musty, old, passe, rancid, rung, rusty, shaft, snare, stagnant, stem, step, stock, stuffy, tasteless, threadbare, timeworn, tired, trite, vapid, weak, worn

STALEMATE arrest, check, crisis, deadlock, draw, impasse, standoff, standstill, tie

STALIN dzhugashvili

henchman beria, yagoda

STALINGRAD tsaritsyn, volgograd

STALK bun, cane, castock, caulis, culm, dog, filament, follow, haulm, hunt, kex, march, pace, pedicel, peduncle, petiole, podetium, prey, prowl, pursue, quill, ratoon, reed, scape, seta, shadow, shaft, shank, spear, spindle, spire, spread, stack, stale, stam, steal, stem, sterigma, stipe(s), straw, stride, strut, stump, swagger, swank, sweep, tail, walk, wride
attached to petiolar
comb. culmi
dry keck, kek
having petiolate
plant axis, haulm, kex, pedicel, petiole, scape, stem
remove strig
ripened straw
short stipe

STALKING *horse* candidate, mask, pretense, red-herring

STALKY clever, slender, wily

STALL alcove, anticipate, arrest, balagan, barn, bin, boose, boosy, booth, bulk, cabinet, carcer, carol, cavesson, check, compartment, conk(out), crib, cub, cubicle, decoy, delay, die, dwell, end, enthrone, fail, fence, halt, hut, idle, induct, loge, manger, mire, niche, pew, pitch, place, pretend, pretense, procrastinate, room, seat, shamble, stable, stand, stash, stasidion, station, stick, stog, stop, tarry, temporize, throne, travis
church pew
division between bail
theater box, fauteuil, loge

STALLION courtesan, horse, paramour, sire, stud
-ass offspring hinny

STALWART bold, brave, brawny, courageous, firm, hardy, healthy, hero, lusty, muscular, partisan, powerhouse, resolute, robust, rugged, solid, sound, stiff, stout, strong(man), sturdy, substantial, tenacious, tough, valiant, valorous, vigorous

STAM amaze, stalk, stump, trunk

STAMEN *comb.* adelphous, andra, androus, andry
group androecium
having aplostemonous, diandrous
part anther, filament, microsporangia
without anandrarious, anandrous

STAMINA endurance, FORCE, grit, guts, nerve, pluck, power, sand, spirit, strength, vigor, vim, vitality, zip

STAMM race, stem, stock, tribe

STAMMER balbutiate, faffle, falter, fribble, hacker, hammer, haw, hem, hesitate, hocker, hotter, maffle, mammer, mant(er), pselism, sputter, stagger, stot, stumble, stutter, titubate, traulism, yammer

STAMP beat, brand, bray, cast, character(istic), chop, clop, clump, crush, die, dink, distinguish, drub, emboss, fix, form, frank, impress(ion), imprint, incuse, incute, inscribe, kind, label, make, mark, mold, name, pace, pestle, postage, pounce, pound, press, print, pulverize, ruff, seal, sigil, sign, sort, stigmatize, stomp, strike, tenor, thresh, token, tramp(le), tread, type, value, walk
background burele
book album
bookbinding block, fillet
border tressoure, tressure
cancelling killer
clay pintadera
collecting philately
collector philatelist
fencing appel
group block
hand canceler
madness timbromania
official chop
out abolish, cancel, dele(te), destroy, end, erase, expunge, exterminate, extinguish, kill, nullify, remove, scotch, scratch
paper pelure
revenue fiscal
sheet part pane
space spandrel
trade in redeem

STAMPEDE blitz, breakaway, charge, debacle, flight,

frighten, panic, riot, rout, run, rush, scamper

STANCE attitude, carriage, distance, foothold, halt, pen, poise, position, posture, room, stand(still), stanza, station, stop
golfer's address

STANCH (See also STAUNCH.) allay, check, close, dam, extinguish, quell, sound, stem, stop, trusty

STANCHION, STANCHEL bar, brace, crotch, crutch, mullion, piton, post, prop, stencil, stent, support

STAND abide, accord, afford, agree, angle, appear, arise, attitude, base, bear, bipod, block, booth, brook, cask, caster, concern, confront, continue, cost, counter, dais, easel, endure, erect, etagere, exist, face, fix, halt, kiosk, last, lectern, locate, maintain, pause, place, podium, poise, pose, post, pulpit, rack, rank, remain, resist, rest, rise, scruple, settle, slant, stall, station, stay, stick, stillion, stomach, stop, submit, suffer, support, sustain, table, tabo(u)ret, teapoy, tolerate, treat, tripod, trivet, tub, undergo, view, zarf
auction block
barrel jib, thrall
behind or by adjoin, back, defend, guarantee, maintain, serve, support
compass binnacle
dresses frippery
drill pipe fourble
fast persevere, persist, resist, stay put
finjan zarf
fireclay crank
for abide, bear, denote, endure, guarantee, mean, permit, represent, sponsor, symbolize, suffer, tolerate, volunteer
guard cover
hawk kestrel
-in alter ego, bear, deputy, pinch-hitter, replacement, ringer, substitute
inability to abasia, astasia
in the way obstruct
off aroint, avaunt, draw, push, recede, resist, stall, tie

on behoove, depend, insist, magnify, rely
on end arise, erect, upend
1-night gig
opposite face, front
ornamental athenienne, epergne, etagere, teapoy, zarf
out acme, a-one, beetle, jut, persevere, project, protrude, superior, supreme, surpass, tops
over delay, postpone
pat dig in, persevere, solid
-patter conservative
printer's bank, frame
raised pergola
sculptor's chassis
shelved whatnot
shooting butt
small tabo(u)ret
still stop, whoa
3-legged teapoy, tripod, trivet
tile-making criss
together agree, cohere, combine, cooperate
top criss
2-legged bipod, duopod
up counter, delay, endure, last, pass, persevere, resist, rise, straighten, treat
up for defend, justify, sponsor, support
STANDARD alem, archetype, assize, banner, base, beacon, beauseant, bracciale, brattach, candlestick, canon, chest, classic, coffer, color, criterion, emblem, ensign, example, flag, frame, ga(u)ge, gonfalon, ideal, labarum, law, mean, measure, median, model, modulus, norm, orthodox, par, paradigm, paragon, pattern, pennant, pennon, pole, post, prescriptive, principle, rule(r), set, square, staple, streamer, suit, support, test, titer, touchstone, toug, type, unit, usual, vexillum, yardstick
-bearer alferez, candidate, ensign, gonfalonier, leader, signifer, staller, vexillary
of measurement metric
of pitch diapason
of quality grade
pert. vexillary
small jack
STANDING capacity, continuing, credit, degree, durable, durability, erect, established, esteem, fixed, foothold, footing, immovable, inert, lasting, motionless, permanent, position, prestige, rank, reputation, settled, situation, stagnant, statant, static, station, status, vertical
alone detached, separate
comb. stato
erect horrent
incoordination astasia
long customary, lasting, traditional
out bold, eminent, extant, jutting, salient
room only sro
social fashion, station
upright orthostatic
STANDISH, MILES *intermediary* john alden
wife rose
STANDOFFISH aloof, cold, cool, coy, reserved, reticent, shy
STANDPOINT angle, attitude, fulcrum, outlook, position, stance, station
STANDSTILL cessation, checkmate, deadlock, halt, impasse, jib, rest, stalemate, stance, stay, stop, tie
STANG ache, acre, bar, beam, carry, hanger, lever, pang, pole, rail, rood, shaft, spear, stick, sting, throb, wound
STANHOPE, PHILIP chesterfield
STANK dam, ditch, drain, pond, pool, reservoir, stang, tank, weak, weir, worn out
STANZA alloeostropha, apartment, ballad, ballata, baston, chamber, dixain, dizain, envoi, huitain, poem, rispetto, room, settaine, stave, stev, strophe, troilet, troilus, verse
2-line couplet, distich
3-line tristich
4-line quatrain
5-line cinquain, pentastich, quintain
6-line hexastich, sestet, sextain
8-line huitan, octave, octet triolet
10-line decalet, dizain(e)
14-line sonnet
irregular alloestropha
last envoi, envoy
part stave, verse

STAPES columella, ossicle, stirrup
STAPLE chaplet, chief, column, commodity, depot, emporium, fiber, fibre, fixed, frame, goods, important, item, loop, main, market, mart, materials, merchandise, nail, pillar, pit, post, principle, prosaic, shaft, source, stitch, storehouse, supply, support, vervelle
roll sliver
STAR ace, actor, actress, asterisk, asteroid, astral, badge, blaze, chief, coryphee, decoration, destiny, dingbat, diva, emphasize, etoile, excel, feature, fortune, giant, headliner, hero(ine), hummingbird, lead, luminary, mullet, orb, ornament, personage, phad, planet, preeminent, present, prima donna, principal, protagonist, satellite, sedge, sphere, stella, sun, super
anise illicium, stinkbush
apple balata, bullytree, caimito, manilkara, sapodilla, shea
belt zodiac
blazing comet
-bloom pinkroot, spigelia
bright alpha, altair, beta, canopus, cor, delta, gamma, nova(e), sirius, spica, sun, vega
chart uranometry
cluster praesepe
comb. aster(o), astr(o), sidero
conjunction syzygy
course arc, orbit
covered with seme
-crossed doomed, ill-fated, unfortunate
distance parsec
divination astrology
dog sept(i), sirius, sopt, sothis
double mizar
emanation blas
evening hesper(us), mercury, moon, venus, vesper
evil, pert. sideral
explosion nova, vulne
facet pane
falling See *shooting*, below.
feather comatula
1st magnitude achernar, acrux, alpha, altair, antares,

cygni, cygnus, deneb, hadar, spica, vega

finch redstart

5-pointed pentacled

flower brodiaea, chickweed, triteleia

followers magi, wisemen

giant aldebaran, arcturus

grass callitriche, cólicroots, starwort

group asterism, cluster, constellation, galaxy, milky way, nebula, spiral

guiding lodestar, polestar

heraldic estoile

hyacinth squill

jelly alga, nostoc, starshot

lights bluet, dove's-foot

mapping uranography

morning daystar, jupiter, lucifer, mars, mercury, phosphor, saturn, venus

multiple epsilon, lyrae, milky way

name meaning asta, esther, estelle, hester, stella

new nova

-nose mole

observation astronomy, uranoscopy

observing instrument armil, astrolabe, telescope

-of-bethlehem eucharis, sleepy-dick, squill, starwort

-of-jerusalem salsify

-of-night pitch-apple

-of-the-earth plantain

officer's pip

ornamental etoile

pattern etoile

pert. antalgol, astral, luminous, planetoid, pointed, sidereal, sphery, stellar, stellate

point node

potential comer

pulsating cepheid

red antares, mars

reed birthwort

royal aldebaran, antares, formalhaut, regulus

sapphire asteria, astrion, astroite

science of astrology, astronomy

-shaped asteroid, etoile

-shaped spicule actine

shooting comet, cowslip, leonid, meteor

-spangled banner author francis scott key

-strewn seme

temporary nova

thistle caltrap, calt(h)rop, knapweed

-throat heliomaster, hummingbird

through difficulty to ad astra per aspera

variable algol, antalgol, caltrap, caltrop, mira, nova, omicron

worship idolatry, sabaism, uranolatry

worshipper sabaist

STAR IN *andromeda (chained lady)* almak, alpherat(z), delta, mirac(h)

aquarius (waterbearer) al bali, ancha, sadachbia, sadalmelik, sadalsund, skat

aquila (eagle) als(c)hain, altair, deneb, difda, gamma, soaring falcon, tar(a)zed

argo aspidiske, canopus, markeb, miaplacidis, milky way, naos

argo divisions carina (keel), malus (mast), puppis (stern), pyxis (mariner's compass, nautical box), vela (sails)

aries (ram) alpha-arietis, botein, el nath, hamal, mesartim, sheratan

auriga (charioteer) alpha-aurigas, beta-tauri, capella, el nath, kids, menkalinan, she-goat

big dipper (charles's wain) See *ursa major,* below.

bootes (herdsman) alkalurops, arcturus, beardriver, canes vanatici, guard-keeper, izar, mirak, muphrid, nekkar, seginus, watcher

cancer (crab) acubens, altarf, asellus, praesepe, tegmine

canis major (big dog) adhara, aludra, dog-star, furud, murzim, sirius, wezen

canis minor (little dog) gomeisa, procyon

canis venatico asterion, chara, corcaroli

capricorn (goat) algedi, dabih, deneb, nashira

carina (keel) canopus

cassiopeia caph, ruchbah, schiedar

centaurus agena, rigil

cepheus alderamin, alfirk, errai

cetus (whale) baten-kaitos,

deneb, dheneb, menkar, mira

columba (dove, noah's dove) phaet(o), wezn

corona (crown) alphecca, gemma, nusakan

corvus (crow) alchiba, algorab, gienah

crater (cup, goblet) alkes

cygnus (swan) albireo, arided, azelfafage, gienah, sadr

delphinus (dolphin) deneb, rotanev, sualocin

draco (dragon) adib, alrakis, alsafi, altais, elasich, etamin, giansar, grumium, juga, nodus secundus, rastaban, thuban

equuleus (horse) kitalpha

eridanus (river) acamar, achernar, ancha(t), angetenar, azha, beid, cursa, keid, theemim, zaurak

gemini (twins) alhena, apollo, castor, hercules, mebsuta, mekbuda, pollux, propus, wasat

hercules cujam, kornephorus, rasalgethi

leon (lion) adhafera, alkhafara, algieba, denebola, duhr, sasalas, regulus, zosma

leporis (rabbit) arneb, nihal

libra (scales) kiffa, zubenelgenubi, zubeneschamali

lyra (lyre) aladfar, shelyak, sulafat, vega, wega

ophiuchus (serpent-bearer) cebalrai, marfic, rasalhague, sabik, yed

orion (hunter) alnilam, alnitak, alnitham, bellatrix, betelgeuse, betelgeux, meissa, mintaka, rigel, saiph

pegasus (winged horse) algenib, alpha andromedae, atik, baham, biham, delta pegasi, enif, enri, great square, homam, markab, matar, menkib, salm, scheat

perseus algenab, algol (medusa-head), alpherat(z), at(t)ik, demon-star

phoenix nair-al-zaurak

pisces (fish) al rischa, difda, fomalhaut

pleiades alcyone, asterope, atlas, celaeno, electra, maia, merops, pleione, sterope, taurus, taygeta

sagittarius (archer) alnasi,

arkab, ascella, kaus, media, nunki, rukbat
scorpius (*scorpion*) acrab al niyat, antares, dischubba, graffias, lesath, shaula
serpent alya, unuk-al-hay
taurus (*bull*) alcyone, aldebaran, asterope, atlas, celaeno, electra, el nath, hyades, maia, merope, pleiad(es), pleione, sterope, taygeta
ursa major alcor, alioth, alkaid, alkphrah, alula, benetmasch, big dipper, dubhe, el kophrah, megrez, merak, mirak, mizar, pha(c)d, phecda, talitha, tania
ursa minor cynosure, kochab, pherkad, polaris, yildun
virgo (*virgin*) almuredin, azimech, porrima, spica, syrma, vindemiatrix, zaniah, zavijava
STARCH amidulin, amulum, amydon, amyl(oid), amylum, arrowroot, arum, backbone, carbohydrate, cassava, curcuma, energy, faecula, farina, fecula, fixature, formality, glucosan, glycogen, manioc, maranta, pentyl, sago, salep, stark, stiffen, stiffness, strength, strong, talipot, vim
animal glucogen
blue smalt
comb. amyl(o)
compound amylose, dextrin
grain nucleus hilum
-like amyloid, amylose, arum
-like substance alantine, inulin, olivil
molecule group amylin
-producing amyliferous
soluble amidin, amidulin
STARCHWORT cuckoopint
STARCHY amylaceous, amyloid, formal, precise, prim, proud, rigid, stiff, thick, unbending, viscid
STARE blaze, boof, bore, bristle, eye(ball), gape, gaup, gawk, gawp, gaze, glare, gleam, glitter, glop, glore, glower, gove, leer, look, ogle, peer, pore, see, shine, starling, type, watch, wonder
foolishly gowk
STARER lorgnette
STARFISH asterias, asteriid, asteroid, astropecten, echin-

oderm, ophiuran, pad, phanerozonium, radiate
arm ray
larva bipinnaria, brachiolaria
STARGAZE daydream, muse
STARGAZER astrologer, astronomer, catfish, kathetostoma, uranologist, uranoscopid
instrument armil, astrolabe, telescope
STARING agape, agaze, aglare, conspicuous, evident, goggle, googly, wide-eyed
STARK bare, barren, buck, cark, complete, crude, desolate, fair, firm, fixed, forte, hard, harsh, inflexible, long, loud, obdurate, powerful, pure, rigid, rough, set, severe, sheer, stalwart, starch, stiff(en), strong, stubborn, tense, unyielding, utter(ly) very, vigorous, wooden
STARKY dry, hard, shriveled, stiff
STARLING chepster, cutwater, mina, myna, oxpecker, pastor, sali, shepstare, shepster, spreeuw, starn(el), staynil, tilyer
group murmuration
pert. sturnine, sturnoid
STARLITE zircon
STARRED *lizard* agama, hardim
STARRY astral, bright, celestial, luminous, shining, sparkling, starny, stellar, stelled, stellate
campion catchfly
START 3 jar, run, shy 4 dart, dash, head, hunt, jerk, jolt, jump, lead, move, open, rush, seed, send, tail, turn 5 begin, birth, debut, dodge, float, flush, found, glent, issue, lever, onset, rally, rouse, sally, scare, shock, spurt, wince 6 actify, attack, boggle, broach, depart, fall to, flinch, fright, handle, ignite, launch, loosen, origin, outset, propel, set off, set out, shrink, source, spring, tee off, twitch 7 actuate, advance, disturb, getaway, impulse, instant, opening, pitch in, produce, propose, provoke, push off, retreat, STARTLE, support 8 activate, displace, handicap, initiate, organize, outburst, shove off, with-

draw 9 advantage, beginning, establish, institute, introduce, originate, strike out 10 inaugurate
again resume
aside dodge, shy, skirt
back blench, flinch, retreat, return
forward advance, brainge
up grow, jump, rise
STARTER catchword, controller, cue, drill, entrant, first, ignition, koji, official, punch, trigger
STARTLE affright, alarm, arouse, astonish, astound, boggle, booger, bustle, consternate, course, disturb, electrify, excite, flinch, fright(en), jar, jolt, rouse, scare, shock, stagger, START, stir, stun, sturt, surprise, take aback, terrify, thrill, unsettle, upset
STARTLING alarming, breathtaking, dramatic, exciting, fearful, restless, shocking, skittish, startly, thrilling
STARVATION famine, penury, want
STARVE clem, desire, destroy, die, disable, famish, fast, freeze, hunger, need, perish, raven, stint, suffer, want, weaken
STARVEACRE hungerweed
STARVED drawn, emaciated, haggard, hungry, meager meagre, pinched, poor, underfed, undernourished
STARWORT aster, astrofel(l), callitriche, chickweed, colicroot, stellaria
STASH cache, end, refuge, secrete, stop, store
STASIS faction, quiescence, slackening, stagnation, stoppage, strife
STATE 3 say 4 acme, ally, aver, avow, case, etat, form, land, mode, mood, pass, pomp, rank, talk, tell, trim 5 class, duchy, estre, phase, posit, power, realm, staat, style, utter, voice 6 affirm, allege, aspect, assert, canopy, canton, colony, crisis, domain, empery, empire, fettle, height, kilter, nation, plight, polity, preach, public, recite, relate, render, report, status, steven, temper, throne

7 account, civitas, country, declare, dilemma, dukedom, earldom, enounce, explain, expound, kingdom, mandate, narrate, posture, quality, quandry, recount, specify, station 8 announce, describe, dominion, eminence, juncture, kingship, position, property, propound, province, republic, toparchy 9 archduchy, community, condition, enunciate, postulate, pronounce, satellite, situation, territory 10 asseverate, government, palatinate, possession, principate, settlement, toptarchia 11 chieftaincy, predicament, seneschalty 12 commonwealth, magnificence, principality, protectorate 13 establishment

based on honor timocracy
benefice plenarty
bound by treaty ally
comb. acy, age, ance, ancy, ence, ency, hood, ness, osis, tude
department foggy bottom
division county, parish, province
explicitly define, itemize, particularize, specify
feudal wei
goddess of vesta
group bundelkand, confederation, country, federation, nation, union
highest supreme, ultimate
house capitol
ideal utopia
member citizen, subject
of affairs case, conjecture, pass
of mind fettle, humor, mood
of neglect limbo
office secretariat
pert. civil, federal, political
police trooper
revert to escheat
symbol caesar
under foreign control colony, dependency, protectorate
under oath allege, testify
STATED avowed, declared, established, express, fixed, formulated, given, measured, phonic, said, uttered
STATELY august, baronial, burly, ceremonious, dignified, formal, grand(iose), haughty, imposing, impressive, kingly, lofty, magis-

terial, majestic, monumental, noble, pompous, portly, proud, regal, solemn, splendid, straight, tall, towering

STATEMENT abstract, account, address, adscription, allegation, argument, assertion, averment, balance-sheet, bill, brief, bulletin, capitulation, comment, crack, declaration, delivery, description, dictum, dixit, edict, explanation, expression, formula, information, invoice, judgment, manifesto, memo, mention, note, observation, precis, premise, pronouncement, proposal, recital, recitation, record, reflection, remark, report, saying, subjoinder, synopsis, testimony, topic, utterance, word

abbreviated precis, resume, synopsis
assumed true premise
authoritative dictum
concise aphorism
defamatory libel, slander
dull bromide, platitude, saw
false lie
financial balance-sheet, budget
introductory foreword, preface, prelude, proem, prolog(ue), prorrhesis
mathematical theorem
meaning of explicans
of belief credo, creed
positive assertion, averment
self-contradictory paradox
self-evident truism
sworn affidavit, affidavy, deposition
unsupported dixit
STATESMAN diplomat, emissary, minister, solon, wealsman
STATESMANSHIP diplomacy, politics, tact
STATIC complaints, disturbance, fixed, inactive, inert, interference, noise, opposition, passive, quiescent, resting, rigid, stable, standing, stationary
STATICE armeria, limonium
STATION appointment, base, calling, camp, caste, cuartel, degree, depot, establish, estate, footing, function, gare, garrison, ground, habitat, install, level, locate, lo-

cation, office, outpost, place, plant, position, post, prestige, range, rank, seat, set, site, situation, sphere, spot, stage, stall, stand (ing), standpoint, status, stop, stratum, tambo, terminal, terminus, venue, work
break commercial
exalted purple
identification call letters
police kotwalee, tan(n)a, thanah
prehistoric piltdown
wagon brake
-wagon part tailgate
STATIONARY arrested, dormant, fixed, immobile, immovable, motionless, permanent, quiescent, sedentary, set, sitfast, stabile, stable, standing, static, still, unchanging
hold lay to
point cusp, spinode
STATIONERY billhead, flimsy, foolscap, ink(stand), pad, paper, papeteries, parchment, pen, pencil, quill, tablet
STATIRA barsine
attendant gigis
husband alexander, artaxerxes, darius
poisoner parysatis
slayer belitaras, melantas
STATISTICIAN compiler, figurer, statist
STATISTICS data, facts, figures, numbers
boundary percentile
STATIUS *poem* thebaid
STATOBLAST bud, gemmule, germ
STATOR jupiter
STATUE acrolith, agalma, bronze, bust, caryatid, cast, effigy, figure, figurine, icon, image, likeness, marforio, mask, monument, orant, pantheum, portrait, sculpture, xoanon
base plinth
fashion sculpt
largest ever colossus of rhodes
living galatea
-lover pygmalion
praying orant
primitive agalma, xoanon
recess niche
small emmy, figuline, figurine, oscar, statuette, tanagra

support entablement, pedestal, plinth
support part socle
upper part bust, torso
weeping niobe
STATUESQUE dignified, majestic, massive, stately
STATURE altitude, development, elevation, eminence, figure, form, growth, height, pitch, posture, tallness
abnormally small nanism
STATUS aspect, caste, class, condition, estate, footing, position, posture, prestige, rank, rating, relation, repute, situation, standing, state, station, walk, yiches, yichus, yihus
high cachet
imperial empery
lower backseat
symbol cadillac, car, club, diamond, mink, rolls royce, silk, swimming pool
STATUTE act, assize, authority, canon, decree, edict, law, legislation, measure, order, ordinance, regulation, rule, tanzimat, treaty
collection code(x), codices
heading title
proposed bill
STAUNCH constant, devoted, earnest, faithful, fast, firm, honest, leal, loyal, reliable, resolute, rocklike, sound, stable, STANCH, steadfast, steady, stiff, stout, sturdy, tried, true
STAUP awkward, clumsy
STAVE baculus, bar, bash, baston, beat, blow, break, burst, cudgel, hurry, knock, lag, letter, line, overcome, pole, pour, rung, rush, shaft, shatter, slat, smash, spill, sprain, staff, stake, stanza, stap, steeve, stick, stop, stove, strip, support, verse, wattle
biblical bands, beauty
bundle shook
groove croze
in break, bulge, burst, open
narrow buck
off delay, fend, prevent, resist
rhyme alliteration
STAVER poser, saunter, totter, worker
STAVEWOOD paradise tree, silver tree

STAVING fine, good, great
STAY abide, abode, allay, arrest, avast, await, balk, base, bide, billet, brace, calm, cease, cessation, check, clasp, continue, control, curb, defer, delay, depend, detain, dwell, endure, found, guy, halt, hinder, hindrance, hook, inhabit, interrupt, lag, last, linger, live, lodge, loiter, mansion, pacify, pause, persevere, persist, postpone, prevent, prop, rely, remain, reprieve, reside, resist, respite, rest, restrain(t), retard, rope, satisfy, slacken, slow, sojourn, stand, stop, strut, support, suspend, sustain, table, tack, tarry, uphold, visit, wait, wire
-at-home recluse
for await, expect
plow restharrow
rope guy
with stick
STAYING lasting, permanent, resident
STAYS bodice, corset jumps, jupes, whalebone
STAYSAIL cheater, jumbo, spitfire
STEAD advantage, assist, avail, benefit, beset, city, farm, hamlet, help, impress, lieu, location, palace, place, position, replace, room, service, situation, spot, suffice, support, throne, town, trace, track
STEADFAST certain, changeless, constant, durable, established, express, faithful, firm, fixed, immovable, lasting, leal, persevering, reliable, resolute, set(tled), stable, staid, sta(u)nch, STEADY, tried, true, unalterable, unchanging, unswerving
STEADING farm(house), homestead, land, site
STEADY beau, brace, calm, canny, cold-blooded, constant, dispassionate, enduring, equable, even(tempered), firm, fixed, girl, guy, impassive, imperturbable, lasting, moderate, passive, periodic, regular, reliable, resolute, safe, sane, sober, solid, stabilize, stable, staid, sta(u)nch,

STEADFAST, stiffen, sturdy, substantial, sweetheart, undeviating, uniform, unwavering
at anchor holsom
STEAK bifteck, broadie, flitch, griskin, hamburg(er), meat, slice, tucket
broiled chateaubriand
cut club, filet, flank, new york, porterhouse, rib, round, rump, shell, sirloin, skirt, spencer, swiss, t-bone, tenderloin
sirloin entrecote
STEAL abduct, abstract, annex, appropriate, bag, bargain, burglarize, burgle, capture, chor, cly, condiddle, cop, creep, crib, crook, defraud, divert, embezzle, extort, filch, finger, fub, glom, gyp, handle, hijack, hook, kidnap, lift, loot, lurk, magg, mana(r)vel, mill, mooch, nick, nim, nip, palm, peculate, pilfer, pillage, pinch, pirate, plagiarize, plunder, poach, prig, purloin, ramp, ratten, rifle, rip off, rob, rung, rustle, scrounge, seize, shanghai, skyugle, slink, snaffle, snare, snatch, sneak, snig, snitch, stalk, stem, swipe, take, theft, thieve, trespass, truff
along slink
a march on anticipate, precede, surprise
away depart, flee, loop, slink
cattle duff, rustle
game poach
one's thunder adopt, ape, appropriate, imitate, thwart
up on becreep
STEALER See THIEF.
STEALTH concealment, covertness, furtiveness, huggermuggery, secrecy, slinkiness, slyness, subterfuge, theft
by stow(n)lins
STEALTHY artful, backstairs, cat-like, cautious, clandestine, covert, cunning, feline, foxy, furtive, privy, secret, skulking, sly, sneaky, surreptitious, thievish, tricky, underhand(ed), wily
STEAM boil, cook, effluvium, energy, evaporate, exhalation, exhale, foam, fog, force, fume, gas, glow,

heat, irritation, miasma, mist, oam, poach, pother, power, reek, roke, smoke, stufa, vapor(ize), vexation
bath sauna
comb. atmo
engine inventor watt
jet soffioni, stufa
lubricator impermeator
organ calliope
pipe riser
roller crush, defeat, overpower, pulverize(r), railroad
shovel digger, navvie, navvy
treatment atmocausis
STEAMBOAT *inventor* fitch, fulton, livingston, rumsey
STEAMER boat, clam, cooker, liner, ship, vessel
cabin texas
duck loghead, racer
STEAMSHIP liner, steamer
route lane
STEATITE lardite, potstone, soapstone, talc
STECH cram, gorge, groan, pant, puff, stink
STEED charger, cob, dobbin, equine, horse, mount, nag, pegasus, roil, stead, stud
STEEK bar, bit, close, fasten, fix, garment, imprison, loop, pace, pain, piece, pierce, prick, put, set, sew, shut, stitch, stop, strike, thread
STEEL acier, armor, bessemer, damascus, damask, fleerish, fusil, harden, inure, invar, iron, metal, plate, prepare, press, stahl, strengthen, sword, tail, terre, toledo, weapon, whittle, wootz
bar anvil, bloom
beam girder
cap capeline, cereveliere
coating barff
convert into acierate
decoration damascene
defect cinderpatch, lap
fire-lighting eslabon
flint, used with fleerish, furison, fusil
gold-inlaid koft(gari)
-gray pigeon's-neck
harden temper
-making process bessemer
mass bloom
metallurgy siderurgy
plating acierage
pour teem
rod burin

slab billet
sphere, magnetized earthkin, terrella
splint tace, tasse
tooth broach
waste cobble
wedge froe
worker blacksmith, farrier, hooker, ironsmith, stickman, strander, stranner
STEELHEAD ruddy-duck, trout
STEELYARD balance, bismer, desemer, dotchin, lever, statera
weight pea
STEEP abrupt, acclinate, acclivitous, acclivous, arduous, ascending, bathe, bluff, bold, bowk, brant, brasque, breakneck, brent, brew, bright, cliffy, climbing, clivose, complicated, costly, dear, decoct, difficult, drenchy, elevation, excessive, exorbitant, expensive, extreme, flashing, gleaming, glittering, headlong, heavy, height, high, hilly, imbue, infuse, lofty, macerate, penetrate, precipice, precipitous, prominent, proud, raised, rapid, render, rennet, ret, rising, saturate, sharp, sheer, soak, sog, sop, souse, stew, stiff, straight, tall, upgrade, uphill, waterlog, wet
in lime bowk
STEEPGRASS butterwort
STEEPLE belfry, fleche, hennin, minaret, rise, spear, spire, staple, tower
top cupola, finial, whale
STEEPLEBUSH hardhack
STEEPLECHASE *hazard* hedge
STEEPLEJACK climber
STEER advice, advise, bestir, bovine, bull(ock), bustle, cattle, con, conduct, confuse, conn, control, direct, disturb, drive, follow, govern, guidance, guide, harsh, haste, helm, hint, injure, lead, luff, manage, mosshorn, noise, operate, oxen, pilot, ply, poke, rough, rouse, rudder, rule(r), severe, spado, starling, start, stem, stern, stiff, stir, stocker, stot, strong, taurine, tip, tolly, trouble, wend, yaw

a middle course straddle
clear of avoid, shun, spurn
flesh beef
hornless not(t)
into wind luff
wild cowbrute, yaw, yew
wildly yaw
young stocker, stot
STEERING aim, direction, government, lively, management, operation, regulation, restless, tendency
device helm, rudder, tiller, wheel
direct con(n)
STEERSMAN boatsetter, canopus, cox(swain), crewman, helmsman, pilot, seacunny, slewer, sternman, wheelman
STEEVE cram, derrick, firm, freeze, lade, obstinate, pack, spar, stiff(en), store, stow, stuff, sturdy
STEG dolt, gander, ninny, stag, stalk
STEIN cup, flagon, mug, pint, schooner, shant
1/8 livre
1/20th pfund
STEIN, GERTRUDE *friend* alice b toklas
STEINBECK, JOHN *character* joad, okie
creation cannery row
dog charlie
home monterey, salinas
STEINBOK antelope, ibes
STELE cippus, gravestone, handle, memorial, monument, pillar, slab, stile, stone
STELL brook, delineate, ditch, drain, establish, fix, pool, prop, shelter, support
STELLA *sidney's* penelope devereux
swift's esther johnson
STELLAR astral, brilliant, celestial, sidereal, starry
STELLED See STARRY.
STEM arise, arrest, axis, base, bine, birn, bole, bow, branch, bulb, bun, cane, caudex, caulicle, caulis, caulome, check, cion, contain, corm, culm, dam, derive, encircle, end, etymon, family, flow, fulcrum, funicule, haulm, issue, origin(ate), pedicel(lus), pedicle, peduncle, petiole, petiolule, proceed, progress, prong, prow, ram, reed, re-

strain, result, rise, root, scape, scapus, shaft, source, spear, spindle, spire, spring, stalk, stanch, steer, sternpost, stipe, stock, stop, straw, street, tamp, tendril, theme, tigella, tigellum, trunk, tube(r)
abnormality spiralism
apex phyllophore
axis caulome
-*bud* blumule
bulblike corm, rhizome, tuber
-*clasping* amplexicaul
climbing bine, tendril, vine
comb. caul(o)
covering ocrea
dry birn
edible eddo
glass baluster
growing on caulicolous, cauligenous, cauline
hollow cane
hookah snake
joint culm, node, phyton
jointed culm
-*leaf angle* axil
-*like* cauliform, stipular
match shaft
mushroom stipe
musical note filum, tail, virgula
ornamental stave
part caulome, epicotyl, hypocotyl, ocrea, pith, stele, xylem
pert. cauline, petiolar, stipular
pipe stapple
pithy cane
prostrate stolon
rudimentary caulicle
sheath ocrea
slender sarmentum
twining See *climbing,* above.
underground bulb, corm, rhizome, tuber
without acaulescent, acauline, acaulose
winder ace, champion, watch
withered birn
STEMMA family tree, genealogy, ocellus, pedigree, scroll
STEMWARE glass, goblet, vitrics
STENCH fector, fogo, halitosis, hogo, malodor, miasm(a), mephitis, odor, putor, reek, smell, stink, taint, whiff
STENCIL *process* pochoir
STEND bound, spring, stride

STENDAHL marie henri de beyle
character fabrice, julien sorel
novel charter house of parma, chartreuse de parme, the red and the black, rouge et noir
retreat civitavecchia
STENOGRAPHER amanuensis, secretary, stenotypist, tachygrapher, typist
STENT bound, extend, extent, levy, rate, refuse, rubble, stretch, tax, tight, value
STENTORIAN clarion, loud, powerful
STEP, STEPS act(ion), advance, dance, degree, expedient, footfall, foothold, gait, gradation, grade, gradin(e), imprint, jog, ladder, measure, move, pace, pas, peg, phase, predella, procedure, progress, rank, rate, rest, rime, round, rundle, rung, scale, spoke, stage, stair, staup, stave, stile, stratlin, stride, string, tiptoe, trace, trample, tread, trip, trot, walk
aside digress, dodge, swerve, yield
ballet See BALLET references.
-*by-step* consecutively, deliberate(ly), graditim
down decrease, descend, mitigate, retard, retire
false hob, slip, snapper, sphalm(a), stumble
flight of gemonies, grece, grice, perron, stairs, stairway
gliding chasse
half semitone
in enter, intercede, interfere, intervene, intrude, mediate, negotiate, shoe, slipper
introductory initiative, rudiment
lively bustle, run, rush, skelp
measurer passometer, pedometer
mining log, stemple
off measure, pace
of ladder round, rung, rundle
on crush, smash, squash
on it hurry, rush, speed
outdoor perron, stile
part nosing, riser, tread
recording device odograph
series of raised gradin(e)
set stile
up accelerate, advance, approach, ascend, augment, boost, increase, lift, magnify, mount, raise, rev, soup, speed
STEPBROTHER beaufrere
STEPHANO *mistress* portia
STEPLADDER trap
STEPMOTHER bellemere, hangnail, noverca
pert. novercal
STEPMOTHERLY harsh, severe
STEPPE See PLAIN.
cat manul
storm buran
STEPSON beaufils
STERCULA bottletree, calool, kurrajong
STEREOPTICON balopticon, magic lantern
STEREOTYPED cliched, conventional, corny, hackneyed, mechanical, shopworn, threadbare, tired, trite, used, worn
STERILE acarpous, antiseptic, arid, asceptic, axenic, bankrupt, bare, barren, dead, dry, exiguous, fruitless, futile, hollow, ineffective, infertile, invalid, meager, meagre, neutral, nugatory, otiose, sanitary, unfruitful, unproductive, useless, vain
STERILITY acyesis, agen(n)esis, aphoria, atocia, barrenness
STERILIZE alter, degerm, disinfect, fumigate, geld, poulardize, sanitize, spay
STERILIZER autoclave, retort
STERLING costly, excellent, genuine, money, penny (weight), precious, silver, splendid, superb, superior, upright, valuable
100,000 pounds plum
STERN abaft, adamant(ine), aft, ascetic, astringent, austere, back, baft, counter, cruel, disciplinary, dour, exact, fierce, forbidding, gloomy, grim, gruff, hard (hearted), harsh, heel, helm, inflexible, mighty, obstinate, poop, puppis, rear, relentless, resolute, rigid, rigorous, rough, rudder, rump, savage, severe, shrewd, spartan, steadfast, steer, stour, strict, stringent, strong, sturdy, sullen, tail,

tiller, torvid, torvous, un-bending, uncompromising, unfeeling, uninviting, un-kind, violent

fast painter, proviso

-foremost awkwardly, backward

ornament aplustre

toward abaff, abaft, aft, bast, caudal, rear(ward)

STERNE, LAURENCE *character* corporal trim, dr slop, toby, tristram shandy

widow wadman, yorick

STERNUM breastbone

comb. ento

STERNUTATIVE ptarmic

STEROL ambrain, amyrin, cholesterol, sterin

STEROPE pleiad

consort ares, oenomaus

parent hippodamia

STET keep, let it stand, retain

STETHOSCOPE auscultator

inventor cammann, laennec

STEVEDORE cargador, dockhand, lader, loader, longshoreman, packer, stower, trimmer, wharfie

STEVEN announce, appoint-(ment), assembly, bespeak, din, doom, howl, judgment, money, noise, outcry, petition, prow, rant, report, roar, season, shout, speech, state, talk, voice

STEVENSON, R. L. *character* ben gunn, hyde, jeckyll, jim hawkins, long john silver

friend gosse

grave apia

home samoa, shramsburg, upolu

novel kidnapped, master of ballantrae, treasure island

samoan name tusitala

STEW (See also *kind,* below.) anger, bathe, bind, boil, brothel, bustle, chafe, confusion, cook, difficulty, dither, dive, drizzle, dudgeon, fret, fume, hash, hothouse, imbue, impasse, impatience, intoxicate, itch, jug, mixture, muddle, olio, olla, pot, predicament, problem, prostitute, puzzle, seethe, simmer, snit, spray, steep, stink, stive, sweat, swelter, vapor, vivarium, worry

base soffrito

kind bouillabaisse, bredi, burgoo, caldera, capilotade, cassoulet, chowder, couscous, curry, daube, etuvee, fricassee, frijoada, goulash, haricot, hash, hoddle, hotchpot, hotpot, matelot, mortreux, mulligan, navarin, olla, paella, pepperpot, pottage, puchero, ragout, stodge, stovies, stuffata

pan cauldron, cocotte, pot, skillet

STEWARD administrator, agent, bailiff, bhandari, butler, caretaker, cellarer, chamberlain, crewman, croupier, curator, custodian, dapifer, dewan, director, diwan, econome, employee, erenach, estateagent, factor, flunky, foreman, garcon, gastaldo, granger, grieve, herenach, khansamah, landreeve, maitre d', majordomo, malvolio, manager, manciple, mormaor, oeconomus, peshkar, proctor, procurator, providore, purveyor, reeve, seneschal, sircar, spencer, stipe, supervisor, supplier, treasurer, victualer, villcus, waiter

ship's flunk(e)y

STEWARDLY careful, frugal, prudent, sparing

STEWED agitated, a l'etuvee, boiled, DRUNK, intoxicated

STHENEBOEA See ANTIA.

STHENELAUS *slayer* patroclus

STHENELE *consort* menoetius

father acastus

son patroclus

STHENELUS *brother* alcaeus

companion diomedes, hercules

consort nicippe

enemy amazons

friend diomedes

grandfather minos

kingdom mycenae

member of epigoni

offspring alcinoe, cycnus, eurystheus, medusa

parent actor, androgeos, andromeda, capaneus, evadne, perseus

STHENIAS athena

STHENIC active, strong

STHENO See GORGON.

STIB dunlin

STIBIUM, STIBNITE antimony

STICHIUS *slayer* hector

STICK 3 bar, bat, fix, gad, gum, jib, log, rod, set 4 balk, bear, bind, brin, buff, cane, clam, club, dolt, glue, halt, hold, hurt, mast, mire, part, pogo, pole, pose, prod, slat, stab, stay, stop, wand 5 abide, baton, botch, brand, caman, cling, demur, fagot, paste, piece, place, shaft, staff, stake, stall, stand, stave, stilt, waddy 6 adhere, atlatl, attach, baffle, battel, billet, boggle, bungle, cement, charge, cleave, cleeky, cohere, cudgel, endure, faggot, fasten, ferule, lubber, mundle, pierce, puzzle, raddle, settle, squail, thrust 7 cammock, compose, hurlbat, kilnrib, kippeen, perplex, scruple, spurtle 8 ashplant, bludgeon, hesitate, obstacle, revolver, tolerate 9 bastinado, blackjack, perforate, pikestaff, stabilize, truncheon

archery wand

bamboo lathee, lathi

basketry league

bent rifle

bundle fag(g)ot, fasces, fascine

-button burdock

by back, defend, support

candy gibby

cleft changan

crooked caman, cammock, gambrel

dog's tail shangan

-ear brand

fast bind, fitcher, jam(b), persevere, resist, seize

fishing cane, gad, pole, rod

forked grom, groom

hockey bulgar, caman, cammock, cummock, doddart, hurl(e)y, shinny

in insert, obtrude, ram, thrust

insect walking-straw, walking-twig

-in-the-mud conservative, fogy, hard-liner, idler, laggard, sink, slowcoach, tory

iron-pointed valet

it out endure, persevere, resist

jumping pogo

knobbed billet
large mock
marking lead
measuring ellwand, ruler, yardstick, yardwand
mountain-climbing alpenstock
odd jay
out beetle, bulge, extrude, jut, overhang, poke, protrude, shoot
pointed fescue, goad
pointing ferule, fescue
polishing buff
prayer paho
round dowel, spindle
small batling
stirring mundle, pooler, potstick, spurtle, swizzler
stout bat, lowder
throwing atlatl, boomerang, hornerah, javelin, squail
-tight bidens, bur-marigold
tobacco lath
together balter, cement, cling, clot, cohere
-to-itive dogged, persevering, persistent, pertinacious, relentless, resolute, retentive, tenacious
up arise, cock, erect, holdup, hump, lift, protrude, rob(bery)
-up man footpad, robber, thief
walking ashplant, cane, gibstaff, jambee, jockey, kebbie, kebby, makila, stilt, waddy, whangee
weighted squail
STICKER adhesive, billposter, bramble, burr, casein, enigma, glue, hinge, jack, knife, label, mopstick, paster, poser, resin, riddle, seal, thorn
STICKIT abortive, botched, failed, imperfect, stuck, unsuccessful
STICKLE agitation, altercate, appease, argue, balk, bargain, boggle, bristly, contend, demur, difficult, falter, haggle, hesitate, higgle, insist, kick, mediate, object, pacify, perplexity, protest, rapid, rough, scruple, separate, shy, steep, vacillate, waver
STICKLEBACK apeltes, baggie, bandie, banstickle, cleavers, ghoster, hackle, minnow, pinfish, pungitius, sharpling

STICKLER arbiter, judge, meddler, mediator, perfectionist, purist, tapist, tyrant, umpire
STICKSEED lapula
STICKUM adhesive, glue, goo(p), gum, paste
STICKY adhesive, bristly, cabby, claggy, clammy, clarty, cledgy, clit, cloggy, dank, difficult, gluey, glutinous, goo(ey), gummy, hot, humid, limy, malmy, messy, moist, mucous, muculent, muggy, pasty, puggy, rough, saccharine, sentimental, slushy, soggy, sultry, tacky, tenacious, thick, treacly, visc(o)id, viscous
fingered larcenous
STIFF adamant(ine), awkward, boardy, budge, bum, cadaver, carcass, carkled, ceremonial, cledgy, cold, conventional, cool, corpse, cramped, deep, dense, difficult, drunk, exorbitant, expensive, firm, fixed, forced, formal, frigid, grave, halting, hard, harsh, high, hobo, inflexible, inspissated, jelled, labored, laborer, laggard, loafer, obstinate, pompous, ponderous, precise, prim, proper, ramroddy, rigescent, rigid, rigorous, robust, set, severe, solid, starchy, stark, steep, steeve, stilted, stout, strong, stubborn, sturdy, tense, tharf, thick, tough, tramp, trig, uneasy, ungainly, unyielding, vagabond, vagrant, wooden, worker
as a poker
-necked bullheaded, contumacious, dogged, dogmatic, inflexible, mulish, obdurate, obstinate, pigheaded, prudish, rigid, stubborn
STIFFEN benumb, brace, cake, gel, harden, inspissate, jell, ossify, rigidify, set, solidify, stabilize, starch, stark(en), steady, tense, tighten, truss
STIFFENER buckram, counter, sizing, starch
STIFLE asphyxiate, blanket, choke, conceal, damp, extinguish, fill, gag, kill, moderate, muffle, muzzle, querken, restrain, smother, spifli-

cate, squelch, stive, stop, strangle, suffocate, suppress, throttle
bone kneepan, patella
STIFLING airless, close, heavy, hot, oppressive, smothery, stuffy, stuvy, suffocating, sultry
STIGMA attaint, bar-sinister, blemish, blot(ch), blur, brand, disgrace, dishonor, fleck, imputation, mark, odium, pore, reproach, scar, shame, slur, smirch, smudge, smutch, speck, splotch, spot, stain, taint, tarnish
heraldic champain
STIGMATIZE befoul, besmear, besmirch, blemish, blot, brand, defame, denounce, discredit, disgrace, mark, smear, taint, tarnish
STILBITE desmine, heulandite
STILE post, stairs, step, style, stylus
STILETTO bodkin, dagger, dirk, eyeleteer, piercer, pointel, stab, stylet
STILL allay, always, appease, but, calm, check, compose, concurbit, constant(ly), continual, cosh, descensory, distillery, drip, dumb, even, gentle, habitual, however, hush(ed), inactive, inert, low, lull, motionless, muffle, mum, mute, nevertheless, noiseless, notwithstanding, pacific, pacify, placid, quench, quiescent, quiet(ude), restful, resting, restrain, serene, shush, silence, silent, soft, soothe, stell, stop, subdue, tranquil (ize), uneventful, uniformly, whist, yet
-hunt search, stalk(ing), stealth
room larder
STILLNESS calm(ness), hush, peace, quiet, rest, silence
STILT bird, clay, crutch, himantopus, kaki, lawyer, leg, limp, longlegs, patten, pile, pogo, pole, post, raise, scatch, shaft, triangle, yeguita
bug berytid
STILTED affected, angular,

artificial, backward, bombastic, bookish, elevated, formal, inflated, literary, lofty, pedantic, pompous, posed, stern, stiff

STIME, STYME glimpse, particle, peer

STIMULANT (See also *kind,* below.) beverage, bracer, drug, energizer, impetus, incentive, incitement, liquor, motive, pickmeup, pickup, roborant, STIMULUS, tonic, urge

heart adrenaline, cardiant, digitalis, epinephrin(e), thialdin(e)

kind adonidin, alcohol, ammonia, amphetamine, arnica, benzedrine, benzoin, caffein, camphor, coffee, dexedrine, digitalis, kola, nikethamide, nux-vomica, pepper, picrotoxin, quassia, quinine, reviver, salts, strychnine, tea, thein(e), tobacco, tonic

respiratory antipyretic, antispasmodic, cardiazol

STIMULATE activate, agitate, animate, arouse, brace, challenge, elate, encourage, energize, enliven, excite, exhilarate, fan, fillip, fire, galvanize, goad, hypo, impel, incite, inflame, instigate, interest, invigorate, irritate, kindle, motivate, move, pique, provoke, quicken, rally, refresh, rouse, seed, sharpen, spark, spur, sting, stir, tickle, tingle, urge, vivify, whet

STIMULATING brisk, chilly, electric, excitant, exciting, exhilarating, invigorating, moving, piercing, provocative, provoking, sensational, stirring, striking, suggestive, tantalizing

STIMULUS cue, fillip, goad, hypo, impetus, incentive, source, spur, STIMULANT, sting

response beneception

sensitivity to heteropathy

threshold limen

STING aculeus, barb, bite, burn, cheat, dart, dupe, exasperate, excite, fang, foin, gall, goad, hurt, impale, injure, irritate, mast, needle, nettle, nip, offend, pain, pierce, pike, pique, pole,

post, pierce, prick(le), shaft, smart, stick, stimulus, stir, tang, tingle, urge, urticate, wound

-ray angler, batfish, lophid, obispo, stephen, trygon, wairepo

STINGER bee, drink, highball, wasp

STINGFISH weaver

STINGING acid, acrid, acrimonious, acuate, aculeate, acuminate, biting, bitter, caustic, hot, irritating, keen, peppery, piercing, prickly, pungent, sharp, smart

ant kelep

STINGO ale, beer, force, kick, liquor, power, vitality, zest, zip

STINGS *sport of* croquet

STINGY avaricious, biting, cheap, cheeseparing, chinchy, chintzy, close (fisted), dree, driech, frugal, grudging, hard (fisted), illiberal, meager, meagre, mean, mingy, miserly, narrow, near, niggard (ly), nipping, parsimonious, pennypinching, penurious, scanty, scotch, scrimy, sharp, skimpy, skinny, sordid, strait, thrifty, tight

STINK ashtunk, odor, outcry, reel, smeech, smell, stech, STENCH, to-do

STINKBERRY buckthorn

STINKBIRD anna, hoa(c) tzin

STINKBUG calicoback

STINKBUSH star-anise

STINKCAT zoril

STINKER asafetida, cigar, fitchew, foumart, fulmar, garlic, jerk, leek, louse, onion, petrel, polecat, reprobate, skunk, zoril

STINKING fetid, foul, fusty, musty, nasty, offensive, punk, putrid, rancid, rank, revolting

STINKPOT albatross, capehen, fulmar, petrel, turtle

STINKWEED ailanthus, cassia, coffee-senna, sandrocket, tree-of-heaven

STINKWOOD buckthorn, dogwood, ocotea, sourgum

STINT assignment, begrudge, bound, cease, cessation, check, chore, delay, desist, end, famish, grist, grudge, job, limit, pinch, re-

strain(t), restrict(ion), sandpiper, scamp, scant(le), screw, scrimp, share, skimp, skinch, snape, starve, stay, stop (page), stunt, task, withhold, work

short snatch

without freely, generously, liberally

STIPE anthopore, caudex, petiole, stalk, steep, stem, support

STIPEND allowance, annat, commenda, compensation, emolument, fee, hire, honorarium, income, pay, pension, prebend, recompense, remuneration, reward, SALARY, screw, subsidiary, tax, wage(s)

STIPPLE dapple, dot, engrave, fleck, paint, speckle, sponge, spot, streak, variegate

STIPULATE agree, article, bargain, condition, contract, covenant, designate, itemize, lay down, name, particularize, postulate, promise, protest, provide, specify

STIPULATION agreement, annex, bargain, bond, clause, compact, condition, contract, postulation, premise, premiss, terms

STIPULE leaf, pinfeather, sheath, stipel, tendril

STIR activity, ado, agitate, agitation, arouse, awaken, beat, blather, blend, bubble, budge, busk, bustle, buzz, carouse, din, disorder, disquiet, disturb (ance), drive, energize, excite (ment), flurry, fuss, galvanize, goad, gog, hoopla, hubbub, impell, incite, inflame, instigate, interest, JAIL, jumble, mix, motivate, move-(ment), noise, poke, pother, prison, prod, proke, provoke, push, quicken, racket, rally, remble, rile, rog, roil, roke, rounce, rouse, roust, rustle, seethe, shift, stang, start(le), stimulate, swizzle, tease, to-do, trouble, tumult, uproar, urge, waken, whip, whisk

about bustle, carouse, knock, porridge, proddle, oatmeal, roust

drink muddle, swizzle

up aggravate, agitate, buzz,

distract, enrage, excite, inflame, kindle, rile, roil, rumble, studdle, teer, tiokle, torment

STIRK boor, bullock, heifer

STIRPS ancestry, family, race, stock

STIRRING active, agitating, bustling, deedful, emotional, eventful, exciting, inspiring, lively, moving, phenomenal, quickening, rousing, stimulating, thrilling, touching

STIRRUP chapelet, clamp, footrest, footstall, iron, stapes, steelbow, strap
bone stapes
hood tapadera, tapadero
oil beating, thrashing
part chapelet, sudadero, tapadero
-shaped stapediform

STITCH (See also *kind*, below.) ache, baste, bit, cantlet, close, contortion, cramp, crick, crochet, embroider, fagot(ing), feston, filling, grimace, hem, join, kink, loop, pain, pang, part(icle), pierce, prick, punto, purl, seam, sew, shred, suture, tack, tailor, throe, thrust, twinge, unite
kind buttonhole, carpet, chain, coral, cord, cross, damask, double, glover's, jours, needlepoint, over-and-over, popcorn, saddle, tricot, twist
knitting cable, feston, purl
raised gros-point
wheel pricker

STITCHBIRD honeyeater, ihi

STITCHDOWN sewround

STITCHER dressmaker, necker, seamer, seamstress, sewer, tailor

STITCHWHILE instant, moment

STITCHWORT allbone, alsine, bird's-tongue, chickweed, easter-bell, headache, lady's-lint, mayflower, paigle, snakeflower, snapjack, snapper, snapwort, thunderflower

STITE nonsense, rebound, stagger

STITHY anvil, forge, smith(er)y, stiddy, studdy

STIVE confine, dust, pack, pen up, smoke, steeve, stew, stifle, stow, suffocate

STIVER bit, bristle, coin, stagger, struggle, strumpet, trifle

STOA colonnade, porch, portico, promenade, verandah, vestibule

STOAT clubster, ermine, futteret, vair, weasel, whitrack

STOB gibbet, pierce, post, stab, stake, stub

STOCAH attendant, clown, menial, servant

STOCK accumulation, ancestry, animals, assets, backlog, banal, bar, bolt, brood, broth, butt, cabbage, cant, capital, carry, cast(e), cattle, certificate, clan, colewort, commonplace, cravat, crop, estoc, extirpate, family, fund, furnish, gillyflower, goods, graze, haft, hand(le), hive, hoard, investment, issue, lay up, line(age), material, matthiola, neckcloth, normal, original, part, peck, plant, progenitor, provide, race, regular, reserve, rhizome, root, security, set, shank, share, source, stack, stake, standard, stem, stirps, stoccado, store, stump, supply, support, swell, tribe, trite, trunk, typical, usual
authorize capitalize
dove pigeon
duck mallard
eagle woodpecker
exchange big board, bolsa, bourse, coulisse, curb, market, wall street
exchange instrument ticker
exchange patron, bear, bull, buyer, seller, trader
exchange term arbitrage, bear, bull, buyer, dow jones, par, seat, trader
father ancestor, progenitor
feed amelcorn, bran(ner), browse, chaff, forage, grain, husk, mast, speltz, wheat
inflated chinese paper
in trade capital, goods, material, merchandise, tool, ware
issue security
jobbing agiotage
language borotuke, salish, siouan
market See *exchange*, above.
meat bouillon, broth
of goods line
pair of cippi, cippus

-pile accumulate, amass, heap up, reserve, save, store
plastic biscuit
preliminary scrip
racial pedigree
railroad granger
report dow jones
room storehouse
-still fixed, motionless, stationary

STOCKADE barracks, barracoom, barrier, boma, bullpen, camp, enclosure, etape, fort(ification), jail, pah, pau, pen, piling, prison, redoubt, tambour, zareba

STOCKBROKER agent, dealer, jobber, principal, trader, stag

STOCKFISH cod, haddock, hake, ling, lutfisk, salpa, spelding, speldron, titling, torsk

STOCKHOLDER grazier, investor, shareholder

STOCKING(S) anklet, bas, bobbysocks, buskin, caliga, hose, hosiery, hushion, moggan, nylons, scogger, shinner, sock, spatterdash, traheen
bishop's buskin, caliga
clock coin, gushet, gusset, quirk
cotton lisle
flaw catch, ladder, run, snag
footless hushion, scogger
material cantrece, cotton, lisle, nylon, silk
ornament clock
part boot, clock, coin, quirk
run ladder
soleless traheen

STOCKMAN breaker, broncobuster, buckaroo, cattleman, cowboy, cowpunch, equerry, farrier, gaucho, groom, herder, herdsman, hostler, neatherd, ostler, oxherd, puncher, rancher(o), ranchhand, swineherd, trainer, vaquero, wrangler

STOCKS catasta, harmans, pillory, shackle

STOCKY blocky, boisterous, bunting, bunty, chunky, cobby, cold, compact, defiant, dumpy, fat, formal, fubsy, headstrong, heavy (set), obese, plump, pursy, rounded, short, solid, squat, stiff, stout, stub(by), stuggy, sturdy, thickset, tubby

STODGE clump, gorging, satiate, satisfy, stuff, tramp, trudge

STODGY bulky, crammed, dull, fogyish, fuddyduddy, heavy, lumpish, obese, old-fogy, satiating, stout, stubby, stuffed, stuffy, stuggy, thick(set), uninspired, viscid

STOG bog, plod, stab, stall, trudge

STOGY boot, brogan, cigar, clumsy, coarse, shoe

STOIC(AL) ascetic, cool, detached, disciplined, hard, impassive, imperturbable, indifferent, pantheist, passive, patient, phlegmatic, spartan, stern, stolid
dogmas paradoxes
founder zeno
philosopher cato, chrysippus, marcus aurelius, zeno
school stoa

STOICISM abstinence, apathy, asceticism, calmness, coolness, dispassion, fortitude, grit, guts, impassivity, indifference, phlegm, pluck, sand, stolidity, tolerance, unconcern

STOIT lurch, stagger, stumble, totter

STOKE coal, eat, feed, fire, fuel, ignite, poke, stab, stick, stir, supply, tend, thrust

STOKEHOLD fireroom
part fiddley

STOKER fireman, firer, teaser

STOLE armil(l), armilla, boa, closestool, cotta, fur, orarion, orary, scarf, staw, stolon, surplice, vestment, wrap

STOLEN furtive, hot, pinched, pirated, secret
goods booty, haul, loot, mainour, pelf, swag
goods receiver fence

STOLID adamant(ine), anesthetic, apathetic, blunt, bovine, brutish, clumse, dense, dull, heavy, impassive, inactive, inert, obtuse, oxlike, passive, phlegmatic, sluggish, steady, stoical

STOLON branch, rootstock, runner, shoot, sobol(e), solenium, stem, wire

STOMA mouth, opening, orifice, ostiole, pore, spiracle

STOMACH abdomen, abide, abomasu, alvus, anger, appetite, arrogance, bear, belly, bingee, bingey, bonnet, bouk, breadbasket, brook, capacity, courage, crappin, craw, crop(py), desire, disgust, dislike, encourage, endure, enrage, gebbie(s), gizzard, gorge, grouf, gut(s), inclination, irritate, kite, kyte, maw, mouth, nauseate, offend, omasum, paunch, poke, pouch, pride, relish, resent, roddikin, spirit, spleen, stand, strength, suffer, swallow, taste, temper(ament), tolerate, tripe, tummy, tumtum, valor, venter, viscera, vitals, wame
1st belly, rumen
2nd bonnet, reticulum
3rd manifold, manyplies, omasum, psalterium
4th abomasum, read, roddikin
ache colic, collywobbles, fantad, gastralgia, gullion, nausea, tormina
animal omasum
comb. abdomino, gastr(o), ventro
entrance pylorus
excision gastrectomy
foulness saburra
inflammation gastritis, linitis
interior, pert. endogastric
opening pylorus
pamperer gastrophile
part omasum
pert. abdominal, celiac, gastral, gastric, gutty, visceral
remedy antacid, anthemis, bromoseltzer, cardiac
sour acor
study gastrology
without agastric, anenterous

STOMACHER broach, echelle, forepart, gimp, placard, plaque, poitrel, truss

STOMACHIC anthemis, berberine, bitters, cordial, cornus, coto, gentian, tonic

STOMACHY irritable, obstinate, paunchy, potbellied, proud, resentful, spirited

STOMP dance, mash, STAMP, step, stump, walk

STONE abacus, achate, adamant(ine), agate, ashlar, attack, bauta, bone, boss, boulder, brash, breccia,

brick(bat), cabochon, calculus, cenotaph, cephas, chaton, cobble, conglomerate, cra(i)g, diamond, domino, egg, endocarp, ezel, face, flag, flint, GEM, geode, granite, gravel, harden, herma, jewel, kill, lapidate, lapis, lith, lump, makiki, marble, marver, memorial, mineral, mirror, monolith, monument, ore, pavement, pebble, pellet, pelt, peridot, pit, rock, rosetta, rubble, sand, sarsen, schist, scoria, scree, sculpture, seed, slate, stanner, stean, steen, talus, trap, throw
abrasive emery, pumice
age eolithic, neolithic, paleolithic, protolithic
age implement arrow, boucher, celt, eolith, neolith
amulet hagstone
ancient galactite
and clay sere
architectural abacus
artificial adamant, albolite, albolith, concrete, granolith, scagliola
ax celt
bag dungeon
base plinth
bench banker
biblical ezel, peter
binding perpend, pierpont, through
blast furnace dam
block assize
bond girder, keystone
bow-ejected jalet
brake parsley-fern, polypody
break cavil, kevel, saxifrage
breaker burster, buster
broken ballast, macadam, rubble
building ashlar, cashel, mitchel, sperone, summer
burial stele
carved cameo, cuvette
casting tymp
cavitied geode
changed to. aglauros, agraulos, anaxarete, calcified, niobe, petrified, polydectes, propoetides
chatoyant tigereye
china petunse
chip gallet, nig, spall, spaul
chisel celt
circle cromlech, gorsedd, peristalith, stonehenge
clay lech

coal anthracite
cobble coggle
coffin cist
comb. lapio, lite, lith(o)
coping capstone, skew, tablet, tabling
crushed gravel, tailings
crystal-lined geode
curlew bankera, burhinus, bustard, thick-knee, willet
curling guard, herd, hog, loofie, potlid
debris talus
desert gibber
devil hellgrammite
dish comal
door rybat
dress dab, nidge, nig, scabble, spall
dressing tool broach, crandell
druid sarsen
drying stillage
eagle etite
ear sagitta
edging setter
engraving cameo, intaglio
famous blarney, braganza, cullinan, dresden, excelsior, florentine, great mogul, green, hope, jonker, jubilee, kohinoor, kohinur, massak, mogul, orloff, pitt, plymouth rock, regent, rosetta, sancy, scone, star of africa, star of the south, stewart, tiffany, vargas
fireback cathud
flat drake, ledger, plat
fly crab, creeper, perla
foundation bedder
14 pound
fragment brash, chips, gravel, ratchel, sand
fruit cob(be), drupe, endocarp, nutlet, paip, pit, putamen, pyrene, seed
gem-cutting adamas
glass-rolling marver
granitic gneiss
grave See GRAVESTONE.
green callais
grinding mano, metate, muller
groove jad
group pile, scree
growing on epilithic
heap ahu, bourock, cairn(e), carn(e), clitter, hurrock, karn, montjoy, scrae, scree, talus, warlock
hewn ashlar, ashler
hoist lewis(son)
hollow druse, geode
holy bear

hopscotch pallall, peever
hurling device catapult, onager, slingshot, trebucket
imitation See *artificial*, above.
kidney nephrite
landmark cairn
lead kevel
-like hard, lithoid
line with stean, steen
loose gibber, glidder
magic agate, alectoria
marker cairn
memorial bauta, cairn, ebenezer, stela, stele
meteoric aerolite, aerolith, angrite, nakhlite
middle honey
money fei
monumental lech, megalith, menhir, stele
nodule auge, geode
of arch keystone
orange sard
ornamental mischio
orpine houseleek
paving brick, cobble, coggle, flag, paver, pitcher, sett, slab, slat
perch ruff(fish)
pert. lapidary, lithic, lithoid
philosopher's adrop, carmot, elixir
pillar herma, monolith, obelisk, stele
platform mastaba
plover dotterel, godwit, thick-knee
precious See GEM.
pyramid-shaped benben
quarry latomy
refuse roach
ring chaton, hololith
rocking logan
roller doughbelly, hogsucker, mammy, minnow, mommy, toter
rolling mick jagger
rough rubble
row parallelith
sacred baetulus, baetyl(us)
shape See *dress*, above.
sharpening emery, hone, whet
shoemaker's lapstone
slab bilith(on), clam, lech, plaque, stele
small dornick, pebble, sneck
softened sap
square ashlar, ashler, quadrel
standing bauta, carnac, massebah, menhir, stele, stennis, stonehenge
stepping goat

stratified flag, slab, slate
sucker lamprey
talisman gamahe
thrower catapult, mangonel, onager, perrier, slingshot, trebucket
to death lapidate, stean, steen
translucent phengite
uncut cabochon, naif
upright See *standing*, above.
veined agate, mexican onyx
wall (See also STONE-WALL.) barrier, obstacle
wall facing ashlar, ashler
work bossage, masonry
worker dorbie, lapicide, mason, slater
writing slate
STONE, EZRA henry aldrich,
STONEBIRD finch, moro, yellowlegs
STONEBITER hawfinch, wolffish
STONEBOAT drag, sledge
STONECHAT blackcap, moortetter, saxicola, thrush, titmouse, wheatear, whinchat
STONECROP bird's-bread, country-pepper, creepingcharlie, goldchain, golddust, orpin(e), prickmadam, rosewood, sedum, tangle-tail
STONECUTTER jadder, lapicide, mason, squareman
disease chalicosis, silicosis
implement chisel, drove, sebilla
STONECUTTING stereotomy
pert. lapidary
STONED blotto, bombed, DRUNK, plastered, ripped, soused, zonked
STONEGALL kestrel
STONEHATCH ringplover
STONEHEAD bedrock
STONEPECKER sandpiper, turnstone
STONESEED gromwell, lithospermum
STONEWALL defensive, determined, filibuster, hard, obstinate, obstruct, perpend, resist, stick, stubborn
STONEWARE basalt, ceramics, earthenware, gres, jasper, pottery
bottle bellarmine
STONEWORT alga, candelabra-plant, chara
STONKER block, delete, foil, kill

STONY adamant, broke, callous, cobby, cold, fixed, hard, inexorable, inflexible, lapidose, malevolent, niobean, petrified, petrous, pitiless, relentless, rigid, rocky, rugged, solid, still

STOOGE act(or), agent, antic, buffoon, comic, foil, fool, henchman, lackey, patsy, servant, slave, zany

STOOK cluster, handkerchief, pillar, sheaf, shock

STOOL base, bench, betray, blab, buffet, chair, coppy, creepie, cricket, crock, currie, decoy, dupe, kneeler, mora, platform, pole, seat, see, shamble, stump, thew, throne, tiller, trest, tripod, tuffet, tumbrel
ball tutball
cucking thew, tumbler, tumbrel, tumbril
cylindrical taboret
foot cricket, hassock, ottoman, tabo(u)ret
pigeon betrayer, canary, decoy, fink, informer, lure, nark, observer, peacher, plainclothesman, ratfink, snitch(er), spy, squealer, stooge, stoolie
support trivet
3-legged trestle

STOOP abase, alight, bend, bow, collar, condescend, coorie, cringe, crouch, degrade, deign, demean, descend, descent, fall, fawn, gallery, gamble, huckle, humble, kneel, lean, overcome, patron(ize), piazza, pillar, platform, porch, pounce, prostrate, rucksey, sink, slant, souse, squat, stake, stump, subject, submit, succumb, supporter, swoop, tilt, veranda, yield

STOP 3 bar, dam, end, gag, jam, nip, nix, tie 4 balk, bind, bode, bung, calk, call, camp, clog, cool, cork, curb, don't, drop, fill, flag, foil, foul, halt, hold, kill, live, mend, pack, plug, quit, rest, shut, sist, slow, stay, stem, weir, whoa 5 avast, basta, belay, block, brake, break, catch, caulk, cease, check, chink, choke, chuck, close, cover, daunt, defer, delay, dwell, hitch, letup, lodge, parry, pause, quell,

sit on, spile, stall, stand, still, stoup, stuff, stump, tarry, tie up 6 anchor, arrest, boggle, cut off, defeat, desist, disuse, finish, hinder, lay off, muffle, reside, scotch, settle, stanch, stymie 7 abandon, caesura, confine, congest, counter, impasse, prevent, put down, run down, shutoff, sojourn, squelch, station, staunch, suspend, turn off 8 blockade, deadlock, knock off, obstruct, postpone, renounce, restrain, suppress, surcease 9 cessation, forestall, frustrate, interrupt 10 standstill 11 destination, discontinue 12 interruption
at the beginning nip in the bud
-block buffer
flow stanch
full period
glottal catch, stod, stoss(ton)
growth blast
last death, destination, end, terminal, terminus
leak ca(u)lk, fother, plug
payment default
short break, cessation, delay, halt, intermission, interval, pause, respite
up barricade, bung, chink, clog, close, cloy, dam, fill, obstruct, obturate, oppilate, plug, sta(u)nch, stuff
voiceless tenuis

STOPCOCK bib(b), turncock

STOPGAP expedient, makeshift, pisaller, resort, shift, substitute, temporary

STOPPAGE arrest, bar, block, cessation, check, cloture, congestion, detention, devall, embargo, halt, hitch, jam, leath, obstruction, shutdown, sitin, strike
comb. stasis
temporary arrest(ment), delay, interception, intermission, interruption, pause, recess

STOPPER beat, bouchon, brake, bung, close, closure, cork, eugenia, fipple, lid, obstacle, obstruction, occludent, pad, plug, spile, stopple, tampion, wad

STOPPLE See STOPPER.

STOPS *game* commit, crazy-eights, enfle, fantan, jig,

matrimony, michigan, newmarket, parliament, play or pay, pope joan, rebouge, saratoga, schwellen, spin (ado)
term comet, dead-hand

STORAGE accumulation, bestowal, dump, preservation, safekeeping
battery plate grid
charge cellarage, demurrage
clamp grave
jar amphora, stamnos
place (See also STOREHOUSE.) ambar, armory, arsenal, attic, bank, barn, basement, bin, bloodbank, bootbox, broomcloset, cachet, cedarchest, cellar, chest, chiffonier, closet, cubbyhole, cupboard, depot, desk, elevator, file, garage, granary, highboy, hopper, loft, magazine, mow, reservoir, safe, shed, silo, trunk, vault, wardrobe, warehouse, yard
prepare for bottle, can, freeze, jerk, pack, preserve, salt, smoke
room closet, larder, lastage, lazaret(te), lazaretto

STORAX balsam, copalm, exudate, gum, lordwood, resin, styrax
comb. styrene

STORE 4 bank, barn, bury, coop, fund, heap, hold, keep, list, lode, mart, mass, save, shop, stow, toko, well 5 amass, cache, depot, etape, fount, hoard, hutch, lay in, lay up, put up, stack, stash, steve, stock, trove 6 accrue, bazaar, bodega, coffer, ensile, garner, gather, girnel, market, memory, pile up, plenty, recond, repair, steeve, supply, tienda, winkel 7 arsenal, bhandar, bottega, canteen, collect, deposit, florist, furnish, grocery, harvest, husband, imberse, provide, reposit, reserve, sutlery 8 boutique, business, credence, cumulate, emporium, exchange, grindery, magazine, pharmacy, put aside, quantity, reserves, salt away, supplies, tendejon, treasure, treasury 9 abundance, livestock, repertory, reservoir, resources,

stockpile, sweetshop, warehouse 10 accumulate, collection, commissary, cumulation, memory bank, provisions 11 supermarket, tattersalls, tobacconist 12 accumulation, commissariat, haberdashery
cargo ste(e)ve
cheap five-and-ten, slopshop
confectioner's bonbonniere, confiserie, sweetshop
fodder ensilate, ensile
food delicatessen, grocer's, grocery, market, meat market, sweetshop
fruit greengrocery
government tesoreira
group chain
hidden bike, cache
large pile, raff, raft
military canteen, commissary
STOREHOUSE (See also *military*, below.) argosy, bank, barn, bhandar, bike, bodega, building, cache(t), camalig, camarin, chalkotheke, closet, conservatory, crib, cupboard, depository, depot, dock, entrepot, etape, godown, gola, granary, hike, lanary, lumberroom, magasin, magazine, mow, panary, pataka, promptuary, repository, reservoir, saddlery, shed, silo, staple, stockroom, thesaurus, treasury, vault, vintry, warehouse, wareroom
military armory, arsenal, commissary, depot, dump, magazine
public depot, etape
raised futtah, pataka, whata
rural barn, crib, granary, mow, shed, silo
subterranean mattamore, palace
wool lanary
STOREKEEPER almacenista, bhandari, greengrocer, grocer, merchant, shopkeeper, steward, storeman
STOREROOM armariolum, armarium, attic, basement, bodega, boxroom, buttery, cave, cellar, dingle, ewery, genizah, gola(h), granary, larder, lazaret, loft, pantry, repository, thalamus, ward
STORIED celebrated, famous, immortal, laureate
STORK, STORK'S adjutant,

argala, ciconia, cigogne, crane, heron, hurgila, ibis, jabiru, maguari, marabou, openbeak, openbill, simbil, wood-ibis
-bill erodium, pelargonium, plant
-like ciconiform, pelargic
pouched adjutant
STORKEN congeal, grow, stiffen, thrive
STORM agitation, anger, assail, attack, bagio, baguio, bayamo, besiege, blast, blizzard, blow, bluster, bombard, borasco, bourasque, brash, bravado, bura(n), burga, calamity, commotion, convulsion, cordonazo, cyclone, disturbance, eruption, explode, flood, fume, fury, gale, gauster, hail, harrycane, houvari, hurricane, khamsin, monsoon, orage, outbreak, outburst, paroxysm, pisachi, pour, rage, rain, rampage, rant, rave, rig, roar, ruckus, rush, samiel, shaitan, siege, simoon, southeaster, sou'wester, squall, stour, tempest, thud, tornado, trouble, tumult, typhoon, upheaval, violence, whirlwind, willywilly, wind
and stress sturm und drang
away from alee
-bird petrel
black karaburan
center eye
country girl tess
detection sferics, spherics
door dingle
dust devil, haboob, khamsin, peesash, shaitan
feature corposant, st elmo's fire
god adad, adda, addu, adrammelech, aloadae, hadad, marut, otus, ramman, rudra, susanoo, teshup
goddess harpy, tempestate
-raiser astagoras
recorder brontometer
rotary cyclone
sand tebbad
severe, peeler, snifter, snorter, tempest, tufan
shelter cyclone-cellar
snow blizzard, buran
thunder chubasco
-trooper brown shirt, fascist, soldier, sturmabteilung

violent elephanta, hurricane, karaburan, tempest
withstand ride out
STORMCOCK fieldfare, missel-thrush, petrel, woodpecker
STORMY agitated, angry, blustery, boisterous, cloudy, cyclonic, dirty, dusty, foul, furious, gurl(y), gusty, nimbose, oragious, procellous, raging, rainy, rampant, riotous, rude, rugged, tempestuous, turbulent, typhonic, violent, wild
cape spirit adamastor
petrel allamonti, allamoth, allamotti, assilag, mitty, spencie, spency, witch
STORY account, adage, allegory, analogy, anecdote, annals, article, canard, chronicle, conte, description, epic, episode, etage, fable, fabrication, fabula, falsehood, fib, fiction, floor, gag, gest, gossip, haggada, history, hoax, jeremiad, joke, legend, lie, lore, mystery, myth, narration, narrative, nouvelle, novel(la), paper, parable, piece, pistle, pitch, plot, prevarication, recital, report, romance, rumor, saga, scenario, screed, script, solar, soler, tale, text, tier, tradition, untruth, version, yarn
absurd bull, canard, hoax, yarn
birth jataka
continued sequel, serial
detective whodunit
exclusive beat, scoop
fiction dime novel, romance
figurative allegory
fish See LIE.
funny or *humorous* joke, knee-slapper
long bull, rigmarole
morbid dreadful
mystery thriller
newspaper feature, lead
old chestnut, dido
part fit
scary chiller
sentimental soap opera, tear jerker
short conte, nouvelle, novelette, novella
tell lie, narrate, tattle, yarn
traditional myth
unconfirmed rumor
untrue canard, lie, whopper

upper attic, garret, hyperoon, penthouse

western horse opera, oater

STORYTELLER aesop, anteri, author, balladeer, bard, conteur, dis(s)our, fibber, jongleur, liar, narrator, raconteur, relater, shanachie, spinner, troubador, writer

STORYTELLING chanachus, fibbing, shanachas

STOT bounce, bound, bull, rebound, stagger, stammer, steer, stoat, stumble, stutter

STOUND ache, apparition, assault, astonish(ment), attack, beat, benumb, blow, bruise, grief, instant, moment, occasion, pang, period, season, sorrow, stun, swoon, thrill, throb, time, twinge

STOUP basin, benitier, bucket, cask, cup, flagon, font, pail, measure, tankard

holy-water aspergillum, aspersorium, benitier, cantharus, kantharos

STOUR agitation, agony, assault, austere, chaff, coarse, difficulty, dust, encounter, excitement, fierce, fit, fog, gale, great, gush, hard(y), hoarse, huge, inflexible, loud, meeting, move, paroxysm, robust, rough, rude, severe, shock, spray, stern, stiff, stir, storm, strong, throe, uproar, vast, violent

STOUSH assault, beat, blow, strike, tirade

STOUT active, ale, arrogant, august, beer, bock, bold, bouncing, brave, brawny, brosy, bulky, bunty, burly, cobby, corpulent, courageous, defiant, energetic, fat, fierce, firm, fleshy, fodgel, forceful, gnat, hard, haughty, horsefly, husky, intrepid, kedge, lager, lusty, obese, obstinate, persistent, plump, porter, portly, powerful, proud, pyknic, resolute, roborean, rogust, rotund, shock, solid, stalwart, sta(u)nch, steadfast, stocky, strapping, strong, stubborn, stuffy, sturdy, substantial, tenacious, thick(set), tough, valiant, vigorous

and rough burly

and short five-by-five, stocky, thickset

-hearted bold, brave, courageous, good, valiant

STOUTH robbery, stealth, theft

and routh plenty

STOVE appliance, bogey, brasero, bukhari, calefactor, chauffer, chul(h)a, cockle, cooker, etna, franklin, furnace, galley, glasshouse, grate, heater, hothouse, hotplate, kiln, latrobe, oven, peach, potbelly, primus, push, range, stave, stew

alcohol etna

charcoal hod

grated chauffer

part broiler, burner, damper, firebox, griddle, oven, pilot

portable barbecue, chauffer, primus

valve damper

warming kangri

STOVEN shoot, sprout, stock, stump

STOVEPIPE *hat* caroline, topper

STOVER bristle, fodder, food, panner, provision, stiffen, stubble

STOW arrange, box, cease, commit, contain, cooper, cram, crop, crowd, cut, dunnage, entrust, fill, grant, hide, hold, lade, load, lodge, mass, pack, place, put, restrain, rummage, slice, steeve, steve, store, stump, trim

STOWE, HARRIET B. *character* little eva, simon legree, topsy, uncle tom

novel uncle tom's cabin

STOWER boathook, pole, round, rung, stevedore, stour

STRABISMUS anoopsia, cast, cockeye, crosseye, heterotropia, squint, tropia

latent heterophoria

STRADDLE bestride, bracket, divaricate, equivocate, hedge, pace, perch, ride, spraddle, sprawl, spread, striddle, stride, trim, waffle, walk

STRADIVARI *home* cremona

teacher amati

STRAFE attack, bomb, cas-

tigate, damage, punish, shell, stray, waif

STRAGGLE draggle, lag, loiter, meander, ramble, roam, rove, sprangle, stray, streel, tarry, wander

STRAGGLER nomad, nuchshlupper, stray, tramp, vagabond

STRAGGLING lagging, ragged, scratchy

STRAIGHT accurate, artless, beeline, brant, candid, clean, continuous, correct, direct(ly), erect, even, fair, fixed, flush, frank, full, genuine, graith, honest, horizontal, lineal, linear, neat, open, perpendicular, plumb, precipitous, rectilinear, reliable, right, rigid, rigorous, sequence, severe, sheer, squarely, stern, streamlined, strict, thorough, true, unbending, unbent, unbowed, unbroken, undeviating, undiluted, undistorted, unerring, uninterrupted, unmixed, unswerving, upright, vertical, virtuous

as an arrow

-backed rigorous, severe, stern

comb. euthy, lineo, orth(o), rect(i)

course as the crow flies, beeline

-haired euthycomic, leiotrichous, lissotrichous

man stooge

out direct, outright, thoroughgoing, unqualified, unrestrained

up and down perpendicular, sheer, vertical

STRAIGHTAWAY anon, aright, bedeen, bedene, directly, downright, forthright, forthwith, immediately, instantly, promptly, right away

STRAIGHTEDGE alidade, ruler, strickle

STRAIGHTEN align, aline, arrange, compose, correct, disentangle, extend, level, order, plumb, rectify, streamline, tidy, unbend, unfold, unravel, untwist, unwind

STRAIGHTFORWARD aboveboard, apert, aright, candid, dexter, direct, even, fair, foreright, forthright, frank, homespun, honest, honorable, impartial, jannock, just, level, open, outright, outspoken, plain, plat, round, sincere, truthful, undeviating, veracious

STRAIN 3 air, hug, rax, sie, sye, tax, try, tug 4 barb, bend, call, curb, dash, harm, haul, heat, heft, hurt, kind, line, mood, pull, push, race, rack, sift, song, sort, tone, tune, urge, vein, work 5 breed, brunt, chafe, clasp, class, clean, demur, drain, heave, labor, shade, sieve, smack, stock, surge, tinge, touch, trace, track, trail, trait 6 colate, effort, fasten, filter, flight, melody, overdo, refine, riddle, screen, SPRAIN, strand, streak, stress, temper, thread, throng, weaken, wrench 7 clarify, descent, embrace, passage, progeny, prolong, squeeze, stretch, tension, torment 8 compress, endeavor, outburst, pedigree, struggle, tendency 9 bloodline, constrict, overexert, percolate 10 exaggerate
blood breed, family, lineage, race, stock
comb. tono
concluding cadence
great exertion, stress, tax, tension, tenterhooks
measurer telemeter

STRAINED distorted, filtered, forced, intense, labored, pent, tense, weakened, wrenched

STRAINER colander, colatorium, colatory, colature, cribble, filter, milsey, milsie, renge, riddle, screen, sieve, sifter, sile, strum, syth, tamis, tammy, thead
coffee grecque
of twigs huckmuck
silver mazarine
wicker thead, thede
woolen tamis, tammy

STRAIT angust, belle-isle, bering, bosporus, canal, channel, close, confine(d), constricted, crisis, definite, difficult(y), euripus, exact(ing), exigency, familiar, fretum, gorge, hampered, hardship, intimate, isthmus, juncture, kersey, kyle, limited, mean, narrow(s),

neck, need, pass(age), phare, pinch, poverty, predicament, ravine, restricted, rigid, rigor(ous), scanty, scrupulous, severe, shard, sound, stingy, strict, stringent, tight
-jacket camisole
-laced blue(nosed), constrained, obstinate, overmodest, overscrupulous, priggish, prim, proper, prudish, puritanic(al), restricted, severe, squaretoed, stiff, strict, stubborn

STRAITEN afflict, break, confine, contract, distress, flatten, hamper, impoverish, limit, pinch, restrict, strap, tighten

STRAITENED crimped, difficult, meager, meagre, narrow, perplexed, pinched, poor, strapped

STRAITS chops, difficulty, extremes, need, press
of gibraltar pillars of hercules

STRAITS SETTLEMENTS
city georgetown, malacca, singapore
coin cent, dollar
measure chupak, gantang, para(h), parrah, pau, pipe, tun
native state johore, labuan, negri-sembilan, pahang, penang, perak, selangor, sungeiujong
region penang
weight bedur, bhara, catty, chee, hoon, koyan, picul, saga, tahil

STRAKE coaming, course, garboard, loiter, move, plank, plate, proceed, rut, saxboard, streak, stretch, strip, stripe, stroll, trough, wale, wander

STRAM bang, gad, knock, slam, walk

STRAMASH break, broil, destroy, disturbance, crash, fracas, racket, smash

STRAND bank, beach, cable, channel, coast, cord, current, desert, fiber, fibre, ground, gutter, lissom, littoral, maroon, ply, praya, quay, region, ripa, rope, sand, sea, shore, sliver, stream, string, thread, tress, weave, wharf, wire
-wolf hyena

STRANDED aground, alone,

castaway, ditched, foundered, grounded, high and dry, isolated, on the rocks, shipwrecked, stuck, swamped, wrecked

STRANGE alien, alter, anomalous, atypic, bizarre, curious, different, eccentric, eerie, eery, erratic, exotic, extraordinary, fanciful, fantastic, fell, ferlie, foreign, frem(d), fresh, marvelous, new, novel, odd, outlandish, outre, peculiar, preternatural, quaint, queer, rare, remove, selcouth, tramontane, unco, unfamiliar, unique, unkenned, unknown, unpracticed, unusual, weird
comb. xeno
to say mirabile dictu

STRANGER abator, alien, come, foreigner, fuidhir, guest, incomer, newcomer, odder, outlander, outsider, peregrin, unco
comb. xeno
fear of misoxeny, xenophobia

STRANGLE bowstring, choke, disable, execute, garrotte, grane, jugulate, kill, paralyse, repress, slay, snarl, squeeze, stifle, suffocate, suppress, throttle
hold chancery, grip, monopoly

STRANGLETARE broomrake, orobanche

STRANGLEWEED dodder

STRANGULLION quinsy

STRAP (See also *kind,* below.) babiche, bar, beat, biَd, birch, bowyang, bretelle, cord, credit, fasten, flagellate, flog, gird, groom, guige, halter, hang(er), lainer, ligature, ligule, lora, patte, punish, rein, sharpen, squilgee, straiten, string, strip, strop, switch, taws(e), thong, tick, tie, toggle, treat, turnback, wristlet
fern hart's-tongue, longleaf
-hanger commuter
kind band, belt, boondoggle, bracelet, bretelle, byard, cribber, enarme, fillet, guige, halter, harness, hasp, jess(e), lanyard, latigo, leash, rein, sendal, tapling
rawhide parfleche

-shaped ligular, ligulate, lorate

STRAPPED broke, penniless

STRAPPING beating, big, blooming, bouncing, hefty, husky, lusty, robust, stout, strong, sturdy, swanking, vigorous

STRASS glass, paste, straw

STRATAGEM artifice, blind, contoise, coup, cunning, device, dodge, execution, expedient, feint, finesse, intrigue, liripipe, liripoop, machination, maneuver, manipulation, play, plot, ploy, policy, quentise, resort, ruse, shift, slaughter, strategics, STRATEGY, stroke, trap, trepan, trick, turn, wile
advantageous waiting game
smart liripipe, liripoop

STRATEGY approach, craft, game, generalship, plan, scheme, STRATAGEM, subtlety, system, tactics

STRATIFICATION bedding, foliation, lamination, layer

STRATOCLES *consort* phylacion
enemy philippides

STRATOSPHERE *study* aeronomy

STRATUM aquafer, bed, caste, class, couch(e), cut, deposit, floor, folium, lap, layer, ledge, pinnel, seam, shelf, station, subsoil, table, tier
edge basset
outcropping basset
pert. erian, stratal, terrane
thin folium, lentil, seam, sheet

STRAUSS *opera* elektra, der rosencavalier, die fledermaus, salome

STRAVAGE saunter, stroll, wander

STRAVINSKY *work* agon, fairy's kiss, firebird, les noces, oedipus rex, orpheus, petrouchka, pulcinella, rake's progress, rite of spring, sacre du printemps

STRAW baku, bhoosa, bit, buri, churchwarden, culm, farthing, fig, gloy, haulm, mote, piece, pipe, remainder, shilf, shiv, sign, snap, stalk, stem, strammel, strew, stubble, trifle, tube, windlin, worthless, yedda

beehive skep
broken bhoosa, bhusa
bundle batten, bolt
coat mino
-colored blond, flaxen, leucous, stramineous
cookery pailles
drinking bombilla
fiddle xylophone
for hats sabutan, sennit
gown bangkok
half-rotten mulch
hat baku, ballibuntl, benjy, boater, leghorn, milan, panama
in the wind omen, probe, sign
kind bangkok, fescue, leghorn, sabutan, sennit, tuscan, windlin
-like stramineous
load barth
mat tatami
mattress palliasse
measure bale, kemple
piece wisp
plaited milan, sennit
rope sime
-splitter quibbler
thatching yelm
threshing floor bhossa
waxed strass
weaving rafia
worm cadbait, caddice, cadew
yellow festucine

STRAWBERRY balloonberry, brandywine, fragaria, fraise, hautboy, prutilla, runner
blite good-king-henry, goosefoot
bog cinquefoil, comarum
bush euonymus, evonymus, fishwood, wahoo
creeping dewdrop
finch amadavat, avadavat
fruit etaerio
geranium See AARON'S beard.
guava feijoa
kind dunlap, klondike, rosacean
liqueur creme de fraise
part acheme, akene
shrub allspice, bubby, calycanthus, cowberry, spicebush, sweetshrub
tassel milkwort
tomato physalis
tree apple of cain, arbutus

STRAWFLOWER bellwort, cornflower, everlasting, uvularia

STRAWSMEAR warbler, whitethroat, wren

STRAY aberr, abnormal, derelict, detached, deviate, digress, divagate, dogie, drift, err, fall, gad, gallivant, incidental, lost, maverick, meander, odd, prowl, ramble, range, roam, rove, sin, straggle(r), swerve, traipse, twist, unrelated, waff, waif, wander, waver, wilder

STREAK band, bar, barre, beam, dash, fleck, groove, layer, line, mark, mood, polish, ray, round, rub, rule, rung, seam, series, shade, shim, slash, smack, smear, smooth, smudge, soupcon, spurt, stipple, strain, stream, stria, string, strip(e), stroke, suggestion, suspicion, touch, tincture, tinge, trace, trait, variegate, vein, vitta
in glass skim
in wood roe
mottled roe
narrow stria
regular stripe

STREAKED alarmed, banded, barred, brindle(d), brooked, finched, laced, lineate, liny, netlike, roey, rowy, spotted, striate(d), strigate, striolate, striped, tabby, variegated, veined, watered, worried

STREAKY laced, liny, mixed, roey, rowy, scovy, uneven, variable

STREAM abound, affluent, bache, batch, beam, beck, blast, binnacle, binocle, blow, bourn(e), branch, brook(let), burn(ie), channel, course, creek, crick, current, drift, emit, flood, flow, flux, fork, fresh(et), gill, gush, issue, khal, kill, lake, millrace, nymph, outburst, outlet, pour, puit, race, rain, ray, rill, rindle, rio, river, rivulet, run, rundle, runnel, sick, sike, sluice, spruit, streak, strone, tide, torrent, train, wadi, watercourse
bed arroyo, billabong, channel, coulee, coulie, donga, draw, streamway, wash
bed hole dump
comb. amni
edge hag

gentle drip, trickle(t)
god neptune
growing in autopotamic
living in amphibian, rheophile
mythical arethusa
of forgetfulness lethe
of song chattahoochee, suwannee, swanee, wabash
ravine ghyl, gill
rushing jet, torrent
small brook(let), coulee, draught, freshet, grindle, rigolet, rill(et), rithe, rivulet, run(dle), runlet, runnel, sick, sike(t), squirt, stripe
source headwater(s)
strong gush, jet, torrent
underground aar, swallet
upper part headwater, source
STREAMER banderol(e), banner(ol), beam, filament, flag, guidon, headline, jet, lappet, pendant, pennant, ribbon, strip, wimple
STREAMLINE modernize, simplify
STREAMLINED clean, efficient, modern, new, sleek, straight, up to date
STREAMLINER express, train
STREEK begin, commence, extend, extent, fall, hasten, progress, reach, speed, stretch
STREET avenue, course, estreat, highway, road, route, rue, strada, terrace, thoroughfare, via, way
arab gamin, urchin, vagabond, waif
cleaner orderly, whitewing
cover slurry
curved crescent
degraded slum
deity agyieus, trivia
fight rumble
financial broad, lasalle, montgomery, spring, threadneedle, wall
hawker coster(monger)
instrument barrel-organ
kind cul de sac, one-way, through, two-way
main artery, avenue, boulevard
market rag-fair
narrow alley, chare, place, ruelle
peddler camelot
refuse fullage, litter
roisterer mun
safety zone island

seller costermonger, huckster
short place
show raree
singer balladier
sweeper mudlark, scavenger, whitewing
sweepings fulyie, fulzie
STREETCAR electric, jigger, tram, trolley
STREETWALKER cruiser, PROSTITUTE, WANTON
STRELITZA bird of paradise
STRENGTH arm, assets, beef, brawn, capacity, concentration, endurance, energy, fibre, foison, force, fortitude, guts, hardihood, hardiness, heart(iness), huskiness, intensity, main, maught, means, might, muscle, muscularity, nerve, potency, power, prime, proof, puissance, resolution, robustness, ruggedness, sinew, soundness, spirit, stalwartness, stamina, sthenia, stoutness, sturdiness, substantiality, thew(s), validity, verdure, vigor, virility, vis, vitality, will
center ganglion
deprive of enervate, unnerve, weaken
diminish dilute
feat of tour de force
loss asthenia
name meaning ethan
of character backbone, fortitude, gristle, grit, guts, sand
personification cratus
poetic puissance
regain rally, rejuvenate, rejuvenesce, revive
source of asset
symbol atlas, bull, goliath, hercules, samson, tarzan
without dowless, infirm, weak
STRENGTHEN arm, beef up, brace, buttress, cleat, comfort, confirm, consolidate, encourage, energize, enforce, fang up, fortify, gird, harden, increase, invigorate, lace, nerve, nourish, prop, quicken, rally, refresh, reinforce, renew, revive, steel, stiffen, stimulate, support, sustain, tone, toughen, vitalize, vivify
with alcohol fortify, lace, spike
STRENGTHENER bracer,

forcemeat, roborant, stimulant, tonic
STRENUOUS active, aggressive, ardent, assiduous, difficult, dynamic, eager, energetic, hard, intense, laborious, live, lusty, pressing, toilsome, urgent, vigorous, zealous
STREPEROUS, STREPENT boisterous, harsh, loud, noisy, turbulent
STRESS accent(uate), afflict, brunt, cadence, constraint, crux, distraint, effort, emphasis, emphasize, eustreff, hit, ictus, insist, meter, pressure, shear, strain, tension, throng, thrust, torsion, urgency, weight
free from anneal, calm
longitudinal, pert. euthytatic
metrical ictus
musical accent, arsis
pert. ictic
STRETCH amplitude, atent, breadth, bridge, burst, compass, continuance, continue, course, crane, direction, distance, distend, distort, duration, eke, elasticity, elongate, enlarge, exaggerate, exercise, exert, expand, expanse, extend, extent(ion), fell, gamut, hang, impair, length(en), magnitude, mantle, overdo, overestimate, period, plain, proceed, prolong(ate), protract, purview, rack, range, ratch, rax, reach, run, size, span, spelder, spread, stent, strain, swage, sweep, tend, tension, term, tighten, tract, walk, widen
-berry greenbrier
cloth tenter
comb. eurysis, tany
injuriously sprain, strain
inning seventh
leather draft, draught, stake
measurer extensometer
neck crane, pillory
out distend, eke, elongate, extend, lie(down), protract, reach, recline, spread, sprawl
wide yawn
STRETCHED craned, elongated, extended, porrect, prolate(d), prone, spread, supine, taut, tense
while drying tentered
STRETCHER angare(e)b,

angarep, cot, frame, gurney, lie, litter, procrustes, rack, spanrail, spreader, stend, stenter, tenter, trolly -*bearer* brancardier

STREW beset, besprinkle, broadcast, cast, diffuse, disperse, disseminate, litter, mess, overlay, raze, scatter, skinkle, spatter, spread, sprinkle, stray, strow

STREWN besprent, dotted, seme

STRIA band, channel, dragline, fillet, groove, line, ridge, streak, striolet, strip(e)
faint striola

STRIATE(D) furrowed, grooved, lined, marked, streaked, strigate

STRICKEN ill, incapacitated, overcome, panicked, panicky, smitten, streaked, terrified, upset, worn out, wounded

STRICT absolute, accurate, ascetic, austere, close, compressed, conscientious, dour, entire, exact(ing), exigent, firm, forbidding, grim, hard (headed), harsh, inflexible, intimate, literal, meticulous, narrow, nice, onerous, oppressive, orthodox, partial, precise, prudish, puritanic(al), relentless, rigid, rigorous, rugged, scrupulous, severe, spartan, stark, stern, straight, strait(laced), stringent, swift, taut, tense, thin-lipped, tight, tough, undeviating, unsparing, vigorous

STRICTURE animadversion, aspersion, blame, censure, condemnation, contradiction, criticism, reflection, sign, spark, touch, trace

STRIDE advance, bestraddle, gait, lamper, pace, parade, progress, stalk, step, straddle, striddle, stroam, stroke, strut, tread, walk

STRIDENT blatant, boisterous, brassy, clamorous, clangorous, discordant, dissonant, grating, grinding, hard, harsh, noisy, raspy, raucous, rough, shrill, squeaky, stridulous, uneven

STRIDULATE chirk, clitter, creak, crick, jangle

STRIFE affray, altercation,

barrat, bate, battle, brawl, broil, chest, clash, combat, competition, conflict, contention, contest, controversy, discord, dissension, exertion, faction, feud, fight, fracas, friction, jehad, jihad, mutiny, quarrel, riot, spat, squabble, stasis, stour, strow, struggle, strut, sturt, tug, variance, war, wrangle
civil stasis
freedom from peace
god loki

STRIG footstalk, rachis

STRIGA bristle, flute, scale, striation

STRIGAL scraper

STRIGOSE bristly, grooved, hispid, rough, sharp

STRIKE 3 bat, bob, bop, box, cob, cop, cut, dab, hew, hit, lam, pat, peg, ram, rap, tap, wap 4 baff, bang, bash, beak, beat, belt, biff, bill, blip, blow, bolt, bump, bunt, butt, cast, clap, clip, coin, cope, cosh, coup, dart, dash, dint, dunt, frap, hook, hurt, lash, mint, nail, peal, pelt, pink, plug, poke, putt, ring, slam, slap, slog, slug, snap, soak, sock, swat, sway, toll, wham, whop, yerk 5 bandy, baste, catch, chime, clash, clout, crack, crunt, devil, douse, dunch, empty, erase, force, gowff, knock, level, lower, paste, plunk, pound, punch, score, shoot, sitin, skite, smack, smear, smite, snick, sound, steal, swack, thump, touch, whack, whale, whang, yield 6 affect, affrap, arrive, assail, attack, batter, borrow, buffet, cancel, glance, hammer, hartel, huelga, larrup, pelter, picket, pommel, punish, revolt, shmeer, stoush, stroke, thrash, thrust, thwack, unload, wallop 7 balance, boycott, clobber, collide, impinge, impress, percuss, unearth, walkout, whample 8 bludgeon, discover, shutdown, slowdown, strickle 9 blackjack, influence, intervene 12 workstoppage
1/4th bushel
1/2 peck
against bump, collide, crash

all of a heap agitate, astonish, astound, startle
and rebound carambole, car(r)om
back get even, retaliate
balance average, equalize, settle, weigh
bargain agree, arrange, settle
-*breaker* blackleg, fink, goon, rat, scab
colors quit, yield
down fell, floor, lay, slay, wend
dumb awe, dumfound, silence, stun
gently bump, dab, nudge, pat, putt
hard bash, clout, devel, dunt, lam, ram, slam, slap, slash, slog, slough, slug
hunger endura
labor sitin, steek, turnout, walkout
obliquely carom
off deduct, discount, erase, improvise, print, separate, sever
on head bean
out begin, cancel, dele(te), efface, elide, eliminate, erase, excudate, fail, fall, fan, go down, miss, obliterate, originate, start, try
prepare to coil
settler arbitrator, mediator
sharply slap, smite, pelt(er)
to and fro bandy
together clash, collide, knack
up begin, emboss, raise, yerk
with fist noddle, plug, pommel, pound, punch
with head buck, butt
with whip jerk, lash, quirk
with wonder astonish, awe

STRIKING appulse, arresting, astonishing, cogent, colorful, commanding, conspicuous, dashing, dramatic, effective, extraordinary, fresh, impressive, knockout, lofty, notable, noticeable, outstanding, potent, prominent, pronounced, remarkable, salient, showy, signal, significant, skelpin, stimulating, surprising, vivid, wonderful

STRINDBERG *work* miss julia, the creditors, the father, tschandala

STRING(S) amentum, band, beige, brace, braid, chain, conditions, cord(on), drove, fiber, filament, file, group,

hoax, jolly, josh, lace, lac(h)
et, langate, length, ligature,
line, nerve, procession,
queue, rope, row, score,
sequence, series, set, snare,
snead, strengthen, stretch,
succession, suit(e), tally,
taum, tendon, thread, tie,
train, twine, wire
along agree, dangle, flatter,
follow
bean haricot, scarletrunner,
snap(per)
bonnet bride
comb. chord
course cordon, guidon,
ledge, table
drum snare
figure art kamut
game cat's cradle
group hank, mop, quartet,
ran, rope, trio
instrument See MUSICAL
INSTRUMENT *stringed.*
knotted macrame
of beads chaplet, necklace,
rosary
of onions reeve, trace
pottery schnurkeramik
put on a enfile
tensile catgut
up hang, lace, lynch
STRINGENT acrimonious,
austere, close, cogent, compelling, compulsory, con-
vincing, exacting, harsh,
limiting, narrow, onerous,
restrictive, rigid, rigorous,
severe, stern, strait, strict,
tight, urgent
STRINGER(S) ba(u)lk, handcuffs, irons, libertine, sleeper, tie, timber, vein
STRINGY capillary, cirrose,
cirrous, fibilliform, fibroid,
fibrous, filamentous, filiform,
flossy, full, funicular, gangling, gluey, lank(y), lean,
ligular, ligulate, long, loose,
ropy, silky, sinewy, spindling, thick, thin, thready,
tough, viscid, viscous, wooly
STRINGYBARK eucalyptus,
pepperminttree, tallowwood
STRIP (See also *kind,*
below.) band, bare, bark,
batten, bleed, border, clear,
culpon, decorticate, denude,
deprive, despoil, devastate,
devest, disarm, disarray,
disfurnish, dismantle, displume, disrobe, divest, exhaust, expose, fascia, flay,
fleece, flense, hild, hull,

husk, impoverish, line, list,
loot, milk, pare, peel, pick,
piece, pluck, plunder, ransack, ravage, remove, ribbon, rifle, rob, runway,
scroll, shave, shear, shred,
skelp, skin, slice, slip, slype,
spill, strake, strap, streak,
stripe, taenia, tape, tear, uncover, undress, unrig,
unrobe, waste, withdraw,
wrest
blubber flense
camouflaging garland
cork spreader
dependent lambeau
dividing cloison
finishing molding
kind apron, batten, belt,
came, cleat, cove, fillet,
ingot, inwale, lath(e), latigo, lead, ligula, rand,
reeve, reglet, rib, ridge,
riem, slat, splent, spline,
splint, stave, thong, tirr,
welt
leveling shim
narrow bandeau, reeve, ribbon, slat, strake, strap, tape
of cloth banner, dutchman,
rind
off flipe, flype, husk, skin,
slipe, tirl
ornamental border, flounce
paper orihon, streamer
-teaser ecdysiast
unploughed gair, hade, headland
wood batten, cleat, footing,
furring, lath, list, slat,
stave, welt
STRIPE band, bar(re), beat,
blow, braid, buddle, character, chevron, cottise, description, fillet, ilk, insigne,
kidney, kind, lash, length,
line, mark, nature, plaga,
ribbon, ridge, rivulet, sort,
streak, stria, strike, STRIP,
stroke, thrust, type, variegate, vitta, wale, weal, welt,
wheal
STRIPED bandy, barred,
bayadere, fasciate, lineate,
paled, pirned, pirny, rowed,
streaked, tabby, tigroid, vit-
tate, waled
bass rockfish, serranid
maple dogwood
STRIPLING adolescent, boy,
chiel(d), lad, shaveling,
shaver, springal, stirra,
yon(u)ker, youth
STRIPPED bare, husked, in-

digent, naked, nude, peeled,
picked, poor
by trickery buncoed, bunk-
oed, fleeced, taken
STRIVE agonize, aim, assay,
attempt, bandy, battle,
buckle, compete, contend,
contest, emulate, endeavor,
essay, exert, fend, fight, hie,
labor, pingle, resist, scuffle,
seek, strain, struggle, tew,
toil, travail, try, tug, tussle,
vie, work, wrestle
for advantage buck
STRIVING ambition, agonistic, combative, conation,
hormic, nisus, straining
STRIX barn-owl, fluting, syrnium, tyto
STROCKLE shovel
STROIL capability, dexterity,
grass, power
STROKE ability, action,
apoplexy, attack, bang, beat,
bell, blow, brush, capacity,
caress, chime, chop, chuck,
coup, coy, dash, dent, ding,
disaster, dunt, effort, feat,
fetch, fit, flip, hit, hurt,
ictus, impact, influence, injury, instant, knock, lick,
line, mark, massage, move-
(ment), pain, palsy, paralysis, pat, peal, pet, power,
putt, rub, seizure, shock,
slew, slice, slive, smit,
smooth, soothe, sound,
spasm, step, strategem,
streak, stride, strut, success,
swing, throb, touch, trait,
wale, welt, whet, whisk,
work
comb. plegia
finishing coup de grace, end-
all
kind baff, birdie, cerif, chop,
eagle, masse, putt, serif,
slice, virgule, wedge, whisk
of bell bong, jowl, knell
of fortune break, luck
of genius tour de force
of luck fluke, hit, strike
repeated patapat
the wrong way annoy, irritate
STROLL amble, dacker,
daiker, dander, flanerie,
gander, idle, lounge,
mos(e)y, promenade, ram-
ble, range, roam, rove,
saunter, soodle, spatiate,
strake, stravage, stray,
stroam, strome, toddle,
traik, tramp, walk, wander

STROLLER actor, baby-carriage, gocart, peddler, pram, shu(i)ler, sulky, tramp, vagrant
STRONG 3 big 4 able, bold, deep, fell, fere, firm, full, gamy, hale, hard, high, rank, vile, wiry 5 acerb, brisk, burly, eager, freck, fresh, great, gross, hardy, heavy, hefty, husky, large, lusty, manly, nasty, nervy, solid, sound, stout, tough, valid, vivid, wight, withy, yauld 6 active, ardent, brawny, buckra, bunkum, cogent, fierce, fortis, hearty, maduro, mighty, potent, rancid, robust, rugged, sinewy, strict, sturdy, virile 7 buirdly, doughty, durable, feckful, fertile, intense, skookum, sthenic, violent, zealous 8 athletic, bouncing, flagrant, forceful, forcible, muscular, powerful, puissant, rigorous, stalwart, striking, superior, vehement, vigorous 9 difficult, effective, efficient, energetic, herculean, important, obstinate, strapping, tenacious, two-fisted 10 boisterous, formidable, passionate, persuasive, productive, rock-ribbed 11 impregnable, influential 12 overpowering
-arm assault, beat(up), beef, coerce, force, power, rob, violence, violent
-arm man bouncer, goon, hood(lum), thug
as brandy, gibraltar, horse, lion, nails, oak, rock, steel
-flavored acrid, pungent, racy, spicy
man See POWERHOUSE.
-minded determined, obstinate, resolute, willful
name meaning andrew
of wing pennipotent
point forte, metier, specialty, talent
-scented fetid, foxy, frowzy, gamey, high, olid, rank
-willed See *-minded*, above.
STRONGBOX case, chest, coffer, deedbox, pete, safe, treasury, vault
STRONGHOLD acropolis, beachhead, bridgehead, bulwark, castle, citadel, FORT, keep, rath, refuge, safe,

sion, TOWER, treasury, zion
STRONGLY bigly, swith(e)
STRONGYLURA agujon, needlefish
STRONTIUM *compound* acanthin, apotome, celestite
STROP hone, sharpen, STRAP, whet
STROPHE alcaic, laisse, sapphic, spiral, stanza, strain
STROPHIUS *consort* anaxibia, astyochia, cydragora
kingdom phocis
parent antiphata, crissus
reared orestes
son astydamia, pylades, scamandrius
STROW confusion, disturbance, strew, strife, turmoil
STROYGOOD spendthrift, wastrel
STRUB despoil, plunder, rob, strip
STRUCK impressed, punished, shut, smit(ten), smote
out cancel(l)ed, deled, deleted, elided, erased, fanned
smartly percussed
STRUCTURE anatomy, architecture, arrangement, build, compagination, composition, conformation, constitution, construction, contexture, edifice, erection, establishment, fabric, feature, form, format(ion), frame(work), gestalt, make(-up), organization, pile, scheme, setup, shape, skeleton, system, texture, unit
abnormal malformation
anatomical apron, bud, carina, crescent
anticlinal swell
arched fornix
body build, frame, physique
calcareous coral
climbing ladder, stairs, steps, stile
conical bullet, pyramid
crownlike corona
curved arch, cupola, dome, geode
filamentous hair
floating raft
funeral catafalque
grammatical syntax
hallowed basilica, bethel, cathedral, chapel, church, shrine, synagogue, tabernacle, temple

high campanile, skyscraper, spire, steeple, tower
human physique
keel-like carina
knee-shaped geniculum
loop-like ansa
many-stoned polylith
member socle
monumental pylon, pyramid, wat
original isogen
ornamental gazebo, kiosk
osseous bone
over obstacles bridge
over water dock, jettee, jetty, jiti, wharf
pert. tectonic
prehistoric bilith(on)
raised altar, cimborio, dais, platform, rostrum, stage
ready to set up prefab (ricated)
sacrificial altar
science of anatomy, angiology, anthropotomy, histology, morphology, osteography, osteology
sheltering cot(e)
sickle-shaped falx
supporting pier
tall See *high*, above.
temporary falsework, scaffold(ing)
tent-like tabernacle
white albedo
STRUGGLE affray, agitation, agon(ize), agony, aim, altercation, assay, attempt, barrace, battle, brawl, broil, brush, buckle, buffet, bustle, compete, contend, contest, cope, deal, discord, dissension, disturbance, duel, effort, endeavor, essay, exert(ion), fend, fight, flounder, founder, frab, fray, grapple, hassle, labor, mutche, peniel, pingle, quarrel, reluct, scraffle, scramble, scuffle, sprunt, stiver, strife, strive, tave, tervee, tew, toil, touse, travail, try, tug, tuilyie, tumult, tussle, tweil, vie, war (fare), widdle, work, wrestle, writhe
along hobble
death agony, throes
spiritual peniel
STRUM pick, play, pluck, plunk, strainer, sulk, thrum, twang, twank
STRUMPET blowen, brim, bulker, callet, cocotte, dol-

lymop, harlot, limmer, PROSTITUTE, stiver, succuba, tart, trollop, wanton, wench

STRUNT dock, liquor, pique, strut, stump

STRUT brace, bracket, brag, bulge, bunton, contention, flaunt, lak, major, nauntle, ostentation, pace, parade, peacock, prance, prink, prop, protrude, stay, stemple, stretch, stride, strife, stroot, support, swagger, swank, swell, wrangle
peacock's lak

STRUTTING swashbuckling

STRYCHNINE *source* nux vomica

STRYMON karasu, strame
consort calliope, euterpe, terpsichore
son rhesus

STUB beat, blockhead, bump, butt, check, counterfoil, coupon, crush, dincher, dolt, drive, end, extirpate, fool, pen, raincheck, remnant, short, sprunt, squat, stocky, strike, stump, tag, tail, tally, thickset

STUBBLE arrish, beard, bristle, bun, eddish, gratten, mane, refuse, remainder, remains, shack, stibble, stump
comb. seti
field arrish, eddish, stibblerig
field, unplowed rowan
tuft of mane

STUBBORN adamant, balky, bulldog, bullheaded, calcitrant, camsteary, coarse, crossgrained, cussed, determined, dogged, firm, fixed, froward, hard, harsh, headstrong, inflexible, intractable, mulish, obdurate, obstinate, opinionated, ornery, persistent, perverse, piggish, pigheaded, recalcitrant, refractory, resistant, resolute, rigid, rough, rude, rusty, sot, stiff, stony, stunkard, stunt, sturdy, tenacious, thrawart, thro, thwart, tough, unyielding, willful, wry
person ass, bitterender, buckie, bullethead, diehard, mule, pighead, roundhead

STUBBORNNESS inflexibility, obstinacy, obstinance, perseverance, perversity, resolution, rigidity, tenacity

STUBBY blocky, chubby, chumpy, chunky, dumpy, fat, heavy, little, podgy, pudgy, punchy, retrousse, short, small, snubbed, snubby, spuddy, squab(by), squat, stocky, stodgy, stuggy, stumpy, thick(set), tubby

STUCCO albarium, cement, plaster

STUCK aground, bemired, caught, enamored, fast, fixed, frozen, grounded, held, impacted, inextricable, jammed, left, mired, packed, stooded, stranded, wedged
-up arrogant, conceited, frosted, haughty, robbed, self-important, snobbish, supercilious, vain

STUD adorn, a(i)glet, ashlar, ashler, bolt, boss, breeder, bulge, bull, chaplet, clout, dot, haras, horse, joist, knob, knop, male, man, nail, ornament, pillar, pin, poker, post, potence, prop, puncheon, rod, scantling, spread, sprinkle, stem, string, stub, stump, support, trunk
farm haras
for shoe hobnail
horse stallion
with jewels engem

STUDENT aggie, auditor, bursar, bursch(e), cadet, catechumen, coed, commoner, disciple, ecolier, educand, eleve, freshman, frosh, fuchs, grind, intern(e), junior, learner, matmid, monitor, neophyte, novice, observer, philomath, plebe, prefect, pupil, scholar, scholastic, schoolman, scolog, semibejan, senior, sizar, soph(omore), swot, tosher, trainee, tyro
account battel
agricultural college aggie
college freshman, frosh, graduate, junior, senior, soph(omore), undergraduate
divinity stibbler, theologian, theologue
1st year fresher, freshman, frosh, fuchs, greenhorn, plebe, rookie
girl coed
graduate fellow, laureate

group academe, academy, class, college, school, seminar, university, varsity
hall common room, union
hardworking dig, grind, plug, sap, smug
high grade alpha
in charge monitor, prefect, proctor
law puisne, punee, stagiary
military cadet, plebe
naval academy cadet, midshipman
pantry stue
residence dorm(itory), fraternity, hostel, house
revel gaudeamus, gaudy
scholarship bursary, fellowship
song gaudeamus igitur
task assignment, homework, term paper, thesis
teacher don, prof(essor), tutor
town oppidan
wandering goliard

STUDIED advised, affected, artificial, calculated, ceremonial, conscious, considered, cool, deliberate, designed, formal, inclined, intentional, learned, measured, painstaking, planned, precious, premeditated, qualified, voluntary, willful

STUDIES academic arts, humanities, science

STUDIO abozzo, atelier, bottega, den, gallery, retreat, room, study
gear easel

STUDIOUS assiduous, bookish, diligent, meditative, profound, reflective, scholarly, scholastic, thoughtful

STUDY abbozzo, account, analyse, analysis, analyze, application, attention, bone (up), bookwork, brainwork, canvass, carol, check, composition, concentration, con(sider), contemplate, cram, croquis, deliberate, den, devise, dig, discuss, document, effort, endeavor, examine, excogitate, exercise, eye, grind, headwork, image, inspect(ion), investigate, investigation, learn, lesson, library, lucubrate, lucubration, meditate, mug, muse, muzz, office, paper, peruse, picture, plan, pochade, ponder, pore, read,

reflect(ion), research, revolve, see, sift, sketch, speculate, stithy, STUDIO, subject, think, thought, tract, treatise, weigh, work
clay bozzetto
closely con(centrate), examine, pore
deep absorption
for exam cram
hard bone, cram, dig, lucubrate, smug, stew, swot
musical etude
optional elective
pert. academic
preliminary sketch
STUFF ability, amount, baggage, bombast, cash, choke, clog, cloth, congest, copy, cram, crowd, devour, distend, eat, element, engorge, essence, fabric, feed, fill, force, gaum, gear, goods, gorge, gormandize, grain, graith, guttle, heroin, junk, lard, line, load, material(s), matter, medicine, narcotics, nonsense, overeat, overload, pack, pad, paste, paunch, potion, press, property, pulse, ram, refuse, rubbish, sate, satiate, steve, stifle, stock, stodge, stop, store, stow, substance, suffocate, supply, surfeit, tack, textile, trash, trivia, wad
coarse baft(a), baftah
folding See MONEY.
full cram, glut, gorge, satiate, stodge
green See MONEY.
hard See DRUG *narcotic.*
inferior mockado
sticky glop, goo(k), goop
worthless gear, hogwash, rot
STUFFER taxidermist
STUFFING bombast, content(s), down, dressing, farce, farcing, feathers, fill(er)(ing), forcemeat, kapok, lining, obstruction, packing, padding, panada, pulu, sawdust, stech, viscera, vitals
STUFFY airless, angry, bombastic, boring, close, dull, fat, frousty, fuggy, heavy, mettlesome, morose, obstinate, old-fogyish, oppressive, perverse, pompous, prim, prosaic, prudish, resolute, stifling, stodgy, stout, straitlaced,

stuggy, suffocating, sulky, sultry, wool(l)y
STUGGY short, stodgy, strong, stubby, STUFFY, sturdy, thickset
STULM adit, entrance, passage(way)
STULTIFY arrest, atrophy, bar, block, check, curb, hinder, inhibit, interrupt, obstruct, restrain, stunt
STULTILOQUY babble, gossip, talk
STUMBLE blunder, boggle, botch, bumble, chance, err, failure, fall, falter, flounder, halper, hamble, happen, lapse, lumper, lurch, offend, scamble, scruple, sin, slip, stagger, stammer, stoiter, stot(ter), stummer, stump, stutter, thrumble, trip
-bum fool
inclined to pecky
STUMP barnstorm, bewilder, block, blunted, butt, campaign, challenge, circuit, clump, dare, dock, doddard, dotard, excursion, foil, hobble, mystify, nonplus, nubbin, pace, part, perplex, piece, pillar, platform, plod, puzzle, rampick, rampike, remainder, remnant, ruin, runt, scrab, skeng, snag, speak, stab, stagger, stool, stoop, stop, strike, stub, stumble, tortillon, tramp, troupe, walk, worn
dead runt
orator campaigner
tree doddard, dotard, nubbin, stock, stoven, zuche
up ante, pay, settle
STUMPY barge, bunty, cash, money, short, stubby
STUN aston(e), astonish, astony, astound, benumb, confound, dammish, daunt, daze, dazzle, deaden, deafen, deave, din, dizzy, dozen, dumfound, muddle, numb, overpower, paralyze, sandbag, shock, silence, stagger, stupefy, stupend, surprise
STUNG bitten, cheated, smarted, taken
STUNNED astonied, deaf, donnard, farchadat, shocked, terrified
STUNNING astonishing, attractive, beautiful, breathtaking, dazzling, fine, gor-

geous, smart, striking, stupefying, terrifying
STUNT abbreviate, abrupt, act, angry, antic, arrest, atrophy, bartani, blast, blunt, caper, catalina, check, craddy, cripple, curtailed, deed, dido, dolphin, dwarf, exploit, feat, hinder, interrupt, joke, limit, performance, ramp, retard, sap, shorten, stamp, stint, stratagem, stubborn, stultify, tour de force, trick, weaken
gymnastic handspring, kip(p)
man acrobat, daredevil, frank tallman
STUNTED dwarf(ed), grubby, pauperitic, runtish, runty, scroggy, scrub(by), scruffy, small, undersized, urled
STUPA chorten, memorial, monument, shrine, temple, tomb, tope, tuft
STUPEFIED bemazed, benumbed, besotted, dazed, dopey, dozzled, languid, mazed, mindless, silly, stunned, stupent, terrified
STUPEFY aston(e), astonish, astony, astound, awe, baze, befuddle, bemuse, besot, bewilder, blunt, confound, confuse, daver, daze, deaden, deave, dope, drug, dull, fall, flabbergast, goof, infatuate, intoxicate, maze, muddle, numb, pall, petrify, shend, shock, soporate, STUN, terrify, torpify
with drink fuddle
STUPENDOUS amazing, astonishing, astounding, enormous, extraordinary, gigantic, great, huge, immense, titanic, vast, wonderful
STUPID anserine, anserous, asinine, bayardly, bete, blank, blind, blockheaded, blunt, booby, bovine, brainless, buffleheaded, buzzard, chumpish, claybrained, clod, crass, daffish, dawkin, dense, doited, doltish, dopey, dowf(art), dull(ard), dumb, dummel, duncical, dunney, duns, empty(pated), fat(headed), fatuous, foolish, glaiket, goosy, gross, gullible, halfbaked, half-witted, hebetate,

ignorant, imbecile, impassive, inept, inert, insensate, lethargic, lolo, loutish, lumpish, mindless, moronic, numskulled, oafish, obtuse, opaque, rattlebrained, senseless, silly, sluggish, sottish, stockish, stolid, sumphy, tavert, thick(witted), thoughtless, torpid, unteachable, urluch, vacant, void, witless

comb. moro

person ass, blinkard, blockhead, blubberhead, blunderbuss, bonehead, boob(y), boodle, boor, bucca, clod, coot, cuif, dimwit, dolt, dullard, erk, fathead, goose, gump, hoit, jukes, kalikeh, kallikak, kolyika, loon, lout, lown, lummox, moke, noodle, nowt, oaf, simp(leton), staumrel, stirk, sumph, tumfie

render hebetate, mope

STUPIDITY amentia, anility, astonishment, betise, blunder, boobery, bopkes, bubkes, chachma, density, dotage, dullness, duncery, folly, hachma, hebitude, idiocy, imbecility, incapacity, indifference, insipience, khaukhma, moronism, morosis, numbness, senility, shtuss, stupor, thickness, vacancy, vacuity

marked stupor

symbol ass, ostrich

STUPOR apathy, asthenobiosis, coma, daze, doldrums, inertia, insensibility, languor, lassitude, lethargy, narcoma, narcosis, numbness, sleep, sopor, stupefaction, stupidity, swarf, swoon, torpidity, torpor, trance

and confusion catatonia

comb. narc(o)

in condition of narcose

pert. carotic

STUPOROUS comatose, dull, inactive, inert, languid, lethargic, listless, obtuse, passive, sluggish, supine, torpid

STUPRATE debauch, ravish, seduce

STURDY brawny, buff, buirdly, burly, enduring, energetic, firm, gid(dy), hardy, healthy, lusty, muscular, obdurate, powerful, resolute, robust, rugged, set,

solid, sound, stable, stalwart, sta(u)nch, steady, stern, sthenius, stiff, stout, strapping, STRONG, stubborn, stupid, substantial, tenacious, thickset, thro, tough, unyielding, vigorous, violent

STURGEON beluga, elops, fish, ganoid, hackleback, hausen, huso, mammose, rubbernose, sterlet

roe caviar(e)

small sterlet

white beluga, huso

STURT annoy, bargain, disturbance, startle, stir, strife, trouble, vex

STUTTER falter, ganch, habble, hack, stammer, stot (ter), stumble

STUTTERING psellism, traulism

STY ascend, aspire, boil, climb, den, enclosure, hordeolum, hovel, hut, ladder, lair, mount, pen, piggery, pigpen, pimple, pustule, quat, rising, shed, slum, soar, stairs, step, stile

STYGIAN chthonian, dark, deathly, ebon, gloomy, hadean, hellish, infernal, inviolable, irrevocable

STYLE air, appellation, approach, art, calendar, call, cast, character, charisma, chic, convention, craze, cry, cut, describe, diction, dub, entitle, fad, fashion, form, genre, gnomon, graver, hubris, key, kind, language, machismo, manner, method, mode, movement, name, needle, oomph, panache, patina, pen, personality, phraseology, polish, pzazz, rage, record, refinement, school, smartness, spicule, swank, system, taste, technic, technique, term, title, ton(e), trend, twig, type, usage, vein, vogue, way, wording

affected euphuism

artistic artifice, dandyism, gothic, gusto

dress getup

having flawless addisonian

inflated fustian

lacking dowdy, fuddyduddy, old-fashioned, shabby

latest craze, dernier cri, kick, trend

lofty epic

oratorical rhetorical

pompous johnsonese

STYLET aciculum, awl, dagger, mandrin, poniard, probe, specillum, stiletto, STYLUS, tool, trocar

surgical trocar

STYLISH alamode, brave, braw, chic, dapper, dashing, doggish, dressy, elegant, fashionable, modish, natty, newfangled, nifty, nobby, popular, posh, smart, snazzy, spruce, swanky, toffish, tony, trendy

STYLITE ascetic, daniel, monk, pillarist, simeon

STYLUS gad, greffe, harpago, pointel, pointer, pyropen, scriber, spicule, STYLET, tracer

point cutter

STYMIE balk, block, check, foil, frustrate, impede, obfuscate, obstruct, stop

STYPTIC alum, amadou, astringent, barometz, emetic, matico, punk, stancher, tannic acid

action anastalsis

STYX hades, hell, lethe, nymph, river

consort pallas

ferryman charon

locale hades

offspring bia, crates, cratus, kratos, nike, zelos, zelus

parent oceanus, tethys

pert. stygian

tributary aornis, cocytus

SUAEDA burroweed, donida, goosefoot

SUANT agreeable, demure, equable, even, grave, placid, quiet, regular, sewan, smooth, steady

SUAVE affable, bland, cordial, courteous, diplomatic, fulsome, genial, glib, glossy, gracious, ingratiating, mannered, oily, pleasing, polite, silky, sleek, slick, smooth, smug, soapy, sociable, unctuous, urbane

SUAVITY amenity, blandness, butter, courtesy, glibness, oiliness, smoothness, softsoap, sweetness, unction, urbanity

SUB auxiliary, grass, subirrigate, submarine, subordinate, substitute, under

SUBASTRAL earthly, mundane, terrestrial

SUBCONSCIOUS psyche, subliminal, supraliminal, unconscious

perception intuition

SUBDIVIDE carve, halve, mince, separate

SUBDIVISION beat, branch, bunda, canton, class(ification), corps, curia, dekan, department, development, dheri, part, phyle, sector, suburb, taluk, township, tract

lateral aisle

SUBDOLOUS artful, crafty, cunning, sly

SUBDUCT deduct, remove, subtract, withdraw

SUBDUE allay, awe, beat, bend, best, bow, break, bridle, calm, captivate, capture, castigate, censor, charm, chasten, conquer, control, convince, crush, defeat, destroy, direct, discipline, dompt, down, foil, humble, lick, lower, manage, master, moderate, muffle, overcome, overpower, quash, quell, reduce, relieve, repress, reprime, restrain, retund, rout, sober, soften, subject, subjugate, suppress, surmount, tame, tone down, trample, vanquish

SUBDUED chaste, conquered, docile, gentle, humble, meek, modest, simple, soft, submiss(ive), tame, timid, tractable

SUBFUSC(OUS) dark, dingy, drab, dull, duskish, dusky

SUBJACENT below, lower, under(lying)

SUBJECT accessible, acquiescent, amenable, apt, argument, bethrall, break, captive, cause, citizen, class, collateral, conditional, content, contingent, course, dependent, dominate, enslave(d), enthrall, feudal, feudary, feudatory, inferior, keep down, leitmotif, liable, liege(man), likely, material, matter, motive, national, noun, obedient, open, prone, provisional, reason, relative, rule, sec-

ondary, sensitive, servant, servile, slave, slavish, study, subdue, subjugate, subordinate, subservient, substance, succursal, susceptible, text, theme, thesis, thrall, topic, tributory, vassal

loyal liege

matter argument, leitmotiv, motive, text, theme, thesis, topic

melodic theme

to predispose, provided, submit

to change amenable, mutable

to choice elective

to demand on call

SUBJECTION bondage, captivity, domination, liability, servitude, slavery, submission, thirling, vassalage

SUBJECTIVE fanciful, illusory, immanent, individual, internal, introspective, introverted, mental, nominative, pectoral, personal, phenomenal, real, submissive, substantial, topical

SUBJOIN add, affix, annex, append, attach, unite

SUBJUGATE beat, break, captivate, conquer, cow, defeat, enslave, foil, lick, master, outwit, overawe, overcome, rout, rule, subdue, SUBJECT, thwart, vanquish

SUBJUGATION bondage, servitude, SUBJECTION

SUBLATE cancel, deny, eliminate, negate, reduce, remove

SUBLEASE farm out, sublet

SUBLEVATE excite, lift, raise

SUBLIMATE divert, elevate, enoble, exalt, glorify, heighten, refine, vaporize

SUBLIMATION abreaction, catharsis, elevation, inhibition, repression, suppression

SUBLIME abstract, delightful, empyreal, exalted, glorious, gorgeous, grand, great, high, ideal, lofty, magnificent, majestic, noble, resplendent, seraphic, solemn, splendid, stately, superb, superior, supreme, top, transcendent, winged

SUBLIMINAL See SUBCONSCIOUS.

SUBLIMITY grandeur, hon-

or, importance, magnanimity, magnificence, majesty, nobility

SUBLUNAR(Y) earthly, mundane, terrestrial

SUBMARINE diver, engulfed, immersed, inundated, pigboat, subaqueous, submersible, u-boat, underwater, warship

atomic narwhal, polaris, swordfish, trident

detector sonar

espionage project jennifer

group wolf-pack

nuclear, 1st nautilus

observation post conning tower

part periscope, snorkel

projectile missile, polaris, torpedo

SUBMERGE baptize, bog, bury, dip, dive, drench, duck, dunk, engulf, flood, hide, immerse, inundate, overflow, plunge, saturate, sink, soak, souse, submerse, swamp, whelm

SUBMERGENCE baptism, burial, dip, dousing, ducking, engulfment, immersion, inundation, onlap, sinking

SUBMERSE See SUBMERGE.

SUBMISS humble, low, obsequious, subdued

SUBMISSION acquiescence, backdown, capitulation, complaisance, compliance, confession, curtsy, defeatism, deference, docility, meekness, nonresistance, obedience, passivity, patience, resignation, servility, subordination, subjection, subservience, surrender, vail, yielding

act of bow, curts(e)y, kneel, salaam

all-out passive obedience

symbol camel

to destiny fatalism

SUBMISSIVE abject, amenable, biddable, buxom, compliant, deferential, demiss, docile, dutiful, humble, meek, menial, obedient, obeisant, passive, pliable, pliant, resigned, servile, slavish, subject, subdued, tame, tractable, weak-kneed, yielding

to wife uxorious

SUBMIT abide, accede, accept, acknowledge, acquiesce, advance, affirm, agree, avale, bear, bend, bow, break, capitulate, cave, cede, comply, defer(to), delate, endure, give in, humor, indulge, knuckle under, lower, moderate, obey, offer, postulate, present, propose, refer, relent, resign, soften, stoop, subdue, subject, succumb, suffer, surrender, temper, truckle, vail, yield
for consideration remit
proposal to move
to buckle(under), obey

SUBNORMAL abnormal, defective, feebleminded, retarded, substandard

SUBORDINATE accessory, accidental, aide, ancillary, appurtenance, assistant, auxiliary, collateral, dependent, exempt, henchman, incidental, inferior, junior, lower, minion, minor, obedient, petty, puisne, second(ary), servant, servient, servile, slave, subdue, subject, submissive, subsidiary, tributary, under

SUBORN adorn, bribe, equip, father, foist, furnish, incite, procure, provide

SUBPOENA penalty, process, summon(s), writ

SUBROGATE See SUBSTITUTE.

SUB ROSA confidentially, covertly, privately

SUBSCRIBE abet, accept, adhere, agree, ascribe, assent, attest, consent, consign, contribute, enroll, give, guarantee, publish, ratify, register, resign, sanction, sign, submit, support, surrender, underwrite, yield

SUBSCRIPTION acceptance, approval, consent, donation, obedience, signature, submission, support
to newspaper abonnement

SUBSECIVE extra, leisure, spare

SUBSEQUENT after, attendant, behind, companion, ensuing, following, future, later, posterior, postnate, retainer, succeeding
comb. rere

to birth postnatal, postpartum

SUBSERVIENCE bondage, inferiority, servility, submission, subordinancy, subordination, truckling

SUBSERVIENT abject, deferential, flattering, fawning, menial, obsequious, oily, servile, slavish, subject, submissive, vassal

SUBSIDE abate, allay, assuage, blow over, calm, cool, decline, decrease, descend, diminish, dwindle, ebb, fall, flatten, gravitate, languish, lapse, lay, peter out, relapse, settle, sink, taper, wane, withdraw

SUBSIDENCE decline, decurrence, dregs, droop, fall(ing), lapse, sediment, settling, sinkage, slump

SUBSIDIARY accessory, accidental, ancillary, auxiliary, branch, bye, contributory, endowed, minor, nonessential, secondary, subordinate, supplemental, supplementary, tributary

SUBSIDIZE abet, aid, finance, give, promote, subvene, support

SUBSIDY aid, alimony, allotment, allowance, annuity, appropriation, assistance, award, bonus, bounty, endowment, gift, grant, payment, pension, stipend, subvention, support, tontine

SUBSIST abide, breathe, continue, desist, endure, exist, fare, feed, hold, live, maintain, obtain, rely, remain, stand, stay, support

SUBSISTENCE accommodation, aliment, allowance, being, continuance, inherency, keep, livelihood, living, maintenance, nurture, persistence, provisions, substance, support, sustenance, sustentation, upkeep
money allowance, batta

SUBSOIL pan, ratchel, shrave, sole
animal gopher, mole, prairiedog

SUBSTANCE additive, affluence, agent, amount, assets, basis, being, body, bottom, burden, capital, component, content, core, element, essence, estate,

fiber, form, foundation, fund(s), gist, ground, heart, import, majority, marrow, mass, material, matter, meaning, means, meat, object, pith, proof, property, purport, quantity, reality, resources, riches, sap, soul, spirit, staple, stuff, subject, substratum, sum(mary), supply, tachlis, texture, thing, topic, wealth
adhesive cement, gloea, glue, paste, sealant, sticker
amorphous ferrite, glass, lignin, pectin, resin, rosin, saponin
animal gelatin
astringent alum, catechu
bitter acid, aloes, aloin, amarine, elaterin, emetine, gall, ilicin, linin
calking berengelite
chemical reagent
colloidal algin, gum
corrosive caustic, lye
dark atrament
dissolved solute
dissolving (re)solvent
eternal adharma, dharma
expansive gas
fatty degras, ergusia, lipoid, smear, suberin
fermenting leaven, mother, yeast
filmy gauze, gossamer
fusible ethal
grinding abrasive
hard adamant, diamond
horny baleen, chitin
hypothetical fluid, inogen, protyl
infusible ceria
narcotic See DRUG.
primordial protyl(e), psychoplasm
protein interferon, iodospongin, meat
simple element
sour acid, vinegar
sticky birdlime, epoxy, glue, goo(p), gum, gurry, paste, size, tar
subtle spirit
transparent cellophane, celluloid, glass
unctuous grease, oil, ointment, salve
vegetable peat, resin, rosin
vital keest
waxy cerin, paraffin
white alanine, alba, elaterin, inulin

SUBSTANDARD bad,

bauch, inferior, lousy, second-rate, shoddy, subnormal, third-rate

SUBSTANTIAL actual, affluent, ample, authoritative, big, bodily, bulky, considerable, dense, firm, genuine, hearty, heavy, important, influential, large, massive, massy, material, meaty, monumental, nourishing, physical, pukka, real, reliable, responsible, rich, sensible, significant, solid, square, stable, steady, stout, strong, sturdy, tangible, tidy, true, valid, vast, wealthy

SUBSTANTIALITY body, corporeity, durability, endurance, firmness, mass, materiality, solidity, stability, strength, SUBSTANCE, tangibility

SUBSTANTIATE actualize, back, bolster, confirm, corroborate, demonstrate, embody, incarnate, materialize, objectify, prove, realize, reify, test, try, validate, verify, warrant

SUBSTANTIVE actual, considerable, definite, direct, enduring, entity, essential, firm, lasting, noun, permanent, pronoun, self-contained, solid

SUBSTITUTE act for, agent, akori, alternate, apology, artificial, beetmister, benchwarmer, change, commute, compound, copy, counterfeit, delegate, deputy, displace, double, dub, dummy, duplicate, enallage, equal, equivalent, ersatz, expedient, exchange, extra, factice, fill-in, ghost, imitation, in lieu, locum-tenens, makeshift, nominate, pinchhitter, postiche, provisional, proxy, quid pro quo, relief, replace(ment), represent, reserve, ringer, secondary, shift, spell, standin, stopgap, subrogate, succedaneum, succenturiate, suffect, supersede, supplant, supply, surrogate, switch, synthetic, temporary, tentative, token, understudy, vicar(ious), vice(regent)

comb. ette, vice

SUBSTITUTION change,

commutation, enallage, ersatz, exchange, interchange, reciprocity, shift, swap, switch

SUBSUME assume, comprehend, cover, deduce, embrace, explain, include, involve, summarize

SUBTERFUGE artifice, blind, chicane(ry), deception, doubledealing, evasion, excuse, expedient, feint, fraud, lie, makeshift, maneuver, mask, pretense, pretext, quirk, recourse, refuge, ruse, shift, stall, stealth, stratagem, tergiversation, trick(ery), voidance

SUBTERRANEAN abysmal, catachthonic, hellish, hidden, plutonic, secret, sunk, underground

SUBTLE abstruse, acute, airy, analytical, argute, artful, astatic, clever, crafty, cunning, deep, delicate, designing, discriminate, elusive, ethereal, exact, exclusive, expert, faint, fine, fragile, hairsplitting, indistinct, ingenious, keen, logical, meticulous, nice, penetrating, perceptive, profound, rare, rarefied, recondite, shrewd, sly, tenuous, thin, wily, wise

point nuance, refinement

SUBTLETY cunning, delicacy, discrimination, exility, finesse, guile, quiddity, quillet

SUBTRACT borrow, deduct, detract, diminish, dock, minus, pull, remove, withdraw, withhold

SUBURB(S) annex, banlieue, barrio, borgo, confines, environ(s), faubourg, hinterland, outskirts, periphery, pettah, poblacion, purlieu, town

SUBVENTION aid, appropriation, grant, SUBSIDY

SUBVERSIVE collaborator, fellow traveler, fifth column, fraternizer, ruinous, saboteur, spy, trojan horse, underground

SUBVERT betray, capsize, corrupt, debase, deceive, demolish, deprave, destroy, gainsay, kill, overthrow, overturn, pervert, raze, re-

verse, ruin, sap, spy, upset, wreck

SUBWAY bmt, cave, irt, metro, railroad, train, tube, underground, underpass

entrance kiosk

fare token

SUCCEED accomplish, achieve, advance, approach, attain, batten, bloom, blossom, bring off, carry off, catch on, click, come after, connect, cotton, descend, devolve, displace, do well, ensue, eventuate, fadge, fare, flourish, follow, gain, get(ahead), go far, graduate, happen, hit it, inherit, make good, manage, occur, pass, prevail, progress, prosper, prove(out), pull off, put across, put over, replace, result, rise, score, supersede, supplant, take, thrive, triumph, weather, win, withstand, work

SUCCESS accolade, accomplishment, achievement, advance, artha, cess, consequence, eclat, eureka, exploit, felicity, fortune, fruition, hit, issue, jackpot, luck, mastery, outcome, progress, prosperity, smash, triumph, victory, walkaway, win, wow

symbol citation, commendation, diploma, emerald, medal, laurel, palm, prize, scalp, token, trophy

SUCCESSFUL blooming, booming, coming, flourishing, fortunate, fruitful, happy, hot, lucky, on top, palmy, prosperous, speedful, thrifty, thriving, triumphant, unbeaten, victorious

person arrive, arriviste, champion, conqueror, parvenu, upstart

SUCCESSION assise, chain, course, diadoche, diadochi, dynasty, family, gradation, line, posterity, progression, row, run, sequence, series, set, stream, string, suit(e), track, train

comb. meta

male, pert. salic

next in line heir

of customers queue

of rulers dynasty

pert. ordinal

SUCCESSIVE after, arow,

consecutive, constant, continual, continuous, discrete, ᶜfollowing, hereditary, incessant, inherited, sequent(ial), serial, seriate
SUCCESSOR calif, caliph, designado, follower, haeres, heir, heres, relief, sub(stitute), tanist
SUCCINCT aphoristic, blunt, brief, brusque, close, compact, compressed, concise, condensed, crisp, curt, direct, laconic, pithy, short, straight, summary, terse
SUCCISA blueball, bluekiss, scabious, teasel
SUCCOR abet, aid, alleviate, assist(ance), befriend, comfort, cure, deliver, help, mitigate, refuge, relief, relieve, rescue, reset, secure, serve, shelter, strengthen, support, sustain
SUCCORY catanche, catnache, cupidone, cupid's-dart
SUCCUBUS asparas, demon, fiend, strumpet, whore
SUCCULENT cactus, echevaria, fleshy, fresh, frim, herb, juicy, luscious, lush(y), mellow, nutritive, pappy, pulpy, rich, sappy, tender, vital, young
SUCCUMB abandon, bow, break, capitulate, cave, crush, defer, die, fail, fall, give in, lose, perish, quail, relent, relinquish, resign, sink, stand, stoop, subdue, submit, surrender, swoon, traik, weary, yield
SUCCURSAL collateral, dependent, secondary, subject, subordinate, tributary
SUCH certain, inferior, kind, like, mediocre, poor, previous, sic(k), siker, similar, some, swich
SUCHNESS bhutatathata
SUCK absorb, aspirate, assimilate, bleed, consume, disappointment, drain, draw, drink, engulf, extract, frustration, imbibe, inhale, liquor, nurse, osculate, plowshare, resorb, rob, sip, suction, swig, tipple, whirlpool
dry drain, impoverish, strip
-egg cuckoo, extortioner, weasel
hole whirlpool
in inhale, lure, sell, swindle,

up absorb, drink, tipple
up to toady, truckle
SUCKER acetabulum, bait, bobolink, bothrium, branch, catspaw, chouse, chub, chupon, cinch, cully, cupule, customer, cutlips, dotterel, dupe, fall-guy, fish, geck, gonotyl, gudgeon, gull, haustorium, humpback, lamprey, loculus, lollypop, mug, mullet, osculum, parasite, patsy, pigeon, pushover, ratoon, redfin, redhorse, scourge, setup, shoot, simpleton, sobol(e), sprout, square, sugar, supper, surculous, thief, victim, yekl
black stoneroller
sailing quillback
SUCKERFISH blackhorse, catostomid, clingfish, hagfish, horsefish, lamprey, lumpfish, moxostoma, pega, redhorse, remora, stoneroller
SUCKLE comfit, feed, foster, lactate, milk, nourish, nurse
SUCTION inhalation, inspiration, intake, snuffle, sucking
pump aspirator
SUDAN nigritia
animal dama, oterop
arab guhayna
bed angareb
beer dolo
capital khartoum, khartum
city alubayd, atbara, elfasher, elgeneina, elobeid, geneina, juba, kassala, khart(o)um, kosti, malakal, meroe, nyala, obeid, omdurman, opari, suakin, wad medani, yei
desert nubian
fetish grigri, suanu
gazelle dama
general abboud
grass garava, garawi
independence movement anyanya
lake chad, tsad
language efe, efik, ewe, ibo, kru, mandango, mandingo, mole, nubian, tshi, vak, vei, yoruba
leader jaafar numeiri
movement anyanya, scorpion
nomad fula(ni), kababish
peak kinyeti
people bagara, bagarra, baggara, balante, bari, beri, bobo, bongo, daza, dinka,

dor, egba, fula(h), golo, gurmantshi, gurusi, hamite, hausa, junje, makari, mandinga, menkiera, mosgu, mossi, nilote, nubiyin, nuer, peul, sarakille, senufo, sere, songhai, songhay, songhoi, sonr(h)ai, surhai, taureg, tibbu, volta
port suakin
president numeiri
range nuba
rebel leader lagu
region darfur, dongola, gezira, kassala, kordofan, segu, sennar
river (white)nile
statesman abboud
stockade zareeba, zeriba
stretcher angare(e)b, angarep
village fashoda
weapon trombash, trumbash
weight habba
SUDARIUM handkerchief, maniple, napkin, veronica
SUDDEN abrupt, accidental, acute, brief, early, hasty, hurried, headlong, immediate, impetuous, impromptu, impulsive, precipitate, precipitous, prerupt, prompt, rash, short, soon, speedy, spurtive, subitaneous, subitous, swift, unexpected, unforeseen, violent
SUDDENLY abruptly, amain, astart, at once, bang, immediately, in a jiffy, in no time, instantly, momently, presto, short, skelp, slapdash, subito, unawares
SUDOR exudation, perspiration, sweat
SUDS beer, bog, bubbles, dregs, filth, foam, froth, lather, marsh, refuse, sapples, scum, soap, yeast
SUE appeal, apply, ask, beg, chase, claim, continue, court, demand, entreat, exact, follow, implore, litigate, petition, plea(d), practice, pray, prosecute, pursue, request, seek, solicit, suit, supplicate, trounce, urge, woo
SUET fat, lard, tallow
comb. stearo
SUEZ *builder* de lesseps
part bitter lakes, port said
SUFFER abide, accept, ache, admit, agonize, ail, allow,

bear, bide, bleed, bow, brave, brook, clem, complain, countenance, cry, dree, encounter, endure, experience, feel, grieve, groan, hurt, leave, let, moan, pain, permit, prove, resist, sink, smart, stand for, starve, stomach, submit, support, sustain, take, thole, tolerate, undergo, writhe

SUFFERANCE connivance, consent, endurance, forbearance, indulgence, leave, misery, pain, passivity, patience, permission, resignation, respite, sanction, tholance, tolerance, toleration

SUFFERER doormat, martyr, patient

SUFFERING adversity, affliction, agony, anguish, bad, bale, care, distress, dolor, dree, extremity, gethsemane, grief, hardship, heartache, ill(ness), loss, misery, misfortune, pain, passion, pathos, rack, sick(ness), sorrow, travail, tribulation, tsoriss, tsouris, tsuris(s), woe, wrake

capable of patible

comb. path(ia), pathic, patho

intense calvary, gethsemane

SUFFICE allow, answer, appease, avail, content, fulfill, furnish, get by, last, meet, permit, qualify, reach, replenish, satisfy, serve, supply

SUFFICIENCY ability, abundance, adequacy, capacity, competency, conceit, enough, fill, plenitude, plenty, plethora, profusion, self-confidence

SUFFICIENT adequate, ample, bastant, comfortable, competent, decent, due, enough, enow, fit, full, good, meet, plentiful, plenty, relevant, responsible, satisfactory, substantial, suitable, valid

not quite meager, scant, skimpy, sparse

SUFFIX add, adjunct, affix, annex, append, attach, ending, sequel

SUFFLAMINATE brake, check, clog, impede, obstruct

SUFFLATE blow up, inflate, inspire

SUFFOCATE accloy, asphyxiate, burke, choke, kill, murder, scumfish, slocken, smoor, smother, stifle, stive, strangle, suppress, throttle

SUFFOLK *horse* leiston, punch

painter constable

SUFFRAGE aid, approval, assent, ballot, franchise, help, petition, prayer, testimony, voice, vote

SUFFUSE bathe, blush, color, cover, diffuse, embay, fill, imbue, infuse, ingrain, penetrate, permeate, pervade, spill, spread

SUFI ascetic, mystic, safawid

community ribat

concept fana

disciple murid

mystic qutb

path tariqat

psychological stages ahwal

saint abdal

SUGAR acrose, agavose, aldose, allose, altrose, azucar, bios, bribe, browning, cane, cassonade, cellobiose, cellose, chitose, cymarose, dextrose, doctor, fructose, fucose, glucose, glutose, glycose, goor, gulose, gur, hexose, idose, ketose, lactose, levulose, lyxose, maltose, money, muscavado, octose, ose, panela, panocha, papelon, penochi, pentose, penuche, piloncilla, pyranose, raab, raffinose, rhamnose, rhodeose, secalose, snow, sorbose, sucre, sucrose, sweeten, sweetness, talose, tetrose, threose, triose, turanose, xylose, zucchero

addition chaptalization

and butter, blend cream

and molasses malada

apple biriba, cherimoya, sweetsop

artificial allose, gulose, lyxose, mannose, saccharin

beet extract betaine, lycine, oxyneurine

beet pulp bagasse

boiling kettle flambeau

bowl sucrier

bowl of the world cuba

brown caraibe, jaggary, jagghery, panela, piloncillo

burnt caramel

bush honeyflower, protea, suikerbosch

candy alphenic, caramel

cane glumal, mattress, milo, ratoon, sorghum, sorgo, sucrose

cane disease eyespot, iliau, redrot, ringspot, sereh, sundew

cane juice liquor

cane residue bagasse, dunder, mare, trash

cane stalk ratoon

cleaning elution

coarse raab

coat with candy, crystallize

comb. sacchar, sucr(o), ose, osid

compound acrose, osamine, triose

crude gur, head, melada, piloncillo

crystalline maltose, rhamnose, tagatose

crystals goor, gur, massecuite

evaporating pan tache

extract betain(e), lucine, oxyneurine

fruit fructose, ketose, levulose

grape dextrose, maltose

having low blood hypoglycemic

inferior bastard

liquid sirup, syrup

loaf conoidal, hill, mountain

lump cube, loaf

measurer saccharimeter

mill central, trapiche, usine

muscle inosite

percentage brix-scale

pill placebo

raw brown, cassonade, gur, muscovado, panocha

refining device cupel, elutor, granulator, tiger

sack bayon

scale ventzke

simple ose

source beet, cane, corn, fruit, grape, maple, milk, sap, sorghum, xylose

substitute honey, saccharin, sorbitol

syrup molasses, treacle

water ambrosia, nectar

SUGARBIRD grosbeak, honeycreeper, sunbird

SUGARHOUSE *part* purgery

SUGARPLUM bonbon, candy, kiss, shadbush, sweetmeat

SUGARY candied, honeyed, saccharin, sweet

SUGGEST adumbrate, advance, advise, allude, arouse, broach, commend, connote, counsel, dictate, hint, imply, import, indicate, indite, infuse, insinuate, inspire, intimate, jog, mean, offer, present, promise, prompt, propose, propound, recommend, refer, remind, seduce, signify, submit, tempt, tout

SUGGESTION advice, allusion, clew, clue, cue, dash, hint, idea, implication, inkling, intimation, notion, proposal, recommendation, reminder, shade, smack, soupcon, supposition, temptation, thought, tinge, tip, touch, trace, whisper

SUGGESTIVE allusive, aniconic, indicative, inferential, insinuating, obscene, off-color, pregnant, provocative, racy, redolent, risque, sexy, significant, smutty, stimulating, symbolic

SUICIDE banzai, felo-de-se, harakari, harakiri, harikari, seppuku, shinju, suttee(ism)
fighter kamikaze
fish fugu
kingdom of japan
leap brodie

SUID(AE) boar, hog, pig, swine

SUIT accommodate, accord, action, adapt, agree, appeal, apt, assort, attire, become, befit, beseem, besit, case, cast, cause, class(ify), clothing, comport, conform, costume, courtship, drape, dress, ensemble, entreaty, fadge, fit, habit, hit, kind, like, litigation, livery, match, order, pair, petition, plea(d), please, prayer, prosecution, request, retinue, rig, satisfy, series, serve, set, sort, sue, suffice, supplication, tailleur, tally, trial, wooing
bathing bikini, maillot, trunks
card See CARD *suit.*
coat click
diving gangava
instigator promovent
maker sarta, sartor, tailor

of mail See ARMOR.

SUITABLE adequate, agreeable, answerable, applicable, apposite, appropriate, apropos, apt, becoming, befitting, compatible, competent, condign, congruous, consistent, consonant, convenient, correct, correspondent, decent, eligible, expedient, feasible, fit(ten), fitting, germane, happy, ideal, idoneal, idoneous, liable, likely, matching, meet, pat, pertinent, proper, relevant, right, satisfactory, seeming, seemly, sortable, sufficient, timely, well, weme
make adapt, prepare

SUITCASE bag(gage), dorlach, duffel bag, flight bag, gladstone, grip, keester, kennebunker, luggage, portmanteau, reticule, satchel, valise

SUITE apartment, catena, chain, chamber, convoy, cortege, court, entourage, escort, flat, followers, group, partita, retinue, rooms, sequel, series, set, staff, train
member of attache

SUITOR admirer, amoroso, appellant, attendant, beau, flame, follower, gallant, lochinvar, lover, petitioner, plaintiff, steady, supplicant, swain, sweetheart, wooer

SUKARNO *dream* nasakom

SULA booby, gannet

SULAWESI celebes

SULCATE cleft, fluted, furrowed, grooved

SULCUS fissure of rolando

SULEIMAN *captain* barbarossa

SULFA miracle-drug

SULFUR See SULPHUR.

SULK(S) boody, bouderie, dort, fantod, fret, frown, frump, furrow, glum(p), grouch, grout, harl, huff, hump, lour, lower, mope, mump(s), pet, plow, pout, scowl, snudge, strum, sulcate, sull, sullens, thurmus

SULKY carriage, cart, chuffy, churlish, crabbed, cranky, cross, doddy, dorty, dour, dull, edgy, fretful, gloomy, glum, gocart, grouchy, huffy, humpy, inert, irrita-

ble, morose, mumpish, peevish, perverse, plow, querulous, saturnine, snuffy, SULLEN, sumphy, surly, techy, testy, touchy
race trot

SULLA See SYLLA.

SULLAGE drainage, dross, filth, mud, pollution, refuse, scoria, scum, sewage, silt, slag

SULLEN alone, baleful, black, boorish, chuff, chumpish, crabbed, cranky, cross, crusty, dismal, dorty, dour, dull, dumpy, fretful, gloomy, glum, grim, grouty, gruff, heavy, inert, intractable, lonely, louring, lowering, melancholy, moody, moping, mopy, morose, mulish, obstinate, peevish, perverse, petulant, pouty, refractory, rusty, saturnine, serious, short, silent, single, sole, solitary, somber, sour, spiteful, stern, stunkard, SULKY, surly, testy, thawn, ugly, unique, wemod

SULLY begrime, besmear, besmirch, black(en), blemish, blot, blur, brand, corrupt, darken, defile, dirty, foul, pollute, seduce, slubber, smear, smirch, smudge, smutch, soil, spoil, spot, stain, tarnish

SULPHATE alum, alunite, alunogen, barite, baryta, beaverite, bianchite, blende, botryogen, brimstone, glauberite, hepar, ilesite, krausite, loweite, mallardite, matte, patronite, picromerite, pisanite, sulphur, vitriol
double alum
calcium gypsum
ferrous copperas
rare krausite

SULPHIDE acanthite, alaskaite, beegerite, blende, bornite, cubanite, galena, germanite, glance, hauerite, hepar, kobellite, orpiment, plagionite, polydymite, proustite, realgar, troilite, zarnec, zarnich
mixture matte

SULPHUR brimstone, quebrith, sulfur, yellow
alloy niello
bacteria beggiatoa

-bottom rorqual, whale
comb. thi(o)
compound thetin
containing thionic
source pyrite
water barege
SULPHURIC *acid* vitriol
SULPHURWEED brimstone-wort
SULTAN calif, caliph, kalif, kaliph, khalif, murad, padishah, ruler, selim, soldan
decree irade
domain soldan
palace seraglio, serai
palace part harem
title padishah
SULTANATE kuwait, mahra, muscat, oman, zanzibar
SULTANESS sowdones
SULTRY close, coarse, damp, erotic, flush, hot, humid, lurid, moist, muggy, obscene, oppressive, passionate, puthery, sensual, smutty, sticky, stifling, still, stuffy, suffocating, sweltering, sweltry, torrid, wet
SULU *island* jolo, siassi
native moro
SUM add, addend, addition, aggregate, all, amount, assembly, calculate, cast(up), complete, compute, count, epitome, epitomize, estimate, figure, foot, fund(s), gathering, gist, height, host, integer, kitty, mass, money, number, numeral, pot, quantity, recap, reckon, solidum, some, subsidy, summary, summit, tale, tot(al), totality, whole
and substance gist, upshot
derived proceeds
forfeited dedit
in briefly
large gob(s), pot
of money account, bundle, pot, savings, take
part augend
small chickenfeed, drab, drib(b)let, smidgen, smitchen
unexpended savings
up add, foot, recapitulate, subsume, summarize, tot, total(ize)
SUMAC ailanthus, anacardium, anam, balinghasay, blood-plum, burtree, karee, myrica, rhus, scotino, shoe-

make, squawbush, tree-of-heaven
climbing poison ivy
SUMATRA *animal* balu, banxring, napu, orang, shrew, siamang, tana, tanu, teledu, tupaia
ape orang(o)utan(g), siamang
camphor borneol
city achin, bonkulin, djambi, indrapoor, jambi, kuala, langsa, medan, natal, padang, pakanbaru, palembang, rengat, solok, uruk
deer napu
deity abu, utu
fiber caloee
gutta siak
island nias, sunda
kingdom achin, atjeh
lake toba
language nias(ese)
measure etto, jankal, paal, pakha, sukat, tub, tung
peak kerintji, leuser
people achinese, batak, batta(k), lampong, malayan, rejang
port bencoolen, benkulen, djambi, padang
raft rakit
river djambi, hari, indragiri, jambi, musi, rokan
silk ikat
squirrel-shrew tana, tanu
strait sunda
volcano merapi
weight candil
wildcat balu
wind bohorok
SUMER eridu, isin, kish, lagash, larsa, uruk
deity abu, allatu, anu, anunnaki, aralu, aruru, enlil, enmeshara, ereshkigal, inanna, kulla, nammu, ninkhursag, ninlil, nintu, utu
demon asag, namtar
dialect emesal
drum ala(l)
people accadian, akkadian
priestess entum
priest-king patesi
ruler gudea
settler guti
writing cuneiform
world of the dead kur
SUMMA treatise, work(s)
theologica author thomas aquinas
SUMMARILY acervatim, shortly
SUMMARIZE abridge, ab-

stract, bridle, calculate, outline, precis, recapitulate, repeat, resume
SUMMARY abridg(e)ment, abstract, arbitrary, argument, breviary, breviate, brief, capitulation, compend(ium), comprehensive, concise, conspectus, digest, epilogation, epitome, extract, general, gist, headnote, immediate, laconic, pithy, precis, prompt, quick, recap(itulation), resume, review, round-up, rundown, short, substance, succinct, sum, syllabus, synopsis, terse, total
SUMMER beam, canicule, dog days, estate, estivo, ete, girder, lintel, timber
bird cuckold, wryneck
cypress kochia
duck garganey
flounder plaice
goddess aestas, carpo
haze calina
herring blackbelly, sockeye-salmon
house alcove, arbor, belvedere, cabana, casino, folly, gazebo, kiosk, pagoda, pandal, pergola, tupek
hyacinth galtonia
late silly season
late, pert. serotinal, serotinous
lilac butterfly-bush, damewort
palace baradari
pert. canicular, estival
rash prickly-heat
residence cabin, cottage, mahal
snipe dunlin
spend estivate
squash cocozelle, pattypan, scallop
tanager redbird
wood latewood
SUMMIT acme, apex, apogee, brow, calotte, cap, climax, comble, crest, crown, culmen, culmination, divide, dod(d), edge, extremity, fastigium, height, knap, limit, maximum, meridian, mountain, peak, pinnacle, pitch, point, roof, spire, tip, top, vertex, zenith
pert. apical
round dod(d)
SUMMON accerse, accite,

advoke, arouse, assemble, beacon, becall, beckon, bid, buzz, call, cite, clepe, command, compel, conjure, convene, convoke, cry, demand, educe, elicit, enjoin, enroll, entreat, evocate, evoke, excite, exorcise, hail, implore, invite, invoke, knell, muster, order, page, prompt, provoke, recall, send for, serve, signal, sist, sound, subpoena, toll, vocate
up collect, gather, recall, remember

SUMMONS ban, beck, call, cital, citation, command, habeas-corpus, monition, nod, signal, subpoena, venire, warning, warrant, writ
to eat soup's on
to war to arms

SUMMULA abridgment, epitome

SUMP bog, cesspool, cistern, dirt, drain, marsh, mud, pit, pool, reservoir, sewer, shower, sink, standage, tank, well

SUMPHISH See STUPID, SULKY.

SUMPTER baggage, burden, driver, mule, pack(horse)

SUMPTUOUS costly, deluxe, elegant, expensive, grand, lavish, luxurious, magnificent, munificent, opulent, prodigal, splendid, stately, superb, wlonk

SUN aldebaran, bask, daystar, dry, elohim, heat, helios, glory, jouskeha, luminary, monstrance, orb, parhelion, phoebus, power, savitar, sol, sonne, splendor, star, surya, tan, titan
and earth, pert. siliterraneous
and moon conjoined sullunar
apartment solarium
asphyxia sunstroke
-bathe apricate, aprication, bask, tan
-bath treatment heliotherapy
bear bruang
beetle amara
bittern carle, caurale, helias
blind awning, um(b)rella
body orbiting comet
-centered heliocentric
circle around aura, corona, halo, sundog
clock sundial
comb. helio, soli

disk aten, aton, c(h)akra
disk center cazim
-dried tiled
drops scabish
envelope aureola, aureole, corona, halo
equatorial equinox
exploding nova
fever dengue
fleck lucule
gall jellyfish
gaseous envelope chromosphere
gem diamond
glasses shades
god abraxas, aditi, adityas, adonis, agni, amen, amon, amun, apollo, asvins, athtar, atmu, aton, atum, baal, babbar, balder, beal, belenus, beli, chepera, dyaus, elagabalus, endymion, frey, hadad, helios, herakhti, hiruko, horus, hyperion, ing, inti, janus, khepera, khepri, lleu, llew, lug(h), ment(u), mithras, mitra, nergal, nigihayahi, ninib, ninurta, osiris, paiva, phaethon, phoebus, reharakhti, rhe, savitar, shamash, shu, sokaris, sol, surya, tem, titan, tonatiuh, tum, utu(g), varuna, vishnu
goddess allat, amaterasu
greatest distance from apsis
grebe finfoot, gruiform, sunbird
halo corona, sundog
halter joshua
hat topee, topi
horse abrax, actaeon, aethon, alsvidur, alsvinn, alsvith, amethea, arvakur, aslo, bronte, eos, erythreos, ethiops, ethon, lampos, phaeton, philoge, phlegon, puroeis, pyrois
king louis xiv
lamp argand
light around See *envelope,* above.
measurer diopter, pyrheliometer
metal gold
mock parhelion
moon and stars host
near heliac
obscuring spissatus
pain hemicrania
parlor solarium
path ecliptic, orbit
personification See *god,* above.

pert. heliac(al), solar
-planets representation orrery
protective device blind(age), havelock, parasol, shade(s), umbrella
ray measurer actinometer
reflector sematrope
regent uriel
resort anguilla, antigua, aruba, bahamas, barbados, bermuda, capri, cayman, conaire, cozumel, curacao, grenada, guadeloupe, guatemala, haiti, honduras, jamaica, martinique, mexico, montserrat, nevis, panama, puerto rico, saba, st barthelemy, st kitts, st lucia, st maarten, surinam, virgin islands
rising herakhti
rising, land of japan, nippon
rose portulaca
satellite planet
son of inca
spider scorpion
spurge cat's-grass, cat's-hair, cat's-milk, churnstaff, sunweed, turnsole, wartweed, wartwort
sweat of the gold
tan merida
tree hinoki, retinispora
turning with eutropic
worship helioculture, heliolatry, sabianism
worshiper heliolater, idolator, parsee, parsi, sabian

SUNAPEE char, saibling, trout

SUNBEAM banana

SUNBIRD cadet, finfoot, mamo

SUNBONNET cresie, kappie, shaker, tilt, ugly

SUNBOW iris

SUNBURN actino, august, beige, dermatitis, greening, heliosis, tan

SUNBURST adust, brooch, ensign

SUNCUP evening-primrose, golden-eggs

SUNDA *island* bali, borneo, celebes, java, lambok, nias, raoul, sumatra, timor

SUNDAE gedunk, ice cream

SUNDAY dimanche, domenica, dominical, exaudi, gaudete, judica, sabbath, trinity
advent, 4th in rorate
ascension exaudi
easter paques, pasqua

easter, before palm sunday
easter, 4th after cantate
easter, 7th after pentecost, whitsun
lent, 5th after judica
lent, mid bragget, laetare
low antipascha, quasimodo
pert. dominical
special easter, palm
SUNDER break, cleave, detach, disally, disjoin, dissever, distract, divide, divorce, part, rend, rip, rive, segregate, sejugate, separate, sever, split, twain, twin(e)
SUNDEW aldrovanda, drosera, eyebright, roridula, youthwort
SUNDIAL ghurry, horologe, lupine, scaphion, solarium
part gnomon, style
pert. gnomonic, sciatheric
point node
SUNDOG halo, parhelion, pekingese, rainbow, windgall
SUNDOWN See SUNSET.
SUNDOWNER captain, drink, hobo, nightcap, tramp, tussocker, vagabond, whaler
SUNDRY apart, asunder, different, divers(e), miscellaneous, respective, several, variegated, various
SUNFISH bigmouth, blackears, bluegill, bluejoe, bream, cichlid, crappie, croppie, flatfish, flier, flounder, flyer, headfish, huro, jellyfish, kivver, lepomis, mola, moloid, moonfish, opah, percoid, pondfish, pumpkinseed, redear, redeye, roach, ruff(e), warmouth, yellowbelly
SUNFLOWER aster, balsamroot, canada, girasole, golden, helianthus, helio (trope), marigold, rockrose, sunfoil, turnsole
state kansas
turned into clytie
SUNG *dynasty founder* chao kuang-yin
SUNK abject, absorbed, concave, couch, downcast, hollow, overcome, seat, subsided, turf
in enforced
SUNLESS blae, gray
SUNLIGHT glare, yang
SUNN ambary, dagga, hemp,

janapa(n), madras, sana(i), sann(hemp)
SUNNA custom, tradition, usage
horse abakur, alsividur, arvakur, aslo
religion mohammedanism
SUNNY auspicious, bright, cheerful, cheery, clear, gay, golden, happy, merry, sanguine, shiny, sparkling, vivacious, warm
SUNRISE aurora, dawn, daybreak, morning, orient, sunup
goddess aurora
song aubade
SUNSET curfew, dusk, e'en, eve(ning), eventide, nightfall, twilight
god endymion, tem, zeus
pert. acronic(al), crepuscular, occasive
reflection alpenglow
state arizona, oregon
SUNSHADE awning, brisesoleil, parasol, roundel, sombrero, tiresol, visor, umbrella
SUNSHINE cheerful(ness), happiness, joy, light, prosperous, sunburst, sunniness, warmth
state florida, new mexico, south dakota
SUNSPOT cloud, facula, flaw, freckle, lucule, macula, penumbra, umbra
SUNSTONE amber, avertine, oligoclase
SUNSTROKE calenture, coup de soleil, heliosis, ictus, siriasis
SUNWEED spurge
SUNWISE clockwise, deasil, deiseal, dessil
SUOMI finland
SUP absorb, consume, dine, drink, eat, feed, liquor, mouthful, sip, snack, sope, sowp, spoonful, swallow
SUPAWN hasty pudding, mush, porridge, sepon
SUPER actor, excellent, extra, first rate, grand, janitor, square, superficial, superior, ultra, watch
SUPERABUNDANCE cataract, cornucopia, excess, flood, gobs, lots, overflow, plenty, plethora, prodigality, redundance, superfluity, surplus
SUPERABUNDANT exces-

sive, exuberant, lavish, luxuriant, overflowing, profuse, rank
SUPERANNUATE age, dismiss, outlast, overyear, pension, retire
SUPERANNUATED aged, anile, antiquated, decrepit, obsolete, old(fogy), out-of-date, passe, retired, senile, stale, stodgy, stuffy
SUPERB colossal, divine, good, grand, elegant, excellent, exquisite, glorious, gorgeous, immense, imposing, lordly, magnificent, majestic, marvelous, noble, peerless, prime, rich, sensational, splendid, stately, sublime, sumptuous, superlative, terrific, tremendous, unrivaled, wonderful
SUPERCHERIE chicanery
SUPERCILIOUS arbitrary, arrogant, cavalier, contemptuous, disdainful, haughty, insolent, lordly, overbearing, proud, snobbish, snooty, toplofty, vain(glorious)
SUPERCILIUM eyebrow, fil(1)et, lintel
SUPERCRESCENT parasitic
SUPERDUPER great, marvelous, wow
SUPEREGO censor, conscience, scruple
SUPEREROGATORY excessive, extreme, free, gratuitous, independent, nonessential, overdone, spare, superfluous, uncalled-for, wanton
SUPERFICIAL apparent, artificial, bird's-eye, careless, casual, cursory, dilettante, dull, empiric(al), empty, exterior, external, facile, flimsy, formal, frivolous, frothy, glib, hasty, hollow, immature, insincere, left-handed, light, magaziny, perfunctory, sciolistic, shallow, silly, simple, slapdash, slight, small, sophomoric, surface, thin, trivial, uncritical, weak
SUPERFINE choice, de luxe, elect, elite, excellent, extra, nice, plush, prime, rich, superior
SUPERFLUITY embellishment, excess, excrescence, extravagance, fat, fluther, frill, frippery, gingerbread,

luxury, overflow, overplus, padding, plethora, prodigality, redundancy, surfeit, surplus

SUPERFLUOUS abnormal, de trop, dispensable, excessive, exorbitant, extra, futile, inessential, lavish, luxus, needless, over, profuse, redundant, spare, supererogatory, surplus, uncalled-for, unnecessary, useless, wasteful, worthless

SUPERHET radio

SUPERHUMAN d(a)emon, divine, extraordinary, herculean, lemurian, miraculous, powerful, puissant, supernatural, titanic, yaktavian

SUPERIMPOSE add, applique, cover, lay, overlay, surprint

SUPERINTEND administer, boss, conduct, conn, control, direct, guide, lead, oversee, preside, regulate, run, supervise

SUPERINTENDENT baleboosteh, baleboss, boss, caporal, captain, caretaker, director, ephor(us), foreman, gaffer, ganger, inspector, intendant, manager, overman, overseer, principal, supervisor, surveyor, swingman, taskmaster, veneur

SUPERIOR abbess, above, ace, a-one, arrogant, assuming, best, better, blue ribbon, boss, capital, cardinal, chief(tain), classy, condescending, cream, director, dominant, domineering, duce, excellent, exceptional, expert, extra, fine(r), forby(e), foreby(e), giltedged, golden, good, grander, great(er), guardian, head, higher(up), larger, leader, liege, mahant, meritorious, mistress, over, palmary, paramount, patronizing, peerless, preeminent, preferable, ranking, select, senior, singular, snobbish, sovereign, splendid, sterling, superb, supercilious, supreme, tops, ultra, upper
lake shining big seawater

SUPERIORITY advantage, ascendency, drop, edge, em-

inence, excellence, gree, height, lead, mastery, odds, power, precedence, predominance, priority, prowess, pull, rank, supremacy
position of domination

SUPERLATIVE acme, apex, banner, best, capital, consummate, crashing, elative, exaggerated, excessive, exorbitant, greatest, highest, incomparable, olympian, optimum, peak, peerless, raving, smashing, splendid, sublime, superior, supreme, surpassing, swinging, transcendent, unexcelled, unsurpassed
absolute elative
comb. est

SUPERMAN triton among the minnows

SUPERNAL celestial, divine, ethereal, heavenly, high, towering

SUPERNATURAL abnormal, d(a)emonic, divine, ethereal, ghostly, hyperphysical, immaterial, incorporeal, magic(al), marvelous, metaphysical, miraculous, numinous, occult, other-worldly, psychic, spectral, spirit-like, spiritual, theurgic, transmundane, unearthly, unworldly, wraith-like, wraithy
being angel, atua, banshee, banshie, bugaboo, d(a)emon, elf(in), fairie, fairy, genie, ghost, ghoul, god, goddess, gremlin, harpy, incubus, jinn(ee), leprechaun, ouphe, spector, spirit, sylph, troll, vampire, wraith
force wakanda

SUPERNUMERARY additional, extra, spare, substitute, superfluous, surplus

SUPERSCRIBE address, direct, mark, write

SUPERSCRIPT superior

SUPERSEDE abandon, annul, defer, desert, discontinue, displace, forbear, omit, override, postpone, refrain, replace, repudiate, spurn, stay, substitute, succeed, supplant, suspend, void

SUPERSTITION aberglaube, fetish, freet, freit, idolatry, magic, shibboleth, voodoo

pert. goetic

SUPERSTITIOUS excessive, freity, idolatrous, magical, punctilious, scrupulous

SUPERVENE add, annex, append, conjoin, ensue, follow, succeed

SUPERVISE administer, boss, chaperone, control, govern, guide, handle, inspect, overlook, oversee, peruse, read, SUPERINTEND, survey

SUPERVISION auspices, care, charge, check, control, direction, eye, jurisdiction, management, oversight, surveillance

SUPERVISOR alytarch, boss, censor, chief, curator, custodian, deskman, director, ephor, floorman, foreman, guide, head, inspector, leachman, manager, master, monitor, onlooker, operator, overseer, proctor, roadmaster, spectator, SUPERINTENDENT, teacher

SUPINE abed, apathetic, careless, couchant, dormant, drowsy, dull, flat, horizontal, idle, inactive, indolent, inert, languid, lazy, lethargic, listless, otiose, passive, prone, prostrate, reclining, recumbent, servile, slothful, slow, sluggish, thoughtless, torpid

SUPPER cuddy, dinner, feed, meal, paschal, sucker, toper
eating coenaculous
pert. cenatory
room cenacle

SUPPLANT crowd out, dismiss, displace, eject, eradicate, expel, extirpate, follow, oust, overthrow, remove, replace, substitute, succeed, supersede, trip, undermine, uproot, upset, usurp

SUPPLANTER *name meaning* jacob, jake, james, jim(my)

SUPPLE agile, bain, complacent, complaisant, compliant, cunning, elastic, fawning, flexible, gentle, limber, lingy, lissom(e), lithe, mollify, nimble, obsequious, oily, plastic, pliable, pliant, resilient, responsive, salve, slamp, sly, soft(en), soothe, springe, springy, submissive, swack, swanky, swiple, wandle, yielding

SUPPLEJACK cane, clematis, kareao, rattan, soapwort

SUPPLEMENT accessory, add(enda), addition, additive, adjunct, annex, appendage, appendix, bolster, codicil, complement, eke, enhance, heighten, improve, intensify, mend, postscript, rider, sequel, tack

SUPPLEMENTARY additional, auxiliary, subsidiary

SUPPLIANT, SUPPLICANT asker, beggar, begging, beseeching, petitioner, pleader, solicitous

SUPPLICATE adjure, appeal, ask, beg, beseech, conjure, crave, entreat, implore, importune, invoke, obsecrate, obtest, petition, plead, pray, request, solicit, sue

SUPPLICATION appeal, ave, craving, entreaty, litany, obtestation, petition, plea, pleading, prayer, request, rogative, solicitation, suffrage, suppliance, vow

SUPPLIER caterer, commissary, furnisher, provider, provisioner, purser, purveyor, quartermaster, source, steward, sutler, victualer

SUPPLIES cache, duffel, estovers, etape, food, gear, goods, ordnance, possessions, provisions, stock, stores, stuff

SUPPLY accommodate, administer, advance, afford, aid, amount, assets, assistance, backlog, capital, cater, dispense, donate, dose, endow, endue, equip(ment), feed, fill, fit, foison, fortify, fret, fund, furnish, give, grist, help, issue, layout, load, means, minister, money, outfit, plenty, prescribe, provide, provision, quantity, reinforce, relay, relief, relieve, reservoir, resource(s), satisfy, spread, staple, stock, store, stuff, substitute, succor, support, temporary, tend, trove, underwrite, well, yield

abundant cornucopia

extra reserve, surplus

hidden cache, hoard

inexhaustible widow's cruse

reserve cushion

rich argosy, bonanza, eldorado

sufficient competence

SUPPORT (See also *kind,* below.) 3 aid, arm, bed, peg, tie 4 abet, arch, back, bank, base, beam, bear, buoy, dade, fend, firm, help, hold, keep, limb, meat, pier, prop, rest, rock, trig, urge 5 appui, asset, atlas, basis, board, brace, carry, cheer, favor, frame, manna, stave, stell, stipe, strut, vouch 6 afford, assist, barrow, bridge, cradle, crutch, defend, endure, living, pillar, pillow, second, shield, steady, timber, uphold, upkeep 7 advance, backing, bearing, bolster, bracket, bulwark, care for, cherish, comfort, confirm, consent, cushion, endorse, finance, fulcrum, further, nourish, nurture, promote, protect, provide, stiffen, sustain 8 approval, buttress, champion, handrail, holdfast, keystone, mainstay, maintain, preserve, reliance, sanction, sepiment, shoulder, sympathy, underpin 9 encourage, grubstake, patronage, patronize, promotion, provision, reinforce, sustinent, vindicate 10 livelihood, permission, strengthen, sustenance, underwrite 11 corroborate, countenance, endorsement, nourishment, subsistence 12 underpinning 13 encouragement

architectural corbel

kind backrest, baluster, bandage, block, brace, buck, easel, floor, frame, framing, fulcrum, guy, heel, hod, jackstay, lap, leg, pedestal, ratline, rib, scaffold, shoe, shroud, skid, splint, staff, stand, stay, stilt, strut, trestle, tripod, trivet

1-legged unipod

partisan barrack

principal backbone

refuse to bolt

slab planch, tray

slight toehold

spike brob

statue pedestal, socle

surgical brace, sling, truss

3-legged tripod, trivet

triangular a-frame

upright jamb, pile, poppet, post, stud

SUPPORTER abettor, adherent, advocate, angel, apostle, associate, backer, booster, champion, cohort, devotee, disciple, enthusiast, espouser, exponent, fan, favorite, follower, garter, henchman, mainstay, partisan, patron, promoter, protagonist, rooter, satrap, second(er), sectary, suspender, sympathizer, upholder, votary, well wisher

comb. crat, ist, ite

SUPPOSE accept, allow, apprehend, assume, believe, calculate, conceive, conclude, conjecture, consider, daresay, deduce, deem, devise, divine, dream, expect, fancy, feel, gather, guess, hold, imagine, imply, incline, infer, intention, judge, opine, posit, predicate, presume, pretend, reckon, repute, say, see, speculate, substitute, surmise, suspect, suspicion, take, theorize, think, trow, understand, ween, wis

SUPPOSED alleged, assumed, conjectural, doubtful, hypothetical, mooted, postulated, presumed, putative, questionable, reputed, **SUPPOSITITIOUS,** surmised, tentative

SUPPOSING altho(ugh), assuming, granting, in case, what if

SUPPOSITION assumption, belief, condition, conjecture, guess(work), hint, hypothesis, idea, implication, impression, inkling, intimation, notion, opinion, postulate, premise, shot, suggestion, supposal, surmise, theory, thesis, view, weening

SUPPOSITITIOUS artificial, assumed, conjectural, fabulous, feigned, hypothetical, illegitimate, illusory, imaginary, putative, reputed, spurious

SUPPRESS arrest, ban, blanket, bottle up, burke, calm, cancel, censor, check, choke, compress, conceal, conquer, cork, crush, cushion, elide, extinguish, forbid, harass, hide, hold in, hush up, inhibit, interrupt, kibosh, kill, lay, leash, moderate, muffle, oppress, overpower, overwhelm, prohibit, put down, quash, quell, quench, ravish, repress, restrain, restrict, smore, smother, squash, squelch, stamp(out), stifle, stop, strangle, subdue, throttle, vanquish, withhold

SUPPRESSION abeyance, abreaction, blackout, blockage, censorship, concealment, control, destruction, elision, fall, inhibition, overthrow, repression, restraint, sublimation

SUPPERATE beal, fester, rankle, ripen, run, weep, wheal

SUPPURATION bealing, boil, coction, diapyesis, matter, pus, pyosis
pert. pyoid

SUPPURATIVE digerent, festering, maturative, purulent, pussy, rankling

SUPREMACY ascendancy, authority, autocracy, control, dominion, headship, influence, mastery, overrule, predominance, preeminence, sovereignty, sway, transcendence
maritime thalassocracy

SUPREME absolute, ace, acme, almighty, best, big, capital, cardinal, chief, crucial, dominant, final, fine, first, foremost, good, great(est), high(est), immense, imperial, important, last, leading, loftiest, magnificent, marvelous, maximal, maximum, meritorious, noble, out of this world, paramount, peerless, preeminent, prime, pure gold, sovereign, special, splendid, stately, sterling, sublime, superb, superior, superlative, terrific, top (drawer), topnotch, transcendent, ultimate, utmost, wonderful
being allah, creator, deity, god, monad
god See GOD *supreme.*
power destiny moros
SUQ bazaar, market, sook

SUR south, tyre
SURCEASE abate, cessation, desist, end, lull, relief, respite, rest, stay, stop
SURCHARGE attack, burden, fill, impost, load, overburden, overcrowd, overload, pack, sate, surfeit, tax, weigh down
SURCINGLE band, belt, cincture, girdle, girth, roller, wanty
SURCOAT cyclas, jupon, kabaya
SURD atonic, deaf, insensate, irrational, mute, radical, senseless, sharp, soften, voiceless
SURE actual, assured, authentic, believing, betrothed, bound, certain(ly), cold, confident, convinced, decided, definite, dependable, destined, dogmatic, enduring, fast, firm, indeed, indubitable, infallible, perfect, positive, promise, real, reliable, reliant, safe, sanguine, secure, sicker, stable, steadfast, steady, strong, true, trustworthy, unerring, unfailing, unfaltering, witter, yes
as death and taxes, fate
-fire certain, dependable, foolproof
-footed agile, secure, spry
SURELY assuredly, atweel, certainly, exactly, fine, firmly, indeed, necessarily, pardie, pardy, positively, really, redly, securely, undoubtedly, wis
SURETY assurance, aval, backer, bail(sman), bond (sman), caution, earnest, engager, gage, guarantee, guaranty, hostage, mainprise, patron, pawn, pledge, safety, security, soverty, sponsor, substitute, token, voucher
contract adpromission, aval, mandatum, sponsion
post bond
SURF breakers, foam, kalema, ocean, sea, spray, swell, waves
boat catamaran
coot scoter
duck coot, scoter
fish alfiona, perch
plant cumaphyte

scoter blossom-bill, boxcoot, pishang, skunktop, surfer
shiner sparada
sound of roar, rote, rut, surge
snipe sanderling
SURFACE apparent, appear, area, arise, blanket, crop out, covering, emerge, envelop, expanse, exterior, face(t), finish, flare up, ground, materialize, meros, nap(pe), outside, pave, plane, plat, rise, shallow, side, skin, stretch, superficial, superficies, texture, top, veneer
comb. plano
configuration topography
curved belly, bulge
dull mat(te)
flat aequor, area, bed, floor, lateral, orlo, pagina, plane, sheet, slab
geometrical conicoid, conoid, cylinder, helicoid, nappe, sphere, tore, toroid
grooved drove
growing on epigenous
hairy nap
inclined cant, descent, ramp, shelving
inner lining
mellowed patina
pert. acrotic, areal, facial, obverse, reverse
plane area, facet
rising above emersed
rough crizzle, stubble
rounded concavity, convexity, lap
small areola, facet
toward ectad
uneven accidented
SURFEIT acrasia, agrote, choke, cloy, congest, cram, crowd, disgust, drench, dull, englut, excess(ive), extravagant, feed, flood, glut, gorge, indulge, intemperate, jade, nausea, nimiety, overdose, pack, pall, plethora, plus, sate, satiate, satiety, satisfy, saturate, sicken, sog, stuff, superfluity
SURFEITED blase, complete, jaded, replete, sated, satiated, sick, stuffed, weary
SURFER patchhead
SURGE arise, ascend, billow, breaker, din, eddy, flow, fountain, growth, gurgitate, gush, jet, mount, pour, ripple, rise, roller, rush,

slacken, slip, soar, source, spring, spurt, swell, tide, tower, wave, whirl

SURGEON (See also MEDICAL and MEDICINE references.) doctor, leech, medico, physician, sawbones
appliance brace, cast, crutch, splint, tampon, tourniquet, truss
compress stupe
drainage tube can(n)ula
dressing cast
file xyster
gauze carbasus
instrument abaptiston, ablator, acus, ankylomele, aspirator, bilabe, bistoury, can(n)ula, catheter, catlin(g), curet(te), cystoscope, drain, ecraseur, fleam, forceps, goosebill, gorget, hemostat, hypodermic, lance(t), leucotome, levator, ligator, microscope, needle, osteoclast, otoscope, pincette, pipette, plessor, probe, rongeur, scala, scalpel, speculum, sphenotribe, stethoscope, stiletto, stylet, syringe, tenaculum, tent, terebellum, torcular, trepan, trephine, trilabe, trocar, tweezers, vectis, vulsellum, xyster
operation resect(ion)
oral stomalogist
puncture centesis
stitch seton, suture
stylet trocar
thread seton

SURGEONFISH acanthurus, barber(o), doctor, medico, sawbones, tang(e)

SURGERY ablation, aciurgy, amputation, biopsy, excision, incision, knife, operation, resection, section
comb. cenosis, chirurgia, ectomy
perform amputate, excise, operate, reduce, resect, section, trepan
specialty anaplasty, orthopedics, plastic, prosthetics

SURGICAL See SURGEON.

SURICATE meerkat, zenick

SURINAM *animal* hyahya
basket pegall
canoe corial
capital paramaribo
cherry pitanga
drink paiwari
fish arapaima
former name dutch guiana

hut benab
indian urukuena
indian woman buckeen
measure ketting
people boni, boschneger, djuka
toad pipa(l)
tree acuyari, bethabara, dal(l)i, genip, icica, lana, mora, quassia
waterfall kaiteur

SURLY abrupt, arrogant, badtempered, bluff, blunt, boorish, chuff, churlish, clumse, crabbed, cranky, cross, crusty, doggish, dour, gloomy, glum, grouchy, gruff, grumpy, gurl(y), haughty, illtempered, irritable, menacing, morose, snappish, snarly, sour, sulky, sullen, testy, touchy, uncivil, unkind, waspish
as a bear

SURMISE allegation, assume, assumption, charge, conceive, conclude, conclusion, conjecture, consider, deduce, deem, fancy, gather, guess, hypothesis, imagine, infer(ence), jalouse, judge, mistrust, opine, presume, presumption, scent, speculation, suppose, supposition, suspect, suspicion, theory, think, weening

SURMOUNT ascend, beat, cap, climb, conquer, crown, culminate, defeat, exceed, excel, hurdle, lick, master, mount, negotiate, outtop, overcome, overgo, overthrow, pass, reduce, rise, rout, scale, subdue, surpass, top, total, tower, transcend, triumph, vanquish, vault, win

SURNAME agnomen, appellation, cognomen, eponym, nickname, patronym(ic), sobriquet

SURPASS amend, antecede, atrede, beat, best, better, cap, cop, cote, dominate, eclipse, exceed, excel, flog, foil, outclass, outdo, outrank, outreach, outsoar, outstrip, outvie, overdo, overtop, SURMOUNT, top, transcend, whap

SURPLICE chrisom, cotta, ephod, pelisse, vestment

SURPLUS additional, balance, epact, excess, extra,

glut, leftover, lumber, over(age), overrun, plenty, plethora, prodigality, remainder, reserve, residue, rest, spare, superabundance, superavit, superfluity, surfeit

SURPRISE alarm, amaze(ment), ambush, astonish, astound, attack, awe, befuddle, bewilder, bombshell, cap(ture), catch, confound, consternate, cop, counterturn, dazzle, detect, disconcert, dumfound, faze, flabbergast, gloppen, nab, nonplus, overcome, overwhelm, perplex, rattle, scare, seize, shock, sneak, startle, strike, stupefy, uncover, waylay, wonder(ment)
exclamation babai, crimine, criminy, gip, gorblimy, gramercy, heavens, hein, heugh, hoo(ch), hunh, juckies, lack, law(ks), lord, odso, suz, tck, wow, zounds

SURPRISING astonishing, awesome, extraordinary, ferlie, striking, unexpected, unlookedfor

SURQUIDRY arrogance, folly, insolence, presumption, pride, wantonness

SURRA(H) anemia

SURREALISM *founder* dali
painter ernst
source dada
style abstract expressionism

SURRENDER abandon(ment), abdicate, addict, back down, bow, buckle, capitulate, capitulation, cave(in), cede, cess(ion), consign, dedition, deliver(y), forgo, forsake, give(up)(way), hand over, kamerad, leave, quit, recede, recession, release, relinquish(ment), remise, remit, render, renounce, renunciation, resign, sacrifice, submission, submit, tender, waive, withdraw, yield

SURREPTION fraud, lapse, misrepresentation, slip, temptation

SURREPTITIOUS bootleg, clandestine, concealed, covert, deceitful, deceptive, furtive, hidden, occult, privy, secret, slinking, sly, sneaky, stealthy, underhand(ed)

SURREY carriage

ornament fringe
section kew
SURROGATE delegate, deputy, replacement, stopgap, subrogate, substitute
SURROUND ambush, band, bar, begird, beleaguer, belt, beset, besiege, blockade, border, bound, brace, cincture, circle, circumfuse, circumscribe, cloister, close, compass, corral, edging, embay, embosom, embrace, encase, encircle, enclasp, enclose, encompass, enfold, engird, enswathe, entrench, envelop, environ, enwrap, flood, fold, gird(le), hedge(in), hem(in), impale, inarm, inclose, infold, inundate, involve, loop, overflow, ring, sphere, swathe, wrap, wreathe
comb. peri
with water enisle
SURROUNDED amid(st), among, bounded, circumfluous, embayed, encircled, encompassed, girt, mid(st)
SURROUNDING(S) ambiance, ambient, amplectant, around, beset(ting), circumjacent, entourage, environment, environs, midst, milieu, neighborhood, range, roundabout, scene, zone
SURT(R) *kingdom* muspelheim, muspellsheim
victim frey
SURTOUT barvar(o)y, cloak, coat, hood, mantle, overcoat
SURVEILLANCE examination, observation, oversight, recon(naissance), scrutiny, stakeout, supervision
SURVEY behold, canvass, consider, conspectus, descry, digest, discern, espy, examination, examine, history, inspect(ion), look, lustrate, map, measure, note, notice, observe, outline, overlook, perceive, peruse, plan, plot, poll, precis, probe, prospect, range, reconnaissance, regard, remark, review, scan, scrutinize, scrutiny, search, see (ing), sketch, study, traverse, treatment, view, vista
SURVEYING geodesy, gromatics

map topo
measurer stratameter
mine latching
nail spad
pert. gromatic
pin arrow
technique backsight, resection
term target
tool alidad(e), caliper, level, odolite, perambulator, rod, setup, stadia, stratameter, tachymeter, theodolite, transit, vernier
SURVEYOR arpenteur, bolo, chainman, clashee, clashy, dial(l)er, gromatic, levelman, lineman, poleman, rodman
SURVIVAL durability, endurance, leftover, outliving, relic(t)
science ecology
SURVIVE abide, continue, endure, exist, last, live, outlast, outlive, outwear, persist, recover, remain, resist, stand, stay, subsist, withstand
SUS ben(e), boar
SUSA *eunuch* gabatha, tharra
founder memnon
inhabitant elamite
SUSAN *blackeyed* coneflower
SUSANNA *defender* daniel
father kilkiah
husband joachim, joakim
SUSANOO, SUSANOWO *daughter* suserihime
harp koto
parent izanagi, izanami
peaceful soul nigimitama
province izumo
sister amaterasu
sword kusanagi
temple atsuta
wicked soul aramitama
SUSCEPTIBILITY capacity, emotion, exposure, feeling, frailty, openness, sensibility, sensitivity, susceptivity
excessive allergy, anaphylaxis
SUSCEPTIBLE allergic, disposed, docile, exposed, feeling, impressionable, inclined, liable, open, patient, pliable, pliant, predisposed, prone, receptive, responsive, sensible, sensitive, softhearted, subject, tolerant, unguarded, unresistant
SUSLIK sisel, spermophile, squirrel

SUSPECT believe, chastise, conjecture, defendant, disbelieve, discredit, distrust(ed), doubt(ed), doubtful, dubious, fancy, guess, heed, hold, jalouse, misdeem, misdoubt, mistrust (ed), note, questionable, respect, suppose, surmise, suspicious, think
SUSPEND adjourn, arrest, bar, batten, blackball, check, condition, continue, dangle, debar, defer, delay, depend, depose, disbar, dismiss, eject, exclude, expel, halt, hang, hinder, hold, intermit, interrupt, oust, overhang, pend(ent), postpone, retard, shut, sist, sling, stay, stop, swing, withhold
SUSPENDED halted, hanging, hovering, hung, inactive, inert, latent, pendant, pendent, pendulous, pensile, poised, tabled
SUSPENDER(S) braces, gallows, galluses, garter, gibbet, hanger, hook, knob, nail, peg, pothook, ring, spar, strap, supporter
SUSPENSE abeyance, alarm, anticipation, anxiety, apprehension, demur, doubt, expectancy, hesitation, impatience, indecision, pause, poise, stagnation, uncertainty, vacillation, waiting
in pending
SUSPENSION abeyance, armistice, breach, break, cessation, cloture, continuance, cutoff, delay, emulsion, halt, hint, infusion, intermission, interruption, pause, recess, respite, rest, shutdown, sist, stay, stop (page), tabling
SUSPICION apprehension, cynicism, dash, distrust, doubt, dubiety, envy, guess, hear, hint, idea, impression, incredulity, inkling, intimation, jealousy, misgiving, mistrust, non-belief, notion, premonition, shade, skepticism, soupcon, strain, streak, suggestion, supposition, surmise, tincture, tinge, touch, trace, umbrage, uncertainty, vein
free from absolve, acquit,

clear, exculpate, exonerate, purge

SUSPICIOUS distrustful, doubtful, doubting, dubious, farfetched, fishy, incredulous, jealous, leary, leery, peery, queer, quizzical, shady, skeptical, smoky, suspect, unbelieving, wary

SUSPICIOUSLY askance

SUSPIRE breathe, respire, sigh

SUSQUEHANNA conestoga
city on binghampton, endicott, harrisburg

SUSTAIN abet, abide, advocate, aid, assist, back, bear, buoy, carry, confirm, console, continue, convey, endure, experience, extend, feed, foster, hold, keep, lengthen, maintain, nourish, nurture, preserve, prolong, prop, protract, retain, sprag, stay, strengthen, succor, suffer, support, tolerate, undergo, uphold, upstay

SUSTENANCE aliment, bread, foison, food, gear, keep, livelihood, living, maintenance, nourishment, nutriment, pabulum, relief, support

SUSU congo, dolphin, fish, gerip, gutta, platanist, soo-soo

SUSURRATE murmur, rustle, sough, whisper

SUTLER provant, provisioner, supplier, vendor, vivandiere
shop canteen, commissary

SUTRA adage, aphorism, precept, rule, scripture

SUTTEE concremation, cremation, immolation, sacrifice, sati, suicide

SUTTER *estate* new helvetia

SUTTUNG *kin* bangi, gunnlod

SUTURE arthrosis, articulation, harmony, joint, junction, pterion, raphe, seam, seton, sew(ing), stitch, union

SUZERAIN khedive, liege, lord, magnate, nobleman, overlord, paramount, potentate, sovereign

SVAHA *husband* agni

SVARGA heaven, paradise

SVAYAMBHUVA *father* brahma

SVELT lissome, lithe, slender, slim, smooth, sylphlike, thin, trim, willowy

SVERIGE sweden

SVIZZERA See SWITZERLAND.

SWAB boor, brush, clean, clown, epaulet, lout(ish), lubber, malkin, mop, oaf, officer, patch, peasant, plunger, reel, sponge, squigee, sway, wash, wipe(r)
-like device badger

SWABBLE reel, rod, SQUABBLE, swash, sway

SWACK beat, blow, cast, drink, fall, intoxicate, nimble, pliant, shrewd, slippery, strike, supple, thrash, throw, treacherous, whack

SWACKING big, large, robust, whacking

SWAD bumpkin, clown, coal, crowd, lump, mass, piece, pod, shell, soldier

SWADDLE band(age), beat, bind, clothe, cudgel, dress, muffle, restrict, swathe, sweel, wrap

SWAG bag, bluey, blusterer, boodle, booty, brag, bundle, cant, fall, festoon, flourish, hang, hollow, inclination, incline, knapsack, list, loot, lucre, lurch, matilda, money, oscillate, pillage, plunder, pool, prize, sag, shiralee, sink, spoils, strut, sway, swing, tip

SWAGE assuage, border, boss, dolly, flatter, groove, jumper, moderate, mouth, shaper, swedge, tool, upset

SWAGGER air, arrogance, bluster, boast, bounce, brag(gadoccio), bravado, brave, bridle, bristle, bully, crow, cuttle, dashing, domineer, fanfaronade, flourish, gauster, hector, lurch, ostentation, pace, panache, parade, peacockery, prance, put on the dog, quarrel, roister, scold, sprose, stagger, strut, stylish, swank, swash(buckle), swell, vaunt
stick See STAFF.

SWAGGERER bantomcock, blimp, boaster, braggart, bucko, cuttle, fanfaron, huff, peacock, pistol, pre-

tender, ruffler, strutter, swanker, swashbuckler

SWAGGERING blustering, huffcap, strutting, swashbuckling, tearcat, thrasonical

SWAGMAN bum, drummer, fence, hobo, stiff, sundowner, tramp, vagabond, whaler
bundle bluey

SWAIN admirer, beau, boy, colin, cuddy, damon, flame, gallant, lad, lover, peasant, rustic, servant, shepherd, spark, squire, strephon, suitor, youth

SWALE board, coolness, lath, marsh, plank(ing), shade, slash, sway, swing, swirl, valley

SWALLOW absorb, accept, arundel, bear, believe, bird, bolt, consume, destroy, devour, digest, disregard, down, drink, eat, endure, engorge, engulf, esophagus, fall for, gobbet, gobble, gullet, gulp, guzzle, hirondelle, imbibe, ingest, ingurgitate, lap, martin, pigeon, progne, recant, resorb, retract, sip, stomach, strip, supress, swelly, swift, take, throat, tolerate, witchuck
changed into chelidon, procne
fish gurnard, trigla
genus delichon, hirundo, progne
heraldic martlet
hurriedly bolt, (en)gorge, gulch, swill
inability to aglutition, aphagia
noisy slurp
pert. hirundine
plover pratincole
up destroy, devour, gulf, swamp
whole flapdragon

SWALLOWING deglutation, glutition
difficulty dysphagia

SWALLOWPIPE gullet, windpipe

SWALLOWTAIL butterfly, papilio, troilus

SWAMI guru, pundit, sage

SWAMP avalanch, bog, crowd, defeat, deluge, empty, engulf, entangle, fen, flat, flood, hollow, lerna, letch, MARSH,

mire, morass, overflow, overwhelm, quagmire, satiate, saturate, sink, slender, slew, sloo, slough, slue, strand, submerge, submerse, sump, surfeit, swale, swang, terai, thin, urman, vlei, vley, wham, whelm, whin
angel thrush
coastal dismal
cottonwood liar
cypress ahuehuete
deer barasingha
dismal pocosin
dogwood buttonbush, cornel, hoptree
fever anemia, malaria
fox francis marion
gas methane, miasma
grass See GRASS *marsh.*
growing in uliginose
hen coot, gallinule, sultanabird
hickory bitternut, pignut
holly bearberry
honeysuckle azalea
hornbeam tupelo
loosestrife peatweed, peatwood
mahogany gunnung
maple box-elder
milkweed dagga
moss sphagnum
oak beefwood, viminaria
orchid snakemouth
ore limonite
pine loblolly
plant cowbane, sola
robin chewink, thrush
squawweed ragwort
sunflower sneezeweed
tree alder, cypress
turnip jack-in-the-pulpit
SWAMPLAND (See also SWAMP.) maremma, muskeg, slash, tundra
SWAMPY boggy, callow, fenny, marshy, moorish, paludal, peaty, poachy, puxy, quashy, queachy, slumpy, spongy, uliginal, uliginous, uvid
cree maskegon
SWAN bird, cob, cygnet, cygnus, declare, elk(e), hooper, northern cross, olor, pen, swear, whooper
bill knob berry
changed into cycnus, jupiter
female pen
flower cycnoches, orchid, swanwort
group bank, game, mark, wedge

-like cygneous
male cob
marking upping
mythological hansa
of avon shakespeare
of cambray fenelon
of eternity hansa
of mantua virgil
of meander homer
river daisy brachycome
star group in milky way
symbol of grace
tail deneb
wild elk(e), hooper, trumpeter
young cygnet
SWANHILD *parent* gudrun, siegfried, sigurd
SWANK active, airs, chic, display, energetic, grandstand, peacock, prance, put on, show off, splurge, stalk, strapping, strut, swagger, swashbuckle, swell
SWANKY active, dashing, limber, lush, luxurious, ostentatious, post, pretentious, rich, smart, stylish, supple, swash
SWAP bandy, bang, bargain, barter, beat, beat, change, cheat, chop, devour, dicker, dismiss, exchange, fall, fire, flop, interchange, pounce, replace, resemble, strike, stroke, swallow, swoop, swop, thrash, trade, truck
SWAPPING big, huge, swooping, whopping
SWARD grass, lawn, rind, skin, sod, swarf, swarth, turf
SWARM abound, assemble, band, bevy, bike, cast, climb, cloud, collection, congregate, crowd, drove, flight, flock, flush, GROUP, herd, hive, horde, infest, jam, migrate, mob, mount, move, multitude, nest, pack, press, rabble, quantity, shin, shoal, snarl, snee, sny, swarve, teem, throng, troop
up ascend, climb, mount
with abound
SWARMING alive, bustling, crawling, crowded, issuing, migrating, packed, teeming
SWART baneful, black(en), blighting, dark, dismal, dun, gloomy, heinous, malignant, swarthy
SWARTHY bistered, bistred, black, dark, dun, dusky,

grimy, moory, morian, murky, swart, tawny
SWASH blow, bluster, cast, channel, clash, dash, drum, fuddled, hogwash, lash, moisten, ripple, soft, sound, splashy, sprinkle, squashy, strike, swabble, swagger, swanky, swatch, swill, wash
SWASHBUCKLER bravo, daredevil, gascon, rogue, ruffian, slasher, soldier, swaggerer, swank
SWASHY insipid, squashy, watery, weak
SWASTIKA charm, cross, fylfot, gammadion, hakenkreuzler, hooked cross, insignia, symbol, talisman, tetraskelion
SWAT ale, blow, clobber, clout, cuff, dehgan, drink, hit, moslem, punch, slap, slug, smite, squat, strike, swot, wallop, wort
SWATH band, crop, reach, row, skin, staddle, strip, stripe, sward, sweep, swipe, trace, track, windrow
SWATHE band(age), bind, bond, clothe, confine, dress, encircle, enfold, envelop, fetter, fold, furl, integument, lap, path, shackle, surround, swaddle, swarf, SWATH, windrow, wrap
SWATTER hitter, scatter, squander, squatter, splash
SWATTLE dissipate, gulp, guzzle, squander
SWAY affect, ascendancy, authority, bias, careen, carry, change, control, convince, deflect(ion), deviate, direct, divert, dominance, dominate, dominion, fall, flap, flounder, fluctuate, govern (ment), guide, hoist, inclination, incline, induce, influence, lean, move, oppress, oscillate, pendulate, persuade, pitch, power, predispose, rock, roll, rotation, rule, shoggie, sovereignty, swabble, sweep, swing, totter, undulate, vacillate, veer, wabble, waver, wield, wobble, yaw
-back lordosis, renguera, warfa
SWAZILAND *city* manzini, mbabane
coin lilangen
founder mswazi, sobhuza

king kbe, ngwe, nyama, sobhuza
language siswati
river komati, mhlatuze, umbuluzi, usutu
SWEAL burn, melt, scorch, singe, waste
SWEAR abuse, affirm, assert, asseverate, attest, aver, avow, bedamn, blaspheme, covenant, curse, damn, declare, dejerate, depone, depose, engage, execrate, invoke, objure, pledge, plight, promise, snum, swow, testify, threaten, vow, vum, warrant
at attack, clash, curse, disagree
by guarantee, rely on, trust
falsely forswear, perjure, rap, slander
for guarantee
off abandon, abstain, forswear, give up, renounce
solemnly dejerate
to secrecy tile
word curse, expletive, oath, profanity
SWEARING blasphemy, cursing, juration, profanity
false perjury
SWEAT bead, bleed, chafe, chuck(a)luck, eject, extort, extract, exude, ferment, fleece, grill, heat, impatience, labor, life(blood), mador, ooze, oppress, overwork, parboil, pawn, perspiration, perspire, pledge, plug, putrefy, shakes, soldier, stew, sudate, sudor, suffer, swelter, swivvet, task, toil, transude, work
abnormal dysidrosis
bath sauna
comb. hidro
excessive hidrosis
foul brom(h)idrosis, osmidrosis
out await, extract, produce
pert. hidrotic, puggy, sudatory, sudoric, sudorous, temescal
-producing diaphoretic, sudoriferous, sudorific
production hidropoiesis
room sauna, sudatorium, turkish bath
SWEATER bolero, bulky, cardigan, gansey, jersey, knittie, pullover, shell, shvitzer, slipon, slipover, sloppy-joe, sweatshirt, top-

per, t-shirt, turtleneck, windbreaker, woolie, woolly
SWEATWEED marshmallow
SWEATY clammy, drenched, laborious, moist, odorous, perspiring, perspiry, puggy, sudoric, sudorous, toilsome
SWEDEN, SWEDISH sverige
actress liv ullman
army landstorm
army conscripts varnpliktige
artist zorn
astronomer angstrom, celsius
auto volvo
battle lund, pultowa
beer dragol
bird, sacred stork
bodyguard drabant
botanist bromel, fresia, linnaeus
buffet smorgasbord
canal gota
capital stockholm
cheese fontina, jarlberg
chemist arrhenius, berzelius, scheele, svedberg, theorell
city arvika, boden, boras, edane, eskilstuna, falkoping, falun, gavle, goteborg, gottenburg, halsingborg, jonkoping, kuruna, linkoping, ludvika, lulea, lund, malmo, norrkoping, nykoping, orebro, pitea, solna, stockholm, umea, uppsala, vasteras, visby, ystad
clover alsike
coin carolin, krona, krone, ore, rigsdaler, skilling
county lan
dance polska
division amt, gotaland, jamtland, laen, lan, norrland, orebro, skane, swealand, uppsala
dramatist strindberg
drink aquavit
dynasty vasa
explorer hedin
farm thorp, torp
fruit cloudberry, hjortron
geographer hedin
giant gilly
god See AESIR and NORSE references.
guard, royal drabant
gulf bothnia
hero wasa
idiom suecism
inventor dalen, ericsson
island got(a)land, o(e)land
king bernadotte, eric, gustavus, oscar, wasa
lake asnen, dalalven, hiel-

mar, jhalmren, malar(en), siljan, ster, vaner(n), vatter(n), vener, wennen, wetter
language, ancient suiogothic
legislature andra-kammaren, diet, forsta, riksdag
liquor control bratt system
manual training sloyd
manufacturer nobel
match taendstikker
mathematician mittag-leffler
measure alar, aln, amar, carat, famn, fathom, fjarding, foder, fot, jumfru, kanna, kapp(e), kappland, kollast, koltunna, last, linje, mil, nymil, oxhuvud, ref, spann, stang, stop, tum, tun(n)land
merit order vasa
milk tatmjolk
money skilling
movie director ingmar bergman
nightingale jenny lind
nobel winner arrhenius
oculist gullstrand
patron god frey
patron saint eric
peak ammar, helags, ovniks, sarjek, sarv
philosopher ihre, swedenborg
physicist dalen
politician arnoldson
port gavle, goteborg, halmsted, halsinborg, lulea, malmo, norrkoping, pitea, stockholm, sundsvall, umea, visby
prime minister branting
province alvsborg, blekinge, elfsborg, gotland, halland, jamtland, kalmar, laen, lan, malmohus, orebro
queen christina
river angerman, dal, gota, kalix, klar, lainio, ljungan, ljusne, lulea, pitea, ranea, tornea, umea, windel
round hambo
scientist swedenborg
sculptor milles
soprano lind, nilsson
sour milk tatmjolk
state religion lutheran(ism)
statesman branting, erlander, essen
tenor bjo(e)rling
theologian soderblom
tokens polleten
tribe geatas
turnip rutabaga

weight ass, carat, centner, last, lispund, lod, mark, nylast, ort, shippound, skalpund, skeppund, sten
wine punch glogg
writer arnoldson, bellman, bergman, carlen, heidenstam, karlfeldt, lagerkvist, lagerlof, strindberg
SWEEP bend, besom, blank, broom, brush, carry, clean, clearance, coast, collect, command, compass, course, crumb, curve, cut, drive, dust(man), expanse, extent, gamut, gather, glide, graze, ken, knapweed, latitude, oar, onslaught, orbit, pillage, purlieu, range, reach, rustle, scavenger, scope, scoundrel, scour, space, speed, spread, strickle, suite, swath, swing, touch, trail, traverse, vacuum, whisk, whitewing, win, wipe
SWEEPBOARD strickle
SWEEPING all-embracing, broad, complete, comprehensive, deviation, general, indiscriminate, motley, rasant, thorough, vast, wholesale, wide
SWEEPINGS dust, fulvie, fulzie, fuzzguzzies, riffraff
SWEEPSTAKES ante, bet, lottery, race
SWEER indolent, loath, niggardly, reluctant, slothful, slow, swear
SWEET agreeable, ambrosial, bonny, candied, candy, caramel, cloying, confectionary, confit, darling, dear, delightful, dessert, douce, doux, dulce(t), easy, fresh, honey(ed), lieblich, lovely, luscious, mellifluent, mellifluous, mellow, melodious, musical, nice, pet, pleasant, pleasing, rich, saccharine, silken, sirupy, smooth, soft, sugarcoated, sugared, sugary, syrupy, winning, winsome
alyssum alison
as honey, sugar
bay beaverwood, brewster, hackberry, laurel, magnolia
betty soapwort
billy goldfinch
brown sugar penuche
calabash kuruba, passionflower
cassava aipi(m), manihot

cherry belladonna, blackchoke, burbank
cicely anise, myrrh
clover bokhara, lotus, melilot
coltsfoot bitterbur, lagwort
comb. gluco, hedy
cypress galingale
fennel finochio, florence
fish ayu, plecoglossus
flag acorus, araca, beewort, calamus, carminative, sedge, tonic
gale baybush, bogbean, buckbean, fleawood, gagel, galewort, gallbush, golden withy, myrica, myrtle
gum alligator tree, amber, bilsted, copalm, liquidambar, storax
hay camel-grass
marjoram oregano
nancy narcissus
orange china, chino
pea catgut, lathyrus, painted lady
pepperbush clethra, soapbush
pinesap beechdrops
potato batata, camote, kumara, manroot, ocarina, patat, yam
potato protein ipomoein
pudding bakewell
rush squinant
shrub spicebush
singer david
-smelling aromatic, fragrant, olent, redolent
-sounding mellifluent, mellifluous, mellow, melodious, merry
-sour agrodolce
spire itea, willow
susan catchfly
-talk butter, cajole, flatter, honeyfogle, persuade, softsoap
-tempered affable, agreeable, amiable, easy
trefoil melilot
violet blaver, fineleaf
walnut shagbark
william dianthus, goldfinch, pink, wren
SWEETBREAD bur(r), inchpin, pancreas, ris de veau, rusk, thymus
SWEETBRIAR bedeg(u)ar, eglantine, horse-bramble, rose
SWEETEN addulce, appease, bribe, cleanse, disinfect, dulcify, edulcorate, flatter,

freshen, mitigate, mollify, mull, purify, relieve, soften, solace, sugar
the pot ante, contribute
SWEETENER cyclamate, honey, molasses, saccharin(e), sirup, sorghum, sorgo, sugar, syrup, treacle
SWEETHEART adorer, agrah, amaryllis, amorosa, beau, beloved, bird, bully, catch, cheri(e), chick, clinah, cooky, courtesan, cummer, darling, dear, delia, doll, doney, doudou, doux, dowsabel, doxy, ducky, dulcinea, enamorato, fellow, flame, gill, girl, gra, heart-throb, honey(bunch), inamorata, jill, joe, judy, ladylove, lass, leman, liebchen, lief, love, lovelass, lover, mistress, moll, orpine, pet, pigeon, querida, sis, spark, sprunny, steady, swain, tootsie, treasure, truelove, valentine, wahine, wanton
SWEETLEAF dyeleaves, laurel, symplocos
SWEETMEAT balushai, bonbon, bucayo, cake, candy, caramel, caraway, cates, claggum, comfit, confection, confetti, confiture, conserve, delicacy, dessert, dolce, dragee, dredge, dulce, goody, hardbake, junket, kiss, loukoum, marchpane, marzipan, penuche, preserve, succade, sugarplum, taffy, toffee, toffy
SWEETSOP annona, annonce, ata, ates, atis, atta, corazon, custard-apple, fruit, tree
SWEETWATER chasselas
SWEETWOOD laurel, ocotea, rosewood
SWELCHIE whirlpool
SWELL amplify, augment, bag, balloon, beal, billow, bloat, blow, blub, bulge, bulk, coxcomb, crescendo, dandy, dilate, din, distend, dome, dude, enhance, enlarge, excellent, expand, extend, fantastic, fine, fop, good, grand, great, grow(th), heave, heighten, hill, increase, inflate, intensify, lengthen, lovely, nob,

plim, prominence, puff, ripple, rise, smart, spark, splendid, strut, stylish, surf, surge, swagger, swank, thrill, tiptop, toff, tony, tumefy, turgesce, wave

cause to binge, emboss

mob pickpocket, swindler, thief

out belly, billow

SWELLDOODLE eggfish, puffer

SWELLFISH bellowsfish, blower, blowfish, pike, puffer, snipe, tambor, trumpetfish

SWELLHEAD braggart

SWELLHEADED conceited, egoist(ic), stuck-up

SWELLING amper, big, blain, blister, bombastic, bouge, bubo, bulge, bump, bunch(y), bunion, chemosis, dilation, distension, distention, dropsy, edema, enlargement, expansion, excrescence, extumescence, fat, gall, intumescence, knot, lump, mouse, node, nodule, pimple, prominence, protuberance, protuberant, puff, pustule, spargosis, struma, sty(e), surgent, swelth, torus, tumefaction, tumescence, tumor, vessicon, wen, wheal

on head cowl

pert. edematose, edematous, nodal

subsidence detumescence

SWELT broil, burn, course, die, faint, melt, perish, scorch, suffocate, SWELTER, swoon

SWELTER bathe, broil, burn, exude, fretting, haste, heat, languish, ooze, oppression, perspiration, perspire, roast, soak, stew, sweat, wallow, welter

SWELTERING burning, hot, humid, muggy, stewy, sultry, torrid

SWERVE avert, bend, bias, climb, deflect, deviate, deviation, digress(ion), diverge, divert, dodge, jouk, reel, retreat, roam, scruple, sheer, shift, shy, sidestep, skew, skid, stray, swarm, swing, tack, totter, turn, veer, wander, warp, yaw

SWEVEN dream, sleep, vision

SWICK betray, blame, cease, cheat, deceit, deceive, disloyalty, fault, fraud, trap, treachery

SWIDGE smart, tingle

SWIETENIA caoba, mahogany

SWIFT abrupt, alert, apodid, apus, bird, collocalia, cypselus, expeditious, fast, fleet, flighty, flit, hasty, headlong, hepialus, immediate, lizard, marlet, precipitate, prompt, quick, rapid, ready, reel, screamer, speedy, squealer, sudden

as arrow, lightning, wind

comb. oxy

-footed aliped, ariel, mercury

SWIFT, JONATHAN *animal* yahoo

character gulliver, varina, vanessa

lady friend esther vanhomrigh, stella, vanessa

pseud. bickerstaff, cadenua, drapier

work battle of the books, GULLIVER'S TRAVELS, journal to stella, tale of a tub

SWIFT, TOM *friend* rover

SWIFTLY amain, apace, fast, hastily, in a flash, in a jiffy, lickety-split, posthaste, rapidly, snelly, speedily, tantivy, trippingly, wightly

SWIFTNESS celerity, fastness, haste, promptitude, speed, velocity

SWIG consume, drink, gulp, rock, suck, swash, swiggle, swill, tackle, toss down

SWILL basket, dash, drench, drink, filth, garbage, guzzle, hogwash, immerse, mess, offal, refuse, rinse, shake, slop(s), slosh, soak, soss, swallow, swash, swig, swish, wash, waste

SWILLBOWL drunkard, sot

SWILLER carouser, dishwasher, glutton, toper

SWIM abound, bathe, crawl, current, dip, fashion, float, glide, levitate, natate, overflow, project, reel, scheme, slip, soom, submerge, swarm, swoon, teem

nude skinny-dip

pert. natatory

stroke back, breast, crawl, dog-paddle, trudgen

suit bikini, maillot, thong, trunks

with the stream conform

SWIMMER bather, bloelia, driver, duck, fish, frogman, leander, mermaid, merman, naiad, natator

underwater diver, frogman, scubadiver

SWIMMING aquatics, blurred, dizzy, flooded, flotant, naiant, natant, natation, natatory, vertigo

appendage fin, nectopod

bell nectophore

belt life-preserver

comb. nect(o)

exhibition aquacade

pert. natatory

pool natatorium, piscina, plunge, tank, therm(e)

sandpiper phalarope

SWIMMINGLY easily, prosperously, smoothly, steadily, successfully

SWINDLE bam(boozle), beat, bilk, bubble, bucket, bunco, bunko, cheat, chisel, chouse, con, cozen, crook, deceive, defalcate, defraud, diddle, dupe, embezzle, estafa, extort(ion), fiddle, finagle, flimflam, foist, forge, fraud, gull, gip, gyp, hoax, hoodwink, hornswoggle, mace, misrepresent, nobble, peculate, pilfer, purloin, rig, rook, scam, screw, sew, skin, steal, sucker, swiz, take, trick, trim, verneuk, victimize, yentz

SWINDLER biter, blackleg, bubbler, cardsharp, cheat, chiaus, chouse, cozener, criminal, crook, fob, gilenyer, gouger, hawk, knave, macer, magsman, rogue, rooker, shark, sharper, shaver, shicer, thief, tramposo, yentzer

decoy barnard

famous brinkle, chadwick, cornfeld, coster, de angelis, estes, goldblum, insull, kreuger, law, lustig, musica, ponzi, reavis, trippet, vesco, weil, wriston

victim esau, sucker

SWINE, SWINE'S (See also *breed,* below.) aper, arctonyx, babir(o)ussa, barrow, ben(e), boar, bushpig, cochon, cur, dolt, fare, far-

row, galt, gilt, grunter, gussie, hog, peccary, pig(gy), pork(er), reprobate, scum, shoat, shote, slattern, sneak, snort(er), sow, suid, sus, tamworth, tantony, warthog, wretch
bread earthnut, truffle
breed berkshire, cheshire, chester, duroc, essex, hampshire, hereford, landrace, mangalitza, poland-china, razorback, suffolk, tamworth, yorkshire
call soss
changed into elpenor, polites
-cote pigsty
cress brass-buttons, buckhorn, carara, coronopus, herb-eve, plantain
disease bull-nose, erysipelas, garget
family setifera
fat lard
female gilt, sow
fennel brimstonewort
fever cholera, rouget
food pannage, slop(s), swill
group herd, sounder
pert. gadarene, porcine
pipe redwing
poison sowbane
red duroc
snout dandelion
succory chicory
symbol of filth, greed, satan
young pig(gy), piglet, shoat, shote
SWINECOTE pigsty
SWINEHERD eumaeus, gurth, stockman
pert. sybotic
SWINESTONE anthraconite
SWING ace, action, alternate, beat, bent, bias, blow, brandish, cadence, cannon, change, control, dangle, engineer, execute, fade, flap, flounder, flourish, fluctuate, gyrate, handle, hang, hurl, impetus, influence, latitude, lilt, lurch, manage, manipulate, meter, oscillate, pace, pendulate, period, pitch, pivot, ply, quiver, range, reel, revolve, rhythm, rock, roll, room, rotate, scope, scourge, shake, shift, showd, slue, spin, suspend, swag, sway, swerve, swivel, syncopate, tempo, thrash, thrust, totter, trend, turn, undulate, veer, vibrate,

wag(gle), wave, wheel, whip, whirl, wield
around jib, pivot, slew, slough, slue, tack
devotee jitterbug
music bebop, boogiewoogie, bop, hep, jazz, jive, rag
musician hepcat
seat transom
wild haymaker
SWINGDEVIL swift
SWINGE beat, blow, burn, chastise, cut, force, impetus, lash, leash, punish, revolve, scorch, scourge, singe, sweep, thrash, whip, whirl
SWINGER hepcat, rogue, sluggard, speculator, vagabond, whirler, whopper
SWINGLE cudgel, lever, separate, scutch(er), swing, swip(p)le, tool
SWINISH beastly, boarish, brutal, brutish, carnal, cruel, gadarene, gross, porcine, sensual, suilline
SWINK drink, drudge(ry), exhaust, grind, labor, slave, toil, travail, work
SWIPE blow, chop, cop, draft, drink, fellow, filch, glom, gulp, hit, lift, pilfer, purloin, rub, snatch, snitch, steal, strike, swape, swath, sweep, swine, wipe
SWIPPER nimble, quick
SWIRE neck, throat
SWIRL birl, boil, crimp, crisp, curl, curve, eddy, gorce, gulf, gurge, gyrate, knot, pirouette, purl, revolve, rotate, snake, swale, sweel, swoosh, twist, wheel, whirl, whorl, wind, wreathe
SWISH birch, cane, flog, hiss, mortar, rustle, smart, strike, swill, whip
tail pheasant
SWISS See SWITZERLAND.
cheese emmentaler, gruyere
dotted lappet
pine mugho
SWITCH azote, beat, birch, branch, cane, change, deflect, derail, divert, exchange, flog, hairpiece, hickory, hit, interchange, jerk, kippeen, larrup, lash, lever, part, postiche, prune, rat(tan), relay, rod, scourge, shift, shunt, sidetrack, sprig, squitch, strap, strike, substitute, swap,

swing, toggle, trade, transfer, tress, trim, turn, twig, veer, whip, whisk, wig
bird ihi
blade chiv, knife, shiv
engine goat
grass black-bent, foxtail
-hitting ambidextrous
part frog, selector
railroad gate, point
setting off
sorrel akeake, chamiso
SWITCHBOARD exchange, panel, pbx
SWITCHMAN shunter
SWITCHTAIL dogfish, sturgeon
SWITH(E) firm, greatly, hasten, hurry, instantly, many, quick(ly), scorch, singe, strong(ly), swift, very (much)
SWITHER agitation, doubt, faint, fall, fluster, hesitate, hesitation, hurl, quandary, rush, scorch, waver, whiz
SWITZERLAND, SWISS helvetia, ladin, schweiz, suisse, svizzera
alps man brison
anatomist peyer
archer william tell
architect le corbusier
army landwehr
ax piolet
balsam riga
bay uri
botanist bauhin, candolle, fries
breeze bornan, rebat
canton aarau, aargau, altdorf, appenzell, basel, basle, bern(e), chur, fribourg, gallen, geneva, geneve, glaris, glarus, graubunden, grisons, lucerne, luzern, neuchatel, neuenberg, nidwald, nyon, obwald(en), sankt, schaffhausen, schwyz, solothurn, st gall(en), tessin, thurgau, ticino, unterwalden, uri, valais, vaud, waadt, wallis, zug, zurich
canton officer amman
capital bern(e)
card game jass
castle chillon
cheese cottage, emmenthaler, gruyere, sapsago, schweizer(kase)
chemist abderhalden, glaser, karrer, reichstein, ruzicka, schonbein, werner

city altdorf, bale, basel, basle, bellinzona, bern(e), biel, brig, chur, coire, fyzabad, geneva, geneve, glarus, herisau, interlaken, lausanne, locarno, lucerne, luzerne, montreux, neuchatel, nyon, sarnen, schaffhausen, schwyz, sion, solothurn, st moritz, surat, thun, vevey, zug, zurich

coin angster, baetzner, blaffert, centime, duplone, franc, hallar, rappe(n)

commune aarau, chur, davos, sion, thun, uster, vevey

composer bloch, honegger, lievermann, martin, raff

conductor ansermet

cottage chalet

dialect ladin

diplomat vattel

district See *canton,* above.

drink cheri-suisse, marmot-chocolat

educator pestalozzi

engineer maillart

flower edelweiss

food benerplatte, raclette

game jass

geologist agassiz

guildhall ruden, saffran, schmiden, waag, zunfthaus

hat alpine

herdsman senn

hero melchthal, william tell, winkelried

historian burchkardt, sismondi

house chalet, riegelhaus

house spirit jack o' the bowl

instrument alphorn

lake ageri, biel(ersee), bienne, brienz, constance, geneva, hallwil, leman, lucerne, lugano, lungern, maggiore, morat, neuchatel, sarnen, sarnersee, thon, thun(ersee), uri, viervald, wallen, zug, zurich

language french, german, italian, ladin, romans(c)h, switzerdeutsch

legislature gross(e)rat, grossrath, landrat(h), landsgemeinde

linguist saussure

magistrate amman, avoyer

mathematician bernoulli, euler, steiner

measure aune, elle, fuss, holz(k)lafter, im(m)i, juchart, klafter, lieue, ligne,

linie, maass, moule, muid, perche, pied, pot, pouce, quarteron, saum, schuh, setier, staab, strich, toise, viertel, zoll

mountain pass albula, bernina, brenner, cenis, furka, gemmi, grimsel, kinzig, lotschen, maloja, st gotthard, simplon, splugen, usteri

neurologist bleuler

nickel batz

oceanographer piccard

painter klee

peak adula, balmhorn, bernina, beverin, blanc, burgenstock, cenis, diablerets, dom, eiger, finsteraarhorn, genis, grimsel, jungfrau, jura, karpf, linard, matterhorn, mont blanc, pilatus, pizela, rheinwaldhorn, righi, rigi, rosa, rotondo, sentis, st gotthard, todi, weisshorn, wetterhorn

people french, german, helvetian, italian, muff, rhartian, romansch, ro(u)mansh, swiss(er)

pert. alpen, alpine, helvetian

physician paracelsus

physicist balmer, bernoulli, bloch, guillaume

physiologist abderhalden, hess

pianist fischer

pine arolla, cembra, mugho

police headquarters urania street

postal district rayon

potherb chard

psychiatrist bleuler, jung

range alps, st gotthard

reformer calvin, zwingli

resort arosa, st moritz, zermatt

river aar(e), arve, broye, doubs, engadine, inn, linth, maggia, pratigau, reuss, rhine, rhone, sarine, saxane, thur, ticino

scientist argand, bernoulli, euler, haller

sculptor giacometti

signal instrument alphorn

sled luge(r)

song yodel

stage designer appia

state canton

surgeon kocher

tennantite binnite

theatrical producer appia

theologian barth, brunner, erastus, lavater, vinet

title banneret, landamman

tunnel cenis, gotthard, loetschberg, simplon

valley aar, emme, engadine, zermatt

watch unit legne

weight centner, fund, pfund, quintal, zugthierlast

wind bise, bize, bruscha

wine dezaley, vevey

wine festival fete des vignerons

writer amiel, anet, constant, ducommun, keller, lavoter, spyri, usteri, wyss

zoologist agassiz

SWIVEL axis, caster, fiddle, gudgeon, hinge, pin, pivot, rotate, swape, swing, swipe, tirret, toggle, traverse, trunnion, turn

SWIVET haste, hurry, flutter

SWIZZLE drink, gulp, guzzle

stick muddler

SWOB See SWAB.

SWOLLEN big, bloated, blobber, blown, blubber(y), bollen, bombastic, brawny, bulbous, bulging, bulgy, distended, elated, enlarged, expanded, fat, gibbose, increased, inflated, pobby, pompous, pretentious, proud, puffy, round, tumid, tumorous, turgid

SWOON attack, blackout, drop, drown, dwa(l)m, ecstasy, faint, keel over, languish, pass out, sleep, sloom, spell, stupor, succumb, swarf, sweb, swelt, swither, syncope

SWOOP blow, dart, descend, dive, pounce, seize, souse, sweep

SWORD (See also *short,* below.) 3 fox, sax 4 bolo, epee, falx, foil, gram, iron, kris, pata, saex, seax, spit, stab, tuck 5 balas, bilbo, blade, bowie, catan, degen, diego, estoc, katar, khand, kukri, ripon, saber, sabre, skean, spada, zashi 6 andrew, bancal, barong, cattan, daisho, damask, dusack, floret, glaive, katana, kukeri, macana, parang, pinker, rapier, rippon, spatha, tesack, toledo, verdun, wafter 7 ascalon, askelon, baldric, balmung, brandon, curtana, cutlass, espadon, estoque, ferrara, fleuret, gladius, joyeuse, machete, malchus, morglay, shabble, sidearm, slasher, spurtle, yashmac 8 acinaces, baselard, basilard, campilan, claymore, damascus, falchion, flamberg, schlager, scimitar, shamshir, spadroon, spitfrog, wacadash, whinyard, yataghan 9 badelaire, brackmard, kamashimo, schiavone, shamsheer, wakizashi 10 tranchefer 12 pappenheimer

-bearer ensiferi, portgla(i)ve, selictal, verger

belt loop hanger

blade web

blunt schlager, wafter

ceremonial tachi

comb. ensi, xiph(o)

counter foil

curved falchion, falx, saber, sabre, scimitar

cut estramacon

dancer matachin

double-edged anelace, ken, khanda, pata, spatha

dueling epee, foil, sharp

engraving hatchment

famous almace, askelon, balmung, colada, corrouge, curteen, excalibar, excalibur, gram, graysteel, khaled

fencing epee, foil, rapier, saber, sabre

grass bulrush, gladdon, neti, sedge, spurry

guard pas d'ane

half forte

handle fuseau, haft, hilt

heel ricasso, talon

lily gladiolus

long colichemarde, rapier, spatha, tuck, whiffle

maker ansias, demosthenes, galas, munifican, wieland

mount alloy shakudo

narrow tuck

of death morglay

of god khaled

of mercy curtana, curteen

part foible, forte, grip, haft, handle, heel, hilt, pas d'ane, pommel, quillon

pointless curtana

put away sheathe

rusty shabble

-shaped ensate, ensiform, gladiate, xiphoid

short acinates, anlace, balas, baselard, basilard, bayonet,

bodkin, creese, cris, dagger, dirk, estoc, hanger, katar, khangar, kukri, langue de boeuf, misericorde, obelisk, pointel, poniard, skean, skene, snee, snickersnee, stiletto, stylet, whinger, whinyard

stroke montanto

symbol of st adrian, st alban

thrust estocada

2-edged pata

2-handed claymore, espadon, spadone, spadroon

weed senna

wooden strickle, waster

SWORDFISH albacore, aus, billfish, boatbill, broadbill, dorado, espada, espadon. forktail, garpike, scombroid, xiphias, xiphioid

feature serra

SWORDPLAY spadroon

SWORDSMAN blade(r), epeeist, fencer, fighter, slasher, thruster

SWORDTAIL grasshopper, helleri, kingcrab

SWORN affirmed, attested, avowed, bound, confirmed, determined, devoted, inveterate, out and out

to secrecy tiled

SWOT dig, grind, labor, plug, student, study, swat, sweat, work

SYBARITE epicure, pleasure-seeker, sensualist, voluptuary

SYBARITIC effeminate, epicurean, luxurious, sensual, sensuous, voluptuous

SYBIL See SIBYL.

SYCAMORE buttonball, buttonwood, cotonier, daroo, flindosa, lacewood, plane tree, plantain, platanus

blight anthracnose

lady of athyr, hathor

SYCOPHANCY calumniation, flattery, tale-bearing

SYCOPHANT accuser, applepolisher, backscratcher, bootlicker, charlatan, clawback, courtier, favorite, fawner, flatterer, flunky, footlicker, groveler, hangeron, informer, jackal, kowtower, lackey, leech, lickspit(tle), parasite, pickthank, shmatte, shmegege, shmotte, slanderer, snob, sponge, stooge, tagtail, talebearer, timeserver, toadeater, toady,

traduce, trencher, truckler, tufthunter, yes-man

SYCOPHANTIC adulatory, fawning, gnathonic, obedient, obsequious, servile, slavish

SYCORAX *son* caliban

SYE drop, fall, scythe, sigh, strain

SYENE ass(o)uan, aswan

SYENITE appinite, trachyte

SYLEUS *slayer* hercules

SYLLA lucius-cornelius

accuser censorinus, virginius

ally cinna, servius

ancestor rufinus

captive copillus, jugurtha

chronicler juba

colleague metellus, pompeius

companion afidius, metrobius, roscius, sorex

conquest mithridates

consort aelia, caecilia, cloelia, ilia, metella, valeria

daughter aemilia, posthuma

enemy lamponius, lepidus, marius, telesinus

friend bocchus, catulus, metrobius

lieutenant albinus, annius, balbus, dolabella, ericius, gabinius, galba, lucullus, metellus, murena, torquatus

nephew nonius

slave chrysogonus

son faustus

son-in-law glabrio, pompey

surname epaphroditus, felix

twins fausta, faustus

SYLLABLE antepenult, penult, prefix, suffix

accented arsis, upbeat

added prefix, suffix

last ultima

last but 1 penult

last but 2 antepenult

lengthening ectasis

music See MUSIC *note.*

omission apocopation, apocope, elision, syncope

pert. dactylic

refrain dildo

short breve, mora

shortening systole

singing tra

stress ictus

unaccented anacrusis, atonic, thesis

SYLLABUS abstract, analysis, breviary, brief, compendium, curriculum, digest, epitome, list, outline, precis, program, summary, synopsis, table, vidimus

SYLLOGISM abduction, analysis, argument, barbara, deduction, enthymeme, epi(e)chirema, figure, lemma, paralogism, reasoning, sorites
part. conclusion, premise
series sorites

SYLPH elf, fairy, fay, hummingbird, pixie, pixy, spirit

SYLVAN arborescent, bosky, braky, copsy, forest(ed), nemoral, rustic, sylvatic, timbered, wild, wooded, woodsy, woody
god faun, pan, satyr

SYLVANITE tellarium, telluride

SYLVESTER cochineal

SYLVIA beccafico, blackcap, figpecker, warbler, whitethroat

SYMAETHIS *consort* faunus
offspring aeis

SYMBIOSIS lichenism, mutualism, nutricism

SYMBOL abbreviation, accent, amulet, apotropaion, attribute, badge, banner, button, caract, ceremony, character, charm, cipher, constant, contribution, creed, crest, cross, device, diagram, eagle, egis, emblem, ensign, exponent, expression, faciend, fetish, figure, flag, hierogram, icon, idol, ikon, image, index, insigne, letter, mace, mandala, mark, maxim, motif, name, neum, note, number, orant, ornament, palatal, palm, pattern, pneume, regalia, representation, seal, shadow, sign (al), similitude, swastika, tablet, talisman, token, totem, trademark, type, word
absolute taikih
group formula
magic caract
of authority badge, baton, crown, fasces, insigne, mace, scepter, star, stripe
sacred cross, hierogram, labrys
study of typology

SYMBOLIC allegorical, allusive, aniconic, denotative, figurative, graphic, imagerial, representative, shadowy, suggestive, typical

SYMBOLISM hieroglyphics,

iconology, totemism, typology

SYMBOLIZE adumbrate, agree, betoken, body, characterize, combine, concur, demonstrate, embody, exemplify, figure, harmonize, illustrate, image, impersonate, indicate, personify, portend, portray, prefigure, represent, shadow, show, signify, stand for, suggest, token, typify, unite

SYME *husband* glaucus

SYMEON *son* john, levi

SYMMETRICAL balanced, coequal, coordinate, equal, even, formal, holohedral, proportional, regular, round, shapely, spheral, spherical, uniform

SYMMETRY balance, conformity, congruity, correspondence, harmony, measure, proportion, regularity, uniformity

SYMPATHETIC accordant, akin, compassionate, compatible, compatient, congenial, congruous, consistent, consonant, gentle, good, gracious, harmonizing, indulgent, kind(ly), kosher, responsive, sensitive, simpatico, soft, tender, understanding, warm(hearted)

SYMPATHIZE agree, answer, commiserate, console, correspond, empathize, match, pity, resemble, share, understand

SYMPATHIZER blackneb, champion, condoler, friend, partisan, subversive, supporter, tsitser
comb. ite

SYMPATHY affinity, agreement, attraction, benevolence, chord, commiseration, compassion, concord, condole(nce), consent, correspondence, echo, empathy, harmony, heart, homopathy, kindness, pity, response, ruth, tenderness, warmth
lack dispathy

SYMPHONIA bagpipe, hurdygurdy, virginal

SYMPHONIZE accord, agree, harmonize

SYMPHONY accord, consonance, harmony, orchestra, overture, ritornel, sinfonia, sonata

SYMPODIUM pseudaxis, sika

SYMPOSIUM banquet, compotation, conference, dialogue, discussion, talk

SYMPTOM alarm, evidence, fever, indication, instance, manifestation, mark, note, omen, prodrome, prognosis, sign(al), stigma, token, warning
group syndrome

SYMTOSIS emaciation, wasting

SYNAGOGUE aljama, assembly, communion, congregation, meeting, proseucha, schul, shul, temple
curtain mechitzah, mehitzan
founder ezra
great anshe keneseth haggedolah
lamp ner-tamid
melodies chazanut, hazanuth
official baal-kore, gabbai(m), hazzan, parnas, rabbi, shammash
platform almemar, alminbar, bema, bimah
pointer yad(ayim)
sephardic snoga
singer cantor
storeroom genizah
tax finta

SYNAPSIS pairing
result meiosis

SYNAXIS congregation, eucharist, feast, meeting, rite, service

SYNCERUS bison, bubalus, buffalo

SYNCHRONIZE accompany, arrange, coexist, concur, contemporize, harmonize, mesh, organize, regulate

SYNCHRONOUS coeval, concomitant, concurrent, contemporary, existing, simultaneous

SYNCLINE downfold

SYNCOPATE contract, jazz (up), jive, rag, swing

SYNCOPE contraction, cotype, elision, faint(ing), haplology, hyphaeresis, suspension, swoon

SYNCRETISM compromise, eclecticism, fusion, reconciliation, union

SYNDIC agent, censor, critic, magistrate, manager, officer, trustee

SYNDICATE association,

cartel, censure, chain, combine, cosa nostra, gang, group, hui, mafia, monopoly, pool, sell, trust, underworld
SYNECTIC connecting, holomorphic, joining
SYNERGISM cooperation, monopoly
SYNERGIST booster, sesamin
SYNOD assembly, conference, congress, conjunction, convention, council, meeting, sobor
part diocese
SYNONYM euphonym, heteronym, homonym, metonym, polyonym
SYNOPSIS abridgment, abstract, analysis, apercu, brief, compendium, conspectus, digest, epitome, outline, plan, precis, prospectus, scenario, statement, summary, SYLLABUS, SYNTHESIS
SYNTAX accidence, grammar, order, system
analyze parse
error solecism
SYNTHESIS abstract, composition, combination, complex, fusion, incorporation, mix, summa, SYNOPSIS, systasis
SYNTHETIC acetate, affected, ampliative, artful, artificial, dialectic(al), ersatz, factitious, man-made, plastic, spurious, substitute, unnatural
SYRACUSE *citizen* archimedes
founder archias
harbor laccius, porto maggiore
merchant aegeon
ruler or *tyrant* agathocles, diocles, dion(ysius), helon, hermocrates, hicetes, hieron(ymus), mamercus, nysaeus, thrasybulus, timoleon
SYRIA, SYRIAN *ancient* aram, aramaean
animal addax, daman, dub(b)
ascetic stylite
bear dub(b)

bishop abba
buried city dura
capital antioch, damascus
church plan triconch
city aleppo, alexandretta, antioch, baalbek, balbec, beirut, beyrouth, busra, calneh, calno, damascus, derra, emesa, halab, hama(h), homs, idlib, jerud, latakia, nawa, palmyra, raqqa, seleucia, ugarit
cloth acca
coin piaster, pound, talent
commandos assaiqa
deity agabal, allat, ashtaroth, baal, elagabal, gad, hadad, mammon, resheph, rimmon
desert hamad
district aleppo, hauran
fabric acca
fanatic baathist
flower juniper, retem
goat angora
governor quirinius, sisinnes
grass johnson
gypsy aptal
hymn writer narsai
king antiochus, benhadad, faisal, hazael, rezin
kingdom tob
lake djeboid, merom, tiberias
language syriac
leader assad, khaddam
mallow okra
meadow abel
measure garava, makuk
metal cloth acca
monk simeon-stylites
paleolithic site jabrud
part amurru, golan, hauran
party baath
peak carmel, hermon, libanus
peasant fellah
people afshar, aissor, amorite, ansairieh, ansarie(h), ansariyah, aptal, aushar, avshar, awshar, druse, khachaturian, nosaris, nusaris, saracen, shemite
plant cumin
port latakia
river asi, barada, euphrates, jordan, knabur, orontes
script peshito, serta
sect druse, druze
shrub retem

silk acca
tetrarchy abilene
weight artal, artel, cola, ratel, rotl, talent
wind simoon
SYRINGA lilac, mock-orange, philadelphus, shrub
SYRINGE douche, filler, gun, hypo, scoot(er), serring, squirt(er)
SYRINX panpipe
changed to reed
pursuer pan
SYRT bog, quicksand
SYRUP claire, dhebbus, eclegma, falernum, glucose, honey, karo, maple, molasses, orgeat, quiddany, sorghum, sweetener, theriaca, treacle
maple sap
starch glucose
SYRUPY sweet, thick, viscid
SYSTASIS See SYNTHESIS.
SYSTEM arrangement, body, bureaucracy, code, complex, credo, design, doctrine, economy, fashion, group, hypothesis, ism, manner, method, mode, network, order(liness), organism, organization, philosophy, plan, principles, procedure, process, project, regimen, regularity, religion, rite, rote, rule, scheme, service, stereo, strategy, syntax, tactics, theory, treatise, universe, way, world
communication circuit, hookup
language grammar, syntax
navigational lanac, shoran
social caste, class
SYSTEMATIC analytical, business-like, logical, methodical, neat, orderly, organized, punctilious, regular
SYSTEMATICS classification, taxonomy
SYSTEMATIZE adjust, arrange, catalog(ue), classify, codify, marshal, methodize, order, organize, regiment, regulate
SZLACHTA gentry, landowner, nobility

T

TAA pagoda
TAAL afrikaans, boer
TAB account, aglet, aiglet, airfoil, bill, check, cost, designate, flap, flash, index, label, lace, latchet, loop, name, pan, pendant, price, reckoning, score, signal, strap, strip, tag, tally, tongue
TABARD cape, chimer, cloak, coat, gown, inn, mantle, pendant, surcoat
inn host baillie, bailly
inn location southwark
TABASHEER bamboo-sugar
TABBY brindled, busybody, calender, cat, dress, fabric, gossip, gown, old maid, puss(y), spinster, streaked, striped, taffeta, tattler, water(ed)
cloth moire, moreen, silk, taffeta, worsted
moth agloosa
TABEBUIA amapa, cedar, gum tree, primavera
TABERNA booth, shelter, shop, tavern, tent
TABERNACLE abode, altar, ambry, box, chantry, church, closet, dove, enshrine, habitation, kirk, niche, pix, pyx, recess, safe, shrine, temple, tent, tomb
architect beseleel, bezaleel
feast succoth
servant nethinim
TABES atrophy, emaciation, locomotor ataxia, wasting
TABETIC, TABID haggard, marcid, mean, poor
TABITHA dorcas, gazelle
TABLE (See also *kind*, below.) analysis, bar, belly, bench, board, booth, buffet, calendar, canon, catalogue, chart, cheveret, committee, consol, counter, credence, cuisine, defer, delay, diagram, facet, fare, feed, flat, food, horizontal, inventory, lamina, list, mensa, menu, palm, panel, pigeonhole, pinax, place, plateau, postpone, poudreuse, presentation, pye, raft, register, roll, roster, rota, schedule,

scheme, shelf, shelve, sheveret, sift, slab, stand, statement, stringcourse, synopsis, tablet, tabulate, teapoy, toilette, workbench
arithmetic tariff
astrological speculum
calculating abacus, list
card basset
centerpiece epergne
circular roundel
cloth tapis
cloth mat dunnage, pardnap
communion altar, credence, credenza
constellation mensa
cover baize, cloth, tapis
decoration candelabra, candlestick, centerpiece, epergne
d'hote prix fixe
dish tureen
dressing toilet(te), vanity
dropleaf butterfly
18th century bouilotte, cheveret, sheveret
expander leaf
folding servette
gambling tapis-vert
game billiards, pool
holy altar
kind card, coffee, console, dressing, dropleaf, gateleg, lampstand, sommo, taboret, trivet
lamp bouillotte
leg baluster
linen cloth, doil(e)y, doyley, napery, napkins, placemat
massage plinth
mountain amba, mesa
musical diagram
night somno
on the above board, candid, frank, open, overt
ornamented pembroke
pert. mensal
philosopher deiphosophist
serving teacart, trolley, wagon
setting cover
shaking slimer
small kursi, stand, tabo(u)ret, teacart, teapoy, tendoor, tendour, wagon
stone dolmen
3-legged teapoy, tripod, trivet

utensils cutlery, flatware, place-setting, silverware
ware china, flatware, haviland, spode
workman's bench, siege
writing carlton, desk, escritoire
TABLEAU drama, list, pageant, picture, portrait, register, representation, scene, schedule, table
TABLELAND altiplanicie, balaghat, bench, kar(r)oo, mere, mesa, pamir, paramo(s), plain(s), plat (eau), puna, puno
TABLET album, aspirin, brass, bred, capsule, cartouch(e), churinga, disk, fa(s)cia, lamina, leaf, lozenge, memorial, monument, pad, panel, pax, pellet, pill, pinax, plaque, sheet, slab, slate, stele, stile, tabule, triptych, troche
comb. pina
medicinal aspirin, disc, disk, jelloid, tabella, tabloid, troche, trochiscus
memorial brass, plaque
stone stela, stele
symbol pax
3-leaved triptych
2-leaved diptych
upright stela, stele
votive pinax
writing codicil, pad, slate, triptych
TABLINUM alcove, recess, room
TABLOID compressed, concentrated, condensed, newspaper, sheet(let), short, summary, synopsis, tablet
TABOO, TABU ban, bar, censure, debar, forbid(den), inhibit, interdict(ion), kapu, nono, ostracism, prohibit (ion), proscription, sacred, tapu, verboten
opposed to noa
TABOR at(t)abal, drum, eardrum, fort, kettledrum, tabret, tambourine, timbre(l)
TABRIZ *ancient* tauris
TABULATE arrange, list, record, schedule
TABULATION analysis,

compilation, registration, scale, scheme
grammatical paradigm
yearly calendar
TACAMAHAC balsam, calaba, calophyllum, galipot
TACANA *indian* arauna, cavina, toromona
TACE silence, splint, tasset
TACHE attach, besmirch, blemish, bond, buckle, clasp, fault, spot, stain, tack, tarnish, teach, tie
TACHEBRUN *master* ganelon
TACHLIS achievement, heart, nub, point, substance
TACHOMETER *reading* rpm
TACHYGRAPHY shorthand, stenography
TACIT allusive, implicit, implied, inferred, noiseless, silent, suggested, understood, unsaid, unspoken, wordless
TACITURN brief, close(lipped) (mouthed), concise, curt, dumb, inhibited, laconic, mum, mute, quiet, reserved, restrained, reticent, secretive, sententious, silent, speechless, still, terse, tight-lipped, tongue-tied, wordless
TACITUS *work* annals, germania
TACK adjoin, agreement, aim, annex, append, attach, baste, basting, beat, bent, board, brad, buckle, busk, cast, catch, clap, clothes, connect, course, deviate, deviation, endurance, fasten, fetch, food, gear, gibe, handle, haul, hook, jib(e), join, laveer, lease, method, nail, path, pin, rack, rider, rope, route, secure, set, shelf, shift, slap, spell, stay, stickiness, supplement, tache, take, tingle, trim, turn, unite, veer, yaw
craftsman's lorimer
glazier's brad
on add, append
room equipment harness
to jibe
to windward trip
2-pointed staple
TACKLE (See also *kind,* below.) accept, angle, apparatus, arms, arrow(s), attack, attempt, burton, collar, cordage, derrick, drink, encounter, equipment, fishfall, food, garnet, gear,

grapple, grasp, halt, halyard, harness, hold, jigger, lineman, materiel, mistress, outfit, paraphernalia, player, purchase, rig(ging), runner, seize, steeve, stop, stuff, swig, taglia, take on, taw, teagle, tools, try, undertake, weapons, yoke
anchor cat(fall)
block burton
fishing le(d)ger, otter, tew
kind block, burton, cat, luff, pulley, runner, windlass, yoke
light jigger
strong cat
watch handy-billy
TACKY adhesive, crude, dowdy, flashy, gaudy, mangy, out-of-date, poky, ratty, seedy, shabby, shaggy, showy, slovenly, sticky, thick, viscid, wreck(ed)
TACSO passiflora
TACT address, amenity, delicacy, diplomacy, discretion, discrimination, feeling, finesse, method, mode, perception, poise, politics, savoir faire, sensitivity, touch, urbanity
TACTFUL diplomatic, discreet
TACTICS maneuver, method, plan, procedure, scheme, stratagem, system, technique
TACTILE tangible, touchable
process barblet
quality texture
TACTION contact, tangency, touch
TACTITE diopside, garnet, limestone, vesuvianite
TACTLESS blunt, boorish, brash, crude, gauche, inconsiderate, indiscreet, obtuse, undiplomatic
TACTOR antenna, feeler
TAD boy, child, hobbledehoy, toad
TADPOLE bullhead, fledgling, larva, merganser, polehead, polliwog, porwigle, powhead
fish forkbeard
TAEL liana, liang
part mace
TAENIA headband, fillet, strip, tapeworm
TAENIATE ribbonlike, stringy, striped

TAFFETA affected, cloth, dainty, delicate, fabric, fastidious, florence, florid, ornate, samite, silk, tabby
TAFFY (See also WELSH *people.*) butterscotch, blarney, cajolery, cambrian, candy, claggum, flattery, gundy, toffee, toffy
TAFT, WILLIAM H. *birthplace* cincinnati, ohio
burial site arlington, virginia
party republican
profession lawyer
vice president sherman
TAG adjunct, aglet, aiglet, appellation, append, attach, bit, catkin, chase, cliche, cue, dagge, epithet, fasten, flap, follow, frazzle, game, heel, identification, join, label, lock, loop, mark, name, pompompullaway, pursue, rabble, rag, shadow, shred, slip, stub, swatch, tab, tail, tally, tap, tatter, term, ticket, tigtag, title, touch, trail, token
end butt, fragment, remnant, scrap
TAGALOG pulahan
child anac(s), bata
deity bat(h)ala
gambling game panguingui
"good" mabuti
language batan, bikol, cham(oro), ibanag, igorot, ilokano, malagasy, manobo, montes, moro, palau, pampango, pangasinan, selung, sulu, tiam, tino, visayan
male lalaqui
mother ina
peasant tao
people malayan, philippino, pulahan
race ita
river ilog
wine alac
TAGETES See MARIGOLD.
TAGRAG rabble, ragged, riffraff, tatter, vagabond, worn
TAGTAIL satellite, sycophant
TAGUS *city on* toledo
TAHITI otaheite, otaheiti
apple ambarella, hevi, macupi
arrowroot pia
canoe pahi
capital papeete
centipede veri
curlew kioea

dialect beche-de-mer
garment maro, pareu
god oro, taaroa
island neighbor See
FRENCH POLYNESIA.
minstrel society areoi, arioi
mulberry aute
peak orohena
plant awapuhi, taro
port papeete
sugar daddy papa choux
woman wahini
TAHOE trout pogy, salmo
TAHR goat, jharral, kras,
tair, tehr, thar
TAHREA parent micah
TAI (See also THAI.) ahom,
khamti, pagrus, porgy,
shan, siamese
TAIHOKO taipei
TAIL abridged, account, appendage, back, behind,
braid, brush, bun(t), ca-
boose, cauda, chase, coda,
conclusion, cue, dock, dog,
dregs, empennage, end, en-
tail(ed), escape, extremity,
eye, fantail, flee, fol-
low(er), fud, fundament,
herd, limitation, limited,
pendant, pole, pursue,
queue, rear, reduced, retinue, reverse, rumple, scut,
shadow, spy, stern, stub,
switch, tag, tally, tax, terminal, train, verso, wreath
animal's bob, b(r)ush, bun,
flag, fud, scut, s(h)ingle,
stern, twist
bird's fan
bushy brush
comb. caud(o), cerc(al),
cerco, uro
comet's beard, stream(er)
dock strunt
double queue-fourche
end caboose, conclusion,
hindermost, last
feather rectrix, sickle
fin, having isocercal
furry scut
having caudate
having long macrurous
having short brevicaudate
having tapering leptocercal
kind bob, bun(t), cauda,
empennage, fud, plume,
scut, stern, streamer, strunt,
twist, wreath
lack of anury
-like caudiform
off decrease, diminish
pert. caudal, caudate, cercal
piece anquera, queue

short bun, scut
stump strunt
tip tag
toward the caudad
train caboose
TAILBOARD endgate, endpiece
TAILLE build, duty, figure,
fit, form, imposition,
impost, levy, shape, style,
tax, waist
TAILLESS acaudal, acaudate,
acaulescent, acauline, acaulose, acaulous, anurous,
ecaudate, excaudate
TAILOR bluefish, botcher,
busheler, cabbage, carzee,
clothier, couturier, darzee,
darzi, draper, fashion, fit,
form, fuller, gorer, herring,
knell, make, pricklouse, sartor, schneider, seamster,
sempster, shepster, snip(per),
snyder, stitch, tailleur, taper, tireman
bird darzee, sutoria
botching jack-snip
goose flatiron, sadiron
itinerant cardooer
lapboard panel
marker french-chalk
muscle sartorius
pert. sartorial
technique stoating
TAILRACE afterbay, channel, flume
TAILS cutaway, formal, swallowtail
TAILSPIN fall, flicker
TAILSTOCK deadhead
TAIN epic(foil), mirror,
taken
TAINO haitian
god zeme, zemi
TAINT accuse, blemish, blot,
brand, characteristic, color,
contaminate, convict(ion),
corrump, corrupt, debauch,
decay, decompose, defect,
defile, detract, dip, disgrace,
dye, fault, flaw, flybow, hit,
hogo, hue, imbue, impair,
infect(ion), infuse, poison,
pollute, putrify, rot, smear,
spoil, spot, stain, stench,
stigma, tarnish, tinge,
touch, trace, vice, vitiate,
weaken
without clean, perfect, pure
TAINTED bad, blown, cankered, corrupt, diseased,
gamy, high, imbued, pindy,
poisoned, rancid, rank, rotten, sappy, spoiled, wemmy

TAIPEI taihoku
TAIWAN (See also CHINA
references.) formosa
capital taipei
city daihoku, kaohsiung,
keelung, shoka, taichung,
tainan, taipei, taiwan
dialect amon, hakka, mandarin
headhunters taiyal
island group matsu, penghu,
quemoy
peak hsinkao, tzukao, yu-
shan
port chilung, kaohsiung,
keelung, takao
river choshui, hualien, ta-
chia, tanshui, wuchi
tribe sekhwan
wine hsao hsing, kaoliang
TAJ MAHAL builder (shah)
jahan
site agra, india
TAKE 3 bag, cop, get, hog,
nab, net, use 4 bear, cull,
gate, glom, grab, haul,
hook, loot, need, skin,
swag, tote, trap 5 adopt,
booty, bring, cadge, carry,
catch, charm, cheat, draft,
fetch, graft, grasp, infer,
photo, pluck, purse, seize,
spell, spoil, steal, strip,
study, touch, trick, usurp,
wrest, yield 6 accept, adhere, allure, arrest, assume,
attach, attack, borrow,
choose, clutch, collar,
derive, endure, gather, income, occupy, pocket,
profit, rip off, secure,
snatch, spirit 7 acquire, attract, bewitch, capture,
catch on, delight, deliver,
enchant, extract, preempt,
procure, receipt, receive, returns, swallow, swindle, unpurse 8 contract, embezzle,
proceeds, receipts 9 apprehend, captivate, fascinate,
transport 10 confiscate, dispossess, photograph 11 appropriate
aback astonish, check, confound, dismay, start(le)
a break relax, rest, vacation
account of consider, inventory, notice, regard, re-
member
a chance gamble, risk, speculate, venture
a crack at See ATTEMPT.
advantage of abuse, avail,
capitalize(on), deceive,

exploit, misuse, move, overreach, profit(from), use
advice hear, heed, listen,
mind
a flier bet, speculate
after emulate, follow, imitate, resemble
alarm boggle, bristle, recoil,
shudder
amiss bridle, misunderstand,
resent
another's place See SUBSTI-
TUTE.
apart demolish, destroy, disassemble, end, ruin
a powder escape, flee, hide,
run
as actual posit
away abduct, abstract,
adeem, adempt, bereave,
call off, convey, deduct
(ion), deprive, derogate,
detach, detract, devest, diminish, dislodge, divest,
eloign, heave, kidnap,
reave, recant, reduce, remove, retract, revoke, seize,
steal, subduce, subtract,
unvest, wrest
back apologize, exchange,
recall, recant, repeal,
repossess, retract, retreat,
return, revoke, withdraw
beforehand preempt
bold attitude brisk
by craft entoil
by force erept, raven, reave,
seize, snatch, usurp
by stealth hook, snitch
by storm assault, attack, besiege, expugn, invade, overcome, overwhelm, seize,
surprise, sweep, triumph
by strategem (en)trap
care achtung, attend, attention, beware, cark, caution,
cuidado, husband, look out,
mind, nurse, reck, watch
(out)
care of accomplish, avenge,
babysit, cope, deal with,
kill, look after, nurse, perform, provide for, punish,
see to, serve, tend, ward,
watch over
census count, list, muster
charge attend, command,
control, direct, lead, manage, rule, run
cognizance acknowledge,
note, notice, recognize, remember
courage brace up
dancing lead out

delight enjoy, revel
down abase, depress, devour,
dismantle, distribute, emaciate, escort, fail, fell, humble, humiliate, lay low,
lower, note, prostrate, rebuke, record, reduce, reprimand, sicken, strike, swallow, withdraw, write
exception demur, disagree,
disapprove, dissent, doubt,
object, qualify, resent,
strain, veto
first preempt
five See REST.
food dine, eat, lunch, sup
for granted accept, assume,
believe, expect, imply, presume, suppose, think
form crystal(l)ize
from deduct, deprive, derive,
derogate, detract, divest,
grab, seize, subtract, wrest
heart brace up, buck up,
cheer up, hope
heed advert, attend, beware,
mind, note, notice, reck,
tent, ware
hold adhere, bite, catch, get,
grab, grasp, influence, obtain, pinch, seize
ill ail, catch, contract, fail,
resent, sicken
in abbreviate, absorb, adhibit, admit, annex, assimilate,
attend, cheat, commence,
comprehend, compress, comprise, contract, deceive, devour, drink, embrace, en-
close, encompass, entail,
entrance, escort, explore,
fence, fool, fraud, furl,
gain, gather, get, hear, include, ingest, mislead, observe, open, outwit, receive,
reduce, scoop, see, shorten,
soak up, trick, understand
in hand attempt, practice,
seize, train, undertake
in sail brail
into account consider, include, remember
into custody See ARREST.
issue deny, dispute, dissent,
oppose
it accept, acquiesce, endure,
resist, suppose, tolerate, understand
it easy idle, relax, rest
it out on abuse, anger,
avenge, beset, harass, punish, rebuke, reprimand
leave congee, decamp, de-

part, excuse, separate, vacation
legally attach
notice advert, heed, observe,
see, witness
off abate, ape, begin(ning),
begone, burlesque, catapult,
copy, countdown, deduct
(ion), depart, deter(mine),
detract, discount, distract,
doff, douse, escape, exterminate, flee, flight, fly, head
for, hie, hurry, imitate, jet,
kill, launch(ing), leave,
lessen, lift, mimic, opening,
outset, parody, remove, reproduce, satire, shuck, soar,
spoof, start, strip, subtract,
withdraw
-off strip runway, tarmac
off suspended list reinstate
on accept, acquire, add,
adopt, agonize, arrogate, associate, assume, challenge,
complain, consort, dare,
embrace, employ, encoun-
ter, engage, fight, fret, fuss,
grieve, hire, mount, oppose,
receive, start, succeed, tackle, undertake, use, worry
one's breath astonish,
frighten, startle, stun, surprise, thrill
one's measure estimate, examine, look, scrutinize, try
one's time dally, dawdle, loiter
one's way wend
orders comply, obey, submit,
yield
out airbrush, copy, date, deduct, dele(te), efface, elide,
eliminate, erase, escort, except, expunge, exterpate,
extract, omit, overcall, remove, scratch, separate, unhitch
out curves straighten
over acquire, appropriate,
arrogate, assume, grab, monopolize, seize, succeed,
usurp
pains be careful, bother,
strive, try
part compete, contribute, engage, fight, join, lead, participate, share, side, sit in
place arise, befall, break,
eventuate, happen, occur,
pass
place again recur
pleasure in admire, enjoy,
fancy
possession acquire, appro-

priate, capture, conquer, distrain, enter, escheat, inherit, seise, seize
prisoner apprehend, arrest, captivate, capture
root grow, influence, settle, stabilize, strike
shape crystallize, emerge, form, jell, materialize
shelter hide, howf, nestle
sides advocate, argue, back, support
some of partake
stock(of) appraise, check, count, estimate, examine, inventory, survey
ten rest
the cake prevail, succeed, win
the count fail, fall, lose
the edge off blunt, dilute, moderate, weaken
the place of replace, second, substitute, supersede, supplant, supply
the pledge abstain, quit, renounce
the stick steer
the veil quit, retire
time dawdle, delay, fabianize, linger, loiter
to avail, care for, desire, like, master, practice, try
to court litigate, sue
to heart feel, resent
to task carpet, challenge, chew out, jack up, punish, rebuke, reprimand, reprove, scold
to wife marry, wed
unawares ambush, astonish, astound, capture, confound, overcome, overwhelm, seize, start(le), surprise
unlawfully embezzle, filch, pilfer, rob, snitch, STEAL, thieve, usurp
up absorb, accept, acquire, adopt, allow, arrest, assume, begin, borrow, buy, check, collect, comprehend, consider, discuss, dissent, elevate, employ, engross, enter, exact, extirpate, fill, gather, include, lift, mount, occupy, patronize, practice, purchase, raise, rebuke, receive, remove, reprimand, resume, review, seize, settle, shorten, start, try, understand, undertake
up again renew, resume
upon oneself assume, pretend, undertake, volunteer

with accept, acknowledge, agree, brook, confess, like, side with
with a grain of salt discount, doubt, question
without authority usurp
TAKEN impressed, occupied, reserved, tain, ton
aback aghast, astonished, blank, surprised
by 2's duple
for granted assumed, tacit
TAKER captor, catcher, pilferer, plagiarist, purveyor, receiver, thief
comb. ceptor
of court action suer
of profits pernor
TAKIN budorcas, gazelle, ruminant
TAKING adoption, adoptive, alluring, appealing, appropriation, attachment, attack, attractive, blight, caption, captivating, catch(ing), charming, contagious, delightful, deprivation, desirable, dispossession, distress, dudgeon, enchanting, fascinating, fit, grasping, infectious, malefic, palsy, pleasing, plight, possession, rapacious, receipt(s), seizure, winning
TAKT beat(s), measure, pulse, tempo
TALA basin, destruction, raid, ruin, tree
TALAK ahsan, divorce, hasan
TALAPOIN animal, monk, monkey, poonghie, quenon
TALAR robe
TALARI pataca, patacoon
TALARIA *footgear of* hermes, mercury
TALAUS *offspring* adrastus, eriphyle
parent bias, pero
slayer melampus
wife lysimache
TALC agalite, conte, mica, soapstone, steatite
TALE (See also *kind,* below.) account, aition, anecdote, ballad, conte, conversation, discourse, edda, epic, esteem, estimation, fable, fabliau, falsehood, fib, fiction, gest(e), gossip, history, information, lai, lay, leed, legend, lie, myth, narrative, novel, recital, reckon, romance, rumor,

saga, speech, spoke, story, sum, talk, yarn
comic fabliau
devised aition
epic tain
false slander
folk nancy, threne
kind allegory, bourd, conte, epic, gest(e), jeremiad, lai, lay, legend, liang, novel(la), roman(ce), saga, storiette, story, yarn
merry bourd
of sorrow iliad, jeremiad
of two cities family manette
pious conte-pieux
short conte, lai
teller author, munchausen, narrator, shanachie, writer, yarner
traditional saga
TALEBEARER blab(ber), blabbermouth, busybody, buzzer, gossip, informer, newsmonger, quidnunc, scandalmonger, snitch, talepyet, tattler, tattletale, telltale, tittletattle
TALENT ability, aptitude, art(istry), attribute, bent, bore, brilliance, calibre, capability, capacity, charisma, cichar, craft, desire, disposition, dower, dowry, endowment, faculty, flair, forte, genius, gift, inclination, instinct, knack, money, moxie, parts, power, property, qualification, riches, skill, specialty, talon, turn, verve, wealth
1/60th mina
1/6000th drachma
natural dower
sale venality
scout bushbeater
special forte
TALENTED able, addicted, clever, disposed, gifted, inclined, skilled
TALIERA palm, tara, tree
TALINUM flameflower, puchero, rock-pink
TALIPES clubfoot, deformity
TALIPOT basketpalm, bookpalm, buripalm, corypha
TALISMAN amulet, charm, fetish, greegree, grigri, ichthus, ichthys, image, magic, mantra, periapt, phylactery, priest, rod, saffi, saphic, scarab, sorcery, staff, stick, symbol, telesm, wand, wishbone

TALK 3 gab, gas, jaw, rap, yak, yap 4 blab, bukh, bukk, bull, carp, chat, chin, coze, gaff, guff, gush, harp, knap, rant, rave, tale, tell 5 argot, argue, chaff, clack, click, drawl, drone, drool, lingo, noise, orate, prate, rally, rumor, scold, speak, spiel, spout, state 6 babble, banter, blague, bleeze, broach, cackle, caquet, confab, drivel, gabble, gibber, gossip, hot air, intone, jabber, jargon, parley, patter, preach, report, sermon, speech, tattle, yabber, yammer 7 address, blabber, blather, chaffer, chatter, comment, confess, descant, diction, discuss, jawbone, lecture, oration, palaver, prattle 8 argument, badinage, chinfest, chitchat, colloquy, converse, dialogue, harangue, jeremiad, language, nonsense, parlance, raillery, repartee 9 amphigory, discourse, phillipic, soliloquy 10 amphigouri, caqueterie, chew the fat, chew the rag, conference, discussion, filibuster, peroration, persiflage, tattletale 11 declaration 12 conversation 13 confabulation, interlocution 14 shoot the breeze

about discuss, gossip, hash, review
abusive hoker, jawing
aimlessly ramble
back answer, repartee, retort, ripost(e), sass
big boast, bounce, brag, rodomontade
boastful bull, gaff, gax, rant
bombastic fustian, twaddle
ceremonious chinchin
comb. logue
common fable, hearsay
complaining carp
confused galimatias, gibberish, nonsense
deliriously rave
desultorily carp, ramble
double nonsense
down belittle, disparage, outlast, silence, simplify
effusively gush, rave
empty ballyhoo, bosh, drivel, gash, gloze, prattle, psilogy
familiar chitchat, confab
fast and idly gnatter, rattle

flattering palaver
fondly bill and coo
foolish babble, bilge, blabber, bosh, buff, buncombe, bunk(um), claver, fraise, gab, gas, gash, goose-cackle, guff, hogwash, patter, poppycock, rigmarole, spiel, stultiloquy, twaddle, wishwash
foolishly blather, blither, drivel, drool, footle, gabble, gibber, gnatter, prattle, sawney, tootle
formal address, lecture, oration, sermon, speech
freely descant
idle blab, buff, chat(ter), chitchat, claver, gaff, gossip, jangle, palaver, twattle, yackety-yack, yakety-yak
idly babble, chatter, chin, gab(ble), gas, gnatter, prate, prattle, tattle, twaddle
imperfectly lisp, stammer, stutter
impudent slackjaw
incoherently babble, chunner, chunter, dander, hotter, mither, moider
indiscretely blab
inflated bluster
insincere banana oil, buncombe, bunkum, cant, claptrap, humbug(gery)
in sleep somniloquy
insolently sass, snash
into convince, persuade
irrationally jabber, rant, rave
monotonously drone
nonsensical blather, folderol, rot
out of dissuade
over confer, consider, convince, discuss, review
persuasively reason
pertly chelp
pompous grandiloquence, hyperbole
pompously harangue, orate
profuse chat, palaver, patter, persiflage
rambling rigmarole
rapid palabra, patter
rapidly gabble, gnatter, jabber
saucy prate, sass, slack
silly claptrap, drivel, gabble, nonsense, prattle, stultiloquence, twaddle
slowly drawl
small brag, buck, bukh, chat,

chin, chitchat, gab, prate, prattle
smooth blarney
to accost, address, apostrophize, buttonhole, harangue, invoke, tutoyer
to no purpose blat
to oneself soliloquize
turgid cant, rant
unintelligible drivel, gibberish, jargon, patter
vaguely woozle
wildly rant, rave

TALKATIVE babblative, babblesome, buzzy, chatty, clamorous, clashy, eloquent, fluent, gabby, garrulous, gash, glib, loquacious, mouthy, multiloquent, prolix, tellsome, verbose, vocal, voluble, wordy

TALKATIVENESS eloquence, garrulity, logorrhea, loquacity

TALKER blellum, buller, camper, chatterbox, jawsmith, magpie, mouthpiece, potgun, proser, speaker, spellbinder, whiffler

TALKFEST brainstorming, bull session, chinfest, confab, dialogue, discussion

TALKING converse, discourse, noration
board ouija
iron gun, rifle
loud noration
machine phonograph, victrola
-to earful, lecture, rebuke, reprimand, scolding

TALL big, bold, bouncing, brave, comely, courageous, craney, deft, docile, excellent, excessive, exorbitant, fine, gangle-shanked, gangling, gangly, great, handsome, high, incredible, lank(y), large, lathy, leggy, lengthy, lofty, long(legged), obedient, ostentatious, proper, quick, rangy, ready, seemly, steep, towering, unbelievable, unusual, vaulting, yielding
person beanpole, daddy longlegs, highpockets, longshanks, spindleshanks, stringbean
story bluster, gossip, lie
timber backwoods

TALLEYRAND *residence* auteuil

TALLITH prayer scarf, prayer shawl
tassels zizith
TALLNESS altitude, procerity
TALLOW arming, candle, fat(ten), grease, lard, marrow, sebum, sevum, suet, taulch
berry locustberry
comb. sebi, stear(o), steat(o)
constituent stearin, suet
dip candle
loaf cabbage
maker chandler
mange seborrhea
pert. stearic
pot fireman
refuse crackling
salt stearate
sediment greaves
shrub wax-myrtle
source suet, wax
tree candlenut, cera, roka
TALLY accord, account, agree, calculate, catalog(ue), chalk, check, coincide, comport, conform, correspond, count(erpart), deal, ditto, enroll, enumerate, equal, estimate, gibe, harmonize, inventory, jibe, label, list, mark, match, mate, notch, numerate, point, reckon(ing), register, roster, run, score, square, suit, swatch, tag, tailyie, tailzie, total
TALLYWAG sea bass
TALMAI *offspring* absalom, maacah
TALMUD commentaries, compendium, debates, gemara
academy yeshibah, yeshiboth, yeshiva(h)
glosses tosaphoth
interpretation gemara, pilpul
parables aggadah, aggadoth
part nezikim, nezikin
prayer abodah
student ba(c)hur
text mishnah
title abba
treatise berakah
TALON chela, claw, clutch, fang, foot, hallux, nail, pounce, sere, spur, unguis, weapon, zipper
TALOS *creator* hephaestus
slayer daedalus
uncle daedalus

TALUK estate, tract, zamindari
TALUS ankle(bone), astragal(us), clubfoot, incline, knucklebone, rubble, scree, slope
TAM balmoral, beret, cap, hat
TAMALE *night* christmas eve
TAMANDUA anteater
TAMAR *brother* absalom
father david
father-in-law judah
husband judah, onan
offspring hur, pharex
TAMARA, TAMORA *consort* aaron, titus
kingdom georgia, imeritia
son alarbus, chiron, demetrius
TAMARACK atle(e), epinette, hackmatack, heath, jhow, larch, larix, lodgepole-pine, mummy-brown
gall tacahout
TAMARIN jacchus, leoncito, marikina, marmoset, pinche
TAMARIND amli, quamachil, sampaloc, silktree
TAMARISK See TAMARACK.
TAMAS darkness, dullness, ignorance, inertia
TAMASHA commotion, display, excitement, fuss, pageant, show, spectacle
TAMBAC See AGALLOCH.
TAMBO corral, cowbarn, inn, stable, tambourine, tavern
TAMBOUR(INE) cup, daira, dove, drum, rikk, taar, tabo(u)r, timber, timbrel
vibrance travale
TAME accoy, accustomed, begin, biddable, boring, break, broach, bust, cadish, calm, check, civilize(d), control, cultivated, curb, daunt, dead, defeat, discipline, docile, domesticate(d), dull, familiar, feeble, gentle, harmless, harness, humble, ineffectual, inert, insipid, inward, man(suete), master, meek (en), mild, milky, moderate, mollify, obedient, overcome, pliable, pliant, prune, servile, soften, stop, subdue(d), subjugate(d), submissive, suppress, tedious,

timid, tractable, train, tunebo, vapid
animal cade, cosset, pet
cheater decoy
hawk man
poison swallowwort
TAMENESS mansuetude, mildness
TAMER *of men* sparta
TAMERLANE *capital* samarkand
grandson ulugebek
people uzbeks
successor ulugbeg
trumpet kerna
TAMIL (See also INDIA.) dravidian, hindu, vellala
capital madras
cast vellala
TAMING OF THE SHREW
author shakespeare
character baptista, bianca, biondello, curtis, grumio, hortensio, kate, katharine, lucentio, petruchio, sly, tranio, vicentio
hero petruchio
heroine kate, katharine
TAMIS strainer, tammy
TAMMANY *man* bucktail, politico
officer sachem, wiskinkie, wiskinky
opponents locofocos
TAMMUZ *beloved* ishtar
progenitors ninazu, ningishzida
sister belili
TAMORA See TAMARA.
TAMP cram, drive, fill, pack, pound, press, pug, ram, stem, stuff
TAMPA *festival* gasparilla parade
TAMPER alter, bribe, change, dabble, fiddle, fix, fool, influence, interfere, machinate, meddle, molest, monkey, plot, potter, puddle, putter, scheme, tinker, tool, touch, trinkle, trouble
TAMPICO *fiber* istle
TAMPION plug, stopper, TAMPON, tampoon, turnpin, wadding
TAMPON dressing, drumstick, plug, tympan
nasal rhinobyon
TAMUS baneberry, bindweed, byrony
TAN ascot, beat, bronze, burn, camp, cure, dress, flog, imbrown, picul, scourge, sunburn, switch,

tanbark, tannin, taw(ny), thrash, wallop
ascot brownstone
color adust, almond, beige, biscuit, bishop, brindle, brown, buff, coconut, dun, ecru, khaki, mocha, oriole, rabbit, tawny, toast
liquor owse
TANA banxring, shrew, tain
TANAGER cardinal, cashewbird, euphonia, firebird, habia, lindo, organist, piranga, redbird, spindalis, warbird, yeni
fruit-eating tanagra
scarlet pocketbird
TANAQUIL *slave* ocrisia
TANBARK algerian, avaram, ross, turwar
tree hemlock, tsuga
TANCEL abuse, beat, thrash, whip
TANCRED *beloved* clorinda, sigismunda
kingdom sicily
squire guiscard(o)
TANDAN catfish, eelfish
TANG aroma, bite, fish, flavor, hint, nip, odor, pang, pierce, piquancy, point, prick, pungency, relish, ring, rockweed, sapidity, savor, scent, seaweed, smack, smell, sting(er), surgeonfish, taste, ting, tooth, trace, twang, zest
dynasty poet lipo
TANGANYIKA See TANZANIA.
TANGELO ugli
TANGENT abutting, ajacent, ajoining, contactual, contiguous, contingent, juxtaposed, meeting, slope, touching
screw worm
TANGENTIAL contiguous, digressive, divergent, erratic
TANGERINE mandarin, naartje
TANGFISH pike, seal, surgeonfish
TANGI dirge, gorge, lamentation, wake
TANGIBLE actual, certain, concrete, corporeal, definite, evident, manifest, material, objective, obvious, palpable, perceptible, physical, real, sensible, solid, specific, substantial, tactile, touchable, tractible, true

TANGIER *feature* casbah
measure kula, mudd
TANGLE argue, balter, brangle, catch, chaparral, confuse, confusion, cot(ter), derange, elf, embrangle, embroil, entrap, fank, fight, foul, furbelow, hamper, hankle, harle, involve, jumble, knot, knurl, mat, momble, mucker, perplex, puzzle, ravel, scrobble, seaweed, shag, share, sharl, sleave, snarl, snirl, taffle, taisch, taissle, tardle, tat, teihte, thrum, trap, twine, weave, wopse
legs hobblebush, liquor
picker turnstone
tail stonecrop
thread snarl
TANGLED afoul, complicated, interlaced, intermeshed, intricate, involved, meshed, sharled, snarly, tousy
mass mat, shag
up haywire
TANGLEFOOT deerweed, heath-aster, liquor, whisky
TANGLEHEAD pili
TANGO argentine, bingo, dance
TANGY appetizing, brisk, flavorful, piquant, pungent, racy, sharp, spicy, zestful, zesty
TANIA eddoes, taro, yautia
TANITH astarte, caelestis, dea
TANK aquarium, bang, basin, bosch, bosh, break, cistern, curvette, grant, hit, knock, lake, landship, mixer, pachuca, panzer, piscina, pond, pool, reservoir, stomach, vat, vehicle, weapon
armored flail, landship, panzer, whippet
part tread, turret
rectangular bowly
runner jacana
town See TOWN *small.*
weapon bazooka
up drink, get drunk, imbibe
TANKARD can, facer, goblet, goddard, hanap, jack, pewter, pottle, stein, stoop, stoup, vessel
leather bombard
TANKED See DRUNK.
TANKER freighter, oiler, ship, vessel

TANNED bronzed, brown, ruddy, sunburned, tawny, toasted
TANNER,   TANNER'S barker, bateman, beamsman, egger, plumper, samar, sixpence, staker, sun
knife grainer
patron saint clement
tree amla, amli, arjan, arjun, coriaria, sumac, tanehaka
wool slipe
TANNHAUSER *beloved* elizabeth, lisaura
cavern venusberg
composer wagner
TANNIN aromadendrin, quercic
source areca, betel, gallnut, sumac, tara, valonia
TANNING beating, browning, curing, flogging
chemical borax, lime
chemical source bomah-nut, quebracho-wood
extract acacia, amaltas, arjan, arjum, bate, cachou, cashoo, catechin, catechu, cutch
gelatin collin
gum angico, kino
machine sammier
method napa
pert. scytodepsic
shrub sumac(h)
solution plumper
substance resorcin(ol), splate
TANOAN *indian* isleta, manso, pecos, picuris, piro, pueblo
TANSY bitterbuttons, cammock, costmary, herb, ragwort, silverweed, tanacetum, tonic
mustard flixweed, fluxweed
ragwort ragweed
TANTALIZE afflict, annoy, attract, badger, bait, bother, excite, harass, harry, interest, jade, plague, suffer, tease, torment, try, vex, worry
TANTALIZING alluring, desirable, interesting, mouthwatering, stimulating
TANTALUS celleret, mycteria
kingdom argos, corinth, lydia
offspring broteas, niobe, pelops
parent jupiter, pluto, thyestes, zeus

wife clytia, dione, eupryto, euryanassa, taygete

TANTAMOUNT alike, equal, equivalent, identic(al), like, same, selfsame, similar, uniform

TANTARA blare, blast, fanfare, noise

TANTIVY gallop, haste(n), headlong, rapid, ride, royalist, rush, speedily, speedy, swift(ly), tory

TANTRA agama, shastra

TANTRUM anger, caprice, conniption(fit), convulsion, fit, huff, miff, outburst, paroxysm, rage, spell, temper, tirrivee, wingding

TANTUM allowance, stint

TANZANIA isle of cloves, tanganyika, zanzibar

capital dar es salaam

city arusha, dar es salaam, dodoma, kigoma, kilwa, korogwe, kwasemangube, lindi, morogoro, moshi, mtawara, mwanza, tabora, tanga, ujiji, wete

commune ujamaa

crater ngorongoro

gorge olduvai

island pemba, zanzibar

lake nyas(s)a, rukwa

language swahili

leader karume, nyerere, sayid

party afro-shrazi

peak kibo, meru

people arusha, bantu, goma, makonde, sambara, sandawe, sukuma, swahili, wabunga, wagogo, wagoma, zongora

port tanga(nyika)

range usambara

river kagera, mbaesa, mbenkuru, pangani, ruaha, rufiji, ruvu(ma), wami

swagger stick fimbo

title sayid

weight farsalah

TAO(ISM) absolute, cosmic order, hsuan-chiao, man, peasant, road, truth, way

characters eight immortals

doctrine tac

founder chang-tao-ling, chuang-tzu, lao-tse, lao-tzu, tien-shin

god jade-emperor, jurojin

head celestial teacher, chang tao-ling, heavenly preceptor

magician mao-ku

philosopher chang-kuo, chuang-chou, chuang-tzu, lao-tse

practice wuwei

TAP ask, bang, bar, beat, blow, bob, borrow, broach, bunt, cast, chuck, cock, crack, dab(ble), dance, decant, draft, drain, draw(off), drum, extract, faucet, fever, fillip, flick, flip, heat, hit, hob, hole, latchet, leach, malaria, nattle, nozzle, nut, obstruction, open, palpate, pat, peck, penance, penetrate, percuss, perforate, pierce, pipe, plug, rap, reprove, sell, signal, snap, snock, sole, sound, spigot, spile, spout, start, strike, tip, tirl, touch, tunk, type, valve, vat

cask strike

cinder bulldog, slag

dance buck-and-wing, toe and heel

down tamp

fencing beat

foot appel

hole floss, mouth

master hob, hub

of tow hurds

on near

TAPA kapa, kikepa, siapo

TAPACOLA turco

TAPE band(age), bind(ing), cassette, dressing, fasten, ferret, fillet, garter, gin, lear, liquor, measure, mole, record, ribbon, scale, secure, string, strip, tie, yarn

fish snake

grass celery-grass, eel grass, wild celery

interruption gap

kind ferret, inkle, lear, scotch, wick

lamp wick

linen inkle

metallic galloon

narrow taste

needle bodkin

red wiggery

transparent scotch

TAPEMAN chainman

TAPER abate, acuminate, candle, cierge, contract, cusp, decrease, diminish, dip, draft, draught, draw in, dwindle, ebb, fade, lessen, lighter, luminary, narrow(ed), pricket, pyramidal, pyramidical, reduce, scarf, sharpen, slack off, snape, spire, subside, trindle, trowel, wane, wick

rod podger

TAPERED, TAPERING barreled, boattail, conical, fusiform, graduated, longicone, pointed, sharp, spiral, spired, spiring, subulate, terete

piece gore, gusset, miter

point acumen

TAPES carpet-shell, clam, venerida

TAPESTRY arras, aubusson, audenarde, bayeaux, beauvais, bruges, carpet, ceiling, coster, dorsal, dorser, dosser, dossier(e), fabric, gobelin, hanging, mortlake, susanee, tapis, textile, verdure

beetle carpet-bug

moth trichophaga

screen ceiling

warp thread lease, liss(e)

TAPEWORM bandworm, cestoda, cestode, coenurus, cystica, davainea, entozoan, flatworm, helminth, hydatid, liguca, platode, platyhelminth, taenia

embryo encopshere

head scolex

infestation scoleciasis

larva bladderworm, coenurus, cysticerus, hydatid, measle, procercoid, proscolex

part bothridium, bothrium, proglottis, strobilla

remedy brayera, embelia, mesenna

sucker osculum

TAPIO *offspring* nyyrikki, tuulikki

wife mielikki

TAPIOCA cas(s)ava, manihot, manioc, salep

globule fisheye

TAPIR anta, anteater, buffalo, bush-cow, danta, kuda, seladang, tennu

TAPIS band, hanging, hide, sash, TAPESTRY

TAPNET basket, frail

TAPPET cam, lever

TAPROOM bar, buvette, inn, pub, saloon, tavern

TAPS *composer* butterfield

1st sounder norton

TAPSTER nickpot, skinker

TAPUYAN *indian* apinage(s), auca, botocudo, bugre, caingang, camacan, caraho(s), cayapa, cayapo, chavante, coroado, ges, gesan, geslan, ghes, goyana, juya, timbira

TAR alchitran, alkitran, asphalt, binder, bluejacket, brea, coat, gob, incite, irritate, jack(y), lute, maltha, mariner, matlow, pavement, pitch, provoke, rating, sailor, salt, salve, seaman, tease, telegram

and feathers plumeopicean, torture

birch daggett

box shepherd

bush yerba santa

camphor naphthalene

extract retene

mineral maltha

product aniline, cre(o)sol, creosote, pyridine, quinoline

smear with pay

TARA brake, dolma, fern, palm, tree

TARADIDDLE liar, lie

TARANAKI *volcano* egmont

TARANTELLA bergamasca, bergamask, dance

TARANTULA hunter, jayhawk, mygalid

TARBOOSH cap, fez, turban

TARDY backward, behind(hand), bustard, delay, detained, dilatory, dreigh, lag(gard), lagging, late (some), off guard, overdue, remiss, retard(ed), slack, slow, unprepared

TARE counterweight, darnel, deduction, discount, leakage, plant, vetch, weed

grass cow-vetch

TARENTE gecko

TARES dregs, filth, refuse, weeds, zizany

TARGET aim, blank, buckler, bull's-eye, butt, cockshy, cut, cymbal, desire, end, goal, limit, mark, niveau, object(ive), pendant, prick, quintain, scope, shield, shred, signal, slice, tassel, tatter, vane

archery clout

center bull's eye, clout, eye, pin(hole)

distance from markshot

game darts

piece scab

rifle bull-gun

ring sous(e)

thrown at cockshut, cocky

towed drogue

unidentified skunk

TARHEEL *state* north carolina

TARIFF cess, charges, customs, duty, excise, impost, rate, revenue, tax, teind, tithe, toll, tribute

act dingley, fordney-mc cumber, payne-aldrich, smoot-hawley, underwood, walker

favorer protectionist

TARKA otter

TARKINGTON *character* penrod, sam

work seventeen

TARN lake, loch, pool

TARNISH besmirch, blemish, blot, brand, canker, cloud, darken, decolor, defile, dim, dirty, discolor, disgrace, dull, fade, injure, obscure, smear, smirch, soil, spoil, spot, stain, stigma, sully, tache, taint

TARO bleeding-heart, caladium, cocco, cocker, coco (root), colocasia, dalo, dasheen, eddo, eddyroot, elephant's-ear, gabe, gabi, kalo, karou, koko, malanga, masi, poi, talo, tania, tanya, tarrow, yautia

paste poi

patch ukelele

root eddo, ginger, kalo

TAROK angehen, mediatore, primavista, primiera, tarochhini, trappola, tresette

term dreier, spadilla, spadille, ultimo

TAROT atout, atutti, chariot, diable, empereur, ermite, estoile, fortitude, imperatrice, juno, jupiter, justice, l'empereur, l'ermite, l'etoile, lune, mat, minchiate, mond(e), naib, pagat, pape, papesse, tarocco

TARP(AULIN) canvas, coat, cover, hat, sailor, seabred

TARPON elops, fish, machete, milkfish, sabalo, savanilla, silverfish, silverking

relative chiro

TARQUIN *slave* ocrisia

son sextus

wife tullia

TARRADIDDLE fib, liar, lie

TARRAGON biting-dragon

TARRIANCE awaiting, delay, hindrance, sojourn

TARROCK gull, tern

TARROW delay, grumble, linger, TARRY

TARRY abide, await, bide, black, bundle, continue, dally, dawdle, defer, delay, detain, endure, fatigue, idle, lag, linger, lodge, loiter, outstay, postpone, remain, rest, retard, soiled, sojourn, stay, stop, unclean, wait, weary

TARSHISH galle

TARSIER lemur

TARSIGER bush-robin, ianthia

TARSUS ankle, digital, foot, hock, pala, shank

birthplace of paul, saul

bone astragal(us), balista, calcis, centrale, cuboid, navicular, talus

governor cleon

insect manus

river cydnus

saint paul, saul

TART (See also *kind*, below.) acerb, acid(ulous), acrid, acrimonious, blunt, bowla, brusque, caustic, curt, cutting, dry, irritable, keen, painful, pastry, pert, pie, piercing, piquant, polynee, prostitute, pungent, saucy, sensitive, severe, sharp, slut, snippy, sour, stew, strumpet, subacid, tender, trollop, turnover, wanton, waspish

candy acid-drop

kind banbury, bowla, flan, tantadlin, turnover

TARTAN boat, check, fabric, highlander, plaid, sett, ship

garb kilt

pattern sett

plaid bracken

trousers trews

TARTAR (See also *people*, below.) argal, argol, argul, calculus, chazar, crank, jung, khazar, khozar, kin, kitan, meletsky, plaque, shrew, vixen

army golden horde

burnt fecula

capital kazan

conqueror tamburlaine, tamerlane, tim(o)ur

drink kumiss

dynasty kin, wei

film plaque, scale

food earth-bread

horse tarpan

horseman cossack

lancer or *militiaman* uhlan, ulan
leader genghis khan
mounted band cahmbul, horde, u(h)lan
noble murza
people alani, bulgar, huns, jung, kalmuck, mongol, shor(tzy), sienpi, soyot, toba, turk
prince agib, chan, khan
royalty agib, khan(ate)
ruler cham
scales beeswing
strait, river into amur
tent balagan
TARTARUS hades, hell, underworld
father aether
jailer campe
offspring echidna, gigantes, typhoeus
prisoners danaids, ixion, sisyphus, titans, tityus
TARTARY See TARTAR.
lamb barometz, lycopodium, moramez
TARTNESS acerbity, acidity, acor, acrimony, asperity, piquancy, sourness
TARTUFFE hypocrite, pretender
benefactor orgon
creator moliere
maid dorine
victim elmire, orgon
TARWEED grindelia, madia, mountain-misery
TARWHINE bream
TARZAN powerhouse, stalwart, strongman
creator edgar rice burroughs
TARZED alschain, soaring falcon, star
TASH disgrace, fabric, fatigue, soil, stain
TASK accounting, assignment, aufgabe, blame, burden, business, censure, char(e), charge, chore, deed, drive, drudgery, duty, employment, enterprise, exercise, fag, feat, function, impose, impost, job, labor, metier, niyoga, nullo, occupation, office, oppress, overburden, overdrive, overtax, overwork, pensum, ramsch, stint, study, sweat, tax, test, toil, tourne, trauchle, travail, undertaking, work
assigned devoir, homework, stent, stint

easy breeze, cinch, pipe, setup, sinecure, snap
hard backbreaker, tall order
impossible aladdin's window
psychological test aufgabe
take to censure, lecture, rebuke, reproach, reprove, scold
TASKMASTER driver, overseer, rawhider, superintendent, tyrant
TASMANIA van dieman's land
animal anteater, echidna, phalanger, tapoa, thylacine, tiger, wolf, wombat
bird pardalote
cape grim
capital hobart
city burnie, devonport, hobart, launceston
convict derwenter
devil dasyurid, sacrophilus
finch firetail
lake echo, sorell, westmoreland
native vand(i)emonian
peak barrow, ben lomond, brown, cradle, drome, grey, humboldt, lomond, nevis, wellington
phalanger tapoa
pine huon
port hobart
river arthur, derwent, esk, gordon, huon, jordan, pieman, tamar
shrub honeywood, peachberry, pinkberry, river-wattle
strait bass
tiger or *wolf* thylacine
tree fitzroya, huon-pine
wolf hyena, thylacine
woman lubra
TASS bowl, cup, haystack, heap, mow, tash
TASSEL befringe, brush, clasp, cordelle, fringe, label, pendent, ribbon, tag, target, tercel, thrum, toorie, torsel, tuft, tussle, undergraduate, zizith
fish threadfin
grass ruppia
tree garrya
TASSO *character* armida, clorinda, olindo, rinaldo, sophronia, tancred
work aminta, jerusalem delivered
TASTE aesthetics, appetite, assay, bit(e), cast, charm, cultivation, dash, decency,

degust, delicacy, discernment, discrimination, drop, elegance, enjoy, experience, experiment, finesse, flavor, gout, grace, gustation, gusto, hint, judgment, lick, liking, little, manner, morsel, niceness, nicety, nip, palate, penchant, perception, pleasure, polish, pree, prove, refinement, relish, sample, sapidity, sapor, savor, scent, sense, shade, sift, sip, smack, smatch, smell, smitch, snack, soupcon, spice, style, suggestion, sup, tang, test, tinge, tint, tongue, touch, trace, trial, try, twang, zest
abnormal parageusia
absence ageusia, ageustia, inelegance
bud papilla, tongue
decided penchant, preference
-delighting friand
fundamental acid, bitter, salt, sour, sweet
good decorum
having agreeable palatable, sapid, sipid
not to one's uncongenial
pert. gustative, gustatory, palatal
perversion malacia
refined elegance
small draught, drop, gulp, nip, sip, snort
strong tang
TASTEFUL aesthetic, apt, artistic, charming, chaste, classical, cultivated, dainty, delicate, esthetic, fine, fit, neat, nice, refined, sipid, TASTY
TASTELESS artless, barbarous, blatant, coarse, crude, dull, faded, flat, flavorless, gauche, graceless, gross, harsh, improper, inaesthetic, inartistic, incorrect, indecorous, inelegant, insipid, lifeless, low, malmy, moan, offensive, outlandish, palling, rude, savorless, slipshod, stale, uncouth, unpolished, unrefined, unsavory, unseemly, vapid, vuglar, watery, waugh, wersh
TASTER cup, pipette, porringer, sample, skewer
TASTY flavorful, palatable, sapid, saporous, savory, TASTEFUL, toothsome

TAT absolute, cloth, crochet, edge, knot, matting, pony, rag, tangle, tap, tattoo, touch
kin isis

TATAR See TARTAR.

TATHAGATA See BUDDHA.

TATLER *author* addison, steele
publisher bickerstaff

TATOU(AY) armadillo, cabassou

TATTER bit, chatter, clitter, gabble, jag, libbet, part, patch, peevish, rag(man), rent, rip, scold, shred, tagrag, target, tear, testy, trollop, wear

TATTERDEMALION clown, ragamuffin, ragged, vagabond

TATTERED beaten, broken, dilapidated, disheveled, dispersed, disrupted, jagged, ragged, routed, shabby, shaggy, slashed, torn

TATTLE babble, betray, blab, chatter, cheep, clatter, clype, disclose, divulge, gash, gossip, inform, jabber, peach, prate, prattle, quatch, reveal, sneak, snitch, squeal, talk, tell, tutel

TATTLER alarm clock, bird, blab, busybody, fish, gambet, gossip, informer, quidnunc, redshank, sandpiper, talebearer, telltale, totanus, watch, willet, yellowleg

TATTOO blare, drum, mark, moko, pink, pitterpatter, pony, pounce, rat-a-tat, rub-a-dub, tafzint
design flash
man with yun

TATU peking

TAU ankh, cross, crucifix, crux, tace

TAUNT affront, aggravate, banter, barrack, censure, chaff, charge, check, chiv(v)y, comeback, crack, criticize, cut, dare, deride, dig, disdain, flaunt, fleer, fling, flout, gibe, gird, glaik, haughty, high, insult, jab, jape, jeer, jest, jibe, joke, mock, needle, nettle, niggle, offend, outrage, pert, poohpooh, provoke, quip, quirk, rag, rally, rap, rebuke, reply, reproach, revile, ridicule, sarcasm, scoff, scold,

scorn, scout, scurrility, slam, slant, slap, slare, slate, sneer, sneest, tall, tease, tempt, twit, upbraid, vex, wipe

TAUPE mole(skin), tan

TAUREG awellimiden

TAURINE bovine, bull

TAUROMACHY bullfight

TAUROPOLOS artemis

TAUROTRAGUS antelope, bongo, eland, oreas, orias

TAURUS bull, constellation, pleiades
commander caesar
gem topaz

TAUT distended, edgy, firm, highstrung, neat, nervous, rigid, severe, snug, stiff, strained, stretched, strict, tangled, tense, tidy, tight, tort, tough, trig

TAUTEN brace, snub, stiffen, swifter, swig

TAUTOG blackfish, chub, labroid, moll, oysterfish

TAUTOGOLABRUS burgall, cunner, perch

TAUTOLOGY periphrasis, pleonasm, redundancy, repetition, verbiage

TAVERN alehouse, bar (room), bierstube, bistro, brasserie, brauhaus, buvette, caback, cabaret, cafe, cantina, gasthaus, hotel, howff, inn, khan, lodge, oasis, ordinary, osteria, pothouse, pub, restaurant, roadhouse, saloon, spa, taberna, tambo, taphouse, taproom, weinstube

TAW alley, beat, dress, flog, glassie, harass, harden, marble, score, scourge, shooter, tan, tav, tew, thrash, torment, toughen, whip

TAWDRY base, blatant, cheap, coarse, flashy, florid, garish, gaudy, gilded, gross, loud, meretricious, obtrusive, pretentious, showy, tasteless, tinsel(ly), vulgar

TAWNY brusk, bullfinch, cervine, dusky, fulvid, fulvous, fusc, indian, jacinth, olive, rubiate, swart(hy), tan(ned), tenne, tigrene
comb. fusco
owl billywix
thrush veery

TAX (See also *kind*, below.) accuse, assess(ment), bur-

den, capitation, cast, censure, charge, contribution, cost, dispute, duty, exaction, exercise, fee, fine, geld, importune, impose, impost, impute, levy, ley, load, murage, oblation, onus, oppress, order, overuse, overwork, prescribe, ratal, rate, reproach, revenue, scot, settle, stent, stipend, strain, task, tenth, tire, tole, toll, tribute, try
assessor stentmaster
avoidance technique shelter, skimming
capitation jizya(h), vergi
collector See *gatherer*, below.
comb. age
ecclesiastic teind, tithe
excessive maltolte
extraordinary auxilium
feudal tallage
gatherer catchpole, catchpoll, exciseman, gabbai, gabeller, poller, qaid, tahsildar, tither
harvest cornbole
head capitation
herring catch lastage
kind 3 cro, soc, vat 4 cess, geld, gift, head, mise, poll, salt, scat, sess, toll 5 finta, lekin, likin, maill, obrok, prest, quint, sales, scatt, stent, toust, vergi, zacat, zakah 6 abkari, abkary, annale, avania, caphar, cedula census, estate, excise, export, extent, fumage, hidage, import, income, jeziah, kharaj, liquor, octroi, octroy, pavage, single, surtax, taille, vinage 7 annates, bonaght, boomage, boscage, burghal, chancer, chevage, chivage, customs, doomage, gabelle, lastage, license, patente, pollage, pontage, prisage, scutage, tallage, terrage 8 alcabala, auxilium, bonaught, carucage, cornbole, danegeld, kernetty, maltolte, nuisance, peshcash, property, romescot, romeshot, screwing, stackage, wheelage 9 ad valorem, severance, surcharge, war profit 10 added value, capitation, chaukidari 11 inheritance, value added, withholding 12 capital gains
land carucage, tenmantale, vergi

liquor abkari

logs boomage

municipal burghal-penny, scot-and-lot

parish purvey

plow carucage

poll capitation, census, head-penny, toll

property rates

protest boston tea party

rate assessment, ratal

salt gabelle

synagogue finta

traveler's caphar

unbelievers' khanaj

walls murage

wood boscage

wool maletolte, maletote

TAXATION accusation, assessment, caption, charge, reproof, revenue, valuation

TAXI cab, crawler, cruiser, fiacre, hack, jinrikisha, jixie, ricksha(w), takeoff

driver cabby, hacker, jehu

meter clock

TAXIDERMIST stuffer

TAXIDERMY nassology

TAXING exhausting, grueling, severe, tiring

TAXIS arrangement, order, ordonnance

TAXONOMY classification, systematics

TAXUS badger, yew

TAYASSU pecari

TAYGETE *consort* zeus

offspring eurotas, lacedaemon

parent atlas, pleione

TAYLOR, ZACHARY old rough and ready, ole rough 'n' ready

birthplace virginia

burial site louisville, kentucky

party whig

profession lawyer

victory buena vista

TAZZA bowl, cup, vase

TCHAIKOVSKY *ballet* nutcracker, sleeping beauty, swan lake

TCHE flute, shrub, vanieria

TEA (See also *kind,* below.) bellywash, beverage, collation, marijuana, party, reception, sociable, social, steep

berry checkerberry, snowberry, wintergreen

black bohea, congo, oopa(c)k, pekoe, souchong, sychee

bowl chawan

box caddy, calin, canister

cake biscuit, crumpet, flipflap, sally lunn, scon(e)

cart trolley

ceremony chanoyu

chest lining calin

coarse bancha

constituent caffeine, theine

dissertation on tsiology

excessive drinker theic

expert taster

extract adenine

flower rose

girl mousmee

green gunpowder, hyson, twankay

high-grade gyokuro

inferior blash, boher

kind assam, bergamot, black, bohea, cambric, camomile, caper, cha(a), chais, chia, congo(u), darjeeling, earl grey, emesa, faham, gowiddie, green, gunpowder, herb, hyson, kat, keemun, lapsang, ledum, lemon balm, mate, miang, oolong, oopack, oopak, orange-pekoe, padra, pekoe, penny royal, ptisan, redroot, sage, salo(o)p, sassafras, souchong, sunglo, tcha, tham, tisane, tsane, tsia, twankay, woodruff, wormseed, yerba

leaves souchong

medicinal camomile, ptisan, sassafras, tisane

plant thea

plant disease copper blight

rolled cha(a), chais, tsia

room cafe, kiosk

rose bon silene, bride

substitute faham

table ambulante, teapoy, tepoy

tree manuka

weak blash, catlap

TEACH amaister, apprise, aral, biteche, catechize, coach, conduct, counsel, cram, direct, discipline, document, drill, edify, educate, endue, enlighten, expound, ground, guide, impart, implant, inculcate, indoctrinate, inform, initiate, instill, instruct, lecture, monitor, nurture, preach, prime, school, show, tache, tell, train, tutor, wisse

edward blackbeard, buccaneer, pirate

TEACHABLE apt, docile, pliable, pliant

TEACHER abecadarian, abecedary, acharya, akun(d), alfaqui(n), alim, amauta, ayudante, biddy, coja, coach, didascalos, director, docent, doctor, dominie, don, educator, gamaliel, guide, guru, hoja, ima(u)m, instructor, khoja, kindergart(e)ner, lecturer, madrih, maestro, magister, master, maulvi, melammed, mentor, mistress, molla(h), moonshee, mujtahid, mulla(h), munshi, murshid, pandit, pedagog(ist), pedagogue, pedant, pir, preacher, preceptor, prof (essor), pundit, rab(bi), reb(be), regent, rhetor schoolmarm, schoolmaster, scribe, shastri, sophist, starets, trainer, tutor, usher

fee minerval

group faculty, nea, professorate, pta, staff

of eloquence rhetor, sophist

of the deaf oralist

of the koran alfaqui(n)

religious acharya, akhoond, akhund, alim, didascalos

TEACHING acousma, acroama, brownism, cacodoxy, dharma, didactic(s), education, guidance, instruction, loring, pedagogics, pedagogy, tuition, tutelage

exoteric acousmata

of a fable moral

of the 12 didache

oral acroama

pert. didactic, pedagogic

science of didactics, pedagogy

TEAHOUSE *site* naha, okinawa

TEAK cocoa, dark, dhak, djati, ebony, endiandra, flindosa, kino, lingoum, puriri, saj, teca, tectona, wood

-like wood angili

TEAKETTLE chafer, cresset, pourie, suke(y), sukie, suky

TEAL bluewing, crick, duck, fowl, garganey, nettion, nyroca, querquedula, sarcelle

group spring

TEAM associate, brace, brood, chain, crew, draft, eleven, faction, five, flock,

franchise, gang, group, join, lineage, nine, offspring, pair, party, progeny, race, random, rig, set, side, span, squad, staff, string, teem, two, yoke
athletic club
harnessed tandem
kind duo, eleven, five, frosh, nine, scrub, second, spike, unicorn, varsity
of horses cartware
supporter fan, rooter
3-horse randem, spike, troika, unicorn
2-horse podanger
up with combine, join
TEAMMATE comrade, co-worker, partner
TEAMSTER bearer, carrier, carter, drayman, driver, skinner, toter, trucker
command gee, haw
président fitzsimmons, hoffa
TEAMWORK collaboration, cooperation, coordination
TEAP See RAM.
TEAPOT cadogan, chawan, samovar, track, urn
cover cosie, cosy, cozy
lidless cadogan
spout beak
TEAR (See also TEARS.) afflict, agitate, bacchanal, binge, break, bust, cleave, dainty, damage, delicate, destroy, disrupt, divide, divulse, drop, explode, fault, fine, flax, flurry, fly, fray, frazzle, hurry, hurt, jag, jamboree, lacerate, lachryma, lament, laniate, larme, mangle, open, outburst, party, passion, pierce, pull, race, rage, remove, rend, rent, revel, rip(ple), rit, rive, run, rush, separate, shatter, shred, skat, skeg, slash, slit, snag, snatch, spalt, speed, split, spree, sunder, tatter, toot, torment, touse, trip, waste, weep, wound, wrench
apart criticize, demolish, discerp, dismantle, divulse, rend, rip(up), shred, tatter, tease
around bustle, rampage, storm
away avulse, strip
bottle lachrymatory
-cat blusterer, ranting, swaggering
down demolish, destroy,

disassemble, discredit, disparage, prostrate, rase, raze, unpile
drop eyewater
gas bromoacetone, lachrymator
into attack, lambaste, undertake
loose extricate
off depart, discerp, start, strip, take
on a doing the town (up brown), painting the town (red)
pert. lachrymal, lachrymatory, lachrymose
pit gland, larmier
-producing substance lachrymator
to pieces criticize, demolish, dilacerate, laniate, shred, tatter, tease, toll
up annul, arac(h)e, assart, cancel, eradicate, essart, extirpate, pluck, scrap
TEARFUL crying, lachrymose, maudlin, moist, sad, snivelly, sorrowful, watery, weeping, weepy, wet, woeful
TEARING avulsion, furious, harrowing, hasty, hurrying, impressive, laceration, ripping, splendid, tremendous, violent
TEARS brine, dew, eyewater, heatdrops, rheum
comb. dacry(o)
excessive flow dacryorrhea
inducing rheumatic
pert. lacrimal
poetic rheum
secretion dacryagogue
TEASE abuse, annoy, badger, bait, ballyrag, banter, beg, bother, bullyrag, caddle, card, chafe, chaff, chevy, chip, chivvy, comb, devil, disturb, fret, gall, guy, harass, hare, harry, hatchel, hector, importune, intimidate, irritate, jog, josh, kib(b)itz, molest, needle, pest(er), pick on, plague, rag, rally, rib, ride, stir, tantalize, tar(r), torment, tout, trouble, twit, vex, wherret, worry
wool comb, toom, tum
TEASEL boneset, comb, dipsacus, huttonweed, manweed, scabiosa, succisa, tassle, thistle
bundle glean

prepare heads of carp
TEASER advertisement, carder, curler, fireman, gull, kicker, skua, sniper, tizeur, willow(er)
TEASING annoying, badinage, banter, chaff, joshing, persiflage, quizzing, raillery
TEATY cross, fretful, peevish
TEBAH *mother* reumah
TEBELDI baobab
TECHED See INSANE.
TECHNICAL fussy, occupational, persnickety, professional, skilled
TECHNICALITY detail, item, nicety, particular, punctilio, specification, subtlety
TECHNIQUE art(istry), capacity, coquille, feat, form, gate, manner, method, procedure, routine, skill, spiccato, system, tactics, usage, way, wrinkle
TECHY choleric, cranky, cross, fretful, irascible, irritable, irritating, peevish, sensitive, splenetic, testy, TOUCHY, vexing
TECK cravat, tie
TECMESSA *consort* ajax
parent teleutas, teuthras
son eurysaces
TECOMA angelin, bignonia, fiddlewood, peroba, roble, shrub, trumpet-creeper
TECTON *son* phereclus
TECUMSEH *brother* the prophet
slayer richard m johnson
TED scatter, spread, theodore, toad, turn, waste
TEDIOUS bored, boresome, boring, colorless, deliberate, dilatory, dingdong, dreary, dree, dreigh, dry, dull, elenge, everlasting, exhausting, flat, hackneyed, harping, humdrum, insipid, irksome, irritable, long(winded), monotonous, noxious, onerous, oppressive, peevish, plebian, poky, preachy, prolix, prosaic, prosy, slow, stale, stuffy, tiresome, tiring, trite, unexciting, vapid, verbose, wearing, wearisome, wooden
TEDIUM boredom, discontent, doldrums, ennui, melancholy
TEE bring, bullhead, cock, draw, lead, mark, precisely,

proceed, target, tight, tozee, witter

-*hee* laugh, snicker, titter

off begin, drive, reprimand, scold

TEEM abound, augment, bear, bristle, burst, bustle, conceive, crawl with, discharge, drain, effect, empty, engender, fetch, fill, generate, lead, multiply, overflow, pour, proliferate, pullulate, rain, resort, shower, swarm, swim, throng, yield

TEEMING abounding, alive with, aswarm, big, bristling, countless, crawling, crowded, fertile, full, gushing, innumerable, numberless, overflowing, packed, plentiful, plenty, populous, pouring, productive, profuse, prolific, rife, studded, swarming, thick, thronged, tumid, uncounted, untold

TEEN abuse, affliction, age, anger, calumniate, damage, distress, grief, harm, hate, hurt, injure, injury, irritate, keen, pain, provoke, reproach, shut, slander, sorrow, suffering, teind, tend, tind, trouble, tune, vex(ation), vexed

-*age* adolescent, hebetic, youthful

-*age social* slumber party

TEENAGE brushwood

TEENER giglet, gossoon

TEENY fretful, little, malicious, miniature, minute, peevish, petite, small, tiny, wee(ny)

TEET peep, pry, snoop

TEETER alternate, change, didder, dither, jiggle, lurch, oscillate, quake, quiver, reel, rock, sandpiper, seesaw, shake, shimmy, sway, tip, totter, tremble, vacillate, waver, wobble

board seesaw

TEETERTAIL sandpiper

TEETH See also TOOTH.

ridge alveole, alveolus

set denture(s)

space between diastema

without edentate

TEETHY biting, crabbed, cross, irritable

TEETING titlark

TEETOTAL absolute, abstain, abstemious, complete, entire

TEETOTALER abstainer, dry, nephalist, nonuser, rechabite, refrainer

TEETOTUM put and take, whirligig

TEEWHAAP lapwing

TEFNUT *brother* shu

consort shu

TEGEA *founder* agamemnon, tegeates

king aleus

TEGEATES *father* lycaon

son limon, scephrus

TEGUA sandal, shoe

TEGUEXIN See TEIOID.

TEGULA alula, appendage, epaulette, pantagium, scapula, squama, squamula, tile

TEGUMENT aril, coat, cover, cortex, membrane, skin, testa

TEGURIUM cabin, hut, shrine

TEICHER bleed, ooze

TEIND tax, tithe(s)

TEIOID ameiva, jacuaru, lizard, racerunner, teguexin, teju

TEIRESIAS See TIRESIAS.

TEJU See TEIOID.

TEKKE, TEKYA carpet, convent, monastery, rug, turkoman

TEKOA *herdsman* amos

TELA bristle, membrane, tissue, web

TELAMON atlantes, atlas, caryatid, column, pilaster, pillar

brother peleus, phocus

consort eriobea, glauce, hesione, periboea, theanira

friend hercules

parent acheus, aeacus, endeis

son ajax, teucer, trambelus

victim phocus

TEL AVIV *newspaper* haaretz

part jaffa, joppa, yafa

TELDRIN chlorpheniramine

TELEDU badger, mammal, skunk, stinkard

TELEGONUS *consort* penelope

parent circe, odysseus, proteus, ulysses

slayer hercules

son italus

victim odysseus, ulysses

TELEGRAM cable, dispatch, flash, message, nightletter, wire(less)

TELEGRAPH *click* dash, dot

code morse

device ticker

inventor marconi, morse

key tapper

kind simplex

operator brass-pounder

part anvil, key, siphon, tapper

plant tick-trefoil

signal dash, dot, semaphore

underwater cable

unit baud, spacer

TELEKINETIC psychic(al)

TELEMACHUS *nurse* euryclea

parent odysseus, penelope, ulysses

son latinus

TELEPATHIC clairvoyant, extrasensory, mentiferous, psychic, spiritualistic, supernatural

TELEPATHY clairvoyance, esp, intuition, telesthesia, telopsis, telurgy

TELEPHASSA *husband* agenor

offspring cadmus, europa, phoenix

TELEPHONE buzz, call, dial, horn, pipe, ring up

book directory

booth call-box

company ma bell

duration meter calculagraph

exchange central, pbx

inventor bell

operator central, phone-girl

receiver cymaphen

washington to moscow hot line

TELEPHONUS bacbakiri

TELEPHUS *consort* astyoche, laodice

foster-father corythus

kingdom mysia

parent auge, hercules

wounded by achilles

TELEPIX wire photos

TELESCOPE abbreviate, abridge, aligner, astrograph, collapse, condense, fieldglass, fold, glass, lens, shorten, siderostat, sight, simplify, spyglass

kind almucantar, cassegrain(ian), collimator, galilean, gregorian, herschelian, newtonian, reflecting, yerkes

mountain palomar, wilson

part eyepiece, lens, mirror, reticle, speculum

TELEVISION boob tube, idiot box, telly, tube, video

adjunct mike, rabbit ears
advertiser sponsor
broadcast telecast, telethon
cable coaxial
camera creepie-peepie, pickup, walkie-lookie
camera boom crane
commercial cowcatcher, message, spot(announcement)
defect flopover, ghost, snow
interference snow
inventor farnsworth, nipkow
network abc, bbc, cbs, nbc, rai
part aerial, knob, screen, tube
program telecast
prompter idiot-board
rating arbitron, hooper, nielsen
recording kinescope
rerun fee residual
serial soap(er)
slide balop
solicitation telethon
summer fare rerun
technician cameraman, monitor, soundman
term adder, bloom, catv, dolly, encoder, evr, ghost, grid, image, instant replay, kinescope, mixer, noise, orthicon, pan, pickup, picture, rain, relay, rerun, scan, scophy, screen, signal, snow, telecast, televise, uhf, vhf, video, vidicon
tube emitron, iconoscope, monoscope, vidicon
union aftra
western horse opera, lancer
TELIS aristotle
TELL acquaint, advertise, advise, affect, affirm, announce, apprise, ascertain, betray, blab, blat, broadcast, bruit, calculate, carp, chat, communicate, confess, count, declare, deem, describe, determine, dictate, discern, disclose, discourse, divulge, enumerate, explain, express, hill, impart, impress, influence, inform, issue, know, matter, mention, mound, narrate, noise, notify, number, own, present, publish, recite, reckon, recognize, recount, regard, relate, render, repeat, report, reveal, review, say, signify, snitch, speak, spread, state, storify, tale,

talk, tattle, teach, utter, value, ventilate, weigh
all confess
in advance caution, warn
off berate, chew out, denounce, enumerate, number, rebuke, reprimand, reprove, scold
on betray, blab, inform, peach, reveal, sing, snitch, squeal, tattle
revelatory facts debunk, expose
secretly whisper
secrets blab, clype
without authority gossip, rumor
TELL, WILLIAM *companion* melchthal
enemy gessler
hero egil(1)
home altdorf, uri
wife edwidge
TELLER banker, cambist, cashier, fabulist, paymaster, potdar, purser, senachie, storier
TELLING cogent, conclusive, convincing, decisive, definitive, effective, eloquent, enumeration, forceful, important, influential, narrative, operative, pertinent, potent, powerful, relation, relevant, revealing, significant, sound, stimulating, striking, timely, trenchant, valid
TELLTALE betrayer, betraying, blab, busybody, clew, clue, hint, indication, indicator, informer, talebearer, tattler, tattletale, timeclock
TELLTRUTH frankness, honesty
TELLURIAN earthly, terrestrial
TELLURIDE altaite, calaverite, hessite, petzite
compound wehrlite, weissite
TELLURIUM *black* nagyagite
source sylvanite
TELLUS *festival* fordicidia
TELSON pleon, segment, somite
TELUGU gentoo, gentu, telinga
TEM atmu, atum, tum
emblem ankh, pschent
TEMA *kin* ishmael
TEMBLOR earthquake, tremor

TEMERARIOUS bold, chance, foolhardy, fortuitous, headlong, headstrong, heedless, rash, reckless, venturesome, venturous
TEMERITY audacity, boldness, brass, cheek, daring, effrontery, foolhardiness, gall, hardihood, impetuosity, nerve, rashness
TEMPER adapt, adjust, allay, alleviate, anger, animus, anneal, appease, assuage, attune, bait, bate, birse, blend, blood, chasten, compromise, control, cool, curb, dander, delay, disposition, fit, fix, govern, hackles, harden, heal, heat, humor, ire, irish, irritation, lighten, make-up, manage, mean, medium, mettle, mingle, mix, moderate, modify, mollify, monkey, mood, nature, neal, personality, planish, qualify, rage, reduce, regulate, relax, relieve, restore, restrain, season, sober, soften, soothe, spell, spirit, spunk, state, steady, tone, toughen, tune, weaken
bad anger, bile, choler, conniption(fit), huff, pet, spleen, tantrum
burst of blowup, boutade, brainge, fit, moorburn, pet, tantrum
having even calm, sedate, staid
kind choler, huff, ire, mood, spleen
leather moisten
metal allay
TEMPERAMENT climate, complexion, composition, constitution, crasis, disposition, gemut, heart, humor, kidney, kind, mind, mood, personality, nature, TEMPER, type
TEMPERAMENTAL constitutional, excitable, froward, headstrong, irritable, moody, sensitive, willful
TEMPERANCE abnegation, abstinence, asceticism, austerity, calmness, combination, conservatism, continence, denial, eschewal, forbearance, frugality, mingling, moderation, prudence, renunciation, restraint, sacrifice, self-con-

trol, self-restraint, sobriety, temperature
organization wctu
symbol of elephant
symbolic color white
TEMPERATE abstemious, balmy, calm, collected, composed, conservative, constant, continent, cool, curbed, dispassionate, equable, even, fair, frugal, gentle, just, lenient, measured, medium, moderate, reasonable, restrained, self-controlled, sober, soft, sparing, steady, stinting, warm
TEMPERATURE calefaction, calescence, compound, constitution, disposition, febricity, fever, heat, hotness, mildness, mixture, moderation, pyrexia, temperament, state
gradient thermocline
line isothere
lowering hypothermia
measurement celcius, fahr (enheit), pyrometry
measurer climatometer, cryometer, thermometer
point solidus
TEMPEST agitate, bayamo, blast, bourasque, commotion, convulsion, drum, excitement, gale, orage, outburst, rage, rout, samiel, squall, storm, thud, tumult, turmoil, upheaval, wind (storm)
author shakespeare
character adrian, alonso, antonio, ariel, caliban, ceres, ferdinand, francisco, gonzalo, iris, juno, miranda, prospero, sebastian, stephano, sycorax, trinculo
deity setabos
slave caliban
villainess sycorax
TEMPESTUOUS boisterous, raging, rugged, stormy, tumultous, turbulent, violent
TEMPLAR barrister, knight, lawyer, mason
battle cry beauseant
enemy saladin
idol baphomet
standard beauseant
TEMPLATE See TEMPLET.
TEMPLE bure, candi, cathedral, cella, chandi, church, covil, deul, dewal, duomo, fane, firja, guaca, haffet, heiau, heraeum, her(a)ion,

hieron, huaca, jinja, jinsha, kiack, kovil, mandir, marae, masjid, mosk, mosque, naos, olympium, pagoda, pantheon, parthenon, pentastylos, rameseum, rath(a), sacrum, sanctuary, sha, shrine, synagogue, taa, tabernacle, teocalli, teopan, tjandi, valhalla, varella, vat, vihara, wat, yashiro
area mandapa
builder micah
cavelike speos
enclosure marae, marai
flower frangipani, plumeria
gateway torii
mound teocalli
of reason notre dame
part cella, naos, pastophorion, pastophorium, pronaos
porch chaori, mantap(p)a
portico narthex
sanctuary penetralia
study naology
tower sikh(o)ra, vomana, ziggurat
vestibule antarala, epinaos, pronaos
TEMPLET, TEMPLATE beam, bezel, gauge, lute, mold, pattern, rake
TEMPO agoge, beat, cadence, coin, measure, meter, pace, pulse, rate, rhythm, speed, takt, time, velocity
change accelerando, ritardando
fluctuating rubato
pert. agogic
rapid presto
slow adagio, grave, lento
TEMPORAL carnal, chronological, civil, earthly, ephemeral, laic, lay, material, mortal, mundane, objective, passing, political, profane, secular, temporary, transient, transitory, worldly
TEMPORARILY for the nonce, in the interim, meanwhile
TEMPORARY acting, ad hoc, ad interim, brief, ephemeral, episodal, episodic, evanescent, fleeting, flying, fugitive, impermanent, interim, makeshift, meanwhile, passing, pro tem, provisional, short, stopgap, substitute, supply, transient, transitory

contrivance makeshift
TEMPORIZE delay, diagonalize, filibuster, negotiate, parley, procrastinate, soothe, stall, tarry, trim, yield
TEMPORIZER drifter, egotist, timeserver, trimmer
religious politique
TEMPT allure, attempt, attract, bait, court, decoy, entice, incite, induce, inveigle, invite, lure, persuade, prevail on, prove, provoke, seduce, solicit, suggest, test, tole, try, woo
TEMPTATION allurement, bait, enticement, inducement, lure, seduction, surrection, testing, trial
TEMPTER devil, enticer, satan, siren
TEMPTING appetizing, enticing, inviting, luring, magnetic, seducting, seductive
TEMPTRESS circe, delilah, lorelei, siren
TEMS(E) sieve, sift
TEN brisque, chang, cheung, decad(e), decem, denary, di(c)ker, dix, icre, indefinitely, iota, many, sawbuck, several, tithe
cents dime
-cent store five and dime, kresge's, woolworth's
comb. dec(a), decem, deka
commandments decalog(ue)
company of decury
-footed decapod
leader of decarch, dekarch, doyen
parts, divided into decameral, decamerous
-percenter agent
plus, comb. teen
-pounder awa, bonefish, bonyfish, cannon, chiro, elops, ladyfish, macabi, skipjack, springer
-sided decagon
-strike score, sensation, success
-stringed decachord
thousand, comb. myri(a)
years decennial
TENABLE believable, defensible, justifiable
TENACE ace-queen, fork, fourchette, king-jack
TENACIOUS adhesive, cledgy, clinging, closefisted, coherent, dogged, fast, firm, glutinous, grasping, leal,

miserly, obdurate, obstinate, opinionated, persevering, persistent, pertinacious, possessive, prehensile, resolute, retentive, stalwart, stanch, steadfast, sticky, stout, strong, stubborn, sturdy, thick, tough, true, viscid, viscous

TENACITY adhesiveness, backbone, coherence, cohesiveness, courage, decision, grit, guts, lentor, mettle, nerve, pluck, resolution, retention, spirit, toughness

TENANCY conacre, estate, holding, house, occupancy, occupation, possession, tenure

TENANT bordar, ceile, chakdar, colibert, cottar, cott(i)er, crofter, customer, dreng(h), dwell(er), feodary, feudary, fuidhir, geneat, homager, householder, inhabit(ant), inmate, kmet, laet, lessee, leud, live, livier, lodger, molman, occupant, occupier, occupy, possess(or), radman, rentee, renter, reside(nt), roomer, saer, socager, socman, sokeman, suckener, tenon, vassal, vavasor, villein
farm croft
feudal leud(e), radknight, socager, vassal, villein
free dreng(h)
inferior pendicler
life liveyer, livier
non-paying cesser
service thirlage
servile gablatores
tribute cens

TENCH cyprinid, penitentiary, tinca

TEND affect, aid, aim, attend, await, bear, bend, burn, care(for), cherish, conduce, contribute, cultivate, dispose, dress, drift, expect, feed, foster, govern, groom, guard, head, impel, incline, influence, kindle, lead, lean, listen, mind, minister, nurse, nurture, point(to), predispose, propend, protect, purpose, reach, serve, shield, stretch, supply, trend, turn, verge, wait, warp, watch
a fire stoke
to rise levitate
toward one point converge

TENDANCE attention, care, ministration, service

TENDENCY addiction, affection, aptitude, aptness, attitude, bearing, bent, bias, cast, conatus, course, current, diathesis, direction, disposition, drift, drive, eonism, genius, impulse, inclination, instinct, knack, leaning, mind, nitency, partiality, pattern, penchant, predisposition, proclivity, proneness, propensity, readiness, samkara, set, slant, temper, tenor, trend, turn, twist, vergency, warp
structural peloria

TENDER aching, administer, advance, affectionate, amatory, amoroso, amorous, apply, approach, attendant, bid, boat, careful, cockboat, considerate, dear, delicate, feminine, fleshly, fond, fragile, frail, gentle, gift, give, gracious, hearty, hoy, humane, immature, intimate, kind, light, loving, merciful, mild, money, nurse, overture, painful, patache, pay, pinnace, piteous, pitiful, precious, prefer, present, proffer, proposal, responsive, sensitive, sentimental, shepherd, soft (hearted), sore, stenter, sympathetic, tart, tenuous, ticklish, tid, touchy, vernal, volunteer, warm(hearted), weak, young, youthful
legal aloi, cash, coin(age), currency, dollar, MONEY, specie
ship's barge, collier, ding(e)y, dinghy, gig, pinnace

TENDERFOOT babe, beginner, cheechaco, cheechako, dude, greenhorn, greenie, innocent, neophyte, newcomer, novice, rookie, rube, shorthorn, tyro

TENDERHEARTED compassionate, human(e), impressionable, kind, soft, sympathetic

TENDERLOIN fil(l)et, stews, undercut

TENDERLY amoroso, cautiously, delicately, effeminately, fondly, gently, softly

TENDERNESS affection,

compassion, delicacy, effeminacy, fondness, gentleness, kindness, mercy, passion, softness, sympathy, yearning

TENDING inclining, leaning
comb. acious, ative, centric, telic

TENDON aponeurosis, c(h)ord, frenulum, muscle, sinew, string, thew
bone sesamoid
comb. teno
inflammation tenositis, thecitis

TENDRIL bine, capreol, cir(h)us, clasp, climber, coil, crook, curl, filament, part, ringlet, root, shoot, sprig, stem, stipule, tenacle, twist, winder
having capreolate
-like pampiniform
pert. cirrate

TENEBRIFIC, TENEBROUS dark, dusky, gloomy, nocturnal, obscure, sad

TENEDOS bozcaada

TENEMENT abode, advowson, apartment, chawl, dwelling, flat, franchise, habitation, holding, house, land, lodging, quarters, praedium, rooms, warren

TENERIFFE canary, wine
volcano teide, teyde

TENES *kingdom* tenedos, troas
parent cycnus, philonome, porclea
slayer achilles
stepmother philonome, phylonome

TENET adoxy, axiom, belief, canon, confession, credo, creed, conviction, decree, doctrine, dogma, faith, mishnah, opinion, paradox, persuasion, principle, view

TENFOLD decuple, denary

TENNANTITE binnite

TENNE hyacinth, orange, tawny

TENNESSEE *capital* nashville
city alcoa, bristol, camden, cedar hill, chattanooga, clarksville, cleveland, dickson, fayetteville, franklin, gallatin, greenbrier, hendersonville, inglewood, kingsport, knoxville, lexington, memphis, morristown, murfreesboro, nashville, oak

ridge, old hickory, paris, pulaski, sparta, springfield
college belmont, bethel, fisk, lambuth, lane, lemoyne, milligan, siena, tusculum, vanderbilt
county cocke, davidson, dyer, giles, grundy, knox, mc minn, miegs, obion, rhea, sevier
dam norris, wilson
flower flag, iris, maypop, passionflower
fort donelson, henry, nashboro
governor, 1st sevier
indian cherokee, chickasaw, shawnee
lake cherokee, douglas, reelfort, wattsbar
name, old franklin
national park shiloh
native whelp
nickname big bend state, old franklin, volunteer state
peak clingman's dome, guyot, lookout
president jackson, polk
range cumberland, smokies, smoky
river caney, cumberland, duck, elk, hiwassee, holston, stone
river rapids muscle shoals
state bird mockingbird
state flower flag, iris, passionflower
state tree poplar
valley authority, part wilson dam
TENNIS *attendant* caddy
ball palm
ball surface nap
champion anderson, arth, ashe, betz, borg, budge, bueno, casals, cooke, dent, doeg, flam, gerulaitis, gonzales, goolagong, hard, hart, hoad, hunt, king, lacoste, laver, mako, marble, moody, nastase, newcombe, osborne, osuna, panatta, pasarelle, perry, ralston, richey, riggs, santana, schroeder, smith, susman, talbert, tilden, travert, wade, wallach, ward, wightman, wills, wright
court wall battery
cup davis
error fault
4 players doubles
game series set
-like game badminton, fives

no score love
old form bandy
player netman
racquet scute
racquet string gut
relative badminton, paddle tennis, ping pong, racquet ball
score ace, adin, deuce, love
shoe keds, plimsol, sneaker
stroke ace, backhand, cannonball, chandelle, chop, cut, dink, let, lob, serve, smash
term advantage, alley, bandy, break, court, cut, dedans, deuce, drive, fault, game, let, match, net, placement, racket, rally, receive, run on, serve, service, set, stroke, toss, volley
tournament site forest hills, wimbledon
TENNYSON *character* bellicent, elaine, enid, enoch arden, hallam, king arthur, maud, ulysses
poem enoch arden, idylls of the king, in memoriam, maud, the princess
TENOCHTITLAN mexico city
TENON coak, cog, dovetail, join, lewis(son), mortise, tooth, tusk, unite
secure by cauk
TENOR baritone, canto, character, condition, course, current, direction, drift, effect, feck, gist, import, inclination, intent, meaning, mood, motion, move, nature, purport, quality, significance, singer, stamp, strength, tendency, tone, transcript, trend
falsetto tenorino
famous caruso
violin alto, violotta
TENPINS newport
TENREC centetes, centetid, hedgehog, hedgepig, tangue
TENSE brace, brittle, constrict, edgy, firm, flex, hard, highstrung, inflexible, intent, jittery, nervous, prolong, rapt, rigid, stiff(en), stout, strained, strait, strict, taut(en), tight(en), time, uneasy, unrelaxed, uptight
grammatical aorist, conditional, future, past, perfect, pluperfect, present, preterit, progressive

TENSILE ductile, elastic, pliant
TENSION anxiety, balance, brunt, discontent, discord, fatigue, force, intensity, isotonia, nerves, potential, pressure, pull, rigidity, stiffness, strain(t), stress, stretching, tautness, torsion, thrust, unrest
device bungee
normal isotonia
relaxing of detente
remedy aspirin, mantra, meditation, miltown, tranquilizer, valium
TENT attention, balagan, big top, cabin, camp, cannat, canopy, canvas, care, chum, cover(ing), crame, darry, dossil, dressing, heed, hinder, hut, kedar, kibitka, leanto, lint, lodge, marquee, marquise, observe, paul, pavilion, pawl, pr(a)etorium, probe, proffer, search, shelter, shool, sparver, taberna, tawn, teld, tender, te(e)pee, test, tienda, tilt, tipi, toldo, tupek, wigwam, wine, witu, yourt, yurt(a), zdarsky
caterpillar malacosoma, webworm
circular kibitka, y(o)urt(a)
covering fly, tilt
dweller arab, bedouin, camper, gypsy, indian, kedar, nomad, scenite, tourist, yuruk
fabric canvas, duck, nylon
live in camp
maker omar khyyam
maker's patron saint paul
peg stake
store crame
TENTACLE antenna, brachium, feeler, hair, horn, pacle, palp, sucker, tendril, tentaculum
branch tentillum
having actinal, dicerous
without acerous
TENTATIVE ad interim, conditional, contingent, dependent, experimental, gingerly, impermanent, makeshift, potential, provisional, substitute, temporary, testing, trial
TENTER foreman, frame, hang, machine, stretch
TENTERHOOK(S) nail, spike, stretcher

on agog, anxious, confounded, edgy, nervous, tense, uneasy

TENTH decima, dime, mill, tax, teind, tithe
anniversary decennial, tin
comb. dec(i)
muse sappho
nerve vagus
part teind, tithe

TENUITY delicacy, exility, faintness, indigence, meagerness, poverty, rareness, rarity, slenderness, thinness

TENUOUS aerial, airy, delicate, ethereal, flimsy, fine, foggy, frail, gaseous, gossamer, insignificant, rare, rarified, slender, slight, slim, subtile, subtle, thin, trivial, unsubstantial, vague, weak

TENURE almoign, bordage, burgage, capite, censive, copyhold, drengage, dynasty, farmage, feu, frankalmoign, freehold, gavelkind, holding, incumbency, jagheer, jag(h)ir, lease, manurance, overland, period, regime, reign, sergeanty, soc(c)age, socmanry, sorehon, sorren, suithold, term, vavasory, venville

TEPEE chum, lodge, tent, tipi, wickiup, wigwam

TEPHROSIA anil, catgut, goat's-rue, herb

TEPID disinterested, indifferent, languid, leu, lukewarm, mild, warm(ish), wlach, wlech

TEQUILA agave, century plant, drink, liquor, mescal

TERA church, monastery

TERAH *father* nahor
son abraham, haran

TERAPH god, idol, image, talisman

TERATHOPIUS bataleur, bateleur, berghaan, eagle

TERATISM abnormality, anomaly, deformity, monstrosity

TERATOMA embryoma, tumor

TERBIUM europium, gadolinium
source monazite

TEREBINTH resin, teil, turpentine

TEREBRA auger, drill, gastropod

TEREBRATION boring, pain, perforation, trephining

TEREDO borer, mollusk, shipworm, woodworm

TERENCE *play* adelphi, andria, eunuchus, hecyra, phormio, the mother-in-law

TERESA *husband* sancho panza
offspring amina

TERETE centric

TEREUS *ally* pandion
changed into hawk, hoopoo
consort procne
father ares, mars
sister-in-law philomela
son itis, itylus, itys

TERGAL aboral, back, dorsal, posterial

TERGITE pygidium, tergum

TERGIVERSATE apostatize, desert, equivocate, evade, lie, oscillate, quibble, retreat, shift, shuffle

TERGIVERSATION about-face, ambiguity, apostasy, deceit, desertion, evasion, reversal, reverse, right-about-face, shift, subterfuge, voltface

TERM (See also TERMS.) administration, age, appelative, articulation, bound(ary), bourn, call, capitulation, conclusion, confine, definition, designate, dub, duration, end, entitle, epithet, epoch, era, express(ion), extent, footing, gnomon, issue, limit, locution, mahalath, morpheme, name, parturition, period, pillar, pochismo, premise, rap, rhema, semanteme, semester, session, space, speak, spell, state, style, syllable, tag, tenure, time, title, usage, utterance, verbalism, vocable, word
academic quarter, semester, seminar, trimester
hyphened compound
misuse of abusion
of imprisonment jolt, lag(ging), stretch
of office regime, tenure

TERMAGANT amazon, barge, boisterous, crone, furious, jade, ptarmigan, quarrelsome, scolding, tumultuous, turbulent, scold, shrew, virago, vixen, witch

TERMINABLE determina-

ble, discontinuing, endable, finish, finite

TERMINAL base, boundary, cathode, closing, concluding, depot, desinent, destination, distal, end(ing), eventual, extreme, extremity, final, imput, input, last, latest, limit, mucro, pole, pothead, railhead, station, ultimate, yard
negative cathode, kathode
positive anode

TERMINALIA anagep, anaguep, araca, arjan, arjun, bahera, broadleaf, griselina, kalumpit, myrobalan, puka

TERMINATE abate, abolish, abort, adjourn, call, cease, close, complete, conclude, confine, cut, direct, discontinue, dismiss, dissolve, end, expire, extinguish, finish, fire, halt, kill, prorogue, restrict, result, stop, wind up

TERMINATION abscission, bound, close, completion, conclusion, decision, desinence, end(ing), exitus, expiry, extremity, finale, finial, finis(h), issue, limit, outcome, period, pruning, result, suffix, terminus, upshot

TERMINATIVE absolute, bounding, concluding, definitive, determining, finitive

TERMINOLOGY glossology, jargon, nomenclature, phrase(ology), vocabulary, wordage
technical cant
universal typocosmy

TERMINUS atlanta, boundary, end, extremity, goal, marker, post, stone, TERMINAL

TERMITE anai, anay, ant, calotermitid, duckant, insect, king, nasute, polilla, worker
fontanel fenestra
larva bushman, rice
soldier nasute

TERMLESS boundless, indescribable, inexpressible, infinite, limitless, nameless, unconditional, unconditioned, unending

TERMS agreement, circumstances, conditions, footing, limitations, means, position, propositions, provisions, relation(ship), standing, state, stipulations

unconditional carte blanche

TERN anous, chirre, darr, fowl, goeland, gygis, kermew, kip, kirmew, lari(d), manusina, medrick, noddy, noio, pearl, picket, pictarnie, pirl, pirr(maw), richelbird, rittock, rixy, scray, seafowl, skeer, skirr, sparling, spurre, starn, stern(a), striker, tarrack, tirracke

black carr-swallow, starn

common rixy, sheartail, tarrack

noddy fulmar, noio, ruddyduck

TERNARY ternion, three (fold), treble, triad, trinity, triple

TERPENE bornane, camphene, camphine, carene, fenchene, limonene, nerol, nopinene, pinene, santene, terebene, thujene

alcohol borneol

TERPSICHORE(AN) choreographic, dancer, dancing, gestic, saltatory

TERRA (See also GAEA.) earth, land, sod, tellus

alba burnt alum, gypsum, kaolin, magnesia

cariosa rottenstone

cotta clayware, earthenware, figurine

daughter mnemosyne, phoebe, rhea, tethys, thea, themis

firma base, earth, estate, mainland

husband uranus

japonica gambir

nobilis diamond

son oceanus

TERRACE balcony, bank, barrow, bench(land), berm(e), chabutra, colonnade, dias, dune, earthwork, embankment, flaw, gallery, grounds, heiau, lawn, linch(et), mesa, mound, offset, parterre, patio, piazza, plain, plateau, platform, pnyx, portico, roof, street, tier, trass, tumulus, veranda, way, xyst

lounging lanai

natural mesa

railed poy

wall podium

TERRAIN area, district,

earth, environment, milieu, sphere

TERRAMYCIN oxytetracycline

TERRAPENE cistudo

TERRAPIN chelonia, coodle, emyd(ian), emys, feuille, potter, redbelly, skilpot, slider, tortoise, turpin, turtle

color feuille

female heifer

male bull

red-billed slider

TERRELLA earth(kin), loadstone, magnet, planet

TERRENE earth(y), ground, land, mundane, realm, terrestrial, worldly

TERRESTRIAL earth(l)y, geal, geophilous, global, human, layman, mortal, mundane, planetal, sublunar(y), subsolar, tellurian, telluric, terrene

TERRET cringle

TERRIBLE abominable, alarming, appalling, astounding, atrocious, awesome, awful, bad, base, beastly, bhairava, contemptible, deplorable, despicable, detestable, dire (ful), dismal, dreadful, egregious, enormous, evil, excessive, extreme, fearful, fell, flagrant, fleysome, formidable, foul, frightening, frightful, fulsome, gast, ghastly, gorgonian, grave, grievous, grim, gross, hateful, heinous, hideous, horrendous, horrible, horrid, horrific, horrifying, infamous, lamentable, morbid, nefarious, noisome, obnoxious, odious, outrageous, pitiable, pitiful, rank, redoubtable, regrettable, sad, scandalous, scary, shameful, shocking, terrifying, tremendous, ugly, unpleasant, upsetting, vile, villainous, woeful, wretched

comb. dino

the bhairava

TERRIER account, diehard, dog, inventory, list, missile, ratter, rattoner, roll, verminer

breed aberdeen, airedale, bedlington, border, boston, bull, cairn, clydesdale, dandie(dinmont), fox, irish,

kerry-blue, lhasa(apso), manchester, norwich, schnauzer, scottish, sealyham, skye, welsh, wirehair, yorkshire

scottish aberdeen, diehard, scottie, scotty, verminer

TERRIFIC agitating, appalling, bang on, exciting, extreme, good, great, superb, supreme, TERRIBLE, tremendous

TERRIFIED afraid, aghast, appalled, astounded, awed, dismayed, frightened, horrified, horrorstruck, pale, panic(k)ed, panic-stricken, panicky, paralyzed, petrified, scared, stunned, stupefied

TERRIFY abast, affray, affright, agitate, agrise, alarm, annoy, appal(l), awe, awhape, bother, bree, browbeat, cow, daunt, destroy, freeze, frighten, horrify, importune, injure, intimidate, petrify, scare, shock, startle, tease, terrorize, torment, upset

TERRIFYING bloodcurdling, fearful, fleysome, frightening, ghastly, hair-raising, hideous, horrible, horrid, petrifying, stunning, stupefying, TERRIBLE

TERRIGENOUS autochthonous, earthborn

TERRITORIAL local, regional, soldier

division amt, arrondissement, bailiwick, banat(e), banlieu(e), beylic, beylik, canton, city, commune, country, county, demesne, department, diocese, district, hundred, lathe, magistracy, metropolis, mofussil, palatinate, parish, pashalic, pashalik, precinct, provence, riding, shire, soke, state, tithing, township, wapentake, ward

TERRITORY area, bailiwick, belt, bounds, colony, confines, district, domain, dominion, enclave, exclave, extent, field, ground, kingdom, land, lebensraum, limits, mandate, march, pashalik, possession, province, quarter, realm, region, scope, seignory, soil, sphere, state, terrain, terrene, tract, zone

lost irredenta
recovery irredentism
shut in enclave

TERROR affray, alarm, anarchy, awe, bete-noir, bugbear, consternation, demon, devil, dismay, disquiet, dread, dreddour, dridder, fear, fray, fright, gorgon, horror, hurlothrumbo, incubus, nightmare, nuisance, ogre(ss), panic, perturbation, pest, trepidation

TERRORISM anarchism, anarchy, despotism, intimidation, nihilism, subjugation, violence

TERRORIST alarmist, apache, goon(da), nihilist, rebel, revolutionary, scaremonger, sicarius, thug

TERRORIZE abash, bulldoze, cow, embarrass, force, harass, intimidate, menace, TERRIFY, threaten, upset

TERSE aphoristic, brief, clearcut, clipped, close, compact, concentrated, crisp, curt, incisive, laconic, neat, pithy, pointed, polished, refined, short, smooth, succinct, summary

TERSENESS brevity, laconism

TERTIARY neozoic, palaeic
comb. trit
epoch cenozoic, eocene, miocene, neocene, oligocene, paleocene, pliocene

TERTULIA club, meeting, party

TERUTERO lapwing

TERVEE struggle, writhe

TESSELLATED checkered, mosaic, tiled

TESSERA abaciscus, abaculus, abacus, cube, die, marble, password, pledge, tablet, tally, tessella, ticket, tile(tte), token, voucher

TEST analysis, analyze, approof, approve, assay, assess, aussage, authenticate, avena, canon, check, control, criterion, crucible, cupel, demonstrate, demonstration, determine, dry run, essay, evaluate, evidence, exam(ination), examine, exercise, experience, experiment, fand, feel, gantlet, grope, inquire, inquiry, investigate, investi-

gation, measure, norm, oral, ordeal, performance, potsherd, pree, probation, proof, prove, question, quiz, sample, scrutiny, shell, standard, study, task, tempt, touchstone, trial, try, verification, verify, will, witness, yardstick
archeological bose
area proving ground
comb. oeca
courage scratch
egg candle
fineness and weight pyx
ground bose
intelligence stanford-binet
meal ewald
medical ascoli, dick, kolmer, pap, patch, rabbit, schick, scratch, wasserman
orally catechise, catechize, examine, quiz
ore assay, van
personality rorschach
pilot scott crogsfield
pot crucible
series ga(u)ntlet
tube buret(te), retort
value assay

TESTA aril(lode), arillus, coating, covering, episperm, lorica, seedcoat, shell

TESTAMENT (See also NEW *testament* and OLD *testament*.) bequest, bible, covenant, dispensation, instrument, quethe, scripture, will, witword

TESTAMENTARY bequeathed, endowed, given, willed

TESTED proven, tried, weighed

TESTER assayer, candler, conner, crown, denierer, headpiece, helmet, prover, sparver, testiere, teston, trier

TESTIFIER deponent, witness

TESTIFY acknowledge, affirm, argue, asseverate, aver, avouch, bear witness, blab, certify, declare, demonstrate, depone, depose, indicate, protest, prove, show, state, swear, vouch, warrant, witness, witten

TESTIMONIAL certificate, character, commendation, compliment, credential, evidence, honor, memorial, monument, ovation, recom-

mendation, reference, scroll, token, tribute, warrant

TESTIMONY admission, affidavit, affidavy, affirmation, allegation, attest(ation), authority, avouchment, compurgation, corroboration, declaration, demonstration, deposition, evidence, profession, proof, recommendation, statement, witness, word

TESTUDO ceiling, cover, lyre, screed, shed, snail, talpa, tortoise, tumor, turtle, vault

TESTY bantam, captious, carping, choleric, cranky, cross, edgy, fretful, hasty, headstrong, irascible, irritable, peevish, petulant, snappish, snappy, splenetic, spunky, tatter, te(t)chy, touchy, tutty, waspish

TETANUS holotonia, lockjaw, trismus
spasm pleurothotonus

TETCHED See INSANE.

TETCHY See TESTY.

TETE See HEAD.
a-tete causeuse, chat, conversation, face to face, facing, intimate, opposite, private, seat, siamoise, side-by-side, sofa, talk, twosome, vis-a-vis

TETHER baikie, bind, cabestro, chain, confine, cord, leash, limit, longe, moor, pastern, picket, range, restrain, rope, scope, shackle, stake, tedder, tie, toggle
-devil bittersweet, matrimony-vine

TETHYS aplysia
brother cronus
consort oceanus
offspring See OCEANUS *offspring.*
parent gaea, terra, uranus

TETRACHORD hypaton, lichanos

TETRACYCLINE achromycin

TETRAD four(fold), quadrivalent, quaternion, tetractys

TETRAGON quadrangle, quadrilateral, quartile, rhombus, square

TETRAGRAMMATON invh, jhvh, jhwh, yhvh, yhwn

TETRAHEDRITE fahlerz, fahlore, panabase

TETRAHYDRIDE germane, stannane

TETRAONID capercaillie, capercailzie, cock-of-the-wood, grouse, partridge, ptarmigan, quail

TETRAZENE buzane

TETRIC acerb, austere, gloomy, harsh, sullen

TETTER blister, complain, dartars, dartre, eczema, fret, gripe, herpes, lichen, pimple, psoriasis, pustule, ringworm, ulcer

TETTERBERRY bryony

TETTERWORT bloodroot, celandine, potentilla, puccoon, tormentil, tumeric

TEUCER *consort* eune
kingdom cyprus, troy
offspring asteria
parent hesione, idaea, scamander, telamon
step-brother ajax

TEUCRIUM ambrose, betony, cat-thyme, germander, poly

TEUTHIS ornytus

TEUTON german, goth

TEUTONIC british, dutch, english, german(ic), gothic, gothonic, nordic, scandinavian, yekke
barbarian goth
deity See AESIR.
demon mara
dwarf god troll
earth midgard, midgarth, mithgarthr
elf king wayland
fate norn, urth
giant wade
hero offa, wudga
homicide morth
land odal
law salic
letter rune
pantheon aesir, asynjur
peace goddess nerthus
princess ildico
sea deity aegir, gymir, hler, ran
seeress albruna
sky god tiu, tiw, tyr(r), zio, ziu
smith wayland, wieland
thunder deity donar, thor
tribe gepidae, germanic, goth(onic), hermiones, heruli, istvacones, lombard, sicambrian, suiones, ubi(i), vindelici
war deity tiu, tiwaz, tyr
water nymph nis

TEW beat, fatigue, fuss, incite, knead, pincers, pull, strive, struggle, taw, tease, teu, tools, tow, tuarn, tue, tuyers, vex, work, worry

TEWEL alley, bore, chimney, flue, funnel, heater, hole, lane, louvre, pipe, tool, tuyere, vent

TEWSOME restless, troublesome

TEXAS *bandit queen* belle star
baseball team rangers
battlefield palo alto
bay corpus christi
bedbug conenose
bronco mustang
buckthorn jujube, lotebush
capital austin
city abilene, alice, amarillo, arlington, austin, bay city, bay town, beaumont, bellaire, big spring, borger, brazos, brownsville, brownwood, bryan, cleburne, corsicana, dallas, del rio, denison, denton, eagle pass, edinburg, el paso, ennis, gail, galveston, garland, grand prairie, greenville, groves, houston, irving, laredo, longview, lubbock, lufkin, marfa, marshall, mcallen, mesquite, midland, odessa, orange, ozona, pampa, paris, pasadena, plainview, port arthur, quanah, richardson, san angelo, san antonio, san benito, san pedro, sherman, sonora, texarkana, tyler, vega, victoria, vidor, waco, weslaco, wichita falls
college baylor, rice, smu, tcu, wiley
cottonwood alamo
county atascosa, bexar, erath, fannin, garza, goliad, hidalgo, refugio, yoakum, zapata, zavala
cowboy jacket chaqueta
fever blackwater, murrain, tristeza
fortress alamo
founder austin
hat stetson, ten-gallon
herb golden-wave
horse mustang
indian adai, alabama, apache, biloxi, caddo, comanche, coushatta, hasinai, jumano, karankawa, kichai, lipan,

querecho, shuman, tonkawa, waco
island padre
itch buffalo mange, cattle mange, scab(ies)
judge, famous roy bean
lake amistad, falcon, texoma
land measure labor
massacre site alamo
millet river-grass
national park big bend
native tejano
nettle sandbur
nickname lone star state
oil boom spindletop
oil town midland, overton
peak el capitan
pioneer austin, houston
plant evening star, sage
poplar alamo
port corpus christi, galveston, houston
president eisenhower, johnson, sam houston
range guadalupe
river brazos, colorado, neches, nueces, pecos, red, rio grande, san jacinto, trinity
saloon jersey lilly
shrub agrito, anagua, anaqua, baretta, bluewood, mejorana
snakeroot birthwort
state bird mockingbird
state flower bluebonnet
state motto friendship
state police rangers
state tree pecan
tree logwood
yomulka ten-gallon hat

TEXT antethem, argument, body, book, content, copy, edition, handwriting, matter, miqra, motive, passage, pericope, purana, script, shakha, subject, theme, tome, topic, variorum, verse, version
advertising copy
in various languages interlinear
letter capital
musical libretto
opera libretta
revision recension
sacred avesta, bible, koran, s(h)ruti
set to music oratorio
variation lection
with notes variorum

TEXTBOOK abecedarium, battledore, cocker, dunce, hornbook, libretto, manual, mc guffey's, primer, reader, scripture, speller

TEXTILE (See also COTTON, FABRIC, SILK, WOOL, etc.) cloth, goods, material, stuff, weaving, woven
dealer mercer
dye brasilein, migrosine
fiber azlon, dacron, nylon
finish plisse
frame for scray
machine loom, poteye, spinning jenny, willow
ornament fagoting
plant refuse hurds
screw pine ara, pandan
worker reeder, reedman, weaver

TEXTURE arrangement, character, cobweb, composition, essence, fabric, feel, finish, grain, knit, make-up, nap, network, pile, quality, structure, surface, textile, tissue, wale, weave, weaving, web, weft(age), woof
cloth wale, warp, woof
having felt-like pannose
having soft malacoid

TEZ pungent, violent

THACKERAY *character* amelia sedley, becky sharp, blanche amory, briggs, clive, dobbin, ethel, george osborne, glorvina, henry esmond, lord steyne, mrs mackenzie, pendennis, pitt crawley, rawdon crawley, rosey
novel barry lyndon, denis duval, henry esmond, newcomes, pendennis, vanity fair, virginians
pseud. charles yellowplush, fitzboodle, titmarsh
tale country paflagonia

THAHASH *mother* reumah

THAI(LAND) land of the free, siam
barge balloen, balloon
cab samlaw, samlo(r)
canal khlong, klong
capital ban(g)kok
city ayudhya, ayuthea, ban(g)kok, chiangmai, khonkaen, kiangmai, lampang, lopburi, phitsanulok, puket, rahaeng, ranong, singora, songkla, sukhotai, thonburi, ubon
coin att, ba(h)t, bia, bullet money, catty, fuang, pynung, salung, satang, tical

"compassion" metta
deer thameng
demon nat
dialect lao
dress panung
dynasty chakri
elephant, golden erawan
fabric siamoise
foreigner farang
fruit camut, mango, papaya, pumelo
game saka, tautem
group kui
king bhum(i)bol, chulalongkorn, mongkut, prahjadhipok, rama
language ahom, kadai, lao, shan, tai
leader kukrit-pramoj, phraruang
measure anukabiet, can, chaimeu, changawn, cohi, kabiet, kammeu, kanahn, ken, kwien, laang, leeng, ngan, niou, niu, nmu, rai, roeneng, sat, sen, sesti, sok, tanan, tang, vouah, wah, yot(e)
nature spirit nat
peak khieo, maelamun
people lao, lawa, shan, siamese, t(h)ai
plain khorat
province monthon
river chaophraya, chi, mekong, menam, meping, mun, nan, ping, yom
ruler (See also *king,* above.) kittikachorn, pibul-songram, sarit-thanarat
straw hat bangkok
temple vat, wat
weight ba(h)t, catty, chang, coyan, f(l)uang, grani, hap(h), kati, klam, klom, pai, pay, picul, pilul, salung, sen, sok, sompay, tamlung, tical

THAIS courtesan, hetaera, prostitute, snail, wanton
composer massenet
consort alexander the great, ptolemy-lagi
son lagus, leontiscus

THAISA *father* simonides
husband pericles
offspring marina

THALASSA, THALATTA eureka

THALASSIC marine, neritic, oceanic, pelagic

THALIA arrowroot, asteroid, bloom, brace, nereid, salpa
consort zeus

sister aglaia, charites, euphrosyne, graces, gratiae
slayer erato

THALLIUM *discoverer* crookes
source crookesite, lorandite

THALLOGEN amphigen

THALLOID frondose

THALLOPHYTE algae, ascolichene, bacteria, fungus, lichen

THALLUS frond, thamnium

THAMAR See TAMAR.

THAMES isis
boat bawley
estuary nore
on south side of transpontine
shore embankment, strand
sight swan
town eton, henley, london, oxford
tributary cherwell, tyburn

THAMYRIS *parent* argiope, philammon
symbol lyre

THAN and, but, nor, then, when

THANA jail, police station, prison

THANATOS death, mors
brother hypnos, sleep
mother night, nyx

THANATOSIS hypnosis, inanition

THANE abthain, attendant, banquo, baron, bodyguard, chief, churl, follower, gesith, macduff, peer, servant, thegn, warrior
estate manor

THANK acknowledge, bless, favor, graceful, gratitude, inquiry, mercy, praise, pray, regracy, remercy, thought
-you-ma'am cahot

THANKFUL agreeable, appreciative, content, grateful, meritorious, pleasant

THANKLESS unappreciated, ungrateful, unlamented, unreturned, unrewarded, unwelcome
person ingrate

THANKS cumshaw, danke (schon), grace, gracias, gramercy, gratitude, grazia, mahalo, merci(beaucoup), much obliged

THANKSGIVING broche, doxology, eucharist, glory, prayer

THAPE gooseberry

THAR behoove, need, tahr, their, there

THARF heavy, rigid, stiff, unbending

THARM belly, catgut, intestine, stomach

THARRHYPAS *son* alcetus

THAT because, but, ceci, cela, cet, hic, ille, lest, quello, questo, qui, tham, thick, thilk, tho, what, when, which, who, yat, yond

is id est, namely, to wit

one ille, quella, quello, questa, questo

THATCH cadjan, datch, face, hair, nipa, sirki, sirky, sting, theek, thrum

grass neti, restio

material reed, rush, straw

palm inodes, nipa, sabal, thrinax

peg scob

roof pole wattle

support wattle

THATCHER crowder, heler, hellier, reeder, thacker

implement gro(o)m, spar, spelk, springle

THAUMAS *consort* electra

daughter arce, harpies, iris

parent gaea, neptune, pontus, terra

THAUMATURGE mage, magician, saint, sorcerer, wizard

THAUMATURGY alchemy, legerdemain, magic, sorcery, witchcraft, witchery, wizardry

THAW deliquesce, dissolve, fuse, liquefy, melt, relax, unbend, warm(th)

THAYER *poem* casey at bat

THC cannabis, hemp

component olivetol, resorcinol

THE there, they, thi, yare

THEA camellia

companion artemis

consort hyperion

parent terra, uranus

ravisher aeolus

THEANO *consort* antenor, pythagoras

father cisseus

offspring agenor, antheus, archelochus, arignote, mnesarchus, myia, telauges

sister hecuba

THEATER area, arena, auditorium, bowl, cavea, cine (ma), circus, coliseum, colosseum, drama, gaff, guignol, hall, hippodrome, house, kino, legit, movie, music hall, odeon, odeum, opera, ozoner, pantheon, playhouse, showboat, showshop, site, spellken, stadium, stage

audience house

award oscar, tony

box baignoire, cubiculum, loge, stall

company cast, repertory, troupe

curtain drop, teaser, tormentor

district broadway, great white way, rialto

elizabethan globe

extra super

floor pit

full sro

goer first-nighter

goer, cheap groundling

group anta, ascap, habima

guide usher

in the round arena

low class gaff

motion picture bioscope, cinema(tograph), kinematograph, movie

notice pan, rave

outdoor arena, drive-in, open-air

part baignoire, balcony, box, circle, coulisse, episcenium, flies, footlight, foyer, gallery, greenroom, loge, parodus, parquet, parterre, pit, platform, proscenium, skene, stage, stall, vraia

pert. broadway, histrionic

pit circle, parquet, parterre

pit spectator groundling

promenade fop's alley

schedule repertoire

sign sro

sports arena

stall See *box*, above.

summer strawhat

trapdoor scruto

valet dresser

variety music hall

vaudeville orpheum

THEATRICAL affected, artificial, campy, ceremonial, dramatic, emotional, emotive, hammy, histrionic, mannered, melodramatic, pompous, pretentious, showy, spectacular, stagy, vivid

THEBAINE paramorphine

THEBE *abductor* zeus

parent asopus, metope

THEBES, THEBAN amphion, cadmean, jocasta, karnak, laius, luxor, niobe, oedipus, pentheus

bard pindar

citadel cadmea

conquerors alexander, epigoni

deity amen(t), amon, amun, cabiri, harmony, mentu, mut, neith

enemy (See also *7 against*, below.) alcmaeon

ensign sphinx

festival agrania

founder cadmus

fountain paraporti

general diogiton, malcitas, pammenes, pelopidas

king amphion, attalus, cadmus, creon, eetion, eteocles, laius, lycus, oedipus, pentheus

lute-player amphion

mayor paser

queen aedon, dirce, jocasta, niobe

rival athens, sparta

river dirce, ismenus

7 against adrastus, amphiaraus, capaneus, hippomedon, parthenopaeus, polynices, tydeus

soothsayer tiresias

wall-builder amphion, zethus

THECA anther, ascus, capsule, case, cell, cup, pyxidium, sac, sheath, sporangium, urn

THEE grow, increase, prosper, thigh, thou, thrive, thyself, you

THEFT abaction, abduction, appropriation, BURGLARY, byrthynsak, caper, crib, embezzlement, extortion, filch(ing), furtum, grab, heist, holdup, job, larceny, michery, peculation, pilferage, pilfery, pillage, pinch(ing), piracy, plagiarism, poaching, proggery, pugging, purloining, ripoff, robbery, scrounging, shoplifting, snitching, stealing, stouth, swiping, thievery

forcible southrief

literary plagiarism, plagiary

pert. kleptistic

-prone furacious

THEIA *brother* hyperion

consort hyperion

offspring eos, helios, selene
parent gaea, uranus
THEM hemen, people, those
THEME antethem, argument, article, base, burden, composition, discourse, dissertation, dux, essay, idea, leitmotif, matter, melody, motif, mythos, paper, scope, song, strain, subject, tema, text, thesis, topic, tract, urlar
literary motif
musical cantus, tema
repeated burden
return to reprise
title lemma
trite cliche
THEMIS euboulos, soteira
consort iapetus, jupiter, zeus
offspring astraea, dice, eunomia, hesperides, horae, irene, moerae, prometheus
parent gaea, terra, uranus
THEMISTE *parent* eurydice, laomedon
son anchises
THEMISTO *husband* athamas
rival ino
THEMISTOCLES *consort* archippe, stesilaus
daughter asia, italia, mnesiptolema, nicomache, sybaris
enemy aristides
eulogist andocides
follower chileus, sicinnus
home magnesia, phrearrhi
kin lysander, phrasicles
parent abrotonon, euterper, neocles
rival architeles, aristides, cimon, epicydes, leobotes, pausanias
son archeptolis, cleophantus, demopolis, diocles, neocles, poleuctus
tribe leontis
victim arthmius
THEN accordingly, after, agin, allora, alors, also, and, anon, besides, despues, donc, dunque, entonces, hence, immediately, next, past, poi, pues, soon, thence, thereat, therefore, whence
and there at once, instantly, now, suddenly
too again
THENCE away, elsewhere, hence, thereafter, therefore
THENCEFORTH forward, thereafter, tomorrow

THEOCRITUS *herdsman* thyrsis
parent philinna, praxagoras
patron ptolemy
teacher asclepiades, philetas
work idyls
THEODOLITE alidade, taipo, transit
THEOLOGIAN churchman, clergyman, cleric, divine, fagih, mujtahid, ulema
authority imam, ulema
famous aquinas, arius, barth, buber, erasmus, fosdick, luther, merton, murray, schweitzer, tillich
THEOLOGY divinity, irenics, kalam, poimenic(s), polemics
THEONOE idothea
aided helen, menelaus
parent proteus, psammathe, thestor
THEOPHANE *consort* poseidon
THEOPHANY epiphany, ghost, incarnation, revelation
THEOPHILUS thistle-shifter
THEORBO arch(i)lute, lute
THEOREM argument, axiom, fundamental, hypothesis, law, lemma, postulate, premise, principle, rule, theory, thesis, topic
THEORETICAL abstract, academic, armchair, closet, conjectural, hypothetical, ideal, impractical, platonic, premised, presumptive, quixotic, speculative, titular
power odyl(e)
THEORIZE hypothesize, reason, speculate, suggest
THEORY abstraction, analysis, assumption, conclusion, conjecture, doctrine, explanation, guess, hypothesis, idea, ism, law, notion, opinion, plan, postulate, premise, principle, scheme, speculation, supposition, system, theorem, thesis
atomic bohr
psychological associationism, behaviorism, gestalt
THEOSOPHY *sect founder* blavatsky
THEOTOKOPOULOS el greco
THEOW bond, servant, servile, slave, thrall
THERAPEUTIC curative, healing, prophylactic

THERAPEUTICS aceology, acology, MEDICINE, THERAPY
THERAPY analysis, cure, gestalt, MEDICINE, psychiatry, remedy, therapeutics, treatment
shock See SHOCK *therapy.*
THERAVADA hinayana
THERE able, ahi, alla, capable, dort(hin), ere, ibi, ready, reliable, sant, that, thence, thither, voila, where(ever), yare, yonder
THEREABOUTS approximately, close, generally, nearby, or so, roughly, roundly
THEREAFTER accordingly, afterward, subsequently, thence, upon
THEREAT hence, then, therefore, thither
THEREFOR in return, pursuant to, so that
THEREFORE accordingly, alors, argal, argo, consequently, considering, daher, deshalb, deswegen, donc, ergo, for that, for this, forthy, hence, igitur, on that account, percio, propter hoc, since, so that, then(ce), thereat, thus(ly), when(ce), wherefore
THEREON after, as a result, at once, besides, forthwith, immediately, mit, moreover, since, upon, withal
THERETO also, besides, moreover
THEREUPON See THEREON.
THEREWITH(AL) and, besides, forthwith, mit, moreover, over and above, thereat, through, together, withal
THERIAC(A) antidote, galena, molasses, treacle
THERM bath, pool, spa, tub
THERMAL erotic, hot, passionate, warm
balance calenture
comb. eury
fever calenture, heatstroke, sunstroke
unit bot, btu, calorie, therm
THERMOMETER *alcohol* cryometer
differential pyroscope
kind black-bulb, calorimeter, celsius, centigrade, dry-bulb,

electric, fahrenheit, hydra, pyrometer, reaumur, register, thermopile, thermostat, wet-bulb

THERMOPLASTIC saran

THERMOPYLAE *attacker* xerxes

defender leonidas

THEROID beastly, brutal, brutish, carnal

THERSANDER *companion* agamemnon

parent argia, polynices

slayer telephus

THERSILOCHUS *slayer* achilles

THERSITICAL abusive, scurrilous

THESAURUS anthology, archives, dictionary, encyclopedia, gallery, garland, lexicon, museum, repository, storehouse, treasure, treasury

compiler roget

THESEUS *birthplace* troezen

consort aegle, anaxo, antiope, ariadne, helen, hippolyte, iope, periboea, perigune, phaedra, phereboea

friend p(e)irithous, pyrithos

helmsman nausithous

grandfather cycnus, damastes, pittheus

grandson ioxus

offspring acamas, demopho(o)n, hippolytus, iphigenia, melanippus, oenopion, staphyllus, thaos

parent aegeus, aethra, poseidon

revels master philostrate

savior ariadne

slayer lucomedes

thread-giver ariadne

victim alycus, antaeus, busiris, cercyon, corynettes, cycnus, domastes, minotaur, pallantids, periphetes, phaea, polypemon, procrustes, sciron, sin(n)is, termerus

THESIS act, article, assumption, dissertation, downbeat, essay, hypothesis, manuscript, monograph, paper, postulate, premise, proposition, statement, subject, supposition, theme, theory, thesicle, tract, topic, treatise

THESPESIA bago, banago, bendy-tree

THESPIAN actor, actress, dramatic, dramatist, imper-

sonator, mime, mummer, performer, player, tragedian, tragic, trouper

maids muses

THESPROTIA *king* aidoneus

queen callidice

river thyamis

THESSALUS *parent* chalciope, hercules, jason, medea

THESSALY *city* larisa, pherae

commander eumelus

district tetrarchy

king admetus, aeolus, deucalion, erysichthon

magistrate tagus

peak ida, oeta, ossa, othrys, pelion, pindus, psiloriti

people dolopes, lapithae, myrmidons

river amphrysian, peneus, spercheus

valley tempe

witch aganice, erichtho

THESTIUS *kingdom* aetolia

offspring althaea, hypermnestra, leda, plexippus, toxeus

parent ares, demonice, euryte, parthaon

THESTOR *offspring* alcmaon, calchas, leucippe, theonoe

parent idmon, laothoe

THESUS *kin* acamas, phaedra

THETIS *consort* peleus

guest dionysus, hephaestus

parent doris, nereus

sisters nereids

son achilles

wooer poseidon, zeus

THEURGIST magician, wizard, wonderworker

THEURGY magic, miracle, occultism, sorcery, wizardry

THEW custom, discipline, form, habit, manner, mode, muscle, oppress, pillory, power, press, quality, resolution, sinew, strength, trait, virtue

THEWLESS feeble, lazy, spiritless

THEWY athletic, muscular, sinewy, strong

THEY men, people, thae, thei, them, those

THIAMINE aneurine, vitamin-b

source grain, liver, peas

THIAZI See THJAZI.

THICK abundant, beamy,

big, blobber, blubber, blunt, broad, brosy, bulky, burly, bushy, chummy, close, clumsy, coarse, compact, concentrated, condensed, confidential, corpulent, crass, crowded, deep, dense, dull, excessive, familiar, fat, firm, friendly, full, greasy, great, gross, grumous, guttural, hard, harsh, hazy, heavy, hoarse, husky, impenetrable, inarticulate, indistinct, intimate, laticostate, lutulent, luxuriant, middle, midst, numerous, obtuse, overgrown, plump, profound, roily, ropy, shaggy, simple, sizy, solid, squat, stocky, stodgy, stout, stupid, teeming, turbid, unbelievable, viscid, viscose, viscous, wide

and short chunky, squat

and thin devoted, unflinching

comb. hadr(o), pachy

-headed See THICK-*witted*, below.

-headed fly conopid

-knee burhinus, bustard, curlew, dikkop, plover

leaf crassula

-lipped blobber, labrose

-skinned callous, imperceptive, insensitive, obtuse, pachyderm(ic)

-toed pachydactyl

-tongued pachyglossal

too incredible, unbelievable

-witted dense, doltish, dull, heavy, numskulled, obtuse, slow, stupid

THICKEN cake, clabber, clot, coagulate, condense, confirm, congeal, crowd, crystalize, curd(le), deepen, dry, dull, fix, flock, gel, harden, increase, inspissate, intensify, keech, jelly, set, solidify, stiffen, strengthen

THICKENING callus, clavate, crassula, ephippium, pachynsis, pycnosis, roux

THICKET bluff, bosc(age), bosh, bosk(et), bosque, brake, brush, bush, canebrake, ceja, chamisal, chamise, chamiso, chaparral, chor, clump, clyfaker, cop(pet), coppice, copse (wood), covert, espinal, firth, frith, gonoph, greave, group, grove, heath, hedge, jungle, mallee, motte, rone, shaw, shola, slick, spinney, tod, tussock, undergrowth, wood(shaw)

THICKHEAD barbet, bird, bluetongue, thickknee, whistler

THICKNESS body, bore, breadth, bulk, cal(l)iper, corpulence, density, diameter, layer, mass, opacity, ply, sheet, stratum, stupidity, viscosity

measurer caliper, micrometer

THICKSET beefy, bulky, chunky, dense, dumpy, fleshy, humpty, obese, plump, portly, pudgy, squat(ty), stocky, stodgy, stout, stub(by), stumpy, thight

THIEF, THIEVES (See also *famous*, below.) 3 dip, gun, pad 4 chor, crib, gilt, lift, mill, prig, rook, thug, whyo, yegg 5 budge, creep, crook, ganef, ganof, ghoul, gonof, gonov, piker, rogue, sansi, scamp, sneak, snoop 6 ackman, arrant, bandit, cannon, cloyer, forger, gozlen, gunman, hooker, klepto, ladron, lifter, looter, micher, nimmer, pirate, rascal, rifler, ripper, robber, snitch, sucker, waster 7 booster, bramble, brigand, burglar, cribber, filcher, footman, footpad, gorilla, grifter, hoodlum, ladrone, lurcher, pincher, poacher, prigger, prowler, rustler, scourer, sharper, slocker, stealer, swagman, yeggman 8 abductor, criminal, cudgeler, cutpurse, gangster, larcener, marauder, picaroon, picklock, pilferer, snatcher, snitcher, swindler 9 buccaneer, cudgelboy, cutthroat, drawlatch, embezzler, hornthumb, larcenist, miscreant, peculator, plunderer, purloiner, road agent, scoundrel, scrounger 10 bushranger, depredator, freebooter, highwayman, pickpocket, plagiarist, sandbagger, shoplifter, thimblerig 11 nightwalker, safecracker 12 kleptomaniac, moll cutpurse

cattle blotter, rustler

clever cannon

comb. klept(o)

crucified dismas

famous ahmed, autoclycus, bill sykes, bonnie, claude duval, clyde, dick turpin, dillinger, fagin, jack sheppard, jesse james, jonathon wild, macheath, mercury, raffles, robert macaire, robin hood, william sutton

gentleman raffles

god mercury

group gang

latin cant, jargon, slang

leader ali

mountain choar

night scourer

on the cross desmas, dismas, dysmas, gesmas

petty hooker, slocker

river ackman, lumper

2nd-story cat-burglar, porch-climber

skillful mercury

tool alderman, crowbar

vagabond waster

wharf tosher

THIEVE See STEAL.

THIEVELESS aimless, bleak, bootless, cold, forbidding, frigid, listless

THIEVERY, THIEVING See THEFT.

THIEVISH depredatory, dishonest, kleptic, larcenous, lightfingered, spoliative

THIGH carve, flank, gammon, ham, hock

bone coxa, femur, ilium

comb. mer(o), merus

hair culotte

muscle gracilis, pectineus, quadratus, quadriceps, vastus

pain meralgia

pert. crural, femoral

THILL blade, fill, limber, plank, shaft, sill

THIMBLE bushing, cap, cringle, cup, ferrule, foxglove, harebell, ring, sew, skein, sleeve, socket, sput, watch

conjurer's goblet

THIMBLEFUL See BIT.

THIMBLERIG cheat, fraud, swindle, trick

THIMBLERIGGER cheat, imposter, swindler

THIMBLEWEED anemone, prairie-clover, rudbeckia

THIN araneous, attentuate(d), bony, cadaverous, decrease, deduct, delicate,

dilute(d), dim, dull, emaciate(d), extenuate(d), faint, fine, flimsy, frail, gaunt, gracile, haggard, infertile, insipid, lank(y), lathy, lean, leggy, lessen, lew, light, little, macilent, meager, melt, papery, pinched, poor, prune, rangy, rare, rarify, scanty, scraggy, scrank, scrannel, scrawny, sheer, shrill, skinny, slender(ize), slight, slim(sy), small, spare, sparse, spindling, spindly, stringy, subtle, superficial, svelt, tenuous, thready, transparent, trim, unbelievable, wasted, water(y), weak, wee, wiry, wispy, withy, wizen

and delicate araneose, araneous

and haggard chitty, gaunt

and withered weazen, wizen

as a lath, rail, rake, skeleton, splinter, wafer

comb. mano, sero, tenui

delicately subtile

man's dog asta

man's wife nora

out chop, deduct, delete, disbud, hoe, peter, prune, single, trim

person beanpole, broomstick, cadaver, gangleshanks, lathlegs, loksh, rattlebones, scrag, shadow, skeleton, slim, spindleshanks, spindling, sylph, wraith

-skinned sensitive, tender, touchy

-textured sleazy

-toned piping, reedy

-worn threadbare

THING (See also THINGS.) act, affair, aim, apparatus, appurtenance, article, assembly, bag, being, bit, business, case, cause, chose, circumstance, concern, cosa, deed, detail, device, dingbat, dingus, end, entity, essence, event, forte, hangup, happening, idea, incident, instrument, item, machine, material, matter, mechanism, metier, notion, noun, object, particular, point, reality, reason, res, slave, story, style, substance, tool, transaction, whatnot

accomplished acta, actum, deed

added addendum, additament, addition, appendix, complement, ell, insert(ion), supplement

admitted datum, element, fact, given, principle

aforesaid ditto

another aliud

assumed implication, postulate, premise, presupposition, stipulation

big humdinger, killerdiller, lallapalooza, lollapalooza

brought into being creation

comb. ance, ancy, ence, ency

consecrated to deity anathema, hieron, sacrum, shrine

contrary to logic alogism

cursed anathema

disgusting chaloshes, khaloshes

done act(a), action, deed, faciend, fact, fait-accompli

edible esculent

enormous monster

extra bonus, bounty, gratuity, lagn(i)appe, lanyap, premium, tip

following sequel

found discovery, trove

holy hagia, kodashim

important ace

indefinite nondescript, so and so

in itself noumenon

insignificant nothing, scrat

legal chose, res

linked in origin cognate

obtained from other thing derivative

old-fashioned antique, snuff

opposite antipode

out of place anachronism

out of time atavism

petty shabble

possessed bird in hand

precious curio, jewel, keepsake, pippin, rarity, relic, treasure

real mccoy

reasoned noumenon

remarkable beaut, lulu

remembered token

sad ruth

sensed phenomenon

silly trimtram

single unit

small See BIT.

stuffy rottock

stunted runt, scrunt, sheeshin

unexpected godsend, serendipity, surprise

unimportant bagatelle, bauchle, bean, fillip, nihil, nonentity, nothing, nought,

picayune, pinhead, plack, res nihili, res nullius, stiver, trifle, trinket

unusual freak, malformation, monstrosity, oddity

worthless tripe

THINGAMAJIG dingbat, doodad, doohickey, doohinkus, gadget, gismo, gizmo, jigger, thingum(a)bob, whatchamacallit, whatsit

THINGS (See also THING.) belongings, chose, clothes, effects, equipment, gear, goods, hushel, possessions, property, realia, trappings, traps, wardrobe, wealth

added addenda

between extremes intermediates

done acta, res-gestae

for sale goods, merchandise, services, wares

gained by purchase aquirenda, aquisition, aquisitum

hidden penetralia

holy hagia

household lares and penates

jumble of conglomeration, mess, muss, potpourri

little fewtrils

living biota

movable chattels, res-mobiles

prohibited taboo, tabu, vetanda

to be done agenda

to see sights

unimportant smatter

worth remembering memorabilia

THINGUMBOB See THINGAMAJIG.

THINK account, allow, analyse, analyze, assess, believe, brood, calculate, care, cerebrate, cogitate, conceive, concentrate, conclude, concoct, conjecture, consider, contemplate, daresay, deduce, deem, deliberate, design, determine, develop, devise, envisage, envision, estimate, expect, fancy, feel, gather, guess, hold, ideate, imagine, infer, intend, judge, mean, meditate, mind, mull, muse, opine, plan, ponder, presume, purpose, puzzle, reason, reckon, reflect, regard, repute, resolve, ruminate, scheme, seem, sepad, sleep on, speculate, stew, study, suppose, surmise, suspect,

trow, understand, view, ween, weigh, wis

according to one's wishes rationalize, thob

alike agree

back recall, recollect, remember, reminisce

better of recant, reconsider, repent

for suppose, suspect

hard brainstorm, ponder, ruminate

highly of admire, approve, esteem, respect

little of disesteem, disregard, relax, scorn, underestimate, underrate

logically reason

moodily brood

of anticipate, consider, imagine, judge, mind, purpense, remember

out cogitate, conclude, contrive, develop, devise, discover, excogitate, perfect, plan, reason, sleep on it, solve

out loud discuss, hypothesize, soliloquize, theorize

over brood, consider, mull, muse

-piece thumb-sucker

proper see fit

tank rand

twice consider, doubt, hesitate, waffle, waver, weigh

up contrive, design, devise, invent, originate

well of See *highly of*, above.

THINKER brain, meditator, mind, philosopher, pundit, sage, solon, sophist, student

creator rodin

THINKING cogitation, conceit, consideration, idea, judgment, opinion, ratiocination, rational, reasoning, reflection, thought(ful)

precisely ratiocinative

THINLY airily, barely, insufficiently, sparse(ly)

THINNESS exiguity, exility, tenuity

THIRD gamma, terce, tertian, three, tierce

comb. tri, trit(o)

-degree cross-examine, grill, torture

estate proletariat

every tertian

in number tertiary

international comintern, komintern

man abel
party catalyst
person, held by in escrow
power cube
-rater mediocrity, piker
THIRL bind, drill, enslave, enthrall, gaunt, hole, hungry, hurl, hurtle, nostril, penetrate, perforate, perforation, pierce, restrict, shriveled, sunken, thin, thrall, thrill, tie, tingle, vibrate, whirl, window, wound
THIRST anadipsia, appetite, covet, crave, craving, desert, desire, dipsosis, drought, drouth, dryness, eagerness, hanker(ing), hunger, long(ing), pine, soif, want, wish, yearn(ing)
absence adipsia, aposia
excessive anadipsia, dipsosis, polydipsia
-producing dipsetic
-producing serpent dipsas
-quenching adipsous, refreshing
THIRSTY adry, arid, avid, dry, eager, keen, parched, sitient, unslaked
THIRTEEN baker's dozen
fear of triakaidekaphobia
THIRTY end, finish, tricenary
-day trigesimal
series of trental
years' war treaty westphalia
THIS cis, esta, haec, here, hic, hoc, latter, questa, questo, thilk, thus, yis
being so therefore
is hoc est
minute at once, immediately, instantly, now, pronto
THISBE *beloved* pyramus
THISNESS haecceity
THISTLE achillea, anacyclus, anaphalis, antennaria, anthemis, aplopappus, arctotis, arnica, artemisia, aster, baccharis, baeria, bedeg(u)ar, bellis, bidens, boebera, boltonia, borrichia, buphthalmum, calendula, calermis, calt(h)rop, cardon, carduace, carduus, carlina, carthamus, centaurea, chaenactis, chaenolobus, cirsium, cnicus, cosmos, dashel, dindle, dyssodia, echinacea, echinops, euthamia, fistle, gutweed, hoyle, layia, milkweed, onopardon, puha,

rauriki, saltwort, saussurea, scolymus, sneezewort, sonchus, spilanthes, teasel, teazel, thorn, waratah
blue chicory, echium, viper's-bugloss
butterfly painted lady, vanessa
-down fluff, pappus
-eater cardophagus, donkey
emblem of scotland
flower ageratum
-like plant artichoke, carlina, teasel
principle cnicin
sage chia
shifter theophilus
sow gutweed
THISTLY prickly, thorny
THITHER distant, farther, there, toward, ulterior, yon(d), yonder, yondward
THJAZI, THJATSI *consort* niord, njord, njorth
daughter skathi
home thrymheim
THOAS deiphilus, thoon
consort myrina, myrine
kingdom calydon, lemnos, pleuron, tauris
offspring hypsipyle, sicinis
parent andraemon, ariadne, bacchus, dionysus, gorge, hypsipyle, jason, theseus
slayer hercules
ward iphegenia
THOCANUS *son* hezekias
THOLE allow, bear, endure, fid, fulcrum, oarlock, peg, pin, suffer
pin fulcrum
THOMAS didymus, the twin, tomcat, waiter
burial site ortona
emblem lance
opera hamlet, mignon
poem fernhill
THOMOMYS camass-rat, geomys, pocket-gopher
THOMSONITE mesole, mesotype, ozarkite
THONG amentum, babiche, brail, cord, girth, knout, lacing, lainer, laniard, lanyard, lash, lasso, lathet, leash, lingel, lingle, lora, quirt, rein, riem(pie), romal, strap, string, thunk, twitch, whang, whank, whip
javelin amentum
-shaped lorate
THOOSA *consort* poseidon
father phorcys
THOR donar, thunar, thunor

adversary king utgardaloki
attendant thialfi
belt meginjard
brother tyr
consort grid, sif
goat chase, crack, crash, grind
hammer miolnir, mjollnir, mjolnir
hammer thief thrym
home bilskirnir, thrudvang, thruheim
palace bilskirnir
parent jord, odin
sanctuary glove of skrymir
servant thialfi
son asvidar, magni, modi, ull(er), ull(u)r
talisman girdle, glove, hammer, iron glove
victim geirrod, hrungnir, hymir, serpent of midgard, thrym
wrestling foe elli, old age
THORAX alitrunk, breast (plate), chest, corselet, cuirass, forebody, pereion, trunk
duct alveus
muscle pectoralis, trapezius
THORAZINE chlorpromazine
THOREAU, HENRY *work* walden
THORITE enalite, orangite
THORN adam's needle, affliction, annoy, babul, bane, barb, beggar's-tick, bramble, briar, brier, brod, burf, cactus, catchweed, cleavers, cockspur, gonake, gonakie, goosegrass, haybote, hurt, needle, nettle, prick(le), retama, spike, spine, sticker, stob, stug, thistle, trouble, urge, vex(ation), yucca
apple datura, haw, jimsonweed, metel, stramonium, stramony
-bearing spinate
broom furze
comb. acanth(o), acanthus, spini
full of briery, scroggy
in-the-flesh bane, pest
-like spinate
pert. spinose, spinous
small spinule
tree acacia, hawthorn, honey-locust, retama, wattle
without anacanthous, spineless
THORNBACK dorn, old maid, raja, ray, roker,

skate, spidercrab, stickleback

THORNBILL tomtit

THORNBUSH crataegus

THORNTAIL hummingbird

THORNY baffling, brambly, briery, bristly, complex, difficult, hard, painful, prickly, scroggy, severe, sharp, spinate, spinose, spiny, stabbing, thistly, troublesome, vexatious *comb.* acanth(o)

THOROUGH absolute, all-inclusive, arrant, au fait, businesslike, careful, clean, clear, complete, comprehensive, concise, consummate, downright, efficient, errant, exact, exhaustive, full, furrow, hotshot, intensive, out-and-out, outright, painstaking, passage, perfect, practical, pure, regular, royal, sound, strict, sweeping, through(out), total, trench, unconditional, unqualified, unreserved, utter, veritable, way, wholehog

THOROUGHBRED accomplished, blooded, blue-blooded, breedy, cultured, educated, elegant, fancy, gentleman, highborn, horse, hot-blooded, lady, noble, pursang, trained, well-bred

THOROUGHFARE alley (way), artery, avenue, boulevard, drive, highroad, highway, parkway, passage, pike, road(way), street, transit, waterway, way

THOROUGHGOING absolute, arrant, complete, errant, hearty, painstaking, proper, profound, radical, true bred, unqualified, zealous

THOROUGHLY absolutely, all, altogether, completely, deeply, heartily, inly, richly, roundly, soaking, thrice, wholly

THOROUGHWAX boneset, hare's-ear

THOROUGHWORT agueweed, boneset, comfrey, eupatorium, hempweed, hoarhound

THORP(E) community, hamlet, town, village

THOS jackal

THOSE them, they, yond

THOTH aahtehuti, dhouti, djehuti, zehuti
consort maat, nehmauit, seshat(a)
invention numbers
master horus, osiris
parent geb, nut
sacred ape aani
son hornub

THOU lei, loro, sie, tha, thee, thousand, toi, usted, voi, vous, you

THOUGH admitting, albeit, and, even if, granting, however, nevertheless, that, yet

THOUGHT anxiety, attention, belief, bit, brainwork, care, cerebration, cogitation, concept(ion), concern, consideration, conviction, counsel, deliberation, distress, expectation, fancy, heed, hope, idea, idee, image, imagination, impression, intellection, intention, judgment, little, meditation, melancholy, mind, notion, opinion, pensee, persuasion, ratiocination, reason(ing), recollection, reflection, rumination, sentiment, strain, study, surmise, theory, thinking, thwart, touch, trace, trifle
bright brainstorm
comb. ideo, logo, noia
continuous meditation
control brainwashing
creative genius, imagination, inspiration
deep in cogitabund
disturbance block
fear of ideaphobia
inability to express asemia, asymbolia
interchange communion
literary pensee
out advised, studied
payment for penny
pert. noetic, phrenic
profound absorption
pure moesis
-reader telepath
science of noetics
speculative metapsychology, philosophy
transference telepathy

THOUGHTFUL abstracted, attentive, careful, circumspect, cogitabund, cogitative, concerned, considerate, contemplative, courteous, deliberative, diplomatic, earnest, grave, intent, judicious, meditative, mindful, moody, museful, pensive, polite, pondering, preoccupied, prudent, rapt, rational, reflective, ruminant, ruminative, serious, sober, solemn, solicitous, speculative, studious, wary, wistful

THOUGHTFULNESS amiability, care, concentration, concern, consideration, grace, gravity, kindness, regard, solicitude, tolerance

THOUGHTLESS aloof, blank, blind, careless, dizzy, fatuous, flighty, foolhardy, giddy, glaiket, glaikit, harumscarum, heedless, improvident, impulsive, inadvertent, inane, inattentive, incogitant, inconsiderate, lightheaded, negligent, ramstam, rash, reckless, remiss, scatterbrained, silly, stupid, supine, tactless, unconcerned, unoccupied, unthinking, unwise, vacant, vacuous, vapid, witless

THOUSAND chi(liad), grand, mil(le)
10 myriad(s)
100 lac, lakh
1,000,000 billion
and countless, numberless
comb. kilo, mill(e), milli
dollars grand
-headed cabbage brussels sprouts
-headed snake s(h)esha
-jacket ribbonwood
-leaf yarrow
-legs galleyworm, millepede
pert. millenarian, millenary
years chiliad, millennian, millennium, milliad

THOUSANDTH millesimal
of centimeter lambda
of inch mil

THRACE, THRACIAN *captain* acamas
city cestos, sestos
conqueror megabazus, sesostris
drinking vessel rhyton
gladiator spartacus
god dionysus, hero, orpheus, salmoxis
goddess bendis, cotys, cotytto
hero orpheus
king acesius, acessamenus, lysimachus, phineus, polymnestor, rhesus, tegyrius

maenad bassara, bassarid
modern name bulgaria
mountaineers bessi
musician orpheus, philammon
neighbors macedonians, scythians
peak haemus
people abderite, bessi, bisaltae, cicones, edomi, getae, gete, satrae, thrax
pert. getic
poet linus, musaeus, orpheus, thamyris
port abdera
priest-king orpheus
princess phyllis
range h(a)emus, rhodope
river aegospotami, hebrus, nestus, strymon
sea aegean
settlement perinthus, selymbria, tomi
virago harpelice
THRALL bondage, bond(s)-man, captive, enslave(d), esne, gurth, oppression, peon, serf, servant, slave (ry), subject, suffering, theow(dom), vassal, villein
THRALLDOM bondage, captivity, serfdom, servitude, slavery, theowdom, thirlage
THRANGITY business, bustle
THRASAEUS *son* apollonius
THRASH bang, baste, beat, belabor, best, bethwack, brandish, bray, buffet, cane, cudgel, defeat, drub, drudge, flail, flog, flourish, lam(baste), maul, pitch, pound, pulverize, pummel, ribroast, rush, smite, stir, strike, surge, swaddle, swap, swinge, tan, threap, THRESH, thwack, toss, towel, toze, trollop, trounce, urticate, wallop, wave, whale, whip, yerk
THRASHER threaper, THRESHER, toxostoma
THRASHING beating, licking, warming, whaling
THRAST constrain, press
THRASYBULUS *father* lycus
ruler of syracuse
THRASYMEDES *parent* anaxibia, nestor
THRAVE bind, bundle, number, quantity
THRAW, THRAWART adverse, agony, anger, back-

ward, crooked, ill-humor, misfortune, peevish, perverse, reluctant, sprain, stubborn, throe, twist(ed), unpleasant, wrench
THREAD(S) (See also *kind*, below.) babiche, bar, basting, bave, bride, cord, cotton, doup, fiber, filament, findings, intersperse, lace, ligature, line, lingel, lingle, lisle, penetrate, pierce, poil, purl, reeve, reticle, screen, stamen, steek, strand, stream, string, tenor, tram, twine, twist, twitter, vein, warp, weft, wind, wire, worm, yarn
assemblage capillitium
ball clew, clowe, clue, glome, wharrow
bind with oop
bits lint, ravelings
buttonhole bar
coarse gimp, gird
coiled cop
comb. mit(o), nema(to)
cone cop
cotton lisle
cross reticle, tram, warp, weft, woof
embroidery cannetille, floss
floating pickover
40 beer, bier
gold cannetille
group beer, copy, dent, split
hard lisle
in shuttle filling, shoot, tram, weft, woof
kind arrasene, bast, bave, cotton, crochet, film, floss, linen, lingel, lingle, nylon, rayon, seton, silk, trame, yarn
length stitch
lengthwise warp
-like fibroid, filamentous, filar, filate, filiform, filose, linear, nemaline, stringy
-like process filum, hair
linen incle, inkle
metal lamp, wire
needle reeve
network capillitium
oakum pledget
on spindle cop
ornamental tassel
partly twined slubber
pert. filum
pulled snag
raveled sleave
refuse bur(r)
separate ravel, shed, sleave, sley

shoemaker's lingel, lingle
silk bave, bur(r), doupioni, filoselle, floss, tram(e)
skein hasp
soft thrum
strong gounau, lisle
surgical seton
-tangle sea-lace
tape inkle
testing device serimiter
warp end, stamen
waxed tacker
weft floss, shot
work with sew
THREADBARE barren, common(place), corny, frayed, hackneyed, impoverished, meager, mean, motheaten, napless, obsolete, pilled, poor, ragged, scanty, sear, sere, shabby, shopworn, stale, thin, trite, worn
THREADFIN alectis, barbu(do), catfish, cobbler, cutlass, herring, kingfish, mangofish, seer(fish), seir(fish), shad, sulea
THREADFISH cobbler, sunfish
THREADFLOWER poinciana
THREADFOOT riverweed
THREADING stringing, winding
THREADWORM filaria, nematode, pinworm
remedy quassia
THREADY feeble, filamentous, slender, slight, stringy, thin, viscid, weak
THREAP, THREEP accusation, affirm, argue, argument, assert, beat, bicker, charge, chide, complain, insist, legend, maintain, press, quarrel, rebuke, report, scold, thrash, threp(e), urge
THREAT attack, bluff, chide, commination, compel, crowd, dare, denunciation, foreboding, imminence, intimidation, maltreat, menace, misery, omen, oppress, peril, press, push, reprove, throng, troop, trouble, urge, vex, warning
futile brutum-fulmen
THREATEN augur, bark, blackmail, bludgeon, bluff, bluster, boast, bulldoze, bully, caution, comminate, cow, denounce, dere, endanger, forebode, foreshad-

ow, fulminate, harass, impend, intimidate, loom, lour, lower, menace, portend, presage, warn

THREATENING angry, baneful, dire, fateful, glum, imminent, impending, looming, loury, menacing, minacious, minatory, minitant, ominous, rampant, sinister, ugly

THREE crowd, drei, gimel, leash, ter(cet), tern(ary), ternion, terzetto, tierce, tre(y), triad, triangle, trio, trois

aces corona, gleek

-angled triagonal, triangular

b's bach, beethoven, brahms

birds nodding-cap, toadflax

-card monte montebank

-card sequence tierce

cards alike gleek

cent piece trime

-choice problem trilemma

-cleft trifid

comb. ter, tri(o), tris, trit

-cornered triangular, triquetrous

-day fever dengue

-dimensional cubic(al), solid, spatial, stereo, thick

estates clergy, commonalty, nobility

-flowered trifloral

-footed tripodal, tripodic

-forked trisulc

friends bamboo, pine, plum

graces aglaia, bloom, brilliance, euphrosye, joy, thalia

group of brelan, cock-eyes, gleek, leash, pairial, tern (ary)(ion), tierce, tre, triad, triangle, triche, tricon, trine, trinity, trio, triple(t), triumvirate, triune, troika

-headed tricephalus

-horse vehicle randem

-hundredth anniversary tercentennial, tricentennial

in one oil, trinity, triune

kingdoms shu-wei

l's latitude, lead, lookout

-layered trilaminar

-leaved arum jack-in-the-pulpit

-leaved liverwort hepatica

-leaved nightshade trillium

-legged stand teapoy, tripod, trivet

-lined trilinear

-lobed trefle, trefoil

-masted vessel frigate, schooner, tern, xebek

miles league

months quarter, trimester

musketeers aramis, athos, porthos

musketeers' author dumas

musketeers' friend d'artagnan

of a kind See THREE *group of.*

-penny piece thrip

-person discourse trialogue

pert. ternal, ternary, thrice, trebal, trine, triple, triply

-piled best, costly, extravagant, wealthy

-pointed tricuspidal

r's reading, rithmetic, riting

-ribbed tricostate

-seeded trispermous

sequence fourchette, tierce

-sided triagonal, trihedral, trilateral, triquetrous

sided figure triangle, trion

signs of being anatta, anicca, dukkha

-spot trey

-square cross, irritable, threefold

-styled trystylous

-toed tridactyl

-toed bird stilt

trees gallows

unities action, place, time

-winged tripterous

wise men balthasar, gaspar, melchior

THREEFOLD ternal, ternary, ternate, thribble, thrice, tierce, treble, trinal, trine, triplasian, triple, triply

THREEP See THREAP.

THREEPENCE joey, thrip, thrum, tickey, tickie, trey

THREESCORE sixty

THREESOME trio

THRENODY coronach, dirge, lament, requiem, threne

THRESH beat, best, cave, cob, flail, flog, frail, mash, pound, pulverize, thrash, whip, winnow

THRESHER beater, combine, flail, tasker

shark fox(fish), whiptail

whale killer

THRESHING *refuse* colder, husk, straw

THRESHOLD beginning, dearn, doorsill, doorstone, drashel, entrance, eve, gate,

groundsel, groundsill, limen, mudsill, outset, portal, sill, sole, start, vestibule

THRICE See THREE.

THRIFT economy, employment, frugality, herb, husbandry, occupation, prosperity, providence, prudence, statice, work

THRIFTLESS extravagant, feckless, improvident, lavish, prodigal, wasteful

THRIFTY canny, careful, chary, economical, forehanded, frugal, miserly, narrow, parsimonious, proper, prosperous, provident, prudent, saving, scrimping, skimpy, small, spare, sparing, thriving, useful

THRILL arouse, bore, cast, delight, dindle, dirl, drill, electrify, enchant, enrapture, excite(ment), fascinate, fidget, flush, flutter, fremitus, frisson, galvanize, girl, glow, hurl, intoxicate, jerk, jollies, kick(s), kindle, nostril, palpitate, pant, perforate, quake, quicken, quiver, rouse, sensation, shake, shiver, squirm, stir, thirl, throb, throw, tickle, tingle, tirl, titillate, transfix, tremble, tremor, tumble, twitch, twitter, vibrate, wiggle, wriggle, writhe, zing

THRILLER fiction, mystery, who-dun-it

THRILLING breathtaking, delightful, electric, exciting, moving, quivering, startling, stimulating, tingling, trembling, vibrant, vibrating

THRIPS blackfly, physopod

THRIVE advance, batten, bloom, blossom, boom, burgeon, chieve, develop, fadge, fatten, flourish, flower, fructify, grow, increase, make good, moise, prosper, prove, storken, succeed, thee, thram, throdden, wax

THRIVEN adult, experienced, grown, prudent, wise

THRIVING bein, bien, blooming, booming, exuberant, grushie, prosperous, thrifty, vigorous

THRO eager, fierce, grow, increase, stubborn, sturdy, through

THROAT channel, crop, entrance, fauces, gorge, gowl, gula, gullet, guzzle, hals(e), inlet, jaws, jugular, jugulum, maw, mouth, mutter, neck, orifice, passage, rictus, swallow, swire, thropple, throttle, utter, voice, weasand

and mouth whistle

clear hawk, hoick, hough

comb. lemo

corolla fauces

covering barb, scarf

infection angina, croup, cynanche, laryngitis, pertussis, quinsy, squinancy, strep, thrush, tonsillitis, tussis

irritation frog, rasp

latch fiador

lozenge cough drop, pastil(le), troche

medicine argyrol

part amygdala, esophagus, glottis, gula, larynx, pharynx, tonsil, trachea, windpipe

pert. esophag(e)al, gular, guttural, jugular

skin dewlap

sore housty, quinsy

spasm gutturotetany

swelling frog

vein jugular

THROATLET boa, pelerine, tippet

THROATWORT bellflower, figwort, foxglove, gayfeather, liatris

THROATY croaky, gruff, guttural, harsh, hoarse, husky, raucous, roupy, stertorous, voracious

THROB ache, beat, drum, dunt, flack, flichter, flutter, leap, palpitate, palpitation, pant, pound, pulsate, pulse, quap, quop, stang, stound, thrill, tick, tingle, tremble, trepidation, vibrate, warch, wark

THROBBING dunt, painful, palpitant, pit-a-pat, resonant, smarting, splitting

THRODDY active, fat, plump, well-grown

THROE ache, agony, anguish, distress, froe, pain, pang, paroxysm, pull, rack, seizure, shower, spasm, stitch, stour, struggle, twinge

THROMBUS clot

THRONE apse, asana, cathedra, chair, exalt(ation),

gadhi, gad(d)i, musnud, power, rank, seat, seggio(la), selle, shinza, sinhasan, sovereign(ty), stall, state, stead, stool, tribune

remove from depose

room aiwan

THRONG army, assemble, assembly, busy, collection, company, congregate, congregation, crew, crowd, crush, distress, flock, gang, gathering, hardship, heap, horde, host, hurried, legion, lurry, mob, multitude, pack, peril, press, rout, shoal, strain, stress, surround, swarm, teem, thrave, threat, thrimp, thrutch, troop

THROSTLE See THRUSH.

THROTTLE burke, check, choke, gag, garrote, gun, kill, muffle, neck, obstruct, paralyze, pedal, seize, smother, stifle, stop, strangle, suffocate, suppress, throat, thropple, valve, windpipe

down slacken, slow

open gun, rev

THROUGH across, along with, among, around, athro, because of, by way of, coffin, complete, concluded, dia, done, during, ended, entirely, final, finished, into, over, past, per(pend), round, sarcophagus, succeed, therewith, thoroughfare, thoroughly, thru, trug, unobstructed, upon, via, washed up, with

and through completely, thorough(ly), utterly

comb. dia, trans

-other confused, disorderly, promiscuous, scatterbrained

THROUGHGANG energy, labor, overhauling, thoroughfare

THROUGHGOING energetic, examination, overhauling, reprimand, reproof, thoroughfare

THROUGHGROW boneset

THROUGHOUT about, always, bedene, bidene, completely, during, entire, everywhere, overall, passim, perfect, sempre, thorough, utterly

THROW afghan, bail, bandy, bear, blow, boa, bombard, bowl, buck, bung, cant,

cast, catapult, chuck, chunk, clap, cob, confuse, conject, coverlet, curve, dart, dash, deal, defeat, discharge, divest, ejaculate, ejaculation, eject(ion), fall, flick, fling, flip, flirt, force, haunch, heave, hinder, hurl, jaculation, jerk, kest, lance, lathe, launch, lob, obstruct, pass, peg, pelt, pepper, pitch, produce, project, propel, prostrate, put, quarrel, quilt, rack, retard, revolve, scarf, serve, service, shed, shoot, shot, shy, skew, skim, sling, snap, soss, spang, sprain, spread, spring, stone, strike, stroke, thrust, thwart, tilt, TOSS, turn, twirl, twist, unseat, vang, venture, volley, waft, wrap, wrench, writhe, yend

about bounce, slosh, tack, thrash

a fit anger, rage, storm

away bandy, bill, discard, dissipate, dodger, doff, dump, eliminate, flyer, fritter, handbill, jettison, leaflet, refuse, reject, squander, unload, waive, waste

back check, defeat, delay, refuse, reject, repel, retort, return, reversal, reverse, revert

ball lace, pitch

cold water deter, discourage, moderate

dice jeff

down abase, cast, defeat, demolish, fell, flatten, fling, floor, overthrow, precipitate, raze, refusal, reject (ion), subvert, thring

down the gauntlet challenge, dare, defy

dust in one's eyes blind, deceive, fool, hoodwink, mislead

for a loss defeat

forcefully bung

free foul

from saddle unhorse

in add, contribute, engage, inject, insert, interpolate, interpose, join

in one's teeth challenge, charge, confront, taunt

in the towel cede, give up, quit, surrender, yield

in with combine, join, unite

into confusion demoralize, disturb, foul up, snafu, snarl, stampede
into disorder clutter, derange, foul up, pie
into ecstasy enrapt, thrill
into the shade beat, eclipse, outshine
lazily lob
light on clarify, explain, illume, illuminate
lowest ambsace, amesace
mud at discredit, slander, smear
off abandon, abate, begin, cast, confuse, deflect, discard, discharge, disconnect, discount, emit, escape, expel, fluster, free, improvise, mislead, mo(u)lt, ·overthrow, reduce, reduction, reject, release, remove, say, shed, slough, unburden, unhorse, unseat
off the track derail, evade, mislead
on don, spread
one's weight bully, grandstand, influence, rule, urge
open dispark
out bounce, chuck, confuse, disbar, discard, disgorge, disjoint, dislocate, dismiss, distance, dump, egest, eject, eliminate, emit, erupt, evict, excrete, expel, extend, extrude, fire, ignore, lade, project, propose, reject, remove, sack, scrap, spout, unfrock
over abandon, discard, ditch, eliminate, forsake, jettison, jilt, relinquish
sideways shy
-stick boomerang
together huddle, join, unite
underhand lob
up criticize, demit, erect, lift, raise, relinquish, rise, spew, taunt, upchuck, vomit
up the sponge quit, relinquish, yield
violently ding, hurtle, smash, sock, spanghew, swack, whither
THROWBACK atavist, reversion, reverter, setback
THROWER chucker, discobolus, flinger, grainsman, hurler, javelinist, pitcher, shotputter, slinger, tipper
THROWING *stick* atlatl, boomerang, trombash, wommera, woomera

THRU See THROUGH.
THRUM beggar, bit, drum, fringe, hum, lout, particle, play, purr, repeat, strum, tangle, tassel, thatch, threads, threepence, thumb, tuft, yarn
THRUSH aphtha, babbler, bellbird, blackbird, breve, chat, chercock, draine, forktail, frush, grive, hermit, hopping-dick, hylocichla, jaypie(t), kickup, mavis, missel, olomao, omao, ousel, ouzel, pitta, pop, prunella, pulish, redstart, redwing, robin, sabia, shagbark, shama, shirl, shrite, soor, sprew, sprue, stonechat, struthio, thickhead, throstle, thrushel, thrustle, turdus, urticate, uzzle, veery, wagtail, whinchat, woodchat
brown shagbark, veery
disease aphtha, sprew, sprue
golden oriole
ground pitta
-like bird thrasher, turdoid
missel draine, mavie, mavis, shrite, skirlcock, skrike, stormcock
pert. turdine
THRUST (See also *in* and *out*, below.) allonge, assault, attack, barge, bear(ing), birr, blow, buck, bump, bunt, burr, butt, cant, clap, clash, collide, cram, crowd, cut, dart(le), dig, drive, elbow, emphasis, energy, extend, feint, foin, force, gird, goad, hurtle, hustle, impetus, interject, intrude, jab, jam, jibe, jog, jolt, jostle, lunge, nudge, onset, penetrate, pierce, poke, poss, power, press (ure), prod, proke, propel, punch, push, ram, shear, shoulder, shove, spread, stab, strain, stress, strike, swing, tension, throng, throw, thrutch, torsion, urge, vigor
against wall mured
aside abstrude, beat, blow, bore, bump, daff, detrude, shove, shuffle
back repel, repulse, retrude
down depress, depulse, detrude, thring
in cram, crowd, enter, insert, interject, interpose, intrude,

jam, pack, penetrate, pierce, plunge, stuff, wedge
lance aventre
out discard, dismiss, expel, extend, extrude, obtrude, protrude, reach, remove
with elbow hunch
with weapon foin
THRYMHEIM *inhabitant* thjazi
THUCYDIDES *opponent* pericles
parent hegesipyle, melesias, olorus, orolus
teacher anaxagoras, antiphon
THUD baff, beat, blow, bump, clop, clump, clunk, crump, doyst, dump, flump, gust, klop, pad, pat, phut, plod, plump, plunk, pound, squelch, swag, tempest, thump, windstorm
muffled kerplunk
THUG apache, assassin, bandit, bruiser, criminal, cuttle, desperado, gangster, goon (da), gorilla, gunman, hood (lum), killer, mohock, rodman, rough(neck), ruffian, yegg
THUJA arborvitae, biota, cedar, sandarac
THULE denmark, iceland, norway
THULIUM yttrium
THUMB digit, feel, finger, handle, hitchhike, mark, paw, phalanx, pollex, soil, thenar, thrum, touch
ball of cushion, thenar
-bird goldcrest
bone lunate
-finger space span
lady's peachwort
-marked commonplace, soiled, used
nose flout
-print feature whorl
-sucker think-piece
through browse, leaf, scan
without epollicate
THUMBS *down* blackball, condemnation, disapproval, dissent, negation, objection, refusal, veto
up affirmative, approval
THUMBSCREW coerce, torture
THUMBSTALL poucer, pouser, thimble
THUMMIM *associate* urim
THUMP bang, beat, blaff, blow, bounce, bump, bunch, clour, clout, crump,

cudgel, defeat, ding, drive, drub, drum, flutter, hammer, hit, knock, lump, palpitate, poke, pommel, pound, pulse, pummel, punish, slap, strike, thrash, throb, thud, thunge, thwack, tunk, whelk, whip, yark, yerk

THUMPER stunner, whopper

THUMPING big, bumping, great, heavy, huge, tattoo, whapping, whopping

THUNDER barrage, berate, boom, bronte, clap, clazon, crack, crash, denounce, din, donner, fouldre, fulmen, fulminate, noise, peal, rage, rant, rattle, roar, roll, threat, vajra

and lighten fulminate

and lightning, pert. ceraunic, fulminous

ax celt

-bearer jupiter, zeus

-bird thickhead

bolt censure, denunciation, fire, fouldre, fulmen, fulminant, fulmination, lightning, sulphur, surprise, vajra

bolt, comb. ceraun(o), keraun(o)

cloud cumulonimbus

comb. bront(o)

egg geode

fear of astrapophobia, brontophobia, tonitrophobia

god adad, donar, hurakan, indra, jupiter, lares, leikung, perkun, taranis, thor, zeus

-like sound brontide

making device broneton, bronteum

master of taramis

peal clap

plant houseleek

pump(er) bittern, drumfish

-smitten goddess semele

sons of boanerges, james, john

sound clap, peal, roar

squall bayamo, vendaval

treatise brontology

tube fulgurite

witch baba

THUNDERER jupiter, london times, thor, zeus

THUNDERFISH catfish, loach, misgurnus, raad

THUNDERFLOWER campion, cornpoppy, stitchwort

THUNDERHEAD cloud, cumulus, omen, warning

THUNDERING big, extraordinary, foudroyant, great, huge, thumping, unusual, whopping

THUNDERSTONE belemnite

THUNDERSTORM bayamo, borasca, borasco, borasque, borrasca, bourrasque, houvari, tempest, tornado

god summanus

recorder brontometer

THUNDERSTRUCK afraid, agape, aghast, astonished, astounded, breathless, confounded, spellbound, surprised

THUNDERWOOD sumac

THUNDERWORM lizard

THUNDERWORT houseleek

THUNGE bang, blow, thump

THURIBLE censer

carrier acolyte, altarboy, thurifer

swing cense

THURIFER acolyte, altarboy

THURIO *rival* valentine

THURROCK drain, hold

THURSDAY *after trinity* corpus christi

40 days after easter ascension day

god of thor

holy skire

THURSE apparition, demon, giant, spirit

THUS accordingly, ainsi, consequently, cosi, dyce, ergo, for instance, hence, ita, sae, sic, similarly, so far, therefore, thiswise, turpentine, yet

far yet

THWACK bang, beat, blow, club, crack, crump, crush, defeat, fill, force, knock, maul, pack, pommel, pummel, rap, strike, thrash, whack

THWART across, adverse, baffle, balk, bar, beat, belabor, bilk, blast, block, blow, checkmate, circumvent, clash, confound, contrair, contravene, counteract, cross(ways), dash, defeat, disappoint, discomfit, disconcert, discountenance, dish, elude, flummox, foil, forestall, frustrate, hinder, hogtie, impede, interpose, oblique, obstruct(ion), op-

pose, opposition, outwit, overcome, perverse, prevent, quarrel, restrain, ruin, saucy, scotch, spike, spite, spoil, stubborn, stymie, transverse, upset

THYATIRA akhisar

THYESTES *brother* atreus

consort aerope

parent hippodamia, pelops

rival atreus

son aegisthus, aglaus

THYLACINE tiger, wolf, yabbi

THYMBRAEUS *father* laocoon

THYMBRIS *consort* zeus

THYME herb-mastic, hillwort, marum, mint, peletre, penny-mountain, serpolet

THYMUS gland, mint, sweetbread

THYROID *deficiency* athyria

disorder myxedema, strumitis

enlargement goiter

hormone thyroxine

projection adam's apple

THYRSIS herdsman, rustic, shepherd

rival corydon

THYRSUS staff, stick, wand

symbol of bacchus, satyr

TIAMAT *consort* apsu, kingu

messenger mummu

TIARA cidaris, coronet, crown, frontlet, gardenia, headdress, lassa, miter

TIBBU berber, daza, teda

TIBER volturnus

ancient name albula, tivoli

city on rome

country etruria

defender horatius

festival portunalia, volcanalia

italian name tevere

patron god vulcan

region beyond trastevere

seaport ostia

swimmer cloelia

tributary anio, nar, nera, teverone

TIBERIAS galilee

TIBET stisang

animal bharal, chiru, dgoba, dzeren, goa, kiang, manul, nahoor, nayaur, oorial, ounce, panda, serow, sha (bo), shou, shue, takin, tanghan, tangun, urial, yak, zebu

antelope chiru, dgoba, dzeren, goa

ass, wild kiang

banner tanka
beast of burden yak
beer chang
brigand khamba
buddhism hamaism
cabinet kashag
cap chuba
capital lassa, lhasa
cat manul
chamberlain phala
chief pombo
city gartok, gyangtse, karak, lassa, lhasa, noh, shigatse, totling
coin tanga
deer shou, shue
dialect balti, bhutanese, bhutani, ladakhi
dog lhasa-apso
ecclesiastic dalai lama
food tsamba
garment chuba
gazelle goa
goat fleece pashm
god chenrezi
hay komal
heaven honorable field
kingdom nepal
lake aru, bam, bum, dagtse, garhur, jagok, jiggitai, kashun, kyaring, mema, nam, seling, tabia, tangra, tengrinor, teriman, tosu, tsaring, yamdok, zilling
lama dalai
language bodskad
leader chime youngdong, dalai lama, rimpoche
monastery benchen, lamasery
monk lama
name for mt everest chomolungma, goddess mother of the world
outcast ragyapa
ox yak
palace potala
peak bandala, kailas, kamet, sajum
people balti, bhoti(y)a, bhutani, bhutia, bodpa, champa, drokpa, drupa, gyarung, khamba, khambu, panaka, sherpa, taghlik, tangut
pony tanghan, tangum, tangun
priest lama
prime minister surkhang
public park lingka
range himalayas, kailas, kunlun
region jyekundo
religion bon(bo), lamaism
religious painting tanka

resident amban
river indus, matsang, nak, nau, sak, salween, song, sutlej, tsangpo
ruler (dalai)lama
ruminant serow, takin
sect bon
sheep bharal, hahoor, nayaur, oorial, sha(bo), urial
"thanks" thujichenja
tribe See *people*, above.
wildcat manul
TIBIA bone, cnemis, flute, shank, shin(bone)
part armilla
pert. cnemial
TIBURON shark, village
TIC correct, jerk, jump, lata(h), nystagmus, spasm, twitch
TICAL baht
TICE ball, entice(ment), lure, yorker
TICINO *capital* bellinzona
TICK acarian, acarid, account, achenes, annulatus, arachnid, argasid, beat, beggarlice, birdfly, boophilus, carapato, chalk, chick, click, cover, credit, crike, dash, dot, fag, flirt, fondle, gar(r)apata, insect, instant, ixodian, ixodid, jar, kade, ked, margaropus, mark, mattress, mianabug, mite, moment, operate, pallet, pat, peak, pest, pick, pike, pinolia, pique, pulse, recur, score, second, sound, speck, spot, strap, talaje, tampan, tap, throb, touch, trust, turicata, whinchat
beak capitellum, capitulum
bird ani, beefeater, oxpecker
fever blue disease
genus argas, cimex, ixodes, margaropus
off check, designate, identify, list, mark, peach, rid
pert. ixodic
study of acarology
trefoil bedstraw, beggarweed, desmodium, sainfoin
venomous pajahuello, tampan
TICKER clock, heart, tikker, timepiece, watch
print-out tape
TICKET (See also *kind*, below.) ballot, billet, card, certificate, coupon, credit, docket, ducat, fiche, iou, label, license, list, notice, pass, permit, placard, plan,

policy, schedule, slate, slip, tag, token, transfer, trust, voucher
complimentary annie oakley, freebie, pass, raincheck
kind one-way, return, round-trip, stopover
lottery horse
of leave parole
part stub
receiver of free deadhead
roundtrip return
scalper iceman
season ivory
sell illegally scalp
speculator iceman, scalper
traffic tag
window guichet
TICKLE amuse, annoy, arouse, beat, capture, caress, chastise, chuck, convulse, cuitle, delicate, delight, difficult, divert, enchant, entertain, excite, gladden, gratify, insecure, itch, nice, please, provoke, regale, squeamish, stir, stroke, take, tease, thrill, tiddle, tingle, titillate, titillation, touch, unstable, unsteady, vellication, wanton, whip
the palm bribe, tip
-toby switch, whip(ping)
weed hellebore
TICKLED amused, glad, gratified, pleased
TICKLISH awkward, brittle, chancy, changeable, critical, delicate, difficult, goosey, insecure, itchy, kittle, nice, precarious, queasy, risky, sensitive, tender, touchy, tricky, trying, uncertain, unreliable, unstable, unsteady
TICKSEED coreopsis, dodder, goldenwave, knotweed, spurry, trefoil
TICKTACK badminton
TICKTACKTOE noughts and crosses
TICONDEROGA *commander* gates
TID childish, fond, (ill)humor, lively, mood, silly, sprightly, tender
TIDAL *creek* estero, estuary, firth
current tiderace
river hudson
strata onlap
wave aigre, bore, eagre, ebb, neap, surge, tsunami

TIDBIT beatille, bonbouche, cate, dainty, delicacy, goody, item, kickshaw, morsel, nibble, nosh, saynete, snack, sunket

TIDDLE fidget, fondle, indulge, pamper, potter, tickle

TIDDLEY small, trivial

TIDDLEYWINK beerhouse, squail

TIDDY babyish, child(ish), girl, tiny, tot, trivial

TIDE agger, befall, chance, continue, current, drift, drive, fair, festival, flood, flow, freshet, happen, help, hour, moment, neap, ocean, opportunity, period, pour, proceed, sea, season, stream, surf, surge, time
double agger
flowing back ebb
gate aboideau
gauge marigraph, thalassometer
low neap
low, pert. neritic
over assist, cover, endure, help, surmount, survive, triumph
retrograde lakie
rising flood

TIDEWATER seaboard, seacoast, shore, strand

TIDINGS advice, evangel, gospel, information, intelligence, message, news, report, rumor, slogan, word

TIDY ample, antimacassar, clean, clear, comely, cover, diligent, donsie, fair, fettle, fix, groom, healthy, kempt, large, mense(ful), methodical, natty, neat, orderly, pinafore, plump, police, prim, redd, seasonable, shipshape, skillful, snod, snug, spick-and-span, spruce, straighten, substantial, systematic, taut, ted, timely, tolerable, tosh, trig, trim, upright, well-kept, worthy

TIDYTIPS aster, flower, layia

TIE (See also *down* and *kind,* below.) allegiance, alligate, anchor, angle, attach, band, beam, beat, bind, bond, brace, break even, bride, bridge, cadge, cast, cement, chain, clinch, condition, connection, constrain(t), constrict, cord,

couple, dead heat, deadlock, draw, equal, even, fasten, FASTENER, influence, join, knot, lace, lash, leash, ligate, link, marry, moor, neckband, nexus, obligation, oxford, pledge, post, refait, relation, rig, rivet, rope, sag, scarf, sheaf, shoelace, sleeper, stalemate, standoff, stop, string(er), tach(e), tape, teck, temper, tether, thrap, tossup, trammel, trice, truss, union, yerk, yoke
down confine, constrict, fetter, hamper, restrain, restrict, secure, shackle
-dyeing bandhnu
fabric rep(p), silk
fast belay
in associate, association, collaboration, combine, connection, join, link, relation(ship)
kind ascot, black, bolo, bow, butterfly, cravat, foulard, four-in-hand, jazzbow, paisley, shoestring, string, teck, wanty, white
leather wanty
off belay, ligate, snub
ornament clip, pin, tack
plate turtle
ready-made teck
sail trice
securely lash, shackle, trammel, truss, yerk
the can to discard, dismiss, fire
together harness, knit, knot, leash, splice, yoke
up bind, bundle, combination, confine, connect(ion), delay, engage, entanglement, hinder, impede, join, knot, ligate, moor, obstruct, pack, red tape, restrain, restrict, rope, secure, snub, stop, strike, tether, trammel, trice, truss, twitchel, wrap

TIED bound, constrained, drawn, equal, even, knotted, neck and neck, square
up busy, encumbered, occupied

TIEN SHAN heavenly mountains

TIER apron, bank, chess, class, course, deck, degree, grade, layer, level, pinafore, rank, row, series, stack, story, stratum, withe

TIERCE cask, lunge, parry,

service, third, three, undersong

TIERGARTEN park, zoo

TIERRA DEL FUEGO *indian* agni, fuegian, ona
strait magellan

TIERRA FIRMA darien

TIETICK pipit

TIFF altercation, argue, bicker(ing), bout, broil, condition, contend, discord, dress, drink, dudgeon, fight, fit, huff, humor, liquor, lunch, miff, mood, order, outburst, peeve, pet, quarrel, row, rumpus, sip, spat, spell, squabble, state, temper, tift, wrangle

TIFFANY flimsy, gauze, glass, lawn, muslin, sieve, sifter, silk

TIFFIN condor, lunch(eon), repast, tea

TIFFLE disarrange, entangle, fray, idle, potter, snarl, trifle, tumble, unravel

TIFT flight, haste, hurry, just, pant, puff, sniff, tiff, whiff

TIG meddle, pat, run, sulks, tag, tamper, touch

TIGER, TIGER'S bully, cat, champ, chati, feline, felis, groom, jaguar, leopard, rake, sher(e), shir, swaggerer, thylacine
bird amadavat, barbet, bittern
cat chati, dasydure, margay, ocelot, serval
cocoa patashte
cub sherbacha
finch amadavat
fish carcharhinus, carcharias, hydrocyon
foot ipomoea
hungry slot machine
-hunting dog dhole
milk gin, liquor
mouth foxglove, snapdragon, toadflax
nut chufa
of france clemenceau
saber-tooth smilodon
shark demoiselle
short-haired bengal
sir shere-khan
snake elap(o)id
symbol of ferocity
the clemenceau
-wolf hyena, thylacine

TIGERWOOD bush-tamarind, jacaranda, machaerium

TIGHT alert, appoint, capable, cheap, close(fisted),

compact, competent, condensed, constant, constricted, cosy, dense, difficult, draw, DRUNK, energetic, faithful, fast, firm, fixed, frugal, grasping, hard, high, impervious, inebriated, intend, intoxicated, mean, miserly, narrow, neat, packed, penurious, ready, rigid, secure, severe, shapely, smart, snug, solid, sparing, stent, stingy, strained, strait, strict, stringent, taut, tee, tense, tiddly, tidy, tipsy, trim
as a drum, tick
-fisted cheeseparing, miserly, niggardly, parsimonious, penny-pinching, penurious, sordid, stingy
-lipped close(mouthed), reserved, reticent, secretive, silent, taciturn, terse, uncommunicative
make See TIGHTEN.
spot fix, jam, mess, pinch, predicament
TIGHTEN astrict, brace, ca(u)lk, cinch, close, constrict, contract, firm, frap, lace, screw, stiffen, straighten, strain, straiten, stretch, tauten, tense, tensify, thrap, wrench
device to toggle, washer, wrench
one's belt economize
ropes frap
strings of drum frap
TIGHTNESS astriction, constriction, snugness, strain, tautness, tenseness, tension
TIGHTROPE *walker* funambulist
TIGHTS breeches, fleshings, pants
TIGHTWAD churl, curmudgeon, fist, miser, niggard, piker, pinchfist, screw, scrooge, skinflint, stingypeter
TIGRANES *brother* guras
city tigranocerta
favorite metrodorus
kin mithridates
kingdom armenia
orator amphicrates
rival lucullus, pompey
royal city artaxata
victim seleucus
wife cleopatra, zosime
TIGRIS *and euphrates region* chaldea

boat goofah, gufa, kufa
city on amara, nineveh
tributary euphrates
TIKE See TYKE.
TIKOR arrowroot, garcinia
TIKVATH *son* jahaziah, shallum
TIL plant, sesame, teel, tilde
TILDE tittle
TILE azulejo, brick, carreau, conduit, domino, drain, favus, hat, headdress, imbrex, kashi, lappet, pam(m)ent, pantile, pavement, pipe, plate, quarrel, quarry, slab, slate(r), tegula, tessera(te)
carved quarl(e)
comb. ostraco
enameled kashi
game dominoes, mah-jongg
glazed azulejo
hexagonal favus
hollow backing
large dalle, quarl(e)
length gauge
-like slaty, tegular
marble dalle
mosaic abaculus, tessera
roofing pantile
rounded crease
square quadrel, quarrel
trimmer zax
work kashi
TILEFISH blanquillo
TILER doorkeeper, heler, hellier, kiln, oven, porter, thief
TILIA basswood, linden
TILL before, box, cash, cash register, casket, charm, cultivate, develop, draw, drawer, dress, entice, even, farm, forwards, gain, husband, labor, land, lentil, lob, moneybox, plough, plow, prepare, seed, set, sow, strive, than, train, tray, treasury, until, unto, when, while, whilst, work
TILLAGE agriculture, aration, crops, farming, gainor, tilture
fit for arable
TILLER agriculturist, bar, bow, farmer, grower, handle, harrower, harvester, helm, hoer, husband(man), killifer, lever, peasant, plowman, rancher, rudder, sapling, shaft, shoot, sprout, stalk, stern, stool, tree
TILON *father* shimon
TILT altercation, argue, aslant, awning, burst in,

canopy, cant, careen, contest, controversy, covering, dispute, duel, empty, fight, forge, heald, heel(d), hield, inclination, incline, joust, kip(p), lean, list, pour, quintain, rush, seesaw, slant, slope, speed, stave, stilt, stroke, tent, throw, thrust, tip, topple, tournament, tourney, unload, upset
-hammer oliver
up cock, upend
TIMAEUS *son* bartimaeus
TIMALIA babbler, thrush
TIMANDRA *brother* castor
consort alcibiades
parent leda, tyndareus
sister clytemnestra, helen, philopoe
TIMARAU buffalo
TIMBER (See also *kind*, below.) batten, beam, bibb, bitt, boat, bracket, build, cahuy, camber, dram, forest, fuel, hurdle, kevel, log, lumber, material, quality, spar, structure, stumpage, trees, wood(en)
bevel snape
block bolt, juggle
coal prop brob
convex camber
curved cruck
cut bunk, fallage, fell, lumber
decay See *rot*, below.
defect collapse, conk, doze, lag, rindgall, shan
end tenon
estimator biltmore stick, cruiser, scaler
floor joist, summer(tree)
foundation batten, sill
framing puncheon
heartwood duramen
heavy balk, beam, rafter
horizontal lintel, reason, stringer
kind cavel, hag, header, joist, kevel, mast, purlin(e), putlog, rafter, rib, sill, spale, stringer, stud, stull, summer(tree)
knee angle breech
length balk, bolt, flitch
length, cut to juggle
mine cog, divider, juggler, lifter, stull
peg coak
perfect freestuff
prop stull
roof lever, rafter, sile

rot doat(y), dote, dotiness, doze

ship's bibb, bitt, bracket, dagger, deadwood, dogshore, futtock, harpin(gs), keel, kevel, knee, lacing, ledge, mast, rib, rung, scroll, snape, spale, spar, spur, standard, stemson, sternson, stocks, wale

slabbed cant

sloping rafter

space between spirket

standing forest, puncheon, spile, stud(ding), stumpage, woods

stout templet

support beam, corbel, girder, ledger, legpiece, stringer, t-bar

tree See TREE timber.

truck wynn

uncut See standing, above.

unit ton

upward curve sny

value stumpage

vertical bitt, jamb

weatherbeaten driki

weight-bearing sleeper

wolf lobo

TIMBERLAND forest, sticks, woodland

TIMBERMAN bracer, carpenter, cruiser, logger, lumberman, sawyer, woodsman

TIMBO ajari, cube

TIMBRE character, clang, color, crest, klang, miter, pitch, quality, resonance, ring, tone

pert. tonal

TIMBREL drum, sistrum, tabo(u)r, tambourine

TIME accent, beat, befall, cadence, clock, control, date, duration, eld, epoch, fare, fuss, happen, hint, leisure, liberty, limit, measure, meter, occasion, opportunity, period, procrastinate, regulate, schedule, season, sele, sithe, spell, steven, stoun(d), tempo, temps, tense, term, tid, tide, watch, weather, yore, zeit

after post

after time often, repeatedly

ahead of early, premature

allowed usance

and again frequently, often, repeatedly

another again

at any when(so)ever

at no never(more)

at same in unison, simultaneously, together

bad bust, crash, depression, downer

being nonce, pro tempore

bill certificate

blossom blutezeit

book chronicle

break hiatus

brief See short, below.

card chronicle

christmas yuletide

clock bundy, recorder, telltale

comb. chron(o), chronous, horo, temp

decisive zero hour

division aeon, age, beat, century, day, decade, eon, epoch, era, fortnight, ghurry, hour, instant, minute, moment, month, recess, season, sec(ond), span, spell, tempo, term, trice, week, year

endless eternity, infinity, perpetuity

fast daylight saving, dst, lent

flies tempus fugit

god cronus, kronos, saturn, zervan, zurvan

gone by ago, auld lang syne, past, yesterday, yesteryear, yore

good ball, barney, bash, fete, frolic, gala, holiday, party, soiree, upper

fixed for payment usance

granted delay, frist, reprieve, stay

happy bust, jamboree, lark, party, revel(ry), soiree, spree, tear

-honored traditional

intervening interim, meantime, meanwhile

long age, blue moon, century, coon's age, dog's age, forever, millenium, month of sundays

machine author h g wells

measurer (See also TIMEPIECE.) micronometer

musical beat, lilt, rhythm, tempo

of day, comb. horo

of depression nadir

of highest strength heyday

of woe wosith

olden eld, syne, yore

opportune tide

out break, breather, elevens, intermission, interval, lull, recess, respite, rest

pert. chronal, eral, horal, temporal

present nonce, now

prosperous boom

right tid

-serving obsequious, temporizing, trimming

short bat, blink, crack, flash, instant, jack robinson, jerk, jiff(y), minute, moment, nick, sec(ond), short shrift, snatch, space, span, spot, stound, throw, tick, tiff, twink(ling), two shakes

single once

table itinerary, schedule, sked

unit, hypothetical chronon

waste boondoggle, dally, dawdle, diddle, flanerie, goldbrick, goof off, idle, laze, loaf, loiter, niggle, potter, putter, tinker, trifle

wrong anachronism

TIMEKEEPER almanac, clock, horologue, metronome, watch

TIMELESS ageless, coeternal, dateless, eternal, eterne, everlasting, interminable, premature, true, undated, unending, untimely, valid

TIMELY appropriate, auspicious, befitting, cogent, convenient, duly, early, expedient, favorable, fit(ting), happy, lucky, meet, pat, prompt, propitious, providential, opportune, seasonable, seasonal, suitable, topical, towardly

TIMEPIECE alarm clock, chronograph, chronometer, chronopher, clepsydra, clock, dial, egg-glass, ghurry, gnomon, horolog(u)e, horologium, hourglass, isochronon, metronome, pendule, repeater, sandglass, stemwinder, stopwatch, souper, sundial, sunwatch, telltake, ticker, turnip, verge, watch, wristwatch

TIMER See TIMEPIECE.

TIMETABLE bradshaw, calendar, schedule

TIMEWORN aged, antiquated, mossgrown, motheaten, out of date, ragged, stale, tired, trite

TIMID afraid, apprehensive, argh, backward, bashful,

bauch, blate, cautious, chary, circumspect, cowardly, diffident, faint(hearted), fearful, fearing, frighty, henny, jumpy, misventurous, modest, mous(e)y, nervous, nesh, pavid, retiring, scaddle, scary, shaky, sheepish, shivery, shrinking, shy, skittery, skittish, startlish, strange, timorous, trembling, trepid, wary, weak
soul caspar milquetoast
TIMIDITY (See also FEAR.) funkiness, jumpiness, shyness, skittishness, timerity, timorousness
symbol hare, sheep
TIMNA *kin* amalek, eliphaz, lotan
TIMOLEON *brother* timophanes
parent demariste, timaenutus, timodemus
ruler of sicily, syracuse
victim timophanes
TIMON cynic, helm, misanthrope, rudder, tiller
flatterer lucius, lucullus, sempronius
friend alcibiades, apemantus, ventidius
of athens character alcibiades, apemantus, caphis, flaminius, flavius, hortensius, lucilius, lucius, lucullus, philotus, phrynia, sempronius, timandra, titus, ventidius
servant flaminius, lucilius, servilius
steward flavius
TIMOR *capital* dili
city atambua, kupang
coin avo, pataca
island lakor, leti, moa, roti
language tetum
TIMOROUS afraid, apprehensive, blenching, fearful, harehearted, quailing, shivering, shrinking, shuddering, terrible, TIMID, trembling, tremulous, trepid
TIMOTHY grass, hay, phleum
colleague paul
grandmother lois
mother eunice
TIMPANO kettledrum
TIMUCUAN *indian* yustaga
TIN box, can(nikin), container, counterfeit, inferior, k(h)atin, kindle, latten, mean, metal, money, pack

(age), pan, petty, pillion, preserve, prillion, shut, spurious, stannum, swell, tind, worthless
alloy babbit, brittania, cassiterite, pewter, terne, tutania
black cassiterite
can destroyer
can island niuafoo
fish torpedo
foil tain
glass bismuth
-lead coat terne
mess dixie, dixy
mineral cassiterite
mine stannary
mine workman spadiard
ore carbona, floran, scove
pan alley group ascap
pert. stannic, stannous
planet jupiter
plate foil, tagger, tain, terne
-pot inferior, paltry, poor, shoddy, third-rate, wretched
pyrites stannite
roofing terne
rubbish stent
shack bidonville
sheet latten, lattin
slag quitter
stone cassiterite
type mezzotint
vessel blickie, blicky
-washing device buddle
worker bungler, tinker, tinner, whitesmith
works stannary
TINAMOU bird, macuca, martinet, partridge, tataupa, ynambu, yutu
TINCAL altincar, borax
TINCT color, dye, hue, imbue, shade, tinged, tint (ed)
TINCTURE admixture, aramaize, argent, arnica, bufo, cast, color(ing), dash, diamond, drug, dye, elixir, extract, imbrue, imbue, infusion, laudanum, mixture, pigment, quality, sable, shade, smack, smattering, stain, strain, suggestion, suspicion, taint(ure), tinge, tint, touch, trace, vein, vestige
black bufo
for sprains arnica
heraldic argent, azure, gules, purpure, sable, vert
TINDER amadou, combustible, firebox, fuel, kindling, punk, sponk, spunk, touchwood

TINE bit, destroy, die, enclose, fang, fine, forfeit, grain(ing), grass, grief, harrow, instant, kindle, knag, lose, offer, pain, perish, plant, point, prong, repair, shut, snag, spike, teen, tind, tiny, tooth, trouble, tub, tynd, vat, vetch
antler crocket, right, surroyal
branch snag
group antler
having 3 tridentate
TINEA barber's itch, ringworm
TINEWEED vetch
TINGE bepaint, cast, chroma, color, dash, discolor, dye, flavor, hue, imbrue, imbue, modify, paint, savor, season, shade, smack, smear, smutch, soo, stain, streak, taint, tinct(ure), tinge, tint, touch, trace
TINGGIAN *tribe* apayao, it(a)neg
TINGLE burn, creep, dirl, excitement, fastening, girl, itch, nail, patch, prickle, pringle, prinkle, ring, smart, stimulate, sting, support, swidge, tack, thrill, tickle, tink(le), tremor, trinkle, vibrate
TINGLING athrill, paresthesia, smarting, thrilling, tremulous, vibrating
TINHORN cheap, fake, flashy, fourflusher, petty, piker, smalltime
TININE enclosure, harrowing, losing
TINK plink
TINKER, TINKER'S auk, beggar, boggle, botch(er), bungler, caird, dabble, fidget, gypsy, jack-of-all-trades, kettler, mackerel, mend(er), mugger, murre, patcher, potter, putter, rascal, repair, rogue, silversides, tramp, traveler, wanderer
bird barbet
dam trible
jargon shelta
weed feverroot
TINKLE chatter, chink, clink, dindle, ding(le), jingle, ring, summon, ting(le), TINKER, trinkle, twinkle
TINKLING grackle, jingling

TINNE *indian* athapascan, chipew(a)yan, montagnard

TINNY bright, brittle, cheap, hard, metallic, rich, thin, wealthy

TINSEL brummagem, clinquant, fake, finery, forfeiture, frippery, gaudy, geegaw, gimcrack, loss, pretentious, glittery, sham, shoddy, specious, splendor, spurious, tawdry, trumpery
cheeks rouge

TINT color, dye, ennue, eye, grain, hue, shade, spraing, tinct, tinge
comb. chrom(o)

TINTYPE daguerreotype, ferrotype, old(fashioned), photo(graph)

TINY atomic, bantam, bitty, diminutive, fine, infant, little, microscopic, miniature, minikin, minute, peewee, petite, SMALL, teeny, wee(ny), weeshy
creature atomy, minimus

TIP apex, apiculus, ba(c)ksheesh, ba(c)kshish, bestow, bonus, b(u)na mano, brush, cant, cap(itulum), careen, cave, cock, counsel, cue, cumshaw, dertrum, douceur, drink, dump, earwig, end, entomion, extremity, foothold, glove-money, gratuity, heel, heeld, held, hint, horn, incline, information, inkling, intoxicate, keel, kickback, knap, lean, list, mucro, overturn, peak, perquisite, pike, pile, point, pouch, pourboire, present, prompt, refuse, reminder, slant, slope, spire, spure, summit, tap, tilt, tiptoe, toe, top, touch, trinkgelt, trip, tup, unload, upset, upturn, vertex, warning, wheeze
comb. acr(o), apic
having sharp aristate
near to apical
off advise, alarm, alert, caution, hint, inform, prompt, tell, warn(ing)
over fall, upset
pointed or small apiculus

TIPCART butt, cocopan, coupe

TIPCAT kitcat, piggie, piggy, pussy

TIPPECANOE william henry harrison

TIPPED banked, canted, crank

TIPPET almuce, amice, cape, fur, liripipe, liripoop, muffler, palatine, patagium, ruff, scarf, sindon, snell, victorine

TIPPLE bib(ber), bibble, dram, drink, fuddle, gill, guzzle, intoxicate, liquor, nip, overturn, pot, puddle, sip(ple), suck, tope, tumble, upset

TIPPLER alcoholic, aleknight, alestake, bibber, carouser, drinker, drunk(ard), pigeon, potator, soak, sot, souse, stricker, toast, toper, tosspot, tumbler, winer

TIPPY smart, stylish, unsteady, wobbly

TIPSTAFF attendant, bailiff, constable, POLICEMAN

TIPSTER dopester, forecaster, informant, insider, speculator, tout(er)

TIPSY bosky, bungfu, DRUNK, ebriose, fuddled, groggy, happy, high, inebriated, merry, nappy, ree, soused, sprung, staggering, tiddly, tight, tozie, unsteady, wet

TIPTAIL sandpiper

TIPTOE alert, cautiously, eager(ly), exalted, expectant(ly), quietly, roused, skip, stealthy, trip, warily, wary

TIPTOP ace, a-one, apex, bang-up, best, bunkum, fine, first-rate, galumptious, good, great, highest, prime, shipshape, sound, star, summit, swell

TIPTOPPER gentleman, lady, nob, swell, toff

TIPUP sandpiper, tilt

TIRADE abuse, denunciation, diatribe, harangue, jeremiad, philippic, screed, speech, stoush, vituperation

TIRE adornment, array, ATTIRE, bore, bush, cloy, decorate, deplete, drain, dress, enervate, exhaust, fag, fatigue, frazzle, gnaw, harass, hoop, invest, irk, jade, labor, moil, overdo, overwork, pall, pinafore, poop(out), pull, raiment, robe, satiate, seize, sicken, tear, tier, trachle, tread,

tucker, vest, vex, wear out, weary
groove sipe
part carcass, casing, rim, shoe, tread, tube
pneumatic, inventor dunlop
remade recap, retread

TIRED all in, aweary, beat, bleary, blown, bucked, bushed, deadbeat, disgusted, done(in), exhausted, fagged, fatigued, forwaked, hackneyed, impatient, jaded, played out, sleepy, spent, stale, tavert, wearied, weary
-looking haggard, toil-worn, wan

TIRELESS assiduous, busy, energetic, indefatigable, persevering, strenuous, strong, unflagging, untiring. unwearied, vigorous

TIRESIAS prophet, soothsayer
daughter manto
parent chariclo, everes

TIRESOME annoying, arduous, boring, borish, bromidic, difficult, dreary, dreich, dull, ennuyant, exhausting, fagging, fatiguing, hard, humdrum, irksome, irritating, monotonous, platitudinous, poky, prolix, prosaic, tame, tedious, trite, uninteresting, vexatious, wearisome, wearying
person bore, bromide, killjoy

TIRHANA *father* caleb

TIRL bout, divest, pluck, rap, rattle, revolve, risp, strip, tap, thirl, thrill, tirr, tirve, turn, twirl, uncover, undress, unroof, unroll, vibrate, vibration, wheel, whirl

TIRZAH *brother* hur

TISAMENUS *enemy* heraclidae
parent hermione, orestes, thersander
realm argos, sparta

TISANE decoction, infusion, medicine, ptisan, tea, tilleul

TISAPHERNES *enemy* agesilaus, xenophon
slayer tithraustes

TISSUE cloth, fabric, fa(s)cia, fiber, gauze, gleba, gossamer, graft, interweave, kleenex, meat, mesh(work), net(work), onionskin, phloem, ribbon, sheer, tela, texture, weave, web(bing)

absence aplasia

animal bone, fat, gelatine, gum, keratin, paxwax, suet

black clypeus

bony ossein, scrag

comb. histo

connective bone, cartilage, fascia, hadrome, leptome, ligament, mestome, reticulum, stroma, tendon

cork suber

death of gangrene, necrosis

decay atrophy, calaplasia, caries

dissection histotomy

fatty grease, lard

framework stroma

fungus centrum

hard bone

hardening sclerosis

horny keratin

human aerenchyma, albedo, diploe, keloid, ligament, strama(ta), tela, tendon

hyphal trama

hypothetical coagulin

layer dartos, elastica, epiblema, fascia, serosa, stratum

-like histoid, telar

lymphoid tonsil

nerve alba, ganglion

oily fat

pert. histoid, telar

plant hadrome, leptome, mestome

reproduction anagenesis

skeletal cartilage

soft flab

study of histology

substance sarcine

thickened callus, corn

tooth gum

transplantation anaplerosis

vegetable armor, bast, lignin, meristem, phloem, xylem

wasting away phthisis

weblike plexus, tela

woody lignin, lignum, vitrain

TISZA *city on* szeged

TIT bird, blow, bluecap, diminutive, draw, girl, horse, hussy, jade, jerk, mesia, mufflin, nag, pin, plug, pull, tap, teat, tee, tite, tug, twit(ch), woman

blue nun, stonechat

for tat equivalent, give and take, interchange, retaliation, revenge

-tat-toe go bang, noughts and crosses

TITA *root* mishmee, mishmi

TITAN astraeus, asura, atlas,

bana, coeus, cresus, creus, crios, cronos, cronus, epimetheus, giant, gigantic, helios, hyperion, iapetus, kronos, leader, magnate, missile, oceanus, pallas, powerhouse, prometheus, s(h)esha, stalwart, sun

female circe, dione, eurynome, leto, maia, mnemosyne, phoebe, rhea, selene, tethys, theia, themis

giant aeg(a)eon, agrios, gyges, kottos, kronos

jailer tartarus

moon of saturn

parent gaea, uranus

1000-armed bana, s(h)esha

war with gods gigantomachy

TITANATE geikielite, isarate, pyrophanite, rutile, warwickite

TITANIA *husband* oberon

planet uranus

TITANIC big, colossal, enormous, giant, gigantic, huge, mammoth, monster, stupendous, vast

TITANITE grothite, lederite, ligurite, sphene

TITANIUM *alloy* anatase, arkansite, blomstrandine, brookite, octahedrite, rutile

ore ilmenite

TITE immediately, promptly, quickly, soon

TITFISH trepang

TITHE assessment, canon, cess, charge, decima(l), decimate, dime, levy, prebend, rate, tariff, tax, teind, tenth, toll, tribute

pert. decimal

TITHING bor(g)h, borrow, decen(n)ary, decime, denary, frankpledge

man borsholder, constable, dean, decurion, tuttiman

TITHONUS *brother* priam

changed to grasshopper

consort aurora, eos

offspring emathion, laomedon, memnon

parent laomedon, strymo

TITHYMALUS caper-spurge

TITI callicebus, callithrix, cliftonia, cyrilla, hapale, ironwood, marmoset, monkey, ora(bassu), ouistiti, petrel, saimiri, teetee, wistit(i)

TITILLATE amuse, attract, delight, excite, interest,

please, stimulate, thrill, tickle, vellicate

TITIVATE cultivate, decorate, dress, smarten, spruce, tidy

TITLARK pipit, teeting

TITLE (See also under countries, e.g. INDIA *title.*) address, appellation, asset, book, call, capitulary, caption, claim, cognomen, deed, designation, dub, epigraph, epithet, equity, flag, ground, handle, head(ing), honorific, identification, inscription, justification, label, legal right, legend, letterhead, lien, LORD, magnate, mark, masthead, merit, motto, muniment, NAME, nomenclature, ownership, parish, placard, play, pretense, pretension, proof, property, rank, reason, right, rubric, RULER, screamer, style, superscription, tag, titulus

acquisition usucapt

archaic sire, sirrah

courtesy illustrissimo

ecclesiastic See CHURCHMAN.

feminine dame, dona, frau (lein), han(o)um, lady, maam, madam(e), mademoiselle, memsahib, milady, missis, missus, mistress, mme, mrs, sahibah, sen(h)ora, senorita, signora, signorina

foreign ag(h)a, aya, baba, bailiff, basha(w), bey, chan, dan, devi, dominus, don, effendi, gaek war, g(h)azi, graf, herr, huzzoor, kaan, kaun, kawn, lars, mian, mir(za), monsieur, mpret, nawob, pacha, pasha, peshwa, ras, sa(i) yid, sen(h)or, sha(h), shereef, sherif, shogun, shree, shri, sidi, sieur, squire, sri, suffee, tuan, von

governmental chairman, governor, justice, mayor, president, prime minister, viceroy

-holder champion

masculine esquire, herr, master, mister, monsieur, mssrs, sahib, sen(h)or, signor(e), signorino, sir, tuan

noble archduke, banneret, baron(et), caballero, cheva-

lier, conte(ssa), count(ess), duke, earl, esquire, knight, LORD, marquis, prince, ritter, sir, viscount
of dignity dan, don, esquire, sir(e)
of respect burra, coja, hodja, khaja, khoja, lief, madam(e), mian, milady, sahib, shri, sidi, sir
page design vignette
pert. nominal, titular
royal abgar, abimilech, ag(h)a, ali, autocrat, bey, caesar, calif, cham, czar, darius, duke, emeer, emir, emperor, empress, ghazi, hospodar, kaiser, khan, khedive, king, landgrave, mikado, nejus, nizam, padishah, pharaoh, prince, princess, principe, prinz, queen, raja(h), shah, shareef, sheik, sultan, tsar
to property deed
TITLING pipit, sparrow, stockfish
TITMOUSE baiolophus, bird, blackcap, bluebitton, bluecap, bushtit, chic(k)adee, colmose, fuffit, goosander, hackmall, hagmall, heckimal, heffel, jacksaw, mag, mufflin, mumruffin, nun, oxeye, parid, parus, psaltiparus, puffer, ragamuffin, sharpsan, sparus, spick, tat, titmall, tomnoup, tomtit, verdin
bearded reedling
blue stonechat, tidife, tidwife, tinnock, tydie
long-tailed bottletit, fuffit, millithrum, pokepudding
pert. parine
small miller's-thumb
TITO broz
foe chetnik, mihailovic
TITOGRAD *former name* podgorica
TITRATE analyze
TITTER giggle, laugh, rather, seesaw, snicker, snigger, sooner, teehee, totter, tremble, twitter, wobble
-totter seesaw, sway, teeter
TITTEREL whimbrel
TITTLE accent, atom, bit, cedilla, gossip, iota, jot, mark, minute, mite, particle, smidgen, smitch, speck, tattle, tickle, tilde, whisper, whit

-tattle busybody, chat(ter), gossip, prate, tattler
TITTLEBAT stickleback
TITTUP caper, frish, gambol, hop, prance
TITULAR cognominal, honorary, honorific, nominal
TITUREL *son* amfortas
TITUS ANDRONICUS *author* shakespeare
brother marcus
character aaron, aemilius, alarbus, bassianus, caius, chiron, demetrius, lavinia, lucius, marcus-andronicus, martius, mutius, publius, quintus, saturninus, sempronius, tamora, valentine
daughter lavinia
kinsman caius, publius, sempronius, valentine
queen tamora
son lucius, martius, mutius, quintus
TITYRA becard, bird
TITYUS *jailer* tartarus
parent elara, gaea, terra, zeus
slayer apollo, artemis, zeus
tormentor vulture
victim leto
TIU ear, tiwaz, tyr
TIVOLI See TIBER.
TIWAZ ear, tiu, tyr
TIZZY dither, dudgeon, pet, sixpence, snit, swiv(v)et
TLACO *2* cuartillo
8 real
TLASCALAN *god* camaxtli
TLEPOLEMUS *kingdom* argos
parent astydamia, astyoche (ia), hercules
slayer sarpedon
uncle and *victim* licymnius
TLINGIT *indian* auk, chilcat, chilkat, koluschan, kolush, sitka, stikine, sumdum, tlinkit, tonga(s), yakutat
TM transcendental meditation
founder maharishi mahesh yogi
TMEMA part, piece, section, segment
TMESIS diacope, metastasis
TMOLUS *consort* omphale, pluto
father proteus
son tantalus
TNT dynamite, explosive, toluene, trinitrotoluene, trinitrotoluol, trotol, trotyl
TO again(st), at hand, beside, close, forward, near,

one, tae, thither, till, toward(s), until, unto, upon, with
a degree rather, somewhat
a high degree amain, largely
all appearances apparently, evidently
all intents and purposes substantially
a man unanimously
and fro alternate(ly), back and forth, changeably, discussion, fluctuant, fluctuation, in and out, libratory, pendulant, pendular, seesaw, shuttlewise, undulant, up and down, vacillation, wibble-wobble, zigzag
a nicety exactly, perfectly
any degree aughtlins
any extent aught
arms aux armes
a sickening degree ad nauseam
a turn exactly, perfectly
be einai, esse(re), etre, ibe, sein, was
be sure all right, certainly, even, indeed, of course
blame at fault, culpable, guilty, liable
boot also, and, besides, over
-deal, -dele distinguish, distribute, divide, separate
-do ado, agitation, bustle, commotion, flurry, fluster, foofaraw, fooster, fuss, hoopla, pother, stir, tarrarom, terrarom, travally, uproar
-draw detract, postpone, protract, pull, rend, tear
each his own suum cique
-fall hanger-on, lean-to, refuge
no avail in vain, unsuccessfully
no purpose amiss
one side abeam, agee, ajee, apart, aside, askew
pieces apart, broken
rights neat, orderly, perfectly, straight, tidy
say no more at least
sheltered side alee
that end hence, therefore
that time until
the alla, aux
the end outrance, throughout, utterly
the left aport, haw
the letter literally
the man ad hominem
the opposite side across

the point across, ad rem, concise, germane, pertinent, pithy, plain(ly), salient, terse

the purpose apropos, pertinent, relevant

the rear abast, astern, backward, behind

the right gee, starboard

this hereto

this place here, hither

victory aboo, abu

which whereto

wit for example, namely, scilicet, videlicet, viz

your health See TOAST drinking.

your heart's content agogo, aplenty

TOA soldier, warrior

TOAD(S) aglossa, agua, alytes, amphibian, anura(n), bufo(nid), charlie, crapaud, crapon, frog, gang(e)rol, hyla, hylid, natterjack, paddo(ck), peeper, pipa(l), pode, puddock, quilkin, rana, reptile, salimentia, spadefoot, tad(e), ted, xenopus

-eater See TOADY.

extract bufagin, bufotalin, bufotenin(e)

-eye cassiterite, tinstone

group knot

horned phrynosoma

kind horned, hyla

largest agua

larva tadpole

-mouth snapdragon

obstetrical alytes

poison phrynin

rush saltweed

spittle cuckoo-spit

-spotted blemished, infamous

-stabber jackknife

symbol of inspiration

tongueless aglossa

trademark wart

TOADFISH angler, cabezon, frogfish, grubby, loricate, midshipman, puffer, sa(r)po, scorpion, sculpin, slim(m)er

TOADFLAX bread-and-butter, brideweed, bridewort, butter-and-eggs, churnstaff, comandra, fluellen, gallweed, gallwort, greenbrier, kicksia, linaria, meadowsweet, ramstead, thesium

TOADPIPE equisetum, horsetail

TOADSTONE bufonite

TOADSTOOL agaric, canker, fungus, morrel, mushroom, puffball

TOADY apple-polish(er), bootlick(er), cajole, cower, crawl, cringe, dependent, earwig, fawn(er), flatterer, flunky, follow, grease, grovel, hanger-on, lackey, lacquey, leech, lickspit(tle), parasite, pawn, serve, shmatte, shmotte, shoneen, sponge, suck, sycophant, tag, truckle(r), tuft-hunter, yes-man, zany

TOAST belle, birsel, bread, brede, brown, bumper, burn, carouse, celebrate, cook, drink, dry, frizzle, health, heat, leep, parch, pledge, propine, roast, rouse, sippet, soak, tan, tippler, warm

and ale swig

bit snippet

drinking a votre sante, bottoms up, brindare, brindisi, cento anni, cheerio, cheers, health, here's mud in your eye, here's to you, kampai, l'chaim, lechayim, proface, prosit, prosperity, salud, salute sante, sk(o)al, vive, waes-hael, wahz-hile, wassail

rhymed brindisi

TOASTMASTER symposiarch

TOBACCO baccer, baccy, bogie, bright, broadleaf, burley, capa, caporal, cowpen, fogus, funky, gagroot, goracco, hand, havana, henbane, knaster, lady nicotine, latakia, leaf, makhorka, maryland, nicotia, nicotine, oronoco, perique, petun, pigtail, regie, salvadora, sana, seedleaf, shag, snout, tabac(um), tabak, terbacker, tobacker, tumbak(i), tumbek(i) turkish, uppowoc, virginia, vuelta, weed

aging fermentation

alkaloid anatabine

ash dottel, dottle

box butt, caddy, doss, humidor, saratoga, skate, sunfish

bundle carrot, hand

caked cavendish, heel

camphor nicotianin, nicotine

cask hogshead

chewing beechnut, cavendish, chaw, crowley, cud, fid, fudgeon, grammas, griffin, heise, mailpouch, navy, pesky, plug, quid, redman, rettenmund, scrap, spit and run, twist

cigarette bull, rag

coarse caporal, scrap, shag

disease blackfire, blackshank, brindle, calico, etch, frogeye, mildew, mosaic, poleburn, walloon, wilt

dried tabacum

dryer oast

factory stemmery

field vega

flavoring petune

frenching phyllodination

frogeye cigar-spot

hard-spun nailrod, pigtail

hookah smoking goracco

indian eyebright, gagroot, pukeweed

inferior boots, bug dust, crumbs, doglegs, lugs, shag

ingredient nicotine

in pipe bowl dottel, dottle, topper

juice ambeer, ambier, praiss

kentucky burley

ladies' cudweed

leaf heart ratoon

leaf miner splitworm

leaf moistener caser, kase

leaves flyings, seconds

leaves, bunch break, hand

leaves, dried tabacum

leftover dottel, dottle, topper

liquid form anatabine

moisture extraction curing

molasses-moistened honeydew

mosaic walloon

offensive mundungo

package sack of dust

paste goracco

pile bulk

pipe billiaro, briar, calabash, calean, chibouk, chibouque, chillum, clay, corncob, cutty, dudeen, dust, fillins, goat-hair, hookah, meerschaum, tumblins

pipe bowl calabash

plug fid, navy, quid

portion quid

pouch doss

process cavendish

pulverized snuff

quid cud, fid

raw leaf

receptacle hooka(h), humidor, narghil(e), pipe

residue dottle

roll carotte, carrot, cigar, nailrod, prick, pudding, segar, stogie

room prizery

ropes bogie

sailor's cornucopia, fair maid, faithful lover

sharp-tasting piperina

shredded shag

small piece carotte, cud, dottel, dottle, fid, fig, quid

smelly mundungus

smoke-hater misocapnist

store smokeshop

symbol blackamoor, highlander, turk, wooden indian

user nicotian

virginia cowpen

worker leafboy, leafgirl, looper

worm hornworm

TOBIAS *angel* raphael

father tobit

foot-swallower fish

friend azarias, raphael

son hyrcanus

wife sarah

TOBIT *kin* ahikar, anael, tobias

obsession interment

wife anna

TOBOGGAN car(r)iole, coast(er), decline, fall, glide, glissade, skid, sled, slide, slither

TOBY cigar, highway, jug, mug, pitcher, road, rob (bery), street, way

creator sterne

TOBYMAN highwayman, robber

TOCHER dot, dower, dowry

TOCO bird, flogging, thrashing, tonguelashing, toucan

TOCSIN alarm, alert, bell, signal, warning

TOD bundle, bush, fox, load, mat, pack, shrub

TODAY aujourd'hui, here, heute, hoc dies, now, oggi, present

TODDLE daddle, dance, diddle, fadge, paddle, saunter, stroll, totter, tottle, waddle, walk

TODDLER child, gangrel, infant, trottie

TODDY drink, grog, sagwire, tass, terry, trot, tuba

bird swallow, weaverbird

cat civet

palm juice sura

TODE boat, haul, sled

TODY flycatcher, robin

TOE(S) bottom, dactyl, digit, drive, end, hallux, journal, minimus, pivot, poulaine, tais, tip, toon, tun

and heel jig, tapdance

bird's heel

-biter tadpole

clip beak

coldness acrocyonosis

comb. dactyl(o), digiti

disease acropathy, ainhum, athetosis

great halux

having abnormal synpelmous

having 6 hexadactyl

-hold bridgehead, foothold, footing

inflammation dactylitis

little minimus

on one's active, alert, busy

pert. digital

plate shod

the mark conform, obey

walking on digitigrade

without adactyl(ous)

TOFF beau, bloke, buck, coxcomb, dandy, dude, fellow, fop, macaroni, nob, spark, swell

TOFFISH brave, braw, chic, dapper, dashing, natty, nifty, nobby, posh, smart, spruce, stylish

TOFT farm, hill, holding, homestead, knoll, messuage

TOG, TOGS clothes, clothing, coat, dress(up), duds, garb, garment

TOGA aba, candida, garb, garment, gown, insignia, robe, trabea

TOGARMA *father* gomer

TOGETHER accompanying, as one, at once, bedene, collectively, concertedly, concurrently, conjointly, continually, en masse, ensemble, in cahoots, insame, joined, jointly, mass, mutually, on end, same, side-by-side, simultaneously, unanimously, union, united(ly), with, yfere

comb. com, con, syn

with alongside, among, and, into, side by side

TOGGLE bolt, bungle, button, chain, cord, cottar, cotter, fasten, frog, key, mend, netsuke, pin, rod, rope, screw, strap, tether

bar fid

iron harpoon

TOGO *capital* lome

city anecho, atakpame, lome, palime, sokode

language or *people* ewe, hausa, kabrais, lotocoli, ouatchi, twi

president grunitsky, olympio

river anie, haho, mono, oti

TOGUE namaycush

TOHU-BOHU chaos, confusion, disorder

TOI *kingdom* hamath

TOIL battle, bilder, broil, buckstall, chore, contend, contention, darg(ue), drudge (ry), effort, ensnare, entangle, entrap, exert(ion), fatigue, fight, grind, industry, labor, mither, moil, muck, net, occupation, overwork, pains, plod, pull, rend, scrat, slave, snare, strain, strife, strive, struggle, sweat, swink, task, till, trap, travail, tug, turmoil, tweil, weary, work

TOILED cultivated, exhausted, tilled, wearied, worn

TOILER drudge, laborer, moiler, slave, worker

TOILET attire, backhouse, biffy, can, costume, dressing table, head, john, latrine, lavatory, loo, necessary, outhouse, parasha, pot(ty), powderroom, primping, privy

case bag, etui, etwee

goods notions

water bay rum, cologne, eau de lavande, perfume

TOILS grip, meshes, net, noose, pitfall, snare, trap, web

TOILSOME arduous, difficult, fatiguing, hard, laborious, moilsome, sweaty, wearisome

TOILWORN beat, exhausted, spent, weary

TOKAY gecko, grape, lizard, tucktoo, wine

lover francis rakoczy ii, frederick the great, louis xiv, sun king

TOKEN accolade, amulet, attribute, auspice, award, badge, beaver, betroth, buck, castor, certificate, check, chip, clew, clue, cointise, collar, copper, counter, coupon, dib, dollar, earnest, emblem, evidence, fare, feature, fetish, footstep, forbysen, garland,

gift, guaranty, hansel, honor, index, indicia, instance, jetton, keepsake, mark, medal, memento, memorial, name, omen, ostent, pawn, pledge, portent, presage, proof, promise, reminder, sample, scrip, sign, signacle, signal, slug, souvenir, substitute, surety, symbol, symptom, tag, tessella, tessera, ticket, trophy, type, voucher, warrant
good luck han(d)sel
of affection accolade, amoret, handsel, mascot
of office badge
of respect accolade, salute
of victory laurel, palm
TOKO flogging, shop, store
TOKOLOSHE spirit, sprite
TOKYO edo, yed(d)o
airport atsugi
department store tsetan
district akasaka, asakusa, ginza, marunouchi, roppongi, shinjuku, shinsekai, tama, ueno, yoshiwara
street ginza
TOLA *son* jahmai, jeriel, jibsam, rephaiah, samuel, uzzi
uncle joseph
TOLBOOTH See TOLL-HOUSE.
TOLCUS *king* pelias
TOLDO hut, tent
TOLEDO blade, sword
archbishop ximenes
TOLERABLE acceptable, adequate, admissible, all right, bearable, decent, endurable, fair, indifferent, mediocre, middling, moderate, passable, presentable, pretty good, respectable, soso, supportable, tarble, tidy
TOLERANCE allowance, charity, clemency, endurance, forbearance, fortitude, grace, impartiality, indifference, indulgence, leeway, leniency, lenity, liberality, long-suffering, mercy, patience, perseverance, remedy, resignation, shere, stoicism, sufferance
religious adiaphorism
TOLERANT benevolent, benign, broad(minded), charitable, clement, forbearing, forgiving, humane, indulgent, lenient, liberal, merciful, open-minded, patient, permissive, soft

TOLERATE abide, accept, allow, bear(with), bow, brook, condone, disregard, endure, humor, ignore, indulge, overlook, resist, stand, stomach, submit, succumb, suffer, support, yield
TOLL allure, annul, assessment, attract, ballastage, berthage, boomage, caphar, cess, chiminage, chum, customs, decoy, drag, due, duty, entice, exaction, excise, fee, impost, invite, jow(l), knell, levy, lure, multure, peage, pedage, pesage, piccage, pike, price, rate, ring, sound, stallage, strike, summon, tallage, tariff, tax, teind, terrage, tithe, tribute, tronage, vacate, weighage, wheelage
comb. age
gatherer collector, customer, publican, taxcollector, taxer
illegal maltolt(e)
weight tronage
TOLLHOUSE cookie, customhouse, hall, jail, market, prison, tollbooth, tolsey, townhall
TOLLY candle, cane, spire, staff
TOLSTOY *character* anna karenina, vronsky
TOLTEC *ruins* tula
TOLUENE diluent, methylbenzene, phenylmethane, tnt
TOLYPEUTES apar(a), armadillo
TOM buck, bull, male, shore, toom, trough
dick and harry everyone, nonentity
long simpleton, sluggard
o'bedlam lunatic, madman, mendicant
pepper liar
tailor stormy petrel
thumb dwarf, meadow-pea, orchis
thumb's giant grumbo
tram jester
TOMAHAWK assail, attack, axe, criticize, cut, hatchet, missile
TOMATO burbank, love-apple, pretty girl
disease blackdot, buckeyerot, dartrose, early-blight, fernleaf, graywall, rhizoctonia
sauce catsup, ketchup
soup gazpacho

TOMB barrow, burial, bury, casket, catacombs, catafalque, cenotaph, chul(l)pa, cist(vaen), crypt, cubiculo, dargah, dokhma, durgah, galgal, grave, guaca, hallcist, huaca, kistvaen, lair, marabout, mastaba(h), mausoleum, mazar, memorial, mole, monument, mound, ossuarium, ossuary, pir, pit, pyramid, reliquary, samadh, sarcophagus, sepulcher, shaft, shrine, speos, stupa, syrinx, tabernacle, taboot, tabut, thole, tholos, tope, tritaph, trough, tumulus, turbe(h), vault
chamber cist, kist, serdab
circular tholos
empty cenotaph
for bones ossuary
guardian anubis
passage to dromos
prehistoric cist(vaen), kist (vaen), kurgan
recess arcosolium
3-chambered tritaph
TOMBAUGH *discovery* pluto
TOMBOY gamine, harlot, hoiden, hoyden, meg, romp, rowdy, strumpet, tomrig
TOMBSTONE barrow, cairn, cenotaph, cromlech, cross, epitaph, footstone, headstone, marker, memorial, monument, peron, shaft, slab, tumulus
TOMCAT gib, podger, thomas
TOMCOD bocaccio, gade, gadid, kingfish, microgadus, smelt, whiting
TOME album, book, letter, volume, work
TOMFOOL blockhead, buffoon, clown, crazy, defective, dolt, flycatcher, foolish, halfwit(ted), rainbird, stupid
TOMFOOLERY buffoonery, foolishness, hell, nonsense, silliness, tommyrot
TOM JONES *author* fielding
character allworthy, blifil, hellamar, honour, lady bellaston, partridge, sophia, square, squire western, thwackum
TOMMY bread, food, fool, loaf, podger, provisions, requin, rod, simpleton, soldier

TOMMYROT nonsense, wahoo

talker kazoo

TOMNODDY, TOMNOODLE dunce, fool, nincompoop, puffin

TOMNOUP See TITMOUSE.

TOMORROW by and by, demain, domani, manana, presently

TOM SAWYER See SAWYER, TOM.

TOMTIT miro, titmouse, treecreeper, wren

TOMTOM drum, gong

TON fashion, heap, lot, mode, style, toun, tunny, vogue, weight

metric millier

TONANT blatant, boisterous

TONE accent, attitude, aura, beep, blend, cadence, cast, character, color, composition, elasticity, energy, expression, feel, harmony, hue, inflection, key, manner, melody, method, modify, modulation, mood, note, pitch, property, quality, resiliency, savor, shade, sound, spirit, strain, style, temper, tendency, tenor, timbre, tint, trend, vein, vigor, voice, way

broken arpeggio, crack

changing cambiata

chord concento

color timbre

combination chord

complex klang

-deafness asonia

-deaf person tin ear

deep bass

down allay, decolor, dim, drab, lower, mellow, moderate, modify, muffle, mute, restrain, soften, soft-pedal, subdue, tame, temper

lack asonia, atony

loud forte

low bass, bourdon

monotonous drone

nasal twang

quality klang(farbe), resonance, timbre

range compass

rapid tremulo

rhythmical cadence

series octave, scale

sharp clang, skirl, tang

single drone, monotone

singsong sough, sugh

succession melody

thin sfogato

unit nil

variation nuance

vibrant twang

whining girn

TONELESS atonic, deaf, gray, mute

TONG association, group, society

TONGA ono, tofua, vavau

capital nukualofa

coin paanga

island haapai, ono, tofua, vavau

king tafa-ahau-topou

queen salote

town neiafu

TONGS feet, grampus, grapple, overalls, pincers, tenail(le), trousers, tueiron, tuyere, tweezers

TONGUE argot, beeweed, bell, chib, clack, clap(per), dialect, flap, glossa, glossus, gossip, idiom, ilokano, isthmus, kabyle, kali(ka), language, lick, lingua, lorriker, neap, neck, pale, parlance, pawl, plectrum, point, pole, prate, projection, reed, shaft, sole, speech, spit, tab, talk, tang, taste, touch, voice, vote

absence aglossia

auld wives' aspen, poplar, tuliptree

bellows gusset

black anthrax

bone hyoid

classical greek, hebrew, latin

coating atter

comb. glosso, linguo

disease agrom, lichenoid

forked, man with liar

forked, pert. fissilingual

in cheek insincerely, mockingly

-lash assail, baste, berate, castigate, censure, jaw, rail, rate, rebuke, reprove, revile, scold, upbraid, vituperate, wig

-lashing censure, comeuppance, dressing-down, jobation, rats, toco

-like languet(te), lingual

-like process ligula

metal pawl

mother vernacular

mucous membrane periglottis

muscle hyoglossus, lingualis

of land langue(t), reach, spit

oxcart cope

part blade, corona, dorsum, papilla, raphe

pert. apical, glossal, lingual

pivoted pawl

projection papilla

sacred pali

serpent's fang

-shaped linguiform, lingulate

shoe flap, kiltie, kilty

3rd calumniator

-tie ankyloglossia

-tied dumb, inarticulate, mum, mute, quiet, silent, taciturn

tip corona

tumor ranula

under hypoglossal

wagon neap, pole

worm acornworm, balanoglossid

TONGUEBIRD wryneck

TONGUEFENCE argument, debate

TONGUEFISH sole

TONGUELESS aglossal, aglossate, dumb, elinguate, mute, speechless

TONIC (See also *kind,* below.) accented, arouser, bracer, bracing, corroborant, elixir, healthy, invigorating, keynote, medicine, nostrum, pep(tic), pickup, pop, quinine, refreshing, remedy, reviver, roborant, stimulant, stressed, vigor

bitter absinthium, anthemis, quinine

kind absinthium, aloe, anthemis, barberry, bayberry, berberis, bitters, boneset, calamus, calombo, canella, catnip, chirata, chiretta, colomba, damiana, dope, fumaria, gentian, gilo, goldenseal, helonias, mahonia, nervine, quassia, quinine, salacin, sambul, soda, tansy, trillium, wormwood

leaf coca

TONIKAN *indian* koroa, tiou, yazoo

TONKA *bean* c(o)umar(o)u, g(u)aiac

TONKAWAN *indian* ervipiame, mayeye, yojuane

TONKIN *capital* hanoi

native tho

TONSIL almond, amygdal(a), gland, kernal, paristhmion

comb. amygdal(o)

disease cynanche, quinsy

enlarged adenoid

operation tonsilectomy, tonsilotomy

pert. amygdaline

TONSILLITIS amygdalitis, antiaditis, laryngitis, pharyngitis, quinsy

TONSURE corona, crown, diksha, rasure, shave, shear

TONSURED bald, clipped, peeled, polled, shaved, shaven, shorn

TONY aristocratic, high class, high-toned, posh, simpleton, smart, swell, toff

TOO also, and, besides, else, excessively, extremely, further(more), likewise, moreover, over(ly), then, trop (po), very, withal

bad alas, averah, disappointing, shameful, terrible, unfortunate

late belated, tardy, untimely

little insufficient, scanty, skimpy

much excess(ive), exorbitant, glut, nimiety, overabundance, satiety, superfluous, surfeit, trop

much, comb. ard, art

small to matter inappreciable

soon premature, untimely

TOODLE capture, coo, pipe

TOODLE-OO See GOODBYE.

TOOL agent, apparatus, appliance, cat's-paw, contraption, contrivance, convenience, convey, creature, device, draw, drive, dupe, equipage, facility, figurehead, fixture, gadget, gimmick, goffer, implement, instrument, jigger, manage, manipulate, means, pawn, polish, puppet, ride, shape, sword, towel, utensil, weapon

abrading file, rasp

bookbinder's gouge

boring auger, awl, bit, brace and bit, bradawl, broach, burr, corkscrew, drill, gimlet, nail-bit, reamer, trepan, trephine, wimble

came-opening ladkin

case trousse

chopping dolabra, mezzaluna

cleaning froe

cultivating harrow, leveler, plough, plow

cutting adz, axe, bezel, bezil, bit, blade, boaster, broad-

ax(e), burin, chisel, die, drove, gouge, graver, hob, knife, plane, razor, reamer, saw, sax, scissors, shears, sye, trepan, whittle

digging shovel, spade, spud, trowel

edge basil, bezel, bezil

edged adz(e), axe, belduque, bill(hook), bistoury, broadax(e), bushwhacker, chisel, cleaver, clippers, colter, gouge, groover, hack, hatchet, hedge-trimmer, hoe, jackknife, knife, lance(t), machete, mattock, panga, pick, plowshare, razor, scalpel, scissors, scoop, scraper, scythe, share, shears, sickle, slotter, snips, tomahawk, wedge

enlarging reamer

excavating pick(ax), shovel

flat spatula

flint microlith

foundry eggsleeker

grass-cutting mower, scythe, sickle, sithe

grinding pestle

gripping clamp, pincers, tongs, vise

handle haft

handle part butt, tang

handle wood cocobolo

holder monitor, turret

lifting jack

mechanic's awl, bar, bevel, bodkin, bradawl, buffer, calipers, crowbar, edger, file, flail, forceps, fork, grapnel, grindstone, hawk, header, jackscrew, lathe, level, monkey, pincers, planer, pliers, puncheon, ram, screwdriver, shaper, spatula, square, stapler, tackle, tamp, tapper, tongs, tweezers, vise

metal-working dolly, lathe, swage

mining gad, pick

planing bullnose, chamfer, dado, rabbet, scraper

plastering trowel

pointed awl, barb, brod, brog, fid, gad, gimlet, pick, stylet

pounding hammer, mallet, pestle, sledge

prehistoric boucher, celt, eolith, macrolith, paleolith

sawing grooverhead

shaping lathe, swage

slate-measuring scantle

smoothing file, plane, sleeker

splitting axe, froe, frow, hatchet

squaring edger

steal ratten

temperer hardener

thief rattener

threading chaser

woodworking adz(e), edgeman, edger, grainer, scauper, scriber, spokeshave

TOOLBOX chest, etui, etwee, kit

TOOLS cutlery, gear, gibbles, hardware, kit, tew

TOOLSHED doghouse

TOOM dump, empty, lank, lean, leisure, pour, stupid

TOON cedar, lim

TOOT bender, blare, blast, blow, carousal, carouse, draft, drink, elevation, fool, gaze, honk, look(out), peep, play, proclaim, pry, revel, shout, sound, spread, spree, sprout, spy, tear, towt, trumpet, tutu

one's own horn boast, brag

plant tutu

TOOTER horn, lookout, spy, trumpeter, watchman

TOOTH (See also TEETH.) appetite, bit, bite, cog, dens, dental, fang, fondness, gam, gear, gum, indent, ivory, jag, joggle, liking, notch, pearl, point, projection, prong, rasp, scrivello, serration, snag(gle), sprocket, tang, taste, teethe, tine, tush, tusk

absence anodontia

ache dentagra, odontalgia

ailment caries, gingivitis, pyorrhea

and nail desperately, earnestly, fiercely, gamely, hard, violently

artificial bridge(work), denture, dummy, plate, pontic, prosthesis

backward displacement retrusion

body dentine

bovine taurodont

canine cuspid, cynodont, dogtooth, eyetooth, holder, laniary, tush

cap crown

coat enamel

comb. dent(i), dento, odont (ia), odonto

covering enamel

cress coralwort

cutting device airbrasive, drill

decay caries, cavity, saprodontia

deposit calculus, plaque, tartar

double grinder, molar

-drawer dentist

edge cusp, dentate, scalprum

enamel amelification

extraction exodontia

facing cusp, enamel

false See *artificial,* above.

filling crown, inlay

for a tooth retaliation, revenge, talion

fungus bear's-head, hydnum

gear addendum, cog, dent, gub, sprocket

grinding bruxism

grinding surface mensa

harrow tine

having all alike isodont

having large macrodont

having one only monodont

having small microdont

horse's divider, nipper

kind baby, bicuspid, canine, carnassial, cutter, impacted, incisor, milk, molar, premolar, sectorial, wisdom

large buck, snag

layer cementum

-like dental, dentate, dentiform, dentoid, fanged, odontoid, snaggled

long fang, tush, tusk

looseness agomphiasis, agomphosis, gomphiasis

malposition anteroclusion, malocclusion

molar wang

moss blephara

part corona, crown, cusp, dentine, enamel, fang, neck, pulp, root(canal), table

pert. dental, molar, odontic

point cusp

premolar bicuspid

projecting buck, snag

pulp nerve

radula uncinus

rash strophulus

replacement bridge

saw serra

scraper dentiscalp

-shaped dentiform

small denticle

socket alveole, alveolus

sower of dragon's cadmus

sprocket wheel gub

steel broach

supernumerary surdent

tissue dentin

violet coralwort

wheel cam, cog, gear, tine

TOOTHED dentate, serrate(d), virgate

comb. odus

formation serra

implement card

irregularly erose

TOOTHLESS agomphious, decrepit, dull, edental, edentate, edentulous, futile, gummy, ineffectual, infantile, morne, weak

TOOTHPASTE dentifrice, prophylactic

TOOTHPICK arkansan, quill

TOOTHSOME agreeable, appetizing, dainty, delectable, delicious, desirable, palatable, pleasing, sapid, saporous, savory, tasty, voluptuous

TOOTHWORT coolwort, coralwort, cress, crowtoe, dentaria, leadwort, pepperroot, plumbago, shepherd's-purse

TOOTS baby, honey, sweetie

TOP ace, acme, acmic, apex, aristocracy, attic, best, bonnet, cap, capital, capote, ceil(ing), climax, command, consummate, cover, cream, crest, crop, crown, culminate, defeat, dome, dominant, dominate, drain, drink, elite, exceed, extreme, face, finial, first class, forelock, foremost, hat, head(most), height, highest, hood, lead, lid, maximum, meridian, outdo, overcome, paramount, peak, pick, pinnacle, preeminent, prune, ridge, roof, skim, summit, supreme, surface, surmount, surpass, tent, tip, top drawer, topple, toy, transcend, tumble, unique, upper(most), upset, vertex, zenith

banana See CHIEF, HEAD, LEADER.

card ace

child's nun

chimney cowl, hood

comb. acro, apico, super

-dressing fertilizer, mulch

hat See HAT *opera.*

-heavy lopsided, tippy, tipsy, unbalanced, unstable, unsteady

hill crest, knag, knap, knoll

-hole excellent, first-class, tip-top

-kick sergeant

-like strobic

limit ceiling

man cob

minnow gambusia, gularis, guppy, helleri, limia, sailfin

off complete, end, fill, finish, wind up

ornament epi, finial, tee

pert. acmic, apical, cacuminal, capital

sail raffe(e)

-shaped turbinate

spinning scopperil

stone capstone

story attic, brain, garret

vehicle calash, capote

TOPAZ physalite, pycnite, pycnium

false cairngorm, citrine

humming bird ani, ava

symbol of fidelity

zodiac sign taurus

TOPCOAT chesterfield, overcoat, reefer, siphonia

TOPE carouse, dogfish, drink, grove, memorial, orchard, shark, shrine, stupa, tomb, tower, wren

TOPEE, TOPI cap, hat, pithhelmet

material sola

wallah european

TOPER boozer, bouser, drunk, shark, soak, sot, souse, tippler, tosspot, trough

TOPFULL brimming

TOPHET chaos, confusion, HELL

TOPI antelope, bubal(e), bubalis, hartebeest, TOPEE

TOPIARY box, clipped, trimmed, yew

TOPIC affair, argument, burden, consideration, gambit, ground, head(ing), issue, item, matter, motif, motive, point, problem, proposition, question, reason, statement, subject, substance, text, theme, theorem, thesis, treatise

TOPICAL limited, local, nominal, particular, restricted, subjective, timely

TOPKNOT braid, bun, chignon, commode, crest, flounder, hair, head(dress), onkos, panache, plume, tuft

TOPLOFTY arrogant, condescending, contemptuous,

disdainful, haughty, supercilious

TOPMOST apical, highest, uppermost

TOPNOTCH ace, a-one, banner, best, crest, excellent, first-class, first-rate, highest, super(ior), supreme, tip-top, unequaled, unsurpassed

TOPNOTCHER ace, a-one, brick, corker, crackerjack, daisy, dandy, darb, dazzler, dilly, expert, firstrater, hero, honey, humdinger, jimdandy, knockout, lulu, one-in-a-million, oner, peach, pip(pin), prodigy, star, trump, winner, wonder

TOPPIECE epi, head, masterpiece, toupee

TOPPING arrogant, fine, frosting, gallant, great, icing, pretentious, proud, sauce, tiptop, whipped cream

baked with au gratin

TOPPLE collapse, fall, founder, jut, lean, overthrow, overturn, somersault, tilt, tip, tumble, upset

TOPS See TOPNOTCH.

TOPSMAN chief, drover, hangman, headman

TOPSOIL kelly

TOPSY-TURVY askew, awry, chaotic, cockeyed, confused, disorderly, inversion, invert(ed), overturned, reelrall, reversed, upset, upsidedown

TOQUE macaco, macaque, munga, rilawa, zati

TOQUILA jipijapa

TOR crag, hill, mound, mountain, peak, pinnacle, taw

TORA antelope, hartebeest, tetel

TORAH law, old testament, pentateuch, precept, revelation, scroll
chanted part maftir
law-giver moses
lesson parashah
place-marker yad
reader maftir

TORCH blaze, brand, cresset, fish, flambeau, flare, flashlight, jack, lamp(ad), lantern, light(er), link, lucigen, luminary, mashal, mullein, mussal, roughie, wase
flower prairie-smoke

frame cresset
lily kniphofia
man linkman
small match

TORCHBEARER daduchus, keryx, lampadephore, linkboy, linkman

TORCHWOOD amyris, balsam, bikkia, boswellia, canarium

TORE knob, persevere, plod, pommel

TOREADOR, TORERO bullfighter, capeador, escamillo, matador, verminion

TORMENT afflict(ion), aggravate, aggravation, agonize, agony, annoy(ance), badger, bait, bale, bane, bedevil, bother, bug, burden, chevy, chivvy, convulse, crucify, curse, devil, discomfort, distort, distress, excruciate, grate, hagride, harass, harrow, harry, hatchel, hector, hell, horror, infest, lacerate, macerate, martyrize, misery, moil, molest, mutche, nightmare, ordeal, pain, pang, persecute, persecution, pest(er), plague, provocation, provoke, punish, purgatory, rack, rag, scarify, scold, scourge, spasm, storm, taw, tear, tease, tempest, terrify, torture, travail, trial, trouble, try, utz, vex, woe, worry, wring
liable to excruciable

TORMENTIL bloodwort, ewedaisy, indianpaint, potentilla, puccoon, redroot, septfoil, tellerwort, turmeric

TORMENTOR baiter, canvas, curtain, executioner, fork, pest, strigil, torturer, toy

TORN broken, lacerated, ragged, reft, rent, ripped, riven, seedy, shabby, split

TORNADO cyclone, hurricane, outburst, squall, storm, travado, twister, typhoon, vortex, whirlwind, windstorm

TORO bull, cavalla, cowfish

TORONTO ft rouille, ft york, hogtown
resident hogtowner

TORP croft, farm

TORPEDO attack, batoid, benumb, bomb, catfish, crampfish, criminal, dam-

age, destroy, electric-ray, end, explode, explosive, firework, fish, gangster, hoodlum, killer, mine, missile, nixie, numbfish, paralyze, petard, ruin, shatter, shell, shoot, sink, wreck
boat catamaran, submarine
damner admiral farragut
fish ray
inventor whitehead

TORPID apathetic, boat, brosy, comatose, dormant, dull, foul, idle, impassive, inactive, inert, languid, lethargic, numb, passive, phlegmatic, slow, sluggish, sodden, stolid, stupid, stuporous, togger

TORPOR accidie, acedia, apathy, coma, doldrums, dormancy, dullness, inanition, indifference, inertia, languor, lassitude, laziness, lethargy, oscitancy, phlegm, sleep, sloth, slumber, stagnation, stolidity, stupifaction, stupor, swoon
comb. narc(o)

TORQUE bee, chain, collar, necklace, sarpe, strain, twist

TORREFY burn, dry, parch, roast, scorch

TORRENT cascade, cataract, cloudburst, deluge, downpour, flood, flow, freshet, niagara, outburst, pour, river, rush, shower, sluice, spate, stream

TORREYA savin, tumion

TORRID ardent, arid, boiling, burning, dried, eager, fiery, hot, inflamed, oppressive, parching, passionate, scorching, steamy, sultry, sweltering, tropical, zealous
zone boundary tropic of cancer, tropic of capricorn
zone island galapagos
zone resident ascian

TORRUBIA blolly

TORSION convolution, didromy, pressure, shear, strain, stress, tension, thrust, tormina, turning, twisting, wrenching

TORSO body, column, figure, trunk

TORT grievance, injury, injustice, libel, offense, toward, twisted, wrong
-feasor actor

TORTIOUS distorted, injurious, misleading, wrongful

TORTOISE bekko, chelonia, chukwa, cooter, ellachick, emyd(ian), galapago, gaper, hicatee, kashyapa, laggard, matamata, mungofa, pelomedusid, shellpad, shellpot, terrapin, testudo, turtle
bearded matamata
beetle cassida, cassidina, chrysomelid
earth-supporting chukwa
flower turtlehead
fresh-water ellachick
genus clemmys, emys, terrapene
land mungofa
pert. chelonian
plant elephant's foot
shell carapace, carey, iridescent, mottled
shell articles bekko
symbol of chastity
tablets kepoukhpai
TORTUOUS anfractuous, bent, circuitous, cranky, crooked, devious, evasive, flexuous, indirect, injurious, labyrinthine, mazy, oblique, roundabout, screwy, serpentine, sinuate, sinuous, spiral, turning, twisting, winding, wriggly, wrongful
TORTURE afflict, agonize, agony, boot, brainwash(ing), break, crucify, cruelty, deform(ation), dismember, distort(ion), draw and quarter, flay, garble, gnarl, grill, impale, injure, keelhaul, kill, maim, mangle, martyr, mutilate, pain, pang, persecute, pervert, picket, pine, punish, rack, scaphism, strappado, suffering, torment, worry, wrong
caldron alfet
instrument alfet, bancacava, barnacle, boot(ikin), bull of brass, equuleus, furca, iron heel, iron maiden, pilliwinks, rack, scarpines, screw, strappado, thumbkin, thumbscrew, tumbrel, wheel
TORTUROUS distorted, excruciating, painful, twisted
TORUS baston, boltel, boutell, bowtel, molding, protuberance, thalamus, tore
TORY conservative, diehard, loyalist, outlaw, peelite, robber, royalist, tantivy

TOSCA *aria* vissi d'arte
victim scarpia
TOSH bathe, bathtub, bosh, drench, familiar, intimate(ly), neat(ly), nonsense, souse, tidy, trash, tub, tush
TOSS agitate, bandy, billow, cant, cast, chance, chuck, clap, cob, commotion, cup, disquiet, disturb, excitement, fillip, flick, fling, flip, flirt, flounder, flurr, harass, heave, hurl, lift, lurch, oscillate, pitch, raise, rear, rock, roll, serve, shag, shy, stir, sway, tave, thrash, thresh, throw, thrust, toast, torfel, torfle, tout, tumble, uplift, wager, wallow, welter, wentle, whemmel
about popple, thrash, thresh
a coin chance, flap, flip, gamble, sky
and turn flounder, thrash, vacillate
away blow
carelessly flip
from side to side ballot
head in derision geck
in interject
off consume, drink, improvise, swap, swop
together scramble
TOSSPOT carouser, dipsomaniac, drinker, drunk (ard), sot, tippler, toper
bottle flagon
TOSSUP equal, even chance, gamble, odds, tie
TOT add, amount, bit, calculate, child, count, cup, drink, item, jot(ting), kid, note, tad, toddle, total, tote, totter
TOTAL abrupt, absolute, account, add(itament), addition, aggregate, all, amount, calculate, cast, complete, comprehensive, concise, count, difference, entire(ty), enumerate, figure, foot(ing), full, global, gross, inclusive, kit and caboodle, mass, number, numeration, omnis, perfect, plenary, product, quantity, reckon, score, sum(ma), summary, summation, summed, tally, thorough, tot(e), tottle, unqualified, utter, whole
TOTALITARIAN absolute, arbitrary, authoritarian, des-

potic, dictatorial, fascist, oppressive, tyrannical
ruler big brother, dictator, hitler, mussolini
TOTALITY aggregate, all (ness), completeness, entirety, eternity, heap, integral, omnitude, whole(ness)
TOTE bag, carry, conduct, convey, count, escort, freight, handbag, haul, lead, purse, reckon, transport
TOTEM emblem, fetish, figure, huaca, pillar, pole, shaft, symbol, zoomorph
group tribe
pole xat
TOTO all, baby, young
TOTONACAN *indian* tepehua
TOTTER brangle, change, coggle, convulse, didder, dither, dodder, dotter, falter, flounder, fribble, joggle, lurch, oscillate, pace, pitch, quake, quaver, reel, rock, seesaw, shake, shimmy, slide, slip, stagger, staver, stoit, swerve, swing, titubate, toit, toss, tremble, vacillate, wamble, waver, weaken, whither, wobble
TOTTERING adverse, aged, changeable, cockerie, declining, greggy, rickety, shaky, threatening, titubant, vacillating, wambling, wavering
TOTTERY crambly, palsied, shaky, unsafe, unsteady, weak
TOTTLE boil, calculate, count, purl, reckon, simmer, toddle, total, totter, whole
TOTUAVA totoaba, weakfish
family member bass, corbina, corvina, croaker, queenfish, spotfin-croaker, yellowfin-croaker
TOU *kingdom* hamath
TOUCAN aracari, guarani, pteroglossus, rhamphastos, toco, tucana
TOUCH 3 act, beg, bit, dab, hit, lap, pat, paw, pet, ply, rap, rub, tag, tap, tat, tig, tip 4 abut, bump, butt, dash, feel, iota, join, kiss, lick, mark, meet, melt, move, palm, palp, rine, sale, skim, test, vein 5 bribe, brush, flash, graze, grope, refer, rival, shade,

shave, smack, stamp, sweep, thumb, trace, trait, trial, verge 6 adjoin, affect, arouse, border, borrow, breath, caress, defect, excite, finger, glance, handle, rebuke, relate, scrape, signal, smutch, strain, streak, stroke, tactus, twinge 7 attaint, concern, contact, feeling, impinge, impress, palpate, pertain, request, soupcon, taction, thought, tweedle, twiddle, vestige, whisper 8 approach, interest, reproach 9 agreement, influence, stimulate 10 impression, manipulate

and go contingent, chancy, desultory, hasty, pending, precarious, risky, sketchy, uncertain

-and-heal st-john's-wort

closely osculate

comb. aphia, hapt(o), tac, thigmo

finishing colophon, copestone, icing

impairment apselaphesia

light stroke

lightly attinge, brush, glance, graze, scuff, skiff, twiddle

loss anaphia

-me-not garden-balsam, impatiens, jewelweed, noli-me-tangere, squirting-cucumber

off explode, ignite, initiate

organ antenna, feeler, finger, hand, palp

pert. haptic, palpable, tactile, tactual

up amend, furbish, improve, polish, repair, rev, rouse

upon concern, review, scan, slight

TOUCHBELL earwig

TOUCHDOWN rouge, score, six

TOUCHED contrite, cracked, dotty, goofy, insane, mad, moved, nutty, pixilated, rancid, tetched

TOUCHING about, adjacent, affecting, against, attingent, concerning, distressing, heartrending, impressive, interesting, moving, pathetic, piteous, pitiable, pitiful, poignant, sad, sympathetic, tangent, tender

lightly libant

single point tangent

TOUCHSTONE basanite, criterion, gauge, lydite, proof,

schist, standard, test, trial, yardstick

beloved audrey

TOUCHWOOD amadou, funk, punk(wood), sponk, spunk, tinder

TOUCHY captious, carping, choleric, cranky, cross, delicate, edgy, feisty, grouchy, huffy, irascible, irritable, kittle, miffy, nervous, peevish, precarious, risky, sensitive, short, snappish, splenetic, sullen, techy, tender, testy, tetchy, thinskinned, ticklish

TOUGH arduous, bruiser, bully(boy), callous(ed), cartilaginous, chewy, cohesive, complicated, coriaceous, difficult, disorderly, dogged, durable, fibrous, firm, glutinous, gristly, hard(ened), hardhearted, hardy, heartless, hickory, hoodlum, indurated, inflexible, infrangible, intractable, inured, knotty, leathery, lusty, obdurate, obstinate, resistant, rigid, robust, ropy, rowdy, ruffian, rugged, rum, seared, severe, shameless, sinewy, stalwart, staunch, steely, sticky, stiff, stout, strict, stringy, strong, stubborn, sturdy, tenacious, thick, unbreakable, unruly, unshatterable, unyielding, uphill, vigorous, violent, viscid, wiry, withy

and lean scragged, sinewy

as cartilage, gristle, leather

it out endure, hang in there, persevere

-minded hardheaded, practical, realistic, shrewd, strong-willed, stubborn, unsentimental, vigorous, willful

proposition chore, difficulty, dilemma, enigma, puzzle

TOUGHEN anneal, brutalize, endure, harden, inure, season, strengthen, taw, temper, tor, train

TOUGHHEAD ruddy-duck

TOUGHNESS fiber, fibre, guts, stomach, strength, tenacity, tuck

TOULOUSE *mayor* capitoul

TOUPEE doily, periwig, peruke, postiche, rug, toppiece, wig

TOUR barnstorm, beat, cir-

cuit, compass, cruise, excursion, expedition, giro, hitch, jaunt, journey, junket, periegesis, perigrinate, period, proceed, range, resort, revolution, round, run, safari, shift, spell, swing, travel, trick, trip, turn, visit

de force feat, stunt

political hustings, soapbox, stump, whistlestop

TOURACO lory, lourie, musophaga, parrot, plantaineater, turacus, turakoo

TOURELLE See TOWER.

TOURING on the go, on the road, travel(l)ing

TOURIST journeyer, pilgrim, traveler, tripper, wayfarer

accommodation autocamp, hotel, inn, motel, motorcourt, parador, posada

TOURMALINE achroite, aphrizite, borosilicate, chrysoberyl, chrysolite, datolite, dravite, s(c)horl, siberite, subsilicate

black s(c)horl

blue indicolite

brown dravite

containing schorly

red rubellite, siberite

TOURNAMENT battle, bonspiel, car(r)ousel, contest, field day, gymkhana, joust, match, meet, sport, tilt, trial, turnerfest

TOURNIQUET bandage, dressing, garrot, turnstile

TOURNURE bustle, contour, grace, outline, pad, poise, turn

TOUSE commotion, dishevel, disturbance, fracas, fuss, pull, rack, rumple, rumpus, struggle, tear, turmoil, tussle, uproar, worry

TOUSLE dalliance, dishevel, disorder, drag, horseplay, pull, rumple, sool, sowl, tear, toozle, tussle

TOUSLED messy, rumpled, towzie, tumbled, unkempt

TOUS(L)Y disorderly, rough, shaggy, tangled

TOUT (See also TOUTER.) canvass, disorder, guard, lookout, peep, peer, praise, reconnoiter, runner, skiv, solicit, spy, tease, tipster, toot, toss, vex, watch

a fait absolutely, completely, entirely, quite

court briefly, brusquely, short, simply

ensemble all together

de suite at once, immediately, successively

le monde everybody, everyone

TOUTER dopester, informant, runner, skiv, solicitor, spy, tipster

TOVE babble, chat, smoke, talk

TOW barge, chain, codilla, cordelle, crib, drag, draw, fiber, filament, flax, hale, haul, hemp, jute, lead, pull, rope, track, tug(boat), yarn

cloth canvas

flax codilla, hards, hurds

hook pintle

rope cordelle, gumline, tew

TOWAI birch, kamahi, tree

TOWARD adversus, afoot, against, anenst, approaching, apt, beside, close to, coming, compliant, facing, favorable, fornent, forward, future, gain, imminent, lateral, left, manageable, menacing, near, obliging, onward, opposite, promising, propitious, tort, tractable, upon, willing, with, ynesche

comb. pros

TOWARDLY affable, compliant, docile, favorable, forward, gentle, kindly, promising, seasonable, thriving, timely, tractable

TOWEL beat, bludgeon, bullet, clean, cloth, cudgel, dry, lambaste, lavabo, napkin, rub, shot, sponge, swab, thrash, vesperal, wipe(r)

fabric bird's-eye, crash, huck(aback), linen, terry (cloth)

hot oshibori

TOWER arise, ascend, aspire, atalaya, babel, barbican, bartizan, bastil(l)e, belfry, bulwark, campanile, castle, chul(l)pa, citadel, colossus, column, command, cupola, defense, derrick, dokhma, dome, dominate, domineer, donjon, elevate, exalt, fleche, fortress, gazebo, gopura, grow, heighten, jail, martello, minar(et), mirador, monument, mount, nuraghe, obelisk, overlook, overtop, pagoda, pilaster,

pillar, pinnacle, prison, pylon, pyramid, raise, reach, rear, redoubt, rise, rondel(le), shaft, shikara, sikar(a), sikhara, skyscraper, soar, spire, spring, steeple, stronghold, stupa, stupe, surge, surmount, surpass, talayot, tope, tor(rion), totem pole, tourelle, tournel, turret, turrion, vimana, ziggurat, zikurat

belfry clogh(e)ad

bell carillon

circular clogh(e)ad, martello

comb. pyro, turri

conning sail

famous babel, eiffel, london, minar, pisa

-like turrical

movable bastille

mustard crucifer

of london warder beefeater

of silence dakhma, dokhma

of strength powerhouse, protector, stalwart, support

over command, dominate, dwarf

pert. turrical

pyramidal sikara, sikhara, sikhra, sikra, vimana

sentinel's guerite

signal bantayan

small bartizan, rondel(le), turret

wind badgir

TOWERING eminent, great, high, huge, imperial, imposing, impressive, lofty, surpassing, tall, violent

TOWHEAD blonde, merganser

TOWHEE bunting, che(e)wink, finch, joree, pipilo

TOWN bayan, borough, bourg(ade), brugh, burg(h), bye, casale, city, deme, exurbia, farm(stead), ham(let), machi, manor, municipal(ity), municipium, oppidum, quivira, shtetl, suburb(ia), urban, van, village

comb. burg, muni, ton, tre

crier bellman

desolated gubat

dweller cit(izen), oppidan

fortified bastide, bastille, borough, burg(h), enceinte

hall cabildo, court, rathaus, signory, stadhouse, tolbooth, tribunal

insignificant podunk

meeting tunmoot

mythical quivira

official alderman, bailie, councilman, grieve, mayor, reeve, selectman

pert. civic, oppidan, urban

plan plat

provincial oppidum

small dullsville, east cupcake, hicksville, hick town, kokomo, main street, onehorse town, podunk, shtet(el), tanktown, whistlestop, wide space(in the road)

talk gossip

unfortified bourgade

walled avila, chester, pargana

witches' salem

TOWNSHIP bayan, borough, community, deme, dorp, parish, treen, vill(age)

TOWNSMAN burgher, cit(izen), cockney, gillie, inhabitant, oppidan, resident, selectman, snob, townee, urbanite, villager, villein

TOWPATH driver, hoggee, hoggy

TOW-ROW fight, racket, rumpus, uproar

TOXEMIA blackleg, blood poisoning, eclampsia, pyemia, septicemia

TOXEUS *parent* althaea, oenus

victim oenus

TOXIC mephitic, miasmal, pestilent(ial), poison(ous), venomous, virulent

TOXIN abrin, bane, botulin, brucin, poison, ricin, venom, virus

TOXOCARA roundworm

TOXOLOGY archery

TOXOPHILITE amor, cupid, eros

TOY (See also *kind*, below.) antic, bauble, butt, caprice, coquet, cuddle, dabble, daff, dalliance, dally, dandle, diminutive, disport, diversion, fancy, flirt, fool, frolic, gewgaw, gimcrack, hobby, instrument, knickknack, lakin, midget, miniature, mistress, nicknack, ornament, pastime, pet, play(thing), recreation, small, sport, trifle, trinket, twiddle, whim

kind ball, bandalore, bat, battledore, blocks, checkerboard, cockhorse, doll (house), football, hobbyhorse, hoop, jack-in-the-box, jackstraw, kazoo, kiddikar, marbles, marionette, pinwheel, puppet, quiz, racket, rattle, rockinghorse, teddybear, teetotum, top, whimwham, yoyo

TOYING, TOYISH fantastic, frivolous, playful, sportive, trifling, trivial, useless, wanton, whimsical

TOYON chamiso, christmas-berry, holly, tollon

TOYWORT shepherd's-purse

TOZIE shawl, snug, tipsy

TRABEATE post-and-lintel

TRABUCO blunderbuss, cigar

TRACE bit, blueprint, braid, breath, cast, clew, clue, copy, course, delineate, diagram, discern, discover, draft, engram, establish, file, follow, footprint, ghost, glimpse, harness, hint, hitch, influence, investigate, line, march, mark, nose out, path, plait, procession, pursue, rack, ramble, record, remainder, reproduce, road, route, run down, rush, scent, series, shadow, sign, sketch, smell out, smidgen, soupcon, speck, spoor, spot, step, stricture, taint, tang, thought, tinge, tint, tittle, token, TRACK, trail, train, traverse, trudge, tug, uncover, vestige, walk, wander
backward unwind
harness theat, treat, tug
memory engram(ma)
origin affiliate, filiate
small ghost, scintil(la), smatch, smidgen

TRACER inquiry, investigator, punch, searcher, seeker, stylus

TRACERY ardish, fanwork, frosting, network, openwork, trailery

TRACHEA gullet, windpipe
crane's trump

TRACHONITIS prince philip

TRACHYTE domine, piperno, syenite

TRACK abature, ascot, course, dog, footprint, hunt, imprint, line, mark, orbit, pad, path, pist(e), print, pursue, rails, road, route, routine, rut, scent, sight,

sign, slot, spectacle, spoor, spur, stalk, stamp, tang, teapot, token, tow, TRACE, trail, traverse, tread, turf, vestige, wake, walk, way, wye
animal's file, foiling, persue, run, slot, spoor, spur, strain
circuit lap
down disclose, discover, ferret out, find, spot, trace
event broad jump, high jump, hurdles, relay, shot put
layer gandy-dancer
man spiker
official judge, referee, starter, timer
off the astray, derailed, divergent
put on another shunt, switch
race cross-country, dash, mile, relay, sprint
railroad approach, gantlet, lead, main line, siding, spur, stub, tangent
rope channel
running oval
ship's wake
temporary shoofly
unit block
walker gandy-dancer
worm's nereite

TRACKER guide, puggi, puggy, tower, trailer, tugboat
method dovap

TRACT area, article, bent, block, book, brochure, bundle, campagna, campaign, campo, cingulum, cru, development, discuss, dissertation, district, drive, doab, duab, duar, duration, ejido, enclave, essay, estate, euripus, expanse, exposition, extent, farmhold, field, frith, gore, grabe, grant, haul, homily, horst, housing, laine, leaflet, hot, mark, pamphlet, part, patch, plot, polder, portion, province, quarter, quillet, region, reserve, royalty, section, sector, space, spread, strath, stretch, subdivision, sweep, terrain, town(site), trait, treat(ise), zone
boggy morass, runn
clayey takyr
cleared j(h)um, joom
cultivated cru
digestive enteron, peptogaster

grassland prairie, veld(t)
irregular gore
open slash, vega
seller colporteur
swampy baygall, flow
treeless steppe
triangular gore
uncultivated desert, waste
upland down(s)

TRACTABLE acquiescent, amenable, bearable, biddable, bitwise, compliant, docile, ductile, endurable, flexible, flexile, malleable, maniable, meek, obedient, plastic, pliable, pliant, subdued, submissive, tame, tangible, toward, willing, yielding

TRACTARIANISM oxford movement, puseyism

TRACTION attraction, draft, draught, drawing, force, friction, haulage, influence, power, towing, transportation, tugging, utility

TRACTOR amphibian, bobtail, bulldozer, cat(erpillar), crawler, creeper, dozer, dragon, duck, grader, halftrack, mule, pedrail, scraper, tank

TRADE action, activity, bandy, bargain, barter, bother, business, buy, cabotage, calling, career, chaffer, change, cheap(en), commerce, coup, course, craft, custom(ers), deal, employment, exchange, forte, fuss, habit, hawk, interchange, job, livelihood, market, material, medicine, method, metier, mister, occupation, pass, path, patronage, patronize, place, position, practice, profession, purchase, pursue, pursuit, repair, rubbish, sale, school, scorse, sell, shop, speculate, stuff, swap, swop, track, traffic, trail, train, tread, troke, truck, turn, vend, vocation, walk, way, work
article commodity, goods, merchandise
association hansa, hanse, nam
combination cartel, g(u)ild, hanse, merger
god vanir
in cauponate, cauponize
-last compliment, flattery

-*mark* biograph, brand, chop, emblem, identification, idiograph, label, logo, symbol
off barter, tossup
on exploit, use
pert. emporeutic
prohibited contraband
secondary avocation, hobby, sideline
votes logroll
wind brisa, briza, monsoon, puno
with patronize

TRADER agent, balija, banya, broker, chapman, chetty, fellmonger, kurveyor, marwari, monger, nepman, operator, sangler, troker, trucker
caste balija, bania(n)

TRADESMAN apronman, artisan, bakal, buyer, cooper, craftsman, dealer, eggler, goladar, merchant, retailer, seller, shopkeeper, storekeeper, tensor
supply goods, inventory, line, stock

TRADING barter, commercial, corrupt, interchange, jobbing, mongery, shopping, venal
post agora, canteen, fort, market, mart, pit, station

TRADITION cabal(a), code, convention, custom, delivery, doctrine, halacha, halakah, heritage, legend, lore, mores, myth, smriti, sunna(h), surrender, threap, usage
indifferent to ahistoric
oral cabala

TRADITIONAL acknowledged, admitted, age-old, ancient, classic, conventional, customary, established, fixed, handed down, historic, immemorial, inveterate, legendary, prescriptive, received, recognized, rooted, time-honored, understood, unwritten

TRADUCE abuse, asperse, blacken, calumniate, decry, deduce, defame, depreciate, derive, derogate, detract, disparage, exhibit, libel, malign, pervert, revile, seduce, slander, transfer, transport, vilify, vituperate

TRAFFIC bargain, barter, broke, business, buy, chaffer(y), commerce, communication, congestion, contact, converse, deal(ings), exchange, goods, industry, interchange, merchantry, mong, movement, path, rabble, sell, track, trade, trail, trash, travel, truck, wander
circle crossway, rotary, roundabout
in cauponate, cauponize
in sacred things simony
jam snarl, squeeze
light blinker, signal, stoplight

TRAGACANTH astragalus, bassorin, gum, tree, whiteleaf
substitute badan

TRAGEDY buskin, calamity, catastrophe, complaint, cothurnus, disaster, drama, misery, misfortune, reverse
father of aeschylus
1st english gorboduc
muse melpomene
personification ate

TRAGIC adverse, black, calamitous, cataclysmic, catastrophic, deplorable, desolate, dire, disastrous, dreadful, fatal, forlorn, grievous, lamentable, melancholy, miserable, mournful, pathetic, pitiful, ruinous, sad, thespian, unfortunate, wretched

TRAGOPAN bird, fowl, monal, pheasant

TRAIK break, fatigue, idle, lounge, misfortune, pest, plague, saunter, stray, stroll, tramp, trudge, wander, waste

TRAIL abature, arbor, chase, comino, crawl, creep, dawdle, degrade, dog, drag (gle), drail, draw, foil, follow, grating, grill, hale, hang, heel, hound, hunt, journey, lag, lattice, linger, loiter, odor, path, piste, protract, pug, pull, run, scent, sledge, slot, spoor, straggle, stream, streel, striggle, sweep, tag, taigle, tail, TRACE, track, traipse, tramp, trapes, trellis, troll, trudge, wake, wander
blazer guide, harbinger, leader, pathfinder, pioneer
boss cattle-driver
descending bahada, batjada
make blaze

marker cairn
wagon rudloff

TRAILER caravan, coach, creeper, detective, flatbed, follower, frogger, gondola, hunter, mobile home, semi, sprag, tracker
court motel

TRAILING creeping, drooping, following, lagging, runner, succeeding

TRAIN (See also *famous* and *kind*, below.) 3 aim, row, set, try 4 beam, file, form, gait, lead, line, rack, rank, rear, tail, tame, turn, wake 5 array, break, breed, chain, coach, dress, drill, force, groom, group, guide, point, raise, ready, slant, staff, suite, teach, track, trail 6 allure, column, convoy, direct, entice, foster, gentle, harden, school, season, series, sequel, sleigh, string 7 break in, bring up, caravan, carrier, correct, cortege, develop, dragnet, educate, improve, nurture, perfect, prepare, qualify, retinue, upbring, work out 8 accustom, artifice, drynurse, exercise, instruct, manifest, practice, rehearse, sequence 9 aftermath, condition, cultivate, followers, following, habituate 10 discipline, housebreak, procession
animals break, gentle
battering artillery
captain conductor
famous bullet, chief, el capitan, fleche d'or, golden arrow, lark, metroliner, north star, orient express, owl, sette bello, sunset limited, superchief, transsiberian, twentieth century limited
fast express, limited, rapido
funeral convoy
hawk afaite
horses manege
kind electric, express, flier, freight(er), funicular, interurban, limited, local, shuttle, special, streamliner, subway, tube, underground
man See RAILROAD *man.*
men crew
overhead elevated
railroad cannonball-express, choochoo, drag, express,

limited, local, pickup, rattler
repair shop roundhouse
robber jesse james, sam bass
sleeper international wagon-lits, pullman
underground See SUBWAY.
TRAINED adept, aimed, bred, broken, cultivated, cultured, domesticated, educated, experienced, gentled, practiced, proficient, seasoned, skilled, taught, veteran
TRAINER breeder, coach, driller, gymnasiarch, handler, lanista, paedotribe, stockman
airplane jeep, link, penguin
TRAINING ascesis, breeding, cultivation, culture, deportment, development, discipline, domestication, drill, education, manners, nurture, practice, theat
center academy
horse dressage, manege
manual sloid, slojd, sloyd
severe ascesis
TRAIPSE flaunt, gad(about), gallivant, meander, promenade, prowl, ramble, range, roam, saunter, slattern, stray, stroll, tramp, trapse, trudge, walk, wander
TRAIT amenity, attribute, characteristic, charm, habit, hallmark, item, knack, lineament, mark, note, peculiarity, property, quality, strain, streak, stroke, touch, tract, vein
TRAITOR apostate, benedict arnold, betrayer, brutus, double-crosser, double-dealer, ganelon, informer, iscariot, judas, knave, lordswike, mugwump, quisling, rat, rusty, snake, squealer, treacher, treasonist, turncoat, warlock
TRAITOROUS betraying, black, corrupt, disloyal, double-crossing, faithless, false, felon, perfidious, recreant, renegade, treacherous, treasonable, treasonous, unfaithful
TRAJAN *arch site* benevento
TRAJECT cast, course, cross(ing), ferry, impell, passage, passing, throw, transportation

TRAJECTORY curve, orbit, path, route, sporabola, way
TRAM align, bench, car, gauge, leg, limb, measure, pickup, rail, shaft, stratagem, streetcar, thread, tranvia, tub, wagon
tier deck
TRAMMEL bind, catch, check, clog, confine, curb, embarrass, encumber, fasten, fetter, hamper, hindrance, hobble, hogtie, hold, impede, impediment, inhibit, intercept, limit, manacle, net, obstruct, pothook, restrain(t), restrict, shackle, stifle, tie
TRAMMELS braids, compass, ellipsograph, gauge, locks, tresses
TRAMONTANE alien, barbarian, barbarous, boor, foreign(er), outland(er), overberg, polestar, stranger, transalpine, wind
TRAMP bagman, beggar, bimbo, bindlestiff, boe, bogtrotter, bum, burly, caird, cramp, crush, drummer, footpad, gang(e)rel, gaycat, gypsy, hake, hike, hobo, jaunt, javel, jocker, journey, landlo(u)per, nomad, pedestrian, picaro, punk, ramble, range, rinther(e)out, roam, rogue, rove(r), ruffler, skellum, snoozer, steamer, step, stiff, strag, stroll, sundowner, swagger, swagman, tinker, traipse, trample, trapes, trapse, tread, tromp, trounce, trowane, trudge, vagabond, vamp, viator, waff(ie), walk, wander, yegg(man)
mark monica, monniker
TRAMPCOCK haystack
TRAMPLE champ, crunch, crush, defoil, domineer, extinguish, hoof, hox, oppress, override, overrun, poach, scamble, scaut, spurn, stamp, subdue, tread, violate
TRANCE alley, amentia, coma, daze, dream, ecstasy, enrapture, entrance, entry, hall, hypnosis, lupa, passage(way), peril, prance, rapture, samadhi, sopor, spellbind, stupor, swoon, tramp, transfixion, travel
induced by music sama

TRANIO *master* lucentio
TRANQUIL bonny, calm (ato), comfortable, composed, cool, easy, equable, gentle, halcyon, lown, mild, pacific, peaceful, placid, quiet, reposeful, restful, serene, smooth, soft, still, undisturbed
TRANQUILIZE allay, alleviate, appease, assuage, becalm, calm, compose, lull, quiet, relax, sedate, settle, soften, soothe, still, unruffle
TRANQUILIZER alcohol, allonal, alurate, amytal, ataras, benzodiazepine, chloralhydrate, chlorpromazine, clonopin, compazine, dalmane, diazepam, doriden, equanil, flurazepam, glutethimide, heroin, librax, librium, lomotil, mellaril, meprobamate, miltown, mogadon, narcotic, opium, oxazepam, pertofrane, phenobarbital, quaalude, rauwolfia, reserpine, seconal, sedative, serax, stelazine, thalidomide, thorazine, tranxene, trilafon, valium, vesprin, vistaril
comb. azepam
pert. bromal
TRANQUILLITY ataraxia, ataraxy, calm(ness), composure, harmony, imperturbability, peace, quiet(ude), rest, sattva, serenity
goddess sattva
TRANSACT accomplish, bargain, bring about, carry on, carry out, compromise, conclude, conduct, deal, dicker, discharge, enact, execute, manage, negotiate, perform, settle, transfer, treat
TRANSACTION act(ion), affair, bargain, business, commercium, contract, deal, deed, discharge, event, mohabat, negotiation, performance, proceeding, report, sale, traffic
unlawful chevisance
TRANSCASPIAN *capital* ashkhabad
TRANSCEND cap, elevate, exceed, excel, outdo, outstrip, overcome, overpass, overstep, overtop, raise, soar, surmount, surpass, top
TRANSCENDENT(AL) ab-

solute, abstract, abstruse, acosmic, banner, categorical, consummate, ethereal, extraordinary, extraterrestrial, finished, heavenly, ideal (istic), incomparable, peerless, preeminent, superior, supranatural, suprarational, supreme, surpassing, ultimate, visionary
meditation founder maharishi mahesh yogi
meditation school maharishi international university
meditation word mantra
TRANSCRIBE compose, copy, duplicate, imitate, impute, paraphrase, reproduce, translate, write
carelessly transcribble
TRANSCRIPT apograph, carbon, copy, double, dupe, duplicate, facsimile, imitation, record, replica, report, reproduction, transumpt
TRANSEPT arm, plage, porch, wing
TRANSFER abalienate, alien(ate), alienation, amorte, amortization, amortize, assign(ment), attorn, carry, cartage, cede, cession, change, commit, communicate, conduct, confer (ment), conferral, consign (ment), contagion, convection, convey(ance), copy, deed, delegate, deliver (ance), delivery, demise, deport, depute, devolve, donation, enfeoff(ment), forward, give, grant, hand(on) (over), impart, let, metastasis, metathesis, migrate, move, negotiate, pass(age), portage, relay, relegate, remove, shift, sign over, succeed, ticket, traduce, transfuse, transfusion, transit(ion), translocation, transmission, transmit(tal), transplant, transposal, transpose, transposition
authority delegate, deputize
design decal
heat convect
homage attorn
legally abalienate, alien-(ate), attorn, convey, deed, lease
TRANSFERABLE alienable, assignable, bequeathable, conveyable, heritable, negotiable, transmissible

TRANSFERENCE assignment, conveyance, delation, demise, devolution, displacement, disposal, empathy, identification, movement, passage, projection, rapport, removal, shift, TRANSFER, transmission, transport
TRANSFIGURATION change, conversion, exaltation, metamorphosis, transformation, transmogrification
TRANSFIGURE change, clarify, convert, deify, enhance, exalt, glorify, heighten, idealize, illumine, intensify, irradiate, magnify, metamorphose, renew, transform, transmogrify, transmute
TRANSFIX dart, hold, impale, nail, perforate, petrify, pierce, pin, pitch, skewer, spear, spellbind, stab (ilize), stick, thrill
TRANSFORM alter, assimilate, catalyze, change, convert, disguise, heterize, modify, permute, revolutionize, shift, TRANSFIGURE, transmute, turn, vary
as if by magic aladdinize
TRANSFORMATION alteration, change, conversion, heterotopia, metabolism, metamorphosis, metaphysis, metasomatosis, mutation, permutation, sea-change, switch, transfiguration, translocation, transmutation, variation, wig
into human form anthromorphosis
TRANSFORMER alembic, booster, changer, converter, dimmer, hedgehog, jigger, teaser
TRANSFUSE diffuse, endue, imbue, indue, infuse, instill, permeate, pour, transfer
TRANSGRESS break, contravene, cross, digress, disobey, encroach, err, exceed, impinge, impose(on), infract, infringe, offend, overgo, overstep, sin, thwart, trespass, violate, wrong
TRANSGRESSION averah, breach, crime, delict(um), error, excursion, fault, incroachment, infraction, infringement, invasion, lapse,

misdeed, offense, scape, sin, slip, trespass, vice, violation
TRANSGRESSOR lawbreaker, offender, sinner
TRANSIENT boarder, brief, casual, changing, ephemeral, evanescent, fleeting, flighty, flitting, flying, fugitive, guest, impermanent, lessee, lodger, migratory, momentary, passing, renter, roomer, shortlived, temporary, TRANSITORY, traveler, wander(ing)
TRANSILIENT discontinuous, saltatory
TRANSISTOR battery
TRANSIT change, conveyance, cross, pass(age), plunge, theodolite, transept, transfer, transportation, travel
part alidade
TRANSITION bridge, change, conversion, evolution, flux, jump, katabolism, leap, metabasis, modulation, passage, rise, segue, shift, turn
TRANSITIVE figurative, intermediate, transitional
TRANSITORY brief, caducous, evanescent, fleet(ing), flying, impermanent, insignificant, passing, temporal, temporary, TRANSIENT, transitive, volatile, whilend
TRANSKEI *capital* umtata
city port of st james
council bunga
leader guzana, kaiser, matanzima
native xhosa(s)
party idi-amin
TRANSLATE carry over, change, construe, convert, decipher, decode, english, enrapture, expound, interpret, paraphrase, ravish, remove, render, reword, TRANSFER, transform, transport
TRANSLATION ascension, cab, crib, horse, jack, key, metaphrase, paraphrase, pony, rendition, thargum, trot, version
TRANSLATOR interpreter, repairer, repeater, turner
TRANSLUCENT bright, brilliant, clear, diaphanous, effulgent, glowing, hyaline, light, limpid, lucid, lumi-

nous, pellucid, radiant, shiny, transparent, transpicuous

TRANSMIGRATION death, deportation, diapedesis, metempsychosis, passing, reincarnation, sam(s)ara, sansara, transformation

TRANSMISSION descent, gear(box), transfer
physiological heredity

TRANSMIT beam, bear, bequeath, broadcast, cable, communicate, conduct, consign, convey, dispatch, enclose, endow, forward, impart, issue, mail, move, phone, post, radiate, remit, remove, render, send, shift, ship, spread, traject, transfer, transport, wire

TRANSMITTING *device* jammer, microphone, mike, radio, sender, television

TRANSMOGRIFY See TRANSFORM.

TRANSMUTATION alternation, change, conversion, evolution, exchange, fluctuation, metamorphosis, transformation

TRANSMUTE change, convert, ennoble, permute, transfer, TRANSFORM, transport, transume
into gold aurify, gild

TRANSOM couch, crossbar, crosspiece, lintel, louver, patible, seat, trave(rse), vane, ventilator, window

TRANSPARENCY clarity, diaphaneity, lucidity, slide

TRANSPARENT bright, candid, clear, crystal(line), diaphane, diaphanous, dioptric, distinct, frank, gauzy, glassy, gossamer, hyalescent, hyaline, lacy, limpid, lucent, lucid, luculent, luminous, lustrous, obvious, open, pellucid, pervious, sheer, shining, shiny, simple, thin, translucent, transpicuous, vitrean, vitreous, vitriform
comb. diaphano
semi fuscohyaline

TRANSPIRE befall, betide, develop, elapse, emit, evaporate, excrete, exhale, hap(pen), leak, occur, pass, perspire

TRANSPLANT displace, em-

igrate, relocate, shift, transfer, transpose

TRANSPORT ardor, back, banish, bear, bewitch, bliss, bring, bus(s), cabotage, captivate, carriage, carry, commit, conduct, convey, convict, delight, deport, ecstasy, enravish, exile, expel, express, extradite, fetch, frenzy, happiness, jag, joy, lug, move, oust, pack, passion, please, portage, porter, rapture, ravish, remove, ride, send, shift, ship, shoulder, take, tote, traduce, transfer, transmit, vessel, waft, whisk
by relay dak, dawk
kind boat, bus, cart, ferry, flute, freighter, horse, oiler, railroad, ship, tanker, train, troopship, van, vehicle, vessel

TRANSPORTATION banishment, bearing, carriage, cartage, convection, conveyance, da(w)k, deportation, drayage, ecstasy, fare, freight, haulage, lation, portage, porterage, railage, removal, ride, shipment, shipping, telpherage, ticket, toting, transit, truckage, waftage
business airline, express, mail, railroading, shipping, steamship, trucking
cost carriage
felonious asporation

TRANSPOSE agitate, change, convert, convey, discompose, disturb, exchange, interchange, invert, rearrange, remove, reverse, swap, transfer, translate, transmute, transport

TRANSPOSITION anagram, change, metathesis, rearrangement, shift, transformation
of sounds spoonerism

TRANSUBSTANTIATION carnification, metusia
believer capernaite
denier berengarian

TRANSUDE excrete, exude, sweat

TRANSVAAL See also SOUTH AFRICA.
capital pretoria
city krugersdorp
conglomerate banket

daisy gerbera
flag vierkleur
gold region rand
gypsy vaalpen
jade grossularite
legislature raad
native takhaar
policeman zarp
president kruger

TRANSVERSE across, alter, athwart, bias, collateral, crossbar, crosswise, diagonal, facing, horizontal, oblique, overthwart, overturn, shortcut, swivel, thwart, transform, trave(rse), versify
baffle bridgewall
bar arch, axle, s(w)ingletree, whiffle, whippletree
pin toggle
rail bearer

TRANSVERSION corruption, crossing, perversion

TRANSVESTITE berdache

TRANSYLVANIA *ruler* vayvode, waywode

TRANTLUM trifle, trinket

TRAP (See also *animal* and *fish,* below.) 3 bag, get, gin, jig, net, pit, tie 4 bait, bind, cage, drop, girn, hook, lime, lure, mesh, nail, plot, putt, ruse, snag, tipe, toil, tree, trip 5 benet, blind, brake, brike, buggy, catch, lasso, mouth, noose, seine, shock, snare, start, swick, swike, toils 6 ambush, cobweb, corner, cruive, detect, enmesh, keddah, lariat, meshes, quilez, snatch, stayer, tangle, trepan, willow 7 baggage, bindset, capture, cunning, deceive, dragnet, ensnare, involve, luggage, pitfall, putchen, putcher, sniggle, springe, startle, trammel 8 birdlime, carriage, coalhole, confound, conibear, deadfall, downfall, entangle, inveigle, separate, surprise 9 caparison, policeman, quicksand, stratagem
animal bownet, creel, eelpot, hatch, pot, tipe, type, web, weel, weir
baited lure
bird scrape
door drop, hatch, pitfall, scruto, slot, vampire, vampyre

fish corral, creel, fyke, kill, leap, weel, weir, willy
for feet caltrops
for unwary pitfall
game hopo
poker sandbag
police dragnet, roadblock
rodent clam, tipe, type
salmon putt
sand bunker
tree jack

TRAPPER decoyer, hunter, lurer, natty bumpo, pointsman, snarer

TRAPPING(S), TRAPS apparel, appurtenances, armory, bardings, belongings, caparison, clothing, decoration, dress, equipage, equipment, finery, fittings, gear, housing, jhool, luggage, ornament, raiment, regalia, toggery, wardrobe
theatrical prop(erty), scenery

TRAPSHOOTING skeet
target clay pigeon

TRASH ashes, baggage, balderdash, blather(y), bosh, bushwa, camelote, claptrap, clog, collar, crop, cul(t)ch, dirt, dreck, dregs, dross, encumber, flummery, gook, halter, hinder, hindrance, jade, jog, junk, kelter, leash, lop(pings), muck (ment), mundungus, nonsense, plod, rabble, raff, rammel, refuse, restrain, retard, riffraff, rot, rubbish, rubble, scrap, sculch, scum, skittles, smachrie, tire, tramp, trivia, troke, trouse, trudge, trumpery, vermin, waste, wrack
can dustbin
pile dump

TRASHY cheap, flashy, flimsy, low, paltry, poor, quisquillian, riffraff, rubbish(y), tacky, toshy, trifling, tripy, trumpery, useless, vain, vile, wasteful, worthless

TRAUMA hurt, injury, shock, stress, wound

TRAVAIL accouchement, agony, anguish, birth, delivery, drudgery, eclipse, effort, grind, harass, journey, labor, pain, pangs, suffering, swink, toil, torment, travois, trouble, work

TRAVEL circle, circuit, commute, course, cruise, emigrate, expedition, fare, fetch, gallivant, globetrot, hie, jaunt, journey, junket, locomote, migrate, mog, motion, move, mush, navigate, odyssey, passage, peregrinate, peregrination, ply, post, ride, roam, roll, run, safari, sail, sashay, stream, stump, torment, tour(ism), track, transit, traverse, trek, trip, troupe, trundle, voyage, walk, wander, wayfare, wend
agent aaa, american express, thomas cook
allowance batta, mileage
authorization passport, visa
by foot backpack, hike, shank, tramp, trudge
day's jornada, journey
fast barrel, streak
guide baedeker, burton, cicerone, de tocqueville, fielding, fodor, halliburton, michelin, murray
over snow mush
pert. viatic
through woods bushwhack
to and fro commute, shunt, shuttle
wandering wanderjahr

TRAVELER, TRAVELER'S agent, argonaut, bagman, camper, commuter, cruiser, drummer, emigrant, explorer, farer, globetrotter, hadji, howadji, itinerant, kilroy, migrant, navigator, nomad, palmer, passenger, pilgrim, rider, sailor, sightseer, swaggie, swagman, tinker, tourist, tramp, transient, trekker, tripper, viator, voyager, wanderer, wayfarer, waygoer
commercial agent, bagman, brinjaree, brinjary, drummer, rider, salesman
deity isis, mercury
famous baedeker, burton, captain cook, christopher columbus, de tocqueville, doughty, fielding, halliburton, henry james, herodotus, kilroy, lowell thomas, magellan, marco polo, mark twain, michelin, munchausen, odysseus, prester john, ulysses
garment balandrana
grass settler's-twine
group cafila, caravan, cavalcade, party, pilgrimage, safari, train
joy beggarbrush, bindwith, clematis, hagrope, oldman's-beard, withywind
money viaticum
saint christopher, julian
schedule itinerary
tree ravenala
wayside shelter cold harbor

TRAVELING circulating, dromomania, errant, moving, peregrinating, stirring, tourism, viatorial, wandering, wanderlust
salesman See TRAVELER *commercial.*
show carnival
stair escalator

TRAVERSE across, argue, barrier, bisect, contradict, controversy, counter(act), cover, cross(ing), crosspiece, crossways, decussate, delineate, deny, discuss, disprove, dispute, divert, examine, ford, gainsay, hinder, impede, inspect, intersect, navigate, oblique, obstacle, obstruct, oppose, pace, partition, pass, patrol, pivot, plane, quarrel, range, rebut, refute, reverse, review, road, rung, screen, shift, stall, stripe, study, subterfuge, survey, swivel, thwart, trace, track, transom, transpierce, travel, trick, turn, wander

TRAVERTINE aragonite, calcite, calcsinter, calctufa, tophus

TRAVESTY burlesque, caricature, comedy, imitation, lampoon, mimic, parody, ridicule, satire
pert. parodic
writer parodist, satirist

TRAVOIS alligator, dray

TRAWL boulter, dragnet, fish, net, pull, seine, trap, troll

TRAWLER bragozzo, pareja

TRAY anguish, batea, betray, bowl, box, case, coaster, fatigue, hod, hurtle, plate, salver, server, trestine, trey, trouble, trough, waiter
circular rounder
crumb voider
fish-drying flake
master king lear

revolving lazy susan
shellfish float
small servet

TREACHEROUS black, catchy, catty, corrupt, dangerous, dastardly, deceptive, disloyal, double-dealing, faithless, false, fickle, insecure, insidious, mutinous, perfidious, perilous, plotting, proditorious, recreant, seditious, shifty, slippery, sly, snaky, swack, traitorous, tricky, twofaced, unfaithful, unreliable, unstable, yellow
person judas, traitor, turncoat

TREACHERY bad faith, dastardy, deceit, disaffection, disloyalty, duplicity, felony, fraud, guile, infidelity, perfidy, swick, tradiment, train, traitory, treason

TREACLE claggum, cure, dibs, goo(p), molasses, remedy, sirup, sweeten(er), syrup, theriac(a)

TREACLEWORT herb, pennycress, thlaspi

TREAD chalaza, cicatricle, crush, dance, employment, footprint, footstep, gait, labor, pace, pack, pad, pit, press, quench, rate, repress, rung, rut, sneak, sole, stamp, step, stride, subdue, thresh, track, trade, trail, traipse, tramp(le), trapes, trapse, trod, volt, walk
clumsily balter, clump
heavily trample, trudge
on one's toes irritate, offend
renewal recap
-softly spurge-nettle
under foot despise, destroy, domineer, subdue, trample

TREADLE chalaza, lever, pedal, propeller, TREAD

TREADMILL routine

TREASON betrayal, collaboration, deception, disloyalty, double cross, lesemajesty, perduellion, perfidy, prodition, rebellion, revolt, sedition, subversion, tradiment, treachery, uprising

TREASONABLE perfidious, traitorous, treacherous

TREASURE appreciate, asthore. boast, cache, capital, catch, cherish, coin, diamond, enrich, esteem, find, fund(s), gem(s), gersum, gold, hoard, jewel, lay up, money, pearl, plum, prize, respect, revere(nce), riches, roon, stock, store(house), thesaur(us), trove, value, venerate, warison, wealth, worth
box hanaper
city el dorado
island author stevenson
island character ben gunn, jim hawkins, livesey, long john silver, pew, trelawney
island inn benbow
little storeen
state montana

TREASURER banker, bhandari, boucher, bowser, bursar, cashier, chamberlain, cofferer, comptroller, controller, curator, defterdar, depository, fisc(al), haznadar, hoarder, hoardward, guardian, paymaster, provisor, purser, receiver, steward, teller, trustee

TREASURY aerarium, anthology, bank, bursary, burse, cashbox, chest, coffer, exchequer, fisc(us), fisk, florilegium, funds, gallery, hordary, locker, moneybox, museum, purse, repository, safe, storehouse, strongbox, thesaurus, thesaury, till(er), tomb, vault
agent t-man
department camera
pert. aerarian
royal fisc, fisk

TREAT address, advise, argue, attend to, bandage, bargain, beano, bleed, blow to, bran, buy, care for, confer(ence), consider, consult, control, deal(with), delight, dight, discuss, dispute, doctor, dose, dress, entertain(ment), expound, favor, feast, feed, garnish, govern, handle, heal, honor, host, immunize, iodize, irradiate, joy, lead, leech, lolly, manage, manipulate, massage, medicament, medicate, minister, negotiate, nurse, parley, party, pay, physic, poultice, prepare, purge, regale, remedy, repast, represent, rub, serve, settle, solutize, solve, stand, study, think, urge, use, weigh, welcome

badly bedevil, crucify, dishonor, flout, frame, illuse, manhandle, manipulate, misuse, scout, snub, spite
comb. ize
roughly bang, grabble, manhandle
tenderly baby, coddle, dandle, favor, fondle, indulge, pamper, spare
with bargain, mediate, negotiate

TREATABLE conciliatory, moderate, pleasant, responsive, tangible, tractable

TREATISE account, agama, almagest, article, book, brochure, catholicon, comment, composition, covenant, description, didactic, discourse, dissertation, donet, ecthesis, essay, exposition, monograph, pandect, speculum, story, study, summa, theme, thesis, tract(ate)
elementary donet, grammar, primer, reader
introduction isagoge
religious hierography, homily, sermon, tract

TREATMENT allopathy, analysis, antidote, antitoxin, biological, chemotherapy, chiropractic, cure, first aid, handling, hydrotherapy, management, medication, naturopathy, practice, regime(n), remedy, therapeutics, therapy, usage, use, x-ray
compassionate clemency, mercy
harsh abuse, cruelty, misusage, severity
unprofessional malpractice

TREATY account, agreement, alliance, armistice, bargain, capitulation, carta, cartel, charter, compact, concord(at), contract, convention, discourse, discussion, entente, league, mise, negotiation, pact, protocol, treatise, truce
free world cento, nato, seato
members allies
site amiens, berlin, bretigny, ghent, karlowitz, lausanne, locarno, london, luneville, nanking, neuilly, nijmegen, paris, prague, pressburg, rapallo, rastatt, saint germain,

sevres, tilsit, troyes, utrecht, versailles

TREBLE acute, descant, highpitched, latten, shrill, soprano, tenor, threefold, triple, triplum, whine

clef gee

TREBUCHET balance, cucking stool, dond(a)ine, sling

TRECULIA breadfruit, mulberry, screwpine

TREE (See also *evergreen, fruit, hardwood,* etc., below.) barrel, bosc(age), bosk(age), cask, corner, cross, cudgel, gallows, gibbet, handle, hang, pedigree, perplex, pole, sapling, seedling, shaft, ship, staff, stake, stick, timber, trap, wood(en)

anacardiaceous cashew, mango, pistachio, sumac

aromatic allspice, aloes, balsam, cedar, clusia, huisache, jasmine, pim(i)ento, sassafras

bamboo-like coleu

bark crut, rhytidome, ross, tan, taps

bear raccoon

big redwood, sequoia

bignoniacious catalpa, primavera

black-varnish theetsee

blinding sap alipata

bombacaceous balsa, baobab

branch angle axil

branches ramage

broad-trunked baobab

bully balata

burned, broken rampick, rampike

cactus saguaro

caucho-yielding See *rubber,* below.

-celandine plume-poppy

cemetery cypress, yew

changed to baucis, daphne, heliads, philemon

citrus citrange, grapefruit, kumquat, lemon, lime, mandarin, orange, shaddock, tangelo, tangerine

clothes costumer, valet

clump See *group,* below.

-cobra mamba

colorful catalpa, jacaranda

comb. dendro(n)

coniferous alder, cedar, cypress, fir, jackpine, larch, pine, thuja, tsuga, yew

cornaceous tupelo

covering See *bark,* above.

-creeper tomtit

crooked scrag

cursed gallows, warytree

cut back dotard, pollard

cypress gilia

cyrillaceous titi

dead dryki, rampick, rampike, runt, snag

decay See *disease,* below.

decayed dotterel

deciduous arjun, taxodium

desert joshua, ocotillo, yucca

devil dita

devil's cotton abroma

disease blacksap, blight, bottomrot, buttrot, footrot, knot, melaxuma, tarspot

drupe-bearing bito

-duck fiddler, yaguaza

dwarf arbuscle, bush, chinquapin, runnel, scrub

dwelling nest

dye anatto, annatto, arnatto, hursinghar, ipil, mora, nagkassar, toon, tua, tui

epiphytic waxflower

euphorbiaceous candlenut

evergreen abelmosk, abies, abroma, agathis, arborvitae, arbutus, ardisia, athel, balsam, baretta, bay, bebeeru, bibiri, bilimbi, calaba, camphor, carob(e), casimiroa, catha, cazaba, cedar, cedrus, celastra, chir, clove, coigue, coihue, conifer, corkfir, cupressus, cypress, deodar, erica, eucalypt(us), everlasting, fir, greenheart, hemlock, holly, holm(oak), juniper, kanagi, kapuka, larch, lemon, loquat, madrona, mapau, mastic, matsu, monkeypuzzle, nectandra, ocote, olax, olive, orange, pine, pittosporum, pondapple, rhododendron, rosebay, sabine, savin(e), spruce, sugi, taraire, tarata(h), tawa, thea, thuja, toatoa, tolu, toyon, tsuga, whort, winter's-bark, yew

expert dendrologist

extinct sigillaria, stringwood

exudation chicle, gum, jelutong, lac, latex, lycium, resin, rosin, sap, tar, xylan

fabaceous (See also LOCUST *tree.*) agati

fallen deadman

family descent, pedigree, stemma

fat-yielding shea

felling allage

fern alsophila, amamau, polypody, pulu

fiber bendy, bentang, bulak, kurrajong, mahoe, majagua, sida, simal, terap

flowering acacia, agati, catalpa, cleaster, elder, ironwood, jacaranda, lehua, mimosa, oleaster, redbud, titi, tulip

fodder mahoe, tagasaste

food akee

forgetfulness lotus

fragrant jasmine

framework espalier

-frog ferreiro, hyla

fruit anag(u)ep, annona, apple, apricot, araca, avocado, bakupari, banana, banyan, bel, biriba, capulin, custard-apple, fig, ga(u)b, genip(ap), gingko, icho, kalumpit, lemon, lime, litchi, loquat, mahis, medlar, olive, orange, papaw, pawpaw, peach, pear, plum, quince, sapota, seckel, tamarind, tangelo, tangerine, tche, terminalia, voavanga

funeral cypress

geneological arbor, jesse

genus abies, acer, citrus, lithocarpus, maba, owenia, quercus, styrax, trema, ulmus

goddess pomona

group bluff, bosc(age), bosk(age), bosque, camp, clump, coppice, copse, flora, forest, glade, grove, hurst, hyrst, mott, nursery, pinetum, shinnery, silva, spinney, stand, stell, sylva, thicket, tope, toll, tump, wood(s)

grower arborist

growing on arboricoline, epidendric

growth layer ring

growth of sylvage

gum acacia, alveary, amapa, babul, balata, banildad, bansalague, bumbo, coolibah, eucalypt(us), gamboge, gimlet, gommier, haw, hyawa, icica, kar(r)i, kikar, kino, mallet, mora, nyssa, owenia, sapodilla, sapota, sapote, sapotilha, sapotilla, satin-walnut, sloe, storax, sunt, tewart, tuart, tupelo, wandoo, xylan, yaya, zapote *hardwood* aalii, acle, agba, alarco, almique, almon, anagap, andoroba, aranga, ash, avodire, bancal, bansalague, banuyo, bethabara, bitternut, brazil(wood), breakax, cadamba, camuning, capulin, caraipe, cariapi, carya, cedar, cocobolo, crabwood, cuya, ebony, elm, ferreum, gee, gidgea, gidgee, gidia, gidjee, gidya(e)a, heartwood, ipil, ironwood, juglans, kaneelharu, lana, lillypilly, loblolly, mabee, mabi, macaasin, madrono, mahogany, maple, muermo, myrsine, narra, ngaio, oak, pecan, pelu, pignut, pinkwood, poon, quebracho, quercus, resak, shagbark, shellbark, sundari, teak, tindalo, ulmo, urunday, walabee, walnut, zante

head coma

heath briar, brier

honey mahua

infernal zaqqum

-inhabiting arboreal, arboricole

in stream sawyer

-jobber woodpecker

juglandaceous hickory, walnut

juice See *exudation*, above.

kangaroo dendrolagus

kapok ceiba

knot burl, gnur, knag, node

koranic zaggum

landmark lopstick

lauraceous camphor, cassiabark, ishpingo, sassafras

left in cutting holdover

leguminous angelique, blackbean, carob, catalpa, dicorynia, hyacinth bean, koko, laburnum, lebbek, tonka bean, wallaba, zebrawood

-like arboreal, arboreous, arborescent, arboresque, dendroid, sylvan

limb bough, branch

lucern tagasaste

malaceous apple, cydonia, hawthorn, malus, medlar, pear, pyrus, quince, shadbush

malvaceous abutilon, althea, gossypium, hibiscus, lacebark, lavatera

many-trunked banyan

measurer saliper, salliper

medic moon-trefoil

medicinal amuyong, quebracho, sassafras, sumac(h), strychnos, wahahe

meliaceous carapa, cedar, cedrela, flindosa, langsat, mahogany

mimosaceous acacia, gama, mimosa, siris

moraceous breadfruit, breadnut, ficus, fig, morus, mulberry, upas

moss climacium, lichen, usnea

moth egger

mothproof cedar

-mouse dendromus, nuthatch, vole

myrtaceous allspice, eucalyptus, eugenia, guava, pim(i)ento, psidium

mythical tuba, yggdrasil

nut akhrot, almendron, almond, chicha, cola, hazel, hickory, pecan, walnut

nymph hamadryad, meliad, meliae

of heaven ailanthus, sumac

of life arborvitae, cypress, date

of sadness hursinghar, nightjasmine

oil bel, ben(ne), candlenut, eboe, mahua, mahwa, poon, supa, tung

oleaceous ash, fraxinus, ligustrum, olive

on wall rider

ornamental asak, asok (a), catalpa, crape myrtle, jacaranda, laburnum, pacay, physicnut, silverbell, ulmus, yellowwood

over 2 ft diameter veteran

oxalidaceous carambola

parasite mistletoe

parasitic aralie, santalum

part bark, bole, branch, knot, leaf, root, sapwood, trunk, twig

-peony moutan

pert. arboreal, arboreous, arborous, cacuminal, dendral, sylvan

pinaceous araucaria, arborvitae, cedar, conifer, fir, hemlock, juniper, kauri, larix, pine, redwood, sequoia, spruce, thuja, tsuga

-planters state nebraska

-planting holiday arbor day

platform machan

pod-bearing catalpa

poisonous bunk, guao, hemlock, ligas, rauwolfia, sassy, tanghin, tanquen, upas

pollard runnel

prune sned

pruner averruncator

quaking leaves aspen

rare joshua

resinous arar, balsam, brea, fir, pine, tacamahac, torchwood

root spurn, tang

rope-making amuyong

round-headed rata

row of stich

rubber caucho, ule

rutaceous aegle, bael, bel, lime, quince, torchwood, wampee

sacred pipal

sapindaceous inkwood, soapberry

sapotaceous acana, almique, bumelia, guttapercha, marmalade tree, sapodilla, shea tree

science silvics

scrub See *stunted*, below.

shade ash, balsam, catalpa, dilly, elm, guama, halesia, hevea, inkwood, joewood, lin(den), maple, oak, poplar, sycamore, teil, umbrella

-shaped arboriform

showy See *ornamental*, above.

shrew tana

silk-cotton bulak, ceiba

small ake(ake), alder, arboret, blolly, box, chanar, cumay, dwarf, emajagua, hardtack, henna, huisache, inkwood, joewood, jojoba, kadamba, kowhai, ngaio, oleaster, seron, snowbell, sourwood, straddle, tche, treelet, treeling

snake boomslang, gimp, lora

softwood abura, ambay, balsa, cork, lin(den)

sparrow weaverbird

sprout sapling, sprig

standing filler

sterculiaceous cacao, cocoa, kolanut, kurrajong, theobroma

streaked wood baria

student arborist

stump doddard, dotard, mock, nubbin, runt, shag, stock, stool, stoop, stoven, stow, zuche

stunted bito, scrab, scrog, scrub, scrunt, windcripple

supporting husband
swamp tupelo
swelling nutgall
tallow candlenut, cera, maffur(r)a, roka
thorny acacia, ambash, ambatch, aroma, aromo, bael, barriguda, bel, bindoree, bito, boogum, brea, bucare, bumelia, catechu, chichicaste, cockspur, colorin, honey, huisache, lavanga, lemon, lime, samohu
tiger leopard
timber 3 ash, dar, fir, ihi, koa, oak, saj 4 acle, anda, baku, cuya, ekki, kaya, kino, miro, pelu, pine, rata, rimu, tala, teak, vera 5 acana, acapu, almon, amaga, amapa, amate, ambay, anjan, araca, banak, birch, carob, cedar, culla, ebano, ebony, erizo, fotui, guijo, hinan, icica, kauri, khaya, kiaki, kokan, lauan, maniu, maple, matsu, narra, pekea, penda, pooli, roble, tenio, timbo, tulip, yacal 6 alagao, alerce, alfaje, alupag, baboen, bacury, banaba, bancal, baobab, barbas, carbon, chupor, cocuyo, cortez, dagame, dukuma, dungon, eperua, espave, freijo, gaboon, gamari, imbuia, jacana, lanete, lebbek, malave, mopane, muermo, piquia, puriri, sandan, satine, shorea, totara, walnut 7 amuguis, becuiba, camagon, caraipi, cedrela, cypress, gomavel, guacimo, guarabu, guayabi, harpula, hollong, koombar, lapacho, licania, mancono, mangeao, mayapis, redwood, shepine, tarairi 8 almaciga, amarillo, axmaster, boarwood, cabreuva, caracoli, cocobolo, crabwood, doncella, etaballi, guatambu, holywood, ironbark, longjohn, mahogany, rasamala, rewarewa, sucupira, tanguile, umburana, zapatero 9 araucaria, axemaster, huamuchil, ivorywood, snakebark, sweetroot, vinhatico 10 billetwood, caimitillo, gasparillo, halmalille, marinheiro, princewood, sir-

vaballi 11 malaanonang, stenocarpus
tissue cambium
toad anuran, hyla, hylid
top See *trim,* below.
trained espalier
treatise silva
trim lap, lop, prune, shrag
tropical See TROPICAL tree.
trunk bole, butt, caber, caudex, mast, stick
trunk, comb. cormo
trunk, trimmed log
trunk, worshipped irminsul
turpentine-yielding terebinth
unarmed albizzia
universe symbol yggdrasil
varnish doon, theetsee
worship arborolatry, dendrolatry
young runnel, sapling, seedling, silva, spring(er), tiler

TREELESS barren
area fellfield
TREENAIL gutta, mooter, nog, peg, pin, spike, trunnel
TREF hamlet, homestead
TREFOIL arch, bedstraw, beggar's-tick, canch, claver, cloverleaf, crowtoe, medic, nonesuch, sainfoin, shamrock, tickseed, trifolium
bog buckbean
burgundy alfalfa, lucerne, medicago
yellow birdsfoot
TREK draw, expedition, journey, migrate, migration, pull, safari, tramp, travel, trip, trudge, wade
TRELLIS arbor, bower, espalier, filigree, fret(work), interlace, lattice(work), pergola, summerhouse, tarlies, tracery, treillage, treille
TREMATODE bilharzia, cercaria, flatworm, fluke, marita, parasite, schistosome, strigeid, worm
TREMBLE aspen, bever, didder, dingle, dirl, dither, dodder, fear, fidget, flicker, flutter, jar, nither, oscillate, palpitate, quail, quake, quaver, quiver, shake, shimmy, shrink, shudder, stagger, thrill, throb, titter, totter, tremor, trepidation, trymle, vibrate, wabble, whither, wince, wobble
TREMBLER buzzer, quaker, vibrator

TREMBLING aquiver, aspen, dither, quaking, quavery, quivery, shaky, shy, timid, tremulant, tremulous, trepid
TREMELLOSE gelatinous, thick, viscid
TREMENDOUS alarming, astounding, awful, big, colossal, dreadful, enormous, extraordinary, frightful, giant, gigantic, great, huge, horrible, immense, large, mighty, momentous, monstrous, monumental, prodigious, stupendous, superb, terrible, terrific, terrifying, titanic, vast
TREMOLITE amphibole, amphibolite, grammatite
TREMOR dindle, earthquake, flutter, heartquake, oscillation, quaver, quiver, ripple, shake, shiver, shudder, temblor, thrill, TREMBLE, upheaval, vibration
earth quake, teleseism
TREMULOUS afraid, agitated, aspen, blubbery, fearful, frightened, nervous, palsied, perturbed, quaky, quivering, sensitive, shaking, shaky, timid, timorous, tingling, tremandò, trembly, tremulant, unsteady, vibrating, wavering
TRENCH approach, aqueduct, border, canal, carve, channel, chase, cut, dike, ditch, drain, encroach, foss(a), furrow, gash, gaw, graff, grave, grip, groove, gully, gutter, haha, infringe, intrude, invade, leat, levee, moat, sap, scar, seuch, seugh, sheuch, sheugh, sike, slash, slice, slidder, tajo, thorough, track, trespass, trig, trough, verge, way
angle zig(zag)
artificial leat
bomb hand-grenade
digger sapper
digging sap
digging tool burgoyne
into extend, pass, penetrate, pertain, reach
irrigation float, sugsloot
mouth vincent's infection
mouth remedy arsphenamine
on adjoin, encroach, trespass, violate
sloping parados
winding boyau
TRENCHANT acrid, acrimo-

nious, acute, biting, caustic, clear(cut), concise, crisp, cutting, distinct, edged, energetic, incisive, keen, mordant, penetrating, piercing, sardonic, scathing, sharp, significant, vigorous

TRENCHER board, carver, food, hanger-on, knife, parasitic(al), plate, platter, roundel, sapper, sponging, sycophant(ic), viands
cap mortarboard

TRENCHERMAN cook, eater, glutton, gormandizer, hanger-on, parasite, sponger

TREND bear(ing), bend, bent, course, current, curve, deviate, direction, disposition, drift, extend, gravitate, inclination, incline, line, motion, movement, progress(ion), revolve, roll, run, set, skirt, slant, strike, style, swing, tend(ency), tenor, tide, tone, turn, veer, vein, vogue, wind
new nouvelle-vague

TREPAN cheat, cut, deceiver, ensnare, entice, entrap, lure, perforate, saw, snare, stratagem, swindle, tool, trap, trephine, trick (ster)

TREPANG balate, beche-de-mer, holothruian, sea-cucumber, sea-slug, swallo(w), teatfish, titfish

TREPID quaking, timorous, trembling

TREPIDATION agitation, alarm, anxiety, aquiver, awe, clonus, concern, confusion, consternation, creeps, didder, dismay, disquiet(ude), disturbance, dithers, dread, excitement, fear, fidgets, flutter, fright, horror, nerves, nervousness, oscillation, palpitation, panic, perturbation, shakes, shivers, stage fright, sweat, terror, tremor, unrest, vibration, worry

TRESPASS breach, butt in, crime, debt, depart, die, encroach, enter, entrench, err(or), fault, furtum, infringe, interfere, interlope, intrench, intrude, invade, misfeasance, obtrude, offend, offense, overloup, overstep, poach, sin, transgress(ion), trench(on), tri-

pet, trover, vice, violate, violation, wrong

TRESS beaucatcher, braid, curl, earlock, elflock, frizz(le), hair, kiss-me-quick, lock, lovelock, mane, mop, plait, ringlet, spitcurl, wimpler
-like comoid

TRESTLE bench, buck, chevalet, clotheshorse, horse, leg, mare, pillar, sawhorse, stool, support, tripod, trivet

TREWS breeches, stockings, trousers

TREWSMAN highlander

TRIAD chord, ternary, three, trinary, trine, trinity, trio, triratna, triune, trivalent

TRIAL adversity, affliction, agony, anguish, approof, assize, attempt, bore, bout, case, check, contest, cross, demonstration, devilment, difficulty, discomfort, distress, doom, effort, endeavor, essay, evidence, examination, exercise, experiment, grief, hardship, harm, harrassment, headache, hearing, hell, inquest, inquiry, inquisition, inspection, investigation, lawsuit, misery, misfortune, nightmare, nuisance, ordeal, pain, pest, plague, pree, probation, procedure, process, proof, proving, provocation, rigor, sample, sorrow, stab, suffering, suit, taste, temptation, test, torment, tournament, tribulation, trouble, try, visitation, woe, worriment, worry
by ordeal dei judicium, ordalium
experimental tentament
inconclusive mistrial
pert. empiric
place venue
preliminary prolusion
session assize(s)
severe acid test, ordeal
waiver cognovit

TRIANGLE affair, apex, delta, pyramid, triad, trigon, trinity, triquet
heraldic gyron
side hypot(h)enuse, leg
type equilateral, eternal, isosceles, obtuse, scalene

TRIANGULAR cuneate, cuneiform, deltoid, hastate,

trigonal, trilateral, wedge-shaped
comb. trigon(o)
course bentinck
decoration pediment
flag gurgee
insert godet, gore, gusset
pert. cuneate, hastate
piece gore, gusset, miter, mitre, quirk, wedge
sail lateen, spinnaker

TRIBE (For tribes of specific countries, see under that country, e.g., AFRICA *native, people,* or *tribe.*) assemblage, cham, cinel, clan, class, family, flock, folk, gens, group, horde, ilk, kind, phyle, race, sept, sib, siol, sort, stock, type
customs study agriology
division clan, family, sept
emblem totem
head chief, dato, datu, patriarch, tribune
lost lamanites

TRIBULATION affliction, agony, distress, misery, oppression, persecution, sorrow, suffering, TRIAL

TRIBULUS burnut, caltrap

TRIBUNAL acuerdo, appellate, areopagus, areopagy, audiencia, bar, bench, board, conference, council, court, curia, esguard, feme, forum, judicatory, judicial, judiciary, majlis, panel, platform, rigsret, seat, tora, townhall, vehm(e)

TRIBUNE apse, bema, chief, dais, demagogue, magistrate, officer, official, platform, pulpit, rostrum, throne, velutis

TRIBUTARY adjuvant, affluent, anabranch, ancillary, arm, auxiliary, billabong, branch, collateral, confluent, effluent, feeder, fork, prong, pup, secondary, subject, subjugated, subordinate, vanquished

TRIBUTE assessment, blackmail, brennage, cain, canon, caratch, caup, chevage, citation, compliment, customs, donation, dues, duty, encomium, eulogy, excise, fee, gift, heregeld, heriot, homage, impost, kain, levy, ovation, panegyric, peskash, praise, rate, recommendation, romescot, rome-

shot, scatt, tariff, tax, testimonial, tithe, toll, trewage
comb. age
feudal brennage, gavel
TRICE bind, blink, blow, despoil, flash, gird, instant, jiffy, moment, pull, second, secure, snatch, stroke, tie, twinkling
up lash, secure, stiffen
TRICHILIA alfaje, mafura
TRICHOCEREUS cactus, cardona
TRICHOMA hair, plica, trichiasis
TRICHOSPORUM blushwort, centaurium
TRICHOSTEMA bluecurls, selfheal, tarweed
TRICK 3 bob, boy, cog, dap, dor, fob, fox, fub, fun, gum, gyp, rig 4 bilk, chaw, dido, dupe, feke, fool, gaff, gaud, geck, gull, hoax, jape, jest, joke, prat, ruse, sell, shab, skin, trap, turn, wile 5 antic, blind, bluff, caper, catch, cheat, craft, creek, cully, dodge, elude, feint, fetch, fraud, gleek, knack, magic, pavie, prank, quick, shift, shtik, skite, slick, spell, spoof, stunt 6 adroit, baffle, begunk, bejape, brogue, cajole, cautel, chouse, craddy, delude, fourbe, hocket, humbug, nimble, palter, shtikl, thwart, trepan, trucco 7 beguile, cantrip, chicane, deceive, ficelle, gimmick, marlock, pretext, shuffle, swindle 8 artifice, flimflam, illusion, intrigue, maneuver, slampamp 9 bamboozle, chicanery, deception, diablerie, prettikin, shell game, stratagem 10 badger game, necromancy, subterfuge 11 espieglerie, hornswoggle, legerdemain, thimble game 12 monkeyshines 13 sleight of hand 16 prestidigitation
card stich
clever liripipe, liripoop
juggler's foist
last stich
old connu
out adorn, decorate, dress, finify, ornament
symbol monkey
TRICKERY artifice, bait, cautel, cheating, chicanery, cunning, deceit, deception,

dodgery, duplicity, fallacy, finery, forgery, fraud, guile, hocus, hokeypokey, humbug, imposture, japery, jookerie, jugglery, knavery, legerdemain, sham, sleight(of hand), wile
comb. ery
victim cully, dupe, gull
TRICKLE depart, distill, dribble, drip, drizzle, drop, exude, filter, flow, guggle, gurgle, leak, murmur, ooze, percolate, percolation, purl, ripple, seep, siggle, spurtle, stillicide, strain, TRICKY, trill, trintle, zigger
TRICKSTER dodger, fox, gull, imposter, joker, nogoodnik, prankster, rascal, sham, sleeveen, slicker, tramposo
TRICKY adroit, artful, catchy, complex, complicated, crafty, crooked, cunning, deceptive, devious, dishonest, dodgy, elusive, fikie, foxy, hookemsnivey, horsefair, insidious, intricate, misleading, oblique, playful, quirky, rowdy, shifty, shrewd, skil(l)ful, skittish, sliddery, slippery, sly, snide, ticklish, treacherous, unreliable, wily
TRICYCLE rantoon, sociable, tandem, tricar, trike
TRIDENT fork, gig, leister, spear, trisul(a), vajra
bearer neptune, poseidon
TRIED constant, dependable, devoted, ettled, faithful, known, proved, reliable, rendered, skilled, stanch, steadfast, tested, true-blue, trustworthy, weighed
TRIESTE *gulf, river into* isonzo
measure orna, orne
TRIFLE ambsace, bagatelle, bauble, bawbee, bean, befool, betise, bit, boondoggle, breath, bubble, button, cent, chatter, continental, coquette, dabble, dally, damn, dawdle, delude, dessert, dibble, doit, doodad, doodle, drop, equivocate, fable, faddle, falderal, farthing, fico, fiddle, fidget, fig, fike, flimflam, flirt, fool, footle, fribble, fritter, frivol, gaud, gewgaw, gimcrack, gossip, hoot, idle,

jest, joke, kickshaw, knickknack, mock, molehill, nicknack, niffnaff, nifle, niggle, nignay, nignye, nonentity, nothing, nullity, palter, peanut, philander, picayune, piddle, pin(head), pistareen, potter, prune, putter, raillery, rap, rien, shucks, song, stiver, straw, thought, toy, traneen, trantlum, trick, trillibub, trimtram, trinket, triviality, truff, tweedle, twiddle, wanton, waste
showy gewgaw
with dandle, delude, niggle, toy
TRIFLING badinage, banal, childish, coquetry, empty, fiddling, foolish, fribble, frivolous, futile, idle, immaterial, inane, insipid, jejune, little, measly, nugatory, paltry, petty, picayune, piddling, piffling, potty, puny, shallow, slight, TRIVIAL, unimportant, vain, vapid, worthless
TRIFOLIUM berseem, bluebonnet, clover, shamrock, trefoil
TRIG active, brisk, chic, chipper, cram, dandy, dapper, debonair, faithful, fill, firm, fop, full, jaunty, lively, methodical, natty, neat, orderly, prim, prop, run, scotch, shipshape, skid, smart, snug, sound, spick and span, spruce, steady, stiff, stop, strong, stuff, support, tidy, trench, trim, trot, trusty, well
TRIGGER block, catch, cause, ignite, initiate, lever, skid, start(er), stimulus, verge
TRIGGERFISH balistes, bessy, cerka, cocuyo, cucuyo, durgon, filefish, oldwench, oldwife, turbot
TRIGGERMAN assassin, bravo, cutthroat, hoodlum, killer
TRIGLA gurnard, gurnet
TRIGLYPH *space between* metope
TRIGO grain, wheat
TRIGON game, harp, lyre, sabbeka, sackbut, sambuca, triangle, trine, triplicity
TRIGONELLA amyris, balsam, baumier, birdsbill,

birdsfoot, calomba, fenugreek, melilot, ocimum

TRIGONOMETRY *function* cos(ine), secant, sine, tangent

TRILL flap, flow, leak, quaver, quiver, ripple, rock, shake, sing, tiralee, tremble, tremolo, trickle, turn, twirl, vibrate, warble

TRILLION *comb.* treg(a)

TRILLIUM bathflower, benjamin, bethroot, birthroot, birthwort, bloodynose, castilleja, medeola, nosebleed, orchid, pigseye, sarah, truelove, trump, wakerobin

TRILOBITE acidaspis, agnostus, ampyx, arthropod, asaphus, calymene, dalmania, dalmanites, eodiscid, horseshoe(crab), illaenus, king crab, olenellus, paradoxides, phacops, proetus, proparia, triarthrus
larva protaspis
shield cephalon

TRIM 3 axe, bob, cut, dub, fix, gay, nig 4 beak, beat, butt, clip, crop, deck, dink, dock, fine, firm, fuss, gash, hack, neat, pare, perk, sned, snod, snug, tack, tidy, trig 5 adorn, cheat, clean, crimp, dress, natty, nifty, order, perky, plash, poise, preen, prink, prune, shear, shrag, sleek, smart, stout, trick 6 adjust, apoise, barber, dapper, defeat, fettle, punish, rebuke, spruce, steady, strong, switch, thrash, wallop 7 balance, ballast, bedizen, chipper, compact, curtail, dispose, flounce, garnish, orderly, reprove, shapely, shorten 8 beautify, chastise, decorate, manicure, ornament, pleasant, regulate, straddle, truncate 9 condition, embellish, excellent, stabilize, temporize, vacillate 10 depreciate

TRIMMER barber, beam, bridle, edger, ligger, rebuke(r), scold, settler, stunner, virago, vixen

TRIMMING accessory, beading, beating, bertha, braid, cape, chicanery, collar, decoration, defeat, falbala, falderal, flots, flounce, frieze, fringe, froufrou, furbelow, garnish, garniture, gimp,

jabot, lace, lacing, ornament, passement(erie), pickadil, purfle, rebuke, reproof, ribbon, rickrack, ruche, ruching, ruffle, sequin, thrashing, trouncing
border g(u)ard

TRIMURTI brahma, s(h)iva, trinity, vishnu

TRINAL three(fold), TRINE, triple

TRINDLE candle, roll, taper, trundle, unroll, wheel

TRINE auspicious, chord, favorable, hang, march, threefold, trene, triad, trigon, trinity, trio, triple, triune

TRINIDAD tobago
asphalt deposit pitch lake
bird cocorico, oilbird
capital port of spain
city arima, labrea, port of spain, siparia
dance shango
gulf paria
music calypso, goombay
point galera
river ortoire
tree mora

TRINIL *race* apeman

TRINITY spiderwort, ternary, threeness, triad, triangle, trias, TRIMURTI, trine, trio, triune
college drink audit-ale
3 parts father, holy ghost, son

TRINKET bauble, bibelot, bijou, breloque, bric-a-brac, chotchke, cup, doodad, fribble, gaud, gewgaw, gimcrack, kickshaw, knickknack, nicknack, ornament, porringer, tahli, tchotchke, toy, trankum, trantlum, trifle, whimwham

TRIO gleek, ternion, terzetto, three(some), triplet, triune

TRIODE *part* cathode, grid, plate

TRIOPAS *offspring* erysichthon, iphimedia
parent canace, neptune

TRIP backheel, blunder, brood, buck, canter, caper, catch, cruise, dance, drive, err(or), excursion, expedition, failure, fall, flight, flock, foot, frisk, hegira, hinder, hop, jaunt, journey, junket, lapse, misstep, mistake, morsel, obstruct, outing, pace, pawl, pilgrimage,

play, ramble, release, run, safari, sin, skip, slip, stroke, stumble, tilt, tour, trap, trek, trot, voyage, wedge
by dog team mush
hammer bellyhelve
hammer operator tilter
-toe hobblebush
up supplant

TRIPE belly, claptrap, entrails, nonsense, paunch, poppycock, rolpens, rubbish, trillibub, vitals
with beef rolpens

TRIPLE hit, tern, third, three-bagger, threefold, thribble, treble, triad, trinary, trine, tripartite, triune
comb. tri, tris
crown tiara
tree gallows

TRIPLET brelan, hemiolia, parial, sibling, tercet, tern(ion), terzina, three, trine, triole, tristich, triune
one of trin(e)

TRIPLETAIL berrugate, black grunt, chobie, flasher, grouper, sama, spadefish, tern

TRIPOD athenienne, brandreth, cat, easel, gridiron, spider, stand, teapoy, trestle, trivet
decorative athenienne, teapoy
part leg, trivet

TRIPOLI barca, cyrenaica, rottenstone, silex, silica, tripel
coin piastre
measure dra(a), drah
ruler dey

TRIPTOLEMUS *invention* plough
offspring demophon
parent celeus, cothonea, gaea, metanira, oceanus, polymnia, trochilus
patroness demeter
shrine eleusis

TRIPTYCH altarpiece, picture, tablet

TRISMUS lockjaw, tetanus

TRISTAN See TRISTRAM.

TRIST(E) depressing, dismal, dull, gloomy, melancholy, sad, sorrowful, tryst, valse

TRISTRAM *beloved* isaude, isault, iseult, isolde, isolt(a), isoude, isult, yseut, ysolde, ysolt
charger passe-brewell
dog leon, lion

foster-father roald, rual
home lyonesse
parent blanchefleur, blancheflor, meliadus, rivalin
uncle mark(e)
victim morolt
villain melot

TRISTRAM SHANDY *author* sterne
character corporal trim, dr slop, lefevre, uncle tody, widow wadman, yorick

TRITE banal, boring, bromidic, common(place), conventional, corny, cut and dried, dull, familiar, flat, frayed, fusty, hackneyed, hoary, inane, insipid, jejune, motheaten, musty, obsolete, old(hat), ordinary, platitudinous, prosaic, rusty, set, shopworn, stale, stereotyped, stock, threadbare, timeworn, tiresome, tritical, trivial, usual, vapid, worn(out)
saying bromide, cliche, corn, platitude, saw

TRITICUM amelcorn, speltz, wheat

TRITON eft, evet, newt, salamander, shell, snail, trumpet
home aegae
parent amphitrite, neptune, poseidon
shell murex
trumpet conch

TRITONIA blazingstar, montbretia

TRITURATE bray, bruise, comminute, grind, pulverize, rub, thrash

TRITURUS molge, newt, salamander

TRIUMFETTA akonge, burbark

TRIUMPH achieve, bellringer, boast, celebration, conquer, conquest, defeat, exalt, exult(ation), festivity, flourish, joy, jubilation, kiki, killing, mastery, overcome, persimmon, prevail, prosper, rout, scalp, sensation, shut out, succeed, success, surmount, trump, victory, weather, win
exclamation grig, heuch, hooch, hooray, hurrah

TRIUMPHANT conqueror, exultant, jubilant, magnificent, rejoicing, successful, victorious

TRIUMVIRATE *1st* caesar, crassus, pompey
2nd lepidus, mark antony, octavius

TRIVET brandise, brandreth, knife, spider, stand, support, teapoy, trestle, trevet, tripod

TRIVIA bit, chaff, claptrap, crossroads, details, diana, doits, foam, frippery, froth, gimcrackery, hecate, minutiae, narrischkeit, pushpin, rubbish, trash, trifles, trumpery

TRIVIAL banal, childish, common(place), doggerel, empty, fidfad, flimsy, foolish, footle, footling, fribbling, frivolous, frothy, futile, idle, inane, insignificant, leger, light, little, meager, mean, measly, nugacious, nugatory, ordinary, paltry, petty, picayune, piddling, puny, shallow, silly, slight, small, superficial, tenuous, thin, tiddl(e)y, tiddy, trifling, trinkety, trite, unimportant, unworthy, worthless

TRIVIUM grammar, logic, rhetoric

TROCHE button, cachunde, coughdrop, lozenge, pastil(e), pill, rotula, tablet, trochiscus

TROCHEE choree, choreus

TROCHILUS crocodilebird, goldcrest, hummingbird, scotia, warbler

TROD footpath, footstep, path, trace, track, tread, walk

TROEZEN *harbor* pogon
king pittheus
native son theseus

TROG bargain, barter

TROGGER peddler, vagrant

TROGLODYTIC spelean

TROGON que(t)zal, tocororo

TROILUS *and cressida, author* chaucer, shakespeare
and cressida, character achilles, aeneas, agamemnon, ajax, alexander, andromache, antenor, calchas, cassandra, cressida, deiphobus, diomedes, hector, helen, margarelon, nestor, pandarus, paris, patroclus, thersites, ulysses
consort cressida

enemy ajax
horse galathe
kin hector, paris
parent apollo, hecuba, priam
rival diomed
slayer achilles

TROJAN (See also TROY.) dardanian, ilian, teucri, troic
horse ambush, ruse, trap
horse builder epeus
horse designer sinon
war cause helen
war, 1st victim protesilaus
war herald periphas
war leader agamemnon, menelaus
war truce violator pandarus
women, author euripedes

TROKE barter, deal, exchange, negotiate, traffic

TROLL allure, angle, bowl, cart, catch, circulate, demon, dwarf, entice, fish, giant, gnome, harl(e), lure, propel, pull, ramble, reel, repetition, revolve, roll, round, routine, run, sing, song, spin, trawl, trolley, trollop, trundle, turn, wag, walk, warble

TROLLER fisherman, moocher, singer

TROLLEY barrow, block, car(riage), cart, caster, handcar, lace, pully, sledge, streetcar, teacart, tram(car), truck, wheel

TROLLOP beat, dange, dollop, doxy, drab, draggletail, floozy, frump, gad, hang, hurry, PROSTITUTE, slattern, slouch, slump, slut, strumpet, thrash, trollimog, trull, wanton, whore

TROLLOPE, ANTHONY *work* ayala's angel, barchester towers, can you forgive her, doctor thorne, orley farm, phineas finn, sir harry hotspur of humblethwaite, the american senator, the belton estate, the claverings, the last chronicle of barset, the pallisers, the prime minister, the warden

TROMBENIK blowhard, braggart, fake, fourflusher, glutton, idler, phony

TROMBONE blunderbuss, busine, gun, horn, posaune, sackbut, sambuke, sliphorn, tram

playing style tailgate
TROMMEL buddle, screen, sieve
TROMPILLO nightshade, prairieberry
TRONDHEIM nidaros
TRONE market, pillory, scale, truant
TROOP(S) army, assembly, associate, band, battery, collection, comitiva, company, consort, crew, crowd, flock, gathering, ging, group, horde, host, legion, lot, march, multitude, parade, party, press, quantity, ressala, risala, rought, rout, school, solak, squad, swarm, throng, tichel, troupe, turm, wered
array parel
assault wave
assembling muster
cavalry cornet
commander captain
concealed ambush
formation column, echelon
light-armed psiloi
position enfilade
provisioner sutler, vivandiere
quarters barracks, camp, cantonment, etape
raise conscript, draft
TROOPER bargeer, bargir, cavalryman, hussar, rutter, soldier, transport
TROPE differentia, irony, metaphor, metonymy, synecdoche
TROPHIMUS *aide to* paul
TROPHONIUS *brother* agamedes
father erginus
TROPHY award, chaplet, crown, cup, edgar, emmy, garland, guerdon, honor, laurel, medal, memento, memorial, oscar, palm, plume, prize, reward, scalp, spoils, token, tony, wreath
TROPIC boundary, circle, limit, solar, zone
of cancer, capricorn
TROPICAL hot, steamy, sweltering, torrid
alligator caiman, cayman
almond malabar
amphibian caecilian
animal aardvark, agama, agouti, alco, anteater, coati, eyra, iguana, peccary, potto, tapir
ant army, driver, legionary
apricot mammea

bat flying-fox
bird ani, bananaquit, boatbill, boatswain, booby, bushshrike, cacicus, coereba, cotinga, frigate, jacmar, jaeger, jalap, manakin, motmot, thickknee, tody, toucan, trogon, wigtail
buckthorn colubrina
cactus bleo, cardoncillo, pitahay, rhipsalis, tasajillo
clay laterite
crustacean boxcrab, calappa
cuckoo ani
disease aden ulcer, ainhum, buba(s), dengue fever, dhobie itch, frambesia, junglerot, pian, pinta, sprue, yaws
dog alco
dolphin inia
drink sangaree
fern adiantopsis, adiantum, alsophila, basket, bird's-foot, blechnum, cheilanthes, maidenhair, nephrolepsis, pellaea, rockbrake, sword
fever breakbone, calenture, dandy, dengue
fiber istle
fiber cloth pina
fish anableps, astropecten, balao, balloon, barb, barracuda, carpetshark, cavalla, cero, chromid, coachman, coelho, danid, gerres, halfbeak, inia, louvar, manta, mojarra, opah, paco, pintado, ray, remora, rivulus, robalo, salema, sargo, scarid, sparid, squetee, tinosa, toro, warsaw
food taro
fruit avocado, balimbing, banana, bastard-fig, breadfruit, canistel, carambola, cashew apple, ciruela, coconut, custard apple, date, durian, guava, inga, jackfruit, kamrakh, lichee, litchi, longan, loquat, mango (steen), papaw, papaya, passion fruit, pawpaw, pineapple, plantain, roseapple, sapodilla, sapote, soursop, sugar apple, sweetsop, tamarind
fungus balanophorace
grass alang, bamboo, bambusa, camalote, canabrava, imperata, vetiver
grunt burrito, roncador
hat terai, topee, topi

herb achimenes, ageratum, altea, amaranth, arisaema, aristolochia, bacopa, barbados lily, billygoat(weed), bloodberry, boerhavis, bouvardia, bramia, caapeba, cajanus, caladium, capsicum, catjang, celosia, cowpea, coxcomb, evea, galinsoga, gesneria, gomphrena, guzmania, indigofera, irongrass, kalanchoe, kosteletzkya, laportea, manyroot, pareria, pigeonpea, piperaca, pothomorphe, puchero, ramtil, red pepper, renealmia, rivina, rupturewort, sage, sesamum, sida, tacca, thunbergia, triumfetta, urena, veronia, zinnia
hummingbird coquette
insect termite
jay motmot
lizard agama, teioid
mallow altea, escoba, temauve
monkey araba
moonseed cissampelos
morning glory monkey-vine
moth anaphe
orchid angraceum, bletia, cattleya, coelogyne, epidendron
palm attalea, corozo, coyol, cycad, euterpe
plant abelmost, abutilon, acanthus, agave, ageratum, alacad, algalia, alocasia, aloe, alonsoa, altea, ananas, angraecum, anthurium, aphelandra, arrowroot, arum, bacchar, banana, billbergia, bleo, bomarea, breadfruit, bromelia, browallia, cacoon, caladium, calalu, canna, capsicum, cassava, cereza, ceriman, cosmos, cowhage, crinum, croton, cube, dal, dasheen, figwort, fuchsia, gardenia, geonoma, hamelia, hibiscus, isoloma, lantana, liana, liane, maholtine, mallow, mangrove, manioc, musa, pepino, pineapple, pinquin, poinsettia, redwithe, rhoeo, romerillo, ruellia, sida, soja, taro, tillandsia, triurid, udo, yautia, yucca, zamia
plant disease blackblight, brownroot
plum icaco
resin copal

shrub aalii, abelia, abrus, abutilon, adelia, anapanapa, ardisia, asis, avicennia, bauhinia, baybay, bignonia, boucardia, broomwood, bursara, byrsonima, camara, capsicum, cestrum, coffee, colima, derris, escambron, fanflower, flueggea, frangipane, frangipani, fuchsia, gooseberry, hamelia, henna, huisache, inga, ipecac, ixora, lantana, lawsonia, lippia, majo, matico, mimosa, mombin, nerium, olacad, peabush, persea, physalis, pilea, poinciana, quina, randia, rapanea, retama, sabia, sida, soapbark, strongbark, toothwort, torolillo, trema, triumfetta, yawweed, zorillo

snake bushmaster, coral, fer de lance, mussurana

snuff cohoba

sore buba

spider nephila

spurge alchornea

starfish astropecten

storm bagio, baguio, bayamo, chubasco, cordonazo, cyclone, hurricane, tornado, typhoon, willywilly

tern noddy

tick talaje

tree 3 apa 4 agba, akee, asak, ates, atta, aulu, bago, ceba, coco, cola, dali, eboe, ekki, etua, guao, inga, mabi, majo, olax, shea, yaya 5 abura, acapu, amate, aniba, anime, arjan, artar, asoka, assai, balsa, banak, bendy, bongo, cacao, cocoa, couma, cycas, dalli, fotui, guama, guara, guava, icica, ilama, jigua, mahoe, mango, maria, nepal, nitta, njave, papaw, pooli, quina, seron, siris, tarfa, unona, uvito, vitex, zorro 6 acacia, achras, andira, annona, arenga, asokaa, baboen, bacury, bakula, balata, banago, banana, baobab, barbas, bustic, calaba, carapa, carica, cashew, cassia, cazaba, cedron, chupon, clusia, colima, dagame, espave, fustic, genipa, hackia, itauba, lebbek, mammee, mombin, panama, papaya, pawpaw, per-

sea, randia, sapota, yautia 7 achiote, angelin, annatto, annonce, anubing, arnatto, attalea, avocado, bactris, calabur, capulin, caulote, copaiba, cowtree, dattock, ehretia, eugenia, gateado, gauzuma, guacimo, lapacho, majagua, rapania, sandbox, soursop, surette, ximenia, xylopia 8 amaranth, amarillo, axmaster, bauhinia, beefwood, bindoree, breadnut, brosimum, camuning, casearia, cecropia, cedrella, cocobolo, corkwood, dividivi, etaballi, fraxinus, funtumia, garcinia, guaiacum, ironwood, mahogany, mangrove, mulberry, muskwood, mutingia, patashte, rosewood, sebesten, silkwood, sucupira, sweetsop, tamarind, zapatero 9 adansonia, axemaster, balanites, billywebb, blackwood, cauchillo, couratari, dalbergia, huamuchil, machineel, marlberry, physicnut, poinciana, quebracho, quinquino, rauwolfia, roseapple, sapodilla, sapotilla, satinleaf, sterculia, theobroma, tibourbou, zebrawood 10 allophylus, anacardium, billetwood, caimitillo, calliandra, chandelier, flamboyant, frangipane, jack-in-a-box, paddlewood, sandalwood 11 canafistulo, candleabrum, flowerfence, trumpetwood 12 barringtonia 13 marmalade tree, peacockflower

vine abrus, abuta, allamanda, bejuco, canavalia, cassabanana, catjang, ceriman, cow(h)age, cowitch, cucurbita, curuba, gooseflower, guaco, ipomoea, liane, moonseed, palay, passiflora, pereskia, thunbergia

weed basketwithe

wildcat eyra

wind antitrade, trade

yam cushcush

TROS *consort* callirrhoe

grandfather dardanus

kingdom phrygia

parent astyoche, callirhoe, erichthonius

son assaracus, ganymedes, ilus

TROT bustle, canter, child, crib, dance, fadge, gallop, hasten, hurry, jog, line, lope, oldster, pace, pad, piaffe(r), pony, rack, run, toddler, tot, translation, trig, walk

along depart, leave

out introduce, manifest, produce, submit

TROTH belief, betroth(al), certie, certy, engagement, faith, fidelity, loyalty, pledge, promise, trogs, trough, truth, veracity, verity

TROTHLESS disloyal, faithless, untruthful

TROTTOIR path, pavement, sidewalk

TROTWOOD, BETSY *nephew* david copperfield

TROUBADOUR bard, blondel, gleeman, jongleur, minnesinger, minstrel, poet, rhym(st)er, scald, scop, singer, sordello, trouvere, vocalist

poem partimen

song alba

TROUBLE abash, ado, adversity, afflict(ion), agitate, agitation, ail, anger, annoy, anxiety, bore, bother(ation), burden, caddle, calamity, care, cark, catastrophe, chagrin, coil, concern, cumber, curse, difficulty, disadvantage, discomfit, discommode, disease, disorder, displeasure, disquiet, distract, distress, disturbance, dither, dretch, drove, drubble, effort, embarrass, exertion, failure, fash, fike, grief, hardship, hassle, headache, heartscald, hell, hoe, hurt, ills, incommode, inconvenience, inflict, irk, kiaugh, labor, load, mar, matter, meddle, misfortune, molest, nuisance, onus, pain(s), perturb, pester, plague, pother, problem, put out, puzzle, rigor, sore, sorrow, stir, storm, sturt, sussy, tease, threat, toil, torment, trachle, trevail, trial, tribulation, turmoil, tweak, unrufe, uproar, upset, vex, wandreth, woe, worrit, worry

-mirth spoilsport

TROUBLED afflicted, anx-

ious, careful, disturbed, dretched, drubly, drumly, fretful, harassed, hassled, in hot water, perturbed, queasy, solicitous, worried

TROUBLEMAKER agitator, bodgie, breedbate, firebrand, gossip, gremlin, hellion, hoodlum, instigator, nuisance, stormy-petrel

TROUBLESOME afflicted, annoying, awkward, bothersome, burdensome, cumbersome, difficult, disquieting, distressing, disturbing, fashious, fikie, grueling, harmful, heavy, hefty, irksome, laborious, onerous, operose, oppressive, painful, perverse, pesky, pestilent, plaguy, refractory, spiteful, sticky, trying, turbulent, uneasy, unruly, untoward, vexatious, wearisome, weighty

TROUBLOUS afflicted, agitated, muddy, restless, stormy, **TROUBLED,** turbulent, turbulous

TROUGH back(et), bakie, basin, bosh, bowl, box, buddle, channel, chase, chute, coffin, conduit, cove, cradle, dail, dale, dike, dorr, drain, dugout, furrow, gutter, hod, hollow, hutch, laver, manger, moat, shute, sink, strake, tank, tom, tomb, toper, tray, trench, trogue, trug, valley, wallow
eaves canal, cheneau
glacial dorr
inclined chute, tom
mining sluice
shallow wooden backet, bakie
sheep-dip dup
smelting bosh
wooden bakie, trogue, trug

TROUNCE assail, beat, canvass, censure, cudgel, defeat, flog, indict, journey, punish, ramble, scold, sue, thrash, tramp, whomp

TROUPE act, barnstorm, cast, company, cuadrilla, group, performers, TROOP

TROUPER actor, mime, mummer, performer, player, thespian

TROUPIAL blackbird, grackle, oriole

TROUSERS bags, bell bottoms, bermudas, bloomers, blue jeans, breeches, breeks,

breekums, britches, buckskins, cords, denims, ducks, dungarees, flannels, galligaskins, hose, jamaica shorts, jeans, jodhpurs, kerseys, kickseys, kicksies, knickerbockers, knickers, levis, moleskins, nankeens, nankins, overalls, pajamas, pantaloons, pants, pedalpushers, pegtops, plus fours, pyjamas, rompers, shintiyan, shorts, slacks, strides, tartans, tights, trews, trunks, tweeds, whites
bottom cuff, turnup
divest of debag
edge crease
foreign calzoneras, shakshear, shalwar, shintiyan, shulwaurs
leg slop
opening fly, placket, spare, zipper
pocket becket, fob, prat
strap bowyang
tartan trews

TROUT alekey, aureolus, aurora, bass, bodieron, boregat, brook(ie), brownie, char(r), coaster, cutthroat, finnoc, galaxiid, gil(l)aroo, greenling, grilse, hardhead, hardtail, herling, kamloops, kelt, kipper, lake(r), longe, lunge, malma, mykiss, namaycush, oquassa, peal, pogy, pounder, quasky, rainbow, saibling, salmo(nd), salter, scurling, sewen, sewin, skirling, siscowet, speckled, splake, squet(ee), steelhead, taimen, togue, trucha, truff, trutta, tuladi, waha, weakfish
-bird plover
blackspotted cutthroat
blueblack oquassa
gray weakfish
group hover
lake longe, lunge, namaycush, splake
parasite sug
pert. truttaceous
rainbow steelhead
red-spotted dolly varden
rock bodieron, boregat, greenling
-shad squeteague
small fingerling, scurling, skirling
tahoe pogy
young whitling

TROUVAILLE find, godsend, windfall

TROUVERE See TROUBADOUR.

TROW barge, belief, believe, boat, catamaran, covenant, expect, faith, fancy, hope, smack, suppose, think, troll, trough, trust

TROWEL darby, dogtail, dredge, float, leaf, llana, scoop, spreader, taper, tool, trewel, trulla
dress with strike
molder's dogtail, leaf, taper

TROWELBEAK broadbill

TROY (See also TROJAN.) hissarlik, iliac, ilian, ilion, ilium, teucrian, troas, truva
ally adamas, amphius, antiphus, aruns, asteropasus, asterope, pelagon, periphetes, phorbas, rhesus, rhigmus, scylaceus
ancestor dardanus
archer philoctetes
augur ennomus
captor agamemnon, charidemus, hercules
chief alcathous
commander antenor
discoverer schliemann
diviner eurydamas
epic aeneid, iliad, odyssey
founder iasion, ilus, tros
herald eumedes
hero aeneas, agenor, ajais, ajax, alcon, amopaon, antimachus, antiphates, dardan, eneas, euphorbus, hector, ialmenus, ilioneus, iphition, namath, palamedes, paris, sthenelaux, xanthus
king laomedon, paris, priam, teucer
mountain ida
people See TROJAN.
priest calchas
prince aeneas, anchises, eneas, hector, helenus, paris
princess ilione
region troad, troas
serpent victim laocoon
site hissarlik
slave sinon
soothsayer calchas, helenus
weight grain, ounce, pennyweight, pound
youth simoisius

TRUANT absent(ee), beggar, hobo, idle, laggard, meecher, micher, straggler, sundowner, tramp, trivant,

trone, trout, vagabond, vagrant
play bum, ditch, miche, skip, trone
TRUCE armistice, break, breather, cease-fire, cessation, compact, halt, lull, pact, pause, pax, peace, relief, reprieve, respite, treve
cry for barla, barl(e)y
flag kartel
TRUCIAL STATES abu dhabi, ajman, dubai, fujaira, gulf sheikdoms, qashran, ras al-khaima, sharjah, sheikdoms, umm al-qaiwain, united arab emirates
language arabic, english, persian
people arabs, baluchis, indians, pakistanis, persians
TRUCK barter, bogie, buggie, buggy, bummer, bunk, business, camion, car(t), carrier, commerce, corf, dance, deal, dolly, dray, drugge, exchange, handcart, haulaway, jeep, lorry, move, negotiate, nonsense, peddle, pickup, potter, produce, rubbish, sleeper, trade, traffic, transfer, transport, trash, trivia, trolley, trundle, van, vehicle, wagon, wheel, wynn
amphibious duck
armored brinks
coal dan
detention of demurrage
driver See TRUCKER.
heavy drug(ge)
lumber drug, wynn
mining barney, corf
towing wrecker
-trailer semi
TRUCKER barterer, driver, gipsy, gypsy, huckster, peddler, teamster
TRUCKLE barter, bend, bootlick, car, castor, cheese, court, cower, cringe, deal, defer, fawn, kneel, knuckle, nuckle, pander, slaver, submit, tag, toady, trail, trundle, wheel, yield
TRUCKLER bootlicker, sycophant, toady
TRUCULENT barbarous, base, belligerent, brutal, cruel, destructive, fell, ferocious, fierce, frightening, harsh, hostile, inhuman, intimidating, mean, menac-

ing, mercenary, savage, scathing, vitriolic
TRUDGE hake, hike, jog, march, pace, plod, slog, stodge, stumble, trace, traipse, tramp, trapes, trapse, trek, wade, walk
TRUE accurate, actual, adjust, aline, authentic, bona fide, certain, constant, correct, dependable, devoted, direct, even, exact, fac(k), factual, faithful, fidele, firm, genuine, germane, good, honest, just, leal, legitimate, level, literal, loyal, official, orthodox, perfect, plumb, precise, proper, pure, real, regular, reliable, resolute, right, scrupulous, sincere, sta(u)nch, steadfast, steady, straight, tried, trustworthy, unerring, unfeigned, upright, valid, veracious, veridical, veritable, vero, very, virtuous, vrai
as the gospel
bill arraignment, indictment
-blue faithful, fidelity, gentleman, loyal(ty), orthodox(y), sta(u)nch
comb. aletho, ortho
love beloved, sweetheart, trillium
name meaning vera
to fact literal
to form characteristic, consistent, realistic, typical
up adjust, regulate
TRUFF deceive, steal, trick, trifle, trout, turf
TRUFFLE earthball, earthnut, fungus, ground-chestnut, mushroom, tuber
hunter hog, pig
TRUISM adage, axiom, banality, bromide, cliche, commonplace, inanity, maxim, platitude, postulate, saw, sooth
TRULL blowze, callet, girl, lass, PROSTITUTE, strumpet, wanton, wench
TRULY accurately, actually, amen, atweel, awat, certainly, dinkum, duly, exactly, faithfully, genuinely, honestly, indeed, justly, legally, properly, really, rightly, sincerely, soothly, syker, truthfully, verament, verily, veritably, witterly, yea

TRUMAN, HARRY *birthplace* lamar, missouri
program fair deal, marshall plan
TRUMP ace, beat, brick, cap, deceive, impose(on), jewsharp, nob, nonplus, outdo, palm off, polt, proboscis, ruff, sound, topnotcher, trachea, TRUMPET, tube
ace tib
card atout, atutti, basta, deckhead, deece, dix, manille, matador, menel, nell, nob, pam, pedro, playboy, polt, ponto, punt, sancho, spadille, tib, tiddy, triumph, triunfo, trombe, turn-up, wenzel
game beast, bridge, comet, dreiblatt, ecarte, euchre, five-hundred, forty-five, hasenpfeffer, julepe, lanterloo, loo, lue, maw, mistigri, nap (oleon), pamphilius, peep, rams, ronda, rounce, triomphe, triumph
hand without chicane
queen bella
up adduce, allege, concoct, devise, fabricate, frame, miscolor, misrepresent
TRUMPERY deceit, deception, finery, fraud, gimcrack, mockado, nonsense, rubbish, showy, trash(y), trickery, trivia, twaddle, weeds, worthless
TRUMPET alchemy, bene, blare, blazon, bozine, buc(c)in(a), bugle, clarion, conch, cornet, horn, kerana, lituus, lure, narsinga, proclaim, salpinx, shofar, slughorn, sourdine, toot, trombe, tube, tulnic, watercup
bell codon, pavillon
blare fanfare, tantara
blow tubicinate
call dian(a), reveille, sennet, taps
creeper bignonia, catalpa, cowhage, foxglove, hellvine, indian bean, tecoma
fish bellowsfish, flutemouth, snipefish, swellfish
flower crossvine, datura, oleander
group fanfare
-like buccinal
-like instrument bugle, sax(aphone), tuba
lily bermuda lily, easter lily

mouth bell, codon, pavillon
mute pipe, so(u)rdine
shell triton
sound blare, clarion
valveless clarino
vine tecoma
TRUMPETER agami, bird, fish, herald, jacamin, latris, perch, pigeon, psophia, swan, tooter, trout, tubicen, yakamik
fish moki(hi)
perch mabo, mado, therapon
TRUMPETWEED boneset, joepye, wild lettuce
TRUMPETWOOD cecropia, imbauba, slothtree
TRUNCATE cut, dock, lessen, lop, premorse, shorten, trunk
TRUNCATED abbreviated, cut(off)(short), deformed, docked, maimed, shortened, stubbed
TRUNCHEON baton, beat, blackjack, club, cudgel, cut, fragment, scepter, splinter, staff, stem, stick, trunk, worm
TRUNDLE bed, bowl, cart, caster, course, departure, hoop, path, propel, revolve, roll(er), rotate, rull, troll, truck(le), tub, twirl, wheel, whirl
tail cur, dog, mongrel
TRUNK bagatelle, baggage, body, bogie, bole, boot, bouk, caber, carcass, chest, chute, coffer, conduit, corpse, corsage, curtail, fishtank, launder, lobsterpot, locker, lop, maim, nose, pipe, pool, proboscis, saratoga, shaft, sluice, snout, soma, stem, stock, stowage, tank, telescope, thorax, torso, truncate, tube
fossil cycad
line mainline, railroad
small hatbox
tree bole, butt, mast, stick
unhewn arigue
way canal
TRUNKFISH aracana, boxfish, chapin, cowfish, ostracion
TRUSS arrange, betake, bind, bracket, bundle, cantilever, costume, cradle, depart, dress, fasten, frock, furl, hang, lade, load, modillion, pack(age), secure, seize, skewer, span, stomacher,

strengthen, support, tie, tighten, tuck in, wap, warren
up kilt
TRUST accredit, assurance, belief, believe, betrothal, care, cartel, certitude, charge, coalition, commenda, commission, commit, confide(nce), conglomerate, consign, consortium, conviction, corner, count, creance, credence, credit, custody, depend(ence), duty, enterprise, equity, expect, faith, fiduciary, hope, keeping, lippen, lite, loyalty, monopoly, pool, promise, reliance, rely, repose, security, slew, syndicate, task, token, trew, trig, trow, truth, zaibatsu
deed mortgage
fund wakf, waqf, wukf
kind charitable, clifford, irrevocable, living, remainder, revocable, testamentary
TRUSTEE agent, depositary, depository, feofee, fiduciary, mutwalli, sindico, treasurer
TRUSTFUL artless, confident, confiding, credulous, devoted, reliant, unquestioning
TRUSTLESS distrustful, treacherous, unreliable
TRUSTWORTHINESS axiopisty, credence, honesty, honor, reliability
TRUSTWORTHY authentic, believable, certain, confidential, confiding, constant, credible, dependable, faithful, fiducial, honest, kosher, plausible, reliable, safe, secure, si(c)ker, solid, sooth, sound, stanch, sure, syker, tried, upright, veracious
TRUSTY confiding, convict, feckful, gentleman, loyal, reliable, staunch, trig,
TRUSTFUL, TRUSTWORTHY
TRUTH actuality, authenticity, beauty, belief, betroth(al), certainty, constancy, exactness, fact, faith, fealty, fidelity, good(s), gospel, horse's mouth, inside(story), integrity, light, loyalty, orthodoxy, pledge, poop, precision, reality, right, sattya,

scoop, sincerity, tao, troth, trust, veracity, veridity, veriment, veritas, verity
blindness to avidya, avijja
comb. aleth(o)
deity alethia, maat, mithras, sattva, una
denial of heresy
drug amobarbital, pentothal, scopolamine, thiopental
ideal christ, dharma
lover philalethist
name meaning alice
path tao
personified alethia, veritas
pert. alethic
seeming verisimilitude
self-evident adage, axiom, truism
study alethiology
symbolic color white
ultimate light, sunyata
universal axiom
TRUTHFUL accurate, candid, fair, frank, guileless, honest, ingenuous, open, outspoken, reliable, scrupulous, sincere, sooth, TRUE, unfeigned, veracious, veridic(al), veritable, very, worthy
TRY adjudge, afflict, aim, annoy, arbitrate, ascertain, aspire, assay, attempt, audition, beset, bid, bother, choose, contest, court-martial, crack, demonstrate, effort, endeavor, erst, essay, ettle, examine, experience, experiment, extract, fling, fraist, grieve, han(d)sel, harass, hear, inspect, irritate, judge, melt, pester, plague, practice, prove, purify, rack, referee, refine, render, sample, screen, search, select, separate, shot, sieve, sift, stab, start, strain, strive, struggle, take a shot at, taste, tax, tempt, test, torment, trial, trouble, undertake, use, venture, vex, whack, work
again repeat, retest
casual fling
hard agonize, strive
one's temper aggravate, annoy, exasperate, irritate
-out audition, check, demonstration, dry run, experiment, practice, rehearsal, test, trial, workout
out fat render
TRYING annoying, bothersome, crucial, difficult, gru-

eling, hard, pestilent(ial), provocative, severe, troublesome

for out to

TRYSAIL spencer

TRYST affair, afflict, agreement, appoint(ment), assignation, beguile, bespeak, betroth(al), date, engagement, fair, fix, gathering, invite, market, meet(ing), order, rendezvous, visit

TSAR See CZAR.

TSARITSYN stalingrad, volgograd

TSEDDODELT, TSEDRAYT confused, crackpot, crank, demented, kook, lunatic, nut, wacky

TSETSE dipteran, gandi, glossina, kivu, trypanosoma
disease encephalitis, nagana, sleeping sickness, trypanosomiasis

TSHI *tribe* akan, akim, akwapim, ashanti, fanti, twi

TSINE benteng, wild ox

TSITSER bystander, clucker, kibbitzer, onlooker, sympathizer

TSO(U)RISS suffering, troubles, woes, worries

T-SQUARE ruler

TSUBA *kind* shitogi
part seppa(dai)

TSUGA hemlock, pine

TSWANA bechuana, chwana, sechuana

TUAMOTU *island* gambier

TUAREG See BERBER.

TUATARA guana, guano, hatterion, iguana

TUATHA *battle* magtuireadh
chief dagda, nuada
enemies fomorians
goddess danu
successors milesians

TUB back, basin, bath(e), boat, bowie, bowl, breaker, bucket, butterball, cask, container, cowl, dan, eshin, fatty, fire engine, firkin, gaal, gawn, gig, gyle, hod, hogshead, keeler, keeve, kid, kimnel, kit, kiver, knap, knop, kooliman, pan, piggin, pot, pulpit, rack, shaub, ship, skeel, soa, soe, tank(ard), tosh, tram, tun, turnel, tynd, vat, vessel, wash
brewer's back, keeve
butter cool
hunter parasite, sponge(r)

laundry washtray
mining corf
ore tina
tanning leach
wooden kimnel, kit, soe, trundle

TUBA bass, beno, bombardon, cloud, euphonium, helicon, horn, liquor, physic nut, samoyed, sap, saxhorn, tree, trumpet, tube
mouthpiece bocal

TUBAL *friend* shylock
kin japheth, noah

TUBALCAIN *parent* lamech, zillah

TUBBY chunky, clumsy, fat, obese, round, stubby, thick

TUBE ampoule, ampul(e), audion, bombilla, bore, bouch, bronchus, buret(te), canal, cannel, cannon, cannula, cartridge, channel, chute, column, conduit, cylinder, diode, drain, duct, fistula, funnel, gullet, hose, main, nozzle, orthicon, penstock, pipe(line), pipet(te), pitot, reed, siphon, sipper, snorkel, stem, straw, subway, tap, telescope, television, tremie, triode, tunnel, uptake
balloon appendix
bone snuffer
distilling tower
efflux adjutage
electrode audion
electronic diode, driver, kylstron, pliotron
fireworks leader
flexible hose
glandular crypt
glass dropper, matrass, pipette, sight, sipper, straw
hollow calcar
honey nectary, siphonet
knitted stocking
paper leader, pastille, straw
pastry cornet
pert. cannular, capillary, tubate
pollen spermary
priming auget
rectifier ignitron
remove by siphon, syphon
silk spigot
speaking gosport
sucking straw
surgical drain
system of pipage
tapering burette
thermometer stem
vacuum audion, diode, dyna-

tron, heptode, hexode, keyer, triode

TUBER annealer, anu, anyu, beet, bulb, clog, creeler, earthnut, eddo, jalap, jicama, murrnong, node, oca, oka, parsnip, pignut, potato, root, rutabaga, salep, sett, shoot, skewerer, sunchoke, taro, truffle, tugui, turnip, wapata, winder, yam(p), yautia

TUBERCLE acrorhagus, cuspule, excrescence, nodule, pearl, projection, prominence, protuberance, stemma, swelling, verruca

TUBERCULOSIS angleberry, clyers, consumption, decline, marasmus, phthisis, scrofula
animal clyers
military granulitis
pert. phthisic
remedy asbolin
test mantoux

TUBFISH gurnard

TUBMAN attendant, barrister, cooper, preacher

TUCHIN *house* yamen

TUCK appetite, beat, blast, blow, consume, cover, cram(p), draw, eat, enclose, energy, estoc, feast, flange, fold, food, gather, gird, hamper, hide, insert, kilt, lap, life, nip, pinch, pleat, pluck, rapier, restrict, ruche, scold, shorten, spirit, stuff, sword, toke, torment, torture, truss, tug, upbraid, wrap
in appetite, consume, cover, devour, eat, feast, insert, jam, retire, spread, stuff, trouss, truss, wrap
-shop confectioner's
up exhaust, fake, fatigue, hang, kilt, wear out

TUCKAHOE arum, indianloaf, orantium, peltandra, poria, virginian

TUCKED *up* contracted, cramped, exhausted, hampered, spent

TUCKER board, bore, chemisette, collar, corder, deplete, exhaust, fag, fatigue, food, fuller, irk, jade, kilter, meals, pleater, rations, tire, weary

TUDOR *ruler* edward, elizabeth, henry, mary
symbol rose

TUESDAY dienstag, mardi, martedi, martes
god tiu, tiw, tyr
shrove mardi gras

TUFA, TUFF limestone, peperino, porodite, santorin, toph, trass, travertine

TUFT aigrette, alula, arbuscule, beard, beat, brush, bunch, clump, cluster, coma, cop, cowlick, crest, down, fetlock, fleck, floccule, flock, forelock, goatee, hulu, imperial, pile, plume, rouse, ruff, scopula, shock, stupa, tassel, thrum, topknot, tussock, wisp
-bearing byssiferous
bristly birse
comb. lophi(o)
downy frieze
feather egret, hulu
hair brush, cowlick, floccus, switch, topknot, tuzz
having crested
-hunter snob, sycophant, toady
on horse's hoof fetlock
ornamental panache
pert. comal, comoge, tappet
wool flock, fob, tusk, tuzz

TUFTED barbate, byssiferous, cespitose, clustered, comiferous, comose, crested, stupose, tappit, topknotted

TUG boat, chain, chug, contend, contest, drag, draw, drudge, effort, exert, hale, harness, haul, hook, labor, lug, maul, ply, pull, rope, strain, strap, strive, struggle, toil, tow(boat), trace, tracker, tuck, tussle

TUI honeyeater, koko, parsonbird, poebird, tuwi

TUITION care, custody, education, fees, guardianship, instruction, payment, protection, teaching

TULE arundo, bulrush, cattail, pickerelweed, reed, scirpus
hen coot, crowduck
potato or root wapatoo

TULIP *cheek* lalla-rookh
disease shanking
kind bouton d'or, breeder, brunnehilde, butterfly, calochortus, cottage, darwin, globe, lilium, lily, parrot, turnsole
orchid cattleya
source bulb

tree aspen, banana-shrub, basswood, canoewood, cucumber, pajagua, poplar, waratah
wood auburn, emu-apple, sour plum

TULLE illusion, kata, lace, mesh, net

TULLIVER, TOM *river* floss
sister maggie

TULSA *university* oral roberts

TUMBLE collapse, confusion, descend, dishevel, disorder, drop, fail, fall, fling, flop, grovel, happen, leap, mess, overthrow, pitch, precipitate, roll, rumple, run, rush, sault, slip, slope, spring, stumble, thrill, throw, tiffle, tipple, topple, toss, tousle, trip, veer, walter, wamble, welter, whemmel, whirl
down dilapidated, jerry-built, ramshackle, rickety, ruined, ruinous, shack, shaky

TUMBLER acrobat, athlete, balancer, barreler, cart, clothes drier, dove, drum(mer), dunker, glass, lever, pigeon, pin, pupa, rattler, roller, rumbler, tippler, toppler, tumbrel

TUMBLEWEED amaranth, bugseed, pigweed, rolypoly

TUMBREL barge, cart, cucking-stool, dumpcart, wagon

TUMEFY inflate, puff, swell

TUMID bloated, bombastic, bulging, bursting, distended, enlarged, fustian, inflated, plethoric, pompous, pretentious, protuberant, rhetorical, teeming, torose, torous, tumescent, turgent, turgid, swollen

TUMMEL commotion, disorder, noise

TUMMOCK brae

TUMMY See STOMACH.

TUMOR acanthoma, adenoma, ambury, amper, anbury, angioma, arrogance, atheroma, beal, blastoma, bombast, botch, bump, cancer, carcinoma, cat's-hair, cavernoma, cementoma, chloroma, chorioma, cyst(oma), dermoid, desmoid, ecchondroma, edema, embryoma, enameloma, enostosis, epulis, fibroid, glioma, gyroma, hematoma,

hepatoma, holdfast, keloid, lipoma, lump, luteoma, lymphoma, melanoma, moro, myeloma, myo(x)ma, neoformation, neoplasm, nevus, nuroma, odontoma, oncosis, osteoma, pap(illoma), phlegmon, phyma, pian, plasmoma, pomposity, psammoma, pustule, ranula, sarcoma, scirrhus, seminoma, swell(ing), teratoma, testudo, thymoma, uloncus, warble, wart, wen, windgall, yaw
benign acanthosis
bone osteoma
bone-marrow myeloma
cancerous carcinoma, sarcoma, scirrhus
comb. c(o)ele, oid, oma(s), omata, oncus
cystic galactocele
dark melanoma
eyelid grando
fatty lipoma
fibrous desmoid, fibroma, keloid
glandular adenoma
liver hepatoma
malignant carcinoma, sarcoma
muscular myoma
operation ancotomy
pert. systemoid
pustular blain
scalp testudo
skin cylindroma, ouch, phyma
small moro, pap, wen
soft ambury, figwart
study of oncology

TUMP carry, clump, drag, heap, hill, stack, tumulus

TUMULT ado, affray, agitation, altercation, babel, bedlam, bluster, bobbery, brawl, bustle, chaos, clamor, clatter, combustion, commotion, confusion, contention, convulsion, din, dirdum, discord, disorder, dissension, distraction, disturbance, emeute, ferment, fight, flurry, fracas, fray, furor, garboil, hubble, hubbub, hurlement, lurry, moil, mutiny, noise, pandemonium, quarrel, rabble, racket, revolt, riot, roust, row, ruction, ruffle, rummage, rumpus, shouting, squabble, steery, storm, strife, struggle, tempest,

turbulence, turmoil, uproar, violence, vociferation, whirl
place of bear garden
TUMULTUOUS agitated, boisterous, confused, disorderly, disturbed, furious, lawless, loud, noisy, riotous, rough, rude, stormy, turbulent, violent
TUMULUS bank, barrow, burian, dune, hillock, mote, mound, sepulchre, terrace, tomb, tump
TUN belly, bowl, carouser, cask, chimney(pot), cup, drink, guzzle, haab, jar, paunch, puncheon, stomach, store, town, tub, vat, vessel
1/3 tertian
1/2 pipe
20 katun
shell fossil dolite
TUNA ahi, albacore, atun, bigeye, bluefin, bluefish, bonita, bonito, eel, kawakawa, maguro, opuntia, pelamyd, prickly-pear, skipjack, thunnus, TUNNY, yellowfin
TUND beat, bruise, cudgel, pound
TUNDRA See PLAIN.
TUNE accordance, adapt, adjust, air, aria, catch, choral(e), correspond, dial, fix, guajira, guaracha, habanera, harmonize, harmony, height, hum, intonation, key, leed, lilt, melisma, melody, melos, modulate, mood, pitch, play, reconcile, round, sonance, song, sound, spring, strain, temper, tone, train
country hoedown
dance anglaise, furiant, galliard, hornpipe
down decrease, moderate, soften
dull dra(u)nt
folk fado
in get with
mournful dirge, dump
out disregard, ignore
out of scordato
TUNEFUL chantant, concordant, dulcet, euphonious, harmonious, melodic, melodious, musical, sweet
TUNER diapason, pitchpipe
TUNGSTEN cals, scheelin, scheelite, wolfram
alloy carboloy

TUNGSTITE ocher, ochre
TUNGUS *tribe* evenk, lamut, olcha, olchi, orochon, orokon
TUNHUANG *landmark* caves of 1000 buddhas, chien fo tung, silk road
TUNIC acton, arisard, bleaunt, blouse, camise, camisia, chimer, chiton, coat, colobium, cotehardie, cyclas, fecket, gandoura, gippo, integument, jama(h), jupe, kabaya, kirtle, mantle, paltock, robe, smock, sticharion, stola, stole, subucula, sukkenye, surcoat, tabard, toga, tunicle
armor hauberk
hooded sovik
medieval gipon, houppelande, jupon
TUNICATE ascidian, botryllus, bulb, salp(a), salpid, urochord
TUNING *fork* diapase, diapason, modulant
hammer key
to lower pitch anesis
unusual scordatura
TUNIS(IA) carthage, ifriqiyah
cape blanc, bon, rasaddar
city beja, bizerte, carthage, djerba, ferryville, gabes, gafsa, grombalia, jendouba, kairouan, kairwan, mateur, monastir, naveul, sfax, sousse, susa, tebourba, tozeur, zaghouan
coin dinar, millime
gulf gabes, hammamet, tunis
island djerba
lake achkel, bizerte, djerid
measure cafiz, mettar, millerole, saa(h), sah, whiba
oasis gafsa
port bizerte, gabes, sfax, sousse, tunis
president bourguiba
resort capbon, djerba
river medjerda
roman colony eljem
ruler bey, dey
weight artal, artel, kantar, ratel, rotl, saa, uckia
wind chile, chilli
TUNNEL adit, bore, burrow, cave, crosscut, dig, excavate, flue, funnel, lair, level, net, passage(way), puka, sap, shaft, smokestack,

snare, subway, tanna, tossut, tube, underpass
disease ancylostomiasis, hookworm
famous arlberg, baltimore, bitterroot, busk-ivanhoe, cascade, cenis, connought, cumberland, detroit, gallitzin, gothard, gunnison, holland, hoosic, lincoln, lotschberg, mont d'or, mont cenis, mt roberts, otira, severn, simplon, spiral, st clair, st gotthard, transandine, wasserfluh
longest simplon
term heading, slope, stope
worker sandhog
TUNNY albacore, amia, mackerel, scombrid, ton, TUNA
roe botarga(o)
young pelamyd
TUP beat, blissom, butt, cuckold, mallet, monkey, ram, tip
TUPAIA banxring, squirrelshrew
TUPA-INCA *father* pachacuti
TUPEK hut, summerhouse, tent
TUPELO gum, nyssa, pepperidge
TUPI(AN) ahnanga, curupira, devil
indian anta, apiaca, araquaju, aueto, bororoan, canoeiro, cocama, mura, omaqua, sirione, tapajo, tupi, xingo, zingu
language abaneeme, guarani, neengatu
snakebird anhinga
TUR aurochs, goat, ibex, pea, urus
TURALDUS *work* roland
TURANIA *people* akkad
TURB clump, crowd
TURBAN bandan(n)a, cap, fez, hat, headdress, kaffiyeh, lungi, mandil, miter, moab, moslem, mundil, pat(t)a, pug(g)ee, scarf, seerband, squash, tolipane, tuffe, tuft, tulipant
embroidered mundil
flower tupli
plume culgee
TURBID cloudy, dark, dense, dirty, disturbed, drovy, drumly, druvy, dull, feculent, foul, g(r)umly, impure, lutulent, misty, mud-

dled, muddy, murky, nasty, obscure, opaque, polluted, riled, ril(e)y, roiled, roily, smoky, thick, unsettled
render roil
TURBINAL scroll-like, spiral(ed), whorled
TURBOT bannock-fluke, bret, brill, filefish, flatfish, flounder, halibut, psetta, triggerfish, whiff
TURBULENCE agitation, bluster, brawl, broil, commotion, disorder, disturbance, ebullition, ferment, frenzy, fume, furore, fury, hubbub, impetuosity, perturbation, rage, rioting, tumult, turmoil, unruliness, uproar
TURBULENT agitated, angry, blustering, blustery, boisterous, chaotic, clamorous, disorderly, frantic, frenzied, furious, gurl, high, infuriated, loud, mad, mutinous, orgiastic, pandemoniac, passionate, raging, riotous, rude, tough, rugged, stormy, tempestuous, troublous, tumultuous, unsettled, violent, wild, yeasty
TURDUS amsel, blackbird, fieldfare, merula, missel, ouzel, robin
TURF cess, clod, cuff, delf, divot, fale, flaught, flaw, fuel, grass, greensward, lawn, peat, peet, plot, pone, scraw, shirrel, sod, sward, track, vag, verdure
accountant bookmaker
cut divot, vell
cutter edge-iron
fuel vag
grass italian rye
hut barabara, barabora
layer flaw
modern astro
pert. cespititious, cespitose
piece tab
roofing scraw
spade slane
TURGENEV *critic* dostoyevsky
enemy tolstoy
friend zola
mistress pauline viardot
work fathers and sons, nest of gentlefolk, sketches of a sportsman, smoke, virgin soil
TURGENT, TURGID bloat-

ed, bombastic, distended, expanded, flatulent, grandiloquent, grandiose, inflated, magniloquent, overblown, pompous, rhetorical, swollen, torose, torous, tumid
style ampollosity
TURK, TURK'S (See also TURKEY.) aga, brute, bugaboo, corsair, horse, kizilbash, konariot, mongol, moslem, muslim, osmanli, ottoman, sart, scimitar, seljuk, sword, ta(r)tar
cap cactus, lily, martagon, moss, teacozy
head cactus, knot
herb herniary
turban tubeflower
TURKESTAN *city* osh
district pamir
lake hara, shor
moslem salar
native kirghiz, sart, usbeg, uzbek
range alai
river ili, kulja
wind afghanets
TURKEY, TURKISH alderman, anatolia, bird, bomb, bustard, dinde, dud, erector, failure, flop, gobbler, meleagris, porte, stag, steg, turquoise
agent kehaya
ambassador elchee
architect sinan
army corps alai, mustahfiz, mustafuz, ordu, seraglio
army officer See *general* and *official*, below.
attendant bostangi, bostanji
-back yellowlegs
barn ambar
bath bagnio, hammam, hothouse, hummum
beard basket-grass
bird wryneck
blossom caltrop
boat caique, caramoussal, caravel, mahone, saic
brandy rakee, raki
breed bourbon-red
buzzard aura, bromvo(g)el, cathartes, gallinazo, johncrow, vulture
cabinet divan
caliph ali, hassan
camp ordu, palanka
candy halvah
cap calpac(k), fez
cape anamur, baba, bafra, helles, hinzir, ince, karatas, kerempe

capital angora, ankara
caravansary imaret, khan
carpet (See also ORIENTAL *rug*.) ghiordes, kilim, konia, konieh, kulah, kurdistan, melas, panderma, seljuk, smyrna, ushak
carriage araba
castle of cotton pamukkale
cavalry hamidieh
cavalryman hamidian, spahee, spahi
chamber oda(h)
chief See *official*, below.
chin wattle
christian raia
city adana, adrianople, aidin, aintab, akhisar, angora, ankara, antakiya, antalya, antioch, aydin, bergama, boghazkoy, broussa, brusa, bursa, caesarie, c(h)archemish, constantinople, corum, diyarbekir, edessa, edirne, elaziz, erzurum, eskisehir, gaziantep, homs, istanbul, izmir, kars, kayseri, konya, malatya, manisa, maras(h), samsun, scutari, sebaste, sert, sestos, seyhan, siirt, sivas, skutari, smyrna, stamb(o)ul, tarsus, tire, tokat, urfa, uskudar, van, zile
coat stambouline
cock bubblyjock, gobbler, stag
coin akcha, akcheh, altilik, altin, altun, asper, beshlik, chequin, chiquin, copper, forint, iklik, kurus, lira, mahbub, mangour, medjidie(h), metallik, onlik, othmany, para, pataque, piaster, pound, rebia, sequin, sultanin, yirmilik, yuzluk, zecchino, zequin, zermahbub
college ulema
colony egypt, tripoli, tunis
commander See *official*, below.
constable kavass
contemplation, state of keyif
council divan, diwan
couplet beyt
court porte
court man bostangi, bostanji
decree firman, hattihumaum, hatti-sherif, ida, irade
delight loukoum
deputy kahaya

district beyoglu, caza, cilicia, ordu, pera, sanjak

division adana, caza, eyalet, vilayet

dollar piaster

draw lottery

dress charshaf, jelick

dressing sage, stuffing

drink airan, boza, mastic, pasha, rakee, raki

dynasty attalus, seljuk

emblem crescent

emir osman

empire khwarazm

envoy elchee

fabric agaric, chekmak, cottonee, terry(cloth)

fief timar

fig elem, elemi

flag alem, horsetail, toug

float kalak

flock rafter

founder kemal ataturk, osman

freehold mulk

gardener bostangi, bostanji

garment dolman, caftan, charshaf

general ag(h)a, gamal, kamal, pasha, seraskier, sirdar

government gate, porte

government residence konak, yali

governor See *official*, below.

grandee bashaw, pasha

grass cleavers

-greek phanariot

guard bostangi, bostanji, soulack

gulf antalya, cos, izmir

harem seraglio, serai

harem ladies kadein

hat calpac(k), fez

hill dagh

hot springs pamukkale

house konak, selamlik

infidel giaour

inn cafeneh, cafenet, imaret, serai

invader ghuz uighur

javelin jereed, jerrid

judge ag(h)a, cadi(lesker), kadi

king mausolus

kingdom, ancient urartu

lady han(o)um

lake beysehir, egridir, shor, tuz, van

language uigur

leader ag(h)a, ahmed, ecevit, kemal ataturk, koruturk, osman, suleyman demirel

legislature national assembly

liquor See *drink*, above.

male cock, gobbler, tom

man ogor

manna trehala

man of war caravel(le)

measure alma, almud(e), arsheen, arshin(e), berri, chinik, djeri(b), donum, dra(a), drah, fortin, guz, halebi, hatt, khat, kile(h), kilo, nocktat, nul, oka, oke, parmack, pik(halebi), zira(i)

messenger chiaus

military camp ordu

military rank bimbashi, binbashi, chaoush, chiaus

minister vizier

monk dervish

mosque jami

mountain pass beilan

mountain ranger alai

musical instrument canoon, canum, crescent, jingling, johnie, kanum, kussir, zither

musket tophaike

non-moslem raia, rayah

non-moslem group millet

oak blackjack, cerris

oarsman bostangi, bostanji

official aali, ag(h)a, ameer, amir, asha, atabeg, atabek, baghaw, bashaw, beg, beglerbeg, bey, bimbashi, binbashi, cadi, chambul, emeer, emir, kadi, kahaya, kaimakam, kehaya, kemal, mir, mudir, mufti, mustasarrif, mute, osmanli, pachi, pasha, reis-effendi, selim, seraskier, sirdar, subashi, subbassa, sultan, visier, vizi(e)r, wali, zaim

official residence konak

page ichoglan

palace serai

parade alai

party justice, national salvation, nsp, republican peoples, rpp

pasty sambouse

pavilion kiosk

pea devil's-shoestrings, harbinger-of-spring, squirrelcorn

peak ala, ararat, bingol, bolgar, dagh, ericyas, hasan, hinis, honaz, kara(cali), murat, murit, suphan

peasant raya

peninsula gallipoli

people afshar, aissor, aushar,

avshar, awshar, azerbaijani, bashkir, dungan, ephthalites, ghuz, karluk, kurd, moslem, muslim, ogor, osmanli, ottoman, raia, sart, taranchi, tartar, tatar, uigur

pepper paprika

pipe chibouk, chibouque

policeman zaptiah, zaptieh

port adalia, alanya, antalya, bodrum, enos, fethiye, foca, iskenderun, ismir, istanbul, izmir, kas, kusadasi, marmaris, mersin, pergamum, samsun, smyrna, trabzon, trebizond, troy

porter hamal

prayer rug kulah, melas, meles

premier menderes

president bayar, gursel, inonu, kemal ataturk, sunay

province angora, eyalet, sert, sirt, vilayet

punishment bastinado

race osmanli

range aladagh, alai, taurus

-red madder

regiment alai, arni

region kurdistan, thrace, troad

relief organization red crescent

religious sect hanafites

religious war crescentade

reservist redif

residence konak, yali

resort ismir, izmir

river aras, araxes, dicle, firat, gediz, granicus, halys, irmak, kizil, kura, maeander, mesta, muradsu, murat, sakarya, sarus, seihun, seyhan, seylan, tigris

robe dolman

rocket cress

rodent alactaga

room selamlik

royal gardener bostangi, bostanji

royal grant firman

rug See *carpet*, above.

ruler See *title*, below.

saber kilig, obolus, staghan, yatag(h)an

sacred law sheriat

sailor galiongee, galionji

sandal charuk

sea aral, marmara

ship See *boat*, above.

slave eunuch, mameluke

soldier(s) alai, arnaout, arnaut, bashibazouk, janizary, nizami, redif

sound gobble(gobble)
spy mahmut
standard alem, toug
statesman bayar, enver-pasha
statue tanzimat
stone novaculite, turquoise
storage place ambar
storm samiel, simoon
student softa
subject raia, rayah
sultan aba, abdul-aziz, ali, amurath, aziz, calif, caliph, hamid, ilderim, mahmud, me(d)jid, mohammed, murad, pasha, selim, soliman, solyman, suleiman
summerhouse kiosk
sweetmeat loukoum
swindler osman
sword See *saber,* above.
sword-bearer selictar
symbol crescent
tambourine daira, daire
tax avania, caphar, vergi
title aali, aga, agha, ahmed, ali(pasha), atabeg, atabek, baba, bashaw, beg, bey, bimbashi, binbashi, calif, caliph, chambul, dey, effendi, emeer, emir, ghazi, kaimakam, khan, mudir, mufti, mutasarrif, pacha, pasha, seraskier, soldan, subashi, subbassa, sultan
tobacco chibouk, chibouque, latakia
toweling terrycloth
town-dwellers sart
treasurer defterdar, haznadar
tribesmen kurds
tribunal mejlis
trousers shakseer
veil maharmah, yashmak
vessel See *boat,* above.
village adana
warship sultana
weight artal, artel, batman, cantar, cequi, cheke, chequi, deuke, dirhem, drachma, dram, kantar, karat, kerat, kile(h), mane, maund, miskal, obolu, ock, oka, oke, quintal, ratel, rotl, rotolo, tcheke, yusdrum
wheat bulgar, indian-corn
whip kurbash
wild bustard, tom
wine doluca, kavak-lidere
writer yasar kemal
young currassow, poult
zither aria, canun
TURKIC See also TURKEY.

language azerbaijani, chagatai, chuvash, jag(h)atai, kermanji, ta(r)tar
TURKISH See TURKEY.
TURKOMEN, TURKMEN (ISTAN) *carpet* afghan, bokhara, tekke, yomud
conqueror attila, ghenghis khan, tamerlane
city ashkhabad, poltoratsk
game buzkashi
game player chopendoz
nomad idgyr
public bath hammam
region karakalpak, kazak, qara-qalpaq, qazaq, uzbeg, uzbek
stove bukhari
tribe ersar, seid, shik, viddhal
TURKU abo
island aland
TURMERIC ango, azafran, bloodroot, curcuma, haldi, huldee, olena, potentilla, puccoon, rea, redroot, saffron, sanguinaria, tetterwort, tormentil, zieria
TURMOIL agitation, bouleversement, broil, brouhaha, buller, chaos, clamor, commotion, confusion, disorder, dispeace, disquiet, disturbance, ferment, garboil, hassle, hurly, labor, makadoo, pandemonium, perturbation, rummage, stir up, tempest, toil, touse, tumult, turbulence, uproar, welter, whirl
TURN 3 act, bow, haw, yaw **4** airt, bear, bend, bias, cant, cast, deal, deed, eddy, form, gift, gyre, skew, slew, slue, sour, spin, tack, tend, time, tirl, tour, veer, vert, walk, wind **5** angle, apply, avert, chare, cramp, crank, crook, curve, favor, flair, guise, hinge, hitch, knack, pivot, refer, scare, sheer, shift, shock, shunt, spell, start, swing, swirl, tarve, trick, troll, twirl, twist, verte, wheel, whirl, whorl **6** attack, change, circle, crisis, curdle, detour, direct, divert, gyrate, invert, orient, period, queeve, recoil, resort, revert, rotate, swerve, swivel, talent, wimple, zigzag **7** burnish, circuit, crinkle, deflect, deviate, digress, distort, diverge, faculty, fer-

ment, journey, reverse, revolve, twingle, venture **8** penchant, tendency, undulate **9** deviation, direction, fluctuate, oscillate, pirouette, reversion, transpose **10** distortion, proclivity, strophosis **11** disposition **12** metamorphose
about alternate(ly), consecutively, merry-go-round, radical, reverse, revolve, rotate, slew, slue, turnstile, volte-face, windlass
against betray, cross, rebel
around about-face, gyre, pivot, reverse, slew, slue, welt, wend
aside avert, daff, deflect, detour, deviate, digress, divert, gee, haw, obliquate, prevent, sheer, shunt, skew, swerve, veer, wry
away abandon, alienate, avert, avoid, decline, deflect, depart, desert, deter, deviate, dismiss, diverge, divert, evade, hield, leave, repel, reverse, revolt, shunt, shy, snub, swerve
back apostate, backslide, coward, defect, desert, evolute, flipe, flype, fold, forsake, head off, inversion, neglect, regress, relapse, repel, retrace, retroverse, return, reverse, revert, tack
backward retroflex
brown tan
buckle turnabout, turnel
color blush, flush, pale
comb. tropo
complete circle, lap
down blackball, decline, deny, fold, invert, lower, negate, refuse, reject, veto
extra bis, bisque, encore, repeat
frontward obvert
in retire
informer blab, squeal
into convert, metamorphose, transform
inward introvert
left haw, port, wynd, wyne
loose discharge, fire, free, liberate, release
lucky break
off accomplish, branch, consign, decay, deflect, detour, discharge, dismiss, distract, divert, extinguish, fork, hang, marry, putrefy, shunt, shut, spoil, stop, withdraw

on actuate, arouse, attack, depend, drug, enthuse, ignite, intoxicate, motivate, shoot up, start
one's back on abandon, avoid, desert, dismiss, flee, quit, refuse, repudiate, snub, spurn
out abandon, appear, arise, array, arrive, assembly, attendance, bear, breed, clean, detour, discharge, dismiss, dispossess, draw, empty, ensue, equip, eventuate, evert, evict, expel, extinguish, fashion, form, fudge, gate, generate, happen, leave, make, oust, outfit, pour, produce, propagate, prove, result, reverse, siding, slew, slue, veer, visit, yield
outward evert, extrorse, extrovert, splay
over capsize, consider, delegate, deliver, evolute, examine, flap, flip, give, handle, hang, invert, keel, meditate, overturn, plow, ponder, reform, relinquish, reverse, revolve, roll, sale, slice, somersault, tip, transfer, tumble, upend, upset, volti
pale blanch, bleach, blench, fade, whiten
rapidly spin, tirl, twirl, whirl
right gee, hap, hup, starboard
round pivot, revolve, rotate, spin
sharp hairpin, switchback, wrench, zigzag
sharply angle
short zag, zig
sour acescent, bleeze, blink, clabber, fox, go off, prill, spoil
tail flee
the corner rally, rebound, recover, recuperate
the edge blunt
to avail, begin, consult, employ, labor, open, refer to, start, undertake, use
turtle capsize
up appear, arise, arrive, attend, chance, crop up, disclose, discover, find, free, happen, hem, increase, materialize, occur, raise, relinquish, shorten, show up, sight, surprise, tack, tilt, trump, virade
upside down cant, invert,

overturn, ransack, whelm, whelve
TURNCOAT apostate, backslider, changeling, deserter, quisling, rat, recreant, renegade, runagate, traitor
TURNED askew, awry, bent, curved, pronate, rancid, skewed, sour(ed), splay, spoiled
away alienated, averse, cathodic, kathodic
back evolute, folded, retrorse
inward varus
on aroused, awakened, enthusiastic, excited, lit, sold, stirred
outward everted, extrorse
over keeled, spilled
spirally sinistrorse
to one side askew, splayed
up acock, retrousse
TURNING about-face, active, anfractuous, angle, bend, circuitous, convolution, corner, crooked, curvy, deviation, divergent, flexure, fold, framing, inclined, retortion, reversal, rotation, shaping, sinuous, spiral, tortuous, versation,, version, winding, w(r)iggly
comb. stropho
point cardo, climax, crisis, decision, landmark, transition
TURNIP(S) baga, blockhead, brassica, chap, crucifer, fellow, kraut, nape, navew, neep, rape, rapeye, rappini, rutabaga, swede, timepiece, turmut, watch
black lion's-leaf
-cabbage kohlrabi, rutabaga
-like napiform, rapaceus
-pate head, noddle, noodle
wild breadroot, navew, rape
TURNIX buttonquail, hemipod(e), ortygan, quail
TURNKEY gaoler, jailer, locksman, screw, warder
TURNOUT arising, attendance, cleaning, clothes, costume, crowd, dress, emptying, equipage, gathering, layby, output, product, rig, setout, strike(r), stroll, walk, wardrobe
TURNOVER bramble, empanada, flapjack, pastry, pie, pirojki, piroshki, shakeup, shawl, shift, spill, tart, upset, volume

TURNPIKE freeway, highway, road, route, stairway, thoroughfare, tollgate
gatekeeper pikeman
TURNPIN tampion
TURNSOLE heliotrope, sunflower, sunspurge
TURNSPIT hastler
TURNSTONE arenaria, calicoback, chicaric, chickenbird, creddock, heartbird, plover, redleg, snipe
relative sandpiper
TURNTABLE lazy susan, nonsync, playback, racer, rotary
TURNUS *beloved* lavinia
brother juturna
parent daunus, venilia
rival and slayer aeneas
TURPENTINE camphine, crape, gal(l)ipot, gumspirit, oleoresin, thinner, thus
bordeaux gal(l)ipot
crude gum-thus
derivative oil, pinene, resin, rosin
pert. terebinthic
resin alk(gum), gal(l)ipot
shrub prairie-dock
state north carolina
tree loblolly, pine, tallowwood, tarata, terebinth
TURPID base, cowardly, low, vile
TURPIN *horse* black bess
sword almace
TURPITUDE abjection, baseness, corruption, corruptness, decadence, degeneracy, degeneration, degradation, depravity, dissolution, evil, fedity, pravity, profligacy, vileness
TURQUOISE blue, calaite, callais, chalchuite
planet saturn
source persia
symbol of prosperity
TURRET bartizan, belfry, butte, cupola, garret, gazebo, guerite, gunhouse, louver, minaret, mirador, monitor, pepperbox, steeple, terret, toolholder, torel, tourelle, tower, turricle
having castellanus, castellated
TURSE bundle, depart, load, pack, truss
TURTLE arrau, cakuama, caret(ta), carey, chelonid, coodle, cooter, creeper,

emyd(ian), emys, flapjack, hawkbill, juniata, jurara, log(ger)head, lyra, matamata, mungofa, ridley, shagtail, slider, snapper, stinkpot, terrapin, testudinate, thurgi, tortoise, tortuga, torup
delicacy calipee, pee, terrapin
enclosure crawl
food ant-egg
freshwater cooter, emyd(ian), pleurodira
genus caretta, chelodina, chelonia, chrysemys, dermochelys, emys, malademys, pelusios, testudo
giant arrau
group bale
hawksbill caret
jelly calipee, pee
loggerhead caretta
marine archelon, caretta, ridley, thalassian
musk stinkpot
old mossback
pert. chelonian
plastron calipee
prehistoric archelon
shell calipash, carapace, caripee, plastron
snapping shagtail, torup
soft-shelled flapjack
TURTLEHEAD balmony, chelone, coghead, snakehead
TUSCANY *city* firenze, florence, greve, leghorn, livorno, lucca, montecatini, pisa, pistoia, prato
cave people belverdians
faction bianchi, black, ghibelline, guelph, neri, white
wine chianti
TUSH canine, georgian, pshaw, tooth, tusk
TUSK beat, cusk, fang, gain, horn, incisor, ivory, razor, stab, tenon, tooth, tuft, tush
boar's razor
elephant's scrivello
TUSKER boar, elephant
TUSSAH cloth, fiber, pongee, shantung, silk(worm)
TUSSIS cough
TUSSLE argument, conflict, contest, controversy, fight, grapple, scuffle, struggle, touse, wrestle
TUSSOCK brush(wood), clump, cluster, hassock, poa, thicket, tuft
grass bulrush, carex, sedge

TUT hassock, hoot, hush, peep, piece, rebuke, rounders, scold, staccato, toot
TUTELAGE guidance, instruction, nurture, oversight, protection, teaching, tutorship, yemsel
TUTELARY *gods* d(a)emon, genii, lares, penates
TUTENAG bid(d)ery, bidree, bidri, bidry, paktong, zinc
TUTOR admonish, coach, cram(mer), cransier, creancer, docent, don, educate, governor, grinder, ground, guard(ian), humor, indulge, instruct(or), keeper, manual, master, mentor, pamper, pangloss, pedagog(ue), preceptor, prime, school, teach(er), textbook
TUTSAN parkleaves, st-john's-wort
TUTTA, TUTTO all, entire, together, whole
TUTTY flower, nosegay, testy
TUTU tupakihi
material tarlatan
TUULIKKI *father* tapio
TUXEDO black tie, dinner jacket, formal, soup and fish
TV See TELEVISION.
TWADDLE,   TWATTLE babble(ment), bosh, drivel, flapdoodle, footle, fustian, gabble, haver, nonsense, piffle, prate, prattle, rot, slipslop, tosh, trash
TWAIN, MARK See CLEMENS, SAMUEL.
TWANG accent, flavor, guess, jangle, pluck, plunk, pungency, slap, sound, strum, surmise, TANG, taste, twangle, twank(le), twinge
TWEAK agitation, distress, feak, harlot, jerk, pang, pinch, pull, snatch, trouble, twig, twinge, twist, twitch
TWEEDLE blare, cajole, play, sing, touch, trifle, TWIDDLE, whistle
TWEEG hellbender
TWEET cheep, chirp, peep, twitter
TWEEZE, TWEESE squeeze, twist, wrench
TWEEZER(S) case, etui, merganser, mullet, nipper, pin-

cer, pincette, pin(her, twirk, twitch, volsella
case bubblebow
TWELFTH *night* epiphany
night author shakespeare
night character andrew aguecheek, cesario, curio, fabian, feste, malvolio, maria, olivia, orsino, sebastian, sir toby belch, valentine, viola
night clown feste
night scene illyria
part uncia
TWELVE dicker, dodecade, dozen
comb. dodeca, duodecim
dozen gross
-month towmont, year
pence shilling
pert. duodecimal
the apostles, disciples
TWELVER imami
TWENTY cooree, corge, kaph, kappa, score
1 blackjack, vanjohn
3 skidoo
4th part carat, karat
5 quartern
8 parakeet
comb. icos(a), icosi
-faced icosahedral
pert. icosian, vicenary, vigesimal, vingtieme
years vicennial
TWERP jerk, pipsqueak
TWIBILL battleaxe, chisel, mattock, tool, weapon
TWICE bis, doffio, doubly, dually, duplicate, encore, replica, twofold
a month bimensal
a year biannual, biennial
-born regenerate, reincarnated
comb. bis, dis, twi
-told hackneyed, trite
-told tale bromide, chestnut, platitude
TWIDDLE fiddle, play, quiver, shake, touch, tremble, trifle, twirl, twist, twitter, vibrate, wriggle
TWIG beat, bough, branch(ling), child, comprehend, cow, detect, discover, fashion, labor, mode, observe, offshoot, part, perceive, pull, rod, sallow, sarment, scion, see, shoot, shred, slip, spray, sprig, stem, stick, stolo(n), style, switch, twist, twitch, understand, virga, waver, withe, withy
bare cow

bloody dogwood
-branch angle axil
bundle barsom, fagot
dried chad
flexible osier
for fuel chatwood
full of roddy
grafting scion
little surcle
made of virgal, wattled
pert. viminal
thatching scollop
willow anaphyte, sallow

TWILIGHT alpenglow, cockshut, crepuscular, dim(mit), dimps, duckish, dusk, evenglome, eve(ning), eventide, gloam(ing), grisping, nightfall, obscure, shaded, twale, ughten
deity helen, phaedra, tem
of the gods gotterdammerung, ragnarok
pert. crepuscular
sleep drug scopolamine
vision scotopia

TWILL caddice, caddis, chino, dungaree, fabric, flute, quill, reed, rib, russel, spool, weave
fabric barragan, beaverteen, bombasine, bombazeen, bombazet(te), bombazine, broadcloth, chino, rep, serge, toile

TWIN akin, carbon, cord, couple(t), didym(o)us, double, dual, duplicate, fellow, gemel, gemini, hemitrope, identical, jumelle, match, mate, pair, siamese, sibling(s), similar, twain, two(fold)
bill doubleheader
brothers alpha and beta, castor, dioscuri, gemini, geminorum, pollux, remus, romulus
city minneapolis, st paul
comb. didymo
crystal macle
-flower linnaea
fraternal dizygotic
gods alcis
kind fraternal, identical
leaf helmetpod
name meaning thomas
one gemel
siamese chang, eng
stars castor, gemini, pollux
surviving vopiscus
the thomas

TWINBERRY honeysuckle

TWINE anamite, bend, coil, convolution, cord, curl, embrace, encircle, hemp, infold, interweave, intort, mingle, mix, part, prolong, revolve, ripple, rope, shine, sisal, skeenyie, snarl, stretch out, string, sunder, tangle, thread, turn, twingle, twirl, twist, veer, warp, weave, wind, wrap, wreathe
bush pinbush
color anamite, dune
fabric net
fiber hemp, henequen, sisal

TWINGE ache, afflict, constrain, lancination, oppress, pain, pang, pinch, pull, qualm, scruple, stitch, throe, tic, touch, tweak, twitch
painful glisk

TWINGLE turn, twine, wind

TWINK chaffinch, chirp, clink, instant, nict(i)ate, punish, thrash, tinkle, TWINKLE, twitter, wink

TWINKLE blink, coruscate, flash, flicker, gleam, glimmer, glint, glisten, glister, glitter, glow, scintillate, shake, shimmer, shine, sparkle, twire, wink(le)

TWINKLING flash, jiffy, minute, moment, second, trice, wink

TWIRL circle, coil, eddy, gyrate, pirouette, pitch, querl, revolve, rotate, spin, swirl, trundle, turn, twiddle, twirk, twist, wheel, whirl, wind, writhe

TWIST appetite, bend, bias, bought, braid, cast, coil, contort, cord, crimk(le), crook(le), curl(icue), curve, dance, deflect, deviate, disposition, distort(ion), extort, facet, falsify, feak, flexure, flourish, fork, gnarl, grind, hankle, hinge, insinuate, intort, kink, knot, lop, meander, misrepresent, nauseate, ply, prune, quirk, scriggle, skew, slew, slue, snake, spin, spiral, squinch, squirm, stray, strophosis, tail, tendril, thraw, thread, tirl, torque, torsion, turn, tweak, tweeze, twig, twine, warp, weave, whirl, wind, woman, wrabbe, wreathe, wrench, writhe, yarn, zigzag
comb. spiri

forcibly wrench, wring
full of kinky, winding
inward intort
oliver See OLIVER TWIST.
one's arm coax, persuade, press(ure)
out of shape contort, warp
the meaning misinterpret
to and fro wrench, wriggle
together braid, cable, raddle, splice

TWISTED askew, awry, buckled, cam, circuitous, cockeyed, crooked, eccentric, gauche, hurled, kinky, knotted, screwy, skew(ed), torse, tortile, turken, wreathed, wrothe, wry
comb. plecto, spiri, strept
spirally torse

TWISTER cyclone, girder, hurricane, liar, lie, mallard, somersault, tornado, typhoon, waterspout, whirlwind, wind(lass)

TWIT accuse, badger, banter, blame, charge, chide, chirp, deride, gibe, gird, hector, jeer, joke, josh, kid, mock, needle, rally, reprehend, reproach, ridicule, scold, sing, snarl, tangle, taunt, tax, tease, twitch, upbraid

TWITCH carp, confuse, convulse, distract, fasten, feak, jerk, jiggle, jump, nip, pang, perplex, pick, pinch, pirn, pluck, pull, quatch, quetch, shake, skid, snatch, squeeze, start, thrill, tic, tie, tit, tug, tweak, tweezers, twinge, twirk, twit, vellicate, wink, wipe, yank

TWITCHETY, TWITCHY fidgety, irritable, nervous, restless, shaky

TWITCHING convulsion, fidgets, jerking, jerks, nerves, palmus, substultus, tic, vellication

TWITLARK pipit

TWITTER chatter, chipper, chirp, dither, garre, giggle, ridicule, quaver, quiver, shake, sing, taunt, thread, thrill, titter, tremble, trepidation, twiddle, twink, TWIT, twittle, whitter

TWITTERY filmy, finespun

TWO beta, binal, binary, binate, both, brace, company, couple(t), deuce, deux, dos, double(ton), duad, dual(istic), duck,

due, duo, dyad, match, mates, pair, span, team, twain, tway, twin(s), yoke, zwei
-bit bush, cheap, inferior, smalltime, unimportant
bits quarter
-bodied bicorporate
-branched bifurcate, biramous
-by-four cramped, insignificant, little, petty, small
-celled bilocular
-chambered bicameràl, biloculine
-colored amphichromatic, bichrome, dichromic
comb. amph(i), ampho, bin(i), diphy, dua, duo, twi
-edged ancipital, sharp
eyes partridgeberry
eyes of greece athens, sparta
-faced ambivalent, deceitful, duplicate, duplicitous, false, hypocritical, insincere, janiform, mealymouthed, treacherous
-fingered bidigitate
-fisted strong, vigorous, virile
-footed biped(al)
-for a deux
-forked bifurcate(d), dichotomous
government by duarchy
-handed ambidextrous, bimanual, bimanous
-headed ancipital, bicapitate, bicephalus, bicipital, bicipitous, dicephalous
-headed, comb. dicrano
-horned bicorn(ed)
in one biune, biunial
-jointed biarticulate
-leaved bifoliate, diphyllous
-legged bicrural
-lipped bilabiate
-master brig, bully, bum
-month period bimester
of a kind brace, couple, pair, team, twins, yoke
parts, comb. dich(o)
parts, pert. bident, bifurcate, bipatrite, dichotomous
-penny ale, cheap, mean, paltry
pert. ancipital, bifarious, binary, didymous, double, dual, duplicate, twice
-pronged dicellate
shakes instant, jiffy, minute, moment, trice
-sided bifacial, bilateral, dihedral, double-faced, duplicate, hypocritical

-spot deuce
-spurred bicalcarate
step paso-doble
-time betray, cheat, deceive, double cross
-toned bicolor
-up swy
-wheeler bicycle, biga, gig
-winged bialate, dipteral, dipterous
TWOFOLD ancipital, bifarious, binal, binary, binate, diad, didymate, didymoid, didymous, diplastic, diploid, double, duad, dual (ly), duplex, duplicate, twice, twin
comb. diphy
TWO GENTLEMEN OF VERONA proteus, valentine
character antonio, eglamore, eglamour, julia, launce, lucetta, pantheno, proteus, silvia, speed, sylvia, thurio, valentine
dog crab
heroine silvia, sylvia
TWOSOME couple, duo, pair
TYBALT *kin* capulet
slayer romeo
victim mercutio
TYCHE fortuna
father oceanus
symbol ball, horn, rudder
TYCHICUS *aide to* paul
TYCOON baron, businessman, capitalist, entrepreneur, executive, industrialist, lord, magnate, mogul, nabob, personage, ruler, shogun, taikun, vip
TYDEUS *companion* adrastus
consort deipyle
enemy amphiaraus, melanippus
half-brother meleager
parent oeneus, periboea
son diomedes, tydides
victim melanippus
TYE bed, case, casket, chain, close, common, enclosure, featherbed, launder, pasture, rope, tie, wash
TYEE chief, taiyi
TYKE boor, bumpkin, child, churl, cur, dog, imp, moppet, peasant, tad, tike, tot, yorkshireman
TYLENOL acetaminophen
TYLER, JOHN *birthplace* charles city, virginia
burial site richmond, virginia
party democratic

TYLOPOD See CAMEL.
TYMPAN crowd, drum, membrane, panel, plate
TYMPANIC *membrane* drumhead, drumskin, myringa
TYMPANITES, TYMPANISM distension, inflation, meteorism
TYMPANY bombast, conceit, turgidness, TYMPANITES
TYNDAREUS *ally* thestius
ancestor lacedaemon
brother hippocoon, icarius
consort leda
offspring castor, clytemnestra, philopoe, timandra
parent batia, gorgophone, oebalus, perieres
stepchild helen(a), pollux
TYPE arrange, attribute, brand, cast, character(istic), class(ify), cupola, cut, description, dome, emblem, example, exemplar, fashion, foreshadow, form, genre, genus, identify, identity, ilk, impression, kidney, kind, letter, make, mark, measure, model, mo(u)ld, nature, norm, order, original, pattern, prefigure, print, represent(ation), sign, sort, species, stamp, standard, stripe, symbol(ize), token, typify, write
bank font, fount
bar basket
blank quad(rat)
block quad
class See *style*, below.
comb. arch
distribute throw
edge bur(r)
face See *style*, below.
48-point canon
frame chase
heavy boldface, ionic
holder pallet
jumbled pie
mold matrix
part beard, body, counter, face, foot, groove, kern, neck, nick, serif, shank, shoulder, stem
raised braille
script ronde
set of font
size agate, bourgeois, brevier, brilliant, canon, cicero, columbian, diamond, didot, elite, english, excel-

sior, minion, nonpariel, paragon, pearl, pica, primer, ruby, trafalgar
slanting italic
spacer quad(rat), slug
stroke serif
style aldine, antique, barnum, baskerville, blackletter, bodoni, boldface, bradley, bruce, bulmer, caledonia, caslon, century, chapel, chaucer, clarendon, cloister, cochin, columbian, cursive, devinne, elzevir, excelsior, french, fullface, futura, garamond, gothic, goudy, granjon, hess, ionic, italic, jenson, kabel, kelmscott, lightface, lydian, microgramma, modern, news, normal, old english, palatino, peignot, primer, roman, ronde, ruby, runic, sans(s)erif, schoolbook, script, standard, stymie, times, tudor, vogue
term case, font, galley, quad
tray galley
weight boldface, extrabold, lightface, standard
TYPEE *sequel* omoo
TYPESETTER caster, compositor, linotype(r), linotypist, mono(type), pressman, printer, typographer
TYPEWRITER *inventor* cahill, glidden, mill, progin, sholes, soute, thurber
part backspace, bail, bale, carriage, key, knotter, platen, ribbon, shift, shuttle, spacebar, spacer, tab(ulator)
type elite, pica
TYPHA blackcap, cattail, flag, reed-mace
TYPHLOSIS blindness
TYPHOID *fever* tabardillo
remedy antipyretic, aspidospermin(e), thaline
TYPHON *burial site* etna
consort echidna

offspring cerberus, chimera, harpies, sphinx
parent tartarus, terra
subduer zeus
TYPHOON baguio, cyclone, gale, gust, hurricane, storm, tornado, twister, (whirl) wind
TYPHUS brill's disease, fever, tabardillo
cause rickettsia
TYPICAL average, characteristic, classic, common, denotative, distinctive, distinguishing, emblematic, figurative, general, generic, ideal, natural, normal, quintessential, peculiar, perfect, regular, representative, stock, symbolic, universal, usual
TYPIFY embody, epitomize, exemplify, figure, illustrate, indicate, prefigure, represent, symbolize
TYPIST amanuensis, clerk, office girl, scribe, scrivener, secretary, stenographer
TYPOEUS *parent* gaea
TYR dyaus, ear, saxnot, thincsus, things, tiu(z), tiw, ziu
parent frigg, hymir, odin
slayer and *victim* garm
wolf fenrir, fenris
TYRANNICAL, TYRANNOUS absolute, arbitrary, authoritarian, autocratic, cruel, despotic, dictatorial, domineering, harsh, imperious, lordly, masterful, oppressive, severe, slavish
TYRANNIZE domineer, oppress, overlord
TYRANNUS cotinga, flycatcher, kingbird, phoebe, pitta
TYRANNY autocracy, despotism, harshness, inclemency, oppression, rigor, severity

TYRANT autarch, autocrat, caesar, czar, dictator, disciplinarian, fuehrer, hitler, martinet, nero, oligarch, oppressor, phalaris, pharaoh, simon legree, slave driver, taskmaster, tsar, tzar, usurper
bird flycatcher, pewee
murder tyrannicide
TYRE *besieger* alexander, nebuchadnezzar
city sour, sur, zor
destroyers moslems
god melcarth, melkarth
king belus, hiram, huram, ithobal
lord acerbas, escanes, helicanus
port sur
prince pericles
princess dido, elissa
TYRO abecedarian, abecedary, amateur, apprentice, beginner, catechumen, colt, dabbler, deb, dilettante, greenhorn, ham, jackaroo, johnny-come-lately, learner, maverick, neophyte, newcomer, novice, probationer, pupil, rabbit, recruit, rookie, tenderfoot, tiro
consort cretheus, enipeus, poseidon
mother-in-law sidero
parent alcidice, salmoneus
son aeson, amythaon, neleus, pelias, pheres
TYROL(IAN) *capital* innsbruck
district trentino
patriot hofer
singing yodel(ing)
TYRRHENIAN etruscan
king mezentius
TYSTE guillemot
TYT(E) See TITE.
TYTO aluco, barnowl, strix
TZAR See CZAR.
TZENTAL *hero* votan
TZIGANE gypsy

U

U university, upsilon
boat submarine
UANG rhinoceros-beetle
UBANGI *feeder* uele
UBERMENSCH overman, superman
UBEROUS abundant, co-

pious, fruitful, plentiful, productive
UBI where(ever)
UBIETY location, placement, position, relation, whereness

UBIQUITOUS almighty, omnipresent
UBIQUITY everywhereness, locality, omnipresence, situation
UCHEAN *indian* yuchi

UDDER bag, dugs, elder, ewer, mama, other, sumen, tid
UELE *tribe* ababua, abarambo, akka, amadi
UFO flying saucer
UGANDA *battalion* mulire
capital entebbe, kampala
cattle ankoli
city entebbe, jinja, kampala, mbale, mombasa
lake albert, edward, george, kioga, kyoga, victoria
language ateso, ganda, luganda, swahili
leader idi-amin, obote
party kabaka-yekka, people's congress
peak elgon
people acholi, ankole, ateso, baganda, bagisu, bahima, bahuma, bakiga, bambute, bantu, basoga, batoro, bunyoro, hima, huma, kopi, lango, lendil, lugbara, nilotic, sudanic, wahima
plateau ankole
port mombasa
province buganda
river aswa, kafu, katonga, pager
ruler idi-amin, omukama
volcano elgon
UGLY awful, bad, base, black, corrupt, crabbed, cranky, cross(grained), dangerous, disagreeable, displeasing, dreepy, evil, foul, frightful, gorgon, grewsome, grotesque, gruesome, heinous, hideous, homely, horrible, hostile, houghly, ill-favored, ill-tempered, inartistic, inelegant, irascible, laidly, loathsome, mean, misshapen, monstrous, nasty, objectionable, offensive, ominous, quarrelsome, repulsive, revolting, scandalous, shade, shocking, sinister, snivy, spiteful, stormy, sullen, sunbonnet, surly, tempestuous, terrible, threatening, toady, ungainly, unlovely, unprepossessing, unsightly, vicious, vile, waspish
person bogle, fright
UGRIAN *language* ostyak
people avar
UHLAN lancer, militiaman, scout, soldier
UIGHUR jagatai

UINTAH *indian* ute
UITLANDER alien, foreigner, outlander
UKASE command, decree, edict, order, proclamation
UKE jarana
UKKO *wife* akka, maaneno, rauni
UKRAINE *assembly* rada
capital kiev
city artemovsk, bakhmut, berdichev, cernauti, kharkov, kherson, kiev, kirovograd, kramatorsk, kreminchug, lvov, nikolaev, odessa, rovno, sumy, ternopol, zaporozhe
coin grivna, schagiv
dance gopak
egg-painting psysanky
holy city kiev
legislature podolia, rada
musical instrument bandura
poems duma
port odessa, yalta
region crimea
river styr
writer franko
UKULELE (See also GUITAR.) taropatch, uke
ULAM *ancestor* gilead
ULCER abscess, angionoma, aposteme, bedsore, canker, chancre, egilops, encauma, fontanel, fossette, kyle, lesion, noma, phagedena, smutch, sore, tetter, ulcuscle
comb. helc(o)
diet sippy
group canker
kind aden, cochin-china, persian, tropical
-like helcoid
remedy bauxite, bisaspore, gibbsite, mordant
repair helcoplasty
science of helcology
ULCERATED, ULCEROUS bad, botchy, cankered, diseased, rotten
ULCERATION bedsore, caries, helcosis
ULCERATIVE diabrotic
ULE castilla, caucho
derivative latex
ULEMA *leader* imam
ULEX furze, ling, shrub
ULIANOC lenin
ULIGINOSE moist, muddy, oozy, swampy, wet
ULLA *son* arah, haniel, rezia
ULLAGE deficiency, dregs, lees, shortage, wantage

ULL(R) *parent* sif
stepfather thor
ULMO muermo
ULMUS See ELMO.
ULNA bone, cubit(al), cubitus, elbow, ell
part ancon, olecranon
ULOTRICHOUS hairy
ULPHIUS *chamberlain* to king arthur
ULSTER *enemy* connacht
hero cuchullain(n)
insurgent steelboy
king conchobor
queen medb
ULTERIOR additional, distant, eventual, farther, further, future, later, remote(r), succeeding, thither, undisclosed, undivulged
ULTIMA farthest, final, last, remotest
thule iceland
ULTIMATE absolute, acme, basic, best, categorical, concluding, conclusive, creme de la creme, dire, elemental, end, eventual, extreme, farthest, final, fundamental, furthermost, furthest, future, last, latest, maximum, primary, remotest, supreme, terminal, tomorrow, total, uttermost, windup
atom monad
fate ananke
unit monad
ULTIMATELY eventually, finally, hereafter
ULTIMATUM condition, demand, objective, offer, order, proposal
ULTRA a-one, best, beyond, excessive, extravagant, extreme, extremist, fanatic (al), forward, radical, superior, top, uncompromising
conservative bourbon, tory
-ultra chic, fashionable, modern, swell
ULTRAMARINE azure, blue
ULTRAMONTANE alien, catholic, foreigner, italian
ULTRAMONTANISM curialism
ULUA caranx, cavalla, fish, papio(pio)
ULULANT howling, plaintive, wailing
ULULATE bellow, cry, hoot, howl, lament, pule, roar, screech, sob, wail, yelp

ULYANOV lenin

ULYSSES See ODYSSEUS.

UMA See DEVI.

UMBEL radius, ray, sertule, sertulum

UMBELLIFER carrot, celery, parsley, parsnip

UMBER brown, chestnut, dusky, omber, partridge, pigment, protect, shade, shadow, sunshade, umbrere, umbrette, visor
bird grayling, umbrette

UMBO beak, boss, elevation, knob, spike, stud

UMBRA dogfish, fish, ghost, minnow, mudfish, nucleus, phantom, shade, shadow, tree, vestige

UMBRAGE anger, annoyance, cloak, disfavor, disgrace, disguise, displeasure, doubt, dudgeon, exasperation, foliage, fury, grudge, huff, ire, irritation, nettling, offend, offense, overshadow, penumbra, pique, pretext, protection, rage, resentment, semblance, shade, shadow, shelter, snuff, suspicion, trace, vexation, wrath

UMBRAGEOUS dubious, jealous, obscure, overshadowed, shaded, shadowy, shady, suspicious

UMBRELLA akokobaatan, anchor, bell, blind, brolly, bumbershoot, bumbersol, chatta, chute, disguise, entout-cas, fittisol, gamp, gingham, kittysol, mush (room), nyankonton, oyokomma, parachute, parasol, payong, pileus, protection, roundel, screen, shade, shelter, sunblind, sunshade, tyrasole
bird caphalopterus, cotinga, cotingid
bush acacia, miljee
finial tee
grass millet
holder stand
maker ferruler
palm canterbury palm, kentia
part rib, stretcher
plant eriogonum, glumal, mayapple, sedge
point ferule
tree acacia, bendy-tree, catalpa, elkwood, ginseng, magnolia, wahoo

UMBRETTE bird, hammerkop, hombre, umber

UMBRIAN iguvine
river tevere, tiber

UMBRIEL *planet* uranus

UMPIRE arbiter, arbitrator, daysman, judge, odd(s)man, ref(eree), stickler, supervise, ump

UMPTEEN innumerable, many

UMQUHILE at times, deceased, erst, former(ly), late(r), once, sometimes, umwhile

UNABASHED audacious, bold, brazen, browless, cool

UNACCENTED atonic, light, soft, unstressed

UNACCEPTABLE dreadful, inadequate, objectionable, obnoxious, repugnant, uninviting, unpleasant

UNACCOMMODATING disobliging, inconsiderate, selfish, thoughtless, uncheerful, unobliging, unwilling

UNACCOMPANIED acappella, alone, bare, single, solo

UNACCOUNTABLE fantastic, inexplicable, inscrutable, irresponsible, mysterious, strange, unexplained, unfathomable, unintelligible

UNACCUSTOMED inexperienced, new, strange, unacquainted, uncommon, unfamiliar, unused, unusual, unwonted, wontless

UNACQUAINTED ignorant, inexperienced, strange, unaccustomed, unaware, uncouth, unknowing

UNADORNED austere, bald, bare, blunt, inornate, mere, naked, plain, restrained, rustic, simple, stark

UNADULTERATED absolute, clear, frank, genuine, honest, neat, pure, sincere, single, true, unalloyed, uncontaminated, unmixed, virgin

UNADVISED imprudent, inconsiderate, indiscreet, rash

UNAFFECTED artless, genuine, honest, informal, ingenuous, insensitive, naive, native, natural, plain, real, rustic, simple, sincere, single, true, unassuming, unbiased, unexcited, unfeigned, uninfluenced, unmoved, un-

pretending, unruffled, untouched

UNAFRAID bold, brave, confident, courageous, defiant, incautious, undaunted

UNALLOYED deep, genuine, pure, undebased, unmixed, unqualified, virgin

UNALTERABLE adamant(ine), fated, immutable, inflexible, irreversible

UNANIMITY accord(ance), agreement, chorus, concert, concord, consensus, consent, harmony, unison

UNANIMOUS agreeing, concordant, concurrent, consentaneous, consentient, harmonious, like-minded, mutual, one, solid, united, whole

UNANIMOUSLY as one, to a man, together, una voce

UNANSWERABLE conclusive, decisive, irrefutable

UNAPPETIZING disgusting, distasteful, loathsome, nasty, repugnant, uninviting, unpalatable

UNAPPRECIATIVE thankless, unfavorable, ungrateful, unthankful

UNAPPROACHABLE aloof, cold, offish, remote, snobbish, standoffish, stately

UNAPT backward, deficient, dull, inappropriate, inept, slow, unaccustomed, unfit, unlikely, unsuitable

UNARMED bare(handed), unbarbed
comb. anopl(o)

UNASKED unbidden, voluntary, willing

UNASSAILABLE impregnable, indomitable, invincible, invulnerable, secure

UNASSUMING diffident, humble, informal, modest, natural, open, plain, retiring, shy, simple, unaffected, unpretentious

UNATTACHED alone, footloose, free, independent, loose, single, stag, uncommitted, unmarried

UNATTRACTIVE frumpish, homely, plain, UGLY, unappealing, unlikely, unpleasant

UNAU sloth

UNAUTHORIZED illegal, illegitimate, unjustified, unlawful, unsanctioned

UNAVAILING bootless, fruitless, futile, gainless, ineffective, ineffectual, sterile, useless, vain

UNAVOIDABLE certain, ineludable, inescapable, inevitable, positive, shunless, sure

UNAWARE blind, heedless, ignorant, innocent, unconscious, unknowing, unmindful, unwary, witless

UNBALANCED deranged, disordered, dotty, fanatic, fruity, insane, irregular, lopsided, mad, nutty, off one's trolley, onesided, topheavy, uneven, unhinged, unsettled

UNBAPTIZED heathen(ish), profane

UNBEARABLE insufferable, insupportable, intolerable

UNBEATEN champion, prizewinning, undefeated, unvanquished, winner

UNBECOMING awkward, clumsy, gauche, improper, indecent, indelicate, indecorous, inept, maladroit, unfitting, unlovely, unmeet, unseemly, unsuitable, unworthy

UNBELIEF agnosticism, atheism, discredence, heresy, incredulity, infidelity, minimifidianism, miscreance, scepticism, skepticism, unfaith

UNBELIEVABLE absurd, implausible, inconceivable, incredible, preposterous, ridiculous, suspicious, thick, thin, tall, untenable

UNBELIEVER agnostic, apikoros, apostate, atheist, doubter, epicoris, free thinker, giaour, heathen, heretic, infidel, kaf(f)ir, pagan, sceptic, scoffer, skeptic

UNBELIEVING cynical, doubtful, dubious, heretical, incredulous, infidel, mistrustful, quizzical, sceptical, skeptical, suspicious, wary

UNBEND condescend, frese, loose(n), relax, repose, rest, slacken, straighten, thaw, uncock, uncrook, unfasten, untie

UNBENDING adamant(ine), angular, inexorable, inflexible, obdurate, obstinate, ramroddy, relentless, resolute, rigid, stark, stern, stiff, straight, stubborn, tharf, unyielding

UNBIASED detached, dispassionate, equitable, fair, impartial, impersonal, just, neutral, objective, unprejudiced

UNBIND absolve, deliver, detach, dissolve, free, loose, release, unchain, undo, unfasten, unfetter, ungird, unleash, untie

UNBLEMISHED fair, faultless, flawless, immaculate, perfect, pure, sound, spotless

UNBLESSED accursed, evil, unconsecrated, unfortunate, unholy, wretched

UNBLOODY incruent

UNBLUSHING brazen, immodest, obscene, shameful, shameless, unseemly

UNBODIED formless, incorporeal, shapeless

UNBOSOM confess, confide, disclose, open, reveal, unbreast

UNBOUNDED huge, immense, infinite, measureless, unchecked, unconfined, uncontrolled, unlimited, unrestrained, wide

UNBRACE carve, disjoint, enfeeble, free, loosen, relax, reveal, undo, weaken

UNBRIDLED abandoned, excessive, free, immoderate, intemperate, licentious, uncontrolled, uncurbed, unreined, unrestrained, unruly

UNBROKEN blank, cerrero, complete, continuate, continuous, dead, direct, endless, entire, flat, flush, intact, perpetual, regular, single, smooth, solid, straight, undug, unimpaired, unplowed, untamed, wild, whole

UNBURDEN alleviate, disclose, disload, ease, empty, free, relieve, reveal, uncharnel, unhamper, unload, unship

UNBURY disclose, disinter, exhume

UNBUXOM disobedient

UNCALLED-FOR absurd, foolish, impertinent, impolite, improper, imprudent, intrusive, needless, sassy, silly, superfluous, uncivil, unjustified, unwanted, unwarranted, wanton

UNCANNY creepy, deathly, eccentric, eerie, eery, eldritch, frightening, ghastly, ghostly, ghoulish, mysterious, odd, preternatural, queer, scary, secrety, spooky, strange, supernatural, unco (uth), unkid, unnatural, weird, wisht

UNCAS *beloved* cora *father* chingachgook *transportation* canoe

UNCEASING constant, continual, continuous, endless, eternal, everlasting, incessant, interminable, perpetual, unending

UNCEREMONIOUS abrupt, bluff, blunt, brusque, casual, curt, familiar, hasty, informal, rough, rude, short, sly, unconventional

UNCERTAIN ambiguous, amphibolic, amphibolous, borderline, brickle, casalty, casselty, casual, catching, chanc(e)y, changeable, changing, confused, confusing, debatable, delicate, diffident, doubtful, dubious, equivocal, erring, fitful, fluk(e)y, frivolous, halting, incalculable, inconstant, indefinite, indeterminate, insecure, irregular, irresolute, obscure, precarious, problematical, shaky, shillyshally, slippery, speculative, ticklish, touch-and-go, tricksy, unconfident, undecided, unpoised, unpredictable, unreliable, unsteady, unsure, vacillating, vague, variable, waugh, wavering, waw, willynilly, wobbly

UNCERTAINTY ambiguity, ambivalence, anxiety, chance, doubt, dubiety, dubiosity, gamble, hesitancy, hesitation, indecision, irregularity, irresolution, maybe, mistrust, oscillation, question, scepticism, scruple, skepticism, suspense, suspicion, vacillation

UNCHANCY dangerous, illfated, ill-omened, inconvenient, unlucky, unsafe, unseasonable

UNCHANGEABLE durable, eternal, fast, stable

UNCHANGING eternal, immutable, inflexible, invariable, permanent, rigid, static, uniform

UNCHARITABLE censorius, harsh, merciless, severe, unkind

UNCHASTE bawdy, frail, impure, lascivious, lewd, light, scarlet, wanton

UNCHECKED free, liberal, rampant, rife, undisciplined

UNCHEERFUL gloomy, grudging, miserable, sad, unhappy

UNCHRISTIAN agnostic, barbarous, exorbitant, heathen, pagan, uncivilized, ungodly

UNCIA inch, ounce, twelfth *12 juger*, libra, litra, pes

UNCINATE hamate, hooked

UNCIRCUMSISED gentile, heathen, infidel, irreligious, unregenerate

UNCIVIL barbarous, bluff, blunt, boorish, brusque, brute, caddish, churlish, crusty, discourteous, disrespectful, gruff, haughty, illbred, ill-mannered, impolite, indecorous, loutish, rude, savage, ungracious, vulgar

UNCIVILIZED barbaric, barbarous, brutal, feral, ignorant, primitive, rude, savage, sylvatic, wild

UNCLAD disrobed, loose, naked, nude, stripped, unclothed, undressed

UNCLE cozen, eam, eme, moneylender, nunka, nunks, nunky, oncle, oom, pawnbroker, sam, swindle, tio, yeme, zio
pert. avuncular
remus author harris
remus character brer rabbit, tarbaby
say submit, yield
toby creator sterne
toby's beloved widow wadman
tom tio-taco
tom's cabin author harriet beecher stowe
tom's cabin character eliza, little eva, simon legree, topsy

UNCLEAN black, corrupt, defiled, DIRTY, foul, immund, impure, pornographic, sinful, soiled, sullied, tref(a), unchaste, vile

UNCLEAR ambiguous, blear(y), blurred, cloudy, confused, dark, dim, equivocal, faint, hazy, indistinct, misty, muddy, murky, nebulous, obscure, roily, subtle, tenuous, vague

UNCLOSE expand, open, reveal, spread, unhasp, unreserved

UNCLOTHE See UNDRESS.

UNCLUTTERED neat, orderly, shipshape, tidy, trim

UNCO awkward, excitement, extraordinary, extremely, foreign, great, news, remarkable, shy, strange(r), tidings, uncanny, uncommon, unknown, unusual, very, weird, wonder

UNCOFT unbought

UNCOIL develop, unfold, unfurl, unlink, unreel, untangle, untwist, unwind

UNCOLORED achromatic, dispassionate, equitable, fair, hueless, impartial, just, objective, unbiased

UNCOMBED disheveled, disorderly, rumpled, tousled, unkempt, untewed

UNCOMFORTABLE awkward, distressing, hot, ill-atease, painful, poor, queasy, self-conscious, sore, sticky, suffering, uneasy, unfele

UNCOMMON choice, eccentric, exceptional, exotic, extraordinary, forby, infrequent, novel, occasional, odd, outstanding, particular, peculiar, queer, rare, remarkable, scarce, seld, singular, special, sporadic, strange, unco, unique, unusual, unwonted

UNCOMMUNICATIVE close(mouthed), dumb, private, reserved, reticent, secretive, silent, taciturn, tightlipped, unfriendly

UNCOMPLETED See INCOMPLETE.

UNCOMPLICATED honest, rural, SIMPLE

UNCOMPLIMENTARY slurring, unfavorable, unflattering

UNCOMPROMISING austere, extreme, firm, grim, immovable, inflexible, intransigent, obstinate, pat, rigid, severe, solid, stead-

fast, stern, strict, stubborn, ultra, unyielding

UNCONCEALED apparent, bare, evident, manifest, open, ouvert, overt

UNCONCERN apathy, coolness, disinterest, dispassion, disregard, inattention, indifference, insouciance, nonchalance, stoicism, tepidity

UNCONCERNED aloof, apathetic, bland, calm, careless, casual, collected, composed, cool, detached, disinterested, dull, emotionless, free, impassive, incurious, indifferent, insensible, insouciant, lackadaisical, nonchalant, open, passive, perfunctory, phlegmatic, serene, stolid, unemotional, unfeeling, uninterested, untroubled, unworried

UNCONDITIONAL absolute, frank, free, positive, simple, thorough, unmitigated, unqualified, unreserved, utter

UNCONFORMITY discontinuity, incongruity, inconsistency

UNCONGENIAL antipathetic, averse, discordant, discrepant, hateful, illnatured, inappropriate, incompatible, incongruous, inconsonant, obnoxious, repugnant, unfriendly, unsympathetic

UNCONNECTED detached, discrete, gappy

UNCONQUERABLE impregnable, indomitable, invictive, invincible, invulnerable, unbeatable

UNCONSCIONABLE corrupt, egregious, excessive, exorbitant, extortionate, outrageous, unprincipled, unreasonable, unscrupulous, wanton

UNCONSCIOUS accidental, asleep, automatic, blotto, cold, comatose, dead, ignorant, impromptu, inadvertant, inanimate, insensible, involuntary, konked, oblivious, out(cold), psyche, senseless, spontaneous, subliminal, torpid, unaware, unheeding, unmindful, unwitting
render stun
state apsychia, blackout, coma, faint, lipothemia, li-

pothymy, narcosis, sleep, stupor, swoon, syncope
UNCONSTRAINED familiar, free, impulsive, natural, simple, spontaneous, unnet
UNCONTRIVED artless
UNCONTROLLED abandoned, arbitrary, capricious, free, impulsive, inconstant, intractable, liberal, obstreperous, refractory, unchecked, unrestrained, wild
UNCONVENTIONAL audacious, bohemian, casual, daring, degage, devious, different, easy, eccentric, far out, free, imaginative, informal, irregular, kooky, loose, nonconforming, offbeat, original, outre, unceremonious, uncommon, unique, unorthodox, unusual
UNCONVINCING false, fishy, flimsy, inconclusive, unpersuasive
UNCOOKED au naturel, raw(ish)
UNCORDIAL cold, distant, hostile, uncongenial, unfriendly, unkind, unsociable
UNCOUNTED inestimable, innumerable, teeming
UNCOUPLE cut, disconnect, dislink, let go, loose, separate, unleash
UNCOUTH alien, awkward, blunt, boorish, clumsy, coarse, crude, desolate, disconsolate, discourteous, dismal, dreadful, heavy-handed, ignorant, loutish, mysterious, odd, offensive, rare, renish, rude, rugged, solitary, strange, tasteless, unacquainted, uncanny, uncivil, uncommon, uncourteous, unfamiliar, ungainly, ungenteel, unked, unkit, unknown, unmannerly, unpolished, unrefined, unseemly, unusual, wonderful *person* bandersnatch, boor, cad, fool, galoot, lout, peasant, tug, yahoo, yokel
UNCOVER bare, betray, denude, detect, dig up, disclose, display, divest, divulge, exhume, expose, open, reveal, show, strike, strip, tirl, tirr, tirve, uncloak, undrape, unearth, unfold, unheal, unhele, unlap, unmuffle, unveil
UNCRITICAL blind, cur-

sory, indiscriminate, naive, pleased, shallow, superficial
UNCROOK open, unbend
UNCTION anele, anointment, auction, balm, chrism, chrismation, chrismatory, enele, flattery, greasing, gush, insincerity, lubrication, oil(iness), ointment, soothing, unguent, viaticum *extreme* chrism
UNCTUOUS adipose, adulatory, bland, buttery, butyraceous, courtly, diplomatic, false, fat(ty), fulsome, greasy, hypocritical, ingratiating, insinuating, lardaceous, lardy, obsequious, oily, oleaginous, oleic, pinguid(inous), politic, salvy, saponaceous, sleek, slick, slippery, smooth, smug, soapy, soothing, suave, suety, tallowy, unguent(ous)
UNCTUOUSNESS hypocrisy, sanctimony, suavity
UNCULTIVATED arid, barbarous, boorish, desert, fallow, feral, raw, savage, untilled, wild
UNCULTURED artless, boorish, brutal, brutish, ignorant, inelegant, philistine, rough, rude, uneducated, unlearned, unpolished, unrefined, vulgar, wild
UNCUS claw, hook
UNDAMAGED bright, fresh, intact, unharmed, unhurt, uninjured, whole
UNDAUNTED audacious, bold, brave, courageous, doughty, fearless, intrepid, persevering, spartan, sta(u)nch, strong, turbulent, unafraid, unbridled, unconquered, unfaltering, valiant, valorous
UNDEAD *ones* nosferatu
UNDECIDED doubtful, dubious, hesitant, inconstant, indefinite, irresolute, moot, pendent, pending, problematical, uncertain, unresolved, unsettled, up in the air, vacillating, wavering
UNDEFEATABLE See UNCONQUERABLE.
UNDEFEATED See UNBEATEN.
UNDEFILED chaste, intact, pure, uncontaminated, virgin
UNDEMONSTRATIVE cold,

constrained, inhibited, laconic, reserved, restrained, reticent
UNDENIABLE certain, clear, evident, incontestible, indisputable, irrefragable, irrefutable, obvious, sure, unanswerable, unquestionable
UNDEPENDABLE casual, frivolous, inconstant, indefinite, indeterminate, precarious, treacherous, uncertain, unreliable, unsafe, unsure, untrustworthy
UNDER alow, aneath, below, beneath, bottom, downtrodden, downward, inferior, infra, inside, less, liable to, lower, neath, nether, planted, short, sotto, sous, subdued, subject, subordinate
a cloud disgraced, doubted, suspected
arms enlisted, enrolled, equipped
a strain jittery, jumpy, nervous, tense
comb. hyp(o), sous, sub(ter)
false colors deceptive(ly)
lock and key guarded, protected, secure(d)
obligation bound, pledged, promised
one's breath aside, sotto voce, whisper
pressure in a bind, squeezed
protest reluctantly, unwillingly
suspicion doubted, suspect
the aegis of guarded, protected, secure(d)
the counter clandestine, covert, illegal, improper, secret, stealthy, unauthorized
the influence drunk, on a trip, on the nod
the weather ailing, drunk, ill, sick
way afoot, at sea, begun, launched, moving, on course, stirring
wraps secret
UNDERBIT earmark
UNDERBODY basquine, corsetcover
UNDERBRUSH See UNDERGROWTH.
UNDERCLOTHES See UNDERWEAR.
UNDERCOAT paint, petticoat, primer, sealer, surfacer

UNDERCOVER cave, clandestine, concealed, covert, deceptive, hidden, protected, secret, stealthy, sub rosa, surreptitious, underhand

agent cia, counterspy, detective, fbi, informer, ogpu, police, spy

UNDERCROFT crypt

UNDERCURRENT eddy, flow, hidden, latent, underrun

UNDERCUT backspin, fillet, jad, kerf, kirve, lame, nick, notch, pool, tenderloin

UNDERDOG loser, victim, zebra

UNDERDONE bloody, blue, incomplete, partial, rare, raw, red

UNDERESTIMATE disprize, minimize, play down, underrate, undervalue

UNDERFALL succumb

UNDERFED drawn, emaciated, haggard, hungry, pinched, poor, starved, thin, undernourished

UNDERFONG circumvent, ensnare, entrap, receive, sustain, undertake

UNDERFOOT abject, base, below, beneath, downtrodden, in the way, low, prop, secretly, support, underpin

UNDERGARMENT See UNDERWEAR.

UNDERGIRD bind, brace, frap, secure, strengthen, support

UNDERGO afford, bare, bear, carry, dree, encounter, endure, experience, partake, pass, serve, stand, submit, suffer, survive, sustain, tolerate, undermine, understand, weaken

UNDERGRADUATE academic, coed, collegian, freshman, frosh, junior, novice, senior, sophomore, student, tassel

UNDERGROUND basement, beneath, cave, cellar, covert, grapevine, hidden, hushhush, hypogeal, hypogeous, metro, private, railroad, resistance, secret, stealthy, subterranean, subversive, subway, sunken, surreptious(ly), train, tube, tunnel, undercover

army haganah

dweller gnome, gopher, mole

explosion camouflet

movement maquis, partisans, resistance, sla

product coal, gas, minerals, oil, ore

ripening geocarpic

stream aar

worker miner, mucker, pitman, sapper

UNDERGROWTH abature, boscage, boskage, brush(et), bushes, bushwood, coppice, covert, frith, garsil, hypotrophy, rammel, rush, thicket, underbrush

UNDERHAND See UNDERLING.

UNDERHAND(ED) backstairs, byhand, circuitous, clandestine, corrupt, covert, crafty, deceitful, dern, dishonest, dishonorable, fraudulent, furtive, hookycrooky, mean, oblique, privy, secret, shabby, shady, sinister, sly, sneaking, sneaky, stealthy, subordinate, surreptitious, tricky, unfair, unjust, unobtrusive, wily

trick backspang, backstab, chicanery

UNDERHUNG lanternjawed, undershot

UNDERLAY bury, eke, foundation, prop, readjust, rectify, support, tap, undercurrent

UNDERLEAF amphigastrium

UNDERLIE bear, smolder, squat, straddle, submit, subtend, support, surrender, yield

UNDERLINE accentuate, emphasize, mark, score, stress, underscore

UNDERLING apprentice, assistant, deputy, helper, inferior, journeyman, menial, second fiddle, second stringer, servant, subject, subordinate

UNDERLYING anterior, basic, behind, cardinal, covert, essential, fundamental, implicit, inate, indispensable, latent, necessary, needful, obscure, prior, radical, requisite, subjacent, substratal

UNDERMANNED shorthanded

UNDERMINE burrow, cave, cripple, demoralize, destroy, dig, disable, discover, drain, enfeeble, erode, excavate, foil, founder, hole, impair, injure, sabotage, sap, spoil, subvert, supplant, thwart, tunnel, wash away, weaken, whittle away, wreck

UNDERMOST bottom, lowest, nethermost

UNDERNE afternoon, lunch, midday, morning, nine o'clock, noon

UNDERNEATH below, beneath, bottom, disguised, hidden, lower, secret, surreptitious

UNDERNIM capture, perceive, rebuke, reprove, seize, take, understand, undertake

UNDERNOURISHED emaciated, starved, thin

state anutraminosa

UNDERPANTS bloomers, briefs, drawers, knickers, pantalettes, panties, shorts, step-ins, teddy

UNDERPASS shaft, sottopassagio, subway, tunnel

UNDERPIN justify, maintain, substantiate, support, vindicate

UNDERPINNING base, foundation, justification, prop, support

UNDERPRIVILEGED depressed, deprived, poor

UNDERPROP support, underpin, uphold

UNDERRATE decry, discount, extenuate, underestimate, undervalue

UNDERSCORE emphasize, italicize, line, mark, stress

UNDERSEA See UNDERWATER.

UNDERSET maintain, prop, provide, strengthen, sublet, support, underlet

UNDERSHIRT camisa, chemise, jersey, linder, semmit, shift, shirt, singlet, skivvies, tee, t-shirt, vest

UNDERSIGN guarantee, ratify

UNDERSIZE(D) dwarf, peewee, runt, scrub, weeny

UNDERSKIRT crinoline, petticoat, slip

UNDERSONG accompaniment, refrain, tierce

UNDERSTAIRS basement, cellar

UNDERSTAND absorb, accept, agree, appreciate, apprehend, assimilate, assume, believe, can, catch on, comprehend, con(ceive), conclude, construe, cotton, decipher, dig(est), discern, divine, explain, fathom, feel, follow, gather, get, grasp, have, infer, intake, intend, interpret, intuit, ken, know, make, master, penetrate, perceive, perstand, pierce, read, realize, reason, sabby, sabe, savvy, see, seize, sense, solve, suppose, take in, think, trow, twig

UNDERSTANDABLE clear, comprehensible, conceivable, exoteric, intelligible, lucent, lucid, luculent, obvious, rational, simple, transparent

UNDERSTANDING acceptance, accord(ant), acumen, agreement, amity, apprehension, astute, attitude, aware, brain(y), capacity, compact, comprehension, concept(ion), contract, diagnosis, discernment, empathy, entente, faculty, feeling, feet, footwear, grasp, grip, humane, idea, indulgent, intellect, intelligence, intelligent, inwit, judgment, ken, knowing, mastery, mind, news, noema, nous, pact, patience, penetration, perception, percipience, reason, sabe, savvy, sense, skillful, sympathetic, sympathy, tolerance, toleration, treaty, vernuft, verstand
lack betise, stupidity
pert. psychic

UNDERSTATEMENT litotes

UNDERSTOOD agreed, assumed, bien entendu, clear, comprehensible, implied, implicit, inferential, lucid, settled, tacit, unsaid, unuttered

UNDERSTUDY double, pinchhitter, replacement, stand-in, substitute

UNDERTAKE accept, adopt, agree, apply, assume, attack, attempt, begin, buckle to, chide, contract, covenant, dare, dive into, embark, embrace, emprise, en-

deavor, engage(in), enter (on), essay, execute, fand, fang, fond, get going, go into, grasp, guarantee, incept, launch, light into, perform, pledge, plunge, postulate, practice, promise, receive, reprove, sail into, seize, set about, tackle, take on, tear into, try, underfong, venture, volunteer, warrant

UNDERTAKER cerer, contractor, embalmer, entrepreneur, funeral director, godfather, godmother, manager, mortician, omer, publisher, rebuker, sponsor, surety, upholder

UNDERTAKING act, adventure, affair, attempt, aval, avowal, business, calling, cautio, charge, chore, covenant, crusade, endeavor, engagement, enterprise, guarantee, job, move, obligation, pledge, project, promise, proposition, pursuit, risk, scheme, task, venture, vocation
risky glitch
written caution(es)

UNDERTOW current, eddy, riptide, vortex

UNDERVALUE decry, depreciate, disprize, disvalue, underrate

UNDERWALK bypath

UNDERWATER subaqueous, submarine, submersed, suboceanic
apparatus caisson, otter, paravane, tremie
boat sub(marine), submersible, u-boat, wreck
cement mass paar
chamber caisson, cave
eye periscope

UNDERWEAR balmoral, bandeau, bloomers, bodice, body linen, bra(ssiere), brief, bustle, bvd's, camiknicker, camise, camisole, chemilonn, chemise(tte), chiton, cilice, combination, corselet, corset, crinoline, cymar, dessous, doublet, drawers, flannels, flimsy, foundation, girdle, hairshirt, heavies, intimates, knickers, linder, lingerie, pannier, pantalettes, panties, pants, petticoat, scanties, shift, shirt, shorts, simar, singlet,

skivies, skivvy, slip, smallclothes, smalls, smock, snuggies, stammel, stays, stepins, tallith, teddy(bear), teeshirt, tournure, underpants, undershirt, undies, unionsuit, unmentionables, vest, waist, woolies
fabric balbriggan, nylon, silk

UNDERWEIGHT angular, bony, lean, rawboned, scrawny, skinny, thin

UNDERWOOD See UNDERGROWTH.

UNDERWORLD (See also HELL.) amenti, antipodes, aralu, blackhand, crime, dewat, duat, gangdom, gangland, hades, hell, jigoku, limbo, mafia, mictlan, mob, neno kuni, orcus, purgatory, rackets, sheol, soko nokuni, syndicate, tartarus, tophet(h), xialba, yakuza, yowo-tsukuni
dwelling in chthonic
ferryman charon
god abida, aidoneus, anubis, apuat, bran, cog, demon, devil, dis(pater), enmeshara, erebus, gwyn(n), hades, hermes, keneloa, manes, mara, minos, mors, nergal, ningishzida, orcus, osiris, pluto, pwyll, rhadamanthus, rot, satan, serapis, thanatos, thantos, titan, tuoni, vediovis, veduis, vejovis, yama, yima
goddess allatu, aralu, belili, cora, dana, danu, demeter, despoina, don, ereshkigal, frigg, fury, gaea, hecate, hel(a), kore, laruna, mania, persephassa, pereshphone, pherephatta, phersephatta, proserpina, prytania, ran, trivia, tuonetar
guardian cerberus
heads, decapitated kaguhana, mirume
judge rhadamanthus, rhadamanthys
messenger namtaru
river acheron, cocytus, lethe, phlegethon, styx
ruler emmahoo, ereshkigal, hades, nergal, pluto, yamaraja

UNDERWRITE advance, agree to, assure, back, confirm, endorse, ensure, finance, foot, guarantee, insure, pledge, promise, ratify, sign, sponsor, submit to, subscribe, support, sustain

UNDERWRITER angel, backer, banker, cosigner, guarantor, insurer, signer, sponsor

UNDESERVED indign, undue, unearned, unmerited, wrong

UNDESIGNING artless, simple, sincere

UNDESIRABLE See UNPLEASANT.

UNDETERMINED aoristic, doubtful, dubious, indefinite, indeterminate, infinite, irresolute, undecided

UNDEVELOPED crude, immature, juvenile, stunted

UNDIES See UNDERWEAR.

UNDIGHT disarray, disordered, undressed, unfasten

UNDIGNIFIED indecorous, informal, unbecoming, unseemly

UNDILUTED neat, plain, pure, raw, sheer, straight, thick, unmixed, unmodified

UNDINE gnome, nix, nymph, spirit, sylph
consort huldbrand

UNDISCIPLINED capricious, inconstant, unruly, untrained, wanton, wild

UNDISCLOSED covert, hidden, sealed, secret, ulterior, unrevealed

UNDISCRIMINATING gross, imperceptive, promiscuous

UNDISGUISED apparent, bald, barefaced, clear, evident, frank, genuine, manifest, obvious, overt, plain, public, unvarnished

UNDISMAYED brave, courageous, onflemed, staunch

UNDISPOSED antagonistic, deranged, ill-conditioned, ill-prepared

UNDISTINGUISHED common, fameless, humble, mediocre, nondescript, unobserved

UNDISTURBED calm, content, peaceful, placid, quiet, serene, smooth, sound, tranquil, unconcerned, unruffled, untroubled, unworried, virgin

UNDIVIDED continuous, en-

tire, one, single, unipartite, whole

UNDO annihilate, annul, battle, betray, break, cancel, cook, decipher, defease, defeat, defeise, demolish, demoralize, destroy, diddle, disappoint, disentangle, dissolve, erase, explain, expound, foredo, free, liberate, loose, nullify, open, release, remove, resolve, reverse, ruin, smash, solve, spoil, spring, unfasten, unravel, untie, untwist, unweave, unwind, unwrap

UNDOER achan, interpreter, seducer

UNDOING annulment, defeat, destruction, downfall, overthrow, reversal, ruin

UNDOMESTICATED feral, ferine, untamed, wild

UNDONE dished, hopeless, lost, neglected, opened, overcome, rare, ruined, unfastened, upset

UNDRESS bare, deprive, despoil, devest, disarray, dishabille, dismantle, disrobe, divest, doff, negligee, peel, shed, strip, tirl, tirr, unattire, unbind, unbusk, unclad, unclothe, undrape, unrig, unrobe, unspoil, unveil

UNDRESSED au naturel, bare, en deshabille, exposed, nude, stark, stripped, uncovered, undight, ungarbed, ungroomed, unkempt

UNDUE exceeding, excessive, exorbitant, extreme, immoderate, improper, inappropriate, inordinate, intemperate, outrageous, preposterous, undeserved, unjustified, unmerited, unsuitable, untimely, unwarranted, wrong

UNDULATE billow, flicker, float, fluctuate, gyrate, gyrose, kelter, oscillate, pendulate, pulsate, ripple, roll, surge, sway, swell, swing, undate, wave, wavy

UNDULATING flexuous, rippling, ripply, rolling, surging, vibrating, wavy

UNDULATION beat, billow, breaker, comber, convolution, crimping, heave, ripple, roll(er), surge,

swell, teeter, tremolo, vibrato, waviness, waving

UNDULY carelessly, excessively, irregularly, unjustly

UNDYING amaranthine, deathless, endless, eternal, everlasting, immortal, immutable, indestructible, lasting, perpetual, unending, unfading

UNEARTH delve, detect, dig up, disclose, discover, exhume, expose, extract, find, reveal, root, search, uncover

UNEARTHLY appalling, awesome, eerie, eery, extreme, ghastly, ghostly, ghoulish, heavenly, immaterial, odd, outlandish, preposterous, preternatural, spectral, supernatural, terrific, uncanny, weird

UNEASINESS anxiety, discomfort, disquiet, distaste, impatience, malaise, qualms, trepidation, trouble, unrest, worry

UNEASY agitated, anxious, apprehensive, awkward, concerned, constrained, cramping, difficult, disagreeable, disturbed, fidgety, fitful, hectic, impatient, inquiet, jittery, jumpy, nervous, overwrought, perturbed, restive, restless, self-conscious, skittish, solicitous, stiff, uncomfortable, unquiet, worried

UNEDUCATED benighted, callow, crude, green, ignorant, illiterate, nescient, raw, rough, rude, simple, uninformed, unlearned, unlettered, unprepared, untaught, untutored

UNEMOTIONAL apathetic, bland, cold, cool, dry, dull, impassive, indifferent, passive, phlegmatic, stoic(al), stony, unconcerned, unfeeling

UNEMPLOYED disengaged, free, idle, inactive, indolent, laid off, leisured, otiant, otiose, unused, vacant
person batlan, batlon

UNENDING age-long, ceaseless, chronic, continuous, endless, eternal, everlasting, termless, timeless, unceasing, undying

UNENDURABLE ephemeral, insufferable, intolerable, unbearable

UNENLIGHTENED benighted, heathen, ignorant

UNEQUAL anisomerous, asymmetrical, different, disparate, disquiparant, ill-balanced, ill-matched, inadequate, inequitable, inferior, insufficient, irregular, odd, partial, topheavy, uneven, unfair, unjust, variable *comb.* anis(o) -sided amphithect

UNEQUALED alone, inimitable, matchless, nonesuch, peerless, perfect, supreme, surpassing, unique, unmatched, unparagoned, unparalleled

UNEQUIVOCAL absolute, candid, clear, conclusive, definite, direct, distinct, explicit, obvious, open, plain, simple, sincere, square, unmistakable, unqualified

UNERRING accurate, certain, correct, deadly, definite, dependable, exact, flawless, inerrant, infallible, perfect, precise, reliable, straight, sure, true, trustworthy, unfailing

UNESSENTIAL dispensable, needless, trivial, unimportant

UNETHICAL corrupt, dishonest, illegal, unprofessional

UNEVEN broken, bumpy, changeable, choppy, coarse, cross-grained, disparate, diverse, erose, erratic, fitful, harsh, hottery, humpy, irregular, jaggy, jolty, odd, ragged, rank, rough, ruffled, rugged, shagged, shaggy, spasmodic, spotty, streaky, unequal, UNFAIR, unjust, unkempt, unlevel, unlike, unpolished, variable, wrong *comb.* anis(o)

UNEXACTING easy-going, uncritical

UNEXCELLED champion, superior, topnotch, unsurpassed

UNEXCEPTIONAL acceptable, general, ordinary, regular, tolerable, usual

UNEXCITED calm, unfluttered, unrattled, unruffled

UNEXCITING banal, bor-

ing, dead, dull, flat, prosaic, tame, trite, unoriginal

UNEXPECTED abrupt, accidental, casual, chance, eerie, impetuous, impulsive, inopine, rare, sudden, surprising, swift, unforeseen, unusual

UNEXPRESSED allusive, covert, implicit, implied, tacit, understood

UNEYED unobserved, unseen

UNFADING amaranthine, deathless, deep-dyed, endless, enduring, everlasting, fast, immarcescible, immortal, imperishable, lasting, perdurable, permanent, perpetual, undying

UNFAILING certain, constant, deadly, dependable, diligent, endless, inevitable, inexhaustible, infallible, reliable, sure, unerring, unflagging, unremitting, unyielding

UNFAIN displeased, reluctant, sorry

UNFAIR biased, bigoted, devious, discriminating dishonest, foul, inequitable, intolerant, jaundiced, partial, prejudiced, shabby, slanted, tyrannical, underhanded, undue, unequal, uneven, unfavorable, unjust, unreasonable, unseemly, wrong (ful)

UNFAIRNESS bias, discrimination, favoritism, foul (play), inequity, injustice, wrong

UNFAITHFUL adulterous, barratrous, corrupt, derelict, disaffected, dishonest, disloyal, false, fickle, inaccurate, inconstant, inexact, infidel, recreant, traitor, untrue, untrustworthy

UNFAMILIAR alien, bizarre, different, fantastic, fresh, ignorant, little-known, new, novel, obscure, recondite, strange, unaccustomed, unacquainted, unknown, unusual, unversed

UNFASHIONABLE distorted, hokey, obsolete, old (fashioned) (hat), outdated, outmoded, passe, shapeless, unshapely

UNFASTEN detach, free,

liberate, loose(n), open, release, unbind, unbolt, unclasp, undight, undo, unfix, unhasp, unhitch, unlatch, unlock, unpinion, unravel, unsteck, untie, untine

UNFATHERED bastard, illegitimate, spurious

UNFATHOMABLE abysmal, abyssal, bottomless, infinite, profound, unintelligible

UNFAVORABLE adverse, backward, bad, contrary, disapproving, foul, hostile, ill, inopportune, low, poor, repulsive, ugly, unappreciative, uncomplimentary, undesirable, unfortunate, unkind(ly), unpromising, unpropitious, untimely

UNFEELING apathetic, apathy, blunt, brutal, callous, cold(hearted), cool, crass, cruel, dispassionate, fell, frigid, frozen, hard, harsh, heartless, impassive, inanimate, indifferent, insensate, insensible, insensitive, numb, obdurate, oblivious, obtuse, passive, phlegmatic, soulless, stoic, stolid, unconcerned, unemotional, unmoved, untouched

UNFEIGNED authentic, bonafide, cordial, genuine, heartfelt, hearty, impulsive, naive, natural, real, simple, sincere, spontaneous, wholehearted

UNFETTER free, liberate, loose, unchain, UNFASTEN, unshackle

UNFILLED blank, empty, VACANT, vacuous

UNFINISHED fragmentary, immature, imperfect, incomplete(d), ragged, raw, unaccomplished

UNFIT bad, disabled, disqualified, impotent, improper, inadequate, inappropriate, inapt, incapable, incompetent, inept, sick, inapt, unhappy, unlikely, unmeet, unqualified, unsuitable, untimely, wisht, wrong

UNFLAGGING assiduous, constant, diligent, energetic, persistent, steady, unfailing, unremitting

UNFLEDGED callow, green, immature, undeveloped

UNFLINCHING calm, persevering, sta(u)nch, steadfast, unshrinking, unwavering

UNFOLD air, blossom, break, deploy, develop, disclose, display, divulge, evolute, evolve, expand, explain, flower, manifest, open, release, reveal, solve, spread, straighten, uncoil, unfurl, unravel, unroll, unwrap

UNFORESEEN accidental, casual, chance, imprevu, lucky, sudden, uncalculated, unexpected

UNFORGETTABLE extraordinary, indelible, memorable, red-letter

UNFORMED amorphous, callow, chaotic, inchoate

UNFORTUNATE adverse, bad, calamitous, cataclysmic, catastrophic, deplorable, doncy, hapless, ill (omened), inauspicious, inept, inexpedient, lamentable, luckless, regrettable, sad, schartzeh, schartzer, sinistrous, tragic, unhappy, unlucky, unsuccessful, unsuitable, untimely, untoward

UNFORTUNATELY nebbech, nebbish, nebech, nebish

UNFOUNDED baseless, falacious, false, groundless, idle, illogical, ungrounded, unreal, unstable, untrue, vain

UNFREEZE See MELT, THAW.

UNFREQUENTED empty, lonely, remote, solitary

UNFRIENDLY alien, aloof, antagonistic, bitter, chill(y), close, cool, frosty, hostile, icy, inimical, malevolent, malign, opposed, self-contained, strange, unsociable *terms* outs

UNFRUITFUL acarpous, barren, futile, ineffective, infecund, infertile, sterile, unproductive, unprofitable, useless

UNFURL break, develop, disclose, display, expand, open, show, slack, spread, unfold, UNROLL, unwind

UNGAINLY awkward, boorish, clumsy, gawky, graceless, leggy, ponderous,

ugly, uncouth, ungraceful, unheppen, weedy

UNGENEROUS grudging, harsh, illiberal, mean, miserly, niggardly, petty, shabby, small-minded, stingy

UNGENTLEMANLY See UNCOUTH.

UNGIRT discinct, loose(d), relaxed, slack, unbind, unknot(ted)

UNGLE claw, hoof, nail, ungula

UNGODLY atrocious, bad, blasphemous, dreadful, evil, execrable, horrid, impious, impure, irreligious, nasty, outrageous, profane, profligate, reprobate, sinful, unchristian, unearthly, unholy, unrighteous, wayward, wicked

UNGOVERNABLE contrary, froward, headstrong, intractable, irrepressible, licentious, perverse, rebellious, refractory, unbridled, uncontrollable, unruly, violent, wild, willful

UNGRACEFUL angular, awkward, clumsy, gawky, halting, hard, inelegant, tasteless, uncouth, ungainly, untoward

UNGRACIOUS blunt, boorish, churlish, curt, disagreeable, discourteous, gruff, illmannered, impolite, inaffable, offensive, rude, snappish, unamiable, uncivil, unfeel, unfele, unmannerly, unpleasant

UNGRAMMATICAL asyntactic, catachrestic, illiterate, incorrect, solecistic

UNGRATEFUL distasteful, inappreciative, repellent, thankless, unkind, unpleasant *person* ingrate

UNGUARDED accessible, careless, defenseless, exposed, incautious, indiscreet, unprotected, vulnerable, weak

UNGUENT aliptic, anoint, balm, cerate, ceroma, chrism, lubricant, ointment, pomade, pomatum, salve

UNGULA claw, foot, hoof, nail, talon

UNGULATE amblypod, ass, bovine, cervine, cony, cow, daman, deer, elephant,

equestrian, equine, goat, hircine, hog, hoofed, horse, mule, pig, porcine, rhinoceros, ruminant, sheep, swine, swinish, tapir *extinct* amblypod(a), toxodontia, typotheria

UNHALLOWED desecrated, evil, impious, improper, impure, indecent, lascivious, licentious, profane, sinful, unholy, wicked

UNHAMPERED See FREE.

UNHANDY awkward, bulky, clumsy, undexterous, unmanageable

UNHAPPINESS calamity, depression, discontent, dolor, grief, ill-fare, melancholy, misery, sadness, sorrow, tristesse, woe

UNHAPPY afflicted, black, blue, calamitous, cheerless, dejected, desolate, discontented, dismal, displeased, distressed, downcast, drear, gauche, glum, hapless, improper, inapt, inept, inexpedient, infestive, joyless, maladroit, melancholy, mirthless, miserable, morose, overcome, painful, rueful, sad, sorrowful, sorry, uncheerful, unfit, unfortunate, unlucky, unmeet, unsuitable, untimely, wo(e) begone, woeful, wretched *person* unsel

UNHARNESS ungear, unhorse, untackle

UNHEALTHY afflicted, dangerous, delicate, diseased, feeble, frail, harmful, ill, infirm, morbid, noxious, queasy, risky, sick(ly), unsanitary, virulent, weak

UNHEARD faint, inaudible, indistinct, strange, surd, unclear, unknown, unprecedented

-of absurd, exceptional, fresh, rare, strange, sui generis, surprising, unique, unknown, unlikely, unprecedented

UNHELP hinder, hindrance

UNHENDE discourteous, rude

UNHEPPEN awkward, ungainly, unskillful, untidy

UNHESITATING believing, bold, confident, steady, unfaltering, unwavering

UNHINGE craze, detach

dislocate, disorient, displace, disrupt, madden, open, unbalance, unfix, unlock, unnerve, unsettle, upset

UNHOARD pilfer, steal, take

UNHOLY See UNGODLY.

UNHORSE dislodge, dismount, evict, free, overcome, overthrow, purl, throw, topple, unharness, unsaddle, unseat

UNHURRIED deliberate, easy, languid, leisurely, slow, sober

UNICORN chilin, howitzer, lilin, monoceros, narwhal(e), reem
-antelope takin
bird screamer
fish filefish, lija, narwal, narwhal(e), unie
plant martinoe
root blazing-star, swamppink
sheep barwal
whale See *fish*, above.

UNICUM oner, UNION

UNIFIED articulate, consolidated, global, joined, UNITED

UNIFORM akin, alike, cloth, consistent, consonant, constant, dun, equable, equal, even, flat, garb, garment, gown, habit, homogeneous, humdrum, identical, insignia, just, level, like, livery, measured, monkey suit, monodromic, orderly, parallel, plain, regalia, regular, robe, same, similar, single, smooth, stable, standard, steady, suit(y), symmetrical, unchanging, unvaried
color olive-drab
cord aiguillette
leather buff
make even, grade, isochronize, level, smooth, stabilize, steady
material chino, khaki
military blues, fatigues, khaki, regimentals, whites
prisoner's stripes
without mufti

UNIFORMITY agreement, consistency, constancy, correspondence, entropy, evenness, harmony, monotony, oneness, regularity, routine, sameness, similarity, smoothness, stability, symmetry

UNIFY articulate, blend, cement, coalesce, combine, compact, concentrate, conjoin, consolidate, fuse, join, merge, organize, systematize, unite

UNIFYING esemplastic

UNILOCULAR monothecal

UNIMAGINABLE absurd, doubtful, extraordinary, fantastic, implausible

UNIMAGINATIVE arid, banal, common, dull, hackneyed, literal, pedantic, prosaic, stupid, trite, unoriginal

UNIMPAIRED entire, fresh, intact, sound, whole

UNIMPASSIONED continent, phlegmatic, placid, prosaic, serene, sober, stoic, stolid, temperate, tranquil, unemotional

UNIMPEACHABLE · blameless, impeccable, irrefutable, irreproachable, pure, undeniable, unquestionable

UNIMPORTANT casual, fribble, frivolous, frothy, immaterial, insignificant, jerkwater, lowly, minor, niggling, null, of no account, paltry, peddling, pettifogging, petty, picayune, piddling, puny, simple, slight, trifling, trinkety, trivial, unworthy

UNINFLECTED anaptotic

UNINFORMED green, ignorant, unaware, unconscious, uninitiated, untold

UNINHABITED desert, desolate, empty, tenantless, unoccupied, untenanted, vacant

UNINHIBITED audacious, bold, daring, expansive, free, shocking, startling, unconstrained, unrepressed, unreserved, venturesome

UNINSPIRED bland, boring, dry, dull, flat, hack, lifeless, prosaic, stodgy, unremarkable

UNINTELLIGENT asinine, blind, brainless, brute, brutish, dull, dumb, foolish, IGNORANT, inapt, inept, irrational, mindless, obtuse, senseless, STUPID, unthinking, unwise, vacant, vacuous, witless

UNINTELLIGIBLE blind, enigmatic, fathomless, incomprehensible, inscrutable,

mystical, opaque, unfathomable

UNINTENDED, UNINTENTIONAL accidental, casual, fortuitous, inadvertent, purposeless, unmeant, unpremeditated, unthinking

UNINTERESTED apathetic, bored, cool, impartial, incurious, indifferent, oblivious, passive, unconcerned, weary

UNINTERESTING arid, boring, drab, dry, dull, flat, insipid, monotonous, prosaic, stale, tedious

UNINTERRUPTED constant, continuous, direct, endless, perpetual, persevering, steady, straight, unbroken

UNINVOLVED aloof, indifferent, withdrawn

UNION (See also CIVIL WAR.) alliance, amalgam(ation), anastomosis, anschluss, artel, ascap, association, blend, bloc, cio, club, coalition, coherence, combination, combine, composite, compound, concert, concord, confederacy, confederation, connection, consonance, copula, ensign, entent, espousal, federation, fusion, gremio, group, guild, hansa, hanse, harmony, integration, jack, jointure, junction, juncture, league, liaison, link(age), local, marriage, matrimony, meeting, merger, oneness, raphe, seam, society, solidarity, synartesis, systasis, tie, trade-guild, trust, unicum, unity, wedlock, yoga, yoking
comb. apsis, gamo
jack See FLAG.
labor afl, cio, hui, ila, ilo, ilgwu, ita, teamsters, twu, uaw
member bluecollar, blueshirt, hardhat
merchants' hansa, hanse
of soviet socialist republics See RUSSIA.
political systasis
seam-like raphe
troops blue, feds, redlegs, yanks
weak rope of sand

UNIQUE alone, bizarre, choice, eccentrate, eccentric, exceptional, extraordinary, fresh, great, incomparable, isolated, lone, matchless, notable, odd, one, only, original, out of the ordinary, particular, peculiar, peerless, queer, rare, single, singular, sole (yne), special, splendid, strange, sui generis, uncommon, unequal, unicum, unusual, weird

UNISON accord, agreement, assent, concord, consonance, harmony, homophony, unanimity, union

UNIT ace, apparatus, arm, branch, bureau, credit, detachment, digit, element, entity, group, individual, ingredient, integer, item, leg, member, monad, one, part, piece, section, squad, syllable, whole, wing

collective commune

fundamental base

hypothetical idic, pangen(e)

of See noun, e.g., ENERGY unit.

pert. monadic

UNITE add, adhere, adjoin, affiliate, affix, agglutinate, alligate, ally, amalgamate, anchylose, ankylose, annex, assemble, associate, attach, band, bind, blend, cabal, cement, centralize, club, coadunate, coalesce, cohere, combine, commix, compound, concentrate, concur, confederate, conjoin, connect, consolidate, consort, converge, couple, embody, fay, federate, fit, fuse, graft, harmonize, hasp, incorporate, integrate, join, knit, knot, link, marry, meld, merge, mingle, mix, pair, pan, piece, rabbet, rally, reconcile, relate, sam(m), seam, sew, solder, soud, splice, tie, unify, wed, weld, yoke

closely cement, cotton, fay, weld

edges rabbet

in opposition gang up on

metals braze, sweat, weld

ropes splice

UNITED allied, bound, combined, commutual, conjoint, conjugate, connate, corporate, fused, harmonious, joined, kindred, one(d), related, tied, unanimous, unified, wedded

comb. gamo

front coalition

UNITED ARAB EMIRATES abu dhabi, ajman, dubai, fujaira, gulf sheikdoms, ras al-khaima, sharjah, sheikdoms, trucial states, umm al-qaiwain

UNITED ARAB REPUBLIC See EGYPT.

UNITED KINGDOM See ENGLAND.

UNITED NATIONS *agencies* fao, icao, ilo, imco, iro, ito, itu, unesco, unicef, unrra, upu, who, wmo

ambassador moynihan, scali, stevenson, young

creation site dumbarton oaks, san francisco

economic commissions ecafe, ece, ecla

headquarters, former lake success

part general assembly, secretariat, security council

president evatt, spaak

secretary general hammarskjold, lie, u thant, waldheim

staff group secretariat

UNITED PROVINCES friesland, gelderland, groningen, holland, overijssel, utrecht, zeeland

UNITED STATES (See AMERICA for *bird, flower, shrub, tree,* etc.) america, columbia, uncle sam

abolitionist blackwell, garrison, john brown, stevens, stowe

actor barrymore, belafonte, belasco, bogart, booth, carnovsky, chaplin, drew, fairbanks, fields, forrest, gable, garrison, gillette, grant, hampden, hardy, herne, hopper, jefferson, laughton, laurel, lindsay, lloyd, lucas, lunt, mansfield, mantell, march, massey, olcot, payne, pidgeon, robeson, robinson, rooney, skinner, sothern, strasberg, tracy, valentino, von stroheim, warfield, welles

actress bankhead, bara, barrymore, carter, claire, cornell, cowl, crawford, cushman, davies, dietrich, dressler, fiske, fontaine, garbo, garland, harlow, harris, hayes, hepburn, le gallienne, marlowe, monroe, perry, pickford, rogers, skinner, swanson, tucker, west

admiral dewey, evans, farragut, halsey, kincaid, leahy, nimitz, raborn, radford, sampson, schley, sims, spruance, stark, wilkes

aeronautical inventor wright

aid policy marshall plan, truman doctrine

air force motto sustineo alas

air force unit See AIR force unit.

airplane superfort(ress)

airplane designer martin, seversky

anarchist sacco, vanzetti

anthropologist benedict, bolton, herskowitz, hooton, kluckhohn, kroeber, leakey, mead, redfield, wissler

antiquary nutting

anti-trust act clayton, sherman

archeologist hewett

architect bacon, benjamin, bragdon, bulfinch, burnham, carrere, cram, davis, fuller, gilbert, goodhue, johnson, kahn, latrobe, l'enfant, maybeck, mckim, mills, post, price, richardson, saarinen, stone, strickland, town, upjohn, van der rohe, walter, white, wright

army officer See *general,* below.

army scout cody

army store post exchange

army surgeon walter reed

art historian berenson, panofsky

artist See *painter* and *sculptor,* below.

assassin booth, czolgosz, guiteau, oswald, sirhan

assassin, would-be fromme, moore

astrologer evangeline adams

astronomer aitken, bowditch, draper, hale, langley, lowell, mitchell, pickering, shapley, todd

astronaut, 1st on moon armstrong

astronaut, 1st in orbit glenn

astronaut, 1st in space shepard

astronaut, 1st walk in space white

astrophysicist abbot

athlete didrikson, owens

author See *dramatist, novelist, poet, writer,* below.

aviator bennett, earhart, hughes, lindbergh, rickenbacker

bacteriologist de kruif, enders, flexner, lazear, salk, zinsser

band leader armstrong, crosby, heidt, kay, lombardo, miller, satchmo, sousa, tucker, welk

banker lehman

bank robber bonny, clyde, dillinger

baseball commissioner chandler, kuhn, landis

baseball player collins, di maggio, feller, gehrig, greenberg, grove, hornsby, johnson, keeler (wee willie), lajoie, mack, mantle, mathias, mays, mcgraw, musial, ruth (babe), sisler, speaker, stengel, wagner, williams

billiards player hoppe

biochemist benedict, bloch, cori, doisy, duvigneaud, kendall, kornberg, lipmann, northrop, ochoa, stanley, szent-gyorgyi, tatum

biographer bowen, bradford, nicolay, sandburg

biologist beadle, jordan, waksman, watson

blind educator helen keller

blues composer gershwin, handy

blues singer ma rainey

bomber flying fort(ress), liberator

book designer rogers

botanist bartram, britton, carver, coulter, gray, phillips

bowler carter

boxer ali, baer, burns, corbett, demsey, jeffries, louis, marciano, moore, patterson, robinson (sugar ray), sullivan, tunney, walcott, willard

bridge expert culbertson, goren, scheinwold

businessman babson, hartferd, hughes, paley, romney, rosenwald, rul, sarnoff, shriver

cabinet department agricul-
ture, attorney general, commerce, defense, health education and welfare, hew, housing and urban development, hud, interior, justice, labor, postoffice, state, transportation, treasury

cabinet-maker phyfe

capital washington, dc

capitalist robber baron

cardinal cooke, cushing, mcintyre, spellman

cartoonist addams, arno, block, briggs, capp, conrad, darling, disney, fisher, goldberg, gould, herblock, hokinson, mauldin, nast, price, steinberg, thurber

cellist piatigorsky

cemetery arlington, forest lawn

channel swimmer ederle

chemist acheson, baekeland, bishop, carothers, flory, frary, hall, harkins, langmuir, lewis, libby, mannes, mark, morley, pauling, piccard, remsen, richards, rumford, seaborg, segre, urey, woodward

chess player fischer, reshevsky

chief justice See *jurist,* below.

choreographer balanchine, d'amboise, de mille, kidd, koner, tharp

civilian organization job corps, peace corps

civil rights leader king, mckissick, rustin, wilkins

clergyman abbott, coffin, cotton, eggleston, fosdick, graham, hale, higginson, holmes, hopkins, mather, peal, pike, sheen, spellman, van paassen, weems, wigglesworth

clockmaker seth thomas

clown kelly

coin (See also *money,* below.) bit, cent, dime, dollar, eagle, mill, nickel, penny, quarter, rosa, stella, trime

comedian allen, benny, burns, chaplin, hope, smothers

commentator cronkite, davis, murrow, reasoner, sevareid, smith, walters

commerce secretary connor, hodges

commission civil service

communist foster

composer antheil, arlen, barber, barry, bennett, bergsma, bernstein, blitzstein, bond, bowles, brubeck, cage, carmichael, carpenter, carter, converse, copland, cowell, crum, damrosch, dekoven, dellajoio, foote, foss, foster, friml, gershwin, glanville-hicks, godowsky, griffes, grofe, hadley, hanson, harris, herbert, herrmann, hillis, kern, lewis, loeffler, loewe, lopatnikoff, macdowell, mannes, menotti, monk, moore, nevin, piston, porter, rodgers, romberg, rome, sessions, sousa, still, stravinsky, taylor, thom(p)son, varese

conductor adler, alessandro, bennett, bernstein, damrosch, dekoven, fiedler, goldovsky, golschmann, hadley, herrmann, hillis, kostalanetz, koussevitzky, leinsdorf, mehta, monteux, ormandy, reiner, rodzinski, rudolf, scherman, schick, schippers, solti, sousa, steinberg, stock, stokowski, szell, thomas, toscanini, wallenstein, walter, weisgall, whiteman

cooking authority beard, child, claiborne, farmer, rombauer

cosmetician arden, lauder, revson, rubenstein

critic agee, atkinson, benchley, benet, bentley, berryman, blackmur, brooks, burke, clurman, cowley, devoto, fadiman, furness, highet, huneker, kerr, krutch, lewisohn, lowes, mencken, more, nathan, phelps, rexroth, schwartz, sherman, spingarn, trilling, van doren, wilson

currency portrait

$1	washington
$2	jefferson
$5	lincoln
$10	hamilton
$20	jackson
$50	grant
$100	franklin
$500	mckinley
$1000	cleveland
$5000	madison
$10,000	chase

$100,000 wilson

cybernetist wiener

dancer astaire, bolger, castle, damboise, de mille, duncan, eglevsky, graham, greco, holm, humphrey, koner, massine, robbins, rogers, slavenska, st denis, tallchief, tharp, weidman

defense department pentagon

defense secretary forrestal, laird, mcnamara

defense system dewline, norad

designer, fashion adrian, cassini, dache, fogarty, halston, trigere

designer, industrial geddes, loewy, wright

detective pinkerton

diplomat adams, austin, bohlen, bowers, bullitt, bunche, burlingame, clay, cushing, davi(e)s, finletter, franklin, gadsden, galbraith, house, izard, leahy, page, reid, richardson, rush, shotwell, taylor, welles, whitney

director cukor, ford, huston, kazan, kulik, mankeiwicz, mann, preminger, schary, stevens, strasberg, vidor, wilder

dramatist akins, albee, anderson, barry, behrman, belasco, cohan, connelly, corwin, course, crothers, dalton, davis, dell, glaspell, godfrey, green, gregory, hard, hecht, hellman, heyward, hillyer, howard, inge, jeffers, kaufman, kelly, kingsley, kirkland, lawson, lindsay, logan, mckaye, miller, odets, o'neill, rice, riggs, schary, sheldon, sherwood, simon, van druten, wilder, williams, young

drummer dodds

dwarf miller, sawyer, tom thumb, warren

economist balch, eccles, george, knight, samuelson, schumpeter, taussig, veblen, weaver

editor bacheller, bentley, blackwell, bok, botkin, curtis, dana, daniels, hale, hearst, hubbard, luce, mcclure, ross, spingarn, steffins, warner

educator adler, alcott, angell, aydelotte, babbitt, bagley, barnard, bates, beadle,

bemis, bloomfield, brewster, butler, conant, cross, dewey, dubois, eliot, engle, finney, ford, gallaudet, gilman, griswold, hutchins, james, johnson, jones, kerr, kirk, locke, mann, mcguffey, moton, neilson, o'shea, palmer, patri, peabody, perry, phelps, pinchot, pusey, sproul, washington, wilbur, willard

emblem eagle

engineer armstrong, bedeaux, bryant, bush, casey jones, cooper, draper, eads, ferris, forney, fuller, fulton, goeghals, lake, l'enfant, sikorsky, steinmetz, stevens, strickland

entomologist harris, say

environmentalist carson

essayist austin, bowen, canby, frank, krutch, lowell, morley, repplier, santayana, smith, white, woollcott

ethnologist boas

etiquette authority post, vanderbilt

evangelist graham, mcpherson, moody, sunday

explorer akelay, andrews, argand, bartlett, beebe, boone, bridger, byrd, clark, cook, ellsworth, hall, lewis, long, macmillan, perry, pike, stefanson

falls multnomah, niagara, seneca, yosemite

farming region corn belt

feminist bloomer

financial center wall street

financier baruch, biddle, cooke, field, gary, gates, gould, harriman, hill, morgan, rockefeller, vanderbilt, young

firearms designer browning

1st child virginia dare

1st novel wieland

1st playwright godfrey

1st president george washington

1st saint john nepomucene neumann, mother cabrini

1st warship hannah

flag old glory, stars and stripes

flagmaker betsy ross

flutist luening

folk hero casey jones, davy crockett, john henry, john-

ny appleseed, paul bunyan, pecos bill

folklorist botkin, dobie, lomas

folk singer baez, guthrie, ives, ledbetter, odetta, seeger

football coach camp, lombardi, rockne, stagg

foreign aid program marshal plan, point four

frigate constitution, old ironsides

frontiersman kit carson

fur trader astor, harmon

general arnold, bliss, bradley, buckner, butler, clark, clay, custer, doolittle, eaker, eisenhower, fremont, funston, gaines, gansevoort, gates, glover, grant, greely, groves, jackson, kearny, lee, lejeune, lemnitzer, long, longstreet, macarthur, marion, marshall, meade, mitchell, patch, patton, pershing, pike, ridgway, schofield, schurz, schuyler, scott, spaatz, stillwell, vandenburg, van fleet, wainwright, wallace, ward, washington

geneticist beadle, bridges

geographer grosvenor

giant bates

glass designer tiffany

gold depository fort knox

golfer hagen, hogan, jones, mangrum, nicklaus, palmer, snead

hero buffalo bill, daniel boone, johnny appleseed, lindbergh, minuteman, paul bunyan

hew secretary califano, celebrezze, finch, gardner, ribicoff, richardson

highest point mount mckinley

historian adams, allen, andrews, bancroft, beard, becker, bemis, breasted, catton, commager, coulter, craven, dodd, durant, elson, fiske, ford, hart, hayes, hofstadter, morison, motley, nevins, parkman, prescott, robinson, schlesinger, shotwell, sparks, turner, tyler, viereck, van loon

horticulturist burbank

hostess elsa maxwell, pearl mesta

hud secretary hill, weaver

humorist ade, armour, artemus ward, bangs, bemelmans, benchley, browne, burgess, cobb, dunne, lardner, locke, nash, neal, nye, smith, thurber, ward, white

illustrator bemelmans, burgess, flagg, gag, geisel, gibson, glackens, kent, lawson, leaf, pennell, pogany, pyle, rockwell, sarg

impresario hurok

indian See under individual states.

indian fighter custer

industrialist carnegie, duke, dupont, firestone, ford, frick, guggenheim, knudsen, slater, taylor

interior secretary bliss, chapman, fall, garfield, hathaway, hickel, ickes, lamar, lane, morton, payne, schurz, seaton, udall, west, work

inventor alexanderson, baldwin, bell, berliner, blake, bryant, colt, cooper, corliss, curtiss, dahlgren, deforest, duryea, eads, eastman, edison, evans, fiske, fitch, franklin, fulton, goodyear, gregg, haynes, hoe, howe, kettering, land, lewis, maxim, mccormack, morse, pullman, pupin, rumsey, singer, sperry, tesla, westinghouse, whitney

irish organization hibernian society, sons of galway

island guam, hawaii, okinawa, pribilof, puerto rico, wake

jazz musician basie, beiderbecke, brubeck, condon, ellington, gillespie, goodman, henderson, herman, hines, lewis, morton, parker, spanier, tatum, teagarden, waller

jazz singer fitzgerald, holiday, teagarden

jet sabre, scorpion

jockey arcaro, shoemaker

journalist alsop, baum, bennett, bierce, block, bok, bowles, broun, bryant, carter, catton, chandler, conley, cox, dana, daniels, felker, freeman, graham, greeley, harris, hearn, hearst, hersey, hoiles, howard, irwin, knight, krock,

lardner, lewis, lippmann, list, locke, lodge, lorimer, luce, mccormick, ochs, o'hara, patterson, pulitzer, pyle, reed, reid, reston, rice, riis, sedgwick, sulzberger, van paassen, white, wolfert

jurist brandeis, burger, byrnes, chase, cooley, hand, holmes, jackson, jay, kent, landis, lindsey, livingston, marshall, paine, reed, rutledge, sewall, stone, story, taney, waite, warren, white, wythe

labor leader abel, beck, bridges, debs, dubinsky, gompers, green, hillman, hoffa, lewis, mcdonald, meany, mitchell, petrillo, quill, randolph, reuther, schneiderman

labor secretary perkins, wirtz

lake champlain, crater, erie, huron, mead, michigan, ontario, superior, tahoe

lawyer (See also *jurist,* above.) arnold, bailey, baker, boyd, cox, darrow, ingersoll, root

legal scholar pound

legislator volstead

lexicographer webster, whitney, worcester

librarian winsor

linguist jakobson

lithographer currier, ives

lowest point death valley

lyricist hammerstein, hart, lerner, porter

magician houdini

martyr crispus attucks, nathan hale

mathematician becker, birkhoff, bowditch, dickson, einstein, godel, peirce, tarski, von neumann, wiener

measure acre, barrel, basket, block, bolt, bushel, carat, chain, cord, decillion, dram, drum, fathom, foot, gallon, gill, hand, hank, heer, hogshead, inch, iron, labor, lea(gue), line, link, mil(e), minim, nail, pace, palm, peck, perch, pint, pipe, point, pole, pool, pottle, prime, quadrant, quart(er), rod, roll, sack, section, skein, span, spindle, square, standard, stran(d), tablespoonful, teaspoonful, thread, ton, township, tub, typp, vara, vat, yard

merchant faneuil, field, filene, girard, grant, kresge, macy, penney, wanamaker, williams, woolworth

methodist bishop, 1st asbury

midget statton

military academy west point

missile See ROCKET *name.*

mobile designer calder

money (See also *coin,* above.) bean, berry, bit, boffo, bone, buck, cartwheel, cent(ury), copper, dollar, fiver, four bits, greenback, iron man, jitney, sawbuck, smacker, ten spot, two bits

monologist draper

motto e pluribus unum, excelsior

movie official hays

movie producer demille, flaherty, goldwyn, griffith, laemmle, selznick, sennett, thalberg, zanuck

musicologist einstein

national memorial washington monument

national park arcadia, arches, big bend, bryce canyon, capital reef, carlsbad caverns, crater lake, everglades, glacier, grand canyon, grand teton, great smoky mountains, guadalupe mountains, haleakala, hot springs, isle royale, kings canyon, lassen, mammoth cave, mesa verde, mt mckinley, olympia, platt, sequoia, shenandoah, shiloh, virgin islands, wind cave, yosemite, zion

national park founder horace albright

native american ami, gringo, indian, johnnie, yankee, yanqui, yuma

naturalist agassiz, akeley, andrews, audubon, baird bartram, beard, beebe, burroughs, fowler, fuertes, muir, seton, thoreau

naval academy annapolis

naval base guantanamo, key west, pearl harbor, san diego

naval officer barry, dahlgren, decatur, dewey, foote, jones, king, lawrence, mitscher, perry, preble, rickover, sherman, sigsbee

naval victory coral sea, manila bay, midway

navigator bowditch

navy secretary adams, bonaparte, daniels, edison, forrestal, knox, welles

nazi propagandist joyce

newspaper publisher block, graham, hearst, mccormick, patterson, scripps, sulzberger

novelist 4 baum, buck, cook, dana, dell, fast, gale, grey, hall, kerr, page, paul, west, wouk 5 alger, allen, beach, boyle, brown, brush, cable, clark, crane, davis, harte, hearn, hecht, hough, hurst, irwin, james, lewis, mcfee, o'hara, smith, stowe, twain, vidal, welty, white, wolfe, wylie 6 algren, bellow, bowles, cabell, capote, cather, corwin, cronin, deland, ferber, fisher, forbes, french, harris, hersey, hughes, jewett, kantor, london, miller, morley, morrow, nathan, norris, porter, steele, strong, styron, suckow, updike, warren, wilder, wister, wright 7 aldrich, allston, burnett, clemens, coryell, costain, cozzens, derleth, douglas, dreiser, ellison, erskine, farrell, freeman, gallico, gardner, garland, glasgow, hammett, herrick, heyward, howells, jackson, kerouac, lafarge, malamud, marquis, nabokov, nordoff, o'connor, richter, roberts, rolvaag, wallace, wharton, wolfert 8 anderson, atherton, bradbury, bradford, caldwell, canfield, crawford, faulkner, glaspell, lewisohn, marquand, mccarthy, michener, mitchell, phillips, rawlings, rinehart, salinger, sinclair, stockton, wambaugh, westcott, williams 9 bacheller, bromfield, churchill, dos passos, hawthorne, hemingway, mccullers, schulberg, steinbeck, stribling 10 fitzgerald, tarkington, van vechten 12 hergesheimer, shellabarger

nuclear sub See SUBMARINE *atomic*.

nun cabrini

nutritionist fletcher, hauser

oceanographer agassiz

oil magnate rockefeller

oldest city st augustine

orator brooks, bryan, douglass, lincoln, webster

orchestra leader See *conductor*, above.

ornithologist audubon

outlaw billy the kid, bonnie, capone, chessman, clyde, dillinger, jesse james, manson, speck, strangler, sutton, zodiac

painter abbey, allston, avery, baziotes, bellows, berman, bingham, bouche, burchfield, cadmus, cassatt, catlin, cole, curry, davi(e)s, dekooning, demuth, duveneck, eakins, evergood, fuertes, fuller, gorky, gottlieb, gropper, grosz, guston, hartley, hassam, hoffmann, homer, hopper, inness, johns, kline, kuhm, kuniyoshi, lafarge, lee, levine, luks, marin, marsh, martin, melchers, millet, moses, motherwell, o'keeffe, peale, pollock, prendergast, rauschenburg, ray, remington, robinson, rothko, ryder, sargent, shahn, sheeler, sloan, speicher, steinberg, stuart, sully, tobey, trumbull, waugh, west, whistler, wood, wyeth

painters' group ash can school

paleontologist osborn

patriot allen, carroll, hale, otis, paine, parker, quincy, revere

peak baldy, cumbre, elbert, helena, hood, katahdin, logan, mckinley, pikes, rainier, shasta, whitney

pediatrician schick, spock

penologist lawes

philanthropist barton, brookings, carnegie, cooper, cornell, eastman, ford, frick, harkness, hopkins, lenox, riis, rockefeller

philologist grandgent

philosopher carnap, dewey, edman, hocking, james, langer, mead, montague, royce, santayana, thoreau, tillich, whitehead

phonetician kenyon

photographer adams, bourke-white, brady, man ray, porter, steichen, stieglitz

physician blackwell, cronin, dick, finlay, flint, gorgas,

hench, keeley, lazear, mayo, minot, parran, reed, richards, robbins, rush, sabin, spock, warren, weller, wood

physicist anderson, bain, bardeen, bethe, brattain, bridgman, compton, condon, davisson, dempster, farnsworth, feynman, gibbs, glasser, goddard, hess, hofstadter, kerst, kusch, lamb, lawrence, lee, mayer, mcmillan, michelson, millikan, mossbauer, nier, oppenheimer, purcell, rabi, schwinger, shockley, stern, szilard, teller, townes, van allen, von bekesy, wigner

physiologist carlson, cournand, erlanger, flint, gasser

pianist bernstein, brubeck, duchin, gottschalk, gould, grainger, gruenberg, hoffmann, horowitz, iturbi, korngold, levant, nero, pennario, rubinstein, sandor, serkin, van cliburn, watts

pioneer appleseed, boone, bowie, calamity jane, carson, clark, cody, crockett, hickok, lewis, sutter

pirate kidd

plateau piedmont

playwright See *dramatist*, above.

poet 3 poe 4 agee, cary, cook, tate 5 adams, aiken, benet, bogan, colum, crane, eliot, engle, frost, guest, moody, moore, plath, pound, reese, story, towne, wylie 6 barlow, bishop, brooks, bryant, bynner, carman, ciardi, coffin, cullen, dunbar, holmes, hughes, kilmer, lanier, lowell, merton, millay, miller, monroe, parker, ransom, riding, seeger, wilbur, wilcox 7 deutsch, freneau, gregory, halleck, hillyer, jarrell, jeffers, johnson, lazarus, leonard, lindsay, masters, rexroth, roberts, roethke, shapiro, stevens, taggard, viereck, whitman, willard, winters 8 berryman, blackmur, cummings, eberhart, fletcher, macleish, robinson, sandburg, schwartz, teasdale, wheatley, whittier, williams 9 bodenheim, dickinson, doolittle, kreymborg, santayana 10 bradstreet, longfellow, untermeyer

political party america first, anti-masonic, bull moose, democratic, federalist, know-nothings, progressive, prohibition, republican, socialist

political reformer coxey

politician bankhead, bell, benton, beverage, bryan, calhoun, cannon, cox, curley, daly, dies, farley, fawbus, hanna, jones, kennedy, landon, long(worth), luce, mccarthy, ribicoff, romney, rush, scranton, smith, stassen, stevens, symington, taft, taylor, timpkins, tweed, van rensselaer, wagner, wallace, watterson, weed, wheeler, williams, willkie

preacher beecher, fosdick

president adams, arthur, buchanan, carter, cleveland, coolidge, eisenhower, fillmore, ford, garfield, grant, harding, harrison, hayes, hoover, jackson, jefferson, johnson, kennedy, lincoln, madison, mckinley, monroe, nixon, pierce, polk, roosevelt, taft, taylor, truman, tyler, vanburen, washington, wilson

president, confederate davis

presidential plane airforce one

president's residence camp david, executive mansion, white house

president's title cinc, commander in chief, the chief

priest flanagan

prison alcatraz, atlanta, leavenworth, lewisburg

producer belasco, cohan, frohman, hayward, lang, mayer, smith, ziegfeld

psychiatrist alexander, brill, fromm, menninger, meyer, sullivan

psychologist baldwin, cattell, gesell, hall, james, koffka, reik, thorndike

public utilities magnate insull

publisher bancroft, bartlett, curtis, godey, goodrich, knight, knox, mccormack, ochs, scripps, sulzberger

quaker jones, penn

rabbi silver

railroad amtrak, at and sf, big four, burlington (and quincy), great northern, illinois central, katy, lehigh, missouri pacific, monon, new york central, norfolk and western, penn central, pennsylvania, rock island, santa fe, southern (pacific), texas pacific, union pacific, western pacific

railroad builder harriman, hill, vanderbilt

range (See also under individual states.) adirondack, appalachian, black hills, cascades, grand teton, great smokies, green, ozark, rockies, sangre de cristo, sierra nevada, smokies, tetons, unita, wasatch

reformer abbott, adler, comstock, cooper, curtis, howe, mott, noyes, osborne, riis, ripley, sinclair, stanton

relief organization aid, care, core, red cross

religious leader campbell, elijah-muhammad, kaplan, king, mcpherson, mott, smith, williams, young

reservist weekend warrior

river (See also under individual states.) alabama, canadian, colorado, columbia, mississippi, missouri, niagara, ohio, shenandoah, st john, st marys, suwannee

saint frances xavier cabrini, john nepomucene neumann, mother elizabeth ann seton

satirist bemelmans, hopkinson

scholar furness, hadas, hamilton, lowes, nicolson, norton

scientist bardeen, becker, bethe, brattain, bridgman, compton, einstein, evans, hooton, lederberg, millikan, nichols, parran, urey, von braun, von karman, waksman

scout daniel boone, kit carson

sculptor akeley, barnard, bartlett, baskin, bertoia, borglum, calder, calin, crawford, davidson, evans, ezekiel, faggi, fraser, french, gabor, greenough, gross, hoffman, lachaise, lipchitz, lippold, macmonnies, manship, nevelson, noguchi, robus,

roszak, saint-gaudens, story, taft

seal motto annuit coeptis

security adviser zbigniew brzezinski

semanticist korzybski

senate investigation watergate

senator baker, benton, beverage, borah, fulbright, goldwater, hannah, humphrey, kefauver, kennedy, la folette, mansfield, mccumber, norris, vandenberg

short-story writer austin, harris, harte, jewett, lardner, london, mccullers, oates, o'connor, o'hara, poe, runyan, saroyan, thurber

showman barnum, todd

silversmith revere

singer alda, anderson, belafonte, callas, crosby, farrar, garden, gluck, jolson, martinelli, mccormack, melchior, nordica, olcott, peerce, pinza, pons, ponselle, presley, price, robeson, russell, schumannheink, sinatra, smith, sumac, swarthout, tibbett, tucker

social worker adams, wald, wright, young

socialist leader debs, thomas

sociologist cooley, lundberg, ogburn, park, parsons, sorokin

soldier gi joe

song writer berlin, bond, carmichael, gershwin, hammerstein, hart, mckuen, porter, rodgers

southernmost city key west

-soviet talks salt

speaker albert, banks, byrnes, cannon, carlisle, clark, dayton, gillett, grow, henderson, hunter, keifer, kerr, macon, martin, mccormack, o'neil, rayburn, stevenson, taylor, thomas, winthrop

stage designer bragdon, geddes, mielziner

state department foggy bottom

state department intelligence operation inr

state secretary acheson, byrnes, dulles, herter, hull, kellogg, kissinger, knox, lansing, marshall, rusk, seward, stettinius, stimson, vance

statesman acheson, adams, bancroft, baruch, blaine, borah, bowles, byrnes, cass, clay, clinton, daniels, douglas, evarts, everett, fessenden, fish, franklin, glass, hamilton, hancock, hay, hopkinson, huntington, huysen, ickes, lehman, livingston, lodge, morris, pinckney, randolph, root, rutledge, schuyler, seward, sherman, stephens, stevenson, tilden, trumbull, vandenberg

states proposed aroostook, forgotonia, jefferson, puerto rico, superior

statistician babson, gallup

submarine polaris, trident, u-boat

suffragist anthony, catt, stone

supersonic aircraft f-111

supreme court justice black, brennan, burger, burton, butler, cardozo, clark, douglas, ellsworth, fortas, frankfurter, fuller, goldberg, harlan, holmes, hughes, iredell, lamar, marshall, mcreynolds, roberts, stewart, stone, sutherland, taft, taney, van devanter, waite, warren, white, whittaker

surgeon beaumont, crile, cushing, long, mayo

symbol eagle, uncle sam

tank xm-1

temperance leader amelia moore, carrie nation

tennis player budge, conners, evert, gibson, gonzales, kramer, marble, tilden, wills

terrorist group sla, symbionese liberation army, weatherman

theologian beecher, edwards, niebuhr, witherspoon

theosophist tingley

13 original states confederation

traitor benedict arnold

traveler bradbury

treasury agent revenuer

treasury secretary dillon, fowler, gallatin, hamilton, mcadoo, mellon, morganthau, simon

treaty, defense anzua, nato, seato

type designer goudy

vice president adams, agnew, barkley, breckinridge, calhoun, clinton, colfax, curtis, dallas, dawes, fairbanks, garner, gerry, hamlin, hendricks, hobart, humphrey, johnson, king, marshall, mondale, morton, sherman, stevens, tompkins, truman, wallace, wheeler, wilson

violinist elman, heifitz, loeffler, menuhin, milstein, morini, spalding, stern, zimbalist

volcano lassen, shasta

war bond liberty loan

war correspondent pyle

war secretary alger, baker, barbour, bell, butler, calhoun, cameron, cass, davis, dearborn, dern, dexter, garrison, hurley, knox, lamont, pickering, root, royall, sherman, stanton, stimson, taft

warship, 1st ironclad merrimac, monitor

weapon, super a-bomb, cruise missile, hydrogen bomb, lance missile, neutron bomb, nuclear bomb

weapons system (See also ROCKET *name*.) dewline, ferreting, norad, rembass, rvp, sotas

weight bag, carat, denier, flask, grain, keg, kip, ounce, pound, quarter, quintal, ton, troy

writer (See also *dramatist, novelist, poet,* above.) abbott, adams, adler, agee, aldrich, allen, anderson, arendt, austin, babbit, bagley, bailey, baker, baldwin, basso, beebe, beecher, beer, bellamy, bemis, bodenheim, bok, bradford, bragdon, brooks, broun, burgess, burke, burroughs, canby, carson, chase, coatsworth, creel, curtis, day, devoto, dewey, eastman, eggleston, frank, fuller, hicks, hindus, irving, kennan, kent, lardner, leaf, lewisohn, lippman, lofting, loos, luce, morley, mumford, paine, parker, peatie, ripley, rourke, seversky, simms, skinner, slocum, smith, steffens, stuart, van loon, weidman, wiggin, young

zionist szold, wise

zoologist agassiz, ditmars, kinsey, morgan

UNITY accord, agreement, bond, coadunation, coherence, communion, concert, concord, cooperation, esemplasy, fusion, harmony, identity, integral, integrity, junction, oneness, singleness, sodality, solidarity, totality, unanimity, uniformity, UNION, unison, whole

UNIVALENT single, unpaired

element monad

UNIVERSAL absolute, all-inclusive, broad, catholic, common, constant, continual, cosmic, cosmogonal, cosmopolitan, diffuse, doctrine, earthly, eclectic, ecumenical, entire(ty), general, generic, global, infinite, mundane, pandemic, philosophy, public, regular, rife, total, unlimited, unrestricted, usual, whole, worldly

doctor alain de lille, albertus magnus, thomas aquinas

joint coupling

remedy panacea

UNIVERSALITY allness, catholicity, completeness, ecumenicity, entirety, generality, omnitude, panacea, totality, ubiquity, worldwideness

UNIVERSE all, brahmanda, cosmos, creation, earth, hiranyagargha, kosmos, loka, macrocosm(os), mankind, mass, megacosm, mundus, nature, olam, plenum, sphere, totality, world

comb. cosmo

controlling principle logos, tien

creator brahma

description cosmography

hub of the boston

pert. cosmic

science cosmology

study of origin cosmogony

system solar

theory cosmism

vine bearberry

UNIVERSITY academy, COLLEGE, corporation, institute, seminary, studium, varsity

bluebrick cambridge, oxford

board regents, senate, syndics

group ivy league

ivy-league brown, columbia, cornell, dartmouth, harvard, pennsylvania, princeton, yale

resident gremiale

scholarship exhibition

student catercap

unprestigious redbrick

wits greene, lyly, nash, peele

UNJUST biased, dishonest, faithless, foul, hard, improper, inaccurate, inequitable, partial, prejudiced, shabby, underhand, undeserved, . unequal, unfair, unright, wrong(ful), wrongful

UNKEELED ratite

UNKEMPT blousy, blowzy, coarse, crude, dilapidated, dirty, disarrayed, disheveled, dowdy, draggled, fat, frowzy, lax, messy, neglected, ratty, rough, ruddy, ruffled, rumpled, schlep (per), scraggly, shaggy, shagrag, shlep(per), slack, slatternly, slipshod, sloppy, slovenly, strubbly, tousled, unclean, uncombed, unimproved, untidy

UNKENNEL disclose, discover

UNKID desolate, ghastly, inconvenient, lonely, odd, strange, uncanny, unkensome, unknown, weird

UNKIND bad, brutal, coldblooded, cruel, degenerate, fell, foreign, harsh, heartless, inhuman(e), paskudne(h), rough, severe, stern, strange, unbenign, uncharitable, uncompassionate, uncordial, ungenerous, ungrateful, unnatural, unsuitable, unsympathetic, vile

UNKNIT destroy, disperse, dissolve, disunite, relax, undo, unravel, untie, weaken

UNKNOWING ignorance, ignorant, unaware, unmindful, unwitting

UNKNOWN anonymous, ignorant, ignotus, incalculable, incognito, nobody, obscure, secret, strange, unaware, unco, unexplained, unfamiliar, unkenned,

unket, unkid, unwist, unwitting

comb. adelo

soldier's tomb arlington

UNLADE discharge, remove, unload

UNLASH See UNFASTEN.

UNLATCH loose, open, unbolt, UNFASTEN, unlace, unsneck, untie

UNLAWFUL bootleg, contraband, illegal, illegitimate, illicit, irregular, lawless, unleeful, unleesome

UNLEARNED borrel, callow, crude, green, gross, ignorant, illiterate, lewd, natural, nescient, prost, raw, uneducated, unlettered, untaught

UNLEAVENED azymous, flat

UNLESS but, except(ing), if not, lest, nisi, nobut, save, without

UNLETTERED See UNLEARNED.

UNLICKED immature, unformed, ungainly

UNLIEF loathsome, unpleasant

UNLIGHTED dark, lampless, sunless, unilluminated

UNLIKE alien, atypical, different, difform, displease, dissimilar, diverse, irregular, mismatched, mismated, sundry, uneven, unrelated, various

UNLIKELY disagreeable, doubtful, dubious, improbable, inconceivable, objectionable, rare, unfit, unheard of, unpromising, unsuitable

UNLIKENESS difference, discordance, discrepancy, dissimilarity, distinction, divergence, variety

comb. ant(i)

UNLIMITED bottomless, boundless, free, indefinite, infinite, limitless, sovran, unbounded, unconfined, undefined, unqualified, unrestricted, untrammeled, vast

authority carte blanche, power of attorney

UNLOAD break, bulk, deliver, deplete, disburden, discharge, disencumber, drop, dump, eject, market, remove, rid, sell, tip, un-

burden, unlade, unpack, unship, unstow

UNLOCK analyze, disclose, discover, free, interpret, open, release, reveal, solve, spread out, unbolt, undo, unfasten, unlatch, unmake

UNLOOKED-FOR chance, happenstance, serendipitous, unexpected, unforeseen

UNLOVELY disagreeable, displeasing, harsh, objectionable, repellent, ugly, unattractive, unpleasant

UNLOVING anerotic, cold, distant

UNLUCKY blackletter, disastrous, dismal, donsie, donsy, fey, foul, hapless, hoodoo, ill-fated, ill-omened, inauspicious, infaust, mischievous, ominous, sad, unfortunate, unhappy, unsuccessful, untimely, untoward

person s(c)hlemiel, shlemi(e)hl

UNLUSTY delicate, disagreeable, dull, listless, objectionable, unhappy, unmanly, unpleasant, weak

UNMACKLY deformed, unshapely

UNMAKE alter, demote, depose, destroy, reduce, ruin, undo, unfasten, unlock

UNMAN appall, awe, crush, emasculate, enervate, exhaust, frighten, monster, sap, sterilize, undermine, undo, unnerve, weaken

UNMANAGEABLE awkward, churlish, disorderly, donsy, randy, refractory, uncontrollable, ungovernable, unruly

UNMANLY cowardly, effeminate, inhuman, savage, sissy, soft, timid, weak, womanish, womanly

UNMANNERLY boorish, coarse, crude, discourteous, impolite, rude, uncivil

UNMARRIED bachelor, celibate, chaste, divorced, one, onlepy, single, sole, spouseless, unwed, widowed

state agamy

UNMASK betray, debunk, disclose, expose, report, reveal, uncloak

UNMATCHED azygous,

odd, peerless, single, unequaled, unique

UNMEASURED boundless, huge, immense, infinite, intemperate, lavish, unlimited, unmeet, unrestrained, unstinting, vast

UNMEET improper, inappropriate, inapt, incompetent, indecorous, unbecoming, unequal, unfit(ting), unhappy, unseemly, unsuitable

UNMENTIONABLE base, improper, unfit, unspeakable

UNMENTIONABLES See UNDERWEAR.

UNMERCIFUL callous, cruel, excessive, extreme, pitiless, ruthless, severe, unkind, unrelenting

UNMERITED undeserved, undue, unearned

UNMINDFUL careless, forgetful, heedless, ignorant, inadvertent, indifferent, neglectful, negligent, remiss, thoughtless, unaware, unconscious, undiscerning, unobservant

UNMISTAKABLE apparent, certain, clear, decisive, evident, express, frank, manifest, obvious, open, patent, plain, simple, transparent, unambiguous, unqualified

UNMITIGATED absolute, arrant, clearcut, gross, mere, out-and-out, outright, perfect, regular, sheer, thorough, unmodified, unqualified

UNMIXABLE immiscible

UNMIXED blank, neat, pure, raw, sheer, sole, straight, unadulterated, unalloyed, undiluted, utter

UNMOVED adamant, apathetic, calm, cool, dead, firm, inert, obdurate, obstinate, resolute, serene, stolid, stony, stubborn, tight, unaffected, unfeeling, unshaken, unshocked, unstirred, untouched

UNNAMED anonymous

UNNATURAL aberrant, abnormal, affected, anomalous, artful, artificial, atypic, bizarre, brutal, callous, car, contrived, counterfeit, eccentric, eerie, eery, forced, grotesque, heartless, illegitimate, inhuman, irreg-

ular, labored, monstrous, perverse, perverted, spurious, stagy, strained, strange, studied, synthetic, unkind, unusual, weird

UNNECESSARY dispensable, excess, expendable, extrinsic, gratuitous, inessential, needless, superfluous, uncalled for, unessential, useless

UNNERVE agitate, bewilder, demoralize, disconcert, discourage, dishearten, distract, enervate, fluster, frighten, perturb, shake, unhinge, unman, unsettle, unstring, upset, weaken

UNNERVED shook, spooked

UNNOOKED guileless

UNNUMBERED countless, infinite, innumerable, many

UNOBSERVANT blind, heedless, obtuse, thick

UNOBSTRUCTED apparent, free, open, panoramic

UNOBTRUSIVE covert, discreet, modest, restrained, retiring, shy, simple

UNOCCUPIED desolate, empty, free, idle, laid off, leisure(d), thoughtless, unemployed, unfilled, uninhabited, untenanted, vacant, void

UNOFFENDING harmless, innocuous

UNOFFICIAL informal, private

UNORGANIZED acosmic, disorderly, dissolute, inchoate, incoherent, messy

UNORIGINAL cliche, copy, hackneyed, secondhand, stereotyped, trite

UNORN coarse, decrepit, feeble, plain, poor, rude

UNORTHODOX heretic, heterodox, left, unconventional

UNOSTENTATIOUS lenten, modest, plain, quiet, restrained, shy, simple, somber

UNPAID arrears, due, honorary, owed, owing, unrevenged, unsettled, volunteer, wageless

UNPAIRED impar, odd, single, unmatched

UNPALATABLE bitter, brackish, distasteful, inedible, rancid, sour, unappetiz-

ing, uninviting, unpleasant, unsavory

UNPARALLELED alone, inimitable, matchless, peerless, singular, unequaled, unique, unmatched, unrivaled

UNPARDONABLE improper, indefensible, inexcusable, irremissible, unforgivable

UNPAY undo

UNPEACE disquiet

UNPEELED pillaged, stripped

UNPEOPLE depopulate

UNPERFECTED incomplete, inexpert, uncompleted

UNPERSUASIVE flimsy, lame, inconclusive, thin, unconvincing

UNPERTURBED calm, still

UNPITYING ruthless, unmerciful

UNPLANNED accidental, chance, impromptu, extemporaneous, spontaneous, unexpected

UNPLEASANT agonizing, annoying, awkward, bad, beastly, bilious, bitter, brackish, disagreeable, displeasing, distasteful, distressing, dreadful, embarrassing, horrible, indecent, intolerable, noisome, objectionable, obnoxious, offensive, oppressive, rancid, repellent, repugnant, repulsive, rotten, scabrous, sour, terrible, unappealing, undesirable, unsavory, unsoncy

most worst

UNPLEASANTNESS *name meaning* naaman

UNPLIGHT evolve, explain, unfold

UNPLOWED fallow, lea, untilled

strip balk, hade, linch

UNPOLICED impolitic, imprudent

UNPOLISHED agrestic(al), boorish, bruit, coarse, crude, dull, gauche, ill-bred, impolite, inelegant, rough, rude, rugged, rustic, savage, tasteless, uncouth, uneven, unrefined, unvarnished, unwaxed, vulgar

UNPOLLUTED clean, clear, pure, uncontaminated, undebased

UNPOPULAR disapproved, disfavored, disliked, distasteful, ignored, misliked, unfavored, unliked

UNPOSED candid, natural

UNPRACTICED fresh, inexpert, off(form), raw, rusty, unskilled

UNPRECEDENTED exceptional, new, novel, remarkable, signal, singular, surprising, unheard of, unique, unusual

UNPREDICTABLE chancy, cranky, erratic, frivolous, uncertain, unforeseen

UNPREJUDICED fair, impartial, objective, unbiased, unbigoted

UNPREMEDITATED accidental, casual, extemporaneous, extempore, extemporized, impromptu, improvised, impulsive, offhand, premature, spontaneous, unintended, unmeant, unplanned, unthinking

UNPREPARED asleep, raw, tardy, unequipped, unfit, unorganized, unprovided

UNPREPOSSESSING illfavored, seedy, ugly, unfavorable

UNPRETENDING, UNPRETENTIOUS candid, easy, frank, genuine, home-like, homey, humble, lowly, modest, natural, open, plain, simple, sincere, sober, unaffected, unassuming, unelaborate

UNPRINCIPLED abandoned, corrupt, dishonest, immoral, lewd, limmer, perfidious, unethical, unscrupulous, wanton
person bounder, cad, heel, reprobate, scamp

UNPRODUCTIVE arid, barren, childless, dead, desert, dry, fallow, fruitless, ineffectual, issueless, lean, sapless, sterile, teemless, uncreative, unfruitful, unprolific, useless, void

UNPROFESSIONAL amateur(ish), laic(al), lay, unskilled

UNPROFITABLE bad, barren, bootless, dead, dry, fruitless, frustraneous, futile, gainless, inutile, seck, unproductive, useless

UNPROPITIOUS adverse, baleful, counter, evil, fateful, ill, inauspicious, inopportune, malign, menacing, ominous, portentous, thrawart, unfavorable, untimely, untoward

UNPROTECTED accessible, dangerous, defenseless, exposed, helpless, naked, open, susceptible, undefended, unguarded, vulnerable

UNPROVED unattested, unsupported, untested

UNPUFF humble

UNPURSE expend, relax, rob, spend, take

UNQUALIFIED absolute, all-out, categorical, clear, complete, decided, decisive, definite, definitive, direct, downright, entire, explicit, express, final, fixed, flat, implicit, inadequate, incapable, incompetent, indisputable, inexpert, mear, mere, outright, perfect, positive, sheer, thorough, total, utter, unable, unconditional, unequivocal, unfit, unlimited, unmistakable, unmitigated, unreserved, unsuitable

UNQUESTIONABLE absolute, assured, believable, certain, clear, decided, decisive, distinct, evident, implicit, indisputable, irrefutable, positive, sure, true

UNQUIET agitated, disturbed, feverish, hectic, jittery, jumpy, perturbed, restless, skittish, tumultuous, turbulent, uneasy, vexed

UNQUOD untold

UNRAVEL confuse, disengage, disentangle, enodate, enode, fathom, feaze, interpret, open, plumb, resolve, separate, solve, tease, tiffle, undo, unfasten, unfold, unknit, untangle, untie, untwist, unwind

UNREADY asleep, awkward, clumsy, hesitant, slow, undressed, unfit, unprepared
the ethelred

UNREAL aeriform, apocryphal, artificial, chaotic, chemic(k), chimeric, counterfeit, delusive, delusory, false, fanciful, fantastic, fictitious, fictive, halluci-natory, ideal, illusive, illusory, imaginary, imagined, impractical, nonexistent, notional, phantasmal, phantom, shadowy, sham, spurious, strange, theoretical, unsubstantial, vague, visionary, weird, whimsical

UNREALISTIC chimeric(al), crackpot, crazy, impractical, quixotic, visionary

UNREALITY chimera, delusion, dream, fancy, fantastry, fantasy, fiction, hallucination, ideality, illusion, invention, makebelieve, mirage, phantasy, pretense, vision

UNREASON *abbot of* lord of misrule

UNREASONABLE absonant, absurd, arbitrary, asinine, awry, blind, brute, capricious, excessive, exorbitant, extravagant, fanatic(al), farfetched, foolish, illogical, immoderate, implausible, inordinate, insane, intemperate, irrational, mad, nonsensical, preposterous, senseless, silly, stupid, undue, unsound

UNREAVE disentangle, loose, unwind

UNREEL develop, uncoil, untwine, unwind

UNREFINED bad-mannered, base, boorish, brutal, coarse, common, crass, crude, earthy, gross, illbred, inelegant, low, natural, raw, ribald, rude, savage, tasteless, uncouth, uncultivated, uneven, unkempt, unpolished, unpurified, vulgar

UNREFLECTIVE glib, heedless, rash, thoughtless

UNREGENERATE bad, carnal, damned, dissolute, evil, godless, graceless, lost, obstinate, profligate, reprobate, shiftless, sinful, unconverted, wicked

UNREHEARSED extemporaneous, extempore, impromptu, spontaneous

UNRELATED alien, dissimilar, foreign, fremd, independent, irrelative, irrelevant, mismatched, mismated, strange, stray, unakin, unallied, unlike

UNRELENTING adamant, cruel, firm, grim, hard, implacable, inexorable, inflexible, iron, merciless, obdurate, obstinate, persevering, persistent, pitiless, rigid, ruthless, severe, stern, stiff, tenacious, unbending

UNRELIABLE capricious, cas(s)alty, cas(s)elty, changeful, corrupt, feckless, fickle, fishy, frivolous, greasy, inconstant, infirm, irresponsible, precarious, shaky, slippery, treacherous, undependable, unsafe, unsure, untrustworthy

UNRELIEVED boring, humdrum, monotonous, plain, tedious, tiresome, unadorned

UNREMITTING assiduous, busy, constant, continual, dogged, everlasting, hard, incessant, persevering, persistent

UNREMUNERATIVE honorary, unpaid, volunteer

UNREQUITED thankless, unreturned, unrewarded

UNRESERVED artless, candid, common, complete, entire, explicit, frank, free, full, guileless, ingenuous, open, sincere, thorough, unbooked, unlimited, unqualified, unrestricted

UNRESISTING acquiescent, passive, yielding

UNRESPONSIVE cold, distant, dumb, frigid, insensitive, reserved, silent, stubborn, unfeeling

UNREST agitation, commotion, disquiet, dysphoria, insurgency, motion, sedition, trepidation, uneasiness

UNRESTRAINED abandoned, at large, audacious, boisterous, broad, capricious, extravagant, familiar, free(hand), inconstant, inordinate, intemperate, lavish, lax, rampant, riotous, uncontrolled, uncurbed, unlimited, unrestricted, wanton, wild

UNRESTRICTED absolute, arbitrary, free, open, sovereign, unlimited, unqualified, unrestrained

UNREVEALED concealed, covered, hidden, latent, masked, untold

UNREVERENT disrespectful, irreverent

UNRIDE cruel, cumbersome, enormous, harsh, immense, numerous, rough, sharp, unwieldy

UNRIGHT imprecise, incorrect, inexact, unjust, wrong

UNRIGHTEOUS evil, piacular, sinful, unfair, ungodly, unjust, unregenerate, wicked, wrong

UNRIGHTEOUSNESS adharma, evil, sin

UNRIPE callow, crude, green, ignorant, immature, precocious, premature, raw, sour, uncured, unfledged, unmatured, unmellow, unseasonable, unseasoned, verdant

UNRIVALED incomparable, matchless, peerless, supreme, unequalled, unparalled

UNRO disquiet, trouble

UNROLL bare, develop, disclose, discover, display, evolute, evolve, exhibit, open, reveal, show, trindle, uncoil, uncurl, unfold, unfurl, unveil, unwind

UNROMANTIC matter of fact, prosaic, realistic

UNROOF tirr

UNRUFE toil, trouble

UNRUFFLED balanced, calm, collected, composed, cool, easy, even, nonchalant, peaceful, phlegmatic, placid, poised, quiet, sedate, serene, smooth, steady, still, stoical, tranquil, unaffected, undisturbed, unexcited, unflustered

UNRULY abandoned, contrary, disobedient, disorderly, feral, fractious, froward, headstrong, insubordinate, intractable, lawless, mutinous, obstreperous, rampant, rebellious, refractory, resistive, restive, riotous, rowdy, roy(e)t, stubborn, troublesome, turbulent, unbridled, uncontrollable, unmanageable, vicious, violent, wanton, wayward, wild, willful

person rantipole

UNSAFE dangerous, doubtful, dubious, hazardous, hot, insecure, perilous, precarious, risky, shaky, tottery, undependable, unreliable, unsound, unsure, untrustworthy

UNSAID implicit, tacit, understood, unexpressed, unuttered

UNSATISFACTORY bad, failing, ill, inadequate, inferior, lame, measly, poor, thin, unpleasing, unsicker, unsuitable, wretched

UNSAVORY disagreeable, displeasing, distasteful, flat, flavorless, insipid, objectionable, offensive, rancid, rank, sour, stale, tasteless, unappealing, unappetizing, unpleasant, vapid, weak, wersh, zestless

UNSAY recall, recant, retract

UNSCATHED unharmed, uninjured

UNSCRUPULOUS brazen, conscienceless, corrupt, devious, dishonest, immoral, indiscriminate, merciless, miscreant, rascally, unethical, unprincipled, untrustworthy

UNSEASONABLE ill-timed, inappropriate, inopportune, unripe, untimely

UNSEASONED green, immature, inexperienced, raw, tasteless, unfinished, unpracticed, unripe, untimely

UNSEAT remove, throw, unhorse

UNSEEMLY hoiden, hoyden, improper, inappropriate, incongruous, incorrect, indecent, indecorous, indelicate, tasteless, unbecoming, unbefitting, uncomely, unfitting, unworthy, vulgar, wrong

UNSELFISH altruistic, big(hearted), charitable, disinterested, freehanded, generous, liberal, ungrudging, unsparing, unstinting

UNSETTLE agitate, confuse, derange, disarrange, discompose, disorder, disorganize, displace, disquiet, distemper, distract, disturb, loosen, move, perturb, shake, stagger, startle, stir, trouble, unbalance, unfix, unhinge, unnerve, upset, vex, weaken

UNSETTLED ambiguous, changeable, desultory, disordered, disorganized, doubtful, dubious, erratic, faltering, fickle, inconstant, insane, irresolute, mad, moot, precarious, problematical, restless, undecided, unoccupied, unpopulated, unstable, unstaid, unsteady, unsure

UNSHAKEN adamant, calm, dogged, erect, firm, resolute, steady, unmoved, unshook

UNSHAVEN bearded, hairy, stubbled, whiskered

UNSHEATHE discase, draw, pull out, remove, withdraw

UNSHOD barefoot, discalcid, shoeless

UNSICKER deceptive, unsure

UNSIDED disordered, messy, untidy

UNSIGHTLY disagreeable, distasteful, hideous, homely, messy, repulsive, ugly, unattractive, unpleasant

UNSIGNED anonymous

UNSKILLED awkward, bungling, clumsy, feckless, green, ignorant, inadept, inexpert, malapert, puisne, puny, raw, rude, schvartz (er)

UNSKILLFUL ambisinister, ambisinistrous, artless, awkward, bungling, bungly, gauche, inept, inexperienced, injudicious, maladroit, unheppen, unreasonable, unseemly

UNSLEEPING alert, assiduous, vigilant, watchful

UNSMART dowdy, dumb, limp, slack, STUPID

UNSOCIABLE farouche, frosty, reserved, retiring, shy, solitary, sullen, timid, unfriendly, withdrawn

UNSOPHISTICATED artless, authentic, callow, candid, crude, frank, genuine, green, guileless, gullible, homespun, inexperienced, ingenuous, innocent, naif, naive, natural, open, plain, pure, shy, silly, simple, unmixed, unworldly

UNSOUND crazy, cronk, decayed, decrepit, defective, diseased, disturbed, dotty, erroneous, fallacious, false, faulty, feeble, flawed, flimsy, frail, hollow, impaired, imperfect, incorrect, infirm, insane, insecure, irrational, light, nonsensical, poor(ish), precarious, rick-

ety, rotten, senseless, shaky, sick(ly), specious, tottering, unbalanced, unhealthy, unreliable, unstable, unsturdy, wracked

UNSPARING bountiful, excessive, generous, handsome, hard, harsh, lavish, liberal, merciless, relentless, severe, strict, unselfish

UNSPEAKABLE abominable, bad, detestable, dumb, hateful, indescribable, ineffable, inexpressible, loathsome, nameless, objectionable, odious, offensive, repulsive, vile

UNSPOKEN implied, ineffable, mute, quiet, secret, silent, tacit, unsaid, unuttered

UNSTABLE astatic, capricious, changeable, choppy, dweeble, ephemeral, erratic, faithless, flickering, flighty, fluctuating, inconstant, insecure, irregular, irresolute, labile, lubric(i)ous, mercurial, mutable, precarious, rickety, shaky, ticklish, tottery, treacherous, unbalanced, unreliable, unsafe, unsettled, unsound, unsteady, vacillating, variable, volatile, wankle, weak, wobbly

UNSTAINED clean, immaculate, pure, spotless, unblemished, unblotched

UNSTEADY capricious, cogglety, coggly, craichy, cranky, doddering, dotty, DRUNK, flickering, fluctuating, fluky, groggy, haveycavey, inconstant, irregular, jiggety, joggly, quavery, ramshackle, reeling, rickety, rocky, SHAKY, staggering, teetery, tippy, tipsy, tittupy, titubant, topheavy, tottery, uneven, unsettled, UNSTABLE, vacilating, variable, waffly, wambly, wayward, weck, weewow(y), wobbly, wonky

UNSTECK unfasten

UNSTRENG weaken

UNSTRING dissolve, loosen, relax, separate, UNNERVE, weaken

UNSTRUNG anxious, discomposed, fearful, nervous, tired, unhinged, unnerved, upset, weakened

UNSTUDIED careless, casual, colloquial, glancing, glib, impromptu, natural, spontaneous, unaffected, unforced, unlabored

UNSUBSTANTIAL fanciful, flimsy, FRAGILE, frail, gimcrack, immaterial, jerrybuilt, light, limp, paltry, rare, sleazy, sleezy, slight, thin, unsound, visionary

UNSUCCESSFUL abortive, bad, disastrous, fruitless, ineffective, ineffectual, stickit, unfortunate, unfruitful, unhappy, unproductive, vain, void

UNSUITABLE bad, gauche, ill-befitting, improper, inappropriate, inapt, inept, unbecoming, undue, unfit, unlikely, unmete, unsatisfactory, untimely

UNSULLIED clean, fair, fresh, innocent, pristine, pure, raw, spotless, unspoiled, virgin(al)

UNSURE dangerous, doubtful, dubious, hazardous, indefinite, indeterminate, insecure, timid, uncertain, unreliable, unsafe, unsicker

UNSUSPECTING artless, credulous, gullible, ignorant, innocent, trusting, unsuspicious

UNSWEAR adjure, recall, recant, retract

UNSWEET dry, sec, sour

UNSWERVING direct, firm, fixed, loyal, persevering, staunch, steadfast, steady, straight, true

UNSYMMETRICAL anisomerous, disproportional, inequilateral, irregular, lopsided

UNSYMPATHETIC aloof, averse, callous, discordant, frozen, hard(hearted), heartless, hostile, incompatible, incongruous, indifferent, indurated, kindless, pitiless, ruthless, stony, unconcerned, unkind, unresponsive

UNSYSTEMATIC confused, disorderly, disorganized, irregular, messy, untidy

UNTAMED brutal, callous, feral, ferine, ferocious, fierce, ramage, ramish, raw, savage, unbroken, unsubdued, warragal, WILD

UNTANGLE extricate, free,

liberate, release, resolve, sleave, solve, unlace, unravel, unsnarl, untwist, unweave

UNTAUGHT ignorant, illiterate, naive, natural, nescient, spontaneous, uneducated, uninstructed, unlearned, unlettered, untutored

UNTAXED scot-free

UNTENABLE baseless, unbelievable

UNTEWED uncombed, untrimmed

UNTHANK displeasure, ill-will, ingratitude

UNTHINKABLE absurd, inconceivable, out of the question

UNTHINKING automatic, brute, careless, casual, feckless, heedless, impulsive, inadvertent, inconsiderate, indelicate, mechanical, outrageous, puerile, rash, spontaneous, tactless, thoughtless, unintended, unmindful, untactful

UNTHRIFT extravagance, extravagant, folly, lavish, wastefulness, worthlessness

UNTHRIFTY extravagant, foolish, improvident, prodigal, profitless, profligate, profuse, ruinous, wanton, wasting

UNTIDINESS clutter(ment), confusion, jumble, litter, mess, muss, rummage, sloppiness, tousle

UNTIDY bedraggled, blowzy, careless, cluttered, disarranged, disheveled, disorderly, disorganized, dirty, dowdy(ish), draggled, draggly, frowzy, frumpy, grubby, littered, messy, poky, rumpled, slipshod, SLOPPY, slovenly, sluttish, tacky, tousled, unheppen, unkempt

person ragamuffin, scarecrow, slob, sloven, slut

UNTIE clear, cut, disclose, disengage, divorce, free, liberate, loose(n), release, resolve, unbind, undo, unfasten, unfold, unknot, unlatch, unloose, unpinion, untwine

UNTIL already, as far as, as yet, before, down to, formerly, gin, hent, hitherto,

pending, so far, still, thus far, till, to date, twell, unto, up to, when, while, whilst

UNTIMELY advanced, early, forward, immature, inappropriate, inauspicious, inconvenient, inexpedient, inopportune, late, precocious, premature, previous, slow, unfavorable, unfortunate, unhappy, unlucky, unpropitious, unseasonable, untoward

UNTIRING busy, diligent, endless, persevering, persisting, sedulous, tireless, unflagging, unwearied, unwearying

UNTOLD boundless, concealed, countless, hushed up, incalculable, infinite, innumerable, myriad(s), secret, smothered, suppressed, teeming, uncounted, uninformed, unnumbered, unrevealed, vast

UNTOUCHABLE bhangi, bhungi, chandala, distant, harijan, loathsome, outcast, panchama, pariah, vile

UNTOUCHED free, fresh, innocent, insensible, intact, pristine, pure, unaffected, unchanged, unharmed, uninjured, unmoved, unscathed, untried, virgin(al)

UNTOWARD awkward, bad, difficult, froward, improper, inauspicious, inconvenient, indecorous, perverse, troublesome, unfavorable, unfortunate, ungraceful, unlucky, unpropitious, unruly, untimely, vexatious, wayward

UNTRAINED callow, green, ignorant, indocile, inexperienced, raw, rude, unbroken, undisciplined

UNTRAMMELED free, loose, unhampered, unlimited

UNTRIED amateur, fresh, green, immature, inexperienced, maiden, unbeaten, untested, untouched

UNTROUBLED cheery, content, easy, pacific, unconcerned, undisturbed

UNTRUE absurd, apocryphal, disloyal, erroneous, faithless, fallacious, false, fictitious, flam, inaccurate, inconstant, incorrect, not

so, perfidious, unfaithful, unreliable, wrong

UNTRUSTWORTHY dishonest, fly-by-night, perfidious, shaky, shifty, sliddery, slippery, treacherous, tricky, uncertain, undependable, unreliable, UNSAFE

UNTRUTH dishonesty, disloyalty, error, fable, fabrication, falsehood, falsity, fib, fraudulence, invention, LIE, mendacity, sklent, story, treachery

UNTRUTHFUL deceitful, deceptive, delusive, dishonest, false, mendacious, misleading, lying, wrong

UNTUTORED See UNTAUGHT.

UNTWINE disentangle, fag, feaze, free, frese, loose(n), ravel, straighten, uncoil, undo, unravel, untangle, untwirl, untwist, unwind

UNUSED derelict, fallow, fresh, idle, mint, unusual, unwonted, vacant, virgin

UNUSUAL aberrant, abnormal, anomalous, atypic(al), bizarre, crazy, curious, distinct, ECCENTRIC, epigene, exceptional, exotic, extraordinary, foreign, freaky, fresh, funny, incongruous, infrequent, marvelous, novel, odd, outre, portentous, prodigious, quaint, queer, rare, recherche, remarkable, seld, singular, special, strange, sui generis, unaccustomed, uncommon, unexpected, unfamiliar, unheard of, unique, unnatural, unwonted

comb. anom(o)

UNUTTERABLE indescribable, ineffable, sacred, unspeakable

UNVARNISHED clear, plain, straightforward, unembellished, unglossed

UNVARYING constant, even, flat, invariable, level, monotonous, permanent, stable, uniform

UNVEIL disclose, reveal, UNCOVER, undrape, unscreen

UNVEILING anacalypsis, dedication, inauguration

UNWARRANTED baseless, undue, unjustified

UNWARY asleep, careless,

heedless, impetuous, incautious, indiscreet, precipitate, rash, reckless, unaware, unexpected, unguarded

UNWASHED canaille, dirty, hoi polloi, proletariat, rabble

UNWAVERING confident, constant, firm, intense, level, persevering, single-minded, solid, stable, staunch, steadfast, steady, sure

UNWEARYING See UNTIRING.

UNWELCOME de trop, intrusive, non grata, thankless, unwanted

UNWELL ailing, crook, evil, ill, sick, wicked

UNWHOLESOME bad, baneful, cagmag, corrupt, decayed, deleterious, dirty, diseased, ill, immoral, insalubrious, morbid, noisome, noxious, pernicious, pestiferous, pestilent, poisonous, rotten, sick(ly), tainted, unclean, unhealthful, unhealthy, unhygienic, wrong

UNWIELDY awkward, bulky, clumsy, cumbersome, cumbrous, great, gross, hippopotamic, hulking, massive, ponderous, restive, ungainly

UNWILLING afraid, averse, backward, begrudging, disinclined, eschewing, grudging, hesitant, indisposed, involuntary, lo(a)th, nolle, recalcitrant, reluctant, slow, unobliging

UNWIND develop, disengage, disentangle, loosen, ravel, relax, straighten, unclue, uncoil, undo, unfurl, unravel, unreave, unreel, unrool, untwist

UNWISE amiss, false, foolish, ill-advised, ill-considered, impolitic, imprudent, inadvisable, incipient, indiscreet, injudicious, insapient, insensate, irrational, senseless, silly, STUPID, thoughtless, unintelligent, witless

UNWITTING accidental, disregarding, ignorant, inadvertent, oblivious, spontaneous, unaware, unconscious, unintended, uninten-

tional, unknowing, unmeant, unthinking, weetless

UNWONTED infrequent, rare, unaccustomed, uncommon, unique, unused, unusual

UNWORLDLY astral, heavenly, holy, immaterial, innocent, naive, nirvanic, provincial, spiritual, unearthly, unsophisticated, weird

UNWORTHY bad, base, beneath(notice), contemptible, despicable, discredit, disgrace, dishonorable, unbecoming, undeserved, undigne, unfit, unimportant, unmerited, unseemly, unsuited, vile, worthless, wretched, wrong

UNWRAP disclose, liberate, open, remove, reveal, uncover, undo, unveil

UNWREST deceitful, feeble, wicked, worthless

UNWRINKLED brant, brent, smooth, unfurrowed

UNWRITTEN blank, oral, parol, spoken, tacit, traditional, verbal, vocal

UNWROUGHT incomplete, raw, rough, uncompleted, undeveloped, unfashioned, unworked

UNYIELDING adamant, brassbound, bulldog, determined, dour, fast, firm, froward, frozen, grim, hard, headstrong, immovable, indomitable, inexorable, inflexible, iron, obstinate, resistant, rigid, rockribbed, stanch, stark, steely, stiff, stubborn, sturdy, tenacious, unbending, uncompromising, unsubmissive

UP about, advance, afoot, ahead, aloft, apiece, arisen, aroused, ascent, astir, at bat, at stake, awake, boost, competent, erect, expired, high(er), increase, mounted, over(head), prepared, raise, removed, rise(n), rouse, skyward, strengthen, toward

against it confounded, frustrated, needy, straitened

all ended, frustrated, ruined

and doing active, aggressive, alert, busy, energetic

and down alternate(ly), changeable, direct, downright, erect, fluctuation, ir-

regular, undulating, uneven, upright, vertical

-and-up frank, honest, open, sincere

comb. ana, ano

high aloft, lofty

in arms alert, aroused, belligerent, ready, resistant, roused, stirred

in the air confounded, undecided, wavering

on current, informed, knowledgeable, skilled

to able, adequate, competent, till, until

to date abreast, au courant, chic, current, fashionable, informed, modern, new, popular, stylish, with it

to one's ears busy, implicated

to this time hereto, hitherto, until, now

UPANISHAD isha, katha

UPAS antiar, chettik, dita

UPBEAT anacrusis, arsis, cheerful, happy, optimistic

UPBRAID abuse, accuse, blame, blast, censure, charge, chew(out), criticize, denounce, denunciate, disgrace, draw, exprobate, jaw, rail, rebuke, reprimand, reproach, reprove, revile, scold, score, shame, taunt, twist, twit, utter, wig

UPBRAIDING epiplexis

UPBRAST burst

UPBRINGING breeding, nurture, rearing, training

UPBUILDING edification, increase

UPCOME arrive, ascent, growth, grow up, outcome, output

UPCOUNTRY achterveld, hinterland, inland, interior, midlands, outback

UPEND defeat, erect, invert, overthrow, overturn, reverse, upset

UPGANG ascent

UPGRADE ascent, elevate, improve, incline, increase, promote, raise, slope

UPHEAVAL agitation, alteration, cataclysm, catastrophe, commotion, convulsion, disturbance, earthquake, revolt, rummage, temblor, tremor, uplift, upthrow

political statequake

UPHILL acclivous, ascending, ascent, difficult, elevated, hard, laborious, rising, tiring, tough, upwards

UPHOLD abet, advocate, affirm, aid, approve, assert, back, bear, bolster, buoy, carry, champion, confirm, conserve, countenance, defend, encourage, endorse, favo(u)r, help, justify, maintain, preserve, raise, sanction, second, stay, support, sustain, vindicate

UPHOLDER adherent, advocate, backer, champion, dealer, defender, supporter, tradesman, undertaker, upholsterer

UPHOLSTER cover, overstuff

UPHOLSTERY *fabric* damask, lampas, mohair, moquette, president, rep, tabaret, tournay

galloon or *gimp* orris

stuffing down, excelsior, foam-rubber, hair, kapok

UPIS artemis, nemesis

UPKEEP cost, maintain, maintenance, overhead, repair, subsistence, support, sustenance

UPLAND coteau, downs, highland, inland, interior, mauka, mesa, plateau, ridge, rural, wold

boneset thoroughwort

hickory shagbark

plover hillbird, papabote, quaily, sandpiper

UPLIFT buoy, boost, collect, elate, elevate(d), elevation, ennoble(d), erect, exalt, glorify, improve, inspiration, inspire, plateau, raise, rock, toss, tower, unheaval, upend, upraise, uprear, upthrust

UPOLU *capital* apia

UPON about, above, against, atop, concerning, into, near, oer, over, sopra, sur, thereon, touching, toward, upward

comb. epi, supra, sur

that thereat, thereupon

which when, whereat, whereupon

UPPBAD bevaring

UPPER above, advanced, berth, bunk, higher, innermost, over, outer, skive, superior, uber, vamp(ey)

case capital

class See SOCIETY.

classman junior, senior

comb. ano

crust See SOCIETY.

hand advantage, control, dominion, influence, mastery, preference

part cap, finial, spire, top

on one's —s indigent, poor, shabby

story brain, head, top

UPPER VOLTA *capital* ouagadougou

language bobo, lobi, mande, mossi, samo

native bissa, bobo, hausa, lobi, mande, mandingo, marka, mossi, puehl, samo, senoufo, tuareg, voltaic, yatenga

peak tema

president yameogo

river sourou

UPPISH, UPPITY arrogant, assuming, drunk, elated, haughty, intoxicated, peevish, presumptuous, pretentious, proud, snobbish, snooty, supercilious, toplofty

UPPOWOC See TOBACCO.

UPRAISE buoy, elevate, encourage, erect, extol, hoist, lift, uplift, uprear

UPRAISED atilt, elevated, encouraged, erected, extolled, improved, lifted, raised, sublime, vertical

UPREAR arise, bring up, build, elevate, erect, exalt, excite, lift, raise, ramp, rise

UPRIGHT aboveboard, anend, bar, candid, cocked, column, conscientious, correct, creditable, direct, elevation, endwise, equitable, erect, estimable, ethical, fair, good, high-minded, honest, honorable, jamb, jannock, just, law-abiding, manly, moral, noble, perpendicular, piano(forte), pier, pile, pitprop, plumb, pole, post, principled, prop, reliable, reputable, respectable, right(eous), scrupulous, sheer, sincere, square, steep, sterling, stile, straight, stud, sturdy, true, trustworthy, unambiguous, upstanding, vertical, virtuous, worthy, yeomanly

comb. orth(o)

UPRIGHTNESS honesty,

honor, probity, rectitude, truth

UPRISE arise, ascend, ascent, dawn, elevation, grow, incline, insurrection, revolt, swell, UPRISING

UPRISER insurgent, mutineer, putschist, rioter

UPRISING acclivity, ado, ascent, babel, clamor, commotion, conflict, confusion, coup, din, disorder, disturbance, emeute, fray, hubbub, insurrection, mutiny, noise, pandemonium, putsch, racket, rebellion, revolt, revolution, riot, tumult, turmoil, uprist

UPROAR ado, agitation, babel, bedlam, bluster, bother, brawl, broil, brouhaha, bustle, callithump, chaos, clamo(u)r, commotion, confusion, convulsion, din, dirdum, disorder, disturbance, donnybrook, dust, embroilment, ferment, foofaraw, fracas, furor, fuss, habble, helterskelter, hoopla, hubble, hubbub, hullabaloo, hurly(burly), melee, moil, noise, outbreak, pandemonium, pother, pudder, racket, randan, rantan, rattle, riot, rippet, roughhouse, rout, row, rowdydow, ruckus, ruction, rumble, rumbullion, rumpus, rut, shindy, shine, squall, stashie, stir, stoun, stour, strife, tintamarre, todo, touse, trouble, TUMULT, turbulence, turmoil

UPROARIOUS boisterous, disordered, funny, loud, noisy, tumultuous, turbulent

UPROOT abate, abolish, demolish, deracinate, destroy, displace, eradicate, exterminate, extirpate, extract, remove, supplant, unplant, weed out, wipe out

UPSET agitate, alarm, anger, angry, anxious, apprehensive, astound, bewilder, bouleverse, cant, capsize, confound, confuse, crush, dash, defeat, demoralize, derange, discomfit, discompose, disconcert, dislocate, dismay, disorder, disorganize, disquiet, distress, disturb, embarrass, fall, flurry, fluster, frantic, ill, invert, irk, irritate(d), keel, nervous, overpower, overthrow, overturn, overwhelm, perturb, pervert, prostrate, quarrel, refute, reverse, revolution, rile, riot, ruffle, shock, shot, spoil, startle, stir, stricken, strike, subvert, throw, thwart, tip(ple), top(ple), undone, uneasy, unnerve, unsettle, unstrung, upend, vanquish

UPSHOT aftermath, conclusion, consequence, consummation, development, effect, end(ing), eventuality, finish, gist, issue, limit, mark, outcome, result, sequel, termination

UPSIDE-DOWN chaotic, crazy, disordered, head over heels, inverted, overturned, topsyturvy, upended

UPSTAGE aloof, arrogant, backward, conceited, offish, outdo, outshine, shy, snobbish, snub, supercilious

UPSTANDING erect, exceptional, honorable, respected, superior, upright, verticle

UPSTART arrivist(e), bounder, cockhorse, dalteen, mushroom, nouveau-riche, origin, parvenu, saffron, skipjack, snob, social-climber, sprout, squirt, would-be

UPSTIR agitate, commotion, incite, stimulate, tumult

UPSURGE boom, increase, inflation, rise

UPSWING growth, improve (ment), increase

UPTAKE apprehension, collection, comprehend, comprehension, flue, help, lifting, pipe, shaft, succor, support, tube, understanding, upcast

UPTIGHT afret, fretful, frustrated, nervous, supercharged, tense

UPTURN capsize, chaos, disorder, improvement, increase, overturn, rise, upheaval

UPWARD(S) above, aloft, ascending, more, over(head), skyward, upways

comb. ana, ano

of about, above, approximately, more than, several

URAEUS asp, ornament, symbol

URAL *city on* magnitogorsk, orsk

language ugric

URALITE amphibole

URAMIL murexan

URANIA aphrodite

consort amphimarus

muse of astronomy

parent mnemosyne, oceanus, tethys, uranus, zeus

son hymen(aeus), linus

symbol globe

URANINITE broggerite, cleveite, nivenite, pitchblende

derivative helium, radium

URANIUM *center* ambrosia lake

compound autunite, becquerelite, betafite, brannerite, ianthinite, uvanite

discoverer klaproth

fission product ploot, plutonium, technetium

instrument fast breeder, nuclear reactor

source carnotite, pitchblende, samarskite, vanadate

yellow diuranate

URANUS ouranos

consort gaea

dethroned by cronus

discoverer herschel

mother gaea, gaia

offspring aegaeon, alcyoneus, aphrodite, briareus, centimanes, coeus, cottus, cratus, crius, cronus, cyclops, furies, gigantes, gyges, hecatoncheires, iapetus, meliae, oceanus, ops, pontus, rhea, titans

satellite ariel, miranda, oberon, titania, umbriel

slayer cronus

URAO mineral, trona

URARTU armenia, van

people khaldian, van(nic)

URBAN burghal, citified, city, civic, downtown, metropolitan, municipal, oppidan, town

division borough, ward

-dwelling urbicolous

friend paul

region mega(lo)polis

URBANE amiable, bland, civil, courteous, cultured, diplomatic, elegant, gracious, mannerly, pleasant, poised, polished, politic, po-

lite, refined, smooth, sophisticated, suave

URCHIN boy, brat, child, elf(ish), gamin, hedgehog, hunchback, imp, keelie, mudlar, nipper, tad, youngster

URD bean, gram, mungo, pyrol, urth

URDE cleche, crossed, pointed

URDU moorish, rekhta, rekhti

URE custom, exercise, haze, inure, mist, ounce, practice, use

UREA carbamide

UREDO hives, rust, urticaria

URFA edessa

URGA ulan-bator

URGE (See also *on*, below.) abet, advise, advocate, allege, animate, appetite, assuade, blandish, brod, coax, compel, constrain, craving, demand, desire, ding, dun, encourage, enforce, enjoin, entreat, excite, exhort, firk, flog, follow, force, goad, hag, hie, high pressure, hound, impel, importune, impulse, impulsion, incite, induce, influence, insist, instigate, intensify, itch, lash, longing, lure, lust, motive, needle, passion, persuade, ply, poke, pray, press(ure), prick, prod, propel, provoke, push, recommend, sic(k), solicit, spur, stimulate, stimulus, strain, sue, threat, verve, whip, yen

on accelerate, busk, chirk, crowd, drive, egg, ert, hasten, hurry, yoick

URGENCY entreaty, haste, insistence, need, pinch, press(ure), stress

URGENT acute, appealing, clamorous, cogent, compelling, constraining, critical, crucial, crying, demanding, dire, exigent, hot, immediate, impelling, imperative, important, importunate, insistent, instant, necessary, oppressive, pressing, rushing, solicitous, stringent

URGING admonition, agitation, encitement, encouragement, exhortation, goad, hortative, prod, quest, spur, suasion, suasive, vehement

URI *son* bezaleel, marmathi
URIAH *commander* david
son meremoth
wife bathsheba
URIAL oorial, sha, sheep
URIEL *adversary* adammelech
URIENS *wife* morgan le fay
URIJAH *kin* meremoth, shemaiah
URIM *associate* thummim
URISK brownie
URLUCH dull, stupid
URN amphora, bury, capanna, capsule, cistern, ewer, grave, jar, jug, kist, pain, pig, pitcher, run, samovar, silex, situla, steen, teapot, theca, vase, vessel
burial ossuary
cinerary canopus, d(e)inos
field cemetery
keno goose
-shaped urceolar, urceolate
URODELA amphibia, caudata, eft, newt, salamander
URSA bear
major big dipper, chariot, great bear, oknari, wag(g)oner
major star groombridge, pointer
minor little dipper
minor star polaris
URSINE arctoid, bearlike
baboon chacma
howler araguato
URSULA, ST *symbol* arrows
URSULINE *founder* angela merici
URSUS See BEAR.
URTH norn, past, wyrd
URTICARIA cnidosis, hives, rash, uredo
URTICASTRUM laportea
URTICATE flog, lash, sting, whip
URUGUAY *capital* montevideo
city artigas, colonia, durazno, florida, maldonado, melo, minas, montevideo, paysandu, rivera, rocha, salto
coin centesimo, peso
department artigas, flores, rivera, rocha, salto, soriano
estuary plata
guerrilla tupamaro
indian yaro
lake merin, mirim
measure cuadra, suerte, vara
poetess ibarbourou
president batlee y ordonez

river cebollary, cuareim, malo, mirim, negro, queguay, tacaurembo, ulimar, yaguaron
soldier jose artigas
terrorist tupamaro
weight quintal
URUNDI *people* barundi
URUS aurochs, bos, tur, ure
URVASI *consort* varuna
USAGE advantage, behavior, ceremony, conduct, convention, custom, experience, fashion, form, habit, halacha, halakah, interest, manner(s), method, practice, principle, procedure, sunna, system, treatment, usance, use, utility, way, wont
comb. nomo
common idiom
correct sumpsimus
USE accustom, adhibition, administer, advantage, appliance, application, apply, avail, bear, behoof, benefit, borrow, cheat, consumption, convert, custom, devote, disposal, disposition, dupe, employ(ment), engage in, enjoy, equity, exercise, exert, expend, exploit, follow, frequent, function, guide, habit(uate), handle, hansel, help, hire, interest, inure, manage, maneuver, manipulate, necessity, need, object, occupy, office, operate, partake of, pertinence, play, ply, practice, profit, purpose, relevance, resort, right, service, stead, take advantage, treat(ment), try, ure, usufruct, usury, utility, utilize, vail, value, wield, work, worth
ill abuse, harm
in current, popular, prevailing, prevalent
refrain from abjure, boycott, disavow, forswear, reject, renounce
to advantage avail
up absorb, consume, deplete, devour, eat, exhaust, expend, fatigue, finish, outwear, sap, spend, tire, waste, wear out
USED accustomed, employed, experienced, secondhand, utilized, wont, worn(out)
to addicted, wont
up beat, exhausted, fagged,

fatigued, gone, infirm, pooped, shot, spent, tired, worn
USEFUL advantageous, applicable, beneficial, convenient, effective, functional, good, handy, helpful, instrumental, invaluable, practical, pragmatic, proficuous, profitable, remunerative, serviceable, suited, thrifty, utile, utilitarian, worthy
USEFULNESS adequacy, avail, benefit, efficacy, merit, practicality, profit, utility, value, worth
USELESS bootless, doless, feckless, footless, fruitless, futile, good-for-nothing, hopeless, idle, inadequate, incompetent, ineffectual, inefficient, inutile, needless, null, otiose, paltry, profitless, purposeless, scrap, scrubby, sterile, superfluous, trashy, unavailing, unprofitable, unutile, vain, valueless, void, waste(ful), worthless
USER See ADDICT.
USHA *beloved* aniruddha
father bana
USHER attendant, chobdar, conduct, direct, doorkeeper, escort, guide, harbinger, herald, huishar, introduce, ischar, lead, marshal, porter, precursor, preface, seat, show, steward, tiler
in begin, inaugurate, precede, prelude
house of lords black rod
USIGE whisk(e)y
USNEA fungus, lichen, moss
USNECH *son* noise
USQUEBAUGH cordial, water of life, whiskey
USSR See RUSSIA.
USTULATE blackened, burned, discolored, scorched, seared
USUAL accepted, accustomed, analogical, average, common(place), consuetudinary, conventional, current, customary, everyday, expected, familiar, frequent, general, habitual, household, natural, normal, ordinary, orthodox, popular, predictable, prescriptive, prevailing, prevalent, realistic, recurrent, regular, regulation, rife, set, stale, stand-

ard, stereotyped, stock, trite, typical, unexceptional, universal, vernacular, vulgar, wonted

USUALLY customarily, for the most part, generally, normally, often

USUI *parent* asher

USURER bleeder, bloodsucker, extortioner, gaveler, harpagon, leech, loaner, moneychanger, moneylender, shark, shylock, sponger

USURP accroach, appropriate, arrogate, assume, confiscate, encroach, grab, grasp, preempt, presume, seize, take, wrest

USURPATION accession, appropriation, custom, dispossession, encroachment, infringement, seizure, usage, use

USURPER despot, tyrant

USURY gavel, gombeen, interest, ocker, overcharge, premium, shylocking, usance

UTA leishmaniasis, lizard, song, tanka

UTAH *canyon* echo
capital salt lake city
city american fork, beaver, brigham, delta, eureka, gunnison, heber, kanab, kearns, lehi, logan, magna, moab, murray, nephi, ogden, orem, price, provo, richfield, salt lake city, tooele, vernal
college weber
county cache, juab, piute, sanpete, sevier, tooele, uintah
gemstone variscite
indian gosiute, paiute, paviotso, piute, uinta(h), ute, yampa
lake great salt, sevier, swan
mine silver king
mormon name deseret
motto industry
national monument capital reef, rainbow bridge
national park bryce canyon, zion
nickname beehive state, mormon state
peak frisco, granite, griffin, hawkins, kings, lena, lion, marvine, navajo, peale, pennell, swasey, trail
plateau tavaputs, wasatch

range cedar, confusion, henry, hogup, terrage, uinta, wahwah, wasatch
river bear, colorado, grand, green, jordan, sevier, weber
silver queen susan bransford, delitch, engalitcheff, emory holmes
state bird seagull
state flower sego lily
state tree spruce
university brigham young

UTENSIL appliance, gadget, IMPLEMENT, instrument, receptacle, TOOL, vessel

UTGARD *ruler* skrymir

UTHER *consort* igraine
son king arthur

UTILITARIAN banausic, beneficial, economic, matter-of-fact, practical, usable, useful

UTILITARIANISM benthamism
expounder bentham, mills

UTILITY adequacy, benefit, efficacy, efficiency, enterprise, function, happiness, profit, service, USE, USEFULNESS, value, worth

UTILIZE consume, employ, exploit, harness, husband, USE

UTMOST best, end, extent, extreme, farthest, final, fullest, greatest, highest, last, limit, main, maximum, outmost, supreme, uttermost

UTO aztec
language piman

UTOPIA (See also PERSIA utopia.) agapemone, annfwn, annwn, arcadia, atlantis, avalon, canaan, cloudland, cockaigne, dixie, dreamland, eden, erewhon, estotilandia, euphoria, fairyland, garden of eden, goshen, happy valley, icaria, land of milk and honey, laputa, lemuria, lotusland, millennium, nauvoo, new jerusalem, nirvana, oceana, paradise, pie in the sky, shangri-la, xanadu, zion
author more
bridge amaurote
city amaurot
giant king grangousier
harrington's oceana

UTOPIAN ambitious, chimerical, edenic, ideal(istic), impossible, impractical, lo-

tus-eater, pretentious, quixotic, unfeasible, visionary
community oneida

UTRAQUIST calixtin(e), hussite

UTRICLE bag, bladder, cavity, cell, perigynium, sac, vesicle

UTRICULARIA bladdersnout, bladderwort

UTTAR PRADESH *city* benares, lucknow

UTTER absolute, air, announce, articulate, bark, bellow, blat, blinking, blurt, broach, bugle, call, circulate, complete(ly), croak, declare, deliver, disclose, divulge, drawl, ejaculate, emit, enounce, entire, enunciate, express, extreme, final, great, growl, grunt, issue, mere, moot, outer, outside, peremptory, perfect, pronounce, publish, pure, rail, remote, reveal, roar, say, sell, sheer, sigh, sound, SPEAK, squeal, stammer, stark, state, strange, talk, tell, thorough, total, unconditional, unqualified, unusual, vanquish, vend, vent, vociferate, voice, warble, wheeze, whimper, whisper, yell
hastily blurt, bolt
indistinctly babble, murmur
loudly blat, call, cry, halloo, shout
softly whisper
tearfully blubber

UTTERANCE articulation, cry, delivery, enunciation, expression, issue, judgment, locution, oracle, parol, phrase, prelation, speech, statement, ultimate
divine oracle
silly drivel, guff, hot air
soft breath, murmur, whisper
voiced sonant
voiceless spirate, surd

UTTERED breathed, oral, said, spoken

UTTERLY absolutely, blankly, cap-a-pie, completely, entirely, every inch, extremely, fully, greatly, merely, over all, quite, sheer, stark, totally, wholly

UTTERMOST See UTMOST.

UTU babbar, compensation,

hoot, retaliation, reward, satisfaction, shamash, wages
UTURUNCO jaguar, werewolf
UVA arrow-cane, fruit, grape *grass* cana-brava, gynerium
UVID moist, wet
UVULA cion, palate, pap of the hass, plectrum, staphyle *comb.* staphyl(o)

UVULARIA bellflower, bellwort, campanula, daffodil, oakesia
UZ *kin* aran, dishan, shem
UZAI *son* palal
UZBEK jagatai
UZZI *parent* bela, tola *son* arna, zerahiah
UZZIAH *builder for* eloth *captain* hananiah

kingdom judah
parent amaziah, harim, jecoliar, levi, zechariah
scribe jeiel
son athaiah, jehonathan, jotham
wife jerushah
UZZIEL *son* amminadab, jesiah, micah

V

V five, victory
VAAGMAR dealfish
VAALITE vermiculite
VAC sarasvati
VACANCY bareness, barrenness, blank, bleakness, chasm, depletion, emptiness, exhaustion, freedom, gap, hole, hollowness, idleness, inanition, inanity, interim, lack, leisure, loneliness, opening, position, space, vacation, vacuity, vacuum, void, want
VACANT abandoned, bare, barren, blank, clear, dead (pan), destitute, disengaged, dull, empty, expressionless, fishy, foolish, free, glassy, hollow, idiotic, idle, imbecilic, inane, lackluster, leisured, open, quiet, silly, stupid, thoughtless, unemployed, unfilled, unintelligent, unreflecting, untenanted, unused, unusual, vacuous, void, wooden
VACATE abandon, abdicate, abrogate, annul, avoid, cancel, depart, disoccupy, empty, evacuate, go away, leave, move, quash, quit, repeal, rescind, resign, void, waive, withdraw, yield
VACATION furlough, holiday, intermission, leave, liberty, recess, respite, rest, sabbatical, spell, weekend *place* beach, camp, city, forest, lake, mountains, ocean, park, resort, seaside, spa *spent working* busman's holiday
VACCINATE immunize, variolate
VACCINE antisepsis, antitoxen, bacterin, biologic, inoculant, inoculum, preventative, preventive, sabin, shot, toxin-antitoxin

administrator epidemiologist
inventor jenner, pasteur, sabin, salk
VACCINIUM bilberry, blackheart, blueberry, huckleberry, whortleberry
VACHELLIA cassie, huisache
VACILLATE alternate, back and fill, boggle, change, dacker, demur, dillydally, dither, falter, flimflam, flipflop, flounder, fluctuate, hem and haw, hesitate, oscillate, palter, pendulate, procrastinate, pussyfoot, quiver, reel, scruple, seesaw, shaffle, shift, shillyshally, shuffle, shuttle, stickle, sway, teeter, totter, trim, vary, wabble, waffle, wag, waver, wobble
VACILLATING doubtful, halting, hesitating, inconstant, variable, wavering
VACILLATION delay, faltering, indecision, irresolution, procrastination, suspense, uncertainty, wavering
VACUITY absence, blankness, gap, hollow, inanity, nihility, nothingness, stupidity, vacancy, vacuum, void
VACUOUS bare, barren, blank, dull, empty, idle, inane, insipid, silly, stupid, unfilled, unintelligent, vacant, void, wishywashy
VACUUM blank, cavity, clean(er), gap, hole, hollow, nothing, pocket, space, sweep(er), vacancy, vacuity, void
pump pulsometer
tube audion, diode, heptode, klvstron, tetrode, valve
VADE MECUM handbook, manual
VADIUM bail, mortgage, pawn, pledge, security

VAGABOND abra(ha)m-man, arab, beachcomber, beggar, bindlestiff, bohemian, brodyaga, bum(mer), canter, cursitor, custroun, faitour, gadling, gamin, gangrel, guttersnipe, gypsy, hobo, homeless, irregular, javel, kern, landlo(u)per, lazzarone, loafer, lorel, losel, nomadic, palliard, picaro, piker, prog(ger), ragamuffin, ragman, rapparee, rascal, rodney, rogue, rove(r), runabout, runagate, shirk, stiff, straggler, sundowner, swagman, swinger, tagrag, tinkler, tramp, truant, turnpiker, VAGRANT, vaurien, waffle, waif, wanderer, wastrel, whipjack
VAGARIOUS capricious, whimsical
VAGARY caprice, conceit, crankum, crotchet, dream, fancy, flagarie, freak, humor, idea, mood, notion, whim(sey)
VAGRANCY indolence, mopery, roguing, wandering
VAGRANT ambulant, arrant, beachcomber, blackguard, bodyaga, bum, caird, capricious, casual, circuitous, circumforaneous, devious, drifter, erratic, gypsy, inconstant, itinerant, landlo(u)per, migratory, moving, nomad(ic), peripatetic, picaro, piker, prowler, roaming, roving, shifting, shu(i)ler, skelder, skilder, stroller, tramp, truant, VAGABOND, vagrom, waff, waif, wandering
VAGUE abstruse, ambiguous, blear(ed), bleary, blind, blurred, blurry, broad, cloudy, confused, cryptic, dark, dim, doubtful, dreamy,

enigmatic, equivocal, evasive, faint, feeble, filmy, foggy, forlorn, formless, futile, fuzzy, general, hazy, ill-defined, imprecise, inarticulate(d), indecisive, indefinite, indeterminate, indistinct, inexact, intangible, lax, light, loose, lost, misty, muddy, nebulous, nonspecific, obscure, opaque, pale, prank, roam, shadowy, sketchy, stray, tenuous, uncertain, unclear, undefined, unfixed, unrecognizable, unsettled, unspecified, vagabond, vagary, vagrant, veiled, wander, weak

VAGUELY darkly, dimly, idly, inanely, uncertainly

VAGUENESS ambiguity, formlessness

VAGUS *pert.* pneumogastric

VAIL advantage, benefit, bow, bride, decline, descend, discent, doff, dole, downflow, drop, fee, gratuity, humble, lower, offering, perquisite, proceeds, profit, return, sink, slope, submit, subside, tip, yield

VAIN arrogant, baseless, biggety, bootless, chimeric(al), conceited, egotistic, empty, evanescent, flimsy, foolish, fruitless, futile, gorgeous, hollow, hopeless, idle, ignorant, ineffective, ineffectual, invalid, nugatory, otiose, overproud, overweening, paltry, petty, priggish, proud, puny, self-complacent, self-important, silly, slight, smug, snooty, sterile, stuck-up, superficial, trifling, trivial, unavailing, unimportant, unrewarded, upstage, useless, vapid, vaunty, vogie, waste(ful), weak, worthless
as a peacock

VAINGLORIOUS arrogant, boastful, conceited, disdainful, egotistic(al), haughty, insolent, proud, self-proud, vaunting

VAINGLORY boasting, bombast, conceit, display, elation, exhibition, gasconade, parade, pomp, pride, rodomontade, show, vanity

VAISHNAVA See VISHNU.

VAISRAVANA See BUDDHA.

VAISYA bais, bice
caste aroras

VAKEEL, VAKIL agent, ambassador, attorney, lawyer, pleader, representative

VAL *father* aguar

VALANCE border, curtain, drapery, edging, flap, palmette, pelmet

VALE adieu, bache, batch, dale, dean, dell, dingle, earth, farewell, glen, goodbye, valley, world

VALEDICTION, VALEDICTORY adieu, apopemptic, farewell, leave-taking, oration, parting

VALENCE adicity, atomism, power, rank, value

VALENTINE card, gift, greeting, love, sweetheart, token
beloved silvia, sylvia
brother orson
friend orsino
kinsman titus andronicus
rival thurio
servant speed
sister margaret
slayer faust
state arizona

VALENTINITE *antimony* bloom

VALERIAN allheal, bennet, capon's-tail, catbed, cetewall, cutheal, helio(trope), jupiter's-beard, nard, panacea, remedy, self-heal, setwall, spikenard, sumbul

VALET andrew, attendant, crispin, flunky, goad, man, servant, sirdar, squire, stick, tireman, wallie
de pied footman
de place guide

VALETUDINARIAN infirm, invalid, patient, sick(ly), weak(ly)

VALHALLA paradise
hall of odin
heroes einherjar
nymphs valkyries
site asgard

VALI *parent* odin, rind(r)

VALIANT aught, bold, brag, brave, courageous, dauntless, doughty, fierce, galliard, hero(ic), intrepid, invincible, lusty, proud, undaunted, stalwart, stout (hearted), sturdy, valorous, wight, wild

VALID authentic, authoritative, binding, bonafide, cogent, convincing, decisive, dejure, effective, efficacious, efficient, eternal, forceful, genuine, good, just, lawful, legal, licit, logical, meritorious, official, potent, pucka, real, solid, sound, substantial, sufficient, telling, trenchant, valuable, veritable, weighty, wellfounded

VALIDATE affirm, approve, attest, authenticate, certify, confirm, constitute, corroborate, establish, legalize, legitimize, ratify, seal, substantiate, verify, witness

VALIDITY authority, bienfonde, cogency, force, justness, robustness, soundness, strength, valence, value, vigor, worth

VALISE bag, case, dorlach, etui, etwee, gladstone, grip, portmanteau, satchel, suitcase

VALIUM benzodiazepine, diazepam

VALJEAN *discoverer* javert
friend marius
protege cosette

VALKYRIE freyja, kara, shieldmay, sigrdrifa, wishmaiden, wishmay
home valhalla
master odin
queen brunhild, brunnehilde, brynhild

VALLATION earthwork, entrenchment, rampart

VALLETTA *native* maltese

VALLEY aijalon, atrio, bache, basin, bolson, bottom(s), canada, canyon, chasm, clough, combe(e), coom(be), coulee, dale, deal, dell, dene, dhoon, dingle, gehenna, ghyll, gill, glack, glade, glen, gorge, goyal, goyle, gulch, hollow, hoya, intervale, laagte, leegte, nemea, ravine, rill(e), rincon, sacco, slade, strath, swale, tempe, vaal, vaalite, vale, wadi, wady, watershed, yunga
biblical baca, gehenna, hela
circular rincon
deep can(y)on
desert bolson
moon's rill(e)

narrow clough, deau, dene, glack, glen, goyle, kloof

of tears baca

open canada

small gull(e)y, laigh, rincon

volcano's atrio

VALLOTA amaryllis, lily

VALLUM earthwork, rampart, wall

VALOR arete, backbone, bravery, chivalry, courage, guts, heroism, merit, mettle, power, prowess, sand, spirit, stomach, strength, tenacity, valuation, value, worth

VALOROUS bold, brave, courageous, daring, dauntless, doughty, gallant, heroic, intrepid, stalwart, stout(hearted), strong, sturdy, tough, valiant, virtuous

VALPARAISO flaming coast

VALUABLE(S) appreciated, costly, dear, gainful, gem(s), helpful, inestimable, jewel(s), precious, priceless, prize(d), profitable, remunerative, serviceable, treasure(d)(s), useful, wallet, worthy

place for arca, safe(deposit), vault

VALUATE appraise, price, VALUE

VALUATION account, appraisal, assessment, census, esteem, estimate, estimation, worth

VALUE account, admire, advance, advantage, amount, appraise, appreciate, apprize, assay, assess, asset, assize(s), avail, average, benefit, calculate, carat, cherish, compute, cost, equity, esteem, estimate, evaluate, excellence, face, feck, fee, figure, import(ance), judge, matter, mean(ing), measure, merit, moment, money, net, opinion, par, pennyworth, praise, price, profit, quantity, rate, reckon, regard, resource, respect, revere, sterling, treasure, utility, venerate, weigh, worth

be worthy of deserve, earn, merit, rate

creation society sokagakkai

determine appraise, assay, rate

equal parity

excessively inflate, overestimate, overrate

full money's worth

highly cherish, prize

limit of derivate

mean average

net reserve

nominal par

philosophy of axiology

reduction depreciation

relative ad valorem

study of axiology

without baff, hollow, miserable, stramineous, threepenny, trashy, unimportant, useless, waste, worthless

VALVE bleeder, cock, cusp, damper, drawgate, epitheca, fang, faucet, gate, intake, kicker, outlet, petcock, piston, poppet, potlid, scallop, sluice, spigot, stopcock, tap, valvula, ventil, tube

musical piston, ventil

part body, bonnet, case, disk, gabpin, handwheel, nut, raphe, spindle, stem, washer

VAMOOSE beat it, begone, decamp, depart, git, lam, scat, scram, skedaddle, skiddoo

VAMP attract, beguile, fireman, flirt, hose, improvise, patch, piece, plod, sock, tramp, upper, VAMPIRE, walk

up concoct, fabricate, furbish, repair

VAMPER bluster, boast, closer, pose

VAMPHORN megaphone

VAMPIRE aluka(h), bat, bloodsucker, demon, dracula, extortioner, extortionist, flirt, ghost, ghoul, lamia, monster, seductress, siren, temptress, trapdoor

VAN advantage, avant garde, baggage car, camper, caravan, carrier, dray, fan, forefront, fourgon, front, head, khaldian, kittereen, lead, lorry, sail, shovel, store, summit, truck, vehicle, wagon, wing, winnow

VANADATE carnotite, psittacinite, turanite, uvanite

compound mottramite, pintadoite, pucherite, pyrobelonite

derivative uranium

VAN BUREN old kinderhook

birthplace and *burial* kinderhook, new york

party democratic

profession lawyer

vice president johnson

VANCOUVER *indian* ahousaht, aht, clayoquot, ehatisaht, nootka, sanetch, songesh, songish, sooke

VANDAL defacer, destroyer, goth, hooligan, hun, plunderer, saracen, teuton

conqueror belisarius, ricimer

conquest rome

idol flins

king gaiseric, genseric

VANDAMME *commander* napoleon

VANDELLIA bitterblain, candiru, catfish

VAN DIEMAN'S LAND See TASMANIA.

VAN DINE, S. S. willard huntington wright

VANDYKE beard, cape, collar, edge, notch, point

VANE blade, bucket, cock, faine, fan(e), feather, flag, flighter, pennon, plate, sail, sight, tail, target, tee, vexillum, weathercock, web, wing

of feather flue, vexillum, web

VANESSA anglewing, butterfly, painted-beauty, polygonia, pyrameis, red admiral

swift's esther von homrigh

VAN GOGH *brother* theo

city arles

painting drawbridge at arles, potato-eaters

VANGUARD advance, avant-garde, beachhead, bridgehead, first line, fore(front), forepost, front, outpost, pioneer, railhead, satellite, spearhead, VAN

VANILLA cloying, coumarin, flavoring, mawkish, orchid, sweetsmelling

-like vine amlong

substitute tonka-bean

wild deer's-tongue, liatris

VANIR See AESIR.

VANISH burst, consume, die, disappear, dispel, dissipate, dissolve, evanesce, evaporate, flee(t), flit, fly, melt, pass, perish, recede, sant, scatter, sink, slide, wede

VANITY air(s), amour-propre, arrogance, bluster,

breath, complacency, conceit, ego(ism)(tism), emptiness, falsity, folly, foppery, futility, ostentation, pomp, pretense, pride, selfesteem, self love, sham, show, vainglory, vainness
case dorine, entoutcas, etui, etwee
fair See SOCIETY.
fair author thackeray
fair character amelia sedley, becky sharp, briggs, dobbin, glorvina o'dowd, osborne pitt crawley, rawdon crawley, steyne
name meaning abel
symbol margery daw, peacock
VANQUISH annihilate, beat, best, confound, confute, conquer, defeat, expel, foil, frustrate, lick, outray, outwit, overcome, overthrow, overwin, reduce, rout, subdue, subjugate, subvert, suppress, surmount, thrash, win, worst
VANQUISHER champion, conqueror, victor, winner
VANTAGE (See also ADVANTAGE.) chance, coign(e), fee, gain, opportunity, perquisite, profit, superiority, surplus
VAPID banal, bland, dead, dry, dull, flat, flavorless, inane, indifferent, insipid, jejune, mawkish, mild, pointless, prosaic, slushy, soppy, spiritless, stale, tame, tasteless, thoughtless, trite, vacant, vacuous, wishywashy
VAPOR (See also VAPORS.) afflatus, afterdamp, air, aura, bluster, boast, bore, breath, brume, bubble, bully, chokedamp, cloud, contrail, damp, depress, dew, effluvium, ether, ewder, exhalation, exhaust, fancy, firedamp, flatus, fog, fume, gas, halitus, haze, illusion, lunt, miasm(a), mist, moisture, nimbus, phantasm, rack, reek, roke, smaze, smog, smoke, smudge, steam, volatile
comb. atmid(o), atm(o)
convert to aerify
foul malaria, mephitis, miasma

frozen frost, hail, rime, sleet, snow
hot lunt
loss boil-off
noxious damp, miasma
pocket cavitation
pressure indicator tonometer
science atmology
VAPORIZE aerate, aerify, atomize, carbonate, dissipate, distill, etherify, etherize, evaporate, fume, fumigate, gasify, reek, smoke, spray, steam, sublimate, volatilize
VAPOROUS airy, chimerical, cloudy, dampish, ethereal, fleeting, foggy, fumish, fumose, gaseous, halituous, humid, indistinct, misty, moist, rare, shadowy, steamy, unreal, unsubstantial, vain, volatile
VAPORS blues, brume, dejection, depression, dumps, gloom, melancholia, melancholy, sadness
VAPORY abject, hypochondriacal, peevish, spiritless, splenetic, wretched
VAPULATE beat, flog, thrash
VAQUERO cowboy, equestrian, herdsman, horseman, querecho, stockman
weapon bola
VARANGIANS ros, rus, russ, variag, waring
VARDI, VARDY opinion, verdict
VARE staff, voar, wand, weasel
VAREC(H) ashes, kelp, seaweed, wrack
VARIABLE aberrant, brockle, capricious, changeable, changeful, choppy, fickle, fitful, flexible, floating, free, inconstant, irregular, irresolute, kittle, mercurial, mobile, mutable, protean, restless, shifting, shifty, spasmodic, unequal, unstable, unsteady, vacillating, wavering
VARIANCE argument, cline, conflict, contention, difference, disagreement, discord, discrepancy, dispute, dissension, diversity, division, separation, strife
VARIANT different, discrepent, divergent, fickle, rest-

less, state, varied, VARIEGATED
VARIATION aberration, adaptation, alteration, change, deflection, deviation, distinction, diversity, error, extreme, heterism, lection, modification, mutation, nuance, shade, shading, switch, tolerance, turn, variety
comb. allo
from normal acatastasia
musical dynamics
recorder auxograph
slight nuance, shade, shading
vowel ablaut, apophony
VARICOSE cirsoid, enlarged, swollen
vein amper
VARIED assorted, daedal, diverse, diversified, manifold, miscellaneous, mixed, several, sundry, variegated, various
bunting prusiano
VARIEGATE band, bar, bespeckle, bespot, blotch, brindle, checker, dapple, diversify, dot, enamel, fleck, freckle, iridize, maculate, marble, mottle, opalesce, pepper, polychrome, rainbow shoot, speckle, splotch, spot, sprinkle, stipple, streak, striate, stripe, tessellate, vary, vein
VARIEGATED assorted, brindled, calico, check(er)ed, clouded, colorful, daedal, dappled, dichroic, different, diversified, faw, flecked, freckled, harlequin, heterogeneous, kaleidoscopic, lyard, lyart, many-colored, marled, mosaic, motley, mottled, multicolor(ed), omnifarious, overshot, painted, particolored, peckled, piebald, pied, pinto, polychrome, prismal, prismatic, proudpied, sheld, shot, skewbald, sorty, speckled, spotted, spotty, sundry, tissued, varicolored, watered
comb. poecilo
VARIETY allotropy, assortment, brand, breed, class, difference, dissimilarity, divergence, diversity, extent, hash, heterogeneity, intermixture, kind, medley, mess miscellany, mixture, mode, multifariousness, omniformity, polymorphism, pot-

pourri, sort, species, strain, stripe, variation, versatility

VARIOLA horsepox, smallpox

VARIOLOUS foveate, pitted

VARIORUM diversion, edition, medley, text

VARIOUS assorted, changeable, different, disparate, distinct, divergent, divers(e), inconstant, manifold, many, miscellaneous, mixed, multifold, multiform, multiple, numerous, several, sunder, sundry, uncertain, variant, varied, variegated, varying

VARISCITE utahite

VARLET attendant, bailiff, boy, coistrel, gippo, jack, jippo, knave, menial, page, paviser, scoundrel, servant

VARMINT amateur, animal, clever, cunning, dashing, reprobate, sharp, smart, sporting, vermin

VARNA caste

member shudra, sudra

VARNISH adorn, coat, cover, dope, embellish, enamel, excuse, extenuate, falsify, fixative, flatter, furbish, glaze, gloss, japan, lacquer, ornament, paint, palliate, pervert, polish, pretext, shellac(k), theetsee, vermeil

black theetsee

coloring an(n)atto, arnatto

ingredient anime, balsamcapivi, copaiba, copal, dammar, elemilac, mastic, resin, rosin

kind enamel, japan, megilp, lacquer, theetsee

source doon, manjak

tree anacardium, rhus, sumac, theetsee, urushi

VARSITY See UNIVERSITY.

VARUNA amburaja, asura, jadapati, jalapati, prajapati, vishnu

consort aditi, ganges, jumna, urvasi

son agastya

steed makara

VARY alter(nate), assort, change, contrast, convert, depart, deviate, differ, digress, disagree, dissent, diverge, diversify, drift, inflect, metamorphose, modify, modulate, oscillate, quarrel,

shift, swerve, transform, vacillate, variate, variegate

VAS duct, pledge, promise, surety, vein, vessel

VASCULAR arterial, capillary, capsular, cystic, highspirited, hot-blooded, locular, passionate, saccular, veinous, venose, venous, ventricular, vesicular

cylinder stele

pert. haemal, hemic

tissue phloem, xylem

VASE amphora, ampulla, ampullula, askos, beaker, boughpot, bowpot, bugelkanne, canopic, casolette, cotula, cotyla, crater, cylix, deinos, dinos, diota, echea, echeion, filler, hydria, jar, jug, kalpis, kotyle, krater, kylix, lekane, lekythos, murrhine, olla, patella, pelike, pitcher, potiche, prochoos, psykter, pyx(is), scyphus, skyphos, stamnos, tambour, tazza, urceole, urn

cinerary canopic, deinos, dinos

decoration lambrequin

handle ansa

jasper murrine

ornamental epergne

painting black figure, red figure

-vine leatherflower

wide stamnos

VASHTI *husband* ahasuerus

VASODILAN isoxsuprine

VASODILATOR k(h)ellin

VASSAL bondman, ceile, chattel, dependent, dominate, feedman, feodary, feudatory, geneat, helot, homager, leud, liege(man), man, minion, peon, retainer, rudiger, rule, sacope, serf, servant, servile, slave, subject, tenant, thrall, vavaso(u)r, villein

group arriere-ban, manred

pert. feudal

VASSALAGE bondage, commendation, courage, dependence, fealty, manred, manrent, prowess, servitude, slavery, subjection, valor

subject to enfeoff

VAST babylonian, big, boundless, broad, capacious, colossal, cosmic, enormous, extensive, giant,

gigantic, great, HUGE, illimitable, immense, infinite, large, mammoth, measureless, mighty, oceanic, prodigious, spacious, stour, substantial, tidy, titanic, tremendous, untold

VASU See VISHNU.

VASUDEVA See KRISHNA.

VASUKI *serpent of* vishnu

VAT ark, bac(k), barrel, beck, blunger, cistern, coom(b), fate, fette, float, gaal, gail, gyle, keel, keeve, keir, kier, ki(e)ve, kimnel, pit, pressfat, saltpit, tank, temple, tine, tub, tun, vessel, wat

bleaching beck, keir, kier

brewing comb, coom(b), cumming, float, keeve, kieve, tun

cheese chessart, chessel, chesset

cooling kelder

evaporating apron, grainer

fermenting coom(b), float, gyle, keel, tun

VA-T'EN begone, scram, vamoose

VATES prophets, seers, soothsayers

VATICAN *basilica* st peter's

chapel sistine

church lateran

pert. papal

resident pope

retreat castel gandolfo

statue laocoon

system curialism

VATICINATE augur, foretell, predict, prophet

VAUDEVILLE olio, review, revue, song, variety, zarzuela

act dance, skit, softshoe, song, turn

minor smalltime

VAUDY cheerful, elated, gaudy, gay, showy, sturdy

VAULT arch, azure, bound, cache, catacomb, cave(rn), ceiling, cellar, clear, compartment, cope, crater, croft, crypt, cupola, curve(t), dome, dungeon, embow, ensphere, fornix, grave, heavens, hurdle, jump, leap, monument, mount, pit, refuge, safe, sky, spring, storehouse, testudo, tomb, treasury, tresor, volto, wowt

architectural barrel, cloister,

coved, cross, fan, groined, lacunar, lierne, ribbed, underpitch, welsh
burial columbarium, crypt, mausoleum, ossuarium, tomb
ceiling lacunar
edge groin
heaven's welkin
intersection groin(ing)
-like forniciform
opening lunet(te)
part voussoir
rib lierne
sky concave, convex, zenith
support ogive, rib, tierceron
underground crypt
VAULTED arched, camerated, concave, cupolar, curved, domed, embowed
recess apse
roof camera
VAULTING aspiring, overweening, pom(m)ado
block buck, horse
VAUNT bluster, boast, brag, crow, display, exalt, exhibit, flaunt, flourish, font, gasconade, glorify, insult, magnify, parade, roister, roose, show, van, voust
VAUNTY boastful, proud, stuckup, vain
VAURIEN wretch
VAYU *son* hanuman
VE *kin* odin
VEADAR adar sheni
VEAL calf, fricando, meat, veau, vitello, vituline
cutlet wiener-schnitzel
delicacy sweetbread
dish ris de veau, scallopine
larded fricandeau, fricando
pert. vituline
VECTOR bearing, course, force, gradient, phasor, rotor
opposite scalar
VEDA, VEDIC See also HINDU and INDIA references.
aeon kalpa
ancestor manu, pitr
ancestor's rite sraddha
angel sura
artisans of gods sraddha
celestial light gods aditya
cloud dragon ahi
composition gayatri
cosmic order rita
dawn gods asvins
demon asura, daitya, dasyus, jalandhara, rakshasas, ravana, sura

dialect pali
dragon ahi
epic ramayana
evil spirit asura, daitya, dasyus
fate dharma
fire god agni, yavishtha
giant bana
goblins rakshasa
god, goddess See INDIA *god* and *goddess.*
god's messenger ghrugi
holy mountain meru
holy river ganga
holy sage rishi
hymn mantra
hymn collection samhita
incarnation avatar
infinity ananta
interpreter agastya
language pali, sanskrit
life breath prana
life elixir amrita
life god varuna
male principle purusha
mantra gayatri
meter gayatri
nonduality advaita
nymph apsaras
philosopher shankara
philosophy advaita
plant, sacred banyan, bo tree, creeper, ephedra, kusa, milkweed, millet, periploca, pipal, sarcostemma, soma, valli
principle r(i)ta
reform church arya-samaj
sage agastya
school of s(h)akha
scripture aranyaka, atharva, bhagavad-gita, brahmana, gayatri, purana, sak(h), sama, upanishad, vedanta
serpent naga
sky serpent ahi
spirit asura
sun god savitar
thunder god indra
underworld patala
universal ego atman
world guardian lokapala
VEDANTA aranyakas, upanishads
philosopher shankara
VEDIC See VEDA.
VEER bias, cast, deflect, depart, deviate, digress, diverge, divert, fetch, glutter, move, pivot, sheer, shift, shy, side, skew, slew, slough, slue, sway, swerve, swing, swoop, trend, tumble, turn, wear, whiffle, yaw

to windward broach
VEERY See THRUSH.
VEGA meadow, plain
constellation lyre
VEGETABLE dull, food, herb(aceous), herbous, legume, leguminous, loment, monotonous, plant(like), stupid, tuberous
alkali potash
antimony boneset
butter avocado
calomel podophyllum
carbonized lignite
casein legumin
caterpillar aweto
cheese bean-curd
dealer costermonger, greengrocer, huckster
diced mirepoix
disease black rot
dish chiffonade, salad, slaw, subgum, zimmis
early hastings, primeur
esculent legume
existence inertia, stagnation
extract amaroid
exudation lac, resin, rosin, sap
fat oil, oleo
ferment yeast
fibrin gluten
finely cut chiffonade
fresh green goods
fuel peat
garnished with printanier
gelatin agaragar, gliadin, norgine
gold saffron
green artichoke, asparagus, bean, broccoli, brussels sprouts, chard, collards, cress, gumbo, lettuce, okra, pea, pepper, romaine, sabzi, scallion, spinach, watercress, zucchini
hybrid garlion
kind (See also *green*, above.) bean, beet, bell pepper, brassica, cabbage, carrot, cauliflower, celeriac, celery, celtuce, cepa, chickpea, chicory, chive, cilantro, chili(pepper), coriander, corn, cos, cucumber, eggplant, endive, escarole, fennel, finocchio, frijole, garbanzo, garlic, greens, gumbo, hominy, horseradish, kale, leek, legume, lentil, lima bean, mushroom, okra, onion, parsley, parsnip, pea, peascod, pepper, pim(i)ento, po-

mato, popcorn, potato, potherb, pumpkin, radish, raoulia, rutabaga, sabzi, salsify, scallion, shallot, soya, soybean, spinach, squash, succory, sugar beet, sweetcorn, sweet potato, tomato, truffle, turnip, udo, watercress, wobbie, yam, yautia
market truck
matter sudd
matter, decayed duff, humus
mixed macedoine
mold humus
onion-like garlic, leek, scallion, shallot
oil See OIL *vegetable.*
oyster salsify
pear chayote
pepsin caroid
pod hull, husk, pease
poison from abrin
rubbish wrack
salad cabbage, celery, chard, cress, cucumber, endive, escarole, garlic, leek, lettuce, parsley, romaine, scallion, shallot, tomato, watercress
sheep raoulia
soup beet, okra, potato
starchy bean, corn, garbanzo, hominy, potato, soya, soybean, sweet potato, turnip, yam, yautia
stunted scrub
sugar-yielding beet
tinder amadou
tomato-like topepo
tops shaw(s)
washer collander
VEGETATE develop, germinate, grow, hibernate, idle, sprout, stagnate
VEGETATION cover, development, flora, green, growth, herb(age), plantage, plants, scrub, verdure
floating sadd, sudd
fragrant smellage
god adonis, amaethon, attis, atys, baal, bacchus, bonuseventus, consus, dagan, dagon, dionysus, enmeshara, esus, faunus, lono, nabu, nebo, ningirsu, ninurta, pan, tammuz, triptolemus
god resurrection anodos
goddess annona, bri(d)get, brigid, carpo, centiotl, ceres, cora, cotys, demeter, despoina, flora, gaea, gaia, isis, kore, nisaba, ops, per-

sephassa, persephone, pomona, proserpina, proserpine, rhea, tellus-mater, thesmophoros, vacuna
scrub brush
VEGETE flourishing, healthy, lively
VEGLIATINO *steed of* orlando
VEHEMENCE ardency, ardor, enthusiasm, fervency, fervor, fire, force, fury, glow, heat, impetuosity, intensity, passion, rage, strength, verve, violence, warmth, zeal
VEHEMENT angry, animose, animous, ardent, boisterous, eager, ferocious, fervid, fierce, FIERY, forceful, frenzied, furious, heated, hefty, hot, impassioned, impetuous, intense, loud, passionate, potent, powerful, raging, strong, truculent, urgent, violent, zealous
VEHICLE (See also AUTO, CARRIAGE, RAILROAD, WAGON.) agency, agent, car, carrier, channel, conveyance, instrument, machine, means, medium, organ, play
amphibious amtrac, buffalo
animal or man-operated 3 ark, bus, cab, car, rig, rut 4 auto, bike, cart, drag, duke, goat, gram, jeep, luge, mail, putt, sled, taxi 5 araba, bogie, brake, break, brett, buggy, coach, cycle, dandy, dilly, dolly, gurry, hurly, jerry, jukta, noddy, ratha, stage, truck, wagon 6 barrow, charet, cisium, dennet, diesel, esseda, gocart, hearse, herdie, hotrod, jingle, jinker, jitney, kosong, randem, reckla, shoful, sledge, sleigh, spider, surrey, telega, trisha, troika 7 bicycle, bounder, chariot, croydon, fourgon, gondola, growler, iceboat, morfrey, omnibus, pedrail, phaeton, ricksha, scooter, shuttle, tallyho, tartana, tumbler, turnout, unicorn, vettura, voiture, volante 8 brouette, brougham, charette, democrat, equipage, handcart, morphrey, ordinary, pushcart, quadriga, rickshaw, tri-

cycle 9 branchard, buckboard, conestoga, stretcher, tarantass 10 germantown, jinrikisha, stagecoach, velocipede 12 doubledecker
armored tank
awkward ark, tub, tug
body bed, box, frame
bullock-drawn ekka
child's bicycle, bike, buggy, gocart, pram, scooter, skateboard, stroller, tricycle, trike, velocipede, walker
covered buggy, caravan, kibitka, landau, sedan, wagon
display gloat, rally
driver autoist, cabby, chauffeur, coachman, engineer, hacker, hackie, jehu, motorist
earth-moving cat, caterpillar, scoop, steam-shovel
emergency ambulance
foot-operated pedicab
4-in-hand tallyho
4-wheeled buckboard, buggy, CARRIAGE, coupe, herdic, quadricycle, wagon, wain
freightyard trapcar
group cortege, fleet, parade
hauling carrus, dray, lorry, sled, tode, tractor, trailer, travoise, truck, tug, van, wagon
military ambulance, buffalo, caisson, duck, jeep, limber, tank
1-horse See CARRIAGE.
1-wheeled monocycle, unicycle
part axle, battery, bonnet, box, brake, bumper, cam, carburetor, chassis, clutch, cylinder, engine, exhaust, fan, flywheel, gearshift, handlebar, hood, ignition, intake, magneto, mudguard, muffler, neap, pedal, piston, plug, radiator, rim, rumble, shaft, sparkplug, spoke, spring, sprocket, thill, throttle, tire, tongue, tonneau, wheel, wiper
passenger airplane, bus, cab, cable car, charabanc, diligence, droshky, fiacre, hack, hackney, hansom, jinrick(i)sha, jinrickshaw, jinriksha, jitney, minibus, omnibus, plane, ricksha(w), streetcar, taxi, train, tram, trolley

poor quality crate, dog, rattletrap
portable cacolet, dandi, dandy, dooley, dooli, howdah, juan, kago, kuruma, litter, muncheel, norimon, palankeen, palanquin, sedan, stretcher, telega, tomjon, tonjon
rickety crate, rattletrap, shandrydan
rider passenger, standee, straphanger
rude kibitka
runnered See VEHICLE *wheel-less.*
running on rails See RAILROAD.
small babybuggy, hinayana, pram, voiturette
snow sled, sledge, sleigh, pung
the great mahayana
2-wheeled barrow, bicycle, caleche, cart, chaise, chariot, cisium, croydon, curricle, dandyhorse, dennet, draisine, essed, gig, herdic, jingle, jinrickisha, moped, reckla, ricksha(w), sulky, tartana, tonga, vinaigrette, volante
wheel-less autosled, bobsled, carro, coaster, cutter, dray, gambo, go-devil, hurdle, iceboat, jampan, jumper, palki, pulka, pung, ship, skate, sled, sledge, sleigh, tode, travoise
VEI *parent* bani
VEIL calyptra, caul, cloak, conceal, cortina, cover (ing), curtain, disguise, endot(h)ys, faille, film, hide, maharmah, mantilla, mask, mesh, net, paranja, pretense, pretext, purdah, screen, shroud, teleblem, velum, vimpa, volet, watcher, weeper, wimple, yashmac, yashmak
bridal carecloth, genista
ceremonial orale
double yashmak
fabric barege, gossamer, net
humeral sudary
papal orale
widow's weeper
worn in church dominicale
VEILED covered, curtained, hidden, incognito, occult, shrouded, vague, velate
VEILLANTIF *steed of* orlando, roland

VEIN amper, axillar(y), azygous, bed, bent, blood-vessel, cava, cavity, channel, comes, costa, crevice, cubital, dash, disposition, drift, fissure, humor, inclination, jugular, kava, kawa, lode, mine, mood, nervure, precava, prester, procedure, profunda, rib, shade, smack, source, strain, streak, stria, stripe, style, subcosta, tang, temper, tendency, tenor, tinge, tone, touch, variegate, varix, vena, venula, wave
abnormality varix
arrangement neuration
comb. phlebo, veno
deep-seated profunda
enlarged varicocele, varicose, varix
fluid blood, ichor
granitic elvan
inflammation phlebitis
injection, pert. intravenous
leading to heart vena-cava
leaf costa, rib
mining bonanza, hilo, ledge, lode, roke, scrin, stringer
pert. marbled, nervose, veinal, venous
portal, pert. pylic
rich bonanza, mother-lode
small veinule(t), venula, venule
space between areola, areole
swollen prester
surgery phlebotomy, venesection
system venation
varicose amper
without avenous
VEINED actinodrome, actinodromous, marbled, nervose
VEINOUS vascular
VEINSTONE gangue, lodestuff, matrix
VEINY cirsoid, phleboid(al), varicose, venose, venous
VELATION concealment, secrecy
VELD(T) See also PLAIN.
camp laager
depression kommetje
sickness heartwater
VELLEITY desire, hope, inclination, volition, will, wish, woulding
VELLICATE nip, pinch, pluck, tic(kle), titillate, twitch

VELLUM membrane, orihon, paper, parchment, skin
packet cutch, kutch
VELOCIPEDE bicycle, dandyhorse, dicycle, draisine, handcar, rantoon, tricycle
VELOCITY celerity, drift, pace, quickness, rapidity, speed, strength, swiftness
measurer cinemograph
unit farad, foot-second, mach, strob, velo
VELOUR soleil
VELVET bagheera, birodo, drink, fabric, gain, panne, profit, surplus, vellute, velour, velure, velveret, winnings, yuzen
ant wasp
breast merganser
bur cat's-tongue, verbena
cotton velveteen
dock elecampane, mullein
grass calfkill, fog, holcus
groundsel geranium
imitation mockado
knife trevet
leaf cissampelos, dagga, mallow, mormonweed, mullein, pareira, tree-mallow
plant mullein
runner water-rail
scoter basque
-weed mallow
VELVETY cottony, downy, glaubrous, glossy, mild, nappy, satiny, sericeous, silken, silky, sleek, slick, smooth, soft, velutinous
VENADA pudu
VENAL bribable, corrupt (ible), hireling, infamous, mean, mercenary, nefarious, rotten, salable, sordid, vendible, venous, vicious
VEND auction, barter, hawk, higgle, huckster, market, merchandise, peddle, publish, sale, sell, trade, transfer, utter
VENDETTA feud, fight, quarrel
VENDOR agent, alienor, butcher, chapman, colporteur, coster(man), hawker, higgler, huckster, merchant, pitcher, pitchman, pullman, seller, trader
VENEER burl, burr, coat (ing), cover(ing), enamel, facade, face, facing, front, gloss, lamina, layer, over-

lay, plate, polish, pretense, sheathe, shell, shook, show
source abura

VENENATE poison(ed), poisonous

VENERABLE aged, ancient, antique, archaic, august, dignified, dread, estimable, hoar(y), honorable, old(en), patriarchal, protean, respected, revered, reverend, reverential, sacred, sage, venerated, vetust, vintage, wise

VENERATE admire, adore, apotheosize, cherish, deify, dread, esteem, fear, honor, love, prize, regard, respect, revere, reverent, sanctify, treasure, value, worship

VENERATED hallowed, holy, respected, sacred, worshipped

VENERATION adoration, awe, cult, devotion, dulia, esteem, honor, obeisance, respect, reverence, worship, zeal
object of relic
religious dulia, latria

VENERIDA carpetshell, clam, mollusk, quahog, venus

VENERY chase, game, hunting, profligacy

VENETIAN (See also VENICE.) blind, cloth, domino, galligaskins, robe, sequin
red siena, sierra
sumac scotino

VENEZUELA *artist* marisol
capital caracas
city aroa, asuncion, atures, barcelona, barinas, barines, barquisimeto, cabello, caracas, carupano, coro, cumana, guanare, guasipati, maracay, maturin, merida, ocumare, san carlos, san cristobal, san felipe, san fernando, san juan, tacupita, trujillo, valencia, valera
coin bolivar, centimo, fuerte, medio, morocota, peso, real, venezolano
copper center aroa
dance joropo
educator bello
fiber erizo
god tsuma
golf paria
hero bolivar
hydroelectric plant guri
indian bare, caquetio, carib,

charoya, guahibo, guarauno, kaliana, maquiritare, motilone, otomaca, pume, timote
lake maracaibo, tacarigua
language pume
leader betancourt
measure estadel, fanega, galon, milla
orchid butterfly, oncidium
patriot miranda
peak concha, cuneva, duida, el pao, icutu, imutaca, masaiti, pao, parima, pava, roraima, yavi
people See *indian,* above.
philologist bello
plain llano
poet bello
port carupano, ciudad-bolivar, cumana, la guaira, la gyayra, maracaibo, puerto-cabello
president gallegos, gomez, leoni
range andes, pacaraima, sierra de merida
revolutionist miranda
river apure, arauca, caroni, caura, cuyuni, guanare, guaviare, meta, orinoco, oritueo, pao, paragua, suapure, ventuari, vichada
snake lora
state apure, aragua, barinas, bolivar, carabobo, cojedes, falcon, guarico, lara, merida, monagas, sucre, tachira, trujillo, yaracuy, zulia
statesman betancourt, bolivar
tree balata
tree fiber erizo
weight bag, libra
writer diaz-rodriguez

VENGEABLE destructive, extraordinary, great, mischievous, tremendous, vindictive

VENGEANCE alastor, evil, harm, mischief, punishment, reprisal, requital, retaliation, retribution, revenge, ultion, vindict, wanion, wrath, wreak, wreck
deity ara, nemesis
inflict wreak
personification alastor

VENIAL allowed, excusable, pardonable, small, trifling, trivial

VENICE, VENETIAN *blind case* headbox
blue cobalt

boat bucentaur, frigatoon, gondola
bridge bridge of sighs, rialto
canal rio
cathedral san marco
church frari, giobbe, giorgio, rocco, santa maria della salute, scalzi, zanipolo
coin bagattino, betso, bezzo, croisat, ducat, gazzetta, giustina, grosso, leonine, marcello, marchetto, matapan, moccenigo, osella, sequin
council forty-one
court quaranty
district rialto
explorers antonio and nicolo zeno
feature gondola
functionary proveditor
glass latticinio, murano
grandee clarissimo
grosso matapan
island burano, certosa, giudecca, grazia, lido, murano, torcello, vignole
lace rosepoint
landmark grand canal, rialto, saint mark's, san marco
magistrate doge, podesta
medal oscella, osela, osselle
merchant of antonio
moneylender shylock
moor othello
nobleman doge, magnifico
of asia bangkok
painter bellini, canaletto, giorgione, guardi, longhi, palma, tiepolo, tintoretto, titian, veronese
red siena, sierra
resort lido
river brenta
song barcarol(l)e
strand lido
sumac scotino, smoketree
symbol winged lion
thoroughfare grand canal
traveler conti, marco polo
treacle theriaca
water street rio
wine measure anfora

VENILIA *husband* daunus
offspring juturna, turnus
parent pilumnus

VENISON biltong, deer, hunting, meat, pem(m)ican, venery
pert. gamy

VENNEL alley, gutter, lane, sewer

VENNER scowl, snarl

VENOM animosity, atter,

bane, crotalin, crotalus, dye, gall, malice, malignity, poison, rancor, spite, taint, toxin, virulence, virus

VENOMOUS attern, attery, baleful, baneful, deadly, malefic, malicious, malignant, mephitic, mischievous, noxious, pestilent, poisoned, poisonous, rancorous, snaky, spiteful, toxic, viperine, virulent

VENT air(hole), aperture, assert, avenue, aver, belch, brand, bung, chimney, diatreme, discharge, disclose, disgorge, divulge, draw, egress, eject, emerge(nce), emission, emit, escape, exit, express, fent, flue, fontanel, hole, inn, issue, market, moffette, opaion, opening, orifice, outfall, outlet, passage, pipe, publish, reek, release, reveal, sale, say, scent, sesperal, smell, snort, snuff, spilehole, spiracle, spout, suspiral, tavern, tewel, utter, vend, ventilate, voice, vomitory, way

VENTER abdomen, belly, cavity, innkeeper, matrix

VENTIDIUS *friend* timon

VENTILATE aerate, aerify, air, cool, discuss, expose, express, fan, oxygenate, puncture, purify, refrigerate, review, shoot, utter, VENT, verbalize, winnow

VENTILATED aereated, aired, cooled, discussed, drafty, draughty, freshened, oxygenated, windy

VENTILATION aerage, aeration, airing, breathing, discussion, exposition, expression, oxygenation, perflation, publicity, utterance
shaft upcast, uptake, windhole

VENTILATOR airshaft, femerell, funnel, louver, transom, window

VENTPIECE breechblock, bushing

VENTRAL abdominal, anterior, h(a)emad, h(a)emal, inferior, sternal

VENTRICLE cavity, chamber, diacoele, fossa, pouch, tricorn

VENTRILOQUISM *to practice* hariolate

VENTRILOQUIST engas-

trimyth, gastriloquist, polyphonist

VENTRIPOTENT edacious, gluttonous, paunchy

VENTURE adventure, ante, assume, attempt, bet, brave, chance, confide, contingency, courage, danger, dare(say), endeavor, enterprise, essay, feeler, flier, fling, flutter, flyer, fortune, gamble, gest(e), hap, hazard, invest(ment), jeopardy, lark, luck, peril, plunge, presume, presumption, project, pursuit, risk(ing), sashay, speculate, speculation, stake, start, test, trust, try, turn, undertake, undertaking, wage(r)

VENTURESOME, VENTUROUS adventurous, aggressive, audacious, bold, brave, chancy, dangerous, daredevil, daring, enterprising, fearless, foolhardy, furthersome, hardy, hazardous, heedless, heroic, intrepid, rash, reckless, resourceful, risky, speculative, stout, temerarious

VENTUROUSNESS courage, daring, errantry, temerity

VENUE arrival, assault, attitude, bout, coming, encounter, ground, hit, lunge, match, onset, place, station, thrust

VENUS, VENUS'S (See APHRODITE for references to goddess.) charm, copper, dione, grace, green, hesperus, love, vert, vesper
basin teasel
chariot monkshood
cup ladyslipper
ear abalone
flytrap dionaea, plant
gem amethyst
girdle cestus
hair fern, maidenhair, spleenwort
metal copper
needle lady's-comb
planet hesperus, lucifer, phosphor
pride bluet
tree myrtle

VENUST beautiful, comely, graceful, elegant

VERACIOUS accurate, honest, precise, reliable, sincere, true, trustworthy,

truthful, truthy, veridical, verily, veritable

VERACITY fidelity, honesty, honor, hsin, integrity, probity, troth, truth, verisimilitude, verity

VERA CRUZ *city* jalapa
indian totonac

VERANDA balcony, galerie, gallery, lanai, loggia, patio, piazza, porch, portico, pyal, stoa, stoop, terrace

VERB rhema, vocable, word
auxiliary can, had, has(t), have, may, might, must, shall, shalt, should, was, will, would
converted to noun gerund
kind active, intransitive, passive, subjunctive, transitive
modifying adverb
mood optative
subject of noun
table paradigm
tense aorist, conditional, future, past, present

VERBAL articulate, exact, expressed, gerund, infinitive, literal, oral, participle, said, spoken, stated, talkative, verbose, vocal, wordy
comb. ance, are, esce, ing, ire, ise
noun gerund

VERBASCUM adam's-flannel, herb, mullein, weed

VERBATIM direct(ly), exact, literal(ly), sic, word for word

VERBENA *family* aloysia, ash-throat, callicarpa, cat's-tongue, lantana, teak, tectona, vervain, vitex

VERBIAGE chatter, diction, prolixity, talk, tautology, verbosity, vocabulary, wordiness, wording

VERBOSE bombastic, diffuse, garrulous, lengthy, longwinded, loquacious, padded, prolix, protracted, redundant, spunout, talkative, tedious, voluble, windy, wordy

VERBOTEN forbidden, prohibited, taboo, tabu

VERDANT bosky, cespitose, fresh, grassy, green, ignorant, mossy, raw, turfy, unripe, unsophisticated, virid

VERDI *opera* aida, caronomel, don carlos, ernani, falstaff, la forza del destino,

luisa miller, masked ball, oberto, ot(h)ello, rigoletto, sicilian vespers, traviata, trovatore, vespri siciliani
role aida, amneris, radames
VERDICT acquittal, answer, award, decision, decree, determination, diagnosis, finding, guilty, judgment, not guilty, opinion, order, penalty, pronouncement, reckoning, report, resolution, ruling, sentence, vardi, word
unfair bum rap
VERDIGRIS aerugo, canker, deposit, drug, film, patina, pigment, rust
VERDIN goldtit, titmouse
VERDUN *fort* douaument, vaux
river meuse
VERDURE freshness, greenery, greenness, growth, health, odor, scent, smell, strength, tartness, vegetation, vigor, viridity
VERECUND bashful, modest, shy
VEREIN association, group, order, society
VERGE bear, border, bound (ary), brim, brink, circlet, circumference, compass, edge, end, incline, limit, lip, marge, margin, merge, range, rim, rod, scope, shaft, skirt, spindle, staff, stick, tend, timepiece, top, trench, trend, trigger, trim, virgate, wand, watch, yard (land)
VERGER churchman, dean, ecclesiastic, garden, justice, official, orchard, wandsman
VERGIL See VIRGIL.
VERIDICAL genuine, truthful, truthtelling, veracious
VERIFY attest, audit, authenticate, aver, bear out, certificate, certify, check, collate, confirm, correct, corroborate, establish, experiment, justify, prove, ratify, settle, substantiate, support, test, try, validate, vouch for, witness
VERILY amen, assuredly, certainly, certes, confidently, faith(ly), indeed, in fact, parde, pardi, pardy, positively, really, truly, yea
VERISIMILITUDE agreement, correspondence, har-

mony, likeness, probability, resemblance, verity
VERITABLE actual, authentic, bonafide, genuine, honest, proper, real, thorough, true
VERITY fact, faithfulness, honesty, reality, troth, TRUTH, veracity, veridity
VERJUICE acidify, acidity, juice, sourness, tartness, varge
VERMICULATE crawling, creeping, insinuating, sophistical, wormeaten, wormy
VERMICULE larva, ookinete, worm
VERMICULITE kerrite, maconite, vaalite
VERMIFUGE anthelmintic, harmal, helminthic, helonias, kamala, kamala, koosin
VERMILLION carmetta, carminette, cinnabar, cochineal, crimson, goya, paint, paprika, pigment, pimento, red, toreador, vermeil, zinober
rockfish rasher
VERMIN bedbugs, bugs, carrion, dregs, filth, fleas, flies, lice, mice, pest, rabble, riffraff, rodents, scum, trash, varmints, weasels
VERMONT *capital* montpelier
city barre, bennington, bountiful, brattleboro, burlington, grafton, newfane, rutland, stowe, winooskie
college bennington, middlebury
county essex, lamoille, orange, orleans
lake caspian, champlain, dunmore, seymour
motto freedom and unity
nickname green mountain state
peak bromley, hogback, mansfield, prospect
president arthur, coolidge
range green, taconic
river connecticut, nulhegan, saxtons, winooskie
state bird hermit-thrush
state flower clover
state tree sugar maple
university norwich
VERMOUTH boissiere, carpano, chambery, chambraise, cinzano, ferrero,

gancia, positano, punt e mes
ingredient artemisia, wormwood
VERNACULAR argot, cant, chaldee, colloquial, common, dialect, folksay, idiom(atic), indigenous, jargon, lingo, native, patois, patter, slang, vulgar
VERNAL fresh, green, mild, spring-like, warm, young, youthful
VERNE *character* fogg, nemo
craft columbiad, nautilus
VERNEUK cheat, con, humbug, skin, swindle, take
VERONA *gentleman* petruchio, proteus, valentine
prince escalus
VERONICA bird's-eye, bluebell, brooklime, charm, fluellen, handkerchief, speedwell, sudarium, veil
VERSAILLES *palace* (grand) trianon
VERSATE oscillate, revolve, turn
VERSATILE accomplished, adaptable, adjustable, allround, ambidexterous, apt, changeable, complete, deft, expert, flexile, handy, many-sided, mobile, ready, reversible, skillful, talented, variable
VERSE (See also *form*, below.) alba, antiphon, ayah, burden, canto, consider, division, elegiac, familiarize, fit, heroic, jingle, line, meter, part, POEM, poesy, POETRY, rann, revolve, rhyme, rime, rune, stanza, stave, stich, strophe, text, turn, uta
2-feet dimeter, dipody
3-feet trimeter, tripody
4-feet tetrameter, tetrapody
5-feet pentameter
6-feet choliamb, senarian, senarius
7-feet heptameter, heptapody
8-feet octameter
10-feet decameter
2-line couplet
3-line tercet
6-line sestet, sestina
14-line sonnet
analyse scan
biblical text
break in c(a)esura
classical iambelegus

comic doggerel, limerick
devotional antiphon(y)
elegiac hexameter, pentameter
end acroteleutic, doxology
form adonic, alexandrine, anap(a)est, couplet, dactyl, dimeter, dipody, distich, elegiac, epode, haiku, heptameter, heptapody, heptastich, heroic couplet, hexameter, hexapody, hexastich, hokku, iamb(ic), ionic, kyrielle, leonine, limerick, logaoedic, monostich, octameter, octastich, octave, pantum, pentameter, pentapody, pentastich, quaternarius, quatrain, sestet, sestina, sextet(te), sloka, spondee, stichos, tercet, tetrameter, tetrapody, tetrastich, trimeter, triplet, tripody, triseme, tristich, trochee, vers libre, villanelle, virelay
group stave, strophe, tercet, tripos
improvised pennill
informal doggerel
light clerihew, limerick
limping scazon
lyric epode
pair couplet
pert. iambic, glyconic, odic, palinodic, poetic
poor doggeral, singsong
unit foot
unmelodious teretism

VERSED able, accomplished, acquainted, adept, aufait, clever, conversant, erudite, experienced, familiar, informed, learned, practiced, proficient, seasoned, skilled, skillful, strong, studied, trained, wise, witty
in, comb. logist

VERSIFIER bard, minnesinger, minstrel, poet (aster), rhymer, rhymester, rimester, scald, scop

VERSIFY berine, berhyme, meter

VERSION account, chronicle, conversion, description, draught, edition, form, interpretation, lection, paraphrase, reading, rendering, rendition, report, sketch, story, translation, transformation, turning

VERSO back, left, reverse

VERSUS against, agin, anti, con, opposite

VERTEBRA acantha, backbone, centrum, chine, metamere, ossicle, spinal column, spine, spondyl(e), whettlebone
ailment spondylocace, spondylitis, spondylizema
comb. spondyl(o)
part atlas, axis, centrum, lamina, pedicle

VERTEBRATE *aquatic* ichthyopsid
class amniote, amphibian, aves, batrachian, bird, craniata, cyclostome, dipnoan, elasmobranch, fish, holocephalan, mammalian, marsupial, ostracoderm, pisces, reptile, sauropsid, selachian, teleost
cold-blooded amphibian, reptile
feathered bird
protein collagen
warm-blooded aves

VERTEX apex, cope, crown, culmination, peak, point, pole, summit, tip, top, zenith

VERTICAL acme, apeak, erect, height, lengthwise, orthal, perpendicular, plumb, rampant, sheer, standing, steep, straight, summit, top, upended, upraised, upright, upstanding, upward, vertex, zenith
elevation altitude

VERTIGINOUS dizzy, giddy, inconstant, revolving, rotary, rotating, rotational, spinning, unstable, vacillating, whirling

VERTIGO confusion, dinus, dizziness, giddiness, instability, megrim, mirligo, scotomy, staggers, tiego, whirling

VERTUMNUS *beloved* pomona

VERTY early, prudent

VERVAIN ashthroat, avicennia, caryopteris, frogfoot, gervao, ironweed, spiraea, verbena

VERVE animation, aptitude, birr, bounce, charisma, dash, elan, elasticity, energy, enthusiasm, feeling, machismo, panache, passion, pep, spirit, talent, ve-

hemence, vigor, vim, vivacity, zest, zip

VERY absolute(ly), actual, assai, awful(ly), boiling, braw, bully, darn(ed), deuced, dooms, enough, especial, even, exact(ly), exceedingly, extremely, genuine(ly), gey, greatly, identical, intensely, lawful, legitimate, living, mainly, majestic, molto, much, muy, peculiar, precise(ly), pretty, proper, quite, real, right, same, sehr, sowan, super, too, tres, true, truly, truthful, unco, utter(ly), veracious, veritable, well, whacking
comb. cat(a), cath, eri, kat(a), kath
light firework, flare, signal
much aplenty, greatly, immensely

VERZIN See BRAZIL.

VESICA bladder
piscis aureole, mandorla

VESICATE blister

VESICLE aerocyst, ampulla, aphtha, bladder, bleb, blemish, blister, bubble, bulge, bulla, bursa, cavity, cell, cyst, float, hollow, hydatid, pomphus, pouch, sac, utricle, vacuole, vesicula
comb. ydatis
pert. bullose, bullous

VESPA See WASP.

VESPER(S) evening, evensong, eventide, hesper, hymn, lychnic, prayer, service, star
for the dead placebo
music magnificat
sparrow grass-finch, groundbird

VESPERTILIAN bat

VESSEL (See also BOAT and SHIP references.) boat, canal, carrier, craft, duct, receptacle, ship, tube, utensil
anatomical artery, capillary, duct, vas(a), vein
armed flute
armored battleship, cruiser, ironside, monitor
assaying cupel
baptismal font
barge-like pangara
bark coolaman, coolamon, killiman
biblical ark

blood aorta, artery, efferent, vein

boat-shaped navicelli

brewer's round, vat

chemical autoclave, beaker, etna, flask, retort, still, test-tube

clay alcarraza, aludel, pankin, stean, steen, urn

clumsy crare, crayer, hag-boat

coal geordie

coasting See SHIP *coastal.*

comb. angio, angium, vaso

condiment caster, cruet

container (See also CON-TAINER.) aftaba, aiguirre, alcarraza, alembic, aludel, ama, amphora, amula, barrel, basin, bocal, boss, bottle, bowl, cadus, can(teen), cask, creamer, crock, cruet, cup, cymaise, decanter, diota, dixy, dubber, etna, firkin, flask, font, hogshead, jar, jug, kettle, lota(h), oenochoe, olla, olpe, pack(age), pan(kin), patera, pitcher, plate, pot, receptacle, rier, stein, tank, urn, utensil, vase, vat, zarf

cooking bain-marie, casserole, double-boiler, pan, pot, roaster, saucepan, skillet, spider, steamer

cup-like zarf

decorative aiguierre

detention of demurrage

distilling cucurbit, matrass, retort, still

draft ga(u)ge

drinking See DRINKING *vessel.*

earthen bayan, pankin, pig

electroplating trough

engine-driven aviso, coaster, collier, droger, lighter, powerboat, speedboat, steamer

eucharistic ama, amula, chrismal, ciborium, columba, flagon, pyx(is)

famous See SHIP *famous.*

fishing crare, crayer, sealer, smack, trawler

flat-bottomed scow

glass balloon, beaker, bocal, decanter, goblet, tumbler, undine, verre

harbor foyboat

heating etna

holy water fat, font, stock, stoop, stoup

horn-shaped holmos

ladling gaun

large tank, tub, vat

large-necked jordan

lateen-rigged dhow, set(t)ee

leather boot, dubber, girba, jack, olpe

long-necked goglet, guglet

lymphatic lacteal

melting grisset

merchant holcad, hoy

mine corb

mortuary bonepot, urn

narrow-sterned pink

oared catur, galley, rowboat, scull

open loom

ore hoppet, lool

perforated leach

perfume atomizer, censer

pert. vasal

pinecone-shaped thyrse

pirate brigantine

pump vangee

rare snow

rib futtock

sacred ama, censer, monstrance, pix, pyx

sailing 3 cat, cog, gig 4 brig, buss, dhow, ꞓ ni, grab, junk, koff, pink, pram, proa, saic, snow, tode, toup, yawl, zulu 5 barge, batal, boyer, bully, casco, dandy, dhoni, foist, ketch, nabay, praam, sapit, scout, setee, sharp, sieve, skiff, sloop, smack, snipe, tjalk, xebec, yacht, yanky, zabra, zebec 6 argosy, baghla, baidak, barque, bawley, bireme, caique, cangia, chebec, corvet, crayer, dogger, gaissa, galiot, hoggie, hooker, lancha, lorcha, lugger, mistic, moleta, praham, pulwar, quoddy, saltie, sambuk, sampan, scaffy, settee, shibar, tartan, tosher, tranky, zebeck 7 baggala, birling, birlinn, bumboat, caravel, carrack, catboat, chebeck, clipper, collier, coracle, corsair, dromond, felucca, frigate, galleon, galliot, geordie, hagboat, lantcha, patamar, pinnace, piragua, pirogue, polacca, pookaun, scooter, shallop, sharpie, trireme, unireme 8 balinger, ballahoo, bilander, cockboat, corvette, dahabeah, keelboat, lanchara, lateener, mackinaw, pinnacle, schooner, skipjack, tongkang 9 bucentaur, cara-

velle, mumblebee, outrigger, sneakboat, trabacolo 10 barkentine, brigantine, downeaster, fourmaster, knockabout, shipentine 11 barquentine, threemaster 12 fore-and-after, square-rigger

saucer-like patera

seed button, pod

serving argyle, argyll, gravyboat, tureen

shallow kiver, panchion, skeel, trendle, trow

shortage ullage

single-masted hoy, lymphad, sloop, tartan

small ampoule, ampul(e), dinghy, gallipot, hoy, jigger, liepot, phial, picard, vedet, vedette, vetlin(g)

square-rigged brig, snow

3-hulled trimaran

3-legged tripod

3-masted bark(entine), frigate, polacre, tern, xebec, zebec(k)

tin billy, blickey, blickie, pail

2-masted bilalo, brig(antine), polacre, yawl, zulu

unseaworthy coffin

warship See NAVY *vessel.*

wooden bakie, barrel, bicker, boss, cappie, cog(ue), cootie, craft, duddie, firkin, kit, kiver, piggin, skeel, soe, stound

VEST apparel, array, attire, benjy, bodice, cassock, clothe, dress, encompass, endow, fecket, furnish, garb, garment, gilet, give, grant, jacket, jelick, linder, robe, surround, tire, undershirt, waistcoat, weskit

-pocket diminutive, little, miniature, small, tiny

woolen gilet, linder, waistcoat

VESTA caca, HESTIA, lighter, match, taper, wax

parent rhea, saturn

priestess vestal virgin

sister ceres, juno

VESTAL chaste, nun, pure, spinster, virgin(al)

virgin tuccia

VESTIARY clothing, robing room, vestibule, vestment, vestry

VESTIBULE antarala, anteroom, atrium, cavity, chamber, ear, entrance (hall)(way), entry(way), epinaos, fossa, foyer, hall, lobby, naos, narthex, passage, porch, portal, portico, prodomos, propylaeum, stoa, threshold, vestiary

VESTIGE clue, clew, dreg, evidence, foot print, fragment, impression, imprint, iota, left-over, mark, print, rack, record, relic, remainder, remains, remnant, shadow, shred, sign, stamp, survival, tag, tincture, token, trace, track, umbra

VESTMENT (See also *religious,* below.) attire, clothing, cover, dress, garb, habiliment, robe, uniform, vestiary
embroidery orphrey
religious abnet, alb(a), almuce, amice, amphibalus, apron, balt(h)eus, bands, beretta, biretta, buskins, calotte, cap(pa), capuche, capuchin, casaque, chasuble, chimer(e), chrisom, cincture, cingulum, clericals, colobium, cope, cotta, cowl, cuculla, dalmatic, epitrachelion, exorhason, fano(n), frock, geneva, gown, gremial, habit, hood, lappet, lawn sleeves, maniple, mantelletta, mantellone, miter, mozzetta, orale, orarion, pallium, parament, pontificals, rabat, r(h)ason, robe, rochet, saccos, sakkos, scapular(y), scarf, shovel-hat, simar, skull-cap, soutane, stole, subcingulum, surplice, tiara, tippet, triple crown, tunic (le), vagas, vakass, ziamrra, zucchetto

VESTRY chapel, clothing, robing room, sacristy, vestiary, wardrobe

VESTURE apparel, clothe, corn, cover(ing), dress, envelop(e), garments, grass, investiture, raiment, robe, seizin, stubble, togs, underwood, vestment

VESUVIAN fusee, lighter, match

VESUVIANITE californite, cyprine, egeran, idocrase, xanthite

VESUVIUS *metal from* humite

VETCH akra, anthyllis, arvejon, astragal, axseed, cat-pea, crowpea, ers, ervil, faba, fecche, fitch, sativa, sicklewort, tare, tinetare, tineweed, vicia
seed rah

VETERAN emeritus, exercised, expert, hardened, old timer, practiced, seasoned, soldier, trained
organization american legion, dav, fidac, vfw

VETERINARY farrier, horse-doctor, leech
pill bolus

VETIVER ben(a), cuscus, grass, khasghas, khuskhus, kuskus

VETO deny, disallow, disapprove, discountenance, forbid(ance), interdict(ion), kill, negate, negative, overrule, prevent, prohibit(ion), quash, refuse, stop, thumbs down

VEX aggravate, anger, annoy, bedevil, bother, bullyrag, burden, cark, chafe, chagrin, chaw, corsie, cotter, disquiet, distress, disturb, exasperate, fash, fike, fret, fry, gall, grate, gripe, hale, harass, harrow, harry, ire, irk, irritate, nettle, perplex, plague, pother, provoke, puzzle, rasp, rile, roil, ruffle, scold, spite, sturt, tease, torment, tout, trouble, worry

VEXATION affliction, agitation, annoyance, anxiety, bane, bore, bother, care, chagrin, cross, discomfort, discontent, disgust, displeasure, distress, evil, fatigue, grief, harassment, irritation, mortification, nuisance, pique, resentment, teen, thorn, tray, trouble, weariness

VEXATIOUS aching, afflictive, aggravating, annoying, chaw, disturbed, fierce, frampold, maddening, pesky, pestiferous, pestilent, provoking, sore, troublesome, troubling, untoward, weariful, worrying

VEXED afflicted, agitated, angry, cross, disturbed, frabous, harassed, grame, grieved, mad, miffed, narky, riled, rily, roily, sore, sorry, waxy, wild, wraw

VEXILLUM banner, company, cross, flag, petal, standard, vane, web

VIA away, begone, passage, per, through, vessel, way

VIABLE feasible, practicable, real, stimulating, vital, vivid, wealthy, workable

VIADUCT bridge, overpass, span, trestle

VIAL ampoule, ampul(e), bottle, caster, cruet, phial, vessel

VIANDS aliment, cate(s), chow, comestibles, diet, eats, fare, fodder, food, grub, provender, provisions, victuals

VIATICUM allowance, communion, eucharist, provisions, unction

VIATOR junketer, tourist, traveler, wayfarer

VIAUD, LOUIS pierre loti

VIBRANT agitated, animated, lively, pulsing, resonant, resounding, ringy, sonorous, thrilling, throbbing, travale, vigorous, virile, vital

VIBRATE beat, brandish, dindle, dirl, flichter, fluctuate, flutter, jar, jiggle, oscillate, palpitate, pulsate, pulse, quake, quaver, quiver, resonate, rock, shake, shimmy, shivver, sway, swing, thrill, throb, tirl, tremble, tremolo, twiddle, undulate, vacillate, view, waver, whirr

VIBRATION dindle, dirl, dither, flutter, fremitus, oscillation, quaver, quiver, temblor, t(h)irl, thrill, tremble, tremolo, trepidation, vacillation
electronic echolocation
measurer tonometer
musical overtone, sonance, tremolo, trill, vibrato

VIBRATOR oscillator, reed, roller, trembler

VIBRISSA barbel, barbule, bristle, feather, feeler, hair, plume, whisker

VIBURNUM arrowwood, bilberry, black-haw, dockmackie, hawthorn, honeysuckle, laurustine, mae, may, sheepberry, snowball, wahoo

VICAR altarist, clergyman, cleric, curate, deputy, par-

son, pastor, priest, proxy, stallary, staller, substitute, viceregent, viceroy
of christ pope
VICARAGE benefice, dues, house(hold), parsonage, pastorate, rectorate, residence, salary, tithes
VICARIOUS delegated, deputed, indirect, substitute(d), sympathetic
VICE blemish, brace, buffoon, corruption, crime, defect, deformity, delinquency, depravity, deputy, device, evil, failing, fault, flow, foible, frailty, grasp, grip, ill, immorality, imperfection, infirmity, iniquity, instead, lubricity, offense, peccability, piacle, place, press, proxy, screw, sin, squeeze, stairway, stead, stopper, substitute, succeeding, taint, transgression, trespass, trick, turn, ungodliness, viciousness, violation, wantonness, wickedness, wrongdoing
gerent ephor
part chuck, jaw
president veep
VICENTIO *son* lucentio
VICEROY anosia, butterfly, exarch, governor, kehaya, nabob, nawab, nazim, prorex, provost, satrap, subah, tsungtu, vali, warden
VICIA bitterfitch, catpea, ers, faba, horsebean, vetch
VICINAL adjacent, near(by), neighborhood, neighboring
VICINITY area, district, environment, environs, locality, nearness, neighborhood, precincts, proximity, region, resemblance, section, sector, vicinage
VICIOUS abnormal, bad, broken, corrupt, cruel, defective, degenerate, depraved, devilish, diseased, evil, faulty, feral, fratched, ill(tempered), immoral, imperfect, impure, incorrect, infamous, malignant, mean, mountainous, nasty, profligate, refractory, rough, rowdy, savage, sinful, skaithy, spiteful, ugly, unruly, vile, violent, vitial, wicked
VICISSITUDE alternation, change, difficulty, inter-

change, mutation, revolution, trouble, woe
VICTIM butt, casualty, chump, cully, dupe, forfeit, goat, gull, hecatomb, loser, mark, martyr, pawn, prey, quarry, raven, ravin(e), sacrifice, sucker, wretch
list toll
sacrificial host, meriah
VICTIMIZE bunco, bunko, cheat, con, cozen, deceive, defraud, kill, swindle
VICTOR champion, conquer, conquistador, destroyer, hero, master, overcome, pancratiast, triumphant, vanquisher, winner
crown bay, garland, laurel, wreath
fish aku, bonito
VICTORIA auto, calash, car(riage), hog, plum, waterlily
birthday empire day
consort albert
falls river zambezi
lake, river into kagera
-land volcano erebus
parent pallas, styx
VICTORIAN antiquated, genteel, grundyite, hidebound, illiberal, modest, narrow, prude, prudish
bottle tree kurrajong
box laurel
lilac sarsaparilla
VICTORINE See TIPPET.
VICTORIOUS ascendant, champion, conquering, triumphant, unbeaten, winning
VICTORY achievement, award, conquest, killing, knockout, landslide, mastery, palm, success, superiority, triumph, walkaway, win(ning)
celebration epinician
costly pyrrhic
cry aboo, abu
deity nike, odin, vacuna, vicapota, victoria, zeus
ode epinicion
sign bidigitation, vee
statue site samothrace
symbol palm, scalp, trophy
unexpected upset
winged nike of samothrace
VICTUAL(S) chow, comestibles, eatables, edibles, fodder, food, grain, grub, provender, provisions, scran,

supplies, viands, vittles, vivers
VICTUALER innkeeper, purveyor, supplier, sutler
VICUNA vigonia
relative llama
VIDAR *father* odin
home landvidi
victim fenrir, fenris
VIDELICIT namely, scilicet, to wit, viz
VIDOCQ *biographer* charles ledru
friend balzac, dumas, gautier
prototype inspector vautrin
publicist eugene sue
VIE bandy, bet, challenge, compete, competition, contend, contest, cope, emulate, envy, fight, hazard, life, match, multiply, oppose, rival(ry), stake, strive, try, wager
VIENNA wien
assailant suleiman
dance valse, waltz
landmark ring
palace schonbrunn
park prater
wine center grinzing
VIETNAM (See also NORTH VIETNAM and SOUTH VIETNAM.) an(n)am, cochin-china
alligator cayman
bull zebu
city binhdinh, hanoi, hue, ngai, ron, saigon
coin dong, piaster
delta mekong
holiday tet
hut hootch
officer khanh
people annamese, bodo, cham, kinh, malay, muong, nung, tay, thai
region annam, cochin, tonkin
river mekong
VIEW advice, appearance, aspect, behold, belief, catch, concept, consider, conspect, contemplate, diorama, examination, expectation, explore, eye(shot), feeling, glimpse, glom, idea, impression, inspect(ion), intention, judgment, ken(ning), landscape, look(out), note, notice, notion, observe, ogle, opinion, outlook, panorama, peek, perceive, picture, prospect, range, regard, representation, re-

spect, scan, scape, scene(ry), scrutinize, seascape, see, show, sight, sketch, spectacle, survey, thought, vista, witness, yew
brief apercu
bring into disclose, open, reveal
closely examine, inspect
distant offscape
extended panorama
from a distance descry, make out
indulgently tolerate
mentally envision
obstruct conceal, hide
open to bare, expose, overt
pleasing eyeful
site belvedere
VIEWER examiner, inspector, observer, onlooker, spectator, superintendent
group audience, crowd, gate, house
instrument binoculars, scope, stereoscope, telescope
VIEWPOINT angle, attitude, ground, outlook, position, reason, sight, slant, stance, stand(point)
VIEWY capricious, ostentatious, pleasing, showy, spectacular, unpractical, visionary
VIGIL agrypnia, care, devotion, eve, fast, lookout, patrol, prayer, sleeplessness, surveillan~e, wake(fulness), watch(man)
VIGILANCE caution, guard, insomnia, jealousy, readiness, vitality, wakefulness, watch
symbol cock
VIGILANT agog, alert, anxious, astir, attent(ive), avid, awake, careful, cautious, circumspect, eager, guarded, keen, observant, openeyed, ready, sharp, surveillant, wakeful, wary, watchful
name meaning gregory
person argus
VIGNETTE decoration, description, design, illustration, picture
VIGOR activity, animation, ardor, birr, blood, bloom, brio, buoyancy, dash, emphasis, energy, esprit, fettle, foison, force, green, hardihood, health, heartiness, impetus, juice, life, lus-

tiness, might, nerve, pep, pith, potency, power, push, robustness, ruggedness, sap, smeddum, snap, soundness, spirit, stamina, sthenia, strength, thrust, tonus, tuck, validity, vim, vir(ility), vitality, zip
deprive of deaden, enervate, sap, weaken
full of energetic, lifesome, peppy
lacking anemic, effete, langorous, weak
lose decline, fag, fail, flag, pine, sag, weaken
period of heyday
VIGOROUS active, athletic, blooming, bouncing, cant, chipper, cogent, drastic, dynamic, eager, effective, energetic, feckful, forceful, forcible, fresh, hale, hardy, healthy, hearty, husky, juicy, lively, lusty, nippy, pithy, potent, powerful, robust, rugged, sassy, solid, sthenic, stour, stout, strapping, strenuous, strong, stubborn, sturdy, thriving, tough, vehement, vibrant, virile, youthful, zealous
VIHARA garden, monastery, temple
VIKING (See also NORSE references.) dane, norseman, scandinavian
VILE abject, bad, base(born), befouled, brutal, brutish, caitiff, cheap, coarse, common, contaminated, contemptible, corrupted, crusty, debased, degraded, depraved, despicable, detestable, dirty, drafty, drasty, evil, fetid, filthy, foul, gross, hateful, immoral, impure, lecher, lewd, loathsome, low, mean, miserable, nasty, nefarious, obscene, odious, offensive, paltry, perverted, poor, repulsive, revolting, sad, sinful, sordid, swinish, terrible, turpid, vicious, wicked, wild, worthless, wretched
VILI *kin* odin
victim ymir
VILIFY abuse, accuse, asperse, assail, attack, bemean, berate, blacken, blaspheme, brand, calumniate, censure, cheapen, chide, debase, defame, degrade, den-

igrate, derogate, despise, detract, disgrace, dishonor, disparage, libel, malign, misuse, objurgate, outrage, rate, reproach, reprove, revile, scold,' slander, slur, smear, stain, traduce, vituperate
VILLA aldea, dacha, datcha, house, manor, mansion, quinta, residence, trianon, villakin, villanette, villino
VILLAGE abadi, alde(i)a (ment), ambalam, barrio, bastide, berewick, borough, bourg(ade), burg, bustee, busti, campody, campong, campoody, casal(e), caserio, castle, clachan, cral, cranford, crossroads, dessa, dorp, douar, dump, ejido, endship, gav, hamlet, hammon, kaik(a), kainga, kampong, kra(a)l, maabara, mir, mission, mouzah, mura, oppidum, pah, pettah, pueblo, rancho, rew, settlement, shtetl, stad(t), stanitza, thorp(e), tolderia, town, vicus, vill(akin), whistlestop, wick
barley-growing berewick
fortified pah
head patel
imaginary cranford
little tiburon
quiet sleepy hollow
VILLAIN baddie, baddy, base, bezonian, blackguard, boor(ish), caitiff, churl, clown, common, criminal, devil, giant, heavy, hoodlum, iago, knave, lout(ish), malefactor, menace, miscreant, misdoer, rascal, reprobate, rogue, ruffian, scamp, scelerat, scoundrel, sinner, slave, varlet, viliaco, vulgar, wick
mythological dragon, giant, ogre
nemesis hero
tradesmark leer, smirk, sneer
VILLAINOUS bad, base, black, corrupt, dastardly, degenerate, depraved, detestable, evil, flagrant, heinous, infamous, iniquitous, knavish, loutish, low, mean, nefarious, outrageous, profligate, rascally, terrible, vicious, vileyns, vulgar, wretched
VILLAINY abuse, boorish-

ness, chicanery, corruption, crime, depravity, devil(t)ry, disgrace, dishonor, evil, feloniousness, illusage, knavery, mischief, miscreancy, pranks, rascality, reprobacy, roguery, wickedness
VILLATIC rural, rustic
VILLEIN bondman, carl, ceorl, churl, cotarius, cotter, esne, helot, peasant, peon, serf, slave, thrall, villager
VILLOUS hairy, nappy, shaggy
VIM animation, dash, drive, elan, energy, esprit, fire, force, gimp, ginger, kick, pep(per), pith, pizzazz, power, pulse, punch, push, pzazz, snap, spirit, stamina, starch, verve, VIGOR, vitality, zing, zip
VINA ben, bin, guitar, harp, pungi
VINCA bluebottle, bluebutton, myrtle, periwinkle, scabious
VINCULUM band, bond, brace, bracket, commissure, frenum, tie, union
VINDICATE absolve, acquit, assert, avenge, claim, clear, corroborate, defend, deliver, deraign, disprove, exculpate, excuse, exonerate, free, guard, justify, maintain, propugn, punish, rationalize, revenge, shield, substantiate, support, sustain, uphold, warrant
VINDICATION apology, defense, justification, revenge, theodicy
VINDICATOR advocate, avenger, champion, defender, vindex
VINDICTIVE avenging, grim, grudgeful, hostile, malicious, malign, merciless, punitive, relentless, retributive, revengeful, spiteful, unforgiving, unrelenting, vengeful
VINE (See also *kind*, below.) grape, rope, runner, trail (er), trailing, twine(r)
cactus ocotillo
comb. ampel(o), viti
covered with ivied
cucurbitaceous amargoso, ampalaya, balm-apple, balsamine, balsam-pear, briony, bryony, momordica

cultivation viticulture
disease pierce's
edible akebi
evergreen bluebell, skyflower
flowering clematis, jasmine, morning-glory, stephanotis, wistaria, wisteria
grape vitis
grower vinitor
herbaceous brunnichia, cacur, galactia, gonolobus, ipomoea, morning-glory, pisum, sechium, tracaulon, zanonia
kind abobra, akas, akebi, alamanda, ampelopsis, araujia, atragene, betel, bindweed, bine, boneset, buaze, bwazi, cacur, chilicothe, convolvulus, cowage, creeper, cucumis, cupseed, cushcush, decumary, dichondra, dodder, dogbane, dolichos, g(h)erkin, gogo, grape, guaco, hedera, hop, ipomoea, ivy, kudzu, lablab, liane, maypop, milkweed, odal, odel, pareira, passiflora, pumpkin, punya, soma, squash, strychnos, tacso, tinetare, tineweed, traveler's-joy, tururi, wisteria, yampee
leguminous cow(h)age, cowitch
matrimony washington's-bower
narcotic serjania, soma
parasite aphid, aphis
parasitic mistletoe
part cirrus, tendril
pest dodder, fretter, phylloxera
plantation viticetum
poisonous serjania
prostrate calabazilla
short bine
study of vinology
support trellis
twining actaea, baneberry, bindweed, bine, bryony, quamoclit, tamus
woody akebia, allamanda, awikiwiki, bejuco, bignonia, cane, clematis, creeper, cupseed, dogbane, ivy, iyo, thunbergia, timbo, traveler's-joy, uncaria, yangtao
VINEGAR acetate, acetum, alegar, beeregar, eisel(l), esill, vinaigre
bottle cruet
comb. acet(o)
-containing acetous

cup acetabulum
dregs mother, mycoderma
eel eelworm
ester acetate
maker acetifier
malt alegar
pert. acetic, acetous
preserve in brine, marinate, pickle
salt acetate
spice tarragon
turn to acetify
VINEGARWEED ambrosia, bluecurls, camphorweed
VINEGARY acerb, acetic, acetose, acetous, acid, bad-tempered, bitter, crabbed, crabby, cross, sharp, sour, unamiable
VINELAND america
discoverer leif ericson, leif erikson
VINEYARD clos, cote, cru, grapery, vinery, wineyard
coveter ahab
owner naboth
property chateau
protector priapus
VINGT-ET-UN macao, macco
VINNY fenny, finny, moldy, veny
VINTAGE antique, archaic, classic, crop, cuvee, gather, harvest, old, outmoded, produce, vendemia, wine, yield
VINYL plastic
ethylene bivinyl, butadiene, erythrene, pyrrolelene
VIOL barbiton, chelys, fiddle, giga, gigue, gudok, gue, quinton, rebab, rebec, ruana, sarinda, sultana, tarau, turr, vielle, violone, voyal
bass viola da gamba
keyboard claviol
tenor viola d'amore
VIOLA alto, pansy, quint, tenor(e), violet
bastarda baritone, barytone
beloved orsino
brother sebastian
da braccio quint
disguised cesario
VIOLATE abuse, assault, betray, break, broach, corrupt, debauch, defile, deflower, defy, desecrate, dishonor, disobey, encroach, flaw, force, harrow, harry, infringe, injure, invade, mistreat, offend, outrage, pol-

lute, profane, ravage, ravish, seduce, spoil, temerate, trample, transgress, trench, trespass, wrong
oath forfeit

VIOLATION abuse, breach, contravention, crime, desecration, disturbance, error, fault, infraction, infringement, injury, irreverence, neglect, offense, outrage, profanation, rapine, scandal, sin, transgression, trespass, vice

VIOLENCE agitation, ardor, assault, bensail, bensall, bensel(l), bensil, blitz, bloodshed, bluster, brunt, brutality, coercion, compulsion, cruelty, duress, ferocity, fervor, fierceness, fire, force, fury, hubris, impetuosity, inclemency, injury, intensity, outrage, passion, profanation, rage, rapine, rigor, riot, ruff, savagery, severity, sharpness, storm, strain, trouble, tumult, uproar, vehemence, viciousness, war, whirlwind

VIOLENT abnormal, acute, ardent, atrocious, bad, berserk, bloodthirsty, bloody, blustery, boisterous, brutal, cruel, cutthroat, demoniac, derf, diabolic, drastic, drunk, enraged, evil, extreme, fierce, fiery, flagrant, forceful, forcible, frantic, frenzied, furious, headstrong, heady, hefty, high, hot, impassioned, impetuous, insane, intense, irate, loud, mad, manic, mighty, passionate, piercing, rabid, raging, rammish, rampage, rough, ruffian, ruftytufty, savage, severe, sharp, slambang, splitting, stern, stoor, stormy, stour, strong, tempestuous, tez, turbulent, unbalanced, unbridled, unnatural, unruly, vehement, vivid, wild
contact anstoss
person beast, beldam, demon, fury, hellcat, hellion, holy terror, hothead, hotspur, shaitan, sheitan, termagant, terror, tiger, virago, vixen, witch

VIOLET anchiete, blaver, butterfly, can(yon), clematis, dahlia, damson, eveque,

fineleaf, grape, hookers, ianthine, johnny(-jump-up), lobelia, mauve, ophelia, prelate, primula, pureayn, purple, wisteria
adder's plantain
-bloom bittersweet, matrimony-vine
bog butterwort, sheepweed
bulbous snowdrop
corporal napoleon
dogtooth adder's-fern, adder's-tongue
dye archil
emblem of athens, napoleon
hooded hookers
madder eveque
perfume ionone, irone, orris
root iridin, orris
-tip butterfly

VIOLIN amati, chrotta, cremona, crouth, crowd, fiddle, fithel, geige, giga, gigue, guarnerius, kemancha, klotz, kroud, rebab, rebec(k), rocta, ruana, sarod, steiner, strad(ivarius), taille, tarau, theyaou, violotta
bow arco
bow necessity rosin
button end-pin
city cremona
direction arco, pizzicato
false note wolf
5-stringed quinton
forerunner rebab, rebec(k)
part bout, bridge, button, eclisse, f-hole, fingerboard, foglietto, neck, nut, peg (box), scroll, soundhole, string, tailpiece, temper-pin
player auer, bull, corelli, elman, enesco, heifetz, kreisler, menuhin, milstein, morini, nero, oistrakh, ole, paganini, perleman, pugnani, stern, szigeti, tartini, viotti, ysaye, zimbalist
-shaped pandurate, panduriform
softening device mute, tonewolf
sound post ame
string gut
tenor alto

VIOLINIST See VIOLIN
player.
1st concertmaster, concertmeister

VIORNA bluebell, clematis, jasmine, jessamine, leatherflower

VIP big cheese, big shot, big wig, boss, captain, chief,

high muckamuck, kingpin, leader, lion, lord, magnate, mogul, notable, poohbah, top banana
group brass, elite

VIPER adder, agkistrodon, ammodyte, asp(ide), ather, atractaspis, bitis, boa, bushmaster, cerastes, daboia, daboya, echis, habu, hagworm, jararaca, jessur, katuka, krait, kupper, mamushi, puffadder, racer, reprobate, reptile, serpent, snake, urutu, wyver
bugloss blue devils, blueweed, cat's-clover, cat's-tail, echium
horned asp, cerastes, wampum-snake
pit rattler, rattlesnake
red copperhead
russell's daboia, daboya
yellow fer-de-lance

VIR action, activity, green, man, vigor

VIRAGO amazon, ambree, barge, beldam(e), bitch, callet, choleria, fury, harridan, hellcat, nag, randy, rixatrix, rounceval, rullion, scold, shrew, spitfire, termagant, trimmer, vixen, witch, xant(h)ippe

VIRAJ *father* brahma

VIREO bird, grasset, greenlet, john-towit, preacher (bird), redeye, teacher, whip-tom-kelly

VIRGATE rigid, rodlike, toothed, twiggy, verge, wandshaped, yard(land), yoke
half mantal

VIRGIL *birthplace* mantua, mincio, mintio
burial site naples
character aeneas, amata, anchises, camilla, corydon, damon, dido, eneas
goatherd damon
language latin
patron maecenas, octavian
pert. maronian
plant baccar, bacchar
surname maro
teacher parthenius, syron
verse form hexameter
work aeneid, bucolics, eclogues, eneid, georgics

VIRGILIA *friend* valeria
husband coriolanus
son marcius

VIRGIN, VIRGIN'S chaste,

damsel, dorothea, first, fresh, girl, idle, lass, madonna, maid(en), miss, modest, new, pucelle, pure, spinster, unalloyed, uncaptured, uncultivated, undisturbed, unsubdued, unsullied, untouched, untried, untrod, vestal, virgo, youthful

bower clematis, honesty, love, moonwort

comb. partheno

huntress artemis

in paradise houri, huri

knight bradamante

mary despoina, madonna, mater-dolorosa, our lady, theotokos

mary mourning pieta

mary's cowslip lungwort

patron saint winifred

pert. parthenian

queen elizabeth

the See *mary,* above.

tree sassafras

vestal tarpeia

warrior camilla

worship mariolatry, parthenolatry

VIRGINAL (See also VIRGIN.) abstinent, celibate, chaste, fresh, green, harpsichord, maidenly, modest, new, pure, raw, spinet, unadulterated, untested

VIRGINIA diemenia, potomophis, snake

battle site bull run, chancellorsville, fair oaks, fredericksburg, manassas, petersburg, richmond, seven pines, spotsylvania, wilderness, yorktown

broomrape beechdrop

capital richmond, williamsburg

city alexandria, appomattox, bedford, bristol, charlottesville, danville, emporia, fairfax, fredericksburg, hampton, hopewell, luray, lynchburg, manassas, marion, martinsville, norfolk, petersburg, pulaski, roanoke, salem, st albans, staunton, tazewell, waynesboro, williamsburg, winchester, yorktown

college averett, hollins, longwood, madison, mary washington, radford, william and mary

colonist fairfax

county accomack, amelia, arlington, bath, bland, culpeper, fauquier, floyd, fluvanna, henrico, loudoun, louisa, page, prince edward, pulaski, roanoke, smyth, surry, tazewell, wythe

cowslip lungwort

creeper amelopsis, ivy, joy, woodbine

cress peppergrass

dam kerr

deer whitetail

epithet mother of presidents

goat's-rue catgut

governor, colonial culpeper, dale, delawarr

grass lyme, terrell

indian appomattoc, manahoac, matchotic, mattapony, meherrin, monacan, nottaway, pamunkey, powhatan, saponi, tutelo

juniper cedar

knotweed jumpseed, tovara

lake kerr, smith

lungwort cowslip

motto sic semper tyrannis

mouse-ear stickseed

native coohee

naval base norfolk

nickname old dominion

peak baldknob, cedar, elliot, rogers

pine loblolly

poke hellebore

port newport news, norfolk, portsmouth, richmond

president harrison, jefferson, madison, monroe, taylor, tyler, washington, wilson

quail bobwhite

range allegheny, blueridge

reel sir roger de coverley

revolt bacon's rebellion

river appomattox, dan, james, potomac, rapidan, rappahannock, roanoke, shenandoah

serpentary snakeroot

settlement jamestown

silk milkweed

snakeroot birthwort, bugbane, sangreeroot, sangrel, snagrel

state bird cardinal

state flower dogwood

state tree dogwood

stickseed soldiers

surrender site appomattox, yorktown

swamp dismal

valley shenandoah

waterleaf shawnee-salad

willow itea, iva

woodcock peewee

VIRGIN ISLANDS santa cruz, st croix, st john, st thomas, tortola, water-isle

capital charlotte-amalie

coin bit, daler, franc

discoverer columbus

native chacha

VIRGINITY celibacy, continence, freshness, honor, maidenhood, newness, pucel(l)age, spinsterhood

deprive of deflower

symbol cora, kore, persephone, vestal

VIRGO virgin

gem diamond

VIRGULARIAN searod

VIRGULE comma, escapement, hyphen, mark, neume, pause, rod, separatrix, slant

VIRIDITY freshness, greenness, liveliness, verdance, verdure, youth

VIRILE forceful, lustful, male, manly, mannish, masculine, masterful, powerful, sound, strong, vigorous, viripotent, vital

VIRILITY force, green, lust, manhood, masculinity, power, prime, strength, vigor, vitality

VIRL perrule, ring

VIROSE fetid, malodorous, poisonous, virulent

VIRTU aesthetics, artistry, excellence, ornament

pieces antiques, bibelot, bijouterie, bricabrac, curio, knickknacks, relic

VIRTUAL constructive, effective, energizing, implicit, latent, potential

VIRTUALLY almost, but, morally, nearly, practically, totally

VIRTUE ability, abnegation, abstinence, arete, bounty, charisma, charity, chastity, conscience, courage, decency, dharma, discipline, efficacy, ethicality, excellence, fidelity, force, goodness, grace, honesty, honor, hsin, immaculacy, industry, integrity, jen, merit, miracle, morality, morals, paramita, piety, power, probity, purity, quality, rectitude, strength, thew, thrift, uprightness, valor, value, worth

cardinal charity, faith, fortitude, hope, justice, prudence, temperance

excellence of noblesse oblige

goddess fides

paragon of saint

science of aretaics

VIRTUOSO adept, aesthete, artist, authority, connoisseur, empiricist, esthete, expert, musician, performer, savant

VIRTUOUS brave, chaste, decent, ethical, faithful, good, honest, honorable, just, modest, moral, noble, potent, pure, righteous, sainted, sincere, straight, thrifty, upright, valiant, valorous, valuable

VIRUDHAKA See **BUDDHA.**

VIRULENCE acridity, acrimony, anger, animosity, choler, gall, hate, hatred, malignancy, malignity, rancor, severity, toxicity, venom, virus, vitriol

VIRULENT acrid, acrimonious, baneful, bitter, deadly, fatal, harmful, hostile, infectious, lethal, malicious, malign, mephitic, miasmic, mortal, noxious, pernicious, pestilent(ial), poisonous, rabid, spiteful, toxic, unhealthy, venomous, violent, virific, vitriolic

VIRUPAKSA See **BUDDHA.**

VIRUS bacillus, bacterium, bane, bug, disease, germ, infection, malice, malignancy, microbe, nucleic acid, pathogen, poison, toxin, venom, virulence

component dna, protein, rna

disease (See also **DISEASE** *virus.*) flu, herpes, influenza, mumps, rabies, rubella, smallpox, variola, yellow fever

form filamentous, rod-like, solid, sperm-like, spherical

pesticide gypsy-moth, heliothis-zea, tussock-moth

preventive interferon

VIS force, peiktha, potency, power, strength, vigor, visit

VISAGE appearance, aspect, confront, countenance, face, front, guise, image, looks,

map, mug, physiognomy, portrait, puss, semblance, show

VIS-A-VIS carriage, face to face, opposite, seat, sofa, tete-a-tete

VISAYAN aklan, aklanon, cebuan(o), malaysian, philippino

island sonia

VISCERA entrails, giblets, guts, haslet, inmeats, innards, insides, internals, intestines, numbles, organs, umbles, vitals

comb. splanchno

edible giblets, haslet

VISCERAL crude, earthy, gut, instinctive, splanchnic

VISCID, VISCOUS gaumy, gelatinous, gluey, glutinous, gobby, gooey, gummous, gummy, heavy, lentous, limy, mothered, mucilaginous, muculent, pasty, ropy, sizy, slimy, smeary, sticky, stodgy, stringy, syrupy, tacky, tarry, tenacious, thick, tough, tremellose

VISCOUNT deputy, lord, noble(man), officer, peer, sheriff

VISCOUS See **VISCID.**

VISE advise, behold, brace, chap, cheek, clamp, consider, cramp, grip, heed, hold, screw, squeeze, tool, winch

part cam, jaw

VISHNU *abode* meru

avatar balarama, bhagavat, buddha, gopal, govind, jagannath(a), juggernaut, kalki, krishna, matsaya, matsyavatara, narasimha, narasimhavatara, narsinh, parashuram, parashurama, rama(chandra), vaman(avatara), varah(avatara), vasu

bearer garuda

biography bhagavata-purana

bow saran

brother balarama

consort bhumidevi, laks(h)mi, radha, sri

curser aniruddha

daughter brahmi

incarnation See *avatar,* above.

paradise goloka

parent devaki

pilgrimage center trivandrum

priest gosain, gusain, luperci

race yadava

saint alvar

sect vaishnava

serpent naga, sesha, vasuki

soul of universe vasu

3 strides air, earth, heaven

vehicle garuda

victim kansa

weapon chakra

worship bhakti

worshipper bhagavata, bhakta, vaishnava

VISIBLE accessible, apparent, bold, discernible, discoverable, eidetic, evident, explicit, exposed, extant, external, glaring, gross, macroscopic, manifest, observable, obvious, open, patent, perceivable, perceptible, revealed, seeable, sighty, unconcealed, unhidden, visual

barely dark, dim, obscure

comb. delo

partly issuant

VISIGOTH *king* alaric, alarik

VISION (See also **EYE** references.) ainsling, apparition, appearance, beauty, chimera, discernment, dream, eyeful, eyesight, fancy, fantad, foresight, ghost, glance, glimpse, hallucination, illusion, image, imagine, ken, knockout, light, look, mirage, nightmare, perception, perspicacity, phantom, photaesthesia, photopia, picture, poem, revelation, see, sicht, sight, specter, spectre, sweven

comb. opto

defect See **EYE** *defect.*

deprive of blind(fold), cele, seal, seel, sele

distance ken

double diplopia

false parablepsia, parablepsis

fantastic fantad, fantod, hallucination

hallucinatory heteroptics

illusory mirage, pseudoplepsis

instrument retina

lacking blind, purblind

measurement optometry

measurer campimeter, diopsimeter, heteroscope, optometer

multiple polyopia

pert. ocular, optic, visual

science ophthalmology, optometry

triple triplopia

VISIONARY aery, air-monger, airy, chimeric(al), daydreamer, delusional, delusive, don quixote, dreamer, dreamy, enthusiast, fanciful, fantastic, fey, heterodox, ideal(ist), idealistic, illusory, illusionist, imaginary, imaginative, impractical, insane, irrational, mopsus, phantast, quixotic, romancer, romantic(ist), seer, shandy, starry-eyed, unreal(istic), utopian(ist), utopographer

VISIT afflict, attend, benefit, bless, call, ceilidh(e), chat, come, conversation, converse, drop in, examine, frequent, gam, haunt, hawk, infest, inflict, inspect (ion), join, meet, punish, resort, scrutinize, see, sojourn, stay, travel, tryst, vizzy
brief call, vis
ceremonial selamlik

VISITATION adversity, affliction, bane, calamity, cross, disaster, dispensation, hardship, inquiry, inspection, judgment, sene, soken, trial, vicissitude, VISIT

VISITOR caller, company, guest, habitue, inspector, patron, transient
book album, register

VISON mink

VISOR aspect, beaver, eye-shade, face, mask, mesail, messenger, spy, umbre(l), umbrere, umbril, visage, visard

VISTA aspect, corridor, outlook, perspective, prospect, range, scape, scene, sight, view, vision

VISTULA *city on* cracow, krakau, torun
tributary bug, drweca, san

VISUAL ocular, ophthalmic, optic(al), perceptible, scopic, seeable, visible, visory

VISUALIZE appear, conceive, envisage, envision, image, imagine, materialize, picture, see

VITAL active, alive, animate(d), basic, capital, cordial, critical, crucial, dynamic, elemental, energetic, essential, exigent, flourishing, fresh, fundamental, imperative, important, in-dispensable, inherent, invigorating, live, lively, living, lusty, momentous, mortal, necessary, needful, organic, radical, requisite, sappy, significant, souled, viable, vibrant, vigorous, virile, weighty, zoetic
force bioenergy

VITALITY activity, animation, bang, being, biosis, bounce, breath, brio, endurance, energy, foison, gusto, health, horme, life, liveliness, machismo, pep, sap, stamina, starch, stingo, strength, vigor, vim, vivacity, zest, zip
lack adynamia, anemia, APATHY, asthenia, lethargy, torpor
lacking exhausted, slow, tired, wornout

VITALIZE activate, animate, energize, enliven, excite, exhilarate, galvanize, inspirit, invigorate, liven, provoke, quicken, stimulate, vivify

VITALS brain, heart, liver, lungs, organs

VITAMIN *a* biosterin, carotene, catotin, ergusia
a source butter, carrot, eggs, oil
b adermin, aneurin, cobalamin, cyanocobalamin, flavin, folic acid, hepatoflavin, lactoflavin, niacin, nicotinic acid, oryzanin, ovoflavin, pyridoxine, riboflavin, thiamine, torulin
b source beans, cereals, eggs, greens, meat, nuts, peas, whey, yeast
c ascorbic acid, cevitamic acid
c source citrus, lemon, orange
d calciferol, cholecalciferol, ergocalciferol, lumisternol
d source ergosterol, sunshine
deficiency anutraminosa, avitaminosis
e tocopherol
e source lettuce, spinach, wheatgerm
g riboflavin
growth biotin
h biotin
k napthaquinone, phylloquinone, phytonadione
k source alfalfa, fishmeal
m folacin, folic acid, pga
p and x citrin
p source lemon, paprika, rose hips

VITEX barbas, chaste-tree, jocote de mico, molave

VITHAR *father* odin
home asgard, vithi
victim fenrir

VITIATE adulterate, annul, cancel, contaminate, corrupt, damage, debase, debauch, defile, deprave, hurt, impair, injure, invalidate, neutralize, pervert, poison, pollute, spoil, taint, violate, void, weaken

VITIOSITY defect(iveness), depravity, fault, vice, viciousness

VITIS See GRAPE.

VITOTAN *indian* mirana, witato

VITREUS glaizie, glassy, green, hard, transparent
copper torbernite
silver argentite
stone apatite

VITRINE cabinet, etagere, showcase

VITRIOL acid, animosity, bluejack, caustic, copperas, sory, sulphate, virulence
blue See COPPER *sulphate.*

VITRIOLIC acerb, acid, acrimonious, barbed, biting, bitter, caustic, mordant, pointed, scathing, sharp, truculent, virulent

VITUPERATE abuse, asperse, assail, bawl out, berate, censure, chide, condemn, curse, execrate, jaw, malign, objurgate, rail, rate, reprove, revile, scold, smear, tonguelash, upbraid, vilify, wig

VITUPERATION abuse, attack, billingsgate, blame, censure, denunciation, invective, railing, rebuke, revilement, tirade

VITUPERATIVE abusive, caustic, critical, insulting, opprobrious, profane, railing, reviling, scurrile, scurrilous, shameful

VITZ gag, humor, mot, wisecrack, witticism

VIUVA rockfish, widowfish

VIVACIOUS active, animated, blithe, breezy, bright, brisk, buoyant, fresh, gay, jocular, jocund, light-hearted, lively, long-lived, merry, playful, sparky, spirited, spo.tive, sprightly, sunny, vigorous, vital, vivace

VIVACITY animation, ardor, brilliance, brio, buoyancy, charisma, dash, elan, energy, fire, force, life, liveliness, longevity, machis(s)mo, pep, personality, sparkle, spirit, sprightliness, verve, vigor, zeal, zest, zip

VIVANDIER provisioner, sutler, vendor

VIVARIUM, VIVARY box, park, pond, stew, terrarium, zoo

VIVA-VOCE examination, oral(ly)

VIVE brisk, forcible, life-like, lively, living, vivid

VIVERRINE civet, falanaka, foussa, genet, linsang, mongoose, musang, suricate

VIVIAN lady of the lake
lover merlin

VIVID active, acute, bright, brilliant, clear, colorful, distinct, dramatic, eloquent, expressive, fresh, garish, glaring, glowing, graphic, intense, keen, live(ly), living, lucid, lurid, outstanding, pictorial, resplendent, rich, sensitive, sharp, shiny, spirited, striking, strong, theatrical, vigorous

VIVIFY activate, animate, arouse, energize, enliven, excite, foment, quicken, refresh, renew, restore, revive, sparkle, stimulate, stir, vitalize, vivificate

VIVRES food(stuff), provisions, viands, victuals

VIXEN barge, catamaran, fox, fury, hag, nag, scold, shrew, spitfire, termagant, trimmer, VIRAGO, witch, woman

VIZ namely, videlicet

VIZARD disguise, mask, visor

VIZIER atabeg, atabek, councilor, governor, minister, officer, official, ras, ruler, satrap, wazir

VLAD dracula

VLEI creek, lake, marsh, swamp

VOCABLE name, term, word

VOCABULARY argot, cant, diction(ary), jargon, language, letters, lexicon, phraseology, phrasing, pochismo, style, terminology, verbiage, wordage, words

VOCAL articulate, choral, clamorous, eloquent, expressive, fluent, glib, intonated, lyric, operatic, oral, phonetic, sententious, sonant, tongued, tonic, uttered, verbal, voiced, voluble, vowel
chink glottis
cord pipe
composition aria, arioso, ballad, ballet, lied, madrigal, motet, song
organ glottis, larynx, syrinx, tongue
stop affricate

VOCALIST alto, baritone, bass(o), cantatrice, cantor, caroler, changer, coloratura, contralto, crooner, meistersinger, melodist, minnesinger, prima donna, singer, solfaist, soloist, songbird, songster, songstress, soprano, tenor, vocalizer, warbler, yodeler

VOCALIZE express, inflect, intone, phrase, say, sing, sound, speak, utter, vent, voice, warble

VOCATION business, call(ing), career, craft, employment, field, following, invitation, line, metier, occupation, profession, specialty, station, summons, trade, work

VOCIFERATE assert, bawl, bellow, clamor, cry, roar, shout, utter

VOCIFEROUS bawling, blatant, boisterous, brawling, clamorous, intense, loud (mouthed), noisy, obstreperous, sounding, strident, turbulent, vehement

VODKA samogon(ka)

VOE bay, creek, inlet

VOGUE acceptance, acceptation, approval, craze, cry, current, custom, dernier cri, fad, fashion, favor, popularity, practice, rage, reclame, repute, rumor, style, trend, way,
in chic, faddy, fashionable, prevailing, smart, stylish, trendy

VOICE air, announce, articulate, assert, broach, choice, communicate, cry, deliver, disclose, divulge, elect, emit, express, fame, impart, intonation, leden, locution, opinion, option, phrase, pipe, preference, proclaim, report, reputation, reveal, rumor, say, singer, sound, speak(er), speech, steven, talk, tell, tone, tongue, utter(ance), vent(ilate), voce, vote, vox, wish
artificial falsetto
box larynx
disorder lisp, rhinolalia, stammer, stutter
female alto, coloratura, contralto, (mezzo)soprano
flourish roulade
high falsetto, soprano, superius, tenor, treble
loss anaudia, anarthria, aphonia, aphrasia, aphthongia
loud megalophonic, megalophonous
male baritone, bass(o), countertenor, falsetto, tenor
middle motetus
natural di petto
of god vox dei
of the people vox populi
pert. phonetic, vocal
principal cantus
quality timbre
quiet sotto, whisper
range alto, baritone, bass(o), coloratura, contralto, falsetto, mezzosoprano, register, soprano, taille, tenor, tessitura, treble
roughness trachyphonia
sound word
stop affricate
stress accent, arsis, ictus

VOICELESS aphonic, aphonous, asonant, atonic, dumb, flated, hard, mum, mute, noiseless, silent, speechless, spirate, surd

VOID abolish, abrogate, abyss, annihilate, annul, bare, barren, blank, cancel, cass, cavity, clear, depart, depleted, destitute, destroy, devoid, discharge, dismiss, drain, egest, emit, emptiness, empty, evacuate, exhausted, foolish, gap, hole, hollow, idle, ineffectual, invalid, lack, lapse, leer, leisure, nothing(ness), null (ify), quash, remove, scatter, shun, space, unemployed, unoccupied, useless, vacancy, vacant, vacate, vacuity, vacuous, vacuum, vain, veto, want(ing), without

VOIDED cleche(e), clechy, discharged

VOLANT current, flounce, flying, light, nimble, quick, shuttlecock, trimmer, volatile

VOLATILE airy, bird, buoyant, capricious, changeable, darting, effervescent, elastic, elusive, ephemeral, erratic, evaporable, fickle, fitful, fleeting, flighty, flippant, flying, fowl, frivolous, fugacious, fugitive, gaseous, giddy, inconstant, light(hearted), lively, mercurial, resilient, scatterbrained, shallow, transitory, volage, volant, vaporescent, vaporous

VOLATILITY flightiness, flippancy, frivolity, gaiety, impermanence, inconstancy, instability, levity, lightness, liveliness

VOLATILIZE atomize, evaporate, exhale, vaporize

VOLCANO, VOLCANIC antisana, apo, asama, askja, asosan, atitlan, cotopaxi, etna, fuego, fugi, fumarole, gede, hood, krakatau, krakatoa, lassen, maunaloa, merapi, orizaba, pelee, popocatepetl, rainier, raun, shasta, spitfire, stromboli, taal, vesuvius, vulcan
apex cone
cinder scoria
crater See *mouth*, below.
eruption, pert. pelean
extinct alagez, alagoz, aragats, asosan, suribachi
fissure mofette
fragments ejecta, ejectamenta
fume mofette
glass australite, obsidian, perlite, pumice
goddess pele
highest active cotopaxi
hill puy
island fa(e)roes, iwo-jima, stromboli
jet soffione
lava lapilli, latite, pumice, salse, scoria, trass, tufa
mound hornito
mouth caldera, crater, fumarole, maar
mud moya, salinelle, salse

part crater, mouth, rim, somma
rim somma
rock andesite, basalt, dacite, feldspar, perlite, pozzuolana, rhyolite, tephrite, terras, trass, tufa
slag cinder, scoria
steam stufa
valley atrio
vent chimney, diatreme, solfatara

VOLE campagnol, craber, cricetid, meadow-mouse, microtus, neofiber, slam
arboreal tree-mouse

VOLGA rha
city on astrakhan, cheboksary, samara, sarai, stavropol, syzran
region capital samara
tributary kama, oka, sura

VOLGAGRAD stalingrad, tsaritsyn

VOLITION accord, choice, conation, decision, determination, election, intent, option, preference, volency, will(ingness)

VOLKSWAGEN beetle, bug, rabbit
home wolfsburg
name people's car

VOLLEY attack, barrage, blast, blizzard, bowl, broadside, burst, cannonade, company, crowd, discharge, drift, fire(at), flak, flight, fusillade, gunfire, platoon, salvo, shellfire, shooting, shot, spray, volee

VOLSCIAN *general* or *king* tullus-aufidius

VOLSUNG *kin* odin, siegfried, sigmund, volsi, waels
oak barnstock, branstock
son sigmund, signy
wife liod

VOLSUNGA SAGA *character* atli, brunhild, brynhild, giuki, grimhild, siegfried, sigurd
sword gram

VOLT ampere, circle, gait, leap, ohm, repolon, tread, turn, watt
unit var

VOLTA *city* bobodioulasso, ouagadougou
river nile

VOLTAIRE arouet
retirement village ferney
work candide, la pucelle,

l'ingenu, nanine, zadig, zaire

VOLUBILITY eloquence, fluency, garrulity, glibness, loquacity

VOLUBLE changeable, eloquent, fickle, fluent, glib, loquacious, oily, revolving, rotating, speechful, talkative, unstable, vocal, wordy

VOLUME aggregate, album, amount, amplitude, book, bouk, bulk, capacity, coil, content, cubage, cubature, dimensions, edition, extent, folio, loudness, magnitude, mass, number, part, power, quantity, range, roll, scroll, size, sonority, space, strength, tome, tonnage, turn, work
diminish decrescendo, turn down
increase crescendo, turn up
measure barrel, bushel, cord, cup, decistere, finger, gallon, gill, hogshead, liter, magnum, minim, peck, pint, quart, stere, tablespoon, teaspoon, ton, yard
measurer stereometer
measurement stereometry

VOLUMINOUS abundant, ample, big, bouffant, bulky, capacious, comprehensive, full, generous, great, large, numerous, spacious, swelling, winding

VOLUMNIA *son* coriolanus

VOLUND See WAYLAND.

VOLUNTARILY freely, spontaneously, willeliche, willes, williche, willingly

VOLUNTARY autonomous, chosen, deliberate, elective, free, impromptu, independent, intentional, optional, postlude, prelude, sortie, spontaneous, unforced, willful, willing
follower antrustion

VOLUNTEER antrustion, enlist, enroll, offer, proffer, stand, tender, worker
state tennessee

VOLUNTEERS OF AMERICA *founder* booth

VOLUPTUARY antinous, pleasure-seeker, sensualist, sybarite

VOLUPTUOUS carnal, comfortable, delicate, delightful, fleshly, gross, hedonistic, indulgent, luscious, lux-

urious, lydian, opulent, pleasant, sensual, sensuous, sultry, sumptuous, sybaritic, wanton
name meaning adin
VOLUPTUOUSNESS delice, luxury
VOLUTE cillery, coil, helix, mollusk, rolled up, scroll, spiral, turn, twist, univalve, whorl
VOMIT bock, boke, bolt, cack, cast, cat, discharge, disgorge, eject, emetic, erupt, evome, heave, jet, keck, regorge, reject, retch, spew, throwup, upchuck, vome, woom
VOODOO bewitch, charm, fetish, hex, hoodoo, magic, obe(ah), obi, sorcerer, sorcery, vodun
charm doll, grigri, juju, mojo (root), obi
culture yoruban
deity eshu, loa, zombi
marauder bourhousse
practice vodun, wanga
priest babalawo
spell mojo
wizard quimboiseur
worshipper hoodooist
VORACIOUS acquisitive, adephagous, bulimic, covetous, eager, edacious, esurient, esurine, gargantuan, gluttonous, grasping, greedy, hungry, immoderate, insatiable, rapacious, ravening, ravenous
VORACITY avarice, edacity, gluttony, greediness, rapacity
VORTEX apex, eddy, gyre, maelstrom, swirl, tornado, waterspout, whirl(pool), whirlwind
VOTARY addict, adherent, buff, devotary, devotee, enthusiast, fan(atic), fiend, follower, habitue, ite, sectary, supporter, zealot
VOTE adopt, aye, ballot, blackball, call, chirotony, chud, con, confer, elect, grant, logroll, name, nay, nod, placet, plebiscite, poll, primary, propose, proxy, suffrage, ' suggest, ticket, voice, yea
against blackball, blacklist, knife, nay, nyet, thumbs down, veto

assenting aye, nod, placet, yea
canvassing ambitus
for approve, aye, confirm, pro, support
receptacle ballot box, situla
right to franchise, suffrage
straw poll, trial balloon
VOTER assentor, balloter, chooser, constituent, elector, poller
group bloc, constituency, electorate, party
illegal nonresident, repeater, underage
VOTIVE consecrated, devoted, vowed
offering amulet, apotropaion, charm, vow
VOTYAK *water spirit* vukutis, vumurt, vununa, vuvozo, yankimurt
VOUCH accredit, affirm, allege, appeal to, approve, assertion, attest, authenticate, authorize, back, certify, cite, clear, confirm, corroborate, declare, depone, depose, endorse, guarantee, maintain, pray, resolve, sanction, second, sponsor, substantiate, summon, support, testify, uphold, verify, vow, warrant, witness
VOUCHER acknowledgment, acquittance, attest, bill, certificate, certify, chalan, check, chit, credential, debenture, note, receipt, recommendation, release, statement, stub, ticket, warrant, witness
VOUCHSAFE accord, acquiesce, allow, award, bestow, beteem, concede, condescend, confer, deign, favor, give, grant, guarantee, oblige, permit, please, present, stoop, witsafe, yield
VOUSSOIR keystone, quoin, springer, wedge
projection ear
VOW affirm, assertion, asseveration, behight, bind, consecrate, declare, dedicate, depose, devote, oath, pledge, profession, promise, protest, snum, supplication, swear, vote, vum, warrant, wish
bound by votary
-maker votist
pert. votal
VOWEL *change* umlaut

contraction crasis, dip(h)-thong
gradation ablaut, apophony
group digram, digraph
-like vocoid
mark breve, macron, tilde
neutral murmur
omission elision
pert. vocal(ic)
point sere
short breve, matra
sign dieresis
sound dental, labial, palatal
strengthening guna
unaspirated lene
unstressed schwa, shwa
VOYAGE caravan, course, crossing, cruise, expedition, jaunt, journey, navigate, passage, pilgrimage, route, run, sail, tour, travel, trip
maiden shake-down, trial-run
VRITRA ahi
VUELTA See TOBACCO.
VULCAN (See HEPHAESTUS.) mulciber, volcanus
festival volcanalia
pert. mulcibirian
son calus, coeculus, servius tullius
VULCANITE ebonite
VULGAR bad, base, blatant, boorish, brazen, broad, caddish, coarse, common (place), crass, crude, customary, dirty, discourteous, earthbred, general, graubyer, graubyon, gross, ill-bred, improper, indecent, indecorous, indelicate, inelegant, lewd, low(bred), mean, obscene, offcolor, offensive, ordinary, philistine, plebian, popular, prost, public, rabble, randy, rank, raw, ribald, rough, rowdy, rude, secular, slangy, slimy, souterly, spicy, suggestive, tabloid, tasteless, tatty, uncouth, ungenteel, unrefined, vernacular, vile, vulgate, woolen
VULGARIAN barbarian, boor, bounder, clodhopper, loudmouth, lowbrow, philistine, savage, slob, swine
VULGARISM See VULGARITY.
VULGARITY bad taste, barbarity, coarseness, foulness, grossness, illbreeding, indelicacy, ostentation, pro-

vincialism, rudeness, shoddy

VULN wound

VULNERABLE accessible, assailable, beatable, conquerable, dangerous, defenseless, exposed, expugnable, liable, penetrable, pregnable, susceptible, unguarded, unprotected, wounding
point achilles heel, button, underbelly

VULNERATE hurt, injure, wound

VULPINE alopecoid, artful, clever, crafty, cunning, foxy, sly, tricky, wily

VULT aspect, countenance, expression, mien

VULTURE aasvogel, arend, aura, buteo, buzzard, condor, corbie, dirtbird, falcon, gallinazo, gier-eagle, graap, grape, griffin, griffon, grip(h)e, gryphon, gyps, harpy, hawk, nekheb(e)t, papa, porphyrion, raptor, sarcogyps, snatch, urubu, zopilote
bearded arend, lammergeier
black atrata, coragyps, urubu
ensign of egypt
symbol of rapine

VUM snum, swear, vow

W

WA kawa, lawa

WAAG grivet, monkey

WABASH *city on* logansport, terre haute
tributary tippecanoe

WABAYO ouabaio

WABBLE See WOBBLE.

WABRON plantain, wayberry

WACHNA cod(fish), eleginus

WACK clammy, damp, eccentric, moist

WACKER alert, wakeful, watchful

WACKY crazy, disordered, eccentric, erratic, foolish, insane, mental, off one's rocker, off one's trolley, screwy, tsedoodelt(eh), tsedrayt(er), wild

WAD bankroll, bundle, compress, fortune, gag, graphite, heap, lead, line, lump, mass, money, pack, pad, piece, pile, pledge, plug, poke, quantity, stopper, stuff, swab, trace, track, tuft, WADI, wealth, wisp, woad, would

WADDLE default, hoddle, pace, poddle, swing, toddle, totter, trample, tread, wamble, wattle, wauchle, widdle, wobble

WADDY attack, beat, cane, club, cowboy, peg, rustler, stick

WADE bathe, dabble, demon, ford, giant, lair, pass, penetrate, plod, plouter, plutter, slog, slosh, walk
into attack, begin, undertake

WADER alectoride, avocet, avoset, boot, coot, crane, egret, flamingo, heron, jacana, snipe, stilt, stork

WADI, WADY bed, channel, gap, gorge, gulley, oasis, ravine, river, stream, valley, wash

WADSET mortgage, pawn, pledge

WAEG kittiwake

WAFER abret, biscuit, cachet, cake, candy, cracker, diaphragm, disk, flatbrod, gaufre, host, lamina, lavash, lozenge, matzoh, obley, oflete, popadam, primer, seal, slice, troche, valve
ash agrimony-bark, aguebark, hop-tree
box pyx
pharmaceutical cachet

WAFF affection, attack, bark, blast, bum, disreputable, flap, flutter, glimpse, gust, inferior, lowborn, odor, paltry, puff, signal, snarl, solitary, vagrant, waft, wag, wave, whiff, woebegone, worthless, wraith, yelp

WAFFLE bark, battercake, blathers, err(or), flap, flutter, gaufre, gofer, yap, yelp

WAFT bear, beckon, blow, breath, buoy, carry, convey, convoy, current, direct, flag, float(ing), gleam, glimpse, gust, levitate, odor, pennant, seal, signal, smell, summon, taste, transmit, transport, turn, wave, waving, w(h)eft, whiff, wraith

WAFTAGE carriage, conveyance, convoy, ferriage, transportation

WAG beckon, begone, brandish, card, chap, clown, depart, droll, farceur, fellow, flag, flourish, gossip, humorist, jester, joker, jokester, lug, move, nickum, nod, nudge, oscillate, punster, roam, rogue, shake, signal, slyboots, stir, sway, swing, tramp, troll, vibrate, waddle, waff, waggle, walk, wander, wave, wiggle, wigwag, wit, wriggle
-tongue chatterbox, gossip

WAGE, WAGES adventure, attempt, batta, bet, bribe, carry on, conduct, contend, emolument, employ, engage, fee, fight, fulfill, gage, gratuity, hazard, hire, hoot, lay, levy, meed, packet, pawn, pay(check), pension, pledge, practice, produce, recompense, remuneration, requital, reward, risk, salary, screw, service, stake, stipend, tunca, utu, venture, WAGER, wedge
attach garnishee
deduct dock
earner breadwinner, employee, laborer, mechanic, proletarian, provider, worker
insurance chomage
war battle, fight

WAGER ante, bet, competition, contest, depone, gage, gamble, hazard, hold, lay, make book, pledge, pot, prize, quinella, raise, risk, set, speculate, stake, stoater, venture, vie, wadge, wedfee
large stoater
made in bad faith levant

WAGES See WAGE.

WAGGISH arch, comic, droll, frolicsome, funny, humorous, impish, jesting, jocose, jocular, jolly, jovial, mischievous, playful, roguish, sportive, witty

WAGGLE beat, best, defeat,

jerk, reel, sway, wabble, wag, wobble, woggle

WAGNER *opera* gotterdammerung, lohengrin, meistersinger, parsifal, rheingold, rienzi, tannhauser, tristan and isolde

role elsa, erda, eva, hagen, isolde, klingsor, kundry, parsifal, rienzi, senta, tristram, tristan, wotan

wife cosima

WAGON araba, black maria, buggy, caisson, camion, car(avan), carriage, carryall, cart, chariot, coach, coaster, conestoga, dilly, dray, fly, fourgon, jerky, landship, lorry, perambulator, plaustrum, prairie schooner, pram, rack, rolley, rully, runabout, spider, telega, tonga, tram, truck, tumbrel, tumbril, van, wain, whitetop

baggage fourgon

bar sheth

bed katel

body bed, buck, punt

covered caravan, conestoga(wain), germantown, van

covering bucksail

driver wainer

-lit sleeper, sleeping-car

load burden, cargo, fother

lumber gilly

maker wainwright, wheelwright

mining rolley, rully, tram

old wain

on the abstaining, abstinent, teetotalling

part axle, blade, clevis, doubletree, neap, pol, rave, sheth, thill, tongue

pert. plaustral

pin clevis

pole disselboom, janker, neap, nib, tongue

shaft blade, fill, limber, nib, stave, thill

shoe drag, skid

springless telega, tonga

tongue neap

train caravan

WAGONER auriga, trekker, wainer, wainman

WAGTAIL barleybird, dishwasher, flutter, flycatcher, lark, laundress, molly, oatear, quaketail, seedbird, waggie, washdish, washer, washtail, wateril, waterthrush

WAH panda

WAHINE female, lady, mistress, sweetheart, wife, woman

WAHLENBERGIA bluebell, campanula, harebell

WAHOO arrowwood, basswood, buckthorn, burningbush, cascara, elm, evonymus, fish, guarapucu, nonsense, ono, peto, quassia, spindletree, tilia, tommyrot, umbrellatree, viburnum

WAHUNSONACOCK powhatan

WAIF castaway, derelict, feeble, flag, foundling, gamin, homeless, ignoble, paltry, pennant, strafe, stray, vagabond, vagrant, waft, wanderer, wastrel

WAIL bawl, bay, bemoan, blubber, caterwaul, croon, cry, deplore, ejulate, grieve, groan, gurl, howl, keen, lament(ation), moan, mourn, plaint, screech, sigh, sob, sough, squall, ullagone, ululate, waul, wawl, weep, whimper, wow, yammer, yell

WAILER *professional* howler, keener

WAILSOME deplorable, grievous, lamenting, plaintive

WAIN cart, chariot, convey, fetch, WAGON, weyne

charles's big dipper, constellation, ursa major

rope trace

WAINMAN bootes, wagoner

WAINSCOT azulejo, base, ceil(ing), cirphis, leucania, line, lining, moth, oak, panel(ing)

WAIREPO stingray

WAIST basque, belt, blouse, bodice, body, bosom, camisa, camisole, carpel, chemise, corsage, dickey, garibaldi, girdle, girth, halter, josie, middle, pierrot, sark, shift, SHIRT, taille, undershirt, undervest, wasp

decoration jabot

WAISTBAND baldric, band, bellyband, belt, cestus, cincture, cummerbund, fascia, girdle, girth, obi, sash

WAISTCLOTH breechcloth, loincloth

WAISTCOAT benjy, camisole, doublet, fecket, gilet,

jacket, jerkin, singlet, veskit, vest, weskit

WAIT abide, ambush, attend, bide, break, dally, defer, delay, endure, entracte, escort, expect, forbear, guard, halt, hautboy, hearken, hesitate, hope, interlude, intermission, linger, lite, loiter, look, oboe, observe, pause, postpone, protect, remain, search, seek, serenader, serve, snare, stay, stop, tarry, trap, watch (fulness)

-a-bit bramble, cockspur, grappleplant, greenbrier, hawthorn, prickly ash

-awhile taihoa, wattle-tree

for abide, expect, keep

impatiently chafe

on accompany, attend, court, escort, follow, help, lackey, perform, serve, visit

on table butle, hash, serve

WAITER attendant, boy, butler, cameriere, carhop, coaster, dapifer, drawer, flunky, garcon, hasher, kellner, kitmudgar, lackey, maitre d'hotel, mozo, pannier, piccolo, salver, servant, server, servitor, steward, tender, thomas, tray, watcher, watchman, waylayer

helper busboy

WAITRESS carhop, hasher, hostess, maidservant, phyllis

WAIVE abandon, abey, abstain, banish, cast, cease, cede, defer, delay, desert, deviate, disclaim, disown, disregard, evade, forbear, forgo, forsake, grant, leave, neglect, pass, postpone, put, quit, refuse, relinquish, remove, renege, renounce, resign, sacrifice, stop, surrender, throw away, turn aside, vacate, wave, yield

WAIVER dismissal, release

WAKA canoe

WAKASHAN *indian* aht, haisla, heiltsuk, kwakiutl, nohuntsik, nootka, somehulitk, wikeno

WAKE arouse, awake(n), excite, funeral, guard, passage, reanimate, revel, revive, rite, rouse, stir, tangi, track, trail, train, vigil, watch, wauk *island* otori

-robin anthurium, arum, calf's-foot, coughroot, cuckoopint, jack-in-the-pulpit, orchid, sara(h), snake-bite, trillium

up arise, arouse, awake(n), disillusion, excite, flicker, rise

WAKEFUL alert, astir, hypnopomic, insomniac, restless, vigilant, wakerife

WAKEFULNESS insomnia, pervigilium, restlessness, vigil(ance)

WAKEN actuate, arouse, call, excite, fire, galvanize, inflame, kindle, motivate, provoke, quicken, rally, rouse, stimulate, stir

WALDEN *author* thoreau

WALDENSIAN leonist, patarin, sabotier

WALE best, bulge, choice(st), choose, choosing, eddying, grain, mark, pick, rib, ridge, select, strake, streak, stripe, stroke, surging, texture, twill, welt, wheal, whelp, WHIP

WALES (See also WELSH.) cambria, cymru

actor williams

ballgame knappan

bard aneurin, merlin, ovate, talies(s)in

bay cardigan, swansea, tremadoc

benefit comorth

buccaneer morgan

cheese caerphilly

chieftain glendower

city aberdare, amlwch, bangor, brecon, caerleon, caernarvon, caerphilly, cardiff, cwmbran, hereford, holyhead, kidderminster, merthyr-tydfil, milford haven, newport, pembroke, rhondda, rhyl, ross, swansea, towyn

county anglesey, brecknoch, cardigan, carmarthen, denbigh, flint, glamorgan, monmouth, montgomery, pembroke, radnor

dead, god of pwyll

district mold, plynlymmon, rhyl

dog cardigan, corgi, pembroke, sealyham, terrier

emblem leek

ensign dragon

epigram englyn

explorer madoc

fabric cardigan

fairyland ann(f)wn

farmer aillt

fine saraad

fish gwiniad, gyniad

giants, land of ysbaddaden

god, goddess See CELT *god, goddess.*

hamlet tref

headland pen

hero culhwch, evnissyen, olwen

hills malvern

island anglesey, caldy, holyhead

island, mythical ann(f)wn

king, legendary bran

lake bala, vyrnwy

language celtic, cymraeg, cymric, keltic, kymric

law galanas

manor commot(e)

measure cantred, cantref, cover, crannoc, lestrad, listred

musical assembly eisteddfod

musical instrument pibcorn

name prefix caer

oatmeal dish flummery

onion chesboll, cibol, ciboule

painter john

patron saint david

peak snowdon

peasant aillt

people brython, cambrian, celt, cymry, kymry, silures, siluridan, taffies

poem azahrot, cywydd

poet dylan thomas, map(es)

port cardiff, carmarthen, holyhead, llanelly, sidney, swansea

prince, legendary idris, kilwich, madoc

psychoanalyst jone

range berwyn, cambrian

rebel glendower

reformer owen

river dee, severn, taff, teifi, teme, towy, usk, vyrnwy, wye

saint bran

sea god bran, dylan

servant aillt

sky god gwydion

stories mabinogi(on)

strait menai

stranger aillt

sun god lleu, llew

symbol leek

tribe awabakal

underworld god gwyn

utopia ann(f)wn

warrior lludd

writer llewellyn, machen, thrale

zone olenus

WALK 3 gad, jog, leg, mog, pad, peg, wag, way 4 beat, fair, foot, gait, gang, hike, hoof, lane, limp, lope, mope, mush, pace, pass, path, paup, plod, rack, ramp, roam, roll, slog, step, trot, turn 5 aisle, allee, alure, amble, ankle, barge, clump, glide, haunt, jaunt, march, mince, mosey, oxter, range, round, route, scuff, stamp, stomp, stram, stray, strut, stump, trail, tramp, tread, troop 6 airing, arcade, avenue, canter, daddle, dander, depart, hobble, loiter, lumber, parade, pasear, prance, ramble, sashay, stride, stroll, toddle, totter, trapes, travel, trudge, wander 7 balteus, circuit, conduct, cramble, dogtrot, gallery, passage, pasture, pathway, saunter, scuffle, shamble, shuffle, stretch, trachle, traipse 8 ambulate, behavior, frescade, navigate, straddle, traverse 9 circulate, esplanade, promenade 10 procesion 11 perambulate, peregrinate 14 circumambulate, constitutional

affectedly mince, prink

aimlessly lurch, mince, paup, poap

arm in arm oxter

away outrun, setup, snap, triumph, victory

beat patrol

clumsily joll, loppet, lurch, shamble, staup, stump

covered arcade, cloister, gallery, mall, porch, portico, stoa

fashionable grecian bend

fast hotfoot, scurry

for exercise hike

gingerly tiptoe

hard stram, trudge

having swinging swivel-hipped

heavily clump, lamper, lumber, plod(ge), stomp, thump, tramp

horizontal balt(h)eus

inability to abasia

inclined ramp

in one's sleep somnambulate

into attack, devour, thrash
lamely hirple, hobble, limp, shuffle
leisurely amble, dander, saunter, stroll
long march
off with pilfer, pinch, STEAL
of life status
on bit part, role, trample
out court, strike
out on abandon, desert, ditch, leave
over trample, triumph, victory, win
pompous strut
public alameda, arcade, esplanade, mall, prado, promenade, xystus
reeling lurch, totter
rolling wallow
shaded alameda, arbor, arcade, mall
softly steal, tiptoe
steadily plod, snoove
stealthy stalk
the chalk conform
the floor pace
-up apartment
waveringly shevel, wabble, wobble
WALKER babybuggy, foot, forester, fuller, gamekeeper, gocart, leg, orthopteron, peddler, pedestrian, prowler, spazierganger, stroller
WALKING afoot, ambulant, ambulatory, gait, oscillating, passant, peripatetic, swinging
adapted for gressorial
comb. ambul(a)
fern camptosorus
meter pedometer
out courtship
papers dismissal
speed increase festination
stick ashplant, bat, blackthorn, cane, crook, crutch, gibby, gibstaff, kebbie, kebby, pikestaff, pricklypear, sloe, staff, stilt, waddy, woodhorse
toad natterjack
tyrant flycatcher
WALL baffle, bailey, barrier, bartizan, bastion, bawn, boil, brick, bulwark, butt, cashel, cliff, dam, digue, dike, dokhma, emure, enclose, enclosure, encompass, escarp, fence, fortify, haha, levee, meure,

mur(al), mure, parapet, paries, partition, pirca, pluteus, pretil, rampart, rebote, redan, reredos, revetment, scarp, seethe, septum, side, spandrel, spina, tambour, traverse, vallum, woghe, wough
board gobo
bracket corbel, sconce
brick rowlock
builder mason
circular cashel
comb. septo
core hearting
covering calcimine, cloth, depreter, distemper, draperies, grout, intonaca, kalsomine, paint, paneling, paper, plaster, tile, vinyl, wallpaper
curved sweep
decorative dado, wainscot
defensive bailey, ballium, rampart, scarp
divided by septate
dividing partition, septum
foundation riprap
grass stonecrop
handwriting graffiti, menemene-tekel-upharsin
hanging arras, picture, tapestry
hawkweed lungwort
highest part crapwa
hollow rowlock
in confine, enclose, mure, separate
inner escarp, partition
inward slope batter
koran alaraf
lining wainscot
log crib
louse bedbug
low bahut, pluteus, podium
lower part dado
masonry revetment
moss stonecrop
opening bole, door, dormer, scupper, transom, window
ornament dado, fresco, hanging, mirror, mo(u)lding, mural, pla(c)que, tablet, tapestry
outer bail, bailey
outside the extramural
part bahut, baseboard, coping, cornice, dado. gable, niche, panel, pier, plinth, rib, skirtingboard, template, templet, wainscot
peat cop
pepper sedum, stonecrop
pert. mural, parietal

plaque otela
plate pan, resen
projecting anta
puddle hearting
recess m(e)use, niche
retaining bulkhead, crib, piling, revetment
roof carrying bahut
rue tentwort
scarped ghat
secondary chemise
stone riprap
sustaining riprap
tax murage
tower meah
wing aileron, pericarp
WALLABA apa, arawak, eperua
WALLABY boongary, kangaroo, macropus, paddymelon, padmelon, petrogale, toolach, whiptail, wurrung, wurrup
bush pinkwood
WALLACE *novel* ben hur
WALLAH agent, fellow, man, master, owner, person, servant, worker
WALLED enclosed, fortified, mural, obvallate, partitioned, protected
WALLET alfarga, alforja, bag, billfold, boget, bouge, bulge, jag(g), knapsack, mail, pack, pocketbook, porte-monnaie, purse, sack, scrip, toolbag
leather pinseal
WALLEYE alewife, dore, exotropia, leucoma, sauger, squint, strabismus, surffish, watcheye, whall
WALLEYED *pike* blowfish, dore, dory, jack, percid, pickerel, puffer, salmon, swellfish
WALLFISH leader
WALLFLOWER bloody-warrior, cheir(inia), cuba, gelofer, gilliver, gillyflower, jacks, keiri, poisonbush, warrior
WALLOON (See also BELGIUM.)
area belgium, brabant, france, hainaut, liege, luxembourg, namur
WALLOP beat, blow, boil, bubble, clobber, clout, comb, dangle, dress(down), flap, flax, flog, flounder, flutter, gallop, groom, hide, hit, impact, jump, larrup, lather, leap, lick, paddle,

palpitation, paste, plunge, pound, punch, shingle, strike, swat, tan, thrash, throb, trim, waddle, welt, whale

WALLOPING beating, bouncing, large, licking, strong, thrashing, whopping

WALLOW billow, crouch, dissipate, enjoy, fade, flounder, grovel, gush, hollow, indulge, insipid, kommetje, lair, lie, loll, nauseous, pit(ch), revel, roll, slosh, sludder, soil, sprawl, surge, swelter, tasteless, toss, tumble, volutate, welter, wither

WALLOWER pinion, trundle

WALLPAPER hanging, tapestry, tenture

measure bolt, roll

WALLY ample, excellent, fine, fondle, gewgaw, indulge, jolly, large, ornament, pleasant, robust, splendid, strong, sturdy, toy

WALNUT acapu, akhrot, bannut, candlenut, emboya, heartnut, imbuia, juglans, nogal, platycarya, poisonwood, shagbark-hickory, tryma

black mockernut, pignut

color taffy

disease melaxuma

husk bolster

skin hull, shell, zest

tree akhrot

tree, changed into carya

white butternut, sycamore

WALPAPI *indian* shoshone, snake, yahuskin

WALRUS bruta, edentata, horse-whale, morse, odobenus, pelagian, pinniped (ian), rosmarine, seacat

herd pod

limb flipper

young pup

WALTON, IZAAK *burial site* winchester cathedral

fishing spot itchen, netherwallop

work compleat angler

WALTY crank, unsteady

WALTZ boston, breeze, dance, flounce, valse, vienna

emperor johann strauss sr

king johann strauss jr

WAMARA clubwood, coffeewood, ebony, ironwood, panococo, swartzia

WAMBLE change, nausea, oscillate, overturn, pace, quiver, ramble, reel, revolve, roll, rumble, seethe, shake, spin, stagger, totter, tumble, twist, wriggle, writhe

-cropped annoyed, humiliated, qualmish, squeamish, vexed

WAMBLY faint, nauseated, shaky, squeamish, unsteady

WAME belly, hollow, room, stomach, wamb, wem, wyme

WAMP duck, eider

WAMPISH fluctuate, swing, wave

WAMPUM amole, beads, cowrie, fadme, fathom, hawok, money, peag(e), roanoke, se(a)wan

WAMUS jacket, wampus

WAN ashen, ashy, black, blake, cadaverous, colorless, dark, deadly, deathly, dim, dusky, fade(d), faint, feeble, frightful, ghastly, gloomy, gray, haggard, haw, languid, livid, lusterless, pale, pallid, pallor, pasty, peaked, sad, sallow, sick(ly), sorrowful, waughy, waxen, weak, worn

WAND baguet, baton, caduceus, cane, cudgel, divining rod, ferula, rhabdos, rod, scepter, shoot, slat, staff, stick, switch, talisman, thyrse, thyrsus, truncheon, twig, verge, virga, wattle, withe

flower galax, sparaxis

magic caduceus, witchhazel

royal mace, scepter

-shaped virgate

short cudgel, truncheon

WANDER aberrate, circulate, cruise, dander, depart, deviate, digress, divagate, drift, dwale, err, gad, gallivant, glaik, haak, haik, hake, jaunt, loiter, mar, maze, meander, mither, moider, moon, pass, peregrinate, prowl, ramble, range, rangle, rave, roam, roil, rove, saunter, scamander, straggle, strake, stray, stroll, swerve, traik, traipse, trapes, travel, traverse, vagabond(ize), vagrate, vague, waive, waver

aimlessly bum, divagate, gad, maunder, meander, moon, slosh, traipse, trapse

desire to dromomania

mentally dander, daver, delire, dwale, dwall

widely peregrinate, range, roam

WANDERER ahaseurus, ancient mariner, arab, bedouin, butterfly, covenanter, drifter, floater, fugitive, gadabout, gypsy, itinerant, landlo(u)per, migrant, palmer, peripatetic, pilgrim, planet, rambler, ranger, roamer, rover, runabout, savitar, scenite, spider, straggler, stray, traveler, truant, tzigane, vagabond, vag(rant), viator, waif, zingaro

name meaning errol

WANDERING aberrant, aberration, abnormal, arrant, astray, bumming, circuitous, delirious, deviant, deviation, devious, discursive, distraught, divagation, drifting, errant, erratic, excursion, floating, footloose, fugitive, gadding, gallivanting, hoboism, incoherent, itineracy, itinerant, journey, landlo(u)ping, meandering, meandrous, migratory, mobile, nomadic, odessey, perambulant, peregrination, planetary, planeticose, rambling, ranging, restless, roaming, roving, shifting, straggling, straying, strolling, trailing, traipsing, transient, travel(ing), truant, vagabond(age), vagrancy, vagrant, vague, vagus, wanderlust

alone solivagant

at will blackberrying, blakeberyed

plant ivy, saxifrage, zebrina

WANDERLUST itchy-foot

symbol open-road

WANDEROO langur, macaca, macaque, monkey, presbytis

WANDLE agile, lithe, supple

WANE abate, absent, age, close, decay, decline, decrease, defect, deficient, deteriorate, diminish, dwindle, ebb, end, fade, incomplete, insufficient, lack, lessen, loss, peter(out), poverty, recede, repine, slack, taper, want(ing), welk, wilt

WANG cheek, king, meadow, molar, prince, ruler, tooth

WANGA charm, fetish, ouanga, philter, sorcery, spell, voodoo, wongah

WANGLE adjust, contrive, extricate, fake, falsify, finagle, maneuver, manipulate, persuade, plot, shake, totter, trick, wag, w(r)iggle

WANHOP misfortune, mishap

WANHORN galingale

WANIGAN chest, coffer, houseboat

WANION curse, plague, vengeance

WANKLE feeble, fickle, irresolute, sickly, unstable, unsteady

WANT absence, aspire, beggary, blemish, choose, covet, crave, craving, defect, deficiency, demand, deprivation, desire, destitution, exact, fail, fall short, famine, fault, forget, gap, hanker, hole, indigence, lack, long, lose, miss(ing), mole, necessity, need, omission, omit, penury, pinch, pine, plight, poverty, privation, require(ment), scarcity, seek, shortage, starvation, starve, straits, thirst, vacancy, void, wish, yearn

WANTAGE deficiency, shortage, ullage

WANTED necessary, needed *by police* hot

WANTING absent, bankrupt, bereft, defective, deficient, destitute, devoid, feeble-minded, imperfect, incomplete, lacking, less, minus, missing, necessary, needy, required, short, shy, without

WANTON 3 bad, bag, gay, pet 4 bawd, doxy, drab, easy, free, jade, lais, lewd, play, rank, slut, tart, wild 5 cadgy, dally, hussy, light, loose, merry, mopsy, nymph, piece, revel, saucy, slack, thais, tramp, trull, waste, wench 6 callet, carnal, chippy, daring, fallen, floozy, frisky, frolic, giglet, giglot, harlot, haunty, hooker, impish, laches, lavish, lively, phryne, pickup,

rigsby, teaser, trifle, unruly, vulgar 7 aspasia, baggage, chowlah, cocotte, delilah, demirep, giggish, haggard, hetaera, immoral, jezebel, kittock, liberal, lorette, lustful, obscene, playful, profuse, rampant, riggish, riotous, roguish, sensual, smicker, trollop, waggish, wayward 8 arrogant, bonaroba, demimond, flagrant, grisette, heedless, inhumane, paramour, petulant, reckless, sensuous, spiteful, sportful, sportive, strumpet 9 abandoned, concubine, dissipate, lecherous, libertine, luxurious, malicious, messalina 10 capricious, frolicsome, inconstant, lascivious, licentious, lubricious, outrageous, profligate, prostitute, refractory, thriftless 11 extravagant, mischievous, mollycoddle, spendthrift 12 concupiscent, unrestrained, unscrupulous 13 inconsiderate, undisciplined

WANTONNESS abandon, folly, pride, sport, surquidry

WANTWIT fool(ish), idiotic, silly

WANTY bellyband, girth, rope, surcingle, tie

WAP bark, bind, blast, blow, bundle, fight, flap, fold, knock, storm, strike, truss, whop, wrap

WAPITI alce, cervid, deer, elk, losh, lush, maral, moose, stag, wampoose, wawaskeesh

WAPPER blink, totter

WAR arms, battle, blitz (krieg), bloodshed, combat, conflict, contend, contest, crusade, endeavor, feud, fight, guerilla, guerra, guerre, harry, hell, hostilities, jehad, jehid, krieg, military, moloch, oppose, strife, strive, struggle, wage, weer
advocate hawk
alarm flap
bird ace, airplane, aviator, tanager
cause of casus belli
chemical agent lewisite
club mace, marree, merai, mere, mulla(h),
comb. machy

correspondent ernie pyle, william howard russell
cross croix de guerre
cry aboo, abu, alala, aux armes, banzai, beauseant, slogan, tora, warison, whoop
engine or *machine* See ENGINE *war.*
equipment armament(s), materiel, munitions
fleet armada
galley cataphract, ramberge
game kriegspiel
gas mustard, phosgene
god anhur(shu), ares, as(s)hur, as(s)ur, camulus, chemos(h), coel, dagda, enyalius, esus, hachiman (daibosatsu), indra, ir(r)a, koel, kumara, mamers, mars, ment(u), montmenthu, nergal, ningirsu, ninurta, odin, ojin, ophois, oro, quirinus, skanda, sutekh, thor, tiu, tiwas, tyr, woden
goddess alea, anahita, anath, anatum, annunit, athena, babd, bella, bellona, bodb, durga, enyo, ishtar, minerva, morrigan, neith, sekhmet, vacuna
-hater antipolemist, dove, pacifist
-hating misopolemical, pacifistic, peace-loving
hawk bailiff, jingo
holy crusade, jehad, jihad
horse campaigner, charger, courser, destrier, leader, oldster, partisan, politician, standby, steed, trooper, veteran
instrument caltrap, caltrop, relocator
kind abc, atomic, biologic (al), chemical, nuclear
-like, name meaning martin
lord tuchun
lover hawk, jingo(ist), militarist
man of nautitus
mighty in bellipotent
of words logomachy
pert. bellicose, belligerent, martial, military, polemical
planet ninurta
restriction blockade
slow sitzkrieg
such is c'est la guerre
symbol of horse
trophy medal, ribbon, scalp
vehicle jeep, tank

zone front

WARBLE carol, chant, chirl, chirm, chirp, croon, descant, maggot, quaver, shake, sing, swelling, trill, tumor, twitter, vibrate, vocalize, wabble, warnel, wormil, yodel

fly botfly, cattlegrub, gadfly, oestrian, oestrid, oxfly

WARBLER beambird, beccafico, blackcap, canary, cape may, chat, chiffchaff, creeper, crombec, eysoge, fantail, fauvette, fitte, furzeling, gerygone, gnatcatcher, grassbird, haysuck, malurine, ovenbird, parula, pettichaps, pincpinc, pipit, pitbird, redstart, reedbird, riroriro, singer, smeu(th), songbook, soufriere, sylvia, tailorbird, titien, trochilus, vocalist, wren, yellowcrown

garden strawsmear

genus cisticola, dendroica, geothlypis, malurus, phylloscopus, seiurus, setophaga

gray riroriro

ground yellowthroat

sedge haytit, mockbird

willow smeu(th)

WARD area, arrondissement, avert, barrio, beware, block, buckler, calpolli, calpul, care, charge, client, contrada, corridor, counsel, custody, defend, defense, dependent, district, division, dread, enclose, fear, fence, fend, fortify, garrison, govern, guard(ian), heir, hundred, imprison, jail, keeping, orphan, parry, pensioner, precinct, prison, protege(e), protect(ion), quarter, repel, rule, safeguard, storeroom, wapentake, wardrobe, warn, watch, world

artemus charles f browne

heeler flunky, follower, hanger-on, henchman, truckler

off averruncate, avert, avoid, balk, bar, block, buff, dodge, end, fence, fend, foil, forestall, forfend, guard, hinder, obstruct, obviate, parry, preclude, prevent, repel, repulse, resist, shield, stave

pert. pupillary

politician heeler

WARDEN alcaide, alcaiyde,

beefeater, caid, castellan, claviger, concierge, constable, curator, custodian, director, disdar, dizdar, gatekeeper, governor, guard(ian), hogmace, jailer, keeper, leatman, mazir, official, overseer, ranger, regent, roland, sexton, superintendent, supervisor, turnkey, viceroy, warner, watchman

WARDER bulwark, caretaker, custodian, guard, keeper, sentinel, staff, stronghold, truncheon, turnkey, WARDEN, watchman

WARDROBE almirah, ambry, apparel, armoire, bonnetiere, cabinet, chamber, closet, clothes(press), clothing, costumes, dressingroom, duds, ensemble, garderobe, layout, livery, locker, outfit, privy, rig(ging), room, trappings, trousseau, turnout, vestry, vestuary

WARDWOMAN maid(servant), tirewoman

WARE amount, avoid, bestow, beware, careful, cautious, chaffer, china, cloth, cognizant, commodity, dishes, earthenware, fabrics, goods, heedful, host, livestock, merchandise, people, pottery, produce, product, prudent, pus, quantity, seaweed, shrewd, shun, spend, spring, squander, stuff, vigilant, warn, wary, waste

china porcelain

enamel bilston

goose brant

WAREHOUSE almacen, bankshall, depository, depot, elevator, entrepot, etape, fondo(u)k, funnduck, godown, magazine, mart, pantechnicon, shed, silo, storage, store(house)

fee storage

room loft

WARES commodities, goods, merchandise, troggin, troke

WARFARE See WAR.

WARIANGLE shrike

WARINESS cautel, caution, distrust, wariment

WARISH cure, defend, heal, protect, recover, rescue

WARISON property, requital, reward, treasure, wealth

WARK ache, pain, throb, work

WAR-LIKE aggressive, armigerous, bellicose, belligerent, bellonian, combative, contentious, fierce, fighty, gladiatorial, hostile, inimical, martial, militant, military, pugnacious, quarrelsome, savage, scrappy, soldierly

WARLOCK conjuror, deceiver, demon, devil, enchanter, giant, impish, liar, magician, malignant, monster, scoundrel, sorcerer, traitor, wizard

WARM affectionate, alive, amorous, angry, ardent, bake, balmy, bask, beek, calescent, calid, caliente, chafe, clement, close, comfortable, compassionate, cook, cordial, devout, eager, excite, fervent, fervid, flog, flushed, fresh, friendly, genial, glowing, gracious, grateful, haimisher, hearty, heat(ed), home-like, hot, humid, irascible, irksome, keen, loving, mild, muggy, near, occupy, overheat, passionate, preheat, reheat, responsive, rich, secure, sincere, summery, sunny, sunshiny, sympathetic, temperate, tender, tepid, thaw, thermal, toasty, tropical, wholehearted, zealous

as toast

-blooded ardent, fervent, impetuous, irascible, quicktempered

-hearted affectionate, compassionate, cordial, friendly, generous, gracious, hearty, kind, loving, sympathetic, tender

moderately tepid

pert. thermal

up accelerate, chafe, exercise, heat, practice, reheat

-up place bull pen

WARMONGER See WAR

lover.

WARMOUTH bigmouth, flatfish, sacalait, sunfish

WARMTH anger, animation, ardor, calidity, elan, emotion, energy, enthusiasm, excitement, fervency, fervor, flash, glow, heat, irritation, lewth, life, passion, sympathy, temperature, tepidity, tepor, vehemence, zeal

gentle tepidity, tepidness, tepor

pert. thermal

-promoting euthermic

sense of thalposis

symbol hearthstone

without chilly, cold, cool, frigid

WARN admonish, advertise, advise, alarm, alert, apprise, avision, caution, command, counsel, exhort, forebode, gardyloo, inform, monitor, notify, portend, premonish, previse, rede, remind, reprehend, signal, threaten, tip off, warrant

WARNER churchwarden, mentor, warden

WARNING admonition, advice, alarm, alert, aposematic, augury, aviso, beacon, beep, beware, blinker, caution, caveat, counsel, deterrent, example, exhortation, flag, foreboding, jiggers, knell, larum, lesson, monition, notice, notification, omen, portent, premonition, premonitor, prodrome, prodromous, reminder, semaphore, siren, summons, symptom, threat

formal alarm, caveat, sos

phrase cheese it, en garde, jiggers, look out, on guard, watch out

signal alar(u)m, alert, beacon, bell, blinker, flare, foghorn, larum, lighthouse, red light, siren, semaphore, tocsin

system antenna, bmews, dew

without unaware(s), unexpected(ly)

WARNISH fortify, garrison, provision

WARP aberration, beat, bend, bias, buckle, cast, choke, contort, contract, corrupt, crook, cup, damage, deflect, deform, distort (ion), dram, eject, emit, expel, fabricate, falsify, fling, geyze, gnarl, hurl, hurt, influence, injure, interweave, intort, kedge, mar, misrepresent, pervert, porry, rope, sediment, shrink, shrivel, skeller, stunt, sway, swerve, thraw, threads, throw, turn, twine, twist, utter, weave,

web, weft, whirl, wriggle, wrinkle, zigzag

thread abb, lea, stamen

WARPED bent, buckled, distorted, gnarled, partial, perverted, twisted, wry

WARRAGAL dingo, dog, ferocious, horse, myall, outlaw, savage, untamed, wild

WARRANT ability, acknowledge, affirm, assert, assurance, assure, attest, authority, authorize, aver, avouch, behight, berat, brevet, cause, certificate, certify, command, commission, commitment, confirm(ation), declare, defend, depose, docket, document, empower, endorse, ensure, foundation, ground(s), guarantee, guaranty, indemnify, indict, justification, justify, license, maintain, mittimus, pass, permit, plevin, precept, promise, protect, prove, reason, refuge, right, safeguard, safety, sanction, save, secure, security, summons, sunnud, swear, testify, voucher, warren, writ

WARRANTED deserved, due, entitled, guaranteed, justified, merited, qualified

WARRANTY authorization, covenant, evidence, guarantee, proof, sanction, support, WARRANT, writ

WARREN conyger, hutch, milldam, privilege, rabbitry, slum, tenement

WARRIN lorikeet, parrot

WARRIOR berne, berserker, brave, champion, cossack, earl, fighter, freik, g(h)azi, hagen, hero, hessian, hummingbird, impi, kemp, marine, martialist, rodomont, sailor, samurai, sannup, shardana, soldier, spahee, spahl, starkad, starkath, toa, vet(eran), wallflower, warfarer, zerbino

biblical ehud, gideon

bloody wallflower

boastful rodomont

class magani, thanes, thegns

female amazon, aslauga, camilla, shieldmay, valkyrie

group army

mythical aslauga

name meaning herman, lewis, louis, ludi, marco, mark, martin

professional condottiere, gladiator, hessian, janizary, mercenary

virgin camilla

winged zetes

WARS OF THE ROSES *battle* bosworth field

opponents lancaster, york

WARSAW *pert.* varsovian

suburb praga

WARSHIP (See also NAVY *vessel.*) bireme, corvette, dreadnaught, dromond, frigate, galleon, monitor, onebank, ram, razee, sultana, sultane, trireme, wafter

beak embolum

deck orlop

1st ironclad merrimac

pert. naval

pilot house conning tower

quarters gunroom

squadron armada, escadrille

WARSLE flounder, struggle, wrestle

WART acrochordon, ambury, blemish, bulge, burl, diminutive, dwarf, ecphyma, epiderma, knot, lump, papiloma, peewee, protuberance, pustule, rat, shrimp, sycoma, tumor, verruca, verruga

cress carara, coronopus

disease canker

flower celandine

grass sunspurge

hog emgalla, macrocephalus

pert. pyrenoid, verrucose, verrucous

snake xenoderm

WARTWEED celandine, devil's-milk, nipplewort, sunspurge

WARWICK *horse* black saladin

WARY alert, attentive, cag(e)y, calculating, canny, careful, cautelous, cautious, chary, circumspect, discreet, distrustful, economical, guarded, hooly, leary, leery, mindful, provident, prudent, scrupulous, shy, skittish, suspecting, suspicious, timorous, vigilant, watchful, wise

WARYTREE gallows

WASH ablution, alluvion, bathe, bog, bowk, buck, buddle, clean, cleanse(r), cohere, creek, daub, deposit, deterge, diluvium, drench, drift, elute, elu-

triate, estuary, fen, flood, flow, flush, gargle, hose, imbue, immerse, lap, lather, launder, laundry, lave, leach, lixiviate, lixivium, losh, manipulate, marsh, moisten, mop, mud, mundatory, overlay, paint, pan, plash, purge, purifier, purify, rinse, ripple, rub, soak, scour, scrub, shampoo, shower, silt, slosh, soap, solution, solvent, splash, sponge, swab, swash, sweat, swob, tint, tub, tye, wet, wort
away erode, gull, purge
basin See *bowl,* below.
bear raccoon
bowl aljofaina, basin, lavabo, lavatory, sink, tub
brew flummery, sowens
leather losh
lightly lave, rinse
-mouth tattler
out abolish, bore, debacle, decolor, discard, elute, erase, fail(ure), flood, flunk
tub flasket
up discard, dismiss, end, finish

WASHCLOTH flannel
WASHDISH wagtail
WASHED *out* ashen, depleted, dilapidated, dispirited, ended, exhausted, faded, pale, played out, spent, spiritless, through, tired, wan
up done, finished, shot, through
WASHER bur(r), circle, clout, cotterel, dhobi, gasket, grommet, lavandera, potwalloper, ring, rondel, rondelle, rove, scrubber, scullion, sourer
leather button
WASHERMAN dhob(ie), lavandero
WASHERWOMAN blanchisseuse, laundress, wagtail
WASHING ablution, cleansing, coat, covering, elution, elutriation, laundry, lavage, scrub, sluice, swashing
machine dashwheel
machine cycle dry, resoak, rinse, soak, spin, wash
WASHINGTON *capital* olympia
city aberdeen, anacortes, bellingham, bremerton, burlington, ephrata, everett,

hoquiam, kennewick, longview, olympia, omak, othello, pasco, port angeles, pullman, puyallup, renton, richland, seattle, spokane, tacoma, vancouver, wallawalla, wenatchee, yakima
college whitman
county asotin, clallam, kitsap, kittitas, skagit, yakima
dam grand coulee
falls snoqualmie
fort lewis
hydroelectric plant ross
indian aht, chehalis, chimakum, chinook, clallam, colville, cowlitz, dwamish, hoh, lummi, makah, nespelim, nisqually, okinagan, palouse, pishquow, puyallup, quaitso, quileute, quinaielt, quinault, sahaptin, salishan, samish, sanpoil, semiahmoo, senijextee, shahaptian, shoalwater, sinkiuse, skagit, skokomish, spokan(e), squaxon, swinomish, tulalip, twano, yakima
lake chelan, washington
nickname chinook state, evergreen state
palm fanleaf
park mt rainier, olympic
peak adams, baker, jack, lemei, logan, moses, rainier, shuksan, simcoe, sloan, stuart, tunk
port bellingham, everett, seattle, tacoma
range blue, cascades, kettle-river, olympics
river columbia, quinault, snake, snohomish, snoqualmie, yakima
sound puget, rosario
state bird willow-goldfinch
state flower rhododendron
state tree hemlock
WASHINGTON, D.C. *airport* dulles, national
architect pierre l'enfant
art gallery corcoran, freer, national, phillips
feature ellipse, mall, white house
museum smithsonian
nickname foggy bottom
park rock creek
river potomac
subway metro
WASHINGTON, GEORGE father of his country

ancestral home newcastle-upon-tyne
biographer parson weems
birth place bridge's creek, virginia, wakefield
burial site mount vernon
grandmother mildred gale
home mount vernon
manse, ancestral newcastle-upon-tyne
party federalist
portraitist peale, stuart
profession surveyor
sculptor houdon
vice-president john adams
victory trenton
wife martha eustis, patsy
winter headquarters morristown, valley forge
WASHY diluted, feeble, frivolous, insipid, loose, oozy, slippery, thin, watery, weak, wet, worthless
WASP (See also *genus,* below.) aculeate, appledrane, appledrone, braconid, cowkiller, cuckoofly, cynipid, dauber, digger, dryinid, eumenid, hornet, jack-spaniard, jiga, masarid, mason, mutillid, philanthid, pompilid, sceliphron, scoliid, serphid, siricio, sphecid, stinger, vespa, vespid, whamp, yellowjacket
genus bembex, odynerus, pepsis, polistes, pompilus, scolia, sphex, tiphia
killer vespacide
nest bike, bink, vespiary
of twickenham alexander pope
pert. vespal, vespine
ruby cuckoofly
sand horseguard
wingless velvet-ant
WASPISH choleric, contrary, cranky, cross, fractious, fretful, huffish, huffy, irascible, irritable, malicious, peevish, pettish, petulant, querulous, slender, snappish, spiteful, testy, touchy
WASSAIL carol, carouse, drink, frolic, glee, lark, merriment, pledge, revel, shindy, song, spree, toast
WASTE (See also *away* and *matter,* below.) 3 eat, gob, sot, ted, use 4 bare, burn, dull, gnaw, loot, lose, loss, ross, ruin, sack, scum, vain, wear, wild 5 blank, chaff, drain, empty, erode, havoc,

scrap, spend, spill, spoil, tabid, use up 6 barren, bezzle, defeat, desert, diddle, dismal, draffy, dreary, expend, gloomy, lavish, lessen, muddle, ravage, ravish, sahara, trifle, unused 7 consume, corrode, destroy, dwindle, exhaust, fribble, fritter, leakage, mullock, neglect 8 decrease, demolish, desolate, diminish, misspend, squander, treeless, unusable 9 cheerless, condiddle, decrement, depletion, devastate, dissipate, fruitless, remainder, shrinkage, worthless 10 deperition, exhaustion, monotonous, wilderness 11 consumption, destruction, deteriorate, dissipation, expenditure, prodigality, uninhabited 12 extravagance, uncultivated

allowance tret

away age, atrophy, bate, decay, disintegrate, dissipate, dwindle, emaciate, fail, macerate, melt, molder, pine, rot, shrink, sweal, traik, wilt, wither

growing in ruderal

lay ravage, ravish, raze, sack, wreck

matter ashes, debris, draff, dregs, dross, garbage, lees, rammel, refuse, rubbish, sadd, sewage, slops, sudd, swill, trash

matter, pert. spodogenous

time boondoggle, dally, dawdle, diddle, drill, idle

WASTEBASKET circular file, hell(box)

WASTED atrophied, cadaverous, careworn, decrepit, deteriorated, dissipated, emaciated, gaunt, haggard, idle, lank, low, pinched, poor, ravaged, skinny, spare, spent, squandered, thin, weak, worn

WASTEFUL dissipative, extravagant, improvident, lavish, prodigal, profligate, profuse, shiftless, spendful, spendthrift, thriftless, wanton

WASTELAND badlands, barren(s), brule(e), brush, burn, bush, curagh, currach, desert, fen, heath, kar(r)oo, marsh, morass,

moor, sahara, swamp, wilderness, wild(s)

author eliot

WASTING atrophia, atrophy, cachexia, colliquation, consumption, malnutrition, marasmus, symtosis, syntectic, syntexis, tabes, tabetic, tabid

WASTREL bum, defective, derelict, idler, losel, nogoodnik, outcast, prodigal, profligate, spendthrift, stroygood, vagabond, waif, weak, wretch

WAT fellow, hare, know, man, monument, rabbit, temple, vat, wet, wot

WATCH ambuscade, ambush, attend, await, bide, chronometer, clock, examine, eye, follow, gaze, glom, guard, heed, horologe, inspect, keep an eye on, look (out), mark, mind, observation, observe, oversee, patrol(ler), period, plot, police, protect, revel, safeguard, scan, scout, see, sentinel, sentry, shield, spial, spy, stare, stemwinder, tend, ticker, ticktick, timepiece, timer, tompion, tour, tout, twig, vedette, vigil (ance), wait, wake(fulness)

alarm tatler, tattler

band wrister, wristlet

chain albert, fob

charm fob

closely scrutinize

crystal lunet(te)

crystal rim basil, bezel, bezil

inferior turnip

movement ebauche

nautical dogwatch, hack

night lichwake, lykewake

out beware, cave

over attend, babysit, care for, guard, keep, supervise, tend, tent

part crystal, escapement, face, fob, hand, jewel, ligne, mainspring, spring, stackfreed, stem, stud

pin dart

striking repeater, tat(t)ler

WATCHDOG al rakim, bandog, bloodhound, cerberus, cur, garm(r), kratim, mastiff, matin

WATCHFUL alert, anxious, attent(ive), canny, careful, cautious, chary, circumspect, guarded, jealous,

prompt, quick, ready, sleepless, tenty, vigilant, wacker, wakeful, wary, waukrife, wideawake

name meaning ira

WATCHFULNESS attention, care, caution, vigilance

WATCHMAKER chronologer, chronologist, horologer, horologist

rouge clinker

WATCHMAN argus, askari, bantay, bellman, charley, chokidar, cityward, gatekeeper, ghafir, guard, heimdallr, keeper, mina, sentinel, sentry, sereno, shomer, talliar, tooter, vedette, vigil, warden, warder

WATCHTOWER atalaya, bantayan, barbican, beacon, garret, lighthouse, lookout, mirador, mizpah, observatory, sentinel, specchie

WATCHWORD alerta, consigne, countersign, cry, ensign, hint, motto, nayword, parole, password, shibboleth, signal, slogan

WATER abyss, adam's ale, agua, aqua, bath, bree, brine, broo, damp(en), diluent, dilute, douse, dowse, drench, eau, flood, flume, hose, infusion, irrigate, juice, lake, liquid, luster, lymph, manipulate, moisten, moisture, ocean, pond, pool, puddle, rain, river, saliva, saturate, sea, soak, solution, sprinkle, squirt, stream, thin, tide, wet

and buttermilk bland

arum dragon

ash agrimony, ague-bark, box-elder, fraxinus

bag bouget, chagul, matara, mussuk, reticulum

baptismal laver

bath bain-marie

bean chinquapin, lotus

bear tardigrade

bearer aquarius

betony bishop's weed, broomwort, bullwort, figwort

bird See BIRD *aquatic.*

blebs pemphigus

boatman backswimmer, corixa

body bahr, bay, deep, gulf, lagoon, lake, loch, mear, mere, oasis, ocean, pond, pool, reservoir, river, sea, spring(s), strait, tank, well

-borne afloat, floating, nautical

bottle beaker, carafe, canteen, decanter, lota, olla, tinaja

brash pyrosis

bubbling sprudel

bucket aam, canakin, can(n)ikin

buffalo bubalus, carabao, kerbau

buffalo-yak offspring dzo

carrier (See also WATERWAY.) aguador, aquarius, aqueduct, barge, bheestie, bheesty, bhisti, cloud, ditch, duct, flume, main, pipe, zanja

cart dilly

cask winger

cavy capybara

celery cursed-crowfoot

centipede hellgrammite

chestnut caltrap, calt(h)rop, ling, saligo, sedge, trapa

chicken gallinule

chickweed blinks

chinquapin bonnet, lotus, nelumbo, rattlenut, wankapin, yoncopin

clock clepsydra, ghurry

closet necessary, petty, privy, sanitary, stool, toilet

cock kora

colly ouzel

color aquarelle, graphic

comb. aqueo, aqui, aquo, hydat(o), hydro

congealed glace, ice, icicle, snow

containing hydrous

containing iron riddam

cooler icer, olla, refrigerant

course See WATERWAY.

cow manatee, seacow

craft See BOAT, SHIP, VESSEL.

cress bilders, brassica, brooklime, carse, eker, kers(e), nosesmart, perro, plant, roripa

crow coot, ouzel, snakebird

crowfoot buttercup, herb

cure hydropathy, hydrotherapeutics, hydrotherapy

deep ballow

deficiency anhydremia, dehydration, drought

deficiency, comb. anhydr(o)

depth draft, draught

depth, measure sound

depth, measurer See *gauge*, below.

developing in hydrarch, hydroponic

dipper calabash

dirty puddle, saur

dock bloodwort, goldenclub

doctor hydropathist

dog barbet, hellbender, mariner, mudpuppy, old salt, otter, retriever, sailor, salamander, spaniel, swimmer, waterrug

drain downspout, eavestrough, scupper

draw lade

-drinker aquabib, hydropot

eagle osprey

element hydrogen, oxygen

elephant hippopotamus

father of mississippi, oceanus

fear of hydrophobia

fearing hydrophobic, hydrophobous

fennel belderroot, edgeweed, oenanthe, starwort

finder dowser

flea cyclops, daphnia, daphnid

fresh, pert. limnetic

fresh, study of limnology

front bank, beach, harbor, lido, playa, shore

frozen frost, ice, sleet, snow

gall jellyfish, rainbow, winddog, windgall

gauge bathometer, fluviograph, hydrometer, marigraph, nilometer, sound(ing lead), udometer

gazing at lecanoscopy

germander mint, scordium

gillyflower featherfoil

glass clepsydra, goblet, tumbler

gnat marsh-treader

god, goddess See SEA *god, goddess.*

grampus hellgrammite

growing in hydrophyte, hydroponic

hardness degree grain

having affinity for hydrophile

hawthorne aponogeton, pondweed

hemlock brook-tongue, cicuta, cowbane, deathin, death-of-man, dropwort, jellica

hen coot, gallinule

hog bush-pig, capybara

hole alberca, charco, dub, lake, oasis, pit, pond, pool, tinaja

holy eau-benite, hyssop

horehound gypsywort

horse hippocampus, hippopotamus, kelpie

ice sherbet, sorbet

in soil holard

jar banga, lota(h), stamnos

jug gamla, gomlah, goolah

king of amazon

kudu sitatunga

lacking See WATERLESS.

leaf brook-flower, shawny

lemon calabash, passionflower

lettuce pondweed, quiapo

lift See *raising device* and *wheel,* below.

-like hydatoid

lily beaverroot, bobbin(s), calla, camalote, candock, cuckoopint, flatterdock, lotos, lotus, nelumbo, nenuphar, nuphar, nymphaea, victoria, wocas, wokas

living rasa

living in amphibian, aquatic, lenitic, lotic, spanipelagic

marshy pokelogan, pokeloken

measurement acre-foot

meter venturi

mill clow

mineral perrier, pullna, selter(s), seltzer, shasta, soda-pop, sprudel, vichy

mint ammi, bishop's-weed, goutweed, wood-betony

moccasin congo, cottonmouth, snake, viper

mold aphanomyce

mole desman, duckbill, platypus

molecule hydrol

moth caddis-fly

neck strait

newt asp, salamander, triton

nozzle rose(head)

nymph(s) aganippe, apas, apsaras, ariel, arsyra, calypso, cassotis, castalia, crenae, cyane, doto, dragonfly, emphydriad, hago, kelpie, kelpy, lily, limnad, naiad, nicker, nix(ie), oceanid, pegae, pirene, potamid, rusalki, salmacis, sprite, tangie, undine

obstruction bar, dam, reef

of life aquavit, brandy, eau de vie, salvation, usquebaugh, whiskey

on the brain hydrocephalus

open polyna

open, pert. limnetic
opossum yapock, yapok
ouzel cinclus, dipper, ducker, piet, thrush
parsnip sium
pepper knotweed, lakeweed
pert. aquatic, aquatile, hydatoid, marine
pig capybara, gourami
pipe calean, duct, hooka(h), hose, hubblebubble, main, narghile, nargile(h), tube
plant See PLANT *aquatic.*
plantain alisma, thrumwort
plug faucet, fireplug, hydrant, spigot, tap, valve
pocket alberga, tinaja
pot fontal
primeval apsu
pure aquapura
rail bidcock, moorhen, oarcock, rallus, runner
-raising device (See also *wheel*, below.) churrus, jantu, noria, pump, ram, sakieh, shadoo(f), siphon, sweep, taboot, tabut
rat arvicola, craber, muskrat, thief, vole, waterrug
receptacle See *vessel*, below.
reddish resp, riddam
reservoir cenote, dam, lake
rights haustus
rough breakers, eddy, rapids, rip, sea, waves
salt brack, brine, seawater
sapphire iolite
scorpion nepa, nepid
sea-bottom abyss
serpent hydra
shamrock buck-bean
sheep roach
sheet nappe
shield brasenia, deerfood, egg-bonnet, fanwort, fishgrass, frogleaf
shoot channel, chute, drip (stone)
skip over dap
snake hydra, hydrus, moccasin, natrix
soapy graith, suds
soil holard
soldier pondwort
sound klop, plash, rote, splash, swish
speedwell brook-pimpernel
spirit or *sprite* See *nymph*, above.
spouting waikiki
starwort callitriche
still keld, lagoon, login
still, pert. lenitic

-strider skater, sketcher, skipper
substance baregin, glairin
sulphur barege
surface epilimnion, ryme
surface movement seiche
sweetened amrit(a)
swirling eddy
thief pirate
thistle teasel
throw on douse, quench
thrush kickup, ousel, ouzel, wagtail, warbler
tiger dytiscid
tree pitcher-plant, sassy
trench ditch, leat
turkey snakebird
vapor fog, mist, steam
vessel aam, aftaba, banga, basin, bottle, bucket, cannikin, canteen, carafe, cowl, croft, cruse, decanter, ewer, flask, font, goblet, jug, lavabo, lota(h), matara, olla, pail, pitcher, stamnos, tinaja, tub
violet featherfoil, hottonia
vole craber
wally batamote
washing lavation
wheel danaide, noria, sageer, sakieh, sakiyeh, turbine, tympanum
wheel part paddle
white rapids
wier lasher
witch dowser
without anhydrous
without, comb. anhydr(o)
yam lattice-plant
WATERBLOOM algae, scum
WATERBRAIN gid
WATERBUCK antelope, chuzwi, cob, defassa, kob
WATERCUP pennywort, pitcherplant, saracenia, trumpets
WATERFALL braid, cascade, catadupe, cataract, chignon, foss, lin(n), lyn, sault, spout
famous angel, bowen, bridal veil, cauvery, chirombo, detti, fincha, gastein, gavarnie, guaira, handegg, handol, harsprang, helena, horseshoe, howick, iguassu, iguazu, kalambo, kegon, krimmler, minnehaha, multnomah, narada, niagara, passaic, ribbon, ruacana, skykjefos, sluiskin, tegula, tower, vettis, victoria, voring, yosemite

WATERFOWL See BIRD *aquatic.*
WATERGATE affair, channel, floodgate, scandal, sluice, valve, watercourse
WATERINESS aqueity, aquosity
WATERING dilution, epiphora, immersion, irrigation, salivation, secreting, sprinkling
device hose, hydrant, nozzle, pump, spray, sprinkler
eye epiphora
place aguada, baden, bath(s), battis, oasis, pool, pump, resort, saloon, seaside, shore, spa, spring, well
-pot shell aspergillum, brechites
WATERISH feeble, flat, juicy, marshy, succulent, WATERY
WATERLESS anhydrous, arid, desert, dry, parched
comb. anhydr(o)
WATERLOGGED edematous, saturated, soaked, soggy, sopping, soppy, steeped, swampy, useless
WATERMARK crown, plimsoll-line, tidemark
WATERMELON anguria, citrul, cucumis, cucurbit, gourd, pepo, peponida, peponium, sandia, skipjack, tsama
WATERPROOF burberry, camlet, canvas, cloth, cravenette, keratol, tarp(aulin), tenting
WATERSHED basin, brow, divide, snowshed, valley
WATERSKIN mashak, matara, mussack, mussick, mussuk
WATERSPROUT canal, cataract, cloudburst, drip(stone), gargoyle, hurricane, jet d'eau, pipe, prester, spate, torrent, trough, twister, vortex
WATERTIGHT dripproof, hermetic, impervious, leakproof, rainproof, sealed, seaworthy, sta(u)nch, theat, thight
make ca(u)lk
WATERWAY 3 bed, geo, gio, ria, rio, run, urn 4 bahr, burn, cove, foss, gill, gote, hahr, khor, kill, lade, leat, linn, lode, moat, pipe, race, sike, vale, wadi, wady,

yora 5 auwai, basin, bayou, bogue, bourn, brook, canal, chute, cleft, cowal, creek, dhoon, ditch, donga, drain, flume, fosse, ghyll, gorge, gulch, gully, hondo, levee, river, zanja 6 arroyo, canada, canyon, course, groove, gutter, nullah, ravine, relais, runlet, runnel, seaway, sluice, spruit, strait, stream, trench, valley, zanjon 7 acequia, aguador, channel, conduit, couloir, culvert, foggara, igarape, rivulet, trinket, zanjona 8 aqueduct, barranca, spillway 9 oceanlane

artificial canal

dray billabong

science fluviology

WATERY aquatic, aqueous, boggy, dilute(d), flabby, fluid, hydrogenous, hydrous, ichorous, insipid, liquid, moist, pale, plashy, serous, skinking, sloppy, soft, soggy, splashy, swashy, tearful, teary, thin, vapid, weak, wet, wishy-washy, zestless

comb. aqueo, aqui, aquo, sero

WATSON, DR *friend* sherlock holmes

statement amazing

WATTLE acacia, barbel, beat, bluebush, boree, caruncle, cooba, dewlap, flap, flog, frith, gill, hackthorn, hurdle, interweave, jollop, jowl, lappet, mulga, plat, rod, sallow, sally, saltbush, salwe, stave, stick, twig, twist, wand, weave, whip, withe

and daub stud and mud

crow kokako

tree acacia, boree, callicoma, cooba(h), myall, silverleaf

WATTLEBIRD coleia, crow, gillbird, honeyeater, iao, manuaq, maomao, miner, moho, turkey

honey-eater iao, manuao

WATUSI bahima

WAUCHLE stagger, struggle, waddle

WAUGH damp, faint, insipid, nauseous, stale, uncertain, wavering, weak

WAUGHY boggy, clammy, faint, wan, weak

WAUKIT callous, horny, matted

WAVE beachcomber, billow, bore, brandish, breaker, chop, comber, convolution, curve, display, divert, eagre, falter, flag, flap, flaunt, float, flood, flourish, flutter, grayback, greet(ing), gust, hairdo, heave, onde, oscillate, ply, quiver, ridge, riffle, ripple, roller, sea, seiche, shake, signal, streak, stripe, surge, sway, swell, swing, tide, tilde, undulate, undulation, vacillate, vein, vibrate, wag, water, waver, whiffle, whitecap, wield, wigwag

comb. cymo, ondo

god dylan

large decuman, surge, tsunami

phenomenon clapotis

recorder ondograph

science kymatology

seismic tsunami

ship poop

swelling brimmer

tidal bore, eager, eagre

top comb, coom, crest, seege

upward motion scend

WAVER balance, balk, boggle, brangle, change, dacker, daiker, dither, falter, flag, flicker, flitter, fluctuate, flutter, hesitate, hover, lisp, oscillate, pendulate, quiver, reel, roam, sapling, scruple, seesaw, shy, stickle, stray, swale, sway, swerve, swing, swither, teeter, totter, undulate, vacillate, veer, vibrate, wabble, waffle, wander, wiggle, wobble

WAVERING desultory, doubtful, dubious, fickle, flexuous, halting, hesitant, inconstant, indecisive, irresolute, lambent, wauch, waugh, wiggly

WAVERLY *author* walter scott

WAVY billowy, buckled, crisp, curly, floppy, fluctuating, fluttery, moire, nebule, onde, ondoyant, repand, ripply, rolling, sinuous, snakey, snowgoose, squiggly, swelling, swirlv. undate, unde(e), undose, undulate, undulating, undulatory, undy

comb. cer

-haired veddoid

WAWASKEESH elk, wapiti

WAX accumulate, adipocere, arise, beat, candle, capping, carnauba, cere(sin), cerin, ceroxyle, cerumen, coccerin, defeat, develop, epilator, fat, flare up, glow, grease, grow(th), gum, increase, klister, lubricant, lubricate, oil, ozocerite, paraffin, pela, pinsane, polish, putty, rage, shine, size, sleek, smooth, spring, suberin, temper, vesta, wage, zietriskite

and lampblack blackball

and oil ceroma

candle bougie, cierge

catcher bobeche

cobbler's code

comb. cero

-covered cerated

creeper milkweed

disk agnus

figure ceroplast

flower epiphyte

gourd ash-pumpkin, benincasa

grave adipocere

-like ceraceous

match vesta

medicinal cerate

mold ceroplast

moth galleria, pyralid

myrtle arrayan, candleberry, candletree

myrtle fruit bayberry

ointment cerate

palm areca, carnauba, copernica

pert. ceraceous, ceral, cerate, cereous

plant hoya

process cerotype

ski klister

substance adipocere, cerin

taper candle, vesta

tree privet, rhus, sumac

yellow ceresin

WAXBILL amadavat, astrild, estrilda, redbill, weaverbird

WAXEN ashen, ashy, ceraceous, ceral, cerated, cereous, drained, gray, impressionable, pale, pallid, pasty, pliable, pliant, shining, smooth, soft, viscid, wan, yielding

WAXWEED cuphea

WAXWING bombycilla, cankerbird, cedar, chatterer, recollet, silktail, waxbird

WAXY angry, mad, vexed, **WAXEN**

WAY 3 cut, use 4 cost, form, gate, lane, line, mode, pass, path, plan, plot, rite, road, rule, tack, tone, wise, wont 5 calle, cause, guise, habit, means, order, point, route, space, stulm, style, track, trail, usage 6 ambage, arcade, artery, aspect, avenue, bypath, career, chemin, course, custom, design, device, manner, method, motion, reason, scheme, sphere, system 7 advance, calling, channel, fashion, feature, freedom, headway, HIGHWAY, journey, passage, process, respect 8 approach, arterial, behavior, distance, district, doctrine, entrance, momentum, pavement, practice, progress 9 condition, direction, expedient, procedure, technique 10 occupation 11 disposition, progression 12 neighborhood 13 modus operandi 14 characteristic
by the apropos, aside, casually, incidentally, indirectly
god hermes
in contact, entrance
in a after a fashion
indirect ambages, bypath, detour
narrow drang
of the cross via dolorosa
on the agate, begun, enroute, launched, started, toward
open the pioneer
out egress, escape, exit, outlet
under in motion, moving, progressing
up high, important, lofty
-wise experienced, sharp

WAYBILL itinerary, passenger-list, willie

WAYFARER dustyfoot, itinerant, nomad, passenger, pilgrim, shuiler, tourist, tramp, transient, traveler, viator, visitor, voyager

WAYFARING *tree* cottoner, viburnum, whitten

WAYGATE departure, headway, passageway, path

WAYLAND volund, wieland
kin egil, wade

WAYLAY ambuscade, ambush, assail, assault, attack, await, belay, beset, forelay,
forestall, forset, obstruct, rob, seize, surprise

WAYMAKER precursor

WAYMAN platelayer, shipwright

WAYMARK ahu, arrow, guidepost, milestone

WAYSIDE verge
stop hostel, inn, motel, parao, posada

WAYWARD capricious, contrary, corrupt, cussed, disobedient, disorderly, errant, erratic, erring, fallen, fickle, fluctuating, fractious, frail, froward, headstrong, inconstant, infirm, intractable, irregular, naughty, peccable, perverse, prodigal, refractory, restive, self-willed, stubborn, unpredictable, unruly, unstable, unsteady, untoward, unvirtuous, wanton, weak, willful

WAYWISER odometer, pedometer, perambulator

WEAK 3 dim, lax, lew, low, wan 4 dull, flat, gone, limp, pale, puny, sely, soft, thin, vain, worn 5 anile, bauch, chirp, crank, crimp, dicky, faded, faint, frail, naish, seely, slack, small, spent, vague, washy 6 anemic, debile, dickey, droopy, effete, feeble, fickle, flabby, flimsy, infirm, limpsy, marcid, quaggy, scream, semmit, slight, squeak, watery 7 brittle, dwaible, dweeble, flaccid, foolish, fragile, insipid, languid, rickety, sapless, shallow, shilpit, spindly, tottery, unsound 8 adynamic, asthenic, decrepit, feckless, helpless, impotent, languent, listless, pithless, scrannel 9 compliant, dissolute, exhausted, impuisant, powerless 10 inadequate, irresolute, languorous, marrowless, nambypamby 11 debilitated, ineffective, vacillating
as a baby, hair, reed
comb. asthen(o), lepto
from hunger leer
-headed dizzy, dull, stupid
-hearted scared, timid
-kneed frail, irresolute, yielding
knees cold feet
-minded daft, dotty, foolish, soft
-muscled amyous
point danger, fault, frailty
-willed pliable

WEAKEN abate, afflict, appall, attenuate, blunt, break, cave in, conk out, cripple, deacon, deaden, debilitate, decay, decline, decrease, delay, depotentiate, depress, devitalize, die, dilute, diminish, disable, disarm, droop, drop, dull, enervate, enfeeble, exhaust, extenuate, fade, fail, fizzle, flag, give out, impair, labefy, languish, lessen, mitigate, moderate, modify, modulate, peter out, pine, play out, poop out, qualify, rebate, reduce, relax, sap, shake, sicken, sink, slacken, temper, thin, undermine, unman, unnerve, unstring, vitiate, wane, waste, water, waver, wilt, wither

WEAKENED decrepit, groggy, invalid, strained, thinned

WEAKENING attenuation, chronic, deadening, debilitation, diluent, dilution, enervation, fatigue, flagging, languor, reduction, thinning

WEAKFISH acoupa, bluefish, chickwit, corvina, cynoscion, drum, salmon, squeteague, totoaba, totuava, trout

WEAKLING baby, canary, chicken, coward, creampuff, dilling, doormat, dotard, droop, jellyfish, ladyfinger, lightweight, milksop, milquetoast, mollycoddle, namby-pamby, pantywaist, puler, pushover, reckling, ribe, sadsack, shilp, sissy, softy, sop, tenderfoot

WEAKNESS achilles heel, acratia, adynamia, anemia, apathy, asthenia, astheny, atonia, atony, cachexia, crack, craze, debility, decay, decrepitude, delicacy, deterioration, dilution, dottiness, emaciation, exhaustion, failing, faintness, fatigue, fault, flimsiness, foible, folly, fondness, fragility, frailty, frangibility, grogginess, impotence, inability, infirmity, instability, languor, lassitude, shakiness,

softness, unsteadiness, wee-wows, wilt
vocal phonasthenia
WEAKY damp, wet
WEAL body politic, choice, choose, commonwealth, happiness, pomp, prosperity, riches, state, stripe, success, wale, wealth, welfare, well-being, welt, wheal, whip
WEALD forest, plain, wold
WEALTH abundance, acquisition, affluence, assets, capital, catallum, dhan, estate, fortune, funds, gold, good(s), graith, happiness, lucre, luxury, mammon, money, opulence, pelf, pile, plenty, possessions, profusion, property, prosperity, resources, richdom, riches, shower, substance, talent, treasure, wad, warison, weal, welfare, worth
accumulated assets, capital, ch(i)evance, estate
comb. pluto
god bhaga, chao of the dark terrace, jambhala, kuvera, plutus, tsaishen, tsengfutsaichen
goddess benten, lakshmi, sarasvati, shree, shri, sri
patron yaksha
personified mammon
pursuit of plutomania
rule by plutocracy
science of aphnology, economics, plutology, plutonomy
source aladdin's lamp, bonanza, golconda
worship plutolatry
WEALTHY abundant, affluent, ample, bien, couthie, fat, flush, full, heeled, independent, loaded, lush, moneyed, opulent, pecunious, plush, pursy, rich, solid, substantial, tinny, well-fixed, well-heeled, well-off, well-to-do
class nabobery, plutocracy, society, zaibatsu
man See MAN *rich.*
name meaning darius
suddenly new-rich, nouveau riche
WEAN ablactate, alienate, baby, child, convert, convince, detach, disaffect, estrange, infant, reconcile,

separate, sever, wayne, withdraw
WEANER calf, fledgling, hogget, lamb
WEAPON (See also specific weapons, e.g., GUN.) arms, beak, claw, implement, spur, talon
axe-like vouge
bearer armiger, fighter, soldier
collection arsenal
hammer-like martel-de-fer
hurling bolo, boomerang
kind adaga, arrow, assagai, axe, baselard, battle-axe, bayonet, bazooka, bilbo, bill(y), blade, blowgun, bola(s), bolo, boomerang, bow, brass knuckles, brickbat, broadsword, cannon, c(h)akra, claymore, club, creese, crossbow, cutlass, dagger, dart, dirk, drudgeon, falchion, falx, fauchard, foil, gisarme, glaive, GUN, halberd, harpoon, hatchet, javelin, jereed, jerrid, katar, knife, kris, kukri, lance, macana, mace, machete, patu, pike, poleaxe, poniard, rapier, saber, scimitar, skean(dhu), SPEAR, spontoon, stiletto, SWORD, toledo, tomahawk, tuck, yataghan
lay down disarm, surrender
medieval morning-star
prehistoric celt
returns to sender atlatl, boomerang, hammer of thor, mjolnir
shafted guisarme
sharpener acutiator
stone-throwing martinet, slingshot
super a-bomb, charged particles, death ray, energy beam, h-bomb, laser beam, missile, ROCKET
without barehanded, unarmed
WEAR abrade, bear, become, care, carry, chafe, clothes, clothing, consume, corrode, decay, decline, decrease, defend, defense, degrade, display, dissipate, don, dress, eat, efface, endure, erode, exhaust, fashion, fatigue, fray, frazzle, fret, garments, grow, guard, impair, last, oppose, progress, protect, remain, rub(off), rust,

scrape, scuff, service, show, spend, spoil, sport, stand, stop, tatter, use, vogue, waste, weary, weather
and tear decay, decrease, erosion, grueling, injury, slite
away abrade, batter, contrive, corrode, dissipate, eat, end, erode, fade, fray, fret, gall, gnaw, pine, rub, rust, scour
down bray, break, fatigue, grind, influence, overcome, persuade, reduce, weary
on continue, endure, grind
out break, consume, decay, dissipate, efface, erase, exhaust, expire, fatigue, harass, jade, outlast, overwork, sha(u)chle, slite, spend, tax, tire, tucker, weary
the pants boss, control, domineer
WEARABLES dress, duds, glad rags, rags, togs
WEARIED See WEARY.
WEARINESS ennui, fatigue, lassitude, tedium
WEARING abrasion, decay, grinding, taxing, tiring, WEARISOME
away attrition, detrition, erosion
WEARISOME annoying, arduous, boring, dismal, dree, dry, dull, exhausting, fatiguing, gloomy, humdrum, irksome, laborious, monotonous, operose, prolix, stupid, tedious, tiresome, tiring, wearing, weary
WEARY all in, blase, bore(d), bush(ed), collapsed, debilitate(d), depress(ed), disastrous, enfeeble(d), exhaust(ed), fag(ged), fatigate, fatigue(d), fed up, forjesket, grieved, impatient, irk(ed) (some), jade(d), languid, pall, peter out, plague(d), puny, sad, sickly, spent, squeal, succumb, surfeited, tedious, tire(d), tiresome, tucker, unfortunate, weak, wear, weigh(down), wilt, worn, wretched
willie featherbedder, idler, laggard, shirker, tramp, vagrant
WEASAND esophagus, gullet, throat, trachea, windpipe

WEASEL arctoid, cane, equivocate, ermine, ferret, futteret, hulda, huldah, huron, inform, marten, mislead, muishond, mustela, mustelle, rasse, ratel, sable, sneak, sto(a)t, taira, tayra, vair, vare, vermin, vormela, wair, ware, whitrack, zoril
cat linsang
coot smew
name meaning huldah
WEASELSKIN money, pocketbook, purse
WEASELSNOUT dead-nettle
WEATHER air, brave, climate, clime, elements, expose, persevere, rain, ride out, shower, snow, storm, sustain, tempest, vicissitude, wear, wind(ward)
-beaten bronzed, damaged, dilapidated, erose, sea-going, tanned, toughened, worn
cock faine, fanacle, fane, impatiens, jewelweed, vane
cold numb
divination by aeromancy
fair slatch
fish loach, misgurnus
forecasting spherics
gall or *gaw* rainbow, sundog
gauge barometer, sonde
good flying cavu
hot dog days
hot, humid sizzard
man forecaster, meteorologist
map line isobar, isogradient, isohume, isoneph, isotach, isotherm
out endure, prevail, recover, survive, triumph
satellite essa, tiros, tyros
science barometry, climatology, meteorology
under the ill, intoxicated, seedy, sick, tipsy, unwell
WEATHERPROOF impervious, rain-repellent, secure, tight
WEAVE braid, complect, contrive, crochet, darn, devise, enlace, entwine, fabric(ate), fashion, interknit, interlace, intertwine, intertwist, interwind, intort, knit, lace, loom, loop, make-up, pla(i)t, plash, pleach, pleat, produce, raddle, reel, shuttle, spin, splice, sway, texture, twill, twine, twist,

unite, warp, wattle, web, woof, wreath, writhe
basket barleycorn
carpet flossa
herringbone shemaka, so(u)-mak
kind broche, camille, cassimere, damask, duchesse, herringbone, jacquard, leno, net, satin, satinet, twill, uni, web
lattice tee
open barege, leno
patterns brocade
twigs wattle
WEAVER drawboy, knitter, kori, loom, penelope, spider, tanti, tapester, webbe, webster, wobster
bobbin pirn
paste buckety, sowens
reed raddle, slay, sleigh, sley, spear
WEAVERBIRD amadavat, avadavat, baya, bengali, bishop, bittern, boonk, botaurus, bottlebump, canary, cardinal, finch, mannikin, maya, munia, nun, oxbird, philetaerus, silverbill, taha, treesparrow, vidua, whidah, whydah
WEAVING (See also LOOM references.) reeling, taniko, texture, tottering
bar temple
beam craneway, tavil, tram
goddess ergane, minerva
implement batten, boat, evener, guideway, heck, lathe, lay, reed, shuttle, sley
machine carder, jacquard, LOOM
pert. textile, textorial
product cloth, fabric, textile
term beam, beer, bobbin, caaming, cop, lappet, lease, lisse, neck, ravel, uni, warp, woof
together plexure
WEAZEN See WIZEN.
WEB bandana, bit, blade, caul, cloth, entangle, fabric, filament, fleece, gossamer, membrane, mesh, net(work), omentum, plait, plate, ply, rete, scheme, snare, spin, structure, tela, texture, tissue, toil, trap, twist, vane, vexillum, weave, weft, wickerwork
comb. hypho
crank throw
eye haw

-foot fenman, oregonian
-footed oary, pal(a)mate, palmiped, ringed, totipal(a)mate
-footed animal beaver, hydromys
-footed bird albatross, avocet, duck(bill), goose, loon, platypus
-foot state oregon
-maker embiid, spider, spineret
pert. pal(a)mate, retial, retiary, reticular, reticulated, ringed, spidery, telarian, telary
tissue tela
WEBBING lobation, network, palama, palmation
WEBER *opera* der freischutz, euryanthe, oberon
WEBSTER, DANIEL ichabod
WED couple(d), engage, espouse, hitch, join, married, marry, mate, merge, pawn, pledge, splice(d), spouse, stake, tie, unite, wager, wive
pert. marital
WEDDED attached, joined, married, matrimonial, spliced, united
WEDDING bridewain, chasseneh, espousal(s), espousement, khasseneh, marriage, matrimony, tial(s), spousal(s), wedlock
anniversary bronze, candy, china, copper, coral, cotton, crystal, diamond, emerald, floral, flower, fruit, gold(en), iron, ivory, jade, lace, leather, linen, paper, pearl, pottery, ruby, sapphire, silk, silver, steel, tin, willow, wooden, wool
canopy chuppa, huppa
gift dot, dow(e)ry, mahr
proclamation banns
symbol rice, ring
WEDGE angle, bar, cake, cam, chock, chuck, cleat, cleave, coign(e), coin, cotter, crowd, cuneus, cusp, embolus, fix, froe, frow, gib, glut, gore, gusset, horn, horse, ingot, interpose, jam, key, kyle, lump, quine, quinnet, quoin, rive, schoche, scotch, shim, slice, sliver, sprag, stow, trip, voussoir, wage
comb. spheno

curved cam
driver beetle
in fix, force, jam(b), push
-shaped cuneal, cuneate,
cuneiform, sphenic, sphenoid, triangular, ulnare
wooden cow, glut, jack
WEDLOCK See MAR-
RIAGE.
WEDNESDAY *source of
name* woden
WEE diminutive, little, microscopic, miniature, minute, peewee, petite, pewee,
small, teeny, tiny, weeny,
weeshie, weeshy, woe,
young
willie winkie william prince
of orange
WEED(S) (See also *kind,
below*.) armor, cheat, chop,
cigar(ette), clear, clothes,
costume, crape, cull, de-
duct, dregs, dress, eradicate,
extirpate, fag, flesh, free,
garb, garment, hoe, junk,
lymphangitis, marijuana,
mourning, pest, purloin, reject, relapse, remove, sarcle, smoke, tares, tobacco,
trumpery, unroot, uproot,
wrack
aquatic callitriche, starwort
aromatic tansy
asthma lobelia
biblical tare
cornfield darnel
free from rode
jimson stramonium
killer herbicide
kind alfileria, ashwort, bur,
burr, candlewick, chadlock,
cockspur, cohitre, cowheat,
cuckold, dandelion, darnel,
datura, dock, dodder, egilops, flannelleaf, forb,
good-king-henry, gosmore,
gravelroot, hogroot, jimson,
joepye, kex, knawel, knotgrass, loco, louk, mallows,
marijuana, maruta, mat-
fel(l)on, mulle(i)n, oxalis,
piripiri, plantain, potentilla,
purslane, sandbur, sealwort,
shim, spurge, tare, toadflax,
tobacco, trumpery, vervain,
vetch
may maruta
medicinal colt's-foot, spurge
out cull, eliminate, extirpate,
extract, sarcle
poisonous loco, nightshade
prickly bur(r), nettle
sacred vervain

WEEDER sarcler
WEEDING *implement*
aberuncator, hoe, spud
WEEDY foul, lanky, lean,
overgrown, rank, scraggy,
ungainly
WEEK(S) hebdomad, ouk,
oulk, semaine, semana, sennet, sennight, septimana,
settimana, swueak, woche,
wok(e)
day feria(le)
feast of pentecost, shabuoth
interval octan, septan
pert. hebdomadary
2 fortnight
WEEKLY hebdomadal, hebdomadary, septenary
WEEL basket, eddy, pool,
trap, well, whirlpool
WEEN belief, believe, conceive, expect(ation), fancy,
guess, imagine, mean, probability, suppose, surmise,
think, vene, wend
WEEP bawl, bend, bewail,
bleed, blubber, boohoo,
complain, cry, drip, droop,
excrete, exude, grieve, keen,
lament, lapwing, leak,
mewl, moan, mourn, ooze,
orp, percolate, piangere,
pleurer, pule, rain, run,
shed, snivel, sob, squall,
squinny, suppurate, wail,
whimper, yowl
WEEPING begrutten, dripping, lachrymose, lacrimal,
lamentation, madidans,
maudlin, pendent, plora-
tion, rainy, tearful, teary,
vagitus, wailful
philosopher heraclitus
sinew ganglion
spruce brewer's, picea
statue niobe
willow babylonian
WEET bird, know, sandpiper,
wet, wit, wryneck
WEEVER catfish, jugular,
stingbull, trachinus
WEEVIL anthonomus, apion,
beetle, billbug, boll, boud,
bruchus, calandra, curculio,
funnel-twister, laria, lota,
picudo, pope, spheno-
phorus, vaquita, weeble,
woodworm
boll picudo
groove scrobe
plum turk
WEEWOW crooked, irregular, sway, twist, unsteady
WEFT fabric, filling, film,

mist, shoot, shute, waif,
warp, web, woof, yarn
threads tram
WEIGH analyze, apportion,
appraise, assess, balance,
bear, burden, calculate,
carry, compare, consider,
contemplate, dispense, esteem, estimate, evaluate,
examine, heave, heft, hoist,
induce, influence, judge, librate, measure, meditate,
muse, oppress, peize, poise,
ponder, rate, reflect, regard,
revolve, stress, study, support, tax, test, think, trutinate, value
anchor cast off, embark,
launch, loose, start, take
off, unmoor
down or *on* afflict, burden,
cumber, depress, encumber,
freight, hamper, harass,
harry, lade, load, oppress,
overbalance, press, sink, sit,
torment, worry
out apportion
WEIGHED advised, bal-
anced, experienced, intentional, laden, measured,
tested, tried
WEIGHING *instrument* balance, beam, scale(s), steelyard, tron(e)
WEIGHT (See also under individual countries.) affliction, authority, avoirdupois,
ballast, beef, bob, burden,
charge, clout, consequence,
consideration, credit, dumbbell, emphasis, fat(ness),
gravity, hammer, heaviness,
heft, impediment, impor-
tance, incubus, influence,
iron, lead, load, mas-
siveness, maund, moment,
net, obesity, onerousness,
onus, oppressiveness, overbalance, pari, peis(e),
plumb, plummet, poise, potency, poundage, power,
pressure, prestige, quin-
cunx, ram, sandbag, seri-
ousness, shot, significance,
sinker, size, stamp, stress,
suttle, value, worth
allowance beamage, bug,
scalage, tare, tret
balance rider
balancing ballast
carat siliqua
chaser miner, prospector
cheese clove, nail
clock peise

cloth flock
coal keel, quintale, ton
coffee mat
comb. bar(o)
false slang
have militate
heavy monkey
inspector sealer
lead pig, plumb
-lifting apparatus barbell
light suttle
loss deduction beamage
measure or *unit* (See also under individual countries.) bale, bushel, carat, crith, decagram, duella, dung, gorraf, gram, hoon, kantar, kat, kilo(gram), kin(tar), last, liang, libra, lingo(e), lispound, lispund, liter, livre, lod, metage, minal, miskal, momme, ounce, perit, picul, pocket, pound, pund, puud, quintal, reba(h), retti, rotl, ruay, se(e)r, stein, talent, tampang, ton(elada), uckia, vis, wey, yava, yin, zar, zolotnik
moneyers' droit
of equal isobaric
official metage
of uniform homobaric
perception barognosis
pert. baric, ponderal, ponderary
producing gravific
remover dieter
sashcord mouse
science barology, metrology
shuffleboard ship
silk drammage, pari
small gerah, gram, mite, rider
spline dolphin
stabilizer balance, ballast
system avoir(dupois), metric, troy
take on fatten
unit See *measure,* above.
varying man, maund
without cipher
wool clove, nail, tod
WEIGHTED burdened, charged, cumbered, encumbered, evaluated, freighted, hampered, incumbered, laden, loaded, oppressed, taxed
WEIGHTY authoritative, big, bulky, burdensome, capital, carking, conclusive, corpulent, cumbersome, distressing, earnest, exacting, fat, grave, great, grievous, heavy, hefty, impressive,

influential, large, leaden, magisterial, massive, massy, material, momentous, onerous, oppressive, ponderous, powerful, serious, severe, significant, sober, solemn, solid, somber, thumping, troublesome, unwieldy, valid
WEIMAR *legislature* reichsrat(h)
WEIR bank, barrier, burrock, cauld, dam, doach, fence, fishpond, garth, gorce, levee, milldam, seine, stank, trap
WEIRD awful, bizarre, charm, curious, deathly, destine, destiny, eccentric, eerie, eery, eldritch, elrische, fate, fearful, fetish, foretell, fortune, inscrutable, macabre, magic(al), mysterious, odd, omen, peculiar, predict(ion), prophecy, queer, secret, soothsayer, spectral, spell, spookish, spooky, strange, supernatural, uncanny, unco, unearthly, unko, warn, wild, wizardly
sisters See NORN.
WEIRDLY fateful, fortunate, ghostly, happy
WEIRDO creep, dingaling, eccentric, freak, oddball, queer
WEISS, ERICH houdini
WEJACK fisher, pekan
WEKA rail(bird), woodhen
WELCOME accept(able), accoil, accueil, admit, adopt, agreeable, benvenuto, bienvenue, congenial, desirable, embrace, entertain, grateful, gratifying, greet(ing), hail, ovation, pleasant, pleasing, receive, reception, salutation, salute, satisfying
WELD acacia, adhere, arc, bind, cement, consolidate, fuse, join, solder, union, unite, wo(a)ld, would
imperfect cold-shut
WELDING *gas* acetylene
implement blowpipe, blowtorch
mixture thermit
WELFARE alms, benison, blessing, charity, cheer, dole, good, happiness, heal(th), plenty, prosper(ity), sele, success, thrive, weal, wellbeing

goddess salus
WELK decrease, dry up, fade, wane
WELKIN air, atmosphere, heaven(s), sky, vault, walkene
WELL acceptable, adequate, ain, artesian, aweel, bene, bien, boil, booly, borehole, bueno, closely, cockpit, compartment, dight, emanate, enough, expertly, fair, favored, fine, fit, flow, font, fortunate, fount(ain), fully, gasser, gay, good, gradely, graithly, gush(er), healthy, hearty, hole, intimately, issue, jet, justly, much, musha, pit, pour, proper, pumper, quite, reservoir, rightly, robust, satisfactory, seethe, shaft, sound, source, spring, spurt, successfully, suitable, sump, tolerable, trig, very, vessel, weal (some), welt, whirlpool, wholesome, wildcat
-adapted apposite, appropriate, germane, pertinent, relevant
-armed prepared, ready
-balanced even, level-headed, proportional, sensible, sober, symmetrical
-behaved courteous, couth, decorous, good, modest, nice, obedient, orderly, polite
-being comfort, eucrasia, eucrasy, eudaemonia, eudaemony, euphoria, felicity, good, happiness, health, prosperity, success, weal, wealth, welfare
borer bellscrew, tiger
-born or *-bred* blooded, civil, cultivated, cultured, eugenic, genteel, gentle(manly), lady-like, noble, pedigreed, polite, refined, regal, rich, royal, thoroughbred
-born, name meaning eugene
-built shapely, solid, strong, sturdy
casing steaning
comb. agath(o), bene
curb puteal
deep artesian
-defined clear, distinct(ive), evident, exact, sharp, strict
-disposed considerate, cordial, fain, friendly
-doer do-gooder, philanthropist

done bien, bravo, bully, crisp, euge, good, ole, overcooked, shabash

-dressed braw, brawlie, brawly(s), chic, fashionable, modish, smart, stylish, trig

-favored fair, handsome, pleasing, pretty, shapely

-fed blowsy, chubby, fat, gawcey, gawsy, heavy

fern venus's-hair

-fixed See RICH, WEALTHY.

-formed eumorphous, seemly, shapely

-founded established, firm, good, logical, plausible, reliable, solid, sound, sturdy, valid, worthy

-groomed chic, clean, neat, sharp, sleek, smart, soigne(e), trig

-grounded See *-founded*, above.

-head fountain, source, spring

-heeled See RICH, WEALTHY.

-informed au courant, au fait, educated, knowing, knowledgeable

-kept clean, neat, spick-and-span, taut, tidy, trim

-known breem, celebrated, common(place), current, eminent, familiar, famous, kenned, notorious, outstanding, popular, prominent, proverbial, public, trite

-liked admired, fancied, popular

lining stean(ing), steen(ing), steyn(ing)

-made affabrous, shapely, solid, sturdy, workmanlike

-named euonymous

-nigh almost, approximately, nearly

nonproductive duster

-off See RICH, WEALTHY.

oil gasser, gusher, spouter, wildcat

-paying lucrative, profitable, remunerative

pert. phreatic

pit sump

pole sweep

-proportioned handsome, tretis

-qualified able, capable, experienced, trained

-read bookish, cultured, learned, literary, studied

rectangular booly, bowly

-rounded chubby, zaftig

sacred zemzem

-timed apt, fitting, happy, opportune, pat, seasonable, timely

-to-do See RICH, WEALTHY.

-versed adept, erudite, knowledgeable, sharp, skilled, smart

-wisher friend

-worn hackneyed, moth-eaten, ragged, stale, threadbare, tired, trite

WELLADAY alack

WELLINGTON *charger* copenhagen

nickname iron duke, old nosey

victory waterloo

WELLS, H. G. *work* ann veronica, history of mr polly, invisible man, marriage, meanwhile, open conspiracy, time machine, tono bungay

WELS sheatfish, waller

WELSH (See WALES for geographic entries.) brythonic, cambrain, celt, cheat, cymraeg, cymric, fudge, kymric, kymry, shirk

drake gadwall

fiddle itch

main cockfight

parsley hemp, noose

rabbit goldenbuck, rarebit

WELSHER absconder, defaulter, delinquent, dodger, levanter, quitter, skedaddler

WELSHMAN blackbass, brython, celt, cymric, fudge, kymric, squirrelfish, taffy

WELT band(elette), beat, blow, border, bruise, bulge, edge, flap, fringe, hem, join, lap, lash, mark, mouse, quilt, ridge, roll, sew, strip(e), stroke, swelling, thrash, turn(over), upset, wale, wallop, weal, whelp, wilt

shoe wattis

WELTER confusion, flounder, grovel, jumble, overturn, pitch, reel, roll, slough, smother, stagger, strive, struggle, toss, tumble, tumult, turmoil, wallow, wilt, wither, writhe

WEM corrupt, flaw, harm, scar, spot, stain, wame

WEMOD angry, peevish, sullen

WEN blemish, clier, clyer, cyst, excrescence, goiter, growth, imperfection, mole, rune, talpa, tumor, wyn(n)

WENCH audry, baggage, blowen, blowze, child, court, damsel, dell, drab, drazel, girl, gouge, hussy, jade, kitty, maid(en), minx, moll, poplolly, prostitute, quean, servant, squaw, strumpet, trollop, trug, trull, wotlink

WEND alter, change, circuit, convert, depart, direct, lusatian, meander, move, overthrow, pass, perambulation, proceed, shift, slav, sorb (ian), steer, translate, travel, turn, vanish, walk, ween

WENDY *dog* nana

friend peter pan

WENROS eries

WENT alley, course, crossroad, device, gode, journey, lane, passage(way), plan, progress, road, way, yede

WENZEL jack, knave

WER fine, husband, man, vassal, warrior, wergild

WERE apprehension, check, difficulty, doubt, dread, guard, peril, perplexity, uncertainty, ward off

WEREWOLF loup-garou, lycanthrope, turnskin, uturuncu, versipel

WERGILD blood money, bloodwite, cro, eric, fine

WERI aweto

WERTHER *beloved* lotte

WESER *city on* bremen, hamein, hamelin

WESKIT See WAISTCOAT.

WESSEX *king* ine, ini

WEST frontier, occident, sty, waste

doctrine manifest destiny

guardian of the virupaksa

queen of the athyr, hathor

WEST AFRICA *anteater* pangolin

antelope grimme, korrigum, royal

baboon drill

bay bight of biafra

chevrotain boomarah

city accra, kumasi, timbuktu

dance ring-shout
deity asia(-bussu), evua, famien, guruhi, kaka-guia, kitabo, legba, mahou, mao, nampa, nyamia, rick-sene, sakarabru, sunguin, wokolo
duiker philantomba
fiber bolobolo
god nyambe, nzambi
gulf guinea
island fernando po
language ewe, kwa
minnow gularis
mongoose kusimanse(1)
monkey cercocebus, mona, patas, potto, talapoin
mortar swish
musician griot
people achango, akim, ashantee, ashanti, bube, bullom, ediya, egbe, ewe, habe, krepi, kru, nama, tshi, yoruba
raid panyar
reedbuck nagor
river gambia
sheep zenu
squall tornado
state ashanti, bambara, biafra, bornu, dagomba, dahomey, fulani, ghana, goldcoast, gonja, hausa, kaarta, liberia, mossi, oyo, sierra leone, tucolor, upper volta, yoruba
storyteller griot
tree abura, akee, almique, bubinga, bumbo, daniella, didelotia, ebony, manilkara, mitragyna, odum, sapele, sassy(wood)
wood aboudikro
W.ESTERN fiction, hesperian, horse-opera, lancer, oater, occidental, ponent, scaean
bird bluebird, flycatcher
clematis virgin's-bower
dialect chinook
fish rainbow trout, steelhead
hackberry paloblanco
hanging necktie party
indian haw, hopi, kaw, oto(e), paviotso, ree, seri, ute
islands hebrides
land hesperia
movie horse-opera, oater
mugwort prairie-sage
pact nato, oas, salt, seato
range cascades
range horse broomtail
spectacle rodeo
wallflower dogbane, prairie-rocket

wheat grass andropogon, bluejoint, bluestem, palmetto
WEST GERMANY (See also GERMANY.) *capital* bonn
city berlin, ludwigshafen, oberhausen, offenbach, oldenburg, saarbrucken
language langobardic
territory saar(land)
WEST INDIES *agave* keratto
angelfish isabelita
apple manzanilla
aroid tania
bark tonic canella
barracuda picudilla
bayberry ausu, auzu
bean frijolillo
bird ani, arar, egret, gaulding, gaulin, heron, mucaro, tania, tody
boat catamaran, droger, droghier, moses
cactus barbados gooseberry, blad(e)apple, bullsucker, opuntia, pereskia, pricklywithe
calabash curuba
carriage kittereen
cavalla green-jack
charm obeah, obi
chief cacique
clingfish testar
cockroach drummer
coin anchor-money, bit, daler, stampee
communal living matelotage
corkwood harefoot
crustacean splitfinger
dialect creole
dish tumtum
dog, wild cimarron
drink sangaree
drum bamboula, bongo, gumbe, gumby
evergreen calaba
fabric guana
fiber cajun
fig jamaica-cherry
fish acedia, aguavina, atinga, bacalao, bang, banner, barracuda, bessy cerka, blackfin, black oldwife, blanco, boga, burfish, carbonero, cero, chopa(blanca), clingfish, cockeye-pilot, coney, cubera, doncella, elephotoxon, guapena, isabetita, lebrancho, marian, matajuela, oldwife, pary, pegador, pelon, peto, phoebe, picudilla, pintado, pompano, puneca, razorfish, redhind, robalo, rockhind, ronco, sa-

lema, scirenga, sesi, snapper, tang, tattler, testar, trachinotus, triggerfish, yellowgrunt
5-pence bit
flavoring cassareep
flea chigoe, chigre
flycatcher pipiri
fruit carambola, genipap, papaya, pa(w)paw, tuna
gar aguijadecasta
gastropod bleeding-tooth
gaulin egret, heron
gherkin bur-cucumber, cucumis
goby mapo
governor bobadilla
grass bahama, bermuda
grouper yellowfish
grunt lobotes, ronco, tripletail
gulf darien, honduras
handkerchief malabar
hemp sisal
herb ass's-foot, coltsfoot, ocra, tronador, vanglo(e)
hummingbird doctorbird, froufrou
hut bohio
idol zeme, zemi
insect drummer, fourmifou
island anguilla, antigua, antilles, aruba, bahamas, barbados, barbuda, bequia, bermuda, bonaire, caribbean, cayman, cuba, curacao, dominica, french guiana, grenada, guadeloupe, guyana, haiti, hispaniola, isle of pines, jamaica, martinique, montserrat, nassau, nevis, puerto rico, robalo, saba, snook, st christopher, st eustatius, st kitts, st lucia, st martin, st vincent, tobago, tortola, trinidad
island group antilles, grenadine, leewards, virgin, windwards
kale malanga
key cay
king cacique
language gullah
liquor mobbie, mobby, rum, taf(f)ia
lizard ameiva, anoli, arbalo
locust algar(r)oba
magic obe(ah), obi
magician quimboiseur
martin agujadecasta
mistletoe gadbush
mojarra patao
morning glory campanilla

moth urania
mullet lebrancho
music calypso
myrtle ausu, bayberry
nut bichy
orchid greenwithe, purplelips
owl mucaro
palm grigri, grugru, prickly-pole, yagua, yaray
peanut pinda
people carib, creole, cuban, ebo(e), fustee, fustie, gullah, mustee, taino
pert. antillean, caribbean
petrel diablotin
pirate blackbeard
plant cankerberry, redwithe
plum jobo
port basseterre, fort de france, pointe-a-pitre, port of spain
prickly pear pinpillow
raiders brethren of the coast
red hind cabrilla
region malabar
remora pega
rhubarb yawweed
rodent agouti, agouty, hutia, jutia
root jim-crow's-nose
sardine bang
scorpion fish rascacio
scrapper caji
sea caribbean, sargasso
shark gata, tiburon
sheephead salema
shrub anil, annatto, barbados cherry, baskethoop, baylavender, cascarilla, cassava, croton, dama de noche, earwort, ebo(e), horsebush, inga, joewood, lagetta, mallotonia, pich, ratwood, rodwood, scarletweed, velvetseed
snail cerion, urocoptis
snake fer-de-lance
snake god zombi
snapper cubera, sesi
snuff maccaboy, maccoboy
sorcery obe, obi, voodoo
spook plateye
squirrelfish matajuelo
stew pepperpot
storm houvari
strait windward passage
sugar works usine
sweetheart doudou
tallowtree cera
taro tania
tonic canella
tortoise hicatee, hiccatee
tree acana, acapu, aceituna, allspice, almacigo, almique,

aloe, andira, angelin, ausubo, balata, balsa, bayberry, bayrum, bitterwood, blolly, bonace, breakaxe, bustic, cabbage, calaba, candlewood, cera, clam-mycherry, cockspur, cocullo, cocuswood, cocuyo, cogwood, courbaril, dilly, doncella, dorewood, drumwood, ebony, genip, gomart, guavaberry, gumbo (limbo), gwazuma, horsebush, inkwood, jacana, jagua, lacebark, libidi, limbo, loblolly, mangrove, manjack, mora, palmiste, papaya, pa(w)paw, pimento, ramoon, ribbonwood, sabicu, santa maria, sapodilla, sapote, sequoia, slogwood, snakebark, starapple, strongbark, touchwood, yacca
treewood galba
vine basketwood, byrony, pelican-flower
vireo john-to-whit
volcano pelee, soufriere
warbler soufriere-bird, titien
wasp jack-spaniard
yam wawwaw
WESTMINSTER *abbey*
builder edward the confessor
abbey section poets' corner
clock big ben
WEST, NATHANAEL *novel* day of the locust, miss lonelyhearts
WESTPHALIA *chief* wittekind
city castrop-rauxel, munster
commune altena
king jerome bonaparte
WEST POINT *father* thayer
island iona
mascot mule
student cadet, plebe, yearling
WEST, REBECCA cicily isabel fairfield andrews
WEST SAXON *earl* godwin
WEST VIRGINIA *capitol* charleston
city beckley, bluefield, clarksburg, fairmont, grafton, keyser, martinsburg, morgantown, parkersburg, ripley, spencer, vienna, weirton, weston, wheeling
college bethany, bluefield, concord, marshall, salem
county barbour, kanawha, mingo, roane, upshur
indian moneton

lake lynn
motto montani semper liberi
mountain man coker
native mountaineer
nickname mountain state, panhandle state
peak spruce-knob
river elk, guyandot, kanawa, monongahela, ohio, potomac
statebird cardinal
state flower rhododendron
state tree maple
WESTWARD bewest, occasive, wessel
WET asop, bathe, bedew, clashy, crazy, dabby, daggle, daggly, damp(en), dank, dewy, drabble, drench(ed), drink, dripping, drunk, flotter, foggy, hose, humid(ity), imbrue, immerse, insane, irrigate, jarble, lax, liquor, mad, madid, mire, misguided, misty, moist(en), moisture, mooth, off, perspire, rain(y), ret, saturate(d), shower, slopped, slottery, soak(ed), soggy, sopping, soppy, souse, splash, sprinkle, sweat, tearful, tipsy, uvid, wash, water(y), waterlogged, wrong
as a fish
behind the ears green, naive, raw
bird chaffinch
-*blanket* bore, dampen, deadhead, depress, discourage, dispirit, drip, jerk, killjoy, kvetch(er), quench, spoilsport
-*bob* boater, rower
comb. hygr(o)
lightly drizzle, sprinkle
-*my-lip* quail
-*nurse* care for, foster, nourish, nurture
one's whistle drink
WETBACK bracero, peon
WETHER calf, dinman, dinmont, eunuch, ram, sheep, wool
lamb pur
WETTING drink, drop, liquid, moiling, nip, tot
WEVET cobweb
WEY agitate, bewail, lament, move, wee, weigh, why
WHACK allowance, attempt, bang, bargain, beat, belt, biff, blow, bop, condition, crack, deal, divide, excel,

fettle, hit, lam(baste), order, part, period, piece, portion, quack, share, slap, state, strike, stroke, swack, thwack, trial, try, turn, whale, whang, whip
down fell
up apportion, divide, divvy, share
WHACKER drover, lie, quaker, whopper
WHACKING big, enormous, great, huge, large, whopping
WHACKY See WACKY.
WHALE abramis, balaena, baleen, basilosaurus, beat, beluga, blackfish, blower, bottlehead, bowhead, cachalot, cet(e), cetacean, doegling, dolphin, drub, excel, finback, gibbar, gibberet, grampus, graso, hardhead, hit, humpback, huse, huso, jubartes, killer, kogia, lash, leviathan, lick, mammal, marsoon, minke, moby dick, mysticete, orc(a), ork, otary, poggy, ripsack, rorqual, scrag, sperm, spouter, strike, sulphurbottom, thrash(er), wallopp, whack, whip, whopper, zalophus, ziphian, ziphioid
-back grain-carrier, steamship, turtleback
beaked bottlehead, doegling
bird gull, petrel, phalarope, turnstone
blowhole spiracle
blubber refuse fritters
boat See WHALER.
bump on head hovel
butcher lemmer
carcass crang, krang, kreng
carcass refuse slumgullion
channel scarf
chase fall
comb. cet(o)
constellation cetus
expert cetologist
fat blubber
female cow
finback graso
food brit, herring, krill, plankton, sprat
forelimb paddle
fossil basilosauros, phocodont
fossil bone cetotolite
gray ripsack
groove scarf
group gam, herd, pod, school

hunter ahab
iron harpoon
killer ceticide, orca
leap breach
male bull
neck blubber cant
nostril blowhole
oil sperm(aceti)
oil cask cardel, rier
pert. bowhead
polar bowhead
raw muktuk
refuse fenks, gurry, twitter
-road sea
school See *group*, above.
science cetology
secretion ambergris
-shark mhor, rhinedon
skin muktuk, sculp
small blackfish, bottlehead, poggy
sperm cachalot, kogia
strip blubber from flense
-sucker remora
tail part fluke
toothed beluga, blackfish, dolphin, killer, narwhal, odentocete, porpoise, sperm, squalodon, zeuglodont
white beluga, hausen, huse, huso
young calf, cub, poggy, shorthead, stunt
WHALEBONE baleen, baya, inflexible, severe, stiff(en)
WHALEHEAD shoebill
WHALER boat, bushman, cetidide, header, hoh, quileute, spouter, sundowner, swagman, whacker, whopper
carousing mallemaroking
cask cardel, rier
cry fall
meeting gam
steerer sluer
WHALING beating, big, extraordinary, great, huge, large, thrashing, whacking, whopping,
inspector specksioneer
profit lay
WHAM marsh, swamp
WHANG bang, beat, blow, chop, chunk, cord, fling, flog, hurl, impact, lump, part, piece, rawhide, slice, strike, strip, thong, thrash, throw, whack
WHANGDOODLE frippery, jackpots, nonsense, poppycock
WHANGEE bamboo, cane, stick

WHARF bank, birth, dock, gare, jetty, key, landing, pantalan, pier, quay, shore, stade, staith, stelling, strand
fish cunner
lumper stevedore
master wharfinger
monkey ligyda
worker longshoreman, stevedore
WHARTON *character* ethan frome
WHAT active, bold, essence, hoot, hote, how, increase, matter, object, partly, portion, quick, quiddity, something, substance, that, thing, when, which, who(ever), why
for punishment, rebuke, whipping, why
have you and so forth
's what fact, life, reality, truth
will be, will be che sara sara
-you-may-call-it thingum(a) bob, thingumajig, thingummy
WHATNOT article, cabinet, etagere, miscellany, object, omnium, shelf, stand, thing
WHEAL mine, pomphus, pustule, ridge, stripe, superate, swelling, urtica, wale, weal, welt, whelk
WHEAT amelcorn, bulgur, burgul, cereal, corn, durra, durum, einkorn, emmer, frume(n)ty, fultz, grain, kanred, kubanka, marquis, pollard, poulard, semolina, soglia, spelt(oid), spica, staple, sujee, suji, triticum
and rye grown together blendcorn, triticale
beard awn
bearded agropyron, rivets
bird chaffinch, horned lark
boiled in milk frumenty, furme(n)ty, furmity
byproduct bran
cake puri
carried by a god spica
chaff or coat bran, husk
cracked groats, semolina
crushed bulgar, burgul
disease alcium, blackchaff, bunt, colbrand, ergot, fungus, mildew, rust, scab, stinking-smut, takeall
duck widgeon
gall cockle
granulated sujee, suji
grass agropyrun, bluestem

hard durum
kind federation, fultz, kanred, kybanka, marquis, squarehead, turkey
-like triticoid
louse aphid
meal at(t)a, flour, semolina
measure boll, bushel, medimnus, trug
middlings semolina, sharps
parched bulgur
pert. vulgare
processed bulgur, burgul, grits, groats, middlings, sujee, suji
product bran, bread, cereal, flour, groats, marcaroni, middlings, oil, pasta, spaghetti
repository bin, elevator, mattamore, silo
rust aecium
scab deaf-ear
sheaf garb
smut bunt, colbrand
state dakota, idaho, illinois, indiana, iowa, kansas, minnesota, missouri, montana, nebraska, ohio, oklahoma, pennsylvania, washington
stubble arrish
substance gluten, protein, starch
thief gromwell
WHEATEAR arling, bill, bird, chack(er), chat, chickell, gorsehatch, horsematch, ortolan, saxicola, snorter, spica, spike, wittall, wittol
WHEEDLE bam, blandish, blarney, cajole, cant, carn(e)y, coax, cog, court, cuittle, entice, flatter, glaver, glose, gloze, humor, importune, induce, influence, ingratitate, inveigle, jelly, lure, palaver, persuade, scrounge, seduce, tease, tweedle, whilly, whine, worm
WHEEL athey, axis, balance, bicycle, big shot, bike, buff(er), bur, carrier, caster, chukker, circle, cog, compass, cycle, disk, dollar, flier, flyer, gear, gudgeon, guide, gyrate, helm, horral, jagger, kuruma, magnate, mogul, noria, orb, pirouette, pivot, pulley, purl, reel, refrain, revolution, revolve, rhomb, roll(er), rota(te), rotator, rowel,

rull, rundle, sheave, spin, sprocket, steersman, stepney, swirl, swivel, torture, tricycle, trilobe, trindle, trolley, truck, trundle, turn, twirl, unilobe, vip, whirl, wildcat, wyle
bent toe-out
bird nightjar
bucket lifter
check brake, chock, cur(r), spoke, sprag
comb. troch(o)
diamond skive
diamond-dusted slitter
drag shoe
execution rat
5th spare
furniture caster
game See ROULETTE.
gear bilobe, driven, helical
grinding shell
grooved pulley, sheave, shiver
interrupter ticker, tikker
knitting burr
lapidary skeif
-like trochal
-like animalcule rotitei
little rotella
lock rewet
locomotive driver
logging catydid, katydid
measurer odometer, perambulator
metal fillet, gear
mill pirn
notched gear
of life zoetrope
ore bouronite, sulphide
part axle, cam, cog, felloe, felly, flange, hob, hub(cap), linchpin, lug, nave, rim, rowel, shoe, speech, spoke, sprag, sprocket, strake, tire
pert. rotal
pointed tracer
polishing bob, buff(er), scaife, skeif
potter's, kind kick, lathe, pedal, power, throw
rim felloe, felly
setting camber
shaft axle
-shaped circular, rotate, rotiform
ship's helm
small horral, truckle
spinning charkha
spinning, part treadle
spiked rowel
spur rowel
swiveling caster, cog
tank bog(e)y, bogie

timepiece balance
toothed cog, gear, pinion, roulette, rowel
torture catharine, catherine
tree paddlewood
turbine rotor
2 pairs cutts
vaned flyer
water See WATER *wheel.*
WHEELBARROW brushdrag, carrier, gurry, handcart, hod, hurlbarrow, pushcart
leg stilt
WHEELER cyclist, nightjar, poler, pusher
-dealer entrepreneur, go-getter, operator, organizer, promoter, shrewdy
WHEELHOUSE paddlebox
WHEELMAN bicyclist, cycler, cyclist, helmsman, pedalist, pilot, steerer
WHEELWRIGHT *stick* spokedog
WHEEZE adage, chestnut, coghle, contrivance, device, dodge, gag, gasp, hint, hoose, hooze, joke, krechtz, murmur, puff, rale, saw, snore, snort, tip, trick
WHELK acne, buccinum, buckie, filk, grub, maggot, papule, periwinkle, pimple, protuberance, pustule, snail, thump, wheal, winkle
WHELM cover, drainpipe, engulf, flood, immerse, overturn, upset
WHELP bear, boy, bulge, child, chit, cub, dog, fledgling, kitling, pup(py), reprobate, rib, ridge, rogue, ship, son, sprocket, tooth, wale, welt, youth
group litter
WHEMMEL confusion, fummle, overturn, toss, tumble, upset, whamble
WHEN also, although, before, come, duration, enough, how soon, since, till, until, what, whereas, whereupon, while
WHENCE antecedent, hence, source, wherefore
WHENEVER any time, as soon as, once
WHERE ubi, whither
WHEREABOUTS bearings, direction, locus, place, post, site, station
WHEREAS although, because, since, while

WHEREBY how, per quod, why

WHEREFORE accordingly, because, forwhy, hence, reason, therefore, whence, why

WHERENESS ubiety

WHEREUPON immediately, soon, when

WHEREWITHAL cash, funds, means, money, resources

WHERRET box, hit, slap, tease, whirrick, worry

WHERRY barge, boat, lighter, rowboat

WHERRYMAN waterstrider

WHET animate, aperitif, appetizer, arouse, attempt, egg, excite, goad, grind, hone, incite, inspire, kindle, occasion, pique, point, preen, provoke, quicken, rouse, sharpen, stimulate, stir, stroke, strop, time, try

WHETHER alternative, choice, either, gin, in case, nevertheless, optionally, provided, where, which

WHETSTONE buhr, bur(r), edger, hone, novaculite, rip, rub, sharpener, straik, strickle, washita, whittle

WHEWL cry, howl, whine

WHEY fluid, milk, pale, pallid, quey, serum, thin, watery, whig, wig
pressed thrutchings

WHICH quilk, that, whatever, whilk, who
at quem
see loc cit, op cit, quod vide

WHICKER bleat, neigh, snig, whinny

WHID fib, frisk, lie, whisk

WHIDAH *bird* redbill, veuve, weaver, whydah

WHIFF blow, boat, drink, exhale, fan, flag, flatfish, fluff, fuff, gust, hint, inhale, instant, jiffy, megrim, odor, puff, quiff, savor, scull, sip, smack, smell, smoke, sniff, snuff, waft, wave, wind

WHIFFLE battle-axe, blow, change, disperse, evade, fife, flicker, flutter, idle, shake, shift, sword, trifle, turn, vacillate, veer, wave(r), weapon, whiffet, whistle

WHIFFLETREE See WHIPPLETREE.

WHIG buttermilk, con-

venanter, curdle, jog, quig, sour milk, whey
opposition royalist, tory
president harrison, taylor

WHILE albeit, although, amuse, as long as, beguile, dawdle, fleet, idle, interim, interval, labor, meantime, once, pains, pass, period, quondam, sometimes, spend, stead, stoun, till, time, until, when, whet, whilom, whilst, wile
a little whilock
away amuse, deceive, divert
within a shortly, soon

WHILK scoter, whelk, which

WHILLY cajole, gull, wheedle

WHILOM at times, erewhile, erstwhile, former(ly), of old, once, past, sometime, while

WHIM bee, boutad, capriccio, caprice, chimera, conceit, crank, crotchet, desire, fad, fancy, fantasy, fegary, fike, flam, freak, gig, hoist, humor, idea, inclination, jinker, maggot, megrim, notion, outbreak, pun, purlicue, quirk, thrum, toy, vagary, whigmaleerie, whims(e)y, widgeon, winch, wrinkle

WHIMBREL curlew, jack, maybird, mayfowl, spow(e), titterel

WHIMPER bleat, blubber, complain(t), cry, girn, grizzle, keen, mewl, mule, murmur, pule, simper, sniffle, wail, weep, whindle, whine, whinge, whinnock, whitter, wimick, yammer

WHIMSEY caprice, craze, drollery, fike, freak, vagary, waggery, WHIM

WHIMSICAL bizarre, bizzarro, capricious, cockle, droll, eccentric, erratic, fanciful, fantastic, freakish, funny, humorous, notional, odd, quaint, queer, singular, strange, whimmy

WHIMSY See WHIMSEY.

WHIN furze, gorse, hoist, restharrow, rock, ulex, wheen, whincow, winch, woodwaxen

WHINCHAT gorsechat, grasschat, saxicola, utick, wheatear

WHINE beg, bleat, cant,

coax, complain, croon, cry, girn, gowl, growl, grumble, meech, mewl, moan, pule, screech, skirl, snivel, sough, vibrato, wail, whewl, whimper, whindle, whinge, wow, yammer, yarm, yaup, yirm, yirn, yowl

WHINER shmegegge

WHINNOCK bottle, cry, complain, pail, WHIMPER

WHINNY bray, hinny, neigh, snort, whicker

WHINSTONE scurdy, trap

WHINYARD hanger, pochard, shoveler, sword, whinger

WHIP 3 cat, hit, mix, taw 4 beat, belt, cast, crop, dick, dust, flog, foam, goad, hurt, jerk, lash, lick, lout, push, rush, stir, taws, urge, wale, wrap 5 azote, binch, churn, cream, drive, flail, froth, impel, knout, outdo, plete, pound, quirt, romal, seize, spank, start, stick, strap, tawse, whale, whisk 6 arouse, chabuk, defeat, hasten, lainer, larrup, pizzle, punish, quippe, scutch, strike, swinge, switch, thrash, wallop 7 agitate, belabor, blister, chabouk, chicote, conquer, cowhide, instant, kurbash, nagaika, rawhide, scourge, sjambok, torment 8 chastise, chawbuck, coachman, confound, emulsify, koorbash, lambaste, overcast 9 expediter 10 blacksnake, discipline, flagellate, tickletoby 13 cat o'nine tails
around twine, weave, writhe
-bearing mastigophoric
comb. mastix
crop guelder-rose, whitebeam
hand advantage, control, dominion, influence
handle crop, stock
horse wand
jockey's bat
mark wale, weal, welt
o r depart, vamoose
part crop, handle, snead, socket, stock
rawhide blacksnake, bullwhack, knout, quirt, sjambok, taws(e), thong
riding crop, dick, quirt
-scorpion grampus, pedipalp, phrynid, tarantula, whiptail

socket snead

3-lash plet(e)

WHIPLASH cosaque, cracker, sealace

WHIPPED chantilly, fouette

WHIPPING *boy* abusee, fall guy, scapegoat

post fork, pillar

WHIPPLETREE heeltree, swinglebar, s(w)ingletree, whiffletree

WHIPPOORWILL antrostomus, chuck-will's-widow, cowpea

boots pitcher-plant

WHIPSTITCH instant, minute, overcast, tailor

WHIPTAIL lizard, scorpion, skua

WHIR bur(r), buzz, commotion, hurry, speed, whizz, zizz

WHIRL agitation, attempt, bustle, cast, circle, commotion, drill, eddy, fun, gurge, gyrate, gyration, gyre, hurl, hurry, merry-go-round, mizmaze, pirouette, reel, revolve, ride, rotate, rotation, round, rush, spin, surge, swirl, trundle, try, tumult, turn, twirl, vortex, wharve, wheel, whorl, winch, wirble

WHIRLBONE hucklebone, kneepan, patella

WHIRLIGIG beetle, carrousel, merry-go-around, rotary, spindle, teetotum, toy

WHIRLPOOL buller, charybdis, eddy, gorce, gourd, gurge, maelstrom, suckhole, swallow, swelchie, swelth, swilkie, swirl, vortex, weel, wiel

WHIRLWIND baguio, cyclone, eddy, maelstrom, rainspout, tornado, twister, waterspout, whirlicane

WHIRLYBIRD helicopter

WHISK agitate, beat, broom, brush, chauri, chowry, collar, cowtail, flisk, foam, hurry, millet, panicle, plane, rustle, seta, speed, stroke, sweep, switch, transport, tuft, whip, whist, wisp

broom ringe

WHISKER awn, barbel, beard, bristle, broom, brush, fan, feeler, fringe, hair, mold, rod, vibrissa

WHISKERS beard, burnsides, dundreary, galways, goatee,

mustache, muttonchops, sideburns, stubble, ziffs

ear to ear galways

WHISKEY, WHISKY athol(e), barleybree, barleycorn, bourbon, busthead, firewater, grog, hooch, irish, liquor, malt, moonshine, popskull, pot(h)een, rotgut, rye, scotch, usquabae, usque (baugh), water of life

and honey drambuie

bootleg moosemilk

cheap redeye

distillery shebang, still

distributer bootlegger

glass of rubdown

illicit moonshine, moosemilk

jack canada jay

maker distiller, moonshiner

poker schnautz

punch facer

source barley, corn, maize, potatoes, rye, wheat

with beer chaser boilermaker

WHISPER advice, aside, breath(e), breeze, buzz, confide, divulge, hearken, hint, mumble, murmur, report, roun, rumor, siffilate, smear, sough, speak, susurr(ate), susurrus, tip, tittle, touch, trace, tutel, whit

WHISPERER backbiter, gossip, slanderer, talebearer, tattler

WHIST (See also *kind*, below.) game, hush, mute, quiet, silence, silent, still, wheesht

authority cavendish, henry jones

coup slam

declaration misere

dummy mort

forerunner post and pair

hand tenace, yarborough

played carelessly bumblepuppy, nineholes

kind biritch, boston, cayenne, preference, vint

term ask, blue peter, bumper, call, dummy, echo, finesse, grand slam, lilies, misere, slam, sneak, solo

WHISTLE birdcall, blare, blow, boo, call, catcall, cuckoo, fife, flute, fussle, hiss, inform, mouth, piccolo, pipe, reed, rustle, screech, siffle, signal, sing, siren, sistle, s(o)ugh, squeal, summon(s), throat,

toot(le), tweedle, wheep, whew, whine, whute

down the wind argue, defame

duck goldeneye

fish rockling

flute sifflot

male wolf-call

pig groundhog, woodchuck

stop campaign, village

WHISTLER flutist, goldeneye, lapwing, marmot, plover, siffleur, widgeon

WHISTLEWING goldeneye

WHISTLEWOOD alder, basswood, maple, rowan

WHIT atom, bit, brass-farthing, doit, grain, hoot, iota, jot, mite, particle, quat, quit, scintilla, scrap, smidgen, smitch, speck, tittle, touch

WHITE alabaster, alba, albedo, albino, albumine, amphetamine, argent, ashen, auspicious, bawn, bianco, blanc(he), blank, bleach, blond, bright, buckra, candent, candid, caucasian, chalky, chaste, civite, clean, colorless, cut, darling, empty, fair, favorable, favorite, fortunate, frosted, hoar(y), honest, honorable, innocent, ivorine, ivory, laban, lacteous, light, lily, milk(y), niveous, pale, pallid, pearly, pure, quat, quit, rime, shining, silver(y), snow(y), spotless, truth, upright, wan, whittle

alder clethra

and smooth ivorine

ant anai, anay, nasute, termite

as chalk, driven snow, milk

as a sheet, swan

becoming albescent, albicant, albication, albification, canescent

blood cell leucocyte

brant snowgoose

bryony cowbind

cedar juniper

clover shamrock

-collar worker accountant, bookkeeper, clerk, salesman, secretary, stenographer, typist

comb. alb(o), leuco

cover rime, snow

devil nailrod

elephant land burma, ceylon, india, siam, thailand

entirely albino

-eye blight-bird, haddock, wall-eyed pike, zosterops

-face baldpate, blaze, horse, teal

feather cowardice, surrender

flag, sign of cowardice, surrender, truce, yielding

-flecked roan

fly homopter, mealywing

friar alsatian, carmelite

goods bedding, linen, sheets, towels

gum tuart

-headed favorite, fairhaired, fortunate, whitecapped

hellebore itchweed

hot burning, torrid

house designer hoban

house groom robb

hun ephthalite

ipecac itoubou

lead ceruse

-livered cowardly, pusillanimous

magic sorcery

man buckra, cachila, fay, paleface

mapou piripiri

mule gin, liquor, moonshine, whiskey

mustard crucifer, kedlock, sinapis

name meaning gwen, gwin(ne), laban, nan(nie), wendy

nile See NILE.

oak roble

plague consumption, phthisis, tuberculosis

poor cracker, yahoo

poplar abele

-rump godwit, wheatear

-rumped sandpiper sanderling

russian republic byelorussia

sauce bechamel

slave prostitute, wanton

snakeroot poolwort, richweed, stevia, whitetop

-spotted bausond

stone granulite

stuff See DRUG *morphine.*

sturgeon beluga

yellowish ivory

WHITEBAIT icefish, salangid, salmonid, smelt

WHITEBEAM aria, mulberry, sorbus

WHITEBELLY grouse, pigeon, widgeon

WHITEBILL coot, junco, sardine

WHITEBOY favorite, leveler, pet

WHITECOAT hairseal, harpseal

WHITEFISH atinga, beluga, blackfin, bloater, bowback, buffaloback, chivey, chub, cisco, coreponus, greyback, humpback, lavaret, marena, menhaden, menomini, pilan, pilot, pollan, powan, salmon, schnabel, tulip, tullibee, vendace

WHITEHEAD feverfew, pigeon, strawworm, surfscoter, takeall

WHITEN albify, besnow, blanch, bleach, blench, dealbate, decolorize, etiolate, fade, frost, gloss, gloze, pale

WHITENER bleach, blu(e)-ing, indigo

WHITENESS albedo, albinoism, argent, cando(u)r, canities, dealbation, etiolation, leucopathy, lunule, pallor, purity

WHITESIDE goldeneye

WHITETAIL deer, hummingbird, wheatear

WHITETHORN hawthorn

WHITETHROAT babillard, eysoge, haysuck, jack, miller, muffet, mufty, muggy, peggy, sparrow, sylvia, warbler, wheybird, whisky

WHITETOP fleabane, snakeroot

WHITEWALL flycatcher, tire

WHITEWASH absolve, acquit, blanch, calcimine, cancel, chicago, clear, conceal, condone, defeat, excuse, extenuate, gloss, gloze, hide, mask, overcome, palliate, parget, rout, sanitize

WHITEWEED daisy

WHITEWING chaffinch, sail, scoter, (street)sweeper

WHITEWOOD canarywood, canella

WHITHER bluster, flurry, hurl, hurry, rush, shake, throw, totter, tremble, where(to), whereunto, whiz

WHITING butterfish, chalk, cod, corvina, hake, kingfish, merlangus, moonfish, odax, sailor's-choice, sillago, tomcod

pout bibfish, blens, kleg

WHITLOW agnail, ancome,

felon, hangnail, panaris, paronychia, runround, sore, whittle

grass anychia, draba, nailwort, saxifrage, shadflower

WHITLOWWORT See WHITLOW *grass.*

WHITRACK futteret, weasel, whittret

WHITSUNDAY pentecost

WHITSUNTIDE pingster, pinkster, pinxter

WHITTIER *poem* barbara frietchie, barefoot boy, ichabod, snow-bound

WHITTLE blanket, carve, cut, destroy, flannel, form, hew, knife, mantle, pare, peach, petticoat, reduce, remove, sculpt, shape, thwite, trim, twite, whet, whitlow

WHIZ, WHIZZ ace, bargain, buzz, corker, deal, expert, hiss, hum, hurry, pirr, purr, rotate, sing, speed, swither, whir(r), wizard, zizz

WHO chi, quo, that, wer, wha, which

WHOA halt, holla, pruh, stop

WHOLE absolute, aggregate, all, assemblage, body, complete, complex(us), corpus, ensemble, entire(ty), essence, everything, gestalt, gross, hale, healed, healthy, intact, integral, mass, perfect, pure, sole, sound, sum, tot, total(ity), tutto, unanimous, unbroken, uncut, undamaged, unimpaired, unity, unmixed, well

as a enbloc, in toto

comb. all, holo, tot(i), toto

-footed candid, frank, ingenuous, intimate

-hearted earnest, complete, cordial, devoted, earnest, genial, gracious, heartfelt, hearty, sincere, unfeigned, ungrudging, unmitigated, unreserved, zealous

number integer, integral

-souled See *-hearted,* above.

WHOLENESS entirety, integrity

WHOLESALE abundant, bulk, commercial, extensive, indiscriminate, lots, massive, sweeping

WHOLESALER jobber, middleman

WHOLESOME benedict, beneficial, benign, clean, favorable, good, halesome, heal-some, healthful, healthsome, healthy, hearty, normal, nutritious, propitious, robust, salubrious, salutary, sane, sanitary, savory, sound, sweet, vigorous

WHOLLY algate(s), all, altogether, completely, directly, entirely, exclusively, fully, hale, in toto, only, outright, quite, roundly, simply, solely, solidly, thoroly, thoroughly, totally
comb. toto

WHOOP bark, bellow, boost, call, campaign, cheer, cough, cry, halloo, hawk, hoopoe, hoot, praise, scream, shout, urge, yell
it up celebrate, play, rampage, roister

WHOOPING great, immense, **WHOPPING**
cough chincough, kinkhost, pertussis

WHOP bang, beat, blow, bump, cast, crack, dash, fall, flop, hit, hurry, knock, pitch, plump, shake, strike, stroke, surpass, thrash, throw, thud

WHOPPER banger, bender, bumper, crumper, fib, jumbo, lie, lolloper, slapper, spanker, story, thumper, walloper, whacker, whapper, whulter

WHOPPING banging, big, enormous, great, HUGE, large, thumping, very, whaling

WHORE See PROSTITUTE, WANTON.

WHOREHOUSE bordello, brothel, stew

WHORL coil, convolution, cycle, disk, flywheel, spiral, turn, verticil, volution, wharve, whirl, wind, wreath
having spired, verticillate

WHORTLEBERRY bilberry, blackheart, blaeberry, fraghan, frawn, hoot, huckleberry, vaccinium

WHY cause, enigma, heifer, how, perche, porque, pourquoi, problem, quey, reason, what for, whence, wherefore

WHYO criminal, footpad, gangster, hoodlum, thief

WICK angle, bay, bend, blowtorch, borough, burner, corner, creek, dairy

(farm), evil, farmstead, kraal, snast(e), snuff, taper, town, village
end snot
imperfection thief, waster

WICKED abandoned, atrocious, bad, black(hearted), caitiff, corrupt, criminal, cross, cruel, cursed, dangerous, darksome, depraved, devastating, devilish, diabolic(al), difficult, dissolute, evil, fierce, flagrant, guilty, heinous, hellish, horrid, ill, immoral, impious, iniquitous, irreligious, lewd, malefic, meschant, miscreant, monstrous, naughty, nefarious, noxious, pernicious, perverted, piky, profane, reprobate, roguish, sinful, sinister, sorry, stern, terrible, unclean, ungodly, unholy, unjust, unlede, unwrest, vicious, vile, villainous, wrong, wroth
person belial, demon, devil, fiend, malefactor, miscreant, monster, satan, sinner, tzaddik, villain
place cesspit, cesspool, den, hotbed, tenderloin
weed hops

WICKEDNESS atrocity, corruption, crime, depravity, devil(t)ry, evil, folly, guilt, improbity, infamy, iniquity, mischief, misdeed, sin(fulness), villainy, wangrace, wrong

WICKER cane, mark, osier, rattan, twig, wike, withe
basket cesta, crate, kipsy, kish, pannier, pegall
cradle bassinet
flask fiasco

WICKERWORK basketry, rat(t)an, twiggen, weel

WICKET arch, door, framework, grating, guichet, heading, hoop, innings, loophole, pitch, ratan, rattan, stall, stump, window
keeper stump(er)

WICKFIELD *clerk* uriah heep

WICKIUP, WIKIUP hut, shelter, wakiup

WICOPY basswood, leatherwood

WIDDLE struggle, waddle, wriggle

WIDDY gallows(bird), hal-

ter, noose, rope, widow, withy

WIDE ample, astray, broad, capable, capacious, comprehensive, deep, distended, expanded, extended, far(off) (reaching), fast, generous, large, lax, liberal, loose, roomy, sharp, slack, spacious, splay, squat, wrong
-awake active, alert, alive, aware, billycock, conscious, flash, fly, hat, informed, insomniac, interested, keen, knowing, leery, nimble, observant, prepared, quick, ready, sleepless, tern, vigilant, watchful
berth latitude
comb. eury(s)
-eyed aghast, amazed, astonished
-jawed eurygnathic
-mouthed amazed, devouring, eurystomatous, greedy, loud, noisy
of the mark apart, awry, deviating, diverging, erroneous, mistaken
open agape, lax, spread
open spaces country, plain(s)

WIDELY abroad, afar, broadly, extensively, far, largely, loosely, uncivilly

WIDEN amplify, broaden, dilate, enlarge, expand, extend, flue, mushroom, ream, splay, spread, stretch, unfold

WIDENESS breadth, expanse, extensiveness, vastness, width

WIDESPREAD all-over, broad, catholic, comprehensive, diffuse(d), epidemic, expatiate, extensive, farflung, general, pandemic, pervasive, prevalent, public, rife, spacious, sweeping, universal

WIDGEON baldpate, bluebill, duck, garganey, goldeneye, goosander, goose, mareca, poacher, simpleton, smee, smew, whewer, whim, zuisin

WIDOW, WIDOW'S almona, begum, bereave, deaconess, deprive, dowager, doweress, kitty, matron, pearl, pot, skat, suttee, tercer, veuve, widdy
bird whidah
cross rockmoss

1st to remarry gorgophone
fish viuva
headdress bandore
mite lepton
monkey titi
pert. vidual
right dower, jointure, mite, quarantine, t(i)erce
suicide suttee
veil bandore
walk lookout

WIDOWHOOD viduage, viduity

WIDTH amplitude, beam, bore, breadth, diameter, expanse, extent, fullness, girth, latitude, scope, span, stretch, wideness
difference in bilge

WIELD bear, brandish, command, conduct, control, cope, determine, direct, employ, exercise, express, flourish, govern, handle, manage, manipulate, ordain, ply, possess, power, prevail, run, sway, swing, touch, use, wave

WIENER frankfurter, hot-dog, sausage, wurst

WIFE better-half, bride, consort, dame, deianira, deidamia, dionyza, donna, eriphyle, esposa, femme, fere, frau(en), frow, gammer, goody, gudewife, guidwife, helpmate, helpmeet, hen, khadija, lady, madame, mate, missis, moglie, mrs, mujer, ranee, rani, rib, senora, signora, spouse, squaw, uxor, wahine, woman
clergyman's curatess
doting on uxorious
faithful evadne, penelope
lord's lady
murder mariticide, uxoricide
nagging harpy, xanthippe
obedient griselda, grisilda
old gammer
patient enid
pert. uxorial, uxoric(al)
property dos, dower, paraphern(lia)
property, pert. extradotal

WIG baguio, bawl out, berate, bobjerom, brutus, caxon, censure, chedreux, cheweler, dignitary, divot, doily, flash, frizz, front, frowze, gizz, hair, jasey, jaw, judge, mat, nightcap, periwig, peruke, postiche,

ramillie, rate, rebuke, reprimand, rogerian, rug, scold, scratch, seal, seedcake, shaytl, sheitel, spencer, tete, top, toupee, tuft, upbraid, vallancy, way, whey
big See MAGNATE.
bushy busby
18th-century adonis, george
frizzled busby
gray grizzle
large bushy buzzwig
maker board-worker, perruquier, peruker, wigger, wigster
netting caul
repair careen
17th-century vallancy
stand barber's block
worn out caxon
worsted jasey

WIGGLE jerk, shake, stagger, thrill, waggle, wangle, wobble, wriggle

WIGGLETAIL tadpole

WIGHT active, bit, brave, creature, fairy, jot, loud, man, nimble, person, powerful, rough, strong, swift, valiant, whit, witch

WIGWAG alternate, signal, to and fro, wave

WIGWAM cabin, dwelling, home, house, hut, lodge, tent, tepee, tipi, weekwam, wickiup

WILD 3 gay, mad, ree 4 daft, keen, lush, rude, wowf 5 amuck, angry, brave, crazy, eager, feral, fiery, giddy, great, rabid, rough, royet, skeer, vexed, wacky, waste, weald, weird 6 absurd, brutal, daring, desert, far out, ferine, fierce, insane, native, raging, renish, savage, stormy, unruly, wanton 7 blatant, breachy, cerrero, erratic, excited, extreme, frantic, furious, natural, rampant, riotous, untamed, valiant, violent 8 aberrant, agrestal, barbaric, desolate, dramatic, ecstatic, fanciful, frenetic, meshugge, primeval, prodigal, reckless, untilled, warragel 9 abandoned, barbarous, different, dissolute, eccentric, fantastic, ferocious, hellicate, inclement, luxuriant, obstinate, primitive, turbulent, unbridled, uncertain, visionary, wasteland 10 boister-

ous, chimerical, distraught, irrational, licentious, profligate, rampageous, refractory, sylvestral, tumultuous, unexplored, wilderness 11 extravagant, tempestuous, uncivilized 12 obstreperous, rambunctious, uncontrolled, uncultivated 14 unconventional, undomesticated
alder goutweed
arum cuckoopint
banana papaw, pawpaw
boar aper, sounder, suid (ian), tusker, wilrone
box indigo, inkberry, randia
card freak
carrot bird's-nest, dill, eltrot, fiddle, hilltrot
cat See WILDCAT.
celery ache, eche, eelgrass, smallage
chervil ass-parsley, gean, hemlock, honewort, milkweed
cinnamon barbasco, canella
coffee feverroot
comb. agrio, ther
crocus pasqueflower
cyclamen sowbread
dog ag(o)uara, cimarron, dhole, dingo, guara, warragal
-eyed crazy, haggard, radical
garlic moly
goat aegagrus, eveck, ibex, markho(o)r, mazame, pasan, tahr, tur
hog babiroussa, peccary
honeybee angelito, dingar
horse brumbie, kumrah, tarpan
irishman tumatakura
jalap mayapple
kale charlock, radish
lettuce butterweed, fireweed
man maniac, savage, wood-(s)man, yahoo, yanigan
marjoram organ(y), origan
masterwort goutweed
mulberry yawweed
musk alfilaria
mustard charlock
oats escapade, peccadillo
olive tree oleaster
onion umbel(la)
ox anoa, buff, reem, yak
parsley eltrot, hilltrot
pear dogberry
pink carolina-catchfly
plantain balisier
plum islay, sloe
potato manroot, wapatoo
pumpkin calabazilla

radish cadlock, runch
rice manomin
rye lyme-grass
sage clary, eyeseed
sheep argali, bighorn, mouflon, nayaur, urial
succory chicory
sweetpea catgut, goat's-rue
thyme brotherwort, hillwort, pennyroyal, serpolet
tobacco gagroot, marijuana, salvadora
valerian avens, bennet, burnet
vanilla liatris
WILDCAT cablewheel, chati, colocola, irresponsible, lynx, margay, serval, unreliable, unsafe, unsound, wagati
WILDE, OSCAR *pseud.* melmoth
work ballad of reading gaol, de profundis, importance of being earnest, lady windermere's fan, picture of dorian gray, salome
WILDEBEEST gnu
WILDER (See also BEWILDER.) perplex, stray, wander
WILDER, THORNTON
work bridge of san luis rey, our town, skin of our teeth
WILDERNESS badlands, barrens, clutter, confusion, country, desert, forest, waste(land), welter, wilds
WILDS bondoc, boondocks, bonnies, bundoc(ks) brush, bush, sticks, WILDERNESS
WILE allure, artifice, beguile, chicanery, choice, choose, cunning, deceit, deceive, deception, duplicity, entice, feint, fraud, guile, lure, maneuver, pass, pauk, pawk, plot, ruse, snare, spend, stratagem, subterfuge, toy, trick(ery), wale, while
symbol spider
WILHELM *last residence* doorn
WILKES *island* ashi
WILL ambition, appetite, behest, bequeath, bequest, choice, choose, codicil, command, conation, decide, decision, decree, design, desire, determination, determine, devise, disposition, document, election, fancy, hest, holograph, inclination, instrument, intend, intent

(ion), leave, lust, mind, mun, opt, order, passion, pleasure, power, prefer (ence), purpose, resolution, resolve, testament, velleity, volitiency, volition, voluntarism, vote, wish
appendix codicil
beneficiary devisee, heir, inheritor
comb. bulia
convey by demise, devise
dying without intestate
good gree
handwritten holograph
ill animus, enmity, envy, hate, hest
loss abulia, abulomania
maker devisee, devisor, legatee, legator, testator, testatrix
-o'-the-wisp elusive, ignisfatuus, illusion, impractical, luminescence, marshfire, nostoc, visionary
power abstention, abstinence, courage, determination, grit, purpose, resoluteness, resolution, self-control, selfdenial, temperance
power, abnormal parabulia
proof of probate
WILLFUL camsteery, camstrairie, decided, deliberate, determined, dogged, feisty, froward, headstrong, impetuous, intended, intentional, mad, mulish, obstinate, opinionated, rash, rebellious, self-willed, stubborn, temperamental, unruly, voluntary, wrong-headed, wry
WILLIAM *beloved* audrey
II rufus the red
II residence doorn
III horse sorrel
III wife mary
IV silly-billy
prince of orange wee willie winkie
WILLIAM TELL *canton* uri
enemy gessler
hero egil
WILLIAM THE CONQUEROR *brother* odo
burial site caen
daughter adela
mother harlotta
wife matilda
WILLIAMS, TENNESSEE
play cat on a hot tin roof, glass menagerie

WILLIES creeps, nervousness, shakes
WILLING accommodating, agreeable, alacritous, amenable, apt, bain, cheerful, compliant, deliberate, delighted, desirous, disposed, eager, enthusiastic, fain, favorable, forward, game, glad, happy, inclined, intentional, longing, minded, obliging, open, pleased, prompt, prone, ready, unforced, voluntary, zealous
or not nolens volens
WILLINGLY cheerfully, frankly, freely, gladly, graciously, lief, lieve, readily, voluntarily
WILLINGNESS acquiescence, alacrity, assent, compliance, consent, enthusiasm, freedom, heart, inclination, volition, zeal
WILLOCK auk, guillemot, piffin
WILLOW bahan, boobyalla, itea, myoporum, osier, salew, salix, sallow, teaser, trap, twilly, wattle, willy, withy, woody, wuddie
basket prickle, willy
black mulefat
bloom gull
cactus rhipsalis
catkin ament, rag, spike
green reseda
grouse ptarmigan
grove holt, osiery, rodham, salicetum
hat salacot
herb basswood, bloodvine, burntweed, epilobe, epilobium, firetop, fireweed, hart's-tongue, leatherwood, pigweed, rosebay, sallybloom, tilia, wicopy
native cooba(h)
-oak bluejack
plaited wicker
purple blacktop
pussy oca
red cornel, osier, salix
shoot sallow
spike See *catkin*, above.
twig sallow, withe
warbler bankjug, muddler, ovenbird, smeu(th), trochil, willy-mufty
wren chiffchaff, peggy
WILLOWWORT loosestrife, persicaria
WILLOWY delicate, flexible, graceful, lissome, pliable,

pliant, slender, slim, slipper, supple, svelt, tall

WILLY basket, favorable, trap, voluntary, wagtail, willing, willow

-nilly bon gre-mal gre, intermittently, necessarily, perforce, uncertain, vacillating

-wicket sandpiper

-willy cyclone, tornado

WILSON, WILSON'S *plover* collier

snipe cachecache, jack, shadbird

tern medrick

thrush veery

warbler blackcap

WILSON, JOHN *pseud.* christopher north

WILSON, WOODROW
birthplace staunton, virginia
burial site washington
mexico policy watchful waiting
party democratic
profession teacher
relative mcadoo, sayre
vice-president marshall

WILT collapse, cower, depression, droop, ebb, fade, fail, faintness, fatigue, flag, languish, perspire, quail, sag, succumb, waste, weaken, weary, wither

WILTED droopy, emarcid, flaccid

WILY arch, artful, astute, cautelous, clever, crafty, cunning, deceitful, designing, devious, foxy, insidious, politic, shrewd, sly, subtle, tricky, versute, winding

WIMBLE active, auger, bore, brace, brisk, gimlet, lively, nimble, pierce, scoop, sludger, sprightly, twist, wibble, wummel

WIMBLEDON *philosopher of* john horn tooke
sport tennis

WIMICK cry, whimper, whine

WIMPLE bend, confuse, curve, deceive, flag, fold, gorget, headdress, hoodwink, meander, plait, ripple, streamer, turn, twist, undulate, veil, wimlunge, wind, wrap, wriggle, wrinkle

WIN accomplish, achieve, acquire, allure, attain, beat, beget, best, captivate, cap-

ture, charm, conciliate, conquer, defeat, derive, drub, dry, earn, entice, furze, gain, get, happiness, harvest, influence, joy, labor, lift, obtain, overcome, persuade, pot, prevail, procreate, procure, profit, raise, reach, reap, redeem, save, secure, skin, subdue, succeed, success, sweep, take(the cake), triumph, vanquish, victory, whin, winnow, won

all tricks capot, slam

away steal

back recover, regain, retrieve

effortless breeze, cinch, snap

favor catch on

narrow squeeze

over bring around, conciliate, convert, convince, defeat, disarm, persuade

WINCE balk, blench, check, cower, cringe, flinch, kick, quail, quatch, quech, quitch, recoil, reel, retreat, shrink, shy, squirm, start, stick(le), winch, writhe

WINCH cathead, crab, crank, haul, hoist, jack, reel, roller, variable, vise, whin, windlass, windle, winze

drum gipsy(head), gypsy (head)

WINCHESTER *college student* wykehamist

WIND (See also *famous,* below.) afflatus, air, bend, blare, blast, blout, blow, bluster, boast, breath(e), breeze, buster, coil, contort, control, convolve, corkscrew, creek, crinkle, crook, curl, current, curve, cyclone, draft, draught, emanation, entwine, exhalation, extricate, fatigue, flatus, flaw, flurry, gale, gust, haul, hoist, insinuate, intort, manage, meander, scent, screw, scud, serpentine, sinuate, snake, slither, squall, squirm, storm, torsion, turn, twine, twirl, twist, vaunt, vine, waft, warp, weave, whiff, whorl, wield, wiggle, worm, wrap, wreathe, wriggle, wring, writhe. zephyr

abeam lask

action eolation

annual etesian, imbat

away from alee

-borne eolic

burst of blout

close to sharp

cold bise, bize, blizzard, bora, brickfielder, bu(r)ster, crivetz, gregale, levanter, mistral, puna, sarsar

comb. anem(o), pneum(a)

cool imbat

debilitating sirocco

deprive of becalm

desert chergui, gibleh, kamsin, samiel, samum, santa ana, simoon, sirocco

dry bohorok, bora, harmattan, leste, trade

dusty afghanets, hamseen, harmattan

east bentu de soli, eurus, leste, levant(er), trade, wabun

equatorial trade

eroded by eolic

erosion eolation

fall katabatic

famous afer, afghanet, barat, belat, bentu de soli, bise, bize, bohorok, bora, boreas, brickfielder, brisa, briza, brubu, bruscha, buran, burga, buster, cape doctor, caurus, chilli, chinook, etesian, euroclydon, eurus, favonius, fo(e)hn, gregale, harmattan, kabibonokka, kona, laveche, leste, levant(er), leveche, minvano, mistral, mudjekeewis, notus, pampero, ponente, puna(leste), puno, samiel, santa(a)na, sarsar, scirocco, seistan, shamal, shawondasee, shimal, simoon, simoon, siroc(co), solano, sures, tedbad, trade(s), tramontana, vayu, wendaval, zonda

-fanner kestrel

father astraeus

-fertilized anemophilous

fierce buster

flow flurry

force scale See WIND *scale,* below.

gauge anemograph, anemometer, cyclonoscope, cyclonometer, sock, vane, ventometer, weathercock

gentle aura, breeze, zephyr

god adad, adda, addou, aeolus, afer, argestes, astraeus, boreas, caecias, caurus, eecatl, eolus, eurus, kaare, kabibonokka, marut, mudjekeewis, niord, njord, notus, ramman, shawondasee, vayu, wabun, zephryus

gust flan, flaw, pirr

head to atry

high rig

hot brick-fielder, burster, buster, chamsin, chinook, fo(e)hn, gibleh, hamseen, harmattan, khamsin, pampero, puna, samiel, santa(a)na, shamal, shemaal, shimal, shumal, simoom, simoon, s(c)irocco, solano, thawer, zonda

in and out crankle, zag, zig, zigzag

indicator telltale

instrument See MUSICAL INSTRUMENT *wind.*

king aeolus

magnets compound

mountain puna

name meaning keith

north aquilo(n), bise, boreas, collada, fo(e)hn, kabibonokka, mistral, seistan, thrascias, tramontana

north, pert. boread, boreal

northeast argestes, bise, bruscha, buran, burga, caecias, euroclydon, grecale, gregal(e), gregau

northwest barat, belat, caurus, corus, etesian, mistral

periodic etesian, monsoon

personified aeolus, afer, aura, boreas, caecias, caurus, eurus, favonius, kabibonokka, mudjekeewis, notus, shawondasee, vayu, volturnus

pert. aeolian, anemonal, oneumatic, vental

polar tramontane

-preventing goddess mefitis

roaring blore

rope woold, worm

scale beaufort

scale author sir francis beaufort

scale details (0) calm, (1) faint air, (2) light air, (3) light breeze, (4) gentle breeze, (5) moderate breeze, (6) fresh breeze, (7) gentle steady gale, (8) moderate gale, (9) brisk gale, (10) fresh gale, (11) hard gale, (12) hard gale, storm

science aerography, aerometry, anemography, ane-

mology, cyclonology, pneumatics

shake anemosis

sock vane

south auster, notus, samoor, s(c)irocco

southeast eurus, sharki, shurgee, solano, volturnus

southwest afer(ventus), africanus, africus, auster, colla, libecc(h)io, libs, pampero, zephyr

storm See STORM.

strength measurer beaufort

strong birr

-swept bleak

tempestuous euroclydon, mistral

thread cheese, quill

tower badgir

trade brisa, monsoom, monsoon

tree bitterwood

tropical trade

up close, coil, complete, completion, conclude, end, finish, reel in, settlement

violent buster, snorter, squall

warm bohorok, chinook, fo(e)hn, santa(a)na, snow eater

west afer, antitrade, favonius, ponent, zephyr

whirling cyclone, typhoon

wool trend

yarn beam, windle

WINDBAG bellows, bomba, braggart, chatterer, chest, lungs, puffcheek, talker

WINDBREAKER abatvent, jacket

WINDED breathless, puffing, pursy, spent

WINDFALL blessing, blowdown, bonanza, boon, buckshee, chance, fluke, godsend, goldmine, gravy, jackpot, legacy, luck, manna, plum, trouvaille, vail

WINDFLOWER anemone, gentian

WINDGALL tumor, vessignon

WINDHOVER kestrel

WINDING ambagious, anfractuous, bend(ing), circuitous, coiled, contortion, convolute, crooked, curve, curving, deceitful, devious, eely, flexible, flexuous, gyratory, helical, helicoid, indirect, intricate, involuted, involved, labyrin-

thian, mazy, meander(ing), meandrous, pliable, reticular, rivose, rivulose, roundabout, serpentine, sigmoid, sinuate, sinuous, snaky, spiral(ling), torsional, tortile, tortuous, tricky, turning, twisting, vermicular, volute, wanlas, whorled, wily, wreathy, wriggly

device capstan, reel, winch, windlass

sheet cerement, shroud, sudary

WINDJAMMER bandsman, bugler, mariner, musician, sailor, ship, talker, trumpeter

WINDLASS artifice, capstan, crab, crank, drawbeam, draw in, fearn, haul, hoist, perplex, reel, shift, stowce, stowse, whim, whin, winch, windle, wink

drum wildcat

WINDLE basket, drift, meander, redwing, reel, snow, waste, whirl, winch, windlass

WINDMILL asterisk, autogiro, helicopter, jumbo, motor, pinwheel, propeller, solitaire

bar uplong

blade vane

fighter don quixote

part awe, cap, curb, sail, vane

pink catchfly

pump gin

sail arm, awe, eie, eighe, fan, flyer, sweep, swift, van

whip sail-arm

WINDOW aperture, balcone, bay, bull's-eye, casement, chaff, couplet, dormer, eye, fanlight, fenester, fenestra, glaze, grille, guichet, inlet, lancet, lantern, lattice, light, lucarne, luthern, mirador, opening, oriel, orifice, oxeye, pane, port(hole), rose, roundel, sash, shutter, skylight, slit, slot, splite, thurle, transom, ventana, wicket, winnock

above door transom

arrangement fenestration

bar jemmy, jimmy

bay fenestra, mirador, oriel

case frame

circular roundel

cover blind, curtain, drapery,

jalousie, lambrequin, portiere, shade, shutter, valance

dormer lucarne, luthern, oxeye

dresser arrayer

dressing facade, front, show, trim

frame casing, sash

glass, to supply impanel

high lancet

leading came

ledge sill

narrow lancet

on the west leningrad, petrograd, st petersburg

opening fenestra, splite

ornamental balcone, fenestrone

oval oxeye

oyster copis

pane light, lozenge, quirk

pane fish flounder, turbot

part came, casing, esconson, frame, leading, ledge, mouse, mullion, muntin, pane, sash, sill, transom

railing balconet(te)

recess embrasure, exedra

recessed oriel

sash chassis

semicircular fanlight

setter glazier

ship's porthole

-shop browse

small fenestella

throwing out of defenestration

ticket grille, guichet, wicket

twin ajimez

weight mouse

WINDPIPE arber, artery, erber, esophagus, guggle, gullet, halse, keacorn, stroup, thrapple, throat, thropple, throttle, trachea, weasand

branches bronchia, bronchioles, bronchus

comb. bronch(i), bronch(o)

disease cynanche

pert. trachean

WINDPOPPY blood drops

WINDROSE poppy

WINDROW bank, furrow, heap, ridge, swath(e), trench

WINDSHIELD paravent

WINDWARD aloof, aweather, weatherly

island grenada, lucia, spice island(s)

side koolau

WINDY aeolistic, airy,

blowy, bombastic, breezy, brisk, changeable, empty, fresh, gustful, inflated, stormy, swale, swift, ventose, verbose, violent

city chicago

WINE ambrosia, aperitif, drink, friend, grapejuice, ichor, kijafa, krama, lunel, masdeau, nectar, oinos, vino, vinum, wein

add sugar to chaptalize

ancient massic

and dine fete, regale

and honey clary, mulse, oenomel

and soda spritzer

and water krasis

aroma bouquet, nose, seve

aromatic tokay

best quadrimum

bibber drunkard, sot, tippler, toper

blended cuvee

body seve

bordeaux barsac, bergerac, bourg, cabernet, carignan, charbono, chateau d'yquem, chianti, claret, cosne, emilion, floirac, glenpara, graves, malbec, margeaux, mataro, medoc, merlot, pontac, sauterne

bottle amphora, balthazar, bota, carafe, clavelin, decanter, fiasco, jeroboam, magnum, methuselah, olpe, salmanazar

bowl lebes

broker courtier

bucket cooler, icer

bulk cuvee

burgundy beaune, beziers, corton, macon, meunier, musigny, pinot, pommard, savigny, tonnerre, volnay

burgundy, white chablis, chardonnay, mersault, montrachet, pouilly-fuisse

cabinet cellaret(te), tantalus

canary aristippus

cask boss, butt, hogshead, leaguer, pipe, tierce, tun, vat

cask crust argol

cellar bodega, catacomb, cave, pitcher-house, tantalus

cheap duji, plonk, pluck, pop, swill

claret lafite, margaux, medoc, st emilion

clarifying fining

collection cellar

coloring, red oenolin

comb. oen(o), vino

component must, stum

cooler glacier

crust See *deposit*, below.

cup ama, amula, chalice, goblet

deposit argol, beeswing, crust, griffe, lees, tartar

dessert malaga, marsala, muscatel, port, sherry, tokay

dipper olpe

disease casse, graisse

divination by oenomancy

dregs marc, salin, vinasse

drink bishop, cardinal, clary, cobbler, kir, mulse, negus, punch, sangria, sillabub, spritzer

dry brut, calcavella, capri, carcavellos, corvo, musigny, riesling, sack, sec, soave, tavel, zinfandel

estate chateau

eucharist krama, krasis

evaporation ullage

excellent vintage

expert oenologist

extra glass backhander

5th cup cup of elijah

film beeswing

glass baccarat, backhander, flute, goblet, roemer, rummer

god bacchus, dionysus, liber

golden bual, sercial

grape named varietal

grower vigneron, viticulturist

grower's saint vincent

harvest vendange, vendemia

hater oenophobist

hot negus, sake, saki, whitepot

house heuriger

inexpensive plonk, sneaky pete, vin ordinaire

in truth in vino veritas

jar askos, cymaise, stamnos

leather bag olpe

light bual, canary, capri, chablis

list card, carte

locked case tantalus

loire muscadet, sancerre, sauvignon blanc, vouvray

lover bacchanal, bacchant, oenophile, oenophilist

madeira bual, canary, gomera, malmsey, marsala, tinta

maker abkari, vigneron, vintner

making, pert. oenopoetic

measure aam, boutylka, butt, liter, pipe, orna, tertian, tun

medicinal preparation mosto

merchant cooper, vintner

mold condition botrytis cinerea, edelfaule, noble rot, pourriture noble

month october

moselle braunegberger, riesling, zeltinger

mulled gluhwein, plotty

new must

noble rot botrytis cinerea, edelfaule, pourriture noble

of the country vin de pays

ordinary plonk, red ink

oxygen, excess in maderisation

palm beno, sagwire

pert. oenological, vinaceous, vinic, vinous, vintage

pitcher oenochoe, olla, olpe

plant cep, rhubarb

pouch chakakoa

press torcular

press god lenaeus

qualities acid, aromatic, astringent, balanced, big, bitter, body, bouquet, breed, bronze, character, clean, cloudy, coarse, color, corky, delicate, dry, earthy, fine, flat, flinty, flowery, fragrant, fresh, fruity, full, great, green, heavy, light, mellow, mild, noble, nose, nutty, perfume, petillant, piquant, premium, ripe, robust, rounded, seve, silky, small, soft, sound, stemmy, sturdy, sweet, tart, thin, weeper, woody, yeasty, young

quality vintage

red alicante, assmannshauser, barbarassco, barbera, barolo, beaujolais, beaune, bordeaux, burgundy, cabernet, carema, chianti, claret, corton, delaware, dolcetto, gattinara, grignolino, haut-brion, hollock, macon, medoc, pommard, port, retsina, richebourg, saint-estephe, tinta, zinfandel

region-named generic

residue marc, stum

revive stum

rhine bacharach, burger, hochheimer, hock, geisenheimer, johannisberg(er), rhenish, riesling, rulander, sylvaner

rice hsao, hsing, sake, saki

rose tavel

saint vincent tournante

scene of miraculous cana

science oenology

season vendange, vendemia, vintage

server sommelier

shop bar, bistro, bodega, bush, cafe, estaminet, saloon

sorghum kaoliang

sparkling asti spumante, champagne, cold duck

spiced bishop, cardinal, hippocras, nectar, negus, pope, sangaree, sangria

spirit brandy, cognac

storehouse vintry

study of oenology, viniculture, vinology

sugar, add to chaptalize

sweet alicant(e), angelica, banyuls, barsac, bucellas, canary, charneco, cotnar, dubonnet, dulce, falerno, iona, lachryma-christi, lunel, madeira, malmsey, malvasia, marsala, masdeu, mosel(le), muscat(el), oporto, pontac, port, sauterne, scuppernong, sherry, tent, tokay, tyre

tasting cup tastevin

tasting, pert. organoleptic

unfermented must

vat cuvee

very best supernaculum

vessel ama, amula, decanter

vinegar esil

white ambonnay, angelica, asti spumanti, barsac, bernkasteler, bucellas, canary, capri, casel, catawba, chablis, chardonnay, conthey, cortese, deidesheimer, dezaleyhock, farness, forst, gewurtztraminer, hock, lacrima-christi, langoon, liebfraumilch, malaga, marcobrunner, marsala, montrachet, muscadet, niersteiner, orvieto, pinot chardonnay, pouilly-fuisse, rhine, riesling, rudesheimer, sack, sancerre, saumur, sauterne, sauvignon blanc, savennieres, sherry, soave, teneriffe, tokay, traminer, verdal, vermouth, vidonia, vouvray

wormwood eisell, vinegar

year vintage

WINEBERRY bilberry, cur-

rant, gooseberry, grape, makomako, raspberry

WING adjunct, aile, ala, alette, alula, annex, arm, bird, branch, carve, cripple, dependence, detachment, disable, dispatch, division, ell, elytron, elytrum, epaulet, extension, faction, fan, fender, flag, flank, fletch, flight, fly, jambe, kind, mudguard, oar, part, pennon, piece, pinion, pinna, point, pteron, sail, send, shoulder, sort, speed, tail, tegmen, tegumen, transport, unit, vane, volet, wound

arrangement alation

beetle's tegman, tegmina, tegumen

brace spar

building alette, ell, jamb(e)

closed plie

comb. pinna

cover elytron, elytrum, shard

divested of dealate

edge aileron

equip with imp

false alula

feather penna, remex, remiges

flap aileron

fluttering whutter

-footed aliped, fleet, mercurial, swift

group ruffle

having short brachypterous, brevipennate

-like alar(y), alate, aliform, aligerous, pteric, pteroid, pterotic, pterygoid

membrane patagium, propatagium

pair shears

part alula

pert. alar(y), alate(d), exrupeal, pennate, pteric, pteroid, pterotic, tegminal

shell auricle, elytron, strombus

single demivol

support cabane

theatre coulisee

triptych volet

under subalary

vestigial alula

WINGED aile, alar(y), alate, aligerous, elevated, fast, hurt, lofty, pennate, penned, pinnate, rapid, soaring, sublime, swift, wounded

being angel, cherub, mercury, seraph

comb. ptene, pteno

deity amor, cupid, eros, mercury, nike
disk feroher
elm wahoo
figure eidolon, idolon, idolum
fruit samara
horse buraq, pegasus
man(n)ikin ker
monster harpy
victory nike of samothrace
warrior zetes
WINGFISH sea-robin
WINGLESS anapterygote, apteral, apterous, apterygial, dealate(d), exalate
victory nike-apteros
WINK bat, blink, flash, flicker, glance, gleam, instant, look, nap, nictate, nictitate, nod, overlook, palpebrate, periwinkle, signal, sleep, slumber, sparkle, twink(le), twinkling, twitch, well, winch, windlass
-and-peep scarlet pimpernel
at bypass, condone, disregard, overlook, pass over, suffer, tolerate
40 catnap
WINKER(S) blinder, blinker, eye(lash), glasses, spectacles
WINKING blepharospasm, nap, sleep, snooze
WINKLE buccinid, busycon, fulgur, periwinkle, snail, twinkle
WINNER ace, bangster, champion, conqueror, earner, faceman, first, high, master, reaper, sleeper, superior, topnotcher, vanquisher, victor
not also-ran, loser
WINNING(S) acquisition, adorable, attractive, booty, captivating, capture, charming, conquest, gain(ing), loot, pot, profit, successful, velvet, victory, winsome
WINNIPEG *waterway* assiniboine
WINNOW air, analyse, analyze, assort, beat, bolt, brandish, char, cull, disperse, eliminate, fan, flap, glean, pick, refine, scatter, screen, select, separate, sieve, sift, strain, wave, wim
WINSOME agreeable, attractive, blithe, bonny, captivating, charming, cheerful, de-

lightful, gay, gracious, lighthearted, lovable, magical, merry, pleasant, pleasing, pretty, sweet, taking, winning
WINTER bise, brume, cold, december, hibernate, hiems, hiver, inverno, year
bark canelo
bloom azalea, witchhazel
bud statoblast
cabbage savoy
cherry alkekengi
cress cassabully
festival brumalia, christmas
flounder blackback
god ull(er), ullur
melon casaba
pear seckel, warden
pert. See WINTRY.
pink trailing arbutus
quarters hibernacle, hibernaculum
sleep hibernation
squash cushaw, hubbard
teal greenwing
vehicle sled, sleigh
WINTERBERRY black alder, canhoop, cassioberry, holly, hoopwood, ilex, prinos
WINTERGREEN boxberry, checkerberry, chinks, dollarleaf, eyeberry, gaywings, ivyberry, jinks, limonium, pipsissewa, pyrola, ratsbane, shinleaf, teaberry
bitter chimaphila
WINTER'S TALE *author* shakespeare
character antigonus, archidamus, autolycus, camillo, cleomenes, dion, dorcas, emilia, florizel, hermione, leontes, mamillius, mopsa, paulina, perdita, polixenes
scene bohemia, sicilia, sicily
WINTRY aged, arctic, boreal, brumal, cheerless, chilling, cold, frigid, hibernal, hiemal, hyemal, icy, sleety, snowy, stormy, white
WINZE curse, passage(way), winch
WIPE beat, blow, brand, brush, cam, cheat, clean, defeat, defraud, destroy, drub, dry, efface, end, erase, expunge, handkerchief, mop, obliterate, pass, rub, sponge, stain, strike, stroke, swab, sweep, swob, taunt, towel, trick
off dust, scuff

out abolish, annihilate, annul, cancel, clear, deduct, demolish, deracinate, destroy, efface, erase, exhaust, exterminate, kill, nullify, obliterate, remove, rescind, ruin, scrub, uproot
the slate clean acquit, pardon
up defeat, destroy, mop, swab, swob
WIPER cam, duster, handkerchief, rag, rheostat, tappet, tooth, towel, tumbler
WIRE bar, brace, bug, cable, circuit, coil, cord, electrify, encircle, fence, filament, finish-line, guy, lametta, lash, lead, ligature, line, litz, oese, pickpocket, reticle, rod, snake, snare, stolon, string(er), telegram, telegraph, thread, tie, trap, whip
bacteriologist's oese
braided litz
brush card
bundle cable
cable wrapping armature
cover sull
cutter pliers, secateur
diameter ga(u)ge
die whirtle, whortle
enameled litz
fence dropper
foil lametta
frayed jagger
gold kinsen
grass bermuda, bluestem, broomroot, nimblewill, poa
grid mesh
group drop
hole hib(b)
kind barbed, live
loop oese
measure mil, stone
nail brad
photos telepix
platinum oese
priming epinglette, picker
-pull influence
rope jackstay
screen backstop
service ins, reuters, upi
silver or gold lametta
spiral coil
splicing taper
surgical stylet
system network, reticle
tap bug
-tapper snoop, swindler
transmit by pipe
twisted headle, heddle
work filigree

WIREDRAW attenuate, defraud, distort, elongate, extort, force, induce, introduce, outwit, over-refine, prolong, protract, spin out, stretch, wrest
WIREHAIR fox terrier
WIRELESS autotelegraphy, phone, radio, selcal, telegraphy
detector perikon
inventor marconi
WIREWORM agriotis, elater, millepede, myriapod
WIRY athletic, cautelous, hardy, sinewy, stringy, thin, tough
WIS certainly, direct, imagine, indeed, instruct, really, show, suppose, think
WISCONSIN bay green
capital madison
city antigo, appleton, ashland, baraboo, beloit, bloomer, boscobel, brookfield, cudahy, eau claire, fond du lac, greenfield, janesville, kenosha, lacrosse, madison, menasha, milwaukee, neenag, oshkosh, portage, racine, ripon, shawano, sheboygan, shorewood, stevens point, superior, waukesha, wausau, wauwatosa
college alverno, beloit, carroll, carthage, ripon, viterbo
county calumet, door, juneau, shawano, vilas, waushara
indian fox, kickapoo, oneida, potawatomi, sac, sauk, stockbridge, winnebago
lake geneva, kenosha, poygan, mendota, wissota
native badger
nickname badger state
peak rib hill, sugarbush, timshill
port green bay, manitowoc
river chippewa, fox, st croix
specialty butter, cheese, dairies
state bird robin
state flower pansy, violet
state tree sugar-maple
WISDOM acumen, capacity, cunning, discretion, foresight, gnosis, hokmah, judgment, knowledge, learning, lore, profundity, prudence, sagacity, sageness, sapience, sattva, sense, shrewdness, sophia, tact, wisure, wit

affector of pseudosopher
divine theomagy
embodiment achamoth, manjusri
esoteric gnosis
god ear, ganes(h)a, mimer, mimir, nabu, nebo, odin, sabu, sin, tat, thoth, toth, tyr
goddess athena, bri(d)git, minerva, pallas, prudence, sais, themis
hater misosophist
human anthroposophy
name meaning sophia
pert. palladian
practical phronesis
supreme prajna
symbol dragon, owl, serpent, solomon
tooth molar
WISE advise, alert, astute, aware, bright, calculating, canny, cautious, circumspect, cognizant, cool-headed, crafty, cunning, deep, dexterous, direct, discerning, discreet, employ, enlightened, erudite, expedient, explain, foxy, gash, guide, heedful, hep, inform(ed), instruct, intelligent, judicious, knowing, learned, lure, maneuver, manner, mode, omniscient, on to, persuade, philosophical, politic, profound, provident, prudent, rational, sagacious, sage, sane, sapient, sensible, sharp, show, shrewd, skilled, skillful, sly, smart, sophisticated, sound, subtle, tactful, tell, thriven, use, versed, wary, way, wily, witty
as a serpent, solomon
guy See WISEACRE.
infinitely omniscient
man (See also GREEK sage.) amauta, balthasar, balthazar, casper, chacham, chachem, confucius, councilor, franklin, gaspar, illuminato, kaham, MAGI, magician, magus, melchior, mentor, merlin, nestor, odysseus, oracle, pansophist, pundit, sage, savant, solomon, solon, thinker, ulysses, witan, wizard
name meaning alvis
one buddha

up advise, learn
WISEACRE dunce, fool, mastermind, prophet, sciolist, simpleton, solonist, wisenheimer, witling
WISECRACK bon mot, gag, jape, jest, joke, kib(b)itz, quip, remark, retort, spoof, vitz, witticism
WISE-LIKE appropriate, becoming, decent, fitting, judicious, sensible
WISELY discretely, heedfully, sagely, skillfully
WISENT aurochs, bison, bonasus, buffalo
WISEWOMAN fortuneteller, midwife, soothsayer, witch
WISH appetite, aspiration, aspire, bewitch, bid, care, command, covet, crave, desire, goal, hanker, hope, imprecate, invocation, invoke, long(for), longing, lust, meadow, petition, pleasure, propose, recommend, request, thirst, vote, want, will
death destrudo
slight velleity
undone rue
WISHBONE crossarm, fourchette, furculum, merrythought, talisman
WISHFUL desirable, desirous, eager, longing, wistful
WISHY-WASHY banal, bland, diluted, feeble, flat, forceless, inane, indecisive, indifferent, insipid, irresolute, jejune, languid, listless, milk-and-water, milky, mushy, nambypamby, pale, sickly, slipslop, thin, trashy, vacillating, vapid, watery, wavering, weak(kneed)
WISP bit, bunch, bundle, cluster, crumple, flock, fragment, handful, ignis-fatuus, luminescence, parcel, rumple, scrap, shred, skiff, tait, tate, tippet, twist, vapor, wap, wase, whisk (broom)
of straw dossil, wap, wase
WISPY cobwebby, diaphanous, filmy, gossamer, sheer, slender, thin
WISTERIA fuji, kidney-bean-tree, kraunhia, purple, violet
WISTFUL desirous, melancholy, mournful, nostalgic,

pensive, sad, thoughtful, wantful, yearning

WISTITI marmoset

WIT, WITS acumen, address, alertness, badinage, belesprit, brain(s), burlesquer, capacities, clown, comedian, comic, cunning, cutup, drollery, erudition, experience, facetiousness, faculties, farceur, gagman, gagster, grain, head, humor(ist), import, intellect, intelligence, irony, jester, joker, judgment, knowledge, learn(ing), madcap, marbles, meaning, mind, quipster, parodist, penetration, perception, pleasantry, prankster, psyche, punner, raillery, reason, repartee, sagacity, salt, sanity, sarcasm, satire, sense(s), sharpness, skill, soul, spark, student, tid, understanding, vyt, wag, white, wisdom, wisecracker, wotte, zany

dim See FOOL.

to indeed, namely, scilicet, truly

WITCH, WITCH'S acrasia, aganice, alp, ani, asuang, babajaga, beldam(e), bruja, canidia, carline, charmer, circe, crone, cummer, demon, dowser, duessa, enchantress, erichtho, fright, fury, giglet, grebe, grimalkin, gyre-carline, hag, hecate, hekate, hellcat, hex, jezebel, jinx, kimmer, lamia, lilith, magician, mara, mare, medusa, minx, ogress, pilwiz, shamaness, shewolf, sibyl, siren, sorceress, spaewife, sycorax, termagant, tigress, versiera, virago, vixen, walkyrie, weird sisters, wizard

assembly sabbat

attendant familiar

bells bluebottle, foxglove

bird ani

brew hellbroth

broom hexenbesen, staghead

cat grimalkin

-charmed spellbound

chick swallow

city endor, salem

dagger athame

doctor bocor, bokor, boolya, boyla, brujo, goofer, guffer, koradji, magician, shaman, sorcerer, wangateur, wizard

gowan dandelion, globeflower

grass couch, foolhay, panic

group coven, covin(e)

hazel divining rod, hamamelis, hornbeam, rowan, wychelm

-hobble cranberry-tree

male demon, devil, warlock, wizard

master magician, shaman, sorcerer, wizard

milk marestail

offspring holdiken

pouch shepherd's-purse

sabbath walpurgis night

symbol black cat, black hat, broomstick

WITCHCRAFT black magic, brujeria, charm, cunning, demonology, diabolism, enchantment, fascination, goety, hexerei, invultuation, magic, necromancy, pishogue, shamanism, sorcery, spell, theurgy, witchery, wizardry

goddess hecate, obeah

jurist sewall

practice bewitch, hex

WITCHWOOD rowantree, spindletree, wychelm

WITE accusation, accuse, blame, censure, counselor, decree, depart, elder, fault, fee, fine, forfeit, guard, guilt, injury, keep, offense, ordain, punishment, reproach, sage, wayte, wit, wrong

WITH accompanying, along (side), amidst, among, and, anent, avec, because of, beside(s), chez, con, coram, cum, given, mid, mit, near to, plus, through, together, toward(s), wight

comb. col, com, cyn, pro, syn

it au courant, current, groovy, hep, mod, stylish, trendy

it, not square

regard to about, anent, concerning

that moreover, provided, thereupon

WITHDRAW abandon, abjure, abscond, absent, abstract, alienate, avoid, back (away)(down), decamp, decline, deduct, depart, deport, derogate, desert, detach, detract, disavow, dis-

engage, distract, divert, drain, escape, evacuate, extract, flee, flinch, fly, forbear, forsake, kick, leave, minish, part, quit, recall, recant, recede, refrain, relinquish, remove, renounce, repeal, resign, restrain, retire, retract, retreat, revel, revoke, scram, scratch, secede, separate, sequester, sever, subduce, subduct, subside, subtract, sunder, surrender, syphon, turn off, unsheathe, vacate, vaik, void, withhold, yield

WITHDRAWAL departure, detachment, diversion, drain, flight, isolation, pullout, recession, regress, removal, retraction, retreat, revulsion, scuttle

from drugs cold turkey

WITHDRAWN aloof, asocial, detached, distant, ingrown, isolated, private, remote, retiring, secluded, shy, unsociable

WITHE band, boomiron, branch, cringle, halter, ring, rope, snare, twig, twist, wattle, wicker, wind, withy

WITHER adverse, adversity, age, air, arefact, atrophy, blast, blight, cotter, decay, decline, desiccate, die, droop, dry, fade, fail, languish, miff, oppose, opposite, parch, resist(ance), rivel, rust, scorch, sear, senesce, sere, shrink, shrivel, wallow, waste, welter, wilt, wizen, wrinkle

WITHERED arid, blasted, corky, dry, haggard, macerated, marcid, poor, shriveled, shrunken, wizened

WITHERING blight, blistering, caustic, contemptuous, marcescent, scathing

WITHHOLD abstain, boycott, bridle, check, conceal, curb, deny, desist, detain, forbear, hide, keep, maintain, postpone, prevent, prohibit, refrain, refuse, repress, reserve, restrain, retain, stint, stop, subtract

WITHIN among, at home, during, enclosed, herein, hidden, included, indoors, inly, inner, inside, interior,

into, intra, internally, inwardly, underneath
comb. end(o), ent(o), eso, intra
reach accessible, close, near, present
WITHOUT bankrupt, bare, bereft, besides, beyond, bout, but(for), deprived (of), devoid(of), except, exempt, external(ly), failing, forlorn(of), free, innocent, lacking, less, minus, missing, outdoors, outside, outwardly, sans, scant(of), senza, short(of), sine, unless, void, wanting
a break continually, continuously
a doubt certainly
cease constantly, continually, continuously
charge complimentary, free, gratis
comb. ect(o), less
end ad infinitum, endlessly, eternally, everlasting, forever, infinitely, lengthily, lengthy
equal peerless
this sine hoc
WITHSTAND abide, bear, bide, combat, confront, contest, contradict, controvert, defy, endure, face, forbear, gainsay, gainstand, hinder, last, obstruct, oppose, oppugn, prevail, prevent, resist, suffer, sustain, thwart, tolerate, weather
WITHY agile, osier, willow, wiry, woodie, woody
WITLESS brainless, crazy, dazed, dull, dumb, fatuous, foolish, gross, heedless, ignorant, indiscreet, insane, mad, pointless, scatterbrained, silly, slap-happy, stupid, thoughtless, unaware, unintelligent, unknowing
WITLOOF chicory, endive
WITNESS affirm, attend, attest(ant), attest(at)or, authority, behold(er), bystander, certificate, certify, compurgator, confirmation, conjuror, decalogue, deponent, evidence, evince, example, informant, kibitzer, martyr, notice, observe, onlooker, passerby, proof, see, signatory, signer, spectator, sponsor, subscribe,

swear, teste, testifier, testify, testimony, understanding, vouch(er)
-box stand
WITS See WIT.
WITTER assure, barb, certain, certify, direct, evident, inform, knowing, mark, sign, sure, tee, token, wise
WITTICISM bon mot, conceit, crack, gag, humor, jape, jest, joke, pleasantry, pun, quip, repartee, sally, squib, vitz, wheeze, wisecrack
WITTING information, intelligence, intentional, judgment, knowingly, knowledge, news, tidings
WITTY amusing, bright, caustic, comic(al), crafty, cunning, droll, facetious, funny, gash, humorous, informed, jocose, jocular, knowing, salty, sharp, smart, versed, waggish, whimsical, wily, wise
saying mot, pun, quip, riposte
WIVER flutter, quiver, tremble, waver
WIZARD adept, archimage, artist, brujo, comus, conjuror, diabolist, diviner, dowser, enchanter, exorciser, exorcist, expert, faust, fiend, great, mage, magical, magician, magus, master, miracleworker, necromancer, pellar, peller, quimboiseur, sage, shaman, shark, sorcerer, thaumaturge, theurgist, virtuoso, warlock, witchman
of the north sir walter scott
WIZARDRY alchemy, magic, sorcery, thaumaturgy, witchcraft, witchery
WIZEN age, contract, dry, dwindle, haggard, languish, poor, reduce, rivel, shrink, shrivel, weasand, weazen, wither
WOAD anilla, cress, dye(stuff), glastum, herb, indigo, isatis, kers, nill, tinge, wad(e)
constituent indigotin
WOADWAXEN alleluia, basebroom, dyeweed, greenbroom, greenwood, whin
WOBBLE boil, change, cockle, didder, dither, hobble, oscillate, quake, qua-

ver, reel, rock, roll, shake, shimmy, shudder, stagger, sway, teeter, titter, totter, tremble, vacillate, wabble, waggle, wauble, waver, wiggle
WOBBLY doubtful, loose, rickety, rocky, shaky, unsteady
WODEHOUSE *character* jeeves
WODEN See ODIN.
WOE affliction, agony, alas, anguish, bale, bane, distress, dole, dolor, evil, grief, grieving, heartache, misery, pain, regret, sorrow, suffering, torture, tribulation, trouble, unhappiness, wae, welladay
WOEBEGONE crestfallen, dejected, desolate(d), disconsolate, downcast, forlorn, low, melancholy, miserable, mournful, rueful, sad, sorry, unhappy, waff, wretched
WOEFUL afflicted, aggrieved, calamitous, deplorable, disconsolate, dismal, distressing, doleful, dolorous, grieved, grievous, lamentable, lugubrious, mean, melancholy, miserable, mournful, paltry, pitiable, plaintive, rueful, ruthful, sad, sorrowful, tearful, terrible, unhappy, wretched
WOGH crooked, perverse
WOLD downs, forest, hill, old, plain(s), upland, wood
WOLF, WOLF'S bolt, cancer, canine, chanco, coyote, devil, devour, fenrir, freki, gere, geri, glutton, gobble, isgrin, kaberu, larva, libertine, loafer, lobo, loup, lupus, philanderer, raven, ravin(e), roue, sigrim, ulcer, wolve, yabbi
brush coyote
comb. lyco
cry howl
ensign of gaul, rome
fictional akela
fish anarhichas, blenny, catfish, lupin, seacat
fist puffball
fox zorro
gait lope
genus canis
head hure, outlaw(ry)
hunter wolver
in sheep's clothing imposter

-like See WOLFISH.
milk spurge
mythological fenris, isegrim, skoll, werewolf
noble, name meaning adolph(us)
pack unit submarine, u-boat
peach tomato
pert. lupine
prairie coyote
spider hunter, ja(e)ger, jayhawk, lycosid, tarantula
symbol of cruelty, ferocity, rapine
timber lobo
tooth premolar
WOLFBERRY bittersweet, buckbush, buttonbush, ceanothus, coralberry
WOLFE, NERO *associate* archie goodwin, fritz
WOLFHOUND alan, borzoi, psovie
WOLFISH feral, ferocious, lupine, rapacious, ravenous, thooid
WOLFSBANE aconite, dogbane, foxbane, monkshood
WOLSEY *birthplace* ipswich
death foreseer mother shipton
son thomas winter
WOLVERINE carcajoy, cougar, glutton, gulo, lurcher, moocher
state michigan
WOMAN (See also *old* and *young*, below.) 3 dam, eve, fem, hag, hen, her, jug, mam, meg, mme, she, teg 4 baby, bibi, bind, bird, boss, burd, cony, dame, dona, fane, flag, frau, frow, gyne, jade, lady, maam, marm, mary, miss, moll, mort, peri, slut, wife 5 belle, broad, china, coney, donna, femme, frail, houri, jatni, lubra, lucky, madam, menad, missy, mujer, quean, queen, skirt, smock, squaw, tagge, twist, unman, vixen, vrouw, wench, yenta 6 burdie, calico, domina, female, gimmer, kimmer, luckie, madame, maenad, maness, matron, milady, missis, mulier, quaeda, senora, sister, tomato, virago, wahine 7 distaff, dowager, partlet, pinnace, placket, sahibah, senhora, signora 8 fraulein, memsahib, mistress, paramour 9 petticoat

aboriginal gin, lubra
abusive fishwife, xant(h)ippe
adviser egeria,
affected cockney, precieuse, prude
aggressive amazon
alluring charmer, dish, dollie, dolly, sheba, siren
apartment boudoir, harem, oda, seraglio, thalamus, zenana
beautiful aphrodite, beauty, belle, charmer, cherub, cleopatra, doll, eyeful, filly, helen, honey, houri, huri, looker, maja, mantrap, musidora, peach, peri, pinup, siren, spark, sylph, venus, zenobia
beloved amanda, inamorata, querida
-bird harpy
bold ramp
brave hellcat, heroine
celibate agapeta, vestal, virgin
-chaser carpet-knight, libertine, lothario, philanderer, romeo, roue, sheepbiter, wolf
cleaning char, daily
coarse beast, blowze, cotquean, randy, rullion
comb. femo, gyn(o)
coolie changar
coy haggard
cremated sati, suttee
dependent clinging vine
deserted agunah
domain distaff
-eater gynophagite
extravagant araminta
fashionable elegante, milady
fat boss, cow, dumpling, fustilugs
1st embla, eve, izanami, pandora
-fish mermaid
foolish dumb-dora
frenzied maenad, menad
garment See GARMENT *woman's.*
general hays, hoisington, penthesilea
gentle dove, lady
gossipy biddy, cat, haik, hake, tabby
group altrusa, amvs, circle, dar, ebell, gaggle, lib, now, peo, pilot, quota, sisterhood, soroptimist, sorority, sorosis, zonta
-hater misogynist

headdress bonnet, nubia, wimple
ill-tempered nag, scold, shrew, termagant, virago, vixen, witch, xant(h)ippe, yenta
immoral flapper, gitch, harlot, rig, slut, tart
inspired phoebad
kept concubine, demimondaine, inamorata, l'irreguliere, mistress, paramour
-killing femicide
lawyer portia
leader doyenne
learned basbleu, blue(stocking), clergess, pundita, seeress
lewd See *loose*, below.
lib leader ellmann, friedan, greer, lupscomb, millet, quigley, steinem, vivrost
little ladykin, wife
loose bag(gage), bimbo, bitch, broad, bummerkeh, chippy, cocotte, courtesan, courtezen, demivierge, drab, dratchell, flap, flirtgill(ian), franion, giglet, giglot, gillot, harlot, hussy, huzzy, jezebel, jilt, kit, limmer, minx, parnel, quean, queen, quiff, rep, slut, tib, troll(op), trub
love of philogyny
-lover philogynist
malicious cat
married better half, beulah, bride, consort, esposa, femme-covert, frau, frow, goody, helpmate, helpmeet, madam, matron, moglie, mujer, mulier, rib, senora, signora, spouse, squaw, vrouw, wife
masculine amazon, androgyne, corquean, rullion
meek grisel(da), grizel
military group spar, wa(a)c, wave, wrac, wraf, wren, wsp
mythological gorgon, medusa
noble contessa, countess, dame, duchess, lady, marchesa, marchioness
objectionable earlin(e), fag(g)ot, gorgon, grimalkin, hag, harridan, shrew, termagant, virago, witch
of low caste dasi
of rank domina, lady
old baba, bat, battle-axe, beldam(e), biddy, cadua, cail-

leach, cailliach, carlin(e), centenarian, crone, cummer, dame, dodo, dowager, fag-(g)ot, fogram, fogrum, fogy, frump, fuddyduddy, fussbudget, gammer, geezer, gib, grandam(e), grandmother, granny, hag, jade, kulu, mother, nagger, picky, spinster, trot, veck(e), wife, witch

old, pert. anicular, anile

organization See *group*, above.

outlaw ella watson, mollie murrill, pearl hart, rose of the cimarron

peacock-tailed alborak

pedantic See *learned*, above.

pert. chit, female, feminine, gynaecic, gynecic, mul(i)ebral

pilot amelia earhart, pancho barnes

pioneer calamity jane

pregnant gravida

presidential candidate victoria woodhull

priggish nice-nelly, prude

quarrelsome catamaran, termagant, virago

religious abbess, beguine, nun

rich barbara hutton, doris duke, helen clay frick, hetty green, jackie onassis, joan payson, queen(elizabeth) (juliana) (wilhelmina)

ruler gubernatrix, matriarch, queen

rustic joan

scarlet (See also *loose*, above.) babylon, london

scolding nag, shrew, xant-(h)ippe

servant abigail, biddy, char, maid, tweeny

short or *stumpy* cutty, trub

shrewish jade, harpy, skellat

single bachelorette, mistress, spinster, virgin

slatternly See *slovenly*, below.

slender sylph

slovenly bag, besom, clatch, dowd(y), drab, draggle-tail, dratchel, fleabag, frump, maux, slattern, sloven, slut, sow, tawpy, trollimog, trollop

spiteful bitch, cat, fury

squat trub

squeamish cockney

staid beldam(e), dowager, lady, matron

stately juno

state of muliebrity

strong amazon, titaness, virago

suffrage leader anthony, catt, mott, pankhurst, stanton, stone

talkative cat, dolly, fizgig, flirt, gad, gossip, hellcat, hen, scold, shrew, termagant, virago, vixen

theatrical actress, chorine, dancer, ingenue, soubrette

unattractive bag, crone, dog, dowd(y), drab, hag, slattern, witch

unmarried bachelor girl, dame, girl, old maid, spinster, unclaimed jewel

unsteady flap

victim dupe, fall guy, gull, sucker

vixenish harridan, viragin, virago

wailing banshee, banshie

wanton See *loose*, above.

warrior amazon, camilla, joan d'arc, valkyrie

widow sati, suttee

wild m(a)enad

wise alruna, alrune, volva

witchlike fata

with 1 child unipara

with 3 children tripara

withered crone

worship of mariolatry

young babe, baggage, beast, bird, bit, brisette, burd, chick(en), chit, dame, damsel, damozel, daughter, dell, demoiselle, doll, drab, filly, flapper, fluff, girl, grisette, heifer, lass(ie), mademoiselle, mlle, nymph(et), pigeon, puss, senorita, sheila, signorina, subdeb, tib, toast, trull, wench, winklot

WOMANHOOD *goddess* hera, juno, mut, sati

personified eimer

WOMANISH, WOMANLY anile, effeminate, female, feminine, gentle, lady-like, modest, petticoat, soft, tender

WOMANIZER amorist, beast, beau, blade, blood, boyfriend, carpet knight, casanova, cavalier, cicesbeo, cosseter, dallier, dandler, don juan, enticer, fancyman, flirt, gallant,

goat, hotspur, ladykiller, lecher, libertine, lothario, lover(boy), madcap, masher, paramour, philanderer, profligate, rake(hell), ram, roue, seducer, sport, stallion, stud, trifler, wolf

WOMANKIND calico, distaff, feminie, muslin, women

pert. muliebral

WOMBAT badger, didelph, groundhog, koala, phascolomys

WON abide, abode, accustom, apartment, city, district, dwell(ing), inhabit, live, one, region, residence, room, town

WONDER admiration, amaze (ment), astonishment, astoundment, awe, bewilderment, confoundment, curiosity, destruction, disbelief, dismay, doubt, dream, esteem, evil, fantasy, fear, ferly, gape, grief, harm, magic(al), marvel, meditate, miracle, muse, perplexity, phenomenon, ponder, portent, prodigy, puzzlement, rarity, reverence, reverie, selcouth, selly, shock, speculate, stare, study, stupefaction, surprise, suspect, think, topnotcher, unco, vision, wrong

at mirate

comb. terat(o), thaumat(o)

7 artemis temple, artemisia mausoleum, babylon gardens, pharos, pyramids, rhodes colossus, zeus statue

7 natural baikal, everest, glacier bay, grand canyon, mammoth caves, victoria falls, yellowstone

state arkansas

struck with aghast, surprised

worker theurgist, wizard

-working miraculous

WONDERBERRY huckleberry, morel, nightshade, solanum

WONDERFUL, WONDROUS admirable, amazing, amusing, astonishing, bonzer, corking, dandy, excellent, extraordinary, fabulous, firstrate, gallant, grand, great, groovy, lovely, marvelous, mighty, miraculous, mirific, prime, splendid, strange, striking,

stupendous, superb, supreme, swell, unique, wizard
name meaning mira, myra
WONDERLAND See PARADISE, UTOPIA.
cat cheshire
girl alice
WONE abundance, custom, hope, manner, one, plenty, resource, usage, wealth, wont
WONKY awry, feeble, off, shaky, unsteady, wobbly, wrong
WONT accustomed, addicted, custom, desire, dwell, fain, habit(uated), haunt, inclined, mole, practice, reside, rule, usage, use(d), want
WOO allure, approach, assail, attract, beg, beseech, bid, chase, coax, court, cultivate, entreat, follow, importune, invite, love, lure, pursue, seek, solicit, spark, splunt, spoon, sue, suit, trail, wale
WOOD(S) (See also TIMBER, TREE.) bois, bongo, boscage, bosk(et), bosky, bosque(t), bush, cask, coppice, cross, enraged, forest, fuel, furious, glade, grove, hurst, hyrst, keg, kindling, lumber, mad(ly)(ness), motte, rage, spinney, stick, stuff, sylvan, thicket, timber, tree(s), treey, violent, weald, woad, wold
agatized shinarump
alcohol methanol, methyl
anemone bowbells, cyme, emony, snowdrop
ball See WOOD *knot.*
balsam-like bongo
bark blondine, sable
bedstraw scotch-mist
bend in sny
betony beefsteakplant, bishopswort, lousewort, watermint
black ebony
blemish catface
block or *brick* chock, chump, dook, nog
bowl kitty, mazer
broom wild-teasel
bundle fagot
burned ash, brae, bray, charcoal
burned over brulee
burnt as perfume agalloch

cabinet work calamander, yew
carpenter's stuff
carver alcimedon, bodger
chopper, poor ali baba
clearing ridding
comb. hyl(o), ligni, ligno, xylo
construct of materiate
convert to lignify
copper olivenite
core ame
-cracker nuthatch
cutting hylotomous
damage dryrot, wetrot
dark acapu, ebony, teak
dealer xylopolist
decay conk, doze
demon lesh(e)y, lesiy, nat
densified staypak
-destroying ligniperdous, xylophagous
duck branchier, canard, goose, merganser, squealer
dust coom(b)
dye brasilein
-eater termite
-eating hylophagous
elastic sycamore
engraving xylograph
feeding on dendrophilous
fiber, pressed masonite
fine-grained brauna, yew
firing easily kindling, punk, sponk, spunk, tinder, touchwood
flexible edder, osier, willow
fort abatis
fossil peucites, pinite
fragrant acuyari, agalloch, aloes, calambac, cedar, mimosa
fringe fumitory
fuel estovers, kindling, log
fungus cytosporina
god See FOREST *deity.*
grain bate, beat
grass bluestem, knotroot
grating babracot
grove hemora
growing in silvicolous, sylvester
growing on epixylous, xylophilous
growth coppice
gum resin, xylan
hard (See also TREE *hardwood.*) alintatao, anjan, ash, avodire, baku, banuyo, cadamba, camara, cocobolo, curupay, dao, dattock, ebony, elm, freijo, gidgee, gidya, hickory, ipil, ironbark, kajugaru, kar(r)i,

kempas, kokra, lana, mahogany, maple, narra, oak, poon, rata, sabicu, sal, teak, walnut, yacal, zante
heart duramen
heavy axe(master), chengal, dao, ebon(y), guayabi, ironwood, quebracho, sucupira
hedge-repairing haybote, tining
hen rail, weka(s), WOODCOCK
hewer picuculo, tree-creeper, WOODPECKER
hoopoe dungbird, irrisor, picarian, whoop(e)
horse trestle, walkingstick
hyacinth bluebell, crow-toe, greggle, harebell, scilla, squill
ibis gannet, gourdhead, ironhead, jabiru, mycteria, stork
imperfection knot-hole
incense agalloch(um), agalwood, aguilawood, aloes, eaglewood, lignaloes
-inhabiting nemoral, sylvan
inlays intarsia
ipecac feverroot
joint taper, tenon
juice sap
knot burl, burr, gnarl, knag, knar, knur(l), nur(l)
layer core, veneer
light balsa, cork, edder, hemlock, osier, poon, willow
lost chippage
louse cheeselip, deathtick, deathwatch, pillbug, slater, sowbug, white-ant
love of hemophily
luminescence foxfire
lustrous boarwood, latine, leza
made of treen
measure cord, fathom
mottled amboina
nettle albany-hemp
no. 1 driver
no. 2 brassie
no. 3 spoon
no. 4 baffy, cleek
nymph arethusa, dryad, grayling, hamadryad, hummingbird, moth, satyr, wintergreen
oily batete
olive collie
passage glade, path, trail
peg bung, fid, nog, skeg, spile, stopper, thole
perfume-yielding agalloch, linaloa

pert. arboreal, ligneous, nemoral, sylvan, treed, treen, xyloid

petrified lithoxyl(e), rockwood

piece or *part* apron, batten, beam, billet, board, brandering, chock, chump, chunk, deal, dingbat, dowel, euphroe, fid, fillet, kip, lath, lipping, nog, panel, peg, plank, reeper, reglet, rib, rig, shim, slat, spile, spline, splint, spoon, sprag, stave, stower, tenon, timber, trippet, waddy

pigeon cushat, ringdove

pile bats, stran(d), woodrick

pimpernel loosestrife

pin See *peg*, above.

pink bosse

pore lenticel

product bucket, carder, cask, churn, dye-tub, firkin, noggin, piggin, runlet, trencher, trough, tub

pussy polecat, skunk

red aranga, banaba, cherry, dungon, kambala, kar(r)i, koa, rata, satine

reddish-yellow guyo

robin miro, thrush, tomtit

rock asbestos

rotten daddock

rush luzula

sacred asherah

sage ambrose, germander

sapele aboudikiro

ship-building angelique, angili, teak

-slave gecko

small bosk, coppice, grove, spinney, thicket

soft agalloch, elkwood, gaboon, gabun, guatambu, kiri

soot product asbolin

sorrel alleluia, alleluja, averrhoa, begonia, bolboxalis, cuckoo(flower), hallelujah, haremeat, hearts, lujula, oca, oxalis, shamrock, stabwort, trefoil

speckled palmyra

spirits methanol, methyl

steward woodreeve

strip batten, lath, slat, spline

striped araroba, fleck, roe

supporting cleat

tar product creosote

thrush bellbird, campanero, maybird, shrike

tinder punk, sponk, touchwood

tissue pleurenchyma

turner bodger, lathe

unfinished deal

valuable ebony, sal, teak

veneer skillet

water-resisting amubis

yellow fustic, guatambu, guyo, haldu, idigbo, kadamba, makassi, umburana

WOODBINE beewort, creeper, eglantine, eglatere, honeysuckle, jasmine, peridot, virginia creeper, widbin

WOODCHAT ianthia, shrike

WOODCHUCK chug, groundhog, marmot, monax, moonack, suslik, wejack, woodpecker

day candlemas

WOODCOCK becasse, bogsucker, dupe, fool, nightflit, pe(e)wee, pewit, philohela, quis, rubicola, shrups, simpleton, snipe, snite, woodpecker

group fall

WOODCUTTER abe lincoln, ali baba, axeman, chopper, hewer, logger, lumberman, sawyer, wood(s)man

WOODED arboreal, arboreous, arborous, bosky, forested, hylean, sylvan, treey

WOODEN awkward, clumsy, deadpan, dry, dull, expressionless, firm, graceless, hard, heavy, inferior, inflexible, insensitive, lifeless, ligneous, obtuse, rigid, sedate, solid, spiritless, sticky, stiff, stolid, stupid, tense, timbered, timbern, treed, treen, ungainly, worthless, xyloid

form ame

-headed dull, stupid

horse babieca, gallows, scaffold, trojan horse

horse builder epe(i)us

WOODKERN outlaw, robber

WOODLAND boscage, forest, hinterland, miombo, spring, timberland, woodlot

WOODMAN bushman, bushwack, bushy, forester, frontiersman, hunter, nomad, pioneer, rustic, scout, silvan, sylvan, sylvestral, trapper, woodchopper, woodcutter

WOODPECKER awl, campephilus, carpenterbird, carpintero, celeomorph, chab,

climber, creeper, dirtbird, eccle, flicker, hecco, heckle, hewel, hewhall, hewhole, hickoryhead, hickwall, hickway, ickle, ivorybill, jynx, kate, kickwall, logcock, nickle, pianet, picarian, picucule, picule(t), picus, pileated, popinjay, rainbird, rainfowl, redhead, sapsuck(er), snapper, speight, spekt, sprite, stormcock, tapper, wallhick, whetile, witwall, woodcock, woodhacker, woodjobber, woodspite, wryneck, yaffle, yockel, yuckle, yukkel, yunx

changed to picus

kind downy, hairy, imperial, pileated, redheaded, spotted

-like bird jacamar, piciform

pert. picine

WOODRUFF asperula, hairhoof, hairof, mugwet, pettymugget, waldmeister, woodrow

WOODS See WOOD.

WOODSERE cuckoospit, dry, unproductive

WOODSHIP madness

WOODSKIN canoe

WOODWAXEN See WOADWAXEN.

WOODWIND See MUSICAL INSTRUMENT *wind*.

key languet, speaker

WOODWORK boiserie, bratticing, carpentry, ceiling, joinery, sloid, slojd, sloyd

instrument scriber

WOODWORKER bodger, cabinet-maker, carpenter, joiner, millman, nailor, paneler, sawyer, turner

implement adze, edger, hammer, lathe, plane(r), router, sapper, saw, shaper, sticker

WOODWORM gribble, termite

WOODY bosky, bushy, frithy, ligneous, lignose, pithy, shady, silvan, sticky, sylvan, treed, treen, withy, xyloid

fiber bast, hemp, xylem

nightshade bittersweet

tongue actinomycosis

WOOER beau, counter, courtier, lover, paramour, suitor, wower

WOOF abb, bark, cloth, fabric, filling, texture, weave, weft, wough

WOOHOO sailfish

WOOL (See FABRIC *wool;* also *kind,* below.) angora, astrachan, astrakhan, breech, broadtail, combing, down, fleece, gare, hair, jersey, kersey, laine, lana, lock, stuff, tomentum, tousle, trick, yarn
bale sarpler
blemish mote
bunting nun's-cloth
carder tozer
clean garnett
coarse abb, cordova, cotta, cowtail, gare, haslock, shag
-colored beige, camel
comb card
comb. erio, lani
cotton caddice, caddis
curled astrakhan
deposit in suint
draw slub
dryer fugal
eater moth
fabric See FABRIC *wool.*
fat anaspalin, degras, lanolin(e), suet, suint, tallow
fell pelt
fiber nep, noil
fine cashmere, kashmir, picklock, spinners, vicuna
grease cake seak
greasy tippy
grower sheep, rancher
highgrade picklock
inferior abb, brokes, cast, cleamer, cowtail, downright, head, livery
kind alpaca, argali, botany, downright, haslock, kashmir, mor(t)ling, mungo, noil, pulu, shag, shearing
king's shatush
knot burl, nep, noil
lamb's wassail
lock of dag, floccus, flock, frib(by), staple, tag, tate
long blue
long-fibered argali, shafty
low grade abb, livery
matted dag, shag
measure butt, fadge, heer
merino botany
mixed hue tum
nap-raising plant teasel
nodule slub
package butt, fadge
pert. fleecy, floccose, lanate, lanose, peronate
pulled slipe
quality blood
rag mungo, shoddy

reclaimed mongo(e), mungo, shoddy
refuse backing(s), cot(t), flock, fud, pinion
roll carding, club, rove, roving
sheep's leg gare
sheets batt(ing)
shreds noil
skirtings broke
soft berlin, cashmere, kashmir
spun yarn
tease out card, tosy, tum
texture nap
thread worsted
unravel tease
watered moreen
weight clove, tod
worker burler, carder, litster, sartor, shedhand, shepster, spinner, teasel(l)er, weaver, webster
wound trend
yarn abb, caddis, eis

WOOLF, VIRGINIA *novel* fluff, jacob's room, mrs dalloway, orlando, the waves, to the lighthouse

WOOLGATHER muse

WOOLGATHERING absentmindedness, brown study, preoccupation, reverie

WOOLY blurred, confused, curlyheaded, fleecy, floccose, flocculent, fluffy, fuzzy, hairy, hirsute, lanate, lanose, peronate, shaggy, sheep, soft, warm
aphid eriosoma
bear woubit
-bent sand grass
butt eucalyptus
croton hogwort
-haired ulotrichous
pyrol urd

WOOZY befuddled, dazed, dizzy, drunk, faint, flabby, flaccid, grotesque, muddled, shaky, strange, trembly

WORCESTER botany bay

WORD(S) account, adage, advice, affirmation, anagram, avowal, cajole, command, comment, communication, countersign, declaration, direction, discourse, express (ion), fame, homonym, honor, idiom, information, language, lip, logos, lyrics, maxim, message, motto, name, news, order, outburst, palabra, parol(e), password, phrase, pledge,

promise, proverb, quarrel, quatch, remark, report, repute, rhema, say, signal, speech, statement, synonym, talk, term, testimony, text, tidings, utterance, vocable, vocabulary, voice
action verb
addition epexegesis
battle altercation, logomachy
blindness alexia, dyslexia
book cyclopedia, dictionary, glossary, lexicon, libretto, speller, thesaurus, vocabulary
break renig
coined neologism, neology
coiner verbarian
colorful slang
comb. log(o), onym, verb(o)
composite symphrase
containing all vowels ambidextrous, eulogia, euouae, miaoued, oisear, uncopyrightable, undiscoverably
containing all vowels in reverse sequence duoliteral
containing all vowels in sequence caesious
containing no vowels crwth, cwm, nth
containing uu continuum, duumvir(ate), mutuum, perpetuum, residuum, triduum, vacuum, zuurveldt
contraction haplology
corresponding analogue
deletion of letter apocope
derived from another paronym
descriptive adjective
difficult jawbreaker
difficulty dyslexia
divine logos
division syllable, tmesis
excessive interest in verbomania
expansion expenthesis
figurative use metonym, trope
flow of loquacity
foolish See NONSENSE.
formation acronym, acrostic, analogue, antonym, heteronym, homonym, metonym, poecilonym, spoonerism, synonym
formation, pert. rhematic
4-letter tetragram
for word exact, literal, verbatim
from initials acronym
game anagrams, categories, charades, coffeepot, ghosts,

hangman, murder, observa-
tion, salvo, scrabble, testimony
group clause, phrase, sentence
history etymology
imitative echoic, onomatope
imitative, use of onomatopoeia
inventer coiner, neologist
last amen, finish, selah,
thirty
long sesquipedalian
made from another anagram
magic abracadabra, eureka,
presto, sesame, shelah
meaning semantics
meaningless drivel, gibberish, nonsense
mishearing otosis
misuse abusage, abusion,
barbarism, bull, catachresis,
heterophemy, impropriety,
lapsus-linguae, malaprop-
ism, solecism, syllepsis
mystical abracadabra, abrasax, abraxas
naming noun
new neologism, neology, ne-
oterism
new meaning trope
of god logos
of honor oath, parol(e),
pledge, promise
of mouth gossip, rumor
of opposite meaning an-
tonym
of same meaning synonym
of same sound homonym,
homophone
of sanction amen, aye, verily, yea, yes
omission of letter aphesis,
apocope, syncope
one, pert. monepic
order morpheme
order inversion anastrope
overabundance of perissol-
ogy, pleonasm, verbiage,
verbosity
pert. lexical
play on pun
put into express, phrase,
speak
puzzle acrostic, anagram,
charade, crossword, rebus
redundant cheville, verbiage
related amphigon
repetition anophora, epistrophe, ploce
root etym(on), radical,
theme
sacred s(h)elah, sesame

same backward and forward
palindrome
same spelling homograph,
homonym
science of linguistics, semantics
scrambled anagram
separation of parts diacope,
tmesis
sign hieroglyphic, ideogram,
logogram, pictograph
similar synonym
slang argot, twag, whid
source etymon
square palindrome
study etymology
substitute metonym, trope
symbol grammalogue, hieroglyphic
the gospel, scriptures
to the wise advice, counsel,
verbum-sap
transposition of letters anagram
unifying copula
WORDINESS lexiphanicism,
logorrhea, loquaciousness,
pleonism, prolixity, sesquip-
edalism, verbiage, verbosity
WORDLESS dumb, silent,
tacit(urn)
WORDS See WORD.
WORDSWORTH *home* dove
cottage, grasmere
poem the excursion, the
prelude, tintern abbey
sister dorothy
WORDY bombastic, diffuse,
garrulous, loquacious, prolix, redundant, rhetorical,
talkative, turgid, verbal,
verbose, voluble, windy
WORK (See also *hard,*
below.) 3 act, fag, job, ply,
run, use 4 book, darg, deed,
duty, feat, form, grub, lead,
move, opus, plan, play,
task, toil 5 cause, chore,
draft, ergon, forte, grind,
labor, pains, solve, stint,
sweat, swink, trade 6 ac-
tion, behave, bubble, ca-
reer, dargue, design,
drudge, effort, excite, harass, induce, manage, me-
tier, potter, strive 7 attempt, calling, execute, exploit, fashion, ferment, mission, operate, ouvrage, pattern, perform, produce,
product, provoke, pursuit,
trouble 8 activity, business,
drudgery, endeavor, exer-

cise, function, industry, interest, maneuver, material,
memorial, monument, posi-
tion, practice, struggle 9
cultivate, influence, operation, treatment 10 ac-
complish, assignment, em-
broidery, employment, ma-
nipulate, manuscript, occupation, profession 11
achievement, performance
additional parergon
against attack, combat, fight,
knife, sabotage
agreement code, contract,
pact
aimlessly dabble, fiddle, piddle, potter, putter, tinker
at ply
bag etui, etwee, reticule
basket caba(s)
bench donkey, siege, template
body oeuvre
-brittle industrious
cessation hartal, sit-in, strike
child's chore
clothes coverall, denims,
jeans, khaki, levis, overalls
comb. erg(o), ergy
day's darg(ue)
divine theurgy
downstairs chare
dull drudgery
evade goldbrick, goof off,
slack(off), snib
fear of ergophobia
final swansong
for beswink, serve
hard char(e), delve, drill,
drudge, exert, labor, louster, lucubrate, mine, moil,
muck, plod, plug, scrabble,
slave, slog, struggle, sweat,
swot, tew, toil, travail, twig,
yerk
horse aver, drudge, percheron, sawhorse, slave, trestle
incomplete ebauche
intermission coffee-break,
elevens
irregularly dabble
labored lucubration
lover ergophile
man of all factotum, handyman, roustabout
mechanical slojd, sloyd
on cajole, coax, importune,
influence, practice, press
(ure), urge
out accomplish, arrange,
block, calculate, design,
develop, efface, elaborate,
erase, evolve, exercise, ex-

haust, plan, range, rehearse, result, solve, train
over brainwash, elaborate, influence, persuade, redo, rehash, revamp, revise
period day, hitch, hour, month, schedule, shift, spell, tour, trick, turn, watch, week
place atelier, bottega, den, ergasterion, factory, forge, lab(oratory), library, mill, officina, plant, shop, smithy, studio, study
put out of See DISMISS.
skilled slojd, sloyd
sloppy mullock
slowly cacanny, dawdle, plod, potter, putter, worm
steadily hammer(away), peg, ply, toil
stoppage huelga, strike
table bench, siege
to excess exhaust, overdo, overtax
together coact, collaborate, connive, cooperate, play ball, team(up)
unit calorie, erg(on), joule, kilerg, manhour, megajoule, rad
unskillfully botch, bungle, fudge, fumble
up advance, agitate, arouse, develop, elaborate, excite, hike, irk, manipulate, plan, provoke, raise, rouse, stir
youthful juvenilia
WORKABLE feasible, maniable, mellow, pliant, practicable, practical, ripe
WORKADAY bread-and-butter, commonplace, everyday, humdrum, ordinary, practical, prosaic, staple
WORKER ant, artificer, artisan, bee, billjim, breadwinner, cager, carpenter, carrier, char(e), cocker, coolie, cooly, craftsman, dayman, doer, employe, esne, factotum, floater, flunky, gibaro, hand, helot, helper, jobber, laborer, lumper, mechanic, menial, navvy, operant, operator, peon, prole, proletarian, roto, servant, toiler, toty, volk, wage-earner, wright
blue-collar stiff
clumsy bungler, cobbler
cunning bezaleel
comb. ergate, ergato
domestic char(e), help, maid

fellow associate, buddy, butty, comrade, confederate, confrere, mate, partner
food tommy
group crew, force, gang, personnel, staff, team, union
hard beaver, drudge, fagger, slogger
head boss, employer, foreman, ganger, manager, master, overseer, super(intendent), supervisor
migrant arkie, boomer, bracero, floater, gastarbeiter, hobo, okie, wetback
non-union blackleg, freerider, rat, scab
objectionable botcher, bungler, featherbedder, scab, scissorbill
part-time kelly girl, rubbler
pert. blue-collar, eratomorphic
skilled artisan
song internationale
unskilled butcher, coolie, cooly, greener, helper, laborer, peon, roustabout
WORKHOUSE almshouse, jail, poorhouse, prison, workshop
WORKING acting, active, alert, busy, decree, effort, endeavor, fermentation, function, going, leavening, manufacture, operating, operation, ordinance, ruffled, running, solution, twitching
class proletariat
insect See ANT, BEE, WASP.
not broken, idle, off, unemployed
order kilter
WORKMAN See WORKER.
WORKMAN-LIKE adept, deft, expert, proficient, skillful
WORKS deeds, engine, factory, insides, mechanism, mill, motor, plant, shop
WORKSHOP See WORK *place.*
WORLD age, brahmanda, career, cosmos, creation, earth, generation, globe, hiranyagarbha, humanity, kingdom, loka, macrocosm, mankind, monde, multitude, nature, people, planet, population, public, quantity, realm, sphere, terra, terre, universe, vale, wadru, ward(e), warl
academic campus

age yuga
ash yggdrasill
before creation of premundane
below inframundane
citizen cosmopolite
comb. cosm(o)
creating cosmopoietic
creator pan-ku
end of kali, ultima thule
external nonego
fashionable grand monde, haut monde, SOCIETY
holder of atlas
lower orcus
miniature microcosm
mother goddess chomolongma
northernmost part thule
of the dead See HELL.
pert. mundane, secular, terrestrial
police interpol
ruler kosmokrator, uranus
serpent ananta
soul anima mundi, atman
spirit weltgeist
view weltanschauung, weltansicht
-weary blase, bored, sated, satiated
-wide ecumenic(al), global, international, pandemic, planetary, universal
wonder, alexandria catacombs
wonder, china great wall
wonder, england stonehenge
wonder, istanbul st sophia
wonder, nankin porcelain tower
wonders, 7 See WONDER 7.
WORLDLY carnal, earthly, fleshly, human, laic, lay, material, mortal, mundane, physical, profane, secular, sophisticated, sublunary, temporal, terrene, terrestrial
WORLD WAR I *air squadron* flying circus
armistice site compiegne
army aef, amex, bef
battle amiens, ardennes, argonne, armentieres, arras, belleau woods, cantigny, caporetto, gallipoli, marne, nancy, roulers, somme, tannenberg, ypres
central powers austria, bulgaria, germany, hungary, turkey
english commander allenby
nurse cavell

u s general black jack pershing
WORLD WAR II *aerial combat* battle of britain
battle anzio, ardennes, arnhem, bastogne, battle of the bulge, belfort, coral sea, guadalcanal, iwo jima, okinawa, remagen, tarawa
conference casablanca, teh-(e)ran, yalta
fortification maginot line
general carlson, clark, eisenhower, macarthur, montgomery, patch, patton, rommel
nazi prison See NAZI *concentration camp.*
soldier, fictitious kilroy
surrender ve-day, vj-day
surrender site reims
underground maquis, partigiani, partisans, resistance
vessel victory ship
WORM (See also CATERPILLAR.) annelid, arter, ascarid, blight, bob, brandlin, cadew, carbora, cercaria, chetapod, crawl, cur, drag(on), enoplan, eri, ess, extract, fluke, grub, helminth, inch, insinuate, larva, leech, leodocid, loa, lug, lurg, lytta, maggot, naid, nema(tode), nereid, palmer, palolo, piper, plaice, reprobate, reptile, rotifer, sabella, sagitta, screw, serpent, setarid, shamir, sinuate, snake, spile, spionid, spy, strongyl, syllid, tagtail, teredo, termite, trematode, triclad, turn, vermes, vermis, wind, wretch, wriggle, writhe
aquatic achaeta, acholoe, amphitrite, annelid, aphrodite, cadew, eunice, gephyrea, leech, lurg, maid, nais, nema, nemertean, nemertine, nereis, polynoid, spionid, whale's-tongue
arrow chaetognath(a)
bait lurg, mad, tagtail
blind orvet
bloodsucking leech
comb. vermi
earth brandling, ersenia
-eaten blighted, decayed, decrepit, old, out-of-date, pitted, ragged, seedy, shabby, vermoulu, weakened, wermethe, wornout, worthless
edible ipo, palolo

eunicid palolo
eye-infecting loa
flat acoela
fluke plaice
fossil scolite
fossil track nereite
genus cirratulus, enchytraeus, filaria, geoplana, nereis
hole piqure
in flatter, interpose, intrude
intestinal acanthocephala, helminth, tapeworm
killer vermicide
lizard amphisbaenid
marine See *aquatic,* above.
measuring (cabbage)looper, inchworm
mud ipo, loa
mythological shamir
nematode aguillula, aphelenchus, ascarid, giant strongyle, palisade, polymyaria, rhabditis, trichina
nemesis early bird
out of elicit, escape, question
parasitic ancanthocephalan, aphelenchus, cestode, filar, tape, trichina
pert. helminthoid, serpentine, vermian, vermicular, vermiculate
round ascarid, nema(tode)
rudimentary limb parapodium
segmented annelid, earthworm, leech
ship's broma, cobra, teredo
silk ailanthus, eri(a)
snail-like slug
study helminthology
symbol of cringing
thread filaria
trematode amphistomum, bilharzia
wood-boring carbora, termite
WORMSEED ambrosia, santonica
WORMWEED pinkroot, spigelia
WORMWOOD absinthe, absinthion, artemisia, composit, cudweed, mingwort, moxa, ragweed
impregnate with absinthiate
WORN abraded, attrite, bedraggled, dilapidated, eaten, effete, hackneyed, impaired, overworked, ragged, secondhand, seedy, sere, shabby, stale, tattered, threadbare, trite, used, wasted, weakened

down abraded, attrite(d), eroded, erose
out banal, beat(en), bleary, bushed, commonplace, consumed, decrepit, enfeebled, exhausted, fatigued, frayed, hackneyed, harassed, impaired, jaded, obsolete, passe, seedy, shabby, shot, spent, stale, tired, trite
WORRICOW bugaboo, bugbear, devil, hobgoblin
WORRIED afraid, annoyed, anxious, apprehensive, care-laden, concerned, fazed, fearful, fretted, harassed, harried, solicitous, streaked, troubled, uneasy
WORRIER fretter, fussbudget, fusser, worrit
WORRIT fidget, trouble, WORRY
WORRY agitate, anguish, annoy, anxiety, apprehension, badger, bait, bedevil, belabor, beset, bother, brood, caddle, care, cark, chafe, chagrin, chevy, choke, concern, cotter, cumber, disconcert, distress, disturb, doubt, fash, faze, fear, fidget, fike, frab, fret, fuss, gally, harass(ment), hare, harry, hatter, hector, hox, lurry, mangle, maul, moil, nag, perturb, pester, plague, pother, reck, rux, shake, solicitude, stew, strangle, tantalize, tear, tease, tew, torment, touse, trouble, try, turmoil, uneasiness, upset, vex, wherrit, worrit
unnecessarily borrow trouble
without carefree
WORSEN aggravate, decay, decline, degenerate, descend, deteriorate, impair, worst
WORSHIP admiration, admire, adoration, adore, awe, baalism, bless, cherish, credit, cult, devotion, dignity, discipline, dulia, elohism, esteem, exalt, hierurgy, homage, honor, hyperdulia, iconism, idolatry, idolize, imagery, latria, love, magnify, namaz, obeisance, observe, praise, pray, prize, puja, renown, repute, respect, revere(nce), ritual, serve, venerate, veneration, worth(iness), yajna

acts of proseynemata
ancestor manism
comb. latry
exclamation of alleluia(h),
deo gratias, halleluiah, hallelujah, hosanna
highest latria
inferior dulia
nature physiolatry
object baal, fetich, fetish,
god, icon, idol, joss, moloch, totem
pert. liturgic(al)
place altar, bethel, cathedral,
chapel, cheder, church,
dom, fane, mosque, sanctuary, shrine, synagogue, tabernacle, temple
public service
star sabaism
WORSHIPER adorer, bhakta,
communicant, devotee, disciple, fetishist, honorer,
hymner, idolater, praiser,
venerator, votary
of fire gheber, gueber, parsee, parsi
WORST ace, bad, beat, best,
conquer, defeat, deteriorate,
foil, last, master, outdo,
overcome, overthrow, quell,
rout, subjugate, terrible,
vanquish
expecter of cynic, pessimist
WORSTED See FABRIC
worsted.
yarn caddice, caddis, crewel,
etamine, fingering, genappe
WORT gail, gyle, krausen,
plant, potherb, swat, tutsan
WORTH account, adva-
lorem, advantage, benefit,
betide, bounty, caliber,
carat, cost, credit, desert,
dignity, eminence, esteem,
estimation, excellence,
homestead, honor, impor-
tance, integrity, merit,
mount, price, property, pro
rata, rated, regard, riches,
splendor, treasure, use(fulness), utility, valor, value,
virtue, wealth
money's bargain, value
sense of dignity, pride, respect
WORTHLESS abject, bad,
baff, base, bitter, brum-
magem, bum, cheesy, con-
temptible, counterfeit,
crummy, draffy, drasty,
drossy, dusty, feckless,
flimsy, fouty, frivolous, futile, gaudy, hollow, idle, ig-

noble, inferior, inutile,
junk(y), losel, loser, mean,
measly, naughty, no good,
nugatory, otiose, paltry,
petty, piddling, pitiful, putrid, raca, rubbishy, scummy, scurvy, shilpit, showy,
trashy, trumpery, undeserv-
ing, unworthy, useless, vain,
valueless, vile, waste,
wretched
object ambsace, refuse,
stiver, trifle
person black sheep, bum,
cur, javel, knave, losel, loser, scalawag, scamp, scapegrace, tramp, wosbird
WORTHWHILE expedient,
invaluable, lucrative, priceless, valuable
WORTHY acceptable, aught,
beneficial, beseeming, big,
celebrity, competent, condign, creditable, dear, deserved, deserving, digne, eligible, entitled, esteemed,
estimable, excellent, ex-
emplary, favorable, fellow,
fit(ting), good, honest, honorable, merited, merito-
rious, noble, pious, profitable, tidy, valuable, virtuous
of belief credible
of praise laudable
WOTAN See ODIN.
WOUGH harm, wall, woof,
wrong
WOULD could, should, wad,
want, weld, wish, wold
that alevai, halevai, if only
WOUND bayonet, breach,
break, bruise, chotchke(leh),
contuse, cut, damage, detriment, distress, exasperate,
foin, gall, ganch, gore, grief,
grieve, harm, hew, hurt, incision, injure, injury, knife,
lacerate, lesion, maim, offend, outrage, pain, pink,
plague, puncture, rist, scar,
scathe, scratch, sore, stab,
sting, tchotchke(leh), tear,
trauma, tsatske(leh), vuln
(us), wing
comb. traumat(o)
discharge gleet, ichor, pus,
sanies, serum
dressing bandage, compress,
gauze, lint, pledget, sphagnum, splint
mark bleb, blister, cicatrix,
scab, scar, welt
pert. vulneral
remedy vulnerary

small prick, scratch
WOUNDWORT allheal, betony, comfrey, hercules,
mint, vetch
WOUWOU camper, gibbon,
wawa(h)
WOW amuse, bark, delight,
excite, hit, howl, mew,
rave, sensation, success,
wail, whee, whine
WRACK avenge, calamity,
cutweed, defeat, destroy,
destruction, downfall, eelgrass, goods, injury, kelp,
mischief, overthrow, persecution, possessions, punishment, raze, refuse, rock-
weed, rubbish, ruin, sea-
ware, seaweed, stretch,
tease, torment, torture,
trash, vengeance, vex,
weeds, WRECK
WRAITH apparition, co-
walker, doppelganger, double, fetch, food, ghost,
phantasm, phantom, phe-
nomenon, provision, shade,
shadow, specter, spectre,
spirit, spook, swarth, vision,
waft
-like spectral
WRAKE enmity, harm, inspect, ruin, suffering,
WRACK
WRANGLE altercate, altercation, argify, argue, argufy, bicker, brabble, brangle, brawl, caffle, cample,
cangle, chide, contend, contest, controversy, dacker,
debate, digladiation, dispute,
fight, haggle, hassle, herd,
jangle, moil, plead, quarrel,
round up, scold, scraffle,
spar, spat, squabble, strut,
threap, tiff, tire, tirrwirr,
yed
WRANGLER camper, cow-
boy, debater, disputant,
fighter, gossip, herdsman,
opponent, stockman
WRAP afghan, barracan, bitt,
blanket, boa, bob, bundle,
burlap, cade, camlet, cape,
cere, cloak, clothe, coat,
coil, conceal, cover, doup,
dress, embale, embrace, encompass, enfold, enshroud,
envelop, fold, furl, gange,
hap, hide, invest, involve,
lap, mail, mantle, moider,
muffle, obscure, overcoat,
pack(age), pelisse, roll,
seize, shawl, sheath, shroud,

stole, strike, surround, swaddle, swathe, twine, veil, wap, wind, witzchoura

WRAPPER bandage, banian, banyan, bark, bathrobe, binder, binding, carton, cover(ing), dressing gown, dust jacket, envelope, envelopment, fardel, galabia, gown, housecoat, jacket, kimono, maharmah, negligee, paper, peignoir, pelisse, pilch, robe, shawl, skin, smock, tillot, undershirt
book jacket

WRAPPING cerement, charta, covering, mantling, pliofilm, wap

WRASSE ballan, bluehead, conner, cook, corkwing, cunner, doncella, fish, goldfinny, hogfish, janizary, labrid, labrus, ladyfish, pigfish, puddingwife, seawife, senorita

WRATH acerbity, acrimony, anger, ardor, choler, dudgeon, exasperation, fury, impetuosity, indignation, ire, irritation, offense, passion, punishment, rage, resentment, sorrowfully, vex, violence

WRATHFUL angry, choleric, furious, grim, incensed, ireful, mad, malignant, passionate, raging, wroth

WRAW angry, caterwaul, miaul, perverse, vexed

WRAY accuse, betray, denounce, expose, reveal

WREATH anadem, band, bank, bay, braid, chaplet, circle(t), coil, coronet, crease, crown(al), drift, festoon, fillet, garland, infula, iresine, kelphyte, laurel, lie, potong, roll, surround, tail, torse, tortil, trophy, turn, weave, whorl, wind, wrinkle
bridle francoa, spiraea

WREATHE bouquet, coil, contort, crown, eddy, encircle, entwine, garland, intwist, revolve, seize, surround, swirl, turn, twine, twist, wrench, wrest, writhe

WREATHED intorted, spiry, tortille, tortive

WREATHY curled, spiral, twisted

WRECK abundance, blast, blight, break, damage, de-

bacle, demolish, desolate, desolation, despoil, destroy, destruction, dilapidate, disable, founder, jade, misfortune, overthrow, plug, racabones, rase, raze, ruin(s), sabotage, shambles, shatter, smash, strand, torpedo, total, undo, vengeance, wrack
debris from flotsam, jetsam

WRECKER plunderer, saboteur

WREN bluecap, cutty, girl, jenny, kinglet, malurine, nannus, peggy, sally, scutty, stag, stipiturus, tidife, tidley, tomtit, tope, troglodytes, tydie, wrannock
crested kinglet
kind cactus, canyon, carolina, house, marsh, reed, rock, sedge, strawsmear, willow, winter

WREN, CHRISTOPHER *cathedral* st paul

WRENCH (See also *kind*, below.) alligator, bedkey, craft, crick, deceit, distort (ion), extort, force, fraud, hurt, jerk, lever, mechanic, misrepresent, pain, pang, perversion, pervert, pipe, pull, rack, rinse, snatch, spanner, sprain, squinch, stillson, strain, stratagem, tear, tool, torture, turn, tweak, twinge, twist, wramp, wrest, wring, yank
kind alligator, box, carriage, lug, monkey, open-end, pin, pipe, screwkey, socket, spanner, stillson, tappet
tuning epitonion

WREST arrest, deflect, dispose, distort(ion), divert, elicit, exact, extort, force, garble, incline, jar, misapply, misinterpret, pervert, pry, rend, ruse, snatch, sprain, squeeze, strain, stratagem, strip, tear, trick, turn, twist, usurp, wrench, wrestle, wring

WRESTLE conflict, contend, exert, fight, grapple, pray, rassle, scuffle, squirm, strive, struggle, thrimble, throw, thrumble, tug, tussle, work, wraxle, wriggle, writhe

WRESTLER fighter, grappler, hiper, matman, mauler, rassler, scuffler

WRESTLING jujitsu, pal(a)estra, wraxling
arena pal(a)estra, ring
attack flying mare
ceremonial sumo
grip full nelson, half nelson, hammerlock, headlock, scissors, stranglehold, toehold, wristlock
hug cornish-lock
maneuver airplane spin, chip, escape, head, spin
school pal(a)estra
term backheel, chancer, click, fall, grapevine, hank, lock, mare, nelson, pin
throw backheel, body-slam, buttock, hipe, hype
unguent ceroma

WRETCH beggar, bezonian, blighter, budmash, bugger, bum, caitiff, camooch, cullion, cur, derelict, dog, down-and-outer, exile, good-for-nothing, hilding, losel, loser, low-lifer, martyr, meschant, miscreant, miser, mucker, outcast, pariah, pauper, pilgarlic, poltroon, rapscalion, recreant, ronion, ronyon, sad sack, scoundrel, scroyle, scullion, skunk, slave, sneak, spridhogue, squall, swine, wastrel, worm

WRETCHED abject, afflicted, base, bum, calamitous, contemptible, crude, dawny, deeny, dejected, desolate, depicable, distressed, forlorn, grievous, low, mean, melancholy, meschant, miserable, niggardly, paltry, parsimonius, pathetic, pitiable, pitiful, poor, sad, shabby, sordid, squalid, terrible, tragic, unfortunate, unhappy, unlede, unseely, vile, woeful, worthless, yemer

WRETCHEDNESS affliction, baseness, calamity, meanness, misery, misfortune

WRICK hurt, sprain, strain

WRIG runt

WRIGGLE bend, dodge, evade, eyebrow, flexion, insinuate, meander, skew, snake, sniggle, squirm, turn, twist, wag(gle), wamble, wangle, widdle, wiggle, wimple, wind, wintle, wrabill, wrestle, writhe, zigzag

WRIGHT artificer, artisan,

carpenter, manufacturer, mechanic, workman
brothers orville, wilbur
brothers' flight kittyhawk
WRIGHT, FRANK L. *school* taliesin
WRIGHT, WILLARD H. *character* philo vance
pseud. s s van dine
WRING chafe, choke, clasp, compress, deflect, distort, elicit, exact, extort, extract, fret, gall, hurt, pain, press, pry, rack, render, screw, squeeze, squirm, strain, strangle, struggle, throttle, torment, torture, twist, wind, wrench, wrest
WRINKLE age, angle, blemish, buckle, cocker, cockle, compress, corrugate, corrugation, crankle, crease, crimp(le), crinkle, crisp(ation), crow's-foot, crumple, curl, draw, fad, fancy, fashion, fold, frizz(le), frumple, furrow, groove, idea, kink, knit, knot, line, lirk, pucker, purse, reeve, ridge, rimple, ripple, rivel(l), ruck, ruga, rugosity, rumple, runkle, rut, scrimp, seam, shirr, snirl, trick
free from erugate
WRINKLED aged, alutaceous, bullate, corrugated, crapey, furrowed, lined, puckered, purfly, rugate, rugose, rugous
WRIST ankle, carpus, instep
comb. carpo
guard bracer
ligament armilla
mark rasceta
pert. carpal
tumor ganglion
WRISTBAND bracelet, cuff, handcuff, manicle, strap
WRISTBONE capitatum, carpal(e), carpus, multangulum, os-magnum, shacklebone, ulna
WRISTLET bracelet, handcuff, muffetee
WRISTWATCH baguet(te)
WRIT breve, brief, brieve, capias, certiorari, cessavit, cosinage, dedimus, deed, detainer, detinue, distringas, elegit, exigent, fierifacias, formedon, injunction, instrument, latitat, mandamus, mandate, mise, mittimus, noverint, order,

pone, praecipe, precept, precipe, prescript, process, quominus, replevin, scripture, subpoena, summons, tales, testatum, teste, tolt, utrum, venire, warranty
execution elegit, outre
server bum-bailiff, elisor, marshal, sheriff
WRITE author, communicate, compile, compose, copy, decree, depict, dictate, direct, draft, empaper, engross, exarate, indite, inscribe, jot, manifold, notate, note, ordain, pen, postil, record, scratch, scrawl, scribble, scribe, scrive, set down, spell, stamp, trace, transcribe, treat, type
beautifully calligraph
down depreciate, describe, disparage, injure, note, popularize, record, sign, simplify
inability to agraphia
letters correspond
off cancel, deduct, depreciate, discount, disinherit, give up on, remove, repeal, subtract
poorly scratch, scrawl, scribble
up advertise, article, commentary, praise, publicity, puff, report, review, story
WRITER amanuensis, annalist, author, baboo, bard, calligrapher, chirographer, chronicler, clerk, columnist, composer, copyer, copyist, correspondent, critic, diarist, dramatist, dramaturge, elohist, epistolarian, essayist, expositor, fabler, fabulist, farce(u)r, gagman, glosser, glozer, hack, humorist, ink-slinger, journalist, lawyer, librettist, lyricist, narrator, notary, novelist, pamphleteer, parodist, pencilpusher, penman, phrase-maker, playwright, poet, proser, pundit, quillpusher, reporter, rhetorician, sagaman, scenarist, scrawler, scribbler, scribe, scrivener, scriver, secretary, stylist, transcriber, yarner
cramp graphospasm, penpalsy
devotional alvar
female bluestocking, newshen, sobsister

for periodical contributor
free-lance creeper
obituary necrologist
prose essayist, novelist, prosaist
WRITHE agonize, bend, coil, contort(ion), convolve, curl, distort, encircle, insinuate, intertwine, misinterpret, squirm, suffer, thrill, turn, twine, twist, wamble, weave, wince, wind, wrabbe, wrench, wrest, wriggle, wry, zigzag
WRITING article, book, calligraphy, chirography, composition, contract, coup-de-plume, deed, diary, document, gravamen, hand, inscription, legend, lettrure, longhand, macrography, makimono, manuscript, micrography, olla, orthography, penmanship, poem, publication, screeve, script, scrivenery, scrivening, spelling, text
ancient boustrophedon, linear-a, linear-b, miniscule
art rhetoric
automatic psychography
bad cacography, cacology
banal pablum
careless scrawl
character cuneiform, hieroglyph, letter, sign, symbol, word
cipher cryptograph(y)
comb. graph(o)
demotic hieroglyphics
difficulty dyslexia
equipment ballpoint, board, chalk, fountain pen, pad, paper, papyrus, parchment, pen(cil), plume, quill, stationery, style, stylus, tablet
equipment case papeteril, standish
excessive interest in graphomania
goddess seshat
inability agraphia
large macrography
master stylist
of doubtful authority apocrypha
on palm leaf olla
original holograph, manuscript, protograph
pert. scribal, scriptorial, scriptory
prophecy from sorte
sacred adigranth, agamas, alcoran, avesta, bhagavad-

gita, bible, codex, decalog(ue), dhammapada, eddas, gospel, granth, haggadah, hagiographa, hagiology, holy writ, koran, oracles, psalms, pseudepigrapha, scripture(s), sutras, talmud, ten commandments, testament, the good book, torah, tripitika, upanishads, vedas, vulgate, zendavesta
secret cipher, code, cryptogram, cryptograph(y), steganography
stroke tag
style cursive, ronde, spencerian, uncial
universal pasigraphy
WRITTEN cursive, destined, ecrit, engrossed, graphic, holograph, inscribed, inscrolled, ket(h)ib, kthibh, literal, longhand, manuscript, pencilled, penned, recorded, scriptural
above super(script), supra(script)
after adscript, postscript
under subscript
WRO angle, corner, nook, passage
WROCLAW breslau
WRONG abuse, agl(e)y, amiss, astray, awry, bad, car, cheat, cockeyed, crime, damage, deceptive, defraud, delusive, err(or), erroneous, evil, fallacious, false, faulty, foul, grievance, harm, hurt, ill, illegal, immoral, improper, impropriety, inaccurate, inappropriate, inapt, incorrect, indecorous, inequitable, inexpedient, infraction, iniquitous, injure, injury, injustice, mala, malum, mischief, misdeed, misleading, mistaken, off, oppress, outrage, persecute, poor, rotten, shame, sin(ful), tainted, tort, transgress(ion), unbalanced, undue, uneven,

unfair, unfit, unjust, unlawful, unseemly, unsuitable, untrue, vice, villainy, violation, wicked, wrong
civil malum, tort
comb. mal, mis
end foremost arsy-varsy
WRONGDOER criminal, faulter, malefactor, miscreant, misdoer, misfeasor, offender, sinner, tortfeasor, transgressor, trespasser, violator
WRONGDOING crime, evil, fault, malefaction, malfeasance, misfeasance, outrage, vice, wickedness
WRONGFUL perverse, tortious, tortuous, unfair, unjust, unlawful, WRONG, wry
WRONGHEADED obstinate, opinionated, perverse, self-willed, stubborn, willful, wry
WROTH anger(ed), angry, cruel, depressed, exasperated, fearful, fierce, heavy, hysterical, incensed, indignant, irate, ired, ireful, mad, perverse, turbulent, upset, violent, wicked, wrathful, wrathy
WROUGHT accomplished, beaten, created, decorated, dressed, elaborated, embroidered, fashioned, formed, manufactured, processed, shaped, spun, worked
up See WROTH.
WRY askew, avert, bend, bias(ed), conceal, contorted, cover, crooked, deflect, deviate, distort(ed), inclined, oblique, pervert, pinch, stray, stubborn, swerve, tend, turn, twist(ed), veil, warped, willful, wrest, wring, writhe, wrongheaded
WRYMOUTH blenny, congo eel, ghostifish, grimace, murgeon

WRYNECK barleybird, cuckoofool, fellingbird, jynx, loxia, nightingale, peabird, siskin, slab, snakebird, summerbird, torticollis, wagtail, weet(bird), woodpecker
WUDGE bunch, clump
WURST See SAUSAGE.
WURTH adore, esteem, glorify, honor, praise, reverence, value, worship
WURTTEMBERG *city* esslingen, heilbronn, stuttgart, ulm
duchy teck
measure imi
river danube, neckar
WYCLIFFE *man* huss(ite), lollard
WYND alley, court, enclosure, haw, lane
WYOMING *capital* cheyenne
cave shoshone
city buffalo, casper, cheyenne, cody, greybull, kemmerer, laramie, lusk, rawlins, sheridan, sundance, worland
county bighorn, goshen, laramie, niobrara, teton, unita
dam shoshone
flower painted cup
indian arapaho, crow, kiowa
lake jackson, yellowstone
national park grand teton, yellowstone
nickname equality state
peak atlantic, cloud, elk, fremont, gannett, grand teton, laramie, moran, sheridan
range absaro(ka), bighorn, black hills, laramie, rattlesnake, teton(s), wind river
river bear, big horn, green, platte, powder, shoshone, snake, yellowstone
state bird meadowlark
state flower (indian)paintbrush
state tree cottonwood

X

XANADU *prince* khan
river alph
XANTHIC, XANTHINE yellow

source madder
XANTHIPPE scold, shrew, termagant, virago
husband socrates

XANTHIPPUS *son* pericles
XANTHIUM arctium, burdock, clotbur, cocklebur, thistle

XANTHOSOMA blue eddoes, calalu, malanga, spoonflower

XANTHOUS mongolian, yellow

XANTHUS *brother* balius
master achilles
parent podarge, zephyr

XEBEC chebec(k), jabeque, shabbak, shabeque, ship, vessel

XENAGOGUE guide

XENARTHRA anteater, armadillo, sloth

XENIA athena

XENICUS bushwren, rockwren

XENIUM dainty, delicacy, fig, gift, present

XENODOCHIUM asylum, hospital

XENOGAMY cross-fertilization, pollination

XENOMORPHIC anhedral

XENON *source* air, atmosphere

XENOPHON attic muse
commander agesilaus, cyrus
estate scillus
parent gryllus
teacher socrates
work anabasis, cyropaedia, hellenica, oeconmicus

XENOPUS toad

XERES jeres, sherry, wine

XEROPHYLLUM beargrass, bear's-thread, sourgrass, turkeybeard, yucca

XEROTIC dry, sec

XEROX copy, reproduce, reproduction

XERXES ahasuerus
aided mordecai
battle salamis, thermopylae
enemy egyptians, greeks
general artabazus, mardonius, masistius
kingdom persia
parent atossa, darius
sister sandauce
slayer artabanus

XIBALDA See HELL.

XIMENA *bridegroom* cid

XINGU *indian* aneto

XIPHIAS broadbill, dorado, swordfish

XIPHOID breastbone, ensiform, xiphisternum

XMAS See CHRISTMAS.

XOSA amakosa, amaxosa, kaf(f)ir

XP christ

X-RAY grenzray, irradiate, photo(graph), picture, radiograph, urogram
hardness measure benoist-scale
inventor roentgen
measurement dosimetry, roentgenometry
measuring device qualimeter, quantimeter

medical use radiopraxis
picture cathodograph, radiograph
principle bragg's law
science radiology, roentgenology
source target
treatment radiotherapy
unit roentgen

X-SHAPED chiasmal, cruciate

XUREL horse-eye-jack, saurel, scad

XUTHUS *consort* creusa
kin achaeus, aeolus, dorus, ion
parent hellen, orseis

XYLAN *product* xylose
source corncob, straw

XYLEM hadrome, tissue, xylogen

XYLOID ligneous, wooden, woody

XYLONITE celluloid

XYLOPHONE balafo, balaphon, gambang, gamelan(g), gigelira, marimba, saron, sticcado, strawfiddle, vibraharp

XYLOSMA manzillo

XYRICHTHYS razorfish

XYRIDALES bristlewort, herb

XYSTUS porch, portico, stoa, terrace, walk

Y

Y wye, ymca, yod, yogh, yok(e)
-shaped hyoid, upsilon

YABBER, YABBLE conversation, jabber, language, talk

YABBI dasyure, marsupial, thylacine, wolf

YABBY crawdad, crawlie, crayfish

YACARE alligator, caiman, cayman, crocodile, jacare

YACHNA See GOSSIP, YENTA.

YACHT boat, cruise(r), dinghy, keelboat, race, sail, ship, yeaghe
jib genoa
kind raceabout
pennant burgee
presidential sequoia

term abaft, aloft, astern, backwind, cheater, cover, guy, halyard, lanyard, leeward, quarter, sheets, spinnaker, spitfire, staysail, tack, to weather

YACK chatter, gossip, joke, laugh, talk, yachna, yachne, yammer, yenta, yente

YAFFLE armful, bark, bird, handful, scold, woodpecker, yelp

YAHOO brute, bumpkin, clown, coarse, lout, peasant, rowdy, rustic, savage
masters houyhnhnms

YAHWE(H) god, jahve(h), jahwe(h), jehovah, yhvh, yhwh

YAK animal, bulbul, klap, poephagus, sarlak, sarlyk, talk, YACK, yammer, zobo
and water-buffalo offspring dzo
crossbreed yakalo, yakattalo

YAKAMIK jacamin, trumpeter

YAKKA labor, toil, work

YAKKER draykop(f), gossip

YAKONAN *indian* siuslaw, yaquina

YAKSHA angel, demon, dryad, fairy, gnome, jinni, ogre, spirit
offering bali

YAKUSHI See BUDDHA.

YAKUT sakha
river lena

YALE bulldog, eli, lock
blue rameses
popular man woodenspoonist

singing group whiffinpoofs
YALTA *palace* livadia
sea black, marmora
YALU *port on* antung
YAM boniata, buckra, cush-cush, hoi, igname, inamia, inhame, jamb, kaawi, kama, lima(lima), potato, sweet potato, tuber, tugui, ube, ubi, uve, uvi, waw waw
bean jicama, kama, sincamas, wayaka
taro koko
tree kurrajong
YAMATO See JAPAN.
YAMEN court, office
YAMMER chatter, clamor, complain, crave, cry, desire, grumble, klap, lament, scold, scream, shot, stammer, wail, whimper, whine, yearn, yell, yomer
YAMP squawroot
YANG brightness, cry, gurjun, honk, light, male, positive, sunlight
opposite yin
YANGKIN dulcimer
YANGTZE kiang
city on nanking
tributary han, kan, min
YANK blow, buffet, draw, hoick, jerk, pull, slap, soldier, twitch
YANKEE american, new englander, northerner, staysail, yanqui
bump pothole
doodle prince rupert
doodle adornment feather, macaroni
doodle author schuckburgh
father of all benjamin franklin
YAP active, apt, bark, bumpkin, chatter, cheep, complain, cry, cur, dog, eager, fool, gab, greenhorn, hoodlum, hungry, keen, mark, mouth, nag, noise, quick, ready, scold, speech, talk, waffle, yawp, yell, yelp
island money fei
YAPOK opossum, oyapock
YARD area, bar, branch, campus, cancha, close, compound, confine, correction, court, enclosure, field, fold, garden, garth, grounds, hoppet, lawn, measure, outgarth, patio, pen, pik, playground, punishment, quad(rangle), rod,

rule, spar, staff, stick, terrace, twig, vara, verge, wand
1/16th nail
5 1/2 rod
20 score
220 furlong
600 heer
1/3 cubic cartload
119.6 square are
4,840 square acre
bird prisoner
enclosed garth, patio
final fell
goods cloth, fabric, material
goods edge selvage
grass bermuda, eleusine, mangrass, st augustine
grassy garston, lawn
part ell, foot, inch, mill
small garth
·YARDAGE (See also YARD *goods*.) distance, extent, length, volume
YARDLAND verge, virgate
·YARDMASTER dinger, trainman
YARDSTICK criterion, gauge, measure, met(e)wand, norm, rule(r), shibboleth, standard, test, touchstone, verge, yaird
YARE active, agile, eager, lively, manageable, nimble, prompt, quick(ly), ready, soon, year
YARM noise, scream, shriek, wail, whine, yell
YARMULKE, YARMELKE skullcap
YARN (See also *kind*, below.) abb, account, anecdote, boucle, caddis, calk, crewel, exaggeration, fabrication, fib, fiber, flax, fleece, floss, fox, garn, inkle, knop, lie, narrative, pirn, saga, silk, slub, spinel, story, strand, tale, tall tale, thread, tow, twist, wool, worsted
acetate estron
ball baggywrinkle, clew, clue
bleached spinel
bundle hank, haul, pad, slip
chafe-reducing puddening
cluster tuft
cotton alaska
count typp
defect corkscrew, singling
elastic lastex
fine light cashmere, kashmir, zephyr
holder cop

irregularity snick
kind acetate, alaska, angora, berlin, boucle, chenille, crewel, dacron, dynel, genappe, merino, saxony, wool(en), worsted, zephyr
length chase, knot, skein, tape
line caburn
linen spinel
looped boucle
measure clew, clue, cophank, denier, hank, hasp, heer, lea, rap, skein, spangle, spindle, typp
metallic tinsel
pound typp
quantity reelipirn
reel niddynoddy, pirn, windle
roll prick
rope soogee
size denier, forty, lea
skein hank, hasp, rap
snarl twit
spindle hasp
spun raband, robbin, ropeband
strong germantown
thick place in slub
2-ply grandelle
uneven boucle
warp abb
waste thrum
winder flier, flyer, pirner
with rubber core lastex
woolen saxony, shetland
worsted crewel, genappe, zephyr
YARR growl, snarl, spurry
YARRAN gidgea, gidya, myall
YARROW achillea, ahartalav, allheal, bloodwort, cammock, herb, maudeline, maudlin, milfoil, sneezewort, weed
YASHMAK asmack, mantilla, veil, yakmak
YATAGHAN balas, knife, saber, scimitar, sword
YATE eucalyptus
YATTER abuse, chatter, clamor, jabber, prattle
YAUD mare, work horse, yade
YAULD able-bodied, active, alert, sharp, strong
YAUP See YAWP, YELL.
YAUPON assi, blackdrink, casina, cassena, cassine, cassioberry, holly, ilex, senna, shrub, tree

YAUTIA cocker, coco, malanga, tania, tanier, taro

YAW bend, blister, curve, deviate, deviation, gape, incline, lesion, lurch, swerve, tack, tumor, turn, yawn, yes, zigzag

YAWL boat, cry, drane, howl, jollyboat, mizzen, schokker, scream, vessel

YAWN boredom, chasm, cleft, desire, dullness, galp, gane, gant, gape, long, mouth, open(ing), oscitate, part, split, stretch, tedium

YAWNING abysmal, abyssal, agape, gaping, hiant, oscitant

YAWP bawl, bellow, complain, cry, gape, noise, scream, screech, shout, squawk, yammer, yap, yaup, yawn, yell, yelp

YAWS frambesia, pian, polypalloma, tubba, tubboe

YAWSHRUB queenroot

YAWWEED morinda, rhubarb

YAYA chaparro, copa, lancewood, protium, tree

YCLEPT called, named, styled

Y-DOUGHT prosperous, thriven

YE the, thee, thou, yea, you

-and-nay ambiguous, doubtful, equivocal, quaker, vacillating

YEAN bear, ean, lamb

YEANLING eanling, fledgling, infant, kid, lamb, newborn, young

YEAR(S) annee, anno, annum, haab, jahr, twelvemonth

2 biennium

5 lustrum, pentad

7 septenary

8 octennial

10 decade, decennary, decenniad, decennium

15 indiction

20 katun

50 jubilee

70 septaugenary

100 age, centenary, centennial, century

1000 chiliad, millennial, millennium, milliad

after year constantly, long (time), repeatedly

day anniversary

fictitious basselian

first onead

hebrew anno hebraico

-in, year-out constantly, continuously

letter hallmark

many age(s)

of mourning annus luctus

of our lord anno domini

of wonders annus mirabilis

part day, month, quarter, raith, season, semester, trimester, week

platonic annus magnus

record annal, calendar, diary

sabbatical jubilee

YEARBIRD horntail

YEARBOOK annual, annuary, serial

YEARLING colt, hornotine, teg

trainer pinhook

YEARLY annual(ly), etesian, perannum, perennial

occurrence anniversary

YEARN ache, aim, aspire, beg, burn, covet, crave, desire, earn, flag, green, grieve, hanker, hone, hunger, irne, long(ing), love, pain, pang, pant, pine, request, sigh, thirst, vex, want, wish, yammer, yen

YEARNING ambition, aspiration, desire, homesick, longing, nostalgia, rennet, tenderness

YEAST agitation, anthogenous, barm, bee(s), emptings, ferment, foam, froth, koji, leaven, lob, rise, rising, scum, sizzing, sots, spume, torula

cake baba au rhum, babka

enzyme lactase

film flor

sweetbread danish, stollen

wild anamite

YEASTY agitated, ebullient, excited, exuberant, foaming, frivolous, frothy, leavening, light, restless, spumy, trivial, youthful

YED fib, lie, quarrel, wrangle

YEDER great, prompt, quick, vehement

YEGG burglar, criminal, hoodlum, robber, safebreaker, thief, thug, tramp

YEKKE pedantic, rigid, teutonic

YEKL See YOKEL.

YELL bawl, bellow, call, cheer, complain, cry, gowl, holler, howl, protest, roar, scream, screech, scronach,

shout, shriek, wail, yammer, yarm, yaup, yelloch, yelp, yowl, yowt

director cheerleader

YELLOW acacia, acier, afraid, almond, aloma, amber, aureate, aureolin, banana, biscuit, blake, blond, chartreuse, chrome, citrine, citron, contemptible, cowardly, craven, crocus, dishonorable, dorado, ecru, eggshell, envious, favel, flavid, flaxen, fulvous, gamboge, gold(en), gull, icterine, icteroid, jasmine, jaundiced, jaune, jealous, jonquil, luteous, lutescent, mean, meline, mimosa, mongolian, mustard, ocher, ochre, orpiment, oxgall, puri, purree, recreant, saffron, sallow, sensational, shell, sulfurous, sunray, treacherous, xanthic, xanthin(e), yolk, yucatan

alder sagerose

alloy aich, brass, similor

antimony daffodil, sunray

archangel dead-nettle

as gold, saffron

avens bennet, burnet, hemlock, valerian

-back mussel, novel

balsam jewelweed

bartonia screwstem

basswood linden, tilia

beak bejan

beard ferdelance

bedstraw crudwort, curdwort, fleaweed

bile choler, humor

bird goldfinch, oriole

boy bankrupt, coin, guinea, quadroon, sovereign

bright saffron

-brown aloma, amber, bran, dun, fulvid, fulvous, manila, pablo, straw, tawny, topaz

buckthorn bogbirch, rhamnus

bugle eve, ground-pine, iva

butter blake

caltrop turkey-blossom

canary meline

catechu gambier

citron mimosa

clintonia blueberry, dogberry

cockscomb rattle

colorblindness xanthocyanopia

comb. chrys(o), flavo, luteo, ochro, xanth(o)

copper chalcopyrite

copperas copiapite
corydalis colicweed
daisy coneflower, rudbeckia
dirt gold
discoloration xanthosis
dog coward, craven, cur, jerk, mongrel
dye amil, annatto, annotto, arnatto, arusa, auramine, flavine
-eyed goldenseal
fever black-vomit, bulam
fever carrier aedes, mosquito
fir douglas-spruce
flag quarantine, warning
foxtail stickers
gentian bitterwort, dandelion, felwort
golden flavid
gowan crowfoot, dandelion
grayish chamois, drab
-green acacia, andover, aqua, artichoke, asphodel, cannon, celadine, celadon, chartreuse, citrine, glaucous, olive, privet, reseda, rifle, serpentine, tarragon, tea, viridian
iris daggers, levers, sedge
jack caranx, flag, jonquil
jacket eucalypt(us), hornet, nembutal, vespa, vespid, wasp
jasmine woodbine
kings orpiment
lead ore wulfenite,
lemon generall
lemur kinkajou
lily leek
mackerel caranx, cavalla, crevalle
metal brass, gold
mombin hogplum
mustard charlock
nelumbo lotus
nutgrass chufa
ocher oxford chrome, sil
oleander exiletree
orange grenadine
oxeye black-eyed-susan
parilla moonseed
pert. xanthic
poll warbler, widgeon
pond lily clote, clots, duck, nuphar
prickle rubia
puccoon goldenseal
quintonia bluebead
race mongols
ratsbane orpiment
rattle cockscomb, lousewort
reddish acorn, agate, alabaster, alesan, apricot, argentina, auburn, aurora, au-

tumn, bark, beige, bismark, blondine, bracken, brazil, buttercup, fallow, lava, manila, mikado, mirador, mocha, nacarat, nacarine, orange, roan, rosewood, sandy, saravan, sudan, tanagra
river hwangho
sculpin dragonet, sea-raven
sea hwang-hai
sea arm pohai
star sneezeweed
startwort elecampane
streak cowardice, timidity
timber aniba, bois de rose
toadflax ramstead
wagtail barleybird, nightingale, oatear, siskin, wryneck
water lily beaverroot, bobbins, brandybottle, cuckoopint, kelp, nuphar, spatterdock, wokas

YELLOWBELLY bream, coward, flatfish, frog, halfcaste, perch, rate, squawfish, sunfish

YELLOWFIN perch, squeteague, trout

YELLOWFISH atka, grouper, ide, orf(e)

YELLOWHAMMER ammer, bunting, finch, flicker, gladdy, gladeye, goldie, gowdy, skite, veldrin, verdin, woodpecker, yeldrin(e), yeldring, yeldrock, yeorling, yite, yoldring, yorlin
state alabama

YELLOWISH amber, beige, buckskin, buff, jaundiced, lutescent, olive, sallow, sandy, tan

YELLOWLEGS killcu, klookklook, plover, tattler, totanus, yelper

YELLOWMAN bumbailiff

YELLOWS charlock, jaundice, jealousy, jeterus, woodwaxen

YELLOWSTONE *park attraction* bears, deer, geyser, old faithful
park hot spring punch bowl

YELLOWTAIL amberfish, bumper, mademoiselle, manhaden, radirubia, rockfish, runner, seriola, snapper

YELLOWTHROAT warbler

YELLOWTOP crownbeard, goldenrod

YELLOWWEED goldenrod, ragwort, rape, sneezeweed

YELLOWWOOD avodire, boxwood, buckthorn, fustoc, gopherwood, mangwe, smoketree, sumac, sweetleaf, virgilia, yellowroot

YELP baff, bark, boast, brag, complain, criticize, cry, demand, greedy, growl, HOWL, kiyi, kvitch, protest, shout, shriek, squeal, wail, yaff(le), yamph, ya(u)p, yawp, yell, yip, youp, yowl

YELPER avocet, redshank, whelp, yellowlegs

YELT gilt, sow

YEME care, govern, guard, heed, observe, regard, solicitude

YEMELESS careless, negligent

YEMEN arabia-felix
ancient kingdom saba, sheba
capital sana(a)
city dahhi, damar, hodeida, mocha, moka, mukha, sana(a), taiz(z)
coffee mocha
coin riyal
gulf aden
people arab(ian), shafai, yemeni, yemenite, zaidi
port aden, hodeida, mocha, moka, mukha
region tihama
ruler imam
sect shia, shiite, sunni
statesman sallal

YEN appetite, coin, craving, desire, hanker, long(ing), lust, nostalgia, one, passion, propensity, urge, want, yearn(ing), yon

YENAN fushi(h)

YENITE ilvaite

YENTA gossip, schlack, schlag, s(c)hlock

YENTZ cheat, defraud, swindle

YENTZER crook, swindler

YEOMAN assistant, attendant, beefeater, churl, clerk, crewman, estatesman, farmer, freeholder, goodman, guidman, journeyman, proprietor, retainer, tenant, warden, workman-like
officer exon

YEP active, alert, bold, smart, vigorous, YES

YEPLY cunningly, eagerly, quickly

YERBA herb, mate, tea
buena san francisco
santa bear's-weed, gumbush, tarbush
YERK arouse, bind, blow, carp, cast, crack, excite, gird, goad, JERK, kick, lash(ing), pierce, press, pull, skylark, snatch, stab, strike, thrash, throw, thud, thump, tie, whip, wrench, yark
YERN(E) briskly, curdle, eagerly, readily, soon, vigorously
YES affirmative, all right(y), aok, aye, certainly, certes, c'est bien, definitely, exactly, indeed(y), ja wohl, je veux bien, mais si, naturellement, of course, okay, okey, oui, positively, precisely, quite, rather, really, right(o), roger, sure(ly), tres bien, true, truly, uh-huh, undoubtedly, verily, vote, yaw, yea(h), yep, yip, yup
-man sycophant, toady
YESTERDAY ayer, heri, hestern, hier, ieri, langsyne, long ago, past
pert. hesternal, pridian
YET again, algate, and, before, besides, but, e'en, etsi, even(tually), finally, further, gate, henceforth, hitherto, howeer, however, moreover, nevertheless, notwithstanding, now, once more, pour, previously, still, tho(ugh), thus far
YEUK ewk, itch(ing), yu(c)k
YEW chinwood, conifer, evergreen, ewe, hemlock, hew, taxus, tree, yaw, yow
pert. taxine
symbol of death, grief
YEX cough, hiccup, sob, yolk
YGERNE *master* king arthur
YICHES, YICHUS prestige, status
YIDDISH See HEBREW references.
YIELD 3 bow, pay, sag 4 bear, bend, cast, cave, cede, cess, cost, crop, emit, give, lose, make, obey, quit 5 admit, agree, allow, avale, bloom, break, breed, bring, defer, forgo, fruit, leave, repay, stoop, waive 6 accede, accept, accord, afford, assent, buckle, forego, im-

part, income, output, profit, relent, render, resign, result, return, reveal, reward, soften, submit, supply, swerve 7 abandon, appease, blossom, concede, consent, crumple, forfeit, furnish, harvest, out-turn, present, produce, product, provide, restore, revenue, succumb, vintage 8 abdicate, back down, collapse, contract, dividend, engender, generate, proceeds, renounce 9 acquiesce, aftermath, surrender 10 capitulate, relinquish 11 acknowledge 12 knuckle under
YIELDING accommodating, bearing, buxom, cession, complaisant, compliant, complying, dedition, docile, ductile, flaccid, limber, malleable, meek, naish, nesh, obedient, plastic, pliable, pliant, productive, recreant, soft, submissive, supple, tractable, tractile, waxy
comb. ferous
YIN dark(ness), female, negative, one, shadow, shang
opposite yang
YIP cheep, complain, growl, outcry, shriek, squeal, YELP, yirr
YIRM, YIRN complain, fret, grimace, groan, smirk, whine
YITE yellowhammer
YIVER eager, greedy
YMIR chaos
cow feeding audhum(b)la
slayer odin, vili, woden
YNAMBU tinamou
YODEL call, carol, refrain, sing, warble
YODH iod, jod
YOGA asceticism, bhakti, hatha, jnana, jog, karma, mysticism, raja, union, yoking
angas, 3 dharana, dhyana, samadhi
attainment samadhi
concentration charana
contemplation smadhi
exercise asana, cobra
founder patanjali
life breath prana
meditation dhyana
posture asana
practices anga
spinal points cakra, chakra
spiritual power kundalini

trance See *angas,* above.
YOGI(NI) ascetic, fakeer, fakir, jnani, jogi, mystic, swami
YOGURT kisselo, madzoon, mleko
YOKE associate, attach, attack, bail, bang(h)y, bond (age), brace, bracket, cangue, clamp, connect, contest, couple, dispute, fight, frame, harness, hitch, inspan, joch, join, link, marry, match, oppress, pair, pillory, poke, restrain, seize, service, servitude, shackle, slavery, tackle, team, tie, two, union, unite, wed, yex
bar skey
comb. zygo
elm hornbeam
-fellow or *-mate* associate, companion, comrade, coworker, husband, mate, partner, spouse, wife
part bow, riem(pie), skey
YOKEL abderite, boor, bumpkin, chawbacon, clodhopper, clown, dzlob, farmer, greenhorn, hayseed, hick, icicle, lout, lubber, peasant, plowboy, putz, rube, rustic, shlub, simpleton, sucker, yekl, yob, yold, zhlob, zhlub
YOKING union, yoga
YOKO ono
YOLD boob, dolt, fool, oaf, shlemiel, simpleton, YOKEL
YOLK center, core, deutoplasm, essence, heart, latebra, lump, nodule, vitellus, yellow, yex
gland vitellarium
having lecithal
having large megalecithal
having small microlecithal
mass latebra
without alecithal
YOND farther, raging, that, those, yon, YONDER
YONDER beyond, distant, farther, that, there, thither, those
YORE ago, ancient, before, eld, erst, formerly, long since, past, yare
YORK *ancient name* eboracum
archbishop scroop
house of, symbol rose
YORKER tice

YORKSHIRE *division* riding
fog velvet-grass
man learoyd, tike, tyke
YORUBA *people* egba
state oyo
YOSEMITE *peak* cathedral
spires, el capitan, half
dome, three brothers
waterfall bridal veil, ribbon,
vernal
YOU lei, les, loro, los, one,
sie thee, thou, toi, usted(es),
voi, vosotros, vous, yez,
youse, yow, yuh
bet assuredly, of course
don't say really
YOUNG breed, brood,
cletch, clutch, diminutive,
early, farrow, fresh, fruit,
fry, get, green, growing,
hatching, ignorant, imma-
ture, inexperienced, jeune,
junior, juvenile, kindle, litter, miniature, new, off-
spring, pliable, raw, small,
spat, spawn, succulent, tender, tyro, undeveloped, vernal, workable, yearling,
YOUTHFUL
animal baby, calf, cub, faun,
foal, fry, kitten, lamb,
puppy, toto
bird chick
bring forth ean, yean
brood fry
camel colt
communist league komsomol
dog pup(py), whelp
pretender prince charlie
problem of generation gap
YOUNGER junior, kid,
puisne, punee
son cadet
YOUNGEST wallydrag
YOUNGLING beginner, neophyte, novice, student,
youth
YOUNGSTER adolescent,
baby, boy, CHILD, colt,
cub, gamin, girl, gossoon,
kid, lad, midshipman,
minor, preadolescent,
shaver, spalpeen, sprig,
stripling, tad, teenager,
teenster, tike, tot, urchin,
younker, YOUTH
YOUNKER dupe, gallant,
gentleman, knight, noble-
man, novice, squire,
YOUNGSTER
YOUR dein, ihr, loro, oure,
owre, suo, suyo, thy, ton,
tuo, tuyo, vos(tro), votre,
vuestro, yourn

YOUTH adolescence, adolescent, bahur, bellringer,
blood, bloom, bochur, boy
(hood), buck, bursch,
cadet, callent, chabo, chiel,
child(hood), codling, en-
dymion, ephebos, ephebus,
fledgling, girl(hood), gossoon, hobbledehoy, hopeful,
hylas, immaturity, infant
(ry), juvenile, juvenility,
juventude, lad, master, matmid, minority, novelty,
page, puberty, pubescent,
recentness, salad days, sapling, shaver, slip, sprig,
springald, squirt, stripling,
swain, teen(ager), teenster,
timtum, young(fry),
YOUNGSTER, younker
beautiful adonis
callow cub
deity apollo, attis, attys,
hebe, ithun
developed bloomer
mythological adonis, apollo,
etana, icarus
name meaning hebe
rude hoyden, squirt
self-confident princox
shelter hostel
silly calf
successful whiz kid
YOUTHFUL adolescent,
beardless, boyish, callow,
childish, early, fresh, girlish, green, immature, juvenile, laddish, maiden(ly),
neanic, new, pubescent,
puerile, unfledged, vigorous,
virgin(al), YOUNG
YOUTHWORT cow-parsnip,
sundew
YOWL, YOWT See YELP.
YTTRIUM dusprosium, erbium, holmium, lutetium,
terbium, thulium, yetter-
bium
source rare earth
YUCA cassava, manioc,
YUCCA
YUCATAN *capital* merida
city campeche, merida, palenque, uxmal
drink balche
indian maya(n)
plant sisal
ruins chichenitza
temple teocalli
tree yaxche
YUCCA adam's needle,
amole, beargrass, bears-
thread, cassava, dasylirion,
datil, izote, joshua, lilium,

palma, palmito, soapweed,
sotol, spanish bayonet, spanish dagger, thorn, yucker
fiber isote, istle, izote
moth pronuba
YUDHISHTHIRA *brother*
See PANDUSSON.
father dharma, pandu
wife draupadi
YUGOSLAVIA dalmatia
alphabet oyrillic
alps dinaric, julian
brandy See *drink,* below.
capital belgrade, beograd
channel narento
city agram, belgrade, beograd, bitola, bitolj, bosna,
budva, cattaro, cetinje, dubrovnik, laibach, ljubljana,
maglaj, maribor, monastir,
morava, mostarnish, novi-
sad, osijek, pirot, prilep,
prizren, pula, ragusa, rijeka,
rtanj, sarajevo, sava, senta,
skop(l)je, split, subotica, titograd, trogir, tuzlar,
uskub, vardar, varsac, vix-
oco, zadar, zagreb, zara
coin dinar, para
commune pec, stip, veles
drink maraska, plum brandy,
rakia, slivovitz
fascist party ustashi
gulf kvarner
island arbe, cres, hvar, pago,
rab, solta, susac, susak
lake scutari
leader djilas, mikhailovitch,
tito
measure akov, danoranja,
donum, khvat, lanaz, mo-
tyka, oka, plaze, ralico,
ralo, rif, stopa
monarch peter
official zupan
peak durmitor, triglav
people croat, serb, slav, slovene
port belgrade, dubrovnik,
kotor, novisad, pola, rieka,
rijeka, spalato, split
range dinaric alps
region banat(e), bosnia, dalmatia, slavonia
republic bosnia, croatia, her-
zegovina, macedonia, mon-
tenegro, serbia, slovenia
river bosna, cazma, danube,
drava, drin(a), ibar, krka,
morava, neretva, raska,
sava, tamis, tis(z)a, vardar,
velika, vrbas
ruler broz, peter, tito
sculptor mestrovic

secret service udba
soprano milanov
statesman broz, tito
weight dramm, oka, satlijk, tovar, wagon
writer andric
YUKIAN *indian* huchnom, wappo
YUKKEL flicker, woodpecker
YUKON *capital* dawson, whitehorse

tributary tanana
YULE See CHRISTMAS.
YUMAN *indian* diegueno, mohave, patayan, tulkepaia, walapai, yavapai
YUMMY attractive, beautiful, delicious, luxurious, savory, tasty
YUM-YUM *consort* nankipoo
friend koko

YUNCA *indian* chimu, chincha
language mochica
YUNNAN *tribe* archang
YUNX wryneck
YURUNA tupian
YUSTAGA timucuan
YUTU partridge, tinamou
Y-WEND change, convert, direct, turn, wend

Z

Z izzard, zed, zero, zeta, zinc, zulu
ZABAD *kin* ephlal, hasum, shimeath
ZABAGLIONE sabayon
ZABBAI *son* baruch
ZABDI *kin* micha, shimei
ZABDIEL *son* jashobeam
ZABUD *friend* solomon
ZAC goat, ibex, zebuder
ZACATE forage, grass, hay, herbage
ZACCHINI human cannonball
ZACCUR *son* hanan, michaiah
ZACHARIAS *father* barachias
son john the baptist, josephus
ZADKIEL *angel of* jupiter
ZADOK *offspring* achim, ahimaaz, jerushah, meshullam, salemus, shallum
ZAFTIG buxom, full-bodied, germinal, juicy, plump, provocative, seminal, wellrounded
ZAGREB (See also YUGOSLAVIA.) agram
ZAGREUS dionysus
ZAHAM *father* rehoboam
ZAIBATSU conglomerate, monopoly, trust
ZAIDAH *son* maan
ZAIRE belgian congo
capital kinshasa
city aketi, bakwanga, baya, boma, butembo, kamina, kasaji, kikwit, kolwezi, lebo, lubumbashi, mutshatsha, sandoa, yangambi
lake kivu, mweru
language kikongo, lingala, swahili, tshiluba
leader mobutu
money zaire

province equator, kasai, katanga, kivu, oriental
range mitumba, ruwenzori, virunga
river aruwimi, congo, dengu, ibina, kasai, likati, lindi, lomami, lualaba, lukuga, lulonga, ruki, ubangi, uele, zaire
volcano nyaragongo
ZAL *consort* rudabah
son rustam
ZAMBALES See PHILIPPINES.
ZAMBEZI *ruler* monomatapa
tributary shire
ZAMBIA northern rhodesia
capital lusaka
city kitwe, luanshya, luapula, mongu, mufulira, ndola
congo kinshasa
falls victoria
lake bangweulu, mwern
language afrikaans, bemba, lozi, luvale, nyanja, tonga
national park luanga valley
president kaunda
province barotseland
range muchinga
river kafue, luangwa, luapula, zambezi
ZAMIA banga, cicad, coontie, cycad
ZAMINDAR landowner, malik, proprietor, tax collector
ZAMINDARI bhaiyachara, pattidari
chief mird(a)ha
ZAMPOGNE bagpipe, panpipe
ZAN zeus
ZANAJA arroyo, canal, ditch, gully
ZANY acrobat, antic, attendant, badaud, buffoon,

clown, comic(al), crazy, fool, gaby, goofy, idiotic, jester, lunatic, mad, merryandrew, nut, sawney, screwball, simpleton, toady, wit, zanni
ZANZIBAR (See TANGANYIKA.) isle of cloves, tanzania
ZAP attack, defeat, destroy, hit, kill, shoot
ZAPATERO boxwood, cerillo, leather-jack, lima, tree
ZARA *father* judah
ZARAEAS *son* eliaonias, mareroth
ZARAH kazoo
ZARATHUSTRA See ZOROASTER.
ZAREATHITES *ancestor* caleb
ZARF cupholder, stand
ZARZUELA bramble, briar, musical comedy, opera, operetta, vaudeville
ZATI macaque, monkey, munga
ZATTU *son* aziza, eliashib, elioenai, jeremoth, mattaniah, zabad
ZAVAN *kin* ezer, jonathan
ZAYAT portico, shed
ZCHUSS estate, legacy, perquisite, right
ZEA corn, maize
ZEAL alacrity, ardor, desire, devotion, dutifulness, eagerness, elan, energy, enthusiasm, feeling, fervor, fire, force, heart, intensity, interest, passion, piety, piousness, relish, soul, spirit, vehemence, verve, warmth, yen, zest
ZEALAND See DENMARK.
ZEALOT adherent, bigot,

buff, devotee, disciple, enthusiast, epideist, fan(atic), follower, partisan, sectary, simon, votarist, votary, voteen, zelator

ZEALOUS ardent, assiduous, avid, burning, cordial, devoted, devout, eager, earnest, enthusiastic, fanatic(al), fervent, fervid, frenetic, hearty, high, hot, impassioned, industrious, intense, intent, jealous, passionate, phrenetic, rabid, serious, sincere, strenuous, vehement, vigorous, warm

ZEBADIAH *kin* elpaal, ishmael

ZEBEDEE *consort* salome
son boanerges, james, john

ZEBOIIM *king* shemeber

ZEBRA butterfly, dauw, heliconius, quagga, soliped
hybrid zebrass, zebrinny, zebrula
opossum thylacine
pert. striped
poison euphorbia
swallow tail ajax-butterfly
-tailed lizard callisaurus

ZEBRAWOOD araroba, gomavel, marblewood, myrtle, nakedwood, zingana

ZEBU brahman, brahmanybull, bramin, yak
hybrid cattabu, zobo, zoh

ZEBULON *father* jacob
son elon

ZECHARIAH *consort* elizabeth, hezekiah
father elam
leader josiah
offspring abijah, jahaziel, john, joiarib, uzziah

ZEDEKIAH *eunuch* ebedmelech
parent chenaanah, hananiah, hasadiah, josiah
son mahseiah

ZEEKOE hippopotamus

ZELION *son* butes

ZELOS *parent* pallas, styx
sister nice

ZEME, ZEMI fetish, huaca, nagual, spirit

ZEN *enlightenment* satori
founder bodhidharma
master roshi
meditation room zendo
paradox koan
priest roshi
question mondo

ZENANA harem, seraglio

ZENAS *friend* paul

ZENDIK atheist, infidel, unbeliever

ZENI(C)K suricate

ZENITH acme, apex, apogee, climax, culmination, height, heyday, meridian, peak, pinnacle, prime, summit, tip, top, vertex
opposite nadir, perigee

ZENO *follower* stoic

ZEOLITE amydaloid, analcime, analcite, brewsterite, chabazite, faujasite, natrolite, silicate

ZEPHANIAH *son* hen, josiah

ZEPHYR aura, breeze, duster, favonius, jersey, shawl, wind

ZEPHYRUS favonius
consort chloris, hyacinth, iris, podarge
parent aeolus, astraeus, aurora, eos
son balius, carpus, xanthus

ZEPPELIN aerostat, airship, balloon, blimp, dirigible, graf

ZERAH *father* judah, revel, simeon
son calcol, dara, ethan, heman, zimri

ZERAHIAH *kin* meraioth, uzzi

ZERO absent, aught, blank, cipher, close, empty, fig, hour, love, nada, nadir, naught, nihil, nil, none, nothing(ness), nought, nulla, nullity, ought, scratch, zilch
hour crisis
in (on) adjust, aim, concentrate, home, take aim

ZERUAH *son* jeroboam

ZERUBBABEL *son* abishai, asahel, joab

ZEST appetite, ardor, charm, delight, elan, enjoyment, enthusiasm, fervor, flavor (ing), glee, gusto, interest, kick, lust, palate, passion, piquancy, pleasure, rapture, relish, savor, spice, spirit, tang, taste, zeal, zip

ZESTFUL breezy, brisk, eager, gay, gutsy, hearty, hot, lively, nippy, peppery, piquant, pungent, racy, sapid, seasoned, snappy, spicy, tangy, zippy

ZETES *brother* calais
enemy harpies
parent boreas, orithyia, poseidon

slayer hercules

ZETHUS *brother* amphion
consort aedon, thebe
parent antiope, zeus
son itylus
victim dirce, lycus

ZEUS aegiochus, agoraeus, alastor, alexikakos, ammon, anchesmius, apemius, aphesius, apomyius, aqueus, atabyrian, cappotas, carius, cataebates, catharsius, cenaean, chthonius, coccygius, cosmetas, croceatas, cronides, cronion, eleutherios, elicius, ephestios, gamelios, hecaleius, herceius, homagyrius, hymettius, hypsistus, ithomatas, jove, jupiter, kronion, lecheates, leucaeus, lycaeus, mechaneus, meilichios, panhellenios, philius, phyxius, pluvius, polieus, semaleus, soter, stator, taranes, teleus, thunderer, tropaean, victor, zan
amour declined thetis
assistant dice, nemesis, themis
attendants curetes, nike
attribute aegis, fulmen
avenger alastor
bird eagle
brother hades, poseidon
companion fides, victoria
consort aegina, aegle, alcmene, anaxithea, antiope, callisto, carme, cassiopeia, danae, demeter, dia, dione, eirene, elara, electra, europa, eurynome, hera, hesione, juno, kore, lamia, latona, leda, leto, maia, mera, metis, mnemosyne, neaera, niobe, nymphs, phthia, protogenia, selene, semele, taygete, thalia, themis, thetis, thyia, thymbris
cupbearer ganymede, hebe
daughters aegle, aphrodite, artemis, astraea, atalanta, ate, athena, britomartis, bura, canens, despoina, dictynna, dike, electra, eris, eunomia, FATES, GRACES, harmonia, hebe, hecate, helen, HORAE, irene, litae, minerva, MUSES, persephassa, persephone, proserpina, proserpine, thriai, venus
enemy enceladus
festival b(o)uphonia, diasia,

didymaea, diipolia, eleutheria, feria, nemean(games)
guard delphyne
home olympus
host baucis philemon
messenger hermes, iris, rumor
nurse amalth(a)ea, cynosura, goat
nymph thisoa
oracle site dodona
parent cronus, kronos, ops, rhea
pert. jovian
priestesses peleiades
priests sell(o)i
sanctuary dodona
satellite callisto, europa, ganymede
shield aegis
sister demeter, hera, hestia
son aeacus, amphion, apollo, arcas, arcesius, ares, argos, argus, atymnius, castor, corinthus, dardanus, dionysus, dioscuri, epaphus, eros, gad, hephaestus, heracles, herakles, hercules, hermes, lacedaemon, locri, minos, myrmidon, olenus, opuns, orchomenus, palici, pan, perseus, pirithous, pollox, rhadamanthus, rhadamanthys, sarpedon, tantalus, targitaus, tityus, vulcan, zethus
victim enceladus, idas
wives (*chronological order*) metis, themis, hera, mnemosyne, eurynome
ZHMUD lithuanian, samogitaian
ZIARA(T) memorial, shrine, tomb
ZIBEB raisin
ZIBEON *son* aiah, anah
ZIBIAH *kin* ahaziah, joash, shaharaim
ZICHRI *kin* amasiah, elishaphat, joel, shimei
ZIG cum, cock, comrade
ZIGGURAT, ZIKURAT pyramid, shrine, tower(of babel)
ZIGZAG alternate, angle, awry, boyau, broken, chevron, crank(le), dancette, flexuous, meander, oscillate, serpentine, snaky, swerve, tack, traverse, turn, weave, wind, wriggle, yaw
ZILCH cipher, nothing, zero
ZILLAH *husband* lamech, lemech

son naamah, tubal-cain
ZILLION gobs, many, numerous
ZILPAH *husband* jacob
son asher, gad
ZIMARRA cassock, simar
ZIMBABWE kraal, rhodesia
ZIMBI cowrie
ZIMMAH *son* joah
ZIMRAN *father* abraham, salu
ZIMRI *slayer* phine(h)as
ZINC *alloy* bidri, brass, oroide, pa(c)ktong, tutenag
blende blackjack, gallium, sphalerite
coat with shradize
color cloud-gray, gray-dawn
compound adamine, adamite, calamine, goslarite, ilesite, tarbuttite, willemite, wurzite
orange cowslip
ore blende, calamine, smithsonite, sphalerite, willemite
slab spelter
spar smithsonite
spinel gahnite
ZING animation, dash, energy, enthusiasm, force, hum, pep, snap, spirit, thrill, vim, vitality, zip
ZINGARO gypsy, nomad
ZINGIBER awapuhi, cardamon, ginger
root cassumun(i)ar
ZINNIA crassina
ZIO tyr
ZION city of god, heaven, holy city, israel, new jerusalem, paradise, utopia
daughter of jerusalem
ZIONIST *clergyman* volivo
founder herzl
leader chaim weizmann, nordau, trumpeldot
organization avukah, ito
underground irgun
ZIP accelerate, dash, elan, energy, force, pep, rush, snap, sparkle, speed, spirit, stingo, vim, zest
ZIPPER fasten(er), slide(r), talon
ZIPPOR *son* balak
ZIPPORAH *kin* eliezer, gershom, jethro, moses
ZIPPY brisk, gay, lively, peppy, snappy, zestful, zesty
ZIRBANIT *lover* marduk
ZIRCON azorite, hyacinth, gem, jargon, malacon(e), malakon, starlite

ZIRSONIUM baddeleyite, brazilite
source zircon
ZITHER autoharp, canon, cimbalom, cither, cittern, cymbalom, galempong, giterne, gittern, kanoon, koto, palempung, rota
harp koto
ZIZ sicily
ZIZA *father* rehoboam
ZIZANY cockle, darnel, tares, wild rice
ZIZITH fringe, sisith, tassels, tsitsith
ZOBAH *king* hadadezer, hadarezer
ZOBEIDE *sister* amina
ZODIAC *division* decan, sign
sign (*1st to 12th*) aries, taurus, gemini, cancer, leo, virgo, libra, scorpio, sagittarius, capricorn, aquarius, pisces
symbol archer, balance, bull, crab, fish, goat, lion, ram, scales, scorpion, twins, virgin, water-carrier
ZOHAR *son* ephron
ZOLA *artist friend* manet
heroine nana
letter j'accuse
rival loti
work debacle, fecondite, germinal, joie de vivre, lourdes, nana, reve, terre, therese raquin, travail, verite
ZOMBIE clown, corpse, dummy, fool, oaf, simpleton
ZONA band, girdle, layer, shingles, zoster
ZONE area, band, belt, berth, cincture, circuit, climate, clime, district, divide, embrace, encircle, girdle, girth, halo, horizon, latitude, layer, locality, longitude, meridian, range, region, section, sector, segment, sphere, stringer, stripe, tract, tropics, ward, zodiac
kind frigid, hemera, temperate, torrid, tropics, variable
safety island, refuge, zebra
ZOO menagerie, tiergarten, vivarium
sound bray
ZOOID bryozoan, cell, coral, hydranth, hydroid, organism, polyp(ide), polypite
ZOOLOGICAL *comb.* acea, bothr(o), bothri(o)
notch crena

poineer cuvier, darwin, huxley, lamarck
ZOOM ascend, chandelle, climb, speed
ZOOPHYTE bryozoan, coral, gorgonian, hydroid, sea anemone, sponge
ZOOT SUITER pachuco
ZOPHAH *son* beera, beri, harnepher, hod, imra, ithan, shamma, shilshah, shual, swah
ZOPHAR *friend* job
ZORAH *native* samson
ZORCHED drunk, juiced, smashed, soused, stoned
ZORELLEAS *daughter* augia
ZCRIL chinche, ictonyx, mariput, polecat, skunk, sorilla
ZOROASTER, ZOROASTRIAN gabar, parsee, parsi, zarathustra
archangels amesha-spenta
book of formulas vendidad, videvdat
commentator zend
convert vishtaspa
creative spirit spentamainyu
demon ahriman, angramainyu, avestan, jeh
follower gheber, ghebre, mazdaist, parsee, parsi
god ahuramazda, o(h)rmazd, ormuzd
good asa
hymn yasht

messiah saoshyant
priest magus
religion mazdaism
revelation vohumano
sacred book avesta, gathas, vendidad, vispered, yasht, yasna, zendavesta
sacred twigs barsom
translation zend
tempter angramainyu
ZOSARA *husband* haman
ZOSTER belt, girdle, shingles, zona
ZOSTEROPS blightbird, white-eye
ZOUAVE soldier, zuzu
ZOUNDS egad, oons, oops, wauns, zoons
ZUCCHETTO calotte, skullcap
ZUFFOLO flageolet, flute
ZUISIN duck, fowl, jishib, sheldrake, widgeon
ZULU bantu, kaffir
army impi
boy unfaan
capital eshowe, ulundi
deity unkulunkulu, uthlanga
general shaka
head man induna
king cetewayo, chaka, dingan, shaka
language bantu
leader black napoleon, buthelezi, ding(a)an, getshwayo, mnyamanashaka
maurauder viti

meeting indaba
people bantu, kaffir, matabele
salutation bayete
soldier impi
spear assagai, assegai
ZUNI *indian* cibolan, shalako
land cibola
mythological being shalako
ZURICH *police headquarters* urania street
ZWIEBACK biscuit, rusk
ZYGADENUS anticlea, camass, saltgrass
ZYGOMA cheekbone, malar
ZYGOMORPHIC monoclinic, monosymmetric
ZYGON bench, fissure, thwart
ZYGOPHYLLACA caltrap, caltrop, guaiacum, kallstroemia, tribulus
ZYGOTE egg, ookinete, oosperm, oospore, sporont
ZYGOUS linked, paired, yoked
ZYME ferment, yeast, zymin
ZYMOGEN proenzyme
ZYMOME glutenin
ZYMOSIS fermentation
ZYMOTIC contagious, fermenting, infectious
ZYRIAN komi
ZYTHEPSARY brewery
ZYTHUM beer